WE 175 BRO

# SKELETAL TRAUMA

## MEDICAL ILLUSTRATORS

*The editors would like to recognize the work of the medical illustrators
listed below who created the beautiful art for the first edition,
much of which has been retained for this new edition:*

Philip Ashley and Denis Lee

*in association with*

Leona Allison
Marie Chartrand
Megan Costello
Charles Curro
Glenn Edelmayer
Theodore Huff
Christine Jones
John Klausmeyer
Valerie Loomis
Larry Ward

*The editors especially wish to thank Theodore Huff,
who created all of the new artwork for this edition.*

*Third Edition*

# SKELETAL TRAUMA

## *Basic Science, Management, and Reconstruction*

## VOLUME TWO

**BRUCE D. BROWNER, M.D., F.A.C.S.**

Gray-Gossling Professor and Chairman
Department of Orthopaedic Surgery
University of Connecticut Health Sciences Center
Farmington, Connecticut
Director, Department of Orthopaedics
Hartford Hospital
Hartford, Connecticut

**JESSE B. JUPITER, M.D.**

Professor of Orthopaedic Surgery
Harvard Medical School
Director, Orthopaedic Hand Service
Massachusetts General Hospital
Boston, Massachusetts

**ALAN M. LEVINE, M.D.**

Professor of Orthopaedic Surgery
University of Maryland School of Medicine
Director, Alvin and Lois Lapidus Cancer Institute
Sinai Hospital
Baltimore, Maryland

**PETER G. TRAFTON, M.D., F.A.C.S.**

Professor and Vice Chairman
Department of Orthopaedic Surgery
Brown University School of Medicine
Surgeon-in-Charge, Orthopaedic Trauma
Rhode Island Hospital
Providence, Rhode Island

**SAUNDERS**
An Imprint of Elsevier Science

**SAUNDERS**
An Imprint of Elsevier Science

The Curtis Center
Independence Square West
Philadelphia, Pennsylvania 19106

Volume 1: Part no. 9997621123
Volume 2: Part no. 9997621131
Two volume set ISBN 0-7216-9175-7

SKELETAL TRAUMA

---

### Notice

Orthopaedic medicine is an ever-changing field. Standard safety precautions must be followed, but as new research and clinical experience broaden our knowledge, changes in treatment and drug therapy may become necessary or appropriate. Readers are advised to check the most current product information provided by the manufacturer of each drug to be administered to verify the recommended dose, the method and duration of administration, and the contraindications. It is the responsibility of the treating physician, relying on experience and knowledge of the patient, to determine dosages and the best treatment for each individual patient. Neither the Publisher nor the editor assumes any responsibility for any injury and/or damage to persons or property arising from this publication.

THE PUBLISHER

---

First Edition 1992. Second Edition 1998.

**Library of Congress Cataloging-in-Publication Data**

Skeletal trauma: basic science, management, and reconstruction / Bruce D. Browner ... [et al.].—3rd ed.
    p. ; cm.
    Includes bibliographical references and index.
    ISBN 0-7216-9175-7 (set)—ISBN 9997621123 (v. 1)—ISBN 9997621131 (v. 2)
    1. Musculoskeletal system—Wounds and injuries. 2. Fractures. I. Browner, Bruce D.
    [DNLM: 1. Fractures. 2. Bone and Bones—injuries. 3. Dislocations.
    4. Ligaments—injuries. WE 175 S627 2003]
    RD731 .S564 2003
    617.4′71044—dc21                                    2001042813

*Acquisitions Editor:* Richard Lampert
*Developmental Editor:* Faith Voit
*Project Manager:* Lee Ann Draud

GW/QWK

Printed in the United States of America

Last digit is the print number:   9   8   7   6   5   4   3   2   1

# CONTRIBUTORS

**Albert J. Aboulafia, M.D., F.A.C.S.**

Assistant Clinical Professor, Department of Orthopaedic Surgery, University of Maryland School of Medicine; Co-Director, Sarcoma Service, Alvin and Lois Lapidus Cancer Center, Sinai Hospital, Baltimore, Maryland

*Pathologic Fractures*

**Annunziato Amendola, M.D., F.R.C.S.(C.)**

Associate Professor, University of Western Ontario, London, Ontario, Canada

*Compartment Syndromes*

**Paul A. Anderson, M.D.**

Associate Professor of Orthopaedic Surgery and Rehabilitation, University of Wisconsin Medical School, Madison, Wisconsin

*Injuries of the Lower Cervical Spine*

**Michael T. Archdeacon, M.D.**

Assistant Professor, Department of Orthopaedic Surgery, University of Cincinnati College of Medicine, Cincinnati, Ohio

*Patella Fractures and Extensor Mechanism Injuries*

**Terry S. Axelrod, M.D.**

Associate Professor of Surgery,
University of Toronto Faculty of Medicine;
Head, Division of Orthopaedic Surgery,
Sunnybrook and Women's College Health Sciences Centre, Toronto, Ontario, Canada

*Fractures and Dislocations of the Hand*

**Craig S. Bartlett III, M.D.**

Assistant Clinical Professor, Orthopaedic Trauma Service, Department of Orthopaedics, University of Vermont College of Medicine, Burlington, Vermont

*Fractures of the Tibial Pilon*

**Michael R. Baumgaertner, M.D.**

Associate Professor, Department of Orthopaedics and Rehabilitation, Yale University School of Medicine; Chief, Orthopaedic Trauma Service, Yale-New Haven Hospital, New Haven, Connecticut

*Medical Management of the Patient with Hip Fracture;*
*Intertrochanteric Hip Fractures*

**Fred F. Behrens, M.D.**

Professor and Chairman, Department of Orthopaedics, UMDNJ—New Jersey Medical School; Chairman of Orthopaedics, UMDNJ–University Hospital, Newark, New Jersey

*Fractures with Soft Tissue Injuries*

**Mark R. Belsky, M.D.**

Associate Clinical Professor of Orthopaedic Surgery, Tufts University School of Medicine, Boston; Chief of Orthopaedic Surgery, Newton-Wellesley Hospital, Newton, Massachusetts

*Fractures and Dislocations of the Hand*

**Stephen K. Benirschke, M.D.**

Associate Professor, Department of Orthopaedic Surgery, University of Washington School of Medicine; Orthopaedic Clinic, Harborview Medical Center, Seattle, Washington

*Foot Injuries*

**Daniel R. Benson, M.D.**

Professor, Department of Orthopaedics, University of California, Davis, School of Medicine; Orthopaedic Surgeon, University of California, Davis, Medical Center, Sacramento, California

*Initial Evaluation and Emergency Treatment of the Spine-Injured Patient*

**Mohit Bhandari, M.D., M.Sc.**

Clinical Research Fellow, St. Michael's Hospital, Toronto, Ontario, Canada

*Fractures of the Humeral Shaft*

**Oren G. Blam, M.D.**

Fellow, Spine Institute, Beth Israel Medical Center, New York, New York

*Fractures in the Stiff and Osteoporotic Spine*

**Michael J. Bosse, M.D.**

Orthopaedic Trauma Surgeon, Orthopaedic Surgery, Carolinas Medical Center, Charlotte, North Carolina

*Orthopaedic Management Decisions in the Multiple-Trauma Patient*

**Robert T. Brautigam, M.D.**

Assistant Professor of Surgery, University of Connecticut School of Medicine, Farmington; Director of Education, Department of Trauma, and Trauma/Critical Care Surgeon, Hartford Hospital, Hartford, Connecticut

*Evaluation and Treatment of the Multiple-Trauma Patient*

**Mark R. Brinker, M.D.**

Clinical Professor of Orthopaedic Surgery, Tulane University School of Medicine, New Orleans, Louisiana; Clinical Professor of Orthopaedic Surgery, Texas Tech University Health Sciences Center School of Medicine, Lubbock; Director of Acute and Reconstructive Trauma, Texas Orthopedic Hospital, Fondren Orthopedic Group, LLP, Houston, Texas

*Nonunions: Evaluation and Treatment*

**Bruce D. Browner, M.D., F.A.C.S.**

Gray-Gossling Professor and Chairman, Department of Orthopaedic Surgery, University of Connecticut Health Sciences Center, Farmington; Director, Department of Orthopaedics, Hartford Hospital, Hartford, Connecticut

*Principles of Internal Fixation; Chronic Osteomyelitis*

**Richard A. Browning, M.D.**

Clinical Professor, Brown University School of Medicine; Anesthesiologist-in-Chief, Rhode Island Hospital, Providence, Rhode Island

*Pain Management following Trauma Injury*

**Frederick W. Burgess, M.D., Ph.D.**

Clinical Associate Professor, Brown University School of Medicine; Attending Anesthesiologist, Rhode Island Hospital, Providence, Rhode Island

*Pain Management following Traumatic Injury*

**Andrew E. Caputo, M.D.**

Clinical Assistant Professor, Department of Orthopaedic Surgery, University of Connecticut Health Sciences Center, Farmington; Co-Director, Hand Surgery Service, Hartford Hospital and Connecticut Children's Medical Center, Hartford, Connecticut

*Principles of Internal Fixation*

**James B. Carr, M.D.**

Clinical Associate, Department of Orthopaedic Surgery, University of South Carolina School of Medicine; Director of Orthopaedic Trauma, Palmetto-Richland Memorial Hospital, Columbia, South Carolina

*Malleolar Fractures and Soft Tissue Injuries of the Ankle*

**Charles Cassidy, M.D.**

Assistant Professor of Orthopaedic Surgery, Tufts University School of Medicine; Chief, Hand and Upper Extremity Service, New England Medical Center, Boston, Massachusetts

*Fractures and Dislocations of the Carpus*

**David L. Ciraulo, D.O., M.P.H.**

Assistant Professor of Surgery, University of Tennessee College of Medicine—Chattanooga Unit; Trauma/Critical Care Surgeon, Chattanooga, TN

*Evaluation and Treatment of the Multiple-Trauma Patient*

**Mark S. Cohen, M.D.**

Associate Professor and Director, Orthopaedic Education, and Director, Hand and Elbow Program, Department of Orthopaedic Surgery, Rush–Presbyterian–St. Luke's Medical Center, Chicago, Illinois

*Fractures of the Distal Radius*

**Christopher L. Colton, M.D., F.R.C.S., F.R.C.S.Ed.**

Senior Consultant in Orthopaedic Trauma, Nottingham University Hospital, Nottingham, England

*The History of Fracture Treatment*

**Leo M. Cooney, Jr., M.D.**

Humana Foundation Professor of Geriatric Medicine, Yale University School of Medicine; Chief, Section of Geriatrics, and Chief, Section of General Internal Medicine, Yale–New Haven Hospital, New Haven, Connecticut

*Medical Management of the Patient with Hip Fracture*

**Charles N. Cornell, M.D.**

Associate Professor, Orthopaedic Surgery, Cornell University Joan and Sanford I. Weill Medical College and Graduate School of Medical Sciences, New York; Chairman, Department of Orthopaedic Surgery, New York Hospital Medical Center of Queens and Flushing Hospital Medical Center, Flushing, New York

*Osteoporotic Fragility Fractures*

**Jerome M. Cotler, M.D.**

Professor, Department of Orthopaedic Surgery, Thomas Jefferson University Hospital, Philadelphia, Pennsylvania

*Fractures in the Stiff and Osteoporotic Spine*

**Charles M. Court-Brown, M.D.**

Professor of Orthopaedic Trauma, Edinburgh Orthopaedic Trauma Unit, Royal Infirmary of Edinburgh, Edinburgh, Scotland

*Femoral Diaphyseal Fractures*

**Bradford L. Currier, M.D.**

Associate Professor and Director, Mayo Clinic Spine Fellowship, Mayo Medical School, Rochester, Minnesota

**Christopher W. DiGiovanni, M.D.**

Assistant Professor, Department of Orthopaedic Surgery, Brown University School of Medicine; Director, Foot and Ankle Service, Rhode Island Hospital, Providence, Rhode Island

*Foot Injuries*

**Sridhar M. Durbhakula, M.D.**

Albany Medical Center, Latham, New York

*Reconstructive Total Hip Replacement after Proximal Femoral Injuries*

**Thomas A. Einhorn, M.D.**

Professor and Chairman, Department of Orthopaedic Surgery, Boston University School of Medicine; Chief of Orthopaedic Surgery, Boston Medical Center, Boston, Massachusetts

*Enhancement of Skeletal Repair*

**Frank J. Eismont, M.D.**

Vice-Chairman and Professor, Department of Orthopaedic Surgery, University of Miami School of Medicine; Co-director, Acute Spinal Cord Injury Unit, Jackson Memorial Hospital, Miami, Florida

*Thoracic and Upper Lumbar Spine Injuries; Gunshot Wounds of the Spine*

**David V. Feliciano, M.D.**

Professor of Surgery, Emory University School of Medicine; Chief of Surgery, Grady Memorial Hospital, Atlanta, Georgia

*Evaluation and Treatment of Vascular Injuries*


**Steven R. Garfin, M.D.**

Professor and Chair, Department of Orthopaedics, University of California, San Diego, School of Medicine, La Jolla, California

*Thoracic and Upper Lumbar Spine Injuries*


**Harris Gellman, M.D.**

Professor and Co-Director, Hand and Upper Extremity Service, Department of Orthopaedic Surgery, University of Miami, Miami, Florida

*Gunshot Wounds to the Musculoskeletal System*


**Gregory E. Gleis, M.D.**

Associate Clinical Professor, Department of Orthopaedic Surgery, University of Louisville School of Medicine, Louisville, Kentucky

*Diagnosis and Treatment of Complications*


**James A. Goulet, M.D.**

Professor, Department of Orthopaedic Surgery, University of Michigan Medical School; Director, Orthopaedic Trauma Service, University of Michigan Hospital, Ann Arbor, Michigan

*Hip Dislocations*


**Andrew Green, M.D.**

Associate Professor, Department of Orthopaedic Surgery, Brown University School of Medicine, Providence, Rhode Island

*Proximal Humeral Fractures and Glenohumeral Dislocations*


**Stuart A. Green, M.D.**

Clinical Professor, Orthopaedic Surgery, University of California, Irvine, School of Medicine, Irvine, California

*The Ilizarov Method*


**Zbigniew Gugala, M.D.**

The Joseph Barnhart Department of Orthopaedic Surgery, Houston, Texas

*Management Techniques for Spinal Injuries*


**Munish C. Gupta, M.D.**

Associate Professor, Department of Orthopaedics, University of California, Davis, School of Medicine; Orthopaedic Surgeon, University of California, Davis, Medical Center, Sacramento, California

*Initial Evaluation and Emergency Treatment of the Spine-Injured Patient*


**Sigvard T. Hansen, Jr., M.D.**

Professor and Chairman Emeritus, Department of Orthopaedic Surgery, University of Washington School of Medicine; Director, Foot and Ankle Institute, Harborview Medical Center, Seattle, Washington

*Foot Injuries; Post-traumatic Reconstruction of the Foot and Ankle*


**Wilson C. Hayes, Ph.D.**

Professor of Exercise and Sport Science and Professor of Mechanical Engineering, Oregon State University; President and Chief Executive Officer, Hayes & Associates, Inc., Corvallis, Oregon

*Biomechanics of Fractures*


**Andrew C. Hecht, M.D.**

Associate Professor of Orthopaedics, Harvard Medical School; Director of Massachusetts General Hospital Spine Surgery Fellowship; Director of Newton-Wellesley Hospital Spine Center, Boston, Massachusetts

*Injuries of the Cervicocranium*


**David L. Helfet, M.D.**

Professor of Orthopaedic Surgery, Cornell University Joan and Sanford I. Weill Medical College and Graduate School of Medical Sciences; Director, Combined Orthopaedic Trauma Service, Hospital for Special Surgery and New York–Presbyterian Hospital, New York, New York

*Fractures of the Distal Femur*


**John A. Hipp, Ph.D.**

Assistant Professor, Baylor College of Medicine; Chief Scientific Officer, Medical Metrics, Inc., Houston, Texas

*Biomechanics of Fractures*


**Lenworth M. Jacobs, M.D., M.P.H., F.A.C.S.**

Professor of Surgery, University of Connecticut School of Medicine, Farmington; Director, Traumatology, Hartford Hospital, Hartford, Connecticut

*Evaluation and Treatment of the Multiple-Trauma Patient*


**David J. Jacofsky, M.D.**

Instructor, Department of Orthopaedic Surgery, Mayo Clinic, Rochester, Minnesota

*Complications in the Treatment of Spinal Trauma*


**Jesse B. Jupiter, M.D.**

Professor of Orthopaedic Surgery, Harvard Medical School; Director, Orthopaedic Hand Service, Massachusetts General Hospital, Boston, Massachusetts

*Fractures and Dislocations of the Hand; Fractures of the Distal Radius; Diaphyseal Fractures of the Forearm; Trauma to the Adult Elbow and Fractures of the Distal Humerus; Injuries to the Shoulder Girdle*


**Timothy L. Keenen, M.D.**

Clinical Associate Professor of Orthopaedic Surgery, Oregon Health Sciences University School of Medicine, Portland, Oregon

*Initial Evaluation and Emergency Treatment of the Spine-Injured Patient*

**James F. Kellam, M.D., F.R.C.S.(C.)**

Director, Orthopedic Trauma Program, and Vice Chairman, Department of Orthopedic Surgery, Carolinas Medical Center, Charlotte, North Carolina; Adjunct Professor of Engineering, Clemson University, Clemson, South Carolina

*Orthopaedic Management Decisions in the Multiple-Trauma Patient; Pelvic Ring Disruptions; Diaphyseal Fractures of the Forearm*

**Choll W. Kim, M.D., Ph.D.**

Department of Orthopaedic Surgery, University of California, San Diego, School of Medicine, La Jolla, California

*Complications in the Treatment of Spinal Trauma*

**Christian Krettek, M.D.**

Director, Trauma Department, Hannover Medical School, Hannover, Germany

*Fractures of the Distal Femur*

**David Kwon, M.S.**

Medical Student, University of California, San Diego, School of Medicine, La Jolla, California

*Osteoporotic Fragility Fractures*

**Joseph M. Lane, M.D.**

Professor of Orthopaedic Surgery and Assistant Dean, Cornell University Joan and Sanford I. Weill Medical College and Graduate School of Medical Sciences; Chief, Metabolic Bone Disease, Hospital for Special Surgery, New York, New York

*Osteoporotic Fragility Fractures*

**Loren L. Latta, P.E., Ph.D.**

Professor and Director of Research, Department of Orthopaedics and Rehabilitation, University of Miami School of Medicine, Miami; Director of Orthopaedic Biomechanics Laboratory, Mt. Sinai Medical Center/Miami Heart Institute, Miami Beach, Florida

*Principles of Nonoperative Fracture Treatment*

**Sebastian Lattuga, M.D.**

Chief Spine Surgeon, Mercy Medical Center, Rockville Center, New York

*Gunshot Wounds of the Spine*

**Paul E. Levin, M.D.**

Assistant Clinical Professor, Department of Orthopaedics, State University of New York at Stony Brook, Stony Brook, New York

*Hip Dislocations*

**Alan M. Levine, M.D.**

Professor of Orthopaedic Surgery, University of Maryland School of Medicine; Director, Alvin and Lois Lapidus Cancer Institute, Sinai Hospital, Baltimore, Maryland

*Pathologic Fractures; Low Lumbar Fractures; Fractures of the Sacrum*

**Ronald W. Lindsey, M.D.**

Professor of Orthopaedic Surgery, The Joseph Barnhart Department of Orthopaedic Surgery, Houston, Texas

*Management Techniques for Spinal Injuries*

**Margaret Lobo, M.D.**

Orthopaedic Resident, Thomas Jefferson University Hospital, Philadelphia, Pennsylvania

*Osteoporotic Fragility Fractures*

**Jay D. Mabrey, M.D.**

Associate Professor of Orthopaedics, University of Texas Health Science Center of San Antonio; Director, Total Joint Service, University Hospital, San Antonio, Texas

*Periprosthetic Fractures of the Lower Extremities*

**Jeffrey W. Mast, M.D.**

Northern Nevada Medical Center, Sparks, Nevada

*Principles of Internal Fixation*

**Joel M. Matta, M.D.**

Clinical Professor of Orthopaedic Surgery, University of Southern California School of Medicine; John C. Wilson, Jr., Chair of Orthopaedic Surgery, Good Samaritan Hospital, Los Angeles, California

*Surgical Treatment of Acetabular Fractures*

**Keith Mayo, M.D.**

Orthopaedic Center, Tacoma, Washington

*Pelvic Ring Disruptions*

**Augustus D. Mazzocca, M.D.**

Assistant Professor, Department of Orthopaedic Surgery, University of Connecticut Health Sciences Center, Farmington, Connecticut

*Principles of Internal Fixation*

**Robert A. McGuire, M.D.**

Professor and Chairman, Department of Orthopedics, University of Mississippi Medical Center, Jackson, Mississippi

*Thoracic and Upper Lumbar Spine Injuries*

**Michael D. McKee, M.D., F.R.C.S.(C.)**

Associate Professor, Division of Orthopaedics, Department of Surgery, University of Toronto Faculty of Medicine; Staff Surgeon and Assistant Medical Director, Trauma Program, St. Michael's Hospital, Toronto, Ontario, Canada

*Trauma to the Adult Elbow and Fractures of the Distal Humerus*

**Robert Y. McMurtry, M.D.**

Professor of Surgery, Division of Orthopaedics, University of Western Ontario Faculty of Medicine and Dentistry; Consultant, Hand and Upper Limb Centre, St. Joseph's Health Centre, London, Ontario, Canada

*Fractures of the Distal Radius*

**Dana C. Mears, M.D., Ph.D.**
Attending Orthopaedic Surgeon, University of Pittsburgh Medical Center—Shadyside Hospital, Pittsburgh, Pennsylvania
*Reconstructive Total Hip Replacement after Proximal Femoral Injuries*

**Michael W. Mendes, M.D.**
Attending Physician, McLeod Regional Medical Center, Florence, South Carolina
*Principles of Internal Fixation*

**Stuart E. Mirvis, M.D., F.A.C.R.**
Professor of Radiology, University of Maryland School of Medicine; Director, Trauma Radiology, University of Maryland R. Adams Cowley Shock-Trauma Center, Baltimore, Maryland
*Spinal Imaging*

**Sohail K. Mirza, M.D.**
Assistant Professor, Department of Orthopaedics and Sports Medicine, University of Washington School of Medicine; Harborview Medical Center, Seattle, Washington
*Injuries of the Lower Cervical Spine*

**Todd D. Moldawer, M.D.**
Co-Director, Spine Fellowship Program, Southern California Orthopedic Institute, Van Nuys, California
*Gunshot Wounds to the Musculoskeletal System*

**Victor A. Morris, M.D.**
Assistant Professor of Medicine, General Medicine, Yale University School of Medicine; Co-Director, Medicine Consult Service, Yale University School of Medicine, New Haven, Connecticut
*Medical Management of the Patient with Hip Fracture*

**Calin S. Moucha, M.D.**
Chief Resident, Department of Orthopaedic Surgery, St. Luke's–Roosevelt Hospital Center and Columbia University College of Physicians and Surgeons, New York, New York
*Enhancement of Skeletal Repair*

**Michael L. Nerlich, M.D., Ph.D.**
Professor, Trauma Surgery, University of Regensburg Medical School; Chairman, Department of Trauma Surgery, Regensburg University Academic Medical Center, Regensburg, Bavaria, Germany
*Biology of Soft Tissue Injuries*

**Tom R. Norris, M.D.**
Department of Orthopaedic Surgery, California Pacific Medical Center, San Francisco, California
*Proximal Humeral Fractures and Glenohumeral Dislocations*

**William T. Obremskey, M.D., M.P.H.**
Assistant Professor of Orthopaedics and Rehabilitation, Division of Orthopaedic Trauma, Vanderbilt University Medical Center, Nashville, Tennessee
*Evaluation of Outcomes for Musculoskeletal Injury*

**Dror Paley, M.D.**
Professor, University of Maryland School of Medicine; Director, Rubin Institute for Advanced Orthopaedics, Sinai Hospital of Baltimore, Baltimore, Maryland
*Principles of Deformity Correction*

**Ed Pesanti, M.D., F.A.C.P.**
Professor, Department of Medicine, University of Connecticut School of Medicine; University of Connecticut Health Center, Farmington, Connecticut
*Chronic Osteomyelitis*

**Michael S. Pinzur, M.D.**
Professor of Orthopaedic Surgery and Rehabilitation, Loyola University of Chicago Stritch School of Medicine, Maywood, Illinois
*Amputations in Trauma*

**Spiros G. Pneumaticos, M.D.**
Assistant Professor, The Joseph Barnhart Department of Orthopaedic Surgery, Houston, Texas
*Management Techniques for Spinal Injuries*

**Andrew N. Pollak, M.D.**
Associate Professor of Orthopaedic Surgery, University of Maryland School of Medicine; Attending Orthopaedic Traumatologist, R. Adams Cowley Shock Trauma Center, Baltimore, Maryland
*Principles of External Fixation*

**Mark A. Prévost, M.D.**
Walker Baptist Medical Center, Jasper, Alabama
*Thoracic and Upper Lumbar Spine Injuries*

**David Ring, M.D.**
Instructor, Department of Orthopaedics, Harvard Medical School; Department of Orthopaedic Surgery, Massachusetts General Hospital, Boston, Massachusetts
*Injuries to the Shoulder Girdle*

**Craig S. Roberts, M.D.**
Associate Professor and Residency Director, Department of Orthopaedic Surgery, University of Louisville School of Medicine, Louisville, Kentucky
*Diagnosis and Treatment of Complications*

**C. M. Robinson, M.D., F.R.C.S.**
Consultant Orthopaedic Surgeon, Royal Infirmary of Edinburgh, Edinburgh, Scotland
*Femoral Diaphyseal Fractures*

**Craig M. Rodner, M.D.**
Department of Orthopaedic Surgery, University of Connecticut Health System, Farmington, Connecticut
*Chronic Osteomyelitis*

**Leonard K. Ruby, M.D.**
Professor of Orthopaedic Surgery, Tufts University School of Medicine; Staff, Hand Surgery, Department of Orthopaedic Surgery, New England Medical Center, Boston, Massachusetts
*Fractures and Dislocations of the Carpus*

**Thomas A. Russell, M.D.**
Professor of Orthopaedic Surgery, University of Tennessee, Memphis, College of Medicine, Memphis, Tennessee
*Subtrochanteric Fractures of the Femur*

**Roy W. Sanders, M.D.**
Clinical Professor of Orthopaedics, University of South Florida College of Medicine, Tampa, Florida
*Patella Fractures and Extensor Mechanism Injuries*

**Augusto Sarmiento, M.D.**
Professor and Chairman Emeritus, University of Miami School of Medicine, Miami; Director, Arthritis and Joint Replacement Institute, Doctors Hospital, Coral Gables, Florida
*Principles of Nonoperative Fracture Treatment*

**Richard A. Saunders, M.D.**
Orthopedic Surgeon, The Glen Falls Hospital, Glen Falls, New York
*Physical Impairment Ratings for Fractures*

**Joseph Schatzker, M.D.**
Professor, University of Toronto Faculty of Medicine; Orthopaedic Surgeon, Sunnybrook Health Science Center, Toronto, Ontario, Canada
*Tibial Plateau Fractures*

**Emil H. Schemitsch, M.D., F.R.C.S.C.**
Professor and Head, Division of Orthopaedic Surgery, St. Michael's Hospital, Toronto, Ontario, Canada
*Fractures of the Humeral Shaft*

**Robert K. Schenk, M.D.**
Professor Emeritus of Anatomy, Histology, and Embryology; Head of the Bone Research Laboratory, Department of Oral Surgery, University of Berne, Berne, Switzerland
*Biology of Fracture Repair*

**David Seligson, M.D.**
Professor and Vice Chair, Department of Orthopaedic Surgery, University of Louisville School of Medicine; Chief of Orthopaedics, University of Louisville Hospital, Louisville, Kentucky
*Diagnosis and Treatment of Complications*

**Randy Sherman, M.D.**
Professor of Plastic, Orthopedic, and Neurologic Surgery, University of Southern California; Chief, Division of Plastic Surgery, Cedars-Sinai Medical Center, Los Angeles, California
*Soft Tissue Coverage*

**D. Hal Silcox III, M.D.**
Cervical, Thoracic, and Lumbar Orthopaedic Spine Surgeon, Peachtree Orthopedic Clinic, Atlanta, Georgia
*Injuries of the Cervicocranium*

**John M. Siliski, M.D.**
Instructor, Harvard Medical School; Orthopaedic Surgeon, Massachusetts General Hospital, Boston, Massachusetts
*Dislocations and Soft Tissue Injuries of the Knee*

**Michael S. Sirkin, M.D.**
Assistant Professor, Department of Orthopaedics, UMDNJ—New Jersey Medical School; Chief, Orthopaedic Trauma Service, UMDNJ–University Hospital, Newark, New Jersey
*Fractures with Soft Tissue Injuries*

**Marc F. Swiontkowski, M.D.**
Professor and Chairman, Department of Orthopaedic Surgery, University of Minnesota, Minneapolis; Chief of Orthopaedic Surgery, Regions Hospital, St. Paul; Staff Orthopaedist, Henepin County Medical Center, Minneapolis, Minnesota
*Evaluation of Outcomes for Musculoskeletal Injury; Intracapsular Hip Fractures*

**P. Tornetta, M.D.**
Department of Orthopaedic Surgery, Boston Medical Center, Boston, Massachusetts
*Femoral Diaphyseal Fractures*

**Peter G. Trafton, M.D., F.A.C.S.**
Professor and Vice Chairman of Orthopaedic Surgery, Brown University School of Medicine; Surgeon-in-Charge, Orthopaedic Trauma, Rhode Island Hospital, Providence, Rhode Island
*Tibial Shaft Fractures*

**Bruce C. Twaddle, M.D., F.R.A.C.S.**
Director of Orthopaedic Trauma, Auckland Hospital, Auckland, New Zealand
*Compartment Syndromes*

**John H. Velyvis, M.D.**
Albany Medical Center, Albany, New York
*Reconstructive Total Hip Replacement after Proximal Femoral Injuries*

**J. Tracy Watson, M.D.**
Professor of Orthopaedic Surgery, Wayne State University School of Medicine; Vice Chief of Orthopaedics, Division of Orthopaedic Traumatology, Detroit Receiving Hospital, Detroit Medical Center, Detroit, Michigan
*Tibial Plateau Fractures*

**Lon S. Weiner, M.D.**
Chief of Pediatrics and Trauma, Lenox Hill Hospital, New York, New York
*Fractures of the Tibial Pilon*

**Thomas E. Whitesides, Jr., M.D.**

Professor of Orthopaedic Surgery, Emory University School of Medicine; Emory University Hospital, Atlanta, Georgia

*Injuries of the Cervicocranium*

**Sam W. Wiesel, M.D.**

Professor and Chair, Department of Orthopedics, Georgetown University, Washington, D.C.

*Physical Impairment Ratings for Fractures*

**Donald A. Wiss, M.D.**

Clinical Professor of Orthopedic Surgery, University of Southern California, Los Angeles; Southern California Orthopedic Institute, Van Nuys, California

*Gunshot Wounds to the Musculoskeletal System*

**Michael J. Yaszemski, M.D., Ph.D.**

Associate Professor of Orthopaedic Surgery and Biomedical Engineering, Mayo Medical School and Mayo Graduate School; Consultant, Department of Orthopaedic Surgery, Mayo Clinic, Rochester, Minnesota

*Complications in the Treatment of Spinal Trauma*

**Bruce H. Ziran, M.D.**

Assistant Professor, Department of Orthopedics, University of Pittsburgh School of Medicine, Pittsburgh, Pennsylvania

*Principles of External Fixation*

**Gregory A. Zych, D.O.**

Associate Professor, University of Miami School of Medicine; Chief of Orthopaedic Trauma and Associate Chairman for Clinical Affairs, University of Miami/Jackson Memorial Hospital, Miami, Florida

*Principles of Nonoperative Fracture Treatment*

# FOREWORD

Trauma has always represented—and still represents—a constant threat to all people, young and old. Administering competent treatment to the injured victim at the earliest opportunity has always been the goal, but only in our own time has this goal actually been achievable, being accorded top priority in our concept of modern trauma surgery. Nowadays, trauma surgery is able to treat most injuries successfully, rehabilitate the patients, and return them to their families, occupational positions, and places in society through a wide variety of specific therapeutic procedures administered by committed personnel employing advanced techniques. Such treatment not only represents a humanitarian service, but also produces substantial economic benefits.

It is surprising that these services provided by trauma surgery have long gone unrecognized by the general public. Musculoskeletal injuries and disorders are the commonest causes of serious chronic pain conditions and physical disabilities that affect hundreds of millions across the globe. Since these conditions do not usually prove fatal, they have failed to grab the attention of the public in the same way in which cardiac disease, cancer, or AIDS has done.

Injuries and disorders of the locomotor system lead to a substantial impairment in the health and quality of life of a large part of the world's population and currently account for more than half of all chronic disorders in patients older than 60 years. But musculoskeletal conditions are not just prominent among elderly patients. More than 40% of young adults experience their first contact with a doctor as a result of injuries and disorders of the locomotor system. Moreover, the latter also account for more than 40% of all cases of unfitness for work or early retirement.

Unfitness for work, becoming an invalid, and premature death among those in gainful employment represent a considerable drain on society's resources. In addition, the proportion of the elderly in our society is growing. In just 8 years' time, there will be more older people than young people under 20 in Europe and North America. As time passes, the situation for these developed nations will become even more dramatic: 25% of the population will be older than 65 in 2020 and 35% just 10 years later in 2030. By that time, 6% of the population will be older than 85 years. The group of over 85-year-olds thus forms the fastest growing segment of the population. This has serious implications for trauma surgery. The number of femoral neck fractures worldwide, for example, is expected to rise from 1.7 million in 1990 to 6.3 million by 2050. Traffic accidents—humankind's tribute to the triumph of technology—are assuming epidemic proportions, especially in the developing nations, and they deprive these countries of a substantial percentage of the already limited medical resources available.

Trauma surgery has undergone tremendous changes over the past 50 years. At the same time, the expectations of patients and society as a whole concerning the possibilities and capabilities of trauma surgery have grown disproportionately. Residual damage as the result of chance is no longer tolerated. Nowadays, patients demand restitution to full health, frequently resorting to all available legal means and other resources. Moreover, like the field of medicine as a whole, trauma surgery is affected by conflicting changes in the paradigms of politics, economics, the legal system, science, and the globalization of information and network structures. The trauma surgeon must also be proactive in dealing with this conglomeration of issues and challenges in order to cope with the present and plan for the future.

The pace at which developments appear and change occurs is accelerating all the time. Flexibility and adaptability are becoming increasingly important. The surgeon faces growing pressure from advances in microelectronics and computer technology. In the field of minimally invasive surgery, whole areas of traditional surgical practice are being rendered obsolete through the use of minirobots, percutaneous surgical and microprobe techniques, and radiologically assisted minimally invasive procedures. Trauma surgery must also ensure that it does not lose out to third parties such as medical technicians and radiologists when it comes to deciding on indications and treatment. Advances in genetic engineering and tissue engineering will play a role in the future prevention and treatment of injuries. The effects of the digital revolution on factors such as work flow and disease management cannot be predicted. Finally, the execution of surgical procedures by programmed machines (e.g., Robot Doc), master-slave systems, or autonomous or semiautonomous systems will take us into completely new territory. Surgical training will also enter a new dimension. Simulation and virtual reality will become a perfectly natural part of modular training. As a whole, trauma surgery across the world will require a new generation of motivated surgeons prepared to view the challenges of the future as an opportunity and tackle them with insight and commitment.

Every surgeon concerned with skeletal trauma requires a comprehensive, up-to-date textbook that addresses the problems encountered in daily practice. *Skeletal Trauma* is now recognized worldwide as one of the most important textbooks in the field. With this work, Bruce D. Browner, Jesse B. Jupiter, Alan M. Levine, and Peter G. Trafton have made an important contribution toward maintaining the highest standards of education for orthopaedic trauma surgeons.

The changes in the management of skeletal trauma since the appearance of the second edition are truly phenomenal. The scope of the third edition has been substantially expanded. The original chapters have been thoroughly revised, and all the latest findings are described in detail.

The major new addition is the inclusion of extensive material on post-traumatic reconstruction. In addition to the diagnosis and treatment of acute injuries, the authors of the anatomic chapters were all asked to add detailed information on the following: nonunion, malunion, osteoporosis, bone loss, and osteomyelitis. New chapters have been added on total joint replacement, fusions, osteotomies, and other reconstructive techniques. The chapter on enhancement of skeletal repair covers some of the new biologic and technical advances.

The new edition also addresses the daily needs of the practicing surgeon and provides answers to a number of common difficult problems. The book also contains valuable information on ways to avoid technical difficulties and pitfalls, and to manage complications. The book is extremely well illustrated, and the figures impress with their clarity and the highlighting of important technical details. The style is easy to understand, clear, and unambiguous. Complex problems are clearly presented.

I am confident that the third edition will surpass the first two editions in terms of popularity. The editors can rest assured that they have made available to all those concerned with skeletal trauma a work of outstanding quality.

*Professor Harald Tscherne*

# PREFACE

The first edition of *Skeletal Trauma: Fractures, Dislocations, Ligamentous Injuries* was written between 1988 and 1991. This represented a unique window for the creation of this text, coinciding with the increased recognition of the special needs of trauma victims. By the mid-1980s, more than 500 regional trauma centers had been established throughout the United States and Canada. The volume and acuity of blunt trauma and associated musculoskeletal injuries reached a high-water mark. The editors and contributing authors for *Skeletal Trauma* had been on the front lines working in the major trauma centers throughout this period. They helped to develop a new operative approach to the treatment of these injuries that stressed early skeletal fixation and rapid mobilization. The incomparable firsthand experience that they gained helped shape their contributions to the text. In the early 1990s, many states adopted the child restraint device and seat belt legislation. Successful initiatives to control driving under the influence of alcohol significantly lowered incidence of motor vehicle crashes. Improvements in automotive design, such as airbags and side rails, continued to reduce the incidence and severity of blunt trauma and complex musculoskeletal injuries. Although there was an alarming increase in injuries and deaths from gunshots in our major cities, penetrating trauma does not usually result in the multiplicity and complexity of skeletal injuries that are caused by vehicular crashes. In addition, managed care contracting practices resulted in the dispersion of trauma patients to community hospitals, often reducing the number of injuries seen in trauma centers. In retrospect, the 1980s provided a unique opportunity for the creation of this text.

The excellent manuscripts provided by our contributing authors and the beautiful illustrations created by the artists were assembled into an outstanding text by the W.B. Saunders production department. In the year of its publication, 1992, it won first prize in medical sciences from the Association of American Publishers as the best new medical book. The text has been widely embraced by orthopaedic and trauma surgeons throughout the world for its clarity and its utility. They have consistently expressed their appreciation of our approach, which stresses the discussion of problem-focus clinical judgment and proven surgical techniques. The textbook has been regarded by surgeons in training and practicing physicians to be a practice resource that can help guide them through the management of the musculoskeletal injuries with which they are confronted. We retained and strengthened this basic philosophy and organization in the second edition. We added new chapters to cover important subjects that were not addressed adequately in the first edition.

In the years since the publication of the second edition of *Skeletal Trauma,* major new global epidemiologic trends have been noted that influence the character of musculoskeletal injuries throughout the world. In the developed market economies, decreased birth rates and increasing longevity have resulted in the aging of the population. Osteoporosis and associated fragility fractures have grown in number and significance. Road safety improvements in these countries, such as pediatric restraint devices, seat belts, drunk driving control, airbags, vehicle design improvements, and enhanced law enforcement, have decreased the number and severity of road traffic injuries. In the developing world, however, there is a growing epidemic of road traffic injuries. Vulnerable travelers such as pedestrians, bicyclists, motorcycle riders, and passengers on overcrowded buses and trucks are the main victims. Annually, 1 million people die on the world's roads and an estimated 24 to 33 million are severely injured or disabled.

To raise awareness of the burden of these and other musculoskeletal disorders, empower patients, expand research and improvements for prevention and treatment of these problems, and engender multidisciplinary cooperation, the years 2000–2010 have been declared the "Bone and Joint Decade" by U.N. Secretary General Kofi Annan. The movement has also been endorsed by the World Health Organization, the World Bank, and the governments of forty nations. Although there have been dramatic advances in biology, pharmaceuticals, technology, and fixation to improve the care of patients with musculoskeletal disorders in wealthy countries, a large portion of the world's population lacks basic health care and has very limited orthopaedic services available. The third edition of *Skeletal Trauma* has been written in recognition of the challenges of our era and is dedicated to the improvement of musculoskeletal trauma care throughout the world in keeping with the spirit of the "Bone and Joint Decade."

For many years, the *Skeletal Trauma* editorial group has discussed the possibility of creating a separate volume for skeletal trauma reconstruction. Our contributing authors and others have gained wide experience in post-trauma reconstruction, but there have been no comprehensive texts written on this subject. In conjunction with our publisher, we have made a decision to incorporate this material into the current edition. As we are limited by the established size of the two volumes, some basic science chapters were deleted and other information was condensed to make room for the new reconstructive material. New chapters were added on perioperative pain management, osteoporotic fragility fractures, chronic osteomyelitis, gunshot wounds of the spine, fractures in the stiff and osteoporotic spine, medical management of patients with hip fractures, total hip arthroplasty after failed primary treatment of fractures involving the hip joint, acute foot injuries, foot injury reconstruction, lower extremity alignment, periprosthetic fractures, and amputations for trauma. Some of the authors from previous editions have continued but have made major revisions to revitalize their work. In other cases, new authors have been recruited to add international perspective and broaden the base of expertise. Minimally invasive plating, an important new technique, is covered by one of its major developers in the chapter on the distal femur. New biologic agents are addressed in an expanded chapter on enhancement of fracture healing.

In addition to discussing the treatment of acute injuries, the authors of the anatomic chapters were asked to expand their scholarly writing to include the management of nonunions, malunions, bone loss, osteomyelitis, and fixation in osteoporotic bone. The use of fusion and arthroplasty in post-traumatic arthritis is described in detail.

The editors have been gratified by comments from surgeons from around the world indicating that *Skeletal Trauma* has been adopted by many trauma centers and orthopaedic training programs as the principal fracture text. We have welcomed their constructive criticism as well as their accolades. Many of the changes in the current edition were made in response to comments from these surgeons and our own residents.

We are grateful to our contributing authors, whose high level of scholarship and dedication to their chapter writing makes this such a readable and useful reference. The pressures of modern medical practice have made these surgeons busier than they were during the writing of the second edition. Together we have refashioned our text to better address readers' needs for information concerning basic science, acute injury management, and post-traumatic reconstruction.

*Bruce D. Browner, M.D.*
*Jesse B. Jupiter, M.D.*
*Alan M. Levine, M.D.*
*Peter G. Trafton, M.D.*

# ACKNOWLEDGMENTS

We have had the pleasure of working with another group of people who have carried on the tradition of excellence established in the first and second editions. We particularly wish to acknowledge Richard Lampert, Publishing Director, Surgery, the driving force behind the project, and Faith Voit, our Senior Developmental Editor. Additionally, we acknowledge the work of Lee Ann Draud, our Project Manager, and Natalie Ware, our former Production Manager, as well as Walt Verbitski, our former Illustrations Coordinator. Without their efforts, we could not have hoped to maintain this level of excellence.

No staff was hired by the editors for the production of this text. Again, we relied on the hard work and dedication of our own personal staffs. We recognize that without their help we could not have upheld our commitment to this project.

Bruce Browner gratefully acknowledges the work of Deb Bruno and Sue Ellen Pelletier, Executive Assistants at Hartford Hospital and the University of Connecticut, respectively. Their creative pursuit of manuscripts and communication with authors and the Saunders staff helped keep the project on schedule.

Jesse Jupiter would like to thank his executive secretary, Richard Perotti, for helping him communicate with the authors and illustrators and for keeping him focused on the task at hand. He expresses his gratitude as well to Michel Tresfort, transcriptionist, for proofreading all of the manuscripts in addition to his regular duties.

Alan Levine would like to especially acknowledge the efforts of his office administrator, Joanne Barker, who has kept him organized and focused and assisted him in communicating with the authors, illustrators, and the Saunders staff. Eileen Creeger has spent numerous hours proofreading manuscripts, galleys, and page proofs as well as checking the accuracy of citations. The other members of the office staff have also contributed in myriad ways. Finally, he would like to thank all of the residents, fellows, and staff at both Sinai Hospital and at the Maryland Shock Trauma Unit, without whom he would never have garnered the experience necessary to effectively contribute to the preparation of this book.

Peter Trafton gratefully recognizes his administrative assistant, Robin Morin, for her invaluable help with communications, copying, and logistics. He also appreciates the continuing support of his colleagues and staff at University Orthopedics, the stimulus and helpful critiques of Brown University's Orthopaedic Surgery Residents, and especially the Brown University Orthopaedic Trauma fellows, whose quest for surgical expertise and understanding remains a daily inspiration.

# CONTENTS

## VOLUME TWO

# SECTION IV

# *Upper Extremity*

SECTION EDITOR

**Jesse B. Jupiter, M.D.**

# CHAPTER 38

# Fractures and Dislocations of the Hand

Jesse B. Jupiter, M.D.
Terry S. Axelrod, M.D.
Mark R. Belsky, M.D.

The hand is a human being's most exquisite organ of direct interaction with the surrounding universe. Each digit of the hand can be viewed in a manner analogous to an entire limb, given its complement of structures; yet nowhere else in the body does function follow form as closely as in the hand. The precision and stability of its small articulations, the fine balance between its extrinsic and intrinsic motors, and the complex tendon mechanisms gliding on their diaphanous beds demand a stable, aligned, supporting skeleton. These gliding structures intimately enveloping the tubular skeleton of the phalanges prove in many cases to be the ultimate determinants of functional outcome after skeletal trauma. Charnley recognized this point when he stated that "the reputation of a surgeon may stand as much in jeopardy from this injury (phalangeal fracture) as from any fracture of the femur."[54]

Fractures involving the tubular bones of the hand are the most frequent of all skeletal injuries.[86, 124, 206, 227, 291, 299, 329] Although failure to achieve union is unusual in phalangeal and metacarpal fractures,[150] prevention of angular or rotational deformity, tendon adhesion, or articular dysfunction continues to challenge even the most experienced surgeon.[293] The economic cost of injuries to the hand is staggering (Table 38–1). Each year in the United States, more than one third of all injuries involve the upper extremity and over 16 million Americans are affected, with more than 500,000 hospitalizations and over 6 million emergency department visits.[161] In the United States, the hand suffers more than 1.5 million fractures and almost 6 million open wounds each year.[185] These injuries result in 16 million lost days of work, $2 billion in lost earnings, and almost $4 billion in cost to industry.[131] The economic burden has been equally documented in Europe. Boehler noted that the compensation paid out for hand injuries in Austria proved to be almost twice that for fractures of the long bones.[23] Tubiana reported that in 1975 in France, hand injuries were responsible for 27% of the total amount paid in disability benefits for all work-related accidents, and the number of lost workdays approached 8 million.[306]

## FUNCTIONAL ANATOMY

Extending out from the carpal arch of the wrist, the four digital metacarpals form the breadth of the hand (Fig. 38–1). The longitudinal and distal transverse arches of the hand pass through the metacarpals, with a common "keystone" in the metacarpophalangeal (MCP) joints (Fig. 38–2). The rigid central pillar of the hand projects through the second and third metacarpals, whereas the thumb and the fourth and fifth metacarpals and their carpometacarpal (CMC) articulations provide the mobile borders of the palm. The deep transverse metacarpal ligaments interconnect the four metacarpals, thereby adding to their internal support.

The metacarpals are tubular bones structurally divided into a base, shaft, neck, and head (Fig. 38–3). The base is designed like a footing at the base of a foundation in that it is nearly twice as wide as the shaft when viewed in the coronal plane. Strong supporting ligaments and the congruent articulations of the trapezoid and capitate make the second and third CMC joints nearly immobile. This arrangement is in contrast to the modified saddle joint that articulates the hamate with the base of the fourth and fifth metacarpals and affords considerable mobility in the anteroposterior (AP) plane.

The metacarpal shaft extends distally with a gentle dorsal convexity. The concave palmar cortex is denser than the dorsal cortex,[176] thus supporting the hypothesis that with functional loading, the palmar side of the metacarpal will experience compressive force in contrast to the tensile stress dorsally.[147]

When viewed in the sagittal plane, the metacarpal head represents a curve of increasing diameter beginning dorsally and extending along the articular surface to the palmar side. When viewed in the coronal plane, the metacarpal head is pear shaped, with the palmar surface extending out of each side (Fig. 38–4). The collateral ligaments of the MCP joint originate dorsal to the axis of flexion and insert broadly along the palmar aspects of the

**TABLE 38–1** ••••••••••••••••••••••••••••••••

Epidemiology of Injuries of the Tubular Bones in the Hand (1975–1976)

| Injury | Number | Days Lost from Work | Restricted Activity (Days) |
|---|---|---|---|
| Metacarpal | 150,000 | 1,157,000 | 3,421,000 |
| Phalanges | 856,000 | 711,000 | 6,244,000 |
| Multiple hand fractures | 22,000 | — | 67,000 |
| Dislocation of the finger | 67,000 | — | 156,000 |

•••••••••••••••••••••••••••••••••••••••

*Source:* Compiled from Kelsey, J.L.; Pastides, H.; Kreiger, N.; et al. Upper Extremity Disorders. A Survey of Their Frequency and Cost in the United States. St. Louis, C.V. Mosby, 1980.

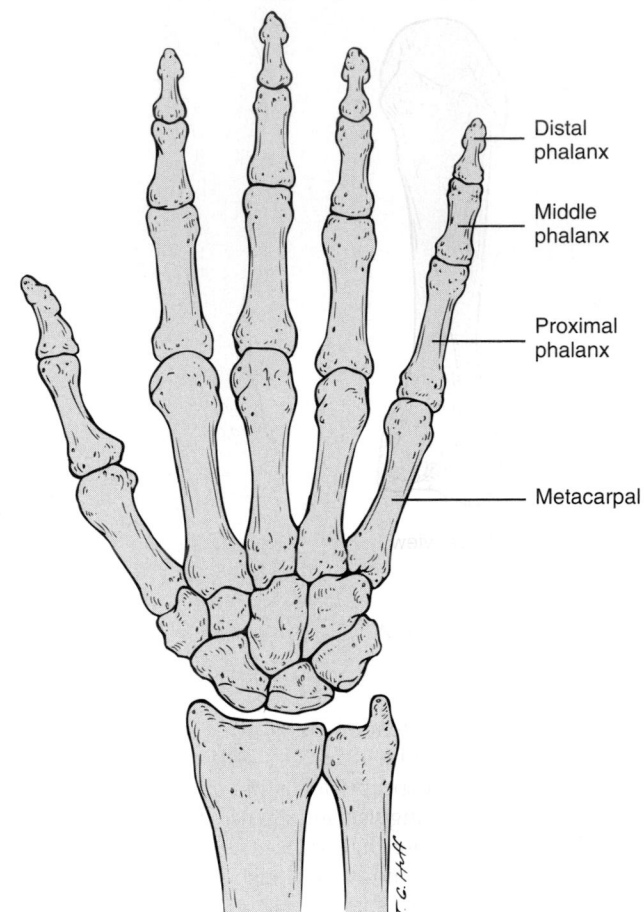

**FIGURE 38–1.** Tubular skeleton of the hand.

proximal phalanges. It is partly because of this eccentric origin of the collateral ligaments on the oddly shaped metacarpal head that the MCP joint is more lax in extension and more stable in flexion. The distal metacarpals are subject to flexion and adduction forces from both the extrinsic flexor muscles and the interosseous muscles in the hand.[153]

The thumb metacarpal is shorter and stouter than the others and is positioned on the trapezium in palmar abduction and pronation to allow for its prehensile functioning. The thumb CMC joint is unique in functioning as nature's universal joint. Some authors have described it as a reciprocally biconcave saddle joint,[119, 166, 220] whereas others have described it as a saddle for a "scoliotic horse."[155] The natural relationship of these reciprocal convex and concave arcs oriented close to 90° apart provides a path for the thumb to abduct, pronate, and flex during its movements in opposition to the digits. Likewise, this complex articulation with its surrounding capsular ligaments provides stability to the powerful thenar and extrinsic muscles that insert onto the thumb (Fig. 38–5).

The thumb MCP articulation is more concentric than the adjacent digital MCP joints and affords nearly equal stability throughout its arc of flexion and extension. The metacarpal head is bicondylar, with the radial condyle slightly larger. This structural difference provides the thumb proximal phalanx with a modest degree of pronation at the final point of pinch.

In distinct contrast to the interconnected metacarpals, the phalanges are isolated skeletal units. The skeletal length of the three phalangeal segments closely follows the ratio of 11.618 (the golden mean) of the Fibonacci series discovered by Leonardo de Pisa (1202 AD).[187] In a distal-to-proximal direction, the length of each phalanx is the sum of the length of the more distal two segments. Accordingly, proximal phalangeal length closely equals the sum of the middle and distal phalanges, with the proximal interphalangeal (PIP) joint axis located exactly at the mathematic center of the digit, thus making it truly the nucleus of digital anatomy and function.[189] This normal skeletal relationship and alignment will keep the intrinsic

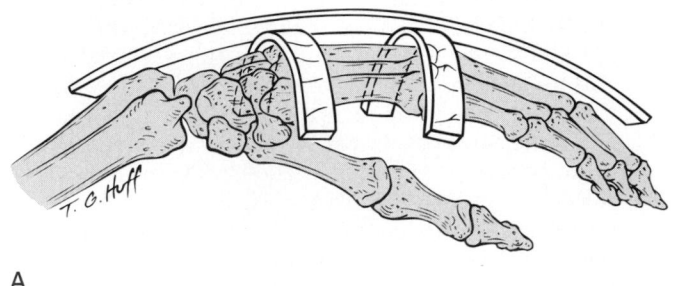

A

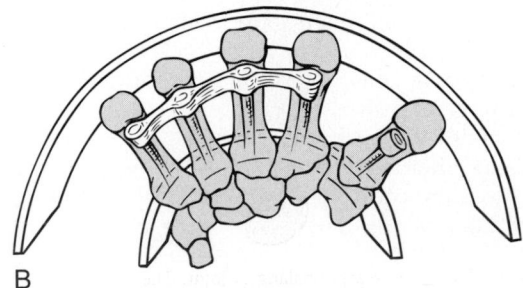

B

**FIGURE 38–2.** The longitudinal (*A*) and transverse (*B*) arches of the hand pass through the metacarpals. The metacarpals are interconnected at their bases by a complex network of ligaments and distally by the deep transverse metacarpal ligament.

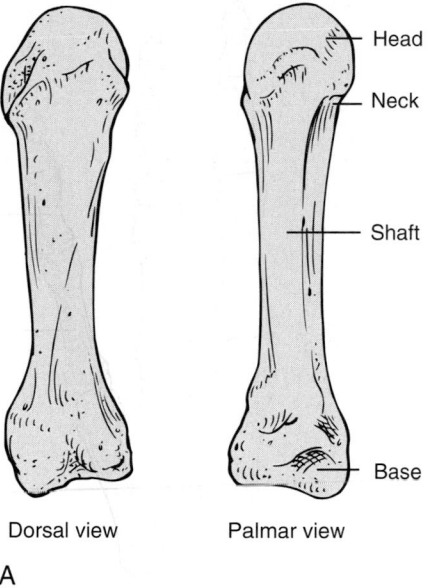

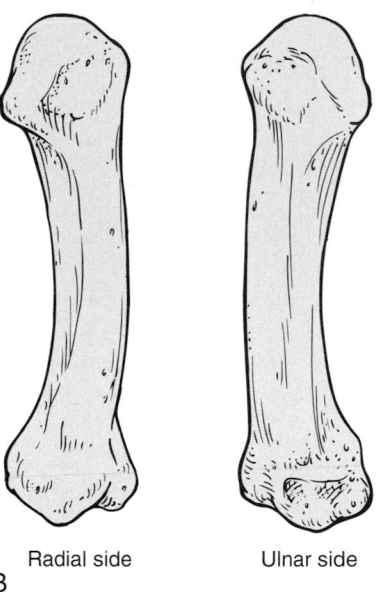

**FIGURE 38–3.** *A, B,* Surgical anatomy of the metacarpal.

and extrinsic muscle-tendon units in equilibrium so that only a minimal amount of force is required to move the digit and maintain a specific locus in space. Alterations in length, rotation, or angular alignment can upset this fine balance and accentuate the dysfunction.

The proximal and middle phalanges can be structurally divided into the base, shaft, neck, and head (condyles) (Fig. 38–6), whereas the distal phalanx differs in having a base, shaft, and tuft. The dorsal surface of the proximal and middle phalanges is straight, and the palmar surface is concave. In contrast to the metacarpal, the phalangeal cortex is thicker dorsally.[278] In normal functional use, the powerful flexor forces suggest that the dorsal side is mechanically subjected to tensile stress. In certain phalangeal fractures, however, this concept may not be applicable

inasmuch as deformities caused by muscle imbalance may subject the dorsum to compressive forces.[127, 269]

Also in contrast to the metacarpals, the digital skeleton is enveloped by the gliding surfaces of the overlying intrinsic and extrinsic tendons. Because of the lack of overlying muscle and minimal subcutaneous fat, the propensity for tendon dysfunction is enhanced after skeletal trauma, as well as the complexity of securely stabilizing the phalangeal skeleton with internal fixation (Fig. 38–7).

The small interphalangeal (IP) articulations are complex both in their form and in their function and are discussed in detail in the sections on PIP joint fractures and dislocations.

## GENERAL PRINCIPLES

Regardless of how innocent a hand fracture may appear, the physician should take care to evaluate pertinent historical factors and then perform a complete physical and radiologic examination.

Before delving into the historical details of the specific hand injury, it is important to determine the occupation and hand dominance of the injured individual. In further establishing the history, details of the mechanism of injury are critical to understanding the patterns of skeletal and soft tissue damage. If machinery has been involved, some details can be of importance in determining the extent of the injury. Such details may include the size of the punches in a punch press, the distance between rollers in a metalworking machine, and so forth.

The patient should be questioned regarding the initial deformities, such as a dislocation that may have already been reduced, open wounds, excessive bleeding, altered circulation to the digit or hand, and symptoms of sensory or motor disturbance.

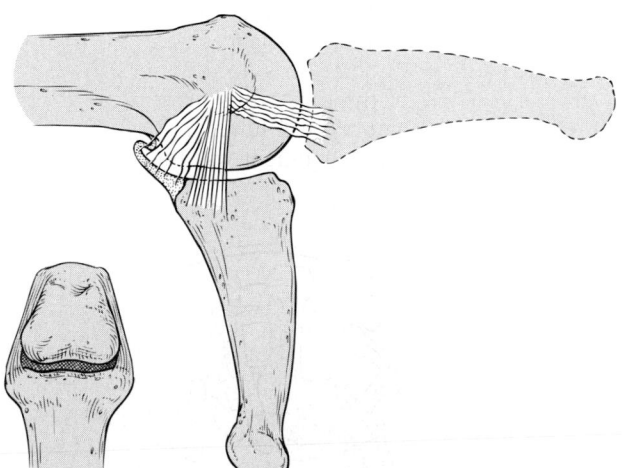

**FIGURE 38–4.** Metacarpophalangeal joint. The metacarpal head is wider on its volar projection and has a curve that increases in diameter in a dorsal-to-palmar direction. Both explain why the collateral ligament is lax in extension and taut in flexion.

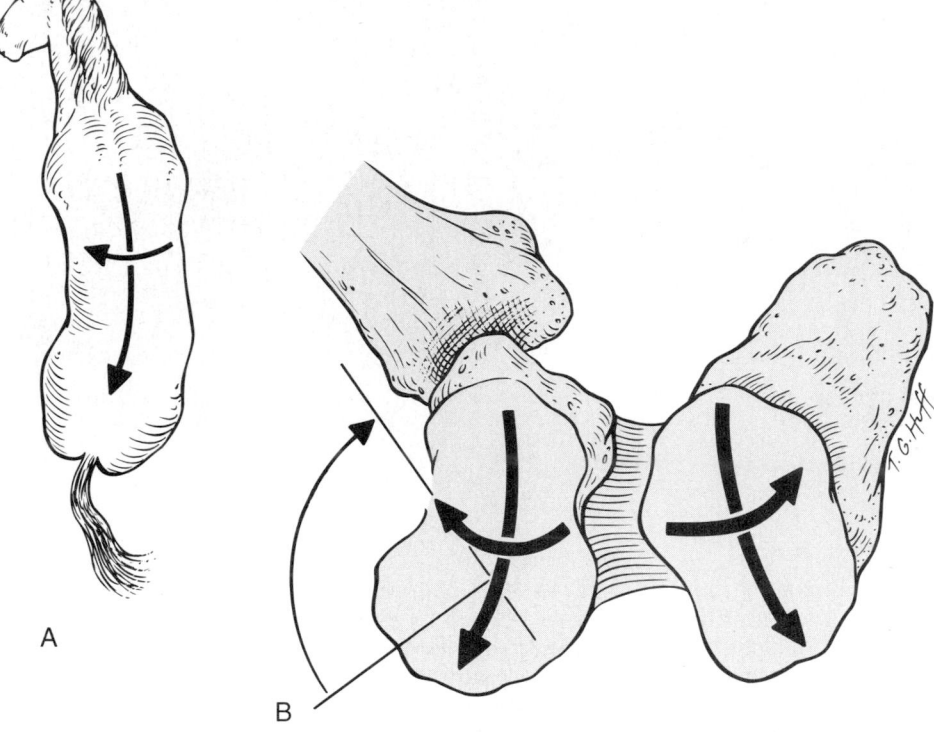

**Figure 38–5.** The thumb metacarpal and its complex "universal joint" articulation with the trapezium (*B*). Some have considered this articulation to be a saddle, whereas others have described it as a saddle for a "scoliotic horse" (*A*).

General questions include any important associated medical illnesses, allergy history, smoking history, and tetanus vaccination status. If the injury occurred in the workplace, appropriate clarification is needed early in the course of treatment.

In patients with any hand fracture or more complex hand trauma, the entire limb must be inspected for more proximal injury. Clothing should be removed to permit both visual and manual inspection of the proximal articulations and skeleton of the upper limb. Any potentially constricting clothing and jewelry, including rings, must be removed.

When evaluating fractures of the metacarpals and phalanges, the examiner must determine the alignment of the digits, both on initial evaluation and, if required, after fracture reduction. Alignment is determined clinically by viewing the relationship of the fingernails with the digits in full extension. The nails should be almost parallel, although in many individuals the distal phalanges of the index and little fingers will angle toward the long finger. Importantly, skeletal alignment must also be assessed with the digits fully flexed. In this position, the fingertips should all point toward the scaphoid tuberosity (Fig. 38–8). The contralateral hand serves as an excellent control for determining angulation and rotation.

Both closed and open skeletal trauma in the hand may have associated trauma to nerves, blood vessels, or tendons. Sensibility is documented by response not only to

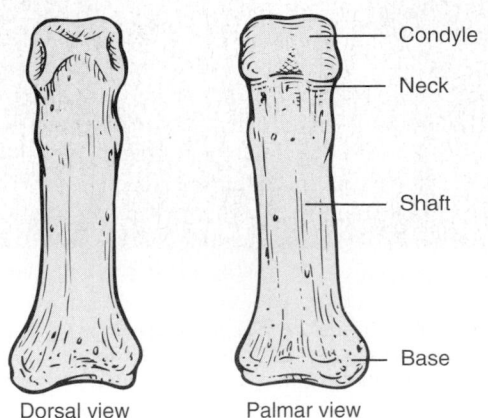

Dorsal view          Palmar view

**Figure 38–6.** Surgical anatomy of the proximal phalanx.

- Condyle
- Neck
- Shaft
- Base

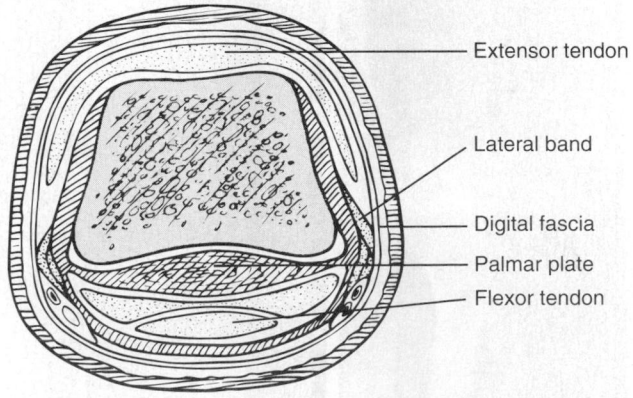

- Extensor tendon
- Lateral band
- Digital fascia
- Palmar plate
- Flexor tendon

**Figure 38–7.** The inherent relationship of the gliding structures to the phalangeal skeleton is seen in this cross-sectional representation of a digit at the proximal phalangeal joint.

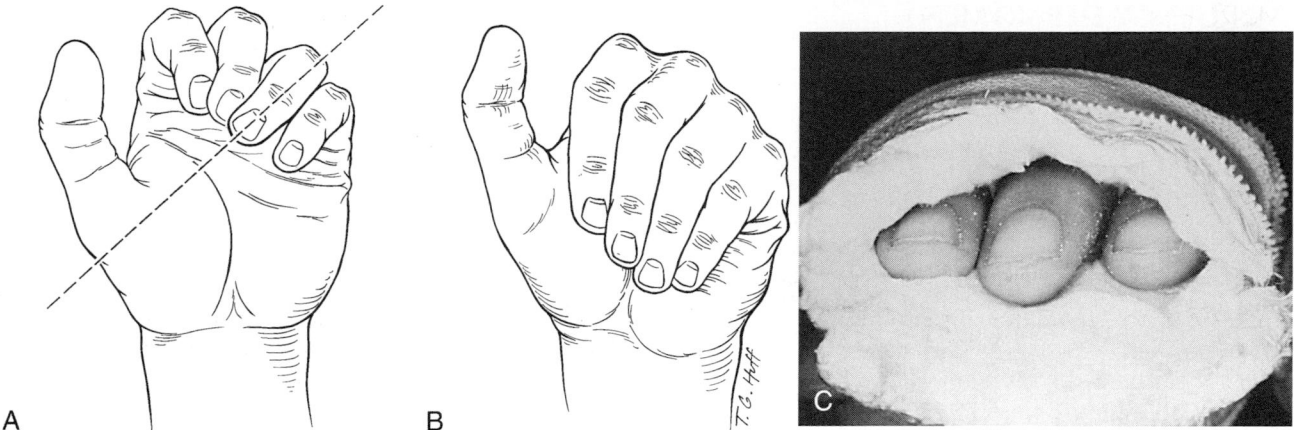

**FIGURE 38–8.** *A,* To determine rotational and angular alignment of the hand skeleton, the nails should be parallel with the digits in extension. *B,* In flexion, the digits should all point to the scaphoid tuberosity. *C,* This 22-year-old man sustained a short oblique fracture of the proximal phalanx of his long finger. Malrotation is seen with the digits in extension.

light touch and pinprick but also to two-point discrimination. Circulation can be determined by visual inspection and documented by timed capillary refill by comparing the capillary refill of the injured digit tested along its paronychial ridge with that of an adjacent digit or a corresponding digit on the other hand.

In the situation of open wounds, minimal inspection is generally warranted. It is preferable to examine the digit distal to the zone of injury to determine the integrity of the vascular, nerve, and tendinous structures. Obvious bleeders should not be clamped in the emergency department to avoid the possibility of irreversible damage to small digital arteries. Bleeding is easily controlled with direct pressure on the open wound.

The integrity of the extensor and flexor tendons to the digits is individually determined, and the physician should palpate along ligament insertions to ensure their integrity.

The tubular skeleton of the hand requires three radiographic views—AP, lateral, and oblique—to accurately assess the position and integrity of these small skeletal units and their articulations (Fig. 38–9). The phalanges must be seen in a true lateral projection, and the injured digit should be isolated to avoid superimposition of the skeletal units of the adjacent digits. A number of specialized radiographic projections have been developed to aid in visualizing specific areas of the skeleton. These projections are discussed in specific fracture sections.

In many cases, anesthesia is required to permit painless assessment of alignment and also to permit closed reduction, if indicated.

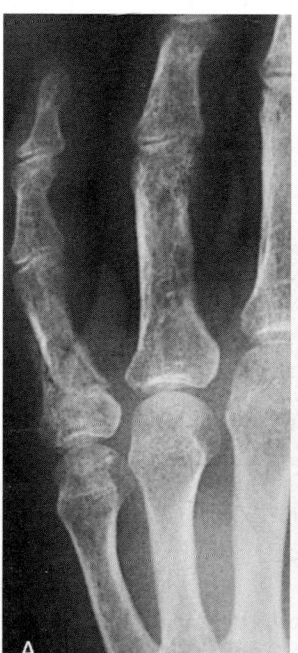
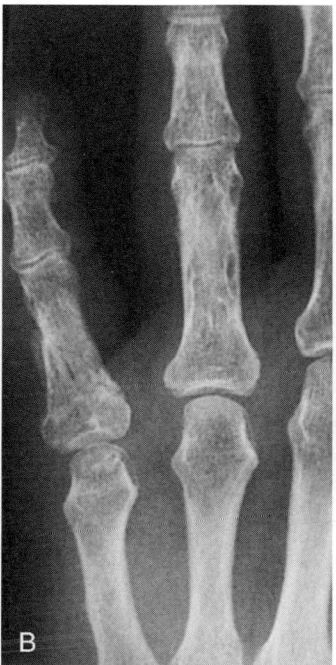
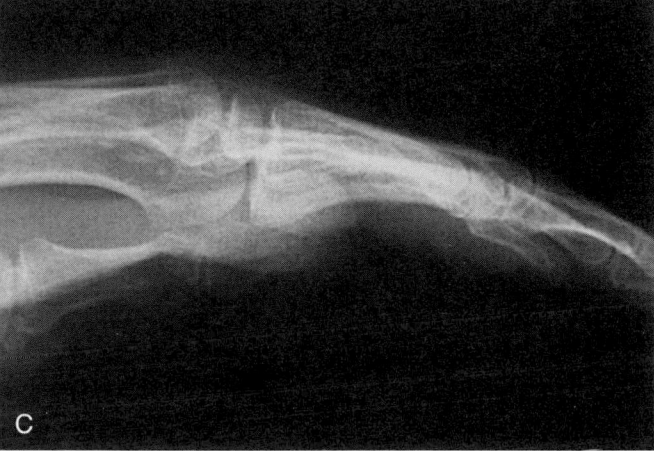

**FIGURE 38–9.** *A–C,* The tubular skeleton in the hand requires three radiographic projections to determine the alignment and joint relationships. This phalangeal fracture was best seen in the oblique projection *(A).*

## EMERGENCY DEPARTMENT ANESTHESIA

For injuries distal to the MCP joint, adequate anesthesia can be obtained with a common digital nerve block of the metacarpal head (Fig. 38–10D). A 25-gauge needle is used to instill 2 to 4 mL of 1% to 2% lidocaine (Xylocaine) or 0.25% to 0.5% bupivacaine (Marcaine), *without epinephrine*. The needle is inserted dorsally between the metacarpal heads until it just tents the palmar skin up. The syringe

should be aspirated to ensure that the injection is not intra-arterial and the needle withdrawn slowly while injecting the anesthetic. Each of the two common digital nerves is blocked separately, and the dorsal skin between puncture sites is infiltrated as well.

Wrist block anesthesia is a little more difficult to perform; however, it offers several advantages for hand and digital injuries. This form of anesthesia can effectively provide a complete sensory block without paralysis of the extrinsic flexor and extensor muscles. Such blocks are necessary to provide voluntary extension and flexion to

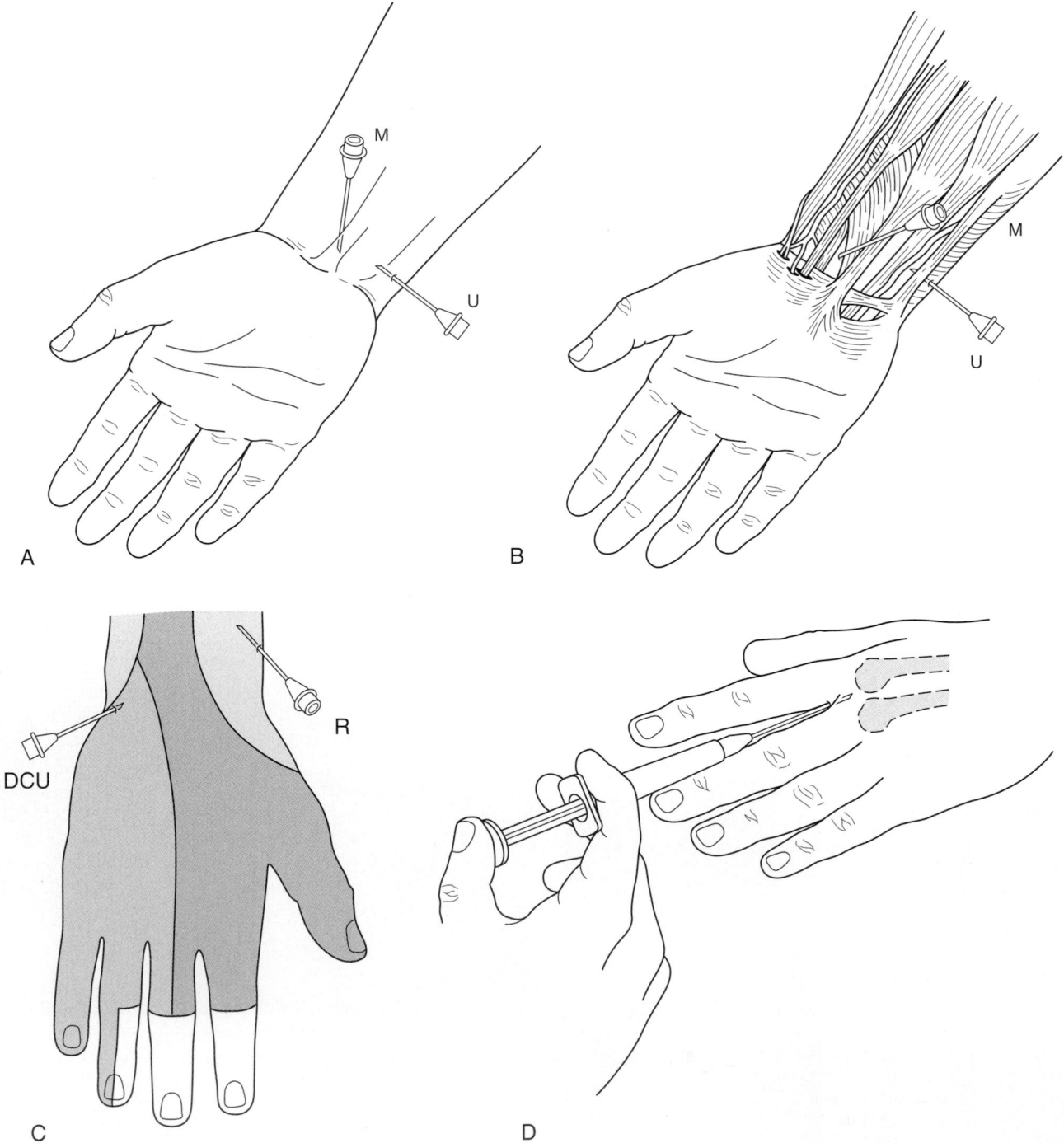

**FIGURE 38–10.** Four types of nerve block at the wrist. *A, B,* Sites of injection to block the median (M) and ulnar (U) nerves at the wrist. *C,* Sites of injection to block the dorsal cutaneous ulnar nerve (DCU) and radial sensory nerve (R) at the wrist. *D,* The common digital nerves can be blocked with an injection through the dorsal webspace.

allow the examiner to determine deformity and assess fracture stability.

To perform a wrist block, the nerves to be anesthetized include the median, ulnar, dorsal sensory ulnar, and superficial radial, either selectively or completely, depending on the bone fractured. A quantity of 5 to 8 mL of either mepivacaine (Carbocaine) or 1% lidocaine is mixed with 0.5% bupivacaine, both without epinephrine. A 5- to 8-inch 25-gauge needle is used. The median nerve is blocked 1.5 cm proximal to the carpal canal, with the injection just radial to and beneath the antebrachial fascia and palmaris longus tendon. This block, when used in conjunction with a superficial radial nerve block, is effective for fractures involving the thumb and the index and long fingers and for some fractures involving the ring finger. The superficial branch of the radial nerve is blocked 3 fingerbreadths above the radial styloid; a transverse wheal will be raised subcutaneously over the radial side of the distal part of the forearm.

The ulnar nerve can be anesthetized with a transverse injection under the flexor carpi ulnaris tendon proximal to the wrist crease. Aspiration is necessary before injection because the ulnar artery runs adjacent to the nerve. To block the dorsal sensory branch of the ulnar nerve, the needle is passed subcutaneously and directed dorsally toward the base of the fifth metacarpal. Ulnar nerve blocks are used for fractures of the little finger ray and in conjunction with median and radial sensory blocks for fractures of the ring finger ray (see Fig. 38–10A to C).

## TREATMENT OF METACARPAL AND PHALANGEAL FRACTURES: CONCEPTS AND GOALS

Hand fractures can be complicated by deformity from no treatment, stiffness from overtreatment, and both deformity and stiffness from poor treatment (Alfred Swanson[299]).

---

**TABLE 38–2**

Goals of Treatment: Fractures of the Hand

Restoration of articular congruity
Reduction of malrotation and angulation
Maintenance of reduction with minimal surgical intervention
Surgically acceptable wound
Rapid mobilization

---

The goal of treatment of fractures of the metacarpals and phalanges includes restoration or preservation of function (Table 38–2). Inherent in this goal is repositioning of a fractured or dislocated bone to a position that will be consistent with function. Whenever possible, articular congruity should be restored. To accomplish this objective, the physician must select a method that will offer the least soft tissue damage and accelerate mobilization of the injured part as soon as fracture stability permits. The choice of method should be determined on the basis of information gained from clinical and radiologic assessment of the fracture.[76, 307]

The vast majority of fractures involving the tubular skeleton in the hand can be effectively treated by an organized, careful, nonoperative approach.[214] Determination of an individual fracture's stability or "personality" is of paramount importance in closed hand fractures inasmuch as it has become increasingly evident that many stable, aligned phalangeal and metacarpal fractures require only limited immobilization and fare better with early return to mobility.[10, 11, 144] Studies by Borgeskov[25] (485 fractures), Wright[326] (809 fractures), and Pun and co-workers[240] (284 fractures) documented the improved results with limited (1 to 2 weeks) immobilization of stable metacarpal and phalangeal fractures of the hand.

A number of factors that can be determined from the initial examination and radiographs will help identify the personality of the fracture. A functional classification should take into account fracture location, pattern, associated soft tissue injury, deformity, and intrinsic stability (Table 38–3). Other pertinent factors include the patient's age, medical condition, socioeconomic status, and motivation.

Hand splintage should always be in the position of immobilization rather than rest.[145, 164] Immobilization involves splinting the wrist in 20° of extension, the MCP joints in 60° to 70° of flexion, and the IP joints in extension. This "safe" position will prevent shortening of the collateral ligaments of both the MCP and the IP joints during the period of immobilization. Improper immobilization of the hand can result in MCP joint extension and IP joint flexion contractures. The thumb metacarpal must be kept in palmar abduction to maintain a functional webspace and prevent an adduction contracture (Fig. 38–11).

In general, stable fractures include closed impacted shaft fractures, fractures with little or no displacement, most distal phalangeal fractures, many isolated metacarpal shaft fractures, and well-aligned fractures that remain in position through a full arc of motion (Table 38–4). Pun and co-workers' radiographic criteria of acceptable align-

---

**TABLE 38–3**

Functional Fracture Parameters: Phalangeal and Metacarpal Fracture Characteristics

| Location | Pattern | Skeleton | Deformity | Soft Tissue | Associated Injury | Reaction to Motion |
|---|---|---|---|---|---|---|
| Base | Transverse | Simple | Angulation | Closed | Skin | Stable |
| Shaft | Oblique | Impacted | Dorsal | Open | Tendon | Unstable |
| Neck | Spiral | Comminuted | Palmar | — | Ligament | — |
| Head (condyle) | Avulsion | Bone loss | Rotation | — | Nerve | — |
| Epiphysis | — | — | Shortening | — | Blood vessel | — |

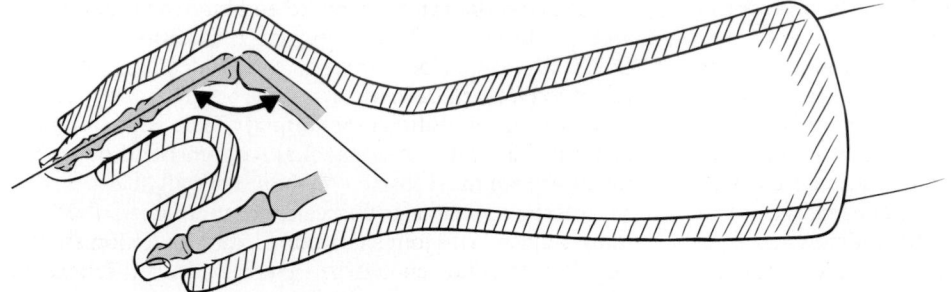

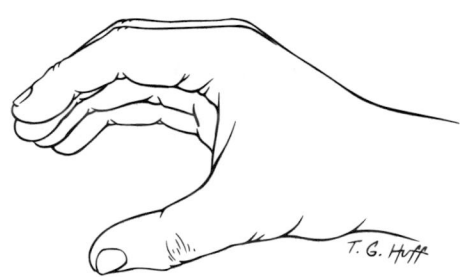

**FIGURE 38–11.** The position of immobilization of the hand involves splinting the wrist in 20° of extension, the metacarpophalangeal joints in 60° to 70° of flexion, and the interphalangeal joints in full extension.

---

| **TABLE 38–4** |
| --- |

**Stable Metacarpal and Phalangeal Fractures**

Impacted fractures
Fractures with little or no displacement
Many isolated metacarpal shaft fractures
Distal phalanx fractures
Fractures without displacement through the arc of digital motion

---

ment of phalangeal and metacarpal fractures include the following[240]:

10° angulation in both the sagittal and coronal planes, except in the metaphysis, where 20° angulation in the sagittal plane is accepted
Up to 45° angulation in the sagittal plane in the neck of the fifth metacarpal
50% overlap at the fracture site
No rotational deformity

---

| **TABLE 38–5** |
| --- |

**Unstable Metacarpal and Phalangeal Fractures**

Multifragmentary (comminuted) fractures
Severely displaced fractures
Short oblique and spiral malrotated fractures
Multiple metacarpal fractures
Subcondylar proximal phalanx fractures
Palmar base middle phalanx fractures
Fractures with associated extensive soft tissue injury
Some fracture-dislocations
Displaced articular fractures
    Bennett's and reverse Bennett's fractures
    Rolando's fracture
    Unicondylar and bicondylar fractures
Complete or incomplete amputations (complex injuries)

---

Similarly, certain fracture patterns tend to be unstable even when anatomically restored by closed manipulation (Table 38–5). These fractures generally require some form of stabilization, but their outcome will often be determined as much by the violence of the original injury, associated soft tissue damage, and contamination as by the method of skeletal reconstruction.[12, 136, 144, 240, 295]

Thus, to achieve the goal of functional restoration, the surgeon must take into account a number of factors related to the fracture and associated injuries and develop a logical treatment approach. The surgeon can choose from a number of treatment methods, including the following[76]:

1. Early motion with or without limited support
2. Closed reduction followed by external support
3. Closed reduction and percutaneous pins
4. Closed reduction and traction or external fixation
5. Open reduction and internal or external fixation

The treatment must be tailored to the demands of the specific personality of the fracture, the surgeon's experience, and the patient's motivation.

## FRACTURE IMMOBILIZATION TECHNIQUES

The fingers are certainly very precious for everybody, but for certain individuals (e.g., musicians, artists) the loss of a finger is perhaps more consequential than the loss of a thigh. In my present opinion, the osteosynthesis of phalangeal fractures must be performed by one of the following techniques: cerclage in the long oblique fractures and transarticular nailing for transverse fractures (Albin Lambotte[172]).

Since the early 1970s, increasingly sophisticated advances have been made in operative techniques for the skeleton of the hand.[6, 15, 33, 73, 142, 207] However, no consensus has been reached regarding the appropriate method of skeletal stabilization for even the simplest of fractures. The development of stable fixation with screws and plates has expanded the application of internal fixation but has by no means replaced plaster splints, casts, or Kirschner wires (K-wires). Surgeons dealing with hand trauma should be well versed in many of these methods to more effectively tailor the treatment to the specific needs of the fracture.[169]

## Phalangeal Fractures: Functional Casting or Extension Block Splintage

Functional casting, or extension block splintage, popularized by Burkhalter and Reyes, takes advantage of the stabilizing forces of the flexor and intrinsic muscles on the phalanges with the MCP joint held in 90° of flexion.[42, 248] It is particularly applicable with closed, palmarly angulated transverse or short oblique phalangeal shaft fractures or impacted base phalangeal fractures that prove stable on reduction. Anatomic reduction and mobilization of the digits neutralize the imbalance of the flexors and extensors, and the intact dorsal extensor mechanism functions as a "tension band" to the palmar cortex.[36, 62] Digital rotation and angulation are largely controlled by having the four digits move together. An Orthoplast custom-fabricated splint will serve the same purpose as a cast or an extension block device. Use of a removable splint requires a compliant patient, however.

### TECHNIQUE

After a metacarpal or wrist block, the fracture is reduced by using a combination of longitudinal traction, hyperextension, and finally, flexion. Angulation and rotation are checked in flexion, and tape is applied as a temporary holding method. The tape is placed longitudinally down the digit, starting at the middle metacarpal level and continuing along the finger to the tip, and then anchored proximally at the wrist. It can be reinforced at the wrist to improve its holding power. This tape keeps the digit flexed 90° at the MCP joint, which is critical for maintaining reduction of this fracture. With the tape in position, the patient has a check radiograph performed. After any required adjustments, a short arm plaster cast is applied with the wrist held in 30° of extension, the MCP joints held in 90° of flexion, and the PIP joints left free. Alternatively, a hand therapist can custom-fabricate a thermoplastic extension block splint with the tape in position to maintain the reduction. The splint holds the hand and digits in exactly the same position as the cast. Once the cast or splint has been applied, the tape is carefully removed. Adjacent finger strapping completes the program and allows some rotational control of the digit. Active digital motion within this fabricated safe arc of movement is encouraged from the onset (Fig. 38–12).

The patient should be monitored clinically and radiographically on a weekly basis for 3 weeks, at which time the cast or splint can be removed and buddy straps applied for an additional 2 to 3 weeks (Fig. 38–13). Lateral tomography may be required to ensure maintenance of reduction during functional casting because lateral radiographs are often difficult to interpret (Table 38–6). Careful attention is paid to rotational alignment during the follow-up visits.

This technique requires careful attention to detail to maintain the MCP joints in flexion; full PIP motion should be allowed and encouraged and adequate follow-up examinations arranged.

If the fracture cannot be held adequately by this closed means, one should move to one of the following methods of additional fixation.

## Kirschner Wires

Pin fixation of a hand fracture was first reported in the American literature by Tennant in 1924.[301] He used a steel phonograph needle for fixation of a metacarpal fracture. Remarkably, more than a half century later, wire fixation is still considered by many to be the gold standard against which other methods of skeletal fixation must be compared.[13, 110, 110, 293] However, a number of real and potential problems exist with the use of K-wires in the hand. These implants are subject to loosening and migration and may require additional plaster immobilization.[21, 196, 199, 310] When the wires are applied in a crossing manner, they can serve to distract the fracture site and delay union. In a study of 23 nonunions of the tubular bones of the hand, the most common cause was improper or ineffective K-wire fixation.[150] Crossed K-wires, commonly inserted openly with retrograde pinning,[83] can distract the fracture. When this technique is used, the K-wires should cross either proximal or distal to the fracture and gain firm anchorage in the proximal and distal metaphysis[266] (Fig. 38–14).

Namba and colleagues identified mechanical factors that influence the holding power of these wires.[219] They found that trocar tips have better penetrating ability and holding power than a diamond tip or a wire cut by hand in the operating room (Fig. 38–15). They also noted improved holding power when the wires were inserted while drilling at lower speeds.

Despite its mechanical and technical shortcomings, a K-wire offers the distinct advantage of percutaneous application, thus avoiding surgical exposure and its attendant soft tissue trauma.[13, 110, 148] In the phalanges, this technique has its widest application in closed unstable diaphyseal, base, and neck fractures. In metacarpal fractures, it can be used effectively for isolated shaft, neck, or base fractures.

K-wires can be inserted in a variety of ways, depending on the configuration of the fracture and surgeon preference. The crossed technique is the most commonly used. Alternatives include two or three parallel wires across the fracture site; longitudinal intramedullary wires, either single or stacked; transarticular intramedullary wires; or a combination of K-wire and interosseous wiring. Transverse and short oblique fractures are well treated with intramedullary methods, long oblique and spiral fractures with the

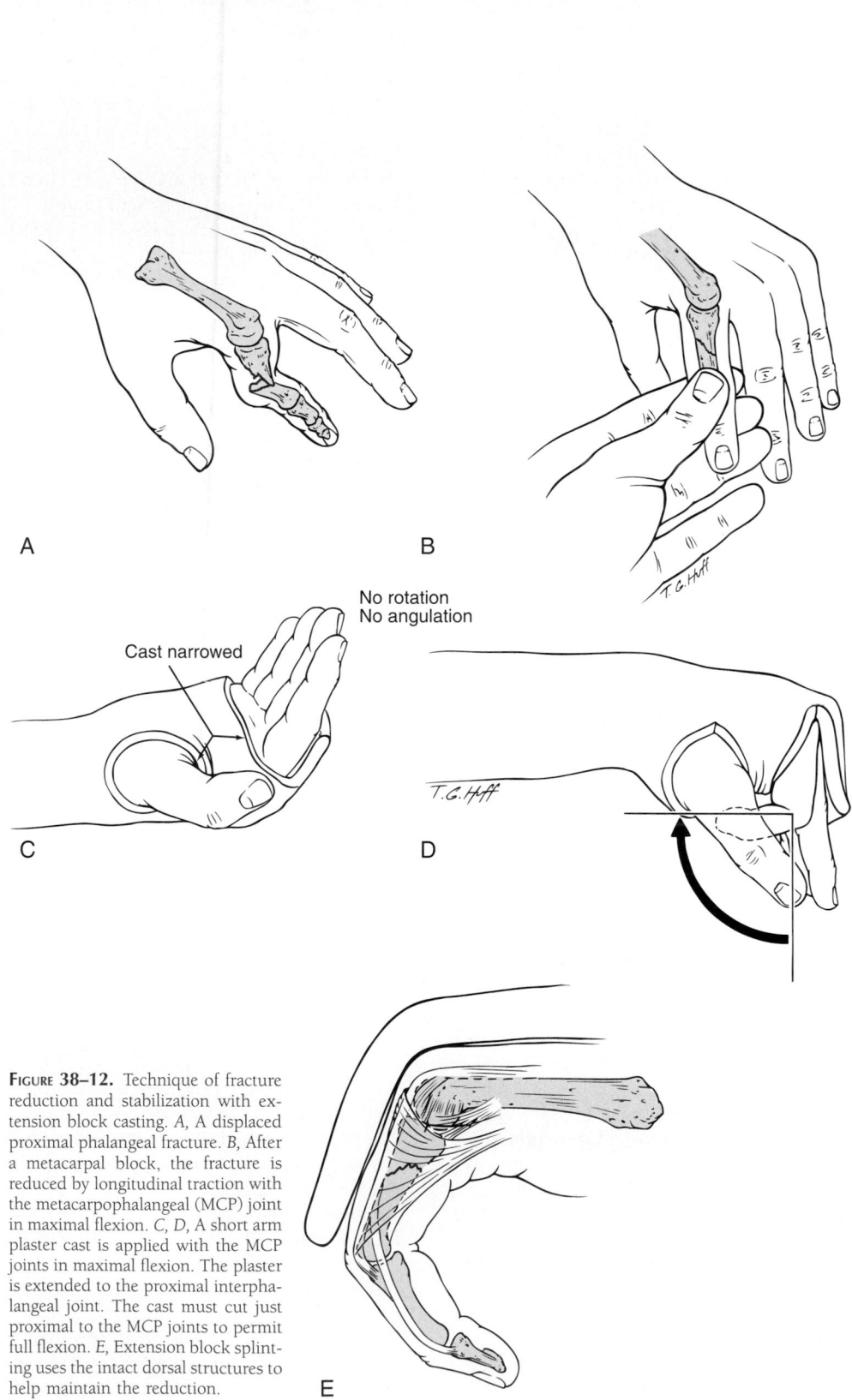

A

B

No rotation
No angulation

Cast narrowed

C                                    D

**FIGURE 38–12.** Technique of fracture reduction and stabilization with extension block casting. *A*, A displaced proximal phalangeal fracture. *B*, After a metacarpal block, the fracture is reduced by longitudinal traction with the metacarpophalangeal (MCP) joint in maximal flexion. *C, D*, A short arm plaster cast is applied with the MCP joints in maximal flexion. The plaster is extended to the proximal interphalangeal joint. The cast must cut just proximal to the MCP joints to permit full flexion. *E*, Extension block splinting uses the intact dorsal structures to help maintain the reduction.

E

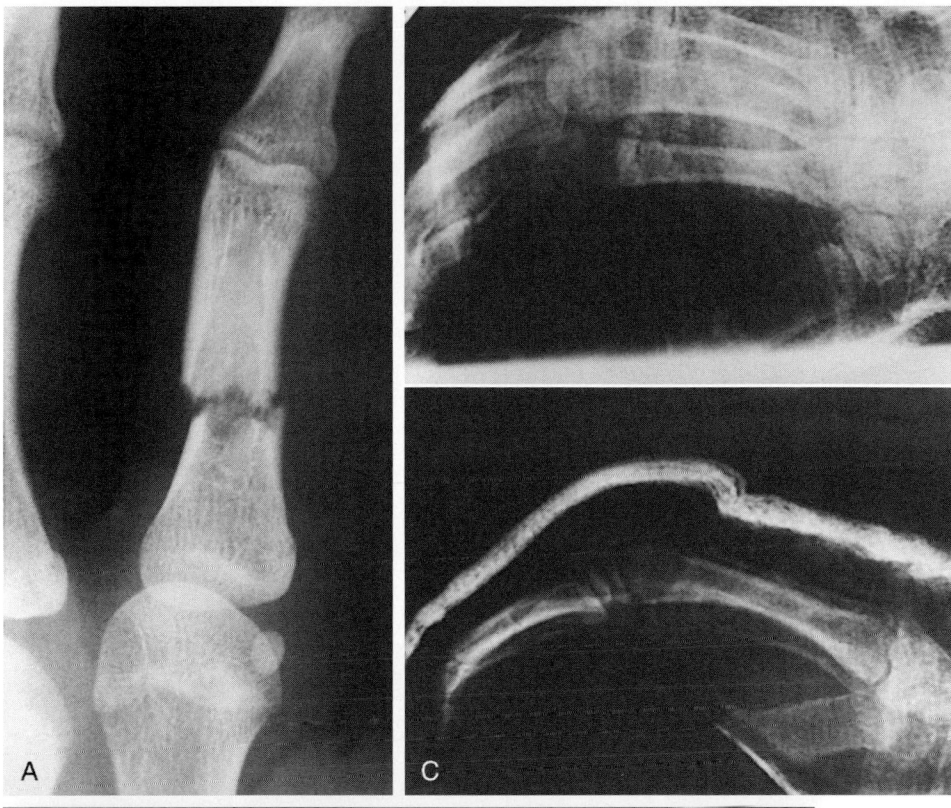

FIGURE 38–13. A, B, A 19-year-old woman sustained a closed displaced proximal phalangeal fracture of the midshaft of her dominant index finger. Closed reduction and extension block casting were performed. C, Fracture union was clinically apparent in 4 weeks and full mobility in 6 weeks.

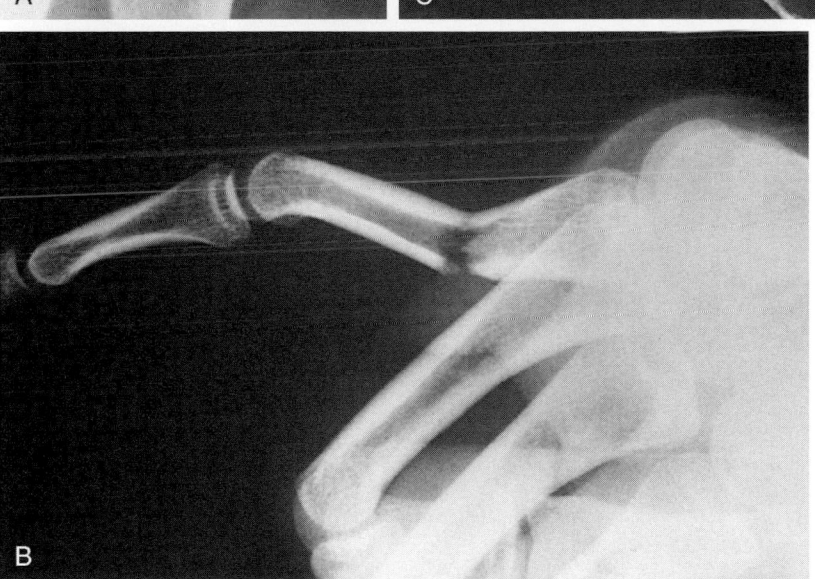

| TABLE 38–6 |
|---|
| Extension Block Casting |

**INDICATIONS**

Closed, dorsally angulated transverse and short oblique shaft fractures and impacted base proximal phalangeal fractures

**ADVANTAGES**

Nonoperative
No instrumentation
Technically simple
Encourages functional motion

**DISADVANTAGES**

Application limited to certain fracture types
Control radiographs difficult to assess

multiple K-wire method, and base fractures with the transarticular intramedullary technique (Fig. 38–16).

## TECHNIQUE

In the proximal phalanges, the technique of closed reduction and percutaneous K-wire fixation involves reduction under wrist block anesthesia and longitudinal traction on the middle phalanx while flexing the MCP joint to 80° and the PIP joint to 45°. For transverse fractures, a 0.035- or 0.045-inch K-wire is passed down the metacarpal head just eccentric to the extensor tendon to avoid tendon adhesion and then directed across the flexed MCP joint down the shaft of the proximal phalanx to the subchondral bone in the head of the phalanx. Some neck

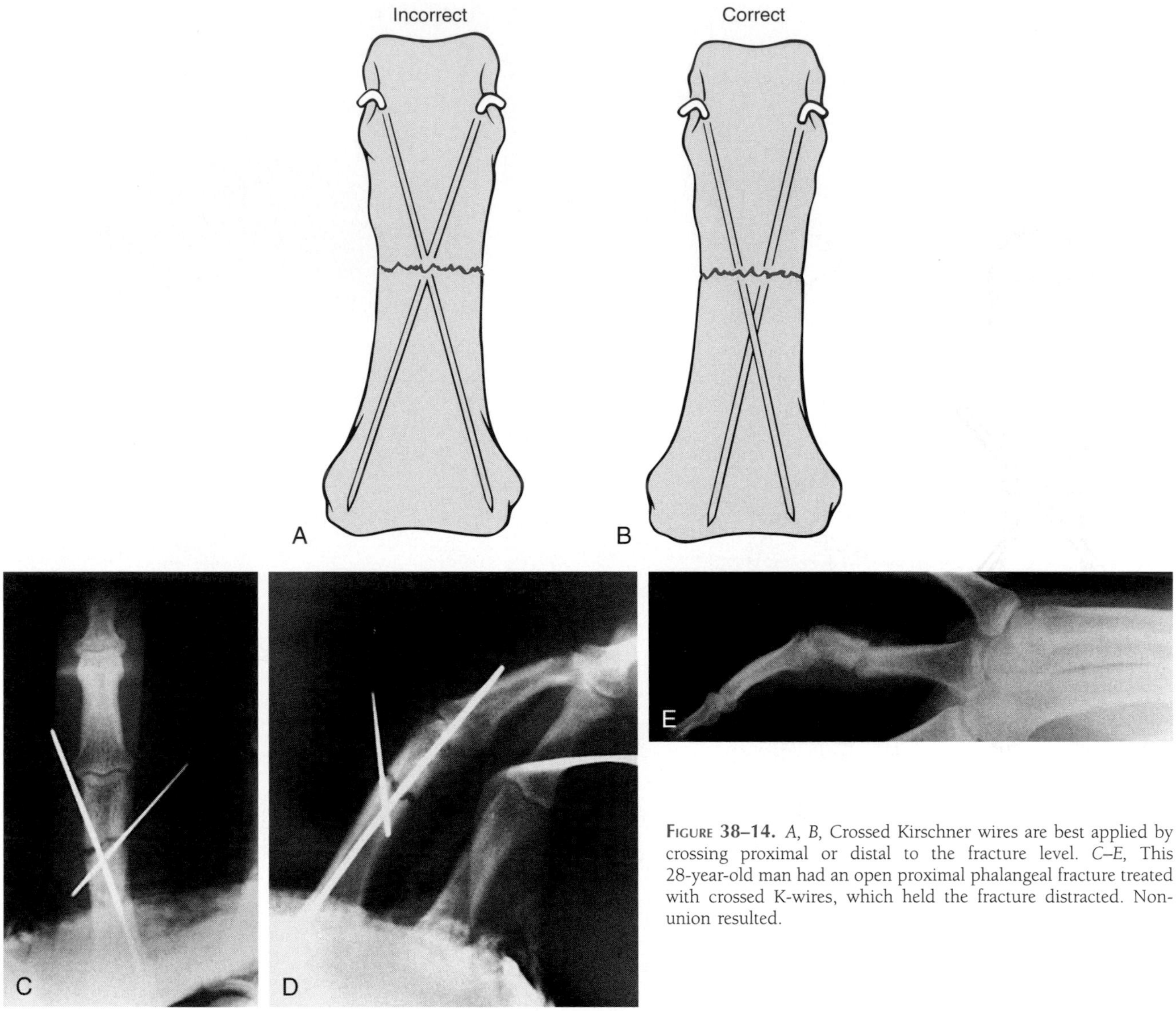

Incorrect

Correct

A

B

C

D

E

**Figure 38–14.** *A, B,* Crossed Kirschner wires are best applied by crossing proximal or distal to the fracture level. *C–E,* This 28-year-old man had an open proximal phalangeal fracture treated with crossed K-wires, which held the fracture distracted. Non-union resulted.

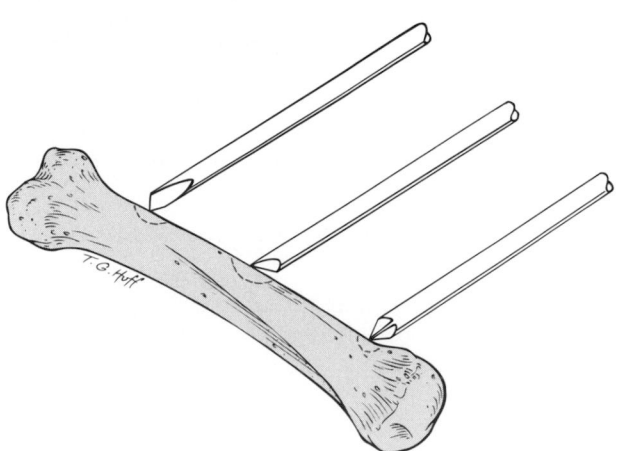

**Figure 38–15.** A trocar-tipped K-wire penetrates the phalangeal cortex more readily than a diamond-tipped wire or a self-cut wire does.

fractures are more unstable and can be treated with two or three 0.028-inch K-wires (Fig. 38–17).

As an alternative, the K-wires can be placed just adjacent to the metacarpal head and sit in the collateral ligament fossa. By hugging the metacarpal head, the wires can be engaged along the lateral borders of the base of the proximal phalanx and passed intramedullary to complete the fixation. This technique avoids transfixion of the joint and will eliminate damage to articular cartilage (Fig. 38–18).

After manipulation, reduction of spiral and oblique fractures is maintained by a towel clamp or pointed reduction clamp to hold the fracture percutaneously. Two or three 0.028-inch K-wires spaced evenly along the fracture's length are directed perpendicular to the long axis of the phalanx and engage both cortices of the phalanx. The wires should be placed as far as possible from each other along the length of the fracture line.

In both pin applications, the pins are left out of the skin and well padded, and a plaster cast is applied with the MCP joint held in flexion. The cast is removed at 3 weeks,

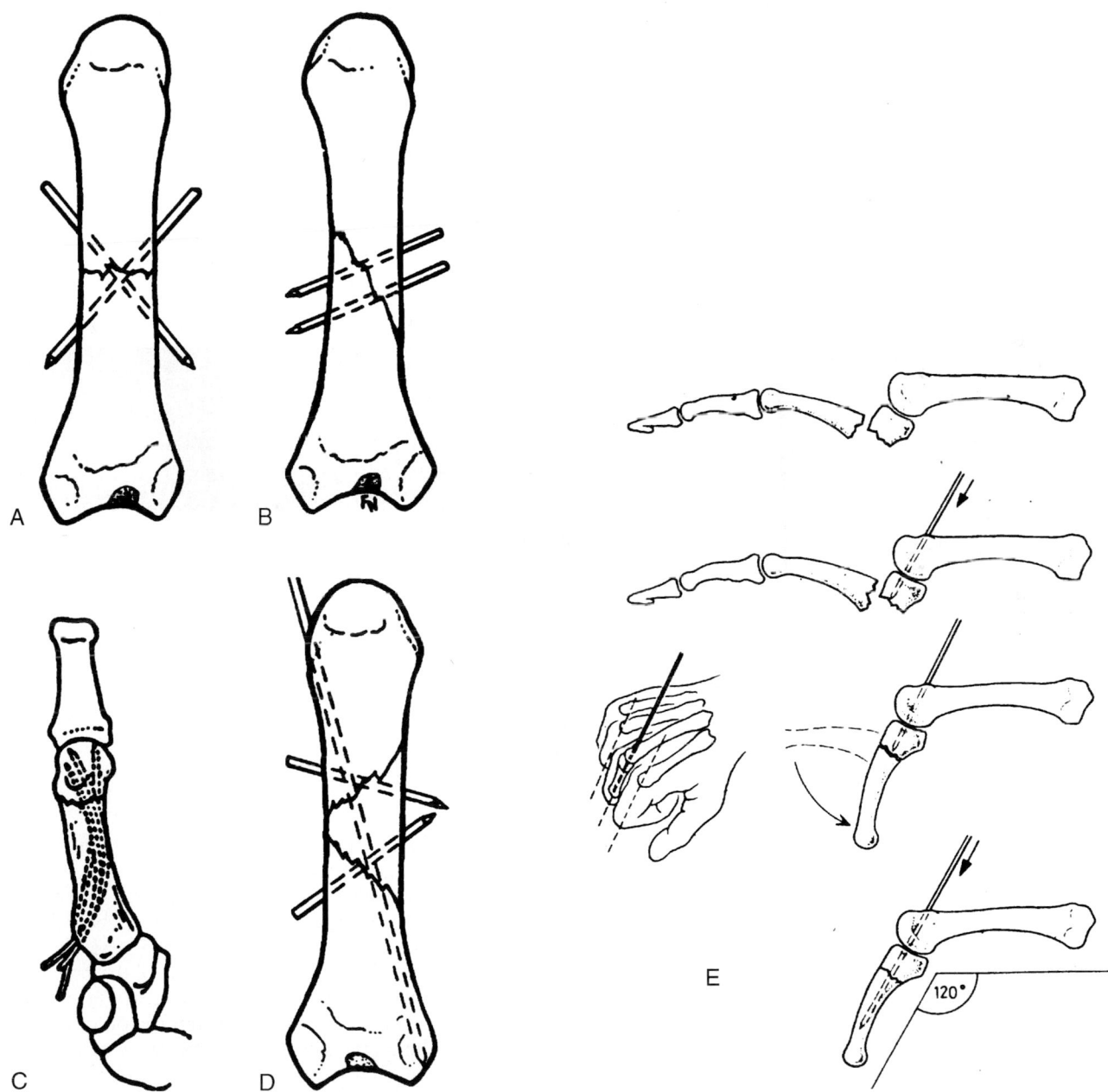

**FIGURE 38–16.** Alternative means of stabilizing with K-wires. *A*, Crossed. *B*, Oblique and parallel. *C*, Intramedullary. *D*, Combined intramedullary and direct. *E*, Transarticular intramedullary pinning.

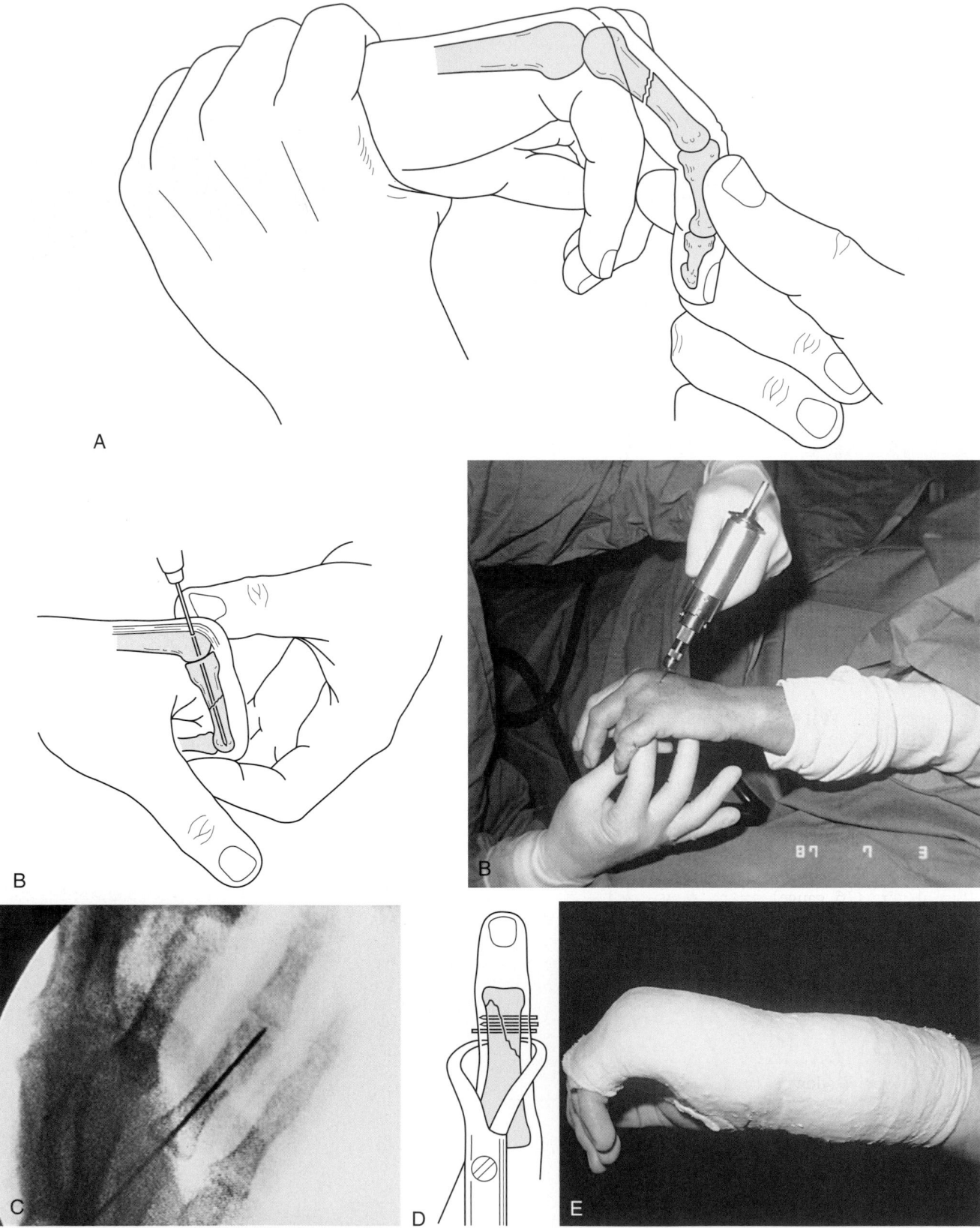

**FIGURE 38–17.** Techniques of closed percutaneous fixation of phalangeal fractures. *A,* The fracture is reduced by longitudinal traction on the middle phalanx with the metacarpophalangeal (MCP) joint flexed 80° and the proximal interphalangeal joint flexed 45°. *B, C,* With transverse fractures, a 0.035- or 0.045-inch K-wire is introduced, under image intensification, into the metacarpal head eccentric to the extensor tendon and is driven down to subchondral bone in the neck. The picture on the image intensifier shows the fracture reduced and held with the longitudinal K-wire. *D,* With oblique fractures, the fracture is reduced with pointed reduction forceps, and two or three 0.028-inch K-wires are passed across the fracture site. *E,* The wires are cut outside the skin and well padded, and a short arm cast is applied with the MCP joint flexed 80°.

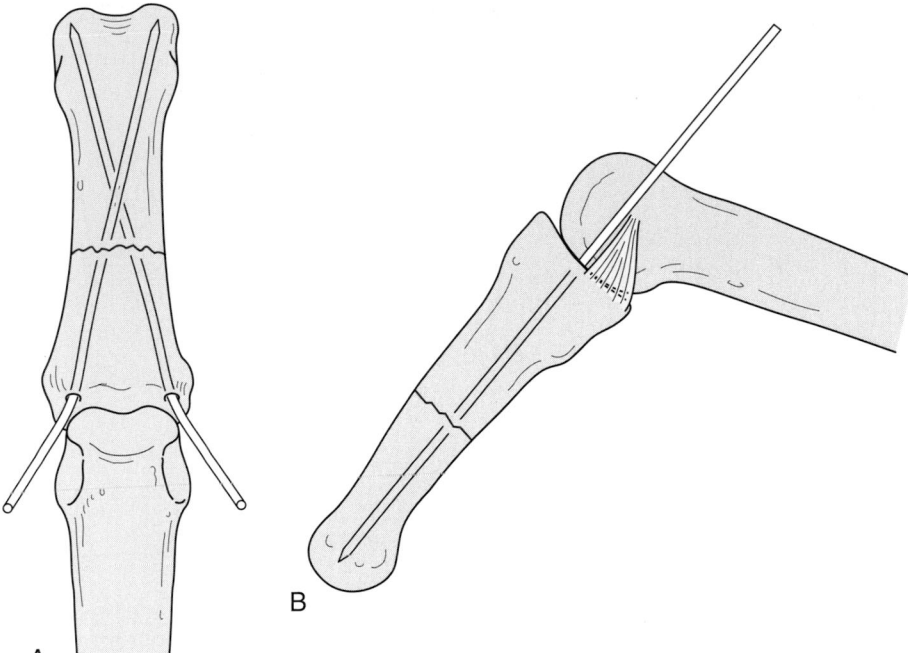

**FIGURE 38–18.** *A, B,* Technique of passing intramedullary K-wires around the metacarpal head to gain access to the base of the proximal phalanx. The wires sit in the recesses medially and laterally for the origin of the collateral ligaments. (*A, B,* Redrawn from Heim, U.; Pfeiffer, K.M. Internal Fixation of Small Fractures, 3rd ed. New York, Springer-Verlag, 1987.)

A

B

and the patient is encouraged to begin digital motion. The longitudinal pins are removed at the time of cast removal, and motion is started. Transversely oriented pins may remain for 1 additional week, with motion begun with the pins in place (Table 38–7).

## Intraosseous Wires

The technique of intraosseous wiring, popularized by Lister,[186] proved effective in certain transverse phalangeal fractures, as well as in avulsion and intra-articular fractures.[106] Its primary application has been in transverse fractures associated with soft tissue injury, replantation, or arthrodesis. The technique involves a small stainless steel loop of wire (26 gauge) passed transversely across the fracture line just dorsal to the midaxis along with an oblique K-wire to neutralize the rotational forces (Fig. 38–19). Although the fixation is stable enough to permit controlled mobilization, the oblique K-wire can cause

---

**TABLE 38–7** . . . . . . . . . . . . . . . . . . . . . . . . . . . .

Kirschner Wire Fixation

---

**INDICATIONS**

Primary: percutaneous fixation of unstable, closed fractures
Secondary: internal fixation of operatively treated fractures

**ADVANTAGES**

Ease of application
Inexpensive; available in different sizes
Requires minimal equipment
Can be applied percutaneously

**DISADVANTAGES**

Weak implant—requires additional support
Can distract a fracture
Subject to loosening and migration

. . . . . . . . . . . . . . . . . . . . . . . . . . . . . . . . . . . . . .

tendon or skin irritation and limit motion (Table 38–8). Zimmerman and Weiland[328] modified this technique by placing two 26-gauge wires perpendicular to each other (Fig. 38–20). This modification, though requiring some additional surgical exposure, is significantly more stable in mechanical testing. In fact, in Vanik and associates' study of the comparative strength of internal fixation techniques, the 90-90 wire technique compared favorably in rigidity with plate fixation[310] (Table 38–9).

## TECHNIQUE

The intraosseous wiring technique, described by Lister as type A wiring, involves drilling two holes with a 0.035-inch K-wire parallel to and 5 mm from the fracture ends and slightly dorsal to the midaxis of the bone. A 26-gauge (No. 0) stainless steel wire is passed through the holes in such a way that the twisted end of the wire will lie on the noncontact side of the digit. Before fracture reduction, a 0.035-inch K-wire is driven obliquely out through the distal cortex until the tip protrudes slightly at the fracture site. The fracture is reduced, and preferably a second surgeon drives the wire into the proximal fragment. The ends of the stainless steel wire are twisted around each other, grasped with a heavy needle holder, and tightened in two steps: the first is to pull on the wire to make it lie snug on the far cortex; the second is to twist the wire to tighten it (see Fig. 38–19).

In patients with intra-articular fractures or smaller avulsion fragments attached to the collateral ligaments, the monofilament wire is passed through soft tissue around the fragment (or through parallel drill holes into larger fragments) and brought to the opposite cortex across the fracture line. The fracture is then reduced and held while the wire is tightened. This approach (type B) avoids devascularization of these small fragments, but its disadvantage is that the wire is tightened against the opposite

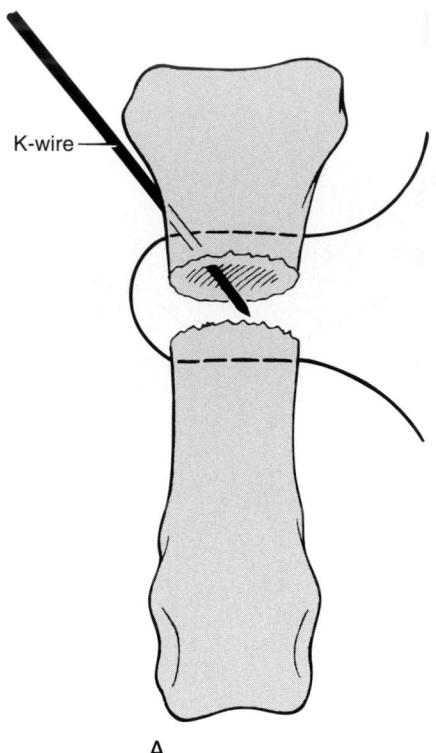

K-wire

A

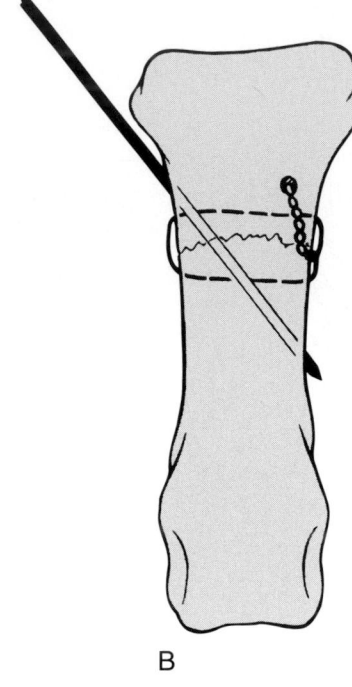

B

**FIGURE 38–19.** Lister's type A intraosseous wiring technique. *A,* A 26-gauge stainless steel wire is passed transversely proximal and distal to the fracture line and just dorsal to the midaxis of the phalanx. A 0.035-inch K-wire is passed obliquely into the distal fragment until the tip is in the fracture line. *B,* The fracture is reduced, the K-wire is passed into the proximal fragment, and the stainless steel wire is tightened. The twisted end can be placed into a drill hole in the cortex.

cortex and thus indirectly at the fracture line (Fig. 38–21 and Table 38–10).

The technique of 90-90 wiring is somewhat more demanding because two sets of holes parallel to the fracture line and 90° apart are required. Precise rotational alignment is necessary before tightening each wire. A 20-gauge hypodermic needle is recommended as a "carrier" for passage of the 26-gauge stainless steel wire. When the wire is passed in a dorsal-to-palmar direction, hyperflexion at the fracture site will improve surgical access. This technique, though more demanding and requiring somewhat greater surgical exposure of the fracture, does offer enhanced stability to permit functional loading of the digit during rehabilitation (see Fig. 38–20).

| TABLE 38–8 |
| --- |
| Intraosseous Wiring: Lister's Type A Technique |

**INDICATIONS**

Open transverse phalangeal fractures
Replantations

**ADVANTAGES**

Technically straightforward
Minimal equipment
Stable fixation for early mobilization

**DISADVANTAGES**

Limited clinical application
Requires surgical exposure
Kirschner wire can limit tendon gliding

## Tension Band Wiring

Intraosseous wiring techniques have been expanded by Belsole and colleagues to take advantage of the inherent mechanical forces that occur in functional loading of the digital skeleton.[16, 17, 113] In a stable state, the phalanges and metacarpals are mainly stressed by bending forces, with less stress occurring as a result of extension, torsion, or axial loading. Such stress results in compressive force on the palmar side and distraction or tensile force dorsally. With a dorsally placed implant, not only are bending and distraction forces neutralized, but the functional loading forces also convert these forces into compressive loads that are active within the plane of the fracture.[147, 269] For any implant to be successful, it must resist torsional and shearing loads. The tension band wiring technique accomplishes these mechanical requirements by placing the small-gauge stainless steel wire above the cortex and strategically wrapped around K-wires, which also serve to interlock the fracture fragments.

### TECHNIQUE

The tension band wiring technique is performed through surgical exposure and is therefore indicated only for unstable fractures not amenable to percutaneous techniques (see Table 38–5). The fracture is reduced and held while 0.035-inch K-wires are inserted. For transverse or short oblique fractures, crossed K-wires are used while 0.035-inch K-wires are inserted, whereas for long oblique or spiral fractures, the K-wires are placed perpendicular to the fracture plane. The wires are cut so that only 1 to 2 mm

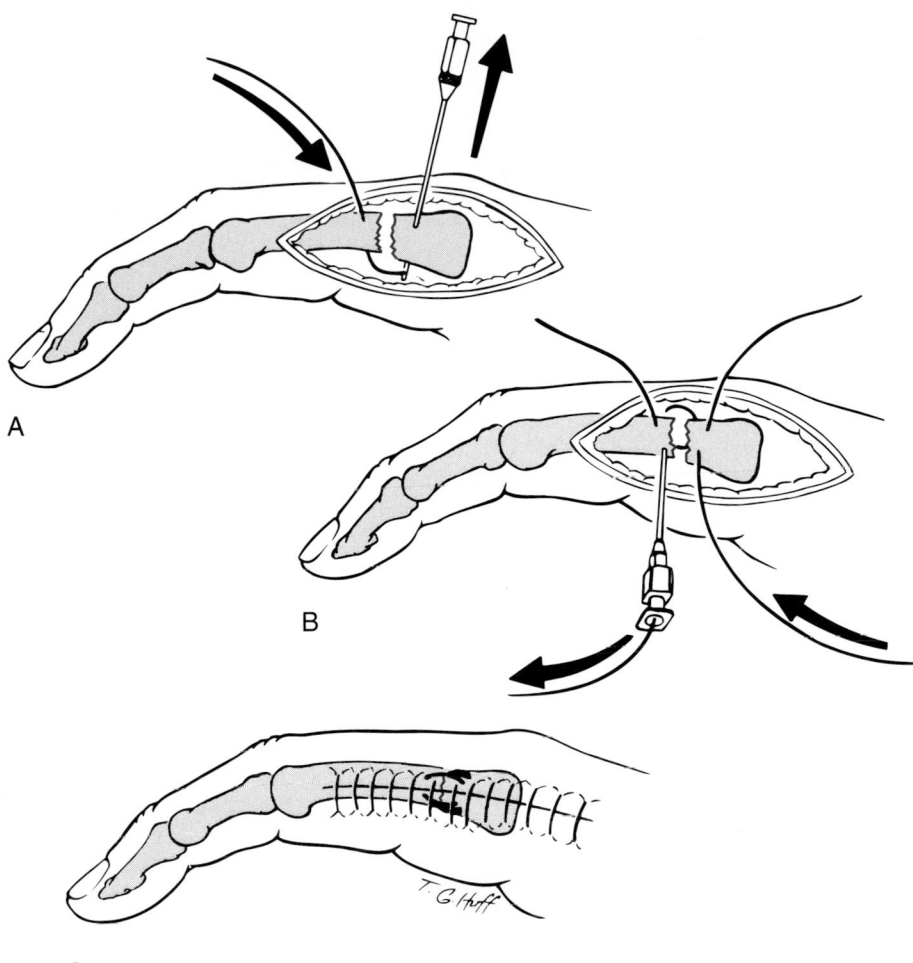

FIGURE 38–20. The 90-90 intraosseous wire technique. *A,* One wire is passed in a dorsal-to-palmar direction with a 20-gauge hypodermic needle. *B,* A second 26-gauge wire is introduced in a similar manner but at a 90° angle to the first. *C,* The fracture is reduced and held to ensure rotational alignment. Both wires are tightened, and the twisted ends are cut short.

protrudes from the cortex on both sides. Whenever possible, the wires should be placed to avoid interference with tendon gliding. The 26- or 28-gauge monofilament stainless steel wire is woven about the ends of the K-wires in a modified figure of eight and twisted tightly (Fig. 38–22). If the fracture is comminuted, several K-wire–stainless steel wire constructs can be made. If cortical defects are present opposite the tension wire, cancellous

bone grafting is recommended before tightening the wire. Active motion should be encouraged within a few days postoperatively because functional loading will promote fracture healing and, importantly, limit postoperative adhesions (Table 38–11).

Advantages of these wiring techniques include speed and ease of application, characteristics that have increasing importance in replantations or complex injuries with multiply devascularized digits. Disadvantages relate to irritation of soft tissue from the K-wires and wire loops and, perhaps more important, the degree of stability achieved. Biomechanical testing indicates that the simple K-wire techniques are quite unstable and, as such, should generally be combined with external support postoperatively. The interosseous wiring and combination techniques are better and may suffice for early unprotected postoperative mobilization, but this advantage remains uncertain. Plate and screw fixation remains the most stable of the internal fixation methods, with strengths approaching that of intact bone.[147, 310]

## Compression Screws

In concept and form, small screws, miniscrews, and plates represent a natural evolution from those used successfully

---

| TABLE 38–9 |
| --- |

**Intraosseous Wiring: 90-90 Technique**

**INDICATIONS**

Open transverse fractures
Replantation
Arthrodesis

**ADVANTAGES**

Biomechanically strong
Low-profile implant
Minimal equipment

**DISADVANTAGES**

Technically demanding
Limited applications
Poor in osteopenic bone

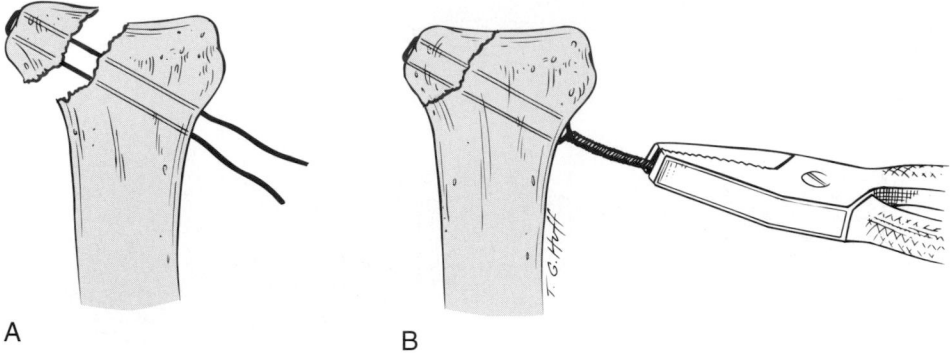

**A**          **B**

**FIGURE 38–21.** Lister's type B intraosseous wiring technique. *A,* A 26- or 28-gauge stainless steel wire is passed through or around the small fragments and brought across the fracture line through the opposite cortex. *B,* The wire is tightened by pulling on the wire to make it lie snug against the fragment and then twisting it.

---

**TABLE 38–10**

Intraosseous Wiring: Lister's Type B Technique

**INDICATIONS**

Intra-articular fractures
Avulsion fractures

**ADVANTAGES**

Limited exposure of the fracture fragment
Maintains vascularity to the fragment
Low-profile implant
Technically straightforward

**DISADVANTAGES**

Indirect wire tightening can limit security of fixation
Poor rotational control
Wire can devascularize ligament

---

**TABLE 38–11**

Tension Band Wiring

**INDICATIONS**

Unstable phalangeal and metacarpal fractures requiring open
  reduction and internal fixation
Failed plates and screws
Diaphyseal fractures with three or four fragments

**ADVANTAGES**

Very stable
Biomechanically sound
Low profile
Simple instruments

**DISADVANTAGES**

Operative exposure may be significant
Technically difficult with certain fracture patterns

---

in the larger skeleton (Fig. 38–23).[217] However, unique anatomic considerations in the hand demand knowledge and experience when applying these implants to the tubular skeleton in the hand. The gliding structures enveloping the digital skeleton are easily compromised by the bulk of the implant, and their location often restricts optimal mechanical placement of the internal fixation. The meager cortical thickness and often small and tenuously vascularized fracture fragments present other challenges to achieving stable internal fixation without devascularization or fragmentation of these fragile fragments.

In spite of their technical complexities, the precision, rigidity, and relatively low profile afforded by these miniscrews have added significantly to the surgeon's ability to manage complex fractures in the hand.[63, 95, 129, 257] In the metacarpals and phalanges, displaced long oblique or spiral fractures or articular fractures involving greater than

25% of the articular surface are excellent indications for screw fixation (Fig. 38–24). In addition, unicondylar and large avulsion fractures are often able to be secured with screws alone. The stability provided by interfragmentary fixation allows for functional rehabilitation even in the most complex of hand injuries (Table 38–12).

The techniques of interfragmentary lag screw fixation are presented in Chapter 10. In the hand, several points should be emphasized. The 2.7-mm screws are best used in the metacarpal base and, in large adults, in the metacarpal shaft. The 2.0-mm screws can be used in smaller metacarpals and in conjunction with 2.7-mm screws, with the smaller screws placed near the apices of the fracture. In the phalanges, 1.5-mm screws are preferable, with 2.0-mm screws used if the threads of the smaller screw "strip" and thus deny adequate cortical purchase.

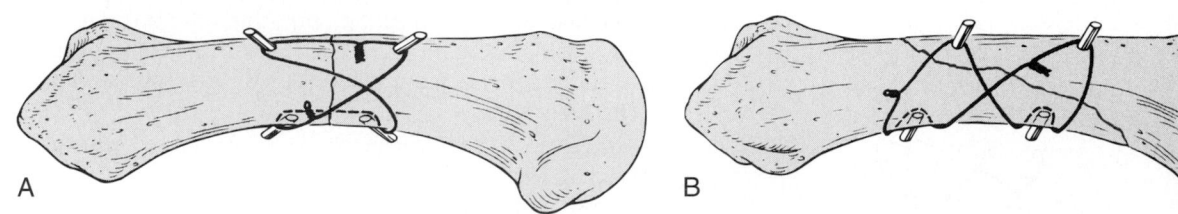

**A**                    **B**

**FIGURE 38–22.** Tension band wiring technique. *A,* For a transverse or short oblique fracture, K-wires are placed in a crossed pattern, and a stainless steel 26-gauge wire is passed around the tips in a modified figure-of-eight pattern. *B,* For spiral or long oblique fractures, parallel K-wires are placed perpendicular to the fracture plane.

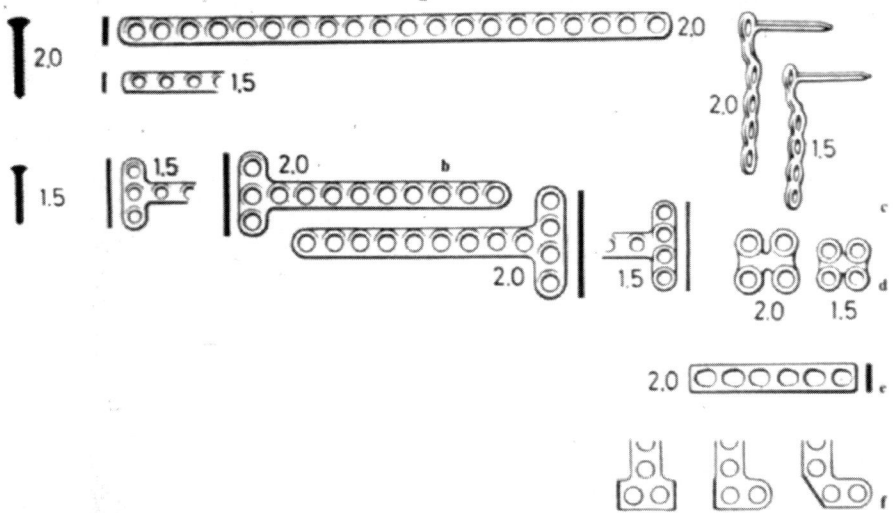

**FIGURE 38–23.** Minifragment implants for hand surgery, including 2.7-, 2.0-, and 1.5-mm implant and screw sizes.

Microscrews are currently available from several manufacturers. These implants were originally used in maxillofacial fracture sets and range in size from 0.8 to 1.2 mm. Microscrews may have a role in small-boned individuals, particularly in the middle and distal phalangeal skeleton.

Small cannulated screws are also now available, but not in sizes less than 2.7 mm. They may play a role in percutaneous fixation of metacarpal base fractures.

The following technical points of application are worth highlighting[37, 127]:

1. Diaphyseal fractures to be fixed by screws alone should have a fracture line at least twice the diameter of the bone.
2. The fracture should be opened and the fracture line inspected to determine the optimal position of the screws and to seek out hidden fracture lines or comminution that will offset screw purchase.
3. The fracture should be anatomically reduced to achieve interlocking of the fracture lines and to maximize the zone of compression.
4. Repeated drilling should be avoided because the lag screw is dependent on the grasp of the screw in the threaded hole.
5. Placing screws only where technically convenient should be avoided. Instead, they should be placed in

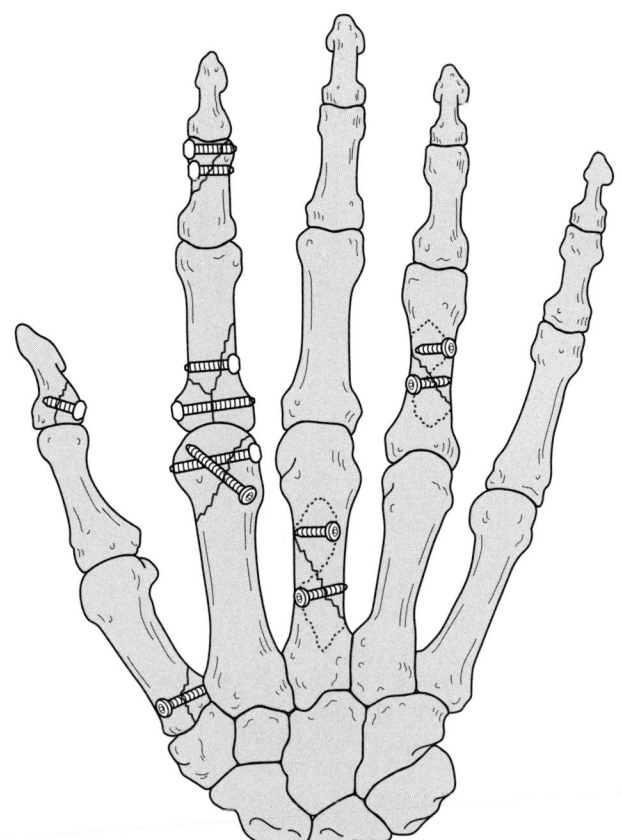

**FIGURE 38–24.** Optimal fracture patterns for interfragmentary screw fixation in the hand.

---

**TABLE 38–12** ....................................................

Interfragmentary Screw Fixation

---

**INDICATIONS**

Displaced spiral or long oblique fractures
Intra-articular fractures >25% of the articular surface
Avulsion fractures

**ADVANTAGES**

Stable fixation for functional rehabilitation
Predictable union when properly applied
Low-profile implant without a need for removal

**DISADVANTAGES**

Technically demanding
Requires operative exposure
Implant and equipment are complex

....................................................

the location that is mechanically most desirable (Fig. 38–25).

6. Screw fixation of a single fragment should be considered only if the fragment is at least three times the thread diameter of the screw.

## Plate Fixation

Although the bulk of a plate is less well tolerated in the hand than elsewhere in the axial skeleton, in a number of complex fractures, fixation with a plate has provided sufficient stability with which to initiate functional rehabilitation. Applications include metacarpal fractures with soft tissue loss, comminuted intra-articular or periarticular fractures, comminuted fractures with shortening or malrotation, and fractures with segmental bone loss. In the phalanges with their enveloping gliding structures, plate application should be limited to fractures with substance loss, intra-articular T condylar fractures, complex fractures (fractures with extensive soft tissue injury or complete amputation), and some fractures with periarticular comminution.

A number of plates have been specifically designed for use in the hand.[95, 127] Metacarpal shaft fractures are stabilized with one-quarter tubular plates and 2.7-mm screws; however, if bone loss is present, a stronger 2.7-mm dynamic compression (DC) plate will be needed.[66] Periarticular fractures are amenable to 2.0-mm condylar plates, 2.7-mm L or T plates, or the newer 2.0-mm three- and four-hole T plates.[38] Similar plate designs with 1.5- and 2.0-mm screws are available for the phalanges. However, the most versatile plate for the phalanges is the 1.5-mm condylar plate.

In contrast to interfragmentary screws, plates will often require removal because their bulk commonly interferes with overlying tendons. If, however, their application permits rapid mobilization and thereby minimizes adhesions, removal should be put into the perspective of allowing for functional restoration along with skeletal healing. The surgeon should reserve plate application, particularly in the phalanges, for only the most complex injuries and fracture patterns.

The small condylar plate has expanded the application of plates in the hand as a result of its versatility, lower profile, and design features[38] (Table 38–13). In the distal metacarpal, the plate is applied on the dorsolateral aspect, which corresponds to the dorsal tubercle of the origin of the collateral ligaments; in the phalanges, sagittal placement of the implant is preferred. The technique of condylar plate application in a bicondylar fracture of the proximal phalanx is discussed in the section Phalangeal Condylar Fractures.

## External Skeletal Fixation

External skeletal fixation of the hand is by no means a new concept.[65, 238] However, small external fixation frames have been developed that offer not only stability but also versatility and the ability to easily make adjustments both intraoperatively and postoperatively.[250, 297] Blunt-tipped pins that are predrilled, swiveling adjustable pin-holding clamps, and compression and distraction units are now available. External fixation was traditionally viewed as applicable only to complex composite injuries in the hand,[93, 271] but the improved design and pin applications have enabled its application in such complex injuries as PIP joint fracture-dislocations and highly comminuted diaphyseal fractures[4, 125, 126] (Table 38–14).

Simple fixators have been constructed with K-wires and acrylic cement. Though adequate for emergency stabilization, their lack of stability has led to pin tract problems and loss of position. The miniature external fixator designed by Henri Jacquet in 1976 has, to a large degree, solved these problems[250] (Fig. 38–26).

### TECHNIQUE

The pinholes are predrilled with 1.5-mm drill bits through a guide. A hand chuck inserts the blunt-tipped, self-tapping 2.0-mm pins. They are attached to pin holders, which can be offset to create more space for the connecting frame in the small skeleton of the phalanges. The pin holders are linked by a connecting rod held onto the pin holders by swiveling clamps that are adjustable in all planes. This feature is particularly effective in the digits because it allows the pins to be placed before reduction of the fracture. The swiveling clamps can have a sliding clamp to permit distraction or compression through the frame. A socket wrench is needed to secure the clamps and pin holders. The frame and connecting rods allow the construction of more varied and, if needed, more complex frame assemblies.

Newer minifixators are available through other manufacturers. Synthes now markets a device that uses 1.25- and 1.6-mm Schantz pins for fixation.

Hotchkiss developed an articulated IP joint external fixator that allows controlled motion through an adjustable arc and can be combined with distraction or compression as needed. This device also allows a choice between active motion, passive manipulative motion (through the screw device), and no motion at all by locking the hinge[134] (Fig. 38–27).

## METACARPAL FRACTURES

Injury to the second through fifth metacarpals, which are interconnected at their bases and necks, can result in significant swelling, pain, and early or late hand dysfunction. Treatment of metacarpal fractures has progressed considerably since the mid-1940s, when nearly all metacarpal fractures were treated by bandaging over a roller bandage with little attempt at fracture reduction.[315] The current approach should be based on fracture location, fracture angulation or displacement, inherent stability, associated soft tissue trauma, and the functional demands of the patient.

Treatment goals specific to the metacarpals include preservation of the longitudinal and transverse arches and prevention of rotational deformity, which will be manifested as overlapping of the digit. Five degrees of

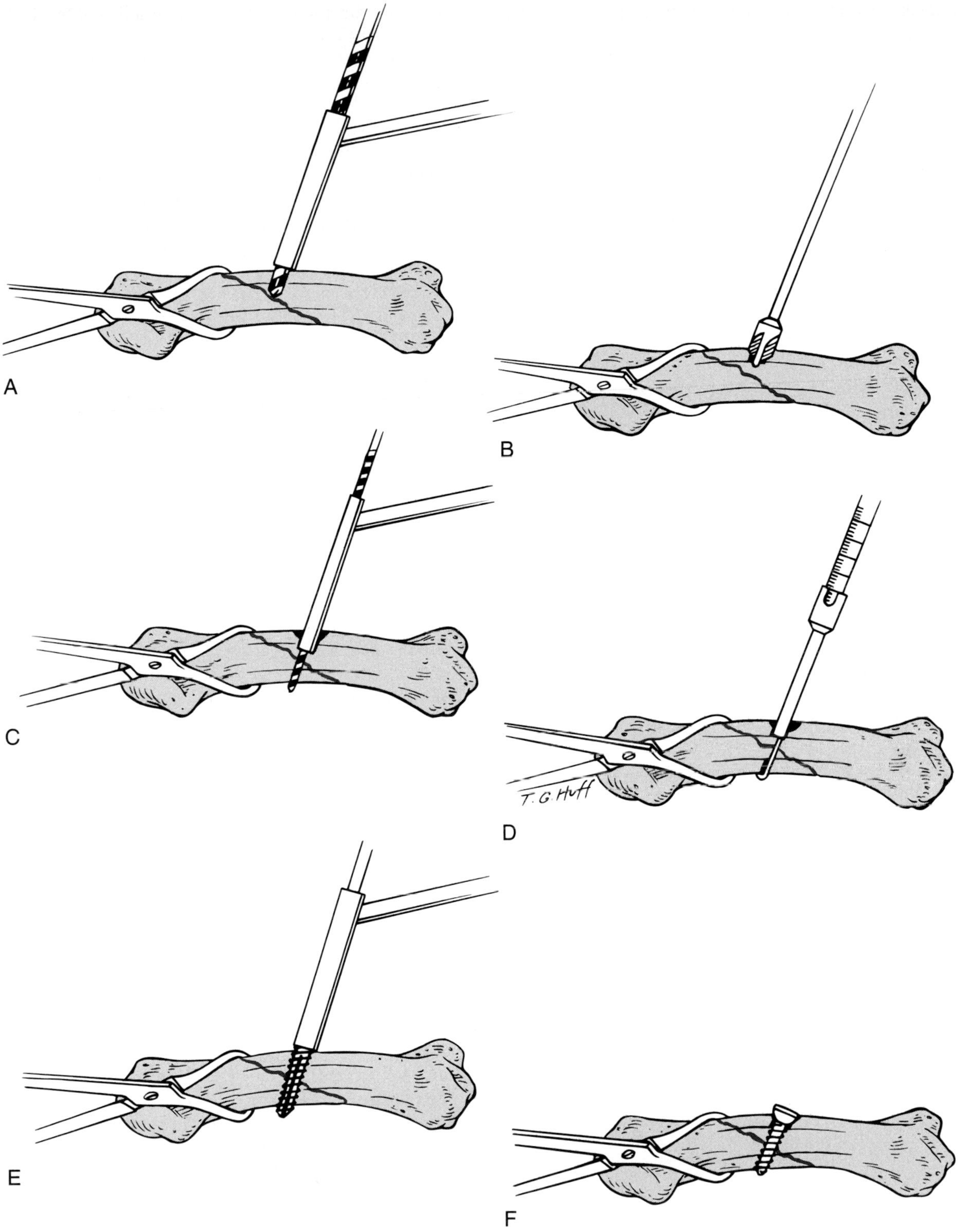

A

B

C

D

E

F

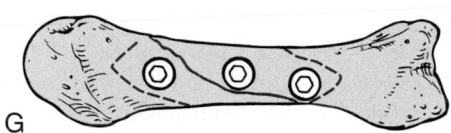

G

**FIGURE 38–25.** Sequence of steps in interfragmentary screw fixation of a spiral metacarpal fracture with 2.0-mm screws. *A,* Overdrill a gliding hole with a 2.0-mm drill bit. Do not drill beyond the first cortex. *B,* Countersink. *C,* Drill across the fracture with a 1.5-mm drill bit and an appropriate drill guide used as an insert sleeve. *D,* Measure the depth. *E,* Tap with a 2.0-mm tap and tap sleeve. *F,* Insert a 2.0-mm lag screw. *G,* Insert the second or third screws like the first, and adjust their positions to conform to the rotational changes in configuration of the fracture.

## TABLE 38–13

### Plate Application

**INDICATIONS**

Complex metacarpal and phalangeal fractures with soft tissue injury or bone loss
Complex intra-articular or periarticular fractures

**ADVANTAGES**

Stable skeletal fixation
Maintains or restores length
Lateral position of the condylar plate permits extra-articular placement

**DISADVANTAGES**

Extreme technical difficulty
Little room for error
Bulk of the implant a problem with overlying tendons

────────────

metacarpal shaft rotation can result in 1.5 cm of digital overlap.[95] Shortening, when 3 mm or less, may be appreciated only by the loss of contour of the metacarpal head during flexion of the MCP joint. When shortening exceeds this amount, however, an imbalance between the intrinsic and the extrinsic tendons may arise. Angulation into flexion is less well tolerated in the radial digits than in the ring and small fingers because of the compensatory mobility of the CMC joints. As a general rule, up to 10° of flexion is tolerable for the index and middle fingers, 20° for the ring finger, and up to 30° for the small finger. Debate continues about the maximal deformity acceptable for metacarpal neck fractures in the small finger. Some authors maintain that up to 70° is acceptable.[225, 282] The greater the flexion deformity, the greater the prominence of the metacarpal head in the palm.

Metacarpal fractures are conveniently grouped according to the anatomic division of the bone: base, shaft, neck,

## TABLE 38–14

### External Skeletal Fixation

**INDICATIONS**

Highly comminuted fractures
Fractures with bone loss
Fractures with extreme soft tissue trauma
Infected fractures
Thumb webspace maintenance
Complex articular fracture-dislocations of the proximal interphalangeal joint

**ADVANTAGES**

Avoids operative manipulation of fracture fragments
Maintains length and alignment during traction without crossing joints
Access to soft tissue care advantageous
Can be applied percutaneously

**DISADVANTAGES**

Complex application
Pins can inhibit gliding structures
Pin tract infection
Traction can delay skeletal healing

────────────

and head. Dobyns and co-workers, in their series of 1621 fracture-dislocations of the hand and wrist, documented 421 metacarpal fractures[76] (Table 38–15).

Imaging for these fractures requires the standard AP, lateral, and oblique radiographic projections. At times, it is difficult to visualize the flexion deformity because of skeletal overlap. In these situations, one can use multiple oblique images obtained with a small fluoroscope, lateral tomography, or computed tomography (CT). However, imaging will not replace careful hand examination in assessing for deformity, especially that of rotation.

# Extra-articular Fractures

## EXTRA-ARTICULAR BASE INJURIES

As a general rule, the interosseous muscles and intrinsically strong CMC capsular and interosseous ligaments provide intrinsic stability to extra-articular fractures at the metacarpal bases.[117] When resulting from direct trauma, extra-articular fractures are frequently impacted and clinically stable. In these cases, supportive splints are indicated. In the setting of more violent trauma, these fractures may be associated with complex soft tissue injuries, and internal fixation with K-wires may be advisable. More stable fixation can be gained with 2.0- or 2.7-mm condylar plates (Fig. 38–28).

## CARPOMETACARPAL FRACTURE-DISLOCATIONS

CMC fracture-dislocations can be more difficult to treat than extra-articular base fractures. These injuries are commonly the sequelae of high-energy trauma and are accompanied by soft tissue swelling. A number of combinations of CMC fracture-dislocations have been reported,[22, 122, 128, 163, 242] although fracture-dislocations of the fifth CMC joint have been described most extensively in the literature.[24, 71, 107, 218]

Severe swelling, pain, and crepitation on examination should alert the physician to the possibility of injury to the CMC joints. Three radiographic views are mandatory inasmuch as the dislocation may not be visible on the AP view and the lateral radiograph may be difficult to interpret because of overlap of adjacent CMC joints. For this reason, 30° oblique radiographs with the forearm both supinated and pronated will accentuate the second and fifth CMC joints, respectively.[160] Lateral tomography and CT scans are especially helpful in confirming the presence of a fracture-dislocation and, more importantly, the extent of the articular disruption (Fig. 38–29).

Fracture-dislocations of the fifth CMC joint, and less so of the fourth, are of particular importance given the mobility of these joints. The fifth and fourth metacarpals articulate with the distal articular surface of the hamate, which is divided by a ridge into two distinct facets. The fifth metacarpal articulation is that of a concave-convex "saddle"-type joint resembling the thumb trapezial metacarpal joint. This type of joint provides the fifth CMC articulation with not only a flexion-extension arc of between 20° and 30° but also a slight rotatory motion that

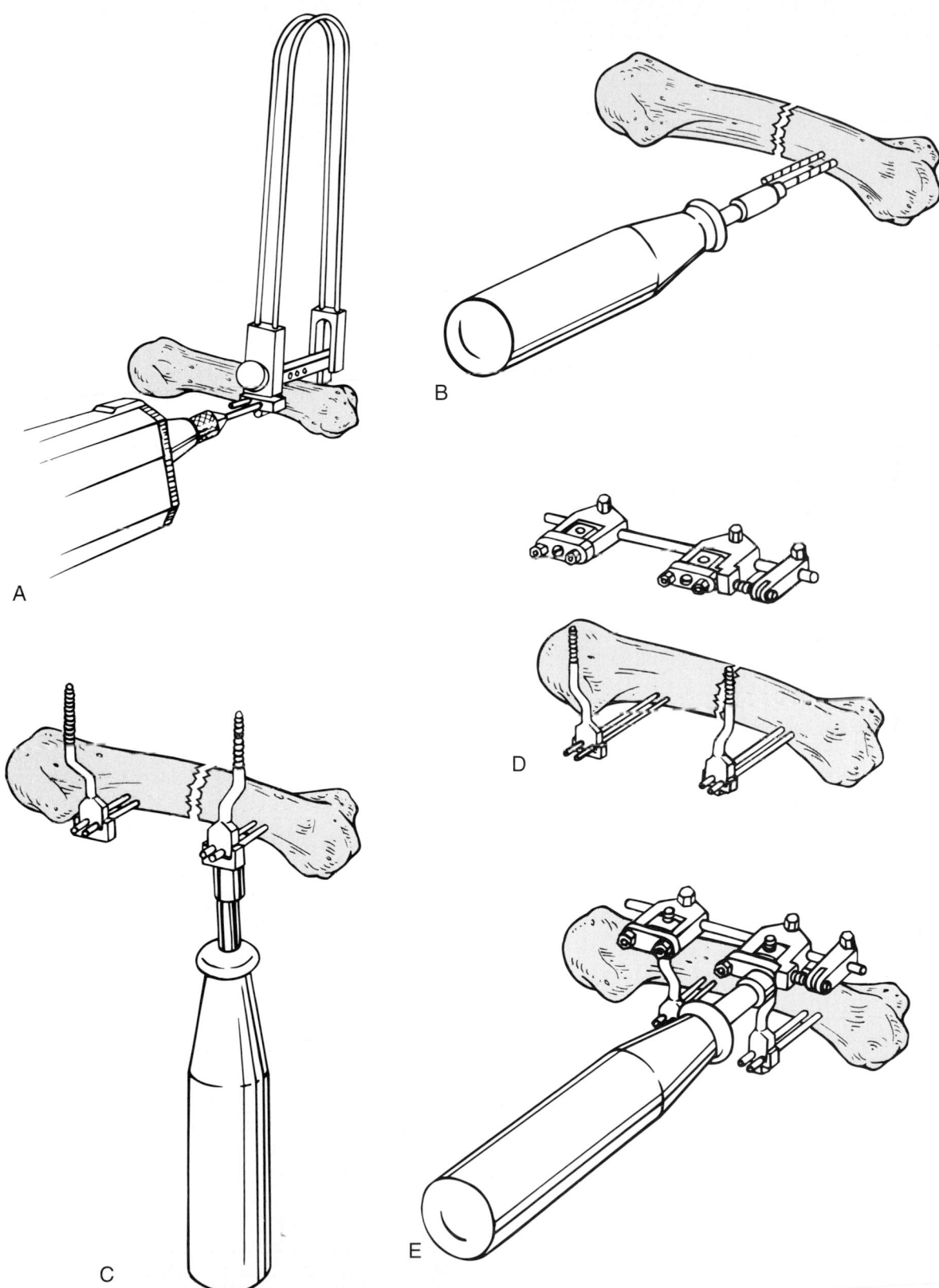

**FIGURE 38–26.** Technique of applying the miniature external fixator of Jacquet. *A,* A drill guide is used to accurately direct the minipins. *B,* The pins are placed with a hand chuck. *C,* The primary connection between the pins and the frame is with offset or straight pin holders. *D,* Simple or sliding swivel clamps link the pin holders to the connecting rod of the frame. *E,* The bolts that connect the clamps to the pin holders and connecting rods are tightened with a socket wrench.

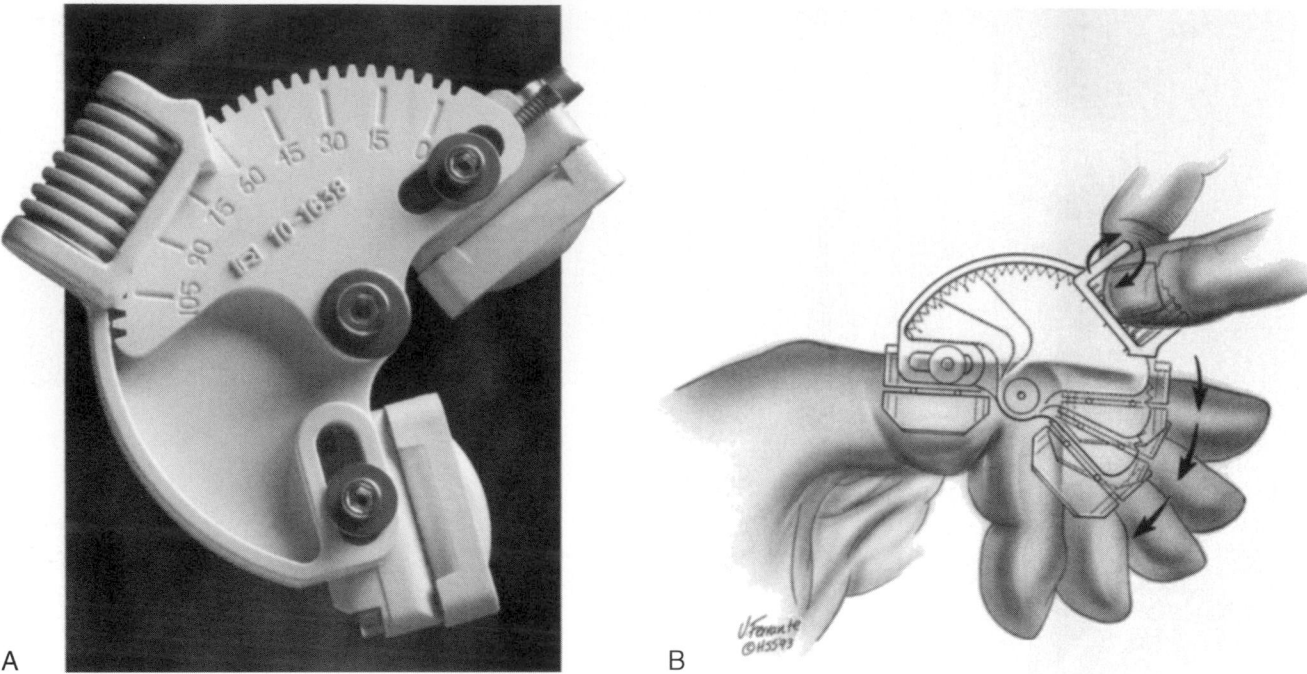

A

B

**FIGURE 38–27.** A Hotchkiss-designed Compass Proximal Interphalangeal Joint Hinge. *A,* Photograph of the device. *B,* The worm gear mechanism allows for active or passive movement. Alternatively, it can be statically locked into place to immobilize the joint. (*A, B,* From Hotchkiss, R.N. Compass Proximal Interphalangeal [PIP] Joint Hinge: Surgical Technique. Product Guide. Memphis, TN, Smith & Nephew Richards, 1993.)

functions to aid the little finger in contact with the thumb.[117, 242] The more radial facet of the hamate is flatter and provides only 10° to 15° of mobility to the fourth metacarpal.

Injuries to these two joints can be the result of a combination of forces, with axially directed forces producing the more comminuted fracture patterns. The extensor carpi ulnaris, which inserts on the base of the fifth metacarpal, acts as a deforming force and accounts to some degree for the instability of these "reverse Bennett" fractures. The deep motor branch of the ulnar nerve passes adjacent to the hook of the hamate and can be traumatized with these fractures.[68, 232]

**TABLE 38–15**

Incidence of Metacarpal Fractures and Dislocations
(*N* = 421)

| Type | Number |
|---|---|
| Neck | 110 |
| Shaft | |
|   Spiral/oblique | 55 |
|   Transverse | 94 |
|   Longitudinal | 1 |
|   Comminuted | 7 |
| Base | 55 |
| Articular head | 32 |
| Condyles (proximal) | 4 |
| Dorsal base | 4 |
| Palmar base | 6 |
| Lateral base | 50* |
| Comminuted | 3 |

*Thirty-seven of these injuries were Bennett's fractures.
*Source:* Compiled from Dobyns, J.H.; et al. J Hand Surg 8:687–690, 1983.

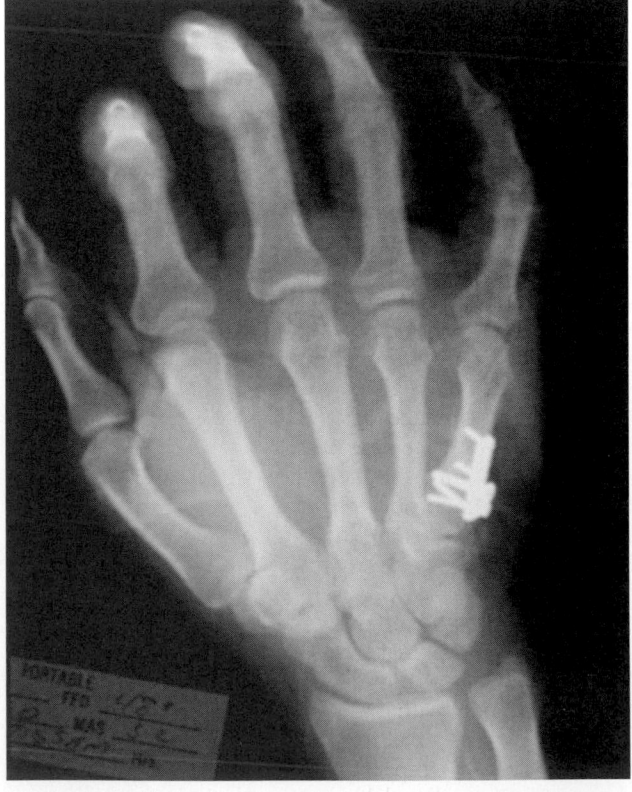

**FIGURE 38–28.** A 28-year-old man sustained a rollover injury to his hand with extensive soft tissue trauma. A 2.0-mm condylar plate was used to stabilize a fracture at the base of the metacarpals. (Courtesy of Dr. Alan Freeland.)

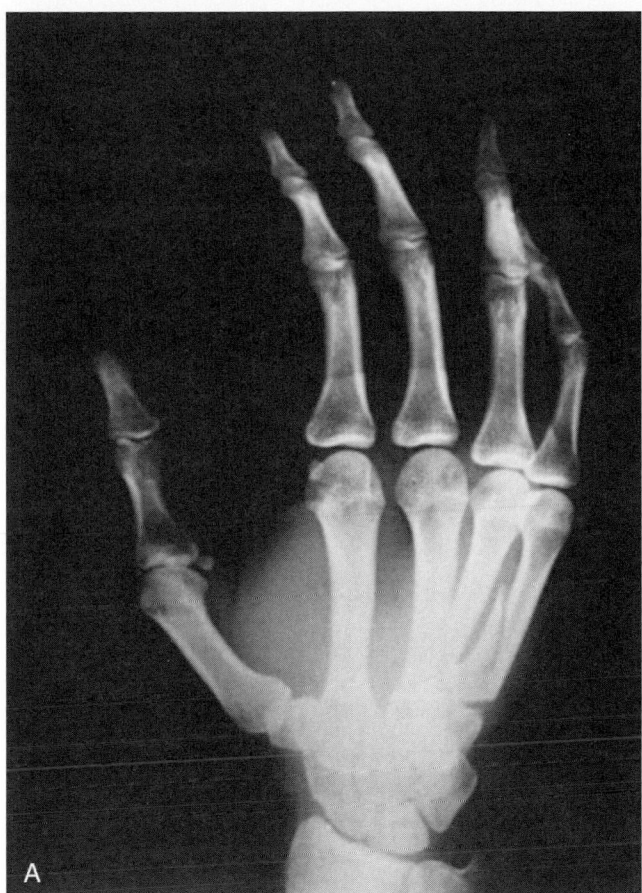

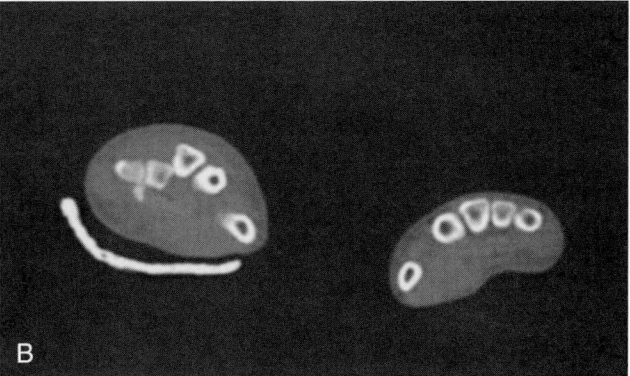

FIGURE 38–29. *A,* An oblique radiograph of a fracture-dislocation of the fourth and fifth carpometacarpal joints. The injury is difficult to interpret on a routine lateral radiograph. *B,* Computed tomography clearly demonstrates the injury when compared with the contralateral side.

As with fractures at the base of the thumb metacarpal, these fractures can be divided into four fracture patterns (Fig. 38–30): epibasal, two part (reverse Bennett's), three part, and comminuted with impaction. Displaced epibasal and two-part fracture-dislocations are readily reduced with longitudinal traction on the fifth metacarpal, followed by manual pressure on the base of the metacarpal. Adequate anesthesia is essential, and finger trap traction may be required to gain skeletal length and maintain the reduction while radiographs are obtained. Because these fractures are unstable, once they are reduced they should be stabilized with two 0.045-inch K-wires placed percutaneously. One pin should be directed across the metacarpohamate joint and the other into the base of the fourth metacarpal. Using a large-bore hypodermic needle as a pin guide will greatly facilitate placement of the pins into the tubular fifth metacarpal. The pins are left out of the skin, and plaster immobilization with an ulnar gutter cast is applied for 6 weeks (Fig. 38–31).

A three-part or comminuted fracture may not reduce as easily with longitudinal traction. It is not uncommon for these fracture-dislocations to be comminuted, particularly when associated with high-energy trauma.[68, 128, 269] Tomography is essential for defining the anatomy of the fracture because impacted articular fragments are not always readily reduced by longitudinal traction. If these fractures are left untreated, symptomatic post-traumatic arthritis can prove problematic, especially in patients who rely on their hands for their livelihood.[57]

Displaced articular fragments are small and exceptionally difficult to reduce and stabilize. For that reason, it is advisable to attempt to reduce the fracture fragments by "ligamentotaxis" with an external fixation device applied to the hamate and metacarpal shaft (Fig. 38–32). If radiographs demonstrate continued displacement of the articular surface, the fragments can be manipulated into place through a limited dorsoulnar incision and secured with 0.028- or 0.035-inch K-wires. As with reduction of impacted articular fractures elsewhere, a metaphyseal defect will exist and should be packed with a small amount of cancellous bone graft obtained from the distal end of the radius (Fig. 38–33). The fixator is left in place for 6 weeks and protected with an ulnar gutter cast or splint.

**Multiple CMC Fracture-Dislocations.** When recognized early, multiple CMC fracture-dislocations are usually reducible by direct manipulation alone or with added longitudinal traction. They are, for the most part, unstable and require percutaneous K-wire fixation with 0.045-inch wires placed obliquely across the CMC joints into the proximal carpal row. Soft tissue swelling is normal. Therefore, a circular plaster cast should be used with caution in the initial postoperative period and is preferably applied once the swelling begins to subside. However, when these complex fracture-dislocations are seen more than 5 to 7 days after injury, they may no longer be amenable to successful closed reduction. Open reduction is best accomplished through longitudinal incisions, which interfere less with venous and lymphatic drainage (Fig.

38–34). Reduction of multiple CMC fracture-dislocations begins with the "keystone" third CMC joint. Again, the reductions are stabilized with K-wires. The patient should be cautioned that these joints may spontaneously fuse or require surgical arthrodesis if painful post-traumatic arthritis ensues.

In the situation of a multifragmentary, displaced intra-articular fracture of the CMC joints, primary arthrodesis becomes an added possibility in management. Arthrodesis is especially helpful for open or complex injuries in which maximal stability is desired from the outset to facilitate hand rehabilitation. The index and middle digit CMC joints have very little normal motion, so arthrodesis of either of these joints will not lead to any major functional hand impairment. Given the mobility of the ring and small finger CMC joints, this option should

not be as readily considered, and preservation of the joint becomes much more important (Fig. 38–35).

## Metacarpal Shaft Fractures

Displacement of isolated closed metacarpal shaft fractures is often limited[147, 242] because the four metacarpal shafts are surrounded by the intrinsic muscles and are linked together proximally and distally by interosseous ligaments. Distally, the deep transverse metacarpal ligaments secure the metacarpal necks together in a slinglike fashion to provide additional support. Transverse fractures will angulate with the apex directed dorsally, and the distal fragment will be pulled palmarward because of the action of the interosseous muscles (Fig. 38–36). Increased palmar

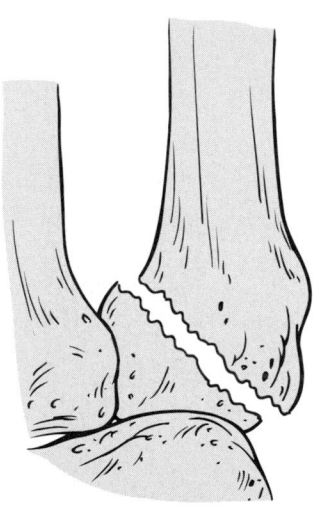

Epibasal

A

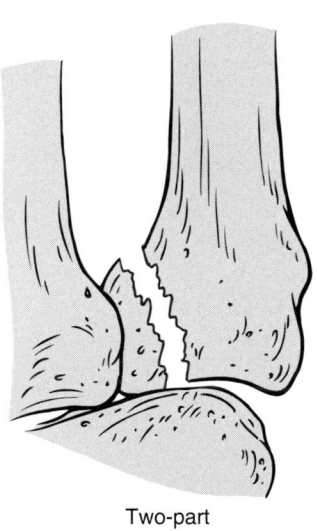

Two-part

B

**FIGURE 38–30.** *A–D,* Four types of fractures of the base of the fifth metacarpal.

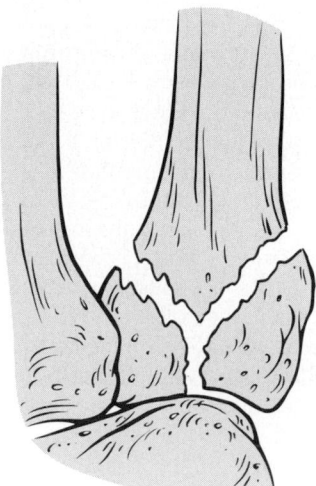

Three-part

C

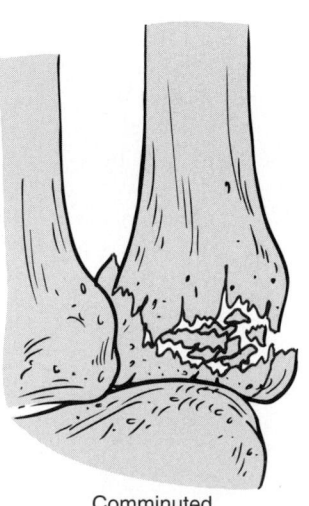

Comminuted with impaction

D

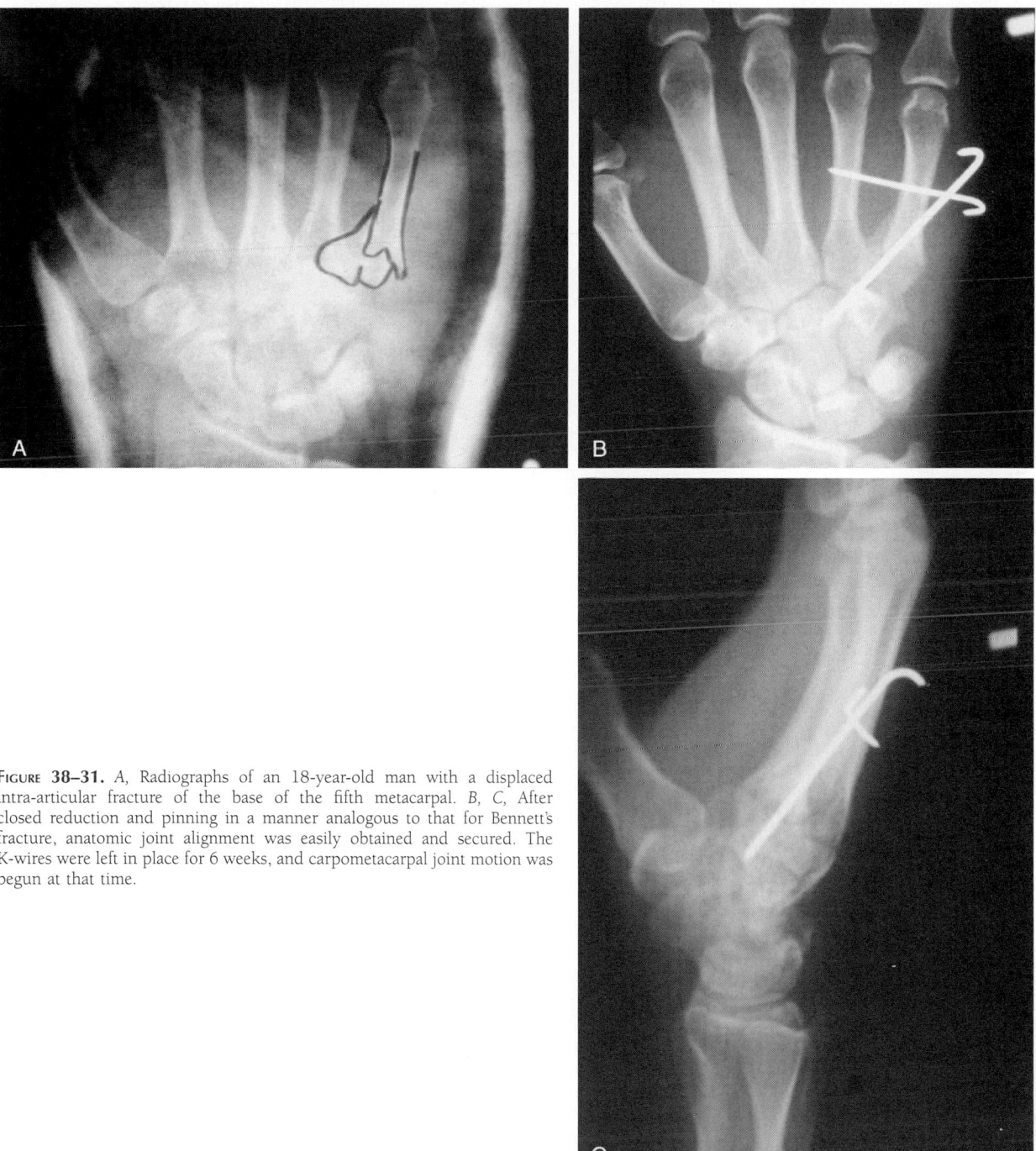

**FIGURE 38–31.** *A,* Radiographs of an 18-year-old man with a displaced intra-articular fracture of the base of the fifth metacarpal. *B, C,* After closed reduction and pinning in a manner analogous to that for Bennett's fracture, anatomic joint alignment was easily obtained and secured. The K-wires were left in place for 6 weeks, and carpometacarpal joint motion was begun at that time.

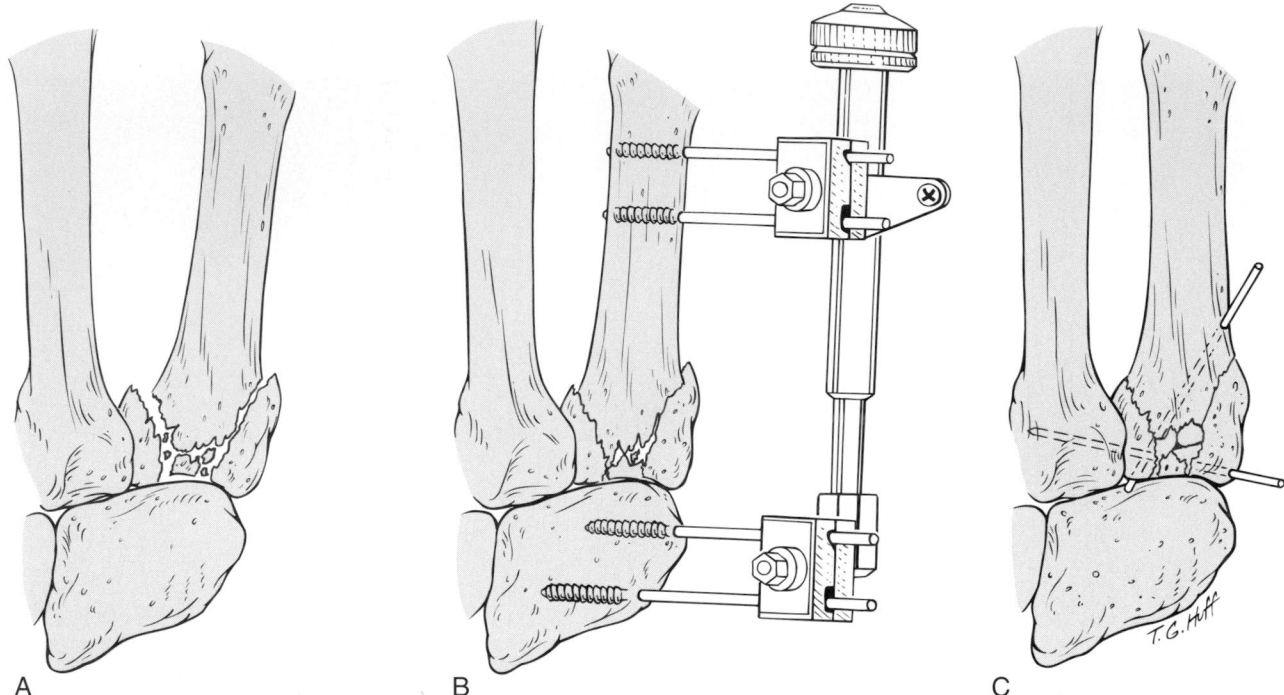

FIGURE 38–32. *A–C,* Three steps in the reduction and fixation of an impacted fifth carpometacarpal fracture-dislocation with a minidistractor.

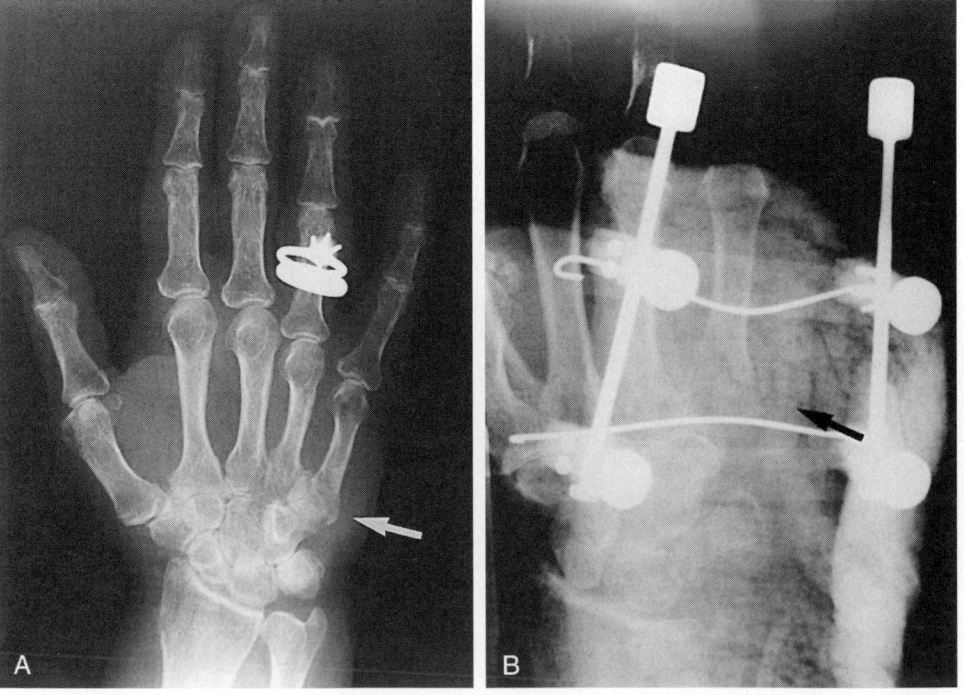

FIGURE 38–33. *A, B,* With a mini-lengthener, a severely comminuted fracture-dislocation of the fifth meta-carpal (*arrows*) was successfully reduced and held with a minidistractor, which was incorporated into a cast.

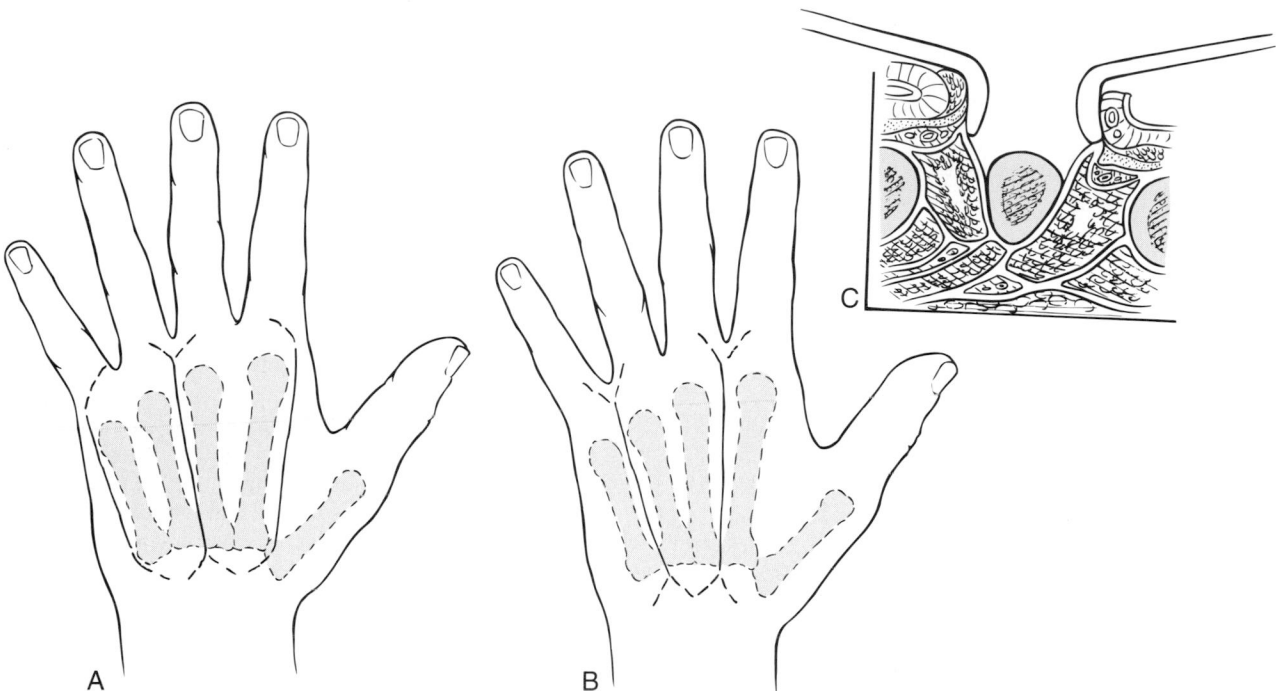

**FIGURE 38–34.** Surgical approaches to the metacarpals. *A,* Incisions for exposure of individual metacarpals. *B,* Incisions for exposure of all four metacarpals. *C,* Exposure of the metacarpal is subperiosteal on the dorsal surface, with care taken to minimize elevation of the interosseous muscles.

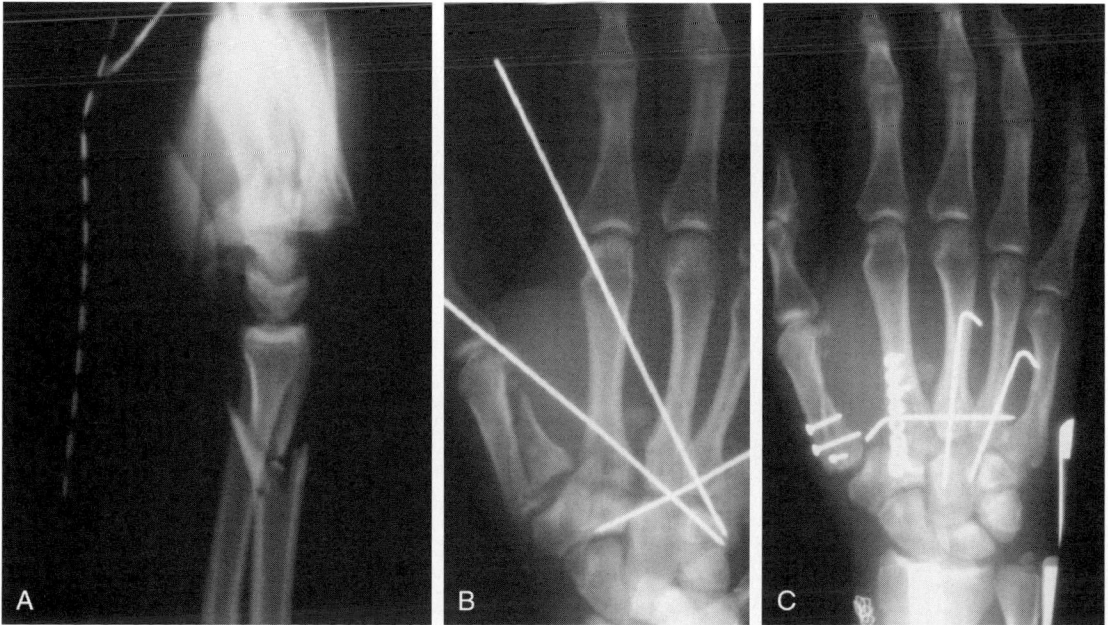

**FIGURE 38–35.** *A,* The dominant hand of a 19-year-old with a crush injury. Injuries consist of a long intra-articular fracture of the thumb metacarpal, a complex fracture-dislocation of the second carpometacarpal (CMC) joint, and simple CMC dislocations of the third and fourth rays. *B,* Initial management was by closed means with percutaneous pinning of the affected joints. Note that the joints are not reduced and the fracture-dislocation of the second CMC joint has extensive intra-articular fragmentation. *C,* After revision and open reduction and primary CMC joint arthrodesis of the second ray with a distal radius bone graft and a plate, open pinning of the third and fourth CMC joints and lag screw fixation of the thumb metacarpal injury were performed.

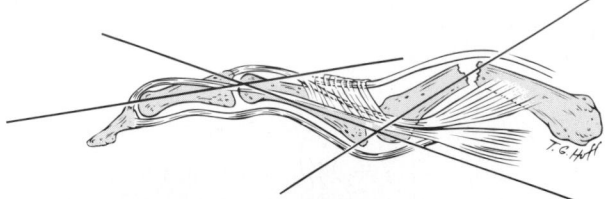

**Figure 38–36.** Transverse metacarpal shaft fractures will angulate with the apex pointing dorsally because of the pull of the interosseous muscles.

displacement of the metacarpal heads can disturb grip, and angulation can result in muscle imbalance with hyperextension at the MCP joint and reduced extension at the PIP joint. The mobile CMC joints of the fourth and fifth metacarpals can accommodate some dorsal-palmar angulation, whereas those of the fixed second and third metacarpals cannot. For metacarpal shaft fractures, up to 20° of dorsal angulation can be accepted for the fourth and fifth metacarpals, but not more than 10° for the second and third.[225, 282] The amount of acceptable angulation for the fourth and fifth metacarpals will be greater when the fracture occurs more distally in the neck.

Oblique fractures tend to shorten, whereas spiral fractures will rotate (Fig. 38–37). Shortening of up to 3 mm is well tolerated and may be apparent only by loss of the normal contour of the metacarpal head with MCP joint flexion. Less tolerance is acceptable with rotational deformity.[95] In general, border metacarpal fractures are less stable than those of the central two metacarpals because of the increased interosseous support of the latter.

## ISOLATED METACARPAL SHAFT FRACTURES

Transverse closed metacarpal shaft fractures with little or no displacement are intrinsically stable and readily treated with a plaster splint or cast for 3 to 4 weeks.[225] The cast is applied with the MCP joint flexed 60° to 70° and carefully molded to provide three points of contact: one over the dorsal apex of the fracture and the other two on the palmar side proximal and distal to the fracture.

If the initial displacement is substantial or the fracture becomes displaced in the cast, percutaneous K-wire fixation should be considered. Several techniques of wire placement are available, and a 0.045-inch smooth K-wire is the wire of choice. A technique particularly suited to the border metacarpals is that of placing one wire proximal and one wire distal to the fracture in a transverse direction into the adjacent metacarpal[171] (Fig. 38–38). This particular configuration was demonstrated by Massengill and colleagues[199] to have significant strength when subjected to biomechanical evaluation. An alternative method is placement of a longitudinal wire with the K-wire introduced through a tuberosity of the metacarpal head and the MCP joint held in flexion. This approach carries the potential problem of the wire interfering with MCP

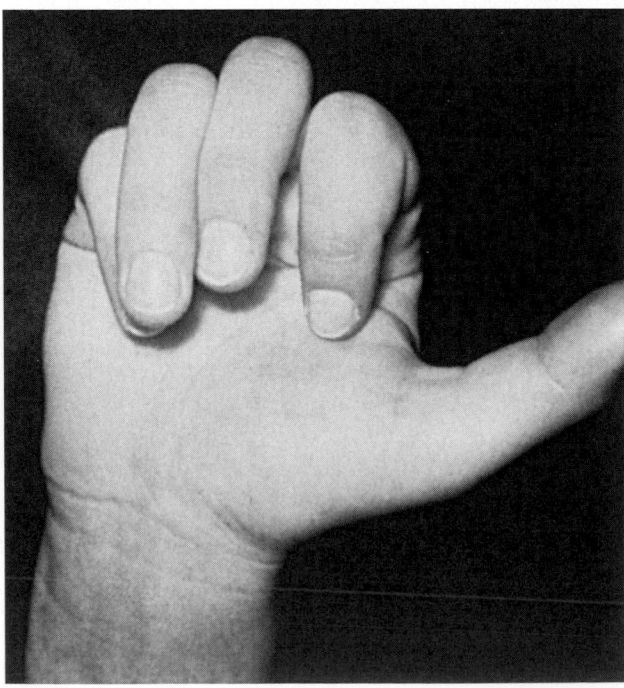

**Figure 38–37.** A malrotated spiral metacarpal shaft fracture can result in disabling digital overlap.

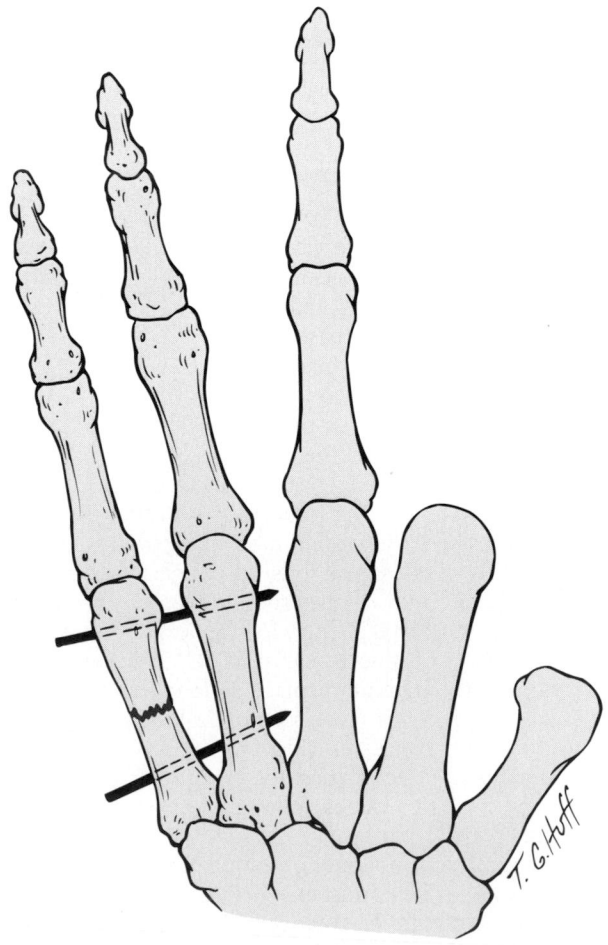

**Figure 38–38.** A displaced transverse metacarpal shaft fracture specifically involving the border metacarpals can be stabilized with 0.045-inch K-wires placed transversely into the adjacent intact metacarpal.

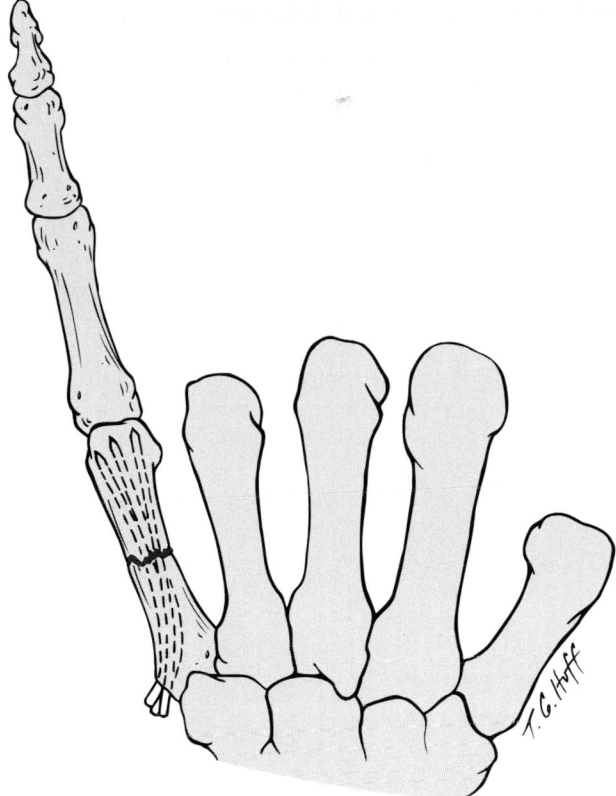

**FIGURE 38–39.** The flexible intramedullary rod technique of Hall is based on filling the medullary canal with curved, smooth-tipped rods passed into the metacarpal through drill holes distant from the fracture site.

joint motion. A third wire technique is that described by Hall,[120] which he termed *flexible intramedullary rodding.* This technique uses a specially designed rod 0.8 mm in diameter and 10 cm long with a rounded tip. Through a 1-cm incision over the base of the metacarpal, several unicortical drill holes are made with a 0.045-inch K-wire. The fracture is reduced under image control, and the flexible rods are introduced through the previously drilled holes and passed across the fracture site into the distal subchondral bone. The position within the shaft is confirmed with the image intensifier. Additional rods are then introduced in a similar manner until the canal is packed with the wires. The rods are cut close to the bone, with only 1 to 2 mm left protruding from the bone. Hall cautions that the portal of entry for the flexible rods should be as far from the fracture as possible to minimize the possibility of the fracture displacing along the path of the rods. This technique is also applicable to displaced metacarpal neck fractures (Fig. 38–39). With all three percutaneous wire techniques, the patient is protected in a plaster cast for 3 to 4 weeks, followed by wire removal and active-assisted motion.

Isolated closed oblique or spiral shaft fractures, if malaligned, will prove unstable after an attempt at closed reduction. Although percutaneous K-wire fixation offers the advantage of a closed fracture technique, it is often exceedingly difficult to obtain adequate fixation to control the rotatory malalignment. In these cases, operative treatment should be considered if angular or rotatory malalignment has occurred (Fig. 38–40).

## MULTIPLE METACARPAL SHAFT FRACTURES

Multiple displaced metacarpal shaft fractures, especially when associated with soft tissue trauma, are an indication for open reduction and internal fixation (ORIF).

**Surgical Approach to the Metacarpals.** Longitudinal extensile incisions are preferable to serpentine or transverse incisions on the dorsum of the hand. The border metacarpals can be approached individually through longitudinal incisions between the second and third or the fourth and fifth metacarpals. The third and fourth metacarpals are approached by making a longitudinal incision between the metacarpals, with the addition of Y-shaped extensions if needed to gain more proximal or distal exposure. When all four metacarpals require exposure, two incisions are made: one between the second and third metacarpals and another between the fourth and fifth (see Fig. 38–34).

The juncturae tendinum interconnecting the common extensor tendons over the distal metacarpals can be split to enhance exposure and then repaired at wound closure. The metacarpals are approached by incising the periosteum longitudinally and exposing the fracture subperiosteally. This technique will minimize disruption of the origins of the interosseous muscles. The exposure should be limited to the extent needed to accommodate the required implant. Small retractors and sharp-pointed fixation clamps are essential to minimize soft tissue trauma (see Fig. 38–34C). The periosteum can at times be closed over the implant.

Skeletal fixation of multiple metacarpal fractures is based on the preference and experience of the surgeon (see Fracture Immobilization Techniques).[72] Our philosophy has been to provide internal fixation that is stable enough to permit functional loading postoperatively and avoid cast immobilization.

Interfragmentary lag screw fixation is the choice of implant for spiral metacarpal fractures. Attention to detail is vital when using these small screws (see Fracture Immobilization Techniques). In large adults, 2.7-mm screws are used, and in smaller individuals, 2.0-mm screws. Screw fixation alone will be successful only if the length of the fracture is at least twice the diameter of the metacarpal and no less than two screws are used. Screw placement is determined by the anatomy of the fracture plane. With two screws, effective resistance to shear and torsional stresses is best achieved with one screw placed perpendicular to the fracture line and another placed perpendicular to the metacarpal shaft. With stable fixation, patients can begin active movement as soon as they are comfortable (see Fig. 38–40).

If problems are noted intraoperatively with the stability of the screw fixation, the tension band wire technique advocated by Belsole and Greene[16] should be considered because it can provide fixation that is stable enough to permit functional rehabilitation without any requirement for a plaster cast.[16, 17]

Short oblique fractures provide an excellent fracture line for interfragmentary screw fixation, but the single screw

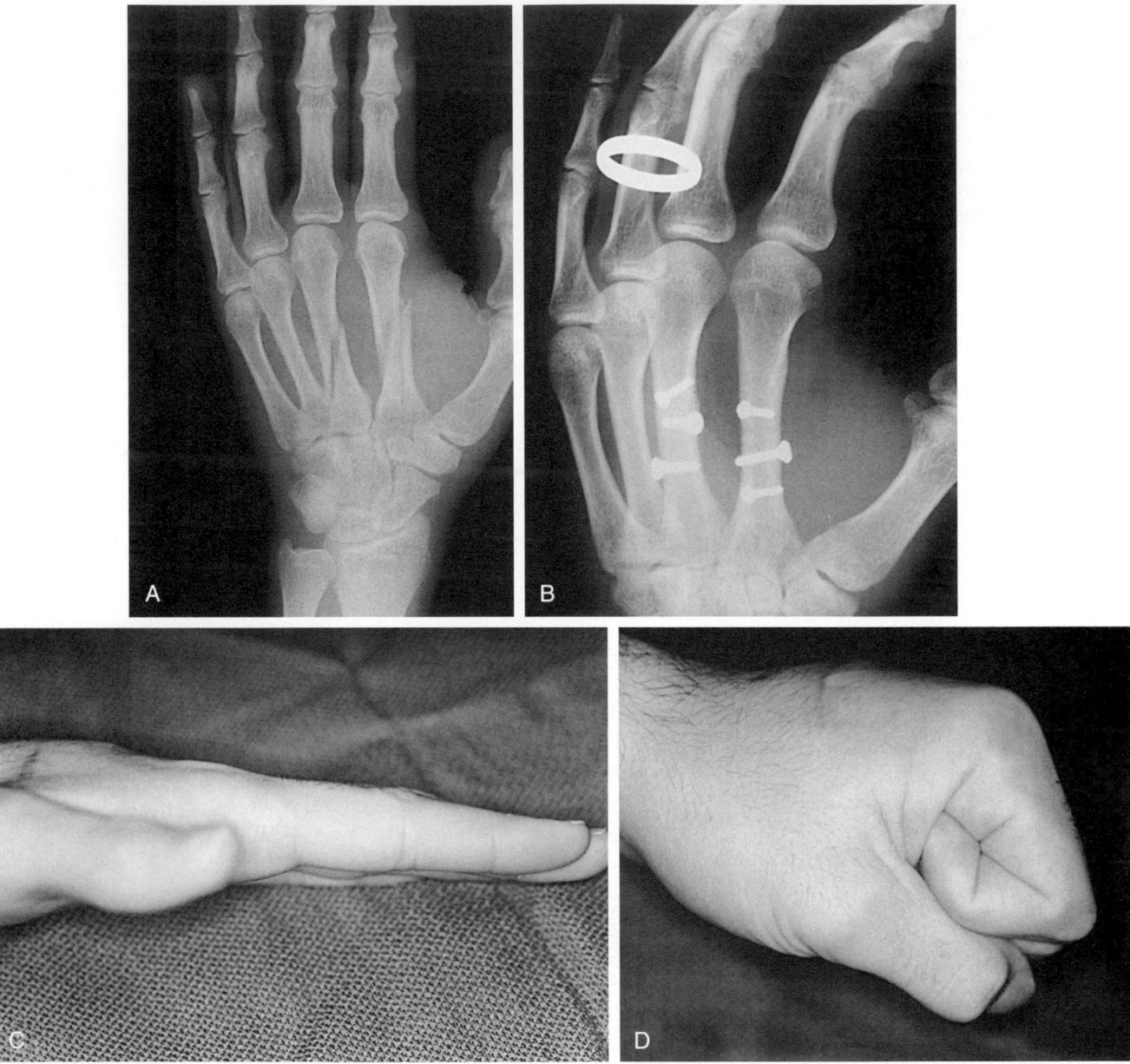

**Figure 38–40.** A 23-year-old man sustained two displaced spiral metacarpal fractures in a rugby match. He presented with a swollen hand and shortening and malrotation of the involved rays. Secure fixation was achieved with interfragmentary lag screws. *A,* A preoperative radiograph demonstrates the long spiral fracture lines. *B,* Anatomic reduction and stable fixation were achieved with carefully placed 2.7- and 2.0-mm lag screws. *C, D,* Full motion was regained.

must be "neutralized" against rotational and shear stress by a plate. The choice of plate must be individualized for the specific location on the shaft. However, as a general rule, the plate should permit two screws (four cortices) proximal and distal to the fracture. In the midshaft, either a one-quarter tubular plate applied dorsally with 2.7-mm screws or a 2.0-mm DC plate with 2.0-mm screws is appropriate for most adult metacarpals. If the fracture is at the proximal third of the metacarpal, a **T** or **L** plate may be the best implant. It is important to first place the screws through the **T** or **L** portion and then fix the screws through the straight portion. If the procedure is done in a reverse manner, rotational deformity will probably occur as the screws are tightened in the **T** or **L** portion (Fig. 38–41).

Depending on the fracture line, a lag screw may be placed either through or independent of the plate. Careful plate contouring is needed to allow the **T** or **L** portion to fit to the metacarpal flare well and prevent torquing and malalignment of the implant with final screw tightening.

Multiple transverse shaft fractures are frequently associated with soft tissue trauma and are well suited to plate fixation (Fig. 38–42). In the absence of comminution and with an intact palmar cortex, again, either the one-quarter tubular plate with 2.7-mm screws or the 2.0-mm DC plate is adequate. In this instance, the implant will function as a tension band plate. It should be overcontoured to sit slightly above the dorsal cortex because when the screws are applied and tightened, the anterior cortex will be compressed. As such, the plate will be under "tensile" stress and will be protected from bending stress.[127]

When faced with comminution, attention must be directed to preserving the remaining soft tissue envelope and any remaining blood supply to the small bone fragments. The concept of biologic plating or indirect reduction is applicable in these situations.[200] The implant itself is used as an internal splint to bridge the multifragmentary segments, with support only proximally and distally. The bone is drawn up to the plate, and the fracture is reduced by traction through the remaining soft tissue attachments. A few isolated additional screws can be placed through the plate to secure the intermediary fragments. With this method, a stronger implant such as the 2.7-mm DC plate should be chosen to stabilize the construct. If the fractures consist of one or two butterfly fragments, an alternative to plate fixation is the tension band wire technique, which will permit each fragment to be individually assembled back onto the diaphysis in a secure fashion. Some caution should be exercised because this technique, though effective, demands particular attention to detail (Fig. 38–43). K-wire fixation alone is difficult with these fractures, often does not provide

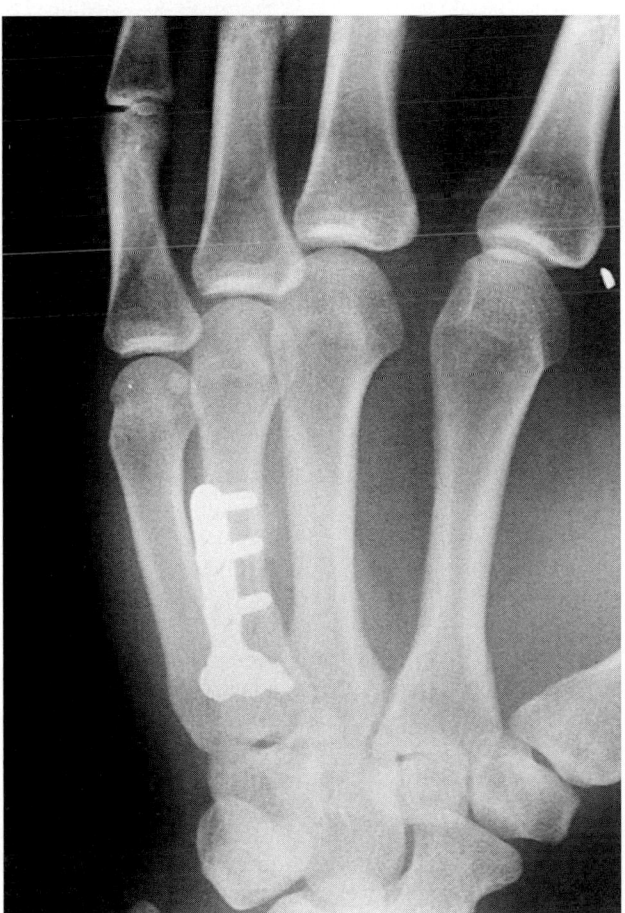

**FIGURE 38–41.** A displaced, malrotated, short oblique fracture of the proximal third of the fourth metacarpal was secured with a T plate. An interfragmentary screw was placed through the plate across the oblique fracture line. (From Jupiter, J.B.; Silver, M.A. In: Chapman, M.W., ed. Operative Orthopaedics. Philadelphia, J.B. Lippincott, 1988, pp. 1235–1250.)

rotational stability, and requires plaster immobilization. The last, in particular, can be unfortunate given the all-too-common soft tissue component of these injuries. K-wire fixation is the least favored method of internal fixation for these fractures.

## METACARPAL FRACTURES WITH BONE LOSS

Metacarpal shaft fractures associated with bone loss are generally only one part of a complex composite skeletal and soft tissue injury. A traditional approach has consisted of maintaining skeletal length with external fixation or intermetacarpal wires, achieving soft tissue closure, and restoring skeletal continuity at a later stage when soft tissue stability is ensured and some mobility is regained in the digital joints.[228]

Along with improvements in the techniques of stable skeletal fixation and soft tissue reconstruction has come recognition that early reconstruction of the skeleton presents a decided advantage in accelerating rehabilitation efforts and minimizing the overall duration of the associated disability. Freeland and colleagues reported excellent results with metacarpal skeletal restoration performed within 10 days of the initial injury.[94] Their protocol is based on extensive wound débridement of all nonviable tissue while maintaining skeletal length and alignment with a number of techniques, including spacer wires, transfixation K-wires, and external fixation devices. A second débridement is performed 3 to 7 days after the first. If the wound appears clean, definitive skeletal reconstruction with an autogenous iliac crest graft and stable internal fixation is performed in conjunction with full-thickness soft tissue reconstruction (see Chapter 13). Freeland and associates reported a high rate of skeletal union without clinical infection.[94] This approach offers distinct advantages in the management of these severe complex injuries. Skeletal length and alignment are more easily ensured without the problems of operating in a contracted, less compliant soft tissue envelope.[52, 255] Union is accomplished by placing the bone grafts in a well-vascularized environment and securely fixing them with more stable internal fixation.[268] Finally, rapid restoration of the skeleton with secure fixation offers the opportunity to start functional rehabilitation, thus minimizing the potential for joint contracture and tendon adhesion.

## Metacarpal Neck Fractures

Fractures at the level of the metacarpal neck are among the most common of all fractures in the hand. Not infrequently, they are the result of a direct impact on the metacarpal head with the hand in a clenched-fist position. Fracture of the fifth metacarpal is by far the most frequent and has become known as a *boxer's fracture*. This description is somewhat misleading because professional fighters are more likely to sustain a second or third metacarpal neck fracture.

Metacarpal neck fractures are impacted on the volar aspect. They always displace with dorsal angulation at the fracture line, and the distal segment, the metacarpal head,

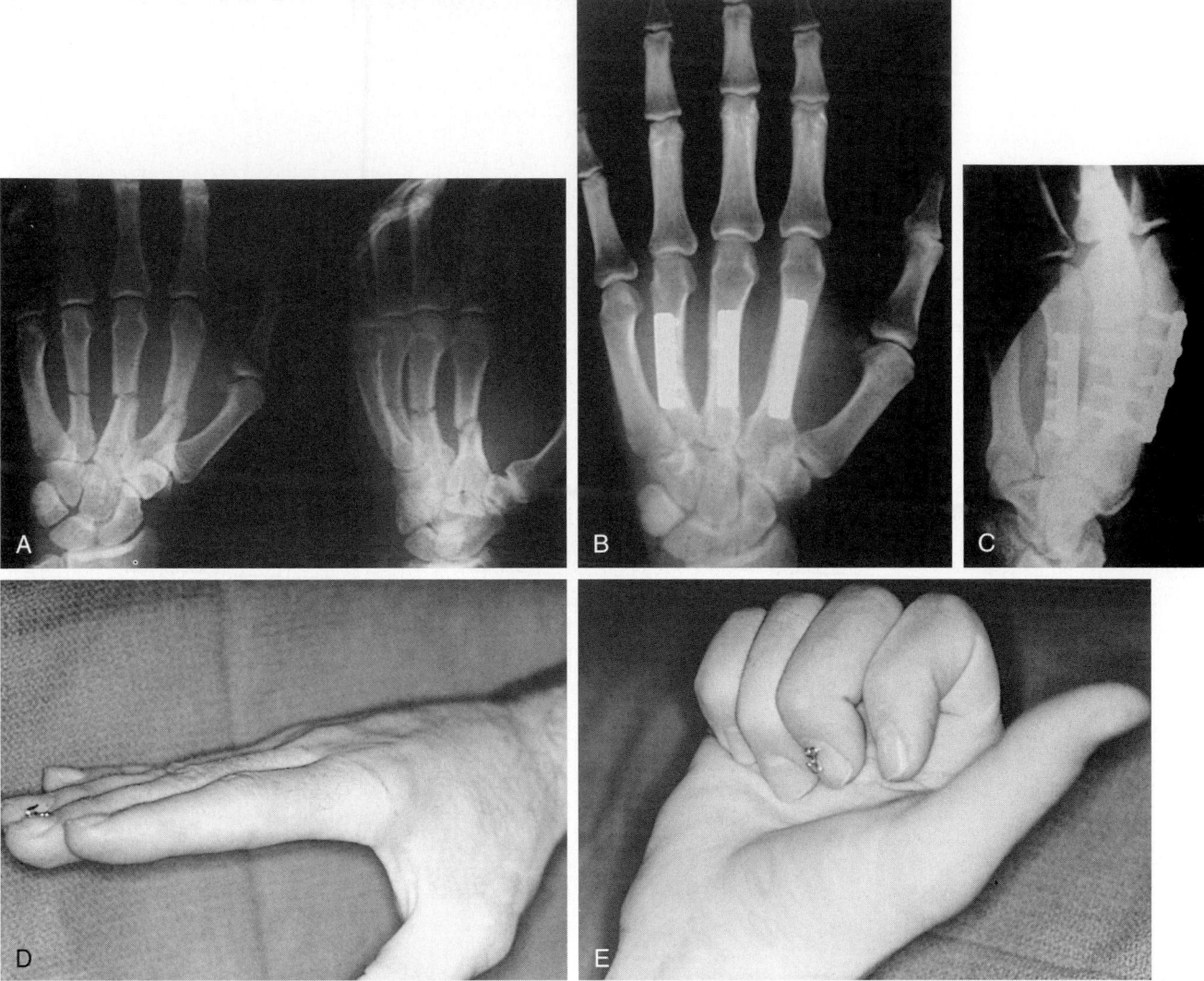

**FIGURE 38–42.** A laborer sustained blunt trauma to his dominant right hand. Massive swelling was associated with three transverse metacarpal fractures. *A,* Anteroposterior (left) and oblique (right) radiographs reveal three transverse metacarpal shaft fractures. Minimal comminution was present. *B, C,* Through two longitudinal incisions, the swelling was decompressed and the fractures stabilized with four-hole one-quarter tubular plates. *D, E,* Active-assisted motion was begun on the first postoperative day along with the application of Coban wraps to diminish swelling. At 2 weeks, the patient had regained nearly full motion. The fracture healed, and the patient returned to his job within 8 weeks postoperatively. (*A–E,* From Jupiter, J.B.; Silver, M.A. In: Chapman, M.W., ed. Operative Orthopaedics. Philadelphia, J.B. Lippincott, 1988, pp. 1235–1250.)

is displaced palmarward. This palmar displacement can lead to an imbalance of the extrinsic tendons manifested as a claw deformity (Fig. 38–44). Physical examination should also ensure that no rotational deformity is present. If the angulation is substantial, the palmar prominence of the metacarpal head may present a problem with grip, especially with hand tools such as a screwdriver or a hammer.

A true lateral radiograph is necessary with these fractures so that the angle of displacement of the distal fragment can be measured. Given the mobility of the fifth and, to a lesser extent, the fourth CMC joints, some angulation at the fracture is acceptable in these two metacarpals. Some authors believe that more than 30° of palmar displacement necessitates an attempt at reduction,[282] whereas others will accept up to 50° of angulation before reduction is considered.[11, 84, 132, 137]

Less disagreement can be found regarding the second and third metacarpals because little, if any compensatory motion is present at their CMC joints. Thus, angulation beyond 10° will probably prove symptomatic. Lateral tomography is of great help when evaluating fractures of these two metacarpals. Metacarpal neck fractures that require no manipulation can be protected in a gutter splint for 2 weeks with the MCP joints flexed beyond 60°.

In the event that the patient has unacceptable palmar displacement of the metacarpal head, closed reduction under either wrist block anesthesia or a direct hematoma block with the MCP joint flexed to 90° is advisable. The proximal phalanx is grasped and used to correct any rotational deformity or palmar angulation; the latter is readily corrected by pushing up on the metacarpal head with the proximal phalanx[88, 143] (Fig. 38–45). A short arm cast or gutter splint is applied with care taken to mold the cast to maintain the MCP joint in 90° of flexion but leave the PIP joint in extension. The splint should be left in place for 3 weeks with a check radiograph obtained 7 to 10 days after reduction. It has become well accepted that the PIP

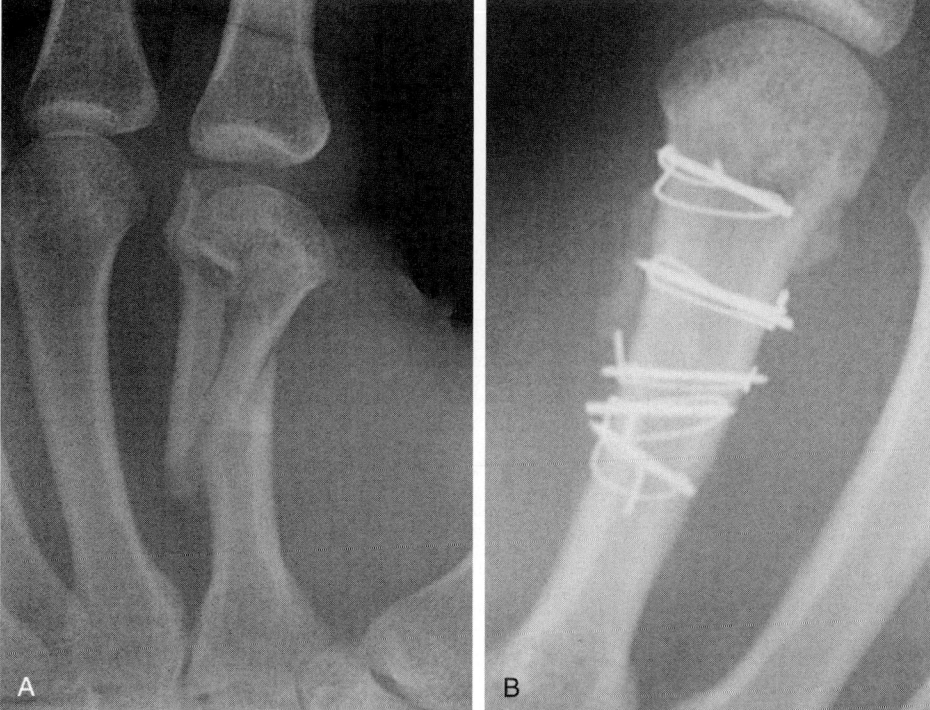

**FIGURE 38–43.** *A, B,* A comminuted metacarpal shaft fracture is reassembled and secured with an arrangement of tension band wires. (*A, B,* Courtesy of Dr. Robert Belsole.)

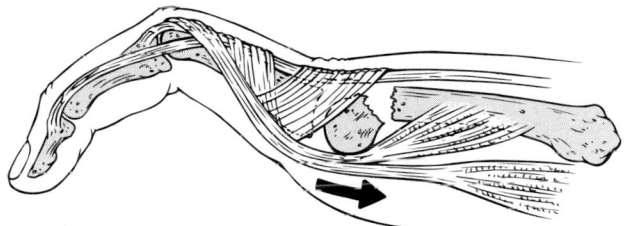

**FIGURE 38–44.** Excess palmar displacement of a metacarpal neck fracture will lead to imbalance of the extrinsic tendons and a claw deformity. The metacarpal head may be felt in the palm and may interfere with grip.

joint should not be held in flexion as initially recommended by Jahss[143] because this position can result in disastrous flexion contracture and even skin loss from pressure necrosis over the joint (Fig. 38–46).

Commercial braces are available that can be used as three-point fixation devices to hold the reduction. Although these braces are quite comfortable, small, and well conceived in principle, problems can arise with their use. Complications from skin necrosis under the contact points of the splint have been reported. Care is advised to check for such problems if these splints are used.[101, 226]

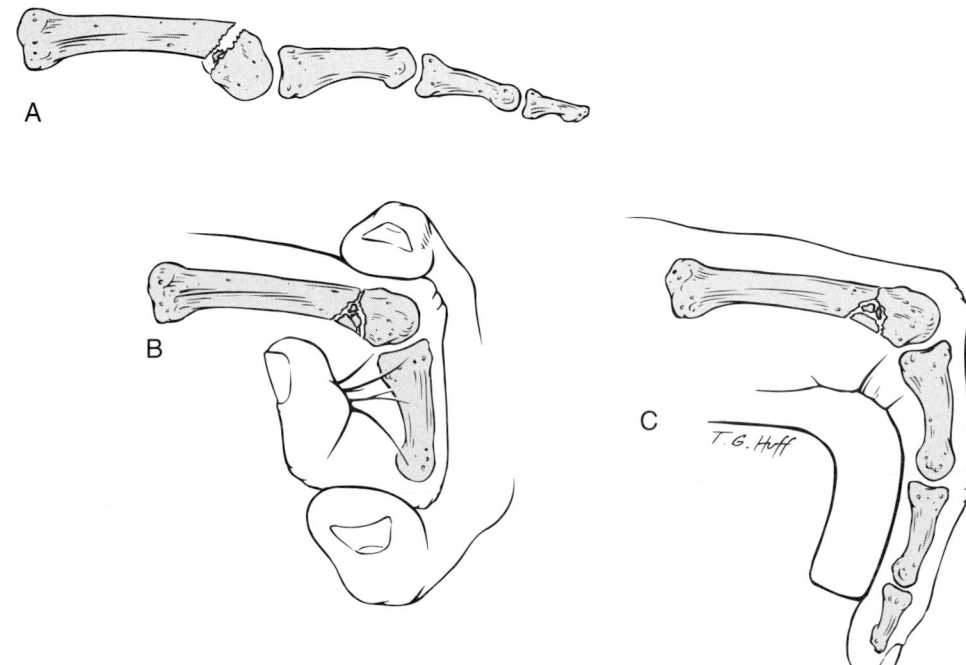

**FIGURE 38–45.** A displaced metacarpal neck can be reduced by flexing the metacarpophalangeal (MCP) joint to 90° and using the proximal phalanx to control rotation and as a lever to push the metacarpal head up. *A,* A displaced neck fracture is generally associated with comminution on the volar surface. *B,* Fracture reduction was accomplished by using the proximal phalanx to push the metacarpal head up. *C,* Immobilization in plaster should place the MCP joint in 70° to 90° of flexion and the proximal interphalangeal joints close to full extension.

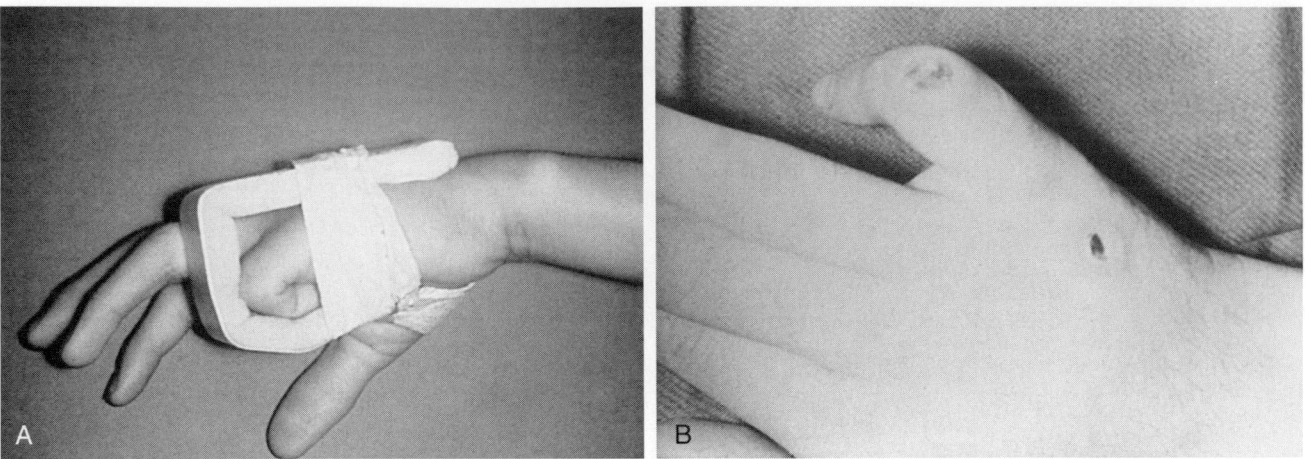

**FIGURE 38–46.** A 40-year-old woman had a displaced boxer's fracture of the fifth metacarpal neck. *A,* The fracture was reduced and held in a splint with the proximal interphalangeal (PIP) and metacarpophalangeal joints in extreme flexion. *B,* A severe flexion contracture of the PIP joint resulted, along with an area of pressure necrosis over the joint. The patient had an unsatisfactory functional outcome.

If a patient is seen with a severely angulated neck fracture of 50° or is initially evaluated 5 to 7 days or more after the injury, it is not likely that the closed reduction will be effectively held in plaster support. In these circumstances, percutaneous wire fixation is recommended. A number of techniques for wire placement exist, as illustrated in Figure 38–47. Our preference is to avoid, if possible, placing pins in or near the gliding structures that

envelope the metacarpal head. The stacked wire technique advocated by Hall[120] allows the pins to be placed through a site distant from the fracture and is recommended for this situation (Fig. 38–48). The metacarpal should be immobilized for 2 to 3 weeks, followed by a removable splint for 1 week.

Rarely is open reduction necessary. On occasion, a patient is first seen 3 to 4 weeks after injury, and closed

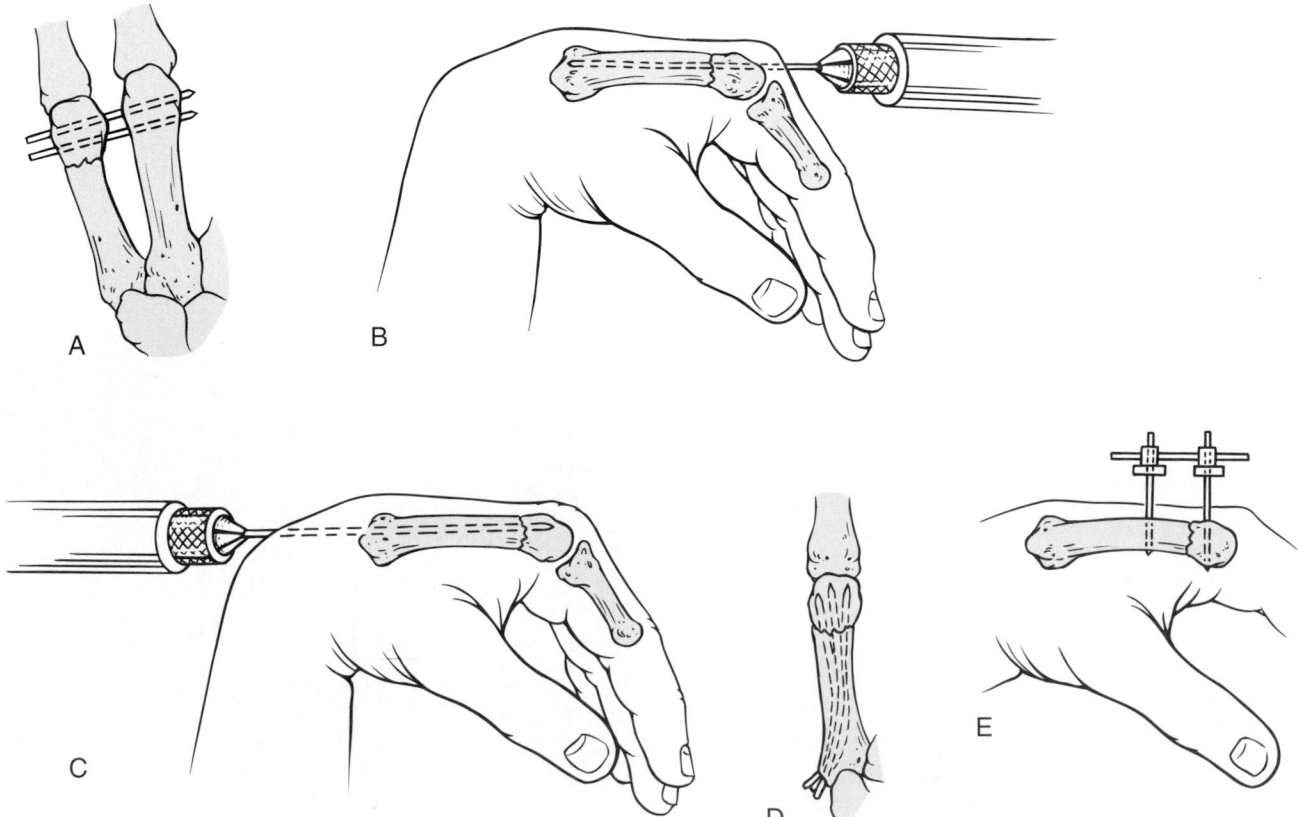

**FIGURE 38–47.** A variety of closed methods of percutaneous pin fixation of metacarpal neck fractures. *A,* Transverse pinning into an intact adjacent metacarpal. *B,* A longitudinal, proximally directed pin placed eccentrically into the metacarpal head. *C,* A longitudinal, distally directed pin. *D,* Multiple stacked pins directed from a proximal window in the base of the phalanx. *E,* Two external fixation pins to aid in and maintain reduction.

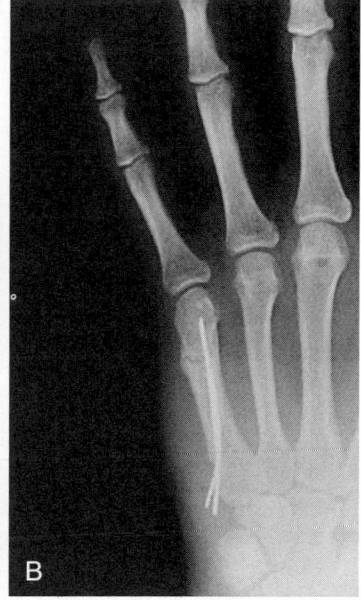

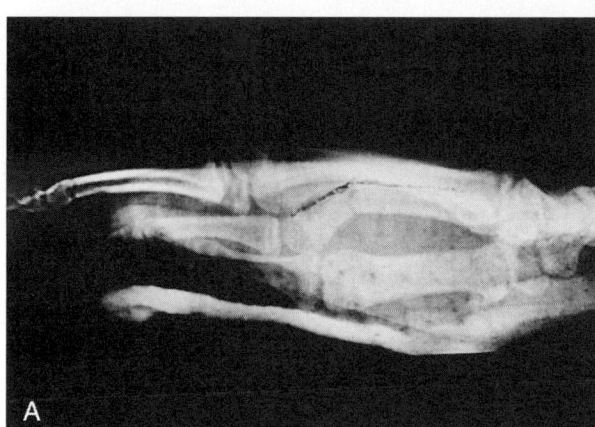

FIGURE **38–48.** A 15-year-old with a fifth metacarpal neck fracture angulated 60° (*A*) was treated by closed reduction and pin fixation introduced from a site proximal to the fracture in the base of the metacarpal (*B*): (*A, B,* From Jupiter, J.B.; Silver, M.A. In: Chapman, M.W., ed. Operative Orthopaedics. Philadelphia, J.B. Lippincott, 1988, pp. 1235–1250.)

manipulation is unsuccessful. In these cases, the fracture is approached through a longitudinal skin incision. The fracture site is also exposed through a longitudinal incision in the extensor mechanism. Our preference for internal fixation is a tension band wire placed around two K-wires (Fig. 38–49). Alternatively, the use of a dorsally applied **T** plate or minicondylar blade plate will work well in this situation. The fracture callus must be mobilized to facilitate reduction and can then be replaced as a local "bone graft" to speed union (Fig. 38–50).

Plates in this anatomic region are best reserved for complex injuries with combined soft tissue and skeletal loss. The 2.7-mm **T** or **L** plate combined with a compact cancellous bone graft has been the implant used most often (Fig. 38–51). The bulk of the implant and screws lying under the extensor tendon mechanism has presented some difficulty in rehabilitation of these gliding structures. This problem has been solved to a large degree with the 2.0- and 2.7-mm condylar plates, which can be applied along the lateral surface of the metacarpal neck and shaft along with a bone graft.

An additional approach in these cases involves external fixation. The technique described by Pritsch and colleagues[239] of placing one pin in the metacarpal head and one in the shaft has been used effectively by these authors even for some closed fractures. Pin loosening and interfer-

FIGURE **38–49.** *A,* A 40-year-old woman was thrown from her horse and sustained a closed, displaced fifth metacarpal neck fracture that was discovered 3 weeks after the injury. *B,* Open reduction was performed, and the fracture was stabilized with a tension band wire passed around two K-wires. Early motion was encouraged because the fixation was mechanically sound.

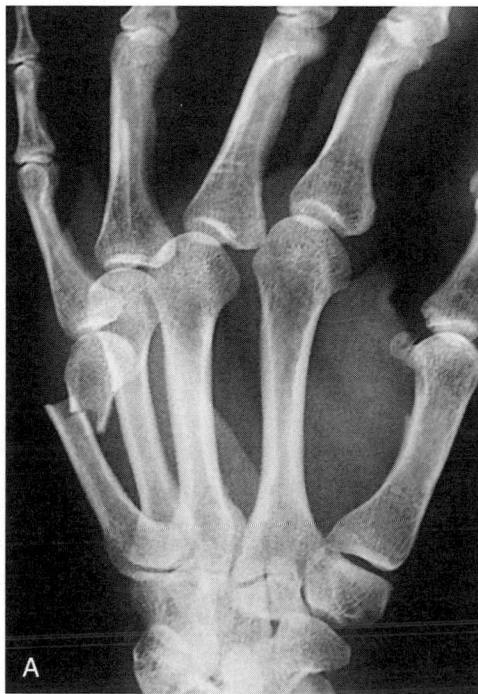
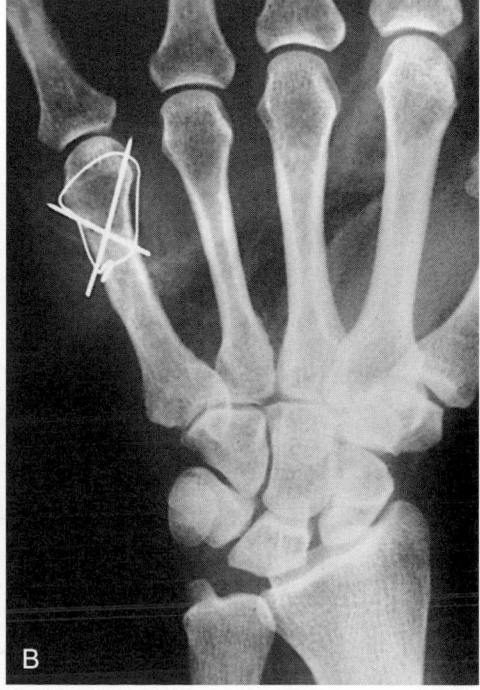

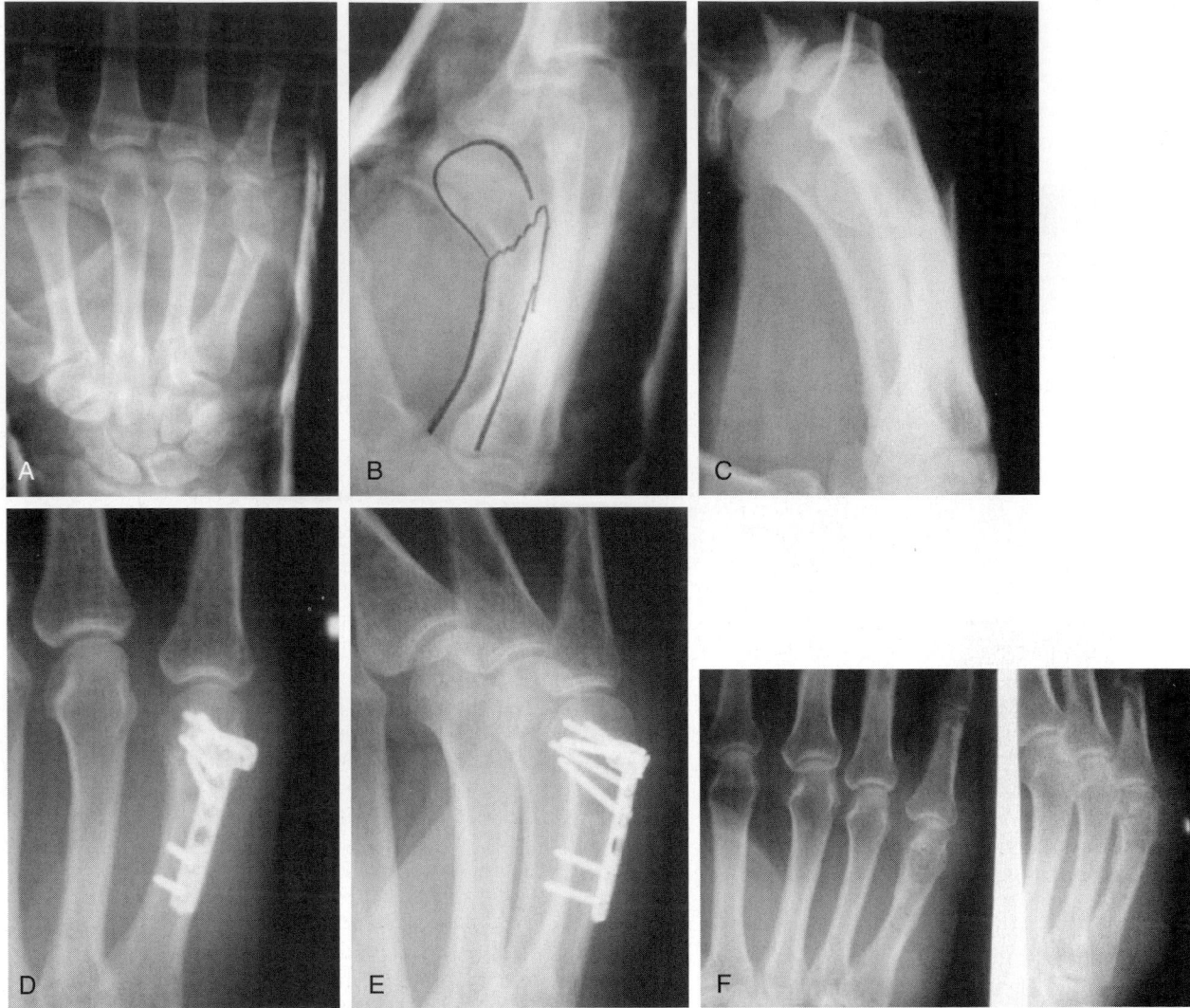

**FIGURE 38–50.** *A, B,* Boxer's fracture showing some malalignment; however, the position was considered acceptable. Cast management was instituted. *C,* At 4 weeks, the fracture had flexed into an 85° deformity. *D, E,* Osteoclasis was performed, followed by reduction and dorsal 2.0-mm T plate internal fixation. *F,* After plate removal, tenolysis, and capsulotomy, full metacarpophalangeal motion was restored without pain.

ence with tendon excursion are the pitfalls with this technique.

## Metacarpal Head Fractures

Intra-articular fractures involving the head of the metacarpal are uncommon injuries. In a review of 250 open and closed articular fractures, Hastings and Carroll found only 16 that involved the metacarpal head and only 5 that were closed injuries.[125] A comprehensive review of 103 such fractures by McElfresh and Dobyns[203] revealed an array of fracture patterns ranging from collateral ligament avulsion fractures to extensive comminuted fractures associated with loss of bony substance. McElfresh and Dobyns divided two-part head fractures into oblique (sagittal) fractures of the metacarpal shaft entering the joint, vertical (coronal) fractures, and horizontal (transverse) fractures (Fig. 38–52). The most common pattern was a comminuted head fracture, which was found in 31 of 103 fractures. The most frequently involved metacarpal was the

second, and these authors postulated that such frequent involvement of the second metacarpal was a result of its border position and lack of mobility at the CMC joint. The increased mobility of the fifth CMC joint puts its metacarpal head in a more flexed position at the moment of a direct axial blow, and as a result, a neck fracture is much more common in this metacarpal.

These injuries may be exceptionally difficult to appreciate on routine radiographs. Lateral radiographs, in particular, are often unrewarding because of overlapping of adjacent MCP joints. Therefore, the Brewerton view has been advocated for these injuries.[175] In this view, the MCP joints are flexed between 60° and 70°, and the dorsal surfaces of the digits lie flat on the x-ray cassette. The x-ray tube is angled 15° in an ulnar-to-radial direction. AP and lateral tomography has an important role not only in confirming the presence of these fractures but also in identifying the specific fracture pattern (Fig. 38–53). CT scanning using fine 1-mm cuts has provided immense help in defining the extent of these injuries.

Small, transverse lacerations proximal to the metacarpal

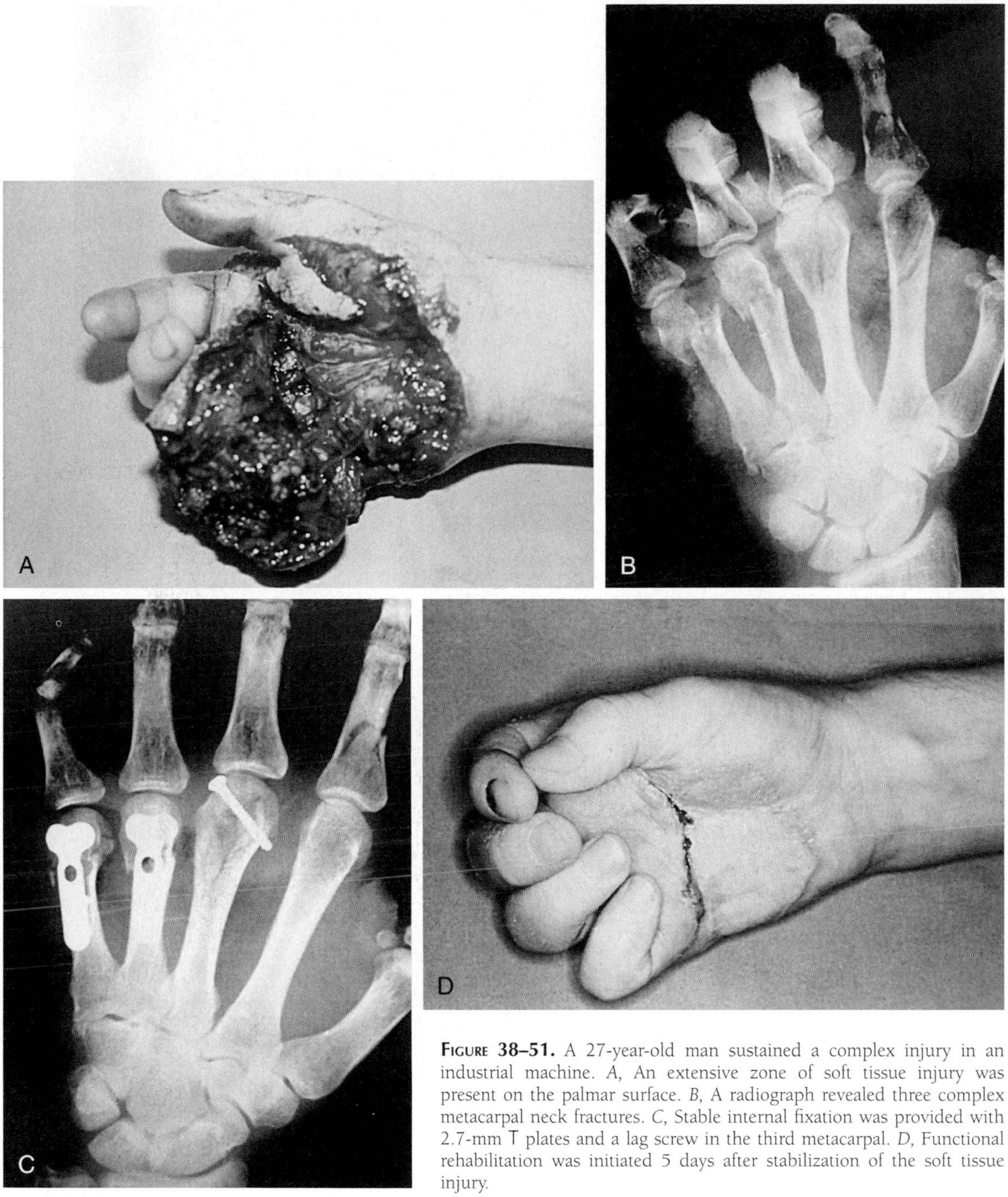

**FIGURE 38–51.** A 27-year-old man sustained a complex injury in an industrial machine. *A,* An extensive zone of soft tissue injury was present on the palmar surface. *B,* A radiograph revealed three complex metacarpal neck fractures. *C,* Stable internal fixation was provided with 2.7-mm T plates and a lag screw in the third metacarpal. *D,* Functional rehabilitation was initiated 5 days after stabilization of the soft tissue injury.

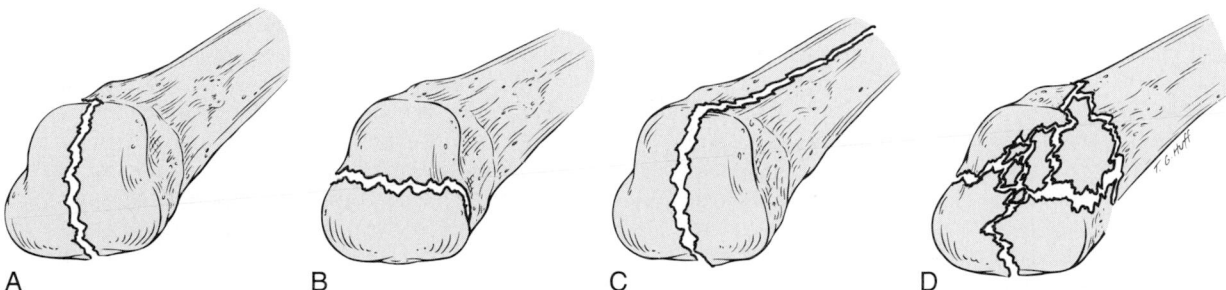

**FIGURE 38–52.** Fractures of the metacarpal head may have several distinct patterns. *A,* Vertical (coronal). *B,* Horizontal (transverse). *C,* Oblique (sagittal). *D,* Comminuted.

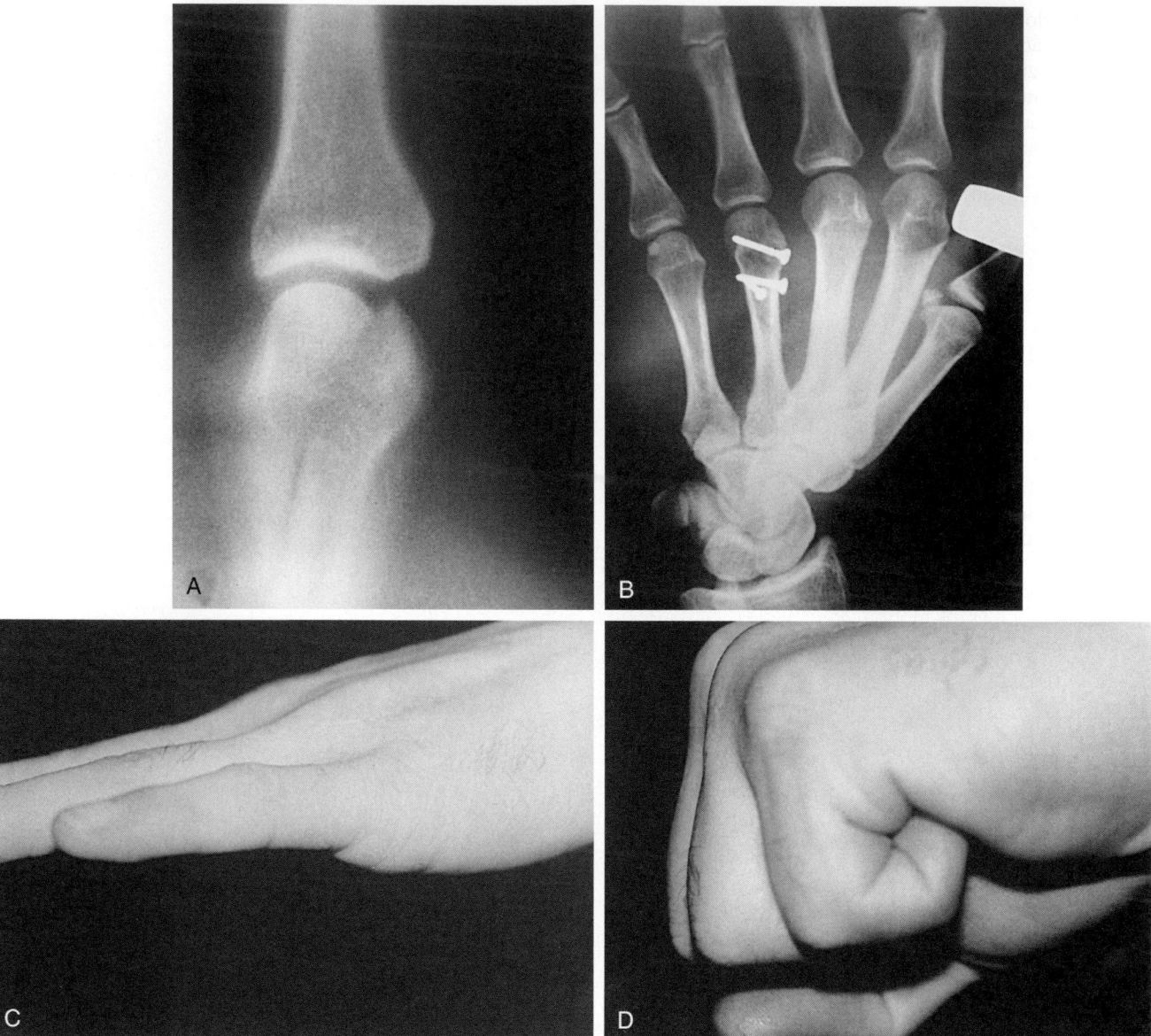

**Figure 38–53.** A 38-year-old man sustained a sagittal metacarpal head fracture of his fourth metacarpal as an extension of a more proximal shaft fracture. *A,* An anteroposterior tomogram clearly demonstrates the articular congruity. *B,* Stable fixation was achieved with carefully placed interfragmentary lag screws. *C, D,* Functional mobility returned within 5 weeks after injury.

head are suggestive of contact with a human tooth. Injuries incurred in fistfights carry a high rate of sepsis if not recognized and treated early with irrigation, débridement, drainage, and intravenous antibiotics.

Closed management with early protected motion will suffice for most undisplaced metacarpal head fractures.

Displaced fractures require special consideration. The goal of treatment of these fractures, as with most intra-articular fractures, involves anatomic restoration and fixation that is stable enough to permit active mobilization. An operative approach to these complex fractures should be considered only if preoperative planning suggests that these goals can be accomplished. Thus, with extensively comminuted fractures, distraction fixation with an external fixation device or early mobilization may be preferable to surgical intervention, which will generally offer little hope of success.

The operative approach is through a dorsal incision with an interval developed between the extensor tendon and the sagittal band. The fracture fragments are gently manipulated, with soft tissue attachments left in place to minimize the risk of devascularizing these tenuous fragments. Hastings and Carroll[125] reported using K-wires for fixation of the small articular fragments. These K-wires, though effective in holding the fragments in place, fail to provide sufficient stability to allow early mobilization. In addition, the pins themselves can irritate the surrounding soft tissue, also limiting mobilization. For these reasons, with large-enough fragments, miniscrews and self-compressing Herbert screw, which can be sunk beneath the chondral surface, have added considerably to the effective operative management of certain of these fractures[162] (Fig. 38–54). Placing the screw heads dorsally and cautiously countersinking them will minimize their impeding tendon mobility. The interfragmentary compression that is achieved results in more predictable union in the restored anatomic position. Multifragmentary fractures with dissociation of the head and shaft fragments require a plate for sufficient stability. The minicondylar plate, which serves as a buttress device, will provide excellent stability and support the articular fragments. A cancellous bone graft taken from either the distal end of the radius or the proximal portion of the ulna will often be needed to provide subchondral support to the elevated articular segments.

A metacarpal head fracture caused by penetrating trauma from a fistfight should be viewed as a highly contaminated wound. Extensive irrigation and débridement are essential, and some may consider leaving the wound open for 24 hours, followed by a second débridement with definitive internal fixation and wound closure.

The most serious complication intrinsic to this unusual fracture is loss of joint motion despite careful operative technique.[197] Avascular necrosis may occur as a result of the initial trauma or from operative intervention. In the series of Hastings and Carroll,[125] the 16 patients with metacarpal head fractures achieved an average postoperative range of motion of +1° to +83° of flexion. In the series of Buechler and Fischer,[38] avascular necrosis developed in 3 of 17 distal metacarpal fixations, all of them performed for intra-articular metacarpal head shear fractures.

## Thumb Metacarpal Fractures

Fractures of the thumb metacarpal are second in frequency only to those involving the fifth metacarpal, and they account for nearly 25% of all metacarpal fractures.[99]

Furthermore, of all thumb metacarpal fractures, more than 80% involve the base.[99, 206] These fractures can be divided into four groups, similar to fractures at the base of the fifth metacarpal (Fig. 38–55 and Table 38–16): epibasal extra-articular, Bennett's, Rolando's, and comminuted. The mechanism of injury in all four types is very similar, that of an axially directed force through a partially flexed metacarpal shaft.

### EPIBASAL FRACTURES

Epibasal extra-articular fractures are more commonly transverse than oblique. The mobility of the trapeziometacarpal will allow as much as 30° of angulation at this level without significant loss of mobility or strength.[112] The vast majority of transverse fractures are stable and require protective cast immobilization in a thumb spica cast for 4 to 6 weeks. If the angulation is greater than 30°, closed reduction and percutaneous K-wire fixation are recommended. Wire placement can be axially directed down the metacarpal shaft and into the trapezium or with two K-wires into the second metacarpal.

An epibasal oblique fracture can be confused with an intra-articular Bennett fracture, and tomography or a fine-cut CT scan may be required to define any articular involvement. If the fracture is displaced, closed reduction and K-wire fixation (as with transverse fractures) should be considered.

### BENNETT'S (TWO-PART) FRACTURE

Intra-articular fractures involving the thumb CMC joints are the most frequent of all thumb fractures[54, 99, 206] and yet have been the source of continued discussion since

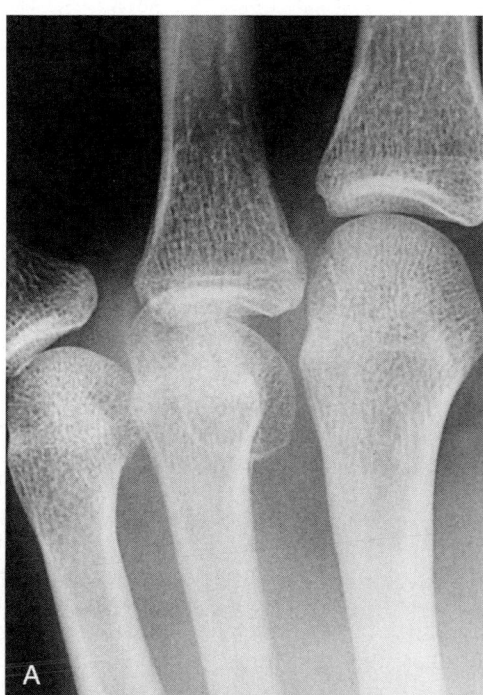
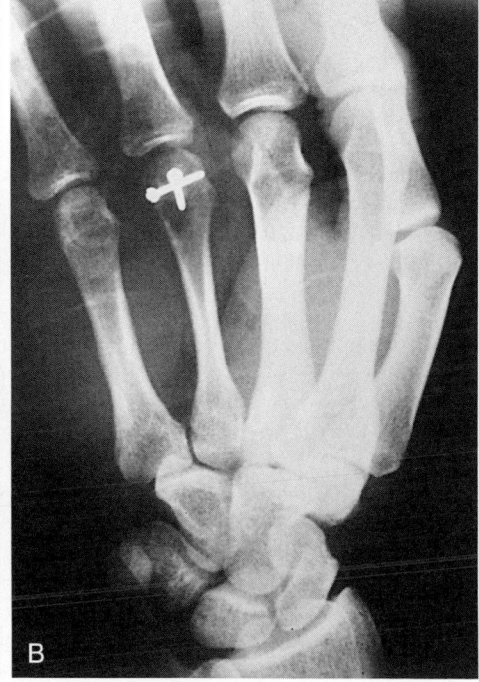

**FIGURE 38–54.** *A, B,* An impacted metacarpal head fracture was operatively reduced and securely fixed with two interfragmentary screws that were carefully countersunk into the dorsal cortex.

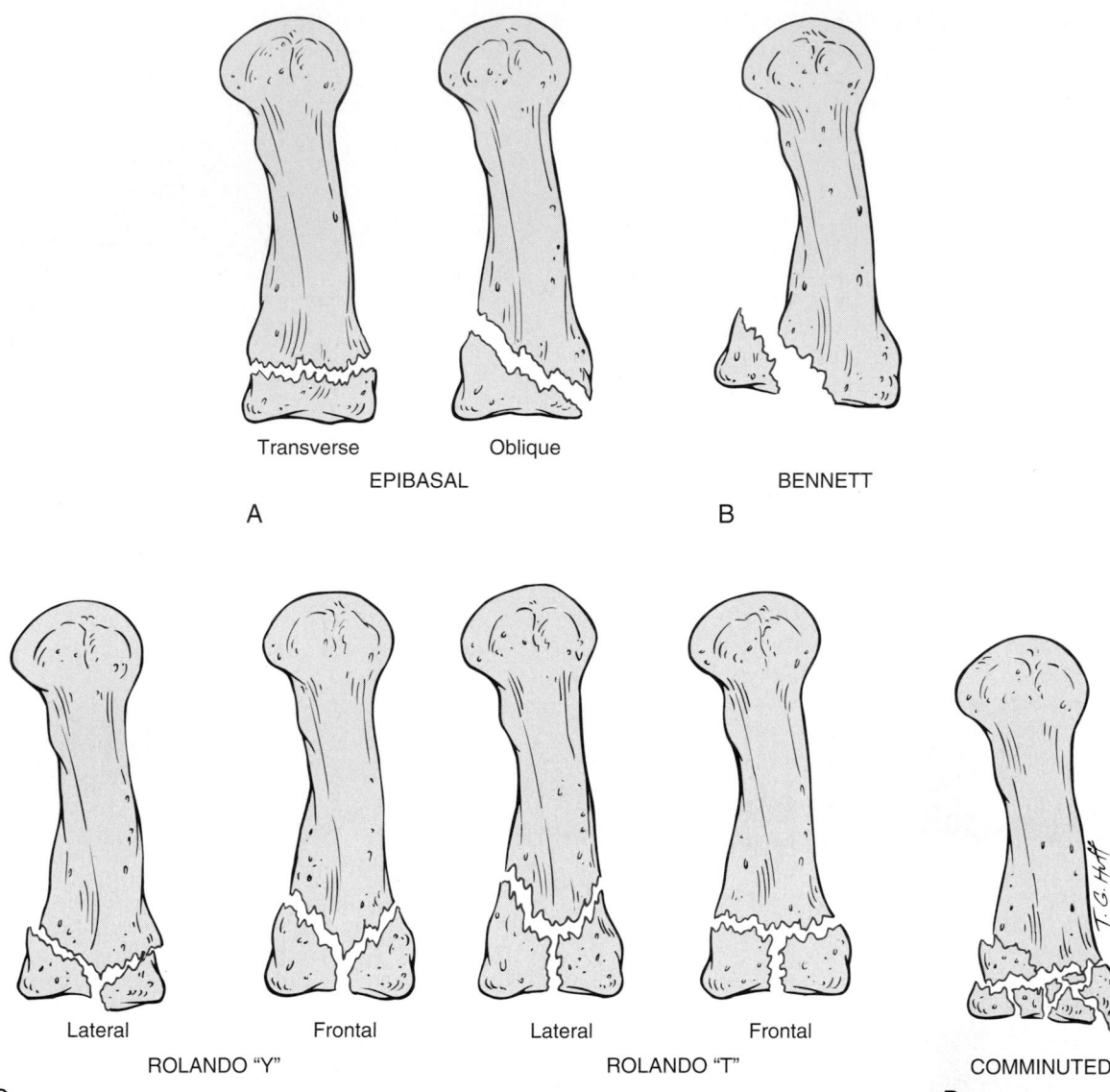

**FIGURE 38–55.** Fractures of the base of the thumb metacarpal can be grouped into four types: epibasal (*A*), Bennett's (*B*), Rolando's Y and T (*C*), and comminuted (*D*).

Bennett first described the fracture in 1882.[18] The mere fact that the literature has offered an exhaustive list of treatment options during the past century reflects the reality that no particular method is ideal for all cases.[32, 49, 102, 112, 237, 258, 283, 304]

**TABLE 38–16**
..........................................

Incidence of Thumb Metacarpal Fractures

| Type | % |
|------|-----|
| Bennett's | 34 |
| Basal | 44 |
| Y/T | 9 |
| Oblique extra-articular | 46 |
| Transverse extra-articular | 29 |
| Diaphysis | 10 |
| Neck/head | 12 |

..........................................

*Source:* Gedda, K.O. Acta Chir Scand Suppl 193:5, 1954.

The CMC joint of the thumb represents two reciprocally interlocked saddles that permit both flexion and extension as well as abduction and adduction.[119, 220, 231, 235] Cooney and co-workers characterized the articular surface as a universal joint with longitudinal and axial rotation limited by its capsule, ligaments, and extrinsic muscle-tendon units.[59, 60] The intracapsular volar oblique ligament is essential as a stabilizing unit of the metacarpal by virtue of the fact that it inserts onto the ulnar articular margin of the volar beak on the ulnar aspect of the metacarpal base. Maximal tension occurs in this ligament with the metacarpal in flexion, abduction, and supination. With Bennett's fracture, the medial volar beak of the first metacarpal is split off. Attached to this fracture fragment is this critical restraining ligament. The result is displacement of the metacarpal base dorsally with rotation into supination by the pull of the abductor pollicis longus. The metacarpal head is also displaced into the palm by the pull of the adductor pollicis[231] (Figs. 38–56 and 38–57).

Bennett's fracture, along with other fractures at the base of the metacarpal, is the result of an axially directed force on the thumb metacarpal while it is partially flexed. Males predominate in almost a 10:1 ratio, and two thirds of these fractures occur in the dominant hand.[231] In Gedda's exhaustive study, nearly half of all Bennett's fractures occurred in patients younger than 30 years.[99]

Because of the thumb metacarpal's oblique orientation in reference to the plane of the palm, routine radiographs of the hand may be difficult to interpret and will often fail to reveal the true extent of the fracture anatomy, as well as subluxation of the metacarpal. A true AP view of this joint can be obtained by using the projection described by Roberts[252] in which an AP view of the thumb is taken with the forearm in maximal pronation and the dorsum of the thumb resting on the cassette. Perhaps of even greater value is the true lateral view advocated by Billing and Gedda.[19] This view is obtained with the forearm flat on the table, the hand pronated approximately 20° with the thumb flat on the cassette, and the x-ray tube angled 10° from vertical in a distal-to-proximal direction (Fig. 38–58). This projection will enable (1) a more exact

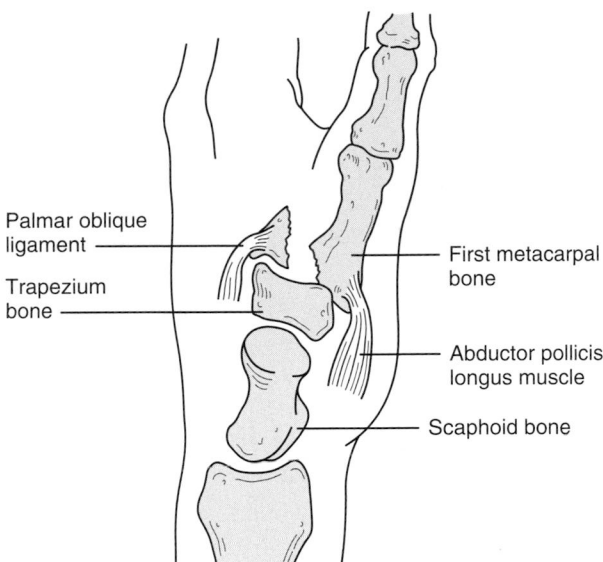

**FIGURE 38–56.** Patterns of force displacement leading to the typical carpometacarpal dislocation of a Bennett fracture. Note that the palmar oblique ligament holds the medial fragment anatomically aligned with the trapezium.

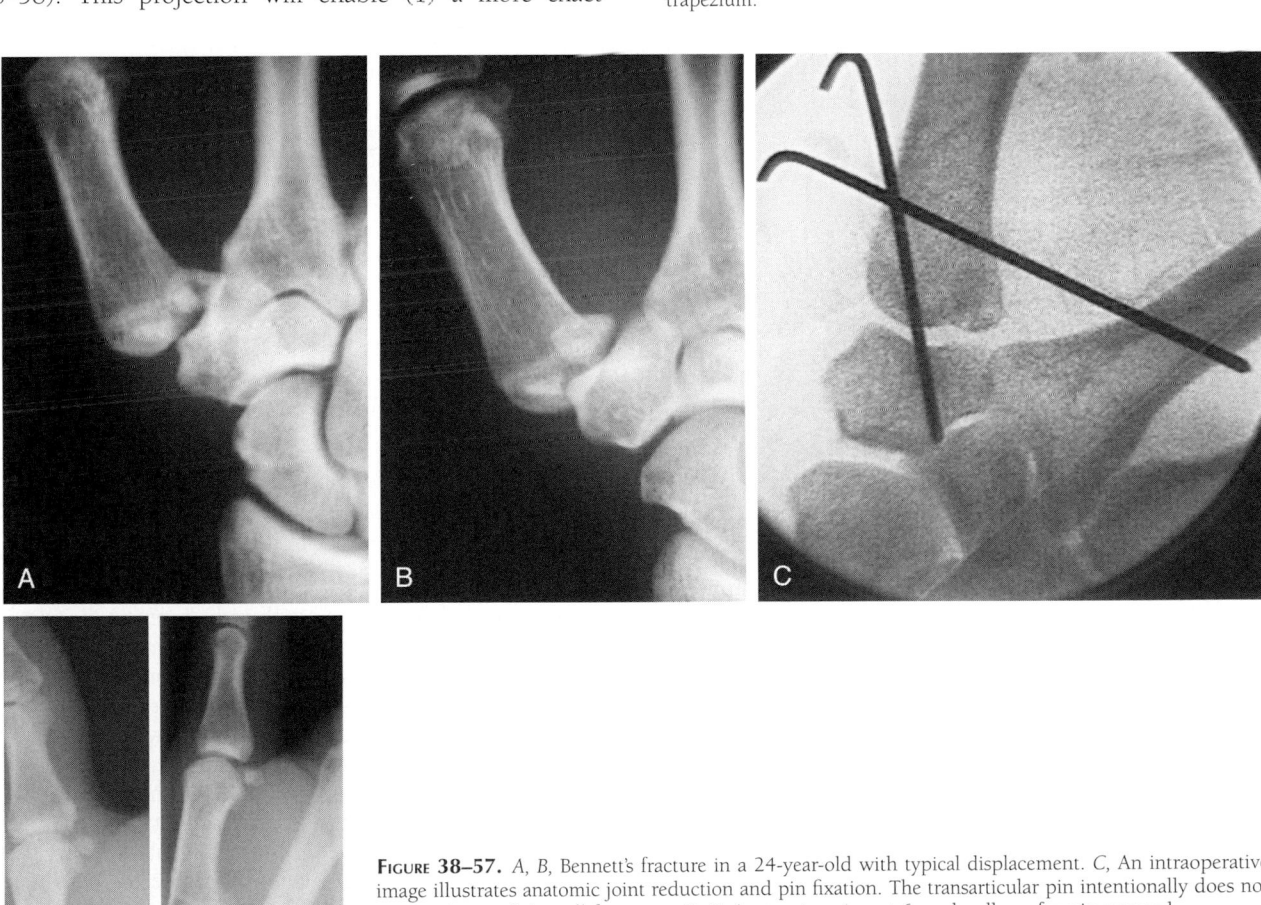

**FIGURE 38–57.** *A, B,* Bennett's fracture in a 24-year-old with typical displacement. *C,* An intraoperative image illustrates anatomic joint reduction and pin fixation. The transarticular pin intentionally does not engage the medial small fragment. *D, E,* Anatomic union at 6 weeks allows for pin removal.

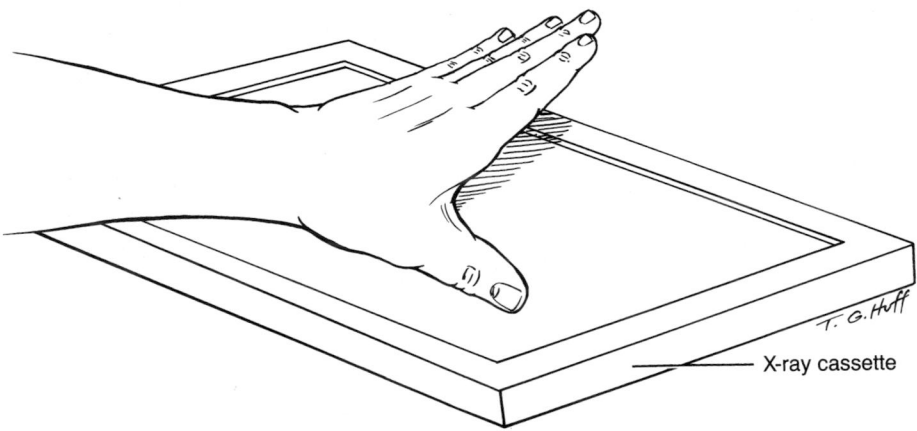

**FIGURE 38–58.** A true lateral radiograph of the first metacarpal trapezial joint is taken with the thumb flat on the cassette, the hand pronated 20° to 30°, and the x-ray tube positioned 10° in a distal-to-proximal direction.

judgment of metacarpal displacement, (2) an estimate of the size and position of the volar fragment, and (3) an estimate of the existing gap between the fragment and the metacarpal base. Tomography is often considered, particularly in cases with a suggestion of impaction at the articular surface.

The optimal method of treating Bennett's fractures is still undecided inasmuch as a vast number of surgeons have used different methods and all have reported good results.[18, 32, 49, 99, 112, 237, 258, 283, 304] This lack of general consensus may well be a result of disagreement about the relationship of the articular anatomy and late results. Although Gedda's data strongly suggested a correlation between persistent fracture displacement and the development of radiographically evident arthritis,[99, 100] such has not been the case in a number of other series.[49, 54, 114, 231, 237, 258, 312] Pellegrini and Burton noted a low percentage (2.8%) of patients who had a past history of a fracture at the base of the thumb and required subsequent surgery for symptomatic osteoarthritis.[230] These authors explained that the weak correlation between anatomic fracture reduction and good functional results was largely a result of the relatively unconstrained nature of this joint. However, they, too, recommended closed reduction and percutaneous pin fixation for injuries with less than 3 mm of fracture displacement and ORIF for fractures with 3 mm or more of displacement.

The solution to this problem may well be found in the description of the fracture patterns by Gedda in 1954[99] and more recently by Buechler[37] (Fig. 38–59). Gedda noted wide variations in the size of the volar ulnar metacarpal beak fragment and in the extent of displace-

ment of the metacarpal on the trapezium, even to the point of complete dislocation. In some instances, he described intra-articular impaction fractures. Buechler[37] identified three features that distinguish one fracture from another, including

1. The location and displacement of the fracture
2. The extent of crush or impaction at the metacarpal base

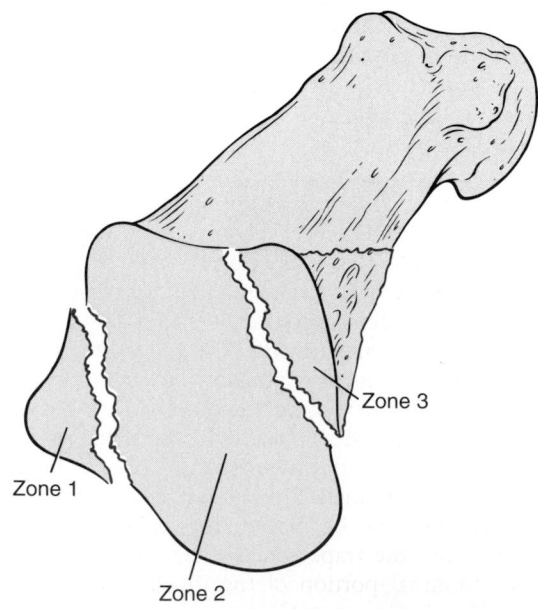

**FIGURE 38–59.** Three zones of articular involvement in Bennett's fractures as proposed by Buechler. Fractures with a displaced, impacted articular surface in zone 2 have the potential for post-traumatic arthritis. In zones 1 and 3, however, post-traumatic arthritis is unlikely.

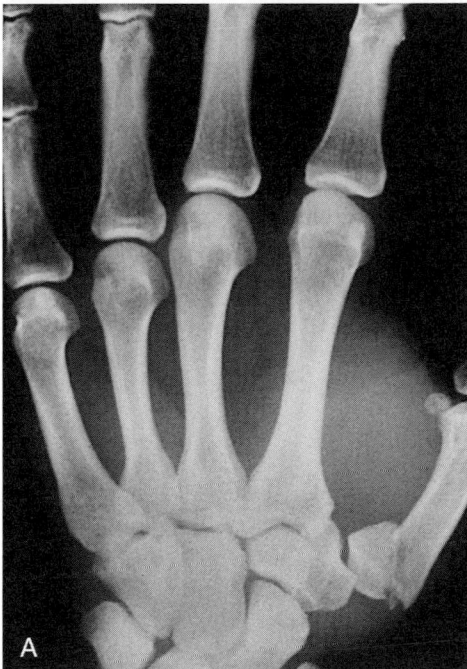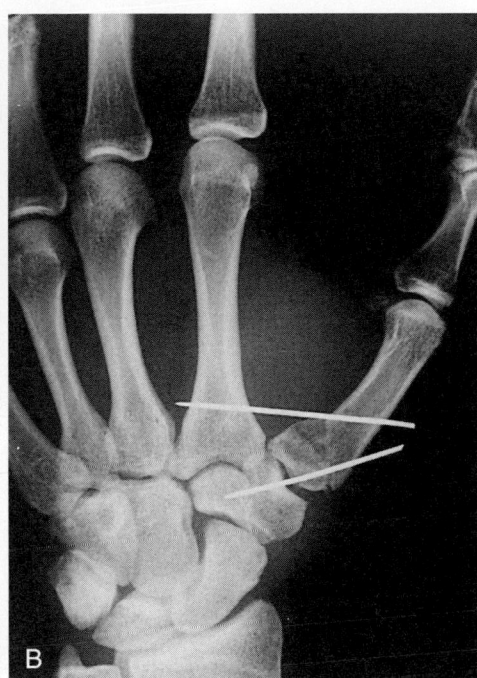

**FIGURE 38–60.** *A*, A 36-year-old man sustained a displaced oblique epibasal fracture of his dominant thumb metacarpal. *B*, The fracture was reduced with traction and manual pressure on the base of the metacarpal and stabilized with 0.045-inch K-wires placed percutaneously.

3. The presence or absence of shearing or impaction injury to the radial side of the articular surface of the trapezium

Buechler also divided the base of the metacarpal into three zones, with the middle zone being the area that will normally be loaded (see Fig. 38-59). If the fracture occurs in the other two zones, later problems will rarely occur. Furthermore, if the fracture lies in the central zone but without impaction of the articular surface, it will also fare well, provided that the metacarpal subluxation is reduced. Only the subgroup of Bennett's fractures associated with a zone of impacted articular surface will be subject to greater shearing forces at the trapezial articulation and the later development of post-traumatic changes.[173]

The approach to a displaced Bennett fracture should therefore be based on the specific nature of the fracture pattern. For the vast majority of fractures in Buechler's zones 1 and 3, as well as those in zone 2 without evidence of impaction, closed reduction and percutaneous pin fixation are our preference (Fig. 38–60). The goal is to reduce and hold the metacarpal base back to the undisplaced ulnar volar fragment. To accomplish this task, it is not usually necessary to open the fracture site—closed manipulation will often work. The reduction is accomplished with longitudinal traction on the end of the thumb, coupled with abduction and extension of the thumb metacarpal. The metacarpal is pronated to bring it into opposition with the nondisplaced palmar fragment, and the base of the metacarpal is manually reduced (Fig. 38–61). K-wires can be placed through the base of the metacarpal into the trapezium and a second wire passed into the proximal portion of the index metacarpal. The second wire helps control rotation and abduction of the thumb (Fig. 38–62). It is not necessary to try to secure the small fracture fragment (Fig. 38–63). Although some studies suggest that cast immobilization alone is effec-

tive,[237] several distinct problems may be encountered with this treatment, including the following:

1. The complexity of providing accurate three-point fixation over the thumb metacarpal and maintaining this contact pressure when soft tissue swelling has diminished
2. The difficulty of monitoring the adequacy of the reduction with radiographs through the cast
3. The poor results reported with cast treatment for fractures initially seen 4 or more days after injury[54, 114]

ORIF of displaced Bennett's fractures is indicated (1) when residual displacement of the joint surface is 2 mm or more after closed manipulative reduction, (2) in cases with radiographic evidence of impaction of the fracture, particularly in Buechler's zone 2 (best identified on tomography), or (3) for individual socioeconomic reasons. A volar incision as described by Gedda and Moberg[100] is used (Fig. 38–64). Care is taken to observe and protect branches of the radial sensory nerve, which can pass toward the palmar side at the base of the thumb. The origins of the abductor pollicis brevis and opponens pollicis are elevated off the proximal aspect of the first metacarpal in a subperiosteal manner. The CMC joint capsule is identified and opened and the fracture hematoma evacuated. The joint is visually inspected to look for free fragments, areas of impaction, or injury to the trapezial cartilage. A dental pick is ideal to gently loosen the hematoma from the fracture site, and reduction can be accomplished with longitudinal traction and manipulation of the metacarpal. A 0.035-inch K-wire will provide provisional fixation of the reduction. If the volar oblique fragment is very small, a second K-wire is used to secure the metacarpal into the second metacarpal, and a cast is worn for 6 weeks.

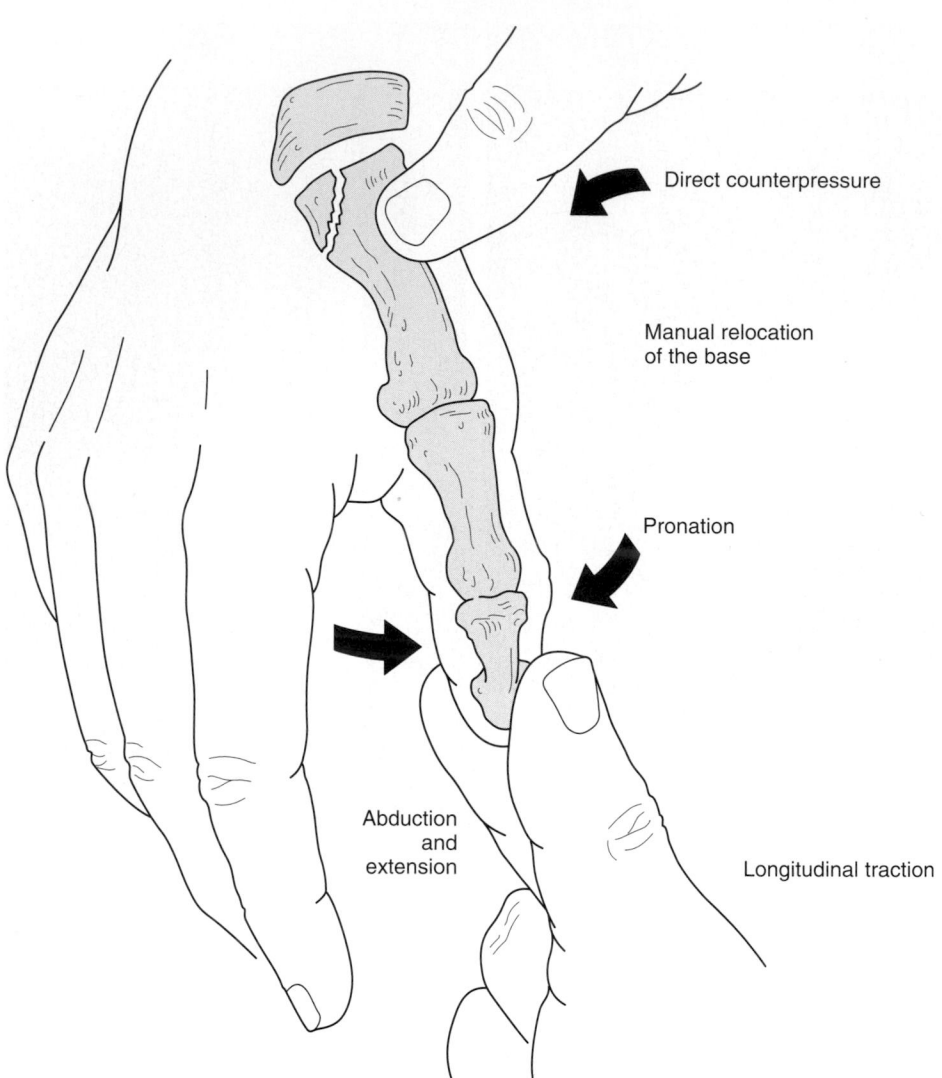

Direct counterpressure

Manual relocation
of the base

Pronation

Abduction
and
extension

Longitudinal traction

**Figure 38–61.** Reduction of a displaced Bennett fracture-dislocation is achieved by longitudinal traction on the end of the thumb coupled with abduction, extension, and pronation of the metacarpal. Manual pressure on the base will aid in its relocation.

With larger fragments, such as those in zone 2, lag screw fixation is indicated.[91] Any impaction of the trapezial articular surface is elevated. If a visible defect is found in the subchondral bone, a small amount of cancellous bone obtained from the distal end of the radius will be necessary to support the elevated articular surface. In judging the size of the screw to be used, the surgeon should bear in mind that the screw's thread diameter should be 30% or less of the width of the cortical surface of the fracture to minimize the risk of fracture of the fragment (see Fracture Immobilization Techniques).[91] The 2.7-mm screw is useful in most cases, and an additional 2.0-mm screw placed in a different direction is advised for large fragments (Fig. 38–65). Radiographs, including a true AP and a lateral view, are obtained to confirm both the accuracy of the reduction and the position of the screw and its length.

The thenar muscles are reattached and the wound closed after release of the tourniquet. A postoperative removable splint is made, and active motion is permitted as soon as comfort allows. Pinching is avoided for 1 month postoperatively, and a return to full functional use can be anticipated by 6 to 8 weeks postoperatively.

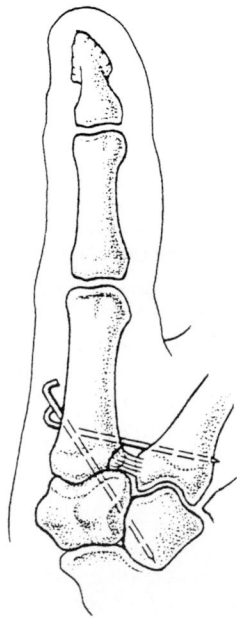

**Figure 38–62.** K-wire pin placement as illustrated clinically in Figure 38–60B. (From Heim, U.; Pfeiffer, K.M. Internal Fixation of Small Fractures, 3rd ed. New York, Springer-Verlag, 1987.)

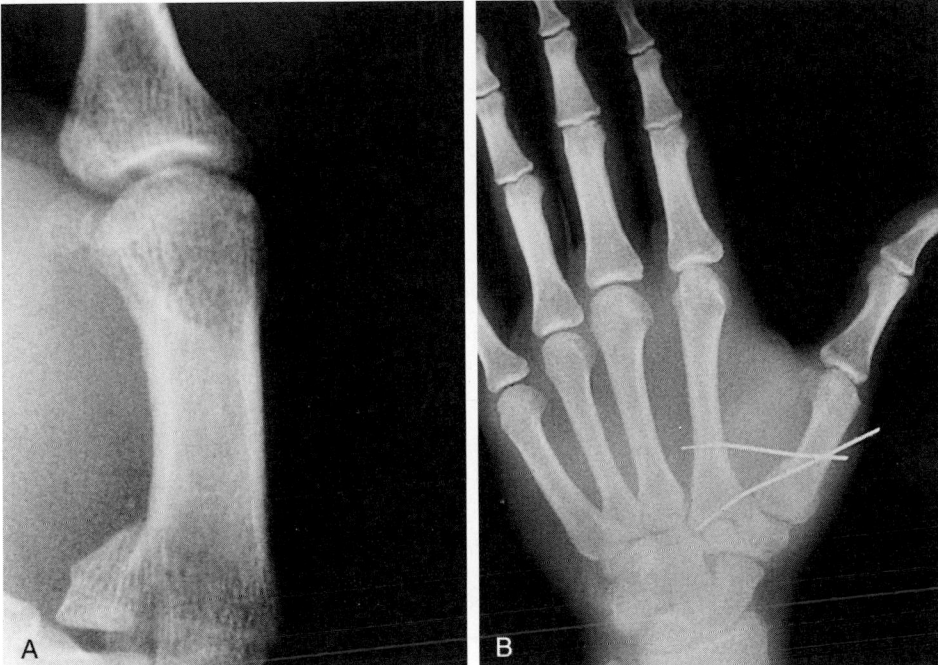

**FIGURE 38–63.** A displaced Bennett fracture-dislocation in a 24-year-old man was treated by closed reduction and percutaneous pin fixation. *A,* Radiograph revealing the Bennett fracture-dislocation. *B,* Two 0.045-inch K-wires stabilize the reduced metacarpal on the trapezium.

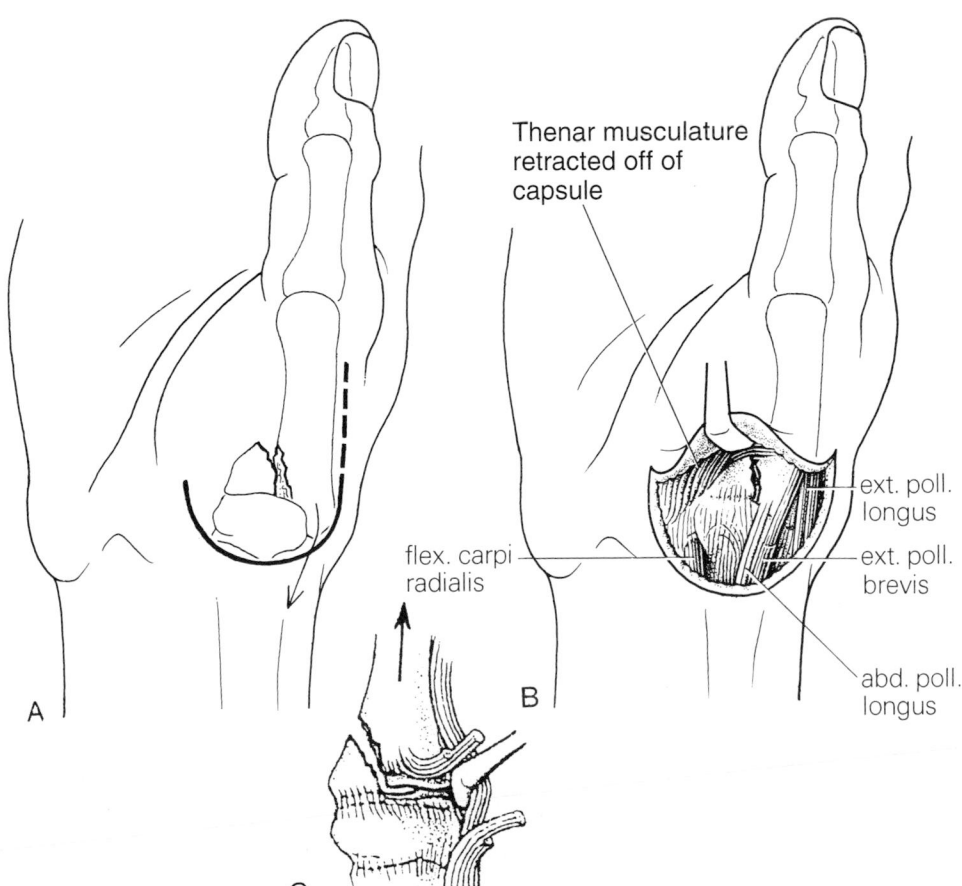

**FIGURE 38–64.** *A–C,* Gedda-Moberg approach to the base of the first metacarpal for fixation of a Bennett fracture. (*A–C,* Modified from Heim, U.; Pfeiffer, K.M. Internal Fixation of Small Fractures, 3rd ed. New York, Springer-Verlag, 1987.)

Thenar musculature retracted off of capsule

ext. poll. longus

ext. poll. brevis

abd. poll. longus

flex. carpi radialis

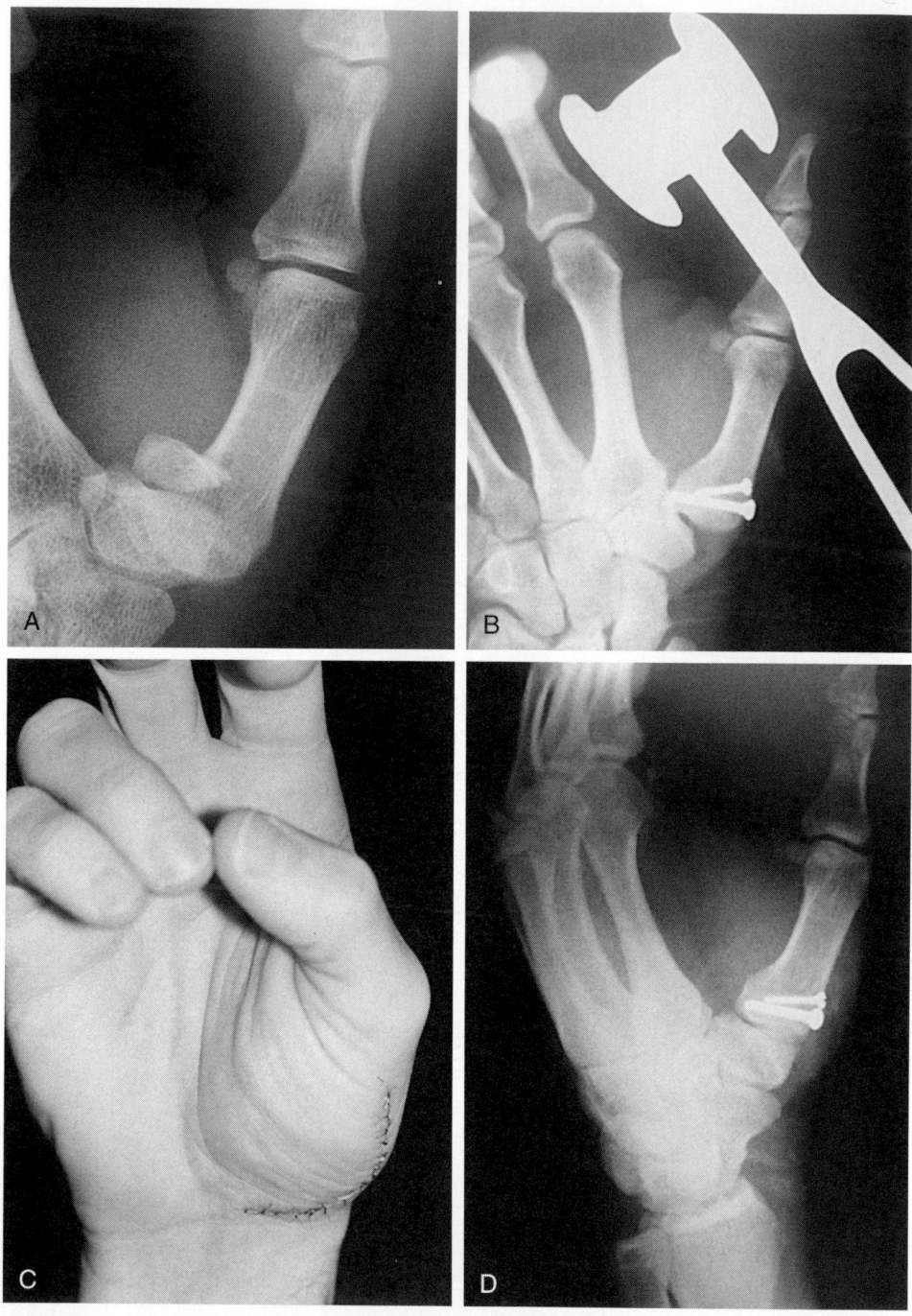

**FIGURE 38–65.** A 37-year-old man, a surgeon, sustained a displaced Bennett fracture-dislocation of his dominant thumb. *A,* Radiograph revealing displacement of the fracture. *B,* Intraoperatively, a large impacted central articular fragment was elevated, and the fracture was reduced and stabilized with 2.7- and 2.0-mm screws. *C,* Mobilization was initiated early postoperatively. *D,* An anatomic and fully functional result was achieved. The surgeon returned to work 2 weeks after the injury.

As outlined previously, lag screw fixation for a simple Bennett fracture does not provide any verified advantage over percutaneous wiring techniques as far as long-term results are concerned. It is substantially more difficult to perform and is more prone to complications. For these reasons, K-wire techniques are favored for most of these injuries.

## ROLANDO'S (THREE-PART) FRACTURE

In 1910, Rolando described the fracture that now bears his name.[254] His publication reported three Y-shaped intra-articular fractures of the base of the thumb. The prognosis for this fracture was described as poor.

Although Rolando's original description was that of a three-part fracture, it seems that this eponymic description has been used by other authors for more comminuted variants[99] (Fig. 38–66). We reserve this description for the uncommon, true three-part intra-articular fracture of the thumb metacarpal. AP and lateral tomography may be required to confirm the anatomy of this fracture, particularly if nonoperative treatment is contemplated. If tomography is not available, radiographs of the thumb taken while longitudinal traction is applied to the metacarpal are advisable.

If radiographic imaging reveals a reconstructible fracture with relatively large bone fragments, we believe that this fracture is best treated by ORIF. The surgical approach is similar to that for Bennett's fracture. The fracture is reduced by longitudinal traction with the two articular fragments manipulated into place. They are provisionally secured with a 0.035- or 0.028-inch K-wire and secured with an interfragmentary 2.0-mm screw. The reconstructed articular fragments can then be secured to the metacarpal shaft with a 2.7-mm **T** or **L** plate[91] (Fig. 38–67). On occasion, one fragment will be impacted and require elevation and support with a cancellous bone graft from the distal end of the radius. Postoperative management is similar to that for Bennett's fracture (Fig. 38–68).

An alternative method that can be considered is traction, either static (with an external fixation device) or dynamic (with a traction wire passed through the base of the metacarpal and out through the first webspace and attached to outrigger traction).[102, 304] Traction through an external fixator applied to the trapezium and the metacarpal shaft can be used in conjunction with limited internal fixation with few screws or K-wires. The traction will decompress the axial loads that cross the joint and neutralize the displacing forces, thereby allowing the minimal internal fixation to perform its role. Finally, both these methods can also be considered as a last resort if difficulty should ensue in applying internal fixation to these small fragments (Fig. 38–69).

## COMMINUTED FRACTURES

Comminuted fractures are exceptionally difficult to treat. Gedda noted post-traumatic arthritis in more than 50% of 14 patients with adequate follow-up.[99] As with the

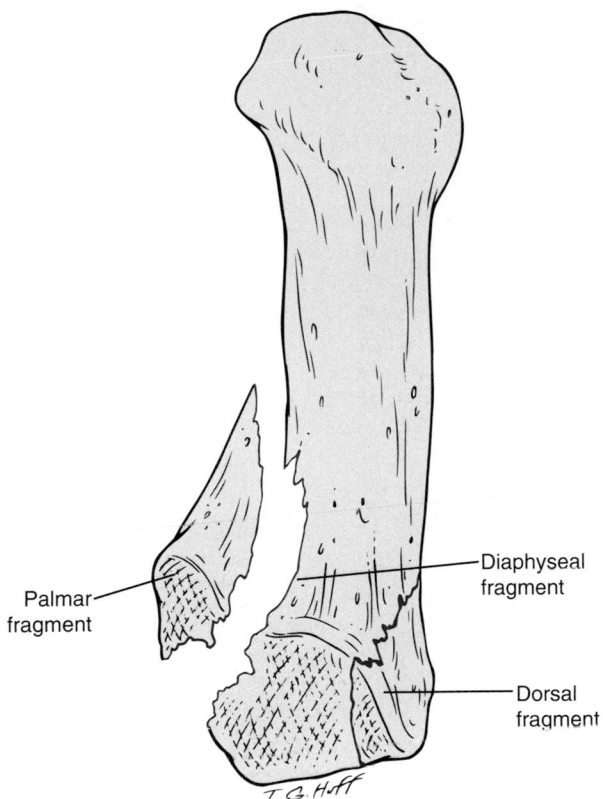

**FIGURE 38–66.** Representation of Rolando's original drawing of the fracture pattern that bears his name.

Palmar fragment

Diaphyseal fragment

Dorsal fragment

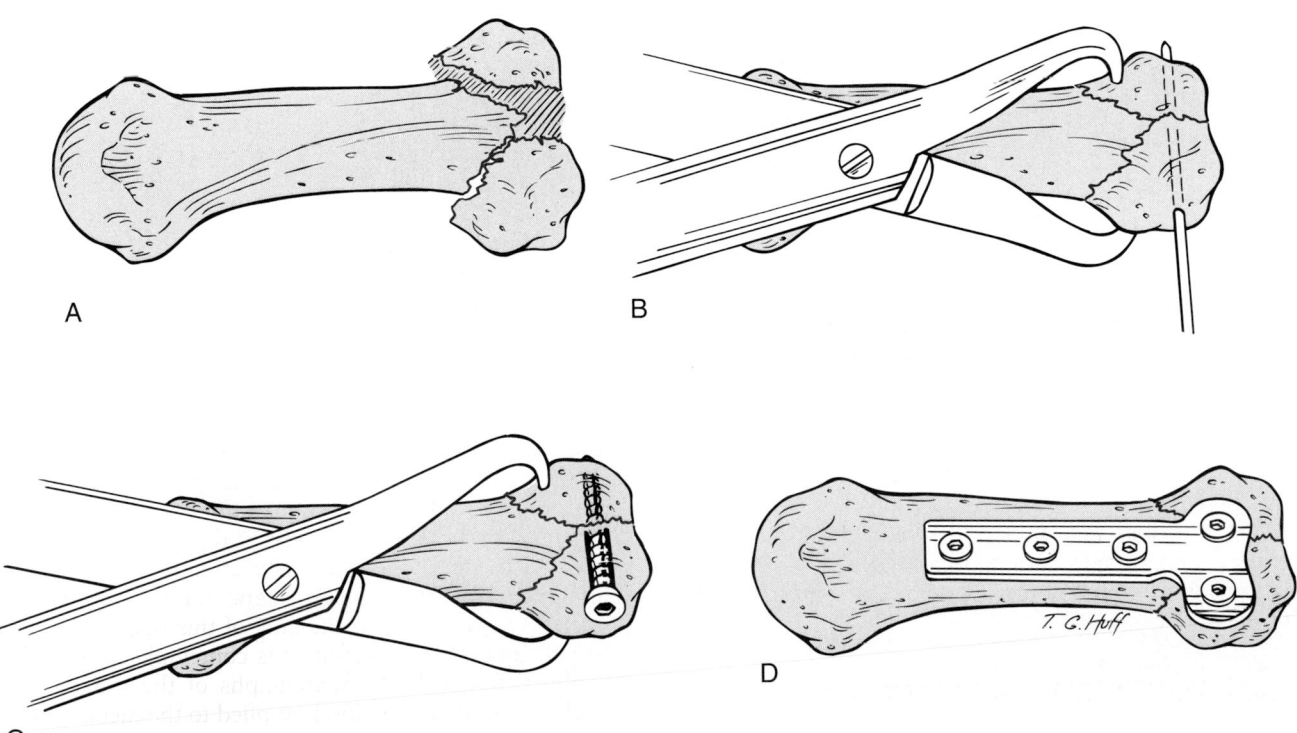

**FIGURE 38–67.** Operative technique of reduction and internal fixation of a three-part Rolando fracture. *A,* Three-part T-type fracture. *B,* Reduction is achieved by longitudinal traction and reduction of the articular fragments. *C,* The articular fragments are secured with an interfragmentary lag screw. *D,* The articular fragments are fastened to the metacarpal shaft with a T or L plate.

Rolando fracture, distraction has become an important factor in the approach to these fractures. If the joint surface is multifragmentary with extensive disruption, it may be very difficult to achieve anatomic reduction. In these situations, simple distraction with an external fixator, adjacent metacarpal pinning, or dynamic traction held with a metacarpal hooked pin and elastic anchored to a distal site ("banjo splint") may provide the best initial management. This latter technique, described by Spangberg and Thoren,[283] counteracts the forces of shortening and varus angulation of the metacarpal neck (Fig. 38–70). Occasionally, once traction is applied, the fractures are reduced by ligamentotaxis, with only a small amount of the joint surface left impacted and nonreduced. Percutaneous manipulation of these fragments may aid in the reduction at minimal cost to the soft tissue envelope. In the situation of minimal comminution and relatively large fragments, we prefer open reduction and use a distractor

intraoperatively to achieve ligamentotaxis reduction of these small fragments.

The surgical approach is similar to that already described. Pins are placed directly into the body of the trapezium and distal metacarpal shaft and attached to a minidistractor. With longitudinal traction applied, the joint fragments can be manipulated into place, secured with 0.028-inch K-wires, and supported with cancellous bone graft. The distractor is left in place for 4 weeks and then removed, and a thumb spica splint or cast is applied for an additional 2 weeks (Fig. 38–71). As an adjunct or an alternative, the traction method entailing the use of a longitudinal K-wire through the first webspace, as described by Thoren,[32, 102, 304] may prove useful.

At times, these fractures are the result of high-energy trauma with associated soft tissue and other skeletal injuries. The miniature external fixator can be used not only as a distractor for the comminuted intra-articular

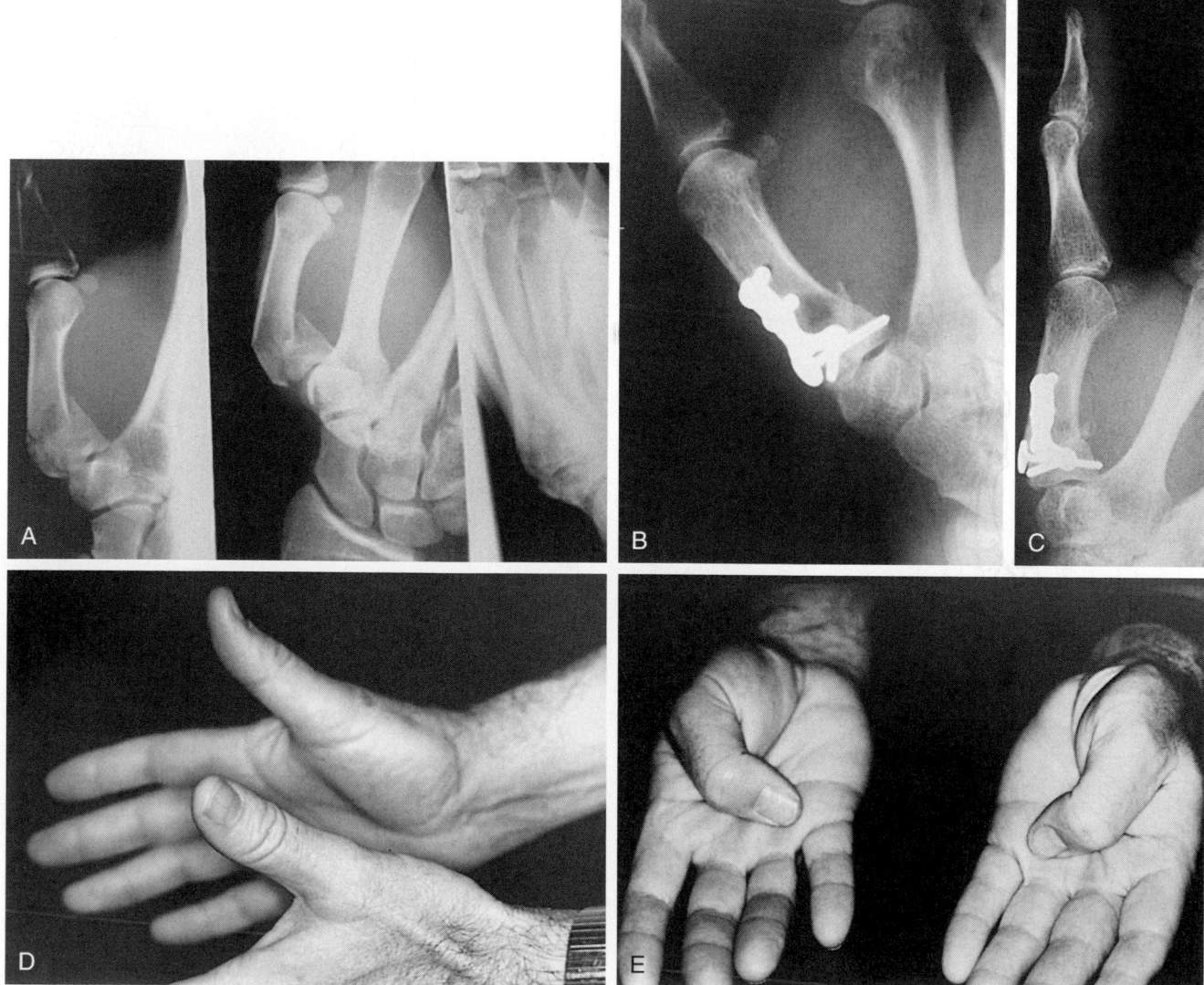

**FIGURE 38–68.** A 42-year-old man with a displaced three-part Rolando fracture at the base of his dominant right thumb. *A,* Radiographs demonstrating the fracture. *B, C,* Open reduction and internal fixation were accomplished. A 2.0-mm lag screw was placed over a washer to stabilize the articular fragments, and the fragments were secured to the shaft with an L plate and 2.7-mm screws. A cancellous bone graft obtained from the distal end of the radius was used to support the reduced articular surface. *D, E,* Full function resulted.

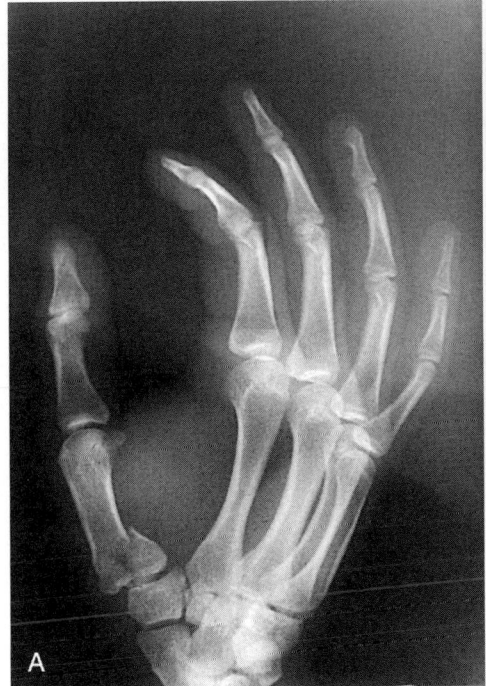 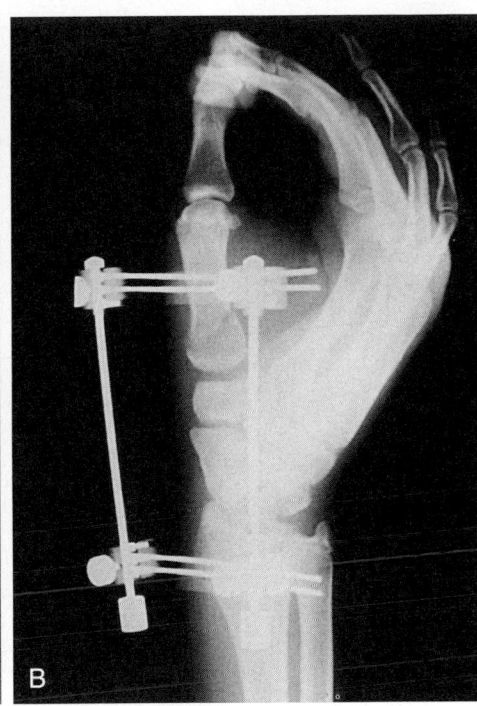

**FIGURE 38–69.** *A, B,* A three-part Rolando fracture was treated by closed reduction and distraction fixation with an external fixation device applied to the radius and thumb metacarpal.

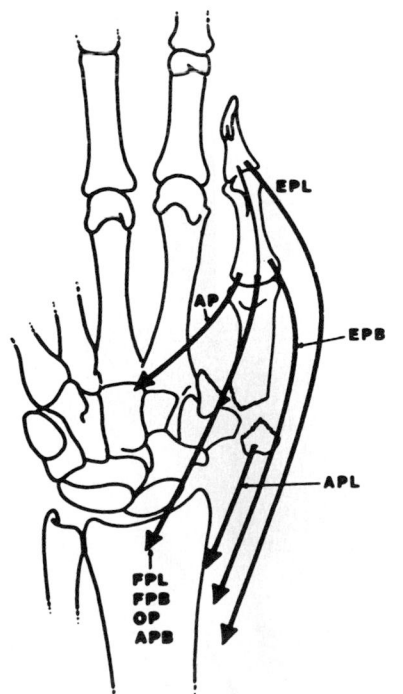 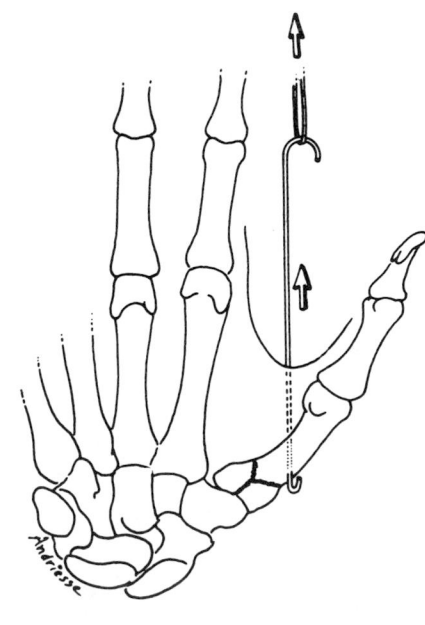

**FIGURE 38–70.** *A,* Illustration of the varus deformity of a Rolando fracture. *Abbreviations:* AP, adductor pollicis; APB, abductor pollicis brevis; APL, abductor pollicis longus; EPB, extensor pollicis brevis; EPL, extensor pollicis longus; FPB, flexor pollicis brevis; FPL, flexor pollicis longus; OP, opponens pollicis. *B,* Oblique wire traction reducing a displaced fracture. (*A, B,* From Breen, T.F.; et al. Hand Clin 4:491–501, 1988.)

A                                B

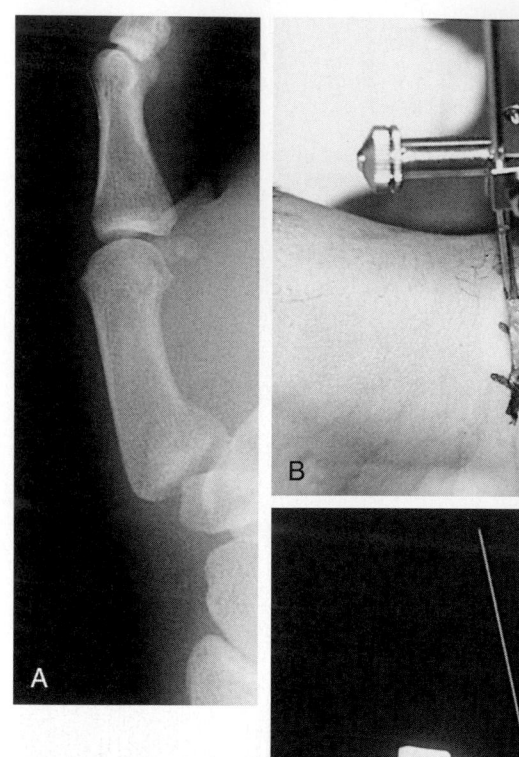

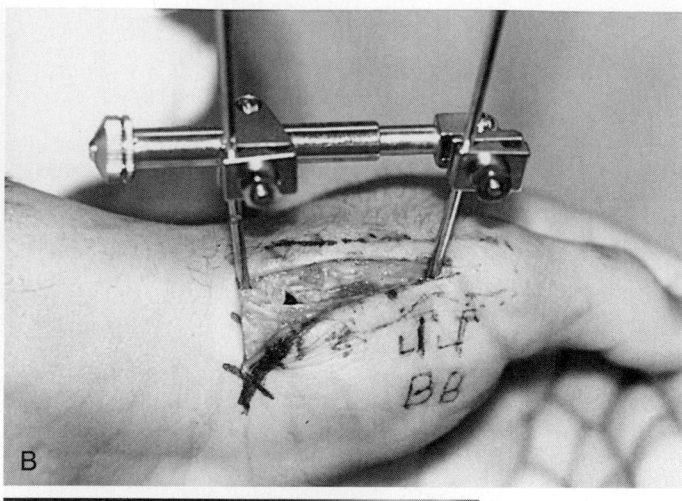

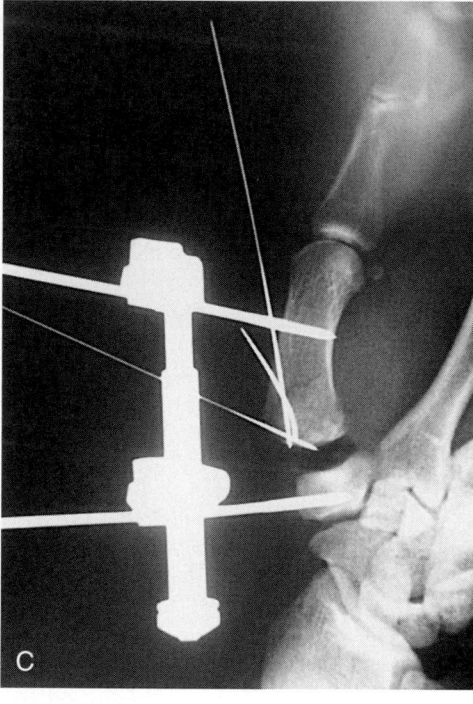

**FIGURE 38–71.** A 19-year-old man sustained a comminuted intra-articular fracture at the base of his dominant thumb. *A,* Radiograph revealing at least four major fragments. *B,* A minidistractor was applied with pins placed in the trapezium and first metacarpal. *C,* The fragments were manipulated into place, secured with small K-wires, and supported with a cancellous bone graft obtained from the distal part of the radius.

fracture but also as an effective means of maintaining the span of the first webspace by connecting the unit to similar pins placed in the second metacarpal[93, 95] (Fig. 38–72).

## PHALANGEAL FRACTURES

### Incidence

Phalangeal fractures are common. Gedda and Moberg, in a series of 2501 fractures of the hand, noted that more than 50% involved the proximal or middle phalanges.[100] In a series of 485 metacarpal and phalangeal fractures, Borgeskov found that 17.3% involved the proximal, 5.7% involved the middle, and 45% involved the distal phalanx.[25] Thomine, in a series of 177 proximal and middle phalangeal fractures, noted that 60% involved the proximal and 40% involved the middle phalanges; the fre-

quency of fracture by location and digit is listed in Table 38–17.[302]

Although phalangeal fractures are common and, in many instances, require little care,[25, 36, 240, 326] the potential for soft tissue adhesion, joint dysfunction, and malunion makes it necessary to define the "personality" of the individual fractures and tailor the treatment accordingly.[58, 135, 173, 280, 286, 294, 299] Little can replace careful completion of the physical examination to detect the presence of malalignment and the potential for late deformity.

### Proximal Phalangeal Fractures

#### EXTRA-ARTICULAR BASE FRACTURES

Fractures at the base of the proximal phalanx in adults can at times prove troublesome. When impacted, they will

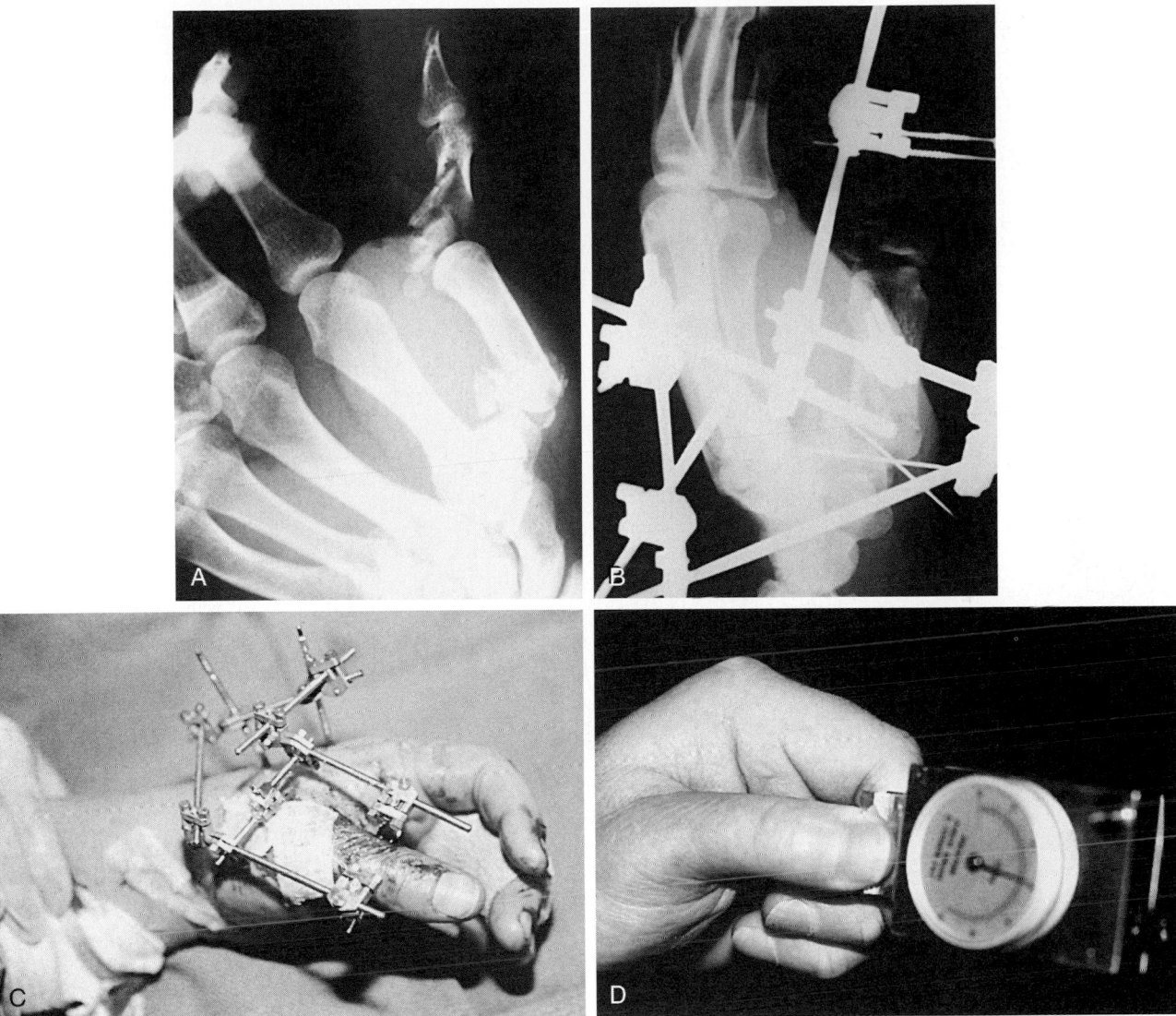

**FIGURE 38–72.** A 30-year-old man suffered a severe multilevel devascularizing injury to his dominant thumb in a press. *A,* Radiograph demonstrating extensively comminuted intra-articular fractures at the base of both the metacarpal and the proximal phalanx. *B,* Distraction fixation was applied to both comminuted fractures, and K-wires were used to secure the fragments of the metacarpal fracture. Bone graft was obtained from the distal end of the radius. *C,* The thumb was revascularized, and the external fixation was connected to pins placed in the second metacarpal. *D,* Excellent function resulted. (*A–D,* From Jupiter, J.B.; Silver, M.A. In: Chapman, M.W., ed. Operative Orthopaedics. Philadelphia, J.B. Lippincott, 1988, pp. 1235–1250.)

| TABLE 38–17 | | |
|---|---|---|
| **Relative Frequency of Phalangeal Fractures** | | |
| | **Proximal** (N = 106) | **Middle** (N = 71) |
| Head | 18 | 12 |
| Neck | 11 | 16 |
| Diaphysis | 72 | 35 |
| Base | 5 | 8 |

*Source:* Thomine, J.M. Les Fractures Ouvertes du Squeulette Digital dans les Plaies de la Main et des Doigts. Actual Chir. Paris, Masson, 1975, pp. 776–780.

commonly angulate in a volar direction at the fracture. If allowed to unite with 25° or more of angulation, digital motion will be impaired as the extensor mechanism becomes shortened, and loss of full extension at the PIP joint will result[62] (Fig. 38–73). The extent of angulation of these fractures may be difficult to judge accurately on radiographs; the angulation may be difficult to see on the lateral projection because of the overlap of adjacent digits, and the AP projection may not reveal much because of superimposition of the skeleton at the fracture line.

Coonrad and Pohlman found that the most common problem with closed reduction and cast treatment was loss of reduction caused by an inadequate degree of MCP joint flexion while in the cast.[62] If the fracture appears stable on reduction, cast immobilization should be considered, provided that the MCP joint is maintained in at least 60° to 70° of flexion (see Fracture Immobilization Tech-

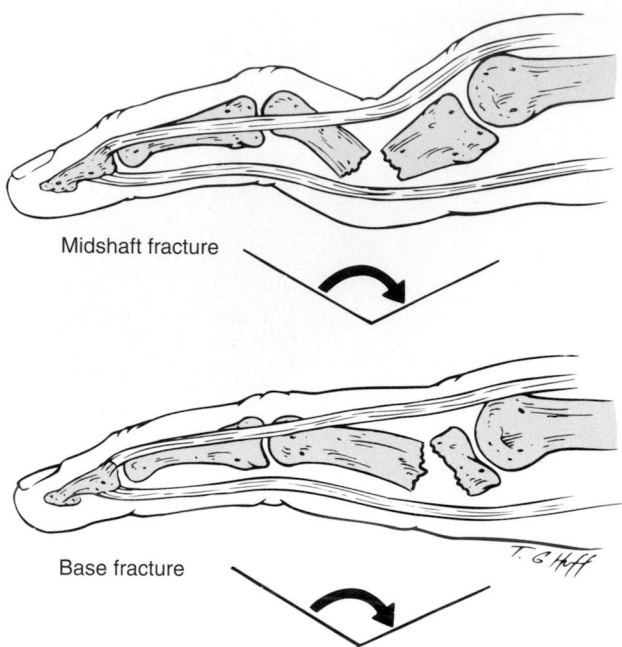

**FIGURE 38–73.** Angulation of fractures of the proximal phalanx may be clinically less apparent at the base than at the mid-diaphyseal (midshaft) level.

niques). If, however, the reduction is unstable or the patient is seen more than 5 to 7 days after injury, closed manipulation and longitudinal percutaneous pinning are recommended (see Fracture Immobilization Techniques). In both cases, the cast is maintained for 3 weeks and followed by active motion, with the digit protected by a buddy strap to the adjacent digit for 2 weeks.

Fractures associated with complex trauma, particularly flexor tendon lacerations, should be treated by stable internal fixation. A small 1.5- or 2.0-mm straight plate applied dorsally under the extensor apparatus is the easiest to manage; however, a 1.5-mm condylar plate applied to the lateral aspect of the phalanx provides fracture stability with less interference to the extensor mechanism than does a plate applied to the dorsal surface.[38]

## INTRA-ARTICULAR BASE FRACTURES

Intra-articular fractures of the base of the proximal phalanx can be subdivided into three types (Fig. 38–74): collateral ligament avulsion fractures, compression fractures, and vertical shaft fractures that extend into the joint. Avulsion fractures are most commonly seen in association with ulnar collateral ligament trauma to the thumb. Compression fractures are the result of an axial load and often have centrally impacted and rotated fragments. Vertical fractures can also have an impacted or split articular fragment.[125]

Avulsion fractures with little or no displacement are readily treated with a buddy strap to the adjacent digit on the side of the injury. When they are displaced, anatomic reduction is important to prevent chronic instability or post-traumatic arthritis. Tension band wiring of these avulsion fractures has proved to have predictable results, offers the advantage of limited soft tissue dissection, and avoids the risk of fragmentation of the fragment.[152] The

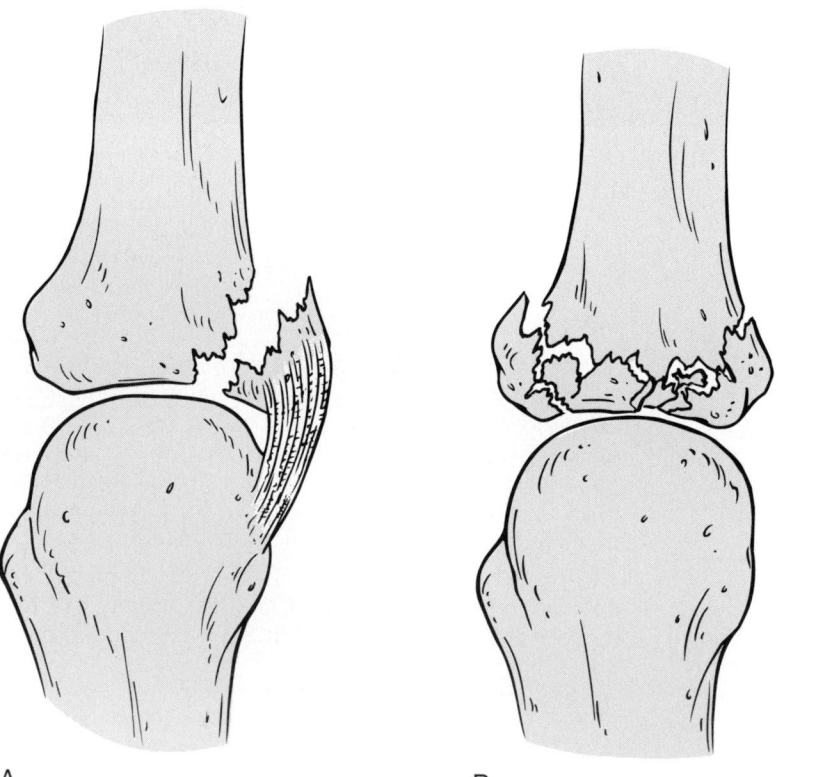
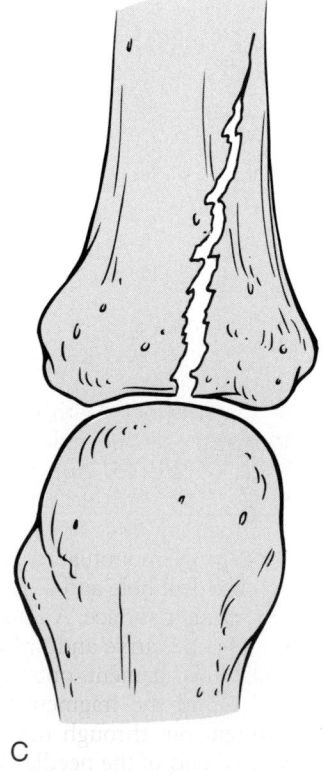

**FIGURE 38–74.** Intra-articular fractures of the base of the proximal phalanx can be classified into three main types: collateral ligament avulsion (*A*), compression (*B*), and vertical shear (*C*).

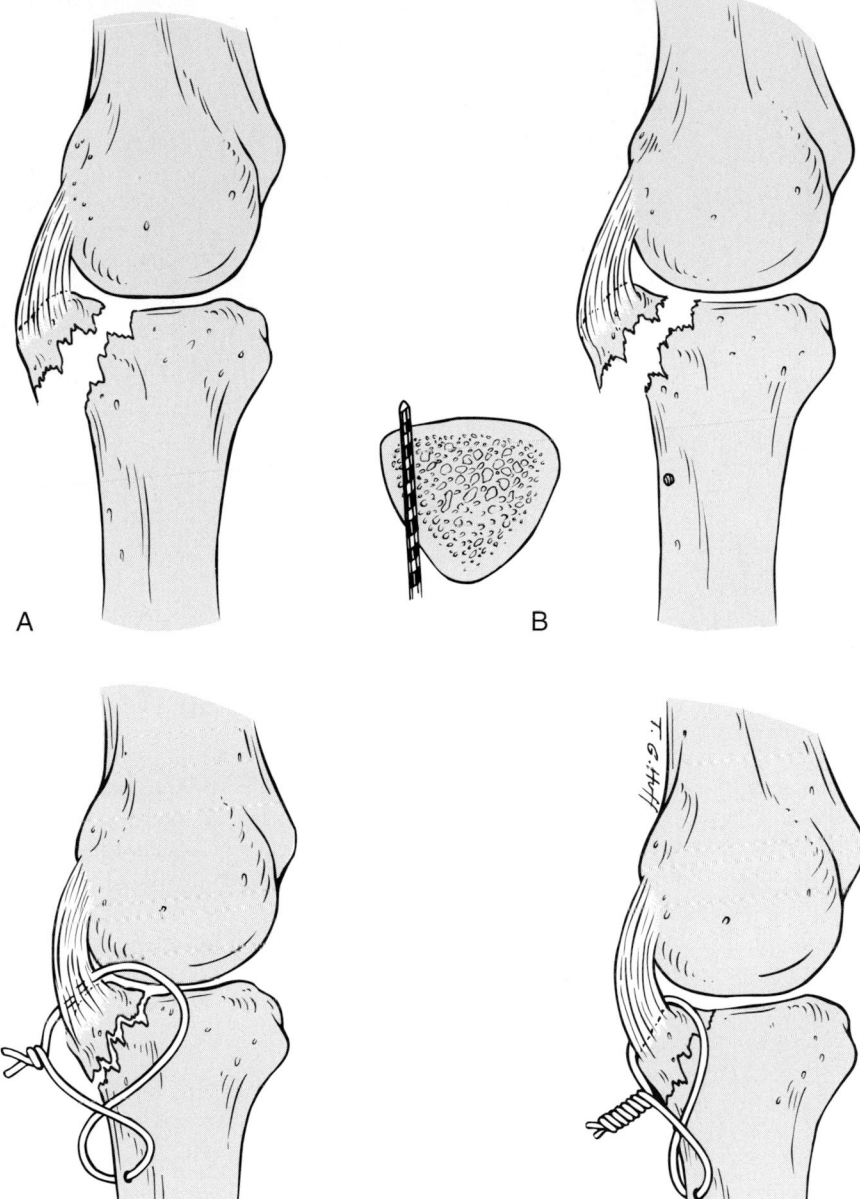

**FIGURE 38–75.** Operative steps in tension wire fixation of collateral ligament avulsion fractures. *A*, Displaced rotated avulsion fracture. *B*, A hole is drilled vertically 1 cm distal to the fracture site. *C*, A 28-gauge stainless steel wire is passed through the hole and through the insertion of the ligament on the fragment. *D*, The wire is tightened, and the twisted end is cut short and bent.

technique involves a dorsal approach that creates an interval between the extensor tendon and the sagittal bands. The joint capsule is opened and the fracture hematoma removed. With gentle manipulation, the fracture fragment can be reduced and the articular surface anatomically aligned. Approximately 1 cm distal to the fracture, a hole is drilled in the proximal phalanx in a dorsal-to-palmar direction with a 0.035-inch K-wire. A 26- or 28-gauge monofilament stainless steel wire is passed through the drill hole and retrieved with curved hemostats from the palmar surface. A 20-gauge hypodermic needle is bent in a gentle curve and passed through the insertion of the collateral ligament onto the fragment. The wire is looped around the fragment in a figure-of-eight fashion and brought out through the ligament by passing it into the beveled end of the needle. With the fragment reduced, the wire is tightened and the twisted end cut short and bent along the phalanx (Fig. 38–75).

A similar approach is possible with comminuted fragments. However, if the fracture is severely comminuted and has multiple tiny fragments, it may be preferable to excise the fragments and reattach the collateral ligament directly to bone. This technique can be performed with the minisuture anchors currently available for this purpose. Alternatively, use of the traditional pull-out suture technique will suffice. The repair can be mobilized after 3 to 4 weeks because healing will not be quite as rapid as that occurring with bone-to-bone repair.

In the situation of a vertical shear fracture, the tension band wiring technique will provide excellent stability; however, an additional K-wire or, preferably, an interfragmentary screw plus a K-wire is necessary.

Postoperatively after the bone stabilization procedures, the patient can begin active motion with the digit protected by a buddy strap to the adjacent digit (Fig.

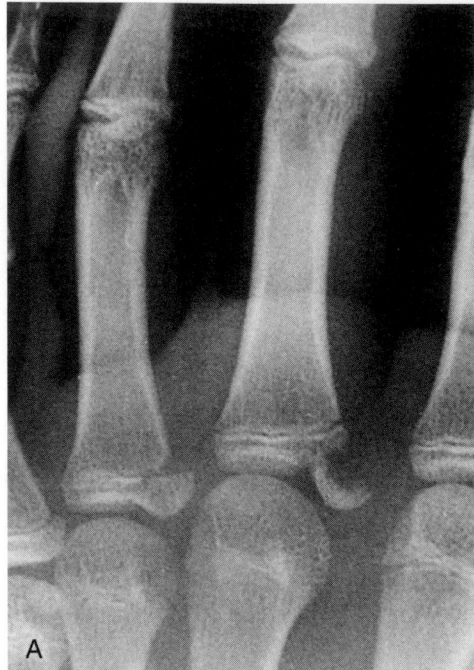 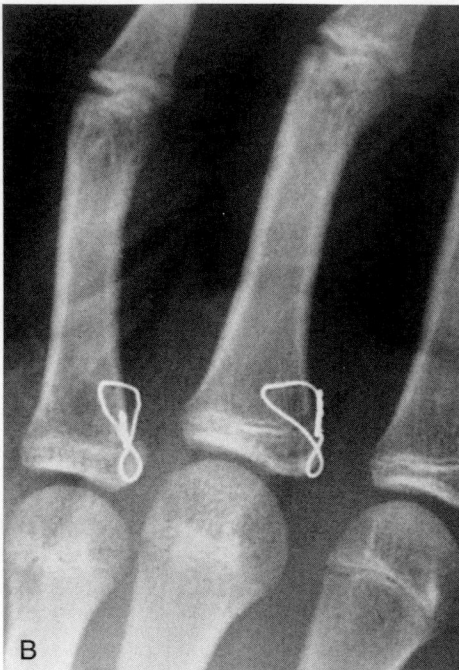

**FIGURE 38–76.** A 15-year-old boy sustained two rotated avulsion fractures at the base of the proximal phalanges of his long and ring fingers. *A,* Radiograph demonstrating the displacement of the avulsion fracture. *B,* The fractures were stably fixed with tension band wires. Full motion was recovered within 2 weeks, and rapid union was noted.

38–76). As mentioned previously, splinting for 3 to 4 weeks is advised for the ligament-to-bone repair.

Compression fractures are not predictably reduced by longitudinal traction because the impacted fragments may be devoid of soft tissue attachments. If displaced sufficiently to result in an intra-articular step-off of greater than 1 to 2 mm or cause an angulatory deformity of the digit, compression fractures may require open reduction and gentle depression of the impacted articular fragments. The

metacarpal head will effectively serve as a template on which the congruity of the articular surface of the proximal phalanx can be built. Cancellous bone graft will be necessary to support the articular fragments. In some instances, interfragmentary screw fixation can be applied, but the defect must be filled with compacted cancellous graft to prevent overcompression of the fragments and loss of congruity of the articular reconstruction[125] (Fig. 38–77). With some complex compression fractures, either

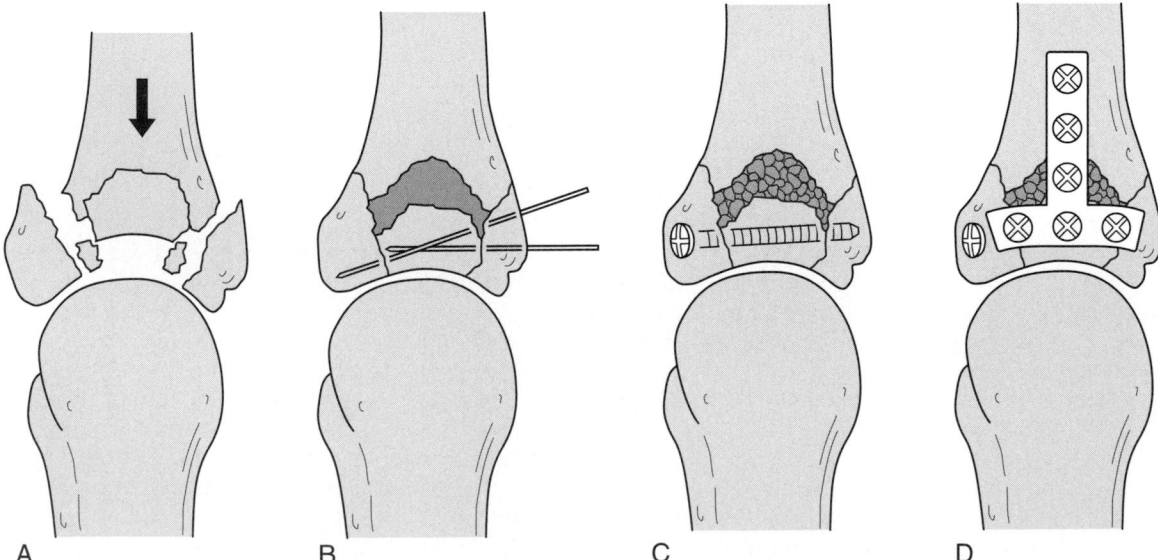

**FIGURE 38–77.** Compression fracture of the base of the proximal phalanx. *A,* Note the central impacted fragment that has driven the medial and lateral joint surfaces apart. *B,* With open reduction, the central fragment is teased back down onto the metacarpal head, and the walls of the fracture are reduced and held with provisional K-wires. *C,* A cancellous bone graft is used to support the reduced joint surface, and a lag screw (or position screw if multiple fragmentation is present) is used to stabilize the joint reconstruction. *D,* A mini-T plate or minicondylar plate is used as a buttress to support the construct and affix the joint fragments to the shaft of the phalanx.

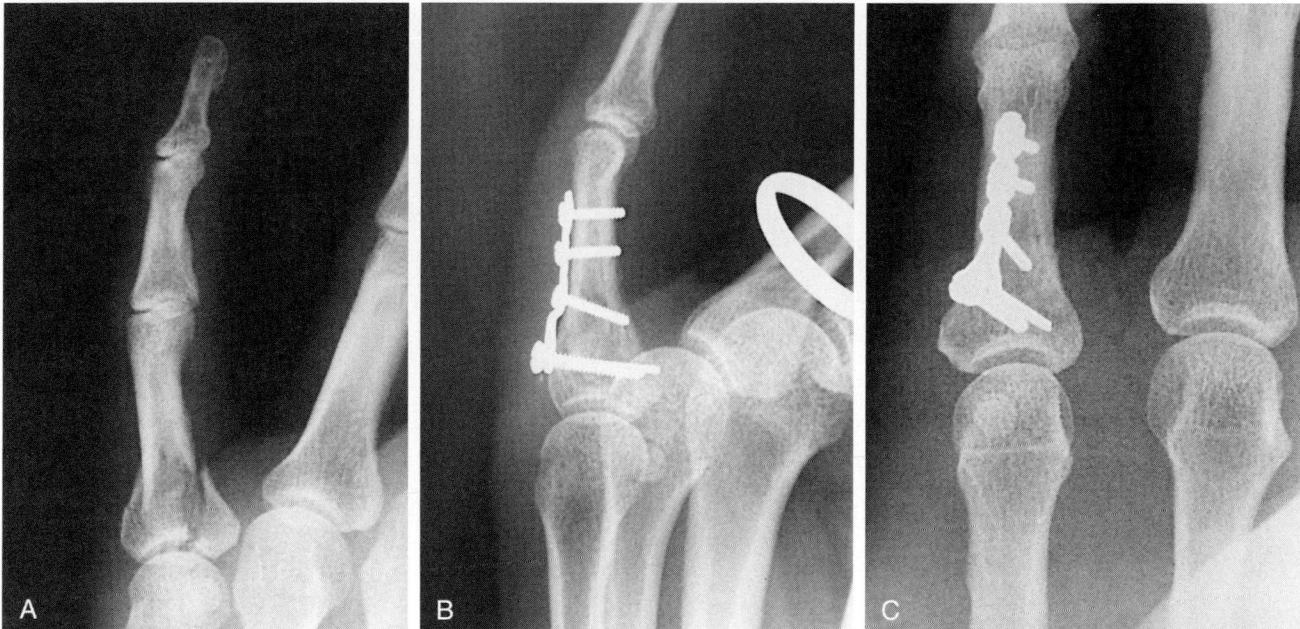

**FIGURE 38–78.** A 35-year-old man fell while skiing and sustained a complex compression fracture of the base of the proximal phalanx of his little finger. *A,* Radiograph demonstrating the disruption of the articular surface. A large impacted central fragment was found. *B, C,* Anatomic reduction, cancellous bone grafting, and a minicondylar plate applied on the lateral surface provided a stable skeletal and articular construct. Motion was begun on the first postoperative day.

a mini-T plate or a minicondylar plate can be applicable because they will serve to both buttress the articular reconstruction and achieve interfragmentary compression through the plate holes (Fig. 38–78).

Vertical fractures can, on occasion, be successfully reduced by longitudinal traction on the phalanx with the MCP joint flexed. If both the articular and the more distal shaft components have been anatomically reduced, percutaneous K-wire fixation under image intensification should be considered. Newer instruments are being developed to allow percutaneous clamp reduction and mini–lag screw fixation. If reduction cannot be achieved with closed methods, ORIF with interfragmentary lag screws is advisable (Fig. 38–79).

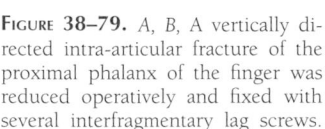

**FIGURE 38–79.** *A, B,* A vertically directed intra-articular fracture of the proximal phalanx of the finger was reduced operatively and fixed with several interfragmentary lag screws.

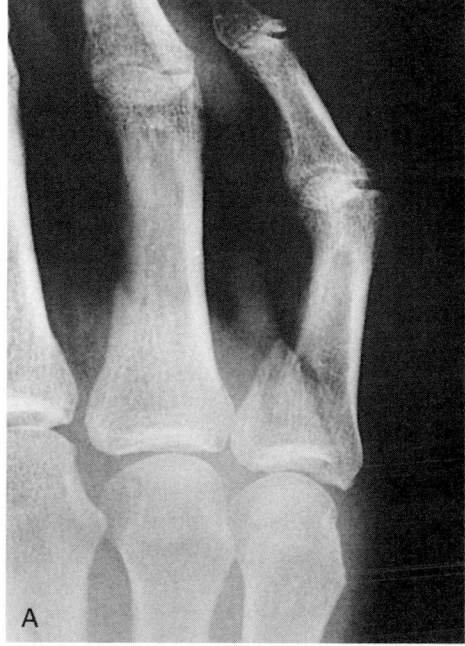
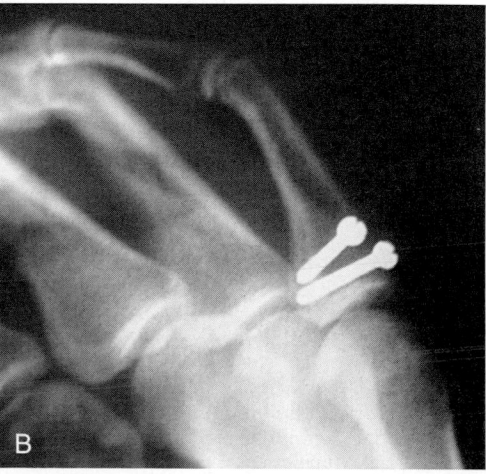

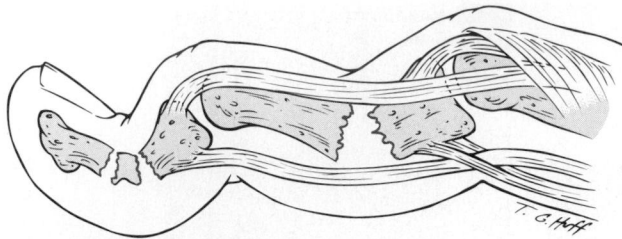

**FIGURE 38–80.** Transverse diaphyseal fractures of the proximal and middle phalanges tend to angulate as a result of the intrinsic and extrinsic muscle forces.

# Proximal and Middle Phalangeal Fractures

## DIAPHYSEAL FRACTURES

Diaphyseal fractures of the proximal and middle phalanges are subject to the deforming influences of both intrinsic and extrinsic muscle forces. These muscle forces and the mechanism of injury are the two major factors determining the fracture pattern.[206]

Transverse fractures have a tendency to angulate with the apex pointed palmarward (Fig. 38–80). With proximal phalangeal fractures, this angulation is due to the insertion of the interosseous muscles on the proximal part of the phalanx; the distal part of the proximal phalanx goes into extension as a result of the pull of the central slip and the lateral bands of the extensor mechanism. With transverse middle phalangeal fractures, the apex of angulation may vary depending on the level of the fracture. Accordingly, a transverse fracture at the proximal third of the middle phalanx may angulate with the apex dorsalward, whereas a fracture beyond the insertion of the flexor digitorum sublimis tendons will tend to angulate with its apex palmarward.

Spiral and long oblique fractures tend to rotate along a longitudinal axis, whereas short oblique fractures may rotate or angulate, or both. Rotational deformities will be evident by evaluation of the fingernails in digital extension and by deviation of the distal phalanges with digital flexion (see Fig. 38–8).

Comminuted diaphyseal fractures, often associated with a greater degree of soft tissue injury, will probably shorten, although shortening may be difficult to judge when the digit is swollen.

In assessing these fractures (see General Principles) for stability, deformity, and associated soft tissue injury, the physician must always bear in mind that stiffness, angular or rotatory deformity, or tendon adhesion will affect the function of not only the involved digit but also adjacent digits, as well as overall hand performance.

**Fractures That Are Closed, Aligned, and Stable.** Treatment options for stable, well-aligned fractures are primarily directed at providing comfort and avoiding lengthy immobilization. Buddy straps to adjacent digits or gutter splints are generally adequate to achieve these intended goals.[11, 240, 292, 326] If early motion is permitted, control radiographs should be obtained within 5 to 7 days to make certain that displacement has not occurred. Healing will take place within 3 weeks clinically, although radiographically it may take as long as 5 weeks to see significant signs of bony union (Table 38–18).

**Fractures That Are Closed, Malaligned, and Stable after Reduction.** For transverse or short oblique fracture patterns, the extension block casting method is effective and should be considered (see Fracture Immobilization Techniques). Because it is mechanically sound, active digital flexion compressive forces are transmitted to the stable palmar cortex while the extensor mechanism and periosteum help hold the fracture in place. Extension block casting not only helps maintain fracture reduction but also maintains the length of the soft tissue envelope and prevents PIP joint stiffness.[42, 248] Four weeks in this splint, followed by 2 weeks of protective buddy-strapping, will be adequate for nearly all closed phalangeal fractures.

For spiral fractures that are stable to motion after reduction, dorsal and volar splints or casts are preferred.

---

**TABLE 38–18**

Treatment of P1 and P2 Diaphyseal Fractures

| Fracture Personality | Treatment Choice | Advantage |
|---|---|---|
| Closed, aligned, stable | Buddy strap | Mobility |
| Closed, malaligned, stable after reduction | | |
|    Transverse/short oblique | Extension block casting | Maintains mobility and length of soft tissues |
|    Spiral | Cast | Minimizes risk of displacement with motion |
| Closed, malaligned, unstable after reduction | | |
|    Transverse, short oblique, spiral | Percutaneous | Maintains length and soft tissue integrity |
| | Kirschner wires | High rate of success and low rate of complications |
|    Highly comminuted | External fixation | Maintains length and soft tissue integrity |
| | | Allows mobility of proximal and distal articulations |
| Closed, malaligned, reduction cannot be obtained | | |
|    Transverse/short oblique | Open reduction and internal fixation | Direct control over fracture |
|    Long oblique/spiral comminuted | | Anatomic alignment possible |
| | Tension band wire | Stable fixation allows early motion |
| | Lag screws | |
| | Plate | |

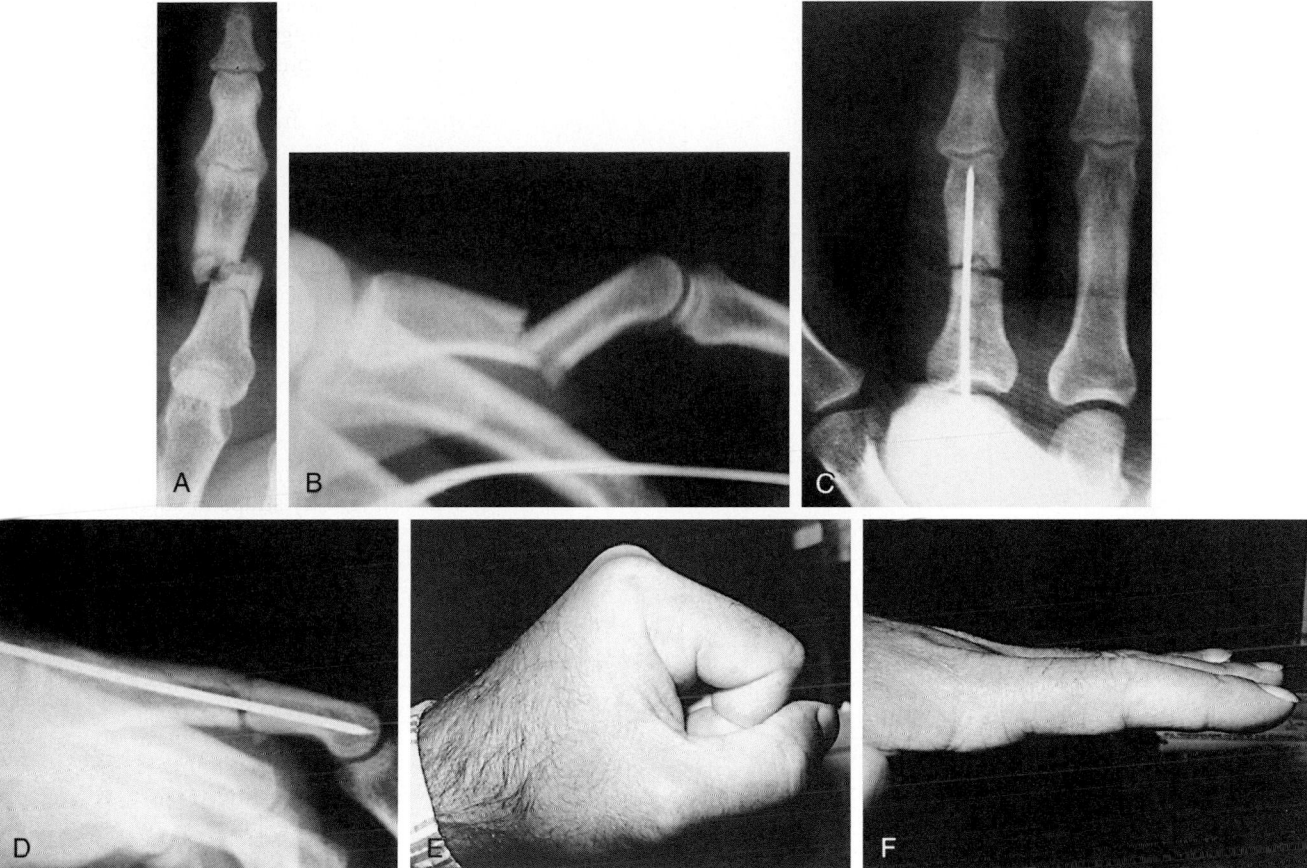

**FIGURE 38–81.** An unstable closed transverse fracture of the proximal phalanx was treated by closed reduction and a longitudinal 0.045-inch K-wire. Anteroposterior (AP) (*A*) and lateral (*B*) radiographs demonstrate the deformity. AP (*C*) and lateral (*D*) radiographs were taken with the fracture reduced and held with a longitudinal K-wire. *E, F,* Full functional recovery was achieved 3 weeks after K-wire removal.

The distal phalanges and fingernails should be visible, and radiographs are suggested 1 and 2 weeks after casting to make certain that malrotation has not occurred.

**Fractures That Are Closed, Malaligned, and Unstable after Reduction.** For the vast majority of fractures that remain unstable after reduction, percutaneous pinning is indicated (see Fracture Immobilization Techniques). Advantages include preservation of the soft tissue envelope surrounding the fracture, maintenance of the resting length of the ligaments and tendons, and limited morbidity. Attention to detail in pin placement, plaster application over the pins, and postoperative management are consistent with efforts to achieve a successful outcome. In most series, results were invariably good, with 90% good to excellent results[13, 110, 148] (Figs. 38–81 through 38–83; see also Table 38–18).

**Fractures That Are Closed, Malaligned, Comminuted, and Unstable after Reduction.** Very comminuted closed fractures are uncommon but can be most difficult to manage. They have a strong tendency to shorten, angulate, and rotate, and casting alone or longitudinal percutaneous K-wire fixation and casting may not sufficiently control the deforming tendencies. External traction through skin, pulp, or wire is unpredictable and fraught with potential problems, including pulp necrosis, pin tract infection, and joint stiffness.

Similarly, operative treatment of these complex skeletal

fractures risks destabilization and devascularization of the small fracture fragments, increased soft tissue trauma, and delayed union or nonunion. Soft tissue adhesions and articular stiffness are common after most operative endeavors on these fractures. Stable fixation with plates will afford an opportunity to minimize these problems with early mobilization, but fixation with screws may be compromised by the extent of the diaphyseal comminution.

For all the preceding reasons, distraction fixation with miniature external fixation devices is preferred in these unusual cases. These devices offer the advantages of maintaining an intact and well-perfused soft tissue envelope, allowing for proximal and distal joint mobility, and being much less technically demanding than internal fixation techniques (see Fracture Immobilization Techniques).[20, 239, 250] The fixator should remain in place for at least 4 and possibly 5 weeks, depending on radiographic evidence of callus formation. A protective splint is advisable for an additional 2 weeks, with only gentle active motion allowed out of the splint during this time (Fig. 38–84; see also Table 38–18).

**Closed and Malaligned Fractures in Which Reduction Cannot Be Obtained.** It is uncommon to not be able to obtain adequate reduction with most acute fractures. However, interposition of soft tissue can block the reduction of some fractures. More commonly, this clinical

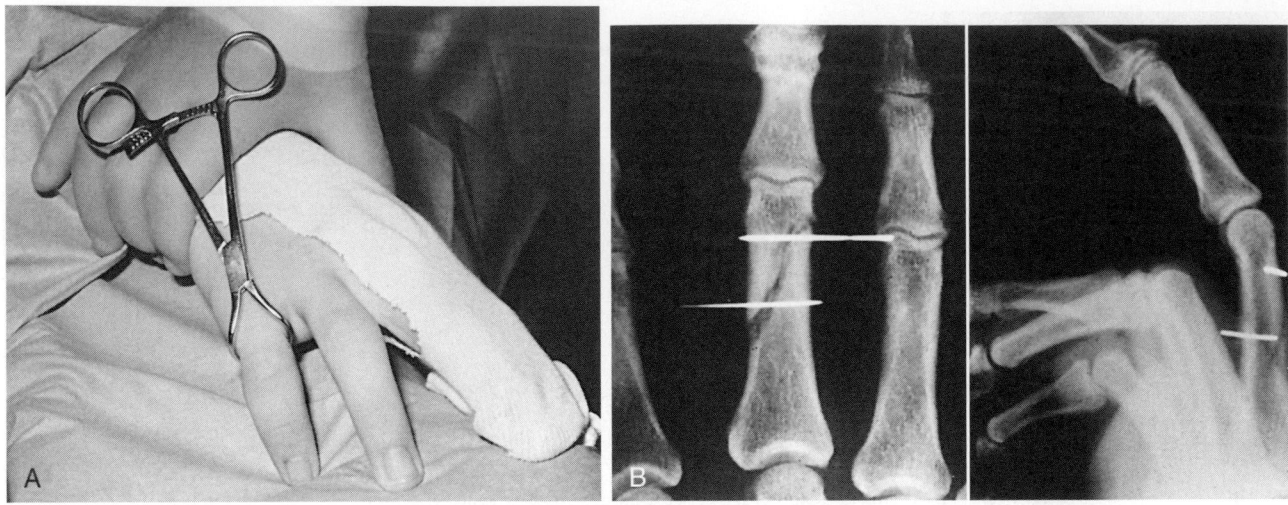

**FIGURE 38-82.** An unstable, closed, long oblique fracture of the proximal phalanx was treated by closed reduction and transverse percutaneous wire fixation with 0.028-inch K-wires. *A,* Under image intensification, the fracture is reduced and held with a pointed reduction clamp. *B,* Stable fixation is achieved with transverse 0.028-inch K-wires.

dilemma will arise when a fracture is seen 2 or more weeks after injury and callus is beginning to form but solid union has not developed. In these conditions, fracture reduction and stable internal fixation may be preferable to waiting and performing an osteotomy, often with an additional need for tenolysis or capsulotomy.

The principles of biologic plating with minimal soft tissue dissection, periosteal strippage, and use of the plate to facilitate reduction are advisable in dealing with these multifragmentary complex fractures.

## SURGICAL EXPOSURE

The proximal and middle phalanges can be approached through either a pure dorsal, a dorsolateral, or a midaxial skin incision. The shaft can be approached either by splitting the central extensor tendon longitudinally or by creating an interval between the lateral band and the extensor tendon. In either case, the periosteum is elevated as a long, wide flap and preserved for later resuturing to help serve as a gliding layer between the implants and the extensor mechanism (Fig. 38–85).

Closed transverse and short oblique fracture patterns involving the proximal and middle phalanges and requiring ORIF are amenable to tension band wiring. This technique offers sufficient stability to allow for early postoperative mobilization yet presents a low profile (see Fracture Immobilization Techniques). This feature is particularly important because the surrounding tendons and soft tissues of the phalanges have little ability to tolerate bulky implants (Fig. 38–86).

Long oblique and spiral fractures are preferably treated with 1.5-mm interfragmentary lag screws (see Fracture Immobilization Techniques).[129] These devices also offer stable fixation without undue bulk (Fig. 38–87).

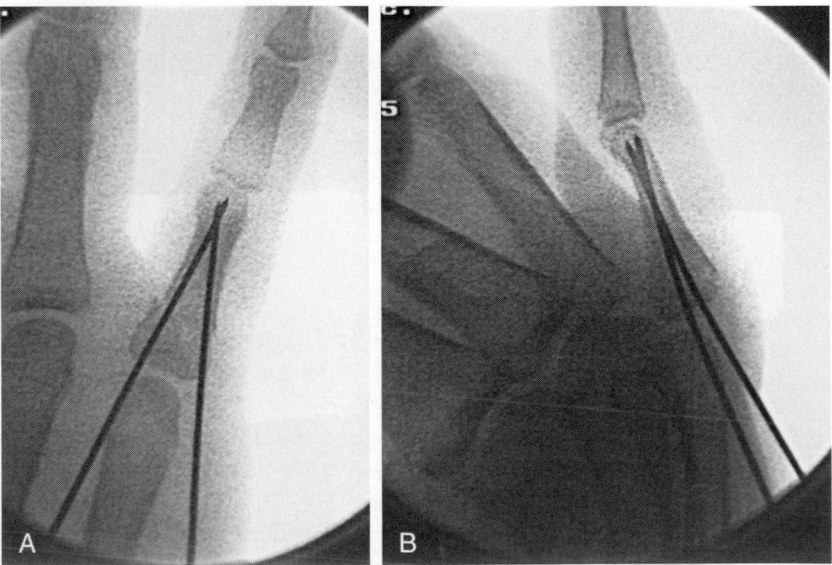

**FIGURE 38–83.** *A, B,* Intraoperative fluoroscopic images of a displaced, unstable base of a proximal phalanx fracture in a 19-year-old. The fracture was initially managed in closed fashion but failed to maintain adequate position. This case demonstrates an intramedullary technique in which the K-wires do not transfix the metacarpal head; rather, they pass on either side and sit in the collateral ligament recesses. The fracture united anatomically.

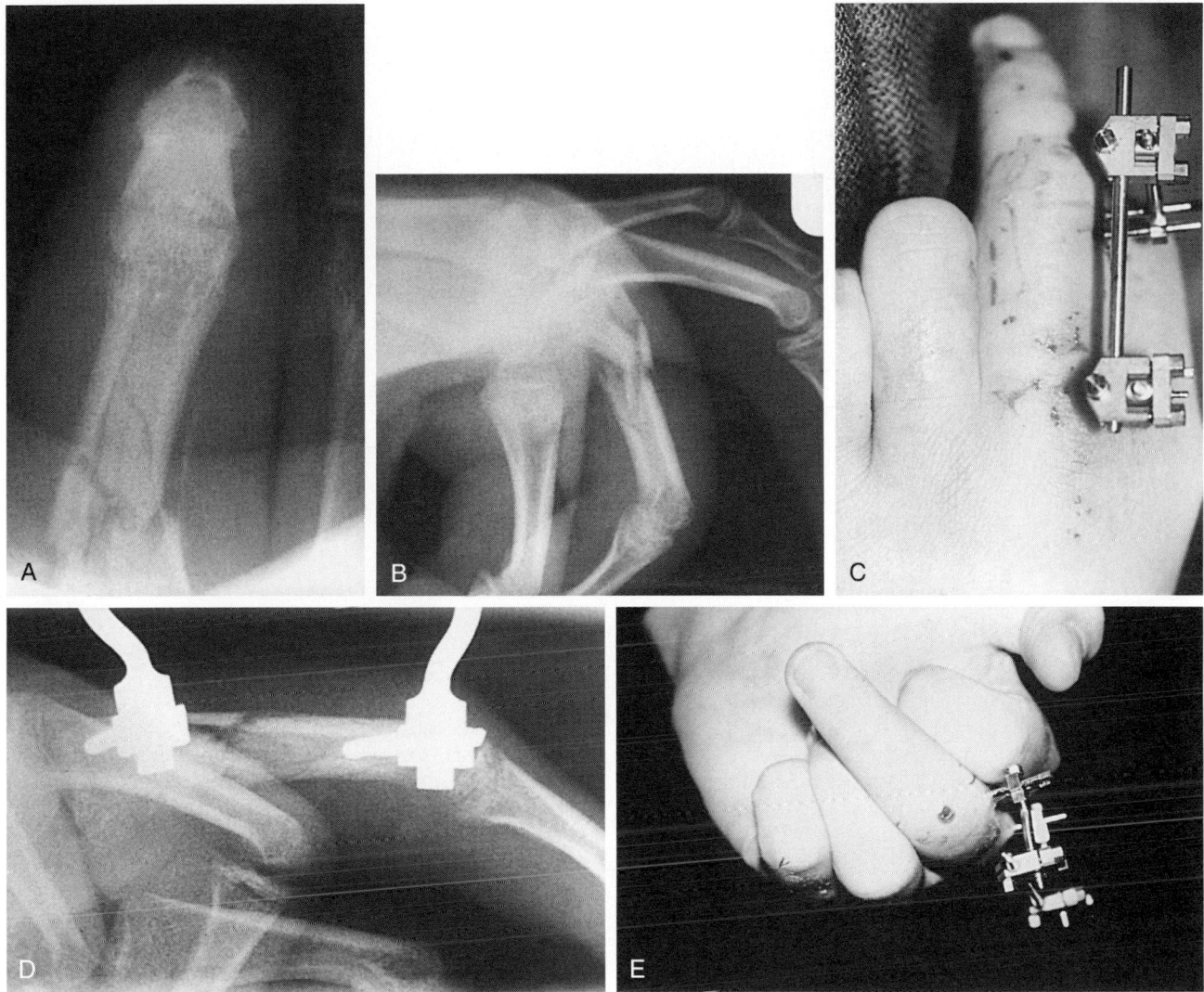

**FIGURE 38–84.** A 16-year-old boy presented 2 weeks after injury with a displaced, closed comminuted fracture of the proximal phalanx of his dominant long finger. Motion of the finger was limited. Anteroposterior (*A*) and lateral (*B*) radiographs revealed an angulated comminuted fracture with early periosteal callus. *C, D,* Under image intensification, a miniature external fixator was applied, with two pins placed in the base and two in the neck. The fracture was reduced, and the pins were connected. *E,* The fixation was stable enough to permit mobilization of the metacarpophalangeal and interphalangeal joints. The fixator was removed 4 weeks after application. *Illustration continued on following page*

If the fracture is comminuted, a plate is indicated to serve as a device to maintain length, alignment, and relative stability. The thicker, stiffer plate designs such as the DC plate can be used dorsally, or alternatively, miniplates or minicondylar plates can be applied along the lateral surface of the phalanx to again minimize interference with the dorsal gliding structures[38, 66, 127, 153, 268] (Fig. 38–88; see also Table 38–18).

## Phalangeal Neck Fractures

Closed fractures involving the phalangeal neck are extremely uncommon in adults, although they can present a most difficult management problem in the pediatric age group. In the latter, these fractures will often rotate dorsally, and it is not uncommon to have soft tissue interposition.[9, 74, 267]

In adults, displaced fractures are readily reduced by closed means but are difficult to control with external splint or cast immobilization. For this reason, percutaneous K-wire fixation is applied either across the MCP joint with the joint in 80° of flexion or through the lateral base of the proximal phalanx (see Fracture Immobilization Techniques).[13] Plaster support is necessary for a minimum of 3 weeks, and the pins should be left in for an additional week (Fig. 38–89).

## Phalangeal Condylar Fractures

### FUNCTIONAL ANATOMY

The condylar configuration of the head of the phalangeal skeleton forms an integral part of a unique hinge articulation. The stability of these joints depends on dynamic and passive factors. Dynamic stability results from joint compressive forces that increase with pinch and

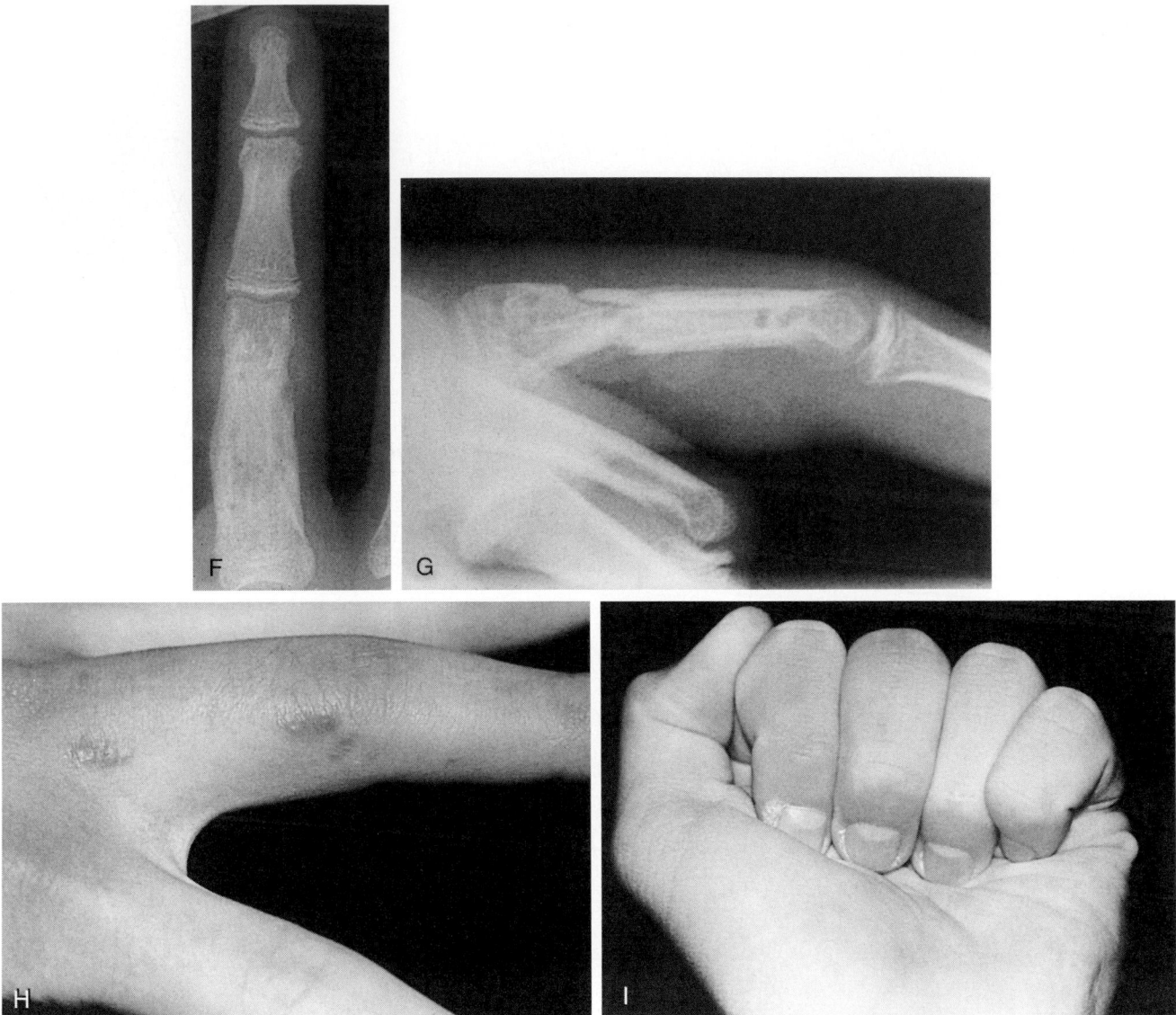

**Figure 38–84** *Continued. F, G,* Radiographs taken at 6 weeks revealed a healed, well-aligned phalanx. *H, I,* Full functional motion was achieved 6 weeks after application of the fixator.

grip actions; these compressive forces increase lateral stability, which in turn depends on the integrity of the articular configurations. If distorted by displaced articular fractures, the joint compressive forces are no longer directed perpendicular to the normal axis of motion and thereby contribute to instability.[31] Passive stability results from collateral ligament tension, which increases with flexion. The true collateral ligament is most important in flexion but is lax in extension, whereas the accessory collateral ligament and volar plate are major stabilizers with the joint in extension.[165, 167]

When viewed end on, the condyles resemble a grooved trochlea (pulley). However, they are asymmetric in shape and contour. The palmar aspect is nearly twice as wide as the dorsal margin. The base of the middle and distal phalanges has an intercondylar ridge and recesses that support articulating condyles, but this arrangement is not completely congruous. This feature allows some rotation

and translation, which affords the digit the ability to better adapt to irregular shapes in grip[31] (Fig. 38–90).

## TREATMENT GOALS

Fractures of the condylar architecture of the head of the phalanges can result in pain, deformity, and loss of motion.[8, 125, 179, 202] Flexion contracture is common after these injuries. Because the function of the IP joints is coordinated in part by a common extensor mechanism, dysfunction of one will nearly always affect the other. Therefore, anatomic repositioning is the goal. With displaced fractures, such repositioning can occasionally be accomplished nonoperatively. More often than not, however, an operative approach is required.[22, 36, 129, 162, 266, 268, 269, 286] The ability to achieve stable internal fixation will add immeasurably to the final outcome.

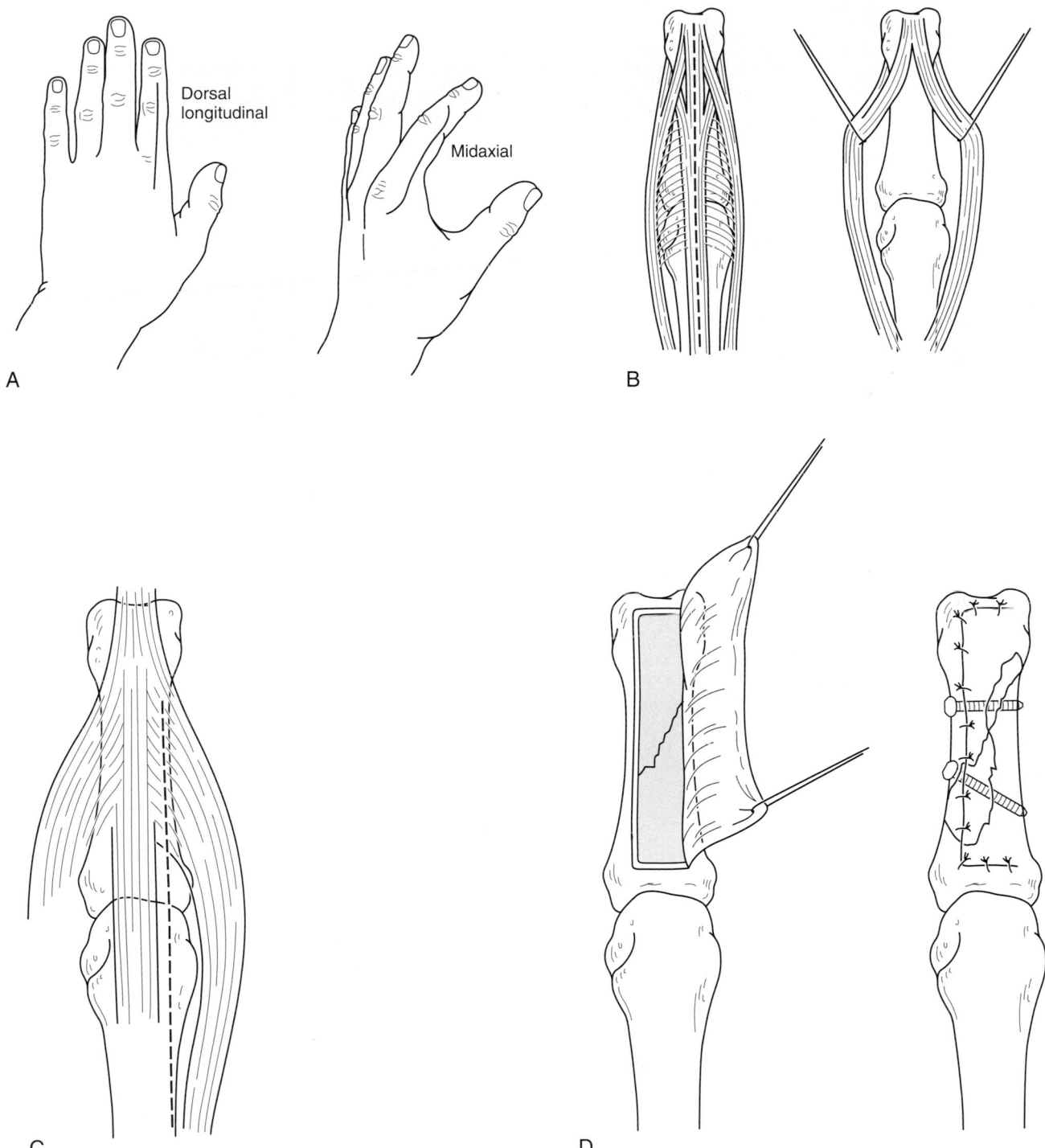

**FIGURE 38–85.** Surgical approach to the proximal phalanx. *A*, A midaxial or dorsal longitudinal skin incision can be used. The diaphysis can be approached through either an extensor-splitting incision (*B*) or an incision creating an interval between the common extensor and the lateral band (*C*). *D*, The periosteum is elevated in a long wide flap that is sutured back into place to cover the implants.

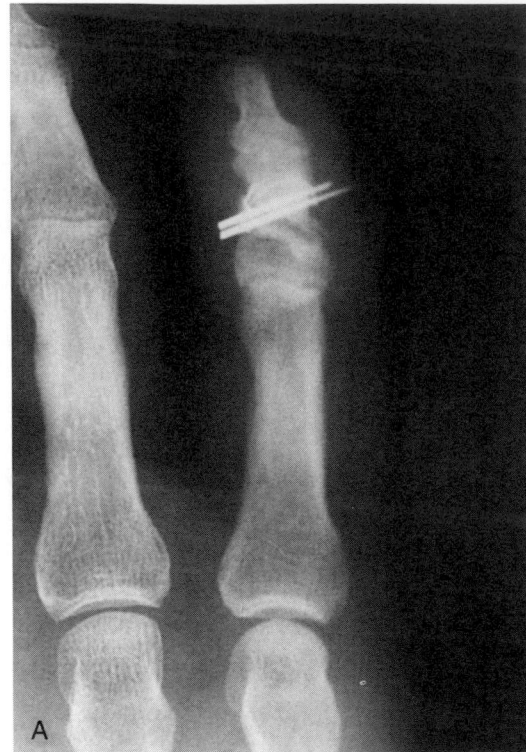

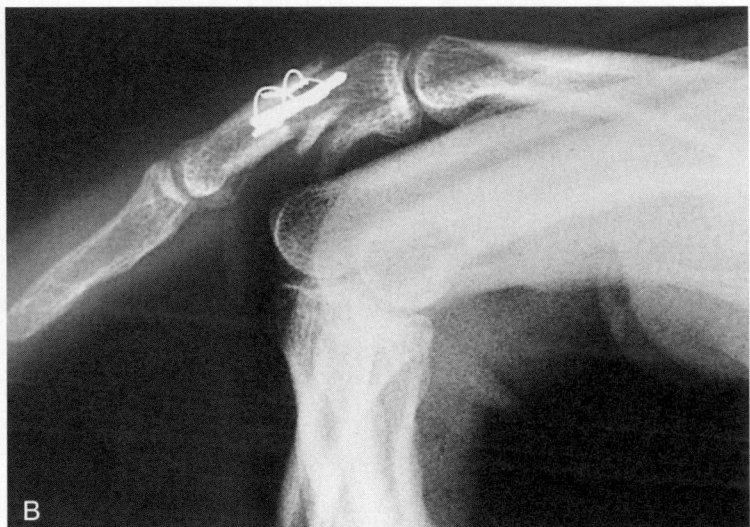

**FIGURE 38–86.** *A, B,* A complex closed shaft fracture of the middle phalanx stabilized with a tension band wire technique.

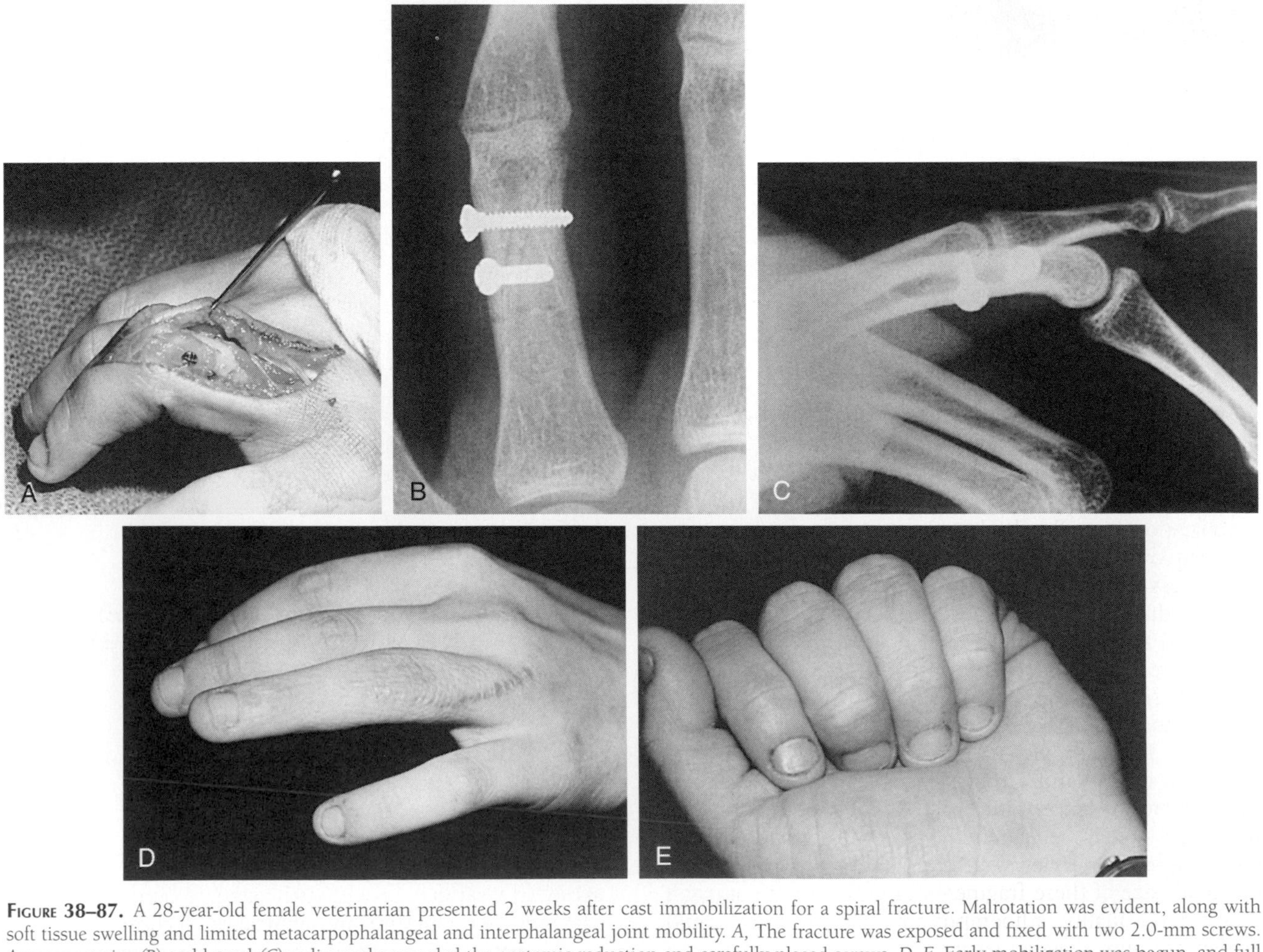

**FIGURE 38–87.** A 28-year-old female veterinarian presented 2 weeks after cast immobilization for a spiral fracture. Malrotation was evident, along with soft tissue swelling and limited metacarpophalangeal and interphalangeal joint mobility. *A,* The fracture was exposed and fixed with two 2.0-mm screws. Anteroposterior *(B)* and lateral *(C)* radiographs revealed the anatomic reduction and carefully placed screws. *D, E,* Early mobilization was begun, and full motion was regained by 6 weeks postoperatively.

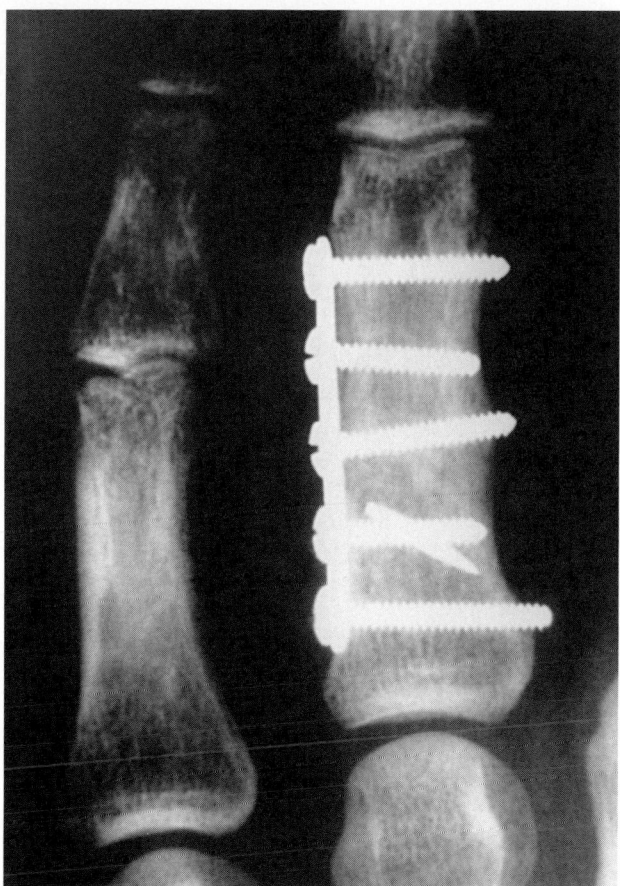

**FIGURE 38–88.** A malaligned proximal phalangeal fracture was stabilized with a miniplate applied along the lateral surface of the phalanx to minimize implant interference with the extensor tendon mechanism. Note the broken drill bit within the bone.

## UNICONDYLAR FRACTURES

Unicondylar fractures are the result of a shearing force and tend to be unstable. Although the fracture may be displaced only in a lateral direction, the attached collateral ligament will frequently cause the condyle to rotate. The latter will lead not only to intra-articular incongruity but also to angular displacement of the more distal phalanx.

Nondisplaced fractures can be treated nonoperatively with a digital splint for 7 to 10 days, followed by protective mobilization (i.e., by buddy-strapping the digit to the adjacent digits). Because of the obliquity of the fracture line, these patients should have repeat radiographs to confirm the anatomic position (Fig. 38–91).

Closed reduction can be considered when a unicondylar fracture is an isolated injury without associated skeletal or soft tissue trauma. Reduction is accomplished by axial traction and by angulating the digit away from the injured condyle. The condyle is compressed with a pointed reduction clamp, and a transverse 0.028-inch percutaneous K-wire is placed into the opposite condyle. The reduction must be carefully confirmed on standard radiographs (three views) in the operating room because the small size of these fragments can mislead the surgeon unless good-quality radiographs are obtained. What could appear as minimal asymmetry in the AP projection may, in fact, represent a malrotation that is more evident on a true

lateral radiograph. When the reduction is anatomic, a true lateral radiograph will have both condyles projected on each other. With malrotation, each condyle will be evident (Fig. 38–92).

Displaced unicondylar fractures are, for the most part, approached operatively because one should have little tolerance for a nonanatomic reduction. The surgical approach is dorsal, and the condyle is exposed by creating an interval between the extensor tendon and the ipsilateral lateral band. Alternatively, the exposure of Chamay is useful, as described later[53] (Fig. 38–93). Once the intra-articular hematoma is evacuated, the anatomy of the fracture can be appreciated. Before reduction, two features should be evaluated. The first is the dimensions of the condylar fragment, particularly in relation to the thread diameter of the screw that is to be used (usually 1.5 mm). Second, the insertion of the collateral ligament is carefully identified so that it can be protected during reduction and internal fixation. The vascularity to the condylar fragment depends in part on the collateral ligament. Thus, undue surgical trauma can lead to avascular necrosis of the fragment.

Reduction is accomplished under direct vision, and provisional fixation is achieved with a transversely directed 0.028-inch K-wire. If the fragment is of sufficient size (see Fracture Immobilization Techniques), a 1.5-mm screw is used. The entry point should ideally be just above and proximal to the origin of the collateral ligament to avoid injury to the ligament and potential avascular necrosis of the condylar fragment (Fig. 38–94). For larger fragments with a longer oblique fracture line, a K-wire should also be used to neutralize shear forces on the screw. In the situation of metaphyseal or diaphyseal extension of the fracture line with fragmentation from the articular segment, it is helpful to use the minicondylar blade plate as either a buttressing or a neutralization implant. The technique is found in the next section, Bicondylar Fractures.

Alternatively, for smaller fragments, two 0.028-inch K-wires or the newer maxillofacial microscrews will be adequate to maintain anatomic reduction.

With the stability afforded by interfragmentary lag screw fixation, mobilization can be started within a few days after surgery. The digit is protected by buddy-strapping to an adjacent digit for 2 to 3 weeks (Fig. 38–95).

## BICONDYLAR FRACTURES

Bicondylar fractures result from compressive loads directly on the head of the phalanx that split the two condyles. The attachments of the collateral ligament to each fragment tend to separate and rotate from each other, thereby making closed reduction exceptionally difficult. However, a surgical approach must not be considered lightly because the exposure may be limited, the fragments small and unstable, and the fixation technically demanding. The 1.5-mm condylar plate has provided a stable implant that resides along the lateral surface of the phalanx, thus avoiding interference with the extensor tendon over the PIP joint (see Fracture Immobilization Techniques).

In some instances, the fracture lines extend more proximally (Fig. 38–96) to allow for stable fixation with

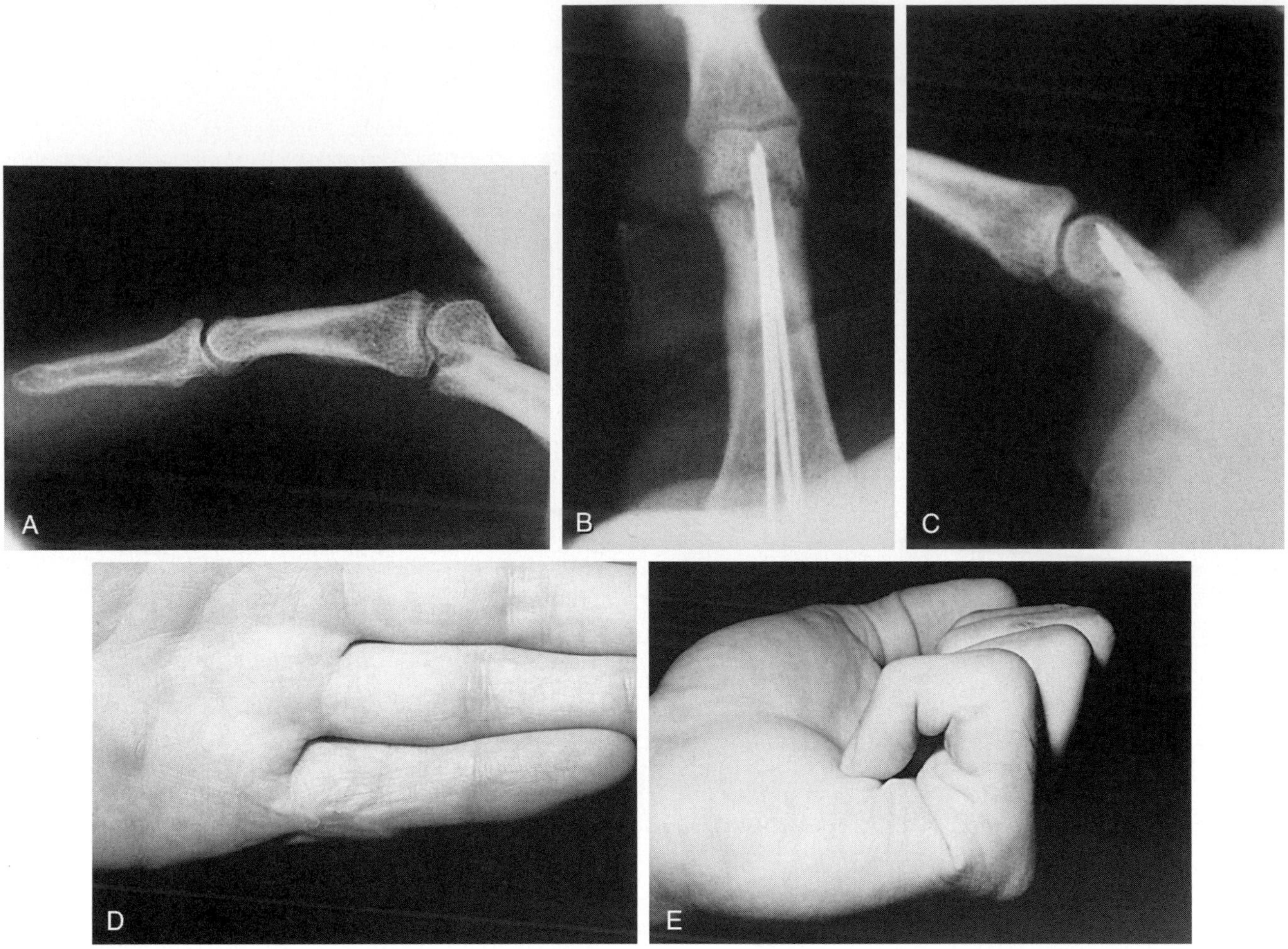

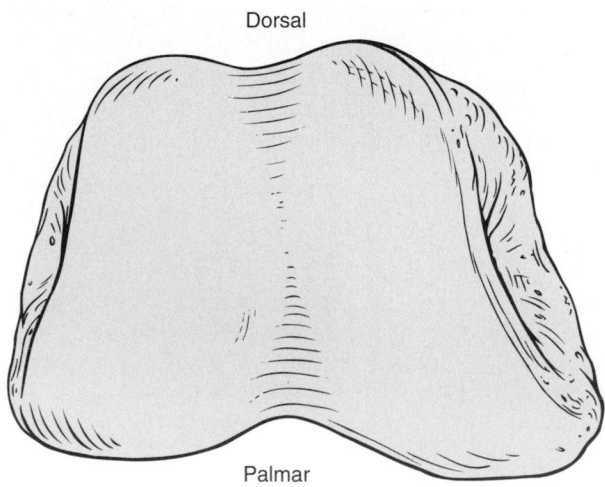

**FIGURE 38–89.** A displaced neck fracture of the proximal phalanx of the little finger was treated by closed reduction and longitudinal percutaneous K-wire fixation. *A,* A lateral radiograph demonstrates a displaced phalangeal neck fracture. Anteroposterior *(B)* and lateral *(C)* radiographs of the fracture were taken after closed reduction and percutaneous wire fixation. The K-wires were left in place for 4 weeks. *D, E,* Nearly full digital motion was regained by 2 weeks after K-wire removal.

Dorsal

Palmar

**FIGURE 38–90.** Condylar arrangement of the head of the proximal phalanx. Note that when viewed end on, the condyles are not symmetric.

interfragmentary screws alone.[191] An alternative technique is a modification of the tension band wire fixation. This technique is a particularly effective last resort if problems arise with plate fixation. Two sets of 0.028-inch K-wires are placed obliquely and distally from each condyle into the opposite, more proximal cortex. The wires should enter the condyles just above the true collateral ligaments but peripheral to the articular cartilage surface. A 30-gauge monofilament stainless steel wire is passed over the points of the K-wire, looped around the condyles and over the dorsum of the phalanx in a figure of eight, and then brought around the proximal protrusion of the K-wires. Each figure of eight is tightened to hold the condyles and thereby avoid rotational deformation. The stainless steel wire passes under the extensor mechanism and sits flat on the phalanx. The fixation gained by this approach is sufficient to permit mobility in the early postoperative period (Fig. 38–97).

The 1.5-mm minicondylar blade plate is ideal for providing stable internal fixation of a displaced bicondylar phalangeal fracture. It can play a role in the fixation of a unicondylar fracture with metaphyseal or diaphyseal extension and dissociation from the articular segment or in

**FIGURE 38–91.** *A,* A minimally displaced unicondylar fracture. The patient was advised to have percutaneous internal fixation; however, surgery was declined. Close observation and splintage were undertaken. *B,* At the 3-week follow-up, no further displacement had occurred, and excellent motion was equally recovered. Weekly follow-up radiographs are needed to ensure that no further displacement has occurred.

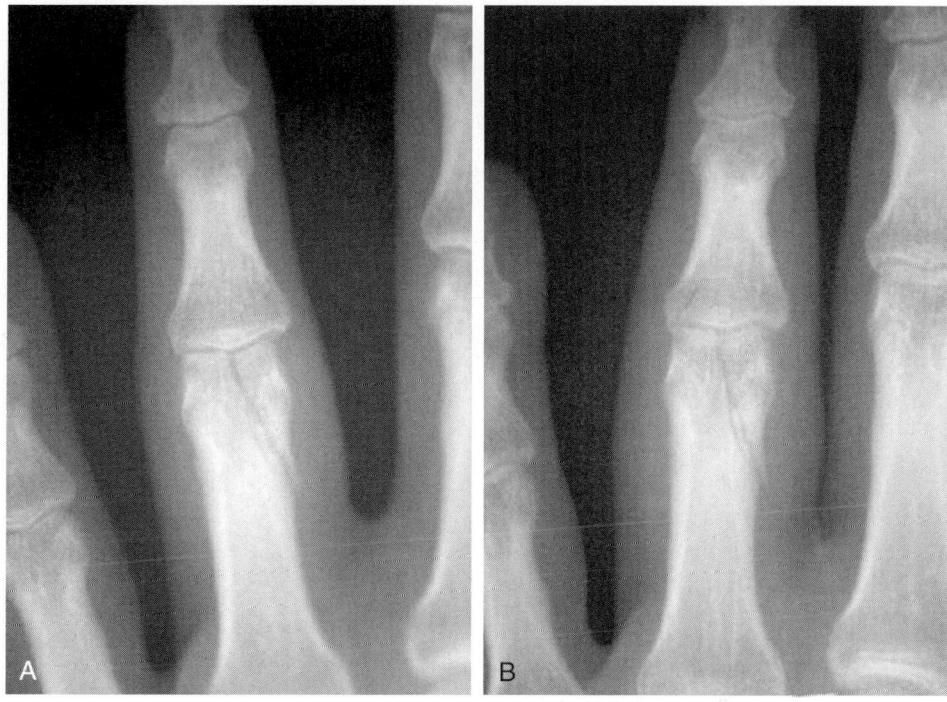

**FIGURE 38–92.** A 26-year-old woman fell while skiing. *A,* Anteroposterior radiograph revealing displacement of the articular surface. *B,* On a lateral film, displacement of the condyles and the interphalangeal joint is evident.

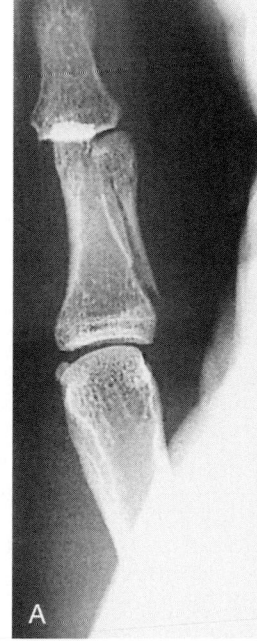
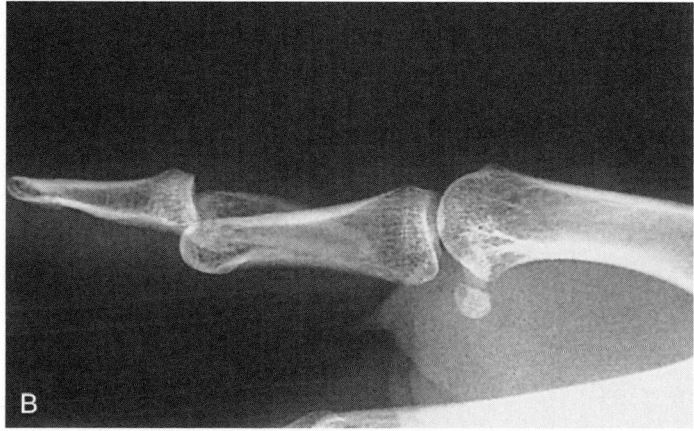

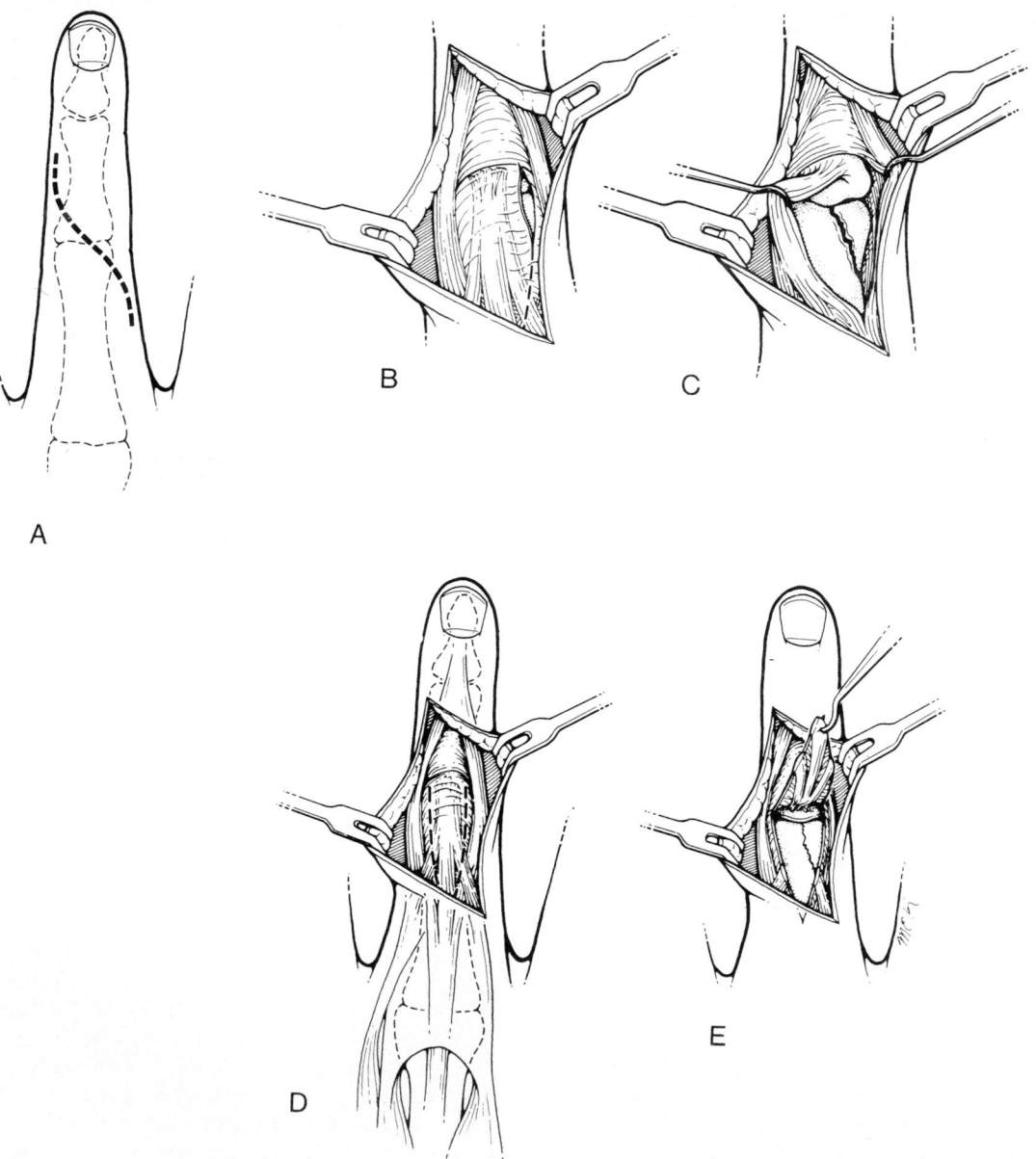

**FIGURE 38–93.** *A*, Typical skin incision for dorsal exposure of the proximal interphalangeal joint. *B, C,* Access to the joint by incising the interval between the lateral band and the central slip. *D, E,* Chamay exposure through a distally based flap of the central slip. (*A–E,* From Freeland, A.E.; Benoist, L.A. Hand Clin 10:239–250, 1994.)

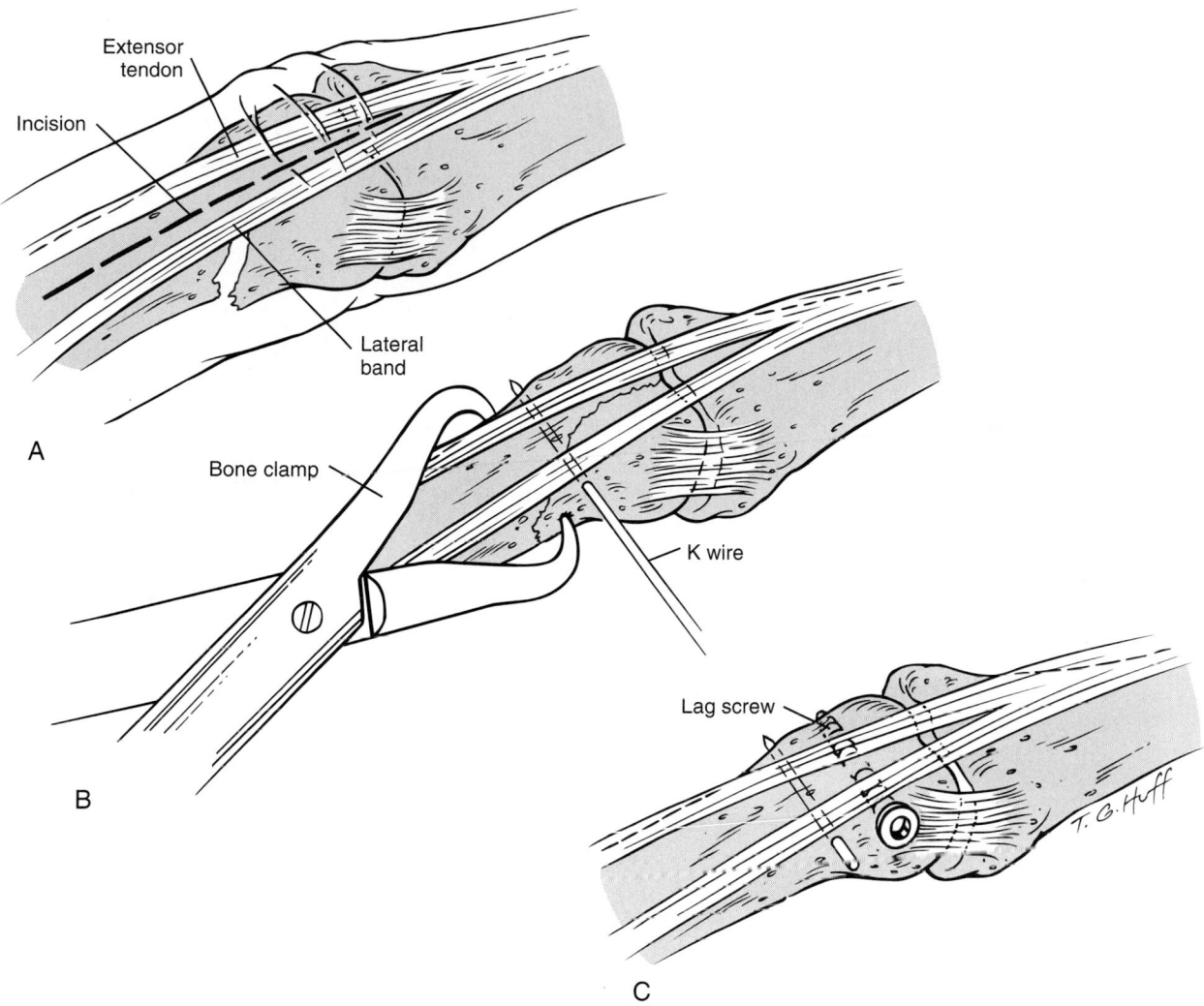

**FIGURE 38–94.** Operative approach to internal fixation of a unicondylar fracture of the head of the proximal phalanx. *A,* The approach is between the extensor tendon and the lateral band. Before reduction, the fragment's dimensions are determined. The fragment must be at least three times the diameter of the intended screw to allow interfragmentary screw fixation to be used safely. *B,* The fragment is reduced and provisionally secured with a 0.028-inch K-wire. *C,* Placement of the screw should be slightly dorsal and proximal to the origin of the collateral ligament. With a large fragment, the K-wire can be left in place to add rotational control.

the fixation of a complex juxta-articular phalangeal fracture (Fig. 38–98).

### Technique

The fracture site is exposed through a midlateral approach or through dorsal exposure as described by Chamay[53] (see Fig. 38–93). The transverse retinacular ligament is reflected to allow surgical access slightly below the lateral band. An area is exposed on the proximal phalangeal condyle for insertion of the blade. A small portion of the origin of the collateral ligament can be elevated off the condyle for ease of application. Such elevation must be conservative to preserve adequate blood supply to the condyle. The intercondylar fracture is reduced and provisionally secured with a 0.028-inch transverse K-wire placed dorsal or palmar to the position at which the blade will be inserted and used as a guide for later placement of the blade. The joint axis is defined with a K-wire, after which the blade hole is drilled with a 1.5-mm drill bit through the appropriate protective sleeve. The depth is measured and the standard 14-mm blade is cut to the

required length with a wire cutter or a small plate cutter. The blade is inserted in the drill hole, the subcondylar part of the fracture is reduced, and the plate's location on the phalangeal shaft is observed. Frequently, the plate will require contouring, which can be done only by removing the plate. The plate is reapplied, and an interfragmentary 1.5-mm screw is placed through the distal hole of the plate adjacent to the blade. The condyles, now reconstructed and well fixed to each other and the plate, are reattached to the shaft, and the plate is secured with 1.5-mm screws. An additional interfragmentary lag screw can be introduced through the oblique hole in the plate just proximal to the blade (Fig. 38–99).

Because of the complexity of these articulations, the meager size and vascularity of the fracture fragments, and the joints' close relationship to the extensor mechanism, these fractures are among the most difficult to manage in the hand. Unstable or improperly placed fixation, excessive soft tissue stripping, and unsupervised postoperative care can all result in an unsatisfactory outcome (Fig. 38–100).

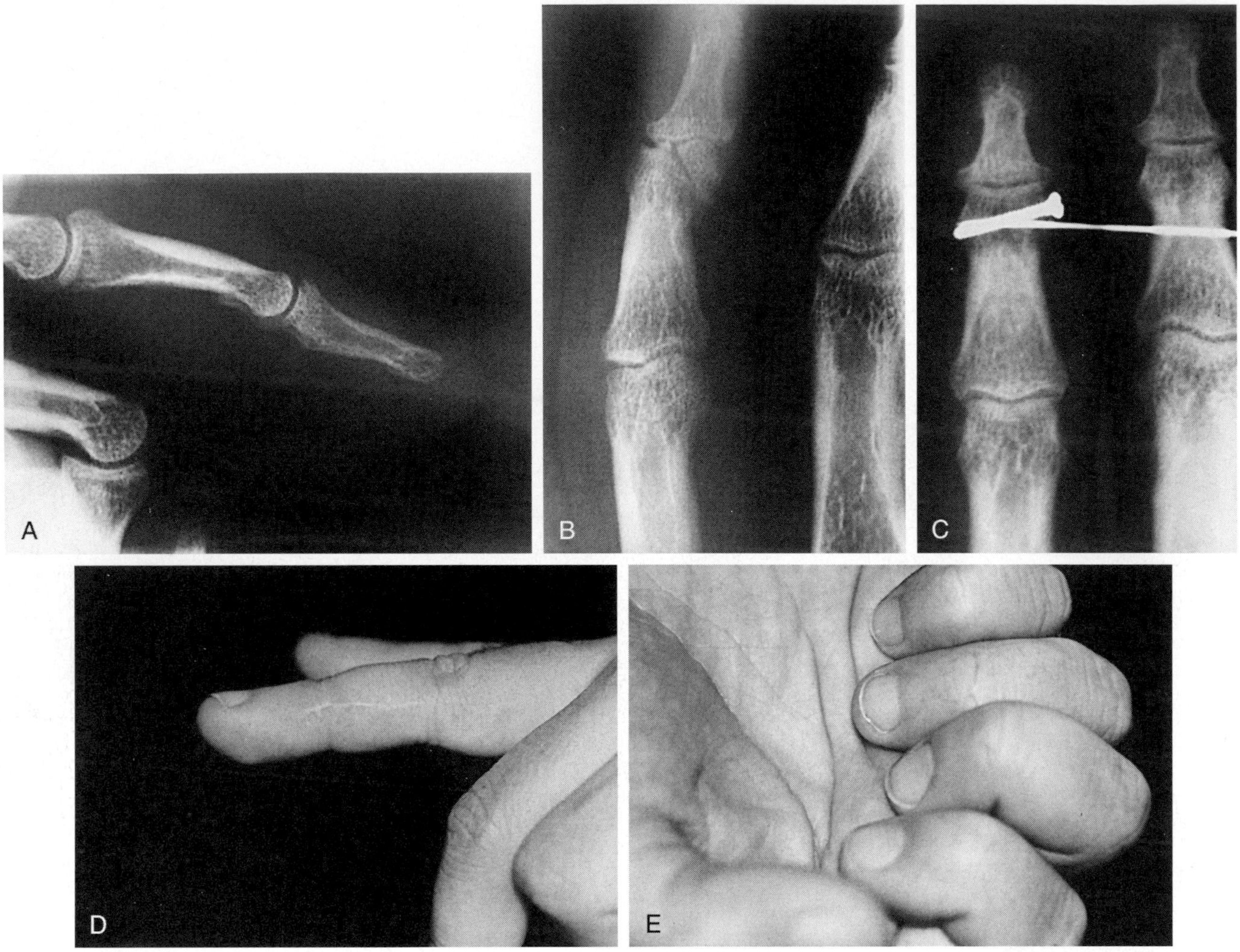

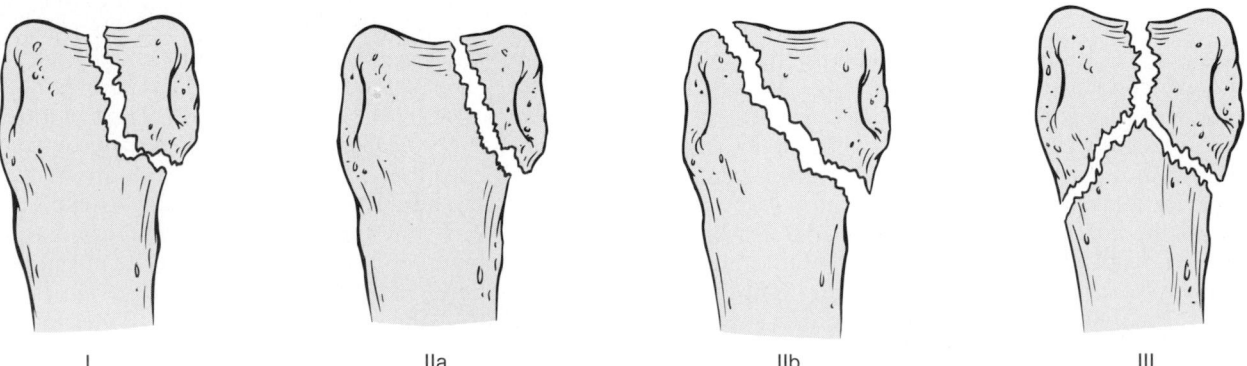

**FIGURE 38–95.** A neurosurgical resident sustained a displaced, rotated condylar fracture of the middle phalanx of his dominant ring finger. Lateral (*A*) and oblique (*B*) radiographs revealed rotation of the condyle. *C*, Open reduction and internal fixation were achieved with a 1.5-mm interfragmentary screw and a 0.028-inch K-wire. *D, E,* Full function resulted, and he returned to surgical duties 2 weeks postoperatively.

I          IIa          IIb          III

**FIGURE 38–96.** London's classification of condylar fractures of the interphalangeal joints.

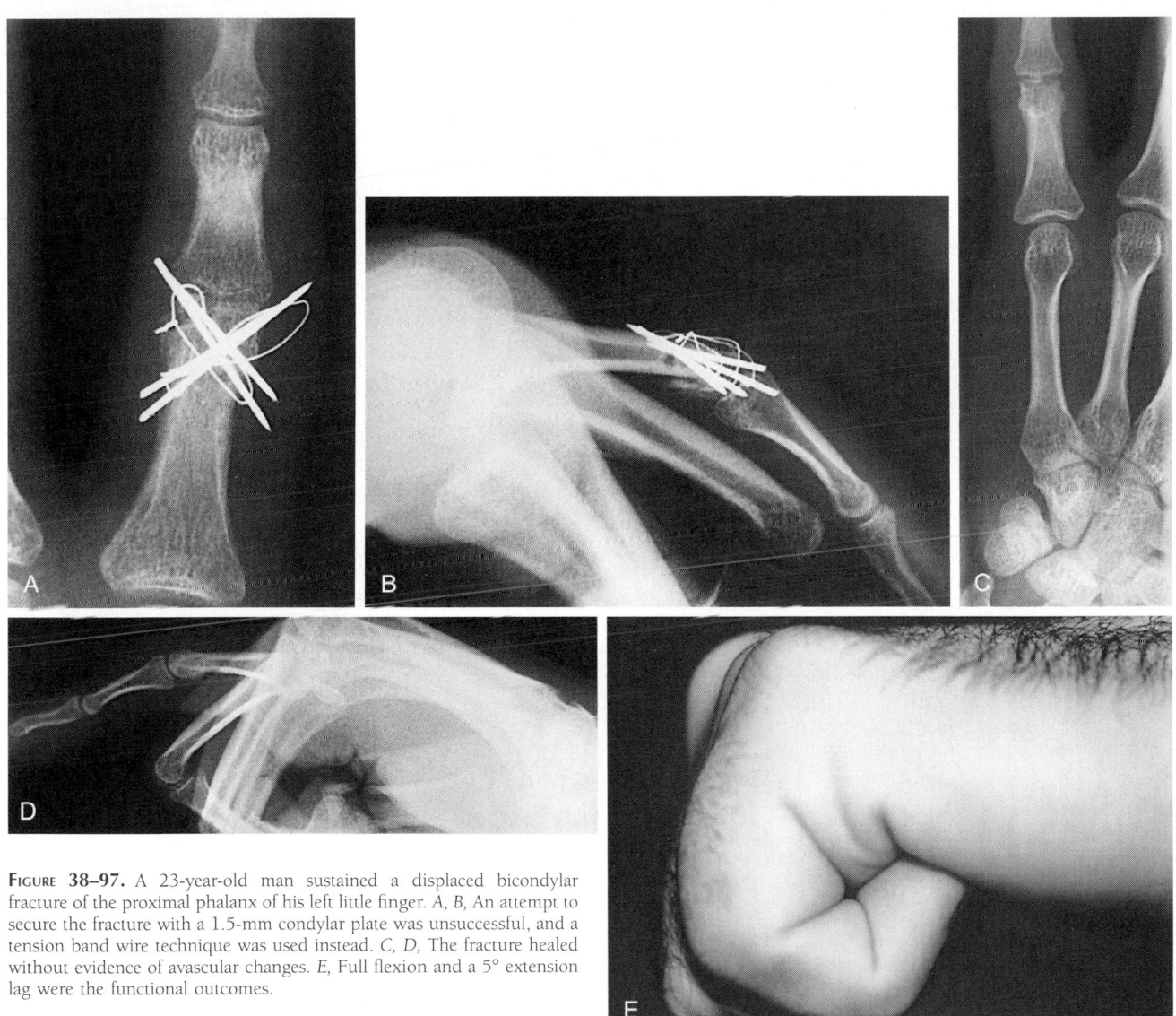

**FIGURE 38–97.** A 23-year-old man sustained a displaced bicondylar fracture of the proximal phalanx of his left little finger. *A, B,* An attempt to secure the fracture with a 1.5-mm condylar plate was unsuccessful, and a tension band wire technique was used instead. *C, D,* The fracture healed without evidence of avascular changes. *E,* Full flexion and a 5° extension lag were the functional outcomes.

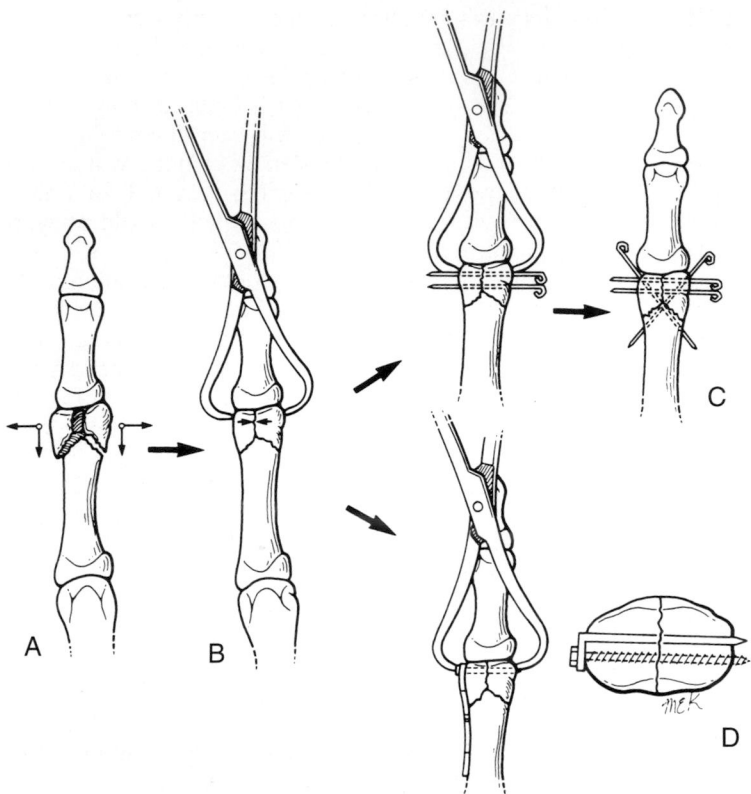

**FIGURE 38–98.** *A,* Surgical technique for reduction and internal fixation of a displaced bicondylar fracture. *B,* A tenacular reduction clamp is used to gently secure the reduction. *C,* K-wire fixation, which can be provisional or definitive. *D,* Providing more stable internal fixation is the minicondylar plate, which will attach the reconstructed, stable joint back to the diaphysis. (*A–D,* From Freeland, A.E.; Benoist, L.A. Hand Clin 10:239–250, 1994.)

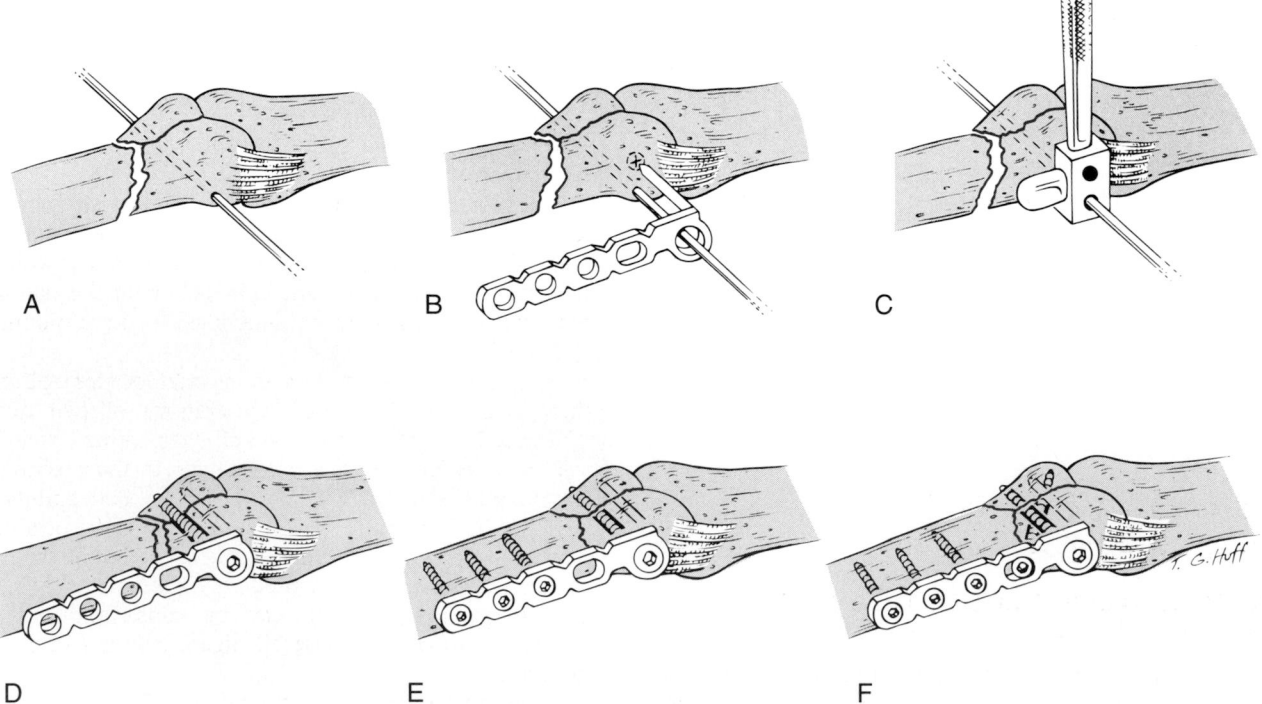

**FIGURE 38–99.** Technique of applying a 1.5-mm condylar plate for a T condylar phalangeal fracture. *A,* The condylar fragments are reduced and held with a 0.028-inch K-wire passed parallel to the line of the joint. *B,* The blade plate is seated over the K-wire, and a seating hole is marked to ideally sit just proximal and dorsal to the origin of the collateral ligament. *C,* With a guide, a 1.5-mm drill bit is used to make a seating hole for the blade. *D,* After contouring the plate to fit the shaft, the blade is introduced and a 1.5-mm screw placed into the condyle in a lag fashion. *E,* The condyles are reduced onto the shaft, and the most proximal screws are placed through the plate. *F,* A final interfragmentary lag screw is introduced obliquely through the most distal hole in the plate for added compression of the articular fragments.

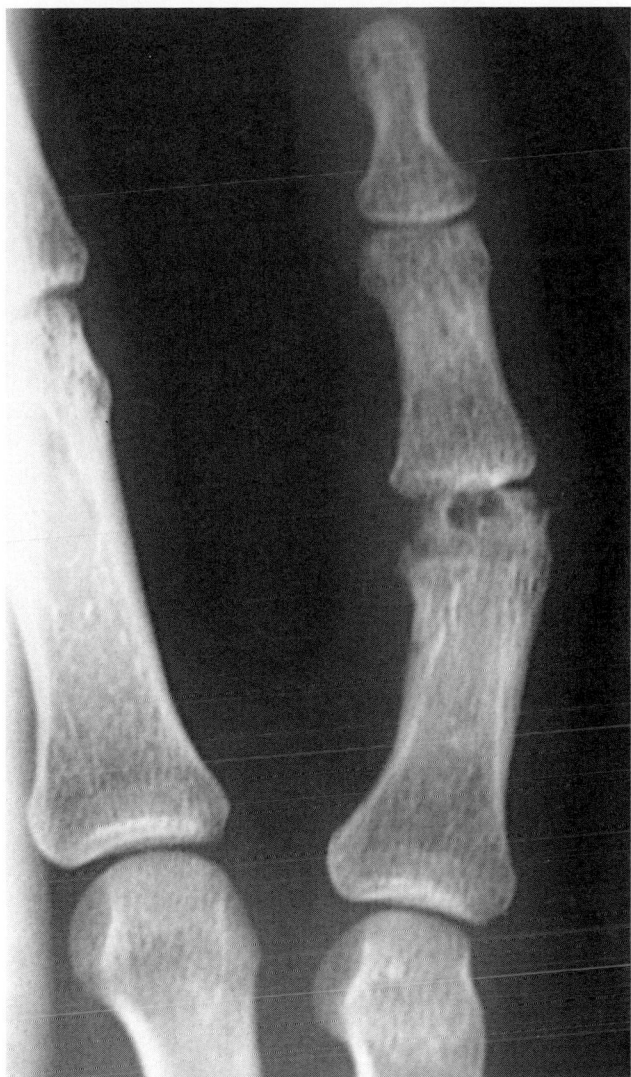

**Figure 38–100.** Excessive soft tissue stripping or a screw that is too large can lead to ischemic changes in condylar fractures. This radiograph reveals changes consistent with subchondral collapse resulting from avascular necrosis after open reduction and internal fixation of a unicondylar fracture.

The complexity of this articular injury increases when combined with soft tissue disruption. The ability to achieve articular restoration and stable fixation has a decided advantage in this setting (Fig. 38–101).

## Fractures of the Proximal Interphalangeal Joint

### FRACTURES OF THE BASE OF THE MIDDLE PHALANX

Fractures involving the articular base of the middle phalanx are the result of an axial load. The specific fracture pattern, as well as the direction and degree of displacement, is determined by the nature of the deforming force.[7, 192]

Fractures of the volar base at the site of attachment of the palmar plate are the most common of these injuries.

These fractures are often confined to only a small portion of the volar lip of the middle phalanx and result from a direct axial load (e.g., a "jammed" finger in a sporting event) (Fig. 38–102). Treatment is often for only comfort and protection. Coban wraps will keep the swelling to a minimum, and a dorsal extension block splint will serve to prevent repeat injury. The splint is required for only 2 weeks, followed by buddy straps, which should be worn an additional 2 to 4 weeks.

Volar fractures associated with dorsal dislocation of the middle phalanx can be classified into those that are stable after closed reduction and those that are unable to be maintained by closed treatment. Schenck developed a new classification system of these injuries that relates fracture extent to joint instability[261] (Fig. 38–103). Stable volar fractures are generally those involving less than 30% to 40% of the articular surface. The stability is a reflection of the attachment of the dorsal part of the true collateral ligament onto the middle phalanx (Fig. 38–104).

The technique advocated by McElfresh and associates[204] involves closed reduction followed by extension block splinting and is best suited for dorsal fracture-dislocations that are stable after reduction with the PIP joint held in a flexed position. It is easily performed under metacarpal block anesthesia. Longitudinal traction and flexion of the PIP joint will reduce the dislocation. A true lateral radiograph must confirm that the dorsal displacement has been eliminated. The digit is allowed to extend slowly until dorsal subluxation recurs; this point is carefully noted. The joint is again reduced and held in flexion 5° to 10° beyond the point at which it redislocated. A short arm cast is fashioned to incorporate a contoured dorsal Alumafoam splint extending dorsally onto the injured digit. The wrist is held in 30° of extension, the MCP joint in 60° to 80° of flexion, and the PIP joint in flexion just beyond its point of instability. Tape is applied to the splint over the proximal phalanx to allow further active flexion of the injured joint. Again, a true lateral radiograph must confirm the reduction.

The patient is seen at weekly intervals and the splint slowly extended over the joint by 10° each week until full extension is achieved. As a rule, the injury will be realigned by 4 to 6 weeks, at which time the splint is removed and buddy straps are applied for an additional 2 to 3 weeks.

Strong suggested an ingenious method for splinting these fracture-dislocations that consists of two dorsal Alumafoam splints bent toward each other over the injured joint to keep the joint resting in the position of flexion, which maintains the reduction.[296] Both splints are taped to the digit, and active flexion exercises are begun. In a manner similar to that described by McElfresh and associates, the joint is extended by 10° on a weekly basis. This technique, however, can be considered only in compliant patients because all digital splints can slip or loosen.

When the fracture involves between 30% and 50% of the base of the middle phalanx, the technique of dorsal block splinting may not be as predictable.[125] In McElfresh and associates' series, only 4 of 17 patients had fracture fragments larger than 30%. For articular fragments that are not comminuted, ORIF has had predictable results. A

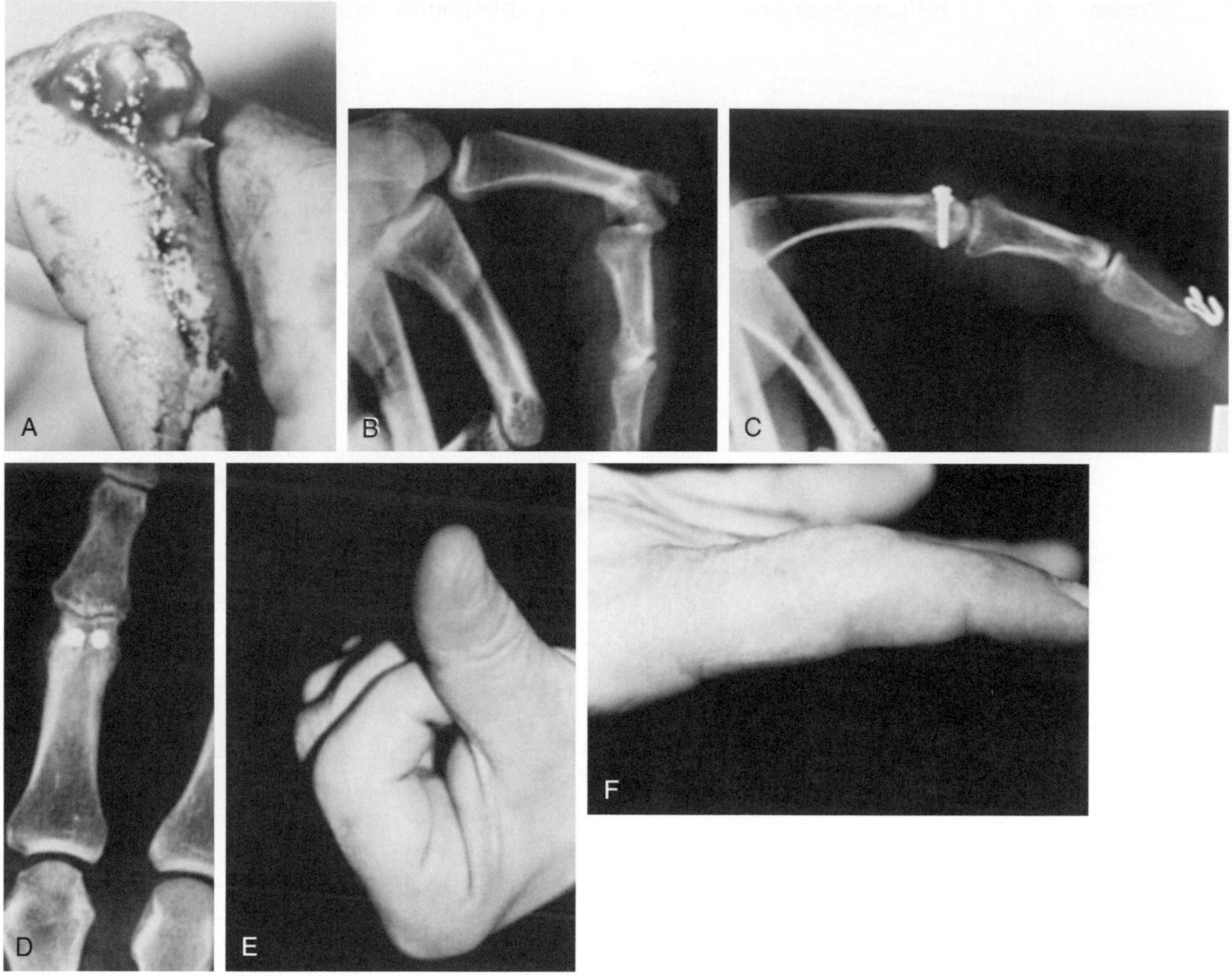

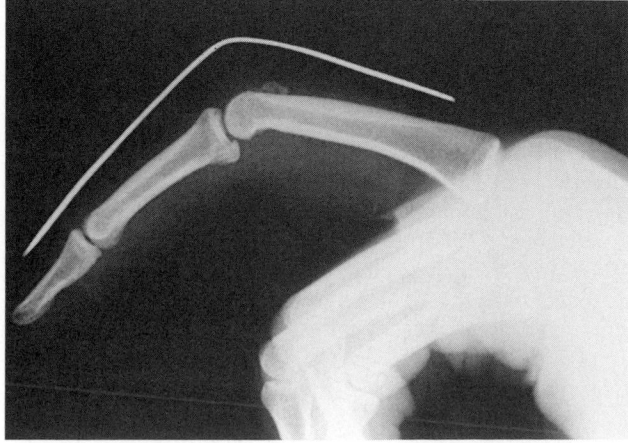

**FIGURE 38–101.** *A,* A 33-year-old man sustained a table saw injury to the dorsum of his left index finger. The extensor mechanism was disrupted, and the articular condyles were vertically and horizontally split. *B,* Lateral radiograph demonstrating the articular disruption. *C, D,* After thorough débridement, the condyles were reduced and internally fixed with two 1.5-mm interfragmentary screws. The extensor mechanism was reconstructed acutely. Radiographs taken at 6 weeks reveal the anatomic restoration without evidence of avascular necrosis. *E, F,* The patient regained nearly full extension and 80° of flexion. Postoperative mobilization was begun 3 weeks after injury to allow for healing of the extensor mechanism.

**FIGURE 38–102.** A 23-year-old woman jammed her finger in a volleyball game. She presented with a painful swollen digit. Radiographs demonstrated a small nondisplaced avulsion fragment on the base of the middle phalanx. Coban wraps and early mobilization with a protective Alumafoam extension block splint led to rapid functional recovery.

midaxial approach affords excellent exposure, and with manual traction on the middle phalanx, the joint can readily be reduced. The internal fixation method should optimally allow early mobilization. Either single-screw fixation or Lister's type B intraosseous wire technique should be considered (see Fracture Immobilization Techniques). Transarticular K-wiring for 3 weeks followed by dorsal block splinting has been effective in some authors' experience.[125, 202, 323]

If the fragments are comminuted and unstable with dorsal block splinting, the options available include dynamic traction and volar plate arthroplasty. Several methods of dynamic traction have been devised, including (1) the dynamic force couple technique designed by Agee,[2] (2) dynamic traction and early passive movement in a circular traction splint (advocated by Schenk[262, 263]), and (3) dynamic external fixation as designed by Hastings and Ernst.[126]

The dynamic traction method involves the insertion of a transosseous traction wire through the head of the middle phalanx. The wire is linked via rubber bands to a

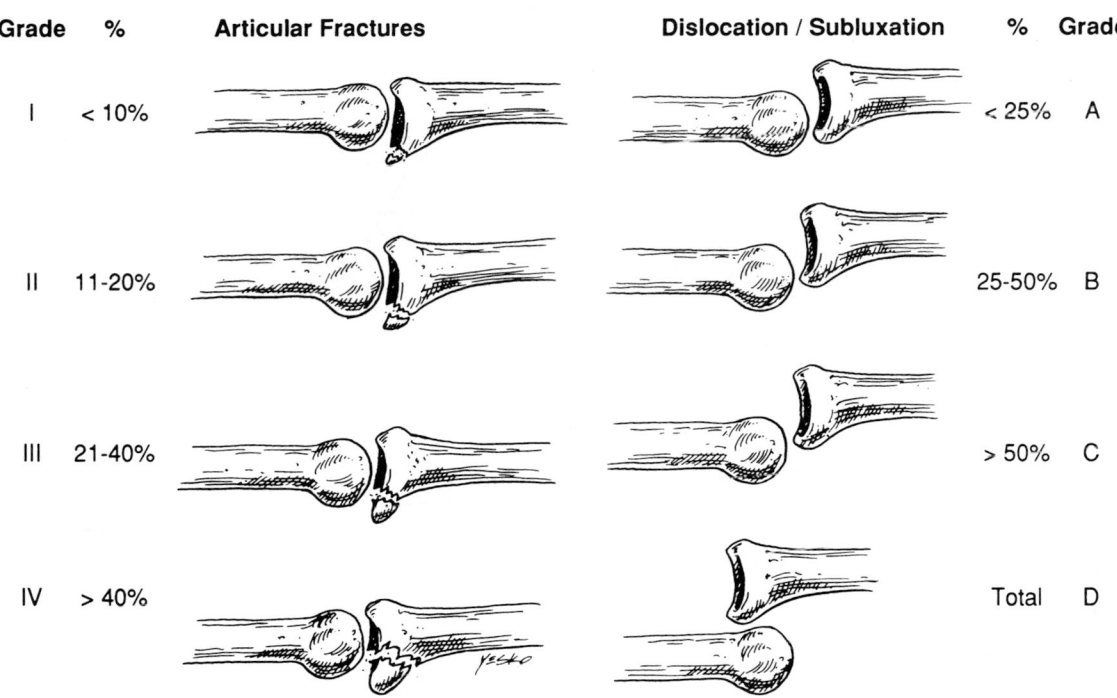

| Grade | % | Articular Fractures | Dislocation / Subluxation | % | Grade |
|---|---|---|---|---|---|
| I | < 10% | | | < 25% | A |
| II | 11-20% | | | 25-50% | B |
| III | 21-40% | | | > 50% | C |
| IV | > 40% | | | Total | D |

**Figure 38–103.** Schenck created a new grading system for fractures and subluxation/dislocation of the proximal interphalangeal joint. The severity of the injury is classified by the grade of the fracture representing the percentage of joint involvement (expressed numerically from I to IV) and the grade of subluxation or dislocation (expressed alphabetically from A to D). An injury can then be classified as grade IIB, for example, which represents a fracture of 11% to 20% of the joint surface and a dislocation of 25% to 50%. (From Schenck, R.R. Hand Clin 10:179–185, 1994.)

movable component on a 6-inch-diameter arcuate splint (Fig. 38–105). Schenck reviewed the original 10 patients of his series treated by this method at 9 years' average follow-up. Joint involvement averaged 63%. The average follow-up range of motion was from 5° of flexion deformity to 92° of flexion, an arc of 87°. All joints remain pain free and otherwise asymptomatic. Further joint remodeling was noted on the longer follow-up of the original series. Other authors have had similar success with this method for fractures with extensive involvement of the articular surface.[70, 215]

In 1987, Agee reported the use of a force couple splint to maintain reduction of an unstable fracture-dislocation of the PIP joint.[2] This splint is somewhat complex to construct; however, when applied correctly, it has produced some excellent results by combining traction and early active motion (Fig. 38–106).

Volar plate arthroplasty has been promoted by Eaton

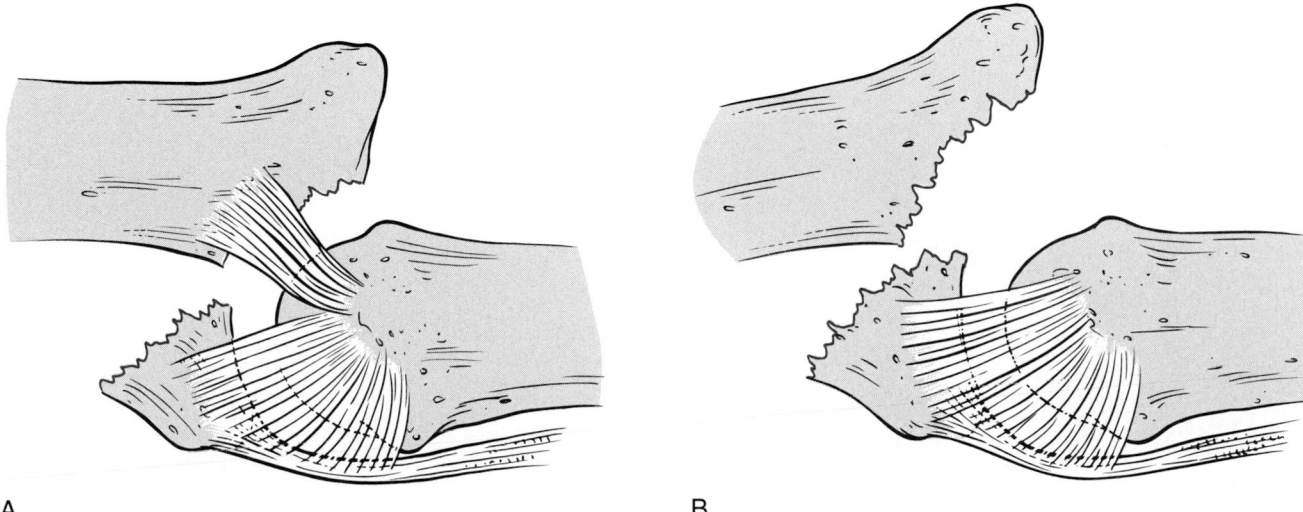

A                                B

**Figure 38–104.** *A, B,* The stability of a displaced dorsal fracture-dislocation is dependent on the collateral ligament. With fragments involving more than 40% to 50% of the volar articular base of the middle phalanx, any attachment of the true collateral ligament is lost.

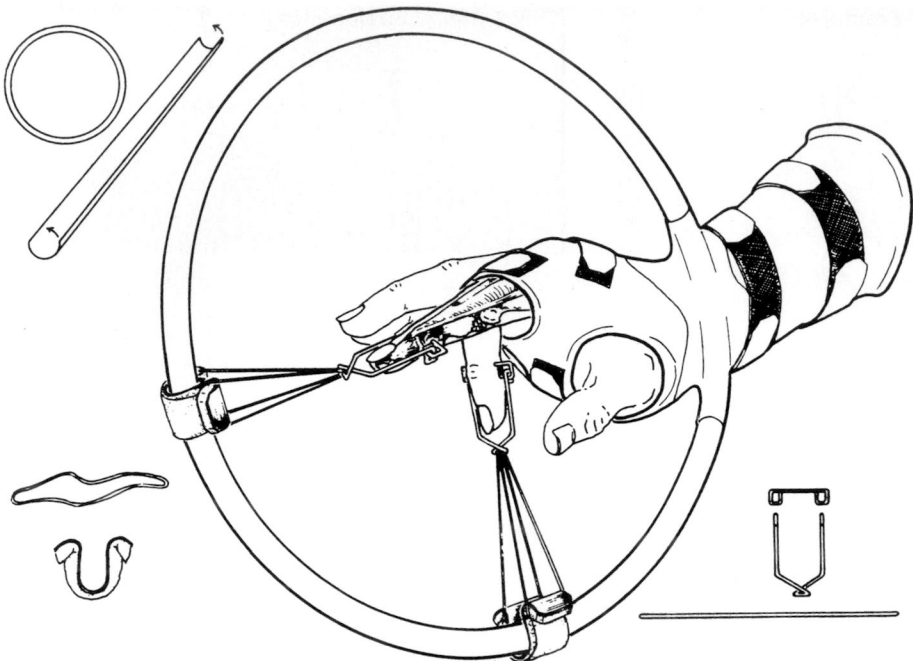

**FIGURE 38–105.** The arcuate splint uses a wire yoke between the transosseous wire and a movable "Dutch girl's hat" component. This dynamic traction allows for in-line traction and active flexion of the injured proximal interphalangeal joint. (From Schenck, R.R. J Hand Surg [Am] 11:850–858, 1986.)

and Malerich for the acute management of this group of injuries.[81] This technique is performed through a palmar approach. The comminuted fracture fragments are resected, and the middle phalanx is reduced. A pull-out wire is woven through the palmar plate, passed out through the fracture site, and secured over the dorsum of the middle phalanx. If the injury is not stable, the joint is held reduced, and an oblique 0.035-inch K-wire is passed across the joint. The wire is left in place for 2 weeks, followed by motion in an extension block splint (Figs. 38–107 and 38–108).

By far the most complex injury pattern is one in which the articular comminution extends beyond 50% of the articular surface of the middle phalangeal base. The fundamental problem in this subgroup of fracture-dislocations is loss of collateral ligament support to the middle phalangeal shaft (see Fig. 38–104). The more distal

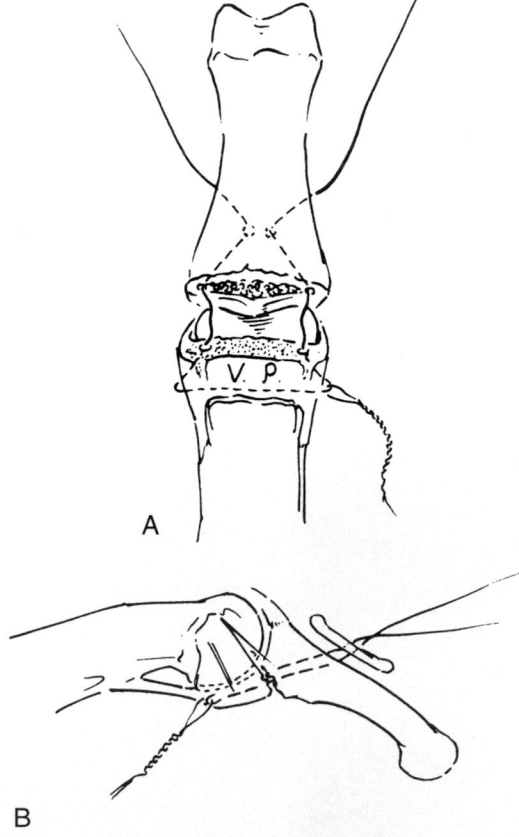

**FIGURE 38–107.** *A*, Surgical technique for arthroplasty with the Eaton volar plate (V.P.). The trough is carefully fashioned at the volar base of the middle phalanx. *B*, A pull-out suture is used to advance the plate securely against the trough and is tied over a dorsal button. For details, see Eaton and Malerich, 1980. (*A, B*, From Eaton, R.G.; Malerich, M.M. J Hand Surg 5:260–268, 1980.)

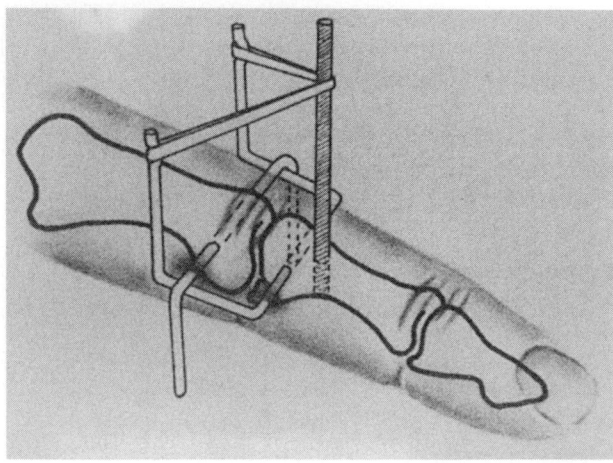

**FIGURE 38–106.** The Agee dynamic force couple splint fully assembled. This construct will hold the joint reduced yet allow full active and passive motion. (From Agee, J.M. Clin Orthop 214:101–112, 1987.)

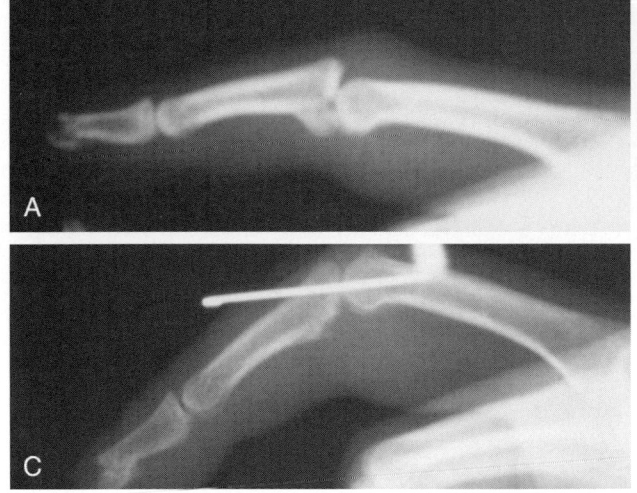

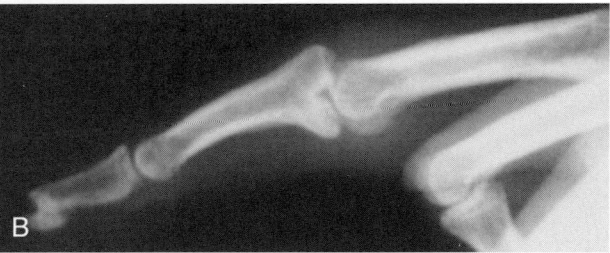

**FIGURE 38–108.** *A,* Initial radiographs of a fracture-subluxation of the proximal interphalangeal joint of a 38-year-old construction worker. *B,* The degree of displacement of the joint was not appreciated, and the patient was treated with only a dorsal Alumafoam splint. The fracture healed with the joint subluxed. The motion was minimal and painful. *C,* Immediate postoperative radiographs after volar plate arthroplasty. Note the resection of the volar fragment, the anatomic joint reduction, and transfixion of the joint with a K-wire in slight flexion. Ultimately, functional range of motion was obtained with an arc of 75° and a 20° flexion deformity of the joint.

attachments of the extrinsic flexor tendons add to the deforming pull on the middle phalanges.[125] Traction, external fixation with or without open reduction, internal fixation, and volar plate arthroplasty are all unpredictable, but the traction "arcuate" splint technique of Schenck has been shown to be effective for these fractures. Traction is applied to a horizontal transosseous wire through the middle or distal phalanx for 6 to 8 weeks. For these complex fractures, Schenck reported an average arc of motion of 87° in 10 patients that was maintained for the 9-year period of recent follow-up.[262, 263] The technique of osteotomy and grafting of the volar fragment to restore a more competent volar buttress, as advocated by Zemel and colleagues, may also have promise in these cases.[327]

Fractures of the base of the middle phalanx with or without dorsal dislocation are common injuries. Unfortunately, a favorable outcome is far from ensured in even the most innocent of injuries. PIP joint stiffness, flexion contracture, and redislocation have all frequently been associated with these articular injuries.

Rarely and perhaps only with open fractures and substance loss, a need may arise for primary arthrodesis of this joint. Alternatively, a nonreconstructible situation in a low-demand individual may lend itself to early reconstruction with a flexible Silastic hinge arthroplasty.

### Fractures of the Dorsum of the Base of the Middle Phalanx

Dorsal avulsion fractures represent a disruption of the attachment of the central slip of the extensor mechanism. These injuries are considered acute boutonnière fractures and treated with extension splinting for up to 6 weeks, with the distal interphalangeal (DIP) joint left free for active motion.

Much less commonly, this injury is associated with volar dislocation of the middle phalanx. An attempt at closed reduction is advisable. If successful, transarticular K-wire fixation is recommended for 3 weeks. The joint should also be splinted in extension and the DIP joint left free. If the dorsal fragment is of sufficient size, ORIF is possible. When open reduction of this fracture is performed, it is advisable to stabilize the repair with a tension band wire because this wire will allow protected early active motion (Fig. 38–109).

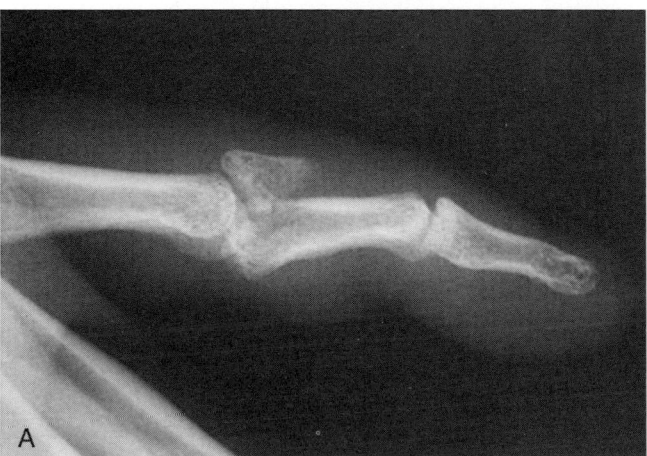

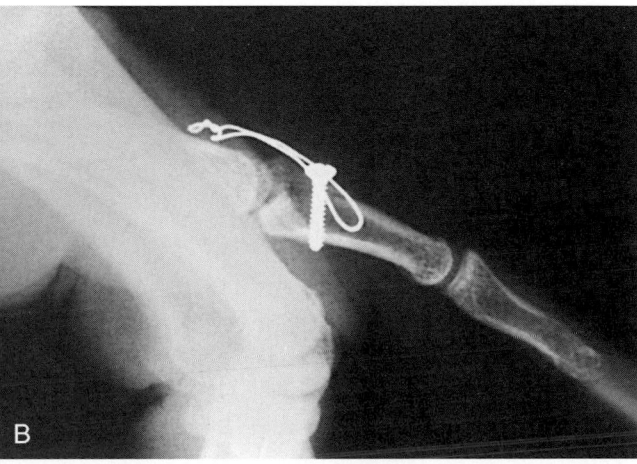

**FIGURE 38–109.** *A,* A 20-year-old man sustained a fracture of the dorsal base of the middle phalanx associated with a volar dislocation. *B,* Open reduction and internal fixation with an interfragmentary screw. An additional tension band wire was directed through a dorsally placed drill hole in the middle phalanx and woven through the central slip to help neutralize the force on the screw.

## Impaction Fractures

A number of specific impaction fracture patterns of the articular surface of the base of the middle phalanges have been outlined in a review by Hastings and Carroll.[125] A direct axial load will produce a central impaction fracture pattern. These injuries are uncommon but can be suitable, in some cases, for operative treatment. As with comminuted articular fractures at the base of the thumb, distraction with an external fixation device will help define the fracture fragments, and it may prove possible to elevate the larger impacted articular fragments and mold them to the corresponding articular surface of the head of the proximal phalanx. Cancellous bone graft must be placed under the elevated joint surface. Unfortunately, some of these impaction fractures are high-energy injuries that offer little hope of functional restoration. Even so, reassembly of the fracture fragments can provide an easier skeletal anatomy on which to perform arthrodesis or arthroplasty (Fig. 38–110).

## Lateral Plateau Fractures

Fractures with eccentric loading result in disruption of the volar side of one of the articular fossae of the base of the middle phalanx. The fragment can be rotated and displaced by the attached collateral ligament. It is not uncommon to find impaction of some part of the articular surface. Instability may be present dorsally, or rotational instability of the digit may be present around the contralateral intact collateral ligament. A surgical approach can achieve restoration of both joint stability and articular anatomy. With larger volar fragments, stable internal fixation is possible with 1.5-mm screws (Fig. 38–111). Another fixation option involves a K-wire and monofilament stainless steel wire (28 or 30 gauge) passed through the attached collateral ligament and around the fragment. If a part of the articular surface should require elevation, a cancellous graft can be used for support of the articular surface (Fig. 38–112).

## Fractures of the Middle Phalanges

The outcome of fractures of the middle phalanges is in general more favorable than that for fractures of the proximal phalanges. This better outcome is mostly due to the fact that the disturbance in DIP joint motion is not nearly as great a functional problem as are similar disturbances in PIP or MCP joint motion.

These fractures are often readily reduced because the stable PIP joint makes manipulative reduction straightforward. With unstable fractures, K-wire fixation is the best choice if the fracture line is amenable. Only with widespread soft tissue trauma should open reduction and stable internal fixation be considered.

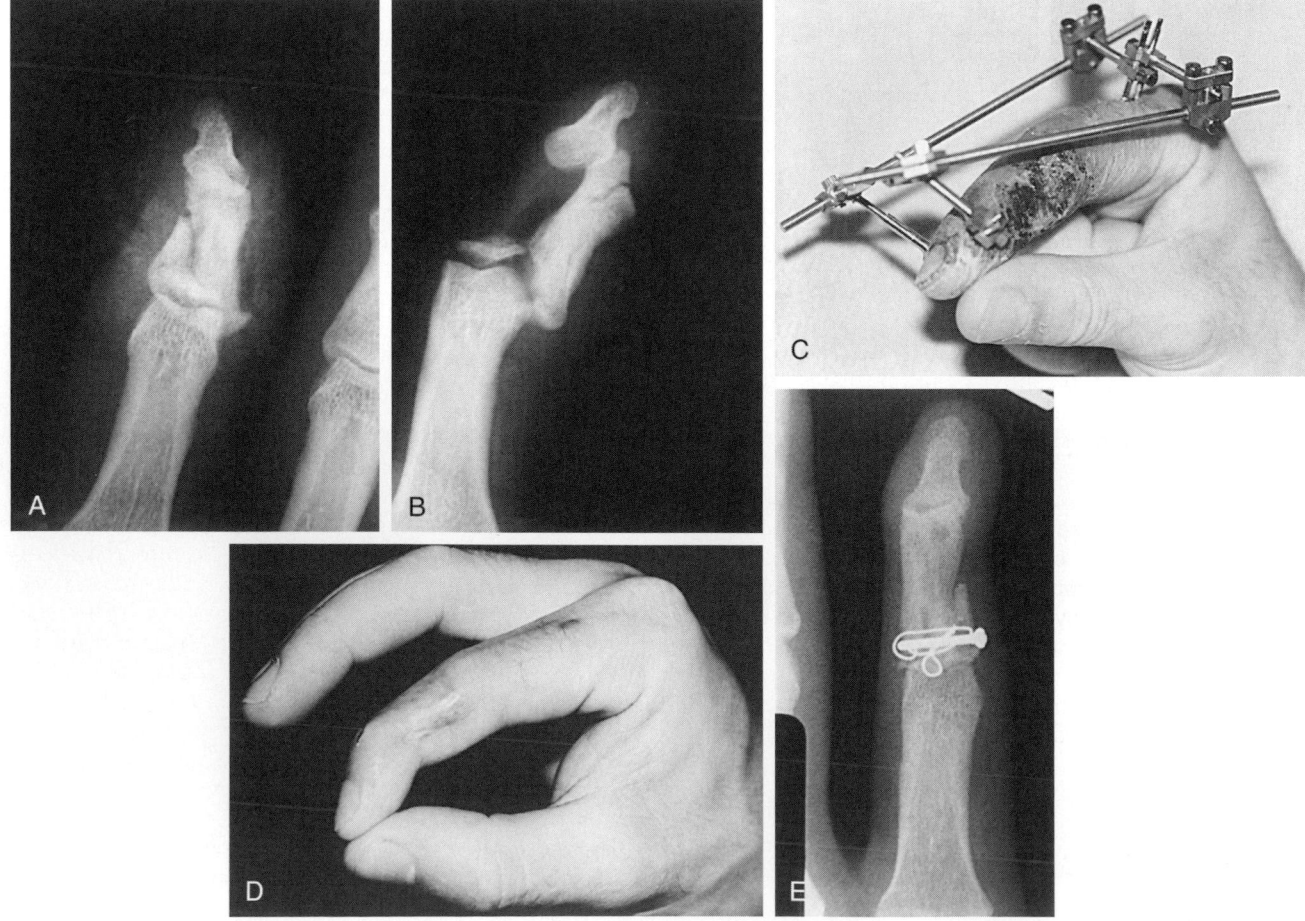

FIGURE 38–110. A 26-year-old man sustained a severe impaction injury of the middle phalanx of his dominant index finger. A, B, Radiographs demonstrate the unfortunate damage to the joint surface. C, A minidistractor was applied, and the joint was reduced and stabilized with internal fixation and a cancellous, distal radial bone graft. D, The joint proved to be stiff, but it was stable and pain free. E, Follow-up radiograph at 6 months.

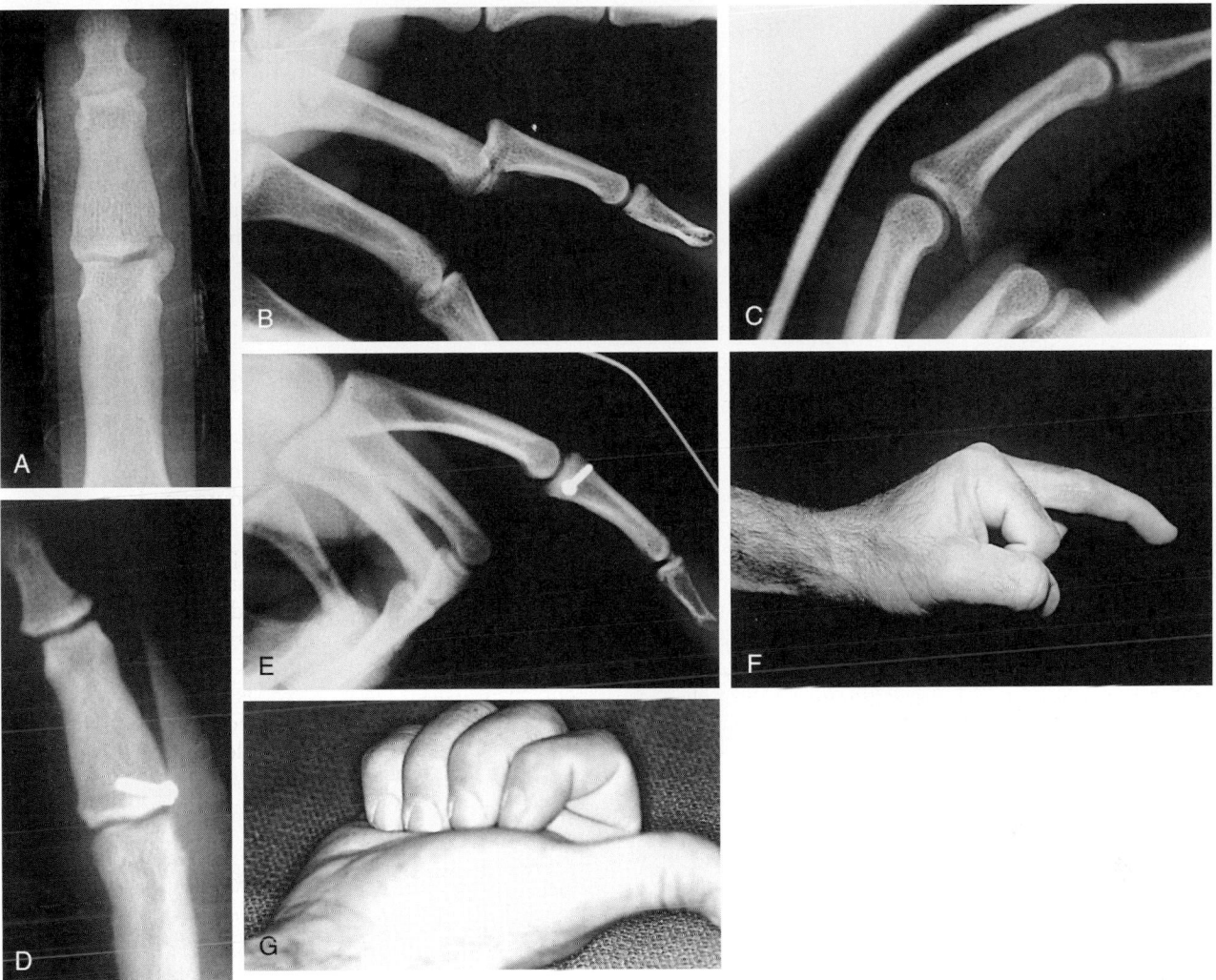

**FIGURE 38–111.** A 21-year-old man sustained a fracture-dislocation of his long finger in a sporting event. Anteroposterior (*A*) and lateral (*B*) radiographs demonstrate the dislocation and the presence of a large volar lateral plateau fracture. *C*, Closed reduction was unsuccessful in reducing the fragment because of displacement by its attached collateral ligaments. *D, E,* Open reduction and internal fixation of the fragment with a 1.5-mm screw achieved both an anatomic joint surface and a stable articulation. Early motion was initiated. *F, G,* Nearly full extension and flexion were regained.

Unicondylar and bicondylar fractures are similar to those of the head of the proximal phalanx, and treatment considerations should mirror those already discussed (see Phalangeal Condylar Fractures). However, the size of the involved segments will be considerably smaller, thereby creating more difficulties in fracture stabilization. The consequences of malunion or arthrosis at the DIP joint are much less than at the PIP joint and are readily managed by joint arthrodesis. As such, if the technical aspects of management of these injuries are overwhelming, it may be better to splint, begin early active motion, or distract the joint with a simple mini-fixator for 3 weeks and deal with the consequences at a later date.

## Fractures of the Distal Phalanx

### ANATOMY

The unique architecture of the human distal phalanx plays an important role not only in overall digital form and function but also in the complexity of its fracture patterns. In addition, the relationship of the distal phalanx with its highly specialized overlying soft tissue envelope often forms the basis for treatment considerations in fractures of this bone.

The broad spadelike distal tuberosity is perhaps the distal phalanx's most distinguishing feature when compared with the structure of the middle phalanx. This so-called ungual tuberosity represents an evolutionary development of the early hominids, perhaps as a result of greater incorporation of pulp use in gripping, as well as an increased reliance on tools.[275] This feature is lacking today in most primates.[298]

The palmar surface of the ungual tuberosity provides the site of attachment of the well-defined fascial bands that separate the distal digital pulp into wedgelike compartments similar to the structure of the heel pad.[141] This particular anatomic arrangement diffuses contact pressure through the conical fat columns, thereby distributing pulp pressure more equally.[275] The overlying nail plate also plays a role in stabilizing the deforming forces on the terminal pulp.

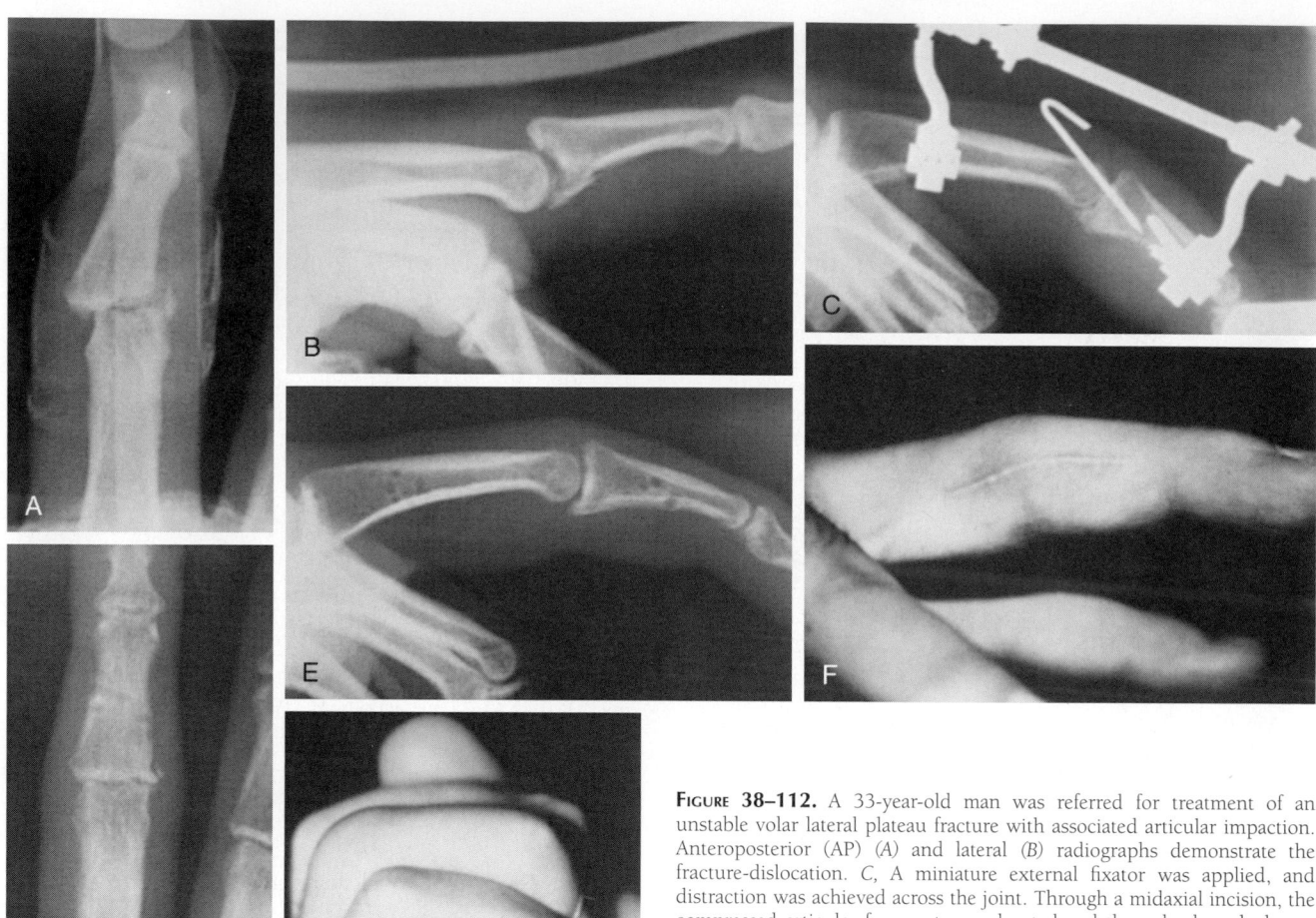

**FIGURE 38–112.** A 33-year-old man was referred for treatment of an unstable volar lateral plateau fracture with associated articular impaction. Anteroposterior (AP) (*A*) and lateral (*B*) radiographs demonstrate the fracture-dislocation. *C,* A miniature external fixator was applied, and distraction was achieved across the joint. Through a midaxial incision, the compressed articular fragment was elevated and the volar lateral plateau fragment reduced. *D, E,* AP and lateral radiographs, respectively, taken 9 weeks postoperatively. *F, G,* The fixator was removed 6 weeks postoperatively, and the patient regained nearly full motion by 9 weeks after surgery.

Spinous processes project on both sides of the ungual tuberosity. These processes serve as anchors for the taut lateral interosseous ligaments arising from the lateral tubercles on either side of the base of the distal phalanx (Fig. 38–113). These ligaments, thought by Shrewsbury and Johnson to be extensions of the osteocapsular portions of the more proximal oblique retinacular ligament, function to protect the neurovascular bundles as they pass dorsally from the pulp to the nail bed.[275] These ligaments also serve to prevent displacement of comminuted tuberosity fractures (Fig. 38–114).

The diaphysis, or waist, of the distal phalanx is less well protected from contact stress than the ungual tuberosity is, and the cortex is considerably thicker. Flat on the dorsal surface, the waist is concave palmarly and creates an ungual fossa unique to hominids.

The base of the distal phalanx offers a prominent crest on the dorsal surface for insertion of the terminal extensor tendon. The tendon firmly adheres to the dorsal joint capsule and extends from the dorsal aspect of one collateral ligament to that of the other. Its fibers blend into the capsule and periosteum and extend virtually to the root of the nail.[157] It is precisely because of these extensive

attachments that variations are observed in the clinical features of the tendinous "mallet" finger. The lateral tubercles on either side of the base are situated near its palmar aspect and serve as the site of attachment for the collateral ligaments of the DIP joint, as well as for the lateral interosseous ligaments. The articular surface is divided into asymmetric concave radial and ulnar recesses separated by a convex intercondylar ridge.[105] This asymmetry corresponds to the asymmetric condyles of the head of the middle phalanx and accounts for the deviation seen particularly in the border digits.[105] On the palmar surface, the flexor digitorum profundus insertion extends distally out onto the midportion of the distal phalanx. The profundus therefore inserts into the entire width of the base of the distal phalanx and blends with the fibers of the palmar plate and periosteum.[157] The fibers of the tendon run in a spiral course, with the superficial fibers attaching to both the sides of the distal phalanx and the lateral tubercles, whereas the deep fibers pass more distally and centrally.[198, 322]

The DIP joint is especially noteworthy in its structural ability to allow passive hyperextension, something not found in the hand of any other member of the Hominidae

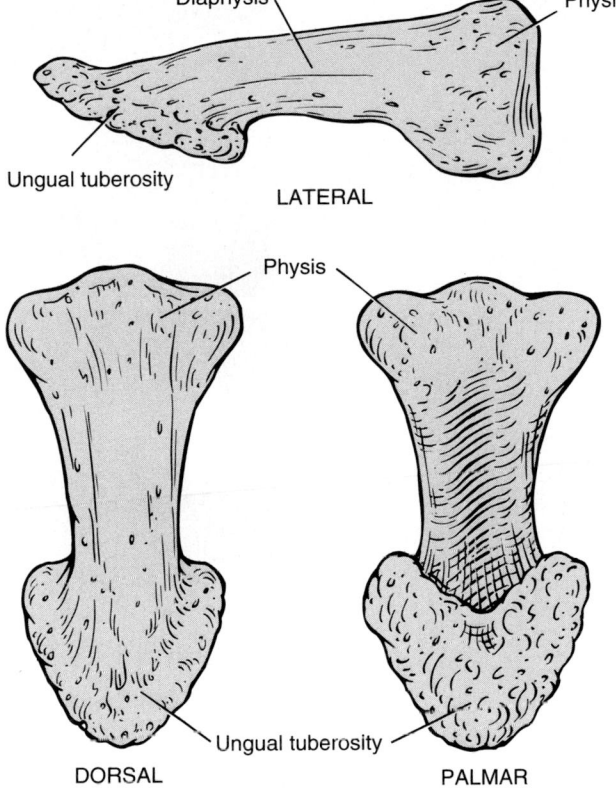

Diaphysis     Physis

Ungual tuberosity

**LATERAL**

Physis

Ungual tuberosity

**DORSAL**     **PALMAR**

FIGURE 38–113. The structure of the distal phalanx is considerably different from that of the proximal and middle phalanges.

except the gibbon's.[308] Such hyperextension is partly due to the fact that the palmar plate, unlike the PIP joint, has a flexible proximal attachment without any "checkreins" onto the middle phalanx.[105] This ability of passive hyperextension allows for pulp-to-pulp pinch, which is unique to humans.

## TYPES OF DISTAL PHALANGEAL FRACTURES AND TREATMENT

The distal phalanx is by far the most commonly fractured bone in the hand and is involved in as many as 50% of all hand fractures in some series.[47, 67] This frequency is not at all surprising when one considers how exposed the terminal parts of the digits are to local trauma. The vast majority of distal phalangeal fractures are the result of a crushing injury, frequently comminuting the bone and often associated with overlying soft tissue or nail bed trauma. The distal phalanx is well supported by fibrous septa and the overlying nail matrix and does not have any tendons spanning the bone as deforming forces.[47] Fractures of this bone will generally heal without undue complications, but physicians must avoid becoming too complacent when treating these injuries because the potential complications can be disabling. Complications include pain, cold weather intolerance, altered sensibility, nail bed and nail deformity, malunion, and even nonunion.[264]

### Classification

Several useful classifications of distal phalangeal fractures have been devised. Kaplan divided the fractures into three major categories[159] (Fig. 38–115): (1) longitudinal split fractures, (2) comminuted fractures (most often associated with overlying soft tissue injury), and (3) transverse fractures, which may have angulatory deformity near the base.

Another and perhaps more useful classification, shown in Table 38–19, is that of Dobyns and co-workers, who subdivide distal phalangeal fractures anatomically as well as by soft tissue injury.[75]

### Treatment Considerations

**Tuft Fractures.** A closed tuft fracture can be exceptionally painful because of inadequate room for fracture hematoma within the compartmentalized pulp space. Release of the subungual hematoma with a heated paper clip or disposable cautery, followed by the application of ice and a protective splint, will provide comfort and support the fracture. A simple splint can be fashioned from the malleable aluminum rims on glass intravenous bottles, covered with adhesive tape, and bent around the distal phalanx to provide both support and protection. Alternatively, a hand therapist can fabricate a simple thermoplastic custom fingertip splint that is supported with Velcro, easily removed and washed, and comfortable for the patient to wear. Commercial varieties such as the Stax splint are also available. Generally, most closed tuft fractures require no more than 3 weeks of splintage.[36]

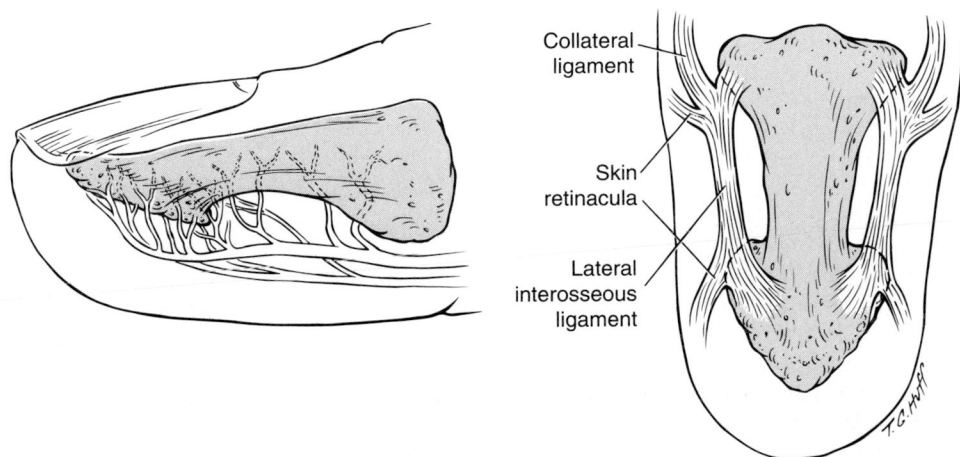

FIGURE 38–114. Anteroposterior and lateral drawings of the distal phalanx demonstrating the lateral interosseous ligaments and neurovascular bundles. These ligaments function to protect the neurovascular bundles as they pass dorsal to the nail bed.

Collateral ligament

Skin retinacula

Lateral interosseous ligament

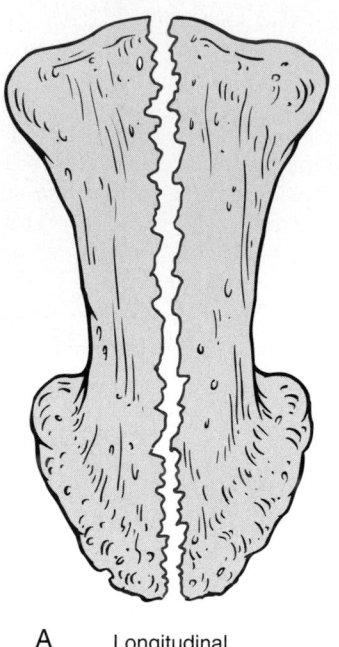

A  Longitudinal     B            C  Transverse

Comminuted

**FIGURE 38–115.** *A–C,* Kaplan's classification of distal phalangeal fractures.

Open tuft fractures are more likely to be unstable because of disruption of the supporting pulp and nail plate. Metacarpal block anesthesia is satisfactory to permit careful débridement, irrigation, and soft tissue repair. Most often, repair of the soft tissue is sufficient to stabilize a tuft fracture, although occasionally a 0.028-inch K-wire will be needed to support a grossly displaced fracture. Oral antibiotics and tetanus prophylaxis are advisable.

It is important to bear in mind that splinting is solely for comfort. Care must be taken to avoid skin necrosis from splints that are too tightly applied. The fingertip will very likely be tender for a considerable number of months after the injury. Radiographic union may take up to 6 months to a year,[75] and the surgeon should be wary of attributing discomfort to delayed union or impending nonunion (Fig. 38–116). Extreme hypersensitivity is more likely the result of crushing of the multiple small terminal branches of the digital nerves. A trained hand therapist should be consulted to formulate a desensitization program for what can be a distressing problem.

**Shaft Fractures.** As with closed fractures of the tuft, the vast majority of closed distal phalangeal shaft fractures are minimally displaced and inherently stable and require limited splintage. Although longitudinal fractures generally heal within 3 to 4 weeks, transverse shaft fractures may take longer, and it is advisable to maintain support until clinical discomfort abates or radiographic union is evident.

Open shaft fractures can prove problematic and are often associated with disruption of the overlying nail bed. In concert with fracture irrigation and débridement, the nail itself should be uplifted and the nail bed inspected. On occasion, the sterile nail matrix may be displaced into the fracture line and thereby provide a block to reduction as well as a potential cause of nonunion. The shaft fracture should be accurately aligned and, if unstable, supported by a longitudinal 0.035-inch K-wire (Fig. 38–117). The sterile matrix is repaired with 7–0 ophthalmic gut under loupe magnification. If the nail itself is in good condition, it can be cleansed with soap and povidone-iodine and

| **TABLE 38–19** | | |
|---|---|---|
| Dobyns and Co-workers' Classification of Distal Phalangeal Fractures | | |
| | **Closed** | **Open** |
| Tuft | Inherently stable<br>Union by 6 to 8 wk | May be unstable with nail bed and pulp injury |
| Shaft | Nondisplaced fractures<br>Union may take longer (8 to 12 wk) | May be unstable<br>Nail bed injury common<br>Nonunion can occur |
| Base (physeal) | May be unstable; closed reduction often required<br>Heals by 6 wk | Eponychium injured<br>May be angulated or malrotated; closed or open reduction often<br>needed |

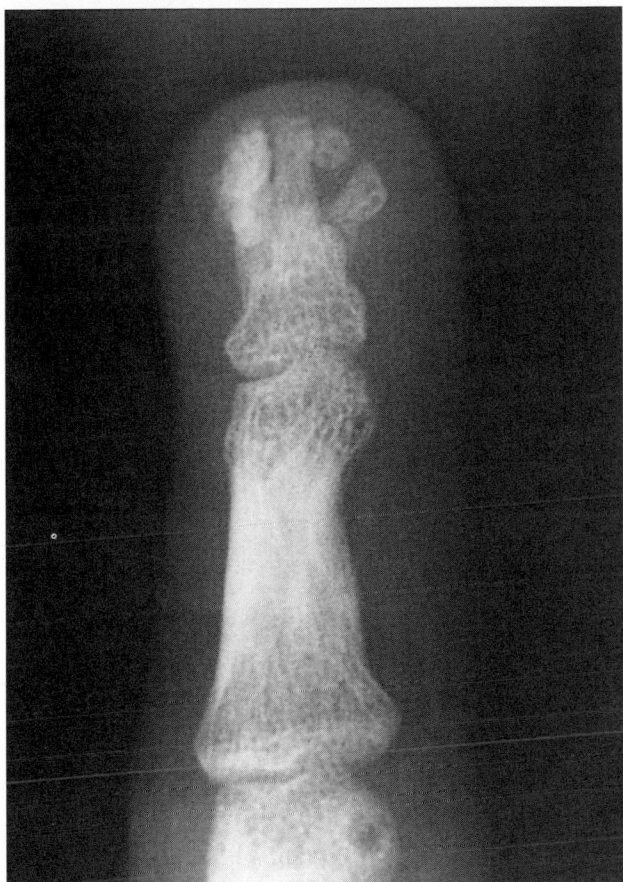

**FIGURE 38–116.** Following a crush injury, a comminuted tuft fracture often demonstrates radiographically a delay in healing. Nonunion, however, is rare.

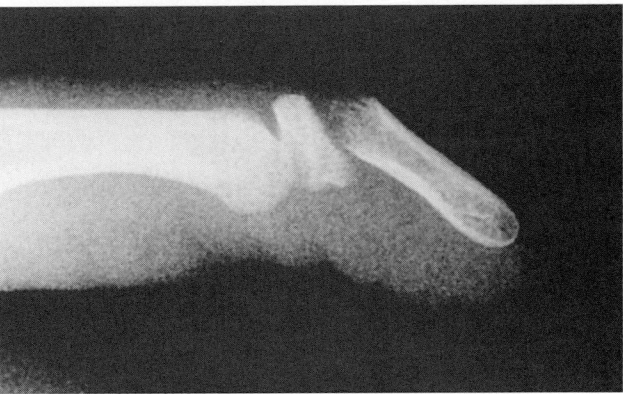

**FIGURE 38–118.** Fractures of the base of the distal phalanx tend to be unstable and will angulate with the apex pointing dorsally.

replaced. Replacement of the nail will help stabilize the fracture and soft tissue repairs, as well as prevent scarring between the eponychium and the nail matrix. A strip of petrolatum-impregnated gauze will also serve this purpose if the nail is not suitable. With either technique, the splint should be left in place for 10 to 14 days. Accurate axial alignment is of some importance to avoid late nail deformity.

**Base (Physeal) Fractures.** Regardless of the extent of the overlying soft tissue involvement, fractures of the base of the distal phalanx tend to be unstable. Subject to the deforming pull of both the extensor and the flexor tendons and not afforded the intrinsic support of the nail and nail plate, these fractures tend to angulate with the apex pointing dorsally (Fig. 38–118).

In adults, a closed fracture at the base of the distal phalanx is best treated by an Alumafoam splint, with the distal fragment and DIP joint kept in extension for a minimum of 4 weeks. Open fractures have the potential for rotational instability. These fractures are commonly seen with severe soft tissue injuries, such as incomplete

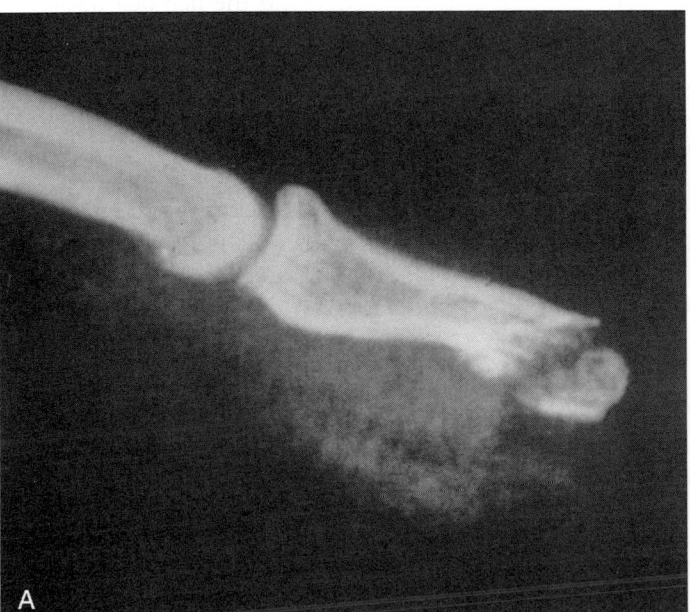

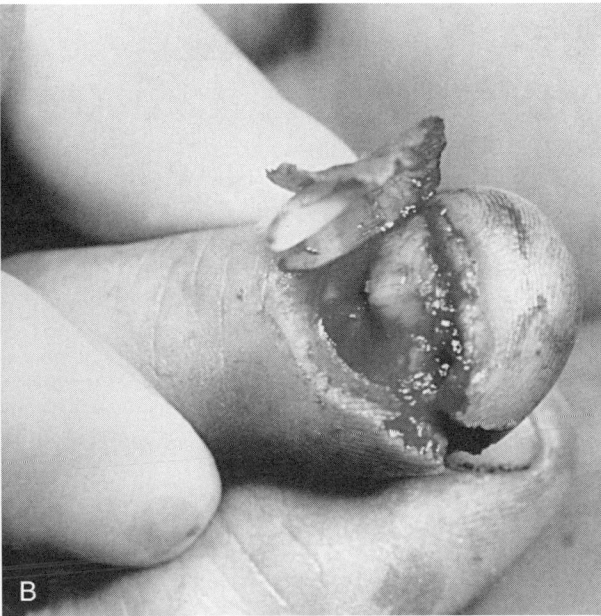

**FIGURE 38–117.** An open distal phalangeal shaft fracture (A) will commonly produce a laceration of the sterile nail matrix (B).

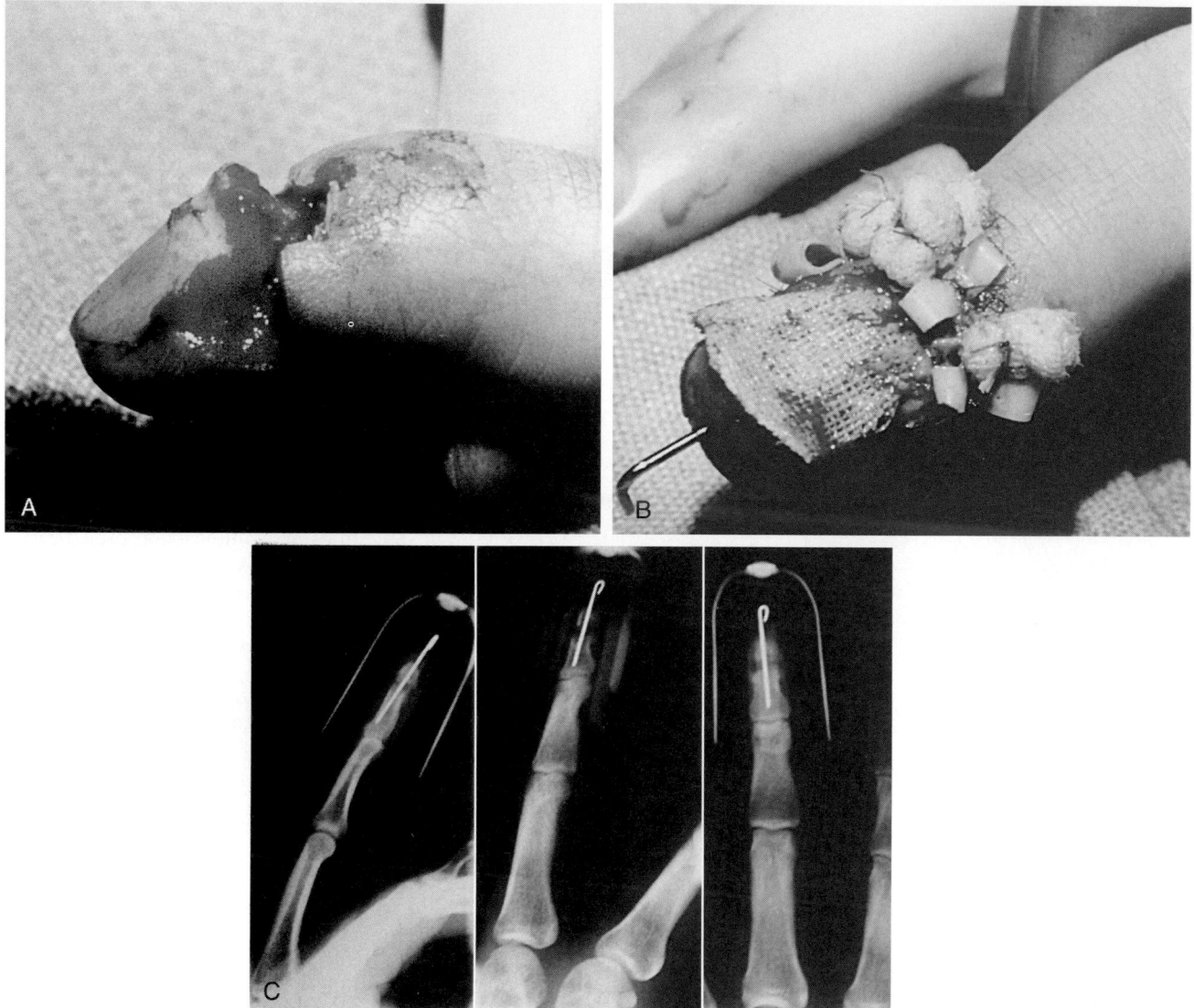

**FIGURE 38–119.** *A–C,* An incomplete amputation was treated with débridement, longitudinal K-wire fixation of the distal phalanx, and repair of the nail bed.

amputations, and are unstable fractures. A 0.035- or 0.045-inch K-wire placed in a retrograde manner will provide adequate internal splintage (Fig. 38–119). Crossing the DIP joint should be avoided unless the proximal fragment is comminuted or fails to allow sufficient purchase of the wire.

When passing a K-wire into the distal phalanx, several technical points are worth mentioning. It should be born in mind that the tuft of the distal phalanx lies just beneath the sterile matrix. The wire is introduced just under the hyponychial fold when passed in an antegrade fashion (Fig. 38–120). If the initial pass of the wire is unsatisfactory, the wire should not be withdrawn because a second pass will quite possibly follow the same hole. Instead, with the initial wire in place, a second wire is directed independently and the initial wire then withdrawn. A 16-gauge hypodermic needle will serve as an effective guide for the K-wire and help prevent the tip of the wire from slipping off the rounded tip of the tuft (Fig. 38–121). Bending the exposed tip of the wire around and onto itself

will create a blunt tip and thus help avoid catching the wire on an object and torquing the fracture site or soft tissue repair (Fig. 38–122).

Two distinct physeal injuries are found in the pediatric age group, depending on the age of the patient (Fig. 38–123). A physeal injury in a preadolescent is most often an open fracture representing a Salter-Harris type I or II physeal separation.[259, 273] These injuries can be mistaken for DIP joint dislocations or mallet injuries. The extensor tendon remains attached to the proximal epiphyseal fragment, whereas the unopposed flexor digitorum profundus pulls the remainder of the distal phalanx into flexion. Not uncommonly, the base of the distal fragment protrudes through the wound and projects over the eponychial fold while the nail and nail plate remain attached to the distal fragment. This injury should not be taken lightly because the potential risks are substantial and include recurrent deformity, premature epiphyseal closure, sepsis, and residual nail deformity.[8, 9, 267, 324]

Adequate anesthesia is mandatory, and general anesthe-

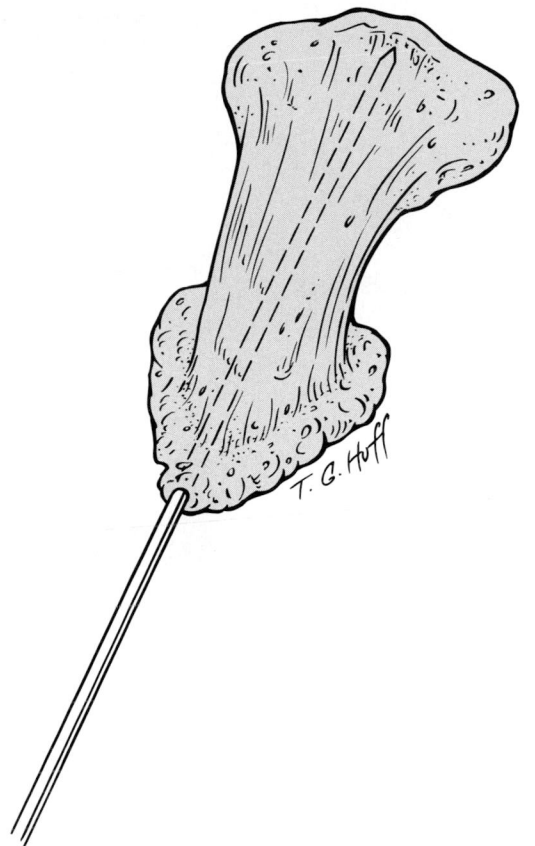

FIGURE **38–120.** K-wire fixation of the distal phalanx involves placement of the wire through the distal tuft just beneath the hyponychial fold.

sia is often required. The fracture site should be gently exposed and thoroughly irrigated. Reduction of the fracture can be accomplished with slight traction and manipulation of the distal fragment and nail into extension, with the nail placed back under the eponychial fold. The nail itself will provide sufficient splintage for the fracture and is best preserved. The use of K-wires should be avoided if possible because a higher incidence of

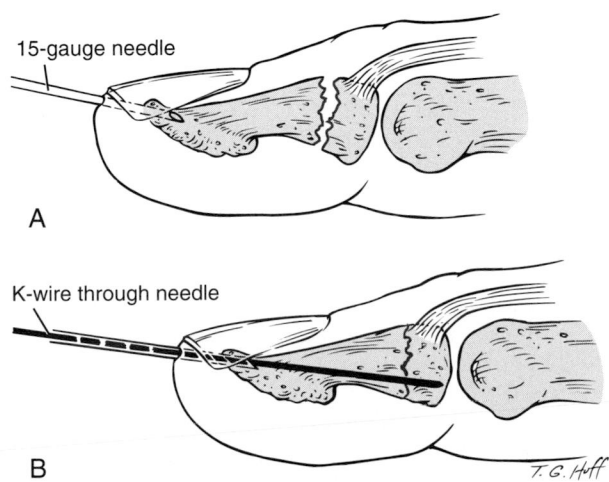

FIGURE **38–121.** *A, B,* A 15-gauge hypodermic needle is an ideal drill guide for K-wire placement into the tuft of the distal phalanx.

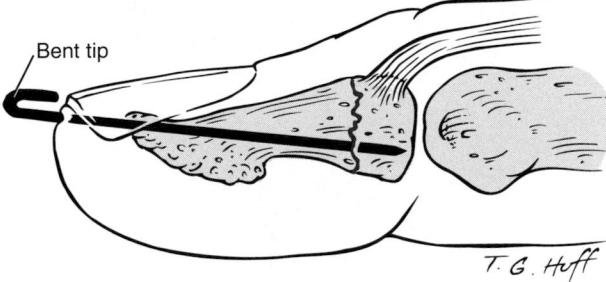

FIGURE **38–122.** Bending of the protruding K-wire in the distal phalanx will avoid catching the wire on objects and torquing the fracture.

infection has been reported with the application of K-wires in these injuries.[249] Although as much as 30° of dorsal or volar angulation can be accepted in a young child (because remodeling will occur), it is preferable to attempt to gain anatomic repositioning. The reduction can be effectively supported with an Alumafoam splint incorporated into a plaster cast and maintained for 4 weeks.

In an older child, the physeal fracture more closely resembles a mallet injury. Closed reduction is achieved by gently extending the distal phalanx. Again, support with an Alumafoam splint incorporated into a cast or with a cast alone may be needed for an active child and should be maintained for 4 weeks (Fig. 38–124; see Mallet Injuries).

### Flexor Digitorum Profundus Avulsion Fractures

A relatively uncommon, but potentially disabling injury is an avulsion fracture of the base of the distal phalanx caused by rupture of the insertion of the flexor digitorum profundus tendon. The mechanism generally involves a hyperextension stress while the involved digit is actively flexed against an object. The ring finger is most often involved, with the classic example being that of a football player grabbing an opponent's jersey while attempting to make a tackle.[43, 116, 320]

The clinical findings include a swollen, painful digit, particularly at the site of avulsion. Ecchymosis may be present. Because the patient can still actively flex the finger at both MCP joints, the injury may be overlooked and considered to be only a "jammed" finger. An inability to initiate DIP joint flexion should alert the examiner to the possibility of this lesion. Three radiographic views—AP, lateral, and oblique—must always be obtained because the fracture fragment, when present, may be only a small flake of bone lying in the soft tissue plane just anterior to the PIP joint (Fig. 38–125).

**Classification.** Several authors have proposed classifications of flexor digitorum profundus avulsion injuries. Leddy and Packer[177, 178] established the following simple, but clinically useful classification (Fig. 38–126):

*Type I:* The tendon has ruptured at its insertion without a bony fragment and has retracted into the palm. Both vincula supplying the tendon have ruptured, with considerable interruption of the vascular supply to the tendon.

*Type II:* The tendon has retracted to the level of the PIP joint and is held there by the intact long vinculum. A

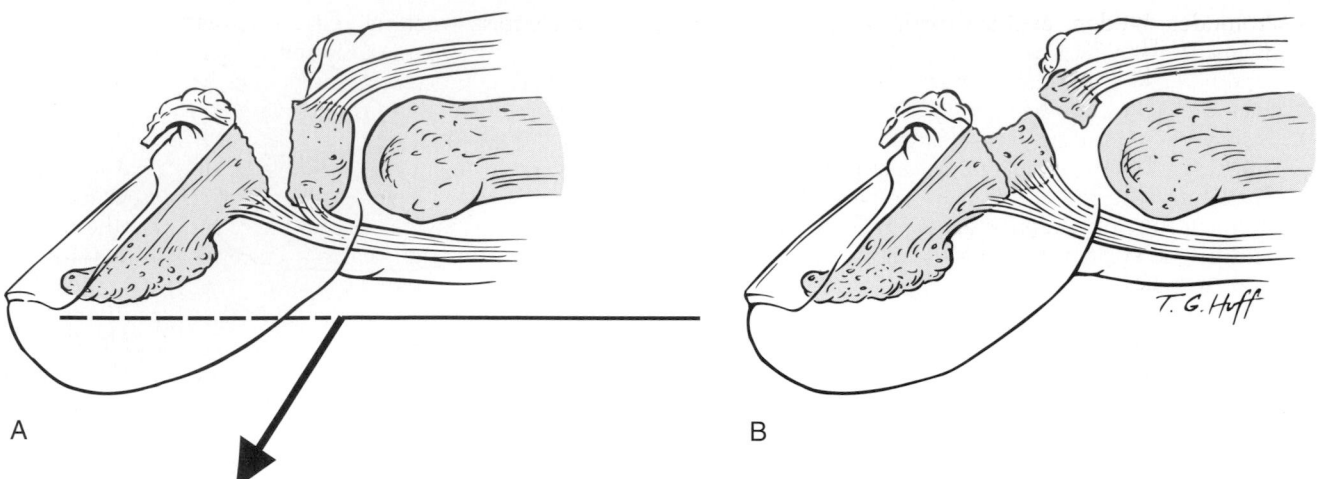

**FIGURE 38–123.** Two distinct physeal injuries of a pediatric distal phalanx include an open Salter-Harris type I or II physeal separation in a younger child (*A*) and a mallet-type fracture in an older child (*B*).

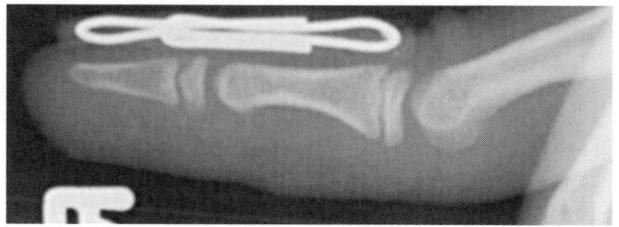

**FIGURE 38–124.** After closed reduction of an epiphyseal separation at the base of the distal phalanx, the digit was immobilized, with a paper clip incorporated into the splint to augment the strength of the splint.

flake of bone from the distal phalanx may be seen on radiographs.

*Type III:* A large bony fragment has been avulsed. Proximal retraction beyond the middle of the middle phalanx is ordinarily prevented by the fourth annular pulley.

Smith suggested an additional type, type IV, in which a fragment of bone is fractured off the volar base of the distal phalanx with simultaneous independent avulsion of the flexor profundus retracted to the base of the proximal phalanx.[281]

Robins and Dobyns proposed the following classification based on the anatomic insertions of the profundus tendon[253]:

1. Profundus tendon avulsion without fracture.
2. Profundus tendon avulsion with a large fracture fragment. Either the superficial or the deep fibers of the tendon insertion, or both, may remain on the fragment or may be stripped off.

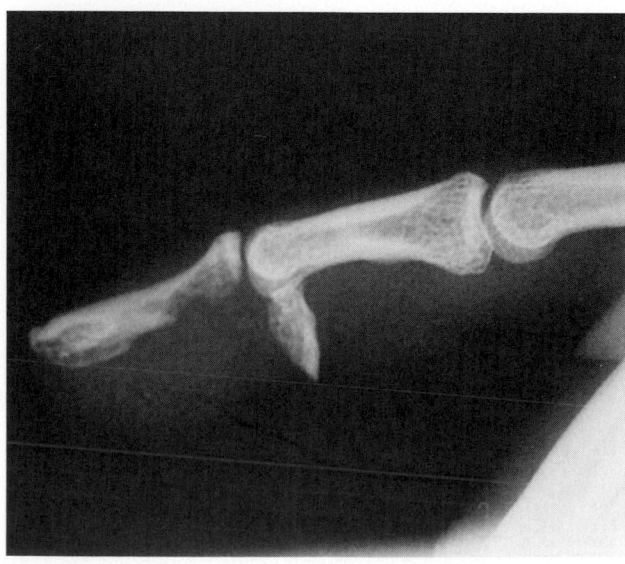

**FIGURE 38–125.** A flexor digitorum profundus avulsion fracture in a 19-year-old man.

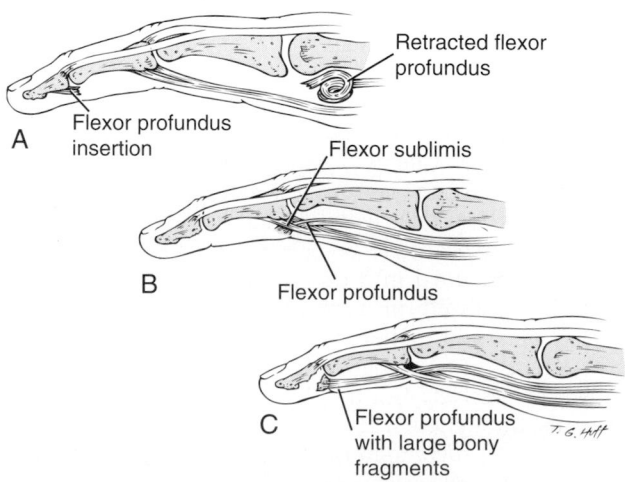

**FIGURE 38–126.** The classification system proposed by Leddy and Packer for flexor digitorum profundus (FDP) avulsion injuries. *A,* Type I: the FDP ruptures and retracts into the palm. *B,* Type II: the FDP ruptures and retracts to the level of the proximal interphalangeal joint. A flake of bone may be present. *C,* Type III: a large bony fragment is avulsed along with the FDP.

3. Profundus tendon avulsion with a small fracture fragment. The deep fibers are stripped off, but the superficial fibers usually remain attached and frequently displace the fragment more proximally.

4. Profundus avulsion with both large and small fracture fragments. The superficial fibers may remain with the small fragment and displace it proximally. The large fragment, free of tendon attachments, remains distally held by the volar plate, collateral ligaments, or fourth annular pulley.

A different entity that could be confused with a profundus tendon avulsion fracture was reported by Bowers and Fajgenbaum.[29] They described a case in which the volar plate of the DIP joint was avulsed from its insertion onto the distal phalanx with a small fragment of bone. The mechanism of injury was a hyperextension force associated with dorsal subluxation of the distal phalanx. Open reduction of the joint and immobilization in 45° of flexion with a K-wire for 4 weeks was recommended.

**Treatment.** The success of treatment can often be directly correlated with the accuracy of the diagnosis and the rapidity of surgical intervention.

Additional factors that influence the outcome include the level to which the tendon retracts, the remaining vascular supply to the avulsed tendon, and the presence and size of bony fragments on radiographs.[177, 178]

With Leddy and Packer type I injuries, the tendon must be retrieved and passed through an intact pulley system back to its point of insertion. This technique can be considered only if the diagnosis has been made within 10 days after injury and before tendon swelling, collagen degeneration, and myostatic contracture occur. Reinsertion after this point could well lead to a significant flexion contracture of both the DIP and PIP joints.

The tendon can be approached through either midaxial or volar zigzag incisions. A small flexible catheter or pediatric feeding tube is helpful in retrieving the tendon back under the intact pulley system and flexor sheath. A distally based osteoperiosteal flap is created in the base of the distal phalanx, and holes are drilled into the distal phalanx, with exit through the overlying nail. A No. 4 monofilament suture can be woven through the end of the tendon and through the drill holes with Keith needles and tied over a sponge and button.

Postoperative care is based, to some degree, on the individual surgeon's bias toward flexor tendon injuries. We have found the passive mobilization program advocated by Duran and associates to be effective in most cases.[79] The hand is maintained in a dorsal blocking splint with the wrist immobilized in midflexion, the MCP joints in approximately 45° of flexion, and the PIP and DIP joints in near extension. A program is designed to permit the patient to passively flex the PIP and DIP joints at 2-hour intervals throughout the day with the hand left in the splint. This program must be closely monitored by a therapist, as well as by the surgeon, and is probably not applicable to an unreliable patient.

If the patient is seen more than 10 days after injury, the options include no treatment, a free graft or staged tendon reconstruction, or a terminal IP joint tenodesis or arthrodesis.

In contrast, when the tendon has retracted only to the level of the PIP joint (Leddy and Packer type II), it may be possible to reinsert these avulsions as late as 6 weeks after injury. The tendon is retrieved and passed under the fourth annular pulley and reinserted into the base of the distal phalanx in a manner similar to that described for type I injuries. The small flake fracture often associated with these injuries may be excised before inserting the tendon back into the distal phalanx. Postoperative treatment is similar to that for type I injuries.

In approaching Leddy and Packer type II avulsion fractures, one must bear in mind the variable fracture patterns as described by Robins and Dobyns.[253] Particular attention should be paid to the preoperative radiograph of the entire digit to recognize an occasional double fracture with the profundus tendon retracted proximally with a small flake of bone. Many of the injuries involving large bony fragments will have associated dorsal subluxation of the distal phalanx. It is not uncommon to find that the avulsed fragment involves a significant portion of the articular surface of the base of the distal phalanx. In general, the prognosis for functional recovery is poorer for patients in whom the tendon insertion has separated from the bony fragment or in whom the base of the distal phalanx is comminuted.[79]

Considerable care is taken to maintain any soft tissue attachments to the fracture fragments, particularly if the profundus insertion is partially separated. The large fragments are prevented from migrating proximally by the fourth annular pulley, and attention should be paid to preserving the integrity of the pulley. Anatomic reduction of the articular surface is mandatory unless the joint surface has been fragmented. In these cases, more often seen in open injuries, consideration can be given to immediate arthrodesis of the distal joint.

Internal fixation with two parallel 0.028-inch K-wires or a single 1.5-mm cortical screw is sufficient (Fig. 38–127). The wires can be removed in 3 to 4 weeks postoperatively. If the tendon has been avulsed, a 4–0 monofilament suture is woven through the tendon end,

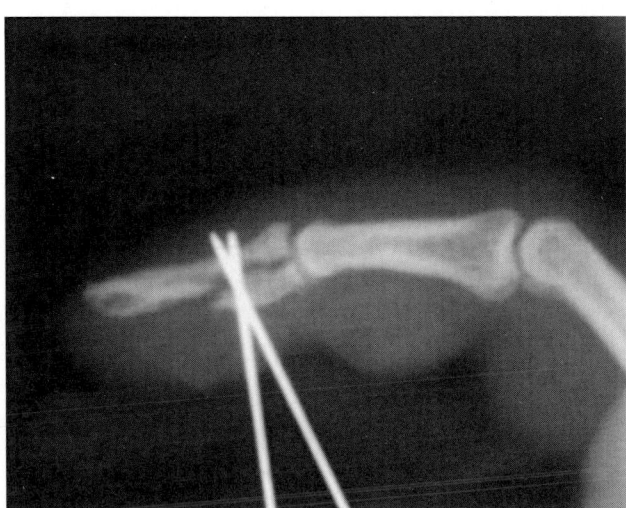

**FIGURE 38–127.** A type III profundus avulsion fracture has been reapproximated and secured with K-wire fixation.

passed dorsally on either side of the distal phalanx through the overlying nail, and sutured over a sponge and button. Sutures should also be placed between the tendon and any available periosteum or fibrous tissue from its original insertion site. Postoperative treatment depends on the extent of tendon disruption from the avulsed fragment. In cases in which the tendon has completely separated from the bony fragment, the digit should be immobilized for 3 weeks. Subsequently, motion can be started under the supervision of a therapist. Sutures can be removed 2 weeks later.

## MALLET INJURIES

The deformity that has come to be known as the *mallet finger* was first recognized in the literature in 1880 by Segond.[270] This injury still engenders considerable disagreement, however, not the least of which concerns its descriptive terminology. Only rarely, in fact, does the digit resemble a mallet. The term *baseball finger*[156] is equally misleading because this sport accounts for only a small percentage of mallet injuries.

The literature is replete with methods and devices for treatment of a mallet injury. The role of surgical intervention is controversial in regard to the indications for surgery and the technique. Even what constitutes a "good" result and what the patient's expectations should be regarding any residual disability remain in question and are subject to continuous reevaluation. However, it is fundamental to establish the type of injury to the terminal extensor mechanism before considering treatment because the underlying pathologic manifestations can vary.

## Tendinous Mallet

A tendinous mallet represents a loss of continuity of the extensor mechanism at the DIP joint. This common injury results from forced flexion against an actively extended digit and occurs not only in sports but also from such minor incidents as putting on socks, washing laundry, or making beds. Less common causes include lacerations on the dorsum of the middle and distal phalanx and a crushing injury over the distal end of the joint that results in a zone of avascular necrosis in the tendon. The latter may be manifested weeks after the initial trauma.

Watson-Jones[314] further defined an extensor tendon injury as including the following three distinct patterns (Fig. 38–128):

1. Incomplete tendon injury caused by stretching of the tendinous fibers. Clinical findings will be a less pronounced droop (15° to 30°) with some ability to actively extend. Extension against resistance, however, will be appreciably weaker than that of the adjacent digit and is usually painful.
2. Complete disruption of the extensor mechanism at its insertion onto the distal phalanx, often with rupture of the dorsal joint capsule. The distal joint will have a more pronounced droop (30° to 60°) and is completely unable to actively extend against gravity. The fact that

MECHANISM

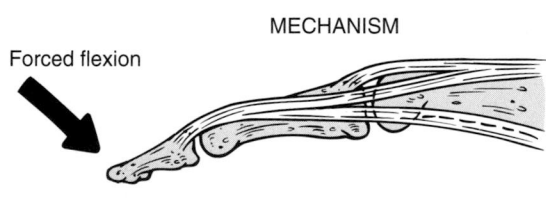

Forced flexion

INJURY

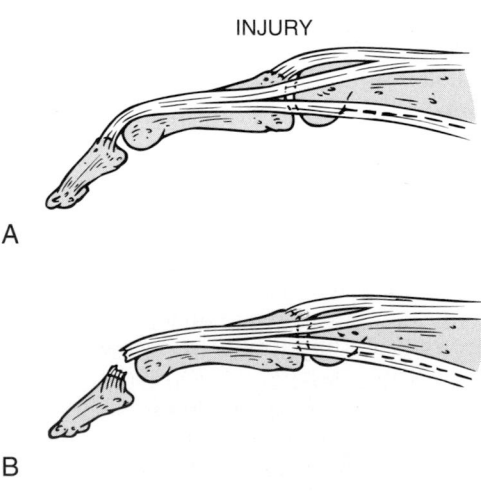

A

B

C

**FIGURE 38–128.** Tendinous mallet injuries were defined by Watson-Jones (1956) to include three distinct patterns: stretching of the common extensor at its insertion (*A*), complete disruption of the extensor mechanism (*B*), and complete disruption of the extensor mechanism with a small "flake" of bone avulsed from the distal phalanx (*C*).

the distal joint is not pulled into more flexion with complete disruption of the extensor mechanism and dorsal capsule has been attributed by Stack to the presence of the oblique retinacular ligament.[174, 285] This explanation, however, has been questioned by Shrewsbury and Johnson, who were unable to consistently define the presence of an oblique retinacular ligament in anatomic dissections.[276, 277] They believed that the collateral ligaments were more likely to be the supporting elements offsetting to some degree the pull of the flexor digitorum profundus.

3. Disruption of the extensor mechanism at its insertion onto the dorsum of the distal phalanx. A small flake of bone is avulsed along with the tendon and is visible on a lateral radiograph. This injury is not considered a mallet fracture and will be effectively treated as a tendinous injury.

## CLINICAL FINDINGS

A closed tendinous mallet finger is more commonly seen in a middle-aged patient, frequently after innocent trauma. In a series of 92 cases, Abouna and Brown[1] noted that 73% of these injuries occurred in the home, 20% at work, and 7% from a sports injury. When seen soon after trauma, the patient's complaints are those of pain and inability to fully extend the terminal joint. Swelling with overlying skin erythema and tenderness is usually present and may in fact mask the flexed posturing of that joint. In some "loose-jointed" individuals, hyperextension will be noted at the PIP joint because of imbalance of the extensor mechanism; this hyperextension leads to increased pull of the extensor on the base of the middle phalanx.

## TREATMENT

It is now generally agreed by most authors that only the DIP joint requires immobilization.[1, 5, 35, 85, 111, 133, 210, 216, 287] Treatment of the three types of tendinous mallet injuries differs only in a shorter duration of immobilization for type I incomplete ruptures.

A small malleable Alumafoam or custom thermoplastic splint contoured to provide three points of contact is recommended in the acute setting. Some authors choose to place the splint on the palmar surface and use tape over the terminus of the joint to maintain its position. A word of caution should be kept in mind regarding positioning the distal end of the joint in excessive hyperextension: the circulation of the skin over the joint can be precarious, and it is wise to make certain that the skin is not blanched on application of the splint to minimize the risk of necrosis.[243] For type I injuries, continuous splinting for a minimum of 4 weeks and preferably 6 weeks is suggested. Six to 8 weeks of continuous splinting, followed by nocturnal splinting for 3 to 4 weeks, is best for type II and III tendinous mallet fingers. Healing of the tendon can be judged by the appearance of the overlying skin and any persistent swelling and tenderness. Given the close proximity of the tendon to the skin, the latter well reflects the healing of the former. If at 6 weeks the skin remains swollen, tender, and erythematous, it is advised that the

splintage be continued for at least another 4 weeks full-time and the situation then be reassessed.

Successful treatment of tendinous mallet injuries can be accomplished even when initially seen 2 to 3 months after injury.[1, 5, 121, 216, 251] In these situations, splintage is required for at least 8 to 12 weeks.

In unusual circumstances, the patient's occupation may be such that splinting is not practical. In these cases, one may consider passing a K-wire across the DIP joint with the wire cut off just below the skin.[51] The risk of pin tract infection, joint sepsis, and osteomyelitis must be considered when making this decision. Given that the small splints can be gas autoclaved, even surgeons can be managed successfully in a nonoperative fashion.

## Bony Mallet

Mallet deformity resulting from a bony injury occurs in association with a fracture of the dorsal articular surface of the distal phalanx (usually one third or greater). The terminal unit of the extensor tendon inserting onto this fracture fragment can no longer function to extend the distal phalanx (Fig. 38–129).

Although splint support of a tendinous mallet is generally agreed on, treatment of a bony mallet remains subject to some debate. To better understand the lack of consensus, it may be best to recognize that different anatomic considerations exist with bony mallet injuries. By individualizing each mallet fracture, the treatment approach can be simplified.

First, a mallet fracture may result from several different mechanisms of injury. Some occur in a manner similar to a tendinous mallet (i.e., forcible flexion of an extended digit with avulsion of a bony fragment of variable size along with its attached extensor mechanism). Others are quite different and instead occur when direct trauma to the tip of an extended digit drives the base of the distal phalanx onto the head of the middle phalanx.[133, 205] This injury may not cause much droop of the terminal phalanx. Rather, this compression type of mallet fracture will have not only displacement of part of the base of the distal phalanx but also impaction of the subchondral bone. These fractures tend to be seen more often in younger individuals and are usually incurred while participating in sports.[133]

A third variant is that caused by a sudden hyperextension force that results in the dorsal aspect of the base of the distal phalanx being impacted against the head of the middle phalanx and producing a dorsal lip fracture and volar subluxation of the distal phalanx. These fractures often involve more than 50% of the articular surface. This injury pattern is particularly difficult to treat because the routine immobilization position of hyperextension will accentuate the subluxation. Open reduction should be considered[127] (Fig. 38–130).

The classification proposed by Wehbe and Schneider identifies the variation in bony mallet injuries, although it does not identify the impacted compression type of injury[319] (Table 38–20). In addition, these authors were able to show excellent results with nonoperative treatment of all types of mallet fractures. Bone remodeling occurred

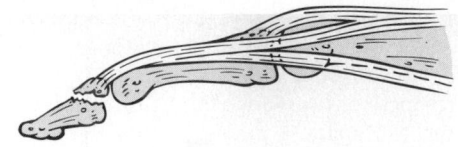

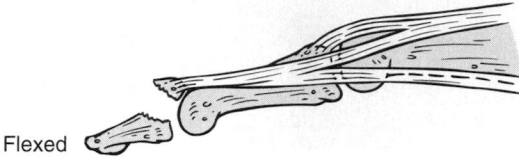

Flexed

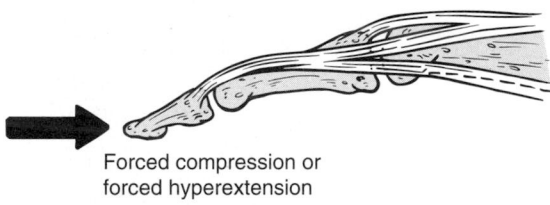

BONY MALLET

Forced compression or
forced hyperextension

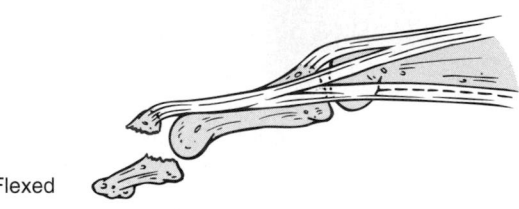

Flexed

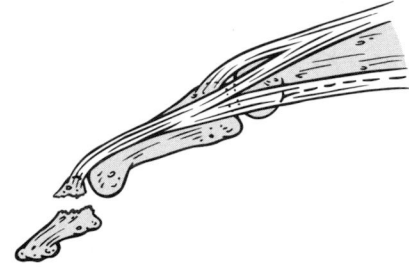

**FIGURE 38–129.** A bony mallet fracture may have a variety of fracture patterns.

in each case, and the articular surface remained preserved. Nearly normal, painless range of motion was achieved in 21 of their 22 patients. They splinted all fractures for 6 to 8 weeks continuously. The only drawback noted by the authors was a residual bump present on the dorsum of the joint.

Although many mallet fractures can be treated nonoperatively, certain fracture types are perhaps more predict-

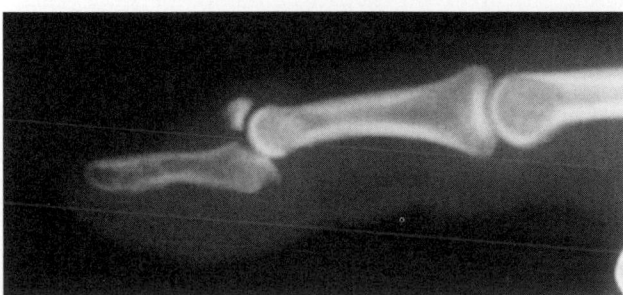

**FIGURE 38–130.** A bony mallet in the little finger of a 36-year-old woman associated with subluxation of the distal phalanx. Operative treatment is indicated.

ably treated operatively, including widely displaced fractures involving 50% or more of the articular surface, fractures associated with volar subluxation of the distal phalanx, and impaction injuries at the base of the distal phalanx. In addition, displaced mallet fractures of the thumb IP joint are probably better treated by operative

| **TABLE 38–20** |
| --- |
| Wehbe and Schneider's Classification of Mallet Fractures |

Type 1: Bony injury of varying extent without subluxation of the joint
Type 2: Fractures associated with joint subluxation
Type 3: Epiphyseal and physeal injuries
Each type is further subdivided into three types:
  A. Fracture fragment less than one third of the articular surface of the distal phalanx
  B. Fracture affecting one third to two thirds of the articular surface
  C. Fracture of more than two thirds of the articular surface

*Source:* Wehbe, M.A.; Schneider, L.H. J Bone Joint Surg Am 66:658–669, 1984.

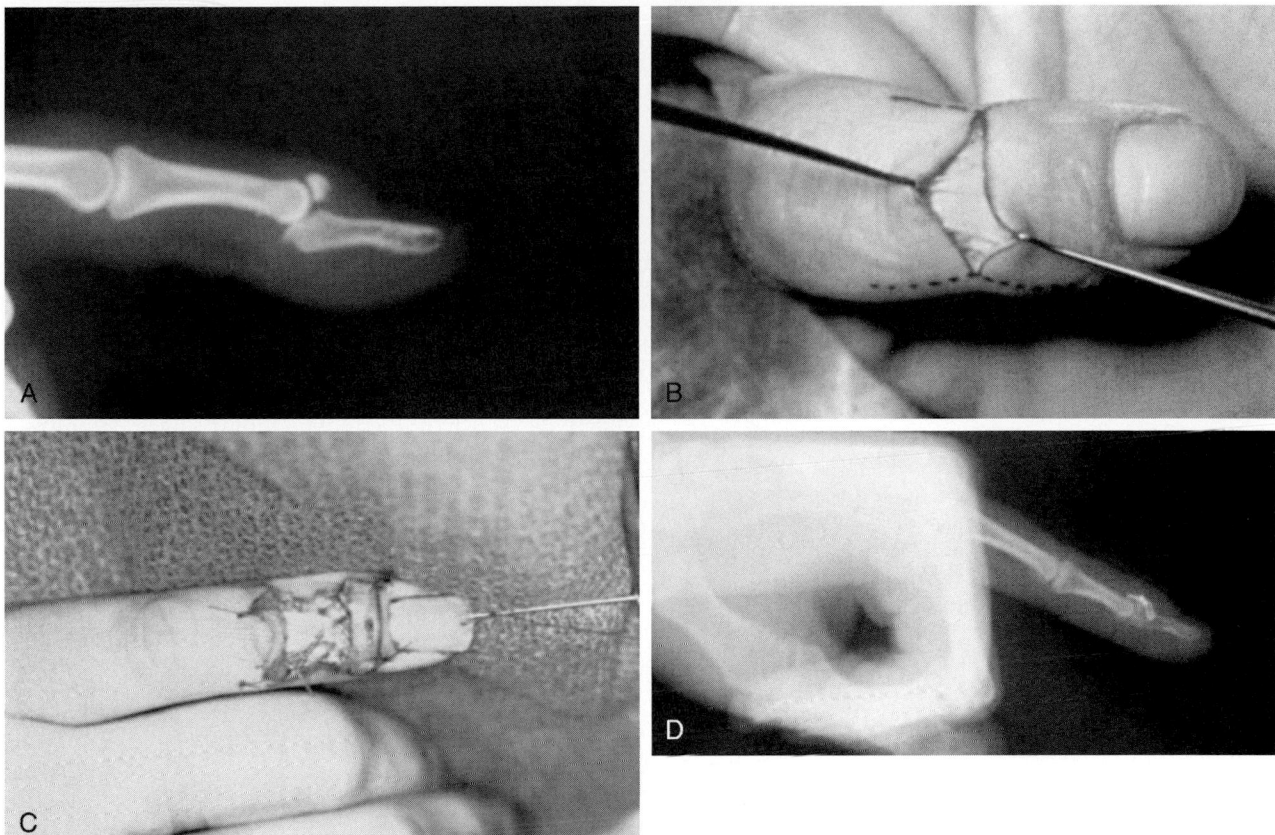

**FIGURE 38–131.** A 25-year-old graduate student sustained a closed displaced mallet fracture associated with displacement of the articular surface despite splint treatment. *A,* Lateral radiograph demonstrating the displaced articular fragment. *B,* Through a dorsal **H** incision, the extensor tendon and attached fragment are readily visible. *C,* After débridement of the fracture hematoma, the articular fragment is reduced under direct vision. A hole is drilled in the distal phalanx distal to the fracture and dorsal to the midaxis of the phalanx. A 30-gauge stainless steel wire is passed through the drill hole, through the insertion of the extensor tendon, and into the bony fragment and tightened in a figure-of-eight fashion. *D,* Excellent fixation is achieved without the risk of fragmentation of the small bony fragment.

means given the potential for displacement by the powerful extrinsic tendons.

A study by Stark and colleagues showed excellent results with operative treatment.[288] These authors gained anatomic reduction and used small K-wires. The technique of tension band wiring has been equally effective in the operative management of these precarious bony fragments.[152] Through a dorsal **H** incision, the fragment is easily identified and reduced after débriding the fracture hematoma. A hole is drilled distal to the fracture line and dorsal to the midaxis of the phalanx, and a 30-gauge monofilament stainless steel wire is passed through the hole and through the insertion of the extensor tendon onto the fracture fragment. When the fragment has been reduced, the wire is slowly tightened while holding the fragment in place to control the possibility of dorsal rotation. Fractures associated with subluxation of the distal phalanx should have a longitudinal K-wire placed across the distal joint for 2 to 3 weeks (Fig. 38–131).

Despite the enthusiasm of some authors for surgical management of these injuries, the surgical approach to such fractures is difficult and fraught with complications.[265] The soft tissue cover is tenuous, the fragment is small and easily fragmented, and joint stiffness is not uncommon. Before making a decision to approach this

fracture operatively, one should carefully assess whether splint treatment is applicable, especially given the success of Wehbe and Schneider[319] with nonoperative management of even the worst of these injuries.

## DISLOCATIONS

Dislocations and ligamentous injuries in the hand are common.[14, 77, 80, 221] Although the PIP joint is most often affected, all the digital articulations are vulnerable, as well as those of the thumb. The spectrum of injury to the ligaments extends from a minor stretch (sprain) to complete disruption.

The deformity caused by a joint dislocation is classified by the position of the distal skeletal unit in relation to its proximal counterpart. Thus, a palmar PIP joint dislocation describes a dislocation in which the middle phalanx is displaced in a palmar direction relative to the proximal phalanx (Fig. 38–132).

Most digital dislocations are the result of an axial load combined with an angular vector of force. The magnitude and direction of the force combined with the position of

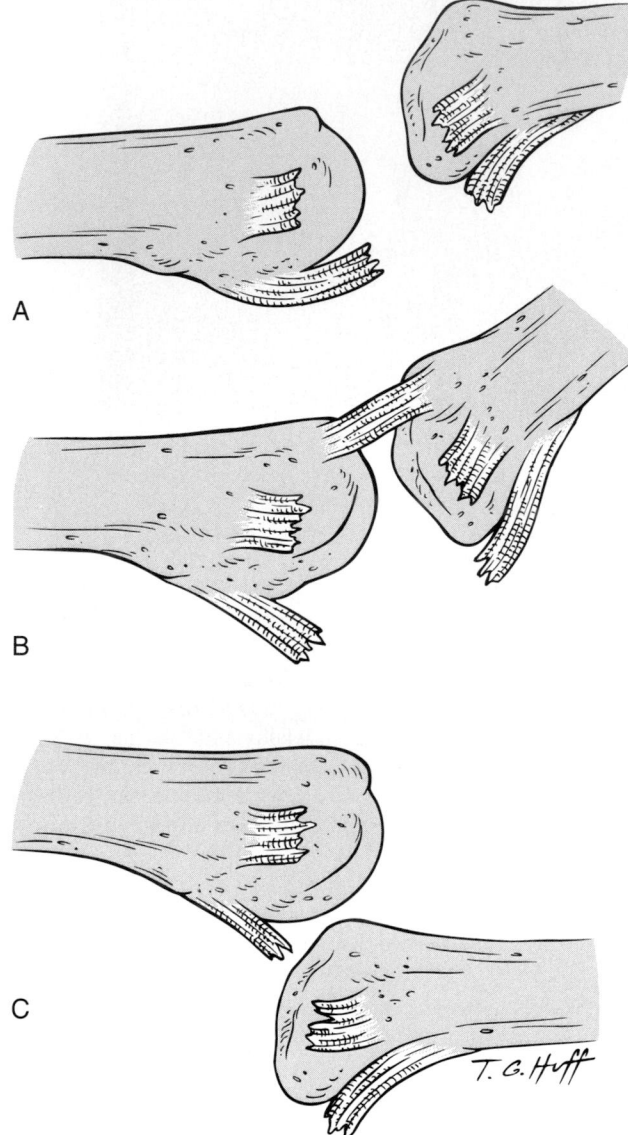

FIGURE 38–132. Dislocations in the hand are classified by the position of the distal skeletal unit in relation to its proximal counterpart. *A*, Dorsal proximal interphalangeal (PIP) joint dislocation. *B*, Lateral PIP joint dislocation. *C*, Palmar PIP joint dislocation.

the joint at the time of injury will determine the type and extent of the dislocation.

## Clinical Evaluation

A dislocation of a small articulation in the hand is ordinarily clinically apparent. Before physical examination, a true lateral radiograph must be viewed to determine whether a fracture is present. The sensibility and circulation of the digit are confirmed, followed by cautious examination of the involved joint. Any laceration must be inspected carefully because a skin "tear" may reflect an open dislocation requiring treatment in the sterile environment of the operating room. If closed reduction or stress testing of the joint is needed, metacarpal block or wrist block anesthesia should be given.

After reduction, joint stability is determined. Eaton suggested that stability be judged both actively and passively.[80] Redisplacement with active motion suggests significant ligamentous disruption. The examiner should gently stress each collateral ligament passively with a laterally directed force and should test the palmar plate with a dorsally to volarly directed force. Angulation or increased mobility, especially in comparison to the same joint on the contralateral hand, reflects disruption of the involved structure or structures.

## Proximal Interphalangeal Joint

Often associated with a jamming injury, ligament injuries and dislocations of the PIP joints are common. Three types of pure dislocations are observed: dorsal, palmar, and lateral (see Fig. 38–132). Closed reduction is the treatment of choice. After local anesthesia induced by a metacarpal head or wrist block, longitudinal traction and manipulation will reduce most PIP joint dislocations. A dislocation with the distal component rotated suggests the possibility of an entrapped flexor tendon around the head of the proximal phalanx. These injuries will not be reducible by closed means and will mandate open reduction with retraction of the involved tendons.

Once the dislocation is clinically reduced, radiographs are mandatory to confirm the position of the joint. Active and passive joint testing will help determine the presence and degree of any residual instability. If instability is observed, especially with active motion, soft tissue interposition should be suspected. Open reduction may be required in these instances.

Dorsal dislocation represents a complete tear of the palmar plate from its insertion on the base of the middle phalanx. Collateral ligament disruption is not uncommon. After closed reduction, we prefer to immobilize the joint with a dorsally placed Alumafoam splint in 10° to 15° of flexion. Once comfortable, the patient can start active flexion while in the splint (Fig. 38–133). In most cases, the splint can be discontinued after 2 weeks and replaced with Velcro buddy straps that hold the involved digit to adjacent digits for an additional 2 weeks. Buddy-strapping is also advisable during athletic activities for at least 6 more weeks.

Lateral dislocations represent rupture of one collateral ligament, as well as the palmar plate. The digit may have both angular and rotational deformity because the middle phalanx may pivot on the intact collateral ligament. After closed reduction, active and passive testing will determine the intrinsic stability of the joint. We ordinarily splint these injuries for 2 to 3 weeks before allowing motion. Buddy straps are advisable for 3 to 4 weeks after removal of the splint.

If reduction cannot be achieved or the postreduction radiograph shows asymmetric widening of the PIP joint space, soft tissue interposition should be suspected. In these cases, the condyle of the head of the proximal phalanx has "buttonholed" through a rent between the lateral band and the central slip of the extensor tendon on the side of the disrupted collateral ligament. Operative intervention is required.[77]

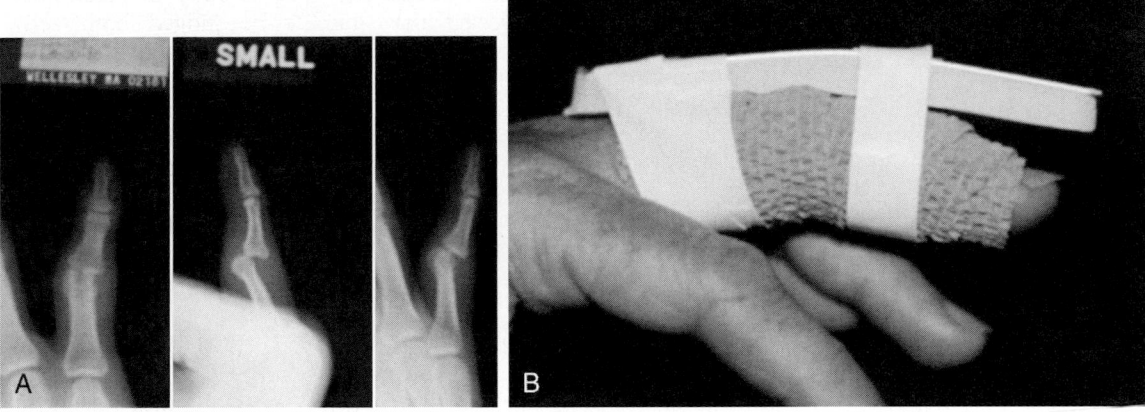

**FIGURE 38–133.** Dorsal dislocation of the proximal interphalangeal joint in an 18-year old man. *A,* Lateral radiographs demonstrate the dorsal displacement of the middle phalanx on the proximal phalanx. *B,* After metacarpal block and closed manipulative reduction, the digit is wrapped with an elastic crepe bandage, and a dorsal extension block Alumafoam splint is applied.

A volar PIP joint dislocation is rare and must be treated in a different manner.[229, 284, 303] In this case, the central slip of the extensor mechanism is injured along with the collateral ligaments and palmar plate. If reduction cannot be achieved or maintained, a boutonnière deformity will result and lead to significant joint dysfunction. Reduction should be performed with the MCP joint held in flexion along with traction and manipulation of the middle phalanx. If reduction is successful, the patient's ability to actively extend the joint is tested. If the patient can extend the joint to within 30° of full extension, a dorsal splint is applied, with the PIP joint kept in full extension but the DIP joint allowed to be mobile. If active extension is not possible, complete disruption of the central slip is probable, and surgical intervention is recommended[77, 303] (Fig. 38–134).

## Distal Interphalangeal Joint

Dislocations of the DIP joints are uncommon. When they do occur, they are more likely to be dorsal than palmar. Although these injuries often involve disruption of both collateral ligaments and the palmar plate, closed reduction can usually be achieved with metacarpal block anesthesia. Splint support for 7 to 14 days with the DIP joint in slight flexion may be all that is needed because these injuries tend to be stable after reduction.

Open injuries require thorough lavage because the joint has been contaminated. Loose soft tissue closure and splinting for 2 weeks should allow adequate soft tissue healing.

Palmar DIP joint dislocations are more difficult to manage because the injury may involve disruption of the insertion of the terminal extensor tendon, as well as disruption of the collateral ligaments and the palmar plate. Postreduction splintage with the joint in extension will be required for a minimum of 8 weeks to allow healing of the extensor tendon.

## Metacarpophalangeal Joint

Dorsal dislocations of the MCP joint are uncommon. They can be difficult to manage because reduction is often blocked by interposed soft tissue (complex dislocation).[77, 80, 158, 194, 221] The clinical picture of a dislocated MCP joint with a dimple in the palmar skin over the metacarpal head should arouse suspicion of a complex dislocation. The index and little fingers are more commonly involved because volar intermetacarpal ligament support is found on only one side of these digits.

Much has been written regarding the pathologic anatomy of a complex MCP dislocation. Kaplan and others suggested that the metacarpal head has "buttonholed" between the flexor tendons and the lumbrical muscle; they recommend a volar surgical approach.[158, 194, 221] However, it is the palmar plate, still attached to the dorsally

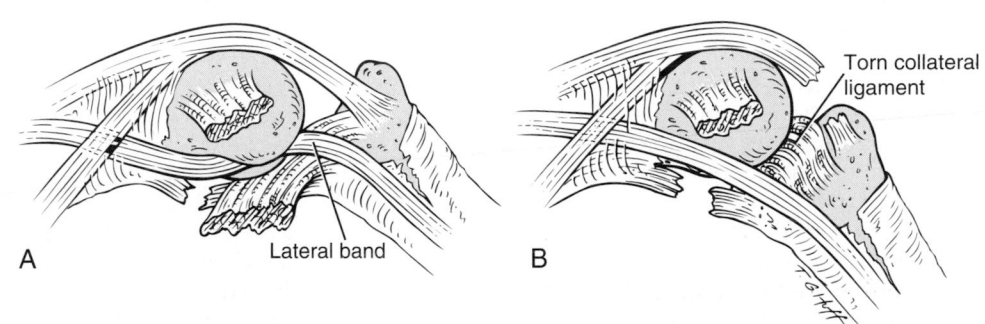

**FIGURE 38–134.** Palmar proximal interphalangeal joint dislocations injure the palmar plate, collateral ligaments, and central slip. *A,* Irreducible palmar dislocation caused by the interposition of a lateral band in the joint. *B,* Irreducible palmar dislocation can also be caused by interposition of the torn collateral ligament.

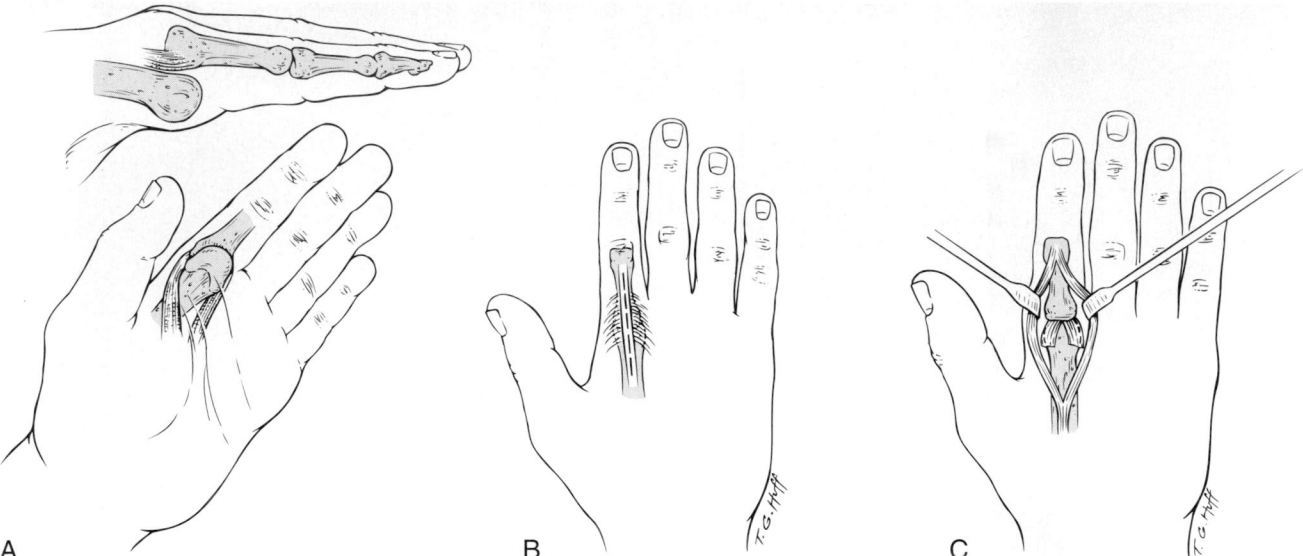

**FIGURE 38–135.** Dorsal dislocation of the metacarpophalangeal joint is considered "complex" inasmuch as closed reduction is rarely successful because of interposition of the palmar plate. *A,* The palmar plate is displaced dorsal to the metacarpal head. In addition, the metacarpal head is "buttonholed" between the flexor tendons and the lumbrical muscle. *B,* Surgical reduction of the complex dislocation is readily accomplished through a dorsal approach splitting the common extensor. *C,* The palmar plate is split longitudinally, followed by atraumatic reduction of the metacarpal.

displaced proximal phalanx, that becomes wedged between the joint surfaces and prevents closed manipulative reduction. For this reason, a dorsal surgical approach proves straightforward and safer because of the limited chance of injury to the digital nerves, which are displaced by the metacarpal head and lie just beneath the palmar skin. After exposing the joint through the dorsal approach, the palmar plate is split longitudinally with a scalpel and retracted to either side with small skin hooks, and the metacarpal head can then be atraumatically reduced (Fig. 38–135). After reduction, the joint is usually remarkably stable, and as such, early mobilization can be encouraged. Postoperatively, all that is required is for the joint to be immobilized in 60° to 75° of flexion for several days, followed by active mobilization in a splint applied dorsally to act as a block to prevent hyperextension. The splint is kept in place for 3 to 4 weeks.

## Thumb

### CARPOMETACARPAL JOINT

Complete dislocation of the CMC joint of the thumb without an associated fracture is very uncommon.[274] It has been thought to be associated with complete disruption of the volar oblique ligament passing from the trapezium to the volar beak of the thumb metacarpal.[7, 80] However, Burkhalter, after surgical exploration of several CMC dislocations, did not find complete rupture of this ligament; instead, he found that the metacarpal rotated in supination out of the capsule of the joint.[41] He suggested that reduction should include maximal pronation of the thumb metacarpal. Once reduced, this joint generally remains quite unstable and is easily redislocated. For this reason, if the reduction has been accomplished by closed means, it is best maintained by percutaneous K-wires

passing from the metacarpal into the trapezium, along with a thumb spica cast for 6 weeks. The reduction must be confirmed radiographically by a true lateral and an AP radiograph (see discussion of Bennett's fracture) (Fig. 38–136).

### METACARPOPHALANGEAL JOINT

Acute ligament injuries to the MCP joint of the thumb are common and are notoriously associated with ski pole injuries.[103] The stability of this joint is related not only to the collateral ligaments, capsule, and palmar plate but also to the actions of the thenar muscles.[59, 61] It is in part because of the thenar muscles' dynamic stabilizing influence that accurate examination of the injured thumb MCP joint may require anesthetic block of these muscles.

The ulnar collateral ligament is far more commonly injured than its radial counterpart. Avulsion fractures may be present in a number of different patterns. The cause of this injury is a sudden valgus stress, often in conjunction with hyperextension of the joint. This pattern of injury occurs when the first webspace of the hand is held firmly against the hard grip of the ski pole by the attached strap and the skier falls away from the "planted" pole. The grip is levered into the webspace and drives the thumb's proximal phalanx into valgus and hyperextension. The onset of pain is immediate.

Physical examination will concentrate on the local features of the injury. Any obvious deformity is noted, local tenderness can be specifically identified, and stability of the collateral ligament complex must be assessed before deciding on management.

Joint stability is tested in full extension as well as in 30° of flexion.[30, 59, 77, 92, 170, 221] The radial and median nerves should be anesthetized at the ~~wrist~~ to provide both analgesia and thenar muscle relaxation. Complete ligament

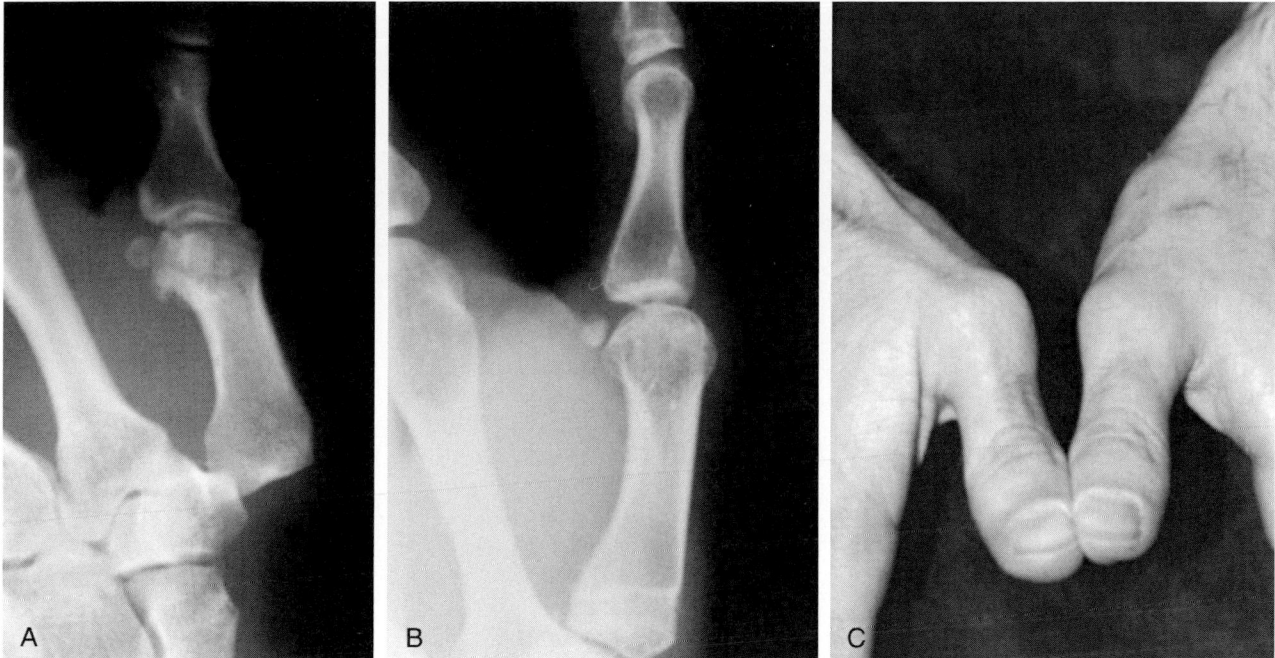

**FIGURE 38–136.** A 20-year-old gymnast presented with pain and limitation of motion in his right thumb 4 weeks after a fall from the parallel bars. *A,* Radiograph revealing complete dislocation of the carpometacarpal joint of the thumb. *B,* Open reduction and stabilization performed with a strip of the flexor carpi radialis tendon. *C,* Excellent long-term stability was noted.

disruption is suspected if the joint can be stressed in a radial direction 25° to 35° beyond a similar stress to the other thumb's MCP joint. This instability should be demonstrated in both full extension and 30° of flexion. More often than not, the presence of ecchymosis will suggest a complete ligament tear as well as volar subluxation of the proximal phalanx, which is seen on a true lateral radiograph. Arthrography and stress testing with radiographic control can be misleading, and we do not recommend these studies for acute injuries.[30]

In 1962, Stener observed at surgery that a completely torn ulnar collateral ligament is often found to be displaced proximally with the adductor muscle aponeurosis interposed between the ligament and its point of insertion[289] (Fig. 38–137). These findings have been confirmed by others and are an indication for surgical

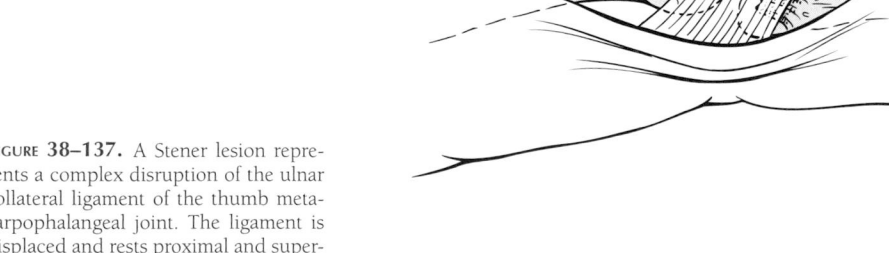

**FIGURE 38–137.** A Stener lesion represents a complex disruption of the ulnar collateral ligament of the thumb metacarpophalangeal joint. The ligament is displaced and rests proximal and superficial to the insertion of the adductor tendon.

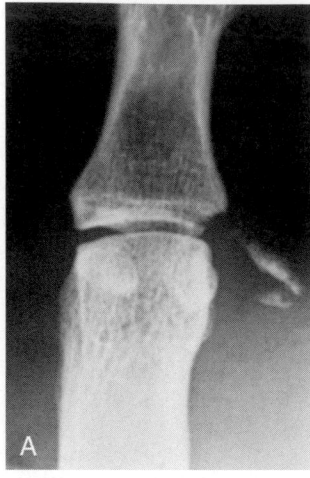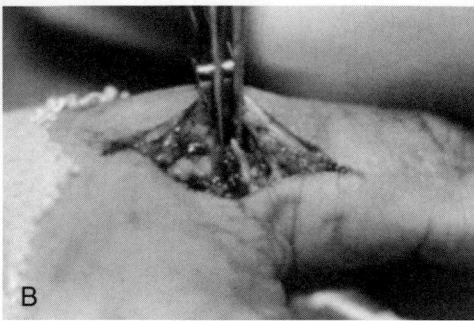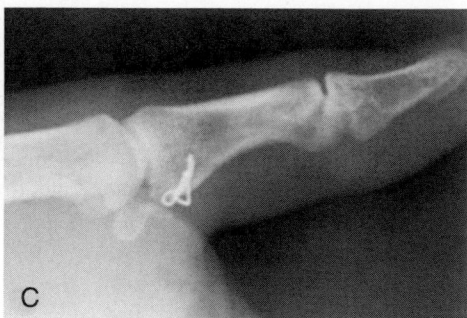

**FIGURE 38–138.** A 34-year-old sustained a skiing injury to the metacarpophalangeal joint of his thumb. *A,* Anteroposterior radiograph showing displacement of the bony attachment of the ulnar collateral ligament. *B,* At surgery, the comminuted fragments were found to be attached to the collateral ligament and displaced proximal to the adductor tendon. *C,* The ligament and its bony fragments were reapproximated and secured with tension wire applied in a figure-of-eight pattern.

exploration if a complete ligament disruption is suspected. The widely displaced position of the collateral ligament will prevent proper healing of the avulsed ligament back to bone, and therefore, adequate stability of the joint will not be restored with closed means of treatment. Pichora and colleagues were able to demonstrate reasonable results with closed management of documented complete collateral ligament ruptures.[234] The vast majority of authors believe that surgical repair is mandatory for a complete lesion. Incomplete tears are treated with a thumb spica cast for 4 to 6 weeks, followed by a removable, hand-based Orthoplast splint protecting against a valgus stress on the healing ligament.

The operative approach is accomplished through a dorsoulnar incision.[79, 289] Care is taken to identify and protect the dorsal radial sensory nerve branches. The adductor aponeurosis is opened longitudinally parallel to the first metacarpal, with a 12-cm edge left for closure. The joint capsule is then observed. Frequently, a dorsal tear of the capsule will be observed. Any additional distal extension of the capsular tear is performed as needed to adequately visualize the site of ligament avulsion and the associated injury to the volar plate. The ligament should be repaired not only to the base of the proximal phalanx at its normal insertion but also to the palmar plate.[77] Repair would be accomplished with direct suture for an in-substance tear (rare). For a typical distal insertion avulsion, the bony site of injury is deepened by curettage or the use of a power bur and the ligament readvanced to the bone site with a pull-out suture technique. Perhaps simpler and associated with fewer skin problems under the button is the use of minisuture anchors. One minianchor is easily embedded into the base of the avulsion site, and the ligament is sutured down to this site with nonabsorbable 1–0 or 2–0 suture. Capsular closure will add to the stability of the repair and is followed by reapproximation of the adductor aponeurosis. The thumb should be immobilized in a thumb spica cast for 4 weeks, followed by protected mobilization with only flexion and extension exercises while the thumb is maintained in a removable splint. Cross-pinning of the joint is rarely required after adequate soft tissue repair has been completed.

Avulsion fractures can be determined on the initial radiographs and can be treated as described for intraarticular base fractures of the proximal phalanges[125, 152] (Fig. 38–138). If minimally displaced, by definition, the collateral ligament will lie in a satisfactory position and will heal with bone-to-bone union. Wide displacement or any associated joint malalignment indicates unacceptable joint instability and dictates surgical management. Generally, the fragment can be reattached as described previously. If the bone injury is severely comminuted and precludes satisfactory internal fixation, it is best to excise the fragments and reattach the ligament directly to bone by using the techniques described previously.

## OPEN FRACTURES

It is worthwhile to address the specific aspects of management of open fractures of the hand in distinction from other skeletal sites. The hand is fortunate to have an excellent macroscopic and microscopic blood supply and, as a result, greater tolerance for open wounds. Nonetheless, careful attention must be paid to the basics of wound care to help prevent the complications of sepsis and infected nonunion of open fractures of the hand.

As identified by Szabo and Spiegel,[300] most infected fractures of the hand and wrist occur after an open fracture with either major soft tissue loss or vascular compromise.

The trauma sustained in an open hand fracture can produce dead, vascularly compromised, or heavily contaminated tissue. The most common "at-risk" wounds are those related to crush injuries, motor vehicle accidents, gunshot wounds, wounds contaminated with lake water, and farm or industrial equipment injuries.

Initial management of all but the most distal of open hand fractures should be performed in the sterile environment of the operating room. All dead and devitalized tissue must be resected, including skin, fascia, muscle, and devascularized small fragments of bone. Once complete débridement has been performed, the bone and soft tissues are irrigated with copious quantities of sterile normal saline solution with or without antibiotics. Usually, 4 to 5 L suffices in the hand. Pulsatile pressurized lavage may have some advantage because of its mechanical débridement effect.

Fracture stabilization in an open fracture situation is critical, which is not to say that all fractures need plating, rather that they require stabilization. Such stabilization reduces ongoing soft tissue injury, bleeding, hematoma formation, and the inflammatory response.[48, 118] In addition, skeletal stabilization will facilitate soft tissue reconstruction and wound coverage.

In the situation of minimal soft tissue contamination and adequate tissue débridement, fracture management will be the same as for a closed fracture of the same location and pattern, as described in the previous sections. The only difference is that bone grafting should probably be delayed until full skin coverage has been achieved. Perioperative antibiotic coverage should follow the guidelines outlined in the section Open Fractures. *Staphylococcus* and *Streptococcus* are the most common offending organisms in the hand, with a recent increase in polymicrobial sepsis with aerobic and anaerobic gram-positive and gram-negative bacteria.[300]

With increasing degrees of soft tissue trauma and associated devitalization of the skeleton, less invasive

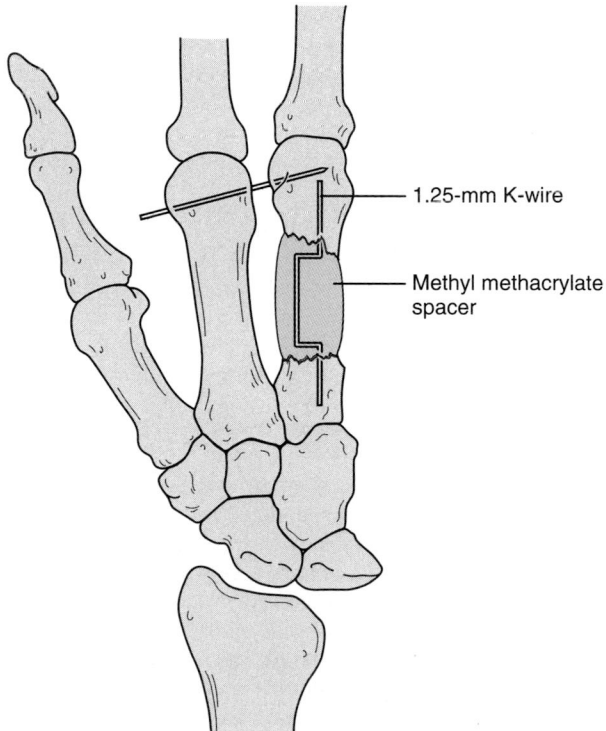

1.25-mm K-wire

Methyl methacrylate spacer

**FIGURE 38–139.** Use of a methyl methacrylate/K-wire construct to fill the dead space in a potentially contaminated severe metacarpal fracture. The bone cement is impregnated with antibiotic powder (gentamicin). The spacer serves to preserve the space needed for later bone grafting and plate reconstruction. The wires maintain metacarpal length and alignment.

means of internal fixation should be considered. External fixation begins to play an increasing role in the stabilization of fractures.

As described by Freeland and associates[93, 94] in the situation of severe wound contamination plus segmental skeletal loss, an antibiotic-impregnated spacer can be created with methyl methacrylate supported by a contoured K-wire as an intramedullary splint (Fig. 38–139). This construct will maintain skeletal length and alignment, fill in potential dead spaces, and help create an excellent tissue site for iliac crest bone grafting in conjunction with rigid internal fixation at secondary or tertiary débridement and reconstruction. Rehabilitation is greatly facilitated in this approach, with all reconstructive procedures being done early on a stable, internally fixed hand skeleton.

Soft tissue reconstructive procedures are of paramount importance, especially the need to obtain adequate skin coverage with local, rotational, pedicled, or free tissue transfers as indicated. The details are not covered in this chapter.

## COMPLEX INJURIES

A *complex injury* represents either a complete amputation or a multisystem injury with devascularization plus variable lesions to major nerves, blood vessels, tendons, bones, muscles, and skin. Specific fracture patterns will mimic those described in the various sections earlier in this chapter. However, with complex injuries, additional considerations, related not only to the fracture configuration but also to the soft tissue injuries, will come into play in determining the ideal fracture management.[56, 69]

### Role of Internal Fixation in Complex Injuries

Freeland and colleagues contributed considerably to our appreciation of the need for stable skeletal fixation in these complex injuries. These authors have identified that stable skeletal restoration is integral to overall wound care and provides the foundation and scaffolding essential for the protection and healing of all soft tissue repairs and reconstruction. Stable anatomic fracture fixation enhances pain control, improves local tissue microperfusion and revascularization, eliminates dead space, contributes to infection prevention, and enhances the probability of fracture healing; it is the keystone for optimal functional recovery.[95]

The goal of fracture management in a complex injury is to achieve maximal skeletal stability in as simple and effective a way as possible and to proceed to management of the soft tissue injuries. As have been described previously, a multitude of techniques are available for stabilizing the skeleton. In a complex injury, the method chosen should be relatively easy and quick to apply and must provide adequate stability to begin immediate rehabilitation of the tendon and soft tissue injuries as dictated by their severity. Which technique is used is somewhat of a personal preference, with many authors

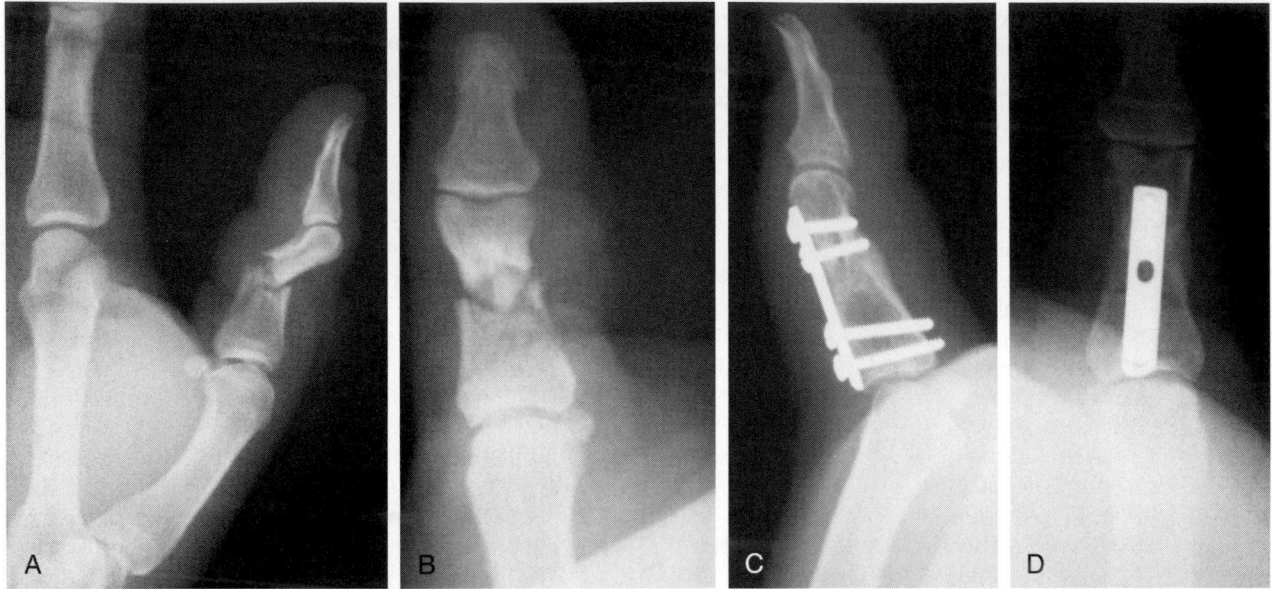

**FIGURE 38–140.** *A, B,* Anteroposterior and lateral radiographs of a complex injury to the dominant thumb with a power saw. Dorsal, ulnar, and palmar skin was transected, as were the flexor tendon, extensor tendon, and one digital neurovascular bundle. The thumb was not avascular. *C, D,* The fracture was shortened slightly, rigid internal fixation was secured with a dorsal 2.0-mm miniplate, and reconstruction of the soft tissue injury was performed. Primary repair of all injured structures was accomplished. Long-term follow-up is excellent, with 85% of normal interphalangeal joint motion on the uninjured side and return of 5-mm moving two-point discrimination on the injured ulnar side.

reporting success with different implants. Zimmerman and Weiland had excellent success with the 90-90 wiring methods,[328] Nunley and co-workers with the mini-H plate,[222] and Lister with the combination wire technique,[186] to mention only a few. A question arises regarding which techniques will afford the skeletal stability required.

Jones, in an excellent review of the biomechanical literature on implant fixation strength, stated that plates and screws provide the most stable form of internal fixation of the hand skeleton, with their strength approaching that of the intact skeleton.[147] However, given the success of other methods, the question still needs to be fully answered.

### Injury Management

After débridement and identification of all injuries, the next step is to deal with the skeletal stabilization needed. The bone ends can be shortened to facilitate rapid skeletal fixation by converting a complex fracture pattern to a simple transverse osteotomy. The advantages of skeletal shortening are obvious. The surgeon has less devitalized tissue to deal with, including bone, wound closure is facilitated, and primary repair, even with substance loss, can be performed for the nerves and vascular structures. These advantages are achieved at the potential cost of an alteration in the basic anatomy and, to some extent, the length-tension relationships of the muscle-tendon units (Fig. 38–140). The use of a simple four-hole 1.5- or 2.0-mm plate is excellent for this purpose, as is the minicondylar plate for juxta-articular injuries. The mini-H plate is also an ideal implant because it can be applied with minimal additional soft tissue dissection.

Once skeletal stability has been achieved, the soft tissue repairs can be built on this scaffolding.

### Expectations

Chen and associates[55] reported on 72 complex injuries to the phalanges and metacarpals treated with miniplates for skeletal stabilization. They reported good results in 46% as determined by outcome criteria of the American Society for Surgery of the Hand. Delayed union occurred in only five fractures, all of which eventually healed. These authors believed that decided advantages could be gained from use of the implants and techniques for complex injuries. As a surgeon becomes more familiar with the use of miniplates, the speed of application improves, complications occur less frequently, and the results improve.

## COMPLICATIONS OF HAND FRACTURE MANAGEMENT

Common complications of hand fracture management include delayed union or nonunion, sepsis, malunion, contracture and stiffness, nerve compression, and post-traumatic osteoarthritis.

Jupiter and colleagues reported on the relatively infrequent complication of nonunion of fractures of the small bones of the hand.[150] Nonunions are rare in closed management of hand fractures. The most common risk for nonunion is that of poor surgical technique in applying K-wire internal fixation. In particular, crossed K-wires that serve to distract the fracture site are a major problem.

Wires that do not cross the fracture site or do not engage bone on both sides of the injury site have also contributed to the development of nonunion.

Nonunion needs to be addressed only when it is associated with a certain level of disability and functional impairment. Many are asymptomatic. The principles of surgical management for nonunion in the hand follow those of the larger skeleton. The offending or broken implants are removed, any dead or contaminated tissue is removed, stable internal fixation is secured with lag screws and plates, and finally, bone grafting is often done to encourage union. Bone grafting may not be needed in a viable, so-called hypertrophic nonunion. Stable internal fixation is mandatory, as is an environment conducive to healing with adequate local blood supply. Soft tissue contractures are released by tenolysis, capsulotomies, or both procedures in an effort to reduce the bending loads applied to the implants and to facilitate maximal functional recovery.

Delayed union may require no more than external skeletal protection with a splint worn full-time until healed. Rarely, if one is concerned about implant failure, early bone grafting and, if indicated, revision of the implant will usually stimulate the occurrence of union.

Sepsis is difficult to manage.[82] The principles follow those for the major long bones. All devitalized tissue is débrided in the operating room. The wounds are left open, and antibiotic beads or a spacer may be helpful. Bone stability is achieved with external or internal fixation. Once the overt infection has been eradicated, bone union can be encouraged with cancellous bone grafting. Soft tissue coverage with vascularized tissue is most helpful in creating an environment conducive to fracture and soft tissue healing. Szabo and Spiegel provided an excellent review of the management of infected fractures of the hand and wrist in 1988.[300]

Malunion is a frequent complication of hand fractures. The most disabling seems to be rotational malalignment of the digit resulting in overlap in flexion (Fig. 38–141; see

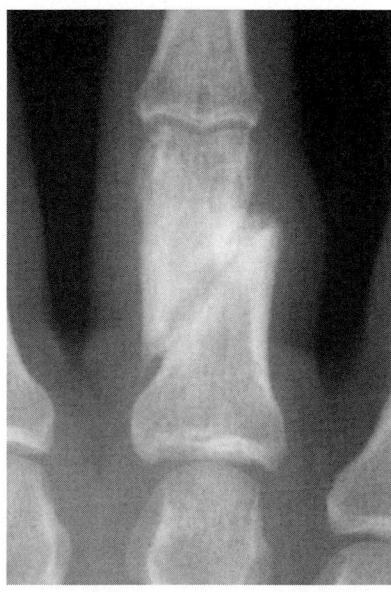

**FIGURE 38–141.** Long oblique proximal phalanx fracture allowed to heal after closed treatment with shortening and rotational deformity.

also Fig. 38–37). Excessive angulation can result in functional impairment, particularly of the index and middle rays. Corrective osteotomy provides a technique to deal with these deformities if adequately symptomatic. Once again, stable internal or external fixation will ensure maintenance of the correction, early functional use of the hand, and a reasonable rate of successful union.[272]

Post-traumatic osteoarthritis can be a frequent complication of articular injuries in the hand. Management depends on the site involved and the symptoms of the individual patient. Standard reconstructive procedures apply to the hand and include débridement, arthrodesis, realignment, or arthroplasty.

The treatment is site specific. Osteoarthritis of the DIP joint is easily treated by arthrodesis using a variety of techniques from Herbert screw fixation to decortication and wire fixation. The PIP joint is less tolerant of fusion; however, fusion remains the mainstay of management for a symptomatic arthritic joint. Arthroplasty may play a role in a low-demand individual, especially for the nonborder digits. The MCP joint is not tolerant of arthrodesis, and as such, Swanson Silastic arthroplasty remains a reasonable option for reconstruction. The CMC joints are generally best dealt with by arthrodesis because no arthroplasty has had success at the nonthumb joints. For the basilar joint of the thumb, ligament interpositional arthroplasty is an excellent reconstructive option, as is functional-position arthrodesis.

Nerve compression syndromes are usually associated with wrist injuries. They are rarely associated with metacarpal fractures, however, and if present, will require decompression and neurolysis.

Contracture and stiffness are frequent complications of fractures of the hand. The mainstays of treatment include progressive static and dynamic splintage until the recovery has plateaued. If the contracture is still unsatisfactory, consideration can be given to tenolysis, capsulotomy, or both as required. MCP joint capsulotomy is perhaps the most frequently required procedure after hand trauma. If implants are in situ, implant removal after fracture union is complete should be considered in conjunction with tenolysis and capsulotomy. This technique will serve to reduce the bulk of immobile mass below the tendons, ease some implant discomfort, and reduce the chance of postoperative re-formation of the adhesions.

## Malunion and Deformity

Deformity is the most common complication noted in metacarpal and phalangeal fractures.[111, 149] When deformity leads to functional loss, corrective osteotomy remains the best treatment option.* The literature available on this subject often consists of small retrospective studies and case reports. The sparse data in the literature may reflect the reluctance of most surgeons to perform corrective osteotomy. With the advent of improved implants for

*See references 26, 34, 39, 58, 78, 108, 109, 146, 182, 183, 193, 195, 208, 211, 233, 236, 241, 244, 245, 256, 272, 305, 309, 311, 317, 325, 327.

stable fixation, complications after osteotomy are uncommon. In addition to post-traumatic deformity, additional indications for corrective osteotomies in the phalanges and metacarpals include epiphyseal injuries, congenital malformations, fixed flexion contractures, chronic joint instability, painful arthritis, paralysis, and nonunion with deformity.[97, 98, 212, 241, 325]

Extra-articular malunion can cause scissoring of fingers, which can adversely affect the function of adjacent digits, including a disturbance in the overall arc of motion, pain secondary to joint malalignment, disturbance in muscle/tendon balance, decreased grip strength, or any combination of these sequelae.[39, 45, 62, 97, 208, 244, 260, 272] Intra-articular malunions can cause joint surface irregularities, which may lead to a block in motion, synovitis, capsular contractures, deformity, or post-traumatic arthrosis (or any combination of these complications).[39, 182, 183, 202, 323, 327] The extent that any of these problems affect function will determine the need for corrective osteotomy.

When first evaluating a malunion, one should strive to obtain an adequate history, including patient age, hand dominance, occupation, mechanism and severity of the initial injury (simple or combined), initial treatment, compliance of the patient, and timing of the treatment. Physical examination should include an evaluation of the skin, assessment of vascular status, determination of range of motion of all the joints in the hand, evaluation of any tendon, ligament, or capsular injuries, and localization of tenderness.

Radiographic examination should include AP, lateral, and oblique radiographs, with comparison films of the normal contralateral side. More complex deformities may require that a true AP and lateral radiograph be obtained proximal and distal to the deformity to later superimpose these films for help in preoperative planning. Deformities involving the joints should be imaged with trispiral tomography, computed tomography, or both. Precise localization of the malunion (extra-articular, intra-articular, combined, epiphyseal, metaphyseal, or diaphyseal); determination of the direction of the deformity (flexion/extension, radial/ulnar deviation, rotation, shortening, or any combination of these deformities); associated soft tissue contracture, deficiency, or neurovascular deficit; and evaluation of skeletal maturity are crucial for both prognosis and treatment. A simple deformity is defined by the problem of being primarily a skeletal malalignment, whereas a complex malunion involves associated soft tissue or articular compromise.

The timing of corrective osteotomy in the treatment of diaphyseal metacarpal and phalangeal malunion involves a number of factors. One can divide the timing of osteotomy into three periods.[39, 151, 182] The first is acute and includes the period when manipulative reduction is still possible (first 7 to 10 days in children and approximately 2 weeks in adults). The second is intermediate and occurs when a fibrocartilaginous or soft bony callus is present (2 to 4 weeks in adults). The third is a mature period when bony union has formed and the soft edema has resolved (4 to 8 weeks). Although most agree that early manipulative reduction (with or without fixation) to correct loss of anatomic position is preferred in the acute phase,[39, 182] whether to perform an osteotomy in the intermediate or mature time period is controversial. Some believe that osteotomy in the intermediate period may further limit active range of motion and lead to poor function.[39] Others think that late osteotomy may be technically more difficult and only delay return of function.[151, 182]

In addition to the time from injury, the timing of osteotomy must take into account the state of the soft tissue envelope and associated joint mobility. Every effort is taken to maximize joint mobility while recognizing that altered tendon balance will limit return of full mobility. Preoperative muscle strengthening will also aid in postoperative rehabilitation.

Less controversy surrounds intra-articular malunion, in which case operative union should be considered as soon as the problem is recognized. The original fracture lines may be appreciated up to 8 to 10 weeks after fracture. After 6 months postinjury, irreversible changes are likely to have developed, so alternative treatment at that point is preferential in most cases.

The type and location of an extra-articular osteotomy for deformity in the metacarpals or phalanges depend on a number of factors. As a general rule, an osteotomy should be performed at the site of the deformity. The type of osteotomy is based on a number of factors, including location, tendon balance, and soft tissue or articular contracture. For the vast majority of pure angular deformities in radial or ulnar deviation, an incomplete osteotomy is suggested.[39, 46, 58, 97, 109, 182, 244, 290, 309] With the exception of those involving the middle or distal phalanges, an opening wedge osteotomy will more predictably restore length, readjust the tension of the extensor mechanism, and require only minimal internal fixation. When length is less of a concern, a closing wedge osteotomy performed with different bur sizes and with the opposite cortex and periosteum left intact to be manually "cracked" will have a high success rate[97] (Fig. 38–142A to F).

For dorsal or volar angular deformities, an opening wedge osteotomy with an interposed bone graft is also preferred. However, one must be mindful of the large deforming forces of the extrinsic muscles, which will necessitate the use of a more sturdy implant.

Pure rotational deformities require a complete osteotomy, which in the vast majority of cases is transverse at the site of the deformity. By the same token, several authors have suggested that pure rotational deformity of the phalanges can be corrected by rotational osteotomy at the metacarpal level.[26, 208, 236, 290, 317] Though conceptually appealing because it offers a less demanding approach and one less likely to cause problems in the complex balance of extrinsic and intrinsic tendons at the phalangeal level, the amount of correction may be limited and a more complex deformity may result.[39] In a cadaveric study, Gross and Gelberman[115] found that the deep transverse metacarpal ligament limited metacarpal rotation to 19° in the index, long, and ring fingers and between 20° and 30° of rotation in the little finger. We have limited our indications for this approach to cases that were complicated by severe soft tissue and articular dysfunction in the involved digit. When indicated, the step-cut osteotomy technique is relatively simple.[195, 233]

When faced with a deformity made complex by multiple directions of deformity or associated tendon and

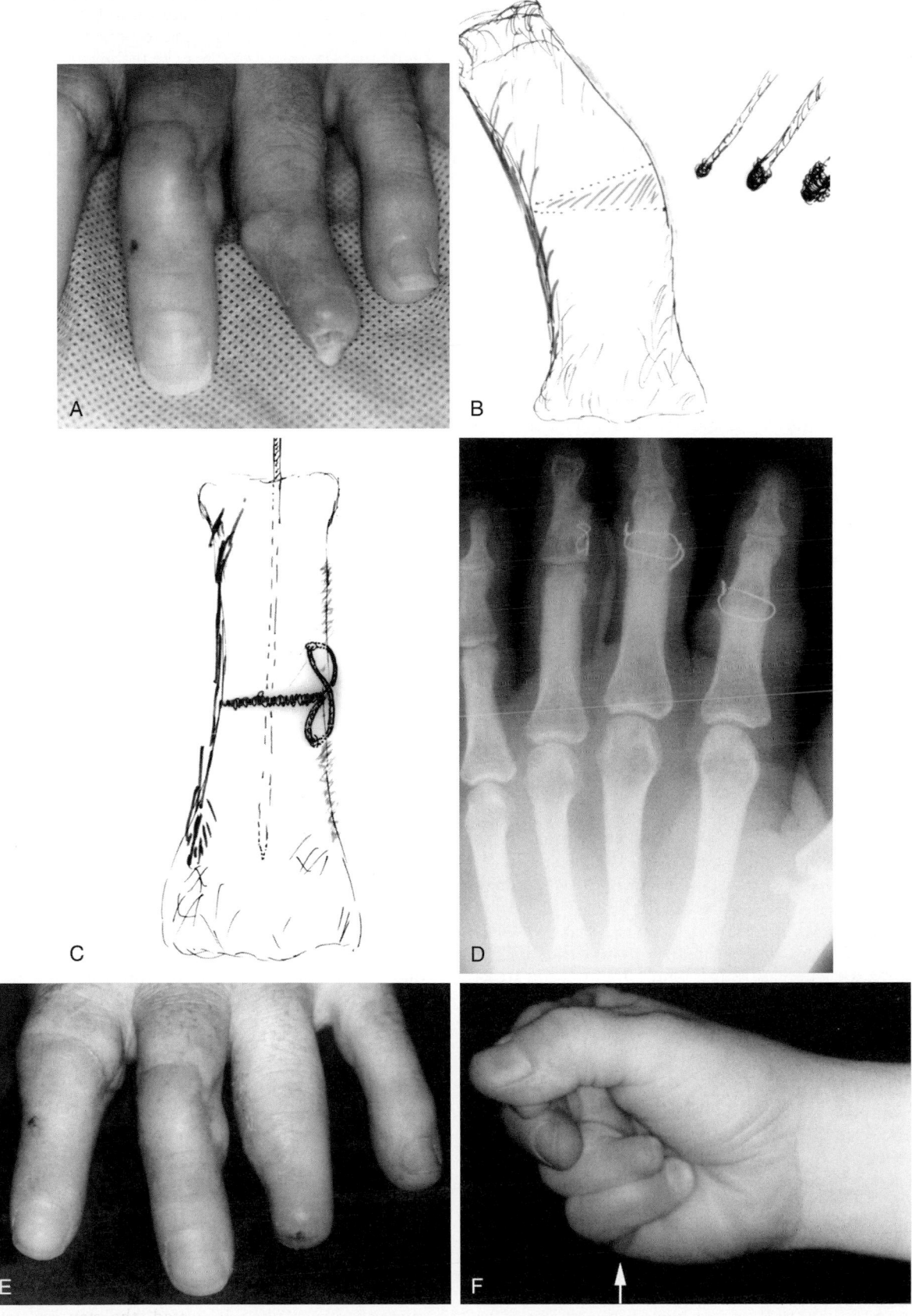

**FIGURE 38–142.** Angular malunion of the middle phalanx of the ring finger of a 42-year-old carpenter who had replantation of the index and long fingers through the proximal interphalangeal joints. *A,* The clinical appearance of the deformity. *B, C,* The preoperative plan of a closing wedge using small burs. Fixation with a tension wire and longitudinal Kirschner wire was proposed. *D,* Anteroposterior radiograph of the union of the osteotomy. *E, F,* The clinical outcome resulted in a return to his preinjury occupation.

articular dysfunction (or both), a complete transverse osteotomy with stable internal fixation and, often, a corticocancellous bone graft will be necessary.

## CORRECTIVE OSTEOTOMY—TACTICS

Preoperative preparation is the key to a successful osteotomy. When performing any corrective osteotomy (metacarpal or phalangeal), preoperative templating is essential.[247] The objective of preoperative tracing of the deformity is to know the precise location for the osteotomy, the graft size needed, and the instrumentation necessary before entering the operating theater.[223]

Proper exposure is important because soft tissue mobilization is crucial to facilitate realignment of the bony fragments after osteotomy. Two sets of reference Kirschner wires are helpful in controlling angular and rotatory deformities. These wires are placed perpendicular to the long axes of the involved bone in a dorsal-to-volar and radioulnar direction, with the distal set of wires also incorporating any rotational deformity. The accuracy of the correction is aided by observing the K-wires become parallel in the frontal, axial, and lateral planes.[39, 269] Complete osteotomies are created with the thinnest blade possible, whereas incomplete osteotomies can be created with small burs.

The choice of osteosynthesis depends on a number of factors. With the exception of a closing wedge osteotomy, in which the opposite soft tissues and periosteum remain undisturbed, corrective osteotomy will benefit from more stable internal fixation and, at times, fixation that is somewhat stronger than that required for an acute fracture involving the same bone. This difference in requirements is due to several factors, including the fact that a corrective osteotomy is performed with a saw that leaves smooth edges, which do not have the stability of an interdigitating fracture line; delay in healing because of the devascularizing effect of the operative procedure and the thermal effects of the saw; and the need for secure bony fixation when associated tenolysis or capsulotomy (or both) is required.

Diaphyseal osteotomies are ordinarily well supported by straight plates preferentially aligned on the lateral side of the bone, whereas juxta-articular osteotomies are better stabilized with condylar plates. The 2.0-mm plates are of sufficient size for the proximal phalanges, 1.5-mm plates for the middle phalanges, and 2.0- or 2.7-mm implants for the metacarpals (Fig. 38–143A to E).

Although the specific features of the postoperative protocol depend on whether associated tendon or articular problems are present, the overall goal after osteotomy is rapid return of digital function. In this light, early mobilization of the digit is encouraged, preferentially under the supervision of a trained hand therapist. The use of dynamic splinting, continuous passive motion, and static extension depends on the complexity of the problem, the stability of the internal fixation, and patient comfort.

When faced with a malunited intra-articular fracture, alternative options other than osteotomy include arthrodesis, implant arthroplasty, and resection of impinging osteocartilaginous spikes.[28, 81, 111, 123, 139, 140, 182, 184, 321] Alternative procedures may be particularly applicable in joints that require stability, such as the thumb IP or MCP joints. Trispiral tomography is extremely useful preoperatively because operative exposure is based on the specific location of the articular incongruity.

## DEFORMITY CORRECTION—PITFALLS

Correction of deformity through osteotomy of the small tubular bones of the hand is a complex reconstructive procedure, often made more so by limited exposure and associated contracted soft tissue or articulations. Among the pitfalls that have been identified as leading to suboptimal results are poor preoperative planning, underestimation of the associated soft tissue problems, imprecise definition of the plane of the deformity, and iatrogenic injury to the overlying tissue.

## METACARPAL MALUNION

Although some deformity often follows metacarpal fractures, operative correction of functional impairment is uncommon.[3, 90, 137, 256] Malunions are most frequently found in the metacarpal neck or with "boxer's fractures." In managing acute fractures, volar angulation of 30° to 50° in the fourth and fifth metacarpals and 10° in the first and second is acceptable.[3, 11, 84, 90, 137, 149] Rotational malunion of up to 10° is also acceptable. If the rotational deformity is greater than 10°, angular deviation of the fingers is likely to occur.[195, 256, 282, 318] Weeks believed that 5° of malrotation causes 1.5 cm of lateral displacement of a fully flexed finger.[318] Because of the greater mobility noted in the fourth and fifth CMC joints, MCP motion is rarely a problem in volar malunions that occur in these digits. However, some patients with a volarly displaced fracture of the metacarpal neck will be dissatisfied because of the prominent metacarpal head noted in the palm, dorsal pain at the fracture site, and a cosmetically unacceptable result.[305] In these instances, a corrective osteotomy will be indicated.

As the malunion gets closer to the center of the diaphysis, the functional and cosmetic outcome worsens. Midshaft malunions that are greater than 20° require correction.[109] As in all malunions, the deformity can be angular, rotational, shortened, or a combination of these deformities. The treatment principles outlined apply to these deformities of the metacarpal diaphysis.[27, 193, 208, 233, 260, 272, 309]

The literature on metacarpal malunion is replete with case reports and retrospective studies.[27, 78, 108, 154, 193, 256, 260, 272, 309] As in all malunions, function remains the primary indication for operative management. Lucas and Pfeiffer retrospectively reviewed the experience of 26 metacarpal osteotomies and found 17 very good, 7 good, and 2 poor results.[193] Pichora and colleagues retrospectively reviewed seven metacarpal osteotomies.[233] All seven patients had bony union by 8 weeks, and alignment was noted to be satisfactory in all cases. MCP motion improved an average of 2.1° ± 9.6° and proximal interphalangeal motion improved 4.0° ± 11.9°.

A few studies have addressed the use of osteotomy for the treatment of intra-articular metacarpal malunion of the fingers.[27, 78, 183] The largest of these studies was a retrospective review of three cases by Duncan and Jupiter.[78] In this review, two of the patients underwent juxta-articular dome osteotomy and one patient was treated with an

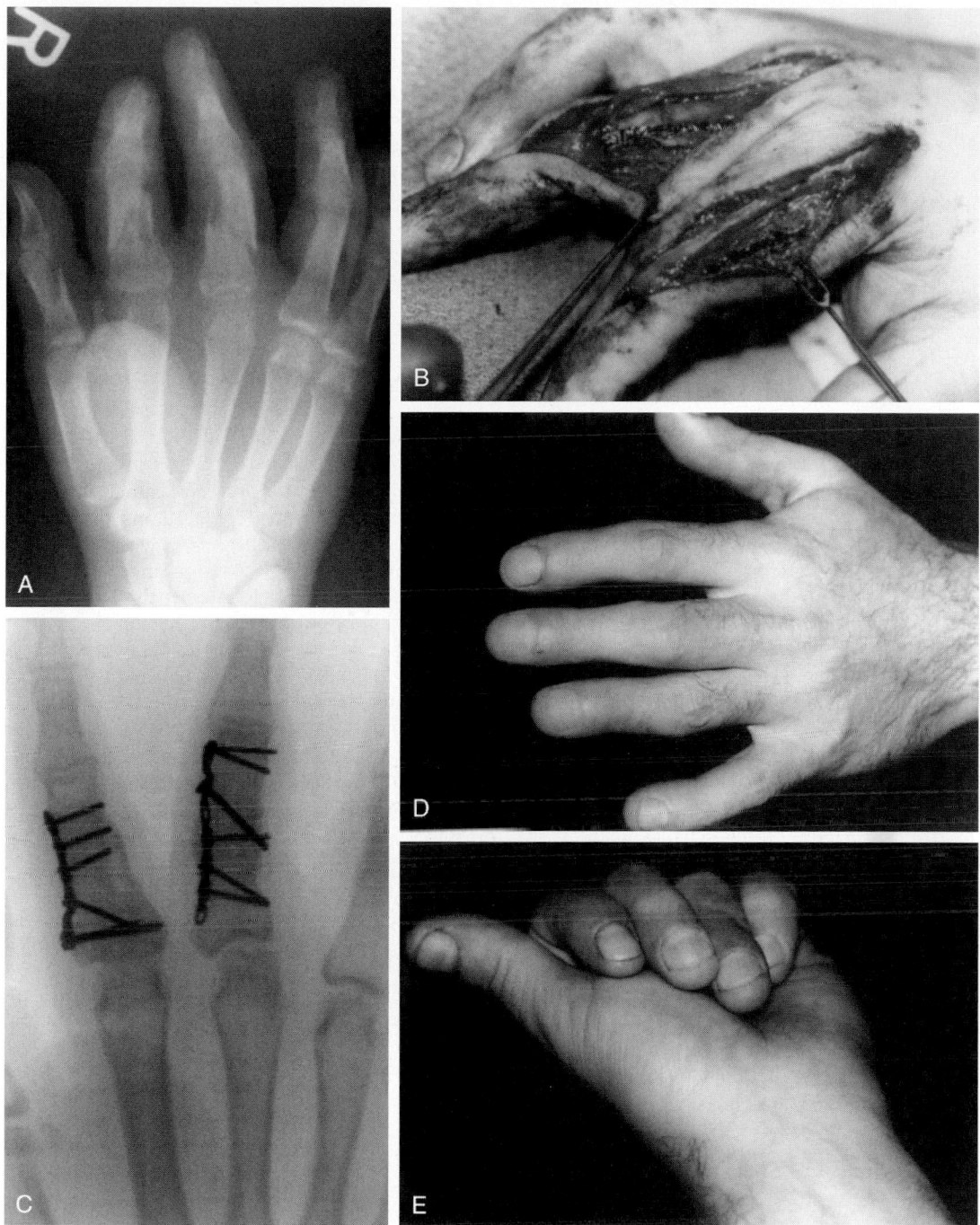

**FIGURE 38–143.** Complex malunion of the proximal phalanges of the index and long fingers of a 19-year-old laborer after open fractures. *A,* Anteroposterior radiograph of the deformity of the index and long fingers. *B,* Operative correction included complex osteotomy, stable condylar plate fixation, extensor and flexor tenolysis, and proximal interphalangeal joint capsulotomy. *C,* Anteroposterior radiographs after union. *D, E,* Satisfactory clinical function.

intra-articular osteotomy. All patients had significant improvement in articular anatomy and function. Because fewer than 10 osteotomies for intra-articular metacarpal malunion have been reported in the literature, it is difficult to draw any concrete conclusions. Nevertheless, the authors in these reviews stress the importance of early recognition and treatment, large enough fragments to allow for stable fixation, compliance with postoperative rehabilitation, and absence of post-traumatic arthrosis.

The thumb is notable for its great mobility. Malunions with shortening or angulation (or both) in the thumb MCP

joint of up to 15° in any plane are often well tolerated.[272] Rotational malposition is poorly tolerated in the thumb and often requires correction. Occasionally, proximal thumb metacarpal malunions of Bennett's fractures may result in subluxation of the trapeziometacarpal joint.

Clinkscales recommended a closing wedge osteotomy to realign the thumb and prevent post-traumatic arthrosis.[58] Others have performed intra-articular osteotomies with good results.[40, 104, 146, 311, 313] As in all intra-articular malunions, if the fracture is noted early, realignment osteotomy is optimal.[46] If post-traumatic arthrosis has already occurred, procedures such as arthrodesis and arthroplasty become necessary.[44, 50, 89, 96, 312]

## PHALANGEAL MALUNION

Although no specific guidelines have been set for when to perform corrective osteotomies, interference with satisfactory hand function remains the critical indication for operative treatment of phalangeal malunions. Often, extra-articular malunions of the thumb phalanges, as well as the middle and distal digital phalanges, cause fewer functional problems than proximal digital phalangeal malunions do.

Phalangeal malunions can be divided into four deforming types: volar angulation, lateral angulation, rotation, and shortening. Combinations of these patterns are most common.[39, 260, 290]

Phalangeal fractures can lead to rotational deformities of the fingers that may be clinically manifested as "scissoring," which is both a cosmetic and functional deformity. Causes include inadequate correction and loss of correction in the splint. Frequently, as little as 10° of rotary deformity may interfere with normal hand function.[88]

Apex volar fractures commonly occur in the proximal phalanx. Such fractures often result in a "pseudoclaw" deformity with a fixed PIP flexion contracture. These deformities are best treated with an opening wedge osteotomy through the malunion site, bone grafting, and rigid internal fixation. Some authors have used closing wedge osteotomies with success.[290]

Lateral angulation usually occurs from bone loss on the ipsilateral side. Early bone grafting may avert this complication, but the local soft tissue environment often precludes early grafting. Just as in apex volar malunions, opening and closing osteotomies have been recommended for these malunions.[39, 109, 111, 244, 290]

Isolated phalangeal shortening often occurs in long spiral, short oblique, and highly comminuted fractures. When closed treatment methods are used, careful close radiographic observation is essential to prevent malunion. When caused by long spiral or short oblique fractures, malunions generally produce difficulty in flexion because of a proximal fragment bone spike. When malunion does occur, it may be possible to perform a simple excision of this spike rather than correct the malunion with an osteotomy.[58, 109, 111, 180]

Management of intra-articular malunions is somewhat controversial. Early malunions (when fracture fragments can be delineated) may be treated by osteotomy and realignment.[39, 183, 202, 323, 327] The results of osteotomy during this early stage have been encouraging. Precise imaging of these complex malunions by tomography is critical in such cases. Operative cases should have large intra-articular fragments, and rigid fixation is preferable. Degenerative arthrosis in the unfractured segment is a contraindication to corrective osteotomy.[111] Although intra-articular osteotomies have been performed up to 15 years after the initial injury, these cases are far more technically demanding.[327]

Most cases involving the PIP joint are due to unreduced old fracture-dislocations.[202, 323, 327] In these cases, the malunion occurs through the middle phalanx. The mechanism of injury is longitudinal compression combined with hyperextension, often seen when a finger is struck by a ball. The size of the volar fragment of the middle phalanx is variable and determines the stability of the dislocation. Surgical steps in correcting this malunion include reduction of the joint and intra-articular fixation in a reduced position, an osteotomy through the base of the middle phalanx, realignment of the volar lip fragment, and bone grafting. Open reduction is performed through a midlateral incision over the PIP joint. The collateral ligament must be released either proximally or distally. The joint can then be hinged open. It is often necessary to strip the dorsal capsule, and occasionally, the opposite collateral ligament must be released for joint reduction. A bone graft can be obtained from the distal end of the radius or the olecranon. After realignment of the volar lip fragment, a pin oriented in a dorsal-to-volar direction can be used to maintain the reduction. Occasionally, the volar fragment is very comminuted, and a pull-out wire may be necessary. The pin holding the joint reduced can be removed at 3 weeks to allow gentle active range of motion. At 6 weeks, the pin maintaining the volar fragment can be removed.

A number of authors have included cases of intra-articular phalangeal malunion in their series of primary intra-articular fracture treatment.[27, 183, 202, 323, 327] Light described correction of intra-articular PIP joint malunion in six cases.[183] All his patients had relief of pain, and all but one patient regained substantial motion. Zemel described 14 cases of chronic PIP joint dislocations treated by osteotomy and bone grafting.[327] Motion improved in his patients from 30° to 68°, with some patients monitored for as long as 10 years. Options in the treatment of intra-articular malunion include juxta-articular osteotomy, extra-articular axial correction, partial arthroscopy, total-joint arthroplasty, and arthrodesis.[81, 184, 208, 321, 327] Occasionally, an intra-articular malunion leads to post-traumatic arthrosis and severe soft tissue injury. These more severe injuries may require amputation[58] (Fig. 38–144A to C).

An unusual finding is a reducible malunion. Fahmy and Harvey used the term "malunited fracture," whereas Green and Rowland call this entity a fibrous malunion.[87, 111] These terms refer to a malunion that is correctible on stress radiographs. Treatment of this entity differs in that closed reduction may be possible with a dynamic flexible external fixator.[111]

In the past 30 years, fewer than 200 instances of corrective osteotomy for phalangeal malunion have been reported in the English literature. Most series are small and therefore make comprehensive understanding of this subject difficult. Pichora and associates retrospectively reviewed 16 phalangeal osteotomies.[233] All 16 had bony union by 8 weeks, and alignment was noted to be satisfactory in all cases. MCP motion improved by an average of 3.7° ± 10°, and PIP motion improved by 3.9° ± 10.5°. van der Lei and colleagues retrospectively reviewed nine patients who were treated for phalangeal malunion.[309] Seven achieved adequate correction of their preoperative deformity with no loss of preoperative motion. Two patients were dissatisfied with their results because of continued digital angulation. Lucas and Pfeiffer retrospectively reviewed the experience with 10 phalangeal osteotomies and noted 6 very good, 1 good, and 3

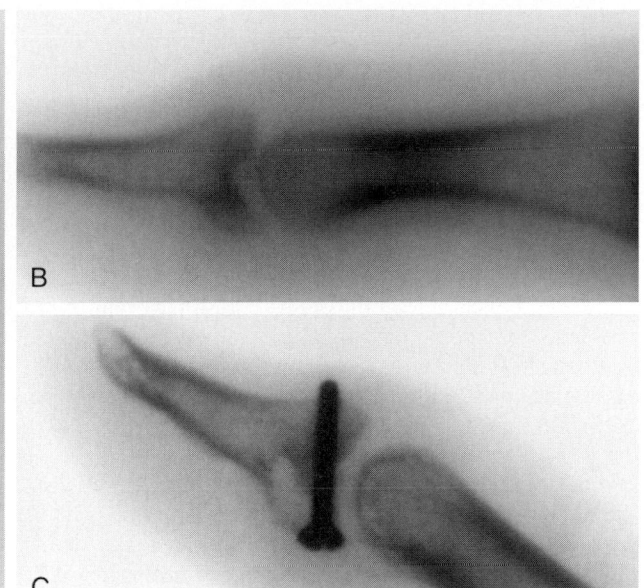

**FIGURE 38–144.** Intra-articular malunion of the base of the distal phalanx in the thumb of a 17-year-old high-school soccer goalie. *A,* Articular radiograph of the impacted articular malunion. *B,* The articular incongruity is well seen on a lateral tomogram. *C,* After intra-articular osteotomy, the defect was separated by an autogenous graft from the distal end of the radius and a small screw.

poor results.[193] They found that the poor results reflected persistent deformity or limited adjacent joint motion. These authors also found that 66% of their patients (metacarpal and phalangeal malunions combined) required removal of hardware. The largest series to date was reported by Buechler and co-workers.[39] They retrospectively reviewed 57 phalangeal malunions treated by osteotomy, rigid fixation, and early motion. Tenocapsulolysis was performed in 50% of the cases. All patients had solid bony union, and 89% achieved a net gain in joint motion. For isolated malunion, good and excellent results were achieved in 96% of the patients.

## MALUNIONS IN CHILDREN

Childhood epiphyseal injuries may lead to metacarpal and phalangeal deformities in adulthood. When the injury occurs near maturity, the deformity may not increase sufficiently to warrant operative intervention. When the injury occurs in early childhood, deformities are often accentuated in adulthood and require realignment osteotomy.[58, 97]

The "booby trap," or subcondylar fracture, noted in children is a neck fracture of the proximal or middle phalanx. These rare fractures often occur in small children, and therefore the reduction is hard to maintain. Moreover, adequate radiographic confirmation of the reduction is difficult in small children with hand immobilization. As always, proper initial treatment will avert progression to more complex malunions. Both open reduction with internal fixation and closed reduction with pin fixation have been advocated as initial treatment.[9, 46, 64, 74, 181, 279] When malunion does occur, open reduction and fixation or excision of the palmar bony spike is often necessary.[45, 212, 279, 290]

Another rare deformity noted in children is a rotational digital deformity caused by finger sucking. Both orthodontic and orthopaedic deformities may develop secondary to finger sucking. These deformities appear to occur in the phalanges and metacarpals. If this habit ends by the age of 6 years (as in a large majority), the dental and digital deformities overwhelmingly resolve. When children continue to suck their fingers past 6 years of age, remodeling is unlikely to resolve the digital deformity, and metacarpal or phalangeal corrective osteotomy is necessary.[190, 241, 245]

## NONUNION

Fractures of the metacarpals and phalanges have a high rate of union, especially when the injury is closed. The incidence of nonunion ranges from 0.2% to 0.7%.[9, 25] The definition of when to consider a fracture a nonunion is controversial. Radiographic union may take up to 1 year, and resolution of symptoms (and healing) varies between patients but may be as short as 3 weeks.[12, 150, 280, 290] Wray and Glunk defined delayed union as the absence of radiographic union at 1 month and nonunion as the absence of union at 3 months.[325] Jupiter and colleagues defined delayed union and nonunion in the metacarpals and phalanges as one entity.[150] This entity is defined as "a lack of bony consolidation in the radiograph and evidence of motion by clinical examination more than four months after the initial injury."[150] This definition is a functional one in that immobilization of the hand for longer than 3 months leads to a functional impairment that may require other reconstructive procedures.[188] If delayed union/nonunion can be diagnosed early, operative management can avert these secondary treatment complications.

As with other bones in the body, nonunion in the hand can be classified as either atrophic or hypertrophic. The classification of Weber and Cech is applicable when evaluating nonunion in the hand.[316] Hypertrophic nonunion is rare in the hand and has been shown to heal by applying stable fixation without disturbing the nonunion.[150, 269] When atrophic nonunion occurs, all fibrous tissue must be removed and supplemental bone grafting may be needed to fill the resultant gap.[290]

Causes of nonunion in the hand include loss of bone

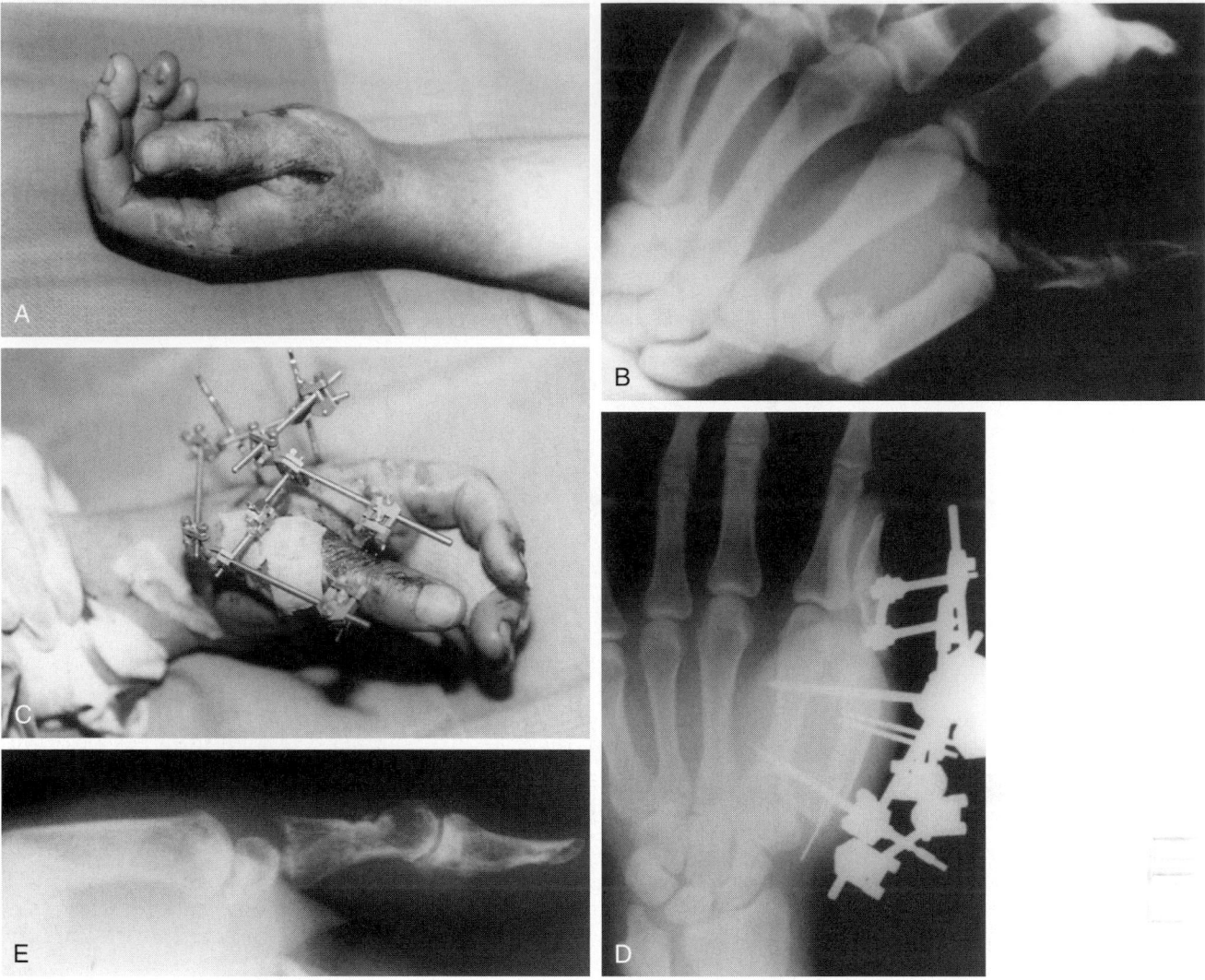

**Figure 38–145.** Complex devascularizing injury to the thumb of a laborer. After skeletal stabilization, nonunion of the proximal phalanx at its base developed. *A,* Initial clinical appearance of the thumb. *B,* The initial radiograph revealed a complex fracture of the base of the metacarpal, as well as the proximal phalanx. *C,* After revascularization, a combination of Kirschner wires and external fixation was used. *D,* Radiograph of the skeletal stabilization. *E,* Nonunion of the base of the proximal phalanx associated with instability during pinch.          *Illustration continued on following page*

substance, inadequate mobilization, fracture distraction (often resulting from inadequate pin fixation or soft tissue interposition), and sepsis.[7, 45, 46, 58, 129, 150, 188, 224, 290] Similar to malunion, indications for operative treatment of nonunion depend on both the symptoms and hand function.

Methods of treatment recommended for nonunion in the hand are similar to those suggested for other parts of the skeletal system and include observation, electrical stimulation, fixation, and fixation with bone grafting.[58, 108, 130, 138, 150, 224, 246, 290] Methods of fixation vary between surgeon and should be individualized to the pathology.[108, 129, 138, 150, 168, 188, 201] In viable nonunions, stable internal fixation is all that is needed. Infected nonunion may benefit from débridement, external fixation, and delayed bone grafting. Finally, patients undergoing tenolysis, capsulotomy, or both procedures may do well enough with stable fixation to allow early motion, as seen in malunions. When a finger is compromised by severe joint stiffness or tendon loss, salvage procedures,

including arthrodesis and amputation, may be indicated[150] (Fig. 38–145A to K).

Distal phalangeal crush injuries often lead to nonunion.[46, 58, 141] The nail plate functions as an external splint and allows stabilization and clinical healing. When a fracture occurs at the base of the distal phalanx, the nail plate is ineffective in providing stability and a painful fibrous nonunion may develop. In these cases, simple K-wires may afford enough stability for healing.[109, 246]

Jupiter and associates retrospectively reviewed 25 consecutive phalangeal and metacarpal nonunions treated by fixation with or without bone grafting.[150] All nonunions healed at an average of 11.4 weeks. In their review, they noted marked clinical improvement in the seven patients treated by internal fixation. In contrast, Wray and Glunk reviewed 13 patients with delayed union, malunion, or nonunion treated by K-pin fixation and found satisfactory results with early motion and K-wire fixation.[325] Regardless of the method of fixation, the goal is still function. If the patient is asymptomatic and uses the

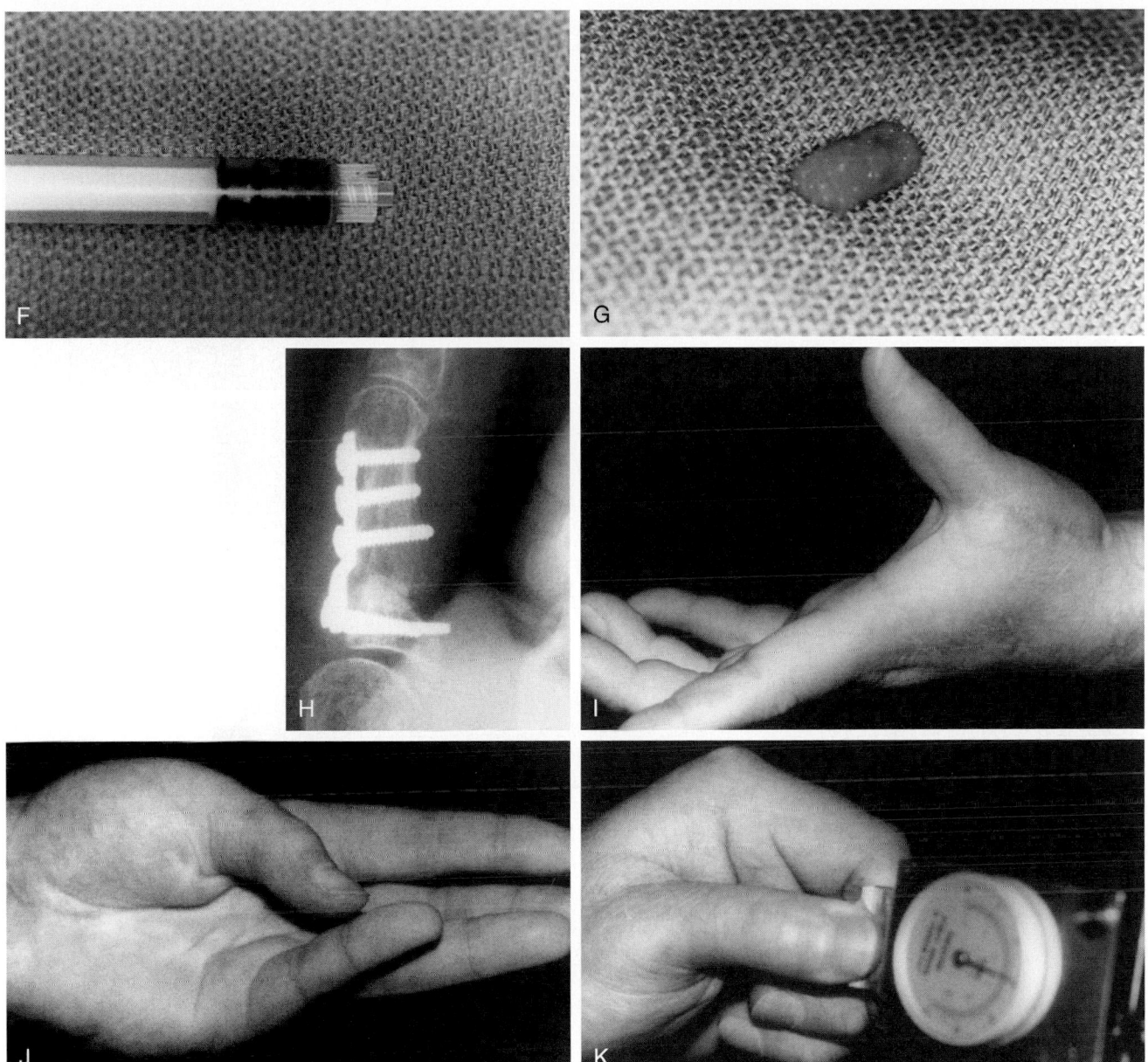

**FIGURE 38–145** *Continued.* F, G, A small compact cancellous graft was created by impacting the cancellous bone in a small syringe. H, Stable fixation was achieved with a condylar plate. I–K, Excellent functional result with maintenance of the thumb-index webspace and stable pinch.

hand without any difficulties, radiographic nonunion should be ignored.

### REFERENCES

1. Abouna, J.M.; Brown, H. The treatment of mallet finger. The results in a series of 148 consecutive cases and a review of the literature. Br J Surg 55:653–667, 1968.
2. Agee, J.M. Unstable fracture-dislocations of the proximal interphalangeal joint of the fingers. Clin Orthop 214:101–112, 1987.
3. Arafa, M.; Haines, J.; Noble, J.; Carden, D. Immediate mobilization of fractures of the neck of the fifth metacarpal. Injury 14:277–278, 1986.
4. Asche, G. Possibility of the para-articular finger fractures with external minifixation. Handchir Mikrochir Plast Chir 16:195–205, 1984.
5. Auchincloss, J.M. Mallet finger injuries: A prospective controlled trial of internal and external splintage. Hand 14:168–173, 1982.
6. Baratz, M.E.; Divelbiss, B. Fixation of phalangeal fractures. Hand Clin 13:541–555, 1997.
7. Bartelmann, U.; Kotas, J.; Landsleitner, B. Causes for reoperation after osteosyntheses of the finger and mid-hand fractures. Handchir Mikrochir Plast Chir 29:204–208, 1997.
8. Barton, N.J. Intraarticular fractures and fracture-dislocations. In: Bowers, W., ed. The Interphalangeal Joints. New York, Churchill Livingstone, 1987, pp. 77–93.
9. Barton, N.J. Fractures of the phalanges of the hand in children. Hand 11:134–143, 1979.
10. Barton, N.J. Fractures and joint injuries of the hand. In: Wilson, J.W., ed. Watson-Jones Fractures and Joint Injuries, 6th ed. Edinburgh, Churchill Livingstone, 1983, pp. 739–788.
11. Barton, N.J. Fractures of the hand. J Bone Joint Surg Br 66:159–167, 1984.
12. Barton, N.J. Fractures of the shafts of the phalanges of the hand. Hand 11:110–133, 1979.
13. Belsky, M.R.; Eaton, R.G.; Lane, L.B. Closed reduction and internal fixation of proximal phalangeal fractures. J Hand Surg [Am] 9:725–729, 1984.

14. Belsky, M.R.; Ruby, L.K.; Millender, L.H. Injuries of the finger and thumb joints. Contemp Orthop 7:39–48, 1983.

15. Belsky, M.R.; Eaton, R.G. Closed percutaneous wiring of metacarpal and phalangeal fractures. In: Tubiana, R., ed. The Hand, Vol. 2. Philadelphia, W.B. Saunders, 1985, p. 790.

16. Belsole, R.J.; Greene, T.L. Comparative strengths of internal fixation techniques. J Hand Surg [Am] 10:315–316, 1985.

17. Belsole, R. Physiologic fixation of displaced and unstable fractures of the hand. Orthop Clin North Am 11:393–404, 1980.

18. Bennett, E.H. Fractures of the metacarpal bones. Dublin J Med Sci 73:72, 1882.

19. Billing, L.; Gedda, K.Q. Roentgen examination of Bennett's fracture. Acta Radiol 38:471–476, 1952.

20. Bilos, Z.J.; Eskestrand, T. External fixator use in comminuted gunshot fractures of the proximal phalanx. J Hand Surg 4:357–359, 1979.

21. Black, D.M.; Mann, R.J.; Constine, R.; et al. The stability of internal fixation in the proximal phalanx. J Hand Surg [Am] 11:672–677, 1986.

22. Bloem, J.J. The treatment and prognosis of uncomplicated dislocated fractures of the metacarpals and phalanges. Arch Chir Neerl 23:55–65, 1971.

23. Boehler, L. Die Technik der Knockenbruchbehandlung. Wien, Aufl. Maudrich, 1951.

24. Bora, F.W., Jr.; Didizan, N.H. The treatment of injuries to the carpometacarpal joint of the little finger. J Bone Joint Surg Am 56:1459–1463, 1974.

25. Borgeskov, S. Conservative therapy for fractures of the phalanges and metacarpals. Acta Chir Scand 133:123–130, 1967.

26. Boteilheiro, J.C. Overlapping of fingers due to malunion of a phalanx corrected by a metacarpal rotational osteotomy—report of two cases. J Hand Surg [Br] 10:389–390, 1985.

27. Bouchon, Y.; Merle, M.; Foucher, G.; Michon, J. Les cals vicieux des metacarpiens et des phalanges: Resultant du traitment chirurgical. Rev Chir Orthop 62:542–555, 1982.

28. Boulas, H.J.; Herren, A.; Buchler, U. Osteochondral metatarsophalangeal autografts for traumatic articular metacarpophalangeal defects: A preliminary report. J Hand Surg [Am] 18:1086–1092, 1993.

29. Bowers, W.H.; Fajgenbaum, D.M. Closed rupture of the volar plate of the distal interphalangeal joint. J Bone Joint Surg Am 61:146, 1979.

30. Bowers, W.H.; Hurst, L.C. Gamekeeper's thumb. Evaluation by arthroscopy and stress roentgenography. J Bone Joint Surg Am 59:519–524, 1977.

31. Bowers, W.H. The anatomy of the interphalangeal joints. In: Bowers, W.H., ed. The Interphalangeal Joint. New York, Churchill Livingstone, 1987, pp. 2–13.

32. Breen, T.F.; Gelberman, R.H.; Jupiter, J.B. Intraarticular fractures of the basilar joint of the thumb. Hand Clin 4:491–501, 1988.

33. Brennwald, J. Bone healing in the hand. Clin Orthop 214:7–10, 1987.

34. Broad, C.P. Non-union of a fractured fifth metacarpal. Postgrad Med J 44:817–818, 1968.

35. Brooks, D. Splint for mallet fingers. BMJ 2:1238, 1964.

36. Brown, P. The management of phalangeal and metacarpal fractures. Surg Clin North Am 53:1393–1437, 1973.

37. Buechler, U. Personal communication, 1989.

38. Buechler, U.; Fischer, T. Use of a minicondylar plate for metacarpal and phalangeal periarticular injuries. Clin Orthop 214:53–58, 1987.

39. Buechler, U.; Gupta, A.; Ruf, S. Corrective osteotomy for post-traumatic malunion of the phalanges in the hand. J Hand Surg [Br] 21:33–42, 1996.

40. Bunnell, S. Surgery of the Hand, 2nd ed. Philadelphia, J.B. Lippincott, 1948, pp. 712–715.

41. Burkhalter, W. Newsletter #18. Denver, American Society for Surgery of the Hand, 1981.

42. Burkhalter, W.; Reyes, P. Closed treatment of fractures in the hand. Bull Hosp Jt Dis 44:145–151, 1984.

43. Burton, R.I.; Eaton, R.G. Common hand injuries in the athlete. Orthop Clin North Am 4:809–838, 1973.

44. Burton, R.I.; Pellegrini, V.D. Surgical management of basal joint arthritis of the thumb, part II: Ligament reconstruction with tendon interposition arthroplasty. J Hand Surg [Am] 11:324–332, 1986.

45. Butler, B.; Neviaser, R.J.; Adams, J.P. Complication of treatment of injuries to the hand. In: Epps CP, ed. Complication in Orthopaedic Surgery, 3rd ed. Philadelphia, J.B. Lippincott, 1978, pp. 359–361.

46. Butler, B.; Rankin, E.A. Complications of hand surgery. In: Epps CP, ed. Complication in Orthopaedic Surgery, 3rd ed. Philadelphia, J.B. Lippincott, 1978, pp. 389–401.

47. Butt, W.D. Fractures of the hand, II. Statistical review. Can Med Assoc J 86:775–779, 1962.

48. Calkins, M.S.; Burkhalter, W.; Reyes, F. Traumatic segmental bone defects in the upper extremity. J Bone Joint Surg Am 69:19–27, 1987.

49. Cannon, S.; Dowd, G.; Williams, D.; et al. A long-term study following Bennett's fracture. J Hand Surg [Br] 11:426–431, 1986.

50. Carroll, R.E. Arthrodeses of the carpometacarpal joint of the thumb: A review of patients with a long postoperative period. Clin Orthop 220:106–110, 1987.

51. Casscells, S.W.; Strange, T.B. Intramedullary wire fixation of mallet finger. Follow-up note. J Bone Joint Surg Am 51:1018–1019, 1969.

52. Chait, C.A.; Cort, A.; Brown, S. Metacarpal reconstruction in compound contaminated injuries of the hand. Hand 13:152–157, 1981.

53. Chamay, A. A distally based dorsal and triangular tendinous flap for direct access to the proximal interphalangeal joint. Ann Chir Main Memb Super 7:179–183, 1988.

54. Charnley, J. The Closed Treatment of Common Fractures, 3rd ed. Edinburgh, Churchill Livingstone, 1974, p. 150.

55. Chen, S.U.; Wei, F.C.; Chen, H.C.; et al. Miniature plates and screws in acute complex hand injury. J Trauma 37:238–242, 1994.

56. Chow, S.P.; Pun, W.K.; So, Y.C.; et al. A prospective study of 245 open digital fractures of the hand. J Hand Surg [Br] 16:138–140, 1991.

57. Clendenin, M.B.; Smith, R.J. Fifth metacarpal hamate arthrodesis for posttraumatic osteoarthritis. J Hand Surg [Am] 9:374–378, 1984.

58. Clinkscales, G.S., Jr. Complications in the management of fractures in hand injuries. South Med J 63:704–707, 1970.

59. Cooney, W.; Chao, E. Biomechanical analysis of static forces in the thumb during hand function. J Bone Joint Surg Am 59:27–36, 1977.

60. Cooney, W.; Lucca, M.; Chao, E.; et al. The kinesiology of the thumb trapeziometacarpal joint. J Bone Joint Surg Am 63:1371–1381, 1981.

61. Coonrad, R.N.; Goldner, J.L. A study of the pathological findings and treatment in soft tissue injury of the thumb metacarpophalangeal joint. J Bone Joint Surg Am 50:439–451, 1968.

62. Coonrad, R.; Pohlman, M. Impacted fractures in the proximal portion of the proximal phalanx of the finger. J Bone Joint Surg Am 57:1291–1296, 1969.

63. Crawford, G.P. Screw fixation for certain fractures of the phalanges and metacarpals. J Bone Joint Surg Am 58:487–492, 1976.

64. Crick, J.C.; Franco, R.S.; Conners, J.J. Fractures about the interphalangeal joints in children. J Orthop Trauma 1:318–325, 1988.

65. Crockett, D.J. Rigid fixation of bone of the hand using K-wires bonded with acrylic resin. Hand 6:106–107, 1974.

66. Dabezies, E.J.; Schulte, J.P. Fixation of metacarpal and phalangeal fractures with miniature plates and screws. J Hand Surg [Am] 11:283–288, 1986.

67. DaCruz, D.J.; Slade, R.J.; Malone, W. Fractures of the distal phalanges. J Hand Surg [Br] 13:350–352, 1988.

68. Dammisse, I.G.; Lloyd, G.J. Injuries to the fifth carpometacarpal region. Can J Surg 22:240–244, 1979.

69. DeBoer, A.; Robinson, P.H. Ray transposition by intercarpal osteotomy after loss of the fourth digit. J Hand Surg [Am] 14:379–381, 1989.

70. Dennys, L.J.; Hurst, L.N.; Cox, J. Management of proximal interphalangeal joint fractures using a new dynamic traction method and early active motion. J Hand Ther 5:16, 1992.

71. Dennyson, W.G.; Stother, I.G. Carpometacarpal dislocations of the little finger. Hand 8:161–164, 1976.

72. Diao, E. Metacarpal fixation. Hand Clin 13:557–571, 1997.

73. Diwaker, H.N.; Stothard, J. The role of internal fixation in closed fractures of the proximal phalanges and metacarpals in adults. J Hand Surg [Br] 1:103–108, 1986.

74. Dixon, G.L., Jr.; Moon, N.F. Rotational supracondylar fractures of the proximal phalanx in children. Clin Orthop 83:151–156, 1972.

75. Dobyns, J.H.; Beckenbaugh, R.D.; Bryan, R.S.; et al. Fractures of the hand and wrist. In: Flynn, J.E., ed. Hand Surgery, 3rd ed. Baltimore, Williams & Wilkins, 1982, pp. 111–180.

76. Dobyns, J.H.; Linscheid, R.L.; Cooney, W.P., 3rd. Fractures and dislocations of the wrist and hand, then and now. J Hand Surg [Am] 8:687–690, 1983.

77. Dray, G.; Eaton, R. Dislocation in the digits. In: Green, D.P., ed. Operative Hand Surgery, 2nd ed., Vol. 1. New York, Churchill Livingstone, 1988, p. 795.

78. Duncan, K.H.; Jupiter, J.B. Intraarticular osteotomy for malunion of metacarpal head fractures. J Hand Surg [Am] 14:888–893, 1989.

79. Duran, R.J.; Houser, R.G.; Coleman, C.R.; Postelwaite, D.S. A preliminary report on the use of controlled passive motion following flexor tendon repairs in zones II and III. J Hand Surg 1:79, 1976.

80. Eaton, R.G. Joint Injuries of the Hand. Springfield, IL, Charles C Thomas, 1971, p. 23.

81. Eaton, R.G.; Malerich, M.M. Volar plate arthroplasty of the proximal interphalangeal joint: A review of 10 years' experience. J Hand Surg 5:260–268, 1980.

82. Ebraheim, N.A.; Biyani, A.; Wong, F.Y.; Cornicelli, S. Management of infected defect nonunion of the metacarpals, a case report. Am J Orthop 26:362–364, 1997.

83. Edward, G.S.; O'Brien, E.T.; Hechman, M.M. Retrograde cross pinning of transverse metacarpal and phalangeal fractures. Hand 14:141–148, 1982.

84. Eigenholtz, S.N.; Rizzon, P.C. Fracture of the neck of the fifth metacarpal bone—is overtreatment justified? JAMA 178:425–426, 1961.

85. Elliott, R.A. Splints for mallet and boutonnière deformities. Plast Reconstr Surg 52:282–285, 1973.

86. Emmett, J.E.; Breck, L.W. A review and analysis of 11,000 fractures seen in a private practice of orthopaedic surgery. J Bone Joint Surg Am 40:1169–1175, 1958.

87. Fahmy, N.R.M.; Harvey, R.A. The "s" quattro in the management of fractures in the hand. J Hand Surg [Br] 17:321–331, 1992.

88. Flatt, A.E. Closed and open fracture of the hand. Fundamentals of management. Postgrad Med 39:17–26, 1966.

89. Foliart, D.E. Swanson silicone finger joint implants. A review of the literature regarding long-term complications. J Hand Surg [Am] 20:445–449, 1995.

90. Ford, D.J.; Ali, M.S.; Steel, W.M. Fractures of the fifth metacarpal neck: Is reduction or immobilization necessary? J Hand Surg [Br] 14:165–167, 1989.

91. Foster, R.J.; Hastings, H., II. Treatment of Bennett, Rolando, and vertical intraarticular trapezial fractures. Clin Orthop 214:121–129, 1987.

92. Frank, W.E.; Dobyns, J.H. Surgical pathology of collateral ligament injuries of the thumb. Clin Orthop 83:102–114, 1972.

93. Freeland, A.E. External fixation for skeletal stabilization of severe open fractures of the hand. Clin Orthop 214:93–100, 1987.

94. Freeland, A.E.; Jabaley, M.E.; Burkhalter, W.E.; Chaves, A.M.V. Delayed primary bone grafting in the hand and wrist after traumatic bone loss. J Hand Surg [Am] 9:22–28, 1984.

95. Freeland, A.E.; Jabaley, M.E.; Hughes, J.L. Stable Fixation of the Hand and Wrist. New York, Springer-Verlag, 1987.

96. Froimson, A.T. Tendon arthroplasty of the trapeziometacarpal joint. Clin Orthop 70:191–199, 1970.

97. Froimson, A.I. Osteotomy for digital deformity. J Hand Surg 6:585–589, 1981.

98. Futami, T.; Nakamura, K.; Shimajiri, I. Osteotomy for trapeziometacarpal arthrosis: 4 (1–6) year follow-up of 12 cases. Acta Orthop Scand 63:462–464, 1992.

99. Gedda, K.O. Studies on Bennett fractures: Anatomy, roentgenology, and therapy. Acta Chir Scand Suppl 193:5, 1954.

100. Gedda, K.O.; Moberg, E. Open reduction and osteosynthesis of the so-called Bennett's fracture in the carpometacarpal joint of the thumb. Acta Orthop Scand 22:249–256, 1953.

101. Geiger, K.R.; Karpman, R.R. Necrosis of the skin over the metacarpal as a result of functional fracture-bracing: A report of three cases. J Bone Joint Surg Am 71:1199–1202, 1989.

102. Gelberman, R.H.; Vance, R.M.; Zakaib, G.S. Fractures at the base of the thumb: Treatment with oblique traction. J Bone Joint Surg Am 61:260–262, 1979.

103. Gerber, C.; Senn, E.; Matter, P. Skier's thumb. Surgical treatment of recent injuries to the ulnar collateral ligament of the thumb metacarpophalangeal joint. Am J Sports Med 9:171–177, 1981.

104. Giachino, A.A. A surgical technique to treat a malunited symptomatic Bennett's fracture. J Hand Surg [Am] 21:149–151, 1996.

105. Gigis, P.I.; Kuczynski, K. The distal interphalangeal joints of the human fingers. J Hand Surg 7:176–182, 1982.

106. Gingrass, R.P.; Fehring, B.H.T.; Matloub, H. Intraosseous wiring of complex hand fractures. Plast Reconstr Surg 66:383–394, 1980.

107. Gore, D.R. Carpometacarpal dislocation producing compression of the deep branch of the ulnar nerve. J Bone Joint Surg Am 53:1387–1390, 1971.

108. Goudot, B.; Voche, P.H.; Bour, C.H.; Merle, M. Osteotsynthese par mini-plaque en "L" des fractures metaphysaires et metaphyso-epiphysaires des metacarpiens et des phalages. Rev Chir Orthop 77:130–134, 1991.

109. Green, D.P. Complication of phalangeal and metacarpal fractures. Hand Clin 2:307–328, 1986.

110. Green, D.P.; Anderson, J.R. Closed reduction and percutaneous pin fixation of fractured phalanges. J Bone Joint Surg Am 55:1651–1654, 1973.

111. Green, D.P.; Rowland, S.A. Fractures and dislocations in the hand. In: Rockwood, C.A.; Green, D.P., eds. Fractures and Dislocations. Philadelphia, J.B. Lippincott, 1984, pp. 317–323.

112. Green, D.; O'Brien, E. Fractures of the thumb metacarpal. South Med J 65:807–814, 1972.

113. Greene, T.L.; Noellert, R.C.; Belsole, R.J. Treatment of unstable metacarpal and phalangeal fractures with tension band wiring techniques. Clin Orthop 214:78–84, 1987.

114. Griffiths, J. Fractures at the base of the first metacarpal bone. J Bone Joint Surg Br 46:712–719, 1964.

115. Gross, M.S.; Gelberman, R.H. Metacarpal rotational osteotomy. J Hand Surg [Am] 10:105–108, 1985.

116. Gunter, G.S. Traumatic avulsion of the insertion of the flexor digitorum profundus insertion in athletes. J Hand Surg 4:461–464, 1979.

117. Gunther, S.F. The carpometacarpal joints. Orthop Clin North Am 15:259–277, 1989.

118. Gustilo, R.B. Management of infected fractures, Part IV. Instr Course Lect 31:18–29, 1982.

119. Haines, R.W. The mechanism of rotation at the first carpometacarpal joint. J Anat 78:44, 1944.

120. Hall, R.F. Treatment of metacarpal and phalangeal fractures in noncompliant patients. Clin Orthop 214:31–36, 1987.

121. Hallberg, D.; Lindholm, A. Subcutaneous rupture of the extensor tendon of the distal phalanx of the finger, mallet finger: Brief review of the literature and report on 127 cases treated conservatively. Acta Chir Scand 119:260–267, 1960.

122. Hartwig, R.H.; Louis, D.S. Multiple carpometacarpal dislocations. J Bone Joint Surg Am 61:906–908, 1979.

123. Hasegawa, T.; Yamano, Y. Arthroplasty of proximal interphalangeal joint using costal cartilage grafts. J Hand Surg [Br] 17:583–585, 1992.

124. Hasting, H. Hand fractures in children. Clin Orthop 188:120–130, 1984.

125. Hastings, H., II; Carroll, C., IV. Treatment of closed articular fractures of the metacarpophalangeal and proximal interphalangeal joints. Hand Clin 4:503–528, 1988.

126. Hastings, H., 2nd.; Ernst, J.M. Dynamic external fixation for fractures of the proximal interphalangeal joint. Hand Clin 9:659–674, 1993.

127. Hastings, H., II. Unstable metacarpal and phalangeal fracture treatment with screws and plates. Clin Orthop 214:38–52, 1987.

128. Hazlett, J.W. Carpometacarpal dislocations other than the thumb: A report of 11 cases. Can J Surg 11:315–322, 1968.

129. Heim, U.; Pfeiffer, K.M. Internal Fixation of Small Fractures, 3rd ed. New York, Springer-Verlag, 1988.

130. Heim, U. The treatment of nonunions in the bones of the hand. In: Chapibal G., ed. Pseudarthroses and Their Treatment. Stuttgart, Germany, George Thieme, 1979, pp. 168–169.

131. Holbrook, T.L.; Grazier, K.; Kelsey, J.; Stauffer, R. The Frequency of Occurrence, Impact, and Cost of Selected Musculoskeletal Conditions in the United States. Chicago, American Academy of Orthopaedic Surgeons, 1984, pp. 1–87.

132. Holst-Nielsen, F. Subcapital fractures of the four ulnar metacarpal bones. Hand 8:290–293, 1976.

133. Honner, R. Acute and chronic flexor and extensor mechanism injuries at the distal joint. In: Bower, W.H., ed. The Interphalangeal Joints. Edinburgh, Churchill Livingstone, 1987, pp. 111–118.

134. Hotchkiss, R.N. Compass Proximal Interphalangeal (PIP) Joint Hinge: Surgical Technique. Product Guide. Memphis, TN, Smith & Nephew Richards, 1993.

135. Howard, L.D., Jr. Fractures of the small bones of the hand. Plast Reconstr Surg 29:334–335, 1962.

136. Huffaker, W.H.; Wray, R.C.; Weeks, P.M. Factors influencing final range of motion in the fingers after fractures of the hand. Plast Reconstr Surg 63:83–87, 1979.

137. Hunter, J.M.; Cowen, N.J. Fifth metacarpal fracture in a compensation clinic population. J Bone Joint Surg Am 52:1159–1165, 1970.

138. Ireland, M.L.; Taleisnik, J. Nonunion of metacarpal extraarticular fractures in children: Report of two cases and review of the literature. J Pediatr Orthop 6:352–355, 1986.

139. Iselin, F. Arthroplasty of the proximal interphalangeal joint after trauma. Hand 7:41–42, 1975.

140. Ishida, O.; Ikuta, Y.; Kuroki, H. Ipsilateral osteochondral grafting for finger joint repair. J Hand Surg [Am] 19:372–377, 1994.

141. Itoh, Y.; Uchinishi, K.; Oka, Y. Treatment of pseudarthrosis of the distal phalanx with the palmar midline approach. J Hand Surg 8:80–84, 1983.

142. Jabaley, M.E.; Freeland, A.E. Rigid internal fixation in the hand: 104 cases. Plast Reconstr Surg 7:288–298, 1986.

143. Jahss, S.A. Fractures of the proximal phalanges. A new method of reduction and immobilization. J Bone Joint Surg Am 20:178–186, 1938.

144. James, J.I.P. Fractures of the proximal and middle phalanges of the fingers. Acta Orthop Scand 32:401–412, 1962.

145. James, J.I.P. The assessment and management of the injured hand. Hand 2:97–105, 1970.

146. Jebson, P.J.L.; Blair, W.F. Correction of malunited Bennett's fracture by intra-articular osteotomy: A report of two cases. J Hand Surg [Am] 22:441–444, 1997.

147. Jones, W.W. Biomechanics of small bone fixation. Clin Orthop 214:11–18, 1987.

148. Joshi, B.B. Percutaneous internal fixation of fractures of the proximal phalanges. Hand 8:86–92, 1976.

149. Jupiter, J.B.; Axelrod, T.S.; Belsky, M.R. Fractures and dislocations of the hand. In: Browner, B.D.; Jupiter, J.B.; Levine, A.M.; Trafton, P.G., eds. Skeletal Trauma, 2nd ed. Philadelphia, W.B. Saunders, 1998, pp. 1225–1342.

150. Jupiter, J.B.; Koniuch, M.; Smith, R.J. The management of delayed unions and nonunions of the metacarpals and phalanges. J Hand Surg [Am] 4:457–466, 1985.

151. Jupiter, J.B.; Ring, D. A comparison of early and late reconstruction of malunited fractures of the distal end of the radius. J Bone Joint Surg Am 78:739–748, 1996.

152. Jupiter, J.B.; Sheppard, J.E. Tension wire fixation of avulsion fractures in the hand. Clin Orthop 214:113–120, 1987.

153. Jupiter, J.B.; Silver, M.A. Fractures of the metacarpals and phalanges. In: Chapman, M.W., ed. Operative Orthopaedics. Philadelphia, J.B. Lippincott, 1988, pp. 1235–1250.

154. Kapandji, A.I. Osteosynthesis using perpendicular pins in the treatment of fractures and malunions of the neck of the fifth metacarpal bone. Ann Chir Main Memb Super 12:45–55, 1993.

155. Kapanji, A.I. Selective radiology of the first carpometacarpal joint. In: Tubiana, R., ed. The Hand. Philadelphia, W.B. Saunders, 1985, pp. 635–644.

156. Kaplan, E.B. Mallet or baseball finger. Surgery 7:784–791, 1940.

157. Kaplan, E.B. Functional and Surgical Anatomy of the Hand, 2nd ed. Philadelphia, J.B. Lippincott, 1965.

158. Kaplan, E.B. Dorsal dislocation of the metacarpophalangeal joint of the index finger. J Bone Joint Surg Am 39:1081–1086, 1957.

159. Kaplan, L. The treatment of fractures and dislocations of the hand and fingers. Technic of unpadded casts for carpal, metacarpal, and phalangeal fractures. Surg Clin North Am 20:1695–1720, 1940.

160. Kaye, J.J.; Lister, G.D. Another use for the Brewerton view. J Hand Surg 3:603, 1978.

161. Kelsey, J.L.; Pastides, H.; Kreiger, N.; et al. Upper Extremity Disorders. A Survey of Their Frequency and Cost in the United States. St. Louis, C.V. Mosby, 1980.

162. Kilbourne, B.C.; Paul, E.G. The use of small bone screws in the treatment of metacarpal, metatarsal, and phalangeal fractures. J Bone Joint Surg Am 40:375–383, 1958.

163. Kleinman, W.B.; Grantham, S.A. Multiple volar carpometacarpal joint dislocations. J Hand Surg 3:377–382, 1978.

164. Koch, S.L. Disabilities of the hand resulting from loss of joint function. JAMA 104:30–35, 1935.

165. Kuczynski, K. The proximal interphalangeal joint. J Bone Joint Surg Br 50:656–663, 1968.

166. Kuczynski, K. Carpometacarpal joint of the human thumb. J Anat 118:119–126, 1974.

167. Kuczynski, K. Lesser-known aspects of the proximal interphalangeal joints of the human hand. Hand 7:31–34, 1975.

168. Lagarev, A.A.; Panfilov, V.M. Bone arthroplasty in ununited fractures, pseudarthroses, and improperly united fractures of the metacarpal bones and the phalanges digitorum manus. Ortop Travmatol Protez 10:44, 1980.

169. Lamb, D. Training in hand surgery. J Hand Surg [Br] 15:148–150, 1990.

170. Lamb, D.W.; Angarita, G. Ulnar instability of the metacarpophalangeal joint of the thumb. J Hand Surg [Br] 10:113–114, 1985.

171. Lamb, D.W.; Abernathy, P.A.; Raine, P.A.M. Unstable fractures of the metacarpal (a method of treatment by transverse wire fixation to intact metacarpals). Hand 5:43–48, 1973.

172. Lambotte, A. Contribution to conservative surgery of the injured hand. Arch FrancoBelges Chir 21:759, 1928.

173. Lamphier, T.A. Improper reduction of fractures of the proximal phalanges of fingers. Am J Surg 94:926–930, 1957.

174. Landsmeer, J.M.F. The anatomy of the dorsal aponeurosis of the human finger and its functional significance. Anat Rec 104:31, 1949.

175. Lane, C.S. Detecting occult fractures of the metacarpal head: The Brewerton view. J Hand Surg 2:131–133, 1977.

176. Lazar, G.; Shulter-Ellis, F.P. Intramedullary structure of human metacarpals. J Hand Surg 5:477, 1980.

177. Leddy, J.P. Avulsions of the flexor digitorum profundus. Hand Clin 1:77–83, 1985.

178. Leddy, L.P.; Packer, J.W. Avulsion of the profundus insertion in athletes. J Hand Surg 4:461–464, 1979.

179. Lee, M.L.H. Intraarticular and periarticular fractures of the phalanges. J Bone Joint Surg Br 45:103–109, 1963.

180. Leonard, M.H. Blocking spur on proximal phalanx [letter]. Hand 13:321, 1981.

181. Leonard, M.H.; Dubravchik, P. Management of fractured fingers in the child. Clin Orthop 73:160–168, 1970.

182. Lester, B.; Mallik, A. Impending malunion of the hand. Treatment of subacute, malaligned fractures. Clin Orthop 327:55–62, 1986.

183. Light, T.R. Salvage of intraarticular malunions of the hand and wrist, the role of realignment osteotomy. Clin Orthop 214:130–135, 1987.

184. Linscheid, R.L.; Murray, P.M.; Vidal, M.A.; Beckenbaugh, R.D. Development of a surface replacement arthroplasty for proximal interphalangeal joints. J Hand Surg [Am] 22:286–298, 1997.

185. Lipton, H.A.; Skoff, H.; Jupiter, J.B. The management of hand injuries. New Dev Med 3:5–42, 1988.

186. Lister, G. Intraosseous wiring of the digital skeleton. J Hand Surg 3:427–435, 1978.

187. Littler, J.W. On the adaptability of man's hand (with reference to the equiangular curve). Hand 5:187–191, 1973.

188. Littler, J.W. Metacarpal reconstruction. J Bone Joint Surg 29:723–727, 1947.

189. Littler, J.W.; Thompson, J.S. Surgical and functional anatomy. In: Bowers, W.H., ed. The Interphalangeal Joints. New York, Churchill Livingstone, 1987, pp. 14–20.

190. Lloyd-Roberts, G.C. Orthopaedics in Infancy and Childhood. London, Butterworth, 1971.

191. London, P.S. Sprains and fractures involving the interphalangeal joints. Hand 3:155–158, 1971.

192. Lubahn, J.D. Dorsal fracture-dislocations of the proximal interphalangeal joint. Hand Clin 4:15–24, 1988.

193. Lucas, G.L.; Pfeiffer, C.M. Osteotomy of the metacarpals and phalanges stabilized by AO plates and screws. Ann Chir Main 8:30–38, 1989.

194. Malerich, M.M.; Eaton, R.G. Complete dislocation of a little finger metacarpophalangeal joint treated by closed technique. J Trauma 20:424–425, 1980.

195. Manketelow, R.T.; Mahoney, J.L. Step osteotomy: A precise rotation osteotomy to correct scissoring deformities of the fingers. Plast Reconstr Surg 68:571–576, 1981.

196. Mann, R.J.; Black, D.; Constine, R.; et al. A quantitative comparison of metacarpal fracture stability with five different methods of internal fixation. J Hand Surg [Am] 10:1024–1028, 1985.

197. Margles, S. Intraarticular fractures of the metacarpophalangeal and proximal interphalangeal joints. Hand Clin 4:67–74, 1988.

198. Martin, B.F. The tendons of the flexor digitorum profundus. J Anat 92:602–608, 1958.

199. Massengill, J.B.; Alexander, H.; Langrana, N.; et al. A phalangeal fracture model—quantitative analysis of rigidity and failure. J Hand Surg 7:264–270, 1982.

200. Mast, J.; Jakob, R.; Ganz, R. Planning and Reduction Technique in Fracture Surgery. Berlin, Heidelberg, Springer-Verlag, 1989.

201. Matev, I. Treatment of ununited fractures of the metacarpal bones and finger phalanges. Ortop Travmatol Protez 27:64–68, 1966.

202. McCue, F.; Honner, R.; Marriott, C.; et al. Athletic injuries of the proximal interphalangeal joint requiring surgical treatment. J Bone Joint Surg Am 52:938–956, 1970.

203. McElfresh, E.C.; Dobyns, J.H. Intra-articular metacarpal head fractures. J Hand Surg [Am] 8:383–393, 1983.

204. McElfresh, E.C.; Dobyns, J.H.; O'Brien, E.T. Management of fracture-dislocation of the proximal interphalangeal joint by extension-block splinting. J Bone Joint Surg Am 54:1705–1710, 1972.

205. McMinn, D.J. Mallet finger and fracture. Injury 12:477–479, 1981.

206. McNealy, R.W.; Lichtenstein, M.E. Fractures of the bones of the hand. Am J Surg 50:563–570, 1940.

207. Melone, C.P. Rigid fixation of phalangeal and metacarpal fractures. Orthop Clin North Am 17:421–435, 1986.

208. Menon, J. Correction of rotary malunion of the fingers by metacarpal rotational osteotomy. Orthopaedics 13:197–200, 1990.

209. Michelinakis, E.; Vourexaki, H. Displaced epiphyseal plate of the terminal phalanx in a child. Hand 12:51–53, 1980.

210. Mikic, Z.; Helal, B. The treatment of the mallet finger by Oakley splint. Hand 6:76–81, 1974.

211. Milka, S.; Wojcik, B. Mikrozespol fixator in treatment of metacarpal malunion (preliminary report). Chir Nargadow Ruchu Ortop Pol 62:21–25, 1997.

212. Mintzer, C.M.; Waters, P.M.; Brown, D.J. Remodelling of a displaced phalangeal neck fracture. J Hand Surg [Br] 19:594–596, 1994.

213. Moberg, E. Three useful ways to avoid amputation in advanced Dupuyten's contracture. Orthop Clin North Am 4:1001–1005, 1973.

214. Moberg, E. Fractures and ligamentous injuries of the thumb and fingers. Surg Clin North Am 40:297, 1960.

215. Morgan, J.P.; Gordon, D.A.; Klug, M.S.; et al. Dynamic digital traction for unstable comminuted intraarticular fractures and dislocations of the proximal interphalangeal joint. Paper presented at the 48th Annual Meeting of the American Society for Surgery of the Hand, Kansas City, MO, September 1993.

216. Moss, J.G.; Steingold, R.F. The long-term results of mallet finger injury: A retrospective study of 100 cases. Hand 15:151–154, 1983.

217. Muller, M.E.; Allgower, M.; Schnieder, R.; Willenegger, H. Preoperative planning and priciples of reduction. In: Manual of Internal Fixation, 3rd ed. Berlin, Springer-Verlag, 1991, pp. 159–176.

218. Nalebuff, E.A. Isolated anterior carpometacarpal dislocation of the fifth finger: Classification and case report. J Trauma 8:1119–1123, 1968.

219. Namba, R.S.; Kabo, M.; Meals, R.A. Biomechanical effects of point configuration in Kirschner wire fixation. Clin Orthop 214:19–22, 1987.

220. Napier, J. The form and function of the carpometacarpal joint of the thumb. J Anat 89:362–369, 1955.

221. Neviaser, R.J. Dislocations and ligamentous injuries of the digits. In: Chapman, M.W., ed. Operative Orthopaedics. Philadelphia, J.B. Lippincott, 1989, pp. 1199–1212.

222. Nunley, J.A.; Goldner, R.D.; Urbaniak, J.R. Skeletal fixation in digital replantation. Use of the "H" plate. Clin Orthop 214:66–71, 1987.

223. O'Donoghue, D.H. Controlled rotation osteotomy of the tibia. South Med J 33:1145–1148, 1940.

224. Ohl, M.D.; Smite, W.S. Treatment of a phalangeal delayed union using electrical stimulation. Orthopedics 2:585–588, 1988.

225. Opgrande, J.D.; Westphal, S.A. Fractures of the hand. Orthop Clin North Am 14:779–792, 1983.

226. Owens, C. Letter to the editor. J Bone Joint Surg Am 73:89, 1991.

227. Packer, G.J.; Shakeen, M.A. Patterns of hand fractures and dislocation in a district general hospital. J Hand Surg [Br] 18:511–514, 1993.

228. Peimer, C.A.; Smith, R.J.; Leffert, R.D. Distraction fixation in the primary treatment of metacarpal bone loss. J Hand Surg 6:111–124, 1981.

229. Peimer, C.A.; Sullivan, D.J.; Wild, D.R. Palmar dislocation of the proximal interphalangeal joint. J Hand Surg [Am] 9:39–48, 1984.

230. Pellegrini, V.D., Jr.; Burton, R.I. Surgical management of basal joint arthritis of the thumb: Part I. Long-term results of silicone arthroplasty. J Hand Surg [Am] 11:309–324, 1986.

231. Pellegrini, V.D., Jr. Fractures at the base of the thumb. Hand Clin 4:87–102, 1988.

232. Peterson, P.; Sack, S. Fracture-dislocation of the base of the fifth metacarpal associated with injury to the deep motor branch of the ulnar nerve: A case report. J Hand Surg [Am] 11:525–528, 1986.

233. Pichora, D.R.; Meyer, R.; Masear, V.R. Rotational step-cut osteotomy for treatment of metacarpal and phalangeal malunion. J Hand Surg [Am] 16:551–555, 1991.

234. Pichora, D.R.; McMurtry, R.Y.; Bell, M.J. Gameskeeper thumb: A prospective study of functional bracing. J Hand Surg [Am] 14:567–573, 1989.

235. Pieron, A.P. The mechanism of the first carpometacarpal (CMC) joint. An anatomical and mechanical analysis. Acta Orthop Scand 148:7–104, 1973.

236. Pieron, A.P. Correction of rotational malunion of a phalanx by metacarpal osteotomy. J Bone Joint Surg Br 54:516–519, 1972.

237. Pollen, A. The conservative treatment of Bennett's fracture-subluxation of the thumb metacarpal. J Bone Joint Surg Br 50:91–101, 1968.

238. Pritsch, M.; Engel, J.; Tsur, H.; Farin, I. The fractured metacarpal neck: New method of manipulation and external fixation. Orthop Rev 7:122–123, 1978.

239. Pritsch, M.; Engel, J.; Frian, I. Manipulation and external fixation of metacarpal fractures. J Bone Joint Surg Am 63:1289–1291, 1981.

240. Pun, W.K.; Chow, S.P.; Luk, K.D.K.; et al. A prospective study on 284 digital fractures of the hand. J Hand Surg [Am] 14:474–481, 1989.

241. Rankin, E.A.; Jabaley, M.E.; Blair, S.J.; Fraser, K.E. Acquired rotational digital deformity in children as a result of finger sucking. J Hand Surg [Am] 13:535–539, 1988.

242. Rawles, J.G., Jr. Dislocations and fracture-dislocations at the carpometacarpal joints of the fingers. Hand Clin 4:103–112, 1988.

243. Rayan, G.M.; Mullins, P.T. Skin necrosis complicating mallet finger splinting and vascularity of the distal interphalangeal joint overlying skin. J Hand Surg [Am] 12:548–552, 1987.

244. Reid, D.A.C. Corrective osteotomy in the hand. Hand 6:50–57, 1974.

245. Reid, D.A.; Price, A.H. Digital deformities and dental malocclusion due to finger sucking. Br J Plast Surg 37:445–452, 1984.

246. Reid, L. Non-union in a fracture of the shaft of the distal phalanx. Hand 14:85–88, 1982.

247. Renner, A.; Santh, E.; Manninger, J. Karreturosteotomien nach fehlstellung verheilten bruchen der mittelhand- und finger-knochen. Handchirurgie 11:213–218, 1979.

248. Reyes, F.A.; Latta, L.L. Conservative management of difficult phalangeal fractures. Clin Orthop 214:23–30, 1987.

249. Rider, D.L. Fractures of the metacarpals, metatarsals, and phalanges. Am J Surg 38:549–559, 1947.

250. Riggs, S.A., Jr.; Cooney, W.P., III. External fixation of complex hand and wrist fractures. J Trauma 23:332–336, 1983.

251. Robb, W.A.T. The results of treatment of mallet finger. J Bone Joint Surg Br 41:546–549, 1959.

252. Roberts, P. Bulletins et memoires de la Societe de Radiologie Medicale de France. 24:567, 1936.

253. Robins, P.R.; Dobyns, J.H. Avulsion of the insertion of the flexor digitorum profundus tendon associated with fracture of the distal phalanx. In: AAOS Symposium on Flexor Tendon Surgery in the Hand. St. Louis, C.V. Mosby, 1975, p. 151.

254. Rolando, S. Fracture de la base du premier metacarpien et principalement sur une variete non encore ecrite. Presse Med 33:303–304, 1910.

255. Rose, E.H. Reconstruction of central metacarpal ray defects of the hand with a free vascularized double metatarsal and metatarsophalangeal joint transfer. J Hand Surg [Am] 9:28–31, 1984.

256. Royle, S.G. Rotational deformity following metacarpal fracture. J Hand Surg [Br] 15:124–125, 1990.

257. Ruedi, T.P.; Burri, C.; Pfeiffer, K.M. Stable internal fixation of fractures of the hand. J Trauma 11:381–389, 1971.

258. Salgeback, S.; Eiken, O.; Carstam, N.; et al. A study of Bennett's fracture—special reference to fixation by percutaneous pinning. Scand J Plast Reconstr Surg 5:142–148, 1971.

259. Salter, R.B.; Harris, W.R. Injuries involving the epiphyseal plate. J Bone Joint Surg Am 45:587–622, 1963.

260. Sanders, R.A.; Frederick, H.A. Metacarpal and phalangeal osteotomy with miniplate fixation. Orthop Rev 20:449–456, 1991.

261. Schenck, R.R. Classification of fractures and dislocations of the proximal interphalangeal joint. Hand Clin 10:179–185, 1994.

262. Schenck, R.R. The dynamic traction method combining movement and traction for intraarticular fractures of the phalanges. Hand Clin 10:187–198, 1994.

263. Schenck, R.R. Dynamic traction and early passive movement for fractures of the proximal interphalangeal joint. J Hand Surg [Am] 11:850–858, 1986.

264. Schneider, L.H. Fractures of the distal interphalangeal joint. Hand Clin 12:277–288, 1994.

265. Schiund, R.; Cooney, W.P.; Burny, F.; An, K. Small external fixation devices for the hand and wrist. Clin Orthop 293:77–82, 1993.

266. Segmueller, G. Principles of stable internal fixation in the hand. In: Chapman, J.M., ed. Operative Orthopaedics. Philadelphia, J.B. Lippincott, 1988, pp. 1213–1218.

267. Segmueller, G.; Schonenberger, F. Fractures of the hand. In: Weber, B.G.; Gruner, C.; Fruehler, F., eds. Treatment of Fractures in Children and Adolescents. New York, Springer-Verlag, 1980, p. 340.

268. Segmueller, G. Indications for stable internal fixation in hand injuries. In: Chapman, M., ed. Operative Orthopaedics. Philadelphia, J.B. Lippincott, 1988, pp. 1219–1233.

269. Segmueller, G. Surgical Stabilization of the Skeleton of the Hand. Baltimore, Williams & Wilkins, 1977, pp. 18–22.

270. Segond, P. Note sur un cas d'arrachment du point d'insertion des deux languettes phalangettiennes de l'extenseur du petit doigt par flexion forcèe del la phalangette sur la phalangine. Prog Med 8:534–535, 1880.

271. Seitz, W.H., Jr. Management of severe hand trauma with a miniexternal fixateur. Orthopedics 10:601–610, 1987.

272. Seitz, W.H., Jr.; Froimson, A.I. Management of malunited fractures of the metacarpal and phalangeal shafts. Hand Clin 4:529–538, 1988.

273. Seyman, N. Juxtaepiphyseal fractures of the terminal phalanx of the finger. J Bone Joint Surg Br 48:347–349, 1966.

274. Shah, J.; Patel, M. Dislocation of the carpometacarpal joint of the thumb. A report of four cases. Clin Orthop 175:166–169, 1983.

275. Shrewsbury, M.M.; Johnson, R.K. Form, function, and evolution of the distal phalanx. J Hand Surg 8:475–479, 1983.

276. Shrewsbury, M.M.; Johnson, R.K. A systematic study of the oblique retinacular ligament of the human finger: Its structure and function. J Hand Surg 2:194–199, 1977.

277. Shrewsbury, M.M.; Johnson, R.K. Ligaments of the distal interphalangeal joint and the mallet position. J Hand Surg 5:214–216, 1980.

278. Shulter-Ellis, F.P.; Lazar, G. Internal morphology of human phalanges. J Hand Surg [Am] 9:490–495, 1984.

279. Simmons, B.P.; Peters, T.T. Subcondylar fossa reconstruction for malunion of fractures of the proximal phalanx in children. J Hand Surg [Am] 12:1079–1082, 1987.

280. Smith, F.L.; Rider, D.L. A study of the healing of one hundred consecutive phalangeal fractures. J Bone Joint Surg Am 17:91–105, 1935.

281. Smith, J.H., Jr. Avulsion of a profundus tendon with simultaneous intraarticular fracture of the distal phalanx—case report. J Hand Surg 6:600–601, 1981.

282. Smith, R.J.; Peimer, C.A. Injuries to the metacarpal bones and joints. Adv Surg 2:341–374, 1977.

283. Spangberg, O.; Thoren, L. Bennett's fracture: A method of treatment with oblique traction. J Bone Joint Surg Br 45:732–739, 1963.

284. Spinner, M.; Choi, B.Y. Anterior dislocation of the proximal interphalangeal joint. J Bone Joint Surg Am 52:1329–1336, 1970.

285. Stack, H.G. Mallet finger. Hand 1:83–89, 1969.

286. Stark, H.H. Troublesome fractures and dislocations of the hand. Instr Course Lect 19:130–149, 1970.

287. Stark, H.H.; Boyes, J.H.; Wilson, J.N. Mallet finger. J Bone Joint Surg Am 44:1061–1068, 1962.

288. Stark, H.H.; Gainor, B.J.; Ashworth, C.R.; et al. Operative treatment of intraarticular fractures of the dorsal aspect of the distal phalanx of digits. J Bone Joint Surg Am 69:892–896, 1987.

289. Stener, B. Displacement of the ruptured ulnar collateral ligament of the metacarpophalangeal joint of the thumb. J Bone Joint Surg Br 44:869–879, 1962.

290. Strickland, J.W.; Steichen, J.B.; Kleinman, W.B.; et al. Phalangeal fractures, factors influencing digital performance. Orthop Rev 11:39–50, 1982.

291. Stern, P.J. Fractures of the metacarpals and phalanges. In: Green, D.P., ed. Operative Hand Surgery, 3rd ed. New York, Churchill Livingstone, 1993, pp. 695–758.

292. Stern, P.J.; Wieser, M.J. Complications of plate fixation in the hand skeleton. Clin Orthop 214:59–65, 1987.

293. Strickland, J.W.; Steichen, J.B.; Kleinman, W.B.; et al. Phalangeal fractures, factors influencing digital performance. Orthop Rev 11:39–50, 1902.

294. Strickland, J.W.; Steichen, J.B.; Kleinman, W.B.; Flynn, N. Factors influencing digital performance after phalangeal fracture. In: Strickland, J.W.; Steichen, J.B., eds. Difficult Problems in Hand Surgery. St. Louis, C.V. Mosby, 1982, pp. 126–139.

295. Strickland, J.W.; Steichen, J.B.; Showalter, J.F. Phalangeal fractures in a hand surgery practice: A statistical review and in-depth study of the management of proximal phalangeal shaft fractures. J Hand Surg 4:285, 1979.

296. Strong, M.L. A new method of extension block splinting of the proximal interphalangeal joint. Preliminary report. J Hand Surg 5:606–607, 1980.

297. Stuchin, S.A.; Kummer, F.J. Stiffness of small-bone external fixation methods: An experimental study. J Hand Surg [Am] 9:718–724, 1984.

298. Susman, R.L. Comparative and functional morphology of hominid fingers. Am J Physiol Anthropol 50:215–236, 1979.

299. Swanson, A.B. Fractures involving the digits of the hand. Orthop Clin North Am 1:261–274, 1970.

300. Szabo, R.; Spiegel, J.D. Infected fractures of the hand and wrist. Hand Clin 4:477–489, 1988.

301. Tennant, C.E. Use of a steel phonograph needle as a retaining pin in certain irreducible fractures of the small bones. JAMA 83:193, 1924.

302. Thomine, J.M. Les Fractures Ouvertes du Squeulette Digital dans les Plaies de la Main et des Doigts. Actual Chir. Paris, Masson, 1975, pp. 776–780.

303. Thompson, J.S.; Eaton, R.G. Volar dislocation of the proximal interphalangeal joint. J Hand Surg 2:232, 1977.

304. Thoren, L. A new method of extension treatment in Bennett's fracture. Acta Chir Scand 110:485–493, 1955.

305. Thurston, A.J. Pivot osteotomy for the correction of malunion of metacarpal neck fractures. J Hand Surg [Br] 17:580–582, 1992.

306. Tubiana, R. Incidence and cost of injuries to the hand. In: Tubiana, R, ed. The Hand, Vol. 2. Philadelphia, W.B. Saunders, 1985, pp. 159–164.

307. Tubiana, R. Evolution of bone and joint techniques in hand surgery. In: Tubiana, R, ed. The Hand, Vol. 2. Philadelphia, W.B. Saunders, 1985, pp. 469–494.

308. Tuttle, R.H. Quantitative and functional studies on the hand of the Anthropoidea. J Morphol 128:309–364, 1969.

309. van der Lei, B.; de Jonge, J.; Robinson, P.H.; Klasen, J.H. Correction osteotomies of phalanges and metacarpals for rotational and angular malunion: A long-term follow-up and a review of the literature. J Trauma 55:902–908, 1993.

310. Vanik, R.K.; Weber, R.C.; Matloub, H.S.; et al. The comparative strengths of internal fixation techniques. J Hand Surg [Am] 9:216–221, 1984.

311. Vasco, J.R. An operation of old unreduced Bennett's fractures. J Bone Joint Surg 29:753–756, 1947.

312. Wagner, C. Transarticular fixation of fracture-dislocation of the first metacarpal carpal joint. West J Surg Gynecol Obstet 59:362–365, 1951.

313. Wagner, C.J. Method of treatment of Bennett's fracture dislocation. Am J Surg 80:230–231, 1950.

314. Watson-Jones, R. Fractures and Joint Injuries, 4th ed. Edinburgh, E. & S. Livingstone, 1956, pp. 645–646.

315. Waugh, R.L.; Ferrazzano, G.P. Fractures of the metacarpals exclusive of the thumb. A new method of treatment. Am J Surg 59:186–194, 1943.

316. Weber, B.G.; Cech, O. Pseudarthrosis. New York, Grune & Stratton, 1976.

317. Weckesser, E.C. Rotational osteotomy of the metacarpal for overlapping fingers. J Bone Joint Surg Am 47:751–756, 1965.

318. Weeks, P.M.; Wray, C. Management of Acute Hand Injuries. St. Louis, C.V. Mosby, 1973.

319. Wehbe, M.A.; Schneider, L.H. Mallet fractures. J Bone Joint Surg Am 66:658–669, 1984.

320. Wenger, D.R. Avulsion of the profundus tendon insertion in football players. Arch Surg 106:145–149, 1973.

321. Wilgis, E.F. Distal interphalangeal joint silicone interpositional arthroplasty of the hand. Clin Orthop 342:38–41, 1989.

322. Wilkinson, J.L. The insertions of the flexor pollicis longus and digitorum profundus. J Anat 87:75–88, 1953.

323. Wilson, J.N.; Rowland, S.A. Fracture-dislocation of the proximal interphalangeal joint of the finger. Treatment by open reduction and internal fixation. J Bone Joint Surg Am 48:493–502, 1966.

324. Wood, V.E. Fractures of the hand in children. Orthop Clin North Am 7:527–542, 1976.

325. Wray, R.C.; Glunk, R. Treatment of delayed union, nonunion, and malunion of phalanges of the hand. Ann Plast Surg 22:14–18, 1989.

326. Wright, T.A. Early mobilization in fractures of the metacarpals and phalanges. Can J Surg 11:491–498, 1968.

327. Zemel, N.P.; Stark, H.H.; Ashworth, C.R.; et al. Chronic fracture-dislocation of the proximal interphalangeal joint—treatment by osteotomy and bone graft. J Hand Surg 6:447–455, 1981.

328. Zimmerman, N.B.; Weiland, A.J. Ninety-ninety intraosseous wiring for internal fixation of the digital skeleton. Orthopedics 12:99–104, 1989.

329. Zur Verth, M. Behandlung der Finger und Handverletzungen. Hefte Z Unfallh, Vol. 6, 1929–1930.

# Fractures and Dislocations of the Carpus

Leonard K. Ruby, M.D.
Charles Cassidy, M.D.

## FRACTURES OF THE SCAPHOID

Scaphoid fractures account for 60% to 70% of all carpal bone fractures[15] and are second only to fractures of the distal radius in frequency of wrist fractures. Almost exclusively, scaphoid fractures occur in young, vigorous men. The diagnosis may be challenging. The course of treatment is often protracted and even under the best of circumstances has a significant impact on these patients, many of whom are engaged in the most productive years of their lives. A recent European study[267] demonstrated that the average time off work following a scaphoid fracture was 6 months. In the United States, it has been estimated that 345,000 scaphoid fractures occur annually[182] and that even with proper treatment at least 5% (17,250) of them fail to unite. The societal impact is considerable. In spite of almost 100 years of experience and an extensive literature, many areas of controversy, especially in regard to treatment, still exist.

### Mechanism of Injury

The scaphoid functions as a link between the proximal and the distal carpal rows via strong ligamentous connections, leaving the scaphoid waist susceptible to fracture.[70, 87, 138, 165, 231] Two different mechanisms can produce fracture of the scaphoid. By far, the more common mechanism appears to involve hyperextension and bending. In elucidating the pathomechanics, Weber and Chao[283] consistently produced scaphoid waist fractures in cadaver wrists by applying an axial load to the radial half of the palm while the wrist was stabilized in 95° to 100° of extension. It is surmised that the proximal pole of the scaphoid becomes fixed in this position by the radius proximally, dorsally, and radially; by the capitate and lunate ulnarly; and by the long radiolunate ligament and the radioscaphocapitate ligament volarly.[17] At the same time, the distal pole is free to translate dorsally with the distal row of carpal bones, which results in fracture, usually through the waist of the scaphoid. The palmar aspect of the bone fails in tension, and the dorsal aspect fails in compression. Smith and co-workers[231] showed that osteotomy of the waist of the scaphoid in cadaver specimens causes a 27° volar angulation of the scaphoid, with consequent collapse deformity of the wrist with extension of the proximal row of carpal bones. This study confirmed the stabilizing link function of the scaphoid—between the proximal and the distal rows—that has been assumed by most investigators based on the anatomy of the scaphoid and on clinical experience.[70, 87, 138, 165, 231]

A less common mechanism of scaphoid waist fracture, termed the *puncher's scaphoid,* was documented recently by Horii and colleagues.[109] In this instance, with the wrist positioned in neutral or slight flexion, force is transmitted axially along the second metacarpal, through the trapezium and trapezoid, resulting in a flexion moment through the distal pole of the scaphoid. The investigators noted a high incidence of open metacarpal head fractures in these patients. Wrist pain in this setting should therefore raise a high index of suspicion for scaphoid fracture.

### Diagnosis

As is often the case in clinical medicine, a strong index of suspicion is the key to early diagnosis.[70, 87, 138, 165, 231] Scaphoid fractures may produce surprisingly little pain, swelling, or limitation of motion.[153] Therefore, if a young adult man presents with a history of a fall on the palm of his hand and pain and tenderness in the anatomic snuffbox, the diagnosis of scaphoid fracture should be assumed until proven otherwise. Tenderness may be localized to the dorsum of the wrist or volar scaphoid tuberosity with proximal or distal pole fractures, respectively.

Radiographic examination is still the best method for determining the presence of a fracture.[161] Indeed, before x-rays were discovered in 1895, fractures of the scaphoid

**FIGURE 39–1.** *A,* A posteroanterior (PA) radiograph showing a scaphoid fracture with no displacement. The fracture is difficult to visualize on this x-ray film. *B,* A PA radiograph of ulnar deviation in which the fracture line is apparent.

were seldom recognized. At the turn of the 20th century, Professor Stimpson of Cornell University Medical School said that simple fractures of this bone were rare and that disability was the usual outcome.[161] Although many different views have been recommended, we find, in common with most researchers, that a standard posteroanterior (PA), an ulnar deviation PA, a true lateral (i.e., radius, lunate, capitate colinear), and a 45° pronation PA view make up a useful initial series. The lateral view is helpful in identifying carpal malalignment often seen in displaced scaphoid fractures. The ulnar deviation and the 45° pronation views position the long axis of the scaphoid more parallel to the radiographic plate and thus the fracture line more parallel to the x-ray beam. Also, ulnar deviation tends to distract the fracture fragments (Fig. 39–1). Both of these factors facilitate visualization of the fracture line.[143]

If these radiographs are equivocal or negative in the face of strong clinical suspicion, further oblique views can be taken. Stecher[243] recommended a PA view that is angled 20° from the vertical from distal to proximal. This too has the effect of directing the x-ray beam more parallel to the

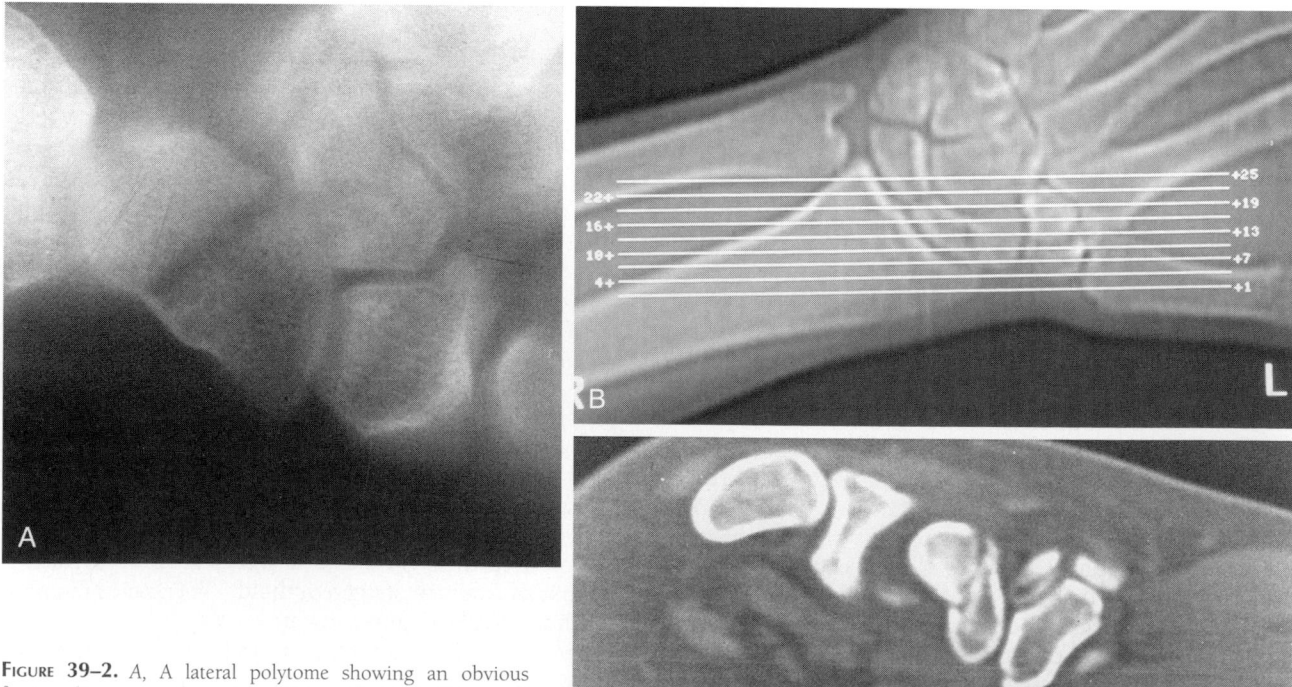

**FIGURE 39–2.** *A,* A lateral polytome showing an obvious fracture line across the waist of the scaphoid. *B,* Computed tomography scout image displaying a scaphoid-sagittal parallel format. *C,* Sagittal scaphoid image demonstrating a scaphoid waist fracture, with angulation.

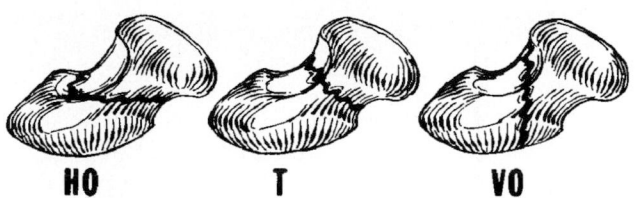

**FIGURE 39–3.** Russe classification of scaphoid fractures. *Abbreviations:* HO, horizontal oblique; T, transverse; VO, vertical oblique. (Reproduced with permission from Taleisnik, J. The Wrist. New York, Churchill Livingstone, 1985. Copyright 1985 Elisabeth Roselius.)

fracture line. If uncertainty still exists after these maneuvers, the patient should be placed in a cast for 2 weeks and the examination repeated.[85] In some instances, even the second x-ray examination is equivocal in spite of the expected resorption at the fracture site,[123] and, in these patients, radionuclide bone scan,[78] polytomography, computed tomography (CT) or magnetic resonance imaging (MRI)[27, 115] can be helpful.[79, 123, 181] The bone scan is the most sensitive but least specific of these procedures. Thus, if the scan results are negative, a scaphoid fracture is ruled out. If the bone scan results are positive, more specific studies such as polytomography (Fig. 39–2A) or CT can be helpful. When ordering the tomographic studies, it is essential to ask the radiologist for images in the sagittal plane of the scaphoid (see Fig. 39–2B) because otherwise cross-sectional views of the wrist are routinely done, and these are very difficult to interpret. In other words, the same principles apply to tomographic views as to plain views. To be most useful, the beam must be parallel to the suspected fracture line or perpendicular to the long axis of the scaphoid. Images should be obtained at 1-mm intervals. Additional information about intercarpal alignment can be gained on the lateral (sagittal) views because the radius-lunate-capitate relationship is well visualized, as is fracture angulation within the scaphoid[213] (see Fig. 39–2C).

## Decision-Making Treatment

Treatment clearly remains the most controversial aspect regarding scaphoid fractures.[36, 152, 161] This is partly because until recently it was not generally appreciated that these fractures may not be isolated injuries and often are only the most obvious sign of a more extensive injury to the wrist. Another confounding factor is the definition of a successful result. Some of the older studies especially have defined a successful result in clinical terms—for example, adequate motion and no significant pain.[152] Although this is not an unreasonable point of view, the best available evidence suggests that the optimal result is more likely obtained if the selected treatment results in a healed scaphoid with normal carpal alignment that can be verified radiologically.

Although no single, universally accepted classification of scaphoid fractures exists, guidelines (Figs. 39–3 and 39–4) exist to help the surgeon design the best course of treatment for a given patient. The fracture can be defined according to several features:

1. *Duration:* Acute fractures are defined as being less than 3 weeks old. Langhoff and Anderson[133] showed that after a 4-week delay, the percentage of bony union with cast treatment decreases markedly. Delayed union is defined as failure to heal by 4 to 6 months. Ununited fractures older than 6 months are considered nonunions.[249] These are, of course, arbitrary definitions, and no one can say with certainty when a delayed union begins or ends.

2. *Location:* The fracture can also be defined anatomically as distal third (pole), middle third (waist), or proximal third (pole). Waist fractures are the most common, accounting for approximately 80% of all scaphoid fractures.[46, 268] Proximal pole and distal pole fractures are seen in 15% and 5% of cases, respectively.

   This classification has prognostic implications. Proximal pole fractures are described as having a poorer rate of healing than more distal fractures, presumably owing to interruption of the blood supply, which enters the bone at or distal to the middle third.[86, 212, 257] Gelberman and Menon[84] showed that the major blood supply is from branches of the radial artery that enter the bone at or distal to the waist at the dorsal ridge. This blood supply accounts for 70% to 80% of the total intraosseous vascularity and 100% of the proximal pole (Fig. 39–5). The osteonecrosis rate for proximal pole fractures approaches 100%.

3. *Orientation:* Russe (see Fig. 39–3)[212] and, later, Herbert and Fisher (see Fig. 39–4)[103] suggested that the plane of the fracture is important and described horizontal oblique, vertical oblique, and transverse fractures; they concluded that vertically oriented fractures are less stable and, consequently, less likely to heal.

4. *Displacement:* Cooney and colleagues[46] and Weber[281] emphasized fracture stability as defined by displacement. Fractures with more than 1 mm stepoff on any view, a scapholunate angle of more than 60°, a lunocapitate angle greater than 15°, or a lateral intrascaphoid angle of more than 20° are considered displaced. Displacement has been shown to affect healing dramatically in conservatively treated scaphoid waist fractures,[46] with nonunion rates as high as 92% being reported.[61]

5. *Comminution:* Comminuted fractures are inherently unstable.

6. *Associated injuries:* Scaphoid fractures commonly accompany perilunate dislocations. These unstable injuries require open reduction and internal fixation (ORIF). The specifics of management are discussed in the carpal dislocations section.

Approximately 5% of distal radius fractures are associated with fracture of the scaphoid.[110] These high-energy injuries usually require surgery.

We agree that displacement and angulation are more important indicators of prognosis than is the plane of the fracture. However, plain radiographs may not be sufficient to determine whether a scaphoid fracture is truly nondisplaced. Some researchers[172, 203] recommend obtaining a

TYPE A:
STABLE ACUTE FRACTURES

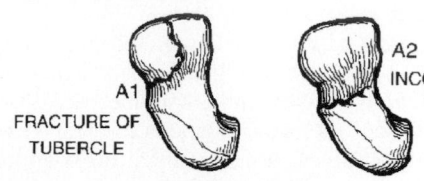

A1
FRACTURE OF
TUBERCLE

A2
INCOMPLETE FRACTURE
THROUGH WAIST

TYPE B:
UNSTABLE ACUTE FRACTURES

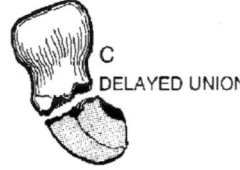

B1
DISTAL OBLIQUE
FRACTURE

B2
COMPLETE FRACTURE
OF WAIST

B3
PROXIMAL POLE
FRACTURE

B4
TRANS-SCAPHOID-
PERILUNATE
FRACTURE DISLOCATION
OF CARPUS

**FIGURE 39–4.** Herbert classification (Herbert & Fisher, 1984) of scaphoid fractures. (Reproduced with permission from Amadio, P.C.; Taleisnik, J. Fractures of the carpal bones. In: Green, D.P., ed. Operative Hand Surgery, 4th ed. New York, Churchill Livingstone, 1999, pp. 809–864.)

TYPE C:
DELAYED UNION

C
DELAYED UNION

TYPE D:
ESTABLISHED NONUNION

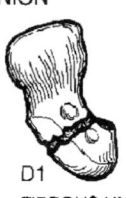 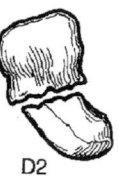

D1
FIBROUS UNION

D2
PSEUDARTHROSIS

scaphoid CT for all waist fractures, citing the high incidence of nonunion, malunion, and avascular necrosis associated with fracture displacement.

In summary, poor prognostic factors for successful nonoperative treatment of scaphoid fractures include late diagnosis, proximal location, displacement or angulation, and, possibly, obliquity of the fracture line. Scaphoid fractures associated with perilunate dislocations are unstable and require internal fixation.

## Nondisplaced Fractures

Cast immobilization remains the mainstay of treatment for nondisplaced scaphoid fractures.[161, 268] The particular type of cast, however, has been the subject of much debate. Almost every wrist position has been advocated, including flexion,[126, 283] extension,[77] radial deviation,[283] ulnar deviation,[126] neutral,[212] and various combinations. Most investigators have recommended including the thumb,[235, 248] whereas others have included the thumb, index, and middle fingers (three-digit cast).[53] Yet others feel that a simple short arm cast is sufficient.[24, 42, 101]

Undoubtedly the most controversial aspect of cast immobilization is the long arm versus short arm debate.[86, 126, 268] The most frequently cited study in this

regard was performed by Gellman and co-workers,[86] who concluded that the time to union was faster (9.5 vs. 12.7 weeks, $P < 0.05$) and the nonunion rate lower (0 vs. 8.7%, not significant) when a long arm thumb spica cast was used for the first 6 weeks of treatment.

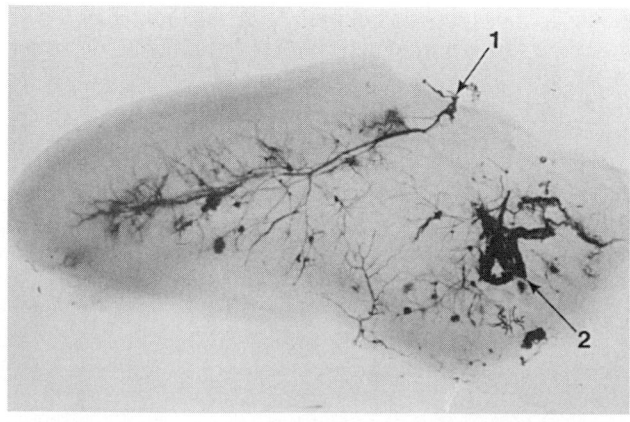

**FIGURE 39–5.** A sagittal section of the scaphoid with the proximal pole oriented to the left. 1, The dorsal scaphoid branch of the radial artery; 2, the volar scaphoid arterial branch. (From Gelberman, R.H.; Menon, J. J Hand Surg [Am] 5:508–513, 1980.)

Part of this diversity in cast immobilization treatment may be because of the consistently successful results (94%–98.5%) reported by several investigators with varying cast treatment of fresh undisplaced fractures.[299] It appears that the exact type of cast is not a critical factor in successful treatment. The goal is to immobilize the fracture as well as possible, and, in our experience, this means a well-fitting cast starting just above the elbow with the wrist in neutral position and including the thumb tip. This allows some flexion and extension of the elbow. The cast is usually changed at 2-week intervals to ensure that it fits snugly. PA, lateral, and ulnar deviation PA radiographs are performed at 6 weeks. If radiographs do not show that the fracture is healed, regardless of the absence of pain, a below-elbow cast is applied for 6 more weeks. If after a total of 12 weeks of immobilization, radiographic examination fails to show unequivocal healing, a CT scan is performed.

There is some evidence that cast immobilization accompanied by electrical stimulation may hasten union.[25, 77] Our experience with electrical stimulation in this setting is limited.

Although the majority of surgeons remain satisfied with cast treatment for nondisplaced scaphoid fractures, there appears to be a growing interest in internal fixation of these fractures. Herbert and Fisher[103] reported a 50% failure rate with nonoperative treatment and suggested that early internal fixation was appropriate for many patients, especially young manual laborers and professional athletes who would not tolerate prolonged cast immobilization. This position was supported by Rettig and associates,[202] whose patients returned to athletics within 6 weeks following scaphoid fixation through a volar approach. As a natural extension, cannulated screws have permitted percutaneous fixation of the scaphoid through a volar[97] or dorsal[228] approach. Adequate long-term follow-up studies are necessary before this type of approach can be generally recommended.

## Displaced or Unstable Fractures

The management of acute, displaced scaphoid fractures is far less controversial. These fractures require surgical treatment. Options include closed reduction and percutaneous pin or screw fixation,[258, 293] arthroscopically assisted pin or screw fixation,[258, 290, 291] and open reduction with either pin[63] or screw fixation.[31, 85, 103] Our preference is ORIF with a cannulated screw. The dorsal approach is reserved for proximal pole fractures. The volar approach is safer for waist or distal 1/3 fractures, because the primary blood supply to the scaphoid is dorsal.[84] Bone graft, when necessary, can usually be obtained from the distal radius. The surgical techniques are discussed in detail in the nonunion section.

## Delayed Union

The location of the scaphoid fracture has a significant impact on time to union. The average healing time ranges from 4 to 6 weeks for tuberosity fractures, 10 to 12 weeks for waist fractures, and 12 to 20 weeks for proximal pole fractures. Therefore, the generally accepted upper limit of "normal" healing time of 4 months[249] must be considered in the context of fracture location.

Some investigators have suggested that noninvasive electrical stimulation be applied for failed treatment.[10, 77] After a review of the experience with electrical stimulation, Osterman and Mikulics[182] concluded that noninvasive methods of electrical stimulation are most appropriately applied to patients who have failed previous bone grafting, have well-aligned waist fractures, do not have significant collapse patterns, and do not have a small proximal fragment or significant arthritis. In the absence of controlled studies showing the efficacy of electrical stimulation,[1] we prefer bone grafting as the next step after failure of cast treatment.

## Nonunion

### OPERATIVE TREATMENT

The decision whether to operate on a scaphoid nonunion is relatively straightforward when the patient is symptomatic. Not infrequently, however, patients present with new onset wrist pain following an injury, and radiographs demonstrate a long-standing nonunion. One could simply advise the patient to splint the wrist, anticipating that the pain will resolve, and the patient return to his asymptomatic ununited state. This is not necessarily true. The question of advising surgery for the patient with an asymptomatic nonunion is a difficult one. The experience of Mack and colleagues,[153] Ruby and co-workers,[209] and Lindstrom and Nystrom[144] showed that scaphoid nonunion results in wrist malalignment and arthritis if left untreated for 5 to 10 years. If surgical treatment of the fracture is selected, the goals of obtaining good alignment of the wrist and scaphoid[7, 119] as well as union should be kept in mind. The techniques of operative treatment of the fracture presently include internal fixation or bone grafting, or both. The salvage techniques are radial styloidectomy,[9] the Bentzon procedure,[13] implant arthroplasty,[233] proximal row carpectomy,[50, 92, 175] either complete[33, 90] or partial arthrodesis,[18, 254, 277] and combinations.

**Bone Grafting.** This is the oldest technique[2] for treating established nonunion or delayed union. The autogenous bone graft serves several purposes. It is osteoconductive and osteoinductive, and it provides a source of osteoprogenitor cells. In addition, it can be used as a structural graft, contoured to fit existing defects or to correct three-dimensional deformity. Donor sites include the iliac crest,[66, 67, 91, 212] distal radius,[28, 71, 91] and proximal ulna.[163] Histomorphometric studies have demonstrated that the quality of cancellous graft is better from the iliac crest than from other sources.[218] An admittedly flawed clinical study by Hull and colleagues[112] confirmed that grafts from the iliac crest were superior to those from the distal radius in the management of scaphoid nonunions. Our preference is to use iliac crest grafts almost exclusively, the exception being the avascular proximal pole nonunion, in which case we prefer to use the vascularized dorsal radius graft, as described by Zaidemberg and colleagues.[297]

Several different methods of bone grafting have been

described over the years.[2, 9, 66, 75, 157, 171, 212, 242] Cortico-cancellous[212] or cancellous[157] interposition grafts and anterior wedge grafts[66] are the most commonly used at the present time. The original Matti technique as described in 1937[157] consisted of excavation of the proximal and distal fracture fragments through a dorsal approach and placement of cancellous graft within these two cavities to act as an internal fixation device as well as a focus for osteogenesis (Fig. 39–6). In 1960, Russe[212] described a volar approach also using cancellous graft, and later he advocated a doubled corticocancellous graft (Fig. 39–7).[91] Because the blood supply of the scaphoid is primarily dorsal, the volar approach is the most popular today. The Matti-Russe–type graft is indicated when the nonunion is not associated with significant dorsal intercalated segment instability (DISI) of the wrist. When DISI is present, an anterior wedge graft after the method of Fisk,[70] Fernandez,[66] or Cooney and associates[48] is the preferred option. Green[91] pointed out that the Matti-Russe technique has a lower success rate when the proximal pole is avascular, as documented by no bleeding of the bone at surgery. In his experience, he had a failure rate of 100% in five patients in whom there was no bleeding of the proximal pole at the time of surgery. He and others have shown that radiographic avascularity is not a reliable indicator of actual vascularity. Our experience with the Matti-Russe method is consistent with that of most investigators, and one can expect 80% to 90% healing rates.[119]

***Technique (Matti-Russe).***[157, 212] A 4- to 5-cm zigzag volar incision is made directly over the flexor carpi radialis tendon ending distally at the tuberosity of the scaphoid.

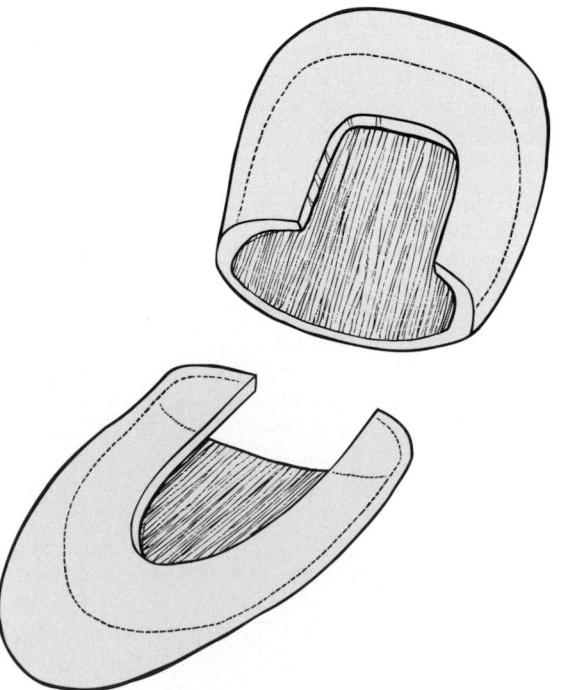

**FIGURE 39–6.** Reproduction of the original drawing of Matti (1937) showing the amount of excavation for a scaphoid nonunion bone graft. This cavity was filled with cancellous bone from the greater trochanter, and the bone graft was pressed carefully into the cavity as a dentist might pack gold into a tooth. (From Verdan, C.; Narakas, A. Surg Clin North Am 48:1083–1095, 1968.)

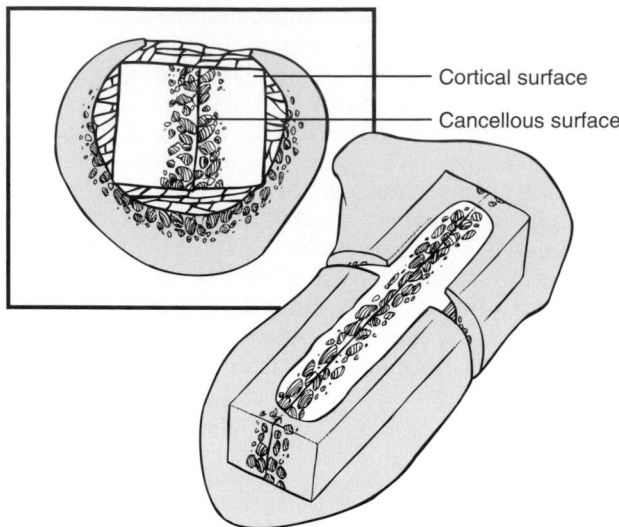

**FIGURE 39–7.** Russe's latest technique using Matti's excavation concept but incorporating corticocancellous graft for improved fixation and a volar approach. (From Green, D.P. J Hand Surg [Am] 10:597–605, 1985.)

One should be careful in dividing the skin not to injure the palmar cutaneous branch of the median nerve, which often lies in the skin flap over the flexor carpi radialis tendon. The flexor carpi radialis is mobilized and retracted ulnarward, and the radial artery is retracted radialward. It is not necessary to isolate the radial artery, although at the distal end of the incision the superficial branch is often visualized and may have to be ligated if the scaphotrapezial joint is to be exposed. The posterior wall of the flexor carpi radialis sheath is divided longitudinally, and the underlying pericapsular fat is exposed. This too is divided, and the multiple vessels in this layer are cauterized with a bipolar instrument. A rolled towel placed under the wrist will provide the extension necessary to visualize the capsule. The exposed volar wrist capsule and volar capsular ligaments are divided sharply, beginning at the distal radius and continuing distally to the scaphoid tuberosity. Care is taken to preserve as much of the extrinsic volar wrist ligament complex as possible.

At this point, the radioscaphoid joint and the entire volar surface of the scaphoid are exposed. The fracture site is usually obvious but, on occasion, a wrinkle in the articular cartilage of the scaphoid may be the only clue. Fingertrap traction and wrist extension will optimize the exposure. An opening is made in the volar nonarticular cortex of the scaphoid at the level of the fracture. The opposing cavities of the two fragments are then excavated. Russe advocated using only hand instruments for this step, but we use the Midas Rex* with a 2× bit for the preliminary curettage and then complete the excavation with straight and curved hand-held curettes. If the proximal pole is very small and avascular, the curettage is carried to the subchondral bone level. Because the articular cartilage is nourished by synovial fluid, the proximal pole is converted into an osteocartilaginous graft. Particular care must be taken not to penetrate the proximal pole if

---

*Midas Rex Pneumatic Tools, Inc., 2925 Race Street, Ft. Worth, TX 76111.

this maneuver is used. After adequate curettage (bleeding cancellous bone is exposed) of both fragments, a properly shaped and sized cancellous graft harvested from the iliac crest is packed tightly into the defect by overdistracting the fragments. Kirschner (K) wires may be used as "joysticks" for this maneuver. Any remaining defect is filled with cancellous bone chips. Stability is then checked by manipulation of the wrist in radial-ulnar deviation and flexion-extension. If the construct is unstable, two parallel 0.045-inch K-wires are inserted from the distal pole across the graft and into the proximal pole. Radiographs should then be taken to ensure proper placement of the wires and alignment of the scaphoid and the rest of the wrist. The volar ligaments and capsule are closed with absorbable 2–0 suture in horizontal mattress fashion. The rest of the closure is routine.

If K-wires are used, they should be cut off under the skin, because they usually need to be retained longer than

6 weeks. A radial gutter splint is applied for 5 to 7 days. This is replaced by a solid, short arm thumb spica cast, changed every 2 to 3 weeks. At 6 weeks postoperatively, radiographs are taken out of plaster. A short arm thumb spica cast is continued for 6 more weeks or until radiographic results indicate that healing is complete. We almost always obtain a CT of the scaphoid to confirm adequate healing.

When angulation is present at the fracture site with concomitant DISI, the Fisk-Fernandez[48, 66, 70] method is most appropriate.

***Technique (Fisk-Fernandez*** (Fig. 39–8)). According to Fernandez[66] and Cooney and associates,[48] it is helpful to measure the normal scaphoid to determine the amount of bone to be resected and the size and shape of the bone graft. A volar wrist approach similar to that in the Matti-Russe technique is used. Although volar angulation at the fracture site makes visualization difficult, wrist

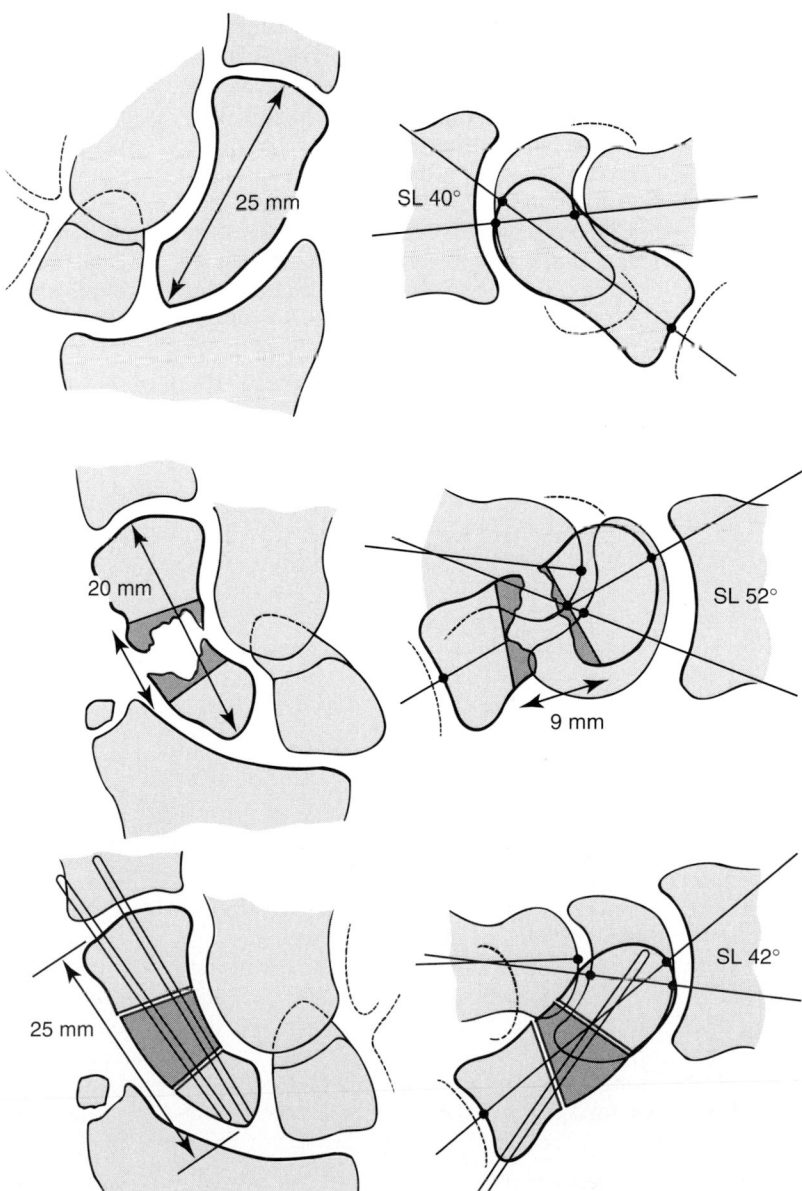

**FIGURE 39–8.** Line drawing illustrating the Fisk-Fernandez grafting technique. *Top,* Reference measurements of the scaphoid length and scapholunate (SL) angle in the uninjured wrist. *Middle,* Degree of deformity requiring correction. *Bottom,* Appropriate length and angulation restored. (Redrawn from Fernandez, D.L. J Hand Surg [Am] 9:733–737, 1984.)

extension and ulnar deviation reveal the fracture. To reduce the DISI deformity of the carpus, a small laminar spreader is placed into the scaphoid fracture site and opened as much as necessary. This maneuver usually reduces the fracture and the carpal instability pattern. Alternatively, one may place 0.054-inch K-wires in the proximal and distal fragments as joysticks and manipulate them into the corrected position. When the carpal collapse is severe, the lunate is first reduced with respect to the radius by palmar translation through the midcarpal joint. A 0.062-inch K-wire is then driven from the radius into the lunate as temporary fixation.[230]

The fracture site is then curetted sufficiently to expose good bleeding cancellous bone on both surfaces. A corticocancellous wedge-shaped bone graft is harvested from the iliac crest. In some patients, the entire scaphoid is shortened, and there is volar and ulnar angulation at the fracture site. This may be due to comminution dorsally at the time of fracture or erosion at the fracture site owing to motion between the fragments.[70] In this situation, once reduction is obtained, there will be a dorsal-ulnar gap as well as a larger volar defect. Therefore, a trapezoid-shaped bicortical graft is trimmed to fit snugly in the defect with the cortical surface anterior. The graft is then placed, and two 0.045-inch K-wires are driven from the scaphoid tuberosity through the distal pole across the graft and into the proximal pole.

If the proximal fragment is very small or has to be extensively curetted because of avascularity, we attempt to place the wires into the lunate to improve fixation. An alternative method for proximal pole fractures is to use a dorsal approach with bone graft and either K-wire[279] or screw fixation.[54] Stability is checked by observing the fracture site while manipulating the wrist. Radiographs are taken in the anteroposterior and lateral planes to check alignment and pin placement. A radial gutter is applied for 7 to 10 days. This is then changed to a short arm thumb spica cast with the wrist in neutral position for 6 weeks; the cast is changed every 2 to 3 weeks. Radiographs and, if necessary, a CT scan are obtained. As indicated, casting is continued for 6 to 9 more weeks until solid union is established by radiographs. This cast is also changed every 2 to 3 weeks.

*Vascularized Bone Grafts.* Over the past 2 decades, increasing attention has been paid to the use of vascularized bone grafts in the management of difficult nonunions. These have included the volar pronator pedicle graft,[124] the dorsal Zaidemberg 1,2 intercompartmental artery pedicle graft[297] (Fig. 39–9), the Fernandez vascular bundle implant,[68] and even the free vascularized iliac crest graft.[188] To date, results using these techniques have been equivalent to those of more conventional nonvascularized methods. We believe that the structural requirements of the graft are more important in graft selection than its vascularity. There clearly does appear to be a role for the dorsal pedicle grafts in the management of well-aligned, proximal pole nonunions.

**Internal Fixation.** The indications for internal fixation have been mentioned and include displaced acute fractures, fractures associated with ligamentous injury, such as trans-scaphoid perilunate fracture-dislocations, delayed union, or nonunion when bone grafting alone is insuffi-

cient to provide adequate internal fixation. A relative indication is inability to tolerate long-term cast immobilization. The internal fixation techniques described include K-wires,[242] screws,[37, 67, 81, 103, 111, 138, 158] and staples,[272] although the last have not achieved much popularity and are not in general use. Of these, K-wires remain the most versatile implant.

The Herbert screw system has been the most popular method of screw fixation,[31, 48, 54, 204, 236] and the results have been encouraging. This device consists of a smooth shaft with threads at both ends with differing pitch. As the screw is advanced, compression is obtained across the fracture site by putting greater pitch in the leading end threads than in the trailing end threads. There is no head on the screw, so the end is countersunk under the cartilage. When the procedure is completed, both ends of the screw are buried and do not interfere with joint motion; thus, the screw need not be removed. Stable internal fixation is provided by this device.[221] Compared with K-wires, however, the technique is demanding and unforgiving.[273] Further, it is necessary to traumatize the scaphotrapezial joint to insert the jig. As noted, very small proximal or distal avascular fragments may not be suitable for fixation with a screw. Herbert and Fisher's results in their original 1984 paper[103] were excellent for acute fractures and delayed union, with sound union verified by radiography achieved in 30 of 33 patients (91%). They had an 80% success rate in nonunion cases (21 failures out of a total of 105). Thus, in established nonunion cases, the Matti-Russe procedure with an 85% union rate reported by several investigators[47, 91, 157, 212] is at least equivalent. The proposed advantage of the Herbert screw is shorter immobilization time. Herbert and Fisher recommend an average of 4 weeks in plaster. Although further experience with the Herbert screw will ultimately determine its place in the surgeon's armamentarium, at present it appears to be an excellent alternative in acute displaced fractures and fracture-dislocations when the prognosis is poor with closed treatment and K-wires may not provide adequate fixation.

Several studies have compared various screws used in

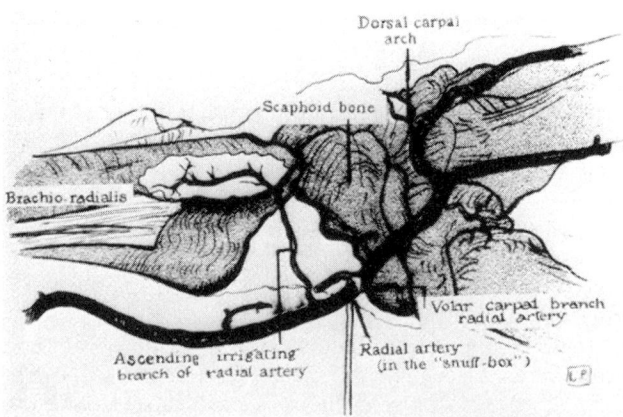

**FIGURE 39–9.** Original drawing of the Zaidemberg 1,2 intercompartmental artery pedicle graft, referred to as the ascending irrigating branch of the radial artery. (From Zaidemberg, C.; Siebert, J.W.; Angrigiani, C. A new vascularized bone graft for scaphoid nonunion. J Hand Surg [Am] 16:474–478, 1991.)

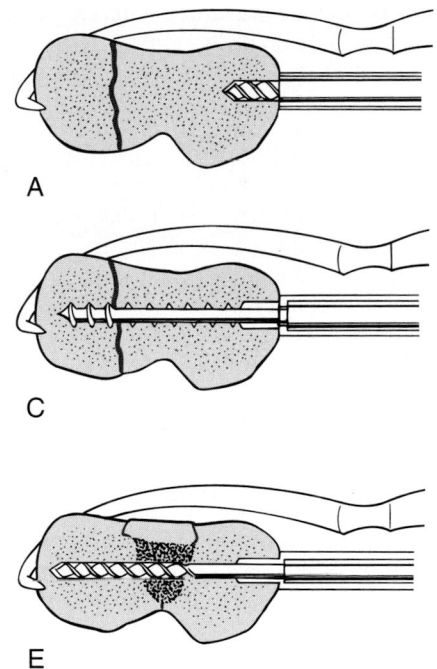

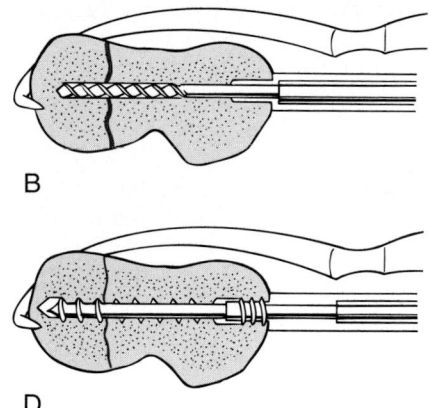

**FIGURE 39–10.** The Herbert screw insertion technique. *A,* The pilot drill for the trailing end of the screw. *B,* The long drill for the leading end of the screw. *C,* The tap for the leading end of the screw. *D,* Inserting the screw. *E,* The screw in use, with a corticocancellous wedge graft to retain scaphoid alignment. (*A–E,* From Herbert, T.J.; Fisher, W.E. J Bone Joint Surg Br 66:114–123, 1984.)

fixation of the scaphoid.[221] Shaw[222] demonstrated that the AO 3.5-mm cannulated screw generates 2.5 times more compression than the Herbert screw. Newport and co-workers[176] concluded that the Howmedica Universal Compression Screw was superior to its competitors. This finding was not supported by Toby and associates,[261] who identified iatrogenic fractures at the screw insertion site using the larger universal compression screw.

In clinical practice, Trumble and colleagues[265] found no difference between the Herbert screw and the cannulated AO screw for scaphoid nonunions. However, they did observe that the location of the screw in the proximal scaphoid was important. Time to union was significantly shorter when the screw was positioned in the central one third of the proximal scaphoid. In summary, attention to technical detail is probably more important than the type of screw.

**Technique (Modified Herbert).**[103] A volar approach similar to that of the Russe technique is used and extended distally to the scaphotrapezial joint (Figs. 39–10 and 39–11). The superficial branch of the radial artery is ligated and divided, and the scaphotrapezial joint is opened transversely. The fracture is then opened, and the ends are prepared as described earlier. If this leaves a large defect, a wedge-shaped corticocancellous graft is harvested from the outer aspect of the iliac crest and inserted. The Herbert jig is placed with the hook around the proximal pole of the scaphoid. The barrel is placed on the distal pole, and the jig is clamped into place. Jig placement is both critical and difficult, with the most common error being placement too near the anterior surface of the scaphoid. To prevent this, it is important to place the proximal hook around to the dorsal surface of the proximal pole.[31] A second reported error is insufficient dissection of the scaphotrapezial joint, which prevents proper placement of the jig barrel as far dorsal as possible.[31] Sometimes, removing bone from the anterior

surface of the trapezium is necessary. If this configuration is unstable or difficult to align, we have found it helpful to place a K-wire through both fragments and the graft (if any) before clamping the jig into place. Radiographs are taken to confirm proper alignment of the wrist, scaphoid, and jig. The large diameter drill is used for the trailing end of the screw, followed by the smaller drill for the leading end of the screw. The tap is used, followed by insertion of the proper length screw as read off the jig. The jig is then removed (see Fig. 39–11). Stability is checked by moving the wrist and checking the fracture site. Closure is accomplished in layers, and a U-shaped above-elbow splint is applied. At 10 to 14 days, the splint is taken off, and sutures are removed. Herbert and Fisher allow motion and a removable splint at this point until healing is complete, as confirmed by radiograph. If a bone graft is used, a short arm cast is applied for 4 to 6 weeks postoperatively.

In the acute fracture or fracture-dislocation, we have found it technically easier and less traumatic to use a dorsal approach and insert the screw from proximal to distal without the jig. A K-wire is used as a guide pin to ensure proper placement and length of the screw. If desired, a conventional 2.7-mm AO screw can also be used to fix the scaphoid. Fernandez[67] reported that 19 of 20 patients achieved union with his technique. We have had 18 of 20 patients achieve union using the cannulated 3.5-mm AO screw for scaphoid nonunions at the waist. The method is technically demanding.

**Technique (AO Cannulated Screw).** The surgical approach and scaphoid preparation are identical to the modified Herbert technique (above). A guide wire is then drilled from distal to proximal across the scaphoid, aiming for the subchondral bone in the center of the proximal pole. Proper wire placement is confirmed fluoroscopically in two planes, and the length is measured. The cannulated 2.5-mm drill bit is advanced to the appropriate depth

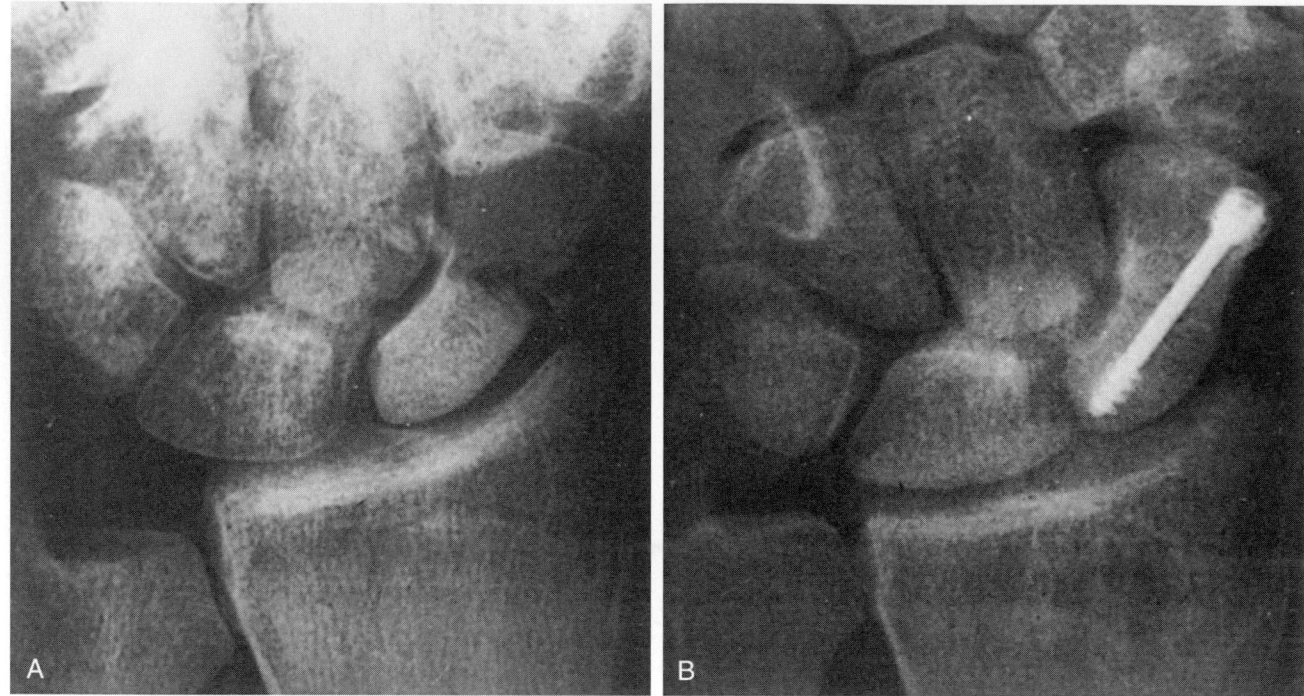

**FIGURE 39–11.** *A*, A preoperative radiograph of a scaphoid waist fracture. *B*, Postoperatively, the fracture fixed with a Herbert screw.

under C-arm guidance. After removal of the drill bit, the appropriate-length cannulated screw is inserted, ensuring that all the threads are across the fracture site. Tapping and countersinking are not necessary. Final radiographs are obtained. Closure and aftercare is as described.

**Salvage Procedures.** If the decision is made not to attempt to achieve union of the scaphoid, there are several alternatives. It should be emphasized that these procedures are usually indicated after failure of primary treatment, which in most cases will have been an operative attempt to gain union. Given the high rate of success in obtaining union with bone grafting techniques, these methods are necessary in relatively few patients.[36]

*Radial Styloidectomy.* This procedure may be indicated as an adjunct to bone grafting or internal fixation, especially when there is osteoarthritis at the articulation between the distal pole and the radial styloid. The excised bone can be used as the graft, and its removal does provide increased exposure of the scaphoid if a radial approach is used. Of course, radial styloidectomy by itself does nothing for the scaphoid nonunion, and if the nonunion is the source of the patient's pain, other measures will have to be undertaken. If one is overzealous in performing radial styloidectomy, the wrist can be destabilized by detaching the origins of the radioscaphocapitate and long radiolunate ligaments.[226] There have been no long-term follow-up reports demonstrating the efficacy of this procedure, and we do not favor its routine use as an isolated procedure.

*Proximal Row Carpectomy.* For the patient who is not a suitable candidate for long periods of immobilization and who has a low demand wrist or whose fracture has failed to heal after bone graft, excision of the proximal carpal row is an option. We prefer this in the older patient, although several investigators reported good results in young manual laborers.[92, 116, 122, 164, 175, 237, 239] Unfortunately,

lunate facet arthritis or capitate arthritis is a contraindication to this procedure. The pattern of arthritis in long-standing scaphoid nonunion is first radius-distal scaphoid pole and then capitate head–proximal scaphoid pole.[209]

Green[92] reported his personal series of proximal row carpectomies in 15 patients with a mean age of 34 years. Follow-up was from 6 months to 6 years, averaging 30 months. Of these 15 patients, 4 were pain-free, 6 had mild discomfort, 3 had moderate pain, and 2 had severe pain. Twelve patients returned to their previous or even heavier work. The range of motion in 13 patients was 39° dorsiflexion, 40° palmar flexion, 31° ulnar deviation, and 5° radial deviation. Strength averaged 83.5% of the opposite side in the dominant wrist in seven patients and 41% of the opposite side in nondominant wrists in six patients. Therefore, Green concludes, quoting McLaughlin and Baab,[164] "whenever motion, even at the price of some weakness and discomfort, is preferable to a strong, painless but stiff wrist," proximal row carpectomy should be considered as an alternative to wrist arthrodesis. We have limited experience with this procedure, because very few of our patients have normal capitate articular surfaces after failed treatment for scaphoid nonunion. Moreover, pain relief is a high priority in our patients.

*Technique* (Fig. 39–12). A longitudinal dorsal skin incision is centered over Lister's tubercle. The extensor retinaculum is incised over the third compartment, carrying this distally into the second compartment. The extensor pollicis longus tendon is retracted radially. A longitudinal capsulotomy is performed, and the capsular-periosteal flaps are elevated radially and ulnarly as far as necessary to expose the entire carpus deep to all the other extensor tendons. The fourth compartment is not opened. The lunate and triquetrum are then removed, using a curved 1/4-inch osteotome as a knife to divide the pericarpal ligaments. A threaded K-wire may be inserted into the carpal bones to facilitate removal. We usually excise only the proximal two thirds of the scaphoid unless there is impingement at the radial styloid on the distal remnant. The head of the capitate is then seated in the lunate facet. If there is instability, a 0.062-inch K-wire is driven transarticularly and kept in place for the first 3 to 4 weeks postoperatively. The wound is closed in layers, leaving the extensor pollicis longus in the subcutaneous tissue. A drain is left in place for 24 to 48 hours. A splint is applied for the first week until swelling subsides, followed by a short arm cast for 4 to 6 weeks. Finger motion is begun and encouraged immediately postoperatively.

A few points deserve emphasis. First, if there are significant articular changes at the head of the capitate or the lunate facet of the radius, this procedure is contraindicated. Second, if there is impingement at the distal third of the scaphoid on the radial styloid, the distal portion of the scaphoid should be removed. If there is still impingement, a limited radial styloidectomy should be done. Third, it is important to preserve the volar wrist ligaments to avoid ulnar translocation of the remaining carpus.

***Arthrodesis.*** Both partial and complete arthrodesis have been recommended for patients who have persistent nonunion, severe arthritis, or extensive avascular necrosis with collapse. Limited arthrodesis options include radioscapholunate,[33, 254, 276] scaphocapitate,[100, 249] and total midcarpal arthrodesis, distal scaphoid excision and proximal pole–lunate–capitate arthrodesis,[269] and scaphoid excision and four-corner arthrodesis.[154, 264] Silicone scaphoid arthroplasty is no longer performed.

Our preference for long-standing scaphoid nonunion, particularly in the setting of advanced arthritis and prior surgery, is total wrist arthrodesis. However, certain vocations, notably plumbing, demand some wrist motion. In addition, patients who are willing to preserve some wrist motion at the expense of mild pain may be candidates for limited wrist arthrodesis. When considering partial fusion, the progression of arthritis must be understood. Fortunately, the radiolunate joint is usually well-preserved, even in long-standing cases.[209] Therefore, motion-sparing procedures that utilize the radiolunate joint may be of value. Our experience with scaphoid excision and four-corner arthrodesis in this setting has been encouraging.

***Technique (Complete Arthrodesis).*** A straight oblique incision is made centered over Lister's tubercle. The extensor pollicis longus tendon is mobilized and retracted radially, and the tubercle is osteotomized. The capsule of the wrist and periosteum over the distal radius is incised, and these layers are elevated subperiosteally to avoid exposing the fourth or fifth compartment extensor tendons. At this point, all joint surfaces to be fused are decorticated using the power burr. We routinely include the third carpometacarpal joint, and the radiocarpal and midcarpal articulations except for the scapho-trapezial-trapezoid joint. The proximal articular surface of the triquetrum, the membranous lunotriquetral (LT) ligament, and the ulnar half of the lunate are also preserved. Cancellous bone graft obtained from the distal radius or iliac crest is packed tightly into the joint spaces. The wrist is then fixed with a prebent AO/ASIF low-profile wrist fusion plate (Synthes Ltd, Paoli, PA)[286] (Fig. 39–13). The wound is closed in layers over a drain. A splint is applied for the first week, followed by a short arm cast until radiographs show consolidation, which usually takes 6 weeks. A personal series of 28 patients attained 75% of normal grip strength and were pain free at an average follow-up of 4 years postoperatively.

### Other Salvage Procedures

***Distal Scaphoid Resection Arthroplasty.***[156] In this procedure, resection of the distal scaphoid fragment and radial styloid presumably eliminates pain from both the nonunion site and radioscaphoid impingement. In their series of 19 patients all with DISI deformity, 13 obtained

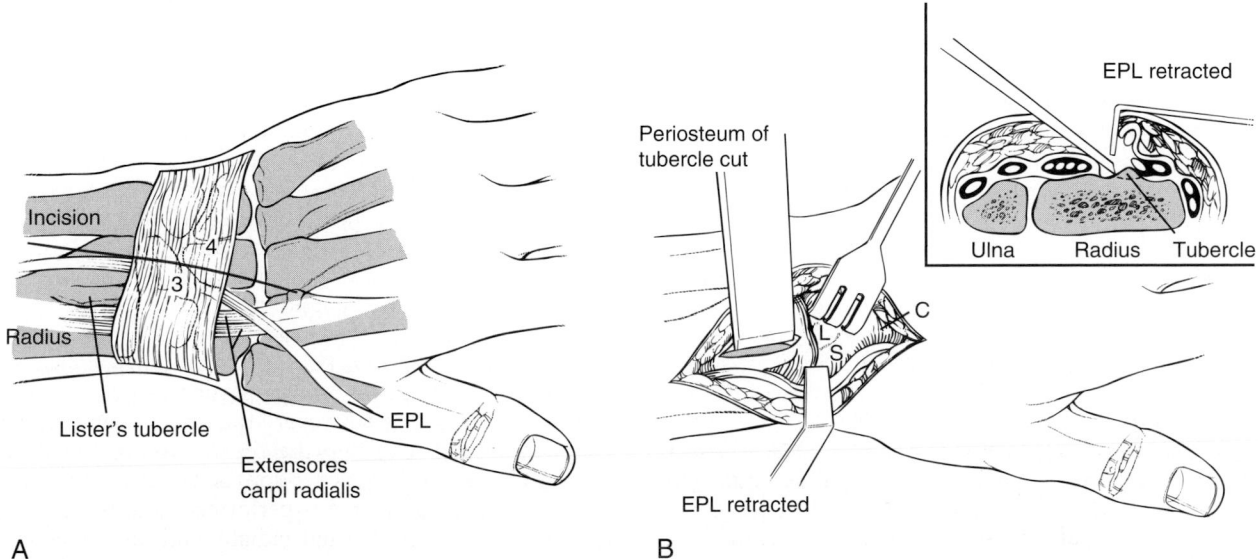

**FIGURE 39–12.** *A, B,* Schematic demonstration of a dorsal approach to the wrist for intercarpal arthrodesis. *Abbreviations:* C, capitate; EPL, extensor pollicis longus; 3, third dorsal compartment (EPL); 4, fourth dorsal compartment (EDC); L, lunate; S, scaphoid. (*A, B,* Redrawn from Weil, C.; Ruby, L.K. J Hand Surg [Am] 11:911–912, 1986.)

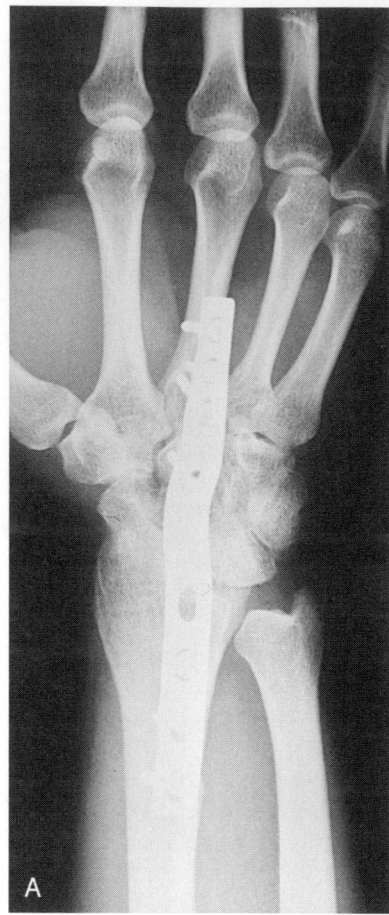

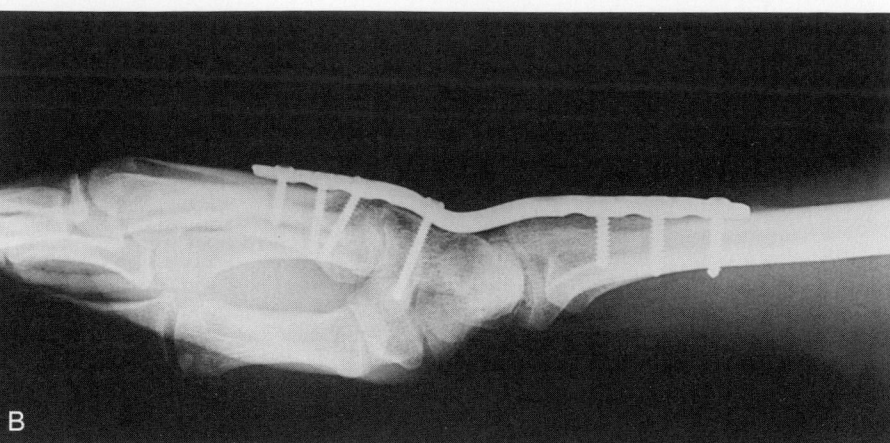

**Figure 39–13.** Anteroposterior (AP) (*A*) and lateral (*B*) radiographs of wrist arthrodesis demonstrating wrist fusion with AO plate.

complete pain relief, and carpal collapse apparently did not progress postoperatively. The investigators felt that capitolunate arthritis was a contraindication to the procedure. We would like to see longer follow-up, especially with regard to carpal collapse, before advocating this intriguing technique.

***Bentzon's Procedure.***[13] A pseudarthrosis is formally created by interposing a soft tissue flap from the dorsoradial aspect of the wrist capsule into the fracture site. The obvious assumption is that the pain in an ununited scaphoid fracture is primarily due to the nonunion itself. Boeckstyns and Busch[23] reported good clinical results in a relatively large series with long-term follow-up, although carpal collapse was seen in the majority of patients. In our opinion, the Bentzon procedure is a good demonstration of the contention that the pain from scaphoid nonunion is due primarily to the nonunion. However, as the progression of arthritis shows, this technique does not restore normal wrist kinematics, and it may be important to do so to prevent radiocarpal arthritis. We have no experience with this procedure.

### Special Situations

***Proximal Pole Fractures.*** As noted earlier, vascular studies by Gelberman and Menon[84] and Taleisnik and Kelly[257] established that fractures through the proximal third of the scaphoid have a high likelihood of devascularizing the proximal fragment, because most of the blood supply enters the bone distal to this level. The proximal pole is covered almost entirely with cartilage and has a poor blood supply apart from its connection to the rest of the scaphoid. Nonetheless, if seen early, these fractures can be treated nonoperatively with a cast until the outcome is obvious. The patient is cautioned that the fracture has a significant chance of nonunion. If nonunion or delayed union does occur, we recommend a cancellous bone graft and internal fixation through a dorsal approach after the method of DeMaagd and Engber.[54] It is particularly important in such areas to perform a thorough and aggressive curettement of the proximal pole to bleeding cancellous bone if present or subchondral bone if not. This is followed by tight packing with cancellous graft (Matti technique) and internal fixation with a screw[6] or K-wires.[279] The same surgical treatment is recommended for avascular necrosis of the proximal pole if there is no collapse or significant arthritis, in spite of limited success in others' experience.[91] Several investigators have recommended vascularized bone grafts for these small proximal pole fractures when the blood supply is marginal or absent.[96, 124, 297] Zaidemberg and co-workers[297] reported on 11 patients who were treated with vascularized bone graft from the dorsal radial aspect of the distal radius based on the ascending irrigating branch of the radial artery in the snuffbox. They had a 100% union rate determined by radiography, and 5 of the patients had previously failed Matti-Russe procedures.

In the setting of collapse of the proximal pole, significant arthritis, or a failed bone graft, several options are available. One can either repeat the bone graft or perform an excision of the proximal fragment with or without replacement with either a tendon[58, 59] or a silicone spacer.[299] According to Zemel and colleagues,[299] 20 of 21 (95%) of these silicone replacement patients had a good clinical result at an average of 5 years postoperatively, although all patients showed some increase in the scapholunate angle and wrist collapse. No silicone synovitis was reported. Watson and Ballet[276] suggested excision of the scaphoid and capitate-hamate-triquetrum-lunate arthrodesis with scaphoid implant. They now recommend not using the implant. We feel that these reports provide evidence that the pain in the presence of a scaphoid nonunion is usually due to the nonunion. Therefore, any procedure that deals with this aspect of the problem should be effective in achieving some degree of pain relief, as evidenced in the Bentzon procedure. However, the altered wrist mechanics inevitably cause arthritis later, which may prove to be symptomatic. To this must be added the now well-known risk of silicone synovitis.[233] We have been reluctant to perform proximal pole excision based on concern for scapholunate dissociation owing to the necessary loss of the stabilizing effect of the scapholunate ligament. We therefore prefer a limited or complete wrist arthrodesis as a salvage for failed bone graft of a proximal pole nonunion.

***Distal Pole Fractures.*** The most common distal pole fracture is an extra-articular avulsion injury of the tuberosity. The small fragment is best visualized on a semipronated view (Fig. 39–14). Cast treatment for several weeks is usually sufficient. In cases of symptomatic nonunion, this fragment may be excised. Distal third fractures of the body of the scaphoid, if fresh and undisplaced, should heal in 4 to 8 weeks with cast treatment.[212] A less common, often subtle, fracture is the distal pole vertical intra-articular fracture,[195] which may be visible only on polytomography or CT scan. If undisplaced, these should be treated with a cast; if displaced, ORIF should be performed. Nonunion in this well-vascularized area is uncommon.[167]

***Author's Preferred Approach.*** For the acute undisplaced fracture, an above-elbow cast including the thumb tip with the wrist in neutral position is applied for 6 weeks and changed at 2 to 3 week intervals. Radiographs are taken at 6 weeks, and if solid union is not evident, a short arm cast is applied and changed every 2 to 3 weeks until a total of 3 to 4 months has elapsed. Radiologic examination is done at 3- to 4-week intervals until solid union is evident and confirmed by polytomography or CT in questionable cases.

For the acute displaced fracture, ORIF is performed with either a Herbert or an Acutrak bone screw or K-wires through the dorsal approach.

For delayed union or nonunion of the undisplaced fracture, cancellous or corticocancellous bone grafting is done through an anterior approach. For displaced nonunion, open reduction is performed through an anterior approach with a wedge or trapezoid-shaped corticocancellous graft with internal fixation. If the fracture is in the proximal third, a dorsal approach is used. When the proximal pole is avascular *and* the overall wrist alignment is normal, we prefer a vascularized distal radius graft with internal fixation.

For a failed bone graft, a repeat bone graft, a scaphoid

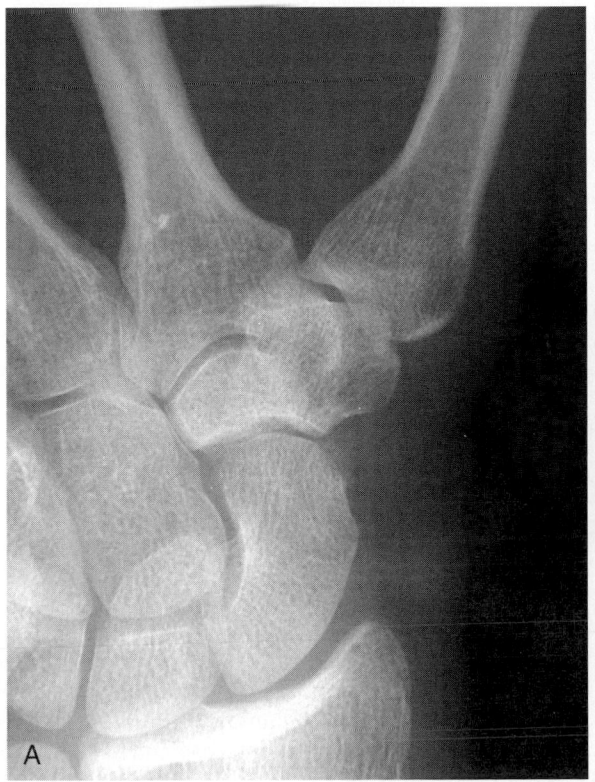

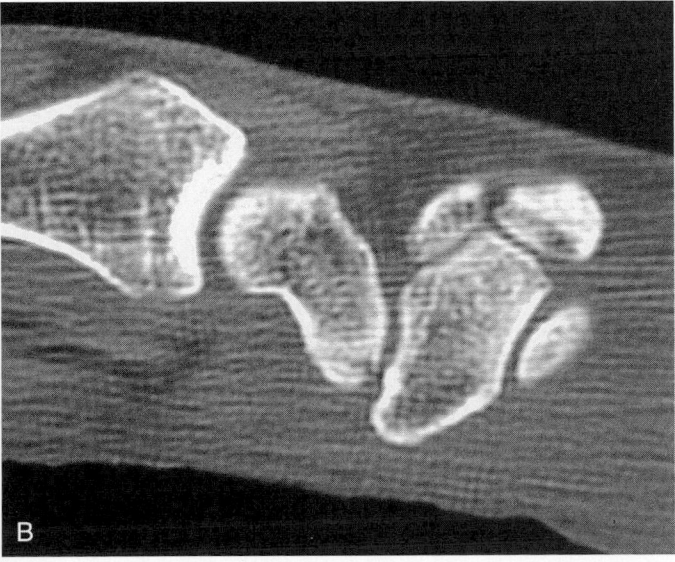

**FIGURE 39–14.** *A, B,* Nonunion of a small distal pole scaphoid fracture. This nonarticular fragment is best visualized on a semipronated posteroanterior view (*A*) or computed tomography scan (*B*). Excision is recommended.

excision and four-corner fusion, or a total midcarpal arthrodesis is performed.

For a symptomatic long-standing nonunion with significant osteoarthritis (usually not present until 10 years or more after the injury), the preferred salvage procedure is total wrist arthrodesis for the high-demand patient. If the arthritis is not particularly symptomatic or is in a low-demand patient, no surgery may be necessary or partial scaphoid excision can be done.[59, 156]

## Lunate Fractures

Excluding Kienböck's disease, acute fracture of the lunate is quite uncommon, accounting for approximately 1% of all carpal fractures.[260] These are usually high-energy hyperextension or axial injuries, and may be associated with distal radius, capitate, or carpometacarpal fractures.[43] However, they may be subtle injuries, evident only on CT scan (see Fig. 39–20), and require a high index of suspicion. Teisen and Hjarbaek[260] have classified acute lunate fractures into five types. Volar pole fractures are the most common and may be associated with volar subluxation of the carpus. Next are marginal fractures, which are stable injuries. Dorsal pole and sagittal and transverse fractures (Fig. 39–15) are quite rare. Surgery is indicated for the displaced body fractures and fracture-subluxations.

## KIENBÖCK'S DISEASE

Ever since Kienböck's original description of lunatomalacia (soft lunate) in 1910,[125] the precise etiology, natural history, and treatment have eluded the best efforts of many investigators.[83] By definition, *Kienböck's disease* is radiologic avascular necrosis of the lunate. It is well accepted that avascularity of the lunate is a part of the process, but whether it is the cause or the result of trauma or fracture is uncertain. Unfortunately, the clinician is frequently faced with the necessity of treating what is often a painful and disabling condition.

## Cause

The loss of the blood supply to the lunate has been attributed to primary fracture,[11] repetitive trauma causing microfracture,[62, 83] or traumatic injury to the ligaments that carry blood to the lunate.[125] It was noted by Hulten[114] in 1928 that there was a statistical association among patients whose ulna appeared shorter than the radius on a PA radiograph of the wrist (Fig. 39–16). This has been termed an *ulnar negative variant*. If the distal articular surface of the ulna is longer than the radius, this is an *ulnar positive variant*. An *ulna neutral variant* exists when the

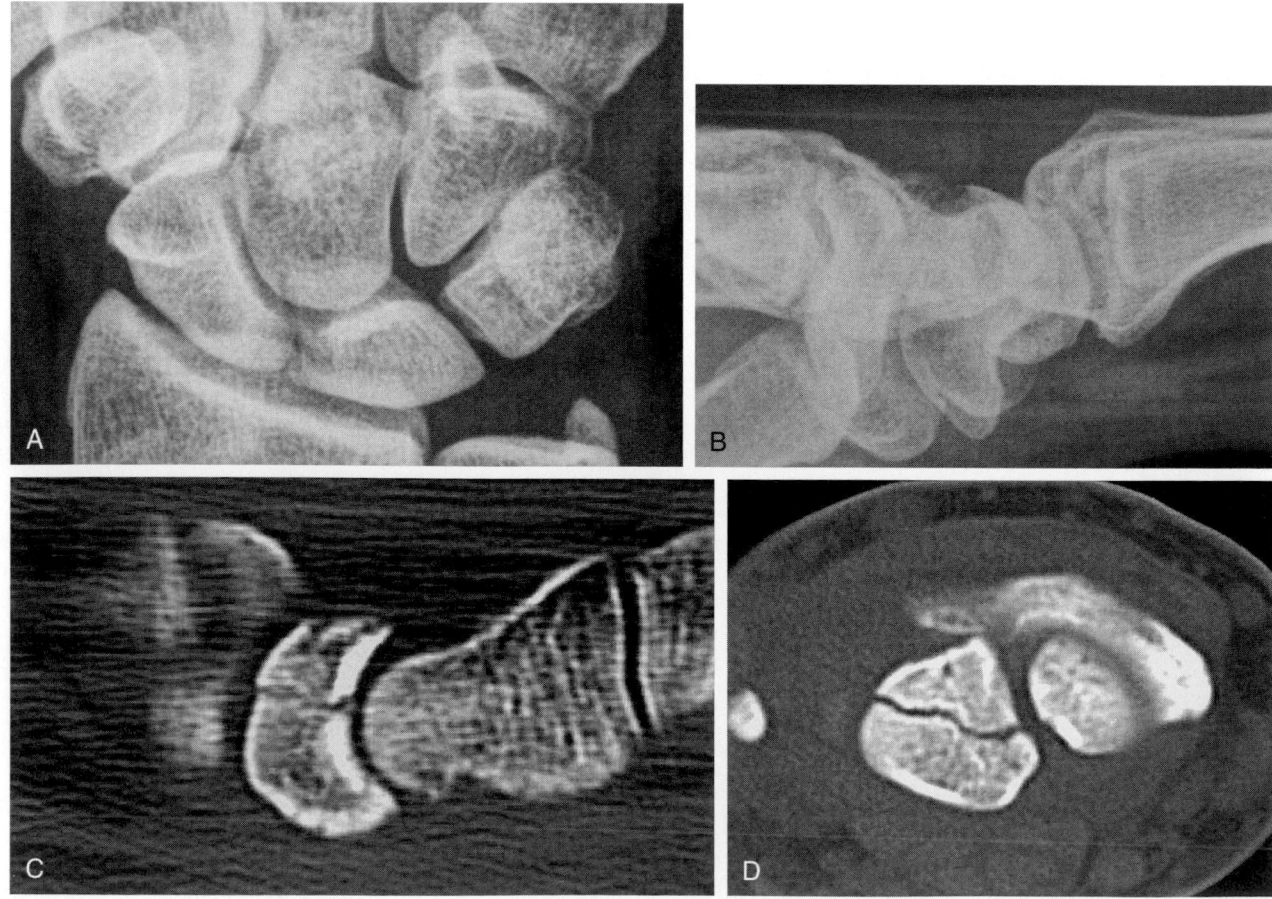

**FIGURE 39–15.** Transverse lunate fracture. *A, B,* Plain radiographs demonstrate some irregularity of the lunate. *C, D,* Axial and sagittal computed tomography images demonstrate the transverse fracture. (*A–D,* Courtesy of Andrew L. Terrono, M.D.)

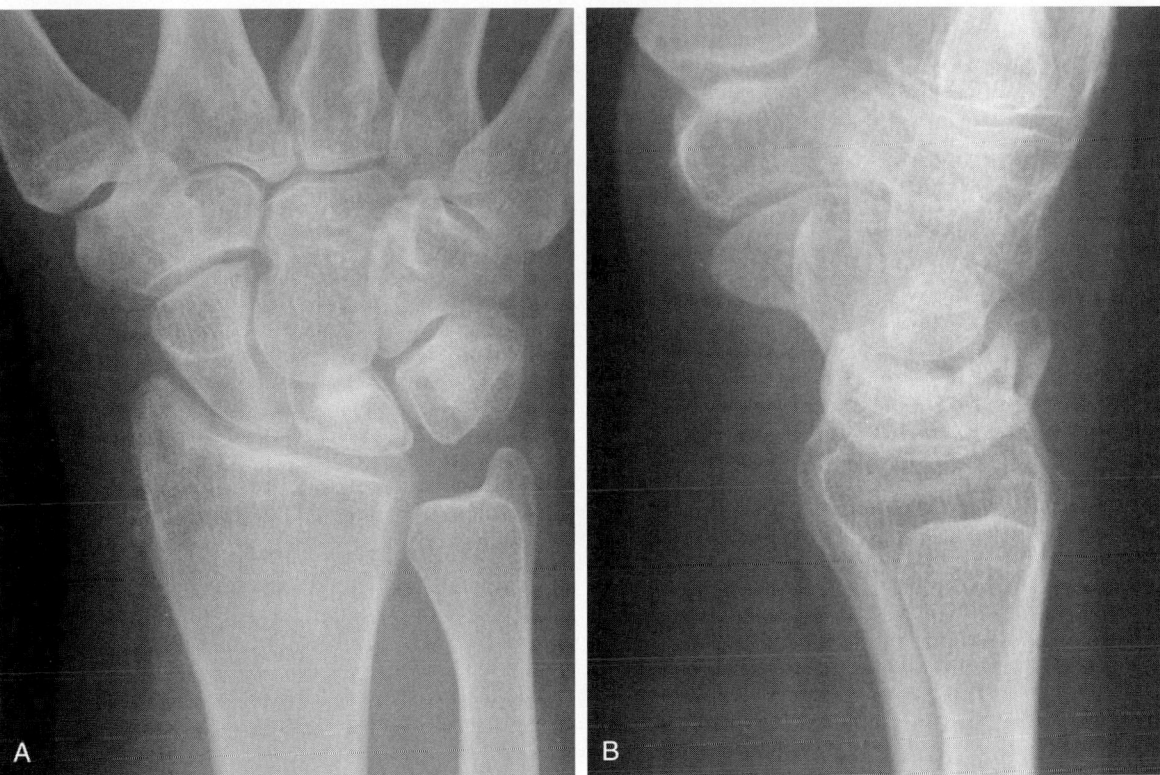

**FIGURE 39–16.** *A, B,* Kienböck's disease. Lunate collapse is present. Ulnar negative variance, as seen here, is a typical feature.

articular surfaces of the radius and ulna are at the same level. Razemon[199] believed that because the radial part of the lunate is supported by the radius and the ulnar part rests on the compliant triangular fibrocartilage, shear stresses are created within the bone that make it more susceptible to fracture. Thus, ulnar negative variance is thought to be causally related to Kienböck's disease by some investigators.[114, 189, 199] It is likely that the cause of Kienböck's disease is multifactorial and that stress, in combination with a precarious blood supply, plays a role in most patients.[255]

## Diagnosis

By definition, the diagnosis is a radiologic one. Very early on the lunate may appear normal, but with time, one sees the typical pattern of sclerosis, loss of lunate height, fragmentation, and, eventually, wrist collapse and arthritis. Clinically, the physician can be suspicious if the patient is a young adult with central dorsal wrist pain and tenderness, swelling, loss of motion, and diminished grip strength. If there is clinical suspicion without radiographic findings, technetium bone scans or MRI scans can be helpful. The presence of ulnar negative variance should raise the possibility of Kienböck's disease. Fractures, usually occurring in the coronal plane, are best seen on polytomography or CT scans. Reinus and co-workers[201] showed that MRI is a very specific technique to show avascular necrosis in carpal bones.

## Treatment

That there is no universally accepted treatment for Kienböck's disease is reflected in the large number of treatment options.[255] Nevertheless, some treatments are applied more commonly than others to this problem, and these are described.

Cast immobilization is no longer considered a useful method for treatment of Kienböck's disease.[64, 238] In a natural history study of sorts, Beckenbaugh and associates[11] in 1980 compared 36 surgically treated patients with 10 patients who were treated nonoperatively. Without surgery, progressive changes were seen radiographically over time (although these changes were not necessarily associated with clinical deterioration).

It appears at present that the modality selected should be based to some degree on the radiologic stage of the process. Stahl[238] and Lichtman and colleagues[140] proposed classifications (Fig. 39–17). It is generally agreed that stage I represents slight sclerosis or fracture; stage II, sclerosis and fragmentation without collapse; and stage III, fragmentation with collapse. Lichtman and colleagues further subdivided stage III into A and B. In stage IIIA, there is lunate collapse but no scaphoid malalignment. In stage IIIB, there is scaphoid malalignment such that it assumes a more vertical position with respect to the lunate and radius. In stage IV, fragmentation, collapse, and arthritis are present.

Surgical options may be divided into stress reduction (unloading), revascularization, replacement of the lunate, and salvage procedures. Stress reduction procedures may

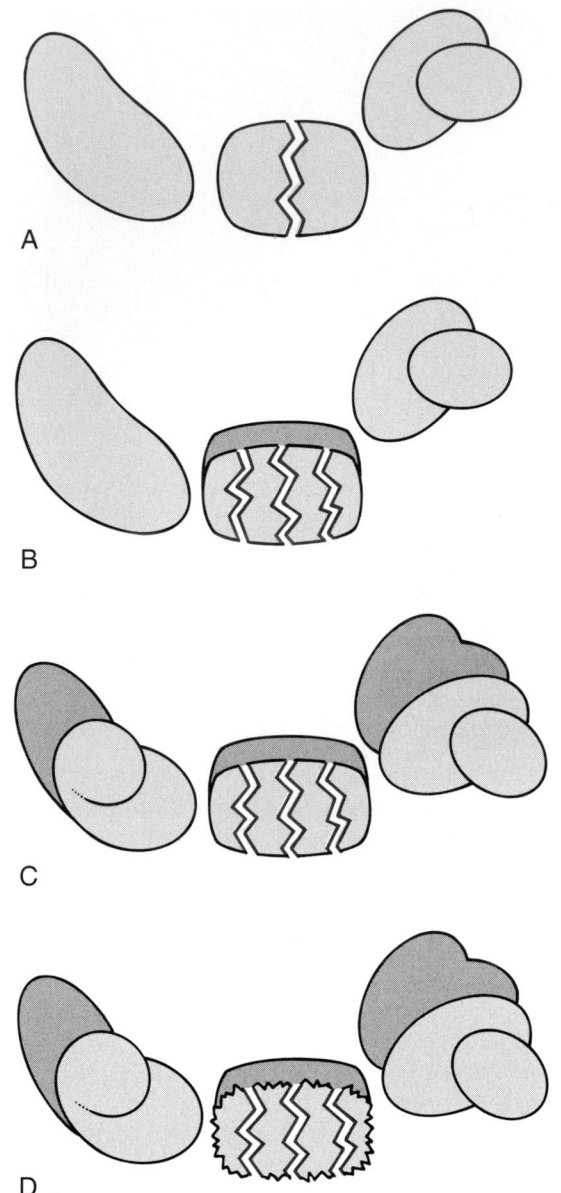

**FIGURE 39–17.** Illustration of the four stages of Kienböck's disease. *A*, Stage I: Sclerosis of the lunate. *B*, Stage II: Sclerosis and fragmentation. *C*, Stage III: Sclerosis and collapse. *D*, Stage IV: Sclerosis, collapse, and intercarpal arthritis. (*A–D*, From Taleisnik, J. The Wrist. New York, Churchill Livingstone, 1985, p. 190.)

be further subdivided into joint leveling procedures (radial shortening, ulnar lengthening), capitate shortening, limited arthrodesis, and distraction. For stage I disease, treatment options include no treatment, cast application, unloading surgery, and open reduction for a recognized fracture. For stage II, unloading procedures, revascularization,[106] and lunate excision with replacement or combinations have been advocated. For stage III, the same options apply, although most investigators state that the prognosis is worse. For stage IV, salvage procedures such as wrist fusion or proximal row carpectomy are recommended for the sufficiently symptomatic patient.

Joint leveling procedures include radial shortening and ulnar lengthening. Almquist[5] summarized the results of

seven series, including his own, in which 69 of 79 patients achieved a successful clinical result with radial shortening. He suggested that this procedure be used only for patients who have "no significant collapse" (i.e., stage I or II) and, of course, ulnar negative variance.

Ulnar lengthening was originally described by Persson in 1950[189] because of problems with radius healing after shortening osteotomy. Armistead and associates[8] reported their experience with this technique and advocated its use in stage II and early stage III patients. They report good results in two series of patients, the second series consisting of 22 patients.[146] There was 1 failure, and 3 patients were lost to follow-up.

More time and experience are necessary to define the role of joint leveling in the management of Kienböck's disease. In an editorial in the *Journal of Hand Surgery* in 1985,[147] Linscheid sounded a cautionary note regarding joint leveling procedures based on his experience of increased wear and degeneration on the ulnar aspect of the lunate, the triangular fibrocartilage, and the triquetrum postoperatively.

Capitate shortening has been suggested by Almquist[5] as a means of unloading the capitate. Horii and colleagues[107] have confirmed that capitate shortening decreases the stress on the lunate by 60%. Obvious concerns regarding iatrogenic avascular necrosis of the head of the capitate have dissuaded us from using this procedure.

Another unloading technique that has several advocates[40, 270] is limited intercarpal arthrodesis. In theory, this procedure decreases the load on the lunate by transmitting it through the fused carpal bones. Watson and Hempton[277] recommended scaphoid-trapezium-trapezoid arthrodesis, whereas Chuinard and Zeman[40] advocated capitate-hamate arthrodesis, and Almquist[5] described capitate-hamate fusion in conjunction with capitate shortening. All these procedures attempt to decrease the normal load on the lunate by transferring it to the other bones of the proximal carpal row. Trumble and colleagues[262] in an in vitro study showed that capitate-hamate fusion was not effective in decreasing lunate load. The joint leveling procedures, scaphoid-trapezium-trapezoid fusion, and scaphoid-capitate fusion were effective in reducing the lunate loading but resulted in a significant decrease in range of motion. Again, Linscheid[147] cautioned that limited wrist arthrodesis alters wrist kinematics extensively and may contribute to later arthritis.

One of the authors of this chapter (LKR) has reported encouraging results with an unloading-revascularization procedure[298] that may be particularly useful in the ulnar-positive patient, for whom radial shortening is contraindicated. The technique involves curettage of the lunate and insertion of cancellous or vascularized bone graft and temporarily unloading the lunate for 6 to 8 weeks with an external fixator. This procedure appears to be most appropriate for persons with stage I or II disease.

Other revascularization procedures for Kienböck's disease are gaining in popularity. Introduced by Hori and co-workers in 1979,[106] the procedure originally involved implantation of a vascular bundle. More recently, Sheetz and colleagues[223] have described a corticocancellous pedicled graft obtained from the distal radius. This technique appears to hold promise and may be most appropriate in conjunction with a joint leveling or unloading procedure.

For advanced disease, lunate replacement has been recommended, using materials as varied as tendon, silicone, acrylic, and Vitallium. Of these, silicone has been the most popular. However, the numerous associated complications, including implant dislocation, progressive carpal collapse,[8] and silicone synovitis,[233] have discouraged its use.

Salvage procedures for advanced Kienböck's disease include wrist denervation, proximal row carpectomy, and limited or total wrist arthrodesis. Some evidence[234] suggests that the results of proximal row carpectomy may not be as good for the Kienböck's population as for the post-traumatic patient.

In our experience, untreated Kienböck's disease most often results in progressive deterioration of the lunate and consequent wrist degeneration.[11] Consequently, for stages I, II, and IIIA, we prefer joint leveling procedures (radial shortening). When ulnar-neutral or ulnar-positive variance exists, we prefer external fixation combined with a vascularized distal radius graft. For stage IIIB, when motion is desirable, we prefer a total midcarpal arthrodesis, acknowledging that the long-term results of this method are not known. Total wrist arthrodesis is indicated for stage IV disease.

### RADIAL SHORTENING

A volar approach is performed at the junction of the middle and distal thirds of the radius. A six-hole 3.5-mm dynamic compression plate is selected and placed in the appropriate position. Two screws are placed distally, and the radius is marked for both the rotational alignment and the proposed osteotomy. The plate is then removed, and a predetermined section of radius is removed between the third and the fourth screw holes to level the radial and ulnar articular surfaces. The plate is replaced, and the remainder of the screws are placed.

A recent technical advance in radial shortening osteotomy has been the oblique osteotomy system of Rayhack. Analogous to his ulnar shortening system,[198] the device includes a cutting jig, which is secured to the radius through the same screw holes that will accommodate the specially designed plate. We have found that this simplifies the procedure considerably.

**Technique (Total Intercarpal Arthrodesis).** Using a dorsal wrist approach, the intercarpal joints are denuded to cancellous bone with a power bur. The wrist is distracted to correct the collapse deformity, and 0.054- or 0.062-inch K-wires are driven across the scaphocapitate, triquetrohamate, and capitate joints. Cancellous bone harvested from the iliac crest is packed tightly into the defects. The wrist is closed in layers, and a U-shaped above-elbow splint is applied. The splint is changed to a solid short above-elbow cast at 1 to 2 weeks, and the sutures are removed. The cast is removed at 6 to 8 weeks, and healing is checked by radiography. If the arthrodesis is successful, the pins are removed and motion is begun.

For stage IV disease, we prefer total radiocarpal and midcarpal arthrodesis. If the radius and capitate articular surfaces are intact, a proximal row carpectomy can be considered. In summary, for stages I, II, and IIIA, we prefer unloading procedures. For stage IIIB, we suggest total intercarpal arthrodesis. For stage IV, we prefer salvage procedures, especially total wrist arthrodesis.

## FRACTURES OF THE CAPITATE

Fractures of the capitate are relatively rare, accounting for 0.8% of 826 carpal injuries reported by Böhler.[24] As with the scaphoid, the intraosseous blood supply to the capitate is retrograde, a factor that undoubtedly contributes to generally unsatisfactory outcomes.[197, 266] Isolated fracture of the waist or proximal portion of the capitate has been reported.[4] More commonly, however, fracture of the capitate occurs in the setting of complex injury patterns.

The association of a capitate fracture with a scaphoid fracture has been termed the *naviculocapitate syndrome*.[245] The cause of this lesion is hyperextension of the wrist, in which the dorsal ridge of the distal radius acts as a fulcrum, fracturing the scaphoid through the waist and the capitate through the neck region. As the wrist continues to hyperextend, the head of the capitate and the proximal fragment of scaphoid rotate together, and the distal portion of the capitate translates dorsally on the proximal pole. When the wrist returns to a neutral position, the distal segment of capitate spins the capitate head by as much as 180° (Fig. 39–18). As a result, the fracture surface of the capitate head comes to lie adjacent to the articular surface of the lunate. Obviously, the capitate will not unite in this malreduced position. This is a difficult diagnosis to make and must be looked for carefully on radiographs (Fig. 39–19). CT may be of value in assessing the degree of displacement and in identifying associated injuries (Fig. 39–20A, B). Once the diagnosis is made, ORIF must be performed.[30, 69]

Cast treatment may be adequate for truly nondisplaced, isolated capitate waist fractures. However, the majority of capitate fractures are displaced or are associated with complex injuries, or both, and require surgery. The capitate is exposed through a dorsal approach. Following anatomic reduction, the fracture is stabilized with multiple K-wires or a headless screw. We prefer to use a mini-Acutrak screw, inserted longitudinally through the head of the capitate and then countersunk.

Complications following capitate fracture include nonunion, malunion, avascular necrosis, and secondary arthritis.[266] As a salvage for avascular necrosis of the capitate head, some investigators have recommended excision of the avascular proximal fragment and fusion of the remaining capitate to the scaphoid and lunate.[30] We successfully performed a capitate-hamate arthrodesis in one case.

## FRACTURES OF THE HAMATE

Fractures of the body of the hamate are uncommon and are often associated with fourth and fifth carpometacarpal fracture-dislocations. CT scanning with sagittal images is

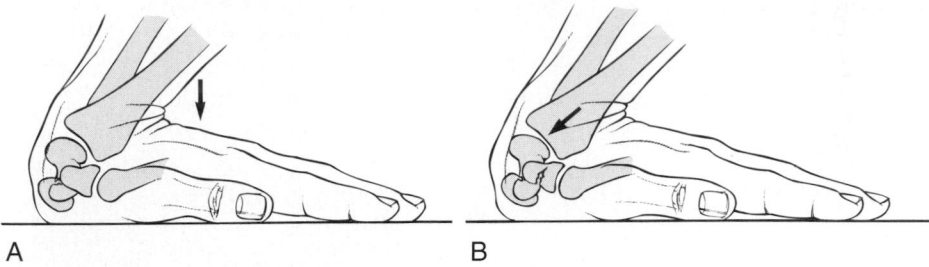

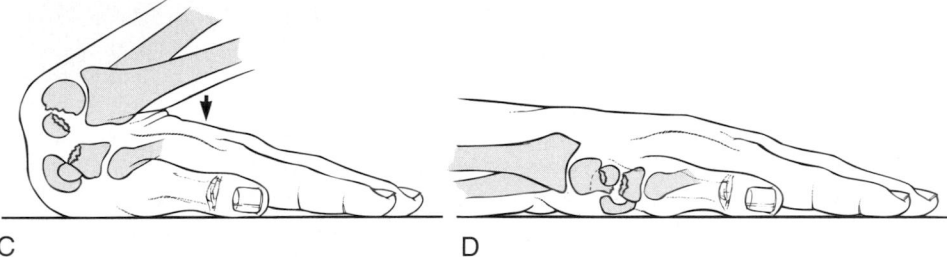

**FIGURE 39–18.** *A–D,* Schematic illustration of the mechanism of injury in the naviculocapitate syndrome.

most helpful. If the fracture is undisplaced and the joint is reduced, closed treatment usually suffices. When the fracture is displaced or unstable, either closed reduction with percutaneous pinning of the joint or ORIF should be performed. Only five cases of isolated hamate body fractures have been reported. ORIF is recommended when there is displacement of the fragment.[180]

Fractures of the hook of the hamate are more common and have attracted attention in the literature because they are a significant and often missed source of disability.[38, 241]

They are especially common in golfers and in tennis, racquetball, and baseball players. The injury is thought to result either from a direct blow to the hamate hook[241] or as an avulsion injury through the transverse carpal and pisohamate ligament attachments to the hamate hook.[20] The physician should suspect the diagnosis if the patient has deep, ill-defined pain in the volar ulnar half of the palm after such an injury. Physical findings include tenderness over the hook of the hamate or dorsoulnar hamate, ulnar nerve symptoms, and, rarely, flexor tendon

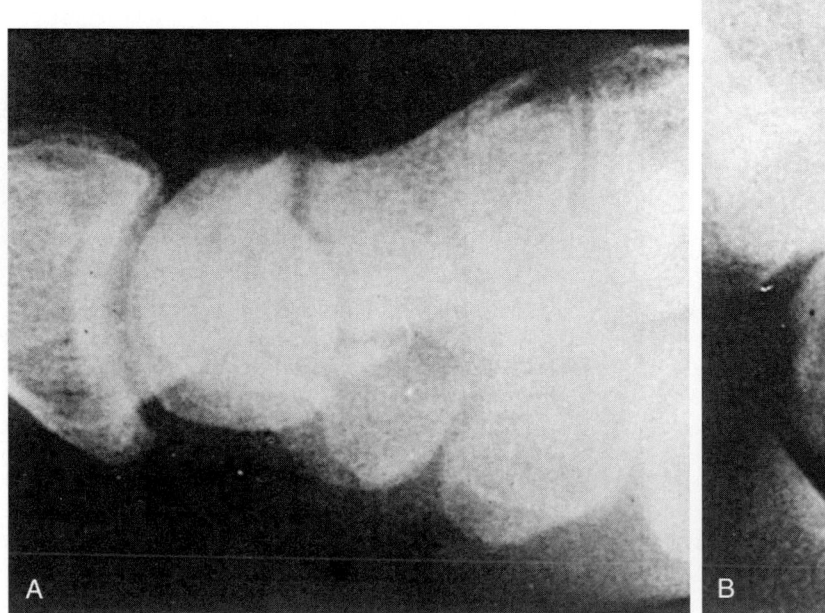

**FIGURE 39–19.** *A,* A lateral radiograph of the carpus demonstrating a naviculocapitate syndrome with the proximal pole of the capitate rotated 180° and the articular surface facing the fracture site. *B,* An anteroposterior view of the wrist demonstrating the naviculocapitate syndrome with the proximal pole of the capitate rotated. (*A, B,* From Monahan, P.R.W.; Galasto, C.S.B. J Bone Joint Surg Br 54:122–124, 1972.)

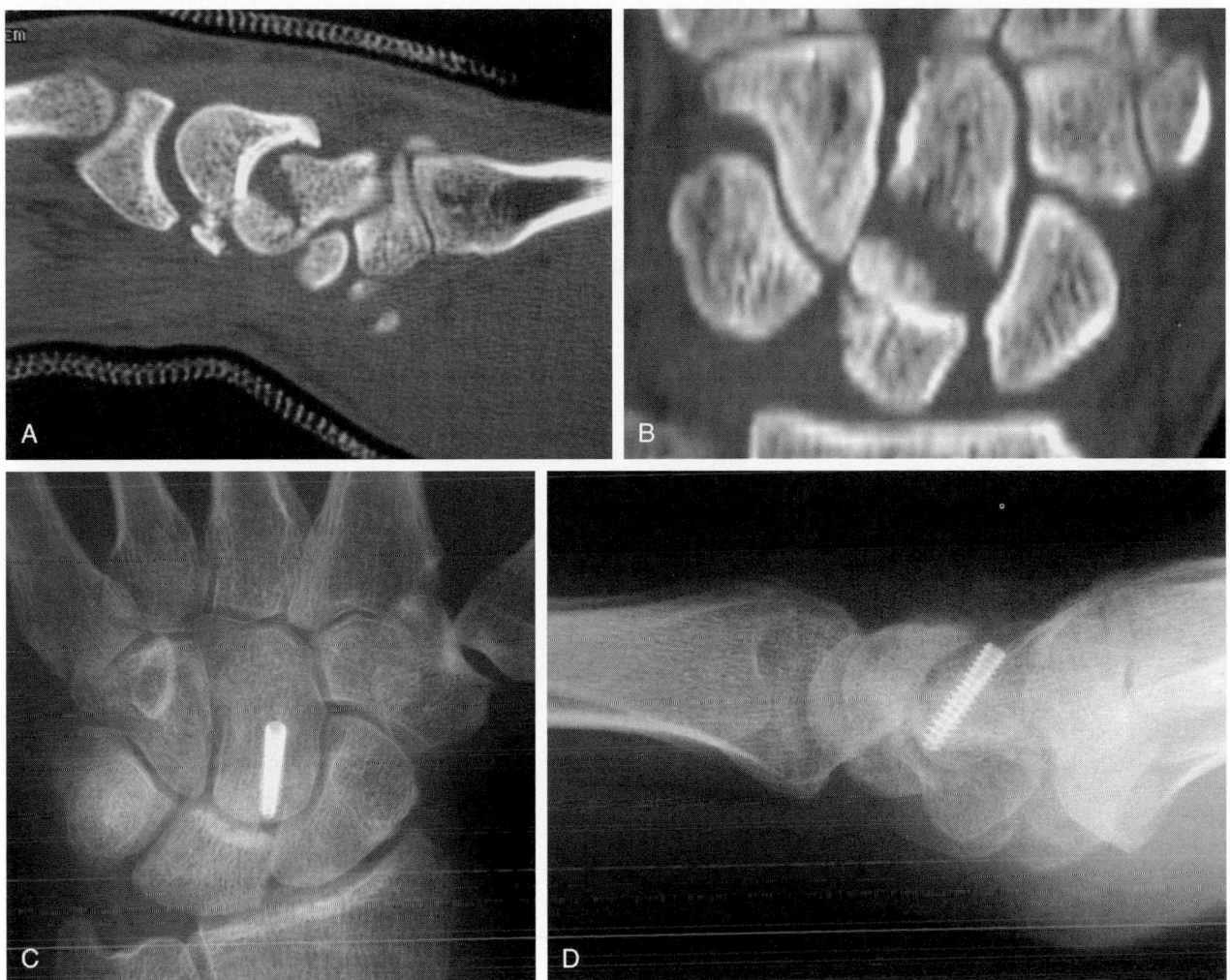

**FIGURE 39–20.** *A, B,* Sagittal and coronal computed tomography images of a displaced capitate fracture-subluxation with an associated volar pole fracture of the lunate. *C, D,* Posteroanterior and lateral radiographs following fixation of the capitate fracture with a mini-Acutrak screw.

rupture.[51] Radiographs may demonstrate this fracture if they are taken in the correct plane, which may be difficult to do. A carpal tunnel view (Fig. 39–21) and a 45° supination oblique view may be helpful. If these are inconclusive, polytomography or CT scans should be used.

Fractures at the base of the hamate hook, particularly when nondisplaced, may heal with cast immobilization. However, fractures near the tip of the hamate hook are more likely to be displaced and are less likely to heal.[30, 74, 118] We reserve internal fixation for acute, displaced fractures of the base of the hamate hook that are large enough for screw placement. However, there seems to be little morbidity from excision of the hook of the hamate. The generally accepted treatment is excision of the fractured hook following a trial of immobilization.[30, 38, 178]

**Technique.** A short longitudinal or zigzag palmar incision is made directly over the hook. The motor branch of the ulnar nerve and the ulnar artery are identified just ulnar to the hook. Subperiosteal dissection is performed around the hamate hook until the fracture site is encountered. The fracture fragment is excised, and the raw surface at the base of the fracture is smoothed and covered with periosteum. Following skin closure, the wrist is splinted for comfort. Gradual resumption of activities is allowed as tolerated. A padded glove may be helpful for the first 4 weeks after initiating grip activities.

## FRACTURES OF THE TRIQUETRUM

Isolated fractures of the triquetrum are the third most common carpal fracture after those of the scaphoid and lunate.[30] The most common type is probably a shear or chisel fracture caused by impingement of the ulnar styloid on the dorsal proximal aspect of the triquetrum when the wrist is forcibly dorsiflexed and ulnarly deviated[137] (Fig. 39–22 A, B). This is seen as a flake of bone on the lateral radiograph (see Fig. 39–22C). Closed treatment with a cast for 4 to 6 weeks is all that is usually required, although these fractures may remain symptomatic for many months. The flake can be excised if symptoms persist.

Triquetral body fracture can occur in association with a perilunate dislocation and requires ORIF. Avascular necrosis has not been reported.

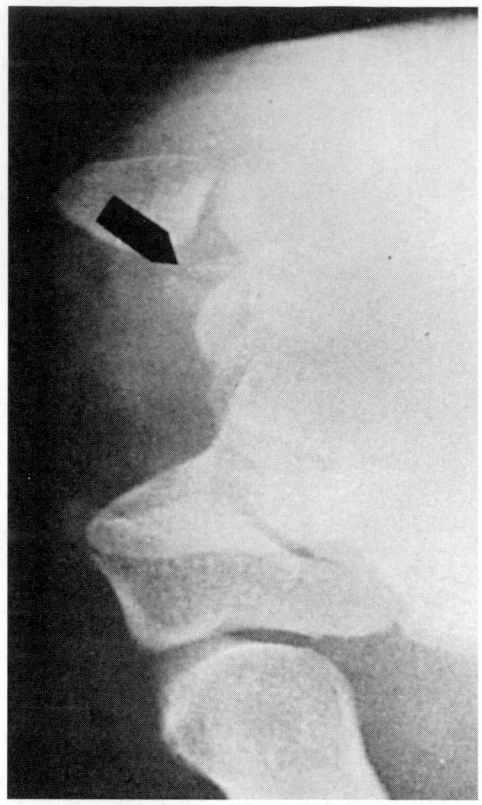

**FIGURE 39–21.** Radiograph of the carpal tunnel demonstrating a split fracture of the hook of the hamate (*arrow*). Lateral tomography and oblique x-ray films might not show this fracture. (From Carter, P.R., et al. J Bone Joint Surg Am 59:583–588, 1977.)

Avulsion fracture of the volar radial portion of the triquetrum is an uncommon injury that represents a serious LT ligament complex disruption.[232] This fracture may be visible only on a PA view with the wrist in radial deviation. If untreated, carpal collapse (volar intercalated segment instability [VISI]) results. We recommend repair or reconstruction of the LT ligament complex.

## FRACTURES OF THE TRAPEZIUM

Isolated trapezium fractures are uncommon injuries, accounting for 2% to 5% of all carpal fractures.[49] There are two types: trapezial body and trapezial ridge fractures. Trapezial body fractures (Fig. 39–23) are the result of a severe axial load to the thumb and appear as either a vertical fracture line or a comminuted, collapsed bone. A 20° pronated radiograph, which places the trapezium into relief, is usually the most helpful. These are intra-articular fractures, and associated metacarpal fracture or subluxation is common. Displaced trapezial body fractures require surgery; both ORIF and traction methods have been described.[26, 49]

The second type is the trapezial ridge fracture (Fig. 39–24). These rare injuries[184] result either from a direct blow, as in a fall on the outstretched hand, or from an avulsion of the flexor retinaculum when the palm contacts a hard surface and the transverse arch is forcibly spread. Diagnosis is suggested by local tenderness and confirmed

by a carpal tunnel view or a CT scan[162] (see Fig. 39–24B). One must have a high index of suspicion, because routine views do not show this fracture. Treatment depends on the location of the fracture. If it is at the tip (type II), a cast for 3 to 6 weeks, molding the first ray into abduction, is sufficient. If it is at the base (type I), early excision of the fracture fragment is recommended because it frequently proceeds to nonunion. If either type results in a painful nonunion, excision should be performed as for ununited fractures of the hook of the hamate.[184] The results of excision are generally good.

## FRACTURES OF THE PISIFORM

These too are relatively uncommon, accounting for 1% to 3% of all carpal bone injuries. Approximately half are associated with fractures of the distal radius, hamate, or triquetrum. Diagnosis is suggested by local pain and tenderness and a history of a direct blow to the ulnar aspect of the hand. Ulnar nerve symptoms may be present. A 30° supination oblique radiograph, carpal tunnel view, or CT scan is confirmatory. Treatment is by short arm cast in 30° of wrist flexion and ulnar deviation for 6 weeks. Late findings include pisotriquetral loose bodies.[246] If painful nonunion or loose bodies develop, pisiform excision is effective. The pisiform is approached through a longitudinal splitting of the flexor carpi ulnaris. Careful subperiosteal excision should be performed, followed by repair of the flexor carpi ulnaris tendon. One should not confuse the presence of an irregular ossification center in the immature patient for a fracture.[26, 30]

## FRACTURES OF THE TRAPEZOID

Owing to the position of the trapezoid as the keystone of the carpal arch and its tight ligamentous connections, trapezoid fractures are exceedingly rare, accounting for 0.2% of all carpal fractures. The mechanism of injury usually involves an axial force through the index metacarpal, although trapezoid fracture can also result from a blast or crush injury.[131, 295] These injuries may be difficult to detect with plain radiographs; CT is recommended. Cast immobilization is usually sufficient. Operative treatment is reserved for displaced fractures or associated ligamentous injury. Dislocation of the trapezoid has also been reported.[244]

## DISLOCATION OF THE CARPUS

### General Considerations

#### FUNCTIONAL ANATOMY

The wrist may be thought of as a mechanical system whose function is to provide motion to and transmit force between the hand distally and the forearm proximally. To accomplish the seemingly contradictory functions of mobility and stability with minimal bulk, the wrist has evolved into a complex of joints among seven bones (the pisiform is a sesamoid for the flexor carpi ulnaris) linked to one another by a complicated set of ligaments. The bony and ligamentous geometry allows this unique joint complex to successfully provide for motion and force transmission. At present, there are two major theories of wrist function.

**Row Theory.** This theory can be summarized as follows: the wrist consists of three proximal (scaphoid, lunate, triquetrum) and four distal (trapezium, trapezoid, capitate, hamate) row bones (Fig. 39–25). This arrangement creates two major joints, the radiocarpal and the midcarpal. The scaphoid, which bridges the two rows, provides a stabilizing link for the midcarpal joints.[56, 69, 72, 150, 208] The proximal row is an intercalated segment between the distal row and the radius–triangular fibrocartilage (TFC) proximally.[56, 69, 132, 208] Although it is composed of rigid elements, the proximal row changes its external configuration by allowing motion among the scaphoid, lunate, and triquetrum, thus providing congruency in all wrist positions.[207] Compressive forces are thought to be transmitted from the distal row to the intercalated segment proximal row and then to the radius–TFC. In Weber's opinion,[282] most of the force is transmitted from the second and third metacarpals to the trapezoid and capitate, then to the proximal two thirds of the scaphoid and lunate, and finally to the radius. Palmer and Werner[187] showed that the amount of force transmitted to the radius is a function of ulnar variance. Their studies showed that in the ulnar-negative variant wrist, 100% of force transmission is through the radius. In a wrist with ulnar-positive variance, 70% of the force is transmitted through the radius, the remainder being borne by the TFC–ulnar head.

**Columnar Theory.** This theory depicts the carpus differently. According to Taleisnik,[251, 252] who reintroduced and modified Navarro's theory,[173] the wrist consists

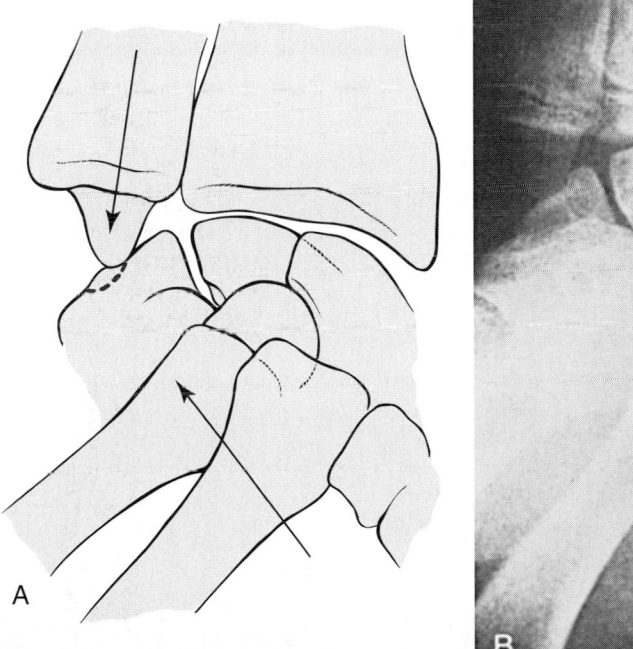

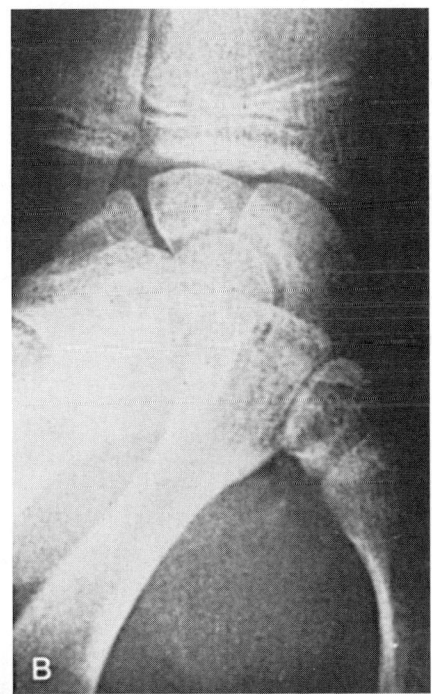

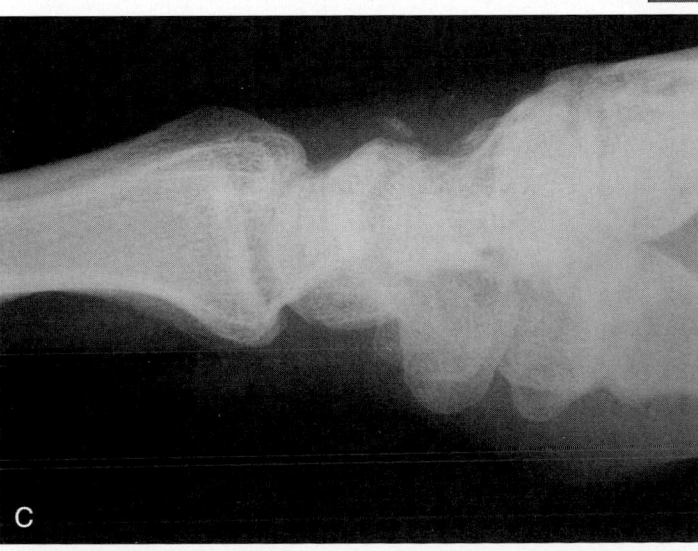

FIGURE 39–22. *A,* Diagram demonstrating the proposed mechanism of the "chisel" fracture of the triquetrum. The arrow along the ulna represents the weight of the torso; the oblique arrow represents the ground force during a fall with the wrist in dorsiflexion and ulnar deviation. *B,* Radiograph demonstrating a chisel fracture of the triquetrum. *C,* Lateral radiograph demonstrating a dorsal triquetral impaction fleck. (*A, B,* From Levy, M., et al. J Bone Joint Surg Br 61:355–357, 1979.)

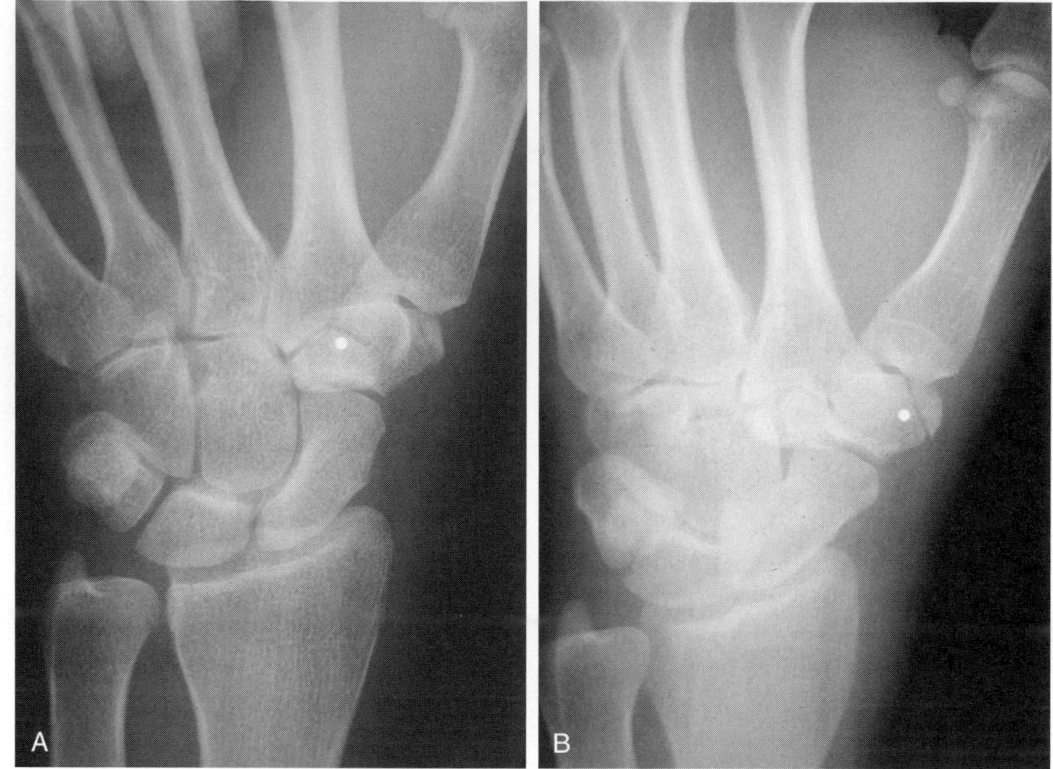

**FIGURE 39–23.** Trapezial body fracture. *A,* The fracture line is not readily apparent on the posteroanterior (PA) view. *B,* The fracture is evident on the semipronated PA view.

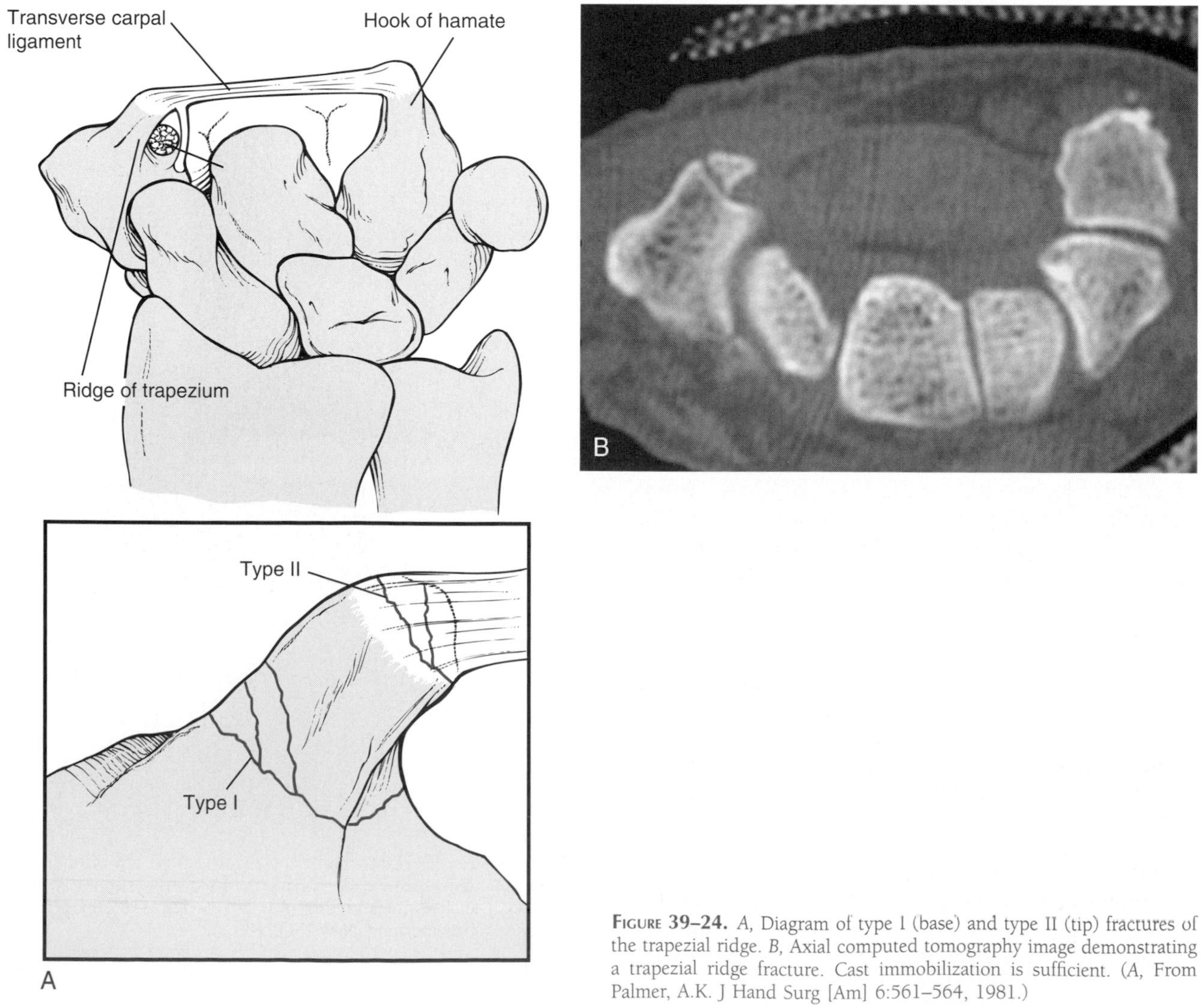

Transverse carpal ligament

Hook of hamate

Ridge of trapezium

Type II

Type I

**FIGURE 39–24.** *A,* Diagram of type I (base) and type II (tip) fractures of the trapezial ridge. *B,* Axial computed tomography image demonstrating a trapezial ridge fracture. Cast immobilization is sufficient. (*A,* From Palmer, A.K. J Hand Surg [Am] 6:561–564, 1981.)

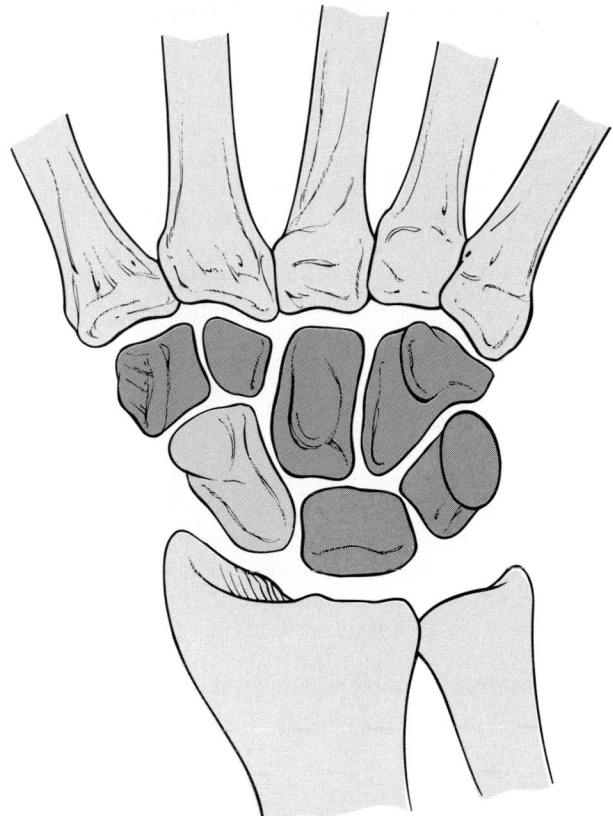

FIGURE 39–25. The row theory of the carpal anatomy. (From Green, D.P. Operative Hand Surgery, 2nd ed., Vol. 2. New York, Churchill Livingstone, 1988, p. 876.)

and the distal V, or deltoid, ligament links the distal row to the proximal row and to the radius. The radioscaphocapitate ligament is the only ligament that spans both rows.

The most important of the volar ligaments are the radioscaphocapitate, the long radiolunate, the short radiolunate, the ulnolunate, and the ulnotriquetral.[251] The distal V, or deltoid, ligament is composed of the scaphocapitate and triquetral-capitate ligaments (Fig. 39–29A). Collectively, the volar ligaments are thought to be important in stabilizing the carpus with respect to the radius and ulna as well as in stabilizing the midcarpal joint. It should be kept in mind that these ligaments are made up of thickenings of the volar wrist capsule and are difficult to identify as distinct structures from the volar surface. The bones of the proximal row are further bound together by the scapholunate interosseous ligament and the lunotriquetral interosseous ligament. The distal row bones are bound even more tightly by their interosseous ligaments (see Fig. 39–29B). True collateral ligaments of the wrist probably do not exist as such and are represented by the tendon sheaths of the first dorsal extensor compartment radially and the sixth dorsal extensor compartment ulnarly.

## WRIST KINEMATICS

There is no general agreement on the exact amount of motion that occurs at the various carpal articulations.[208, 214, 282] This is because these motions are small in

of three columns (Fig. 39–26). The central column comprises the lunate proximally and the capitate and the rest of the distal row distally and is the primary flexion-extension column. The mobile radial column is made up entirely of the scaphoid, and the ulnar or rotation column consists of the triquetrum. It is our opinion that the row theory best fits the available data.

**Ligament Anatomy.** The carpal bones are linked to one another and to the metacarpals and forearm by a complicated set of ligaments. Taleisnik,[251] Mayfield and colleagues,[159] and Berger and associates[16, 17] studied this area extensively, and their work forms the basis for our current understanding. In brief, there are three sets of ligaments: the dorsal capsular, volar capsular, and interosseous ligaments. The two dorsal capsular ligaments—the dorsal intercarpal (DIC) and the dorsal radiocarpal (DRC)—are relatively thin, forming a lateral V configuration (Fig. 39–27). The DIC helps to provide transverse stability to the proximal row, and the DRC helps to stabilize the proximal row to the radius, preventing ulnar translation. Together, the DIC and DRC appear to function as a dorsal radioscaphoid ligament, indirectly stabilizing the proximal pole of the scaphoid.[271] The volar ligaments are intracapsular and are best seen from inside the joint with an arthroscope. They can be thought of as forming a V within a V, with a weak area between them that overlies the capitolunate joint and is called the *space of Poirier* (Fig. 39–28). The proximal V links the carpus to the forearm,

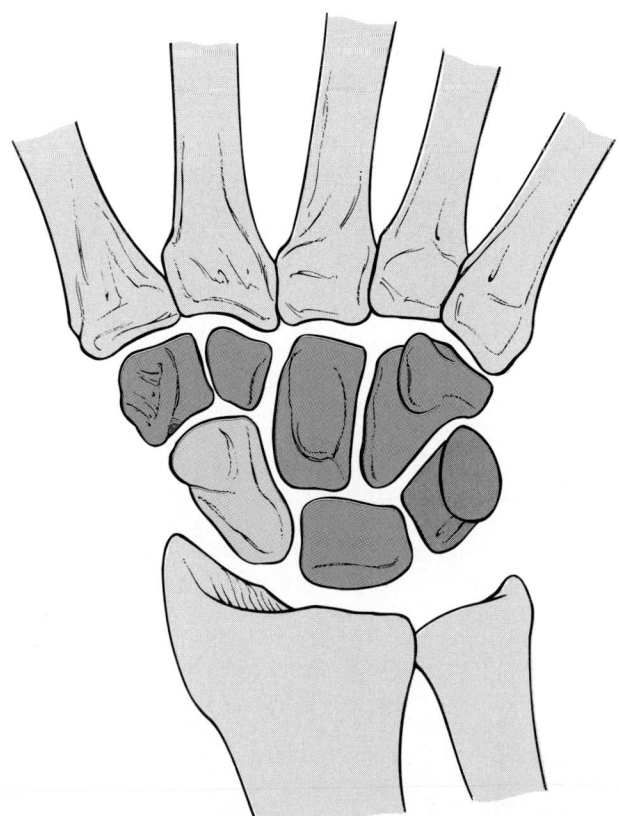

FIGURE 39–26. The columnar theory of the carpal anatomy. (Redrawn from Lichtman, D.M., et al. Ulnar midcarpal instability—Clinical and laboratory analysis. J Hand Surg [Am] 6:515–523, 1981. By permission of Churchill Livingstone, New York, 1981.)

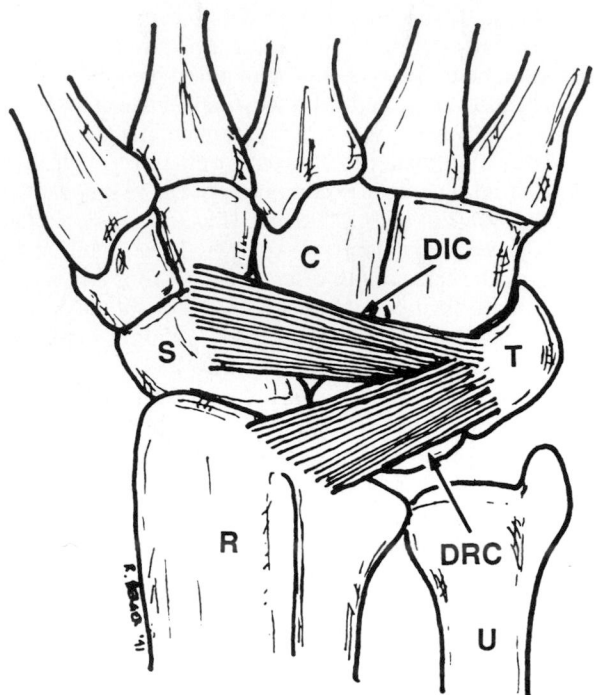

**Figure 39–27.** The extrinsic dorsal ligaments of the wrist. Schematic of the carpal region from a dorsal perspective. *Abbreviations:* C, capitate; DIC, dorsal intercarpal ligament; DRC, dorsal radiocarpal ligament; R, radius; S, scaphoid; T, triquetrum; U, ulna. (From Berger, R.A.; Garcia-Elias, M. In: An, K.N.; Berger, R.A.; Cooney, W.P. III, eds. Biomechanics of the Wrist Joint. New York, Springer-Verlag, 1991, p. 10.)

amplitude and occur primarily in rotation and are therefore very difficult to visualize by traditional means, including radiography. Given the inherent difficulties in obtaining in vivo measurements,[211] much of the foundation for our understanding of wrist kinematics has been based on cadaveric specimens.[208] A recently described technique of noninvasive bone registration using CT has shed some light on wrist kinematics in the living subject.[292] This novel technique will likely refine our understanding of normal and pathologic wrist motion.

Total wrist flexion and extension are made up approximately equally by motion at the midcarpal and radiocarpal joints. However, the midcarpal joint contributes more to flexion (62%) than the radiocarpal joint, as the wrist moves from neutral to full flexion. Conversely, as the wrist moves from neutral to full extension, the radiocarpal joint contributes more (62%) than the midcarpal joint. Further, wrist radial-ulnar deviation is contributed to by motion at the midcarpal and radiocarpal joints, with the majority (55%) of this motion occurring at the midcarpal joint (Fig. 39–30). As the wrist moves from radial to ulnar deviation, the proximal row extends as well as deviates ulnarly. As the wrist moves from ulnar to radial deviation, the proximal row flexes and deviates radially. The distal row also translates dorsally in ulnar deviation and volarly in radial deviation. This translation may be the cause of proximal row extension and flexion.[282] Simultaneously, small amplitude motions occur between the bones of each row. All these motions are normally smooth and integrated, allowing total wrist motion to be synchronous and flowing. We agree with Destot[55] that the proximal carpal

row functions as a variable geometry intercalated segment between the distal row and the radius–TFC.[207]

Because the primary wrist motors all insert into the metacarpals, all wrist motion is controlled by the bony configuration and ligamentous attachments of the carpals. The exact mechanism by which these displacements occur is not well established. Some investigators[282] believe that the triquetrohamate articulation exerts the major control, whereas others[56] believe that the scaphoid and its attachments are most important. At present, a descriptive analysis is the most that can be offered. In 1972, in a seminal article, Linscheid and colleagues[150] described what was then known about carpal mechanics and emphasized the importance of the proximal row as an intercalated segment. They also pointed out some clinically useful radiographic measurements. In a true lateral radiograph of the normal wrist, the long axis of the scaphoid when measured against the long axis of the lunate was found to be 47° with a range of 30° to 60° (Fig. 39–31). Further, the radius, lunate, and capitate long axes are colinear or with slight volar flexion of the lunate. If the lunate is dorsiflexed with respect to the radius, DISI is said to exist (Fig. 39–32A). Conversely, if the lunate is palmar flexed with respect to the radius, VISI is present (see Fig. 39–32B). This nomenclature assumes that the lunate is

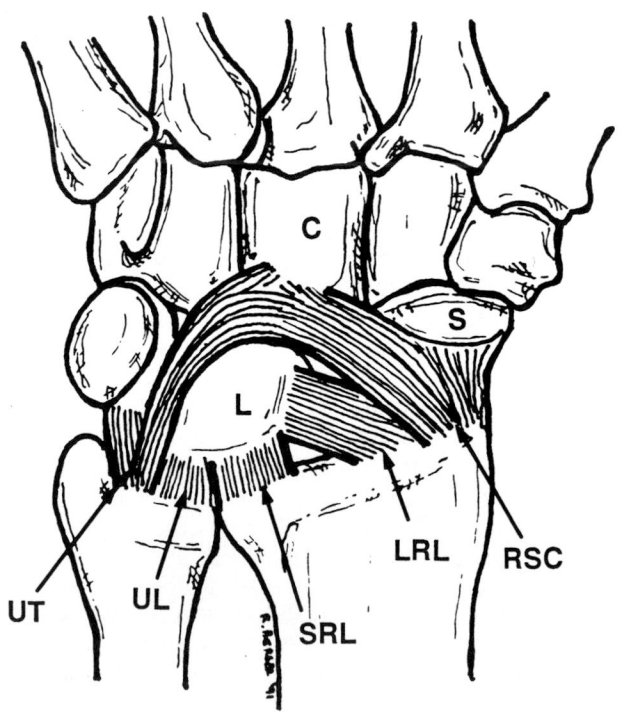

**Figure 39–28.** The extrinsic volar wrist ligaments. Schematic of the carpal region from a palmar perspective with the extrinsic palmar carpal ligaments illustrated. *Abbreviations:* C, capitate; L, lunate; LRL, long radiolunate ligament; RSC, radioscaphocapitate ligament; S, scaphoid; SRL, short radiolunate ligament; UL, ulnolunate ligament; UT, ulnotriquetral ligament. Note how the medialmost fibers of the RSC ligament arch around the distal aspect of the palmar horn of the lunate to interdigitate with fibers from the UL/UT complex to form the arcuate ligament, which supports the head of the capitate. Only a small percentage of fibers from this complex insert into the body of the capitate. (From Berger, R.A., Garcia-Elias, M. In: An, K.N.; Berger, R.A.; Cooney, W.P. III, eds. Biomechanics of the Wrist Joint. New York, Springer-Verlag, 1991, p. 6.)

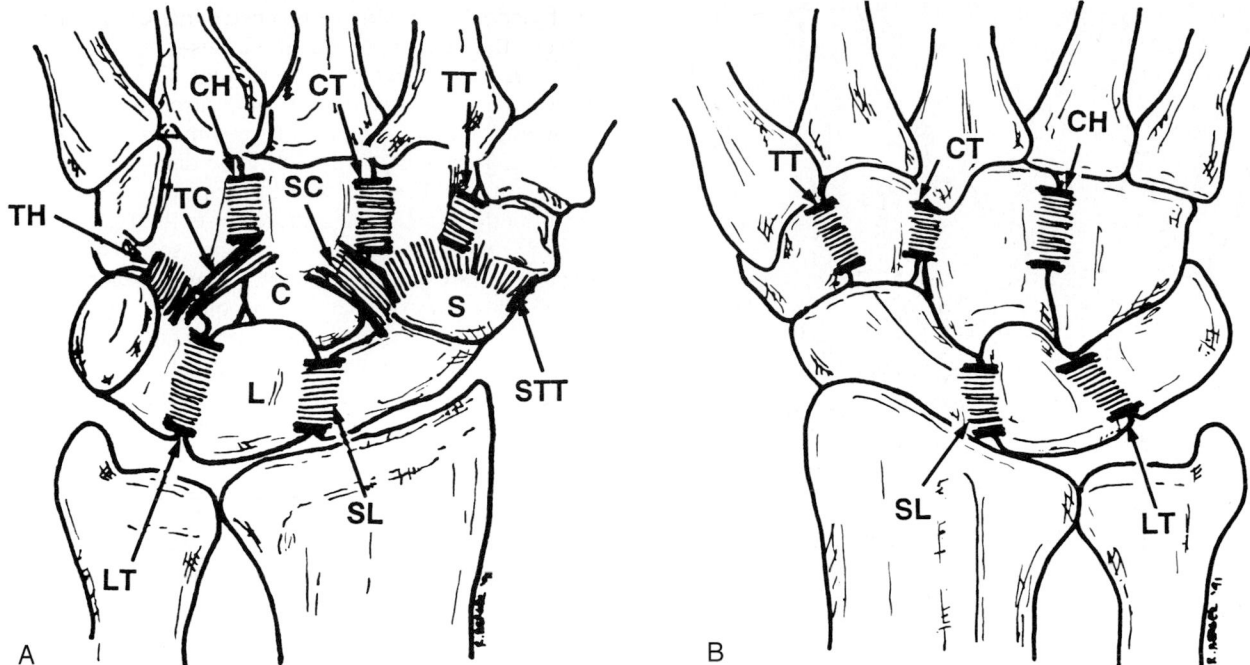

**FIGURE 39–29.** *A,* Schematic of the carpal region from a palmar perspective showing the palmar intrinsic ligaments. *Abbreviations:* C, capitate; CH, capitohamate ligament; CT, capitotrapezoid ligament; L, lunate; LT, lunotriquetral ligament; S, scaphoid; SC, scaphocapitate ligament; SL, scapholunate ligament; STT, scaphotrapeziotrapezoid ligament; TC, triquetrocapitate ligament; TH, triquetrohamate ligament; TT, trapeziotrapezoid ligament. SL, LT, TT, CT, and CH represent the palmar aspects of the interosseous ligaments connecting bones within the proximal and distal carpal rows. STT, SC, TC, and TH represent the intrinsic ligaments that span the midcarpal joint on the palmar side. *B,* Schematic of the carpal region from a dorsal perspective showing the dorsal intrinsic ligaments. *Abbreviations:* CH, capitohamate ligament; CT, capitotrapezoid ligament; LT, lunotriquetral ligament; SL, scapholunate ligament; TT, trapeziotrapezoid ligament. The only dorsal ligament consistently found that crosses the midcarpal joint is the dorsal intercarpal ligament, not shown in this drawing. (*A, B,* From Berger, R.A.; Garcia-Elias, M. In: An, K.N.; Berger, R.A.; Cooney, W.P. III, eds. Biomechanics of the Wrist Joint. New York, Springer-Verlag, 1991, pp. 6, 13.)

representative of the proximal row and therefore the entire intercalated segment. These patterns (DISI and VISI) are commonly seen in clinically important wrist instabilities. Youm and Flatt[296] defined *carpal height* as the distance between the base of the third metacarpal and the distal articular surface of the radius. They further defined the *carpal height ratio* as this distance divided by the length of the third metacarpal. A normal ratio is 0.54 ± 0.03 (Fig. 39–33). Thus, a wrist exhibiting longitudinal collapse DISI or VISI from whatever cause would have a decreased carpal height measurement and a decreased carpal height ratio.

## MECHANISM OF INJURY

Most clinically important carpal dislocations and fracture-dislocations are axial compression-hyperextension injuries, resulting from falls onto the outstretched hand. The exact amount of force and its direction of application as well as the strength and stiffness of the wrist structures determine the precise nature of the injury. A very common pattern is one in which the distal row is displaced dorsal to the proximal row. For this to occur, there must be a failure of the connecting structures between the two rows, and this may be a scaphoid fracture or tear of the scapholunate interosseous ligament as occurs in a scapholunate dissociation. If the force is more severe, a complete perilunate dislocation may occur, wherein the energy of the injury is not dissipated until the LT interosseous ligaments are torn as well.

An attempt to reproduce these mechanisms in vitro was made by Mayfield and co-workers.[160] They loaded cadaver wrists to increasing degrees of destruction and demonstrated four stages of perilunate instability, which they termed *progressive perilunate instability* (Fig. 39–34). The mechanism of injury was extension, ulnar deviation, and intercarpal supination. Thus, stage I is scapholunate instability caused by tearing of the scapholunate interosseous ligament and the long radiolunate ligament; this corresponds clinically with scapholunate dissociation. Stage II includes lunate capitate subluxation caused by the injury propagating through the volar capitolunate capsule (space of Poirier). Stage III includes lunate-triquetral dislocation caused by the injury continuing through the LT interosseous ligament. Stage IV is lunate subluxation with respect to the scaphoid, capitate, triquetrum, and radius owing to tearing of the dorsal radiolunate capsule, which allows the lunate to rotate anteriorly into the carpal canal based on its intact short radiolunate ligament. Therefore, volar dislocation of the lunate is the ultimate in perilunate instability.

It should be emphasized that these studies did not produce isolated ulnar side instabilities. The mechanisms for these were studied by Horii and associates[108] and Viegas and colleagues.[270] Horii[108] demonstrated in cadavers that complete sectioning of the LT interosseous ligament alone altered wrist kinematics but did not cause VISI. If the capsular ligaments (dorsal radiotriquetral and dorsal intercarpal) were also sectioned, static VISI was produced.

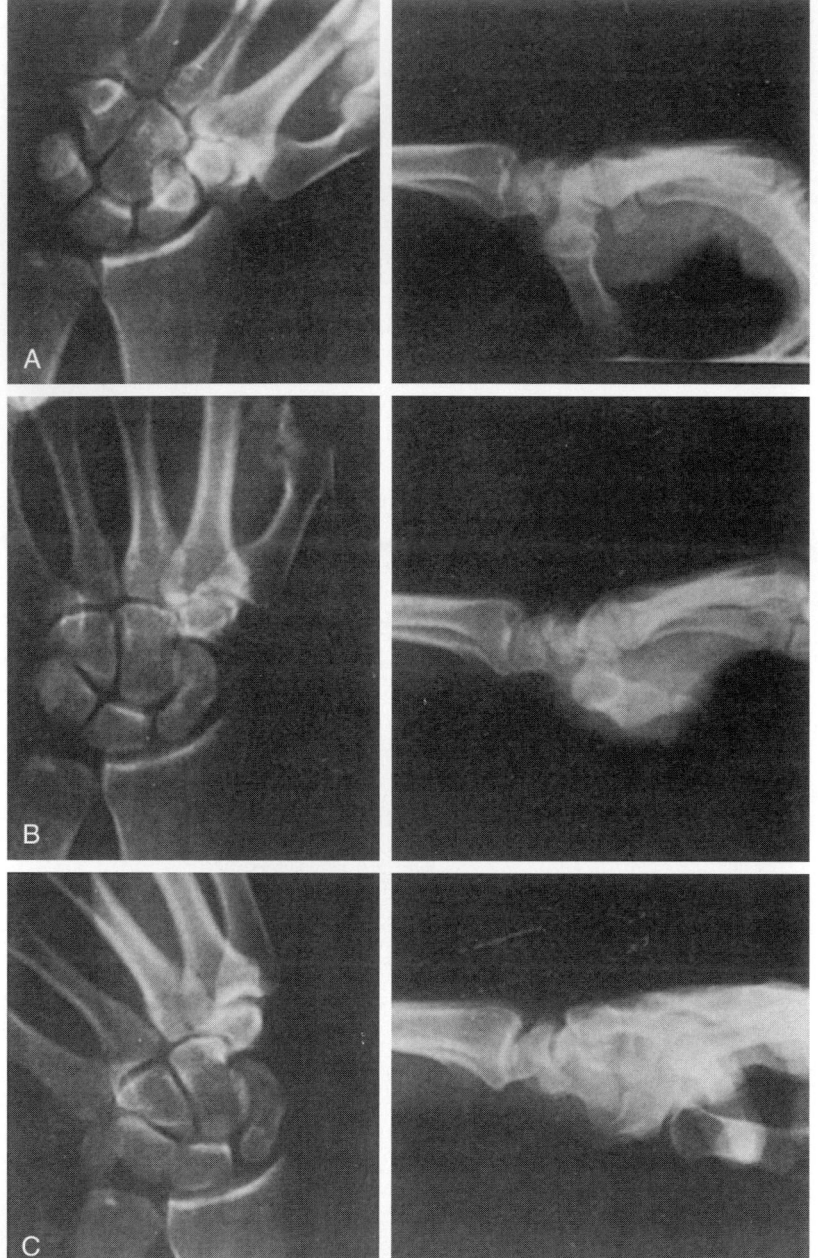

FIGURE 39–30. *A,* In radial deviation, the proximal carpal row deviates toward the radius, translates toward the ulna, and flexes as seen by visualizing the lunate on the lateral radiograph. *B,* With the wrist in neutral, the capitate, lunate, and radius are nearly colinear. *C,* In ulnar deviation, the proximal row deviates toward the ulna, translates toward the radius, and extends as visualized by the lunate on the lateral radiograph.

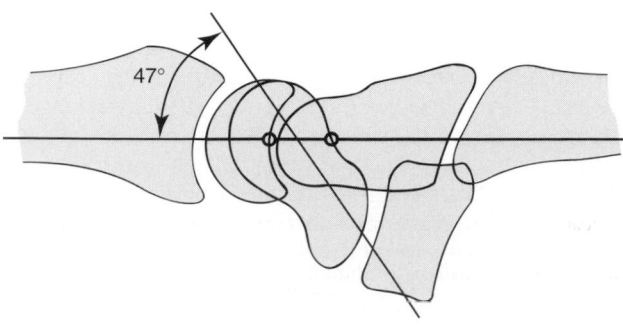

FIGURE 39–31. The normal scapholunate angle as represented in the original drawings from Linscheid and co-workers. (From Linscheid, R.L., et al. J Bone Joint Surg Am 54:1612–1632, 1972.)

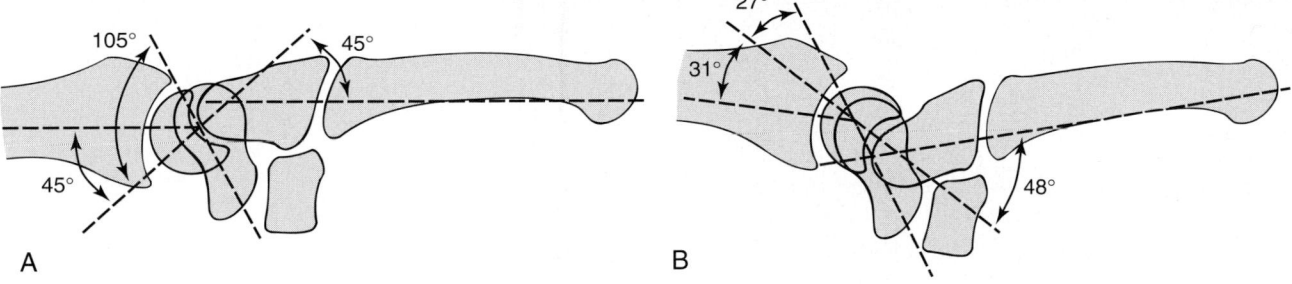

**FIGURE 39–32.** *A,* Dorsal intercalated segment instability. The scapholunate angle is high (105°), the capitolunate angle is high (45°), and the radiolunate angle is high (45°). The intercalated segment is represented by the lunate. *B,* Volar intercalated segment instability. The scapholunate angle is low (27°). (*A, B,* From Linscheid, R.L., et al. J Bone Joint Surg Am 54:1612–1632, 1972.)

Larsen and co-workers[134] devised a carpal instability classification that takes into account six categories: chronicity, constancy, cause, location, direction, and pattern. For example, a case of scapholunate instability could be classified as (1) acute (<1 week); (2) static (demonstrated on plain radiographs); (3) traumatic; (4) midcarpal, scapholunate; (5) DISI; and (6) carpal instability dissociative. They suggested that by better classifying wrist instabilities, surgeons will be able to compare various treatment methods. Our preference is to abbreviate this scheme to (1) cause, (2) anatomy, (3) severity, and (4) time (CAST). Therefore, using the same example, scapholunate instability could be (1) traumatic; (2) midcarpal DISI, dissociative, scapholunate; (3) static; and (4) acute.

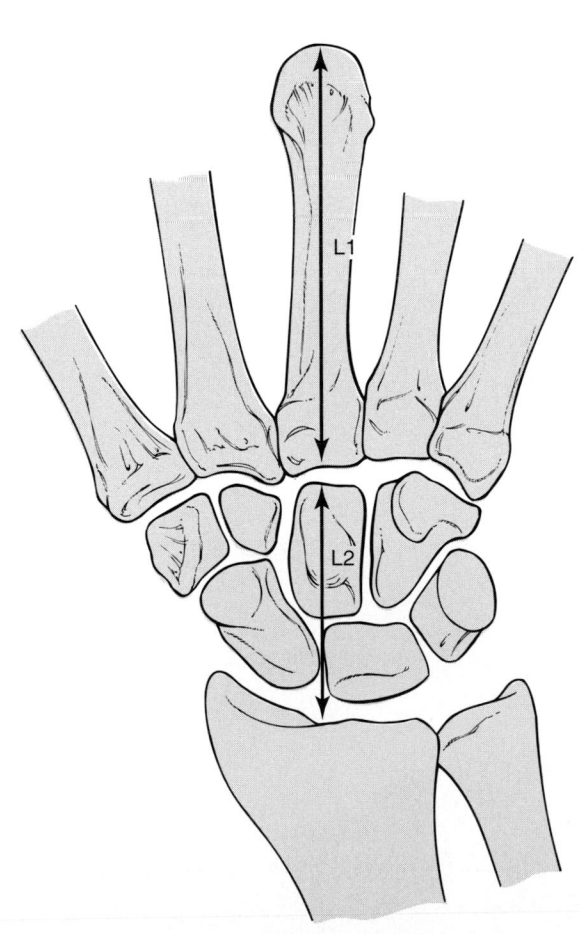

**FIGURE 39–33.** Measurement of the carpal height index. The distance (L2) from the radiocarpal line to the base of the third metacarpal is divided by the length of the third metacarpal (L1). The normal index is 0.54 ± 0.3 mm. (Redrawn from Youm, Y.; Flatt, A. Clin Orthop 149:21–32, 1980.)

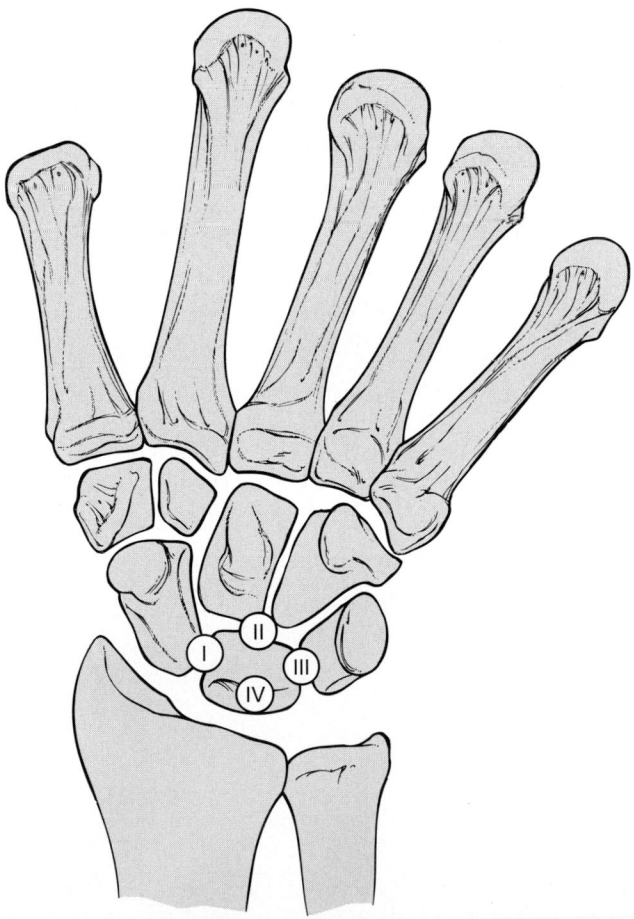

**FIGURE 39–34.** The pathomechanics and progressive perilunar instability pattern demonstrated by Mayfield and co-workers. I, Scaphoid instability with respect to the lunate; II, scaphoid plus capitate instability with respect to the lunate; III, scaphoid plus capitate plus triquetrum instability with respect to the lunate; IV, lunate dislocation. (From Mayfield, J.K., et al. J Hand Surg [Am] 5:226–241, 1980.)

## DIAGNOSIS

The severe instabilities that are obvious on routine radiographs are relatively easy to diagnose (static); whereas subtle instabilities may manifest as wrist pain with normal radiographs are difficult. Approach patients with these symptoms by keeping in mind that not all instabilities are painful and not all painful wrists are due to instability.[207]

### History

In the history, one should look for an episode of trauma such as a fall on the outstretched hand. The patient should be asked about "clicks" or "clunks." The patient can sometimes localize the exact point of pain. Knowing the type of activity that worsens the symptoms is helpful.

### Physical Examination

The unaffected wrist should be used as a reference. Observe for swelling and abrasions that may provide a clue as to the mechanism of injury. Palpate for tenderness of the first dorsal compartment (de Quervain's tenosynovitis), the anatomic snuffbox (scaphoid fracture), the first carpometacarpal joint (arthritis), the scapholunate interval (scapholunate ligament tear or ganglion), the LT joint (LT ligament tear), the dorsal radius (fracture), the radioulnar joint (instability), the extensor carpi ulnaris tendon (tendonitis or subluxation), and the extensor carpi ulnaris–flexor carpi ulnaris interval (ulnar impingement on the carpus, triangular fibrocartilage tear). Volarly, palpate the pisiform (fracture, arthritis) and the hook of the hamate (fracture). Active and passive motion of the wrist should be recorded, and one should note any dyssynchronous movements or "clunks." Range of motion may or may not be reduced. Measurement of grip strength on both wrists is also very important, as any significant wrist disease usually reduces grip strength.

### Stress Tests

Numerous maneuvers have been described to localize wrist pathology. In the dorsal and volar shift test, the forearm is stabilized with one hand and the wrist translated dorsally and volarly with the other hand. It is normal to be able to subluxate the wrist volarly (midcarpal joint) but not dorsally. Instability to dorsal translation is suggestive of scapholunate pathology (Fig. 39–35). A popular test for scaphoid instability is the scaphoid shift[275] (Fig. 39–36). As described by Watson, the scaphoid shift is a provocative maneuver, with a positive test result eliciting pain as well as demonstrating instability. Easterling and Wolfe[57] have shown a high false-positive rate (32%) with this test, and therefore, the findings must be taken in the context of the patient.

Other stress tests are useful for localizing ulnar-sided wrist pathology. In the ulnocarpal stress test,[76] the examiner applies an axial stress while rotating the forearm as the wrist is held in maximal ulnar deviation. A related maneuver, the ulnar carpal shift test, is performed by simultaneously pushing the ulnar head down and pushing the ulnar carpus up (Fig. 39–37). A positive test result elicits pain; both tests are helpful in identifying ulnar impingement syndromes and TFC tears.

The triquetrolunate ballottement test[200] appears to be more specific for LT tears. The lunate is stabilized with one hand and the triquetrum is passively shifted dorsally and palmarly with the other hand, which may elicit pain.

The midcarpal shift test has been described by Lichtman and colleagues[142] to diagnose nondissociative midcarpal instability. While stabilizing the forearm in pronation, the examiner exerts a palmarly directed force onto the patient's wrist and ulnarly deviates the wrist maximally. Lichtman has graded the degree of instability based on the degree of palmar midcarpal translation and the degree of clunking.[65]

Although none of these physical examination maneuvers is difficult to perform, it takes a great deal of experience to interpret the results. It is very helpful to examine the normal wrist first as a baseline.

## RADIOGRAPHY

When ordering diagnostic studies for wrist instability, one must remember that the views generally represent static images of a dynamic problem.

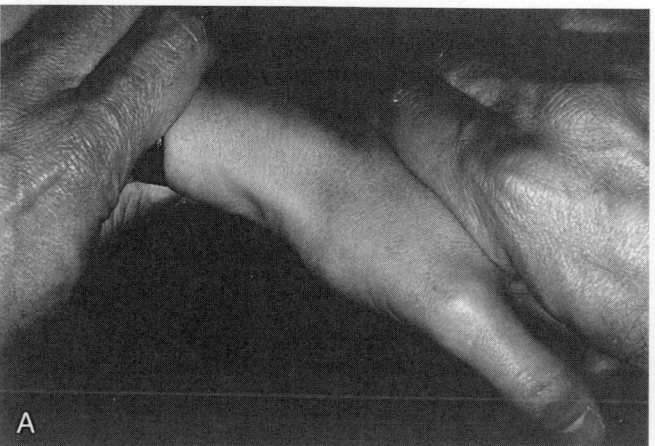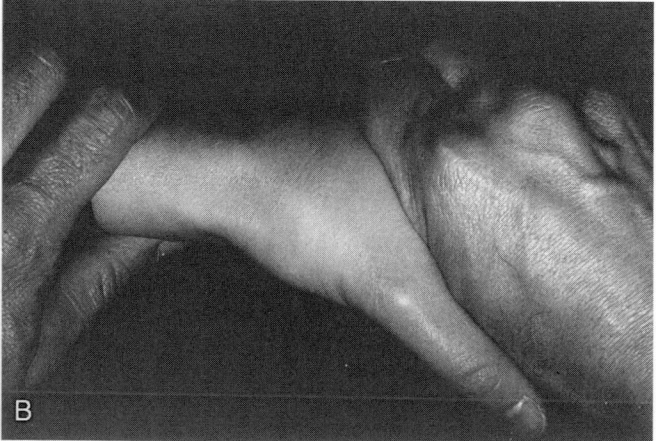

**FIGURE 39–35.** *A,* Volar shift test. The examiner stabilizes the distal forearm and simultaneously pushes the hand in the volar direction. Normally, a painless "shift" is felt by the examiner and patient. This generally represents midcarpal laxity and should be tested against the normal side. *B,* Dorsal shift test. The examiner stabilizes the distal forearm with one hand and simultaneously pushes the hand dorsally. Normally, very little motion is felt. In patients with dorsal intercalated segment instability, increased motion or pain, or both, compared with the findings on the normal side, is a positive finding.

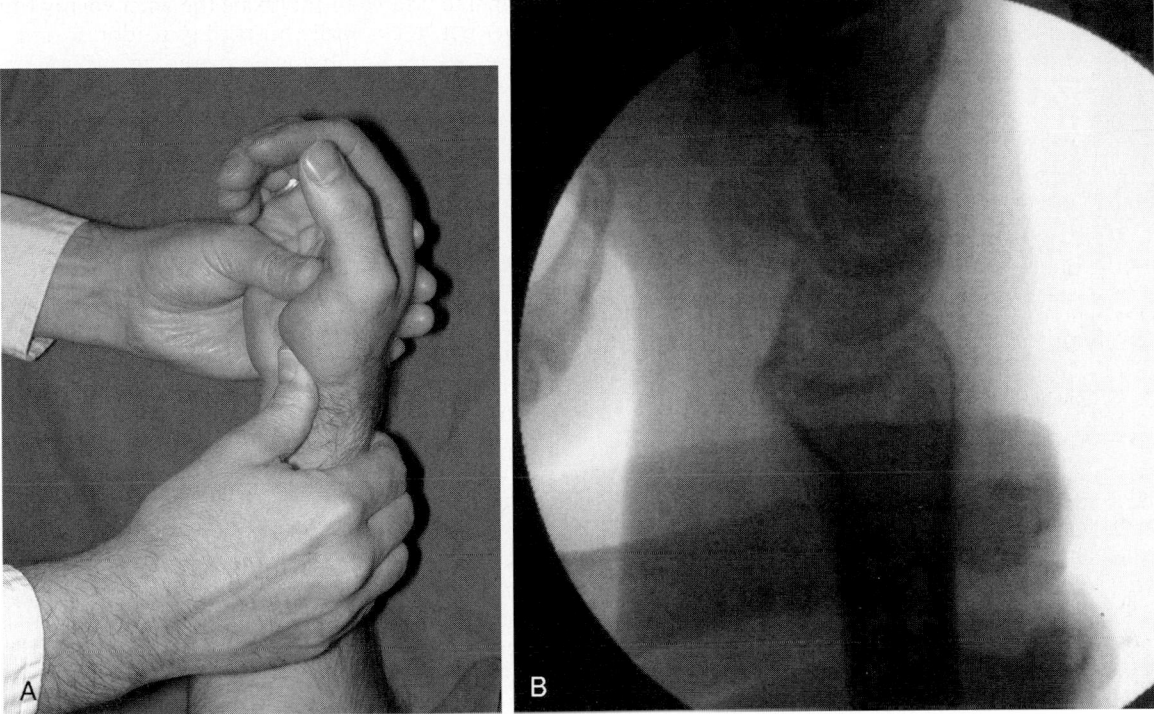

**FIGURE 39–36.** The scaphoid shift test (Watson et al, 1988). *A,* Dorsally directed pressure is applied to the scaphoid tuberosity with the examiner's thumb as the wrist is moved from ulnar to radial deviation. With scapholunate instability, the proximal pole is thought to sublux dorsally out of the scaphoid fossa. When the pressure on the scaphoid is released, the scaphoid abruptly reduces back into the fossa, and a clunk is felt. *B,* Lateral stress radiograph demonstrating dorsal subluxation of the scaphoid.

**Routine Views.** The mainstay of diagnosis remains radiography. Routine views should include PA, true lateral, and a 45° pronation view. The third metacarpal should be perfectly aligned with the radius in all views. Bellinghausen and associates[12] pointed out that three smooth lines can be drawn on a normal PA view of the wrist. If these lines are broken, an instability can be suspected. The proximal line describes the proximal articular surfaces of the proximal row, the middle line describes the distal articular surfaces of the proximal row, and the distal line outlines the proximal articular surfaces of the distal row (Fig. 39–38). On the PA view, increased overlap of a carpal, especially the lunate, to the capitate should be sought. If the lunate presents a triangular as opposed to quadrilateral appearance, perilunate instability may be suspected. The scaphoid normally appears elongated. If it appears foreshortened and demonstrates a "ring" bicortical density, it has become abnormally vertical with respect to the radius,

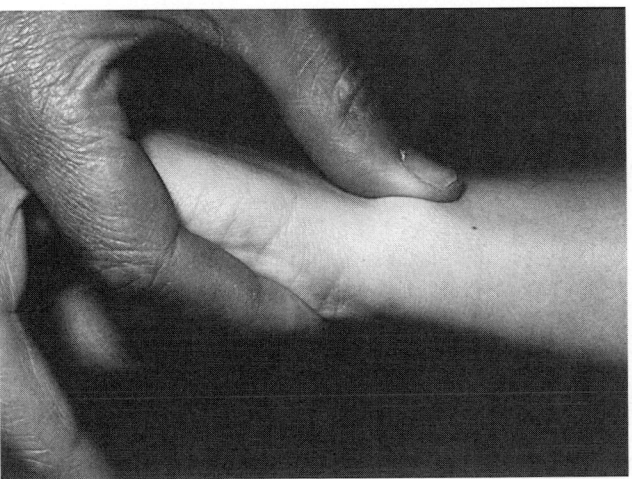

**FIGURE 39–37.** Ulnar carpal shift test. The examiner pushes down on the ulnar head and up on the pisiform. If the test result is positive, pain is felt by the patient in the extensor carpi ulnaris and flexor carpi ulnaris interval. This may be found in cases of ulnar-carpal impingement.

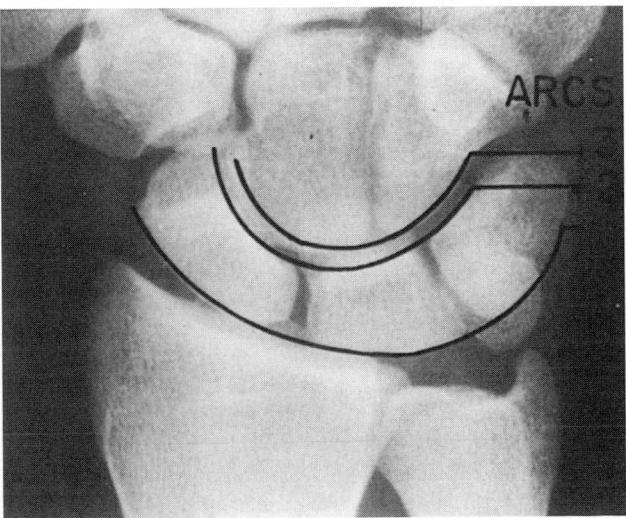

**FIGURE 39–38.** In the normal wrist, three smooth arcs can be drawn on the anteroposterior radiograph. If there is a break in any of these three lines, an intracarpal malalignment should be strongly suspected. (From Bellinghausen, H.W., et al. J Bone Joint Surg Am 65:999, 1983.)

as occurs in both scapholunate dissociation and VISI. The examiner should check also for increased space in the scapholunate interval (>3 mm in scapholunate dissociation) and should assess carpal height[296] (see Fig. 39–33). On the lateral view, as has already been discussed (see Figs. 39–31 and 39–32), any disruption of the normal colinear relationship of the capitate, lunate, and radius should be noted.[88] Also, the scapholunate angle should be measured to check for scapholunate dissociation (angle > 60°) or VISI pattern (angle < 30°). It must be emphasized that because of the normal flexion and extension of the proximal row in radial and ulnar deviation, all measurements must be made on radiographs in which the third metacarpal is aligned parallel to the long axis of the radius in all planes.

**Other Views.** If the results of the routine radiographs are normal and the clinician suspects an instability, a stress or motion series may be helpful.[88] These views include a PA in radial deviation, neutral, and ulnar deviation; a clenched fist anteroposterior (which accentuates scapholunate diastasis); and a lateral in radial deviation, neutral, and ulnar deviation. These additional views are often routinely obtained when instability is subtle. However, Levinsohn and Palmer[136] reported a 65% false negative rate even with this complete series.

*Cineradiography.* Cineradiography can be helpful when the static film results are normal or suspicious but not conclusive.[196] These views are most useful when the radiologist has a clear idea of what is being looked for or when the surgeon performs the studies with the radiologist. The wrist is actively or passively moved in radial and ulnar deviation and examined in the PA and lateral and oblique planes. Evidence of dyssynchronous motion is sometimes found. Traction and stress views performed under fluoroscopy may help to clarify subtle findings.

*Arthrography.* There has been a good deal of experience with this modality, as reported by Kricun,[130] Palmer and co-workers,[186] Schwartz and Ruby,[219] Herbert and colleagues,[102] and Cooney.[45] The method allows identification of scapholunate and triquetrolunate interosseous ligament tears, triangular fibrocartilage tears, synovitis, occult ganglia, and large cartilage defects (Fig. 39–39). However, it can be misleading, because in addition to false-positive and false-negative results,[102] the demonstration of a scapholunate interosseous or lunotriquetral interosseous ligament communication does not necessarily mean that the patient's symptoms are related to these findings. This is partly because the interosseous ligaments have a thin membranous central portion that probably does not contribute significantly to ligament stabilizing function. After the age of 50 years, these tears become increasingly common,[166] and the arthrogram becomes even less useful. The study is most meaningful in the normal younger wrist, especially in patients younger than 20 years of age. It is important to note, as well, that a negative result does not exclude significant wrist pathology. Chung and associates[41] found a negative predictive value of only 20% compared with that of arthroscopy.

**Bone Scan.** Scintigraphy may be of value as a screening test. When results are normal, the study effectively excludes fracture or significant synovitis. The

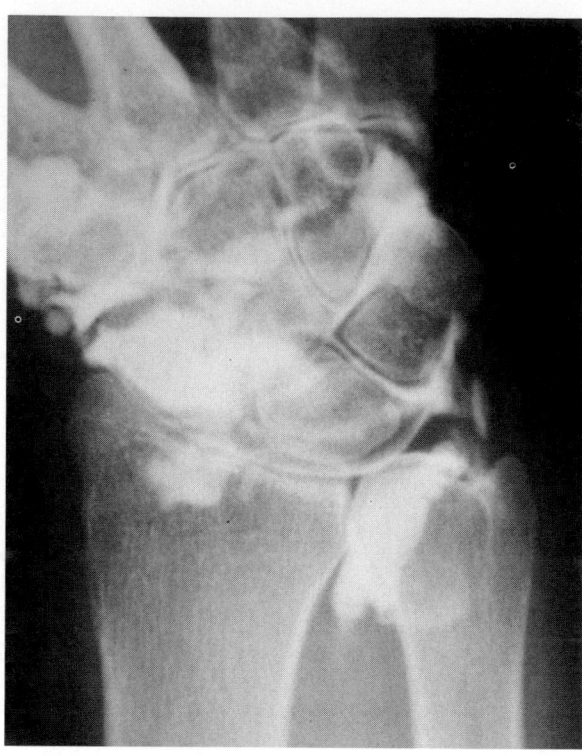

**FIGURE 39–39.** Wrist arthrogram. Radiocarpal injection demonstrating flow into both the midcarpal joint and distal radioulnar joint, indicating lunotriquetral interosseous ligament and triangular fibrocartilage tears.

sensitivity may be as high as 98% for complete interosseous ligament tears, but the test is of little value in identifying TFC and partial interosseous ligament tears.[191] By itself it is not useful in diagnosing carpal instability but may furnish objective evidence of an abnormality. If results are negative, severe wrist disease is less likely.

*Polytomography and Computed Tomography.* At present, these tests may be useful for measuring more clearly subtle changes in the capitolunate and radiolunate angles on the lateral views.[151] They are very useful for diagnosing fractures and malunited scaphoid fractures.[193]

*Magnetic Resonance Imaging.* Historically, attempts to visualize torn ligaments by MRI have been largely unsuccessful. Johnstone and co-workers[121] reported a sensitivity of 37% and 0% in identifying scapholunate and LT interosseous ligament tears, respectively. The investigators concluded that MRI is unhelpful in the investigation of carpal instability. Advances in technology may hold promise, although the recommended dedicated coil, a 1.5-T magnet, three-dimensional volume acquisition, and gradient-recalled echo sequence[216] are not available in many centers. In one European center, three-compartment MR arthrography using a dedicated coil was reported to have a sensitivity of 97% in detecting full-thickness ligament tears.[217] With the average scanner, dorsal midcarpal synovitis may be the only "footprint" of instability.[99] Of course, MRI is very helpful in diagnosing avascular necrosis.[263]

*Arthroscopy.* Over the past several years, wrist arthroscopy has become the standard diagnostic study[44] for wrist instability.[175, 177, 178, 205, 240, 284] Ruch and colleagues[211] have devised an arthroscopy-based classification of wrist ligament injuries. Several researchers have also described treatment of wrist instabilities using the arthroscope.[22, 210, 211, 287]

Our experience with wrist arthroscopy has been very favorable, with few complications and a high degree of success in diagnosing obscure causes of wrist pain. One should examine the wrist under anesthesia *before* introducing the arthroscope. Through the radiocarpal 3,4 portal, the surgeon should inspect for osteochondral injury, damage to the volar extrinsic ligaments, and tears or redundancy in the scapholunate interosseous ligament. The LT ligament is best visualized from one of the ulnar portals; our preference is the 6R portal. Midcarpal joint arthroscopy is essential, as it may reveal subtle stepoff or rotation between the lunate and scaphoid and/or triquetrum not appreciated in the radiocarpal joint. Although valuable as a diagnostic tool, arthroscopic management of wrist instability is largely limited to débridement of partial thickness ligament tears.[240] We have had some encouraging early results with arthroscopically assisted thermal shrinkage of ligaments and capsule. However, the long-term benefit of this technique remains unproven.

In summary, our present approach to the patient with wrist pain is a systematic history and physical examination, paying particular attention to the magnitude and location of the pain, and includes the various stress tests. Next, we perform plain radiographs and, if we suspect a subtle instability, stress radiographs. If the diagnosis is still in doubt, we usually recommend wrist arthroscopy if instability or ligament tear is most likely. If we suspect avascular necrosis, MRI is the next examination. If we suspect fracture, a CT scan is ordered.

## Specific Dislocations

### PERILUNATE DISLOCATIONS AND FRACTURE-DISLOCATIONS

As described earlier, these injuries[93, 179] represent the ultimate stage in perilunate instability (Mayfield stage IV) (Fig. 39–40). Perilunar instability may be purely ligamentous (lesser arc injury) or a combination of osseous and ligamentous injuries (greater arc injuries). If the force of injury traverses a carpal bone, resulting in fracture, the prefix *trans-* is used. Therefore, dorsal perilunate, volar lunate, transradial styloid, trans-scaphoid, trans-scaphoid transcapitate, and transtriquetral perilunate dislocations are variations of the same injury. The most common of these is the trans-scaphoid perilunate dislocation, accounting for 60% of all perilunate dislocations.[80, 104] All the soft tissue structures connecting the lunate to the rest of the carpus are torn. The short radiolunate and ulnolunate ligaments remain intact. The capitate and the rest of the carpus come to lie dorsal to the lunate. Depending on the degree of injury, the lunate either is in its normal position with respect to the radius and the rest of the carpus dorsal (dorsal perilunate dislocation) or is anteriorly displaced and rotated, with the capitate and other carpal bones in more or less normal relationship to the radius (lunate dislocation).

### Diagnosis

Perilunate dislocations result from high-energy trauma, such as a motor vehicle accident or a fall from a significant height. These patients often have associated injuries, and it is not uncommon for the wrist injury to be overlooked. When seen acutely, the wrist is swollen, and wrist and digital motion are limited. Median nerve dysfunction is common, especially with a lunate dislocation. When seen late, patients complain of wrist pain but may exhibit a remarkable degree of wrist motion. In addition to median neuropathy, late findings may include ulnar neuropathy and flexor tendon ruptures.[247]

Standard wrist radiographs are sufficient to make the diagnosis, although the dislocation may be missed by the uninitiated, because the PA view may appear to be relatively normal. As pointed out by Green and O'Brien,[95]

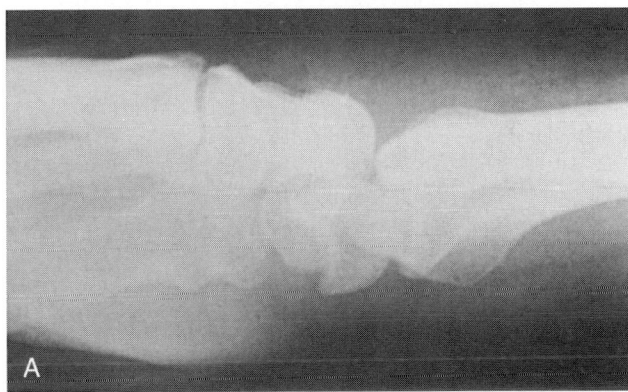

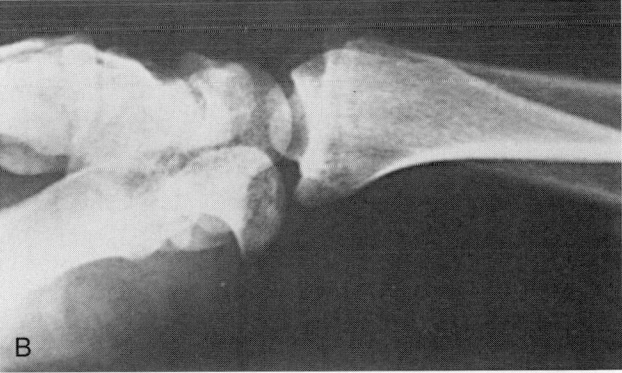

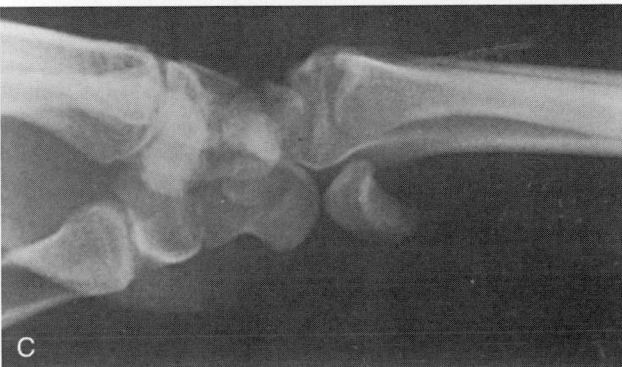

**FIGURE 39–40.** In a patient with a carpal dislocation, the initial lateral radiograph may depict a configuration at any point in the spectrum of injury. *A,* Dorsal perilunate dislocation. *B,* An intermediate state. *C,* Volar lunate dislocation. (*A–C,* From Green, D.P. Operative Hand Surgery, 2nd ed., Vol. 2. New York, Churchill Livingstone, 1988, p. 885.)

the lateral radiograph is the key, with the finding being loss of colinearity of the radius, lunate, and capitate. In a dorsal perilunate dislocation, the capitate rests on top of the lunate. In a volar lunate dislocation, the lunate pivots around the intact short radiolunate ligament and faces anteriorly, a finding termed the *spilled teacup sign*.[95] The capitate migrates proximally and sits in the lunate fossa. On the PA view, overlap of the carpal bones and loss of carpal height are evident. The lunate assumes a triangular shape as it flexes. Associated fractures may be identified. Traction radiographs obtained before reduction may provide additional information about the extent of injury.

## Treatment

In the acute setting, early closed reduction is mandatory. Reduction reduces pain and minimizes swelling, digital stiffness, and the risk of median nerve dysfunction. Definitive treatment, however, remains controversial. Treatment options include cast immobilization, percutaneous pin fixation,[291] and ORIF through a dorsal,[3, 34, 35] volar,[94, 253] or combined dorsal-volar[56, 80, 104] approach. Reports of cast treatment for perilunate dislocations date back to the 1920–1940 era. There is now general consensus that the risk of late instability from cast treatment alone is unacceptably high. Percutaneous fixation has been advocated by some,[291] but precise reduction is difficult to achieve by closed manipulation. Osteochondral fragments with loose bodies are also frequently present. In addition, some investigators[93] feel that ligament repair is a necessary element of treatment. In our opinion, percutaneous pinning has a role in treating the severely injured patient in whom open management is contraindicated.

ORIF is the preferred method of treatment of many investigators, including ourselves. However, there has been controversy regarding the best surgical approach. Campbell and colleagues[34] reported having used a dorsal approach in nine patients and a volar approach in four patients, all without the complication of avascular necrosis. These investigators preferred the dorsal approach, noting that (1) it is usually necessary to remove scar tissue in the lunate space, and (2) it is easier to visualize and align the carpal bones through a dorsal approach. Dobyns and co-workers[56] advocated a dorsal and volar approach to repair the volar ligaments. Green and O'Brien[94] and Taleisnik[253] also recommend a volar approach to effect ligament repair. Adkinson and Chapman[3] reported good results with a dorsal approach only, indicating that it is not necessary to suture the volar ligaments if bony reduction is achieved and maintained with K-wires.

Our preference is to treat these injuries using ORIF with K-wires through a dorsal approach. If the patient has a median neuropathy, we also perform a volar incision to release the flexor retinaculum, explore the nerve, and repair the volar wrist capsule. However, in our experience, the dorsal approach alone is adequate to reduce and fix the dislocation, and suture repair of the volar ligaments is not absolutely necessary.

The end result is influenced by the timing of reduction, and earlier is better. Although successful results have been reported in isolated cases as late as 4 to 5 months after injury,[94] the best results are seen when definitive treatment

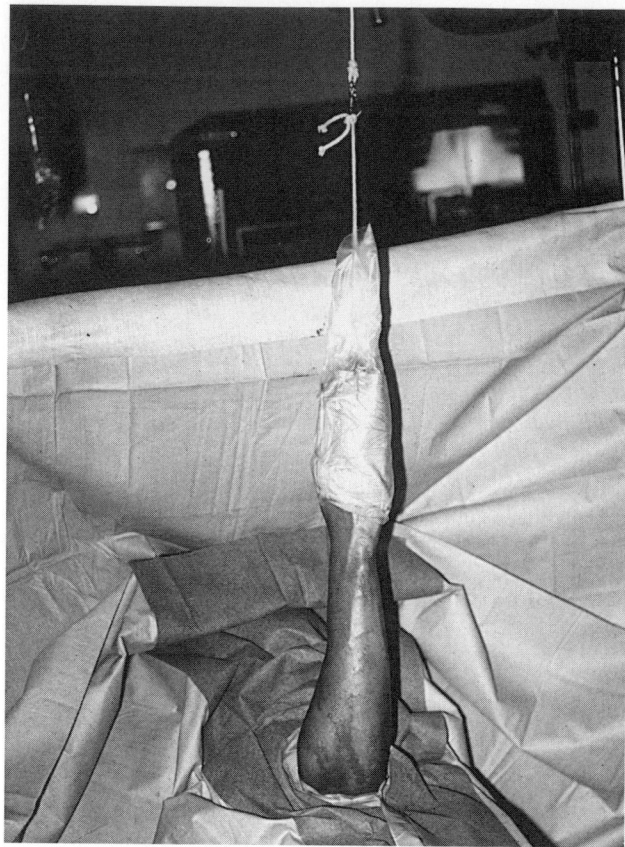

**FIGURE 39–41.** The patient is supine with the upper arm taped to an arm board. The hand is suspended through finger traps to an overhead pulley system, and weight (2.25 to 3.15 kg) is applied.

is performed within 1 to 2 weeks. Most patients will gain approximately 50% of normal motion, and some stiffness is the rule.[94]

**Closed Reduction Technique.** Closed reduction is best accomplished under regional or general anesthesia. Longitudinal traction is applied for 10 minutes using finger traps with 10 to 15 lb of counterweight on the upper arm.[73] We prefer to use the wrist arthroscopy setup with 6 kg of weight applied to the thumb, index, and middle fingers by finger traps through the shoulder holder* (Fig. 39–41). Alternatively, one can use end-of-the-table traction. Green and O'Brien[94] recommend PA and lateral radiographs at this point to better delineate the extent of injury. The finger traps are then removed, and a closed reduction maneuver as described by Tavernier is performed.[259]

The surgeon simultaneously applies longitudinal traction and extends the wrist with one hand while stabilizing the lunate volarly using the thumb of the other hand. The wrist is then gradually flexed, pushing the capitate over the dorsal pole of the lunate. A short arm thumb spica cast is applied with the wrist in slight flexion, and postreduction radiographs are obtained. The arm is then put in a short arm thumb spica cast with the wrist in slight palmar flexion, and postreduction radiographs are obtained.

**Percutaneous Pinning Technique.** This is a difficult

---

*Dyonics Inc., 160 Dascomb Road, Andover, MA 01810.

technique. Our method is to have an assistant stabilize the forearm while the surgeon holds the hand, placing his or her thumb over the dorsum of the capitate. Then, while exerting a volar translation force on the capitate, a single 0.062-inch smooth K-wire is driven proximally from the capitate into the lunate. This stabilizes the capitolunate relationship. Image intensifier or routine radiographs are taken to check reduction and wire position. If satisfactory, the proximal pole of the scaphoid is pushed down (dorsal to volar) while the surgeon drills a single 0.062-inch K-wire through the snuffbox across the scaphoid into the capitate and a second 0.062-inch K-wire from the scaphoid into the lunate. One of us (CC) prefers to stabilize the LT joint with a K-wire as well. The reduction and wire placement are checked radiologically. If satisfactory, the wires are cut just below the skin. A U-shaped above-elbow splint is applied for the first week until swelling subsides, followed by a short above-elbow thumb spica cast for a total of 12 weeks of immobilization. The cast is changed every 2 to 3 weeks to minimize the likelihood of pin loosening. If closed reduction fails or percutaneous fixation is not successful, ORIF is indicated. As mentioned previously, we prefer ORIF over percutaneous fixation as the initial treatment in most situations.

**Open Reduction Internal Fixation Technique.** Use the straight dorsal approach already described in the section on Fracture Treatment. After the extensor pollicis longus is retracted radially, the entire dorsal carpus is in view, because the dorsal capsule has been torn and stripped off the radius by the injury. The proximal pole of the scaphoid and capitate is easily visualized, and the lunate is hidden underneath. Reduction is obtained by applying traction through the hand and pushing up on the lunate anteriorly after clearing the lunate space of soft tissue. Reduction of the lunate can be facilitated by placing a blunt periosteal elevator between the capitate head and the lunate and levering the lunate up dorsally. Any small osteochondral fragments are removed, and the capitolunate relationship is aligned and stabilized by translating

the capitate volarly and driving a smooth 0.062-inch K-wire across the lunate into the capitate from a proximal to a distal direction. It is also helpful to radially deviate the capitate on the lunate approximately 10° before pinning. The scaphoid is reduced to the lunate by pushing down firmly on the proximal pole of the scaphoid and radially deviating the wrist. K-wires can be used as joysticks, clamping a bone reduction forceps around them to close the scapholunate gap. One 0.062-inch K-wire is driven through the scaphoid into the capitate, and a second wire is driven through the scaphoid into the lunate. Another wire is passed from the triquetrum into the lunate (CC). Radiographs are taken to assess reduction and pin placement. One of the authors (CC) prefers to repair the scapholunate ligament with suture anchors. Closure is accomplished in routine fashion, although the dorsal capsule may be badly damaged and irreparable. A U-shaped above-elbow splint is applied with the wrist in neutral position and is changed to a short arm thumb spica cast at 1 week. The cast is changed at 2- to 3-week intervals for a total of 10 to 12 weeks of immobilization. Following pin removal, intensive therapy is begun. Motion is emphasized initially, followed by strengthening exercises.

## TRANS-SCAPHOID PERILUNATE DISLOCATION

Trans-scaphoid perilunate dislocation (Fig. 39–42) occurs by a mechanism very similar to that in dorsal perilunate dislocation, except the energy is transmitted through the waist of the scaphoid instead of through its ligamentous attachments to the lunate. The technique of closed reduction is the same as that for dorsal perilunate–volar lunate dislocation. Unfortunately, even with excellent initial reduction, the scaphoid usually angulates and the wrist collapses into DISI, with the proximal row and proximal pole of the scaphoid angulated dorsally and the distal pole of the scaphoid and distal row angulated volarly. Consequently, we agree with

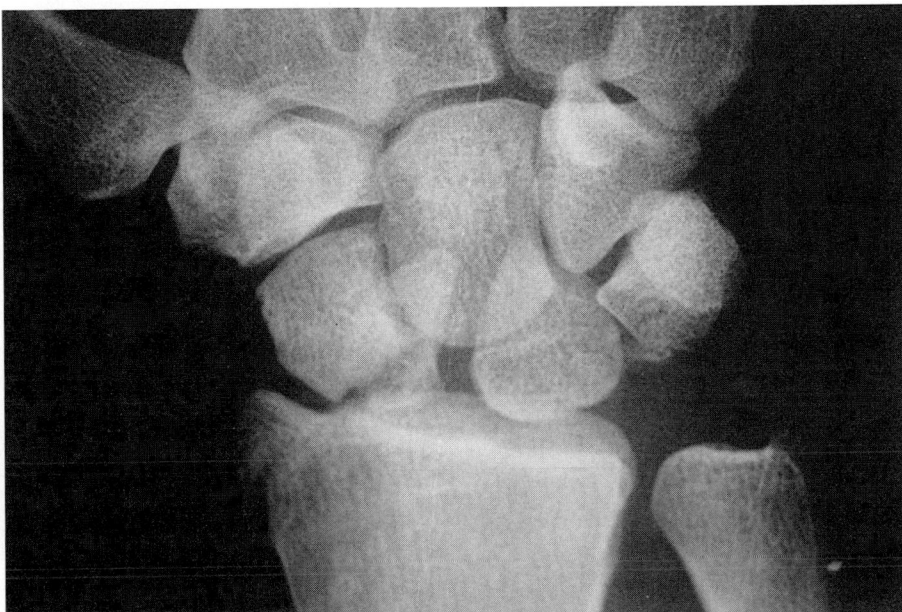

**FIGURE 39–42.** A trans-scaphoid perilunate dislocation with an associated radial styloid fracture.

other investigators[34, 35, 94, 169] that early ORIF is the treatment of choice.

The specific technique is controversial. As with simple perilunate dislocations, volar, dorsal, and combined approaches have been recommended. We use a dorsal approach just as for the dorsal perilunate dislocation and for the same reasons. The disadvantage of this method is that if there is comminution of the volar cortex of the scaphoid, it is difficult to add a bone graft to maintain scaphoid alignment after reduction. Also, the volar ligaments cannot be repaired. Often, just as in a dorsal perilunate–volar lunate dislocation, the question becomes moot because a carpal tunnel release must be done to decompress the median nerve.

**Technique—Dorsal Approach.** A straight dorsal incision is made, centered a few millimeters ulnar to Lister's tubercle. The extensor pollicis longus is retracted radially, and the dorsal wrist capsule is mobilized radially and ulnarly. (It will have been stripped off the carpus and distal radius by the injury.) The head of the capitate will come into view with the distal pole of the scaphoid. Any blood and fibrin are removed from the scapholunate fossa, and traction is applied to the hand. The lunate and the attached proximal pole of the scaphoid are pushed up (dorsal), and the capitate and distal scaphoid fragment are pushed down (volar) over the dorsal pole of the lunate. Again, this maneuver can be facilitated with a blunt periosteal elevator placed in the fracture site and used as a lever. Reduction and stability are checked clinically by radially and ulnarly deviating the wrist. Even though the reduction may appear stable, we routinely use internal fixation because of the high risk of later malalignment. Two methods are useful, and the easiest is to employ K-wires. After reduction, two 0.054-inch or 0.045-inch smooth K-wires can be placed from the proximal pole of the scaphoid across the fracture site through the distal pole and then drawn distally until the ends are in the subchondral bone in the proximal pole, so as not to project into the radioscaphoid joint. After radiographs confirm anatomic reduction of the fracture

and proper placement of the wires, the wound is closed and a U-shaped above-elbow splint is applied for 1 week. This is followed by a short above-elbow thumb spica cast for 6 weeks and then a short arm thumb spica cast for another 6 weeks or until the scaphoid is healed radiologically. The wires usually have to be removed by 3 months, as they tend to become loose.

An alternative method of internal fixation is the Herbert screw, which has the advantages of providing better internal fixation without protruding wires and may obviate the need for long-term cast immobilization (Fig. 39–43). The only drawback is the exacting technique required, because the jig cannot be used with a dorsal approach. For the experienced operator, the screw may be the preferred method.

If the volar cortex of the scaphoid is comminuted or if the patient is seen 2 to 3 weeks after the injury with established DISI collapse, an initial volar approach is preferable.

**Technique—Volar Approach.** A skin incision is made over the flexor carpi radialis tendon, which is exposed and retracted ulnarly. The radial artery is protected. The dorsal sheath of the flexor carpi radialis is incised longitudinally, and pericapsular fat is divided. The anterior capsule of the wrist is divided, and the proximal pole of the scaphoid and the lunate are visualized. Fibrin and clot are removed from the fracture surface and dorsally as far as possible by placing traction on the hand. This should expose the distal fragment of the scaphoid and the head of the capitate. The proximal fragment is pushed dorsally while the distal fragment is pulled volarly. If reduction is successful, internal fixation or bone graft, or both, can be performed. We recommend bone graft if the volar cortex of the scaphoid is sufficiently comminuted to preclude anatomic reduction and adequate fixation. Because a volar approach does not allow good visualization of the critical scapholunate-capitate relationship, radiologic assessment or a dorsal incision will have to be made. Internal fixation is then performed either by driving two 0.045-inch

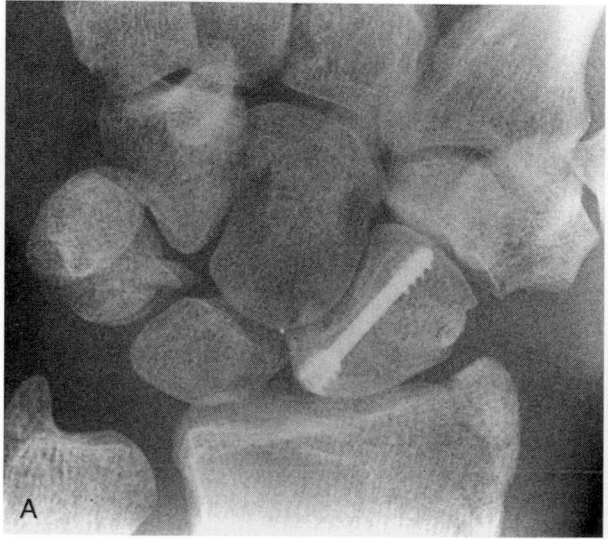
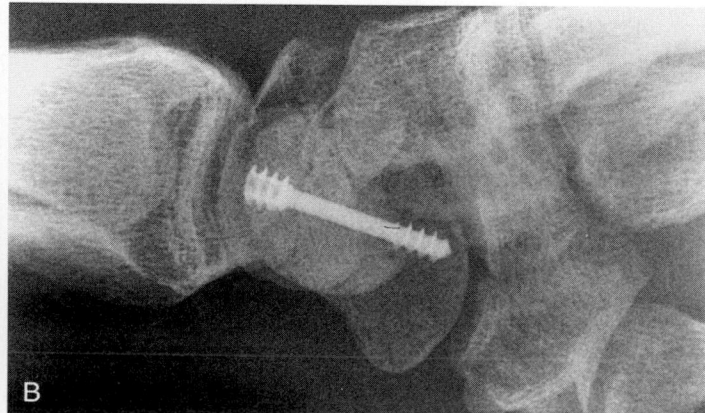

**FIGURE 39–43.** *A, B,* Anteroposterior and lateral postoperative radiographs demonstrating a Herbert screw used to fix the scaphoid fracture in a patient with a trans-scaphoid perilunate dislocation. The screw has been placed in retrograde fashion through the dorsal approach without the jig.

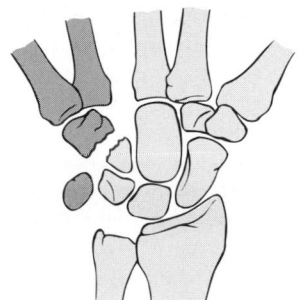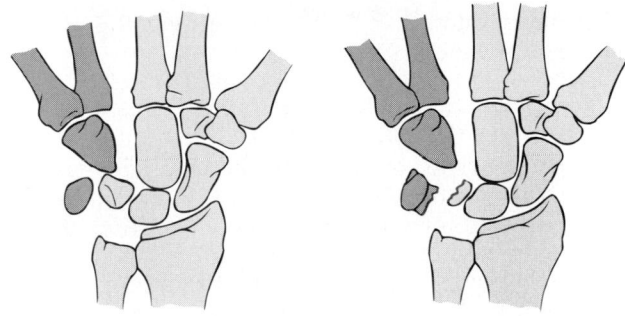

**FIGURE 39–44.** The three patterns of capitate-hamate diastasis described by Garcia-Elias and colleagues. (Redrawn from Garcia-Elias, M., et al. J Bone Joint Surg Br 67:289, 1985.)

smooth K-wires from distal pole to proximal pole or by using the Herbert screw or other screw technique as already described in the treatment of scaphoid fractures. Closure is routine, and aftercare is as already described for the dorsal approach. Again, stiffness is a common sequela of these injuries, and so vigorous and prolonged rehabilitation is necessary.

It is not rare to have an accompanying radial styloid fracture, in which case these injuries are termed *transradial trans-scaphoid fracture dislocations*. If the radius fracture is large and in one piece, it should be treated by internal fixation, because it may contribute to ligamentous and bony stability of the radiocarpal joint. If it is small or comminuted, excision is a reasonable option.

## TRANSTRIQUETRAL PERILUNATE FRACTURE-DISLOCATION

In some carpal dislocations, the plane of injury propagates ulnarly not between the lunate and triquetrum but through the triquetrum. The proximal portion of the triquetrum stays with the lunate, and the distal fragment displaces dorsally with the capitate and distal row analogous to the trans-scaphoid perilunate dislocation. Treatment is the same as for the perilunate dislocation, and the triquetral fracture will be reduced automatically. We recommend ORIF of the fracture and the carpus through a dorsal approach.

## CAPITATE-HAMATE DIASTASIS

If a hand is severely crushed, a cleavage plane may be created between the capitate and hamate and the third and fourth metacarpals (Fig. 39–44). This injury propagates proximally through the triquetrum or between it and the hamate. The diagnosis is easy to overlook, and one should be suspicious in a patient with divergence between the middle and the ring fingers when the hand has been crushed. The injury is best visualized on a PA view. It is important to reduce and fix this diastasis, as failure to do so destroys the transverse arch of the hand and causes rotational malalignment of the fingers. Primiano and Reef[194] performed carpal tunnel release and internal fixation in their four patients. Garcia-Elias and co-workers[79] summarized all 13 cases reported in the literature up to 1985, including 4 of their own patients, and concluded that closed reduction produced good long-term results.

## SCAPHOLUNATE DISSOCIATION

This entity may be defined as dyssynchronous movement of the scaphoid with respect to the lunate. Although the scaphoid is the most mobile bone in the proximal row, its motions are normally similar in direction and amplitude to those of the lunate and triquetrum.[208] If this synchronous motion with respect to the lunate is lost, scapholunate dissociation is said to exist.[150] There is no general agreement as to which ligaments are the most important in stabilizing the scaphoid to the lunate, but evidence exists to support the idea that several structures are important in this regard, especially the scapholunate interosseous ligament.

The scapholunate interosseous ligament is composed of three distinct regions: a relatively thin palmar ligament, a fibrocartilaginous proximal (membranous) portion, and a thick dorsal ligament[14] (Fig. 39–45). Of these, the dorsal fibers are the strongest and clinically the most important.[15] As previously described, the mechanism of injury usually involves hyperextension, ulnar deviation, and intercarpal

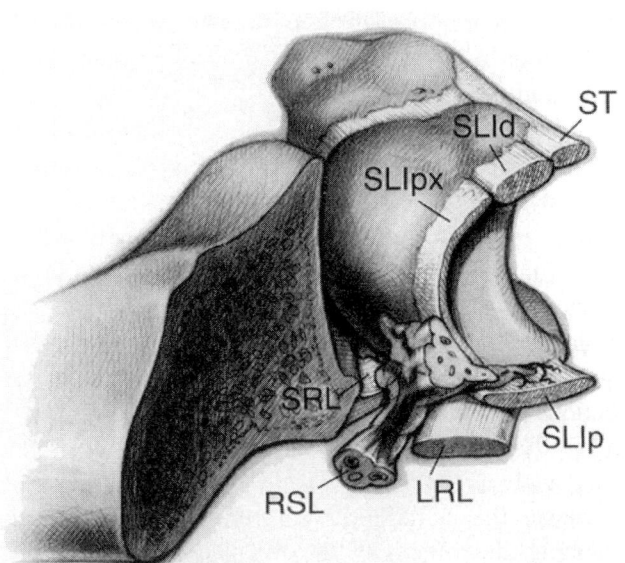

**FIGURE 39–45.** Illustration of the scapholunate interosseous ligament. With the scaphoid removed, three subdivisions of the scapholunate interosseous (SLI) ligament are evident: dorsal (d), proximal (px), and palmar (p). *Abbreviations:* LRL, long radiolunate ligament; RSL, radioscapholunate ligament; SRL, short radiolunate ligament; ST, dorsal scaphotriquetral (or intercarpal) ligament. (Reproduced with permission from Berger, R.A. The gross and histologic anatomy of the scapholunate ligament. J Hand Surg [Am] 21:170–178, 1996.)

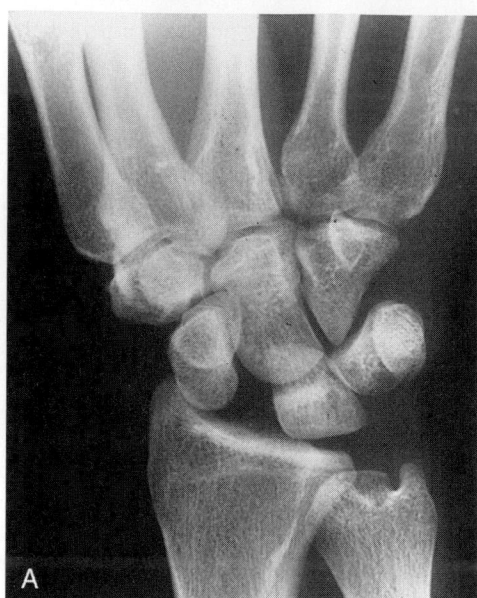
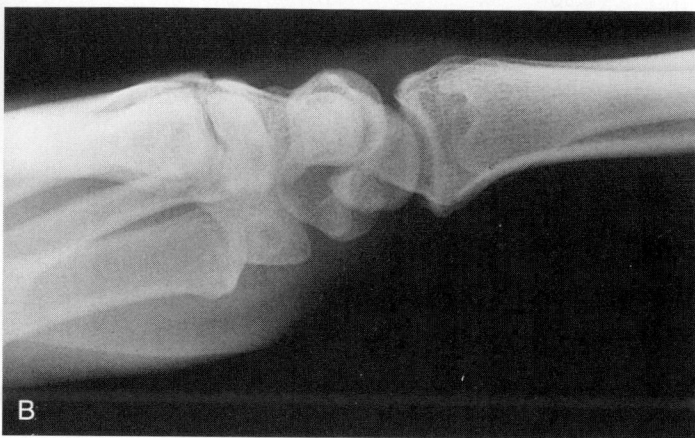

**FIGURE 39–46.** *A, B,* Anteroposterior and lateral radiographs of scapholunate diastasis.

supination. In the scapholunate interval, the force of injury propagates from the palmar to the dorsal direction. Disruption of the palmar and proximal regions alone produces only minor alterations in wrist kinematics. Complete disruption of the scapholunate ligament is required to produce static deformity.

With a complete scapholunate tear, the scaphoid assumes a more vertical (flexed) position, and the lunate and triquetrum extend. As a result, overall contact between the scaphoid and the radius is diminished,[32] becoming concentrated at the distal pole and radial styloid and the proximal pole and dorsal lip of the radius. These are the initial sites for the development of arthritis. Abnormal contact between the capitate and lunate eventually results in arthritis at that articulation.

Watson and colleagues[278, 280] have classified the spectrum of scapholunate instability into four types: predynamic, dynamic, static, and scapholunate advanced collapse.[276] Predynamic instability is defined as localized pain over the scapholunate joint with a positive scaphoid shift test result (see stress tests) and normal radiographic results, including stress views. The existence of this entity remains controversial. In dynamic instability, abnormalities are seen only on stress radiographs. This would be seen, for example, with a partial scapholunate tear. In static instability, the diagnosis is clear on plain radiographs. Long-standing static instability results in extensive degenerative arthritis or a scapholunate advanced collapse (SLAC) wrist.

Scapholunate dissociation can also be seen in conjunction with distal radius fractures. Arthroscopically, the incidence has been found to be as high as 31%.[82] Radiographically, the incidence is probably about 5%.[170] Cast treatment alone does not appear to be adequate in this setting.[250]

### Diagnosis

A wide spectrum of symptoms and findings may be present, depending on the age and severity of the injury and associated problems.[150] A history of a hyperextension injury is sought, although not always found. Symptoms include radial dorsal wrist pain, weakness of grip, limited motion, and a clicking or popping sensation with use. Swelling may be present. Tenderness is localized to the dorsal scapholunate interval or dorsal rim of the radius. There will often be a positive dorsal shift test result with increased pain at the capitate head as it subluxates dorsally out of the lunate concavity. The scaphoid shift test[274] should produce pain and demonstrate instability.

Radiographs should include a PA and lateral in neutral wrist position, with the third metacarpal parallel to the radius. Comparison radiographs are often helpful. Findings of static instability on the PA radiograph (Fig. 39–46A) include the following:

1. An increased scapholunate joint space (the so-called Terry Thomas sign). A gap of more than 3 mm is suspicious, and a gap of more than 5 mm is diagnostic of a scapholunate tear.[168]
2. The "scaphoid ring" sign.[39] When the scaphoid is flexed, the tuberosity is superimposed on the waist, producing a cortical ring or oval. To be considered positive, the distance between the ulnar corner of the scaphoid and the edge of the ring should be less than 8 mm.[21] This finding indicates only that the scaphoid is abnormally flexed and is therefore not specific for a scapholunate tear.
3. Reduction in carpal height. The carpal height ratio is decreased (<0.54).
4. Increased overlap of the lunate on the capitate with a more triangular shape of the lunate.
5. The triquetrum is also dorsiflexed, giving it a wider appearance.

Findings on the lateral view include the following (see Fig. 39–46B):

1. The scapholunate angle is greater than 60°.[150]
2. The lunate and triquetrum are dorsiflexed with respect to the radius and capitate (DISI). The lunate-

capitate angle is reversed from the normal 0° to 15° palmar flexion of the lunate. An angle of more than 10° dorsal is considered abnormal.

3. The V sign of Taleisnik. Normally, the palmar margins of the scaphoid and radius assume a C-shape. When the scaphoid is abnormally flexed, these cortical surfaces form a V-shape.[255]

If the diagnosis is not evident from the results of the routine radiographs, a stress series is ordered. This includes a radial and ulnar deviation PA view and an anteroposterior clenched fist view. The latter view places the opposing facets of the scaphoid and lunate parallel to the x-ray beam, accentuating any scapholunate gap. Additional studies include cineradiography, arthrography, MRI, and arthroscopy. Cineradiography may help to clarify confusing physical findings. Arthrography can be helpful in the younger patient; its limitations have been highlighted earlier. The sensitivity of the routine MRI in detecting scapholunate tears is poor (37%)[121]; we have not found MRI to be useful in this setting.

Wrist arthroscopy has become the diagnostic procedure of choice to confirm clinically suspected dynamic scapholunate instability.[45] The scapholunate interosseous ligament, radioscapholunate ligament, radiolunate ligament, and scaphoid, lunate, and radial proximal articular surfaces can all be directly visualized through the radiocarpal 3,4 portal. As already noted, the midcarpal portal often provides the best view of a scapholunate gap (or stepoff). The degree of instability is classified according to the method of Geissler and colleagues[82] (Table 39–1).

### Treatment

This issue is best considered in terms of management of the acute or chronic condition, as the methods and prognosis for each differ.[252] It should also be pointed out

**TABLE 39–1** ● ● ● ● ● ● ● ● ● ● ● ● ● ● ● ● ● ● ● ● ● ● ● ● ●

Arthroscopic Classification of Tears of the Intracarpal Ligaments

| Grade | Description |
|-------|-------------|
| I | Attenuation or hemorrhage of the interosseous ligament as seen from the radiocarpal space. No incongruency of carpal alignment in the midcarpal space. |
| II | Attenuation or hemorrhage of the interosseous ligament as seen from the radiocarpal space. Incongruency or stepoff of carpal space. There may be a slight gap (less than the width of the probe) between carpal bones. |
| III | Incongruency or stepoff of carpal alignment as seen from both radiocarpal and midcarpal space. Probe may be passed through the gap between carpal bones. |
| IV | Incongruency or stepoff of carpal alignment as seen from both radiocarpal and midcarpal space. There is gross instability with manipulation. A 2.7-mm arthroscope may be passed through the gap between carpal bones. |

● ● ● ● ● ● ● ● ● ● ● ● ● ● ● ● ● ● ● ● ● ● ● ● ● ● ● ● ● ●

Reproduced with permission from Geissler, W.B.; Freeland, A.E.; Savoie, F.H.; et al. Intracarpal soft tissue lesions associated with an intra-articular fracture of the distal end of the radius. J Bone Joint Surg Am 78:78:357–365, 1996.

that two of the most prominent authorities on the wrist, Linscheid and Dobyns, stated that "treatment of this condition is seldom satisfactory."[148] Unfortunately, our own experience supports their conclusion.

**Acute Scapholunate Dissociation.** These injuries are often missed and in fact may be relatively asymptomatic initially. If, however, one does see an acute injury, most investigators, including ourselves, recommend ORIF. In our hands, closed reduction has never succeeded. The difficulty of closed reduction in this injury is probably owing to the paradox of the scaphoid.[159] To close the scapholunate gap, radial deviation of the wrist, which compresses the scapholunate joint, should be done. However, this causes the scaphoid to assume a more vertical position, thereby increasing scapholunate angulation. Conversely, to align the scaphoid more horizontally, ulnar deviation of the wrist should be performed, which distracts the scapholunate joint, increasing the gap. Nonetheless, it may be possible to accomplish closed reduction with the maneuvers described later.

Several researchers[145, 179] have advocated closed reduction and percutaneous pin fixation using the image intensifier. Others[210, 289] have recommended arthroscopically assisted reduction and pinning. In Whipple's series,[289] clinical and radiographic success was achieved in 85% of the patients when the symptoms were of fewer than 3 months' duration and the preoperative scapholunate gap was less than 3 mm more than that of the normal side. Otherwise, only 53% had an acceptable result. We believe that wrist arthroscopy is useful in the diagnosis and management of *dynamic* scapholunate instability associated with *partial* scapholunate ligament tears. Acute, complete scapholunate tears are best treated with ORIF.

*Closed Reduction and Percutaneous Pinning Technique.* After adequate axillary block or general anesthesia, the capitolunate joint is reduced by volar translation and radial deviation of the capitate on the lunate by pushing volarly and radially on the patient's hand while stabilizing the forearm. This is very similar to the volar shift test (see Fig. 39–35A). The assistant then drives a 0.062-inch smooth K-wire across the capitolunate joint, and its position is checked by fluoroscopy. Next, the scaphoid is reduced by 15° to 20° of radial deviation, and simultaneous downward (anteriorly directed) pressure is applied over the proximal pole of the scaphoid. A second 0.062-inch smooth K-wire is introduced across the scaphocapitate joint and a third wire across the scapholunate joint. If the reduction is difficult, temporary K-wires may be placed into the dorsal aspects of the lunate and scaphoid for use as "joysticks." Again, reduction and wire placement are checked radiologically. The wires are cut under the skin. After an initial 1 week of U-shaped thumb spica splinting, a solid short arm thumb spica cast is applied and continued for 8 to 10 weeks and changed at 2- to 3-week intervals. Alternative methods of wire placement have been described, including two pins through the scaphoid to the capitate and two pins through the scaphoid to the lunate.[179] Dobyns and co-workers[56] suggest one pin through the radius into the lunate and a second pin through the radius into the scaphoid.

*Authors' Preferred Method.* Our preference is open reduction through a dorsal approach and pin placement as described previously for closed reduction and percutaneous pinning. In addition, if there is significant scapholunate interosseous ligament to repair, No. 0 nonabsorbable horizontal mattress sutures are placed, if possible, through bone to reconstruct the scapholunate interosseous ligament.[56] This technique is especially useful if the scapholunate interosseous ligament is avulsed from its attachment to the rim of the scaphoid, as it often is. Occasionally, we will use a bone anchor in the proximal pole of the scaphoid to reinforce the repair. Aftercare is the same as for closed reduction and percutaneous fixation.

**Chronic Scapholunate Dissociation.** The dividing line between acute and chronic is not distinct but is arbitrarily drawn at 3 weeks by some[253] and at 3 months by others.[145] The majority of scapholunate tears fall into this category. Rather than focus on time, Lavernia and colleagues[135] have suggested that we consider the quality of the ligament, the reducibility of the joint, and the presence of arthritis as the critical factors in determining the feasibility of ligament repair. The treatment of subacute and chronic scapholunate dissociation remains controversial and difficult, and the results are unpredictable. No single procedure has been uniformly successful in treating this problem.[89] Numerous soft tissue and bony techniques have been recommended.

*Soft Tissue Methods.* These include scapholunate ligament repair, capsulodesis, and tendon grafts. The preferred option for treatment of chronic instability is the same as that for acute instability—open reduction through a dorsal approach, pinning of the three key carpals (i.e., capitate, lunate, and scaphoid), and repair of the scapholunate interosseous ligament. However, the ligament is often of poor quality.

DIRECT LIGAMENTOUS REPAIR. Lavernia and associates[135] described a combination ligament repair and dorsal capsulodesis. Following the prerequisites of good quality ligament, reducibility, and minimal arthritis, they found that the interval between injury and surgery was not important. They had 90% good-to-excellent results in 21 patients, with the major limitation being a 15° loss of wrist flexion. Attention to detail, with anatomic reduction of the carpus and meticulous repair of the ligament, is essential.

DORSAL CAPSULODESIS. Blatt[21] described a soft tissue technique that does not rely on reconstruction of the scapholunate ligament and recreation of the scapholunate linkage that Linscheid recommended.[145] Rather, the Blatt procedure creates a dorsal capsulodesis that realigns, or "horizontalizes" the scaphoid with respect to the radius (Fig. 39–47). The wrist is exposed through a dorsal approach, dissecting a proximally based 1-cm wide flap of dorsal capsule. The scaphoid is then reduced and pinned to the capitate with a single 0.045-inch K-wire. A trough is created in the distal dorsal pole of the scaphoid, and the flap is attached with a suture anchor or a pullout wire led volarly. Motion is begun when the cast is removed at 2 months. The K-wire is removed at 3 months. Recent modifications of the dorsal capsulodesis procedure have been developed that utilize the dorsal intercarpal ligament.[149, 229] We feel that dorsal capsulodesis may have a role in the management of *dynamic* scapholunate instability. We have no experience with this technique for chronic scapholunate dissociation.

TENDON GRAFTS. Various ligament reconstructions using

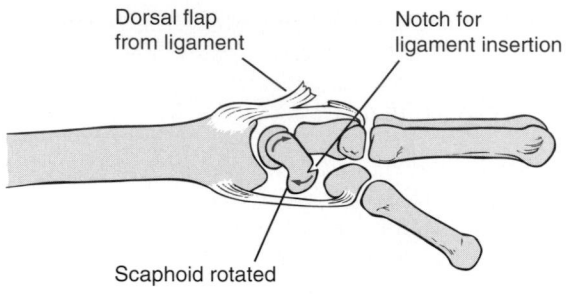

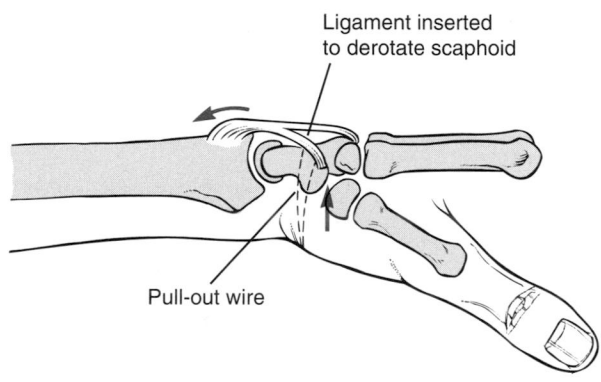

**FIGURE 39–47.** Blatt's technique of dorsal capsulodesis for chronic rotary subluxation of the scaphoid. (Redrawn from Blatt, G. Hand Clin North Am 3:81–102, 1987.)

tendon grafts have been described. These are complicated, technically demanding procedures with unpredictable results. Dobyns and Linscheid and their colleagues[56, 185] described a method using drill holes in the scaphoid and lunate through which is passed a strip of extensor carpi radialis brevis or longus tendon in an attempt to reconstruct the scapholunate interosseous ligament and restore the scapholunate linkage. They emphasize several technical points: (1) careful drilling of the holes to avoid fractures, (2) passage of good quality tendon graft, (3) over-reduction of the radiolunate-capitate and scaphoid joints and using three K-wires to maintain reduction, and (4) postoperative immobilization with the K-wires for 6 to 8 weeks followed by part-time splinting for an additional 6 weeks.

Another type of tendon graft has been proposed by Brunelli and Brunelli[29] that utilizes half of the flexor carpi radialis. They feel that incompetence of the scapho-trapezial-trapezoidal ligaments is a critical feature of scapholunate instability that must be addressed in ligament reconstruction. Consequently, the distally based graft is passed volarly over the scapho-trapezial-trapezoidal joint and then through the scaphoid tuberosity. The graft exits dorsally and is attached to the dorsal aspect of the distal radius. K-wires are removed after 30 days, at which time motion is begun. We have no experience with this technique.

BONE-LIGAMENT-BONE GRAFTS. Extrapolating from the success of such constructs in knee reconstruction, several investigators[52, 225, 285] have developed bone-ligament-bone techniques for scapholunate ligament reconstruction. Donor sites have included extensor retinaculum over Lister's tubercle[225, 285] and the navicular–first cuneiform ligament.[52] In one series,[285] only two of five patients with static instability had significant improvement. We await long-term follow-up on larger series.

***Intercarpal Arthrodesis.*** Because of the difficulty with and variable results of soft tissue procedures, some investigators have proposed various limited intercarpal arthrodeses to stabilize the wrist.

SCAPHOLUNATE ARTHRODESIS. This procedure appears to be a logical solution to the problem of chronic scapholunate dissociation, because it addresses the key feature of this instability directly. Unfortunately, several surgeons who have had experience with it report low arthrodesis rates.[98, 105] Nonetheless, clinical improvement and radiologic reduction can be achieved even in the face of nonunion. In common with all surgery for chronic scapholunate dissociation, no large series have reported uniformly good results.

*Technique.* Expose the proximal half of the scaphoid, lunate, and capitate through a dorsal approach. Using a power bur or hand instrument, create cavities in the adjacent articular surfaces of the scaphoid and lunate. Reduce or overreduce the capitate to the lunate as described for reduction of acute dissociation. Pin this joint with a 0.062-inch K-wire from capitate to lunate. Reduce the scaphoid to the lunate, and pin this joint and the scaphocapitate joint with 0.062-inch K-wires. Alternatively, a scapholunate screw can be used. Follow this by tightly packing the scapholunate joint with cancellous bone graft harvested from either the distal radius or the iliac crest. Close in routine fashion and apply a U-shaped above-elbow splint for 1 week, followed by a short arm cast for 10 weeks that should be changed at 2- to 3-week intervals. Then remove the wires and begin range of motion exercises followed by strengthening exercises. Total rehabilitation usually takes 4 to 6 months.

SCAPHOLUNATE-CAPITATE ARTHRODESIS.[206] This technique improves the fusion rate and solves the instability problem.

However, there is at least a 50% loss of motion, and late changes may occur at the nonarthrodesed joints. In our hands, total intercarpal fusion, including the scaphoid, lunate, capitate, triquetrum, and hamate, has added nothing to the morbidity and has been predictable over the short term.

*Technique.* Expose the wrist through a dorsal third compartment subperiosteal approach, as already described, being careful not to expose the common digital extensor tendons. Remove cartilage and subchondral bone to expose cancellous bone at all the intercarpal joints. Reduce the wrist, taking care to preserve anatomic alignment of the proximal articular surface of the proximal row and preserve the external dimensions of the wrist. Stabilize all the intercarpal joints with 0.062-inch smooth K-wires. Pack all the denuded surfaces tightly with cancellous bone harvested from the iliac crest. Close in layers over a drain. Place the wrist in a U-shaped above-elbow splint, which should be changed at 48 hours. Apply a solid short arm cast at 1 week, and change it every 2 to 3 weeks until 6 to 8 weeks have passed or radiography has confirmed that solid union has occurred; then begin rehabilitation. It will require 3 to 6 months for the patient to return to heavy activity.

SCAPHO-TRAPEZIAL-TRAPEZOID ARTHRODESIS. This is a bony method to treat the vertical collapse pattern of the scaphoid. As with Blatt's technique, there is no attempt to restore scapholunate linkage. Watson and Hempton[277] popularized this arthrodesis, although it was first described by Peterson and Lipscomb[190] in 1967 (Fig. 39–48). Both Watson and Hempton[277] and Kleinman and associates[129] described acceptable clinical results with this technique. Kleinman[128] emphasized the change in wrist kinematics that occurs and reported 11 complications in his series of 41 patients. As with the Blatt dorsal capsulodesis procedure, the rationale here is to prevent the scaphoid from assuming the vertical position that allows

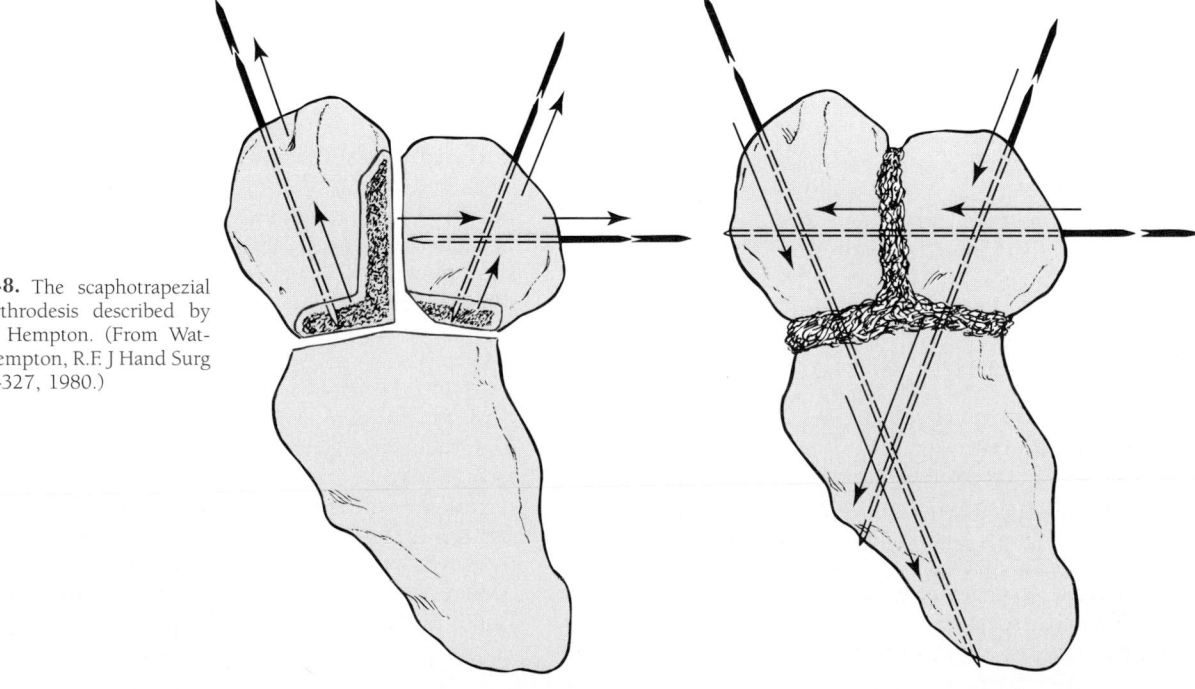

**FIGURE 39–48.** The scaphotrapezial trapezoid arthrodesis described by Watson and Hempton. (From Watson, H.K.; Hempton, R.F. J Hand Surg [Am] 5:320–327, 1980.)

the proximal pole to sublux dorsally out of the radial facet, with consequent arthritis and midcarpal collapse. More experience with this procedure is reported than with any of the other arthrodesis operations,[60, 73, 117] but our personal experience has not been uniformly satisfactory and we no longer use it.

*The Watson Technique.*[274] This begins with a transverse incision made over the dorsoradial aspect of the wrist over the scaphoid. Nerves and tendons are retracted, and the scaphoid, trapezium, and trapezoid are exposed with a transverse incision through the wrist capsule. The articular surfaces of the distal scaphoid, proximal trapezium, proximal trapezoid, and trapezial trapezoid joints are denuded of cartilage. Bone graft is harvested from the distal radius through a second transverse incision between the first and the second extensor compartments. The three bones are then aligned properly with the scaphoid at 45° to the long axis of the radius, and the normal external configuration at the three bones is preserved. At least three 0.045-inch K-wires are prepositioned: one to cross each prepared articular surface and left protruding at the joint surface. To secure proper scaphoid position, two more K-wires are driven across the scaphoid into the capitate after aligning the proximal pole to the lunate. Cancellous bone is packed into the joints, and the wires are driven across. Cortical bone is added. Radiographs are taken to confirm proper alignment and wire placement. No pins should cross into the radius or ulna. The wires are cut under the skin and a bulky dressing applied with a long arm splint. At 10 days, a long arm cast is applied, including the index and middle fingers. Four weeks postoperatively, this is removed, and a short arm cast is applied. Finger motion is encouraged. At 8 weeks, if radiographs demonstrate satisfactory healing, the pins are removed and a light volar splint is applied. Range of motion of the wrist is begun. At 9 weeks, all immobilization is stopped, and full activity is begun.

*Authors' Preferred Methods.* For the patient with acute scapholunate instability, we prefer open reduction and soft tissue repair to attempt to restore the scapholunate linkage, as described by Linscheid and others. For the subacute and chronic problem, we also attempt a soft tissue reconstruction of the scapholunate linkage using locally available ligament. This usually means placing drill holes in the scaphoid and threading No. 0 nonabsorbable sutures in horizontal mattress fashion into the ligament remnant on the lunate. The capitolunate relationship is reduced and pinned with a single 0.062-inch K-wire. The scaphoid is reduced to the lunate and fixed with two pins: one from the scaphoid to the capitate and one from the scaphoid to the lunate. The sutures are tied. A dorsal capsulodesis is performed by imbricating the dorsal radiotriquetral ligament as part of the closure. The pins are cut off under the skin and left in place for 3 months. Protected radiocarpal motion is begun at 6 weeks, and full motion is encouraged after the pins are removed at 12 weeks. If the patient is young and has a high-demand wrist and there is no reconstructable scapholunate ligament, we offer the patient a total intercarpal arthrodesis (LKR) or scaphoid excision and four-corner fusion (CC) not including the radiocarpal or carpometacarpal joints. Total wrist arthrodesis is a fairly reliable solution in the multiply operated wrist.

## LUNOTRIQUETRAL DISSOCIATION

Disruption of the LT ligament complex may be seen in several settings. As mentioned earlier, LT dissociation occurs in perilunate and lunate dislocations. In this instance, the LT tear is addressed as part of the global instability (see "Perilunate Dislocations and Fracture-Dislocations"). At the other end of the spectrum, LT tears may be seen in the setting of chronic atraumatic ulnar-sided wrist pain. When associated with a relatively long ulna (ulnar-positive variance), repetitive overload to the ulnar side of the wrist leads to degeneration of the TFC, chondromalacia of the ulnar head and ulnar aspect of the lunate, and LT tear. This condition has been termed *ulnar impaction syndrome.* Surgical management should include ulnar shortening.

Finally, acute LT ligament complex injury may occur as an isolated finding. The mechanism for LT tears appears to be different from that of perilunate dislocation. In fact, the combination of wrist extension, *ulnar* deviation, and intercarpal *pronation* has been termed the *reverse perilunate mechanism.*[200] Three stages of LT instability have been described.[270] When the injury is limited to the LT interosseous ligament, no instability is seen. Accompanying injury to the volar LT ligament results in dynamic instability. Extension of the tear into the dorsal radiotriquetral ligament results in static VISI.

### Diagnosis

Clinically, there may be a history of a dorsiflexion or twisting injury to the wrist followed by ulnar-sided wrist pain. On physical examination, there is point tenderness over the LT joint[111] and a positive stress test result. This test, as described by Reagan and co-workers,[200] consists of stabilizing the lunate with one hand while shifting the triquetrum dorsally and palmarly with the other. Pain is elicited, and increased motion or crepitus may be perceived by the examiner. Other causes of ulnar-sided wrist pain should be considered, including a TFC injury, triquetral impaction fracture, and extensor carpi ulnaris tendonitis.

Routine radiographic results are normal in the majority of cases. Even with complete tears, an LT gap is not seen. Occasionally, however, the PA view may demonstrate a stepoff at the proximal and distal LT joints (Fig. 39–49). This represents a break in the proximal row line, as described by Gilula and Weeks,[88] accentuated by ulnar deviation. Ulnar variance should be measured. On the lateral view, a VISI pattern may be seen. Arthrography may show contrast flow between the triquetrum and the lunate plus the stepoff, as noted on the plain views. The limitations of arthrography have been mentioned earlier. MRI is not currently useful in the diagnosis of LT tears.

Wrist arthroscopy has become the study of choice to confirm clinically suspected LT tears.[45] The LT tear is best visualized through the 4,5 or 6R radiocarpal portal. An LT stepoff may be seen through the midcarpal portal. The degree of instability is classified according to the method of Geissler and co-workers[82] (see Table 39–1).

### Treatment

In the absence of static deformity, suspected acute LT tears are initially treated nonoperatively with cast immobilization.[200] This treatment appears to be successful in the majority of cases. For refractory pain, wrist arthroscopy and débridement of the membranous LT ligament with[183] or without[210, 287] LT pinning is 80% to 100% successful.

For chronic pain referable to an LT tear (without VISI), several surgical options are available, including capsulodesis,[21] LT arthrodesis,[127, 174, 192] ligament reconstruction, and ulnar shortening osteotomy.[19, 113, 192] Aside from one technique paper,[21] little has been written regarding capsulodesis for this problem. Attempts at LT arthrodesis have produced variable results. Pseudarthrosis rates as high as 57% have been reported,[127, 174, 227] even using screw fixation.[220] Furthermore, successful LT fusion does not guarantee pain relief.[174, 192] A 20% to 30% loss of wrist motion is expected. Our personal experience with LT arthrodesis has been disappointing.

LT ligament reconstruction has been recommended by several investigators.[200, 224] One version[224] of this technically demanding procedure utilizes a distally based strip of extensor carpi ulnaris, weaving this through drill holes in the triquetrum and lunate. The investigators of this technique reported excellent pain relief in eight of nine patients, and the range of motion actually improved 9%. We have no experience with this technique.

Ulnar shortening osteotomy is a popular alternative for LT tears without static instability.[19, 113, 192] This procedure offers several advantages: (1) it is an extra-articular procedure; (2) the resultant tightening of the ulnar carpal ligaments may help stabilize the LT joint; (3) a 2.5-mm shortening decreases the ulnocarpal joint force from 20% to 4%[187]; and (4) decompression of the ulnar aspect of the wrist may alleviate symptoms referable to TFC tears and lunatomalacia, which often accompany LT tears. Ulnar shortening has proved to be a predictable procedure in our hands.

**Authors' Preferred Method.** For acute traumatic ulnar-sided wrist pain with normal radiographic results, we prefer cast immobilization with clinical reevaluation at 2-week intervals. In the rare instance when an acute complete LT injury (without VISI) is highly suspected, we perform percutaneous LT pinning with two or three 0.045-inch smooth K-wires under radiographic and arthroscopic control. The pins are left in place for 6 to 8 weeks. For subacute instability, we prefer arthroscopic LT ligament débridement without pinning. For chronic instability, especially in the setting of ulnar-positive or ulnar-neutral variance, we prefer ulnar shortening osteotomy, using the method of Rayhack and associates.[198] If VISI is present, we prefer scaphoid-capitate-lunate-triquetrum-hamate (total midcarpal) arthrodesis (LKR) or scaphoid excision and four-corner arthrodesis (CC).

## MIDCARPAL INSTABILITY

Lichtman[141] and Dobyns[56] and their co-workers pointed out that in some patients, especially those with lax ligaments, there is a sudden shift of the entire proximal row into extension during wrist ulnar deviation and into flexion in radial deviation. There is no evidence of dissociation (no interosseous ligament disruption) within the proximal row. They termed this condition *nondissociative carpal instability*. Patients may complain of a painful clunk (termed the *catch-up clunk*) with ulnar deviation and pronation and may be able to voluntarily demonstrate it. The midcarpal shift test[142] reproduces their symptoms. Routine radiographic results may be normal or may demonstrate a static VISI deformity (Fig. 39–50). Cineradiology is of potential value in equivocal cases. Arthrography results will be normal; MRI may occasionally demonstrate nonspecific dorsal midcarpal synovitis.[99] Wrist arthroscopy is not recommended except to rule out other painful conditions.

Treatment at present remains challenging. Most investigators favor a trial of splinting, forearm strengthening, and activity modification. For refractory symptoms, surgical management options include joint leveling procedures, soft tissue stabilization, and intercarpal arthrodesis. Radial shortening or ulnar lengthening is an option for the ulnar minus patient with mild symptoms, the theory being that the ulnar head–TFC will support the ulnar side of the wrist.[294] We have no experience with the procedure in this setting. Soft tissue procedures have included volar[120] and combined volar-dorsal[142] approaches. Johnson and Carrera[120] described a volar soft tissue repair technique in which the interval between the radioscapholunate and the radiolunotriquetral is tightened, obliterating the space of Poirier. Lichtman and associates[142] described repair of the dorsal and volar arcuate (V) ligaments. As Lichtman and colleagues point out,[139] these soft tissue procedures are destined to fail in moderate-to-severe cases. Limited intercarpal arthrodesis procedures have included triquetrum-hamate or four-corner fusions.[139] Midcarpal arthrodesis should be curative in this condition but may be excessively aggressive.

**Authors' Preferred Approach.** We recommend extensive nonoperative treatment, concentrating on forearm strengthening and avoidance of aggravating activities. If this fails, we suggest a soft tissue reconstruction first, except in severe cases. Total midcarpal arthrodesis or scaphoid excision and four-corner fusion are recommended for refractory cases.

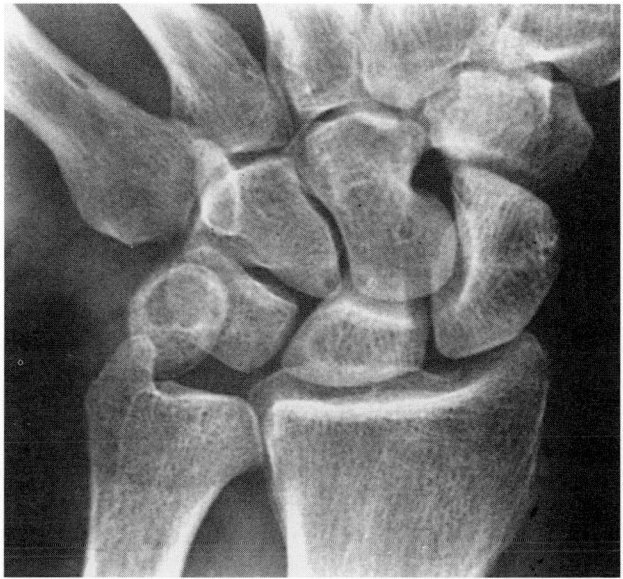

**FIGURE 39–49.** Radiograph of a patient with triquetrolunate instability. Note the triquetrolunate stepoff in ulnar deviation.

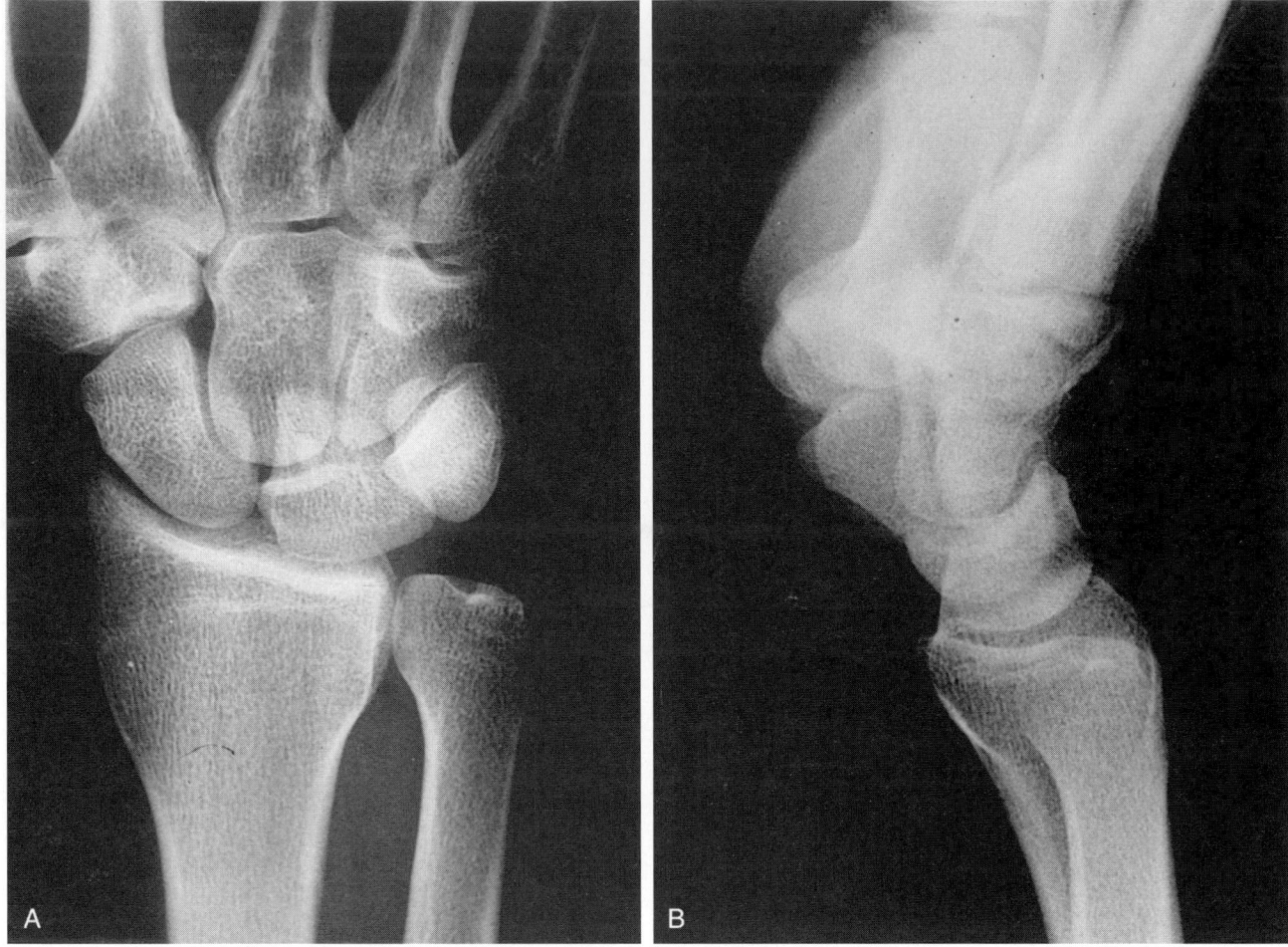

**Figure 39–50.** *A, B,* Volar intercalated segment instability, nondissociated (volar midcarpal instability).

## REFERENCES

1. Adams, B.D.; Frykman, G.K.; Teleisnik, J. Treatment of scaphoid nonunion with casting and pulsed electromagnetic fields: A study continuation. J Hand Surg [Am] 17:910–914, 1992.
2. Adams, J.D. Fracture of the carpal scaphoid. A new method of treatment with a report of one case. N Engl J Med 198:401–404, 1928.
3. Adkinson, J.W.; Chapman, M.W. Treatment of acute lunate and perilunate dislocation. Clin Orthop 164:199–207, 1982.
4. Adler, J.B.; Shafton, G.W. Fractures of the capitate. J Bone Joint Surg Am 44:1537–1547, 1962.
5. Almquist, E.E. Kienböck's disease. Hand Clin North Am 3:141–148, 1987.
6. Alnot, J.Y.; Bellan, N.; Oberlin, C.; De Cheveigne, C. Fractures and nonunions of the proximal pole of the carpal scaphoid bones: Internal fixation by a proximal to distal screw. Ann Chir Main 7:101–108, 1988.
7. Amadio, P.C.; Berquist, T.H.; Smith, O.K.; et al. Scaphoid malunion. J Hand Surg [Am] 14:679–687, 1989.
8. Armistead, R.B.; Linscheid, R.L.; Dobyns, J.H.; Beckenbaugh, R.D. Ulnar lengthening in the treatment of Kienböck's disease. J Bone Joint Surg Am 64:170–178, 1982.
9. Barnard, L.; Stubbins, S.G. Styloidectomy of the radius in the surgical treatment of nonunion of the carpal navicular. J Bone Joint Surg Am 30:98–102, 1948.
10. Bassett, C.A.L.; Mitchell, S.K.; Gaston, S.R. Pulsing electromagnetic field treatment in ununited fractures and failed arthrodesis. JAMA 247:623–628, 1982.
11. Beckenbaugh, R.D.; Shives, T.C.; Dobyns, J.H.; Linscheid, R.L. Kienböck's disease: The natural history of Kienböck's disease and consideration of lunate fractures. Clin Orthop 149:98–106, 1980.
12. Bellinghausen, H.W.; Gilula, L.A.; Young, L.V.; Weeks, P.M. Posttraumatic palmar carpal subluxation. Report of two cases. J Bone Joint Surg Am 65:998–1006, 1983.
13. Bentzon, P.G.K.; Randlov-Madsen, A. On fracture of the carpal scaphoid: A method for operative treatment of inveterate fractures. Acta Orthop Scand 16:30–39, 1945.
14. Berger, R.A. The gross and histologic anatomy of the scapholunate ligament. J Hand Surg [Am] 21:170–178, 1996.
15. Berger, R.A.; Imeada, T.; Berglund, L.; An, K.N. Constraint and material properties of the subregions of the scapholunate interosseous ligament. J Hand Surg Am 24:953–962, 1999.
16. Berger, R.A.; Kauer, J.M.G.; Landsmeer, J.M.F. Radioscapholunate ligament: A gross anatomic and histologic study of fetal and adult wrists. J Hand Surg [Am] 16:350–355, 1991.
17. Berger, T.A.; Garcia Elias, M. General anatomy of the wrist: Ligamentous anatomy. In: An, K.N.; Berger, R.A.; Cooney, W.P. III, eds. Biomechanics of the Wrist Joint. New York, Springer Verlag, 1991, pp. 5–14.
18. Bertheussen, K. Partial carpal arthrodesis as treatment of local degenerative changes in the wrist joints. Acta Orthop Scand 52:629–631, 1981.
19. Bilos, Z.J.; Chamberland, D. Distal ulnar head shortening for treatment of triangular fibrocartilage tears with ulna positive variance. J Hand Surg [Am] 16:1115–1119, 1991.
20. Bishop, A.T.; Beckenbaugh, R.D. Fracture of the hamate hook. J Hand Surg [Am] 13:135–139, 1988.
21. Blatt, G. Capsulodesis in reconstructive hand surgery. Dorsal capsulodesis for the unstable scaphoid and volar capsulodesis following excision of the distal ulna. Hand Clin North Am 3:81–102, 1987.
22. Bleton, R.; Alnot, J.Y.; Levane, J.H. Arthroscopy therapeutic possibilities in the chronic painful wrist: Report of a series

of 27 cases in 55 arthroscopies. Ann Chir Main 12:313–325, 1993.

23. Boeckstyns, M.E.H.; Busch, P. Surgical treatment of scaphoid pseudarthrosis: Evaluation of the results after soft tissue arthroplasty and inlay bone grafting. J Hand Surg [Am] 9:378–382, 1984.
24. Böhler, L. The Treatment of Fractures, 4th ed. Baltimore, William Wood, 1942.
25. Bora, F.W., Jr.; Osterman, A.L.; Woodbury, D.F.; Brighton, C.T. Treatment of nonunion of the scaphoid by direct current. Orthop Clin North Am 15:107–112, 1984.
26. Botte, M.J.; Gelberman, R.H. Fractures of the carpus, excluding the scaphoid. Hand Clin North Am 3:149–161, 1987.
27. Breitenseher, M.J.; Metz, V.M.; Gilula, L.A.; et al. Radiographically occult scaphoid fracture: Value of MR imaging in detection. Radiology 203:245–250, 1997.
28. Brunelli, G.A.; Brunelli G.R. A personal technique for treatment of scaphoid non-union. J Hand Surg [Br] 16:148–152, 1991.
29. Brunelli, G.A.; Brunelli, G.R. A new surgical technique for carpal instability with scapho-lunar dissociation: Eleven cases. Ann Chir Main Membr Super 14:207–213, 1995.
30. Bryan, R.S.; Dobyns, J.H. Fractures of the carpal bones other than lunate and navicular. Clin Orthop 149:107–111, 1980.
31. Bunker, T.D.; McNamee, P.B.; Scott, T.D. The Herbert screw for scaphoid fractures. J Bone Joint Surg Br 69:631–634, 1987.
32. Burgess, R.C. The effect of rotary subluxation of the scaphoid on radio-scaphoid contact. J Hand Surg [Am] 12:771–774, 1987.
33. Campbell, C.J.; Keokarn, T. Total and subtotal arthrodesis of the wrist. J Bone Joint Surg Am 46:1520–1533, 1964.
34. Campbell, R.D.; Lance, E.M.; Yeoh, C.B. Lunate and perilunar dislocations. J Bone Joint Surg Br 46:55–72, 1964.
35. Campbell, R.D., Jr.; Thompson, T.C.; Lance, E.M.; et al. Indications for open reduction of lunate and perilunate dislocations of the carpal bones. J Bone Joint Surg Am 47:915–937, 1965.
36. Carrozzella, J.C.; Stern, P.J.; Murdoc, R.A. The fate of failed bone graft surgery for scaphoid nonunions. J Hand Surg [Am] 14:800–806, 1989.
37. Carter, P.R.; Benton, L.J. Treatment of scaphoid fractures and scaphoid nonunion with Herbert compression screw. Exhibit. American Society for Surgery of the Hand, Annual Meeting, Las Vegas, NV, February 1985.
38. Carter, P.R.; Eaton, R.G.; Littler, J.W. Ununited fracture of the hook of the hamate. J Bone Joint Surg Am 59:583–588, 1977.
39. Cautille, G.P.; Wehbe, M.A. Scapho-lunate distance and the cortical ring sign. J Hand Surg [Am] 16:501–503, 1991.
40. Chuinard, R.G.; Zeman, S.G. Kienböck's disease: An analysis and rationale for treatment by capitate-hamate fusion. J Hand Surg [Am] 5:290, 1980.
41. Chung, K.C.; Zimmerman, N.B.; Travis, M.T. Wrist arthrography versus arthroscopy. A comparative study of 150 cases. J Hand Surg [Am] 21:591–594, 1996.
42. Clay, N.R.; Dias, J.J.; Costigan, P.S.; et al. Need the thumb be immobilized in scaphoid fractures? A randomised prospective trial. J Bone Joint Surg Br 73:828–832, 1991.
43. Cohen, M.S. Fractures of the carpal bones. Hand Clin 13:587–599, 1997.
44. Cohen, M.S. Ligamentous injuries and instability patterns. In: Light TR, ed. Hand Surgery Update 2. Rosemont, IL, American Academy of Orthopaedic Surgeons, 1999, pp. 97–106.
45. Cooney, W.P., III. Evaluation of chronic wrist pain by arthrography, arthroscopy and arthrotomy. J Hand Surg [Am] 18:815–822, 1993.
46. Cooney, W.P.; Dobyns, J.H.; Linscheid, R.L. Fractures of the scaphoid: A rational approach to management. Clin Orthop 149:90–97, 1980.
47. Cooney, W.P., III; Dobyns, J.H.; Linscheid, R.L. Nonunion of the scaphoid: Analysis of the results from bone grafting. J Hand Surg [Am] 5:343–354, 1980.
48. Cooney, W.P., III; Linscheid, R.L.; Dobyns, J.H.; Wood, M.B. Scaphoid nonunion: Role of anterior interpositional bone grafts. J Hand Surg [Am] 13:635–650, 1988.
49. Cordrey, L.J.; Ferrer-Torells, M. Management of fractures of the greater multangular. J Bone Joint Surg Am 42:1111–1118, 1960.
50. Crabbe, W.A. Excision of the proximal row of the carpus. J Bone Joint Surg Br 46:708–711, 1964.
51. Crosby, E.B.; Linscheid, R.L. Rupture of the flexor profundus tendon of the ring finger secondary to ancient fracture of the hook of the hamate. J Bone Joint Surg Am 56:1076–1078, 1974.

52. Davis, C.A.; Culp, R.W.; Hume, E.L.; Osterman, A.L. Reconstruction of the scapholunate ligament in a cadaver model using a bone-ligament-bone autograft from the foot. J Hand Surg [Am] 23:884–892, 1998.
53. Dehne, E.; Deffer, P.A.; Feighney, R.E. Pathomechanics of the fracture of the carpal navicular. J Trauma 4:96–114, 1964.
54. DeMaagd, R.L.; Engber, W.D. Retrograde Herbert screw fixation for treatment of proximal pole scaphoid nonunions. J Hand Surg [Am] 14:996–1003, 1989.
55. Destot, E. Injuries of the Wrist: A Radiological Study. London, Ernest Benn, 1925.
56. Dobyns, J.H.; Linscheid, R.L.; Chao, E.Y.S.; et al. Traumatic instability of the wrist. Instr Course Lect 24:182–199, 1975.
57. Easterling, K.J.; Wolfe, S.W. Scaphoid shift in the uninjured wrist. J Hand Surg [Am] 19:604–606, 1994.
58. Eaton, R.G. Personal communication, 1990.
59. Eaton, R.G.; Akelman, E.; Eaton, B.H. Fascial implant arthroplasty for treatment of radioscaphoid degenerative disease. J Hand Surg [Am] 14:766–774, 1989.
60. Eckenrode, T.F.; Louis, D.S.; Greene, T.L. Scaphoid-trapezium-trapezoid fusion in the treatment of chronic scapholunate instability. J Hand Surg [Am] 18:815–822, 1993.
61. Eddeland, A.; Eiken, O.; Hellgren, E.; Ohlsson, N.M. Fractures of the scaphoid. Scand J Plast Reconstr Surg 9:234–239, 1975.
62. Eiken, O.; Niechajev, I. Radius shortening in malacia of the lunate. Scand J Plast Reconstr Surg 14:191–196, 1980.
63. Ender, H.G.; Herbert, T.J. Treatment of problem fractures and nonunions of the scaphoid. Orthopedics 12:195–202, 1989.
64. Evans, G.; Burke, F.D.; Barton, N.J. A comparison of conservative treatment and silicone replacement arthroplasty in Kienböck's disease. J Hand Surg [Br] 11:98–102, 1986.
65. Feinstein, W.K.; Lichtman, D.M.; Noble, P.C.; et al. Quantitative assessment of the midcarpal shift test. J Hand Surg [Am] 24:977–983, 1999.
66. Fernandez, D.L. A technique for anterior wedge-shaped grafts for scaphoid nonunions with carpal instability. J Hand Surg [Am] 9:733–737, 1984.
67. Fernandez, D.L. Anterior bone grafting and conventional lag screw fixation to treat scaphoid nonunions. J Hand Surg [Am] 15:140–147, 1990.
68. Fernandez, D.L.; Eggli, S. Nonunion of the scaphoid. Revascularization of the proximal pole with implantation of a vascular bundle and bone grafting. J Bone Joint Surg Am 77:883–893, 1995.
69. Fick, R. Über die Bewegungen in den Handgelenken. Abh Math-Phys Cl Sachs Ges Wis (Leipzig) 26:419–467, 1901.
70. Fisk, G.R. Carpal instability and the fractured scaphoid. Ann R Coll Surg Engl 46:63–76, 1970.
71. Fisk G.R. Non-union of the carpal scaphoid treated by wedge grafting. Abstract. J Bone Joint Surg Br 66:277, 1984.
72. Fisk, G.R. The wrist. J Bone Joint Surg Br 66:396–407, 1984.
73. Fortin, P.T.; Louis, D.S. Long-term follow-up of scaphoid-trapezium-trapezoid arthodesis. J Hand Surg [Am] 18:675–681, 1993.
74. Foucher, G.; Schuind, F.; Merle, M.; et al. Fractures of the hook of the hamate. J Hand Surg [Br] 10:205–210, 1985.
75. Friedenberg, Z.B. Anatomic considerations in the treatment of carpal navicular fractures. Am J Surg 78:379–381, 1949.
76. Friedman, S.L.; Palmer, A.K. The ulnar impaction syndrome. Hand Clin 7:295–310, 1991.
77. Frykman, G.K.; Taleisnik, J.; Peters, G.; et al. Treatment of nonunited scaphoid fractures by pulsed electromagnetic field and cast. J Hand Surg [Am] 11:344–349, 1986.
78. Ganel, A.; Engel, J.; Oster, Z.; Farine, I. Bone scanning in the assessment of fractures of the scaphoid. J Hand Surg [Am] 4:540–543, 1979.
79. Garcia-Elias, M.; Abanco, J.; Salvador, E.; Sanchez, R. Crush injury of the carpus. J Bone Joint Surg Br 67:286–289, 1985.
80. Garcia-Elias, M.; Irisarri, C.; Henriquez, A.; et al. Perilunar dislocation of the carpus: A diagnosis still often missed. Ann Chir Main 5:281–287, 1986.
81. Gasser, H. Delayed union and pseudarthrosis of the carpal navicular: Treatment by compression screw osteosynthesis. J Bone Joint Surg Am 47:249–266, 1965.
82. Geissler, W.B.; Freeland, A.E.; Savoie, F.H.; et al. Intracarpal soft-tissue lesions associated with an intra-articular fracture of the distal end of the radius. J Bone Joint Surg Am 78:357–365, 1996.

83. Gelberman, R.H.; Bauman, T.D.; Menon, J.; Akeson, W.H. The vascularity of the lunate bone and Kienböck's disease. J Hand Surg [Am] 5:272–278, 1980.

84. Gelberman, R.H.; Menon, J. The vascularity of the scaphoid bone. J Hand Surg [Am] 5:508–513, 1980.

85. Gelberman, R.H.; Wolock, B.S.; Siegel, D.B. Fractures and non-unions of the carpal scaphoid. J Bone Joint Surg Am 71:1560–1565, 1989.

86. Gellman, H.; Caputo, R.J.; Carter, V.; et al. Comparison of short and long thumb-spica casts for non-displaced fractures of the carpal scaphoid. J Bone Joint Surg Am 71:354–357, 1989.

87. Gilford, W.W.; Bolton, R.H.; Lambrinudi, C. The mechanism of the wrist joint with special reference to fractures of the scaphoid. Guys Hosp Rep 92:52–59, 1943.

88. Gilula, L.A.; Weeks, P.M. Posttraumatic ligamentous instabilities of the wrist. Radiology 129:641–651, 1978.

89. Goldner, J.L. Treatment of carpal instability without joint fusion. Current assessment. Guest editorial. J Hand Surg [Am] 7:325–326, 1982.

90. Graner, O.; Lopes, E.I.; Carvalho, B.C.; et al. Arthrodesis of the carpal bones in the treatment of Kienböck's disease, painful ununited fractures of the navicular and lunate bones with avascular necrosis, and old fracture dislocations of carpal bones. J Bone Joint Surg Am 48:767–774, 1966.

91. Green, D.P. The effect of avascular necrosis on Russe bone grafting for scaphoid nonunion. J Hand Surg [Am] 10:597–605, 1985.

92. Green, D.P. Proximal row carpectomy. Hand Clin North Am 3:163–168, 1987.

93. Green, D.P. Carpal dislocations and instabilities. In: Green, D.P., ed. Operative Hand Surgery, 2nd ed., Vol. 2. New York, Churchill Livingstone, 1988, pp. 875–938.

94. Green, D.P.; O'Brien, E.T. Open reduction of carpal dislocations: Indications and operative techniques. J Hand Surg [Am] 3:250–265, 1978.

95. Green, D.P.; O'Brien, E.T. Classification and management of carpal dislocations. Clin Orthop 149:55–72, 1980.

96. Guimbertceau, J.C.; Panconi, B. Recalcitrant nonunion of the scaphoid treated with a vascularized bone graft based on the ulnar artery. J Bone Joint Surg Am 72:88–97, 1990.

97. Haddad, F.S.; Goddard, N.J. Acute percutaneous scaphoid fixation: A pilot study. J Bone Joint Surg Br 80:95–99, 1998.

98. Hastings, D.E.; Silver, R.L. Intercarpal arthrodesis in the management of chronic carpal instability after trauma. J Hand Surg [Am] 9:834–840, 1984.

99. Hausman, M. Imaging for wrist instability problems. Presented at the American Society for Surgery of the Hand, Seattle, WA, 2000.

100. Helfet, A.J. A new operation for ununited fractures of the scaphoid. J Bone Joint Surg Br 34:329, 1952.

101. Herbert, T.J. The fractured scaphoid. St. Louis, Quality Medical Publishing, 1990.

102. Herbert, T.J.; Faithfull, R.G.; McCann, D.J.; Ireland, J. Bilateral arthrography of the wrist. J Hand Surg [Br] 15:223–235, 1990.

103. Herbert, T.J.; Fisher, W.E. Management of the fractured scaphoid using a new bone screw. J Bone Joint Surg Br 66:114–123, 1984.

104. Herzberg, G.; Comtet, J.J.; Linscheid, R.L.; et al. Perilunate dislocations and fracture-dislocations: A multicenter study. J Hand Surg [Am] 18:768–779, 1993.

105. Hom, S; Ruby, L.K. Attempted scapholunate arthrodesis for chronic scapholunate dissociation. J Hand Surg [Am] 16:334–339, 1991.

106. Hori, Y.; Tamai, S.; Okuda, H.; et al. Blood vessel transplantation to bone. J Hand Surg [Am] 4:23–33, 1979.

107. Horii, E.; Garcia-Elias, M.; An, K.N.; et al. Effect of force transmission across the carpus in procedures used to treat Kienböck's disease. J Hand Surg [Am] 15:393–400, 1990.

108. Horii, E.; Garcia-Elias, M.; An, K.N.; et al. A kinematic study of lunotriquetral dissociation. J Hand Surg [Am] 16:355–362, 1991.

109. Horii, E.; Nakamura, R.; Watanabe, K.; Tsunoda, K. Scaphoid fracture as a "puncher's" fracture. J Orthop Trauma 8:107–110, 1994.

110. Hove, L.M. Simultaneous scaphoid and distal radius fractures. J Hand Surg [Br] 19:384–388, 1994.

111. Huene, D.R. Primary internal fixation of carpal navicular fractures in the athlete. Am J Sports Med 7:175–177, 1979.

112. Hull, W.J.; House, J.H.; Gustillo, R.B.; et al. The surgical approach and source of bone graft for symptomatic non-union of the scaphoid. Clin Orthop 115:241–247, 1976.

113. Hulsizer, D.; Weiss, A.P.; Ackelman, E. Ulna-shortening osteotomy after failed arthroscopic debridement of the triangular fibrocartilage complex. J Hand Surg [Am] 22:694–698, 1997.

114. Hulten, O. Über anatomische variationen der handgelenkknochen. Acta Radiol 9:155–168, 1928.

115. Hunter, J.C.; Escobedo, E.M.; Wilson, A.J.; et al. MR imaging of clinically suspected scaphoid fractures. Am J Roentgenol 168: 1287–1293, 1997.

116. Inglis, A.E.; Jones, E.C. Proximal row carpectomy for diseases of the proximal row. J Bone Joint Surg Am 59:460–463, 1977.

117. Ishida, O.; Tsai, T.M. Complications and results of scapho-trapezio-trapezoid arthrodesis. Clin Orthop 287:125–130, 1993.

118. Jensen, B.V.; Christensen, C. An unusual combination of simultaneous fracture of the tuberosity of the trapezium and hook of the hamate. J Hand Surg [Am] 15:285–287, 1990.

119. Jiranek, W.A.; Ruby, L.K.; Millender, L.B.; et al. Long-term results after Russe bone grafting: The effect of malunion of the scaphoid. J Bone Joint Surg Am 74:1217–1228, 1992.

120. Johnson, R.P.; Carrera, G.F. Chronic capitolunate instability. J Bone Joint Surg Am 68:1164–1176, 1986.

121. Johnstone, D.J.; Thorogood, S.; Smith, W.H.; Scott, T.D. A comparison of magnetic resonance imaging and arthroscopy in the investigation of chronic wrist pain. J Hand Surg [Br] 22:714–718, 1997.

122. Jorgensen, E.C. Proximal row carpectomy. J Bone Joint Surg Am 51:1104–1111, 1969.

123. Jorgensen, T.M.; Andresen, J.; Thommesen, P.; Hansen, H.H. Scanning and radiology of the carpal scaphoid bone. Acta Orthop Scand 50:663–665, 1979.

124. Kawai, H.; Yamamoto, K. Pronator quadratus pedicled bone graft for old scaphoid fractures. J Bone Joint Surg Br 70:829–831, 1988.

125. Kienböck, R. Concerning traumatic malacia of the lunate and its consequences: Degeneration and compression fractures. Translation of 1910 article. Clin Orthop 149:4–8, 1980.

126. King, R.J.; MacKenney, R.P.; Elnur S. Suggested method for closed treatment of fractures of the carpal scaphoid: Hypothesis supported by dissection and clinical practice. J Soc Med 75:860–867, 1982.

127. Kirschenbaum, D.; Coyle, M.P.; Leddy, J.P. Chronic lunotriquetral instability: Diagnosis and treatment. J Hand Surg [Am] 18:1107–1112, 1993.

128. Kleinman, W.B. Management of chronic rotary subluxation of the scaphoid by scapho-trapezio-trapezoid arthrodesis. Hand Clin North Am 3:113–133, 1987.

129. Kleinman, W.B.; Steichen, J.B.; Strickland, J.W. Management of chronic rotary subluxation of the scaphoid by scapho-trapezio-trapezoid arthrodesis. J Hand Surg [Am] 7:125–136, 1982.

130. Kricun, M.E. Wrist arthrography. Clin Orthop 187:65–71, 1984.

131. Kuhlmann, J.N.; Fournol, S.; Mimoun, M.; Baux, S. Fracture of the lesser multangular (trapezoid) bone. Ann Chir Main Memb Super 5:133–134, 1986.

132. Landsmeer, J.M.F. Studies in the anatomy of articulation. I. The equilibrium of the "intercalated" bone. Acta Morphol Neerl Scand 3:287–303, 1961.

133. Langhoff, O.; Anderson, J.L. Consequences of late immobilization of scaphoid fractures. J Hand Surg [Br] 13:77–79, 1988.

134. Larsen, C.F.; Amadio, P.C.; Gilula, L.A.; Hodge, J.C. Analysis of carpal instability: Description of the scheme. J Hand Surg [Am] 20:752–764, 1995.

135. Lavernia, C.J.; Cohen, M.S.; Taleisnik, J. Treatment of scapholunate dissociation by ligamentous repair and capsulodesis. J Hand Surg [Am] 17:354–359, 1992.

136. Levinsohn, E.M.; Palmer, A.K. Arthrography of the traumatized wrist. Correlation with radiography and the carpal instability series. Radiology 146:647–651, 1983.

137. Levy, M.; Fischel, R.E.; Stern, G.M.; Goldberg, I. Chip fractures of the os triquetrum. J Bone Joint Surg Br 61:355–357, 1979.

138. Leyshon, A.; Ireland, J.; Trickey, E.L. The treatment of delayed union and nonunion of the carpal scaphoid by screw fixation. J Bone Joint Surg Br 66:124–127, 1984.

139. Lichtman, D.M.; Bruckner, J.D.; Culp, R.W.; Alexander, C.E. Palmar midcarpal instability: Results of surgical reconstruction J Hand Surg [Am] 18:307–315, 1993.

140. Lichtman, D.M.; Mack, G.R.; MacDonald, R.I.; et al. Kienböck's disease: The role of silicone replacement arthroplasty. J Bone Joint Surg Am 59:899–908, 1977.

141. Lichtman, D.M.; Schneider, J.R.; Swafford, A.R. Midcarpal instability. Presented at the 35th Annual Meeting of the American Society for Surgery of the Hand, Atlanta, GA, February 4–6, 1980.

142. Lichtman, D.M.; Schneider, J.R.; Swafford, A.R.; et al. Ulnar midcarpal instability—Clinical and laboratory analysis. J Hand Surg [Am] 6:515–523, 1981.

143. Lindgren, E. Some radiological aspects of the carpal scaphoid and its fractures. Acta Chir Scand 98:538–548, 1949.

144. Lindstrom, G.; Nystrom, A. Natural history of scaphoid nonunion with special reference to "asymptomatic" cases. J Hand Surg [Br] 17:697–700, 1992.

145. Linscheid, R.L. Scapholunate ligamentous instabilities (dissociations, subdislocations, dislocations). Ann Chir Main 3:323–330, 1984.

146. Linscheid, R.L. Ulnar lengthening and shortening. Hand Clin North Am 3:69–79, 1984.

147. Linscheid, R.L. Kienböck's disease. Editorial. J Hand Surg [Am] 10:1–3, 1985.

148. Linscheid, R.L.; Dobyns, J.H. Athletic injuries of the wrist. Clin Orthop 198:141–151, 1985.

149. Linscheid, R.L.; Dobyns, J.H. Treatment of scapholunate dissociation. Hand Clin 8:645–652, 1992.

150. Linscheid, R.L.; Dobyns, J.H.; Beabout, J.W.; Bryan, R.S. Traumatic instability of the wrist. J Bone Joint Surg Am 54:1612–1632, 1972.

151. Linscheid, R.L.; Dobyns, J.H.; Young, D.K. Trispiral tomography in the evaluation of wrist injury. Bull Hosp Joint Dis Orthop Inst 44:297–308, 1984.

152. London, P.S. The broken scaphoid bone: The case against pessimism. J Bone Joint Surg Br 43:237–244, 1961.

153. Mack, G.R.; Bosse, M.J.; Gelberman, R.H.; Yu, E. The natural history of scaphoid nonunion. J Bone Joint Surg Am 66:504–509, 1984.

154. Mack, G.R.; Kelly, J.P.; Lichtman, D.M. Scaphoid non-union. In: Lichtman, D.M., ed. The Wrist and Its Disorders. Philadelphia, W.B. Saunders, 1997, pp. 234–267.

155. Maitin, E.C.; Bora, F.W., Jr.; Osterman, A.L. Lunatotriquetral instability: A cause of chronic wrist pain. Proceedings of the American Society for Surgery of the Hand, Annual Meeting, San Antonio, TX, 1987. J Hand Surg [Am] 13:309, 1987.

156. Malerich, M.; Clifford, J.; Eaton, R.; Littler, J.W. Distal scaphoid resection arthroplasty for the treatment of degenerative arthritis secondary to scaphoid nonunion. J Hand Surg [Am] 24:1196–1205, 1999.

157. Matti, H. Über die behandlung der navicular fraktur und der refractura patellae durch plombierung mit spongiosa. Zentralbl Chir 64:23–53, 1937.

158. Maudsley, R.H.; Chen, S.C. Screw fixation in the management of the fractured carpal scaphoid. J Bone Joint Surg Br 54:432–441, 1972.

159. Mayfield, J.K.; Johnson, R.P.; Kilcoyne, R.F. The ligaments of the human wrist and their functional significance. Anat Rec 186:417–428, 1976.

160. Mayfield, J.K.; Johnson, R.P.; Kilcoyne, R.K. Carpal dislocations: Pathomechanics and progressive perilunar instability. J Hand Surg [Am] 5:226–241, 1980.

161. Mazet, R., Jr.; Hohl, M. Conservative treatment of old fractures of the carpal scaphoid. J Trauma 1:115–127, 1961.

162. McClain, E.J.; Boyes, J.H. Missed fractures of the greater multangular. J Bone Joint Surg Am 48:1525–1528, 1966.

163. McGrath, M.H.; Watson, H.K. Late results with local bone graft donor sites in hand surgery. J Hand Surg [Am] 6:234–237, 1981.

164. McLaughlin, H.L.; Baab, O.D. Carpectomy. Surg Clin North Am 31:451–461, 1951.

165. Melone, C.P., Jr. Scaphoid fractures: Concepts of management. Clin Plast Surg 8:83–94, 1981.

166. Mikic, Z.D.J. Arthrography of the wrist joint. An experimental study. J Bone Joint Surg Am 66:371–378, 1984.

167. Mody, B.S.; Belliappa, P.P.; Dias, J.J.; Barton, N.J. Nonunion of fractures of the scaphoid tuberosity. J Bone Joint Surg Br 75:423–425, 1993.

168. Moneim, M.S. The tangential posteroanterior radiograph to demonstrate scapholunate dissociation. J Bone Joint Surg Am 63:1324–1326, 1981.

169. Moneim, M.S.; Hofammann, K.E., III; Omer, G.E. Transscaphoid perilunate fracture dislocation. Clin Orthop 190:227–235, 1984.

170. Mudgal, C.S.; Jones, W.A. Scapho-lunate diastasis: A component of fractures of the distal radius. J Hand Surg [Br] 15:503–505, 1990.

171. Murray G. End results of bone grafting for nonunion of the carpal navicular. J Bone Joint Surg 28:749–756, 1946.

172. Nakamura, R.; Imaeda, T.; Horii, E.; et al. Analysis of scaphoid fracture displacement by three-dimensional computed tomography. J Hand Surg [Am] 16:485–492, 1991.

173. Navarro, A. Anatomia y fisiologia del carpo. An Inst Clin Quir Cir Exp 2:161–248, 1936–1937.

174. Nelson, D.L.; Manske, P.R.; Pruitt, D.L.; et al. Lunotriquetral arthrodesis. J Hand Surg [Am] 18:1113–1120, 1993.

175. Neviaser, R.J. Proximal row carpectomy for posttraumatic disorders of the carpus. J Hand Surg 8:301–305, 1983.

176. Newport, M.L.; Williams, C.D.; Bradley, W.D. Mechanical strength of scaphoid fixation. J Hand Surg 21B:99–102, 1996.

177. North, E.R.; Meyer, S. Wrist injuries: Correlation of clinical and arthroscopic findings. J Hand Surg 15A:915–920, 1990.

178. North, E.R.; Thomas, S. An anatomic guide for arthroscopic visualization of the wrist capsular ligaments. J Hand Surg 13A:815–822, 1988.

179. O'Brien, E.T. Acute fractures and dislocations of the carpus. Orthop Clin North Am 15:237–258, 1984.

180. Ogunro, O. Fracture of the body of the hamate bone. J Hand Surg [Am] 8:353–355, 1983.

181. Olsen, N.; Schousen, P.; Dirksen, H.; Christoffersen, O.K. Regional scintimetry in scaphoid fractures. Acta Orthop Scand 54:380–382, 1983.

182. Osterman, A.L.; Mikulics, M. Scaphoid nonunion. Hand Clin North Am 4:437–455, 1988.

183. Osterman, A.L.; Seidman, G.D. The role of arthroscopy in the treatment of lunatotriquetral ligament injuries. Hand Clin 11:41–50, 1995.

184. Palmer, A.K. Trapezial ridge fractures. J Hand Surg [Am] 6:561–564, 1981.

185. Palmer, A.K.; Dobyns, J.H.; Linscheid, R.L. Management of posttraumatic instability of the wrist secondary to ligament rupture. J Hand Surg [Am] 3:507–532, 1978.

186. Palmer, A.K.; Levinsohn, E.M.; Kuzma, G.R. Arthrography of the wrist. J Hand Surg [Am] 8:15–23, 1983.

187. Palmer, A.K.; Werner, F.W. Biomechanics of the distal radioulnar joint. Clin Orthop 187:26–35, 1984.

188. Pechlaner, S.; Hussl, H.; Konzel, K.H. Alternative operationsmethode bei Kahnbeinpseudarthrosen. Prospektive studie. Handchirurgie 19:302–305, 1987.

189. Persson, M. Causal treatment of lunatomalacia. Further experiences of operative ulna lengthening. Acta Chir Scand 100:531–544, 1950.

190. Peterson, H.A.; Lipscomb, P.R. Intercarpal arthrodesis. Arch Surg 95:127–134, 1967.

191. Pin, P.G.; Semenkovich, J.W.; Young, V.L.; et al. The role of radionucleotide imaging in the evaluation of wrist pain. J Hand Surg [Am] 13:810–814, 1988.

192. Pin, P.G.; Young, V.L.; Gilula, L.A.; Weeks, P.M. Management of chronic lunotriquetral ligament tears. J Hand Surg [Am] 14:77–83, 1989.

193. Posner, M.A.; Greenspan, A. Trispiral tomography for the evaluation of wrist problems. J Hand Surg [Am] 13:175–181, 1988.

194. Primiano, G.A.; Reef, T.C. Disruption of the proximal carpal arch of the hand. J Bone Joint Surg Am 56:328–332, 1974.

195. Prosser, A.J.; Brenkel, I.J.; Irvine, G.B. Articular fractures of the distal scaphoid. J Hand Surg [Br] 13:87–91, 1988.

196. Protas, J.M.; Jackson, N.T. Evaluating carpal instabilities with fluoroscopy. AJR Am J Roentgenol 135:137–140, 1980.

197. Rand, J.A.; Linscheid, R.L.; Dobyns, J.H. Capitate fractures. Clin Orthop 165:209–216, 1982.

198. Rayhack, J.M.; Gasser, S.I.; Latta, L.L.; et al. Precision oblique osteotomy for shortening of the ulna. J Hand Surg [Am] 18:908–918, 1993.

199. Razemon, J.P. Étude pathogenique de la maladie de Kienböck. Ann Chir Main 1:240–242, 1982.

200. Reagan, D.S.; Linscheid, R.L.; Dobyns, J.H. Lunotriquetral sprains. J Hand Surg [Am] 9:502–514, 1984.

201. Reinus, W.R.; Conway, W.F.; Totty, W.G.; et al. Carpal avascular necrosis: MR imaging. Radiology 160:689–693, 1986.

202. Rettig, A.C.; Kollias, S.C. Internal fixation of acute stable scaphoid fractures in the athlete. Am J Sports Med 24:182–186, 1996.

203. Ring, D.; Jupiter, J.B.; Herndon, J.H. Acute fractures of the scaphoid. J Am Acad Orthop Surg 8:225–231, 2000.

204. Robbins, R.R.; Carter, P.R. Iliac crest bone grafting and Herbert screw fixation of nonunion of the scaphoid with avascular proximal poles. J Hand Surg [Am] 20:818–831, 1995.

205. Roth, J.H.; Haddad, R.G. Radiocarpal arthroscopy and arthrography in the diagnosis of ulnar wrist pain. Arthroscopy 2:234–243, 1986.

206. Rotman, M.B.; Manske, P.R.; Pruitt, D.L.; Szerzinski, J. Scaphocapitolunate arthrodesis. J Hand Surg [Am] 18:26–33, 1993.

207. Ruby, L.K. Carpal instability. J Bone Joint Surg Am 77:476–487, 1995.

208. Ruby, L.K.; Cooney, W.P.; An, K.N.; et al. Relative motion of selected carpal bones: A kinematic analysis of the normal wrist. J Hand Surg [Am] 13:1–10, 1988.

209. Ruby, L.K.; Stinson, J.; Belsky, M.R. The natural history of scaphoid nonunion: A review of 55 cases. J Bone Joint Surg Am 67:428–432, 1985.

210. Ruch, D.S.; Poehling, G.G. Arthroscopic management of partial scapholunate and lunotriquetral injuries of the wrist. J Hand Surg [Am] 21:412–417, 1996.

211. Ruch, D.S.; Siegel, D.; Charbon, S.J.; et al. Arthroscopic categorization of intercarpal ligamentous injuries of the wrist. Orthopedics 16:1051–1056, 1993.

212. Russe, O. Fracture of the carpal navicular. Diagnosis, nonoperative treatment and operative treatment. J Bone Joint Surg Am 42:759–768, 1960.

213. Sanders, W.E. Evaluation of the humpback scaphoid by computed tomography in the longitudinal axial plane of the scaphoid. J Hand Surg [Am] 13:182–187, 1988.

214. Sarrafian, S.K.; Melamed, J.L.; Goshgarian, G.M. Study of wrist motion in flexion and extension. Clin Orthop 126:153–159, 1977.

215. Sasaki, T. Lunate body fracture. J Japan Soc Surg Hand 8:635–639, 1991.

216. Scheck, R.J.; Kubitzek, C.; Hierner, R.; et al. The scapholunate interosseous ligament in MR arthrography of the wrist: Correlation with non-enhanced MRI and wrist arthroscopy. Skeletal Radiol 26:263–271, 1997.

217. Scheck, R.J.; Romagnolo, A.; Hierner, R.; et al. The carpal ligaments in MR arthrography of the wrist: Correlation with standard MRI and wrist arthroscopy. J Magn Reson Imaging 9:468–474, 1999.

218. Schnitzler, C.M.; Biddulph, S.L.; Mesquita, J.M.; Gear, K.A. Bone structure and turnover in the distal radius and iliac crest: A histomorphometric study. J Bone Miner Res 11:1761–1768, 1996.

219. Schwartz, A.; Ruby, L.K. Wrist arthrography revisited. Orthopedics 5:883–888, 1982.

220. Sennwald, G.R.; Fischer, M.; Mondi, P. Lunotriquetral arthrodesis: A controversial procedure. J Hand Surg [Br] 20:755–760, 1995.

221. Shaw, J.A. A biomechanical comparison of scaphoid screws. J Hand Surg [Am] 12:347–353, 1987.

222. Shaw, J.A. Biomechanical comparison of cannulated small bone screws: A brief follow-up study. J Hand Surg [Am] 16:998–1001, 1991.

223. Sheetz, K.K.; Bishop, A.T.; Berger, R.A. Arterial blood supply of the distal radius and its potential use in vascularized pedicled bone grafts. J Hand Surg [Am] 20:902–914, 1995.

224. Shin, A.Y.; Battaglia, M.J.; Bishop, A.T. Lunotriquetral instability: Diagnosis and treatment. J Am Acad Orthop Surg 8:170–179, 2000.

225. Shin, S.S.; Moore, D.C.; McGovern, R.D.; Weiss, A.P. Scapholunate ligament reconstruction using a bone-retinaculum bone autograft: A biomechanical and histological study. J Hand Surg [Am] 23:216–221, 1998.

226. Siegel, D.B.; Gelberman, R.H. Radical styloidectomy: An anatomical study with special reference to radiocarpal intracapsular ligamentous morphology. J Hand Surg [Am] 16:40–44, 1991.

227. Siegel, J.M.; Ruby, L.K. A critical look at intercarpal arthrodesis: Review of the literature. J Hand Surg [Am] 21:717–723, 1996.

228. Slade, J.F. Arthroscopic aided percutaneous fixation of scaphoid fractures. Presented at the American Society for Surgery of the Hand, Seattle, WA, 2000.

229. Slater, R., Jr.; Szabo, R.; Bay, B.K.; Laubach, J. Dorsal intercarpal ligament capsulodesis for scapholunate dissociation: Biomechanical analysis in a cadaver model. J Hand Surg [Am] 24:232–239, 1999.

230. Smith, B.S.; Cooney, W.P. Revision bone grafting for nonunion of the scaphoid. Clin Orthop 327:98–109, 1996.

231. Smith, D.; Cooney, W.; An, K.N.; et al. The effects of simulated unstable scaphoid fractures on carpal motion. J Hand Surg [Am] 14:283–290, 1989.

232. Smith, D.K.; Murray, P.M. Avulsion fracture of the volar aspect of the triquetral bone of the wrist: A subtle sign of carpal ligament injury. AJR Am J Roentgenol 166:609–614, 1996.

233. Smith, R.J.; Atkinson, R.E.; Jupiter, J.B. Silicone synovitis of the wrist. J Hand Surg [Am] 10:47–60, 1985.

234. Sotereanos, D.G.; Varitimidis, S.E.; Riano, F.A. Proximal row carpectomy: Results in Kienböck's disease versus scapholunate advanced collapse. Presented at The American Society for Surgery of the Hand, Seattle, WA, 2000.

235. Soto-Hall, R.; Haldeman, K.O. The conservative and operative treatment of fractures of the carpal scaphoid (navicular). J Bone Joint Surg 23:841–850, 1941.

236. Sprague, H.; Carter, P.; Osterman, L.; et al. Use of the Herbert screw for scaphoid fractures. Orthop Trans 9:176, 1985.

237. Stack, J.K. End results of excision of the carpal bones. Arch Surg 57:245–252, 1948.

238. Stahl, F. On lunatomalacia (Kienböck's disease). A clinical and roentgenological study, especially on its pathogenesis and the late results of immobilization treatment. Acta Chir Scand 95(Suppl 126):133, 1947.

239. Stamm, T.T. Developments in orthopaedic operative procedures. II. Excision of the proximal row of the carpus. Guys Hosp Rep 112:6–8, 1963.

240. Stanley, J.K.; Trail, I.A. Carpal instability. J Bone Joint Surg Br 76:691–700, 1994.

241. Stark, H.H.; Jobe, F.W.; Boyes, J.H.; et al. Fracture of the hook of the hamate in athletes. J Bone Joint Surg Am 59:575–582, 1977.

242. Stark, H.H.; Rickard, T.A.; Zeme, N.P.; Ashworth, C.R. Treatment of ununited fractures of the scaphoid by iliac bone grafts and Kirschner wire fixation. J Bone Joint Surg Am 70:982–991, 1988.

243. Stecher, W.R. Roentgenography of the carpal navicular bone. AJR Am J Roentgenol 37:704–705, 1937.

244. Stein, A.H., Jr. Dorsal dislocation of the lesser multangular bone. J Bone Joint Surg Am 53:377–379, 1971.

245. Stein, F.; Siegel, M.W. Naviculocapitate fracture syndrome: A case report. New thoughts on the mechanism of injury. J Bone Joint Surg Am 51:391–395, 1969.

246. Steinmann, S.P.; Linscheid, R.L. Pisotriquetral loose bodies. J Hand Surg [Am] 22:918–921, 1997.

247. Stern, P.J. Multiple flexor tendon ruptures following an old anterior dislocation of the lunate: A case report. J Bone Joint Surg Am 63:489–490, 1981.

248. Stewart, M.J. Fractures of the carpal navicular (scaphoid): A report of 436 cases. J Bone Joint Surg Am 36:998–1006, 1954.

249. Sutro, C.J. Treatment of nonunion of the carpal navicular bone. Surgery 20:536–540, 1946.

250. Szabo, R.M. Overview of scapholunate instability. Presented at the American Society for Surgery of the Hand, Seattle, WA, 2000.

251. Taleisnik, J. The ligaments of the wrist. J Hand Surg [Am] 1:110–118, 1976.

252. Taleisnik, J. Posttraumatic carpal instability. Clin Orthop 149:73–82, 1980.

253. Taleisnik, J. Scapholunate dissociation. In: Strickland, J.W.; Steichen, J.B., eds. Difficult Problems in Hand Surgery. St. Louis, C.V. Mosby, 1982, Ch. 39.

254. Taleisnik, J. Subtotal arthrodeses of the wrist joint. Clin Orthop 187:81–88, 1984.

255. Taleisnik, J. The Wrist. New York, Churchill Livingstone, 1985.

256. Taleisnik, J. Fractures of the carpal bones. In: Green, D.P., ed. Operative Hand Surgery, Vol. 2, 2nd ed. New York, Churchill Livingstone, 1988, pp. 813–873.

257. Taleisnik, J.; Kelly, P.J. The extraosseous and intraosseous blood supply of the scaphoid bone. J Bone Joint Surg Am 48:1125–1137, 1966.

258. Taras, J.S.; Sweet, S.; Shum, W.; et al. Percutaneous and arthroscopic screw fixation of scaphoid fractures in the athlete. Hand Clin 15:467–473, 1999.

259. Tavernier, L. Les deplacements traumatiques du semilunaire. Lyon, These, 1906, pp 138–139.

260. Teisen, H.; Hjarbaek, J. Classification of fresh fractures of the lunate. J Hand Surg [Br] 13:458–462, 1988.

261. Toby, E.B.; Butler, T.E.; McCormick, T.J.; Jayaraman, G. A comparison of fixation screws for the scaphoid during application of cyclical bending loads. J Bone Joint Surg Am 79:1190–1197, 1997.
262. Trumble, T.; Glisson, R.R.; Seaber, A.V.; Urbaniak, I.R. A biomechanical comparison of the methods for treating Kienböck's disease. J Hand Surg [Am] 11:88–93, 1986.
263. Trumble, T.E. Histologic and magnetic resonance imaging correlations in Kienböck's disease. J Hand Surg [Am] 15:879–884, 1990.
264. Trumble, T.E.; Bour, C.J.; Smith R.J.; et al. Intercarpal arthrodesis for static and dynamic volar intercalated segment instability. J Hand Surg [Am] 13:396–402, 1988.
265. Trumble, T.E.; Clarke, T.; Kreder, H.J. Non-union of the scaphoid: Treatment with cannulated screws compared with Herbert screws. J Bone Joint Surg Am 78:1829–1837, 1996.
266. Vander Grend, R.; Dell, P.C.; Glowczewskie, F.; et al. Intraosseous blood supply of the capitate and its correlation with aseptic necrosis. J Hand Surg [Am] 9:677–680, 1984.
267. van der Molen, A.B.; Groothoff, J.W.; Visser, G.J.; et al. Time off work due to scaphoid fractures and other carpal injuries in the Netherlands in the period 1990 to 1993. J Hand Surg [Br] 24:193–198, 1999.
268. Verdan, C.; Narakas, A. Fractures and pseudarthrosis of the scaphoid. Surg Clin North Am 48:1083–1095, 1968.
269. Viegas, S.F. Limited arthrodesis for scaphoid nonunion. J Hand Surg [Am] 19:127–133, 1994.
270. Viegas, S.F.; Patterson, R.M.; Peterson, P.D.; et al. Ulnar-sided perilunate instability: An anatomic and biomechanic study. J Hand Surg [Am] 15:268–278, 1990.
271. Viegas, S.F.; Yamaguchi, S.; Boyd, N.L.; Patterson, R.M. The dorsal ligaments of the wrist: Anatomy, mechanical properties, and function. J Hand Surg [Am] 24:456–468, 1999.
272. Warner, W.C.; Freeland, A.E.; McAndrew, J.C. The scaphoid staple for stabilization of selected fractures and nonunions. Orthop Trans 4:18–19, 1980.
273. Warren-Smith, C.D.; Barton, N.J. Nonunion of the scaphoid: Russe graft vs. Herbert screw. J Hand Surg [Br] 13:83–86, 1988.
274. Watson, H.K. Symposium on the wrist. Presented at the annual meeting of the American Academy of Orthopaedic Surgeons, Newport Beach, CA, 1984.
275. Watson, H.K.; Ashmead, D., IV; Makhlouf, M.V. Examination of the scaphoid. J Hand Surg [Am] 13:657–660, 1988.
276. Watson, H.K.; Ballet, F.L. The SLAC wrist scapholunate advanced collapse pattern of degenerative arthritis. J Hand Surg [Am] 9:358–365, 1984.
277. Watson, H.K.; Hempton, R.F. Limited wrist arthrodesis. I. The triscaphoid joint. J Hand Surg [Am] 5:320–327, 1980.
278. Watson, H.K.; Ottoni, L.; Pitts, E.C.; et al. Rotary subluxation of the scaphoid: A spectrum of instability. J Hand Surg [Br] 18:62–64, 1993.
279. Watson, H.K.; Pitts, E.C.; Ashmead, D., IV; et al. Dorsal approach to scaphoid nonunion. J Hand Surg [Am] 18:359–365, 1993.
280. Watson, H.K.; Weinzweig, J.; Zeppieri, J. The natural progression of scaphoid instability. Hand Clin 13:39–50, 1997.
281. Weber, E.R. Biomechanical implications of scaphoid waist fractures. Clin Orthop 149:83–89, 1980.
282. Weber, E.R. Concepts governing the rotational shift of the intercalated segment of the carpus. Orthop Clin North Am 15:193–207, 1984.
283. Weber, E.R.; Chao, E.Y. An experimental approach to the mechanism of scaphoid waist fractures. J Hand Surg [Am] 3:142–148, 1978.
284. Weiss, A.P.; Akelman, E.; Lambiase, R. Comparison of the findings of triple-injection cinearthrography of the wrist with those of arthroscopy. J Bone Joint Surg Am 78:348–356, 1996.
285. Weiss, A.P.C. Scapholunate ligament reconstruction using a bone-retinaculum-bone autograft. J Hand Surg [Am] 23:205–215, 1998.
286. Weiss, A.P.C.; Hastings, H. Wrist arthrodesis for traumatic conditions: A study of plate and local bone graft application. J Hand Surg [Am] 20:50–56, 1995.
287. Weiss, A.P.C.; Sachar, K.; Glowacki, K.A. Arthroscopic debridement alone for intercarpal ligament tears. J Hand Surg [Am] 22:344–349, 1997.
288. Weiss, A.P.C.; Weiland, A.J.; Moore, J.R.; Wilgis, E.F.S. Radial shortening for Kienböck's disease. J Bone Joint Surg Am 73:384–391, 1991.
289. Whipple, T.L. The role of arthroscopy in the treatment of scapholunate instability. Hand Clin 11:37–40, 1995.
290. Whipple, T.L. Stabilization of the fractured scaphoid under arthroscopic control. Orthop Clin North Am 26:749–754, 1995.
291. Whipple, T.L. The role of arthroscopy in the treatment of wrist injuries in the athlete. Clin Sports Med 17:623–634, 1998.
292. Wolfe, S.W.; Neu, C.; Crisco, J.J. In vivo scaphoid, lunate, and capitate kinematics in flexion and in extension. J Hand Surg [Am] 25:860–869, 2000.
293. Wozasek, G.E.; Moser, K.D. Percutaneous screw fixation for fractures of the scaphoid. J Bone Joint Surg Br 73:138–142, 1991.
294. Wright, T.W.; Dobyns, J.H.; Linscheid, R.L.; et al. Carpal instability non-dissociative. J Hand Surg [Br] 19:763–773, 1994.
295. Yasuwaki, Y.; Nagata, Y.; Yamamoto, T.; et al. Fracture of the trapezoid bone: A case report. J Hand Surg [Am] 19:457–459, 1994.
296. Youm, Y.; Flatt, A. Kinematics of the wrist. Clin Orthop 149:21–32, 1980.
297. Zaidemberg, C.; Siebert, J.W.; Angrigiani, C. A new vascularized bone graft for scaphoid nonunion. J Hand Surg [Am] 16:474–478, 1991.
298. Zelouf, D.S.; Ruby, L.K. External fixation and cancellous bone grafting for Kienböck's disease. J Hand Surg [Am] 21:743–753, 1996.
299. Zemel, N.P.; Stark, H.H.; Ashworth, C.R.; et al. Treatment of selected patients with an ununited fracture of the proximal part of the scaphoid by excision of the fragment and insertion of a carved silicone rubber spacer. J Bone Joint Surg Am 66:510–517, 1984.

# CHAPTER 40

# Fractures of the Distal Radius

Mark S. Cohen, M.D.
Robert Y. McMurtry, M.D.
Jesse B. Jupiter, M.D.

Fractures of the distal radius are extremely common, accounting for one sixth of all fractures seen in the emergency department.[74, 83, 135] The greatest frequency occurs in two age groups, those 6 to 10 years of age and those between 60 and 69 years old.[4] These fractures occur more commonly in women than in men, increase in frequency with advancing age, and result from low-energy falls more often than from high-energy trauma.

Although Colles first described the distal radius fracture in 1814, considerable controversy remains regarding the classification, appropriate treatment, and anticipated outcome of these injuries. Colles initially stated that the wrist would eventually gain "perfect freedom in all of its motions and be completely exempt from pain" after this fracture.[40] This perpetuated the concept of distal radius fractures as a homogeneous group of injuries that could be treated nonoperatively with an expected good functional outcome.

It is now appreciated that well over half of these fractures involve either the distal radioulnar or the radiocarpal joint and that conventional reduction by traction or manipulation may not restore distal articular anatomy. Furthermore, many of these fractures, although initially reducible by manipulation, may be inherently unstable and may collapse with simple cast immobilization. More recent reports have confirmed a direct correlation between late functional results and residual deformity. Emphasis has shifted toward efforts to restore articular congruency and bony anatomy of the distal radius using operative means when appropriate.

## FUNCTIONAL ANATOMY

The distal end of the radius forms the anatomic foundation of the wrist joint. The flare of the radial metaphysis begins approximately 2 to 3 cm proximal to the radiocarpal joint. The articular surface of the distal radius is divided into two articular facets for the scaphoid and lunate by a longitudinal sagittal ridge (Fig. 40–1). The ulnar surface of the distal radius has a separate articular facet, the sigmoid notch, for the seat of the ulna. It is here that forearm rotation takes place as the radius and carpus rotate around the ulna. The triangular fibrocartilage spans from the distal edge of the radius to the base of the ulnar styloid process, stabilizing the distal radioulnar joint and supporting the ulnar carpus.

The normal distal radius articular surface inclines radially between 22° and 23° in the frontal plane[52, 66, 160] (Fig. 40–2). The joint surface slopes palmward between 4° and 22°, with an average palmar inclination of 10° to 12°.[66] This is best appreciated on a true lateral radiograph. Radial length refers to the distance between the tip of the radial styloid process and the distal articular surface of the ulnar head.[68, 132, 155] The average radial length is 11 to 12 mm. Ulnar variance is the relative length between the head of the ulna and the articular surface of the distal radius. This measurement must be taken from a neutral rotation posteroanterior (PA) radiograph because forearm rotation affects the relative length from the distal radius to the ulna.[58, 138] The average ulna and radius end within 1 mm of one another.[72] These anatomic parameters have become well accepted in the radiographic evaluation of distal radius fractures (see Fig. 40–2).[37, 52, 68, 109, 146, 155, 166, 167]

## CLASSIFICATION

Classification systems serve as a basis for treatment and provide a means to evaluate the outcome of different treatment procedures.[129] Perhaps in no other area of skeletal injury have eponyms enjoyed such longevity as in fractures of the distal radius.[140] Classification of these fractures as Colles, Smith, or Barton fractures continues in

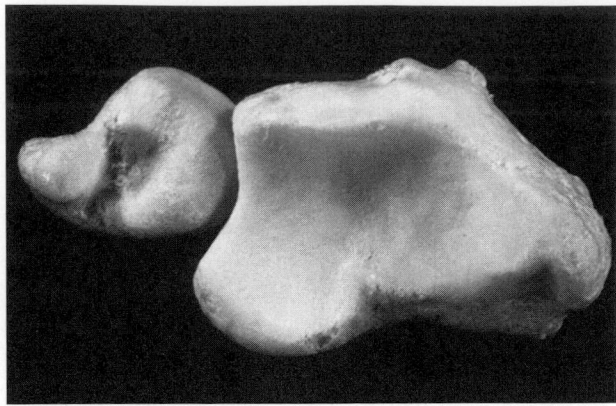

FIGURE 40–1. Anatomic specimen of the distal radius articular surface of a right wrist. Note the triangular facet for the scaphoid and the lunate facet, which is elongated in an anteroposterior dimension. These facets are separated by a sagittal ridge.

clinical practice and in the literature. However, most distal radius fractures do not fall into the simple extra-articular patterns described by Colles and Smith. The use of these terms has led to conflicting data with regard to treatment recommendations and expected outcome.

Since the 1960s, a number of classification schemes have been developed in an attempt to describe more accurately the variety and extent of fracture patterns of the distal radius.[68, 109, 132] In 1967, Frykman established a system of classification that identified involvement of the radiocarpal and distal radioulnar joints as well as the presence or absence of a fracture of the ulnar styloid.[67] Although this system has been used by many investigators, it fails to identify the extent of intra-articular injury or the degree of displacement or dorsal comminution. Simple low-energy fractures with minimal angulation and shortening are classified together with high-energy fractures that involve multiple displaced fragments. This system, therefore, has little value as a treatment guide or a predictor of outcome.

Fernandez[60] and Jupiter and Fernandez[91] have developed a more useful classification based in part on the mechanism of injury. It reflects an expanded understanding of the various fracture patterns:

1. *Bending*—metaphysis fails under tensile stress (Colles, Smith)
2. *Compression*—fracture of the joint surface with impaction of subchondral and metaphyseal bone (die-punch)
3. *Shearing*—fractures of the joint surface (Barton, radial styloid)
4. *Avulsion*—fractures of ligament attachments (ulna, radial styloid)
5. Combinations of 1 through 4—high-velocity injuries

Melone introduced the concept that fractures of the distal radius often follow a similar pattern with respect to intra-articular fragmentation.[124] He described four basic components of these fractures that are common and identifiable: (1) the radial shaft, (2) the radial styloid (scaphoid facet of the distal radius), (3) the dorsal aspect of the lunate fossa, and (4) the palmar aspect of the lunate fossa. The lunate fossa fragments are pivotal to both

radiocarpal and distal radioulnar joint function and are termed the *medial complex*. A large percentage of so-called extra-articular fractures have nondisplaced intra-articular components that occur within these guidelines. Using these fragments as a guide, Melone classified intra-articular fractures into five types based on the extent of comminution and separation of the fragments.[124, 125]

The most detailed of the classification systems is the AO system (Fig. 40–3). This scheme is organized in order of increasing severity of the osseous and articular lesions. The classification divides distal radius fractures into extra-articular (type A), partial articular (type B), and complete articular (type C). Each type is then subdivided into three groups. Type C, for example, can be divided into $C_1$ (simple articular and metaphyseal fracture), $C_2$ (simple articular with complex metaphyseal fracture), and $C_3$

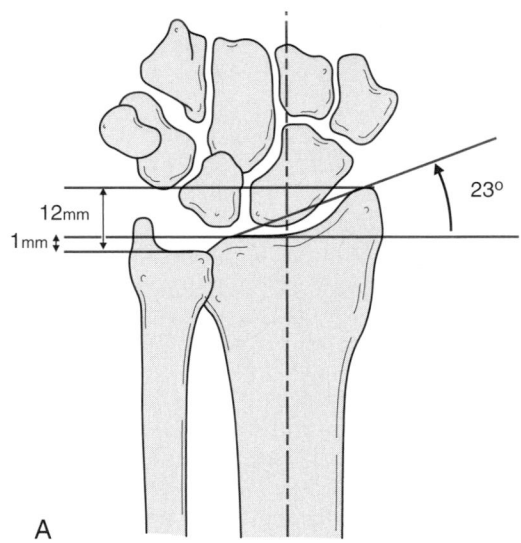

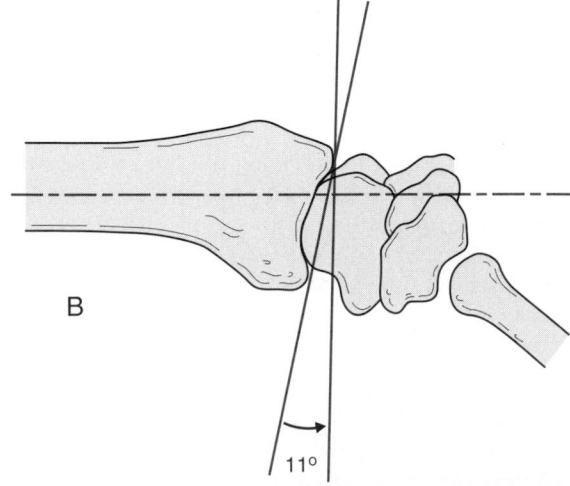

FIGURE 40–2. *A*, Measurements of radiographic parameters of the distal radius and ulna. Radial inclination, measured off the perpendicular to the radial shaft, averages 23°. Radial length is the difference in length between the ulnar head and the tip of the radial styloid (average 12 mm). Ulnar variance depicts the difference in length between the ulnar head and the ulnar aspect of the distal radius (shown as 1 mm ulnar-negative). *B*, Palmar tilt, as determined on the lateral radiograph, averages 11°.

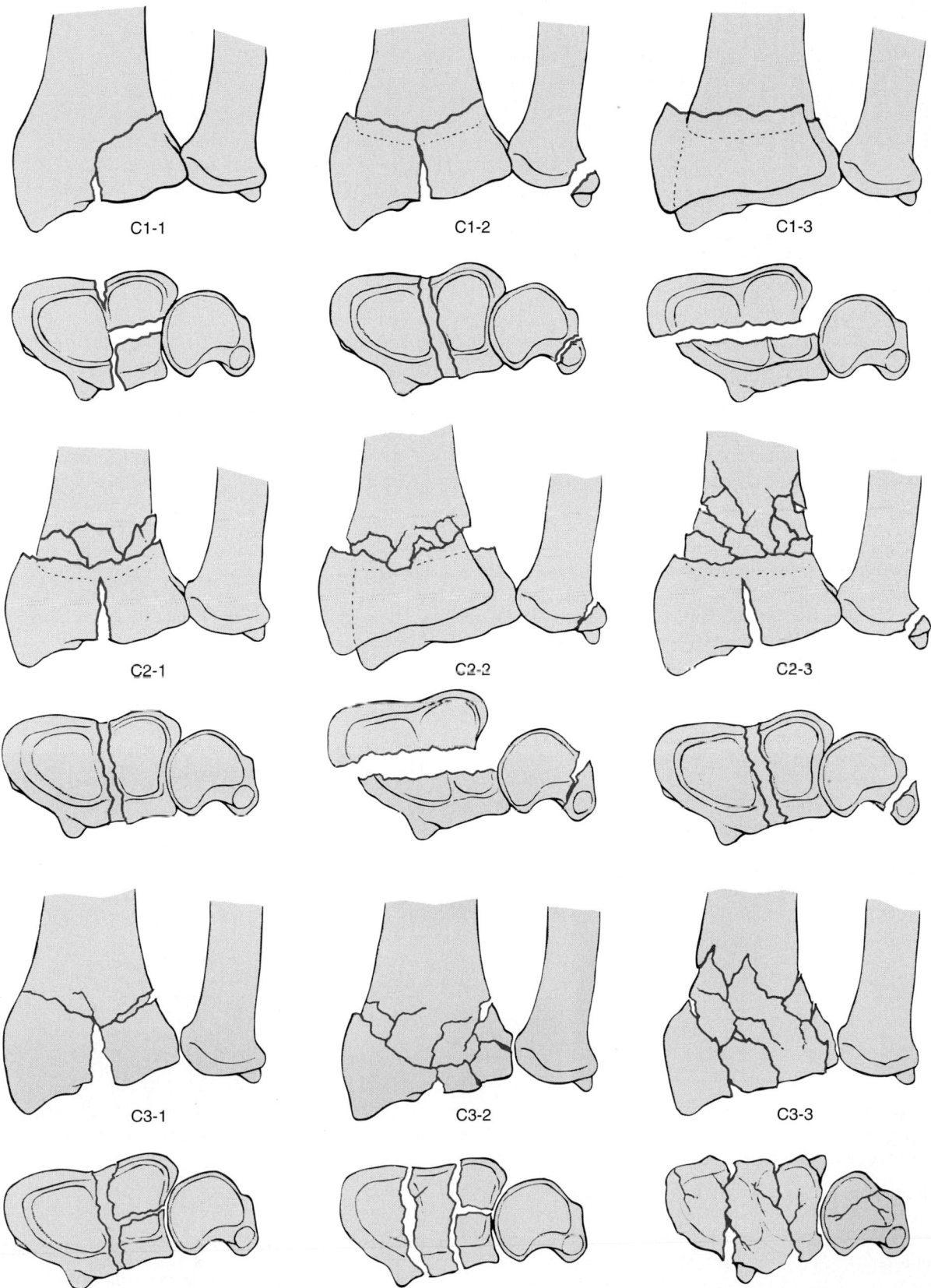

**FIGURE 40–3.** The AO classification of complete articular distal radius fractures.

(complex articular and metaphyseal fractures). These groups, in turn, can be further subdivided into subgroups reflecting the morphologic complexity, difficulty of treatment, and prognosis. Several studies have shown reliability and consistency in the ability of different assessors to agree on fracture type, but to lesser extent on group and subgroup[6, 64, 104] (see Fig. 40–3).

Classification of fractures by anatomic type using the number of fracture "parts" was introduced as a more clinically useful scheme by which to describe fractures of the distal radius.[90, 120] This system is used in this chapter. It uses the fracture fragment principles of Melone but expands these to include extra-articular and intra-articular fracture patterns. For the purposes of this classification, a part is defined as a fragment of bone of sufficient size to be functionally significant and capable of being manipulated or internally fixed.

## Extra-articular Fractures

Extra-articular fractures are those that do not affect either the radiocarpal or the distal radioulnar joint. These are two-part fractures (involving the radial shaft and the articular segment), and they characteristically occur in the distal 3 to 4 cm of the radius. If they are displaced, there must be a certain degree of injury or disruption of the distal radioulnar joint, unless there is a fracture of the ulna proximal to the distal radioulnar joint (Fig. 40–4). Two-part extra-articular fractures can be associated with a minimal or a marked degree of dorsal comminution. The degree of initial displacement and comminution deter-

mines whether these injuries will be stable once reduced (see later discussion).

## Intra-articular Fractures

Intra-articular injuries include any fracture that extends into the radiocarpal or radioulnar joint and is displaced more than 1 to 2 mm. These fractures are further subdivided into fractures with two, three, four, and five or more parts.

The most common of the two-part intra-articular fractures are the simple transverse bending fractures, which enter the distal radioulnar joint but do not involve the radiocarpal articulation. Although these are often referred to as extra-articular fractures, they do disrupt the sigmoid notch of the distal radius and can lead to dysfunction of the distal radioulnar joint (pain and limitation of forearm rotation). Distal radioulnar joint involvement should not be overlooked in fractures of the distal radius.

Two-part intra-articular fractures that involve the radiocarpal joint include the dorsal and palmar Barton fractures. These are typically associated with radiocarpal subluxation. The radial styloid (chauffeur's) fracture and the dorsoulnar impacted (die-punch) fracture are also in this category. A critical factor regarding these injuries is that the opposite portion of the radiocarpal joint remains intact and therefore in continuity with the remainder of the radius (Fig. 40–5).

The three-part intra-articular fracture typically involves the lunate and scaphoid facets of the distal radius, which

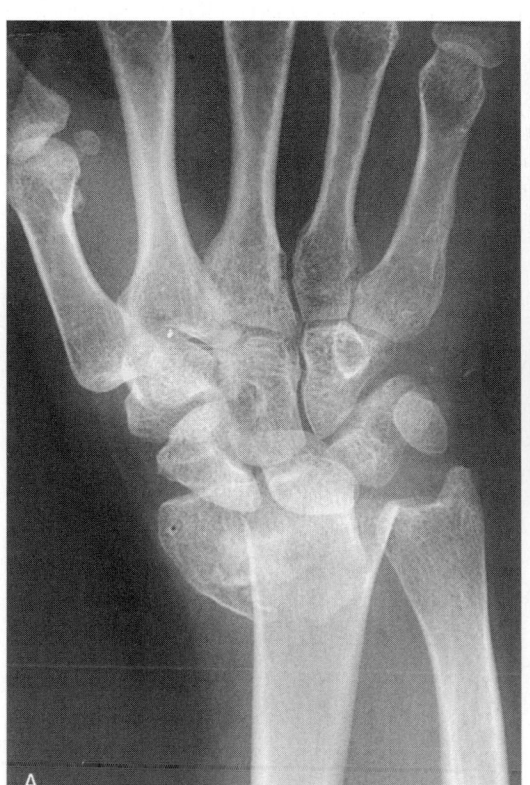

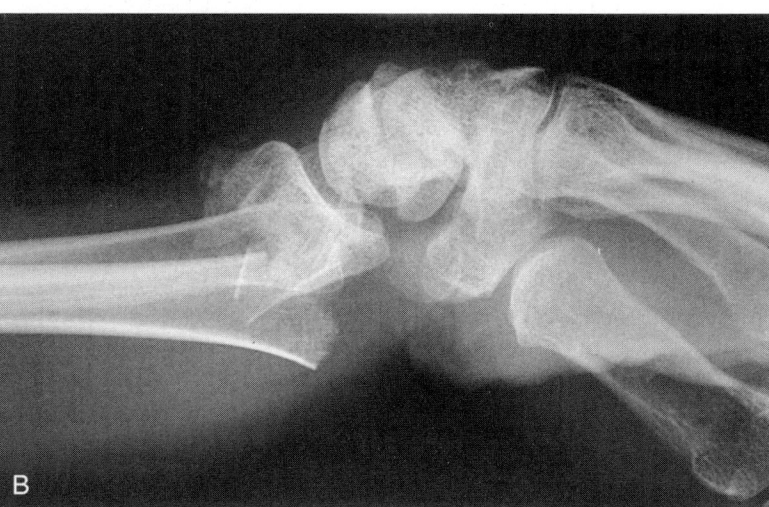

**FIGURE 40–4.** Posteroanterior (*A*) and lateral (*B*) radiographs of an extra-articular fracture of the distal radius with significant displacement and disruption of the distal radioulnar joint.

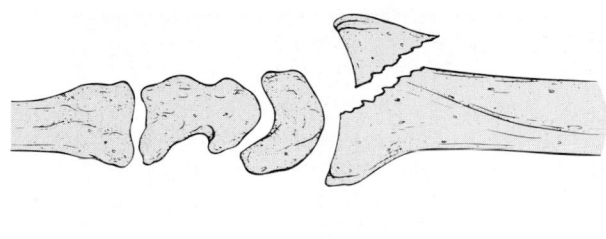

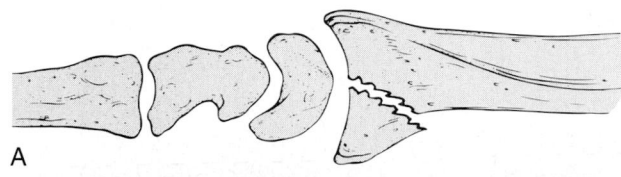

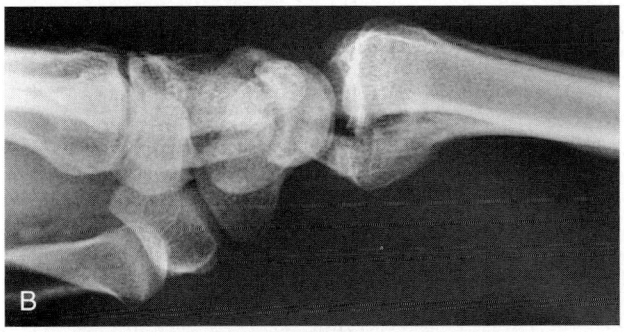

**FIGURE 40–5.** The two-part fracture. *A*, Artist's depiction of the dorsal and palmar Barton fracture-subluxation. *B*, Lateral radiograph of a volar Barton fracture. These are inherently unstable injury patterns associated with shear forces.

are split by a longitudinal fracture line. These fragments are displaced both from each other and from the proximal radius (Fig. 40–6). The lunate facet is particularly critical, because it articulates not only with the radiocarpal joint but also with the distal radioulnar joint. This fracture is analogous to the medial complex fracture described by Melone.[124, 125]

The four-part intra-articular fracture is the same fracture as the three-part fracture with further separation of the lunate facet into dorsal and volar fragments. In general, any displaced intra-articular fracture extending into the lunate facet in the coronal plane (as seen on the lateral radiograph) must also be associated with a fracture extending into the distal radioulnar joint (Fig. 40–7).

The intra-articular fracture with five or more parts comprises a wide variety of high-energy distal radius fractures. At times the extent of disruption of the joint surface precludes direct manipulation or fixation.

## RADIOGRAPHIC ASSESSMENT

The basic imaging techniques used in the evaluation of distal radius fractures are plain radiography, anteroposterior (AP) and lateral tomography (or computed axial tomography), and fluoroscopic examination performed

with the patient under anesthesia. Most distal radius fractures can be adequately assessed with good-quality radiographic views. These are required to define the "personality" of the fracture, which includes the degree of initial displacement and the intrinsic stability of the fragments. The importance of the initial radiographs in the determination of fracture stability should be mentioned.

In addition to standard PA and lateral views, additional radiographs are often essential.[72] Directing the lateral view 20° to 25° from distal to proximal improves visualization of the distal radius articular surface.[114] The partially supinated oblique PA view allows evaluation of the dorsal facet of the lunate fossa (i.e., dorsomedial facet) (Fig. 40–8). The partially pronated oblique PA view best projects the radial styloid (Fig. 40–9). Oblique views frequently reveal intra-articular extension or displacement not appreciated on standard frontal and lateral projections. The importance of good-quality radiographs (out of a splint if necessary) cannot be overemphasized in planning treatment. Inadequate radiographs and subsequent poor fracture characterization have contributed, in part, to the difficulty in comparing results among various treatment methods for these injuries.

Trispiral or computed tomography[38, 89, 148] can be valuable in accurately defining anatomic disruption, particularly for intra-articular fractures with multiple components (Fig. 40–10). This technique permits a clear definition of the fragments and their displacement. Often, centrally impacted fragments cannot be appreciated on plain radiographs. Sagittal and coronal tomographic views allow clear visualization of these fragments and almost always reveal greater comminution and displacement than can be appreciated on plain radiographs.

A significant amount of information can be obtained by performing a fluoroscopic examination with the patient under regional or general anesthesia. At times, there may be difficulty determining the precise nature of the fracture with routine radiographs. Cast or splint material may further obscure fracture detail. This usually occurs in highly comminuted or displaced fractures. A fluoroscopic examination under traction may permit a greater understanding of the fracture and indicate a treatment method more specifically tailored to meet the needs of the fracture. It is not uncommon for operative decisions such as those regarding the need for open reduction and inspection of the joint surface or application of a palmar buttress plate to be made at the time of surgical intervention, when more detailed images can be obtained.

## DETERMINATION OF STABILITY

Most distal radius fractures can be reduced initially by manipulative closed reduction. This technique uses ligamentotaxis (fracture reduction through intact ligaments) to restore anatomic relationships.[14] Stability of a fracture is best defined as its ability to resist displacement after it has been manipulated into an anatomic position. In addition to the anatomic type, a number of local factors contribute to fracture stability, including the degree of metaphyseal

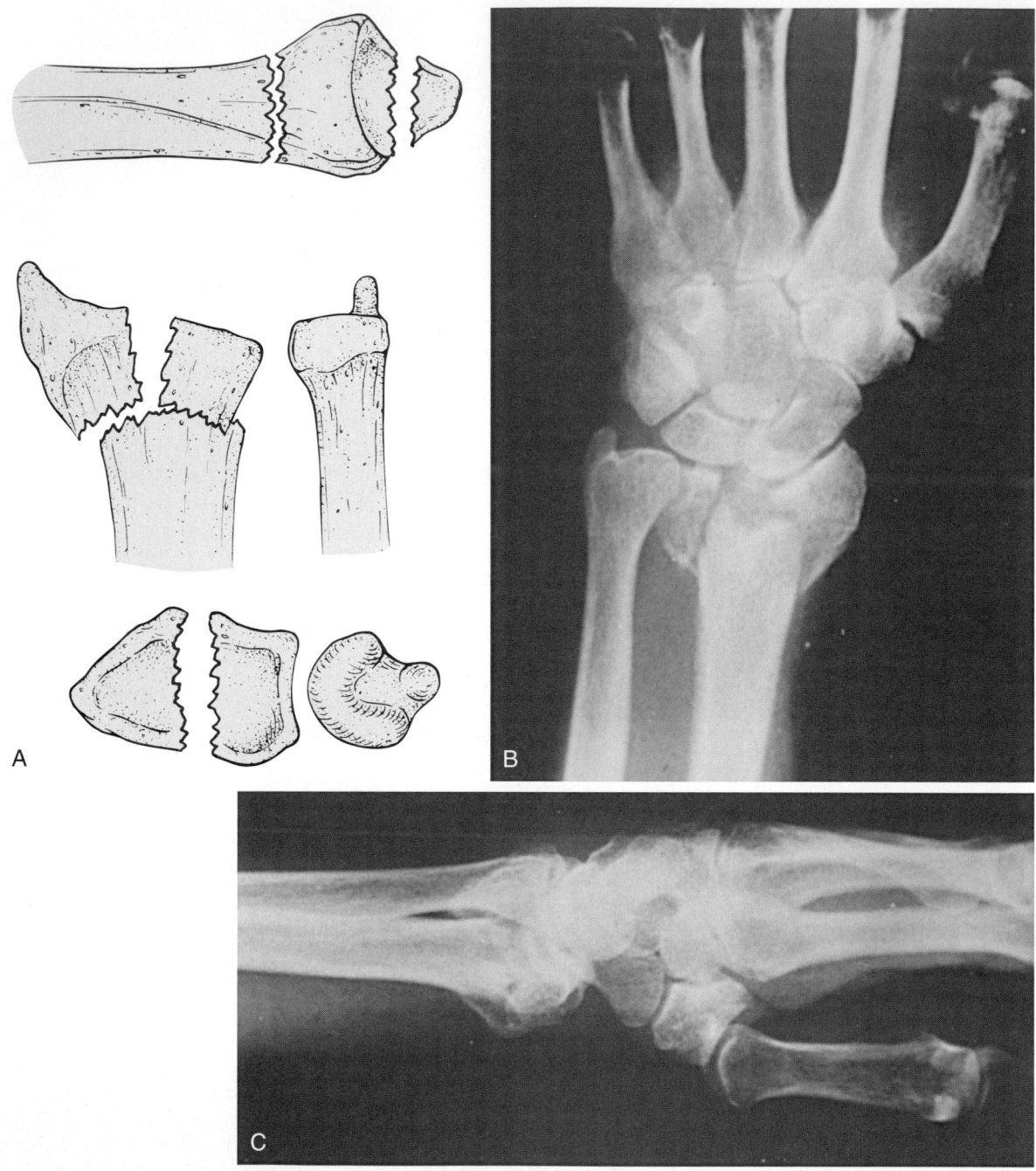

**FIGURE 40–6.** The three-part fracture. Artist's sketch (*A*) and posteroanterior (*B*) and lateral (*C*) radiographs of a three-part fracture. Note the separation of the radial styloid (scaphoid facet) from the entire lunate facet of the distal radius.

comminution, the quality of the bone, the energy of the injury, and the degree of initial displacement.

Comminution, or fracture fragmentation, tends to increase with both the energy of the injury and the patient's age. Most investigators believe that the extent of cortical comminution is of particular importance in predicting the intrinsic stability of fracture reduction.* Bone quality reflects the underlying skeletal osteopenia and has a direct

relation to the fracture's tendency to shorten and the ability of the bone to achieve a strong interface with implants such as Kirschner wires (K-wires) or metal plates and screws. Fractures of the distal radius are more common in postmenopausal women, and the quality of the bone has a direct relation to treatment options. The difficulty of maintaining reduction with wires or internal fixation influences treatment decisions in this group of patients.

The energy imparted to the bone and soft tissues at the time of injury also affects fracture stability. Fractures of the distal radius most often result from a fall on the outstretched hand and involve relatively low energy.

*See references 29, 33, 34, 37, 45, 48, 52, 75, 88, 146, 160, 171, 182, 186, 187.

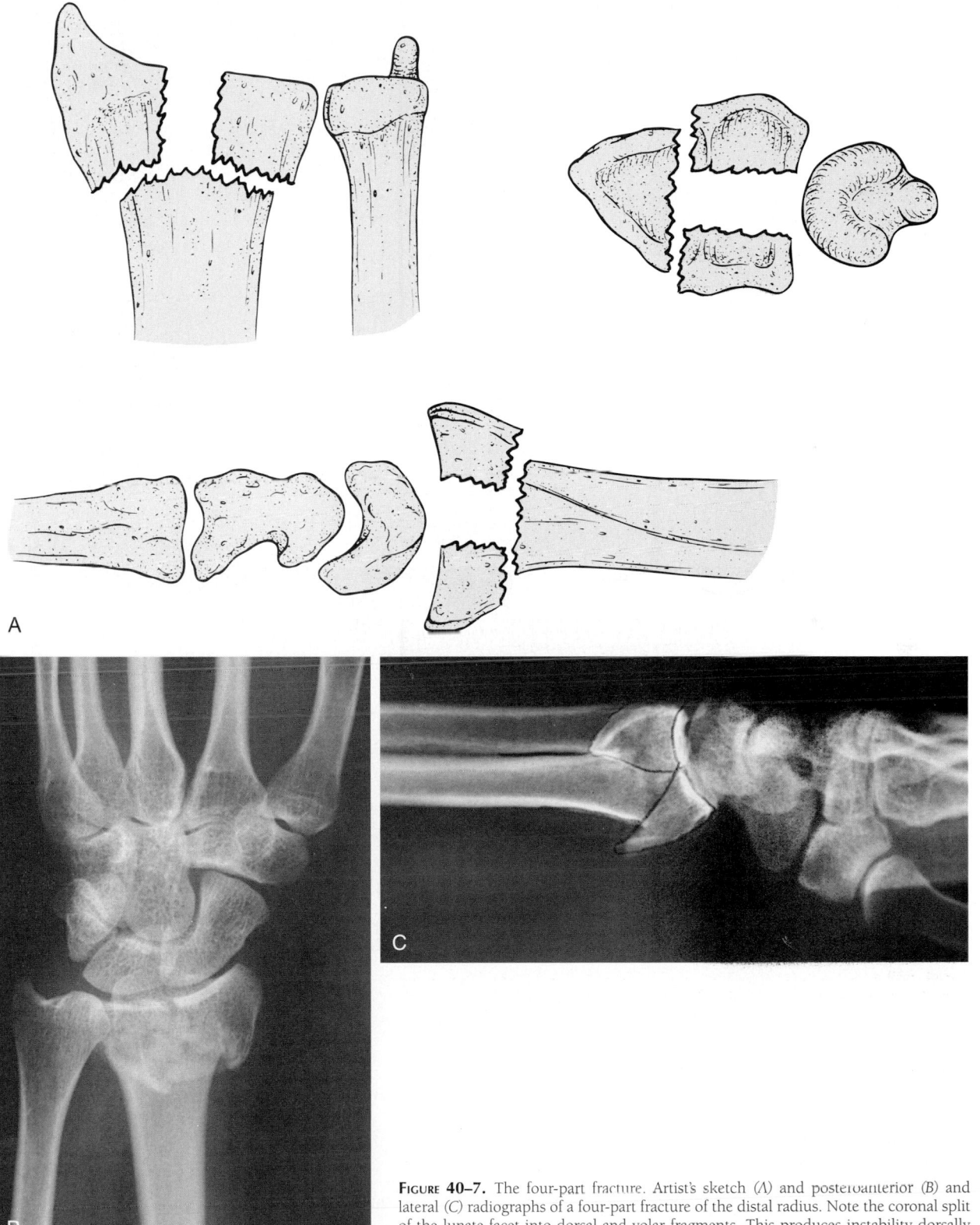

**FIGURE 40–7.** The four-part fracture. Artist's sketch (*A*) and posteroanterior (*B*) and lateral (*C*) radiographs of a four-part fracture of the distal radius. Note the coronal split of the lunate facet into dorsal and volar fragments. This produces instability dorsally and volarly and most commonly requires a combined dorsal and palmar approach.

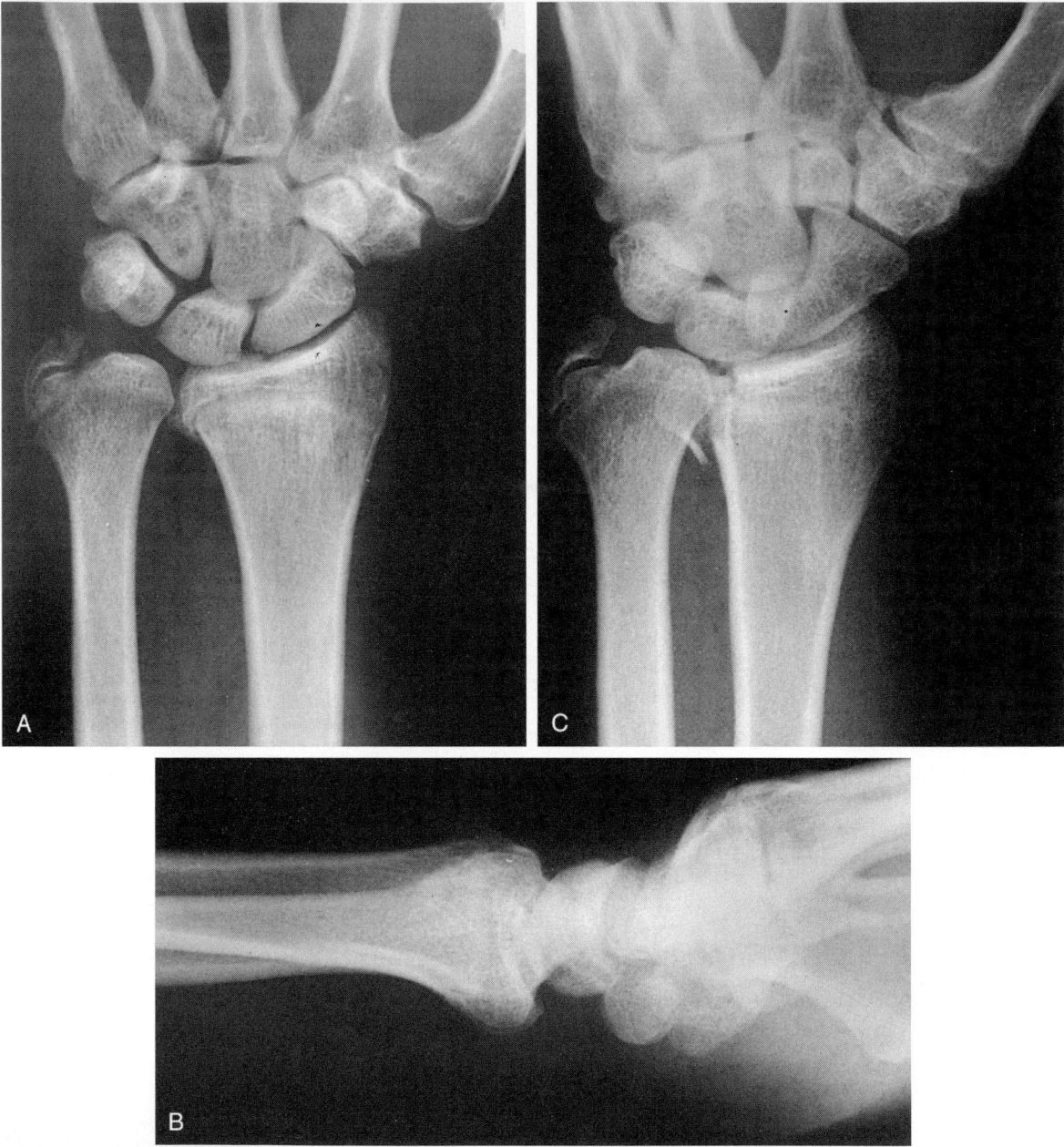

**FIGURE 40–8.** Posteroanterior (*A*) and lateral (*B*) views of the distal radius of a 50-year-old laborer after a fall. There is an old ulnar styloid deformity with no obvious injury to the radius. *C,* Partially supinated oblique radiograph reveals displaced dorsal portion of the lunate facet (die-punch fracture).

These, as previously noted, are found more frequently in postmenopausal women with localized or generalized osteoporosis. In contrast, young adults tend to incur high-energy injuries, which correspondingly present more difficulties in management.* Greater degrees of displacement, comminution, and subsequent instability are present with high-energy injuries.

Displacement refers to the extent to which the bone or joint, or both, have been disrupted from the normal alignment. The greater the extent of displacement, the more likely it is that soft tissue stripping and instability

---

*See references 10, 22, 35, 94, 101, 124, 125, 144, 156, 176.

are also present.[45] The degree of initial fracture displacement must be considered in evaluating treatment options. In addition, the treating physician must bear in mind the correlation between the extent of displacement and associated swelling or neurovascular compromise.

In an attempt to define more precisely the unstable distal radius fracture, Cooney and co-workers considered those fractures widely displaced with extensive dorsal comminution, a dorsal angulation of 20° of more, or extensive intra-articular involvement to have a significant chance of redisplacement after reduction.[45] Weber extended this concept to include any fracture in which the

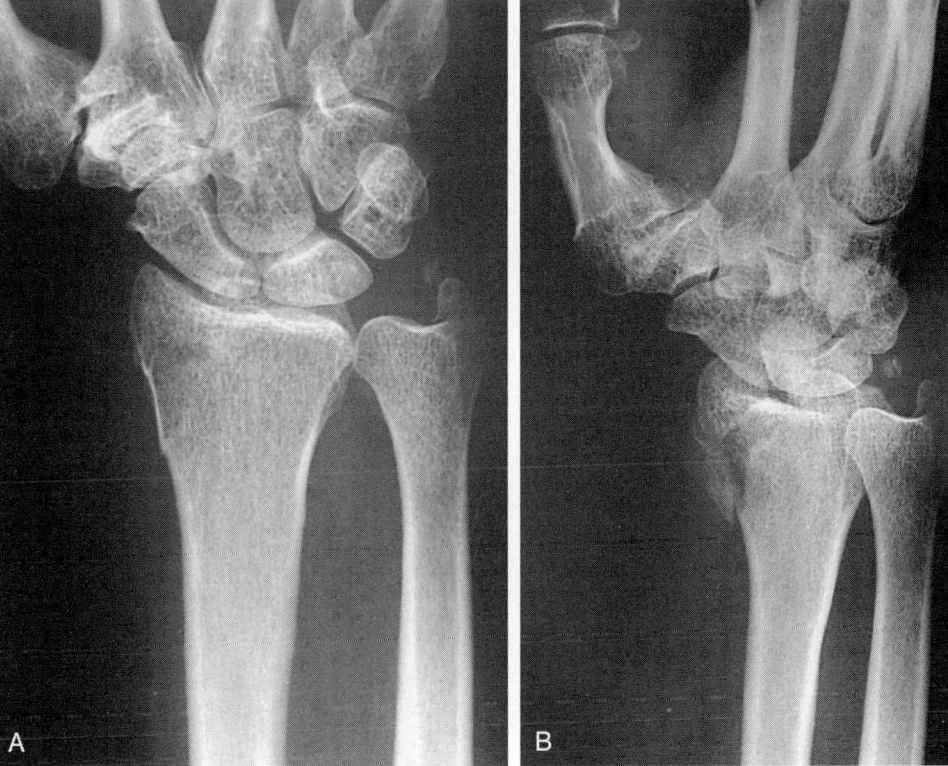

**FIGURE 40–9.** *A,* Posteroanterior view of the distal radius, revealing no obvious fracture. *B,* Partially pronated oblique radiograph demonstrates displaced radial styloid fracture. This view best projects the radial styloid process.

dorsal comminution is seen to extend volar to the midaxial plane of the radius on a lateral radiograph.[186] LaFontaine and associates suggested five factors that indicate instability of distal radius fractures: (1) initial dorsal angulation greater than 20°, (2) dorsal metaphyseal comminution, (3) radiocarpal intra-articular involvement, (4) associated ulnar fractures, and (5) patient age older than 60 years.[106] Last, Abbaszadegan and colleagues suggested that instability is present if the initial radiograph reveals more than 4 mm of impaction or axial shortening.[1] It is clear from this discussion that absolute guidelines with respect to fracture stability have yet to be established. Each local factor contributes to stability, and a judgment must be made with respect to the ability to maintain fracture reduction in a splint or cast. Borderline fractures treated nonoperatively must be observed closely with repeat radiographs to evaluate displacement.

## RELATION OF ANATOMY TO FUNCTION

Controversy exists regarding the precise relation between distal radius residual deformity and functional results. For example, it is well recognized that adequate wrist function and absence of pain can coexist with radiographic deformity after a distal radius fracture in low-demand individuals.[31, 166, 195] However, even studies that have observed successful outcomes that did not correlate with anatomic restoration have noted that objective results may be inferior to the subjective assessment of the patient.[5, 143, 166] Furthermore, a number of retrospective studies have suggested a direct relation between residual deformity and disability.*

---

*See references 12, 37, 45, 48, 68, 75, 109, 118, 122, 146, 155, 160, 168, 174, 175, 182, 184.

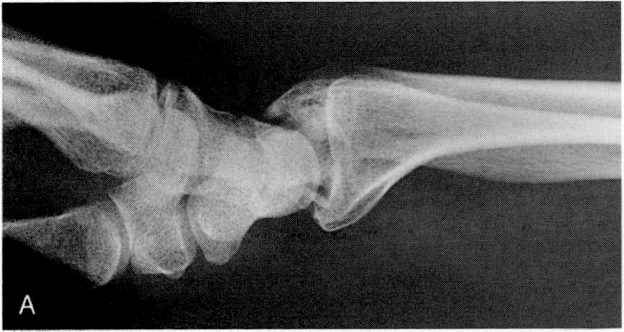
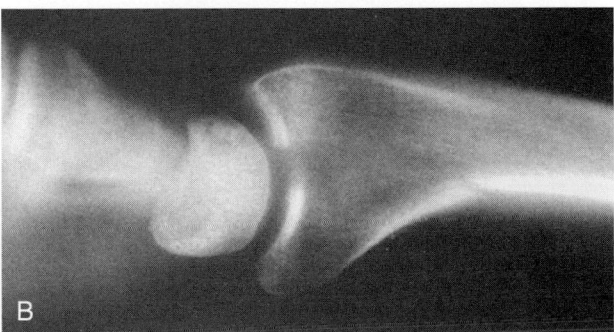

**FIGURE 40–10.** *A,* Lateral radiograph of a distal radius fracture. The articular surface and anatomy of fracture are difficult to visualize. *B,* Lateral tomographic slice identifies volarly displaced fragment with volar translation of the carpus (Barton fracture).

Loading patterns across the wrist are affected by very minor changes in distal radial geometry. Axial loads at the radiocarpal joint are normally distributed primarily onto the radius (82%), with additional loading at the distal ulna through the triangular fibrocartilage complex (18%).[136, 137] At approximately 10° of dorsal tilt of the distal radius, the load bearing across the radiocarpal joint begins to change significantly. For example, at 20° of dorsal tilt the ulna bears 50% of the load and the radiocarpal forces become dorsally shifted and concentrated at the scaphoid articular facet.[126, 165] At 45° of dorsal tilt, the ulna bears 67% of the axial load across the wrist. As little as 2.5 mm of radial shortening also significantly shifts force loading to the distal ulna (from 18% to 42% of total load).[97, 137, 142, 180] This additionally disturbs the relationships and the forces at the distal radioulnar joint,[24, 99, 188] which manifests as pain and limitation in forearm rotation (in addition to ulnocarpal impingement). These biomechanical parameters support the need for more aggressive approaches to restore anatomic relationships after fracture of the end of the radius.

Several contemporary prospective studies have focused on the relation between anatomy and function. Howard and co-workers, in a study comparing external fixation and plaster immobilization, found that functional results had a significant relation to the quality of the anatomic restoration and were less influenced by the method of immobilization.[85] These findings were confirmed in additional prospective studies by van der Linden and Ericson,[182] Porter and Stockley,[146] and Jenkins and associates.[88] In each of these studies function, as reflected in grip strength and endurance, was impaired if the fracture healed with more than 20° of dorsal angulation or less than 10° of radial inclination. Radial shortening was associated in some cases with disruption of the distal radioulnar joint.

Residual intra-articular incongruence also has implications for late functional results and the development of degenerative arthrosis. Although mild articular involvement in low-energy fractures in older postmenopausal women has little impact on the generally favorable outcome found with these patients,[67, 109, 146] this is not necessarily the case in younger, more vigorous persons. Impacted intra-articular fractures have received more attention in recent years, because failure to reduce these fractures to within 2 mm of articular congruity, especially in young adults, will probably lead to symptomatic post-traumatic arthritis.*

Articular impaction fractures in younger patients are more often the result of high-energy trauma and can be associated with a spectrum of injuries, including carpal instability,[18, 101, 124] disruption of the distal radioulnar joint, and local soft tissue trauma. With greater understanding of the pathomechanics of these fractures has come the recognition that conventional manipulation or reduction by traction may not adequately reduce many of these impacted or rotated articular fractures and may not restore intracarpal ligament dissociations.

A number of studies have highlighted the importance of the distal radioulnar joint in the overall functional outcome after distal radius fracture.[44, 67, 74, 127] This joint can be affected both by diastasis resulting from direct injury and by residual deformity of the distal radius. Although Darrach's procedure of distal ulna excision was initially met with a high degree of enthusiasm, a predictable successful outcome has not always been achieved.[16, 21, 56] Distal ulnar instability[16, 21] and weakness[21, 59] have tempered the interest in distal ulna excision, thus placing importance on restoration of the distal radioulnar joint anatomy after fracture in more active individuals.

Given the fact that most distal radius fractures occur either in young patients with the potential for remodeling or in older patients with generally lower functional demands, it is not surprising that in most large clinical series the majority of patients do relatively well.† Problems do exist, however, particularly with the high-demand wrist. Bacorn and Kurtzke evaluated a large number of patients with work-related distal radius fractures and found an average disability of 24% of the involved limb and no disability at all in only 3% of cases.[12]

## TREATMENT

### Patient Considerations

The initial selection of treatment options after fracture of the distal radius must be made in the context of the patient's needs and functional requirements. Similar fractures in the dominant wrist of a 20-year-old athlete and in the nondominant wrist of a 72-year-old nursing home patient do not necessarily dictate similar treatment. Patient evaluation should take into consideration a combination of age, occupation, handedness, and lifestyle requirements. It must not be based solely on the chronologic age of the patient. The patient's psychologic outlook and associated medical conditions should also be considered.

The workup of a patient with a distal radius fracture should consist of a careful medical history, general physical examination, and routine laboratory testing. The coexistence of life-threatening injuries or long-standing systemic illnesses may represent a relative contraindication for more invasive management. A history of substance abuse or recurrent poor compliance also represents a relative contraindication to complicated treatment options. Appropriate treatment requires matching a patient's needs and the character of the fracture with the best treatment alternative.

An example of a patient with a high loading expectation is a laborer or someone frequently involved in recreational sporting activities. The loads borne on the distal radius and ulna in normal functional activities have never been accurately defined. Brand and associates[23] calculated the potential force generated by the forearm musculature to be approximately 500 kg. Young, active patients would be expected to have high loading of the distal radius with vigorous activities over many years. Anticipated functional loading should influence treatment far more than the age

---

*See references 11, 13, 22, 32, 35, 94, 101, 124, 125, 144, 156, 176, 185.

†See references 31, 34, 37, 45, 48, 49, 52, 54, 67, 68, 75, 87, 88, 107, 109, 113, 132, 143, 146, 155, 159, 166, 171, 174, 182.

of the patient. Efforts should be concentrated on restoration of distal radius geometry and articular congruency in these more active individuals.

## Options

The methods for treatment of fractures of the distal radius include above-elbow and below-elbow cast immobilization, percutaneous pins and cast immobilization, external fixation with or without percutaneous pins, limited or formal open reduction, and autogenous bone graft supplementation. In dealing with complex fractures, a combination of these methods is often required. The advantages and disadvantages of the various procedures are presented in Table 40–1.

## EXTRA-ARTICULAR FRACTURES

### Stable Fractures

Closed reduction with cast immobilization remains the accepted method of treatment for approximately 75% to 80% of distal radius fractures that are considered inherently stable.[42, 68, 90, 109] Stable fractures are generally those that are undisplaced or only minimally displaced and impacted at the time of presentation. As previously stated, significant initial displacement and dorsal comminution are signs of inherent instability.

With a stable extra-articular fracture, a simple below-elbow or sugar-tong splint molded over the fracture site suffices in most patients. The splint remains in place for the first week after fracture reduction and is then replaced by a cast. Digital motion is stressed throughout the healing phase. Follow-up radiographs at 1 and 2 weeks are necessary to monitor any displacement within the cast. Because of diminished soft tissue swelling and atrophy from disuse, several new, well-molded casts are required during the typical 5- to 6-week period of immobilization.

Despite the widespread acceptance of cast immobilization, questions remain as to the optimal position for immobilization and the need to extend support above the elbow. Several studies have addressed these issues in a prospective manner,[139, 143, 168, 182] looking at different positions of the hand and wrist,[182] functional bracing with the forearm in supination versus short arm splints,[158, 159, 168] and long arm versus short arm casts.[143] Neither position of immobilization nor extension above the elbow appeared to influence the anatomic outcome to any noteworthy degree in these studies. This suggests that maintenance of fracture alignment depends mostly on the inherent characteristics of a given fracture (e.g., initial displacement, comminution, bone quality). We therefore tend to favor short arm cast immobilization for stable distal radius fractures.

Loss of reduction of fractures during cast or splint immobilization is not uncommon, and remanipulation has been reported. Unfortunately, two retrospective studies found displacement to recur in 46% and 67% of cases following remanipulation.[39, 123] A greater likelihood of retaining the reduction was noted in younger patients and in those fractures remanipulated between 7 and 15 days after the initial reduction,[39, 109] but the failure rate was still quite substantial. Thus, loss of reduction in a cast is a sign of fracture instability, and consideration should be given to more aggressive treatment if warranted by the patient's functional requirements.

### Unstable Fractures

A number of treatment options exist to offset the loss of reduction in an unstable extra-articular distal radius fracture in a patient in whom the maintenance of anatomy is deemed important. These include percutaneous pinning of the distal fragment,[34, 48, 52, 171] immobilization of the limb with pins incorporated in plaster,[29, 33, 37, 75, 160, 187] metal external skeletal fixation devices, and, rarely, open reduction and internal fixation.[7, 35, 45, 85, 86, 150, 162, 183]

#### PERCUTANEOUS PINS

Extra-articular fractures with displacement and extensive comminution are amenable to percutaneous pinning of the fracture fragments and application of a cast. Although it was advocated as early as 1952 by De Palma,[48] Clancey[34]

---

**TABLE 40–1**

Treatment Procedures for Distal Radius Fractures

| Procedure | Advantages | Disadvantages |
|---|---|---|
| **Cast** | | |
| Below elbow | Simple, rapid, accessible | Poor control in presence of axial instability or intra-articular displacement |
| Above elbow | As above | As above |
| Percutaneous pins | Maintains fracture alignment | Requires supplemental cast or external fixator; pins migrate; pins require removal |
| External fixator | Maintains length and neutralizes displacement forces | Indirect control of intra-articular fragments |
| **Open reduction** | | |
| Limited | Direct manipulation of fragments; simpler and less invasive than formal open reduction | Achieves alignment, not stability; must be supplemented with external fixator |
| Full | Direct control, allows visualization of joint surface and alignment | Higher morbidity; technically difficult with three parts or more |
| Bone graft | Excellent for supporting articular fragments | Supplementary only; donor site morbidity |

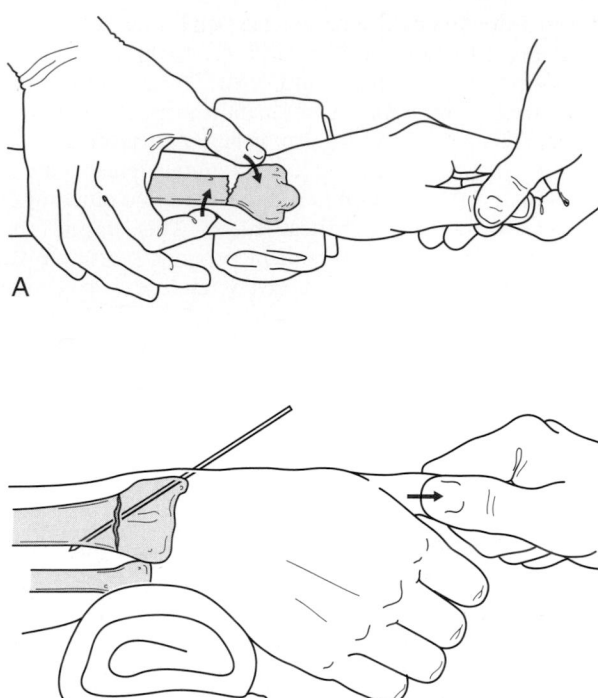

**FIGURE 40–11.** *A,* Technique of percutaneous pinning of a distal radius fracture begins with fracture reduction. This is maintained with dorsal pressure applied to the distal fragment and counterpressure applied to the radial shaft while the wrist is ulnarly deviated over a towel roll. *B,* The first pin is placed through the radial styloid and directed ulnarly to exit the ulnar cortex of the radial shaft. A second pin is begun at the dorsoulnar corner of the radius and directed volarly and radially. Pin fixation is performed under fluoroscopic guidance. (*A, B,* Redrawn from Benoist, L.A.; Freeland, A.E. J Hand Surg [Br] 20:82–96, 1995.)

and Benoist and Freeland[17] more recently reported on displaced, unstable fractures treated by percutaneous pin fixation. Anatomic position was maintained in 28 of 30 patients reported by Clancey and in the majority of those reported by Benoist and Freeland with minimal complications. This technique, however, has less optimal results in high-energy, complex fractures. Benoist and Clancey recommended supplemental bone grafting in this subset of injuries. Fractures associated with soft tissue problems that would preclude a circular cast are also a relative contraindication to this treatment method. Percutaneous pinning can effectively be combined with external fixation in these cases, as discussed later.

The technique of percutaneous pinning involves an image intensifier. Regional anesthesia is preferred. If the fracture is treated within 5 to 7 days after injury, manipulative reduction should be all that is required to restore radial length and a normal volar tilt. The reduction is accomplished with traction, ulnar deviation and dorsal pressure applied to the distal fragment, and counterpressure on the volar cortex of the radial shaft (Fig. 40–11). Reduction is held while two crossed 0.062-inch K-wires are placed to secure the fracture position. These are introduced percutaneously with a power wire driver. Pins smaller than 0.062 inch in diameter provide minimal resistance to torsion and bending forces.[131]

The first K-wire is introduced at the tip of the radial

styloid just dorsal to the first extensor compartment,[173] with positioning guided by the image intensifier. Optimal placement requires an angle of approximately 45° with the long axis of the radius on the PA view and aiming of the wire slightly dorsal on the lateral view, because the styloid sits just anterior to the midaxis of the radius. The second K-wire is inserted into the dorsoulnar corner of the distal part of the radius between the fourth and fifth extensor compartments. This wire, by necessity, passes across the fracture line at an angle of approximately 45° on the AP view and slightly more vertical from dorsal to palmar on the lateral view. It is critical to make certain that both K-wires are advanced to penetrate the cortex of the radial shaft proximal to the zone of metaphyseal comminution. The accuracy of the reduction and the placement of the wires are confirmed with fluoroscopic or plain radiographic imaging (Fig. 40–12).

Both K-wires are cut beneath the skin, and a circular plaster or fiberglass cast is applied (with the tourniquet deflated). Again, digital motion is important and should be begun immediately. Follow-up radiographs are taken at 5 to 7 days to ensure maintenance of reduction and to apply a new, well-fitting cast. At approximately 5 to 6 weeks the pins are removed, and at approximately 6 weeks the cast is changed to a wrist splint, which allows wrist range-of-motion exercises with interval splinting for comfort and support.

Although most fractures do not redisplace with this method, poor osteoporotic bone or excessive dorsal comminution may lead to settling or pin migration with loss of reduction. Even while the wrist is casted, there are compressive loads that cross the wrist with daily activities. Therefore, fractures treated with this method must be monitored closely. If signs of instability exist at the time of pin fixation or if bone quality is very poor (and maintenance of alignment is deemed important for a given patient), consideration should be given to placement of a rigid external fixator to better neutralize compressive forces across the fracture (see later discussion).

## PINS AND PLASTER

Pins placed in the metacarpal and forearm bones, initially advocated by Böhler in 1929,[20] reached widespread popularity after the encouraging report of Green, who in 1975 documented 86% good to excellent results.[75] However, Green noted a significant incidence of both minor and major complications during the period of treatment, with pin-related problems involving one third of patients. More recent studies have verified a substantial incidence of complications associated with this technique, and for this reason we have abandoned it.[29, 33, 187]

## EXTERNAL SKELETAL FIXATION

External skeletal fixation is now very commonly used in the treatment of distal radius fractures. This can be attributed, in part, to the recognized problems associated with pins and plaster, and to improvements in frame design and pin application.[86, 130, 162] If instability exists and the maintenance of length and alignment are deemed important, particularly in the presence of soft tissue problems, we favor the application of an external fixator. A number of retrospective studies have reported favorable results with external fixation.[7, 45, 86, 130, 151, 183, 187, 196] Two prospective, randomized studies comparing external fixation with cast immobilization for unstable distal radius

fractures documented external fixation to be superior in maintaining fracture position and with respect to overall hand function.[85, 88]

Although improved pin application techniques, including open and more strategic pin placement, have dimin-

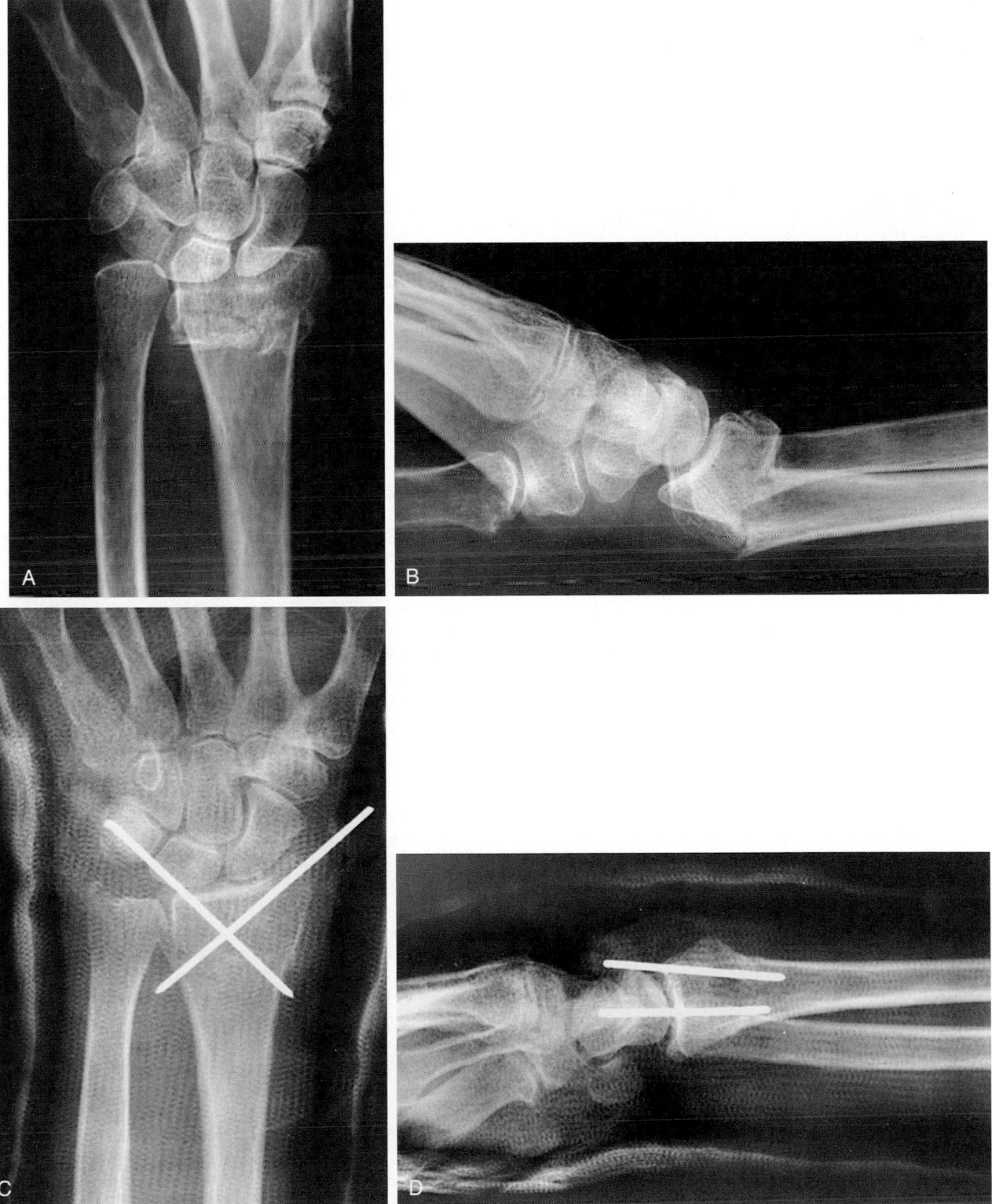

**FIGURE 40–12.** Posteroanterior (*A*) and lateral (*B*) radiographs of a displaced and comminuted unstable two-part distal radius fracture. *C, D,* This was treated with percutaneous pin fixation and a cast.

ished the incidence of pin-related problems,[86, 130, 162] the potential for permanent loss of wrist motion has remained a concern. Cooney and co-workers[45] reported minimal loss of motion in patients observed for 2 years or longer. Other investigators have recommended decreasing the amount of radiocarpal distraction after 3 weeks, limiting the duration of fixation by adding percutaneous pins or autogenous bone graft,[11, 107, 162] or using hinged fixators to afford wrist motion while traction is maintained.[35] Interest in the dynamic external fixation concept has been tempered by the complexity of the operative protocol and a prospective study that showed greater loss of reduction, more complications, and no benefit in wrist motion with this procedure, compared with those in static external fixation.[169]

When applied in conjunction with percutaneous pins or bone grafting through a limited exposure, the external fixation device can be removed as early as 4 to 5 weeks after application.[26, 107] Protected wrist motion is begun at approximately 6 weeks, with interval splinting for comfort and support. If applied without adjuvant treatment, the device is best left in place for 6 to 8 weeks, until union has occurred.

The technique of applying external fixation depends on strict attention to detail. The placement of the fixator pins can be accomplished before fracture reduction, but this alters the skin tension on the pins once the fracture is reduced. This problem can be avoided by obtaining an adequate reduction before placement of the external fixator pins. Supplemental K-wire fixation, as outlined previously, is a simple means of maintaining reduction before the fixator is applied. In this way, the external fixator functions as a rigid neutralization device and is not the sole means of maintaining fracture position. This technique requires less distraction across the wrist by the fixator (which is deleterious both to digital motion and perhaps ultimately to wrist motion) to maintain reduction. The addition of supplemental K-wires also significantly improves fracture stability, thereby facilitating union.[53, 181, 189]

The locations of the external fixator pins can be marked over the index metacarpal and distal forearm before application (Fig. 40–13). Forearm pins are best placed just proximal to the first dorsal compartment outcropper muscles, along the dorsoradial forearm between the extensor carpi radialis and brevis tendons. The metacarpal pins should be placed approximately 45° off the horizontal plane of the palm to permit retroposition of the thumb. We advocate small incisions, which afford protection to the radial sensory nerve branches and allow central pin location with the bone. In hard cortical bone of young adults, predrilling with a 2.0-mm drill bit is helpful when using the 2.5-mm threaded half (Schanz) pins. In older persons, predrilling is not necessary. By placement of pins at a slight angle, a greater degree of thread can be maintained within the narrow diaphysis of the second metacarpal.

After placement of the pins, an external frame is constructed and secured with slight radiocarpal distraction and the wrist in near-neutral position. Care must be taken to release the skin tension about the Schanz pins at completion to avoid local skin necrosis and subsequent

pin tract problems. Although superficial pin tract infections are not uncommon, the majority respond to local antibiotics and local wound care, and osteomyelitis is rare.[3, 100] Following fixator placement, digital motion must begin immediately, including the thumb. Patients often feel more secure if the wrist is supported in a palmar splint during fixator wear. This can be applied by an occupational therapist who monitors digital motion, edema, and pin tract care during the healing phase.

For unstable extra-articular injuries with large distal fragments, there are reports of placing the distal external fixator pins into the distal fragment without bridging the wrist.[121] In this way, earlier motion and return of function can be restored.

## OPEN REDUCTION

Open reduction for extra-articular fractures is indicated in rare instances in which the aforementioned methods are unsuccessful. This most often occurs in two circumstances. The first relates to very distal, metaphyseal-diaphyseal oblique fractures, which actually represent a distal Galeazzi fracture (see Chapter 41). The second circumstance involves a patient presenting 2 to 3 weeks after injury, at which time closed manipulation is no longer possible owing to early healing. Open manipulation of the fracture becomes necessary, either through a limited exposure or using a full open technique. The limited technique uses a small incision centered directly over the fracture, in a position determined by fluoroscopy.[69] An elevator is then used to break up the early callus and manipulate the distal fragment. If the resultant dorsal defect is significant, it can be filled with pure cancellous bone graft (or a bone graft substitute) to facilitate healing and provide support against dorsal collapse. Pin fixation with or without a neutralizing external fixator is indicated in this setting.

## INTRA-ARTICULAR FRACTURES

### Stable Fractures

Treatment of the stable intra-articular fracture that enters either the distal radioulnar or the radiocarpal joint follows the same principles as for the stable extra-articular fracture. Care must be taken to watch these injuries closely, because initially minimally displaced fractures with intra-articular extension can collapse and displace in a cast (Fig. 40–14). As previously outlined, intra-articular extension into the radiocarpal joint is itself a sign of potential fracture instability. Weekly radiographs must be obtained until the fracture proves to be stable.

### Unstable Fractures

The most common intra-articular distal radius fracture is that which disrupts the distal radioulnar joint without radiocarpal joint displacement, for example, the simple two-part bending fracture. These are treated like the

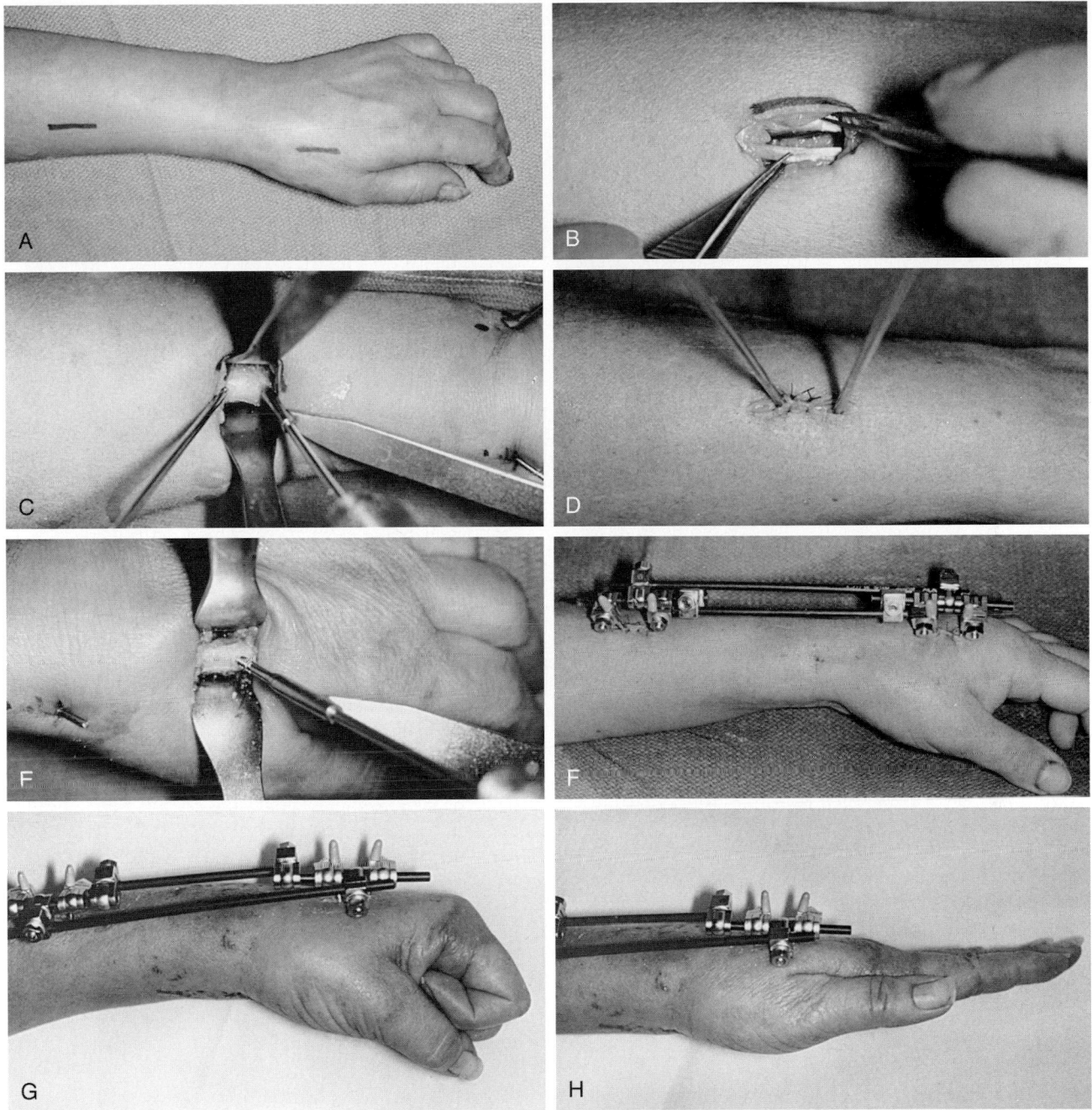

**FIGURE 40–13.** Technique of external fixator application. *A,* Pin sites are marked over the dorsoradial radius and the index metacarpal. *B,* Radial pins are placed between the tendons of the extensor carpi radialis longus and brevis just proximal to the first compartment outcropper muscles. *C,* Homan retractors and drill guides protect the soft tissues. *D,* Pin sites are loosely closed while easily sutured without the frame in place. *E,* The index metacarpal pins are placed through a small open incision, allowing direct visualization and central pin placement within the bone. Branches of the radial sensory nerve must be protected in each of these incisions. *F,* The fixator is then assembled. Early digital flexion (*G*) and extension (*H*) should be stressed during fixator wear.

unstable extra-articular fractures with a combination of pins, cast or external fixator immobilization, and, rarely, open reduction. Care must be taken to ensure an adequate reduction of the sigmoid notch of the distal radius. Often, the unstable transverse distal fracture translates radially and settles with loss of radial inclination. This will lead to incongruity at the distal radioulnar joint. This tendency must be countered by ulnar deviation in addition to distraction and palmar translation at the time of fracture reduction. Radiography or fluoroscopy performed with the forearm in neutral or zero rotation is the only way to properly evaluate the distal radioulnar joint after reduction.[58, 138] Nondisplaced intra-articular fracture lines involving the radiocarpal joint are often present in these injuries and can be percutaneously pinned if deemed potentially unstable.

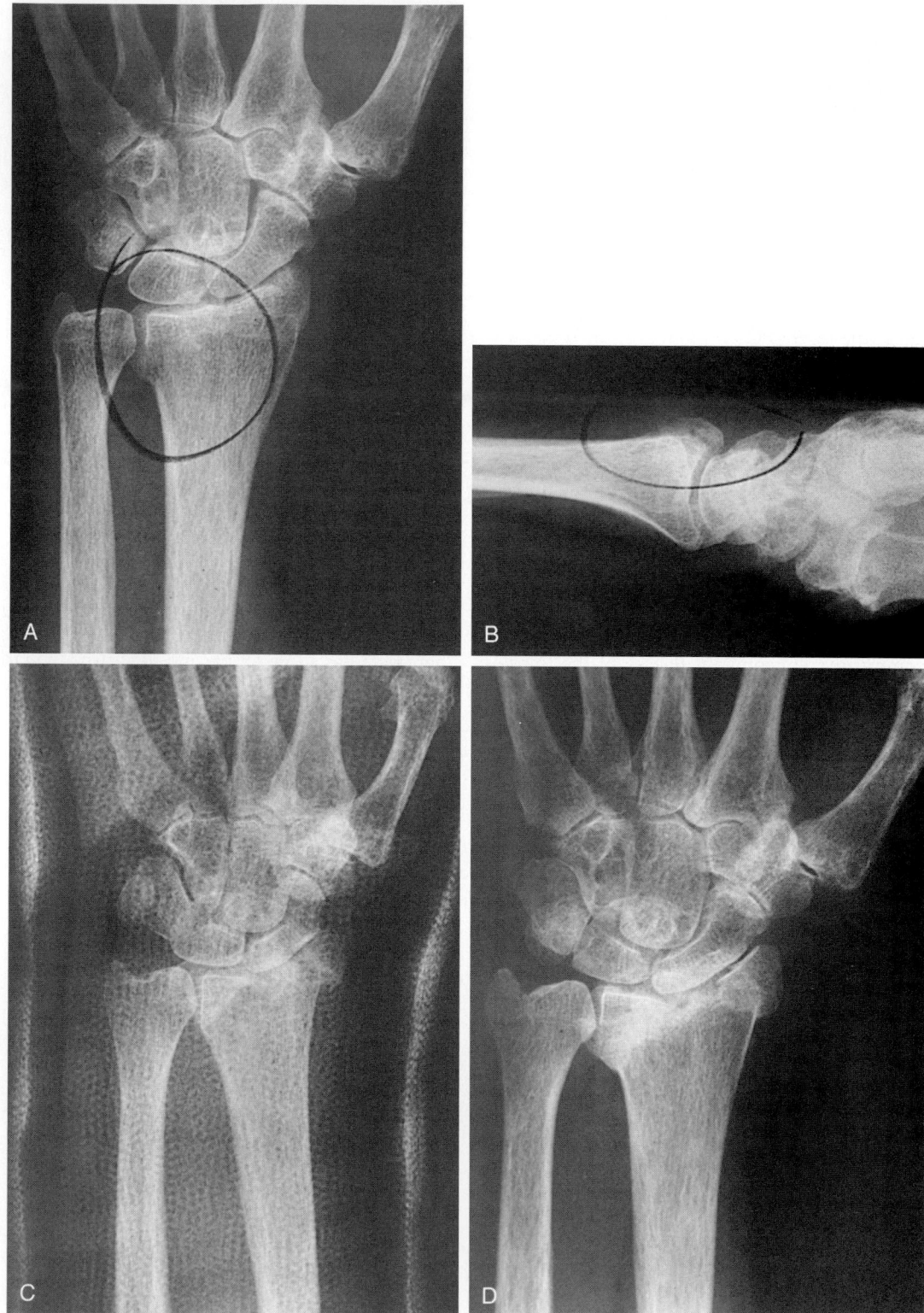

**Figure 40–14.** Posteroanterior (*A*) and lateral (*B*) views of a nondisplaced but intra-articular fracture of the distal radius in a 65-year-old individual. A cast was applied, and the patient was seen 4 weeks later in the office. *C, D,* Radiographs at that time revealed intra-articular displacement and collapse that occurred in the cast. Intra-articular fractures, even with minimal displacement, must be observed closely.

## TWO-PART RADIOCARPAL FRACTURES

The higher-energy, shearing, two-part radiocarpal fracture-dislocations (Barton, reverse Barton) require relocation of the joint to ensure wrist function and to prevent post-traumatic arthritis.[47, 57, 92, 139, 179] Although in some cases anatomic reduction is possible by closed means, these fractures are extremely unstable and usually redisplace if treated by casting alone. The anterior fracture-dislocation (Barton fracture) is far more common than its dorsal counterpart. Radiocarpal fracture-dislocations occur more commonly in younger persons with stronger bone that proves amenable to supporting the reduction with small buttress plates.[47, 57, 139, 179]

Given the small size of the articular fragment, the limited surgical access, and the associated overlying soft tissue structures, the operative approach to the shearing fracture can be difficult. Adequate preoperative planning is essential, and tomography is sometimes useful to further define the fracture anatomy.

The injury should be approached based on the direction of dislocation to allow precise identification and reduction of the displaced articular fragment. For example, an anterior fracture-dislocation is best approached through an anterior incision. With most volar Barton fractures, the surgical incision is placed radially and dissection is carried down through the flexor carpi radialis tendon sheath (Fig. 40–15). This exposure necessitates retraction of the median nerve and carpal canal contents ulnarly. We generally recommend a concomitant release of the transverse carpal ligament if any preoperative median nerve symptoms exist. This can easily be accomplished through a separate palmar incision.

An alternative approach involves exposure more ulnarly, bringing the flexor tendons, median nerve, radial artery, and flexor carpi radialis laterally.[80, 120] This wider exposure has the advantage of offsetting the potential for persistent retraction on the median nerve during the procedure. The transverse carpal ligament is routinely released, allowing a wider zone of mobility for the soft tissue structures.

Whichever exposure is chosen, the pronator quadratus is next visualized as it blankets the volar aspect of the distal radius (see Fig. 40–15). This muscle is usually incised at its radial insertion (leaving a soft tissue rim for repair) and elevated ulnarward. Homan or small Bennett retractors allow for excellent exposure of the anterior distal radius. Traction applied with the aid of an assistant or finger traps and weights hung over the end of the operating table is helpful to distract the carpus distally and allow reduction of the palmar and proximally displaced articular fragment. Care must be taken during the manipulation because the anterior cortex often has nondisplaced longitudinal fracture lines, which should not be disturbed.

Once the anterior fragment is reduced, an anterior buttress plate is applied. These plates are precontoured for the anterior flare of the distal radius. AP K-wires are used for provisional fixation. These can be placed through the plate or just distal to the plate at the distal articular rim. Plate position is verified under fluoroscopy in both the AP and lateral planes before the screws are placed. Because this plate is functioning in a buttress fashion, it is not mandatory to place screws through the distal fragment. A well-contoured plate will maintain reduction. In the sturdier bone of younger adults with a single, large anterior fragment, however, intrafragmentary screws can aid in the stability of the reduction.

Articular congruence is usually verified fluoroscopically or with intraoperative plain radiographs. Care should be taken not to transversely incise the important volar radiocarpal ligaments. Undue exposure and dissection of the volar capsular ligaments can lead to instability of the fracture fragments, devascularization of the metaphyseal fragment, and potential intracarpal instability. If visualization of the joint surface is required, this must be performed through a separate, limited dorsal approach. The distal radius articular surface can be properly assessed only from a dorsal exposure.[80]

After application of the volar plate, a careful evaluation of the radial styloid must be performed to determine whether it is separately involved. This often requires a semipronated PA fluoroscopic view. A volar buttress plate does not stabilize the radial styloid, and even a nondisplaced styloid fracture can subsequently displace as a result of the pull of the brachialis.[79] If a fracture line is present, the radial styloid should be secured with an additional K-wire or screw (Fig. 40–16).

The pronator quadratus is next reapproximated at its radial insertion, allowing coverage of a portion of the plate. Often the pronator muscle cannot be brought back fully over the plate. This is of little consequence, because the hardware has a low profile and lies flush along the anterior cortical surface and thus does not interfere with flexor tendon function.

With the less common dorsal fracture-dislocation, a longitudinal incision is used and the distal radius is exposed through the third dorsal compartment (Fig. 40–17).[80] The retinaculum is opened, the extensor pollicis longus is retracted, and subperiosteal dissection is carried out ulnarly and radially. In this way, the fourth compartment subsheath that contains the digital extensor tendons is not disturbed. Traction is again helpful for reduction and visualization of the joint surface. The application of an implant in this region is more complicated as a result of the intrinsic relation of the gliding extensor tendons to the dorsal skeleton. If plates and screws are used in this area, it is often necessary to remove them after fracture union is ensured. This can be done as early as 3 to 4 months after surgery. The longitudinal (and not the transverse) capsular incision is then closed and the retinaculum is repaired, transposing the extensor pollicis longus tendon dorsally (see Fig. 40–17).

## TWO-PART IMPACTED FRACTURES

Two-part impacted fractures result from impaction of the distal radius articular surface, primarily by the lunate. These can be either isolated injuries or part of a more complex three-part or four-part fracture pattern. Saito and Shibata[156] described isolated displacement of the entire lunate facet from the radial styloid (medial cuneiform fracture). This is similar to the ulnar fragment seen in the typical three-part distal radius fracture. Scheck coined the term *die-punch fragment* to refer to a shear fracture of

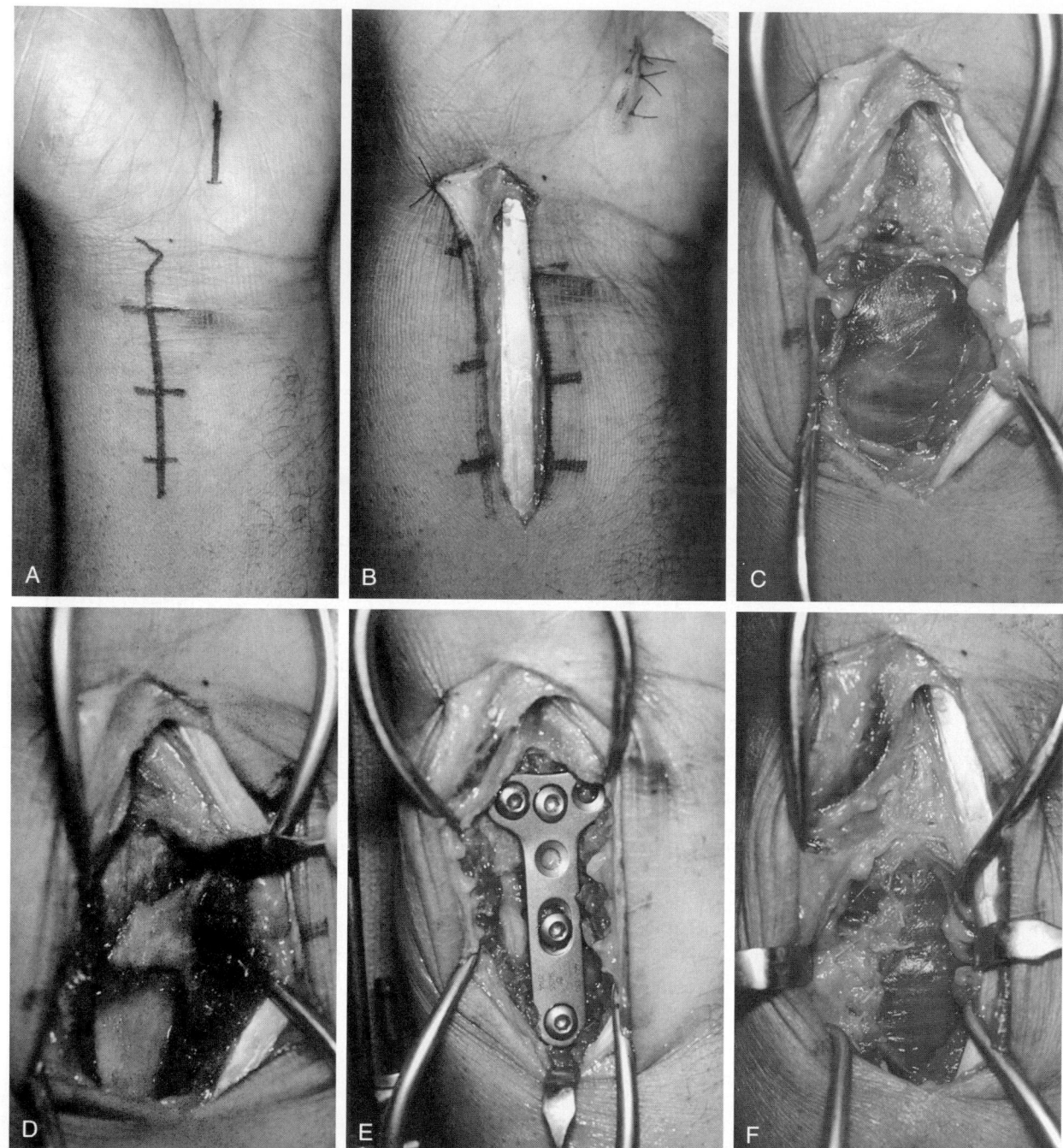

**Figure 40–15.** Intraoperative photographs outlining the steps of a palmar approach to the distal radius through the more common radial interval in a left wrist. *A,* The incision is drawn directly over the palpable flexor carpi radialis (FCR) tendon. *B,* The FCR sheath is opened. *C,* The tendon is retracted ulnarly, revealing the pronator quadratus, which covers the distal aspect of the radius. Note that it is not necessary to expose the radial artery with this approach. *D,* The pronator quadratus has been released radially (leaving a tag for later repair) exposing the palmar surface of the distal radius. *E,* A palmar plate has been applied. *F,* The pronator muscle has been repaired covering the plate. It is not always possible to anatomically repair the pronator quadratus muscle.

the dorsal portion of the lunate facet.[160] This is analogous to the dorsoulnar fragment that is seen in four-part injuries. Often these fragments cannot be adequately reduced by ligamentotaxis alone, and open methods are necessary.

Two-part isolated volar fractures may also occur secondary to palmarly directed shearing forces on the articular surface. These are similar to the volar Barton fractures but do not involve the entire anterior aspect of

the articular surface and therefore may not be associated with radiocarpal subluxation. Volar marginal fractures can involve isolated displacement of the anterior part of the radial styloid or the anterior aspect of the lunate facet.

Isolated volar marginal fractures involving the scaphoid or lunate facet of the distal radius are treated like the volar Barton fracture. Through an anterior approach, the fracture is reduced and a buttress plate is applied. Often, stable internal fixation can be obtained, allowing early rehabilitation of the wrist (Figs. 40–18 and 40–19).

Articular two-part impacted fractures involving the dorsal portion of the lunate facet (die-punch fracture) or the entire lunate facet (medial cuneiform fracture) may be managed with a combination of external skeletal fixation and a limited open technique.[10, 69] After fixator application, a small longitudinal dorsal incision can be made, and the impacted fragment can be elevated from the metaphyseal side using fluoroscopy without direct visualization of the joint surface. The fragment is supported with K-wires, which can be introduced transversely from the radial styloid. Dorsal-to-palmar wires are added if necessary.

Care must be taken not to enter the distal radioulnar joint. The external fixator functions to neutralize longitudinal forces that can cause fracture displacement or settling (Fig. 40–20).

If the reduction is not deemed satisfactory under image intensification, the incision can be extended and the joint can be inspected directly. This allows direct manipulation of the fragment and ensures anatomic reduction of the articular surfaces. If a large metaphyseal defect is created after fracture reduction, pure cancellous autograft can be used to fill the gap and to buttress the reduced facet. When needed, this can be obtained from the iliac crest or from the ipsilateral olecranon process.[25] Donor bone graft site

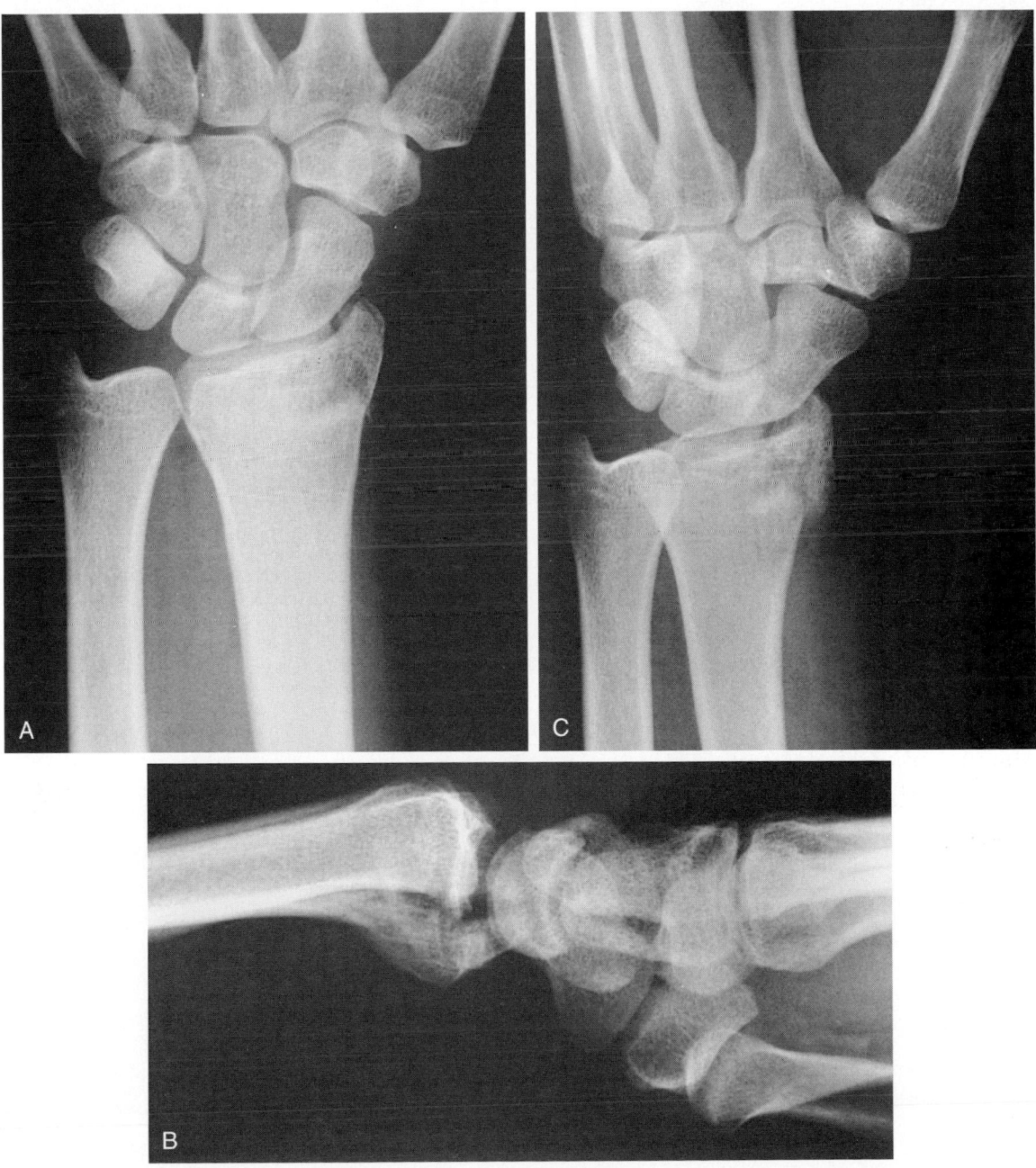

**FIGURE 40–16.** Posteroanterior (*A*), lateral (*B*), and semipronated oblique (*C*) views of a volar Barton fracture. The partially pronated oblique film best depicts the minimally displaced radial styloid component.

*Illustration continued on following page*

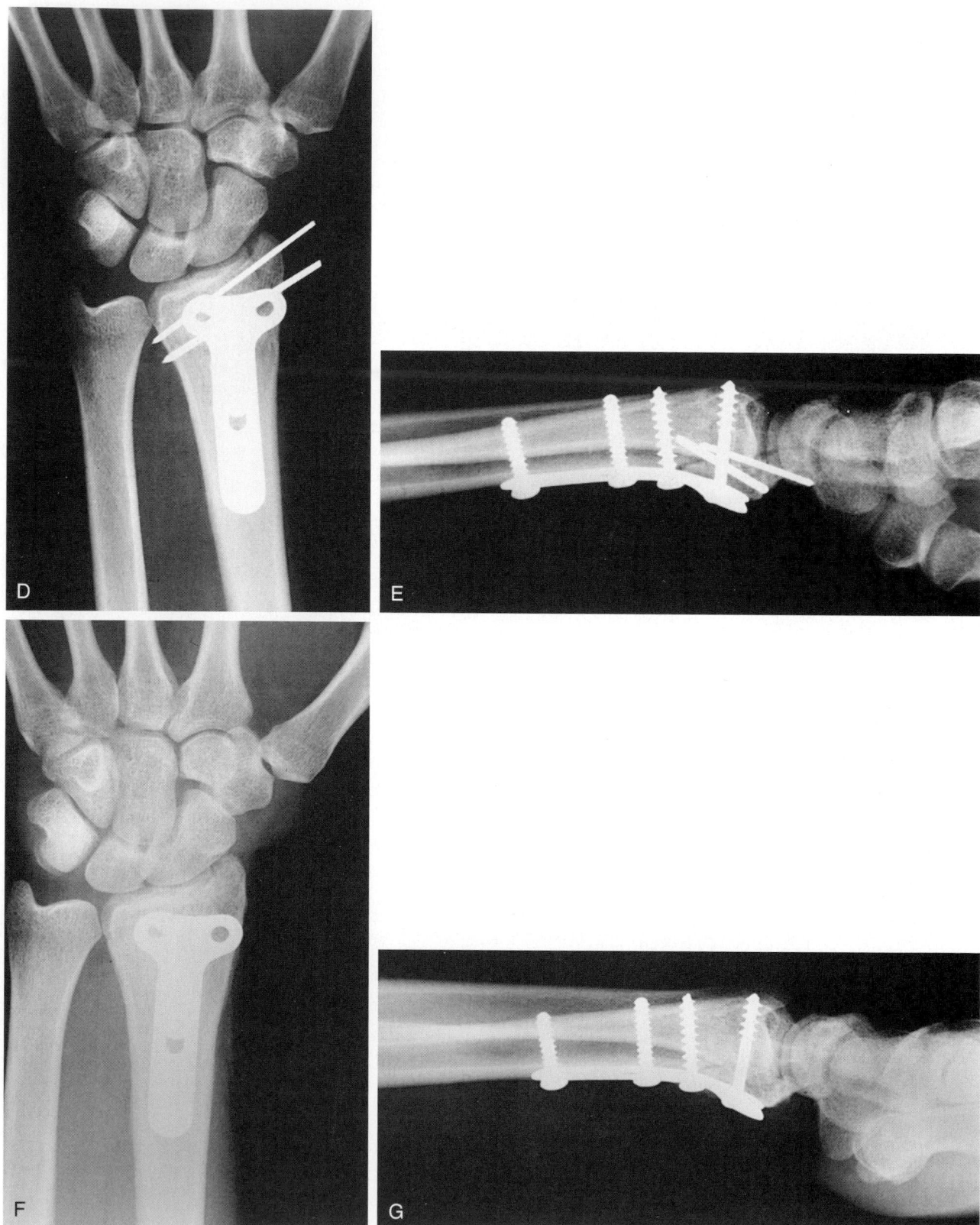

**FIGURE 40–16** *Continued. D, E,* This fracture was stabilized with a volar buttress plate and two Kirschner wires for the radial styloid. The styloid fragment can displace owing to the pull of the brachialis muscle if not secured. Final posteroanterior *(F)* and lateral *(G)* views.

morbidity must be discussed with the patient before surgical intervention.

## TWO-PART RADIAL STYLOID FRACTURES

With greater understanding of the ligamentous architecture of the distal radius it has become apparent that some styloid fractures represent part of a ligamentous injury to the volar carpal and intercarpal ligaments. The association of scapholunate interosseous ligament disruptions with radial styloid fractures is discussed later. Anatomic repositioning of radial styloid fractures is important not only

for restoration of the articular surface but also for preservation of the ligamentous architecture. Although these fractures may occur as one part of a three- or four-part distal radius fracture, the isolated radial styloid fracture is often caused by high-energy trauma in younger adults.

Displaced radial styloid fractures can often be reduced by closed means, but they are inherently unstable, shearing-type fractures and as such are best secured with internal fixation. Simple K-wires and a cast will suffice. Alternatively, more stable fixation can be obtained with conventional or cannulated interfragmentary compression

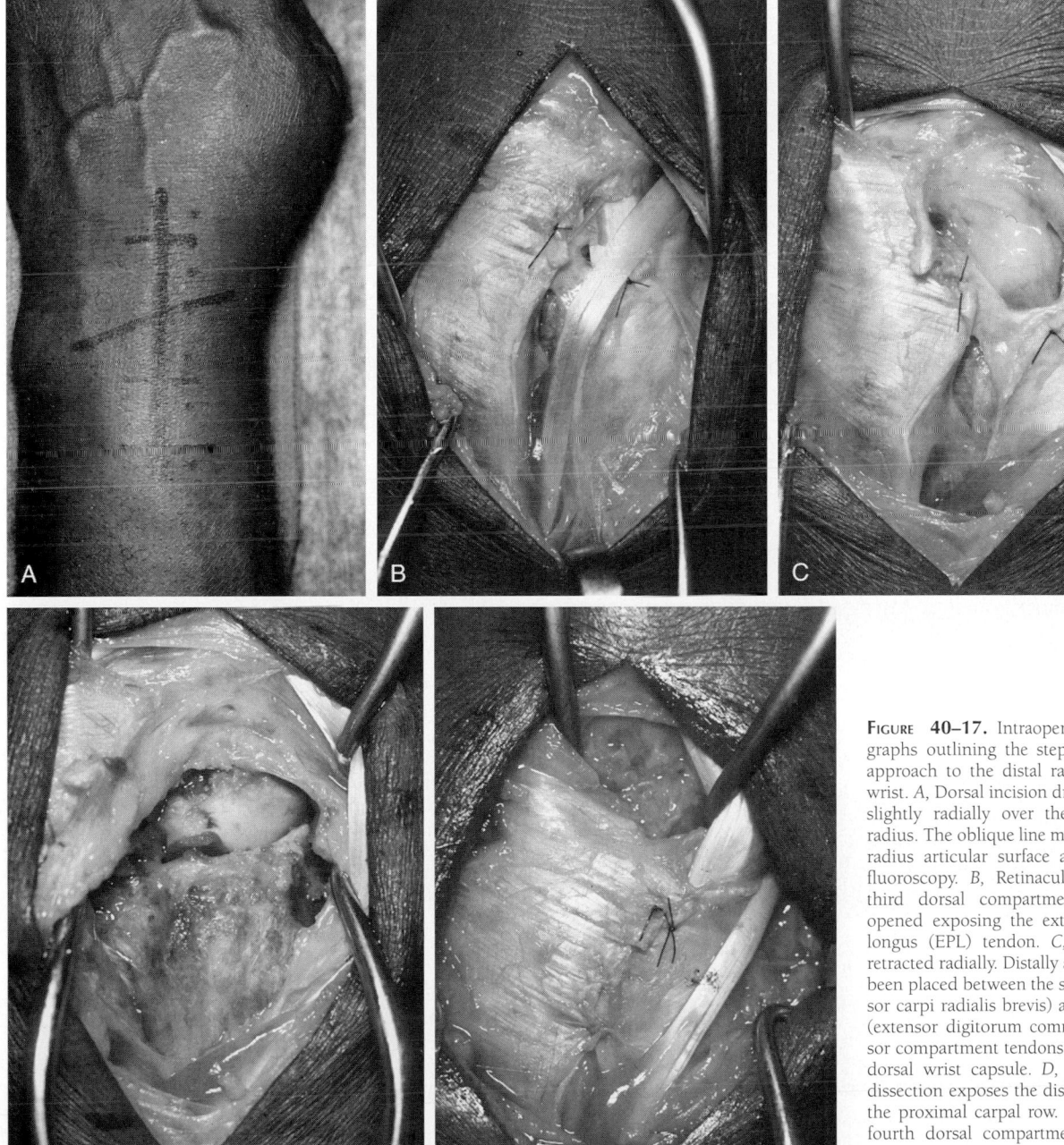

FIGURE 40–17. Intraoperative photographs outlining the steps of a dorsal approach to the distal radius in a left wrist. *A,* Dorsal incision drawn centered slightly radially over the axis of the radius. The oblique line marks the distal radius articular surface as defined by fluoroscopy. *B,* Retinaculum over the third dorsal compartment has been opened exposing the extensor pollicis longus (EPL) tendon. *C,* The EPL is retracted radially. Distally a retractor has been placed between the second (extensor carpi radialis brevis) and the fourth (extensor digitorum communis) extensor compartment tendons to expose the dorsal wrist capsule. *D,* Subperiosteal dissection exposes the distal radius and the proximal carpal row. Note that the fourth dorsal compartment subsheath has not been violated. *E,* Following reduction, the retinaculum is anatomically repaired, leaving the EPL dorsally in a protected position.

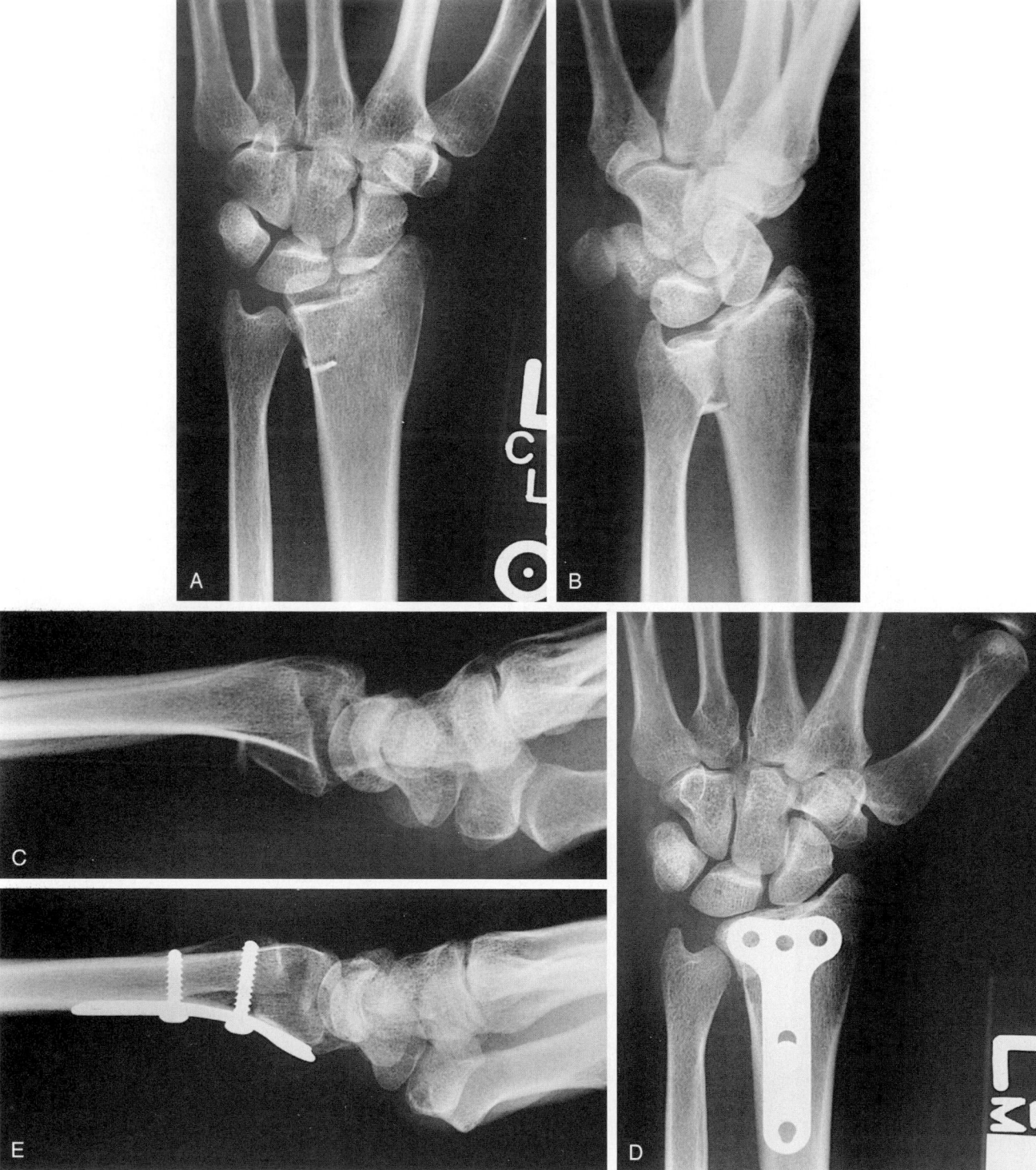

**FIGURE 40–18.** *A–C,* Radiographs depicting volar marginal shear fracture of the lunate facet only. *D, E,* This was stabilized with a volar buttress plate similar to that placed for the volar Barton fracture.

screws. Screws should ideally be placed perpendicular to the fracture plane to maximize compression and prevent shear. Subcutaneous dissection is recommended when using screws to avoid injury to the dorsal sensory radial nerve branches.

If anatomic repositioning cannot be achieved by traction, a K-wire can be percutaneously introduced into

the styloid fragment and used as a lever to aid in reduction. The styloid fragment often requires distraction, flexion, and pronation to obtain reduction (i.e., the opposite of the original deforming force).

If reduction by closed means proves unsuccessful or if significant metaphyseal comminution exists behind the fragment (from styloid fractures associated with axial

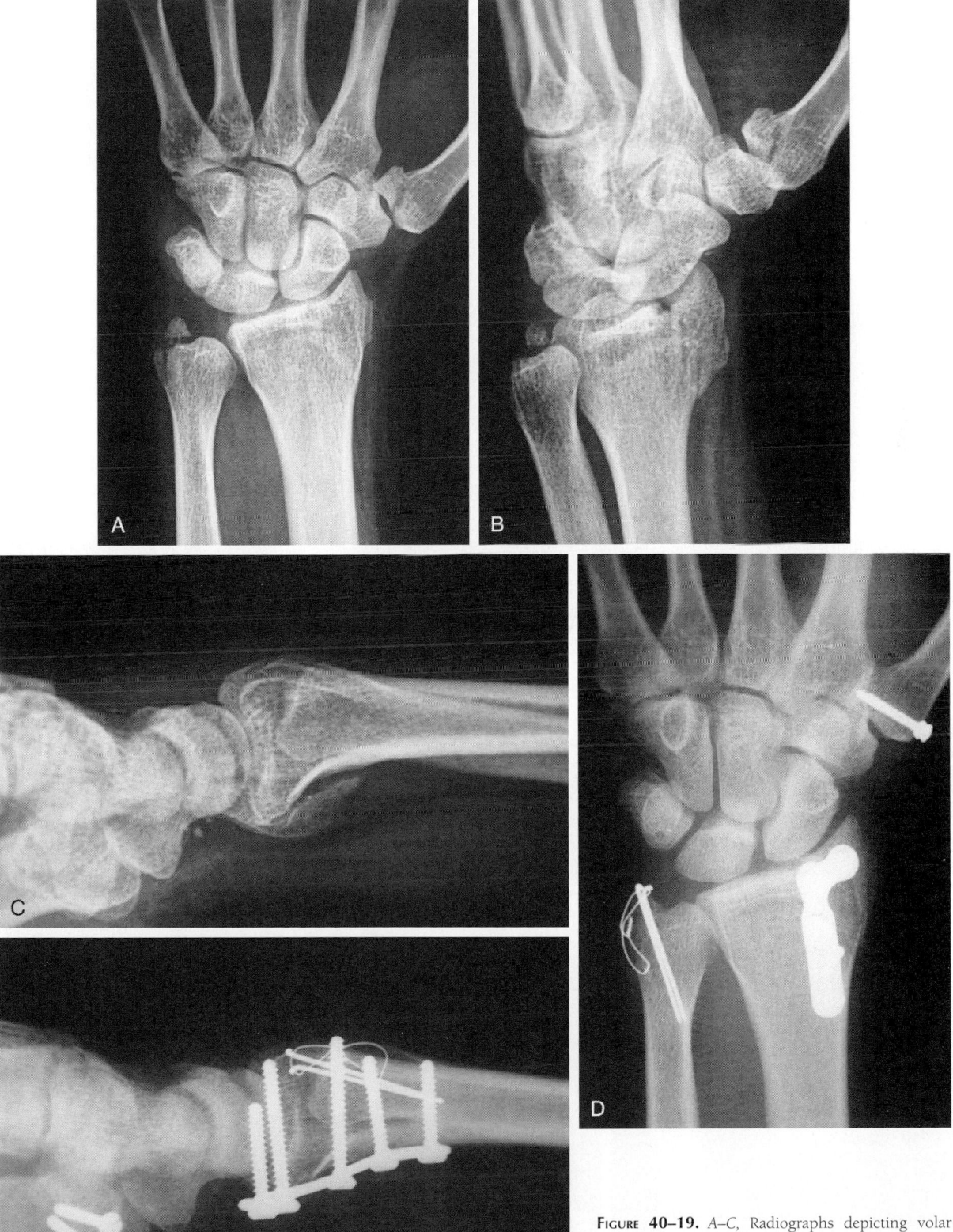

**FIGURE 40–19.** *A–C,* Radiographs depicting volar marginal shear fracture of the scaphoid facet only. *D, E,* This was stabilized with a 2.7-mm L plate. Note that the ulnar styloid base fracture is stabilized with a tension band wire technique.

compression), open reduction is necessary. This is best accomplished through a more radial incision, with dissection carried between the first and second dorsal compartments.[80] As with the displaced lunate facet fragment, an external fixator is helpful to neutralize longitudinal deforming forces in comminuted, compression-type styloid injuries (Fig. 40–21). Bone graft again can be used to fill in metaphyseal defects when appropriate.

## THREE-PART INTRA-ARTICULAR FRACTURES

As articular fractures become more complex it is common to use combined treatments, including external fixation, limited open reduction, and K-wires with or without bone graft. In three-part fractures, the lunate and scaphoid facets are separate fragments and are displaced from each other and from the proximal radius. Sometimes these fragments can be manipulated into anatomic position by closed means, using direct traction (ligamentotaxis), bone reduction clamps, and periosteal elevators. The fracture fragments, if anatomically repositioned, can be stabilized with percutaneous K-wires, and external fixation can be employed to maintain axial length. If any question remains regarding reduction of the articular surface, a limited or more formal open dorsal approach is required. If sizable metaphyseal defects exist after reduction and are deemed to impart instability to the elevated fragments, they can be filled with cancellous autograft.

## FOUR-PART INTRA-ARTICULAR FRACTURES

The four-part intra-articular fracture is an extension of the three-part fracture, with further separation of the lunate facet into dorsal and palmar fragments. The medial fragments make up the medial complex, which possesses strong ligamentous attachments to the carpus, ulnar styloid, and distal radioulnar joint.[124, 125] Displacement of this complex alters the function of both the radiocarpal and distal radioulnar joints.

Because of its soft tissue attachments, the anterior lunate facet fragment is characteristically displaced more severely than its dorsal counterpart and may not be amenable to manipulative reduction by closed means. When it is displaced, traction applied for reduction tends to extend the palmar fragment (through the stout radiocarpal ligaments) and to flex the dorsal fragment, leading to a more pronounced deformity. In this situation, instability exists in both dorsal and palmar directions. A palmar buttress plate is then required to restore palmar cortical stability and counteract the tendency for the palmar fragment to rotate into extension. Once the palmar articular fragment is stabilized, it can act as a scaffold to allow elevation and reduction of the dorsal lunate facet (Fig. 40–22). External fixation is often necessary to neutralize forces and maintain the soft tissue length during the course of treatment.

Treatment of the displaced four-part fracture usually begins with the placement of an external fixator. Because a dorsal approach is frequently required, care should be

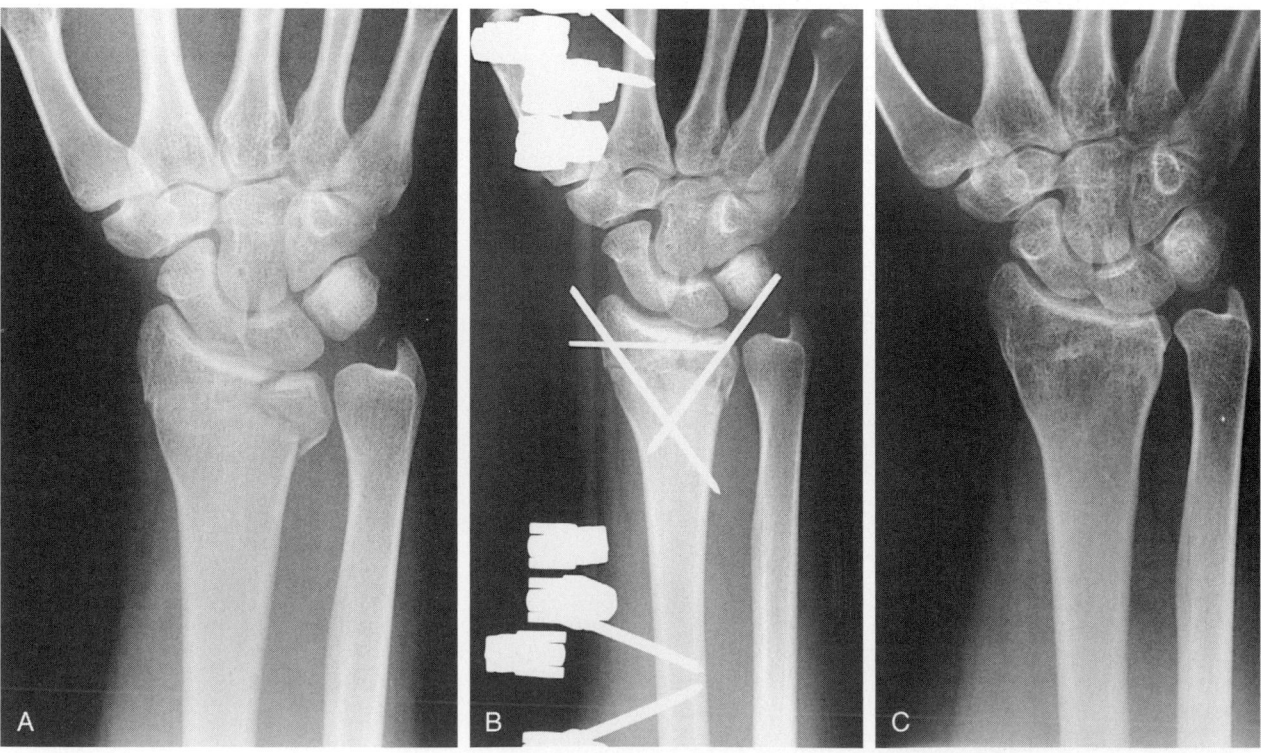

**Figure 40–20.** *A,* Two-part medial cuneiform fracture involving impaction and displacement of the entire lunate facet of the distal radius. *B,* A limited open reduction was required with an external fixator to neutralize forces across the articular surface. *C,* Final radiograph following pin and fixator removal.

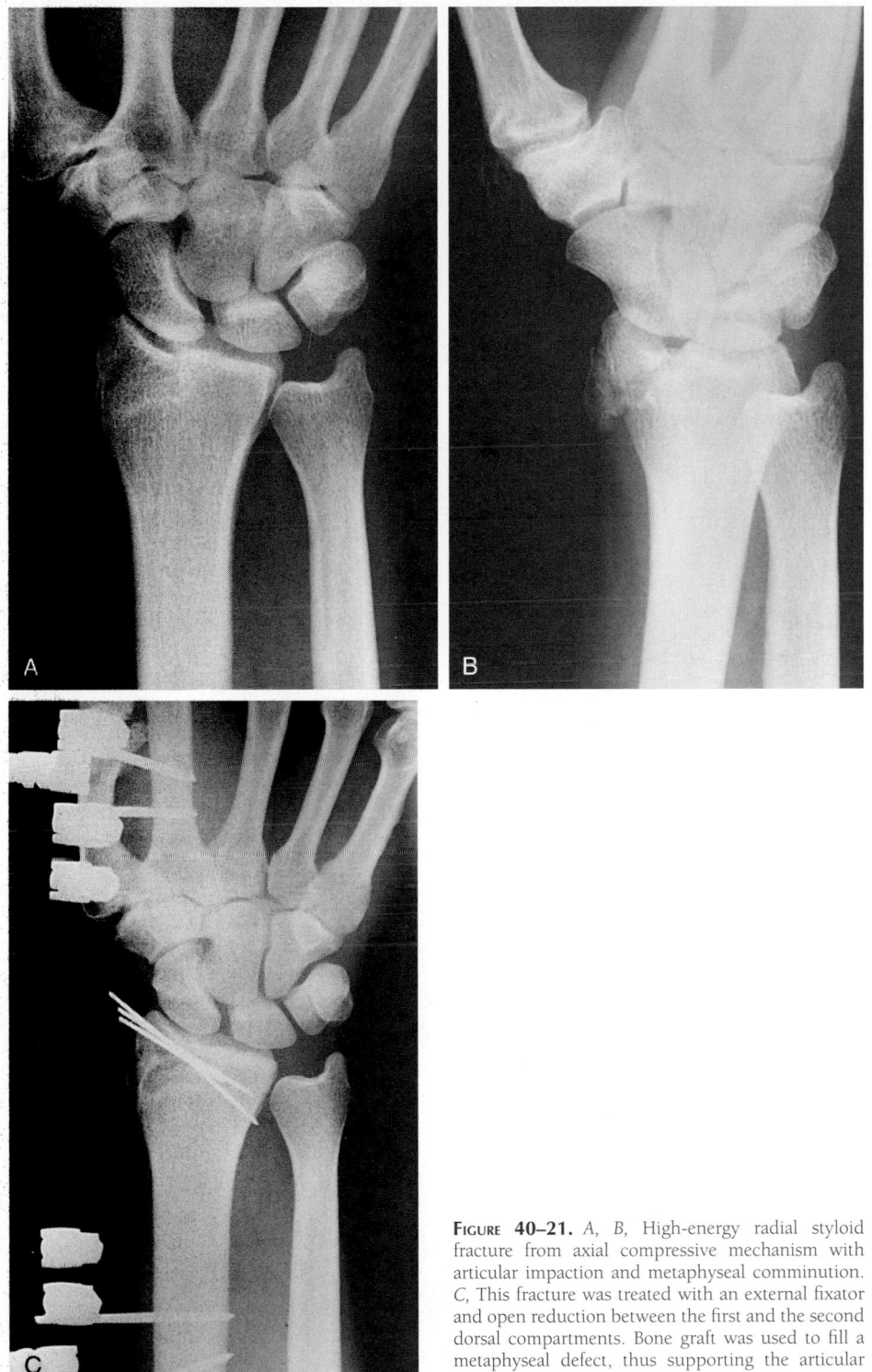

**FIGURE 40–21.** *A, B,* High-energy radial styloid fracture from axial compressive mechanism with articular impaction and metaphyseal comminution. *C,* This fracture was treated with an external fixator and open reduction between the first and the second dorsal compartments. Bone graft was used to fill a metaphyseal defect, thus supporting the articular surface.

taken to angle the pins radially enough to allow for a dorsal exposure. Often, the decision as to whether a palmar buttress plate is required can be made only after an attempted closed reduction performed with the patient under anesthesia. If the palmar cortex is not unstable and reduces with traction, a volar approach may not be required. More commonly, however, the volar cortex rotates with distraction, as previously mentioned. A palmar ap-

proach similar to that used for the volar Barton fracture is then required.

Several factors make placement of this palmar plate more difficult than in the simple two-part anterior fracture-dislocation. First, the volar cortex by definition has a longitudinal fracture line separating the free radial styloid component. This radial styloid fragment cannot be adequately visualized and reduced from the palmar side.

In addition, nondisplaced longitudinal palmar fracture lines are often present and must be protected. These, in addition to the displaced dorsal lunate facet fragment with associated dorsal comminution, make screw placement into the distal volar fragment virtually impossible.

Once the palmar plate is applied and the volar cortex stabilized, the radial styloid and dorsal lunate facet can be reduced to this scaffolding. An attempt can be made at closed reduction using pointed clamps and image intensification. Often, however, reduction requires a limited or more formal open dorsal approach through the third compartment. Impacted and displaced articular fragments are elevated and stabilized with K-wires or less commonly with a second dorsal plate.[63]

Frequently, comminution and displacement are greater than appreciated on fluoroscopy. The radial styloid must be translated distally and pronated to align with the volar-ulnar fragment. Stabilization usually requires additional Kirschner pins. One pin must be placed to capture the radial styloid and secure it to the radial shaft. This diminishes the tendency for the radial shaft to converge with the distal ulna, leading to distal radioulnar joint incongruity. Cancellous bone graft is used if metaphyseal defects exist that may structurally lead to articular settling (Fig. 40–23).

## INTRA-ARTICULAR FRACTURES WITH FIVE OR MORE PARTS

Intra-articular fractures with five or more parts are associated with higher-energy trauma and are often associated with concomitant skeletal or soft tissue injuries.[10, 22, 94, 101, 123, 144] The severity of these injuries is reflected in the fact that after treatment, most patients, although improved functionally, have some residual limita-tion in wrist mobility and in grip strength.[10, 22, 94, 125, 144] Several studies have suggested that restoration of the articular anatomy is the most critical factor in obtaining a good functional result and preventing late post-traumatic arthritis.[10, 22, 101, 123, 124, 144]

The surgical management of these fractures is particularly difficult and is associated with significant early and late morbidity. Preoperative planning, including AP and lateral tomography, is often helpful. In these cases, care must be taken to assess the injury to the soft tissues. If undue swelling is present, reduction can be accomplished and definitive surgery delayed. An extensive surgical procedure in the presence of severe soft tissue swelling is fraught with its own complications.

As with the four-part intra-articular fractures, the surgical approach is dictated by the displacement of the fracture fragments. Some injuries have severe fragmentation and comminution of the articular surface without significant volar cortical disruption. These can be approached dorsally after length has been restored and compressive forces neutralized with an external fixator (Fig. 40–24). In higher-energy fractures, fragments may be displaced in both directions, requiring a combined dorsal and palmar approach. Some fractures have articular fragmentation too extensive to permit open reduction and internal fixation of the articular surface. Often, an early or delayed radiocarpal fusion is required in this situation.[178]

Although there is growing enthusiasm for the operative approach to the complex articular distal radius fracture, both the surgeon and the patient must be aware that complications can be significant. These include loss of fixation, median neuritis, reflex sympathetic dystrophy, wound problems, and late post-traumatic arthritis.[10, 15, 94, 144]

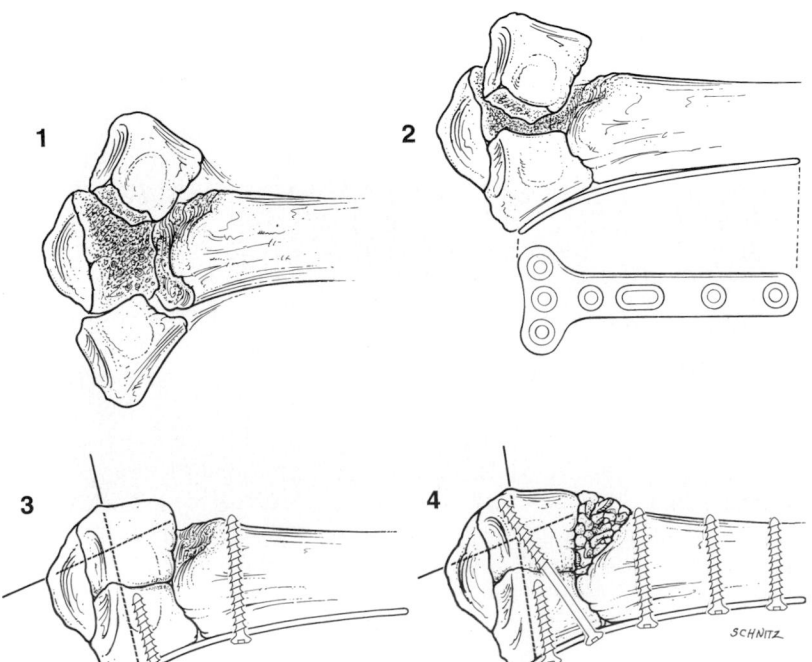

**Figure 40–22.** Sequence for reconstruction of the four-part fracture (1). Reduction begins with a volar buttress plate to restore palmar cortical stability (2 and 3). The dorsal lunate facet is then reduced to this scaffold with supplemental bone graft added to fill potentially unstable metaphyseal defects (4). The radial styloid must also be reduced and secured. (From Hastings, H. Adv Op Orthop 2:227–277, 1994.)

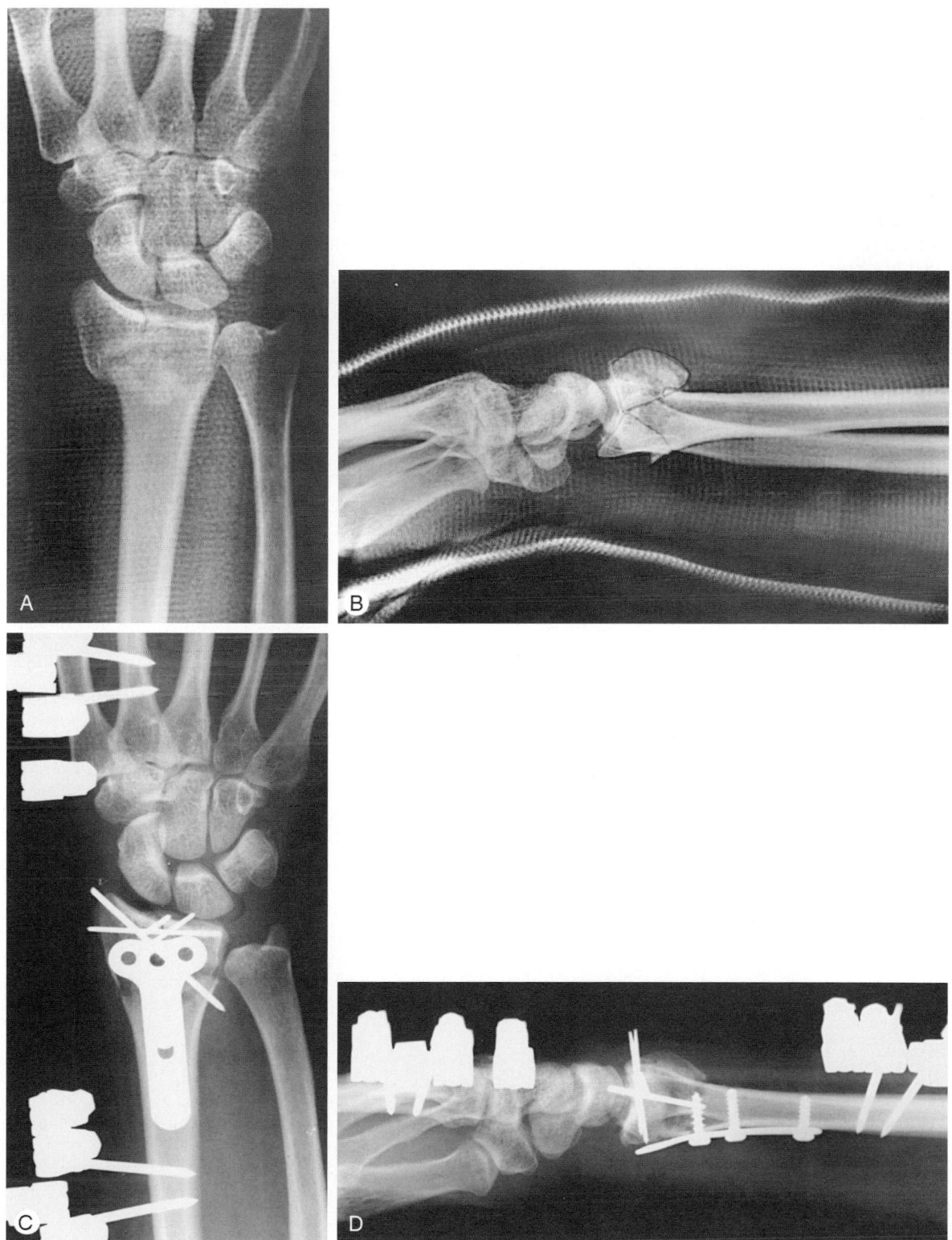

**FIGURE 40–23.** Postreduction posteroanterior (*A*) and lateral (*B*) views of a four-part fracture of the distal radius. *C, D,* This was treated with external fixation, a palmar plate, and a limited open reduction through a dorsal approach.

*Illustration continued on following page*

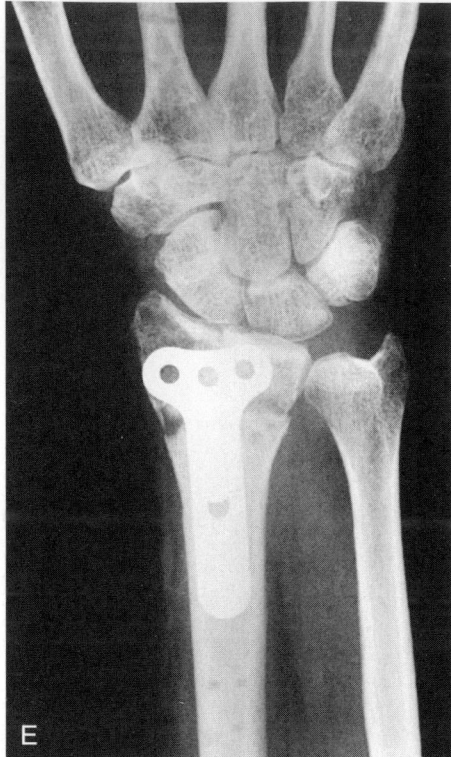
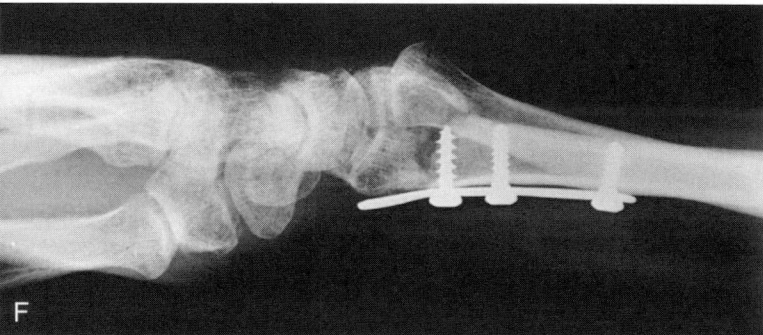

**FIGURE 40–23** *Continued. E, F,* Final radiographs with fixator and pins removed.

## ASSOCIATED INJURIES

### Ulnar Styloid Fractures

Fractures of the ulnar styloid are common, occurring in 50% to 70% of fractures of the distal radius.[12, 67, 109] Most of these are small avulsion fractures involving the tip of the ulnar styloid. Several reviews have shown that the presence or lack of union of these avulsion fractures does not significantly affect late functional results.[28, 109, 174]

Fractures at the very base of the ulnar styloid, however, can involve instability of the distal radioulnar joint.[111] In these injuries, the ulnar insertion of the triangular fibrocartilage is disrupted at the ulnar fovea. If they are associated with gross instability of the distal radioulnar joint as determined clinically, these ulnar styloid base fractures should be reduced and stabilized.[62, 163] Open reduction with internal fixation is usually required. Dissection is carried between the flexor and extensor carpi ulnaris, with care taken to identify and protect the dorsal sensory ulnar nerve branches. A small fragment screw or a tension band wire technique is used for fixation (Fig. 40–25; see also Fig. 40–19).

More proximal ulnar fractures involving the ulna head and neck often require reduction and stabilization. These occur in only 3% to 6% of cases.[19] A 2.7-mm minifragment condylar blade plate is helpful in fixation of these injuries.

### Carpal Injuries

Falls on the outstretched hand can lead both to fractures of the end of the radius and to bone and soft tissue injuries within the carpus proper. The triangular fibrocartilage is almost always disrupted if the initial fracture angulation exceeds 25° to 30° in the sagittal plane.[142] Several arthroscopic evaluations have also identified concomitant injuries to the volar radiocarpal and the scapholunate interosseous wrist ligaments in a large percentage of patients.[46, 77, 110, 111, 128, 149] These injuries range from central, stable ligament perforations to complete ligament ruptures with potential for resultant carpal instability. Fractures of the radial styloid resulting from tension forces and those that split the scaphoid and lunate articular facets are highly associated with scapholunate ligament disruptions (Fig. 40–26).

These occult soft tissue injuries may in part be responsible for continued discomfort after distal radius fractures even when bony architecture has been restored. Careful radiographic evaluation of carpal bone alignment is mandatory in the evaluation and treatment of distal radius fractures. Carpal instability may been seen in the initial postreduction radiographs, or it may become apparent only later, under physiologic loading. It can also manifest after application of an external fixator, because the scaphoid translates distally under traction if the scapholunate ligament is completely disrupted (Fig. 40–27). Carpal bone instability detected early requires open reduction and internal pin fixation.[128]

Carpal bone injuries can also accompany fractures of the distal radius, because they result from a similar injury mechanism.[134] These fractures are easily missed because attention is drawn to the obvious radius deformity. Nondisplaced carpal fractures usually require no additional treatment because the methods used for immobilization of the radius are sufficient. The scaphoid is an

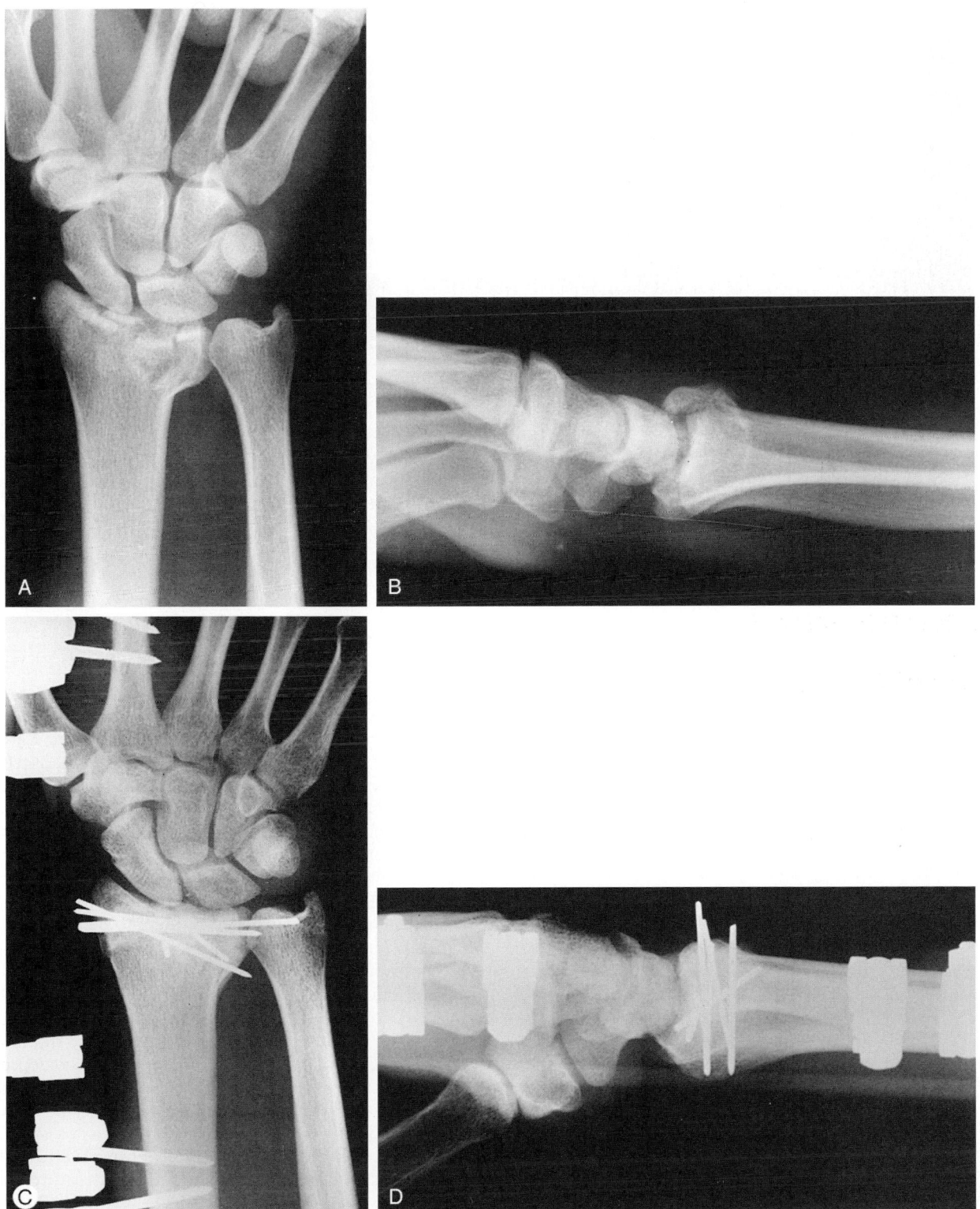

**FIGURE 40–24.** *A,* High-energy impaction-type distal radius fracture with multiple parts. *B,* Note maintenance of the palmar cortex. *C, D,* Operative reduction was performed with multiple pins through a formal open dorsal approach with an external fixator and metaphyseal autograft.

*Illustration continued on following page*

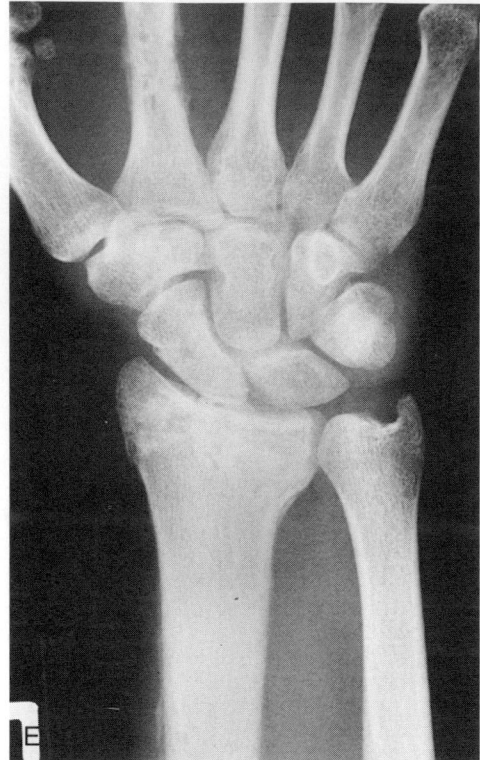
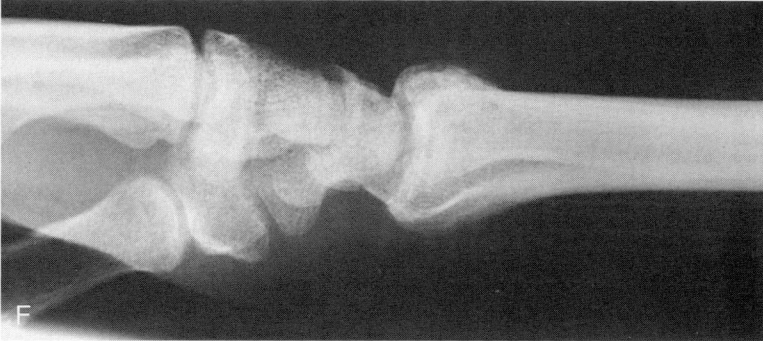

**FIGURE 40–24** *Continued. E, F,* Final radiographs with pins and fixator removed.

exception because of the long period of immobilization required for healing of this bone. Internal fixation is usually indicated for scaphoid fractures in this setting to allow mobilization of the wrist after the distal radius fracture has healed (Fig. 40–28).

## COMPLICATIONS

### Nerve Injuries

Median nerve dysfunction is the most commonly observed complication in most series of distal radius fractures.* Although acute compartment syndromes do occur,[116] the majority of these are nerve contusions or stretch injuries that do not require immediate surgical intervention. Sensation must be evaluated before and after fracture reduction in the emergency room setting. If median nerve sensation is mildly impaired on presentation, it can usually be observed clinically. Often, fracture reduction with proper immobilization is all that is required for nerve recovery. If a nerve deficit, even an incomplete one, is associated with a fracture requiring surgical intervention, nerve release is indicated at that time.

When progressive sensory loss ensues after a distal radius fracture with severe unremitting pain, a compartment syndrome must be considered.[116] Initial treatment requires loosening of the wrapping used for

immobilization and elevation of the wrist to heart level. If this does not lead to symptom resolution, a release of the carpal canal is indicated. Carpal canal pressure measurement can be helpful in this setting.[122] If swelling is significant along the volar distal forearm, the release should include the antebrachial fascia proximal to the wrist flexion crease.[108]

Median nerve symptoms can also be seen late after fractures of the distal radius. This is especially true in dorsally angulated malunions, which can mechanically tent the nerve.[8, 67, 108, 175] Late carpal tunnel symptoms often respond to a cortisone injection into the carpal canal. If this does not adequately resolve symptoms, transverse carpal ligament sectioning may be indicated.

In the setting of increasing pain, swelling, loss of joint mobility, or paresthesias during the healing phase, an impending dystrophy should be considered. Atkins and co-workers observed that these symptoms were more common than previously thought in association with distal radius fractures.[9] Lynch and Lipscomb[115] and Stein[172] noted the strong possibility that median nerve compression is a common precursor of reflex sympathetic dystrophy. Stein observed significant improvement with median nerve decompression in four patients with signs of reflex dystrophy after a distal radius fracture. Most investigators agree that early recognition of median nerve compression is important in the prevention of long-term impairment.[9, 12, 67, 109, 115, 119, 172]

Ulnar nerve embarrassment is much less frequently associated with distal radius fractures. It is more common in higher-energy open injuries. Most of these are nerve

---

*See references 8, 44, 67, 84, 103, 115, 119, 143, 170, 175.

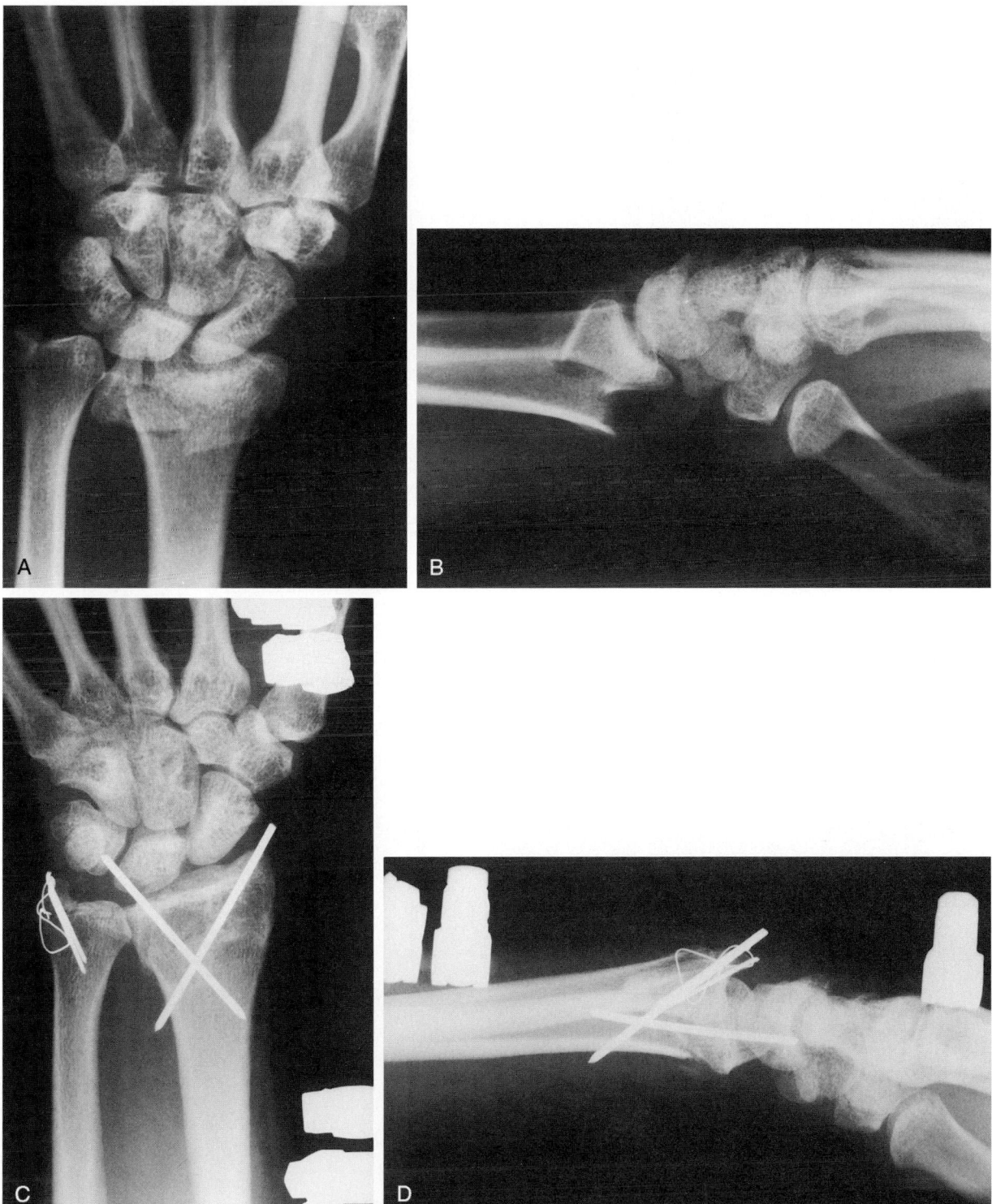

**FIGURE 40–25.** Posteroanterior (*A*) and lateral (*B*) radiographs of a high-energy distal radius fracture associated with a base of the ulnar styloid fracture. Following reduction and pinning with external fixation, the ulnar styloid fragment remained displaced and gross distal radioulnar joint instability was present. *C, D,* Tension bend wire fixation of the ulnar styloid base fracture reestablished stability of the distal radioulnar joint.

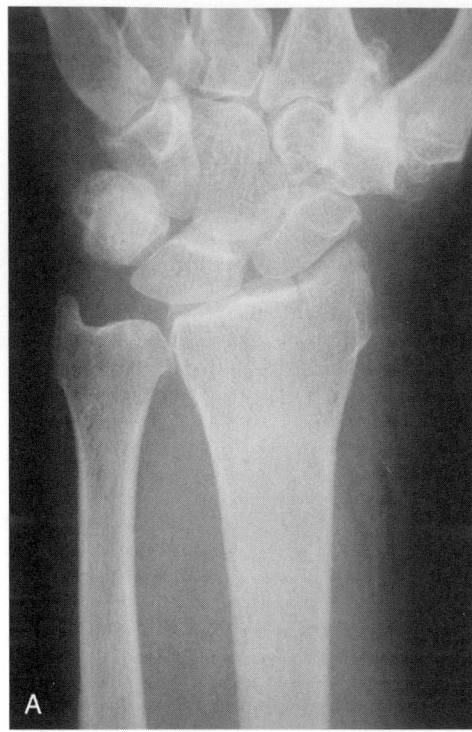
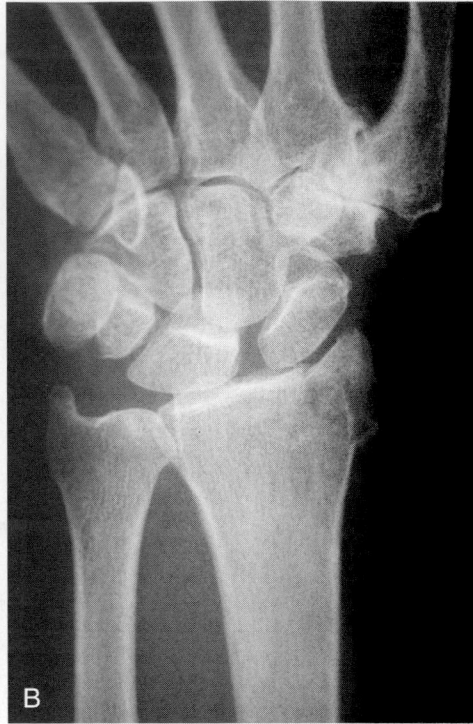

FIGURE 40–26. *A*, Posteroanterior radiograph revealing an apparent nondisplaced oblique fracture of the radial styloid. This was immobilized in a cast. *B*, Follow-up radiograph 1 week later reveals the fracture displacement. This has unmasked an obvious associated scapholunate ligament disruption. Scapholunate ligament tears are associated with radial styloid fractures, as both occur by similar mechanisms.

contusions or stretch injuries that resolve with conservative care.[103]

## Tendon Adhesions and Ruptures

Early digital motion must be emphasized after distal radius fractures, regardless of the treatment method used. Care must be taken when applying any splint or casting material

to end at the proximal metacarpophalangeal joint palmar flexion crease, to allow for unrestricted digital motion. This is important because motion not only limits tendon adhesions but also functions to reduce digital soft tissue swelling. Early digital stiffness should be treated aggressively with appropriate occupational therapy.

Tenosynovitis most often affects the tendons of the first dorsal compartment (de Quervain's disease). Tendon ruptures occur rarely but almost exclusively involve the

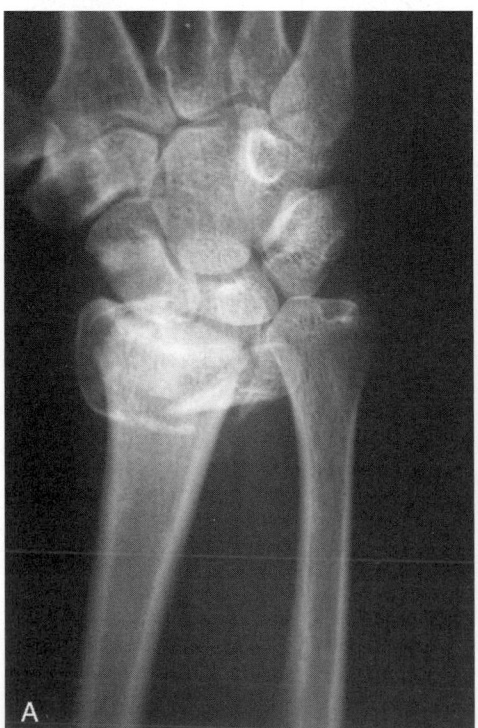
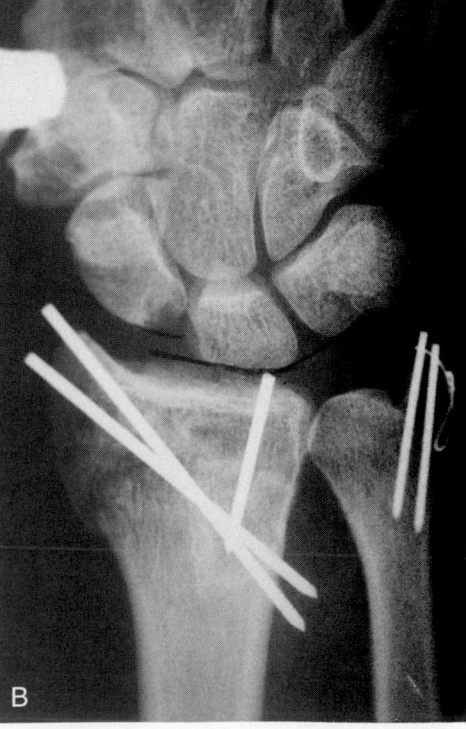

FIGURE 40–27. *A*, Posteroanterior radiograph depicting a high-energy distal radius fracture. *B*, After application of traction by an external fixator, a scapholunate ligamentous injury is evident. This manifests as a break in the contour of the proximal carpal row due to distal translation of the scaphoid. The scaphoid will migrate distally under traction if the scapholunate ligament is incompetent.

extensor pollicis longus tendon.[31, 50] These most commonly occur within 8 weeks after the traumatic event but can be seen late after fracture healing. Controversy exists regarding the exact cause of the rupture, but it probably represents a combination of mechanical and ischemic mechanisms. Although direct end-to-end repair is usually not possible because of tendon attrition and retraction, transfer of the extensor indicis proprius can reliably restore thumb extensor function after rupture.

## Malunion

Malunion of distal radius fractures may be extra-articular in the metaphyseal region or intra-articular with residual joint surface incongruity. Extra-articular malunion most commonly occurs in the direction of fracture displacement, namely, with dorsal angulation of the articular surface, shortening, and loss of radial inclination. A supination deformity of the distal fragment is common as

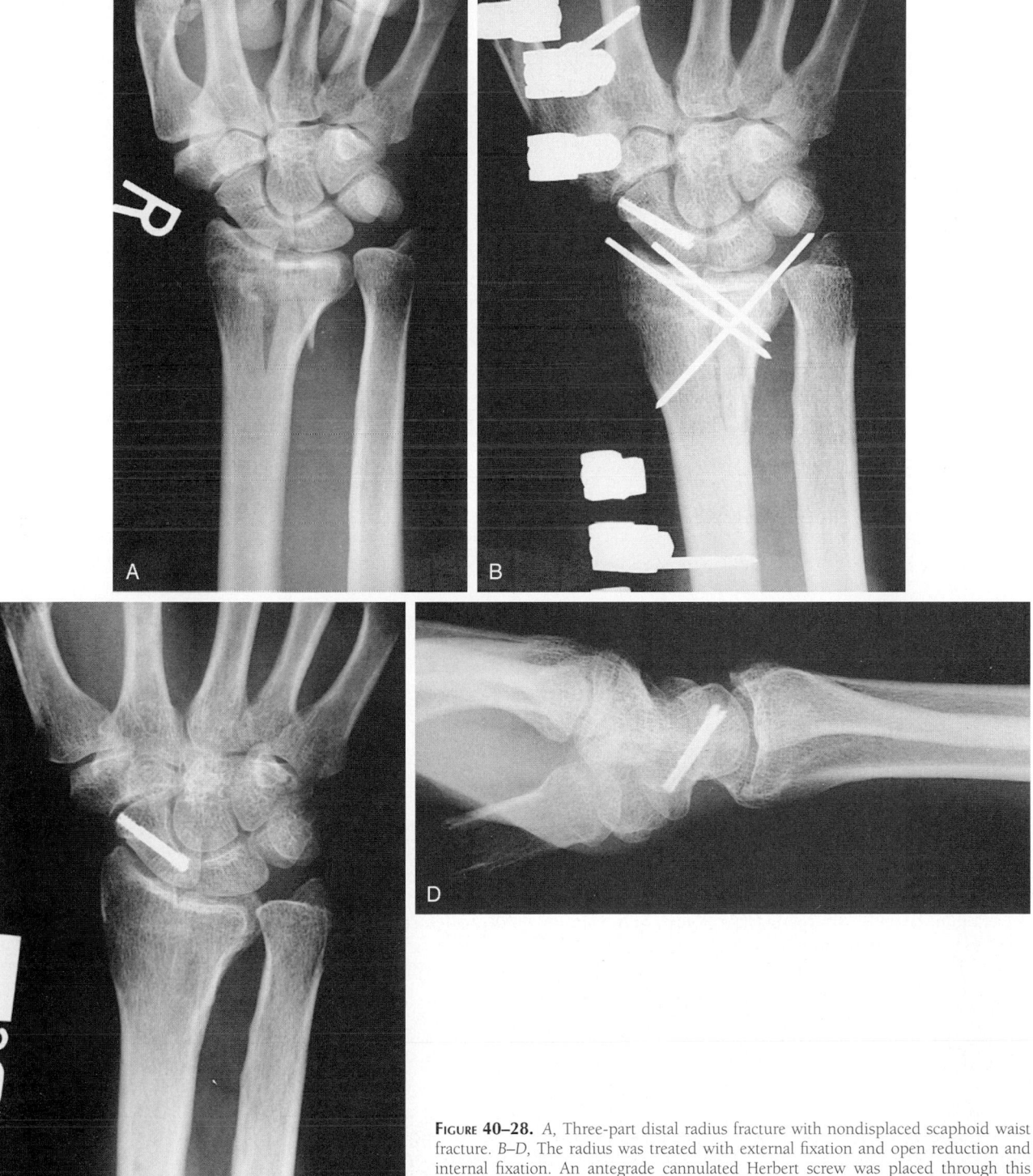

**FIGURE 40–28.** *A,* Three-part distal radius fracture with nondisplaced scaphoid waist fracture. *B–D,* The radius was treated with external fixation and open reduction and internal fixation. An antegrade cannulated Herbert screw was placed through this approach, stabilizing the scaphoid. Wrist motion was begun at 6 weeks after the operation.

well. As previously outlined, malunion significantly affects the biomechanical forces across the radiocarpal and distal radioulnar joints. Furthermore, dorsal angular malunion changes the flexion-extension arc and leads to limited palmar flexion and exaggerated wrist extension. It can also lead to radiocarpal pain secondary to dorsal subluxation of the carpus and to midcarpal pain in young, active individuals (extrinsic midcarpal instability).[18, 59, 93, 177] Radial shortening leads to ulnocarpal abutment and problems with forearm rotation.

Adequate wrist function with minimal symptoms can occur despite significant radiographic deformity. This result is more common, however, in persons with low functional requirements. A corrective radial osteotomy for an extra-articular malunion is usually indicated in younger patients who require anatomic restoration of the distal radius for specific functional requirements and who would be expected to have late degenerative arthritis because of their deformity. The presence of more than about 15° to 20° of dorsal angulation is probably an indication for osteotomy in young, active persons. It is also indicated in older patients if the radius deformity is determined to be responsible for radial-sided wrist symptoms that would not be expected to improve with an ulnar-sided wrist reconstructive procedure (e.g., Darrach excision, ulnar shortening osteotomy, hemiresection arthroplasty).[62, 133] Approximately half of patients who undergo radial osteotomy require an additional ulnar-sided wrist procedure to address the distal radioulnar joint abnormality.[61]

Distal radius osteotomy requires careful preoperative planning. The goals are restoration of the alignment of the distal radius articular surface and the distal radioulnar joint surface to restore mechanical balance, improve function and decrease articular cartilage stress concentration. Contraindications to osteotomy alone include advanced arthrosis, fixed carpal malalignment, extensive osteoporosis, and limited functional capacity of the patient. In established malunions, it is helpful to allow some return of mobility and soft tissue equilibrium before reconstruction. However, earlier surgical intervention has been shown to be technically easier and reduces the overall period of disability when compared with that in delayed reconstruction.[95]

From a technical standpoint, templates are very helpful in preparation for surgery. The majority of dorsally angulated malunions are treated with a dorsal opening wedge osteotomy through a posterior approach. Reduction is aided by K-wires placed perpendicular to the articular surface and the radial shaft. The osteotomy cut is made as close to the apex of the deformity as possible, parallel to the articular surface. In many cases with more simple deformities, the volar cortex and periosteum may be left intact and the distal fragment may be hinged open dorsally (and radially), restoring length and palmar tilt (Fig. 40–29). This can be facilitated with the use of a lamina spreader. In cases requiring significant restoration of length as well, an AO small distraction device can be utilized intraoperatively to obtain gradual correction while maintaining stability between fragments (Fig. 40–30). In long-standing deformities, release or Z-lengthening of the brachioradialis tendon may be required to obtain adequate correction.

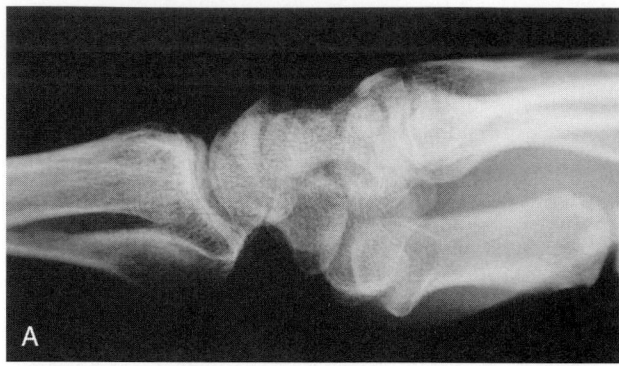

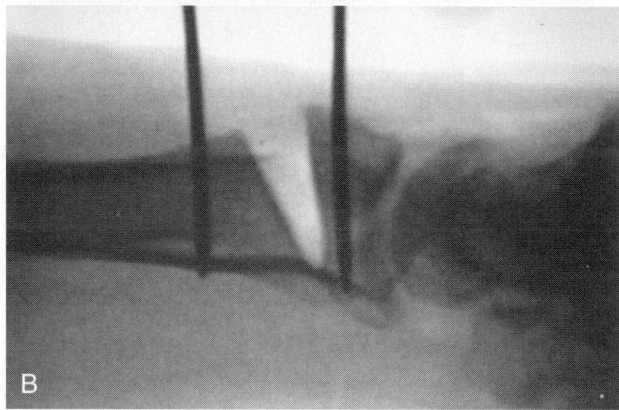

FIGURE 40–29. A, Lateral radiograph revealing dorsally angulated radius malunion following fracture. B, In this case, restoration of length and tilt was possible with an opening wedge osteotomy maintaining integrity of the palmar cortex for stability. Note the K-wires used intraoperatively to guide the reduction.

Once the reduction is complete, provisional fixation can be accomplished with smooth K-wires. A dorsal plate is then applied to maintain the correction. Although compression-resistant corticocancellous grafts are traditionally used to fill the dorsal defect, with the use of more stable dorsal plate fixation systems, pure cancellous autograft has been shown to be equally effective following distal radius osteotomy without loss of correction (see Fig. 40–30).[154]

An alternative technique for a dorsally angulated malunion involves a palmarly based closing wedge osteotomy without bone graft supplementation (Fig. 40–31).[147] This technique is most often indicated in older individuals when the sigmoid notch of the distal radius is incongruous. The closing wedge osteotomy realigns the radiocarpal and midcarpal joints, but it does result in relative shortening of the radius. Concomitant distal ulna resection is therefore required (see Fig. 40–31).

In palmarly angulated malunions, the distal fragment is typically shortened, flexed, and pronated. Limited forearm rotation, especially supination, is common. Diminished mechanical advantage of the extrinsic flexor tendons may contribute to loss of grip strength. Principles of correction are similar to those for dorsally malunited fractures. A palmar approach is utilized with extension and supination of the distal fragment (Fig. 40–32). Intraoperative fluoroscopy is essential owing to the inability to visualize the radiocarpal joint surface from the palmar approach. Bone graft is placed in the palmar defect with internal fixation applied to the anterior surface of the radius.[112, 164]

Osteotomy for established intra-articular malunion is very technically demanding. It involves careful re-creation of the fracture into the joint and is indicated only in select cases in the absence of degenerative changes.[117, 193] Early arthrodesis may be required when the articular surface cannot be adequately restored.[178]

Although motion and pain relief are typically improved following corrective osteotomy, reconstruction does not restore anatomy and function to "normal" in the majority of cases.[64] A subset of patients have pathologic carpal malalignment that does not correct following successful osteotomy of the radius.[82] This underscores the importance of preventing malunion in the initial treatment of these injuries.

## Nonunion

Nonunion of distal radius fractures is extremely rare.[78, 161] Nonunion occurs most commonly in elderly patients with multiple medical conditions. Inadequate immobilization and a peripheral neuropathy (Charcot joint) predispose patients to this complication. Overdistraction of fracture

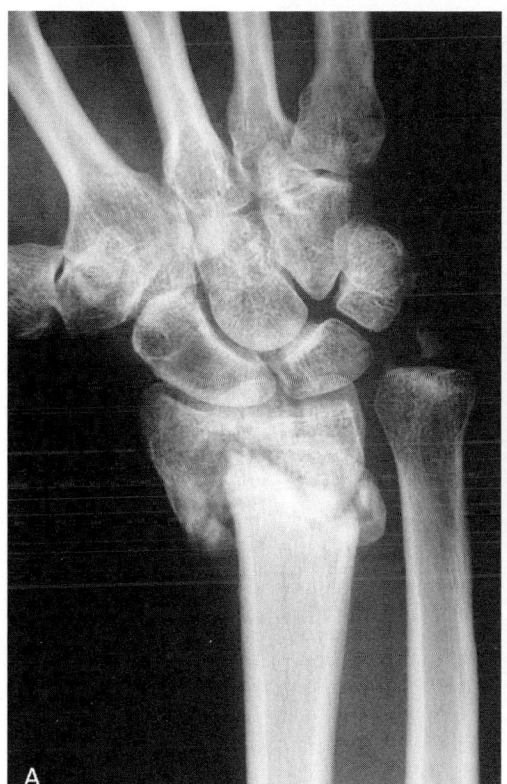

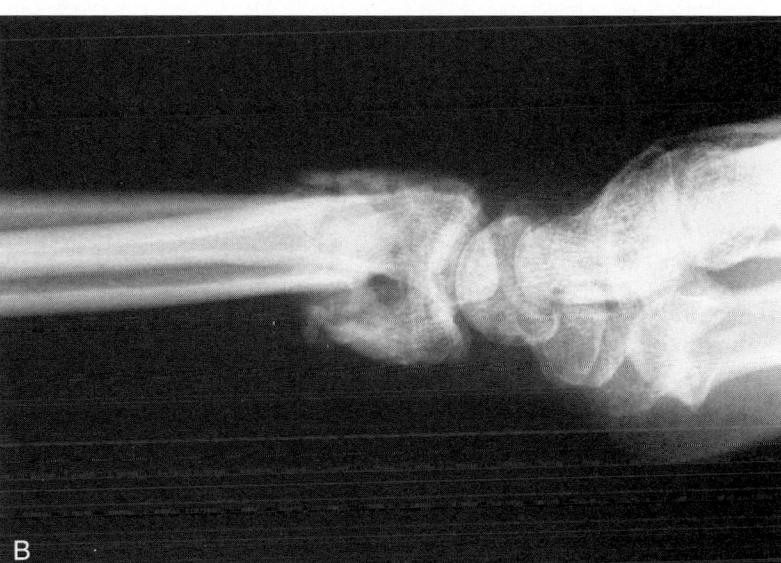

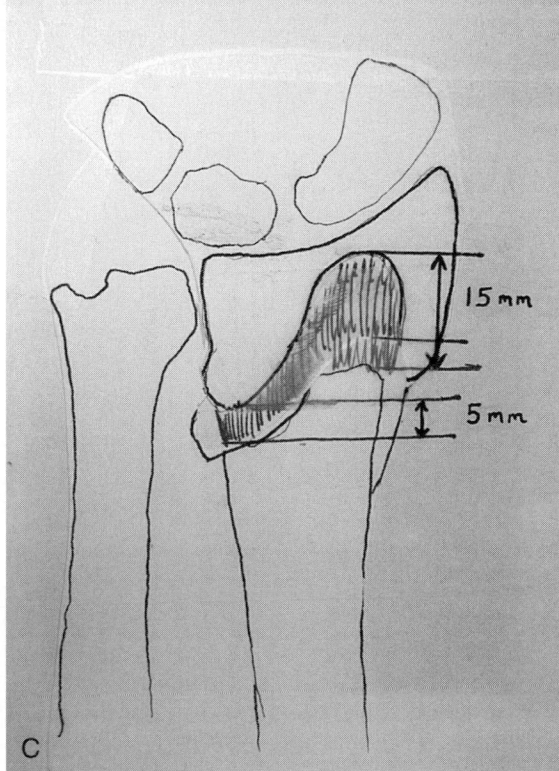

**FIGURE 40–30.** Posteroanterior (*A*) and lateral (*B*) radiographs revealing malunion with significant shortening of the right radius. *C*, Template depicting the correction required to restore radial length.

*Illustration continued on following page*

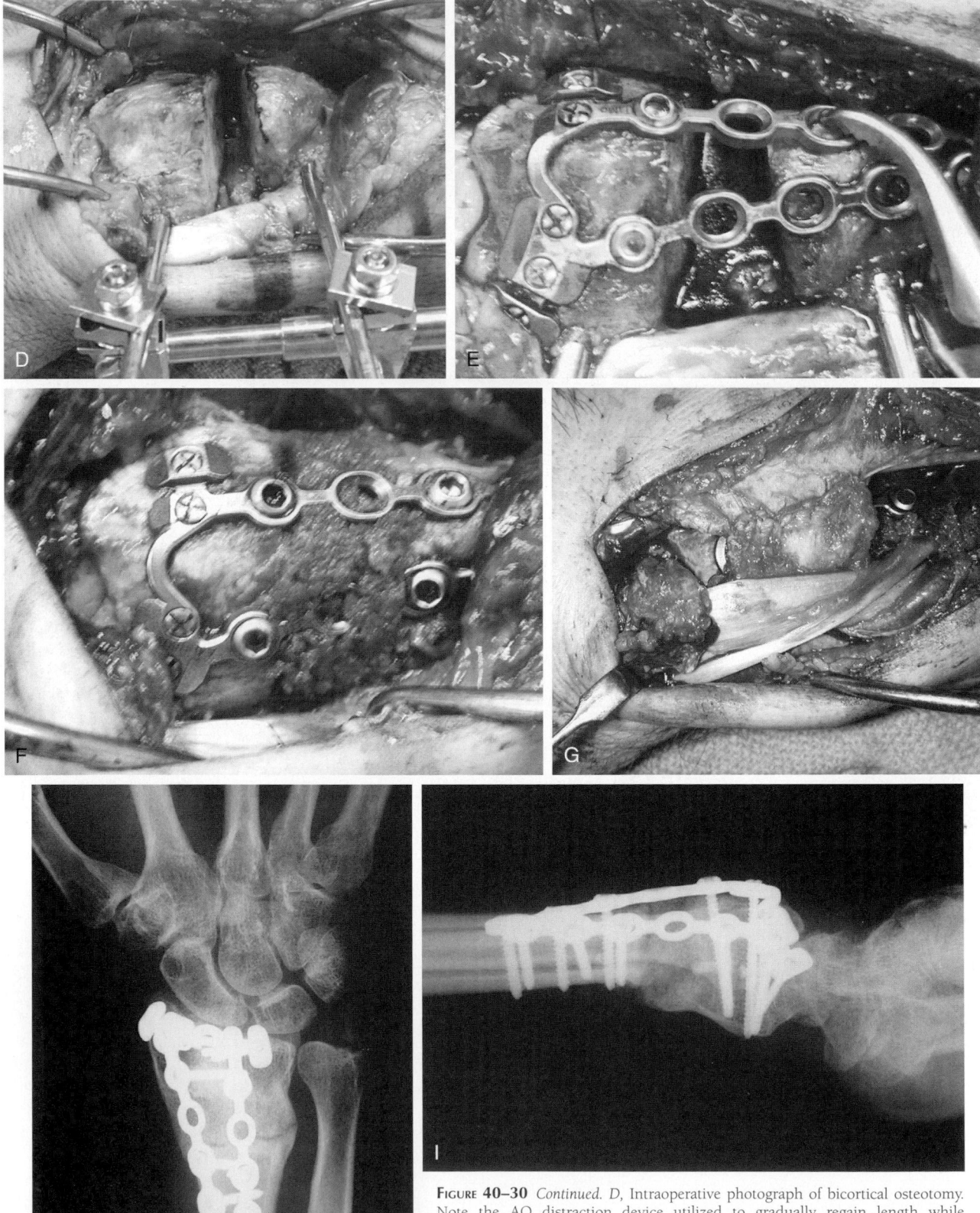

**FIGURE 40–30** *Continued. D,* Intraoperative photograph of bicortical osteotomy. Note the AO distraction device utilized to gradually regain length while maintaining stability between the fragments. *E,* Placement of a dorsal Π plate to maintain the reduction. *F,* The osteotomy defect has been filled with pure cancellous bone graft. With the stability of newer plating systems, corticocancellous grafts are often not required. *G,* Soft tissue closure over the plate. Note that the radial retinaculum has been passed beneath the wrist extensor tendons to decrease the potential for extensor tendon irritation from the plate. Follow-up radiographs (*H, I*).

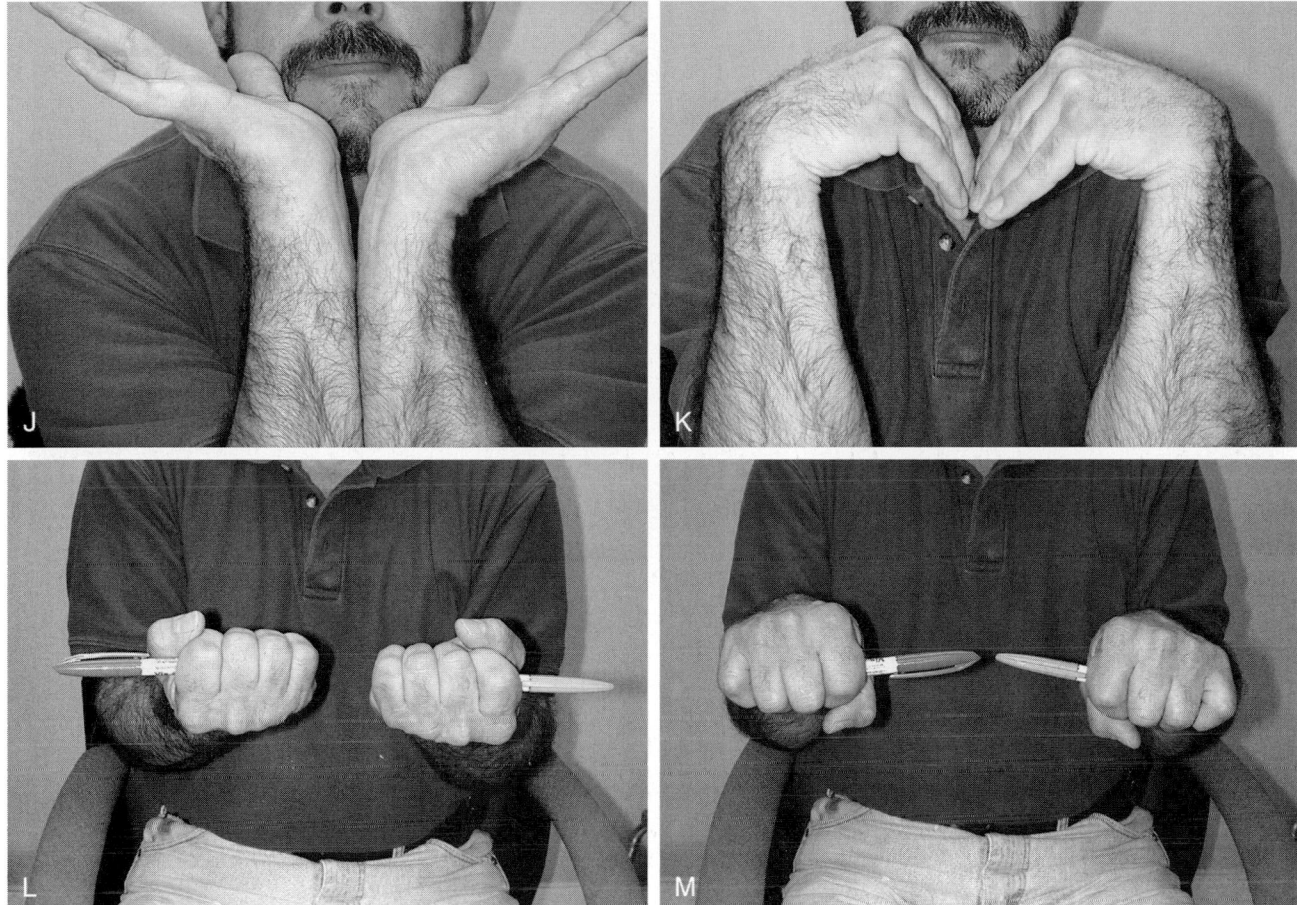

FIGURE **40–30** *Continued.* Motion of the wrist (*J, K*) and forearm (*L, M*).

fragments with the use of an external fixator is an additional cause.

Treatment of a distal radius nonunion requires many of the procedures used in the treatment of complex acute fractures. Included in these are bone graft, internal fixation, and external fixation when appropriate. In the elderly patient with poor bone stock and a small distal fragment, arthrodesis may be required to restore stability to the wrist.

## EVALUATION OF OUTCOME

Significant variability exists in the reported outcomes of distal radius fractures. This can be explained in large part by the wide variation in fracture patterns, the numerous methods of radiologic and clinical evaluation, and the duration from injury to follow-up. Most investigators have relied on the evaluation system of Gartland and Werley,[68] who modified McBride's demerit point system based on disability evaluation charts.[118] These systems evaluate a number of subjective, objective, and radiologic parameters but lack some objectivity. For example, demerit points are assigned for an observer's assessment of residual deformity or radiologic changes, despite an absence of subjective symptoms or functional loss. Objective evaluation is not quantitative and provides no comparison with the contralateral side. Sarmiento and associates[158] modified these systems, adding evaluation of grip strength and loss of pronation. Lucas and Sachtjen[113] further modified the system by adding more specific criteria for hand dysfunction, including median nerve compression, reflex sympathetic dystrophy, and digital stiffness.

Several investigators have expressed concern that the Gartland and Werley system does not provide an accurate measure of functional outcome. Porter and Stockley[145] developed a functional index that measures grip strength, angular and rotational movement of the hand and wrist, and functional movements performed against resistance and compares them with similar measurements on the contralateral wrist. Functional evaluation was extended further by McQueen and Caspers,[122] who incorporated a number of tests used for interpreting hand dexterity, grip strength and endurance, tasks of daily living, and pain and aesthetic parameters. Bradway and colleagues[22] used the evaluation scale of Green and O'Brien,[76] which proved more stringent with respect to evaluation of motion and strength but did not take into account radiologic outcome. In their series of patients treated operatively, 56% had a good-to-excellent result by this evaluation system, compared with 81% by the Gartland and Werley system.

Contemporary literature reflects the recognition that an accurate interpretation of outcome after distal radius

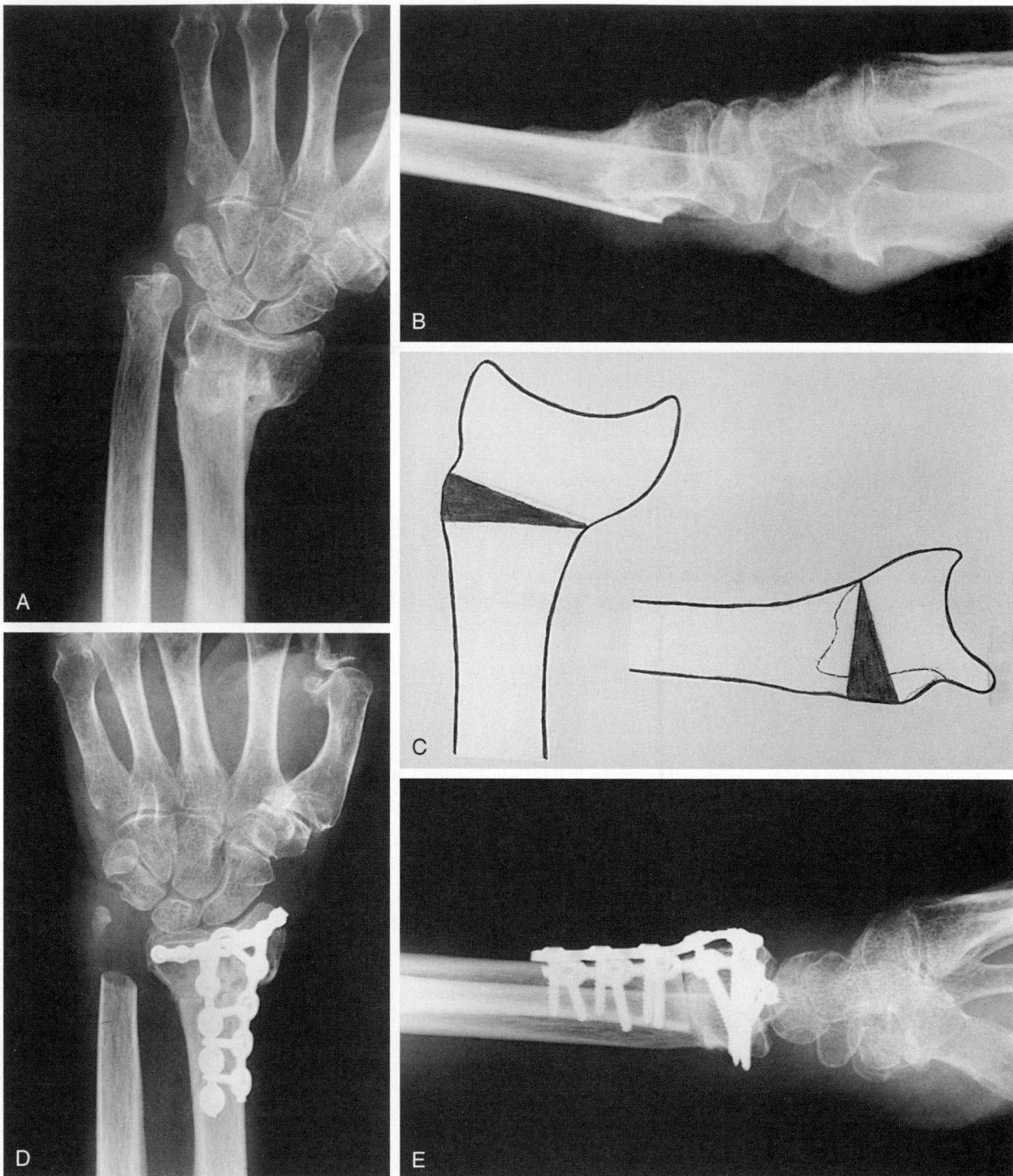

**FIGURE 40–31.** Posteroanterior (*A*) and lateral (*B*) radiographs of a severe malunion deformity in a 72-year-old low-demand individual. Note the loss of radial height with reversal of the radial inclination and distal radioulnar joint incongruity. *C,* Preoperative design of a biplanar volar and ulnar closing wedge osteotomy of the distal radius. This is an alternative to the more complicated opening osteotomy. Bone graft is not required. Postoperative posteroanterior (*D*) and lateral (*E*) radiographs following osteotomy. A closing wedge osteotomy results in radial shortening, necessitating a Darrach excision of the distal ulna.

fractures must take into account a host of parameters reflecting an enhanced understanding of functional anatomy and the functional requirements of the individual patient.

## FUTURE CONSIDERATIONS

### Bone Replacement Materials

Pure cancellous autograft is the material most commonly used to fill large metaphyseal defects that could lead to articular collapse and malunion. A variety of bone substitute materials (e.g., calcium phosphate–based ceramics) are also available. Each has advantages and disadvantages in terms of cost, osteoinductive and osteoconductive properties, ease of use, and degree of mechanical support.[55, 81, 105, 191] These materials obviate the need for a donor bone graft site but are inferior to pure cancellous bone graft in their ability to incorporate and provide early structural support.

A process has been developed for the formation of the mineral phase of bone in situ.[36, 41, 55] This involves combination of an inorganic calcium and phosphate to form a paste that can be injected into a fracture site. The material begins to harden within minutes, forming a cement that ultimately reaches 10 times the strength of cancellous bone and one half the strength of cortical bone in compression. Over time, it is remodeled in vivo and replaced by host bone in a manner identical to that for native bone. Placement of this cement into the dorsal metaphyseal defect following reduction provides a stable buttress supporting the distal articular fragment (Fig. 40–33).[96, 102, 194]

A prospective, randomized multicenter study was conducted comparing the use of this injectable cement with conventional treatment methods in displaced fractures of the distal radius.[27] A total of 323 patients were randomized to receive either the cement (with or without pins) or pins, with a cast or external fixator per the surgeons' preference. Patients treated with cement were allowed to begin range of motion and rehabilitation at 2 weeks, compared with 6 to 8 weeks for the controls.

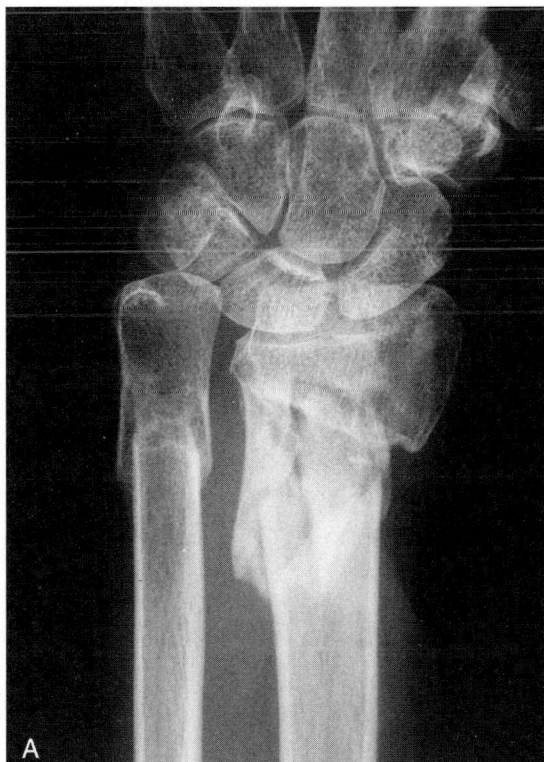

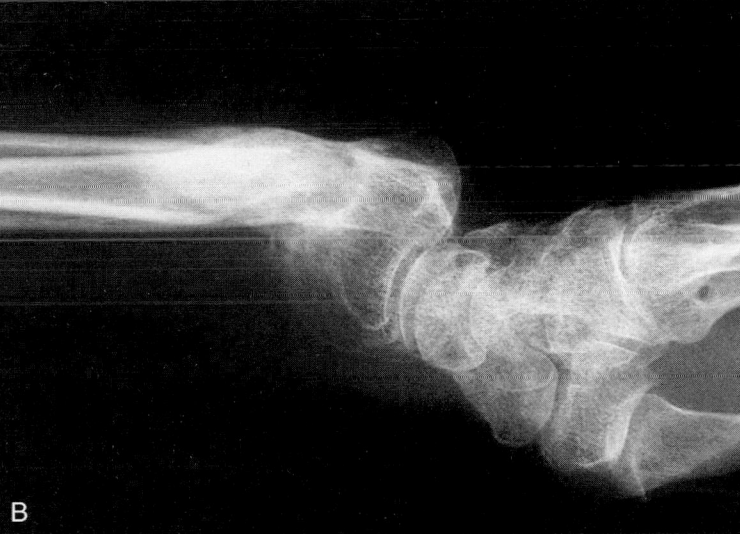

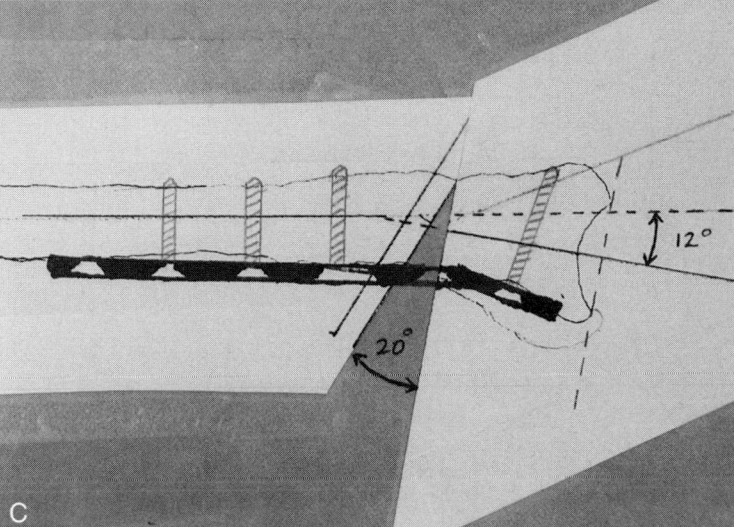

FIGURE **40–32.** Posteroanterior (*A*) and lateral (*B*) radiographs depicting palmarly angulated malunion of the distal radius following fracture. This typically results in flexion and pronation of the distal fragment with loss of forearm rotation. *C*, Template design of osteotomy correction.

*Illustration continued on following page*

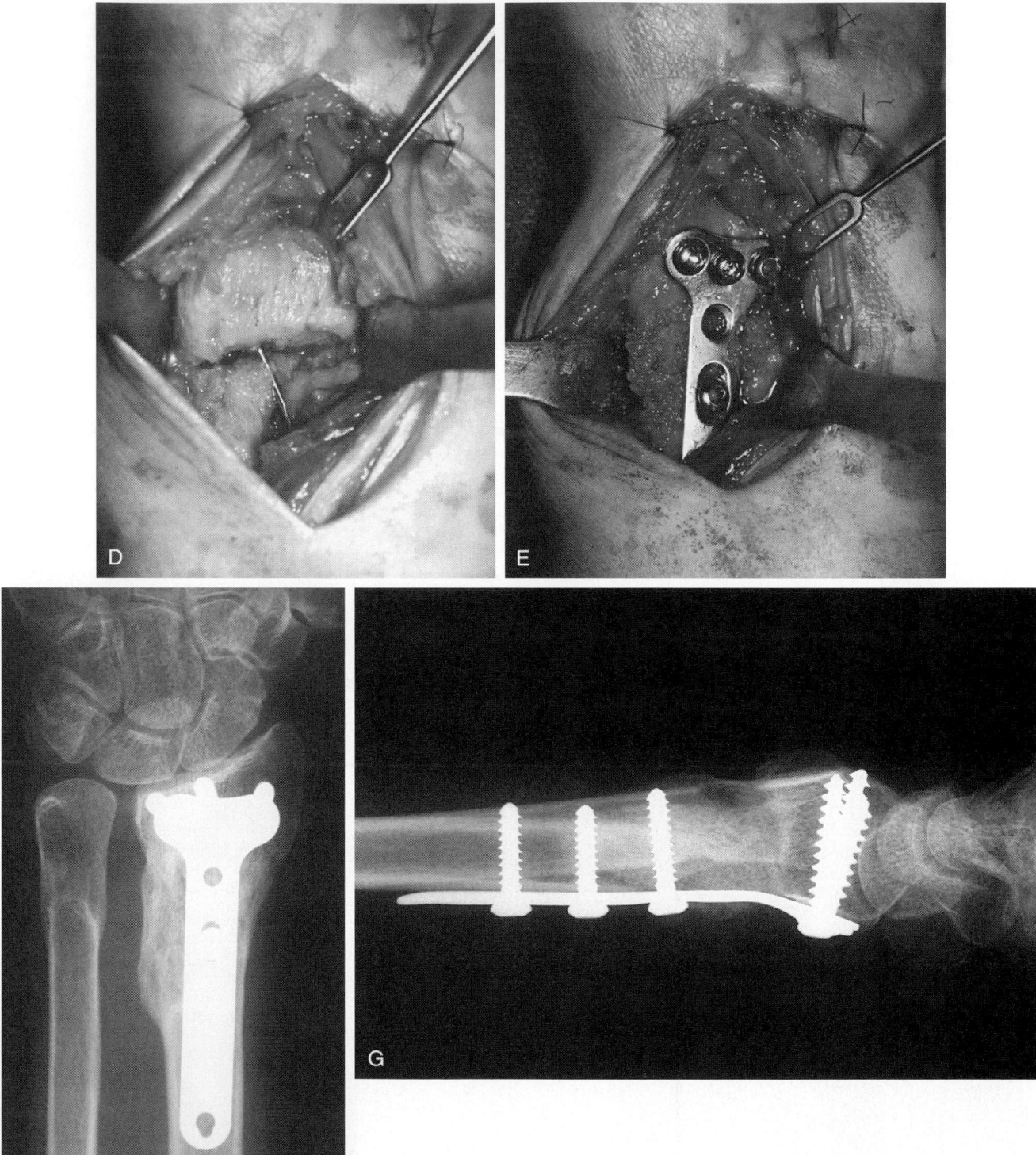

**FIGURE 40–32** *Continued. D,* Intraoperative photograph depicting palmar approach with provisional K-wire fixation following osteotomy and reduction. *E,* A palmar **T** plate has been applied and pure cancellous autograft used to fill the osteotomy defect. Follow-up radiographs (*F, G*).

Results revealed improved motion, strength, hand use, and social and emotional function in the cement-treated patients at 6 to 8 weeks. By 3 months, results were similar in all parameters. Radiographic analysis showed no differences between groups at follow-up, and there were no adverse effects observed directly related to the cement.

A second prospective study reported similar findings in individuals older than 50 years.[157] Thus, the use of a metaphyseal bone replacement material with mechanical integrity permits earlier mobilization of the wrist with more rapid return of function and may be particularly beneficial in older patients with osteoporotic bone.

Long-term outcome appears to be similar to that with conventional treatment methods.

## Specialized Plating Systems

Because of the intrinsic relation of the extensor tendons to the dorsal cortex of the distal radius, dorsally applied plates are prone to extensor tendon adhesions and impaired tendon gliding. Newer, low-profile plating systems are now available for the treatment of distal radius fractures. One system utilizes a mesh π-plate design that allows for the placement of multiple screws and locking pins to stabilize small metaphyseal and juxta-articular bone fragments[153] (see Figs. 40–30 and 40–31). Another involves a preshaped dorsally applied T-plate design with recessed screw holes.[30] Alternative plate designs use smaller low-profile implants placed radially and dorsally at 50° to 70° to one another to better buttress the "columns" of the radius.[141] Preliminary results with this technique are encouraging.[152] Finally, palmar plates with fixed-angle or distally locking screw design are being developed to allow stable fixation without the problems associated with dorsal plates.[193]

Early, stable fixation of selected distal radius fractures with internal fixation may allow for more rapid rehabilitation and less morbidity after these injuries. However, the results must still be compared with those using conventional methods with a proven track record, such as external fixation.[98] Currently, dorsally applied plates are most often used for malunions of the distal radius and for fractures treated late, when more limited approaches are no longer an option. Plate removal is often required following union.

## Arthroscopically Guided Reduction

Several investigators have used arthroscopic methods as a less invasive means of accurately reducing articular displacement.[2, 43, 46, 51, 70, 71, 190] This technique allows evaluation of the joint surface without the need for an extensive dorsal exposure. Arthroscopic treatment of distal radius fractures, however, is much more complicated than simple elective wrist arthroscopy without fracture. Visualization is more difficult, and complications from fluid extravasation can be significant. This technique should be performed only by physicians who are very experienced with arthroscopic techniques of the wrist. It is yet to be determined whether the limited morbidity achieved with a well-performed dorsal exposure warrants the added operative time, equipment, and potential morbidity of arthroscopy in the acutely fractured distal radius.

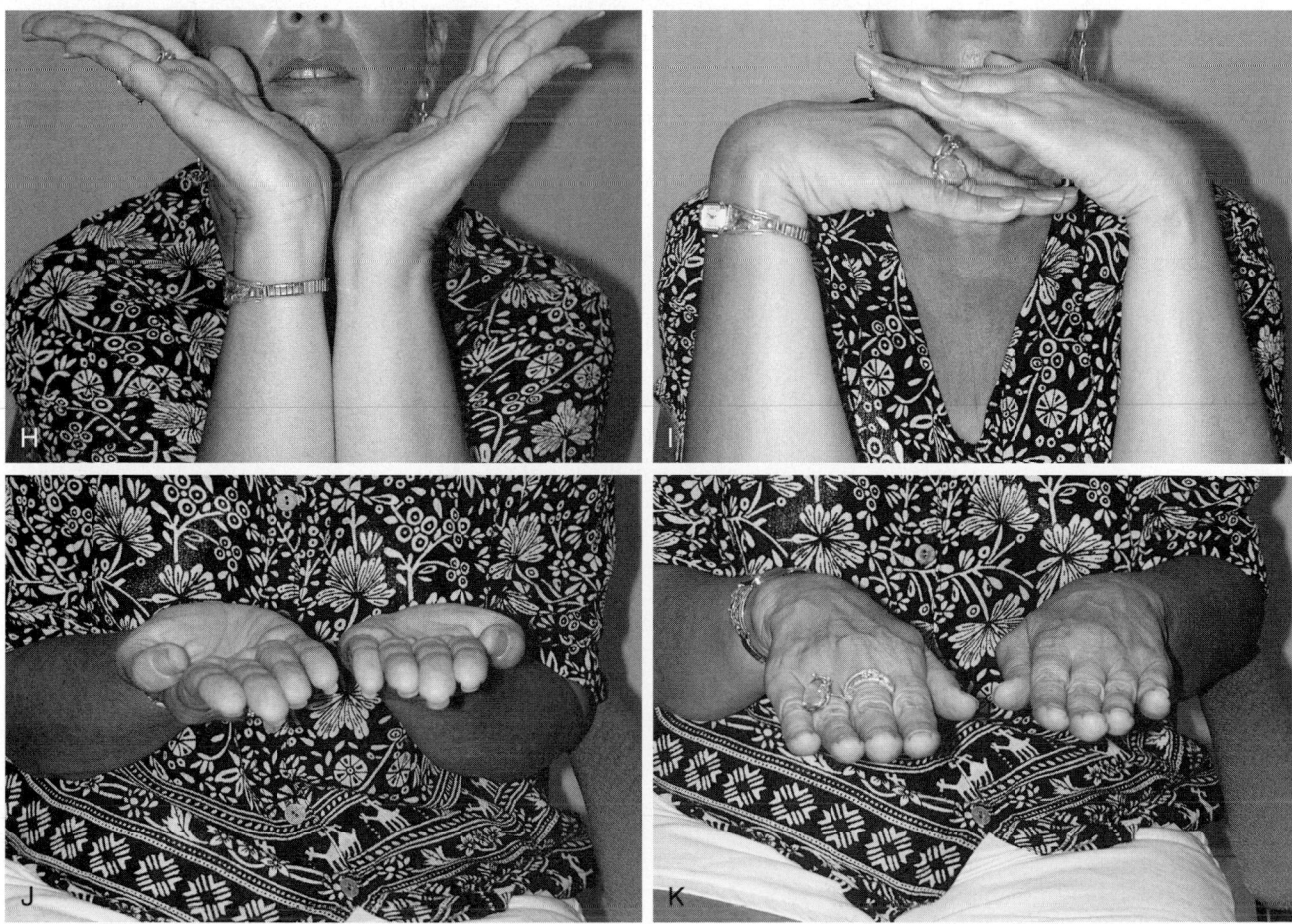

**FIGURE 40–32** *Continued.* Motion of the wrist (*H, I*) and forearm (*J, K*).

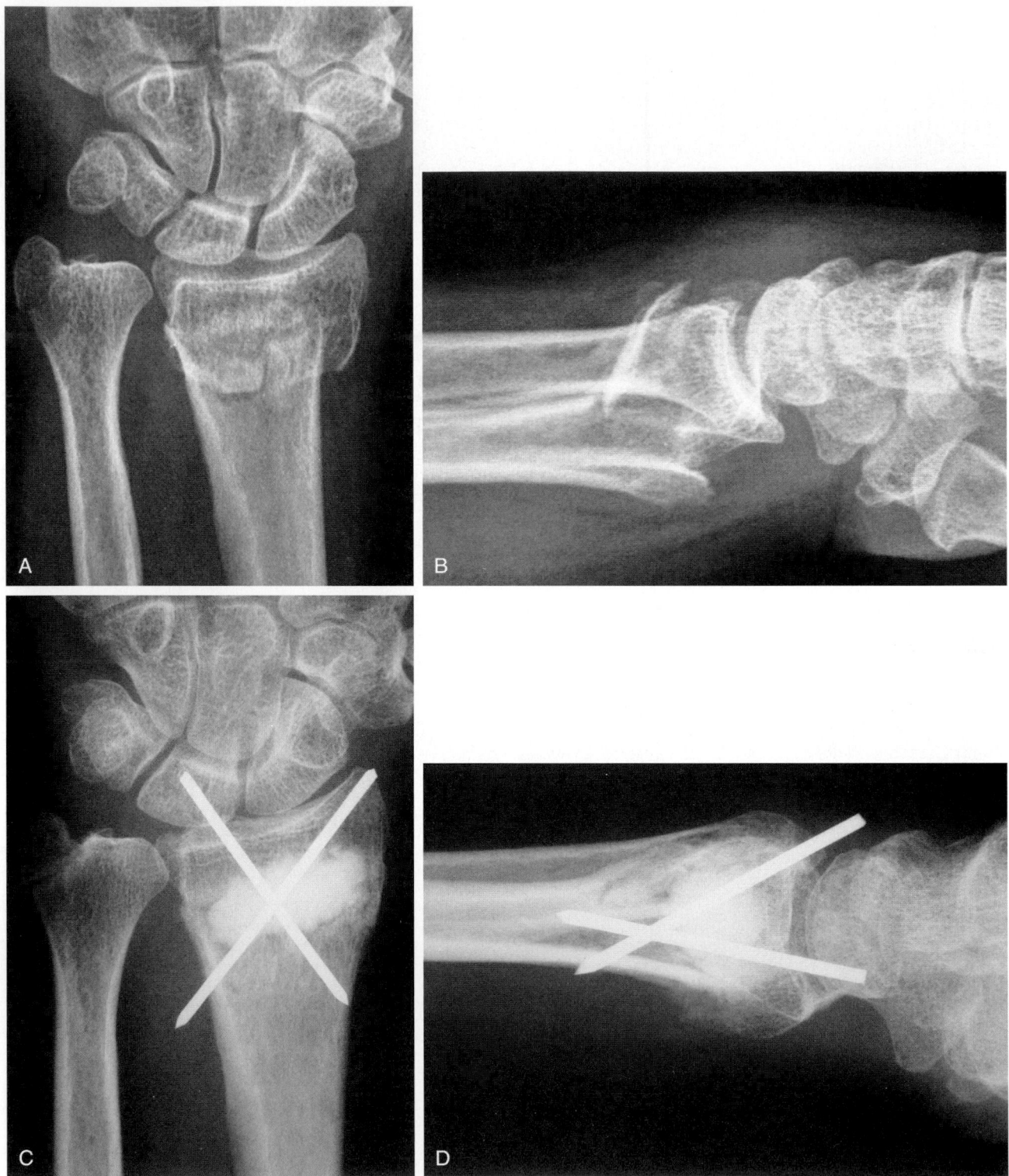

**Figure 40–33.** Posteroanterior (*A*) and lateral (*B*) radiographs of an unstable distal radius fracture. *C, D,* Postoperative radiographs following reduction and stabilization with K-wires and a carbonated apatite cement used to fill the metaphyseal fracture defect.

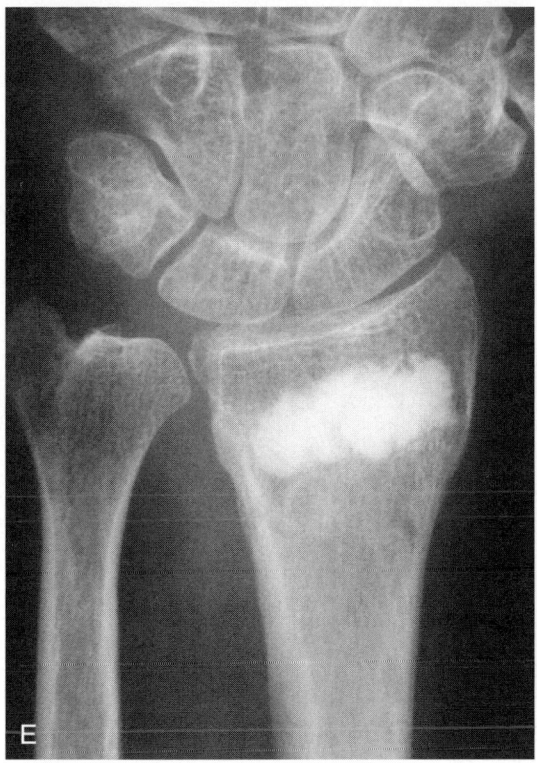
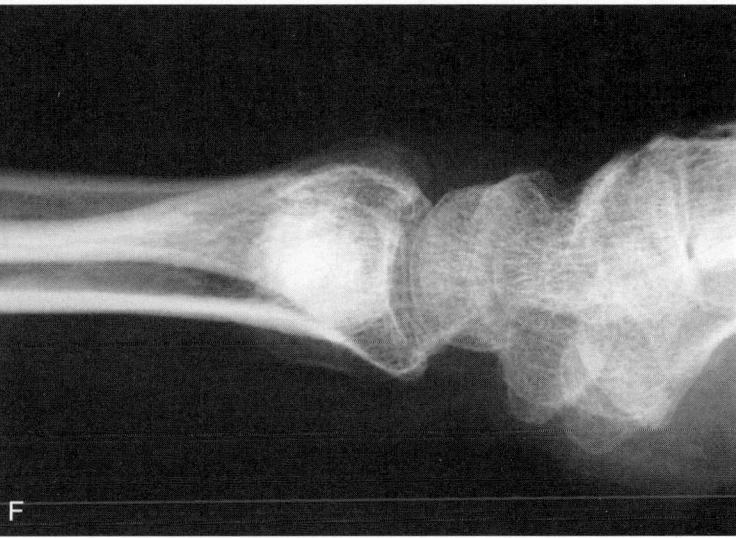

**FIGURE 40–33** *Continued. E, F,* Follow-up radiographs show maintenance of reduction despite an early range of motion program. This bone replacement material hardens, providing a supportive buttress for the distal fragment. It may be particularly beneficial in older patients with osteoporotic bone, allowing an earlier return to function.

## SUMMARY

Fractures of the distal radius are common, particularly in older persons. A favorable outcome, even in the presence of mild residual deformity, can be anticipated in most patients with low functional requirements. More aggressive intervention is becoming recognized as more appropriate in higher-demand, younger individuals. As expressed by Edwards and Clayton in 1929, "What would be considered a good result in an old arthritic patient might be deplored as a comparative failure in a young working man."[54]

Treatment must be individualized to the given fracture pattern, energy of injury, associated problems, quality of bone, functional requirements, and patient compliance far more than simply to the chronologic age of the individual. The restoration and maintenance of anatomy enhance the potential for a full functional recovery. Attention to detail and careful patient follow-up are critical, whether simple cast immobilization, external skeletal fixation, or a formal open reduction with internal fixation is used.

### REFERENCES

1. Abbaszadegan, H.; Johnsson, U.; von Sivers, K. Prediction of instability of Colles' fractures. Acta Orthop Scand 60:646–650, 1989.
2. Adolfsson, L.; Jorgsholm, P. Arthroscopically-assisted reduction of intra-articular fractures of the distal radius. J Hand Surg [Br] 23:391–395, 1998.
3. Ahlborg, H.G.; Josefsson, P.O. Pin-tract complications in external fixation of fractures of the distal radius. Acta Orthop Scand 70:116–118, 1999.
4. Alffram, P.A.; G'doran, C.H.B. Epidemiology of fractures of the forearm. J Bone Joint Surg Am 44.105–114, 1962.
5. Altissimi, M.; Antenucci, R.; Fiacca, C.; Mancini, G.B. Long-term results of conservative treatment of fractures of the distal radius. Clin Orthop 206:202–210, 1986.
6. Andersen, D.J.; Blair, W.F.; Steyers, C.M., Jr.; et al. Classification of distal radius fractures: An analysis of interobserver reliability and intraobserver reproducibility. J Hand Surg [Am] 21:574–560, 1996.
7. Anderson, R.; O'Neill, G. Comminuted fractures of the distal end of the radius. Surg Gynecol Obstet 78:434–440, 1944.
8. Aro, H.; Koirunen, J.; Katevuo, K.; et al. Late compression neuropathies after Colles' fractures. Clin Orthop 233:217–225, 1988.
9. Atkins, R.M.; Duckworth, J.; Kanis, J.A. Algodystrophy following Colles' fracture. J Hand Surg [Br] 14:161–164, 1989.
10. Axelrod, T.J.; McMurtry, R.Y. Open reduction and internal fixation of comminuted intra-articular fractures of the distal radius. J Hand Surg [Am] 15:1–11, 1990.
11. Axelrod, T.; Paley, D.; Green, J.; McMurtry, R.Y. Limited open reduction of the lunate facet in comminuted intra-articular fractures of the distal radius. J Hand Surg [Am] 13:372–377, 1988.
12. Bacorn, R.W.; Kurtzke, J.F. Colles' fracture: A study of 2,000 cases from the NY State Workmen's Compensation Board. J Bone Joint Surg Am 35:643–658, 1953.
13. Baratz, M.E.; DesJardins, J.D.; Anderson, D.D.; Imbriglia, J.E. Displaced intra-articular fractures of the distal radius: The effect of fracture displacement on contact stresses in a cadaver model. J Hand Surg [Am] 21:183–188, 1996.
14. Bartosh, R.A.; Saldana, M.J. Intra-articular fractures of the distal radius: A cadaveric study to determine if ligamentotaxis restores radiopalmar tilt. J Hand Surg [Am] 15:18–21, 1990.
15. Bass, R.L.; Blair, W.F.; Hubbard, P.P. Results of combined internal and external fixation for the treatment of severe AO–C3 fractures of the distal radius. J Hand Surg [Am] 20:373–381, 1995.
16. Bell, M.J.; Hill, R.J.; McMurtry, R.Y. Ulnar impingement syndrome. J Bone Joint Surg Br 67:126–129, 1985.

17. Benoist, L.A.; Freeland, A.E. Buttress pinning in the unstable distal radius fracture. J Hand Surg [Br] 20:82–96, 1995.

18. Bickerstaff, D.R.; Bell, M.J. Carpal malalignment in Colles' fractures. J Hand Surg [Br] 14:155–160, 1989.

19. Biyani, A.; Simison, A.J.M.; Klenerman, L. Fractures of the distal radius and ulna. J Hand Surg [Br] 20:357–364, 1995.

20. Böhler, L.B. Die funktionelle Bewegungsbehandlung der "typischen Radiusbrueche." M'dunch Medi Wochenschr 20:387, 1923.

21. Bower, W.H. The distal radioulnar joint. In: Green, D.P., ed. Operative Hand Surgery, 2nd ed. Philadelphia, J.B. Lippincott, 1988, pp. 939–989.

22. Bradway, J.; Amadio, P.C.; Cooney, W.P. Open reduction and internal fixation of displaced, comminuted intra-articular fractures of the distal end of the radius. J Bone Joint Surg Am 71:839–847, 1989.

23. Brand, P.W.; Beach, R.B.; Thompson, D.E. Relative tension and potential excursion of muscles in the forearm and hand. J Hand Surg [Br] 3:209–219, 1981.

24. Bronstein, A.J.; Trumble, T.E.; Tencer, A.F. The effects of distal radius fracture malalignment on forearm rotation: A cadaveric study. J Hand Surg [Am] 22:258–262, 1997.

25. Bruno, R.J.; Cohen, M.S.; Berzins, A.; Sumner, D.R. Bone graft harvesting from the distal radius, olecranon and iliac crest: A quantitative analysis. J Hand Surg [Am] 26:135–141, 2001.

26. Cannegieter, D.M.; Juttmann, J.W. Cancellous grafting and external fixation for unstable Colles' fractures. J Bone Joint Surg Br 79:428–432, 1997.

27. Cassidy, C.; Jupiter, J.; Delli-Santi, M.; et al. Norian SRS versus conventional therapy in distal radius fractures: Minimum one-year follow-up on 323 patients. American Society for Surgery of the Hand 54th Annual Meeting, Boston, September, 1999.

28. Castaing, J. Les fractures recentes de l'extremité inferieure du radius chez l'adulte. Rev Chir Orthop 50:581, 1964.

29. Carrozzella, J.; Stern, P.J. Treatment of comminuted distal radius fractures with pins and plaster. Hand Clin 4:391–397, 1988.

30. Carter, P.R.; Frederick, H.A.; Laseter, G.F. Open reduction and internal fixation of unstable distal radius fractures with a low-profile plate: A multicenter study of 73 fractures. J Hand Surg [Am] 23:300–307, 1998.

31. Cassebaum, W.H. Colles' fracture. A study of end results. JAMA 143:963–965, 1950.

32. Catalano, L.W. III; Cole, R.J.; Gelberman, R.H.; et al. Displaced intra-articular fractures of the distal aspect of the radius. Long-term results in young adults after open reduction and internal fixation. J Bone Joint Surg Am 79:1290–1302, 1997.

33. Chapman, D.R.; Bennett, J.B.; Bryan, W.J.; Tullos, H.S. Complications of distal radius fractures: Pins and plaster treatment. J Hand Surg [Am] 7:509–512, 1982.

34. Clancey, G.J. Percutaneous Kirschner wire fixation of Colles' fractures. J Bone Joint Surg Am 66:1008–1014, 1984.

35. Clyburn, T.A. Dynamic external fixation for comminuted intra-articular fractures of the distal end of the radius. J Bone Joint Surg Am 69:248–254, 1987.

36. Cohen M.S.; Whitman, K. Calcium phosphate bone cement—The Norian skeletal repair system in orthopedic surgery. AORN J 65:958–962, 1997.

37. Cole, J.M.; Obletz, B.E. Comminuted fractures of the distal end of the radius treated by skeletal transfixion in plaster cast: An end result study of thirty-three cases. J Bone Joint Surg Am 48:931–945, 1966.

38. Cole, R.J.; Bindra, R.R.; Evanoff, B.A.; et al. Radiographic evaluation of osseous displacement following intra-articular fractures of the distal radius: Reliability of plain radiography versus computed tomography. J Hand Surg [Am] 22:792–800, 1997.

39. Collert, S.; Isacson, J. Management of redislocated Colles' fractures. Clin Orthop 135:183–186, 1978.

40. Colles, A. On the fracture of the carpal extremity of the radius. Edinb Med Surg J 10:182–186, 1814.

41. Constantz, B.R.; Ison, I.C.; Fulmer, M.T.; et al. Skeletal repair by in situ formation of the minimal phase of bone. Science 267:1796–1799, 1995.

42. Cooney, W.P. Management of Colles' fractures. Editorial. J Hand Surg [Br] 14:137–139, 1989.

43. Cooney, W.P.; Berger, R.A. Treatment of complex fractures of the distal radius: Combined use of internal and external fixation and arthroscopic reduction. Hand Clin 9:603–612, 1993.

44. Cooney, W.P.; Dobyns, J.H.; Linscheid, R.L. Complications of Colles' fractures. J Bone Joint Surg Am 62:613–619, 1980.

45. Cooney, W.P.; Linscheid, R.L.; Dobyns, J.H. External pin fixation for unstable Colles' fractures. J Bone Joint Surg Am 61:840–845, 1979.

46. Culp, R.W.; Osterman, A.L. Arthroscopic reduction and internal fixation of distal radius fractures. Orthop Clin North Am 26:739–748, 1995.

47. De Oliveira, J.C. Barton's fractures. J Bone Joint Surg Am 55:586–594, 1973.

48. De Palma, A.F. Comminuted fractures of the distal end of the radius treated by ulnar pinning. J Bone Joint Surg Am 34:651–662, 1952.

49. Dias, J.J.; Wray, C.C.; Jones, J.M.; Gregg, P.J. The value of early mobilization in the treatment of Colles' fractures. J Bone Joint Surg Br 69:463–467, 1987.

50. Dobyns, J.H.; Linscheid, R.L. Complications of treatment of fractures and dislocations of the wrist. In: Epps, C.H., Jr., ed. Complications in Orthopaedic Surgery. Philadelphia, J.B. Lippincott, 1978, pp. 271–352.

51. Doi, K.; Hattori, Y.; Otsuka, K.; et al. Intra-articular fractures of the distal aspect of the radius: Arthroscopically assisted reduction compared with open reduction and internal fixation. J Bone Joint Surg Am 81:1093–1110, 1999.

52. Dowling, J.J.; Sawyer, B., Jr. Comminuted Colles' fractures. Evaluation of a method of treatment. J Bone Joint Surg Am 34:651–662, 1952.

53. Dunning, C.E.; Lindsay, C.S.; Bicknell, R.T.; et al. Supplemental pinning improves the stability of external fixation in distal radius fractures during simulated finger and forearm motion. J Hand Surg [Am] 24:992–1000, 1999.

54. Edwards, H.; Clayton, E.B. Fractures of the lower end of the radius in adults. BMJ 1:61–65, 1929.

55. Einhorn, T.A. Current concepts review: Enhancement of fracture healing. J Bone Joint Surg Am 77:940–956, 1995.

56. Ekenstam, F.; Engkvist, O.; Wadin, K.; et al. Results from resection of the distal end of the ulna after fractures of the lower end of the radius. Scand J Plast Reconstr Surg 16:177–181, 1982.

57. Ellis, J. Smith's and Barton's fractures: A method of treatment. J Bone Joint Surg Br 47:724–727, 1965.

58. Epner, R.A.; Bowers, W.H.; Guilford, W.B. Ulnar variance: The effect of wrist positioning and roentgen filming technique. J Hand Surg [Am] 7:298–305, 1982.

59. Fernandez, D.L. Correction of post-traumatic wrist deformity in adults by osteotomy, bone grafting and internal fixation. J Bone Joint Surg Am 64:1164–1178, 1982.

60. Fernandez, D.L. Avantbras segment distal. In: M'dueller, M.E.; Nazarian, S.; Koch, P., eds. Classification AO des Fractures: Les Os Longs. Berlin, Springer Verlag, 1987, pp. 106–115.

61. Fernandez, D.L. Radial osteotomy and Bowers arthroplasty for malunited fractures of the distal end of the radius. J Bone Joint Surg Am 70:1538–1551, 1988.

62. Fernandez, D.L. Reconstructive procedures for malunion and traumatic arthritis. Orthop Clin North Am 24:341–363, 1993.

63. Fitoussi, F.; Ip, W.Y.; Chow, S.P. Treatment of displaced intra-articular fractures of the distal end of the radius with plates. J Bone Joint Surg Am 79:1303–1312, 1997.

64. Flinkkila, T.; Nikkola-Sihot, A.; Kaarela, O.; et al. Poor interobserver reliability of AO classification of fractures of the distal radius. Additional computed tomography is of minor value. J Bone Joint Surg Br 80:670–672, 1998.

65. Flinkkila, T.; Raatikainen, T.; Kaarela, O.; Hamalainen, M. Corrective osteotomy for malunion of the distal radius. Arch Orthop Trauma Surg 120:23–26, 2000.

66. Friberg, S.; Lindstrom, B. Radiographic measurements of the radiocarpal joint in normal adults. Acta Radiol (Stockh) 17:249, 1976.

67. Frykman, G. Fracture of the distal radius including sequelae: Shoulder hand finger syndrome, disturbance in the distal radioulnar joint and impairment of nerve function. A clinical and experimental study. Acta Orthop Scand Suppl 108:1–155, 1967.

68. Gartland, J.J., Jr.; Werley, C.W. Evaluation of healed Colles' fractures. J Bone Joint Surg Am 33:895–907, 1951.

69. Geissler, W.B.; Fernandez, D.L. Percutaneous and limited open reduction of the articular surface of the distal radius. J Orthop Trauma 5:255–264, 1991.

70. Geissler, W.B.; Freeland, A.E. Arthroscopically assisted reduction of intra-articular distal radial fractures. Clin Orthop 327:125–134, 1996.

71. Geissler W.B.; Freeland, A.E. Arthroscopic management of intra-articular distal radius fractures. Hand Clin 15:455–465, 1999.

72. Gelberman, R.H.; Salamon, P.B.; Jurist, J.M.; Posch, J.L. Ulnar shortening in Kienböck's disease. J Bone Joint Surg Am 57:674–676, 1975.

73. Gelberman, R.H.; Szabo, R.M.; Mortensen, W.W. Carpal tunnel pressures and wrist position in patients with Colles' fractures. J Trauma 24:747–749, 1984.

74. Golden, G.N. Treatment and programs of Colles' fracture. Lancet 1:511–514, 1963.

75. Green, D.P. Pins and plaster treatment of comminuted fractures of the distal end of the radius. J Bone Joint Surg Am 57:304–310, 1975.

76. Green, D.P.; O'Brien, E.T. Open reduction of carpal dislocation: Indications and operative techniques. J Hand Surg [Am] 3:250–265, 1978.

77. Hanker, G.J. Arthroscopic evaluation of intra-articular distal radius fractures. Presented at the Annual Meeting of the American Society for Surgery of the Hand, Orlando, Florida, 1991.

78. Harper, W.M.; Jones, J.M. Nonunion of Colles' fracture: Report of two cases. J Hand Surg [Br] 15:121–123, 1990.

79. Hastings, H. Treatment of complex distal radial fractures. Adv Op Orthop 2:227–277, 1994.

80. Hastings, H.; Leibovic, S.J. Indications and techniques of open reduction: Internal fixation of distal radius fractures. Orthop Clin North Am 24:309–326, 1993.

81. Herrera, M.; Chapman, C.B.; Roh, M.; et al. Treatment of unstable distal radius fractures with cancellous allograft and external fixation. J Hand Surg [Am] 24:1269–1278, 1999.

82. Hinzpeter, D.A.; Jupiter, J.B.; Moreno, R.; Roberge, C. Carpal alignment after corrective osteotomy for malunited fractures of distal radius. Presented at the American Society for Surgery of the Hand 54th Annual Meeting, Boston, September, 1999.

83. Hollingsworth, R.; Morris, J. The importance of the ulnar side of the wrist in fractures of the distal end of the radius. Injury 7:263–266, 1976.

84. Hove, L.M. Nerve entrapment and reflex sympathetic dystrophy after fractures of the distal radius. Nerve entrapment and reflex sympathetic dystrophy after fractures of the distal radius. Scand J Plast Reconstr Surg Hand Surg 29:53–58, 1995.

85. Howard, P.W.; Stewart, H.D.; Hind, R.E.; Burke, F.D. External fixation or plaster for severely displaced comminuted Colles' fractures? J Bone Joint Surg Br 71:68–73, 1989.

86. Jakob, R.P.; Fernandez, D.L. The treatment of wrist fractures with the small AO external fixation device. In: Uhthoff, H.K., ed. Current Concepts of External Fixation of Fractures. Berlin, Springer Verlag, 1982, pp. 307–314.

87. Jenkins, N.H. The unstable Colles' fracture. J Hand Surg [Br] 14:149–154, 1989.

88. Jenkins, N.H.; Jones, D.G.; Johnson, S.R.; Mintowt-Czyz, W.T. External fixation of Colles' fractures: An anatomical study. J Bone Joint Surg Br 69:207–211, 1987.

89. Johnston, G.H.; Friedman, L.; Kriegler, J.C. Computerized tomographic evaluation of acute distal radius fractures. J Hand Surg [Am] 17:738–744, 1992.

90. Jupiter, J.B. Current concepts review: Fractures of the distal end of the radius. J Bone Joint Surg Am 73:461–469, 1991.

91. Jupiter, J.G.; Fernandez, D.L. Comparative classification for fractures of the distal end of the radius. J Hand Surg [Am] 22:563–571, 1997.

92. Jupiter, J.G.; Fernandez, D.L.; Toh, C.L.; et al. Operative treatment of volar intra-articular fractures of the distal end of the radius. J Bone Joint Surg Am 78:1817–1828, 1996.

93. Jupiter, J.B.; Masem, M. Reconstruction of post-traumatic deformity of the distal radius and ulna. Hand Clin 4:377–390, 1988.

94. Jupiter, J.B.; Lipton, H. Operative treatment of intra-articular fractures of the distal radius. Clin Orthop 292:48–61, 1993.

95. Jupiter, J.B.; Ring, D. A comparison of early and late reconstruction of malunited fractures of the distal end of the radius. J Bone Joint Surg Am 78:739–748, 1996.

96. Jupiter, J.B.; Winters, S.; Sigman, S.; et al. Repair of five distal radius fractures with an investigational cancellous bone cement: a preliminary report. J Orthop Trauma 22:110–116, 1997.

97. Kazuki, K.; Masakata, K.; Shimazu, A. Pressure distribution in the radial carpal joint measured with a densitometer designed for pressure sensitive film. J Hand Surg [Am] 16:401–408, 1991.

98. Kapoor, H.; Agarwal, A.; Dhaon, K. Displaced intra-articular fractures of distal radius: A comparative evaluation of results following closed reduction, external fixation and open reduction with internal fixation. Injury 31:75–79, 2000.

99. Kihara, H.; Palmer, A.K.; Werner, F.W.; et al. The effect of dorsally angulated distal radius fractures on distal radioulnar joint congruency and forearm rotation. J Hand Surg [Am] 21:40–47, 1996.

100. Klein, W.; Dee, W.; Rieger, H.; et al. Results of transarticular fixator application in distal radius fractures. Injury 31(suppl. 1):71–77, 2000.

101. Knirk, J.L.; Jupiter, J.B. Intra-articular fractures of the distal end of the radius in young adults. J Bone Joint Surg Am 68:647–659, 1986.

102. Kopylov, P.; Jonsson, K.; Thorngren, K.G.; Aspenberg, P. Injectable calcium phosphate in the treatment of distal radial fractures. J Hand Surg [Br] 21:768–771, 1996.

103. Kozin, S.H.; Wood, M.B. Early soft tissue complications after fractures of the distal part of the radius. J Bone Joint Surg Am 75:144–153, 1993.

104. Kreder, H.J.; Hanel, D.P.; McKee, M.; et al. Consistency of AO fracture classification for the distal radius. J Bone Joint Surg Br 78:726–731, 1996.

105. Ladd, A.L.; Pliam, N.B. Use of bone-graft substitutes in distal radius fractures. J Am Acad Orthop Surg 7:279–290, 1999.

106. LaFontaine, M.; Hardy, D.; Delince, P.H. Stability assessment of distal radius fractures. Injury 20:208–210, 1989.

107. Leung, K.S.; Tsang, H.K.; Chiu, K.H.; et al. An effective treatment of comminuted fractures of the distal radius. J Hand Surg [Am] 15:11–17, 1990.

108. Lewis, M.H. Median nerve decompression after Colles' fracture. J Bone Joint Surg Br 60:195–196, 1978.

109. Lidstrom, A. Fractures of the distal radius: A clinical and statistical study of end results. Acta Orthop Scand 41:1–118, 1959.

110. Lindau, T.; Adlercreutz, C.; Aspenberg, P. Peripheral tears of the triangular fibrocartilage complex cause distal radioulnar joint instability after distal radial fractures. J Hand Surg [Am] 25:464–468, 2000.

111. Lindau, T.; Arner, M.; Hagberg, L. Intra-articular lesions in distal fractures of the radius in young adults. A descriptive arthroscopic study in 50 patients. J Hand Surg [Br] 22:638–643, 1997.

112. Linder, L.; Stattin, J. Malunited fractures of the distal radius with volar angulation: Corrective osteotomy in six cases using the volar approach. Acta Orthop Scand 67:179–181, 1996.

113. Lucas, G.L.; Sachtjen, K.M. An analysis of hand function in patients with Colles' fractures treated by Rush rod fixation. Clin Orthop 155:172–179, 1981.

114. Lundy, D.W.; Quisling, S.G.; Lourie, G.M.; et al. Tilted lateral radiographs in the evaluation of intra-articular distal radius fractures. J Hand Surg [Am] 24:249–256, 1999.

115. Lynch, A.C.; Lipscomb, P.R. The carpal tunnel syndrome and Colles' fractures. JAMA 185:363–366, 1963.

116. Mack, G.R.; McPherson, S.A.; Lutz, R.B. Acute median neuropathy after wrist trauma: The role of emergent carpal tunnel release. Clin Orthop 3:141–146, 1994.

117. Marx, R.G.; Axelrod, T.S. Intra-articular osteotomy of distal radial malunions. Clin Orthop 327:152–157, 1996.

118. McBride, E.D. Disability Evaluation, 4th ed. Philadelphia, J.B. Lippincott, 1948.

119. McCarroll, H.R., Jr. Nerve injuries associated with wrist trauma. Orthop Clin North Am 15:279–287, 1984.

120. McMurtry, R.Y.; Jupiter, J.B. Fractures of the distal radius. In: Browner, B.; Jupiter, J.; Levine, A.; Trafton, P., eds. Skeletal Trauma. Philadelphia, W.B. Saunders, 1992, pp. 1063–1094.

121. McQueen, M.M. Redisplaced unstable fractures of the distal radius. A randomized, prospective study of bridging versus non-bridging external fixation. J Bone Joint Surg Br 80:665–669, 1998.

122. McQueen, M.; Caspers, J. Colles' fracture: Does the anatomic result affect the final function? J Bone Joint Surg Br 70:649–651, 1988.

123. McQueen, M.M.; MacLaren, A.; Chalmers, J. The value of remanipulating Colles' fractures. J Bone Joint Surg Br 68:232–233, 1986.

124. Melone, C.P., Jr. Articular fractures of the distal radius. Orthop Clin North Am 15:217–236, 1984.

125. Melone, C.P., Jr. Open treatment for displaced articular fractures of the distal radius. Clin Orthop 202:103–111, 1986.

126. Miyake T.; Hashizume H.; Inoue H.; et al. Malunited Colles' fracture: Analysis of stress distribution. J Hand Surg [Br] 19:737–742, 1994.

127. Mohanti, R.C.; Kar, N. Study of triangular fibrocartilage of the wrist joint in Colles' fracture. Injury 11:321–324, 1980.

128. Mudgal, C.; Hastings, H. Scapholunate diastasis in fractures of the distal radius: Pathomechanics and treatment options. J Hand Surg [Br] 18:725–729, 1993.

129. Müller, M.E.; Nazarian, S.; Koch, P.; eds. Classification AO des Fractures: Les Os Longs. Berlin, Springer Verlag, 1987.

130. Nakata, R.Y.; Chand, Y.; Matiko, J.D.; et al. External fixators for wrist fractures: A biomechanical and clinical study. J Hand Surg [Am] 10:845–851, 1985.

131. Naidu, S.H.; Capo, J.T.; Moulton, M.; et al. Percutaneous pinning of distal radius fractures: A biomechanical study. J Hand Surg [Am] 22:252–257, 1997.

132. Older, T.M.; Stabler, E.U.; Cassebaum, W.H. Colles' fracture: Evaluation of selection of therapy. J Trauma 5:469–476, 1965.

133. Oskam J.; Bongers K.M.; Karthaus A.J.; et al. Corrective osteotomy for malunion of the distal radius: The effect of concomitant ulnar shortening osteotomy. Arch Orthop Trauma Surg 115:219–222, 1996.

134. Oskam, J.; DeGraaf, J.S.; Klasen, H.J. Fractures of the distal radius and scaphoid. J Hand Surg [Br] 21:772–774, 1996.

135. Owen, R.A.; Melton, L.J.; Johnson, K.A.; et al. Incidence of a Colles' fracture in a North American community. Am J Public Health 72:605–613, 1982.

136. Palmer, A.K. Fractures of the distal radius. In: Green, D.P., ed. Operative Hand Surgery, 2nd ed. Philadelphia, J.B. Lippincott, 1988, pp. 991–1026.

137. Palmer, A.K. The distal radioulnar joint. Hand Clin 3:31–40, 1987.

138. Palmer, A.K.; Glisson, R.R.; Werner, F.W. Ulnar variance determination. J Hand Surg [Am] 7:376–379, 1982.

139. Pattee, G.A.; Thompson, G.H. Anterior and posterior marginal fracture dislocations of the distal radius. Clin Orthop 231:183–195, 1988.

140. Peltier, L.F. Fractures of the distal end of the radius: An historical account. Clin Orthop 187:18–22, 1984.

141. Peine, R.; Rikli, D.A.; Hoffmann, R.; et al. Comparison of three different plating techniques for the dorsum of the distal radius: A biomechanical study. J Hand Surg [Am] 25:29–33, 2000.

142. Pogue, D.L.; Viegas, S.F.; Patterson, R.M.; et al. Effects of distal radius fracture malunion on wrist joint mechanics. J Hand Surg [Am] 15:721–727, 1990.

143. Pool, C. Colles's fracture. A prospective study of treatment. J Bone Joint Surg Br 55:540, 1973.

144. Porter, M.L; Tillman, R.M. Pilon fractures of the wrist: Displaced intra-articular fractures of the distal radius. J Hand Surg [Br] 17:63–68, 1992.

145. Porter, M.; Stockley, I. Functional index: A numerical expression of post-traumatic wrist function. Injury 16:188–192, 1984.

146. Porter, M.; Stockley, I. Fractures of the distal radius: Intermediate and end results in relation to radiologic parameters. Clin Orthop 220:241–251, 1987.

147. Poser, M.A.; Ambrose, L. Malunited Colles' fractures: Correction with a biplanar closing wedge osteotomy. J Hand Surg [Am] 16:1017–1026, 1991.

148. Pruitt, D.L.; Gilula, L.A.; Manske, P.R.; Vannier, M.W. Computed tomography scanning with image reconstruction in evaluation of distal radius fractures. J Hand Surg [Am] 5:720–727, 1994.

149. Richards, R.S.; Bennett, J.D.; Roth, J.H.; Milne, K., Jr. Arthroscopic diagnosis of intra-articular soft tissue injuries associated with distal radial fractures. J Hand Surg [Am] 22:772–776, 1997.

150. Riis, J.; Fruensgaard, S. Treatment of unstable Colles' fractures by external fixation. J Hand Surg [Br] 14:145–148, 1989.

151. Rikli, D.A.; Kupfer, K.; Bodoky, A. Long-term results of the external fixation of distal radius fractures. J Trauma 44:970–976, 1998.

152. Rikli, D.A.; Regazzoni, P. Fractures of the distal end of the radius treated by internal fixation and early function. A preliminary report of 20 cases. J Bone Joint Surg Br 78:588–592, 1996.

153. Ring, D.; Jupiter, J.B.; Brennwald, J.; et al. Prospective multicenter trial of a plate for dorsal fixation of distal radius fractures. J Hand Surg [Am] 22:777–784, 1997.

154. Roberge, C.; Ring, D.; Jupiter, J. Comparison of structural and nonstructural bone graft for distal radius osteotomy. Presented at the American Society for Surgery of the Hand 54th Annual Meeting, Boston, September 1999.

155. Rubinovich, R.M.; Rennie, W.R. Colles' fracture: End results in relation to radiologic parameters. Can J Surg 26:361–363, 1983.

156. Saito, H.; Shibata, M. Classification of fractures at the distal end of the radius with reference to treatment of comminuted fractures. In: Boswick, J.A., Jr., ed. Current Concepts in Hand Surgery. Philadelphia, Lea & Febiger, 1983, pp. 129–145.

157. Sanchez-Sotelo, J.; Munuera, L.; Madero, R. Treatment of fractures of the distal radius with a remodellable bone cement: A prospective, randomized study using Norian SRS. J Bone Joint Surg Br 82:856–863, 2000.

158. Sarmiento, A.; Pratt, G.W.; Berry, N.C.; Sinclair, W.F. Colles' fracture: Functional bracing in supination. J Bone Joint Surg Am 57:311–317, 1975.

159. Sarmiento, A.; Zagorski, J.B.; Sinclair, W.F. Functional bracing of Colles' fractures: A prospective study of immobilization in supination vs. pronation. Clin Orthop 146:175–183, 1980.

160. Scheck, M. Long-term follow-up of treatment of comminuted fractures of the distal end of the radius by transfixation with Kirschner wires and cast. J Bone Joint Surg Am 44:337–351, 1962.

161. Segalman, K.A.; Clark, G.L. Un-united fractures of the distal radius: A report of 12 cases. J Hand Surg [Am] 23:914–919, 1998.

162. Seitz, W.H., Jr.; Putnam, M.D.; Dick, H.M. Limited open surgical approach for external fixation of distal radius fractures. J Hand Surg [Am] 15:288–293, 1990.

163. Shaw, J.A.; Bruno, A.; Paul, E.M. Ulnar styloid fixation in the treatment of post-traumatic instability of the radial ulnar joint: A biomechanical study with clinical correlation. J Hand Surg [Am] 15:712–720, 1990.

164. Shea, K.; Fernandez, D.L.; Jupiter, J.B.; Martin, C., Jr. Corrective osteotomy for malunited, volarly displaced fractures of the distal end of the radius. J Bone Joint Surg Am 79:1816–1826, 1997.

165. Short, W.H.; Palmer, A.K.; Werner, F.W.; Murphy, D.J. A biochemical study of distal radial fractures. J Hand Surg [Am]12:529–534, 1987.

166. Smaill, G.B. Long-term follow-up of Colles' fracture. J Bone Joint Surg Br 47:80–85, 1965.

167. Solgaard, S. Classification of distal radius fractures. Acta Orthop Scand 56:249–252, 1985.

168. Solgaard, S.; Binger, C.; Soelund, K. Displaced distal radius fractures. Arch Orthop Trauma Surg 109:34–38, 1989.

169. Sommerkamp, T.G.; Seeman, M.; Silliman, J.; et al. Dynamic external fixation of unstable fractures of the distal part of the radius. J Bone Joint Surg Am 76:1049–1161, 1994.

170. Sponsel, K.H.; Palm, E.T. Carpal tunnel syndrome following Colles' fracture. Surg Gynecol Obstet 121:1252–1256, 1965.

171. Stein, A.H., Jr.; Katz, S.F. Stabilization of comminuted fractures of the distal inch of the radius: Percutaneous pinning. Clin Orthop 108:174–181, 1975.

172. Stein, A.H. The relation of median nerve compression to Sudek's syndrome. Surg Gynecol Obstet 115:713–720, 1962.

173. Steinberg, B.D.; Plancher, K.D.; Idler, R.S. Percutaneous Kirschner wire fixation though the snuff box: An anatomic study. J Hand Surg [Am] 20:57–62, 1995.

174. Stewart, H.D.; Innes, A.R.; Burke, F.D. Factors affecting the outcome of Colles' fracture: An anatomical and functional study. Injury 16:289–295, 1985.

175. Stewart, H.D.; Innes, A.R.; Burke, F.D. The hand complications of Colles' fractures. J Hand Surg [Br] 10:103–106, 1985.

176. Szabo, R.M.; Weber, S.C. Comminuted intra-articular fractures of the distal radius. Clin Orthop 230:39–48, 1988.

177. Taleisnik, J.; Watson, H.K. Midcarpal instability caused by malunited fractures of the distal radius. J Hand Surg [Am] 9:350–357, 1984.

178. Terral, T.G.; Freeland, A.E. Early salvage reconstruction of severe distal radius fractures. Clin Orthop 327:147–151, 1996.

179. Thompson, G.H.; Grant, T.T. Barton's fractures–reverse Barton's fractures: Confusing eponyms. Clin Orthop 122:210–221, 1977.

180. Trumble, T.; Glisson, R.R.; Seaber, A.V.; Urbaniak, J.R. A biochemical comparison of the methods for treating Kienböck's disease. J Hand Surg [Am] 11:88–93, 1986.

181. Trumble, T.E.; Wagner, W.; Hanel, D.P.; et al. Intrafocal (Kapandji) pinning of distal radius fractures with and without external fixation. J Hand Surg [Am] 23:381–394, 1998.

182. van der Linden, W.; Ericson, R. Colles' fracture: How should its displacement be measured and how should it be immobilized? J Bone Joint Surg Am 63:1285–1291, 1981.

183. Vaughn, P.A.; Lui, S.M.; Harrington, I.J.; Maistrelli, G.L. Treatment of unstable fractures of the distal radius by external fixation. J Bone Joint Surg Br 67:385–389, 1985.

184. Villar, R.N.; Marsh, D.; Rushton, N.; Greatorex, R.A. Three years after Colles' fracture. J Bone Joint Surg Br 69:635–638, 1987.

185. Wagner, W.F., Jr.; Tencer, A.F.; Kiser, P.; Trumble, T.E. Effects of intra-articular distal radius depression on wrist joint contact characteristics. J Hand Surg [Am] 21:554–560, 1996.

186. Weber, E.R. A rational approach for the recognition and treatment of Colles' fractures. Hand Clin 3:13–21, 1987.

187. Weber, S.C.; Szabo, R.M. Severely comminuted distal radial fracture as an unsolved problem: Complications associated with external fixation and pins and plaster techniques. J Hand Surg [Am] 11:157–165, 1986.

188. Werner, F.W.; Murphy, D.J.; Palmer, A.K. Pressures in the distal radial ulnar joint: Effect of surgical procedures used for Kienböck's disease. J Orthop Res 7:445–450, 1989.

189. Wolfe, S.W.; Austin, G.; Lorenze, M.; et al. A biomechanical comparison of different wrist external fixators with and without K-wire augmentation. J Hand Surg [Am] 24:516–524, 1999.

190. Wolfe, S.W.; Easterling, K.J.; Yoo, H.H. Arthroscopic-assisted reduction of distal radius fractures. Arthroscopy 11:706–714, 1995.

191. Wolfe, S.W.; Pike, L.; Slade, J.F. III; Katz, L.D. Augmentation of distal radius fracture fixation with coralline hydroxyapatite bone graft substitute. J Hand Surg [Am] 24:816–827, 1999.

192. Wolfe, S.W.; Swigart, C.R.; Grauer, J.; et al. Augmented external fixation of distal radius fractures: A biomechanical analysis. J Hand Surg [Am] 23:127–134, 1998.

193. Wright, T. Osteotomy for distal radius malunion. Tech Hand Upper Extrem Surg 4:222–235, 2000.

194. Yetkinler, D.N.; Ladd, A.L.; Poser, R.D.; et al. Biomechanical evaluation of fixation of intra-articular fractures of the distal part of the radius in cadavera: Kirschner wires compared with calcium-phosphate bone cement. J Bone Joint Surg Am 81:391–399, 1999.

195. Young, B.T.; Rayan, G.M. Outcome following nonoperative treatment of displaced distal radius fractures in low-demand patients older than 60 years. J Hand Surg [Am] 25:19–28, 2000.

196. Zanotti, R.M.; Louis, D.S. Intra-articular fractures of the distal end of the radius treated with an adjustable fixator system. J Hand Surg [Am] 22:428–440, 1997.

# CHAPTER 41

# Diaphyseal Fractures of the Forearm

Jesse B. Jupiter, M.D.
James F. Kellam, M.D., F.R.C.S.(C.)

The supporting skeleton and articulations of the upper extremity serve to position its terminal unit, the hand, in space. In the adult, exacting management of diaphyseal fractures of the radius and ulna is necessary to ensure forearm motion. These injuries can even be viewed as intra-articular fractures with the forearm "joint" providing supination and pronation. Unsatisfactory treatment can lead to loss of motion as well as muscle imbalance and disability of hand function.[44, 85, 124]

The inherent difficulties in the management of forearm fractures have long been recognized.[8, 35, 62, 106, 134] With the exception of Evans,[44] most investigators have been unable to achieve acceptable results in the adult forearm fracture with closed reduction and plaster cast immobilization.[8, 13] Even in Evans' series, there was a loss of more than 50° of forearm rotation in almost 30% of patients. Hughston[62] noted an exceptionally high rate of unsatisfactory results in isolated displaced radius (Galeazzi) fractures. Charnley,[26] writing in his classic book emphasizing the nonoperative method of fracture care, recommended operative treatment of adult forearm fractures.

Early operative efforts had disappointing outcomes that were caused by inadequate methods of internal fixation as much as any other factor. Knight and Purvis[74] reported on a high rate of nonunion with inadequate plate fixation despite additional plaster immobilization. Smith and Sage[133] developed a specific intramedullary nail for the radius and ulna. Their approach required open reduction and an above-elbow cast for 3 months, yet a nonunion rate of almost 7% was observed. Marek[83] modified the nailing approach, developing a square nail and changing the insertion point in the radius from the styloid to Lister's tubercle. An operative exposure and above-elbow cast were required. Although union was described as 100%, an unsatisfactory functional outcome was observed in 22%.

Perhaps in no other area of the appendicular skeleton has plate fixation had as dramatic an impact as in diaphyseal fractures of the adult forearm. Burwell and Charnley[22] published a landmark paper in 1964 in which they reviewed 218 fractures in 150 patients treated with noncompressing Burns or Sherman plates. Even with these now antiquated plates, the authors noted excellent results, provided that the plates were at least 3.5 inches long and had six or more screws and that fracture comminution did not exceed 50% of the cortical diameter. Plaster immobilization was infrequently used.

The advent of the compression plate originated by Danis in 1947 extended the percentage of predictable functional outcome after forearm plating.[32] In 1975, Anderson and colleagues[3] published their experience using the principles of stable fixation put forth by the Association for the Study of Internal Fixation (AO/ASIF) and noted union in 97.9% of radius fractures and 96.3% of ulna fractures treated with compression plates. Their results have subsequently been duplicated by a number of other investigators,* thus making compression plating of forearm fractures the standard by which all other treatments must be measured.

## GOALS OF TREATMENT

To ensure maximal functional outcome, the goals of treatment of forearm fractures should be (1) anatomic reduction of the skeleton, restoring bone length, rotation, and the interosseous space, and (2) secure fixation of the skeleton to enable early soft tissue rehabilitation.

## CLASSIFICATION OF DIAPHYSEAL FOREARM FRACTURES

To be useful, a classification must document a number of factors, including fracture location, fracture pattern, soft tissue involvement, and proximal or distal radioulnar joint (DRUJ) involvement.

---

*See references 53, 56, 59, 77, 87, 98, 105, 114, 115, 120, 145.

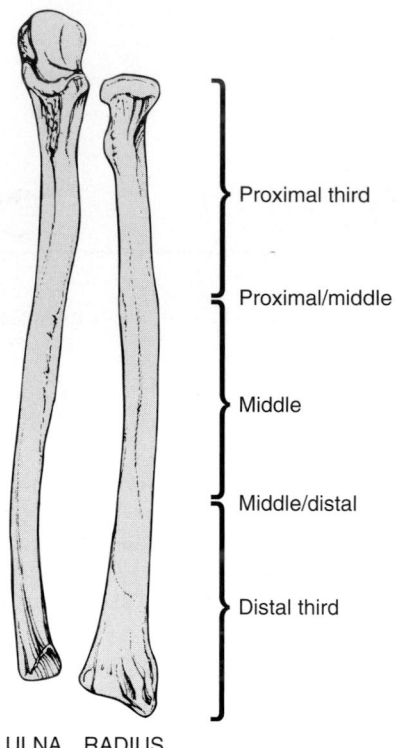

Proximal third

Proximal/middle

Middle

Middle/distal

Distal third

ULNA   RADIUS

FIGURE 41–1. Division of the forearm skeleton into thirds for surgical classification.

The forearm has been considered by many to be divided into thirds for operative considerations (Fig. 41–1). The proximal third of the radius extends from the radial tuberosity to the beginning of the radial bow. The middle third includes the radial bow to the point at which the diaphysis begins to straighten. The distal third of the radius extends out to the metaphyseal flare. The ulna, by contrast, is relatively straight and can be divided into thirds solely on the basis of linear dimensions (see Fig. 41–1). Finally, the enveloping and interconnecting soft tissues must always be considered in identifying patterns of forearm injury.

To address the need for greater specification in forearm fracture classification, the Comprehensive Classification of Fractures, developed by Müller and colleagues,[96] has been adopted by most investigators (Fig. 41–2). The acceptance of this system will become increasingly important as trauma centers compare results of treatment protocols.

## TREATMENT

### Nonoperative Indications

In the adult forearm fracture, the primary indication for nonoperative treatment is the isolated ulnar shaft fracture that has resulted from a direct blow (nightstick fracture) (Fig. 41–3). Even if the fracture is displaced by 25% to 50% of the shaft width, the ulna can be stabilized effectively with a long arm plaster cast for 8 to 10 weeks or with a functional fracture brace. The latter has been reported by Sarmiento and associates[121, 122] to maintain

the anatomic position of the bone successfully when a carefully made interosseous mold is used in the brace.

Displacement, particularly shortening, when located in the distal third of the ulna, can result in deformity of the articulation of the DRUJ. This possibility must be carefully monitored for in fractures that are treated nonoperatively.

With nondisplaced radial shaft fractures, nonoperative treatment may prove successful provided that the anatomic bow of the radius is maintained. The time to healing may be prolonged because the intact ulna prevents coaptation of the radius fracture.

### Operative Treatment

Displaced fractures of the forearm diaphysis are best treated operatively. This treatment has been most predictably accomplished with plate fixation and early functional rehabilitation. However, despite widespread acceptance of plate fixation, a number of issues remain in question. These include timing, surgical technique, surgical approaches, fixation techniques, indications for ancillary bone graft, and postoperative management. With the exception of certain isolated ulnar fractures, all displaced fractures of the diaphysis of the radius or ulna (or both) are managed by open reduction and internal fixation.

#### TIMING

Although at one point it was suggested that operative intervention should be delayed to ensure a higher rate of union,[133] this is no longer considered necessary. To the contrary, early operative treatment permits decompression of the fracture hematoma and reduction of the fracture fragments, thus minimizing soft tissue trauma.[46, 51, 95] Even many open forearm fractures have now been shown to be safely treated by immediate operative treatment (see "Open Fracture").[25, 36, 64, 90] However, there are some situations, such as polytrauma or a compromised soft tissue envelope, in which surgery is best delayed to allow either systemic or local conditions to improve.[79, 109, 129]

#### SURGICAL TECHNIQUE

Most fractures of the forearm can readily be approached with the patient supine and the upper limb abducted onto a hand table. In this position, however, it is necessary to flex the elbow to gain access to the ulnar shaft. This factor has encouraged some surgeons to operate with the patient in the prone position. The ulna is approached with the forearm in pronation, and the radius is approached with the forearm supinated. However, this position may prove uncomfortable with regional block anesthesia and may increase the anesthetic risk in a medically compromised patient.

The use of a pneumatic tourniquet is advisable in most cases. The exception is situations in which the soft tissue envelope is extremely traumatized (see "Open Fracture"). Avoidance of tourniquet-induced ischemia aids the surgeon in assessing the viability of the compromised skeletal muscle during the surgical approach and débridement.

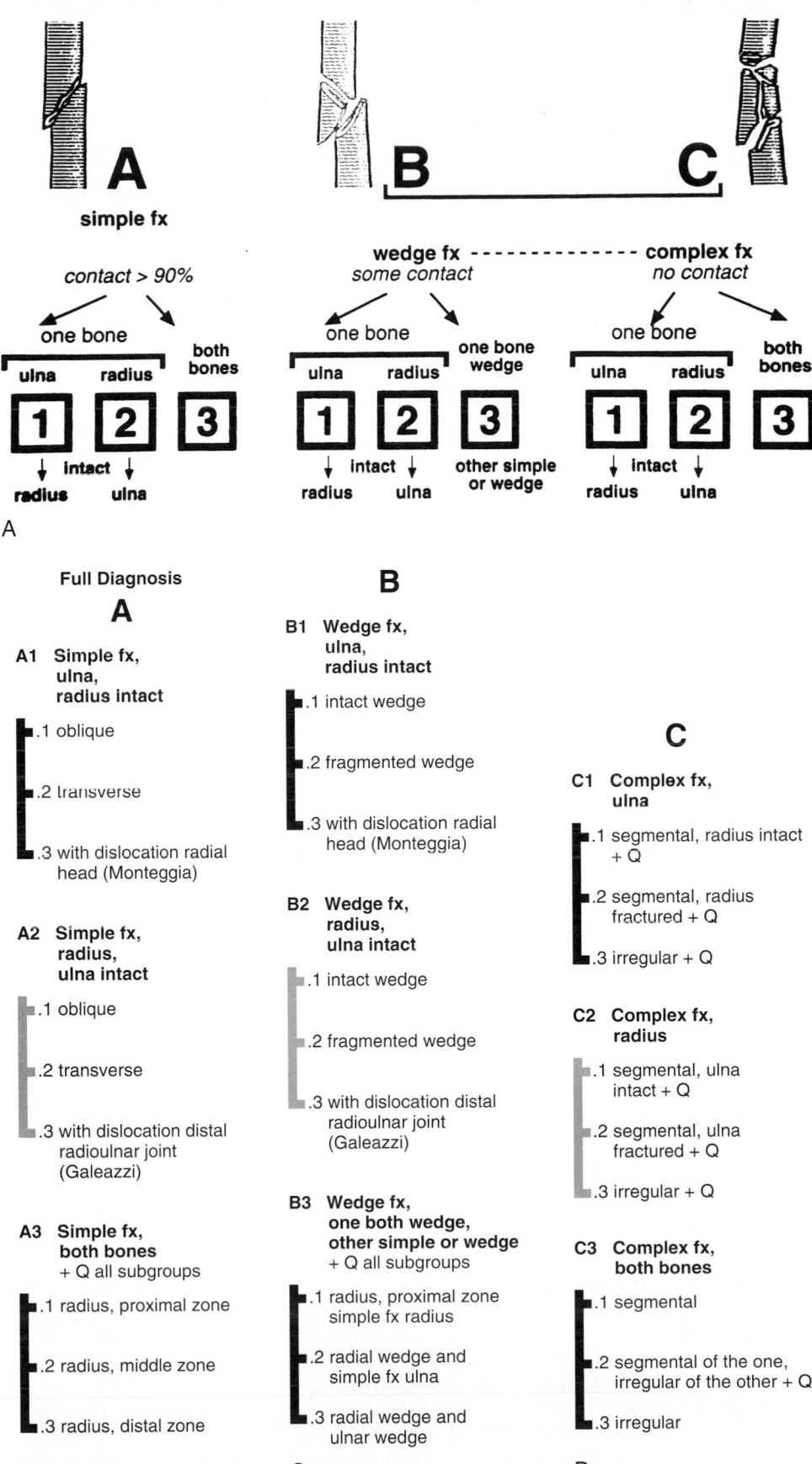

FIGURE 41–2. *A,* Comprehensive fracture (fx) classification types. *B,* Comprehensive fracture classification groups and subgroups of simple extra-articular diaphyseal fractures. *C,* Comprehensive fracture classification of groups and subgroups of wedge-type fracture. *D,* Comprehensive fracture classification of groups and subgroups of complex forearm diaphyseal fractures.

*Illustration continued on following page*

**Qualifications = Q**

**A3 + B3:**
1) without dislocation
2) with dislocation radial head
   (Monteggia)
3) with dislocation distal radioulnar joint (Galeazzi)

**C1.1:**
1) without dislocation
2) with dislocation radial head
   (Monteggia)

**C1.2:**
1) simple
2) wedge

**C1.3:**
1) radius intact
2) radius simple
3) radial wedge

**C2.1:**
1) without dislocation
2) with dislocation distal radioulnar joint (Galeazzi)

**C1.2:** 1), 2) idem to **C1.2**
**C2.3:**
1) ulna intact
2) ulna simple
3) ulna wedge

**C3.2:**
1) bifocal of radius,
   irregular of ulna
2) bifocal of ulna,
   irregular of radius

**FIGURE 41–2.** *Continued E,* Comprehensive classification of fracture
qualifications.

| General Qualifications: | 7) bone loss | 8) partial amputation | 9) amputation |

E

When a tourniquet is used, it is best left inflated for 90 to 120 minutes at most. The tourniquet should always be released before wound closure to ensure control of bleeding.

## SURGICAL APPROACHES

The wide variability of fracture patterns and soft tissue trauma makes it vital that the surgeon become familiar with several surgical approaches to the forearm skeleton.[27]

### Radius

Two general approaches have been advocated for the diaphysis of the radius: the anterior approach as described by Henry[58] and the dorsal approach of Thompson[144]

(Table 41–1). The anterior approach is extensile, permitting ready extension across the elbow or onto the hand; presents a flat surface of the radius distally; and is ideal when fasciotomies are required. When the proximal radius is approached anteriorly, however, the surgeon is confronted with the major neurovascular structures of the forearm as they fan out anteriorly in front of the elbow.

The dorsal or Thompson approach is advantageous in that it is essentially subcutaneous for the distal half of its course. The proximal radius is readily approached as well, with only the common extensors covering the bone. Furthermore, the plate can be applied along the dorsoradial cortex or "tension" side. The disadvantages include limited access to the anterior surface in the event a fasciotomy is required, vulnerability of the posterior inter-

**FIGURE 41–3.** *A, B,* Minimally displaced nightstick fracture of the ulna treated effectively with a long arm functional brace. Note the early callus.

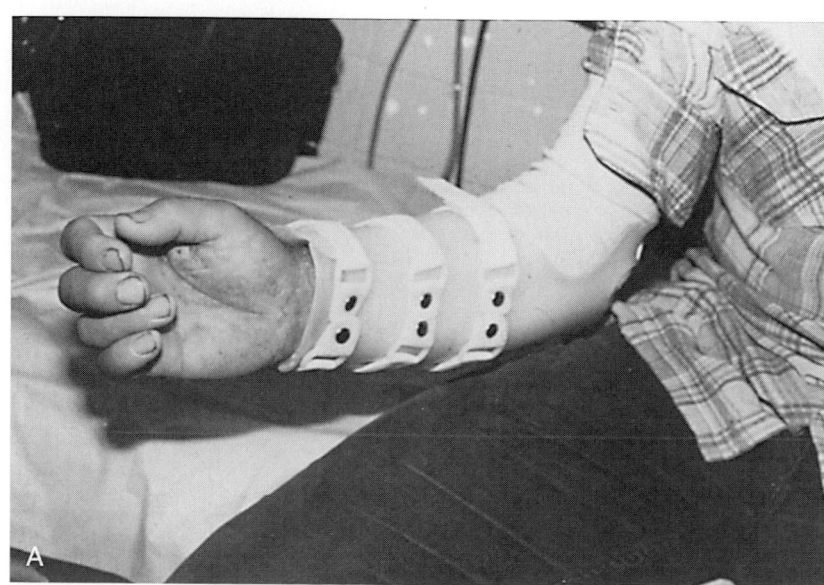

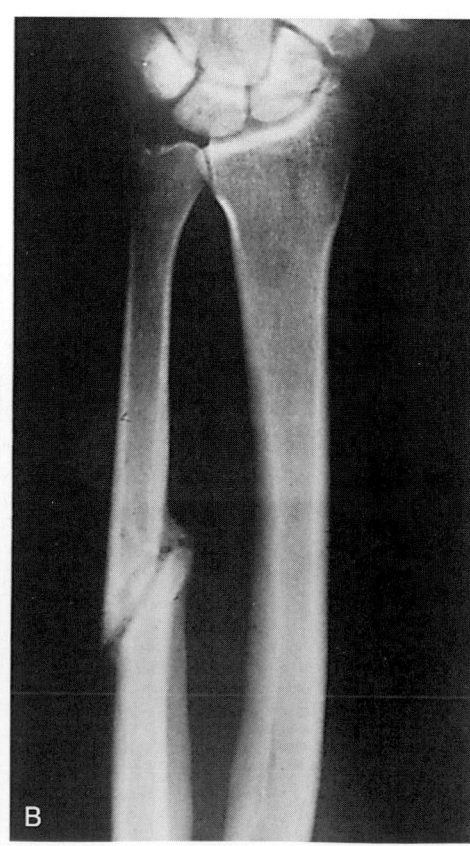

**TABLE 41–1** ...............................................................................................

Surgical Approaches to the Radius

| Approach | Advantages | Disadvantages | Recommendation |
|----------|-----------|---------------|----------------|
| Anterior (Henry) | Extensile; allows fasciotomy | Proximity of neurovascular structures | Proximal third, distal fractures |
| Posterior (Thompson) | Easy; plate on tension side | Not extensile | Middle third fractures |

osseous nerve to injury in the proximal third exposure, and the fact that it is not truly an extensile approach.

**Anterior or Henry Approach.** In the anterior approach, the patient is positioned supine with the arm abducted and forearm supinated. To approach the proximal radius, an incision is made starting at the lateral bicipital sulcus, extending across the elbow flexion crease, and distal to the middle forearm. The brachioradialis muscle is identified, and the fascia along the medial border is incised (Fig. 41–4A). The lateral cutaneous nerve of the forearm is protected. The brachioradialis is retracted laterally, and the biceps and brachialis tendons are identified and retracted medially. The lacertus fibrosus must be divided. The radial nerve can be visualized at this juncture. The branches of the nerve can be identified, with the superficial sensory branch tracking over the supinator and passing distally into the forearm and the posterior interosseous nerve entering the supinator muscle (see Fig. 41–4B). With the forearm maximally supinated, the supinator muscle is dissected off the proximal radius while the posterior interosseous nerve is protected within the two layers of the muscle. With the supinator detached, the brachioradialis and extensor carpi radialis longus and brevis can be mobilized radially to identify much of the radial shaft (see Fig. 41–4C).

For more distal extension, the incision is carried distally 1 fingerbreadth lateral to the edge of the biceps to the radial styloid. The fascia is split longitudinally along the ulnar border of the brachioradialis. This muscle, as well as the remainder of the mobile wad, can be taken radially. On the undersurface of the brachioradialis can be seen the superficial branch of the radial nerve. The radial artery can also be identified at this point, lying on top of the flexor digitorum superficialis and across the pronator teres. The radius can be pronated, directing the surgeon to complete access to the dorsoradial surface (see Fig. 41–4C). If dissection must extend distally to the carpal tunnel, the palmaris longus serves as a landmark in the identification of the median nerve, which lies between it and the flexor carpi radialis. The palmaris longus and the median nerve can be retracted radially, with the superficial and deep flexors taken ulnarly. Doing so reveals the pronator quadratus, which is elevated off the radius from its radial side. Complete access to the radius is gained from the distal articular margin into the forearm.

Closure of the anterior approach is straightforward. The only muscles that ordinarily require reattachment are the supinator proximally and the pronator quadratus distally, the remainder fall into place. The deep fascia is never closed. The subcutaneous tissue and skin are closed over a suction drain (Fig. 41–5A to H).

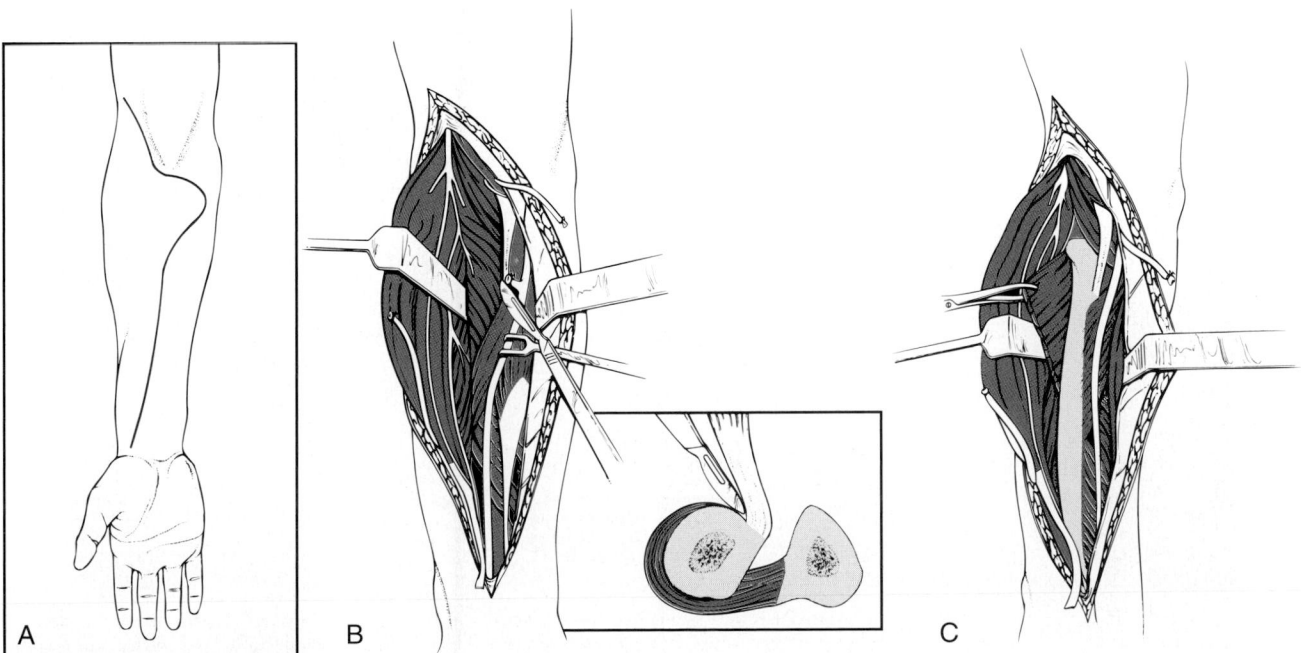

**FIGURE 41–4.** Anterior surgical approach to the radius. *A,* The surgical incision starts at the lateral bicipital sulcus, extends across the elbow flexion crease, and passes distally along the medial border of the brachioradialis muscle. *B,* With the forearm maximally supinated, the supinator muscle is dissected off the proximal radius. The posterior interosseous nerve is protected within the two layers of the muscle. *C,* With the supinator detached, the brachioradialis and radial wrist extensors are readily mobilized to expose much of the radial diaphysis.

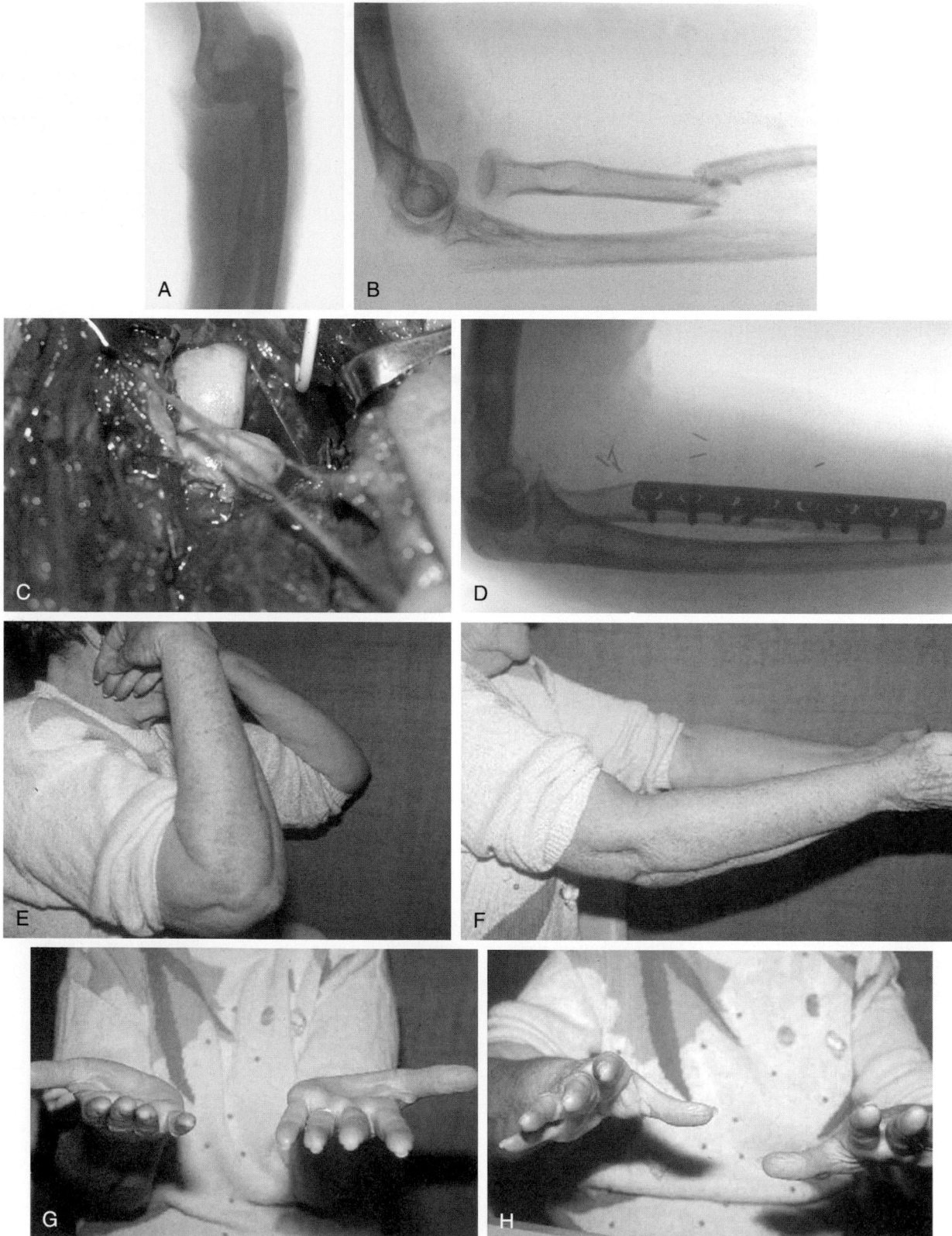

**FIGURE 41–5.** *A–H,* A 60-year-old woman with a proximal third radius fracture associated with dislocation of the radiocapitellar joint. *A* and *B,* The anteroposterior and lateral radiographs of the fracture-dislocation. *C,* The fracture and elbow were exposed through an anterior surgical approach. *D,* Stable plate fixation with a limited contact dynamic compression plate on the radius. *E–H,* Excellent functional result.

**Dorsolateral or Thompson Approach.** The dorsolateral approach is best suited to fractures of the proximal and middle thirds of the radius. The patient is positioned supine with the shoulder abducted and the arm resting on a hand table. The incision extends from the lateral epicondyle of the humerus along the dorsal border of the mobile wad of Henry (the extensor carpi radialis brevis and longus and brachioradialis muscles) down to the radial styloid. The length of incision is determined solely by the fracture. The fascia between the digital extensors and mobile wad is split. This interval is sometimes more apparent distally where the outcropping muscles of the thumb cross over the radius. Often a fibrous band can be identified between the extensor carpi radialis brevis and extensor digitorum communis. This seam is developed proximally in the direction of the lateral epicondyle to expose the supinator in the proximal third of the forearm (Fig. 41–6A).

At this point, the posterior interosseous nerve has pierced the supinator anteriorly and is running at right angles to the muscle's fibers. The nerve can be identified by separating the fibers of the supinator at a level approximately 3 fingerbreadths distal to the radial head (see Fig. 41–6B). The radius is next supinated to identify the insertion of the supinator muscle, which is elevated off the radius. The posterior interosseous nerve has entered the muscle more proximally and is protected as the muscle is elevated. Ready access has now been gained to the proximal and middle thirds of the radius.

To expose the distal third, the surgeon must identify the exact location of the superficial radial nerve as it passes between the brachioradialis and digital extensors. The outcropping muscles of the thumb cross obliquely over the radius at this level. These are readily elevated to permit a plate to be placed beneath them. The remainder of the radius distally is virtually subcutaneous.

Wound closure with the dorsal approach can be accomplished through closure of only the subcutaneous tissue and skin over a suction drain.

## Ulna

The ulna lies in a subcutaneous position throughout its length in the forearm. The only structure of significance that crosses the ulna is the dorsal cutaneous branch of the ulnar nerve, which passes onto the dorsal surface of the flexor carpi ulnaris muscle approximately 6 to 8 cm proximal to the ulnar styloid. Consequently, when an incision is made along the distal third of the ulna, care must be taken to identify and protect this nerve.

To approach the ulnar shaft, an incision is made parallel and just slightly dorsal or volar to its palpable crest. The extensors are detached from the dorsal crest of the ulna. A

FIGURE **41–6.** Dorsolateral approach to the radius. *A,* The surgical approach extends between the extensor carpi radialis brevis and the extensor digitorum communis, exposing the supinator muscle in the proximal third of the forearm. *B,* The supinator muscle is elevated off the radius, providing access to the proximal and middle thirds of the radius.

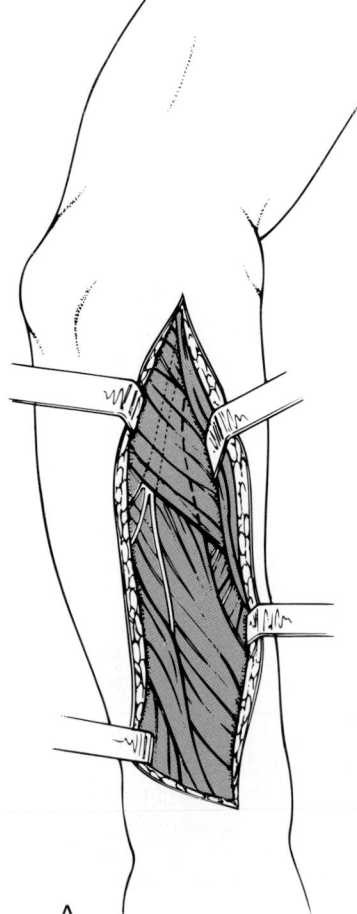

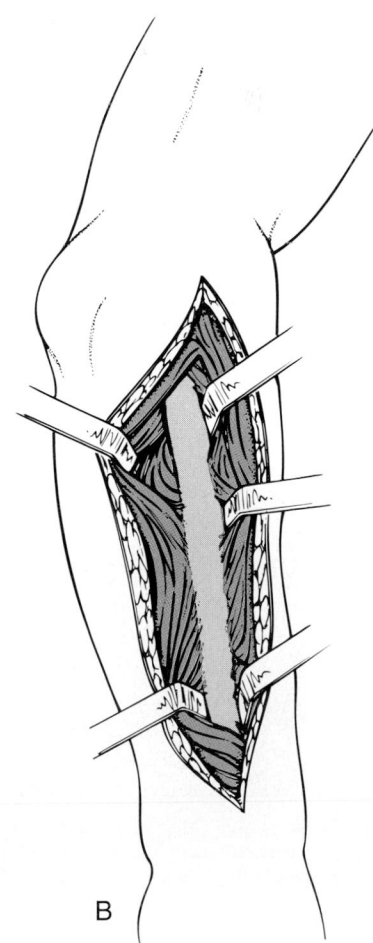

A                                B

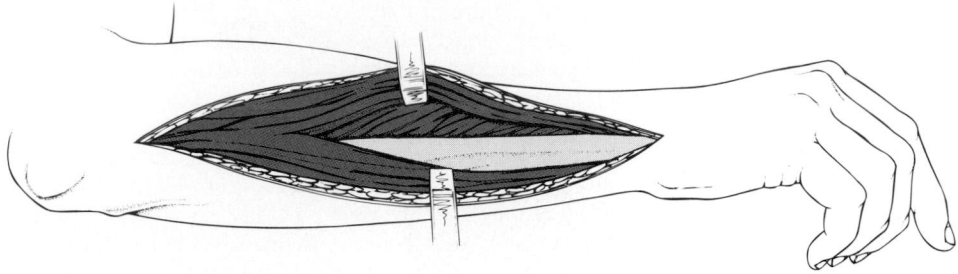

FIGURE 41–7. The surgical approach to the ulnar diaphysis is made parallel and just dorsal or volar to the palpable crest of the shaft.

plate can be applied on either the flexor or extensor surface, depending on the fracture configuration and the preoperative plan. This incision can be extended proximally to expose the olecranon or distal humerus. The ulnar nerve at this juncture must be identified and protected (Fig. 41–7).

## REDUCTION TECHNIQUES

The forearm is a two-bone structure; reduction and fixation of one bone present significant difficulty in obtaining reduction of the other bone. Consequently, it is advisable to expose both fractures and reduce the less comminuted fracture first, holding it provisionally with a plate and two clamps. Doing so establishes length and facilitates reduction of the second fracture. Provisional fixation is applied to the second bone, and radiographs are obtained. When exposing an isolated diaphyseal fracture, assessment of the proximal and distal articulations is mandatory.

Alternatively, comminuted fractures can be reduced by the techniques of indirect reduction, whereby longitudinal traction is applied to the bone using either a small distractor (Fig. 41–8) or the plate itself[84] (Fig. 41–9A to H).

The fracture reduction can be controlled in a number of ways. The simplest way is to visualize the interdigitation of the fracture line and the contour of the diaphysis. Visualization may not be easy with an extremely comminuted fracture. In this instance, after provisional fixation of both fractures, supination and pronation of the forearm are

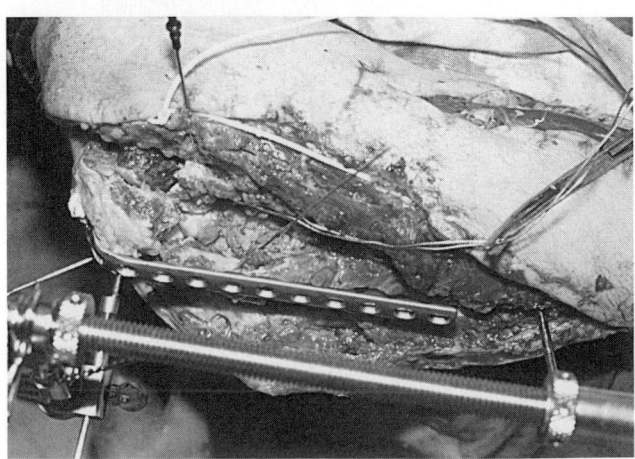

FIGURE 41–8. A comminuted fracture of the proximal ulna is reduced by the technique of indirect reduction using a small distractor.

tested. If full forearm rotation has been restored, the reduction should be considered acceptable and a functional result can be anticipated. If forearm rotation is not complete, the fracture must be reduced again and rotation rechecked. Radiographic control of the reduction is mandatory.

### Plate Application

The plate that has gained widespread acceptance is the 3.5-mm dynamic compression (DC) plate. In most cases, a plate of adequate length, applied with appropriate technique, is of sufficient strength to support functional loading while the fracture heals. At least eight cortices above and below the fracture are usually required, except in the case of a pure transverse fracture, which is effectively held with six cortices on each side (Fig. 41–10). In cases of comminution, 10- or 12-hole plates are recommended (Fig. 41–11).

The development of indirect reduction techniques (by Mast and co-workers[84]) and a more "biologic" approach to plate fixation of forearm fractures have been enhanced by newer plate designs, such as the limited contact DC plate.* This plate features a structured undersurface, improving the local blood supply under the plate; even stiffness; longitudinal undercut screw holes, allowing 40° of tilting of screws in the long axis of the plate; uniform spacing of screw holes, permitting easy shifting and exchanging of plates of different lengths; symmetric plate holes, allowing more versatility in handling complex fracture patterns; and a more trapezoidal shape (Fig. 41–12).

What has become evident is that the blood supply to the diaphyseal skeleton is very sensitive to the external contact of standard compression plates. As part of the stability of plate fixation is derived from friction between the plate and underlying bone, this continued contact results in areas of necrosis in the cortex under the plate. These observations have led not only to implants with less surface contact with the underlying bone but also to newer designs in which the screws lock into the plate, thus creating an internal "splint." With the development of these implants, which have reduced the area of plate contact to small points isolated from each other, it was recognized that by fixing the screw heads within the plate, the length of the screws could be reduced to unicortical fixation (Fig. 41–13A to D). It is quite likely that the standard plate used in the near future will combine both locked screws and bicortical fully threaded standard screws.[118]

*Synthes, Ltd., Paoli, PA.

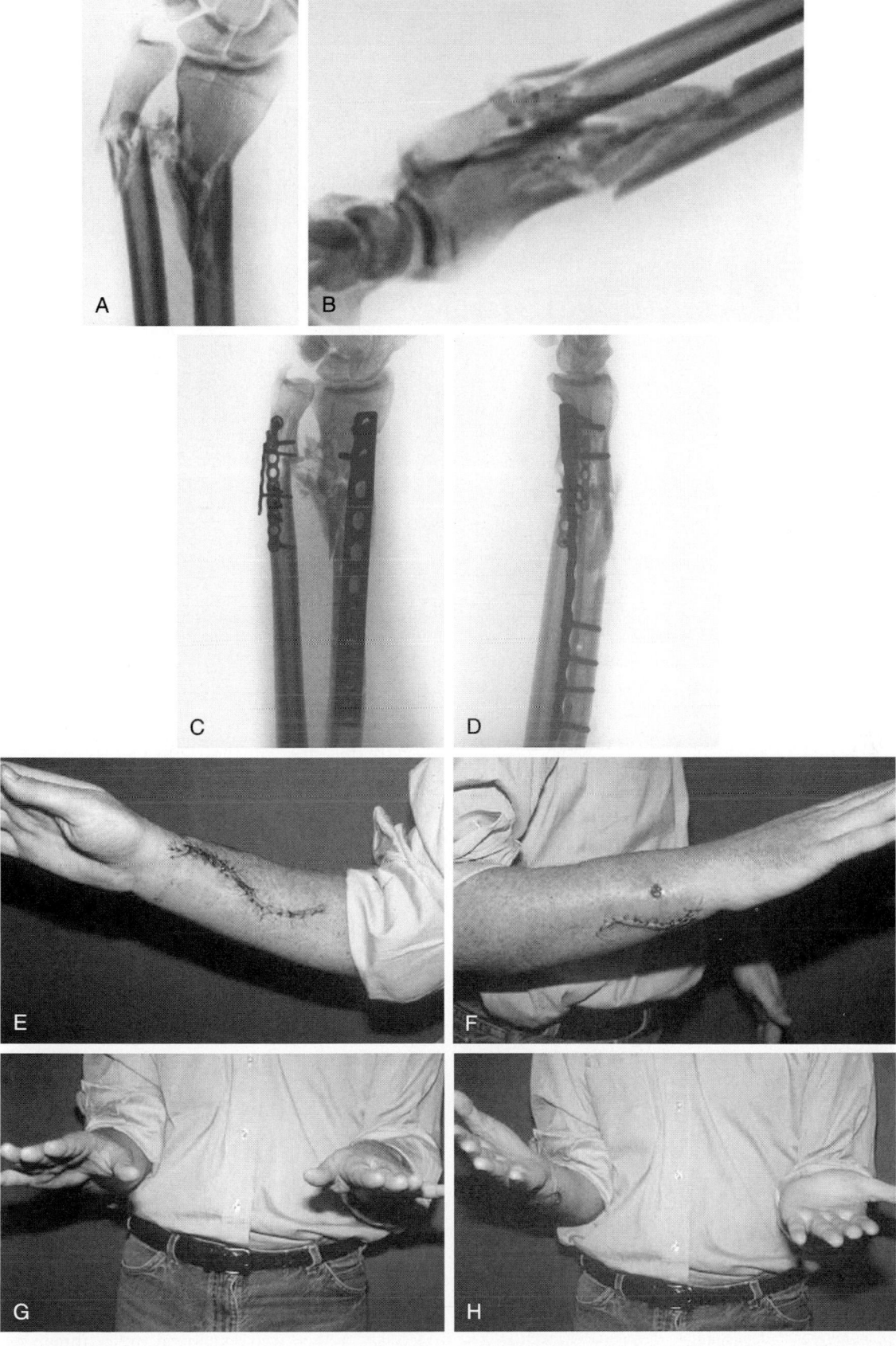

**FIGURE 41–9.** *A–H,* A comminuted distal third forearm fracture caused by an accidental gunshot in a 31-year-old male. *A, B,* Anteroposterior and lateral radiographs of the comminuted fractures. *C, D,* A bridge plate was applied on the radius using a small distractor to reduce the fracture and restore length and small plates applied to the ulna. *E–H,* Excellent function was achieved, as the stability permitted early motion.

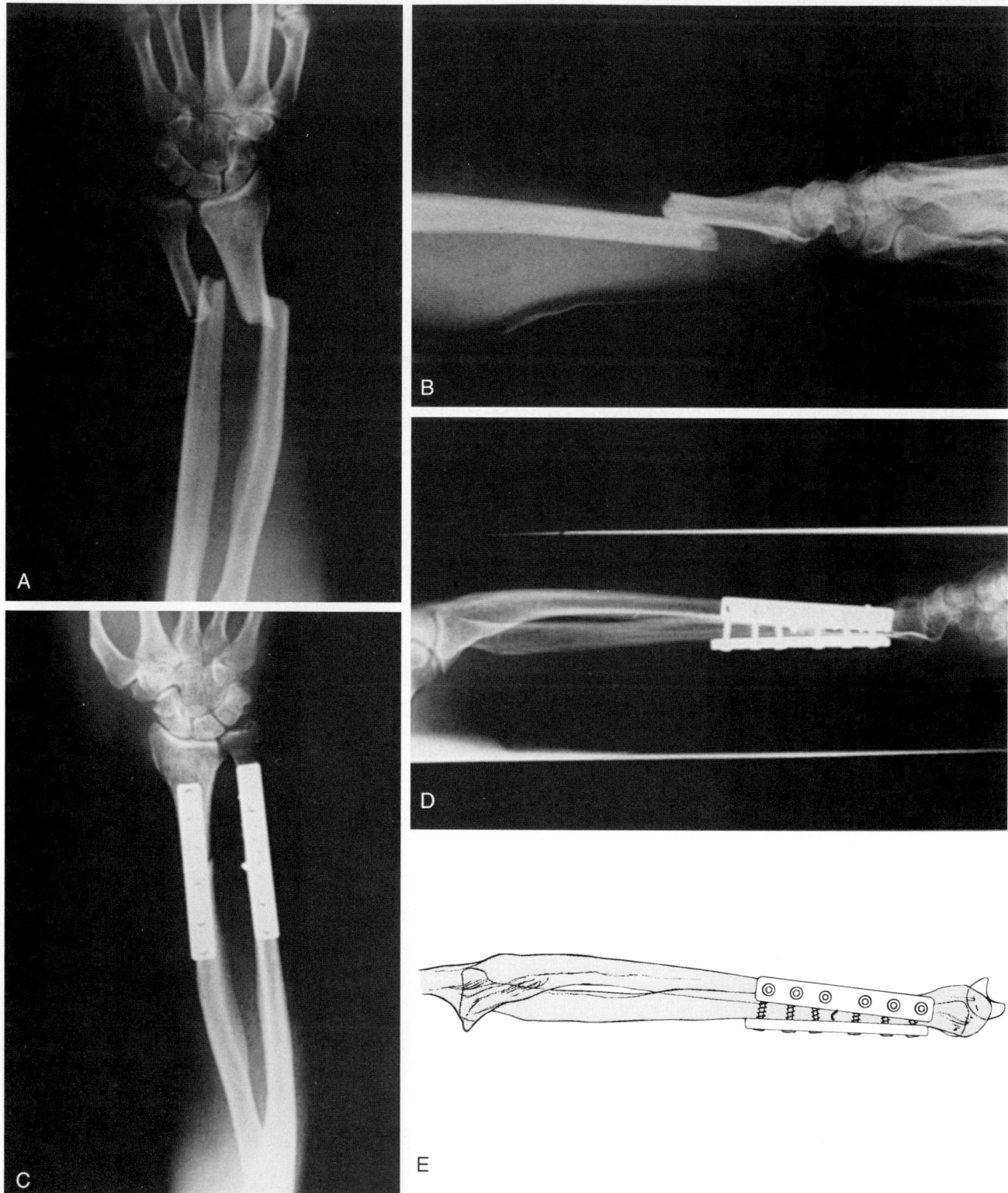

**Figure 41–10.** A 32-year-old construction worker sustained a transverse fracture of the distal third of both the radius and the ulna of his right (dominant) limb. *A, B,* Transverse fractures of both the radius and the ulna at the junction of the middle to distal third of the forearm seen in anteroposterior and lateral radiographs. *C, D,* The fractures were each stabilized with six-hole 3.5-mm dynamic compression plates with an excellent functional outcome. *E,* Schematic of the internal fixation.

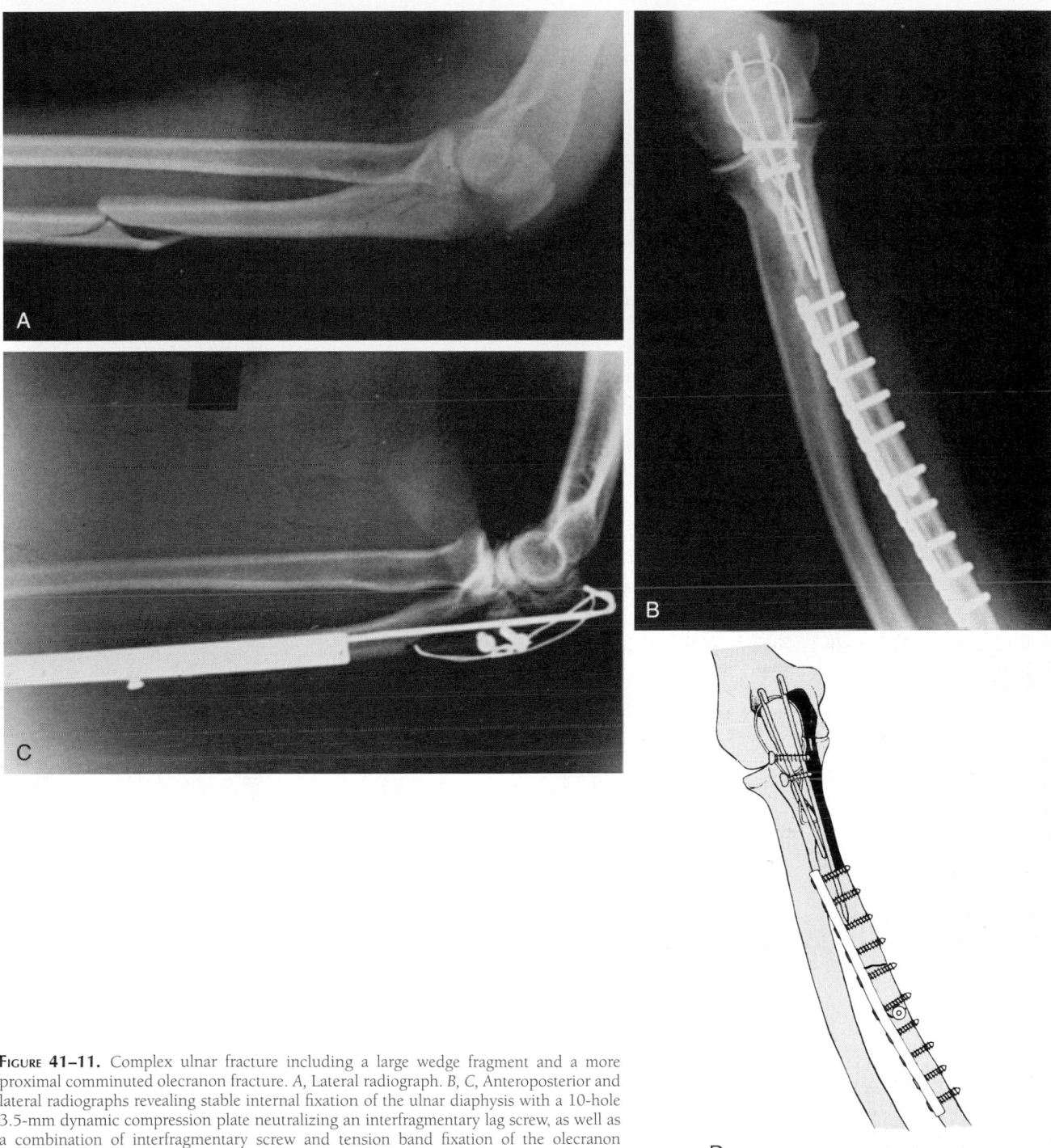

**FIGURE 41–11.** Complex ulnar fracture including a large wedge fragment and a more proximal comminuted olecranon fracture. *A,* Lateral radiograph. *B, C,* Anteroposterior and lateral radiographs revealing stable internal fixation of the ulnar diaphysis with a 10-hole 3.5-mm dynamic compression plate neutralizing an interfragmentary lag screw, as well as a combination of interfragmentary screw and tension band fixation of the olecranon fracture. *D,* Schematic of the fixation.

Whenever possible, an interfragmentary screw is added, either through the plate or in conjunction with the implant (Fig. 41–14). In pure transverse fractures, this addition is not possible. In fractures with an oblique configuration, the plate is precontoured to sit slightly (1 mm) off the shaft over the fracture (Fig. 41–15A). The fracture is reduced, and the plate is applied by placing one screw in the fragment that has its obliquity facing away from the plate (see Fig. 41–15B). This allows the fragment, with its spike directly under the plate, to be pulled into the

plate and fracture when compression is applied by the insertion of the load screw in the other fragment (see Fig. 41–15C). After this, a screw is placed as an interfragmentary lag screw through the plate and across the oblique fracture line (see Fig. 41–15D and E).

Spiral fractures are optimally fixed with the use of interfragmentary screw fixation over the length of the spiral. These screws serve as the primary means of achieving compression of the fracture. A plate is then applied as a neutralization plate, spanning the fracture

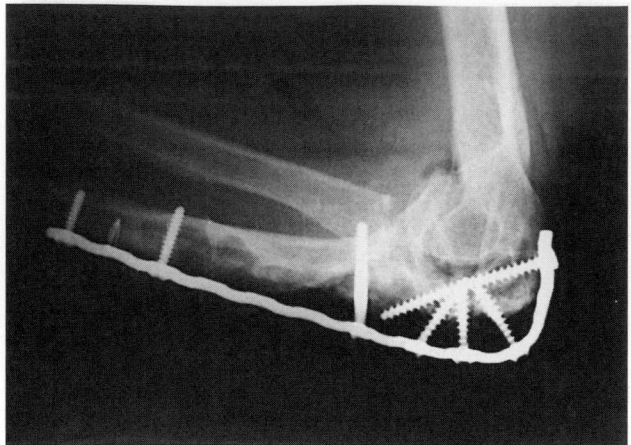

FIGURE 41–12. The limited contact dynamic compression plate is a versatile plate that is ideally suited for forearm fracture or nonunion fixation. Here it is applied for a proximal ulna nonunion.

lines. The plate should be long enough to have screws in at least six cortices of cortical bone on either side of the fracture (see Fig. 41–14).

The management of comminuted fractures is more difficult.[31] The first priority is to preserve the soft tissue attachments to the comminuted fragments. The approach to the skeleton should be extraperiosteal except at the fracture site. In the badly comminuted fracture, the surgeon should avoid attempting to reduce all the fragments and instead should use the plate to maintain length and alignment; the plate in this case functions as a bridge plate (see Fig. 41–9). The more extensive the comminution, the greater the length of plate required to provide stable fracture fixation. The use of a distractor can prove invaluable in gaining length without extensive stripping of the bone fragments[84] (Fig. 41–16). Cancellous bone

grafting should be performed at this time. As a rule, if the loss of cortical contact opposite the plate is greater than one third or if absolute stability cannot be ensured, cancellous bone grafting is indicated.

Segmental fractures can prove problematic.[31, 130] Two plates can be used if one plate is not long enough. When applying two plates to the bone, one should be at a right angle to the other (Fig. 41–17). The ulna, being a straight bone, is more amenable to intramedullary nailing to stabilize a segmental fracture.

The ulnar plate is most easily applied to the flat medial border, whereas the location of the plate on the radius depends to a large degree on the surgical approach. For fractures of the proximal and middle thirds, the radial plate is ordinarily applied on the anterior or dorsolateral surface. The flat anterior surface of the distal radius is the preferred surface for fractures of the middle or distal third.

## INDICATIONS FOR ANCILLARY BONE GRAFT

As a rule, cancellous bone grafting is recommended whenever comminution or bone loss has prevented an anatomic reduction of the fracture fragments. The recommendation of Anderson and colleagues[3] to use bone grafts if more than one third of the diaphyseal cortex is deficient has become widely accepted. In fact, the use of cancellous grafts in comminuted fractures has resulted in union rates comparable to those for closed, noncomminuted fractures.[25]

The anterior iliac crest is an excellent source for graft, although the distal radius or olecranon can provide adequate cancellous graft for most fractures. Great care must be taken to avoid placing graft across the interosseous space, especially with fractures of both forearm bones located at the same level, in order to prevent development of a synostosis.

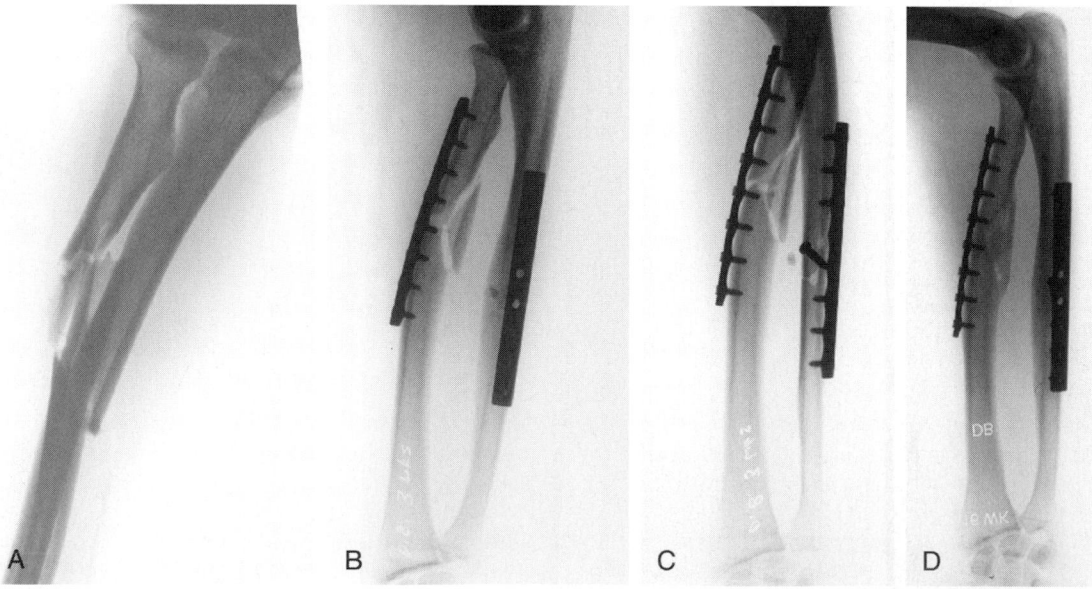

FIGURE 41–13. A–D, A complex forearm fracture in a 38-year-old man was treated with point contact plates with unicortical screws. A, The initial fracture. B, Immediate postoperative radiographs. Note that no attempt was made to secure fixation of the comminuted fragment of the radius. C, Radiograph at 6 weeks. D, Radiograph at 4 months. Note the incorporation of the butterfly fragment.

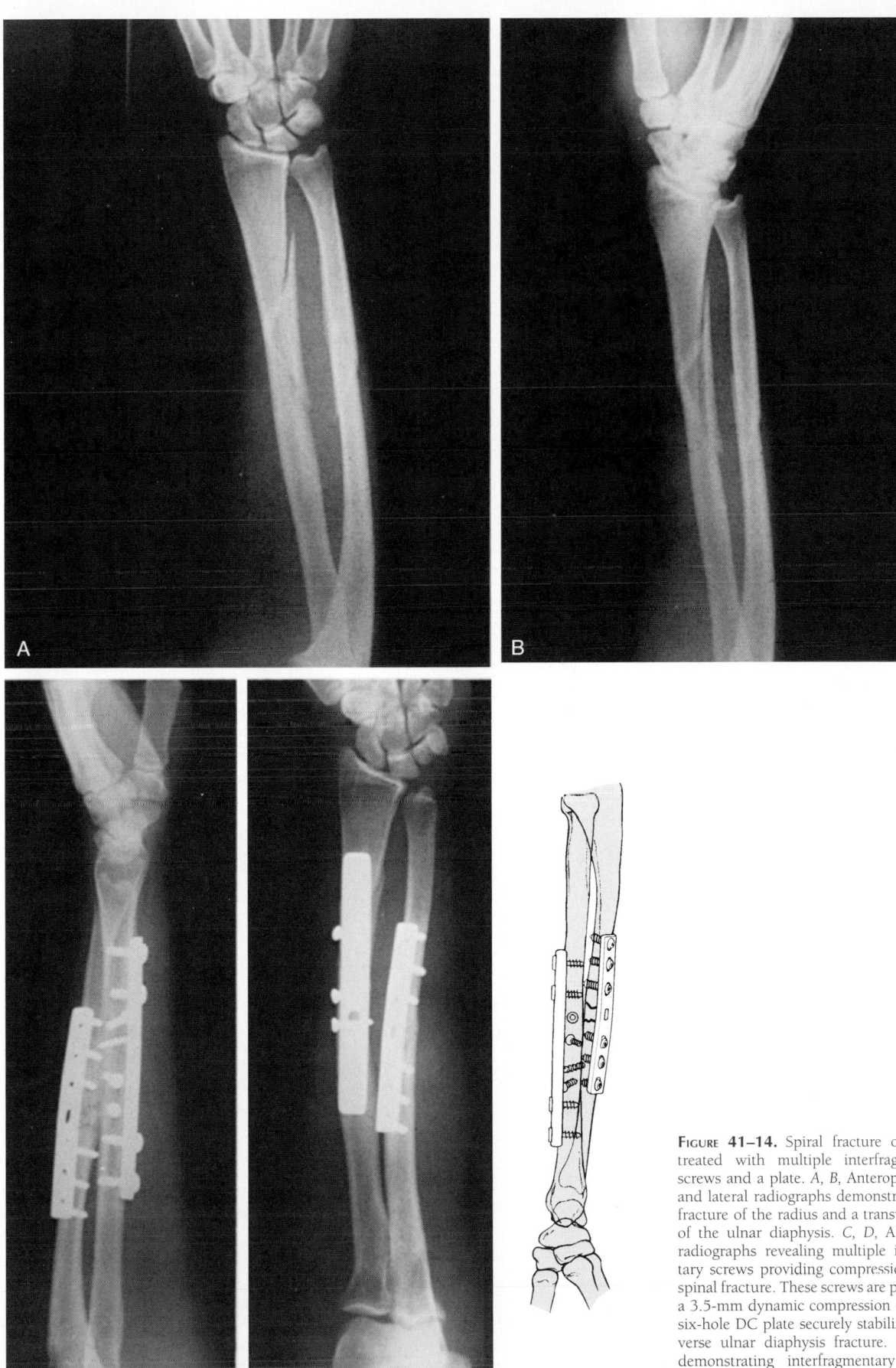

**FIGURE 41–14.** Spiral fracture of the radius treated with multiple interfragmentary lag screws and a plate. *A, B,* Anteroposterior (AP) and lateral radiographs demonstrating a spiral fracture of the radius and a transverse fracture of the ulnar diaphysis. *C, D,* AP and lateral radiographs revealing multiple interfragmentary screws providing compression across the spinal fracture. These screws are protected with a 3.5-mm dynamic compression (DC) plate. A six-hole DC plate securely stabilizes the transverse ulnar diaphysis fracture. *E,* Schematic demonstrating interfragmentary lag screws placed across the spiral fracture with a neutralization plate applied.

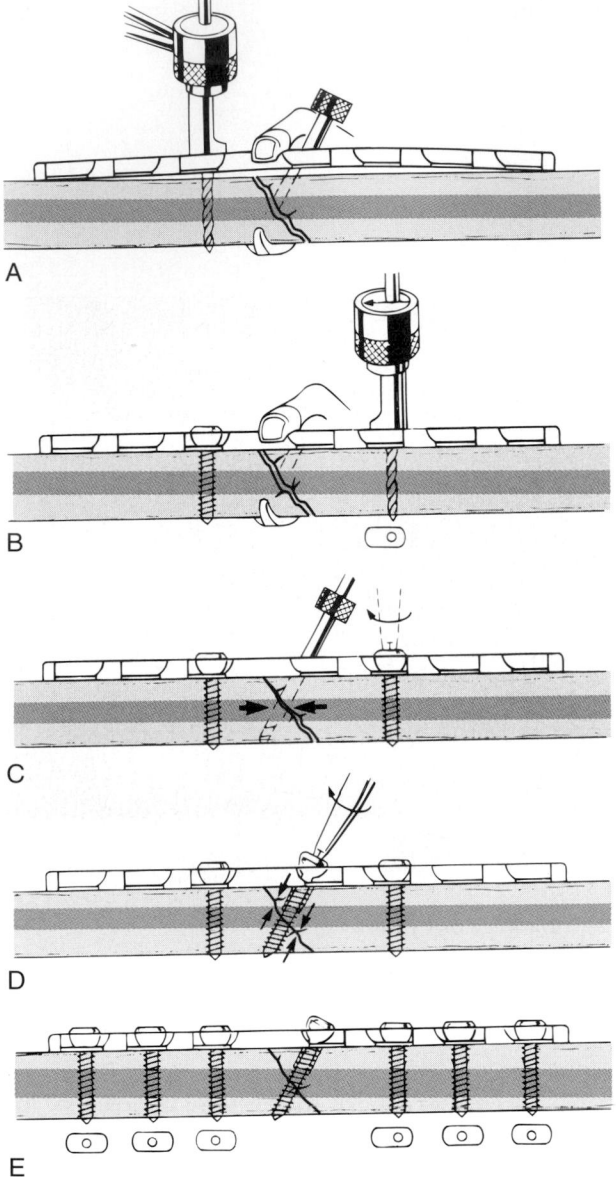

**FIGURE 41–15.** Schematic representation of the technique of applying a dynamic compression plate to an oblique forearm shaft fracture. *A,* The plate is precontoured to sit 1 mm off the shaft over the fracture site. The fracture is reduced, the plate is held with a clamp, and a screw is applied in a neutral mode in the fragment, which has its obliquity facing away from the plate. The gliding hole for an interfragmentary lag screw through the plate can next be drilled with a 3.5-mm drill bit. *B,* A screw is next applied in the load or compression position in the opposite fragment, which will allow this fragment to be pulled into the plate when compression is applied. *C,* The interfragmentary lag screw is then placed through the plate by drilling the far cortex with a 2.5-mm drill bit, tapping it with a 3.5-mm tap. *D,* A screw of appropriate length is placed. *E,* The remainder of the screws are applied through the plate.

In the setting of high-energy trauma or gunshot wounds, bone loss may be significant.[29, 40, 54, 64, 79] Either acutely or after soft tissues have stabilized, a plate can be applied to ensure skeletal length and rotation and to maintain the interosseous space. In 7 to 10 days a cancellous graft can be used to span the defect. Rapid incorporation usually ensues, given the well-vascularized environment in the forearm (Fig. 41–18).

## WOUND CLOSURE

At the completion of internal fixation, the tourniquet is deflated and hemostasis ensured. Wounds should never be closed under undue tension. Rather, it is advisable to leave the wound open and return to the operating room in 48 to 72 hours for either delayed closure or split-thickness skin grafting. In the interim, the wounds are covered with moist saline dressings.

With extensive soft tissue loss, flap coverage may be required.[36, 64] In our experience, the open forearm fractures are treated with internal rather than external fixation because this best ensures not only union but also maintenance of the functional anatomy.

## POSTOPERATIVE MANAGEMENT

Closed, diaphyseal fractures treated with plate fixation are usually supported with a resting forearm plaster splint for the patient's comfort. Active digital and elbow motion is encouraged from the onset. Forearm rotation can be initiated after the patient is comfortable and wound healing is ensured, usually within 3 to 5 days after surgery. If any question exists regarding the stability of the internal fixation or the patient's reliability, external functional bracing should be instituted in a manner such as that advocated by Sarmiento and associates[121] (see Fig. 41–3A and B). This bracing provides excellent support of the forearm skeleton through a careful interosseous mold created in the splint, yet permits functional use of the extremity.

In general, forearm fractures treated with plate fixation heal within 3 to 4 months. During this period, the patient should be permitted to use the extremity for activities of daily living, avoiding only heavy lifting and sports. After radiographic union has occurred, the patient may resume a normal lifestyle. Radiographic findings of callus, resorption at the fracture site, or implant loosening should alert the treating physician to the possibility of instability of the internal fixation.

## OPEN FRACTURE

The enhanced functional results achieved by anatomic skeletal restoration of forearm fractures have extended the application of plate fixation to the management of most open forearm fractures. Clinical studies by Moed and co-workers[90] and Chapman and colleagues[25] have documented a low rate of late infection: 1 of 79 fractures in 50 patients and 2 of 129 fractures in 87 patients, respectively. The results of these studies and the experience of many other centers have shown that infection and nonunion after internal fixation of open forearm fractures are uncommon.*

The management of the open fracture demands meticulous attention to detail in regard to both the soft tissue and the skeleton. Cultures are obtained before débridement and are followed by broad-spectrum antibiotics and

---

*See references 22, 29, 35, 36, 39, 53, 58, 64, 78, 79.

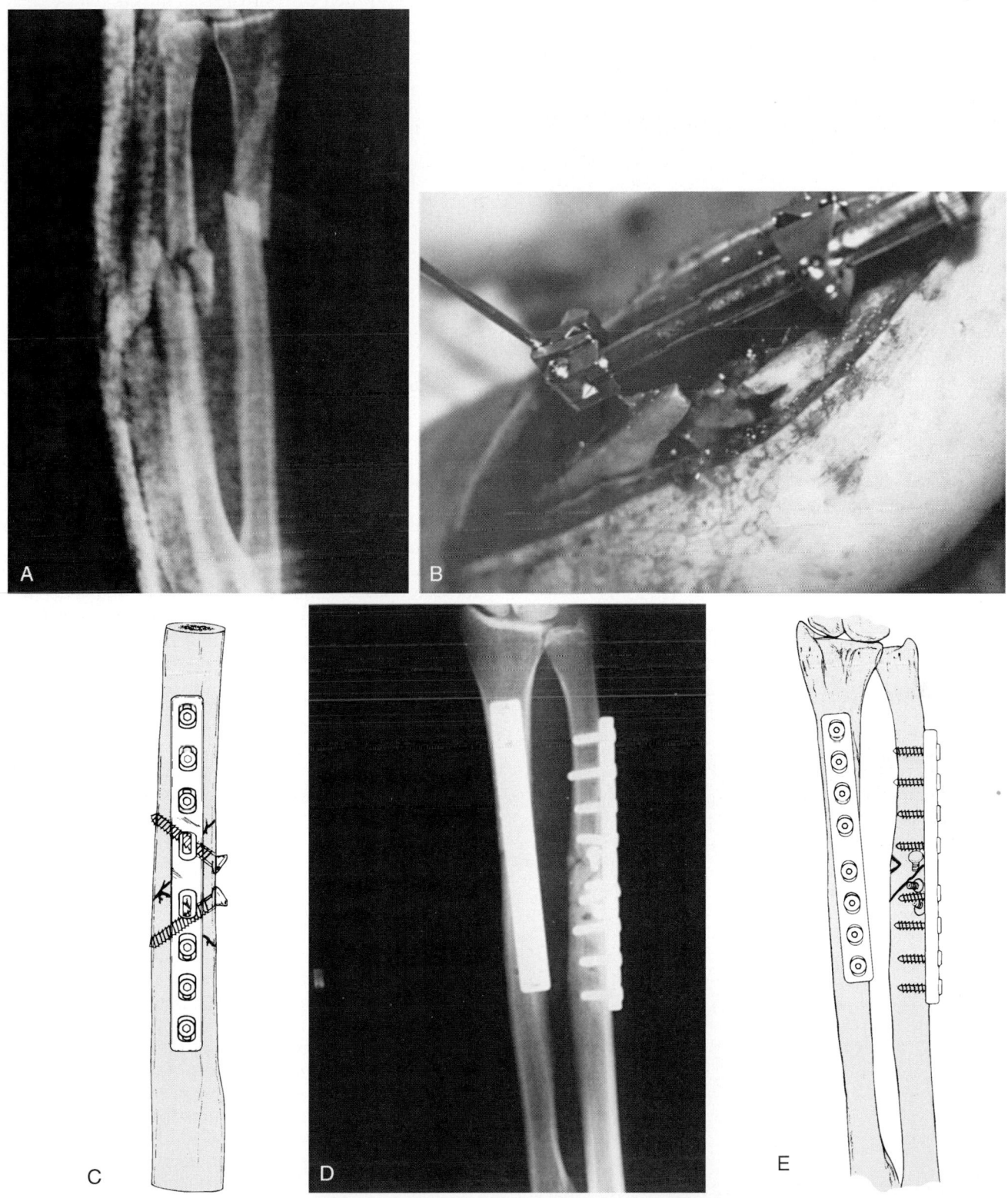

**FIGURE 41–16.** An open comminuted both-bone forearm fracture that occurred in a 27-year-old physician. *A*, Anteroposterior radiograph demonstrating a comminuted ulnar and radial fracture. *B*, A minidistractor was applied to the ulnar shaft to distract the major fragments while the smaller fragments were teased into place. *C*, Schematic of the distractor in place. *D*, The fragments were fixed securely with interfragmentary lag screws, and eight-hole DC plates were applied to both ulnar and radial fractures. *E*, Schematic of the plates in position.

*Illustration continued on following page*

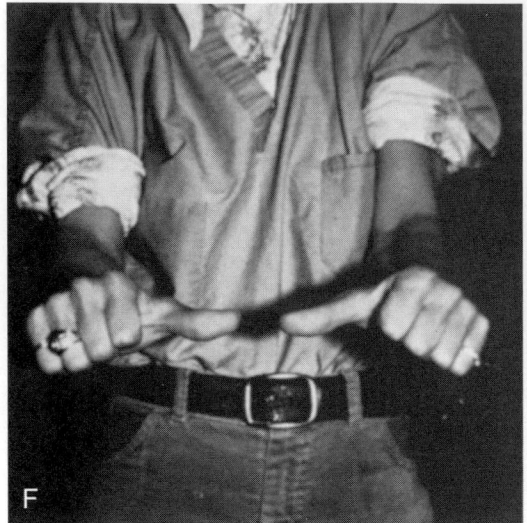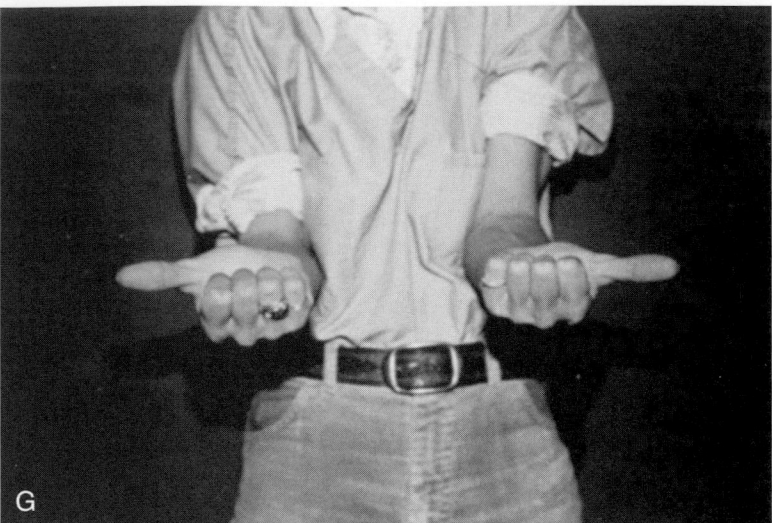

FIGURE 41–16. *Continued   F, G,* Normal function resulted.

appropriate tetanus prophylaxis. A tourniquet is applied but not necessarily inflated in those wounds with extensive skeletal muscle trauma. Mechanical débridement, lavage, and direct débridement of the fracture ends through extensile exposures form the foundations of wound care. All devascularized tissue, including loose fragments of bone, should be excised. Anatomic reduction of the

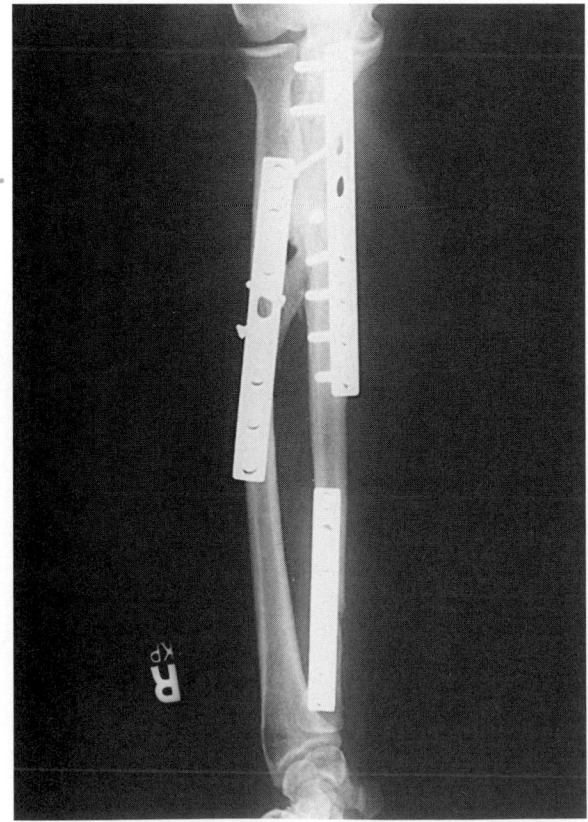

FIGURE 41–17. A segmental open grade III fracture was treated by indirect reduction and two dynamic compression plates with restoration of length and skeletal alignment. Note the interosseous synostosis.

fractures is followed by plate fixation, with placement of the plates under viable soft tissue coverage whenever possible. The surgically created wounds can be closed, leaving the traumatic wounds open. Antibiotics are usually continued for 2 days postoperatively (Fig. 41–19).

Depending to some degree on the extent of the wound, the nature of the contamination, and the associated injuries, a second look is recommended at 48 to 72 hours after operation. At that point, definitive wound closure can be considered. Delayed primary closure or split-thickness skin grafting can be done in most Gustilo grade 1 or 2 wounds. In wounds with extensive soft tissue loss or exposed plates, remote pedicled or microvascular flaps are required (see Chapter 15). At the time of definitive wound closure, cancellous iliac crest graft should be considered for fractures with bone loss or comminution opposite the plate.[25, 54, 90]

For patients with extensive soft tissue loss, extreme contamination, or polytrauma, there may be occasions when internal fixation should be delayed.[79, 81, 127, 131] The application of external fixation or skeletal traction through a metacarpal pin helps to maintain skeletal length and alignment and soft tissue length until the patient is returned to the operating room for a repeated wound débridement. At that point, a judgment can be made to convert the internal fixation if the wound appears clean (Fig. 41–20). The combination of rigid skeletal fixation, meticulous soft tissue care, early wound closure, and liberal use of cancellous bone grafts not only reduces the incidence of complications with these severe injuries but also maximizes functional recovery.[54, 64, 78, 90]

## SPECIFIC LESIONS

### Distal Third

Fractures involving the distal third of the forearm are difficult to treat. Situated at the junction of the diaphysis and metaphysis, these fractures are unstable and offer a limited zone in which secure fixation can be achieved with plates and screws.

A particularly troublesome fracture is the short oblique fracture of the radius (Fig. 41–21). Often comminuted, it is inherently unstable and not infrequently associated with disruption of the DRUJ. It is viewed by some as just a metaphyseal fracture, and so external skeletal fixation spanning the fracture into pins in the metacarpals has been advocated. With this technique, the fixation must remain at least 8 weeks to offset the likelihood of settling or displacement (Fig. 41–22), which is even more likely if the fracture is comminuted. It is our preference to advise open reduction and internal fixation with a plate acting as a buttress plate (Fig. 41–23). The management of associated DRUJ disruption is identical to that outlined with the Galeazzi fracture.[45]

Fractures of the ulnar shaft at this level can also lead to functional limitations if allowed to shorten or angulate, thereby altering the mechanics of the DRUJ.

## Galeazzi Fracture

Isolated fractures of the distal third of the radius can prove troublesome. Commonly referred to as the Galeazzi fracture,[48] they have also been called the reverse Monteggia fracture,[147] Piedmont,[62] or Darrach-Hughston-Milch[123] fracture. Whatever the eponym, the distinguish-ing feature of the fracture is the associated subluxation or dislocation of the DRUJ.

The Galeazzi fracture is uncommon, with an incidence varying from 3%[153] to 6%[48, 92, 121] of all forearm fractures. Although it is commonly thought to result from an axial load on a hyperpronated forearm,[88, 119, 128, 136, 148, 153] the mechanism has never been reproduced in laboratory models.[47, 61, 93] It is more common in males,[35, 88, 92] and its clinical features include pain and deformity at the DRUJ in association with a fracture of the radial shaft, most often at the juncture of the middle and distal thirds. The DRUJ disruption has also been observed to occur with isolated proximal or middle third fractures of the ra-dius.[37, 39, 67, 73, 75, 88, 99, 105, 106] Because there may be substantial soft tissue swelling, the diagnosis must be confirmed radiographically. The radius fracture commonly has a short, oblique pattern, often angulated dorsally on the lateral view and shortened on the anteroposterior radiograph (Fig. 41–24).

The following radiographic findings suggest traumatic disruption of the DRUJ in the presence of an isolated fracture of the radial diaphysis[2, 21, 92]:

1. Fracture of the ulnar styloid at its base
2. Widening of the DRUJ space as seen on the anteroposterior radiograph
3. Dislocation of the radius relative to the ulna seen on a true lateral radiograph
4. Shortening of the radius beyond 5 mm relative to the distal ulna

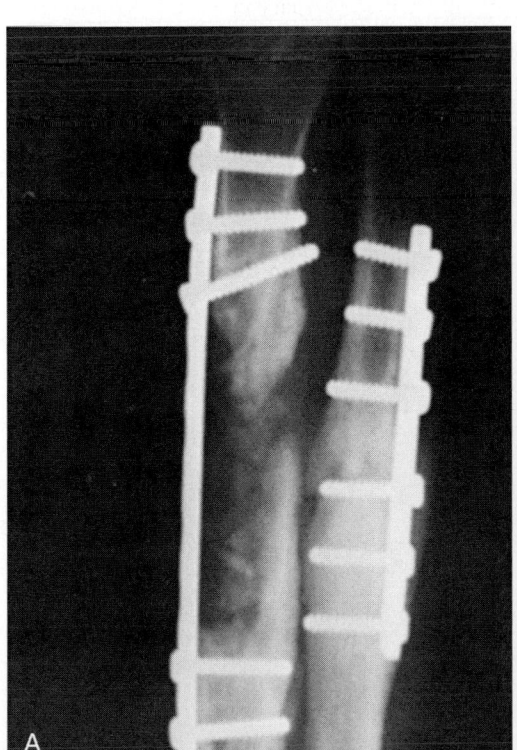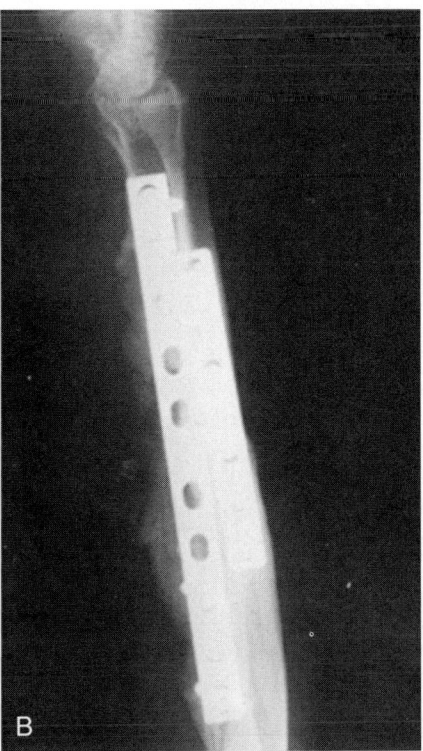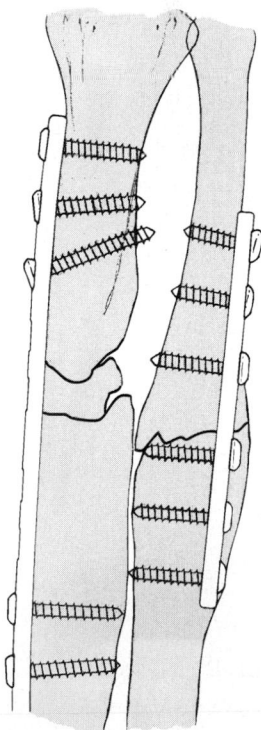

**FIGURE 41–18.** A 28-year-old man sustained a high-energy injury to his right forearm with extensive skeletal and soft tissue loss. After extensive débridement, the ulna was stabilized with a six-hole dynamic compression plate. A groin flap was elevated and inset to cover the soft tissue defect. Ten days later, the radius was brought to length with a distractor, and a strut plate was applied; the defect was filled with cancellous iliac crest graft. Anteroposterior (*A*) and lateral (*B*) radiographs 4 weeks after operation demonstrate early incorporation of the cancellous graft. *C*, Schematic illustration of the internal fixation.

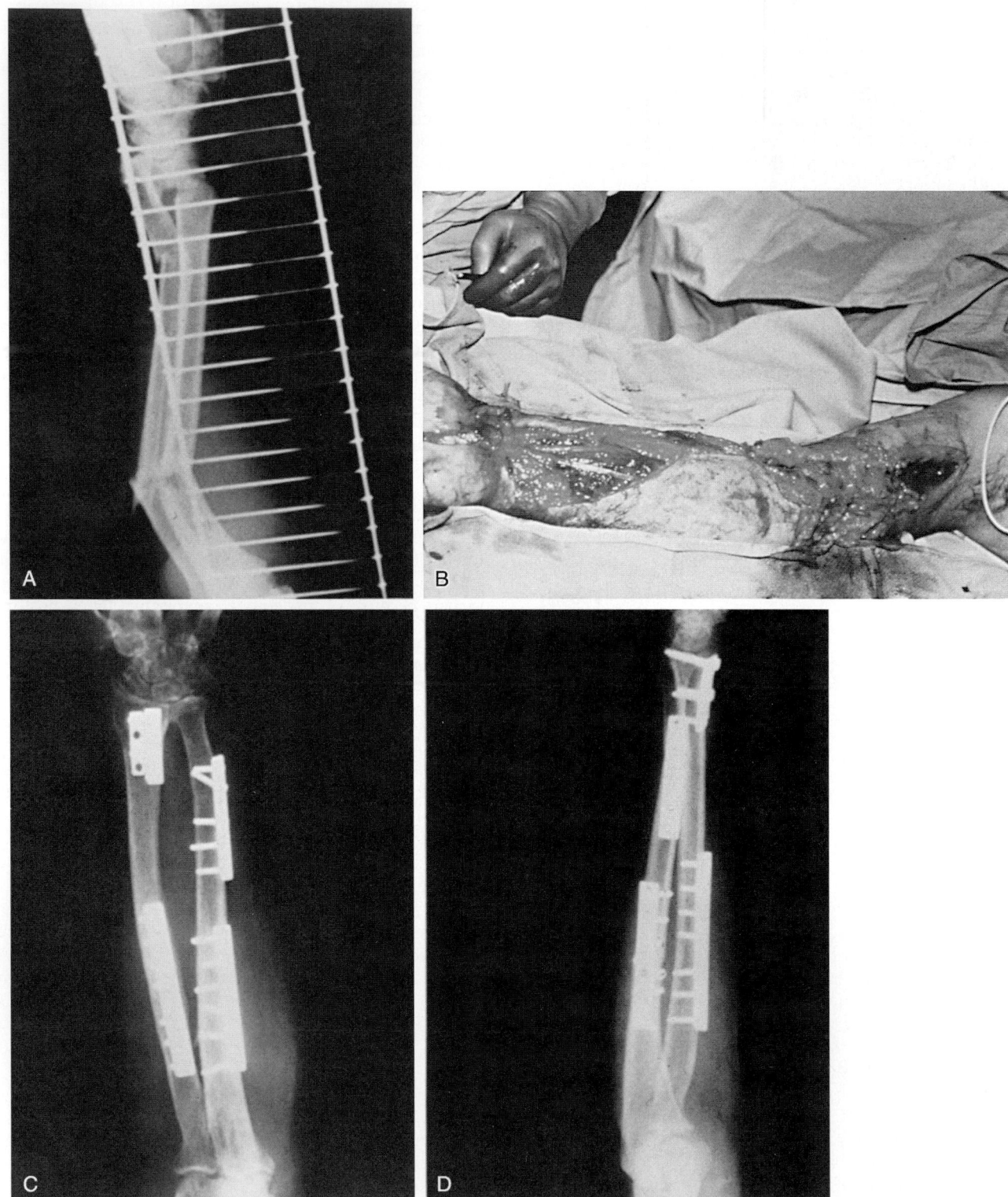

**FIGURE 41–19.** A 60-year-old laborer had his right (dominant) arm crushed in a press. *A,* Radiograph revealing segmental fractures of the radius and ulna, both of which were open. *B,* Extensive débridement and forearm decompression were achieved through an anterior approach. Anteroposterior (*C*) and lateral (*D*) radiographs reveal segmental plating of the fractures. Excellent function resulted.

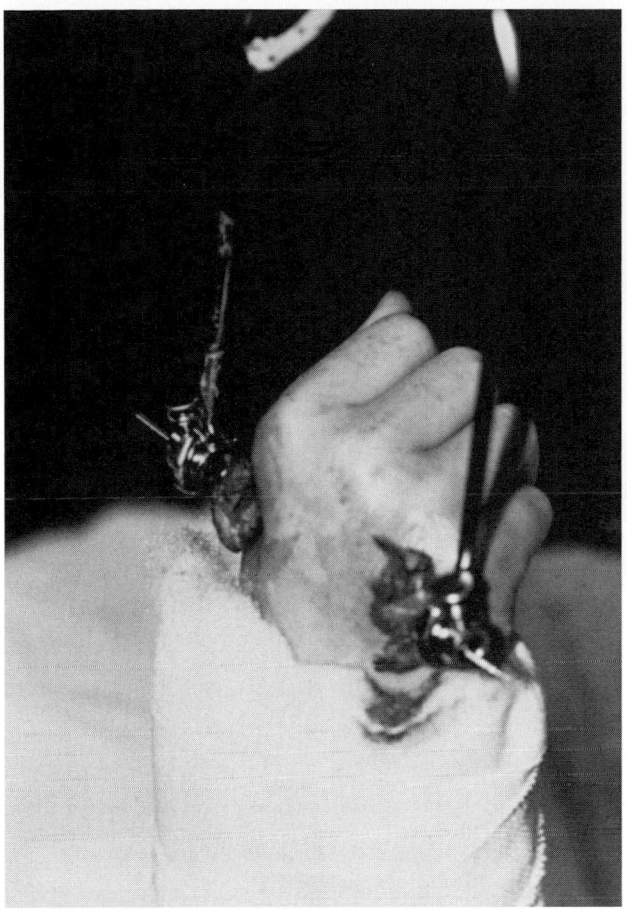

FIGURE **41-20.** A heavily contaminated open forearm fracture that occurred in a horse stable and was treated with extensive débridement and temporary skeletal traction with a pin placed through the second and third metacarpals.

## TREATMENT

It is generally recognized that a Galeazzi fracture is best treated operatively. Campbell noted this in 1941, terming the Galeazzi fracture "a fracture of necessity."[140] The difficulties with nonoperative treatment were subsequently confirmed in 1957 by Hughston,[62] who identified unsatisfactory results in 35 (92%) of 38 cases treated by closed reduction and plaster immobilization. He identified several deforming forces that are not adequately controlled by plaster. These include the muscle pull of the brachioradialis, pronator quadratus, and thumb extensors and the weight of the hand. Although his criteria for a satisfactory result were strict (comprising union, anatomic alignment, no loss of length, no subluxation of the DRUJ, and no limitation of forearm rotation), succeeding clinical studies have supported his observations.[75, 88, 92, 126, 153]

The distal third of the radius is readily approached through the anterior (Henry) exposure. Stable internal fixation is most reliably achieved through compression plate fixation with a minimum of five and preferably six screws. Medullary nails or smaller plates may not control the deforming forces and have been associated with delayed union and nonunion.[35, 37, 139]

After the anatomic reduction has been secured and the plate has been provisionally applied with two screws, radiographs are obtained in both the anteroposterior and true lateral planes to control the DRUJ. If reduction has been achieved, stability is tested clinically with rotation of the forearm (Fig. 41-25). If the reduction is stable throughout full forearm rotation, there is no need for postoperative immobilization and early functional rehabilitation.

If reduction of the DRUJ can be achieved but proves unstable with forearm rotation, two options are available. In cases in which there is an associated fracture of the ulna styloid at its base, open reduction and fixation of the styloid with Kirschner wires or a small screw can effectively stabilize the DRUJ in some cases[88] (Fig. 41-26). If the reduction is stable clinically, the forearm should be immobilized in supination by an above-elbow cast brace for 4 to 6 weeks to allow soft tissue healing. If no styloid fracture is present, the distal ulna can be transfixed to the radius with one or two 0.062-inch Kirschner wires left for 4 weeks. The forearm should also be immobilized in supination by an above-elbow cast brace during this time (Fig. 41-27).

In the unlikely event that the DRUJ cannot be reduced, a soft tissue block should be suspected.[12, 24] The DRUJ can be approached through a dorsal incision and the source of the block identified and removed. In most reported cases, the extensor carpi ulnaris tendon has been the cause of the irreducible DRUJ (see Fig. 41-19B). Instability of the DRUJ may also result from failure to recognize the injury, in part because of inadequate radiographs taken postoperatively or intraoperatively.

## COMPLICATIONS

Complications of the Galeazzi fracture are not uncommon; Moore and co-workers[92] reported a 39% incidence in 36 patients. The complications include nonunion, malunion, infection, instability of the DRUJ, refracture after plate removal, and nerve injury associated with the operative treatment. Nonunion or malunion is most commonly reported in association with the use of plaster casts and inadequate internal fixation.[92, 123, 139]

The radial nerve is the nerve most frequently injured. In Moore's series, six dorsal sensory nerves and one posterior interosseous nerve were injured.[92] Of the six dorsal sensory nerve injuries, three occurred with an anterior approach and three with a dorsal approach. In four of six cases, the nerve was not identified at the time of surgery.

## Monteggia Lesion

Fracture of the proximal ulna with a dislocation of the radial head bears the eponym of Monteggia, who first described this association in Milan in 1814.[91] Bado[6, 7] coined the term *Monteggia lesion* to encompass a number of traumatic lesions having in common disruption of the radiohumeroulnar joint in conjunction with a fracture of the ulna at any level.

Although much has been published regarding the various presentations, treatment options, and complications, the Monteggia lesion remains a relatively uncommon

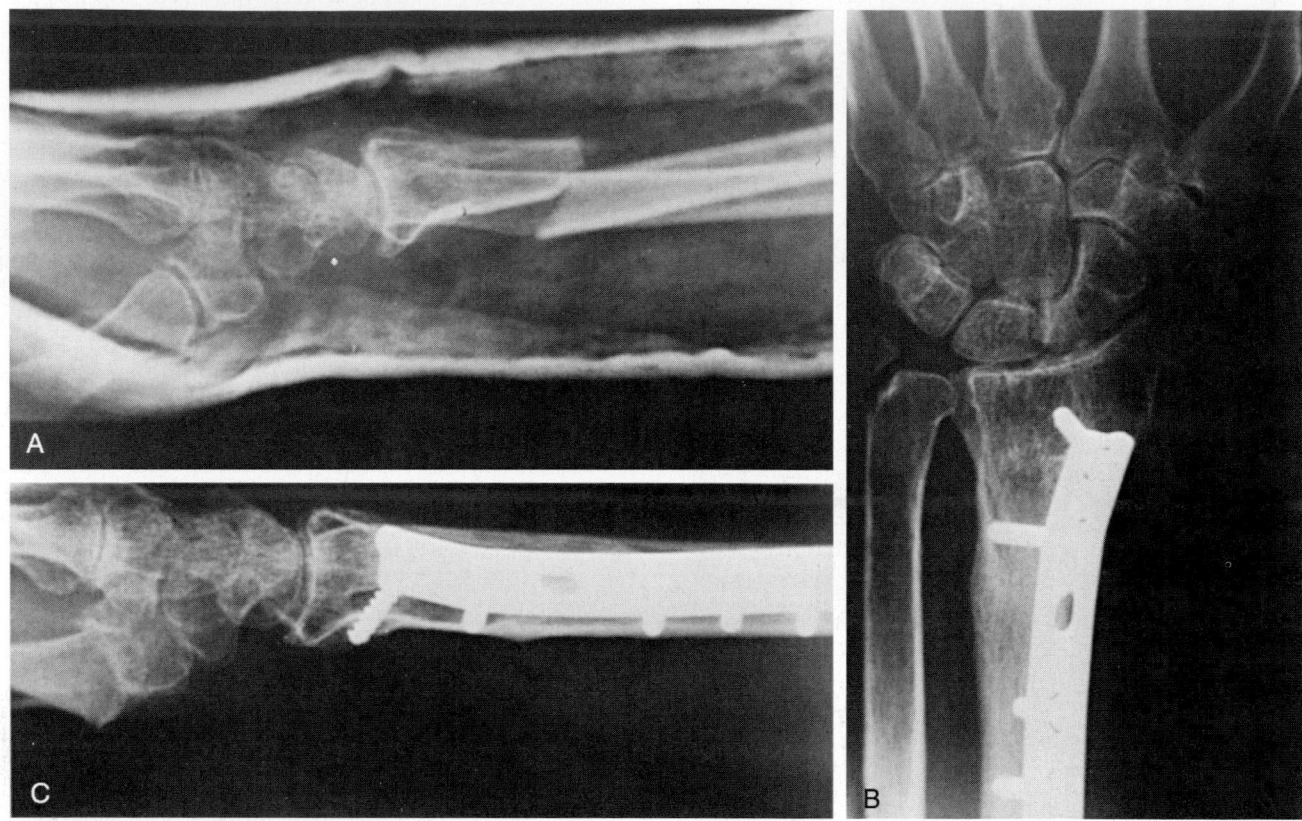

**FIGURE 41–21.** A short oblique fracture of the distal radius in a 56-year-old man. The fracture was initially treated with a cast. However, a follow-up radiograph *(A)* revealed an unsatisfactory alignment. Anteroposterior *(B)* and lateral *(C)* radiographs 1 year after plate fixation with a 4.5-mm dynamic compression plate. Full function resulted.

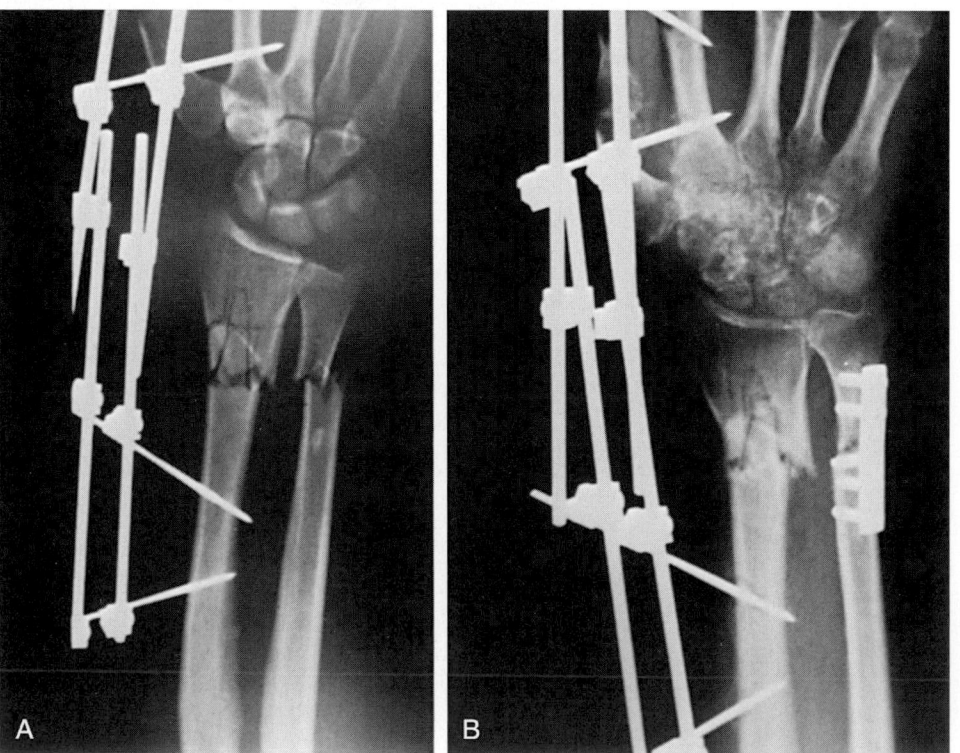

**FIGURE 41–22.** A comminuted fracture of the distal radius and ulna in a 50-year-old woman. *A,* The fracture was initially treated with skeletal fixation with the pins placed in the proximal radius and metacarpals. *B,* The ulnar fracture was stabilized with a five-hole dynamic compression plate, but the radius was maintained in the external fixator. Settling occurred at the fracture site with disruption of distal radioulnar joint function.

injury, its incidence varying between 1% and 2% of all forearm fractures.[20, 22, 23, 105, 106, 123] Problems arise in understanding of these lesions in part because few surgeons have a wide experience. The literature can also be misleading because a number of series combine adult and pediatric injuries.

It has become acceptable to categorize Monteggia fractures in terms of the direction of the dislocation of the head of the radius: anterior, posterior, or lateral. The ulnar fracture has characteristically been located at the junction of the proximal and middle thirds, although it is not unusual for it to occur proximal or distal to this. The apex of angulation of the ulnar fracture is in the same direction as the displacement of the radial head (Fig. 41–28). Bado[6] expanded the categories to include a fourth group: anterior dislocation of the radial head with a fracture of both the ulna and the radius at the proximal third of the forearm.

The type I anterior lesion was long thought to be the result of a direct blow to the posterior aspect of the forearm, which fractures the ulna and forces the radial head anteriorly.[132, 135] However, Evans[43] was able to create this lesion in cadavers with a hyperpronation force on the forearm with the humerus held fixed in a vise. He postulated that this injury was instead the result of a fall on the outstretched hand with the forearm fixed in maximal pronation. Rotation of the torso on this fixed, pronated forearm results in fracture of the ulna; the radius is forced into hyperpronation and is levered anteriorly by the forearm of the fractured ulna.

The anterior dislocation (Bado type I) has been considered the most common type, constituting as much as 60% to 80% of all Monteggia lesions in some series[15, 135] (see Fig. 41–28A). The posterior and lateral dislocations have been considered to be less common. However, because these series tend to combine both adult and pediatric injuries, the published incidences may not apply universally in adult trauma centers.[110]

In series of Penrose[101] and of Pavel and associates,[100] the posterior presentation proved more common than had been previously recognized (see Fig. 41–28B). The investigators identified three distinct components of this injury: (1) a comminuted fracture of the proximal ulna near the coronoid, frequently including a triangular or quadrangular fragment; (2) posterior dislocation of the proximal radius; and (3) a triangular chip fracture of the anterior aspect of the radial head, resulting from a shearing injury against the capitellum (Fig. 41–29A and B). Penrose[101] believed that this lesion more closely resembled a variation of a posterior dislocation of the elbow, except that in this

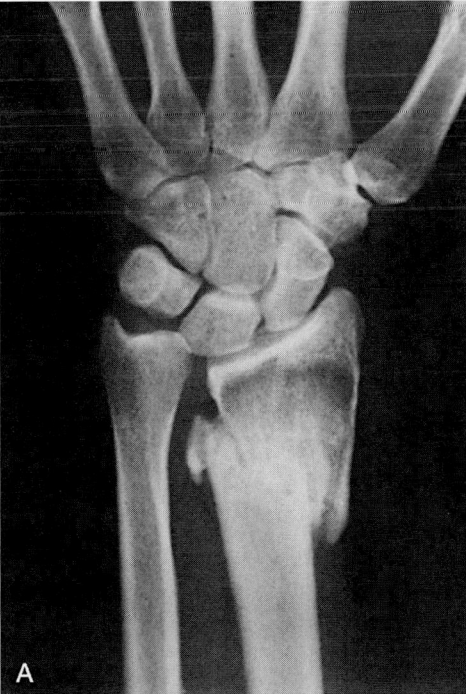
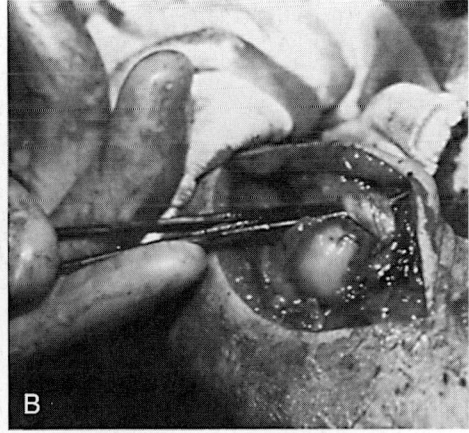
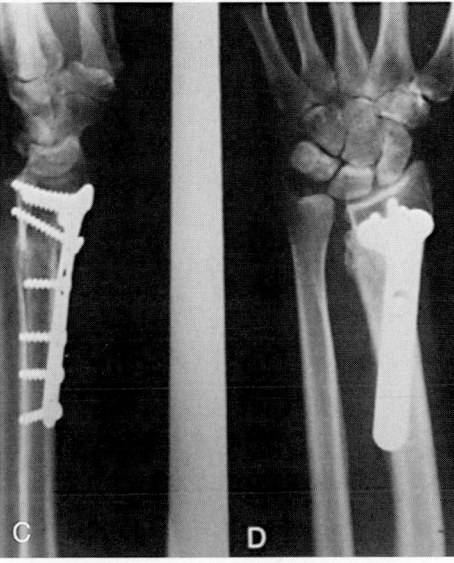

**FIGURE 41–23.** A 32-year-old woman with multiple injuries had this short oblique radius fracture treated in a splint for 6 weeks. *A,* Anteroposterior radiograph demonstrating a short oblique distal radius fracture with shortening and disruption of the distal radioulnar joint. *B,* At surgery, the extensor carpi ulnaris was found interposed between the ulnar head and the distal radius. *C* and *D,* The fracture was taken down, and the bone fragments were lengthened and secured with a 4.5-mm T plate. Residual disruption of the distal radioulnar joint remained, limiting the forearm rotation to 30% of normal.

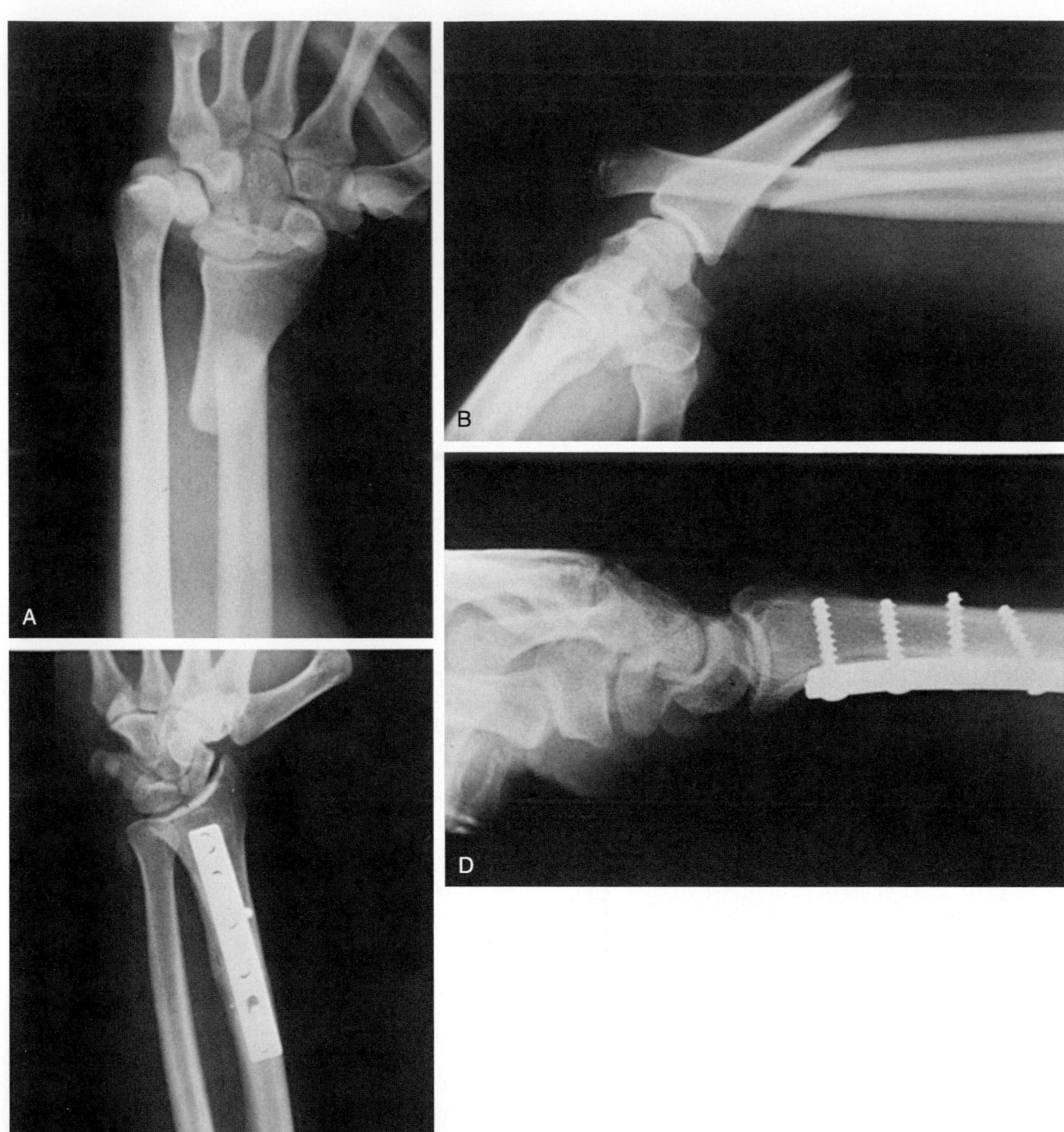

**FIGURE 41–24.** A 20-year-old laborer fell 20 feet from a scaffolding, sustaining an open Galeazzi fracture. Anteroposterior (*A*) and lateral (*B*) radiographs reveal a gross disruption of the distal radioulnar joint and a short oblique fracture of the radius at the junction of the middle and distal thirds. *C, D,* After wound débridement, the radius was stabilized with a six-hole 3.5-mm dynamic compression plate with one screw used through the plate as an interfragmentary lag screw across the oblique fracture. The distal radioulnar joint proved stable when the radius was reduced.

case the ligamentous attachments of the elbow prove stronger than the ulnar shaft. To prove this theory, he placed cadaver humeri on a rigid support with the elbow at 60° of flexion and the forearm in moderate pronation. A direct blow was given across the wrist, resulting in posterior dislocation of the elbow. When the upper anterior surface of the ulna was notched, a similar force consistently produced the posterior Monteggia lesion he

observed clinically. Unlike the anterior Monteggia lesion, which occurs frequently in the pediatric age group, this lesion is more likely to be seen in a middle-aged adult and typically results from a fall on the outstretched hand with the elbow flexed approximately 60° and the forearm pronated about 30°. At the Massachusetts General Hospital from 1981 to 1988, 20 adult Monteggia fractures were treated surgically; 14 were this posterior variant.[69]

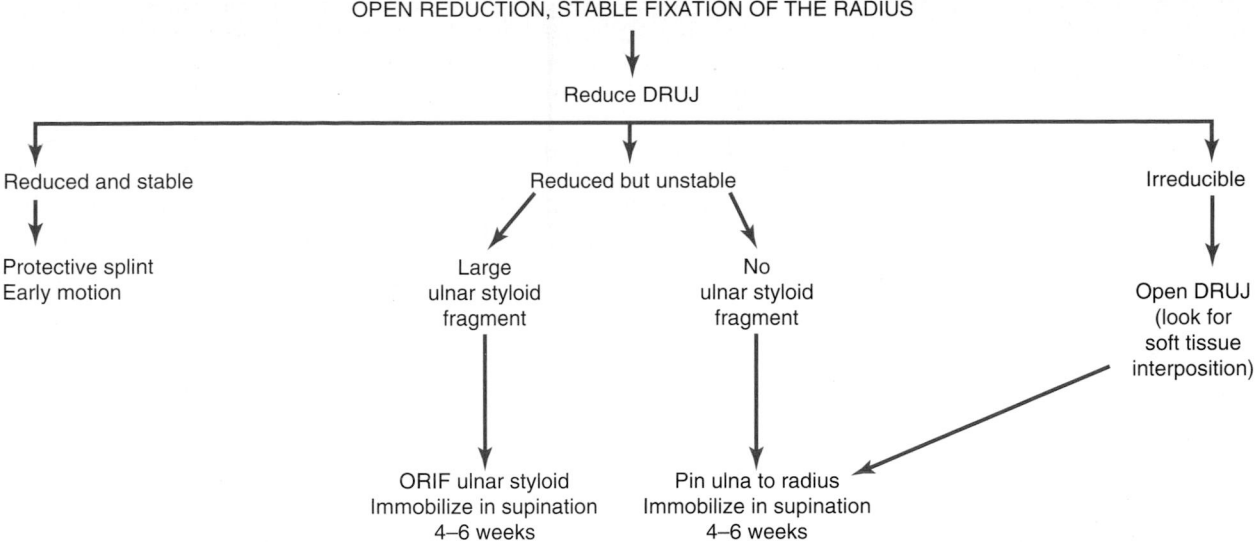

OPEN REDUCTION, STABLE FIXATION OF THE RADIUS

Reduce DRUJ

Reduced and stable → Protective splint / Early motion

Reduced but unstable → Large ulnar styloid fragment → ORIF ulnar styloid / Immobilize in supination / 4–6 weeks

Reduced but unstable → No ulnar styloid fragment → Pin ulna to radius / Immobilize in supination / 4–6 weeks

Irreducible → Open DRUJ (look for soft tissue interposition)

**FIGURE 41–25.** Treatment algorithm for Galeazzi fractures. *Abbreviations:* DRUJ, distal radioulnar joint; ORIF, open reduction and internal fixation.

The third type of Monteggia fracture, that with a lateral displacement of the radius, has been identified in both pediatric and adult patients. It has been attributed to a primary adduction force[103] or a force of both angulation and rotation.[97] This lesion has been associated with radial nerve trauma.[136] The clinical presentation with all Monteggia lesions is a painful elbow that resists attempts at elbow flexion, extension, or forearm rotation. The neurovascular status must be evaluated; associated posterior interosseous, anterior interosseous, and ulnar nerve lesions have all been reported.[42, 63, 69, 80, 128, 138]

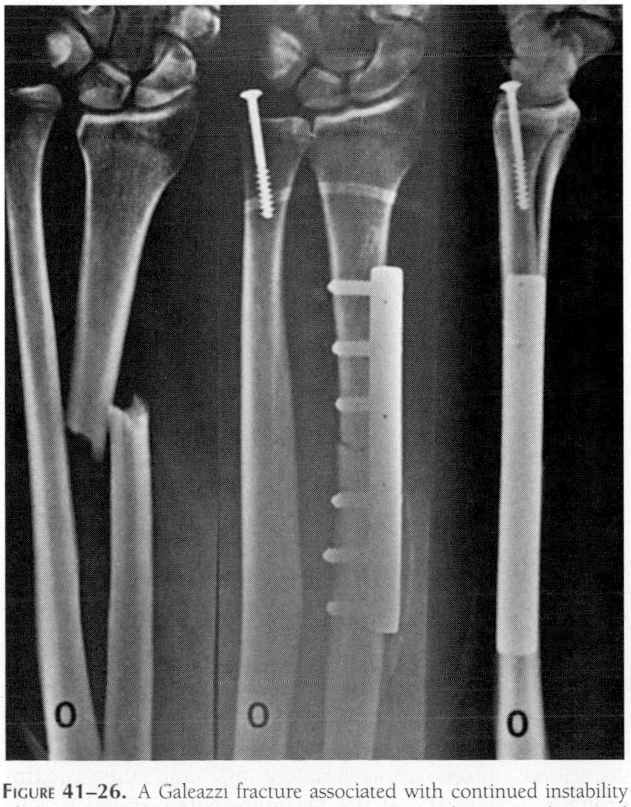

The Monteggia lesion may be misdiagnosed on the initial examination.[111] Whereas the ulnar fracture is readily apparent, the radial dislocation can be overlooked. Several factors account for this.[52] The injury is uncommon and therefore is not always suspected. With associated soft tissue swelling or deformity about the elbow, the position of the radial head can be difficult to assess. In addition, the radial head may have been reduced when the ulna fracture was splinted. The radiographs may not be adequate if they are centered on the ulna fracture and miss the elbow.

In the presence of an isolated forearm diaphyseal fracture, the clinician must always anticipate the possibility of injury to the other bone. A line drawn through the radial shaft and head should touch the capitellum in any position of flexion or extension of the elbow if the radial head is correctly located.[86]

Closed treatment remains standard for most pediatric fractures. In the adult displaced Monteggia lesion, operative reduction and stable fixation are mandatory. The ulnar fracture must be anatomically reduced and securely stabilized in order to ensure accurate repositioning of the radial head. In most instances, this is best accomplished with a plate, although excellent results have sometimes been observed with intramedullary rods.

After operative fixation has been achieved, the surgeon must ensure the stability of the radial head by fully flexing and extending the elbow and rotating the forearm, preferably under image intensification. Instability of the radial head or incomplete reduction usually suggests a malreduction of the ulnar fracture,[123] especially with a posterior lesion. A comminuted metaphyseal ulnar fracture, unless rigidly secured, tends to flex at the fracture site, levering the radial head posteriorly. In these fractures, a plate applied on the dorsal surface of the ulna better ensures an anatomic reduction and functions mechanically as a tension band (Fig. 41–30).

**FIGURE 41–26.** A Galeazzi fracture associated with continued instability of the distal radioulnar joint despite anatomic reduction and internal fixation of the radius. When fixation of the large styloid fragment was achieved, the joint proved stable.

If the radial head cannot be relocated despite an anatomic reduction of the ulna (<10% of cases), the incision should be extended as a Boyd-Thompson approach, reflecting the anconeus, extensor carpi ulnaris, and supinator muscles from the ulna and exposing the radiocapitellar joint.[16] Soft tissue interposition is likely to be the source of the inability to reduce the radial head; it can involve the joint capsule, the annular ligament, or, in some instances, the posterior interosseous nerve.

Boyd and Boals[15] described a procedure to stabilize the radial head by reconstructing a new annular ligament using a strip of forearm fascia elevated from distal to proximal. Our experience and that of others[106] has been that this is rarely, if ever, necessary and is fraught with the possibility of residual scarring and loss of forearm rotation.

In a radial head fracture, the fracture fragment may also serve to block reduction or elbow motion. A large, single fragment is best fixed internally, whereas a smaller fragment should be excised. A comminuted radial head represents one of the indications for a radial head arthroplasty.[112]

Complications of Monteggia lesions are many and can be disabling.[89] They include loss of motion, malunion, nonunion, and nerve palsy, which most often involves the posterior interosseous nerve. The prognosis is good, with recovery beginning within 6 to 8 weeks after injury.[63] If

there is no evidence of nerve function by that time, exploration is advisable. Tardy radial nerve palsy has been reported with long-standing radial head dislocation and has responded well to nerve exploration and radial head excision.[4, 80]

Malunion can follow failure to diagnose the radial head dislocation, inadequate reduction of the ulnar fracture, or unstable internal fixation. When it is recognized, consideration can be given to osteotomy of the ulna and plate fixation. In long-standing deformities, radial head resection may be necessary.

Nonunion of the ulnar fracture almost always reflects inadequate skeletal fixation. In the absence of infection, union is readily achieved with a plate applied on the dorsal (tension) surface and, in some instances, supplemented by an iliac crest bone graft (Fig. 41–31).

## COMPLICATIONS

### Plate Removal and Refracture

Concerns regarding stress protection of the bone under a plate, stress concentration at the end of the plate, and the patient's discomfort have led many to recommend removal

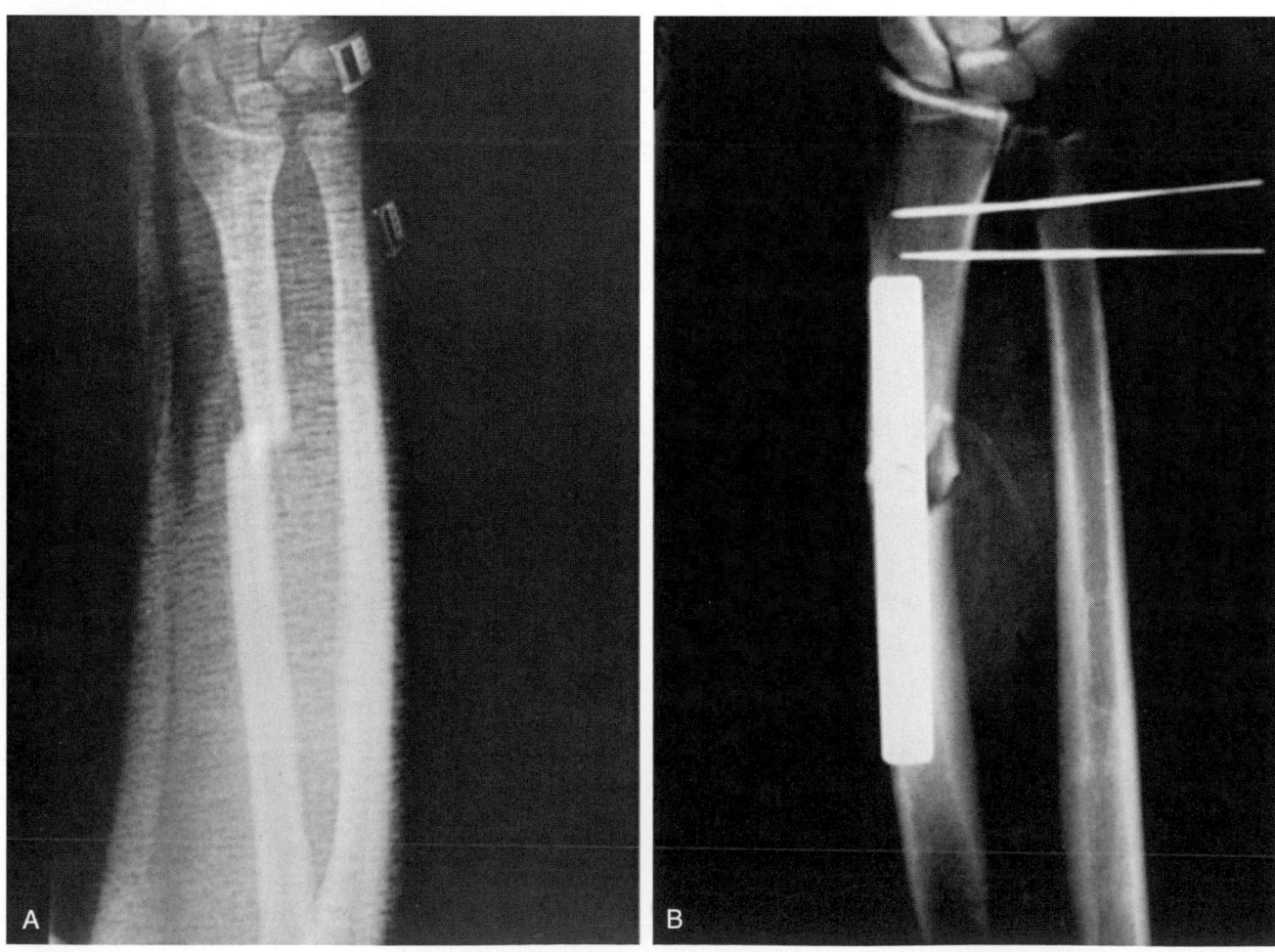

**FIGURE 41–27.** *A,* Despite stable fixation of the radius fracture, the distal ulna remained unstable even with the forearm supinated. *B,* Therefore, the ulna was stabilized to the distal radius with two Kirschner wires for 4 weeks.

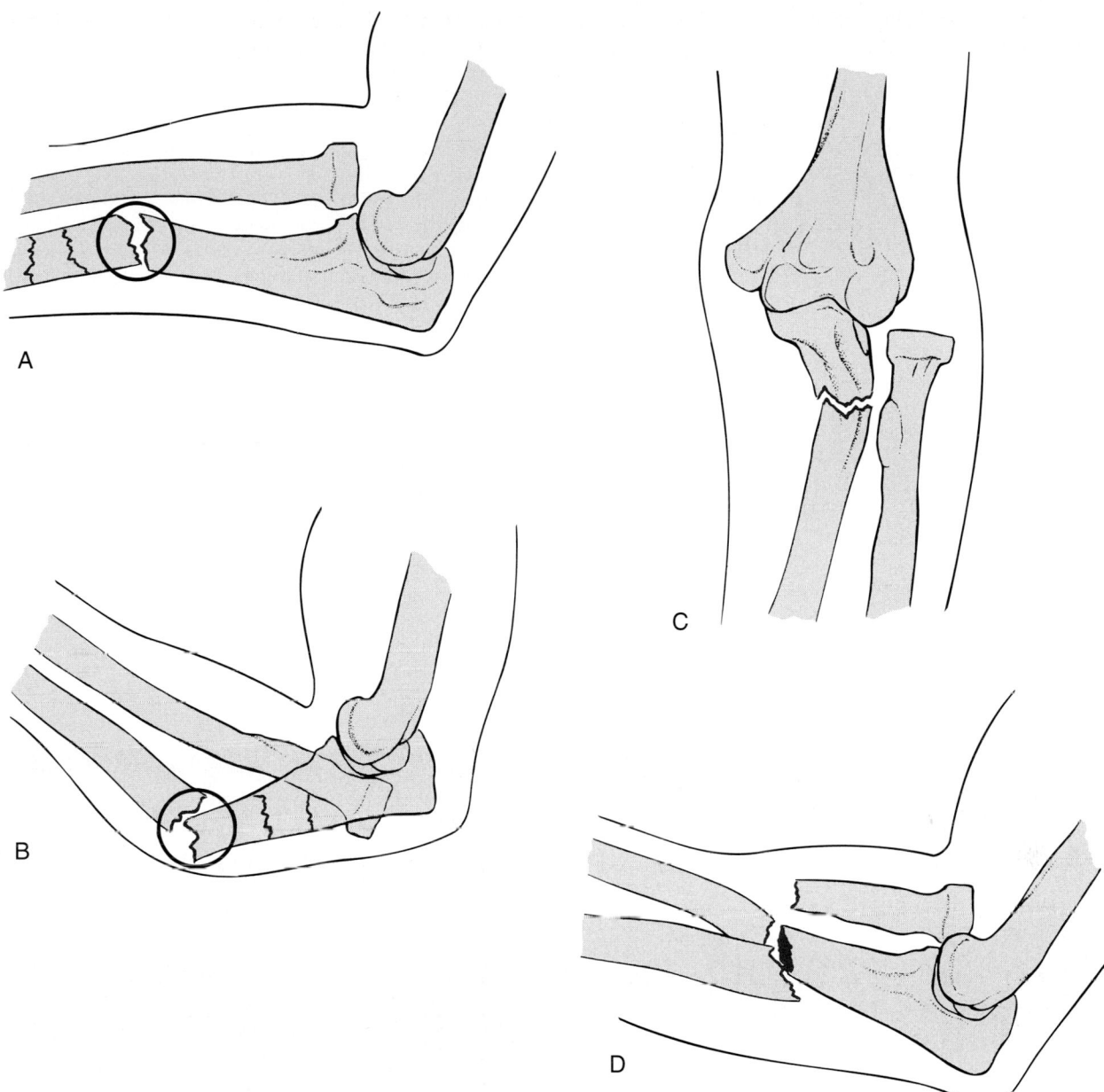

**FIGURE 41–28.** The classification of Monteggia lesions by Bado. *A,* Type I: Anterior angulation of the ulnar fracture and anterior dislocation of the radial head. *B,* Type II: Posterior angulation of the ulnar fracture and posterior dislocation of the radial head. *C,* Type III: Fracture of the proximal ulna metaphysis and lateral dislocation of the radial head. *D,* Type IV: Anterior dislocation of the radial head and fracture of the radial and ulnar shafts.

of forearm plates. The actual incidence of a fracture occurring beyond a plate is unknown, but it does pose a problem to the athlete involved in contact sports.

Plate removal, however, is not without complications.[11] The frequency of refracture after forearm plate removal has been reported to be less than 4% in some series[25, 35, 76] and as high as 25% in others.[34, 55] The basis for this wide variation of incidence is better understood when the number of factors that contribute to refracture is analyzed. Premature plate removal (<1 year after injury), delayed union or nonunion, and inadequate technique were identified by Deluca and colleagues[34] and by Hidaka and Gustilo[60] as causes of refracture.

Bone loss under a plate was long thought to be induced by a mechanical unloading of the bone (stress protection)

by the implant. It has now been demonstrated by Perren and co-workers[102] that the initial porosis observed under a plate is the result of local circulatory disturbance and necrosis followed by bone remodeling. According to these observations, plate removal should be considered only after the remodeling is complete and the cortex under the plate has returned to a near-normal condition. Rosson and associates[116, 117] have suggested that remodeling under a plate requires 18 to 21 months after application.

Given these observations, it has become our policy not to recommend routine removal of the plates. If plates are to be removed, there should be radiographic evidence of cortical remodeling under the plate, which often requires 2 years from the time of plating. For the high-demand athlete, if a decision is reached to remove the plate, it should be done only after cortical bone remodeling is evident radiographically. After plate removal, the forearm should be protected with a functional forearm brace for 6 weeks, and return to activity should occur 3 to 4 months after plate removal.[113]

If pain is the reason for plate removal, the surgeon must identify whether the pain is at the site of the original fracture. Should this be the case, adequate imaging, including radiographs and tomographs, should be obtained to define the status of fracture healing.

## Synostosis

Cross union between the forearm bones, first described by Gross in 1864,[55] has subsequently been identified in conjunction with almost every form of forearm trauma.[14, 119, 149, 150] Although it is more common with fractures of the middle and proximal thirds, the distal forearm is not entirely spared this troublesome complication (Fig. 41–32).

The true incidence of cross union secondary to forearm fractures is difficult to determine accurately because not all reported series address this issue. Vince and Miller[149] reviewed 2381 reported forearm fractures in the literature and identified a combined incidence of approximately 2%.

The incidence may be higher with Monteggia fractures, particularly those involving both forearm bones along with dislocations of the radial head.[17, 145]

A number of etiologic factors have been implicated in the formation of cross unions, but the most likely causes include high-energy trauma with open fractures,[5, 19, 82, 104] infection,[23] multiple trauma with head injuries,[49, 149] and delayed (i.e., by several weeks) internal fixation.[10, 41, 134, 149] Less common factors are nonanatomic reduction with narrowing of the interosseous space, onlay bone grafting, and the use of screws that are too long and cross the interosseous membrane.[14, 28, 74]

Although there have been no studies specifically identifying measures to prevent synostosis, it would appear that both open and closed fractures that are treated early with stable internal fixation and mobilized in the early postoperative period have little risk of developing cross union.[53, 57, 59]

The loss of forearm rotation caused by post-traumatic radioulnar synostosis substantially impairs the function of the entire upper limb. In the past, unpredictable results after operative excision led to recommendations to use interposed materials after excision of the synostosis. The material recommended included muscle, silicone rubber sheets, and fat grafts.[125] Experience with low-dose radiation to prevent heterotopic ossification after reconstructive surgical procedures about the hip has led to similar

FIGURE 41–29. *A*, Schematic of a posterior Monteggia lesion. The features of this fracture-dislocation include (1) comminuted fracture of the proximal ulna near the coronoid, (2) posterior dislocation of the proximal radius, and (3) triangular chip fracture of the radial head resulting from shearing against the capitellum. *B*, Lateral radiograph of a posterior Monteggia lesion in a 36-year-old man.

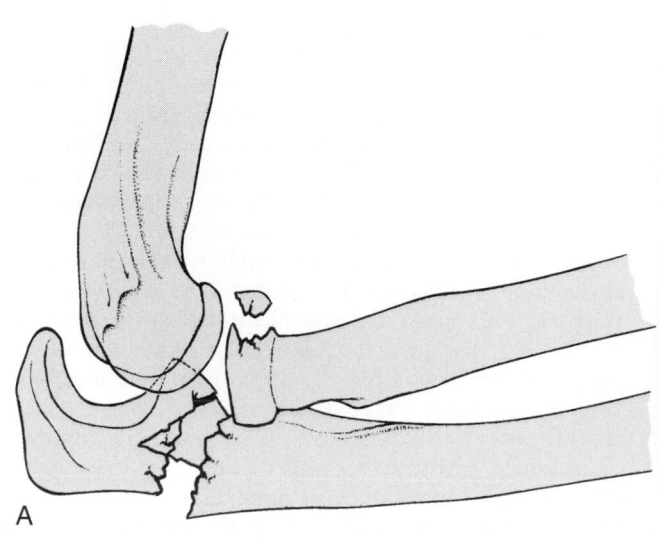

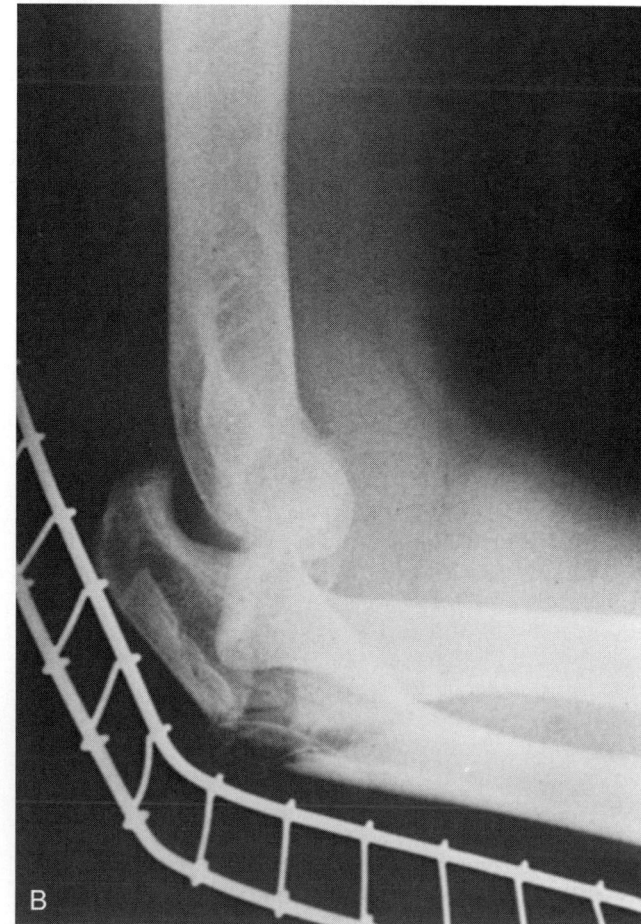

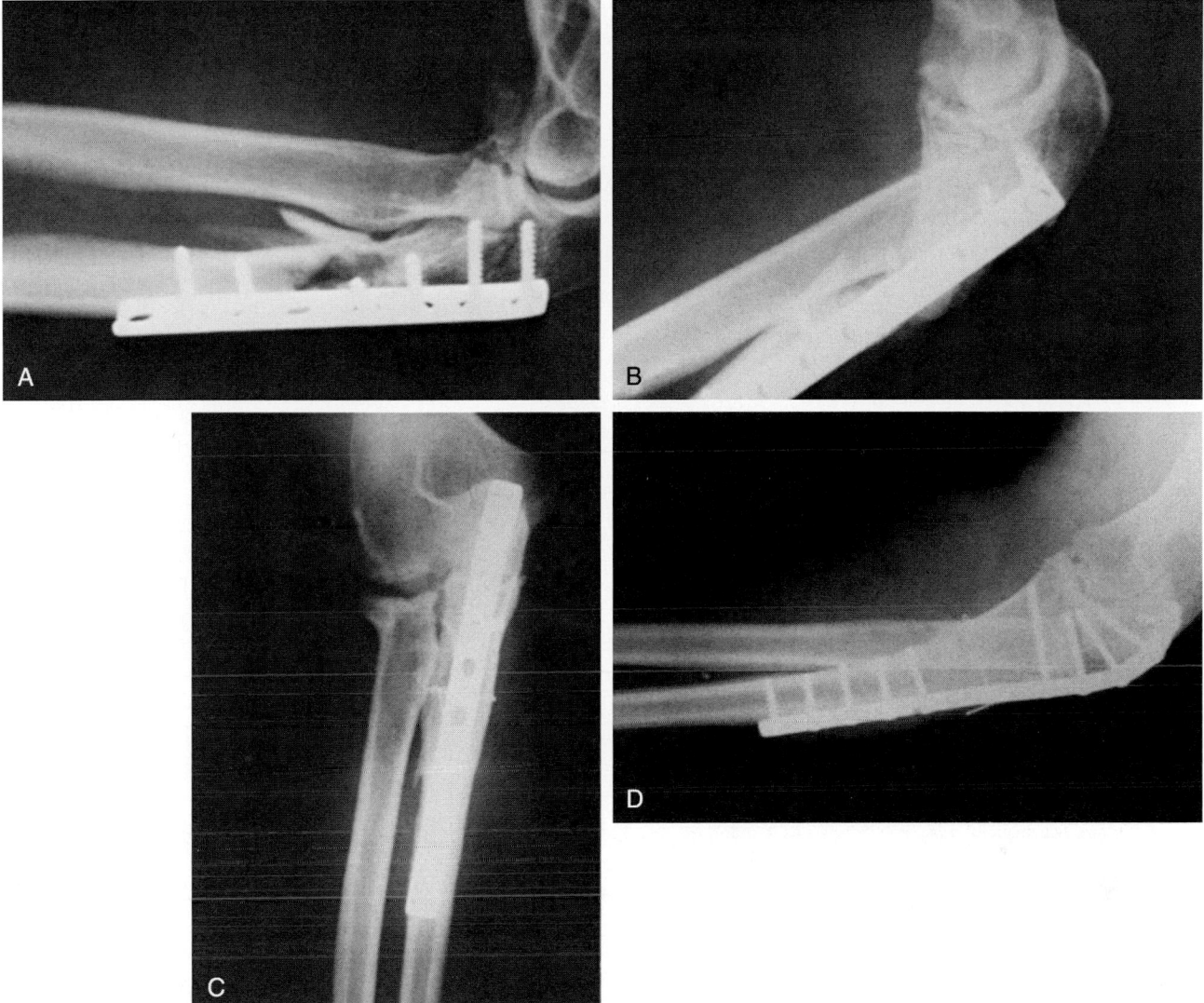

**FIGURE 41–30.** A 44-year-old man had a posterior Monteggia lesion treated with a plate applied to the lateral surface of the ulna. Incomplete reduction of the radial head was noted. *A*, Lateral radiograph showing inadequate skeletal fixation with the plate. Note the persistent posterior subluxation of the fractured radial head. *B*, The fracture displaced with the inadequate fixation. Anteroposterior (*C*) and lateral (*D*) radiographs 5 months after revision surgery including placement of a 12-hole 3.5-mm dynamic compression plate on the tension side and radial head resection.

applications after synostosis resection in the forearm with favorable results.[1, 30]

Although excision of the synostosis in the distal or middle forearm has been well accepted, in the past there was pessimism about the operative approach in the proximal third of the forearm. One of us (JBJ) reported on favorable results of resection of proximal radioulnar synostosis in 18 limbs of 17 consecutive patients.[71] The resection was performed on average 19 months after injury, although eight patients had their surgery less than 12 months after injury. It has become evident that successful treatment can be achieved as early as 6 months after injury combined with adjuvant postexcision radiation. In this group of 17 patients, recurrence was noted in only 1 patient who had an associated closed head injury. The average forearm rotation in the other 17 limbs was 139°. No neurovascular problems were noted (Fig. 41–33).

## Neurovascular Injury

Most major vascular injuries associated with forearm fracture involve a single arterial laceration and do not threaten the viability of the hand. Some studies have suggested that repair of the damaged vessel in this situation may not be worthwhile because thrombosis may result from backflow from the patent artery.[66, 68]

Median, ulnar, and radial nerve palsies have been reported in association with forearm fractures.[63, 94, 138] One of the most common nerve injuries is a posterior interosseous nerve palsy in association with a Monteggia fracture-dislocation.[63, 136, 138] Nerve palsy associated with forearm fracture usually represents a neurapraxic injury caused by nerve contusion or traction and remits spontaneously. Rarely, a nerve becomes trapped in the fracture site or is even transected by a sharp fracture fragment.[94] In general, early nerve exploration in the management of a fracture-associated nerve deficit is not indicated unless there is a change in the neurologic examination after reduction, there is an associated vascular injury or open wound, or the fracture is irreducible.[128] Most forearm fractures are treated operatively, and a nerve exploration can usually be performed without considerable additional surgical trauma.

Most neural injuries, even those associated with high-velocity bullet wounds, recover spontaneously.[40, 68, 78, 128, 131] Nerve exploration can be carried out during the initial irrigation and débridement. Even with early exploration, however, the extent of nerve damage can be difficult to determine. In the case of complete nerve transection, the nerve ends can be sutured to adjacent soft tissue to prevent retraction. Delayed repair is performed after the wound is cleaned and adequately débrided.

Complex combined neurovascular injury is but one of the adverse sequelae of severe mangling upper extremity trauma. The approach to vascular injuries is modified somewhat by the presence of an associated nerve lesion because there is some evidence to suggest that recovery of nerve function is improved by optimization of blood flow.[68, 79] Hand viability may be maintained even if both radial and ulnar arteries have been damaged because, in addition to the dual major arterial supply to the forearm, there are a number of longitudinally oriented collateral vessels in the upper extremity.[66] If both major arteries are damaged in the presence of associated nerve injury, it is recommended that both be repaired, regardless of the apparent vascular status of the hand, in order to optimize nerve recovery. If one major supplier remains intact and provides adequate perfusion to the entire hand (as determined by a timed Allen test), the damaged artery need not be repaired.

Vascular repair should follow fracture stabilization if feasible (often by temporary means such as external

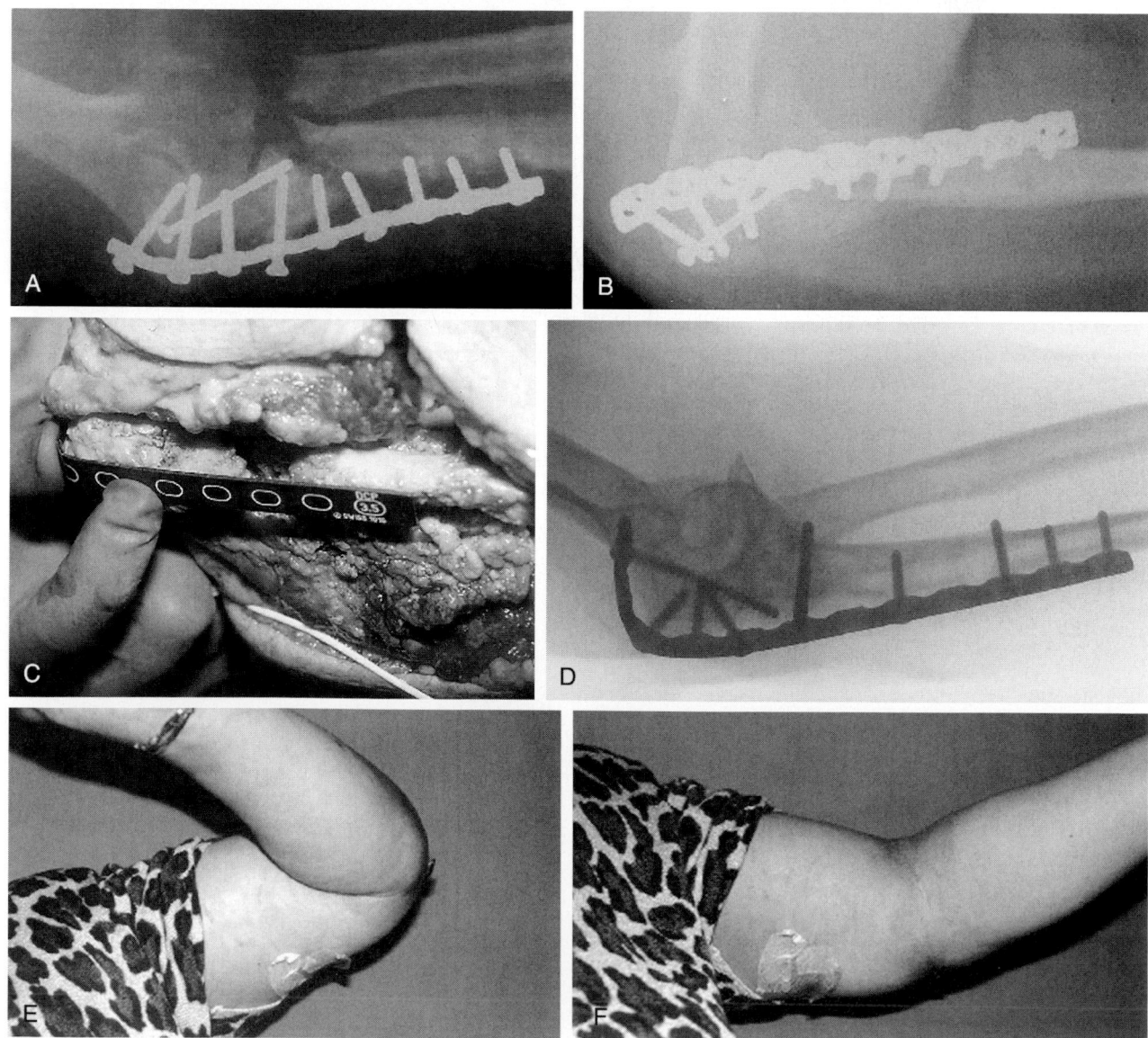

**Figure 41–31.** *A–F,* A 67-year-old schoolteacher with a nonunion of the ulna after operative treatment for a posterior Monteggia variant. *A, B,* Two radiographic views of the unstable nonunion. *C,* Following plate removal and débridement of the synovial nonunion, a malleable template is applied for guidance in contouring the plate.

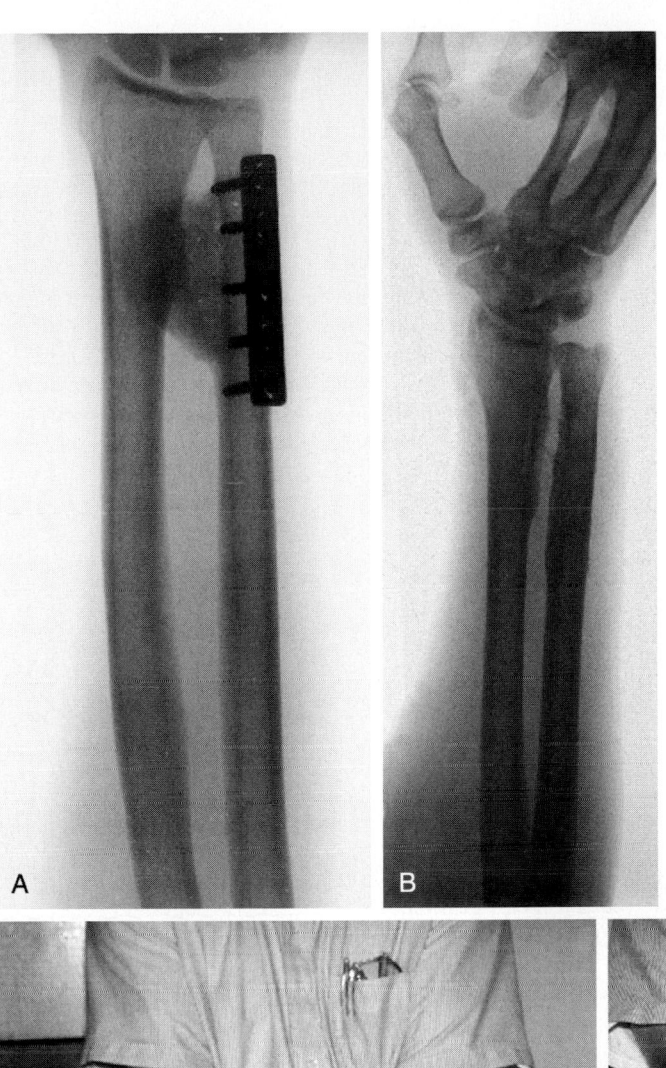

**FIGURE 41–32.** *A–D*, A distal third post-traumatic radio-ulnar synostosis after open reduction and internal fixation of an unstable ulnar fracture. *A*, The synostosis is easily visualized. *B*, Radiograph after plate removal and excision of the synostosis. *C, D*, Excellent forearm rotation.

fixation) in order to provide protection of the repaired vessel. After revascularization, compartment pressures should be checked and fasciotomies performed as indicated.[50]

In many cases, patients with severe mangling upper extremity injury may best be served by early amputation. However, upper extremity prosthetics provide a poor substitute for upper extremity function, and most reasonable attempts at limb salvage are worthwhile.[68, 79] In addition to the judgment of the treating surgeon (based on history, examination, radiologic studies, and operative exploration), consideration of the mangled extremity score is useful in determining the appropriateness of primary amputation.

Operative treatment of forearm fractures exposes the patient to the risk of iatrogenic nerve injury. A neurapraxic superficial radial nerve palsy can occur because this nerve

is retracted laterally along with the brachioradialis when the proximal radius is approached. Rarely, the nerve, and sometimes the nearby radial artery, is damaged during the approach. This damage can be avoided by routinely visualizing and protecting these structures. Central to both the anterior (Henry) and dorsal (Thompson) approaches to the radius is protection of the posterior interosseous nerve. This nerve enters through the supinator muscle; unless it is protected by maximal supination of the forearm during subperiosteal elevation of the supinator muscle (with the volar approach) or direct visualization during the dorsal approach, it is at risk of being damaged.

Treatment of chronic regional pain syndrome (reflex sympathetic dystrophy) has focused on early, aggressive therapy and interruption of the abnormal sympathetic activity by direct block or systemic pharmacologic means.

Nerve blocks, such as a stellate ganglion block for sympathetic maintained pain of the upper extremity, can provide excellent short-term relief, allowing aggressive therapy and possibly facilitating recovery. Pharmacologic therapy (with alpha-adrenergic blockers such as phenoxybenzamine) can be effective but is associated with undesirable side effects.

Yet, experience has demonstrated that if the sympathetic maintained pain is associated with a definable nerve lesion, an operative approach consisting of a combination of repair, reconstruction or lysis (or both) of the involved nerve, and rotation of a local muscle flap intended to enhance the blood supply to the area of injury and minimize scarring can be efficacious.[65]

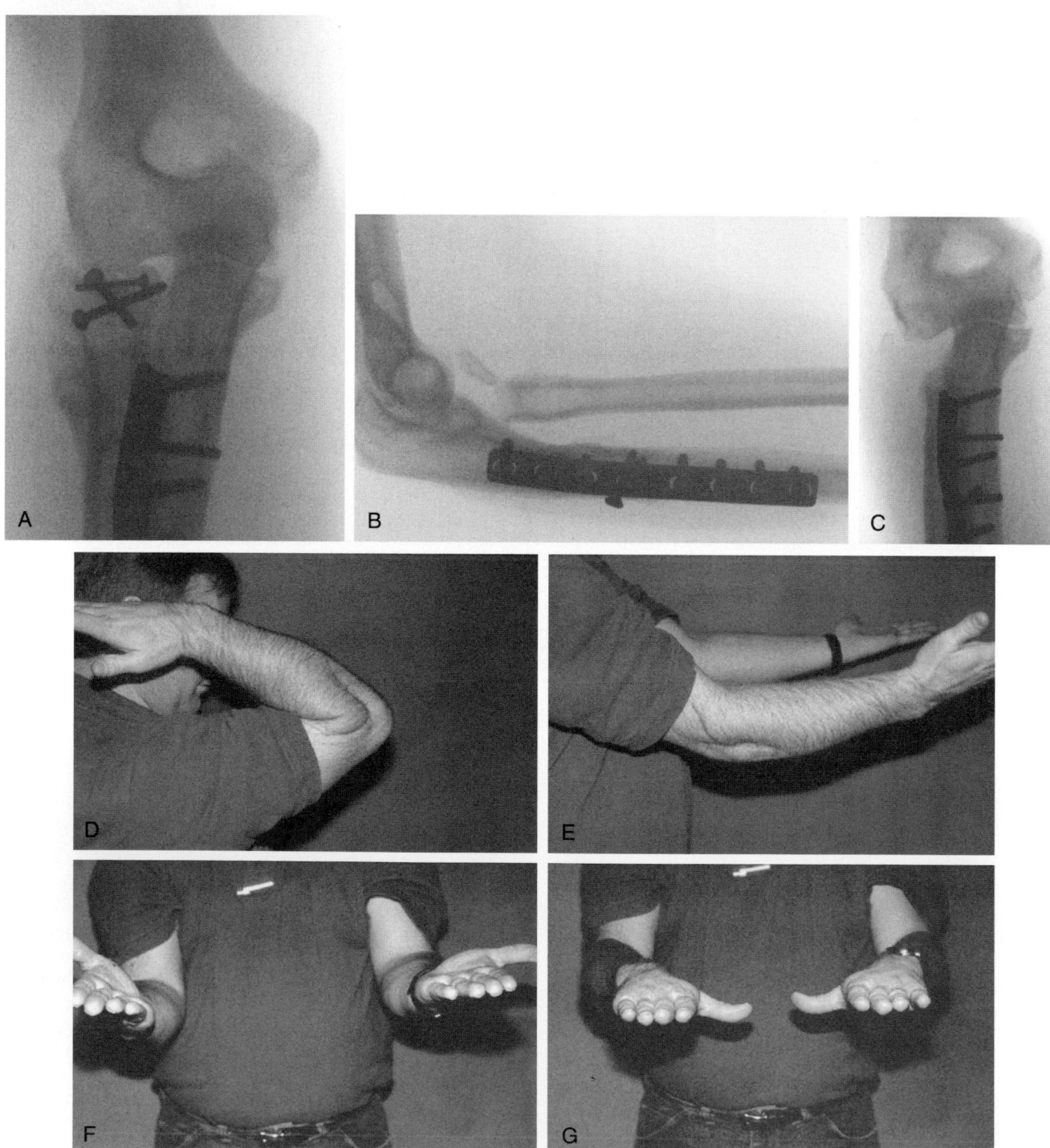

**FIGURE 41–33.** *A–G,* Post-traumatic proximal radioulnar synostosis following complex forearm fracture. *A,* Anteroposterior radiograph demonstrates the extensive synostosis extending from the radial neck to beyond the radial tuberosity. *B, C,* Radiographs after resection of the incongruous radial head and proximal radioulnar synostosis. *D–G,* Excellent function.

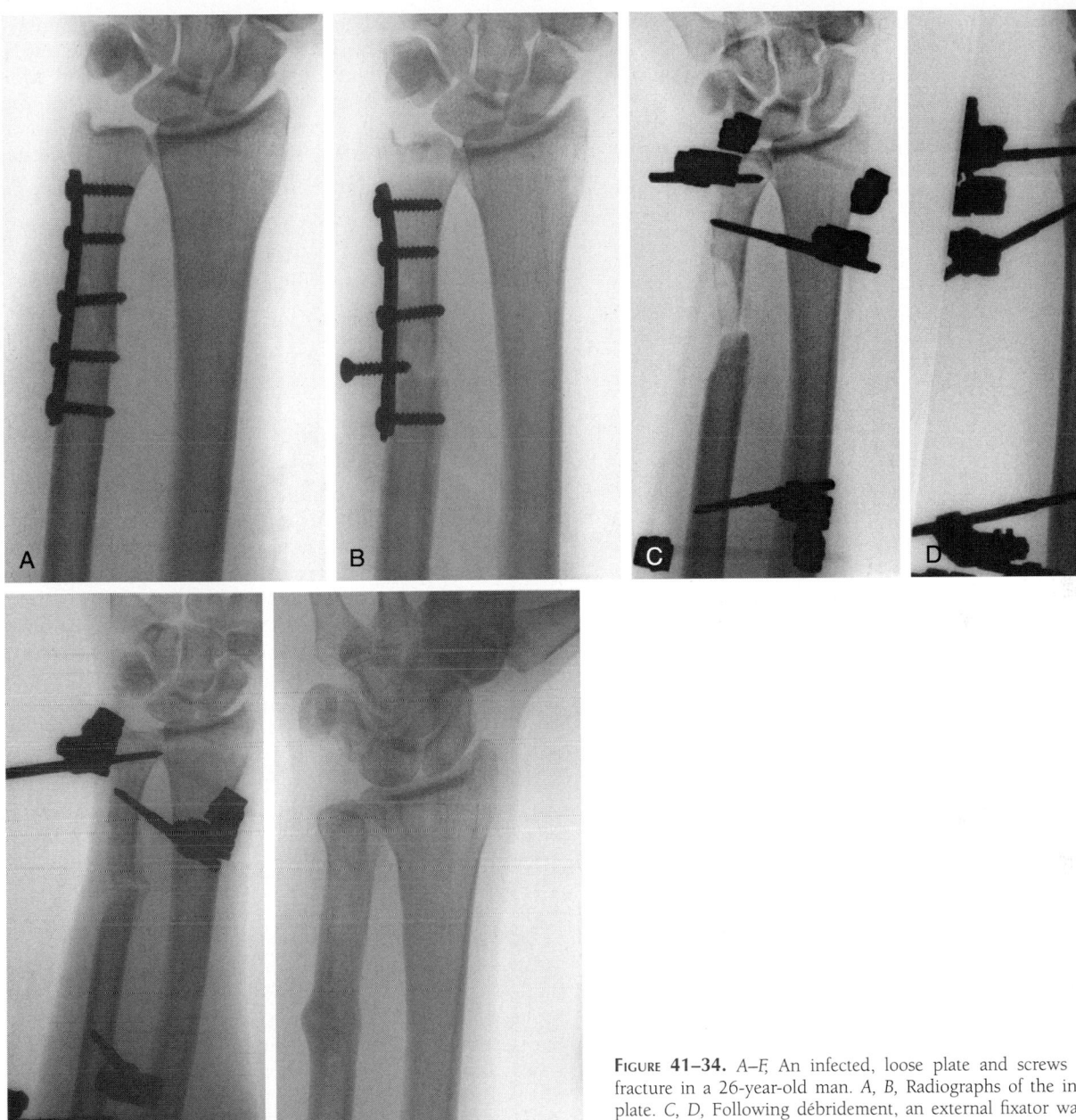

**FIGURE 41–34.** *A–F,* An infected, loose plate and screws on an ulnar fracture in a 26-year-old man. *A, B,* Radiographs of the infected, loose plate. *C, D,* Following débridement, an external fixator was used. *E,* A cancellous graft was applied. *F,* Excellent union and full function at 3 months.

## Infection

At one time there was concern regarding the risk of introducing infection in conjunction with operative treatment of a forearm fracture. However, with current operative techniques and implants (including perioperative antibiotic prophylaxis), infection after operative treatment of closed fractures is uncommon.[3, 25, 87] Furthermore, reports have cited an acceptably low rate of infection in open forearm fractures treated by immediate plate-and-screw fixation (0% to 3%).[25, 36, 64, 78, 90] Adequate débridement and copious irrigation are requisite with this approach and should be repeated frequently until a clean,

healthy soft tissue bed is achieved. Surgical wounds are closed primarily and traumatic wounds by delayed primary closure after adequate wound definition by serial débridement (Fig. 41–34).

If infection occurs, its eradication does not necessarily depend on implant removal. As long as bone fragments and soft tissues are well vascularized, stable internal fixation facilitates wound care and helps maintain length, alignment, range of motion, and overall function without hindering treatment of the infection. After successful eradication of the infection (with organism-specific antibiotics and local wound care), the wound can be irrigated and closed.

## Infection and Bone Defect

On occasion, sequential débridement of an uninfected forearm fracture results in a bone defect. When the defect is associated with a poorly vascularized, contracted, and unstable soft tissue envelope, the bone reconstruction can prove more complicated. Operative approaches based upon nonvascularized autogenous or allogeneic bone grafting may not be applicable because their use is dependent upon the surrounding soft tissue to revascularize the transplanted bone graft.[72] Prior infection is also a threat.[137]

We have found, however, in certain situations in which the overlying soft tissue envelope is well vascularized that substantial defects up to 6 cm can be reconstructed using the technique described by Weber and Brunner[151] of the "wave plate" and autogenous iliac crest cancellous autograft. The wave plate is constructed using a standard plate that is contoured to sit off the bone just proximal and distal to the site of the defect (Fig. 41–35). Use of a small distractor helps to minimize additional soft tissue dissection and devascularization. This plate concept is consistent with the overall emphasis on biologic internal fixation. The contour of the wave plate serves not only to optimize the vascularity of the underlying bone but also to distribute the cyclic forces across a broader one on the plate, reducing the risk of plate failure.[108] The space created by the contour also permits greater access of the autogenous graft to revascularization from the surrounding soft tissue.

Another alternative in the reconstruction of composite skeletal and soft tissue defects after radical débridements for infected fractures is that of the vascularized fibular graft taken either with overlying muscle alone or as a composite osteoseptocutaneous autograft.[72, 152] This approach enables, in a single operative procedure, the reconstruction of a diaphyseal segment of bone with similar dimensions of the radius or ulna along with a vascularized soft tissue envelope (Fig. 41–36). Jupiter and co-workers reported on nine patients treated for composite defects with an average length of fibular transplant of 7.9 cm and average size of associated fasciocutaneous component 11.8 by 5.9 cm. At an average follow-up of 24 months, all but one of the patients had radiographic evidence of bone union at both junctions. No patient had symptoms referable to the donor leg, and six returned to their preinjury occupation.

The distraction-histogenesis method developed by Ilizarov provides an alternative for the reconstruction of composite skeletal and soft tissue defects; however, this approach is complex, lengthy, and associated with numerous complications.[143] This technique can be used to realign and lengthen soft tissue contracture before autogenous bone grafting (Fig. 41–37).

## Nonunion

In the past, closed treatment of both-bone forearm fractures in adults was associated with a substantial rate of nonunion.[13, 18] Nonunion was associated with poor reductions in which minimal apposition of the fracture fragments was obtained and held. Therefore, open reduction with or without internal fixation has been advocated for inadequate or unstable reductions.

Early attempts at internal fixation (including sutures, wires, screws, small plates, and intramedullary wires or pins) provided minimal fracture stabilization, and prolonged cast immobilization was required.[74] All of the disadvantages of operative treatment, including additional soft tissue trauma, devascularization of fracture fragments, and the risks of infection and iatrogenic neurovascular injury, were added to the problems of prolonged immobilization. Among forearm fractures undergoing operative treatment (i.e., fractures irreducible by closed means), the rate of nonunion remained high, and functional outcomes were dismal.[33, 74]

In 1957, Smith and Sage[133] published the disappointing results of early attempts at intramedullary fixation of forearm fractures with a variety of pins and nails. Use of Kirschner wires, associated soft tissue injury, and delayed treatment were all associated with an increased risk of nonunion. Caden[23] recorded similarly poor results with Rush pin fixation.

After studying cadaver radii, Sage[119] introduced a nail with proximal and distal angulations and a triangular cross section in an attempt to improve restoration of radial bow and rotational stability. Complications included nail protrusion, splitting of the cortex, rupture of the extensor pollicis longus tendon, synostosis, and radial nerve palsy; 11.1% of fractures failed to unite within 6 months, in many cases because of technical errors and complications. Marek[83] reported 100% union with the use of a square nail; however, he defined union clinically, had a very short follow-up in many cases, and described many fractures as requiring well over 6 months to heal. Despite continued interest in intramedullary nailing and the periodic introduction of new nail designs, it remains a technically demanding procedure, prone to difficulties and complications.[57]

Improvements in plate-and-screw fixation have almost eliminated nonunion in forearm fractures. Initial improvements were noted with the use of larger plates such as the Eggers slotted plates.[9, 38] In 1964, Burwell and Charnley[22] noted that nonunion was far less common when plates 3.5 inches in length were used. With the addition of interfragmentary compression by the AO/ASIF group,[96] the only problem fractures remaining were those with substantial bone loss or comminution.[3, 25, 29, 35, 53, 98, 120, 142] Primary bone grafting of such fractures has further reduced the risk of nonunion.[3, 25] Also of note, Chapman and colleagues[25] found that the use of 3.5-mm DC plates did not increase the rate of nonunion over that seen with traditional 4.5-mm plates.

The current rate of nonunion is less than 2% when the proper technique is utilized in compliant patients.[25] Nonunions are ascribed to technical errors such as the use of plates of inadequate size (e.g., semitubular plates) or length, inadequate reduction, and failure to use bone grafting for comminuted and open fractures.[70, 77, 139]

One of us (JBJ) reviewed an experience of 44 consecutive nonunions of diaphyseal forearm fractures treated over a 15-year period. Twenty-four involved the radius alone, 11 the ulna, and 9 both bones. The average age of the patients was 38 years. Thirty-four fractures were the result of high-energy trauma, with 24 associated with open

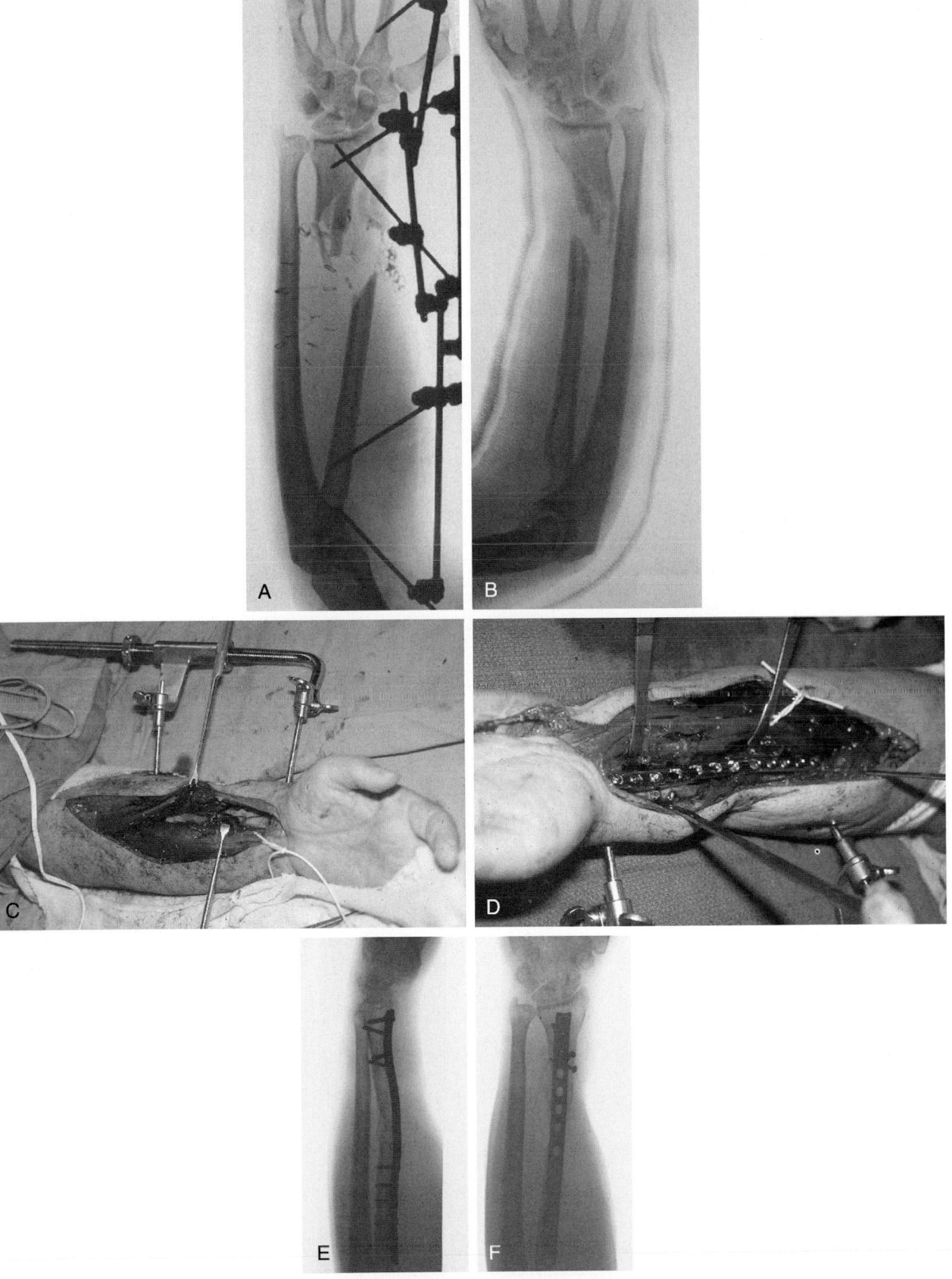

**FIGURE 41–35.** *A–F,* A 47-year-old man had an open forearm fracture that became infected and required extensive bone grafting and realignment. *A,* The radiograph at 4 weeks after débridement and external fixation. *B,* The patient was referred at 10 weeks after injury with loss of length. *C,* Intraoperative distraction allowed realignment and control over adequate plate length for a wave plate. *D,* The wave plate applied with a cancellous bone graft bridging the gap. *E* and *F,* Radiographs at 4 months reveal complete incorporation of the cancellous graft. Excellent forearm rotation was gained.

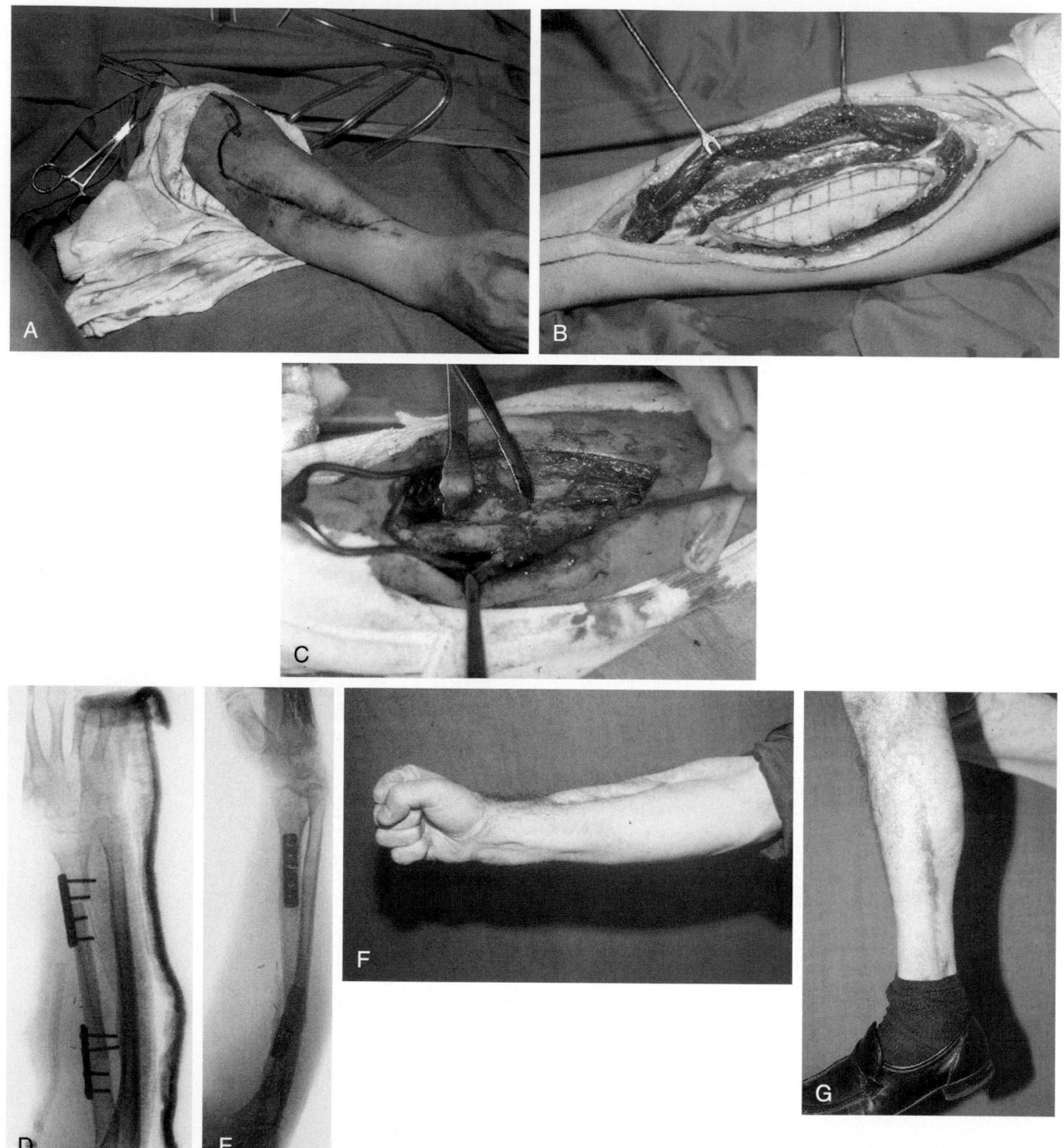

**FIGURE 41–36.** *A–G*, A complex infected nonunion of the radius in a 37-year-old man. *A*, The clinical appearance of the wound. *B*, Débridement led to a 7-cm defect of the radius. *C*, A vascularized fibula with overlying skin was harvested. *D*, *E*, Radiographs of the graft in place. *F*, *G*, Excellent function with little donor site morbidity.

wounds. The main complaint of the patients was severe functional disability. Twenty patients had associated infection. All nonunions healed after operative treatments comprising stable internal fixation and autogenous cancellous bone grafting in all but two hypertrophic nonunions. Forearm rotation averaged 60 to 70° of supination and 60 to 70° of pronation. All patients noted improved function (Fig. 41–38).

## Malunion

With the success of modern plate-and-screw fixation of forearm fractures, malunion has proved to be one of the most important determinants of functional outcome.[107] Historically, a good reduction was regarded as one in which apposition of the fracture fragments of both bones without visually obvious deformity had been achieved.

Substantial angulation and rotation of fragments were commonplace. Limitation of supination and pronation resulted from impingement between the malunited radius and ulna, rotational malunion, cross union, and narrowing and contracture of the interosseous membrane in addition to the stiffness resulting from prolonged immobilization[146] (Fig. 41–39).

The problem of rotational malunion was emphasized by Evans,[44] who noted that inadequate or unstable rotational reduction was a source of severe limitation of supination or pronation, or both. In severe angular malunion, especially when the apices of angular malunion are convergent, radioulnar impingement may occur. Subsequent studies of the effect of angular deformity on pronation and supination in cadaver forearms (performed by advocates of closed treatment) demonstrated progressive loss of forearm rotation with increasing angular deformity.[85, 141] The authors concluded that limitation of rotational movement is acceptable (<20%) in closed reductions with 10° or less of combined deformity of the radius and ulna; this represents essentially a near-perfect reduction and is very difficult to achieve.

The importance of restoring the normal anatomic radial bow was emphasized by advocates of closed treatment and intramedullary nailing of forearm fractures.[119] Schemitsch and Richards,[124] reporting on the effect of malunion after plate-and-screw fixation, demonstrated an important relation between restoration of the normal magnitude and location of the maximal radial bow and functional outcome (Fig. 41–40).

The effects of prolonged immobilization on limitation of forearm motion were minimized in their study by the use of modern plate fixation in all patients and early postoperative mobilization in most. Accounting for the effects of associated soft tissue injury, ipsilateral fracture, or complications in forearm rotation, they demonstrated that failure to restore the location and magnitude of the radial bow to within 4% to 5% of that of the normal arm was associated with a greater than 20% loss of forearm rotation. Grip strength was also reduced with malunited fractures. They suggested that attention to restoration of the radial bow (including comparison with the uninjured forearm in difficult cases) and appropriate contouring of the plate should help to maximize functional outcomes (Fig. 41–41).

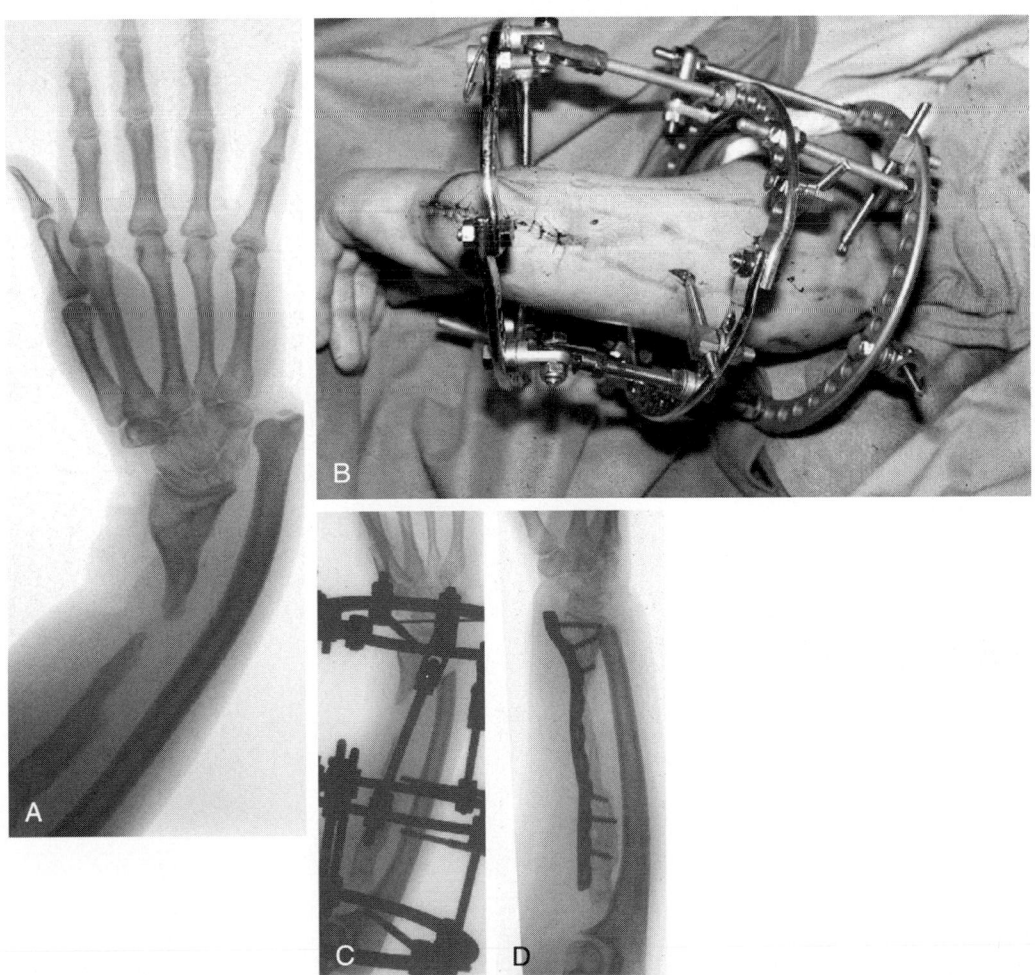

**FIGURE 41–37.** *A–D,* A complex reconstructive problem in a 32-year-old woman involving bone loss, severe deformity, and disruption of the distal radioulnar joint after fracture and infection as a child. *A,* The severe deformity is apparent on the anteroposterior radiograph. *B,* Ilizarov techniques were used to gain length and alignment. The distal ulnar was resected. *C, D,* A wave plate and autogenous bone graft were successful in achieving reconstruction of the radius.

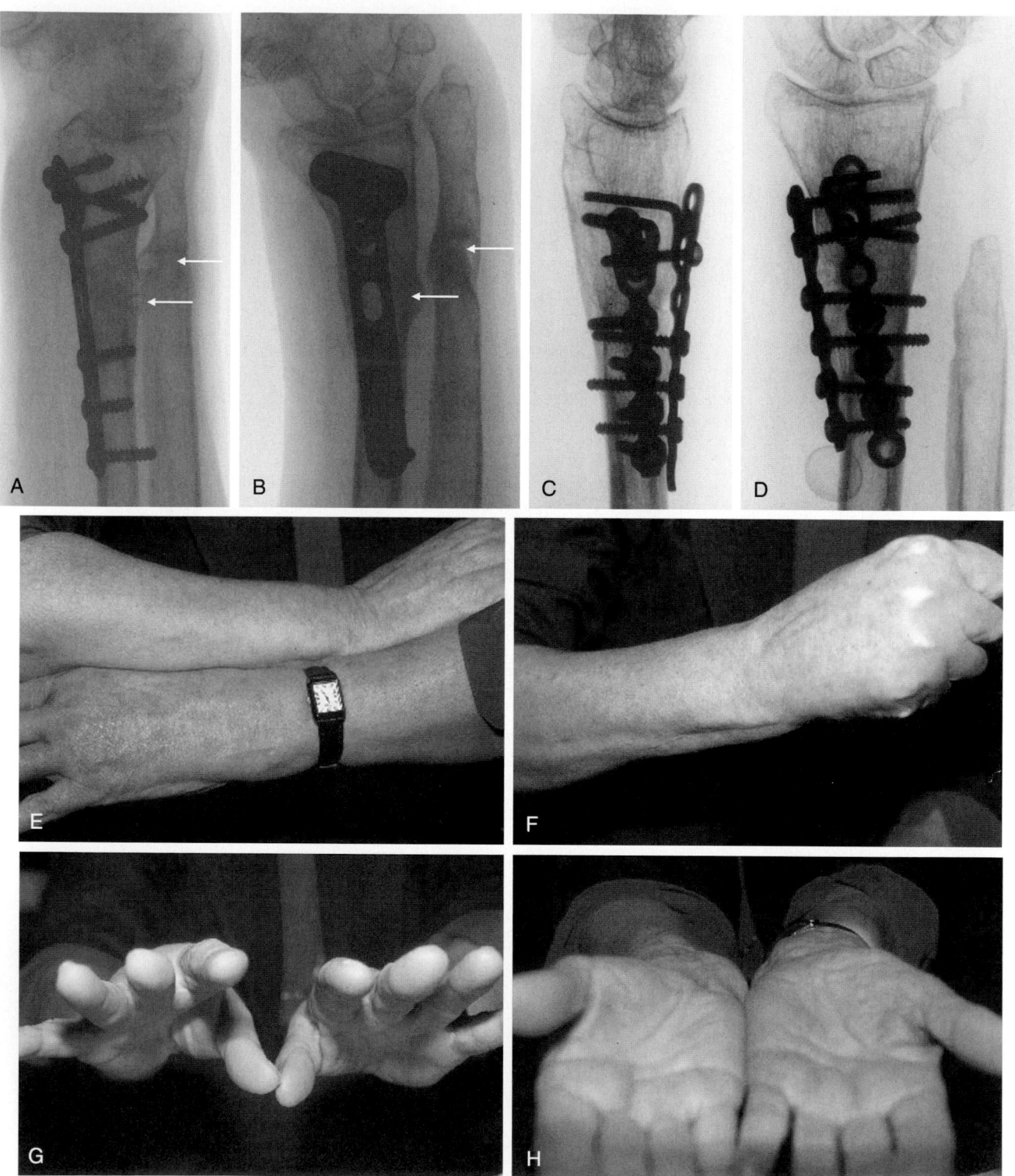

**Figure 41–38.** *A–H,* A painful nonunion in a 75-year-old active woman who had two prior surgical attempts at fracture union. *A, B,* Anteroposterior and lateral radiographs of the ununited radius and ulna. Note the severe disruption of the distal radioulnar joint. *C, D,* Union of the radius was achieved with two orthogonally placed 2.7-mm condylar plates. The distal ulna was used as the source of an autogenous bone graft. *E–H,* Excellent function resulted.

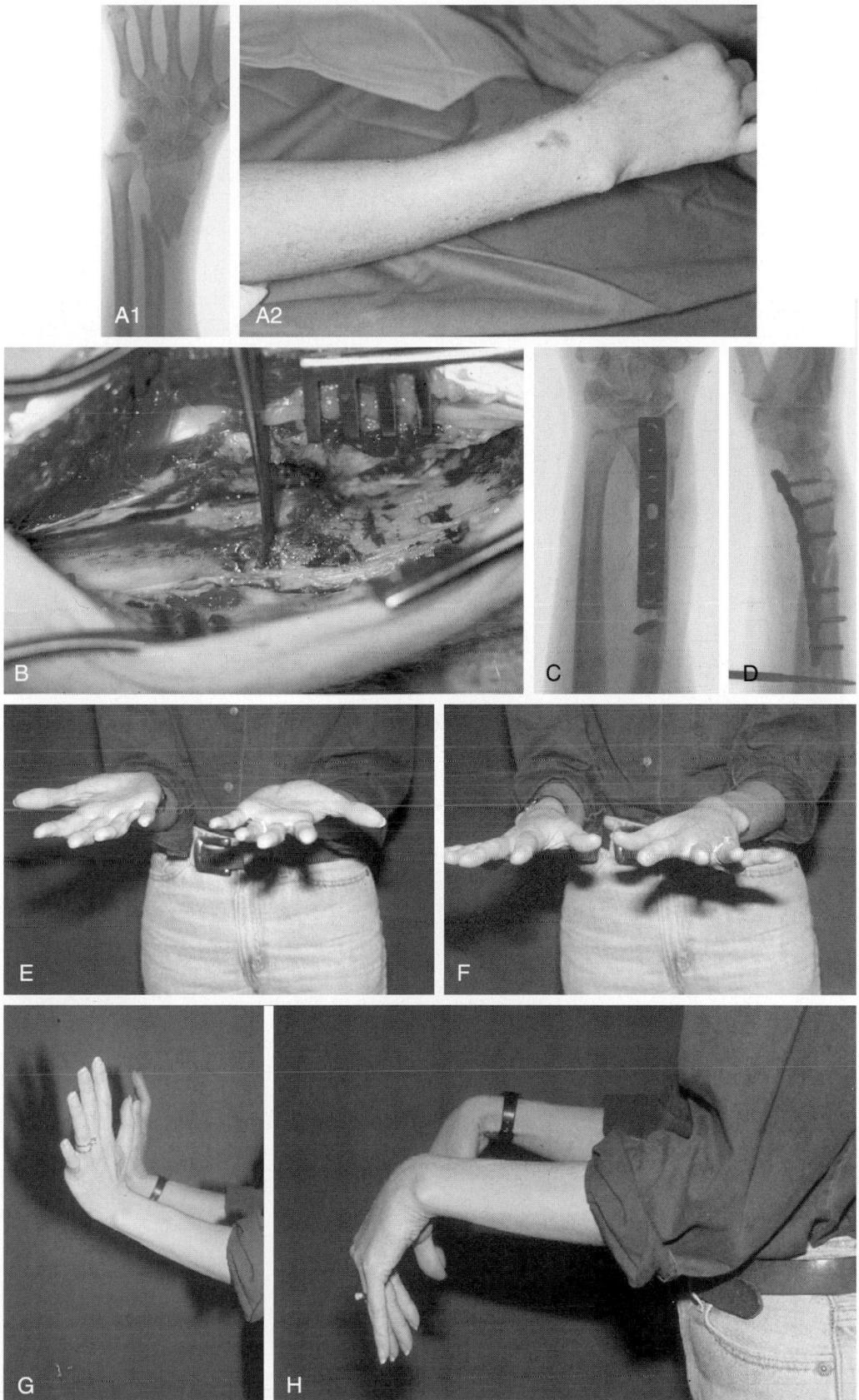

**FIGURE 41–39.** *A–H,* A malunited Galeazzi fracture 4 months after injury in a 29-year-old woman. *A,* The anteroposterior radiograph of the skeletal deformity. Note the disrupted distal radioulnar joint. *B,* The original fracture line was re-created with an osteotome. *C, D,* A distractor was used to regain length and a limited contact dynamic compression plate applied. The proximal distractor pin is still present (intraoperative radiograph). *E–H,* Full function was restored.

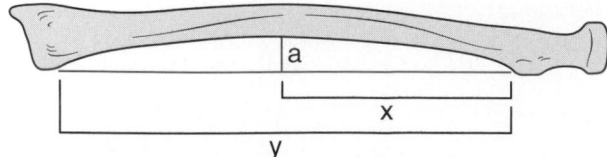

Maximum radial bow = a (mm)

Location of maximum radial bow = x/y × 100

**FIGURE 41–40.** The technique of Schemitsch and Richards for measuring the amount and location of the maximal radial bow. The amount is determined by drawing a line from the bicipital tuberosity to the most ulnar aspect of the radius at the wrist. A perpendicular line is drawn from this line to the radius at the point of maximal radial bow, and the distance is measured in millimeters. The location of the maximal radial bow is determined by dividing the distance from the bicipital tuberosity to the point of maximal bow by the length of the entire line. The value is expressed as a percentage.

## ASSESSMENT OF OUTCOME

Normal function and skeletal union are the goals of treatment of adult forearm fractures. Therefore, any assessment of outcome must address these criteria as well as associated complications. The assessment criteria of Anderson and colleagues[3] continue to provide a reliable means of identifying outcome and allow a more accurate comparison of the results of different studies (Table 41–2).

In their series of 330 acute fractures in 244 patients, Anderson and colleagues[3] recorded 85% satisfactory or excellent results. Union rates were 97.9% within an average of 7.4 weeks for radial fractures and 96.3% within 7.3 weeks for ulnar fractures. Infection occurred in 2.9% of cases and nonunion in 2.9%. In this series, 4.5-mm DC plates were used for the most part.

In a later series using the same grading system, Chapman and colleagues[25] evaluated 129 diaphyseal

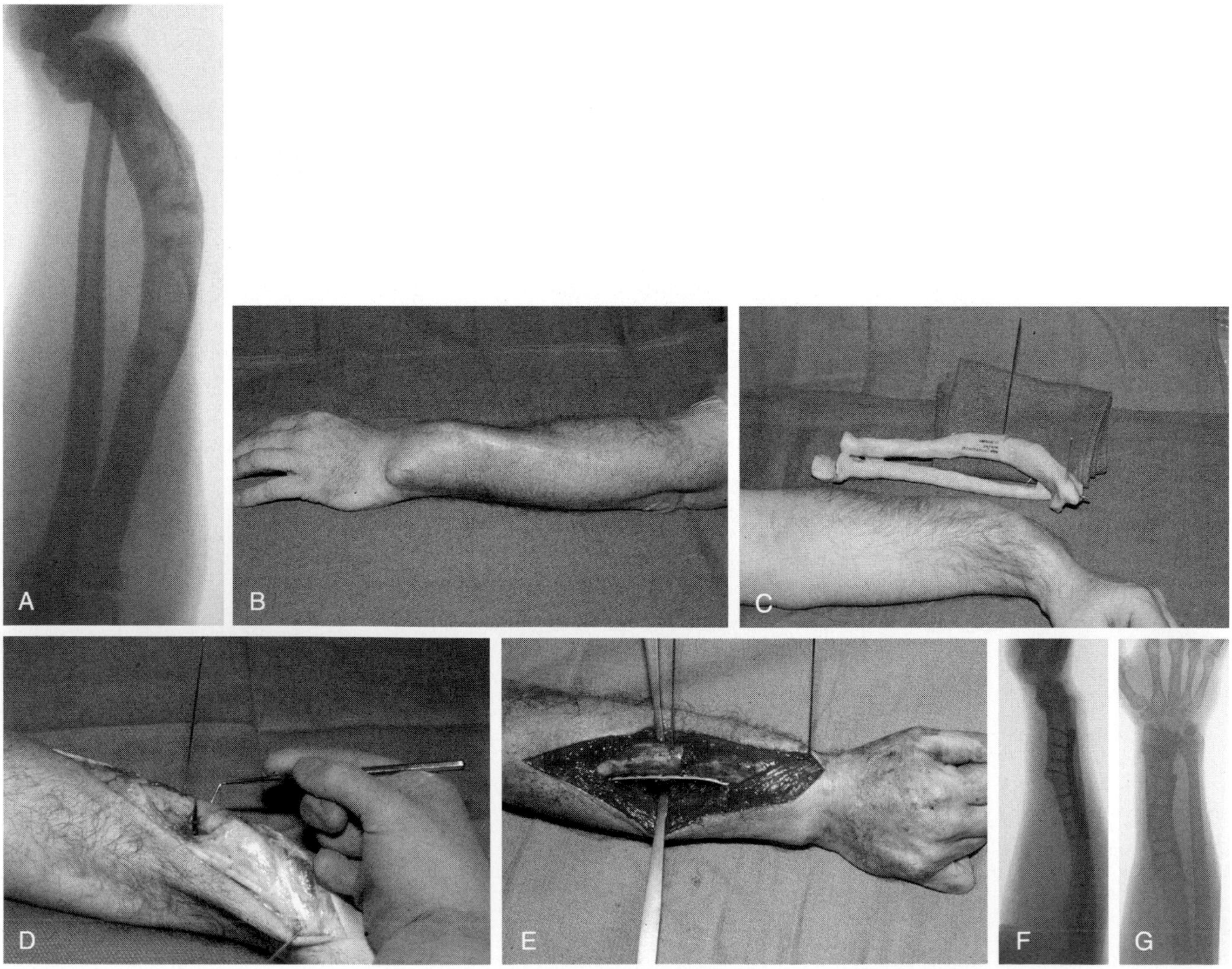

**FIGURE 41–41.** *A–G*, A complex malunion of the radius in a 62-year-old man with Paget's disease following several fractures. *A*, The presenting lateral radiograph of the severe deformity. *B*, The clinical appearance. *C*, A bone model was made from computed tomographic scans and used for preoperative planning. *D*, The deformity was corrected through a single oblique cut. *E*, A contoured plate is applied. *F, G*, Radiographs of the corrected deformity.

**TABLE 41–2**

Outcome Evaluation Scale

| Rating | Outcome |
|---|---|
| Excellent | Union with <10° loss of elbow or wrist flexion or extension and <25% loss of forearm rotation |
| Satisfactory | Union with <20° loss of elbow or wrist flexion or extension and <50% loss of forearm rotation |
| Unsatisfactory | Union with >30° loss of elbow or wrist flexion or extension and >50% loss of forearm rotation |
| Failure | Malunion, nonunion, or unresolved chronic osteomyelitis |

*Source:* Anderson, L.D., et al. J Bone Joint Surg Am 57:287, 1975.

forearm fractures. They used primarily 3.5-mm DC plates; union was recorded in 98% of fractures, and 92% of patients achieved a satisfactory or excellent result. Infection was found in 2.3% of cases.

In other reports on the higher rates of complications associated with plate fixation of forearm fractures,[34, 139] the authors emphasized that the source of most complications is lack of attention to detail, errors in judgment, or errors in technique.

## REFERENCES

1. Abrams, R.A.; Simmons, B.P.; Brown, R.A. Treatment of posttraumatic radioulnar synostosis with excision and low dose radiation. J Hand Surg [Am] 8A:703, 1993.
2. Alexander, A.H.; Lichtman, D.M. Irreducible distal radioulnar joint occurring in a Galeazzi fracture. Case report. J Hand Surg [Am] 6:258, 1981.
3. Anderson, L.D.; Sisk, T.D.; Tooms, R.E.; Park, W.I., III. Compression-plate fixation in acute diaphyseal fractures of the radius and ulna. J Bone Joint Surg Am 57:287, 1975.
4. Austin, R. Tardy palsy of radial nerve from a Monteggia fracture. Injury 7:202, 1976.
5. Ayllon-Garcia, A.; Davies, A.W.; Deliss, L. Radioulnar synostosis following external fixation. J Hand Surg [Br] 18:592, 1993.
6. Bado, J.L. The Monteggia lesion. Clin Orthop 50:71, 1967.
7. Bado, J.L. The Monteggia Lesion. Springfield, IL, Charles C Thomas, 1962.
8. Bagley, C.H. Fracture of both bones of the forearm. Surg Gynecol Obstet 42:95, 1926.
9. Baker, G.I.; Burkhalter, W.E.; Barclay, W.A.; Eversmann, W.W. Treatment of forearm shaft fractures in long slotted plates. J Bone Joint Surg Am 51:1035, 1969.
10. Bauer, G.; Arand, M.; Mutschler, L. Posttraumatic radioulnar synostosis after forearm fracture osteosynthesis. Arch Orthop Trauma Surg 110:142, 1991.
11. Bednar, D.A.; Grandwilewski, W. Complications of forearm plate removal. Can J Surg 35:428, 1992.
12. Biyani, A.; Bhan, S. Dual extensor tendon entrapment in Galeazzi fracture-dislocation. A case report. J Trauma 29:1295, 1989.
13. Bolton, H.; Quinlan, A.G. The conservative treatment of fractures of the shaft of the radius and ulna in adults. Lancet 1:700, 1952.
14. Botting, T.D.J. Posttraumatic radio-ulnar cross-union. J Trauma 10:16, 1970.
15. Boyd, H.B.; Boals, J.C. The Monteggia lesion. Clin Orthop 66:94, 1969.
16. Boyd, H.B. Surgical exposure of the ulna and proximal third of the radius through one incision. Surg Gynecol Obstet 71:87, 1940.
17. Brady, L.P.; Jewett, E.L. A new treatment of radioulnar synostosis. South Med J 53:507, 1960.
18. Brakenbury, P.H.; Corea, J.R.; Blakemore, M.E. Nonunion of the isolated fracture of the ulnar shaft in adults. Injury 12:371, 1985.
19. Breit, R. Posttraumatic radioulnar synostosis. Clin Orthop 174:149, 1983.
20. Bruce, H.E.; Harvey, J.P.; Wilson, J.C. Monteggia fractures. J Bone Joint Surg Am 56:1563, 1974.
21. Bruckner, J.D.; Lichtman, D.M.; Alexander, A.H. Complex dislocations of the distal radioulnar joint: Recognition and management. Clin Orthop 275:90, 1992.
22. Burwell, H.N.; Charnley, A.D. Treatment of forearm fractures in adults with particular reference to plate fixation. J Bone Joint Surg Br 46:404, 1964.
23. Caden, J.G. Internal fixation of fractures of the forearm. J Bone Joint Surg Am 43:1115, 1961.
24. Cetti, N.E. An unusual cause of blocked reduction of the Galeazzi injury. Injury 9:59, 1977.
25. Chapman, M.W.; Gordon, J.E.; Zissimos, A.G. Compression plate fixation of acute fractures of the diaphysis of the radius and ulna. J Bone Joint Surg Am 71:159, 1989.
26. Charnley, J. The Closed Treatment of Fractures, 3rd ed. New York, Churchill Livingstone, 1961.
27. Corea, J.R.; Brakenbury, P.H.; Blakemore, M.E. The treatment of isolated fractures of the ulnar shaft in adults. Injury 12:365, 1981.
28. Crenshaw, A.H. Campbell's Operative Orthopaedics, 7th ed. St. Louis, C.V. Mosby, 1987, p. 94.
29. Crowie, R.J. Fractures of the forearm treated by open reduction and plating. Br J Surg 44:263, 1956.
30. Cullen, J.P.; Pellegrini, V.D.; Miller, R.J.; Jones, J.J. Treatment of traumatic radioulnar synostosis by excision and postoperative low-dose radiation. J Hand Surg [Am] 19:394, 1994.
31. Dabezies, E.J.; Stewart, W.E.; Goodman, F.G.; Deffer, P.A. Management of segmental defects of the radius and ulna. J Trauma 11:778, 1971.
32. Danis, R. Théorie et Pratique de l'Osteosynthèse. Paris, Masson, 1947.
33. DeBuren, N. Causes and treatment of nonunion in fractures of the radius and ulna. J Bone Joint Surg Br 44:614, 1962.
34. Deluca, P.A.; Lindsey, R.W.; Rowe, P.A. Refracture of bones of the forearm after the removal of compression plates. J Bone Joint Surg Am 70:1372, 1988.
35. Dodge, H.S.; Cady, G.W. Treatment of fractures of the radius and ulna with compression plates: A retrospective study of one hundred and nineteen fractures in seventy eight patients. J Bone Joint Surg Am 54:1167, 1972.
36. Duncan, R.; Geissler, W.; Freeland, A.E.; Savoie, F.H. Immediate internal fixation of open fractures of the diaphysis of the forearm. J Orthop Trauma 6:22, 1992.
37. Edwards, G.S.; Jupiter, J.B. Radial head fracture with acute radioulnar dislocation: Essex-Lopresti revisited. Clin Orthop 234:61, 1988.
38. Eggers, G.W.N. Internal contact splint. J Bone Joint Surg Am 30:40, 1948.
39. Eglseder, W.A.; Hay, M. Combined Essex-Lopresti and radial shaft fractures: Case report. J Trauma 34:310, 1993.
40. Elstram, J.A.; Pankovich, A.M.; Eqwele, R. Extra-articular low-velocity gunshot fracture of the radius and ulna. J Bone Joint Surg Am 60:335, 1978.
41. Emery, M.A. The incidence of delayed union and nonunion following fractures of both bones of the forearm in adults. Can J Surg 8:285, 1965.
42. Engber, W.D.; Keene, J.S. Anterior interosseous nerve palsy associated with a Monteggia fracture. Clin Orthop 174:133, 1983.
43. Evans, E.M. Pronation injuries of the forearm with special reference to anterior Monteggia fractures. J Bone Joint Surg Br 31:579, 1949.
44. Evans, E.M. Rotational deformities in the treatment of fractures of both bones of the forearm. J Bone Joint Surg 27:373, 1945.
45. Faierman, E.; Jupiter, J.B. The management of acute fractures involving the distal radioulnar joint and distal ulna. Hand Clin 14:213, 1998.
46. Failla, J.M.; Amadio, P.C.; Morrey, B.F. Posttraumatic proximal radioulnar synostosis: Results of surgical treatment. J Bone Joint Surg Am 69:1208, 1989.
47. Frykman, G. Fracture of the distal radius including sequelae: Shoulder hand finger syndrome, disturbance in the distal radioul-

nar joint and impairment of nerve function. A clinical and experimental study. Acta Orthop Scand 108(Suppl):1, 1967.

48. Galeazzi, R. Ueber ein besonderes Syndrom bei Verletzungen im Bereich der Unterarmknocken. Arch Orthop Unfallchir 35:557, 1934.

49. Garland, D.E.; Dowling, V. Forearm fractures in the head-injured adult. Clin Orthop 176:190, 1983.

50. Gelberman, R.H.; Garfin, S.R.; Hergenroeder, P.T.; et al. Compartment syndromes of the forearm: Diagnosis and treatment. Clin Orthop 161:252, 1981.

51. Gelberman, R.H.; Zakaib, G.S.; Mubarak, S.J.; et al. Decompression of forearm compartment syndromes. Clin Orthop 134:225, 1978.

52. Giustra, P.E.; Killoran, P.J.; Furman, R.S.; Root, J.A. The missed Monteggia fracture. Radiology 10:45, 1974.

53. Grace, T.G.; Eversmann, W.W., Jr. Forearm fractures: Treatment by rigid fixation with early motion. J Bone Joint Surg Am 62:433, 1980.

54. Grace, T.G.; Eversmann, W.W., Jr. The management of segmental bone loss associated with forearm fractures. J Bone Joint Surg Am 58:283, 1976.

55. Gross, S.D. A System of Surgery, 3rd ed. Philadelphia, Blanchard & Lea, 1864, p. 916.

56. Hadden, W.A.; Reschauer, R.; Seggl, W. Results of AO plate fixation of forearm shaft fractures in adults. Injury 15:44, 1983.

57. Hall, R.H.; Bugg, E.I.; Vitolo, R.E. Intramedullary fixation of fractures of the forearm. South Med J 45:814, 1982.

58. Henry, W.A. Extensile Exposures, 2nd ed. New York, Churchill Livingstone, 1973, p. 100.

59. Hicks, J.H. Fractures of the forearm treated by rigid fixation. J Bone Joint Surg Br 43:680, 1961.

60. Hidaka, S.; Gustilo, R.B. Refracture of bones of the forearm after plate removal. J Bone Joint Surg Am 66:1241, 1984.

61. Hotchkiss, R.N.; An, K.; Sowa, D.T.; et al. An anatomic and mechanical study of the interosseous membrane of the forearm: Pathomechanics of proximal migration of the radius. J Hand Surg [Am] 14:256, 1989.

62. Hughston, J.C. Fracture of the distal radius shaft: Mistakes in management. J Bone Joint Surg Am 39:249, 1957.

63. Jessing, P. Monteggia lesions and their complicating nerve damage. Acta Orthop Scand 46:601, 1975.

64. Jones, J.A. Immediate internal fixation of high energy open forearm fracture. J Orthop Trauma 5:272, 1991.

65. Jupiter, J.B.; Seiler, J.G.; Zienowicz, R. Sympathetic-maintained pain (causalgia) associated with a demonstrable peripheral nerve lesion. J Bone Joint Surg Am 76:1376, 1994.

66. Jupiter, J.B.; Kleinert, H.E. Vascular injuries in the upper extremity. In: Tubiana, R., ed. The Hand, Vol. 3. Philadelphia, W.B. Saunders, 1988, p. 593.

67. Jupiter, J.B.; Kour, A.K.; Richards, R.R.; et al. The floating radius in bipolar fracture-dislocation of the forearm. J Orthop Trauma 8:99, 1994.

68. Jupiter, J.B. Nerve injury associated with devascularizing trauma. In: Gelberman, R.H., ed. Operative Nerve Repair and Reconstruction. Philadelphia, J.B. Lippincott, 1991, pp. 679–686.

69. Jupiter, J.B.; Leibovic, S.J.; Ribbans, W.; Wilk, R.M. The posterior Monteggia lesion. J Orthop Trauma 5:395, 1991.

70. Jupiter, J.B.; Ruedi, T. Intraoperative distraction in the treatment of complex nonunions of the radius. J Hand Surg [Am] 17:416, 1992.

71. Jupiter, J.B.; Ring, D. Operative treatment of post-traumatic proximal radioulnar synostosis. J Bone Joint Surg Am 80:248, 1998.

72. Jupiter, J.B.; Gerhard, J.; Guerrero, J.; et al. Treatment of segmental defects of the radius with use of the vascularized osteocutaneous fibular autogenous graft. J Bone Joint Surg Am 79:542, 1997.

73. Khurana, J.S.; Kattapuram, S.V.; Becker, S.; Mayo-Smith, W. Galeazzi injury with an associated fracture of the radial head. Clin Orthop 234:70, 1988.

74. Knight, R.A.; Purvis, G.D. Fractures of both bones of the forearm in adults. J Bone Joint Surg Am 31:755, 1949.

75. Kraus, B.; Horne, G. Galeazzi fractures. J Trauma 25:1093, 1985.

76. Labosky, D.A.; Cermak, M.B.; Waggy, C.A. Forearm fracture plates: To remove or not to remove. J Hand Surg [Am] 15:294, 1990.

77. Langkamer, V.G.; Ackroyd, C.E. Internal fixation of forearm fractures in the 1980s: Lessons to be learnt. Injury 22:97, 1991.

78. Lenihan, M.R.; Brien, W.W.; Gellman, H.; et al. Fractures of the forearm resulting from low velocity gunshot wounds. J Orthop Trauma 6:32, 1992.

79. Levin, L.S.; Golder, R.D.; Urbaniak, J.R.; et al. Management of severe musculoskeletal injuries of the upper extremity. J Orthop Trauma 4:432, 1990.

80. Lichter, R.L.; Jacobsen, T. Tardy palsy of the posterior interosseous nerve with a Monteggia fracture. J Bone Joint Surg Am 57:124, 1975.

81. Lyritis, G.; Ioannidis, T.; Hartofylakidis-Garofalidis, G. The influence of timing and rigidity of internal fixation on bony union of fractures of the forearm. Injury 15:53, 1982.

82. Maempel, F.Z. Posttraumatic radioulnar synostosis: A report of two cases. Clin Orthop 186:182, 1984.

83. Marek, F.M. Axial fixation of forearm fractures. J Bone Joint Surg Am 43:1099, 1961.

84. Mast, J.; Jakob, R.; Ganz, R. Planning and Reduction Techniques in Fracture Surgery. New York, Springer-Verlag, 1989.

85. Matthews, L.S.; Kaufer, H.; Garver, D.F.; Sonstegard, D.A. The effect on supination-pronation of angular malalignment of fractures of both bones of the forearm. J Bone Joint Surg Am 64:14, 1982.

86. McLaughlin, H.L. Trauma. Philadelphia: W.B. Saunders, 1959.

87. Mih, A.D.; Cooney, W.P.; Idler, R.S.; Lewallen, D.G. Long-term follow-up of forearm bone diaphyseal plating. Clin Orthop 299:256, 1994.

88. Mikic, Z.D. Galeazzi fracture-dislocations. J Bone Joint Surg Am 57:1071, 1975.

89. Modabber, M.R.; Jupiter, J.B. Current concepts review: Reconstruction for post-traumatic conditions of the elbow joint. J Bone Joint Surg Am 77:1431, 1995.

90. Moed, B.R.; Kellam, J.F.; Foster, J.R.; et al. Immediate internal fixation of open fractures of the diaphysis of the forearm. J Bone Joint Surg Am 68:1008, 1986.

91. Monteggia, G.B. Instituzione Chirurgiche, 2nd ed. Milan, G. Maspero, 1813–1815.

92. Moore, T.M.; Klein, J.P.; Patzakis, M.J.; Harvey, J.P., Jr. Results of compression plating of closed Galeazzi fractures. J Bone Joint Surg Am 67:1015, 1985.

93. Moore, T.M.; Lester, D.K.; Sarmiento, A. The stabilizing effect of soft tissue constraints in artificial Galeazzi fractures. Clin Orthop 194:189, 1985.

94. Morris, A.H. Irreducible Monteggia lesion with radial nerve entrapment. J Bone Joint Surg Am 56:1744, 1974.

95. Mubarak, S.J.; Owen, C.A.; Hargens, A.R. Acute compartmental syndromes: Diagnosis and treatment with the aid of the wick catheter. J Bone Joint Surg Am 60:1091, 1978.

96. Müller, M.E.; Allgöwer, M.; Schneider, R.; Willenegger, H. Manual of Internal Fixation, 2nd ed. Berlin, Springer-Verlag, 1979.

97. Mullick, S. The lateral Monteggia fracture. J Bone Joint Surg Am 33:543, 1977.

98. Naiman, P.T.; Schein, A.J.; Siffert, R.S. Use of ASIF compression plates in selected shaft fractures of the upper extremity: A preliminary report. Clin Orthop 71:208, 1970.

99. Odena, I.C. Bipolar fracture-dislocation of the forearm. J Bone Joint Surg Am 34:968, 1952.

100. Pavel, A.; Pitman, J.M.; Lance, E.M.; Wade, P.A. The posterior Monteggia fracture: A clinical study. J Trauma 5:185, 1965.

101. Penrose, J.H. The Monteggia fracture with posterior dislocation of the radial head. J Bone Joint Surg Br 33:65, 1951.

102. Perren, S.M.; Cordey, J.; Rahn, B.A.; et al. Early temporary porosis of bone induced by internal fixation implants. Clin Orthop 232:139, 1988.

103. Pollen, A.G. Fractures and Dislocations in Children. Edinburgh, Churchill Livingstone, 1973.

104. Razeman, J.P.; Decoulx, J.; Leclair, H.P. Les synostoses radiocubitales posttraumatiques de l'adulte. Acta Orthop Belg 31:5, 1965.

105. Reckling, F.W.; Cordell, L.D. Unstable fracture-dislocations of the forearm: The Monteggia and Galeazzi lesions. Arch Surg 96:999, 1968.

106. Reckling, F.W. Unstable fracture-dislocation of the forearm (Monteggia and Galeazzi lesions). J Bone Joint Surg Am 64:857, 1982.

107. Richards, R.R. Chronic disorders of the forearm. J Bone Joint Surg Am 78:916, 1996.

108. Ring, D.; Jupiter, J.B. Wave plate osteosynthesis in the upper extremity. Tech Hand Upper Extremity Surg 1(3):168, 1997.

109. Ring, D.; Jupiter, J.B. Mangling upper limb injuries in industry. Injury 30:SB5, 1999.
110. Ring, D; Jupiter, J.B.; Simpson, N.S. Monteggia fractures in adults. J Bone Joint Surg Am 80:1733, 1998.
111. Ring, D.; Jupiter, J.B.; Sanders, R.W.; et al. Transolecranon fracture-dislocation of the elbow. J Orthop Trauma 11:545, 1997.
112. Ring, D.; Jupiter, J.B. Current concepts review: Fracture-dislocation of the elbow. J Bone Joint Surg Am 80:566, 1998.
113. Ring, D.; Jupiter, J.B. Complications of forearm fractures in adults. In: McQueen, M.; Jupiter, J.B., eds. Radius and Ulna. London, Butterworth, 1999, pp. 119–137.
114. Rosacker, J.A.; Kopta, J.A. Both bone fractures of the forearm: A review of surgical variables associated with union. Orthopaedics 4:1353, 1981.
115. Ross, E.R.S.; Gourevitch, D.; Hastings, G.W.; et al. Retrospective analysis of plate fixation of diaphyseal fractures of the forearm bones. Injury 20:211, 1989.
116. Rosson, J.W.; Petley, G.W.; Shearer, J.R. Bone structure after removal of internal fixation plates. J Bone Joint Surg Br 73:65, 1991.
117. Rosson, J.W.; Shearer, J.R. Refracture after removal of plates from the forearm: An avoidable complication. J Bone Joint Surg Br 73:415, 1991.
118. Ruedi, T.P.; Murphy, W.M., eds. AO Principles of Fracture Management. Stuttgart, AO Publishing–Thieme, 2000.
119. Sage, F.P. Medullary fixation of fractures of the forearm: A study of the medullary canal of the radius and a report on 50 fractures of the radius treated with a prebent triangular nail. J Bone Joint Surg Am 41:1489, 1959.
120. Sargent, J.P.; Teipner, W.A. Treatment of forearm shaft fractures by double-plating: A preliminary report. J Bone Joint Surg Am 47:1475, 1965.
121. Sarmiento, A.; Cooper, J.S.; Sinclair, W.F. Forearm fractures: Early functional bracing. A preliminary report. J Bone Joint Surg Am 51:297, 1975.
122. Sarmiento, A.; Latta, L.L. Closed Functional Treatment of Fractures. New York, Springer-Verlag, 1981.
123. Schatzker, J.; Tile, M. The Rationale of Operative Fracture Care. Berlin, Springer-Verlag, 1987.
124. Schemitsch, E.H.; Richards, R.H. The effect of malunion on functional outcome after plate fixation of fractures of both bones of the forearm in adults. J Bone Joint Surg Am 74:1068, 1992.
125. Schneider, C.F.; Leyra, S. Siliconized Dacron interposition for traumatic radioulnar synostosis: Case report. J Med Assoc Ala 33:185, 1964.
126. Schneiderman, G.; Meldrum, R.D.; Bloebaum, R.D.; et al. The interosseous membrane of the forearm: Structure and its role in Galeazzi fractures. J Trauma 35:879, 1993.
127. Schuid, F.; Andrianne, Y.; Burny, F. Treatment of forearm fractures by Hoffman external fixation. Clin Orthop 266:197, 1991.
128. Seigel, D.B.; Gelberman, R.H. Peripheral nerve injuries associated with fractures and dislocations. In: Gelberman, R.H., ed. Operative Nerve Repair and Reconstruction. Philadelphia, J.B. Lippincott, 1991, p. 619.
129. Shea, K.G.; Fernandez, D.L.; Casillas, M. Fixation methods in contaminated wounds and massive crush injuries of the forearm. Hand Clin 13:737, 1997.
130. Simpson, S.; Jupiter, J.B. Complex fracture patterns of the upper extremity. Clin Orthop 318:43, 1995.
131. Slauterbeck, J.R.; Britton, C.; Monheim, M.S.; Clevenger, F.W. Mangled extremity severity score: An accurate guide to treatment of the severely injured upper extremity. J Orthop Trauma 8:282, 1994.
132. Smith, F.M. Monteggia fractures: An analysis of twenty-five consecutive fresh injuries. Surg Gynecol Obstet 85:630, 1947.
133. Smith, H.; Sage, F.P. Medullary fixation of forearm fractures. J Bone Joint Surg Am 39:91, 1957.
134. Smith, J.E.M. Internal fixation in the treatment of fractures of the shaft of the radius and ulna in adults. J Bone Joint Surg Br 41:122, 1959.
135. Speed, J.S.; Boyd, H.B. Treatment of fracture of the ulna with dislocation of the head of the radius (Monteggia fracture). JAMA 115:1699, 1940.
136. Spinner, M.; Freundlich, B.D.; Teicher, J. Posterior interosseous nerve palsy as a complication of Monteggia fractures in children. Clin Orthop 58:141, 1968.
137. Spira, E. Bridging of bone defects in the forearm combined with intramedullary nailing. J Bone Joint Surg Br 36:642, 1954.
138. Stein, F.; Grabia, S.L.; Deiffer, P.A. Nerve injuries complicating Monteggia lesions. J Bone Joint Surg Am 53:1432, 1971.
139. Stern, P.J.; Drury, W.J. Complications of plate fixation of forearm fractures. Clin Orthop 175:25, 1983.
140. Stewart, M. Discussion of paper. J Bone Joint Surg Am 39:264, 1957.
141. Tarr, R.R.; Garfinkel, A.I.; Sarmiento, A. The effects of angular and rotational deformities of both bones of the forearm: An in vitro study. J Bone Joint Surg Am 66:65, 1984.
142. Teipner, W.A.; Mast, J.W. Internal fixation of forearm fractures: Double plating versus single compression (tension band) plating. A comparative study. Orthop Clin North Am 11:381, 1980.
143. Tetsworth, K.; Krome, J.; Paly, D. Lengthening and deformity correction of the upper extremity by the Ilizarov technique. Orthop Clin North Am 22:689, 1991.
144. Thompson, J.E. Anatomical methods of approach in operations on the long bones of the extremities. Ann Surg 68:309, 1918.
145. Tile, M.; Petrie, D. Fractures of the radius and ulna. J Bone Joint Surg Br 51:193, 1969.
146. Trousdale, R.T.; Linscheid, R.L. Operative treatment of malunited fractures of the forearm. J Bone Joint Surg Am 73:894, 1995.
147. Valande, M. Luxation en arrière du cubitus avec fracture de la diaphyse radiale. Bull Mem Soc Nat Chir 55:435, 1929.
148. Vesely, D.G. The distal radioulnar joint. Clin Orthop 51:75, 1967.
149. Vince, K.G.; Miller, J.E. Cross-union complicating fractures of the forearm: Part I. Adults. J Bone Joint Surg Am 69:640, 1987.
150. Watson, F.M., Jr.; Eaton, R.G. Post-traumatic radio-ulnar synostosis. J Trauma 18:467, 1978.
151. Weber, B.G.; Brunner, C. Special Techniques in Internal Fixation. Berlin, Springer-Verlag, 1982.
152. Weiland, A.J. Current concept review: Vascular bone transplants. J Bone Joint Surg Am 63:166, 1981.
153. Wong, P.C.N. Galeazzi fracture dislocation in Singapore 1960–1964: Incidence and results of treatment. Singapore Med J 8:186, 1967.
154. Yong-Hing, K.; Tchang, S.P.K. Traumatic radio-ulnar synostosis treated by excision and a free fat transplant: A report of two cases. J Bone Joint Surg Br 65:433, 1983.

# CHAPTER 42

# Trauma to the Adult Elbow and Fractures of the Distal Humerus

PART I    *Trauma to the Adult Elbow*

Michael D. McKee, M.D., F.R.C.S.(C.)  •  Jesse B. Jupiter, M.D.

The elbow is the intermediate articulation of the upper extremity, and it connects the brachium to the forearm and hand. The joint has three distinct articulations—the radiocapitellar, ulnotrochlear, and proximal radioulnar joints—all contained in one synovium-lined capsule. This cubital complex acts to position the forearm and hand in space and serves a vital load-carrying function.

Two degrees of freedom of motion exist: flexion and extension centered in the ulnotrochlear joint and pronation and supination through the radiocapitellar and proximal radioulnar articulations in conjunction with the distal radioulnar joint (DRUJ). This unique arrangement represents the evolutionary adaptation of the bipedal mammalian forelimb for the tasks of manipulation and prehension. A greater understanding of the functional anatomy of the elbow can be gained from a brief evolutionary perspective.

As mammal-like reptiles evolved around 280 to 180 million years ago, the forelimb became drawn into the torso (Fig. 42–1). The distal end of the humerus was composed of two large, bulbous condyles separated by a shallow groove, whereas at the proximal end of the ulna, a low longitudinal ridge formed for articulation between the condyles. This condylar arrangement reflected the greater weight-bearing requirement of the forelimb along with an increasing degree of flexion and extension. The straight medial margin of the radial head resulted in limited axial rotation of the radius, whose major function was weight bearing[58] (Fig. 42–2).

The ancestral prosimians (premonkeys) that existed 100 to 35 million years ago adopted a tree-living habitat, and one can observe a greater specialization of the forelimbs for climbing.[17] The intercondylar groove of the distal part of the humerus assumed more of a pulley shape, and a deepened greater sigmoid notch and anterior shelflike projection (a primitive coronoid process) developed in the proximal end of the ulna. These changes reflected a shift in the burden of weight bearing and stability from the radius to the humeroulnar articulation. This functional transition, along with a more oval radial

head, allowed for a slightly increased range of forearm rotation.[155] The hominoid apes (25 to 12 million years ago) represented a more advanced stage of primate evolution in which locomotion was characterized by a predominance of arm swinging, or brachiation. The trochlea became wider and deeper with the creation of a more congruent ulnotrochlear joint that became the major determinant of mediolateral stability. With the stabilizing and weight-bearing role of the radiocapitellar joint virtually eliminated, the circular radial head became capable of providing a full range of forearm rotation in any degree of elbow flexion or extension. The hand could now be placed into a vast number of positions during brachiation.[72, 88]

The evolutionary split between the ancestral apes and the early humans probably occurred from 15 to 6 million years ago. As bipedalism evolved, the upper extremity came to be used primarily for prehension and manipulation. The architecture of the contemporary human elbow, however, differs from that of the ancient and modern apes only in small proportional measurements (see the section on the distal end of the humerus).[46, 134]

The importance of elbow mobility to upper extremity function cannot be underestimated, as evidenced by the functional limitations experienced by patients with an elbow arthrodesis as opposed to those with a wrist or shoulder arthrodesis.

## RADIAL HEAD FRACTURES

Fractures of the head of the radius are relatively common injuries and are found in nearly 20% of all elbow trauma.[61, 144, 167] Although much has been written regarding the management of these fractures, confusion and debate regarding optimal treatment continue.[220, 253] Support can be found for virtually every type of treatment, from prolonged immobilization to operative fixation and rapid functional loading. With greater

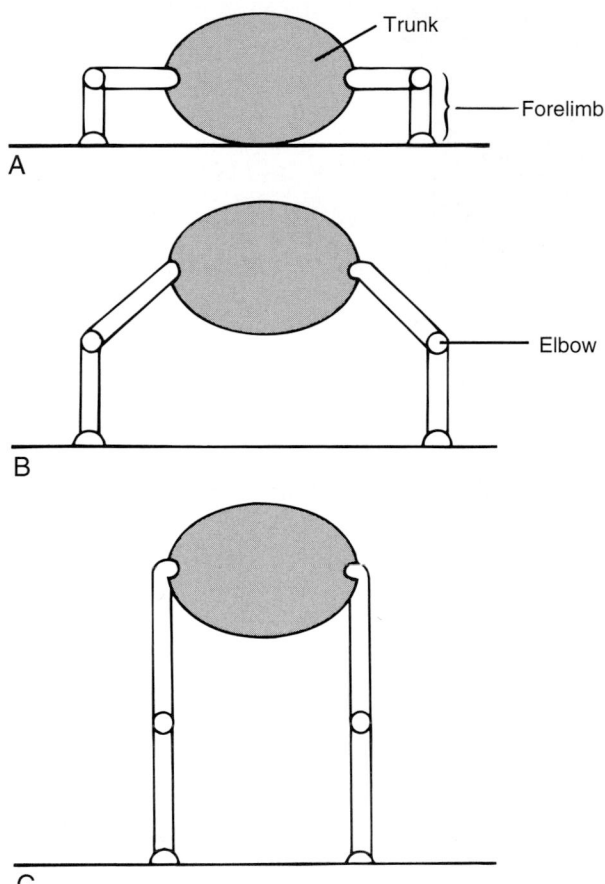

**FIGURE 42–1.** During the process of evolution, the forelimb became drawn into the torso.

recognition of fracture patterns and associated soft tissue injuries, as well as improved methods of fracture fixation, the simplistic universal approach of radial head excision for fractures requiring operative care has become subject to increasing scrutiny.[70] The radial head is an important secondary stabilizer of the elbow, and it is clear that radial head excision alone is contraindicated in certain situations in which extensive damage to the primary stabilizers of the elbow has occurred.[26, 115]

Loss of strength resulting from loss of the proximal part of the radius,[107] valgus instability,[104] early recurrent elbow instability, and proximal migration of the radius leading to wrist pain[156] have all been observed clinically with radial head excision in the trauma setting.[26, 115] Studies of static loading across the elbow have suggested that as much as 60% of the force is transmitted across the radiocapitellar articulation,[3, 4, 48, 166] although Morrey and associates found transmission of force during physiologic muscle contracture to be considerably lower than that reported with static loading.[106] The extent of the radial head's role in resisting valgus stress has been disputed by a number of investigators.[55, 104, 105, 122, 143] However, it is reasonable to state that the radial head is a secondary stabilizer to valgus stress, with the primary restraint being the medial collateral ligament. The role of the radial head in resisting valgus stress becomes predominant with rupture or insufficiency of this ligament. Thus, pathologic valgus instability results if the radial head is resected when concomitant injury to the medial collateral ligament has occurred.[107, 108] In this situation, every effort should be made to preserve or replace the radial head. Similarly, the stabilizing role of the radial head may become predominant with concomitant injury to the interosseous membrane or DRUJ (the Essex-Lopresti lesion), and resection in this situation may result in proximal migration of the radius.[34, 103]

Clinically, the radial head also plays a role in anteroposterior stability if other structures are damaged (such as in the "terrible triad of the elbow," see later), and resection can contribute to posterior instability[37, 115, 131] (Fig. 42–3).

In summary, in isolated lesions involving the radial head, treatment can focus on the head itself, and if the radial head is not reconstructible, excision is reasonable. If other injuries are present (and they must be considered to be present until proved otherwise by the treating clinician), radial head reconstruction or replacement is indicated.

**FIGURE 42–2.** Major stages in the structural development of the elbow. The *left* drawing in each frame represents the distal end of the humerus (ventral surface facing the interior); the *right* drawing is the corresponding radius and ulna rotated 180°. *A,* Primitive terrestrial quadruped elbow (345 to 230 million years ago). *B,* Early mammal-like reptiles (280 to 180 million years ago). *C,* First mammalian elbows (230 to 180 million years ago). *D,* The prosimian (premonkey) elbow (135 to 100 million years ago). *E,* Primitive anthropoid monkey elbow (35 to 25 million years ago). *F,* Hominoid ape elbow (25 to 12 million years ago). (*A–F,* Modified from Jenkins, F.A. Am J Anat 137:281–298, 1973.)

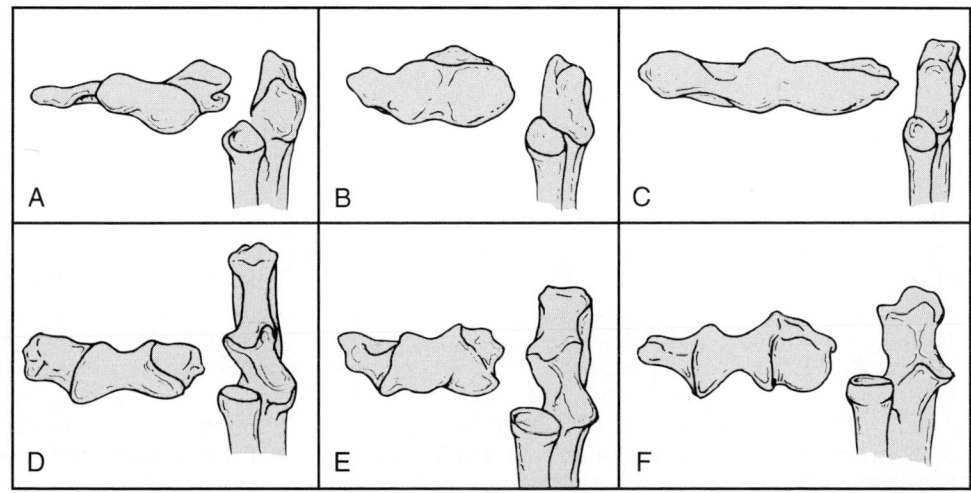

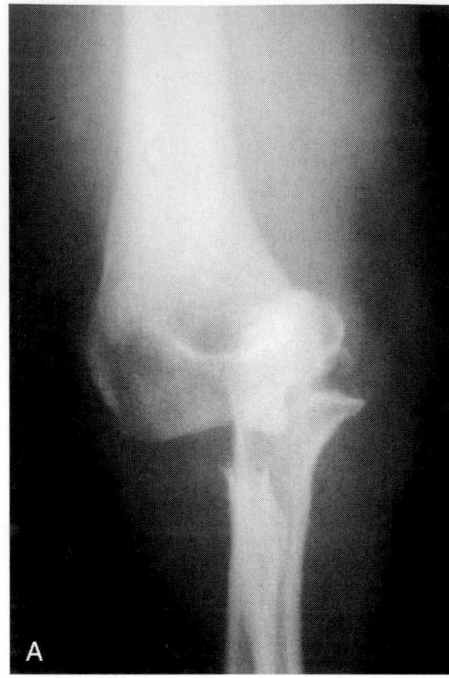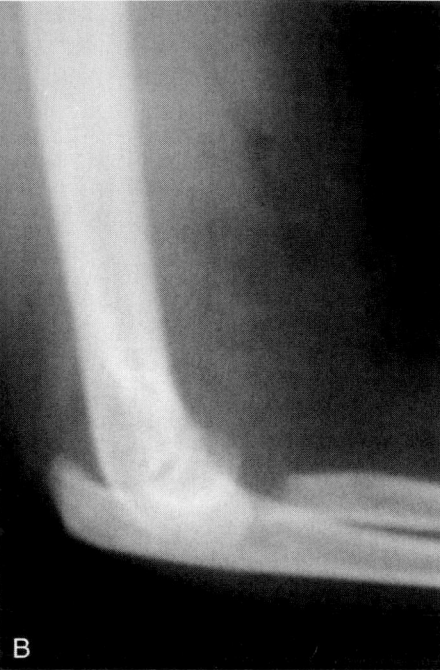

**FIGURE 42–3.** This 56-year-old woman suffered a dislocation of the elbow associated with a type I coronoid fracture and a comminuted radial head fracture. The treating surgeon excised the radial head, as well as the coronoid fragment. The elbow redislocated in the immediate postoperative period, as seen on anteroposterior *(A)* and lateral *(B)* radiographs. Radial head excision alone is contraindicated in most elbow fracture-dislocations.

**TABLE 42–1**

Scharplatz and Allgöwer's Classification of Elbow Injuries

Fractures and fracture-dislocations resulting from axial forces
Transverse olecranon fractures
Comminuted olecranon fractures
Transverse or comminuted olecranon fractures with anterior dislocation of the radius and ulna
Transverse or comminuted olecranon fractures with anterior dislocation of the radial head (atypical Monteggia)
Fractures of the ulnar shaft with anterior dislocation of the radial head (Monteggia)
Fractures of the coronoid process with posterior dislocation of the olecranon
Fractures resulting from transverse and lateral forces
Marginal fracture of the radial head
Marginal fracture of the radial head with disruption of the distal radioulnar joint

*Source:* Modified from Scharplatz, D.; Allgöwer, M. Injury 7:143–159, 1976.

## Mechanism of Injury

The early experimental efforts of Thomas and later of Oldeberg-Johnson[117] suggested that radial head fractures were the result of a fall on an outstretched hand with the forearm in pronation. The axial load can be of varying force and direction, and a variable amount of valgus force is inherent in these injuries, so a variety of associated soft tissue and skeletal injuries can result.[158, 159] These injuries are seen in 30% of patients with radial head fractures and include carpal fractures,[67] DRUJ and interosseous membrane disruption,[28, 32, 34, 87, 156] Monteggia fracture-dislocations, capitellar fractures,[118, 130] and soft tissue injury about the elbow (especially medial and lateral collateral ligament injuries). A retrospective review of patients from the Mayo Clinic with radial head fractures and distal radioulnar disruption (termed *radioulnar dissociation*) showed a 14% success rate in patients in whom the wrist injury was not recognized versus an 80% success rate

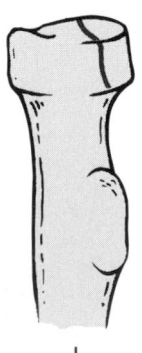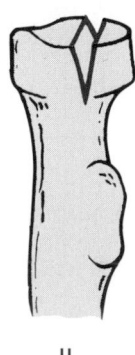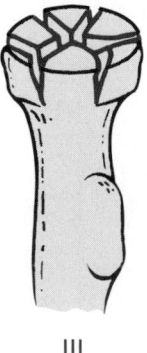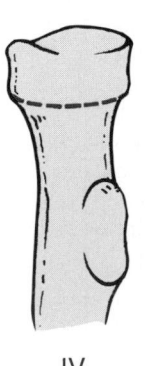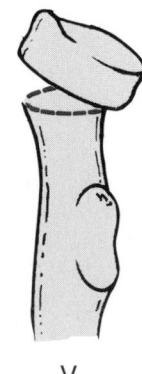

I          II          III          IV          V

**FIGURE 42–4.** Classification system of Bakalim for radial head fractures.

in those with proper initial diagnosis and treatment.[161] This report illustrates the critical importance of early recognition of associated forearm or wrist pathology.

## Classification

Classification of radial head fractures has undergone considerable evolution. Scharplatz and Allgöwer classified injuries about the elbow into two major groups on the basis of the direction of force of the injury[139]: (1) those resulting from pure axial forces and (2) those secondary to forces leading to varus or valgus displacement (Table 42–1). Early classifications of radial head fractures by Carstam,[19] Bakalim[9] (Fig. 42–4), and Mason[84] (Fig. 42–5) were based solely on radiographs and failed to take into account associated injuries. Johnston added a fourth category to Mason's classification in that he identified fractures associated with elbow dislocation.[61] This latter association has also been documented by a number of authors.[11, 25, 42, 103]

Because routine radiographs will project the radial head only in a two-dimensional profile, it is likely that some overlap exists within the arbitrary limits of these classifications. The ideal classification scheme would be reproducible, have low intraobserver and interobserver variability, and relate directly to treatment and prognosis. At the present time, however, no "ideal" classification exists.[15] More recent interest in internal fixation of articular fractures has extended to the radial head and has stimulated the development of classification systems that will prove to be of value when comparing the results of series of operative treatments (Fig. 42–6). Any classification scheme should include a detailed description of associated injuries, which is of critical importance in deciding on treatment.

## Diagnosis

### HISTORY AND PHYSICAL EXAMINATION

Tenderness or swelling over the lateral surface of the elbow or limitation of active or passive elbow or forearm motion should alert the examiner to the possibility of a radial head fracture. Careful palpation of the forearm may reveal tenderness along the course of the interosseous membrane. Obvious DRUJ instability, pain with stressing of the joint, or wrist pain by history is suggestive of an Essex-Lopresti lesion. Pain on the medial side of the elbow or a history of dislocation with spontaneous reduction suggests a concomitant injury to the medial collateral ligament. The history is important and may suggest a severe valgus injury with damage to the medial collateral ligament. The elbow is carefully examined for a block to rotation or flexion/extension. The use of an intra-articular local anesthetic may assist in this maneuver.

### RADIOGRAPHS

Routine anteroposterior (AP) and lateral radiographs may not provide an accurate representation of the individual

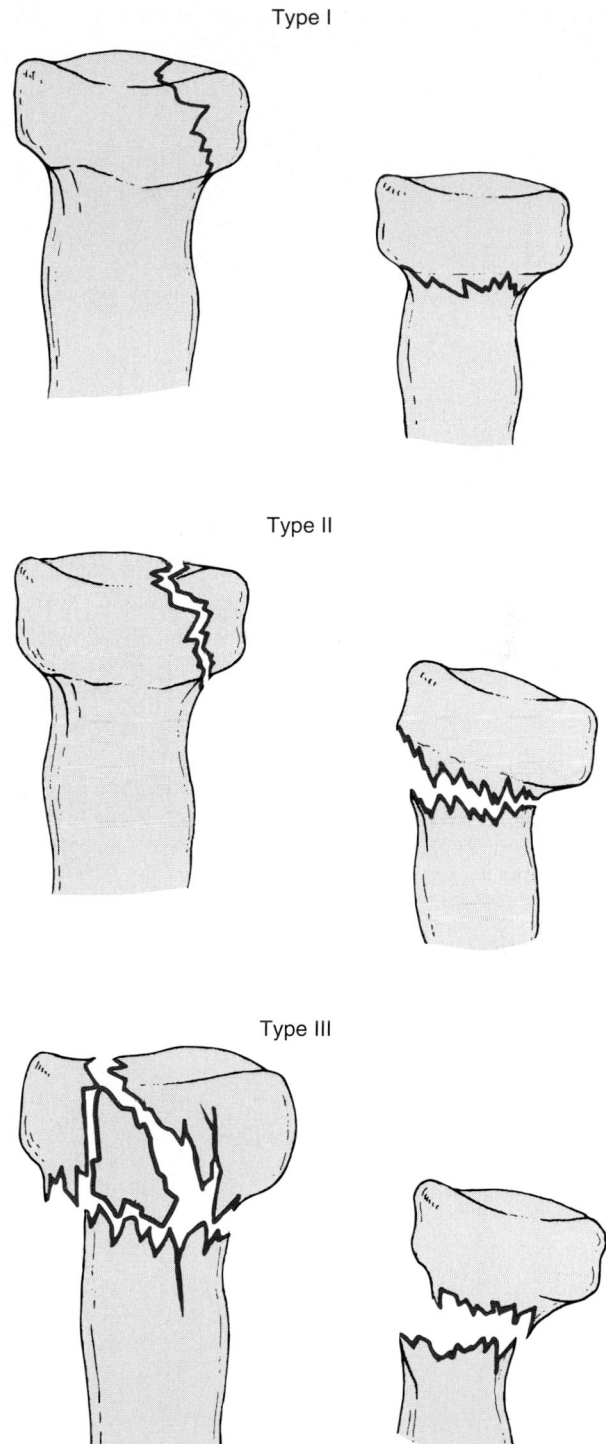

**FIGURE 42–5.** Modified Mason classification system for radial head fractures.

fracture pattern. In a patient with an appropriate clinical history and examination, elevation of the anterior and posterior fat pads (the so-called sail sign) by an intra-articular hemarthrosis may be the only clue to an undisplaced radial head fracture (Fig. 42–7). Skaggs and Mirzayan showed in follow-up radiographs that 76% of children with this sign had evidence of fracture.[147] The

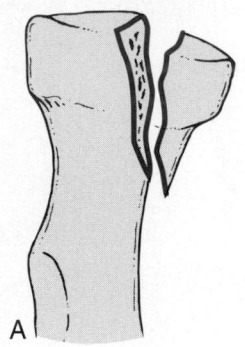 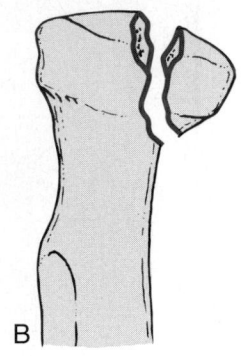 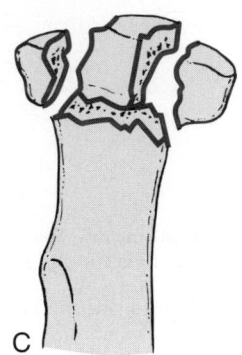

**Figure 42–6.** Classification system of Schatzker and Tile for radial head fractures. *A,* Type I: wedge. This fracture may be displaced or nondisplaced. *B,* Type II: impaction. Part of the head and neck remains intact. The fracture is tilted and impacted, and comminution is variable. *C,* Type III: severely comminuted. No portion of the head and neck remains in continuity; comminution is severe.

radiographic view described by Greenspan and Norman is recommended in cases in which accurate identification of the fracture pattern will influence the method of treatment.[45] This so-called radiocapitellar view is accomplished by positioning the patient as for a lateral radiographic view, but angling the tube 45° toward the shoulder. A recent magnetic resonance imaging (MRI) investigation by Starch and Dabezies has demonstrated that injury to the interosseous membrane or blood or fluid along this membrane can be detected accurately.[148] This promising finding may help in objectively identifying these injuries early and aid in treatment decision making (Fig. 42–8).[8] For instance, radial head excision alone would be contraindicated in patients who had identifiable injury to the interosseous membrane on MRI.

## JOINT ASPIRATION

Aspiration of the radiocapitellar joint is of value not only in confirming the diagnosis of radial head fracture but also in reducing associated discomfort. It can prove invaluable in determining whether a bony block to forearm or elbow motion has occurred as a result of displacement of the fracture. For many, a block to motion after aspiration of an intra-articular hematoma and injection of local anesthetic is an indication for surgery.[141] The technique, as described by Quigley, is performed under aseptic conditions. The forearm is pronated to minimize

the possibility of trauma to the radial nerve, and the needle is introduced through the center of a triangle formed by the radial head, the tip of the olecranon, and the lateral epicondyle.[125] Aspiration of the hemarthrosis accompanied by instillation of a local anesthetic can be done through the same needle (Fig. 42–9). In one study by Fleetcroft, improved results were noted in nondisplaced or minimally displaced radial head fractures when the joint was aspirated and early mobilization encouraged versus early mobilization alone.[36] However, a prospective, controlled trial of 60 cases failed to show any long-term advantage with this technique, and intra-articular infection is a potential risk.[53] Thus, its use can be supported mainly for diagnostic purposes and acute pain relief.

## Treatment

Although these fractures are considered by many to be relatively benign injuries, the outcome can be disappointing. The unsatisfactory results are a reflection not just of the treatment rendered but also (and more likely) of the nature of the original trauma and associated injuries. It is therefore of fundamental importance to define the presence or absence of other soft tissue or skeletal injuries and classify the fracture accordingly. Most fractures prove to be isolated events and can be effectively treated by conservative means.

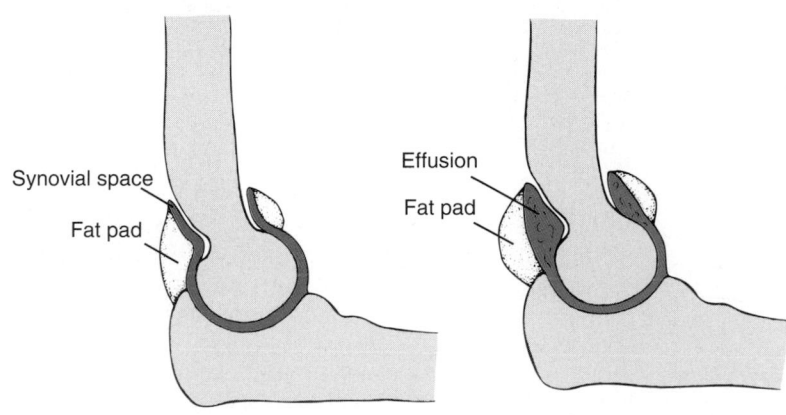

**Figure 42–7.** With an intra-articular effusion, the fat pads will be displaced and become visible on radiographs.

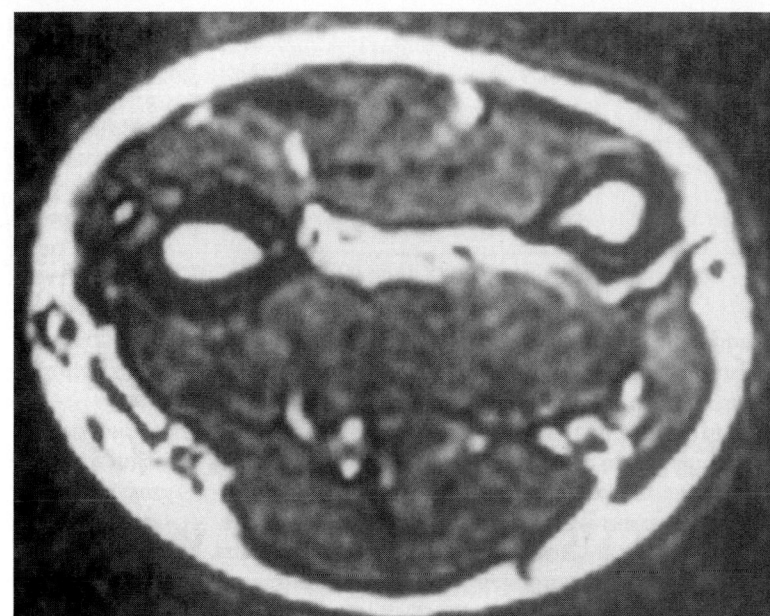

**FIGURE 42–8.** Increased signal intensity along the interosseous membrane seen on a magnetic resonance imaging examination (T2-weighted image) of a patient with an Essex-Lopresti lesion. This finding demonstrates the utility of this type of imaging technique in the diagnosis of interosseous membrane injury in complex elbow/forearm trauma. (From Starch, D.W.; Dabezies, E.J. J Bone Joint Surg Am 83:235–242, 2001.).

## RADIAL HEAD FRACTURE: NO OR MINIMAL DISPLACEMENT

Radial head fractures with no or minimal displacement consist of articular fractures with little or no separation or impaction (Fig. 42–10). Well-aligned, impacted radial neck fractures can also be included in this group.

Concern for residual loss of elbow motion has led many to recommend early mobilization of the forearm and elbow for these "stable" fractures.[1, 53, 83, 168] Several studies have in fact suggested improved results, including shorter disability time and enhanced elbow mobility along with early functional motion after minimally displaced radial head fractures.[53, 168] Early mobilization, however, should

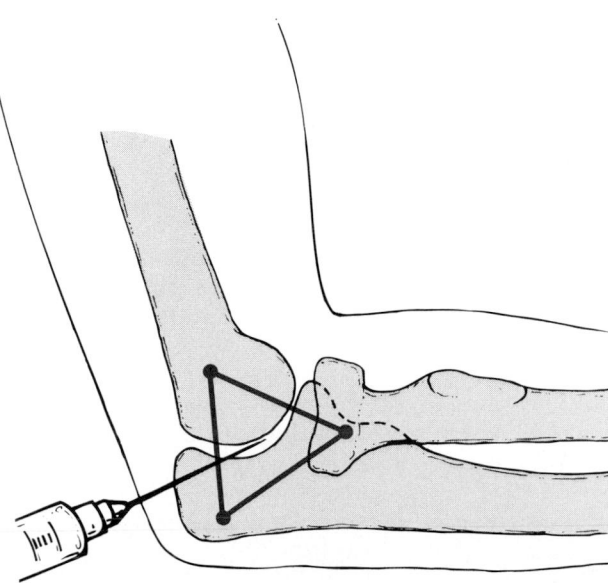

**FIGURE 42–9.** Aspiration of the radiocapitellar joint is performed with a needle introduced through the center of a triangle formed by the radial head, the tip of the olecranon, and the lateral epicondyle.

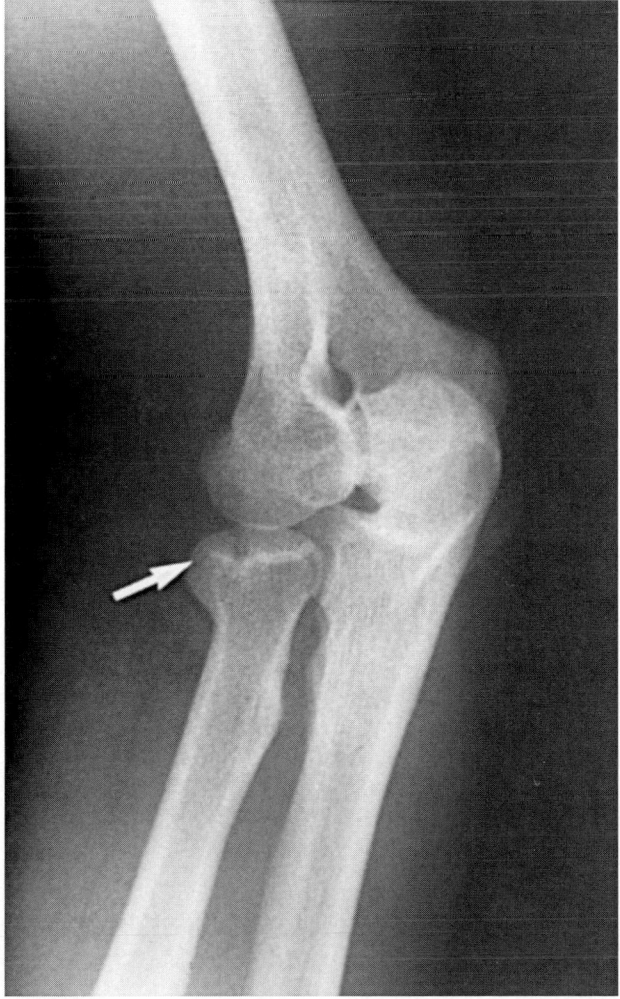

**FIGURE 42–10.** A minimally displaced radial head fracture (*arrow*) can be treated with splinting, provided that a block to forearm or elbow motion is not present.

be considered cautiously when the fracture involves a large segment of the articular surface. In a series reported by Radin and Riseborough,[126] displacement and resultant loss of mobility occurred in some instances of "stable" fractures involving more than one third of the articular surface that were permitted freedom of motion early after injury.

### Treatment Recommendation

Early mobilization should be considered for "stable" fractures that involve less than one third of the articular surface or for fractures in elderly, low-demand individuals. In active individuals, however, fractures involving more than a third of the articular surface should be treated with splint or sling support for a minimum of 2 weeks, followed by protected functional activities for an additional 7 to 10 days. The prognosis for this group is generally good, although Mason reported that one third of the patients in a large series lost an average of 7° of extension.[84] Displacement of the fracture, though uncommon, is associated with a poor result.[126] If displacement is noted, prompt operative repair is indicated.

## TWO-PART DISPLACED RADIAL HEAD FRACTURES

Opinions are diverse regarding the approach to management of two-part displaced radial head fractures, in part because this fracture pattern can vary in the amount of articular surface involved, the extent of impaction of the fracture fragment, the presence or absence of comminution in the radial neck, and associated soft tissue involvement (Fig. 42–11).

### Treatment Recommendation

It is of fundamental importance to assess the amount of forearm rotation and elbow flexion. When no block to motion exists and no palpable incongruity of the articular surface is present, conservative treatment with a splint will generally provide a good result.[102] If, however, a definable block to motion is demonstrated, operative intervention should be considered. At this point, the presence of associated soft tissue or skeletal trauma becomes an essential factor in the decision-making process. Examination under anesthesia, examination after intra-articular injection of local anesthetic, and stress radiographs are helpful in establishing the diagnosis.[103]

**Displaced Two-Part Fractures without Associated Injury.** Displaced two-part fractures without associated injury are preferably treated by open reduction and internal fixation (ORIF).[131] Although good results have been reported after excision of the radial head for these fractures, some studies have noted proximal migration of the radius[87, 149, 156] and a reduction in grip strength.[107]

Improvements in small-implant design and application have made internal fixation of the radial head more reliable.[11, 113, 142, 162] The surgical approach is through a standard lateral incision with identification of the interval between the anconeus and the extensor carpi ulnaris muscles. Through a longitudinal capsulotomy, the fracture hematoma is débrided to expose the fracture fragments. Most often, the fracture involves the anterolateral portion of the radial head, which makes it accessible to reduction

and provisional fixation with Kirschner wires (K-wires).[61] One or two (countersunk) 2.0- or 2.7-mm screws or self-compressing Herbert screws afford sufficient stability to permit postoperative functional mobilization. The differential pitch of the threads of the Herbert screw provides a modest amount of interfragmentary compression, but a more important feature is the ability to countersink the implant beneath the articular rim of the radial head (Fig. 42–12).

It should be noted, however, that the comminution is frequently greater than expected from the preoperative radiographs, so in most series, definitive fixation of the fracture is carried out in approximately 70% of the patients for whom it was intended. The remainder require radial head excision (and/or replacement).

Although most of the margin of the radial head is covered by cartilage for articulation with the proximal end of the ulna, the joint has an arc of approximately 110° that is "nonarticular." This nonarticular area, or "safe zone," can be difficult to determine intraoperatively. A recent cadaver study showed that a plate applied directly laterally on the radial head and neck with the arm in a neutral position would not impinge on the proximal radioulnar joint.[245] Once the fixation is applied, the range of rotation should be checked before closure.

The lack of soft tissue attachment to radial head

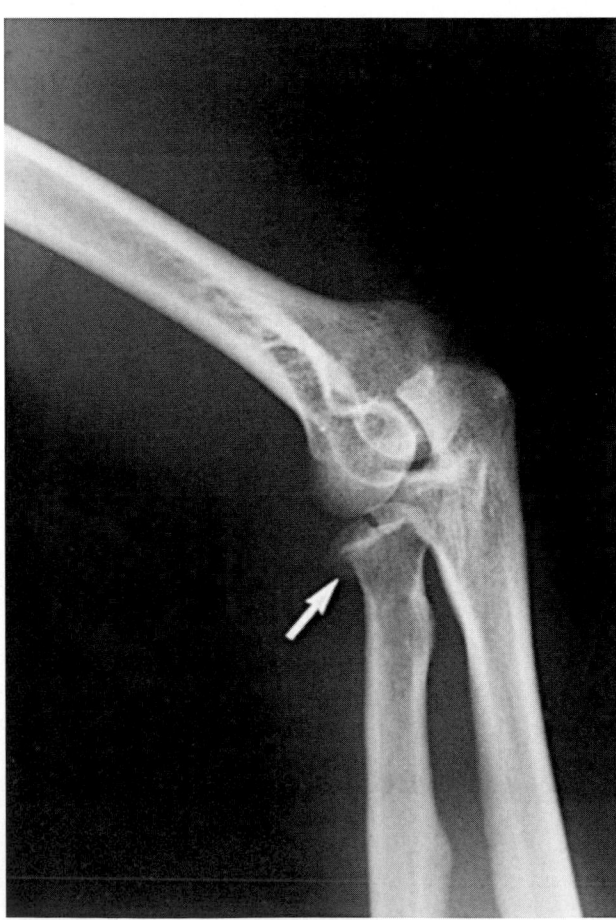

**FIGURE 42–11.** A two-part radial head fracture (*arrow*) can vary widely in the extent of articular surface involved, the amount of displacement, the degree of radial neck involvement, and associated soft tissue injury.

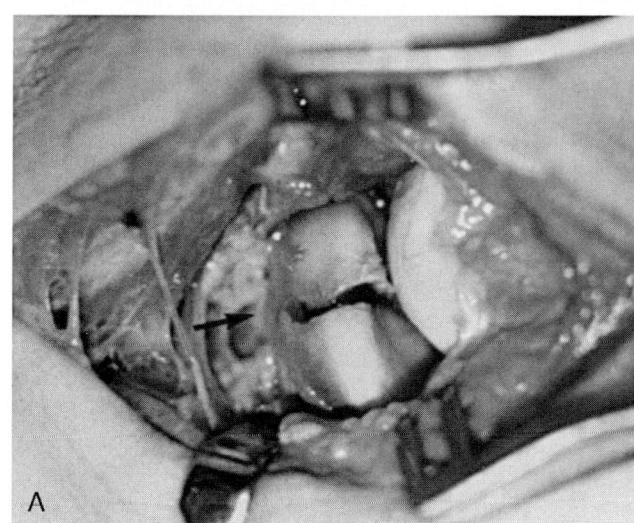 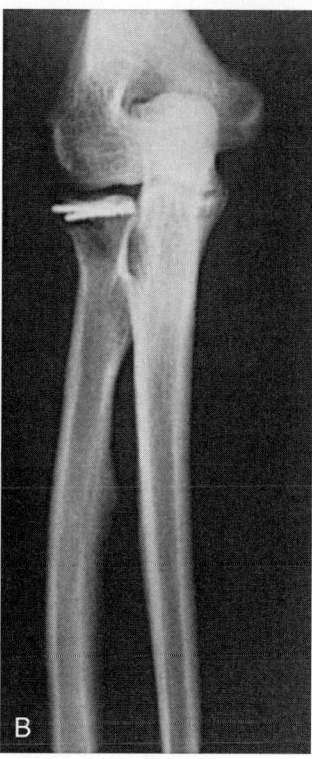

FIGURE 42–12. A 38-year-old woman sustained a displaced two-part radial head fracture. On examination, a palpable block to forearm rotation was appreciated. *A,* An intraoperative photograph shows the extent of articular displacement. *B,* The fracture was secured with two Herbert screws. Full motion was regained within 1 week postoperatively.

fragments would seem to argue against routine fixation because of concern about avascular necrosis and nonunion. However, small fragments heal routinely with a low incidence of necrosis, presumably being revascularized by "creeping substitution" from adjacent vascular bone. An injection study by Yamaguchi and colleagues revealed a direct intra-articular blood supply entering the noncartilaginous portion of the head, as well as blood supply from the intraosseous vessels[173] (Fig. 42–13A and B). This separate supply may help explain the low incidence of avascular necrosis, even when the entire radial head is fractured and devoid of soft tissue attachments. Patel and Elliott reported radiographic survival of a radial head that was fractured and completely free in a fracture-dislocation of the elbow.[121] After reconstruction with a plate and bone graft, the radial head united; at a 2-year follow-up the radial head was viable and the patient had an elbow range of motion of 10° to 130°. Other authors have described the utility of reconstruction of the radial head in this situation as a biologic spacer that can be removed later if nonunion or avascular necrosis intervenes, once sufficient ligamentous healing has occurred to restore elbow stability.[120]

If the articular fragment is impacted and requires elevation for restoration of the articular surface, a small defect will be produced beneath the elevated fragment. This defect is best filled with cancellous bone graft, which is readily available from the lateral epicondyle of the humerus.

**Displaced Fracture with Soft Tissue Injury.** When a displaced two-part radial head fracture is associated with dislocation of the elbow or disruption of the DRUJ and interosseous membrane, preservation of the radial head becomes a higher priority (Fig. 42–14). If internal fixation

of the fracture is not feasible, several treatment options exist. For fracture fragments involving less than a third of the surface of the head, excision of the fragment is one option.[19] However, when dealing with larger fragments, the results of partial radial head excision are inferior to complete radial head excision.[27] Other options include replacement of the head with a prosthesis or exploration and repair of the medial ligament complex of the elbow in conjunction with radial head resection.[25, 49, 50, 103]

Prosthetic replacement offers the advantages of more normal articular relationships, pain relief, intrinsic stability, and elimination of proximal migration of the radial shaft.[50, 151] A radial head implant can also assist in providing the proper "tension" for lateral ligament repair performed for concomitant lateral instability after elbow dislocation. Several drawbacks were associated with the previously popular prosthetic designs made of silicone. In the first place, studies by Carn and co-workers[18] suggested that the silicone rubber prosthesis is too flexible and is thus unable to transmit physiologic forces from the proximal end of the radius to the capitellum; consequently, it fails in its function as a static spacer. A second problem can result from fracture of the silicone prosthesis and resultant particulate synovitis, which lead to local pain and further implant loosening.[44, 171] For this reason, the current standard is the use of metallic implants, which are mechanically more stable, are more durable, and do not produce inflammatory changes in the elbow.

The technique of metallic radial head replacement is similar to that of silicone arthroplasty. The head is resected at the metaphyseal flare, with preservation of the integrity of the annular ligament by preserving as much of the radial neck as possible (Fig. 42–15). The cut edges are smoothed to allow secure seating of the prosthesis, and an implant

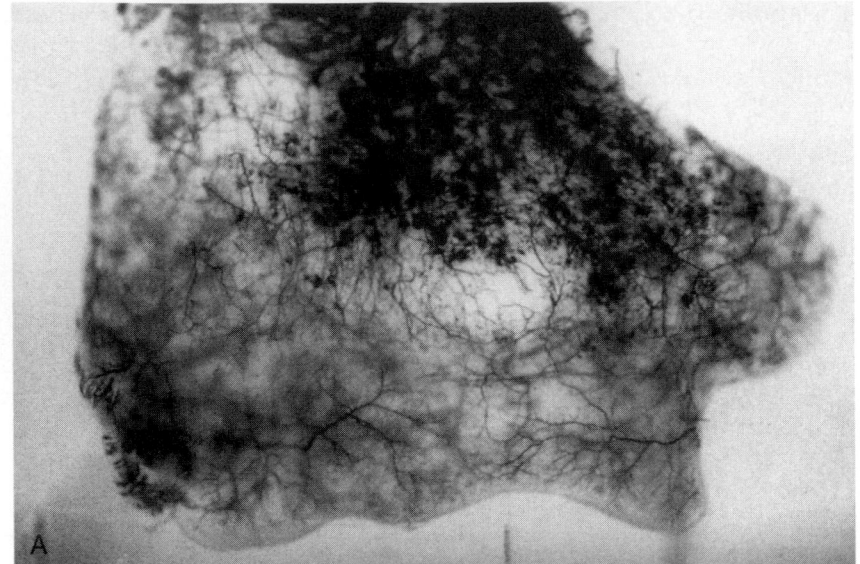

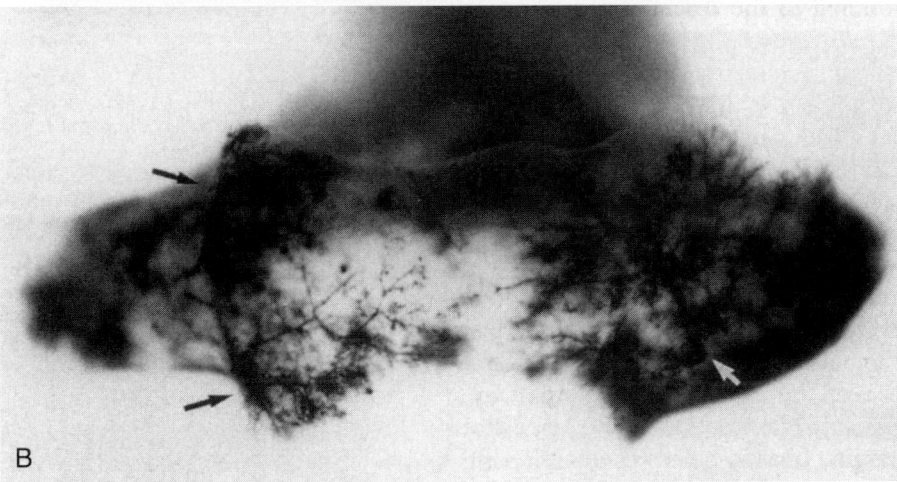

**FIGURE 42–13.** *A* and *B*, The blood supply of the distal end of the humerus and elbow, as demonstrated by an India ink/latex injection technique. Note the sparse nature of the blood supply to the trochlea. (From Yamaguchi, K., et al. J Bone Joint Surg Am 79:1653–1661, 1997.)

that matches the size of the native radial head is used. A smaller implant may not have optimal stability, and a larger one may impinge and thereby reduce motion. The stem of the prosthesis should be inserted directly down the medullary canal of the proximal end of the radius. Typically, when a radial head prosthesis is used, enough instability is present that displacing the proximal part of the radius sufficiently to insert the implant is not a problem.

Much has been said in the literature regarding the timing of surgery for radial head fractures.[220] Some have believed that any surgery should be performed expeditiously to avoid heterotopic ossification and myositis ossificans,[42, 56, 160] whereas others have recommended that surgery be considered within the first week after injury.[19, 84] It is likely that the timing of the actual surgery is less important than both the nature of the original injury and the manner in which the surgery is executed. Because the main complication is heterotopic ossification, consideration may be given to the use of a prophylactic agent effective against heterotopic ossification (e.g., indomethacin, radiation) when performing radial head excision or repair in predisposed patients (e.g., those with extensive

muscle damage, concomitant neurotrauma, or revision procedures).[97]

## COMMINUTED FRACTURES OF THE RADIAL HEAD

More commonly associated with higher-energy trauma, comminuted fracture patterns are rarely amenable to stable internal fixation. Soft tissue swelling and ecchymosis suggest the likelihood of capsular, brachial, or ligamentous injury, including a dislocation that has undergone spontaneous reduction.[60] Capitellar fractures, Monteggia fracture-dislocations, and wrist and forearm injuries may also accompany a comminuted radial head fracture.[130] In view of the possibility of significant soft tissue trauma, the timing of surgery in this setting may be of more significance. However, in general, our approach is to deal with the injury in a definitive manner as promptly as feasible. Occasionally, one may encounter an indication (patient or fracture) for early postinjury mobilization and delayed (beyond 6 weeks) radial head excision.[10, 149]

Although radial head resection is the most commonly performed procedure for comminuted fractures, it has been observed to be associated with instability and late post-traumatic arthritis when performed in the setting of disruption of the medial collateral ligament or interosseous membrane[28, 32, 34, 62, 87, 100, 156] (Fig. 42–16). A recent study by Sanchez-Sotelo and associates examined the effect of immediate radial head excision in elbow dislocations that had comminuted radial head fractures. Instability necessitated postoperative immobilization for a mean of 23 days, and two patients required transarticular pinning.[138] Although the short-term results seemed reasonable, the authors admitted that the 80% rate of radiographic degenerative change at a mean of 4.6 years postoperatively was "worrisome" in this young patient population (mean age, 39 years).

In general, results are better with radial head replacement and the early motion that is possible because of the improved stability. Harrington and associates reported the long-term (mean of 12.1 years) follow-up of 20 unstable elbow fracture-dislocations in which a comminuted radial head fracture was treated with a metallic prosthesis. They had 16 good and excellent and only 2 poor results.[49] Popovic and coauthors described 11 similar cases in which a metallic bipolar radial head prosthesis was used; no revisions were required and only one poor result occurred.[121] In both series, the improved stability afforded by the metallic radial head allowed early motion, which enhanced the functional result and range of motion.

In general, excision alone is contraindicated when injury to either the collateral ligament or interosseous membrane of the elbow is diagnosed. Replacement or reconstruction is indicated in these cases because severe early instability can result (see Fig. 42–3).

### Treatment Recommendation

In the setting of a low-energy injury, an elderly patient, or a lack of physical findings suggestive of associated soft tissue disruption, resection of the radial head alone is a straightforward approach that in most instances is not associated with long-term sequelae.[23] Janssen and Vegter reported 20 good and excellent results in 21 elbows that had a comminuted radial head fracture treated by early excision. Their follow-up ranged from 16 to 30 years, but it is important to point out that elbows with associated injuries (i.e., dislocation) were excluded.[57] More than half the patients had radiographic evidence of proximal migration of the radius of 1 to 3 mm, but only a few had any (mild) wrist symptoms.

If, however, medial collateral ligament instability or disruption of the DRUJ is observed (the Essex-Lopresti lesion), treatment should consist of either internal fixation of the radial head or prosthetic replacement (Fig. 42–17). After radial head reconstruction or replacement, the elbow should be tested for valgus stability, and manual testing of the stability of the DRUJ should be carried out. Should valgus instability be observed, exploration and repair of the medial collateral ligament complex are recommended.

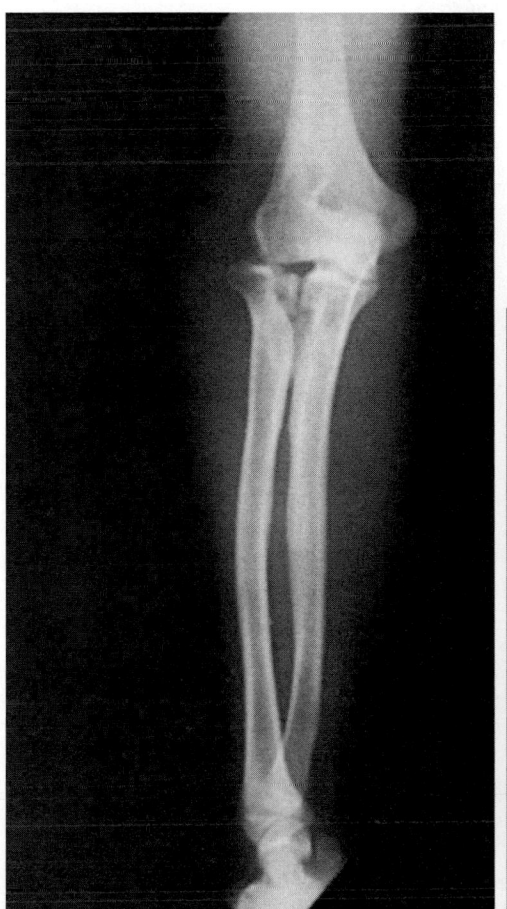
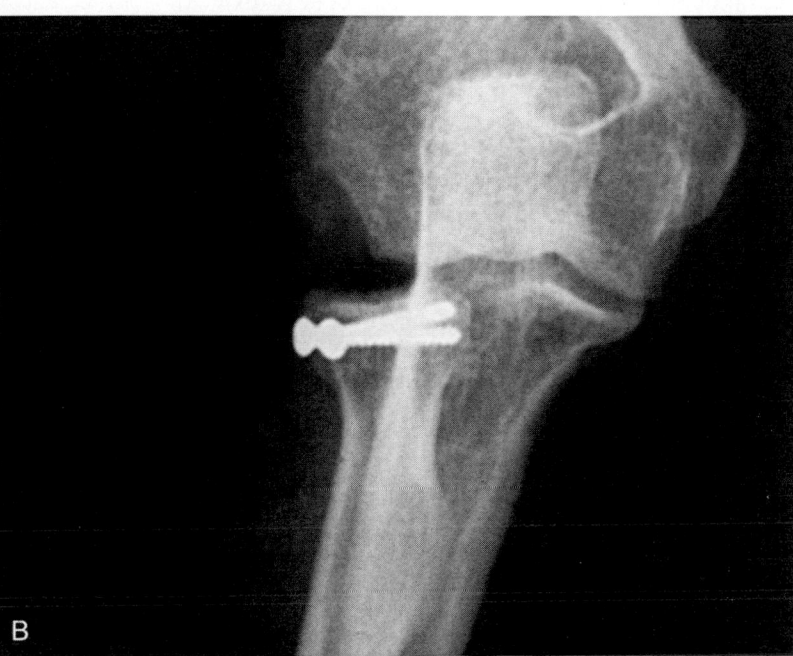

**FIGURE 42–14.** A 27-year-old man sustained a high-energy injury to his right dominant extremity. *A,* Pain was noted at his distal radioulnar joint, and a displaced two-part radial head fracture was seen on the radiograph. *B,* Open reduction plus internal fixation was performed with two 2.7-mm screws.

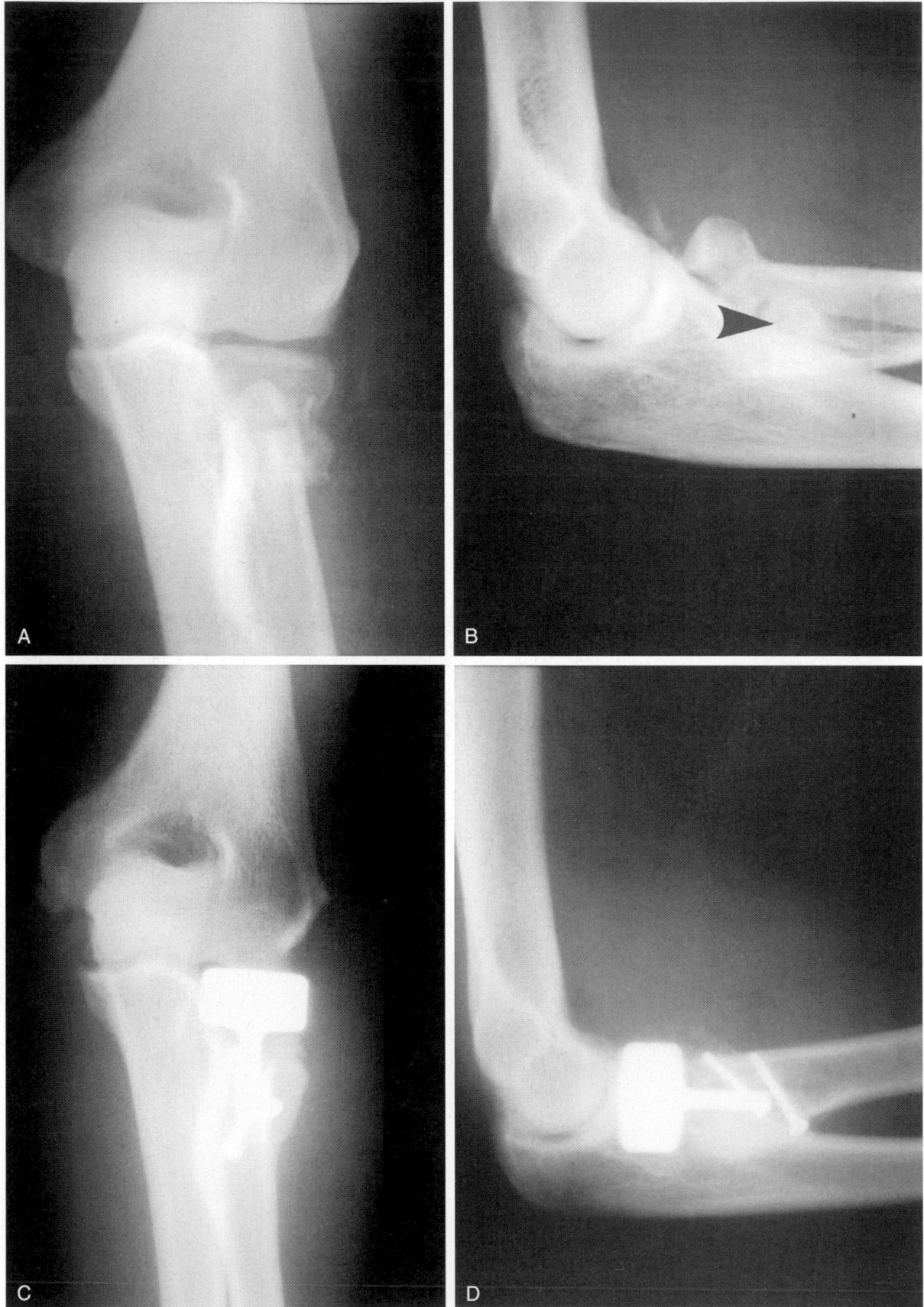

**FIGURE 42–15.** *A, B,* Anteroposterior and lateral radiographs of the elbow of a 32-year-old man after a fall with a severe valgus injury. A comminuted radial fracture can be noted, and one fragment has been driven down the radial neck and has split it *(arrowhead). C, D,* After the fragments of the radial head were removed, gross valgus instability (indicating concomitant medial collateral ligament injury) was present. Stability was restored by lag screw fixation of the radial neck fracture followed by replacement with a metallic radial head.

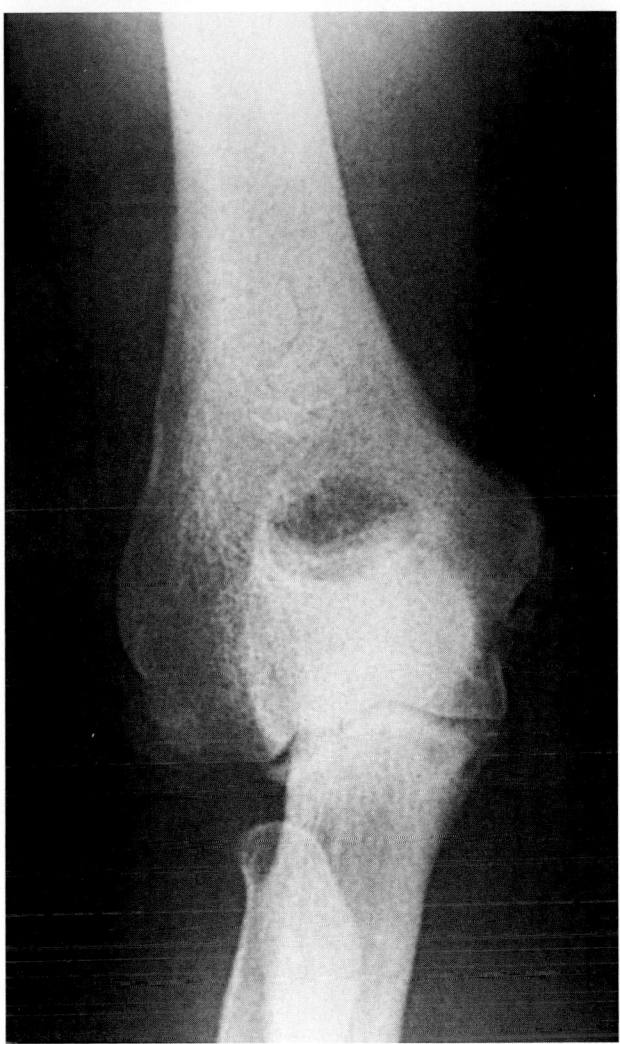

FIGURE 42–16. A 50-year-old man presented 2 years after a fracture-dislocation of his elbow, which was initially treated by closed reduction and radial head resection. Pain, instability, and symptoms of ulnar neuritis were observed. The radiograph demonstrates evidence of ulnohumeral arthritis.

Suture anchors placed in the medial column of the distal end of the humerus can be used to reattach the avulsed medial collateral ligament.[43] Similarly, if distal ulnar instability is present, it is best to pin the ulna to the radius with the forearm in supination. Elbow flexion and extension can then be initiated, with the K-wire left in place for 4 to 6 weeks[161] (Fig. 42–18).

One recent study described the results of treatment of elbow dislocations associated with radial head fractures that were treated by open reduction, radial head stabilization, and ligament repair followed by early motion.[37] Frankle and colleagues described 17 elbow dislocations treated with early surgery for associated radial head fractures. Nine radial heads were repaired and eight were replaced. At the conclusion of the procedure, the disrupted lateral collateral ligament complex was repaired in all cases and the elbow examined. Six elbows required additional stabilization through medial ligament repair, hinged external fixation, or both. All elbows were treated postoperatively with immediate range-of-motion rehabilitation, and the results were good.

## Complications

Complications associated with radial head fractures can be divided into two major categories: (1) those associated with the fracture and (2) those arising after radial head excision.

For the most part, the complications of nonoperative treatment are loss of motion and pain, with loss of full extension being the most common. These complications have generally been reported in association with the more complex comminuted radial head fractures and, rarely, with the minimally displaced variant.

Reported complications with radial head excision are well documented and include loss of grip strength,[28, 32, 34, 153, 156] pain at the wrist,[87] valgus instability,[55, 122, 143] heterotopic ossification,[160] and post-traumatic arthritis of the trochlea-olecranon articulation.[100, 103]

## CORONOID FRACTURES

Fracture of the coronoid process has been identified in as many as 10% to 15% of elbow dislocations.[128, 145] Along with acting as the anterior buttress of the greater sigmoid notch of the olecranon, the base of the coronoid provides attachment for both the anterior bundle of the medial collateral ligament and the middle portion of the anterior capsule.[128]

## Classification

Regan and Morrey classified these fractures into the following three types based on their physical size[128] (Fig. 42–19):

Type I: Avulsion of the tip
Type II: A single or comminuted fracture involving 50% or less of the coronoid
Type III: A single or comminuted fracture involving more than 50% of the coronoid

## Mechanism of Injury

Previously, type I and even some type II fractures were called "avulsion" fractures and were described as having been produced by avulsion from the capsule and brachialis muscle. Several lines of investigation suggest that this reasoning is erroneous. First, the tip of the coronoid can clearly be seen during elbow arthroscopy or arthrotomy with no soft tissue attachment, as has been confirmed by Neill Cage and co-workers in an anatomic study.[111] Second, studies by Amis and Miller have shown that the indirect force caused by axial loading produces a shear effect that is the mechanism behind most coronoid

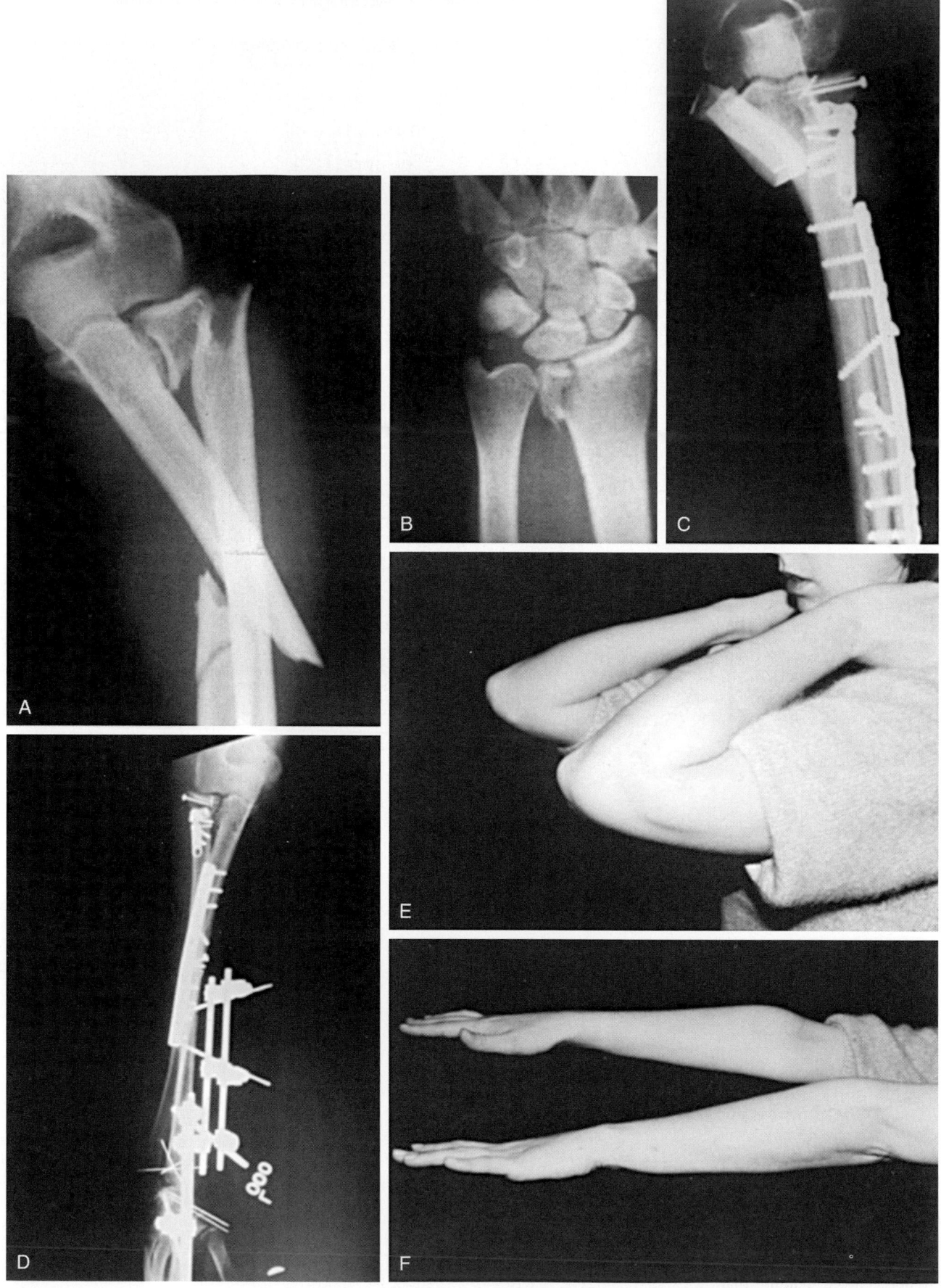

**FIGURE 42–17.** A 24-year-old woman was involved in a high-energy motorcycle accident. Multiple fractures were noted in her left dominant limb. *A*, A radiograph demonstrated complex radial head and neck fractures. *B*, Fractures were also noted to involve the ulnar shaft, distal end of the radius, scaphoid, and capitate. Disruption of the distal radioulnar joint was also present. *C*, Open reduction plus internal fixation of the radial head and neck was performed with an interfragmentary 2.0-mm screw, two threaded 0.028-inch Kirschner wires, and a minifragment T plate. *D*, The remainder of the forearm injuries were treated with internal and external fixation. *E* and *F*, Postoperatively, the patient regained full elbow flexion and extension.

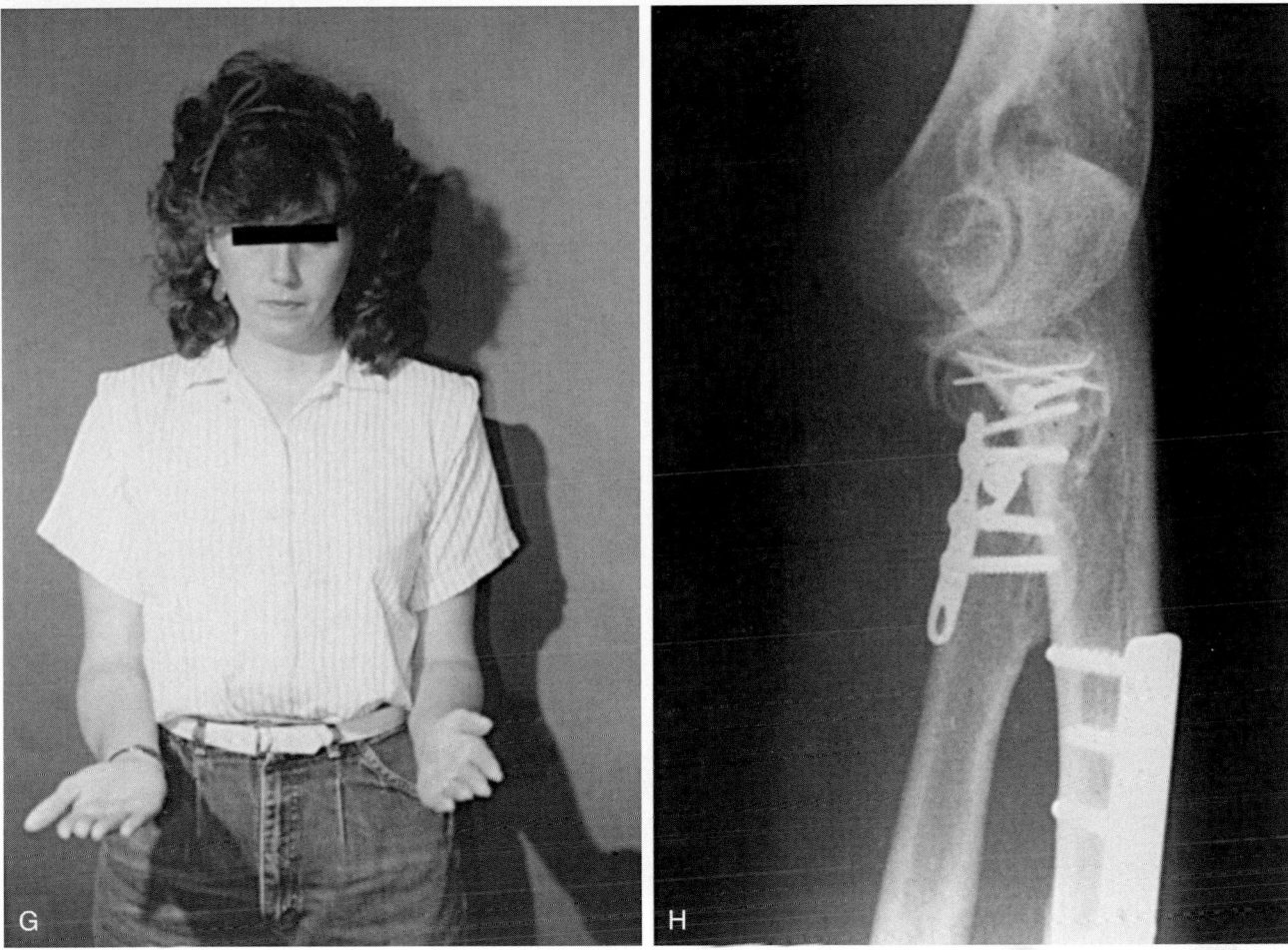

**FIGURE 42–17** *Continued. G,* Forearm supination was limited because of residual disruption of the distal radioulnar joint. *H,* Radiographs revealed excellent union, with calcification noted in the pericapsular tissues. (*A–H,* From Jupiter, J.B. J Hand Surg [Am] 11:279–282, 1986.)

fractures.[5] Third, the morphologic similarity between isolated coronoid fractures and those seen in episodes of elbow fracture-dislocation strongly supports a shearing mechanism of injury. In fact, many authorities believe that the presence of a coronoid fracture is pathognomonic of an episode of elbow instability.[115] Thus, although repair or fixation of a type I coronoid fracture may not be indicated on a mechanical basis, it has significance in terms of the mechanism of injury and possible soft tissue injury.[157]

## Biomechanics

An increasing amount of study has been devoted to the coronoid process because it has become apparent that it plays a significant role in elbow stability. Closkey and colleagues performed a biomechanical analysis of axial loading of the elbow in various positions of flexion after resection of varying amounts of the coronoid process. They found that elbows with a fracture involving greater than 50% of the coronoid became displaced in a posterior direction more readily than did those with a fracture involving less than 50% of the coronoid.[20] This finding was especially true, even with the collateral ligaments intact, when the elbow was flexed more than 60°. This study helps explain why elbow injuries associated

with (unrepaired) type III coronoid fractures have a poor prognosis, and it supports the current trend toward fixation of these fractures in an effort to restore stability.[10, 20, 23, 26]

The soft tissue attached to the base of the coronoid consists of the anterior capsule and brachialis anteriorly and the insertion of the medial collateral ligament medially. These soft tissue structures may also be important in restoring elbow stability, independent of the mechanical effect of the bony fragment. Terada and coauthors reported on three patients who had the so-called terrible triad of the elbow, which consists of fracture of the coronoid, fracture of the radial head, and dislocation of the elbow. Despite repair of the radial head fracture and ligaments, these patients suffered recurrent posterior instability until the "small" coronoid fragment was repaired.[157] The improved stability seen in these patients was probably due to restoration of the associated soft tissue structures.

## Treatment

Regan and Morrey, as others, identified more instability and complications with elbow dislocations associated with displaced major coronoid process fractures.[76, 128, 145] In

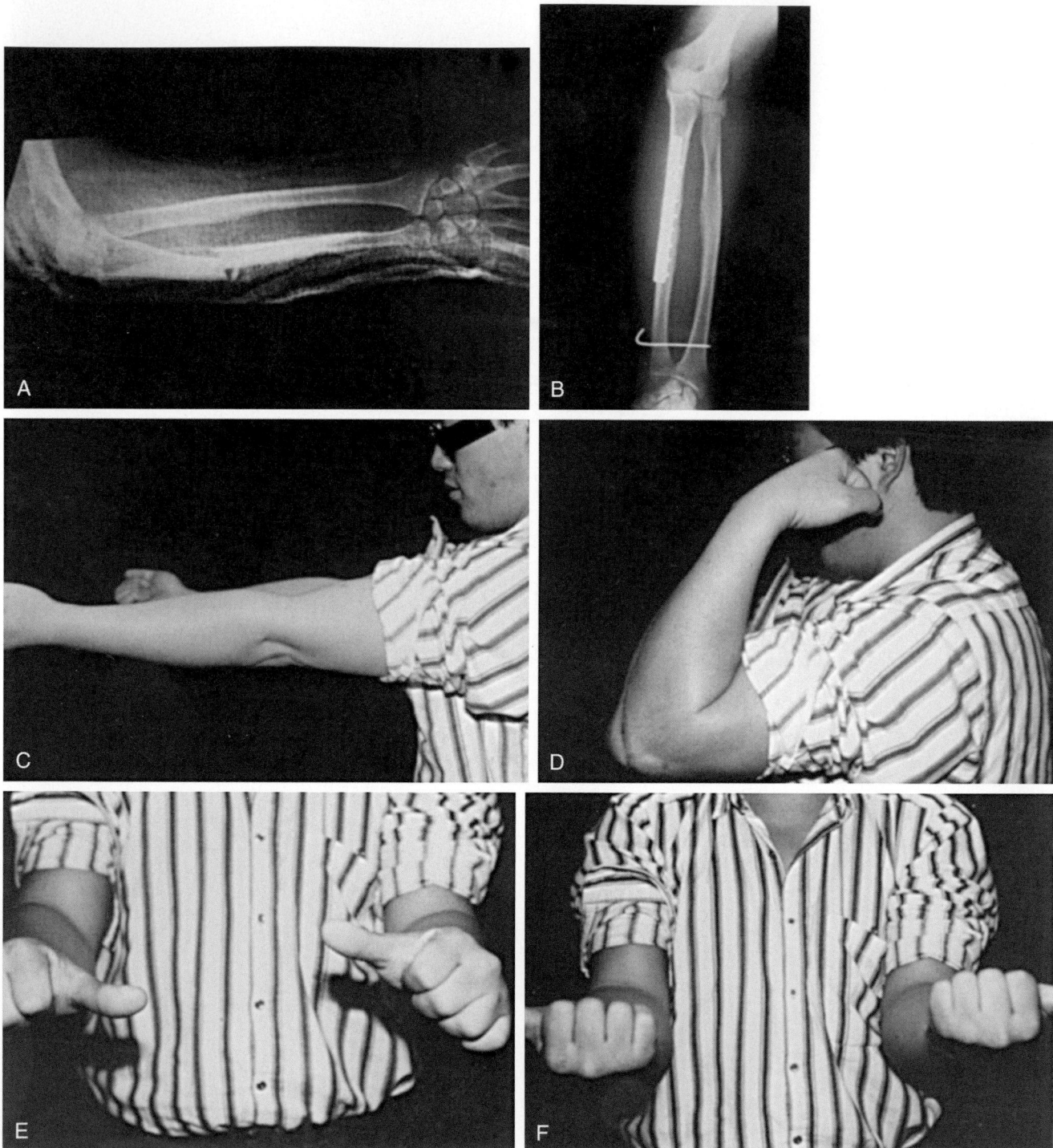

**Figure 42–18.** A 28-year-old man sustained a high-energy injury to his left upper extremity. *A,* A radiograph reveals a comminuted, displaced radial head fracture, an ulnar shaft fracture, a distal radial fracture, and disruption of the distal radioulnar joint. *B,* After resection of the comminuted radial head fragments and plate fixation of the ulna, a silicone radial head prosthesis was placed. In addition, with the forearm in supination, the distal end of the ulna was pinned to the radius. Full elbow motion (*C, D*) and nearly full forearm motion (*E, F*) resulted.

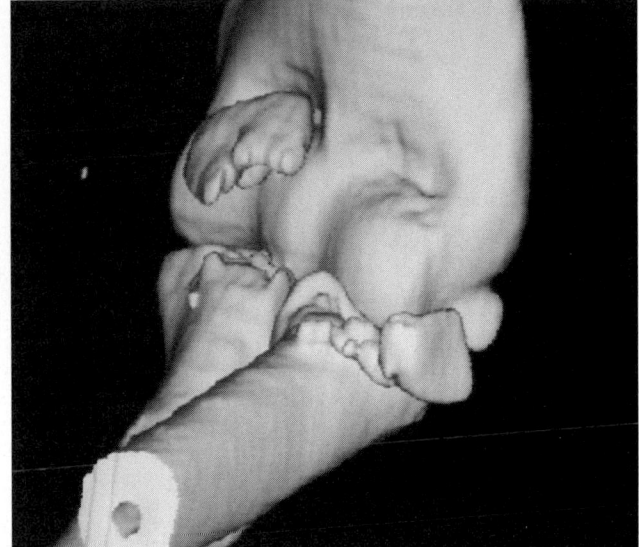

**FIGURE 42–20.** Three-dimensional computed tomographic reconstruction of the "terrible triad" of the elbow demonstrating how a larger coronoid fragment remains in place in the coronoid fossa as the remaining proximal ends of the ulna and radius dislocate or subluxate.

the past in these situations, it was recommended that a longer duration of immobilization (3 to 4 weeks) in greater flexion is preferable to surgery, but such treatment may not produce concentric reduction of the elbow and may result in loss of full mobility and a permanent elbow flexion contracture. The complications of coronoid fracture fixation include the possibility of the development of myositis ossificans as a result of surgical dissection within the brachialis muscle. Our preference in these situations is to consider surgical stabilization of the displaced coronoid fracture at the time of the initial treatment, followed by protected mobilization for 5 to 7 days postoperatively. A hinged orthosis may protect against varus-valgus instability during the early phase of ligament healing.

Although typically remaining in place in relation to the coronoid fossa of the distal end of the humerus, a displaced coronoid fracture that provides a block to full elbow motion is another indication for operative reduction and surgical stabilization of these injuries (Fig. 42–20).

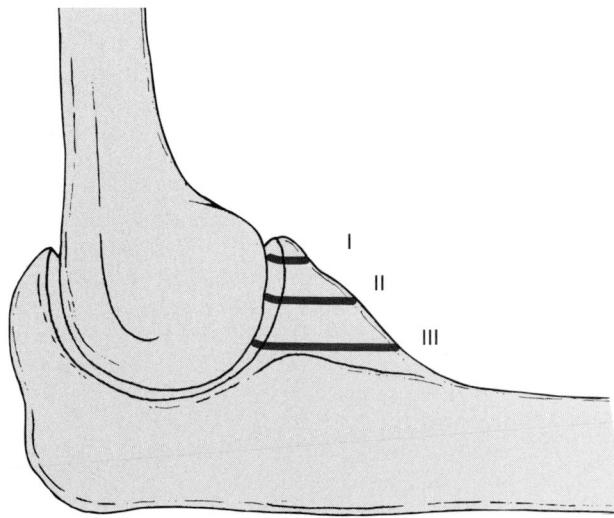

**FIGURE 42–19.** The coronoid fracture has been classified into three types by Regan and Morrey.

## THE "TERRIBLE TRIAD" OF THE ELBOW

Hotchkiss coined the term "terrible triad of the elbow" to describe the triumvirate of elbow dislocation, radial head fracture, and coronoid fracture.[54] The afflicted elbow is prone to early recurrent instability, chronic instability, and post-traumatic arthritis and earns its nickname honestly. Although few reports have dealt with this entity in isolation, numerous series of elbow fracture-dislocations or radial head fractures contain patients with this injury pattern, and the results are uniformly poor. For instance, in one series, only 4 of 13 patients had a satisfactory outcome. Those who underwent resection of the radial head had a 90% rate of unsatisfactory outcome.[115]

Treatment of this injury is directed toward each injured component in sequential fashion (Fig. 42–21A to D). Radial head excision alone is contraindicated and radial head reconstruction or replacement is performed, followed by repair of the coronoid fracture if possible. Essentially three methods may be used to reduce and fix the coronoid fragment. If the fragment is too small to support internal fixation, a "lasso" of nonabsorbable suture can be passed over the top of the fragment and any attached anterior capsule and brought out through drill holes in the ulna. Second, if the fragment is large enough to be captured by a screw, a cannulated screw inserted from the posterior aspect of the ulna, with the fracture under direct vision from the inside of the joint, can be used to fix the fracture. Such fixation can often be accomplished by using the limited exposure from the lateral arthrotomy, especially if the radial head has been resected (before radial head replacement). Third, if this procedure is too difficult, the fracture can be accessed directly from an anteromedial approach, which can be facilitated by disruption of the medial soft tissue structures (medial collateral ligament, flexor-pronator mass) often seen in these injuries.

After fixation of the coronoid and radial head fractures, the lateral collateral ligament complex (which is typically

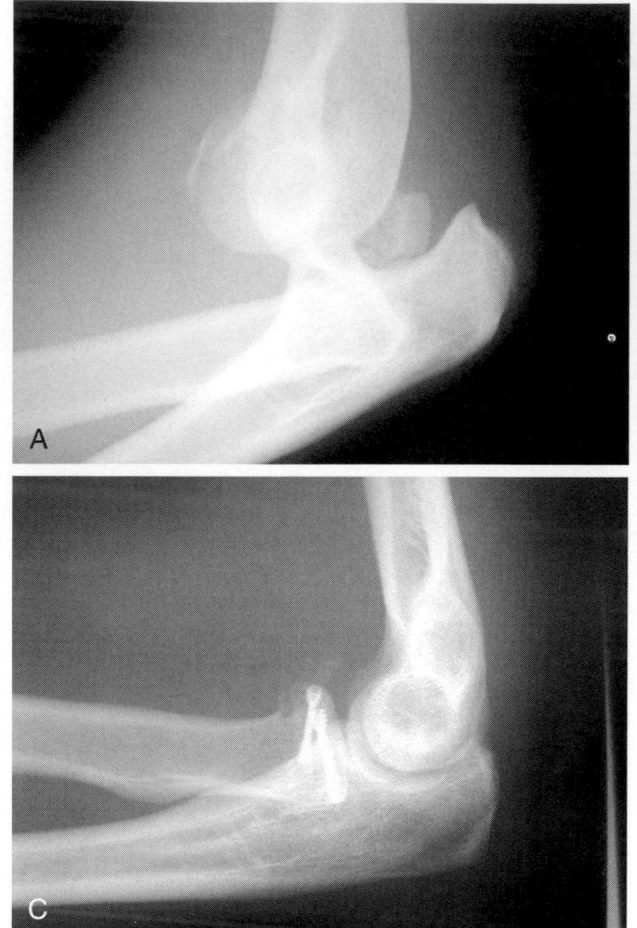

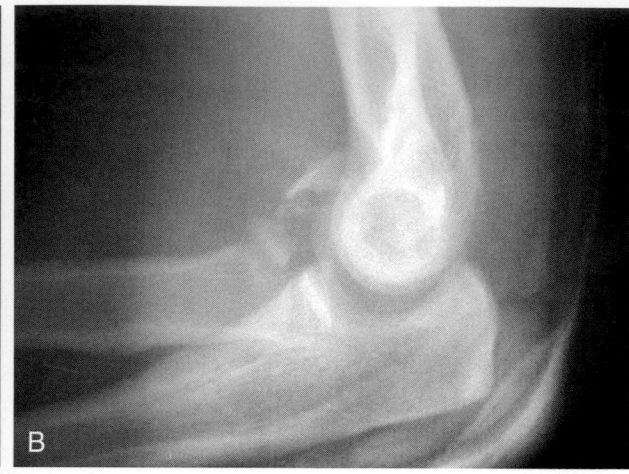

**FIGURE 42–21.** *A,* Lateral radiograph of the "terrible triad" of the elbow consisting of elbow dislocation, a radial head fracture, and a coronoid fracture. *B,* After closed reduction, the radial head is not concentrically reduced, the ulnohumeral joint space is increased, and the coronoid fragment remains displaced. *C,* These injuries are inherently unstable after closed reduction because of the limited soft tissue or bony constraint to posterior translation.

avulsed from the lateral epicondyle) is secured with suture anchors or drill holes through bone (Fig. 42–22).

## OLECRANON FRACTURES

The olecranon is the proximal articulating unit of the ulna. Together with the coronoid process, the olecranon forms the greater sigmoid notch, which in turn articulates with the trochlea of the distal end of the humerus. This articulation provides the flexion/extension movement of the elbow joint, and its intrinsic architecture adds to the stability of the elbow. The triceps tendon inserts onto the olecranon with extension both medially and laterally to insert onto the periosteum of the proximal end of the ulna, as well as the fascial envelope of the proximal part of the forearm. The ulnar nerve passes through the cubital tunnel beneath the medial epicondyle of the distal end of the humerus to exit along the medial aspect of the olecranon and enter the volar aspect of the forearm between the two heads of the flexor carpi ulnaris.

The subcutaneous position of the olecranon renders it vulnerable to direct trauma. Fracture patterns can be the result of a number of different mechanisms, including a direct blow, a fall on an outstretched hand with the elbow in flexion, or higher-energy trauma, which is associated with radial head fractures or elbow dislocation.[139, 151, 170]

Fractures of the olecranon are intra-articular injuries and as such are often manifested as swelling, pain, and an effusion. The fracture itself may be palpable. A true lateral radiograph is necessary for accurate identification of the plane of the fracture, the number of fracture fragments, and the extent of articular disruption. A radiocapitellar view may be of help if the patient appears to have a concomitant injury or displacement of the radial head.

A number of classifications of olecranon fractures have been described, with only modest variation. The type of fracture is the single most important factor in determining the optimal type of treatment. Although surgeons have traditionally looked to apply one form of treatment for all olecranon fractures, it has become quite apparent that the mechanical characteristics of the various fracture patterns differ and that not all are amenable to one single method.

Colton[24] classified olecranon fractures into two major groups: undisplaced (type I) and displaced (type II). A type I undisplaced fracture is defined as having less than 2 mm of separation and no increase in displacement with flexion to 90°, and the patient is able to extend the elbow against gravity (Fig. 42–23). Colton further subdivided displaced fractures into type IIA, avulsion; IIB, oblique and transverse; IIC, comminuted; and IID, fracture-dislocations.

Schatzker[140] addressed the mechanical considerations of fractures, with specific reference to the requirements placed on internal fixation. He considers transverse fractures (occurring at the deepest point of the trochlear notch) to be either simple (two fragments) or complex (involving comminution or depression of the articular surface). A separate group includes oblique fractures, which extend distally from the midpoint of the trochlear notch. These fractures prove less stable with tension band wiring alone. His final group consists of comminuted fractures, which may include (1) fractures of the coronoid process, (2) fractures extending distally beyond the midpoint of the trochlear notch, and (3) fractures or dislocations of the radial head (Fig. 42–24).

The goals of treatment of olecranon fractures should include the following objectives[16]: articular restoration, preservation of motor power of extension, stability, avoidance of stiffness, and limitation of possible associated complications. Nondisplaced fractures, though uncommon, can be effectively treated by immobilization of the limb in a long arm splint or cast with the elbow flexed 90° for 4 weeks. A radiograph should be obtained in 7 to 10 days to ensure that displacement of the fracture has not occurred.

## Displaced Fractures

### TREATMENT RECOMMENDATION

Displaced fractures require operative treatment. Avulsion fractures of the proximal part of the olecranon, though in reality extra-articular fractures, should be treated operatively because they disrupt the insertion of the triceps mechanism. These fractures are more common in the elderly, and operative treatment consists of suturing the triceps back to the proximal end of the ulna with strong, nonabsorbable suture material placed through drill holes.[135, 165] A tension band wire can be used to reinforce the repair.

Two types of treatment exist for displaced intra-articular olecranon fractures: ORIF or fragment excision and triceps reconstruction. The evolution of these very divergent approaches can be more clearly understood by reviewing the history of olecranon fracture treatment. Interest in operative treatment was generated by the poor results produced by immobilization, initially recommended with the elbow in extension, which led to loss of motion. This approach was then followed by immobilization in flexion, which resulted in displacement of the

fragments and weak extension.[29] Subsequently, starting with Lister in 1883, innovative surgeons began to use a variety of techniques and materials to securely stabilize the olecranon to permit functional motion and avoid displacement.[78, 86, 109, 163, 169, 174] Although each technique was advocated enthusiastically, none proved satisfactory for each type of fracture pattern. This limitation in part stimulated the concept of fragment excision and triceps reattachment.[31] Popularized by McKeever and Buck,[96] this technique has gained acceptance by some authors, particularly for elderly patients.[2, 41, 135]

In determining which treatment should be used for a displaced olecranon fracture, the classification system of Schatzker is of great help. Despite some authors' enthusiasm for excision of the olecranon, in certain fractures this method is not advisable, including fractures associated with elbow instability, avulsion of the coronoid, and comminution extending toward the distal aspect of the olecranon and fractures in younger individuals with high functional demands. In a biomechanical model, An and associates[6] confirmed the important stabilizing function of the olecranon and noted that the proximal portion of the olecranon has a greater effect on joint constraint than had generally been appreciated.

## Transverse Fractures

### TREATMENT RECOMMENDATION

A transverse fracture, whether simple or involving comminution or depression of the articular surface, is amenable to repair by the mechanically effective tension band fixation technique. This technique is based on placement of a wire loop dorsal to the midaxis of the ulna. In this position, the tensile or distraction forces at the fracture site are transformed into compressive forces. Two K-wires are used as an internal splint to offset the rotational and angular displacement forces. The K-wires are placed in parallel and extend in a proximal dorsal–to–distal anterior direction to just catch the anterior cortex of the ulna distal to the fracture line (Fig. 42–25). This technique will offset some of the reported difficulties of the K-wires backing out and causing discomfort and limitation of motion.[59, 82, 110] Placement of the wire loop is fundamental to the

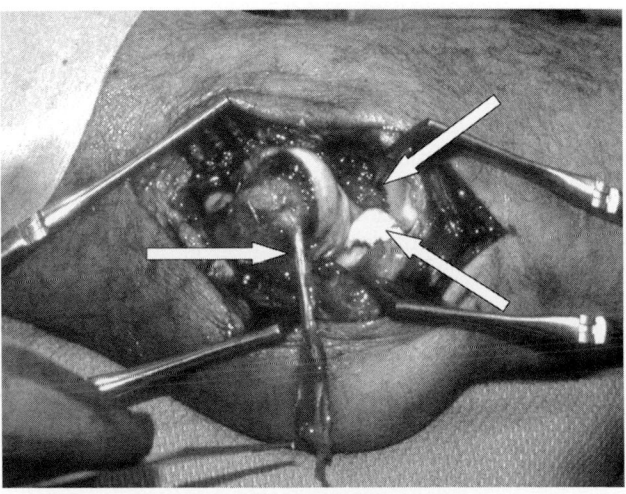

**FIGURE 42–22.** Intraoperative photograph after a lateral incision in an elbow that has sustained a "terrible triad" injury. Note the extensive lateral soft tissue injury, with disruption of the lateral collateral ligament and posterolateral capsule (*arrow*). The tip of the coronoid is fractured and wedged in the joint and is preventing reduction (*arrow*), and a radial head fracture is present (*arrow*).

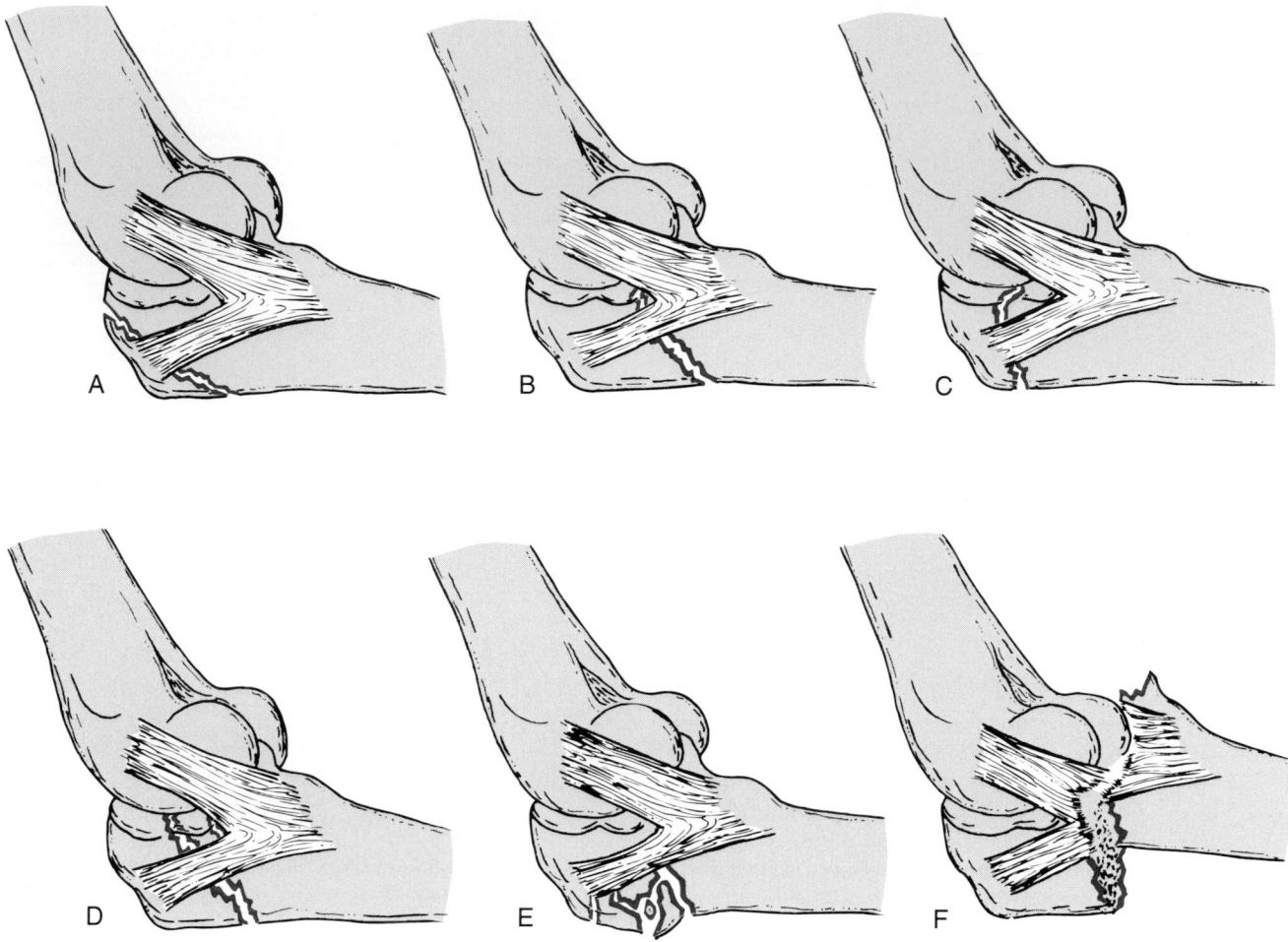

**FIGURE 42–23.** Colton's classification of olecranon fractures. *A,* Avulsion. *B,* Oblique. *C,* Transverse. *D,* Oblique with comminution. *E,* Comminuted. *F,* Fracture-dislocation.

effectiveness of the technique. A hole is drilled with a 2.0-mm drill bit dorsal to the midaxis of the ulna and at least 2.5 to 3 cm distal to the fracture for placement of the tension band wire. As a rule, the distance spanned by the wire from the fracture should be at least equal to the distance from the fracture to the tip of the olecranon. The tension band wire is passed deep to the triceps tendon and held in place by the two parallel K-wires, which are bent around the tension wire as they are impacted into the proximal end of the ulna (Fig. 42–25). The tension wire is carefully tightened with the elbow in extension. This technique results in a slight over-reduction of the fracture at the articular surface that disappears as the elbow actively flexes.

A transverse fracture with depression of the articular surface should have the articular surface elevated and, if possible, secured with an interfragmentary screw. At times, cancellous bone will be needed to support the articular restoration. Such bone is readily available from the lateral epicondylar area of the distal end of the humerus. A tension band will effectively protect the articular elevation and permit early active functional aftercare (Fig. 42–26).

Oblique fractures should have, whenever possible, an interfragmentary lag screw placed across the fracture line. This compression screw can be neutralized against rota-tional or translational forces either by a tension band wire or by a dorsally applied plate (Fig. 42–27).

Displaced comminuted fractures that extend to and include the coronoid process present the most difficult of all olecranon fractures to treat by internal fixation. At times, as a result of high-energy trauma, these fractures can be associated with instability of the elbow. Because of the comminution, the tension band wiring technique will not be effective for these fractures.

These fracture patterns typically include a triangle-shaped coronoid fragment, which is important for stability. It is wise to fix this fragment with an interfragmentary compression screw and work through the main fracture line for exposure. Once this fragment is fixed, the main olecranon fracture is repaired (Fig. 42–28A to C). Plate fixation on the dorsal surface is necessary. The plate, a 3.5-mm dynamic compression, reconstruction, or one-third tubular plate, can be contoured to project proximally around the tip of the olecranon. A review by McKee and colleagues of the use of the limited-contact dynamic compression (LCDC) plate in the upper extremity has shown this particular design to be advantageous in this situation.[94] The lower profile and improved contourability of the LCDC plate are ideal for the proximal end of the ulna and do not sacrifice strength or the use of compres-

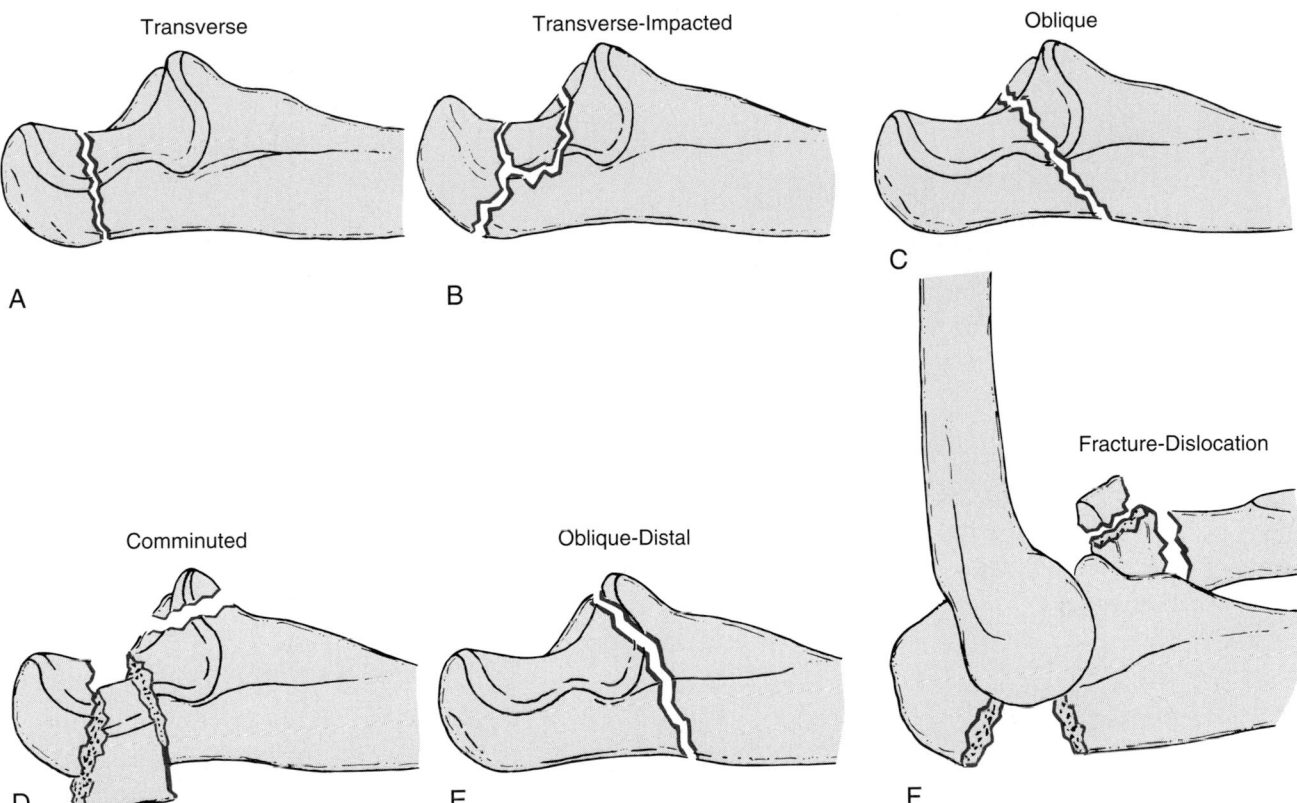

**FIGURE 42–24.** Schatzker's classification system of olecranon fractures. *A,* Transverse. *B,* Transverse-impacted. *C,* Oblique. *D,* Comminuted. *E,* Oblique-distal. *F,* Fracture-dislocation.

**FIGURE 42–25.** A transverse olecranon fracture is optimally treated by a tension band wire technique. Note the placement of the two parallel K-wires in a dorsal proximal–to–anterior distal direction to engage in the anterior cortex. Such placement minimizes the problem of K-wire migration.

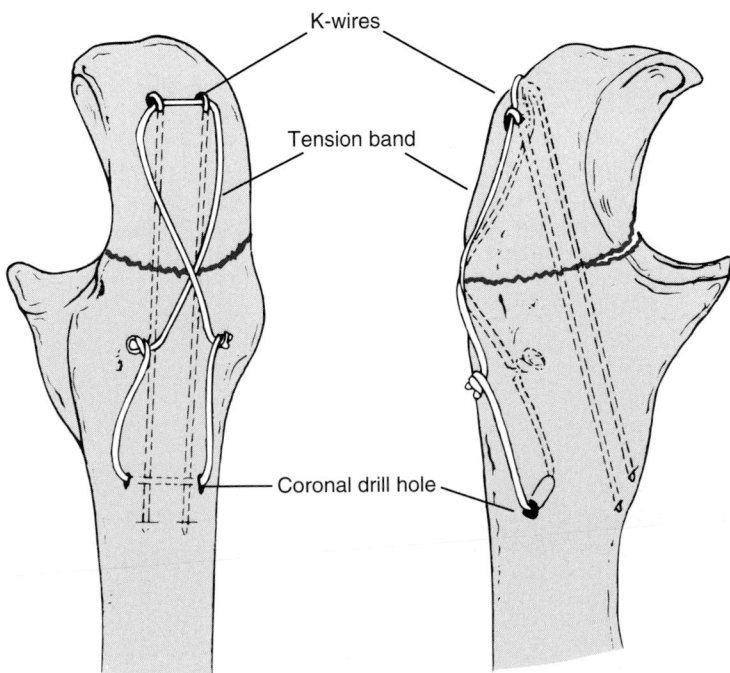

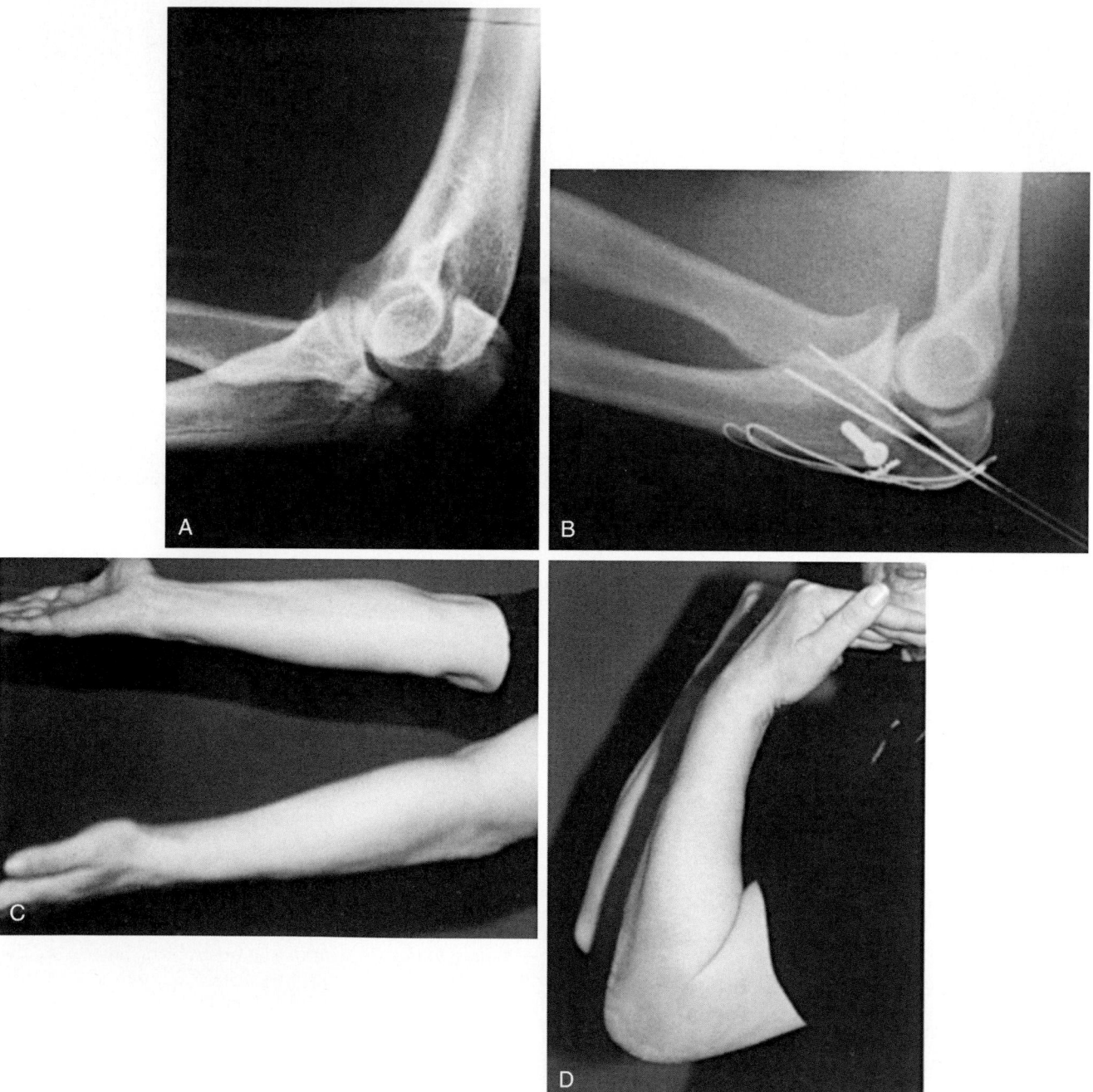

**Figure 42–26.** A 38-year-old woman sustained an impacted transverse olecranon fracture. *A,* A lateral radiograph reveals an impacted transverse olecranon fracture. *B,* After elevation of the major articular fragment, an interfragmentary lag screw was inserted. A double tension band loop secured the comminuted dorsal ulnar cortex. Note the oblique position of the K-wires just before bending the wires. *C, D,* Full flexion and extension were achieved within 3 weeks after injury.

FIGURE 42–27. *A, B,* An oblique olecranon fracture was fixed with an interfragmentary lag screw, a tension band wire, and two K-wires.

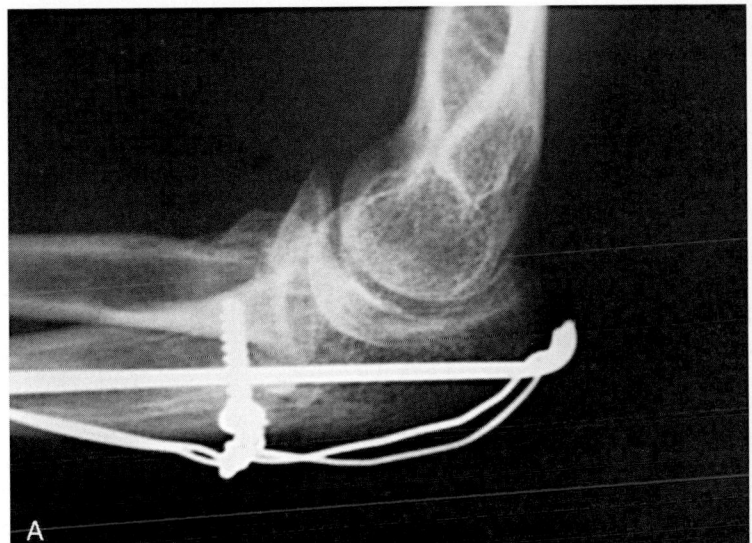
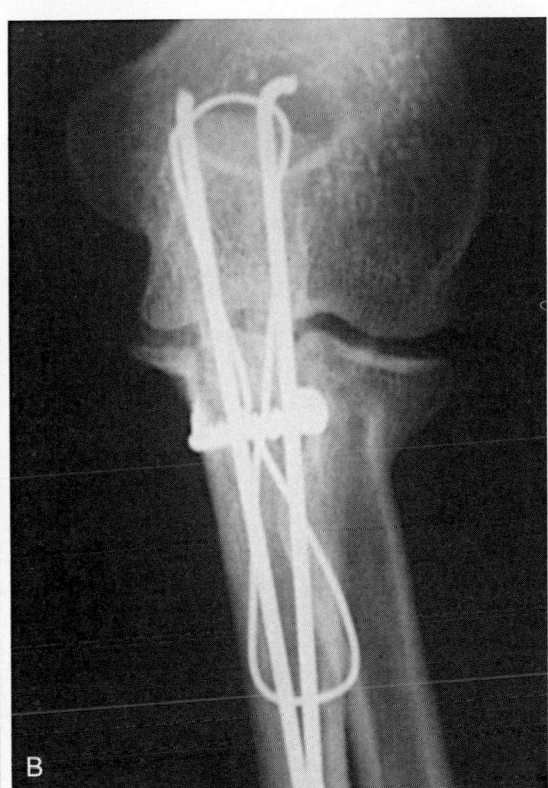

sion holes when compared with the dynamic compression plate (Fig. 42–29). The proximal contouring of the plate will enhance the holding power of the screws in cancellous bone because they will now be inserted in two directions.

Cancellous bone graft should be used to help support the articular reconstruction and to fill in any defects in the cortex opposite the plate (Fig. 42–30). Difficulty in maintaining secure fixation of olecranon fractures, particularly comminuted fractures in the elderly population, has led some authors to continue to advocate olecranon excision and reattachment of the triceps.[26, 41] In a low-demand elbow, this technique has proved effective even with as much as two thirds of the olecranon excised, provided that no instability is present (Fig. 42–31). Studies by Gartsman and co-workers,[41] in which function and mechanical strength were evaluated, suggested that elbow strength after excision and triceps reattachment is equal to that with internally fixed olecranon fractures. Strength was significantly less, however, after both procedures than in the contralateral uninjured control elbow. Yet in the series of Gartsman and co-workers, the technique of internal fixation varied and the elbow was immobilized, thus delaying functional aftercare of the patient. It remains to be demonstrated whether excision plus triceps reattachment is functionally as effective as properly executed internal fixation combined with early postoperative rehabilitation.

## Complications

Complications specific to fractures of the olecranon include loss of elbow flexion and extension, malunion,

nonunion, and post-traumatic arthritis. Lack of extension is not uncommon in traumatic injuries about the elbow, although it has not generally been a major factor with olecranon fractures.[33]

Loss of reduction is an uncommon complication and more likely to occur as a result of misdiagnosis when a Monteggia-type injury with a proximal ulnar fracture is mistaken for a simple olecranon fracture. In this situation, the tension band is poorly suited to resist the angular forces acting at the fracture site, and redisplacement often occurs.[68] Treatment by revision to a dorsally applied plate is usually successful.

Nonunion has been reported in a number of series of olecranon fractures, although it, too, is uncommon. More often than not, treatment will be successful with a plate applied dorsally to function as a tension band.

Post-traumatic arthritis can be problematic because the sigmoid notch–trochlea articulation is important in providing intrinsic stability to the elbow. Fortunately, it is not a common occurrence.

## DISLOCATION OF THE ELBOW

Dislocation of the elbow accounts for 20% of all dislocations, second only to those of the glenohumeral and finger joints. Elbow dislocations occur most commonly in younger individuals, with the peak age of occurrence between 5 and 25 years. Along with disruption of the joint capsule and restraining ligaments, accessory injuries are not uncommon and include skeletal injuries such as radial

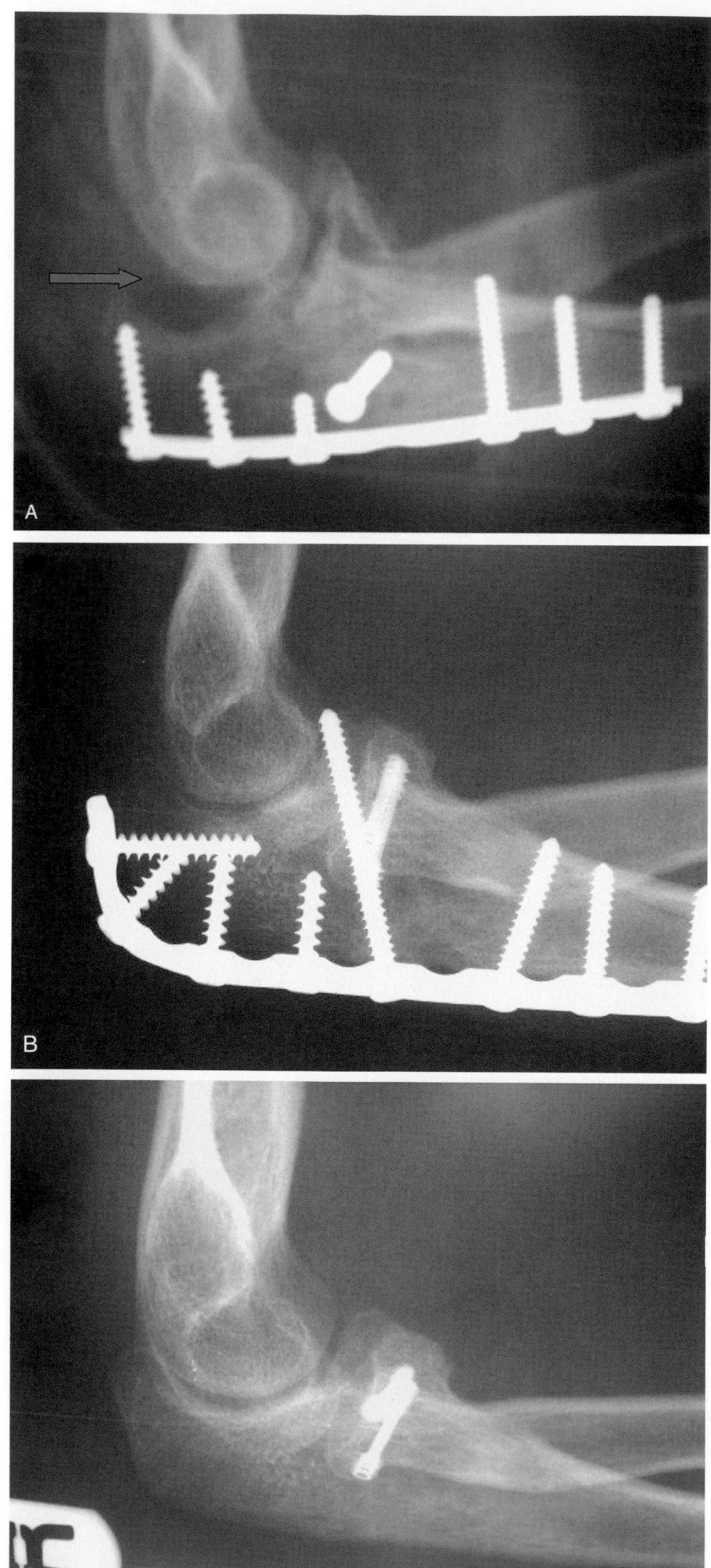

**FIGURE 42–28.** *A,* Lateral radiograph of a complex proximal ulnar fracture in which the coronoid fragment was not repaired; posterior subluxation of the elbow resulted. *B,* After repeat fixation with a screw directed into the coronoid fragment for stabilization and repair of an unrecognized radial head fracture. *C,* The final result after hardware removal reveals concentric reduction of the joint.

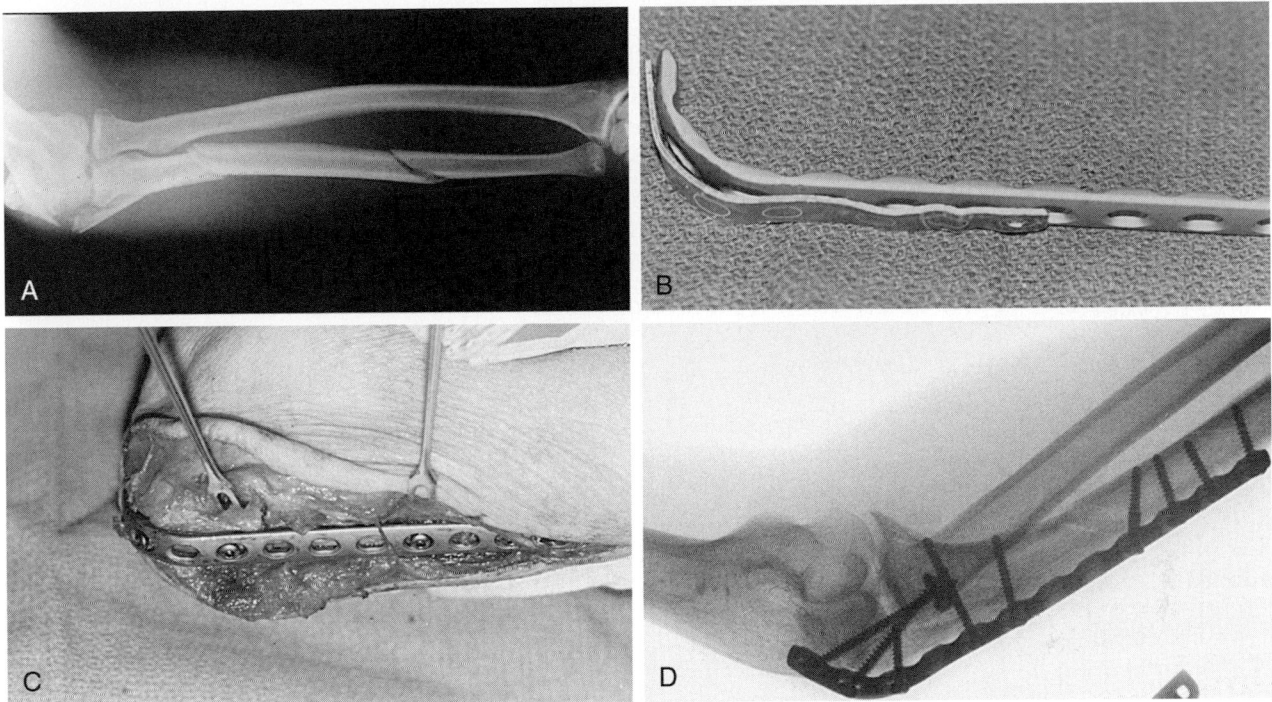

**FIGURE 42–29.** *A,* A high-energy comminuted olecranon fracture associated with an ulnar shaft fracture in a 28-year-old man involved in a motor vehicle accident. *B,* Intraoperative contouring of a limited-contact dynamic compression (LCDC) plate to the template. The plate contours evenly, both at and between the screw holes, thereby giving a smooth profile without abrupt angulation. *C,* Intraoperative photograph showing the application of a plate to the proximal end of the ulna. *D,* Postoperative lateral radiograph showing contouring of the LCDC plate to the proximal part of the ulna.

head or neck fractures (see Radial Head Fractures), capitellar injury, avulsion of the coronoid process of the ulna,[128, 145] and avulsion of the medial or lateral epicondyles in younger individuals. Associated soft tissue injuries can involve vascular compromise[77, 79, 152] or neurologic trauma,[39, 85, 123, 127, 146, 150] with the latter usually involving stretch injury to the median or ulnar nerve.

Although elbow dislocation may be diagnosed clinically, swelling often obscures the bony landmarks about

the elbow (Fig. 42–32). Because supracondylar distal humeral or associated fractures must also be considered, radiographic examination is essential.

Radiographic studies will define the type of dislocation. Dislocation of both the radius and the ulna together is by far the most common type and can be posterior, medial, lateral, or anterior to the distal end of the humerus. The radius and ulna can also dislocate in divergent directions. Dislocation of either the radius or the ulna alone has been reported but is exceptionally uncommon (Fig. 42–33).

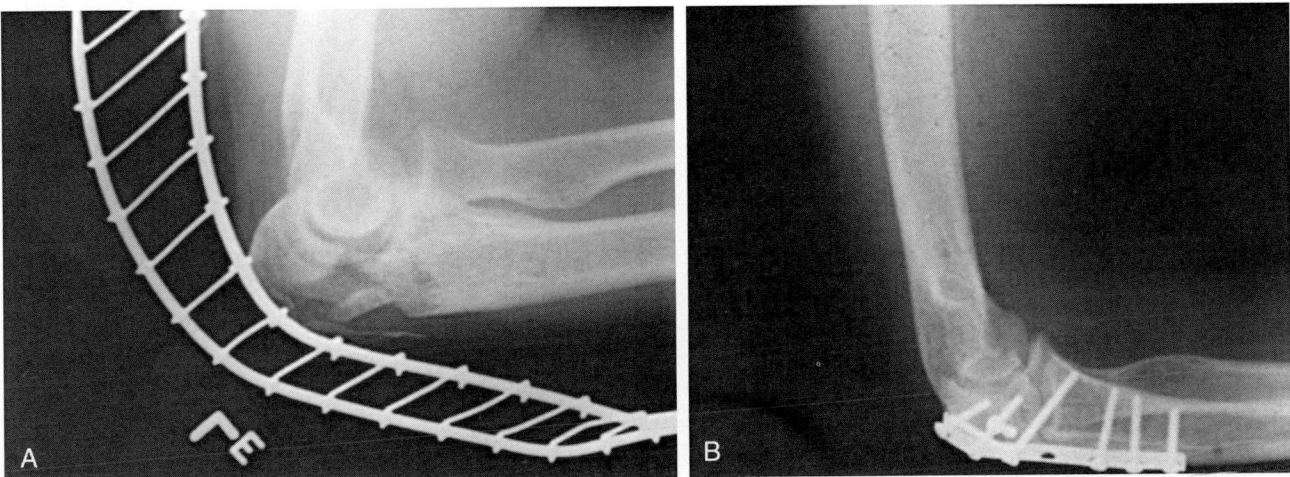

**FIGURE 42–30.** A 55-year-old woman fell 10 feet off a ladder and landed directly on her left elbow. *A,* A lateral radiograph reveals an extensively comminuted olecranon fracture extending to the very distal aspect of the semilunar notch. *B,* The fragments were carefully teased into place and held with interfragmentary screws and a contoured, 3.5-mm one-third tubular plate. Note how the plate conforms to the shape of the proximal aspect of the olecranon and the screws are directed at various angles.

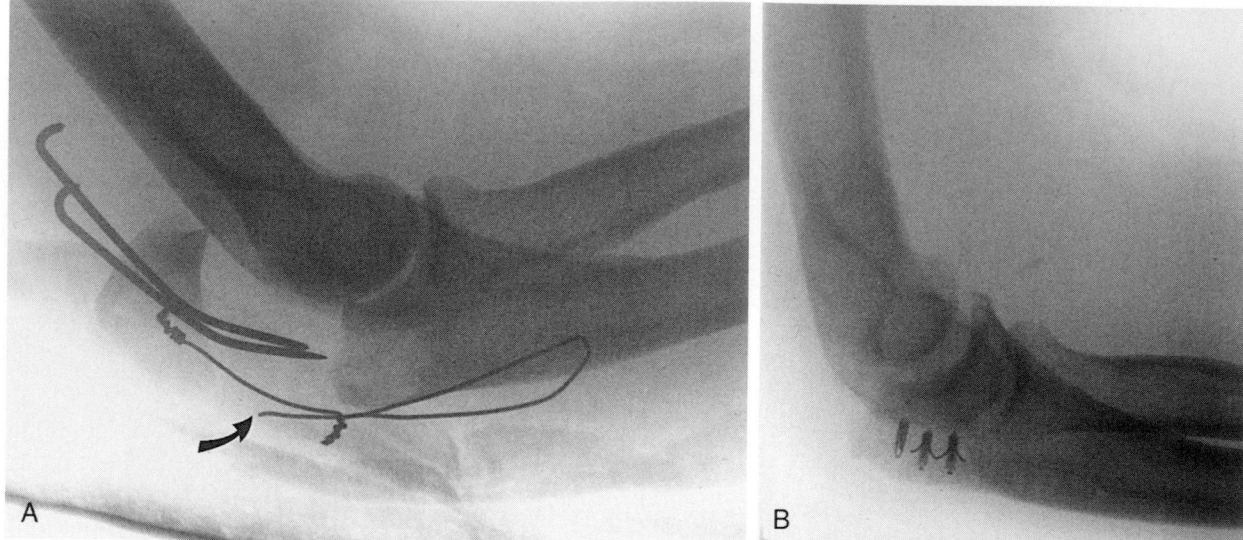

**FIGURE 42–31.** *A,* A lateral radiograph of failure of fixation of an olecranon fracture in a noncompliant 58-year-old diabetic patient illustrates a broken wire loop *(arrow)* and backing out of K-wires. *B,* Treatment was excision of the olecranon fragment and reattachment of the triceps to bone with suture anchors. Elbow stability was not affected.

A posterior or posterolateral dislocation is found in more than 80% of all elbow dislocations.[71, 77, 133] Two theories have been promoted to explain the mechanism of this injury. The hyperextension theory suggests that force is taken on the hand with the elbow extended.[51, 76] The olecranon thus impinges on the olecranon fossa, with further energy levering the ulna and radius from their capsular constraints. The brachialis muscle may be torn and the coronoid process fractured from a shearing mechanism as the elbow subluxates or dislocates. Continued extension force results in the tearing of the epicondylar attachments of the capsule and ligaments, and in some instances an abduction force results in injury to the radial head or capitellum.

The second theory suggests that the dislocation occurs with the elbow slightly flexed and subject to axial compressive loading.[118] The radial collateral ligament and lateral capsule tear, with resulting posterior dislocation of the forearm on the humerus.

Whatever the mechanism, in a posterior or posterolateral elbow dislocation, the distal end of the humerus drives through the anterior capsule and brachialis, with the final position of the forearm dependent to some degree on the direction of the force. True lateral or anterior dislocations are extremely rare and are often a result of violent avulsion or distraction forces (such as those seen in industrial accidents). In anterior dislocations the soft tissue injury may be severe because it may be the result of a violent blow to the olecranon. Such is also often the case with divergent dislocations in which the radius is displaced from the ulna and both are dislocated from the humerus.

## Treatment

The goal of treatment of any elbow dislocation is restoration of articular alignment as expeditiously and atraumatically as possible. Before any reduction, careful neurovascular assessment must be performed to document any sensory or motor deficit. Although an elbow dislocation can often be reduced without any anesthetic, especially before soft tissue swelling has advanced, it is preferable to perform the reduction under regional or general anesthesia to minimize the force required.

Several methods have been described for reduction of common posterior dislocations.[74, 76, 99, 112, 119] Perhaps the most predictable is that of gentle traction applied to the forearm with countertraction on the brachium. Residual

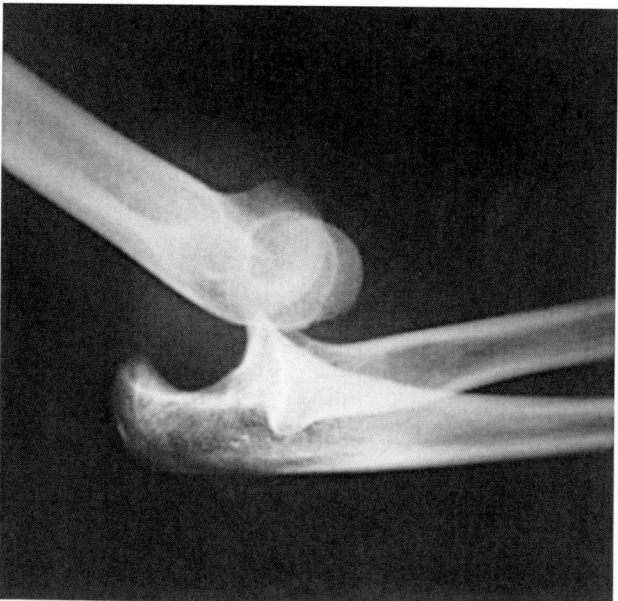

**FIGURE 42–32.** A 26-year-old woman who was 6 months pregnant fell on her outstretched left arm. Radiographs were not obtained at the time of injury because of her pregnancy. As a result of persistent pain and swelling about her left elbow, she sought medical attention 1 week after injury. Radiographs revealed complete posterolateral dislocation of her elbow, which had remained dislocated for 1 week.

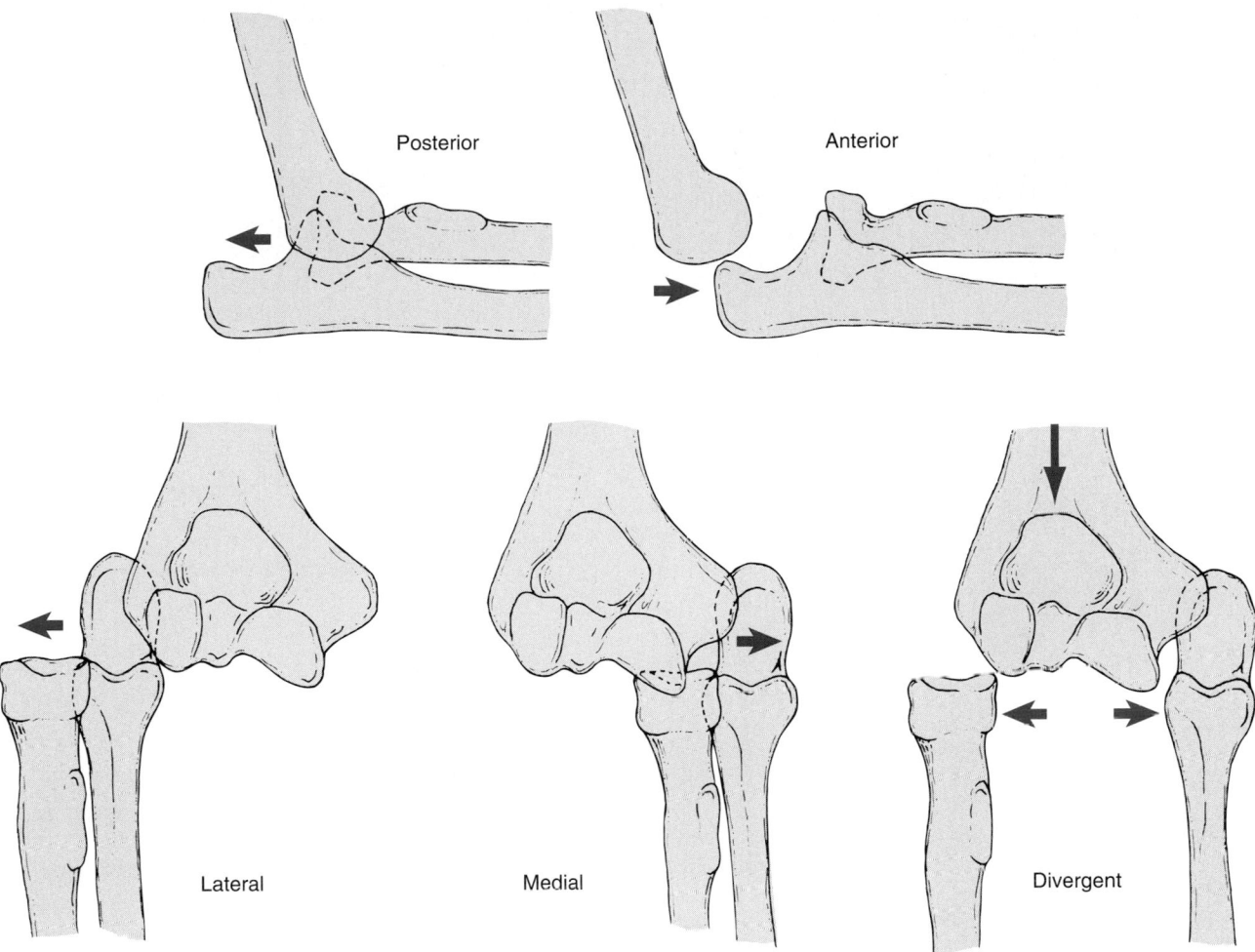

**FIGURE 42–33.** An elbow dislocation is defined by the direction of the forearm bones.

medial or lateral displacement of the elbow joint can be corrected, followed by gentle flexion of the forearm. The reduction is often appreciated by a palpable and occasionally audible "clunk." Undue force is counterproductive, and care should also be taken to not hyperextend the forearm too vigorously to minimize additional trauma to the brachialis muscle. After manipulation, the reduction is confirmed by both radiographs and examination. It is important to obtain both lateral and AP films to ascertain whether the reduction is accurate. The elbow should be ranged from full extension to full flexion to ensure that no block to motion exists and to document any instability in the plane of motion. In addition, the elbow is subjected to varus and valgus stress both in full extension and in moderate flexion. For the more unusual medial or lateral dislocations, more sustained traction and countertraction will be required. Rotation of the forearm may also aid in reducing the translational displacement (Fig. 42–34).

It is not unusual to see small flecks of bone or actual avulsion fractures of the medial and lateral epicondyles in conjunction with elbow dislocations. A recent study by Kobayashi and colleagues examined 12 patients with such injuries (half had associated dislocations, half had subluxations). Although the study was retrospective, the eight patients treated by simple closed reduction and motion at

a mean of 3 weeks did as well as the four patients treated by operative repair.[73] This paper suggests that the presence of an associated avulsion fracture should not influence management to a great degree; if a concentric closed reduction can be achieved, early motion should be initiated and operative repair deferred.

## Postreduction Management

With the elbow held at 90°, a well-padded splint is applied. Adequate access to the hand and wrist is mandatory to permit careful monitoring of neurovascular status. In the event of signs or symptoms suggesting vascular compromise or neurologic dysfunction, forearm compartment pressure measurements should be performed at once at the bedside (see Chapter 12). Arterial inflow can also be documented at the bedside with digital cuff impedance plethysmography or formal arteriography.

In cases in which no instability was noted after reduction, only 7 to 10 days of immobilization is needed, followed by a program of active exercises out of a removable splint. For elbows with a tendency toward redislocation during stress in the operating room, it is advisable to continue immobilization for 2 to 3 weeks.

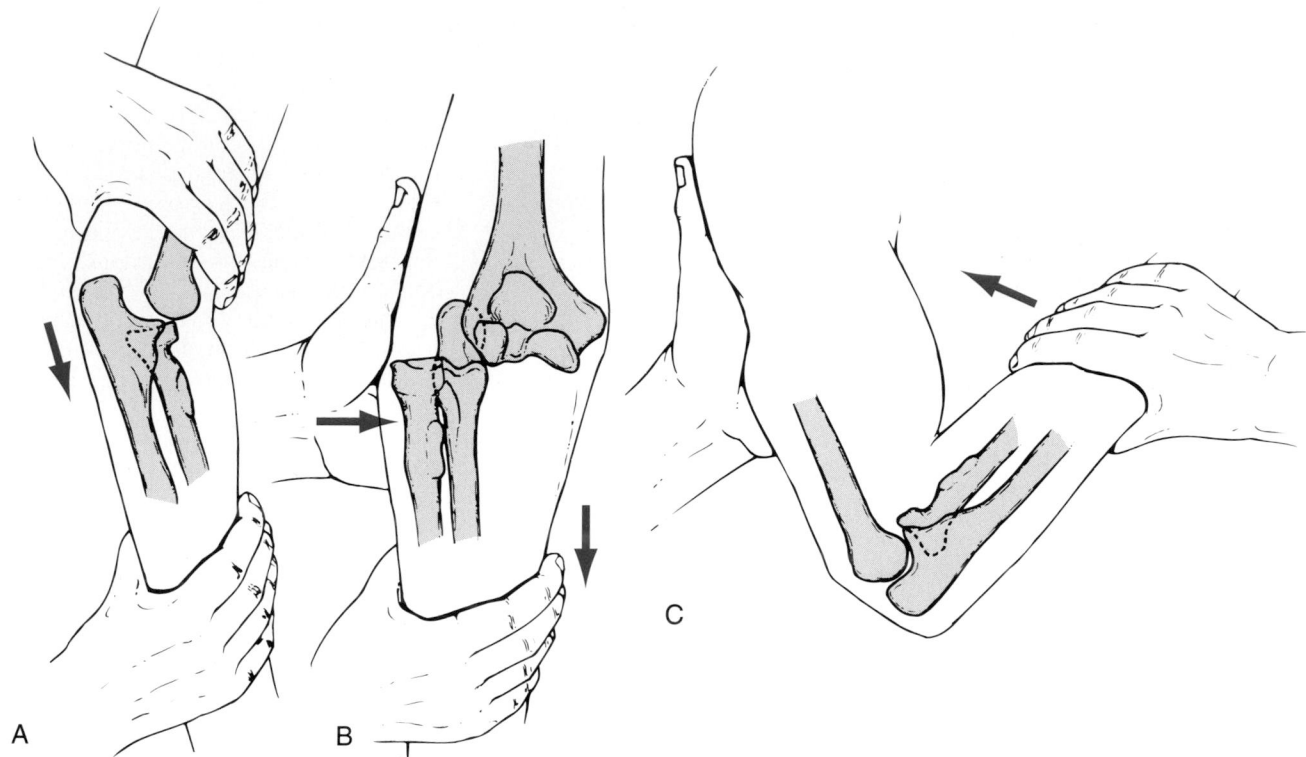

**FIGURE 42–34.** Reduction of a posterior elbow dislocation consists of longitudinal traction (*A*), correction of lateral or medial displacement (*B*), and flexion of the elbow (*C*).

Control radiographs are necessary within 3 to 5 days after reduction to make certain that the joint remains congruent.[66] Immobilization beyond 3 weeks will have significant adverse effects, particularly residual loss of motion and elbow flexion contractures.[63, 64]

Open reduction of simple (without fracture) elbow dislocations is rarely indicated. In fact, a prospective study by Josefsson and associates demonstrated no significant difference between the results of operative and nonoperative treatment of simple dislocations.[66] However, studies of surgical treatment have revealed the extent of soft tissue injury, even with uncomplicated dislocations.[24, 30, 56, 80] Complete rupture of the medial collateral ligament has been described in nearly all cases and disruption of the lateral collateral ligaments in most. In addition, extensive injury to the anterior capsule and brachialis muscle is common. Nonetheless, most simple elbow dislocations are stable once reduced. This finding supports the biomechanical studies of Morrey and co-workers,[104, 107] who demonstrated that as much as 50% of elbow stability is provided by the congruent articulations of the trochlea and olecranon.

A number of investigations have suggested a favorable long-term outcome after simple elbow dislocations.[63, 65, 66, 77, 98, 112, 124] Josefsson and colleagues,[63] in a review of 52 patients seen an average of 24 years after injury, found that more than 50% had no residual symptoms. No complaints were related to instability, although 19 patients had some loss of motion, and follow-up radiographs revealed no loss of the articular space in most, although periarticular calcification was seen in 76%.

Favorable results are not as common with elbow dislocations associated with fractures of the radial head, olecranon, or coronoid process. Radial head fracture has been observed to occur in 5% to 10% of all elbow dislocations,[76] and the outcome of these fractures is considerably worse than that of simple radial head fractures.[1, 25, 61, 103, 160] As a general principle, when displaced periarticular fractures contribute to joint instability, they should be fixed to enhance concentric reduction and early motion[115, 131] (Fig. 42–35). Complications have included loss of motion, post-traumatic arthritis, instability, and ulnar neuritis. Myositis ossificans has been noted in some studies.[160] When faced with a radial head fracture associated with humeroulnar dislocation, effort should be made to maintain the radial head either through ORIF or with a metallic prosthesis. If maintenance of the humeral head is not possible and instability to valgus stress is obvious in the operating room after excision of the radial head, a medial incision plus repair of the medial collateral ligament is advisable.

Dislocations associated with olecranon fracture can be exceptionally complex injuries and may be the result of high-energy trauma with extensive soft tissue injury. In this setting, myositis may be more likely to develop. As with any complex intra-articular fracture, joint reconstruction and early mobilization should be the goals of treatment, although these objectives may not always be possible when soft tissue reconstruction is necessary (Fig. 42–36). Additionally, posterior radiocapitellar dislocations can occur with fracture of the olecranon, and these dislocations can prove surgically challenging as well (see forearm posterior Monteggia lesions in Chapter 41).

Considerably more uncommon are medial, lateral, divergent, and pure radial head dislocations. The clinical finding of a distorted elbow despite normal length of the brachium and forearm should raise suspicion of a medial or lateral elbow dislocation.[124] The radiograph will show the distal end of the humerus to be completely uncovered from its normal articulation with the greater sigmoid notch. The method of reduction has already been described (see Treatment under Elbow Dislocation).

A divergent dislocation, which is exceptionally uncommon, is usually associated with more violent trauma. In this injury, the ulna is dislocated posteriorly, and the radial head and radius are dislocated anteriorly. Closed, manipulative reduction should be attempted, but repositioning of the radius may prove problematic and typically requires open reduction. Careful preoperative and postoperative assessment of neurovascular status is mandatory with this complex injury.

Traumatic radial head dislocation without a concomitant ulnar fracture is extremely rare in adults, but isolated anterior and posterior dislocations have been described.[14, 52, 136, 137] Closed reduction by means of longitudinal traction with the elbow in extension, followed by forearm supination while maintaining direct pressure over the radial head, has been recommended,[14] although open reduction may be necessary.

## Complications

Complications of elbow dislocations can be disabling and include recurrent instability (acute or chronic), stiffness, myositis ossificans, heterotopic calcification, and neurovascular dysfunction.[40, 71, 127, 132]

Although most elbow dislocations can be successfully managed with closed reduction and early motion, a small but significant percentage exhibit early recurrent instability. The elbow dislocation in these cases is more likely to have been caused by high-energy trauma (motor vehicle trauma, industrial accident, fall from a height) and may have an associated fracture of the coronoid or radial head. The lack of concentric reduction on initial postreduction radiographs is often the first clue that a stability problem exists. Because prolonged immobilization in extreme positions to maintain stability can be hazardous and usually results in elbow stiffness, the goal of treatment should be surgical restoration of stability followed by early motion. This objective can be accomplished by fixation of associated fractures, ligament reconstruction, and early protected motion.

Eygendaal and co-workers examined 41 elbows a mean of 9 years after posterolateral dislocation treated in closed fashion.[35] They found that elbows with persistent medial instability had worse elbow and pain scores and more radiographic degenerative changes. Thus, the lack of restoration of medial stability (greater degree of primary injury, failure of the normal healing process) is probably one reason for a poor outcome after this injury.

## Hinged External Fixation

When conventional surgical treatment is insufficient to restore elbow stability, alternative treatments are available. Reports describing the use of hinged external fixators about the elbow to maintain stability and yet provide early motion have demonstrated promising results in these challenging cases[22, 92] (Fig. 42–37). These fixators have replaced the older technique of transarticular pinning, which was associated with complications that included pin breakage, loss of reduction, and severe stiffness (Fig. 42–38). Cobb and Morrey[22] described the use of a hinged

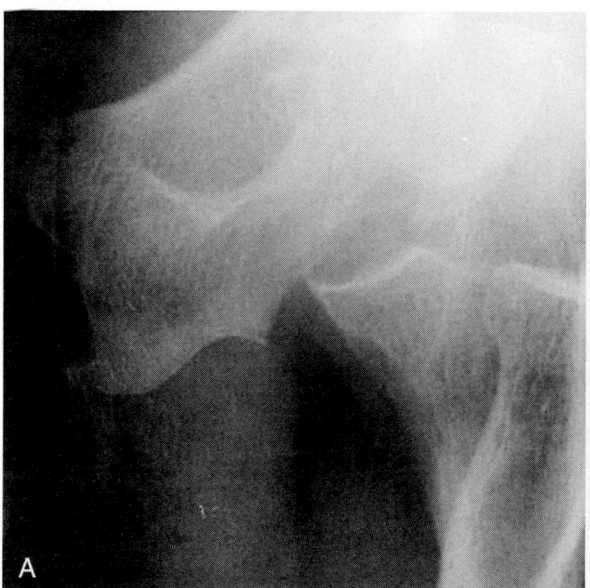 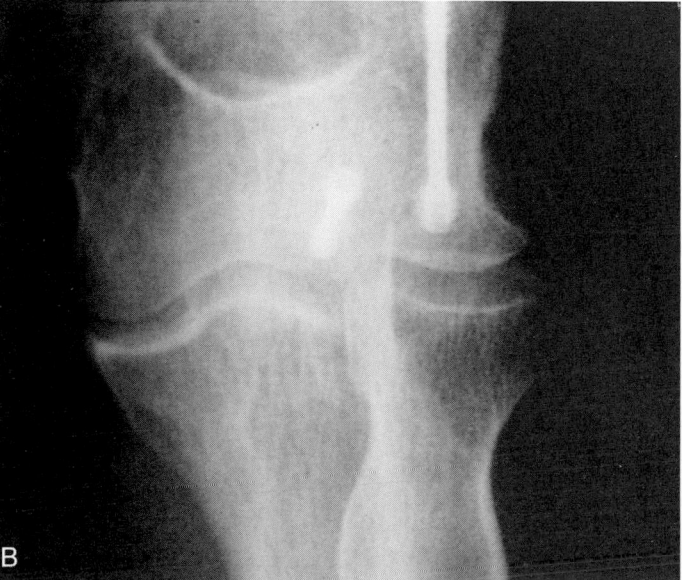

**FIGURE 42–35.** A 64-year-old woman fell on her outstretched arm. *A,* She suffered a displaced capitellar/lateral column fracture associated with elbow dislocation. *B,* Rigid internal fixation with Herbert screws restored joint congruity and stability and allowed early motion, thereby enhancing the functional result.

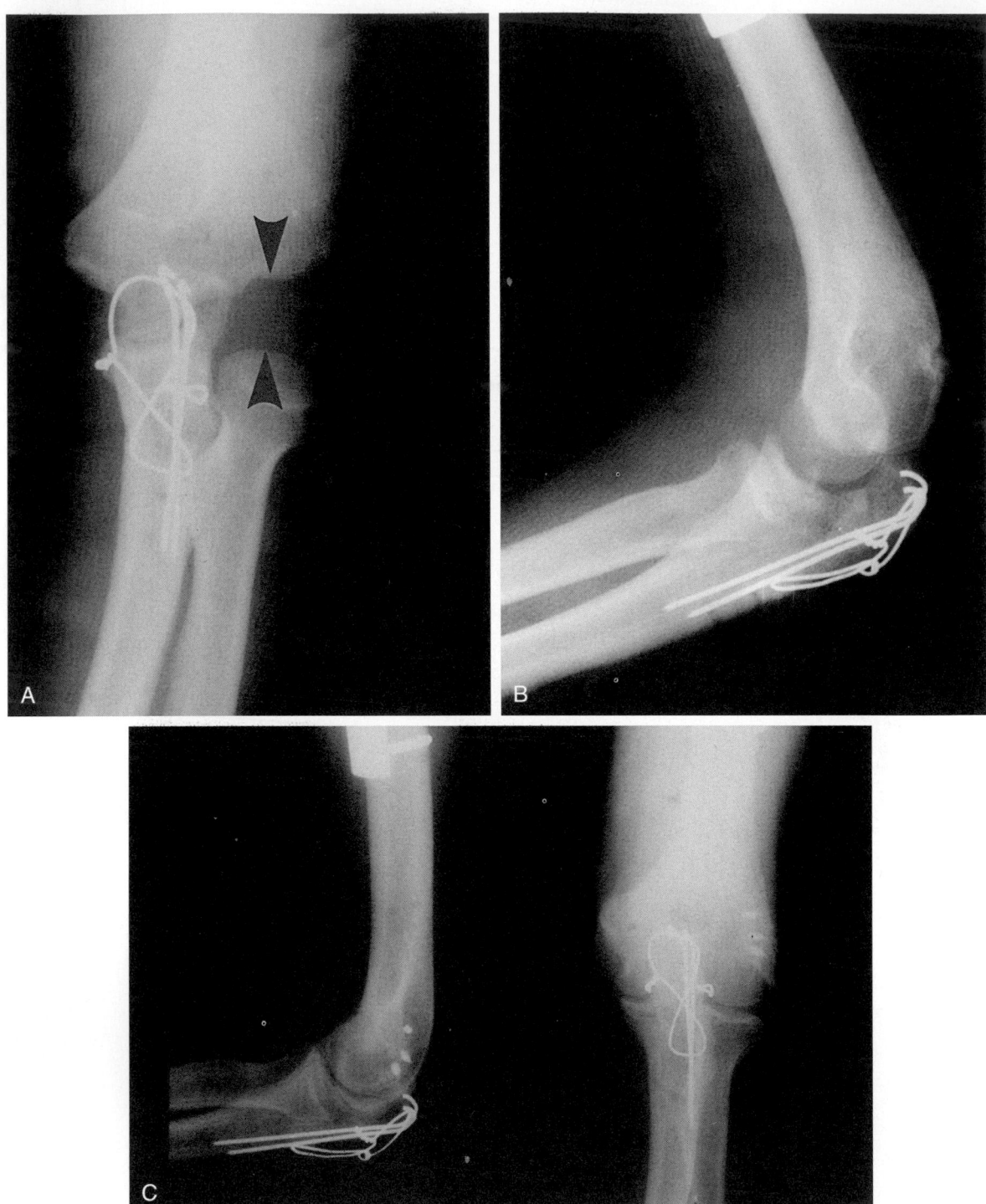

**FIGURE 42–36.** This 24-year-old man was involved in a high-speed motor vehicle accident in which he suffered multiple fractures, including a humeral shaft fracture, a displaced olecranon fracture, and an elbow dislocation of his left arm. The humeral shaft fracture was plated and the olecranon fracture repaired with a tension band technique. Four weeks postoperatively, the patient displayed clear signs of instability consisting of widening of the radiocapitellar joint space and incongruity of the ulnohumeral articulation. The elbow was grossly unstable on physical examination. *A,* Anteroposterior radiograph of the elbow demonstrating a widened radiocapitellar joint space *(arrows). B,* Lateral radiograph illustrating opening of the ulnohumeral articulation. *C,* The patient was treated by repeat open reduction of the joint, reconstruction of the lateral ligamentous structures with suture anchors on the lateral column, protection of the repair with a hinged elbow external fixator, and early motion. Radiographically, the joint is congruous at the 3-month follow-up.

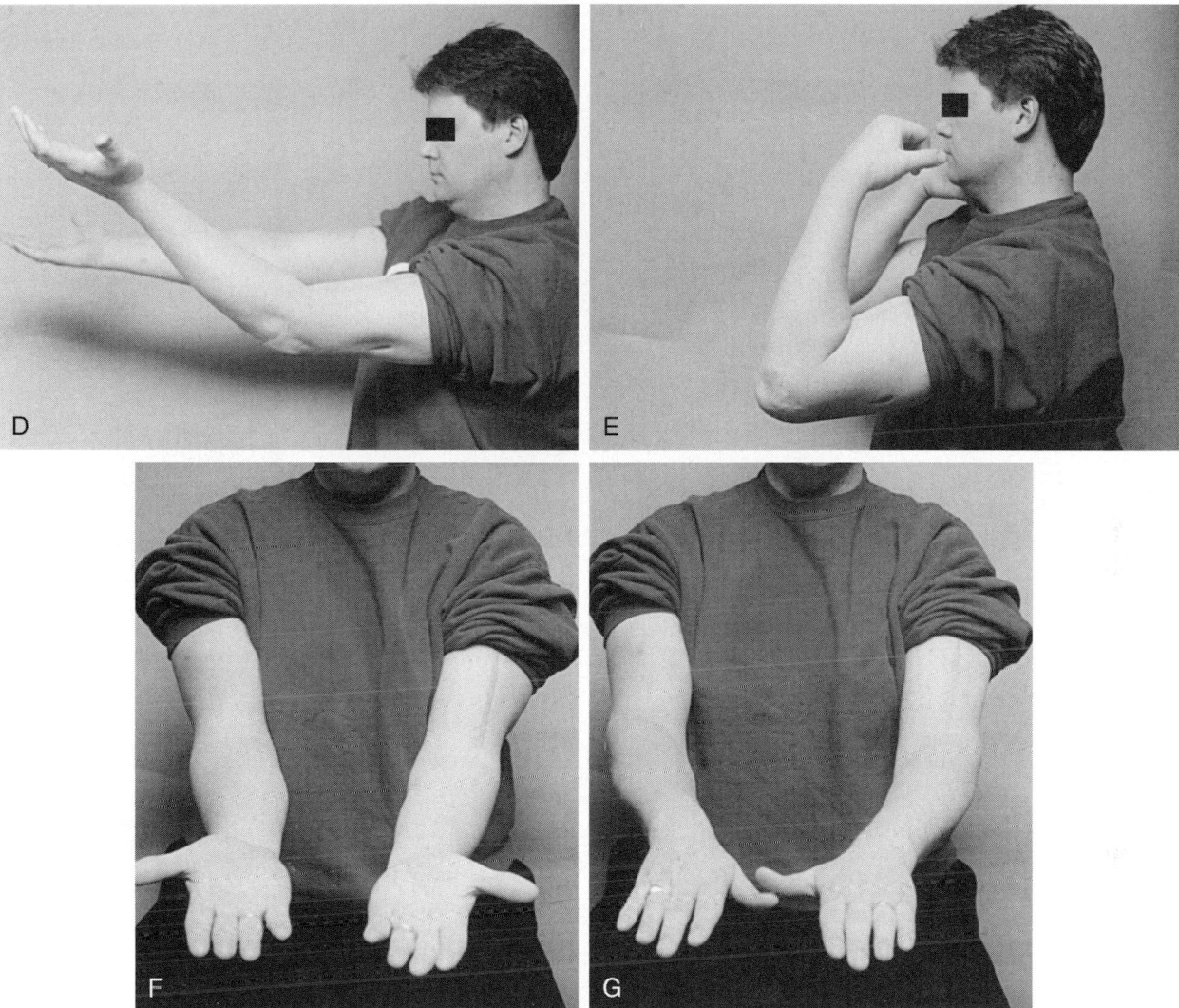

**FIGURE 42–36** *Continued. D–G,* The patient has a range of motion from 30° to 130° and full rotation, and the joint is clinically stable.

fixator to restore concentric stability yet allow early motion in eight cases of recurrent elbow instability associated with fractures. McKee and colleagues described a similar series of 16 elbows, typically those in which initial treatment had failed or associated fracture comminution made stable repair technically impossible.[89] Good results (with an average flexion-extension arc of over 100°) were achieved, along with restoration of concentric elbow stability. Wyrsch and associates had similar results with the same device.[172] From these series it would appear that the main indications for the use of these devices are (1) when conventional surgical treatment (ligament repair, radial head fixation/replacement, etc.) is unable to produce an elbow stable enough to allow early motion and (2) in the treatment of patients who present late, often after failure of primary treatment.

The key to successful treatment with these devices is the insertion of a temporary pin through the center of the axis of rotation of the elbow, which is the basis of hinge construction. The hinge is placed on this temporary pin and then attached to the humerus and ulna through half pins. If the pin at the center of rotation is malaligned,

nonconcentric motion and increased resistance will occur and compromise the final result. Madey and co-workers performed a biomechanical study and found that malpositioning of the hinge axis by as little as 10 mm produced a 10-fold increase in resistance to motion, thus highlighting the importance of accurate hinge placement.[81] The center of the axis of rotation of the elbow runs through the center of the capitellum and exits medially just inferior and anterior to the medial epicondyle. The ulnar nerve must be protected during insertion of the axis pin.

Recurrent or "habitual" dislocation is uncommon but can be exceptionally difficult to treat. A number of causes have been postulated to account for this chronic instability, including attenuation of the collateral ligaments, residual articular defects in the trochlear or semilunar notch, nonunion of a large coronoid fracture, and failure of the anterior capsule to heal.[154] Osborne and Cotterill postulated the cause to be located on the lateral side and devised a repair based on this supposition.[118] More recently, the condition of *posterolateral rotatory instability* of the elbow was defined by O'Driscoll and colleagues.[114] This post-

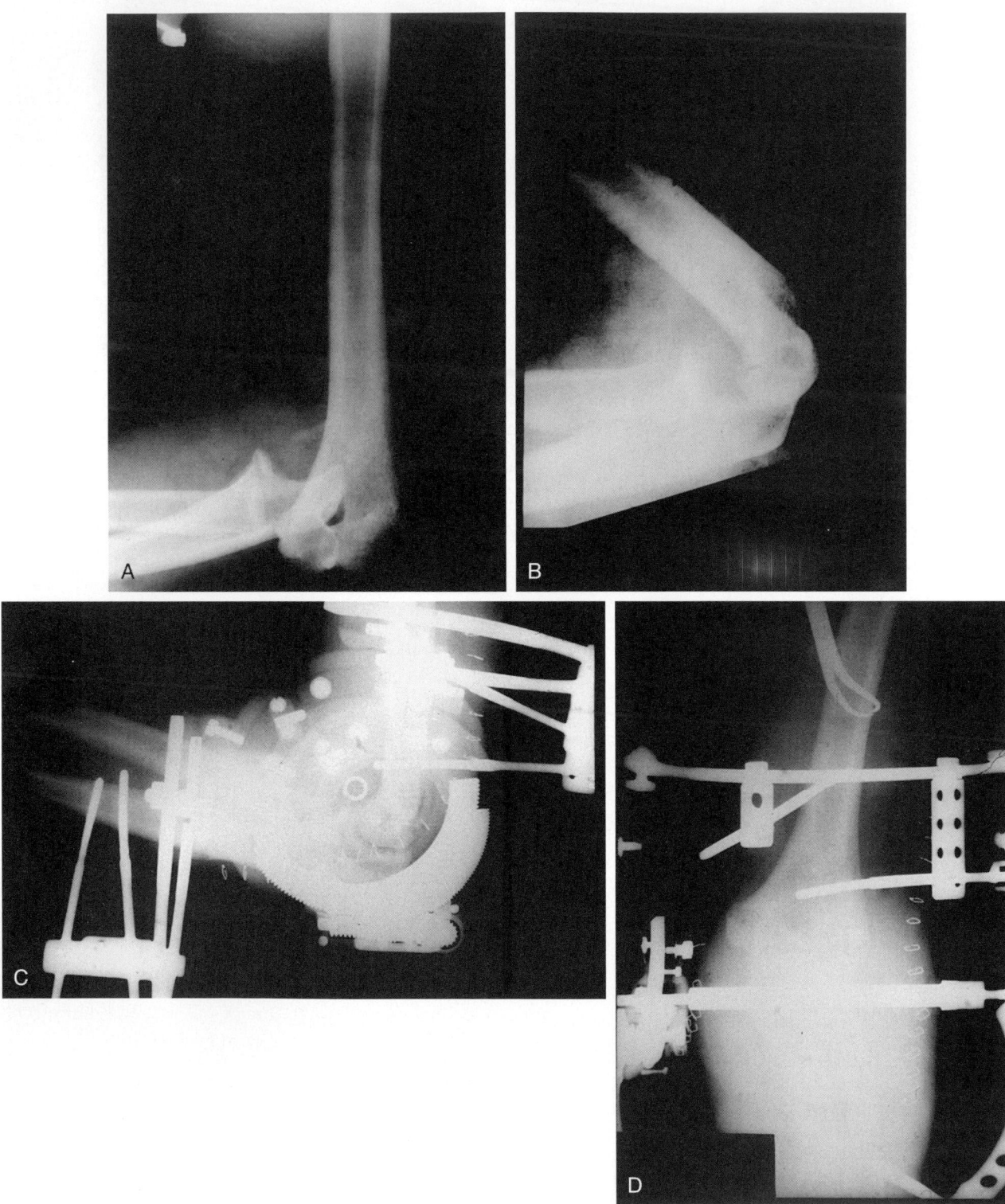

**FIGURE 42–37.** *A,* This 22-year-old man was involved in an accident in which his arm was caught in a logging machine. The patient suffered numerous soft tissue abrasions and lacerations to his upper extremity. Preoperative radiographs revealed an anterior elbow dislocation. *B,* A postoperative radiograph after an attempt at closed reduction under general anesthesia demonstrated residual anterior subluxation of the elbow with incongruity of the joint. *C, D,* Subsequent open reduction revealed severe soft tissue stripping from the distal end of the humerus. The patient was treated by open reduction of the elbow, transposition of the ulnar nerve, and reconstruction of both the medial and lateral ligaments. Radiographs showed accurate elbow reduction, and a hinged external fixator was applied to protect the stability of the elbow and allow early motion.

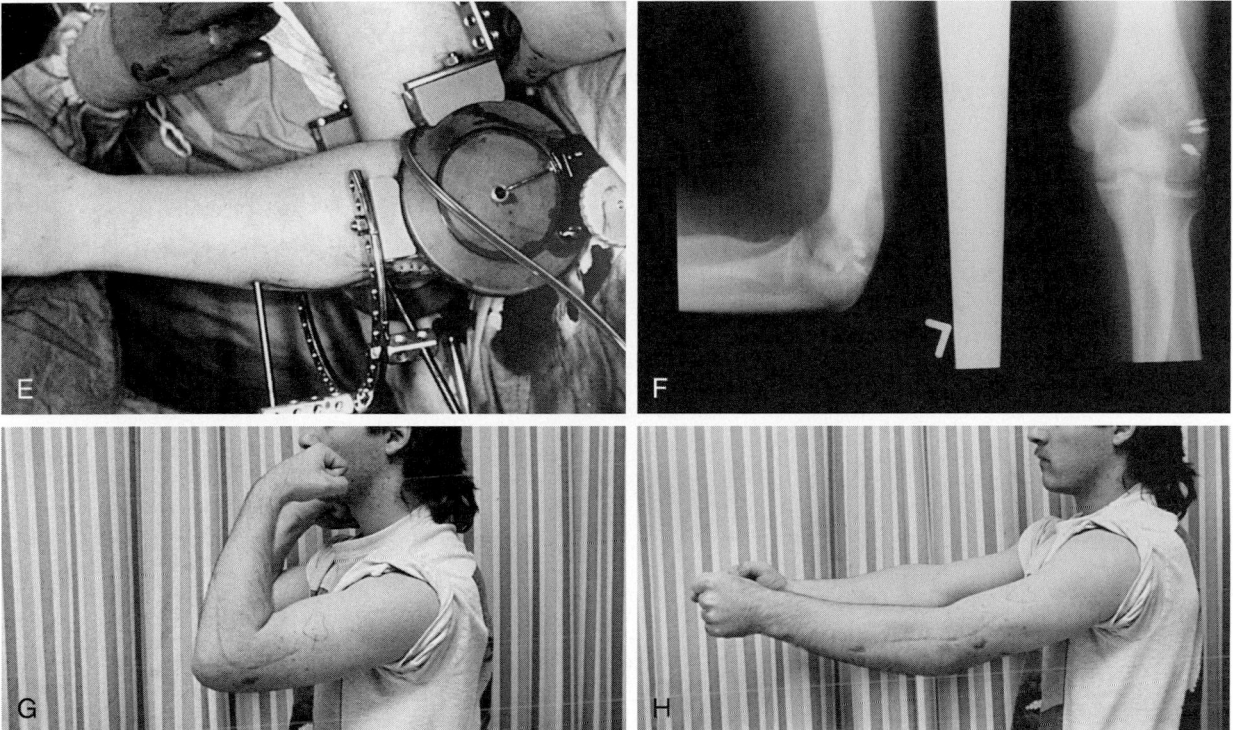

**FIGURE 42–37** *Continued. E,* Intraoperative photograph after application of the fixator. *F,* Postoperative follow-up radiographs at 3 months showed maintenance of the congruous reduction of the joint. *G, H,* Clinical follow-up at 3 months revealed a functional range of motion, full rotation, and a stable elbow.

traumatic condition results from a deficient lateral collateral ligament and causes the radial head and proximal end of the ulna to rotate off the distal end of the humerus in a posterolateral direction (Fig. 42–39). Treatment is directed at repair or reconstruction of the lateral collateral ligament.[116]

As the pathology of recurrent elbow subluxation/dislocation is more clearly defined, a number of previously described surgical procedures are beginning to be of historical interest only. Milch[101] placed a tibial bone block into the tip of the coronoid, whereas Reichenheim[129] described transfer of the biceps tendon into the region of the coronoid, through a drill hole, and out the dorsal aspect of the ulna. Kapel[69] described the creation of a "cruciate" ligament with a strip of the triceps aponeurosis left attached distally and a similar strip of the biceps tendon brought through the brachialis into a hole drilled into the olecranon fossa. Arafiles[7] described a similar concept using a strip of free tendon graft. Osborne and Cotterill[118] recommended reattaching what they believed to be a deficient posterolateral capsule and lateral collateral ligament to a roughened area along the lateral aspect of the distal end of the humerus, similar to the reconstruction recommended by O'Driscoll and Morrey.[116] This type of repair is rapidly becoming the standard surgical treatment of this disabling condition.

Schwab and co-workers[143] focused their attention more on the role of the medial collateral ligament and advised either surgical reattachment or reconstruction with a free tendon graft. This technique is especially useful in patients with associated symptomatic valgus instability.

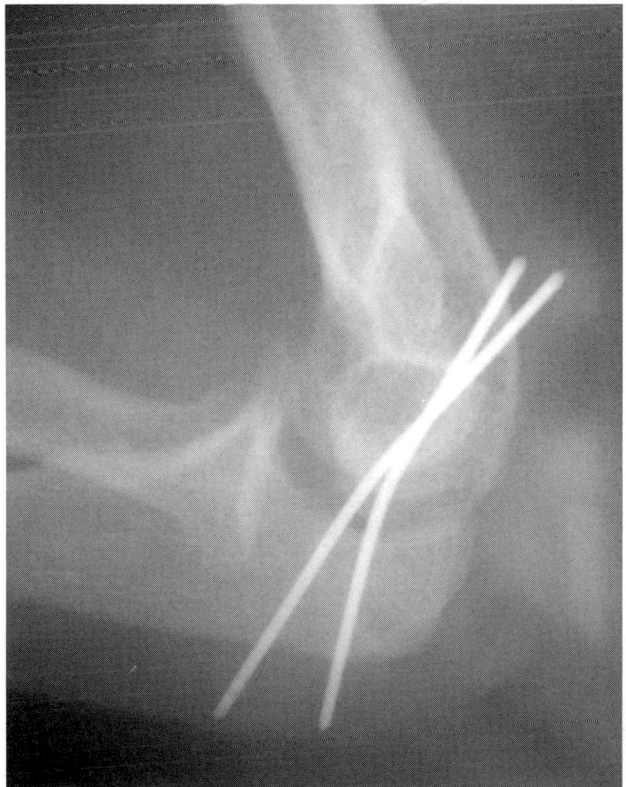

**FIGURE 42–38.** Lateral radiograph of an unstable elbow treated by transarticular pinning. The pins have bent, and the elbow is not concentrically reduced (the radial head is directed posterior to the capitellum, and the ulnohumeral joint space is widened). With the development of hinged fixators for the elbow that maintain stability yet allow early motion, this technique has become obsolete in most cases.

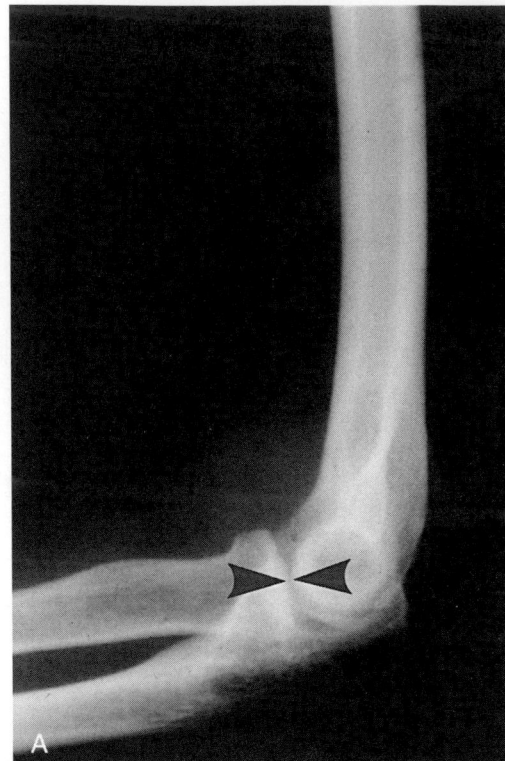

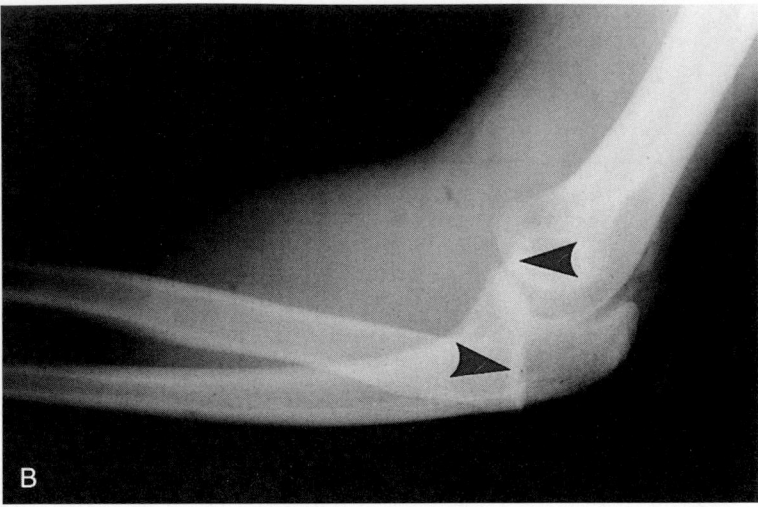

**FIGURE 42–39.** This 32-year-old patient suffered an elbow dislocation while wrestling with a friend. After closed reduction and treatment in a cast for 2 weeks, he was allowed early range of motion. The patient subsequently began to complain of a sense of instability, weakness, and "clicking" in his elbow. *A,* A standard lateral radiograph revealed concentric reduction *(arrows). B,* A radiograph taken with supination and valgus stress demonstrated posterolateral subluxation of the radial head *(arrows).* This abnormality is due to posterolateral rotatory instability after elbow dislocation.

## PART II    *Fractures of the Distal Humerus*

Michael D. McKee, M.D., F.R.C.S.(C.)  •  Jesse B. Jupiter, M.D.

## DISTAL HUMERAL ANATOMY

### Functional Anatomy

The elbow can be characterized as a hinge joint in that it has only a single axis of rotation.[213] By definition, it is a constrained joint. In the case of the elbow, the ulna rotates with respect to the humerus around a transverse axis. The cylindrical part of the elbow, which consists of the semilunar notch of the proximal part of the ulna, articulates around the trochlea of the distal end of the humerus, the central axis of this joint (Fig. 42–40).

The term *trochlea* is derived from the Greek word meaning *pulley,* although to the modern eye it appears more like a spool. The trochlea functions effectively as the articulating axis of the joint by virtue of its being held between two bony columns, much like the ends of a spool of thread that are held between the thumb and index finger (Fig. 42–41). The end of the skeleton of the humerus splits in a wishbone fashion to form the two columns that support the trochlea. By interconnecting with these divergent columns, the terminal part of the elbow joint most resembles a triangle. This factor is fundamental in understanding the proper mechanics of intra-articular

distal humeral fractures. With disruption of any one of the three arms of this triangle, the entire construct is weakened more than what might be expected.[223] This issue is important and helps explain why instability results after internal fixation of fractures unless all three arms of this triangle are effectively stabilized (comminuted fractures of the distal end of the humerus are best fixed with plates on both the lateral and medial columns).

However, defining the distal humeral articulation as a triangle based on the trochlea ignores the capitellum. There are reasons to consider the capitellum and its articulation with the radius as a joint separate from the elbow (i.e., the ulnotrochlear joint). Mechanically, the radiocapitellar joint contributes to the function of forearm rotation and is independent of elbow flexion and extension. In short, it is possible to have an arthrodesis of the elbow joint and yet have full forearm rotation. Furthermore, if this joint is eliminated (e.g., with removal of the radial head), elbow flexion and extension are not typically affected.

On viewing the distal end of the humerus from a posterior aspect, the trochlea and its articular surface are readily appreciated to be centrally located between the lateral and the medial distal humeral columns from which the trochlea is suspended.[178] On the other hand, the capitellum is not seen, and only on viewing the distal portion of the humerus from the anterior surface does it become apparent that the capitellum represents the cartilage-covered anterior surface of the end of the lateral column. It may well be best to view it as such rather than as an integral articular part of the distal end of the humerus and elbow joint. It can be removed from the distal part of the humerus traumatically or surgically and not interfere with the structural integrity of the "distal humeral triangle." However, malunion of a capitellar fragment proximally can inhibit flexion of the elbow as the radial head impinges at the site of the obliterated radial fossa (see Surgical Anatomy). Because the radius and ulna are closely linked, restriction of movement of one bone has an indirect effect on the other.

Although the ulnotrochlear joint behaves as a hinge joint with a single axis of rotation, the motion of the elbow appears to be more complex clinically. This complexity may partly be a result of the fact that the trochlear axis is not parallel to any ordinate body axis and the consequent forearm projection of elbow extension/flexion actually traverses several sagittal planes. In fact, the forearm always remains within a single plane, one that is oblique to the sagittal and coronal planes of the body. The trochlear axis with respect to the longitudinal axis of the humerus is approximately 94° in valgus in males and 98° in females (Fig. 42–42). In addition, the trochlear axis is externally rotated between 3° and 8° with respect to a line connecting the medial and lateral epicondyles.[213] This orientation therefore places the forearm in a slight degree of external rotation when the elbow is in 90° of flexion (Fig. 42–42).

This normal valgus position of the elbow is commonly referred to as the *carrying angle* of the elbow. Functionally, the combination of external rotation and valgus allows the positioning of objects away from the body when they are held with the elbow in extension. When this concept is considered in depth, it becomes clear that with the elbow

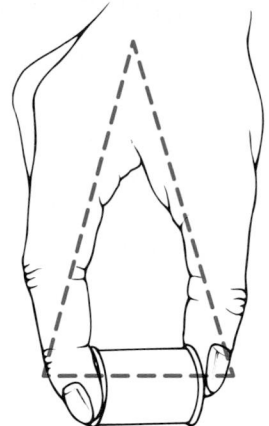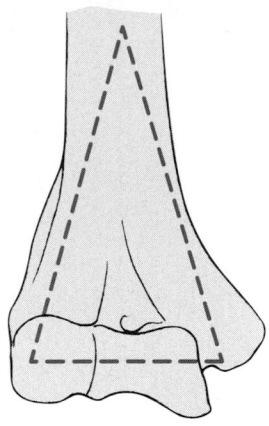

FIGURE 42–41. The trochlea functions as the articulating axis of the distal end of the humerus. It is held between two bony columns much like the ends of a spool of thread held between the thumb and the index finger.

in full extension, an object is truly suspended rather than carried. This action puts the shoulder girdle musculature at a mechanical disadvantage in that the lever arm of the upper extremity is located at a substantial distance. Any attempt to hold an object away from the body leads to fatigue of the shoulder abductors within a few seconds.

A second source of confusion with the common rationale for a carrying angle is the fact that if a heavy object is held in the hand with the elbow in extension, the laws of physics dictate that the center of gravity of the object must be precisely below the center of rotation of the shoulder. The positioning of the "pendulum" that is holding this object really has very little to do with the ultimate position of what the pendulum is suspending (Fig. 42–43). Thus, one generally sees the trunk of the body tilted, which is functionally more efficient than it would be if the elbow had a greater carrying angle. A final argument against the stated purpose of the carrying angle is that in functional activities of the upper extremity, the angle is really manifested only in the anatomic position (i.e., with the humerus in neutral rotation and the forearm

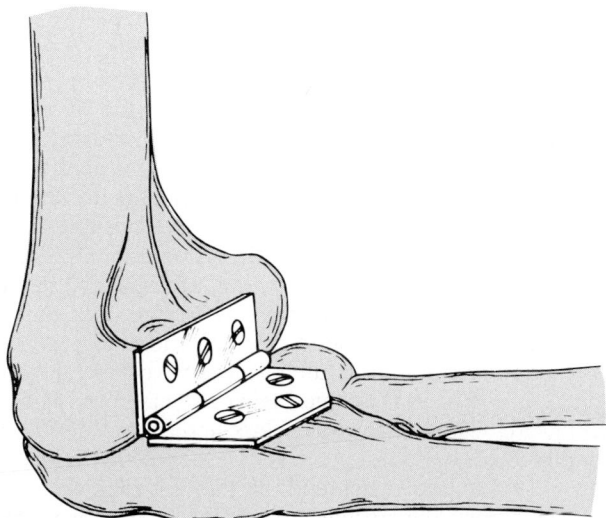

FIGURE 42–40. The elbow is a true hinge joint with a single axis of rotation.

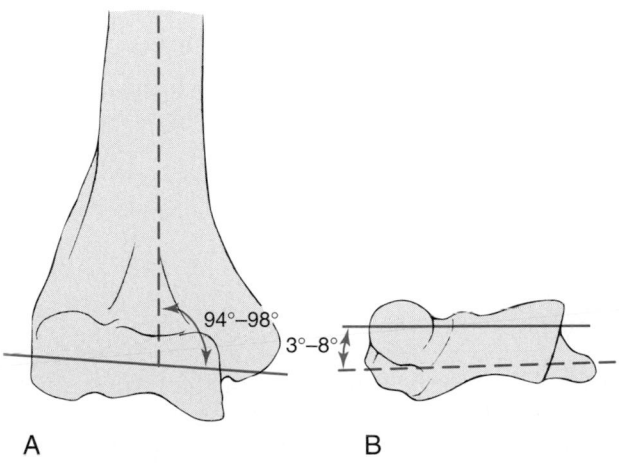

FIGURE 42–42. The axis of the trochlea is in valgus with respect to the longitudinal axis of the distal end of the humerus (A) and in internal rotation with respect to the transverse axis (B).

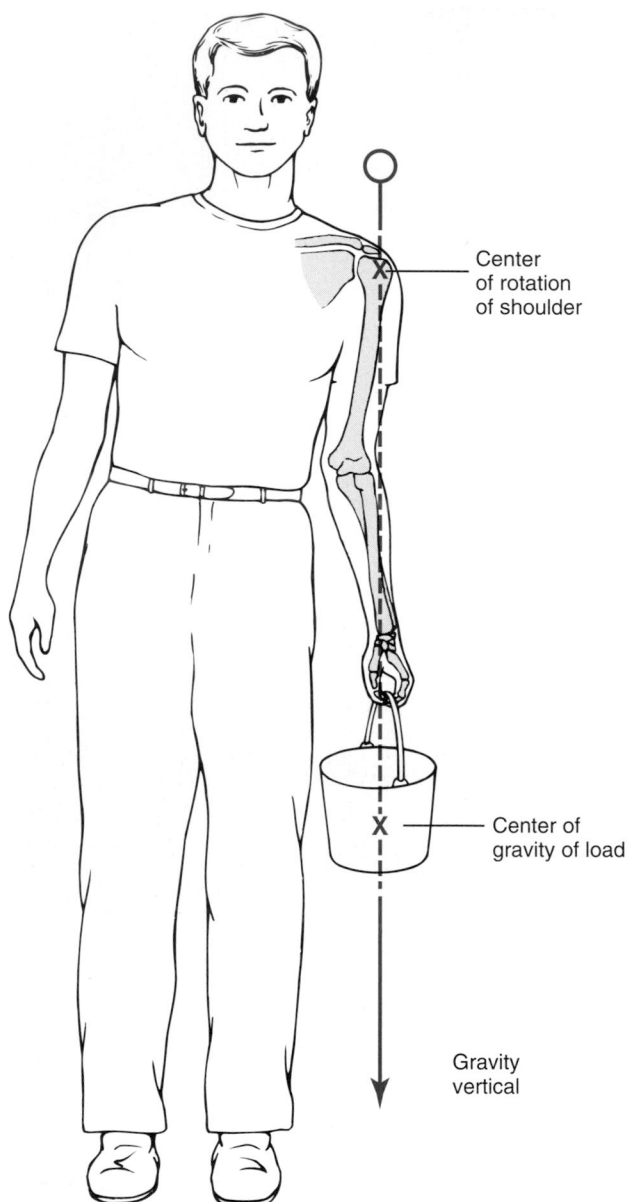

Center
of rotation
of shoulder

Center of
gravity of load

Gravity
vertical

**FIGURE 42–43.** With the elbow in full extension, an object held is truly suspended rather than carried.

in full supination). In fact, this position is rarely assumed in activities of daily living. The most common posturing of the upper extremity for carrying objects is with the humerus in 45° of internal rotation, the forearm in 45° of supination, and the limb left in position with the palm facing the thigh. Little elbow angulation is apparent in this position.

## Surgical Anatomy

When viewed from a posterior approach, which is the standard surgical view, the humeral shaft is divided into longitudinal medial and lateral columns. These columns terminate distally at the point where the transversely oriented trochlea connects them. The medial column ends approximately 1 cm proximal to the distal end of the

trochlea, whereas the lateral column extends to the distal aspect of the trochlea (Fig. 42–44), where its cartilage-covered anterior surface forms the capitellum.

Bounded by the triangular structure of the distal end of the humerus is a similarly triangular depression, the olecranon fossa. This fossa accommodates the proximal tip of the olecranon in full elbow extension. The intramedullary canal of the humerus tapers to an end 2 to 3 cm proximal to the olecranon fossa, and the humerus becomes very thin distally between the medial and the lateral columns. Up to 6% of patients may have an actual bony defect in this area termed a *septal aperture* (a normal anatomic variant). A layer of fatty tissue, the posterior fat pad, is normally contained within the olecranon fossa. This fat pad is sandwiched between two layers of the posterior joint capsule (i.e., the fibrous layer, which is superficial to the fat pad, and the synovial layer, which is deep).[221] In the presence of an intra-articular effusion, the fat pad is displaced posteriorly and will become visible on a lateral radiograph as the so-called posterior fat pad sign (see Fig. 42–7). Recent work has confirmed that the presence of a "fat pad" sign is associated with a fracture in approximately 76% of cases (in children).[147] In normal elbow extension, the fat pad becomes displaced to permit room for the tip of the olecranon. This displacement, which is posterior as well as superior, is also visible if a lateral radiograph of the extended elbow is obtained. After trauma or surgery, this posterior fat pad will at times become fibrotic or adhere to the olecranon fossa and contribute to the commonly noted loss of full elbow extension after major trauma to the elbow.

The medial and lateral columns are not as apparent from an anterior perspective (see Fig. 42–44), primarily because of the lack of a counterpart to the deep olecranon fossa to put the columns in relief. However, a small coronoid fossa is located just proximal to the trochlea and an even smaller radial fossa just proximal to the capitellum. These two fossae are separated by a longitudinal ridge of bone that continues distally with the lateral lip of the trochlea. This longitudinal ridge and the lateral trochlear lip form the anatomic division between the lateral and the medial columns. The coronoid fossa and trochlea are situated between the two columns and form a symmetric intercolumnar arch (see Fig. 42–44). The medial column begins at the medial border of this arch.

The medial column of the distal end of the humerus diverges from the humeral shaft at an approximately 45° angle. The proximal two thirds of this column is cortical bone. The distal third of the column represents the medial epicondyle,[224] which is composed of cancellous bone and is ovoid in cross section. The medial and superior surfaces of the medial epicondyle serve as the origins of the flexor muscle mass of the forearm. The medial epicondyle additionally serves as the origin for the anterior and posterior bundles of the ulnar (medial) collateral ligament.[181, 196, 199, 231, 256] This anatomic fact has significance with regard to elbow stability: accurate reduction and fixation of a medial epicondylar fracture fragment helps restore elbow stability.

It is of surgical importance to recognize that the inferior surface of the medial epicondyle is available for the placement of internal fixation. The ulnar nerve, which

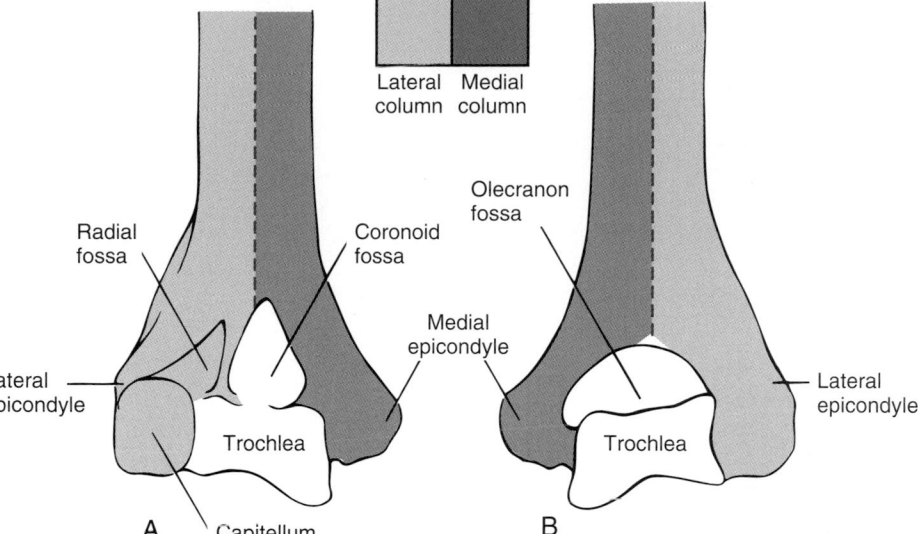

**FIGURE 42–44.** Anterior (A) and posterior (B) views of the medial and lateral columns of the distal third of the humerus.

runs in the cubital tunnel below this structure, can be transferred anteriorly, and the entire posterior medial column can be used for the placement of internal fixation. Because no articulations are present on the anterior aspect of the medial column, screws can penetrate anteriorly and not interfere with articular function. The triangular shape of this medial column should be kept in mind because it affords excellent purchase for screws. The screws should be directed somewhat medially to obtain purchase on the anteromedial cortex, which is more substantial. When the bone stock of the medial column is poor distally, plates can be contoured to "cradle" the medial epicondyle and aid in fracture reduction (Fig. 42–45).

The lateral column of the distal end of the humerus diverges from the humeral shaft at the same level as the medial column but is subtended at an approximately 20° angle with reference to the axis of the humeral shaft. The proximal half of this column is cortical bone, with the posterior aspect being broad and flat and ideal for accepting a plate. The distal half of the lateral column is cancellous bone, which is somewhat more complex from both an anatomic and a surgical point of view. From the posterior view, this part of the lateral column begins at the level of the middle of the olecranon fossa. As it extends distally, it begins to gradually curve anteriorly. The anconeus muscle covers the lateral column as it follows the curvature of the adjacent trochlea. At the most distal point of this curve, the capitellar cartilage begins. It represents the distal limit that would allow internal fixation posteriorly, and transgression of this point with fixation can result in impingement of the radial head. The concept of the columnar structure of the distal end of the humerus is important when considering where to place internal fixation because the anterior aspect of the lateral column cannot be seen directly from the posterior view. One must bear in mind that the trochlea lies *between* the two columns, whereas the capitellum is *part* of the lateral column. It therefore follows that the olecranon and coronoid fossae associated with the trochlea are intercolumnar, whereas the radial fossa associated with the capitellum is part of the lateral column. The radial fossa is

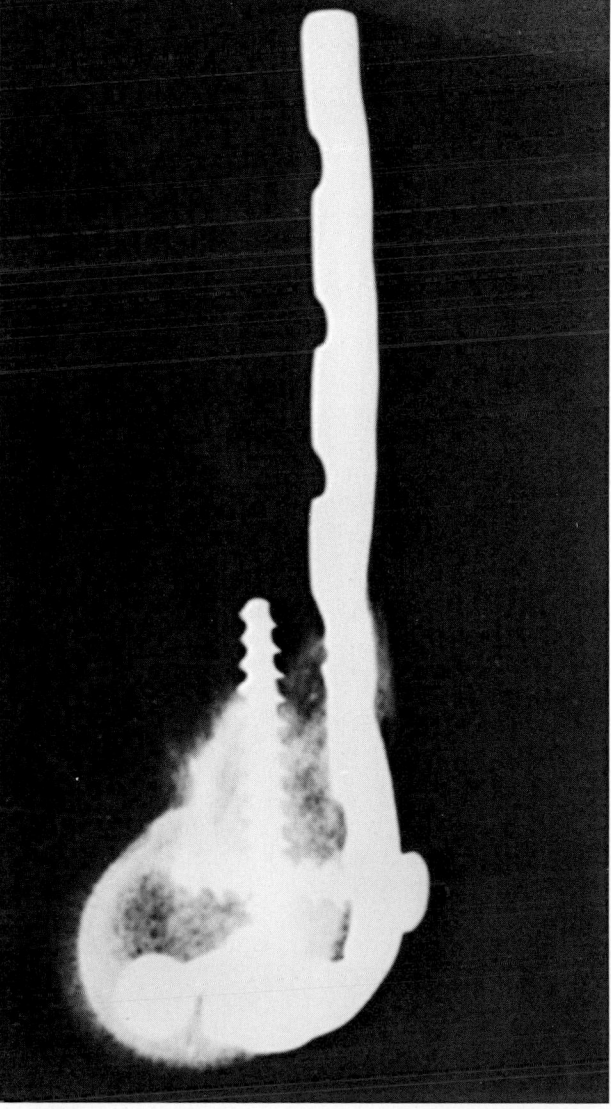

**FIGURE 42–45.** The medial epicondyle can be "cradled" by a 90° bend in the plate. The two distal screws will be perpendicular to each other and thereby provide a mechanical interlocking construct.

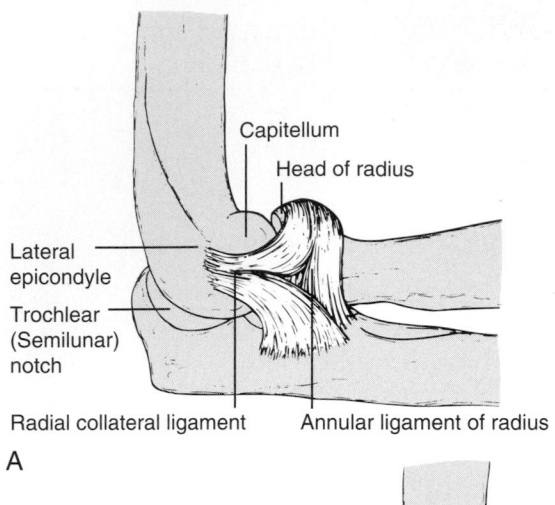

Capitellum

Head of radius

Lateral epicondyle

Trochlear (Semilunar) notch

Radial collateral ligament    Annular ligament of radius

A

**Figure 42–46.** Lateral (*A*) and medial (*B*) views of the collateral ligaments of the elbow.

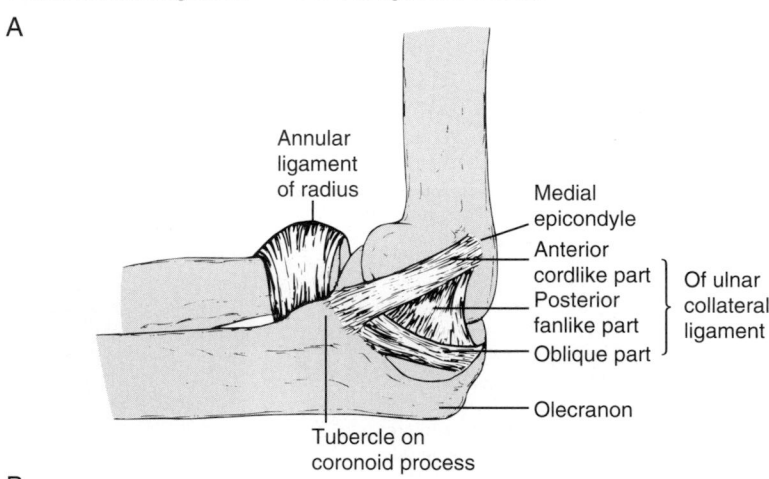

Annular ligament of radius

Medial epicondyle

Anterior cordlike part

Posterior fanlike part

Oblique part

} Of ulnar collateral ligament

Olecranon

Tubercle on coronoid process

B

vulnerable to screw penetration when applying internal fixation to the posterior aspect of the lateral column.

When viewed from the anterior surface, a rough ridge of bone is seen projecting laterally farther along the lateral column from its proximal tubular portion. This bone is the lateral supracondylar ridge. The brachioradialis and extensor carpi radialis longus muscles originate from this ridge, which ultimately blends distally with the lateral epicondyle. The lateral epicondyle, though smaller than its counterpart on the medial side, is the point of origin of the lateral collateral ligament of the elbow.[199] This ligament is not as distinct as its medial counterpart but is part of a lateral ligamentous complex that blends with the common extensor origin and the annular ligament.[237] The anterior fibers of the lateral collateral ligament insert on the supinator crest of the proximal end of the ulna. The lateral collateral ligament complex is the primary constraint against posterolateral instability of the elbow; accurate reduction of this fragment helps prevent instability in this plane. The common extensor muscle origin arises from the lateral tip of the epicondyle posterior to the radial portion of the lateral collateral ligament (Fig. 42–46).

Medially and anteriorly, the lateral column is bounded by the longitudinal ridge. Proceeding distally, the column indents to form the shallow radial fossa. Just below this fossa, the capitellum juts out anteriorly as a hyaline cartilage–covered, incomplete hemisphere. The midpoint

of this hemisphere is directly anteriorly and is an arc of only 180° in the sagittal plane. This arc must be compared with an articular arc of 270° for the trochlea. The rotational center of the capitellum is displaced between 12 and 15 mm in front of the humeral shaft axis and is aligned with the trochlear axis. Thus, the ulna and radius flex and extend coaxially.

The trochlea is the intercolumnar "tie rod." It has the form of a spool and is composed of medial and lateral lips with an intervening sulcus. The sulcus articulates with the semilunar notch of the proximal end of the ulna, and the adjacent lips offer medial and lateral stability to this simple articulation. The anterior and distal aspects of the lateral trochlear lip have a different radius of curvature than the medial lip, thus changing the symmetry of the trochlea. This asymmetry gives the impression that the trochlea is mechanically complex. Although many have thought that this asymmetric shape positions the ulna in a different axis from flexion to extension,[256] London[213] has shown that it is part of a pure and simple hinge joint. However, as the elbow moves through its flexion-extension arc, normal kinematics allow for 3° to 4° of varus or valgus laxity in response to applied force.[229, 236] Thus, the elbow does not function as a tightly constrained joint but has a mild degree of varus-valgus laxity, which has been described as a "sloppy hinge" that some elbow arthroplasty designs emulate. As depicted in Figure 42–47, when the trochlea is viewed end on and the "missing" anterolateral and posteromedial lips are "filled in," it can be seen to be a symmetric spool.

The anatomic division of the *condyle* has been absent in this description. Although entrenched in the anatomic and orthopaedic literature, this term may well represent a pathologic description rather than a true anatomic division. The word *condyle* comes from the Greek word *kondylos,* which means *knuckle* and can be defined as a rounded projection of bone.[189] Although this term accurately describes the distal end of the femur or the head of the metacarpals, no obvious structures anatomically lend themselves to this term in the distal end of the humerus. For this reason, we have chosen to not define the condyle as part of the delineated anatomic divisions of the distal end of the humerus; instead, we will use it to describe skeletal disruption of the distal part of the humerus.

## Blood Supply

Although the bone of the distal end of the humerus is rarely affected by avascular necrosis (compared with the proximal end of the humerus), preservation of the blood supply can be important for a variety of clinical reasons, including improved fracture healing. A recent cadaver study by Yamaguchi and colleagues involving an India ink/latex injection technique showed that the blood supply of the distal part of the humerus follows a consistent pattern in both the intraosseous and extraosseous circulation[173] (see Fig. 42–13*A* and *B*). The blood supply of the elbow was organized into three arcades: medial, lateral, and posterior. The medial arcade is formed by the superior and inferior ulnar collateral arteries and the posterior ulnar recurrent artery. The lateral arcade is formed by the radial and middle collateral, radial recurrent, and interosseous recurrent arteries, whereas the posterior arcade is derived primarily from the medial and lateral arcades. The intraosseous circulation is derived mainly from perforating vessels from these arcades, thus suggesting that careful preservation of these vessels may enhance the blood supply and, by logical extension, fracture healing. The importance of preserving such vessels would be especially true for the "watershed areas" (such as the trochlear groove) that were identified as having sparse circulation.

| TABLE 42–2 |
| --- |
| Classification of Distal Humeral Fractures |

I. Intra-articular fractures
  A. Single-column fractures
    1. Medial
      a. High
      b. Low
    2. Lateral
      a. High
      b. Low
    3. Divergent
  B. Bicolumn fractures
    1. T pattern
      a. High
      b. Low
    2. Y pattern
    3. H pattern
    4. λ pattern
      a. Medial
      b. Lateral
    5. Multiplane pattern
  C. Capitellum fractures
  D. Trochlear fractures
II. Extra-articular intracapsular fractures
  A. Transcolumn fractures
    1. High
      a. Extension
      b. Flexion
      c. Abduction
      d. Adduction
    2. Low
      a. Extension
      b. Flexion
III. Extracapsular fractures
  A. Medial epicondyle
  B. Lateral epicondyle

## GENERAL CLASSIFICATION

Traditional classifications of fractures of the distal end of the humerus have centered on the anatomic concept of the terminal end of the humerus structured as condyles (hence the terms *supracondylar, condylar, transcondylar,* and *bicondylar* fractures).[255] As discussed, the distal end of the humerus is more precisely described and understood as two diverging columns supporting an intercalary articular surface (i.e., the trochlea). By changing the term *condyle* to *column,* the general fracture categories will be maintained and the fractures more accurately described (Table 42–2).

## SINGLE-COLUMN FRACTURES

Single-column fractures are rare and account for only 3% to 4% of distal humeral fractures.[181, 210] Lateral-column fractures are more common than medial column fractures.[181, 224, 234] These fractures traverse either the medial or the lateral column and extend distally through the intercolumnar portion of the distal end of the humerus. The separated fragment represents the distal portion of the fractured column along with the adjacent part of the

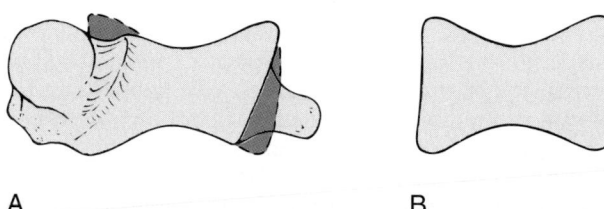

**FIGURE 42–47.** *A,* The trochlea viewed end on. *B,* The anterolateral and posteromedial lips are "filled in," and as a result, the trochlea resembles a symmetric spool.

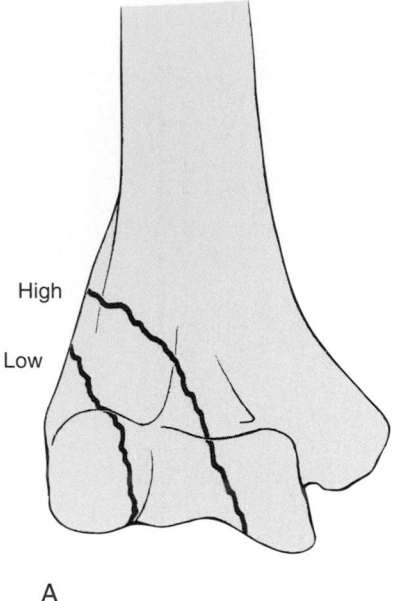
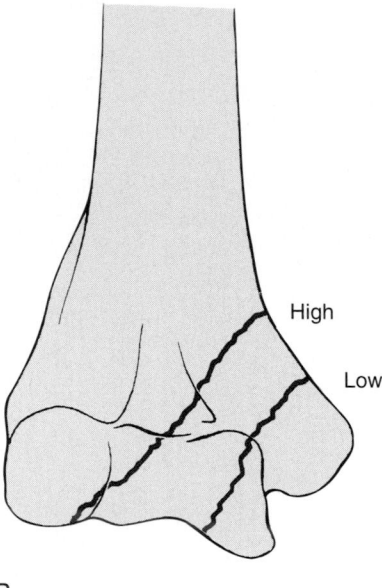

High

Low

High

Low

A                                    B

FIGURE 42–48. Single-column fractures of the distal end of the humerus. A "high" fracture involves most of the trochlea and is unstable because the ulna is displaced with the fracture fragment. "Low" fractures are inherently stable.

trochlea. In fact, the extent of the trochlea that separates with the columnar fragment is directly related to how high proximally or how low distally the columnar fracture is. The higher the fracture, the larger the trochlear fragment that separates with the column (Fig. 42–48). These fractures can occur as part of a fracture-dislocation of the elbow, and accurate reduction of the lateral condyle and its associated soft tissue structures (lateral collateral ligament, common extensor origin) is vital to the restoration of elbow stability.

## Classification

Single-column fractures have traditionally been thought to be condylar fractures, with the classification of Milch considered standard.[181, 188, 224, 234] Milch divided the fractures into two types based on whether the "lateral wall of the trochlea" remained attached to the main mass of the humerus (type I) or fractured away from it (type II). He considered the type II pattern to be a fracture-dislocation because of displacement of the radius and ulna along with the fracture fragment. On the basis of this notion, he suggested that type I injuries may be treated nonoperatively, whereas type II injuries fare better with operative intervention.[224]

It has been our impression that displacement has less to do with the fracture involving the lateral trochlear ridge than with which fragment has the greater capsular attachment and whether either of the collateral ligaments is ruptured.[181]

The present classification is based on our columnar concept of the distal end of the humerus. Two basic categories of single-column fractures may be differentiated, depending on which column is dissociated from the remainder of the humerus. The level of the fracture (proximal or distal) in reality represents a continuum, but it is useful to categorize these injuries as high or low.

High fractures share the following characteristics:

1. The fractured column includes most of the trochlea.
2. The ulna and radius follow the displacement of the fractured column.
3. Internal fixation is reliable and technically straightforward because sufficient skeleton is available for placement of internal fixation devices in the distal fragment.

Low fractures, on the other hand, have opposite characteristics.

Another type of single-column fracture of the distal end of the humerus has been described by Kuhn and co-workers.[211] This fracture, which has been termed a *divergent* single-column fracture, occurs in adolescents who have a large fossa or septal aperture between the olecranon and the coronoid fossa.[195] The authors proposed that an impaction injury drives the olecranon proximally and splits the medial and lateral columns in a divergent fashion, with the fracture exiting high on the respective bony column (Fig. 42–49). This mechanism is probably an inherent part of many bicondylar distal humeral fractures.

## History and Physical Examination

The mechanism of fracture has been well delineated in past studies. Milch[224] suggested that these fractures may be caused by an abduction or adduction force, but this mechanism has never been definitively supported. The fracture may be the result of a motor vehicle accident,[182] a direct blow to the elbow, or a fall on an outstretched hand. The elbow becomes swollen and painful, and movement is restricted. High fractures are clinically more unstable than low fractures and may occur as an apparent varus or valgus deformity.[250] A collateral ligament injury may be associated with the fracture[188] but may not be apparent until after internal fixation of the fracture.

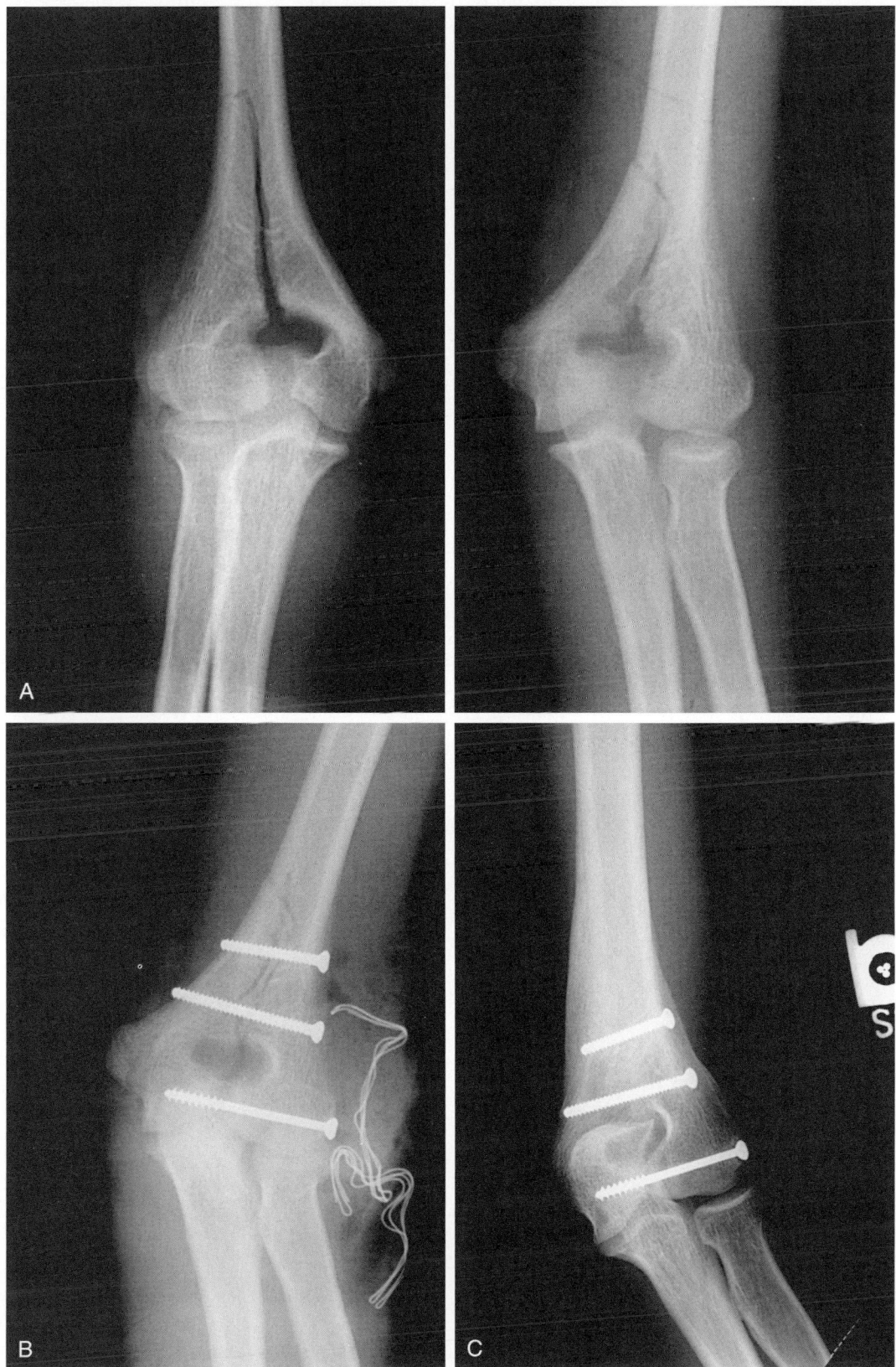

**FIGURE 42–49.** *A*, Radiographs of "divergent" distal humeral fractures sustained by a 15-year-old boy predisposed to such fractures by a supracondylar septal aperture. These fractures occurred 1 year apart. *B*, Intraoperative radiograph showing anatomic reduction and fixation of the fracture with multiple lag screws in the left elbow. *C*, Solid, bony union 6 months after surgery.

Typically, however, the ligament is attached to the fracture fragment and is incompetent because of loss of its bony origin rather than an in-substance tear. The neurovascular status of the distal end of the extremity must be evaluated and documented in both high and low single-column fractures.

Standard AP and lateral radiographs of the elbow are often sufficient to diagnose a single-column fracture. A view of the radial head and capitellum may be necessary to differentiate a lateral-column fracture from a capitellar fracture.[198] This view may also uncover an occult radial head fracture. Tomographic or computed tomographic (CT) scans may be of additional value in precisely defining the skeletal and articular injuries in more complex cases.

## Management

Although these injuries, both high and low, are intra-articular fractures, some authors continue to advocate closed reduction for low fractures.[181] Disadvantages of closed treatment of any intra-articular elbow fracture include prolonged immobilization, the potential for early or late displacement, and residual incongruity of the articular surface, leading to instability and post-traumatic arthritis.

We believe that displaced single-column fractures are best treated by ORIF followed by early mobilization of the elbow, but in certain situations, internal fixation may not be advisable, such as in a polytraumatized patient in whom extensive peripheral surgery may not be indicated at the time of initial stabilization and long bone skeletal management. In these cases, closed reduction with splinting of the fracture in 90° of elbow flexion can be considered. Definitive fixation can be delayed until the patient is medically optimal. To promote joint stability, with fractures of the lateral column the forearm should be maintained in pronation, whereas with fractures of the medial column, the forearm should be maintained in supination.[181, 188]

When considering a surgical approach, the surgical planning, technique, and postoperative regimen are similar to those described for bicolumn fractures, with only a few exceptions. These exceptions include the fact that the ulnar nerve does not generally need anterior transposition with lateral-column fractures. In restoration of the mechanical integrity of the distal humeral triangle, a single plate is typically needed in addition to distal transtrochlear screw fixation. Divergent single-column fractures are best treated with interfragmentary screws between the two columns because muscular forces tend to pull the trochlea proximally and push the two columns apart, thereby resulting in failure of closed treatment.[211]

Postoperative care and rehabilitation are essentially the same as those for bicolumn fractures, and the reader is referred to the following section.

## BICOLUMN FRACTURES

Bicolumn fractures are the most common type of distal humeral fracture and the most difficult to treat. The fracture disrupts each component of the distal humeral triangle (see Functional Anatomy), thereby resulting in dissociation of each column from the other and from the proximal humeral shaft.

## Incidence

Statistics regarding the incidence of bicolumn fractures vary widely in the literature from a low of 5%[209] of all distal humeral fractures to a high of 62%.[214] In terms of the overall incidence of skeletal fractures, they are uncommon. Of 4536 consecutive fractures treated at the Massachusetts General Hospital in one clinical study, only 14 (0.31%) were bicolumn fractures.[214] However, it would appear that the incidence of this fracture is increasing both in the elderly population as their numbers and general activity level increase and in younger, high-energy trauma patients as improved vehicular restraint mechanisms and trauma care programs translate into increased survival for persons with severe appendicular trauma.

## Mechanism of Injury

Although many authors have considered bicolumn fractures to be the result of the distal end of the humerus being "wedged" apart by the olecranon,[183, 193, 251] this mechanism has not been duplicated in mechanical studies. In cadaver studies performed at the University of Southern California biomechanical laboratories, a direct force applied to the olecranon with the elbow flexed 90° repeatedly resulted in transverse olecranon fractures. Only with the elbow flexed beyond 90° were bicolumn fractures produced (Fig. 42–50).

## Associated Injury

Although sporadic reports of associated neurologic or vascular injury with closed bicolumn fractures have appeared, such injuries are exceptionally uncommon.[176, 183] Open bicolumn fractures are not uncommon, especially in high-energy vehicular or industrial trauma, and an incidence varying from 20% to as high as 50% in some series has been noted.[194, 208, 223] War-related fractures, such as blast injuries and fractures from high-velocity gunshot wounds, are commonly associated with injuries to adjacent bony and soft tissue structures. These injuries may require specialized treatment (see later).[75]

## Classification

Considerable modifications to the classification of bicolumn fractures have been made since Reich's original description in 1936 of T and Y fracture classifications.[239] Riseborough and Radin in 1969 subdivided these fractures into four categories based on separation, rotation, and comminution of the distal articular fragments.[241] With increased interest in the surgical approach to these fractures has come a realization that these classifications do not accurately reflect the extent of the injury or help in

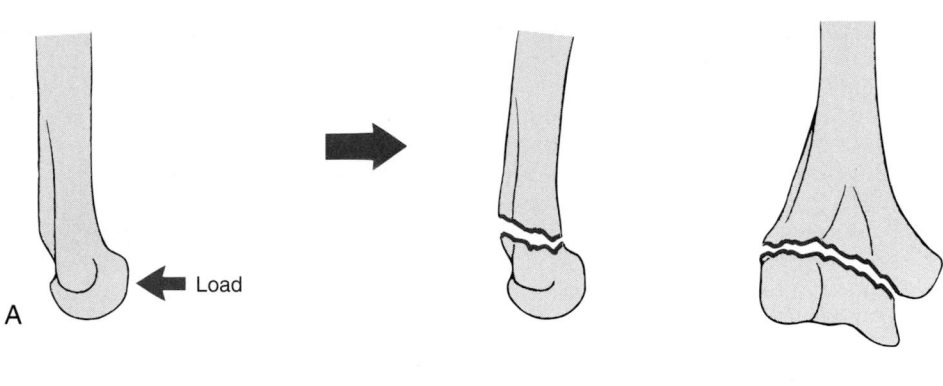

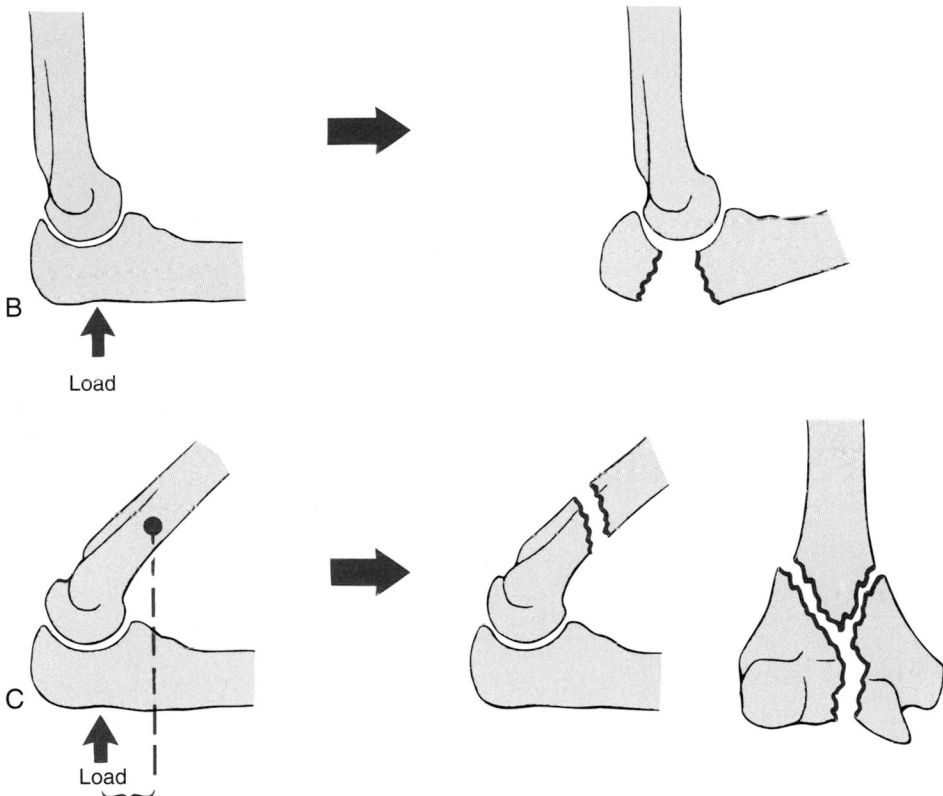

FIGURE 42–50. Fracture patterns about the elbow commonly reflect the magnitude and direction of the force of injury. *A,* A transcolumn fracture results from an axial load directed through the forearm with the elbow flexed 90°. *B,* An olecranon fracture often represents a direct impact on the olecranon with the elbow flexed 90°. *C,* An intercondylar fracture of the distal end of the humerus occurs with an axial load on the olecranon and the elbow flexed 90°.

surgical planning. The AO/ASIF (Association for the Study of Internal Fixation) classification has expanded the definition of the intra-articular components, but it, too, is lacking in identifying the anatomy of the columnar involvement.

The following classification system addresses the specific characteristics of the various types of bicolumn fractures to help in the preoperative planning of internal fixation:

1. *High T fracture.* A transverse fracture line divides both columns proximal to or at the upper limits of the olecranon fossa (see Fig. 42–62A).
2. *Low T fracture.* This fracture is among the most common and the most difficult to treat. A transverse line crosses the olecranon fossa usually just proximal to

the trochlea, with relatively small distal fragments being formed (see Fig. 42–63A).
3. *Y fracture.* In this pattern, oblique fracture lines cross each column and join in the olecranon fossa to form a distal vertical line. The oblique fracture lines and the large fragments with broad fracture surfaces make this fracture a relatively straightforward one to treat with internal fixation (see Fig. 42–64A).
4. *H fracture.* In this pattern, the medial column is fractured above and below the medial epicondyle. The lateral column is fractured in a T or Y configuration. The trochlea is thus rendered a free fragment and is also at risk for avascular necrosis. This fracture pattern may be the most difficult to treat (see Fig. 42–65A).
5. *Medial λ (lambda) fracture.* The most proximal fracture line exits medially, with the lateral fracture line being

distal to the lateral epicondyle, and only a small zone is left for internal fixation on the lateral side (see Fig. 42–66A).

6. *Lateral λ fracture.* This fracture pattern is similar to an H fracture without the lateral-column fracture. Though technically not a true bicolumn fracture (because the medial column remains intact), it still requires fixation approaches similar to those for bicolumn fractures (see Fig. 42–67A).

7. *Multiplane fracture.* This complex fracture consists of the standard T-type distal humeral fracture along with another fracture line in the coronal plane. In addition to standard fixation, Herbert screws countersunk through the articular cartilage aid in fixation[206] (see Fig. 42–68).

Ideally, a classification system should be reproducible, guide treatment, and correlate with prognosis and outcome. Many traditional fracture classification schemes have come under increased scrutiny as a result of perceived deficiencies in all three of these features. Wainwright and colleagues used a group of orthopaedic surgeons, radiologists, and orthopaedic trainees to investigate the interobserver (different observers at the same time) and intraobserver (same observers at different times) reliability of the three most popular classification systems for distal humeral fractures.[164] They found that although the Riseborough and Radin system had "moderate" agreement, only half the fractures examined could be classified. The complete AO system and the Jupiter/Mehne scales could be applied to all fracture types, but their agreement was only "fair." If the AO scale was simplified by restricting it to "type," agreement improved to "substantial," but this category is a very simplified one that adds little to guide treatment or predict outcome. It is clear that the ideal classification system remains to be determined.

## Clinical Features

Commonly, the elbow is swollen and may be deformed. The arm may also appear shortened because of proximal migration of the distal fragment and arm.[181] The neurovascular status must be carefully checked. Additionally, the posterior soft tissue envelope should be inspected carefully and examined for the possibility of an open wound, which is present in more than a third of cases.[180, 194, 208, 223, 250] Typically, such a wound is posterior or posterolateral and is created by the sharp end of the humeral shaft as the condyles split away and the shaft traverses the extensor mechanism and skin[91] (Fig. 42–51).

Standard AP and lateral radiographs generally provide an adequate projection of the fracture pattern. In the operating room, an AP view with traction on the arm can further define the intra-articular aspect of these fractures, especially when a high degree of comminution is present. CT scanning is rarely of benefit.

## Treatment

Until the 1970s, the vast majority of studies dealing with this fracture tended to approach these injuries in

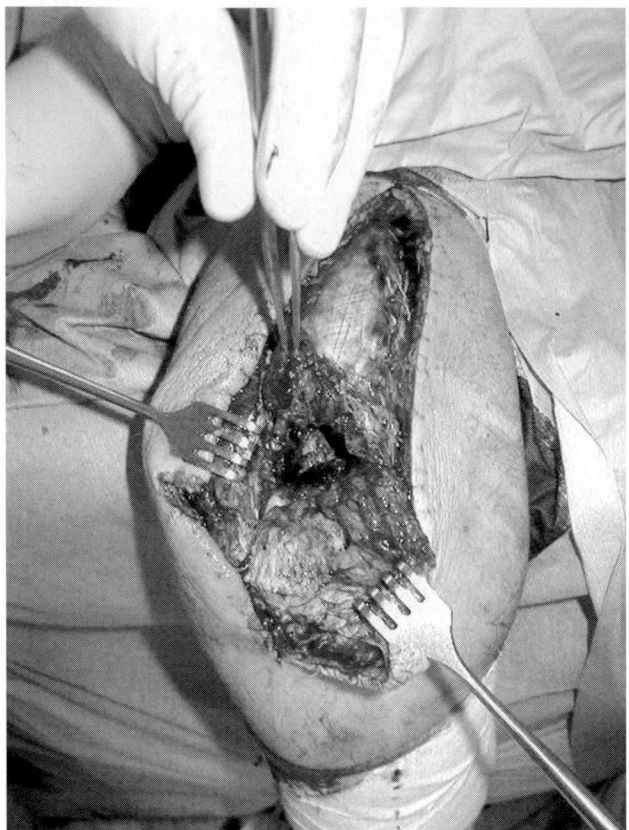

**FIGURE 42–51.** Intraoperative photograph of a traumatic defect in the triceps muscle/tendon created by protrusion of the humeral shaft after an open supracondylar humeral fracture. It is logical to incorporate this defect into a triceps-splitting type of approach rather than create a second extensor mechanism injury immediately adjacent to it by performing an olecranon osteotomy. This defect can be anticipated when a posterior open wound is seen preoperatively.

one of two ways: conservative or operative. The conservative approach ranged from no treatment to traction methods and casting.[180, 209, 227, 239, 257] Operative approaches were based on surgical exposure and limited internal fixation. The results of these treatment methods are difficult to analyze because the rating systems used were quite different and frequently quite broad. For example, an excellent result could include, in some cases, a 60° flexion contracture.[184] Riseborough and Radin expressed the general consensus well in their review published in 1969 when they stated, "Open reduction and adequate internal fixation is not easy, and seemed to offer little chance of a good outcome"[241] (Fig. 42–52). The technical difficulties with operative treatment of these fractures have been confirmed by other authors as well.[193, 209, 214, 226, 227, 246, 250, 251]

In 1985, Jupiter and colleagues[208] reported on 39 fractures treated by ORIF in one AO center in Switzerland. Thirteen patients had excellent results and 14 had good results, with the conclusion being that ORIF can provide a predictable outcome and offer a chance at functional restoration, even in elderly patients. These results have subsequently been confirmed in other studies.[194, 223] These authors have shown that the key to surgical success lies in obtaining enough stability that early postoperative motion can be instituted, which usually entails fixation with plates and screws on the medial and lateral columns. Because of the triangular shape of the distal end of the humerus, it is important to reestablish the longitudinal stability of both columns. Restoration of stability typically means that a plate should be used, although a lag screw may suffice if interdigitation of a single fracture line is possible. K-wire fixation alone rarely provides sufficient stability in these difficult fractures.[216, 219] Prolonged immobilization (greater than 3 to 4 weeks) after surgical intervention has been shown to result in unacceptable stiffness.[252]

## PREOPERATIVE PLANNING

Ideally, surgery should be performed as soon as possible, preferably within 2 to 3 days of the fracture. Special consideration is required for polytraumatized patients. A molded posterior splint or overhead traction can be used to stabilize these injured limbs while the more serious systemic injuries are treated.

The surgical strategy is planned preoperatively and depends on the fracture type as determined by good-

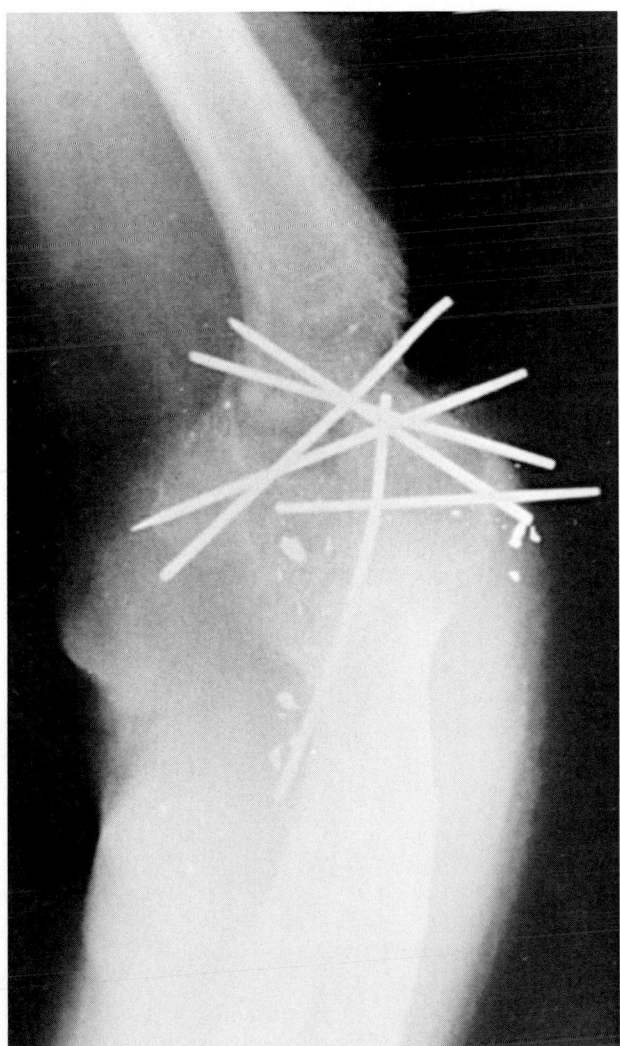

**FIGURE 42–52.** Flexible wire fixation of complex distal humeral fractures does not provide sufficient stability to allow early mobilization and can result in loss of reduction and limited motion.

quality radiographs. A full complement of instrumentation, including plates and screws of differing size, should be available when contemplating surgical stabilization of these fractures. A sterile arm tourniquet, fine dissecting instruments, and a sharp osteotome complete the surgical equipment necessary for these procedures.

General anesthesia is preferred because these surgical procedures can prove lengthy, and an iliac crest bone graft may be required. The lateral decubitus position is a versatile one that allows exposure of the iliac crest and the entire arm[223] without the potential problems incurred with the patient in a prone position[203] (Fig. 42–53). With the patient placed in the lateral position and the sterile tourniquet high on the arm, an 8- to 10-inch roll of folded drapes can be tucked between the arm and the chest wall to suspend the arm for ease of access. Alternatively, a padded bolster may be attached to the table and the arm draped over it.

## OPERATIVE TECHNIQUE

### Surgical Approach

The patient is positioned in the lateral decubitus position with the affected side up and the arm draped over a bolster or folded drapes. Alternatively, the patient can be positioned supinely and the affected arm draped and brought across the chest. A longitudinal incision is made over the posterior aspect of the arm beginning 15 to 20 cm proximal to the tip of the olecranon, curving slightly medially at the elbow to skirt the olecranon, and returning to the midline and extending approximately 5 cm distal to the tip of the olecranon (Fig. 42–54). The ulnar nerve is dissected free for a distance of 6 to 8 cm proximal to the cubital tunnel and 5 cm distal to the cubital tunnel. Because internal fixation is usually necessary in the vicinity of the cubital tunnel and medial epicondyle, the ulnar nerve is transposed anteriorly to the medial epicondyle in the subcutaneous plane. The fascia over the flexor carpi ulnaris is split, and the muscle is divided to allow the nerve to rest without tension in its new position.

The preferred approach to the distal end of the humerus is posterior ("the front door to the elbow is through the back"). This approach provides the best exposure of the joint, is extensile both proximally and distally, and minimizes interference with neurovascular structures. However, the extensor mechanism intervenes and must be dealt with. Essentially, one has two choices for dealing with the extensor mechanism: an osteotomy of the olecranon or a soft tissue procedure of the triceps, which can include splitting or reflecting the triceps insertion. The advantages of osteotomy include unparalleled exposure of the joint and its proven track record, which make it the gold standard against which other approaches must be compared. Disadvantages include the increased time of the procedure, a significant complication rate (delayed union, nonunion), and a high rate of irritation postoperatively from the subcutaneous hardware used to fix the osteotomy.[95] Advantages of the triceps-splitting approach are its technical ease, the ability to use the intact trochlear notch of the proximal end of the ulna as a template against which to gauge fracture reduction and check range of motion, the lack of implanted hardware, and the potential

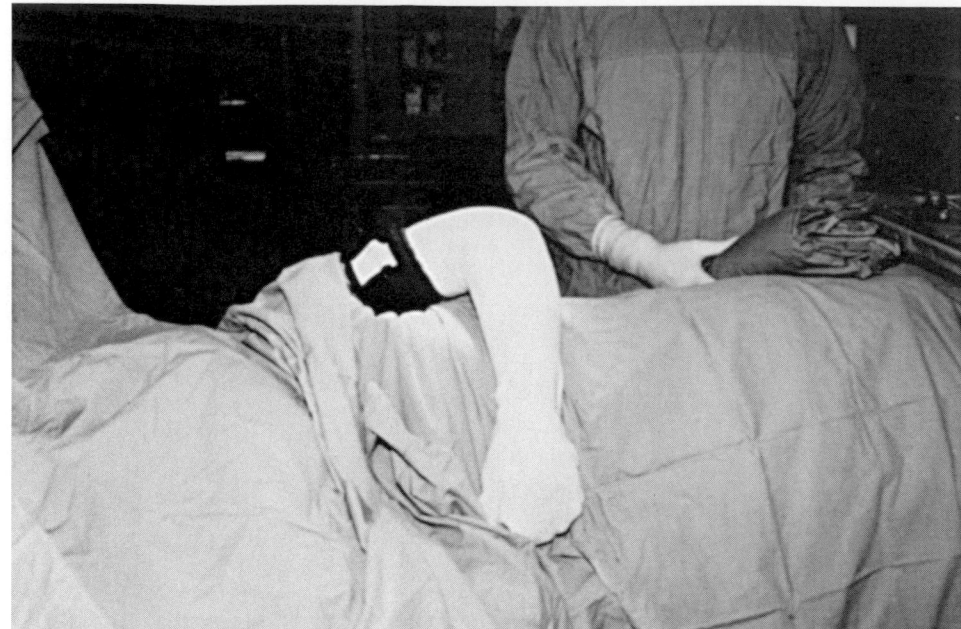

FIGURE 42–53. The lateral decubitus position provides a versatile approach to fractures about the elbow. Exposure of the entire arm as well as the iliac crest is facilitated.

to proceed with elbow arthroplasty (in older patients) if necessary (Fig. 42–55A to D). It was previously thought that splitting the triceps muscle would have a detrimental effect on its strength. However, a recent study by McKee and colleagues compared objectively measured elbow extension strength in 25 patients who had either a triceps-splitting or olecranon osteotomy approach for the treatment of a displaced intra-articular fracture of the distal end of the humerus.[95] No difference was found in elbow extension strength, which was approximately 75% of the opposite intact side in both groups (Fig. 42–56A and B).

At the conclusion of the triceps split or peel, the triceps tendon should be reattached to the olecranon with interrupted, nonabsorbable sutures through drill holes in the bone. Such reattachment helps prevent postoperative detachment of the tendon.

To perform an osteotomy, the triceps insertion is isolated and the distal part of the triceps separated from the adjacent soft tissues. The joint capsule is freed from both sides of the olecranon, with only the attachment of the triceps tendon remaining. Gauze is passed through the trochlear notch of the ulna to act as a suspensory sling and provide countertraction during the course of the olecranon osteotomy. The osteotomy can be performed with either a fine-bladed saw or a sharpened, thin osteotome. If a saw is chosen, the osteotomy should be completed with an osteotome, which will produce a more irregular surface for later reduction and fixation. The osteotomy is directed either perpendicular to the long axis of the shaft of the ulna in a transverse manner or in a chevron fashion with the apex pointing distally. The advantages of the latter are the ease of repositioning after completion of the distal humeral fixation and the broader surface of cancellous bone for more rapid union. Predrilling of the olecranon can be considered if the surgeon chooses to use a large screw such as a 6.5-mm cancellous screw (Fig. 42–57).

Once the osteotomy of the olecranon is completed, the olecranon and triceps are wrapped in moist gauze and retracted proximally to expose the fracture. The fracture surfaces and small fracture fragments are gently débrided of hematoma and irrigated with pulsed lavage to help clear the hematoma atraumatically. At this point, consideration

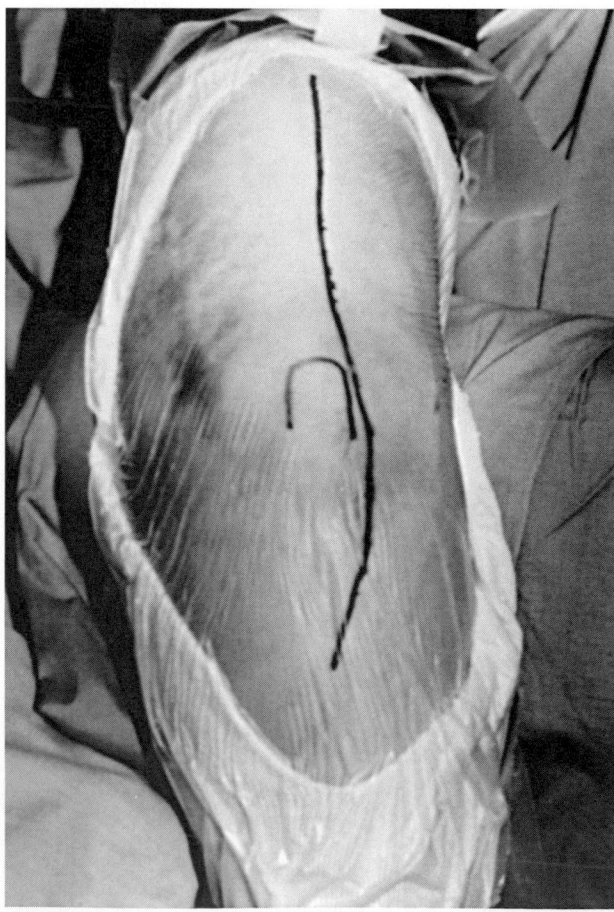

FIGURE 42–54. The skin incision for fractures of the distal part of the humerus is extensile and skirts just around the tip of the olecranon.

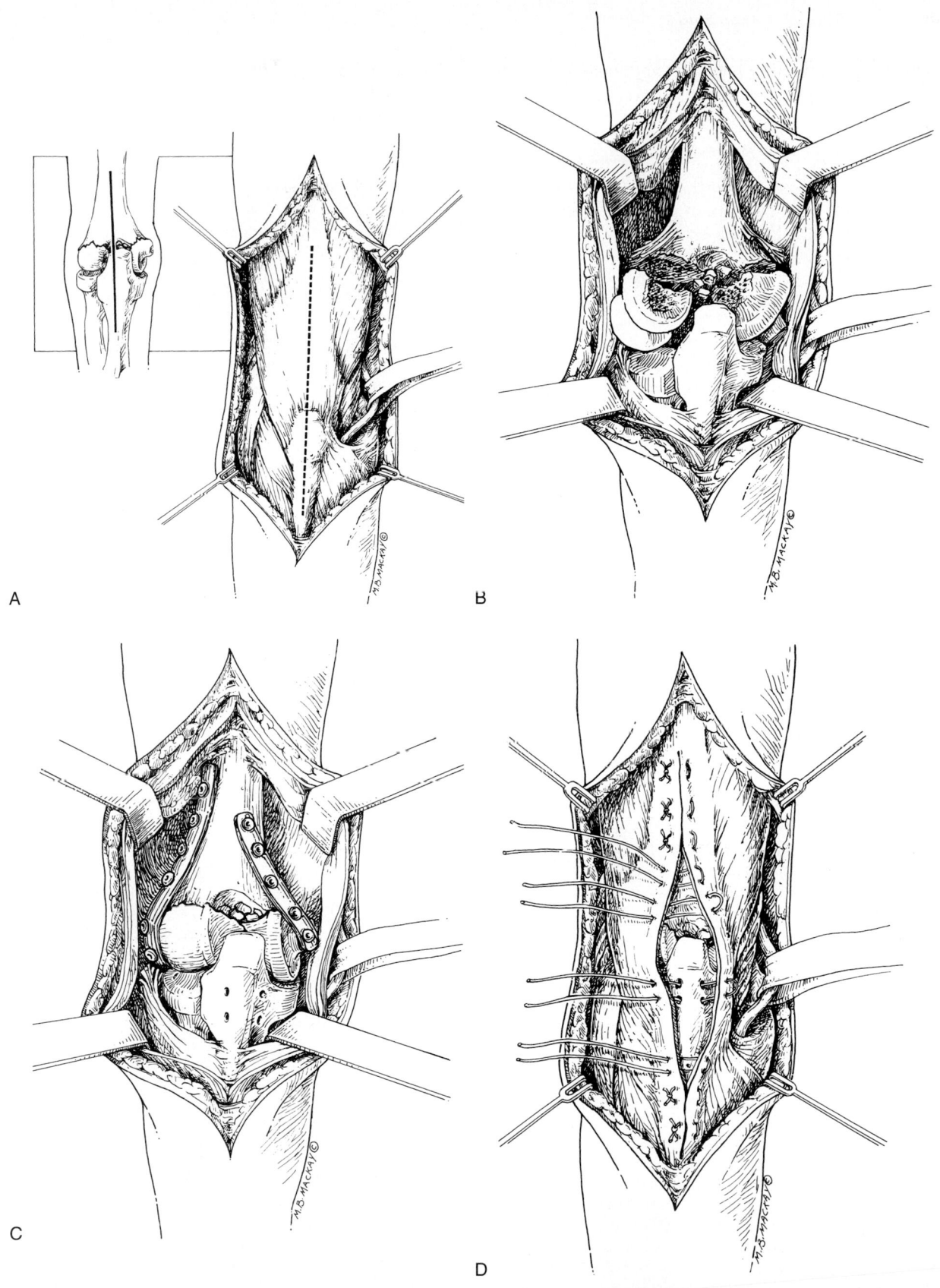

**FIGURE 42–55.** The triceps-splitting procedure for the treatment of distal humeral fractures. *A,* Posterior view of the left elbow after skin incision and subcutaneous dissection. The *dotted line* represents the planned incision through the triceps muscle and tendon. The ulnar nerve is identified and protected throughout the procedure with a Penrose drain. *B,* Exposure of the fracture site after a midline split of the triceps muscle and tendon. It is important to reflect the tendon sharply off the olecranon and preserve a contiguous layer medially and laterally to be reattached at the conclusion of the procedure. Visualization of the anterior aspect of the joint can be improved by flexing the elbow or grasping the olecranon with a towel clip (or both) and pulling posteriorly. *C,* Posterior view of the elbow after fixation of a bicolumnar, intra-articular distal humeral fracture with plates on both the medial and lateral columns. Holes have been drilled through the olecranon for reattachment of the triceps. At this point, elbow range of motion and fracture reduction can be assessed. Because the olecranon is still intact, any narrowing of the trochlear groove (i.e., through overcompression of a comminuted fracture) can be readily determined by extending the elbow and observing olecranon/trochlea articulation. *D,* Closure of the triceps split with interrupted sutures, including sutures placed through drill holes in the olecranon. (From McKee, M.D., et al. J Bone Joint Surg Br 82:1701–1707, 2000.)

is given to the approach to reduction and internal skeletal fixation.

### Fixation

The principle of fixation of these fractures is to anatomically reconstruct and stably secure each side of the distal humeral triangle. It must be remembered that these fractures prove difficult to fix securely for a number of anatomic reasons, including the following:

1. The distal fragments are small and limit the number of screws that can be placed.
2. The distal fragments are cancellous bone, which also presents a problem in gaining stable purchase with screws.

3. The hardware must avoid the articular surfaces and three fossae to maintain full motion.
4. The complex skeletal and articular geometry in this area makes plate contouring difficult.

Although modifications must be made depending on the specific fracture patterns, the principles of internal fixation apply to all fracture types. A standard fixation is illustrated in Figure 42–58. Fractures of the trochlea can be secured with an interfragmentary compression screw. However, the surgeon must be careful to not overcompress the trochlear notch if the fracture is comminuted. In this instance, the screws need to be inserted in a noncompression mode. The trochlear "tie rod" is then reconstructed back onto the medial and lateral columns with plates. A

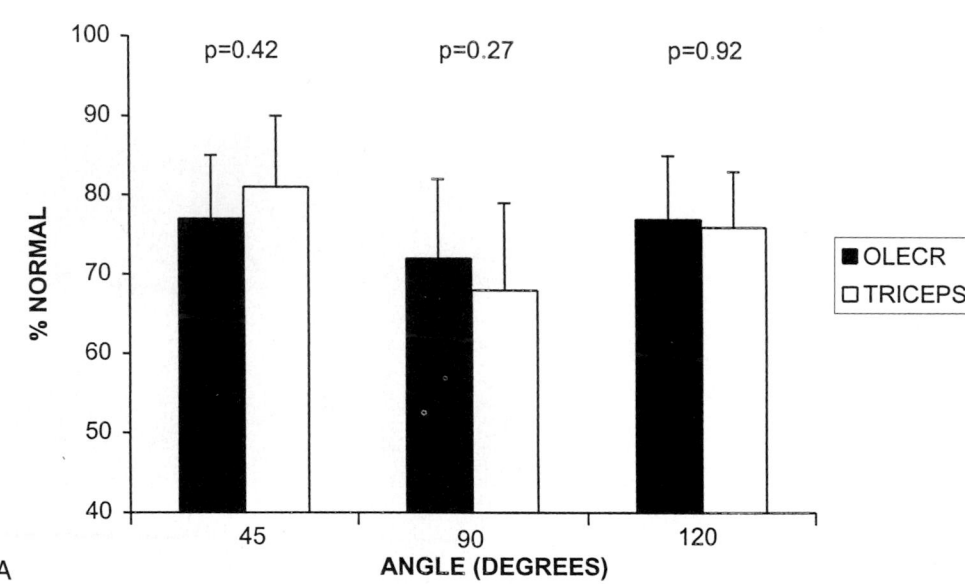

A

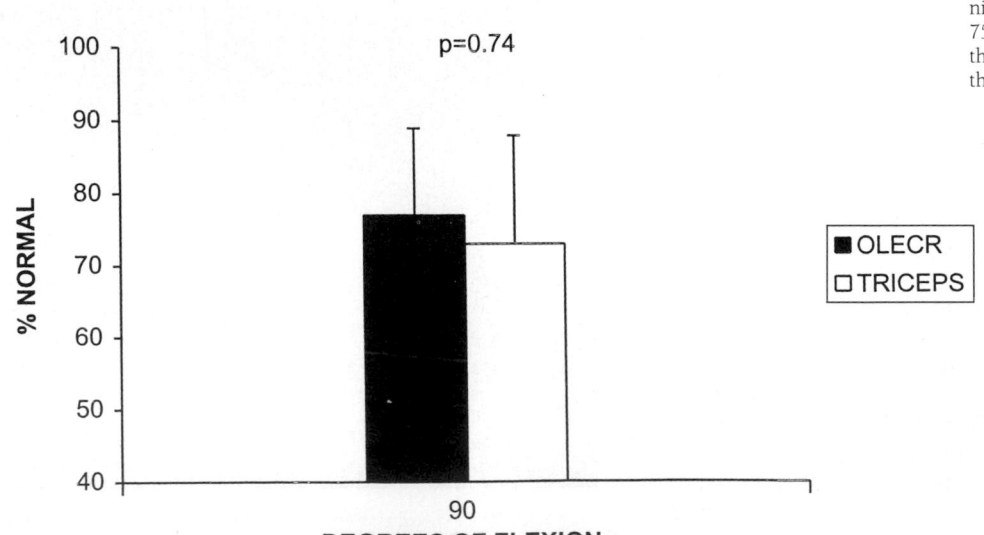

B

FIGURE **42–56.** Objectively measured isometric muscle strength after operative repair of intra-articular distal humeral fractures through a posterior approach involving either an olecranon osteotomy (OLECR) or a triceps-splitting (SPLIT) approach. Values are a percentage of the opposite normal side. *A,* Extension strength at 45°, 90°, and 120° of elbow flexion. No difference is noted between the two groups. *B,* Interestingly, elbow flexion strength has significantly decreased to approximately 75% of normal despite the fact that the elbow flexors are not involved in the surgical approach.

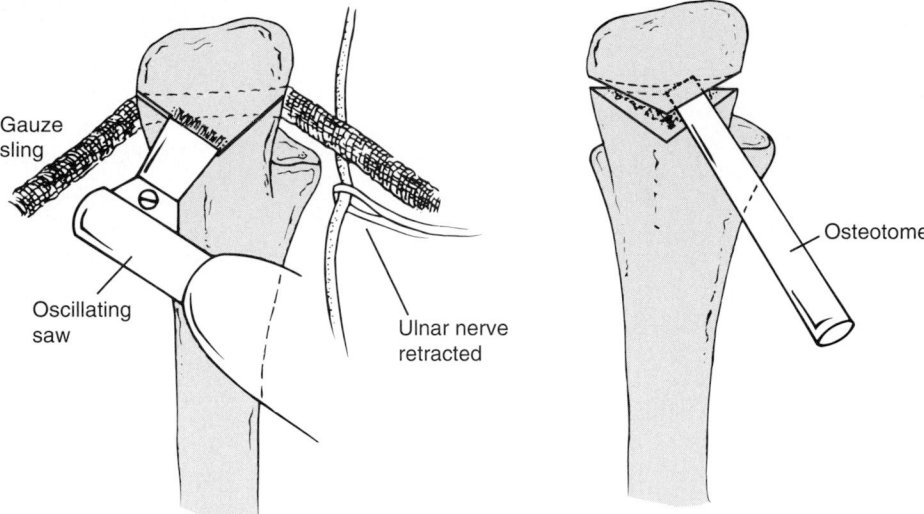

**FIGURE 42–57.** An olecranon osteotomy made in a chevron fashion allows for greater ease in repositioning and provides a broader surface of cancellous bone for healing.

Gauze sling

Oscillating saw

Ulnar nerve retracted

Osteotome

reconstruction plate offers distinct advantages in the distal end of the humerus because it can be bent in three dimensions to match the complex geometry of the distal humeral columns. The medial epicondyle can be "cradled" by a 90° bend in the distal part of the plate (see Fig. 42–45). This bend is achieved by placing two instruments in the adjacent holes at the distal part of the plate and applying torque (Fig. 42–59). Thus, the two distal screws will be perpendicular and provide a mechanical interlocking construct, the strength of which exceeds the combined pull-out strength of each of the screw threads.

The lateral plate is applied as distally as possible until it almost abuts the posterior border of the capitellar cartilage. The most distal screw is directed proximally to avoid the capitellum and to provide a mechanical interlocking construct (Fig. 42–60). The biomechanical strength of the plates is improved by placing them 90° to each other. If both plates are positioned posteriorly such that the weak dimension of the plate is in the plane of motion of the elbow, fatigue failure of the plate or plates can occur should fracture healing at the metaphyseal-diaphyseal junction be delayed. This result is more likely if two pelvic reconstruction plates or weaker one-third tubular plates are used.

The order of fixation varies and must be tailored to the individual fracture pattern. At times, it may be advisable to fix the longer fracture planes first, which ordinarily involves one of the columns. One other basic principle that should be maintained is to contour the plates and fix them in a distal-to-proximal direction because the distal plate position is the most critical to maximize distal screw purchase. Precontoured plates can also be used to help "cradle" smaller distal bony fragments or to maintain position of the fragments when bone quality and screw purchase are poor[252] (Fig. 42–61). The precontoured "J" or Dupont plate designed for the lateral column is especially useful in severely comminuted fractures. When anatomic reconstruction is not possible, the lateral column can be matched to fit the plate, which helps re-create the

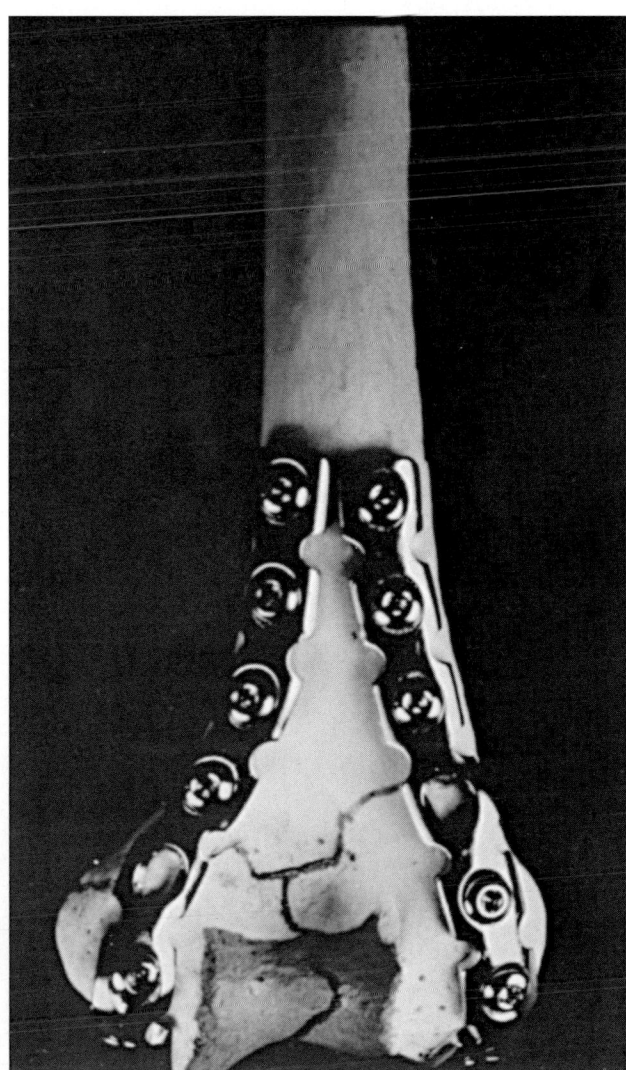

**FIGURE 42–58.** Two-column fixation of the distal end of the radius with contoured 3.5-mm reconstruction plates.

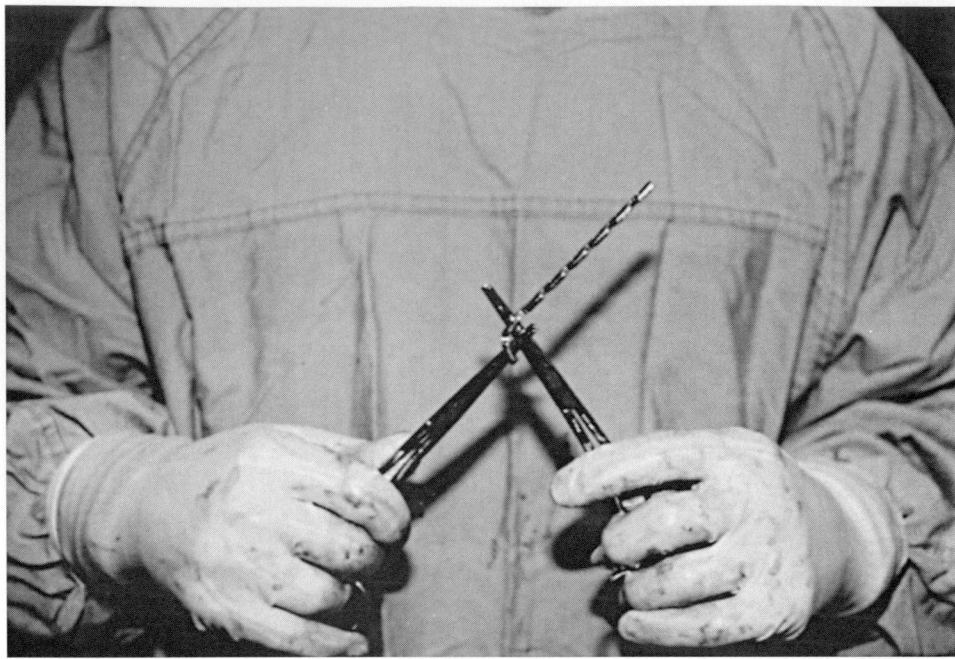

FIGURE **42–59.** A reconstruction plate can be bent by placing two Kocher clamps in the distal two holes.

natural anterior curvature of the lateral column of the distal end of the humerus (Fig. 42–62A to C).

### Fixation of Specific Fracture Types

**High T Fracture.** A high T fracture is the simplest to securely fix because the distal fragments are relatively large. The vertical fracture line is the longest, so it is generally fixed first with a transverse lag screw (Fig. 42–63).

**Low T Fracture.** A low T fracture is the most common, and a particular problem is often fixation of the lateral fragment. For this reason, the medial column is ordinarily fixed first because this column proves to be the most straightforward to fix. The medial column can be secured to the lateral column by a long malleolar screw placed through the distal plate hole, with purchase achieved more proximally in the lateral column. The lateral column can be secured with a plate that is twisted sagittally around the lateral column (Fig. 42–64).

**Y Fracture.** The oblique fracture planes permit interfragmentary compression screws. In a Y fracture, plates have to function only as neutralization plates (Fig. 42–65).

**H Fracture.** In principle, the trochlear fragment must be realigned onto the distal columns. The three distal fragments are reduced with pointed reduction forceps onto

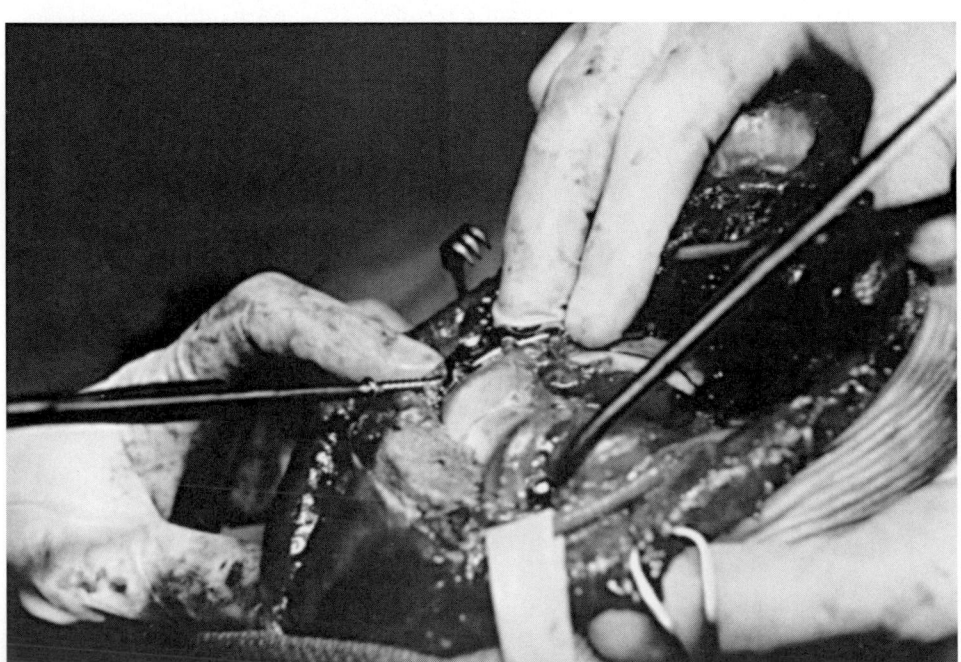

FIGURE **42–60.** The plate on the posterior aspect of the lateral column can extend distally onto the posterior aspect of the distal column.

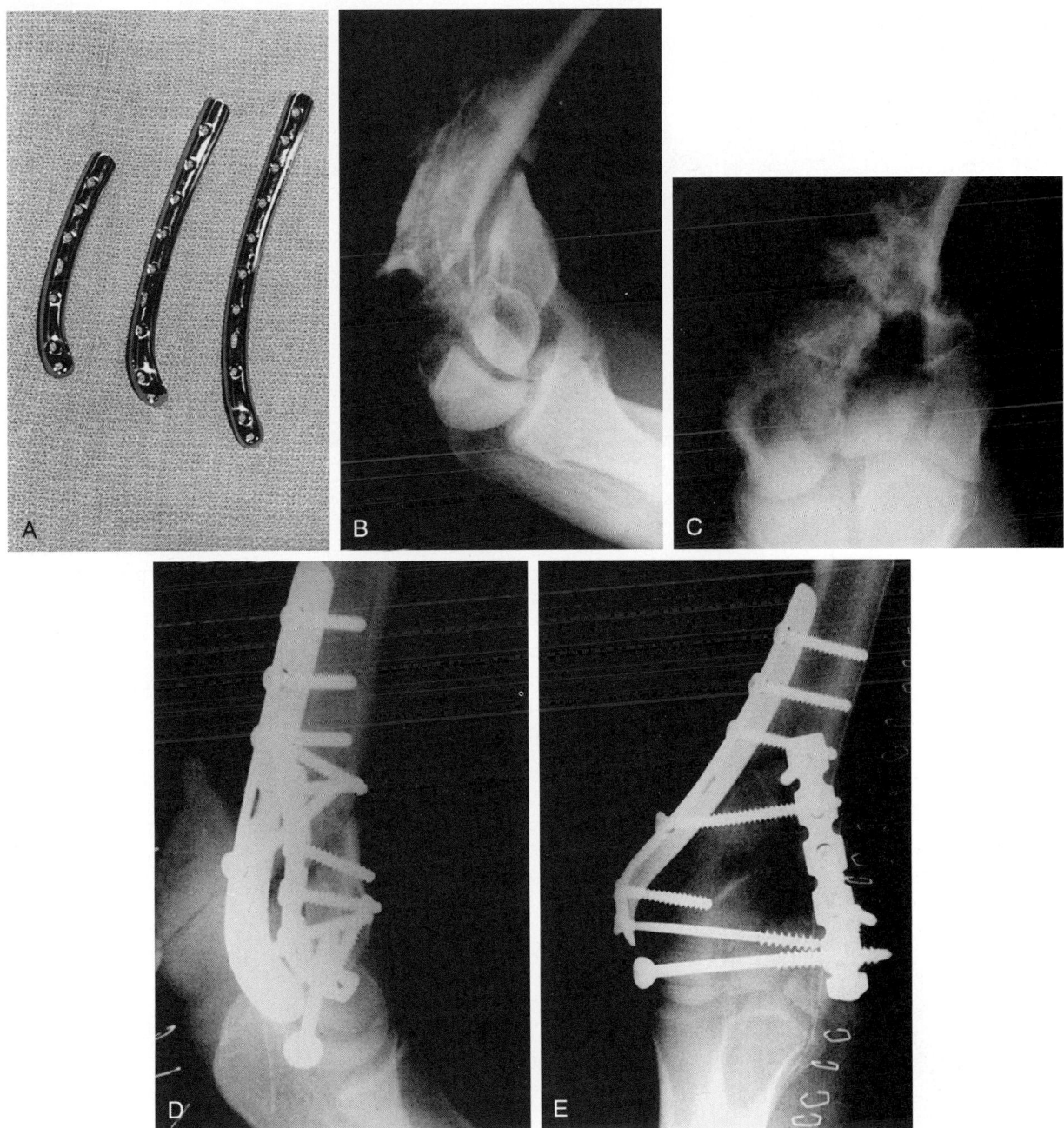

**FIGURE 42–61.** *A,* The "Dupont" plate is a precontoured lateral column plate designed for comminuted distal humeral fractures. This plate is useful in that it allows the distal lateral column of the humerus to be reconstructed to the plate, thus correctly reestablishing the proper curvature of the distal lateral column and capitellum. *B, C,* Preoperative radiographs of a comminuted, high-energy distal humeral fracture. *D, E,* Postoperative radiographs showing application of the precontoured "Dupont" plate.

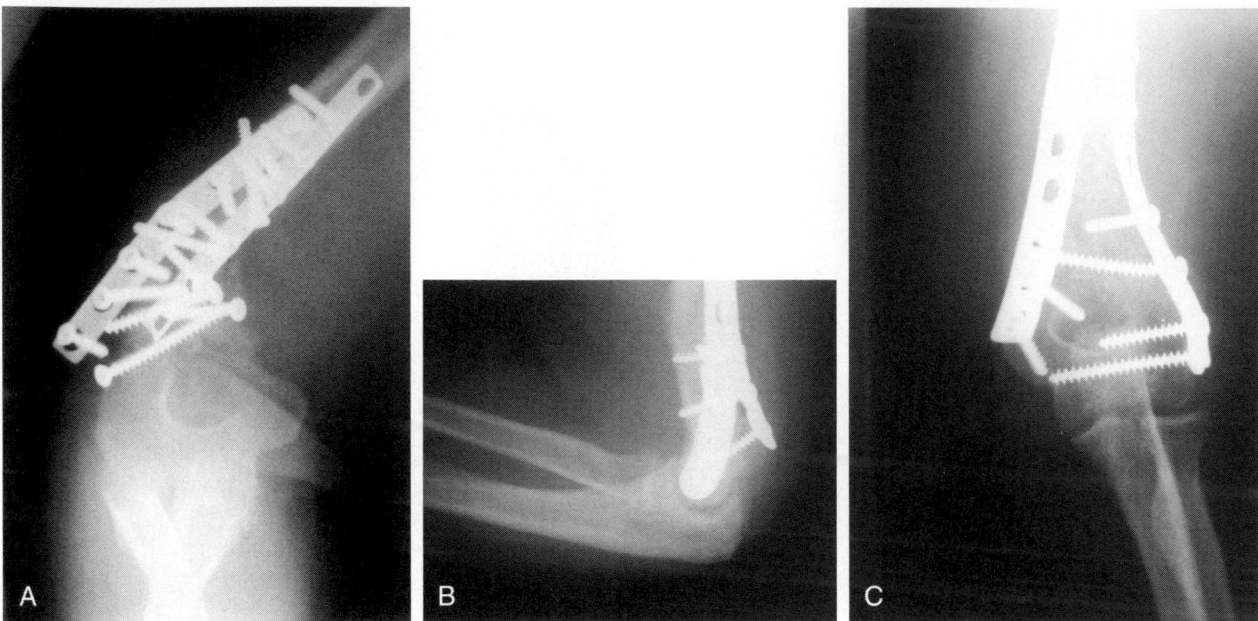

**Figure 42–62.** *A,* Anteroposterior radiograph of early fixation failure after operative repair of a distal humeral fracture. The plate fixation does not extend far enough distally. *B, C,* Solid healing after salvage with a precontoured "Dupont" plate laterally and limited-contact dynamic compression plate medially. The rigidity and precontoured design of the plate are useful in the revision situation when exact anatomic reconstruction of the fracture fragments is obscured by time and previous surgery.

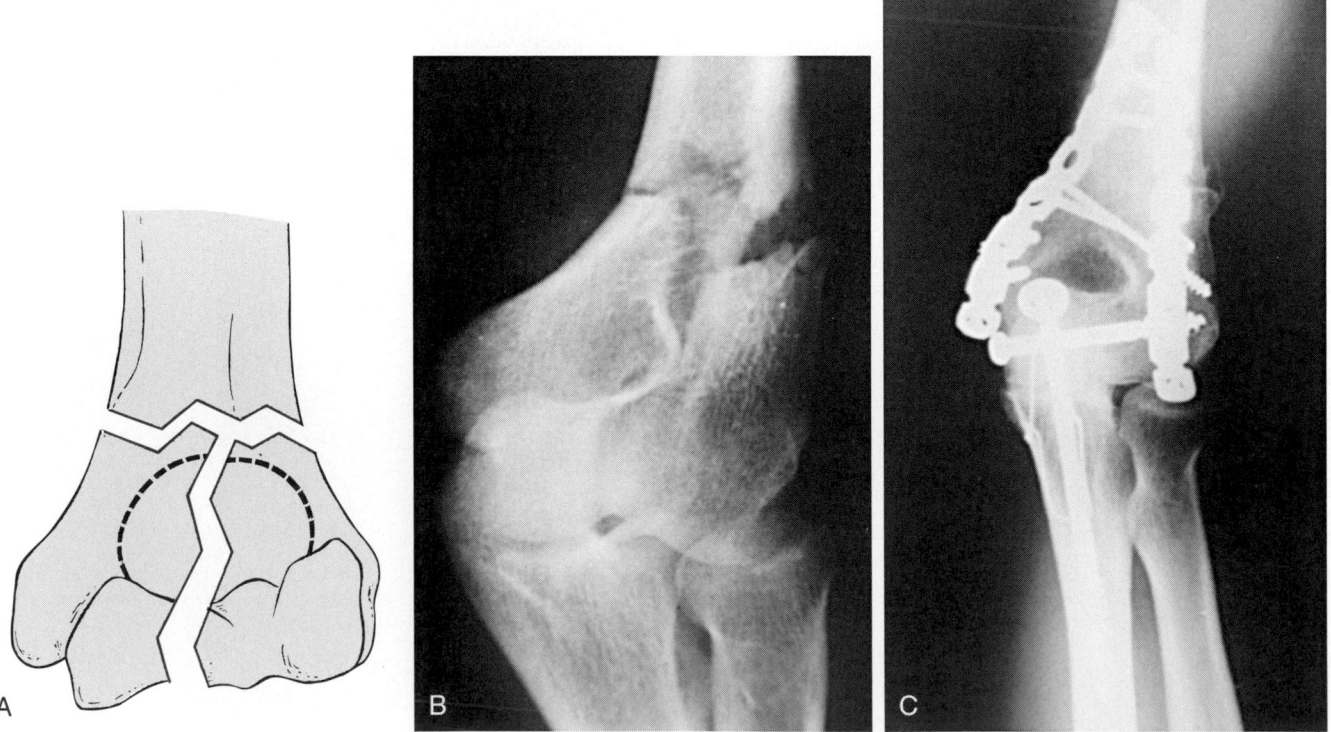

**Figure 42–63.** *A–C,* A high T fracture is the most straightforward bicolumn fracture to secure with internal fixation because the distal fragments are large.

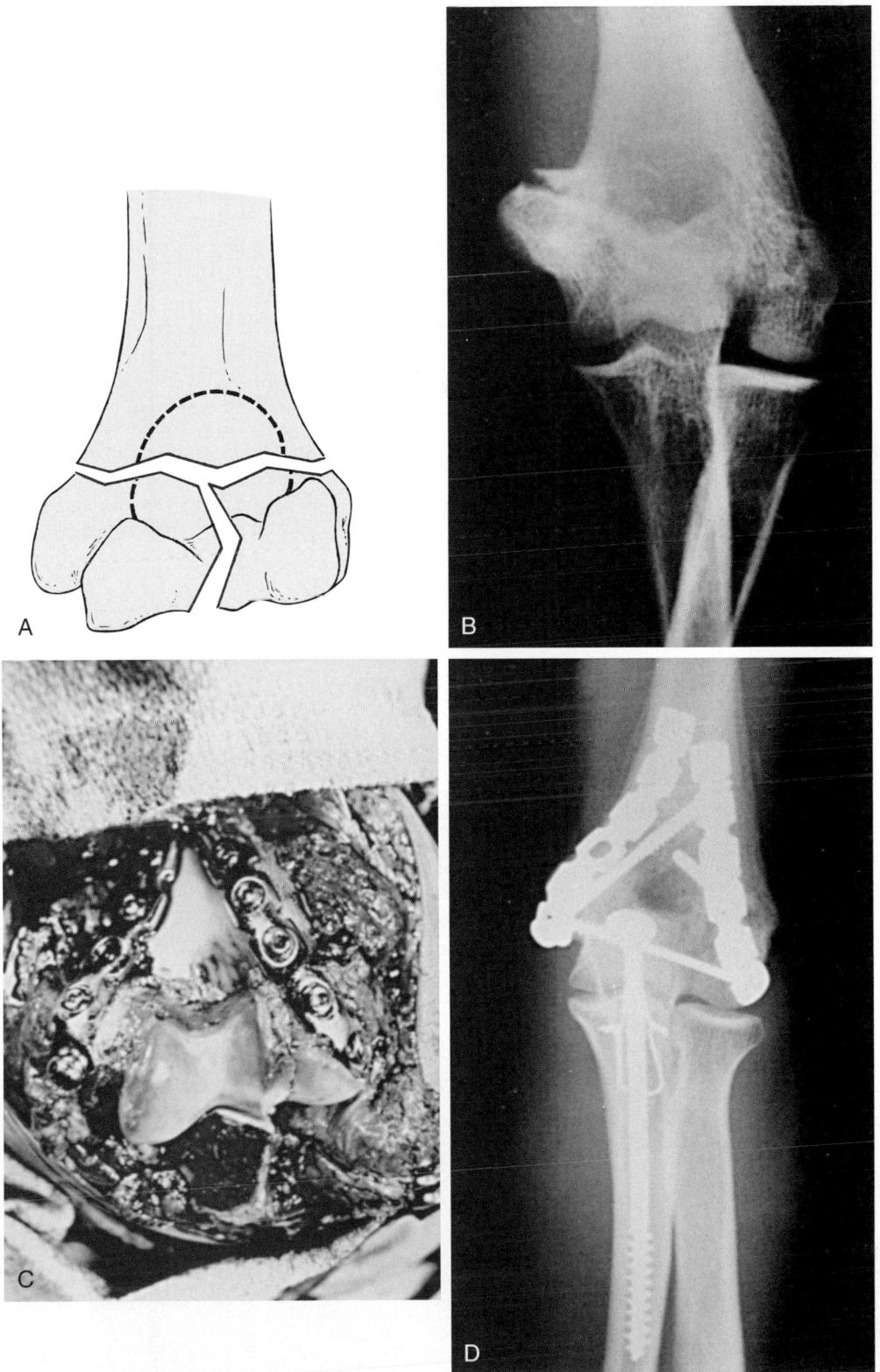

**FIGURE 42–64.** *A, B,* Low T bicolumn fracture. *C,* Intraoperative view of internal fixation of a low T fracture. Note that both plates extend distally along the columns of the distal end of the humerus. *D,* Radiograph of internal fixation of a low T bicolumn fracture.

the two upper columns. A temporary transverse K-wire is helpful in stabilizing the trochlea and preventing displacement of the fragments when the interfragmentary 4.0- or 6.5-mm screw is introduced. The medial and lateral columns are secured in the previously described manner (Fig. 42–66).

**Medial λ Fracture.** The difficulty with a medial λ fracture is the minimal purchase area available in the lateral fragment. Additionally, the medial trochlear fragment is too small for screw purchase, such as what can be done with low T fractures. The lateral column can be secured with two 4.0-mm screws to bring the capitellum to the medial column and achieve distal transverse fixation. Two lateral 4.0-mm screws then secure the same fragment to the lateral plate to provide fixation of the entire lateral column. The medial column is secured with a standard 3.5-mm reconstruction plate (Fig. 42–67).

**Lateral λ Fracture.** In lateral λ fractures, the trochlea is a free fragment, as in the H fracture, but the medial column is intact; therefore, effort can be directed primarily toward securing the trochlear fragment onto the medial column. Standard plate fixation may be used on the medial column. The two distal holes of the plate are overdrilled with a 3.5-mm drill bit to allow passage of 4.0-mm cancellous screws. The distal plate can be twisted sagittally to place the two distal screw holes onto the medial aspect of the trochlea. The two 4.0-mm screws are then directed transversely through the plate holes into the trochlea and the capitellum. Both screws secure the plate and lag the distal fragments together. The proximal portion of this plate is secured to the medial column in standard fashion. Lateral-column fractures of this type can readily be fixed with standard plate technique (Fig. 42–68).

**Multiplane Fracture.** This unique fracture pattern described by Jupiter and associates consists of a well-recognized T-type distal humeral fracture with the added component of a coronal fracture of the anterior aspect of the trochlea.[206] Thus, fracture lines are located in the transverse, sagittal, and coronal planes (Fig. 42–69). The fractures were fixed through a posterior approach by osteotomy of the olecranon. The coronal portion of the fracture was fixed with Herbert screws countersunk into the articular cartilage of the trochlea. The sagittal component of the fracture was then fixed with interfragmentary screws and the articular assembly fixed to the bony columns with 3.5-mm reconstruction plates. This rigid fixation allowed early motion in each case, which contributed to the good results seen in their series (100% union, no avascular necrosis, average arc of motion of 104°).[206]

**Open Fractures of the Distal End of the Humerus.** Although treating intra-articular fractures of the distal end of the humerus is inherently challenging, the complication rate and complexity of the injury increase significantly when such fractures are associated with soft tissue wounds. Open fractures in this area are typically a result of high-energy trauma such as motor vehicle accidents, industrial injuries, and falls from a height. Associated injuries are often found in the same limb and can influence management, as do the nature and location of the open wound.

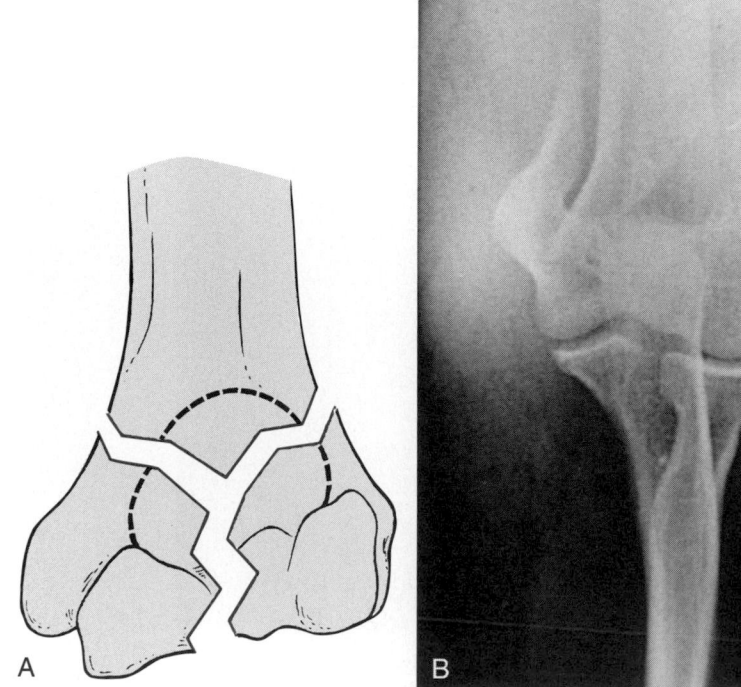
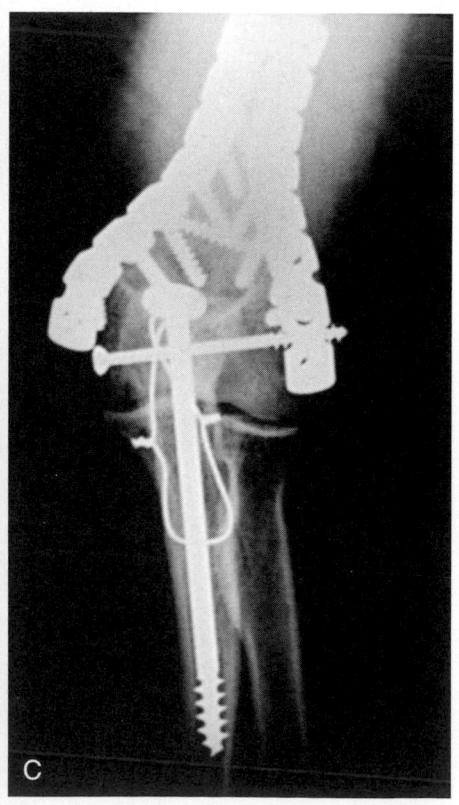

FIGURE 42–65. *A, B,* A Y bicolumn fracture has oblique fracture planes that permit intrafragmentary compression of screws across the fracture line. *C,* Stable fixation of a Y bicolumn fracture.

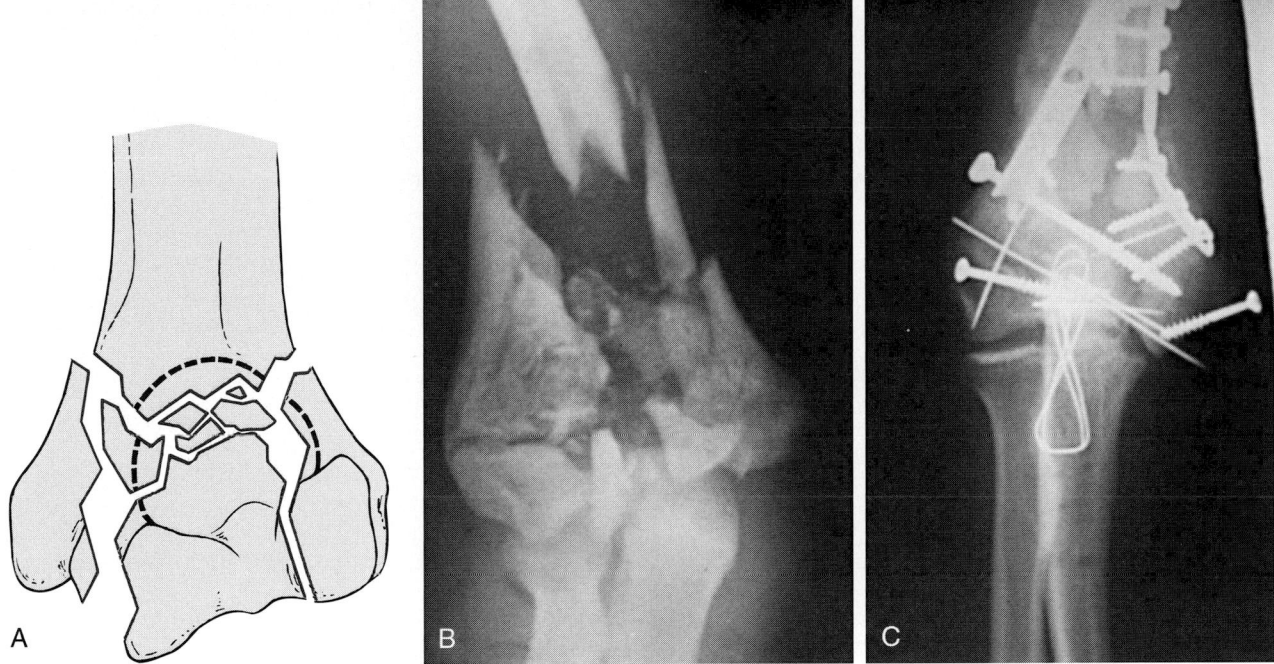

**FIGURE 42–66.** *A, B,* An H fracture is the most complex of the bicolumn fractures. *C,* Stability was achieved with internal fixation. Final elbow motion was 125° of flexion and 40° of extension.

The open wound is usually made by the sharp end of the humeral shaft as the condyles fracture off and the sharp projection of the distal end of the humerus pierces the surrounding soft tissue. If the wound is anterior, the brachial artery and median nerve are at risk, and a careful neurovascular examination should be performed. Although anterior wounds are commonly seen in children with an extension type of injury, recent studies have suggested that posterior wounds are more likely in adults and are usually produced as a result of a direct blow on the flexed elbow or sustained as the elbow flexes from a fall on the hand.

A posterior wound has significance in terms of treatment. To pierce the skin on the posterior aspect of the

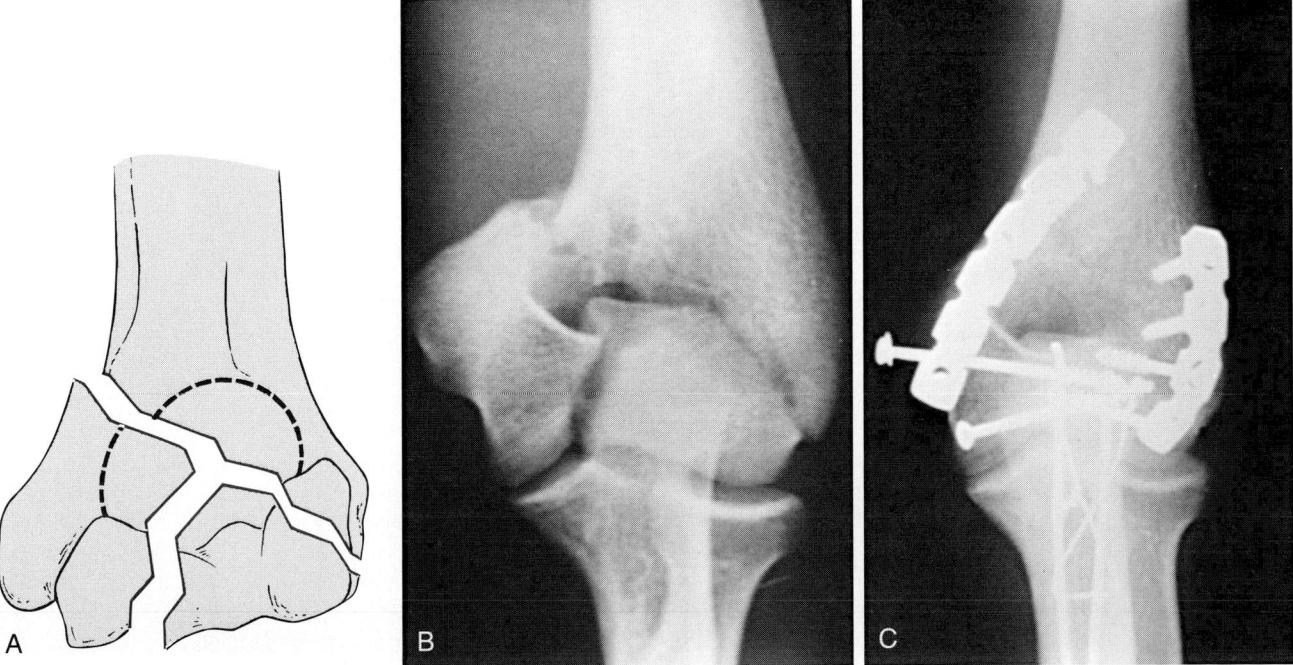

**FIGURE 42–67.** *A, B,* Medial λ bicolumn fracture. *C,* Internal fixation of a medial λ bicolumn fracture.

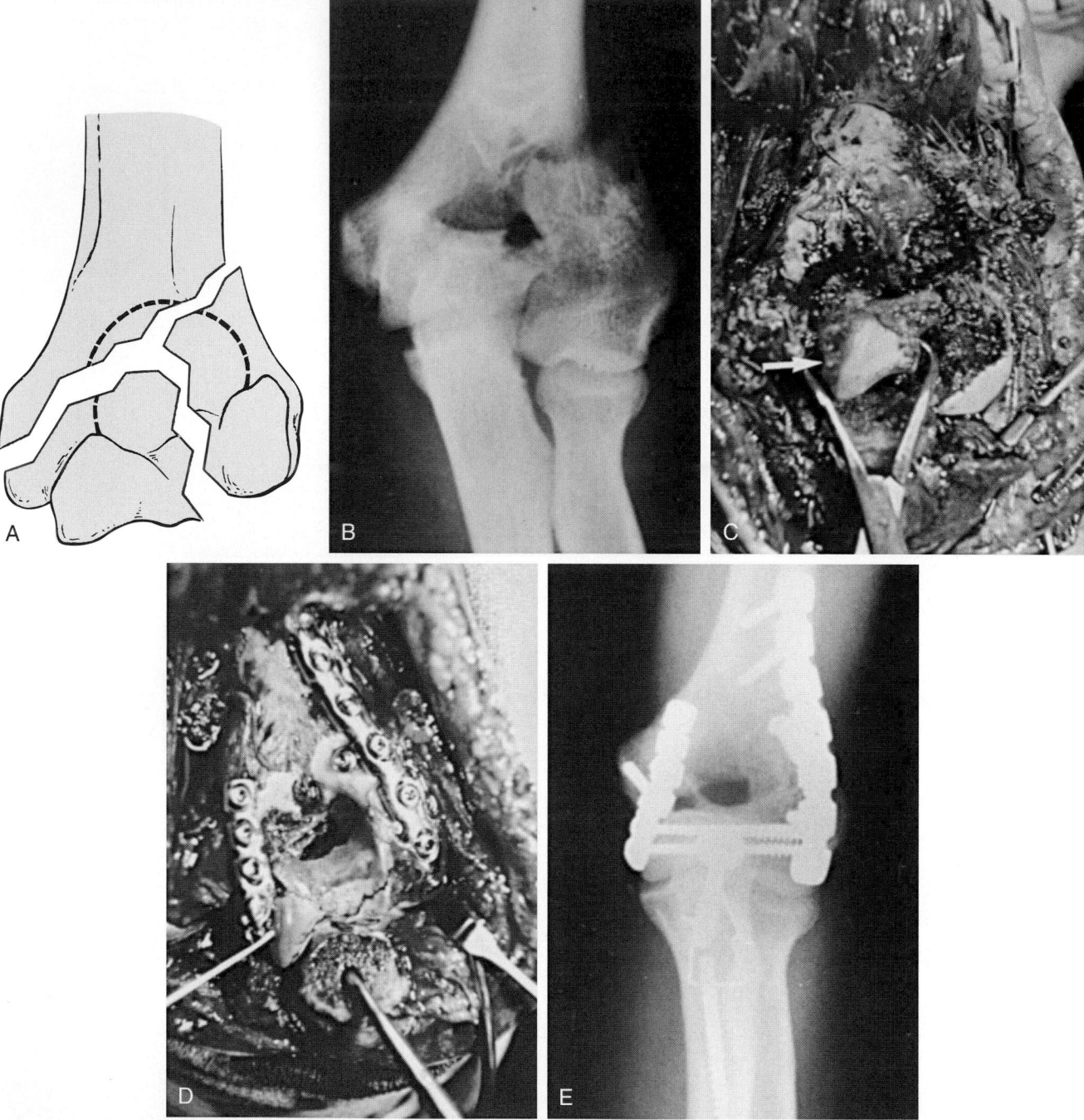

**FIGURE 42–68.** *A, B,* Lateral λ bicolumn fracture. *C,* Intraoperative view of the trochlea *(arrow)* held with a pointed clamp. It is completely devoid of soft tissue attachment. *D,* Intraoperative view of a lateral λ fracture after reassembling trochlear fragments and securing the construct back to the humeral column. *E,* Radiograph of internal fixation of a lateral λ fracture.

elbow, the shaft must have traversed the triceps muscle or tendon. If such is the case, it is logical to use the rent or defect in the triceps and incorporate it into the approach rather than violating the extensor mechanism a second time with an olecranon osteotomy immediately adjacent to the injury. In a similar vein, a significant amount of impacted dirt and debris may be found in the end of the humerus, which should therefore be carefully cleaned and débrided.

Few reports in the literature have described this specific injury. McKee and coauthors reported on 26 open intra-articular fractures of the distal end of the humerus treated with immediate irrigation, débridement, and ORIF through a posterior approach.[91] The infection rate was 11%, although only one patient required a reoperation for infection. The 13 patients who had a triceps split with incorporation of any triceps defect into the approach had better Disabilities of the Arm, Shoulder, and Hand (DASH; 18 versus 30, $P = .06$) and Mayo Elbow Performance (85 versus 74, $P = .05$) scores, with a trend toward improved range of motion (102° versus 92°), than did those who had an olecranon osteotomy. Their conclusion was that immediate ORIF was a safe and reliable method and that the triceps-splitting approach was superior to the olecranon osteotomy approach (Fig. 42–70A to C). Mostafavi and Tornetta reported good results with external fixation for open fractures of the humeral shaft and distal end of the humerus caused primarily by gunshots. However, although this technique allows realignment of frac-

tures with no or little intra-articular displacement, it is not conducive to the reconstruction of comminuted intra-articular fractures.[233]

### Total-Elbow Arthroplasty for Distal Humeral Fractures

As the clinical results and techniques associated with total-elbow arthroplasty (TEA) are refined, investigators are attempting to determine the role of TEA in the

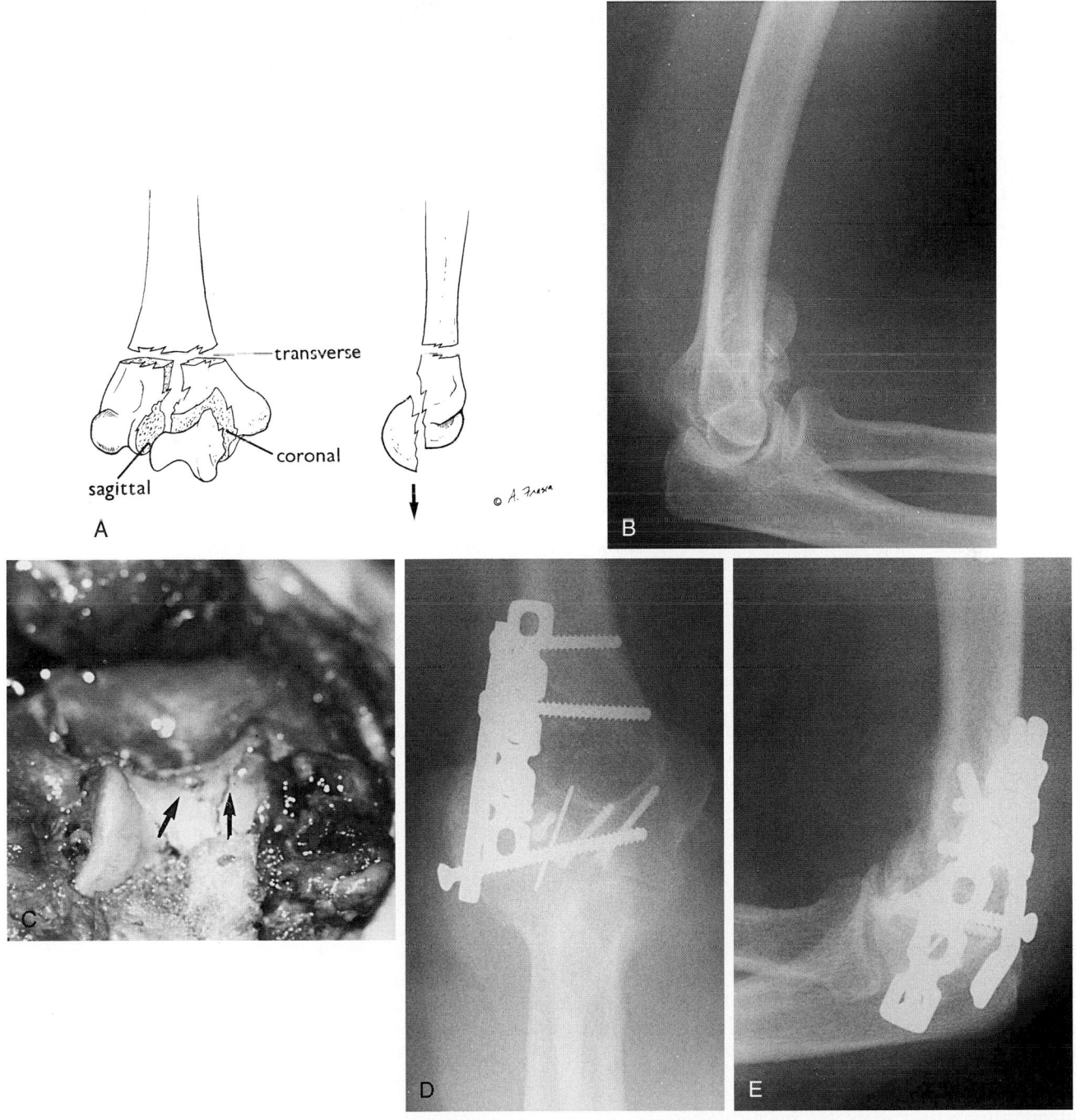

**FIGURE 42–69.** *A,* Schematic of a multiplane fracture of the distal end of the humerus that includes fracture lines in the sagittal, coronal, and transverse planes. A free segment of the trochlea is created in the coronal plane. *B,* A 59-year-old woman fell on her outstretched hand and sustained this complex intra-articular fracture of the distal part of the humerus. *C,* An intraoperative view clearly shows the coronal split of the trochlea secured with two Herbert screws *(arrows).* A plate and corticocancellous graft were placed along the lateral column. *D, E,* Stable fixation was achieved with a good functional result 1 year after surgery.

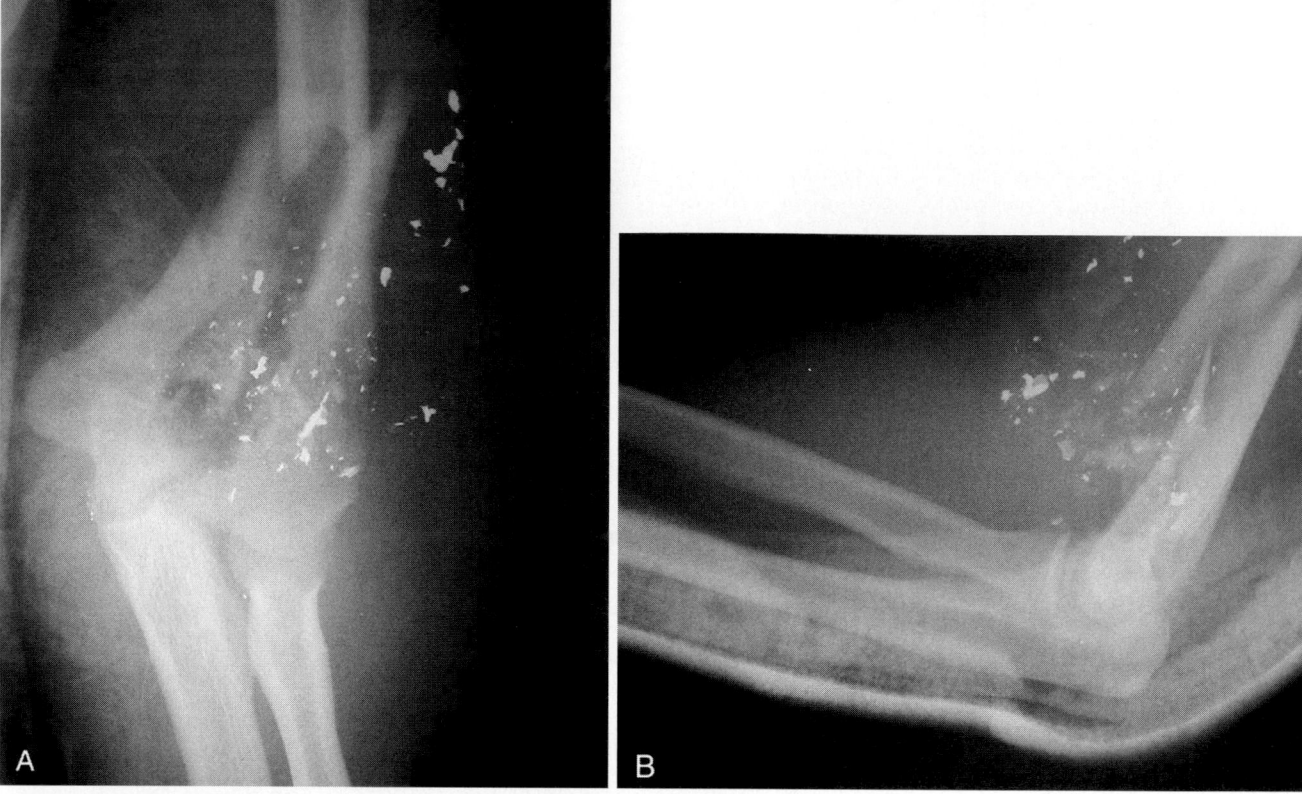

**FIGURE 42–70.** *A, B,* Preoperative anteroposterior and lateral radiographs of a supracondylar humeral fracture caused by a gunshot with an associated radial nerve palsy. From the track of the bullet, a defect in the triceps was anticipated.

treatment of acute fractures of the distal end of the humerus.[235] Like joint replacement for other periarticular fractures (shoulder, hip), TEA has several advantages when dealing with comminuted fractures in osteoporotic bone or in patients with preexisting elbow pathology (Fig. 42–71). It allows for immediate motion, provides immediate stability, and eliminates the potential complications of nonunion, malunion, and avascular necrosis. Because of the lack of bony support usually found with these fractures, a semiconstrained prosthesis is preferable to a resurfacing arthroplasty. This option should be considered for older, low-demand patients when preoperative radiographs lead the treating surgeon to suspect that either poor bone quality or fracture comminution will make conventional fixation extremely difficult (Fig. 42–72A to D).

This technique should be restricted to surgeons with extensive experience in performing elbow arthroplasty for elective elbow reconstruction. A triceps-reflecting approach rather than an olecranon osteotomy should be used if it is contemplated that the fracture is so comminuted that TEA may be necessary. Otherwise, an olecranon osteotomy may compromise the insertion and stability of the ulnar component. Moreover, it is possible in this situation to perform TEA without detaching the triceps from the olecranon. Because it has been shown that the humeral condyles may be safely resected without affecting the longevity or stability of the (semiconstrained) prosthesis, it is advantageous to remove the distal fracture

fragments and create a "working space" distally. This technique allows insertion of the humeral and ulnar components by simply reflecting the triceps from the distal end of the humerus and leaving the triceps insertion intact (Fig. 42–73A to E). This measure further decreases operative time, posterior pain, and swelling and essentially eliminates the possibility of triceps dehiscence.

Another significant concern regarding humeral condylar resection in the setting of acute fractures is the possible negative effect that it would have on forearm, wrist, and hand strength from loss of the bony origins of the flexor pronator mass and the common extensors. This effect can be minimized by reattachment of these structures in a continuous sleeve to the proximal soft tissue during closure. A recent study involving objective muscle strength testing in a group of 32 patients with TEA by McKee and associates did not show any significant differences in forearm rotation or wrist or grip strength between patients with and without condylar resection.[93] Both groups had forearm and grip strength that was approximately 70% of the normal, uninvolved side.

Apart from a number of technique-related articles, at the present time only two reports have described the use of this technique. Cobb and Morrey reported on 21 elbows that had sustained intra-articular distal humeral fractures and were treated with semiconstrained TEA.[21] They had 15 excellent and 5 good results with only 1 revision at a mean of 3.3 years postoperatively. It should be noted that

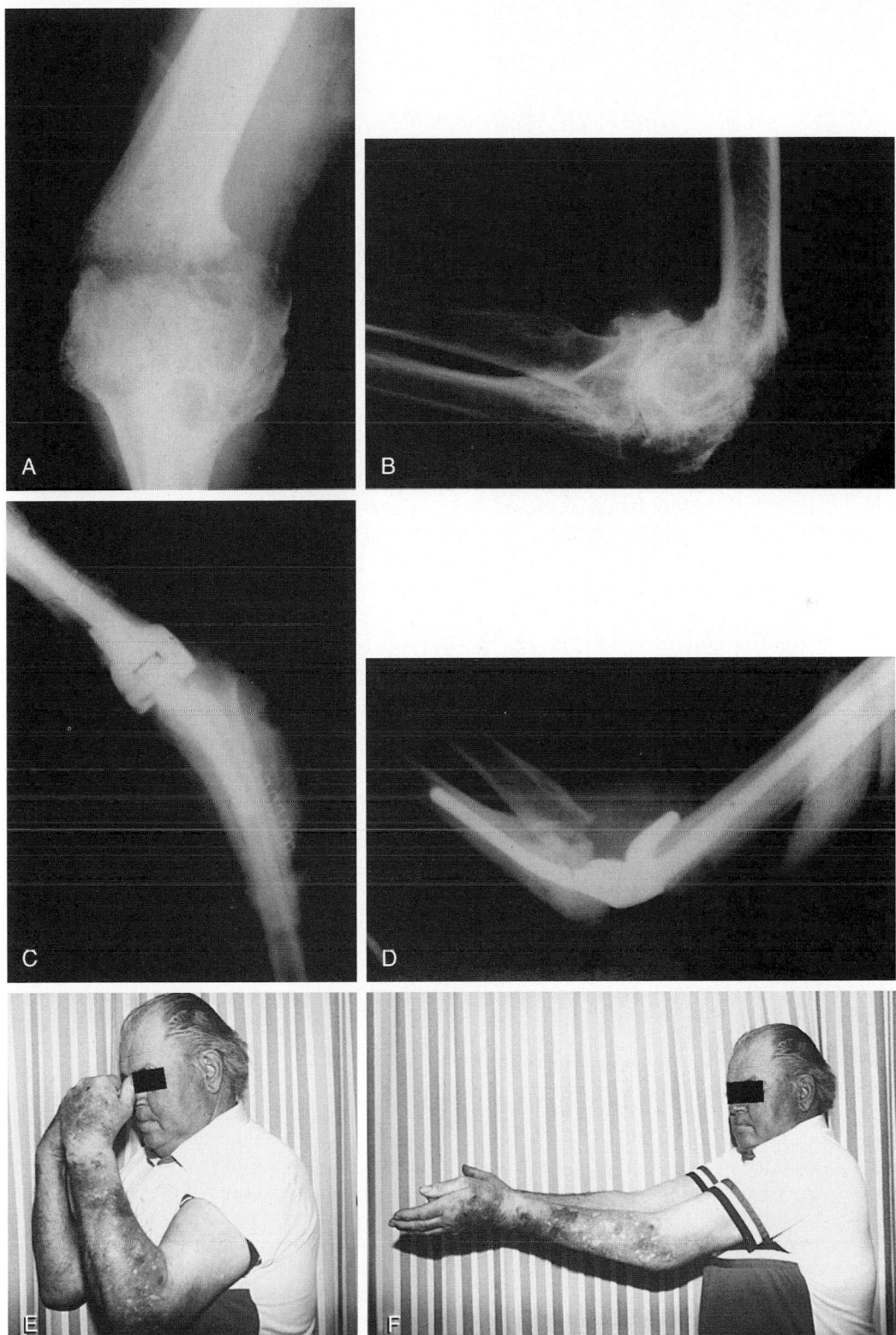

**FIGURE 42–71.** A 55-year-old farmer had a long history of pain and stiffness in his left elbow. The patient subsequently fell onto his outstretched arm and suffered immediate pain in his elbow. *A, B,* Preoperative anteroposterior and lateral radiographs reveal severe arthritic change in the elbow with an accompanying supracondylar distal humeral fracture. Fixation of the fracture would leave the patient with a painful elbow and place severe stress on the fixation because of the adjacent stiff joint. *C, D,* Postoperative radiographs reveal a semiconstrained total-elbow arthroplasty in good position. This design of the elbow arthroplasty is especially advantageous in that it allows for resection of the entire distal humeral fragment without compromising elbow stability. This result would not have been possible with an unconstrained design. *E, F,* Postoperative function showing pain-free, improved elbow flexion/extension. Rotation was normal.

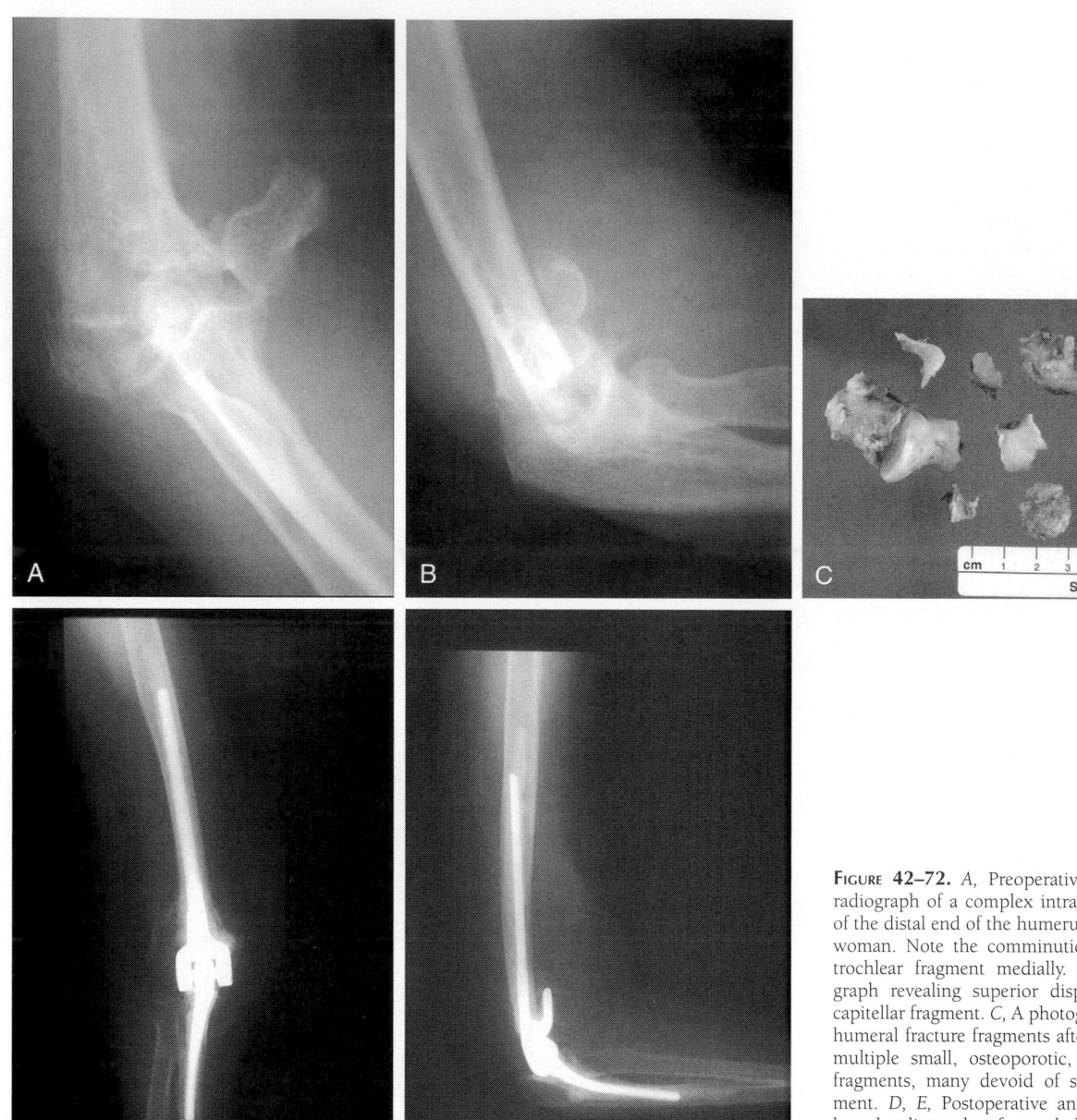

**FIGURE 42–72.** *A,* Preoperative anteroposterior radiograph of a complex intra-articular fracture of the distal end of the humerus in a 75-year-old woman. Note the comminution and displaced trochlear fragment medially. *B,* Lateral radiograph revealing superior displacement of the capitellar fragment. *C,* A photograph of the distal humeral fracture fragments after excision shows multiple small, osteoporotic, cartilage-covered fragments, many devoid of soft tissue attachment. *D, E,* Postoperative anteroposterior and lateral radiographs of a total-elbow arthroplasty. A semiconstrained design is important in this case because of loss of the usual bony and soft tissue stabilizers.

these were relatively "low-demand" patients with a mean age of 72 years and half had rheumatoid arthritis. In the only comparative study, Frankle and colleagues reported on a series of 24 elderly women (mean age of 73 years) with displaced intra-articular fractures of the distal end of the humerus, half of whom underwent ORIF and half of whom were treated with semiconstrained TEA.[38] The results (as measured by the Mayo Elbow Performance Score) were superior in the TEA group (11 excellent, 1 good) when compared with the ORIF group (4 excellent, 4 good, 1 fair, 3 poor), and 3 patients in the ORIF group required revision to TEA. However, both these studies were retrospective. A properly conducted prospective randomized trial comparing TEA and ORIF would be

ideal. At present, it would appear that TEA is a technique with a great deal of promise for the treatment of displaced intra-articular fractures of the distal end of the humerus, although its exact role remains to be defined.

**Reattachment of the Olecranon Osteotomy.** The olecranon osteotomy can be secured either with a 6.5-mm screw placed over a washer (see Olecranon Fractures), as well as incorporation of a tension band wire, or with two K-wires. One must be cautious when using 6.5-mm screws in individuals with excessively large or narrow ulnar canals. In the former, the screw may not obtain good purchase, especially in older individuals with poor cancellous bone, and in the latter, the screw may bind between the two cortices before fully seating and consequently leaving it standing proud. In either situation, a K-wire/ tension band technique is preferred. The surgeon should be able to put the elbow through a full range of motion without obstruction by hardware or demonstration of fracture instability (Fig. 42–74). A small suction drain is placed in the depths of the wound, and the wound is closed in layers. A sterile, bulky, soft dressing and a posterior molded splint are applied. The drain can be removed 24 hours postoperatively, and the patient can be started on a program of active exercises as soon as the wound appears stable. Immobilization should be consid-

ered for comfort only. A sling can provide sufficient stabilization and avoid the potential postoperative stiffness that may come from prolonged immobilization. The patient can rest the elbow on a padded tabletop, concentrate on relaxing the biceps muscle, and let the elbow extend over a period of 15 to 20 seconds. Extension is alternated with active flexion, also exerted over a 15- to 20-second period.

As radiographs demonstrate bone healing, usually within 4 to 6 weeks, the patient is permitted to perform active extension exercises and to slowly add resistance to

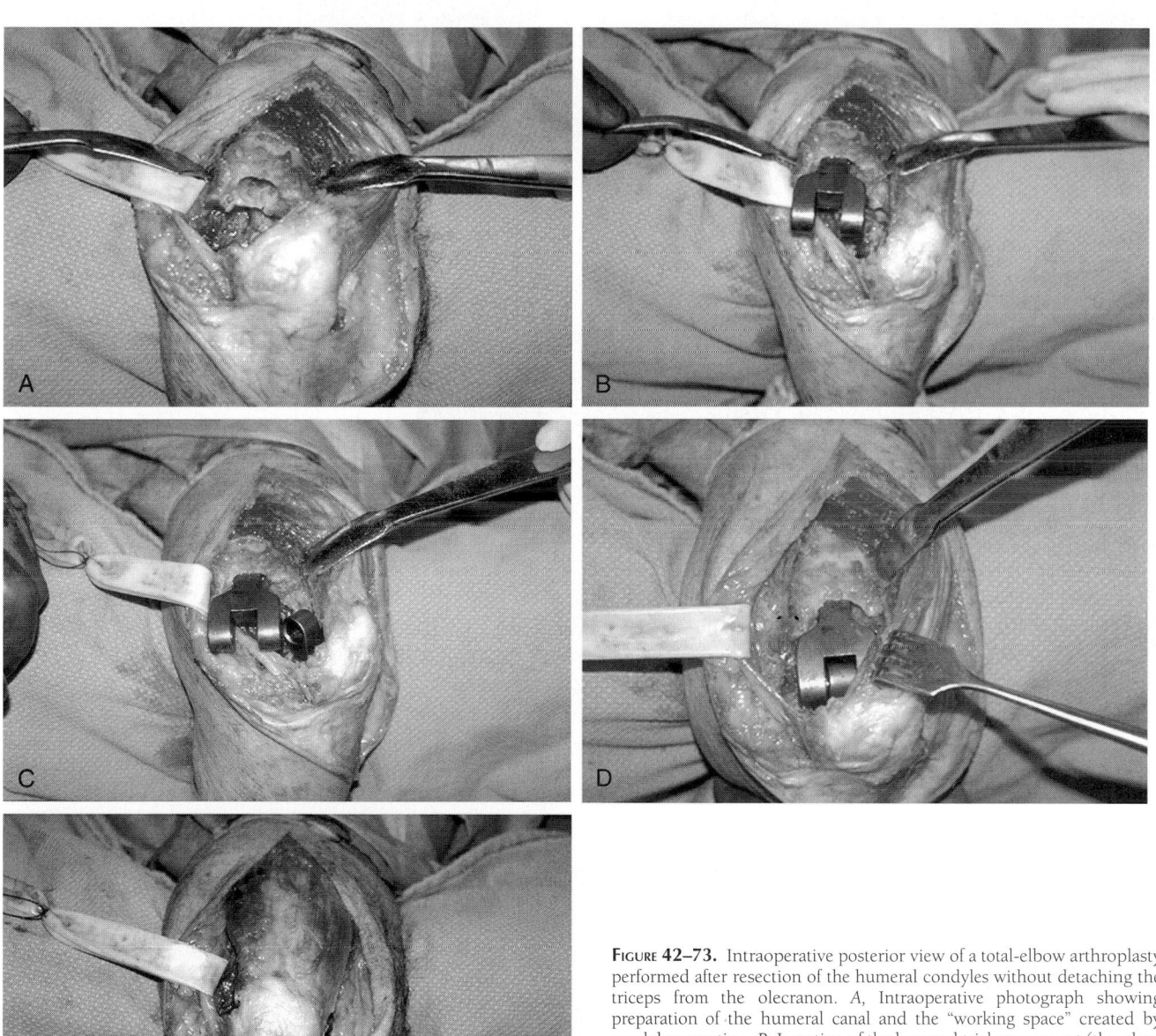

**FIGURE 42–73.** Intraoperative posterior view of a total-elbow arthroplasty performed after resection of the humeral condyles without detaching the triceps from the olecranon. *A,* Intraoperative photograph showing preparation of the humeral canal and the "working space" created by condylar resection. *B,* Insertion of the humeral trial component (the ulnar nerve is identified and protected by a Penrose drain). *C,* Insertion of the ulnar trial component, which is facilitated by forearm pronation. *D,* Reduction of the trial components with the triceps retracted to reveal the articulation. *E,* Final position with the triceps insertion intact and uninterrupted. This approach can reduce posterior pain and swelling and facilitate rehabilitation, and it essentially eliminates the possibility of triceps dehiscence.

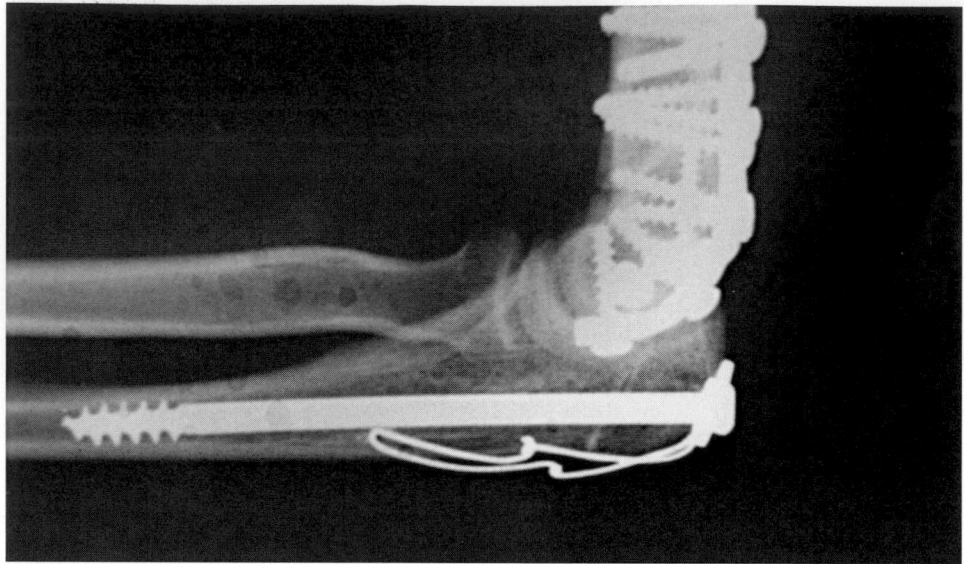

FIGURE **42–74.** An olecranon osteotomy can be secured either with a 6.5-mm screw placed over a washer or with a tension band wire technique.

active flexion and extension exercises. Passive exercises by the patient in both extension and flexion can be started, but the patient is instructed to stretch only to the point of discomfort, not to the point of pain.

## Evaluation of Outcome

Commonly accepted parameters of elbow function include the following[231]:

1. Range of motion
   a. Elbow extension (normal, 0°)
   b. Elbow flexion (normal, 140° to 150°)
   c. Forearm supination (normal, 85°)
   d. Forearm pronation (normal, 75°)
2. Strength
   a. Elbow flexion
   b. Elbow extension
   c. Grip

Most activities of daily living can be performed in a range of 30° to 130°,[223, 232] with a 100° arc of forearm rotation about the neutral axis. Lack of extension is more easily compensated for than lack of flexion.

It is now recognized that the traditional measures of a successful outcome after operative repair of fractures in the upper extremity may not accurately reflect the patient's satisfaction with the outcome. In the past, "surrogate" measures of success such as radiographic parameters or range of motion have been heavily relied on. It is now well recognized that the emphasis should be placed on the patient's rather than the surgeon's perception of success. Newer assessment tools that are patient oriented have been shown to be valid, reliable, and reproducible indicators of a patient's own feelings regarding the success or failure of surgical intervention in the upper extremity.[218, 238] These studies include both limb-specific measures such as the DASH and general health status instruments such as the SF-36. These scores also allow comparison between different interventions (elective, emergency) on different joints (elbow, shoulder, etc.). The physical function and pain portions of such scales have been shown to correlate well with standard scores of shoulder and elbow function.[238] The DASH is a 30-item validated, responsive, patient-completed questionnaire for patients with upper limb disorders.[14, 30] A DASH score of 0 indicates normal, pain-free function; a score of 100 indicates complete impairment of the upper extremity.[14] Despite apparent "surgical" success, these scales may reveal significant residual disability and correlate more closely with a patient's ability to return to activities of daily living and recreational or occupational pursuits.

## Anticipated Results and Complications

In predicting final outcome, it is often not the fracture pattern that determines the ultimate outcome but the energy absorbed by the elbow in the initial trauma.[12, 208, 223] High-energy injuries such as sideswipe injuries, falls from a height, motor vehicle trauma, and gunshot wounds all result in greater soft tissue trauma, leading to scarring and diminished range of motion. This section will deal with the anticipated results after ORIF of a displaced intra-articular distal humeral fracture.

### RANGE OF MOTION AND STIFFNESS

Early mobilization is the key to restoring a functional arc after operative repair. The combination of fracture, ORIF, and prolonged casting results in stiffness. It has been shown that immobilization for longer than 3 weeks after operative fixation culminates in stiffness and loss of functional range of motion.[252] Thus, it is imperative that sufficient stability be achieved intraoperatively to allow early motion (typically in 24 hours at the author's institution). The mean arc of flexion-extension reported in the literature after ORIF of displaced intra-articular fractures of the distal end of the humerus is between 100° and 110° if all patients are included.[194, 208, 223] Patients with a high-energy injury usually lose more motion than do patients with lower-energy injuries. Flexion generally returns first, usually within 2 months. Extension returns more slowly, and the final outcome may not be reached until 4 to 6 months.[194, 223] It is typical for patients to have a residual flexion contracture after this injury despite optimal treatment; the contracture averages 20° to 25° in most series. Severe stiffness is occasionally seen, but as long as the fracture has healed and intra-articular alignment is good, this type of elbow can be salvaged by hardware removal and elbow release. Heterotopic ossification can complicate these injuries in patients who are also head injured. Consideration should be given to the use of some form of prophylaxis, such as indomethacin or radiation therapy, in this situation.

Supination and pronation are essentially unaffected by bicolumn fractures, particularly when the fracture is mobilized early.[176, 180, 184, 192, 202, 227, 239] However, in patients with any associated forearm injury or prolonged immobilization, even forearm rotation may be affected, typically as a result of extensive intra-articular adhesions.

## STRENGTH

Exertional pain may be expected in about 25% of patients after this type of injury, especially with heavy activity or repetitive flexion-extension of the elbow. The pain does not appear to be related to the energy of trauma, the range of motion, or radiographic arthrosis.[208, 223] It would appear that this phenomenon may be due to muscle weakness.

McKee and co-workers examined a series of 25 patients who had undergone successful ORIF of a displaced intra-articular fracture of the distal end of the humerus and performed objective muscle strength testing of the elbow a mean of 37 months after injury.[95] Both elbow extension and flexion strength were decreased to approximately 75% of the opposite normal side. Interestingly, although all fractures were fixed through a posterior approach, flexion strength was diminished to a degree similar to extension strength. Because the elbow flexors were not violated during the surgery, the results may indicate that the diminution in strength is an inherent component of the injury rather than a result of the approach. It may also explain the easy fatigability, lack of endurance strength, and muscle pain and cramping that many patients experience when they attempt to return to heavy occupational or recreational pursuits.

The type of posterior approach used, either an olecranon osteotomy or a triceps-splitting procedure, had no effect on extension strength. This type of testing helps provide an objective level of strength impairment after such injuries.

## FAILURE OF FIXATION

Failure of fixation most often results from a lack of secure fixation of the plates and screws at the time of surgery. K-wires or smooth pins alone rarely provide adequate fixation after the open reduction of distal humeral fractures in adults (see Fig. 42–52). Fixation failure is usually seen at the junction of the distal articular fracture patterns and the humeral shaft. Clinically, fixation failures are accompanied by pain, decreased range of motion, and radiographic evidence of implant loosening or breakage. If the elbow is left as is, nonunion can be anticipated.[208] If the internal fixation breaks or pulls out from the bone or if the fracture fragments become displaced into a position that is not acceptable for ultimate function, early reoperation should be considered. If, however, the loosening is noted at an early stage without complete disruption of the reconstruction, cast immobilization can be considered. Such immobilization offers the possibility of obtaining union, but at the expense of loss of mobility and ultimate elbow stiffness.

## NONUNION AND MALUNION

Though uncommon, nonunion can be disabling because of pain, loss of motion, and associated ulnar neuropathy (see later).[175, 183, 205, 208, 223] It is more likely to occur with fractures resulting from high-energy trauma or as a result of fixation failure, often caused by inadequate internal fixation (Fig. 42–75). Operative repair of these lesions is technically demanding because of poor bone stock, distortion of local anatomy, associated ulnar neuropathy, previously implanted hardware, and extensive periarticular fibrosis. The goals of treatment must be restoration of elbow function, osseous union, and acceptable alignment. If the patient is an active individual and has sufficient bone stock and preserved articular cartilage, reconstruction with bone grafting is the preferred approach. Surgical tactics include wide exposure, mobilization and neurolysis of the ulnar nerve, soft tissue release, bony realignment, stable fixation, and autogenous bone grafting. Fixation must be secure enough to allow early motion, or recurrent stiffness may result. Series by McKee and co-workers[219] and by Jupiter and Goodman[207] reported the average elbow arc of motion to be over 100° after successful reconstruction of complex intra-articular malunion or nonunion of the distal end of the humerus. In addition, gratifying results in terms of pain relief and restoration of ulnar nerve function were noted. Observation of these patients did not, in general, reveal progression of post-traumatic arthrosis (Fig. 42–76; see Chapter 20).

For older, low-demand patients with deficient bone stock or advanced arthritic change, TEA is a reasonable option. Patients must be evaluated carefully for preexisting infection; if such infection is not present, several authors report good results with this technique.[229, 230] A semiconstrained prosthesis such as the Coonrad-Morrey elbow replacement has advantages in that it is less reliant on soft tissue or bony support than are unconstrained or resurfacing arthroplasties. Thus, this prosthesis can be used in patients with greater degrees of bone loss or deformity without any risk of subsequent instability (Fig. 42–77). Morrey and Adams reviewed 36 patients with an average age of 68 years at a mean of 50.4 months after semiconstrained TEA for distal humeral nonunion. These authors reported satisfactory results in 86% of the patients, with an average postoperative arc of motion of 111° and a 13% reoperation rate.[228] Other reports have yielded similar results.[229]

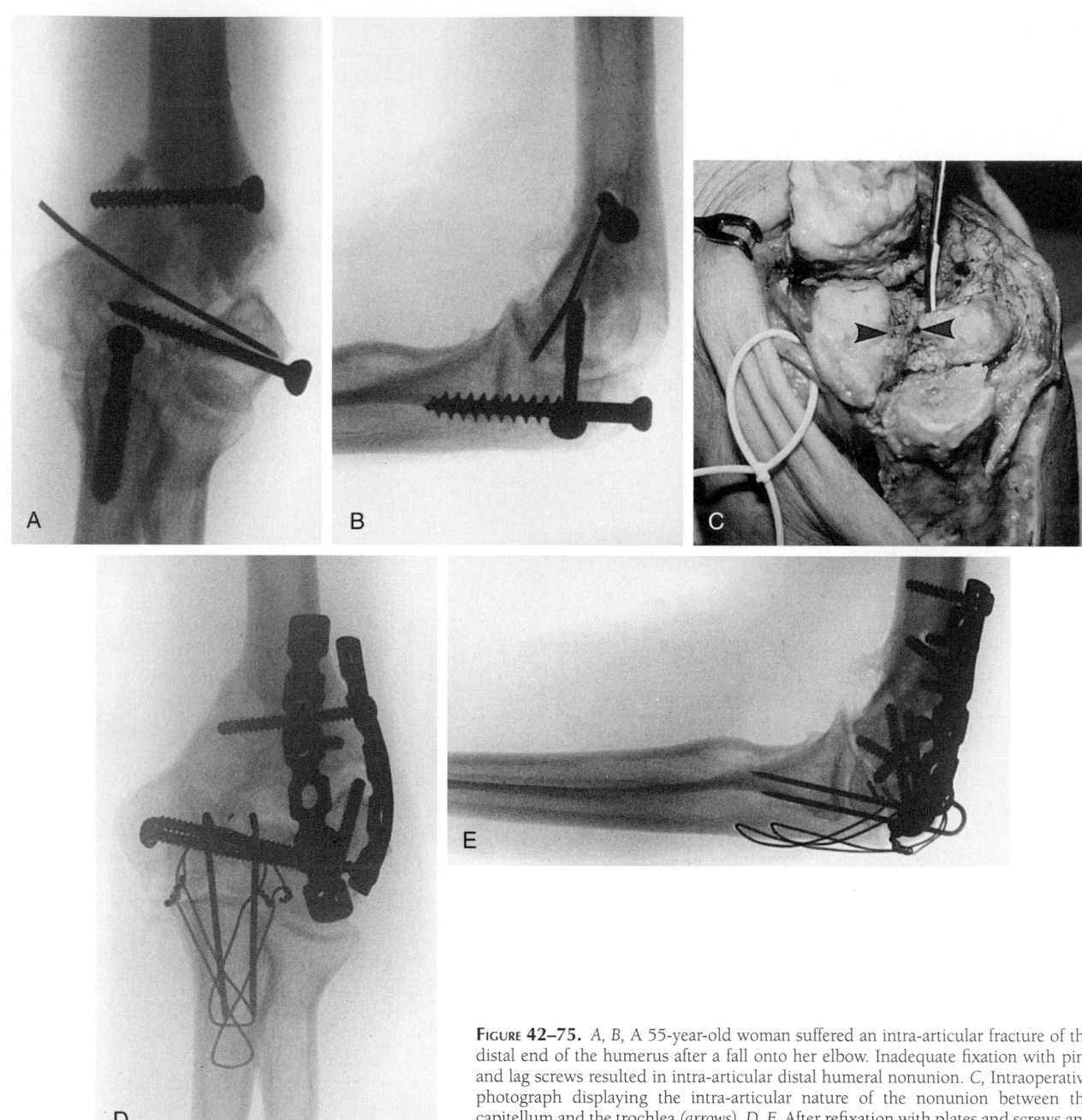

**FIGURE 42–75.** *A, B,* A 55-year-old woman suffered an intra-articular fracture of the distal end of the humerus after a fall onto her elbow. Inadequate fixation with pins and lag screws resulted in intra-articular distal humeral nonunion. *C,* Intraoperative photograph displaying the intra-articular nature of the nonunion between the capitellum and the trochlea *(arrows). D, E,* After refixation with plates and screws and a corticocancellous iliac crest bone graft, joint contour has been restored.

## NONUNION OF AN OLECRANON OSTEOTOMY

Nonunion of an olecranon osteotomy has been recognized by a number of authors.[175, 208, 223] Fixation failure has been associated with the use of a number of different types of techniques, in part because the osteotomy, with its smooth "fracture" planes, is intrinsically less stable. The use of a chevron-shaped osteotomy should diminish the incidence of this complication. The apex of the chevron should point distally so that the osteotomized olecranon will not split. Nonunion is treated by repeat osteosynthesis; a plate applied along the subcutaneous border of the ulna is preferable, and a bone graft may be required. If the initial osteotomy involves only the proximal part of the olecranon and the nonunion fragment is relatively small,

excision of the fragment and reattachment of the triceps tendon can also be considered.

## INFECTION

Despite the fact that a substantial number of these fractures are open and the surgery is long and complicated, infections are uncommon. Infection rates in the literature range from 0% to 6%.[176, 179, 180, 183, 194, 208, 223] They have been described more commonly in grade 3 open wounds but have not been associated with one type of treatment more than another. If the fixation is stable, repeated irrigation plus débridement is indicated; many of these fractures have bone loss that will require grafting at a later date when the wound is clean.

## INSTABILITY

Given the degree of severity of injury to the elbow seen in most displaced distal humeral fractures, the incidence of postoperative instability is surprisingly low, probably because of the fact that the medial and lateral collateral ligaments to the fractured condyles are intact and that once the bone is reduced and stabilized, the elbow is inherently stable. Moreover, because of the degree of scarring and fibrosis seen after this injury, stiffness is the usual clinical problem as opposed to instability. Hall and colleagues reported one patient in whom acute elbow instability developed after fixation of a severe, open distal

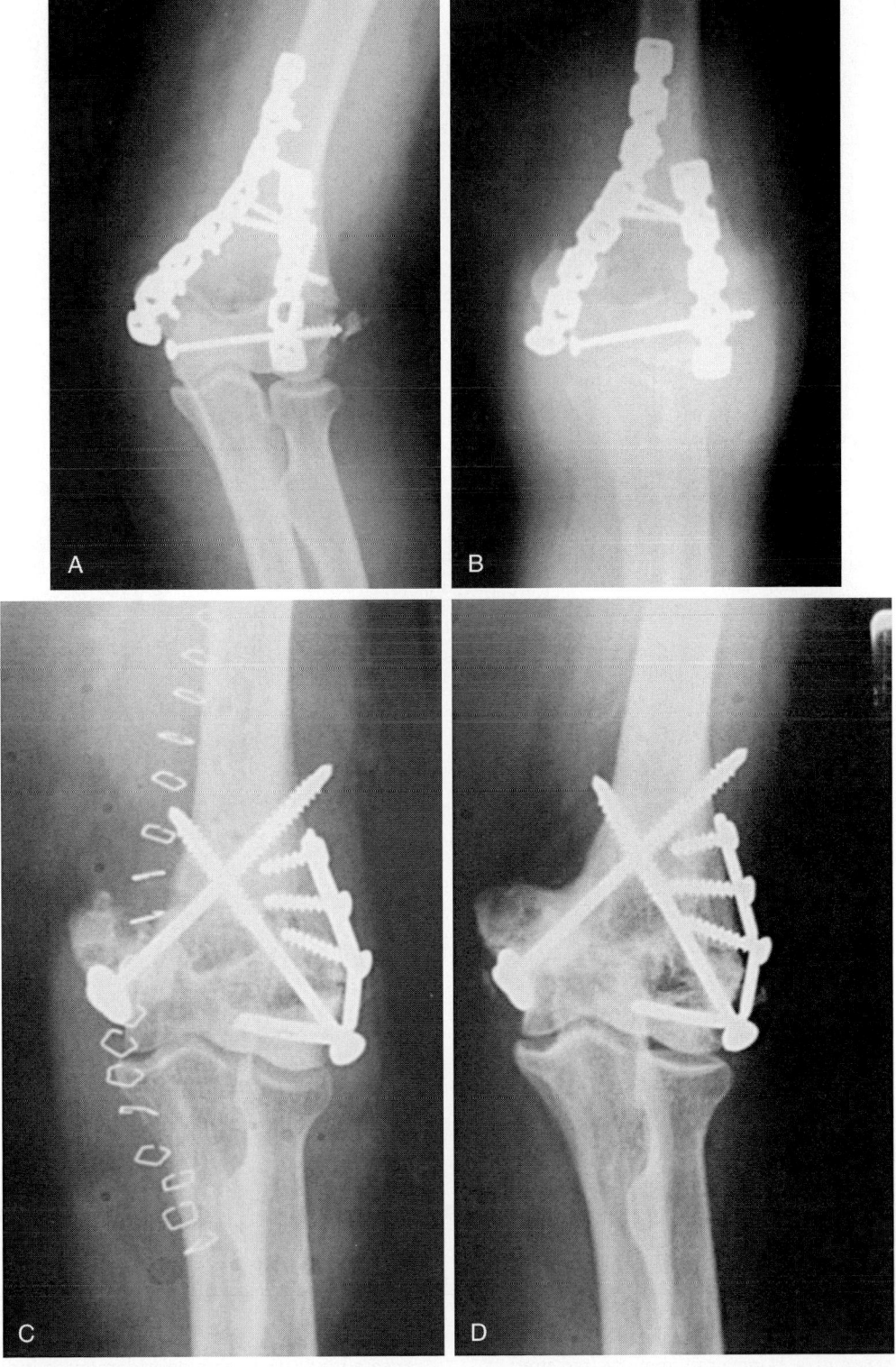

**FIGURE 42–76.** *A,* A bicolumn fracture was internally fixed with two plates and an interfragmentary screw. *B,* Five months postoperatively, instability of the fixation and nonunion were noted. *C,* Stable fixation of the nonunion with a contoured plate along the lateral column. *D,* Radiograph 12 months after fixation of the nonunion.

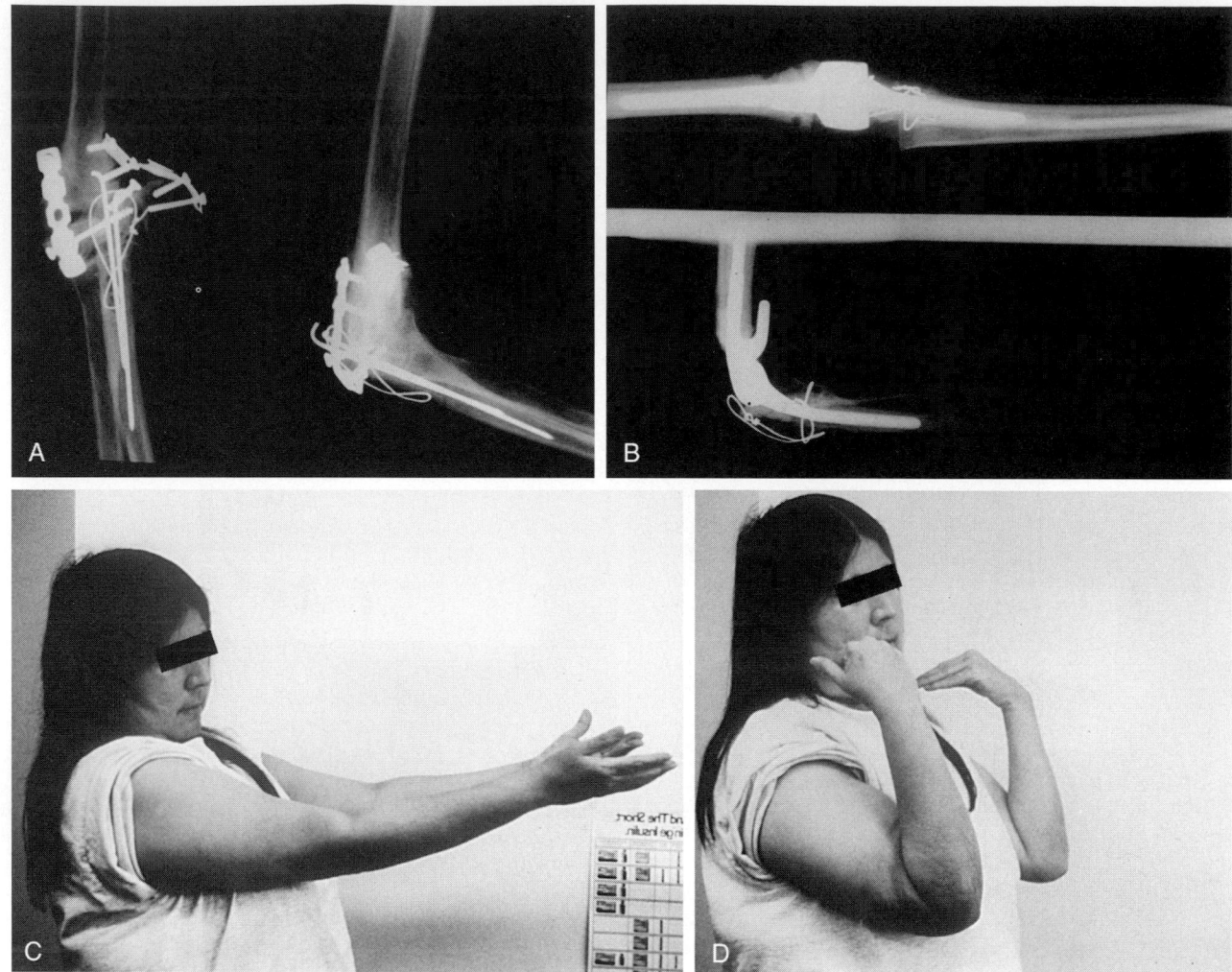

**FIGURE 42–77.** *A,* This 35-year-old woman with a previous history of rheumatoid arthritis affecting her elbows suffered a displaced supracondylar distal humeral fracture after a fall. She subsequently underwent internal fixation with lag screws through a posterior approach along with an olecranon osteotomy. A painful pseudarthrosis resulted, and radiographs revealed nonunion, broken implants, and loss of joint space. *B,* The patient subsequently underwent total-elbow arthroplasty with a semiconstrained Coonrad-Morrey prosthesis. Fixation of the olecranon with a tension band wire technique was necessary because of olecranon osteotomy nonunion. *C, D,* An excellent functional result was achieved. The patient had mild pain with excessive activity but was able to return to work as a cashier.

humeral fracture.[47] It was probably the result of failure to accurately reduce the lateral condylar fragment. Treatment with a hinged elbow external fixator was successful in reestablishing elbow stability and a functional range of motion.

## ULNAR NERVE PALSY

Ulnar neuropathy is often one of the most disabling sequelae of distal humeral fractures and has been reported in a number of series of operatively treated distal humeral fractures.[180, 182, 194, 208] Operative manipulation of the nerve, inadequate release, impingement or injury by bony fragments or hardware, and postoperative fibrosis (especially with prolonged elbow immobilization) can all contribute to this problem. Fortunately, these lesions rarely involve transection of the nerve, and good results can be obtained with ulnar neurolysis. McKee and co-workers

reported a series of 20 patients who had ulnar neurolysis for post-traumatic ulnar neuropathy at the time of concomitant elbow reconstruction.[90] The average Gabel and Amadio score for ulnar nerve function improved from 3.2 points preoperatively to 6.5 points postoperatively, which corresponded to 1 excellent, 17 good, and 2 poor results. The poor results were associated with failure of the underlying elbow reconstruction. Of 14 patients who had intrinsic muscle weakness preoperatively, 12 recovered grade V power and 2 recovered grade IV power, as classified by the Medical Research Council.[222] Though much improved, these patients did not have normal function, thus making it most important to adequately mobilize and protect the nerve at the time of the original surgery to minimize the risk of this complication. Many authors recommend placing the nerve anteriorly at the conclusion of the procedure, away from implanted hardware and bony fragments.[208]

# FRACTURES OF THE CAPITELLUM

Capitellar fractures are extremely rare. It is estimated that they account for 1% of all elbow fractures and about 6% of all distal humeral fractures.[181] Although slight variations in fracture patterns can be noted, these injuries are essentially a shear fracture in a coronal plane that displaces the capitellum from the lateral column of the distal end of the humerus. This fracture has been described as occurring more frequently in females than males.[186, 197] Capitellar fractures may be associated with radial head fractures, as well as with posterior elbow dislocations.[181, 212]

Most capitellar fractures are "complete" fractures as originally described by Hahn[200] and Steinthal[247] in the 19th century. This fracture has been called the *Hahn-Steinthal fracture* in subsequent literature.[177, 191, 242] A second, less common type involves only the shell of the anterior cartilage of the capitellum with a thin layer of subcondylar bone. This lesion has been called the *Kocher-Lorenz fracture*.[177, 191, 197, 212, 242]

A more contemporary and more useful classification is that proposed by Bryan and Morrey.[181] Type I fractures are complete fractures of the capitellum; type II, the more superficial lesions of Kocher-Lorenz; and type III, comminuted capitellar fractures (Fig. 42–78). A fourth type of capitellar fracture, the *coronal shear fracture,* has been characterized by McKee and associates.[217] This fracture, as the name suggests, is a shearing fracture of the anterior surface of the distal end of the humerus such that the capitellum and a major portion of the trochlea, including the lateral trochlear ridge, become separated as one fragment (Fig. 42–79). An isolated case has been reported by Stricker and co-workers[248] in a child. These fractures exhibit a characteristic radiographic feature, the "double-arc" sign, which represents the subchondral bone of the capitellum and the lateral trochlear ridge.

## Clinical Features

Historically, this injury occurs in middle-aged or elderly patients. The symptoms are similar to those of a radial head fracture: swelling and tenderness localized along the lateral aspect of the elbow. Pain is noted with forearm rotation.

Standard AP and lateral radiographs demonstrate the

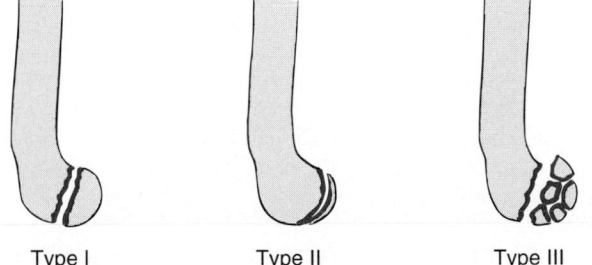

**FIGURE 42–78.** Fractures of the capitellum can be divided into type I, a complete capitellar fracture; type II, the more superficial lesion of Kocher-Lorenz; and type III, a comminuted capitellar fracture.

fracture in most cases. At times, this fracture may be confused with a displaced lateral epicondylar fracture. Type II fractures are more difficult to diagnose because the extent of subcondylar bone involvement may be minimal. A radial head–capitellum view is helpful in these cases.[198] Tomographic and CT scans have also been used to delineate these fractures.

As with all elbow trauma, careful examination of the wrist and shoulder is mandatory.

## Treatment

Because this fracture is uncommon, it would be unusual for any individual to have extensive clinical experience. The literature reflects a wide variety of recommendations, extending from closed treatment[185, 191, 197, 240] to surgical excision[177, 215] and ORIF.[186, 190, 212, 214] Although closed reduction has been described, if the fracture is displaced, successful reduction and maintenance of reduction are unpredictable. Some authors have advocated excision of the fracture fragment,[191] although one study of 11 fractures treated by excision and monitored for an average of 5 years noted that results were unsatisfactory.[197] With the evolution in small-fragment fixation methodology, ORIF of these fractures has gained favor.[182, 203, 212, 214]

**Type I.** Consideration should be given to closed reduction with this fracture pattern. However, the timing of surgery is critical if closed reduction is contemplated. It should be done as soon as possible, with general or regional anesthesia to afford complete muscle relaxation. With the patient in the supine position, traction is applied by an assistant to the supinated forearm with the elbow held at 90° of flexion. Downward pressure by the surgeon's thumb is applied to the capitellar fragment.[185] If successful anatomic reduction is achieved, the elbow should be immobilized in a well-molded posterior splint or long arm cast for a minimum of 3 to 4 weeks, after which active, assisted range-of-motion exercises can be initiated. Success with closed treatment is contingent on achieving anatomic or near-anatomic reduction.

If closed reduction proves unsuccessful or a span of several days has elapsed from the time of fracture, ORIF should be considered (Fig. 42–80). A lateral approach is recommended, with the incision begun 2 cm proximal to the lateral epicondyle and extending 3 to 4 cm distal to the radial head. The common extensor origin is detached with a sharp osteotome and reflected distally to expose the lateral elbow joint. The capitellar fragment is reduced, temporarily held in place with sharp reduction forceps, and provisionally secured with a K-wire. Internal fixation can be achieved with 2.0-mm miniscrews used in a lag fashion or 4.0-mm cancellous screws placed in a posterior-to-anterior direction. A Herbert screw may also be used in these cases, its advantage being that it can be buried underneath the cartilage in subcondylar bone.

Care is taken to avoid damage to the radial nerve, which lies between the brachioradialis and brachialis muscles. The most likely cause of damage is excessive soft tissue retraction while gaining the exposure.

Should the fixation prove secure, postoperative mobilization can be initiated as soon as tolerated. Should the

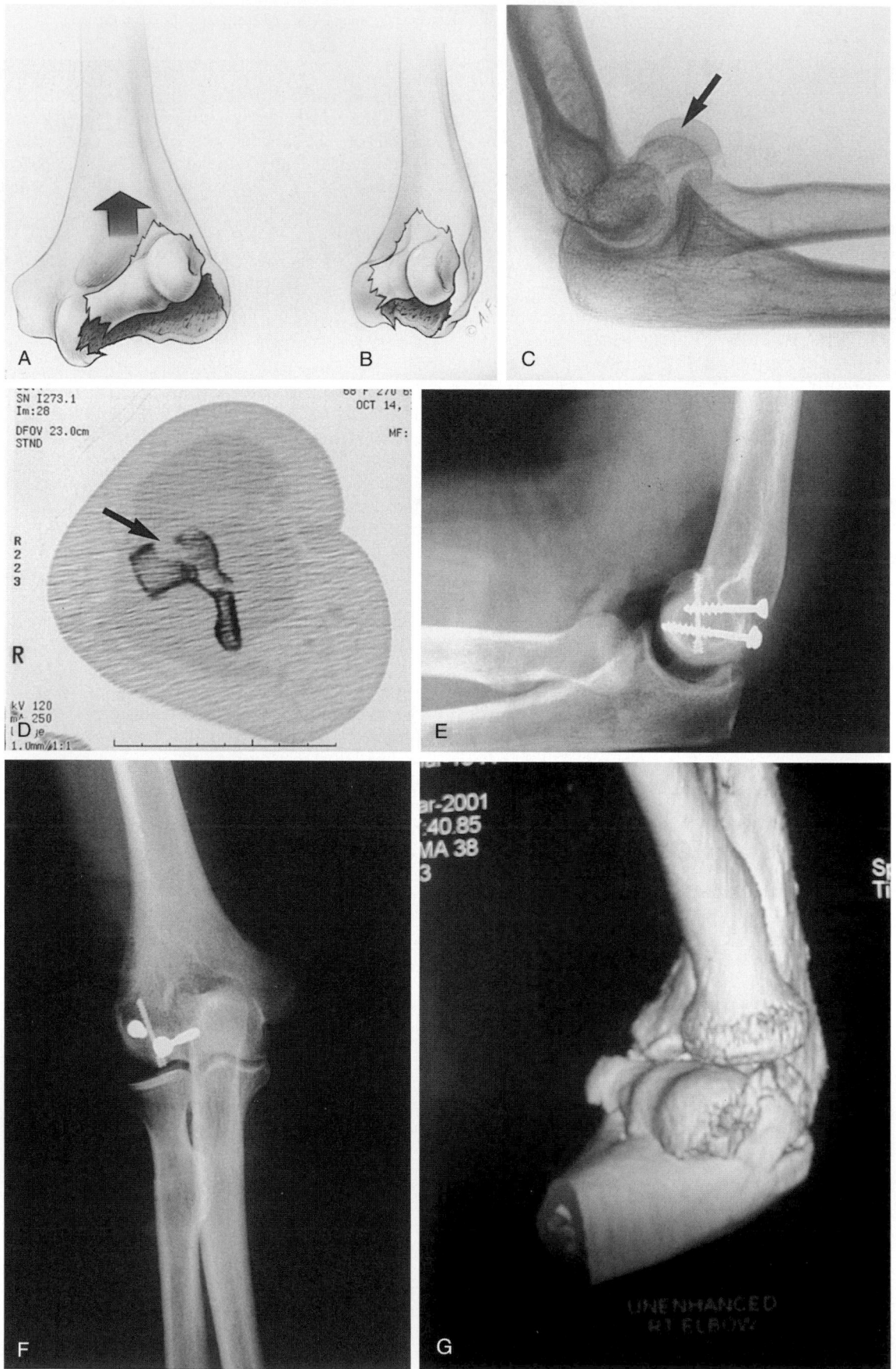

**FIGURE 42–79.** Coronal shear fracture of the distal end of the humerus. *A, B,* Diagram showing separation, proximal migration, and rotation *(arrow)* of the distal fragment, which includes most of the anterior joint surface. *C,* Oblique view from the lateral aspect showing the characteristic double-arc sign *(arrow)*. One arc represents the subchondral bone of the capitellum and the other the lateral ridge of the trochlea. *D,* Preoperative computed tomographic scan made through the distal end of the humerus in an axial fashion showing the coronal fracture line *(arrow)* involving both the capitellum and the lateral ridge of the trochlea. Postoperative lateral *(E)* and anteroposterior *(F)* radiographs show the anatomic reduction and internal fixation obtained with Herbert and 4.0-mm AO screws. The patient had a good result, with an elbow score of 92 points (Morrey scale) at the 1-year follow-up evaluation. *G,* Three-dimensional CT scan reconstruction of a coronal shear fracture. Note the medial extension.

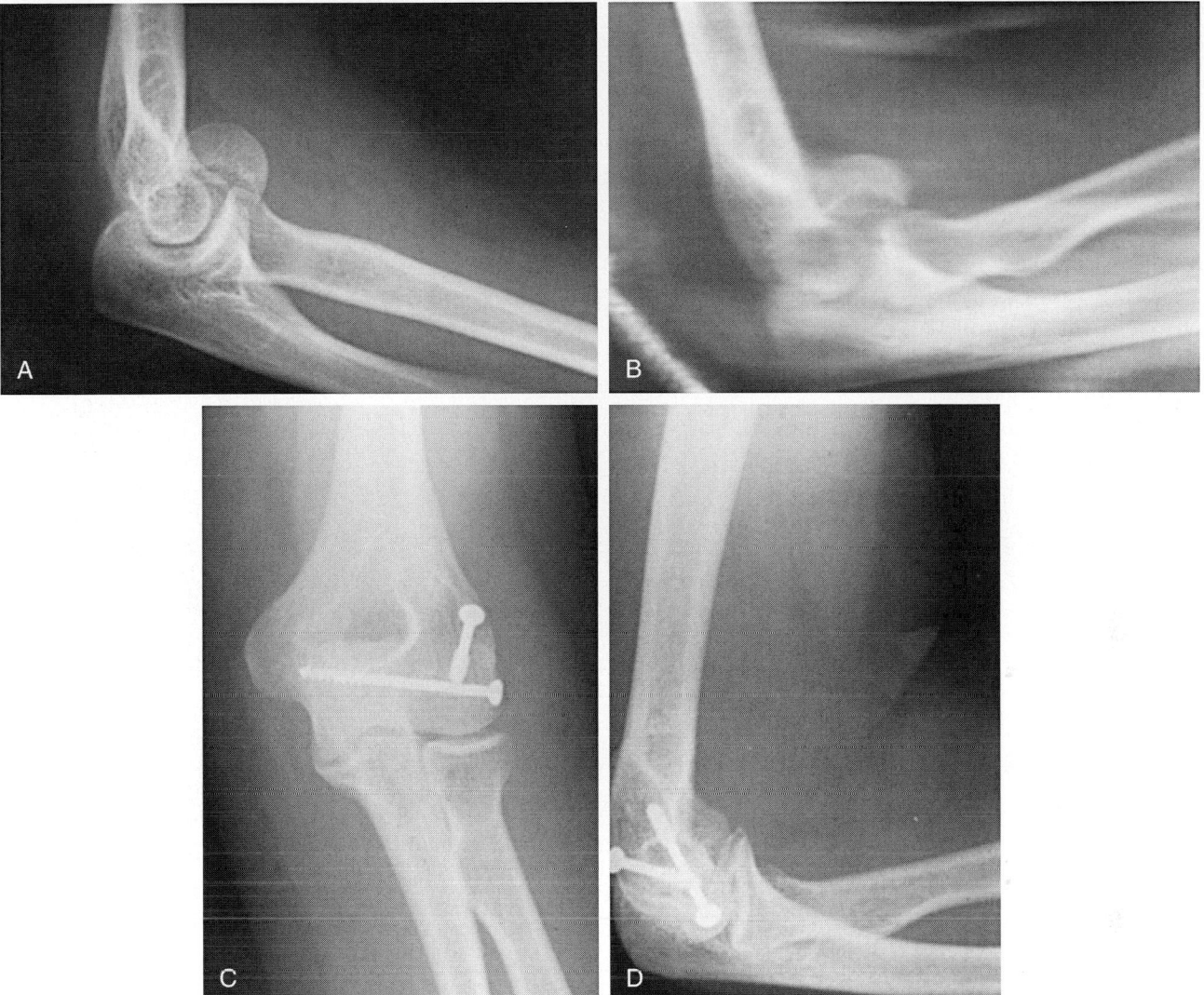

**FIGURE 42–80.** Displaced type I capitellar fracture in a 28-year-old woman. *A*, Lateral radiograph demonstrating rotational displacement of the capitellum. *B*, Lateral tomography provides an excellent picture of the extent of displacement. *C, D,* Through a lateral approach, anatomic repositioning and stable fixation were achieved with two screws. Full motion was regained.

fixation not prove rigid, it is necessary to support the elbow for 3 to 4 weeks in a posterior splint or cast.

**Type II and Type III Fractures.** Internal fixation of shear fractures or comminuted fractures is not easily accomplished. In most cases, excision of the fragments is advisable. The surgical approach is the same as that for type I fractures, and the techniques of exposure and resection are straightforward. Again, it is advisable to consider surgery as early as possible after the injury. The results of excision can be expected to be good in the short term,[177, 191] but long-term results have been less favorable because of loss of motion or instability.[186, 191, 197]

**Type IV Fractures.** Internal fixation is recommended for type IV fractures. Failure to anatomically reduce these fractures would leave the anterior aspect of the distal end of the humerus incongruous and potentially destabilize the elbow because of displacement of the lateral trochlear ridge. Fixation is best accomplished through a lateral approach, and Herbert screws countersunk through the cartilage can augment fixation[217] (see Fig. 42–79).

## Complications

The principal complication to be expected from a capitellar fracture is loss of elbow motion,[186, 197] which has been associated more with fragment excision than with ORIF.

A less common complication is avascular necrosis of the capitellar fragment.[177, 181] It is likely that avascular necrosis of capitellar fractures is more common than generally appreciated, but it may not become apparent clinically or radiologically because of rapid revascularization of the small fragment. In the event that avascular necrosis does occur and becomes symptomatic, delayed excision is indicated.[197]

Malunion is uncommon, but failure on the part of the patient to seek treatment or the treating physician to recognize this injury can result in this complication (Fig. 42–81). Usually, severe restriction in elbow flexion results. Treatment consists of excision of the fragment with anterior soft tissue release.

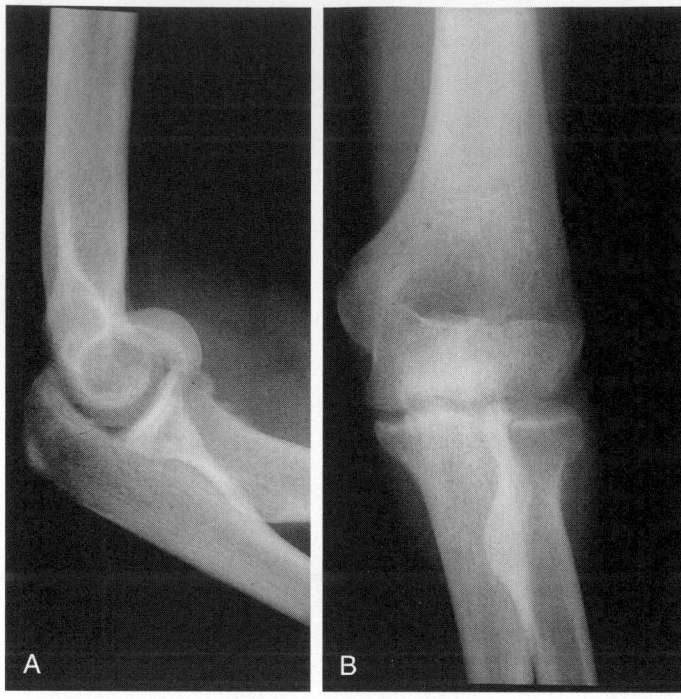

**FIGURE 42–81.** *A, B,* This patient fell on his elbow and sustained a capitellar fracture. Although offered surgery at another institution, he declined. When evaluated at our institution approximately 9 months after injury, the patient had an established malunion of the capitellar fragment with severe restriction of elbow flexion.

Finally, an additional complication is a nonunion of the capitellar fragment. Should the nonunion prove to be painful or associated with significant loss of elbow motion, excision of the capitellar fragment along with soft tissue elbow release through a lateral approach can improve overall function.

## EXTRA-ARTICULAR INTRACAPSULAR FRACTURES: TRANSCOLUMN FRACTURES

### Pathologic Anatomy

Transcolumn fractures traverse both columns of the distal end of the humerus without violating the articular surface. Although the fracture line may be above the olecranon fossa, it is usually somewhat lower and may in fact represent an intracapsular fracture. These fractures occur in four basic patterns: high, low, abduction, and adduction.

The high and low fractures can be further subdivided into extension and flexion patterns. We have categorized these fractures into the following subgroups (Fig. 42–82):

*High extension fracture.* The fracture line is oblique and extends from a posterior proximal position to a low anterior position with posterior displacement.
*High flexion fracture.* The fracture line is oblique; it begins proximally anteriorly and extends distally with anterior displacement.
*Low extension fracture.* The fracture is slightly oblique or transverse with posterior displacement.
*Low flexion fracture.* The fracture line is slightly oblique or transverse with anterior displacement.

*Abduction fracture.* The fracture line is oblique with a lateral proximal–to–distal medial direction. Lateral displacement is present.
*Adduction fracture.* The fracture line is oblique, with the line extending in a proximal medial–to–distal lateral direction with medial displacement.

### Incidence

These fractures are more common in pediatric patients and are rare in adults. Figure 42–83, which represents a compilation of statistics from several references,[181, 188, 204, 243] illustrates that transcolumn fractures are exceptionally uncommon. High extension fractures are the most frequent of the transcolumn fractures.

### Diagnosis

Transcolumn fractures are most often the result of a fall. Extension fractures have been believed to be associated with a fall on the outstretched hand with a posteriorly directed force on the distal end of the humerus.[182] Conversely, flexion fractures have been thought to result from an anteriorly directed force on the posterior aspect of the distal end of the humerus.[249] Adduction and abduction fractures result from axial loading on the distal part of the humerus with an additional varus or valgus component. A patient with the flexion pattern may also give a history of direct trauma over the posterior aspect of the distal end of the humerus, usually with the elbow flexed.[188, 227, 244]

A transcolumn fracture is manifested as noticeable swelling in the elbow area, and deformity may be appreciated if the fracture is displaced. Posterior displacement may be apparent with extension fractures and anterior displacement evident with flexion fractures.

The vascular supply of the extremity must be checked expeditiously. Though uncommon, brachial artery injury may occur with any of these fracture patterns but particularly with the extension pattern. In the presence of excessive swelling at the fracture site and diminished or absent distal pulses, arteriography should be considered.

An assessment must also be made of the compartments in the forearm.[254] Finally, neurologic status must be checked because injury to all three of the major nerves has been documented. The radial and median nerves have more commonly been associated with extension injuries, whereas the ulnar nerve has been associated with flexion fractures.

Routine AP and lateral radiographs are generally

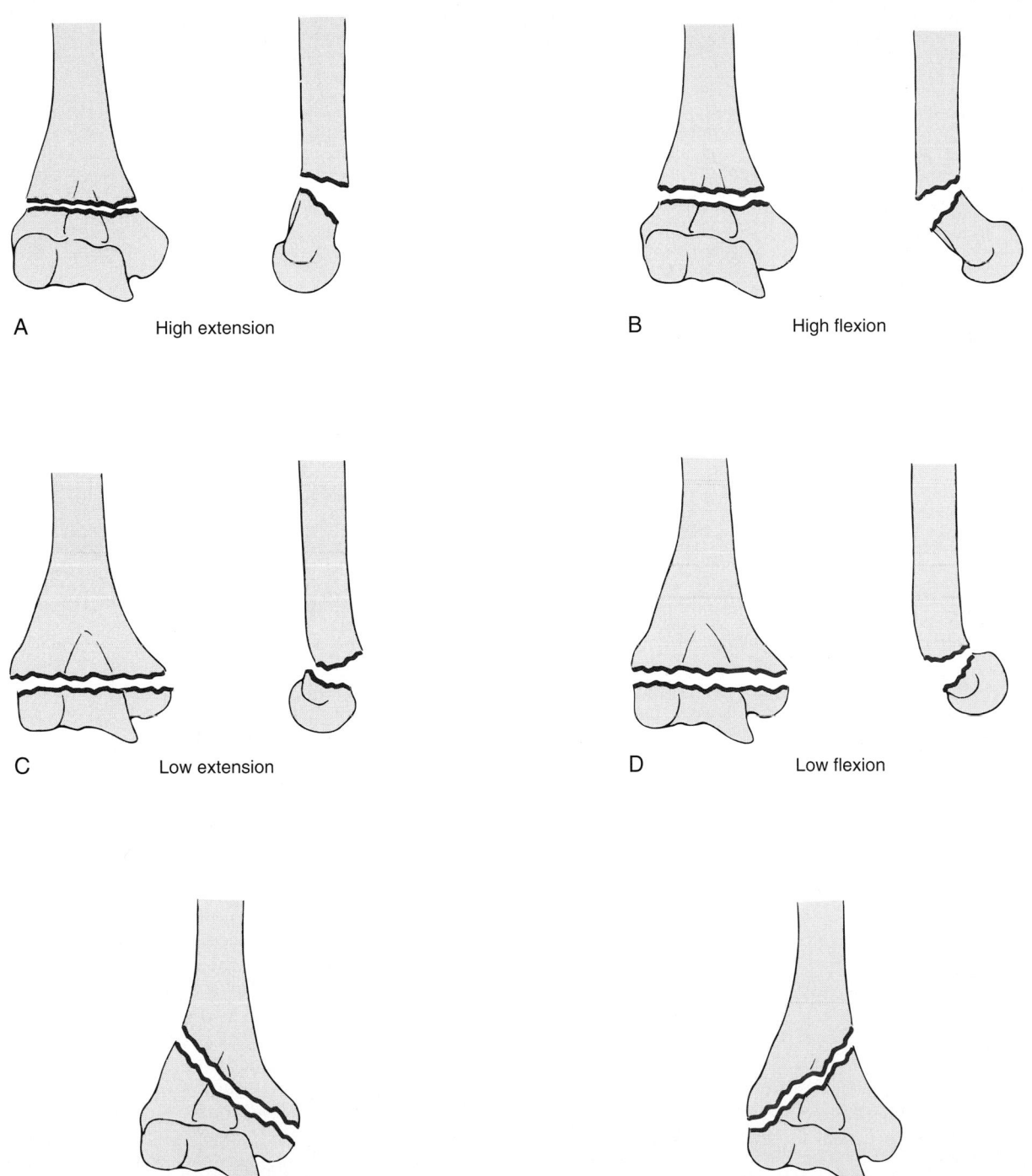

A    High extension

B    High flexion

C    Low extension

D    Low flexion

E    Abduction

F    Adduction

**FIGURE 42–82.** *A–F,* Transcolumn fractures. These fractures occur in four basic patterns: high, low, abduction, and adduction. The high and low fractures can be further subdivided into extension and flexion patterns. When compared with other fractures of the distal end of the humerus, transcolumn fractures are uncommon.

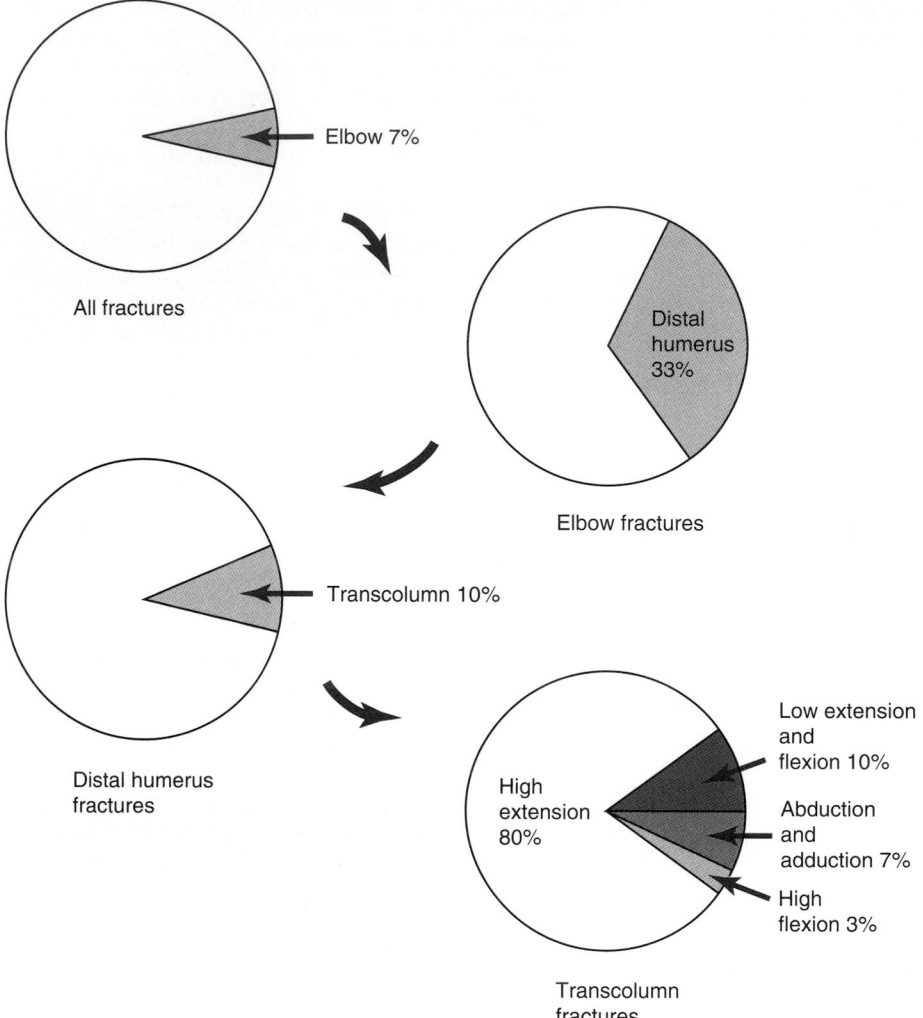

**FIGURE 42–83.** The relative incidence of various fractures of the distal end of the humerus. Note the rarity of transcolumn fractures.

adequate to define a transcolumn fracture. The AP radiograph alone will differentiate a low or high fracture pattern, even in the presence of an oblique fracture line. However, it may not be able to differentiate between a transcolumn fracture and a bicolumn injury. Such differentiation is particularly important because a bicolumn fracture is a much more common injury. Lateral radiographs will distinguish a flexion pattern from an extension pattern and will also identify the extent of the obliquity of the fracture plane. More advanced imaging techniques such as tomographic and CT scans may be helpful but are not usually necessary.

## Management

The literature is relatively limited with regard to studies specifically dealing with these fractures. For the most part, they have been included in papers related to adult bicolumn fractures[184, 193, 208, 227, 256] or in those describing general elbow trauma.[179, 187, 201, 249] In the past, most authors advocated closed reduction and plaster immobilization of these fractures.[190, 204, 214, 225, 254] However, current indications for closed reduction of an adult transcolumn fracture are limited and include patients who are

poor surgical risks and fractures associated with pathologic conditions that limit stable internal fixation. The standard treatment of this fracture in adults is accurate ORIF, if possible.

The techniques of closed reduction are the same as those for any fracture. With extension fractures, the extended position of the distal fracture fragment should be maintained while traction is applied to the humerus and countertraction applied to the distal part of the arm. The surgeon uses both thumbs in pushing the distal fragment distally and anteriorly. Reduction is checked either with fluoroscopy or with AP and lateral radiographs. If satisfactory reduction is achieved, the elbow is extended to between 10° and 20° of maximal flexion and placed in a well-padded but well-molded splint.

Flexion fractures are more difficult to maintain in a reduced position with a posterior molded splint. In these cases, the cylinder cast technique described by Sultanpur may be more effective.[249] This technique is designed to maintain a posterior force on the distal humeral fragment with the forearm flexed, which is achieved by having a well-molded forearm cast "shoving backward" on the forearm with a counterforce provided by the posterior portion of a cylinder arm cast. The arm cylinder portion is initially applied while traction is maintained directly on the humeral epicondyle. The elbow, at this juncture, is in flexion. When the cast hardens, the surgeon places one hand posteriorly to support the cast while pushing the patient's forearm posteriorly with the other hand to reduce the fracture. The forearm plaster is applied to complete a circumferential long arm cast. Complications associated with closed reduction of these fractures include damage to the brachial artery, which can be the result of hyperflexion, particularly in the setting of significant soft tissue swelling. Should arterial damage occur, the elbow must be extended until the distal pulses can be appreciated. If damage to the brachial artery is suspected, an intraoperative arteriogram is recommended.

In the event that closed manipulation fails to achieve or maintain a reduction, a number of authors have advocated olecranon traction, either overhead[226] or sidearm.[181] Percutaneous pin fixation, though very successful in the pediatric age group, has not gained widespread application in adults. Because fixation is not stable with this technique,

the fracture must be immobilized for a period of 4 to 6 weeks, which may result in prolonged or permanent elbow stiffness. For this reason, this technique is not recommended unless bone quality, patient compliance, or both make ORIF impractical.

## PERCUTANEOUS FIXATION

Indications for percutaneous fixation include a low transcolumn fracture with osteoporotic bone or any other transcolumn fracture in which reduction cannot be attained and the patient's condition or the clinical situation is not appropriate for ORIF. With the patient in the supine position, the fracture is reduced as previously described. Image intensification is of tremendous help in both reduction and pin placement. With the elbow maintained in 90° of flexion, smooth pins are placed from each epicondyle across the fracture line into the opposite cortex. The pins are directed at a 35° to 45° angle through the

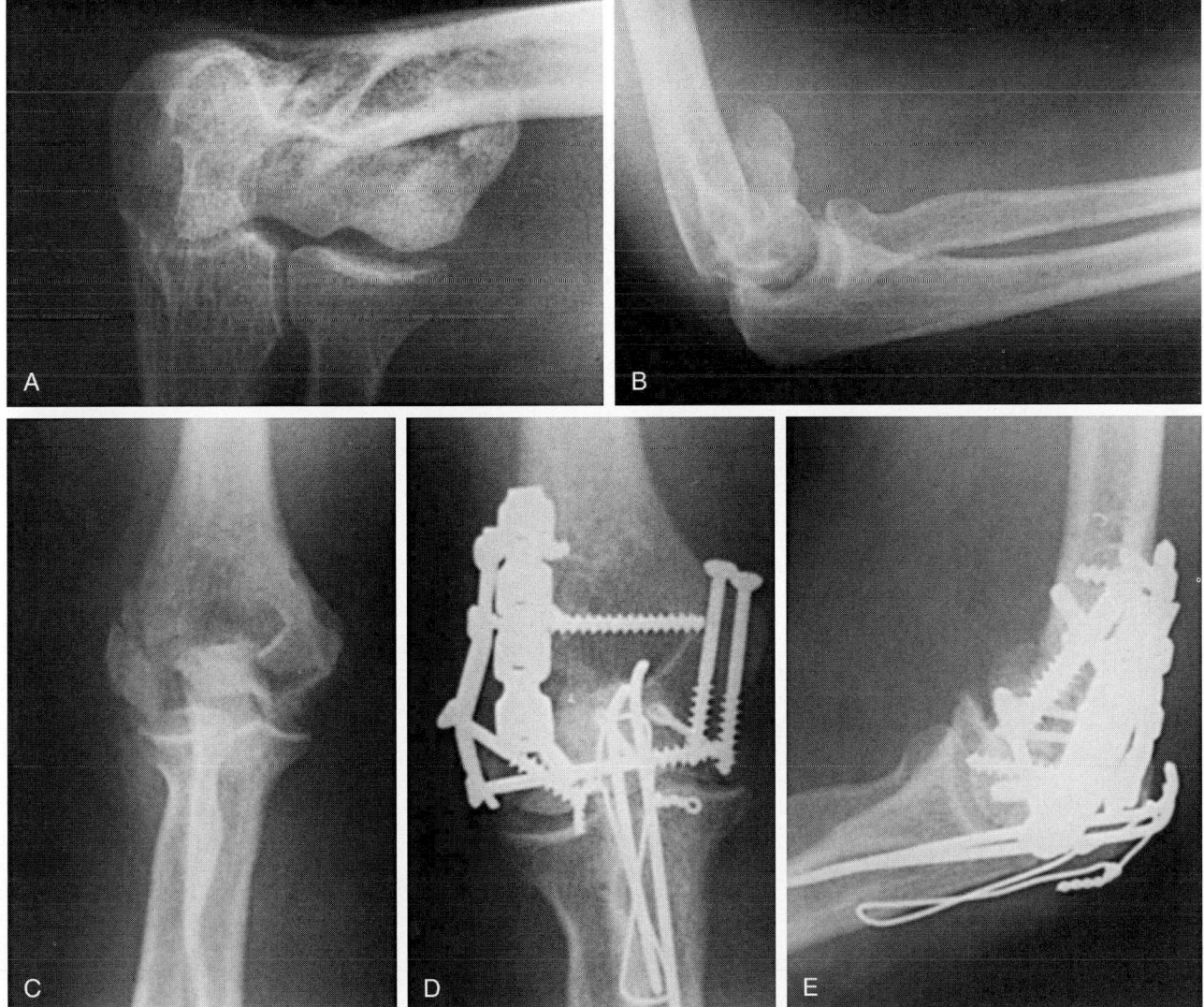

**FIGURE 42–84.** A 50-year-old woman fell while hiking and landed on her elbow. Anteroposterior (AP) (*A*) and lateral (*B*) radiographs demonstrate the displaced transcolumn fracture. *C,* An AP radiograph with traction applied to the forearm provides a clearer picture of the fracture pattern. *D, E,* Through an olecranon osteotomy, the articular fragments were secured with screws and plates; fixation was secure enough to permit postoperative mobilization.

longitudinal axis of the humeral shaft. A right-handed surgeon will find it easier to insert the lateral pin first in a right distal humeral fracture and the medial pin first in a left distal humeral fracture.[204] If radiographs confirm satisfactory fracture reduction and pin placement, the pins are cut off so that they protrude just outside the skin. Any skin tension around the pins must be liberally released. Skin edges compressed by a pin are prone to the development of localized cellulitis. The pin tract wounds are covered with antibiotic ointment, and a well-molded posterior splint is applied with the elbow in 90° of flexion and the forearm held in neutral rotation.

Potential complications with this approach especially involve damage to the ulnar nerve. This complication can be avoided either by identifying the nerve directly or by using smooth pins introduced from the anterosuperior medial epicondyle, thus avoiding the cubital tunnel.

Once the postoperative swelling has diminished, conversion from a posterior splint to a long arm cast is accomplished. The pins can be removed without any anesthesia in the office between 4 and 5 weeks postoperatively. Depending on fracture stability and the radiographic appearance of union, the extremity may be further immobilized in a cast or, if it appears stable, protected in a sling.

## OPEN REDUCTION AND INTERNAL FIXATION

For the most part, a well-planned and executed internal fixation will offer the patient the most favorable chance of union, as well as function. We believe that this treatment should be considered in all adult displaced transcolumnar fractures unless the patient's general condition contraindicates surgery or the surgeon does not think that stable fixation can be achieved. The timing, technique, and postoperative care of transcolumnar fractures are identical to those of bicolumnar fractures, with one exception: the two columns do not have to be fixed to each other distally. Such elimination of the need for distal columnar fixation in fact facilitates the internal fixation (Fig. 42–84).

Postoperative care after stable internal fixation of transcolumnar fractures is identical to that for bicolumn fractures. Controlled mobilization under the supervision of a therapist is an integral part of the overall treatment program.

## REFERENCES

### Trauma to the Adult Elbow

1. Adler, J.B.; Shafton, G.W. Radial head fractures: Is excision necessary? J Trauma 4:115–136, 1964.
2. Adler, S.; Fay, G.F.; MacAusland, W.R., Jr. Treatment of olecranon fractures: Indications for excision of the olecranon fragment and repair of the triceps tendon. J Trauma 2:597–602, 1962.
3. Amis, A.A.; Dowson, D.; Wright, V. Elbow joint force predictions for some strenuous isometric actions. J Biomech 8:765–775, 1980.
4. Amis, A.A.; Dowson, D.; Wright, V.; Miller, J.H. The derivation of elbow joint forces and their relation to prosthesis design. J Med Eng Technol 3:229, 1979.
5. Amis, A.A.; Miller, J.H. The mechanisms of elbow fractures: An investigation using impact tests in vitro. Injury 26:163–168, 1995.
6. An, K.N.; Morrey, B.F.; Chao, E.Y.S. The effect of partial removal of proximal ulna on elbow constraint. Clin Orthop 209:270–279, 1986.
7. Arafiles, R.P. Neglected posterior dislocation of the elbow: A reconstruction operation. J Bone Joint Surg Br 69:199–203, 1987.
8. Arvidson, H.; Johansson, O. Arthrography of the elbow joint. Acta Radiol 43:445, 1955.
9. Bakalim, C. Fractures of radial head and their treatment. Acta Orthop Scand 42:320, 1970.
10. Broberg, M.A.; Morrey, B.F. Results of delayed excision of the radial head after fracture. J Bone Joint Surg Am 68:669–674, 1986.
11. Broberg, M.A.; Morrey, B.F. Results of treatment of fracture-dislocation of the elbow. Clin Orthop 216:109–119, 1987.
12. Broudy, A.; Jupiter, J.; May, J.W., Jr. Management of supracondylar fracture with brachial artery thrombosis in a child: A case report and literature review. J Trauma 19:540–543, 1979.
13. Bunker, T.D.; Newman, J.H. The Herbert differential pitch bone screw in displaced radial head fracture. Injury 16:621–624, 1985.
14. Burgess, R.C.; Sprague, H.H. Posttraumatic posterior radial head subluxation. Clin Orthop 186:192–194, 1984.
15. Burstein, A.H. Fracture classification systems: Do they work and are they useful [editorial]? J Bone Joint Surg Am 75:1743–1744, 1993.
16. Cabanela, M. Olecranon fractures. In: Morrey, B.F., ed. The Elbow and Its Disorders. Philadelphia, W.B. Saunders, 1987.
17. Campbell, B.G. Human Evolution: An Introduction to Man's Adaptations, 2nd ed. Chicago, Aldine, 1974.
18. Carn, R.M.; Medige, J.; Curtain, D.; Koenig, A. Silicone rubber replacement of the severely fractured radial head. Clin Orthop 209:259–269, 1986.
19. Carstam, N. Operative treatment of fractures of the upper end of the radius. Acta Orthop Scand 19:502–526, 1950.
20. Closkey, R.F.; Goode, J.R.; Kirschenbaum, D.; Cody, R.P. The role of the coronoid process in elbow stability. J Bone Joint Surg Am 82:1749–1753, 2000.
21. Cobb, T.K.; Morrey, B.F. Total elbow arthroplasty as primary treatment for distal humeral fractures in elderly patients. J Bone Joint Surg Am 79:826–832, 1997.
22. Cobb, T.K.; Morrey, B.F. Use of distraction arthroplasty in unstable fracture dislocations of the elbow. Clin Orthop 312:201–210, 1995.
23. Coleman, D.A.; Blair, W.F.; Shurr, D. Resection of the radial head for fracture of the radial head. J Bone Joint Surg Am 69:385–392, 1987.
24. Colton, C.L. Fractures of the olecranon in adults: Classification and management. Injury 5:121–129, 1973–1974.
25. Conn, J., Jr.; Wade, P.A. Injuries of the elbow: A ten-year review. J Trauma 1:248–268, 1961.
26. Copf, F.; Holz, V.; Schauwecker, H.H. Biomechanische Probleme bei Ellenbogenluxationen mit Frakturen am Processus coronoideus und Radius koepfchen. Langenbecks Arch Chir 350:249–254, 1980.
27. Crenshaw, A.H. Fractures of the shoulder girdle, arm, and forearm. In: Crenshaw, A.H., ed. Campbell's Operative Orthopaedics. Toronto, Mosby–Year Book, 1992, pp. 1031–1033.
28. Curr, J.; Coe, W. Dislocation of the inferior radioulnar joint. Br J Surg 34:74–77, 1946.
29. DeLee, J.C.; Green, D.P.; Wilkins, K.E. Fractures and dislocations of the elbow. In: Rockwood, C.; Green, D.P., eds. Fractures and Dislocations. Philadelphia, J.B. Lippincott, 1985, pp. 559–652.
30. Duerig, M.; Mueller, W.; Ruedi, T.P.; Gauer, E.F. The operative treatment of elbow dislocation in the adult. J Bone Joint Surg Am 61:239–244, 1979.
31. Dunn, N. Operation for fracture of the olecranon. BMJ 1:214–215, 1939.
32. Edwards, G.; Jupiter, J.B. The Essex-Lopresti lesion revisited. Clin Orthop 234:61–69, 1988.
33. Ericksson, E.; Sahlen, O.; Sahdahl, V. Late results of conservative and surgical treatment of fracture of the olecranon. Acta Chir Scand 113:153–166, 1957.
34. Essex-Lopresti, P. Fractures of the radial head with distal radioulnar dislocation. J Bone Joint Surg Br 33:244–247, 1951.
35. Eygendaal, D.; Verdegaal, S.H.M.; Obermann, W.R.; et al. Postero-lateral dislocation of the elbow joint. J Bone Joint Surg Am 82:555–560, 2000.
36. Fleetcroft, J.P. Fractures of the radial head: Early aspiration and mobilization. J Bone Joint Surg Br 66:141–142, 1984.
37. Frankle, M.A.; Koval, K.J.; Sanders, R.W.; Zuckerman, J.D. Radial head fractures associated with elbow dislocations treated by immediate stabilization and early motion. J Shoulder Elbow Surg 8:355–361, 1999.

38. Frankle, M.A.; Sanders, R.W.; DiPasquale, T. A comparison of ORIF vs. primary total elbow arthroplasty in the treatment of intra-articular fractures of the distal humerus in females greater than sixty-five years of age. Paper presented at the American Shoulder and Elbow Surgeons' 15th Annual Open Meeting, Anaheim, California, February 7, 1999.

39. Galbraith, K.A.; McCullough, C.J. Acute nerve injury as a complication of closed fractures or dislocations about the elbow. Injury 11:159–164, 1979.

40. Garland, D.E.; O'Halloren, R.M. Fractures and dislocations about the elbow in the head injured adult. Clin Orthop 168:38–41, 1982.

41. Gartsman, G.M.; Sculco, T.P.; Otis, J.C. Operative treatment of olecranon fractures—excision or open reduction with internal fixation? J Bone Joint Surg Am 63:718–721, 1981.

42. Gaston, S.R.; Smith, F.M.; Baab, D.D. Adult injuries of the radial head and neck: Importance of time element in treatment. Am J Surg 78:631–635, 1949.

43. Goble, E.M. The development of suture anchors for use in soft tissue fixation to bone. Am J Sports Med 22:236–239, 1994

44. Gordon, M.; Bullough, P.G. Synovial and osseous inflammation in failed silicone-rubber prostheses. J Bone Joint Surg Am 64:574–580, 1982.

45. Greenspan, A.; Norman, A. The radial head capitellar view: Useful technique in elbow trauma. AJR Am J Roentgenol 8:1186–1190, 1982.

46. Gregory, G.K. The humerus from fish to man. Am Mus Novit 1400:1–54, 1949.

47. Hall, J.; Schemitsch, E.H.; McKee, M.D. Use of a hinged external fixator for elbow instability after severe distal humeral fracture. J Orthop Trauma 14:442–448, 2000.

48. Halls, A.A.; Travill, A. Transmission of pressures across the elbow joint. Anat Rec 150:243–248, 1964.

49. Harrington, I.J.; Sekyi-Otuu, A.; Barrington, T.W.; et al. The functional outcome with metallic radial head implants in the treatment of unstable elbow fractures: A long-term review. J Trauma 50:46–52, 2001.

50. Harrington, I.J.; Tountas, A.A. Replacement of the radial head in the treatment of unstable elbow fractures. Injury 12:405–409, 1981.

51. Hassman, G.C.; Brunn, F.; Neer, C.S. Recurrent dislocation of the elbow. J Bone Joint Surg Am 57:1080–1084, 1975.

52. Heidt, R.S., Jr.; Stern, P.J. Isolated posterior dislocation of radial head. Clin Orthop 168:136–138, 1982.

53. Holdsworth, B.J.; Clement, D.A.; Rothwell, P.N. Fractures of the radial head—the benefit of aspiration: A prospective controlled trial. Injury 18:44–47, 1987.

54. Hotchkiss, R.N.; Fractures and dislocations of the elbow. In: Rockwood, C.A., Wilkins, K.E., King, R.E., eds. Rockwood and Green's Fractures in Adults, 4th ed., Vol. 1. Philadelphia, J.B. Lippincott, 1996, pp. 929–1024.

55. Hotchkiss, R.N.; Weiland, A.J. Valgus stability of the elbow. Orthop Trans 10:224, 1986.

56. Jacobs, R.L. Recurrent dislocation of the elbow joint: A case report and review of the literature. Clin Orthop 74:151–154, 1971.

57. Janssen, R.P.A.; Vegter, J. Resection of the radial head after Mason type-III fractures of the elbow: Follow-up at 16 to 30 years. J Bone Joint Surg Br 80:231–233, 1998.

58. Jenkins, F.A. The functional anatomy and evolution of the mammalian humeroulnar articulation. Am J Anat 137:281–298, 1973.

59. Jensen, C.M.; Olsen, B.B. Drawbacks of traction-absorbing wiring (TAW) in displaced fractures of the olecranon. Injury 17:174–175, 1986.

60. Johansson, O. Capsular and ligament injuries of the elbow joint. Acta Chir Scand Suppl 287:1–159, 1962.

61. Johnston, G.W. Follow-up of one hundred cases of fracture of head of the radius with a review of the literature. Ulster Med J 31:51–56, 1962.

62. Josefsson, P.O.; Gentz, C.F.; Johnell, O.; Wendeberg, B. Dislocation of the elbow and intraarticular fractures. Clin Orthop 246:126–130, 1988.

63. Josefsson, P.O.; Johnell, O.; Gentz, C.F. Long-term sequelae of simple dislocation of the elbow. J Bone Joint Surg Am 66:927–930, 1984.

64. Josefsson, P.O.; Gentz, C.F.; Johnell, O.; Wendeberg, B. Dislocation of the elbow and intraarticular fractures. Clin Orthop 246:126–130, 1989.

65. Josefsson, P.O.; Johnell, O.; Wendeberg, B. Ligamentous injuries in dislocations of the elbow joint. Clin Orthop 222:221–225, 1987.

66. Josefsson, P.O.; Gentz, C.F.; Johnell, O.; Wendeberg, B. Surgical versus nonsurgical treatment of ligamentous injuries following dislocations of the elbow joint. J Bone Joint Surg Am 69:605–608, 1987.

67. Jupiter, J.B. The management of fractures in one upper extremity. J Hand Surg [Am] 11:279–282, 1986.

68. Jupiter, J.B.; Leibovic, S.J.; Ribbans, W.; Wilk, R.M. The posterior Monteggia lesion. J Orthop Trauma 5:395–402, 1991.

69. Kapel, O. Operation for habitual dislocation of the elbow. J Bone Joint Surg Am 33:707–714, 1951.

70. Keon-Cohen, B.T. Fractures at the elbow. J Bone Joint Surg Br 48:1623–1639, 1966.

71. Kini, M.G. Dislocation of the elbow and its complications. J Bone Joint Surg 22:107–117, 1940.

72. Kluge, A.G. Chordate Structure and Function, 2nd ed. New York, Macmillan, 1977, pp. 179–269.

73. Kobayashi, Y.; Oka, Y.; Ikeda, M.; Munesada, S. Avulsion fracture of the medial and lateral epicondyles of the humerus. J Shoulder Elbow Surg 9:59–64, 2000.

74. Lavine, L. A simple method of reducing dislocations of the elbow joint. J Bone Joint Surg Am 35:785–786, 1953.

75. Lerner, A.; Stahl, S.; Stein, H. Hybrid external fixation in high-energy elbow fractures: A modular system with a promising future. J Trauma 49:1017–1022, 2000.

76. Linscheid, R.L. Elbow dislocations. In: Morrey, B.F., ed. The Elbow and Its Disorders. Philadelphia, W.B. Saunders, 1985, pp. 414–432.

77. Linscheid, R.L.; Wheeler, D.K. Elbow dislocations. JAMA 194:1171–1176, 1965.

78. Lister, J. An address on the treatment of fracture of the patella. BMJ 2:855, 1883.

79. Louis, D.S.; Ricciardi, J.E.; Spengler, D.M. Arterial injury: A complication of posterior elbow dislocation. A clinical and anatomical study. J Bone Joint Surg Am 56:1631–1636, 1974.

80. Mackay, I.; Fitzgerald, B.; Miller, J.H. Silastic replacement of the head of the radius in trauma. J Bone Joint Surg Br 61:494–497, 1979.

81. Madey, S.M.; Bottlang, M.; Steyers, C.M.; et al. Hinged external fixation of the elbow: Optimal axis alignment to minimize motion resistance. J Orthop Trauma 14:41–47, 2000.

82. Maeko, D.; Szabo, R.M. Complications of tension-band wiring of olecranon fractures. J Bone Joint Surg Am 67:1396–1401, 1985.

83. Mason, J.A.; Shutkin, N.M. Immediate active motion in the treatment of fractures of the head and neck of the radius. Surg Gynecol Obstet 76:731–737, 1943.

84. Mason, M. Some observations on fractures of the head of the radius with a review of one hundred cases. Br J Surg 42:123–132, 1954.

85. Mateo, I. A radiological sign of entrapment of the median nerve in the elbow joint after posterior dislocation: A report of two cases. J Bone Joint Surg Br 58:353–355, 1976.

86. McAusland, W.R. The treatment of fractures of the olecranon by longitudinal screw or nail fixation. Ann Surg 116:293–296, 1942.

87. McDougall, A.; White, J. Subluxation of the interior radioulnar joint complicating fracture of the radial head. J Bone Joint Surg Br 39:278–287, 1957.

88. McHenry, H.M.; Corruccini, R.S. Distal humerus in hominoid evolution. Folia Primatol 33:227–244, 1975.

89. McKee, M.D.; Bowden, S.H.; King, G.J.; et al. Management of recurrent, complex instability of the elbow with a hinged external fixator. J Bone Joint Surg Br 80:1031–1036, 1998.

90. McKee, M.D.; Jupiter, J.B.; Bosse, G.; Goodman, L. Outcome of ulnar neurolysis during post-traumatic reconstruction of the elbow. J Bone Joint Surg Br 80:100–105, 1997.

91. McKee, M.D.; Kim, J.; Kebaish, K.; et al. Functional outcome after open supracondylar fracture of the humerus: The effect of the surgical approach. J Bone Joint Surg Br 82:646–651, 2000.

92. McKee, M.D.; King, G.; Patterson, S.; Richards, R.R. The compass elbow hinge for complex, acute elbow instability. Paper presented at the annual meeting of the Canadian Orthopaedic Association, Quebec City, Canada, May 25–29, 1996.

93. McKee, M.D.; Pederson, E.; Pugh, D.M.W.; et al. The effect of

condylar resection on strength and functional outcome following semi-constrained total elbow arthroplasty. Paper presented at the annual meeting of the Canadian Orthopaedic Association, London, Canada, June 7, 2001.

94. McKee, M.D.; Seiler, J.G.; Jupiter, J.B. The application of the limited contact dynamic compression plate (LCDCP) in the upper extremity: An analysis of 114 consecutive cases. Injury 26:661–666, 1995.

95. McKee, M.D.; Wilson, T.L.; Winston, L.; et al. Functional outcome following surgical treatment of intra-articular distal humeral fractures through a posterior approach. J Bone Joint Surg 82:1701–1707, 2000.

96. McKeever, F.M.; Buck, R.M. Fractures of the olecranon process of the ulna. JAMA 135:1–5, 1947.

97. McLaren, A.C. Prophylaxis with indomethacin for heterotopic bone after open reduction of fractures of the acetabulum. J Bone Joint Surg Am 72:245–247, 1990.

98. Mehlhoff, T.L.; Noble, P.C.; Bennett, J.B.; Tullos, H.S. Simple dislocation of the elbow in the adult. Results after closed treatment. J Bone Joint Surg Am 70:244–249, 1988.

99. Meyn, M.A.; Quigley, T.B. Reduction of posterior dislocation of the elbow by traction on the dangling arm. Clin Orthop 103:106–108, 1974.

100. Mikic, Z.D.; Vukadinovic, S.M. Late results in fractures of the radial head treated by excision. Clin Orthop 181:220–228, 1983.

101. Milch, H. Bilateral recurrent dislocation of the ulna at the elbow. J Bone Joint Surg 18:777–780, 1936.

102. Miller, G.K.; Drennan, D.B.; Maylahn, D.J. Treatment of displaced segmental radial head fractures: Long-term follow-up. J Bone Joint Surg 63:712–717, 1981.

103. Morrey, B.F. Radial head fracture. In: Morrey, B.F., ed. The Elbow and Its Disorders, 2nd ed. Philadelphia, W.B. Saunders, 1993.

104. Morrey, B.F.; An, K.N. Articular and ligamentous contributions to the stability of the elbow joint. Am J Sports Med 11:315–319, 1983.

105. Morrey, B.F.; An, K.N. Functional anatomy of the ligaments of the elbow. Clin Orthop 201:84–90, 1985.

106. Morrey, B.F.; An, K.N.; Stormont, T.J. Force transmission through the radial head. J Bone Joint Surg Am 70:250–256, 1988.

107. Morrey, B.F.; Chao, E.Y.; Hui, F.C. Biomechanical study of the elbow following excision of the radial head. J Bone Joint Surg Am 61:63–68, 1979.

108. Morrey, B.F.; Tanaka, S.; An, K.N. Valgus stability of the elbow: A definition of primary and secondary constraints. Clin Orthop 265:187–195, 1991.

109. Müller, M.E.; Allgöwer, M.; Schneider, R.; Willenegger, H. Manual of Internal Fixation, 2nd ed. New York, Springer-Verlag, 1979.

110. Murphy, D.F.; Greene, W.B.; Dameron, T.B. Displaced olecranon fractures in adults. Clin Orthop 224:215–223, 1987.

111. Neill Cage, D.J.; Abrams, R.A.; Callahan, J.J.; Botte, M.J. Soft tissue attachments of the ulnar coronoid process. An anatomic study with radiographic correlation. Clin Orthop 320:154–158, 1995.

112. Nevasier, J.S.; Wickstrom, J.K. Dislocation of the elbow: A retrospective study of 115 patients. South Med J 70:172–173, 1977.

113. Odenheimer, K.; Harvey, J.P., Jr. Internal fixation of fractures of the head of the radius. J Bone Joint Surg Am 61:785–787, 1979.

114. O'Driscoll, W.W., Bell, D.F., Morrey, B.F. Posterolateral rotatory instability of the elbow. J Bone Joint Surg Am 73:440–446, 1991.

115. O'Driscoll, S.W.; Jupiter, J.B.; King, G.J.W.; Hotchkiss, R.N. The unstable elbow. J Bone Joint Surg Am 82:724–738, 2000.

116. O'Driscoll, S.W., Morrey, B.F. Surgical Reconstruction of the Lateral Collateral Ligament. Master Techniques in Orthopaedic Surgery. New York, Raven, 1994.

117. Oldeberg-Johnson, G. On fractures of the proximal portion of the radius and their causes. Acta Radiol 3:45, 1924.

118. Osborne, G.; Cotterill, P. Recurrent dislocation of the elbow. J Bone Joint Surg Br 48:340–346, 1966.

119. Parrin, R.W. Closed reduction of common shoulder and elbow dislocations without anaesthesia. Arch Surg 75:972–975, 1957.

120. Popovic, N.; Gillet, P.; Rodriguez, A.; Lemaire, R. Fracture of the radial head with associated elbow dislocation: Results of treatment using a floating radial head prosthesis. J Orthop Trauma 14:171–177, 2000.

121. Patel, V.R.; Elliott, D.S. Salvage of the head of the radius after fracture-dislocation of the elbow. J Bone Joint Surg Br 81:306–308, 1998.

122. Pribyl, C.R.; Kester, M.A.; Cook, S.D.; et al. The effect of the radial head and prosthetic radial head replacement on resisting valgus stress at the elbow. Orthopedics 9:723–726, 1986.

123. Pritchard, D.J.; Linscheid, R.L.; Svien, H.J. Intraarticular median nerve entrapment with dislocation of the elbow. Clin Orthop 90:100–103, 1973.

124. Protzman, R.R. Dislocation of the elbow joint. J Bone Joint Surg Am 60:539–541, 1978.

125. Quigley, T.B. Aspiration of the elbow joint in treatment of fractures of the head and neck of the radius. N Engl J Med 240:915–916, 1949.

126. Radin, E.L.; Riseborough, E.J. Fractures of the radial head. J Bone Joint Surg Am 48:1055–1064, 1966.

127. Rana, N.A.; Kenwright, J.; Taylor, R.G.; Rushworth, G. Complete lesion of the median nerve associated with dislocation of the elbow joint. Acta Orthop Scand 45:365–369, 1974.

128. Regan, W.; Morrey, B. Fractures of the coronoid process of the ulna. J Bone Joint Surg Am 71:1348–1354, 1989.

129. Reichenheim, P.P. Transplantation of the biceps tendon as a treatment for recurrent dislocation of the elbow. Br J Surg 35:201, 1947.

130. Reith, P.L. Fractures of the radial head associated with chip fractures of the capitellum in adults: Surgical considerations. South Surg 14:154, 1948.

131. Ring, D.; Jupiter, J.B. Fracture-dislocation of the elbow. J Bone Joint Surg Am 80:566–580, 1998.

132. Roberts, J.B. The surgical treatment of heterotopic ossification of the elbow following long-term coma. J Bone Joint Surg Am 61:760–763, 1979.

133. Roberts, P.H. Dislocation of the elbow. Br J Surg 56:806–815, 1969.

134. Romer, A.S.; Parsons, T.S. The Vertebrate Body, 6th ed. Philadelphia, W.B. Saunders, 1986.

135. Rowe, C. The management of fractures in elderly patients is different. J Bone Joint Surg Am 47:1043–1059, 1965.

136. Ryu, J.; Pascal, P.E.; Levine, J. Posterior dislocation of the radial head without fracture of the ulna: A case report. Clin Orthop 168:136–138, 1982.

137. Salama, R.; Wientroub, S.; Weissman, S.C. Recurrent dislocation of the head of the radius. Clin Orthop 125:156–185, 1977.

138. Sanchez-Sotelo, J.; Romanillos, O.; Garay, E.G. Results of acute excision of the radial head in elbow radial head fracture-dislocations. J Orthop Trauma 14:354–358, 2000.

139. Scharplatz, D.; Allgöwer, M. Fracture-dislocation of the elbow. Injury 7:143–159, 1976.

140. Schatzker, J. Olecranon fractures. In: Schatzker, J.; Tile, M., eds. The Rational Basis of Operative Fracture Care. New York, Springer-Verlag, 1987.

141. Schatzker, J. Fractures of the radial head. In: Schatzker, J.; Tile, M., eds. The Rational Basis of Operative Fracture Care. New York, Springer-Verlag, 1987.

142. Schmueli, G.; Herold, H.Z. Compression screwing of displaced fractures of the head of the radius. J Bone Joint Surg Br 63:535–538, 1981.

143. Schwab, G.H.; Bennett, J.B.; Woods, G.W.; Tulles, H.S. Biomechanics of elbow instability: The role of the medial collateral ligament. Clin Orthop 146:42–52, 1980.

144. Schwartz, R.P.; Young, F. Treatment of fractures of the head and neck of the radius and slipped radial epiphysis in children. Surg Gynecol Obstet 57:528–537, 1933.

145. Selesnick, F.H.; Dolitsky, B.; Haskell, S.S. Fracture of the coronoid process requiring open reduction with internal fixation: Case report. J Bone Joint Surg Am 66:1304–1306, 1984.

146. Sharma, R.K.; Covell, N.A.G. An unusual ulnar nerve injury associated with dislocation of the elbow. Injury 8:145–147, 1976.

147. Skaggs, D.L.; Mirzayan, R. The posterior fat pad sign in association with occult fracture of the elbow in children. J Bone Joint Surg Am 81:1429–1433, 1999.

148. Starch, D.W.; Dabezies, E.J. Magnetic resonance imaging of the interosseous membrane of the forearm. J Bone Joint Surg Am 83:235–242, 2001.

149. Stephen, I.B.M. Excision of the radial head for closed fracture. Acta Orthop Scand 52:409–412, 1981.

150. Strange, F.G.St.C. Entrapment of the median nerve after dislocation of the elbow. J Bone Joint Surg Br 64:224–225, 1982.

151. Stugh, L.H. Anterior dislocation of the elbow with fracture of the olecranon. Am J Surg 75:700–703, 1948.

152. Sturm, J.T.; Rothenberger, D.A.; Strate, R.G. Brachial artery disruption following closed elbow dislocation. J Trauma 18:364–366, 1978.

153. Swanson, A.B.; Jaeger, S.H.; LaRochelle, D. Comminuted fractures of the radial head: The role of silicone implant replacement arthroplasty. J Bone Joint Surg Am 63:1039–1049, 1981.

154. Symeonides, P.P.; Paschaloglov, C.; Stavrov, Z.; Pangalides, T. Recurrent dislocation of the elbow: Report of three cases. J Bone Joint Surg Am 57:1084–1086, 1975.

155. Szaly, F.S.; Dagosto, M. Locomotor adaptations as reflected on the humerus of paleogene primates. Folia Primatol 34:1–45, 1980.

156. Taylor, T.K.F.; O'Connor, B.T. The effect upon the inferior radioulnar joint and excision of the head of the radius in adults. J Bone Joint Surg Br 46:83–84, 1964.

157. Terada, N.; Yamada, H.; Seki, T.; et al. The importance of reducing small fractures of the coronoid process in the treatment of unstable elbow dislocation. J Shoulder Elbow Surg 9:344–346, 2000.

158. Thomas, T.T. A contribution to the mechanism of fractures and dislocations in the elbow region. Ann Surg 89:108, 1929.

159. Thomas, T.T. Fractures of the head and the radius. An experimental study and recent report of cases. Univ Penn Med Bull 18:184–197, 221–234, 1905.

160. Thompson, H.C., III; Garcia, A. Myositis ossificans: Aftermath of elbow injuries. Clin Orthop 50:129, 1967.

161. Trousdale, R.T.; Amadio, P.C.; Cooney, W.P.; et al. Radioulnar dissociation: A review of twenty cases. J Bone Joint Surg Am 74:1486–1497, 1992.

162. Vierhout, R.J.; Oostvogel, H.J.M.; Van Vroonhoven, J.M.V. Internal fixation of the head of the radius. Neth J Surg 35:13–16, 1983.

163. Wadsworth, T.G. Screw fixation of the olecranon after fracture or osteotomy. Clin Orthop 119:197–201, 1976.

164. Wainwright, A.M.; Williams, J.R.; Carr, A.J. Interobserver and intraobserver variation in classification systems for fractures of the distal humerus. J Bone Joint Surg Br 82:636–642, 1999.

165. Wainwright, D. Fractures of the olecranon process. Br J Surg 29:403–406, 1941–1943.

166. Walker, P.S. Human Joints and Their Artificial Replacements. Springfield, IL, Charles C. Thomas, 1978, pp. 182–183.

167. Watson-Jones, R. Fractures and Other Bone and Joint Injuries, 2nd ed. Baltimore, Williams & Wilkins, 1941.

168. Weseley, M.S.; Barenfeld, P.A.; Eisenstein, A.L. Closed treatment of isolated radial head fractures. J Trauma 23:36–39, 1983.

169. Willenegger, H. Problems and results in the treatment of comminuted fractures of the elbow. Reconstr Surg Traumatol 11:118–127, 1969.

170. Wolfgang, G.; Burke, F.; Bush, D.; et al. Surgical treatment of displaced olecranon fractures by tension band wiring technique. Clin Orthop 224:192–204, 1987.

171. Worsing, R.A.; Engber, W.D.; Lange, T.A. Reactive synovitis from particulate Silastic. J Bone Joint Surg Am 64:581–585, 1982.

172. Wyrsch, R.B.; Seiler, J.G.; Weikert, D.R.; et al. Early experience with the compass elbow hinge: A retrospective review. Orthop Trans 21:442, 1997.

173. Yamaguchi, K.; Sweet, F.A.; Bindra, R.; et al. The extraosseous and intraosseous arterial anatomy of the adult elbow. J Bone Joint Surg Am 79:1653–1661, 1997.

174. Zuelzer, W.A. Fixation of small but important bone fragments with a hook plate. J Bone Joint Surg Am 33:430–436, 1951.

**Fractures of the Distal Humerus**

175. Ackerman, G.; Jupiter, J. Nonunion of fractures of the distal end of the humerus. J Bone Joint Surg Am 70:75–83, 1988.

176. Aitken, G.K.; Rorabeck, C.H. Distal humeral fractures in the adult. Clin Orthop 207:191–197, 1986.

177. Alvarez, E.; Patel, M.; Nimberg, P.; et al. Fractures of the capitellum humeri. J Bone Joint Surg Am 57:1093–1096, 1975.

178. Anson, B.J.; Maddock, W.G., eds. Callander's Surgical Anatomy. Philadelphia, W.B. Saunders, 1958.

179. Böhler, L. The Treatment of Fractures, 5th ed., Vol. 1. New York, Grune & Stratton, 1956.

180. Brown, R.F.; Morgan, R.G. Intercondylar T-shaped fractures of the humerus: Results in ten cases treated by early mobilization. J Bone Joint Surg Br 53:425–428, 1971.

181. Bryan, R.S.; Morrey, B.F. Fractures of the distal humerus. In: Morrey, B.F., ed. The Elbow and Its Disorders. Philadelphia, W.B. Saunders, 1985, pp. 302–339.

182. Bryan, R.S. Fractures about the elbow in adults. Instr Course Lect 30:200–223, 1981.

183. Bryan, R.S.; Bickel, W.H. "T" condylar fractures of the distal humerus. J Trauma 11:830–835, 1971.

184. Cassebaum, W.H. Open reduction of T and Y fractures of the lower end of the humerus. J Trauma 9:915–925, 1969.

185. Christopher, F.; Bushnell, L. Conservative treatment of fractures of the capitellum. J Bone Joint Surg 17:489–492, 1935.

186. Collert, S. Surgical management of fractures of the capitellum humerus. Acta Orthop Scand 48:603–606, 1977.

187. Conwell, H.E.; Reynolds, F.C., eds. Key and Conwell's Management of Fractures, Dislocations, and Sprains, 7th ed. St. Louis, C.V. Mosby, 1961.

188. DeLee, J.C.; Green, D.P.; Wilkins, K.E. Fractures and dislocations of the elbow. In: Rockwood, C.A., Jr.; Green, D.P., eds. Fractures, 2nd ed. Philadelphia, J.B. Lippincott, 1984.

189. Dorland's Illustrated Medical Dictionary, 24th ed. Philadelphia, W.B. Saunders, 1965.

190. DePalma, A.F. The Management of Fractures and Dislocations, Vol. 2. Philadelphia, W.B. Saunders, 1970.

191. Dusuttle, R.; Coyle, M.; Zawalsky, J.; Bloom, H. Fractures of the capitellum. J Trauma 25:317–321, 1985.

192. Eastwood, W.J. The T-shaped fracture of the lower end of the humerus. J Bone Joint Surg 19:364–369, 1937.

193. Evans, E.M. Supracondylar Y fractures of the humerus. J Bone Joint Surg Br 35:381–385, 1953.

194. Gabel, G.T.; Hanson, G.; Bennett, J.B.; et al. Intraarticular fractures of the distal humerus in the adult. Clin Orthop 216:99–107, 1987.

195. Glanville, F.U. Perforation of the coronoid olecranon in septum humeroulnar relationships in Netherlands and African populations. Am J Phys Anthropol 26:85–92, 1967.

196. Grant, J.C.B. Grant's Atlas of Anatomy, 6th ed. Baltimore, Williams & Wilkins, 1972.

197. Grantham, S.A.; Norris, T.R.; Bush, D.C. Isolated fracture of the humeral capitellum. Clin Orthop 161.262–269, 1981.

198. Greenspan, A.; Norman, A. Radial head–capitellum view: An expanded imaging approach to elbow injuries. Radiology 164:272–274, 1987.

199. Guyot, J. Atlas of Human Limb Joints. Berlin, Springer-Verlag, 1981.

200. Hahn, N.F. Fall von einer besonderes Varietät der Frakturen des Ellenbogens. Z Wund Geburt 6:185, 1853.

201. Hamilton, F.H. A Practical Treatise on Fractures and Dislocations, 8th ed. Philadelphia, Lea Brothers, 1891.

202. Hasner, E.; Husky, J. Fractures of the epicondyle and condyle of the humerus. Acta Chir Scand 101:195, 1951.

203. Heim, V.; Pfeiffer, K.M. Small Fragment Set Manual. Berlin, Springer-Verlag, 1982.

204. Jones, K.G. Percutaneous fixation of fractures of the lower end of the humerus. Clin Orthop 50:53–69, 1967.

205. Jupiter, J.B. Complex fractures of the distal part of the humerus and associated complications. J Bone Joint Surg Am 76:1252–1263, 1994.

206. Jupiter, J.B.; Barnes, K.A.; Goodman, L.J.; Saldana, A.E. Multiplane fracture of the distal humerus. J Orthop Trauma 7:215–220, 1993.

207. Jupiter, J.B.; Goodman, L.J. The management of complex distal humerus nonunion in the elderly by elbow capsulectomy, triple plating, and ulnar nerve neurolysis. J Shoulder Elbow Surg 1:37–46, 1992.

208. Jupiter, J.B.; Neff, U.; Holzach, P.; Allgöwer, M. Intercondylar fracture of the humerus. J Bone Joint Surg Am 67:226–239, 1985.

209. Keon-Cohen, B.T. Fractures at the elbow. J Bone Joint Surg Am 48:1623–1639, 1966.

210. Knight, R.A. Fractures of the humeral condyle in adults. South Med J 48:1165–1173, 1955.

211. Kuhn, J.E.; Louis, D.S.; Loder, R.T. Divergent single-column fractures of the distal part of the humerus. J Bone Joint Surg Am 77:538–542, 1995.

212. Lansinger, O.; More, K. Fractures of the capitellum humeri. Acta Orthop Scand 52:39–44, 1981.

213. London, J.T. Kinematics of the elbow. J Bone Joint Surg Am 63:529–536, 1981.

214. MacAusland, W.R.; Wyman, E.T. Fractures of the adult elbow. Instr Course Lect 24:165–181, 1975.

215. Mazel, M.S. Fracture of the capitellum. J Bone Joint Surg 17:483–488, 1935.

216. McKee, M.D.; Jupiter, J.B. A contemporary approach to the management of complex fractures of the distal humerus and their sequelae. Hand Clin 10:479–494, 1994.

217. McKee, M.D.; Jupiter, J.B.; Bamberger, H.B. Coronal shear fractures of the distal end of the humerus. J Bone Joint Surg Am 78:49–54, 1996.

218. McKee, M.D.; Jupiter, J.B.; Bosse, G.; Hines, L. The results of ulnar neurolysis for ulnar neuropathy during posttraumatic elbow reconstruction. Orthopaedic Proceedings. J Bone Joint Surg Br 77(Suppl):75, 1995.

219. McKee, M.D.; Jupiter, J.B.; Toh, C.L.; et al. Reconstruction after malunion and nonunion of intraarticular fractures of the distal humerus. Methods and results in 13 adults. J Bone Joint Surg Br 76:614–621, 1994.

220. McLaughlin, H.L. Some fractures with a time limit. Surg Clin North Am 35:555, 1955.

221. McVay, C.B. Surgical Anatomy, 5th ed., Vol. 2. Philadelphia, W.B. Saunders, 1971.

222. Medical Research Council. Aids to the Examination of the Peripheral Nervous System. London, Her Majesty's Stationary Office, 1976.

223. Mehne, D.K.; Matta, J. Bicolumn fractures of the adult humerus. Paper presented at the 53rd Annual Meeting of the American Academy of Orthopaedic Surgeons, New Orleans, 1986.

224. Milch, H. Fractures and fracture-dislocations of the humeral condyles. J Trauma 4:592–607, 1964.

225. Milch, H. Fracture Surgery: A Textbook of Common Fractures. New York, Hoeber, 1959.

226. Miller, O.L. Blind nailing of the T fracture of the lower end of the humerus which involves the joint. J Bone Joint Surg 21:933–938, 1939.

227. Miller, W.E. Comminuted fractures of the distal end of the humerus. J Bone Joint Surg Am 46:644–656, 1964.

228. Morrey, B.F.; Adams, R.A. Semiconstrained elbow replacement for distal humeral nonunion. J Bone Joint Surg Br 77:67–72, 1995.

229. Morrey, B.F.; Adams, R.A. Semiconstrained elbow replacement arthroplasty: Rationale, technique and results. In: Morrey, B.F., ed. The Elbow and Its Disorders, 2nd ed. Philadelphia, W.B. Saunders, 1993.

230. Morrey, B.F.; Adams, R.; Bryan, R.S. Total replacement for posttraumatic arthritis of the elbow. J Bone Joint Surg Br 73:607–612, 1991.

231. Morrey, B.F.; An, K. Functional anatomy of the ligaments of the elbow. Clin Orthop 201:84–89, 1985.

232. Morrey, B.F.; Askew, L.J.; Chao, E. A biomechanical study of normal functional elbow motion. J Bone Joint Surg Am 63:872–877, 1981.

233. Mostafavi, H.R.; Tornetta, P., III. Open fractures of the humerus treated with external fixation. Clin Orthop 337:187–197, 1997.

234. Niemann, M. Condyle fracture of the distal adult humerus. South Med J 70:915, 1977.

235. O'Driscoll, S.W. Prosthetic elbow replacement for distal humeral fractures and nonunion. Oper Techn Orthop 4:54–57, 1994.

236. O'Driscoll, S.W.; An, K.N.; Korinek, S.; Morrey, B.F. Kinematics of elbow semi-constrained total elbow arthroplasty. J Bone Joint Surg Br 74:297–299, 1992.

237. O'Driscoll, S.W.; Horii, E.; Morrey, B.F.; Carmichael, S.W. Anatomy of the ulnar part of the lateral collateral ligament of the elbow. Clin Anat 5:296–303, 1992.

238. Otsuka, N.Y.; McKee, M.D.; Liew, A.; et al. Functional outcome following treatment for nonunion of the humerus. Paper presented at the annual meeting of the Canadian Orthopaedic Association, Halifax, Canada, June 4, 1995.

239. Reich, R.S. Treatment of intercondylar fractures of the elbow by means of traction. J Bone Joint Surg 18:997–1004, 1936.

240. Rhodin, R. Treatment of fractures of the capitellum. Acta Chir Scand 86:475, 1942.

241. Riseborough, E.J.; Radin, E.L. Intercondylar T fractures of the humerus in the adult. A comparison of operative and nonoperative treatment in twenty-nine cases. J Bone Joint Surg Am 51:130–141, 1969.

242. Simpson, L.A.; Richards, R.R. Internal fixation of a capitellar fracture using Herbert screws. Clin Orthop 209:166–169, 1986.

243. Siris, I.E. Supracondylar fractures of the humerus. Surg Gynecol Obstet 68:201–222, 1939.

244. Smith, F.M. Surgery of the Elbow, 2nd ed. Philadelphia, W.B. Saunders, 1972.

245. Soyer, A.D.; Nowotarski, P.J.; Kelso, T.B.; Mighell, M.A. Optimal position for plate fixation of complex fractures of the proximal radius: A cadaver study. J Orthop Trauma 12:291–293, 1998.

246. Speed, J.S. Surgical treatment of condylar fractures of the humerus. Instr Course Lect 7:187–194, 1950.

247. Steinthal, D. Die isolirte Fraktur der eminentia Capetala in Ellenbogengelenk. Zentralb Chir 15:17, 1898.

248. Stricker, S.J.; Thomson, J.D.; Kelly, R.A. Coronal plane transcondylar fracture of the humerus in a child. Clin Orthop 294:308–311, 1993.

249. Sultanpur, A. Anterior supracondylar fracture of the humerus (flexion type): A simple technique for closed reduction and fixation in adults and the aged. J Bone Joint Surg Br 60:383–386, 1978.

250. Suman, R.K.; Miller, J.H. Intercondylar fractures of the distal humerus. J R Coll Surg Edinb 27:276–281, 1982.

251. VanGorder, G. Surgical approach in supracondylar "T" fractures of the humerus requiring open reduction. J Bone Joint Surg 22:278–292, 1940.

252. Waddell, J.P.; Hatch, J.; Richards, R.R. Supracondylar fractures of the humerus: Results of surgical treatment. J Trauma 28:1615–1621, 1988.

253. Watson-Jones, R. Fractures and Joint Injuries, 4th ed., Vol. 2. Baltimore, Williams & Wilkins, 1955.

254. Whitesides, T.E., Jr.; Hanley, T.C.; Morimoto, K.; Harada, H. Tissue pressure measurements as a determinant for the need of fasciotomy. Clin Orthop 113:443, 1975.

255. Wickstrom, J.; Meyer, P.R. Fractures of the distal humerus in adults. Clin Orthop 50:43–51, 1967.

256. Warwick, R.; Williams, P.C., eds. Gray's Anatomy, 3rd ed. Philadelphia, W.B. Saunders, 1980.

257. Zagorski, J.B.; Jennings, J.J.; Burkhalter, W.E.; et al. Comminuted intraarticular fractures of the distal humeral condyles: Surgical vs. nonsurgical treatment. Clin Orthop 202:197–204, 1986.

# Fractures of the Humeral Shaft

Emil H. Schemitsch, M.D., F.R.C.S.C.
Mohit Bhandari, M.D., M.Sc.

Fractures of the humeral shaft are relatively common injuries. Over 66,000 fractures of the humerus occur annually in the United States and account for over 363,000 days in the hospital.[134] Best estimates from the literature suggest that humeral shaft fractures represent approximately 3% of all fractures.[2, 31, 37, 40, 47, 52] Although most of these fractures can be treated nonoperatively, indications for operative intervention have been well reported.* Ultimately, optimal results depend on matching the treatment alternative with the character of the fracture and the needs of the patient. Defining the character of a humeral shaft fracture mandates a knowledge of basic anatomy and function.

## ANATOMY

The shaft of the humerus extends from the upper border of the insertion of the pectoralis major to the supracondylar ridge distally. The cylindrical proximal end of the humerus assumes a more triangular shape in its distal third. Three borders divide the humeral shaft into three surfaces (Fig. 43–1): the anterior border, which extends from the greater tuberosity proximally to the coronoid fossa; the medial border, which extends from the lesser tuberosity to the medial supracondylar ridge; and the lateral border, which extends from the posterior aspect of the greater tuberosity to the lateral supracondylar ridge. The anterolateral surface features the deltoid tuberosity and the sulcus for the radial nerve and profunda brachii artery. The anteromedial surface forms the floor of the intertubercular groove. The anterolateral and anteromedial surfaces blend distally, at which point they provide the origin for the brachialis muscle. The posterior surface contains the spiral groove for the radial nerve and the origin of the medial and lateral heads of the triceps[31, 62, 74, 76, 104] (see Fig. 43–1).

*See references 1–28, 30–47, 52–62, 68–70, 75, 78–90, 94, 96, 104, 106, 110–116, 118–126, 128, 129, 135, 137, 146–164, 166–175.

The medial and lateral intermuscular septa divide the arm into anterior and posterior compartments. The biceps brachii, coracobrachialis, brachialis, and anconeus muscles, the brachial artery and vein, and the median, musculocutaneous, and ulnar nerves are contained in the anterior compartment. The triceps brachii and the radial nerve constitute the posterior compartment (Fig. 43–2).

The blood supply to the humeral diaphysis arises from branches of the brachial artery. One or more nutrient vessels may emanate from this artery, the profunda brachii artery, or the posterior humeral circumflex artery to course distally and provide the intramedullary circulation. The periosteal circulation likewise depends on these vessels, multiple small muscular branches, and the arterial anastomosis about the elbow. Care must be taken to avoid disruption of both the intramedullary and the periosteal circulation during operative fracture management.[31, 62, 74, 76, 105]

## BIOMECHANICAL CONSIDERATIONS

Analysis of fractures of the humeral diaphysis reveals the effect of muscular forces acting on the shaft at varying levels (Fig. 43–3). In fractures occurring above the insertion of the pectoralis major, the proximal fragment is displaced into abduction and external rotation as a result of the action of the rotator cuff musculature (see Fig. 43–3A). Fractures occurring in the interval between the insertion of the pectoralis major proximally and the deltoid insertion distally result in adduction of the proximal fragment and proximal and lateral displacement of the distal fragment (see Fig. 43–3B). Fractures distal to the insertion of the deltoid muscle result in abduction of the upper fragment and proximal displacement of the distal fragment by unopposed muscle contraction[52] (see Fig. 43–3C).

The energy absorbed by the humerus during a fracture is an important determinant of the amount of displace-

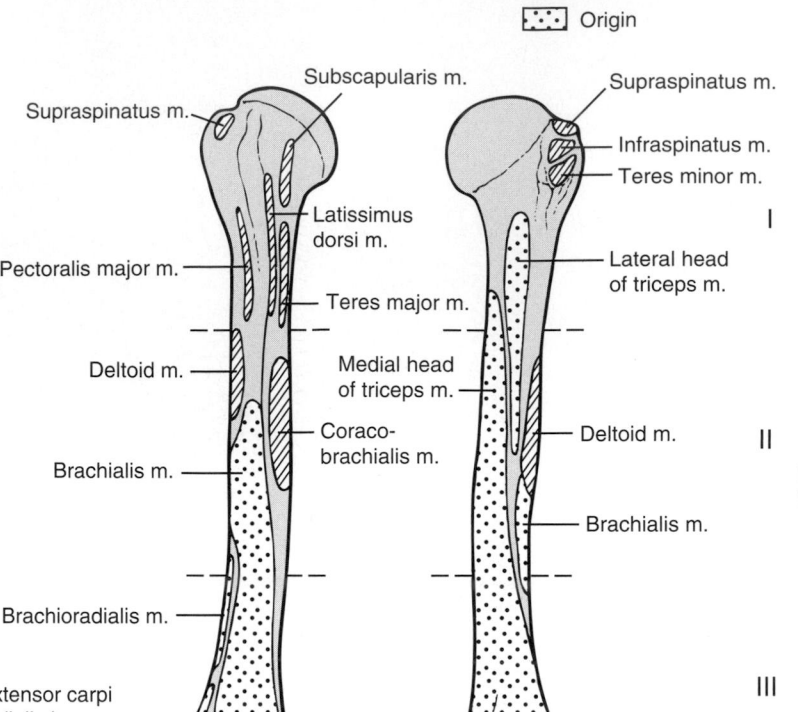

Legend:
▨ Insertion
⠿ Origin

**Anterior view labels:**
- Supraspinatus m.
- Subscapularis m.
- Pectoralis major m.
- Deltoid m.
- Brachialis m.
- Brachioradialis m.
- Extensor carpi radialis longus m.
- Common extensor tendon
- Latissimus dorsi m.
- Teres major m.
- Medial head of triceps m.
- Coraco-brachialis m.
- Pronator teres m.
- Common flexor tendon

**Posterior view labels:**
- Supraspinatus m.
- Infraspinatus m.
- Teres minor m.
- Lateral head of triceps m.
- Deltoid m.
- Brachialis m.
- Anconeus m.
- Flexor carpi ulnaris m.

ANTERIOR          POSTERIOR

I
II
III

**FIGURE 43–1.** Shaft of the humerus showing the division into three surfaces.

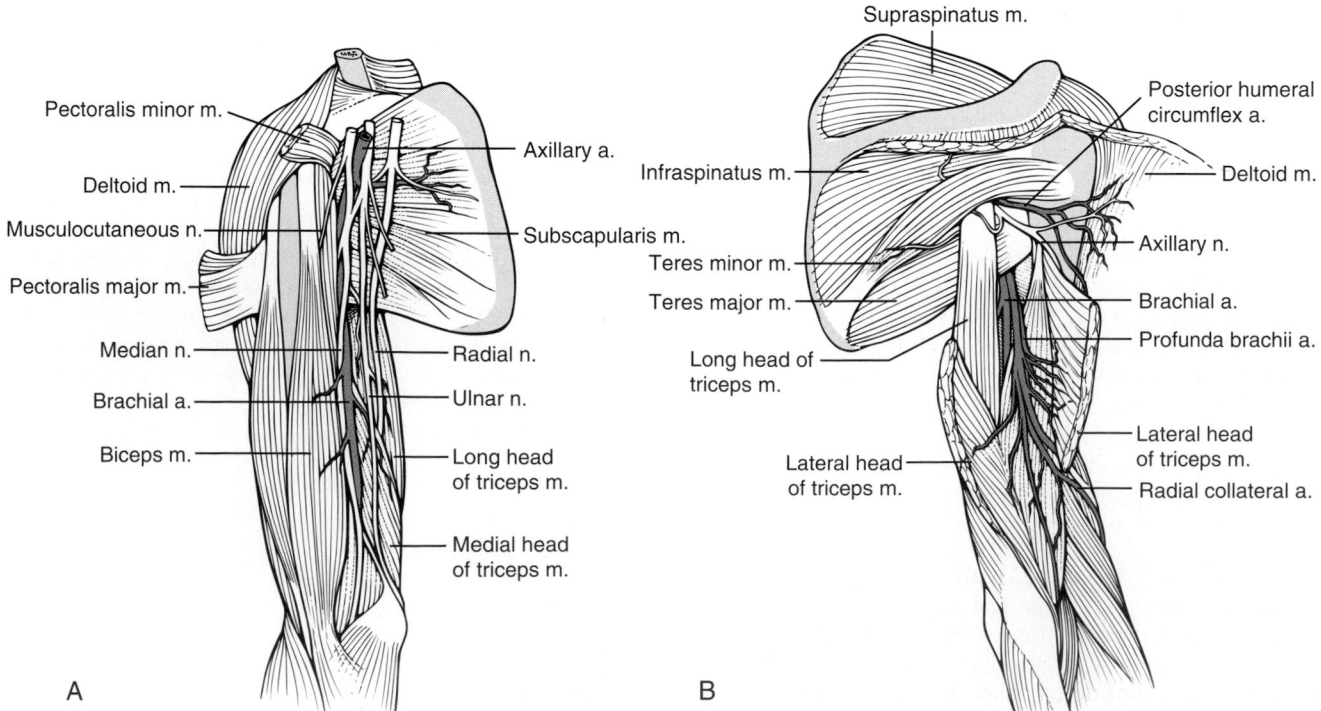

**A labels:**
- Pectoralis minor m.
- Deltoid m.
- Musculocutaneous n.
- Pectoralis major m.
- Median n.
- Brachial a.
- Biceps m.
- Axillary a.
- Subscapularis m.
- Radial n.
- Ulnar n.
- Long head of triceps m.
- Medial head of triceps m.

**B labels:**
- Supraspinatus m.
- Infraspinatus m.
- Teres minor m.
- Teres major m.
- Long head of triceps m.
- Lateral head of triceps m.
- Posterior humeral circumflex a.
- Deltoid m.
- Axillary n.
- Brachial a.
- Profunda brachii a.
- Lateral head of triceps m.
- Radial collateral a.

A          B

**FIGURE 43–2.** The muscular and neurovascular structures of the upper part of the arm are divided into anterior and posterior compartments.

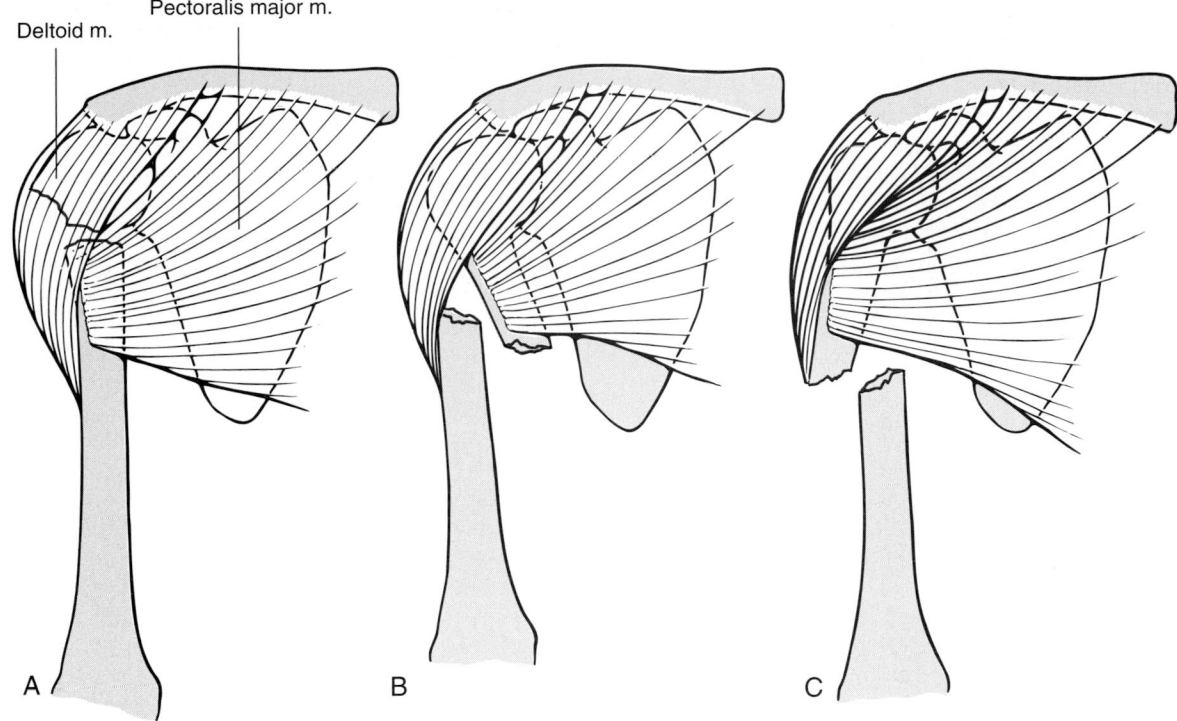

Deltoid m.        Pectoralis major m.

A        B        C

**FIGURE 43–3.** The muscular attachments to the shaft of the humerus cause different degrees of displacement, depending on the level of the fracture. *A,* The proximal fragment is abducted and externally rotated by the rotator cuff musculature in fractures occurring above the insertion of the pectoralis major. *B,* The deltoid muscle displaces the distal fragment proximally and laterally in fractures occurring proximally, between its insertion and that of the pectoralis major. *C,* Fractures distal to the insertion of the deltoid muscle result in abduction of the proximal fragment.

ment. Low-energy fractures may be held in position by the internal splinting effect of the intermuscular septa. The weight of the arm aids in preserving alignment and length in these low-velocity injuries. High-energy fractures result in comminution of the bone and disruption of the soft tissues, with loss of this internal splinting effect.

A consideration other than location of the fracture and the amount of energy absorbed or dissipated in the injury is the mobility of the shoulder and the elbow joints, which tends to minimize the effect of post-traumatic angulation and rotational deformities. Klenerman showed experimentally that the musculature around the humerus will accommodate 20° of anterior angulation and 30° of varus angulation without compromising function or appearance.[97] The normal mobility in the shoulder and elbow joints will compensate for this degree of deformity. The humerus can easily accept 15° of malrotation and still function fully. The amount of shortening that can be accepted in fractures of the humerus without loss of significant function is approximately 3 cm.

## CLASSIFICATION

The classification of humeral shaft fractures has commonly been based on the nature and location of the primary fracture lines, an estimation of the kinetics of the injury (low versus high energy), and associated soft tissue trauma. When considered collectively, these factors represent the unique "personality" of the fracture (Table 43–1).

| TABLE 43–1 |
| --- |
| Classification of Humeral Shaft Fractures |

Anatomic location
  Above the pectoralis major insertion
  Below the pectoralis major insertion, above the deltoid insertion
  Below the deltoid insertion
Fracture Personality (direction and character of the fracture)
  Transverse
  Oblique
  Spiral
  Segmental
  Comminuted
Associated soft tissue injury (Gustilo)
  Open
    Grade 1
    Grade 2
    Grade 3
  Periarticular injury
    Glenohumeral
    Elbow joint
  Nerve injury
    Radial nerve
    Median nerve
    Ulnar nerve
  Vascular injury
    Brachial artery
    Brachial vein
Intrinsic conditions of the bone
  Normal
  Pathologic
  Metabolic
  Metastatic
  Infectious
  Incomplete fractures

The approach of Epps and Grant[52] and that of Bone[17] have been combined and modified to provide a useful system.

Transverse fractures that are not internally splinted by the intramuscular septa may be difficult to control, whereas oblique fractures usually unite without difficulty. Spiral fractures in the distal third (Holstein-Lewis fracture) may produce a radial nerve injury.[75] Segmental injuries are also difficult to control, and delayed union of one or both fracture sites is common. Displaced transverse fractures may be difficult to reduce because of interposed muscle or nerve, especially in the distal third and less commonly in the middle third, and such fractures exhibit slower healing. Comminuted fractures, which are associated with soft tissue injury, are difficult to manage by internal fixation but unite well with nonoperative fracture management.

Associated soft tissue injuries may dictate the mode of treatment.[66, 67] Gustilo grade I (low energy, wound less than 1 cm) and grade II (moderate energy and soft tissue damage, wound greater than 1 cm) open fractures respond well to stable internal fixation and soft tissue care, whereas grade III (high energy, wound greater than 10 cm) injuries may call for external fixation.[17, 22, 64–67, 90] Open injuries with associated nerve or vascular damage may require stabilization to protect the repair of these structures.[39, 117, 133, 138, 139]

However, interobserver agreement among surgeons in applying the Gustilo classification has been limited.[24] Brumback and Jones reported an average 60% agreement among 245 orthopaedic surgeons in applying the Gustilo classification to 12 open fracture cases.

Because the variables presented in Table 43–1 are largely descriptive, their usefulness in clinical research and outcome studies may be limited. The AO classification is a well-accepted anatomic classification scheme for humeral shaft fractures (Fig. 43–4). Briefly, fractures are categorized as simple (type A), wedge (type B), or complex (type C). Each of these types is further subcategorized to refine the anatomic nature of the fracture. In general, types A, B, and C represent a spectrum of increasing fracture severity. Although information on the reliability of this system is limited, the AO classification, in general, has been met with low interobserver agreement.[112, 157, 173] Extrapolating from studies on other fractures, the AO classification has achieved only fair to moderate agreement ($\kappa = 0.34$ to $0.53$).[112, 157, 173] When the AO classification is simplified into its component parts, however, its reliability does improve.[173]

## DIAGNOSIS

### History and Physical Examination

Humeral shaft fractures typically result from falls, twisting injuries, penetrating injuries, and pedestrian or motor vehicle crashes. Often, the specific traumatic event is clear. In a multiply traumatized patient, a history is infrequently available from the patient because of the patient's medical condition and associated injuries. In such situations, delineating the mechanism of injury provides important clues to the nature of the patient's injuries.

Previous studies have suggested that fractures of the humerus are associated with other fractures of the upper and lower extremity.[3] Specifically, among 733 motor vehicle occupants with an Injury Severity Score greater than 12, 6.3% sustained fractures of the humerus. These fractures were found to be significantly associated with fractures of the forearm/hand, femur, tibia, and ankle/foot.[3] In addition to the mechanism of injury, information pertaining to co-morbidities such as previous neurologic injury, metabolic bone disease, malignancy, or lower extremity injuries (requiring use of the upper extremities for ambulation) should be obtained from either the patient or family members.

Prioritization of the physical examination largely depends on the nature of the traumatic event. Isolated blunt trauma to the humerus in an otherwise alert patient should result in direct attention to examination of the injured arm. However, a multiply traumatized patient involved in a motor vehicle collision should be prioritized according to the principles of Advanced Trauma and Life Support (ATLS).[6] After a primary survey consisting of assessment of the patient's airway and protection of the cervical spine, evaluation of breathing, circulatory resuscitation, control of hemorrhage, and assessment of disability, attention to the injured extremity can proceed.

The neurovascular status of the entire limb should be evaluated at multiple levels. Careful motor and sensory examination of the radial, ulnar, and median nerves is essential. The soft tissue compartments of the arm and forearm should be examined, and the possibility of a compartment syndrome should be considered. The shoulder and elbow joints should be carefully evaluated. Abrasions, lacerations, or puncture wounds on the arm should raise suspicion of an open injury necessitating emergency management.

Identification of humeral shaft fractures may also fulfill another important purpose—to serve as a marker for organ injury. Just as one previous study found femoral fractures to be a marker for small-bowel injuries,[3] a subsequent study reported that humeral shaft fractures were significantly predictive of liver injury in multiply injured patients.[4] These injuries typically occurred from lateral impact motor vehicle collisions resulting in right-sided humeral shaft fractures. Therefore, the obvious finding of a humeral shaft fracture should alert the surgeon to proceed with a careful examination for detection of intra-abdominal pathology.

### Radiographic Examination

Standard radiographic evaluation of the humerus should include two views taken at 90° to one another, with the shoulder and elbow joints included in each view.

In pathologic fractures, other studies such as technetium-labeled bone scans, computed tomograms, and magnetic resonance images are often necessary to delineate the extent of disease.

Ultrasonography may have promise in the diagnosis of long bone fractures. An evaluation of 163 individuals

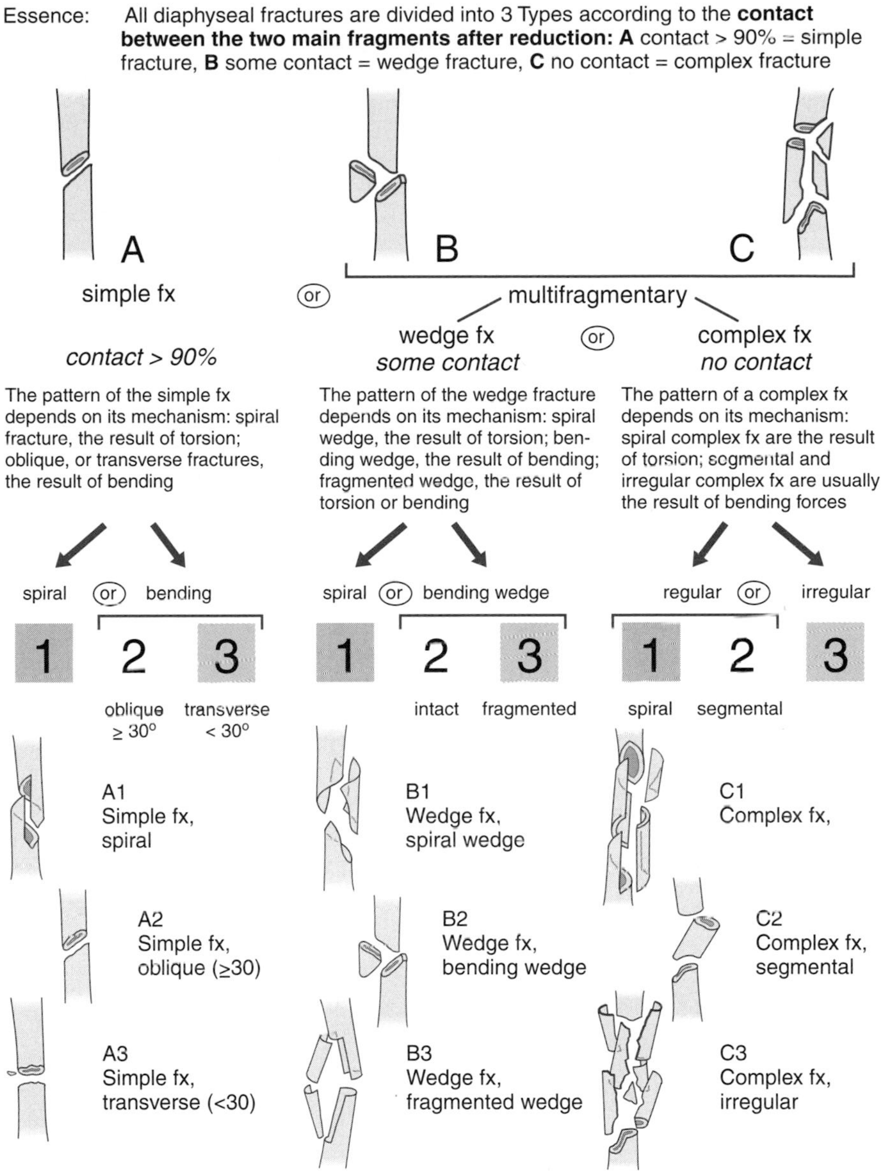

Essence:  All diaphyseal fractures are divided into 3 Types according to the **contact between the two main fragments after reduction: A** contact > 90% = simple fracture, **B** some contact = wedge fracture, **C** no contact = complex fracture

A

B

C

simple fx      (or)      multifragmentary

*contact > 90%*    wedge fx    (or)    complex fx
*some contact*              *no contact*

The pattern of the simple fx depends on its mechanism: spiral fracture, the result of torsion; oblique, or transverse fractures, the result of bending

The pattern of the wedge fracture depends on its mechanism: spiral wedge, the result of torsion; bending wedge, the result of bending; fragmented wedge, the result of torsion or bending

The pattern of a complex fx depends on its mechanism: spiral complex fx are the result of torsion; segmental and irregular complex fx are usually the result of bending forces

spiral  (or)  bending          spiral  (or)  bending wedge          regular  (or)  irregular

**1  2  3**            **1  2  3**            **1  2  3**

oblique  transverse          intact  fragmented          spiral  segmental
≥ 30°     < 30°

A1
Simple fx,
spiral

B1
Wedge fx,
spiral wedge

C1
Complex fx,

A2
Simple fx,
oblique (≥30)

B2
Wedge fx,
bending wedge

C2
Complex fx,
segmental

A3
Simple fx,
transverse (<30)

B3
Wedge fx,
fragmented wedge

C3
Complex fx,
irregular

**FIGURE 43–4.** AO classification of fractures of the humeral diaphysis. (From The Comprehensive Classification of Fractures. Bern, Switzerland, M.E. Müller Foundation, 1997.)

Definitions

**Simple fracture:** A single circumferential disruption of the diaphysis. Small cortical fragments which represent less than 10% of the circumference are ignored since they are of no significance for the treatment or prognosis
  -**spiral:** A result of torsion
  - **oblique:** The angle of the fracture line with a perpendicular to the long axis of the bone is equal to or greater than 30
  -**transverse:** The angle of the fracture line with a perpendicular to the long axis of the bone is less than 30. Usually a small wedge of less than 10% of the circumference can be detected
**Wedge fracture:** A multifragmentary fracture of the diaphysis with one or more intermediate fragment(s) in which after reduction there is some contact between the main fragments
  -**spiral:** is also called a "butterfly fragment" or a third fragment fracture
  -**bending:** Mostly caused by a direct blow. Therefore the soft tissue lesion is here more severe than in a spiral wedge fracture
  -**fragmented:** A wedge fx when after reduction the main fragments are still in some contact
**Complex fracture:** A multifragmentary fracture of the diaphysis with one or more intermediate fragments in which after reduction there is no contact between the main proximal and distal fragments
  -**spiral:** involving multiple and usually large intermediate fragments of spiral pattern
  -**segmental:** A fracture at two levels (bilocal) or three levels (trilocal). After reduction the intermediate fragment(s) make contact with more than 50% of the circumference of each of the main fragments
  -**irregular:** A diaphyseal fracture with a number of intermediate fragments without any specific pattern usually accompanied by severe soft tissue lesions

with 224 suspected fractures revealed excellent correlation with radiographs for humeral and femoral fractures.[77] Ultrasound was found to have a specificity of 83% and a sensitivity of 100% for detecting humeral fractures. These percentages correspond to a negative likelihood ratio (i.e., the likelihood of no fracture given a negative test) of 0.2 and a positive likelihood ratio that exceeds 100 (both of which result in large changes in the likelihood of a fracture). Based on this study, surgeons using ultrasound can be confident that a negative test essentially rules out a fracture and a positive test rules in a fracture.

## MANAGEMENT

Historically, fractures of the humeral shaft have been associated with a high incidence of nonunion. On this very topic, Klenerman in 1982 wrote, "It is a pity that in some parts of the world a trend of recent years has been to operate more and more readily on recent fractures of the humerus, sometimes relying on totally inadequate techniques of internal fixation without sufficient external protection, thus causing established nonunion of the fracture."[98] However, during the past 2 decades, advances in operative stabilization techniques and optimization of fracture bracing have led to a significant decline in nonunion rates.[8, 96, 116, 124, 125, 150, 171, 174]

Several variables must be considered before formulating a treatment plan. The fracture pattern, degree of soft tissue injury, associated neurologic injury, patient age, comorbidity, and patient compliance should be considered together to optimize treatment success and limit the risk of complications.

However, significant fracture deformity indicates a need for open reduction and operative stabilization. In all cases, fracture management is combined with early motion and rehabilitation of the injured extremity to limit problems associated with fracture disease.

## Nonoperative Treatment

Most humeral shaft fractures can be managed nonoperatively, with expected union rates approaching 100%.[92, 150, 151] Sir John Charnley wrote, "It is perhaps the easiest of the major long bones to treat by conservative methods."[98] The generally good outcomes with nonoperative treatment may be due, in part, to tolerance of malunion in the arm. As mentioned, Klenerman showed that 20° of anterior angulation and 30° of varus angulation are well tolerated by the musculature around the humerus.[97] The humerus can tolerate up to 3 cm of shortening as a result of overriding fracture fragments with little functional deficit.[97]

Functional fracture bracing has largely replaced all other procedures as the treatment of choice for these injuries. Typically, a coaptation splint or hanging arm cast is used until the immediate postfracture pain has subsided, usually in 3 to 7 days. A functional fracture brace is then applied. Other methods of nonoperative management include the Velpeau dressing, sling and swathe, abduction splint, shoulder spica cast, and skeletal traction. The relative advantages and disadvantages of each alternative are presented in Table 43–2.

**TABLE 43–2**

Nonoperative Treatment of Humeral Shaft Fractures

| Treatment Method | Advantages | Disadvantages | Indications |
| --- | --- | --- | --- |
| Hanging arm cast | Helps restore length<br>Can control angulation through loops at the wrist | Patient must stay erect or semierect<br>Distraction can lead to nonunion<br>Limits range of motion of the hand, wrist, elbow, and shoulder | Mostly used for initial treatment to obtain reduction in a shortened fracture<br>Usually changed to functional bracing after an initial period of treatment |
| Coaptation splint | Inexpensive<br>Easy to apply<br>Allows motion of the hand and wrist | May allow shortening of the fracture<br>Axillary irritation<br>Angular union in obese patients | Initial management of nondisplaced or minimally displaced fractures<br>Usually changed to functional bracing |
| Velpeau's dressing/ sling and swath | Can be useful in unmanageable children or elderly patients who are uncooperative | Restricts motion to all joints<br>Potential for skin maceration | Used as initial treatment in uncooperative children or elderly patients |
| Abduction cast/splint | No clear advantages | Poorly tolerated, awkward position with rotator cuff pressure | Always listed as an option in textbooks, but no clear indication for its use |
| Skeletal traction | Can be used in recumbent patients<br>Can be used with large soft tissue defects and allows access to wounds | Requires patient cooperation<br>Risk of infection<br>Requires close supervision<br>Potential for ulnar nerve injury | Rarely used because it has no clear advantage over external fixation |
| Functional fracture bracing | Allows motion of all joints<br>Lightweight and well tolerated<br>Decreased nonunion rate | Is not useful for initial reduction or bringing fracture out to length | The current gold standard for most shaft fractures after an initial period in a hanging cast or coaptation splint |

*Source:* Degnan, G. In: Baratz, M.E., ed. Orthopaedic Surgery: The Essentials. New York, Thieme, 1999, p. 317.

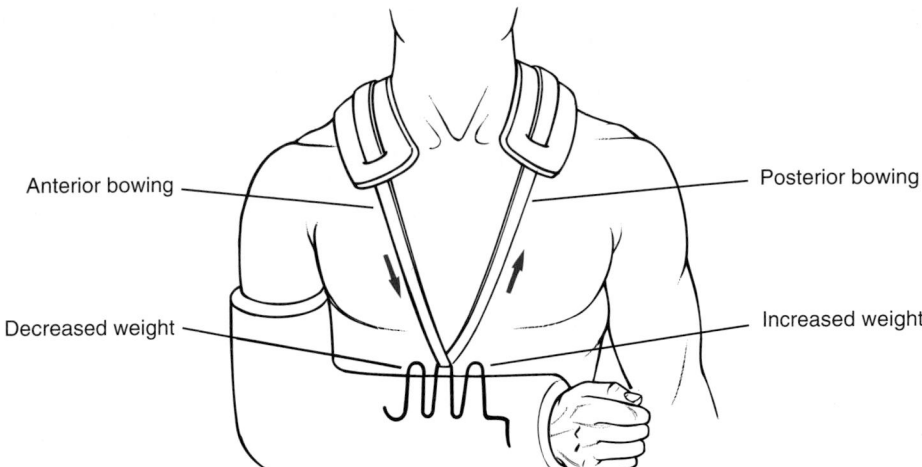

FIGURE 43–5. A hanging arm cast is used both to obtain reduction of the fracture and to allow union in this reduced position.

Anterior bowing    Posterior bowing
Decreased weight    Increased weight

## HANGING ARM CASTS

The hanging arm cast technique, introduced by Caldwell in 1933, remains a standard management technique for humeral shaft fractures.[26, 27, 79, 104] The indications for use of a hanging arm cast include displaced midshaft humeral fractures with shortening, particularly fractures with an oblique or spiral pattern. Use of the hanging arm cast is not indicated for transverse fractures because of the potential for distraction and healing complications.

Specific principles should be followed when using this technique: (1) a lightweight cast should be used, (2) it should extend from 2 cm proximal to the fracture across the elbow joint to the wrist with the elbow at 90° and the forearm in neutral rotation, (3) the cast must be secured at the wrist by wire or plaster loops[26, 27, 79, 96, 104, 137] (anterior/posterior and varus/valgus alignment at the fracture site is controlled by the attachment of the suspension strap to these loops) (Fig. 43–5), and (4) the patient should ensure that the arm is always in a dependent position.

Most surgeons use the hanging arm cast to achieve reduction in the first week after the fracture and replace it with a functional brace until healing occurs. However, if one chooses to continue with a hanging arm cast until healing, frequent reevaluation with weekly radiographs is necessary during the first month. Overdistraction of the fracture is always a risk with this technique. Patients should be allowed to begin active-assisted shoulder and hand exercises within the tolerance of their pain. Isometric exercises for the remainder of the arm are also recommended for optimal results. With careful patient selection and proper technique, union rates of 93% to 96% can be achieved with this technique.[26, 27, 79, 96, 104, 137]

## VELPEAU DRESSING/SLING AND SWATHE

Gilchrist described an inexpensive, easily applied device for immobilization of the shoulder and humerus.[61] A similar, but more restrictive device is the sling and swathe dressing (see Fig. 43–7), which is most useful for nondisplaced or minimally displaced fractures in children younger than 8 years or in elderly patients who

are unable to tolerate other methods of management. Pads composed of various materials can be placed in the axilla to control the angulation of the fracture site. These splints serve as load-sharing devices and rely heavily on the inherent soft tissue integrity around the fracture to maintain stability.[107] The Velpeau dressing is seldom used and should be replaced with a functional fracture brace as soon as possible without compromising the patient.

## COAPTATION SPLINT

A coaptation splint (i.e., sugar tongs or U splint) supplemented with a collar and cuff is often used to acutely splint humeral shaft fractures that are minimally displaced or not suitable for a hanging arm cast.[16, 34, 46] The arm should be covered with a stockinette and supplemental padding before plaster application. Care should be taken to ensure that the plaster extends over the deltoid, around the elbow, and up to the axilla.

Modifications to the technique of applying this splint have been reported. One such modification includes extension of the plaster beyond the deltoid to the base of the neck around to the axillary fold.[156] This technique requires an additional strap around the chest to prevent slippage. The patient can expect motion of the hand and wrist (limited at the elbow). Close follow-up is necessary to identify potential pitfalls such as axillary irritation, shortening of the fracture, displacement, and pain.

## ABDUCTION SPLINT—SHOULDER SPICA CAST

Though used infrequently, a plaster or Orthoplast splint supporting the arm in abduction has been advocated for certain humeral shaft fractures.[73, 162] The primary indication may be for situations in which closed reduction of the fracture requires significant abduction and external rotation of the upper extremity. However, in such situations, operative stabilization of the fracture is frequently performed. Disadvantages of these splints include the unusual and awkward position of the arm, immobilization of the shoulder, and pressure on the rotator cuff.

## SKELETAL TRACTION

Skeletal traction is rarely indicated. However, it can be used in patients who must remain recumbent or have extensive soft tissue injuries requiring open wound care (these situations are presently more suited for operative stabilization). When used, skeletal traction is applied through a transolecranon Kirschner wire or Steinmann pin. The pin should be inserted in a medial-to-lateral direction to minimize the risk of ulnar nerve injury.[52]

## FUNCTIONAL BRACING

Sarmiento and colleagues pioneered the concept of functional bracing of humeral fractures in 1977.[150] A functional brace is an orthosis that achieves fracture reduction through soft tissue compression. Though initially designed as a wraparound sleeve, current braces use an anterior shell with a contour for the biceps tendon and a posterior shell with a triceps contour to ensure adequate compression and support for the fracture. One of the shells is designed to fit inside the other, and Velcro straps hold the brace in proper position. These straps can be tightened as swelling decreases over time. Although the original braces of Sarmiento and co-workers were custom fabricated, prefabricated braces are readily available and commonly used (Fig. 43–6).

Fractures stabilized by Velpeau slings or hanging casts should be converted to functional braces within 3 to 7 days when the acute pain and swelling have subsided. Slings can be used initially but should be discontinued as soon as feasible because they lead to varus and internal rotation deformities. Patients are allowed to use the injured extremity as much as tolerated. The distal sleeve of the brace is fashioned to avoid the medial and lateral

epicondyles and permit free elbow motion. Abduction should be limited to 60° to 70° until fracture healing has progressed and is evident on radiographs. The brace should be worn for at least 8 weeks and can be discontinued if the patient exhibits pain-free abduction with radiographic evidence of fracture healing. Union rates of 96% to 100% have been reported with these devices[8, 116, 150] (Fig. 43–7).

Sarmiento and colleagues reported the largest series of patients with diaphyseal humeral fractures treated by functional bracing.[151] Of 922 patients treated with functional braces, these investigators were able to gain follow-up data on 620 (67%). All patients were treated in standard fashion. Briefly, the extremity was initially stabilized in a coaptation splint or above-elbow cast for a mean of 9 days, after which a prefabricated brace was applied and supplemented with a collar and cuff. Patients were instructed to begin pendular exercises and combine active/passive range of motion after splint application. Closed fractures (465, 75%) healed at a median of 9.5 weeks, whereas open fractures (155, 25%) healed at a median of 14 weeks. Ninety-seven percent of the fractures healed without complications. Nonunion developed in nine patients (6%) with open fractures and seven patients (<2%) with closed fractures. The final angular deformities were cosmetically acceptable in most instances (87% healed in <16° varus angulation; 81% healed in <16° anterior angulation). Four patients (<1%) suffered a refracture after treatment.

Despite the promising results reported by Sarmiento and coauthors, complications of functional bracing include angular deformities. Patients at risk for varus angular deformities include obese females with pendulous breasts. However, the cosmetic defect associated with this varus angulation is often masked in such patients. Daily hygiene is also of paramount importance to prevent skin maceration during the course of splinting.

Contraindications to the use of a functional brace include (1) massive soft tissue injury or bone loss, (2) an unreliable or noncompliant patient, and (3) an inability to obtain or maintain acceptable fracture alignment. In these situations, alternative treatment strategies should be considered.

## Operative Treatment

Although nonoperative treatment can be successful in most humeral shaft fractures, operative intervention is indicated in special circumstances, including (1) failure of closed reduction, (2) intra-articular extension, (3) neurovascular compromise, (4) associated ipsilateral forearm and elbow fractures (Fig. 43–8), (5) segmental fractures, (6) pathologic fractures, (7) open fractures, (8) fractures in polytraumatized patients, (9) bilateral humeral shaft fractures, and (10) periprosthetic fractures (Fig. 43–9) (Table 43–3). Given the relative propensity for delayed union in transverse or short oblique fractures managed nonoperatively in an active individual, these fracture patterns may be relative indications for surgery.[153] Alternatives to operative stabilization include intramedullary

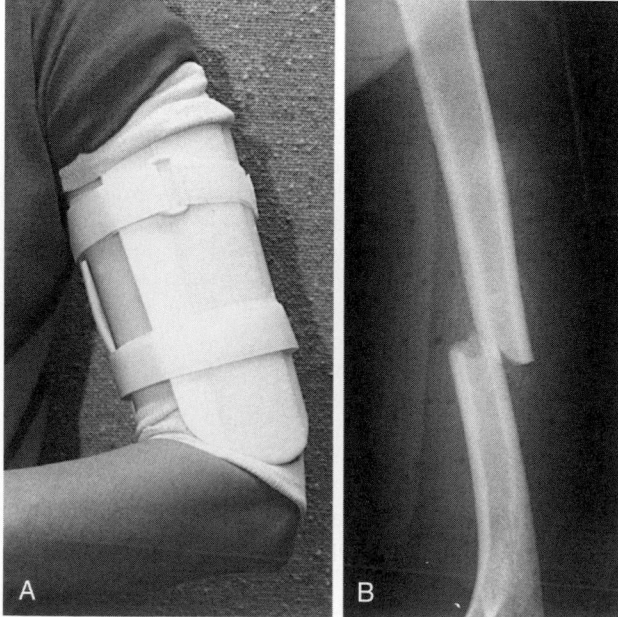

**FIGURE 43–6.** *A,* A humeral fracture brace uses hydraulic force to maintain fracture alignment while allowing mobilization of the entire upper extremity. *B,* Radiograph showing bone apposition in a functional fracture brace.

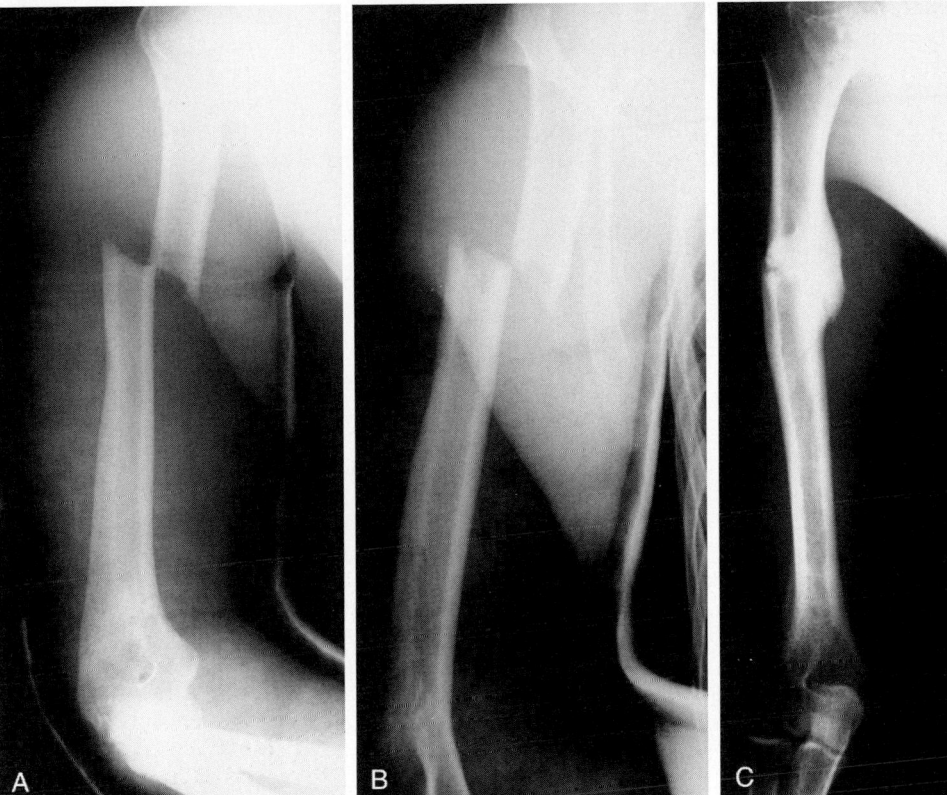

**FIGURE 43–7.** *A, B,* Humeral shaft fracture with significant displacement initially treated in a hanging cast and then converted to a humeral fracture brace. *C,* Radiograph showing a well-aligned fracture after removal of a functional fracture brace.

nailing, compression plating and screw osteosynthesis, and external fixation.[71]

## PLATE OSTEOSYNTHESIS

### Surgical Approaches for Plating of the Humerus

Several approaches to the shaft of the humerus[31, 74, 76, 119, 121, 130] may be used and include an extended lateral approach, an anterolateral approach, a posterior approach, and an anteromedial approach. Of these, the anterolateral and posterior approaches are most often used for operative stabilization of fractures of the humerus.[76] Generally, fractures of the proximal two thirds are exposed by an anterolateral approach. When radial exploration is required, a straight lateral approach can be used. Isolated fractures in the distal half of the humerus can be approached posteriorly. The anteromedial approach is seldom used because of the potential for significant neurovascular injury.

**Anterolateral Approach.** The anterolateral approach is most often used for fractures of the proximal and middle thirds of the humeral shaft (Fig. 43–10), but it can also be used for distal fractures. Furthermore, the radial nerve is generally located with greater ease in distal fractures when the anterolateral approach is used. The patient is placed supine with padding under the shoulder to support the scapula. The arm is draped free to allow access to the neck, shoulder, elbow, and forearm. The shoulder is abducted 45° to 60°.

Surface landmarks include the coracoid process, the deltopectoral groove, the lateral bicipital sulcus, and the lateral epicondyle. The skin incision can begin 5 cm distal to the coracoid process and pass along the deltopectoral groove. The incision continues along the lateral border of the biceps to within 7.5 cm of the elbow joint. The superficial and deep fascia is divided, with care taken to protect the cephalic vein. The humerus is approached between the deltoid and the pectoralis major muscles proximally. Distally, the biceps is mobilized medially to expose the brachialis muscle. Deep dissection is performed longitudinally through the brachialis (lateral to its midline) to expose the humerus. Innervation of the brachialis muscle is preserved during this approach inasmuch as its lateral portion is supplied by the radial nerve and the medial portion by the musculocutaneous nerve. Flexion of the elbow, along with partial anterior detachment of the medial brachialis origin, can facilitate improved visualization of the humerus. As it winds around the humeral shaft, the radial nerve is protected by the lateral half of the brachialis muscle. In its most distal extent, the approach continues between the brachialis medially and the brachioradialis laterally. Care must be taken to avoid injury to the radial nerve laterally and the lateral antebrachial cutaneous nerve medially.[76]

**Posterior Approach.** The posterior approach is a triceps-splitting approach that exposes the humeral shaft from the olecranon fossa to the middle third of the humerus. The posterior approach is most useful in isolated fractures of the distal end of the humerus (Fig. 43–11). This approach is also indicated when revision or repair of radial nerve injury is necessary.

The patient is placed in the prone or lateral position with the arm abducted 90° over an elbow rest. The arm is draped free to allow access to the elbow and shoulder joints. A straight skin incision is aligned from the posterolateral edge of the acromion to the tip of the olecranon. Typically, this incision begins at the free border of the deltoid and ends 4 cm proximal to the tip of the olecranon. Proximally, the interval between the long and lateral head of the triceps is identified and dissected

bluntly. Distally, sharp dissection is required to divide the triceps tendon. The lateral brachial cutaneous nerve should be preserved. The medial (or deep) head is split in the midline to expose the humerus. At the proximal extent of the medial head, the profunda brachii and radial nerve run along the spiral groove and should be identified and

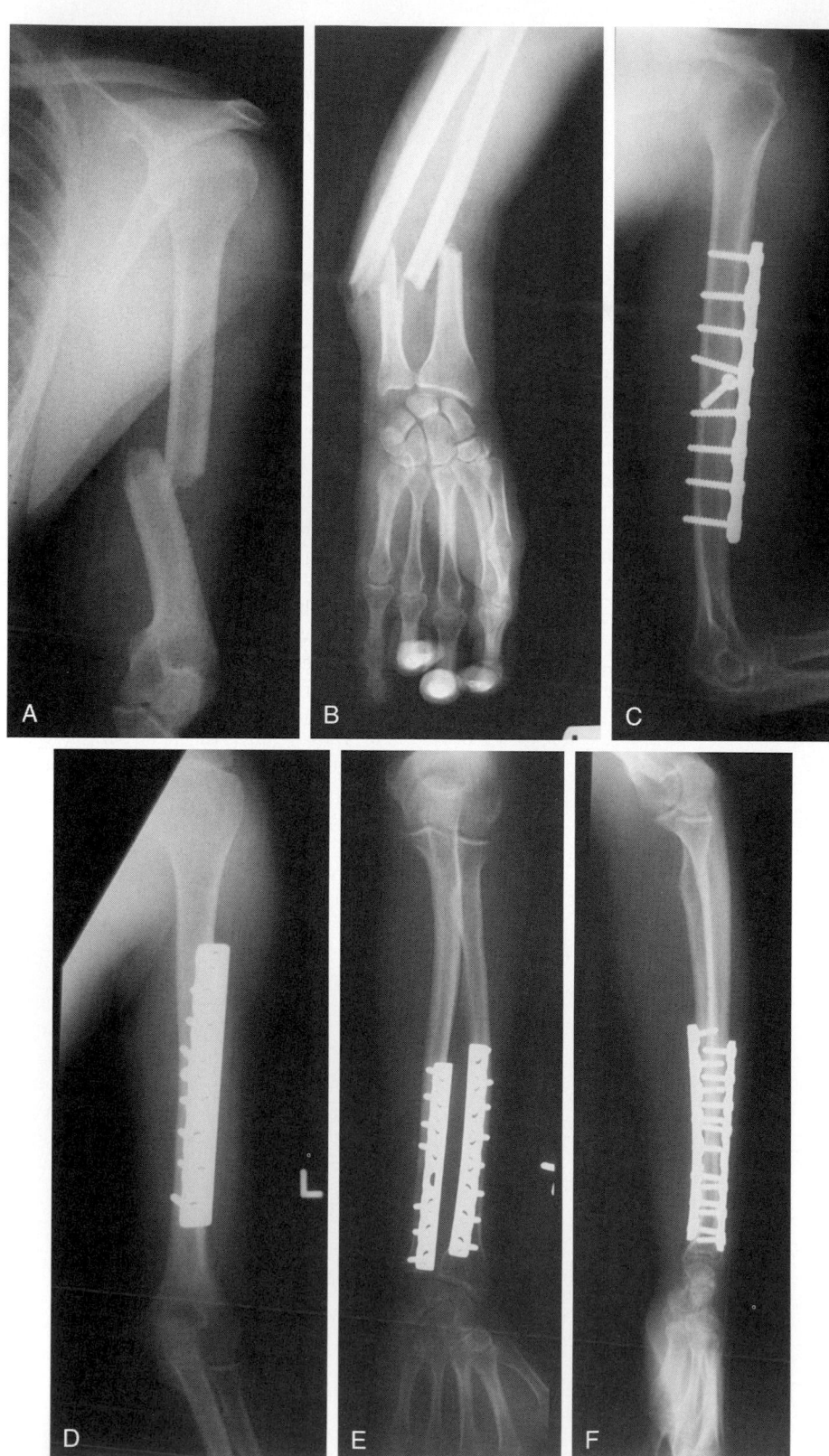

**FIGURE 43–8.** *A*, Radiograph showing a displaced humeral shaft fracture. *B*, Radiograph showing an ipsilateral both-bone forearm fracture. *C, D,* Radiographs showing open reduction and internal fixation of the humerus with a limited-contact dynamic compression plate and lag screws. *E, F,* Radiographs showing open reduction and internal fixation with a limited-contact dynamic compression plate for the radius and ulna.

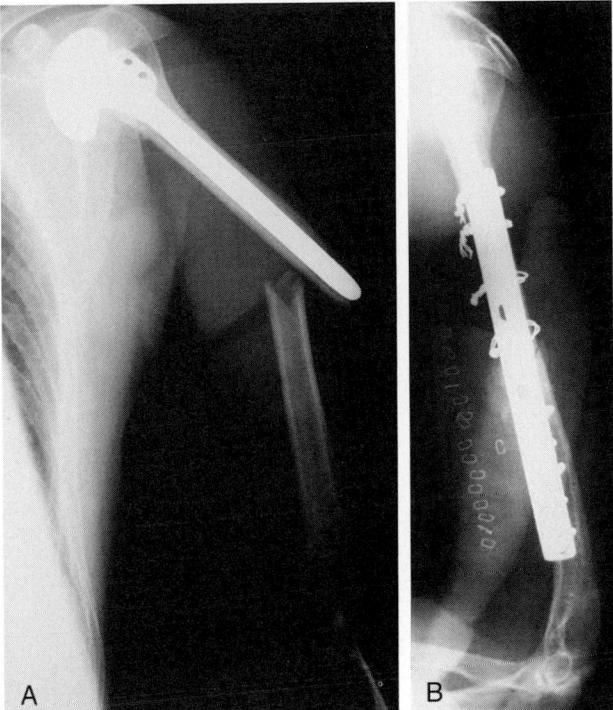

**FIGURE 43–9.** *A,* Radiograph showing a periprosthetic humeral shaft fracture. *B,* Open reduction and internal fixation by means of a dynamic compression plate with screw fixation distally and cerclage wire fixation proximally.

protected. Proximal dissection is limited by the axillary nerve and the posterior humeral circumflex vessels.

The obvious disadvantage to this approach is danger to the radial nerve and profunda brachii vessels because they directly cross the path of the incision.[76]

**Lateral Approach.** The extended lateral approach takes advantage of the lateral approach to the elbow and applies it more proximally.[119] The patient can be placed supine and the distal two thirds of the humerus exposed in the intermuscular plane between the triceps and anterior arm muscles. Thus, the radial nerve can be visualized

**TABLE 43–3**

Indications for Surgical Intervention

**EXTREMITY INDICATIONS**

Failed closed treatment
  Loss of reduction
  Poor patient tolerance/compliance
Open fracture
Vascular/neurologic injury
Segmental fractures
Floating elbow (associated fractures of the forearm)
Associated intra-articular fractures
Associated injuries to the brachial plexus
Chronic problems (nonunion, malunion, infection)

**PATIENT INDICATIONS**

Bilateral fractures
Pathologic fractures
Parkinson's disease
Polytrauma
  Head injuries
  Burns
  Chest trauma
  Multiple fractures

*Source:* Adapted from Lange, R. In: Levine, A., ed. Orthopaedic Knowledge Update: Trauma. Rosemont, Il, American Academy of Orthopaedic Surgeons, 1996.

throughout its distal course in the arm. Moreover, if required, the incision can be extended proximally in a posterior triceps-splitting exposure or an anterolateral extension (through the deltopectoral interval).

**Anteromedial Approach.** The anteromedial surface of the humeral shaft can be approached posterior to the intermuscular septum along a line extending proximally from the medial epicondyle (Fig. 43–12). The ulnar nerve must be freed from the triceps muscle and retracted medially. The triceps is then separated from the posterior surface of the medial intermuscular septum and adjacent humeral shaft. The median nerve and brachial artery are at risk during the exposure. This approach is rarely used in fracture stabilization; however, indications do include fractures with vascular injury.

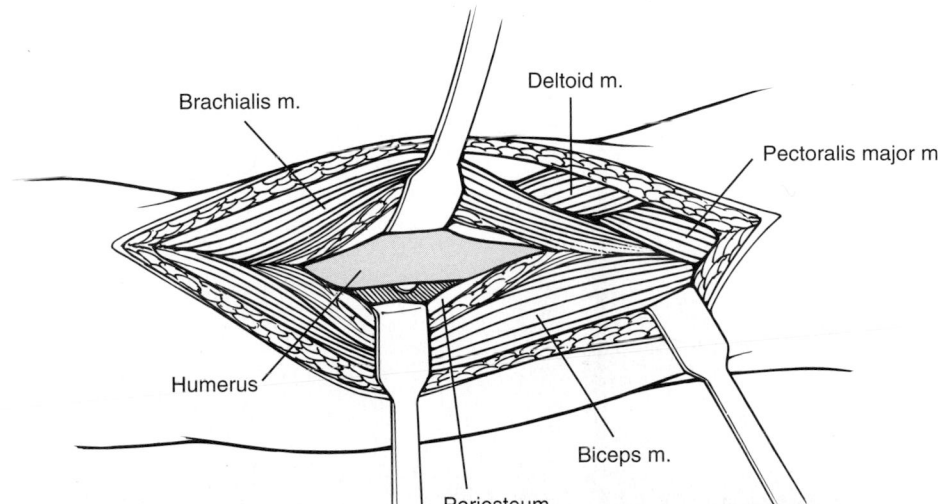

**FIGURE 43–10.** Anterolateral approach to the humeral shaft.

Brachialis m.

Deltoid m.

Pectoralis major m.

Humerus

Biceps m.

Periosteum

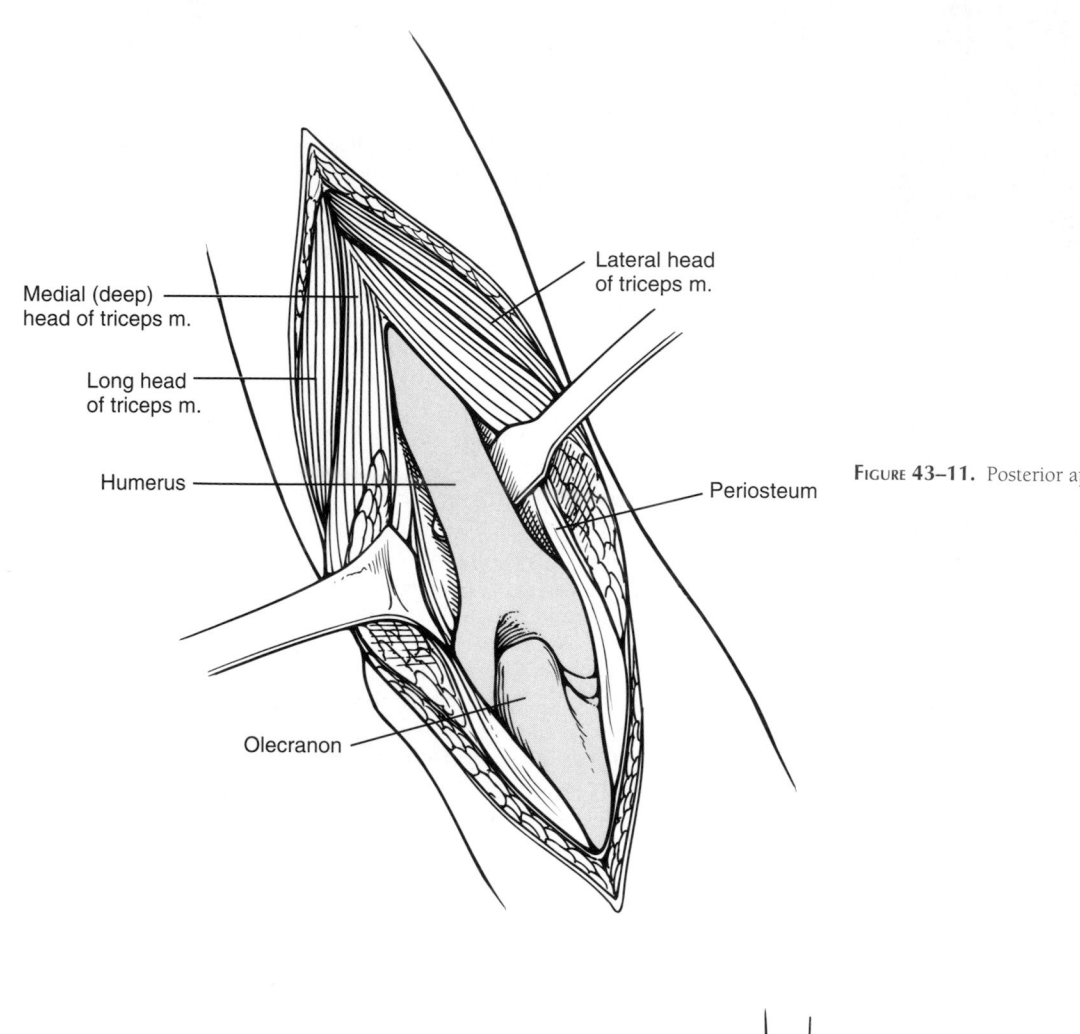

Medial (deep) head of triceps m.

Long head of triceps m.

Humerus

Olecranon

Lateral head of triceps m.

Periosteum

**FIGURE 43–11.** Posterior approach to the humeral shaft.

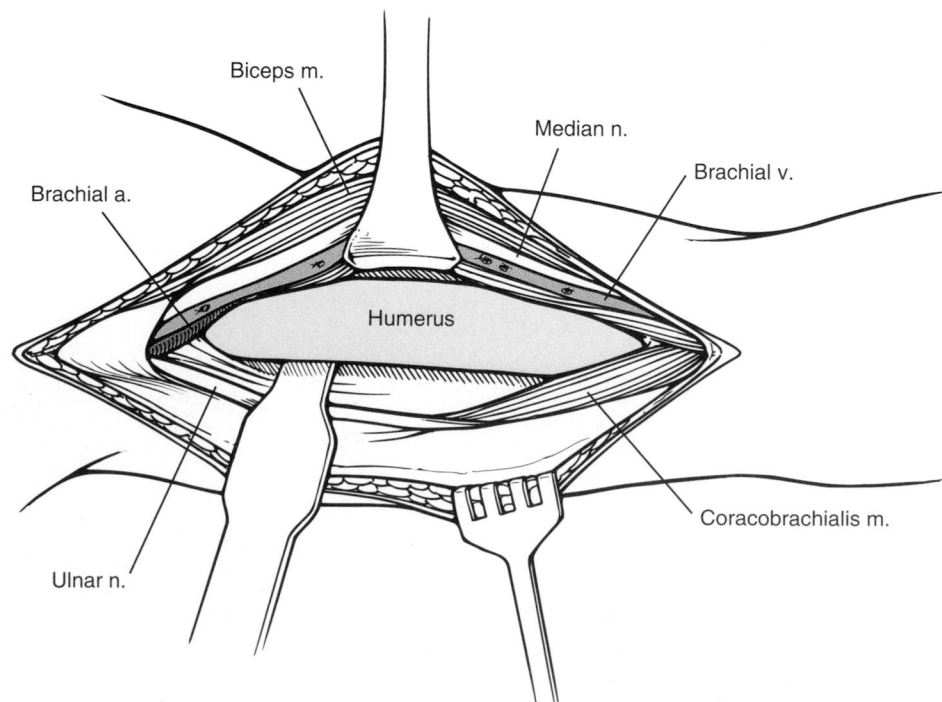

**FIGURE 43–12.** Anteromedial approach to the humeral shaft.

Brachial a.

Biceps m.

Median n.

Brachial v.

Humerus

Ulnar n.

Coracobrachialis m.

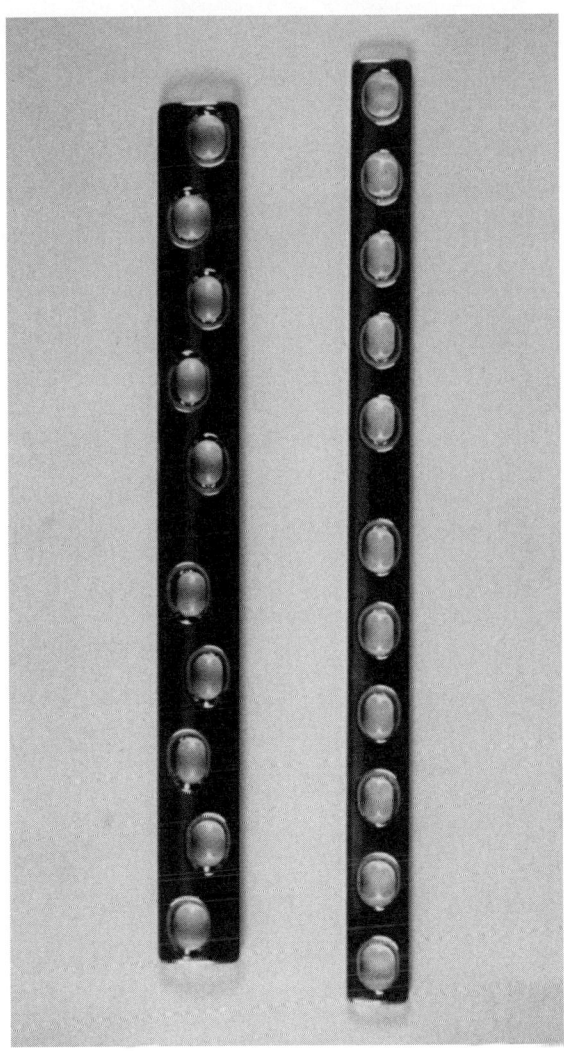

FIGURE 43–13. The broad 4.5-mm dynamic compression plate shown on the *left* has staggered screw holes to prevent longitudinal fissuring of the humerus. The small 4.5-mm dynamic compression plate on the *right* is used in individuals with narrow lumen.

## Technique of Plate Osteosynthesis

**Preoperative Plan.** When surgical treatment is indicated, a preoperative plan should consider the "personality" of the fracture and the condition of the soft tissue envelope. The location of the fracture dictates the surgical approach. As a general rule, fractures of the proximal two thirds of the humeral shaft can be approached with an anterolateral incision, whereas a posterior approach provides facile exposure of distal humeral fractures. Posterior plating of distal humeral fractures is recommended because the humerus is flat posteriorly, the plate can be applied further distally without compromising elbow function, and screw application is easier posteriorly than anteriorly.[153]

**Biomechanical Considerations.** Because the humeral shaft is prone to splintering, screw fixation alone should never be accepted. Moreover, longitudinal fissuring of the humerus can be prevented by the use of a broad 4.5-mm dynamic compression (DC) plate with staggered screw holes (Fig. 43–13). Occasionally, in individuals with

narrow humeri, a small 4.5-mm DC plate can be used. The difficult transition zone in distal humeral diaphyseal fractures can be effectively stabilized with two 3.5-mm DC plates. The optimal method for internal fixation of fractures in the distal end of the humerus has been evaluated in a number of studies.[83, 155, 179] Using cadaveric humeri, Schemitsch and colleagues found that with cortical contact, two plates placed medial and lateral (or at 90° to each other) provided maximal fixation rigidity.[154, 155] In a similar study, Jacobson and coauthors reported that among five different plate constructs (including triple plating), a medial pelvic reconstruction plate combined with a posterolateral DC plate provided the greatest rigidity (in both the sagittal and coronal planes).[83] Although a lag screw is the most efficient method of achieving secure interfragmentary compression in spiral and oblique fractures, it is not strong enough to withstand torque and bending forces. Accordingly, we suggest the addition of a neutralization plate to protect the lag screw fixation. In transverse fractures, primary interfragmentary compression is achieved with a DC plate. The stability of the fixation is greatly enhanced if an interfragmentary screw can be placed across the fracture through the plate. In all operative stabilizations of the humeral shaft, it is essential that a minimum of six and preferably eight cortices (a minimum of three to four screws) be penetrated both above and below the fracture site for adequate fixation (Fig. 43–14).

**Technique.** Provisional reduction of the fracture should be accomplished after exposure and evacuation of any hematoma. Stabilization can be achieved with reduction clamps or Kirschner wires. Whenever possible, lag screw fixation should be included as part of the overall fracture plan. A broad 4.5-mm DC plate contoured to adequately fit the shaft is applied. Extreme care should always be taken to ensure that the radial nerve is not beneath the plate before application. In transverse fractures, the plate is applied in compressive mode. Moreover, prebending (prestressing) the plate will be of further help in preventing a gap in the fracture when the screws are inserted. In spiral or oblique fractures, provisional interfragmentary lag screw fixation maintains the reduction, and the plate is applied to neutralize rotational and bending forces around the fracture. Radiographic confirmation of the reduction should be obtained both in the provisional stabilization phase and before skin closure.[17, 69, 113, 124–126, 170]

Postoperatively, patients with stable internal fixation can begin range-of-motion exercises at the shoulder and elbow in the first week and progress as tolerated. By convention, patients are not allowed to bear weight until 4 to 6 weeks after surgery. However, Tingstand and colleagues, in an observational study of 83 humeral shaft fractures,[168] reported nonsignificant differences in malunion and union rates in patients who progressed with immediate weight bearing and those who did not.

## Special Considerations in Humeral Plating

**Risk to Neurovascular Structures.** The radial nerve is always at risk during open reduction and plate fixation, so care should be taken to ensure that the radial nerve is identified before application of a plate. During plating, surgeons must confirm that the radial nerve is away from the plate and not accidentally compressed between the plate–bone interface.

**Stress Risers and Bone Blood Flow.** Fracture at the end of a plate is a well-recognized complication.[48] Attempts to reduce the stress riser effect at the end of plates have led to the use of unicortical screws at the end holes in plated fractures. However, Davenport and colleagues, in a biomechanical comparison of unicortical and bicortical fixation of distal screws in DC plates, did not find any apparent benefit to the use of unicortical screws.[44] The use of unicortical screws in this experiment did not increase torsional strength but did compromise stiffness. McKee and associates reported a 97.3% success rate with limited-contact DC (LCDC) plates in 114 consecutively treated patients with fractures of the upper extremity.[115] The LCDC plate offered advantages in facile contouring to bone and the theoretical long-term benefit of decreased stress shielding[115] (Fig. 43–15). The effect of plate osteosynthesis on blood flow and cortical bone porosity has been investigated.[84, 95] Jain and coinvestigators evaluated the efficacy of LCDC plates over DC plates in cortical bone blood flow and bone remodeling.[84] Using a canine segmental fracture model, they found a trend toward increased new bone formation with LCDC plates. Ultimately, it was the injury itself and not the type of implant that influenced the outcome.[84]

**Poor Bone Quality.** Poor-quality bone poses additional challenges in achieving stable fixation. Cement augmentation of screw fixation has been a strategy to address this problem. An alternative approach in osteoporotic bone may be the use of Schuhli locking nuts. Jazrawi and colleagues evaluated the biomechanical stability of plate constructs with Schuhli nuts in an osteoporotic humerus fracture model.[85] Schuhli nut augmentation led to a 3-fold increase in stability with cyclical torsional loading and a 1.3-fold increase in four-point axial bending when compared with standard screw fixation. These biomechanical properties were not significantly different from those of cemented augmented screws. In addition to the strategy presented by Jazrawi and associates, the use of strut allografts to augment fixation has been reported.[88, 176, 177] For instance, a combination of intramedullary fibular grafting combined with AO compression plates to achieve quadricortical fixation has yielded fracture healing rates of up to 89% in bone severely compromised by osteoporosis.[176, 177] Proximal humeral shaft fractures (with extension into the metaphysis) in patients with poor bone stock can be approached with a blade plate construct. Palmer and colleagues used interlocked blade plates customized by bending standard AO dynamic compression plates[131] and reported union rates of 100%. These principles can be used for both fresh fractures and nonunion (Figs. 43–16 and 43–17).

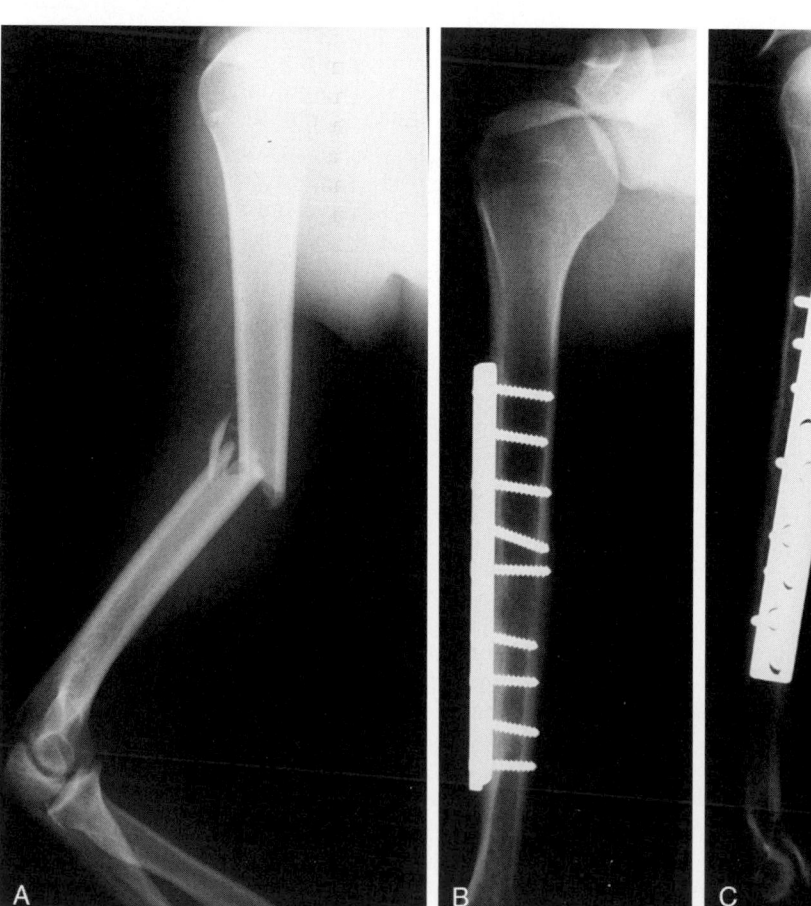

FIGURE 43–14. A, Displaced humeral shaft fracture in a multiple-trauma patient. B, C, Open reduction and internal fixation with a dynamic compression plate.

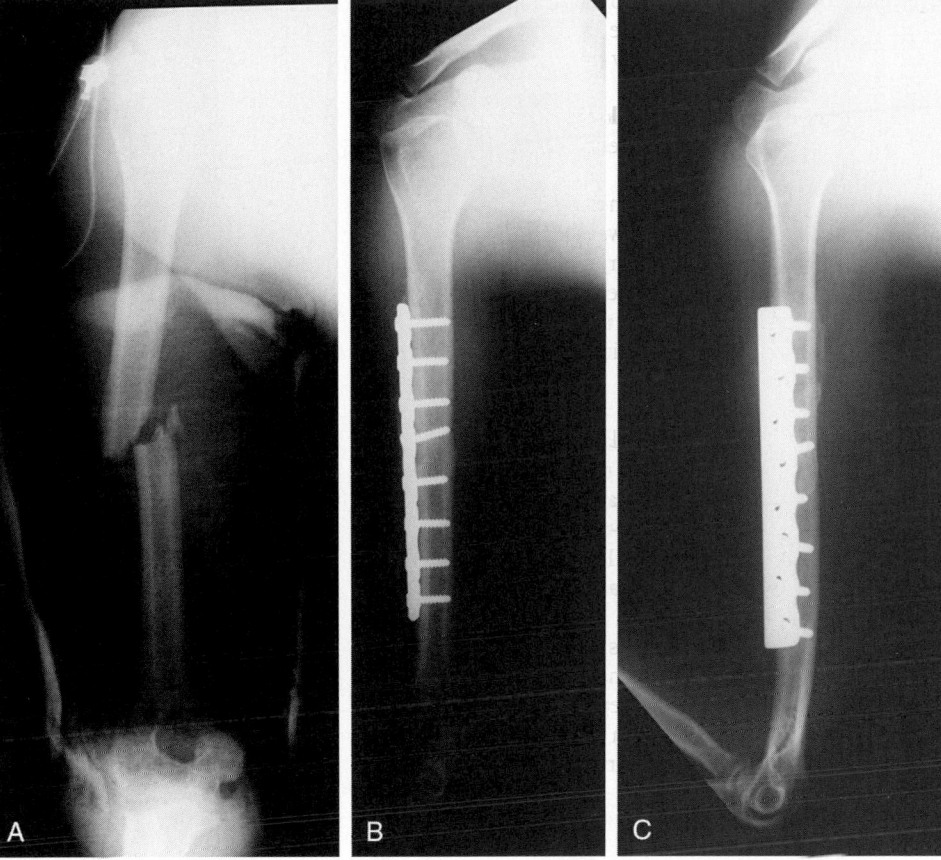

**FIGURE 43–15.** *A,* Displaced humeral shaft fracture in a patient with bilateral humeral shaft fractures. *B, C,* Open reduction and internal fixation with a limited-contact dynamic compression plate. The fracture is well aligned and well healed.

## INTRAMEDULLARY NAILING

The popularity of intramedullary fixation has been fueled, in part, by the successful management of lower extremity long bone fractures. Historically, various types of devices have been used for intramedullary nailing, including multiple Hertzog wires, the straight Küntscher cloverleaf nail (which may be inserted either antegradely or retrogradely into the humerus), tibial nails, and commercially available humeral interlocking intramedullary nails. The humeral intramedullary nails can be divided into expanding fin (interference fit, e.g., the Seidel nail or Truflex) and interlocking (e.g., Russell-Taylor [Smith and Nephew], compressing interlocking [Synthes]).

Although all indications for surgery can be applied to closed intramedullary nailing of the humerus, some circumstances may be better suited to nails, including segmental fractures, fractures in osteopenic bone, and pathologic and impending pathologic fractures. Contraindications to closed intramedullary nailing include humeral fractures associated with neurologic deficit, open Gustilo grade III fractures, fractures with bone loss, and established atrophic nonunion. An open intramedullary nailing technique should be used if this treatment option is selected.

### Biomechanical Considerations in Intramedullary Nailing

Mechanically, intramedullary nails offer several advantages over plates and external fixators. Intramedullary nails are subjected to smaller bending loads than plates are because they are closer to the mechanical axis than the usual plate position on the external surface of the bone.[5, 103] Intramedullary nails can also act as load-sharing devices in fractures with cortical contact.[5, 103] Moreover, the stress shielding commonly seen with plates and screws is minimized with intramedullary nails.[103]

Zimmerman and colleagues compared the biomechanical properties of distal fin locking nails (Seidel), solid interlocking nails, and flexible nails in cadaveric humeri with experimental transverse midshaft fractures.[179] When compared with plated humeri, the torsional properties of the solid interlocking nails were equivalent; however, solid interlocking nails offered greater bending rigidity and stiffness than plates did. Moreover, solid interlocking nails had significantly greater torsional and bending strength than did either the distal fin or flexible nail constructs.[179]

With the increasing popularity of retrograde humeral nailing, investigators have sought to identify the appropriate indications for its use based on biomechanical parameters.[108] In distal humeral shaft fractures, retrograde nails have shown significantly more initial stability and higher bending and torsional stiffness than is the case with antegrade nails. The opposite has been observed in proximal humeral shaft fractures: antegrade nails demonstrated clearly superior biomechanical properties. As one might expect, both antegrade and retrograde nails have exhibited similar properties in midshaft humeral fractures.[108]

### Antegrade Humeral Intramedullary Nailing

**Indications.** The antegrade approach is commonly used for fractures involving the proximal and middle thirds of the humerus; however, distal third fractures can also be treated with antegrade humeral nails. Nails with a curved upper segment are generally inserted through the greater tuberosity and should not be used in very proximal shaft fractures. Fractures less than 5 to 6 cm from the greater tuberosity are contraindications to the use of such nails.[140] Straight nails are inserted in line with the intramedullary canal and are suitable for proximal shaft fractures. However, these nails do so at the cost of violating the rotator cuff and lateral articular cartilage.

Accurate assessment of canal diameter is imperative in the preoperative plan for the following reasons: (1) the humerus does not tolerate reaming well,[140] (2) some nails are available in only one size (i.e., the Seidel nail, Howmedica), and (3) excessive reaming may have potential drawbacks (i.e., cortical necrosis).

**Anatomy.** The incision is typically made anterolateral to the acromion. Lateral or posterior placement of the incision increases the risk of fracture of the proximal end of the humerus on nail insertion. A deltoid-splitting approach is used, and the subdeltoid bursa is exposed and excised to visualize the supraspinatus tendon. The deltoid

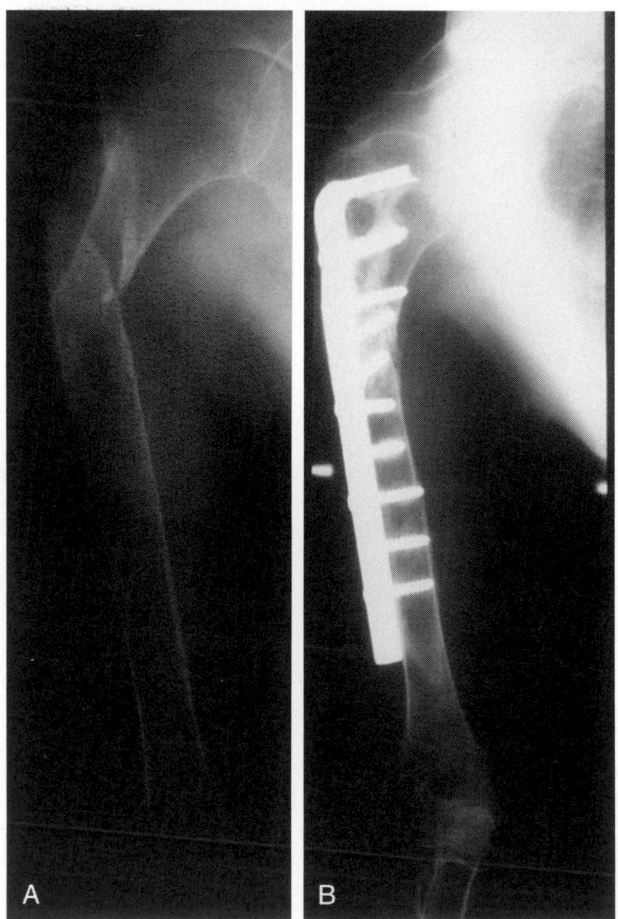

**FIGURE 43–16.** *A,* Radiograph showing atrophic nonunion of a proximal humeral shaft fracture. *B,* Open reduction and internal fixation with a blade plate and cement augmentation of screw fixation.

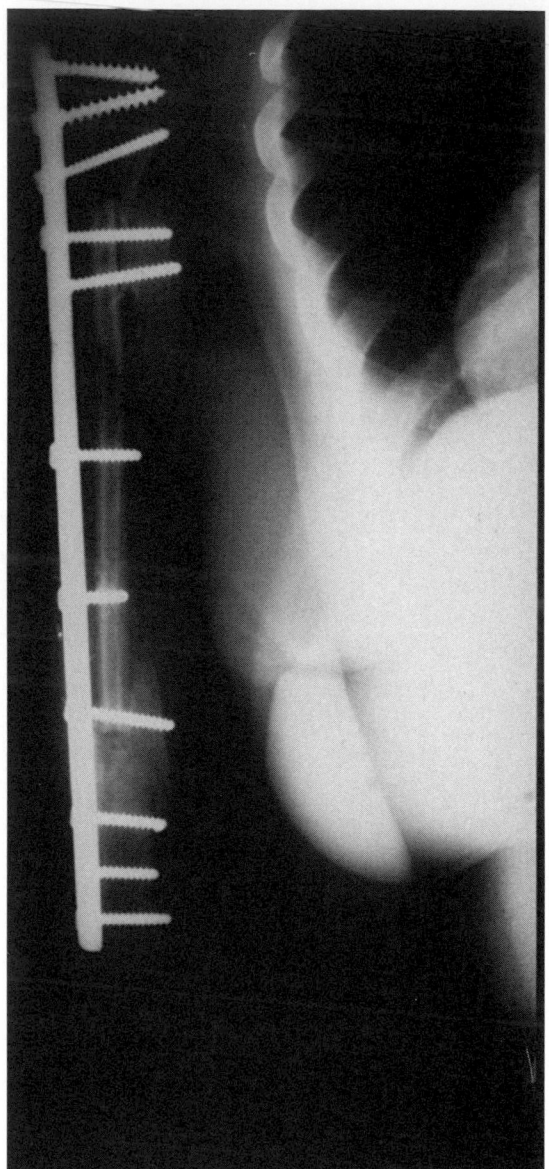

**FIGURE 43–17.** Strut fibular allograft used to augment fixation in a patient with significant humeral bone loss.

should not be incised farther than 4 to 5 cm distally to avoid injury to the axillary nerve. The supraspinatus tendon is incised in line with its fibers with the arm adducted and flexed across the chest. The entry portal is based just medial to the greater tuberosity. The potential drawback with a lateral portal is that the lack of linear access to the humeral canal necessitates additional medial tearing of the rotator cuff as the nail is inserted. After nail placement, care must be taken to repair the supraspinatus tendon.

Reimer and colleagues described an anterior approach to antegrade humeral nailing from anatomic dissections.[141] An incision anterior to the acromion is made with the shoulder extended to 30°. The coracoacromial ligament is incised to allow direct access to the humeral canal. This entry portal has the potential advantage of avoiding damage to the rotator cuff, as observed with a conventional surgical approach.

The incision for the distal locking screws is based lateral to the biceps tendon. The tendon is retracted medially, with care taken to protect the branches of the lateral antebrachial cutaneous nerve. Injury to the anterior interosseous nerve may also occur during anteroposterior insertion of distal interlocking screws in the antegrade approach. These injuries are usually transient and resolve in a period of weeks to months.

**Technique.** The patient is placed on a beach chair or similar reclining support. The patient is then brought to the edge of the radiolucent table and a roll placed underneath the scapula. The shoulder should easily extend to 30° to expose the humeral head from beneath the acromion.

The C-arm may be positioned in one of three ways most convenient to the surgeon: (1) on the unaffected side of the patient, (2) at the head of the patient with the C-arm moved parallel to the humerus, or (3) perpendicular to the patient on the affected side with the swing of the C-arm in line with the patient. The arm is prepared and draped free in the sterile field. Anteroposterior views of the humerus are obtained with the arm anatomically positioned. Gentle rotation can also be used to project a lateral view. A graduated ruler may be positioned on the arm to determine the appropriate length of nail required.

Fracture reduction can be accomplished with gentle longitudinal traction and manual manipulation. However, excessive traction and manipulation increase the risk of neurologic injury. Mills and colleagues reported their experience with somatosensory evoked potential (SSEP) monitoring during closed humeral nailing.[120] By using baseline radial and median SSEPs as a guide, these investigators were able to accurately identify neurologic problems that necessitated a change in the surgical plan. An absence of radial nerve signal in one patient led to an open procedure that revealed radial nerve entrapment within the fracture site.

The proximal starting point is facilitated by the use of a guide wire. An awl is introduced over a previously placed guide wire at the junction of the lateral third of the humeral head and the lateral articular surface. This starting position is directly in line with the intramedullary canal but should be confirmed by fluoroscopy.

Intramedullary reaming can be used to facilitate insertion of the selected nail. When reaming is chosen, surgeons must ensure that cortical contact at the fracture site is achieved before passage of the reamer. Cortical fracture gaps place the radial nerve at risk of injury when the reamer is passed across the fracture. Unreamed nails must be passed by hand or very gentle tapping. We have previously reported that reaming before nail insertion significantly increases muscle and surrounding soft tissue blood flow when compared with unreamed nails and that this increase persists for up to 6 weeks.[154] Utvag and co-workers confirmed these findings in a rat femoral fracture model.[169] An increase in blood flow to the soft tissues may also improve cortical blood flow. Grundnes and colleagues demonstrated increases in cortical blood flow up to five times control after reamed nailing of rat femurs.[65] The degree of reaming may also be important in optimizing patient outcomes. Our work has shown that in

fractures that compromised circulation (i.e., segmental fractures), limited reaming led to the smallest degree of cortical porosity when compared with standard reaming or controls.[81]

Because distraction of the fracture is a potential risk during nail insertion, care must be taken to ensure that the fracture is reduced. Compression can also be facilitated through the nail.[15] The humeral nail selected is usually 8 to 9 mm in diameter. Young patients often have a smaller-diameter intramedullary canal that requires reaming before nail placement; in older patients with a larger-diameter intramedullary canal, an unreamed 9-mm humeral nail can often be used. It is important to ensure that the proximal end of the nail is buried within the substance of the humeral head to limit shoulder impingement.

Distal fixation can be achieved by interlocking screws or interference fit. To ensure rotational stability, we recommend screw fixation at each end of the nail to control rotation (Fig. 43–18).

In contrast to the laterally based distal locking screw fixation in femoral and tibial nailing, humeral nails are distally locked in either a posterior-to-anterior (safest in terms of nerve proximity),[148] anterior-to-posterior, or lateral-to-medial direction; however, the difficulty in placing most multiply injured patients in the prone position limits use of the posterior-to-anterior approach. When the lateral approach is used, care must be taken to use blunt dissection to bone to ensure that the radial nerve is away from the drill. Polymethyl methacrylate can improve fixation but should be avoided and used only when interlocking fixation is not possible.[29] The interlocked screws are placed through the rod under C-arm control.[17, 33, 99–102, 170–175]

### Retrograde Humeral Intramedullary Nailing

**Indications.** Fractures involving the diaphysis and distal third of the humeral shaft are best managed by retrograde intramedullary nailing.

**Anatomy.** The distal end of the humerus is approached by a 5-cm incision centered over the posterior aspect of the lower part of the arm. The triceps is dissected to bone. Care is taken to ensure that the dissection to bone is proximal to the olecranon, but well distal to the spiral groove and radial nerve (Fig. 43–19). The medullary canal is entered with a 4.5-mm drill bit through the posterior cortex 1.5 to 2 cm above the olecranon fossa (Fig. 43–20). Strothman and colleagues evaluated the relative loss in strength of the humerus that results from creation of the entry portal.[164] They reported 29% and 45% reductions in torque to failure with metaphyseal and olecranon fossa entry portals, respectively. This study has important implications in postoperative rehabilitation.

**Technique.** The patient is placed either supine, prone, or in a lateral decubitus position on a regular operating table. Whichever position is used, hyperflexion of the elbow must be possible to ensure insertion of the nail parallel to the humerus. This entry portal is enlarged with a router and over-reamed to allow passage of the reamer in line with the humeral shaft. Sequential reaming over a ball-tipped guide can progress in a retrograde manner until the desired canal diameter is achieved. It is essential to use

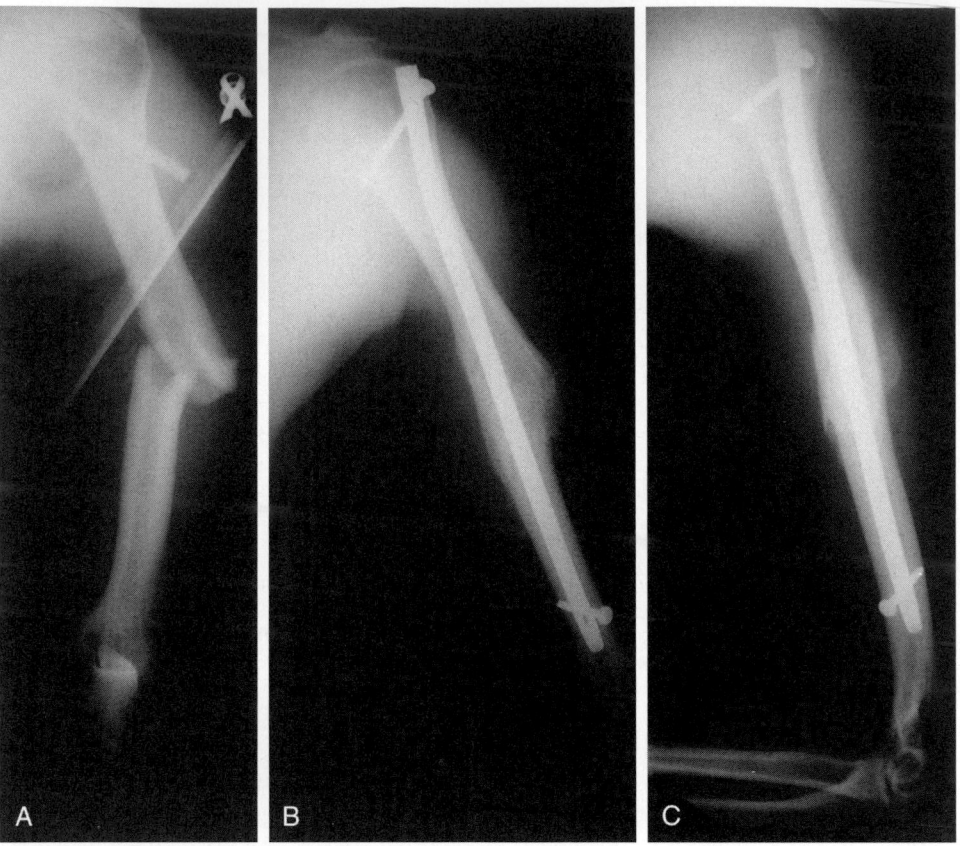

**FIGURE 43–18.** *A,* Displaced humeral shaft fracture in a multiply traumatized patient. *B, C,* Closed reduction and internal fixation with a statically locked intramedullary nail.

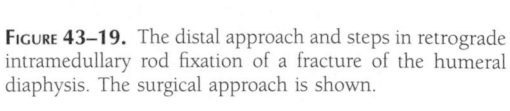

**FIGURE 43–19.** The distal approach and steps in retrograde intramedullary rod fixation of a fracture of the humeral diaphysis. The surgical approach is shown.

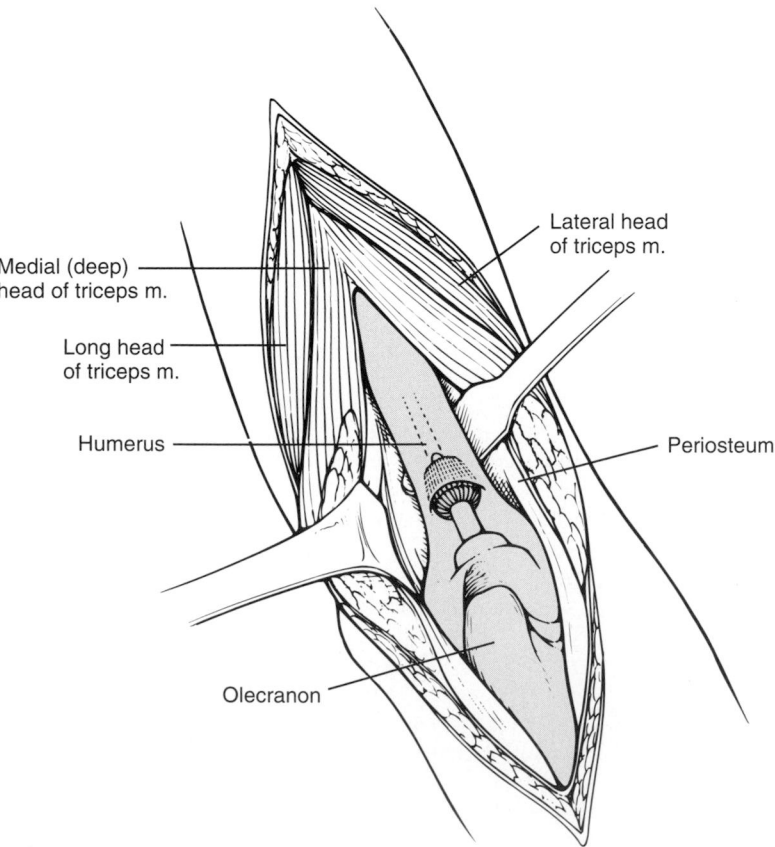

interlocking screws, or one screw above the olecranon fossa, to block the nail in its distal portion so that dislodging or backing out does not occur.[17, 100–102, 170–174] If unreamed nails are used, they should not be inserted until the fracture fragments are reduced to prevent injury to the radial nerve. The intramedullary nail is finally passed into the shaft of the humerus up to a point 1 to 1.5 cm from the humeral head.

It is important to consider nail characteristics when planning insertion of either a reamed or unreamed nail. The Synthes nail is a solid titanium alloy nail available in 6.7-, 7.5-, and 9.5-mm diameters (length, 190 to 325 mm). The nail can accommodate three distal locking screws (3.4 or 3.9 mm in diameter). Conversely, the Russell-Taylor nail is a stainless steel nail available in a solid 7-mm diameter or cannulated 8- and 9-mm diameters (length, 180 to 300 mm). Interlocking can be achieved by self-tapping screws (4.0 mm) proximally and distally through slots at either end of the nail. Blum and co-workers compared two humeral retrograde nails (Synthes AO unreamed nail, Russell-Taylor nail) in a cadaveric transverse humeral shaft fracture model.[14] They attributed the significantly greater torsional resistance in the unreamed nail to its nail–bolt interface (circular holes versus slots).

### Flexible Intramedullary Devices

Flexible intramedullary devices such as Ender pins, Hackethal nails, Rush rods, Nancy (Prevot) nails,[172] and more recently, Kirschner wires[136] have been used in the management of humeral shaft fractures (see Fig. 43–21). Advantages of these devices include ease of application and speed of insertion. Brumback and associates[23] reported the best results with retrograde insertion through an entry portal located proximal to the olecranon fossa. One should be aware, however, that flexible intramedullary nails do not provide rigid fixation; they do not prevent fracture shortening, nor do they provide significant rotational control. Multiple rods should be placed to increase stability of the fracture site. A functional brace should be used in conjunc-

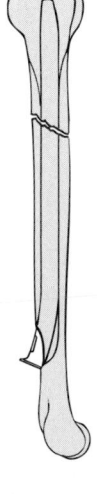

**FIGURE 43–20.** The posterior cortex is entered 1.5 to 2 cm proximal to the olecranon fossa with a 4.5-mm drill bit and then enlarged.

tion with these devices to prevent fracture displacement.[23, 45, 52, 68, 128, 129, 135, 150]

### Special Considerations with Intramedullary Nails

Potential injury to neurovascular structures during intramedullary nailing of the humerus can be divided into three main areas: (1) risk to the radial nerve from canal preparation and nail insertion, (2) risk to the axillary nerve from proximal locking, and (3) risk to the radial, musculocutaneous, and median nerves and brachial artery from distal locking. Ferragos and colleagues performed a comprehensive overview of complications after fractures of the humeral shaft.[53]

**Risk to the Axillary Nerve.** Most nailing systems use a lateral-to-medial proximal locking technique.[8, 19, 25, 46, 49, 52] Riemer[140] recommended that the anteroposterior approach be avoided because penetration of the posterior cortex with either a screw or drill bit places the main trunk of the axillary nerve in jeopardy. Similarly, extreme internal rotation of the arm may jeopardize the nerve, even with lateral-to-medial locking. The axillary nerve lies approximately 5 to 6 cm distal to the tip of the acromion.[47] Lateral-to-medial locking screws placed proximal to this level should not injure the nerve, but the more distal of the two proximal locking screws in some nail designs may be in very close proximity to it. Because the axillary nerve usually arborizes at the lateral margin of the humerus, smaller (proximally directed) branches may be inadvertently injured.[21, 40, 47] This unrecognized phenomenon may help explain some of the shoulder pain and dysfunction seen after antegrade nailing. In general, however, proximal locking with a standard locking jig-sleeve-trocar system appears safe if performed in a lateral-to-medial direction within 5 cm of the edge of the acromion. Although it is necessary to engage the medial cortex to enhance screw stability, overpenetration should be avoided because of possible damage to the axillary nerve.

With retrograde nail insertion, the main trunk of the axillary nerve is in danger from overpenetration of anterior-to-posterior proximal locking screws. To prevent this complication, some authors have advocated that retrograde insertion of the nail not extend proximal to the surgical neck (ending ideally in the proximal end of the shaft)[30] or that only nail designs with lateral-to-medial proximal locking at the end of the retrograde nail be used.[25, 47]

**Risk to the Musculocutaneous and Median Nerves.** Given the failure of intramedullary expansion bolts or the intrinsic nail design to provide adequate rotational control, most nail designs rely on one or two distal locking screws for stability.[28, 49] Although a number of different authors have recommended a variety of insertion techniques or approaches, one thing is clear: given the proximity of important nervous structures, their variable position, the varying position of the tip of the nail, and the lack of any clearly visible or palpable landmarks or "safe zones," percutaneous insertion of distal locking screws through "stab" incisions is dangerous.[34] Rupp and coauthors described direct injury to the musculocutaneous nerve with the anteroposterior approach and increased risk to the median nerve/brachial artery bundle in smaller patients.[148] In separate anatomic studies, Port[40] and Faruqui[21] delineated the risk to the radial nerve with lateral-to-medial locking. In general, the radial nerve is in jeopardy with the lateral-to-medial approach, and the median nerve, musculocutaneous nerve (and lateral cutaneous branch), and brachial artery are at risk from the anteroposterior approach. Regardless of the nail design or technique selected, these screws should be inserted under direct vision through incisions large enough to protect local nerves and vessels. For anteroposterior locking distally, dissection lateral to the biceps tendon is recommended. Despite these risks, iatrogenic nerve palsy from distal locking screws is rare; the few cases reported have been transient in nature with full spontaneous recovery.[30, 32, 56]

Although use of the posteroanterior approach for distal locking is probably safest in terms of nerve proximity, it is impractical to perform in patients in the supine or lateral position. The difficulties inherent in placing multiply injured patients (who represent a large percentage of those undergoing fixation of humeral fractures) in the prone position limits the use of this approach.

**Risk to the Radial Nerve.** Crolla and colleagues, Ingman and Waters, and Rommens and associates reported only one case each in large series of 30 to 40 patients.[42, 82, 144] Each palsy was transient, and no permanent injury occurred. Other series have not reported any radial nerve injuries at all.[8, 23, 25, 52, 55] The only reported incident of a nerve injury with permanent sequelae was a musculocutaneous nerve palsy in a patient sustaining an open fracture with transient radial nerve injury; the patient underwent unplanned bone grafting for iatrogenic comminution after introduction of the nail.[56]

The potential for radial nerve injury can be minimized during closed nailing of the humerus by ensuring accurate reduction of the fracture (no gap) before passage of the reamers or the nail and by avoiding reaming in areas of comminution where the nerve is closely apposed to the bone.

**Insertion Site Morbidity at the Shoulder.** The insertion of intramedullary nails inevitably leads to some symptomatology at the insertion site.[9, 26–28, 49] Despite a number of modifications in technique ranging from "mini" incisions at the edge of the rotator cuff to formal open cuff incision and subsequent repair,[27, 30, 45, 55, 56] insertion of humeral nails through the shoulder can lead to pain and stiffness.

The disparity in the literature regarding the incidence and severity of shoulder impingement and persistent pain is probably due to differences in surgical technique, the method of assessment, and the adequacy of follow-up. In 1991, Habernak and Orthner[27] reported that 18 of 19 patients had "full" shoulder function by 6 weeks postoperatively after antegrade Seidel nailing. However, 8 years after publication of their original article, in a letter to the editor withdrawing their support for the Seidel nail, they reported that they had not assessed shoulder function at all in their original paper, and they thought that the antegrade approach through the rotator cuff "inevitably" caused damage.[28] Whereas Reimer[140] described excellent shoulder function in 17 of 18 patients, Hems[30] reported that only 60% of patients regained excellent shoulder function

as measured by the Neer Shoulder Score, and Robinson[49] reported that 12 of 17 fracture patients had unsatisfactory or poor shoulder function after antegrade nailing. This dismal outlook was supported by Ingman and Waters,[82] who stated that "all patients treated by the shoulder approach had significant restriction of active shoulder flexion." Similarly poor outcomes were reported by Varley.[56] Recent evidence from randomized trials suggests that shoulder impingement and subsequent pain occur in one in five patients treated by antegrade humeral nailing (see Table 43–5).

Careful repair of the rotator cuff incision and deltoid split, as well as insertion of the nail below the surface of the humeral head so that it is not proud, can help reduce the incidence of impingement. Various proximal entry points for the nail have been described; Riemer described superior shoulder function after a more anterior insertion point with sectioning of the coracoacromial ligament.[140] It would also appear prudent to avoid the "avascular" portion of the rotator cuff during insertion of the nail. However, despite excellent technique, certain subgroups are at risk for this complication: older patients, patients with preexisting shoulder pathology, and patients with ipsilateral shoulder injuries.[2, 19, 30, 58]

Removal of a previously inserted and well-seated antegrade humeral nail has additional problems. Not only is the rotator cuff subject to the risk of further damage during nail removal, but removal does not guarantee pain relief.[38] For all of the aforementioned reasons, interest in retrograde nail insertion is increasing.

**Insertion Site Morbidity at the Elbow.** Because of the potentially high rate of complications from the antegrade approach, the retrograde approach to the humerus has become increasingly popular. Ingman and Waters[82] reported that in 30 patients managed by retrograde nailing, only 1 lost greater than 30° of elbow extension. Lin and colleagues[108] reported on 39 fractures of the humeral shaft treated by retrograde nailing with a locking nail. Though initially inserted through a supracondylar approach, problems with angulation at the fracture site and iatrogenic fracture of the distal end of the humerus led them to abandon this entry site and instead use a starting point in the olecranon fossa. In the series of 39 fractures treated by retrograde nailing, Rommens and associates reported that five patients (13%) had moderate or poor elbow function at follow-up.[144]

Our experience with this technique is limited; however, it is clear that an entry site hole of significant size must be made to allow entry of the nail. After nail insertion, this defect lies at the end of the implanted nail and represents a significant stress riser. However, insufficient scientific evidence is available at present to refute or recommend the retrograde approach over the antegrade approach. Evidence from randomized trials does suggest that the retrograde approach is associated with a lower risk of reoperation than the antegrade approach is (probably because of the significant reduction in shoulder problems).

**Narrow Canal Diameter.** Although it is our experience that the intramedullary nailing of narrow-diameter humeral canals is extremely difficult, only one report in the literature has looked specifically at this issue. In a series of 40 patients undergoing intramedullary nailing with the Seidel nail, Reimer and colleagues[141] noted a dramatically increased complication rate (58% versus 4%) in patients with a canal diameter of 9 mm or less when compared with those with a canal diameter of 10 mm or more. This finding represented a 93% reduction in the risk of complications in patients with canal diameters greater than (or equal to) 10 mm. Complications such as iatrogenic comminution, infection, and nonunion could therefore be avoided (Fig. 43–21).

Although intramedullary reaming of cancellous bone may be relatively innocuous or even beneficial in most circumstances, reaming of cortical bone thins and weakens the cortex. Cortical reaming, in conjunction with the increased heat produced, damages the endosteal blood supply of the bone and, if done excessively, can lead to complete architectural alteration of the endosteum and prevent revascularization. This effect is amplified in the humeral canal, whose architecture, with its distal taper and lack of metaphyseal flair, does not allow dissipation of the pressure head or debris created by the reamer.

Failing to ream adequately, however, can increase the risk of comminution or fracture distraction, which is poorly tolerated in the humerus. Although a "tight" distal fit was thought to be necessary for proper purchase of the Seidel expansion bolt,[46, 55, 56] it is not required for nail systems that rely on distal interlocking. Newer systems also have a variety of smaller nail sizes, including 7-, 8-, and 9-mm nails that can be used in patients with smaller canal diameters.[1, 25, 52] Thus, it seems prudent to carefully examine preoperative radiographs of the involved humerus; if the canal diameter is such that excessive cortical reaming will be required to accommodate the available intramedullary implant, an alternative method of fixation should be selected.[8, 25, 52] Smaller-diameter implants such as Ender nails can also be effective in such circumstances.[12, 57]

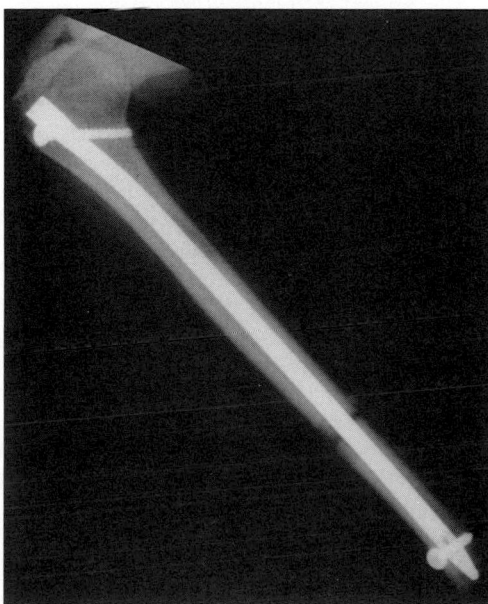

**FIGURE 43–21.** Humeral shaft fracture treated with intramedullary nailing of a narrow-diameter humeral canal. The fracture was nailed with 2 mm of distraction and at 6 months shows no evidence of fracture healing.

If canal size does not permit reaming, the nail can be inserted in an unreamed fashion. Reports comparing lockable, smaller-diameter unreamed humeral nails with standard reamed nails by Blum and associates[15] (nonunion, 10% in reamed versus 7% in unreamed canals) and Achecar and Whittle (nonunion in 1 of 17 reamed versus 0 of 17 unreamed canals) do not show any significant differences between the two groups in terms of union or implant failure.[1] With the preliminary data available, it appears that reaming is not essential to produce union, and given the improved mechanical strength of newer small-diameter nails, implant failure is a reduced clinical concern.

**Iatrogenic Comminution.** The introduction of a large-diameter intramedullary nail into a fractured humerus can lead to comminution of the existing fracture or insertion site. The rate of iatrogenic comminution in previous reports ranged from 7% to 20%,[30, 52] with most not jeopardizing fixation.[17, 38] Comminution of the fracture or insertion site can result in fixation failure and future functional impairment. Barnes and Shuler reported an overall complication rate of 46% that included iatrogenic comminution jeopardizing stability and healing.[2] Robinson and colleagues used the Seidel nail and reported a 10% rate of comminution, a 17% rate of proximal nail migration, and an overall implant failure rate of 10%.[49] Ingman and Waters,[82] in a series of 41 fractures, reported a 10% rate of iatrogenic comminution, with functional impairment occurring in one case. In Varley's[56] series, 5 of 23 nail insertions resulted in significant fracture comminution, with four patients requiring unplanned open surgery to provide additional stabilization. Many of these problems occurred before the widespread availability of narrower-diameter (7, 8, and 9 mm) implants, which to a large degree has eliminated this problem.

Currently, a major concern is fracture at the site of nail insertion seen with the retrograde approach, especially when using nails designed for antegrade insertion. Simon and colleagues reported a 10% incidence of supracondylar fractures during "Marchetti" retrograde nail removal.[158] This complication has caused some authors to switch from a supracondylar starting point to one with a "straighter shot" at the humeral canal from the olecranon fossa.[33] It remains to be seen whether newer nail designs specifically tailored to retrograde insertion will limit such fractures.[8]

**Fracture at the End of the Implant.** A well-recognized drawback of plated diaphyseal fractures is the risk of fracture at the end of the implant because of the stress riser effect of the screws at the end of the plate or refracture after implant removal.[7, 22, 31] This problem was largely eliminated in the lower extremity by the introduction of locking intramedullary nails. It was postulated that such would also be the case in the humerus after the use of similar intramedullary devices. However, a fundamental difference is seen in the intramedullary canal of the humerus and that of the tibia or femur. Rather than having a capacious metaphyseal flare, the humeral canal tapers to an end above the olecranon fossa. Thus, the tip of an intramedullary implant ends in diaphyseal, rather than metaphyseal bone. The combination of a long rigid implant ending in diaphyseal bone and adjacent cortical

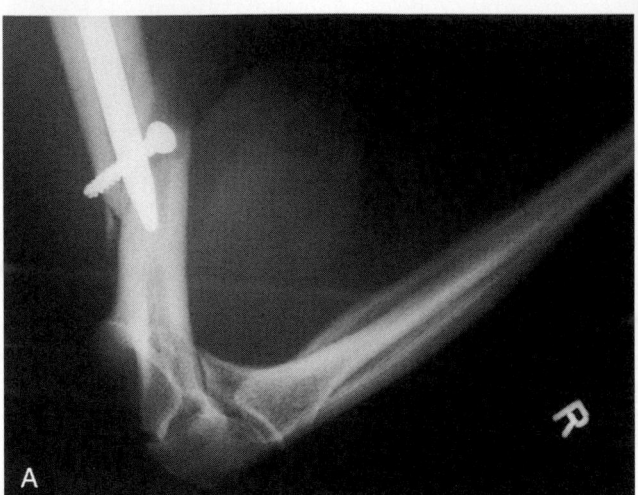
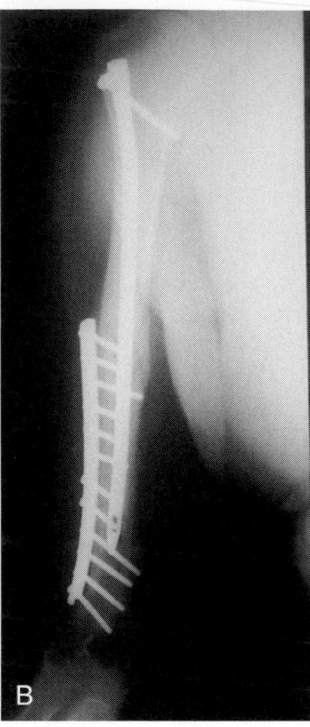

**Figure 43–22.** *A,* Humeral shaft fracture treated with a locked intramedullary nail. Note the fracture at the end of the implant. *B,* Open reduction plus internal fixation was performed with difficulty with a lateral small-fragment plate.

holes drilled for locking screws is biomechanically disadvantageous (Fig. 43–22).

It is unclear whether design modifications of the nail or locking screws are likely to reduce the incidence of this complication. Careful technique is critical, especially avoidance of drilling cortical holes that "miss" the locking holes and leave an unfilled cortical defect.

Because of the limited number of cases described, it is difficult to make treatment recommendations for fractures at the end of locking humeral nails. However, previous reports suggest that the healing potential of fractures located at the tip of humeral intramedullary implants is poor and that interposition of distal locking screws at the fracture site further complicates matters.[11] These fractures bear a close resemblance to the "Holstein-Lewis" fracture configuration, and injury to the radial nerve has been reported during attempts at closed reduction.[31] Thus, it would seem reasonable to either remove the locking screws and implant, followed by reduction of the fracture and maintenance of the reduction by either casting or plating, or leave the implant in situ with plating and screw fixation around the nail.

## PLATING VERSUS INTRAMEDULLARY NAILING: CLINICAL RESULTS

### Nonrandomized Trials

Several observational studies published in the literature have evaluated reports of the use of plates and intramedullary nails (rigid and flexible) (Table 43–4). In studies (*n* = 438 patients) examining outcomes after plate osteosynthesis of humeral shaft fractures, no shoulder or elbow problems were noted. Moreover, nonunion, postoperative

nerve palsy, or infection developed in less than 5% of the patients. Comparatively, in studies evaluating antegrade humeral nails (*n* = 466 patients), shoulder problems developed in 20% of patients and 10% suffered a nonunion. If we assume that these studies were conducted in more or less the same manner and pool the overall results, the relative risk of nonunion and shoulder impingement with plating is 0.46 (i.e., 4.6%/10%) and 0 (0/20%), which means that plating will reduce the risk of having a nonunion by 54% ([1 − 0.46] × 100) when compared with antegrade humeral nailing. Moreover, plating will essentially reduce the risk of shoulder problems to zero when compared with antegrade humeral nailing.

### Randomized Trials

Although observational studies are helpful in generating hypotheses about a particular treatment, biases inherent in their design limit their validity. A better estimate of the "true effect" of plating versus nailing can be achieved through a randomized design, blinding of outcome assessment, concealment of treatment allocation, and complete follow-up of patients. The effect of plating and intramedullary nailing of humeral shaft fractures has been reported in a number of small randomized trials (Table 43–5). These trials have met most of the criteria important in limiting bias. When considered together, plate fixation resulted in a reoperation rate of 6% versus 18% for intramedullary nail fixation, which means that plates reduced the risk of a subsequent surgery by 66% when compared with plates. Moreover, for every eight patients treated with a plate rather than a nail, one reoperation can be prevented (number needed to treat = 1/difference in risk = 1/[0.18 − 0.06] = 8).

**TABLE 43–4** ...............................................................................................

Clinical Results from Nonrandomized Trials: Plating versus Nailing

| | Sample Size | Shoulder Problem | Elbow Problem | Nonunion | Nerve Palsy | Infection |
|---|---|---|---|---|---|---|
| **PLATES** | | | | | | |
| Bell | 39 | 0 | 0 | 2 | 1 | 1 |
| Dabezius | 44 | 0 | 0 | 1 | 2 | 0 |
| Heim | 127 | 0 | 0 | 7 | 2 | 4 |
| Vander Griend | 36 | 0 | 0 | 1 | 1 | 2 |
| Foster | 36 | 0 | 0 | 0 | 0 | 2 |
| Paris | 156 | 0 | 0 | 9 | 8 | 3 |
| **Total** | **438** | **0%** | **0%** | **20 (4.6%)** | **14 (3.2%)** | **12 (2.7%)** |
| **RIGID INTRAMEDULLARY NAILS (ANTEGRADE)** | | | | | | |
| Crolla | 30 | 6 | 0 | 1 | 0 | 1 |
| Ikpeme | 20 | 3 | 0 | 1 | 0 | 0 |
| Riemer | 28 | 6 | 0 | 0 | 0 | 0 |
| Riemer | 40 | 2 | 0 | 3 | 0 | 3 |
| Robinson | 27 | 13 | 2 | 7 | 1 | 2 |
| Kopfl | 111 | 19 | 0 | 5 | 8 | NA |
| Cox | 37 | 6 | 0 | 4 | 0 | 1 |
| Flinkkila | 126 | 25 | 0 | 21 | NA | NA |
| Lin | 47 | 12 | 0 | NA | NA | NA |
| **Total** | **466** | **92 (19.7%)** | **2 (0.4%)** | **42 (9%)** | **9 (1.9%)** | **7 (1.5%)** |
| **RIGID INTRAMEDULLARY NAILS (RETROGRADE)** | | | | | | |
| Rommens | 39 | 3 | 5 | 2 | 1 | 0 |
| **Total** | **39** | **7.7%** | **12.8%** | **5.1%** | **2.6%** | **0** |
| **FLEXIBLE INTRAMEDULLARY NAILS** | | | | | | |
| Brumback | 63 | 3 | 3 | 1 | 0 | 1 |
| Hall/Pankovich | 86 | NA | 0 | 1 | 0 | 0 |
| Henley | 49 | 0 | 1 | 1 | 0 | 1 |
| Peter | 39 | 0 | 0 | 3 | 1 | 0 |
| Qidwai SA | 29 | 0 | 2 | 3 | NA | NA |
| **Total** | **266** | **3 (1.1%)** | **6 (2.2%)** | **9 (3.4%)** | **1 (0.4%)** | **2 (0.8%)** |

## ANTEGRADE VERSUS RETROGRADE INTRAMEDULLARY NAIL INSERTION

Although comprehensive information regarding the insertion technique is limited in published randomized trials, they contain adequate details to determine reoperation rates in these subgroups. Thus, when plates are compared with retrograde insertion of intramedullary nails, their relative benefit is less (relative risk reduction, 42%) than with antegrade insertion (relative risk reduction, 72%). This finding suggests that retrograde nail insertion is probably more advantageous than the antegrade approach in limiting reoperations.

## External Fixation

External fixation is infrequently used, problematic, and generally reserved for fractures that present contraindications to other types of treatment. The external fixator is a load-sharing device that depends on the rigidity of the pin

**TABLE 43–5** ...............................................................................................

Clinical Results from Randomized Trials: Plating versus Nailing

| | Sample* | Shoulder Problem | | Nonunion | | Nerve Palsy | | Infection | | Reoperation | |
|---|---|---|---|---|---|---|---|---|---|---|---|
| | | *Plate* | *Nail* | *Plate* | *Nail* | *Plate* | *Nail* | *Plate* | *Nail* | *Plate* | *Nail* |
| **RIGID NAILING** | | | | | | | | | | | |
| Chapman | 46/38 | 0 | 6 | 3 | 2 | 2 | 1 | 3 | 0 | 4 | 6 |
| McCormack | 23/21 | 0 | 3 | 1 | 2 | 0 | 3 | 0 | 1 | 1 | 7 |
| Bolano | 14/14 | 1 | 6 | 1 | 4 | — | — | — | — | — | — |
| **Total** | **83/73** | **1** | **15** | **5** | **8** | **2** | **4** | **3** | **1** | **5** | **13** |
| **FLEXIBLE NAILING** | | | | | | | | | | | |
| Rodriguez-Merchan | 20/20 | 0 | 0 | 0 | 1 | 0 | 0 | 1 | 0 | — | — |

*Figures are totals for plates/nails.

and frame to maintain fracture alignment.[107] The major indications for external fixation include severe open fractures with extensive soft tissue and bone loss, associated burns in which easy access to the limb is required, infected nonunion, extensively comminuted fractures in patients requiring mobilization, and possibly patients with ipsilateral fractures of the humerus, radius, and ulna (the floating elbow).[22, 63, 89] Ruland suggests that post-traumatic radial nerve palsy is a further indication for external fixation.[147] The major advantage of external fixation is that it allows management of associated soft tissue injuries. External fixation can influence fracture callus formation by dynamization, distraction, or compression. In general, however, the fixator should be used as provisional stabilization until alternative treatment can be substituted (i.e., functional brace or internal fixation).

Two pins are placed above and below the fracture after radiographic confirmation of fracture alignment.[22, 63] The pins should engage both cortices and be in the same plane. To minimize soft tissue and neurovascular injury, each pin should be inserted under direct visualization. If radial nerve injuries occur during fracture manipulation,[90] immediate exploration is indicated. External fixation is often complicated by pin tract infection and, to a lesser extent, by nonunion.[63] These sequelae can be avoided with meticulous pin care by the patient, adherence to proper technique, and adjustment of the fixator to provide compression when indicated.

Marsh and colleagues reported their experience in 15 patients with open humeral shaft fractures treated with a monolateral external fixator.[111] Four patients (26%) required reoperations (two needed reapplication of the external fixator, two required revision to plates with bone grafting). Pin tract infections developed in eight patients (53%), all of which resolved with local skin care and antibiotics.

Mostafavi and Tornetta evaluated 18 patients treated with external fixators for open fractures of the humerus. At an average of 34 months' follow-up, they reported good to excellent function in 67% (12/18) of the patients. Complications in this group of patients included two late fractures after fixator removal, three malunions, and eight pin tract infections.[122]

## COMPLICATIONS

### Radial Nerve Injury

Radial nerve palsy may occur in up to 18% of closed humeral shaft fractures.[50, 60, 93, 113, 133, 175] Most of these palsies are essentially neurapraxias, with 90% of patients recovering within 4 months of the injury with conservative treatment.[133] The timing of the injury has important implications in patient management. The presence of a radial nerve palsy at the time of fracture is not an indication for surgery. In certain instances, however, exploration is indicated. For example, the sudden onset of a new palsy after initial fracture management may represent a laceration of the nerve or, more commonly, nerve interposition between fracture fragments during manipulation and treatment. In this situation, operative nerve exploration is mandatory.[60, 133] Occasionally, a delayed radial nerve palsy may occur. Chesser and Leslie reported entrapment of the radial nerve by the lateral intermuscular septum 3 months after a humeral shaft fracture.[36]

Because the radial nerve can be injured during operative exposure and fixation of the humerus, it is essential for surgeons to understand its relationship with surgically identifiable landmarks. Bono and colleagues, in a study involving dissection of 50 cadaveric upper extremities, reported that the radial nerve was located 17 ± 2.3 cm from the proximal end of the humerus and 16 ± 0.4 cm from the distal end of the humerus.[18]

In the complete absence of clinical evidence of return of function, radial nerve dysfunction should be evaluated 6 weeks after injury by electromyography and nerve conduction studies. The search for objective evidence of return of function should be directed toward motor response, primarily in the brachioradialis and extensor carpi radialis longus and brevis muscles. If action potentials are present, conservative management can be continued. However, if denervation fibrillation or complete denervation is noted on these tests, electromyographic and nerve conduction studies should be repeated at 12 weeks (3 months). If no recovery is seen by 3 months, surgical exploration plus repair, with or without cable grafts, is indicated.

These same principles apply when palsies develop after intramedullary nailing. Closed intramedullary nailing has been associated with a low rate of nerve injury.[19, 32, 50] However, if nailing is to be undertaken, we recommend exploration of the nerve when a preoperative palsy is present. No clear recommendations can be made at the present time with regard to patients whose preoperative nerve function is unclear (i.e., head-injured patients); SSEP monitoring has been reported in this situation and may prove to be useful.[16] In most cases in which a nerve palsy has developed after closed nailing, close observation is indicated because complete recovery can be expected, particularly if no gap was present at the fracture site during nail insertion or intramedullary reaming.[16, 35, 50] In the absence of clinical or electrophysiologic evidence of recovery by 3 or 4 months, exploration is mandatory.

Neurapractic radial nerve injury is most often associated with transverse fractures of the humeral shaft. In the authors' experience, 90% to 95% of these patients recover within 4 to 6 months of injury. Special situations requiring primary operative exploration of the nonfunctional radial nerve include open fractures, fractures associated with penetrating injuries, and radial nerve injury associated with a spiral oblique fracture of the mid to distal third of the humerus (Holstein-Lewis fracture).[50, 60, 75, 93, 113, 133, 175] However, conservative treatment of Holstein-Lewis fractures plus radial nerve injury has been favorable. Sarmiento and co-workers treated 85 patients with extra-articular, comminuted distal humeral fractures (18% of which had associated nerve injury) with prefabricated braces.[152] All nerve injuries resolved and 96% of the fractures united without infection. Sanders and colleagues reported a 55% incidence of nerve disruption in 12 patients with nerve deficits associated with open humeral shaft fractures. Of these 12 patients, only one third recovered (presented at the 16th Annual Meeting of the Orthopaedic Trauma Association, October 12, 2000).

Primary repair of the injured nerve and open reduction and stable fixation of the humeral fracture should be carried out at the time of exploration. Muscle should be interposed between the fracture site and the nerve repair to prevent incorporation of the repaired nerve into the bone-healing response.

## Vascular Injury

Though uncommon, injury or laceration of the brachial artery can be associated with fractures of the humeral shaft. The risk of vascular injury increases in open fractures or with penetrating injuries.[39, 117, 137, 139] If arterial injury is suspected, arteriography should be used to determine the site of injury and the specific vascular repair needed. Vascular reconstruction should be considered an absolute indication for stable fixation of the fracture, either with plate-and-screw stabilization or by external fixation. Primary control of hemorrhage can usually be accomplished by direct pressure while the patient is prepared for surgery. At surgery, the vessel should be explored and repaired and the fracture stabilized. A medial approach to the humeral shaft will facilitate both vessel exploration and internal fixation. In general, bone stabilization should precede arterial reconstruction. Fasciotomy of the arm, forearm, and hand may be necessary when flow has been reestablished.

## Nonunion

### PATHOPHYSIOLOGY

At the pathologic level, a nonunion is a fracture bridged with soft tissue. The characteristics of the tissue in the fracture gap reflect the local mechanical and nutritional factors that predominate in the early weeks after the fracture. Nonunion is classified as hypervascular (hypertrophic) or avascular (atrophic) based on its ability to incite a biologic reaction. Hypertrophic nonunion, with a predominance of fibrocartilage in the gap, can be effectively managed by stabilization alone. However, atrophic nonunion, with a fibrous tissue gap, often requires bone grafting.

### RISK FACTORS

Evaluation of patients with a humeral nonunion should include a thorough history and physical examination. Although no consensus has been reached, most surgeons agree that humeral fractures should unite within 4 months. Factors associated with delay in healing and ultimately

with an increased risk of nonunion include proximal and distal fractures of the humerus, a transverse fracture pattern, fracture distraction, soft tissue interposition, and inadequate immobilization.[56] Evidence from randomized trials (see Table 43–5) suggests that nonunion rates of 5% and 10% can be anticipated with plates and intramedullary nails, respectively. The higher rates of nonunion after nailing may be due to overdistraction of the fracture during nailing. Distraction of the fracture is especially deleterious, and many authorities suggest (and some nail systems have been designed for) distal locking first, followed by "back-slapping" of the nail before proximal locking to produce compression at the fracture site[25, 49, 52] (Fig. 43–23).

## TREATMENT ALTERNATIVES

Treatment objectives for patients with a humeral shaft nonunion are to reestablish fracture alignment, promote fracture union, and restore physical function. Treatment options include both nonoperative (i.e., functional bracing, ultrasound, electrical stimulation) and operative measures (i.e., internal or external fixation with or without bone grafting). However, compression plating with bone grafting is probably the most effective method for the treatment of established nonunion. The basic principles of treatment of nonunion include (1) maintenance of osseous stability, (2) preservation of vascularity, (3) correction of deformity, and (4) eradication of infection (if present).

### Intramedullary Nailing

The treatment of nonunion after locked humeral nailing does not appear to be analogous to similar problems seen in the lower extremity (Fig. 43–24). In a series of 21 patients in whom nonunion of the humeral shaft developed after locked nailing, exchange nailing, routinely effective for tibial and femoral nonunion of a similar nature, was successful in only 4 of 10 cases.[38] Although no other report specifically addresses this issue, descriptions of exchange nailing for nonunion that appear as part of other series parallel our findings. Robinson and colleagues[49] reported treating five cases of humeral nonunion after Seidel nailing with over-reaming and exchange nailing; persistent failure to achieve union was seen in three of the five. McKee found that open reduction plus internal fixation with bone grafting, though technically difficult, was highly successful, with union achieved in all nine cases of nonunion after locked humeral nailing treated in this manner.[38] Chapman also reported an identical success rate in three similar cases.[33] Although caution must be exercised when comparing the results of two different treatments in a retrospective review, it would appear that open reduction plus internal fixation with bone grafting is superior to exchange nailing in this clinical scenario.[38]

Wu and Shih compared 35 cases of humeral shaft nonunion treated by plating (19 patients) or antegrade interlocked nailing (16 patients). Plate fixation resulted in an 89.5% union rate within 4.5 ± 1.7 months, and

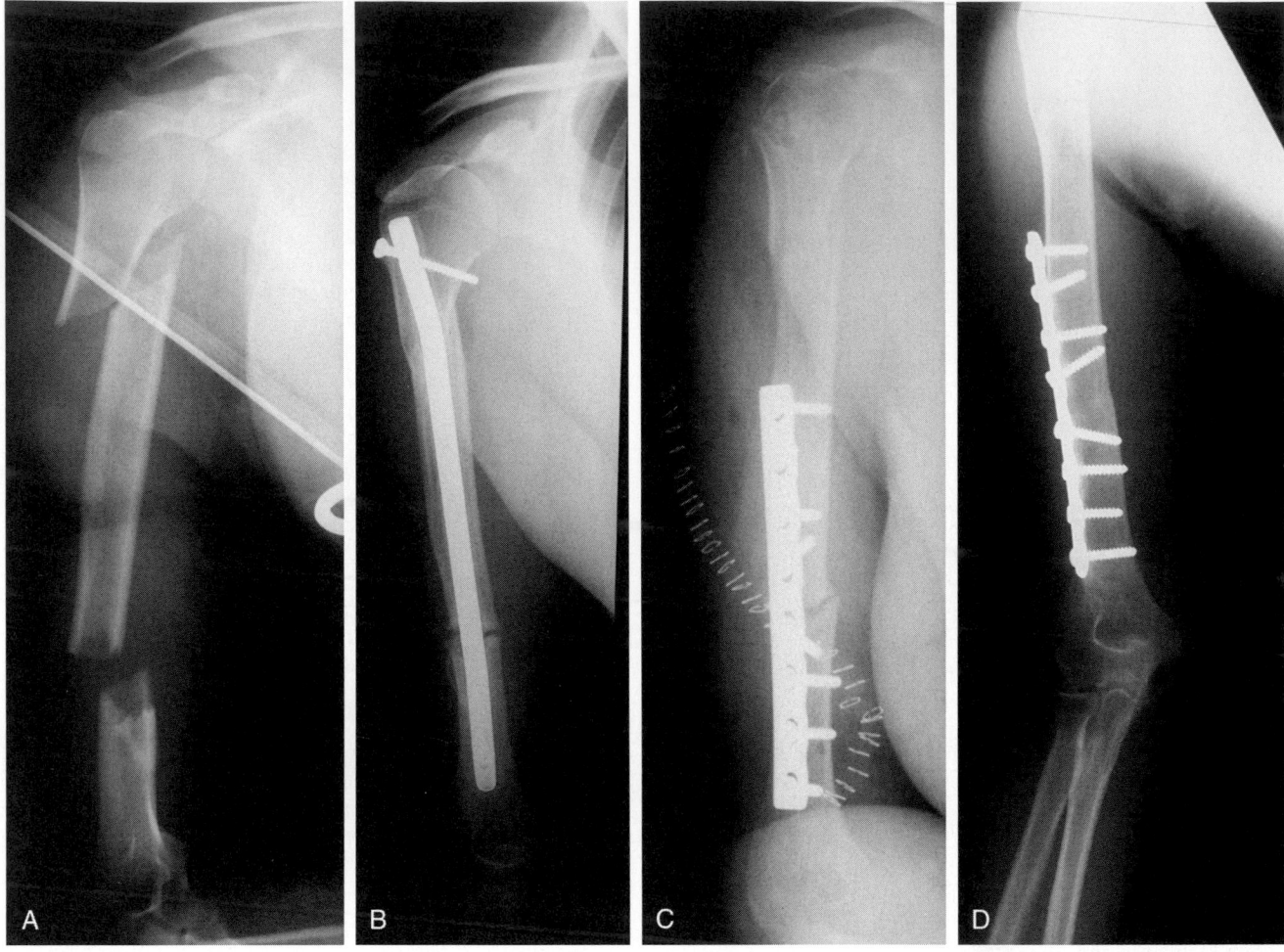

**FIGURE 43–23.** *A,* Radiograph showing a segmental humeral fracture in a multiply traumatized patient. *B,* The fracture was stabilized with a locked intramedullary nail. The proximal fracture has healed, but in the distal fracture, nonunion has developed. Note the radiolucency around the nail. *C,* The nonunion was managed by removal of the nail and fixation with a compression plate. Note the significant morbidity of the insertion site resulting from removal of the nail. *D,* Healing of the nonunion after compression plating.

antegrade nailing resulted in an 87.5% union rate within 4.4 ± 1.8 months.[178] Interestingly, patients who had plate fixation sustained almost twice as many complications as those managed by interlocked nailing (21% versus 12%).

### Plating

In an attempt to improve union rates with plates and limit complications, Ring and colleagues evaluated the utility of a bridge (wave) plate technique for humeral shaft nonunion. They successfully achieved fracture union in 14 of 15 (93%) patients with atrophic nonunion of diaphyseal humeral fractures (mean length of the bony defect, 3.0 cm) by using autogenous cancellous bone grafting and a bridging plate (wave plate).[142] Although wave plate osteosynthesis may have relative advantages over standard plating techniques in ease of application, it has not been shown to be biomechanically superior to standard plating.[91]

Billings and Coleman reported excellent results in 10 patients with pseudoarthroses of the humerus after a

fracture.[13] They used compression plating and a tricortical iliac crest bone graft anchored rigidly across the fracture site with screws. With this approach, these authors achieved 100% union rates. Barquet and colleagues reported successful union in 24 of 25 (96%) cases of aseptic humeral shaft nonunion with a combined regimen of decortication, internal fixation with a broad DC plate, and autologous cancellous bone grafting.[10]

Ring and coinvestigators modified standard plating techniques in the treatment of 22 elderly patients with nonunion after initial plate fixation.[143] In each patient, at least one modification of the standard technique of plate-and-screw fixation was needed as a result of osteopenia. To enhance fixation, their standard protocol incorporated the use of a long plate (with an average of 11 holes and an average length that was 76% of the length of the bone), a plate with a blade (used in 13 patients), and replacement of loose, 4.5-mm cortical bone screws with 6.5-mm cancellous bone screws (12 patients). Spiked nuts (Schuhli nut, Synthes) that lock the screws to the plate and create a solid point of fixation analogous to a blade were incorporated into the protocol when they became available (used in six patients). In five limbs, the nonunion was associated with an osseous defect that could not be addressed by shortening of the bone alone. Three of these limbs were stabilized with a plate that had been contoured to stand away from the bone at the site of nonunion (so-called wave plate osteosynthesis), and the remaining two limbs were stabilized with a combination of intramedullary and extramedullary plates. In one of these two limbs, the extramedullary plate was contoured (that is, a wave plate). The fracture united in 20 (91%) of the patients.[143]

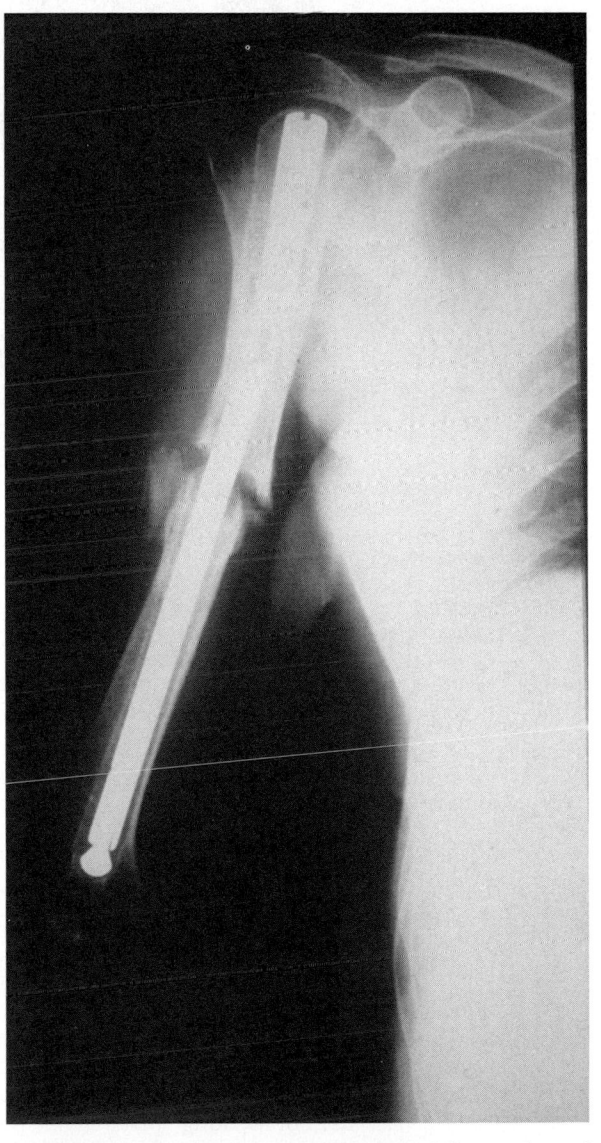

**FIGURE 43–24.** Humeral nonunion after intramedullary nailing of a humeral shaft fracture. Note the significant radiolucency indicative of significant bone loss around the nail both proximally and distally. Also note that the nail is deep in the humeral head, so removal of the hardware will be difficult and cause significant morbidity at the insertion site.

## SPECIAL ISSUES

### Open Fractures

Open fractures of the humeral shaft should be managed by using the same principles as for any open long bone fracture. A sterile dressing should be placed over the open wound, the arm splinted, and appropriate antibiotic coverage administered along with tetanus prophylaxis. The patient should be taken emergently to the operating room for formal débridement with extension of the skin wound to completely expose the zone of injury. Débridement begins with the superficial tissue and extends to the deeper soft tissues and eventually to the fracture site. All necrotic and devascularized tissue must be excised and the wound irrigated by pulsatile lavage. Grade I open injuries can be treated as closed fractures after débridement, whereas fractures with more severe soft tissue damage should be stabilized to allow better management of soft tissue. Both plates and screws and external fixators have been used successfully in the treatment of open humeral shaft fractures. Interest has also been shown in the use of interlocked humeral nails in the treatment of open fractures. Patients with higher-energy soft tissue and osseous injuries should return to the operating room within 48 hours for a "second-look" débridement. Early soft tissue coverage is preferable; bone grafting can be performed at 6 weeks, if necessary, once the wound is clean, closed, and dry (Fig. 43–25).

### Pathologic Fractures

When pathologic conditions affect the humeral shaft, the strength of the cortical bone is decreased.[35, 60, 106] The cause of the underlying disease (e.g., metastatic tumor) may compromise union of the fracture and result in delayed union or nonunion if nonoperative methods of management are used.[109, 132] Internal fixation is often necessary to decrease the associated morbidity and to obtain union. Single and dual plates have the disadvantage of relying on the screw–bone interface for stability. Unreamed intramedullary devices, such as Rush rods or Ender pins, provide poor rotational control and do not prevent distraction of the fracture fragments, but they may act as an internal splint of sufficient strength to obtain union.[33, 80, 149, 175] A reamed intramedullary rod with interlocked fixation usually provides the best stabilization of these injuries.[171] Once the fracture is stabilized, treatment of the underlying pathologic condition can be accomplished[59, 97, 106] (see Fig. 43–22).

## CONCLUSIONS

Fractures of the humeral shaft are relatively common injuries. Although most of these fractures can be treated nonoperatively, optimal results depend on matching the treatment alternative with the character of the fracture and

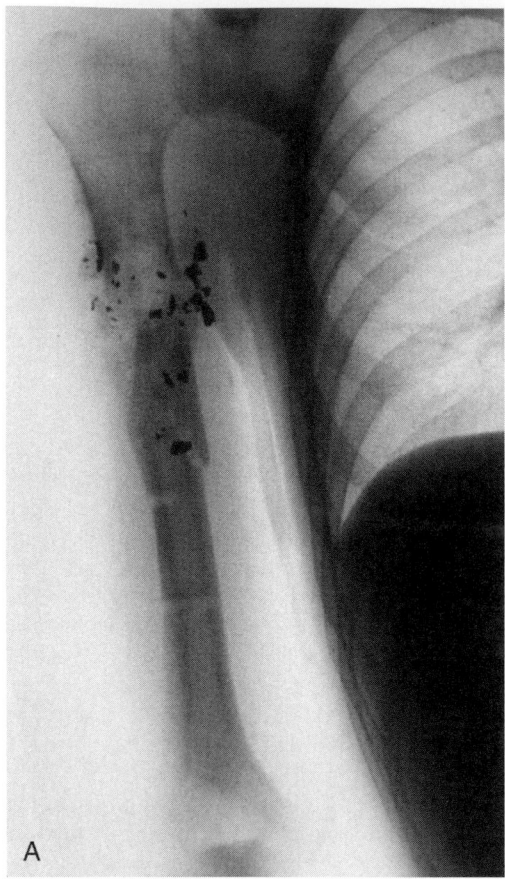
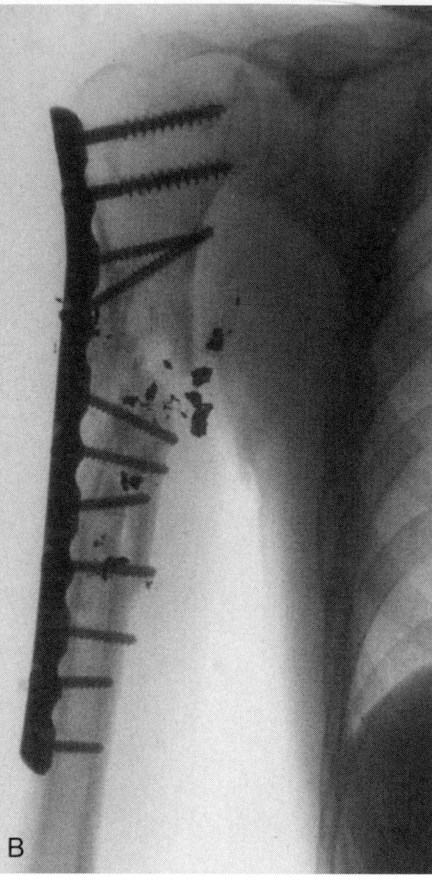

**FIGURE 43–25.** *A,* Radiograph showing an open humeral shaft fracture secondary to a gunshot wound initially stabilized by external fixation. *B,* The patient has subsequently undergone stabilization with plate fixation.

the needs of the patient. If open reduction is chosen, plate fixation remains the gold standard method of internal fixation for displaced humeral shaft fractures.

## REFERENCES

1. Ackerman, G.; Jupiter, J.B. Nonunion of fractures of the distal end of the humerus. J Bone Joint Surg Am 70:75–83, 1988.
2. Adams, J.C. Outline of Fractures. Edinburgh, E. & S. Livingstone, 1968.
3. Adili, A.; Bhandari, M.; Lachowski, R.; et al. Organ injuries associated with femoral fractures: Implications for severity of injury in motor vehicle collisions. J Trauma 46:386–391, 1999.
4. Adili, A.; Bhandari, M.; Dunlop, R.B.; Schemitsch, E.H. Humeral shaft fractures as predictors of intra-abdominal injury in motor vehicle collision victims. Paper presented at the Canadian Orthopaedic Association, Edmonton, Alberta, 2000.
5. Allen, W.C.; Piotrowski, G.; Burstein, A.H.; Frankel, V.H. Biomechanical principles of intramedullary fixation. Clin Orthop 60:13–20, 1968.
6. American College of Surgeons. Advanced Trauma Life Support (ATLS) Manual. Chicago, American College of Surgeons, 1993, pp. 17–46.
7. Baker, D.M. Fractures of the humeral shaft associated with ipsilateral fracture dislocation of the shoulder: Report of a case. J Trauma 11:532–534, 1971.
8. Balfour, G.W.; Mooney, V.; Ashby, M. Diaphyseal fractures of the humerus treated with a readymade fracture brace. J Bone Joint Surg Am 64:11–13, 1982.
9. Banks, S.W.; Laufman, H. An Atlas of Surgical Exposures of the Extremities. Philadelphia, W.B. Saunders, 1964, pp. 63–97.
10. Barquet, A.; Fernandez, A.; Luvizio, J.; et al. A combined therapeutic protocol for aseptic nonunion of the humeral shaft: A report of 25 cases. J. Trauma 29:95–98, 1989.
11. Bell, M.J.; Beauchamp, C.G.; Kellam, J.K.; McMurtry, R.Y. The results of plating humeral shaft fractures in patients with multiple injuries. J Bone Joint Surg Br 67:293–296, 1985.
12. Bennett, G.E. Fractures of the humerus with particular reference to nonunion and its treatment. Ann Surg 103:994, 1936.
13. Billings, A.; Coleman, S.S. Long-term follow up of persistent humeral shaft nonunions treated with tricortical bone grafting and compression plating. Iowa Orthop J 19:31–34, 1999.
14. Blum, J.; Machemer, H.; Baumgart, F.; et al. Biomechanical comparison of bending and torsional properties in retrograde intramedullary nailing of humeral shaft fractures. J Orthop Trauma 13:344–350, 1999.
15. Blum, J.; Machemer, H.; Hogner, M.; et al. Biomechanics of interlocked nailing in humeral shaft fracture: Comparison of 2 nail systems and the effect of interfragmentary compression with the unreamed humeral nail. Unfallchirurg 103:183–190, 2000.
16. Böhler, L. The Treatment of Fractures. Supplementary Volume. New York, Grune & Stratton, 1966.
17. Bone, L. Fractures of the shaft of the humerus. In: Chapman, M.W., ed. Operative Orthopedics, Vol. 1. Philadelphia, J.B. Lippincott, 1988, pp. 221–234.
18. Bono, C.M.; Grossman, M.G.; Hochwald, N; Tornetta, P. Radial and axillary nerves. Anatomic considerations for humeral fixation. Clin Orthop 373:259–264, 2000.
19. Boyd, H.B. Symposium: Treatment of ununited fractures of the long bones. J Bone Joint Surg Am 47:167, 1965.
20. Boyd, H.B.; Anderson, L.D.; Johnston, D.S. Changing concepts in the treatment of nonunions. Clin Orthop 43:37, 1965.
21. Boyd, H.B.; Lipinski, S.W.; Wiley, J.H. Observation on nonunion of the shaft of the long bones with a statistical analysis of 842 patients. J Bone Joint Surg Am 43:159, 1961.
22. Brooker, A.F.; Edwards, C.C. External Fixation—The Current State of the Art. Baltimore, Williams & Wilkins, 1979.
23. Brumback, R.J.; Bosse, M.J.; Poka, A.; Burgess, A.R. Intramedullary stabilization of humeral shaft fractures in patients with multiple trauma. J Bone Joint Surg Am 68:960–969, 1986.

24. Brumback, R.J.; Jones, A.L. Interobserver agreement in the classification of open fractures of the tibia. The results of a survey of two hundred and forty-five orthopaedic surgeons. J Bone Joint Surg Am 76:1162–1166, 1994.

25. Burney, F.; Demolder, V.; Hinsen Kamp, M.; Posquin, C. The treatment of fractures of the humeral shaft with external fixation. Paper presented at the Seventh International Symposium on External Fixation, Avignon, France, 1980.

26. Caldwell, J.A. Treatment of fractures in the Cincinnati General Hospital. Ann Surg 97:161, 1933.

27. Caldwell, J.A. Treatment of fractures of the shaft of the humerus by hanging cast. Surg Gynecol Obstet 70:421, 1940.

28. Cameron, B.M. Shaft Fractures and Pseudarthroses. Springfield, IL, Charles C. Thomas, 1966.

29. Cameron, H.U.; Jacob, R.; MacNab, I.; Pilliar, R.M. Use of polymethyl methacrylate to enhance screw fixation in bone. J Bone Joint Surg Am 57:655–656, 1975.

30. Campbell, W.C. Ununited fractures of the shaft of the humerus. Ann Surg 105:135, 1937.

31. Carroll, S.E. A study of the nutrient foramina of the humeral diaphysis. J Bone Joint Surg Br 45:176–181, 1963.

32. Cave, E.A. Fractures and Other Injuries. Chicago, Year Book, 1958.

33. Chapman, M.W. Closed intramedullary nailing of the humerus. Instr Course Lect 32:324–328, 1983.

34. Charnley, J. The Closed Treatment of Common Fractures. Baltimore, Williams & Wilkins, 1961.

35. Cheng, D.S.; Seitz, C.B.; Eyre, H.J. Nonoperative management of femoral, humeral, and acetabular metastases in patients with breast carcinoma. Cancer 45:1533–1537, 1980.

36. Chesser, T.J.; Leslie, I.J. Radial nerve entrapment by the lateral intermuscular septum in trauma. J Orthop Trauma 14:65–66, 2000.

37. Christensen, S. Humeral shaft fractures: Operative and conservative treatment. Acta Chir Scand 133:455, 1967.

38. Comfort, T.H. The sugar tong splint in humeral shaft fractures. Minn Med 56:363–366, 1973.

39. Connolly, J. Management of fractures associated with arterial injuries. Am J Surg 120:331, 1970.

40. Conwell, H.E.; Reynolds, F.C. Management of Fractures, Dislocations and Sprains, 7th ed. St. Louis, C.V. Mosby, 1961.

41. Coventry, M.B., Laurnen, E.L. Ununited fractures of the middle and upper humerus: Special problems in treatment. Clin Orthop 69:192–198, 1970.

42. Crolla, K.M.P.; de Varis, L.S.; Clevers, G.J. Locked intramedullary nailing of humeral fractures. Injury 24:403–406, 1993.

43. Dameron, T.B.; Grubb, S.A. Humeral shaft fractures in adults. South Med J 74:1461–1467, 1981.

44. Davenport, S.R.; Lindsey, R.; Leggon, R.; et al. Dynamic compression plate fixation: A biomechanical comparison of unicortical and bicortical distal screw fixation. J Orthop Trauma 2:146–150, 1988.

45. DeGeeter, L. Treatment of diaphyseal humeral fractures by percutaneous pinning. Acta Chir Belg 69:198, 1970.

46. DePalma, A.F. The Management of Fractures and Dislocations. Philadelphia, W.B. Saunders, 1970.

47. Doran, F.S.A. The problems and principles of the restoration of limb function following injury as demonstrated by humeral shaft fractures. Br J Surg 31:351, 1944.

48. DiMaio, F.R.; Haher, T.R.; Splain, S.; Mani, V. Stress-riser fractures of the hip after sliding screw plate fixation. Orthop Rev 21:1229–1231, 1992.

49. Doty, D.B.; Treiman, R.L.; Rothschild, P.D.; Gaspar, M.R. Prevention of gangrene due to fractures. Surg Gynecol Obstet 125:284, 1967.

50. Duthie, H.L. Radial nerve in osseous tunnel at humeral fracture site diagnosed radiographically. J Bone Joint Surg Br 39:746, 1957.

51. Epps, C.H., Jr.; Adams, J.P. Wound management in open fractures. Am Surg 27:766, 1961.

52. Epps, C.H., Jr.; Grant, R.E. Fractures of the shaft of the humerus. In: Rockwood, C.A., Jr.; Green, D.P.; Bucholz, R.W., eds. Rockwood and Green's Fractures in Adults, 3rd ed., Vol. 1. Philadelphia, J.B. Lippincott, 1991, pp. 843–869.

53. Farragos, A.F.; Schemitsch, E.H.; McKee, M.D. Complications of intramedullary nailing for fractures of the humeral shaft: A review. J Orthop Trauma 13:258–267, 1999.

54. Fenyo, G. On fractures of the shaft of the humerus. A review covering a 12-year period with special consideration of the surgically treated cases. Acta Chir Scand 137:221–226, 1971.

55. Fisher, D.E. Nonunions of the humeral shaft. Minn Med 55:395–403, 1972.

56. Foster, R.J.; Dixon, G.L.; Bach, A.W.; et al. Internal fixation of fractures and nonunions of the humeral shaft. J Bone Joint Surg Am 67:857–864, 1985.

57. Friedman, R.J.; Smith, R.J. Radial nerve laceration twenty-six years after screw fixation of a humeral fracture. J Bone Joint Surg Am 66:959–960, 1984.

58. Gallagher, J.E.; Black, J.R. Humeral intramedullary nailing—a new implant. Injury 16:374–376, 1985.

59. Ganz, R.; Isler, B.; Mast, J.W., Jr. Internal fixation technique in pathological fractures of the extremities. Arch Orthop Traumatol Surg 103:73–80, 1984.

60. Garcia, A., Jr.; Maeck, B.H. Radial nerve injuries in fractures of the shaft of the humerus. Am J Surg 99:625–627, 1960.

61. Gilchrist, D.K. A stockinette Velpeau for immobilization of the shoulder girdle. J Bone Joint Surg Am 49:750–751, 1967.

62. Goss, C.M., ed. Gray's Anatomy, 25th ed. Philadelphia, Lea & Febiger, 1950.

63. Green, S.A. Complications of external skeletal fixation. In: Uhthoft, H.K., ed. Current Concepts of External Fixation. Heidelberg, Springer-Verlag, 1982, pp. 43–52.

64. Gregersen, H.N. Fractures of the humerus from muscular violence. Acta Orthop Scand 42:506–512, 1971.

65. Grundnes, O.; Utvag, S.E.; Reikeras, O. Restoration of bone flow following fracture and reaming in rat femora. Acta Orthop Scand 65:185–190, 1994.

66. Gustilo, R.B.; Anderson, J.T. Prevention of infection in the treatment of 1025 open fractures of the long bones. Retrospective and prospective analysis. J Bone Joint Surg Am 58:453–458, 1976.

67. Gustilo, R.B.; Simpson, L.; Nixon, R.; Ruiz, A. Analyses of 511 open fractures. Clin Orthop 66:148–154, 1969.

68. Hall, R.F.; Pankovich, A.M. Ender nailing of acute fractures of the humerus. J Bone Joint Surg Am 69:558–567, 1987.

69. Hampton, O.P., Jr.; Fitts, W.T., Jr. Open Reduction of Common Fractures. New York, Grune & Stratton, 1959.

70. Harris, W.H.; Jones, W.N.; Aufranc, O.E. Fracture Problems. New York, Grune & Stratton, 1959.

71. Henley, M.B.; Monroe, M.; Tencer, A.F. Biomechanical comparison of methods of fixation of a midshaft osteotomy of the humerus. J Orthop Trauma 5:14–20, 1991.

72. Hoglund, E.J. A new method of applying autogenous intramedullary bone transplants and of making autogenous bone screws. Surg Gynecol Obstet 24:243–246, 1917.

73. Holm, C.L. Management of humeral shaft fractures. Fundamental nonoperative technics. Clin Orthop 91:132–139, 1970.

74. Hollinshead, W.H. Anatomy for Surgeons, Vol. 3. New York, Hoeber-Harper, 1958.

75. Holstein, A.; Lewis, G.B. Fractures of the humerus with radial nerve paralysis. J Bone Joint Surg Am 45:1382–1388, 1963.

76. Hoppenfeld, S.; De Boer, P. Exposures in Orthopedics. Philadelphia, J.B. Lippincott, 1984, pp. 47–75.

77. Hubner, U.; Schlicht, W.; Outzen, S.; et al. Ultrasound in the diagnosis of fractures in children. J Bone Joint Surg Br 82:1170–1173, 2000.

78. Huckstep, R.L. Fibula replacement of humerus. J Bone Joint Surg Br 65:101, 1983.

79. Hudson, R.T. The use of the hanging cast in treatment of fractures of the humerus. South Surg 10:132, 1941.

80. Hupel, T.M.; Weinberg, J.A.; Aksenov, S.A.; Schemitsch, E.H. Effect of unreamed, limited reamed, and standard reamed intramedullary nailing on cortical bone porosity and new bone formation. J Orthop Trauma 15:18–27, 2001.

81. Hunter, S.G. The closed treatment of fractures of the humeral shaft. Clin Orthop 164:192–198, 1962.

82. Ingman, A.M.; Waters, D.A. Locked intramedullary nailing of humeral shaft fractures. J Bone Joint Surg Br 76:23–29, 1994.

83. Jacobson, S.R.; Glisson, R.R.; Urbaniak, J.R. Comparison of distal humerus fracture fixation: A biomechanical study. J South Orthop Assoc 6:241–249, 1997.

84. Jain, R.; Podworthy, N.; Hupel, T.M.; et al. Influence of plate design on cortical bone perfusion and fracture healing in segmental tibial fractures. J Orthop Trauma 13:178–186, 1999.

85. Jazrawi, L.M.; Bai, B.; Simon, J.A.; et al. A biomechanical comparison of Schuhli nuts or cemented augmented screws for plating of humeral fractures. Clin Orthop 377:235–240, 2000.

86. Johansen, K.; Bandyk, D.; Thiele, B.; Hansen, S.T. Temporary intraluminal shunts: Resolution of a management dilemma in complex vascular injuries. J Trauma 22:395–402, 1982.

87. Junkin, H.D. The Topography of Pins, Precision Pinning of Fractures. Bloomington, IN, American Fracture Association, 1971.

88. Jupiter, J.B. Complex nonunion of the humeral diaphysis: Treatment with a medial approach, an anterior plate, and a vascularized fibular graft. J Bone Joint Surg Am 72:701–707, 1990.

89. Jupiter, J.B. The treatment of complex nonunions of the humeral shaft with a combination of surgical techniques. J Bone Joint Surg Am 72:701–707, 1990.

90. Kamhin, M.; Michaelson, M.; Waisbrod, H. The use of external skeletal fixation in the treatment of fractures of the humeral shaft. Injury 9:245–248, 1977.

91. Karnezis, I.A. Biomechanical considerations in biological femoral osteosynthesis: A study of bridging and wave plating techniques. Arch Orthop Trauma Surg 120:272–275, 2000.

92. Keller, A. The management of gunshot fractures of the humerus. Injury 26:93–95, 1995.

93. Kettlekamp, D.B.; Alexander, H. Clinical review of radial nerve injury. J Trauma 7:424, 1967.

94. Key, J.A.; Conwell, H.E. Fractures, Dislocations and Sprains. St. Louis, C.V. Mosby, 1956.

95. Klaue, K.; Fengels, I.; Perren, S.M. Long term effects of plate osteosynthesis: Comparison of four different plates. Injury 31(Suppl):51–62, 2000.

96. Klenerman, L. Fractures of the shaft of the humerus. J Bone Joint Surg Br 48:105–111, 1966.

97. Klenerman, L. Experimental fractures of the adult humerus. Med Biol Eng 7:357, 1969.

98. Klenerman, L. Injuries of the arm. In: Wilson, J.N., ed. Watson-Jones Fractures and Joint Injuries. Edinburgh, Churchill Livingstone, 1982, pp. 576–582.

99. Kunec, J.R.; Lewis, R.J. Closed intramedullary rodding of pathologic fractures with supplemental cement. Clin Orthop 188:183–186, 1984.

100. Küntscher, G. The Küntscher method of intramedullary fixation. J Bone Joint Surg Am 40:17, 1958.

101. Küntscher, G. Intramedullary surgical technique and its place in orthopaedic surgery: My present concept. J Bone Joint Surg Am 47:809, 1965.

102. Küntscher, G. Practice of Intramedullary Nailing. Springfield, IL, Charles C. Thomas, 1967.

103. Kyle, R.F.; Schaffhausen, J.M.; Bechtold, J.E. Biomechanical characteristics on interlocking femoral nails in the treatment of complex femoral fractures. Clin Orthop 267:169–173, 1991.

104. LaFerte, A.D.; Nutter, P.D. The treatment of fractures of the humerus by means of hanging plaster cast—"hanging cast." Ann Surg 114:919, 1941.

105. Laing, P.G. The arterial supply of the adult humerus. J Bone Joint Surg Am 38:1–105, 1956.

106. Lancaster, J.M.; Koman, A.L.; Gristina, A.G.; et al. Treatment of pathologic fractures of the humerus. South Med J 81:52–55, 1988.

107. Lewin, J.D.; Murthy, V.L. Humeral diaphysis or midshaft fractures. In: Hoppenfeld, S.; Murthy, V.L., eds. Treatment and rehabilitation of fractures. Philadelphia, Lippincott Williams & Wilkins, 2000, pp. 104–119.

108. Lin, J.; Inoue, N.; Valdevit, A.; et al. Biomechanical comparison of antegrade and retrograde nailing of humeral shaft fracture. Clin Orthop 351:203–213, 1998.

109. MacAusland, W.R., Jr.; Wyman, E.T. Management of metastatic pathological fractures. Clin Orthop 73:39–51, 1970.

110. Mann, R.; Neal, E.G. Fractures of the shaft of the humerus in adults. South Med J 58:264–268, 1965.

111. Marsh, J.L.; Mahoney, C.R.; Steinbronn, D. External fixation of open humerus fractures. Iowa Orthop J 19:35–42, 1999.

112. Martin, J.S.; Marsh, J.L.; Bonar, S.K.; et al. Assessment of the AO/ASIF fracture classification for the distal tibia. J Orthop Trauma 11:477–483, 1997.

113. Mast, J.W.; Spiegel, P.G.; Harvey, J.P.; Harrison, C. Fractures of the humeral shaft. Clin Orthop 12:254–262, 1975.

114. Mazet, R., Jr. A Manual of Closed Reduction of Fractures and Dislocations. Springfield, IL, Charles C. Thomas, 1967.

115. McKee, M.D.; Seiler, J.; Jupiter, J.B. The application of the limited contact dynamic compression plate in the upper extremity: An analysis of 114 cases. Injury 26:661–666, 1995.

116. McMaster, W.C.; Tivnon, M.C.; Waugh, T.R. Cast brace for the upper extremity. Clin Orthop 109:126–129, 1975.

117. McNamara, J.J.; Brief, D.K.; Stremple, J.F.; Wright, J.K. Management of fractures with associated arterial injury in combat casualties. J Trauma 13:17–19, 1973.

118. Mears, D.C.; Maxwell, G.P.; Vidal, J.; et al. Clinical techniques in the upper extremity. In: Mears, D.C., ed. External Skeletal Fixation. Baltimore, Williams & Wilkins, 1983, pp. 458–520.

119. Mills, W.J.; Hanel, D.P.; Smith, D.G. Lateral approach to the humeral shaft: An alternative approach for fracture treatment. J Orthop Trauma 10:81–86, 1996.

120. Mills, W.J.; Chapman, J.R.; Robinson, L.R.; Slimp, J.C. Somatosensory evoked potential monitoring during closed humeral nailing: A preliminary report. J Orthop Trauma 14:167–170, 2000.

121. Modabber, M.R.; Jupiter, J.B. Operative management of diaphyseal fractures of the humerus. Clin Orthop 347:93–104, 1998.

122. Mostafavi, H.R.; Tornetta, P. Open fractures of the humerus treated with external fixation. Clin Orthop 337:187–197, 1997.

123. Müller, M.E. Treatment of nonunions by compression. Clin Orthop 43:83, 1965.

124. Müller, M.E.; Allgöwer, M.; Willenegger, H. Technique of Internal Fixation of Fractures. New York, Springer-Verlag, 1965.

125. Müller, M.E.; Allgöwer, M.; Schneider, R.; Willenegger, H. Manual of Internal Fixation. New York, Springer-Verlag, 1970.

126. Naiman, P.T.; Schein, A.J.; Siffert, R.S. Use of ASIF compression plates in selected shaft fractures of the upper extremity. A preliminary report. Clin Orthop 71:208–216, 1970.

127. Newman, A. The supracondylar process and its fracture. AJR Am J Roentgenol 105:844, 1969.

128. Nummi, P. Supramid pin in medullary fixation. A follow-up study of fracture patients examined after more than 10 years. Acta Chir Scand 137:67–70, 1971.

129. Nummi, P. Intramedullary fixation with compression for the treatment of fracture in the shaft of the humerus. Fixation with Supramid pin and two Vitallium screws. Acta Chir Scand 137:71–73, 1971.

130. O'Brien, P.J.; Guy, P.; Blachut, P. Humeral shaft fractures—open reduction internal fixation. In: Wiss, D., ed. Master Techniques in Orthopaedic Surgery—Fractures. Philadelphia, Lippincott-Raven, 1998, pp. 63–80.

131. Palmer, S.H.; Handley, R.; Willet, K. The use of interlocked customized blade plates in the treatment of metaphyseal fractures in patients with poor bone stock. Injury 31:187–191, 2000.

132. Parrish, F.F.; Murray, J.A. Surgical treatment for secondary neoplastic fractures—a retrospective study of 96 patients. J Bone Joint Surg Am 52:665–686, 1970.

133. Pollock, F.H.; Drake, D.; Bovill, E.G.; et al. Treatment of radial neuropathy associated with fractures of the humerus. J Bone Joint Surg Am 63:239–243, 1981.

134. Praemer, M.A.; Furner, S.; Price, D.P. Musculoskeletal Conditions in the United States. Park Ridge, IL, American Academy of Orthopaedic Surgeons, 1992, p. 116.

135. Pritchett, J.W. Delayed union of humeral shaft fractures treated by closed flexible intramedullary nailing. J Bone Joint Surg Br 67:715–718, 1985.

136. Qidwai, S.A. Treatment of humeral shaft fractures by closed fixation using multiple intramedullary Kirschner wires. J Trauma 49:81–85, 2000.

137. Raney, R.B. The treatment of fractures of the humerus with the hanging cast. N C Med J 6:88, 1945.

138. Rich, N.M.; Baugh, J.H.; Hughes, C.W. Acute arterial injuries in Vietnam: 1,000 cases. J Trauma 10:359–369, 1970.

139. Rich, N.M.; Metz, C.W.; Hutton, J.E.; et al. Internal versus external fixation of fractures with concomitant vascular injuries in Vietnam. J Trauma 11:463–473, 1971.

140. Riemer, B. Humeral shaft fractures—intramedullary nailing. In: Wiss, D., ed. Master Techniques in Orthopaedic Surgery—Fractures. Philadelphia, Lippincott-Raven, 1998, pp. 81–94.

141. Riemer, B.L.; D'Ambrosia, R.; Kellam, J.F.; et al. The anterior acromial approach for antegrade intramedullary nailing of the humeral diaphysis. Orthopedics 16:1219–1223, 1993.

142. Ring, D.; Jupiter, J.B.; Quintero, J.; et al. Atrophic ununited diaphyseal fractures of the humerus with a defect: Treatment by wave-plate osteosynthesis. J Bone Joint Surg Br 82:867–871, 2000.

143. Ring, D.; Perey, B.; Jupiter, J. The functional outcome of operative treatment of ununited fractures of the humeral diaphysis in older patients. J Bone Joint Surg Am 81:177–190, 1999.

144. Rommens, P.M.; Verbruggen, J.; Broos, P.L. Retrograde locked nailing of humeral shaft fractures. J Bone Joint Surg Br 77:84–89, 1995.

145. Rosen, H. The treatment of nonunions and pseudarthroses of the humeral shaft. Orthop Clin North Am 21:725–742, 1990.

146. Ruedi, T.; von Hochsetter, A.H.C.; Schlumpf, R. Surgical Approaches for Internal Fixation. Heidelberg, Springer-Verlag, 1984, pp. 15–41.

147. Ruland, W.O. Is there a place for external fixation in humeral shaft fracture. Injury 31(Suppl):27–34, 2000.

148. Rupp, R.E.; Chrissos, M.G.; Ebraheim, N. The risk of neurovascular injury with distal locking screws of humeral intramedullary nails. Orthopedics 19:593–595, 1996.

149. Rush, L.V.; Rush, H.L. Intramedullary fixation of fractures of the humerus by the longitudinal pin. Surgery 27:268, 1950.

150. Sarmiento, A.; Kinman, P.B.; Calvin, E.G.; et al. Functional bracing of fractures of the shaft of the humerus. J Bone Joint Surg Am 59:596–601, 1977.

151. Sarmiento, A.; Zagorski, J.B.; Zych, G.A.; et al. Functional bracing for the treatment of fractures of the humeral diaphysis. J Bone Joint Surg Am 82:478–486, 2000.

152. Sarmiento, A.; Horowitch, A.; Aboulafia, A.; Vangsness, C.T. Functional bracing for comminuted extra-articular fractures of the distal third of the humerus. J Bone Joint Surg Br 72:283–287, 1990.

153. Schatzker, J. Fractures of the humerus. In: Schatzker, J.; Tile, M., eds. The Rationale for Operative Fracture Care, 2nd ed. Berlin, Springer-Verlag, 1996, pp. 83–94.

154. Schemitsch, E.H.; Kowalski, M.J.; Swiontkowski, M.F. Soft tissue blood flow following reamed versus unreamed locked intramedullary nailing: A fractured sheep tibial model. Ann Plast Surg 36:70–75, 1996.

155. Schemistch, E.H.; Tencer, A.F.; Henley, M.B. Biomechanical evaluation of methods of internal fixation of the distal humerus. J Orthop Trauma 8:468–475, 1994.

156. Shantharam, S.S. Tips of the trade #41: Modified coaptation splint for humeral shaft fractures. Orthop Rev 20:1033, 1039, 1991.

157. Siebernock, K.A.; Gerber, C. The reproducibility of classification of fractures of the proximal end of the humerus. J Bone Joint Surg Br 73:1751–1755, 1993.

158. Simon, P.; Jobard, D.; Bistour, L.; Babin, S.R. Complications of Marchetti locked nailing for humeral shaft fractures. Int Orthop 23:320–324, 1999.

159. Sisk, D.T. Fractures and fracture dislocations of the shoulder and humerus. In: Gossling, H.R.; Pillsbury, S.L., eds. Complications of Fracture Management. Philadelphia, J.B. Lippincott, 1984, pp. 301–306.

160. Spak, I. Humeral shaft fractures—treatment with a simple hand sling. Acta Orthop Scand 49:234–239, 1978.

161. Stern, P.J.; Mattingly, D.A.; Pomeroy, D.L.; et al. Intramedullary fixation of humeral shaft fractures. J Bone Joint Surg Am 66:639–646, 1984.

162. Stewart, M.J.; Hundley, J.M. Fractures of the humerus. A comparative study in methods of treatment. J Bone Joint Surg Am 37:681–692, 1955.

163. Stewart, M.J. Fractures of the humeral shaft. In: Adams, J.P., ed. Current Practice in Orthopaedic Surgery. St. Louis, C.V. Mosby, 1964.

164. Strothman, D.; Templeman, D.C.; Varecka, T.; Bechtold, J. Retrograde nailing of humeral shaft fractures: A biomechanic study of its effects on the strength of the distal humerus. J Orthop Trauma 14:101–104, 2000.

165. Taylor, J.C. Delayed union and nonunion of fractures. In: Crenshaw, A.H., ed. Campbell's Operative Orthopaedics, 8th ed., Vol. 2. St. Louis, Mosby–Year Book, 1992, pp. 1329–1332.

166. Terry, R.J. A study of the supracondyloid process in the living. Am J Phys Anthropol 4:129, 1921.

167. Thompson, R.G.; Compere, E.L.; Schnute, W.J.; et al. The treatment of humeral shaft fractures by the hanging cast method. J Int Coll Surg 43:52–60, 1965.

168. Tingstand, E.M.; Wolinsky, P.R.; Shyr, Y.; Johnson, K.D. Effect of immediate weightbearing on plated fractures of the humeral shaft. J Trauma 49:278–280, 2000.

169. Utvag, S.E.; Grundnes, O.; Reikeras, O. Effects of degrees of reaming on healing of segmental fractures. J Orthop Trauma 12:192–199, 1998.

170. Vander Griend, R.A.; Tomasin, J.; Ward, E.F. Open reduction and internal fixation of humeral shaft fractures. J Bone Joint Surg Am 68:430–433, 1986.

171. Vander Griend, R.A.; Ward, E.F.; Tomasin, J. Closed Küntscher nailing of humeral shaft fractures. J Trauma 25:1167–1169, 1985.

172. Wachtl, S.W.; Marti, C.B.; Hoogewoud, H.M.; et al. Treatment of proximal humerus fracture using multiple intramedullary flexible nails. Arch Orthop Trauma Surg 120:171–175, 2000.

173. Wainwright, A.M.; Williams, J.R.; Carr, A.J. Interobserver and intraobserver variation in classification systems for fractures of the distal humerus. J Bone Joint Surg Br 82:636–642, 2000.

174. Ward, E.F.; White, J. Interlocked intramedullary nailing of the humerus. Orthopedics 12:135–141, 1989.

175. White, R.R.; Ward, E.F. Küntscher nailing of the humerus. In: Seligson, D., ed. Concepts in Intramedullary Nailing. New York, Grune & Stratton, 1985, pp. 219–233.

176. Wright, T.W.; Miller, G.J.; Vander Griend, R.A.; et al. Reconstruction of humerus with an intramedullary fibular graft. J Bone Joint Surg Am 75:801–807, 1993.

177. Wright, T.W. Treatment of humeral diaphyseal nonunions in patients with severely compromised bone. J South Orthop Assoc 6:1–7, 1997.

178. Wu, C.C.; Shih, C.H. Treatment for nonunion of the shaft of the humerus: Comparison of plates and Seidel interlocking nails. Can J Surg 35:661–665, 1992.

179. Zimmerman, M.C.; Waite, A.M.; Deehan, M.; et al. A biomechanical analysis of four humeral fracture fixation systems. J Orthop Trauma 8:233–239, 1994.

# CHAPTER 44

# Proximal Humeral Fractures and Glenohumeral Dislocations

## PART I  *Essential Principles*

Tom R. Norris, M.D. • Andrew Green, M.D.

Glenohumeral dislocations and proximal humeral fractures account for most traumatic skeletal shoulder girdle injuries.[12, 71] Because these injuries may have a dramatic socioeconomic and functional impact, timely and accurate evaluation and diagnosis are essential to selecting appropriate management. A full understanding of the relevant anatomy, principles of tissue healing, and appropriate rehabilitation is crucial to maximizing outcome.

Nordquist and Petersson[71] noted significant differences in the mechanisms and types of shoulder girdle injury in children, adults, and the elderly population when they reviewed 504 consecutive cases. In their study, 87% of injuries in children were clavicular fractures and 50% were the result of play or sports accidents. Among patients aged 15 to 64 years, one third of the injuries were proximal humeral fractures, one third were clavicular fractures, and one sixth were primary glenohumeral dislocations. Most of these injuries were the result of motor vehicle accidents or athletic trauma. In individuals older than 65 years, 81% of the injuries were proximal humeral fractures. About 60% of the injuries in the elderly population were the result of a low-energy indoor fall.

Fractures and dislocations of the proximal end of the humerus and glenohumeral joint encompass a broad range of clinical problems. Although some are straightforward, others present significant treatment challenges. Isolated shoulder girdle injuries are usually recognized and evaluated early, but some injuries are missed, ignored, or trivialized in the polytrauma setting. A comprehensive approach to an injured patient requires recognition of the critical importance of restoration and preservation of shoulder girdle function after traumatic injury.[76]

The goal of this chapter is to review the relevant anatomy, biomechanics, epidemiology, classifications, evaluation, management, complications, and outcomes of treatment of acute glenohumeral dislocations and proximal humeral fractures and fracture-dislocations.

## RELEVANT ANATOMY AND BIOMECHANICS

To comprehend the pathologic changes caused by proximal humeral fractures and fracture-dislocations and glenohumeral dislocations, it is important to understand the developmental and normal adult anatomy of the glenohumeral joint.

The proximal part of the humerus develops from three centers of ossification. In infants, the proximal end of the humerus is spherical, and the epiphyseal plate is convex inferiorly with its apex posterior and medial to its center.[24] The epiphysis of the central articular segment of the humeral head appears within 4 to 6 months of birth.[41] The epiphysis of the greater tuberosity appears at approximately 3 years and that of the lesser tuberosity by 5 years. The three centers of ossification coalesce between 4 and 6 years of age and fuse with the humeral metaphysis between 20 and 23 years[41] (Fig. 44–1).

Codman recognized that proximal humeral fractures in adults occur along the lines of the old physeal scars, with injury patterns involving the four segments[13, 66] (Fig. 44–2). These segments include the articular segment; the lesser tuberosity with the subscapularis attached; the greater tuberosity with the supraspinatus, infraspinatus, and teres minor tendons attached at their respective facets; and the shaft of the humerus.

The humeral head is normally retroverted 35° to 40° relative to the epicondylar axis of the distal end of the humerus.[23] The shoulder joint is not located in the sagittal or coronal plane of the body, and scapular-plane motion occurs 35° to 40° anterior to the coronal plane. This arrangement has important implications for imaging, repair and reconstruction, and rehabilitation.

The average adult humeral head has a radius of curvature of 22 to 25 mm.[45] The most cephalad surface of the articular segment is on average 8 mm above the greater tuberosity. The size of the humeral head determines the

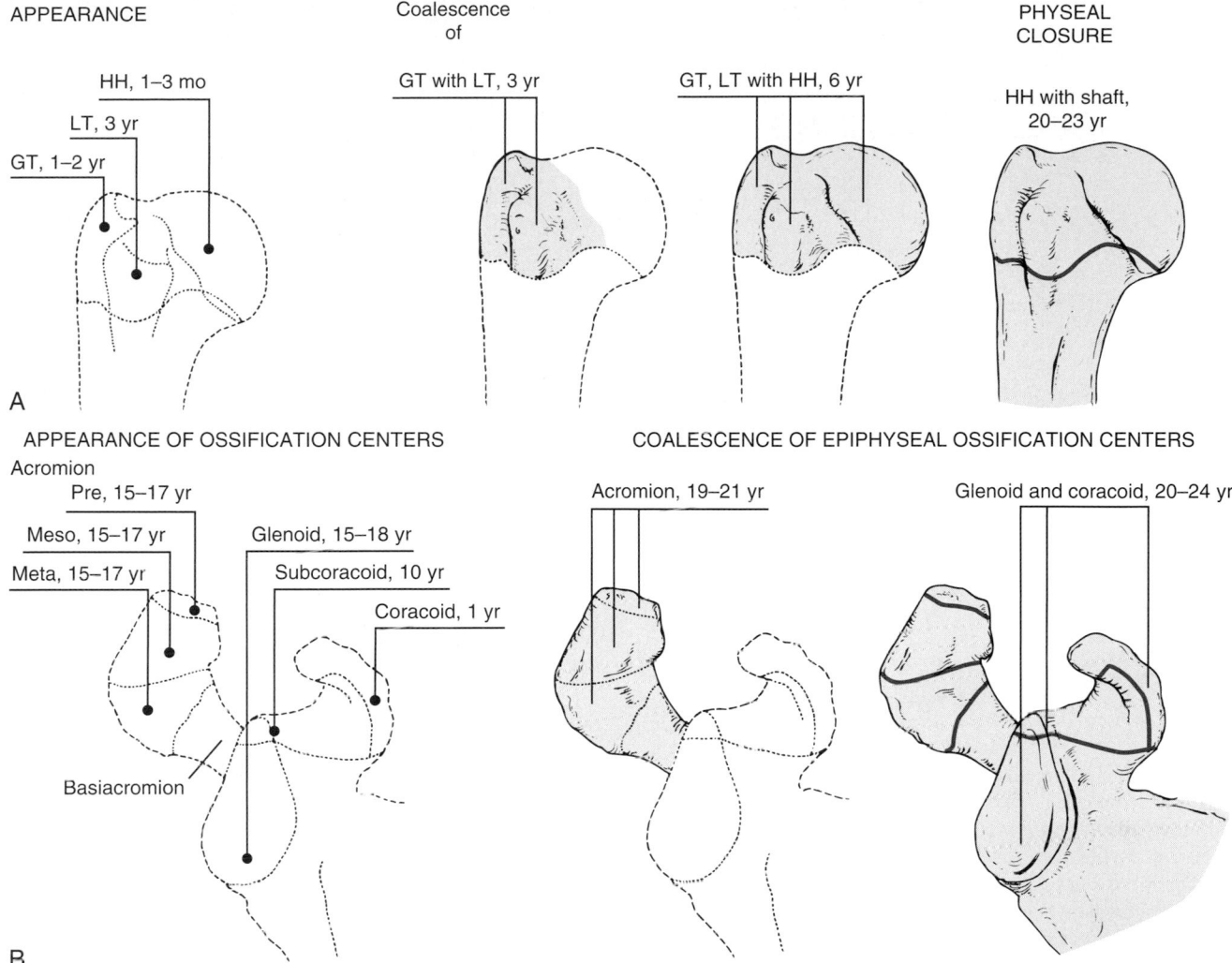

APPEARANCE

HH, 1–3 mo
LT, 3 yr
GT, 1–2 yr

Coalescence of

GT with LT, 3 yr

GT, LT with HH, 6 yr

PHYSEAL CLOSURE

HH with shaft, 20–23 yr

A

APPEARANCE OF OSSIFICATION CENTERS

Acromion
Pre, 15–17 yr
Meso, 15–17 yr          Glenoid, 15–18 yr
Meta, 15–17 yr          Subcoracoid, 10 yr
                        Coracoid, 1 yr
Basiacromion

COALESCENCE OF EPIPHYSEAL OSSIFICATION CENTERS

Acromion, 19–21 yr          Glenoid and coracoid, 20–24 yr

B

**FIGURE 44–1.** Appearance and closure of ossification centers about the glenohumeral joint. *A,* Proximal end of the humerus. *B,* Acromion, coracoid, and glenoid. The basiacromion was present at birth. *Abbreviations:* GT, greater tuberosity; HH, humeral head articular segment; LT, lesser tuberosity; Meso, mesoacromion; Meta, meta-acromion; Pre, preacromial epiphysis. (*A, B,* Redrawn from Hodges, P.C. AJR Am J Roentgenol 30:809, 1933.)

lateral displacement of the greater tuberosity and the rotator cuff insertions and has an effect on the kinematics of the glenohumeral joint. Anatomic alterations such as those that accompany humeral head collapse or superior greater tuberosity malunion can lead to major disruptions in motion.

Although the glenoid is congruent with the humeral head, the surface area of the glenoid is only 25% to 30% of the humeral head and thus provides for very little skeletal stability.[95]

The glenoid labrum is a wedge-shaped soft tissue structure attached to the glenoid rim. The superior aspect of the labrum is intimately associated with the tendon of the long head of the biceps brachii. Inferiorly, the labrum has a blunted edge and is firmly attached to the glenoid rim.[19, 26] The labrum increases the depth of the glenoid fossa by about 50%.[43] Histologically, the labrum is a transitional structure between the hyaline articular cartilage of the glenoid and the fibrous glenohumeral capsule. It is predominantly fibrous except at its attachment to the glenoid rim, where it is fibrocartilagi-

nous.[19, 62, 81] The labrum becomes fibrous as it blends into the capsule.

The intact humeral head is the fulcrum through which the deltoid, the rotator cuff, and the long head of the biceps act to provide power for elevation of the arm while stabilizing the humeral head within the glenoid. The active power of the rotator cuff serves to protect the passive ligamentous stabilizers from overstretching or tearing.[54] Rotation and elevation are lost if the head fulcrum is destroyed by fracture, dislocation, osteonecrosis, or surgical resection.

Most of the direct blood supply to the humeral head comes from the arcuate artery supplied by the anterior humeral circumflex artery, which arises from the third division of the axillary artery just above the teres major muscle[31, 50] (Fig. 44–3). The arcuate branch ascends lateral to the biceps groove and enters the humeral head in the biceps groove to provide the major blood supply to the articular segment of the humeral head. The posterior humeral circumflex artery also sends branches to the greater tuberosity posteromedially in the area of the

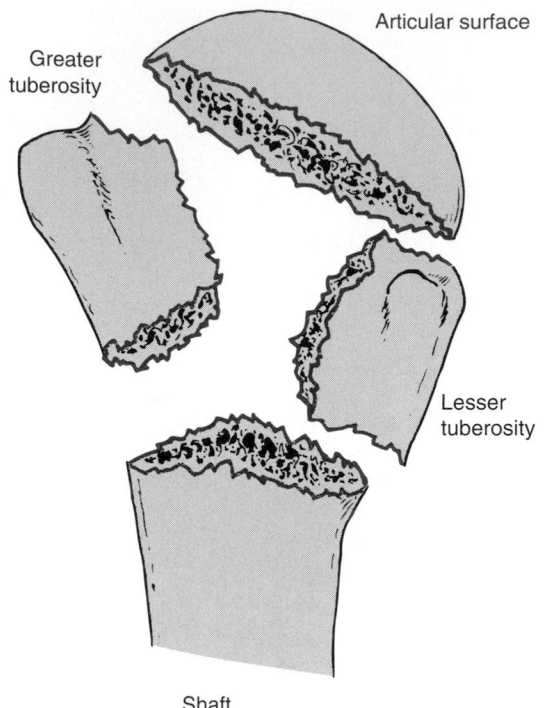

**FIGURE 44–2.** Codman's classification of four-segment proximal humeral fractures.

capsular insertion.[31, 50] To a lesser extent, blood supply is provided through the rotator cuff tendon insertions on the tuberosities and through the capsule. Vessels in the medial portion of the capsule presumably maintain blood supply to the articular segment in valgus-impacted four-part fractures.[8] Injury to the axillary artery or to the ascending branches by fracture or surgery is associated with an increased incidence of osteonecrosis.

The glenohumeral joint has the greatest range of motion of any joint in the body. The loose ligaments that allow this motion provide a passive restraint against instability. They are primarily effective at the extremes of glenohumeral motion. Unlike the discrete ligamentous structures of other joints, the glenohumeral ligaments represent thickenings within the capsular tissues. The most important of these structures is the inferior glenohumeral ligament complex, with anterior and posterior bands on either side of an axillary pouch.[62, 91, 99] The anterior band travels from the humeral neck inferiorly up along the anterior glenoid rim. It becomes confluent with the anterior glenoid labrum in the anteroinferior quadrant of the glenoid. When taut in abduction and external rotation, it is the primary shoulder stabilizer. Traumatic anteroinferior glenohumeral dislocation most commonly injures the anteroinferior labrum and anteroinferior glenohumeral ligament complex. The much less well developed posterior band of the inferior glenohumeral ligament travels superiorly from the humeral neck to the posterior glenoid rim to join the posterior glenoid labrum (Fig. 44–4).

The clinical significance of the superior labrum, superior and middle glenohumeral ligaments, and coracohumeral ligaments is not as well defined. The superior glenohumeral ligament attaches at the apex of the superior labrum, along with the tendon of the long head of the biceps brachii, and at the base of the coracoid. The middle glenohumeral ligament attaches along the anterior aspect of the glenoid neck. Detachments of the superior labrum (superior labrum anterior and posterior [SLAP] lesions) and superior and middle glenohumeral ligaments are associated with instability. The rotator cuff interval, including the coracohumeral and superior glenohumeral

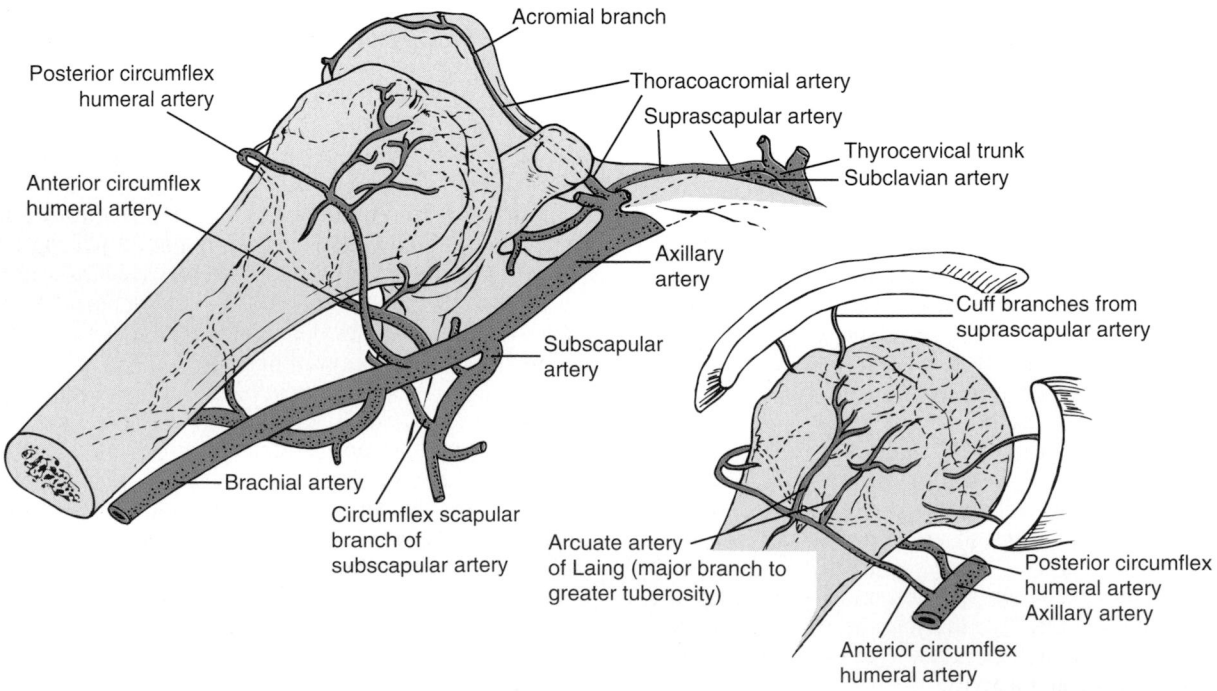

**FIGURE 44–3.** Vascular supply to the shoulder region.

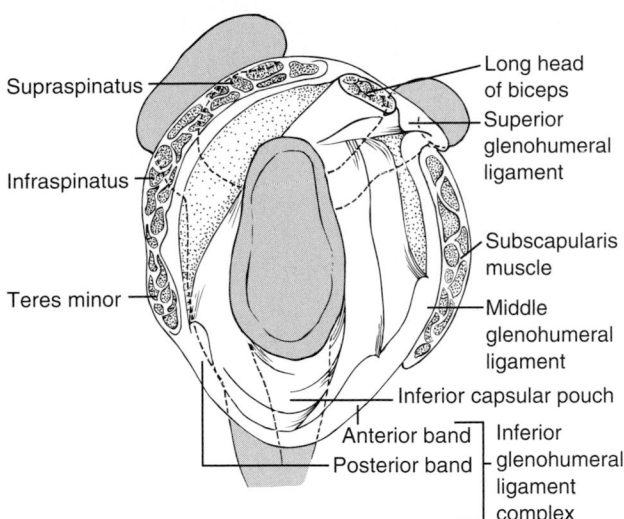

**FIGURE 44-4.** Glenoid cavity. Relationship of the glenohumeral ligaments, the rotator cuff, and the tendon of the long head of the biceps. (Redrawn from Hodges, P.C. AJR Am J Roentgenol 30:809, 1933.)

ligaments, resists inferior translation of the adducted humerus and prevents posterior dislocation in the positions of flexion or abduction and external rotation.[37] The coracohumeral ligament has a role in preventing inferior instability and restraining external rotation. The latter effect is commonly seen in adhesive capsulitis and shoulder contractures.

When visualized arthroscopically, the inferior glenohumeral ligament is the most consistent ligament discerned.[60, 62, 91, 99] The glenoid labrum is the site of attachment of the inferior glenohumeral ligament. The middle glenohumeral ligament attaches medial to the labrum and more superiorly on the glenoid neck. It has some variation. The superior glenohumeral ligament is not consistently visible.

Approximately two thirds of full overhead shoulder motion occurs through the glenohumeral joint, and one third occurs through the scapulothoracic articulation.[44, 47, 83] The humeral head fulcrum is lost if the articulation is destroyed or the articular surface is discarded. With loss of this fulcrum, rotation is lost, as well as elevation and abduction. For full overhead elevation, external rotation with an intact humeral head fulcrum is necessary.[68]

For normal function, the shoulder requires power and strength, which are derived from the coordinated interaction of at least 26 muscles, including the scapulothoracic, scapulohumeral, and thoracohumeral muscles. Although the shoulder is not subjected to the same type and magnitudes of load as the hip and knee and has been described as a non–weight-bearing joint, it is load bearing. The forces generated by the muscles that cross the glenohumeral articulation are substantial. When the arm is held in 90° of abduction, the joint reaction force equals 90% of body weight.[82] These forces understandably increase with resisted activity.

The rotator cuff and deltoid each provide approximately 50% of the power needed for overhead lifting.[15, 44] These structures, combined with the scapular stabilizing muscles, allow positioning of the arm in space with power and precision. Dynamic glenohumeral stability is primarily provided by the rotator cuff muscles and tendons and by the long head of the biceps (Fig. 44–5). Lippett and colleagues[54] demonstrated that stability is related to the depth of the concave glenoid fossa and the magnitude of compressive force generated by the rotator cuff, thus confirming the role of the rotator cuff as a dynamic stabilizing mechanism. The scapular stabilizing muscles assist in glenohumeral stability by maintaining the glenoid as a stable fulcrum for the proximal end of the humerus.[60] This function is disturbed when rotator cuff tearing accompanies glenohumeral dislocation. Disruption of any of these intricate mechanisms can result in pain and shoulder dysfunction.

Even small changes between the head and the deltoid insertion can significantly alter the deltoid length-tension ratios.[69, 105] The effective deltoid contraction may be spent reducing an inferior humeral head subluxation, with little contraction left for elevation power (Fig. 44–6).

The shoulder girdle muscles also influence the degree and direction of displacement of the fracture fragments. The pull of the supraspinatus, infraspinatus, and teres minor muscles results in superior and posterior displacement of the greater tuberosity. The subscapularis muscle displaces the lesser tuberosity medially. The deltoid, pectoralis major, latissimus dorsi, and teres major muscles cause displacement of the humeral shaft.

## Neurovascular Anatomy

The brachial plexus and peripheral nerves are intimately associated with the glenohumeral joint and shoulder girdle. Although true anatomic anomalies are uncommon, considerable variation can be seen in the exact relationship of the peripheral nerves and other shoulder girdle structures. Burkhead and co-workers[9] have shown that the distance of the axillary nerve from the midportion of the acromion is on average 5.4 cm in females and 6.2 cm in males. Glousman and colleagues[32] demonstrated that the standard recommendation to limit splitting of the deltoid fibers to 5 cm distal to the acromion would lead to crossing of the axillary nerves in 44% of females.[32] The musculocutaneous nerve has been demonstrated to enter the coracoid muscles anywhere from 2 to 8 cm from the coracoid.[29] The motor branches of the supraspinatus muscle are about 3 cm medial to the supraglenoid tubercle, and the motor branches of the infraspinatus are about 2 cm from the posterior glenoid rim.[102]

The vascular supply of the shoulder girdle is derived from the subclavian artery and the rich arborization of arteries that originate from the axillary artery (see Fig. 44–3). These vessels include the suprascapular, thoracoacromial, subscapular, and circumflex anterior and posterior humeral arteries. The suprascapular and posterior humeral circumflex are in close proximity to the suprascapular and axillary nerves, respectively.

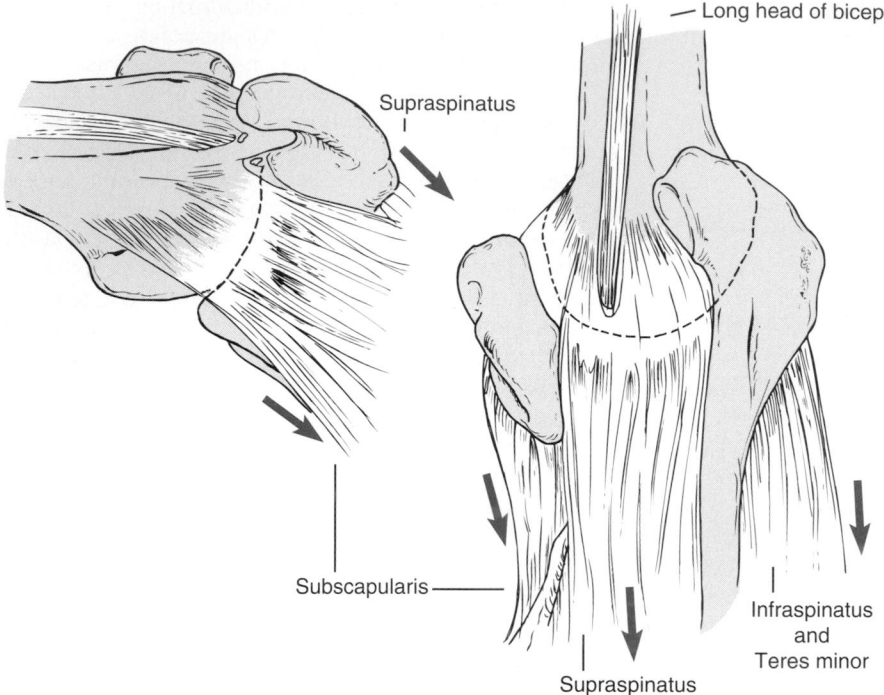

FIGURE **44–5.** Rotator cuff forces on the proximal end of the humerus provide dynamic stability—by centering the head in the glenoid and preventing abnormal glenohumeral translation—and rotate the arm. The rotator cuff provides 50% of the power for arm elevation and 90% of the power for external rotation.

## EVALUATION OF AN ACUTELY INJURED SHOULDER

### History

A detailed history should obtain information related to the patient's health, activity level, and the specifics of the injury.[76] The general history includes the patient's age, sex, hand dominance, occupation, hobbies, and how the injured extremity is used in daily life. A good understanding of the patient's general health (e.g., whether osteoporosis or any condition is present that might interfere with wound or fracture healing) is of critical importance. The incidence of osteoporosis increases rapidly after middle age, especially in women. Osteoporosis has serious implications in terms of maintenance of reduction with traditional techniques of internal fixation. Expectations regarding postoperative activities should also influence the type of treatment. In some patients, a previous shoulder

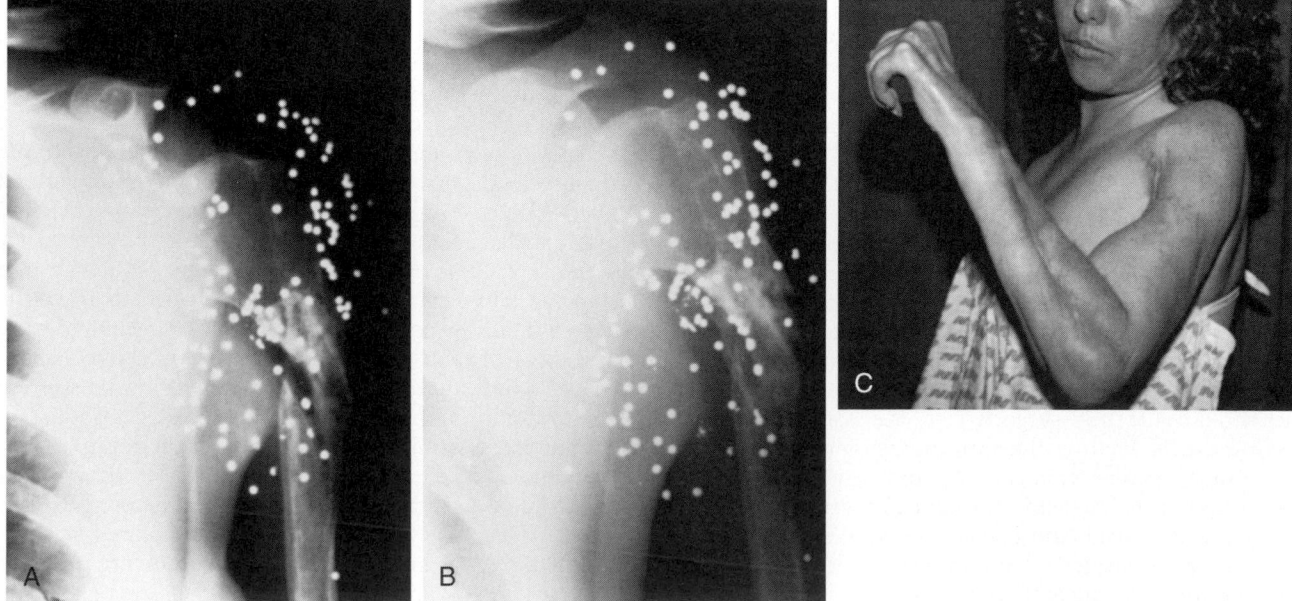

FIGURE **44–6.** Inferior instability from bone loss in the proximal end of the humerus. *A*, Loss of 5 cm of bone between the deltoid origin and its insertion followed a shotgun blast. *B*, Effective deltoid muscle contraction is spent on reduction of the humeral head with little left for arm elevation. *C*, Volkmann's ischemic contracture resulted from the axillary artery injury.

injury may have occurred, and such a history of shoulder problems can potentially complicate any new acute injury.

An assessment of the motivation and psychologic well-being of the patient and the patient's ability to understand and follow postoperative directions during a potentially long and complicated rehabilitation is necessary.[76] If these assessments change later in the course of treatment, modifications in the type of immobilization, supervised therapy, and explicitness of directions can be made.

The mechanism of injury (i.e., whether the trauma was mild, moderate, or violent) is an important factor that should be determined in conjunction with the physiologic status of the patient. The extent of vascular and neurologic compromise and the time of onset of these potentially rapidly deteriorating symptoms must be monitored frequently. The position of the arm and the direction of force determine the direction of glenohumeral dislocation.

## Physical Examination

A complete physical examination requires visualization of all the injured anatomic parts. On occasion, the shoulder girdle is examined superficially in the acute setting and the patient then sent to the radiology department for plain radiographs, which will not substitute for a careful physical examination. Adequate exposure of the shoulder girdle and upper extremity is required. A gown is placed to cover the breasts and below the shoulders for women; men are disrobed from the waist up. An examining table in the middle of the room permits evaluation of a seated patient from the front, the side, or behind. In the supine position, other muscles can be relaxed, and the patient can be made more comfortable during this portion of the evaluation.

Deformity is more common with dislocations and displaced fractures. Dislocations about the shoulder are associated with visible or palpable depressions in the skin and underlying soft tissue. With an anterior dislocation, the humeral head is anterior, medial, and inferior. A sulcus is visible and palpable posteriorly and laterally beneath the acromion. With posterior dislocations, the coracoid becomes prominent, an anterior sulcus is present, posterior prominence can be noted, the arm is usually held in adduction and internal rotation, and the axis of the humerus is directed posteriorly. Inability to externally rotate the arm is the classic physical finding associated with posterior dislocation. As a result, the palm of the hand cannot be turned up despite the fact that the forearm can be supinated. In the rare subspinous posterior dislocation, the arm is held in abduction. Fracture-dislocations may be less apparent than isolated dislocations.

In proximal humeral fractures, the deltoid and soft tissue may mask significant fracture displacement or dislocation. Swelling and obesity can also obscure any alteration in skeletal landmarks. The examiner must have a high index of suspicion for skeletal injury to avoid errors in diagnosis. Swelling and ecchymosis may not be present in the acute period but may develop with time. By approximately 48 hours after injury, ecchymosis can be seen to extend across the chest or down to the elbow.

Other areas are evaluated before addressing the proximal humeral fracture. The cervical spine is assessed for any tenderness and pain with motion. If the status of the cervical spine is uncertain, cervical spine radiographs are obtained before any movement of this area. Direct tenderness over fresh or healing fractures has always been a useful clinical sign for the ribs, clavicle, acromion, and humerus and often indicates the area of concern. Pain or tenderness may be elicited indirectly with motion or with longitudinal compression or distraction.

Occasionally, it is necessary to assess the degree of humeral shortening. The length of the arm from the posterior of the acromion to the olecranon tip can be measured and compared with the opposite side. Shortening between the deltoid origin and its insertion is especially important. Maintenance of length of the deltoid is essential if this muscle is to function adequately.

Neurologic evaluation is carried out for all components of the upper extremity. Gentle motion and isometric contractions are generally sufficient to allow palpation of individual muscle groups as a screening test for muscle integrity and nerve supply. In the absence of ipsilateral forearm and hand injuries, radial, median, and ulnar nerve function can be assessed without disturbing the proximal humeral fracture. An attempt is made to evaluate the biceps, the triceps, the three divisions of the deltoid, the spinati, the pectoralis, the latissimus dorsi, and the trapezius muscles. Dermatomal sensory patterns are recorded, but unfortunately, sensibility in the axillary nerve distribution in the lateral aspect of the arm is not a reliable test for determining the presence of axillary motor function. It is important to remember that neurovascular injuries occur in 5% to 30% of complex fractures of the proximal end of the humerus.[3, 25, 78, 92] After 50 years of age, the incidence of nerve injury with proximal humeral fracture-dislocation was greater than 50% in one reported study. The axillary nerve is the most commonly injured peripheral nerve. In addition, axillary nerve injury often occurs in combination with other peripheral nerve injuries. Some of these combined injuries are infraclavicular brachial plexus injuries. Unfortunately, recovery of associated nerve injuries is often incomplete.

Early deltoid muscle atony with inferior subluxation of the humeral head can occur and must be distinguished from an axillary nerve injury. Electromyography (EMG) and nerve conduction studies at the time of injury may exclude previous injury and give a baseline for comparison 3 weeks later when the studies are repeated to assess the extent of nerve involvement.[96] Early EMG may identify evidence of previous denervation. Nerve conduction studies before wallerian degeneration can confirm nerve continuity. A careful and detailed neurologic examination should be possible if the patient is cooperative. The findings will usually provide enough information to accurately determine the location and extent of neurologic injury.

In the distal part of the involved limb, the color, capillary refill, and radial pulse are examined and compared with those of the uninjured upper extremity. More detailed vascular evaluation is undertaken if arterial injury is suspected. Vascular injuries are less commonly associated with shoulder girdle trauma than neurologic injuries are. Most significant vascular injuries are arterial (Fig. 44–7). The collateral circulation may mask an arterial injury, and the distal pulses may be intact. Clinical ischemia may be absent initially.[51, 53, 58] An expanding axillary hematoma suggests a vascular injury. Arm positioning can compromise vascularity by extrinsic compression of a major vessel. Doppler pressures should be assessed in patients with any possibility of a vascular injury, and any abnormalities should be further evaluated with arteriography. Venous injuries are less common and rarely discussed. Nonetheless, venous laceration can cause

significant local bleeding. Subclavian thrombosis can be identified with duplex ultrasonography and venography.

Complicated injuries, especially in the polytrauma setting, and those involving open fractures are splinted, and much of the evaluation that does not require the patient's subjective input or attempt to demonstrate muscle function can be delayed until the patient's condition is stabilized or the patient is taken to the operating room for treatment of associated injuries.

Several helpful clinical signs in the evaluation of closed fractures include an estimation of the stability of the fracture and whether a dislocation is present. With gentle

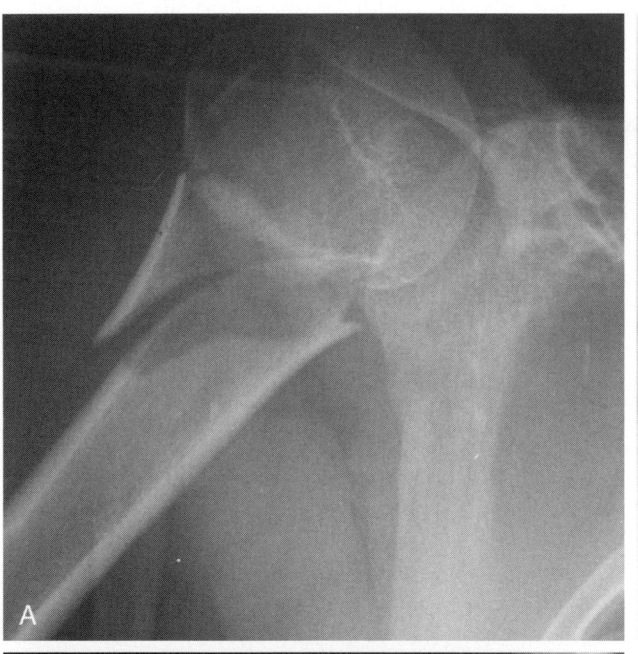

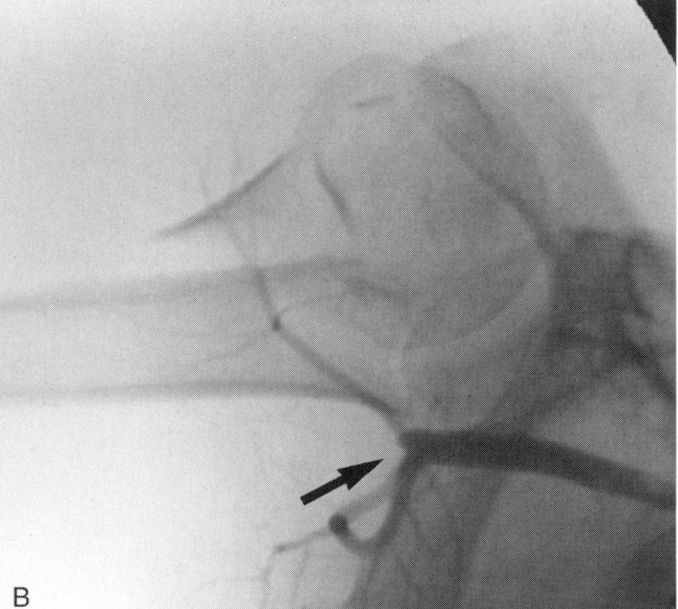

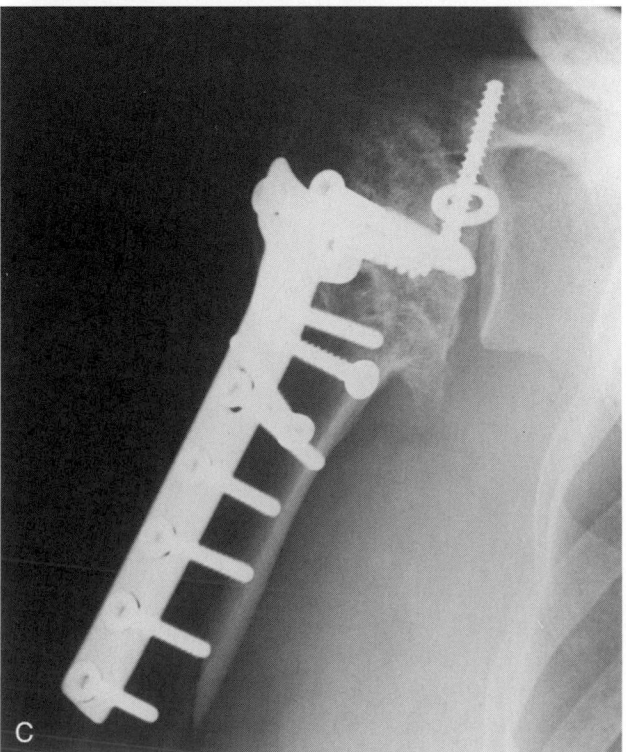

**FIGURE 44–7.** Radiographs of the shoulder of a 28-year-old man who was injured when he fell down a flight of stairs. *A,* He sustained a displaced surgical neck fracture of the proximal end of the humerus. His radial pulse could not be palpated despite satisfactory perfusion of the hand. *B,* An arteriogram demonstrated occlusion of the axillary artery *(arrow)* associated with the proximal humeral fracture. At exploration, the axillary artery was found entrapped at the fracture site. *C,* The fracture was reduced and fixed with a plate and screws. Four years later, the patient had symptomatic avascular necrosis.

AP in scapular plane.

Arm supported in sling.

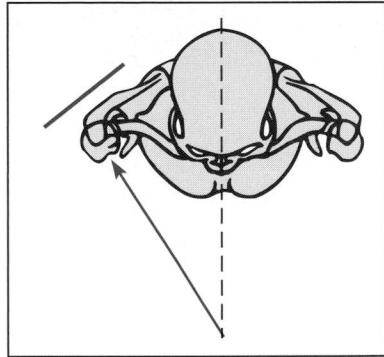

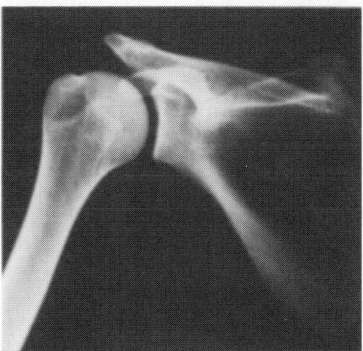

No overlap of head and glenoid.

Lateral in scapular plane.

Arm supported in sling.

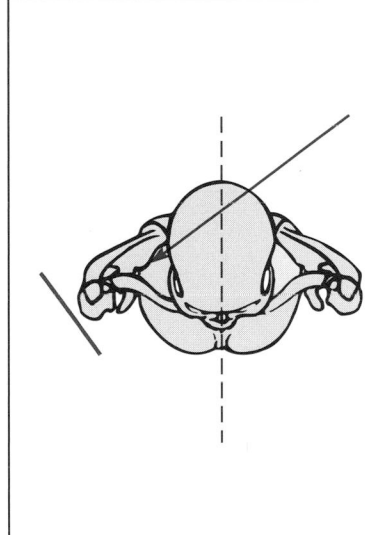

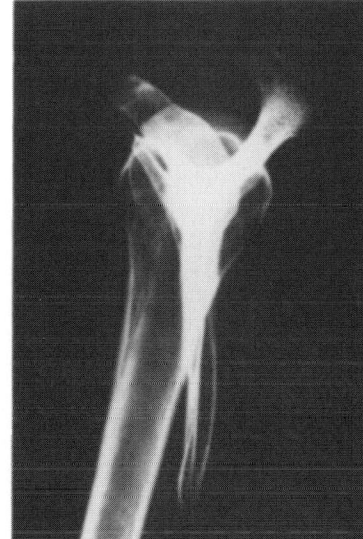

90° to AP.

Head in center of glenoid.

Identify anterior and posterior displacement.

Identify greater tuberosity displacement.

Evaluate shape of acromion for cause of impingement or cuff tears.

Emergency axillary.

Arm is gently abducted.

Tube at the hip.

Involved shoulder supported on pad.

Arm holds IV pole or is supported by assistant.

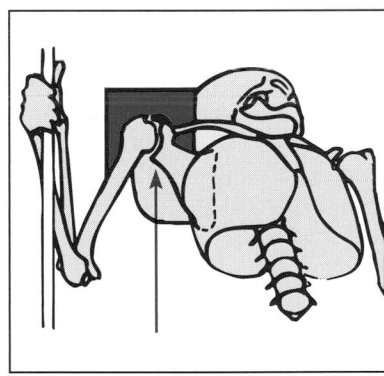

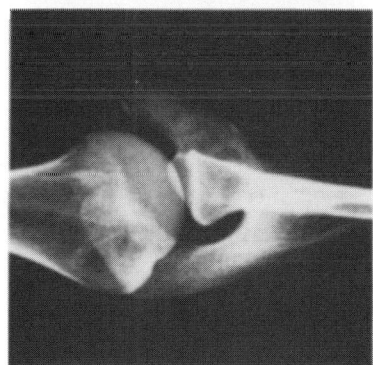

Evaluate glenoid for uneven wear or rim fractures.

Identify anterior and posterior dislocation.

Identify displaced tuberosities.

Identify unfused acromial epiphysis.

**FIGURE 44–8.** Trauma series views. (From Norris, T.R. In: Chapman, M.W.; Madison, M., eds. Operative Orthopaedics. Philadelphia, J.B. Lippincott, 1988, pp. 203–220.)

longitudinal traction, damage to the neurovascular structures would not be anticipated. When the humerus is grasped at the elbow and the arm gently rotated, an assessment can be made regarding whether the humeral head rotates with the shaft. With careful manipulation and longitudinal traction, crepitus is a common finding with a displaced or unstable fracture unless soft tissue interposition has occurred. The lack of crepitus with a displaced fracture and an inability to obtain an accurate closed reduction suggest soft tissue interposition. When dislocation is present, it is difficult to rotate the arm.

## Imaging

The glenohumeral articulation lies between the sagittal and the coronal planes of the body. In the elective setting, a complete plain radiographic evaluation includes five views of the shoulder—the three right-angle views of the trauma series[67, 75] (true anteroposterior [AP], axillary lateral, and Y view) (Fig. 44–8) and AP views in internal and external rotation. Computed tomography (CT), three-dimensional reconstructions, additional plain radiographic imaging, arthrography, ultrasonography, and magnetic resonance imaging (MRI) all provide further definition of shoulder injuries.

Precise radiographs are critical to establish an accurate diagnosis in shoulder trauma.[97] All too often, injuries are missed because the only radiographs obtained were AP views in the plane of the body rather than in the plane of the scapula. In these views, overlapping structures preclude full definition of the injuries.

## FIVE SCREENING RADIOGRAPHIC VIEWS

### Trauma Series (Three Views)

Glenohumeral congruity and reduction and the relationship of the four segments to each other are defined in three-dimensional space with three right-angle trauma series views[67, 75] (see Fig. 44–8). These views are taken relative to the scapular plane rather than the coronal plane of the body. The scapular AP view centered on the glenohumeral joint is a 30° posterior oblique view. The glenohumeral joint space is defined clearly. In the absence of subluxation or dislocation, the humeral head should not overlap the glenoid, in contradistinction to the AP rotational views taken in the sagittal plane of the body. Alternative views for posterior head displacement are taken in a 30° to 45° posterior oblique plane, with 45° to 60° caudal angulation.[48, 100]

The axillary lateral radiograph is the most useful in assessing the position of the humeral head relative to the glenoid. Although anterior dislocations can easily be distinguished on AP and lateral scapular views, subluxations, fracture-dislocations, and dislocations in the posterior direction are more difficult to diagnose.[39]

Posterior fracture-dislocations and displaced greater tuberosity fractures are the most commonly missed fractures of the proximal end of the humerus, usually because an axillary lateral projection is not obtained. The axial view is more difficult to perform but will avoid missing these less common injuries.[30] Although it can be difficult to position the shoulder because of pain or body habitus, many positions and projection techniques can be used to obtain a good axillary lateral image.[49] If the AP position of the humeral head or the position of the greater tuberosity is at all uncertain, a CT scan should be obtained.

In acute trauma, an assisted axillary view is obtained with gentle longitudinal traction applied at the elbow and minimal abduction and slight shoulder flexion. This position can be maintained with a soft foam pad. The radiographic plate is placed at the top of the shoulder with the edge against the neck. The tube at the hip is directed cephalad and medial, with enough scapula visualized to estimate accurate glenoid version, adequately depict humeral head articular and glenoid rim fractures, and appreciate any subluxations or dislocations. The patient can also be supine and hold an intravenous pole or can be positioned on the opposite, uninjured side[33, 49, 75, 88] (see Figs. 44–8 and 44–21C).

The axillary view and specific modifications are the best views with which to evaluate the articular surface of the humeral head and glenoid. Head-splitting fractures are often optimally visualized on the axillary lateral radiograph. Defects in the humeral head, glenoid fractures, and

**FIGURE 44–9.** Bloom-Obata modified axial view. (Redrawn from Bloom, M.H.; Obata, W.G. J Bone Joint Surg Am 49:943–949, 1967.)

fractures of the coracoid base, distal part of the clavicle, and acromion are also well visualized on axial projections.[40]

The Bloom-Obata modified axial view was specifically devised to determine the presence of posterior dislocation or fracture-dislocation[4] (Fig. 44–9). No manipulation of the arm is necessary. This position is difficult for elderly kyphotic patients, who often have trouble leaning backward over the x-ray table.

Another axillary modification is the West Point axillary view, which is used to visualize the anteroinferior glenoid rim[88] (Fig. 44–10). Anterior glenoid rim fractures or the ectopic calcification in many anteroinferior labral detachments with instability can be delineated with this view.[74, 88]

The lateral scapular view is taken at right angles to the scapular AP view; thus, at a 60° anterior oblique angle, the beam parallels the scapular spine. The head overlaps the glenoid evenly and entirely to sit in the center of a Y formed by the scapular spine and coracoid superiorly and the scapular body inferiorly (Fig. 44–11). In this projection, an anterior dislocation is easily appreciated. More information is added regarding tuberosity and shaft displacement. Avulsed greater tuberosity fragments that may overlap the humeral head in the AP views can usually be seen posterior to the head on the Y view. Slight scapular malpositioning leads to confusion when defining the status of the humeral head. The use of fluoroscopy in positioning the patient enables an inexperienced technician to superimpose the axillary and vertebral borders of the scapula. Once superimposed, the humeral head is centered on the glenoid in a normal shoulder.

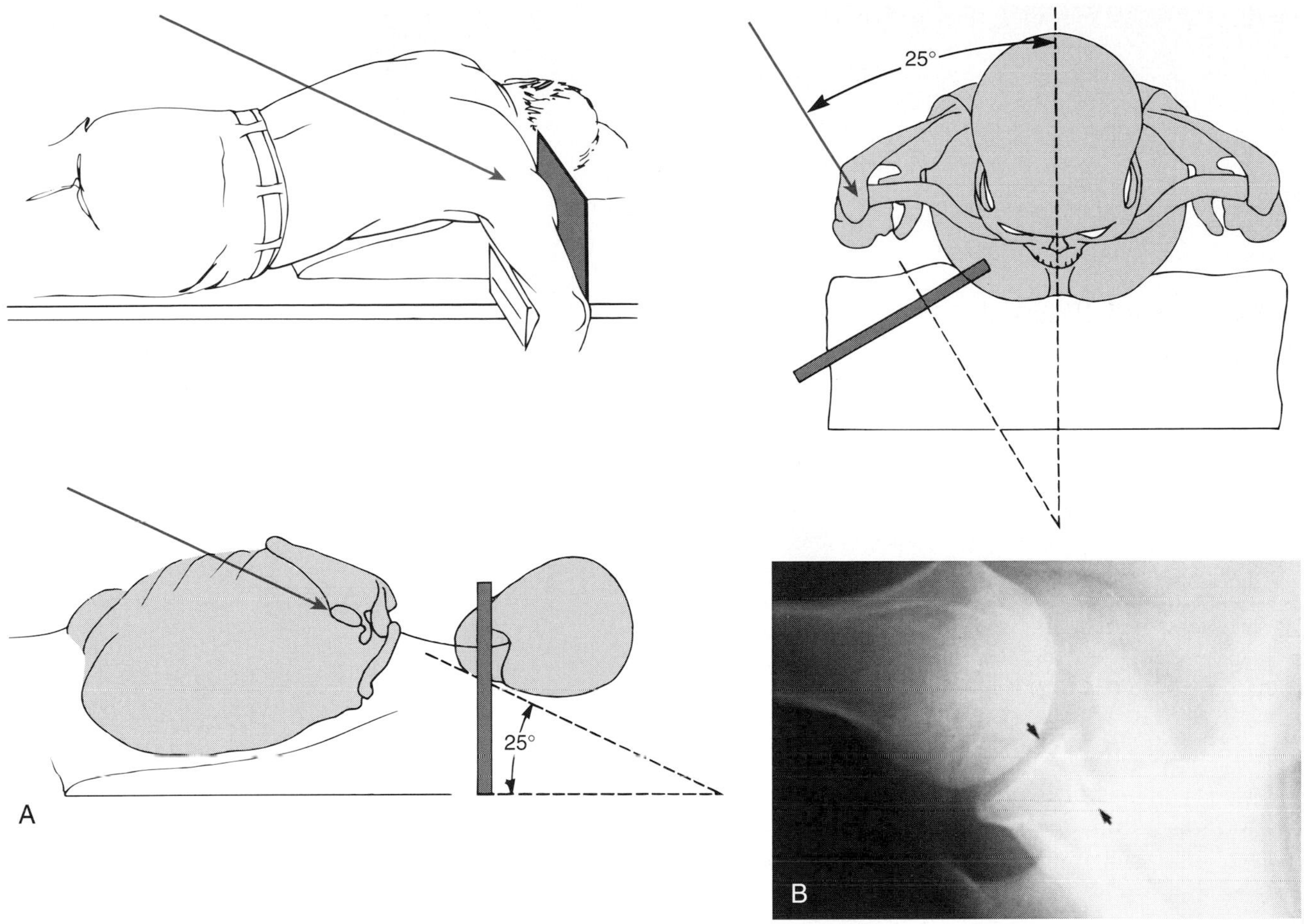

**Figure 44–10.** West Point axillary view to visualize the anteroinferior glenoid rim for evidence of labral detachment or a rim fracture. *A,* Radiographic evaluation. *B,* Anteroinferior rim fracture *(arrows)* after anterior dislocation.

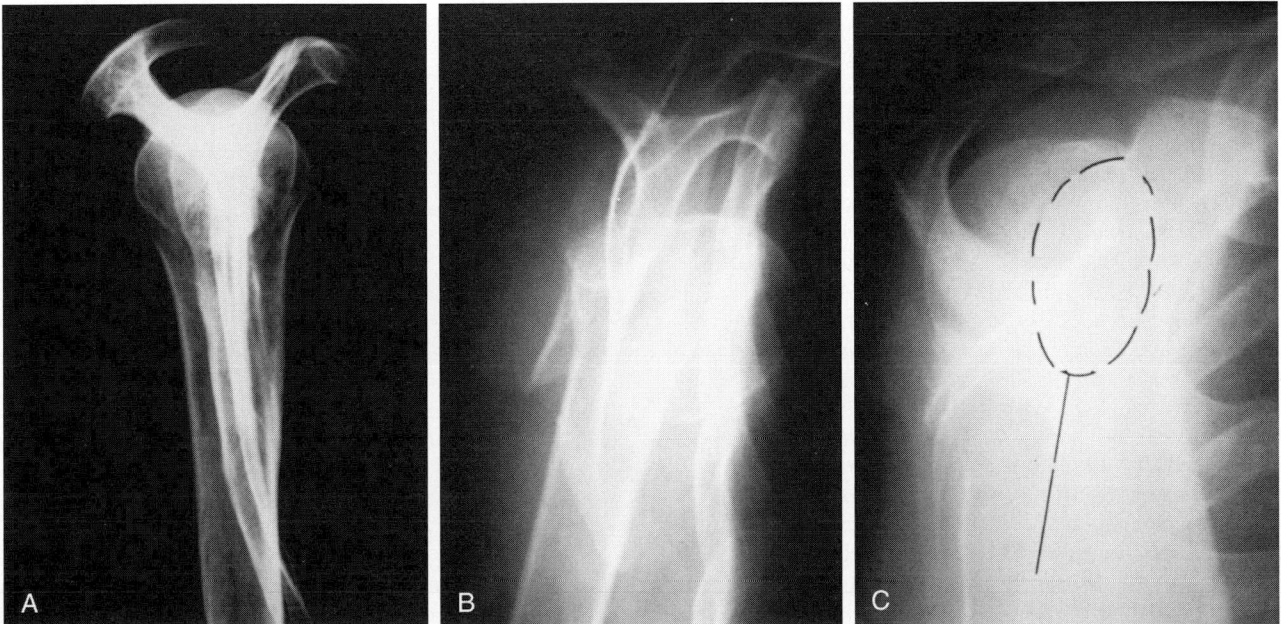

**Figure 44–11.** *A,* Lateral or scapular Y views. The humeral head is centered on the glenoid located at the junction of the coracoid process, scapular spine, and scapular body. *B,* In an anterior dislocation with a two-part surgical neck fracture and axillary nerve palsy, the humeral head is anterior to the glenoid in a subcoracoid position. *C,* In a posterior fracture-dislocation, more of the head is posterior to the glenoid at the center of the scapular Y. Slight scapular rotation makes diagnosis by this view alone difficult.

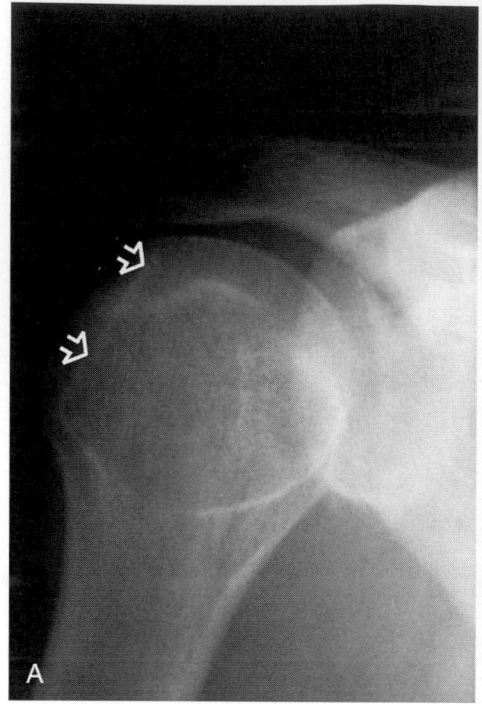
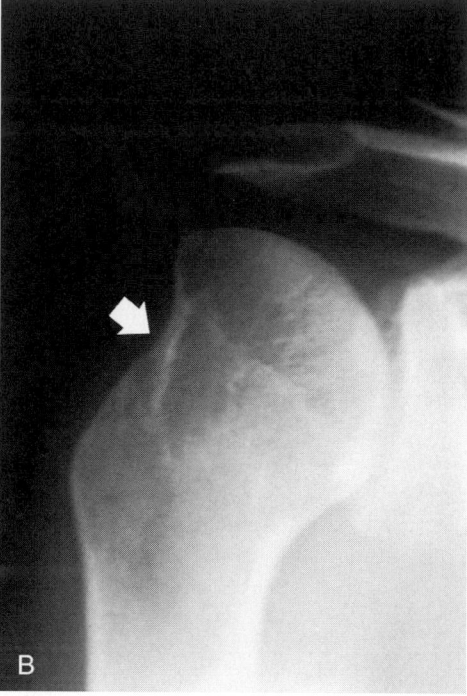

FIGURE 44–12. Examples of pathologic findings seen with rotational anteroposterior views after anterior dislocation and reduction. *A,* Internal rotation. A Hill-Sachs posterolateral humeral head impression fracture can be noted. *B,* External rotation. The greater tuberosity is missing from its normal location on the humerus after a displaced two-part greater tuberosity fracture and anterior dislocation.

### Rotational Anteroposterior Views (Two Views)

When the head moves with the shaft, particularly in late cases of nonunion or malunion, internal and external rotational views in the AP plane supplement the three-view trauma series to make up the five standard screening views recommended for routine shoulder evaluation (Fig. 44–12). The AP in internal rotation and the Stryker notch views are the two projections most likely to demonstrate a posterolateral humeral head impression fracture (Hill-Sachs lesion).[36, 40, 88]

In the external rotation view, the greater tuberosity is normally seen. When it is absent, the axillary view is mandatory to locate any tuberosity fragment that might be retracted by the spinatus muscles toward the base of the scapular spine. This fragment may be difficult to appreciate on the AP view because of superimposition with the humeral head.

Overpenetrated rotational AP and lateral scapular views are useful to locate calcium deposits. Occasionally, rotator cuff avulsion with a small fragment of tuberosity can be confused with a calcium deposit (Fig. 44–13).

AP views in the sagittal plane of the body do not adequately demonstrate posteromedial displacement, and a posterior fracture-dislocation is frequently missed.[20, 28, 33, 39] Overlap of the head and glenoid is expected on an AP view taken in the sagittal plane of the body, but it is indicative of a posterior dislocation or fracture-dislocation in the true AP view (Fig. 44–14).

The importance of accurate classification and diagnosis of proximal humeral fractures has been emphasized.[14, 38, 64] Inadequate evaluation often leads to error in diagnosis and inappropriate treatment. A detailed history, physical examination, and plain radiographs form the basis of any shoulder evaluation.[74, 76, 77] Of all the classes of shoulder disorders, fractures are perhaps the most

dependent on accurate radiographic imaging technique. The three views of the shoulder trauma series (glenohumeral AP, axillary lateral, and scapular lateral) should be obtained in all cases of shoulder injury.[77] If only two views can be obtained, the true AP and axillary lateral are the most informative.

## COMPUTED TOMOGRAPHY

CT scanning is an adjunctive method for evaluating complex proximal humeral fractures. When CT scans and standard radiographs were compared, CT scans were superior in assessing the location of fracture lines, displacement of fracture fragments relative to their normal position,

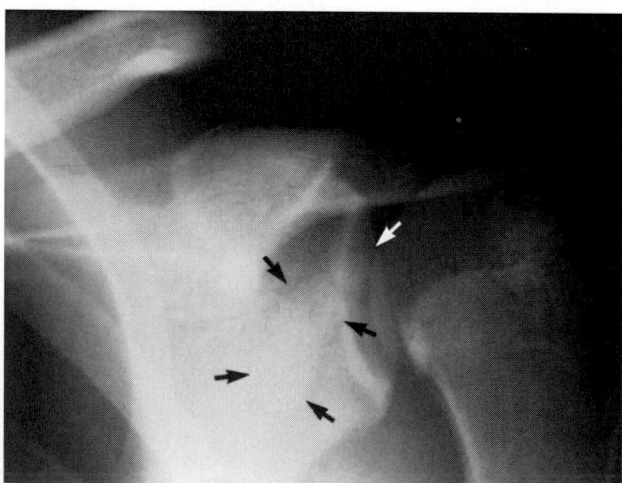

FIGURE 44–13. Isolated lesser tuberosity fracture with medial retraction (*arrows*). The displaced tuberosity could be confused for calcific tendonitis.

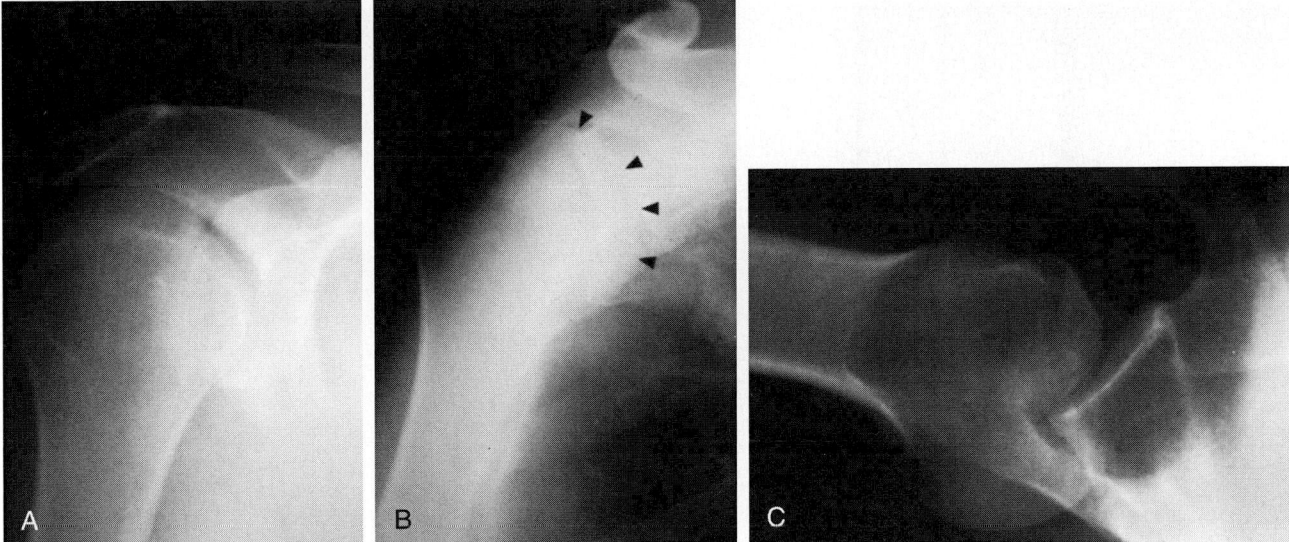

**FIGURE 44–14.** Anteroposterior radiographs. *A,* In the sagittal plane of the body (missed posterior dislocation). *B,* In the sagittal plane of the scapula, overlap of the head and glenoid (*arrowheads*) indicates a dislocation. *C,* Axillary or computed tomography scans are the best views for diagnosing posterior dislocation or fracture-dislocation.

rotation of the humeral articular surface, and fractures of both the glenoid and humeral head.[11, 27, 61, 74–76] Castagno and coauthors[11] reported that the CT findings altered the treatment method in 15 of 17 patients. In six of the eight patients undergoing surgery, unsuspected abnormalities guided the type of surgical treatment. In this study, craniocaudal displacement was not as well demonstrated as horizontal displacement when these views were reconstructed in the axial plane.

In contrast, Burnstein and associates found that the addition of CT scans was associated with only a slight increase in intraobserver reliability and no increase in interobserver reproducibility. The interobserver reproducibility of the senior shoulder surgeons regarding diagnosis and treatment did not change when CT scans were used in addition to plain radiographs.[10] Nevertheless, CT scans can be especially useful in evaluating complex fractures or malunion.[72, 73] CT is superior to MRI in depicting bony detail (Table 44–1).

CT scans have also been used to evaluate shoulders for signs of glenohumeral instability, including glenoid rim fractures, Hill-Sachs lesions, and when arthrography is added, capsulolabral pathology.[93]

MRI is now readily available in the United States. Nonetheless, it is rarely indicated in the acute evaluation of a shoulder fracture. However, if plain radiographs fail to demonstrate a fracture and the clinical course is not progressing satisfactorily, MRI can be used to demonstrate an occult nondisplaced fracture, most commonly a greater tuberosity fracture, rotator cuff tearing, or occult articular injury.[56, 86] Patten and colleagues reported that ultrasonography can also identify occult nondisplaced greater tuberosity fractures.[79]

### Three-Dimensional Imaging

Three-dimensional reconstruction from CT scans is readily available and allows visualization of the fracture from any direction and in real time to determine the position and displacement of the fracture fragments. This technique gives the treating surgeon an unparalleled opportunity to make an accurate diagnosis and plan for reconstruction. We have found three-dimensional imaging to be useful in occasional patients with especially complex fractures. Three-dimensional models can be produced and are of more use in reconstructive cases with fracture malunion or abnormal and eccentric wear of the glenoid[72, 73] (Fig. 44–15).

## ROTATOR CUFF EVALUATION

Wide displacement of the tuberosities suggests rotator cuff tearing. Anterior shoulder dislocations in patients older than 40 years are most commonly associated with avulsion of the posterior superior rotator cuff (supraspinatus and infraspinatus). Imaging studies used to evaluate the rotator cuff include ultrasonography, arthrography, and MRI.

Ultrasonography is the least expensive, no radiation is used, and the other shoulder can easily be imaged for comparison. Experience with ultrasonography in North America has been varied, and the results are operator

---

| **TABLE 44–1** |
| --- |
| Common Uses for Computed Tomography |

Nondisplaced fracture
Greater or lesser tuberosity displacement
Four-part fracture
Posterior fracture-dislocation
Avascular necrosis with collapse
Tuberosity malunion
Glenoid version evaluation
Loose bodies

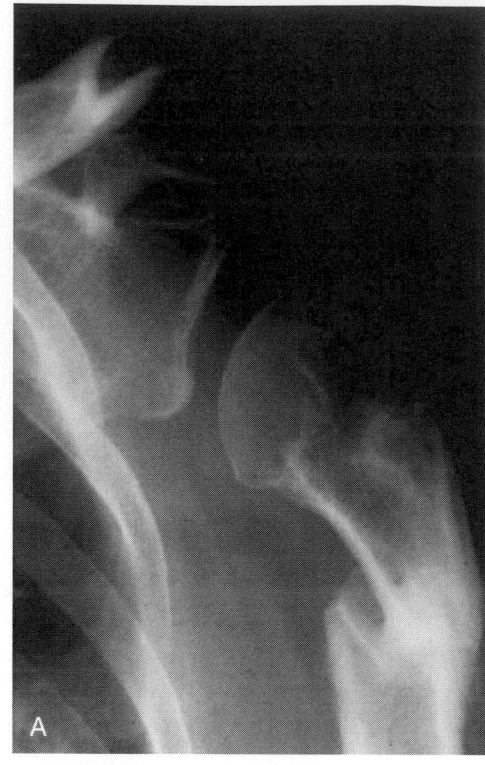
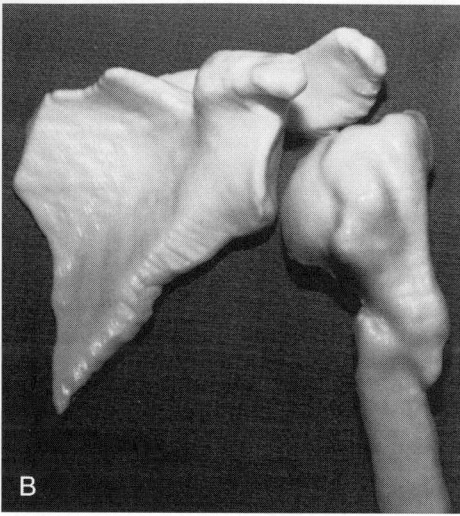

FIGURE **44–15.** Three-part fracture with malunion of the greater tuberosity and loss of humeral length. *A,* Anteroposterior radiograph showing varus malunion. *B,* Three-dimensional reconstruction confirms varus malunion through the upper part of the shaft, inferior subluxation of the humeral head, and poor position of the greater tuberosity directly over the humeral shaft. Late prosthetic reconstruction required biplanar osteotomy of the greater tuberosity and repositioning lower than the articular surface and more laterally. (*A, B,* From Norris, T.R. In: Watson, M., ed. Surgical Disorders of the Shoulder. London, Churchill Livingstone, 1991, pp. 473–510.)

dependent.[55] A study by Teefey and co-workers reported high sensitivity and specificity for the detection of rotator cuff tears.[98]

Historically, arthrography was considered the gold standard for determining the presence of a full-thickness rotator cuff tear.[34, 52, 59] However, it is not as helpful as clinical examination or MRI in evaluating the size of the tear or demonstrating evidence of chronic pathology such as atrophy on physical examination or fatty replacement of muscle on MRI.[46]

Recent advances in MRI technology and the proliferation of scanners have made MRI the standard test for evaluation of the shoulder for rotator cuff pathology. MRI provides the best-quality imaging and has high sensitivity, specificity, and accuracy for detection of rotator cuff pathology.[46]

## FLUOROSCOPY

Fluoroscopy is rarely used but has distinct advantages in positioning the patient for radiography, in determining motion at a delayed union or nonunion site, and in evaluating stability in cases in which the degree of stability is the determining factor for open reduction and internal fixation (ORIF).[74]

## DIFFERENTIAL DIAGNOSIS

The differential diagnosis of proximal humeral fractures and glenohumeral dislocations includes muscle contusion or sprain, rotator cuff tear, brachial plexus injury, infection, disruption of the axillary artery, neuropathic arthropathy,

and thrombosis of the axillary vein. Imaging studies combined with the history and physical examination enable differentiation of these injuries.

## SURGICAL TREATMENT OF PROXIMAL HUMERAL AND GLENOHUMERAL INJURIES

Operative treatment of an injured shoulder requires detailed and complete knowledge of the anatomy of the shoulder girdle. Shoulder anatomy is complicated and can be treacherous for inexperienced or occasional shoulder surgeons. Few shoulder injuries require immediate or emergency surgery. In most cases, surgery is performed when the patient is medically stable and the surgeon and operating room are ready and adequately equipped. All necessary fixation devices and prostheses should be in the operating room before the patient is anesthetized.

## Anesthetic Considerations

Either general anesthesia or an interscalene nerve block can be used for closed reduction or open surgical procedures on the shoulder girdle. When general anesthesia is used, it is important to be able to paralyze the patient to relax the muscles around the shoulder and facilitate retraction and exposure. Many centers specializing in shoulder surgery have extensive experience with interscalene nerve blocks[6, 17, 80, 103] (Fig. 44–16). Regional anesthesia avoids the potential cardiac complications associated with general anesthesia, as well as the often unpleasant side effects of general anesthesia, and has not been associated with a significant incidence of complications. Additionally, some benefit may be derived from the preemptive analgesia (before the surgical procedure) that the block provides. Importantly, the nerve block provides substantial postoperative pain relief and eliminates the need for large narcotic doses immediately after surgery. Success with regional anesthesia for shoulder surgery depends on having anesthesiologists experienced in these techniques.

## Intraoperative Imaging

Intraoperative radiographs are required for adequate evaluation of the operative treatment of proximal humeral fractures and fracture-dislocations. Obtaining quality images is particularly challenging in these cases because the patient is often positioned in the beach-chair or semisitting position and the plane of the glenohumeral joint is oblique. Image intensification is very useful in that it allows greater flexibility in obtaining the correct projection and multiple images can be obtained without having to wait for films to be developed. Biplanar radiography or image intensification is difficult but can be facilitated with proper patient positioning. If surgery is performed with the patient in the supine position, a radiolucent table can be used. In the beach-chair position, most standard operating room tables can be set up so that an image intensifier can be used.

## Positioning

A Gelfoam mattress is placed on the operating table to provide additional padding and protection of bony prominences. The patient is positioned supine in the beach-chair position for anterior and superior approaches, and the lateral decubitus position is used for most posterior approaches. The upper section of a standard operating room table is replaced with a padded articulating

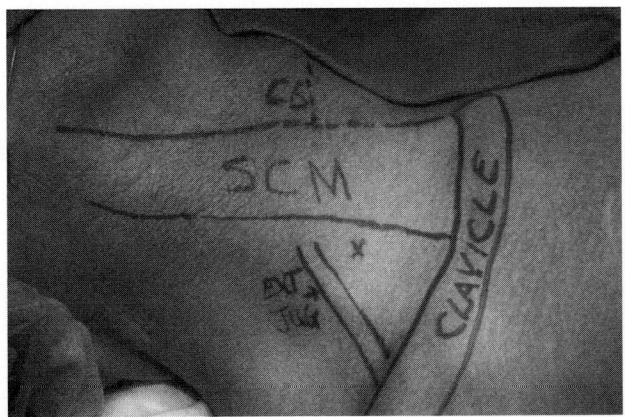

**FIGURE 44–16.** Interscalene nerve block with superficial anatomic landmarks. *Abbreviations:* EXT JUG, external jugular vein; SCM, sternocleidomastoid.

headrest (Fig. 44–17) that is adjusted to position and support the head so that the cervical spine is slightly flexed and deviated to the opposite side approximately 10°. Such positioning gives more exposure superiorly in the region of the neck. The patient is positioned to the side of the table so that the arm can be extended vertically off the edge. The scapula is padded forward with a gel bolster. A narrow gel pad can be placed over the taped eyes. A towel is wrapped around the head to exclude the hair and anesthesia tubes from the operative field. Anesthesia tubing is positioned away from the operative field. The contralateral arm and both legs and heels are positioned and padded to protect the skin and peripheral nerves.

If an autogenous bone graft (in addition to what is available in the surgical field) may be necessary, two potential donor sites are the ribs and the anterior iliac crest. A bolster under the hip makes the anterior iliac crest more prominent and facilitates exposure. Harvesting bone from the opposite anterior iliac crest permits simultaneous shoulder surgery. However, if the ipsilateral iliac crest is the donor site, the patient will be able to hold an assistive device for ambulation with the uninjured arm. The latter is preferred.

The surgical fields are scrubbed with bactericidal soap and then rinsed with saline solution or alcohol. An adherent SteriDrape is applied high on the neck with the tails toward the axilla to isolate the surgical field.

The shoulder and upper extremity are suspended from the wrist and prepared with iodine solution or an iodine preparation. The forearm and hand are wrapped in sterile towels and an impervious stockinette and secured with a sterile elastic wrap. Prophylactic antibiotics are given before the skin is incised and continued for 24 to 48 hours. The Cell Saver can be used if significant blood loss is anticipated.[4] The skin incision is marked and the exposed skin covered with adherent SteriDrape. A sterile articulating arm positioner is extremely helpful during the procedure because it can be used to precisely position the arm. This device facilitates exposure and positioning for imaging and frees the assistants' hands (Fig. 44–18).

## Surgical Approaches

The surgeon needs to be familiar with three approaches to the shoulder. The deltopectoral approach can be used for most fractures.[21, 67] The superior approach gives access to the subacromial space without any need for transacromial osteotomy or detachment of the middle deltoid origin.[22, 65] Occasionally, a posterior approach is necessary for posterior and inferior glenoid fractures or a malunited greater tuberosity fracture, but this approach is seldom necessary for ORIF of acute proximal humeral fractures or for prosthetic replacement.[94, 104]

### DELTOPECTORAL APPROACH

The incision for the deltopectoral incision begins at the distal third of the clavicle, passes just lateral to the coracoid, and extends to the deltoid insertion (Fig. 44–19). Occasionally, a more cosmetic incision can be made in Langer's lines from the coracoid process to the

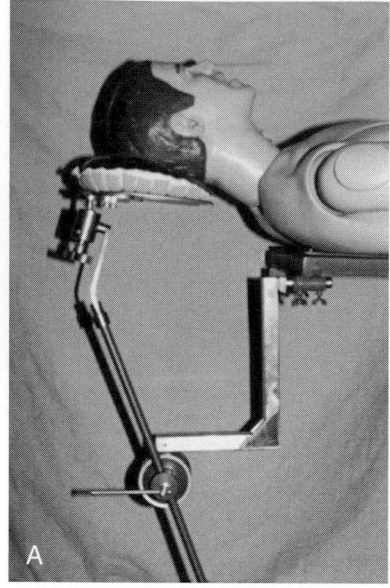

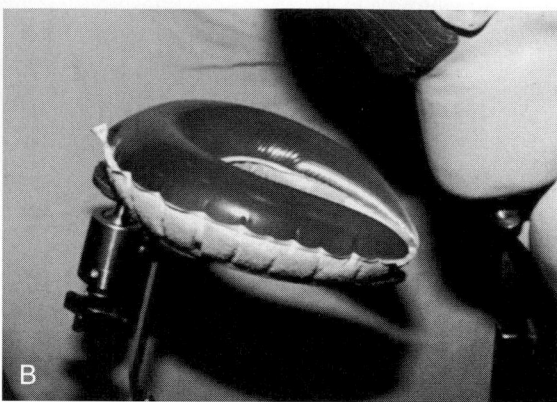

FIGURE **44–17.** *A,* McConnell headrest. The headrest is adjusted and can be positioned through a series of universal joints to protect the cervical spine. *B,* The gel pads provide secure fixation with minimal, evenly distributed pressure holding the head and neck.

axilla. The cephalic vein is preserved and retracted laterally with the deltoid muscle. Care is taken at the upper end of the deltopectoral interval to avoid disrupting crossing branches of the cephalic vein. The clavipectoral fascia is incised to expose the subscapularis tendon and lesser tuberosity. Careful blunt dissection under the deltoid and in the subacromial space improves exposure. Richardson retractors or an abdominal Balfour retractor is used to retract the deltoid laterally and cephalad and the intact coracoid muscles medially. Self-retaining retractors should be used with caution to avoid iatrogenic nerve injury. Abduction of the arm and release of the anterior 1 cm of the deltoid insertion and the upper half of the pectoralis major insertion provide more tissue relaxation and wound exposure if necessary. The coracoid muscles are left intact and the coracoid is not osteotomized to protect the brachial plexus. Although the coracoacromial ligament can be incised to improve exposure, we preserve it whenever possible. The axillary nerve is palpated medially and inferior to the subscapularis muscle, as well as under the deltoid muscle. Care is taken to protect it throughout the procedure. The tendon of the long head of the biceps is the key landmark in the approach to the proximal part of the humerus.

For a two-part surgical neck fracture, the glenohumeral joint rarely needs to be opened. For a posterior dislocation in which the articular deficit in the head is less than 20%, an opening through the subscapularis is used; however, if the deficit is between 20% and 40%, osteotomy of the lesser tuberosity enables transfer of the lesser tuberosity into the humeral head deficit.

In three-part fractures, the joint is already exposed by avulsion of one of the tuberosities. The rotator cuff interval between the subscapularis and the supraspinatus can be extended medially to improve access to the glenohumeral joint. Frequently, a finger placed into the glenohumeral joint can be used to assess the articular surface of the humeral head.

In four-part fractures, both tuberosities are usually separated, but in the rare instance in which they are still intact at the biceps groove, the groove is osteotomized and the cuff opened through the rotator interval.

## SUPERIOR APPROACH WITH OR WITHOUT ANTERIOR ACROMIOPLASTY

The superior approach incorporates a split in the deltoid (Fig. 44–20*A*). When acromioplasty is not involved in the

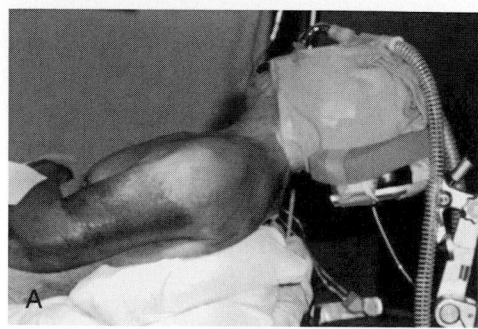

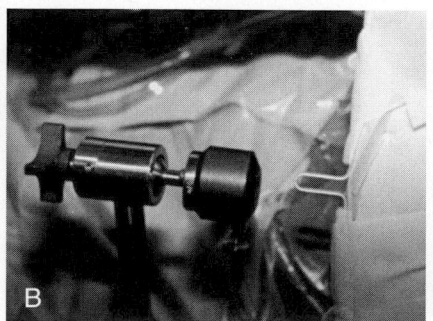

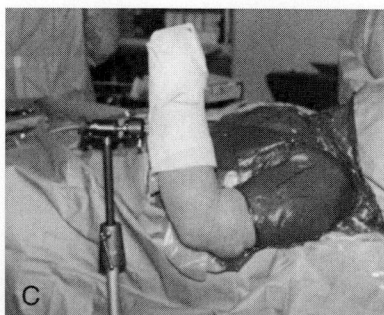

FIGURE **44–18.** The semi-Fowler beach-chair position for anterior and superior approaches to the shoulder. *A,* The cervical spine is protected in slight flexion. The headrest permits superior exposure of the shoulder girdle. *B,* The McConnell arm positioner attached to the forearm enables the arm to be positioned in any rotation or elevation (*C*).

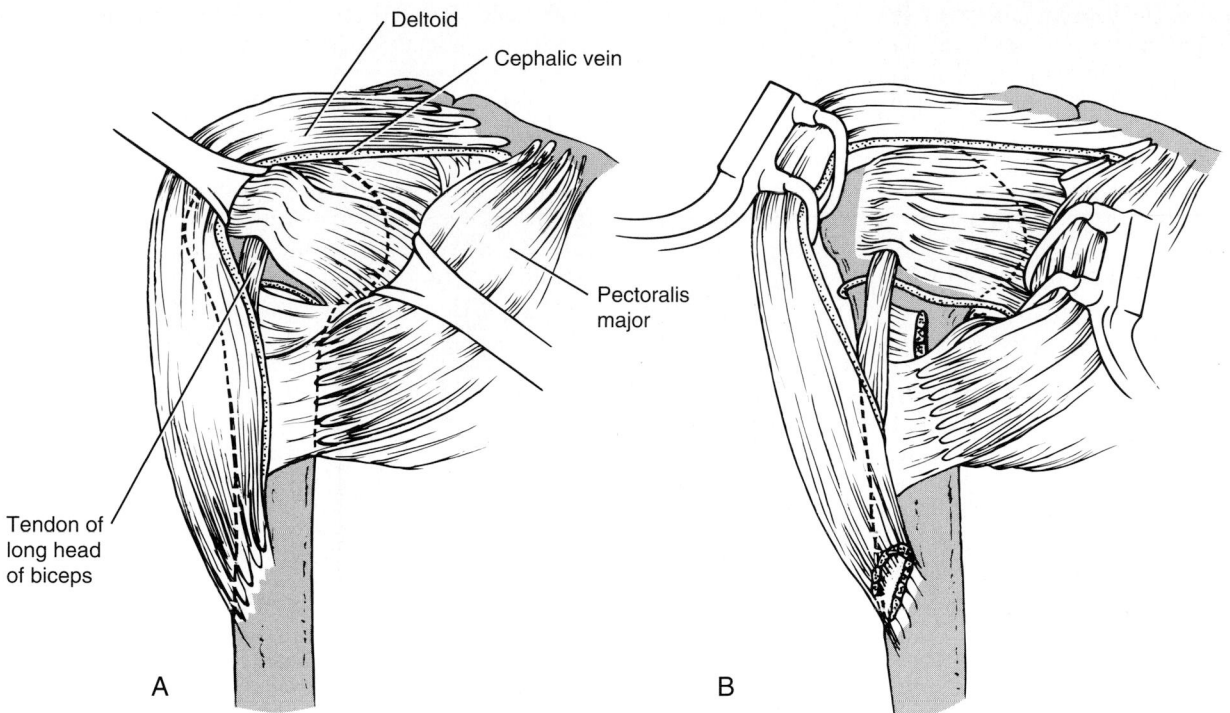

Deltoid

Cephalic vein

Pectoralis major

Tendon of long head of biceps

A

B

**FIGURE 44–19.** The deltopectoral approach preserves the cephalic vein. The coracoid is left intact to protect the brachial plexus. Richardson retractors (*A*) or self-retaining Balfour retractors (*B*) maintain exposure to the proximal end of the humerus.

operative procedure, an incision is made over the lateral border of the acromion along Langer's skin lines. The skin and subcutaneous tissue are elevated medially and laterally in full thickness to give wide exposure. The deltoid is split laterally from a point just posterior to the anterolateral corner of the acromion and posterior to the tendinous raphe between the anterior and the middle deltoid. The

acromial branch of the thoracoacromial artery is coagulated. Small Richardson retractors are placed to retract the deltoid. Care is taken to avoid splitting the deltoid any more than 4 or 5 cm lateral to the acromion to prevent injury to the axillary nerve.[9, 32] Any underlying hemorrhagic bursa is excised. A stay suture can be placed at the distal portion of the deltoid split, 5 cm below the

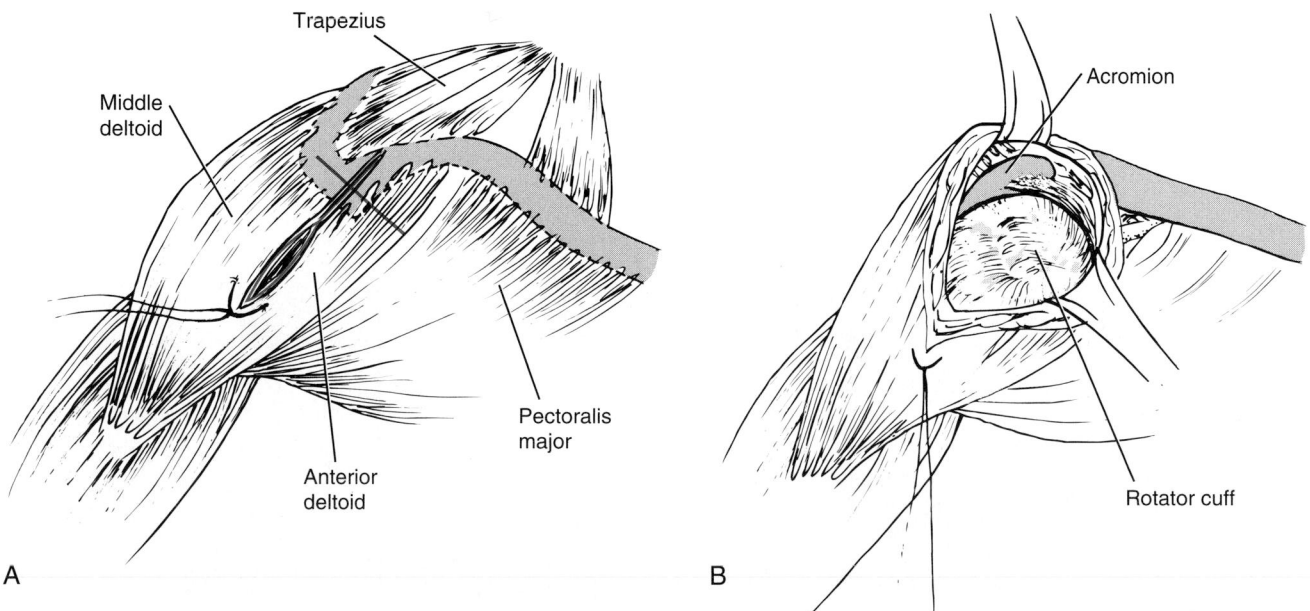

Trapezius

Middle deltoid

Anterior deltoid

Pectoralis major

Acromion

Rotator cuff

A

B

**FIGURE 44–20.** *A,* Superior approach with a deltoid split but without anterior acromioplasty. *B,* Approach for anterior acromioplasty. The skin incision follows Langer's skin lines over the top of the acromion and perpendicular to the deltoid split.

acromion, to prevent injury to the axillary nerve. This operative approach is commonly used for greater tuberosity fractures. With some isolated greater tuberosity fractures, a superior approach with a lateral deltoid split may be sufficient.

When the procedure includes anterior acromioplasty, an incision is made over the midportion of the acromion along Langer's skin lines and paralleling the AP direction of the acromion (see Fig. 44–20B). The incision is carried from the posterior third of the acromion down beyond the anterior edge of the acromion, midway to the coracoid. After undermining circumferentially, a split is made in the deltotrapezius fascia over the anterior of the acromion 5 to 10 mm posterior to the anterior acromial margin. It is continued down into the deltoid fibers similar to the deltoid-splitting incision. The acromial branch of the thoracoacromial artery is coagulated. The anterior deltoid is elevated off the anterior of the acromion, and Sharpey's fibers are preserved with the deltoid for later attachment. The coracoacromial ligament is simply released from the acromial attachment and not excised. Elevating the anterior deltoid off the acromion improves exposure because the deltoid can be retracted more with less risk of injuring the axillary nerve.

Longitudinal traction on the arm enhances visualization of the subacromial space. Visualization may also be aided with a flat Darrach elevator in the subacromial space to push the humeral head inferiorly. An osteotome or chisel is used to remove spurring and undersurface prominence of the anterior of the acromion. The goal of acromioplasty is to create a flat undersurface.[65] Care is taken to remove spurring at the deltoid origin laterally or medially at the acromioclavicular joint. If arthritic, the distal end of the clavicle is excised to enable adduction of the arm without contact between the clavicle and the medial aspect of the acromion. Scar and adhesions in the subacromial and subdeltoid bursa are released to provide access to the rotator cuff and tuberosities. At the end of the procedure, the anterior deltoid is reattached to the acromion with nonabsorbable transosseous sutures.

The superior approaches are used for ORIF of greater tuberosity fractures and some three-part fractures and valgus-displaced four-part fractures.

## POSTERIOR APPROACH

In most cases, the posterior approach (Fig. 44–21) to the shoulder is performed with the patient in the lateral decubitus position. A beanbag or hip arthroplasty positioning system is used to support the patient. A soft gel bolster is placed underneath the upper chest wall to protect both the brachial plexus and the dependent

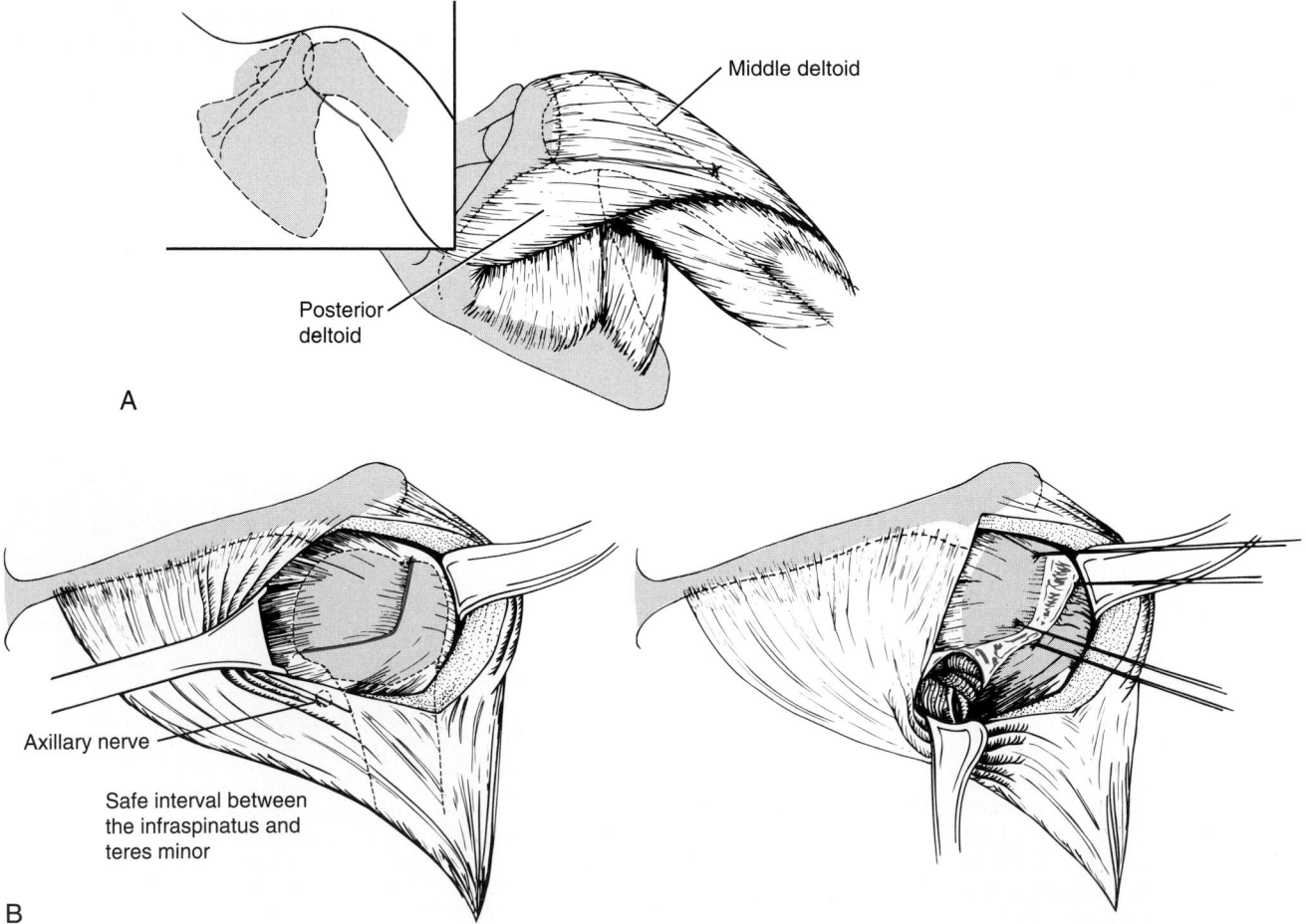

**FIGURE 44–21.** *A,* Posterior approach, longitudinal incision. The posterior of the deltoid is split up to 8 cm from the acromion to expose the infraspinatus and teres minor. *B,* Vertical infraspinatus arthrotomy with any horizontal component at the internervous plane between the infraspinatus and teres minor.

shoulder. The head is secured to a gel-padded headrest. The arm is positioned with a sterile articulating arm holder from the opposite side of the table.

Our preferred posterior incision is vertical and follows Langer's lines; it starts about 2 or 3 cm medial to the posterolateral corner of the acromion and extends caudad to a point just medial to the axilla. If necessary, this incision can be extended medially along the scapular spine or superiorly over the top of the shoulder. After undermining the skin and subcutaneous layer, the deltoid is split between 6 and 8 cm from the level of the posterior spine of the scapula, with care taken to not injure the axillary nerve. Additional exposure can be gained by releasing the deltoid origin from the scapular spine in the medial and lateral directions. Alternatively, the arm can be abducted and the inferior border of the deltoid carefully retracted in a cephalad direction. The latter provides exposure to the posterior of the scapula and the lateral scapular border. The critical point in the exposure is the location and protection of the axillary nerve plus its branches along the undersurface of the deltoid and to the teres minor. Exposure to the posterior aspect of the glenohumeral joint is gained by splitting the infraspinatus muscle[94] and tendon or by opening the interval between the infraspinatus and teres minor.[104]

The posterior approach is generally used for scapular body and glenoid fractures; however, it has been used for prosthetic shoulder arthroplasty.[83]

# OUTCOME EVALUATION

Recent trends in clinical medical practice have emphasized the importance of outcome evaluation. Numerous orthopaedic rating systems have been described. Originally, most systems were formulated to assess the outcome of specific surgical procedures, but more recent work has emphasized the importance of using measures of general health status and site- and disease-specific outcome to evaluate the results of treatment.

Early shoulder evaluation scores were developed to assess the results of specific shoulder procedures. The Neer score was devised to evaluate the results of shoulder arthroplasty[69]; the Rowe score evaluates the results of repair of shoulder instability.[90]

More recently, several outcome evaluation systems for assessing the shoulder have been developed, including the Constant-Murley score, the American Shoulder and Elbow Surgeons score, and the Disability Arm, Shoulder, and Hand (DASH) questionnaire. In addition, other rating systems have been proposed.

The Constant-Murley score evaluates pain, ability to perform activities of daily living, shoulder motion, and abduction strength. Additionally, the score is normalized to age.[18] It is the only measurement tool that was subjected to validation in its original publication.[16] Conboy and associates[16] studied the Constant-Murley score and raised questions about its validity for generic evaluation of all shoulder disorders.

The original American Shoulder and Elbow Surgeons shoulder evaluation form provides an organized format to record subjective and objective data. It was not intended to be used for calculation of a composite score.[2] This work has been updated and evaluated in field tests.[87] More recent work on outcome evaluation emphasizes subjective patient parameters.

The DASH evaluation was developed by the American Academy of Orthopaedic Surgeons in conjunction with the Institute for Work and Health of the University of Toronto and member organizations of the Council of Musculoskeletal Specialty Societies.[1] It includes patient-reported domains such as symptoms, function, expectations, satisfaction, and quality of life and is designed to be a broadly applicable outcome instrument for the upper extremity.

The general health status of orthopaedic patients is most commonly evaluated with the Short Form 36 (SF-36) questionnaire.[101] The SF-36 Health Survey was developed as an abbreviated form of the Medical Outcomes Study Survey, which assesses 40 physical and mental health concepts. It is a generic measure because it assesses health concepts that represent basic human values relevant to functional status and well-being. The eight scales of the SF-36 Health Survey assess the physical and mental aspects of behavioral functioning, perceived well-being, social and role disability, and personal evaluation of health in general.[34]

Outcome evaluation of proximal humeral fractures is complicated by the fact that premorbid assessment is not available. Thus, using outcome evaluation tools that are designed to assess treatment of chronic shoulder conditions such as glenohumeral arthritis and rotator cuff tearing may not be valid. Comparison to the unaffected extremity is usually helpful, as is consideration of age-matched normal function.

## REFERENCES

1. American Academy of Orthopaedic Surgeons. Disabilities of the Arm, Shoulder, and Hand. Rosemont, IL, American Academy of Orthopaedic Surgeons, 1995.
2. Barrett, W.P.; Franklin, J.L.; Jackins, S.E.; et al. Total shoulder arthroplasty. J Bone Joint Surg Am 69:865–872, 1987.
3. Blom, S.; Dahlback, L.O. Nerve injuries in dislocations of the shoulder joint and fractures of the neck of the humerus: A clinical and electromyographic study. Acta Chir Scand 136:461–466, 1970.
4. Bloom, M.H.; Obata, W.G. Diagnosis of posterior dislocation of the shoulder with the use of Velpeau axillary and angle-up roentgenographic views. J Bone Joint Surg Am 49:943–949, 1967.
5. Bovill, D.F.; Norris, T.R. The efficacy of intraoperative autologous transfusion in major shoulder surgery. Clin Orthop 240:137–140, 1989.
6. Brems, J.J.; Yoon, H.J.; Tetzlaff, J. Interscalene block anaesthesia and shoulder surgery. Paper presented at the American Shoulder and Elbow Surgeons Sixth Open Meeting, New Orleans, February 11, 1990.
7. Brewer, B.J. Aging of the rotator cuff. Am J Sports Med 7:102–110, 1979.
8. Brooks, C.H.; Revell, W.J.; Heatley, F.W. Vascularity of the humeral head after proximal humerus fractures. J Bone Joint Surg Br 75:132–136, 1993.
9. Burkhead, W.Z.; Scheinberg, R.R.; Boc, G. Surgical anatomy of the axillary nerve. J Shoulder Elbow Surg 1:31–36, 1992.
10. Burnstein, J.; Adler, L.M.; Blank, J.E.; et al. Evaluation of the Neer system of classification of proximal humerus fractures with computerized tomographic scans and plain radiographs. J Bone Joint Surg Am 78:1371–1375, 1996.
11. Castagno, A.A.; Shuman, W.P.; Kilcoyne, R.F.; et al. Complex fractures of the proximal humerus: Role of CT in treatment. Radiology 165:759–762, 1987.

12. Cave, E.A. Fractures and Other Injuries. Chicago, Year Book, 1958.
13. Codman, E.A. The Shoulder. Boston, T. Todd, 1934.
14. Cofield, R.H. Comminuted fractures of the proximal humerus. Clin Orthop 230:49–57, 1988.
15. Colachis, S.C., Jr; Strohm, B.R.; Brecher, V.L. Effects of axillary nerve block on muscle force in the upper extremity. Arch Phys Rehabil Med 50:647–654, 1969.
16. Conboy, V.B.; Morris, R.W.; Kiss, J.; Carr, A.J. An evaluation of the Constant-Murley shoulder assessment. J Bone Joint Surg Br 78:229–232, 1996.
17. Conn, R.A.; Cofield, R.H.; Byer, D.E.; et al. Interscalene block anaesthesia for shoulder surgery. Clin Orthop 216:94–98, 1987.
18. Constant, C.R.; Murley, A.H.G. A clinical method of functional assessment of the shoulder. Clin Orthop 214:160–164, 1987.
19. Cooper, D.E.; Arnoczky, S.P.; O'Brien, S.J.; et al: Anatomy, histology, and vascularity of the glenoid labrum. J Bone Joint Surg Am 74:46–52, 1992.
20. Craig, E.V. Importance of proper radiography in acute shoulder trauma. Minn Med 68:109–112, 1985.
21. Crenshaw, A.H. Surgical approaches. In: Crenshaw, A.H., ed. Campbell's Operative Orthopaedics, 7th ed. St. Louis, C.V. Mosby, 1987.
22. Cubbins, W.R.; Callahan, J.J.; Scuderi, C.S. The reduction of old or irreducible dislocations of the shoulder joint. Surg Gynecol Obstet 58:129–135, 1934.
23. Cyprien, J.M.; Vasel, H.M.; Budet, A.; et al. Humeral retrotorsion and glenohumeral relationship in the normal shoulder and in recurrent anterior dislocation (scapulometry). Clin Orthop 175:8–17, 1983.
24. Dameron, T.B.; Reibel, D.B. Fractures involving the proximal humeral epiphyseal plate. J Bone Joint Surg Am 51:289–297, 1969.
25. de Laat, E.A.T.; Visser, C.P.J.; Coene, L.N.; et al. Nerve lesions in primary shoulder dislocations and humeral neck fractures. J Bone Joint Surg Br 76:381–383, 1994.
26. DePalma, A.F.; Callery, G.; Bennett, G.A. Shoulder joint: Variational anatomy and degenerative lesions of the shoulder joint. Instr Course Lect 6:255, 1949.
27. Deutsch, A.L.; Resnick, D.; Mink, J.H. Computed tomography of the glenohumeral and sternoclavicular joints. Orthop Clin North Am 16:497–511, 1985.
28. Dorgan, J.A. Posterior dislocation of the shoulder. Am J Surg 89:890–900, 1955.
29. Flatow, E.L.; Bigliani, L.U.; April, E.W. An anatomical study of the coracoid muscles. Clin Orthop 244:166–171, 1989.
30. Flinn, R.M.; MacMillan, C.L., Jr.; Campbell, D.R.; Fraser, D.B. Optimal radiography of the acutely injured shoulder. J Can Assoc Radiol 34:128–132, 1983.
31. Gerber, C.; Schneeberger, A.; Vinh, T.S. The arterial vascularization of the humeral head. An anatomical study. J Bone Joint Surg Am 72:1486–1494, 1990.
32. Glousman, R.E.; Seltzer, D.; Tibone, J.E. Anatomy of the axillary nerve and its relationship to deltoid splitting surgical approaches. Paper presented at the American Shoulder and Elbow Surgeons Closed Meeting, Williamsburg, Virginia, 1993.
33. Golding, F.C. The shoulder. The forgotten joint. Br J Radiol 35:149–158, 1962.
34. Goldman, A.B.; Ghelman, B. The double contrast shoulder arthrogram: A review of 158 studies. Radiology 127:655–663, 1978.
35. Hall, M.C.; Rosser, M. The structure of the upper end of the humerus with reference to osteoporotic changes in senescence leading to fracture. Can Med Assoc J 88:290–294, 1963.
36. Hall, R.H.; Isaac, F.; Booth, C.R. Dislocations of the shoulder with special reference to accompanying small fractures. J Bone Joint Surg Am 41:489–494, 1959.
37. Harryman, D.T.; Sidles, J.A.; Harris, S.L.; Matsen, F.A., III. The role of the rotator interval capsule in passive motion and stability of the shoulder. J Bone Joint Surg Am 74:53–66, 1992.
38. Hawkins, R.J.; Angelo, R.L. Displaced proximal humeral fractures: Selecting treatment, avoiding pitfalls. Orthop Clin North Am 18:421–431, 1987.
39. Hawkins, R.J.; Neer, C.S., II; Pianta, R.M.; Mendoza, F.X. Locked posterior dislocation of the shoulder. J Bone Joint Surg Am 69:9–18, 1987.
40. Hill, H.A.; Sachs, M.D. The grooved defect in the humeral head: A frequently unrecognized complication of dislocations of the shoulder joint. Radiology 35:690–700, 1940.
41. Hodges, P.C. Development of the human skeleton. AJR Am J Roentgenol 30:809, 1933.
42. Horak, J.; Nilsson, B.E. Epidemiology of fracture of the upper end of the humerus. Clin Orthop 112:250–253, 1975.
43. Howell, S.M.; Galinat, B.J. The glenoid-labral socket: A constrained articular surface. Clin Orthop 243:122–125, 1989.
44. Howell, S.M.; Imobersteg, A.M.; Seger, D.H.; Marone, P.J. Clarification of the role of the supraspinatus muscle in shoulder function. J Bone Joint Surg Am 68:398–404, 1986.
45. Iannotti, J.P.; Gabriel, J.P.; Schneck, S.L.; et al. The normal glenohumeral relationships: An anatomical study of one hundred and forty shoulders. J Bone Joint Surg Am 74:491–500, 1992.
46. Iannotti, J.P.; Zlatkin, M.B.; Esterhai, J.L.; et al. Magnetic resonance imaging of the shoulder: Sensitivity, specificity, and predictive value. J Bone Joint Surg Am 73:17–29, 1991.
47. Inman, V.; Saunders, M.; Abbot, C. Observations on the function of the shoulder joint. J Bone Joint Surg Am 26:1–30, 1944.
48. Kornguth, P.J.; Salazar, A.M. The apical oblique view of the shoulder: Its usefulness in acute trauma. AJR Am J Roentgenol 149:113–116, 1987.
49. Lahde, S.; Putkonen, M. Positioning of the painful patient for the axial view of the glenohumeral joint. Rontgenblatter 38:380–382, 1985.
50. Laing, P.G. The arterial supply to the adult humerus. J Bone Joint Surg Am 38:1105–1116, 1956.
51. Lim, E.V.A.; Day, L.J. Thrombosis of the axillary artery complicating proximal humeral fractures. J Bone Joint Surg Am 69:778–780, 1987.
52. Lindbolm, K. Arthrography and roentgenography in ruptures of tendons of the shoulder joint. Acta Radiol 20:548–561, 1939.
53. Linson, M.A. Axillary artery thrombosis after fracture of the humerus: A case report. J Bone Joint Surg Am 62:1214–1215, 1980.
54. Lippett, S.B.; Vanderhooft, E.; Harris, S.L.; et al. Glenohumeral stability from concavity compression: A quantitative analysis. J Shoulder Elbow Surg 2:27–35, 1993.
55. Mack, L.A.; Gannon, M.K.; Kilcoyne, R.F.; et al. Sonographic evaluation of the rotator cuff: Accuracy in patients without prior surgery. Clin Orthop 234:21–27, 1988.
56. Mason, B.J.; Kier, R.; Bindleglass, D.F. Occult fractures of the greater tuberosity of the humerus: Radiographic and MR imaging findings. AJR Am J Roentgenol 172:469–473, 1999.
57. McLaughlin, H.L.; Cavallaro, W.V. Primary anterior dislocation of the shoulder. Am J Surg 80:615, 1950.
58. McQuillan, W.M.; Nolan, B. Ischemia complicating injury. J Bone Joint Surg Br 50:1090, 1970.
59. Mink, J.H.; Harris, E.; Rappaport, M. Rotator cuff tears: Evaluation using double-contrast shoulder arthrography. Radiology 157:621–623, 1985.
60. Morgan, C.D.; Rames, R.; Snyder, S.J. Arthroscopic assessment of anatomic variations of the glenohumeral ligaments associated with recurrent anterior shoulder instability. Orthop Trans 16:770–771, 1992–1993.
61. Morris, M.E.; Kilcoyne, R.F.; Shuman, W.; Matsen, F., III. Humeral tuberosity fractures: Evaluation by CT scan and management of malunion. Orthop Trans 11:242, 1987.
62. Moseley, H.F.; Overgaard, B. The anterior capsular mechanism in recurrent anterior dislocation of the shoulder: Morphological and clinical studies with special reference to the glenoid labrum and the glenohumeral ligaments. J Bone Joint Surg Br 44:913–927, 1962.
63. Moseley, J.B.; Jobe, F.W.; Pink, M.; et al. EMG analysis of the scapular muscles during a shoulder rehabilitation program. Am J Sports Med 20:128–134, 1002.
64. Müller, M.E.; Allgöwer, M.; Schneider, R.; Willenegger, H. Manual of Internal Fixation. Berlin, Springer-Verlag, 1991.
65. Neer, C.S., II. Anterior acromioplasty for the chronic impingement syndrome in the shoulder: A preliminary report. J Bone Joint Surg Am 54:41–50, 1972.
66. Neer, C.S., II. Displaced proximal humeral fractures: I. Classification and evaluation. J Bone Joint Surg Am 52:1077–1089, 1970.

67. Neer, C.S., II. Fractures about the shoulder. In: Rockwood, C.A.; Greene, D.P., eds. Fractures in Adults. Philadelphia, J.B. Lippincott, 1984.
68. Neer, C.S., II. Prosthetic replacement of the humeral head: Indications and operative techniques. Surg Clin North Am 43:1077–1089, 1970.
69. Neer, C.S., II; Watson, K.C.; Stanton, F.J. Recent experience in total shoulder replacement. J Bone Joint Surg Am 64:319–336, 1982.
70. Neviaser, R.J.; Neviaser, T.J.; Neviaser, J.S. Anterior dislocation of the shoulder and rotator cuff rupture. Clin Orthop 291:103–106, 1993.
71. Nordquist, A.; Petersson, C.J. Incidence and causes of shoulder girdle injuries in an urban population. J Shoulder Elbow Surg 4:107–112, 1995.
72. Norris, T.R. 3D (CEMAX) reformation in the evaluation of complex glenoid wear of fracture. Paper presented at the Sixth Annual Meeting of the American Shoulder and Elbow Surgeons, Orlando, Florida, November 1987.
73. Norris, T.R. Bone grafts for glenoid deficiency in total shoulder replacements. In: The Shoulder. Proceedings of the Third International Conference on Surgery of the Shoulder. Tokyo, Professional Postgraduate Services, 1987, pp. 373–376.
74. Norris, T.R. Diagnostic techniques for shoulder instability. Instr Course Lect 34:239–257, 1985.
75. Norris, T.R. Fractures and dislocation of the glenohumeral complex. In: Chapman, M.W.; Madison, M., eds. Operative Orthopaedics. Philadelphia, J.B. Lippincott, 1988, pp. 203–220.
76. Norris, T.R. History and physical examination of the shoulder. In: Nicholas, J.A.; Hershman, E.B., eds. The Upper Extremity in Sports Medicine. St. Louis, C.V. Mosby, 1990.
77. Norris, T.R.; Green, A. Imaging modalities in the evaluation of shoulder disorders. In: Matsen, F.A., III; Fu, F.H.; Hawkins, R.J., eds. The Shoulder: A Balance of Mobility and Stability. Rosemont, IL, American Academy of Orthopaedic Surgeons, 1993, pp. 353–368.
78. Pasila, M.; Jaroma, H.; Kiviluoto, O.; Sundholm, A. Early complications of primary shoulder dislocations. Acta Orthop Scand 49:260–263, 1978.
79. Patten, R.M.; Mack, L.A.; Wang, K.Y.; Lingel, J. Nondisplaced fractures of the greater tuberosity of the humerus: Sonographic detection. Radiology 1982:201–204, 1992.
80. Peterson, D.O. Shoulder block anesthesia for shoulder reconstruction surgery. Anesth Analg 64:373–375, 1985.
81. Podromos, C.C.; Ferry, J.A.; Schiller, A.J.; Zarins, B. Histological studies of the glenoid labrum from fetal life to old age. J Bone Joint Surg Am 72:1344–1348, 1990.
82. Poppen, N.K.; Walker, P.S. Forces at the glenohumeral joint in abduction. Clin Orthop 135:165–170, 1978.
83. Poppen, N.K.; Walker, P.S. Normal and abnormal motion of the shoulder. J Bone Joint Surg Am 58:195–201, 1976.
84. Reckling, F.W. Posterior fracture-dislocation of the shoulder treated by a Neer hemiarthroplasty with posterior surgical approach. Clin Orthop 207:133–137, 1986.
85. Reeves, B. Experiments on the tensile strength of the anterior capsular structures of the shoulder in man. J Bone Joint Surg Br 50:858–865, 1968.
86. Reinus, W.R.; Hatem, S.F. Fractures of the greater tuberosity presenting as rotator cuff abnormality: Magnetic resonance demonstration. J Trauma 44:670–675, 1994.
87. Richards, R.; An, K.N.; Bigliani, L.U.; et al. A standardized method for assessment of shoulder function. J Shoulder Elbow Surg 3:347–352, 1994.
88. Rokous, J.R.; Feagin, J.A.; Abbott, H.G. Modified axillary roentgenogram: A useful adjunct in the diagnosis of recurrent instability of the shoulder. Clin Orthop 82:84–86, 1972.
89. Rose, S.H.; Melton, L.J., III; Morrey, B.F.; et al. Epidemiologic features of humeral fractures. Clin Orthop 168:24–30, 1982.
90. Rowe, C.R.; Patel, D.; Southmayd, W.W. The Bankart procedure: A long-term end result study. J Bone Joint Surg Am 60:1–16, 1978.
91. Schwartz, R.E.; O'Brien, S.J.; Warren, R.F.; Torzilli, P.A. Capsular restraints to anterior-posterior motion of the shoulder. Orthop Trans 12:727, 1988.
92. Seddon, H.J. Nerve lesions complicating certain closed bone injuries. JAMA 135:11–15, 1947.
93. Seltzer, S.E.; Weissman, B.N. CT findings in normal and dislocating shoulders. J Can Assoc Radiol 36:41–46, 1985.
94. Shaffer, B.S.; Conway, J.; Jobe, F.W.; et al. Infraspinatus muscle-splitting incision in posterior shoulder surgery: An anatomic and electromyographic study. Am J Sports Med 22:113–120, 1994.
95. Soslowsky, L.J.; Bigliani, L.U.; Flatow, E.L.; et al. Articular geometry of the glenohumeral joint. Clin Orthop 285:181–190, 1992.
96. Sunderland, S. Nerves and Nerve Injuries, 2nd ed. New York, Churchill Livingstone, 1978.
97. Szalay, E.A.; Rockwood, C.A., Jr. Injuries of the shoulder and arm. Emerg Med Clin North Am 2:279–294, 1984.
98. Teefey, S.A.; Hasan, S.A.; Middleton, W.D.; et al. Ultrasonography of the rotator cuff. A comparison of ultrasonographic and arthroscopic findings in one hundred consecutive cases. J Bone Joint Surg Am 82:498–504, 2000.
99. Turkel, S.J.; Panio, M.W.; Marshall, J.L.; Girgis, F.G. Stabilizing mechanisms preventing anterior dislocation of the glenohumeral joint. J Bone Joint Surg Am 63:1208–1217, 1981.
100. Wallace, W.A.; Hellier, M. Improving radiographs of the injured shoulder. Radiography 49:229–233, 1983.
101. Ware, J.E. SF-36 Health Survey: Manual and Interpretation Guide. Boston, The Health Institute, New England Medical Center, 1993.
102. Warner, J.P.; Krushell, R.J.; Masquelet, A.; Gerber, C. Anatomy and relationships of the suprascapular nerve: Anatomical constraints to mobilization of the supraspinatus and infraspinatus muscles in the management of massive rotator cuff tears. J Bone Joint Surg Am 74:36–45, 1992.
103. Winnie, A.P. Interscalene brachial plexus block. Anesth Analg 49:455–466, 1970.
104. Wirth, M.A.; Butters, K.P.; Rockwood, C.A., Jr. The posterior deltoid-splitting approach to the shoulder. Clin Orthop 296:92–98, 1993.
105. Yosipovitch, Z.; Tikkva, P.; Goldberg, I. Inferior subluxation of the humeral head after injury to the shoulder. J Bone Joint Surg Am 71:751–753, 1989.

PART **II**    *Proximal Humeral Fractures and*
*Fracture-Dislocations*

Andrew Green, M.D.    •    Tom R. Norris, M.D.

Even with the most expert treatment, proximal humeral fractures and fracture-dislocations can result in pain, weakness, stiffness, and loss of function. Thus, it is important to avoid complications of treatment. In the acute setting, temporary loss of function of one upper extremity is a tremendous handicap. Some elderly patients will require home care assistance or even temporary nursing home care. In some polytrauma patients with axial skeletal or lower extremity injury, a shoulder girdle injury can be the determining factor in the patient's ability to perform independent transfers or ambulate. In adolescents and young adults, it interferes with all activities but is most noticeable in sports. In the active middle-aged group, these fractures may interfere with work, recreation, sports, and basic activities of daily living.

The associated injuries and long-term sequelae of fracture healing and joint injury can have a significant impact on outcome. Loss of humeral length with secondary deltoid weakening, traumatic arthritis, acute or chronic dislocations, rotator cuff tears with tuberosity displacement, nerve injuries, and vascular injuries add to the fracture complications. A number of reconstructive options can be used to treat nonunion, malunion, and post-traumatic glenohumeral arthritis. However, the results of late treatment are inferior to those of successful primary treatment.[12, 61, 188]

## EPIDEMIOLOGY

Proximal humeral fractures account for 4% to 5% of all fractures.[230] Although they may occur in any age group, with the earliest noted at the time of birth, an increased frequency occurs in older middle-aged and elderly individuals[96, 206] because of the age-related increase in osteoporosis.[80, 127]

Rose and colleagues studied 586 fractures of the humerus that occurred in 564 of the 53,000 residents of Rochester, Minnesota, during a 10-year period.[206] Overall, fractures of the proximal end of the humerus accounted for 45% of the initial fractures and 69% of the recurrent fractures. In adults, the incidence of proximal humeral fracture was lowest in the third decade of life and increased in both sexes until the age of 50 years. Thereafter, the incidence continued to increase, but the female-to-male ratio was 4:1. The greatest number of fractures in adult men appeared during the active ages between 30 and 60 years, whereas in women a dramatic increase was noted after menopause.

In a study of 565 proximal humeral fractures in 500,000 people, Kristiansen and co-workers found that 77% of the fractures in all age groups occurred in women.[127] Again, this high frequency of fractures in women was thought to be a result of advanced osteoporosis. Jensen and associates[108] demonstrated that the frequency of osteoporotic fractures varied inversely with bone mineral content. Proximal humeral fractures more reliably correlate with bone fragility than do fractures of the spine, upper part of the femur, pelvis, or distal end of the radius.[96, 108]

Consequently, with advancing age, less trauma is required to produce a fracture of the proximal end of the humerus. In patients younger than 50 years, the most common causes of proximal humeral fractures involve violent trauma such as falls from heights, motor vehicle accidents, and athletic injuries. In patients older than 50, a fracture can result from minimal to moderate trauma, such as a fall from the standing position or even direct impact.[108] Seventy-six percent of fractures involving the surgical neck of the humerus, the most common site of fracture, occur in individuals older than 65.[244]

Epidemiologic studies demonstrate that the incidence of proximal humeral fractures is increasing as a result of increased life expectancy.[3] Kannus and associates studied all proximal humeral fractures in patients admitted to Finnish hospitals between 1970 and 1993.[112] They found a steady increase in the age-specific incidence of proximal humeral fractures in males and females at all ages. Based on population trends, they predicted that the number of proximal humeral fractures would increase exponentially for the next 20 to 30 years.

## MECHANISMS OF INJURY

When the history of the shoulder injury can be recalled, it often reveals one or a combination of mechanisms occurring to produce a fracture of the proximal end of the humerus. A direct blow to the anterior, lateral, or posterolateral aspect of the humerus can result in fracture. In younger patients, such a blow might occur in a motor vehicle or skiing accident, whereas in older individuals, it may occur simply from a fall from standing height or less.

An axial load transmitted to the humerus through the flexed elbow or through the extended hand and forearm when the elbow is locked in extension can also result in fracture. The displacement of the distal fragment depends on the position of the hand and elbow at the time that the axial load is applied. Indirect forces are brought into play in a fall on an outstretched abducted arm. The greater tuberosity is unable to clear the acromion, and the humeral neck levers against the acromion to produce fracture,

fracture-dislocation, or dislocation, depending on the relative strength of the bone and surrounding ligaments.[177] Combinations of rotational forces and forward, backward, or lateral positioning of the arm have been deduced by the history given or by the resultant position of the fracture fragments in an effort to understand what forces could be applied to achieve closed reduction.[229, 249]

The violent muscle contraction that occurs in grand mal seizures and electrical shock can cause fractures and fracture-dislocations of the shoulder. The large internal rotators and adductors of the arm easily overpower the external rotators and thereby result in a locked posterior fracture-dislocation.[14] Fractures caused by seizure or electrical shock occur at an incidence of 1% to 3%.[117, 122, 213] Kelly reported that shoulder fractures occurred 4 times for each 10,000 convulsions induced, or 6.8 fractures per 1000 patients treated.[117]

Convulsive seizures are the most common cause of bilateral posterior fracture-dislocations of the shoulder. They may occur either as locked head impression fractures or as comminuted fracture-dislocations.[47, 142, 145]

Pathologic fractures result from local tumor, such as multiple myeloma or metastatic tumor, or from metabolic disorders.[160] The mechanism of fractures in these patients is closely related to the destruction of cortical bone. Identification of pathologic lesions plus prophylactic treatment of impending fractures is the most efficacious approach to management.

It is important to recognize the amount of trauma involved in proximal humeral fractures. Motor vehicle accidents, falls from heights, falls at high speed (e.g., as in skiing), and high-velocity gunshot wounds usually produce more severe injuries with more extensive associated injury and thus have important implications for treatment and outcome.

## ASSOCIATED INJURIES

### Rotator Cuff Tear

In general, acute rotator cuff tears do not occur in association with proximal humeral fractures. In older individuals, preexisting rotator cuff tears are more common. Nevertheless, acute rotator cuff tears can occur and have a significant impact on outcome. Marked greater tuberosity displacement suggests the presence of a rotator cuff tear. A longitudinal tear at the rotator interval between the supraspinatus and the subscapularis is the most common injury and can occur with displacement of either tuberosity.

### Ipsilateral Upper Extremity Fractures

Ipsilateral upper extremity fractures are uncommon. They most often occur in the setting of multiple trauma or severe multifocal upper extremity injury. In severe trauma, multiple fractures of the ipsilateral extremity may occur in addition to the proximal humeral fracture. They can be missed in the polytrauma setting because of the overwhelming significance of other injuries. Pierce and Hodurski[200] reported that in 21 patients who sustained ipsilateral radial and ulnar fractures, more than 50% experienced residual nerve injury, including injury to the brachial plexus and radial and ulnar nerves. These fractures of the proximal third of the humerus were associated with poor results. Shaft and more distal humeral fractures may have an unsuspected associated proximal humeral fracture or fracture-dislocation[114] (Fig. 44–22).

Ipsilateral humeral shaft fractures present a challenging problem. In elderly patients with inferior bone quality, achieving skeletal stability with operative treatment is a challenge. Closed intramedullary rodding is an option if the proximal end of the humerus is not comminuted. In some cases, closed treatment is the best option and can be very successful (Fig. 44–23). In younger patients with good bone quality, other operative techniques are also appropriate.

Associated wrist and elbow fractures occur in elderly patients who fall onto an outstretched hand. Rehabilitation of the shoulder is difficult in this situation because of pain and injury in the distal end of the upper extremity.

### Nerve Injuries

The infraclavicular brachial plexus and peripheral nerve branches lie anteromedial to the glenohumeral joint and are subject to injury with anterior glenohumeral dislocations, fracture-dislocations, and fractures involving the surgical neck of the humerus. Injury may occur either from direct contact with the fracture fragments or from stretching.[31] Nerve injuries are more common with fracture-dislocations. Greater tuberosity fracture-dislocations are most frequently accompanied by an isolated axillary nerve injury.[221]

When diagnosed by electromyography (EMG), the prevalence of axillary and other nerve lesions in glenohumeral dislocations and humeral neck fractures is 20% to 30%. In patients older than 50 years, it is as high as 50%.[8, 51, 197] Stableforth[227] reported brachial plexus injuries in 6.1% of patients with four-part proximal humeral fractures, only one third of whom made a complete recovery.

Traumatic brachial plexus injuries can be classified as either infraclavicular or supraclavicular.[1, 31, 172, 232] In a review of 420 operative procedures for brachial plexus palsy, 25% of the injuries were infraclavicular and 75% were supraclavicular. Fifteen percent of the 420 operative cases were at double levels.[1] Ninety percent of the injuries occurred in patients aged 15 to 30 years and were the result of automobile or motorcycle accidents. Anterior or inferior shoulder dislocations cause most isolated axillary nerve and posterior cord lesions. In Alnot's series,[1] 80% of the isolated axillary nerve lesions were neurapraxias that recovered in 4 to 6 months. However, in Seddon's series,[220] only 44% of patients had complete recovery, 12% had incomplete recovery, and 44% had no recovery. Violent downward and backward movement of the shoulder causes brachial plexus stretch injuries, and multiple trauma involving fractures of the clavicle, scapula, or upper part of the humerus causes diffuse lesions of

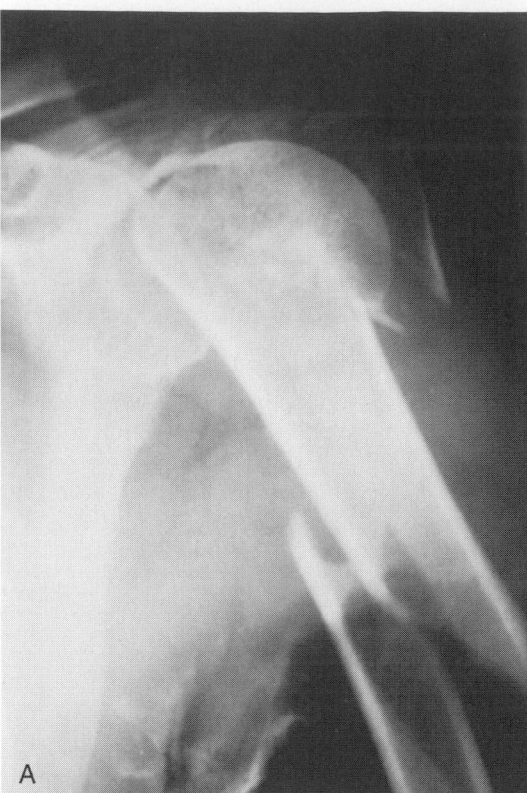

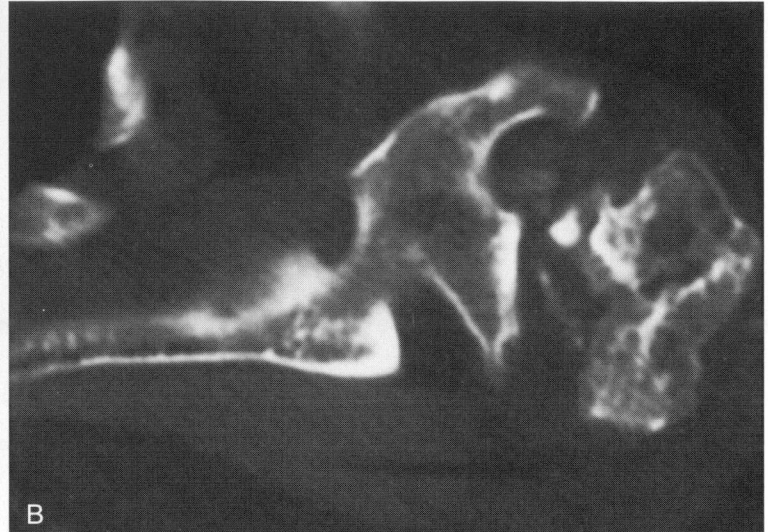

**FIGURE 44–22.** *A,* Three-part greater tuberosity proximal humeral fracture combined with a midshaft diaphyseal fracture. *B,* Treatment of the diaphyseal fracture alone resulted in severe glenohumeral arthritis that later required prosthetic arthroplasty.

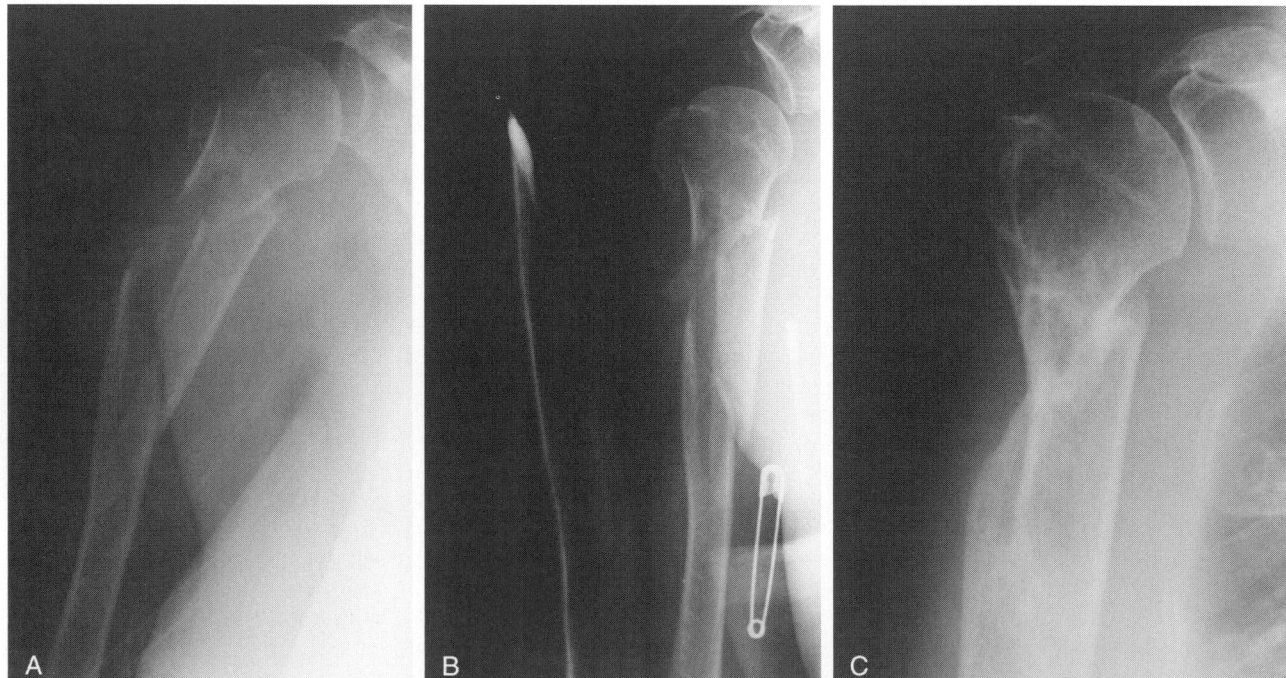

**FIGURE 44–23.** *A,* Comminuted proximal humeral fracture involving the greater tuberosity and surgical neck and extending distal to the deltoid tuberosity of the dominant arm of an active 86-year-old woman. *B,* Treatment with a coaptation splint and collar and cuff immobilization. Passive motion was begun once early healing had been achieved. *C,* One year after injury, the fracture is in anatomic alignment and has completely healed with nearly full active shoulder motion and recovery of all shoulder function.

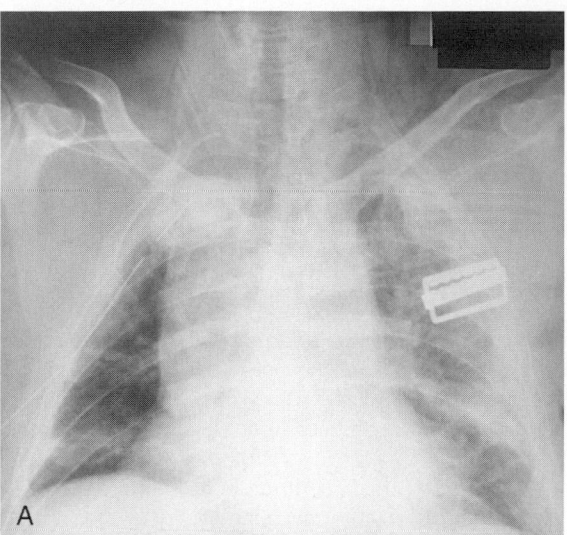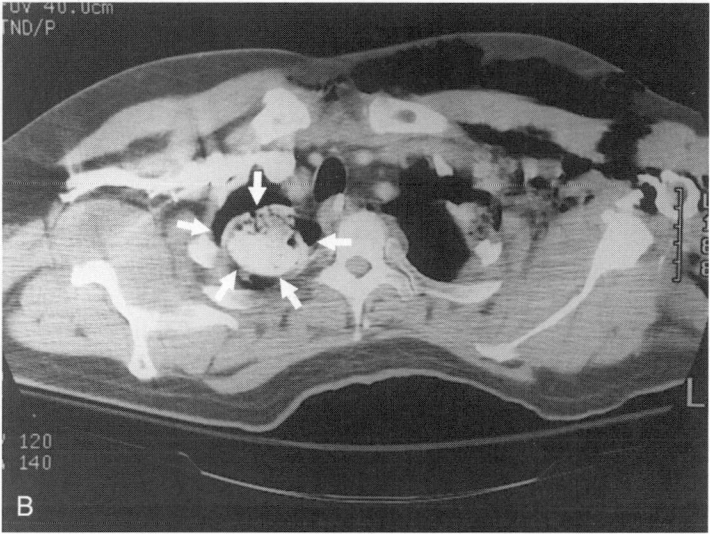

**FIGURE 44–24.** *A,* A 64-year-old man had a contralateral intrathoracic fracture-dislocation of the proximal end of the humerus. The humeral head passed through the mediastinum into the pleural cavity. An associated brachial plexus injury was present, as well as avulsion of the latissimus dorsi and pectoralis major tendons from the humerus. The humeral head is seen in the left upper lung field. *B,* A CT scan shows the humeral head *(arrows).* The humeral head was excised with thoracoscopy. (From Eberson, C.P.; Ng, T.; Green, A. J Bone Joint Surg Am 82:105–108, 2000.)

the trunks and terminal branches, as well as vascular damage. The axillary nerve in the quadrilateral space, the suprascapular nerve at the suprascapular notch adjacent to the coracoid, and the musculocutaneous nerve are injured most frequently.

Nerve injuries can be easily missed because pain and immobilization can make examination difficult in the early post-traumatic period. Sensory loss does not always accompany an axillary nerve lesion.[5, 8] Unfortunately, recovery of associated nerve injuries is often incomplete. Although persistent deltoid palsy from an axillary nerve lesion is rare, a long delay before reinnervation obviates complete recovery. Muscle transfers for deltoid paralysis as a late salvage procedure have had poor results. For this reason, Narakas[171] and others[19, 31, 220] advocate exploration of infraclavicular nerve lesions early after very severe trauma.

## Vascular Injuries

Vascular injuries are rarely associated with proximal humeral fractures. However, the consequences of a missed injury can be so devastating that early evaluation of the vascular status of the upper extremity is a priority. Arteriosclerosis predisposes the elderly population to arterial injury. Proximal humeral fractures have resulted in occlusion, rupture, thrombus formation, and pseudoaneurysms of the axillary artery.[91, 137, 146, 159, 226, 236, 257] Axillary artery injury has been reported in approximately 5% of four-part proximal humeral fractures.[227] Swelling and the collateral circulation may mask the extent of the vascular injury. The peripheral pulses, including the radial artery, should be palpated. However, even in the presence of an axillary artery injury, the radial pulse may be palpable because of the extensive collateral circulation around the shoulder. Other signs of vascular injury include paresthesias, pallor or cyanosis, and an expanding hematoma.

Paresthesias may be secondary to poor distal circulation and suggest a vascular injury. The key to avoiding complications is early diagnosis and treatment.[89, 257]

If a vascular injury is suspected, Doppler ultrasonography and arteriography should be performed (see Fig. 44–7). If vascular repair or reconstruction is indicated, the fracture is stabilized with internal or external fixation before definitive vascular repair. A temporary vascular shunt can be placed to restore peripheral perfusion while the fracture is stabilized. If the ischemia time is prolonged, prophylactic fasciotomies of the arm and forearm should be considered. Serial Doppler examinations postoperatively are then necessary to detect occlusion[257]; otherwise, thrombosis, ischemia, and compartment syndrome may result (see Fig. 44–6C).

## Other Injuries

Chest wall damage[227] has been reported in 2.5% of four-part fracture and fracture-dislocation injuries. Intrathoracic dislocations of the humeral head combined with surgical neck fractures of the humerus, pneumothorax, and pneumohemothorax have been reported with proximal humeral fractures.[83, 198] Displacement as remote as the retroperitoneum and contralateral thoracic cavity has also been reported (Fig. 44–24).[52, 251] In these circumstances, appropriate evaluation to identify associated injuries is required.

## FRACTURE CLASSIFICATION

During the past century, a variety of classification schemes have been used to describe proximal humeral fractures. Most have been inadequate and usually fail to differentiate fracture severity in a meaningful manner. Consequently, it has been difficult to compare the results of most of the early literature on proximal humeral fractures and fracture-dislocations. Despite voluminous experience with these fractures, treatment of these injuries is controversial.

Classification by the anatomic level of fracture[9, 120] did not consider the importance of fracture anatomy or differentiate between more serious displaced lesions and nondisplaced fractures. Classification according to the mechanism of injury, proposed by Dehne,[43] has undergone many modifications.[45, 62, 93, 242] Neer points out that adduction and abduction fractures of the proximal part of the humerus can both be diagnosed in the same injury, depending on the position of the arm at the time that the radiograph is obtained.[174] Thus, the usefulness of this classification is limited.[175] The details of fracture anatomy are not assessed, and clinical management cannot be dictated by the classification because outcome cannot be specifically correlated with the mechanism of injury.[119]

Codman[30] noted that most proximal humeral fractures occur along the lines of the former physes of the proximal end of the humerus. Codman[30] and deAnquin and deAnquin[42] emphasized vascular considerations and their importance to fractures involving the articular segment of the proximal end of the humerus. Neer,[174] realizing this importance, made Codman's four-segment classification clinically useful by emphasizing the degree of displacement or angulation of an anatomic segment. Neer correlated this classification scheme with outcome in a retrospective study of a large series of proximal humeral fractures. This classification attempts to predict the effect of displacement on rotator cuff function, glenohumeral biomechanics, and vascularity of the articular segment (Fig. 44–25).

Neer's classification system is based on the position of the articular segment, the greater and lesser tuberosities, and the humeral shaft. Displacement is determined by the pull of the muscles and tendons that are attached to the various segments.

The first segment is the articular surface. A fracture may displace it through the anatomic neck level or split the head segment, or both. Displacement of the articular segment is determined by the severity of the injury rather than by any soft tissue attachments.

The second segment is the greater tuberosity with its muscle and tendon units, which consist of the supraspinatus, infraspinatus, and teres minor. These muscles serve to abduct and externally rotate the head in a surgical neck fracture or three-part lesser tuberosity fracture. In a two- or three-part greater tuberosity fracture, the tendons attached to the greater tuberosity pull it medially and posteriorly. This segment is often comminuted, and there may be differences in size, location, and the number of rotator cuff tendons involved with the fracture fragments.

The third segment consists of the lesser tuberosity with the attached subscapularis tendon. This tendon opposes or balances the forces of muscles attached to the greater tuberosity and rotates the head internally. The fourth segment is the shaft at the subtuberous or surgical neck level.

When this classification was originally presented in 1970, it stressed that with accurate imaging studies, fractures of the proximal end of the humerus could be classified as displaced or nondisplaced. According to Neer, a fracture is considered displaced if any major segment is displaced 1 cm or more or angulated greater than 45°.[174] He defined six different variations of displaced proximal humeral fractures.

## One-Part Fractures

Empirically, comminuted fractures without displacement of 1 cm are less likely to have disrupted soft tissue or injury to the blood supply to the articular segment. These injuries are referred to as *one-part fractures* or *minimally displaced fractures* in which the periosteum, joint capsule, and rotator cuff attachments hold the fracture fragments together.[30] Stable nondisplaced fractures are treated nonoperatively (i.e., with early functional exercises to avoid stiffness), whereas displaced fractures are considered for closed reduction, open reduction, or prosthetic replacement.

## Two-Part Fractures

*Two-part fractures* involve displacement of one segment. Two-part greater tuberosity fractures and surgical neck fractures are the most common. Two-part lesser tuberosity and isolated anatomic neck fractures are very rare. A two-part fracture involving a tuberosity often occurs in association with glenohumeral dislocation. An innocent-appearing isolated greater tuberosity avulsion may accompany an anterior shoulder dislocation in which the dislocation has spontaneously reduced before the radiograph was taken. If the tuberosity is in anatomic position, the fracture would be classified as a one-part fracture in this classification.

When isolated two-part lesser tuberosity fractures occur, posterior dislocation should be taken for granted until accurate imaging studies can disprove it. An axillary radiograph or computed tomography (CT) scan establishes the diagnosis.

Studies of malunion of the greater tuberosity and malposition of the tuberosity from a varus surgical neck malunion indicate a need to evaluate these lesions more carefully.[105, 186, 191] The limit of 1-cm displacement or 45° angulation is too generous for classifying the lesion as nondisplaced, especially when the tuberosity is superior to the articular surface. With elevation of the arm, the displaced or malpositioned greater tuberosity can impinge in the subacromial space. McLaughlin considered 0.5-cm superior displacement of the greater tuberosity a significant lesion worthy of open reduction.[156] More recently, Park and colleagues suggested that fractures with 3 mm of displacement should be reduced in athletes and heavy laborers involved in overhead activity.[196]

## Three-Part Fractures

*Three-part fractures* involve displacement of three segments: usually the head, the shaft at the surgical neck, and one tuberosity. The muscle pull through the intact

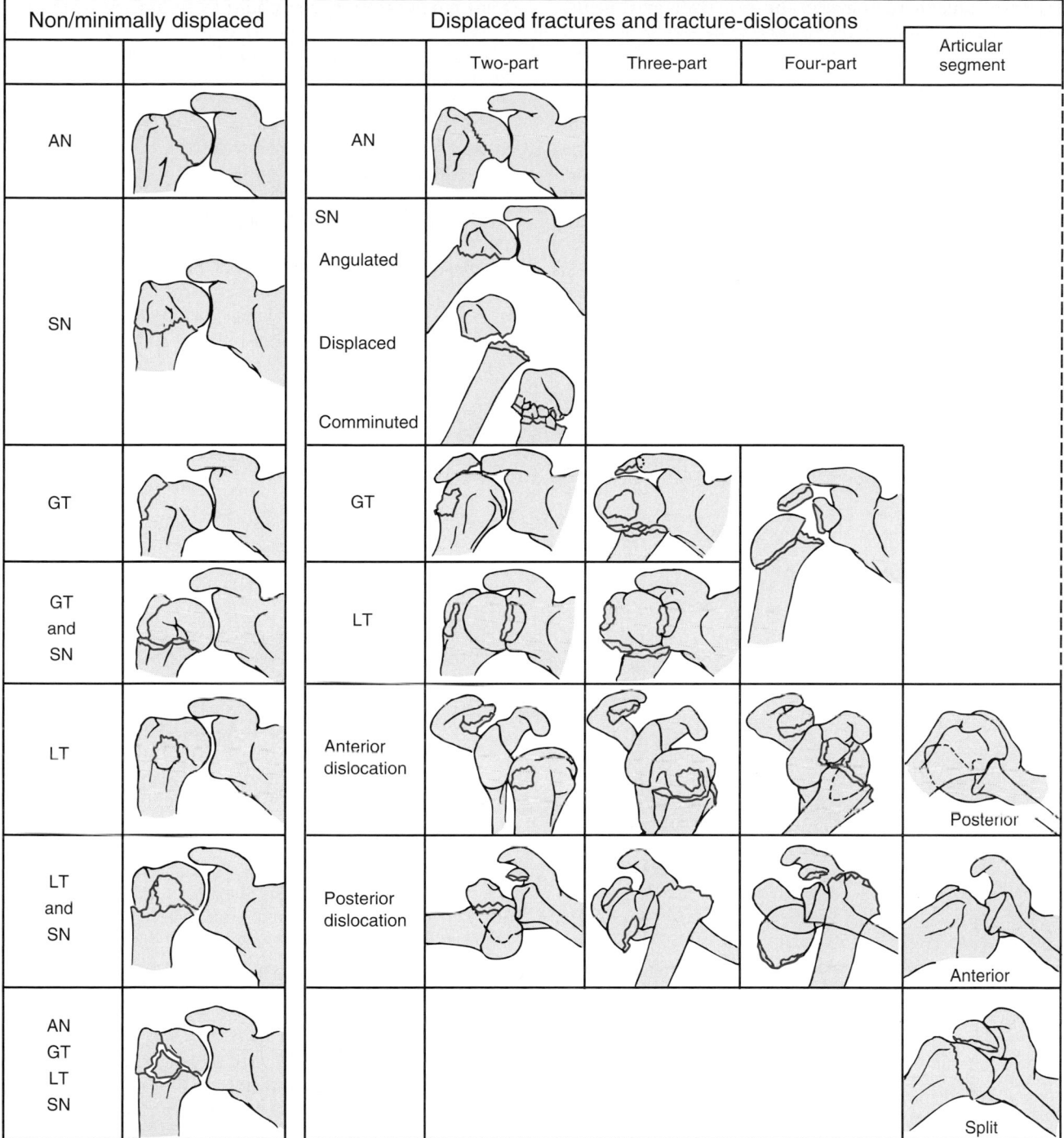

**Figure 44–25.** Four-part classification for fractures and fracture-dislocations. *Abbreviations:* AN, anatomic neck; GT, greater tuberosity; LT, lesser tuberosity; SN, surgical neck.

tuberosity is unopposed, and the articular surface rotates to face the avulsed tuberosity. For example, in a three-part greater tuberosity fracture, the subscapularis muscle attached to the intact lesser tuberosity will rotate the head posteriorly. These fractures can be best visualized in the axillary or lateral scapular views, in which the articular surface faces posteriorly and the shaft is disengaged (Fig. 44–26). In a three-part lesser tuberosity fracture, the infraspinatus and teres minor muscles attached to the

intact greater tuberosity rotate the articular surface to face anteriorly[2, 29, 85, 174, 175, 201] (Fig. 44–27).

## Four-Part Fractures

In *four-part fractures,* all the segments are displaced. The articular segment may be impacted on the upper part of the shaft, displaced laterally into the subdeltoid space, or dislocated anteriorly or posteriorly. The external rotators and supraspinatus pull the greater tuberosity posteriorly and superiorly. The lesser tuberosity is retracted anteromedially. The pectoralis major pulls the humeral shaft medially and anteriorly, whereas the deltoid inserting below the surgical neck tends to pull the shaft into an adducted position (Fig. 44–28). Several recent reports have distinguished valgus-impacted four-part fractures from typical four-part fractures[106] (Fig. 44–29). The valgus position of the articular segment suggests that the inferior medial capsular attachments and some of the vascular supply to the articular segment may be intact.[17]

With the exception of the articular segment, classification is based on the fate of the major segments rather than on the number of fracture lines or the mechanism of injury. Articular impression fractures and head-splitting fractures are considered separately.

## Fracture-Dislocation

In *fracture-dislocations,* the articular segment with or without attached tuberosities is dislocated from the glenoid. Two-, three-, or four-part fractures may accompany an anterior, posterior, or lateral dislocation of the articular surface. Anteroinferior displacement of the articular segment is the most common. In this position, the humeral head lies within or against the brachial plexus and axillary artery, an anatomic arrangement that significantly increases the likelihood of neurovascular injury.[31, 156]

Posterior articular impression fractures, referred to as *Hill-Sachs lesions,* occur with anterior glenohumeral dislocations.[95] The posterior articular surface is crushed on the anterior glenoid rim. Similarly, impression fractures of the anterior articular surface, sometimes referred to as *reverse Hill-Sachs lesions,* result from the posterior glenoid rim

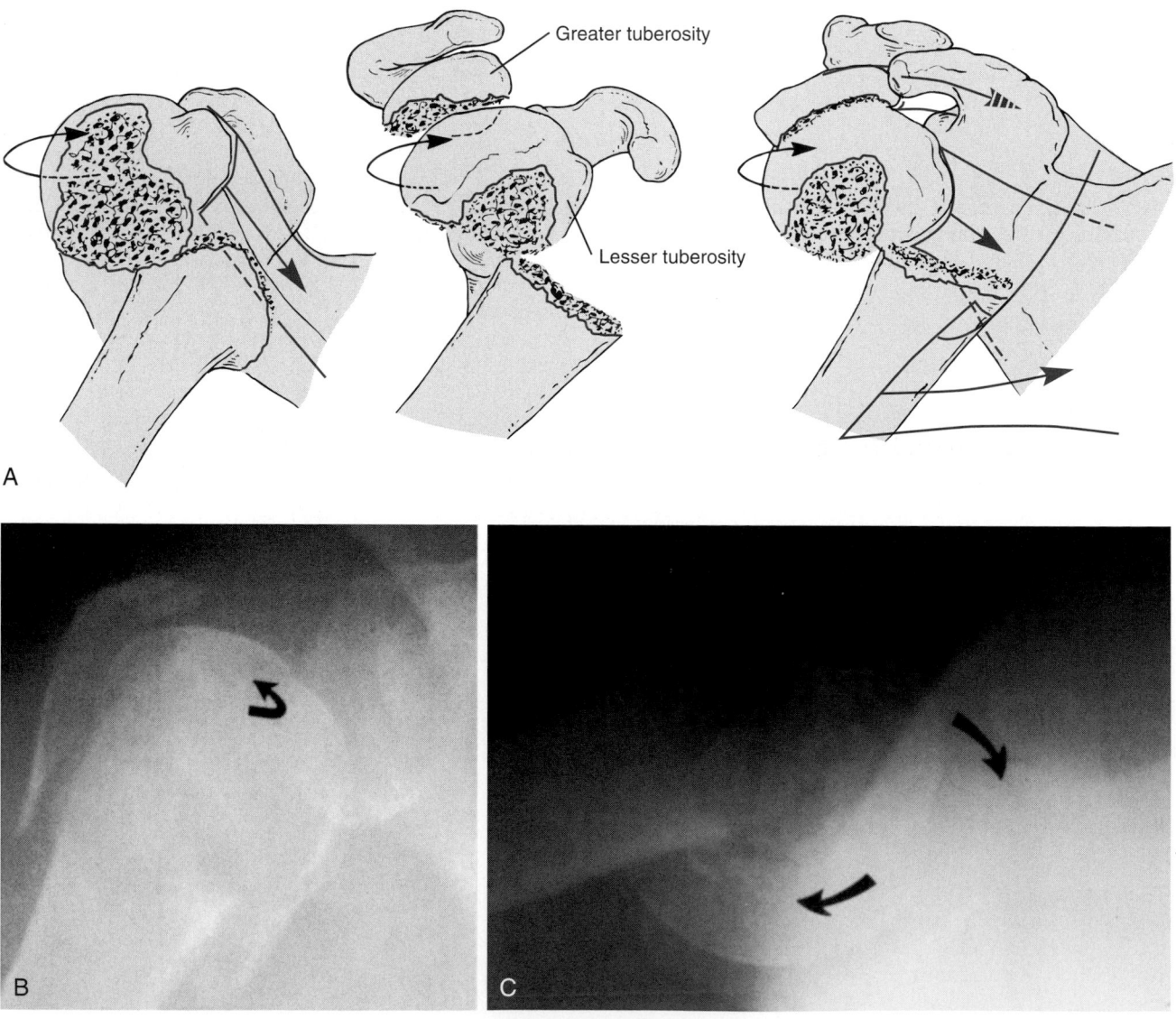

**FIGURE 44–26.** *A–C,* Three-part greater tuberosity fracture. The pectoralis displaces the unimpacted shaft anteriorly and medially. The greater tuberosity is retracted by the spinatus and teres minor muscles. The articular segment is rotated posteriorly by the intact subscapularis. A rotator interval tear is evident. *Arrows* indicate the direction of tuberosity displacement with muscle pull.

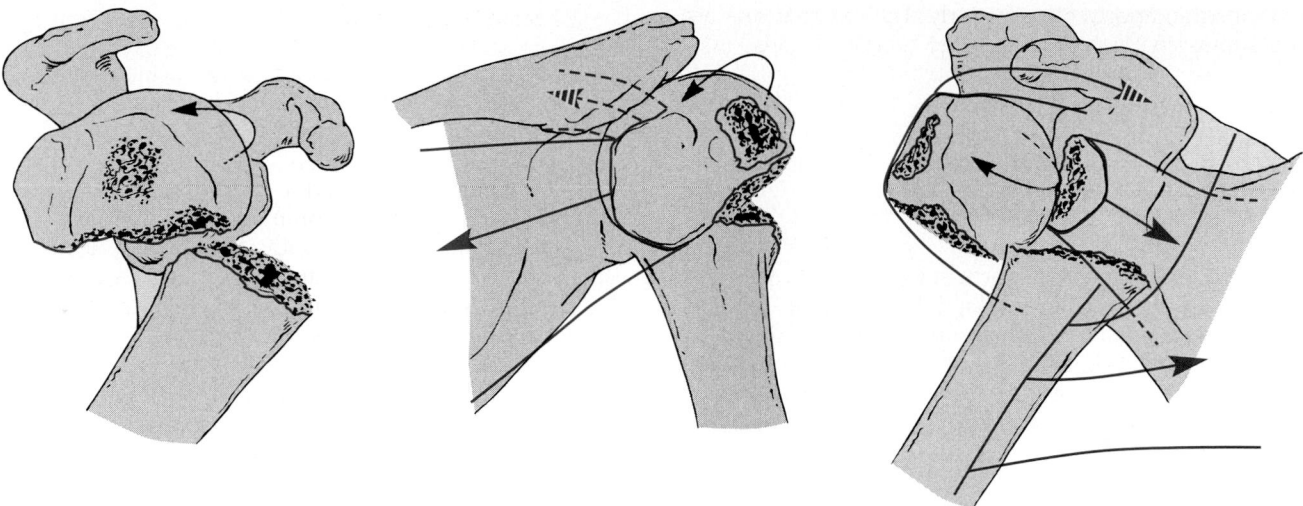

FIGURE 44–27. Three-part lesser tuberosity fracture. The intact spinatus and teres minor muscles attaching to the greater tuberosity rotate the articular segment anteriorly. The avulsed lesser tuberosity and displaced shaft no longer balance the head in neutral rotation. A rotator interval tear is present. *Arrows* indicate the direction of tuberosity displacement with muscle pull.

compressing the anterior articular surface in a posterior fracture-dislocation.

## Head-Splitting Fractures

Head-splitting fractures involve comminution of the articular surface. A double articular contour seen on plain radiographs is a subtle finding that indicates more serious articular injury (Fig. 44–30).

## Role of Classification

In Neer's original classification,[174] group I fractures were categorized as nondisplaced and group II through VI

fractures as displaced. Group II involved displacement of the anatomic neck, group III involved variations of a surgical neck fracture, group IV involved fractures of the greater tuberosity, group V involved those of the lesser tuberosity, and group VI involved fractures associated with dislocations. This classification combines two-, three-, and (potentially) four-part greater tuberosity fractures in group IV; similarly, in group V, the two-, three-, and (potentially) four-part lesser tuberosity fractures are combined. In group VI, all fracture-dislocations are combined, whether they are two, three, or four part and associated with anterior or posterior dislocations. Such grouping would not be a problem if each of the segment classifications were noted when comparing results, but unfortunately, many subsequent articles discussed results in terms of the overall groupings rather than by the number of parts.

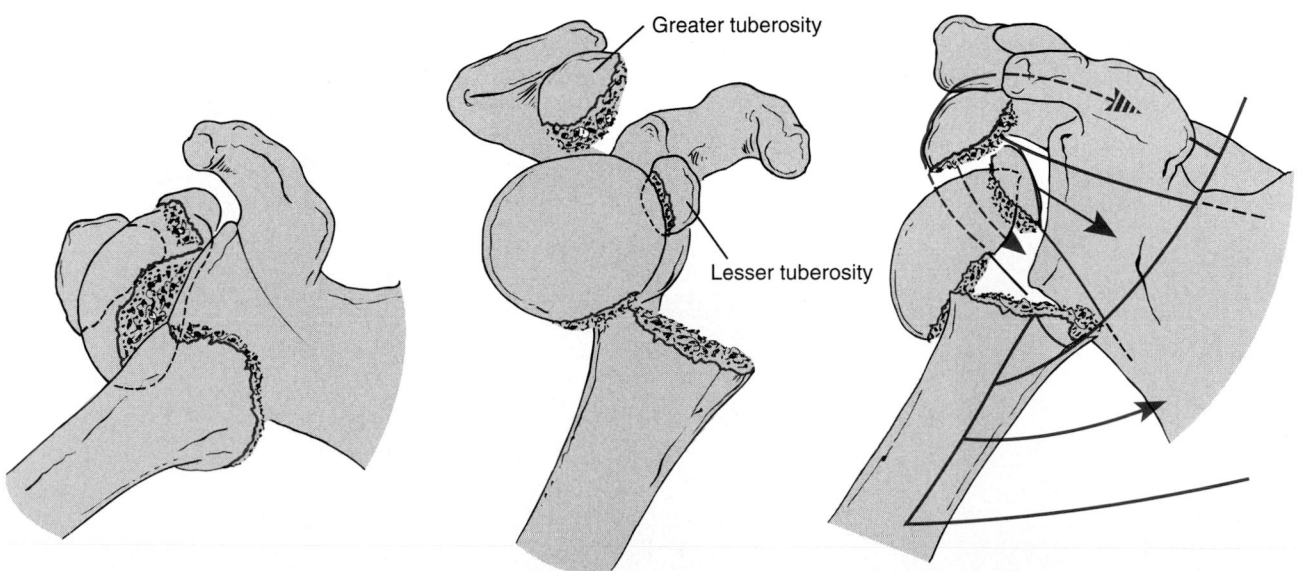

FIGURE 44–28. Four-part fracture. The shaft and tuberosities are displaced by their muscle attachments. The articular segment can be dislocated or subluxed in an anterior, posterior, inferior, or lateral direction, or it may be impacted on the upper part of the shaft. The vascular supply to the articular segment is disrupted. A rotator interval tear may have occurred. *Arrows* indicate the direction of tuberosity displacement with muscle pull.

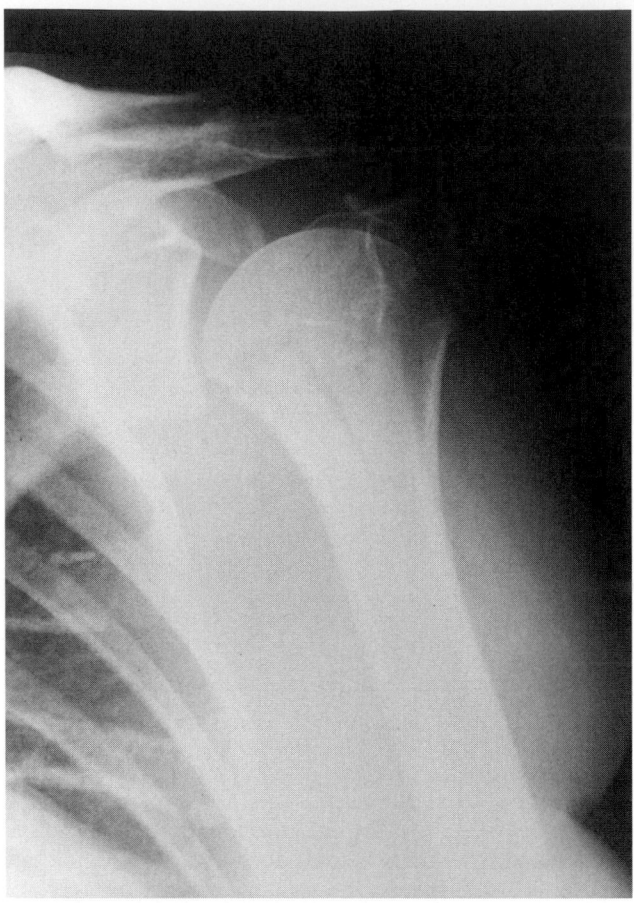

**Figure 44–29.** Valgus-impacted proximal humeral fracture.

In subsequent revisions of the classification, Neer dropped the concept of groups and emphasized the four-part concept.[177] Bigliani[6] has expanded the Neer classification to include humeral head-splitting and impression fractures (see Fig. 44–25).

Jakob and colleagues[105] criticized the Neer classification for not having adequate subgroupings for detailed analysis and documentation. They argued that the displacement classification had not been established clinically or experimentally. For example, they noted that a valgus-impacted four-part fracture might continue to have viability of the articular surface or acceptable function despite avascular necrosis (AVN). The Neer classification does not consider this specific injury in a separate category. In addition, classification of a displaced anatomic neck fracture, a two-part fracture, did not emphasize the seriousness of the anticipated and almost universally disastrous complication of AVN.

The Comprehensive Classification of Fractures, which is endorsed by the AO/Association for the Study of Internal Fixation (ASIF) and the Orthopaedic Trauma Association, attempts to arrange fractures in increasing order of severity[170] (Fig. 44–31). Three types of proximal humeral fractures are differentiated (types A, B, and C). Type A consists of unifocal extra-articular (two-segment) fractures; type B, bifocal extra-articular (three-segment) fractures; and type C, anatomic neck or articular segment fractures. Each type includes three fracture patterns, with nine subgroups for each type of fracture. The subgroup classification indicates the degree of displacement. Although this system allows detailed study of many fractures and their variables, when compared with the Neer classification, it has not solved the issues raised.[223] It can be more confusing and difficult to use than the Neer system.

Interpretation of shoulder radiographs is difficult. Although Neer[174] defined *significant displacement* as either 1 cm or 45°, a certain amount of judgment is involved in the evaluation of radiographs. The significant interobserver and intraobserver variation noted in the interpretation of radiographs of displaced proximal humeral fractures may affect the choice of treatment and eventual outcome.[16, 222, 223] Similar problems with the precision of radiographic interpretation have been noted with the

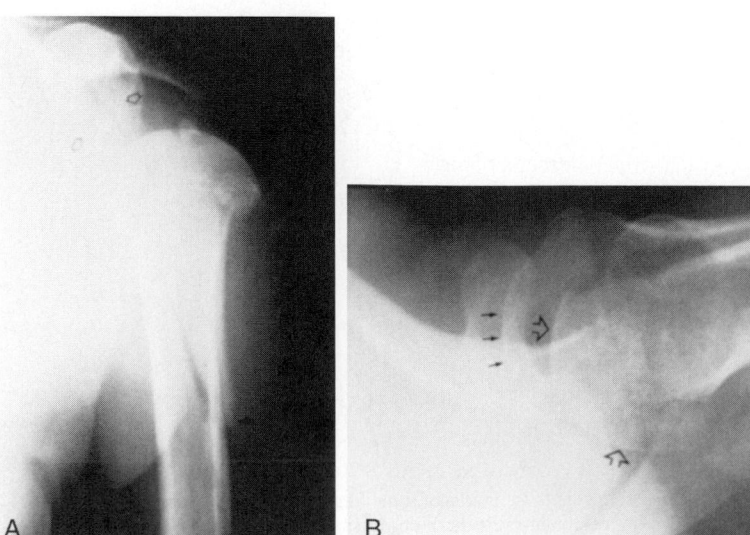

**Figure 44–30.** Head-splitting fracture. *A,* Anteroposterior radiograph. *B,* Axillary radiograph. The double articular contour indicates a displaced split of the humeral head.

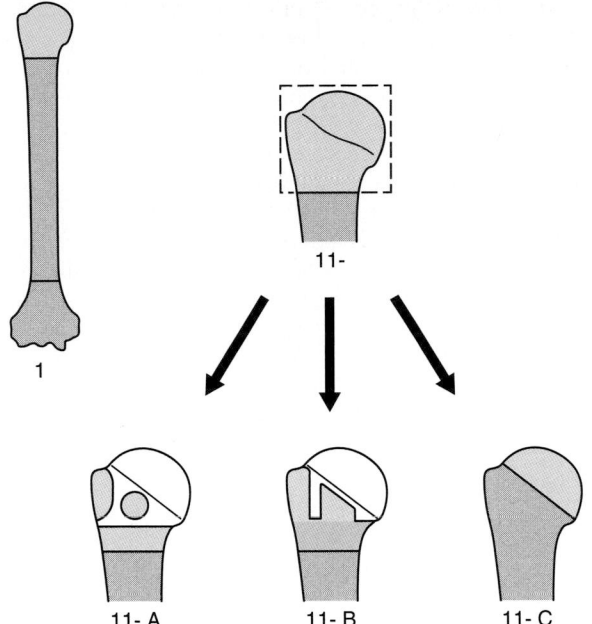

FIGURE 44–31. AO classification of proximal humeral fractures. The classification includes three types (A to C) with nine different fracture subgroups in each type. The A subgroup includes unifocal extra-articular fractures, the B subgroup consists of bifocal extra-articular fractures, and the C subgroup includes fractures of the anatomic neck or articular segment.

AO/ASIF classification. The decision of whether to perform surgery to achieve restoration of normal anatomy is invariably affected by this confusion.

The benefit of the addition of CT scans to plain radiographs has been studied.[21, 224] Bernstein and colleagues demonstrated a slight increase in intraobserver reliability but no increase in the interobserver reproducibility.[21] The interobserver reproducibility of the responses of the senior shoulder surgeons regarding diagnosis and treatment did not change when CT images were used in addition to plain radiographs. Sjödén and associates concluded that even with CT scans, the reproducibility of proximal humeral fracture classification with the Neer and AO systems was limited.[224] Nevertheless, they found that intraobserver reproducibility was better among shoulder specialists and also better with Neer's classification.

Three-dimensional imaging is advocated by some authorities. This technique provides even better definition of the pathoanatomy. Nevertheless, Sallay and co-workers found that the addition of three-dimensional imaging did not improve the reliability of identifying the precise pathoanatomy of proximal humeral fractures.[212] They stated that the problem with classification does not rest with the classification system but instead is "the result of vague criteria for identifying fractured parts and determination of displacement and angulation."

Plain radiographs remain the basis for the classification of proximal humeral fractures. The most important aspect of classification is to determine whether sufficient displacement is present to warrant consideration of operative treatment. Unfortunately, poor interobserver reproducibil-

ity undoubtedly results in problems with treatment selection and significantly limits our ability to make comparisons between different studies.

## MANAGEMENT

### General Principles

Management of fractures of the proximal end of the humerus has undergone an evolution. The early literature is replete with good results from a variety of treatment methods. However, these studies were often biased by the fact that the fractures were not well differentiated or classified and outcomes were not critically assessed. Emphasis on evaluating fracture displacement and vascularity, refinement of surgical techniques, clarification of outcome goals, and improvements in rehabilitation are likely to facilitate the evaluation of treatment approaches and improve the outcome of treatment of proximal humeral fractures.

Early treatments included traction, hanging casts, and abduction casts.[22, 23, 97, 99, 133, 221, 229, 250] Although these nonoperative techniques are primarily of historical interest, in rare settings they are appropriate. Abduction casts and splints to bring the distal fragment to the proximal one are not recommended. The deforming forces of the pectoralis major and latissimus dorsi, which pull the shaft anteriorly and medially, are actually increased with abduction[24, 177] (Fig. 44–32). Furthermore, isolated abduction casts can be heavy and uncomfortable and prevent early

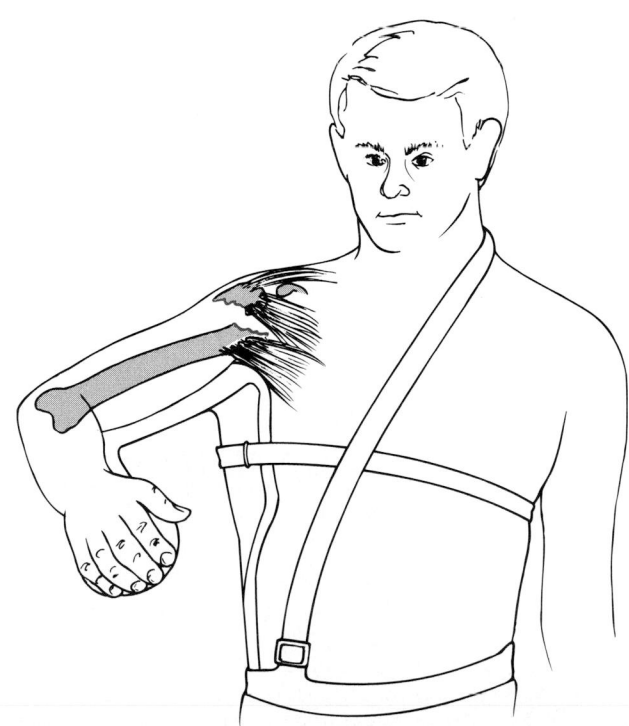

FIGURE 44–32. Deforming forces of the pectoralis in abduction. The pectoralis pulls the humeral shaft toward the chest while it displaces the fracture at the surgical neck.

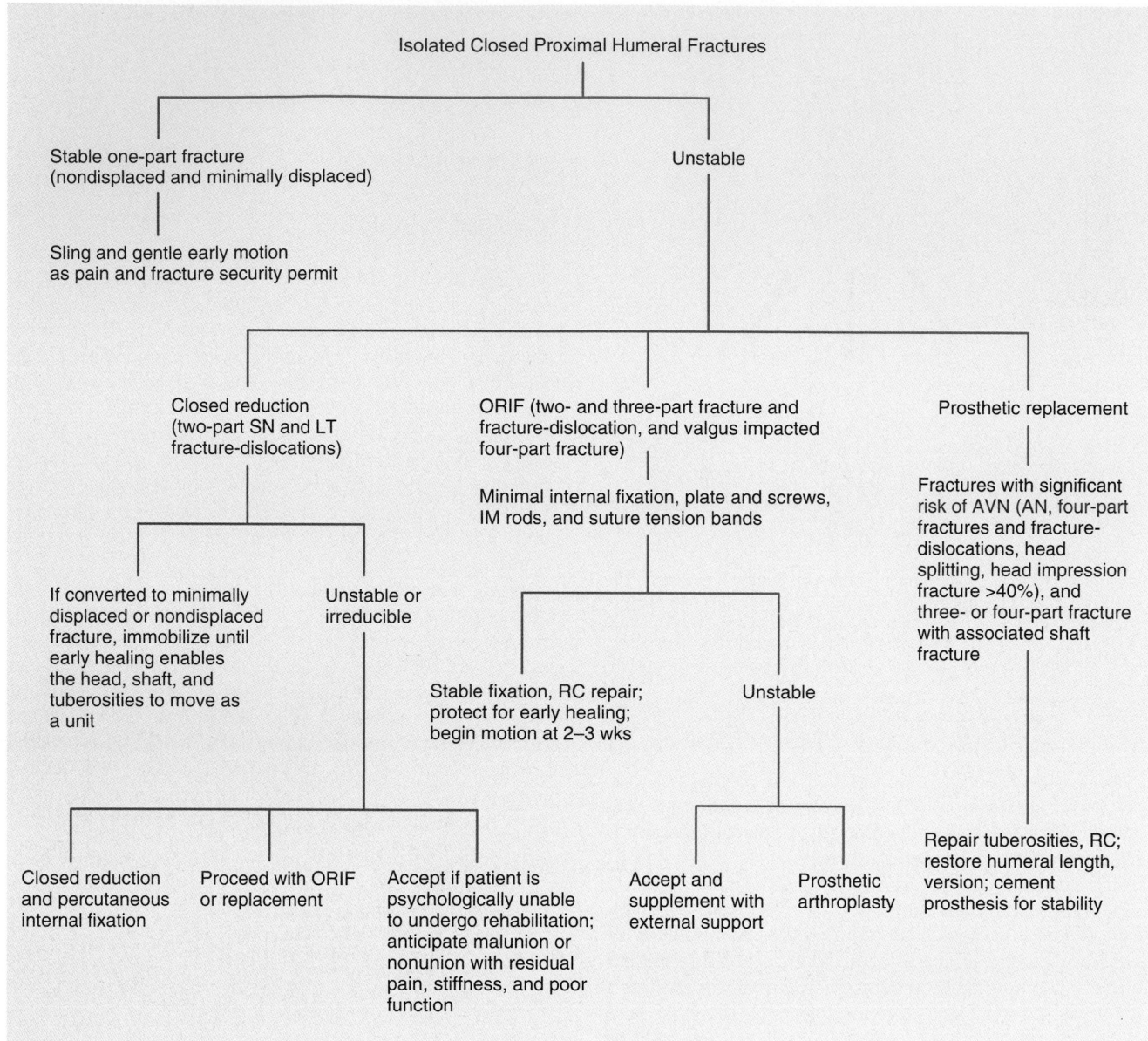

**Figure 44–33.** Algorithm for isolated closed proximal humeral fractures. *Abbreviations:* AN, anatomic neck; AVN, avascular necrosis; IM, intramedullary; LT, lesser tuberosity; ORIF, open reduction and internal fixation; RC, rotator cuff; SN, surgical neck.

assisted motion. Additional deforming forces are added as the arm extends posteriorly when the patient is supine.[45, 54, 99, 184]

Traction, overhead or at the side, through an olecranon pin for surgical neck fractures[23, 118] is reserved for patients who are confined to bed with multiple injuries. Neviaser[184] preferred adduction and flexion of the arm, whereas Callahan[24] proposed keeping the arm at the side for epiphyseal fractures. With improvements in operative treatment, these techniques have largely been abandoned.

Current treatment options include nonoperative measures (usually a sling with early motion),[18, 55, 63, 64, 140, 205] closed reduction and a sling, closed reduction and internal fixation,[103, 169] external fixation,[129, 130, 132, 225] a variety of open reduction and internal fixation (ORIF) techniques (sutures, intramedul-

lary devices, plates, screws, staples, or pins),* prosthetic arthroplasty,† and rarely, excision of the humeral head with or without repair of the rotator cuff[110, 111] and primary arthrodesis. Displacement of the fracture fragments remains the major determinant of treatment (Fig. 44–33).[7, 32, 84, 174, 175]

Fifty percent to 80% of proximal humeral fractures are nondisplaced or minimally displaced and stable.[105, 124, 174, 175] These fractures are managed nonoperatively. In general, closed reduction is possible for two-part surgical neck fractures unless soft tissue interposition has

---

*See references 39, 58, 85, 128, 169, 202, 207, 215, 228, 231, 241, 245, 254.

†See references 42, 46, 53, 61, 70, 72, 88, 115, 126, 150, 175, 182, 203, 235, 239, 247.

occurred. Reduction (open or closed) and internal fixation are used for most two- and three-part fractures and some four-part fractures, and prosthetic replacement is used for most four-part fractures, some three-part fractures in osteoporotic patients, and fractures with comminution of the articular segment.

The realization that a poor result after primary treatment of a displaced fracture of the proximal end of the humerus is very difficult to reconstruct adds to the significance of the initial treatment selected.[4, 11, 61, 188, 235] Bony and soft tissue anatomy must be restored early in unstable or displaced fractures to achieve success.

Malunion, nonunion, and AVN, the most common complications of nonoperative treatment, result in limited shoulder motion and weakness and can cause persistent disabling pain and shoulder dysfunction. These problems can be prevented with successful open treatment. However, operative treatment should not be taken lightly because many of the worst complications result from unsuccessful surgical attempts. In some cases, co-morbid factors render nonoperative treatment the most appropriate treatment despite substantial displacement.

## Considerations for Polytrauma Patients

Proximal humeral fractures and fracture-dislocations in victims of multiple trauma pose difficult treatment problems. The care of more life-threatening visceral injuries, head injuries, axial skeletal injuries, and lower extremity injuries takes precedence over most shoulder girdle and upper extremity injuries. Fractures of the proximal end of the humerus in polytrauma are more likely to be associated with ipsilateral skeletal injuries, neurovascular injuries, and soft tissue injuries (Fig. 44–34). Forearm fractures have a higher incidence of nerve injury within that extremity than do isolated proximal humeral fractures alone. Finally, patients with multiple trauma are often unable to actively participate in shoulder rehabilitation to the same extent as an individual with an isolated shoulder girdle injury.

Proximal humeral fractures may be splinted during the evaluation of other injuries to prevent additional injury. Life-threatening visceral injuries take priority in early evaluation and management. Head injuries are associated with an increased incidence of myositis ossificans in the

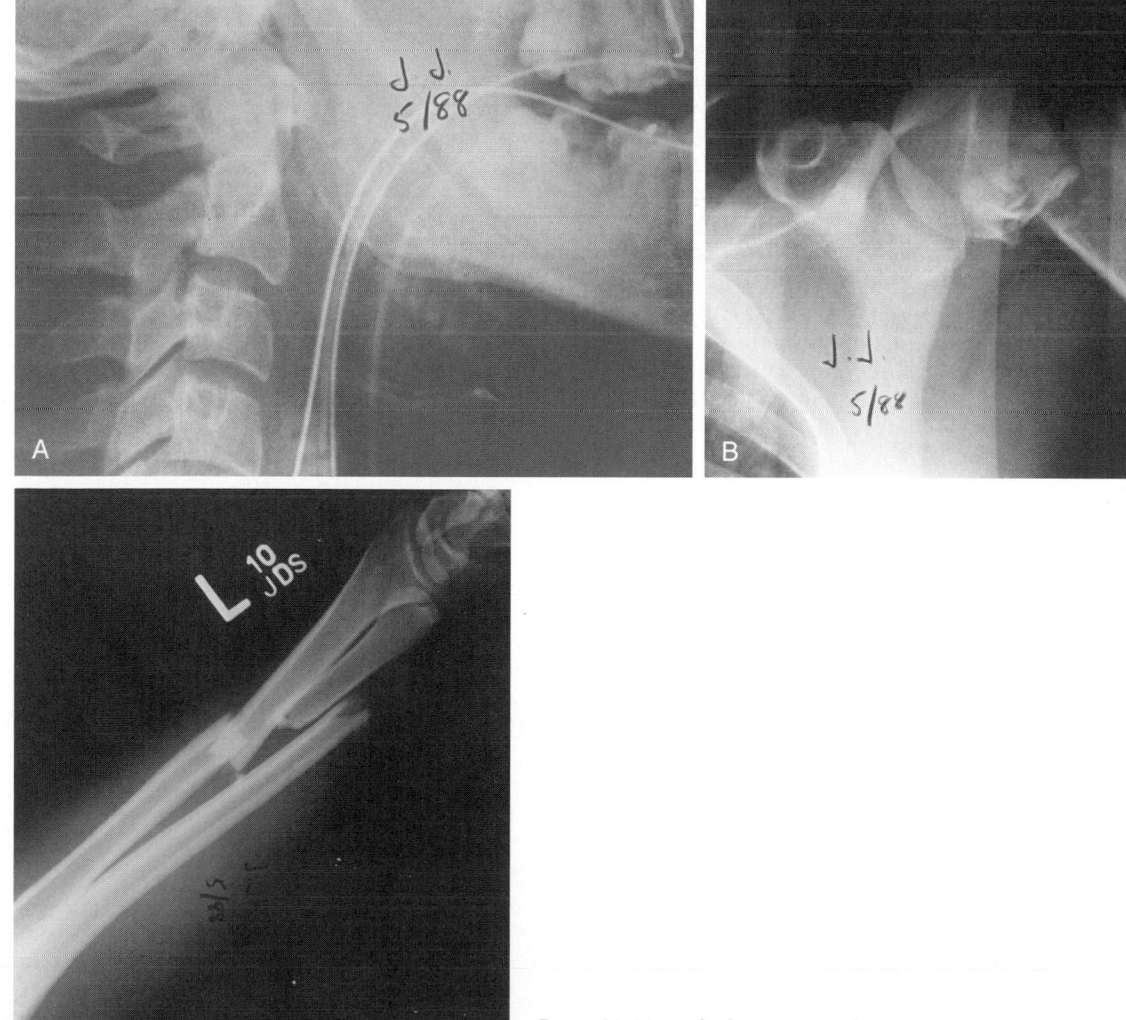

**FIGURE 44–34.** Multiple injuries in this trauma patient included a C2 cervical spine fracture (A), a comminuted fracture of the surgical neck of the humerus (B), and ipsilateral both-bone forearm fractures (C).

region of the extremity fracture. These regions should be stabilized to prevent unnecessary additional soft tissue injury and minimize the incidence of heterotopic ossification.

When associated neurovascular injuries are present, reduction of any dislocations and operative stabilization of unstable fractures permit early repair of the neurovascular structures. Arterial injuries should be provisionally shunted. The fractures should then be stabilized. This sequence prevents excessive manipulation of the definitive vascular repair. Management of fractures associated with nerve injury is still controversial. An adequate examination to screen for any neurologic deficit is important before manipulation of the fracture for closed reduction. If the fracture is open, the nerve can be explored at the time of wound débridement and fracture stabilization. Scapulothoracic dissociation is a rare, but devastating injury that must be considered in patients with severe shoulder girdle trauma.[193, 210]

Although the necessity for meticulous repair of many proximal fractures is seldom questioned, an attitude of benign neglect still abounds with regard to major fractures of the glenohumeral joint. In high-energy fractures of the proximal end of the humerus associated with other serious injuries, the proximal humeral fracture is often overlooked or neglected.[219] Such fractures do not do well with this form of care.[32, 140, 174, 175, 211, 219, 227] Proximal humeral fractures are often overlooked or can be confused with brachial plexus injuries; therefore, imaging procedures should be undertaken and should be of sufficient quality to obtain the information desired concerning fractures and dislocations.

The AO/ASIF group, among others, has advocated stable internal fixation for displaced periarticular and intra-articular fractures.[217] ORIF is recommended for open fractures and fractures with vascular injuries. Other fractures can be treated once the patient is stabilized. Sling immobilization, splinting, traction, and external fixation can be used to temporarily immobilize or stabilize a fracture that will require operative treatment. Any definitive operative repair will be subjected to increased stress in a patient with multiple injuries who has difficulty with independent mobilization. It is sometimes prudent to delay operative treatment of a shoulder injury until the patient is able to transfer out of bed without use of the injured upper extremity.

With multiple injuries to the same extremity, to both humeri, or to other areas, stabilization of proximal humeral fractures simplifies care and permits earlier mobilization. It would be difficult to splint the arm to the chest wall in a patient with a flail chest because such splinting would interfere with ventilation and care of the chest injury.

Open fractures of the shoulder girdle are managed in the same fashion as other open fractures. Treatment begins with débridement and irrigation of an adequately exposed wound, prophylactic antibiotics, skeletal stabilization with either temporary external fixation or definitive internal fixation,[225] and delayed soft tissue closure. Open proximal humeral fractures are rare and usually the result of penetrating or high-energy blunt trauma.

Adequate radiographs are essential to avoid misdiagnosis. Between 50% and 80% of posterior fracture-dislocations are missed by the initial examining physician despite numerous publications that highlight this fact.[50, 87] In the multiple-trauma setting, shoulder fractures, fracture-dislocations, and articular fractures of the glenoid are missed or neglected until more serious life-threatening cranial, thoracic, and abdominal injuries have been treated. Ironically, the shoulder lesions may be the most debilitating residual injury after all others have healed.[101, 154]

## Proximal Humeral Fractures

A variety of treatment options have been described for proximal humeral fractures, as outlined in the categories listed in Table 44–2. Many factors must be considered, including those specific to the patient and the "personality" of the fracture. Such factors include the activities, health, and wishes of the patient; the risks and benefits of treatment; and the effectiveness of the possible treatment methods. The surgeon should be familiar with the specialized techniques of shoulder surgery and its prolonged aftercare.

Some fractures are difficult to treat in the acute setting with operative reconstruction involving either fixation or prosthetic arthroplasty. However, they are much more difficult to reconstruct later after the development of subacromial, capsular, and muscular scarring, fixed retraction of the tuberosities and rotator cuff, malunion or nonunion, osteonecrosis of the humeral head, and neurologic injury.

Preoperative planning and preparation require assessment of the patient's health, neurovascular examination, and determination of the potentially injured structures. The neurovascular evaluation may be supplemented with EMG and nerve conduction studies, Doppler ultrasonography, or arteriography. Plain radiographs in at least three planes are used to classify the fracture and determine its stability. CT scans can supplement routine plain radiographs and help clarify the fracture anatomy, thereby assisting in deciding whether to operate and in planning

---

**TABLE 44–2** ..............................................

Treatment Options for Fractures of the Proximal Humerus

---

Sling
Closed reduction and sling
    Coaptation splints
    Hanging arm cast
Percutaneous pinning
External fixation
Open reduction and internal fixation
    Suture or wires—simple repair or tension band fixation
    Intramedullary rods
        Rush
        Ender
        Mouridian nail
        Humeral locking nail
    Tension band and intramedullary Ender rods
    Screws
        Plates and screws
Prosthetic arthroplasty

..............................................

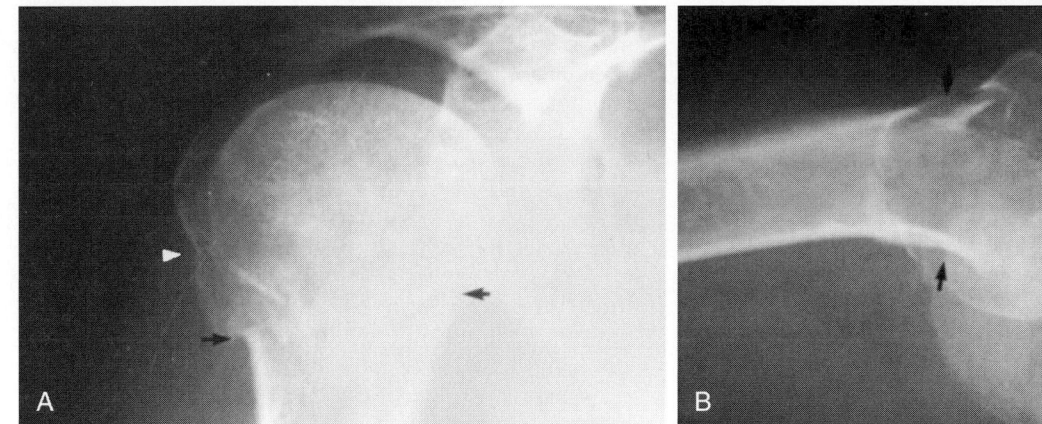

**FIGURE 44–35.** One-part nondisplaced surgical neck fracture *(arrows)*. *A,* Anteroposterior view. *B,* Axillary view.

for repair.[165] A full assortment of plates, screws, intramedullary rods, and prostheses should be available to the surgeon because the type of treatment may change intraoperatively (e.g., when internal fixation is not secure or when additional fractures are displaced during the operation).

For most cases, an interscalene block with or without general anesthesia is preferred. In some cases, closed reduction can be performed with intravenous sedation. If general anesthesia is precluded for medical reasons in an elderly patient, the operation can be done with an interscalene block.[15, 34] However, this block is contraindicated when a patient has a suspected neurologic injury preoperatively. It is more difficult for the surgeon to test the patient's neurologic status in the early postoperative period after regional anesthesia. Good muscle relaxation by block or general anesthesia is especially important. Full muscle relaxation helps facilitate exposure of the fracture.

Contraindications to surgery include poor patient health or rehabilitation potential (such as a patient with dementia) and the surgeon's inexperience with the procedure or the treatment of potential complications.

## NONDISPLACED OR ONE-PART FRACTURES

One-part fractures are nondisplaced or only minimally displaced (less than 0.5 cm when the fracture involves the greater tuberosity or 1 cm between any of the other segments) and angulated less than 45° (Fig. 44–35).[174] Their prevalence ranges between 47% and 85% of all proximal humeral fractures.[29, 80, 105, 124, 174, 206] The rotator cuff and periosteum and the long head of the biceps maintain these fractures in position. Most of these nondisplaced or minimally displaced fractures are impacted or stable. Special care is taken to avoid overly aggressive passive exercises that might displace a fracture that would otherwise eventually undergo uncomplicated healing. Some stiffness is anticipated, and therefore a balance between mobilization and protection should be kept in mind.

### Treatment

Indications for treatment are the same for all stable undisplaced fractures of the proximal end of the humerus. The arm is placed in a sling or sling and swathe for comfort and support. Early, gentle, passive range of motion, beginning with pendulum exercises, is started once the humeral head and shaft have been demonstrated to move together. Impacted, stable fractures can be moved immediately. Stable fractures move as a unit regardless of the degree of comminution. With unstable fractures, early fracture healing must occur before motion can be initiated. This category includes displaced fractures that are converted to nondisplaced or minimally displaced fractures by closed reduction. In most cases, these reduced fractures are not stable. If the fracture does not move as a unit, excessive early motion may result in nonunion or malunion. Particular care should be taken to avoid displacement of tuberosity fragments as a result of inappropriate early activity.

Unimpacted surgical neck fractures are protected in a sling with the arm at the side until the humeral head and shaft rotate in unison. Pendulum exercises may then be added until the union has sufficient strength to allow more aggressive passive and active motion and strengthening exercises. These fractures are at risk for further displacement and nonunion when treated with distraction, when rotational exercises are begun too early, or when manipulations are used to treat a stiff shoulder.

The weight of the arm alone provides 10 to 15 lb of distraction force, which can be supported by a sling or collar and cuff to reduce and maintain the position of the fracture.[45] A hanging arm cast giving additional distraction has been successfully used by several authors.[22, 23, 97, 99, 133, 242, 250] Unfortunately, application of this cast requires some fine-tuning because hanging casts can be problematic. In many patients, a heavy hanging arm cast can distract the surgical neck fracture site. Additionally, the upper aspect of the cast is distal to the level of the fracture and creates an increased lever arm at the apex of the fracture, thus increasing the likelihood of malunion or nonunion.[92, 177] Fractures of the proximal end of the humerus are difficult to immobilize with casts and can be effectively treated with a simple sling.

### Aftercare and Rehabilitation

Rehabilitative exercises are advanced as fracture healing progresses. A sling is worn to support the arm. Early deltoid isometric exercises are helpful in reliable patients, and once the fracture is stable, phase I passive exercises can be started. Rehabilitation is advanced as tolerated and as fracture healing is ensured.[205] Active motion exercises and strengthening are initiated at about 6 weeks after injury. Pulley and supine passive range-of-motion exercises can be instituted 4 to 6 weeks after the injury. Supplemental isometrics are added by 4 to 6 weeks. Active exercises commence at 6 to 8 weeks if healing permits. Frequent clinical and radiographic evaluations are important to assess progress and ensure that no displacement has occurred.

The most common long-term problem is residual loss of glenohumeral motion. To some degree, the increased scapulothoracic motion gained through rehabilitation can compensate for this loss. Subacromial impingement is not uncommon after healing of a nondisplaced greater tuberosity fracture. Scarring that follows subacromial hemorrhage or that forms over the area of fracture healing effectively narrows the subacromial space. Continuation of rehabilitation exercises should be encouraged for at least 6 months after injury. Despite the seemingly benign nature of these injuries, arm function is often significantly impaired, especially in the elderly population.[124] Closed treatment has yielded satisfactory results in 90% of undisplaced fractures.

For nondisplaced fractures, lingering stiffness and a weather-related ache may continue; permanent stiffness sometimes occurs.[29, 124] Longer immobilization times for undisplaced fractures result in a longer period of physical therapy and disability.[29, 124]

Closed treatment can be associated with complications. Treatment by traction is associated with a high nonunion rate.[109] In Jones and colleagues' series, 9 of 13 fractures (69%) were reducible by closed means, but only 5 of 13 (38%) healed.[109] Two of the fractures healed with reduction and closed pinning, but closed reductions were associated with nerve injury, further fracture displacement, and conversion to more unstable fractures with two or more components. An approximately 75% incidence of satisfactory results was noted with closed treatment by other authors.[29, 140, 227, 233] Malunion blocks motion and can cause weakness and disabling pain. Caution is suggested in accepting short-term follow-up. Although a satisfactory radiographic appearance may be observed at 1 year,[199] the humeral head may collapse over the ensuing years with a poor final result.[59, 128, 140, 175, 227, 231]

## ONE-PART FRACTURE WITH DISLOCATION

When dislocations are associated with nondisplaced or minimally displaced one-part fractures, additional care must be taken during reduction if displacement of the fracture is to be avoided.[94] General anesthesia or an interscalene block provides more adequate relaxation for reduction. Consideration should be given to open reduction to ensure gentle atraumatic fracture reduction.

## DISPLACED FRACTURES

An algorithm for displaced fractures requires considerations specific to individual patients, such as their medical health, the quality of the bone, and the overall ability of the patient to cooperate with the necessary postoperative rehabilitation program (see Fig. 44–33). Most patients will follow specific instructions, whereas in extreme cases, immobilization that cannot be removed (i.e., a fiberglass shoulder spica cast) is required in the early healing periods if compliance is a serious issue.

In general, fractures that can be treated by closed reduction do not involve large tears of the rotator cuff or significant displacement of the greater tuberosity. Fractures that are treated by open reduction require assessment and then protection of any remaining blood supply to the humeral head. Prosthetic replacement is preferred for three-part fractures in osteoporotic patients, for most four-part fractures, and for head-splitting fractures. Fractures with dislocations have more severe soft tissue injury.

Nonoperative treatment or closed treatment of displaced fractures has yielded disappointing results.[64, 162, 233] Satisfactory results are obtained in 75% to 85% of reducible two-part surgical neck fractures, 50% of greater tuberosity fractures, and less than 10% of four-part fractures and fracture-dislocations.[29, 32, 54, 233] Thus, most authors recommend that displaced fractures be treated with operative techniques. The primary goal of operative reduction and internal fixation is to reestablish normal anatomy with enough stability to allow early range of motion and facilitate recovery and rehabilitation. Prosthetic replacement offers a predictable procedure for establishing early stability for more comminuted or complicated displaced proximal humeral fractures.* In some cases, stabilization and fixation of an unstable fracture can facilitate early recovery by reducing pain and preventing additional soft tissue injury. Nevertheless, operative treatment is not always the best treatment of displaced proximal humeral fractures. Patients who are unable to participate in the extensive rehabilitation, such as elderly individuals or alcoholics, and patients with substantial medical co-morbidities frequently do not benefit from operative treatment and are far more likely to have complications of surgical treatment.

Many techniques of internal fixation have been described, including heavy nonabsorbable sutures, wire, screws, staples, blade plates, buttress plates, Kirschner wires, Steinmann pins, Mouridian rods, Rush rods, Ender rods, and various combinations.† Treatment is determined and affected by a variety of factors, including the fracture type, patient age and activity level, bone quality, and experience of the surgeon.

Some series report a high incidence of complications of ORIF, including malunion, nonunion, hardware displacement, infection, shoulder stiffness, and AVN.[59, 138, 186, 191] Various studies have reported malunion rates as high as 16%, residual hardware impingement in 15.6%, infection in 12.5%, AVN in 12.5%, and hardware loosening requiring removal in 6%.[149] Kristiansen and Christensen[128] reported that 55% of their patients observed for 2 to 7 years had an unsatisfactory result. Unfortunately, comparison of the results of many of the reported studies is difficult, and few prospective well-controlled studies have been conducted.

---

*See references 53, 72, 75, 88, 126, 131, 150, 173, 175, 177–179, 181, 185, 187, 203, 227, 235, 238, 239.
†See references 7, 28, 36, 39, 49, 58, 79, 85, 90, 92, 99, 103, 119, 128, 136, 160, 161, 168, 169, 175, 181, 185, 190, 191, 199, 202, 207, 215, 217, 227, 228, 231, 233, 234, 241, 245, 254.

Neer[174, 175] reported a 75% incidence of AVN in four-part fractures treated with ORIF. Lee and Hansen noted that AVN can occur up to 3.5 years after the injury, thus indicating that long-term follow-up is necessary.[138] Keene and colleagues demonstrated that fracture deformity correlated with motion and the functional result.[116]

As a result of their experience, Sturzenegger and co-workers[231] recommended "minimal osteosynthesis" with simple screws and tension bands in an effort to avoid injury to the blood supply of the articular segment. They reported that AVN occurred in 34% of their patients in whom plate fixation was used for three- and four-part fractures. A resurgence of interest in the techniques of closed or open reduction and minimal internal fixation offers great promise.

Several studies report that late reconstruction of displaced proximal humeral fractures is difficult and that the outcomes are limited.[4, 44, 61, 188, 235] The belief that prosthetic arthroplasty is an easy salvage option if initial closed treatment or ORIF fails is incorrect. Even though the results are satisfactory, with reduction of pain and consequent functional improvement, the results are inferior to those of successful primary treatment by any method, including primary shoulder arthroplasty.

Although only 20% of proximal humeral fractures have generally been considered to be displaced or minimally displaced,[177, 206] Jakob and coauthors[105] reported that 53% of proximal humeral fractures were displaced. Thus, the more serious or displaced fractures may be more common than previously thought.

## FRACTURE FIXATION

The fact that so many different internal fixation techniques are available supports the opinion that a single technique cannot be used exclusively for any specific fracture pattern. Comminution and osteopenia often affect the stability or rigidity of any fixation technique. Good bone is the exception, and techniques that achieve interfragmentary and axial stability without excessive soft tissue dissection are most likely to be successful.

Screw fixation is often unsuccessful because of poor purchase in the humeral head. The best screw fixation can be achieved in the central aspect of the articular segment.[143] Screw fixation of the greater tuberosity is prone to failure because although the screw may have purchase in the humeral head articular segment, the fragile tuberosity may become displaced around the screw. Heavy suture fixation is often used. Sutures can be placed through the bone or around the tuberosity fragments at the rotator cuff insertion. The latter is usually a stronger technique.

Metaphyseal comminution is particularly problematic. With medial comminution of the surgical neck, it is especially difficult to maintain humeral length and the position of the articular segment. Varus malunion is a common sequela of comminution at the medial aspect of the surgical neck. Intramedullary fixation and fixed-angle plate-and-screw devices can improve axial stability. In all cases, extraneous dissection should be avoided to preserve vascularity to the articular segment.

Several recent biomechanical studies have evaluated the strength and stability of a variety of fixation techniques.

Most demonstrate that the addition of axial stability enhances the fixation of proximal humeral fractures. Instrum and colleagues found that the strength of fixation of a surgical neck osteotomy of the proximal end of the humerus fixed with a blade plate fashioned from a semitubular plate was superior to fixation with an AO T plate.[102] Koval and co-workers studied the stability and ultimate strength of 10 different fixation techniques for surgical neck fractures of the proximal end of the humerus.[125] T plate–and-screw fixation was the strongest fixation in nonosteopenic bone, followed by Ender rods with tension band fixation. In osteopenic specimens, fixation with four Schanz pins (one pin through the greater tuberosity) followed by the T plate and screws provided the strongest fixation. Tension band fixation was the weakest in both groups.

Wheeler and Colville compared the biomechanics of fixation of three-part proximal humeral fractures with percutaneous pinning and locked intramedullary rodding.[246] The intramedullary device that they tested provided greater resistance to angular displacement under cyclical loading, as well as greater failure torque, stiffness, energy absorption, and angular displacement, than did fixation with multiple pins.

Williams and associates evaluated the effect of the addition of intramedullary Ender rod fixation to figure-of-eight wire fixation for fixation of a surgical neck osteotomy of the proximal end of the humerus.[248] The addition of two Ender rods increased the maximal torsional load by 1.5 times. In addition, they did not find a significant correlation between the mean maximal load and bone mineral density of the specimens.

These studies assess the fixation strength of fracture models and do not take into account the effect of the surrounding soft tissues, which are injured to a variable extent and can provide a varying degree of support and stability. Nevertheless, they provide a basis for understanding the role of fixation techniques when treating proximal humeral fractures.

## TWO-PART FRACTURES AND FRACTURE-DISLOCATIONS

Chun and coauthors[28] reported on a series of 141 two-part proximal humeral fractures, including 113 surgical neck fractures, 24 greater tuberosity fractures, 2 anatomic neck fractures, and 2 lesser tuberosity fractures. Most of the cases, 71%, were treated with a sling and early rehabilitation.

### Anatomic Neck Fractures

Isolated anatomic neck fractures of the proximal part of the humerus are extremely rare and account for only 0.54% of proximal humeral fractures.[105, 177] Displaced anatomic neck fractures cause complete disruption of the blood supply to the articular segment of the humeral head.[17] Indications for treatment of these fractures are displacement or dislocation.

No cases of successful closed reduction or closed pinning for isolated, displaced, or dislocated anatomic neck fractures with long-term follow-up have been reported. Closed reduction has resulted in malunion and collapse.[177] In older individuals, the preferred treatment is

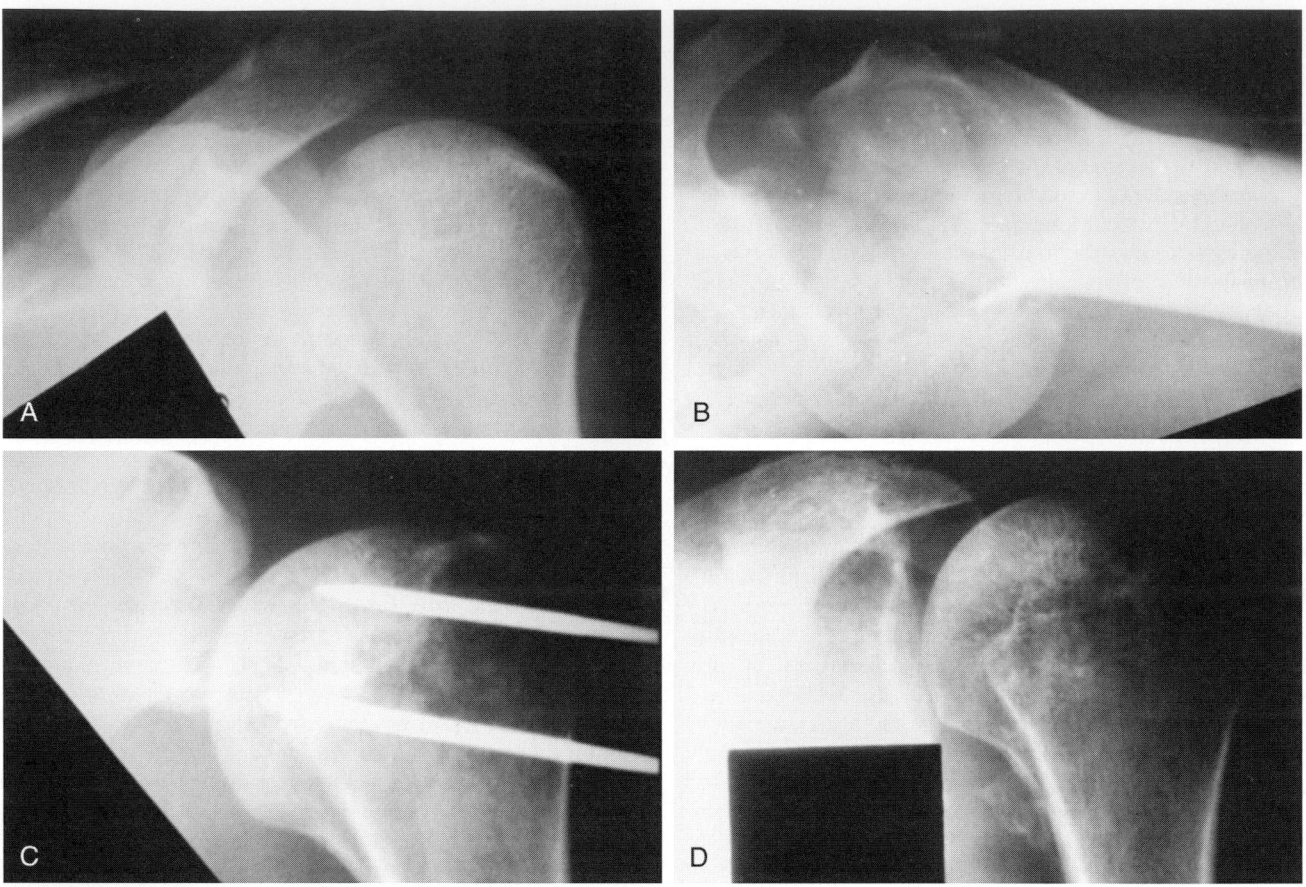

**FIGURE 44–36.** Posterior dislocation with a two-part fracture-dislocation of the anatomic neck. *A,* The anteroposterior view was not diagnostic for the first three orthopaedic surgeons assessing this fracture-dislocation. *B,* An axillary view demonstrating posterior head displacement enabled the diagnosis to be established. *C,* Open reduction and internal fixation with two Steinmann pins. *D,* Four-month follow-up with pin removal at 6 weeks shows good early healing of the articular segment. Longer follow-up will be needed to ensure that late collapse with avascular necrosis does not occur. *(A–D,* Courtesy of Charles A. Rockwood, Jr., M.D.)

early prosthetic replacement to avoid the malunion and collapse that is almost certain to occur when the blood supply to the articular segment has been disrupted. Alternatively, open reduction plus minimal internal fixation with screws or pins is considered for younger patients.

In either case, ORIF or humeral head replacement, a deltopectoral approach is used. In some cases, the humeral head can be reduced by elevating it from a valgus position. An instrument such as a bone tamp can be inserted through a window in the metaphysis. When the articular segment is more displaced, an opening in the subscapularis and anterior capsule 1 cm from their insertion on the lesser tuberosity allows full visualization of the humeral head and, if necessary, the glenoid. The humeral head is positioned anatomically under direct vision. Screws, Kirschner wires, or Steinmann pins are inserted through the tuberosities up into the head. Under direct vision, the arm can then be externally rotated to ensure that the articular cartilage has not been penetrated by hardware (Fig. 44–36).

If the humeral head is dislocated, a bone hook can be used to pull laterally on the upper humeral shaft with the arm in some flexion and abduction to relax the deltoid. This technique gives sufficient room to retrieve the displaced or dislocated articular segment. Once it has been

anatomically positioned, it can be fixed with Steinmann pins, Kirschner wires, or screws. Any wires or pins should be monitored carefully and removed if they break or begin to migrate or when healing permits, usually by 6 weeks.[149] Intraoperative complications to avoid include fragmentation of the head and penetration of the fixation through the articular surface. If secure fixation is not achieved or the articular surface is fragmented, this procedure should be abandoned and converted to humeral head replacement (Fig. 44–37).

An autogenous or autologous bone graft or synthetic bone substitute can be used to fill the metaphyseal region under the articular segment in those with significant osteopenia or loss of bony support as a result of the trauma.

Pins left through or just under the skin surface are removed 6 to 8 weeks after surgery. Screws are left in place permanently unless the humeral head begins to collapse. If screw penetration through the articular surface is discovered, the patient is returned to surgery early. The screw can be replaced with a shorter screw or removed.

The deltopectoral approach without deltoid detachment is ideal for humeral head replacement. The fracture occurs along the scar of the old epiphyseal line. If any bony deficiency is noted, the humeral head is used as additional bone graft. Usually, the metaphyseal bone is present for support and rotatory control of the prosthesis. The subscapularis is opened 1 to 2 cm medial to its insertion on the lesser tuberosity. The elbow is lowered off the operating table to extend the arm at the shoulder, and the shaft is pushed upward in the deltopectoral interval. Anatomic prosthetic reconstruction is preferred. To preserve the normal 30° to 40° of retroversion, the lateral fin of the humeral head prosthesis is positioned posterior to the biceps groove.

A trial reduction is then performed. Tension is estimated in planning for cuff closure. The trial component is removed, and sutures are placed to close the rotator cuff before final placement of the prosthesis and then retracted out of the way. The prosthesis is cemented if a good press fit cannot be obtained.

### Surgical Neck Fractures

Displaced proximal humeral fractures most commonly involve the surgical neck.[28, 174] These fractures account for 60% to 70% of all proximal humeral fractures in adults and about 20% of displaced fractures.[105] The shaft fragment may be impacted, angulated, displaced anteriorly and medially by the pull of the pectoralis, comminuted, occur with or without extension into the tuberosities, or be associated with anterior dislocation of the shoulder.

Frequently, these fractures are unstable after closed reduction because of comminution or soft tissue interposition. The long head of the biceps, the subscapularis, or the deltoid muscles are the most commonly interposed tissues.

A hanging arm cast can distract the fracture site or cause undesirable angulation and result in a high incidence of malunion or nonunion.[191] Although a hanging arm cast may provide distraction early at the fracture site, as the muscles fatigue, it may overpull. Furthermore, when the patient lies down, any potential benefit it may have is lost.

Operative treatment of these fractures varies and depends on the architecture of the fracture, the extent of comminution, and whether a stable closed reduction can be maintained. In polytrauma patients, fractures benefit from reduction and internal fixation to permit ease of care and earlier secure mobilization.

**Impacted and Angulated.** Impacted surgical neck fractures are generally angulated with the apex directed anterolaterally. The posterior periosteal hinge may be intact. Although impacted fractures were not considered in the AO classification, in the absence of avulsion of a tuberosity,[105] they form one of the three important types described by Neer for displaced two-part surgical neck fractures. Angulated fractures account for approximately 26% of displaced proximal humeral fractures, and a significant percentage of them occur with fractures extending up into one or both tuberosities.[105] If these fractures are stable, consideration should be given to accepting the deformity, with the understanding that elevation will be lost in direct proportion to angulation of the fracture.[116] A varus malunion with the greater tuberosity rotated up into the subacromial space will not be tolerated well by an active patient or by one who needs overhead elevation.[109, 177, 180]

**Displaced and Unstable.** Some surgical neck fractures are stable once they are reduced. Reduction can be achieved with longitudinal traction in flexion and adduction and application of a posterior force on the upper part of the humerus. They are immobilized with the arm at the side in a sling or sling and swathe for 3 to 6 weeks. Once the head and shaft rotate as a unit, gentle pendulum exercises may be started. Eighty percent of these fractures will heal more or less in approximately 6 weeks,[109] and then gentle passive stretching exercises may be added. Light resistive exercises may begin at 10 to 12 weeks and are advanced as tolerated. Scheck considered a surgical neck fracture ununited if "the fragments did not move as a unit after a minimum of eight weeks."[218]

Indications for internal fixation include unstable fractures or polytrauma. In the latter setting, stabilization of proximal fractures provides for easier care, pain relief, and earlier rehabilitation.

***Closed Reduction.*** At the time of closed reduction, the surgeon should be prepared for the possibility of an open reduction. These fractures may be reduced after the

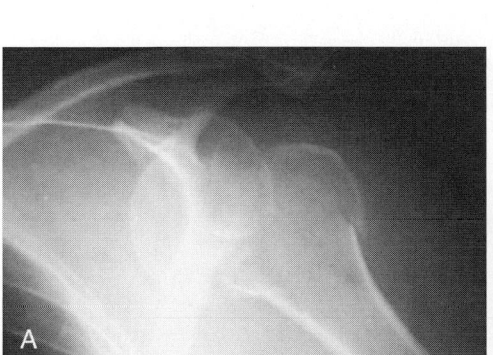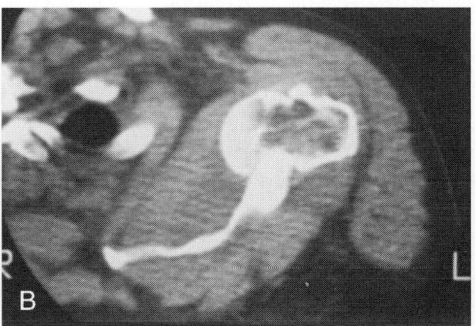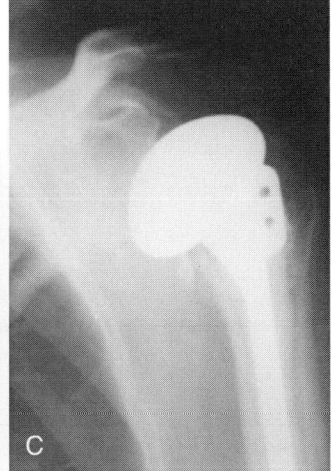

**FIGURE 44–37.** Two-part anatomic neck fracture–anterior dislocation. *A,* Anteroposterior view with an anatomic neck fracture and nondisplaced greater tuberosity fracture. *B,* Computed tomographic scan demonstrating anterior dislocation of the articular surface. *C,* Postoperative prosthetic replacement.

administration of intramuscular or intravenous pain medication and muscle relaxants or, preferably, under general anesthesia or an interscalene block (which results in better muscle relaxation). Fluoroscopic imaging is helpful to rapidly obtain radiographs for assessment of the reduction. Varus angulation is corrected with longitudinal traction and gentle arm pressure in a lateral-to-medial direction at the fracture site and with forward flexion and adduction of the arm to relax the pectoralis and latissimus dorsi. Once the fracture is disimpacted and realigned, upward compression at the elbow may reimpact the fracture for a stable closed reduction. The arm is lowered to the side and immobilized in a sling or a sling and swathe.

In rare cases when surgery is not possible or must be delayed, olecranon pin traction can be used to achieve reduction. The arm is flexed and adducted to relax the deforming muscle forces of the pectoralis major. This technique has disadvantages in that the patient is confined to bed and the traction must be monitored to maintain reduction and avoid overdistraction of the fracture. If the ultimate goal is anatomic reduction of the fracture, early surgical treatment is the best option.

If the fracture cannot be maintained in a reduced position, some form of fixation should be used, either closed pinning or ORIF. Percutaneous fixation should also be considered after stable closed reduction to prevent loss of reduction and to allow earlier rehabilitation (Fig. 44–38) if surgical fixation is not feasible or if unstable immobilization with the shoulder abducted is an option (Fig. 44–39).

***Closed Reduction and Percutaneous Pinning.*** Closed reduction plus percutaneous internal fixation is ideal

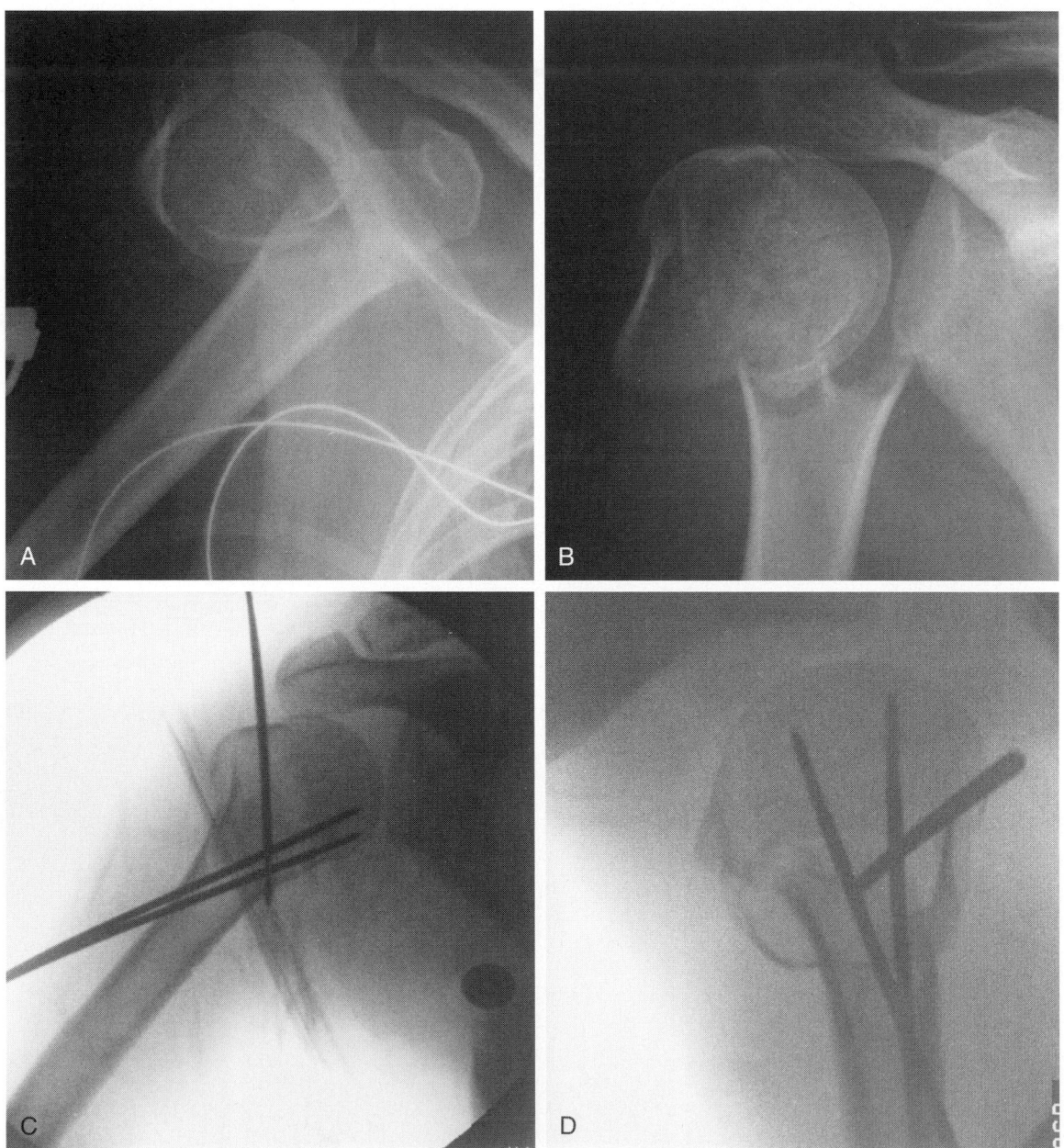

**FIGURE 44–38.** *A, B,* Radiographs of a severely displaced surgical neck fracture in a 38-year-old woman who was injured when a tree fell on her. She also had a T8 fracture-dislocation, rendering her paraplegic. *C, D,* Anteroposterior and axillary radiographs after treatment by closed reduction and percutaneous pin fixation.

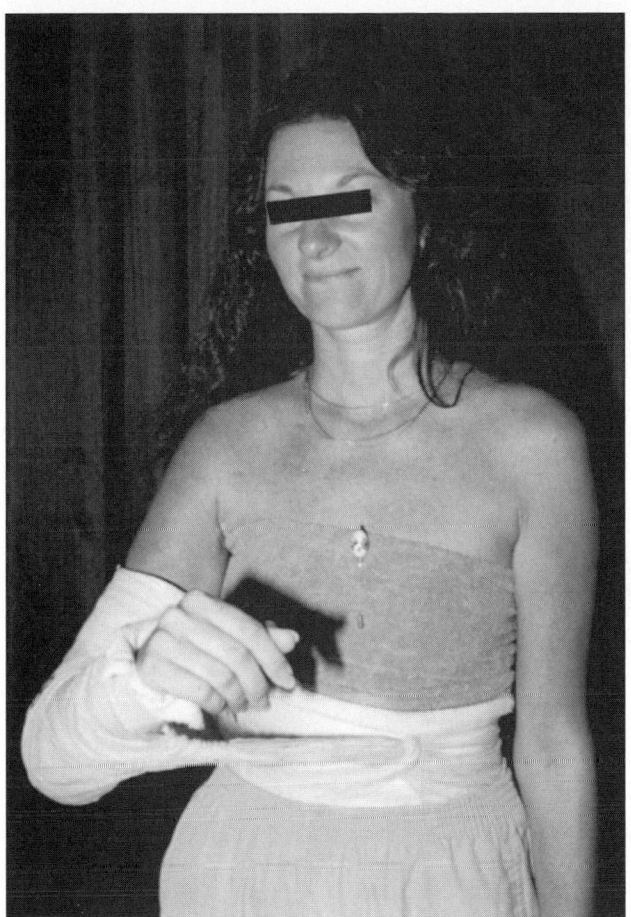

**FIGURE 44–39.** Postoperative position for a two-part surgical neck fracture.

for reducible surgical neck fractures. Positioning the patient supine on a radiolucent table permits easy biplanar imaging. An articulating shoulder-arm positioner (McConnell, Orthopaedic Manufacturing, Greenville, TX) is used to hold the arm during the procedure. Reduction is

performed as described previously. Terminally threaded 2.5-mm pins are drilled through the deltoid tuberosity and into the humeral head. Final advancing is done by hand to place the pins into subchondral bone. Care is taken to spread the pins for more stable fixation and to avoid penetration of the articular surface. A pin through the upper aspect of the greater tuberosity directed into the medial calcar area increases the stability of the fixation. Care must be taken to avoid injuring the axillary nerve, which passes about 5 cm distal to the acromion in the region of the anterior and middle deltoid. Relative contraindications to this technique are surgical neck and metaphyseal comminution.

Either the pins can be cut short and buried under the skin, or they can be left out of the skin. With the latter technique, meticulous pin care is required. If any sign of pin infection is noted, the pin should be removed and the infection treated with oral antibiotics. The greater tuberosity pins are removed 4 weeks after surgery and the distal pins 6 weeks after surgery.

Once the fracture has been rendered stable, essential aftercare includes sling support for 4 to 6 weeks. Gentle pendulum exercises can be started 2 to 3 weeks after fixation. No exercises are begun unless the head and shaft rotate in unison. Manipulation of the arm with excessive force before completion of fracture healing is to be avoided. Although the surgeon, the patient, and the treating therapist are understandably eager to reestablish glenohumeral motion to avoid long-term stiffness, early aggressive physical therapy has been a frequent cause of proximal humeral nonunion at the surgical neck[191] (Fig. 44–40).

The patient can graduate to progressive stretching and active resistive exercises at approximately 6 weeks. It may take 9 to 12 months to regain maximal range of shoulder motion, strength, and endurance.

**Open Reduction.** A small number of these fractures are irreducible because of interposition of soft tissues, including the long head of the biceps, the subscapularis, or the deltoid muscles (Fig. 44–41),[69, 107, 155] or because of comminution. Occasionally, these fractures are reducible

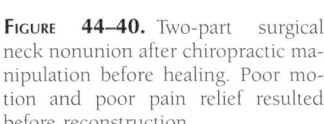

**FIGURE 44–40.** Two-part surgical neck nonunion after chiropractic manipulation before healing. Poor motion and poor pain relief resulted before reconstruction.

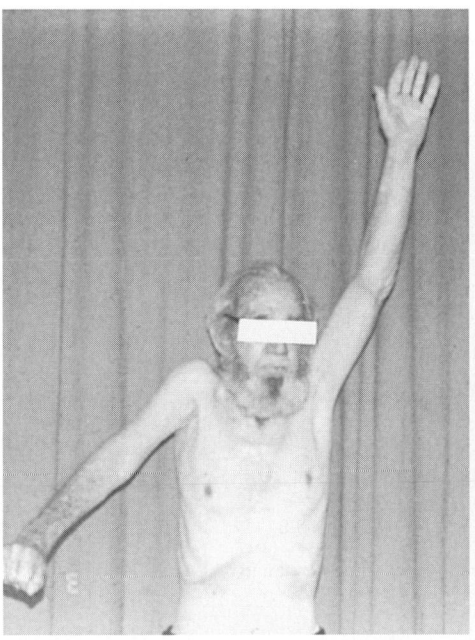
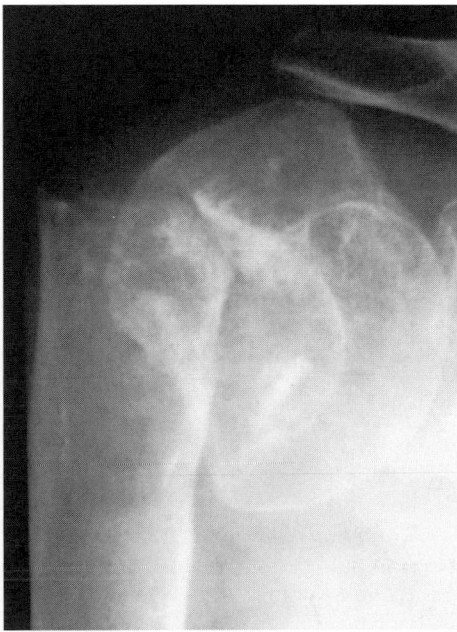

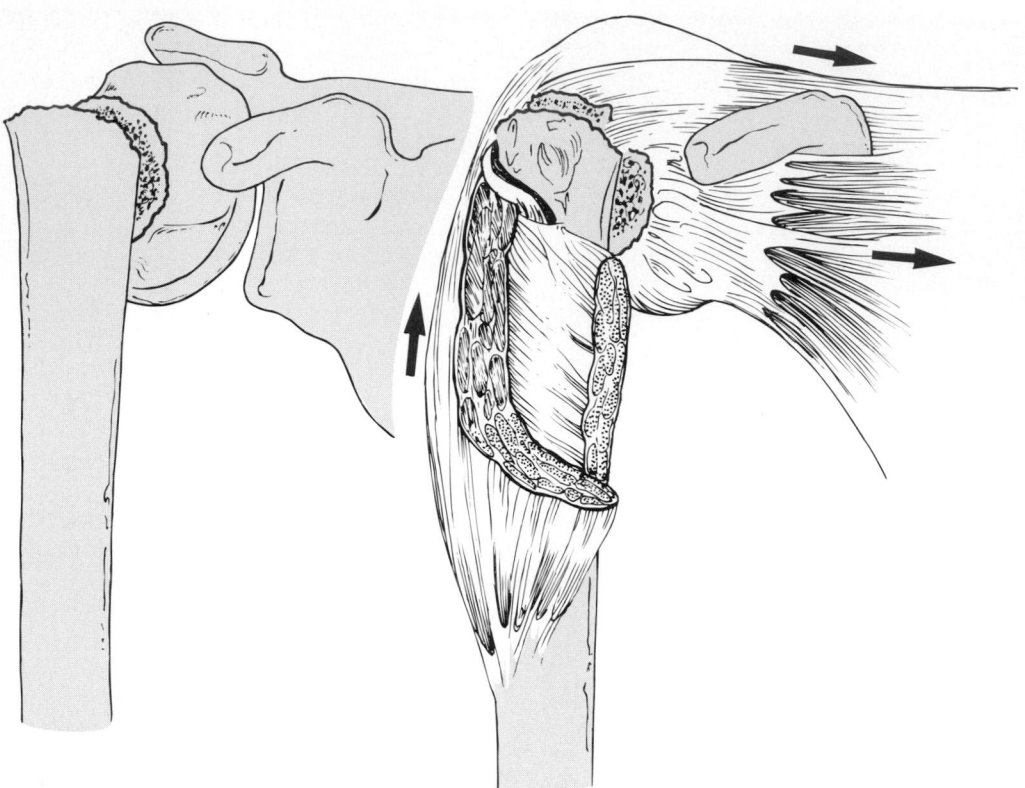

**FIGURE 44-41.** Interposition of the long head of the biceps in a surgical neck fracture precludes stable reduction. Unless the long head is removed, nonunion will result at the fracture site.

but become redisplaced as soon as the surgeon releases the tension holding the fracture. At this point, options for treatment include closed pinning,[79, 103, 130, 141] external fixators,[130, 132] and ORIF.[2, 7, 39, 168, 185] Preoperative imaging studies are obtained to assess osteoporosis, rule out a dislocation, and identify any additional fractures (especially nondisplaced comminution) in preparation for surgery. Care is taken to not displace otherwise minimally displaced or nondisplaced fragments preoperatively or intraoperatively. In fractures that are irreducible or appear to be reducible but are unstable, interposed soft tissue is often found at the fracture site during open reduction.

Current techniques for ORIF include percutaneous pinning, figure-of-eight tension band fixation with wire or heavy nonabsorbable suture, intramedullary rod fixation placed antegrade or retrograde, a combination of tension band and intramedullary rod fixation, and fixation with plates and screws.

***Plate-and-Screw Fixation.*** Traditional techniques of plate-and-screw fixation assumed extensive soft tissue dissection. In reality, plate-and-screw internal fixation does not require extensive soft tissue dissection and stripping. The fracture can be reduced with indirect techniques and the plate applied to the proximal end of the humerus. Unfortunately, the screws often do not hold well in the cancellous bone of the humeral head. Instead of predrilling the screw holes with a drill bit, a smaller K-wire can be used to improve screw fixation. Smaller cancellous screws often have better purchase than larger screws do because more threads engage the cancellous subchondral bone.

This technique is even more difficult in an elderly patient with osteoporosis. Plates, when secure, provide fixation for early rehabilitation but should be used with caution in patients with osteoporosis (Fig. 44–42). Traditional plate-and-screw fixation should be reserved for younger patients with good bone. A small-fragment cloverleaf plate (Synthes) can be modified to permit multiple-screw fixation without causing hardware impingement in the subacromial space[56] (Fig. 44–43).

Fixed-angle plates, such as a 90° blade plate or an angled semitubular or dynamic compression plate, can also be used. These plates do not rely on the screw–plate interface for stable fixation of the proximal segment of the humerus.

The three most common complications of plate-and-screw fixation are impingement of the hardware on the acromion, loosening and loss of reduction, and AVN.

In special cases, replacement of the humeral head will be beneficial for two-part fractures with a small osteoporotic head in an elderly patient.

***Combined Ender Rod and Tension Band Fixation.*** This procedure is performed under general anesthesia or an interscalene block with the patient in the beach-chair position. The patient is positioned high on a standard operating table and to the side so that the arm can be lowered over the edge for placement of the intramedullary rods through a deltopectoral approach.

Open reduction is accomplished through a deltopectoral approach. Interposed soft tissue is removed from the fracture site. This tissue may consist of the deltoid, when

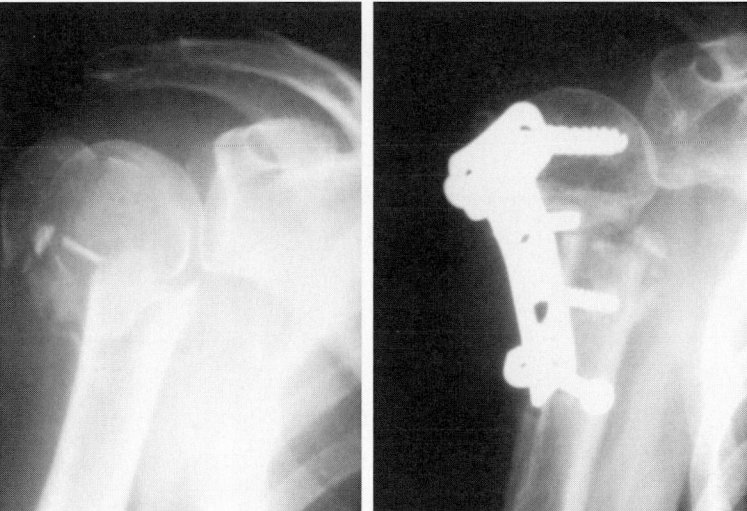

**FIGURE 44–42.** Two-part surgical neck fracture with a nondisplaced greater tuberosity fragment. Plates and screws pulled out of soft bone during the two operative attempts at open reduction and internal fixation.

the distal fragment has passed through it on the initial displacement, or the subscapularis or long head of the biceps (see Fig. 44–41). Holes for the modified Ender rods are made at the articular junction with the greater tuberosity (Fig. 44–44). Alternatively, Rush rods with a suture hole through the top hook, as modified by Watson,[241] can be used. Placement of these rods and the accompanying tension band sutures is technically demanding but provides intramedullary fixation, tension band compression over the fracture site, and sutures to keep the rods from migrating proximally.

With a suture passer, a no. 5 nonabsorbable braided suture is passed down one intramedullary entrance point and out the adjacent one proximally. This suture serves as

the top portion of the figure-of-eight tension band repair. The two free suture ends are passed through the top smooth rounded holes of the modified Ender or Rush rods.

A second set of holes are drilled in the shaft at a distance from the fracture site equal to that of the entrance point of the intramedullary rods. The figure-of-eight suture then crosses the fracture site for maximal tension band compression. One of the sutures is passed through the distal two drill holes in the shaft, which will later permit suture tying distal to the fracture site. The next two sutures are passed through one of the distal drill holes and up the intramedullary portion of the shaft beyond the fracture site. One suture is then passed through each of the proximal intramedullary rod entrance holes, through

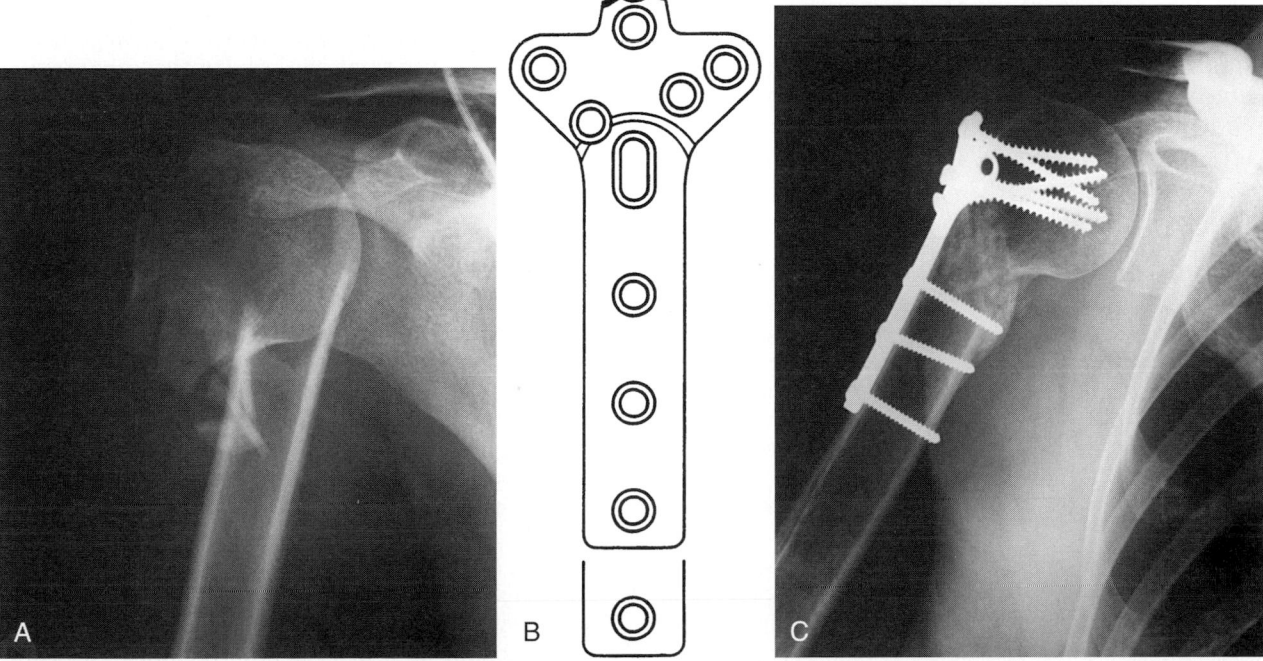

**FIGURE 44–43.** *A*, Radiographs of a 47-year-old woman who sustained a displaced surgical neck fracture when she was struck by a motor vehicle. *B*, Modification of a small-fragment cloverleaf plate (Synthes). *C*, Follow-up radiographs demonstrated the healed surgical neck fracture.

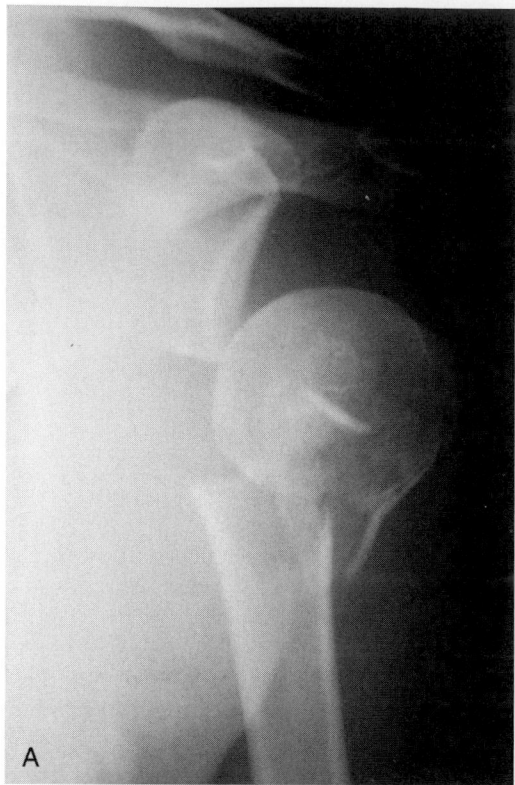
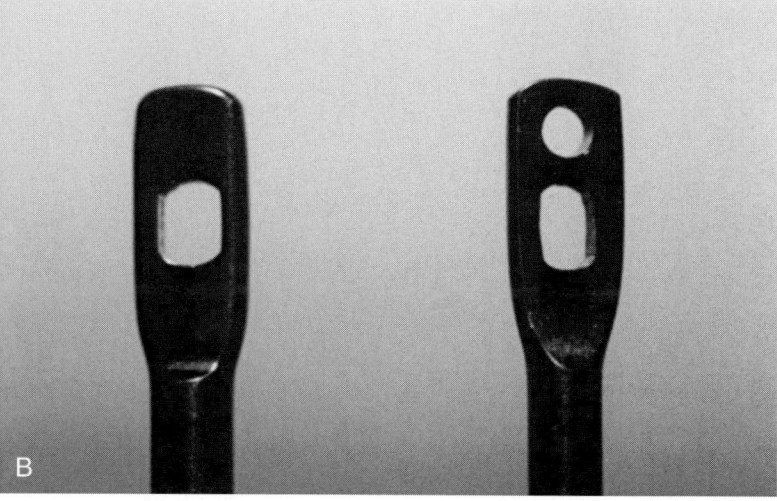

**Figure 44–44.** Technique of Ender intramedullary fixation combined with a tension band for a two-part surgical neck fracture. *A,* Unstable two-part surgical neck fracture with inferior humeral head subluxation. *B,* Modification of the Ender rod with a small superior hole for no. 5 nonabsorbable suture.

the eyelet of the Ender rod, and back down through the same intramedullary hole to be used for that rod. Both sutures subsequently exit distal to the fracture site through the opposite transverse hole drilled for the inferior portion of the tension band suture.

The intramedullary rods are passed down through their proximal entrance holes beyond the fracture site and into the intramedullary canal of the distal fragment. The fracture is anatomically reduced, and the rods are inserted just beneath the cortical entrance point proximally. The sutures through each rod are tied distally to prevent the rod from later being pulled in a superior direction by the tension band suture (see Fig. 44–44D). This technique ensures that no hardware impingement will occur, thus eliminating the need for later hardware removal. The tension band suture is tied tightly to provide secure fixation, and the compression across the fracture site permits early motion.

Fracture security is tested before closing the wound. The patient is placed in a sling, and pendulum exercises are initiated on the first postoperative day. With secure fixation, passive motion may be started in the early postoperative period, as discussed in the section on rehabilitation (see Fig. 44–44E and F).

Alternative techniques for intramedullary rod fixation include the use of narrow rods passed retrograde from the distal end of the humerus and locked intramedullary rods.[78] The former are less likely to maintain anatomic reduction, especially in patients with metaphyseal com-

minution. Locked antegrade rods are associated with subacromial problems. However, they are a good option in cases with significant comminution at the surgical neck level that extends more distally. Any soft tissue interposition is more easily removed by a direct or antegrade approach.

***Open Reduction and Percutaneous Pinning.*** The fracture is exposed through the deltopectoral approach, and the fragments are manipulated and reduced with minimally invasive techniques to preserve soft tissue attachments and vascularity (Fig. 44–45). Terminally threaded 2.5-mm pins are drilled through the deltoid tuberosity and up into the humeral head as described in the technique of closed reduction and percutaneous pinning. Additional fixation is gained with pins placed through the greater or lesser tuberosities and with wire, cable, or suture tension bands. Internal fixation can also be achieved with screws.

***Closed Intramedullary Rodding.*** Closed intramedullary rodding is a more recently developed technique for the operative treatment of displaced or unstable surgical neck fractures. Disadvantages of antegrade rodding include postoperative rotator cuff problems. Advantages include the fact that the procedure does not further disrupt the soft tissue envelope of the proximal end of the humerus and the rod is more centrally placed within the humerus. Stable fixation can be obtained, which facilitates early rehabilitation.

**Metaphyseal Comminution.** Surgical neck fractures with metaphyseal comminution denote a greater degree of

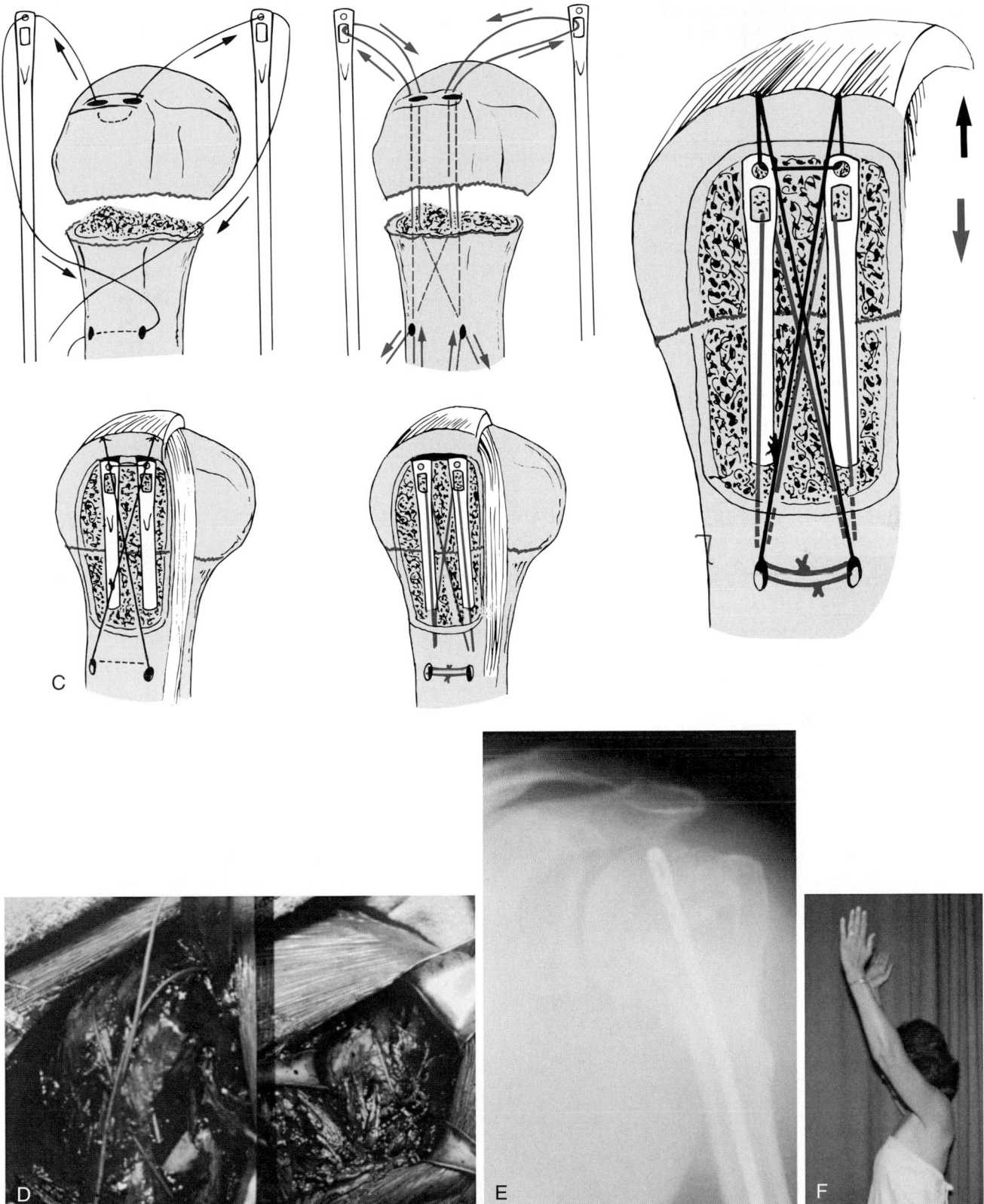

**FIGURE 44–44.** *Continued. C,* Technique of open reduction and internal fixation of two- and three-part surgical neck fractures with modified Ender rods. The superior hole is used for a figure-of-eight tension band. Additional sutures through the rods and secured through drill holes beyond the fracture site preclude migration of the rods into the subacromial space. *D,* Conversion of an unstable two-part surgical neck fracture to a stable one-part fracture that permits early motion. *E,* Satisfactory fracture healing 6 months postoperatively. *F,* Near-normal motion for elevation.

trauma and are more difficult to manage. The comminution can extend varying distances down the shaft. The intact rotator cuff holds the head in neutral rotation, whereas the pectoralis may pull one segment of the shaft in a medial direction. If placed in internal rotation with the forearm and hand against the abdomen, the fragments twist and collapse with shortening, the head may be pushed into a varus position by the upper part of the shaft, and an undesirable malunion or nonunion can result.

Closed pinning is not usually possible. A hanging arm cast has a tendency to lever anteriorly at the fracture site and thereby lead to nonunion or malunion. A posterior plaster slab beginning over the top of the shoulder and extending to the hand has less of a tendency to angulate the fracture than a hanging cast does. Coaptation splints or a fracture brace that extends over the lateral aspect of the shoulder can be used to maintain reduction and provide additional rotational control.

In patients with polytrauma, these fractures are even more difficult to manage by closed means. We prefer to achieve early anatomic reduction secured by internal fixation rather than risk malrotation, shortening with collapse, nonunion, or malunion, followed by a more difficult secondary reconstruction in a stiff, painful shoulder.

Antegrade intramedullary rod fixation combined with tension band sutures provides good axial stability. Heavy absorbable cerclage sutures can be used to secure the intermediate fragments with the attached pectoralis major and latissimus dorsi. The fracture fragments can be manipulated to ensure that the cerclage sutures do not include any neurovascular structures. Standard Rush rods should not be used because they have a propensity to migrate cephalad before fracture healing (Fig. 44–46). Locked rigid antegrade rodding provides the most stable fixation, but it also introduces problems related to violation of the subacromial space and rotator cuff.[144] Alternative internal fixation techniques include the Mouridian intramedullary rod with screw fixation into the head,[168] the AO cloverleaf or buttress plate and screws,[90] the AO 90° blade plate, and retrograde passage of flexible nails.[78, 81, 195] In all techniques, metaphyseal comminution, especially at the calcar region, is problematic and

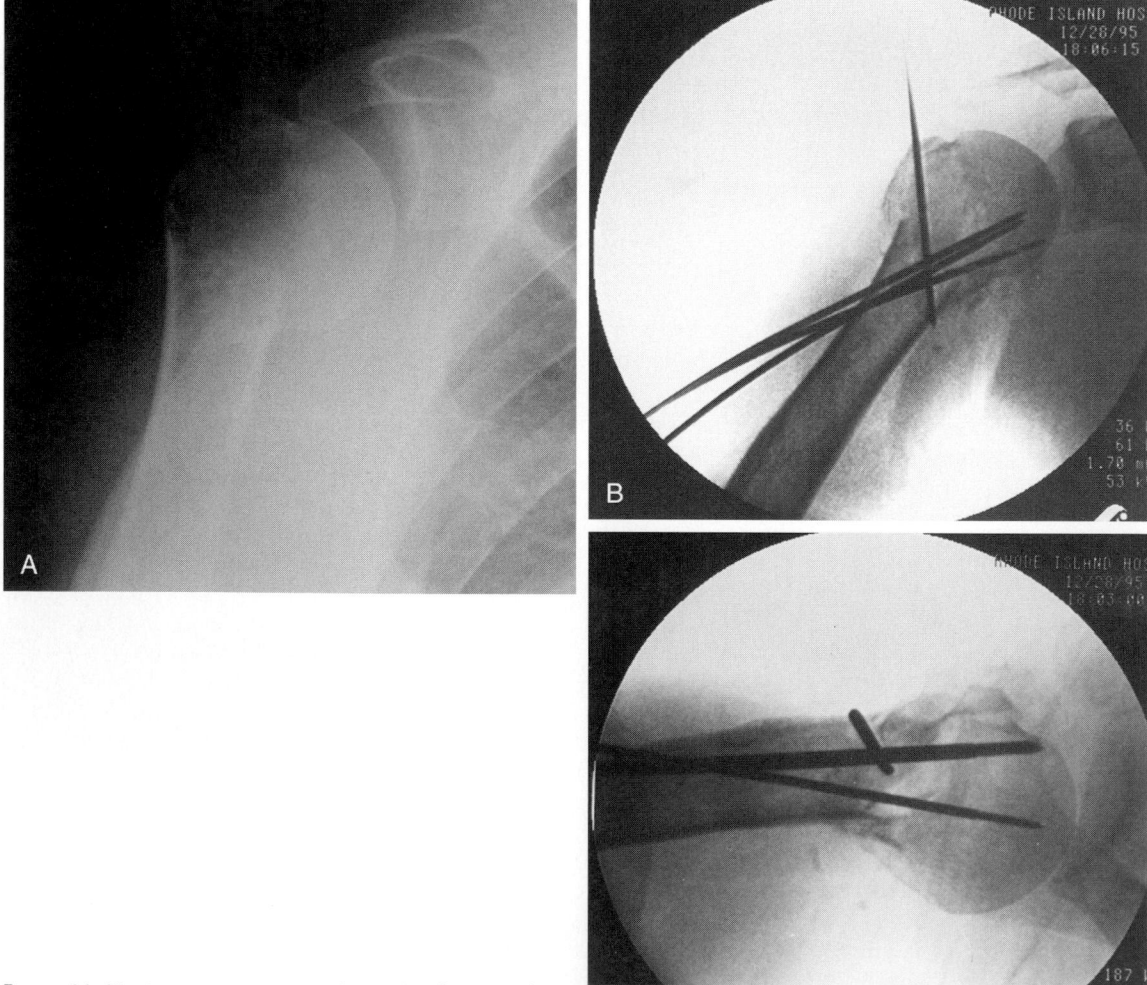

**FIGURE 44–45.** *A,* Anteroposterior radiograph of a severely angulated surgical neck fracture of the dominant arm of a 30-year-old hairdresser. *B, C,* Closed reduction was not possible, so open reduction plus percutaneous pinning was performed.

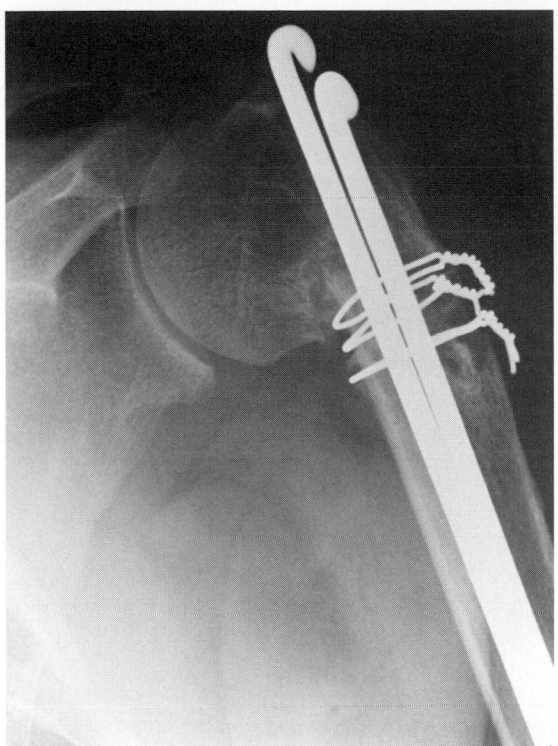

**FIGURE 44–46.** Radiographs of a 41-year-old man who sustained a displaced surgical neck fracture of the proximal end of the humerus when he was struck while riding a bicycle. The initial treatment of open reduction and internal fixation with a Rush rod and cerclage wiring resulted in nonunion of the surgical neck and palsy of the axillary nerve.

requires special attention. We prefer either locked rigid antegrade rods or a 90° blade plate.

Once the fracture is stabilized, aftercare is as described for other two-part surgical neck fractures treated by open reduction. Progress may be somewhat slower if the fragments are thought to lack stability.

**Surgical Neck Fracture with Glenohumeral Dislocation.** Glenohumeral dislocations with displaced surgical neck fractures are rare. This injury is associated with an increased risk of injury to the axillary artery or brachial plexus when compared with isolated surgical neck fractures alone. The neurovascular status must be carefully assessed and documented before reduction.

Closed reduction can be attempted with arm traction in flexion and adduction. In most of these dislocations, the humeral head is anterior, and it can be gently reduced with fingertip pressure. Any maneuvers that compress the brachial plexus (e.g., a socked foot in the axilla for countertraction) should be avoided.

ORIF is appropriate if closed reduction is difficult or the patient has a neurologic injury. The deltopectoral approach is used, similar to the technique for two-part surgical neck fractures. An anteriorly dislocated humeral head may require dissection off the brachial plexus. A bone hook is used to retract the humeral shaft laterally with the arm in forward flexion. The head is then gently manipulated off the brachial plexus and from the glenoid rim back into the joint.

A surgical neck fracture associated with posterior glenohumeral dislocation is even more uncommon. Even when the surgical neck fracture is nondisplaced, open reduction through the deltopectoral approach should be used to avoid displacement of the surgical neck fracture.

As with any dislocation in individuals older than 40 years, the chance of subscapularis avulsion occurring anteriorly or rupture of the supraspinatus and infraspinatus superiorly and posteriorly is significant. If found, the ruptured tendons are repaired back to their bony insertion through transosseous tunnels or with suture anchors and nonabsorbable sutures.

Fixation of a surgical neck fracture can be achieved with any of the variety of techniques described in the previous section.

Deltoid atony from trauma is more likely to occur after fracture-dislocation. The arm should be supported to reduce any inferior subluxation. Persistent inferior subluxation may be indicative of a nerve injury, rotator cuff tear, or humeral shortening (Figs. 44–47 and 44–48).

Rehabilitation for these fractures is prolonged and often underestimated. The initial emphasis is placed on gentle passive motion, followed by progressive active stretching and strengthening 6 to 8 weeks after injury.

### Greater Tuberosity Fractures

Two-part greater tuberosity fractures account for about 15% of displaced proximal humeral fractures with or without anterior dislocation[105] (Fig. 44–49). Chun and colleagues[28] found that displaced greater tuberosity fractures accounted for 26 of 141 two-part fractures. Greater tuberosity fracture occurs in 10% to 33% of anterior shoulder dislocations.[155, 166, 208, 243] It is the most common isolated fracture occurring in skiers.[243] Codman described it as one of the worst proximal humeral fractures because the supraspinatus is pulled off with the fracture.[30]

Anatomically, the greater tuberosity has separate facets for the supraspinatus, infraspinatus, and teres minor insertions. A rotator cuff tear is likely to be present in cases with more severe displacement of any or all of these facets. The more common displacement in the elderly population is a small fragment that retracts into the subacromial space with a supraspinatus tear. In a young patient, both the spinatus and the teres minor muscles retract the entire tuberosity posteriorly toward the spinoglenoid notch. This fragment may be difficult to see on an AP view, but in external rotation, the greater tuberosity will appear to be missing. Lateral scapular and axillary views visualize the displaced tuberosity. Additional evaluation with CT scans to determine the degree of displacement is indicated if operative treatment is being considered. CT more accurately depicts tuberosity displacement in the posterior and medial direction but can underestimate displacement in the superior direction.[26]

Despite Neer's criteria for displacement, most authors agree that the shoulder has very little tolerance for displacement of the greater tuberosity.[58, 158, 196] McLaughlin suggested that displacement greater than 5 mm is problematic.[158] More recently, Park and co-workers suggested that fractures with 3 mm of displacement should be reduced in athletes and heavy laborers who are involved in overhead activity.[196] In view of the fact that the greater

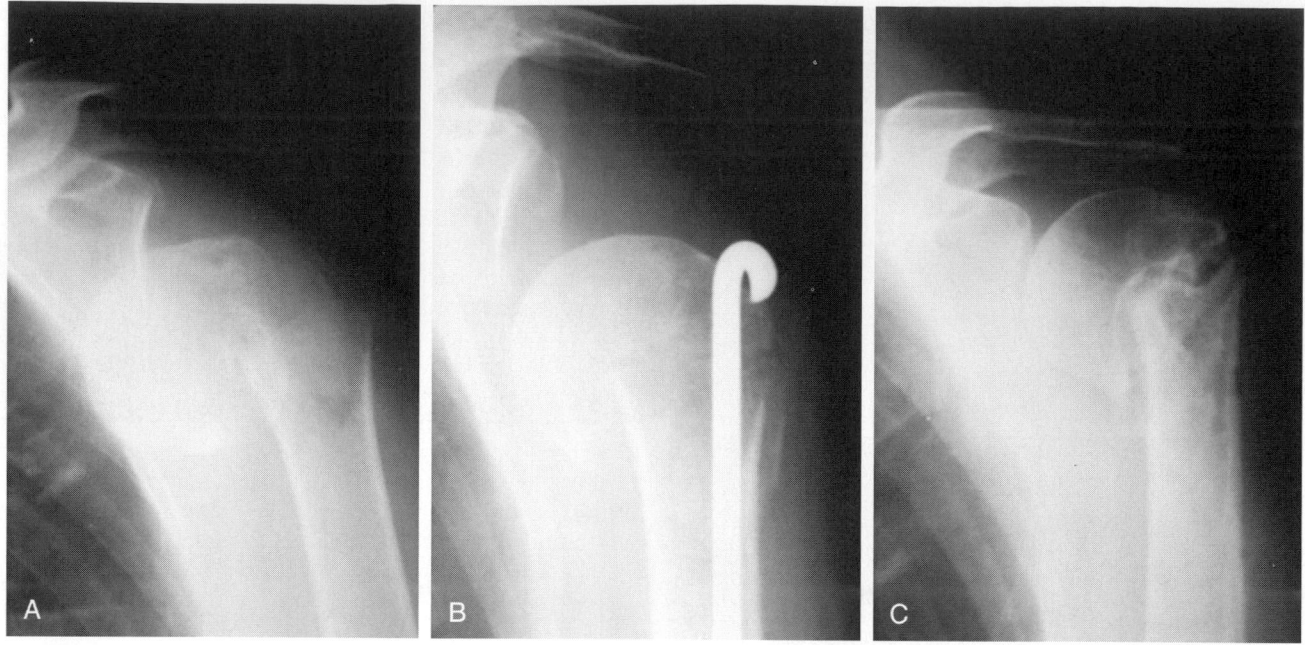

**FIGURE 44–47.** Two-part surgical neck fracture and anterior dislocation with associated axillary nerve injury noted after previous attempts at closed reduction. *A,* Injury film. *B,* Appearance after open reduction and internal fixation with an intramedullary rod and a figure-of-eight suture tension band. Initially, inferior humeral head subluxation was noted, but it resolved as the axillary nerve recovered (*C*).

tuberosity is on average 8 ± 3.2 mm below the top of the articular segment, it appears that even small amounts of displacement can affect shoulder function.[100]

The effect of the direction of displacement is important. Superior displacement that causes subacromial outlet impingement is less tolerated than posterior displacement. Thus, although many authors have used 1 cm as an indication for open reduction of a displaced greater tuberosity fracture, such displacement is excessive.[27, 44, 45, 156, 167, 174–177, 209, 242] Current indications for operative treatment include displacement greater than 5 mm and displacement at or above the most superior point of the articular surface of the humeral head.[155, 240]

Late impingement can occur even with nearly anatomically reduced fractures because of scar tissue formation.

Early surgery is preferred to avoid scarring and fixed retraction of the rotator cuff. A malunited greater tuberosity will block elevation or external rotation and thereby result in a stiff, weak, and painful shoulder. With time, the articular segment can soften, and with late treatment, a humeral head or total-shoulder replacement might be required (Fig. 44–50).

Acute displaced fractures are accessed through the superior deltoid-splitting approach (Fig. 44–51). The hemorrhagic bursa is excised. Nonabsorbable braided no. 2 or 5 sutures are placed through the rotator cuff at its

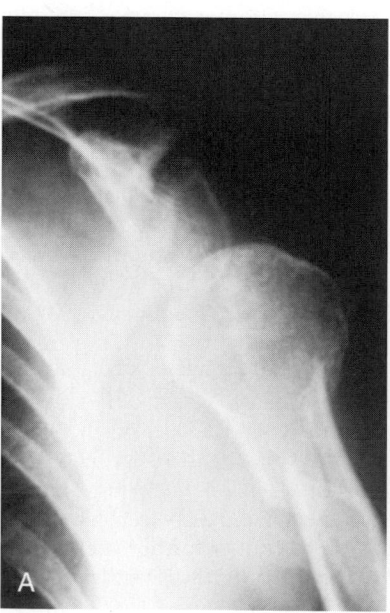

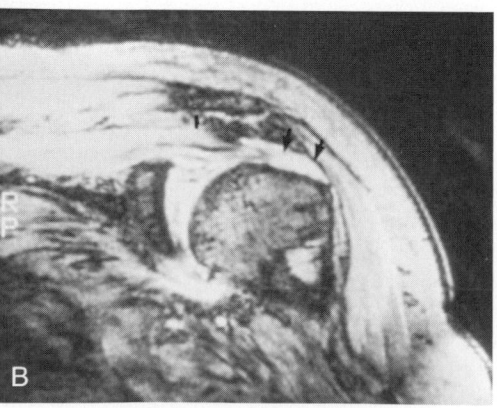

**FIGURE 44–48.** *A,* Inferior glenohumeral subluxation is frequently associated with an acute fracture, bone loss, deltoid paresis, or a massive cuff tear. Two and one-half months after fracture, the persistent subluxation was secondary to muscle atony, and a supraspinatus tendon avulsion was demonstrated by magnetic resonance imaging (MRI). The electromyelogram was normal. Scanograms demonstrated only a 1-cm loss of humeral length through the fracture site. *B,* MRI showing the rotator cuff tear (*arrows*).

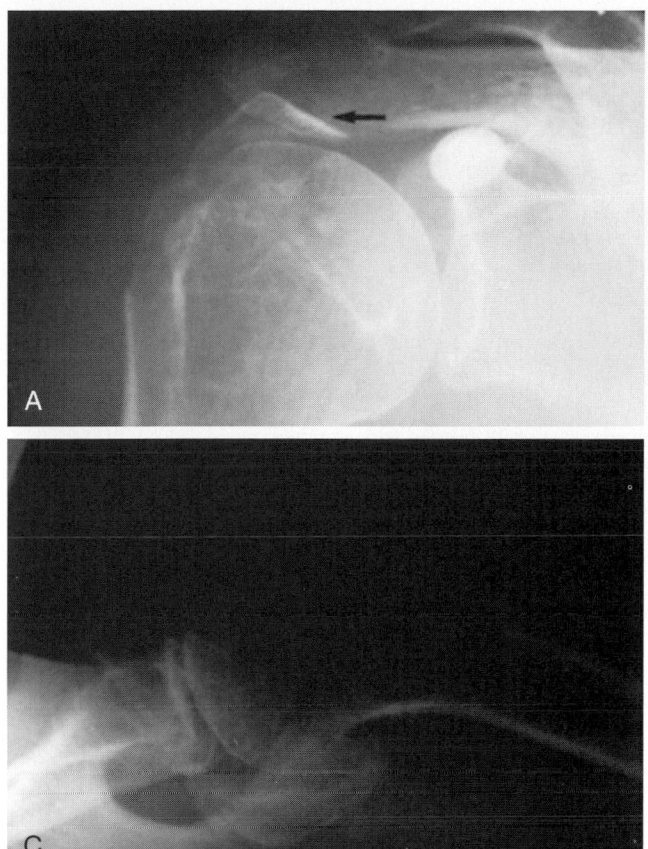

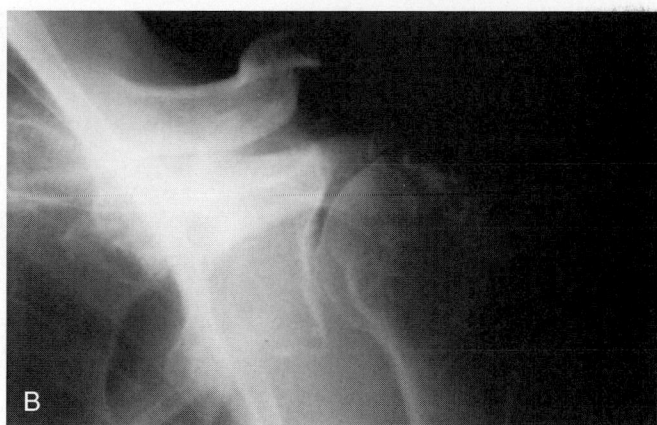

FIGURE **44–49.** Two-part greater tuberosity fracture with a rotator cuff tear. *A,* Two-part greater tuberosity avulsion involving the supraspinatus along with superior tuberosity retraction *(arrow).* Anteroposterior *(B)* and axillary *(C)* views of a neglected two-part greater tuberosity avulsion were obtained. The avulsion led to traumatic arthritis with posterior retraction of the greater tuberosity.

attachment to the greater tuberosity to facilitate mobilization of the tuberosity fragment. The humerus is rotated and abducted to allow anatomic repositioning of the fragment. Drill holes are made around the distal and anterior periphery of the fracture edge, and the greater tuberosity is fixed in place with multiple sutures. Sutures can be placed through the bone or around the greater tuberosity fragment at the rotator cuff insertion. The later technique reduces the chance that the fragment will be further crushed or that the suture will pull through a comminuted and osteoporotic bone fragment. The bone-tendon junction provides better fixation than an osteoporotic bone fragment does. We prefer no. 5 nonabsorbable suture. When severe comminution is present, the suture is placed into the tendon with a locking technique. Ideally, the cortical edge of the fragment can be aligned with the edge of the fracture bed on the proximal part of the humerus.[18] Suture that is placed in a figure-of-eight fashion across the fracture helps prevent over-reduction of the greater tuberosity[68] (Fig. 44–52F). Alternatively, wires or cables can be used for fixation.[58] The tuberosity may need to be trimmed to inset the fragment below the level of the humeral articular surface.

If operative treatment is required, the glenohumeral joint should be inspected to identify injury to the labrum and glenoid rim. In younger patients, a glenoid rim fracture or labral tear should be repaired.

Although screws and washers have been used for internal fixation of greater tuberosity fractures,[90] this technique is often complicated by loss of reduction because the bone quality of the tuberosity and screw purchase in the articular segment are poor. In addition, intra-articular screw penetration is a possible risk.[258]

Intraoperative complications to avoid include displacement of a nondisplaced or minimally displaced fracture at the surgical neck. Gentle manipulation, support of the humerus, and minimal rotatory torque protect the surgical neck. The fracture fixation can stabilize the surgical neck fracture if necessary.[185]

Aftercare is similar to that for one-part fractures; it begins with sling immobilization and early pendulum exercises and proceeds to advancing exercises at 4 to 6 weeks as tuberosity union progresses.

**Two-Part Greater Tuberosity Fractures Associated with Anterior Dislocation.** Greater tuberosity fractures occur in up to one third of anterior shoulder dislocations.[82, 155, 166, 208, 243] In some cases, the glenohumeral joint reduces spontaneously before emergency treatment and imaging documentation. In approximately two thirds of cases, the greater tuberosity reduces anatomically when the glenohumeral joint is reduced.[158]

Closed reduction of subcoracoid anterior dislocations is discussed in detail in the shoulder dislocation section. Excessive abduction or rotation with reduction increases the likelihood of trapping the greater tuberosity displaced under the acromion or fracturing the surgical neck. Once the shoulder is reduced, the extent of displacement of the tuberosity is assessed to determine further treatment. Operative and postoperative management is described in the previous section.

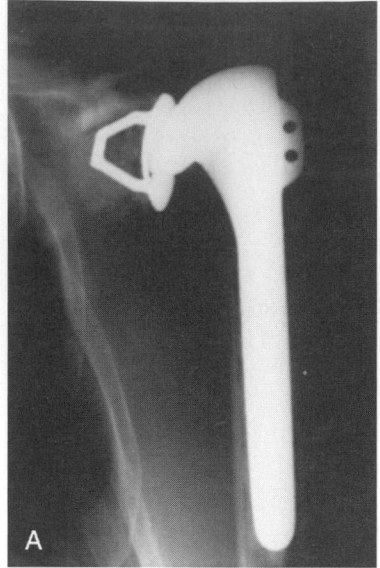

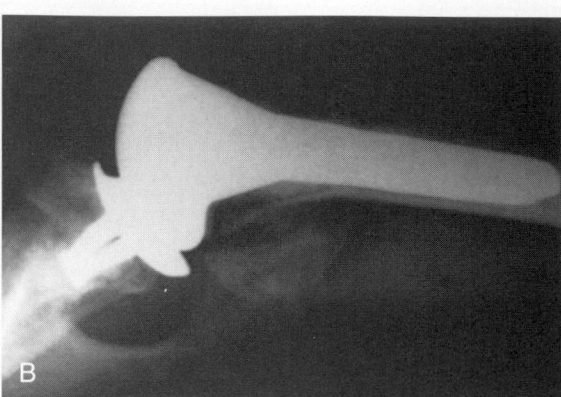

**FIGURE 44–50.** Two-part greater tuberosity fracture nonunion with traumatic arthritis treated by total-shoulder replacement with a short head prosthesis to permit reapproximation of the tuberosity. *A*, Anteroposterior view. *B*, Axillary view.

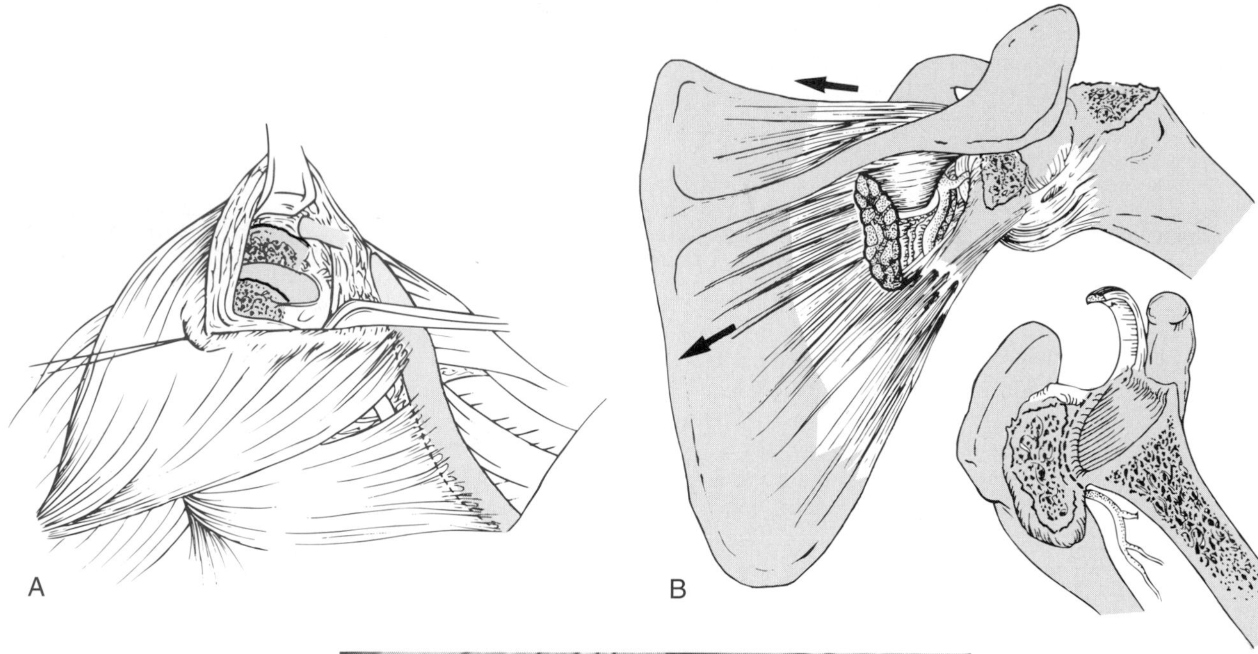

**FIGURE 44–51.** Two-part greater tuberosity fracture. *A*, The operative approach for a retracted greater tuberosity fragment necessitates splitting the deltoid fibers at the juncture of the anterior and the middle deltoid. For chronic or massive tuberosity avulsions, the anterior acromioplasty approach is used. *B*, The greater tuberosity is mobilized by release of bursa and scar superficially and by release of the posterior and superior glenohumeral capsule. The suprascapular nerve at the spinoglenoid notch can be injured by overaggressive dissection and release of the capsule. *C*, Traction sutures are passed around the tuberosity through the rotator cuff for mobilization and late repair as the tuberosity is replaced on the upper part of the humerus.

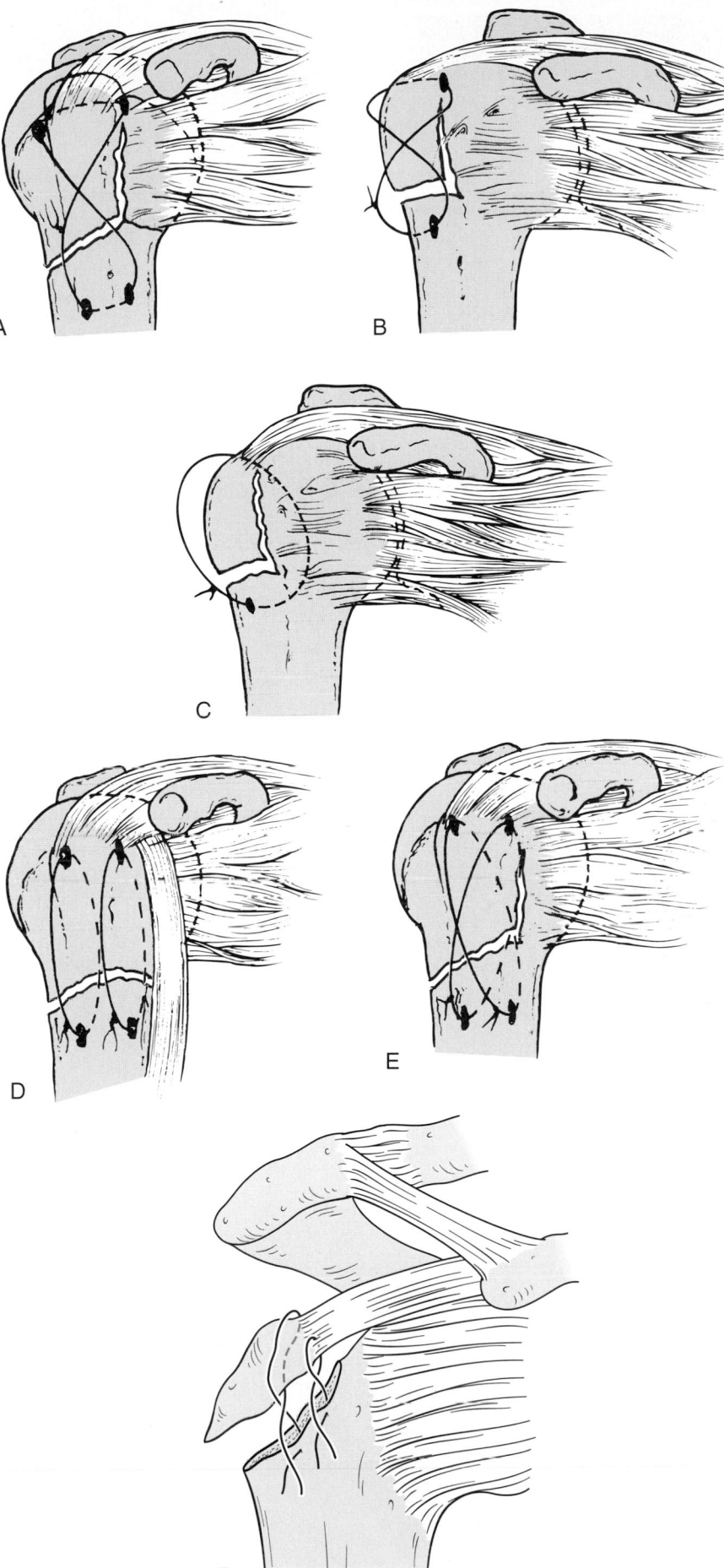

**FIGURE 44–52.** *A, B,* This suture does not include the tuberosity. It is passed through the soft tissue (rotator cuff), differentiated in *B,* in which the bone and cuff are included. In *A,* the suture may erode the cuff. *C,* Suture passage that includes the cuff insertion and tuberosity for good proximal holding power. The rotator cuff interval is closed between the supraspinatus and the subscapularis. *D,* Simple vertical or crossed sutures (shown in *E*) are satisfactory as long as the cuff is included. *E,* A suture through the tuberosity without including the hard bone at the cuff insertion may cut through the bone. *F,* A suture crossed through the fracture site prevents over-reduction of the greater tuberosity fracture.

Several scenarios account for the position of the greater tuberosity after anterior fracture-dislocation. The tuberosity fragment can be embedded in the glenohumeral capsular sleeve from which the humerus has dislocated.[155] On reduction, the tuberosity fragment assumes an anatomic position. In these situations, a tear of the rotator cuff interval may not have occurred and the reduction reapproximates any capsular stripping (Fig. 44–53A to E).

The greater tuberosity can remain displaced in patients with a tear in the rotator cuff interval. On reduction of the humeral head dislocation (see Fig. 44–53F to G), the tuberosity becomes displaced superiorly if the supraspinatus alone is involved (see Fig. 44–53H) or posteriorly toward the spinoglenoid notch if the supraspinatus, infraspinatus, and teres minor are involved. Early reduction and repair of the rotator cuff and tuberosity are essential to optimize shoulder function[155] (see Fig. 44–53F to H).

Less commonly, the greater tuberosity fractures and is displaced with the anteriorly dislocated humeral head. On reduction of the dislocation, the tuberosity is not accurately reduced (see Fig. 44–53I). This problem can occur with a rotator cuff tear from the tuberosity. Diagnostic tests

to evaluate the status of the rotator cuff and early treatment are indicated[155] (see Fig. 44–53J).

Finally, if the bicipital groove is fractured, the biceps tendon can dislocate posteriorly and prevent reduction[69, 107, 155] (see Fig. 44–53K). Open reduction is necessary to remove the interposed long head of the biceps before reduction of the fracture-dislocation.

If operative treatment is required, the glenohumeral joint should be inspected to identify injury to the labrum and glenoid rim. In younger patients, these injuries should be repaired.

### Lesser Tuberosity Fracture

Isolated two-part lesser tuberosity fractures are rare and account for only 0.27% of all proximal humeral fractures and 0.5% of displaced fractures.[105] The fracture may be confused with calcific tendinitis (Fig. 44–54). Although it can be clinically insignificant in the absence of a posterior dislocation,[177] displacement can cause internal rotation weakness, limitation of internal rotation, or coracoid impingement. The clinical relevance of displacement of the lesser tuberosity is not known because of the rarity of this fracture.

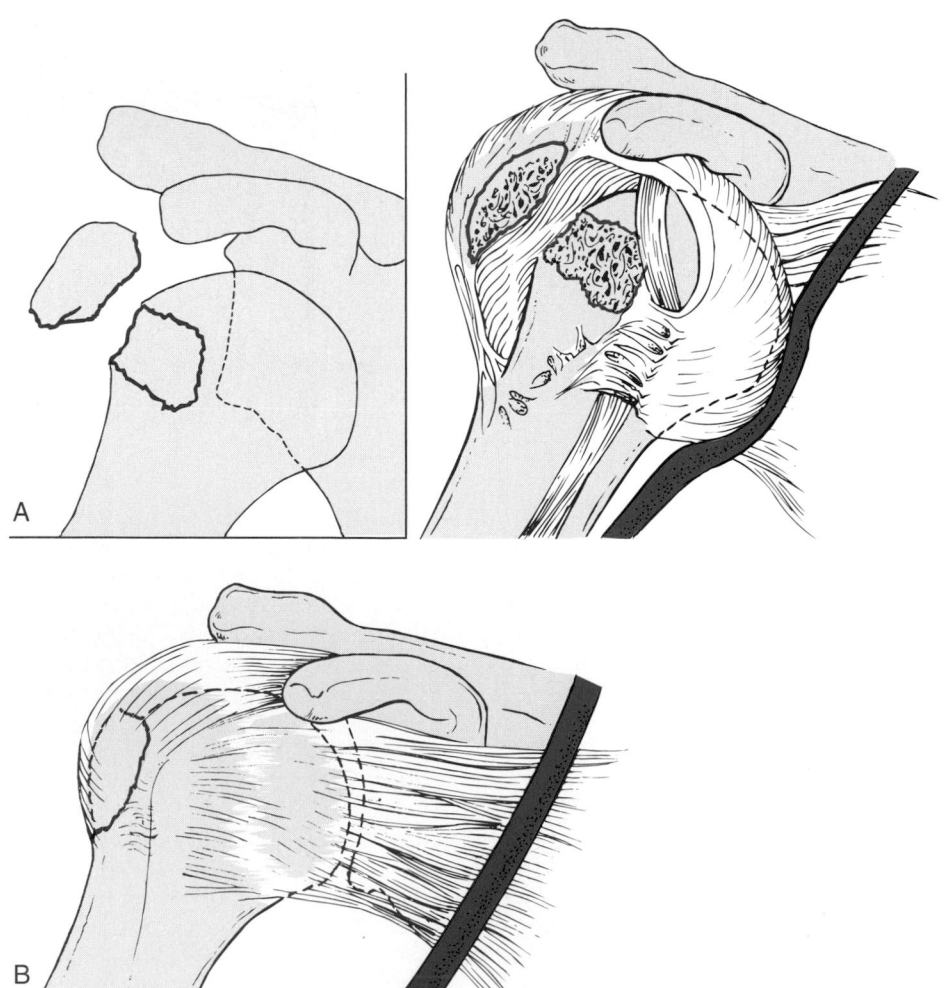

**FIGURE 44–53.** Variations of pathology in two-part greater tuberosity fractures associated with anterior shoulder dislocations. *A* to *E*, Capsular stripping without a rotator cuff tear. *A*, Anterior dislocation with displacement of the greater tuberosity allowed by capsular stripping in the absence of a rotator cuff tear. *B*, Anatomic reduction of the tuberosity with reduction of the shoulder dislocation and closure of the capsular envelope.

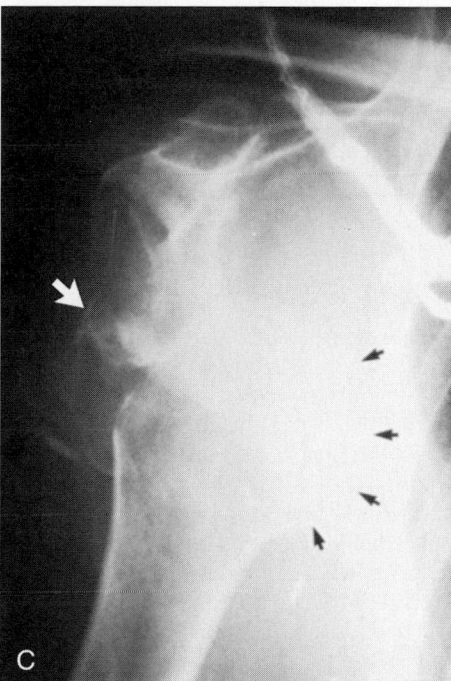

**FIGURE 44–53** *Continued. C, D,* Clinical examples of the pathologic conditions depicted in *A* and *B* with no cuff tear on arthrography *(E)*.

*Illustration continued on following page*

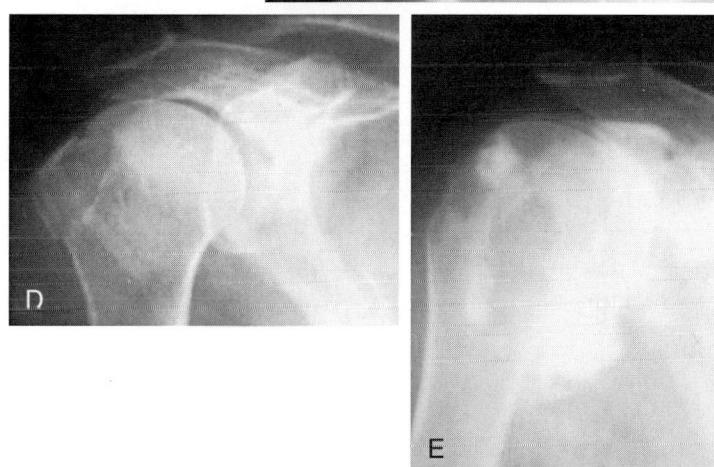

In the absence of an associated posterior dislocation, treatment consists of early sling protection, followed by early gentle motion to prevent stiffness. With displacement of more than 1 cm, ORIF may be considered. If a portion of the articular surface accompanies the lesser tuberosity, malunion with a block to internal rotation may occur. In this case, ORIF is recommended (Fig. 44–55).

Preoperative planning, aside from caring for other associated injuries, requires adequate imaging studies to evaluate displacement of the tuberosity, involvement of the articular surface, and possible associated nondisplaced fractures at the surgical neck or missed posterior dislocations. The typical AP shoulder radiograph may not clearly demonstrate a displaced lesser tuberosity that overlies the proximal part of the humerus.

A technique for repair with screw fixation is shown in Figure 44–56. If the articular surface is not significantly involved, screw fixation is used—or suture fixation when screw fixation is not adequate (Figs. 44–57 and 44–58). The deltopectoral approach is used for repair, with the

coracoid muscles left intact. Special care is taken to preserve the anterior circumflex humeral vessels and protect the axillary nerve at the inferior border of the subscapularis. Sutures are placed through the subscapularis insertion around the lesser tuberosity. Deep sutures are placed through drill holes in the humeral head and pass from the avulsion site to the greater tuberosity (see Figs. 44–57 and 44–58). If necessary, the lesser tuberosity is thinned to facilitate more accurate inset into the fracture bed and prevent coracoid impingement. The sutures are tied and tested for security. The rotator cuff interval is closed, and then the glenohumeral joint is evaluated for stability before a layered closure (see Fig. 44–57).

Postoperatively, a sling is worn for 4 to 6 weeks. Pendulum exercises are started the first postoperative day, with progression to supine passive elevation and external rotation and to standing internal rotation. Isometric external rotation and deltoid exercises can be initiated early after surgery. By 6 weeks after surgery, active use is permitted.

**Two-Part Lesser Tuberosity Fracture with Posterior Dislocation.** Posterior dislocation is associated with a lesser tuberosity fracture in 1.3% of all displaced proximal humeral fractures[105]; thus, it occurs more frequently than an isolated lesser tuberosity fracture. Unfortunately, unless adequate imaging studies in the axial plane are obtained, the dislocation may be missed. As in all dislocations, the incidence of nerve injury is higher than with fractures alone. Preoperative planning includes careful documentation of neurovascular status and axillary views or CT scans to assess the amount of articular surface involvement. These fractures may also be associated with a nondisplaced fracture of the surgical neck.

General or interscalene block anesthesia is recommended to lessen the chance of displacing other fractures. If the surgical neck is not fractured, closed reduction is attempted. The arm is brought into forward flexion and adduction. With longitudinal traction and pressure on the humeral head from behind, the posterior dislocation is reduced while lowering the arm. An image intensifier is used to facilitate documentation of the reduction.

Once the fracture is reduced, closed treatment presents a challenge. Better apposition of a displaced lesser tuberosity is expected if the arm is internally rotated. However, in this position the shoulder may redislocate. The more important lesion to treat is the dislocation.

Immobilization in 10° external rotation and 10° extension with the arm at the side allows the posterior capsule to heal. If the lesser tuberosity displacement is significant, it should be treated with ORIF as described earlier. In patients with an associated surgical neck fracture, open reduction is necessary. With the patient in the beach-chair position and under general anesthesia or an interscalene nerve block, the lesser tuberosity is identified through the deltopectoral approach. Traction sutures are passed around the lesser tuberosity, and a Darrach elevator or Fukuda retractor is placed across the glenoid to gently lever the humeral head back into the joint. Gentle external rotation allows placement of a flat elevator under the head. Once the humeral head is reduced, the lesser tuberosity is repaired, and the arm is supported with a cast or brace at the side in 10° of extension and 10° of external rotation for 4 to 6 weeks to allow the posterior capsule to heal.

Variations in operative findings may require alternative treatment. In patients with an anterior articular impression fracture of up to 40% of the entire humeral articular surface, two options are available. The first is to transfer the lesser tuberosity into the defect and fix it with a screw.[177, 180] Alternatively, a segmental osteochondral allograft can be used to replace large anterior humeral head defects.[35, 66] Larger head defects that involve greater than 40% of the articular surface are treated with primary

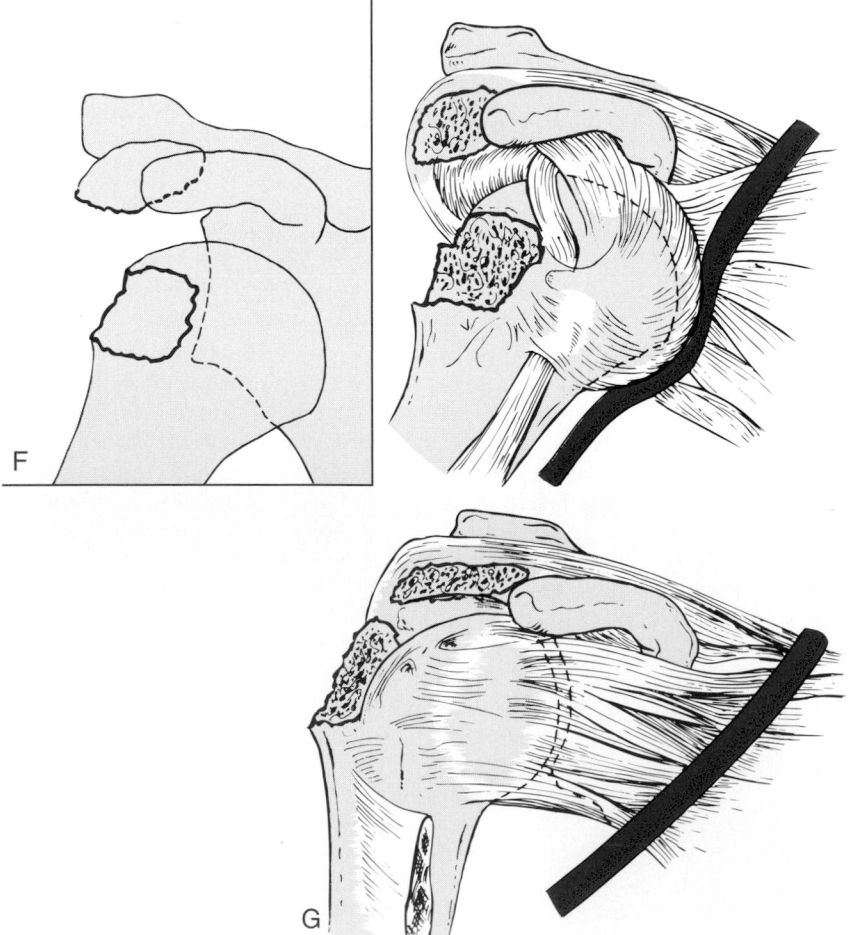

**FIGURE 44–53** *Continued. F to H,* Greater tuberosity avulsion associated with a longitudinal rotator cuff interval tear between the subscapularis and the supraspinatus. *F,* Anterior dislocation and greater tuberosity fracture with a longitudinal tear of the rotator cuff at the rotator interval between the supraspinatus and the subscapularis. *G,* Persistent greater tuberosity retraction superiorly with a supraspinatus tear after closed reduction.

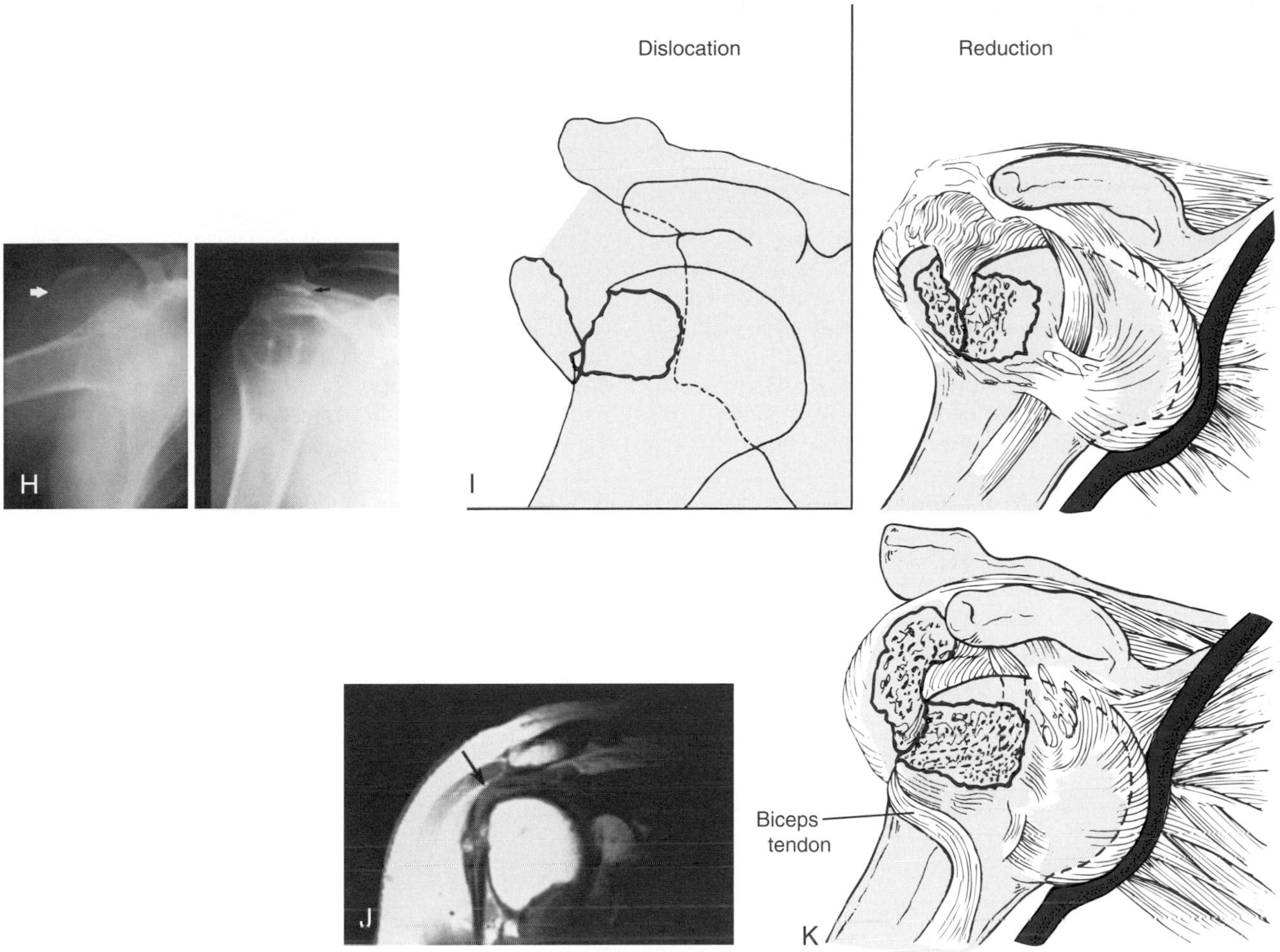

Dislocation                    Reduction

**FIGURE 44–53** *Continued. H,* Clinical radiograph of *F* and *G. I,* Incomplete tuberosity displacement with the cuff detached from the tuberosity leading to a persistent tear on reduction. *J,* Magnetic resonance imaging documentation of persistent cuff avulsion from the anatomically reduced greater tuberosity. *K,* Greater tuberosity fracture or tear of the transverse humeral ligament, or both, permits interposition of the long head of the biceps, which precludes closed reduction.

arthroplasty.[70] More detailed discussion of the treatment of posterior fracture-dislocation is presented in the section on glenohumeral dislocation.

The timing of surgery influences the treatment. In late cases, scarring precludes safe closed reduction. With later treatment, degenerative joint changes may necessitate humeral replacement or possibly total-shoulder replacement. Active rather than passive range-of-motion exercises immediately after cast removal enable earlier rehabilitation. Forceful rotation is avoided. As with any

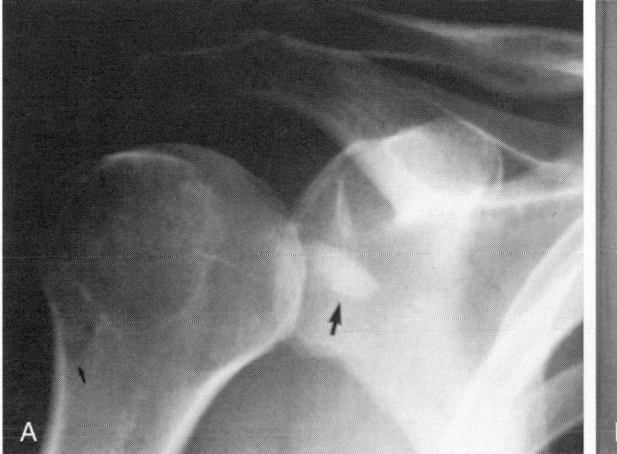
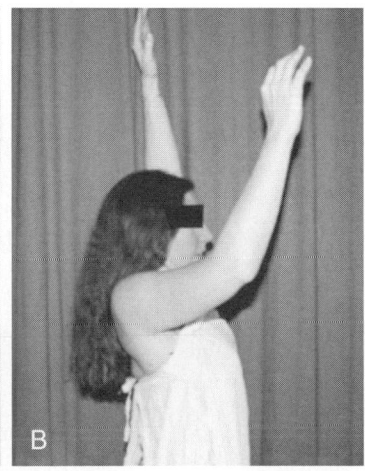

**FIGURE 44–54.** Two-part lesser tuberosity fracture resulting in late stiffness. *A,* Lesser tuberosity avulsion *(arrow)* could be confused with a calcium deposit. *B,* Restricted elevation 9 months after closed fracture treatment.

posterior dislocation, elevation in the scapular plane is preferable to straight shoulder flexion in early rehabilitation because it avoids undue stress on the posterior capsular tissues.

### Results of Two-Part Fracture Treatment

**Surgical Neck Fractures.** Although surgical neck fractures are common, they infrequently require operative treatment. Consequently, few reports have described the results of operative treatment. Chun and colleagues treated 90% of surgical neck fractures with conservative methods.[28] Ninety-three percent of those treated with a sling had an acceptable functional result. Jaberg and associates included 29 two-part surgical neck fractures in a series of proximal humeral fractures that were treated by closed reduction and percutaneous pinning.[103] They reported 14 excellent, 4 good, and 8 fair results (62% excellent and good results). Cuomo and coauthors reported 70% good and excellent results in 14 two-part fractures but did not comment on the number of cases in which intramedullary rods were used.[39]

**Greater Tuberosity Fractures.** Despite the relative frequency of displaced greater tuberosity fractures, especially in association with anterior glenohumeral dislocation, the results of treatment are not commonly reported. Fortunately, most displaced greater tuberosity fracture-dislocations reduce anatomically with reduction of the glenohumeral dislocation.

Closed treatment of displaced two-part greater tuberosity fractures generally leads to a poor outcome. Depending on the physician's experience, displacement of the greater tuberosity has been associated with poor results if the tuberosity remains displaced between 0.5 and 1.5 cm or more.[116, 162, 175] Clifford reported good results in only 50% of fractures, whereas 100% of fracture-dislocations had poor results with closed treatment.[29] McLaughlin found that patients who had greater than 1 cm of displacement had significant disability and that even patients with between 0.5- and 1-cm displacement had a prolonged recovery, with 20% requiring a reconstructive procedure.[158] Although Young and Wallace reported good and acceptable results in seven patients treated nonoperatively,

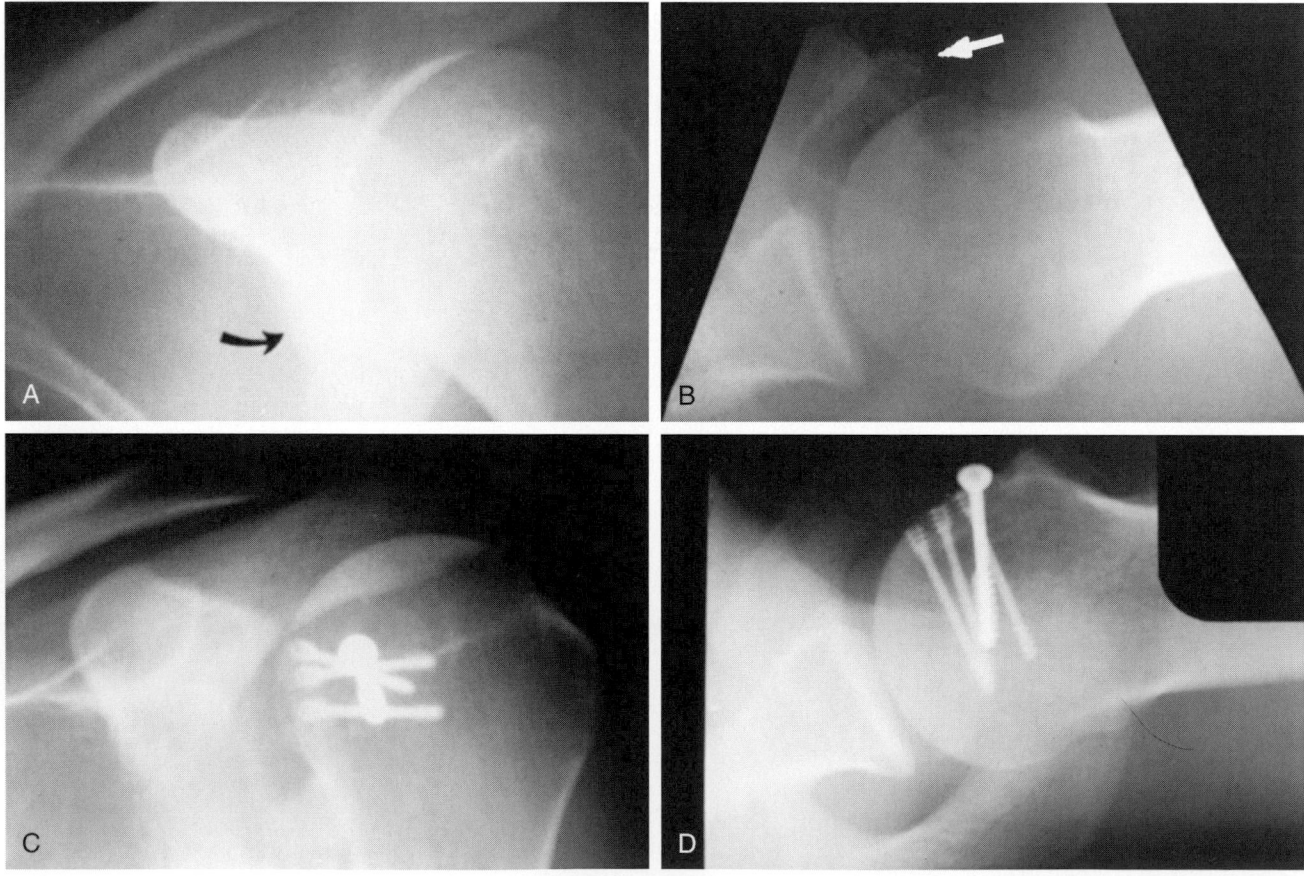

**FIGURE 44–55.** Herbert screw fixation of head-splitting fracture. *A* and *B*, Anteroposterior (AP) and axillary radiographs of a 25-year-old patient in whom a motor vehicle accident caused multiple injuries: a grade II open femoral fracture and a displaced lesser tuberosity fracture (*arrow in A*) that included a 1.5- × 2.0-cm anteroinferior articular fragment. A separate fragment of the lesser tuberosity formed the upper medial aspect of the biceps groove. *C* and *D*, AP and axillary radiographs taken 7 months postoperatively. A deltopectoral approach was used to elevate the subscapularis from the capsule. The articular surface was anatomically reduced, provisionally fixed with Kirschner wires, and then permanently fixed with three Herbert screws 1 to 2 mm below the articular surface (one medially for compression and one each in the superior and inferior capsular reflection). A 4.0-mm cancellous screw was placed extracapsularly to restore the lesser tuberosity and biceps groove. Seven months later, full painless range of motion was restored without avascular necrosis or hardware loosening. (*A–D*, From Lange, R.H.; et al. Orthopedics 9:1393–1398, 1986.)

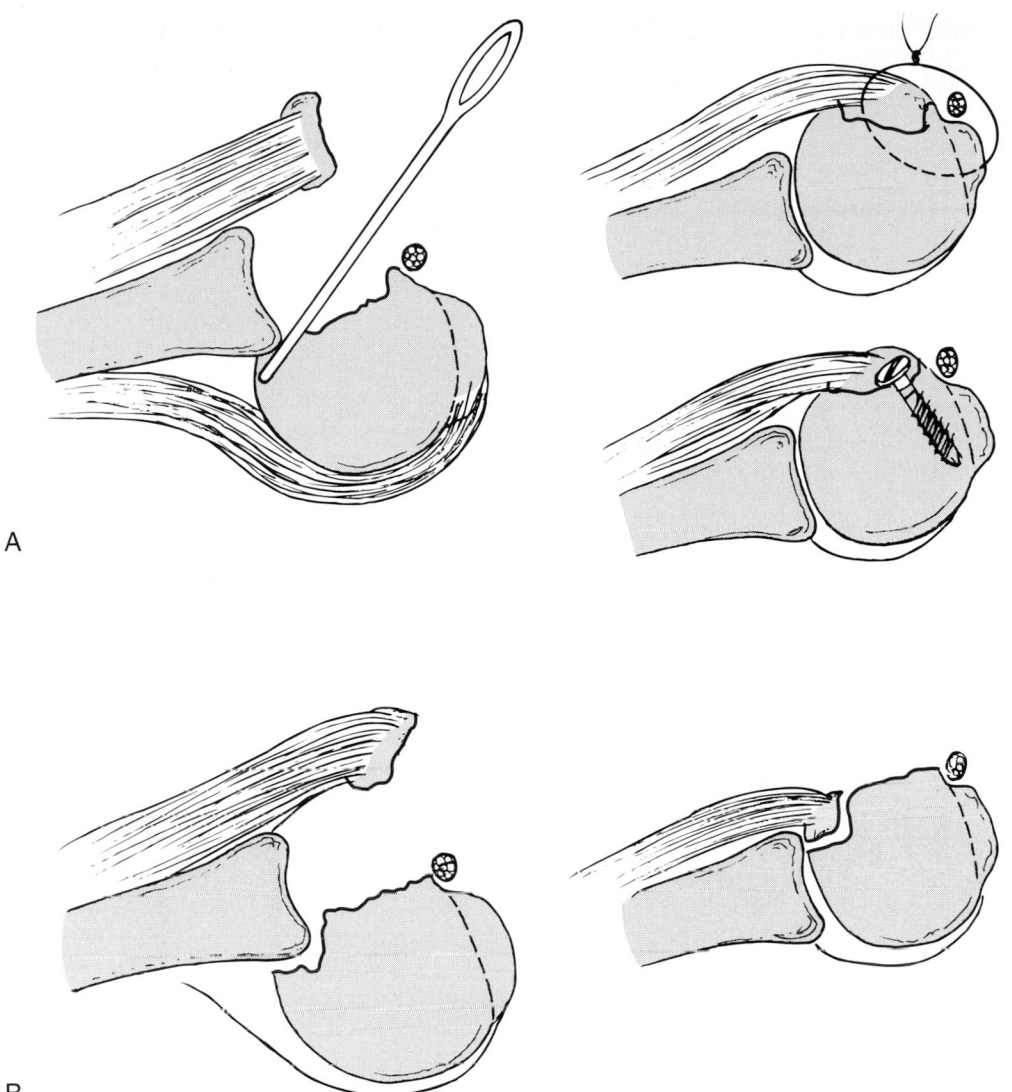

**FIGURE 44–56.** Technique for repair of a two-part lesser tuberosity fracture with posterior dislocation. *A,* A Darrach or flat elevator is used to dislodge the posteriorly dislocated head. A suture or screw secures the tuberosity back to its premorbid position. *B,* The lesser tuberosity is transferred into the anterior humeral head impression fracture associated with the posterior dislocation and repaired with sutures or screws.

they did not use stringent criteria for shoulder motion.[256] Nevertheless, their patients were satisfied with the function of their shoulder and reportedly had no pain.

Only a few published follow-up studies have addressed the surgical treatment of displaced fractures. Jakob and coauthors reviewed a series of 930 operatively treated proximal humeral fractures that included only 17 isolated displaced fractures of the greater tuberosity.[105] They did not report the results of treatment. Paavolainen and colleagues reported good results when they fixed six displaced fractures of the greater tuberosity with screws.[194] Among the 141 two-part proximal humeral fractures reviewed by Chun and co-workers were 24 cases of greater tuberosity fracture.[28] They treated 10 of the greater tuberosity fractures with ORIF and 8 with screws and reported the results of 11 cases. Although they achieved one excellent, seven good, and three fair results, they did not specify whether these were the result of operative or nonoperative treatment. Flatow and colleagues reported 100% good and excellent results with ORIF of the greater tuberosity through an anterosuperior deltoid-splitting approach.[58]

## THREE-PART FRACTURES AND FRACTURE-DISLOCATIONS

In three-part fractures, the shaft and one tuberosity are displaced. The incidence varies in reported series from 3% to 29% of displaced proximal humeral fractures without dislocation.[105, 174, 177] Treatment options include benign neglect and early motion,[92] closed reduction and immobilization for 3 to 4 weeks,[84] ORIF,* and prosthetic replacement.[32, 70, 88, 175, 177, 185, 187, 235]

*See references 2, 29, 71, 77, 79, 85, 86, 128, 174, 175, 184, 194, 201, 215, 231, 233.

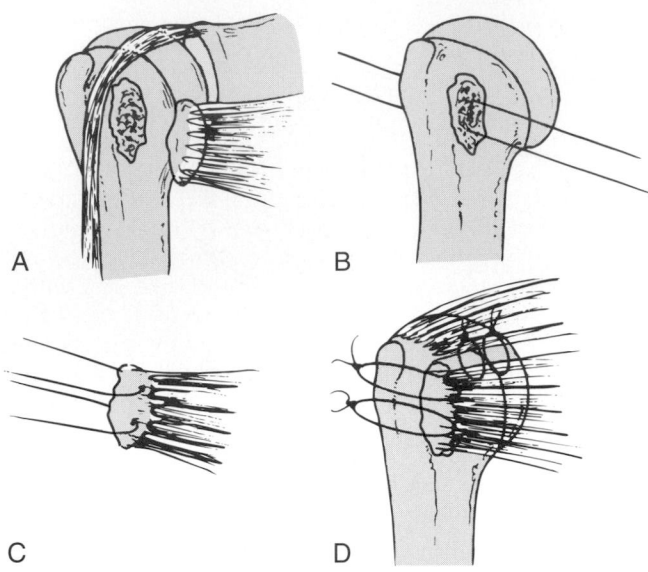

**Figure 44–57.** Suture fixation of a lesser tuberosity fracture. *A* to *C,* Heavy suture is placed through the subscapularis insertion site and then passed through the humeral head. *D,* The rotator cuff interval is repaired.

Closed treatment is indicated in patients for whom anesthesia is deemed unsafe, for some elderly patients with limited goals, or for those with alcoholism or a similar disorder who are unable to cooperate with postoperative rehabilitation. Although the likelihood of a satisfactory result with closed treatment is less than 50%, in some patients, especially the elderly, a result that achieves limited goals is satisfactory.[32, 140] Limitation of shoulder motion and function as opposed to pain is the usual late problem. Although Schai and associates reported better results with ORIF of three-part fractures than with conservative treatment, they also found that the results of conservative treatment of three-part fractures were generally satisfactory.[216]

Whereas preservation of vascularity to the articular segment is critical regardless of the technique of internal fixation, bone quality is the most important consideration in selecting the method of internal fixation. As is frequently the case, patients with three-part fractures and fracture-dislocations are often elderly and very osteopenic. In addition to the previously noted indications for closed treatment, contraindications to ORIF include osteoporosis or an inability to achieve satisfactory fixation. Severe osteopenia is an appropriate indication for prosthetic arthroplasty.

AVN rarely occurs after a three-part fracture unless the fracture has been treated by ORIF. The nondisplaced tuberosity often maintains the integrity of the intertubercular sulcus, thus protecting the arcuate artery, and provides a vascular anastomosis to the articular segment.

### Three-Part Greater Tuberosity Fractures

The shoulder is approached through the deltopectoral approach. The tendon of the long head of the biceps is identified and used as a guide to the proximal humeral anatomy. Care is taken to avoid dissecting around the tendon to preserve the vascularity to the articular segment. The displaced tuberosity is retrieved with traction sutures. Nonabsorbable sutures are placed through the rotator cuff insertion on the tuberosity for manipulation and reduction of the fracture relative to the humeral head, the other tuberosity, and the shaft. Several options may be used for fixation, including percutaneous pins,[103, 130] suture or wire[85] with or without intramedullary support,[39, 185] and plates and screws.[215, 231]

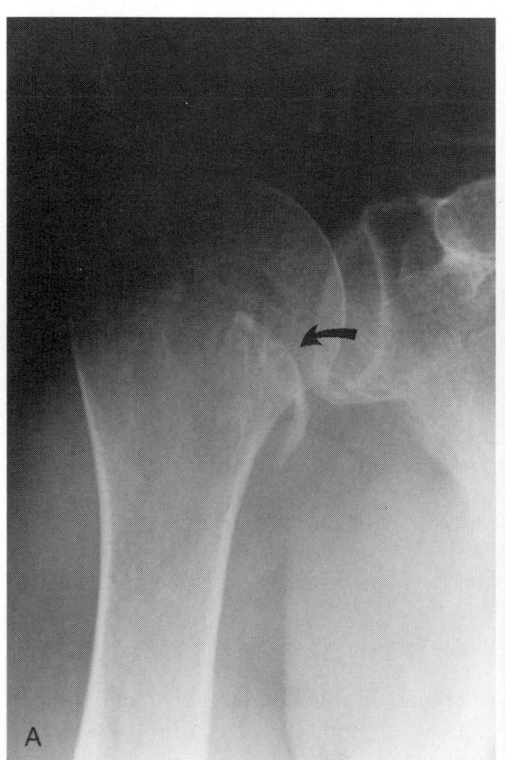
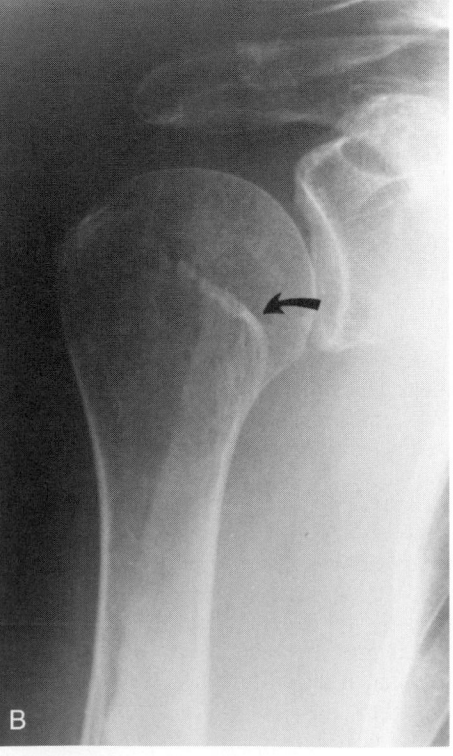

**Figure 44–58.** *A,* Anteroposterior radiograph of a displaced lesser tuberosity fracture *(arrow).* At surgery, a tear of the supraspinatus tendon was noted along with dislocation of the tendon of the long head of the biceps under the lesser tuberosity. *B,* The lesser tuberosity was reduced *(arrow)* and fixed anatomically with heavy nonabsorbable suture, the biceps tendon was relocated, and the supraspinatus tendon was repaired. The patient regained full active motion, strength, and function.

The technique for suture or wire fixation requires fracture reduction first between the tuberosities and the head.[85] Hawkins and coauthors described passing two 14-gauge colpotomy needles through the subscapularis and lesser tuberosity, through the head, and out through the greater tuberosity.[85] The malrotation of the head on the shaft is reduced. Two holes are drilled through the anterior of the humeral shaft below the greater and lesser tuberosity and deep to the biceps tendon. Two 20-gauge wires or no. 5 nonabsorbable braided sutures are used. The first is passed through the shaft and crosses the fracture in a figure of eight centered on the surgical neck fracture with one end through the colpotomy needle. This needle is then removed and the suture tied securely. The process is repeated with a second figure of eight through the second colpotomy needle, thereby converting this injury to a stable one-part fracture. Alternatively, no. 5 nonabsorbable sutures are placed by passing the attached heavy needle through drill holes in the lesser tuberosity and humeral head fragments. The sutures or wire should be passed under the biceps tendon. If the tendon is included in the repair, it will not glide in the bicipital groove during shoulder motion. If the biceps is fixed by tenodesis, the intra-articular segment should be resected to prevent limitation of external rotation. The rotator cuff interval tear is repaired. Stability is checked as the shoulder is passed through a full range of motion (Fig. 44–59A).

Intraoperative difficulties include a rotator cuff tear that requires mobilization and repair, as well as less than adequate holding power in soft bone. The suture can be woven into the rotator cuff to reduce the tendency for pull-out. Supplemental intramedullary rods with tension band closure between both tuberosities add additional stability with vertical fixation to the shaft and horizontal fixation to the intact tuberosity[123, 125, 248] (see Fig. 44–59B).

Although wire can be tied more securely than no. 5 suture, it has a tendency to cut through osteopenic bone and a propensity to break, and migration of the pieces poses a significant problem.[149, 177]

Plates (cloverleaf small-fragment, fixed-angle blade, and large-fragment T or L plates) provide another option in a younger patient. However, the possibility of postoperative hardware impingement and the additional surgical exposure with the resultant increased incidence of AVN make plates less desirable.[79, 231] When these fractures occur in elderly individuals, osteopenia is a relative contraindication to plate-and-screw fixation[85] (Fig. 44–60).

Prosthetic replacement is preferred in some elderly osteopenic patients when open reduction cannot ensure stable fixation and early mobilization of the shoulder. The lesser tuberosity is separated from the articular segment to create a four-part fracture, and reconstruction is carried out as described in the next section.

### Three-Part Lesser Tuberosity Fractures

Three-part fractures with displacement of the lesser tuberosity are much less common than those with displacement of the greater tuberosity. By virtue of the attachment of the lesser tuberosity, the articular surface is rotated anteriorly by the intact external rotators. Indications for and principles of surgery are the same as those for a three-part greater tuberosity and surgical neck fracture.

Careful evaluation is required to avoid missing a posterior fracture-dislocation.

### Prosthetic Shoulder Replacement

In very osteopenic older individuals, prosthetic arthroplasty can provide more secure fixation than ORIF can. When the osteopenia is severe, even the technique of suture fixation for a three-part fracture may not provide enough fixation stability. For a combined three-part fracture and midshaft fracture, operative treatment with a long-stem prosthesis and use of the resected head as a bone graft is an option that can simplify surgery and postoperative care. It also eliminates the risk of AVN, the need for hardware removal, and the risk of loosening or hardware impingement that is more common with plates and screws (Fig. 44–61).

### Fracture-Dislocations

Three-part fracture-dislocations occur in two patterns: anterior dislocation with a greater tuberosity fracture and posterior dislocation with a lesser tuberosity fracture. When compared with typical three-part fractures, fracture-dislocations have a greater incidence of acute neurovascular injury and late AVN after closed or open fixation.

With a displaced anterior three-part greater tuberosity fracture-dislocation, the subscapularis and anterior capsule may still provide some blood supply to the articular surface. Closed reduction is possible in forward flexion and gentle abduction, but open reduction through a deltopectoral approach is a more gentle approach that allows for accurate tuberosity repair, rotator cuff closure, and derotation of the head relative to the shaft. The surgical techniques and aftercare are described in the section on three-part fractures. Three-part lesser tuberosity fracture–posterior dislocations are often not well appreciated. An axillary view or CT scan may be necessary to diagnose displacement of the tuberosity, as well as the posterior dislocation.

The security of the repair for three-part fractures treated by internal fixation or prosthetic replacement and fixation of the tuberosity is determined at surgery. In most cases, the arm is placed in a sling at the side, and early pendulum motion is begun shortly after surgery. More aggressive stretching is avoided for the first 3 weeks; otherwise, fracture displacement can occur. A 45° abduction brace is used for 4 to 6 weeks if the tuberosity repair is under tension. Passive shoulder elevation and external rotation can be initiated even with abduction immobilization.[235]

Active range of motion begins at 6 to 8 weeks and light resistive exercises at 12 weeks. Six to 12 months of daily stretching and long-term therapy will be necessary to maximize the functional outcome. Hardware is removed if breakage, loosening, migration, or impingement occurs.

### Results

Some reports suggest that closed treatment of three-part fractures is associated with minimal to moderate pain and limited shoulder motion.[109] Prominence of the greater tuberosity above the articular segment and angulation at the surgical neck cause limitation of elevation. Rotation is limited by post-traumatic adhesions and malrotation at the surgical neck. Leyshon[140] reported 70% satisfactory results of nonoperative treatment of three-part fractures, whereas

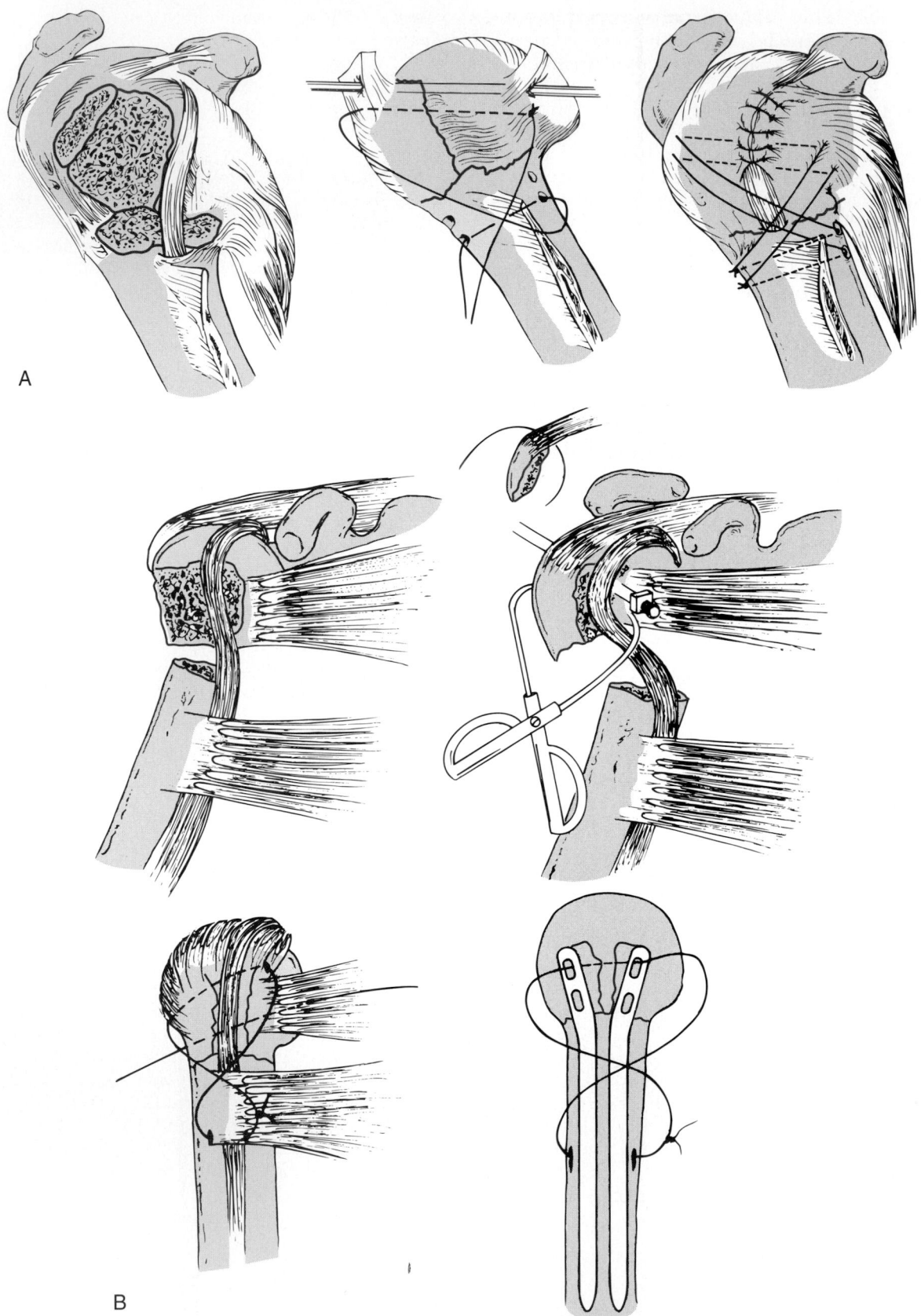

**FIGURE 44–59.** Techniques of three-part fracture fixation. *A,* Tension band fixation. *B,* Tension band combined with intramedullary rods. (*A, B,* Modified from Hawkins, R.J.; et al. J Bone Joint Surg Am 68:1410–1414, 1986.)

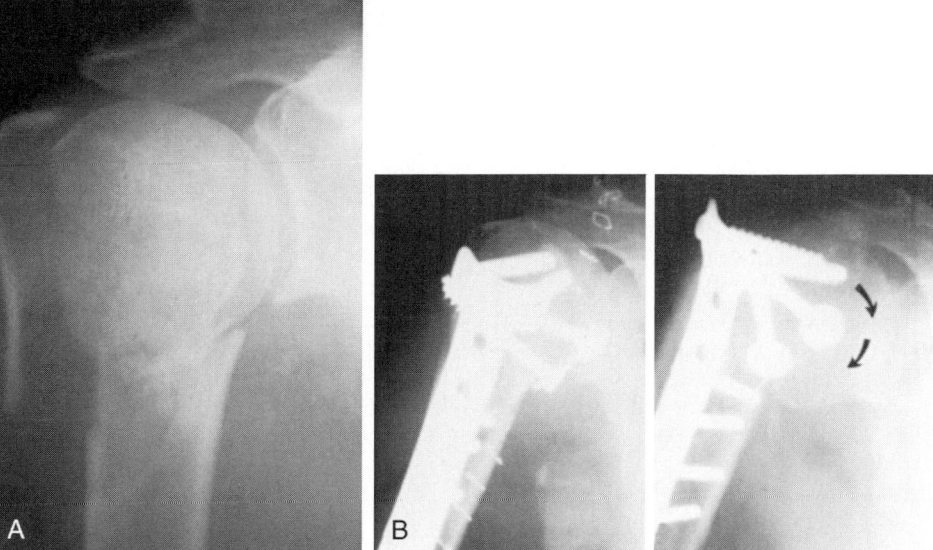

**FIGURE 44–60.** Poor screw-and-plate holding power in elderly patients with osteoporotic bone. *A,* Injury film showing a three-part greater tuberosity fracture. *B,* Postoperative radiographs immediately and at 4 weeks showing loss of fixation *(arrows)* and displacement of the humeral head fragment.

Neer[174] reported only 15% satisfactory results. More recently, Schai and colleagues[216] reported that the results of conservative treatment of three-part fractures were generally satisfactory.

Assuming that the tuberosities are accurately reduced and maintained without healing complications, the results of ORIF are good to excellent in about 80% of the cases reported.[39, 85, 116, 128, 175, 215, 231, 254] The reported average motion is about 130° total elevation and 30° external rotation.[85]

Savoie and coauthors reported satisfactory results in 12 three-part fractures treated by ORIF with an AO/ASIF large-fragment buttress plate.[215] Eleven of 12 underwent ORIF. Nine had a 2-year follow-up. A slightly better range of motion was noted in the five patients in whom an anterior acromioplasty was combined with open reduction of the fractures. This small group averaged 130° elevation and 35° external rotation.

Hawkins and colleagues reported the results of 14 three-part fractures treated with the tension band technique described earlier.[85] The average motion was 126° active elevation, 29° active external rotation, and passive internal rotation to the second lumbar level. Reoperations included prosthetic replacement after AVN and removal of broken and prominent wires.

Cuomo and associates reported satisfactory results in all of the three-part fractures in their series.[39] They used the Ender rod technique described earlier when comminution or instability of the surgical neck region was present.

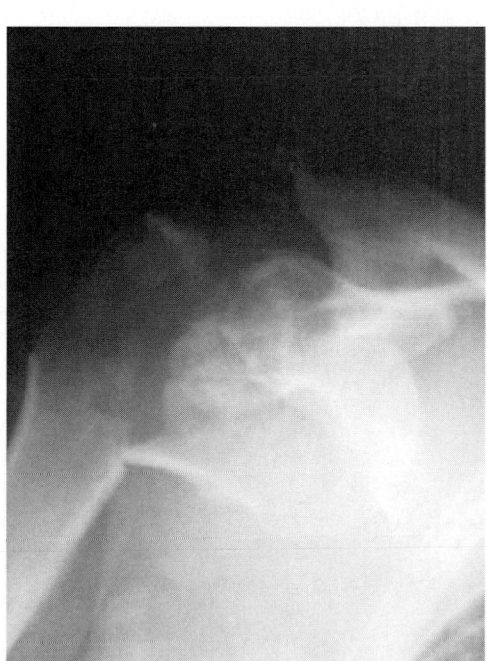
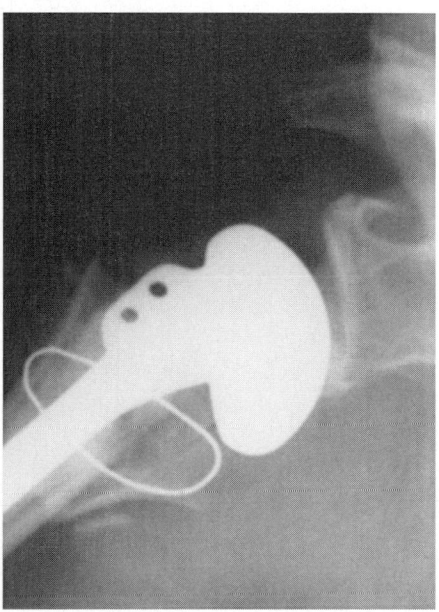

**FIGURE 44–61.** Three-part fracture with anterior dislocation of the articular surface plus comminution of the upper part of the shaft. Reconstruction of the tuberosity around a humeral head replacement cemented out to proper length enabled earlier motion with less risk of avulsion of the tuberosity as encountered with other forms of open reduction and internal fixation.

Zyto and co-workers compared the outcome of closed treatment and ORIF with minimal fixation in a randomized prospective study of elderly patients with mostly three-part fractures. The authors found that the type of treatment had no significant effect on outcome.[259]

Prosthetic replacement for three-part fractures has been reported by several authors.[70, 180, 185–187, 191, 235] It is usually reserved for older patients with poor-quality bone.

After ORIF of three-part fractures with plates and screws, the incidence of humeral head AVN, malunion, and nonunion is significant.[186, 191, 231] AVN occurs in approximately 14% of three-part fractures after closed treatment and in up to 25% after open treatment.[231] Minimal internal fixation is associated with a fivefold decrease in the AVN rate when compared with ORIF with plates and screws.[231]

## FOUR-PART FRACTURES AND FRACTURE-DISLOCATIONS

In most four-part fractures, the articular segment is completely separated from its blood supply. The articular segment may be displaced anteriorly, posteriorly, laterally, or inferiorly or crushed. Both tuberosities are separated from the head and shaft and from each other. In rare instances, the tuberosities are still joined at the biceps groove, but these injuries are still treated as four-part fractures (Fig. 44–62). Rotator cuff tears are relatively uncommon in shoulders with three- and four-part fractures. A longitudinal tear in the rotator cuff interval is sometimes present, and some patients have a preexisting rotator cuff tear.

Neer[174, 175] was the first to clearly demonstrate that

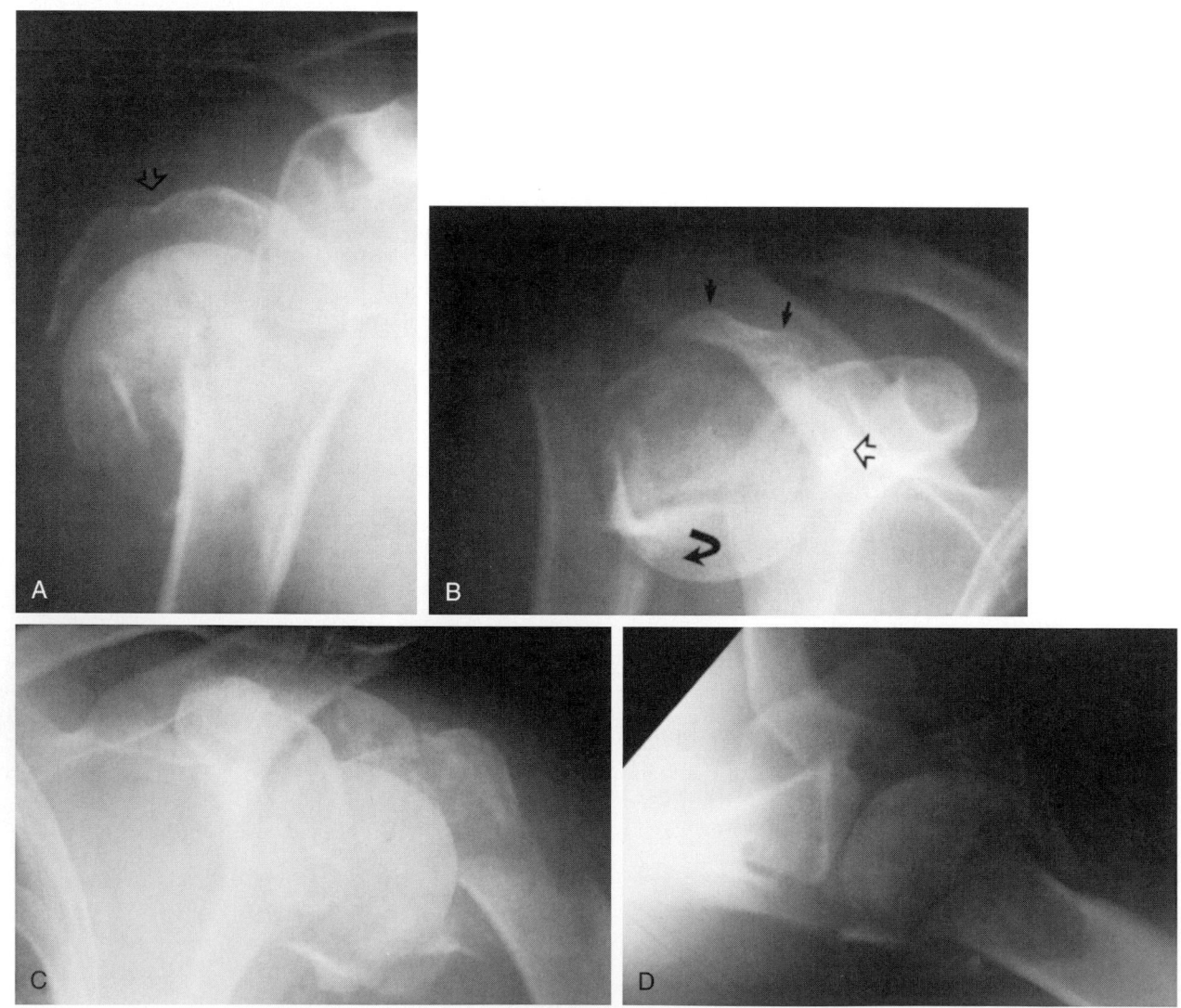

**FIGURE 44–62.** Four-part fracture. *A,* Lateral dislocation of the humeral head and a surgical neck fracture, with the tuberosities still joined at the biceps groove *(arrow)* without attachment to the articular segment. *B,* The patient has a posterior dislocation of the humeral head *(curved arrow)*, the lesser tuberosity *(open arrow)* is an isolated fragment, and the greater tuberosity fracture *(closed arrows)* has included the biceps groove. *C,* Anterior dislocation with the head resting on the brachial plexus. *D,* Axillary view after open reduction without tuberosity repair before prosthetic replacement.

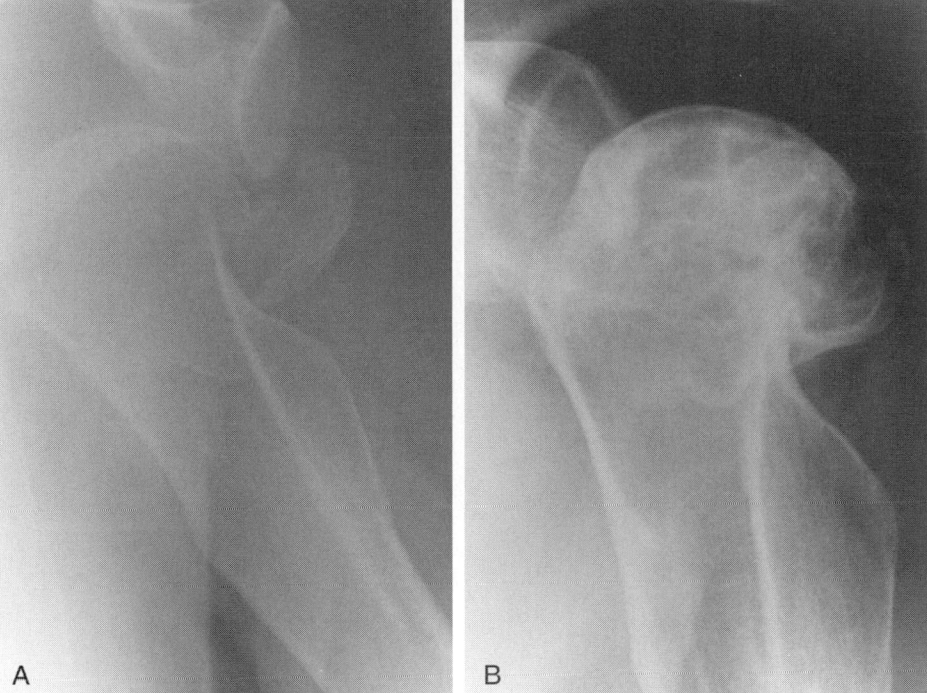

**FIGURE 44–63.** *A,* Anteroposterior radiographs of a four-part anterior fracture-dislocation in a 57-year-old man. *B,* Closed treatment of this injury resulted in avascular necrosis of the articular segment, malunion of the proximal end of the humerus, pain, and dysfunction.

nonoperative treatment of four-part fractures and fracture-dislocations often leads to a poor outcome (Fig. 44–63). Subsequently, most orthopaedic surgeons have agreed that operative treatment should be considered for four-part fractures when the patient is medically able to tolerate surgery and can participate in postoperative rehabilitation. In most cases, treatment involves prosthetic replacement of the articular segment. Numerous series have demonstrated that prosthetic arthroplasty gives consistently satisfactory results with good pain prevention, although the functional results have varied.*

ORIF of four-part fractures and fracture-dislocations remains a controversial subject. In younger individuals, this technically difficult surgical procedure has a role. Most reports of traditional methods of ORIF have demonstrated satisfactory results in about 50% of cases. Recent emphasis on closed reduction and percutaneous fixation, as well as less invasive techniques of ORIF, may lead to improved results. In valgus-impacted four-part fractures, the blood supply to the articular segment may be preserved through the medial capsular tissues.[17, 105, 106, 202]

Whether by ORIF or prosthetic replacement, surgery is indicated to restore the glenohumeral anatomy. Techniques that permit early motion are advantageous. ORIF is frequently discussed but seldom performed for these fractures. Unstable fixation, hardware complications, AVN, and nonunion contribute to the poor results with efforts to preserve the articular segment. The results of techniques

involving minimal dissection are promising. The results of humeral head replacement are predictable, but the issue of prosthetic and functional survivorship in young patients has not been well addressed.

### Authors' Preferred Treatment

Our treatment approach to four-part fractures is as follows. Humeral head replacement is the preferred treatment of most four-part fractures and all four-part fracture-dislocations in older patients. In younger active patients with good bone, ORIF is performed for valgus-impacted fractures and selected other four-part fractures on the basis of activity level, occupation, and rehabilitation potential. Obviously, individualization is important and difficult to put into an algorithm.

**Open Reduction and Internal Fixation.** The major problem with ORIF of four-part fractures has been an inability to achieve stable fixation, with subsequent loss of reduction and malunion. The results of traditional methods of ORIF of four-part fractures have been unsatisfactory in at least 50% of cases.[128, 175, 231] Nonetheless, the use of humeral head replacement in young individuals has long-term implications concerning the durability of the implant and the need for revision surgery.

ORIF with minimal dissection and limited internal fixation is technically challenging (Figs. 44–64 and 44–65). The deltopectoral approach provides the best access for the procedure and permits easy conversion to humeral head replacement if ORIF is not possible. The tuberosities are controlled with heavy nonabsorbable sutures, and the rotator cuff interval is opened to gain access to the glenohumeral joint.

*See references 42, 46, 70, 72, 88, 126, 175, 182, 216, 227, 235, 252.

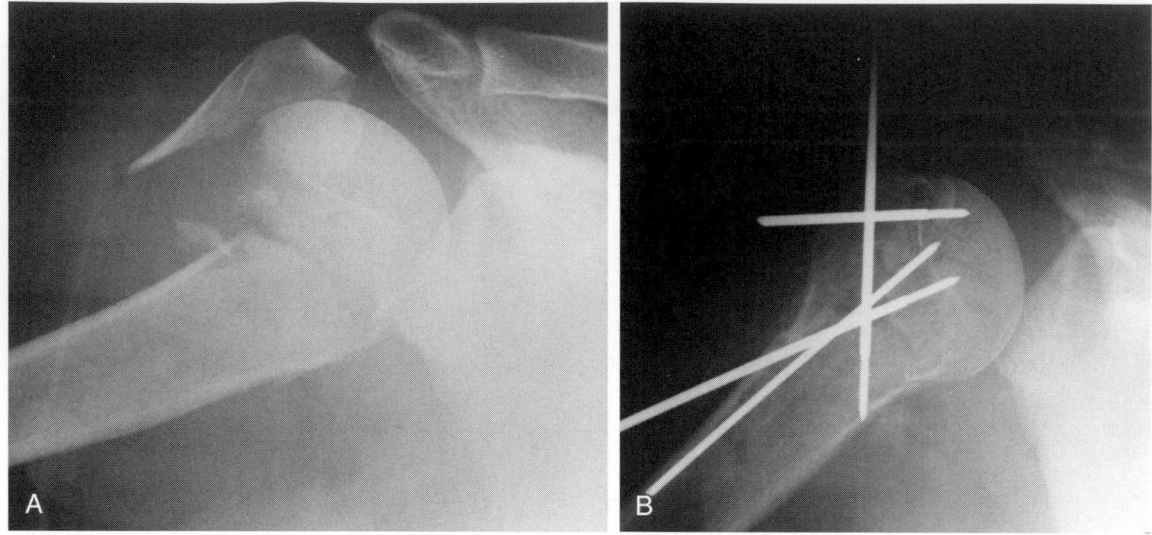

**FIGURE 44–64.** *A,* Four-part fracture of the dominant arm of a 32-year-old man involved in a motorcycle accident. Other injuries included a closed femoral shaft fracture and closed ankle fracture-dislocation. *B,* Open reduction and limited internal fixation achieved a nearly anatomic reduction.

The articular segment is reduced by carefully levering it back into the normal varus position. It is reduced against the glenoid, and then the humeral shaft is positioned appropriately. The articular segment can be fixed to the upper part of the shaft with terminally threaded 2.5-mm pins that are drilled in a cephalad and medial direction from the deltoid tuberosity. The metaphyseal void may need to be packed with autogenous or autologous corticocancellous bone graft to support the articular segment. Alternatively, screws can be used for fixation of the articular segment to the shaft or to the tuberosities.

The tuberosities are pulled down below the articular margin and fixed to each other and the humeral shaft. Heavy suture, wire, or cable can be used to secure the tuberosity reduction. Additional fixation of the greater tuberosity can be achieved with a pin drilled from above and down into the upper medial aspect of the humeral shaft. The pins can be cut short and buried beneath the skin or left out for easier removal. Pin infections can be a problem with either technique, so fixation that does not require pins is preferable.

A sling is used for the first 6 weeks after surgery. If percutaneous pins are used, shoulder motion is initially delayed. During the first 3 weeks, elbow, forearm, wrist, and hand exercises are performed several times each day to avoid distal stiffness. At about 4 weeks after surgery, the pins placed through the greater tuberosity are removed and pendulum circumduction exercises are initiated. The other pins are removed after 6 weeks. More aggressive rehabilitation is then initiated. If pins are not used, pendulum motion can be initiated earlier in cases in which the fixation is stable enough.

True valgus-impacted four-part proximal humeral fractures are a special variation of displaced fractures. The tuberosities are usually spread proximally as the articular segment is impacted into the valgus position. At the metaphyseal aspect of the fracture, the tuberosities are often still attached to the surgical neck. When the articular segment is reduced, the tuberosities can be pushed back into position and the reduction is very stable. Bone graft or substitute packed under the articular segment provides additional support. Minimal internal fixation with interosseous suture or wire is usually sufficient fixation.[106]

**Humeral Head Replacement.** Prosthetic arthroplasty is the preferred treatment of most four-part fractures. Earlier surgery is preferred to lessen the likelihood of stiffness and heterotopic bone formation. Initial reports suggested that surgery should be performed in the first 48 hours.[179] However, this time frame is not really necessary, and surgery is performed as soon as it can be scheduled.

Preoperative planning should include a careful assessment of the patient's neurovascular status, medical condition, and fracture architecture. When swelling and pain make it difficult to clinically assess nerve status, EMG and nerve conduction studies can be obtained. Nerve injuries are more common than reported and probably account for some of the poor results. Radiographs of the contralateral shoulder and humerus can be used preoperatively to determine how far above an identifiable point on the upper part of the shaft the prosthesis should rest. Such comparison is particularly helpful in late reconstructive cases.[76]

The deltopectoral approach is used for humeral head replacement (see Surgical Approaches). The cephalic vein is preserved and retracted laterally with the deltoid. The clavipectoral fascia is incised. The coracoid is not osteotomized, and the coracoid muscles are left intact. Abduction of the arm and release of the anterior 1 cm of the deltoid insertion and the upper half of the pectoralis provide more exposure if necessary without detachment of the deltoid origin (Fig. 44–66).

Special care must be taken to protect the brachial plexus and peripheral nerves if the humeral head is dislocated anteriorly. Only blunt instruments should be used for dissection in this area to expose the articular segment. The jagged fracture edges are gently freed from the surrounding soft tissue, and the humeral head is excised.

The tendon of the long head of the biceps is the key landmark. It is identified as it emerges from under the pectoralis major insertion in the bicipital groove. The transverse humeral ligament is transected, and the rotator cuff interval is opened. The coracohumeral ligament can be released to help mobilize the tuberosities, and the lateral edge of the coracoacromial ligament can be released to improve exposure. Heavy traction sutures are placed through the rotator cuff insertions on the tuberosities; these sutures hold better than drill holes in the bone. The articular segment is retrieved and saved as potential bone graft.

If a prominence is noted on the anterior acromion or inferior spurring is seen at the acromioclavicular joint, they are removed with a bur, osteotome, or rongeur before humeral head replacement. These areas are visualized with relaxation of the deltoid in abduction. The deltoid insertion is elevated with sharp dissection or electrocautery in preparation for the acromioplasty. If the deltoid is inadvertently released, repair is accomplished after the acromioplasty with sutures through the remaining acromion.

The glenoid is examined for evidence of articular surface abnormalities, fractures, or labral pathology. A significant glenoid fracture must be stabilized with internal fixation to ensure stability of the glenohumeral joint after replacement. Alternatively, a glenoid component can be used if the glenoid cannot be repaired or the patient has preexisting arthritis.

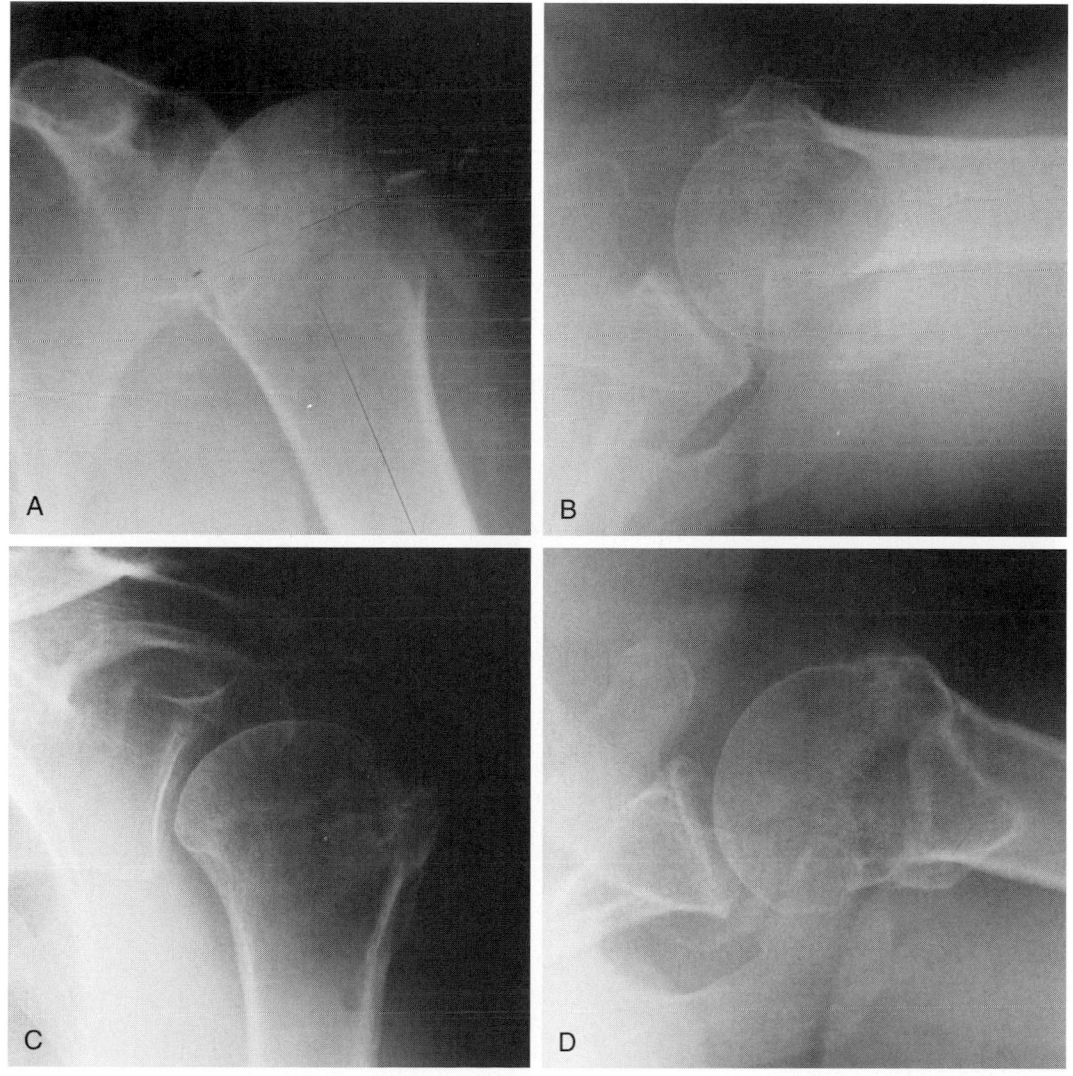

**FIGURE 44–65.** *A* and *B,* True anteroposterior and axillary lateral radiographs of a valgus-impacted four-part fracture that occurred in a 67-year-old woman. The fracture was treated by open reduction and limited internal fixation. *C* and *D,* The position of the articular segment was not altered because it was firmly impacted and stable. The tuberosities were reduced and fixed with heavy nonabsorbable suture.

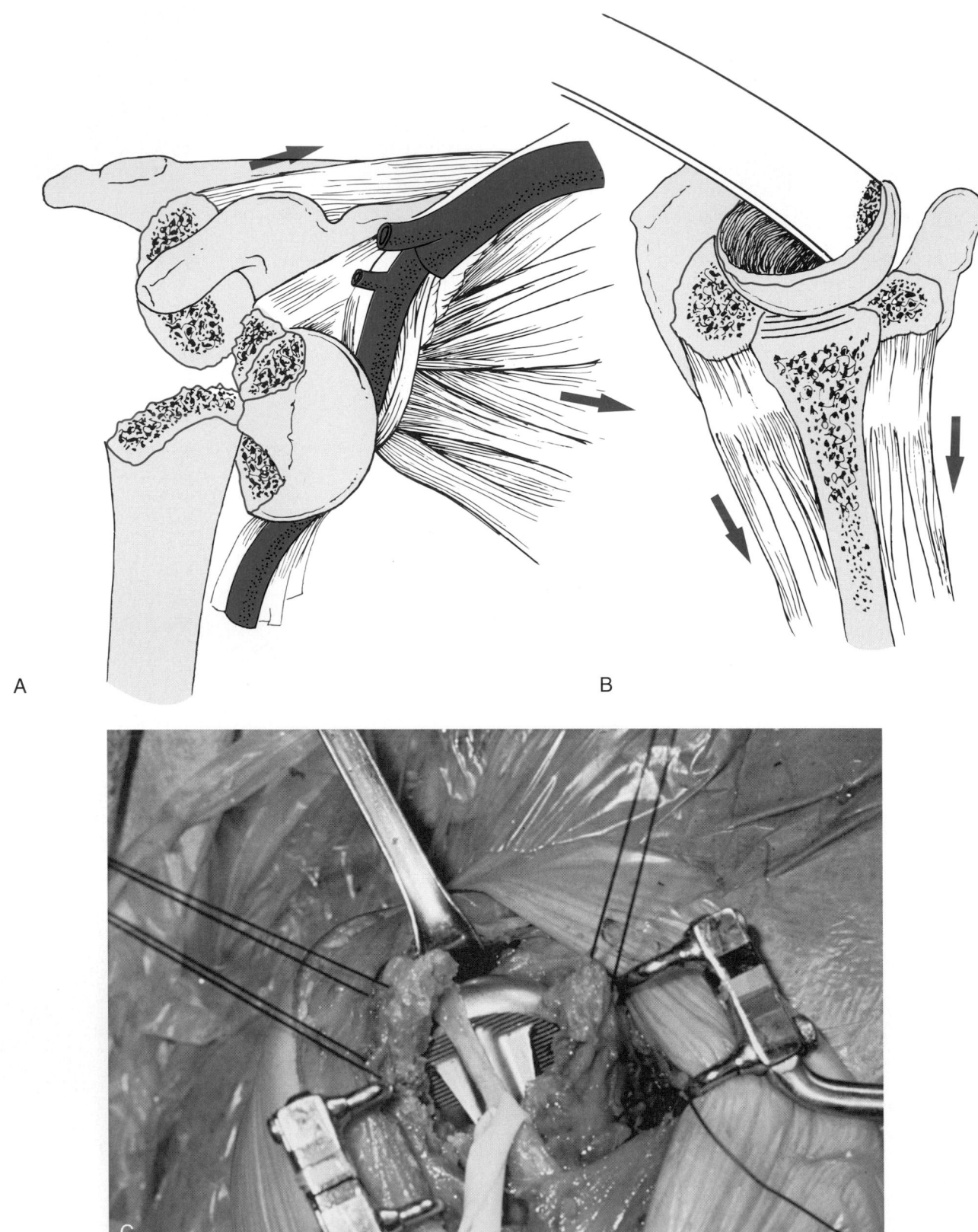

A

B

C

**FIGURE 44–66.** Technique of prosthetic replacement for four-part fractures. *A,* The articular segment is avascular and may rest on the brachial plexus. Rotator cuff muscles displace the tuberosities. The pectoralis, deltoid, and gravity displace the shaft. *B,* An axial view demonstrates medial retraction of the tuberosities by their respective muscle attachments. In this illustration, the displaced head has been reduced. *C,* Operative photograph demonstrating identification of the biceps, mobilization of the tuberosity and cuff, and reduction of the trial humeral head to preserve humeral length.

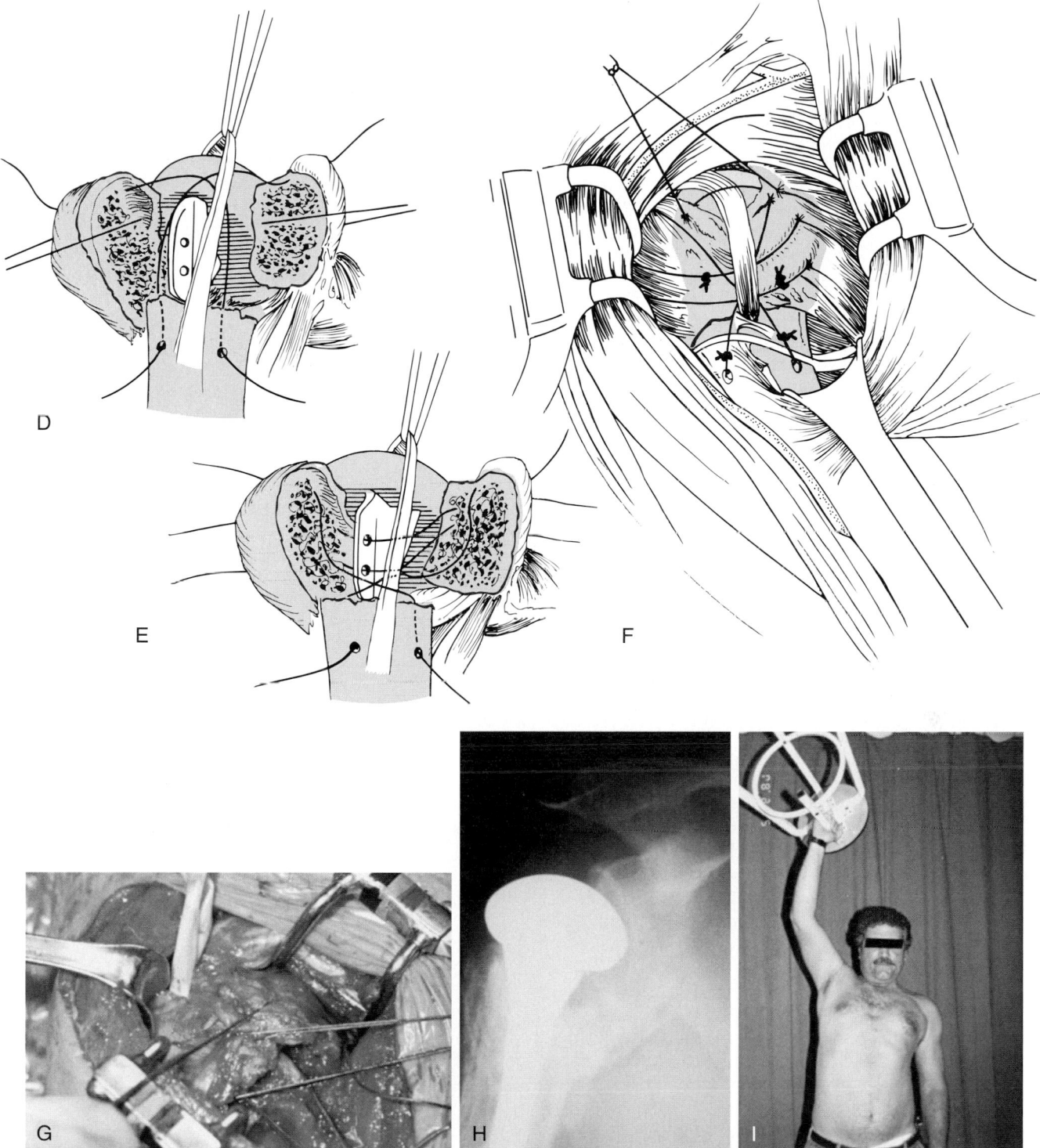

**Figure 44–66** *Continued. D,* The long head of the biceps at the rotator interval is a key structure in identifying displacement of the lesser and greater tuberosities. Traction sutures are placed through the rotator cuff tendons at the insertion site on the tuberosities both for horizontal repair of the tuberosities to each other and to the humeral component and for vertical repair to the humeral shaft. During trial reduction, the proper height for the humeral component is determined by observing the position relative to the humeral calcar and glenoid, the tension in the long head of the biceps tendon, and the ability to close the rotator cuff around the implant. Note that the tuberosities make up a significant portion of the upper part of the shaft. *E,* Once the prosthesis has been cemented in proper version and height, the tuberosities are approximated under the articular surface and above the diaphysis with horizontal and vertical fixation. *F,* Sutures preplaced in the rotator cuff interval are tied. *G,* Reapproximation of the tuberosities in the operative setting. *H,* Mild heterotopic bone formation did not preclude a satisfactory result. *I,* Four-year clinical follow-up with good strength and mild restriction of motion.

The humeral shaft is delivered into the deltopectoral interval by extending the arm off the table and pushing upward at the elbow. The surgical neck area is examined for comminution. The medial calcar area is used as a bony landmark for proper seating of the humeral component. The humeral shaft is sized by inserting axial reamers into the intramedullary canal. A trial humeral implant is then placed with the lateral fin slightly posterior to the biceps groove and the inferior edge of the medial aspect of the head portion at least at the height of the medial calcar. A sponge packed into the intramedullary canal helps maintain the position of the implant. Alternatively, some implant systems have fracture jigs to maintain the position of the trial component. Version can be determined from the relationship between the head component and the palpable humeral epicondylar axis, as well as by assessing the position of the head relative to the externally rotated arm (Fig. 44–67). Final adjustments in implant height can be made during surgery on the basis of tension of the soft tissues, including the long head of the biceps and the rotator cuff.

Common errors to avoid include removing too much bone and resting the prosthesis too low on the shaft without leaving room for the tuberosities. This mistake can result in inferior subluxation of the humeral head because the deltoid myofascial sleeve is rendered too long. Unless the prosthesis restores humeral length, it will be unstable with the functionally weakened deltoid. Too much retroversion will make it difficult to reposition the greater tuberosity, whereas less than the normal 30° to 35° of retroversion fosters anterior instability. Increased anteversion should be selected in patients with posterior fracture-dislocation.

Before preparing for cementing the humeral implant, the humerus is readied for fixation of the tuberosity. Holes are drilled in the shaft so that vertically oriented sutures can be used to repair the tuberosities. A trial reduction is then performed. The mobilized tuberosities with cuff attachments are fitted below the level of the articular portion of the component. This technique avoids impingement of the greater tuberosity and adds length to the upper part of the shaft. The tuberosities can be held together with a towel clip while determining proper head height. With the trial prosthesis out, sutures to repair the rotator cuff interval are placed but not tied.

The humeral component should be cemented in all fracture cases because it is impossible to achieve an adequate press fit in such cases. Soft polymethyl methacrylate cement is injected into the medullary canal. We do not use cement restrictors or pressurization and instead rely on bone-cement-implant fixation at the metaphyseal-diaphyseal juncture. During cementing of the prosthesis, the tuberosities are not forced over the humeral head; otherwise, their pressure could cause the humeral component to subside inferiorly or drift into a varus position before hardening of the cement. During cement hardening, cement is removed from above the shaft level.

The space between the cemented prosthesis and the shaft is filled in by the tuberosities. Autogenous bone graft from the humeral head can be packed under the tuberosities and at the tuberosity-shaft juncture to enhance bone healing. Initial tuberosity fixation is achieved with sutures passed circumferentially around the medial aspect of the prosthesis and the tuberosities (Fig. 44–68). The sutures around each tuberosity are also passed through holes in the prosthetic fins. The vertical sutures in the shaft secure each tuberosity. The preplaced sutures for the rotator interval are tied, and the security of the repair is evaluated. Limits of motion determined intraoperatively are used to guide postoperative rehabilitation.

The deltopectoral interval is closed. The use of a suction drain is optional and should be based on the appearance of the wound. After subcutaneous and subcuticular skin closure, the arm is placed in a sling unless additional relaxation of the greater tuberosity repair is desirable. For these patients, a 45° abduction immobilizer is used.

Most contemporary replacement systems are modular. Modular humeral head replacement permits a more accurate anatomic reconstruction. In addition, the modular component potentially facilitates revision surgery.[48, 163]

Essential aftercare includes ample postoperative support with early physician-guided passive range of motion begun the day after surgery. Active-assisted range of motion is initiated once early healing has occurred, usually by 6 weeks. Isometric exercises are added at 6 weeks and isotonic exercises at 12 weeks. At 3 months after surgery, most patients should be able to do their regular everyday activities. The end result, achievement of maximal motion and function, usually takes about 12 months.

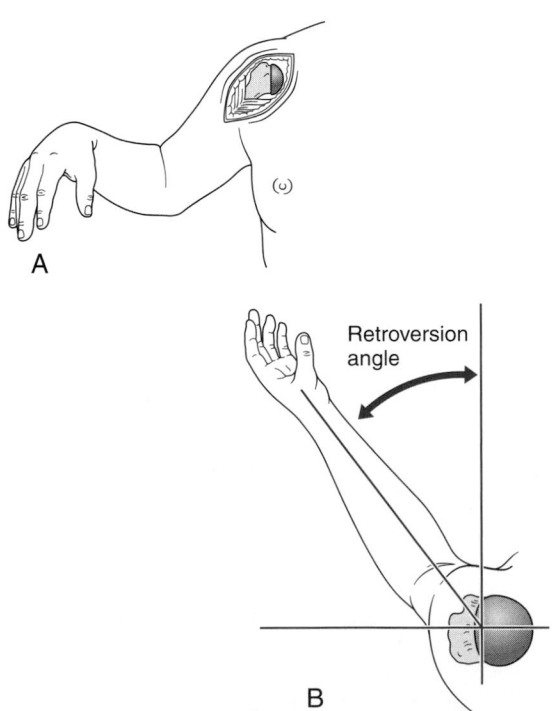

**FIGURE 44–67.** Humeral component version can be determined relative to the forearm axis. The undersurface of the humeral head or implant collar is aligned perpendicular to the floor, and the position of the forearm is noted to estimate the amount of retroversion.

### Results

Good or excellent results are rarely obtained with closed reduction of four-part fractures and fracture-dislocations.[140, 175, 227] Before the introduction of prosthetic replacement, late treatment of these injuries, with or without excision of the humeral head, yielded poor results.[184, 249]

The results of ORIF are generally satisfactory in less than 50% of cases.[29, 104, 128, 175, 231] Isolated reports of revascularization of the humeral head after ORIF indicate satisfactory healing.[121, 199] Unfortunately, many of the cases referenced in the literature often have not been true four-part fractures with isolation of the articular fragment, and follow-up is not sufficient to rule out late osteonecrosis.[32, 59, 138] Hagg and Lundberg noted a 74% rate of AVN when ORIF was used for these fractures.[79] Darder and coauthors[41] reported the results of ORIF in 33 patients with four-part fractures. Using Neer's criteria, 11 excellent, 10 satisfactory, 10 unsatisfactory, and 2 poor results were achieved. AVN developed in nine patients, seven of whom had fracture-dislocations.

Most authors agree that pain relief is achieved in more than 90% of patients after prosthetic replacement but that the results vary with regard to function, motion, and strength.[247] For example, Kraulis and Hunter[126] reported satisfactory results in only 2 of 11 patients after prosthetic replacement, whereas Neer and McIlveen reported nearly 90% excellent results with an improved technique using the deltopectoral approach and better rehabilitation.[182] This technique has become the preferred method of most surgeons.* The best functional results are achieved in active and motivated patients, usually those younger than 65 years at the time of surgery. Green and colleagues recently reported greater than 90% patient satisfaction in a prospective outcome study of humeral head replacement for proximal humeral fractures.[73]

Although the results seem to endure with time, long-term follow-up is not detailed enough to assist in counseling a young patient. Potential long-term problems include glenoid arthritis, rotator cuff deterioration, and implant failure.

The long-term results of open reduction and minimal internal fixation techniques for valgus-impacted four-part fractures are not yet available, but the early results are promising.[106]

In summary, closed reduction plus nonoperative treatment has not been satisfactory for four-part fractures and fracture-dislocations. Such treatment results in stiffness, persistent pain, and functional disability.[29, 119, 174, 175, 227] Reconstructive procedures in which the humeral head is retained often fail, particularly when the head collapses later from AVN.[119, 175, 227] Patients treated with prosthetic replacement have consistently had better pain relief and improved function, strength, and range of motion than those treated nonoperatively or operatively with humeral head excision or ORIF.

Although many authors argue that a second procedure

---

*See references 6, 42, 46, 70, 72, 84, 115, 150, 175, 185, 187, 201, 227, 235, 252.

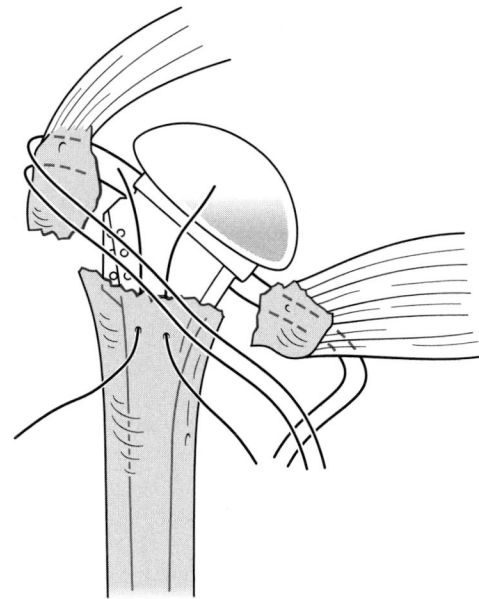

**Figure 44–68.** The tuberosity fixation is secured with circumferential sutures passed around the medial aspect of the prosthesis, sutures around the tuberosities and prosthesis, and sutures around the tuberosities and through drill holes in the shaft (red).

can be performed to replace the humeral head if AVN or post-traumatic arthritis occurs, the situation is usually more complex. In addition to AVN, malunion of the tuberosities has usually occurred.[61, 188, 235] In most cases, we prefer to treat four-part proximal humeral fractures and fracture-dislocations primarily with a prosthesis to avoid the late problems of nonoperative treatment or ORIF. Factors contributing to a successful outcome after early prosthetic replacement,[182] as compared with a previous series,[175, 178] include the following: the deltoid is intact, normal length of the shaft is restored for stability and muscle strength, retroversion of 30° to 40° with proper length of the head provides stability, the tuberosities and the cuff are repaired with nonabsorbable sutures below the articular surface, and gentle passive motion is started early whereas active motion is delayed until the tuberosities have healed. Indications for ORIF in younger patients with good bone quality are not well defined. If it is attempted, vigilant follow-up is mandatory to identify problems early when they can be corrected.

## HUMERAL HEAD-SPLITTING FRACTURES

Humeral head-splitting fractures may occur with or without dislocation. A distinction must be made between fractures in which a portion of the articular segment is attached to a tuberosity and those in which the articular segment is fragmented. Operative treatment is recommended to restore articular congruity. In the former situation, the fracture is treated according to the techniques described in previous sections. Articular fractures with large fragments and no comminution are amenable to ORIF. Prosthetic replacement is preferred in older patients and those with comminution to avoid articular incongruity and AVN, as well as to begin early rehabilitation (Fig. 44–69).

## PATHOLOGIC FRACTURES

Most pathologic fractures are the result of metastatic neoplasm. Lancaster and coauthors reported on 57 humeral fractures or impending humeral fractures in patients with inoperable cancer.[135] Involvement of the humerus above the surgical neck is best treated by cemented prosthetic humeral head replacement. Fractures below the surgical neck of the humerus have been treated with intramedullary fixation. Rods that have proximal and distal locking mechanisms are preferred. Cement augmentation is used with some neoplasms. Healing occurs by 4 months.[135, 168] Local irradiation is used postoperatively for radiosensitive tumors (Fig. 44–70).

## Follow-up and Rehabilitation

### IMMOBILIZATION

After fractures of the proximal end of the humerus, the arm is routinely protected in a sling between times of exercise. Adequate support is required for bone and soft tissue healing. In some cases, a 45° abduction immobilizer is required to relax the greater tuberosity repair. Avoiding early stress on the cuff and tuberosity repairs during the first 6 weeks decreases the incidence of tuberosity and cuff dehiscence.[32, 235]

In posterior fracture-dislocations, postoperative instability is a concern. The arm is protected in the gunslinger position with the arm at the side and the shoulder in 15° extension and external rotation for 4 to 6 weeks to allow the posterior capsule to heal.

Many patients have difficulty at night and should avoid resting completely supine for several weeks. We recommend that patients sleep in a reclined position either propped up on pillows or in a reclining chair.

### MOBILIZATION

When the fracture is fixed securely, including after humeral head replacement, immediate passive motion is possible. At surgery, the surgeon determines the safe range of motion, which then guides the early postoperative exercises. For example, passive internal rotation would be avoided if the greater tuberosity or infraspinatus repair is tenuous.

Some have recommended continuous passive motion to facilitate early rehabilitation.[38] However, no study has conclusively demonstrated that continuous passive motion offers significant long-term benefit. Most patients are discharged within 1 or 2 days of their surgery, and thus little time is left for in-hospital continuous passive motion. The current home units are cumbersome and impractical for an individual who has only one functioning upper extremity. Most importantly, reliance on a machine seems to shift the responsibility for the rehabilitation away from the patient. The best results are achieved with motivated patients who understand the mechanics and goals of the rehabilitation program.

Exercises and mobilization are slow. Unfortunately, exercises cannot exceed the weakest combined suture and tissue strength. Mason and colleagues[151, 152] demonstrated that tendon repair strength is less at 10 to 12 days after surgery than on the day of repair. By 3 weeks, the repair is again as strong as when the sutures were first placed. Full strength of bone and soft tissue healing are achieved many months after injury or surgery. Accordingly, precautions are recommended long afterward.

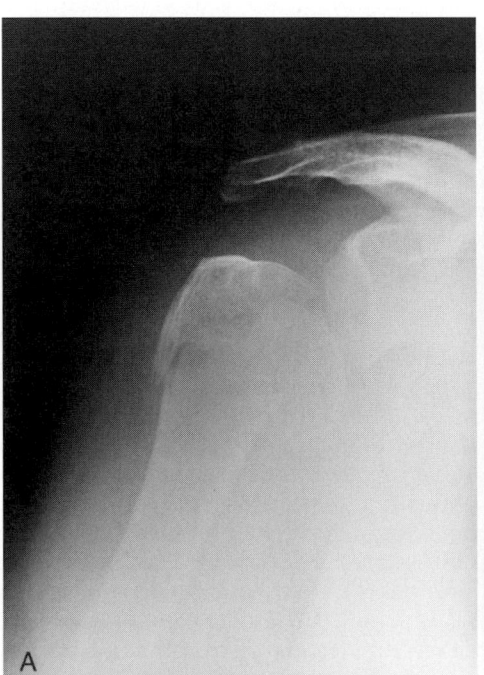
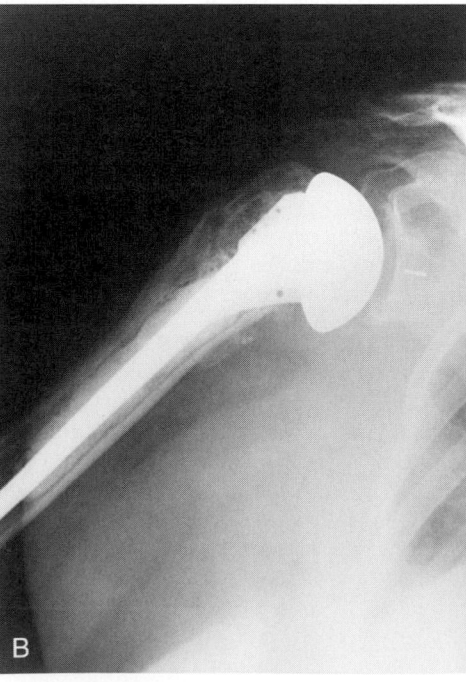

**Figure 44–69.** *A,* Plain radiographs of a 67-year-old woman who fell and sustained a head-splitting proximal humeral fracture. She had a history of shoulder pain and crepitance. *B,* At surgery, she was found to have significant glenoid arthritis and was consequently treated with a total-shoulder replacement.

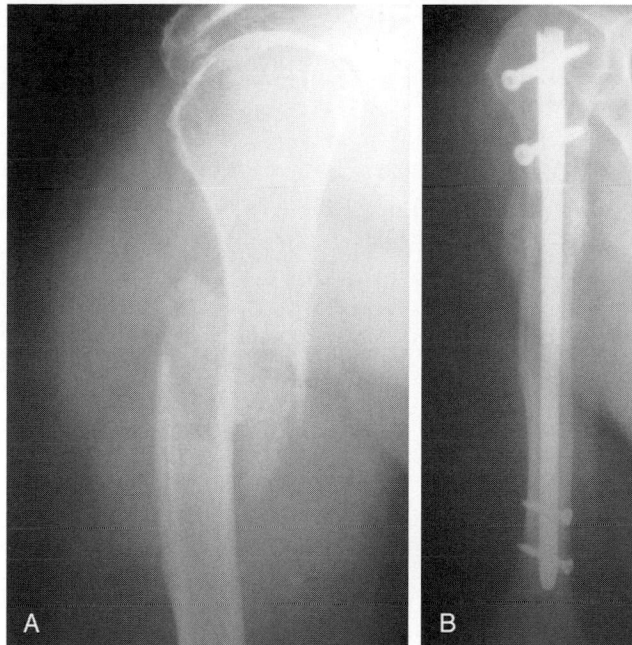

**FIGURE 44–70.** *A,* Pathologic fracture through an area of metastatic breast cancer. *B,* Healing is evident after treatment with an intramedullary rod and postoperative radiation therapy.

The surgeon should determine the length of immobilization, the amount of mobilization, and the appropriate exercises. Earlier passive motion after complex fractures leads to improved results.[180, 182] Physician-directed exercises are divided into three phases.[98]

### Phase I Exercises

Phase I begins with pendulum circumduction and passive-assisted stretching exercises to avoid capsular contracture and adhesions in the subacromial, subdeltoid, and scapulothoracic gliding planes (Fig. 44–71). Early application of ice after surgery decreases swelling and pain. Later, moist heat is used before the exercise sessions. Exercises for short periods several times daily are preferred to extended exercise sessions, which can cause more swelling and pain.

In this first phase, the surgeon, a therapist, or a family member assists the patient in stretching for elevation and rotation. The shoulder can be ranged in forward elevation, external rotation, internal rotation, and horizontal adduction. Later, the patient can do these exercises alone. Abduction in the coronal plane is avoided. During external rotational stretching with the elbow kept at a right angle, the forearm serves as a fulcrum for shoulder rotation. Arm extension behind the back is combined with internal rotation to reach up the back. In general, two principles are followed: (1) stretching is better accomplished with heat and relaxation, and (2) distraction is less painful than compression for joint mobilization.

Gentle deltoid and periscapular isometric exercises (Fig. 44–72) to stimulate muscle rehabilitation but avoid tension on the repair begin early after injury and are advanced after 6 weeks.

### Phase II Exercises

In phase II exercises (Fig. 44–73), active motion plus progressive stretching is encouraged. The combination of passive assistance with elimination of gravity by using a pulley or the opposite arm is initiated to avoid excessive stress on the healing fracture and rotator cuff. The greatest force across the joint generated by muscle contraction is at 90° elevation. Therefore, through this midrange, assisted motion is beneficial. Methods of gradually transferring the load in the operated arm without overstressing the early healing process are demonstrated in Figure 44–74.

Strengthening exercises with light isometric resistance begin in phase II. True isotonic strengthening is delayed for up to 3 months and is reserved for phase III.[32, 235]

Overhead stretching is advanced from pulley exercises to exercises in which individuals can use their own weight to guide how much stretch is applied. All too often an individual may tighten to protect against a hard stretch applied by the surgeon or therapist. Overhead stretching can be done from a stable door or from a device such as a yachting cleat mounted on the wall. Just as with sit-ups, where knee flexion flattens and protects the lower part of the back, overhead stretching requires the back to be rounded with the hips forward. Otherwise, back pain results from apparent shoulder motion that is actually induced by extending the lumbar spine.

### Phase III Exercises

Phase III exercises involve heavier resistance exercises and the incorporation of isotonic and isokinetic strengthening exercises. Terminal stretching to obtain the last 15° of motion and to stretch a tightened posterior capsule often provides a surprising decrease in the residual aching so commonly present after shoulder injuries (Fig. 44–75).

## DURATION OF DISABILITY

The duration of disability after proximal humeral fractures is often grossly underestimated.[29, 180] Many authors believe that no significant improvements in function occur after 6 months.[55, 119, 139, 148, 164, 256]

Motion may be recovered early with one-part fractures, but realistically, 6 to 12 months may be needed for maximal recovery of comfort, mobility, and strength after these and more complex fractures.[32, 85, 124, 180] Endurance is the last element of strength to recover. A weather-related ache and pain from stiffness may persist. Among the many potential complications that may occur in the operative and nonoperative management of displaced humeral fractures, pain, stiffness, and shoulder dysfunction may be permanent.[227]

Individuals with isolated fractures at the proximal end of the humerus will need some assistance in daily care. For an elderly individual who may normally require the assistance of canes or crutches for ambulation, residence in an extended care facility, in a nursing home, or with relatives should be considered. In these individuals with significant limitations, nonoperative treatment is preferred to hasten return to usual activity status.

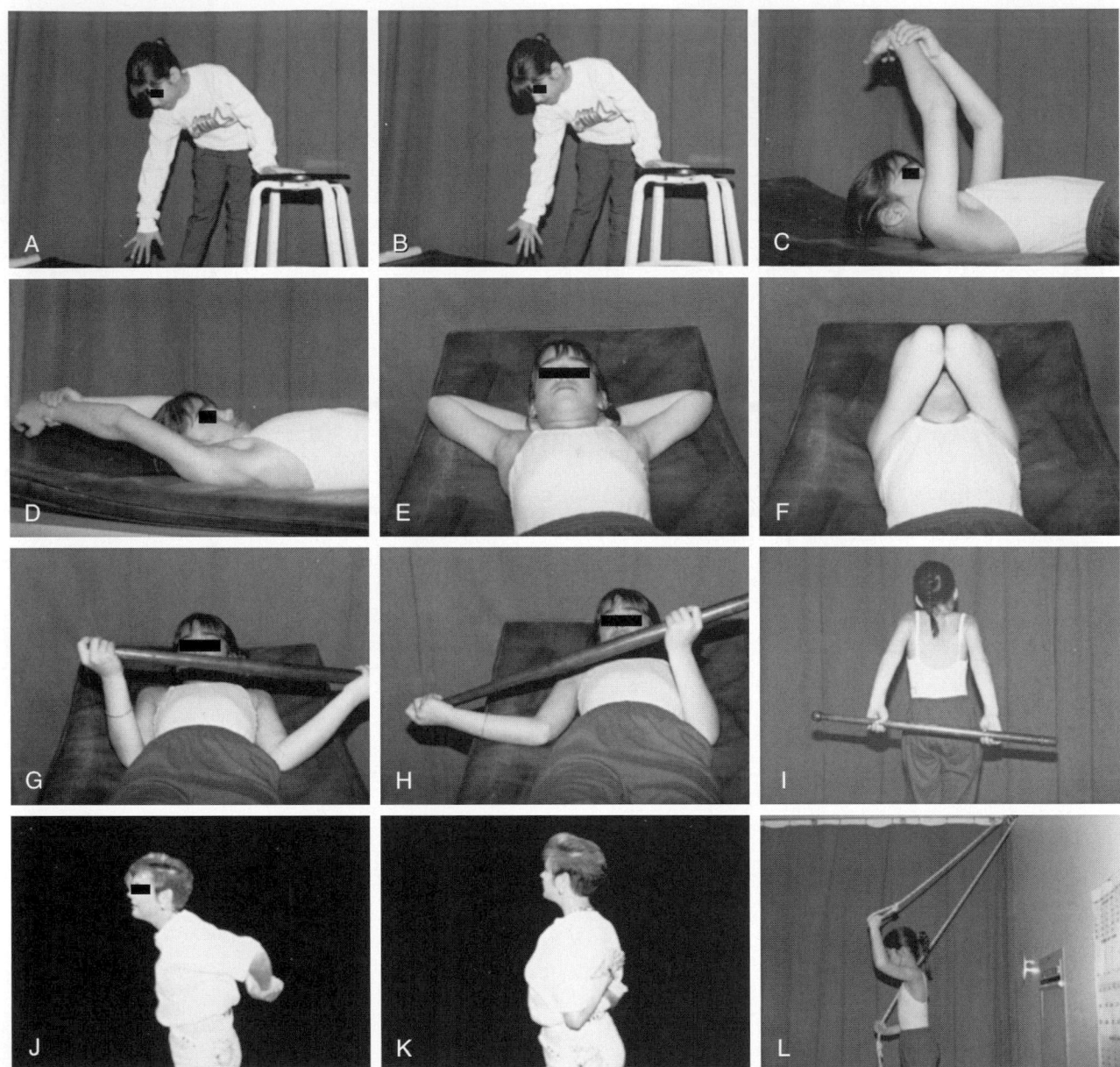

**FIGURE 44–71.** Phase I rehabilitation exercises include passive-assisted exercises to maintain range of motion by preventing strong bursal and capsular adhesions. These exercises are done several times a day for short periods to avoid unnecessary fatigue and soreness. *A, B,* Pendulum circumduction exercises are begun with gravity-assisted elevation and the body supported with the unoperated hand on a stable stool or counter. The arm is gently rotated in external rotation with the palm facing backward and in internal rotation with the palm facing upward. It can be moved downward in a clockwise or counterclockwise manner and supports active use of muscle and the muscle repairs. *C, D,* Supine passive elevation is performed with the assistance of the unoperated arm (or by the therapist or physician) with slight distraction at the shoulder joint. *E, F,* When 120° of passive elevation is obtained, external and internal rotation stretching can be started with the hands locked behind the neck. *G, H,* Supine passive external rotation with a stick or cane is performed with the elbow at a right angle to permit the forearm to serve as a fulcrum for shoulder rotation. This maneuver is performed with a slow, steady stretch, deep breaths with an open mouth for relaxation, and additional stretching within the security of the repair and pain tolerance. *I–K,* Internal rotation is begun first by shoulder extension behind the back with the aid of a stick. The hands are moved closer on the stick until the unoperated hand can grab the wrist of the operated arm. Use of the stick is then discontinued and the arms are extended, followed by flexion of the arms with the "hitchhiking thumb" brought up the back for maximal internal rotation. *L,* Passive-assisted elevation with a pulley permits gentle flexion once active-assisted motion is permitted. The arm is then elevated to its maximal degree, and the unoperated arm allows the operated arm to share the load as the arm is lowered. The overhead arm provides partial support as a means of early strengthening.

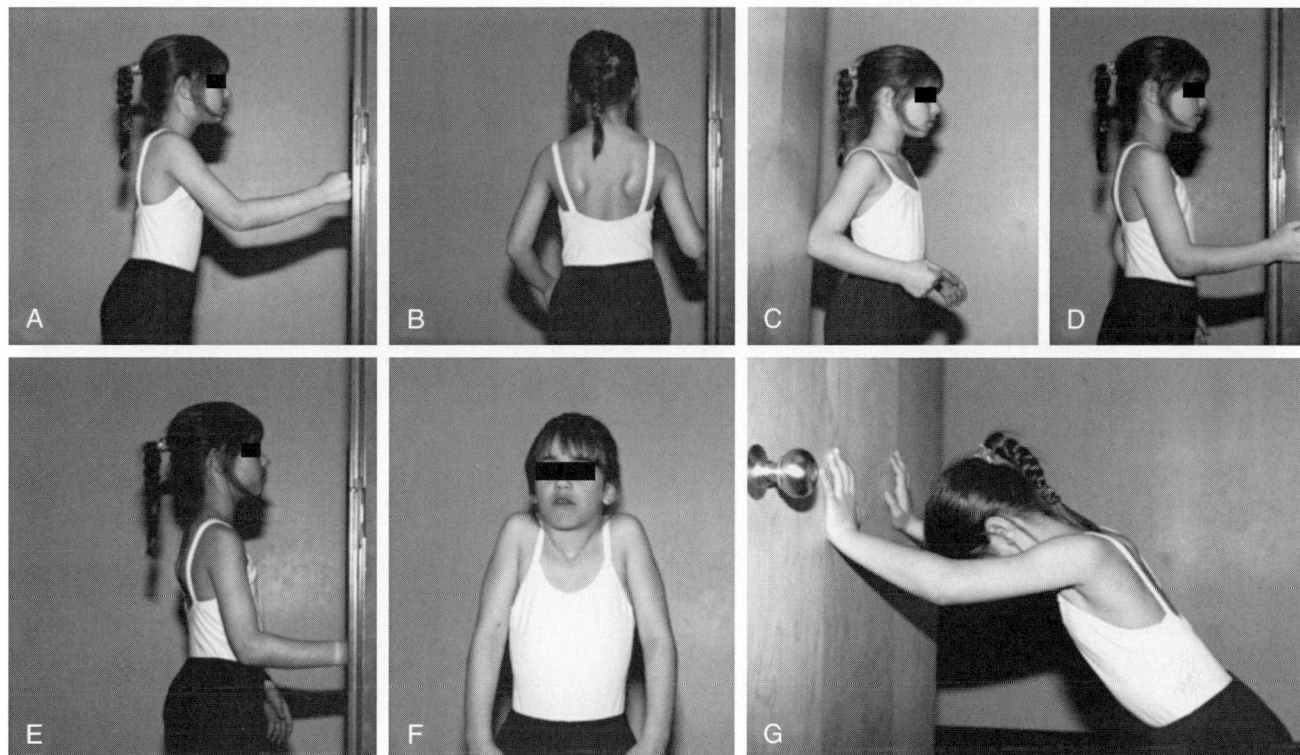

**FIGURE 44–72.** Isometric exercises for triphasic deltoid strengthening. *A*, Anterior deltoid. *B*, Middle deltoid. *C*, Posterior deltoid. Internal rotation (*D*) and external rotation (*E*) are started at the end of phase I exercises to prevent loss of muscle bulk. Scapular stabilization exercises are used for the trapezius (*F*), and pushups are added for the rhomboids and serratus (*G*).

## OUTCOME ASSESSMENT

Evaluation of the outcome of shoulder disorders is the focus of most clinical research. Most studies have concentrated on the treatment of atraumatic disorders, and no outcome measure has specifically been designed to evaluate the outcome of shoulder fractures.

A recent study demonstrated that the outcome of nonoperative treatment of nondisplaced proximal humeral fractures is limited. The outcome was fair or poor in 23% of cases.[124] Consequently, it is not surprising that the results of operative treatment of proximal humeral fractures are frequently less than optimal. In addition, although the majority of proximal humeral fractures are nondisplaced or minimally displaced and treated nonoperatively, most of the recent orthopaedic literature is concentrated on operative treatment.

Studies of operative treatment of more severe proximal humeral fractures report variable outcomes. It is difficult to determine why some studies report better outcomes than others. Varying patient populations and observer bias are undoubtedly factors. Studies that use modern outcome assessments tend to report poorer outcomes for ORIF in more complex fractures, especially four-part fractures.

Documentation and assessment of results after proximal humeral fractures and fracture-dislocations present a unique challenge. Rating systems throughout the literature vary widely among authors. Considerable confusion has arisen because types of fractures are often grouped together for evaluation of individual or combined treatments. Nondisplaced fractures are not always separated from displaced fractures. Little of the older literature is relevant because fracture types and treatments are not separated for analysis. Unfortunately, many contemporary authors still cannot agree on how to measure motion (e.g., elevation may be described as abduction in the coronal plane of the body or the coronal plane of the scapula or as flexion in the sagittal plane of the body; external rotation is reported by some with the arm at the side and by others in 90° of abduction).

The factors that enable us to define the natural history of a specific fracture type, as well as the response to nonoperative or operative management, begin with an adequate fracture classification based on careful imaging and operative findings. Parameters evaluated during and after treatment include pain, range of motion, strength, stability, function, patient satisfaction, radiographic documentation of fracture healing, anatomic restoration, the need for additional operative procedures, and economic factors.

Most studies assess the results of treatment with categoric rating scales. The numeric rating scales have various biases because different authors weight categories differently.[174, 175, 182, 183, 214] For example, Sante[214] did not describe how much elevation was required for a satisfactory result, Knight and Mayne[119] chose 60°, and Neer and McIlveen[182] considered less than 90° to be unsatisfactory.

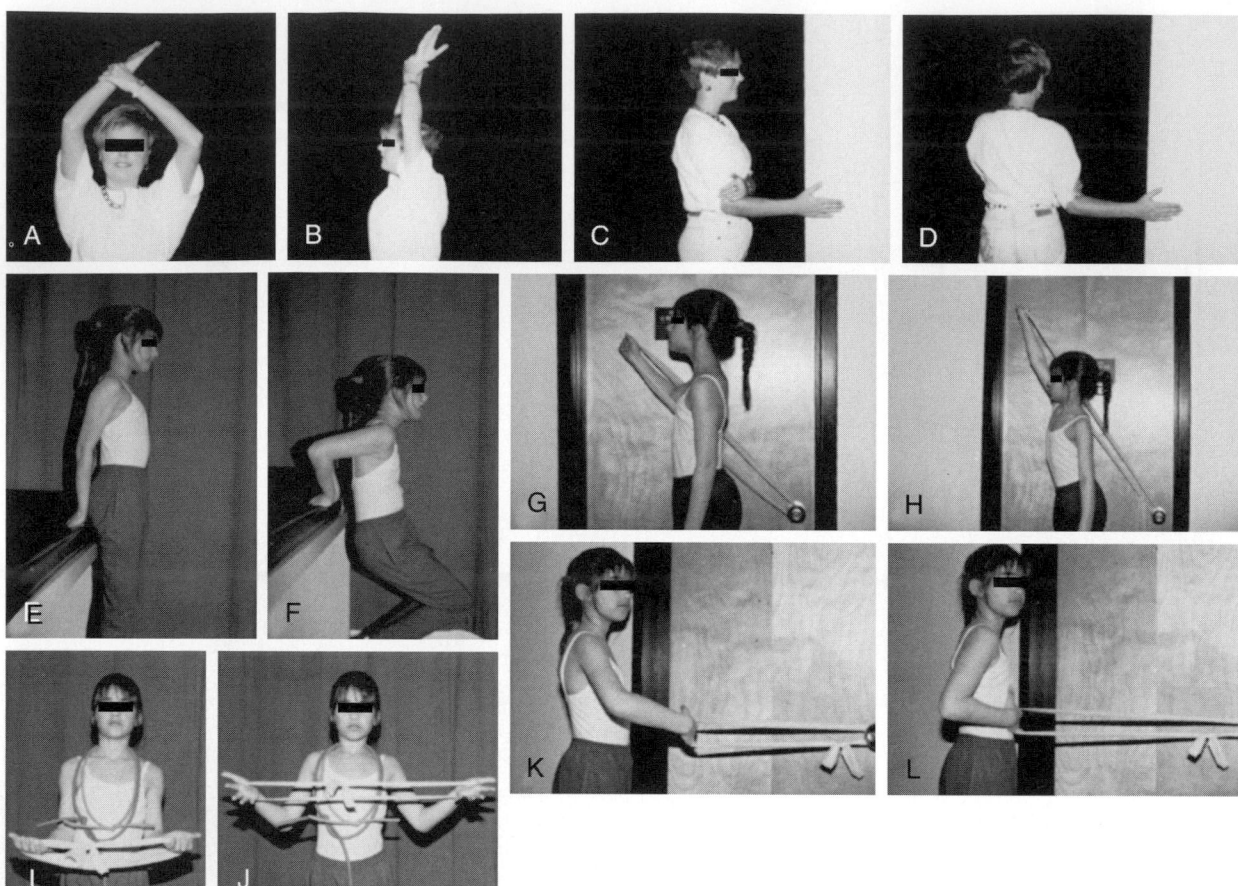

**FIGURE 44–73.** Phase II exercises include early active- and passive-assisted elevation and external and internal stretching. *A, B,* Phase II stretching in early strengthening for elevation. *C, D,* External rotation in a doorway. *E, F,* Internal rotation with the hands behind the back as the patient does deep knee bends. All these exercises are intended to provide more forceful stretching in these three directions. Active exercises for elevation performed by using rubber resistors on a door for the anterior deltoid (*G, H*), external rotation (*I, J*), and internal rotation (*K, L*) can be done with different strength resistors or wall weights for a pulley. The anterior deltoid–strengthening exercises in a forward plane avoid the impingement that might occur in abduction with residual stiffness. With the external rotation–strengthening exercises, the hands are pushed apart equally and are farther apart than the elbows for maximal effect. If the elbow is kept forward for internal rotation strengthening, the pectoralis and internal rotators are exercised, whereas if the elbow is brought backward, the posterior deltoid shares more of the load.

**FIGURE 44–74.** Combined active and assisted pulley strengthening.

Neer proposed a 100-point rating system in 1970 (Table 44–3) to evaluate shoulder arthroplasty for fractures.[174, 175, 182] The result was considered excellent when the patient was enthusiastic about the operation and had full use, active elevation to within 35° of the normal side and rotation to within 90% of the normal side, and no significant pain. A satisfactory result occurred when the patient was satisfied, had no more than occasional pain or weather-related aches, and had good function for daily use, active elevation above the horizontal, and rotation within 50% of normal. An unsatisfactory result was anything less than a satisfactory result. In a previous report, Neer and colleagues[181] included a limited-goals category for patients with massive cuff, bone, or neurologic deficits and in whom reconstruction was believed to be appropriate for pain relief but rehabilitation was directed more to stability than motion. This type of category may be more beneficial in fracture analysis than consideration of these more difficult cases with the overall group. Otherwise, one might tend to view all failures as being in a "limited-goals" category.

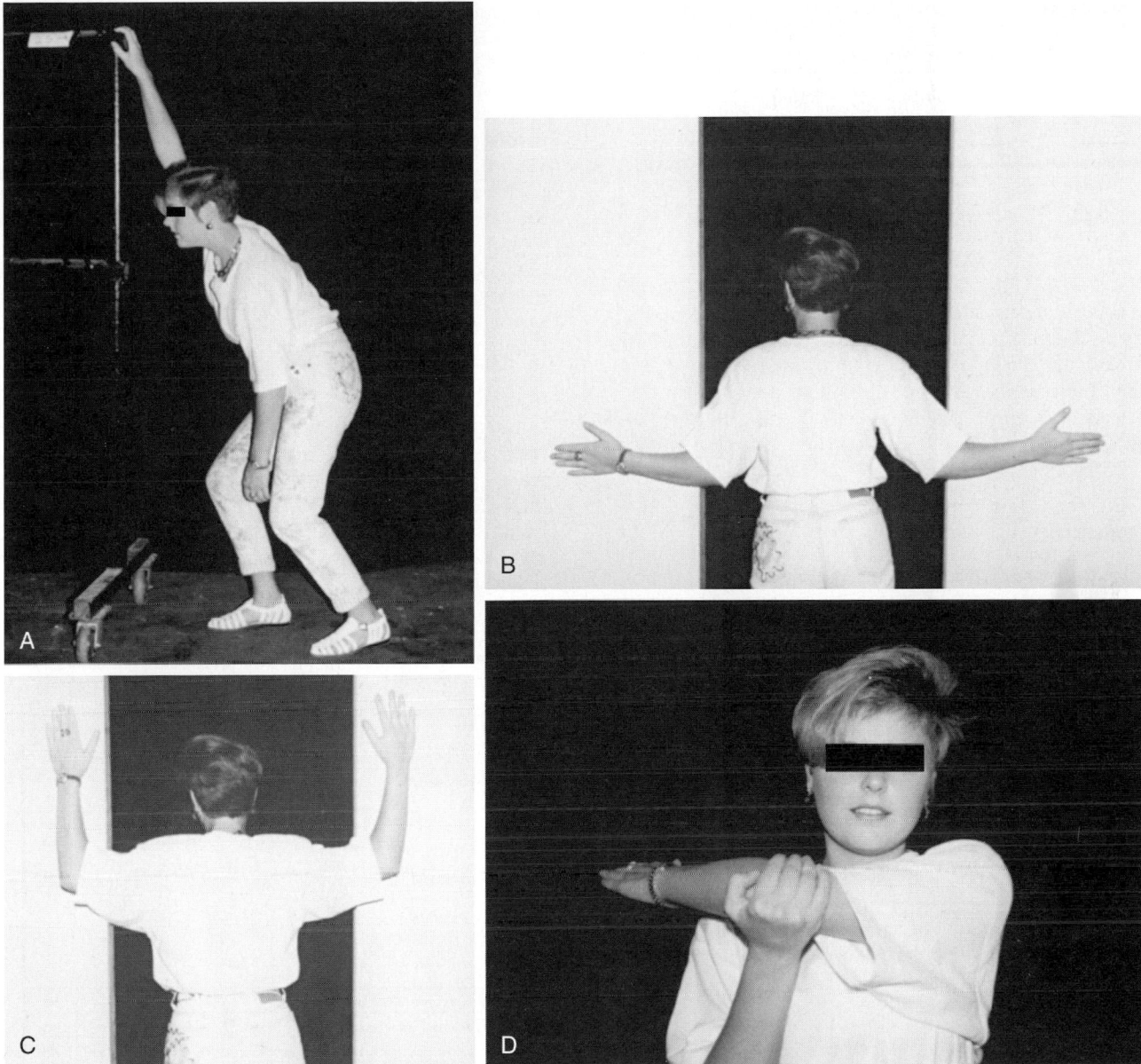

**FIGURE 44–75.** Phase III exercises. More advanced stretching with the arm on the end of a door is accomplished by leaning forward at the waist, rounding the back, and providing a distraction force through the glenohumeral joint by lowering the body as the axilla moves forward and downward. Overhead elevation by arching the lower part of the back is avoided to protect the lumbar spine (*A*). External rotation with the arms at the side (*B*) and abduction and external rotation with the arms overhead (*C*) can be accomplished by leaning through a doorway. *D,* Adduction with stretching of the arm across the chest stretches the posterior capsule, which relieves a form of secondary impingement and also improves the patient's ability to sleep on the operated shoulder. Phase III active strengthening exercises use increasing resistance with surgical tubing, wall weights over a pulley, free weights, and Nautilus and Cybex equipment in the same four basic directions for strengthening and stretching (i.e., elevation, external and internal rotation, abduction). Heat applied before exercise assists in relieving stiffness. Ice applied before exercise assists in relieving pain, decreases swelling, and acts as a local anesthetic.

The American Shoulder and Elbow Surgeons presented a standardized method for assessing shoulder function in 1994 (Fig. 44–76).[204] Recent emphasis on outcome analysis has focused on patient perception of outcome, but few studies of fracture treatment have used modern outcome methods. Green and associates found that patient self-assessment of outcome and satisfaction correlated with the more traditional assessment of results.[74]

## COMPLICATIONS

Complications after proximal humeral fractures are not uncommon. Because these fractures are difficult to manage with any form of treatment, it is critical to make an accurate diagnosis, use safe and simple treatment techniques when possible, and be aware of the likelihood

**TABLE 44–3** • • • • • • • • • • • • • • • • • • • • • • • • • • • • • • • • • • • • •

Neer 100-Point Rating System

| Category | Points | Rating |
|----------|--------|--------|
| Pain | 35 | 90–100: Excellent |
| Function | 30 | 80–89: Satisfactory |
| Motion | 25 | 70–79: Unsatisfactory |
| Anatomy | 10 | <70: Failure |

of complications after specific forms of treatment for a given fracture or fracture-dislocation. The following subsections include specific discussion of the most common complications of proximal humeral fractures. The last section of this chapter includes a more detailed discussion of late reconstruction after proximal humeral fractures.

## Nonunion

Nonunion after surgical neck fractures is most commonly associated with nonoperative treatment. It is promoted by traction at the fracture site, inadequate immobilization or fixation, and early range of motion before secure fracture healing (see Fig. 44–40). Soft tissue interposition that prevents reduction and an inability to maintain reduction are additional causes.[191]

Treatment of nonunion depends on the segments involved and whether traumatic arthritis has developed. With nonunion of the greater tuberosity, mobilization and lateral advancement to the anatomic position require that the capsule be freed from the glenoid and labrum and the rotator cuff from superficial scarring. The tuberosity is often trimmed for a better fit but should not be excised. In long-standing neglected cases, reduction of the tuberosity to its normal position may not be possible. Greater tuberosity nonunion with small fragments can be excised and the rotator cuff advanced to the tuberosity for repair.

Surgical neck nonunions are ideally treated by ORIF with intramedullary Ender rods or a fixed-angle blade plate. Supplemental bone graft is required for atrophic nonunion. However, in many cases the humeral head is excavated from long-standing nonunion, and purchase in osteoporotic bone is poor. For these cases, cemented humeral head replacement with excision of the remaining articular fragment is the preferred technique. The excised humeral head is packed as bone graft for the

**SHOULDER ASSESSMENT FORM**
AMERICAN SHOULDER AND ELBOW SURGEONS

| Name: | | Date |
| Age: | Hand dominance:  R   L   Ambi | Sex:    M    F |
| Diagnosis: | | Initial Assess?  Y  N |
| Procedure/Date: | | Follow-up:   M;   Y |

A

**PATIENT SELF-EVALUATION**

| Are you having pain in your shoulder? (circle correct answer) | Yes | No |

Mark where your pain is

| Do you have pain in your shoulder at night? | Yes | No |
| Do you take pain medication (aspirin, Advil, Tylenol etc.)? | Yes | No |
| Do you take narcotic pain medication (codeine or stronger)? | Yes | No |
| How many pills do you take each day (average)? | | pills |

How bad is your pain today (mark line)?
0 |___|___|___|___|___|___|___|___|___|___| 10
No pain at all                          Pain as bad as it can be

B

| Does your shoulder feel unstable (as if it is going to dislocate)? | Yes | No |

How unstable is your shoulder (mark line)?
0 |___|___|___|___|___|___|___|___| 10
Very stable                               Very unstable

C

Circle the number in the box that indicates your ability to do the following activities:
0 = Unable to do; 1 = Very difficult to do; 2 = Somewhat difficult; 3 = Not difficult

| ACTIVITY | RIGHT ARM | LEFT ARM |
|----------|-----------|----------|
| 1. Put on a coat | 0  1  2  3 | 0  1  2  3 |
| 2. Sleep on your painful or affected side | 0  1  2  3 | 0  1  2  3 |
| 3. Wash back/do up bra in back | 0  1  2  3 | 0  1  2  3 |
| 4. Manage toiletting | 0  1  2  3 | 0  1  2  3 |
| 5. Comb hair | 0  1  2  3 | 0  1  2  3 |
| 6. Reach a high shelf | 0  1  2  3 | 0  1  2  3 |
| 7. Lift 10 lbs. above shoulder | 0  1  2  3 | 0  1  2  3 |
| 8. Throw a ball overhand | 0  1  2  3 | 0  1  2  3 |
| 9. Do usual work - List: | 0  1  2  3 | 0  1  2  3 |
| 10. Do usual sport - List: | 0  1  2  3 | 0  1  2  3 |

D

**FIGURE 44–76.** *A–H,* The American Shoulder and Elbow Surgeons' standardized form for assessment of shoulder function. (*A–H,* From Richards, R.R.; et al. J Shoulder Elbow Surg 3:347–352, 1994.)

**PHYSICIAN ASSESSMENT**

| RANGE OF MOTION | RIGHT | | LEFT | |
|---|---|---|---|---|
| Total shoulder motion<br>Goniometer preferred | Active | Passive | Active | Passive |
| Forward elevation (Maximum arm-trunk angle) | | | | |
| External rotation (Arm comfortably at side) | | | | |
| External rotation (Arm at 90° abduction) | | | | |
| Internal rotation (Highest posterior anatomy reached with thumb) | | | | |
| Cross-body adduction (Antecubital fossa to opposite acromion) | | | | |

E

**SIGNS**

0 = none; 1 = mild; 2 = moderate; 3 = severe

| SIGN | Right | Left |
|---|---|---|
| Supraspinatus/greater tuberosity tenderness | 0 1 2 3 | 0 1 2 3 |
| AC joint tenderness | 0 1 2 3 | 0 1 2 3 |
| Biceps tendon tenderness (or rupture) | 0 1 2 3 | 0 1 2 3 |
| Other tenderness - List: | 0 1 2 3 | 0 1 2 3 |
| Impingement I (Passive forward elevation in slight internal rotation) | Y   N | Y   N |
| Impingement II (Passive internal rotation with 90° flexion) | Y   N | Y   N |
| Impingement III (90° active abduction - classic painful arc) | Y   N | Y   N |
| Subacromial crepitus | Y   N | Y   N |
| Scars - location | Y   N | Y   N |
| Atrophy - location: | Y   N | Y   N |
| Deformity : describe | Y   N | Y   N |

F

**INSTABILITY**

0 = none; 1 = mild (0 - 1 cm translation)
2 = moderate (1 - 2 cm translation or translates to glenoid rim)
3 = severe (> 2 cm translation or over rim of glenoid)

| | | |
|---|---|---|
| Anterior translation | 0  1  2  3 | 0  1  2  3 |
| Posterior translation | 0  1  2  3 | 0  1  2  3 |
| Inferior translation (sulcus sign) | 0  1  2  3 | 0  1  2  3 |
| Anterior apprehension | 0  1  2  3 | 0  1  2  3 |
| Reproduces symptoms? | Y   N | Y   N |
| Voluntary instability? | Y   N | Y   N |
| Relocation test positive? | Y   N | Y   N |
| Generalized ligamentous laxity? | Y   N | |

Other physical findings:

Examiner's name:

_____Date

H

**STRENGTH**
(record MRC grade)

0 = no contraction; 1 = flicker; 2 = movement with gravity eliminated
3 = movement against gravity, 4 = movement against some resistance; 5 = normal power.

| | Right | Left |
|---|---|---|
| Testing affected by pain? | Y   N | Y   N |
| Forward elevation | 0  1  2  3  4  5 | 0  1  2  3  4  5 |
| Abduction | 0  1  2  3  4  5 | 0  1  2  3  4  5 |
| External rotation (Arm comfortably at side) | 0  1  2  3  4  5 | 0  1  2  3  4  5 |
| Internal rotation (Arm comfortably at side) | 0  1  2  3  4  5 | 0  1  2  3  4  5 |

G

**FIGURE 44–76** *Continued*

nonunion site at the tuberosity and surgical neck levels.[190, 191]

Nonunion after failed treatment of three- or four-part fractures is more difficult to treat than the original acute fractures. The best treatment is prosthetic replacement cemented out to length and reconstruction of the rotator cuff and tuberosities. Replacement of the glenoid is considered if it is also involved and good rotator cuff closure can be obtained.

## Malunion

Malunion after proximal humeral fractures can occur at the surgical neck and the greater tuberosity. It is usually the result of inadequate closed or open reduction or loss of reduction secondary to failure of fixation. This complication is most common with the use of plate and screws in osteoporotic proximal humeral bone stock.

Malunion is problematic because of stiffness, blocked motion, traumatic arthritis, and loss of length as a result of collapse at the fracture site. In the absence of traumatic arthritis, a malunited greater tuberosity can be treated by osteotomy and repositioning below the articular surface. Adhesions must be released superficial and deep to the tuberosity and rotator cuff. If the greater tuberosity is adherent to the articular surface, the articular cartilage may be damaged enough to require a humeral head or total-shoulder replacement. Postoperatively, abduction splinting in approximately 45° for the first 3 to 4 weeks protects the tuberosity fixation while allowing for early bone and fibrous healing.

The typical surgical neck malunion has varus angulation. Surgical neck malunion with anterior angulation of the shaft or prominence of the greater tuberosity can result in a rotator cuff tear because of erosion against the coracoacromial outlet (Fig. 44–77). Valgus malunion secondary to tight tension band repair and collapse in the

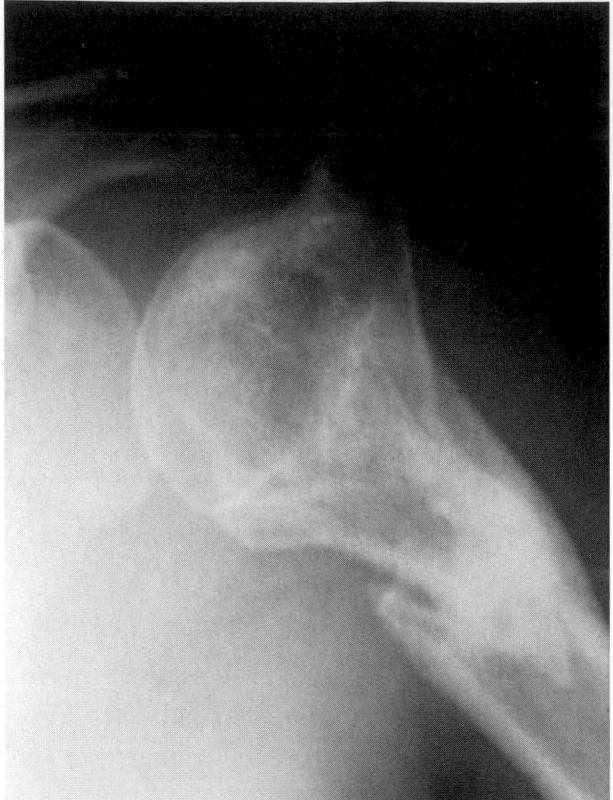

**Figure 44–77.** Varus malunion at the surgical neck rotates the greater tuberosity superiorly. The prominent tuberosity blocks elevation and concomitantly exposes the supraspinatus to more impingement wear.

absence of combined intramedullary fixation has also been reported.[231]

Osteotomy for a surgical neck malunion is technically difficult. The axillary nerve must be dissected free and protected. A closing or opening wedge osteotomy, mobilization of the anatomic planes, fixation out to proper length, and adequate fixation to permit early motion may all be necessary for a satisfactory result. If traumatic arthritis has occurred, consideration is given to accepting the malunion as is, with loss of elevation, or replacing the humeral head. The latter simplifies adjustment of head height and early fixation in preparation for rehabilitation.

## Avascular Necrosis

Injury to the ascending branch of the anterior humeral circumflex artery can result in AVN.[67, 134] AVN rarely occurs after nondisplaced or two-part fractures, occasionally occurs after three-part fractures, and is most common after four-part fractures treated in closed or open fashion. ORIF of complicated three- and four-part fractures with techniques that require more extensive soft tissue stripping seem to increase the incidence of AVN. Sturzenegger and colleagues found that the incidence of AVN was five times greater with plate-and-screw fixation techniques than with the more simple pinning and tension band techniques.[231] Some reports of treatment of four-part fractures without

the development of AVN have appeared,[121] but longer-term follow-up is required because the sequelae of AVN may take several years to develop and cause clinically significant problems. Lee and Hansen noted an intact humeral head at 2 years that later collapsed 3.5 years after treatment.[138]

The clinical manifestations of AVN are often insidious, with gradually worsening shoulder pain and dysfunction. Some patients with AVN and collapse of the humeral head have only mild to moderate symptoms, but most have substantial dysfunction. The clinical relevance of post-traumatic AVN was investigated by Gerber and co-workers,[65] who reviewed 25 patients with post-traumatic AVN of the humeral head. Overall shoulder function according to the Constant score was 51% of that of an age- and sex-matched normal control group. The clinical outcome was related to anatomic alignment of the healed proximal end of the humerus. They noted that a proximal humeral fracture that is at risk for AVN has to be reduced anatomically. If anatomic reduction cannot be obtained, other treatment such as humeral head replacement should be considered.

Core decompression plus bone grafting, which has been used to treat AVN associated with steroid use or sickle cell anemia, might be a consideration for preventing later collapse. Magnetic resonance imaging can be used to demonstrate the location and extent of involvement of the articular segment when planning the procedure. The goal is to stimulate revascularization of the necrotic segment of bone before collapse and the development of articular incongruity. With collapse of the humeral head from AVN, hardware penetration into the joint may hasten traumatic arthritis.[147, 185, 231, 258]

Replacement of the humeral head early rather than waiting until the collapse is severe has advantages (Fig. 44–78). With more extensive collapse, the humeral head can envelop the glenoid and cause further limitation of motion and damage to the articular surface of the glenoid. Intervention before hardware penetration through a collapsing head or severe muscle and capsular contraction can avoid more complex procedures such as subscapularis lengthening or glenoid replacement. Long-standing AVN will probably require both to provide optimal pain reduction and functional restoration (Fig. 44–79).

## Nerve Injury

Nerve injury may occur at the time of fracture, with closed reduction, or after surgical treatment. Brachial plexus injury requires careful and repeated clinical, EMG, and nerve conduction studies for assessment. The most common isolated nerve injured is the axillary nerve. Injuries to the musculocutaneous and suprascapular nerves are less common. If recovery does not begin by 3 months, exploration is warranted. If the nerve is severed or ruptured, both anterior and posterior approaches are necessary. Sural nerve grafting is the treatment of choice.

For long-standing suprascapular nerve injuries, latissimus dorsi transfer for external rotation power may be indicated. Tendon transfers for complete loss of the

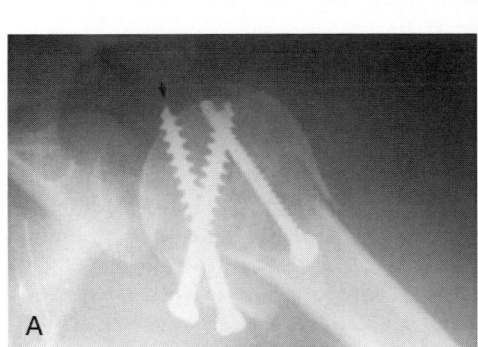
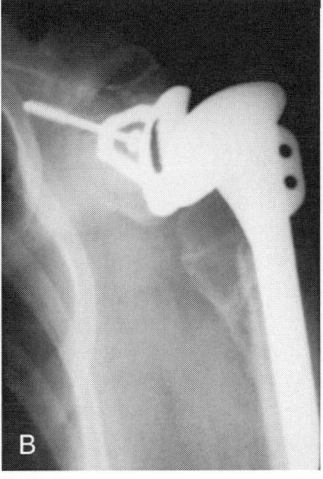

FIGURE 44–78. Complications of open reduction with screw fixation. *A*, Open reduction and internal reduction of a three-part fracture with an intra-articular screw. *B*, Advanced glenoid erosion was treated with a glenoid bone graft from the humeral head at the time of prosthetic replacement, with restoration of function and relief of pain (*C*).

axillary nerve are not very successful, but for isolated loss of the anterior deltoid alone, reapproximation of the pectoralis and middle deltoid has proved valuable.

Most patients recover sufficient muscle strength so that muscle and tendon transfers are not required. Shoulder stiffness is a more common problem and can be avoided with careful attention to rehabilitation.

## Vascular Injury

Successful management of serious vascular injury requires early diagnosis and treatment.[226] Clinical signs and diagnostic tests have been discussed previously. With advancing age, arteriosclerosis increases the risk of vascular injury from minor trauma. Complications in the treatment of vascular injury include compartment syndrome and infection (see Fig. 44–6C).

## Joint Stiffness and Adhesive Capsulitis

Shoulder stiffness or loss of motion is a relatively common sequela of proximal humeral fractures. In many cases, the limitations are mild and not clinically significant enough to require operative management. Loss of motion occurs with prolonged immobilization and is best avoided by initiating early range-of-motion exercises. Unfortunately, even satisfactory radiographic evidence of healing may accompany a poor functional result if immobilization is prolonged. Loss of motion can also be the result of malunion of the proximal end of the humerus and glenohumeral joint

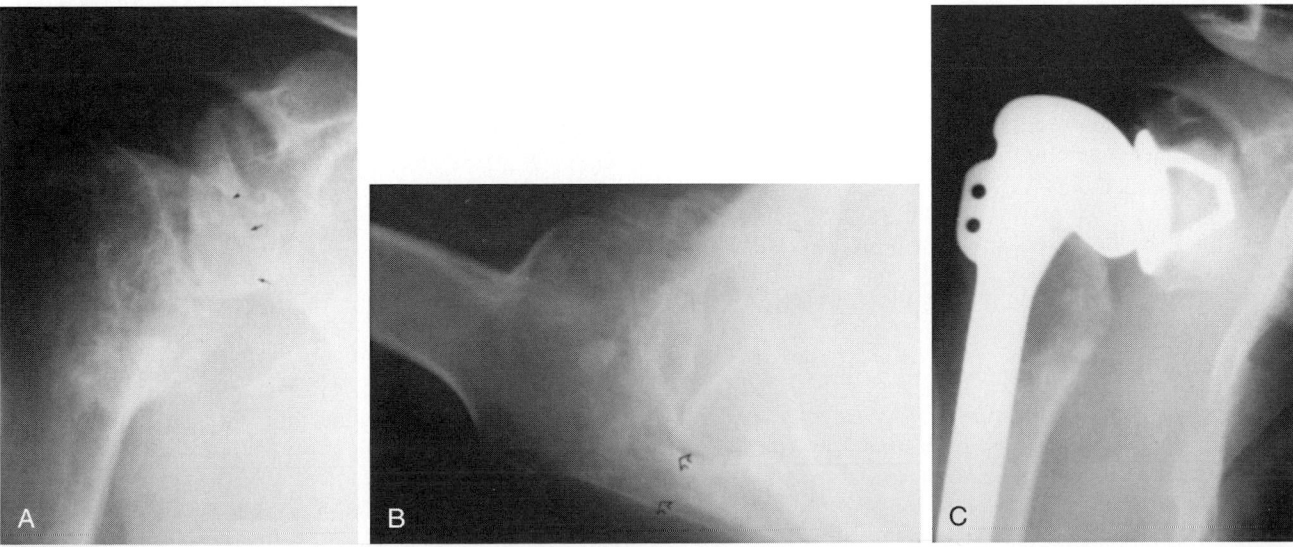

FIGURE 44–79. Late results of closed treatment of a head-splitting fracture at 10 years with disabling pain and only scapulothoracic motion. *A* and *B*, The enlarged humeral head cavity (*arrows*) captures the glenoid and locks on the posterior rim. *C*, With an intact rotator cuff, a prosthetic replacement provides the needed fulcrum for motion and relief of pain.

incongruity. When a fracture has healed anatomically, stiffness is the result of scarring and capsular contracture.

Malunion of the greater or lesser tuberosities causes limitation of external and internal rotation, respectively. The greater tuberosity can impinge against the posterior glenoid and the lesser tuberosity can impinge against either the anterior glenoid or the coracoid process. Superior malunion of the greater tuberosity can cause limitations in humeral abduction or elevation. Surgical neck malunion usually results in loss of elevation and rotation.

Scar and adhesions occur in the bursal and capsular structures. Once fracture stability has been achieved, stretching exercises are the mainstay of treatment for 3 to 6 months. If hardware removal is required in patients with shoulder stiffness, open lysis of adhesions with release of scar and contracture, release of the coracohumeral ligament and inferior glenohumeral capsule, and gentle open manipulation under anesthesia followed by an intensive physical therapy program is indicated. If removal of hardware is not required, therapy might be considered for 6 to 9 months before open release. Arthroscopic release can be considered for stiffness after closed fracture treatment with no or minimal malunion.[20] Arthroscopy permits a minimally invasive evaluation of the articular surfaces. The anterior, posterior, and inferior capsular surfaces, as well as the rotator cuff interval, can be released. In addition, subacromial and subdeltoid adhesions can be released and débrided.

Closed manipulation under anesthesia should be considered with caution because of the possibility of significant risk, including redisplacement of the fracture, new fracture in osteopenic bone, or dehiscence of the rotator cuff.[231] Manipulation under anesthesia is not recommended. Open or arthroscopic release 6 to 12 months after surgery, combined with removal of any prominent hardware, has proved to be effective when necessary.

## Rotator Cuff Tear

A postoperative rotator cuff tear is seen with early unprotected active motion or aggressive passive motion before healing. It can also occur with manipulation under anesthesia and with prominent greater tuberosity malunions that chronically impinge under the acromion.

## Deltoid Dehiscence

Deltoid dehiscence or other problems with the deltoid origin occur after anterior acromioplasty, lateral acromionectomy, or a transacromial approach to the shoulder. With an anterior acromioplasty approach, the deltoid is repaired with nonabsorbable sutures and protected for 4 to 6 weeks. Lateral acromionectomy has been discarded as an operative approach. The transacromial approach is not recommended because it can result in nonunion or malunion. Anterior deltoid detachment can occur after an anterior superior approach if the deltoid repair is not secure or adequately protected.

## Inferior Subluxation of the Glenohumeral Joint

Inferior subluxation after a fracture of the proximal end of the humerus occurs in 10% to 20% of patients.[57, 237] After ORIF, inferior subluxation is anticipated in all patients initially[175]; in the absence of nerve injury, diminished muscle tone as a result of fatigue is the most commonly recognized cause.[37, 57, 113] Inferior subluxation also occurs after fractures of the glenoid, tears of the capsule or ligament, dislocation of the shoulder with nerve injury, isolated brachial plexus injury, and postoperatively when adequate sling support is not provided.[255] Nontraumatic causes include stroke or hemiplegia, poliomyelitis, ligamentous laxity, brachial neuritis, neoplastic compression of the brachial plexus, septic arthritis, neuralgic amyotrophy, hemophilic hemarthrosis, and rheumatoid arthri-

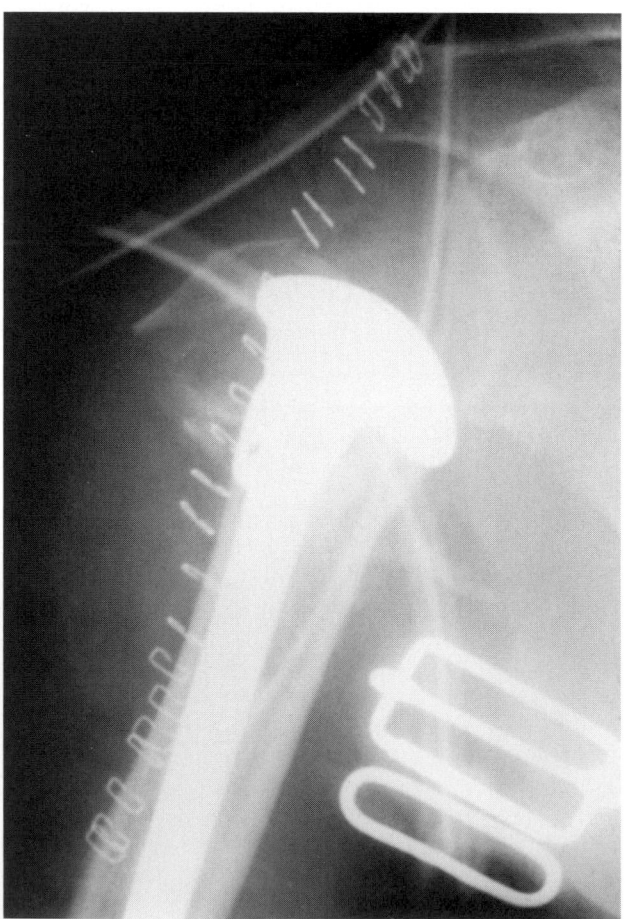

**FIGURE 44–80.** Four-part fracture with early tuberosity dehiscence. The technical error was in seating the prosthetic keel on the upper part of the shaft without restoring humeral length. This mistake resulted in inferior instability and promoted tuberosity dehiscence.

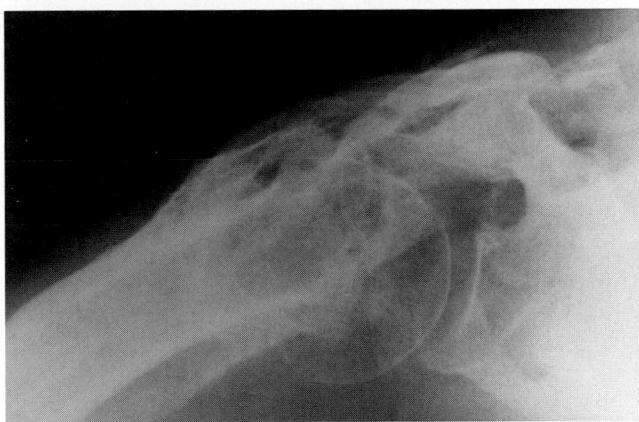

**FIGURE 44–81.** Axillary lateral radiograph demonstrating extensive heterotopic ossification after anatomic open reduction and internal fixation of a displaced four-part proximal humeral fracture that occurred in a high-speed motor vehicle accident. The patient had the functional equivalent of a glenohumeral arthrodesis. The surgery was delayed because of other injuries. The patient had no glenohumeral motion. The ossification bridges from the acromion to the humerus within the deltoid and from the coracoid to the humerus.

tis.[10, 255] Complete recovery is anticipated in most cases. The humerus is supported with a sling to reduce the inferior subluxation. Isometric exercises for the deltoid and rotator cuff muscles are begun early. EMG studies may be considered for patients thought to have nerve injuries. Operative causes of inferior subluxation include axillary nerve injury and failure to restore full humeral length between the deltoid origin and its insertion (Fig. 44–80).

## Heterotopic Ossification

Clinically significant heterotopic ossification is an uncommon complication that is reported in up to 10% of proximal humeral fractures[174] (Fig. 44–81). Many authors warn against delayed operative treatment of proximal humeral fractures because of concern for heterotopic ossification. The severity of the traumatic injury is also an important factor. Fortunately, in most cases the heterotopic ossification does not affect that result. It is more common in fracture-dislocations, but repeated unsuccessful closed reduction or delay in treatment may also contribute.[174] Heterotopic bone can be a significant problem after head injury. Removal of the heterotopic ossification should be considered only if the ossification is mature (e.g., with sharp cortical margins) rather than active (e.g., with a fluffy radiographic appearance). Such maturity rarely occurs before 6 months. Low-dose radiation treatment at the time of excision is thought to prevent recurrence.

## Recurrent Dislocations

Recurrent shoulder instability may be expected with persistent labral or glenoid rim avulsions.[82, 185] Treatment involves repair of the capsule back to the glenoid. Loss of humeral length, use of a prosthetic head that is too small, malunion of a humeral head, or malrotation of a prosthetic replacement can each result in shoulder instability.

Dehiscence of the rotator cuff superiorly and posteriorly is manifested as anterosuperior subluxation, anterior dislocation, or rarely, inferior subluxation. Avulsion of the subscapularis may be associated with either anterior dislocation or recurrent posterior instability. Nerve injuries or muscle atony may produce inferior subluxation. Identification of the cause of the shoulder instability is essential in formulating the correct reconstructive plan.

## Additional Fractures

Additional unanticipated fractures may result from conversion of a nondisplaced fracture to a displaced fracture at the time of closed or open treatment, or they may occur at the shaft level with intraoperative reduction. The newly created fractures alter the course of treatment. If an intraoperative shaft fracture occurs at the time of ORIF, plating of the shaft fracture, intramedullary fixation, and fixation with a long-stemmed humeral component are potential treatment options.[189] The long-stemmed humeral component is preferred for patients with three- or four-part fractures because both levels can be fixed without the extensive dissection that might be required with the application of plates and screws[25] (Fig. 44–82).

Periprosthetic fractures at the distal tip of the prosthesis are difficult to treat.[13, 253] Closed reduction is not easily controlled with casts or fracture braces. Open treatment alternatives include plate fixation of the fracture, a cortical allograft strut and cerclage wire or cable fixation, and revision arthroplasty with a long-stemmed humeral prosthesis.

## Complications of Prosthetic Replacement

Complications or poor results are relatively common after prosthetic replacement for proximal humeral fracture. Implant selection can have a significant effect on the results. Although a larger head provides better leverage, cuff closure may not be possible and the shoulder may be stiff from overstuffing the joint. In contrast, a smaller prosthetic head allows easier closure of the rotator cuff. If the head is too small, the shoulder may be unstable because of the lax capsule and rotator cuff. Fortunately, most of the current implant systems have multiple head sizes to facilitate anatomic reconstruction of the humeral head.

Loosening of a cemented humeral stem is relatively

uncommon. Loosening and subsidence are more common when the humeral stem is uncemented.

If the humeral prosthesis is placed too low, the length of the humerus has not been restored (see Fig. 44–80). Techniques used in assessing prosthetic height include preoperative scanograms, evaluation of the tension in the intact long head of the biceps and rotator cuff at the time of closure,[75] and fracture jigs.[10]

Incorrect version of a prosthesis can result from placement in malrotation or postoperative loosening after inadequate stem fixation. Placement of a prosthesis in a varus position is not uncommon when the prosthesis is placed on top of the shaft without restoring height. Low head placement relative to the greater tuberosity results in impingement with loss of motion.

Revision of a humeral prosthesis is one of the most difficult orthopaedic procedures to perform. Modular prostheses facilitate revision surgery as long as the humeral stem is well positioned. If it is not well positioned, removal of the prosthesis and cement is required. In rare cases when the prosthesis has been placed in a varus position or when the greater tuberosity has healed over the center of the humeral shaft, there is a danger of placing a new prosthesis in a varus position with the stem through the shaft. Revision of a failed prosthesis can be exceedingly difficult if the prosthesis has been cemented in poor position. Neither monoblock Neer prosthetic components nor modular components fare well when a cemented prosthesis is malpositioned. Unfortunately, just changing a modular head does not correct the problem, and removal and repositioning of the stem are necessary. In revising one-piece humeral components, a shorter or narrower stem can be recemented out to proper height for correction of version, but if an angular deformity is present, removal of the cement enables more accurate placement of the new prosthetic component.

For a satisfactory outcome, revision requires attention to all potential deficits. The prosthesis should be at the proper height and version with secure rotator cuff

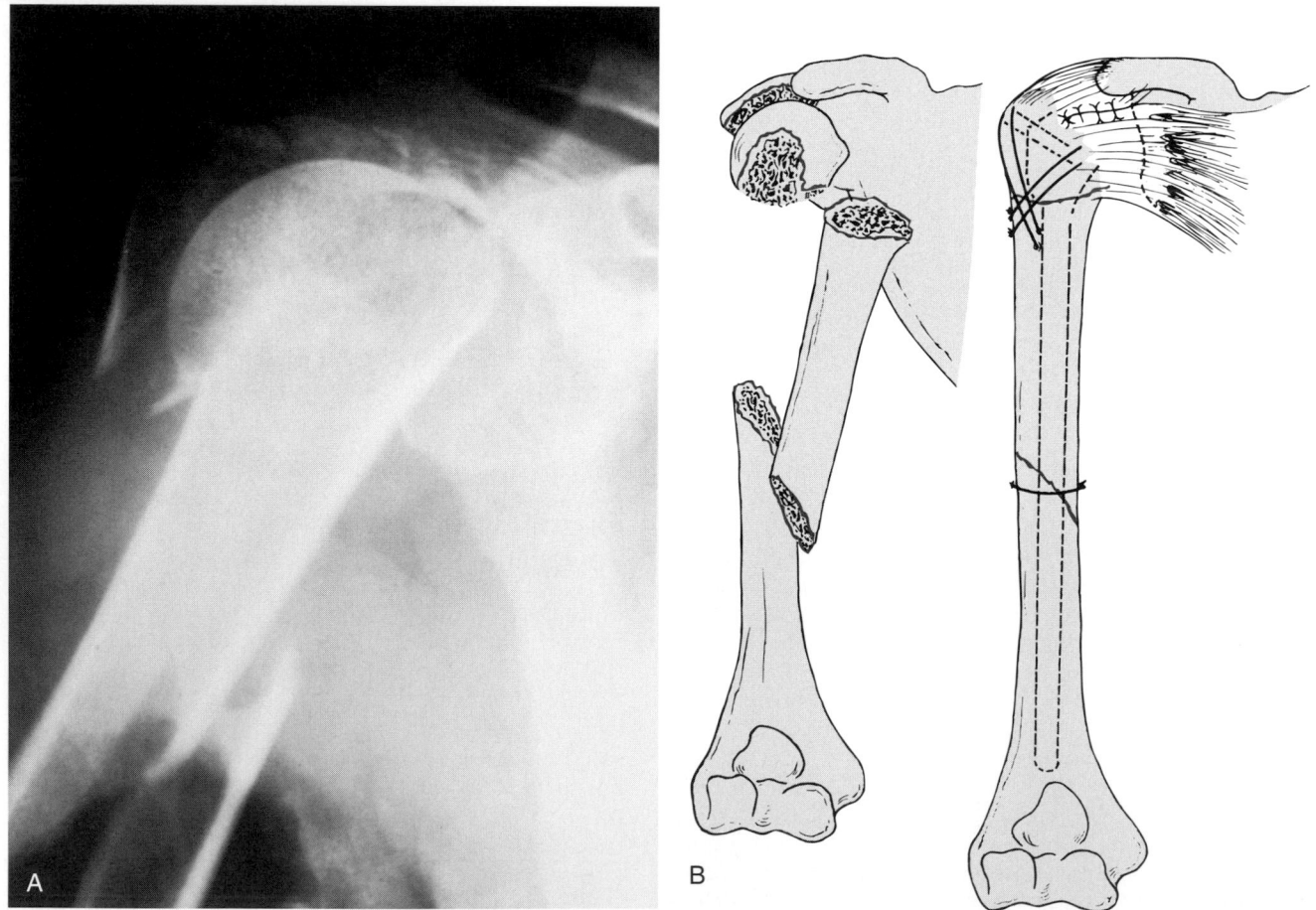

**FIGURE 44–82.** Long-stem prosthesis. *A,* Three-part fracture of the proximal end of the humerus with a diaphyseal midshaft fracture. *B,* Reconstruction of the cuff and tuberosities and fixation of the shaft fracture with a long-stem prosthesis. (*B,* Redrawn from Norris, T.R.; McElheney, E. Semin Arthroplasty 1:138–150, 1990.)

| TABLE 44–4 |
| --- |

## Complications of Humeral Head Prosthetic Replacement

Loosening with subsidence, spinning, or pistoning
  Malposition
  Version: anteverted with anterior instability; retroverted with
    posterior instability
  Too low, with instability
  Too high, with impingement
  Varus: head low, stem out of shaft; narrow stem in large shaft
Soft tissue and bone
  Dehiscence of tuberosities, rotator cuff, or deltoid
  Dislocation or subluxation
  Infection
  Heterotopic bone
  Nerve injury
  Humeral shaft bone defects with loss of length
  Tuberosity excision
  Tuberosity malunion
  Contractures
  Intra- or postoperative humeral shaft fracture at distal prosthetic
    stem
  Inadequate aftercare and rehabilitation

reconstruction. Bone deficits require grafting. Ample postoperative protection and support are necessary until sufficient healing has occurred to begin motion. Complications of prosthetic replacement are summarized in Table 44–4.

## CONCLUSION

Proximal humeral fractures are common injuries; treatment of most is straightforward and uncomplicated. Displaced fractures are less common, and their treatment is more challenging. Many pitfalls must be avoided by the patient and surgeon during the course of treatment. Emphasis is placed on complete and accurate diagnosis and the selection of safe and simple techniques for restoration of musculoskeletal anatomy and shoulder girdle function. Limited dissection and limited internal fixation techniques are best suited for displaced proximal humeral fractures. Prosthetic arthroplasty has proved to be of considerable value in treatment of the more serious comminuted proximal humeral fractures and in the late reconstruction of malunions, nonunions, and traumatic arthritis.

## REFERENCES

1. Alnot, J.Y. Traumatic brachial plexus palsy in the adult: Retro and infraclavicular lesions. Clin Orthop 237:9–16, 1988.
2. Bandi, W. Zur operativen Therapie der Humeruskopfundhalsfrakturen. Unfallheilkunde 196:38–45, 1976.
3. Bengner, U.; Johnell, O.; Redlund-Johnell, I. Changes in the incidence of fracture of the upper end of the humerus during a 30 year period: A study of 2125 fractures. Clin Orthop 231:179–182, 1988.
4. Beredjiklian, P.K.; Iannotti, J.P.; Norris, T.R.; Williams, G.R. Operative treatment of malunion of a fracture of the proximal aspect of the humerus. J Bone Joint Surg Am 80:1484–1497, 1998.
5. Berry, H.; Bril, V. Axillary nerve palsy following blunt trauma to the shoulder region: A clinical and electrophysiological review. J Neurol Neurosurg Psychiatry 45:1027–1032, 1982.
6. Bigliani, L.U. Fractures of the proximal humerus. In: Rockwood, C.A., Jr.; Matsen, F.A., III, eds. The Shoulder. Philadelphia, W.B. Saunders, 1990, pp. 278–334.
7. Bigliani, L.U. Treatment of two and three-part fractures of the proximal humerus. Instr Course Lect 38:231–244, 1989.
8. Blom, S.; Dahlback, L.O. Nerve injuries in dislocations of the shoulder joint and fractures of the neck of the humerus: A clinical and electromyographic study. Acta Chir Scand 136:461–466, 1970.
9. Bohler, L. Die Behandlung von Verrenkungsbruchen der Schulter. Dtsch Z Chir 219:238–245, 1929.
10. Boileau, P.; Walch, G.; Krishnan, S.G. Tuberosity osteosynthesis and hemiarthroplasty for four part fractures of the proximal humerus. Tech Shoulder Elbow Surg 1:96–109, 2000.
11. Boileau, P.; Walch, G.; Trojani, C.; et al. Sequelae of fractures of the proximal humerus: Surgical classification and limits of shoulder arthroplasty. In: Walch, G.; Boileau, P., eds. Shoulder Arthroplasty. Berlin, Springer-Verlag, 1999, pp. 349–358.
12. Bosch, U.; Skutek, M.; Fremery, R.W.; Tscherne, H. Outcome after primary and secondary hemiarthroplasty in elderly patients with fractures of the proximal humerus. J Shoulder Elbow Surg 7:479–484, 1998.
13. Boyd, A.D.; Thornhill, T.S.; Barnes, L. Fractures adjacent to humeral prostheses. J Bone Joint Surg Am 74:1498–1504, 1992.
14. Breederveld, R.S.; Patka, P.; Dwars, B.J.; VanMourik, J.C. Shoulder injury caused by electric shock. Neth J Surg 39:147–148, 1987.
15. Brems, J.J.; Yoon, H.J.; Tetzlaff, J. Interscalene block anaesthesia and shoulder surgery. Paper presented at the Sixth Open Meeting of the American Shoulder and Elbow Surgeons, New Orleans, February 11, 1990.
16. Brien, H.; Noftall, F.; MacMaster, S.; et al. Neer's classification system: A critical appraisal. J Orthop Trauma 38:257–260, 1995.
17. Brooks, C.H.; Revell, W.J.; Heatley, F.W. Vascularity of the humeral head after proximal humerus fractures. J Bone Joint Surg Br 75:132–136, 1993.
18. Brostrom, F. Early mobilization of fractures of the upper end of the humerus. Arch Surg 46:614, 1943.
19. Burge, P.; Rushworth, G.; Watson, N. Patterns of injury of the terminal branches of the brachial plexus. J Bone Joint Surg Br 67:630–634, 1985.
20. Burkhart, S.S. Arthroscopic subscapularis tenolysis: A technique for treating refractory glenohumeral stiffness following open reduction and internal fixation of a displaced three-part proximal humerus fracture. Arthroscopy 12:87–91, 1996.
21. Bernstein, J.; Adler, L.M.; Blank, J.E.; et al. Evaluation of the Neer system of classification of proximal humerus fractures with computerized tomographic scans and plain radiographs. J Bone Joint Surg Am 78:1371–1375, 1996.
22. Caldwell, J.A. Treatment of fractures in the Cincinnati General Hospital. Ann Surg 97:174–177, 1933.
23. Caldwell, J.A.; Smith, J. Treatment of unimpacted fractures of the surgical neck of the humerus. Am J Surg 31:141–144, 1936.
24. Callahan, D.J. Anatomic considerations. Closed reduction of proximal humeral fractures. Orthop Rev 13(3):79–85, 1984.
25. Campbell, J.T.; Moore, R.S.; Iannotti, J.P. et al. Periprosthetic humeral fractures: Mechanisms of fracture and treatment options. J Shoulder Elbow Surg 7:406–413, 1998
26. Castagno, A.A.; Shuman, W.P.; Kilcoyne, R.F.; et al. Complex fractures of the proximal humerus: Role of CT in treatment. Radiology 165:759–762, 1987.
27. Cave, E.A. Fractures and Other Injuries. Chicago, Year Book, 1958.
28. Chun, J.M.; Groh, G.I.; Rockwood, C.A., Jr. Two-part fractures of the proximal humerus. J Shoulder Elbow Surg 3:273–287, 1994.
29. Clifford, P.C. Fractures of the neck of the humerus: A review of the late results. Injury 12:91–95, 1981.
30. Codman, E.A. The Shoulder. Boston, T. Todd, 1934.
31. Coene, L.N.; Narakas, A.O. Surgical management of axillary nerve lesions, isolated or combined with other infraclavicular nerve lesions. Periph Nerve Repair Regen 3:47–65, 1986.
32. Cofield, R.H. Comminuted fractures of the proximal humerus. Clin Orthop 230:49–57, 1988.
33. Cofield, R.H. Total shoulder arthroplasty with the Neer prosthesis. J Bone Joint Surg Am 66:899–906, 1984.
34. Conn, R.A.; Cofield, R.H.; Byer, D.E.; et al. Interscalene block anaesthesia for shoulder surgery. Clin Orthop 216:94–98, 1987.

35. Connor, P.M.; Boatright, J.R.; D'Alessandro, D.F. Posterior fracture-dislocation of the shoulder: Treatment with acute osteochondral grafting. J Shoulder Elbow Surg 6:480–485, 1997.

36. Cornell, C.N.; Levine, D.; Pagnani, M.J. Internal fixation of proximal humerus fractures using the screw-tension band technique. J Orthop Trauma 8:23–27, 1994.

37. Cotton, F.J. Subluxation of the shoulder—downward. Boston Med Surg J 185:405–407, 1921.

38. Craig, E.V. Continuous passive motion in the rehabilitation of the surgically reconstructed shoulder: A preliminary report. Orthop Trans 10:219, 1986.

39. Cuomo, F.; Flatow, E.L.; Miller, S.R.; et al. Open reduction and internal fixation of two and three-part displaced surgical neck fractures of the proximal humerus. J Shoulder Elbow Surg 1:287–295, 1992.

40. Dameron, T.B., Jr. Complications of the treatment of injuries to the shoulder. In: Epps, C.H., ed. Complications in Orthopaedic Surgery, 2nd ed., Vol. 1. Philadelphia, J.B. Lippincott, 1986, pp. 273–274.

41. Darder, A.D.; Darder, A., Jr.; Sanchis, V.; et al. Four-part displaced proximal humerus fractures: Operative treatment using Kirschner wires and tension band. J Orthop Trauma 7:497–505, 1993.

42. deAnquin, C.L.; deAnquin, A. Prosthetic replacement in the treatment of serious fractures of the proximal humerus. In: Bayley, I.; Kessel, L., eds. Shoulder Injury. Berlin, Springer-Verlag, 1965, pp. 206–217.

43. Dehne, E. Fractures of the upper end of the humerus: A classification based on the etiology of trauma. Surg Clin North Am 25:28–47, 1945.

44. DePalma, A.F. Surgery of the Shoulder, 2nd ed. Philadelphia, J.B. Lippincott, 1973.

45. DePalma, A.F.; Cantilli, R.A. Fractures of the upper end of the humerus. Clin Orthop 20:73–93, 1961.

46. Des Marchais, J.E.; Morais, G. Treatment of complex fractures of the proximal humerus by Neer hemiarthroplasty. In: Bateman, J.E.; Welsh, R.P., eds. Surgery of the Shoulder. Philadelphia, B.C. Decker, 1984.

47. Din, K.M.; Meggitt, B.F. Bilateral four-part fractures with posterior dislocation of the shoulder. J Bone Joint Surg Br 65:176–178, 1983.

48. Dines, D.M.; Warren, R.F. Modular shoulder hemiarthroplasty for acute fractures. Surgical considerations. Clin Orthop 307:18–26, 1994.

49. Dingley, A.; Denham, R. Fracture-dislocation of the humeral head: A method of reduction. J Bone Joint Surg Am 55:1299–1300, 1973.

50. Dorgan, J.A. Posterior dislocation of the shoulder. Am J Surg 89:890–900, 1955.

51. Ebel, R. Uber die Ursachen der axillaris parese bei Schulterluxation. Msche Unfallheilk 76:445–449, 1973.

52. Eberson, C.P.; Ng, T.; Green, A. Contralateral intrathoracic displacement of the humeral head. A case report. J Bone Joint Surg Am 82:105–108, 2000.

53. Edelman, G. Immediate therapy of complex fractures of the upper end of the humerus by means of acrylic prosthesis. Presse Med 59:1777–1778, 1951.

54. Einarsson, F. Fractures of the upper end of the humerus: Discussion based on follow-up of 302 cases. Acta Orthop Scand Suppl 32:10–209, 1958.

55. Ekstrom, T.; Lagergren, C.; von Schreeb, T. Procaine injections and early mobilization for fractures of the neck of the humerus. Acta Chir Scand 130:18–24, 1965.

56. Esser, R.D. Treatment of three- and four-part fractures of the proximal humerus with a modified cloverleaf plate. J Orthop Trauma 8:15–22, 1994.

57. Fairbank, T.J. Fracture-subluxation of the shoulder. J Bone Joint Surg Br 30:454–460, 1948.

58. Flatow, E.L.; Cuomo, F.; Maday, M.G.; et al. Open reduction and internal fixation of two-part displaced fractures of the greater tuberosity of the proximal part of the humerus. J Bone Joint Surg Am 73:1213–1218, 1991.

59. Fourrier, P.; Martini, M. Posttraumatic avascular necrosis of the humeral head. Int Orthop 1:187–190, 1977.

60. Freundlich, B.D. Luxatio erecta. J Trauma 23:434–436, 1983.

61. Frich, L.H.; Sojbjerg, J.O.; Sneppen, O. Shoulder arthroplasty in complex acute and chronic proximal humeral fractures. Orthopedics 14:949–954, 1991.

62. Funsten, R.V.; Kinser, P. Fractures and dislocations about the shoulder. J Bone Joint Surg 18:191–198, 1936.

63. Garceau, G.J.; Coglang, S. Early physical therapy in the treatment of fractures of the surgical neck of the humerus. J Indiana Med Assoc 34:293–295, 1941.

64. Geneste, R.; Durandeau, A.; Gauzere, J.M.; Roy, J. Closed treatment of fracture dislocations of the shoulder joint. Rev Chir Orthop 66:383–386, 1980.

65. Gerber, C.; Hersche, O.; Berberat, C. The clinical relevance of posttraumatic avascular necrosis of the humeral head. J Shoulder Elbow Surg 7:586–590, 1998.

66. Gerber, C.; Lambert, S.M.; Allograft reconstruction of segmental defects of the humeral head for treatment of chronic locked posterior dislocation of the shoulder. J Bone Joint Surg Am 78:376–382, 1996.

67. Gerber, C.; Schneeberger, A.; Vinh, T.S. The arterial vascularization of the humeral head: An anatomical study. J Bone Joint Surg Am 72:1486–1494, 1990.

68. Gerber, C.; Warner, J.P. Alternatives to hemiarthroplasty for complex proximal-humeral fractures. In: Warner, J.P.; Iannotti, J.; Gerber, C., eds. Complex and Revision Problems in Shoulder Surgery. Philadelphia, Lippincott-Raven, 1997, pp. 215–243.

69. Goldman, A.; Sherman, O.; Price, A.; Minkoff, J. Posterior fracture dislocation of the shoulder with biceps tendon interposition. J Trauma 27:1083–1086, 1987.

70. Goldman, R.T.; Koval, K.J.; Cuomo, F.; et al. Functional outcome after humeral head replacement for acute three and four-part proximal humerus fractures. J Shoulder Elbow Surg 4:81–86, 1995.

71. Goss, T.P. Proximal humeral fractures revisited. Orthop Rev 16:17–24, 1987.

72. Green, A.; Barnard, W.L.; Limbird, R.S. Humeral head replacement for acute, four-part proximal humerus fractures. J Shoulder Elbow Surg 2:249–254, 1993.

73. Green, A.; Lippitt, S.B.; Wirth, M.A. Outcome of humeral head replacement for displaced proximal humerus fractures: A prospective, multi-center study. Paper presented at the Annual Meeting of the American Academy of Orthopaedic Surgeons, 199

74. Green, A.; Lippitt, S.B.; Wirth M.A. Patient self-assessed outcome after humeral head replacement for acute complex proximal humerus fracture. Paper presented at the Annual Meeting of the American Academy of Orthopaedic Surgeons, 2001.

75. Green, A.; Norris, T.R. Humeral head replacement for four-part fractures and fracture-dislocations. Operative Tech Orthop 4:13–20, 1994.

76. Green, A.; Norris, T.R. Imaging techniques in glenohumeral arthritis. Clin Orthop 307:18–26, 1994.

77. Gristina, A.G. Symposium: Management of displaced fractures of the proximal humerus. Contemp Orthop 15:61–93, 1987.

78. Habernek, H.; Schneider, R.; Popp, R.; et al. Spiral bundle nailing for subcapital humeral fractures: Preliminary report of the method of Henning. J Trauma 46:400–406, 1999.

79. Hagg, O.; Lundberg, B.J. Aspects of prognostic factors in comminuted and dislocated proximal humeral fractures. In: Bateman, J.E.; Welsh, R.P., eds. Surgery of the Shoulder. Philadelphia, B.C. Decker, 1984.

80. Hall, M.C.; Rosser, M. The structure of the upper end of the humerus with reference to osteoporotic changes in senescence leading to fracture. Can Med Assoc J 88:290–294, 1963.

81. Hall, R.F., Jr.; Pankovich, A.M. Ender nailing of acute fractures of the humerus. J Bone Joint Surg Am 69:558–567, 1987.

82. Hall, R.H.; Isaac, F.; Booth, C.R. Dislocations of the shoulder with special reference to accompanying small fractures. J Bone Joint Surg Am 41:489–494, 1959.

83. Hardcastle, P.H.; Fisher, T.R. Intrathorax displacement of the humeral head with fracture of the surgical neck. Injury 12:313–315, 1981.

84. Hawkins, R.J.; Angelo, R.L. Displaced proximal humeral fractures: Selecting treatment, avoiding pitfalls. Orthop Clin North Am 18:421–431, 1987.

85. Hawkins, R.J.; Bell, R.H.; Gurr, K. The three-part fracture of the proximal part of the humerus. J Bone Joint Surg Am 68:1410–1414, 1986.

86. Hawkins, R.J.; Gurr, K. A review of 3-part displaced proximal humeral fractures: Operative vs. nonoperative management. Orthop Trans 8:87, 1984.

87. Hawkins, R.J.; Neer, C.S., II; Pianta, R.M.; Mendoza, F.X. Locked posterior dislocation of the shoulder. J Bone Joint Surg Am 69:9–18, 1987.

88. Hawkins, R.J.; Switlyk, P. Acute prosthetic replacement for severe fractures of the proximal humerus. Clin Orthop 289:156–160, 1993.

89. Hayes, M.J.; Van Winkle, N. Axillary artery injury with minimally displaced fracture of the neck of humerus. J Trauma 23:431–433, 1983.

90. Heim, U.; Pfeiffer, K.M. Internal Fixation of Small Fractures. Technique Recommended by the AO/ASIF Group. New York, Springer-Verlag, 1987, pp. 85–106.

91. Henson, G.F. Vascular complications of shoulder injuries: A report of two cases. J Bone Joint Surg Br 38:528–531, 1956.

92. Heppenstall, R.B. Fractures of the proximal humerus. Orthop Clin North Am 6:467–475, 1975.

93. Hermann, O.J. Fractures of the shoulder joint with special reference to the correction of defects. Instr Course Lect 2:359–370, 1944.

94. Hersche, O.; Gerber, C. Iatrogenic displacement of fracture-dislocations of the shoulder. J Bone Joint Surg Br 76:30–33, 1994.

95. Hill, H.A.; Sachs, M.D. The grooved defect in the humeral head: A frequently unrecognized complication of dislocations of the shoulder joint. Radiology 35:690–700, 1940.

96. Horak J.; Nilsson, B.E. Epidemiology of fracture of the upper end of the humerus. Clin Orthop 112:250–253, 1975.

97. Hudson, R.T. The use of the hanging cast in treatment of fractures of the humerus. South Surg 10:132–134, 1941.

98. Hughes, M.; Neer, C.S., II. Glenohumeral joint replacement and postoperative rehabilitation. Phys Ther 55:850–858, 1975.

99. Hundley, J.M.; Stewart, M.J. Fractures of the humerus: A comparative study in methods of treatment. J Bone Joint Surg Am 37:681–692, 1955.

100. Iannotti, J.P.; Gabriel, J.P.; Schneck, S.L.; et al. The normal glenohumeral relationships. An anatomical study of one hundred and forty shoulders. J Bone Joint Surg Am 74:491–500, 1992.

101. Imatani, R.J. Fractures of the scapula: A review of fractures. J Trauma 15:473–478, 1975.

102. Instrum, K.; Fennell, C.; Shrive, N.; et al. Semitubular blade plate fixation in proximal humeral fractures: A biomechanical study in a cadaveric model. J Shoulder Elbow Surg 7:462–466, 1998.

103. Jaberg, H.; Warner, J.J.P.; Jakob, R.P.; Percutaneous stabilization of unstable fractures of the humerus. J Bone Joint Surg Am 74:508–515, 1992.

104. Jager, M.; Wirth, C.J. Luxationstrummerfrakturen des Humeruskopfes-Resektion oder Refixation der Kopffragemente? Unfallheilkunde 84:26–32, 1981.

105. Jakob, R.P.; Kristiansen, T.; Mayo, K.; et al. Classification and aspects of treatment of fractures of the proximal humerus. In: Bateman, J.E.; Welsh, R.P., eds. Surgery of the Shoulder. Philadelphia, B.C. Decker, 1984.

106. Jakob, R.P.; Miniaci, A.; Anson, P.S.; et al. Four-part valgus impacted fractures of the proximal humerus. J Bone Joint Surg Br 73:295–298, 1991.

107. Janecki, C.J.; Barnett, D.C. Fracture-dislocation of the shoulder with biceps tendon interposition. J Bone Joint Surg Am 61:142–143, 1979.

108. Jensen, G.F.; Christiansen, C.; Boesen, J.; et al. Relationship between bone mineral content and frequency of postmenopausal fractures. Acta Med Scand 213:61–63, 1983.

109. Jones, A.R.; Brashear, H.R.; Dameron, T.B. Surgical neck fracture of the humerus with severe displacement: Factors related to union. Orthop Trans 11:457, 1987.

110. Jones, L. Reconstructive operation for nonreducible fractures of the head of the humerus. Ann Surg 97:217–225, 1933.

111. Jones, L. The shoulder joint—observations on the anatomy and physiology with analysis of reconstructive operation following extensive injury. Surg Gynecol Obstet 75:433–444, 1942.

112. Kannus, P.; Palvanen, M.; Niemi, S.; et al. Increasing number and incidence of osteoporotic fractures of the proximal humerus in elderly people. BMJ 313:1051–1052, 1996.

113. Kapandji, I.A. The Physiology of Joints. New York, Churchill Livingstone, 1970, pp. 40–41.

114. Kavanaugh, J.H. Posterior shoulder dislocation with ipsilateral humeral shaft fracture. Clin Orthop 131:168–171, 1978.

115. Kay, S.P.; Amstutz, H.C. Shoulder hemiarthroplasty at UCLA. Clin Orthop 228:42–48, 1988.

116. Keene, J.S.; Huizenga, R.E.; Engber, W.D.; Rogers, S.C. Proximal humerus fractures: A correlation of residual deformity with long-term function. Orthopedics 6:173–178, 1983.

117. Kelly, J.P. Fractures complicating electroconvulsive therapy and chronic epilepsy. J Bone Joint Surg Br 36:70–79, 1954.

118. Key, J.A.; Conwell, H.E. Fractures, Dislocations, and Sprains, 5th ed. St. Louis, C.V. Mosby, 1951.

119. Knight, R.A.; Mayne, J.A. Comminuted fractures and fracture-dislocations involving the articular surface of the humeral head. J Bone Joint Surg Am 39:1343–1355, 1957.

120. Kocher, T. Beitrage zur Kenntnis Einiger Praktisch Wichtiger Fracturenformen. Basel, Carl Sallman Verlag, 1896.

121. Kofoed, H. Revascularization of the humeral head: A report of two cases of fracture-dislocation of the shoulder. Clin Orthop 179:175–178, 1983.

122. Kolb, L.; Vogel, V.H. The use of shock therapy in 305 mental hospitals. Am J Psychiatry 99:90, 1942.

123. Koval, K.J.; Blair, B.; Takei, R.; et al. Surgical neck fractures of the proximal humerus: A laboratory evaluation of ten fixation techniques. J Trauma 40:778–783, 1996.

124. Koval, K.J.; Gallagher, M.A.; Marsicano, J.G.; et al. Functional outcome after minimally displaced fractures of the proximal humerus. J Bone Joint Surg Am 79:203–207, 1997.

125. Koval, K.J.; Sanders, R.; Zuckerman, J.D.; et al. Modified tension band wiring of displaced surgical neck fractures of the humerus. J Shoulder Elbow Surg 2:85–92, 1993.

126. Kraulis J.; Hunter, G. The results of prosthetic replacement in fracture-dislocations of the upper end of the humerus. Injury 8:129–131, 1976.

127. Kristiansen, B.; Barfod, G.; Bredesen, J.; et al. Epidemiology of proximal humeral fractures. Acta Orthop Scand 58:75–77, 1987.

128. Kristiansen, B.; Christensen, S.W. Plate fixation of proximal humeral fractures. Acta Orthop Scand 57:320–333, 1986.

129. Kristiansen, B.; Kofoed, H. External fixation of displaced fractures of the proximal humerus. J Bone Joint Surg Br 69:643–646, 1987.

130. Kristiansen, B.; Kofoed, H. Transcutaneous reduction and external fixation of displaced fractures of the proximal humerus. J Bone Joint Surg Br 70:821–824, 1988.

131. Krueger, F.T. Vitallium replica arthroplasty of shoulder: Care of aseptic necrosis of proximal end of humerus. Surgery 30:1005–1011, 1951.

132. Kyle, R.F.; Conner, T.N. External fixation of the proximal humerus. Orthopedics 11:163–168, 1988.

133. LaFerte, A.D.; Nutter, D.P. The treatment of fractures of the humerus by means of a hanging plaster case—"hanging cast." Ann Surg 114:921–930, 1941.

134. Laing, P.G. The arterial supply to the adult humerus. J Bone Joint Surg Am 38:1105–1116, 1956.

135. Lancaster, J.M.; Koman, L.A.; Gristina, A.G.; et al. Pathologic fractures of the humerus. South Med J 81:52–55, 1988.

136. Lange, R.H.; Engber, W.D.; Clancy, W.G. Expanding applications of the Herbert scaphoid screw. Orthopedics 9:1393–1398, 1986.

137. LeBorgne, J.; LeNeel, J.C.; Mitland, D. Les lesions de l'artere axillaire et de ses branches consecutives à un traumatisme fermé de l'épaule. Ann Chir 27:587, 1973.

138. Lee, C.K.; Hansen, H.R. Posttraumatic avascular necrosis of the humeral head in displaced proximal humeral fractures. J Trauma 21:788–791, 1981.

139. Lentz, W.; Meuser, P. Treatment of fractures of the proximal humerus. Arch Orthop Trauma Surg 96:283–285, 1980.

140. Leyshon, R. Closed treatment of fractures of the proximal humerus. Acta Orthop Scand 55:48–51, 1984.

141. Li, X.R.; Wang, C.W.; Tao, P.X. Internal fixation by percutaneous pinning for the treatment of fracture of surgical neck of humerus. Acta Acad Med Wuhan 4:236–240, 1984.

142. Liebergall, M.; Mosheiff, R.; Lilling, M. Simultaneous bilateral fractures of the femoral necks and the proximal humeral heads during convulsion. Orthop Rev 17:819–820, 1988.

143. Liew, A.S.; Johnson, J.A.; Patterson, S.D.; et al. Effect of screw placement on fixation in the humeral head. J Shoulder Elbow Surg 9:423–426, 2000.

144. Lin, J.; Hou, S.M.; Hang, Y.S. Locked nailing for displaced surgical neck fractures of the humerus. J Trauma 45:1051–1057, 1998.

145. Lindholm, T.S.; Elmstedt, E. Bilateral posterior dislocation of the shoulder combined with fracture of the proximal humerus. Acta Orthop Scand 51:485–488, 1980.

146. Linson, M.A. Axillary artery thrombosis after fracture of the humerus: A case report. J Bone Joint Surg Am 62:1214–1215, 1980.

147. Lower, R.F.; McNiesh, L.M.; Callahan, J.J. Complications of intraarticular hardware penetration. Complications Orthop May/June 1989, pp. 89–93.

148. Lundberg, B.J.; Svenungson-Hartwig, E.; Wikmark, R. Independent exercises vs. physiotherapy in nondisplaced proximal humerus fractures. Scand J Rehabil Med 11:133–136, 1979.

149. Lyons, F.R.; Rockwood, C.A. Migrations of pins used in operations on the shoulder: Current concepts. J Bone Joint Surg Am 72:1262–1267, 1990.

150. Marotte, J.H.; Lord, G.; Bancel, P. L'arthroplastie de Neer dans les fractures et fractures-luxations complexes de l'épaule: A propos de 12 cas. Chirurgie 104:816, 1978.

151. Mason, M.L.; Allen, H.S. The rate of healing of tendons: An experimental study of tensile strength. Ann Surg 113:424, 1941.

152. Mason, M.L.; Shearon, C.G. The process of tendon repair: An experimental study of tendon suture and tendon graft. Arch Surg 25:615, 1932.

153. Matsen, F.M., III; McLean, D. The shoulder database—University of Washington shoulder and elbow service. American Shoulder and Elbow Surgeons Committee to the American Academy of Orthopaedic Surgeons, February 1990.

154. McGahan, J.P.; Rab, G.T.; Dublin, A. Fractures of the scapula. J Trauma 20:880–883, 1980.

155. McLaughlin, H. Common shoulder injuries. Am J Surg 3:282–295, 1947.

156. McLaughlin, H. Trauma. Philadelphia, W.B. Saunders, 1959.

157. McLaughlin, H.; Cavallaro, W.V. Primary anterior dislocation of the shoulder. Am J Surg 80:615, 1950.

158. McLaughlin, H.L. Dislocation of the shoulder with tuberosity fracture. Surg Clin North Am 43:1615–1620, 1963.

159. McQuillan, W.M.; Nolan, B. Ischemia complicating injury. J Bone Joint Surg Br 50:1090, 1970.

160. Michaelis, L.S. Comminuted fracture-dislocation of the shoulder. J Bone Joint Surg 26:363–365, 1944.

161. Milch, H. The treatment of recent dislocations and fracture-dislocations of the shoulder. J Bone Joint Surg Am 31:173–180, 1949.

162. Mills, H.J.; Horne, G. Fractures of the proximal humerus in adults. J Trauma 25:801–805, 1985.

163. Moeckel, B.H.; Dines, D.M.; Warren, R.F.; Altchek, D.W. Modular hemiarthroplasty for fractures of the proximal part of the humerus. J Bone Joint Surg Am 74:884–889, 1992.

164. Moriber, L.A.; Patterson, R.L., Jr. Fractures of the proximal end of the humerus. J Bone Joint Surg Am 49:1018, 1967.

165. Morris, M.E.; Kilcoyne, R.F.; Shuman, W.; Matsen, F., III. Humeral tuberosity fractures: Evaluation by CT scan and management of malunion. Orthop Trans 11:242, 1987.

166. Moseley, H.F. Athletic injuries to the shoulder region. Am J Surg 98:401–422, 1959.

167. Moseley, H.F. Shoulder Lesions, 3rd ed. Edinburgh, E. & S. Livingstone, 1969.

168. Mouradian, W.H. Displaced proximal humeral fractures: Seven years' experience with a modified Zickel supracondylar device. Clin Orthop 212:209–218, 1986.

169. Müller, M.E.; Allgöwer, M.; Willenegger, H. The Technique of Internal Fixation of Fractures. Segmuller, G., trans. New York, Springer-Verlag, 1965.

170. Müller, M.E.; Nazarian, S.; Koch, P.; et al. The Comprehensive Classification of Fractures of Long Bones. New York, Springer-Verlag, 1990, pp. 54–63.

171. Narakas, A. Brachial plexus surgery. Orthop Clin North Am 12:303–323, 1981.

172. Narakas, A. Surgical treatment of traction injuries of the brachial plexus. Clin Orthop 133:71, 1978.

173. Neer, C.S., II. Articular replacement for the humeral head. J Bone Joint Surg Am 37:215–228, 1955.

174. Neer, C.S., II. Displaced proximal humeral fractures: I. Classification and evaluation. J Bone Joint Surg Am 52:1077–1089, 1970.

175. Neer, C.S., II. Displaced proximal humeral fractures: II: Treatment of three-part and four-part displacement. J Bone Joint Surg Am 52:1090–1103, 1970.

176. Neer, C.S., II. Four-segment classification of displaced proximal humeral fractures. Instr Course Lect 24:160–168, 1975.

177. Neer, C.S., II. Fractures about the shoulder. In: Rockwood, C.A.; Greene, D.P., eds. Fractures in Adults. Philadelphia, J.B. Lippincott, 1984.

178. Neer, C.S., II. Indications for replacement of the proximal humeral articulations. Am J Surg 89:901–907, 1955.

179. Neer, C.S., II. Prosthetic replacement of the humeral head—indications and operative techniques. Surg Clin North Am 43:1077–1089, 1970.

180. Neer, C.S., II. Shoulder Reconstruction. Philadelphia, W.B. Saunders, 1990.

181. Neer, C.S., II; Brown, T.H.; McLaughlin, H. Fracture of the neck of the humerus with dislocation of the head fragment. Am J Surg 85:252–258, 1953.

182. Neer, C.S., II; McIlveen, S.J. Humeral head replacement with tuberosity and cuff reconstruction for 4 part displacement: Current results and technique. Rev Chir Orthop 74(Suppl 2):31, 1988.

183. Neer, C.S., II; Watson, K.C.; Stanton, F.J. Recent experience in total shoulder replacement. J Bone Joint Surg Am 64:319–336, 1982.

184. Neviaser, J.S. Complicated fractures and dislocations about the shoulder joint. Instr Course Lect 44:984–998, 1962.

185. Norris, T.R. Fractures and dislocation of the glenohumeral complex. In: Chapman, M.W.; Madison, M., eds. Operative Orthopaedics. Philadelphia, J.B. Lippincott, 1988, pp. 203–220.

186. Norris, T.R. Nonunions of the proximal humerus. Paper presented at the Fourth International Conference on Surgery of the Shoulder, New York, October 4–7, 1989.

187. Norris, T.R. Unconstrained prosthetic shoulder replacement. In: Watson, M., ed. Surgical Disorders of the Shoulder. London, Churchill Livingstone, 1991, pp. 473–510.

188. Norris, T.R.; Green, A.; McGuigan, F.X. Late prosthetic shoulder arthroplasty for displaced proximal humerus fractures. J Shoulder Elbow Surg 4:271–280, 1995.

189. Norris, T.R.; McElheney, E. The role of the long-stemmed humeral head prosthesis in treatment of complex humeral fractures and in revision arthroplasty. Semin Arthroplasty 1:138–150, 1990.

190. Norris, T.R.; Turner, J.A. Surgical treatment of nonunions of the upper humerus shaft in the elderly. Orthop Trans 9:44, 1985.

191. Norris, T.R.; Turner, J.A.; Bovill, D.F. Nonunion of the upper humerus: An analysis of the etiology and treatment in 28 cases. In: Post, M.; Hawkins R.J.; Morrey, B.F., eds. Surgery of the Shoulder. St. Louis, C.V. Mosby, 1990, pp. 63–67.

192. Oni, O.O. Irreducible acute anterior dislocation of the shoulder due to a loose fragment from an associated fracture of the greater tuberosity. Injury 15:138, 1983.

193. Oreck, S.L.; Burgess, A.; Levine, A. Traumatic lateral displacement of the scapula: A radiographic sign of neurovascular disruption. J Bone Joint Surg Am 66:758–763, 1984.

194. Paavolainen, P.; Bjorkenheim, J.M.; Slatis, P.; Paukku, P. Operative treatment of severe proximal humeral fracture. Acta Orthop Scand 54:374–379, 1983.

195. Pankovich, A.M. Update 1987—flexible intramedullary nailing of long bone fracture: A review. J Orthop Trauma 1:78–95, 1987.

196. Park, T.S.; Choi, I.Y.; Kim, Y.H.; et al. A new suggestion for the treatment of minimally displaced fractures of the greater tuberosity of the proximal humerus. Bull Hosp Jt Dis 56:171–176, 1997.

197. Pasila, M.; Jaroma, H.; Kiviluoto, O.; Sundholm, A. Early complications of primary shoulder dislocations. Acta Orthop Scand 49:260–263, 1978.

198. Patel, M.R.; Pardee, M.L.; Singerman, R.C. Intrathoracic dislocation of the head of the humerus. J Bone Joint Surg Am 45:1712–1714, 1963.

199. Pettine, K.A. Open reduction and internal fixation of four-part fractures of the proximal humerus. Contemp Orthop 19:49–54, 1989.

200. Pierce, R.O.; Hodurski, D.F. Fractures of the humerus, radius, and ulna in the same extremity. J Trauma 19:182–185, 1979.

201. Post, M. Fractures of the upper humerus. Orthop Clin North Am 11:239–252, 1980.

202. Resch, J.; Beck, E.; Bayley, I. Reconstruction of the valgus-impacted humeral head fracture. J Shoulder Elbow Surg 4:73–80, 1995.

203. Richard, A.; Judet, R.; Rene, L. Acrylic prosthetic construction of the upper end of the humerus for fracture-subluxations. J Chir 68:537–547, 1952.

204. Richards, R.R.; Kai-Nan An, A.; Bigliani, L.U.; et al. A standardized method for the assessment of shoulder function. J Shoulder Elbow Surg 3:347–352, 1994.

205. Roberts, S.M. Fractures of the upper end of the humerus: An end result study which shows the advantage of early active motion. JAMA 98:367–373, 1932.

206. Rose, S.H.; Melton, L.J., III; Morrey, B.F.; et al. Epidemiologic features of humeral fractures. Clin Orthop 168:24–30, 1982.

207. Rosen, H. Tension band wiring for fracture dislocations of the shoulder. Chirurgie Orthopédique et Traumatologie: 12ème Congress de SICOT. Amsterdam, Excerpta Medica, 1973, pp. 939–941.

208. Rowe, C.R. Prognosis in dislocations of the shoulder. J Bone Joint Surg Am 38:957–977, 1956.

209. Rowe, C.R.; Marble, H. Shoulder girdle injuries. In: Cave, E.F., ed. Fractures and Other Injuries. Chicago, Year Book, 1958.

210. Rubinstein, J.D.; Ebraheim, N.A.; Kellam, J.F. Traumatic scapulothoracic dissociation. Radiology 157:297–298, 1985.

211. Ruedi, T.; Moshfegha, A.; Pfeiller, K.M.; Allgöwer, A. Fresh fractures of the shaft of the humerus: Conservative or operative treatment? Reconstr Surg Traumatol 14:65–74, 1975.

212. Sallay, P.I.; Pedowitz, R.A.; Mallon, W.J.; et al. Reliability and reproducibility of radiographic interpretation of proximal humerus fracture pathoanatomy. J Shoulder Elbow Surg 6:60–69, 1997.

213. Samuel, E. Some complications arising during electrical convulsive therapy. J Ment Sci 89:81, 1943.

214. Sante, H.E. Fractures about the upper end of the humerus. Ann Surg 80:103–114, 1924.

215. Savoie, F.H.; Geissler, W.B.; Vander Griend, R.A. Open reduction and internal fixation of three-part fractures of the proximal humerus. Orthopedics 12:65–70, 1989.

216. Schai, P.; Imhoff, A.; Preiss, S. Comminuted humeral head fractures: A multicenter analysis. J Shoulder Elbow Surg 4:319–330, 1995.

217. Schatzker, J.; Tile, M. The Rationale of Operative Fracture Care. New York, Springer-Verlag, 1987, pp. 31–70.

218. Scheck, M. Surgical treatment of nonunions of the surgical neck of the humerus. Clin Orthop 167:255–259, 1982.

219. Scott, A.C.; Buckle, R.; Browner, B.D.; Hildreth, D.H. High-energy proximal humerus fractures: Fracture patterns and results of treatment. Orthop Trans 13:42, 1989.

220. Seddon, H.J. Nerve lesions complicating certain closed bone injuries. JAMA 135:11–15, 1947.

221. Sever, J.W. Fracture of the head of the humerus: Treatment and results. N Engl J Med 216:1100–1107, 1937.

222. Sidor, M.L.; Zuckerman, J.D.; Lyon, T.; et al. The Neer classification system for proximal humerus fractures: An assessment of interobserver reliability and intraobserver reproducibility J Bone Joint Surg Am 75:1745–1750, 1993.

223. Siebenrock, K.A.; Gerber, C. The reproducibility of classification of fractures of the proximal end of the humerus. J Bone Joint Surg Am 75:1751–1755, 1993.

224. Sjödén, G.O.J.; Movin, T.; Guntner, P.; et al. Poor reproducibility of classification of proximal humerus fractures. Additional CT of minor value. Acta Orthop Scand 68:239–242, 1997.

225. Smith, D.K.; Cooney, W.P. External fixation of high-energy upper extremity injuries. J Orthop Trauma 4:7–18, 1990.

226. Smyth, E.H.J. Major arterial injury in closed fracture of the neck of the humerus: Report of a case. J Bone Joint Surg Am 51:508, 1969.

227. Stableforth, P.G. Four-part fractures of the neck of the humerus. J Bone Joint Surg Br 66:104–108, 1984.

228. Stableforth, P.G. Open reduction and internal fixation of displaced four-segment fractures of the proximal humerus. Operative Tech Orthop 4:26–30, 1994.

229. Stewart, M.J.; Hudley, J.M. Fractures of the humerus: A comparative study in methods of treatment. J Bone Joint Surg Am 37:681–692, 1955.

230. Stimson, B.B. A Manual of Fractures and Dislocations, 2nd ed. Philadelphia, Lea & Febiger, 1947.

231. Sturzenegger, M.; Fornaro, E.; Jakob, R.P. Results of surgical treatment of multifragmented fractures of the humeral head. Arch Orthop Trauma Surg 100:249–259, 1982.

232. Sunderland, S. Nerves and Nerve Injuries, 2nd ed. New York, Churchill Livingstone, 1978.

233. Svend-Hansen, H. Displaced proximal humeral fractures: A review of 49 patients. Acta Orthop Scand 45:359–364, 1974.

234. Szyszkowitz, R.; Seggl, W.; Schleifer, P.; Cundy, P.J. Proximal humerus fractures: Management techniques and expected results. Clin Orthop 292:13–25, 1990.

235. Tanner, M.W.; Cofield, R.H. Prosthetic arthroplasty for fracture and fracture-dislocations of the proximal humerus. Clin Orthop 179: 116–128, 1982.

236. Theodorides, T.; de Keizer, G. Injuries of the axillary artery caused by fractures of the neck of the humerus. Injury 8:120–123, 1976.

237. Thompson, F.R.; Winant, E.M. Comminuted fracture of the humeral head with subluxation. Clin Orthop 20:94–97, 1961.

238. Valls, J. Acrylic prosthesis in a case with fracture of the head of the humerus. Bal Soc Orthop Trauma 17:61, 1952.

239. Vander Ghirst, M.; Houssa, R. Acrylic prosthesis in fractures of the head of the humerus. Acta Chir Belg 50:31, 1951.

240. Warren R. In: Gristina, A.G., ed. Symposium: Management of displaced fractures of the proximal humerus. Contemp Orthop 15:61–93, 1987.

241. Watson, K.C. Modification of Rush pin fixation for fractures of the proximal humerus. Paper presented at the Annual Meeting of the American Shoulder and Elbow Surgeons, Santa Fe, New Mexico, November 3–5, 1988.

242. Watson-Jones, R. Fractures and Joint Injuries, 5th ed., Vol. 2. Baltimore, Williams & Wilkins, 1955.

243. Weaver, J.K. Skiing-related injuries to the shoulder. Clin Orthop 216:24–28, 1987.

244. Wentworth, E.T. Fractures involving the shoulder joint. N Y J Med 40:1282, 1940.

245. Weseley, M.S.; Barenfeld, P.A.; Eisenstein, A.L. Rush pin intramedullary fixation for fracture of the proximal humerus. J Trauma 17:29–37, 1977.

246. Wheeler, D.L.; Colville, M.R. Biomechanical comparison of intramedullary and percutaneous pin fixation for proximal humeral fracture fixation. J Orthop Trauma 11:363–367, 1997.

247. Willems, W.J.; Lin, T.E. Neer arthroplasty for humeral fracture. Acta Orthop Scand 56:394–395, 1985.

248. Williams, G.R., Jr.; Copley, L.A.; Iannotti, J.P.; Lisser, S.P. The influence of intramedullary fixation on figure-of-eight wiring for surgical neck fractures of the proximal humerus: A biomechanical study. J Shoulder Elbow Surg 6:423–428, 1997.

249. Wilson, J.C.; McKeever, F.M. Traumatic posterior (retroglenoid) dislocation of the humerus. J Bone Joint Surg Am 31:160–172, 1949.

250. Winfield, J.M.; Miller, J.; LaFerte, A.D. Evaluation of the "hanging cast" as a method of treating fractures of the humerus. Am J Surg 55:228–249, 1942.

251. Wirth, M.A.; Jensen, K.L.; Agarwal, A.; et al. Fracture-dislocation of the proximal part of the humerus with retroperitoneal displacement of the humeral head. A case report. J Bone Joint Surg Am 79:763–766, 1997.

252. Wretenberg, R.; Ekelund, A. Acute hemiarthroplasty after proximal humerus fracture in old patients. A retrospective evaluation of 18 patients followed for 2–7 years. Acta Orthop Scand 68:121–123, 1997.

253. Wright, T.W.; Cofield, R.H. Humeral fractures after shoulder arthroplasty. J Bone Joint Surg Am 77:1340–1346, 1995.

254. Yamano, Y. Comminuted fractures of the proximal humerus treated with hook plate. Arch Orthop Trauma Surg 105:359–363, 1986.

255. Yosipovitch, Z.; Tikkva, P.; Goldberg, I. Inferior subluxation of the humeral head after injury to the shoulder. J Bone Joint Surg Am 71:751–753, 1989.

256. Young, T.B.; Wallace, W.A. Conservative treatment of fractures and fracture-dislocations of the upper end of the humerus. J Bone Joint Surg Br 67:373–377, 1985.

257. Zuckerman, J.D.; Flugstad, D.L.; Teitz, C.C.; King, H.A. Axillary artery injury as a complication of proximal humeral fractures: Two case reports and a view of the literature. Clin Orthop 189:234–237, 1984.

258. Zuckerman, J.D.; Matsen, F.A. Complications about the glenohumeral joint related to the use of the screws and staples. J Bone Joint Surg Am 66:175–180, 1984.

259. Zyto, K.; Ahrengart, L.; Sperber, A.; Tornkvist, H. Treatment of displaced proximal humerus fractures in elderly patients. J Bone Joint Surg Br 79:412–417, 1997.

# PART III    *Glenohumeral Dislocations*

Andrew Green, M.D.  •  Tom R. Norris, M.D.

Our modern knowledge and understanding of glenohumeral dislocation has roots in antiquity. Shoulder dislocations were described in the Edwin Smith Papyrus about 3000 BC.[17] Paintings on a wall of the tomb of Ramses II appear to depict closed reduction of a shoulder dislocation.[68, 111] At the height of ancient Greek civilization, Hippocrates clearly described glenohumeral dislocation, recommended closed manipulation, and discussed operative treatment of recurrent dislocation.[111, 118]

In recent years, major advances in our understanding of the various components and mechanisms of glenohumeral stability have helped clarify many of the issues related to the clinical manifestation of glenohumeral instability.[87] Technologic advances in musculoskeletal imaging and surgical instrumentation and new surgical procedures have had a significant impact on the treatment of glenohumeral instability. Critical evaluation of long-term outcomes will determine the value of these advances in the management of glenohumeral dislocations and instability.

The glenohumeral joint is the most mobile and most commonly dislocated major joint. The tremendous range of motion is achieved at the expense of intrinsic skeletal stability. Kazar and Relovszky[76] found that 45% of dislocations involve the shoulder. In a large series of shoulder injuries, Cave and co-workers[24, 25] noted that 86% of shoulder dislocations were glenohumeral dislocations. In contrast to the hip, which has a constrained socket, stability of the glenohumeral joint is dependent on the respective static and dynamic soft tissue constraints of the labrum and glenohumeral ligaments and the rotator cuff.[87]

Although the literature on the subject of shoulder dislocation is extensive, only a few good epidemiologic studies have been conducted.[62, 65, 110, 133] Hovelius reported that the incidence of shoulder dislocations between the ages of 18 and 70 years in Sweden was 1.7%.[62] Most studies have noted a two to five times greater incidence of

dislocations in males than females. Although glenohumeral dislocations are commonly associated with the young and athletic, they occur at all ages and in almost equal numbers before and after the age of 45 years.[62, 96, 124] The greatest number of initial dislocations occur between 10 and 20 years of age.[124] Shoulder dislocations rarely occur in children, and approximately 5% of patients with traumatic anterior dislocation have an open proximal humeral epiphysis.[145]

Patient age has been demonstrated to be the most important determinant of the anatomic pathology, complications, and prognosis of glenohumeral dislocations.[61, 64, 65, 124] For example, recurrent dislocation is rarely a problem in older individuals and, when it occurs, is usually the result of rotator cuff tear or subscapularis rupture. However, associated fractures, rotator cuff injuries, and neurovascular injuries are more common in older individuals.[21, 72–74, 112]

The focus of this chapter is acute glenohumeral dislocations. The evaluation of acute shoulder injury is discussed in the first part of this chapter. Here, the classification, mechanism of injury, pathology, associated injuries, complications, and treatment of acute glenohumeral dislocations are addressed. Treatment of glenohumeral fracture-dislocations is discussed in detail in the second part of this chapter.

## DIRECTION OF DISLOCATION

**Anterior.** The vast majority of glenohumeral dislocations are anterior (Fig. 44–83). In Rowe's series, 98% of dislocations were anterior and 2% were posterior.[123, 124] Many authors have discussed the different positions of the humeral head in anterior dislocations.[122] Subcoracoid dislocations are the most common, followed by subglen-

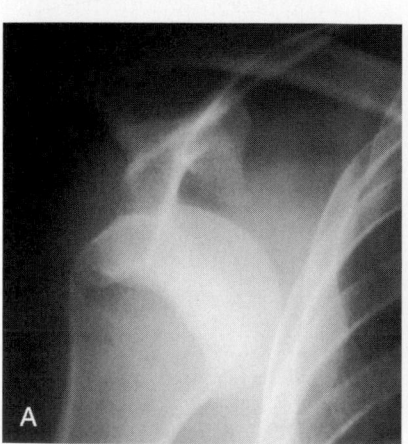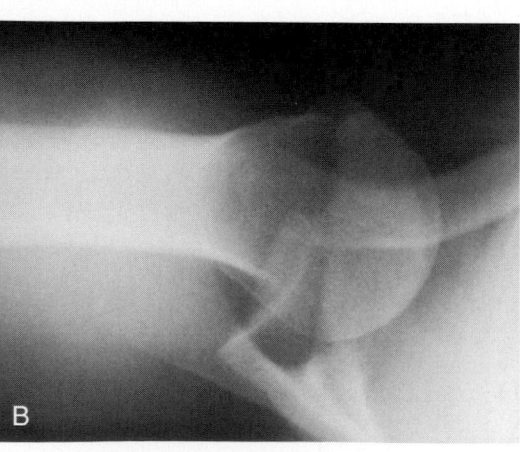

**FIGURE 44–83.** *A,* Anteroposterior shoulder radiograph demonstrating glenohumeral dislocation. *B,* The anterior position of the humeral head is confirmed on an axillary lateral radiograph.

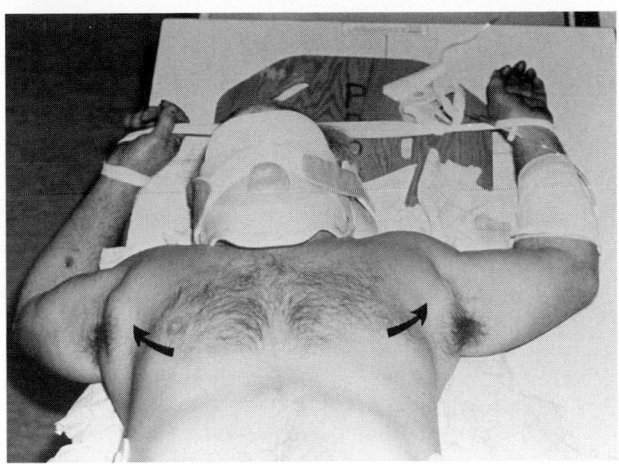

**FIGURE 44–84.** This patient sustained bilateral luxatio erecta after a ladder collapsed under him and both shoulders were hyperabducted. He was splinted with the shoulders dislocated and transported to a trauma center. The humeral heads are prominent in the axilla (*arrows*).

oid, subclavicular, and intrathoracic. Intrathoracic dislocations are exceedingly rare.[38a, 47, 148]

**Posterior.** Posterior glenohumeral dislocations are very rare. They can be either subacromial, subglenoid, or subspinous. Subacromial posterior dislocations are the most common. Most posterior dislocations are considered to be locked posterior fracture-dislocations, with the posterior glenoid rim embedded in the anterior aspect of the articular segment of the humeral head[37, 55, 95] (see Fig. 44–14). Less commonly, a posterior dislocation can spontaneously reduce. Lesser tuberosity fractures and anterior Hill-Sachs or impression fractures are a sign of posterior dislocation.

**Inferior.** Inferior glenohumeral dislocation, or luxatio erecta, is uncommon and usually results from severe trauma.[42] A few bilateral cases have been reported (Fig. 44–84).

**Superior.** Superior dislocations are even more uncommon.[38] As the humeral head is displaced upward, fracture of the acromion, clavicle, coracoid process, and humeral tuberosities or separation of the acromioclavicular joint may occur. Traumatic superior dislocation should be differentiated from the anterior superior instability that can occur with chronic massive rotator cuff tearing or after surgical disruption of the coracoacromial arch.

## ANTERIOR GLENOHUMERAL DISLOCATION

### Mechanism of Injury

Most acute first-time anterior glenohumeral dislocations are the result of a significant injury such as might occur from athletic trauma or a fall. In Rowe's series of over 500 shoulder dislocations, 95% of the dislocations were classified as traumatic.[124] The actual type of trauma is very

age dependent. In the younger age groups, athletic injuries are common, whereas in older persons, dislocations are often the result of falls.[57]

Most dislocations are induced by indirect mechanisms. Anterior dislocations are usually caused by varying degrees of abduction, extension, and external rotation forces on the arm. Occasionally, anterior dislocation can result from a direct blow to the shoulder. Inferior dislocation is the result of a hyperabduction force that levers the proximal end of the humerus against the acromion and out of the glenoid inferiorly. Less commonly, initial shoulder dislocations can be the result of minimal trauma. This mechanism is more frequent in children and young adolescents.

## Pathology

Throughout the orthopaedic literature of the 20th century, the "essential lesion" of recurring anterior glenohumeral dislocation has been a topic of interest. Perthes[114] and Bankart[10, 11] are credited with identifying the importance of detachment of the labrum and the anterior glenohumeral capsule from the anterior rim of the glenoid (Fig. 44–85). Until recently, knowledge of the prevalence of labral detachment and capsular disruption was ascertained only from surgical exploration. Injury to these structures in acute initial anterior glenohumeral dislocations has been demonstrated with various radiographic imaging techniques and arthroscopy.[9, 60, 69, 121, 141]

Ribbans and co-workers[121] evaluated acute primary anterior dislocation with computed arthrotomography. They found damage to the anterior labrum in all patients younger than 50 years and in 75% of those older than 50 years. Magnetic resonance imaging (MRI), which has a

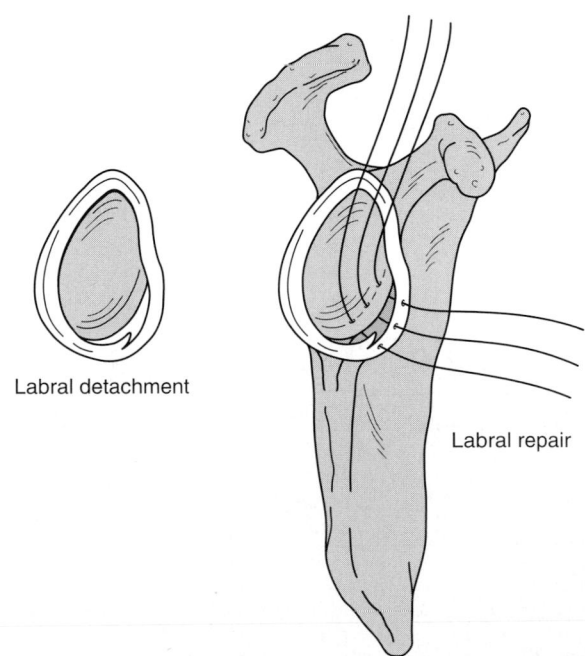

Labral detachment

Labral repair

**FIGURE 44–85.** Drawing with the anteroinferior labrum detached from the glenoid and surgical repair of the glenoid labrum with sutures passed through bone tunnels in the glenoid rim.

high degree of accuracy, is now commonly used to evaluate labral and capsular anatomy.[69]

Arthroscopy provides the opportunity to directly visualize the pathology of glenohumeral dislocations without disrupting the normal anatomic state. Arthroscopic examination demonstrates anatomic pathology in much better detail than possible with any other imaging technique. Hintermann and Gachter[60] evaluated 212 shoulders with shoulder arthroscopy; 184 (87%) had anterior labral tears, 168 (79%) had ventral capsule insufficiency, 144 (68%) had Hill-Sachs lesions, 116 (55%) had glenohumeral ligament insufficiency, and 30 (14%) had complete rotator cuff tears. Baker and associates[9] arthroscopically evaluated 45 shoulders in patients younger than 30 years within 10 days of acute initial dislocation. They defined three groups of patients based on the pathology and degree of

instability. Six shoulders (13%) had capsular tears but no labral lesions and thus had injuries that were considered stable. Eleven shoulders (24%) had capsular tears and partial labral detachment, and the injuries were mildly unstable. Twenty-eight shoulders (62%) had capsular tears with labral detachment and were grossly unstable (Fig. 44–86).

Cadaveric investigations have clarified the significance of the various glenohumeral ligaments and the glenoid labrum in maintaining stability.[66, 87, 101, 129, 135, 143, 144] The anterior band of the inferior glenohumeral ligament is the most important ligamentous constraint to anteroinferior dislocation and instability. Nonetheless, these studies have not yet completely explained anterior glenohumeral instability. Speer and colleagues demonstrated that an isolated anterior labral detachment does not result in

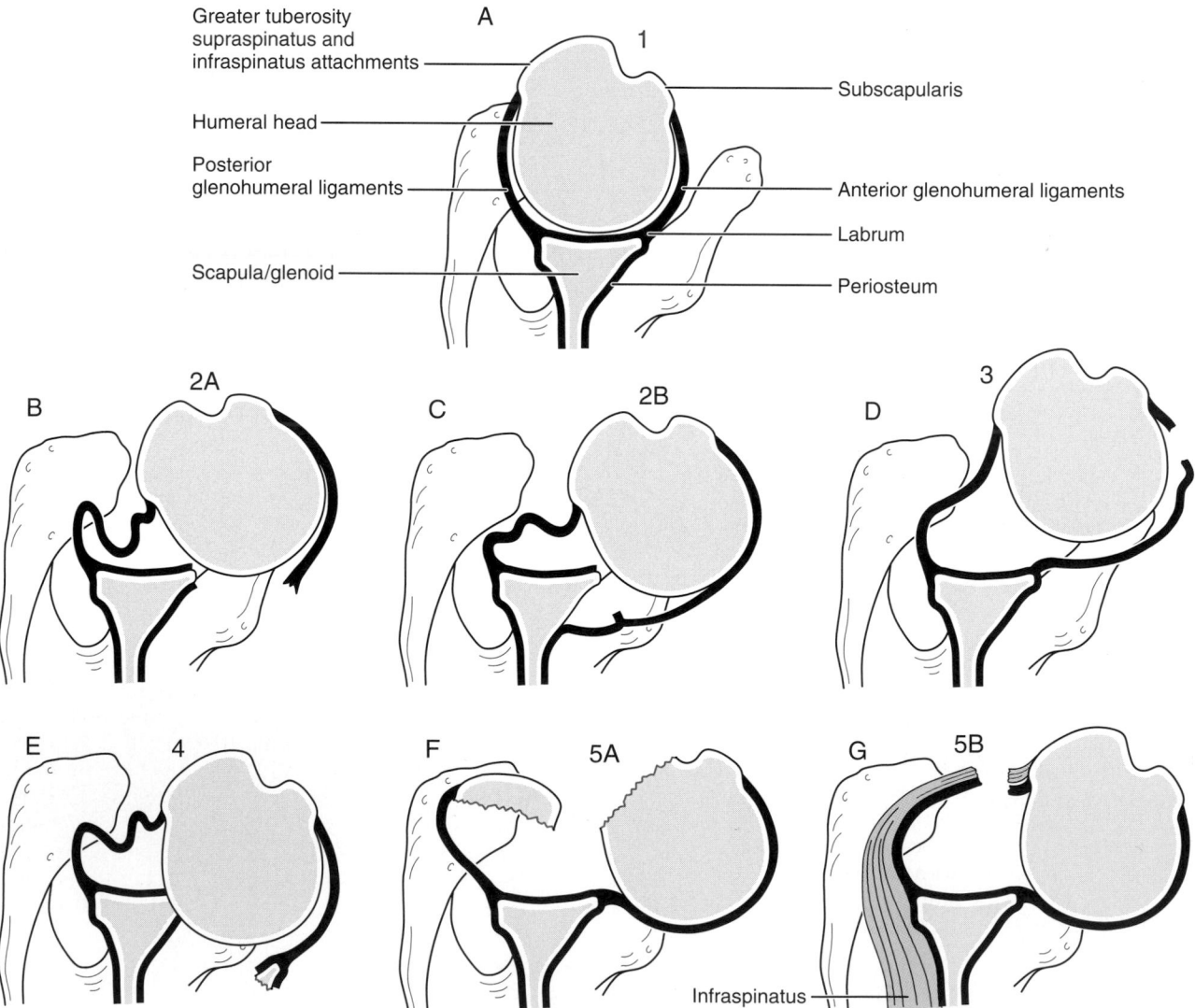

**Figure 44–86.** Diagram of an axial view of the most common pathology that occurs with anterior glenohumeral dislocation. *A,* Normal glenohumeral anatomy. *B,* Anterior labral detachment from the glenoid rim. *C,* Anterior labral detachment in which the periosteum of the anterior neck of the scapula remains attached to the labrum. *D,* Disruption of the glenohumeral capsule and anterior ligaments at the humeral insertion. Such disruption occurs in about 15% of traumatic anterior glenohumeral dislocations. *E,* Fracture of the anterior glenoid rim. *F,* Avulsion of the greater tuberosity. This finding is more common in older patients and occurs in up to one third of traumatic anterior glenohumeral dislocations. *G,* Posterior capsular disruption and rotator cuff tear (infraspinatus).

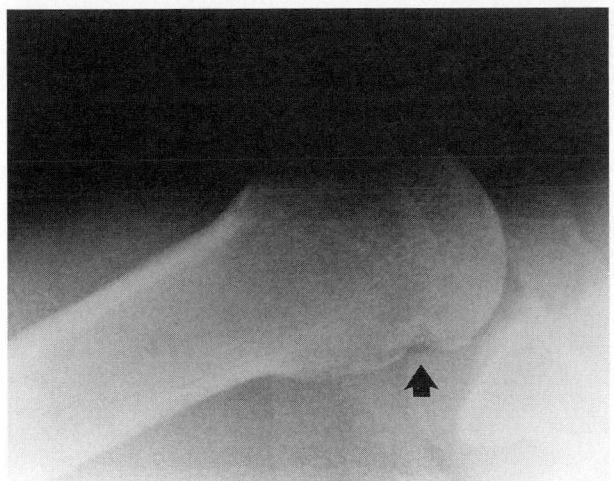

**FIGURE 44–87.** Axillary lateral radiograph of a patient with recurrent anterior glenohumeral dislocations. A Hill-Sachs lesion is located in the posterior aspect of the humeral head *(arrow)*, and the humeral head is subluxated anteriorly.

glenohumeral dislocation. Their study suggested that capsular stretching in addition to labral detachment is the cause of anterior inferior instability.[135]

In the earlier literature, humeral head defects, or Hill-Sachs lesions, were often implicated as a factor in recurrent glenohumeral dislocations[59] (Fig. 44–87). Although lesions of the posterolateral aspect of the articular segment of the humeral head are common, they are not usually considered the "essential lesion" of glenohumeral dislocation and do not require specific treatment. However, Hill-Sachs lesions are not insignificant. Hovelius and colleagues[63] noted a statistically significant association with recurrence in shoulders with Hill-Sachs lesions on initial radiographs after primary dislocation.

The role of the subscapularis muscle and tendon has been debated in the older literature.[35, 36, 138] Correction of abnormalities of the subscapularis formed the basis of the Putti-Platt and Magnusen-Stack procedures. However, significant injuries to the subscapularis, such as tendon rupture, are rarely associated with acute anterior glenohumeral dislocations.

## Associated Injuries and Complications

In addition to the capsulolabral pathology that was discussed earlier, a number of other shoulder girdle injuries are associated with anterior glenohumeral dislocation. Fractures, rotator cuff tears, and nerve and vascular injuries are all more common in older patients.[7, 72, 74, 134, 147]

### FRACTURES

Greater tuberosity and glenoid fractures are the most common fractures associated with acute anterior glenohumeral dislocation.[53, 65, 78, 94, 123, 124] Impression fractures of the humeral head have been discussed previously and are not considered to have a significant impact on treatment or outcome. Coracoid fractures are uncommon but have been reported in association with anterior glenohumeral dislocation.[92]

### Greater Tuberosity Fractures

Greater tuberosity fractures and rotator cuff tears represent the posterior mechanism of anterior dislocation.[30] They accompany 10% to 33% of anterior glenohumeral dislocations and more commonly occur in older patients.[60, 94, 124, 130]

Closed reduction usually reduces the greater tuberosity to its anatomic position.[50] After reduction, the shoulder is immobilized in a sling. Pendulum circumduction exercises and passive external rotation are initiated 2 weeks after reduction. Active motion or use of the shoulder girdle is delayed until 6 weeks after injury to allow enough fracture healing to avoid displacement of the greater tuberosity. Recurrent dislocations do not occur after anterior glenohumeral dislocation with avulsion of the greater tuberosity.

The limit of acceptable displacement of the tuberosity has been debated. Neer[102] defined significant displacement as 1 cm, whereas McLaughlin[94] considered 0.5 cm to be significant. Even anatomically reduced fractures can cause impingement syndrome from scarring in the subacromial space.

Greater tuberosity comminution, rotator cuff tearing, and soft tissue interposition are causes of failure of closed reduction. Operative treatment of displaced greater tuberosity fractures is discussed in detail in the section on proximal humeral fractures.

### Glenoid Rim Fractures

Glenoid rim fractures accompany about 5% of initial anterior glenohumeral dislocations.[8, 81, 124] Small rim avulsions are much more common and have less immediate clinical significance than larger fractures do. Larger glenoid rim fractures are more likely to occur with direct trauma to the lateral aspect of the shoulder that forces the humeral head against the glenoid.[8] Such a mechanism usually involves considerable trauma and generally occurs in younger patients. The same mechanism in older patients is more likely to cause a proximal humeral fracture.

Invariably, the fracture involves the anteroinferior aspect of the glenoid and disrupts the stabilizing function of the anteroinferior labrum and inferior glenohumeral ligament.[8] Displaced glenoid rim fractures are more likely to lead to recurrent dislocation by virtue of the fact that the attached capsule and labral tissues remain displaced and glenohumeral congruity is disrupted. A 62% recurrence rate was reported in Rowe's series.[124] Malunion of a large fragment can cause significant glenohumeral incongruity and lead to post-traumatic arthritis. We consider the presence of a large displaced anterior glenoid fracture to be an indication for open reduction and internal fixation (ORIF)[81] (Fig. 44–88).

The goal of operative treatment is to restore congruity of the articular surface of the glenoid and anatomically reattach the labrum and ligaments. This objective is most easily achieved through a deltopectoral approach. Separating the subscapularis tendon from the anterior capsule

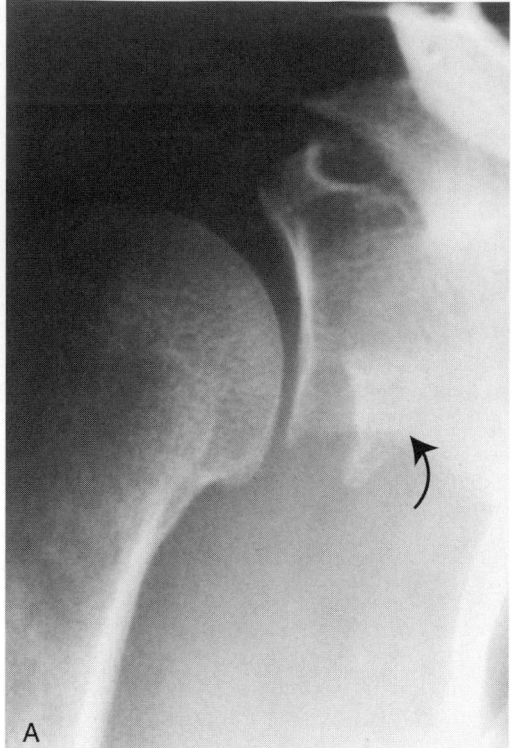

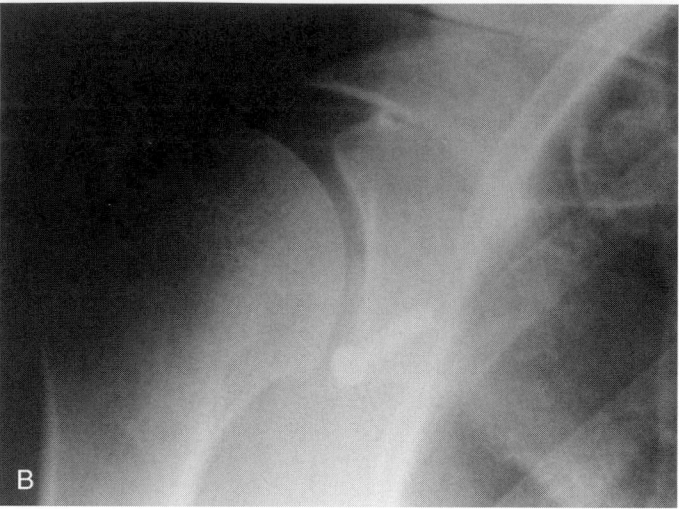

**Figure 44–88.** *A,* Displaced fracture of the glenoid rim after anterior glenohumeral dislocation *(arrow). B,* The fragment was reduced and fixed with a 3.5-mm cortical screw.

and opening the capsule medially, as described by Bankart, provides the best access to the displaced glenoid fragment. Alternatively, a subscapularis-splitting approach with medial capsulotomy can be used to expose an anterior glenoid fracture. Small, cannulated screws and bioabsorbable pins or pegs can be helpful when attempting to fix a glenoid fragment in the deep and confining surgical exposure. If the fragment is too comminuted to accept a screw, two alternatives are available. If it is relatively small, less than 20% of the articular portion of the glenoid, the fragment can be excised and the labrum and capsule repaired directly to the remaining glenoid. Alternatively, the capsulolabral complex and bony fragments can be reattached to the glenoid with suture anchors. Anchors designed for cancellous bone are preferred for this repair.

### Coracoid Process Fractures

Several cases of coracoid fracture associated with anterior glenohumeral dislocation have been reported.[92] The mechanism of injury has been presumed to be either direct impact of the humeral head against the coracoid or strong contraction of the coracoid muscles. The cases we have treated have involved the tip of the coracoid. The amount of displacement can be assessed with computed tomography. The significance of a displaced coracoid fracture is unclear, and we do not recommend ORIF unless surgery is being considered for a concurrent shoulder injury or posterior displacement of the coracoid would cause subcoracoid impingement.

## ROTATOR CUFF TEARS

Rotator cuff tears occur with anterior dislocation far more often than generally suspected. The association of rotator cuff tearing with primary anterior glenohumeral dislocation reflects the age-related degeneration and weakening of the rotator cuff tendons.[18] Reeves demonstrated that the strength of the labral attachment increases into the second decade of life and then remains constant throughout life.[120] In older patients, the rotator cuff tendons are the weaker structure. Thus, whereas anterior glenohumeral dislocation causes disruption of the medial attachment of the glenohumeral ligaments in young patients, rotator cuff tearing is common in older patients. Craig termed this age-related difference the *posterior mechanism of anterior dislocations.*[30]

The incidence of rotator cuff tearing in conjunction with anterior dislocation has been determined with arthrography.[119, 121] Ribbans and co-workers demonstrated that 63% of their patients older than 50 years had full-thickness rotator cuff tears.[121] None of the younger patients had rotator cuff tearing. The true incidence of acute rotator cuff tears is difficult to determine because of the well-known prevalence of tears even in the asymptomatic shoulders of older individuals.[131]

Rotator cuff tearing that occurs with anterior dislocation can be extensive and often involves complete avulsion of the supraspinatus and infraspinatus tendons.[30, 96, 106, 107] Patients with external rotation weakness invariably have disruption of the infraspinatus and are unlikely to ever recover this function without operative repair. Less commonly, the subscapularis tendon is disrupted with or without the supraspinatus and infraspinatus tendons.[44, 105] The biceps tendon can be ruptured or dislocated.

Careful clinical assessment and a high index of suspicion are crucial to the recognition of rotator cuff tearing associated with dislocation. The combination of an inability to actively elevate the arm and external rotation weakness is highly suggestive of massive rotator cuff tearing. External rotation weakness and external rotation lag signs are indicative of a large rotator cuff tear. The lift-off and belly-press maneuvers are signs of subscapularis disruption. Early identification of a large rotator cuff tear is important if surgical repair is a consideration. Early repairs are much easier and yield better results than do delayed attempts to repair massive, retracted, and scarred rotator cuff defects.[13] The best candidates for early surgery are physiologically younger active individuals with external rotation weakness or subscapularis disruption.

Although arthrography[48, 85] can accurately determine the presence of full-thickness tearing, we prefer MRI because of its ability to accurately define the extent of injury,[69] including the size of the tear, the degree of tendon retraction, involvement of the subscapularis and biceps tendons, and assessment of muscle tissue quality.

The long-term outcome of rotator cuff tearing associated with anterior dislocation has not been determined. Most studies have evaluated only the results of operative repair. Bassett and Cofield found that the results of early repair of acute rotator cuff tears were better than those of delayed repair.[13] No studies have compared the outcome of repair with nonoperative treatment.

Many factors must be considered. Patient motivation and expectations are the most important. Assessment of physiologic age and previous activity level can help in determining appropriate outcome goals. In fact, many patients do well with nonoperative treatment. The outcome of nonoperative treatment is determined by the associated pathology, functional demands of the patient, and the ability to participate in rehabilitation. The most significant long-term problem is weakness rather than pain. Despite weakness and even loss of external rotation strength, shoulder elevation can be achieved with the deltoid. Loss of external rotation strength but preservation of elevation or abduction strength after a massive rotator cuff tear is explained by the fact that the infraspinatus muscle provides 90% of external rotation strength whereas the deltoid provides 50% of the strength of elevation.[27, 67]

The integrity of the subscapularis and biceps tendons is critical to the function of a rotator cuff–deficient shoulder. Loss of the normal contour and mass of the biceps muscle belly indicates rupture or dislocation of the tendon of the long head of the biceps. Loss of the stabilizing and head depression function of the biceps tendon is particularly problematic. Disruption of the subscapularis tendon and anterior capsule can result in recurrent anterior dislocation.[105]

Axillary nerve injury can mimic rotator cuff tearing. However, even in the presence of deltoid weakness or paralysis, rotator cuff tearing must be considered.[107] The combination of shoulder dislocation, rotator cuff tear, and axillary nerve injury has been called the *unhappy triad*.[52, 75]

Early aggressive rehabilitation is our preferred treatment in older, less healthy, less motivated, and potentially less cooperative patients. In these individuals, rehabilitation is begun as soon as comfort permits. The occasional younger active patient who is treated nonoperatively can also achieve a satisfactory outcome. Careful attention to rehabilitation is critical so that operative intervention is not inappropriately delayed if function does not improve. The recovery achieved within the first few weeks will predict the eventual outcome.

Most experienced shoulder surgeons recommend early operative repair of large acute rotator cuff tears in active healthy individuals. Bassett and Cofield[13] and Hawkins and associates[54] noted that the results of delayed repair of acute rotator cuff tears are worse than those of early repair. At delayed surgery, it is difficult to mobilize the scarred and retracted tendons. Nonetheless, pain relief is usually predictable even if strength and active motion cannot be completely restored.

## NERVE INJURIES

The position of the brachial plexus and peripheral nerves of the upper extremity places these structures at considerable risk of injury when glenohumeral dislocation occurs. Careful clinical examination before and after reduction of glenohumeral dislocation is essential for identification of a nerve injury. Brachial plexus and axillary nerve injuries are the most common.

The axillary nerve is tethered both anterior and posterior to the glenohumeral joint. As it branches from the posterior cord and passes through the quadrilateral space to innervate the deltoid muscle, it is particularly vulnerable to injury. Milton[100] discussed the potential mechanisms of axillary nerve injury as a result of glenohumeral dislocation and attempts at reduction. Abduction of the arm and inferior displacement of the humeral head place the nerve under tension. In abduction, the nerve can also be crushed against the taut tendon of the long head of the triceps. Shoulder reduction with traction and internal rotation is especially dangerous. With internal rotation, the tension in the axillary nerve is increased as the nerve winds around the proximal part of the humerus. External rotation of the arm relaxes the axillary nerve.

Nerve injuries have been identified in 32% to 65% of patients with dislocation and are more common in older patients and when an associated fracture is present.[15, 34, 78, 112, 113, 142] By physical examination, Pasila and associates[112] identified nerve injuries in 29% of patients who were older than 50 years. Electrophysiologic testing reveals an even greater incidence of nerve injury.[88] Blom and Dahlback[15] reported a 36% incidence of nerve injury with glenohumeral dislocation. deLaat and co-workers[34] identified nerve injuries in 32% of dislocations. Toolanen and associates[142] found a 65% incidence of nerve injury in patients older than 40 years. Rotator cuff injury may also be associated with nerve injury in older patients.[52, 75] The prognosis is worse in older patients with nerve injury.[113] Patients with nerve injuries are more likely to have limited motion and significant symptoms at follow-up. This finding is in contrast to the conclusions of Leffert and Seddon's study of infraclavicular brachial

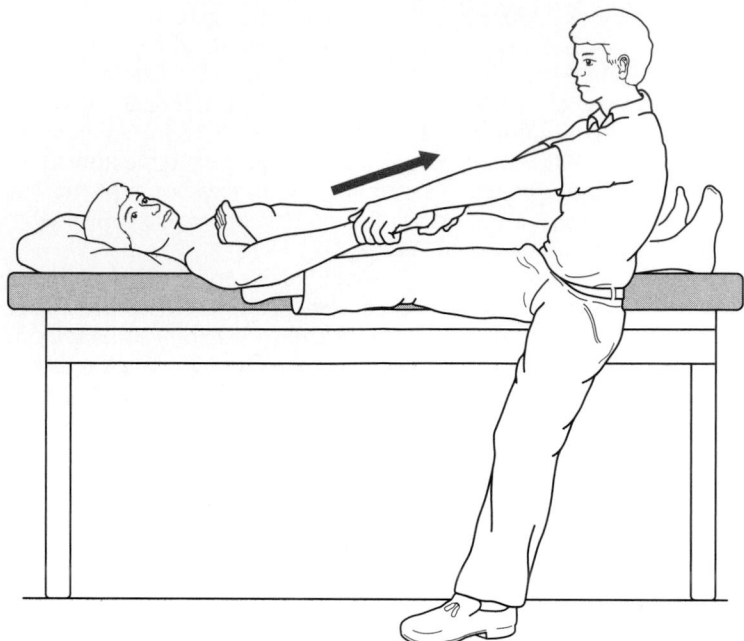

**FIGURE 44–89.** Hippocratic technique of closed reduction of anterior glenohumeral dislocation. The foot is placed against the proximal end of the humerus, and longitudinal traction is applied to the upper extremity. (Redrawn from Rockwood, C.A. In: Rockwood, C.A.; Green, D.P., eds. Fractures in Adults, Vol. 1. Philadelphia, J.B. Lippincott, 1984.)

plexus injuries. These researchers reported that such injuries are usually associated with good recovery.[84]

## VASCULAR INJURY

Although vascular injury rarely accompanies glenohumeral dislocation, it is a potentially devastating problem that if unrecognized, can necessitate amputation of the upper extremity. Many case reports emphasize the importance of early recognition of this injury.* Vascular injury is more common in older individuals who have atherosclerotic vessels.

## Treatment

### CLOSED REDUCTION

A variety of methods of closed reduction of anterior glenohumeral dislocation have been described. Some have existed for centuries. The Edwin Smith Papyrus records that the ancient Egyptians were experienced in treating fractures and dislocations of the shoulder.[17] Illustrations in the tomb of Ramses II have been interpreted as depicting reduction of the shoulder with the Kocher method. The Hippocratic technique described in the *Corpus Hippocrates* advocates longitudinal arm traction with the heel in the axilla.[111, 118]

Thomas wrote that reduction of shoulder dislocation in preanesthetic times was often accompanied by significant morbidity.[139] Neurovascular injuries were common complications of these often traumatic closed reductions of glenohumeral dislocations. The Hippocratic method was predominant for about 2000 years[19] (Fig. 44–89). It involves longitudinal traction on the arm and a reducing

counterforce against the humeral head in the axilla, usually applied with the heel of the foot or balls of various size. During the past 150 years, many other methods of manipulative reduction, most less traumatic, have been devised and popularized.†

The common goal of all techniques is to disengage the humeral head from the glenoid rim. The various methods can be classified as either traction or leverage techniques. The least traumatic reductions are achieved with adequate relaxation and analgesia.

The Kocher method is performed with the physician standing at the side of the supine patient[79] (Fig. 44–90). Traction is applied to the patient's arm by holding the elbow. The right elbow is held with the right hand and vice versa. The humerus is rotated externally and the elbow is moved up toward the chest. Once the shoulder is reduced, the hand is brought to the opposite shoulder. Though highly successful, the Kocher maneuver has been associated with neurovascular complications and humeral fractures and is not generally recommended.

Traction plus countertraction is preferred by Rockwood[122] (Fig. 44–91). The patient is supine with a sheet placed around the chest to apply countertraction. The arm is carefully pulled in the direction of the deformity. Gentle rotational motions of the arm can help disengage the humeral head from the glenoid.

The Stimson technique is an adaptation of the technique for reduction of posterior hip dislocation[136] (Fig. 44–92). The patient is positioned prone, and the arm is allowed to hang down. Some authors recommend applying traction with about 10 lb of weight. Some form of relaxation is usually required.

Several studies have highlighted the advantages of the Milch technique[14, 82, 98, 127] (Fig. 44–93). It is relatively

---

*See references 3, 12, 20, 31, 32, 38, 46, 51, 89, 146.

†See references 2, 14, 29, 33, 70, 79, 80, 82, 90, 98, 116, 127, 136.

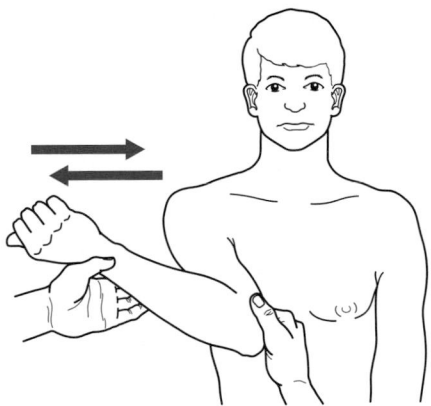

**FIGURE 44–90.** The Kocher maneuver. (Redrawn from Manes, H.R. Clin Orthop 147:200–202, 1980.)

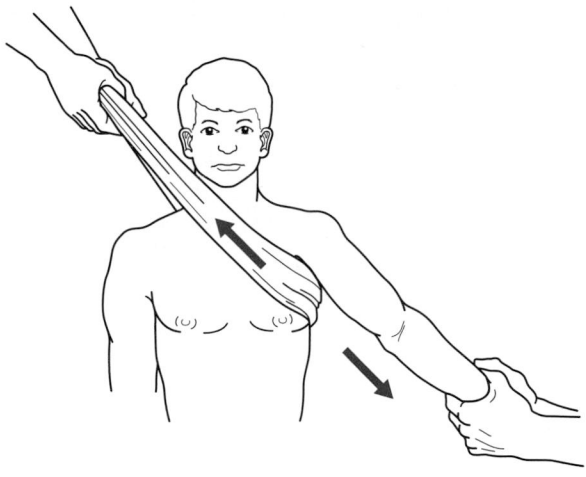

**FIGURE 44–91.** Traction-countertraction technique of reduction of anterior glenohumeral dislocation. (Redrawn from Rockwood, C.A. In: Rockwood, C.A.; Green, D.P., eds. Fractures in Adults, Vol. 1. Philadelphia, J.B. Lippincott, 1984.)

atraumatic, has a high success rate, and is well tolerated by patients. Beattie and associates[14] described performing reductions with the patient prone. The right hand of the physician is placed in the axilla of the dislocated right shoulder, and the physician's left hand holds the patient's hand. The patient's arm is gently abducted and pressure is applied to the humeral head. When the arm is fully abducted, it is externally rotated and gentle traction is applied to reduce the humeral head. These researchers had a 72% initial success rate with the Milch technique as compared with a 70% initial success rate with the Kocher technique. They considered the Milch technique to be less traumatic. However, the success rate of the Milch technique decreased significantly when the dislocation was more than 4 hours old. Russell and colleagues[127] reported an 89% success rate with the Milch technique. Only 31% of their patients required analgesics or muscle relaxants. Lacey and Crawford[82] described a modification of the Milch technique in which the patient is positioned prone. McNair[97] reported a 90% success rate with an average reduction time of 20 minutes when using the prone modification of the Milch technique. The time to reduction and failure rates were increased in older patients.

Scapular manipulation is even less traumatic.[2, 80] Most descriptions are very similar to the prone modification of the Milch technique (Fig. 44–94). Rather than externally rotating the humerus, scapular manipulation effectively internally rotates the glenoid to disengage the humeral head. The patient is placed prone, and 5 to 15 lb of traction is applied to the arm. Once relaxation is obtained, the inferior angle of the scapula is raised and rotated medially and the superior aspect is rotated laterally. This technique generally requires excellent relaxation. Anderson and co-workers[2] and Kothari and Dronen[80] respectively reported 92% and 96% success rates with no complications.

The time from dislocation to treatment is an important determinant of the difficulty of reduction. The goal of all reduction attempts is to relocate the shoulder as soon as possible without inflicting additional injury. Rang quoted Hippocrates: "Reduction is to be effected, if possible, immediately whilst still warm, otherwise as quickly as it can be done, for reduction will be a much quicker and easier process for the operator and a much less painful one for the patient if effected before the swelling comes on."[118]

Early reduction is usually achieved when a dislocation occurs during organized athletics and trained personnel are available to provide treatment. Unfortunately, other than cases of spontaneous reduction, treatment of most glenohumeral dislocations is delayed until the patient is

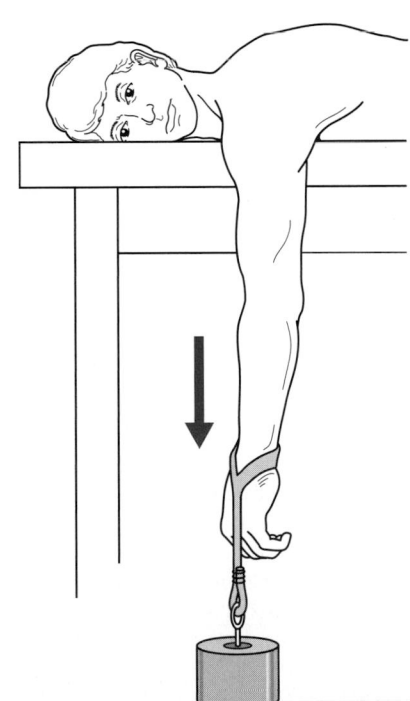

**FIGURE 44–92.** Stimson technique. (Redrawn from Rockwood, C.A. In: Rockwood, C.A.; Green, D.P., eds. Fractures in Adults, Vol. 1. Philadelphia, J.B. Lippincott, 1984.)

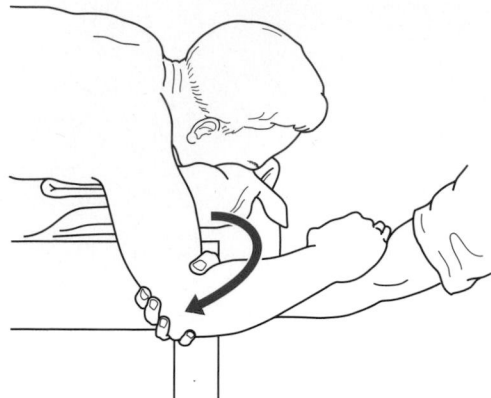

**Figure 44–93.** Milch technique of closed reduction of anterior glenohumeral dislocation with the patient prone. The arm can be manipulated in the same manner with the patient supine. (Redrawn from Lacey, T., II; Crawford, H.B. J Bone Joint Surg Am 34:108–109, 1952.)

evaluated in an emergency treatment facility. In a busy urban hospital, it is not unusual for reduction to be performed by an inexperienced physician several hours after the injury. By the time that most patients are evaluated and treated, considerable pain and muscle spasm have occurred. Consequently, many reductions require some form of anesthetic or muscle relaxation.

Parenteral narcotics and sedatives are the most commonly used medications. Reports have also demonstrated the benefits of intra-articular local anesthetics.[86, 93, 137] The concept is analogous to the use of a hematoma block for closed reduction of a distal radial fracture. These studies demonstrate that carefully monitored use of intra-articular lidocaine is safe. Intra-articular lidocaine avoids the common complications of intravenous medication (oversedation, nausea, and vomiting) and significantly shortens the duration of time spent in the emergency department.

The technique, well described by Matthews and Roberts,[93] involves insertion of a 1.5-inch, 20-gauge needle on a 30-mL syringe into the shoulder joint from a lateral position slightly inferior to the edge of the acromion. The needle is directed slightly caudad, toward the glenoid. The joint is aspirated before injecting 20 mL of 1% lidocaine without epinephrine. This technique provides excellent analgesia and relaxation. The humeral head can usually be guided into reduction with very gentle traction on the arm and fingertip pressure on the humeral head.

In unusual cases, greater relaxation is required. An interscalene block avoids the risks and side effects of general anesthesia.[56, 151] An interscalene block or general anesthesia should be considered for all chronic dislocations and cases in which nondisplaced proximal humeral fracture is suspected. In these situations, greater muscle relaxation may help avoid iatrogenic fracture displacement.[58]

Occasionally, anterior glenohumeral dislocations are irreducible by closed means even with adequate anesthesia. Soft tissue interposition is a rare cause that requires open reduction. Delayed evaluation of shoulder dislocations is an indication for closed reduction under anesthesia

or open reduction. Any dislocation for which the time or mechanism of injury is unknown should be presumed to be chronic. Chronic anterior dislocations most commonly occur in elderly, debilitated patients.[43, 128] Unconscious patients or those with polytrauma are another group that may have an unrecognized dislocation.

Closed reduction of chronic dislocations must be done with great care, minimal trauma, and complete muscle block (either an interscalene block or general anesthesia and paralysis). The risk of neurovascular injury and fracture is considerable. The typical elderly patient has osteopenia of the proximal end of the humerus and scarring that tethers nerves and atherosclerotic vessels. If closed reduction is not possible, open reduction can be attempted. Open reduction also has significant risk. The anatomy becomes distorted and scarred such that in some cases, the surgical risk may outweigh the benefits of open reduction. Schulz and associates[128] reported that 9 of 10 chronic dislocations left unreduced had a satisfactory result. When the dislocation is of long-standing duration and significant articular surface damage is present, consideration should be given to primary prosthetic arthroplasty.[117]

## IMMOBILIZATION

The appropriate duration of shoulder immobilization after anterior glenohumeral dislocation is controversial and has been the subject of many studies and review articles. The underlying concepts that form the basis of the standard recommendations include the specific pathology, understanding of soft tissue healing, and the natural history of dislocations. Large studies can be cited to support either recommendation in this controversy.

Several studies have demonstrated that the duration of immobilization, especially in younger patients, is a factor

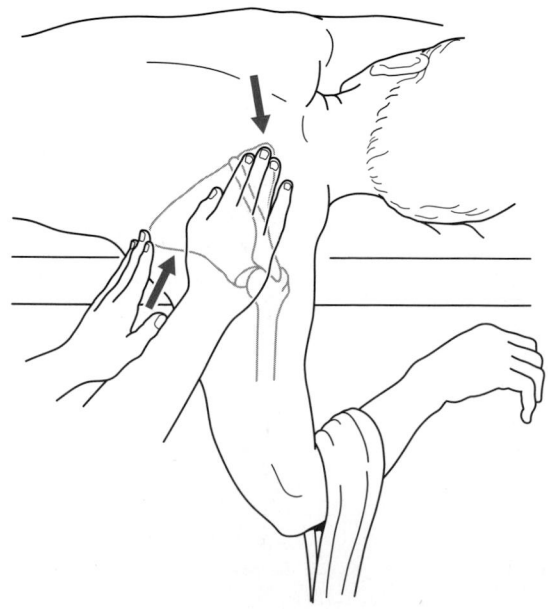

**Figure 44–94.** Scapular manipulation technique for closed reduction of anterior glenohumeral dislocation. (Redrawn from Anderson, D., et al. Clin Orthop 164:181–183, 1982.)

in the incidence of recurrence.[78, 124, 125, 132, 152] Most authors recommend up to 6 weeks of immobilization for younger individuals. The duration of immobilization should be less for older patients. Rowe's study[124] demonstrated that recurrence inversely correlated with the duration of immobilization. Kiviluoto and co-workers[78] studied 226 patients prospectively up to a 1-year follow-up. The 127 patients older than 50 years had 1 week of immobilization. Of the 99 patients younger than 50 years, 53 had 1 week of immobilization and 46 had 3 weeks of immobilization. Among the patients younger than 50 years, the recurrence rate for 1-week immobilization was 50% versus 25% for 3-week immobilization. Simonet and Cofield[132] recommended avoidance of athletics for 6 weeks after acute primary anterior glenohumeral dislocation.

In contrast, other large studies refute the idea that immobilization after initial anterior dislocation is beneficial. Henry and Genung[57] evaluated 121 patients with an average age of 19 years and found that the use and length of immobilization had no effect on the recurrence rate. Hovelius and colleagues[63] reported the most comprehensive and detailed long-term evaluation of the role of immobilization. At the 10-year follow-up in a prospective randomized study, they found that the duration of immobilization had no effect on the recurrence rate.

The role of rehabilitation after primary anterior glenohumeral dislocation has not been comprehensively studied. Aronen and Regan[6] studied 20 Navy midshipmen and concluded that an aggressive rehabilitation program with adherence to restrictions reduced the incidence of redislocation.

Our approach to the management of primary traumatic glenohumeral dislocation is as follows. We recommend 3 weeks of shoulder immobilization for patients younger than 30 years. Older patients, generally those 45 years or older, are only briefly immobilized for comfort. No arbitrary cutoff age is enforced, and other factors such as the extent of trauma, activity level, whether the dominant extremity was injured, and the degree of contralateral glenohumeral laxity are considered. With advancing patient age, consideration of concomitant rotator cuff injury dictates the need for early imaging of the rotator cuff.

We use a progressive rehabilitation program that emphasizes reconditioning and strengthening of the rotator cuff and scapular muscles. Isometric exercises are initiated during the period of immobilization, and resistive strengthening is progressed thereafter. The position of abduction and external rotation is avoided for at least 12 weeks. Ideally, return to risky activities is delayed until motion and strength are recovered. Shoulder harnesses may be helpful in preventing recurrence in athletic activities such as football and downhill skiing.

## Recurrence

Recurrent glenohumeral instability is the most common sequela of primary anterior dislocation. A variety of factors have been studied and a range of recurrence rates reported.

The vast majority of recurrences occur within 2 years of the initial dislocation.[61]

The effect of immobilization on recurrence was discussed under Immobilization. This topic is controversial. In contrast, the undisputed, most consistent factor related to recurrence is the age of the patient at the time of initial dislocation. The recurrence rate is inversely related to the age of the patient.

Patients younger than 20 years have a recurrence rate of 64% to 100%. Skeletal immaturity is associated with 100% recurrence if the original mechanism is traumatic.[91] In contrast, atraumatic recurrent dislocations in the very young often resolve. Rowe and Sakellarides[125] reported a 94% recurrence rate in patients younger than 20 years, whereas a 64% recurrence rate was reported by Hovelius and associates in patients younger than 22 years.[61, 64] Henry and Genung[57] reported an 88% recurrence rate in 121 patients with an average age of 19 years. Sixty-one percent of the recurrences occurred within the first 6 months of the initial dislocation. Simonet and Cofield[132] reported a 66% recurrence rate in patients younger than 20 years.

The recurrence rate declines steadily with advancing age. Rowe reported recurrence rates of 79% for individuals aged 21 to 30 years, 50% for those aged 31 to 40 years, and 14% for patients older than 40 years.[124] Hovelius[61] reported the incidence of recurrence after 5 years' follow-up of a prospectively evaluated group of first-time dislocators. The recurrence rates were 64% in patients younger than 22 years, 53% in those 23 to 29 years, and 19% in those 30 to 40 years old. In the youngest cohort, 25% of the patients had their first recurrence between 2 and 5 years after the initial dislocation. Simonet and Cofield[132] reported a 40% recurrence rate in patients 20 to 40 years and no recurrences after age 40.

## Early Instability Repair

Early surgical repair after primary anterior glenohumeral dislocations is rarely indicated. At a 10-year follow-up of primary anterior glenohumeral dislocations, Hovelius and coauthors[63] reported that only 22.7% of patients had undergone surgical reconstruction. Occupational and vocational requirements, including heavy manual and overhead labor and high-caliber athletics,[4, 149] are the main indications for early instability repair. Arciero and associates[4] compared the outcomes of acute arthroscopic Bankart repair and a protocol of immobilization and rehabilitation in a group of U.S. Military Academy cadet-athletes. The rate of recurrence was significantly reduced in the operative group after an average 32 months of follow-up. However, given our knowledge of the natural history of anterior glenohumeral dislocations and the wide range of reported success rates for arthroscopic repair,[49, 83] surgical treatment of primary dislocations remains controversial. Primary arthroscopic capsule and labral repair is considered for young patients with occupational or athletic requirements that necessitate a stable shoulder (Fig. 44–95). Open repair with anatomic labral or ligament repair[10, 11, 140] or capsular shift[103] is generally reserved for recurrent dislocations.

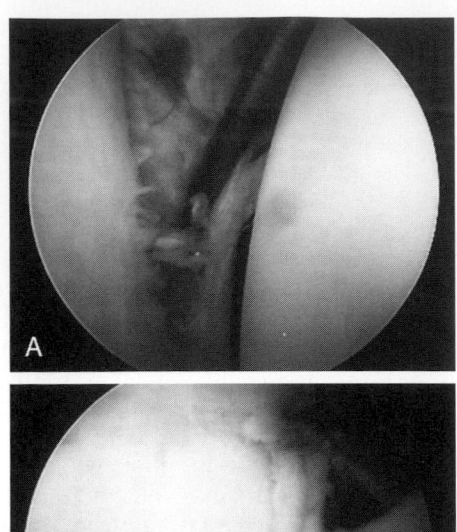
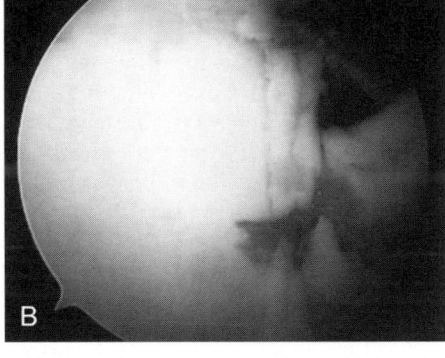

**FIGURE 44–95.** *A,* Arthroscopic visualization of anteroinferior labral detachment after a first-time anterior glenohumeral dislocation in a college soccer goalie. *B,* Because of the patient's athletic demands, primary arthroscopic repair was performed.

## POSTERIOR DISLOCATION

Posterior glenohumeral dislocations and instability are uncommon problems. Posterior dislocations represent approximately 2% of all glenohumeral dislocations.[124] The major clinical significance of posterior dislocation relates to the frequency of errors in diagnosis that result in significant delays in treatment and permanent disability.[54, 104, 105, 126, 150] Despite recurrent warnings about missed injuries, many posterior fracture-dislocations remain undiagnosed.

In the early part of the 19th century, Cooper referred to posterior dislocation when he wrote, "it is an accident which cannot be mistaken."[5] Nonetheless, in reported series of posterior dislocations, little improvement has been noted in the diagnostic accuracy of the initial treating physician. In 1949, Wilson and McKeever[150] reported that in 6 of 11 cases the correct diagnosis was missed during the initial evaluation. Nearly 4 decades later, Rowe and Zarins[126] found that 79% of chronic posterior dislocations were unrecognized by the initial treating physician and that posterior dislocation was nearly twice as common as chronic anterior dislocation. Nearly all the patients reviewed by Hawkins and co-workers[55] had a delay in diagnosis.

Posterior dislocations commonly occur as a result of adduction and axial loading of the shoulder or a direct blow to the anterior aspect of the shoulder. These dislocations also characteristically occur as a result of violent muscle contraction during seizures or electrocu-tion.[1, 22] Seizure is the cause of posterior dislocation in up to 50% of reported cases.[5] In fact, posterior fracture-dislocation can be the first sign of the presence of a seizure disorder.

Posterior dislocations can be subacromial, subglenoid, or subspinous. Subacromial posterior dislocations are the most common. Most posterior dislocations are locked with the posterior glenoid rim embedded in the anterior aspect of the articular surface of the humeral head. This anatomic position creates an anterior impression fracture in the articular segment, the so-called reverse Hill-Sachs lesion.

### Diagnosis

Awareness of the possibility of posterior glenohumeral dislocation or fracture-dislocation is the key to making the diagnosis. The history is often classic, especially when a seizure has occurred.[1] The physical examination is notable for posterior shoulder prominence, flattening of the anterior of the shoulder, prominence of the coracoid process, limitation of glenohumeral elevation, inability to externally rotate the arm, and inability to rotate the palm upward (Fig. 44–96). The possibility of bilateral involvement should be considered, especially in those who have had a seizure or have been electrocuted.[41, 99] The diagnosis is confirmed by an axillary lateral radiograph or variations of this projection.[16, 55] If this view cannot be obtained, a computed tomographic scan is indicated. Various authors have described subtle clues for detecting posterior dislocation. Cisternino and colleagues[26] emphasized the trough line. Reliance on anything other than an axial image, however, is inappropriate.

In chronic cases, patients have limited motion and functional difficulties as their major problem. They have frequently been treated as though they have a frozen shoulder, without success. Pain is often only mild.[55]

### Treatment

Treatment of posterior dislocations depends on timely diagnosis and the size of the anterior impression fracture. Invariably, the posterior capsule is stretched by the injury. Acute traumatic posterior glenohumeral dislocation without an associated fracture is uncommon. Posterior labral detachment is noted in 10% to 15% of shoulders undergoing posterior instability repair.[115] Acute posterior glenohumeral dislocation and chronic locked posterior dislocation are the focus of this chapter.

When the humeral head defect is less than 20%, closed reduction is attempted under adequate local anesthesia, intravenous sedation, or general anesthesia. Minimal resistance from the patient is essential to achieve reduction and avoid additional fracture of the proximal end of the humerus.[58] The arm is flexed forward, internally rotated, and adducted to disengage the head from the posterior glenoid rim. With longitudinal traction and anterior pressure on the humeral head from behind, reduction is achieved. The arm is externally rotated, lowered to the side, and then immobilized in 15° extension and 15° external rotation for 4 to 6 weeks in a light fiberglass cast or prefabricated brace. This position relaxes the posterior capsule and allows initial healing in a shortened position. Contraindications to closed reduction are a fixed dislocation that is not easily reducible or an undisplaced fracture at the surgical neck or tuberosity.

Complications or problems related to closed reduction include an inability to reduce the humeral head with closed treatment, enlargement of the head defect, a shaft fracture, and posterior instability after reduction.

Open reduction is performed through an anterior deltopectoral approach, which permits evaluation of the anterior impression fracture. The humeral head is carefully disengaged from the posterior aspect of the glenoid with a wide flat elevator.

When considering closed or open reduction of a posterior fracture-dislocation, the risks of redislocation, intraoperative fracture, and nerve injury and the possible need for a humeral head replacement at the time of surgery or later should be considered. Displacement of previously nondisplaced fractures changes the treatment indications to those for the new type of displaced fracture encountered.

With head impression fractures between 20% and 40%, closed reduction can be attempted (Fig. 44–97). However, larger impression fractures have a greater chance of redislocation. Alternatively, transfer of the subscapularis tendon into the impression defect, as described by McLaughlin, or Neer's modification in which the lesser

tuberosity is transferred is effective in preventing recurrent posterior dislocation.[40, 55, 102, 109] The lesser tuberosity is osteotomized to convert it to a two-part lesser tuberosity fracture (Fig. 44–98; see also Fig. 44–56). In acute cases, the operative technique and rehabilitation are as described for two-part lesser tuberosity fractures. The results of tuberosity transfer have been superior to those of subscapularis transfer alone.[55]

Rotational osteotomy of the humerus is another option. Keppler and co-workers[77] recommended this treatment when the humeral head defect is less than 40% and the articular cartilage is healthy. The osteotomy ensures that the humeral head defect is always anterior to the glenoid during normal motion. However, this procedure limits external rotation.

Gerber and Lambert[45] reported a limited, but promising experience with femoral head allograft to reconstruct large humeral head defects. More recently, humeral head allograft has been used to reconstruct large defects in patients with an otherwise intact humeral articular surface.[28]

When the humeral head defect is large or greater than 40% or when significant degeneration of the articular surface has occurred, humeral head or total-shoulder replacement with rotator cuff balancing and reconstruction is indicated.

In chronic cases, it is more likely that a replacement will

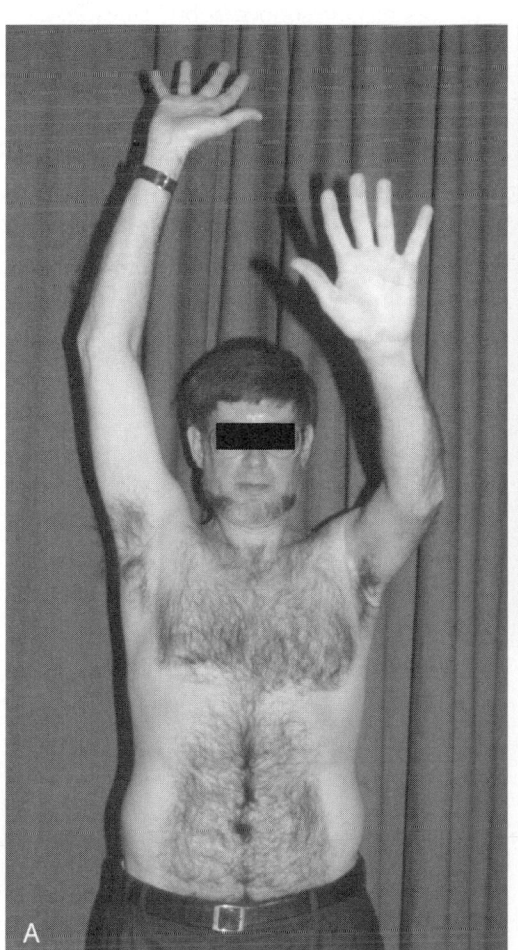
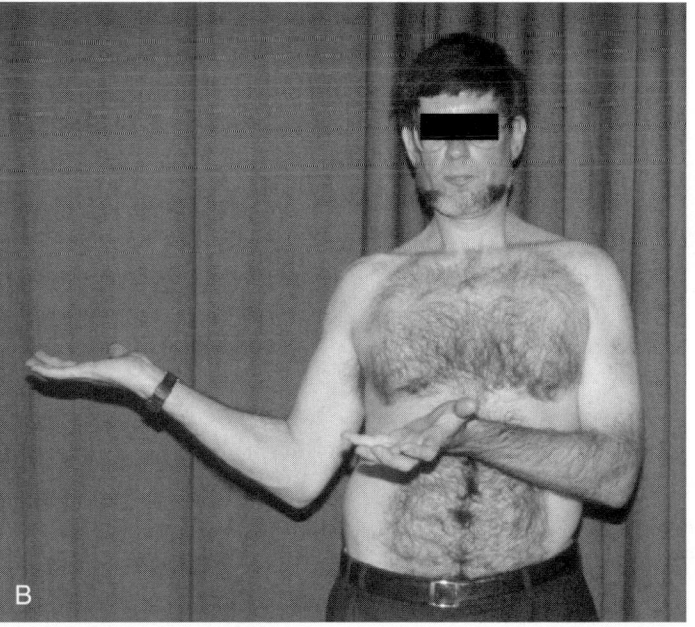

**FIGURE 44–96.** Physical examination of a posterior fracture-dislocation classically reveals limited elevation (*A*) and external rotation (*B*).

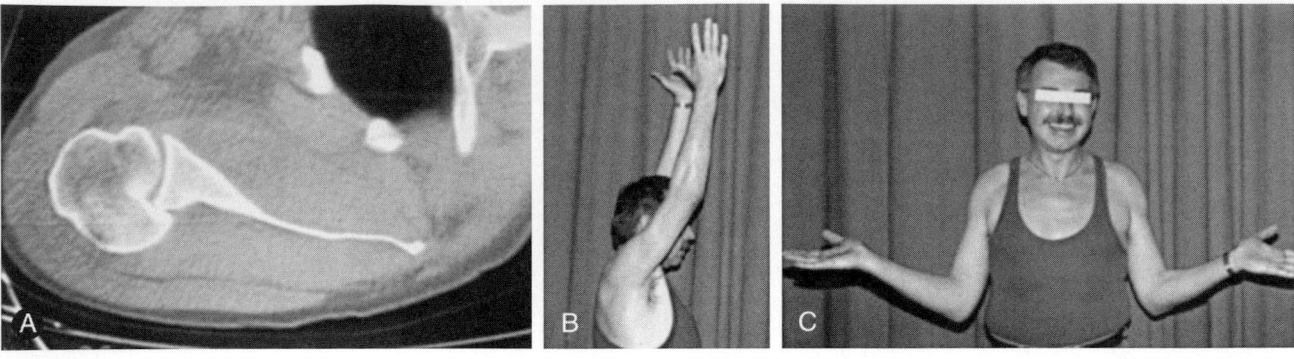

**FIGURE 44–97.** Posterior fracture-dislocation of the humeral head. *A,* Computed tomography demonstrates posterior dislocation and an anterior impression fracture. This injury responded to closed reduction and became stable when immobilized in a lightweight fiberglass waistband cast with the arm in 15° extension, 10° abduction, and 15° external rotation for 5 weeks. *B, C,* Three months after injury, the shoulder is stable with good return of elevation and rotation.

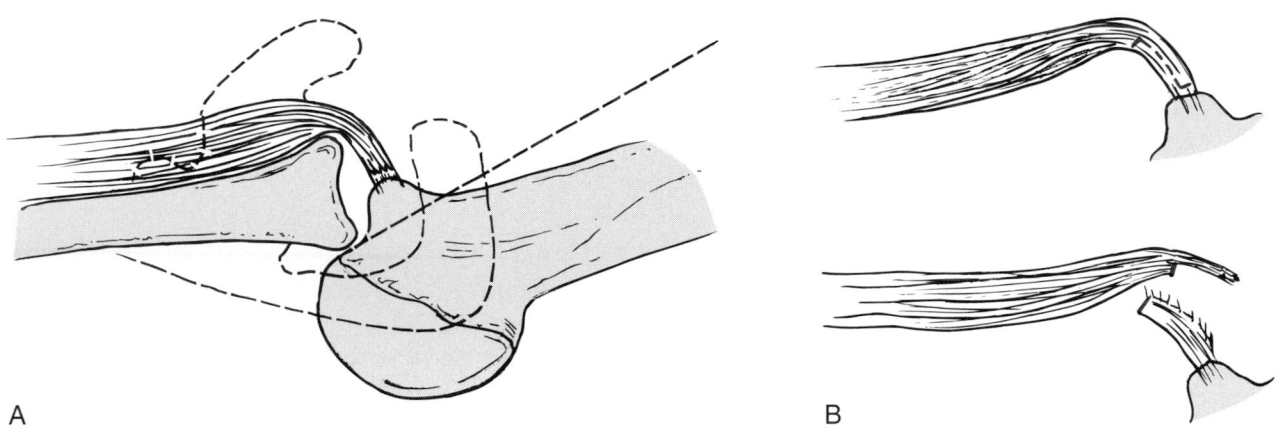

**FIGURE 44–98.** *A,* Lesser tuberosity osteotomy permits transfer of the tuberosity into an anterior head defect. *B,* Alternatively, subscapularis lengthening permits latitude at the time of closure for adjusting the tension and reestablishing external rotation. With a subscapularis and capsule contracture, each centimeter of lengthening permits an additional 20° of external rotation.

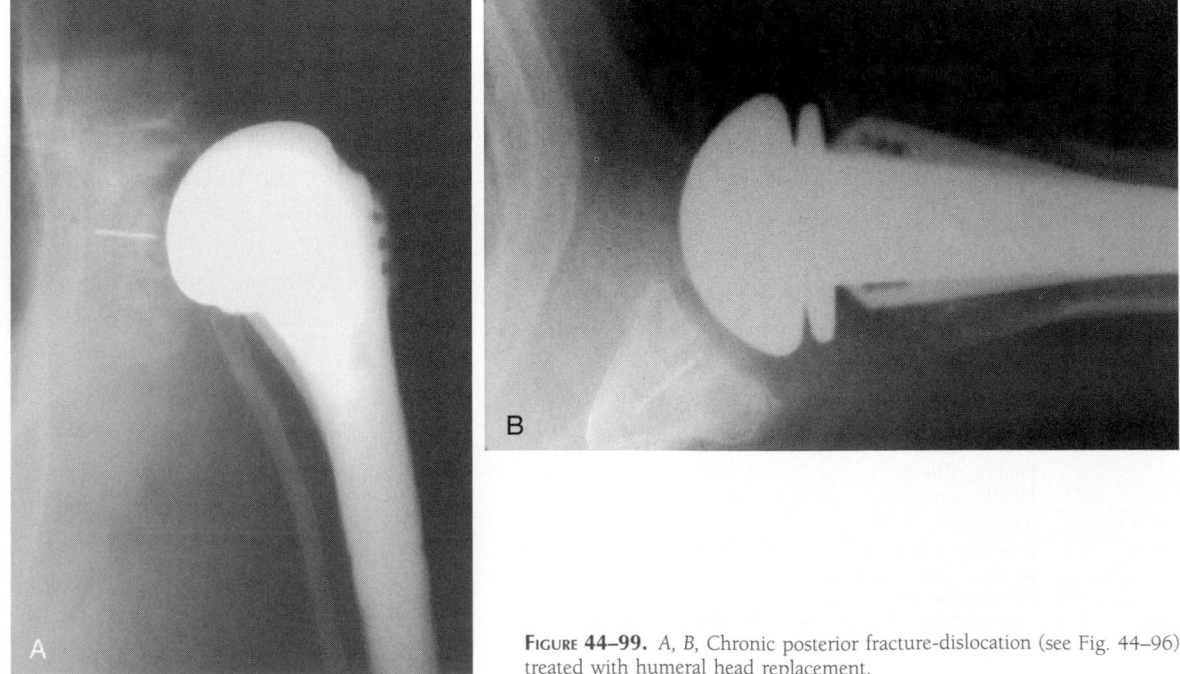

**FIGURE 44–99.** *A, B,* Chronic posterior fracture-dislocation (see Fig. 44–96) treated with humeral head replacement.

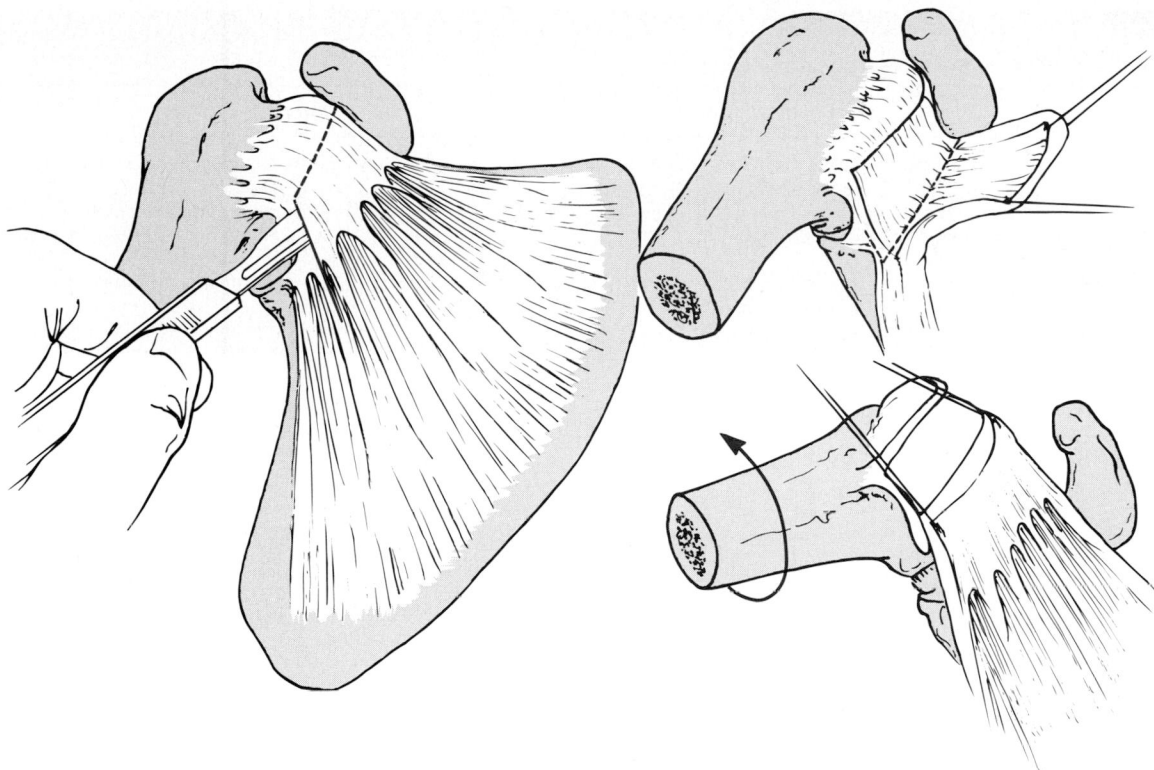

**FIGURE 44–100.** Coronal-plane Z-plasty of the subscapularis and capsule. (From Norris, T.R. In: Watson, M., ed. Surgical Disorders of the Shoulder. London, Churchill Livingstone, 1991, p. 496.)

be necessary because of degeneration of the articular surface[55, 104, 117] (Fig. 44–99). Rather than osteotomizing the lesser tuberosity, a subscapularis coronal-plane Z-plasty preserves the tuberosity while providing the option of lengthening a contracted subscapularis (Fig. 44–100; see also Fig. 44–98B). In addition, the humeral component should be positioned with less retroversion to maintain glenohumeral stability.

When good stability is restored with prosthetic replace-

ment, passive pendulum exercises and abduction and external rotation are begun early. The posterior capsule is not stressed early. The shoulder is immobilized with the arm at the side and the shoulder externally rotated about 15° for 4 to 6 weeks[23] (Tables 44–5 and 44–6). Active exercises commence at 4 to 6 weeks postoperatively and advance to isotonic strengthening at 3 months. It may take 9 to 12 months for maximal range of motion and strength to develop.

**TABLE 44–5**

Preferred Treatment of Proximal Humeral Fractures and Fracture-Dislocations

| Approximate Incidence (%) | Type* | Closed Reduction | ORIF | Indications for Prosthetic Replacement |
|---|---|---|---|---|
| 50–80 | One part nondisplaced | | | |
| 10 | Two part | LT, SN | GT irreducible or unstable SN | AN in older adult |
| 3 | Three part | Rare | LT, GT | LT or GT with osteoporosis or unstable after ORIF |
| 4 | Four part | | Valgus impacted, four part in young patient | Most four-part fractures |
| | Fracture-dislocation | Two-part A and P in absence of RCT | Two part with cuff tear, three-part A or P (some) | Some three-part A or P, most four part |
| | Head splitting | | Rare—simple fracture | Most cases |
| | Head impression | <20%, early | 20–40% with tuberosity transfer into defect | >40% chronic dislocations |

*Displaced fractures are those with greater than 1-cm displacement and more than 45° angulation. Greater tuberosity fractures with greater than 0.5-cm displacement superiorly are now considered displaced.

*Abbreviations:* A, anterior dislocation; AN, anatomic neck, articular surface free segment; AVN, avascular necrosis; GT, greater tuberosity, shaft displaced at the surgical neck; LT, lesser tuberosity; MU, malunion; NU, nonunion; ORIF, open reduction and internal fixation; P, posterior dislocation; RCT, rotator cuff tear; SN, surgical neck; TA, traumatic arthritis.

**TABLE 44–6**

Common Pitfalls in Prosthetic Replacement for Fractures

| Problem | Potential Result | Solution |
|---|---|---|
| Prosthesis too low | Functionally weakens deltoid, inferior subluxation | Place tuberosities between shaft and head or bone graft to full humeral height |
| Prosthesis stem too narrow | Loosening, pistoning or spinning | Larger stem or cement fixation |
| Uncemented prosthesis without metaphyseal bone support | Loosening | Always cement humeral stem in acute fracture treatment |
| Prosthesis in varus | Greater tuberosity prominent, impingement, shaft penetration | Redirect prosthesis at proper height and version |
| Subsidence | Greater tuberosity prominent, impingement | Cement at proper height, bone graft PRN |
| Too much retroversion | Difficult GT attachment, posterior instability | Correct version, cement PRN |
| Too much anteversion | Anterior instability | Correct version, cement PRN |
| Tuberosity avulsion | Cuff retear, weakness, loss of elevation | Delay rehabilitation, trim tuberosity for fit, vertical and horizontal repair, bone graft |
| Intraoperative shaft fracture below prosthesis stem | Unstable fracture | Long-stem prosthesis with or without cement |

*Abbreviations:* GT, greater tuberosity; PRN, as necessary.

## REFERENCES

1. Ahlgren, O.; Lorentzon, R.; Larrson, S.E. Posterior dislocation of the shoulder associated with general seizures. Acta Orthop Scand 52:694–695, 1981.
2. Anderson, D.; Zvirbulis, R.; Ciullo, J. Scapular manipulation for reduction of anterior shoulder dislocations. Clin Orthop 164:181–183, 1982.
3. Antal, C.S.; Conforty, B.; Engelberg, M.; Reiss, R. Injuries to the axillary artery due to anterior dislocation of the shoulder. J Trauma 13:564–566, 1973.
4. Arciero, R.A.; Wheeler, J.H.; Ryan, J.B.; McBride, J.T. Arthroscopic Bankart repair versus nonoperative treatment for acute, initial anterior shoulder dislocations. Am J Sports Med 22:589–594, 1994.
5. Arndt, J.H.; Sears, A.D. Posterior dislocation of the shoulder. AJR Am J Roentgenol 94:639–645, 1965.
6. Aronen, J.G.; Regan, K. Decreasing the incidence of recurrence of first-time anterior shoulder dislocations with rehabilitation. Am J Sports Med 12:283–291, 1984.
7. Astley, T.M. Dislocation of the shoulder in the elderly. J Bone Joint Surg Br 68:676, 1986.
8. Aston, J.W.; Gregory, C.F. Dislocation of the shoulder with significant fracture of the glenoid. J Bone Joint Surg Am 55:1531–1533, 1973.
9. Baker, C.L.; Uribe, J.W.; Whitman, C. Arthroscopic evaluation of acute initial anterior shoulder dislocations. Am J Sports Med 18:25–28, 1990.
10. Bankart, A.S.B. Recurrent or habitual dislocation of the shoulder joint. BMJ 2:1132–1133, 1923.
11. Bankart, A.S.B. The pathology and treatment of recurrent dislocation of the shoulder joint. Br J Surg 26:23–29, 1938.
12. Baratta, J.B.; Lim, V.; Mastromonaco, E.; Edillon, E. Axillary artery disruption secondary to anterior dislocation of the shoulder. J Trauma 23:1009–1011, 1983.
13. Bassett, R.W.; Cofield, R.H. Acute tears of the rotator cuff. Clin Orthop 175:18–24, 1983.
14. Beattie, T.F.; Steedman, D.J.; McGowan, A.; et al. A comparison of the Milch and Kocher techniques for acute anterior dislocation of the shoulder. Injury 17:349–352, 1986.
15. Blom, S.; Dahlback, L.O. Nerve injuries in dislocations of the shoulder joint and fractures of the neck of the humerus. Acta Chir Scand 136:461–466, 1970.
16. Bloom, M.H.; Obata, W.G. Diagnosis of posterior dislocations of the shoulder with use of Velpeau axillary and angle-up roentgenographic views. J Bone Joint Surg Am 49:943–949, 1967.
17. Breasted, J. The Edwin Smith Papyrus. Chicago, University of Chicago Press, 1930.
18. Brewer, B.J. Aging of the rotator cuff. Am J Sports Med 7:102–110, 1979.
19. Brockbank, W.; Griffiths, D. Orthopaedic surgery in the sixteenth and seventeenth centuries: 1. Luxations of the shoulder. J Bone Joint Surg Br 30:365–375, 1948.
20. Brown, F.W.; Navigato, W.J. Rupture of the axillary artery and brachial plexus palsy with anterior dislocation. Clin Orthop 60:195–199, 1968.
21. Brown, J.T. Nerve injuries complicating dislocation of the shoulder. J Bone Joint Surg Br 34:526, 1952.
22. Carew-McColl, M. Bilateral shoulder dislocations caused by electric shock. Br J Clin Pract 34:251–254, 1980.
23. Cautilli, R.A.; Joyce, M.F.; Mackell, J.V., Jr. Posterior dislocations of the shoulder: A method of postreduction management. Am J Sports Med 6:397–399, 1978.
24. Cave, E.F. Fractures and Other Injuries. Chicago, Year Book, 1961.
25. Cave, E.F.; Burke, J.F.; Boyd, R.J. Trauma Management. Chicago, Year Book, 1974, p. 437.
26. Cisternino, S.J.; Rogers, L.F.; Stufflebam, B.C.; Kruglik, G.D. The trough line: A radiographic sign of posterior shoulder dislocation. AJR Am J Roentgenol 130:951–954, 1978.
27. Colachis, S.C., Jr.; Strohm, B.R.; Brecher, V.L. Effects of axillary nerve block on muscle force in the upper extremity. Arch Phys Rehabil Med 50:647–654, 1969.
28. Connor, P.M.; Boatright, J.R.; D'Alessandro, D.F. Posterior fracture-dislocation of the shoulder: Treatment with acute osteochondral grafting. J Shoulder Elbow Surg 6:480–485, 1997.
29. Cortes, C.V.; Garcia-Dihinix, C.L.; Rodriquez, V.J. Reduction of acute anterior dislocations of the shoulder without anesthesia in the position of maximum muscular relaxation. Int Orthop 13:259–262, 1989.
30. Craig, E. The posterior mechanism of acute anterior shoulder dislocations. Clin Orthop 190:212–216, 1984.
31. Cranley, J.J.; Krause, R.F. Injury to the axillary artery following anterior dislocation of the shoulder. Am J Surg 95:524–526, 1958.
32. Curr, J.R. Rupture of the axillary artery complicating dislocation of the shoulder: Report of a case. J Bone Joint Surg Br 52:313–317, 1970.
33. Danzl, D.F.; Vicario, S.J.; Gleis, G.L.; et al. Closed reduction of anterior subcoracoid shoulder dislocation: Evaluation of an external rotation method. Orthop Rev 15:311–315, 1986.
34. deLaat, E.A.T.; Visser, C.P.J.; Coene, L.N.J.E.M.; et al. Nerve lesions in primary shoulder dislocations and humeral neck fractures. J Bone Joint Surg Br 76:381–383, 1994.
35. DePalma, A.F. Surgery of the Shoulder, 2nd ed. Philadelphia, J.B. Lippincott, 1973.
36. DePalma, A.F.; Cooke, A.F.; Prabhakar, M. The role of the subscapularis in recurrent anterior dislocation of the shoulder. Clin Orthop 54:35–49, 1967.
37. Dimon, J.H., III. Posterior dislocations and posterior fracture-dislocation of the shoulder: A report of 25 cases. South Med J 60:661–666, 1967.

38. Drury, J.K.; Scullion, J.E. Vascular complications of anterior dislocation of the shoulder. Br J Surg 67:579–581, 1980.

38a. Eberson, C.P.; Ng, T.; Green, A. Contralateral intrathoracic displacement of the humeral head. A case report. J Bone Joint Surg Am 82:105–108, 2000.

39. Farrugian, P.D. Superior glenohumeral dislocation: A case report. Injury 16:489–490, 1985.

40. Finkelstein, J.A.; Waddell, J.P.; O'Driscoll, S.W.; Vincent, G. Acute posterior fracture-dislocations of the shoulder treated with the Neer modification of the McLaughlin procedure. J Orthop Trauma 9:190–193, 1995.

41. Fipp, G.J. Simultaneous posterior dislocation of both shoulders. Clin Orthop 44:191–195, 1966.

42. Freundlich, B.D. Luxatio erecta. J Trauma 23:434–436, 1983.

43. Ganel, A.; Horoszowski, H.; Heim, M.; et al. Persistent dislocation of the shoulder in elderly patients. J Am Geriatr Soc 28:282–284, 1980.

44. Gerber, C.; Krushell, R.J. Isolated rupture of the subscapularis muscle: Clinical features in 16 cases. J Bone Joint Surg Br 73:389–394, 1991.

45. Gerber, C.; Lambert, S.M.; Allograft reconstruction of segmental defects of the humeral head for treatment of chronic locked posterior dislocation of the shoulder. J Bone Joint Surg Am 78:376–382, 1996.

46. Gibson, J.M.C. Rupture of the axillary artery following anterior dislocation of the shoulder. J Bone Joint Surg Br 44:114–115, 1962.

47. Glessner, J.R. Intrathoracic dislocation of the humeral head. J Bone Joint Surg Am 42:428–430, 1961.

48. Goldman, A.B.; Ghelman, B. The double contrast shoulder arthrogram: A review of 158 studies. Radiology 127:655–663, 1978.

49. Grana, W.A.; Buckley, P.D.; Yates, C.K. Arthroscopic Bankart suture repair. Am J Sports Med 21:348–353, 1993.

50. Green, A.; DaSilva, M. Closed treatment of two-part greater tuberosity fracture dislocations. Unpublished data.

51. Gugenheim, S.; Sanders, R.J. Axillary artery rupture caused by shoulder dislocation. Surgery 95:55–58, 1984.

52. Guven, O.; Akbar, Z.; Yalcin, S.; Gundes, H. Concomitant rotator cuff tear and brachial plexus injury in association with anterior shoulder dislocation: Unhappy triad of the shoulder. J Orthop Trauma 8:429–430, 1994.

53. Hall, R.H.; Isaac, F.; Booth, C.R. Dislocations of the shoulder with special reference to accompanying small fractures. J Bone Joint Surg Am 41:489–494, 1959.

54. Hawkins, R.J.; Bell, R.H.; Hawkins, R.H.; Koppert, G.H. Anterior dislocation of the shoulder in the older patient. Clin Orthop 206:192–195, 1986.

55. Hawkins, R.J.; Neer, C.S.; Pianta, R.M.; Mendoza, F.X. Locked posterior dislocation of the shoulder. J Bone Joint Surg Am 69:9–18, 1987.

56. Heffington, C.A.; Thompson, R.C. The use of interscalene block anesthesia for manipulative reduction of fractures and dislocations of the upper extremities. J Bone Joint Surg Am 55:83–86, 1973.

57. Henry, J.H.; Genung, J.A. Natural history of glenohumeral dislocation—revisited. Am J Sports Med 10:135–137, 1982.

58. Hersche, O.; Gerber, C. Iatrogenic displacement of fracture-dislocations of the shoulder. J Bone Joint Surg Br 76:30–33, 1994.

59. Hill, H.A.; Sachs, M.D; The grooved defect of the humeral head: A frequently unrecognized complication of dislocations of the shoulder joint. Radiology 35:690–700, 1940.

60. Hintermann, B.; Gachter, A. Arthroscopic findings after shoulder dislocation. Am J Sports Med 23:545–551, 1995.

61. Hovelius, L. Anterior dislocation of the shoulder in teenagers and young adults: Five year prognosis. J Bone Joint Surg Am 69:393–399, 1987.

62. Hovelius, L. Incidence of shoulder dislocation in Sweden. Clin Orthop 166:127–131, 1982.

63. Hovelius, L.; Augustini, B.G.; Fredin, H.; et al. Ten year prognosis of primary anterior dislocation of the shoulder in the young. J Bone Joint Surg Am 78:1677–1684, 1996.

64. Hovelius, L.; Eriksson, K.; Fredin, H.; et al. Recurrences after initial dislocation of the shoulder: Results of a prospective study of treatment. J Bone Joint Surg Am 65:343–349, 1983.

65. Hovelius, L.; Lind, B.; Thorling, J. Primary dislocation of the shoulder: Factors affecting the two-year prognosis. Clin Orthop 176:181–185, 1983.

66. Howell, S.M.; Galinat, B.J. The glenoid labral socket: A constrained articular surface. Clin Orthop 243:122–125, 1989.

67. Howell, S.M.; Imobersteg, A.M.; Seger, D.H.; Marone, P.J. Clarification of the role of the supraspinatus muscle in shoulder function. J Bone Joint Surg Am 68:398–404, 1986.

68. Hussein, M. Kocher's method is 3000 years old. J Bone Joint Surg Br 50:669–671, 1968.

69. Iannotti, J.P.; Zlatkin, M.B.; Esterhai, J.L.; et al. Magnetic resonance imaging of the shoulder. J Bone Joint Surg Am 73:17–29, 1991.

70. Janecki, C.J.; Shahcheragh, G.H. The forward elevation maneuver for reduction of anterior dislocations of the shoulder. Clin Orthop 164:177–180, 1982.

71. Jardan, O.M.; Hood, L.T.; Lynch, R.D. Complete avulsion of the axillary artery as a complication of shoulder dislocation. J Bone Joint Surg Am 55:189–192, 1973.

72. Johnson, J.R.; Bayley, J.I.L. Early complications of acute anterior dislocation of the shoulder in the middle-aged and elderly patient. Injury 13:431–434, 1982.

73. Johnson, J.R.; Bayley, J.I.L. Loss of shoulder function following acute anterior dislocation. J Bone Joint Surg Br 63:633, 1981.

74. Johnson, J.R.; Bayley, J.I.L. The early complications of anterior dislocation in the middle aged and elderly patient. In: Bayley, J.; Kessel, L., eds. Shoulder Surgery. Berlin, Springer-Verlag, 1982, pp. 79–83.

75. Kay, S.P.; Yaszemski, M.J.; Rockwood, C.A., Jr. Acute tear of the rotator cuff masked by simultaneous palsy of the brachial plexus. J Bone Joint Surg Am 70:611–612, 1988.

76. Kazar, B.; Relovszky, E. Prognosis of primary dislocation of the shoulder. Acta Orthop Scand 40:216–224, 1969.

77. Keppler, P.; Holz, U.; Thielemann, F.W.; Meinig, R. Locked posterior dislocation of the shoulder: Treatment using rotational osteotomy of the humerus. J Orthop Trauma 8:286–292, 1994.

78. Kiviluoto, O.; Pasila, M.; Jaroma, H.; Sundholm, A. Immobilization after primary dislocation of the shoulder. Acta Orthop Scand 51:915–919, 1980.

79. Kocher, T. Eine neue reductions Methode für Schulterverrenkung. Berlin Klin 7:101, 1870.

80. Kothari, R.U.; Dronen, S.C. Prospective evaluation of the scapular manipulation technique in reducing anterior shoulder dislocations. Ann Emerg Med 21:1349–1352, 1992.

81. Kummel, B.M. Fractures of the glenoid causing chronic dislocation of the shoulder. Clin Orthop 69:189–191, 1970.

82. Lacey, T., II; Crawford, H.B. Reduction of anterior dislocation of the shoulder by means of the Milch abduction technique. J Bone Joint Surg Am 34:108–109, 1952.

83. Landsiedl, F. Arthroscopic therapy for recurrent anterior luxation of the shoulder by capsular repair. Arthroscopy 8:296–304, 1992.

84. Leffert, R.D.; Seddon, H. Infraclavicular brachial plexus injuries. J Bone Joint Surg Br 47:9–22, 1965.

85. Lindbolm, K. Arthrography and roentgenography in ruptures of tendons of the shoulder joint. Acta Radiol 20:548–561, 1939.

86. Lippit, S.B.; Kennedy, J.P.; Thompson, T.R. Intraarticular lidocaine versus intravenous analgesia in the reduction of dislocated shoulders. Orthop Trans 15:804, 1991.

87. Lippit, S.; Matsen, F.A. Mechanisms of glenohumeral joint instability. Clin Orthop 291:20–28, 1993.

88. Liveson, J.A. Nerve lesions associated with shoulder dislocation: An electrodiagnostic study in 11 cases. J Neurol Neurosurg Psychiatry 47:742–744, 1984.

89. Majeed, L. Pulsatile haemarthrosis of the shoulder joint associated with false aneursym of the axillary artery as a late complication of anterior dislocation of the shoulder. Injury 16:566–567, 1984.

90. Manes, H.R. A new method of shoulder reduction in the elderly. Clin Orthop 147:200–202, 1980.

91. Marans, H.J.; Angel, K.R.; Schemitsch, E.H.; Wedge, J.H. The fate of traumatic anterior dislocation of the shoulder in children. J Bone Joint Surg Am 74:1242–1244, 1992.

92. Martin-Herrero, T.; Rodriguez-Merchan, C.; Munuera-Martinez, L. Fractures of the coracoid process: Presentation of seven cases and review of literature. J Trauma 30:1597–1599, 1990.

93. Matthews, D.E.; Roberts, T. Intraarticular lidocaine versus intravenous analgesic for reduction of acute anterior shoulder dislocations: A prospective randomized study. Am J Sports Med 23:54–58, 1995.

94. McLaughlin, H.L. Dislocation of the shoulder with tuberosity fracture. Surg Clin North Am 43:1615–1620, 1963.

95. McLaughlin, H.L. Locked posterior subluxation of the shoulder. Surg Clin North Am 43:1621–1622, 1963.

96. McLaughlin, H.L.; Cavallaro, W. Primary anterior dislocation of the shoulder. Am J Surg 80:615–621, 1950.

97. McNair, T.J. A clinical trial of the "hanging arm" reduction of dislocation of the shoulder. J R Coll Edinb 3:47–53, 1957.

98. Milch, H. Treatment of dislocation of the shoulder. Surgery 3:732–740, 1938.

99. Mills, K. Simultaneous bilateral posterior fracture dislocation of the shoulder. Injury 6:39–41, 1974.

100. Milton, G.W. The circumflex nerve and dislocation of the shoulder. Br J Phys Med 17:136–138, 1954.

101. Moseley, H.F.; Overgaard, K. The anterior capsular mechanism in recurrent anterior dislocation of the shoulder: Morphological and clinical studies with special references to the glenoid labrum and the glenohumeral ligaments. J Bone Joint Surg Br 44:913–927, 1962.

102. Neer, C.S., II. Shoulder Reconstruction. Philadelphia, W.B. Saunders, 1990.

103. Neer, C.S., II.; Foster, C.R. Inferior capsular shift for involuntary inferior and multidirectional instability of the shoulder: A preliminary report. J Bone Joint Surg Am 62:897–908, 1980.

104. Neviaser, J.S. The treatment of old unreduced dislocation of the shoulder. Surg Clin North Am 43:1671–1678, 1963.

105. Neviaser, R.J.; Neviaser, T.J. Recurrent instability of the shoulder after age 40. J Shoulder Elbow Surg 4:416–418, 1995.

106. Neviaser, R.J.; Neviaser, T.J.; Neviaser, J.S. Anterior dislocation of the shoulder and rotator cuff rupture. Clin Orthop 291:103–106, 1993.

107. Neviaser, R.J.; Neviaser, T.J.; Neviaser, J.S. Concurrent rupture of the rotator cuff and anterior dislocation of the shoulder in the older patient. J Bone Joint Surg Am 70:1308–1311, 1988.

108. Neviaser, T.J. Old unreduced dislocations of the shoulder. Orthop Clin North Am 11:287–294, 1980.

109. Nicola, F.G.; Ellman, H.; Eckardt, D.; Finermann, G. Bilateral posterior fracture-dislocation of the shoulder treated with a modification of the McLaughlin procedure. J Bone Joint Surg Am 63:1175–1177, 1981.

110. Nordquist, A.; Petersson, C.J. Incidence and causes of shoulder girdle injuries in an urban population. J Shoulder Elbow Surg 4:107–112, 1995.

111. Pagnani, M.J.; Warren, R.F. The history of anterior shoulder instability: Evolution of principles and treatment: I and II. Contemp Orthop 27:347–354, 465–471, 1993.

112. Pasila, M.; Jaroma, H.; Kiviluoto, O.; Sundholm, A. Early complications of primary shoulder dislocations. Acta Orthop Scand 49:260–263, 1978.

113. Pasila, M.; Kiviluoto, O.; Jaroma, H.; Sundholm, A. Recovery from primary shoulder dislocations and its complications. Acta Orthop Scand 51:257–262, 1980.

114. Perthes, G. Ueber Operationen bei der habituellen Schulterluxation. Deutsch Z Chir 85:199–227, 1906.

115. Pollock, R.G.; Bigliani, L.U. Recurrent posterior shoulder instability: Diagnosis and treatment. Clin Orthop 291:85–96, 1993.

116. Poulsen, S.R. Reduction of acute shoulder dislocations using the Eskimo technique: A study of 23 consecutive cases. J Trauma 28:1382–1383, 1988.

117. Pritchett, J.W.; Clark, J.M. Prosthetic replacement for chronic unreduced dislocations of the shoulder. Clin Orthop 216:89–93, 1987.

118. Rang, M. Anthology of Orthopaedics. Edinburgh, E. & S. Livingstone, 1966, p. 225.

119. Reeves, B. Arthrography of the shoulder. J Bone Joint Surg Br 48:424–435, 1966.

120. Reeves, B. Experiments on the tensile strength of the anterior capsular structures of the shoulder in man. J Bone Joint Surg Br 50:858–865, 1968.

121. Ribbans, W.J.; Mitchell, R.; Taylor, G.J. Computerized arthrotomography of primary anterior dislocation of the shoulder. J Bone Joint Surg Br 72:181–185, 1990.

122. Rockwood, C.A. Fractures and dislocations about the shoulder: II. Subluxations and dislocations about the shoulder. In: Rockwood, C.A.; Green, D.P., eds. Fractures in Adults, Vol. 1. Philadelphia, J.B. Lippincott, 1984.

123. Rowe, C.R. Anterior dislocations of the shoulder: Prognosis and treatment. Surg Clin North Am 43:1609–1614, 1963.

124. Rowe, C.R. Prognosis in dislocations of the shoulder. J Bone Joint Surg Am 38:957–977, 1956.

125. Rowe, C.R.; Sakellarides, H.T. Factors related to recurrences of anterior dislocation of the shoulder. Clin Orthop 20:40–48, 1961.

126. Rowe, C.R.; Zarins, B. Chronic unreduced dislocations of the shoulder. J Bone Joint Surg Am 64:494–505, 1982.

127. Russell, J.A.; Holmes, E.M.; Keller, D.J.; et al. Reduction of acute anterior shoulder dislocations using the Milch technique: A study of ski injuries. J Trauma 21:802–805, 1981.

128. Schulz, T.J.; Jacobs, B.; Patterson, R.L., Jr. Unrecognized dislocations of the shoulder. J Trauma 9:1009–1023, 1969.

129. Schwartz, R.E.; O'Brien, S.J.; Warren, R.F.; Torzilli, P.A. Capsular restraints to anterior-posterior motion of the shoulder. Orthop Trans 12:727, 1988.

130. Seradge, H. Dislocations of the shoulder with tuberosity fracture. Surg Clin North Am 43:1615–1620, 1963.

131. Sher, J.S.; Uribe, J.W.; Posada, A.; et al. Abnormal findings on magnetic resonance images of asymptomatic shoulders. J Bone Joint Surg Am 77:10–15, 1995.

132. Simonet, W.T.; Cofield, R.H. Prognosis in anterior shoulder dislocation. Am J Sports Med 12:19–24, 1984.

133. Simonet, W.T.; Melton, L.F.; Cofield, R.H.; Ilstrup, D.M. Incidence of anterior shoulder dislocations in Olmstead County, Minnesota. Clin Orthop 186:186–191, 1984.

134. Sonnabend, D.H.; Treatment of primary anterior shoulder dislocation in patients older than 40 years of age. Clin Orthop 304:74–77, 1994.

135. Speer, K.P.; Deng, X.; Borrero, S.; et al. Biomechanical evaluation of a simulated Bankart lesion. J Bone Joint Surg Am 76:1819–1826, 1994.

136. Stimson, L.A. An easy method of reduction of dislocation of the shoulder and hip. Med Record 57:356, 1900.

137. Suder, P.A.; Mikkelsen, J.B.; Hougaard, K.; Jensen, P.E. Reduction of traumatic primary anterior shoulder dislocations with local anesthesia. J Shoulder Elbow Surg 3:288–294, 1994.

138. Symeonides, P.P. The significance of the subscapularis in the pathogenesis of recurrent anterior dislocation of the shoulder. J Bone Joint Surg Br 54:476–483, 1972.

139. Thomas, H.O. Fractures, Dislocations, Disease, and Deformities of the Bones of the Trunk and Upper Extremities. London, H.K. Lewis, 1887.

140. Thomas, S.C.; Matsen, F.A. An approach to the repair of glenohumeral ligament avulsion in the management of traumatic anterior glenohumeral instability. J Bone Joint Surg Am 71:506–513, 1989.

141. Tijmes, J.; Loyd, H.M.; Tullos, H.S. Arthrography in acute shoulder dislocations. South Med J 72:564–567, 1979.

142. Toolanen, G.; Hildingsson, C.; Hedlund, T.; et al. Early complications after anterior dislocation of the shoulder in patients over 40 years: An ultrasonographic and electromyographic study. Acta Orthop Scand 64:549–552, 1993.

143. Townley, C.O. The capsular mechanism in recurrent dislocation of the shoulder. J Bone Joint Surg Am 32:370–380, 1950.

144. Turkel, S.J.; Panio, M.W.; Marshall, J.L.; Girgis, F.G. Stabilizing mechanisms preventing anterior dislocation of the glenohumeral joint. J Bone Joint Surg Am 63:1208–1217, 1981.

145. Wagner, K.T.; Lyne, E.D. Adolescent traumatic dislocations of the shoulder with open epiphyses. J Pediatr Orthop 3:61–62, 1983.

146. Weile, F.; Fjeldborg, O. Lesions of the axillary artery associated with dislocation of the shoulder. Acta Chir Scand 137:279–281, 1971.

147. Wenner, S.M. Anterior dislocations of the shoulder in patients over 50 years of age. Orthopedics 8:155–157, 1985.

148. West, E.F. Intrathoracic dislocation of the humerus. J Bone Joint Surg Br 31:61–62, 1949.

149. Wheeler, J.H.; Ryan, J.B.; Arciero, R.A.; Molinari, R.N. Arthroscopic versus nonoperative treatment of acute shoulder dislocations in young athletes. Arthroscopy 5:213–217, 1989.

150. Wilson, J.C.; McKeever, F.M. Traumatic posterior (retroglenoid) dislocation of the humerus. J Bone Joint Surg Am 31:160–172, 1949.

151. Winnie, A.P. Interscalene brachial plexus block. Anesth Analg 49:455–466, 1970.

152. Yoneda, J.B.; Welsh, R.P.; MacIntosh, D.L. Conservative treatment of shoulder dislocation in young males. In: Proceedings and Reports of Universities, Colleges, Councils, Associations and Societies. J Bone Joint Surg Br 64:254–255, 1982.

PART **IV** *Post-traumatic Reconstruction of Proximal Humeral Fractures and Fracture-Dislocations*

Andrew Green, M.D. • Tom R. Norris, M.D.

Although the outcome of most proximal humeral fractures is satisfactory, a few patients have persistent problems that may require or benefit from subsequent surgical treatment. In most instances, a combination of several problems lead to poor results and make late treatment very difficult. These problems include nerve injury, scarring and shoulder stiffness, deltoid injury, malunion, nonunion, avascular necrosis, and post-traumatic arthritis. Even though most patients who undergo late reconstructive surgery after a proximal humeral fracture have a satisfactory outcome, the results are usually limited when compared with successful primary treatment of proximal humeral fractures. The focus of this chapter is to review the indications, technical considerations, and results of late operative reconstruction after proximal humeral fracture.

## EVALUATION

When patients have problems after primary treatment of proximal humeral fractures, several factors are frequently involved in the failure. Identification of these factors requires a comprehensive and detailed evaluation. Details of the original injury and initial neurologic status, the original treatment and rehabilitation, and the current issues must be elucidated. Past medical records should be reviewed because they often provide information that is critical to the decision-making process. Such information may include details about the neurologic status, surgical findings, and rehabilitation. A thorough physical examination includes assessment of passive and active shoulder motion, muscle condition and strength, and neurovascular status. Radiographic evaluation should include five plain radiographs—true anteroposterior, anteroposterior internal and external rotation, outlet or Y view, and axillary lateral views—as well as computed tomographic (CT) scans to assess the anatomy of malunions. Because of the high incidence of neurologic injury, electrodiagnostic studies should be routinely considered as part of the evaluation. Complete knowledge of the pathoanatomy helps in planning further treatment and can provide prognostic information about the potential outcome of treatment.

## PROSTHETIC ARTHROPLASTY

Among the various indications for shoulder replacement, late reconstruction after proximal humeral fractures is less common than replacement for primary glenohumeral arthritis and acute fracture. Shoulder pain and dysfunction with associated post-traumatic glenohumeral arthritis are the primary indications for late prosthetic arthroplasty. Post-traumatic arthritis results from articular incongruity, avascular necrosis and collapse of the humeral head, intra-articular hardware, and long-standing joint stiffness, which can cause degeneration of the articular surfaces. Post-traumatic arthritis is a relatively uncommon sequela of proximal humeral fractures because most fractures do not involve the articular surface of the humerus.

In some cases, mild articular surface irregularity of the humerus can be tolerated. The authors accept a maximum of 2 to 3 mm of articular displacement when performing open reduction and internal fixation (ORIF). It is possible that some degree of acute articular incongruity can be reshaped with early motion exercises. In addition, the location of incongruity is important. More substantial incongruity of the humeral head is likely to cause problems because of the complexity of global shoulder motion. Incongruity at the periphery of the articular segment such as occurs with some tuberosity fractures will affect the end range of shoulder motion.

Once substantial articular damage and significant symptoms have occurred, the best treatment is shoulder arthroplasty. Options of mostly historical interest include resection arthroplasty and shoulder arthrodesis.[5, 28] In the early stages of injury, before the glenoid articular surface is damaged, humeral head replacement can be performed. Glenoid replacement is indicated in those with damage to the articular surface and an intact rotator cuff. Replacing the humeral head early rather than waiting until the collapse is severe with involvement of the glenoid (see Fig. 44–80) has definite advantages. In early treatment, humeral head replacement is all that is needed. Later treatment often requires glenoid replacement and more extensive soft tissue release to overcome the contracture (see Fig. 44–81). Humeral head replacement avoids the problem of failure of the glenoid component.

Complicating the problem is the fact that post-traumatic arthritis rarely occurs in isolation and is often associated with malunion of the tuberosities and surgical neck of the humerus.[1, 2] In some cases, complex malunion without glenohumeral arthritis is also best treated with prosthetic arthroplasty. In these situations, either the multiple osteotomies that would be required to reconstruct the proximal end of the humerus would devascularize the articular segment, or the internal fixation would be so compromised that stable fixation cannot be achieved.

The primary goal of prosthetic reconstruction is anatomic reconstruction of the proximal part of the humerus. The anatomic parameters of the proximal end of the humerus have been defined by cadaver studies[12] (Fig. 44–101 and Table 44–7). The mean radius of curvature is approximately 24 mm (range, 18 to 28 mm), and the mean

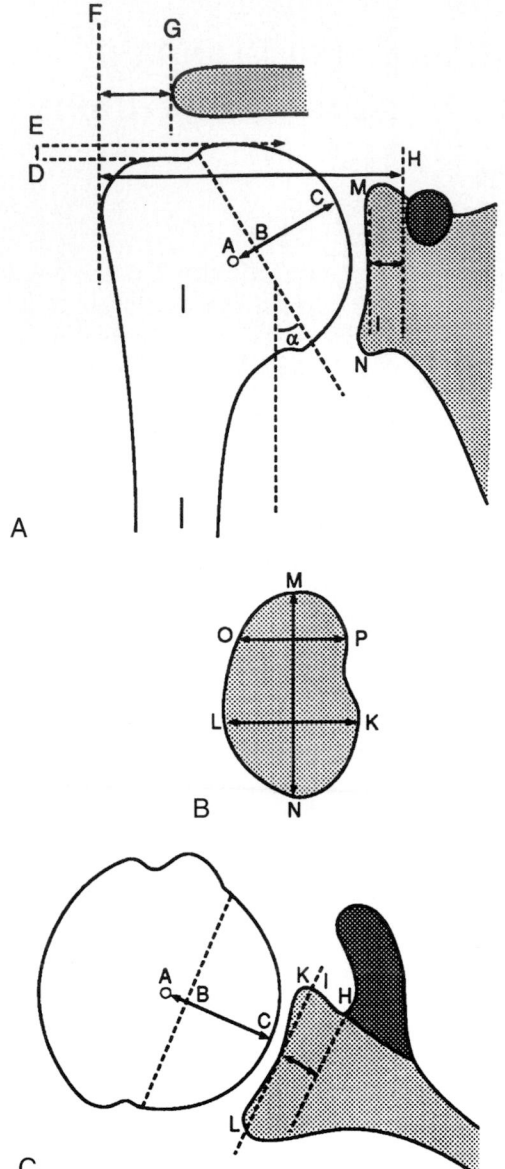

**Figure 44–101.** Anatomic landmarks and parameters of the glenohumeral anatomy and relationships to the acromion and glenoid.

Restoration of humeral length is an uncommon, but important consideration. If the humerus is too short, the deltoid myofascial sleeve does not have enough tension to function properly, and the humeral head will tend to have fixed inferior subluxation. Preoperative comparative radiographs, such as scanograms, can be obtained to plan the reconstruction.[19]

Failure to re-create the normal anatomic parameters of the proximal end of the humerus can have a significant effect on the results of prosthetic arthroplasty. The humeral head offset affects the range of motion and subacromial contact. Humeral head size and volume affect glenohumeral motion and translation. Nevertheless, reconstruction of normal proximal humeral anatomy is often very difficult.

Boileau and colleagues proposed a classification of post-traumatic proximal humeral anatomy. They differentiated between intracapsular problems that do not require greater tuberosity osteotomy and extracapsular problems that require osteotomy and repositioning of the greater tuberosity[3] (Fig. 44–102).

## Technique

The standard anterior deltopectoral approach is used for shoulder arthroplasty. Deeper dissection is usually difficult because of scarring of the previously injured or operated soft tissues. Shoulders with previous open surgery are usually more scarred. Considerable care is required to identify normal tissue structures such as the conjoined tendon, axillary nerve and brachial plexus, and the biceps tendon. In shoulders that have previously undergone surgery, the conjoined tendon is often scarred to the proximal end of the humerus. In addition, all scarred soft tissue planes, including subacromial, subdeltoid, and subcoracoid adhesions, should be released to improve

articular thickness ranges from 15 to 19 mm. The radius of curvature and thickness are proportionate and correlate with humeral shaft length and patient height. The mean lateral humeral offset is 56 mm (range, 43 to 68 mm). The height of the greater tuberosity is 6 to 8 mm above the top of the articular surface.

Although mean humeral head retroversion is recognized to be 30° to 40°, the variation is actually considerable and ranges from approximately 10° to 50° of retroversion.[23] Unlike primary prosthetic arthroplasty for glenohumeral arthritis, it is often difficult to determine what the normal version is for a patient with a proximal humeral malunion. Attempting to re-create 30° to 40° of retroversion is the best approach unless issues of glenohumeral instability warrant variation from the mean. Such issues would include increasing retroversion in patients with a tendency toward anterior instability or increasing anteversion in those with posterior instability.

**TABLE 44–7**

Glenohumeral Sizes and Relationships

| Parameter | Distance | Location in Fig. 44–101 |
|---|---|---|
| Radius of curvature of the humeral head | | |
|   Coronal plane | A–C | A |
|   Axial plane | A–C | C |
| Thickness of the humeral head | | |
|   Coronal plane | B–C | A |
|   Axial plane | B–C | C |
| Dimensions of the glenoid | | |
|   Superior-inferior | M–N | A and B |
|   Anterior-posterior (top) | O–P | B (cadavers only) |
|   Anterior-posterior (bottom) | L–K | B and C |
| Neck-shaft angle | — | A |
| Joint line of the glenoid | H–I | A and C |
| Lateral humeral offset | F–H | A |
| Distance from the greater tuberosity to the lateral acromial process | F–G | A |
| Distance from the humeral head to the greater tuberosity | D–E | A |

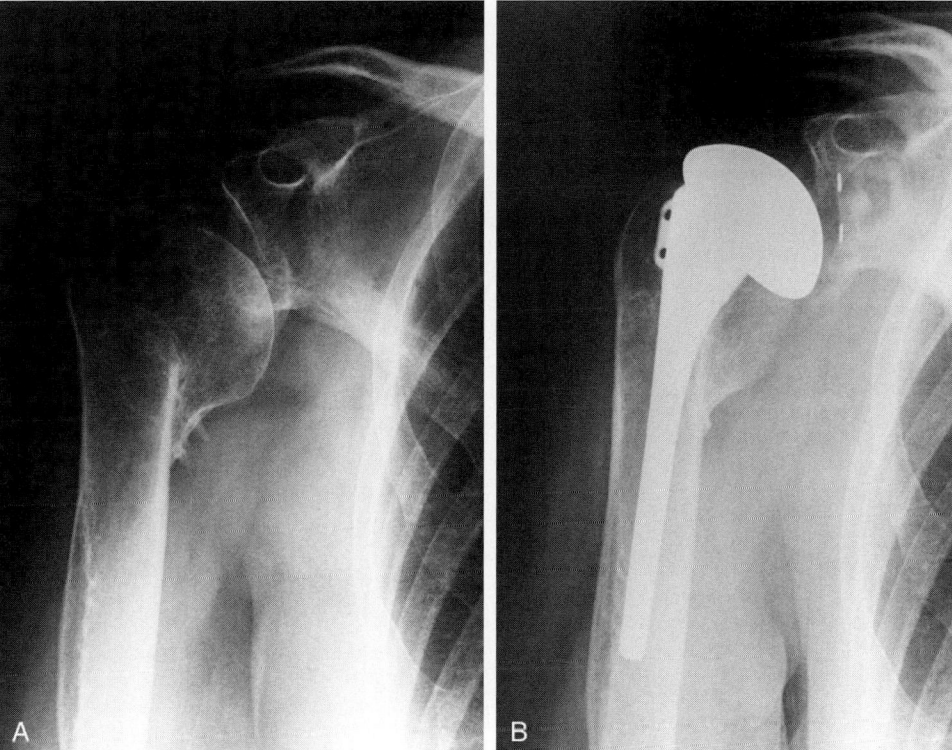

**FIGURE 44–102.** *A,* True anteroposterior radiograph of a 62-year-old woman who had closed treatment of a head-splitting proximal humeral fracture. The glenoid was incongruent. *B,* The shoulder was reconstructed with a total-shoulder replacement. The inferiorly displaced segment of the humeral head was left in place, and the humeral component was seated in the anatomically correct position. The greater tuberosity did not require osteotomy.

shoulder mobility. The axillary nerve is at risk when dissecting under the deltoid. It can be protected by beginning the subdeltoid release proximally and distally and initially avoiding the area 4 to 5 cm distal to the acromion.

Once the anatomy is defined, the approach to the glenohumeral joint is determined by the extent of subscapularis and anterior capsular contracture, as well as the presence of malunion or nonunion of the tuberosity. The lesser tuberosity can be osteotomized, or the subscapularis can be released or lengthened. Capsular releases are imperative to restore motion. During inferior capsular release the axillary nerve must be identified and protected. If extensive dense scarring is seen in the region of the axillary nerve, it is probably safer to avoid the tedious dissection required to expose it and instead simply steer clear of the nerve. Malunion of the greater tuberosity often requires an osteotomy. In some cases, the malunited proximal humeral fracture is converted to a four-part fracture, and the standard procedure for humeral head replacement for acute fracture is followed (Fig. 44–103). The technique of humeral head replacement for four-part fractures is described in detail in Part II of this chapter.

The subscapularis tendon and anterior capsule can be lengthened with a coronal-plane Z-plasty (see Fig. 44–52) or directly elevated off the tuberosity and reattached closer to the articular margin. Elevating it from the anterior scapular neck plus releasing it from the base of the coracoid further mobilizes the subscapularis tendon and muscle. Osteotomy of the greater tuberosity can be performed before excision of the articular segment. The tuberosity and rotator cuff are mobilized as a unit. Ideally, an anatomically sized head is selected for the prosthesis, and effort is made to obtain adequate soft tissue release

rather than undersize or oversize the components. In some cases, a smaller humeral head is necessary because the tuberosity or capsule cannot be adequately mobilized (see Fig. 44–50).

If an osteotomy of the tuberosities is performed, the humeral component should be cemented. If the reconstruction requires only osteotomy of the articular segment, the humeral component can be press-fit.

## NONUNION

Nonunion of the proximal end of the humerus is relatively uncommon and typically involves the greater tuberosity or the surgical neck. The muscular forces acting on the different segments of the proximal part of the humerus promote the nonunion. In addition, traction at the fracture site, inadequate immobilization or fixation, failure of internal fixation, soft tissue interposition, and premature range of motion before secure fracture healing contribute to the development of nonunion[22] (see Figs. 44–39, 44–61, and 44–78). Treatment of the nonunion depends on the segments involved and whether traumatic arthritis has developed.

### Greater Tuberosity Nonunion

Greater tuberosity nonunion is relatively uncommon, and most cases occur when the tuberosity is displaced posteriorly. Treatment is difficult because of the contracted rotator cuff and capsule. Axillary lateral radiographs may not provide sufficient detail to demonstrate the nonunion,

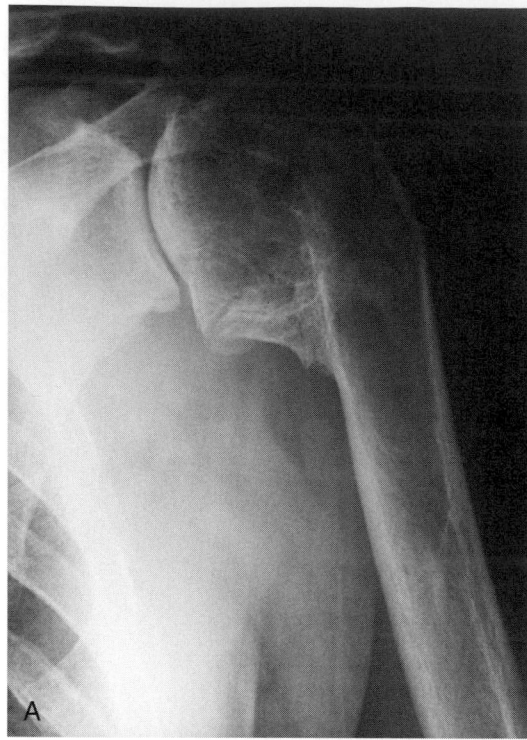
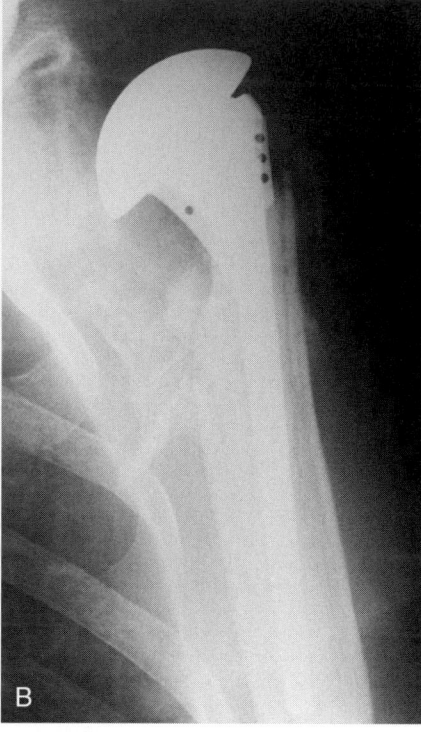

**FIGURE 44–103.** *A,* True anteroposterior radiograph of a 64-year-old man who sustained a proximal humeral fracture 20 years earlier. He sought medical attention for worsening pain and limited motion. *B,* The shoulder was reconstructed with a humeral head replacement and tuberosity osteotomies.

but CT scans provide better detail. Maximal mobilization with lysis of adhesions and capsular release is required to reposition the tuberosity fragment and avoid excessive tension on the repair (Fig. 44–104). Postoperatively, the repair should be protected with abduction bracing to avoid internal rotation and adduction. Additionally, internal rotation and adduction motion exercises should be delayed for 6 weeks until early bone healing has occurred. In long-standing, neglected cases, reduction of the tuberosity to its normal position may not be possible.

## Surgical Neck Nonunion

Nonunion of the surgical neck most commonly occurs after closed fracture treatment. It can be treated with either ORIF or prosthetic arthroplasty. In general, these nonunions are atrophic, and in many cases, a synovial nonunion has developed with communication between the nonunion site and the glenohumeral joint. Surgical neck fractures that do not consolidate within 6 to 8 weeks are very likely to progress to nonunion. Scheck considered a

surgical neck fracture ununited if "the fragments did not move as a unit after a minimum of eight weeks."[24]

Preoperative assessment should include standard plain radiographs, and humeral length can be evaluated by comparison with the normal unaffected humerus. Shortening should be avoided because it might result in fixed inferior subluxation of the humeral head.

ORIF can be performed with intramedullary rods such as Ender rods or a fixed-angle blade plate and supplemental autogenous bone graft[7, 14] (Fig. 44–105). In the elderly population, ORIF is frequently impossible because of poor bone quality. In some cases, the head is excavated from long-standing nonunion and erosion by the humeral shaft. Consequently, fixation purchase in the small remaining osteoporotic proximal segment is poor. Intramedullary bone grafting with an autogenous corticocancellous peg was reported by Walch and associates[29] (Fig. 44–106). This technique increases the bone surface contact area and improves the fixation strength of screws placed into the humeral head.

Alternatively, reconstruction of a surgical neck nonunion can be achieved with prosthetic arthroplasty (Fig.

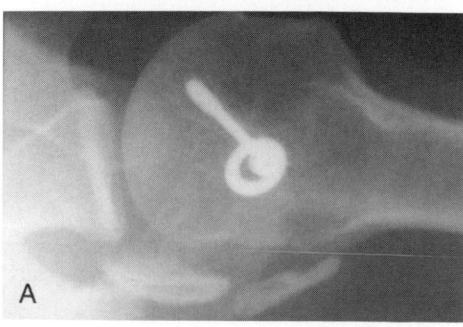
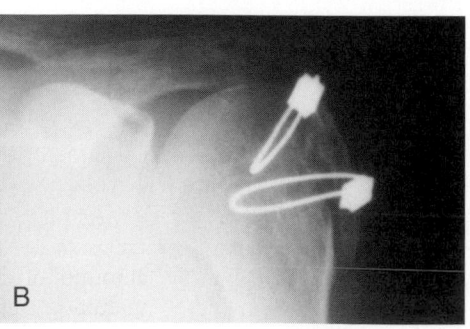

**FIGURE 44–104.** *A,* Greater tuberosity nonunion that resulted after open reduction and internal reduction (ORIF) with a screw and washer. *B,* Treated by ORIF with cables and heavy suture to secure the repair.

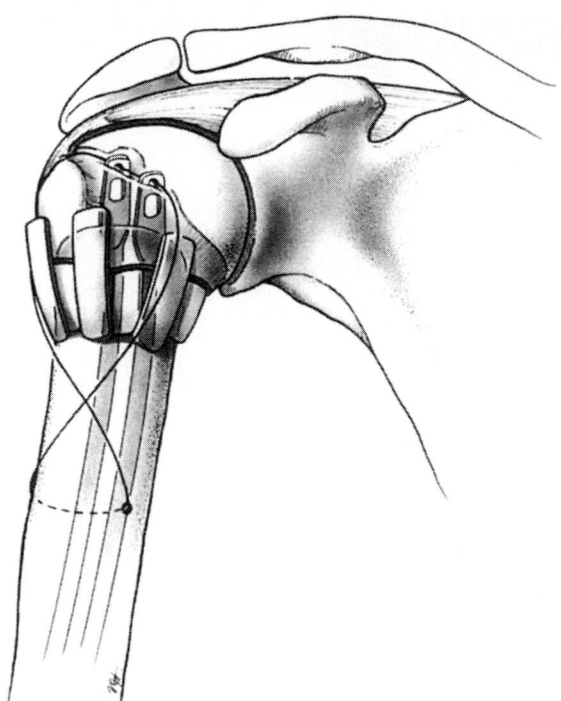

**FIGURE 44–105.** (From Duralde, X.A., et al. J Shoulder Elbow Surg 5:169–180, 1996.)

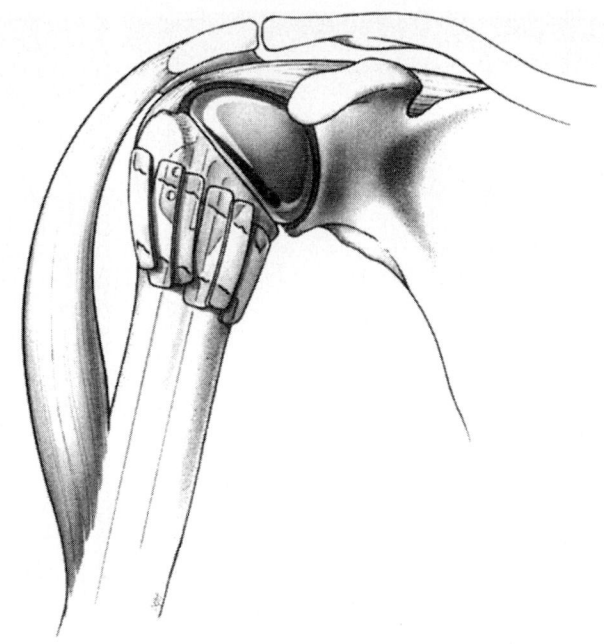

**FIGURE 44–107.** (From Duralde, X.A., et al. J Shoulder Elbow Surg 5:169–180, 1996.)

44–107). In these cases, a cemented humeral head replacement with excision of the remaining articular fragment and preservation of the tuberosities is the preferred technique. A standard deltopectoral approach is used. Careful dissection around the surgical neck is required to protect the axillary nerve both medially, inferior to the subscapularis tendon, and laterally on the deep surface of the deltoid muscle.

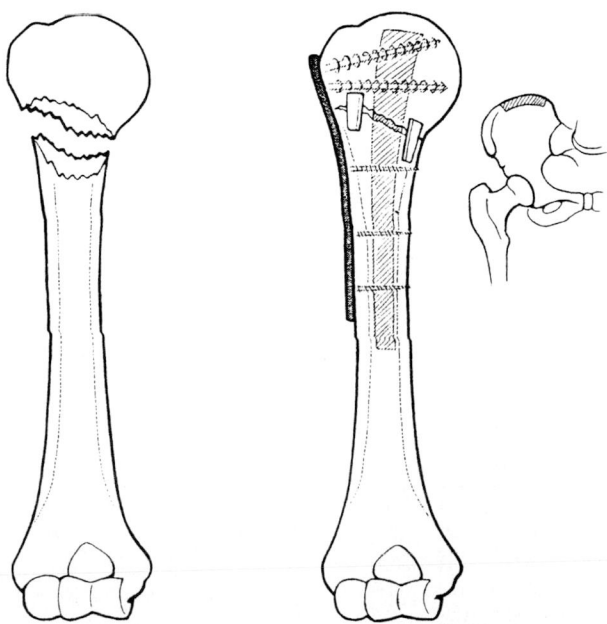

**FIGURE 44–106.** (From Walch, G., et al. J Shoulder Elbow Surg 5:161–168, 1996.)

Essentially, the proximal end of the humerus is converted to a four-part fracture. An osteotome is used to separate the greater and lesser tuberosities at the biceps groove, and the articular segment is excised. Care is taken to preserve tuberosity fragments that are large enough to promote good bony healing. Once the tuberosities have been separated, the capsule is released so that the tuberosities and rotator cuff tendons can be mobilized. Subsequently, the standard procedure for humeral head replacement for proximal humeral fractures is followed. The excised humeral head is morselized and packed as bone graft for the nonunion site at the tuberosity and surgical neck levels[19, 20] (Fig. 44–108).

Earlier treatment of surgical neck nonunion improves the likelihood of achieving a satisfactory result. After long-standing nonunion, the rotator cuff muscles become more contracted and dysfunctional. Long-standing nonunion is also more likely to be associated with degeneration of the articular surface of the glenoid and require total-shoulder replacement.

## MALUNION

Malunion of proximal humeral fractures usually occurs at the greater tuberosity and the surgical neck. It can develop after closed treatment or from loss of reduction secondary to inadequate fixation. The clinical impact of malunion is variable. Some surgical neck malunions cause limitation of motion, but little in the way of pain, and are thus easily accepted by many older patients. In contrast, even small amounts of displacement can render a greater tuberosity malunion significantly symptomatic.

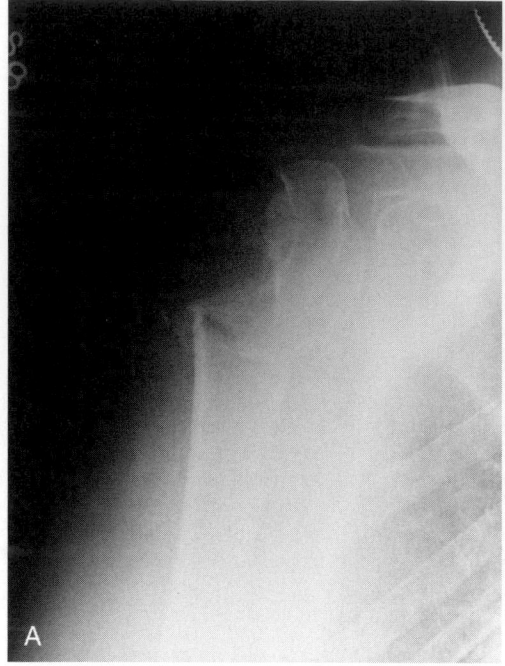
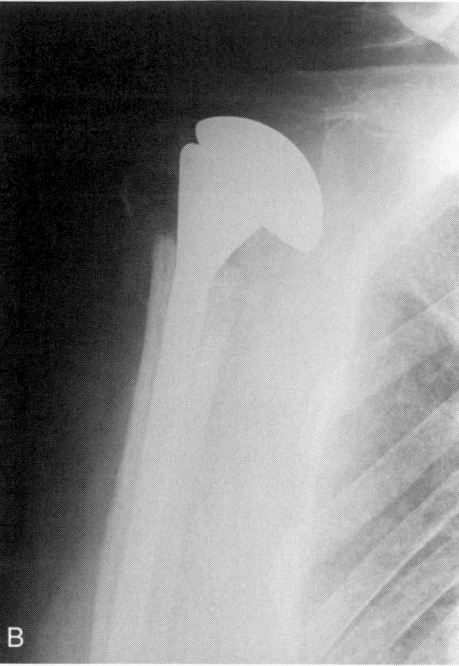

**Figure 44–108.** *A*, Surgical neck nonunion resulted after nonoperative treatment in an elderly woman. *Arrows* outline the cavitation of the humeral metaphysis. *B*, Follow-up radiographs with anatomic reconstruction of the tuberosities and the articular segment with a cemented modular humeral prosthesis.

Anatomic detail needs to be defined with clear imaging. Five plain radiographic views, including true anteroposterior, anteroposterior views in internal and external rotation, an outlet view, and an axillary lateral view, generally provide enough information to plan a surgical reconstruction. In some cases, a CT scan is required to clarify the position of the greater tuberosity relative to the articular segment, as well as the relationship of the articular segment to the glenoid.

Malunions are problematic because of stiffness, blocked range of motion, traumatic arthritis, and humeral shortening. Malunion of the greater and lesser tuberosities causes limitation of external and internal rotation, respectively. The greater tuberosity can impinge against the posterior glenoid or acromion, whereas the lesser tuberosity can impinge against either the anterior glenoid or the coracoid process. Superior malunion of the greater tuberosity can cause limitations in humeral abduction or elevation. Surgical neck malunion usually results in loss of elevation and some loss of rotation. In the absence of traumatic arthritis, surgical treatment of a proximal humeral malunion usually involves corrective osteotomy. Complex malunions of both the greater tuberosity and the surgical neck may require prosthetic arthroplasty to successfully reconstruct the shoulder (Fig. 44–109).

Symptomatic articular incongruity without arthritis can be treated with osteotomy. If the incongruity is the result of malunion of the greater or lesser tuberosity, osteotomy of the tuberosity can be performed.

## Greater Tuberosity Malunion

Pain is the primary indication for surgical management of tuberosity malunion. Patients with painless limitation of motion do not commonly seek medical evaluation. Late treatment of displaced greater tuberosity fractures is very difficult because the rotator cuff and capsule are usually scarred and stiff and difficult to mobilize.

The rotator cuff and tuberosity are mobilized laterally for repair to the proximal end of the humerus. The rotator interval is closed between the subscapularis and the supraspinatus (see Fig. 44–51; see also Fig. 44–53). An abduction brace or cast may be required to relax the repair for the first 6 weeks.

Correction of a malunited greater tuberosity usually requires an osteotomy with repositioning at a more anatomic level below the articular surface. Two operative approaches may be used: the deltopectoral or the superior deltoid-splitting approach. If arthritis is not an issue or a need for replacement is not anticipated, the superior deltoid-splitting approach is used because it creates more room for the tuberosity. The retracted greater tuberosity and its cuff attachments are freed superficial to the cuff from the acromion and deltoid. On the deep surface, the capsule is released from the glenoid without detaching the labrum or disturbing the origin of the long head of the biceps. The rotator cuff interval is opened, and the coracohumeral ligament is released at the coracoid base. If the greater tuberosity is adherent to the articular surface, a humeral head or total-shoulder replacement may be necessary. Postoperatively, abduction splinting in approximately 45° for the first 4 to 6 weeks protects the tuberosity fixation while allowing for early bone and fibrous healing. If mobilization is difficult, a compensatory loss of internal rotation may occur.

Although no series have specifically reported the results of operative treatment of isolated greater tuberosity malunion or nonunion, several papers comment on the difficulty and limited results.[1, 15, 22] In a series of cases of prosthetic humeral head replacement for post-traumatic arthritis and malunion, Tanner and Cofield found that redisplacement was a common problem when they performed tuberosity osteotomy.[27] Norris and co-workers recommended anterior acromioplasty, mobilization of the tuberosity nonunion, and fixation with heavy suture placed at the rotator cuff insertion.[22] Johnson and Bayley performed late repair of four displaced greater tuberosities and noted limited success but improved pain and function.[13]

In rare cases, treatment can involve excision of the prominent bone and repair of the rotator cuff. Occasionally, when the tuberosity is displaced and malunited, a concomitant rotator cuff tear is present. In this situation, the prominent portion of the tuberosity can be excised and

the rotator cuff repaired with standard techniques (Fig. 44–110). However, if the rotator cuff is intact, tuberosity osteotomy with contracture release is preferred because of the potential for bone-to-bone healing.

## Surgical Neck Malunion

Surgical neck malunion is more common, although it is often not as clinically significant. It usually involves varus angulation of the proximal end of the humerus with some

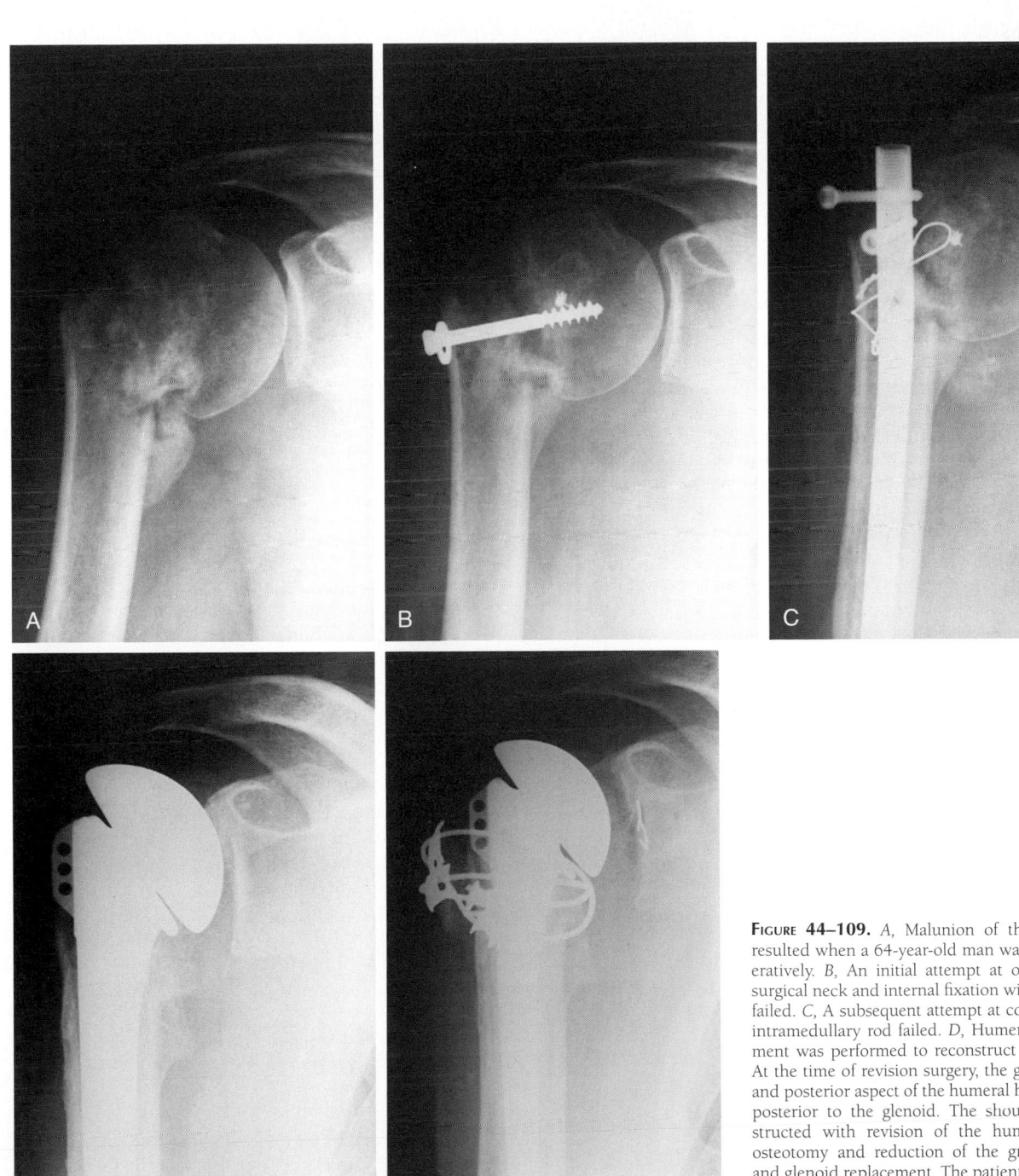

**FIGURE 44–109.** *A,* Malunion of the surgical neck resulted when a 64-year-old man was treated nonoperatively. *B,* An initial attempt at osteotomy of the surgical neck and internal fixation with a single screw failed. *C,* A subsequent attempt at correction with an intramedullary rod failed. *D,* Humeral head replacement was performed to reconstruct the shoulder. *E,* At the time of revision surgery, the greater tuberosity and posterior aspect of the humeral head were locked posterior to the glenoid. The shoulder was reconstructed with revision of the humeral prosthesis, osteotomy and reduction of the greater tuberosity, and glenoid replacement. The patient had elimination of pain but limited active elevation. In this case, successful treatment required correction of all the anatomic problems.

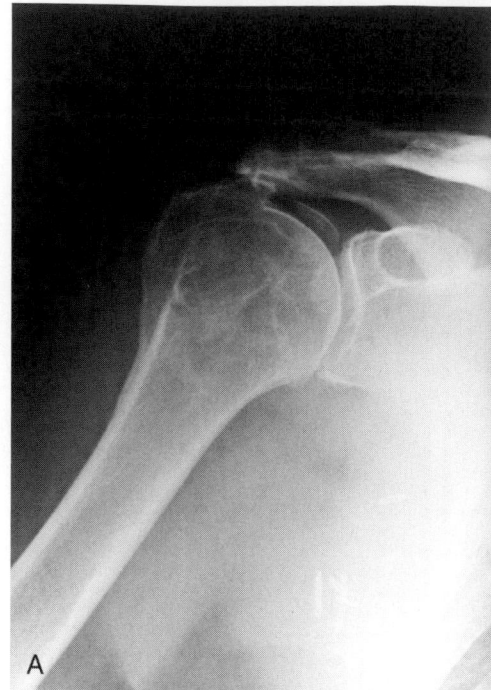

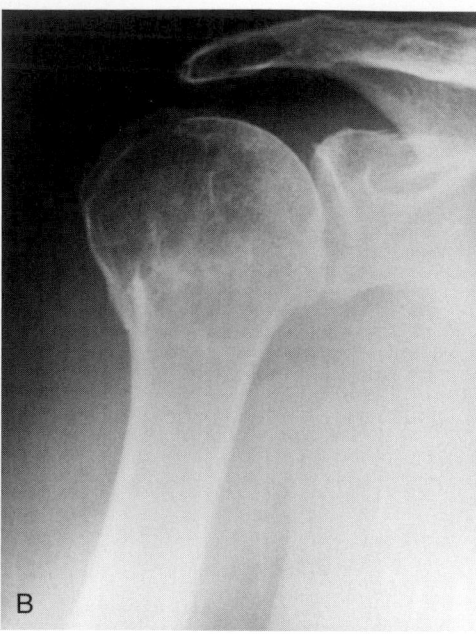

**FIGURE 44–110.** *A,* Greater tuberosity malunion in an elderly female patient. She had a large acromial spur and a large rotator cuff tear that involved the supraspinatus and infraspinatus tendons. *B,* Successful treatment was achieved with arthroscopic acromioplasty and greater tuberoplasty.

degree of apex anterior angulation. Pain is generally the result of coracoacromial arch impingement, and the loss of motion correlates with the degree of angular deformity. Unfortunately, acromioplasty alone is not usually successful in treating these patients. A corrective osteotomy is the best approach to the management of these cases.

Osteotomy for a surgical neck malunion is technically difficult (Fig. 44–111). The axillary nerve must be dissected free and protected. A closing wedge osteotomy, mobilization of the anatomic planes, fixation out to proper length, and adequate fixation to permit early motion are all necessary for a satisfactory result. Internal fixation with a 90° angled blade plate provides secure fixation. If post-traumatic arthritis has occurred, a prosthetic replacement should be considered. The use of an intraoperative image intensifier facilitates the osteotomy. The humerus is rotated until the maximal surgical neck angulation is visualized. A closing wedge osteotomy is then performed to correct this angulation. Alternatively, a dome osteotomy can be used. Provisional fixation with K-wires is achieved before definitive rigid internal fixation. Soft tissue contracture can be addressed with extra-articular releases and dissection. Intra-articular capsular contracture can be released by opening the glenohumeral joint anteriorly through the subscapularis tendon.

Some surgical neck malunions with anterior angulation of the shaft or a prominent greater tuberosity result in entrapment of the greater tuberosity. The superiorly malunited tuberosity can cause erosion of the rotator cuff (see Fig. 44–79). Correction of a three-part greater tuberosity malunion requires correction of both the surgical neck and the tuberosity malunion. Failure to correct the greater tuberosity malunion may limit the outcome. If complete correction is considered, the articular surface should be evaluated to be sure that it is intact.

If the articular surface is already degenerative, shoulder arthroplasty should be performed.

## RESULTS

When compared with the number of published series that have reported the results of humeral head replacement for acute fractures, few studies have reported the results of late reconstruction of proximal humeral fractures. Several studies of humeral head replacement for proximal humeral fractures include cases with delayed treatment. Bosch and associates reviewed the results of 25 patients who had humeral head replacement for three- and four-part proximal humeral fractures.[4] They found a moderate correlation between the time from injury to surgery and outcome. Movin and colleagues evaluated 29 proximal humeral fractures treated by humeral head replacement: 18 acute and 11 late.[16] The results were worse than in other series, but the outcomes were not affected by the timing of surgery. Frich and co-workers reported better pain relief with early arthroplasty for four-part fractures than after surgery delayed for longer than 4 months.[9] They also reported problems with instability in the late group.

Only a few studies have reported the results of late prosthetic reconstruction after proximal humeral fractures. Norris and coauthors reported a retrospective study of 23 patients who underwent late prosthetic reconstruction of the shoulder after proximal humeral fractures.[20] Although patient satisfaction and pain reduction were predictably satisfactory, functional restoration was variable, and the results were inferior to those of primary humeral head replacement for acute proximal humeral fractures in the authors' experience. Beredjiklian and colleagues reported a retrospective study of operative treatment of malunion of the proximal end of the humerus.[2] Among the 39 patients, a number of different initial injuries were seen. The initial treatment was closed without internal fixation in 32 cases. Thirty-three of the patients were younger than 65 years at the time of operative reconstruction. Seventy-nine percent had combined osseous and soft tissue abnormalities. Based on the criteria of slight or no pain, active elevation greater than 90°, and functional capacity of at least 50% of normal, 69% had a satisfactory result. They found a satisfactory result to be correlated with surgical correction of all osseous and soft tissue abnormalities. Sperling and co-workers reported the long-term results of shoulder arthroplasty in patients younger than 50 years.[26] Of 108 patients, 35 had traumatic arthrosis. Twenty-eight were managed by humeral head replacement, and 7 had total-shoulder arthroplasty. The results included 6 excellent (17%), 10 satisfactory (29%), and 18 unsatisfactory (51%) outcomes. The shoulders that were treated with hemiarthroplasty for traumatic arthrosis were more likely to undergo revision than were those with rheumatoid arthritis, the other major diagnosis.

Boileau and colleagues reported the largest series of late prosthetic reconstruction after proximal humeral fractures.[3] They reviewed the results of 71 cases. With use of the Constant score, the functional results were excellent in 11 (16%), good in 19 (26%), average in 18 (25%), and poor in 23 (33%). In patients with nonunion of the surgical neck or severe malunion of a tuberosity, the results were significantly worse. Dines similarly found that patients who did not require a greater tuberosity osteotomy had better results.[6]

Gerber and associates evaluated the clinical relevance of post-traumatic avascular necrosis and reported that the clinical outcome correlated with the precision of the anatomic alignment.[10] Patients with anatomic reductions had better late outcomes. Duralde and co-workers treated 31 shoulders with malunions and found that the results were inferior to the results of acute ORIF of proximal humeral fractures. They also found that patients whose initial treatment was closed had better results than did those who had malunion after ORIF.[8]

Even fewer reports of the results of treatment of surgical neck nonunion have been published. Healy and colleagues evaluated the results of treatment of 25 patients with nonunion of the surgical neck.[11] The best results were obtained with ORIF and bone grafting. They used a tension band construct that included the rotator cuff and proximal end of the humerus with plate/shaft fixation. Overall, only 48% (12 of 25 patients) had good results. Nayak and co-workers treated 17 patients who had nonunion of the surgical neck.[17] Ten patients had tension band fixation with Rush rods and bone grafting, and 7 underwent humeral hemiarthroplasty. Eleven of the 17 patients had a fair or poor result. Although pain relief and functional improvement were similar in both groups of patients, 8 of the 10 patients in the internal fixation group required removal of the hardware. Duralde and associates treated 20 patients with nonunion of a fracture of the surgical neck of the humerus.[7] Ten had humeral head replacement and 10 were treated by ORIF and bone grafting. The results were excellent in five (25%), satisfactory in six (30%), and unsatisfactory in nine (45%). Patients initially treated nonoperatively had better results than did those initially treated with internal fixation. Fifteen major complications occurred, 11 of which necessitated reoperation. Overall, they found that surgical reconstruction for nonunion of the surgical neck of the humerus usually results in significant improvement in pain, but only modest improvement in function. Walch and co-workers used an intramedullary bone peg, internal fixation, and cancellous bone grafting to treat 20 patients

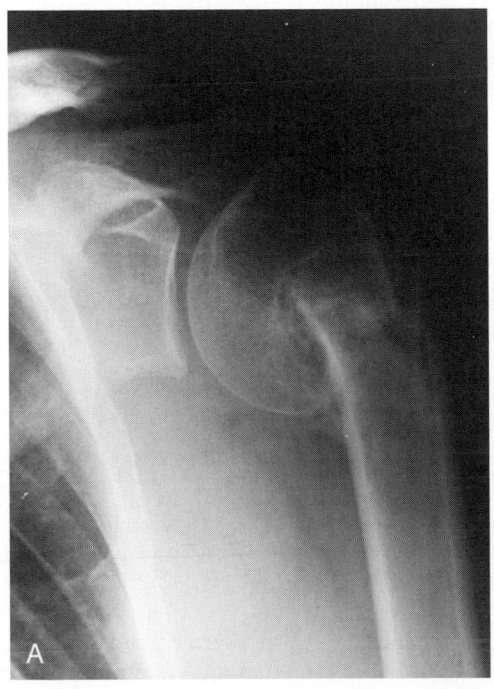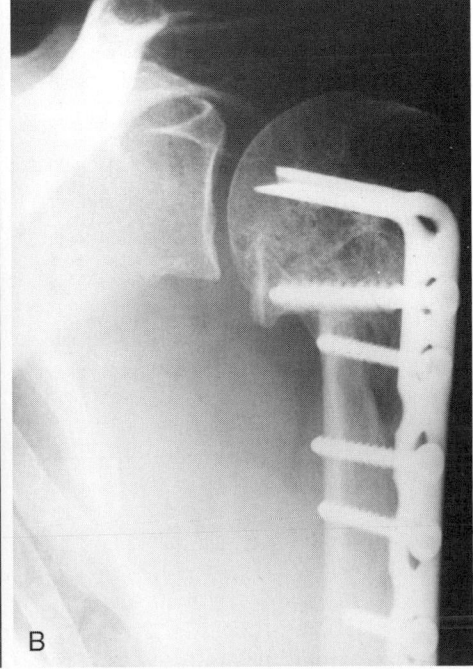

**FIGURE 44–111.** *A,* True anteroposterior radiograph demonstrating a surgical neck malunion. The patient had pain and limited motion. *B,* Reconstruction was performed with a closing wedge osteotomy and internal fixation with a 90° angled blade plate. This treatment resulted in minimal pain and nearly normal shoulder elevation.

with nonunion of the surgical neck. They achieved union and patient satisfaction in 95% of these cases.[29] Simpson and Jupiter reported a 100% union rate of surgical neck nonunions after ORIF with a 90° angled blade plate and an autogenous iliac crest bone graft.[25]

## SUMMARY

Although late reconstruction for failure of primary treatment of proximal humeral fractures can reduce shoulder pain and improve function, these procedures are technically difficult with increased complication rates and less favorable outcomes than the best procedure done primarily.[2, 3, 9, 19, 27] Most late reconstruction involves prosthetic replacement. Glenoid replacement is performed when the glenoid is significantly involved and the rotator cuff is intact or can be reconstructed. Isolated tuberosity or surgical neck malunion can be treated by osteotomy and internal fixation.

## REFERENCES

1. Beredjiklian, P.K.; Iannotti, J.P. Treatment of proximal humerus fracture malunion with prosthetic arthroplasty. Instr Course Lect 47:135–140, 1998.
2. Beredjiklian, P.K.; Iannotti, J.P.; Norris, T.R.; Williams, G.R. Operative treatment of malunion of a fracture of the proximal aspect of the humerus. J Bone Joint Surg Am 80:1484–1497, 1998.
3. Boileau, P.; Walch, G.; Trojani, C.; et al. Sequelae of fractures of the proximal humerus: Surgical classification and limits of shoulder arthroplasty. In: Walch, G.; Boileau, P., eds. Shoulder Arthroplasty, Berlin, Springer-Verlag, 1999, pp. 349–358.
4. Bosch, U.; Skutek, M.; Fremery, R.W.; Tscherne, H. Outcome after primary and secondary hemiarthroplasty in elderly patients with fractures of the proximal humerus. J Shoulder Elbow Surg 7:479–484, 1998.
5. Cofield, R.H.; Briggs, B.T. Glenohumeral arthrodesis. Operative and long term functional results. J Bone Joint Surg Am 61:668–677, 1979.
6. Dines, D.M. Post-traumatic changes of the proximal humerus: Malunion, nonunion, and osteonecrosis. Treatment with modular hemiarthroplasty or total shoulder arthroplasty. J Shoulder Elbow Surg 2:11–21, 1993.
7. Duralde, X.A.; Flatow, E.L.; Pollock, R.G.; et al. Operative treatment of nonunions of the surgical neck of the humerus. J Shoulder Elbow Surg 5:169–180, 1996.
8. Duralde, X.A.; Rodosky, M.W.; Pollock, R.G.; et al. Operative treatment of malunions of the proximal humerus. J Shoulder Elbow Surg 4(Suppl):11, 1995.
9. Frich, L.H.; Sojbjerg, J.O.; Sneppen, O. Shoulder arthroplasty in complex acute and chronic proximal humeral fractures. Orthopedics 14:949–954, 1991.
10. Gerber, C.; Hersche, O.; Berberat, C. The clinical relevance of posttraumatic avascular necrosis of the humeral head. J Shoulder Elbow Surg 7:586–590, 1998.
11. Healy, W.L.; Jupiter, J.B.; Kristiansen, T.K.; White, R.R. Nonunion of the proximal humerus. A review of 25 cases. J Orthop Trauma 4:424–431, 1990.
12. Iannotti, J.P.; Gabriel, J.P.; Schneck ,S.L.; et al. The normal glenohumeral relationships. An anatomical study of one hundred and forty shoulders. J Bone Joint Surg Am 74:491–500, 1992.
13. Johnson, J.R.; Bayley, J.I.L. Early complications of acute anterior dislocation of the shoulder in the middle-aged and elderly patient. Injury 13:431–434, 1982.
14. Jupiter, J.B.; Mullaji, A.B. Blade plate fixation of proximal humeral nonunions. Injury 25:301–303, 1994.
15. McLaughlin, H.L. Dislocation of the shoulder with tuberosity fracture. Surg Clin North Am 43:1615–1620, 1963.
16. Movin, T.; Sjoden, G.O; Ahrengart, L. Poor function after shoulder replacement in fracture patients. A retrospective evaluation of 29 patients followed for 2–12 years. Acta Orthop Scand 69:392–396, 1998.
17. Nayak, N.K.; Schickendantz, M.S.; Regan, W.D.; Hawkins, R.J. Operative treatment of nonunion of surgical neck fractures of the humerus. Clin Orthop 313:200–205, 1995.
18. Neer, C.S. II. Glenohumeral arthroplasty. In Neer, C.S., II, ed. Shoulder Reconstruction. Philadelphia, W.B. Saunders, 1990, pp. 222–234.
19. Norris, T.R. Unconstrained prosthetic shoulder replacement. In: Watson, M., ed. Surgical Disorders of the Shoulder. London, Churchill Livingstone, 1991, pp. 473–510.
20. Norris, T.R.; Green, A.; McGuigan, F.X. Late prosthetic shoulder arthroplasty for displaced proximal humerus fractures. J Shoulder Elbow Surg 4:271–280, 1995.
21. Norris, T.R.; Turner, J.A. Surgical treatment of nonunions of the upper humerus shaft in the elderly. Orthop Trans 9:44, 1985.
22. Norris, T.R.; Turner, J.A.; Bovill, D.F. Nonunion of the upper humerus: An analysis of the etiology and treatment in 28 cases. In: Post, M.; Hawkins R.J.; Morrey, B.F., eds. Surgery of the Shoulder. St. Louis, C.V. Mosby, 1990, pp. 63–67.
23. Pearl, M.L.; Volk, A.G. Retroversion of the proximal humerus relevant to prosthetic replacement arthroplasty. J Shoulder Elbow Surg 8:151–162, 1995.
24. Scheck, M. Surgical treatment of nonunions of the surgical neck of the humerus. Clin Orthop 167:255–259, 1982.
25. Simpson, N.S.; Jupiter, J.B. Reconstruction of nonunion of the proximal humerus with a custom blade plate: Result of 17 consecutive cases. J Shoulder Elbow Surg 6:182, 1997.
26. Sperling, J.W.; Cofield, R.H.; Rowland, C.M. Neer hemiarthroplasty and Neer total shoulder arthroplasty in patients fifty years old or less: Long-term results. J Bone Joint Surg Am 80:464–473, 1998.
27. Tanner, M.W.; Cofield, R.H. Prosthetic arthroplasty for fracture and fracture-dislocations of the proximal humerus. Clin Orthop 179:116–128, 1982.
28. Tillmann, K.; Braatz, D. Results of resection arthroplasty and the Benjamin double osteotomy. In: Kolbel, R.; Helbig, B.; Blauth, W., eds. Shoulder Replacement. Berlin, Springer-Verlag, 1987, pp. 47–50.
29. Walch, G.; Badet, R.; Nové-Josserand, L.; Levigne, C. Nonunions of the surgical neck of the humerus: Surgical treatment with an intramedullary bone peg, internal fixation, and cancellous bone grafting. J Shoulder Elbow Surg 5:161–168, 1996.

# CHAPTER 45

# Injuries to the Shoulder Girdle

David Ring, M.D.
Jesse B. Jupiter, M.D.

Fractures and dislocations of the shoulder girdle are usually treated nonoperatively. In fact, operative treatment of clavicular fractures has traditionally been associated with healing problems and hardware-related complications, and operative treatment of scapular fractures has been considered challenging and risky. Optimal management of these injuries is based on careful selection of injuries for operative treatment and meticulous operative technique.

## ANATOMY

The clavicle and scapula link the upper limb with the axial skeleton, and the clavicle is linked to the scapula through the strong coracoclavicular and acromioclavicular ligaments. Although it was once believed that the clavicle rotated with respect to the scapula,[122, 123] experiments involving the insertion of Kirschner wires into awake volunteers have demonstrated that these two bones form a tightly linked unit.[92, 259] Elevation-depression, protraction-retraction, and rotation of the clavicle through the sternoclavicular articulation are associated with corresponding movements of the scapula with respect to the thorax.

Animals that bear weight on their forelimbs do not have clavicles.[18, 50, 72, 164, 229, 230] The absence of a clavicle improves running and agility on four limbs. In such animals, the scapula is stabilized to the thorax by numerous powerful muscles. Clavicles are present in brachiating animals and apparently serve to help hold the upper limb away from the trunk to enhance more global positioning and use of the limb.

The clavicle has been considered by some to be an expendable bone.[108] Although children with congenital absence of the clavicle adapt surprisingly well[88, 175] and patients with tumors or infections treated by clavicular resection sometimes function adequately,[55, 79, 107, 108, 280, 311] both have difficulty with overhead activities requiring strength or dexterity. Patients with clavicular resection may also have brachial plexus irritation related to instability of the clavicular fragments. Patients with a trapezius palsy do particularly poorly without a clavicle.[311] We believe that the evolutionary process has determined an important function for the clavicle and always strive to preserve the length and alignment of the clavicle.

The sternoclavicular and acromioclavicular joints are both diarthrodial articulations (hyaline articular cartilage–covered and synovium-lined mobile joints) with intervening fibrocartilage discs. Both joints lack inherent osseous articular stability and are maintained by strong ligaments. The acromioclavicular joint is very unusual in that negligible motion occurs through the joint and yet degenerative arthritis is common, particularly after trauma. The function of the acromioclavicular articulation is unclear. Patients with acromioclavicular or coracoclavicular fusion or coracoclavicular screw fixation have full or nearly full shoulder motion.[43, 138, 139, 259] All the motion between the shoulder girdle and the axial skeleton must therefore occur at the sternoclavicular joint. Motion at this joint is commonly thought to be 35° of elevation-depression, 35° of protraction-retraction, and 50° of rotation, as reported by Inman[122]; however, these figures are inconsistent with the common view that 60° of the 180° of shoulder abduction occurs through the shoulder girdle, which would imply that the sternoclavicular joint provides at least 60° of elevation-depression. The sternal epiphysis does not ossify until the midteenage years and is very difficult to visualize on plain radiographs.[222] It closes as late as 25 years in normal adults,[128, 222, 295] and some have argued that many apparent dislocations of the sternoclavicular joint may actually be physeal fractures.[90, 221, 222] This controversial point does not affect management of these injuries.

Ligament-cutting studies in cadavers suggest that the coracoclavicular ligaments limit superior displacement of the clavicle and the acromioclavicular ligaments limit posterior displacement.[96, 267, 301] The capsuloligamentous covering of the acromioclavicular ligament is most stout superiorly. Because one of the complications of distal clavicular excision is posterior displacement of the clavicle with impingement on the scapular spine, many surgeons emphasize preservation of the acromioclavicular ligament, particularly superiorly.[30, 91]

The clavicle is named for its S-shaped curvature, with an apex anteromedially and an apex posterolaterally, similar to the musical symbol clavicula[191] (Fig. 45–1). The larger medial curvature widens the space for passage of neurovascular structures from the neck into the upper extremity through the costoclavicular interval. The transition from medial to lateral curvature occurs at approximately two thirds the length of the bone as measured from its sternal end, a site that roughly corresponds to both the medial limit of attachment of the coracoclavicular ligaments and the entrance point of the main nutrient artery of the clavicle.[222]

The clavicle is made up of very dense trabecular bone lacking a well-defined medullary canal. In cross section, the clavicle changes gradually between a flat lateral aspect, a tubular midportion, and an expanded prismatic medial end.[11] The peculiarities of both its curvature and its cross-sectional anatomy, as well as its bony structure, become important when intramedullary fixation of the clavicle is being considered.[261]

The clavicle is subcutaneous throughout its length and makes a prominent aesthetic contribution to the contour of the neck and upper part of the chest. The supraclavicular nerves run obliquely across the clavicle just superior to the platysma muscle and should be identified and protected during operative exposure to offset the development of hyperesthesia or dysesthesia over the chest wall.

In displaced fractures and ununited fractures of the clavicle, the most common deformity includes shortening, drooping, adduction, and internal rotation of the shoulder girdle (Fig. 45–2). We find it useful to refer to this characteristic deformity as *ptosis of the shoulder,* after Leffert (personal communication). The forces contributing to persistence or worsening of deformity after fracture include the weight of the shoulder as transmitted to the distal fragment of the clavicle, primarily through the coracoclavicular ligaments, and the deforming forces of

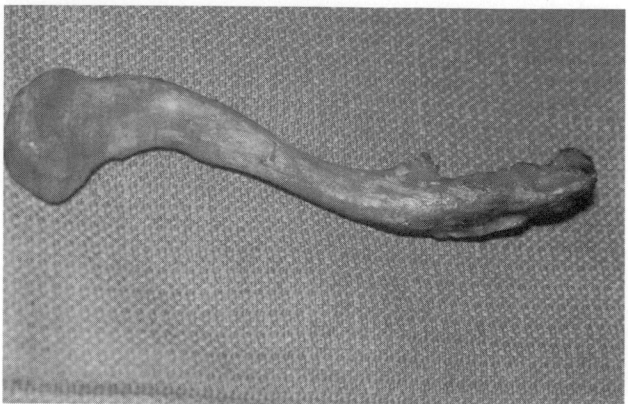

**FIGURE 45–1.** This human clavicle stripped of all soft tissue shows the S shape of the bone, the flattening laterally (left-hand side of picture), and the relatively weak transition point between the middle and lateral thirds.

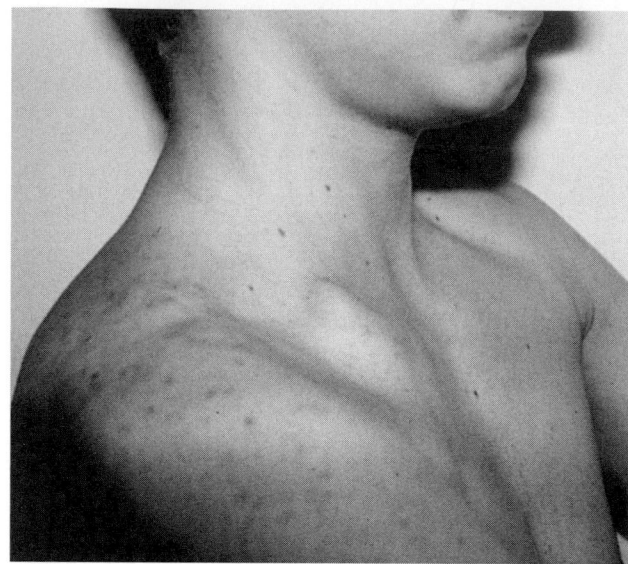

**FIGURE 45–2.** Shortening, drooping, adduction, and internal rotation of the shoulder develop in many patients with clavicular nonunion or malunion. Like Leffert, we refer to this deformity as ptosis of the shoulder girdle.

the attached muscles and ligaments. The medial fragment is elevated by the clavicular head of the sternocleidomastoid muscle, which inserts onto the posterior aspect of the medial portion of the clavicle. The pectoralis major contributes to adduction and inward rotation of the shoulder.[201]

It is not surprising that the middle third is the most common site of clavicular fracture in that the midportion is the thinnest and narrowest portion of the bone; it represents a transitional region of the bone, both in curvature and in cross-sectional anatomy, which makes it a mechanically weak area, and it is the only area of the clavicle that is not supported by ligamentous or muscular attachments. It is possible that this anatomy was selected during evolution because clavicular fracture protects the brachial plexus during difficult births (shoulder dystocia).[225]

In view of the intimate relationship of the clavicle to the brachial plexus, the subclavian artery and vein, and the apex of the lung, it is surprising that injury to these structures in association with fracture of the clavicle is so uncommon. Brachial plexus palsy may develop weeks or years after injury as a result of compromise of the costoclavicular space by hypertrophic callus, with or without malalignment of the fracture fragments.* Narrowing of the costoclavicular space because of malunion or nonunion can also lead to dynamic narrowing of the thoracic outlet.[9, 14, 31, 52, 89, 167, 190, 238, 285] Prolonged compression of vascular structures can likewise be problematic.[61, 105, 145]

The scapula is a broad thin bone that serves as the origin or insertion for at least 18 different muscles. It also supports the upper extremity through its articulation with the humerus at the glenoid. The glenoid is a very narrow and shallow concavity that relies on the surrounding

---

*See references 82, 120, 131, 137, 178, 187, 249, 263, 302, 314.

labrum, ligaments, and muscle-tendon units for stability. The acromial and coracoid processes have enlarged during the evolutionary process, presumably to provide an origin for more powerful and mechanically efficient upper extremity musculature, as well as give the inherently unstable glenohumeral joint a measure of stability.[122]

## SHOULDER SUSPENSORY COMPLEX

Although most isolated fractures of the clavicle and scapula are thought to be relatively straightforward to treat effectively, combined injuries are regarded as more troublesome and are more readily considered for operative treatment.[102, 116, 159] An anatomic concept that has been developed to facilitate understanding of these issues is the superior shoulder suspensory complex.[102] This complex consists of two struts (the clavicle and the lateral portion of the scapular body) linked by a combined bony and soft tissue ring (Fig. 45–3). The ring is composed of the coracoid process, coracoclavicular ligaments, distal end of the clavicle, acromioclavicular ligaments, acromion, and glenoid process. It is argued that disruption of this complex at two sites will be far more problematic than disruption at one site. Common examples of double disruptions include complete acromioclavicular dislocation (e.g., disruption of the coracoclavicular and acromioclavicular ligaments), a displaced fracture of the lateral aspect of the clavicle (i.e., coracoclavicular ligament injury

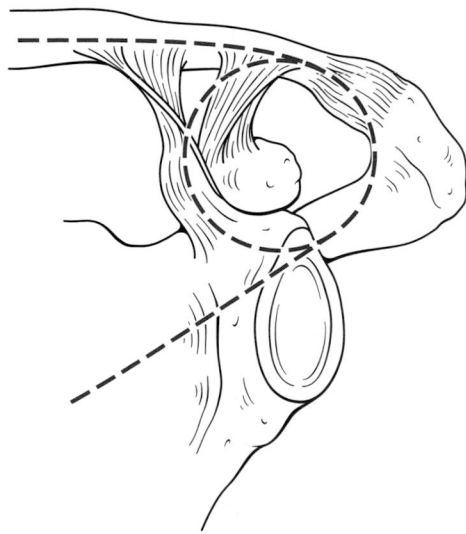

**FIGURE 45–3.** Goss has introduced the concept of the shoulder suspensory complex. The link between the trunk and the upper limb is conceptualized as two struts (the clavicle and the lateral border of the scapula) connected to a bone-ligament ring. Injury to one component of the complex usually does well with nonoperative treatment. Operative treatment is more often considered for double disruptions of the complex. (From Goss, T.P. In: Iannotti, J.P.; Williams, G.R., eds. Disorders of the Shoulder: Diagnosis and Management. Philadelphia, Lippincott Williams & Wilkins, 1999, pp. 597–637.)

and fracture of the distal part of the clavicle), and fracture of the clavicle associated with fracture of the glenoid neck or scapulothoracic dislocation. Although the role of operative treatment of these injuries is debated, each poses more substantial risk to shoulder function than do injuries that disrupt only one aspect of the shoulder suspensory complex.

## STERNOCLAVICULAR JOINT DISLOCATION

Injuries to the sternoclavicular joint are unusual. The ligaments that stabilize the joint are so strong that a substantial force is necessary to dislocate it. The most common sources of sternoclavicular dislocation are motor vehicle accidents and sports injuries.[114, 185, 203, 224, 304] The mechanism of injury is believed to be compression of the shoulder (i.e., a direct medial load on the point of the shoulder) with either forced protraction (causing posterior dislocation) or forced retraction (causing anterior dislocation) of the shoulder girdle.[114, 185] Anterior dislocations are much more common than posterior dislocations.[203, 304] A direct blow to the clavicle—such as when one player falls on top of another—can also cause posterior dislocation of the sternoclavicular joint. It is possible that some of these injuries represent physeal fractures because the medial clavicular physis can remain open well into adulthood[90, 221, 222]; however, in practice, this distinction is difficult and often impossible to make and does not seem to be important (Fig. 45–4A).

The diagnosis of sternoclavicular joint dislocation is usually straightforward and based on the findings of tenderness, swelling, ecchymosis, and deformity. Radiographs are extremely difficult to interpret, even when both sternoclavicular joints are included or special oblique views are used. The most popular alternative view is the so-called serendipity view—a 40° cephalic tilt view of both sternoclavicular joints.[259] Computed tomography should be used to characterize the injury by verifying the direction and displacement of the injury and checking for associated fractures (see Fig. 45–4).

Sternoclavicular joint dislocations represent high-energy chest wall injuries. The thorax and shoulder girdle should be inspected for associated injuries, pneumothorax ruled out, and the neurovascular status of the arm carefully evaluated. Inspection for associated injuries is particularly important in posterior dislocations because the medial part of the clavicle is driven backward toward the trachea, esophagus, and major vascular structures (Fig. 45–4B). Although injury to these structures is uncommon, it is wise to have a thoracic surgeon available when reduction is attempted because an injury to one of these structures could be catastrophic.

Manipulative reduction is usually successful if performed within 48 hours after the injury. General anesthesia and complete muscle paralysis are needed to overcome muscle spasm associated with pain. With the patient supine, a roll is placed between the scapulae to facilitate retraction of the shoulder girdle. Lateral traction is applied

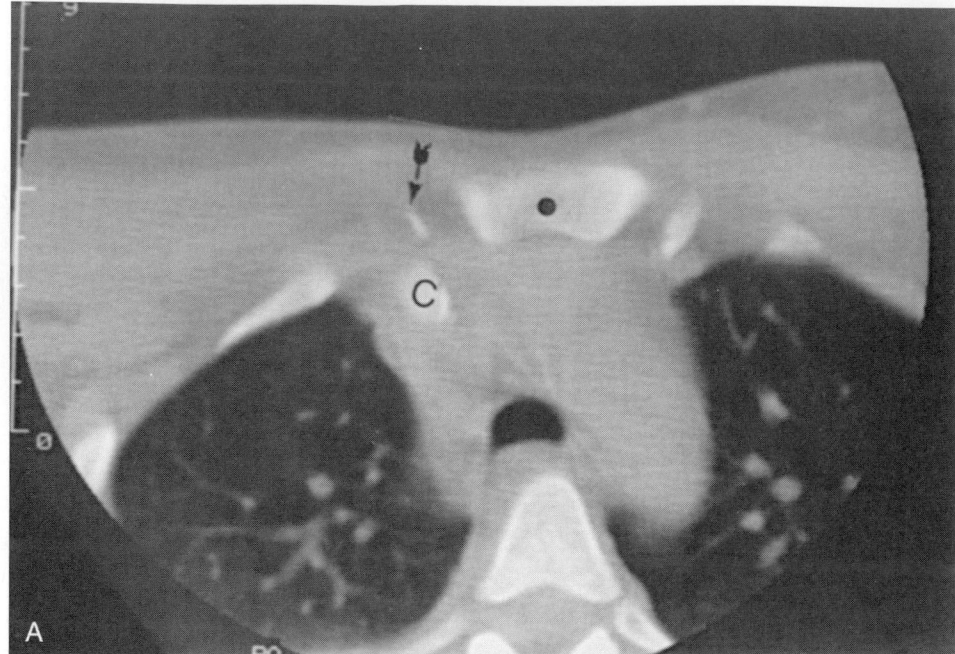

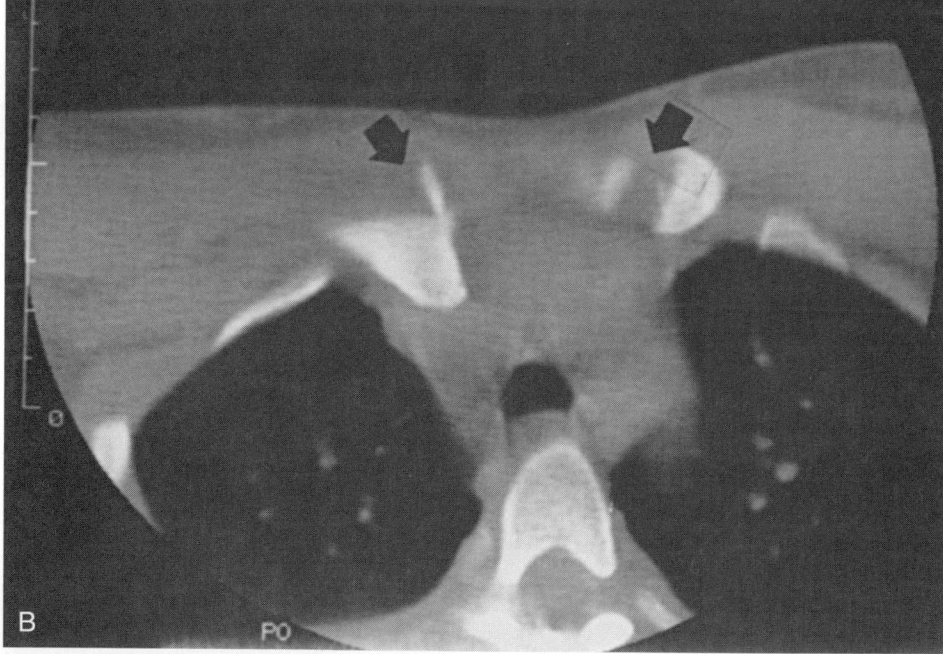

**FIGURE 45–4.** *A,* Computed tomographic (CT) scan of posterior sternoclavicular joint dislocation in a young adult. The sternum *(dot)* and the medial clavicular epiphysis *(arrow)* maintain their normal relationship, and the clavicle (C) is displaced posteriorly. *B,* CT scan of posterior sternoclavicular dislocation. The clavicle is compressing the underlying brachiocephalic vein. The sternoclavicular joint spaces on the uninjured and injured sides *(arrows)* are well demonstrated.

to the arm with the shoulder in 90° of abduction while an assistant places countertraction on the torso (Fig. 45–5*A*). The arm is then extended to retract the shoulder girdle. Reduction usually creates an audible pop and is obvious. It is occasionally necessary to grasp the clavicle and manipulate it directly, particularly with posterior dislocations (see Fig. 45–5*B*). The skin can be cleansed and a sterile towel clip applied if the clavicle is difficult to grasp with the hand (see Fig. 45–5*C*).

When manipulative reduction is successful, the shoulder girdle is immobilized in a sling or figure-of-eight bandage for 6 weeks while the ligaments begin to heal. If open reduction is required, some surgeons favor stabilizing

the joint,* whereas others suggest resecting the medial 1 to 1½ inches of the clavicle and securing it to the first rib.[259] Regardless of which approach is selected, smooth wires should not be used to stabilize the joint because of the potential for migration of these wires into the thorax.[168]

Problems after this injury include instability or arthrosis of the sternoclavicular joint. Reconstructions using fascia lata,[4, 8, 140, 165, 186, 281] the subclavius tendon,[42, 166] or other tendon grafts have been suggested for instability. Painful arthrosis of the sternoclavicular joint has been treated with medial clavicular excision.[15, 34, 183, 186, 242]

---

*See references 10, 23, 38, 39, 41, 65, 66, 81, 111, 166, 171.

# ACROMIOCLAVICULAR JOINT DISLOCATION

Dislocations of the acromioclavicular joint represent varying degrees of disruption of the ligamentous connections between the clavicle and scapula. Treatment considerations focus on the potential for symptoms related to arthrosis of the acromioclavicular joint or displacement and instability of the clavicle. Nonoperative treatment is favored in most cases because patients with complete loss of ligamentous association between the clavicle and scapula and complete displacement of the acromioclavic-

ular joint usually have excellent shoulder girdle function.[126, 133, 169, 287, 294, 303]

Most acromioclavicular injuries are the result of a fall on the point of the shoulder. The diagnosis is usually based on the mechanism of injury and localization of swelling, ecchymosis, tenderness, and deformity to the acromioclavicular joint. Classification of these injuries has attempted to distinguish the degree of ligament injury as seen on radiographs.[4, 296] Minimal displacement is believed to represent partial ligament tearing or a sprain (type 1). Superior displacement less than half the width of the clavicle is believed to represent complete tearing of the acromioclavicular ligaments with partial tearing of the

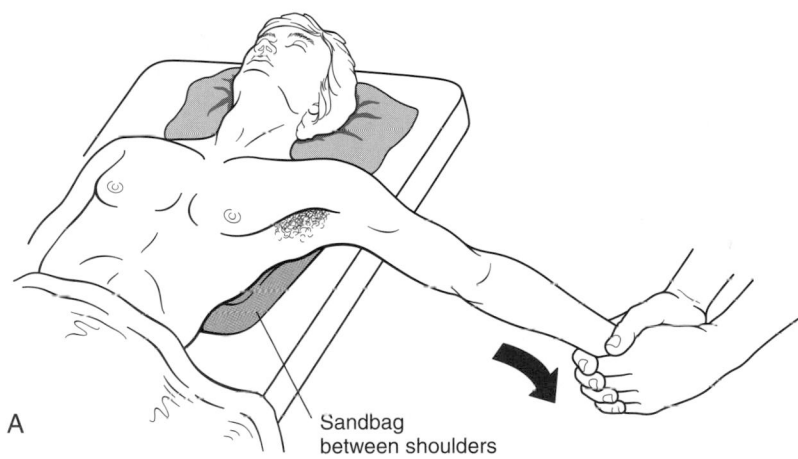

**FIGURE 45–5.** Manipulative reduction of sternoclavicular dislocation under general anesthesia. *A*, With a support placed between the scapula, lateral traction is applied. *B*, Direct manipulation of the clavicle or application of a towel clip (*C*) is occasionally necessary.

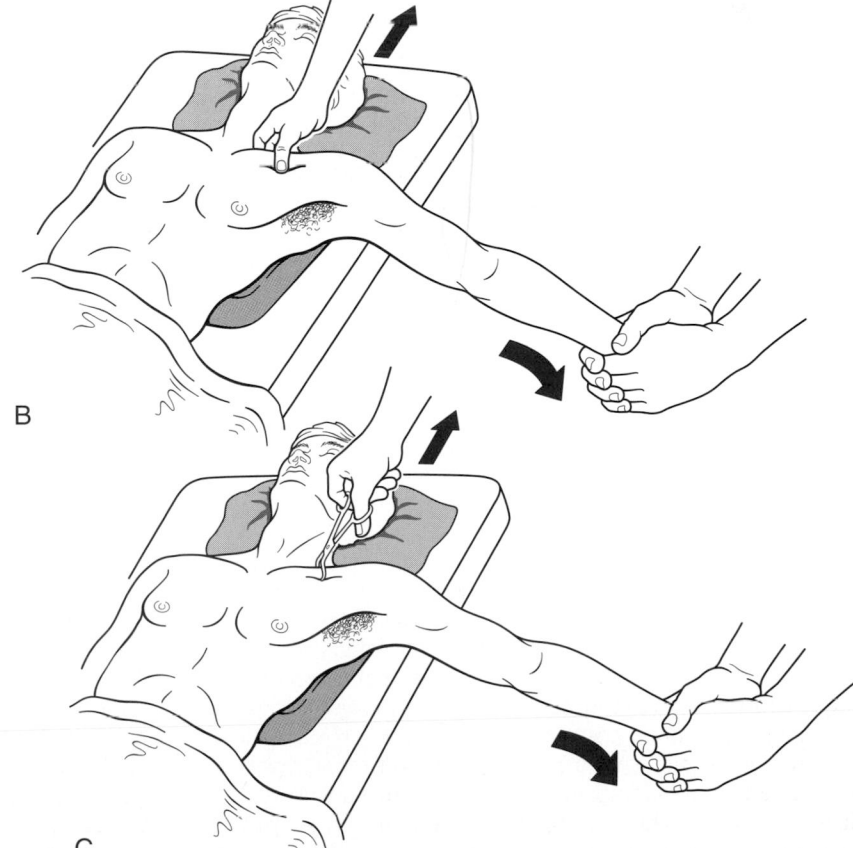

coracoclavicular ligaments (type 2). Injuries with greater displacement represent complete tearing of all the ligaments (type 3). In the past, stress radiographs (taken with weights supported by the hands) were used to evaluate many apparent type 2 injuries to look for complete injury to the coracoclavicular ligaments (type 3).[16, 25, 259] Because most surgeons now treat both type 2 and type 3 injuries nonoperatively, this distinction is no longer thought to be important and stress radiographs are not advised.

Three additional categories have been introduced to help distinguish more severe injuries in which operative treatment might be warranted.[259] Posterior displacement of the clavicle (type 4) is more likely to create chronic symptoms from impingement of the clavicle on the scapular spine and is usually treated operatively. Not only is extreme superior displacement less aesthetic, but the prominent clavicle is also more vulnerable and therefore more likely to be symptomatic. Such extreme superior displacement is usually associated with extensive stripping of the trapezius, pectoralis major, and deltoid muscles (type 5). Inferior displacement of the clavicle (type 6) is a rare type of injury resulting from a direct downward blow.

Nonoperative treatment is generally aimed at relieving symptoms (sling, ice, analgesics) and has been referred to as "skillful neglect."[259] Manipulative bracing (e.g., the so-called Kenny-Howard brace) is cumbersome and painful, may cause pressure necrosis of the skin, and is therefore not recommended. Athletes often return to play within a few days or weeks, even with type 3 injuries.

Operative treatment consists of a combination of ligament repair with or without reinforcement (e.g., transfer of the coracoacromial ligament) and either acromioclavicular or coracoclavicular fixation. The acromioclavicular joint can be fixed with wires,[260] screws, or a hook plate (a plate that attaches with screws to the distal end of the clavicle and bends through the acromioclavicular joint and under the acromion). Coracoclavicular fixation is performed with screws,[27, 138, 139] wires,[3, 16] stout sutures or tape,[58, 97, 133, 202, 219] or suture anchors.[67] Most of the complications of operative treatment are related to fixation. Smooth wires are particularly risky because of their potential for migration.[168] Sutures and tape can erode the clavicle or coracoid.[58, 97, 219] The risk of arthrosis related to placement of fixation devices through the acromioclavicular joint is uncertain.[287] Some surgeons believe that arthrosis of the acromioclavicular joint is inevitable because it is impossible to restore the normal alignment and stability of the joint, and a few recommend excising the distal portion of the clavicle as part of the initial treatment.[220]

Reconstructive procedures address arthrosis of the acromioclavicular joint, instability and impingement of the clavicle, or both. Relatively stable acromioclavicular joints (type 1 and type 2) that have become painful and arthrotic can be treated by distal clavicular excision. This procedure can be done by either open means or arthroscopically. With either method, it is important to try to preserve the superior acromioclavicular ligament. When the excision is performed in open fashion, use of a capsular incision in line with the clavicle, limited excision (about 5 mm), and repair of the ligaments during closure of the wound should

help limit impingement.[30] If the clavicle is unstable (type 3, 4, 5, or 6), excision of the distal part of the clavicle should be augmented by attempts to stabilize the remaining stump, which is usually done by transferring the coracoacromial ligament to the distal end of the clavicle and providing internal stabilization with one of the techniques mentioned earlier.[305]

# FRACTURES OF THE SCAPULA

Fractures of the scapula threaten shoulder girdle function in three ways: (1) injury to the glenoid with malalignment can contribute to instability or arthrosis of the glenohumeral joint, (2) malalignment through the scapular neck can contribute to dysfunction of the rotator cuff and shoulder girdle musculature, and (3) malalignment of the scapular body can cause painful scapulothoracic crepitation. However, the indications for operative intervention are tempered by the difficulty in establishing criteria for unacceptable alignment and by the risks and technical difficulties of operative treatment in this area.

## Operative Exposure

### ANTERIOR

For anterior exposure of glenoid fractures, a standard deltopectoral exposure is used. On occasion, it is sufficient to open the rotator interval or split the subscapularis in line with its fibers. Otherwise, the subscapularis is taken down and a retractor placed in the glenohumeral joint (e.g., Fukada) to retract the humeral head.

### POSTERIOR

Posterior exposure is less familiar to most orthopaedic surgeons. The patient is usually placed in a lateral position with the shoulder and trunk allowed to droop forward slightly. For exposure of the glenoid, a horizontal or vertical skin incision can be made with the creation of skin flaps. The deltoid is split in line with its fibers, and the infraspinatus and teres minor are exposed. The infraspinatus can be either partially or completely detached and later reattached, or it can be split or the interval between the infraspinatus and teres minor developed, depending on the extent of exposure required. To gain access to the inferior margin of the scapular body, a vertical skin incision must be used. The interval between the infraspinatus and teres minor is developed medially, and the origin of the long head of the triceps is detached. The surgeon must take care to protect the suprascapular and axillary nerves.

### SUPERIOR

If access to the superior glenoid is inadequate through either anterior or posterior exposure, the skin incision can be extended superiorly over the angle between the spine of the scapula and the acromioclavicular joint. The trapezius and supraspinatus can then be split in line with their fibers to provide some access to the superior glenoid.

## Fractures of the Glenoid

Goss,[101] in a modification of the classification scheme of Ideberg and colleagues,[121] described six fracture types with numerous subtypes (Fig. 45–6). The critical distinctions seem to be between anterior and posterior glenoid margin fractures that can compromise the stability of the glenohumeral joint (types Ia and Ib), fracture of the inferior glenoid (type II), fracture of the superior glenoid (types III, IV, and Vb), and multifragment fractures (types Va, Vb, and VI). Impaction fractures of the glenoid fossae tend to create a transverse split with either inferior or superior fragments and, on occasion, both. Several factors have been suggested to contribute to these patterns, including concentration of compressive forces in the central region, orientation of the subchondral trabeculae in the transverse plane, and an indentation along the anterior rim of the glenoid.[103] The latter two characteristics are probably related to embryonic formation of the glenoid from separate superior and inferior ossification centers.

### TYPES Ia AND Ib: FRACTURES OF THE ANTERIOR AND POSTERIOR MARGINS OF THE GLENOID

Fractures of the anterior or posterior margin of the glenoid (types Ia and Ib) may cause instability of the glenohumeral articulation. Recurrent or irreducible stability necessitates operative treatment, but when the glenohumeral joint is concentrically reduced, the indications for surgery are less clear. One guideline suggested by DePalma was that fractures with more than 10 mm of displacement and involving more than one fourth of the anterior glenoid rim or one third of the posterior rim were prone to instability and merit operative treatment.[66] Each fracture and patient should be evaluated individually. We have found three-dimensional computed tomography to be very useful in characterizing the fracture for guidance in management (Fig. 45–7).

For anterior fractures, exposure is performed through a standard deltopectoral approach with mobilization of the

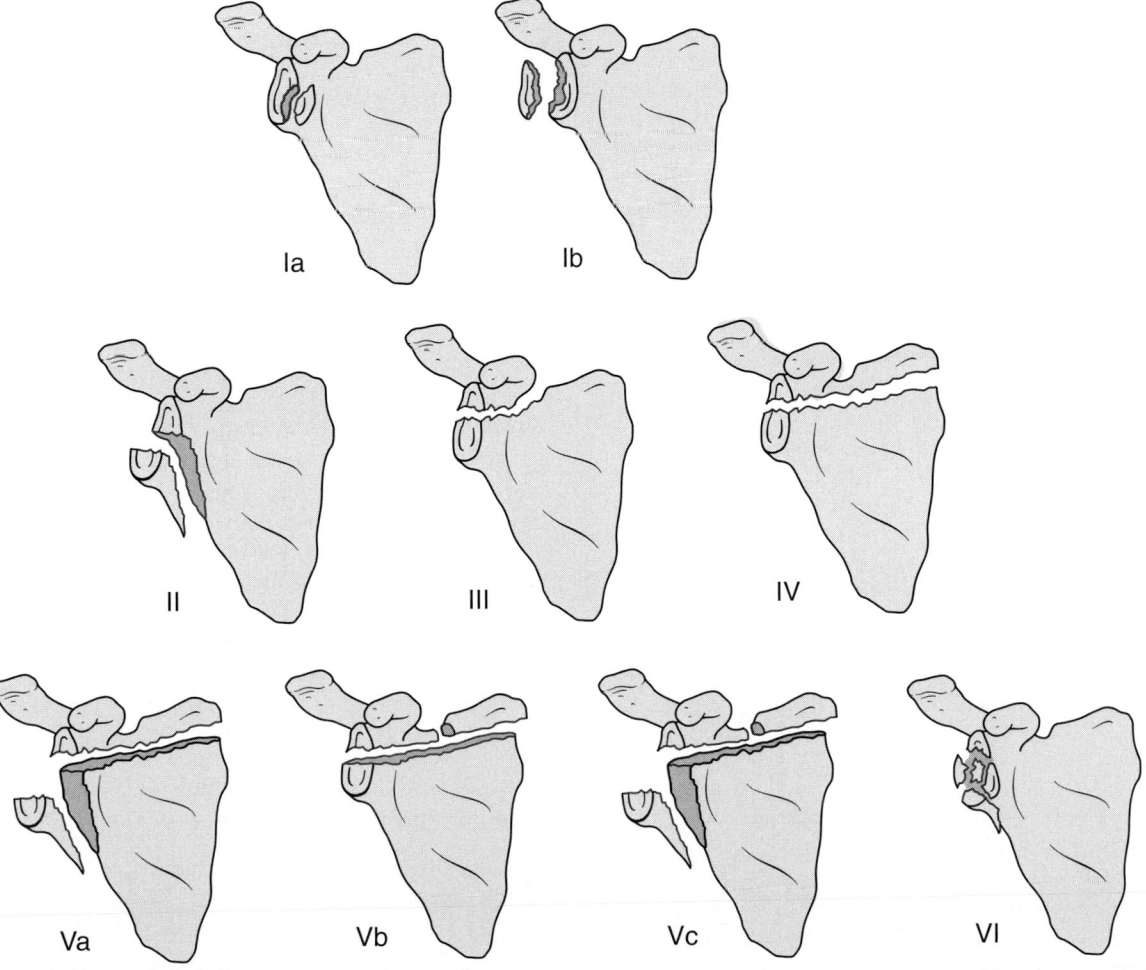

**FIGURE 45–6.** The Goss classification of glenoid fractures. (From Goss, T.P. In: Iannotti, J.P.; Williams, G.R., eds. Disorders of the Shoulder: Diagnosis and Management. Philadelphia, Lippincott Williams & Wilkins, 1999, pp. 597–637.)

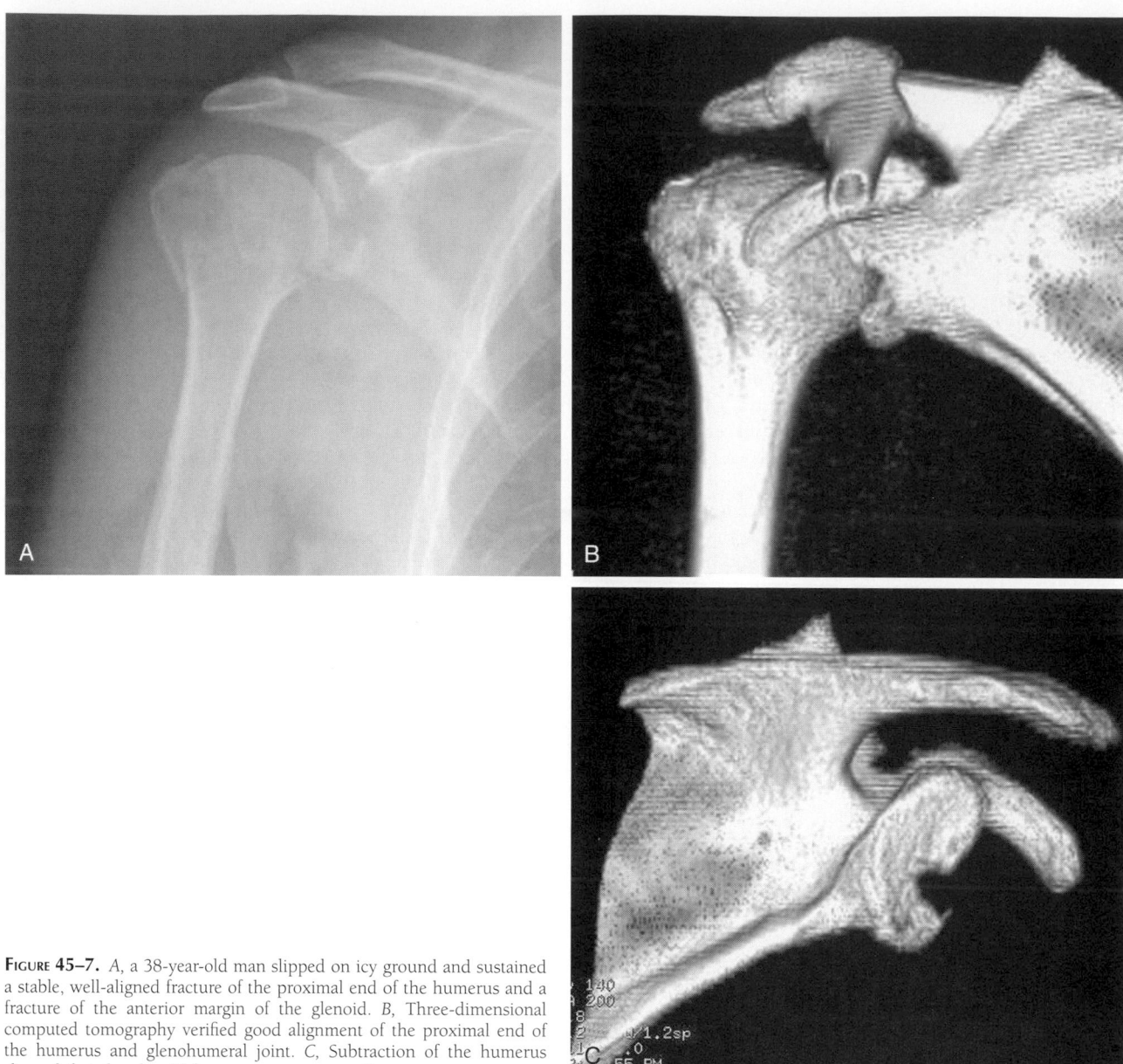

**FIGURE 45–7.** *A,* a 38-year-old man slipped on icy ground and sustained a stable, well-aligned fracture of the proximal end of the humerus and a fracture of the anterior margin of the glenoid. *B,* Three-dimensional computed tomography verified good alignment of the proximal end of the humerus and glenohumeral joint. *C,* Subtraction of the humerus showed that the glenoid fragment was very small.

subscapularis muscle. For posterior fractures, a posterior glenohumeral exposure is used with mobilization of the infraspinatus. A large fragment can be fixed with two screws, but smaller fragments or comminuted fragments might require a buttress plate with smaller screws. On occasion, it may be necessary to excise the fragments and apply a corticocancellous graft from the iliac crest to restore stability.

## TYPE II: FRACTURES OF THE INFERIOR GLENOID

When the inferior glenoid is fractured, the humeral head usually remains concentric with the remaining glenoid. Instability (i.e., nonconcentric reduction of the humeral head with the remaining glenoid) is an indication for operative treatment. In the absence of instability, indica-

tions for operative treatment are less clear. The commonly accepted cutoff for acceptable displacement of the articular surface is 5 mm, but the basis for this cutoff is meager.[101] A single large fragment may be straightforward to realign and secure. Multifragmented fractures will prove more challenging, and operative treatment may not improve the results.

## TYPES III, IV, AND Vb: FRACTURES OF THE SUPERIOR GLENOID

Superior glenoid fractures with wide displacement are unusual because numerous structures impede displacement (Fig. 45–8). Five millimeters is reported as the acceptable cutoff—in other words, marked displacement should be present before operative treatment is considered. Other factors that might lead one to consider operative treatment include a neurovascular injury or double disruption of the shoulder suspensory complex. If suprascapular nerve palsy is suspected, it is recommended that an electromyogram be obtained to verify the diagnosis.[76, 201, 279] If a nerve injury is documented, some surgeons recommend operative treatment to decompress the nerve and provide the best chance for recovery.

If this injury is part of a wider injury to the shoulder suspensory complex, realignment of the other injured components (e.g., a displaced clavicular fracture) may restore acceptable alignment to the glenoid fragment and thus make operative treatment of the glenoid unnecessary.[116, 117, 159] When direct treatment of the glenoid fragment is elected, this region can be accessed through an anterior or posterior exposure. Three-dimensional computed tomography might help plan the best approach. Kirschner wires can be used to manipulate and provisionally reduce the fracture, but definitive fixation is achieved with cannulated screws.

### TYPES Va, Vb, AND VI: MULTIFRAGMENTED FRACTURES

The greater the number of fragments that the fracture creates, the less likely that operative treatment will improve the ultimate result. If the inferior and superior fragments are sizable but the glenoid neck is not fragmented, plate-and-screw fixation through a posterior operative exposure could be considered (Fig. 45–9). Multifragmented fractures are often treated symptomatically (e.g., sling and swathe). Some believe that early passive gravity-assisted mobilization (e.g., pendulum exercises) will help improve alignment of the fragments and the overall result.[103]

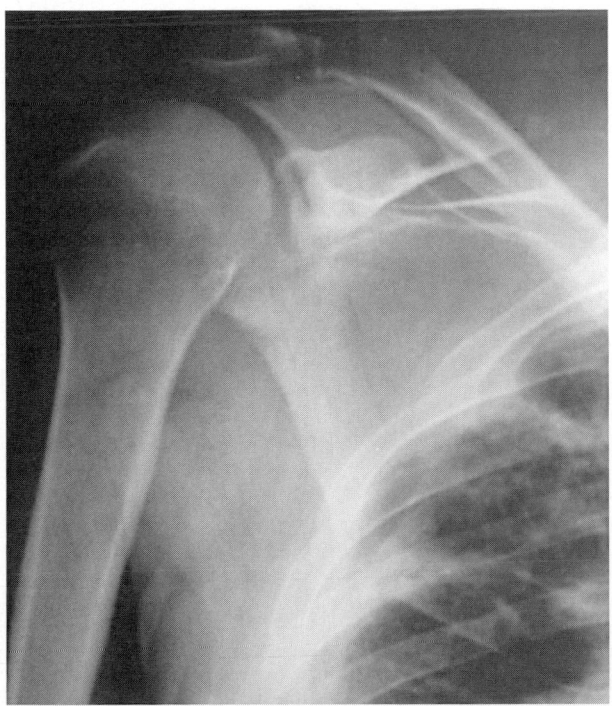

**FIGURE 45–8.** Superior fractures of the glenoid rarely have substantial displacement.

## Fractures of the Glenoid Neck

As with other scapular fractures, substantial displacement (10 mm) and angulation (40°) of the glenoid neck are accepted before operative intervention is considered.[1, 110, 211, 317] Very widely displaced fractures will cause dysfunction of the rotator cuff and shoulder girdle musculature and may contribute to impingement.[1, 110] Classification systems have distinguished fractures according to the superior exit point (lateral to the coracoid, medial to the coracoid, or through the scapular body), but these differences have little impact on management.[1, 110]

When these fractures are associated with a displaced fracture of the clavicle, the combined injury has been termed a "floating shoulder."[116, 159] If the glenoid neck is initially in poor alignment, realignment and stable fixation of the clavicle may restore adequate alignment of the scapula and obviate surgical intervention at that site.[116, 159]

When operative treatment of the glenoid neck is required, it is best performed through a posterior exposure. Ideally, a plate is applied across the fracture. Fixed angle plates such as a 2.7-mm condylar plate or 3.5-mm combination plates (Synthes) may prove useful for gaining fixation of the metaphyseal bone of the glenoid, and two plates can be used at slightly different angles. Alternatively, cannulated screws may be used.

## Fractures of the Scapular Body

Scapular body fractures heal readily and do not merit operative intervention. Nonetheless, painful scapulothoracic crepitation related to a bony prominence from the scapula will occasionally develop (Fig. 45–10). If it is sufficiently symptomatic, operative intervention to remove a painful excrescence may be warranted.

## Fractures of the Coracoid and Acromion Process

Fractures of the coracoid and acromion process are relatively uncommon, and no compelling argument has been made in favor of operative treatment. As with other fractures of the scapula, only very displaced fractures in patients who place high demands on their shoulder should be considered for operative fixation.

## FRACTURES OF THE CLAVICLE

Most orthopaedic surgeons regard the clavicle as a relatively agreeable and cooperative bone. Fracture of the clavicle is common, and it has long been thought that the bone's inherent reparative capacity leads to rapid healing with little more than symptomatic treatment.[261] Deformity has been described as merely a cosmetic concern because function is satisfactory despite malunion.[209] It has been suggested by many that primary operative intervention is

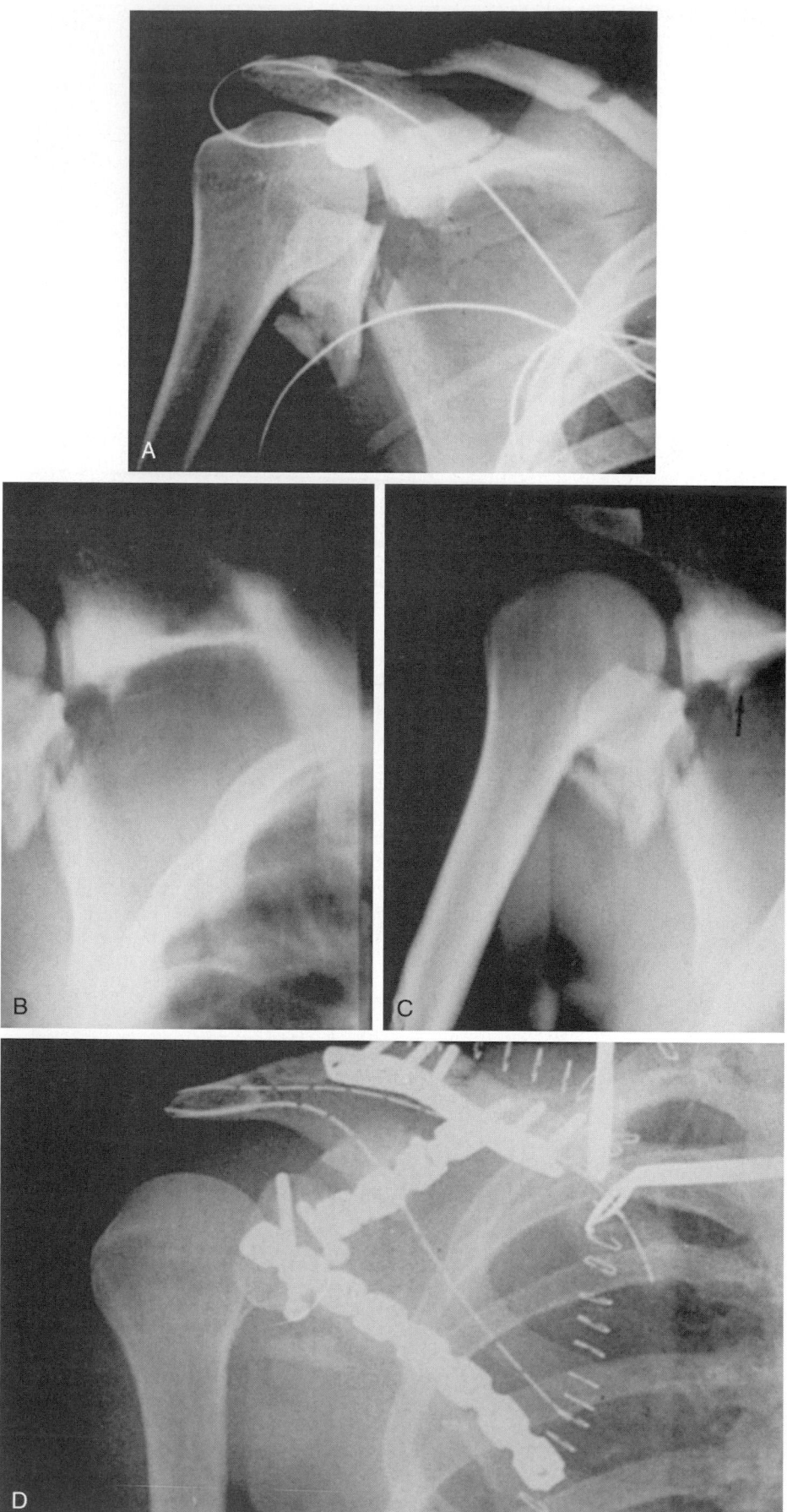

**Figure 45–9.** *A–C*, This complex intra-articular fracture of the glenoid was characterized by separation into large simple fragments. *D*, The fragments were realigned and stabilized with two lag screws and two plates. (Courtesy of Dr. Roy Sanders.)

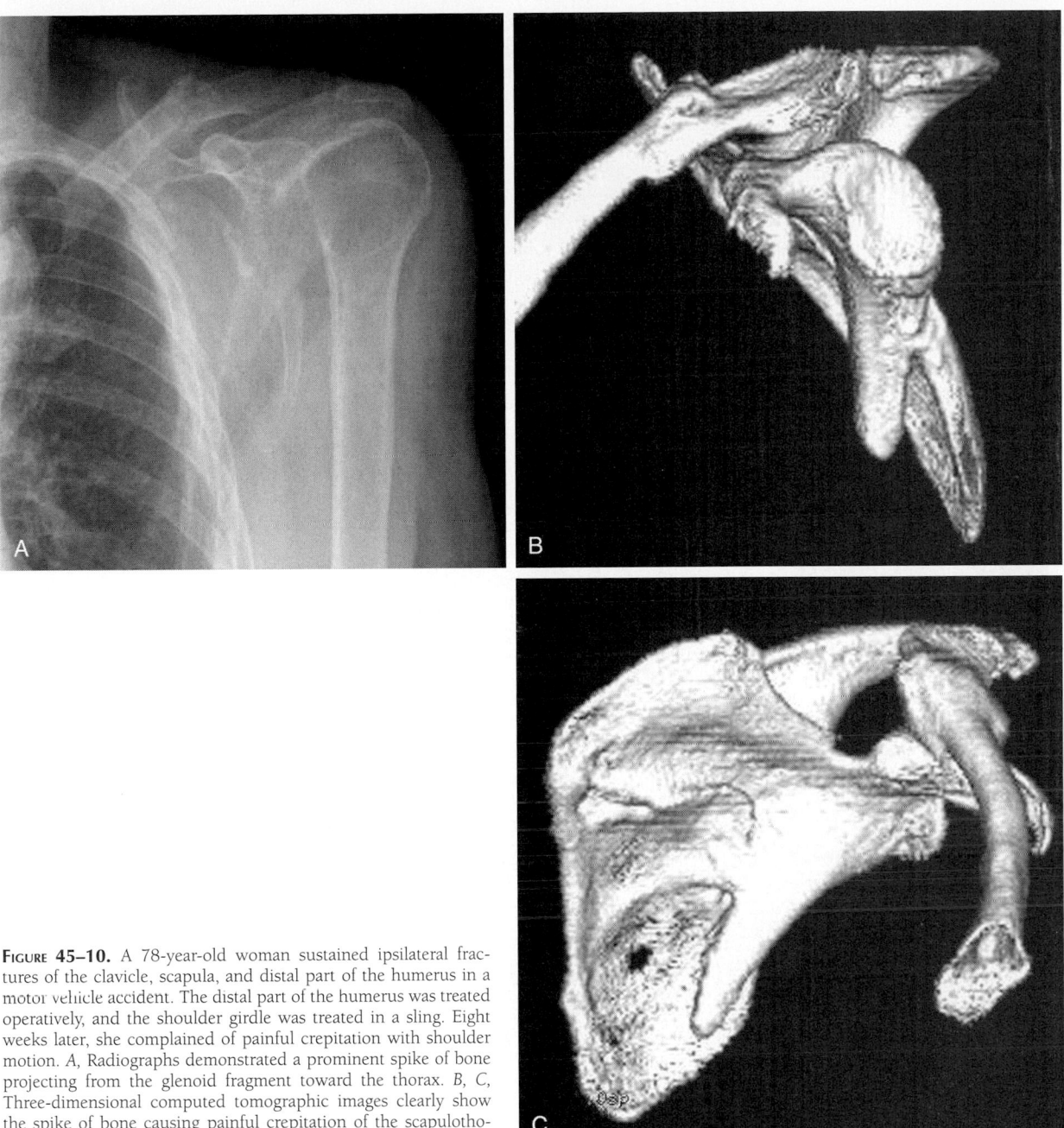

**FIGURE 45–10.** A 78-year-old woman sustained ipsilateral fractures of the clavicle, scapula, and distal part of the humerus in a motor vehicle accident. The distal part of the humerus was treated operatively, and the shoulder girdle was treated in a sling. Eight weeks later, she complained of painful crepitation with shoulder motion. *A,* Radiographs demonstrated a prominent spike of bone projecting from the glenoid fragment toward the thorax. *B, C,* Three-dimensional computed tomographic images clearly show the spike of bone causing painful crepitation of the scapulothoracic articulation.

meddlesome and only makes things worse.[198, 261] Despite the proximity of major vascular, nervous, and cardiopulmonary structures, associated injury is uncommon.

One may have reason to question some of these established beliefs. Our understanding of clavicular fractures and clavicular function is based for the most part on only a modest amount of recorded data. A large percentage of clavicular fractures occur in children and heal readily with remodeling of the deformity.[216, 288] Failure to evaluate these fractures separately from displaced fractures in adults has clouded the issues.

Interest in clavicular nonunion is relatively new,[20] and it has been demonstrated that displaced fractures of the middle portion of the clavicle can be troublesome injuries in adults.[131, 174, 309, 310] Failure of the bone to unite after these injuries can lead to progressive shoulder deformity, pain, impaired function, and neurovascular compromise. Malunion may also contribute to weakness, pain, and neurovascular compromise.[24, 18, 86, 87, 237] Data on displaced distal clavicular fractures in adult patients have demonstrated sufficient difficulty in healing to consider primary operative treatment.[78, 198–201] Recent investigations focusing on the results of treatment of widely displaced high-energy midclavicular fractures in adult patients suggest that this subset of fractures may also be prone to nonunion and delayed union.[119, 256, 309]

## Classification and Epidemiology

The traditional division of the clavicle into thirds[4, 200, 201, 261] seems arbitrary given that most fractures occur near the junction of the middle and distal thirds.[288] Other authors have suggested division of the clavicle into fifths, with the middle three fifths representing midclavicular fractures and the lateral fifths representing distal clavicular fractures.[256] The use of fractional divisions may not adequately distinguish fractures with injury to the coracoclavicular ligaments.

Neer defined fractures of the lateral aspect of the clavicle as being lateral to the medial limit of the trapezoid ligament.[200] He distinguished fractures of the distal end of the clavicle with intact coracoclavicular ligaments (type 1) from those associated with tearing of these ligaments and wide displacement of the fracture fragments (type 2).[200] The wide displacement and instability of type 2 fractures place them at greater risk for nonunion (Fig. 45–11).

Rockwood's distinction of distal third fractures with intact (type IIA) or disrupted (type IIB) coracoclavicular ligaments is confusing because of the lack of a clear distinction between type IIA fractures and more distal midclavicle fractures.[257, 258]

In unusual instances, fractures of the distal end of the clavicle may be unstable in the absence of ligamentous injury. This situation occurs when both of the coracoclavicular ligaments remain attached to an inferior fracture fragment that lacks attachment to either of the primary medial or lateral fragments.[233]

Neer noted in his initial report that distal clavicular fractures are occasionally associated with extension into the acromioclavicular joint, and he classified such fractures as type III.[199, 200] It has been suggested that some injuries diagnosed as type I acromioclavicular joint separation may in fact be intra-articular distal clavicular fractures and that post-traumatic osteolysis of the distal end of the clavicle[126, 170, 247] occurs in part as a result of an undetected intra-articular fracture.[57, 201]

Fractures of the medial end of the clavicle are uncommon and, almost without exception, are treated symptomatically. Craig subdivided these injuries into minimally displaced (type I), displaced (type II), intra-articular (type III), physeal separation (type IV), and comminuted (type V) fractures.[57] Fractures in this region of the clavicle are so uncommon that the patterns of medial clavicular injury have rarely been described and studied, and it remains unclear how different fracture patterns influence treatment and prognosis.

Robinson reviewed 1000 fractures of the clavicle treated at the Royal Infirmary of Edinburgh over a 6-year period.[256] He divided the clavicle into fifths and labeled fracture of the medial fifth as type 1, or medial clavicular fracture; fracture of the lateral fifth as type 3, or lateral clavicular fracture; and fracture of the middle three fifths as type 2, or midclavicular fracture. For midclavicular fractures he applied subclassifications that distinguished displacement greater than the width of the bone and segmental comminution of the fracture fragments (Fig. 45–12). For medial and lateral clavicular fractures he distinguished displacement and articular involvement (Fig. 45–13). Of interest are the facts that the incidence of medial clavicular fracture was 1 per 100,000 per year as compared with 20 for midclavicular and 8 for lateral clavicular fractures, that midclavicular fractures were more often than not displaced by a ratio of 2.7 to 1, and that lateral clavicular fractures were more frequently displaced by a ratio of nearly 2 to 1. Ten percent of displaced midclavicular fractures had delayed or arrested healing, and 6% were treated operatively. None of the nondisplaced fractures had healing problems. Segmental comminution of the fracture was also a risk factor for nonunion, with 5% of noncomminuted fractures failing to heal versus 11.5% of comminuted fractures. Forty-four percent of displaced lateral clavicular fractures had healing problems, and 14% were treated operatively.

Other recent studies of the epidemiology of clavicular fractures found an incidence closer to 50 per 100,000 per year and suggest that lateral clavicular fractures are increasingly common in the elderly who have a simple fall from a standing height.[216, 218, 256] In another study, two thirds of patients with a lateral clavicular fracture were alcoholics.[212]

## Mechanism

In adolescents and adults, clavicular fractures in all regions typically result from a moderate- or high-energy traumatic impact, such as that caused by a fall from a height, motor vehicle accident, sports injury, blow to the point of the shoulder, or rarely, direct injury to the clavicle.[216, 218, 256]

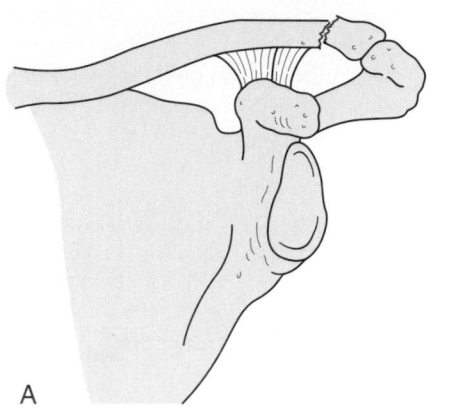

A

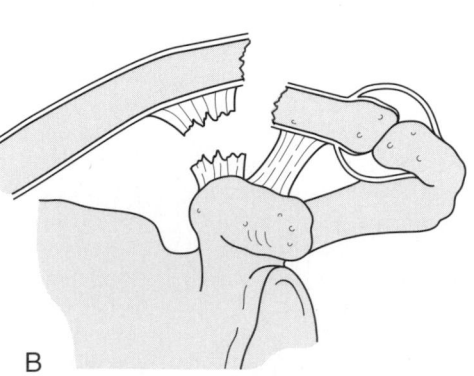

B

**FIGURE 45–11.** When the distal end of the clavicle is fractured, the ligaments may either remain intact and serve to maintain apposition of the fracture fragments (*A*, type I) or rupture and allow wide displacement of the fragments (*B*, type II). (*A, B,* Redrawn from Rockwood, C.A.; Green, D.P., eds. Fractures, 4th ed., Vol. 1. Philadelphia, J.B. Lippincott, 1996.)

Cortical Alignment Fractures (Type 2A)          Displaced Fractures (Type 2B)

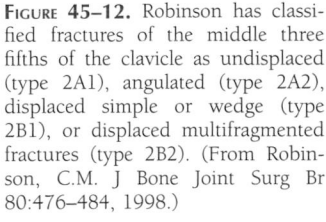

FIGURE 45–12. Robinson has classified fractures of the middle three fifths of the clavicle as undisplaced (type 2A1), angulated (type 2A2), displaced simple or wedge (type 2B1), or displaced multifragmented fractures (type 2B2). (From Robinson, C.M. J Bone Joint Surg Br 80:476–484, 1998.)

Undisplaced (Type 2A1)

Simple or wedge comminuted (Type 2B1)

Angulated (Type 2A2)

Isolated or comminuted segmental (Type 2B2)

In older persons, clavicular fractures usually occur after low-energy trauma such as a simple fall.

It has become clear that the clavicle fails most commonly in compression.[19, 93, 268, 282] Failure in compression is seen after falls onto the shoulder and direct blows to the point of the shoulder. A direct blow to the clavicle, which can occur in sports in which sticks are wielded (e.g., lacrosse[277]), may also fracture the clavicle. Although a fall onto the outstretched hand has traditionally been considered a common mechanism of midclavicular fracture,[4] recent observations bring this assumption into question.[282]

Stanley and colleagues[282] studied 122 of 150 consecutive patients who sought treatment at two hospitals in Sheffield for a fractured clavicle and provided a detailed account of their injury: 87% resulted from a fall onto the shoulder, 7% from a direct blow to the point of the shoulder, and 6% from a fall onto an outstretched hand. A fall onto an outstretched hand was the apparent mechanism of 5 (6.3%) of 79 midclavicular fractures and 2

(5.9%) of 34 distal clavicular fractures, thus suggesting that a direct injury to the shoulder is the most common mechanism of clavicular fracture at all sites. These authors hypothesized that even patients who recall their injury as a fall onto an outstretched hand may have fallen secondarily onto the shoulder. This second impact may have been the injuring force, and an isolated fall onto an outstretched hand may actually be an unusual mechanism of injury.[282]

## Evaluation

The diagnosis is usually straightforward and based on the mechanism of injury, the location of swelling and ecchymosis, and the findings of deformity, tenderness, and crepitation. Open clavicular fractures are uncommon, even after high-energy traumatic injury, and are usually the result of a direct blow to the clavicle. Tenting of the skin by one of the major fracture fragments or by an intervening fragment of comminuted bone is not uncom-

Cortical Alignment Fractures (Type 3A)          Displaced Fractures (Type 3B)

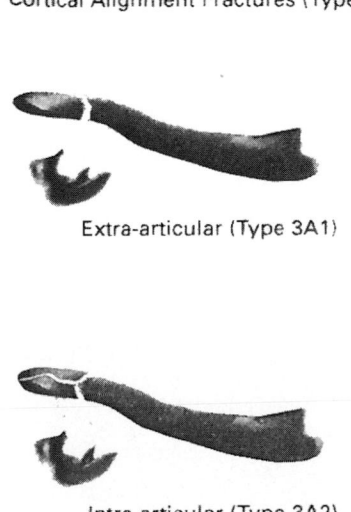

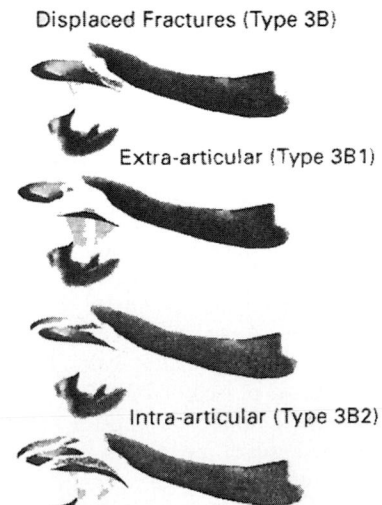

Extra-articular (Type 3A1)

Extra-articular (Type 3B1)

FIGURE 45–13. Robinson has classified fractures of the lateral fifth of the clavicle as undisplaced extra-articular (type 3A1), undisplaced intra-articular (type 3A2), displaced extra-articular (type 3B1), or displaced intra-articular fractures (type 3B2). (From Robinson, C.M. J Bone Joint Surg Br 80:476–484, 1998.)

Intra-articular (Type 3B2)

Intra-articular (Type 3A2)

mon, but a true threat to the integrity of the skin is unusual.[248, 256]

Neurovascular injury,[120] pneumothorax,[69, 172, 184, 314] and hemothorax[261] have been reported in association with fracture of the clavicle, but these sequelae are uncommon. In contrast to late dysfunction of the brachial plexus after clavicular fracture, a situation in which medial cord structures are typically involved, acute injury to the brachial plexus at the time of clavicular fracture usually takes the form of a traction injury to the upper cervical roots. Such root traction injuries generally occur in the setting of high-energy trauma and have a relatively poor prognosis.[13, 154, 273]

The prevalence of pneumothorax in association with fracture of the clavicle is often quoted as being 3 based on Rowe's study of more than 600 fractures at Massachusetts General Hospital.[261] In that study, Rowe did not distinguish between moderate- and high-energy injuries, and he did not distinguish isolated fractures from injuries associated with an ipsilateral scapular fracture or dissociation from the thorax or with ipsilateral upper rib injuries. The presence of these associated injuries indicates an injury mechanism of extremely high energy.[73, 74, 116, 151, 159, 253, 308] Pneumothorax and hemothorax are more common in this situation and are more likely to result from a generalized chest wall injury than from a direct injury to the apical pleura by the fractured clavicle.[69, 172, 184, 314] Nonetheless, evaluation for possible pneumothorax by physical examination and by close inspection of an upright film that includes the ipsilateral upper lung field is important.

Vascular injuries may not always be apparent. They may consist of an intimal injury or a small puncture wound and can become evident after weeks to years in the form of an aneurysm, pseudoaneurysm, or thrombosis of the involved vein or artery.

When a clavicular fracture occurs in the setting of a high-energy traumatic injury (e.g., motor vehicle accident, fall from a height), evaluation of life-threatening lesions takes precedence. Major vascular disruption can occur in association with fracture of the clavicle, but it is extremely rare.* Injury to the thoracic duct has also been reported.[17, 35] Death after a tear of the subclavian vein with a subsequent pseudoaneurysm was recorded in the famous case of the death of Sir Robert Peel.[68, 149] Arterial thrombosis may occur after intimal injury.[124, 153, 300] Most vascular injuries associated with clavicular fractures occur in combination with scapulothoracic dissociation, which has been compared with a closed forequarter amputation.[73, 74, 151, 226, 262]

Evaluation of the vascular status of the upper extremity should include an assessment of relative temperature and color in comparison to the uninvolved extremity. Because of the extensive collateral blood supply to the upper extremity, these factors may appear normal despite the presence of a major vascular injury. A difference in peripheral pulses or blood pressure between injured and uninjured upper extremities may be the only clue that a vascular injury is present. If the limb is threatened or if persistent, unexplained hemorrhage is occurring, angiog-

raphy can help detect and localize any vascular injury and thereby assist in definitive management.

Compression[60, 84, 120, 189, 250] and even thrombosis[162, 270, 283] of the subclavian vein can occur in the early postinjury period. Pulmonary embolism has been reported in the setting of subclavian vein thrombosis after clavicular fracture.[283]

## Radiographic Evaluation

An anteroposterior (AP) view of the clavicle identifies and localizes most clavicular fractures, and it should differentiate displaced from nondisplaced or minimally displaced fractures. The radiographic film should be large enough to evaluate both the acromioclavicular and the sternoclavicular joint, as well as the remainder of the shoulder girdle and the upper lung fields.[261] Oblique views can be used to further gauge the degree and direction of displacement.[245, 261] Quesada recommended 45° caudad and cephalad views, which he believed would facilitate evaluation by providing an orthogonal projection.[245] In practice, a single 20° to 60° cephalad-tilted view provides an adequate second view because interference with thoracic structures is minimized. Medial clavicular fractures may be difficult to characterize on this view, and computed tomography is often necessary.

Evaluation of distal clavicular fracture displacement in the AP plane requires a different set of radiographs because cephalad-tilted and caudad-tilted views are hindered by overlap of the bones of the shoulder and overexposure of the distal end of the clavicle and often fail to accurately depict the degree of displacement. Neer suggested a stress view (with 10 lb of weight in each hand) to evaluate the integrity of the coracoclavicular ligaments and 45° anterior and posterior oblique views to gauge displacement.[199]

A combination of both AP and cephalad-caudad obliquity has been advocated in the evaluation of midclavicular fractures.[251, 307] The so-called apical oblique view (tilted 45° anterior and 20° cephalad) may facilitate the diagnosis of minimally displaced fractures (e.g., birth fractures, fractures in children).[307] Ultrasound is also a sensitive diagnostic tool in the evaluation of birth fractures.[135]

The abduction lordotic view (Fig. 45–14), taken with the shoulder abducted above 135° and the central ray angled 25° cephalad, is useful in evaluating the clavicle after internal fixation.[251] Abduction of the shoulder results in rotation of the clavicle on its longitudinal axis, which causes the plate to rotate superiorly and thereby expose the shaft of the clavicle and the fracture site under the plate (Fig. 45–15).

## Management of Specific Injuries

### MIDCLAVICULAR FRACTURES

*Nonoperative Treatment*

Surviving writings from ancient Greece and Egypt document that for more than 5000 years humans have been concerned primarily with the deformity rather than the

---

*See references 56, 64, 68, 70, 106, 120, 127, 177, 179, 197, 217, 235, 286.

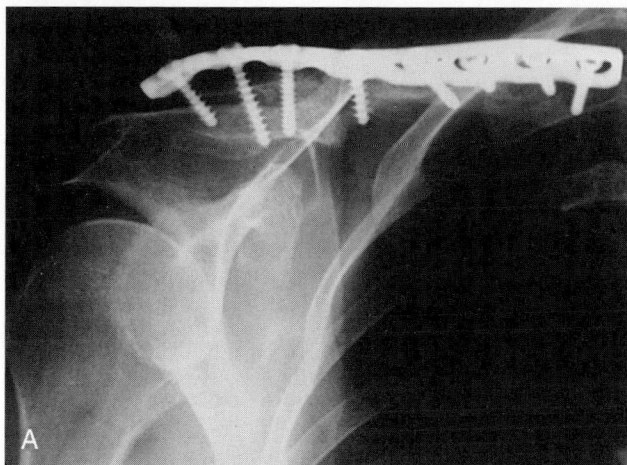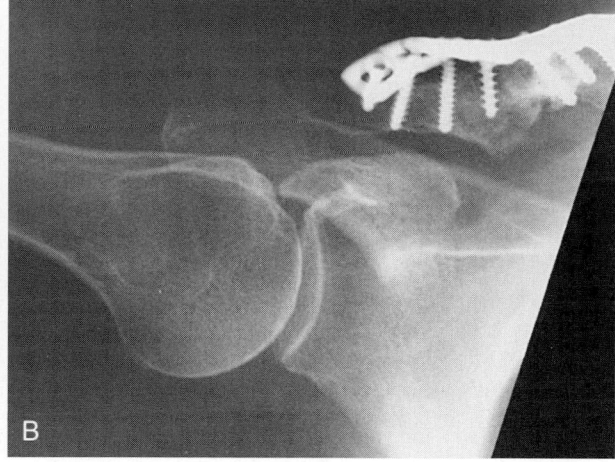

**FIGURE 45–14.** The abduction lordotic view (B) takes advantage of the rotational motion of the clavicle with abduction of the shoulder to provide an alternative view of the clavicle. This radiographic projection is useful for visualizing the fracture site under the plate, which is often obscured in the routine anteroposterior view (A).

healing of fractures of the clavicle.[2, 32] In fact, the method of closed reduction of clavicular fractures described in the Edwin Smith Surgical Papyrus differs little from methods used today.[32]

Closed reduction of clavicular fractures is rarely attempted because the reduction is usually unstable and no reliable means of providing external support is available. The reduction maneuvers described resemble those used for sternoclavicular joint dislocations.[32, 54, 231, 246, 299]

Of the many appliances that have been devised in an attempt to effect or maintain closed reduction and thereby minimize the deformity associated with fracture of the clavicle, most have proved to be cumbersome, painful, or even dangerous.[209] Dupuytren in 1839[71] and Malgaigne in 1859[173] argued that deformity of the clavicle was inevitable and emphasized use of the simplest and most comfortable method of treatment; for Dupuytren, treatment consisted of placing the arm on a pillow until healing occurred.[71]

Nonetheless, devices intended for the maintenance of reduction and immobilization of clavicular fractures have remained popular and commonly take the form of either a figure-of-eight bandage, with or without a sling,

and on rare occasion, a figure-of-eight plaster (Billington yoke[21]) or a shoulder spica cast.[4, 231, 246, 261] Those who agree with Dupuytren and Malgaigne that accurate reduction plus immobilization of clavicular fractures is, as stated by Mullick, "neither essential nor possible,"[93, 94, 158, 160, 194, 269] advocate the use of a simple sling for comfort and forego any attempt at reduction.

The advantage of the figure-of-eight bandage is that the arm remains free and can be used to a limited degree. Disadvantages include increased discomfort,[5, 93, 94] the need for frequent readjustment and repeat office visits,[5, 181] and the potential for complications, including axillary pressure sores[101, 239] and other skin problems,[5] upper extremity edema and venous congestion,[5, 181, 194] brachial plexus palsy,[268] worsening of the deformity,[93, 181, 194] and perhaps an increased risk of nonunion.[310]

A few investigations have compared treatment with a figure-of-eight or reducing bandage with the use of a simple sling or supporting bandage.[5, 158, 181, 282] Although the details of patient selection and evaluation in these investigations remain unclear because of the meager data published, the authors claim to have found no difference in regard to shoulder function,[5, 158, 181] residual deformity,[5, 181] or time to return to full range of motion and full activity.[282]

Even though the clavicle is one of the most commonly fractured bones, very little in the way of stringent, detailed analysis of clavicular fracture data has been performed. The existing literature regarding nonoperative treatment consists of relatively few series,[53, 86, 93, 158, 261, 268] relatively limited studies comparing specific treatment measures,[5, 181, 282] descriptions of technique,[21, 54, 112, 142, 231, 299] anecdotal observations,[94, 194, 209, 246] and general reviews.[4, 117, 204–206, 241]

Few reports have attempted to evaluate the relationship between residual deformity and shoulder function.[86, 87, 214, 223, 227] Eskola and associates[86] invited all 118 patients treated for fracture of the clavicle at Helsinki University Central Hospital in 1982 to return for evaluation 2 years after injury. Among the 89 who showed up for follow-up examination, 24 (27%) had either slight pain on

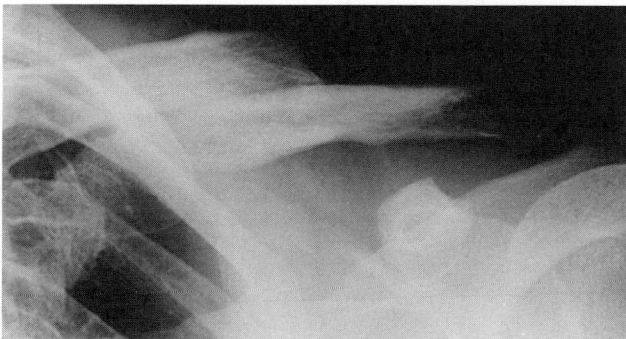

**FIGURE 45–15.** Anteroposterior radiograph demonstrating healing of a clavicular fracture with 2 cm of overlap. This patient had restricted shoulder motion and required osteotomy for restoration of clavicular length.

exercise or restricted shoulder movement, and 4 had major functional problems. Primary fracture displacement and shortening of the clavicle, as compared radiographically with the uninvolved side at the 2-year follow-up, were used as measures of deformity. Among the 15 patients with primary fracture displacement of more than 15 mm at the time of injury, 8 (53%) had pain with exercise after 2 years, whereas only 12 (16%) of the remaining 74 patients had pain, a difference found to be statistically significant by chi-square analysis ($P = .02$). Among 47 patients with demonstrable shortening at follow-up, 17 (36%) had pain with exercise as compared with 3 (7%) of 42 patients without shortening ($P = .02$ by chi-square analysis) (Fig.

45–16). Based on these findings, the authors recommended reduction of the deformity associated with displaced clavicular fractures, particularly with regard to shortening. However, this conclusion may be questioned on the grounds that the fractures that are more displaced are those that are associated with higher-energy traumatic injury, which can be expected to do worse regardless of the residual deformity. Nonetheless, the fact that 27% of these patients reported pain during exercise or restricted shoulder movement after 2 years suggests that there is room for improvement.

Nordqvist and colleagues found that 15-mm or greater shortening of the clavicle did not measurably affect mobil-

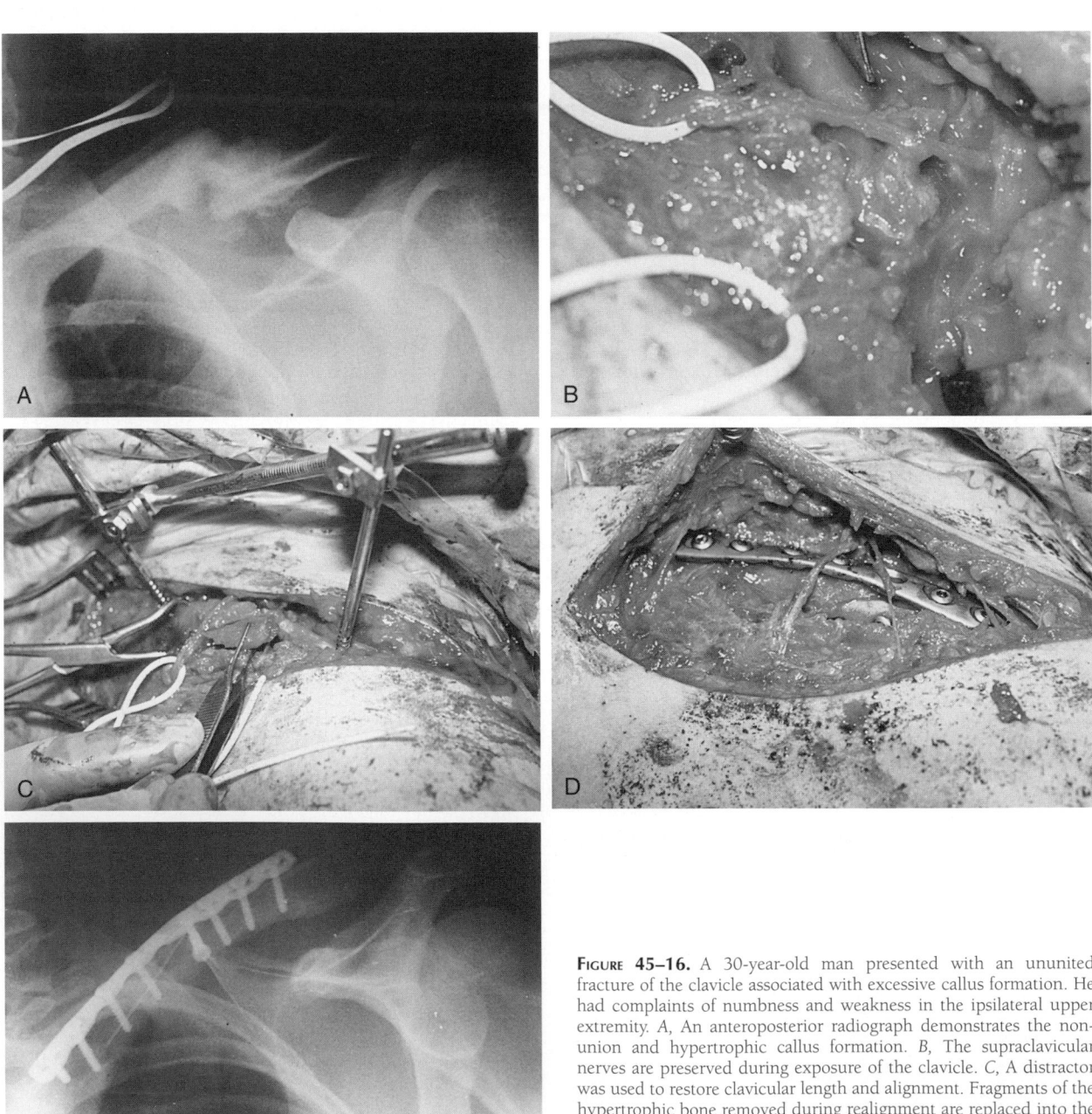

**FIGURE 45–16.** A 30-year-old man presented with an ununited fracture of the clavicle associated with excessive callus formation. He had complaints of numbness and weakness in the ipsilateral upper extremity. *A,* An anteroposterior radiograph demonstrates the non-union and hypertrophic callus formation. *B,* The supraclavicular nerves are preserved during exposure of the clavicle. *C,* A distractor was used to restore clavicular length and alignment. Fragments of the hypertrophic bone removed during realignment are replaced into the wound. *D,* The clavicle is then stabilized with a 3.5-mm limited-contact dynamic compression plate. *E,* Postoperative radiograph demonstrating restoration of length and alignment of the clavicle and stable plate fixation.

ity, strength, or Constant score in 16 adult patients.[214] Oroko and associates found that 3 of 13 adults with healed clavicular fractures and 15-mm or greater shortening had diminished Constant scores, but in each case the disability was explained by factors other than the shortening.[227] We believe that shortening of the clavicle does affect function of the shoulder girdle but that these effects are subtle, difficult to measure, and probably only important in patients who place substantial demands on their shoulder.

### Operative Treatment

Operative treatment of clavicular fractures has traditionally been discouraged. Early reports documented that the clavicle heals readily and predictably unless primary operative treatment is undertaken.[198, 261] According to Neer, only 3 (0.1%) of 2235 patients with midclavicular fractures treated by closed methods failed to heal whereas nonunion developed in 2 (4.4%) of 45 treated with immediate open reduction and fixation.[198] Rowe found a 0.8% incidence of nonunion after closed treatment versus 3.7% after initial open treatment.[261] Interpretation of these numbers should be tempered by the likelihood of a selection bias, with more complex fractures being treated operatively.

With the development of more predictable implants, some interest has been shown in the use of primary operative treatment.[95, 141, 156, 208, 228, 240, 272, 274, 318] The good results with open reduction, internal fixation, and bone grafting of clavicular nonunion that have been documented in recent reports also support the contention that internal fixation of the clavicle, when performed properly, should not impede healing.[22, 131, 174]

Zenni and colleagues[318] treated 25 of 800 fractures of the clavicle seen over an 8-year period operatively. Their indications for operative treatment included fracture of the distal third of the clavicle with coracoclavicular ligament disruption, severe angulation that threatened the integrity of the overlying skin, and comminution of a fracture of the middle third of the clavicle. They used a threaded intramedullary wire for fixation, and all of the fractures united after the initial operative procedure. They recommended, as additional indications for primary operative treatment, neurovascular compromise resulting from compression by fracture fragments and an inability to tolerate prolonged immobilization (e.g., because of an associated neuromuscular disorder).

A number of authors have reported good results after plate fixation of open clavicular fractures, clavicular fractures with severe angulation that prevented closed reduction, and clavicular fractures in patients with multiple traumatic injuries, especially in the setting of ipsilateral upper extremity trauma or bilateral clavicular fracture.[37, 141, 148, 228, 240, 272] In particular, scapulothoracic dissociation and the so-called floating shoulder, which represents a combination of displaced clavicular and scapular neck fractures, are believed by some to be good indications for open reduction and plate-and-screw fixation of the clavicular fracture.[73, 74, 102, 116, 151, 159, 253]

Khan noted no nonunions in 19 patients treated by primary plate fixation.[141] Schwarz and co-workers used 2.7-mm plates and reported nonunion in 3 of 36 patients, which they attributed to use of a plate of inadequate length.[272] Poigenfurst and colleagues had extensive experience with plate fixation of fresh clavicular fractures and reported nonunion in 5 (4.1%) of 122 patients treated operatively.[240] They, too, related the failures to technical errors, including the use of a plate of inadequate length or strength and devitalization of fracture fragments during operative exposure. Shen and associates[274] reported nonunion in 7 (3%) of 232 patients treated by plate fixation. All the nonunions occurred in displaced fractures with segmental comminution (Robinson type 2B2). One was related to infection and the other six to technical errors. Böstman and colleagues reported five deep infections, six hardware failures, and three nonunions in 103 patients treated by plate fixation.[26] The use of a plate of inadequate strength and size was responsible for most of the plate-related complications.

External fixation has also been used for fixation of the clavicle. In a study by Schuind and colleagues,[271] good results were obtained in 15 fresh midclavicular fractures and in 5 delayed unions. However, in view of the rarity of severe soft tissue injury in this area, the role of external fixation remains unclear.[59]

### Authors' Preferred Treatment

Nondisplaced and minimally displaced fractures of the midclavicle require little more than symptomatic treatment.[261] Such treatment is best achieved with a simple sling, which can be supplemented by a swathe component if necessary for added comfort early after injury. Most of these nondisplaced fractures occur in children, who heal quickly, and although they may not be compliant with sling wear, they usually self-regulate their activity level until healing has progressed and merely require more gentle handling during the healing period.[261] The clavicle typically heals sufficiently to discontinue protection within 3 to 4 weeks in young children, 4 to 6 weeks in older children, and 6 to 8 weeks in adults.[261] Limitation of activity to reduce the risk of refracture is usually encouraged for a minimum of 8 weeks after clinical and radiographic union.

Indications for operative fixation of clavicular fractures remain uncertain. The indications that we would consider are uncommon and include open fracture, scapulothoracic dissociation,[73, 74, 151] the so-called floating shoulder injury,[102, 116, 159, 253] and associated major vascular injury for which an open approach will be necessary for vascular repair. Complex clavicular injuries involving dislocation or epiphyseal separation at the articulations of the clavicle in addition to clavicular fracture might benefit from open reduction and internal fixation (ORIF) and should be considered individually.[80, 150, 155, 292, 313] Likewise, rehabilitation of associated ipsilateral upper extremity lesions may be facilitated by operative fixation of the clavicle. In the absence of these indications, nonoperative treatment remains our preference.

It is often stated that ORIF should be considered if the skin is threatened by pressure from a prominent clavicular fracture fragment; however, it is extremely rare for the skin to be perforated from within.[248] In the rare event of a vessel or nerve injury requiring repair, the clavicular fracture can be used to improve access for the repair and then fixed internally.

A malaligned fracture that is causing brachial plexus

compression[82, 178, 187, 249, 263, 302] should be treated by open realignment and internal fixation (see Fig. 45–16).

We prefer plate-and-screw fixation when performing ORIF of the clavicle. Before the advent of AO/Association for the Study of Internal Fixation (ASIF) techniques, the small, thin plates that were used gave poor results,[261] which led many to prefer intramedullary fixation with wires or screws.[33, 148, 152, 190, 195, 207, 236, 261, 264] The theoretical difficulties of intramedullary fixation of the clavicle—because of the curvature, high density, and poorly defined intramedullary canal of the bone[261]—have not been described in practice.[22, 45, 318] Intramedullary devices have been altered in attempts to prevent the complications associated with pin migration; threaded pins, pins with heads, and pins bent at the ends have been used. However, even threaded and bent pins can migrate, particularly if they break.[22, 45, 196, 217, 318] The potential advantage of intramedullary fixation—namely, a smaller, more cosmetic scar—is disputable considering that the incision required for open reduction is not a great deal smaller than that required for plate fixation and that a second, more lateral scar is necessary for implant removal. Perhaps the greatest disadvantage of intramedullary fixation is its inability to control the rotational forces experienced by the clavicle, which makes postoperative immobilization necessary in most cases.

Our technique for internal fixation of the clavicle is as follows.[163, 278] The patient is placed in a semisitting (beach-chair) position (Fig. 45–17A). The opposite iliac crest is routinely prepared and draped. An incision is made parallel and just inferior to the long axis of the clavicle (see Fig. 45–17B and G). The crossing supraclavicular nerves are identified under loupe magnification and preserved (see Fig. 45–17C). The goals of alignment and apposition of the fracture fragments can often be achieved without stripping the periosteum and surrounding musculature from the bone by using a small distractor. This device helps control the fragments and aids in obtaining the desired length and alignment while obviating the need for devascularizing and potentially dangerous circumferential clamps in many cases (see Fig. 45–17D).

We apply a 3.5-mm limited-contact dynamic compression plate (LCDC plate, Synthes) to the superior aspect of the clavicle. A minimum of three screws should be placed in each major fragment (see Fig. 45–17E). If the fracture pattern is amenable, placement of an interfragmentary screw greatly enhances the stability of the construct (see Fig. 45–17F). When the vascularity of the fragments has been preserved, no bone graft is needed. When extensive stripping or gaps have occurred in the cortex opposite the plate, one might consider the addition of a small amount of autogenous iliac crest cancellous bone graft. If the skin condition is suitable, wound closure is accomplished in atraumatic fashion with a subcuticular suture. (see Fig. 45–17G).

Our current practice, provided that we are confident with the security of fixation, is to use a sling for patient comfort during the initial 7 to 10 postoperative days. Thereafter, the arm can be used for functional activities with the arm at the side and the sling used only as needed. Passive shoulder pendulum exercises are sometimes used. Active forward flexion and abduction are initiated between 6 and 8 weeks after injury. Once healing is demonstrated, progressive strengthening exercises are permitted. Return to all occupational duties and recreational pursuits is usually possible by 3 months after operative treatment.

In most cases, plate removal is unnecessary. When patients request plate removal for cosmetic or comfort reasons, we advise waiting at least 12 and preferably 18 months from the time of injury and verifying reconstitution of the cortex under the plate with an abduction lordotic view.

## DISTAL CLAVICULAR FRACTURES

Fractures of the distal end of the clavicle with little or no displacement are treated symptomatically with a sling. Although some cases of nonunion have been reported after such fractures,[215] the chance of nonunion is extremely low, and symptoms are variable.

Displaced distal clavicular fractures, on the other hand, are recognized as the only general type of clavicle fracture for which routine primary operative treatment should be considered. This indication is based on the work of Neer[199–201, 215] and others,[78, 215] who found that 22% to 33% of these fractures fail to unite after nonoperative treatment. An additional 45% to 67% require longer than 3 months for healing of the fracture.[78, 200]

Good results have been reported with the operative treatment of type 2 fractures by a variety of techniques.[78, 85, 100, 118, 200, 306] A few authors have reported acceptable results with nonoperative treatment[188, 215] and have stated that the few nonunions that become symptomatic can be treated with a reconstructive procedure at a time remote from the injury, if necessary.

Neer and others recommended stabilization of displaced distal clavicular fractures with two Kirschner wires inserted retrogradely into the distal fragment through the fracture site.[188, 199–201, 215] Two wires are used to control rotation. The wires are passed through the acromioclavicular joint and the acromion and out the skin on the lateral aspect of the shoulder and then passed into the medial fragment, bent to decrease the risk of migration, and cut beneath the skin. Shoulder motion must be restricted to prevent pin breakage and migration. Others have used a single wire,[115, 233, 261] threaded wires,[115] or screws,[115, 204–207] and some have made a point of avoiding the acromioclavicular joint.[233] Caution was urged in a report by Kona and colleagues,[144] who noted high rates of both nonunion and infection with transacromial wire techniques.

Alternative techniques for operative fixation of distal clavicular fractures include coracoclavicular screw fixation,[6, 27, 78] transfer of the coracoid to the clavicle,[46, 90, 136] and other coracoclavicular fixation.[100, 118, 306] The AO/ASIF group recommended use of a tension band wire construct in which two Kirschner wires enter on the superior aspect of the clavicle to avoid the acromioclavicular joint.[113] In addition, they suggested consideration of a small plate, particularly a small T-shaped plate, with one of the screws directed into the coracoid.[113] A specially designed plate that is contoured so that its distal limit curves under the acromion through the acromioclavicular joint has also been used.[113]

We prefer the tension band wire technique and proceed

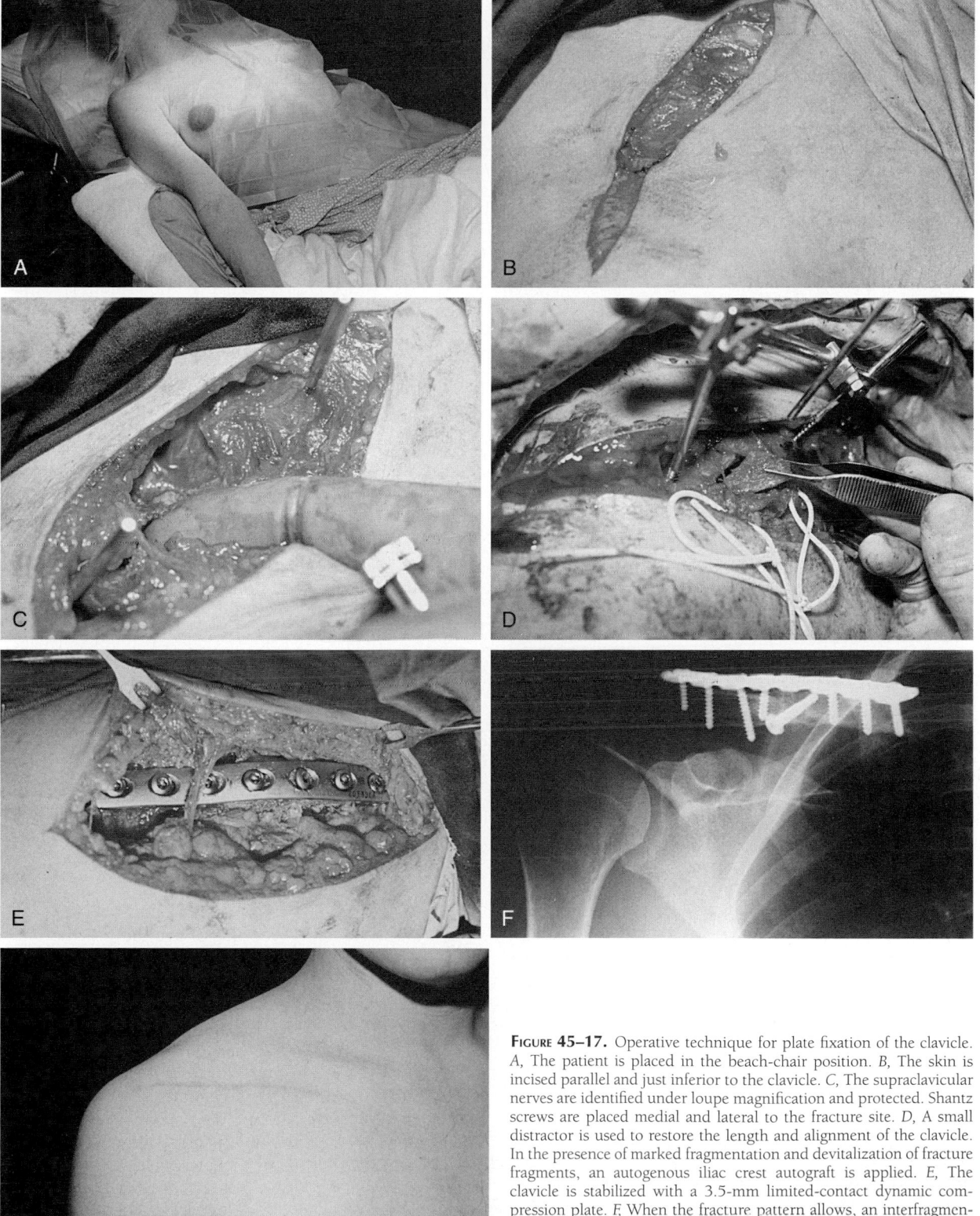

**FIGURE 45–17.** Operative technique for plate fixation of the clavicle. *A,* The patient is placed in the beach-chair position. *B,* The skin is incised parallel and just inferior to the clavicle. *C,* The supraclavicular nerves are identified under loupe magnification and protected. Shantz screws are placed medial and lateral to the fracture site. *D,* A small distractor is used to restore the length and alignment of the clavicle. In the presence of marked fragmentation and devitalization of fracture fragments, an autogenous iliac crest autograft is applied. *E,* The clavicle is stabilized with a 3.5-mm limited-contact dynamic compression plate. *F,* When the fracture pattern allows, an interfragmentary lag screw is used to achieve compression between the fracture fragments. *G,* Hypertrophy of the scar is uncommon.

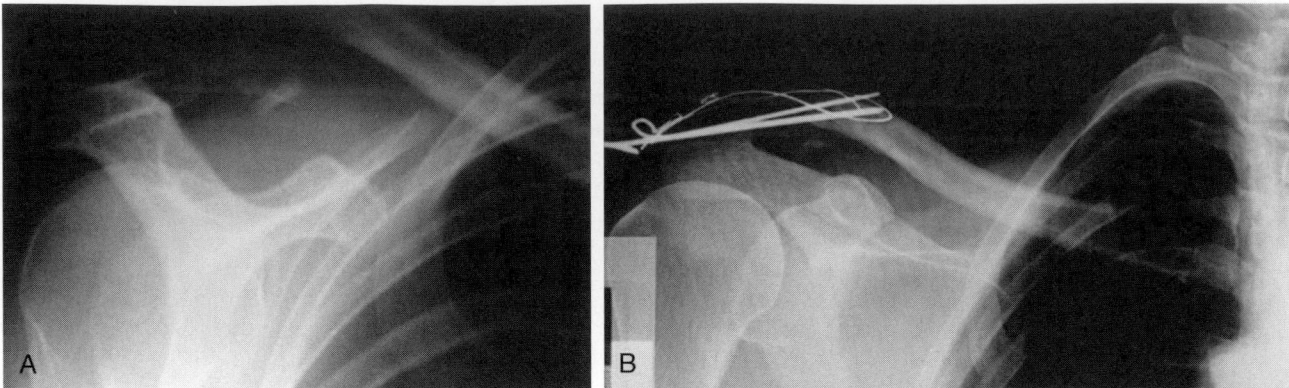

**Figure 45–18.** *A,* A 55-year-old woman sustained a comminuted type II fracture of the distal end of the clavicle in a motor vehicle accident. *B,* Fixation was achieved with two transacromial Kirschner wires exiting through the thick dorsal cortex of the medial fragment in combination with a tension band wire.

as follows. The distal end of the clavicle and acromion are exposed through an incision parallel to the clavicle, and skin flaps are fashioned. Provisional fracture reduction can be held with a transacromial Kirschner wire. Definitive fixation consists of two stout, smooth Kirschner wires passed through the outer edge of the acromion and angled obliquely across the acromioclavicular joint and fracture to gain purchase in the solid cortex of the dorsal aspect of the clavicle medial to the fracture (Fig. 45–18). An 18-gauge wire is then looped through a drill hole medial to the fracture and around the tips of the wires, which are bent 180°, turned downward, and impacted into the acromion. If either the trapezoid or the conoid ligament is torn and identified, an attempt is made to perform a suture repair. The wound is closed over a suction drain. Postoperative management differs from that for a midclavicular fracture in that the patient is maintained in a sling for a minimum of 4 to 6 weeks.

## MEDIAL CLAVICULAR FRACTURES

Medial clavicular fractures are uncommon, and most practitioners have limited experience treating them. The literature offers little more than case reports, most describing medial physeal separation injuries.[38, 98, 132, 161, 243, 316] Although some authors recommend ORIF,[38, 243] most advocate nonoperative treatment initially, with resection of the medial part of the clavicle if symptoms persist.* In view of the risks attendant with insertion and migration of implants in this region, we rarely consider operative treatment. Displaced fractures must be evaluated with computed tomographic scanning to be certain that posterior displacement of the fragments does not present a threat to neurovascular structures at the base of the neck.

## Complications

### NONUNION AND MALUNION

Until recently, the rate of nonunion of nonoperatively treated fractures of the clavicle was consistently below

3%.[86, 146, 158, 198, 261, 268, 288] Recent studies suggest that the rate of delayed union and nonunion may approach 10% to 20% in widely displaced, comminuted fractures in adults.[119, 213, 256, 309]

In series of patients with established symptomatic nonunion, Jupiter and Leffert,[131] as well as others,[174, 266, 310] found that the degree of displacement of the fracture fragment was the most important risk factor for nonunion. Displacement reflects more severe soft tissue injury, decreased stability, and limited apposition of fracture fragments. The role of soft tissue interposition remains unclear.[125, 174] With the use of contemporary techniques, nonunion after operative treatment is unusual and generally due to a plate of inadequate length or thickness[240, 272, 274] (Fig. 45–19).

Patients with an ununited clavicle are likely to have specific complaints related to deformity, which consists of adduction, shortening, and internal rotation of the shoulder; altered shoulder function as a result of deformity or pain; or local compression of the underlying brachial plexus or vascular structures.[131, 266] Occasionally, patients

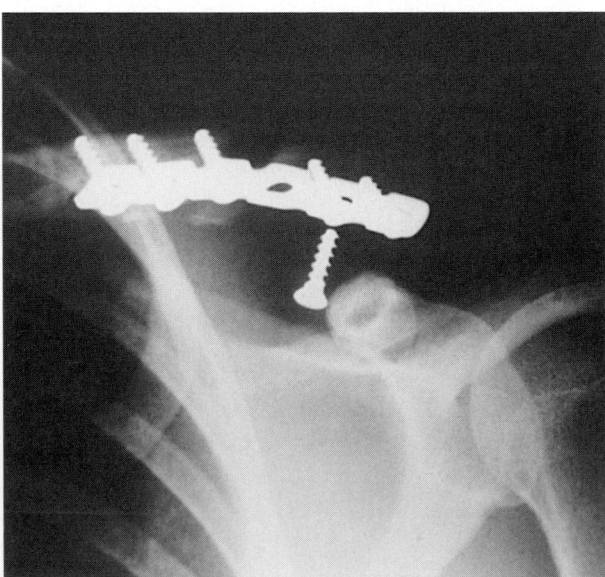

**Figure 45–19.** Implant loosening and nonunion are typically related to inadequate plate size and length.

---

*See references 4, 38, 53, 57, 86, 117, 158, 161, 201, 261, 316.

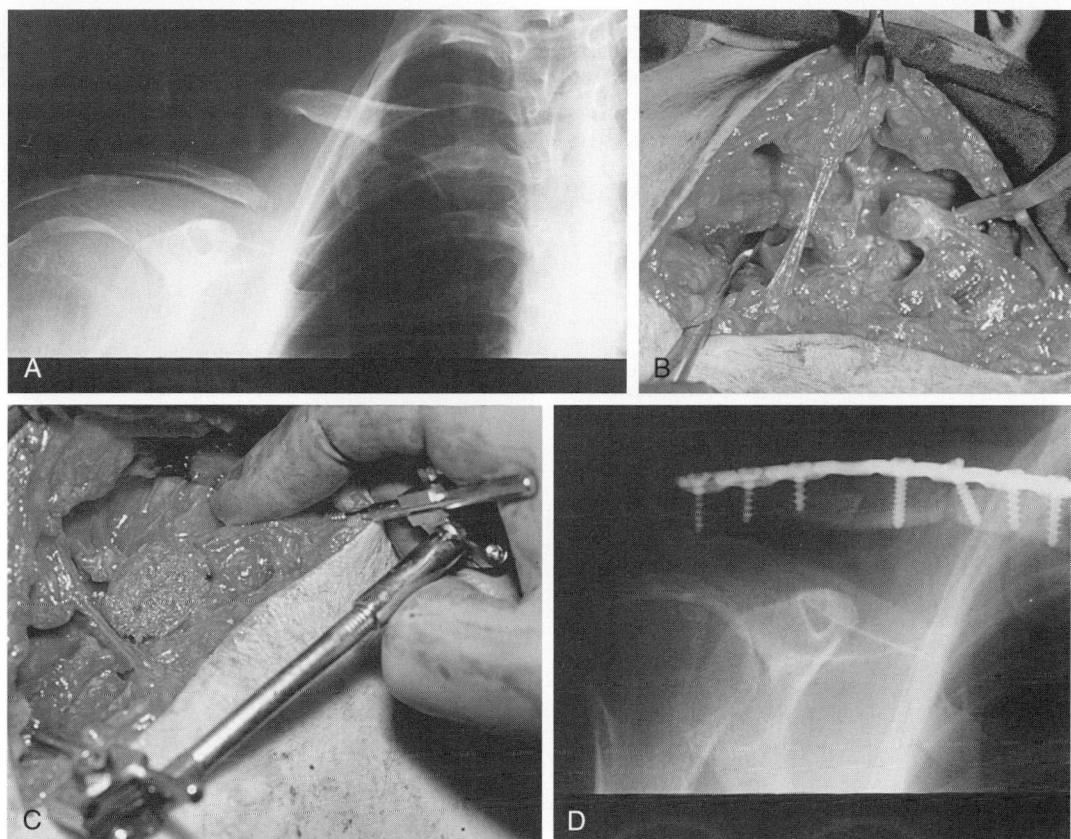

**FIGURE 45–20.** A 56-year-old woman had complaints of increasing shoulder pain, stiffness, and deformity after injuring her clavicle at 14 years of age. *A*, An anteroposterior radiograph demonstrated an ununited fracture of the clavicle with widely displaced, atrophic fragments. *B*, The supraclavicular nerves were identified under loupe magnification and protected throughout the operative procedure. *C*, A distractor was used to restore anatomic length and alignment of the clavicle, and a tricortical bone graft from the iliac crest was used to bridge the residual bony defect. *D*, One of the screws through the plate is transfixing the bone graft.

are initially evaluated for treatment decades after the original injury,[129, 131, 254, 310] perhaps in part because they were previously advised that nothing operative could or should be done (Fig. 45–20).

Neurovascular problems that may accompany clavicular nonunion include thoracic outlet syndrome,[9, 14, 31, 52, 89, 167, 192, 238, 285] subclavian artery or vein compression[61, 145] or thrombosis,[61, 105, 315] and brachial plexus palsy.[44, 120, 131, 137] The prevalence of neurovascular dysfunction in patients with clavicular nonunion has varied widely in reported series from as low as 6% to as high as 52%.[129, 131, 143, 310]

In the treatment of clavicular nonunion, we prefer to distinguish between reconstructive procedures, in which the goals of relief of pain and neurovascular compression and enhanced function are sought through restoration of the alignment and continuity of the clavicle, and salvage procedures, in which the clavicle is resected, contoured, or avoided altogether (e.g., first-rib resection[60]), with the limited goal of relief of symptoms. Although treatment of clavicular nonunion with electrical stimulation has been attempted,[36, 51, 63, 196] indications for its use are limited. Symptomatic clavicular nonunion typically has elements of both shoulder deformity and dysfunction, as well as neurovascular compromise, which are not addressed by electrical treatment.[196]

With the advent of improved techniques of stable fixation, the results of reconstructive procedures have improved to the point that salvage operations are now largely of historical interest.[278] The only situation in which we would consider partial resection of the clavicle is a chronically infected clavicle in a medically compromised patient or a very distal clavicular nonunion. A small distal clavicular fragment can be resected and the coracoclavicular ligaments securely attached to the outer end of the medial fragment.[278]

Treatment of clavicular nonunion has evolved from screw fixation of tibial or iliac crest bone grafts,[12, 20, 99, 266] to intramedullary fixation,[129, 176, 198, 289] which still has a few advocates,[22, 45, 83, 312] to the current preferred method of rigid plate-and-screw fixation.* Our preference for plate fixation and our operative technique and rehabilitation protocol have already been described. A few points regarding the treatment of midclavicular nonunion deserve further discussion.

In hypertrophic nonunion, the exuberant callus can be resected and saved for use as a bone graft, thus making harvest of an iliac crest graft unnecessary in some cases. The nonunion site does not require débridement because

---

*See references 7, 28, 29, 62, 75, 77, 88, 130, 131, 134, 143, 174, 193, 223, 244, 254, 255, 265, 278, 293, 297, 310.

the fibrocartilage progresses to union after stable internal fixation. If the fracture line is oblique, it is sometimes possible to secure the fragments with the use of an interfragmentary screw in addition to a superiorly placed plate. If lengthening is desired, the oblique fracture can be mobilized before inserting the lag screw.[28]

Atrophic nonunions have sclerotic ends with interposed fibrous tissue, whereas pseudoarthroses have a false synovial joint. Resection of the ends of the fracture fragments and the intervening tissue is required in both situations. In this case, a small distractor often proves invaluable to help control the fragments and to attain the desired length and alignment (Fig. 45–21A). A sculptured tricortical iliac crest bone graft is useful to ensure restoration of length and alignment and to promote healing (see Fig. 45–21B).

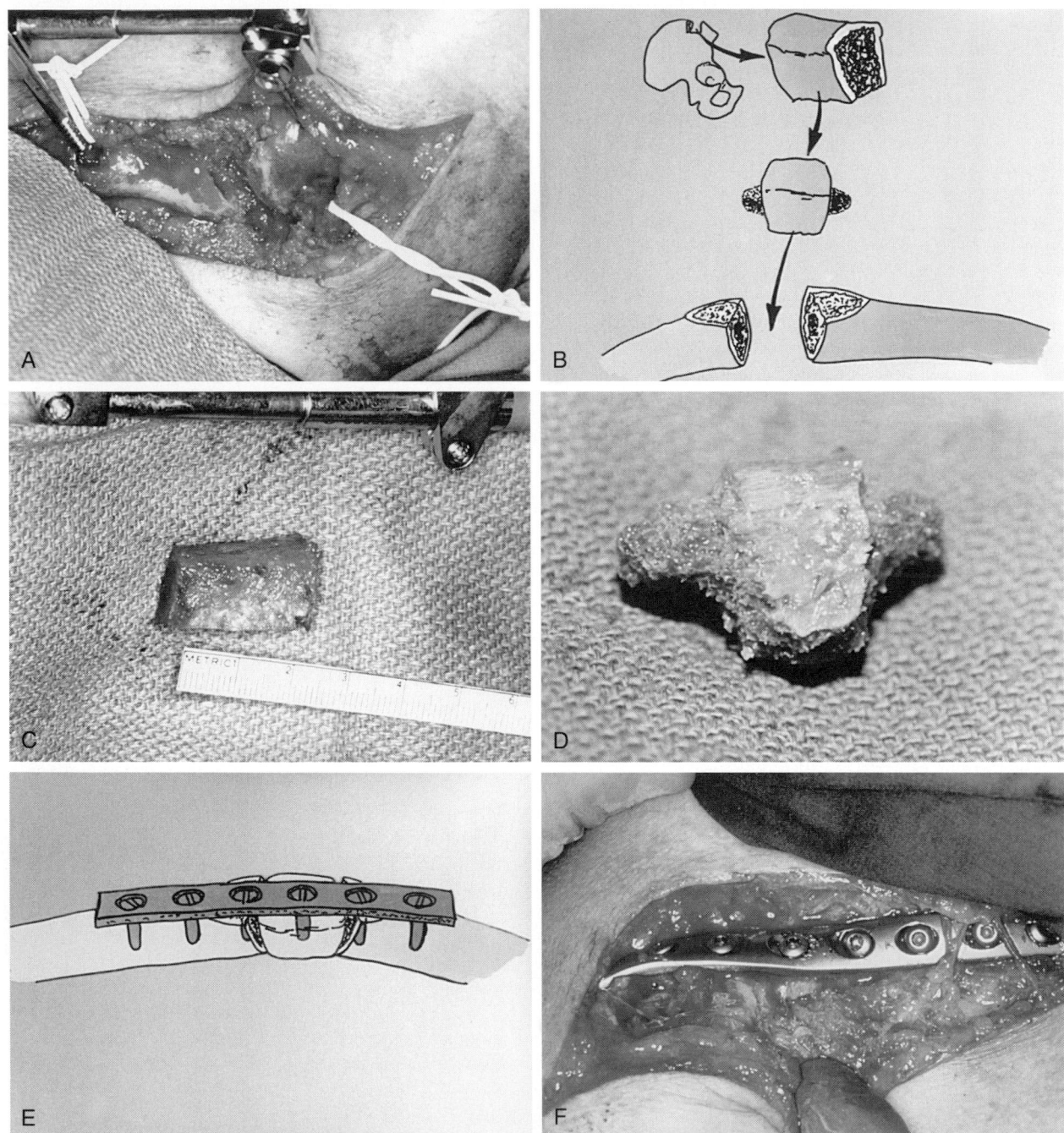

**FIGURE 45–21.** Sculpting of a tricortical iliac crest autograft allows interdigitation of the graft with the fracture fragments, thereby increasing the stability of the construct and limiting callus formation. *A,* After resection of the nonunion back to viable bone and distraction of the clavicle to restore length and alignment, a substantial bony defect is common. *B,* A tricortical graft is harvested from the iliac crest, and cancellous pegs are sculpted at the medial and lateral aspects. The medullary canals of the fracture fragments are opened with a drill, and the pegs interdigitate with the fragments. *C,* The harvested iliac crest graft before sculpturing. *D,* The graft after sculpturing. *E,* Interdigitation of the graft with the fracture fragments provides a measure of stability by facilitating plate fixation. One of the screws transfixes the plate. *F,* Radiograph with the graft in place and stabilized with a limited-contact compression plate.

We harvest the iliac graft from the crest through an oblique incision along the midpoint of the ilium. The crest is exposed subperiosteally, and a tricortical section measuring 1.5 times the anticipated size of the final graft is removed with either osteotomes or a small oscillating saw (see Fig. 45–21C). The graft is then sculptured to create large cancellous pegs at each end that plug into the medullary canals of the clavicular fragments (see Fig. 45–21D). This interdigitation increases the stability of the construct and facilitates plate fixation. The graft is positioned so that the dorsal cortical margin of the iliac crest lies on the inferior surface of the clavicle to afford better purchase for a screw and more resistance to bending forces at the nonunion site. Additional cancellous graft from the iliac crest is compacted into the medullary canals of each fragment before final impaction of the corticocancellous segmental graft.

A 3.5-mm LCDC plate is then applied with a minimum of three screws in each major fragment and a single screw transfixing the graft. Compression is applied to both surfaces of the graft to enhance early stability and healing with little callus formation (see Fig. 45–21E and F). The wound is closed with a subcuticular suture over suction drainage.

Although malunion has traditionally been considered primarily a cosmetic concern,[209] some have reported difficulties in shoulder function in patients with overriding of clavicular fragments.[86, 87] In addition, compression of underlying neurovascular structures has been reported in association with malaligned clavicular fractures as a result of narrowing of the costoclavicular space* and compression of the brachial plexus or the subclavian artery or vein.[44, 61, 105, 120, 131, 137, 145, 314] Malunited fractures may typically give rise weeks or months after the injury to neuromuscular symptoms from proliferative callus.[9, 52, 82, 89, 249, 263, 302]

Osteotomy for symptomatic malunion of the clavicle is becoming more commonplace.[24, 18, 237] The malunion is osteotomized through the plane of deformity, realigned with the use of a small distractor, and secured with a plate and screws (Fig. 45–22).

## NEUROVASCULAR COMPLICATIONS

Acute neurovascular complications are rare; they typically occur in association with scapulothoracic dissociation[56, 120, 197] or are unrelated to the clavicular fracture (e.g., brachial plexus traction injury).[120, 154] Neurovascular dysfunction caused by narrowing of the thoracic outlet can occur within the first 2 months after injury when the fracture is malaligned or many months or even years later as a result of hypertrophic callus in the setting of nonunion.

Further mention should be made of thrombosis and pseudoaneurysm of the subclavian or axillary artery or the subclavian vein at a time remote from the injury. In patients seen late with symptoms of atrophy and cold intolerance of the involved upper extremity, axillary or subclavian artery thrombosis most likely represents acute occult intimal injury,[120, 124, 153, 276, 300] but it may also result from compression in a narrowed costoclavicular space.[291] Cerebral embolism has been reported after subclavian artery thrombosis in this setting.[315]

True aneurysms of the subclavian artery may occur as poststenotic aneurysms when the costoclavicular space is narrowed.[64, 290, 291, 315] Displaced clavicular fracture fragments may very rarely cause a small perforation injury of the subclavian artery. Occasionally, a pseudoaneurysm may cause brachial plexus dysfunction months to years later as a result of compression.†

Subclavian vein thrombosis may also occur in relation to compression or intimal injury.[162, 270, 283] Pulmonary embolism may likewise occur in this setting.[270]

Neurovascular symptoms related to compression by hypertrophic nonunion have been mistaken in the past for sympathetically maintained pain (shoulder-hand syndrome).[238] Damage to the supraclavicular nerves can cause anterior chest wall pain.

## REFRACTURE

Repeat fracture of the clavicle usually occurs after premature resumption of full activity, in particular, contact sports. Because the typically vigorous healing response of the clavicle results in a rapid decrease in pain and return of shoulder function, overenthusiastic patients often ignore their physicians' admonitions to avoid contact sports for at least 2 to 3 months after healing of the fracture. Refracture after plate removal is unusual if the plate remains in place for at least 12 to 18 months after healing of the fracture.[240, 278]

## COMPLICATIONS OF OPERATIVE TREATMENT

Despite the proximity of important anatomic structures beneath the clavicle, intraoperative complications are rare. Eskola and co-workers reported tearing of the subclavian vein, pneumothorax, air embolism, and brachial plexus palsy, all in a single patient during dissection of a clavicular nonunion.[87] On the other hand, wires and pins[168] show a remarkable ability to migrate once inserted and may ultimately be found in the abdominal aorta,[196] the ascending aorta,[210] the aorta and pericardium (causing fatal tamponade),[49] the pulmonary artery,[157] the mediastinum,[40] the heart,[234] the lung[180, 182, 232, 252, 298] (sometimes the opposite lung[252]), or the spinal canal.[217] A patient evaluated by Kremens and Glauser[147] brought in a Steinmann pin that he reported having expectorated 1 month after fixation of his medial clavicular fracture.

Some authors have had problems with superficial and deep infections,[26, 240] but other authors have had little trouble with infections after plate fixation.[37, 131, 141, 148, 174, 228, 240, 272]

Many authors cite hypertrophic scar formation as one of the potential complications of operative treatment of clavicular fractures,[141] particularly the proponents of intramedullary fixation, who advocate a more longitudinal incision in alignment with Langer's lines.[205, 206] We have had no particular problem with cosmetically displeasing scars.

*See references 9, 14, 31, 52, 82, 89, 167, 178, 187, 192, 238, 263, 285, 302.

†See references 47, 56, 104, 109, 120, 197, 275, 284, 286, 314.

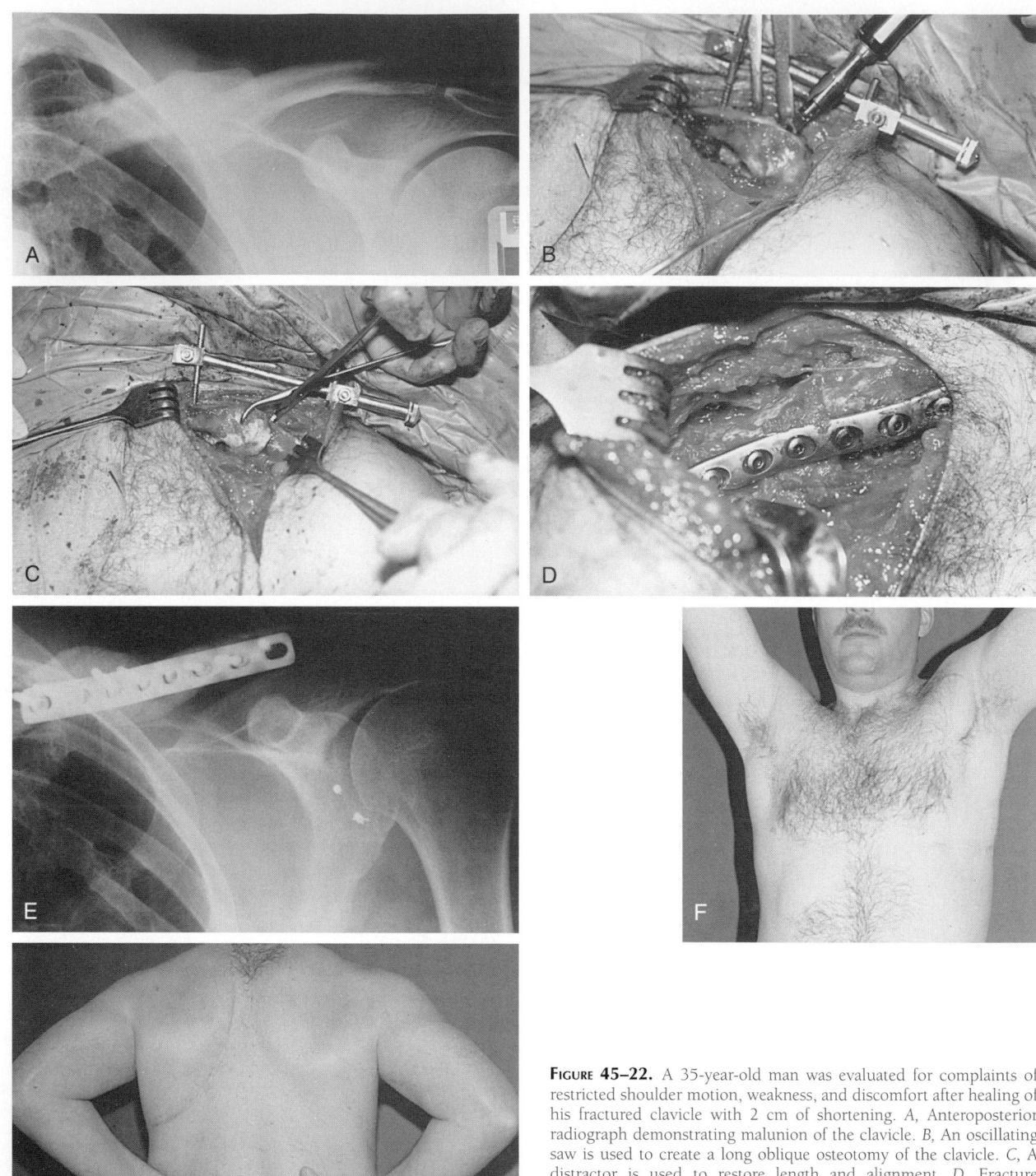

**FIGURE 45–22.** A 35-year-old man was evaluated for complaints of restricted shoulder motion, weakness, and discomfort after healing of his fractured clavicle with 2 cm of shortening. *A,* Anteroposterior radiograph demonstrating malunion of the clavicle. *B,* An oscillating saw is used to create a long oblique osteotomy of the clavicle. *C,* A distractor is used to restore length and alignment. *D,* Fracture reduction forceps help maintain alignment while an anterior plate incorporating an interfragmentary screw is applied. *E,* Radiograph demonstrating stable plate fixation with restoration of clavicular length. *F, G,* Nearly full shoulder motion was obtained postoperatively.

## REFERENCES

1. Ada, J.R.; Miller, M.E. Scapular fractures—analysis of 113 cases. Clin Orthop 269:174–180, 1991.
2. Adams, C.F. The Genuine Works of Hippocrates. Baltimore, Williams & Wilkins, 1939.
3. Alldredge, R.H. Surgical treatment of acromioclavicular dislocation. Clin Orthop 63:262–263, 1969.
4. Allman, F.L. Fractures and ligamentous injuries of the clavicle and its articulation. J Bone Joint Surg Am 49:774–784, 1967.
5. Andersen, K.; Jensen, P.O.; Lauritzen, J. Treatment of clavicular fractures. Figure-of-eight bandage versus a simple sling. Acta Orthop Scand 57:71–74, 1987.
6. Ballmer, F.T.; Gerber, C. Coracoclavicular screw fixation for unstable fractures of the distal clavicle. A report of five cases. J Bone Joint Surg Br 73:291–294, 1991.
7. Ballmer, F.T.; Lambert, S.M.; Hertel, R. Decortication and plate osteosynthesis for nonunion of the clavicle. J Shoulder Elbow Surg 7:581–585, 1998.

8. Bankart, A.S.B. An operation for recurrent dislocation (subluxation) of the sternoclavicular joint. Br J Surg 26:320–323, 1938.

9. Bargar, W.L.; Marcus, R.E.; Ittleman, F.P. Late thoracic outlet syndrome secondary to pseudarthrosis of the clavicle. J Trauma 24:857–859, 1984.

10. Barth, E.; Hagen, R. Surgical treatment of dislocations of the sternoclavicular joint. Acta Orthop Scand 54:746–747, 1983.

11. Basmajian, J.V. The surgical anatomy and function of the arm-trunk mechanism. Surg Clin North Am 43:1471–1482, 1963.

12. Basom, W.C.; Breck, L.W.; Herz, J.R. Dual grafts for non-union of the clavicle. South Med J 40:898–899, 1947.

13. Bateman, J.E. Nerve injuries about the shoulder in sports. J Bone Joint Surg Am 49:785–792, 1967.

14. Bateman, J.E. Neurovascular syndromes related to the clavicle. Clin Orthop 58:75–82, 1967.

15. Bateman, J.E. The Shoulder and Neck. Philadelphia, W.B. Saunders, 1978.

16. Beardon, J.M.; Hughston, J.C.; Whatley, G.S. Acromioclavicular dislocation: Method of treatment. Am J Sports Med 1:5–17, 1973.

17. Beatty, O.A. Chylothorax: Case report. J Thorac Surg 6:221–225, 1936.

18. Bechtol, C.O. Biomechanics of the shoulder. Clin Orthop 146:37–41, 1980.

19. Bennett, E.H. The mechanism of fractures of clavicle. Ann Surg 1:293–303, 1885.

20. Berkheiser, E.J. Old ununited clavicular fractures in the adult. Surg Gynecol Obstet 64:1064, 1937.

21. Billington, R.W. A new (plaster yoke) dressing for fracture of the clavicle. South Med J 24:667–670, 1931.

22. Boehme, D.; Curtis, R.J., Jr.; DeHaan, J.T.; et al. Non-union of fractures of the mid-shaft of the clavicle. Treatment with a modified Hagie intramedullary pin and autologous bone-grafting. J Bone Joint Surg Am 73:1219–1226, 1991.

23. Booth, C.M.; Roper, B.A. Chronic dislocation of the sternoclavicular joint: An operative repair. Clin Orthop 140:17–20, 1979.

24. Bosch, U.; Skutek, M.; Peters, G.; Tscherne, H. Extension osteotomy in malunited clavicular fractures. J Shoulder Elbow Surg 7:402–405, 1998.

25. Bossart, P.J.; Joyce, S.M.; Manaster, B.J.; Packer, S.M. Lack of efficiency of weighted radiographs in diagnosing acute acromioclavicular separation. Ann Emerg Med 17:47–51, 1988.

26. Böstman, O.; Manninen, M.; Pihlajamaki, H. Complications of plate fixation in fresh displaced midclavicular fractures. J Trauma 43:778–783, 1997.

27. Bosworth, B.M. Acromioclavicular separation: A new method of repair. Surg Gynecol Obstet 73:866–871, 1941.

28. Boyer, M.I.; Axelrod, T.S. Atrophic nonunion of the clavicle. Treatment by compression plate, lag-screw fixation and bone graft. J Bone Joint Surg Br 79:301–303, 1997.

29. Bradbury, N.; Hutchinson, J.; Hahn, D.; Colton, C.L. Clavicular nonunion. 31/32 healed after plate fixation and bone grafting. Acta Orthop Scand 67:367–370, 1996.

30. Branch, T.P.; Burdette, H.L.; Shahriari, A.S.; et al. The role of the acromioclavicular ligaments and the effect of distal clavicle resection. Am J Sports Med 24:293–297, 1996.

31. Braun, R.M. Iatrogenic compression of the thoracic outlet. Johns Hopkins Med J 145:94–97, 1979.

32. Breasthead, J.H. The Edwin Smith Surgical Papyrus: Published in Facsimile and Hieroglyphic Transliteration and Commentary in Two Volumes, Vol. 1. Chicago. University of Chicago Press, 1930.

33. Breck, L.W. Partially threaded round pins with oversized threads for intramedullary fixation of the clavicle and the forearm bones. Clin Orthop 11:227–229, 1958.

34. Breitner, S.; Wirth, C.J. Resection of the acromial and sternal ends of the clavicle. Z Orthop 125:363–368, 1987.

35. Brewer, L.A.I. Surgical management of lesions of the thoracic duct. Am J Surg 90:210–227, 1955.

36. Brighton, C.T.; Pollack, S.R. Treatment of recalcitrant non-union with a capacitively coupled electrical field. A preliminary report. J Bone Joint Surg Am 67:577–585, 1985.

37. Bronz, G.; Heim, D.; Pusterla, C.; et al. Die stabile Claviculaosteo-synthese. Unfallheilkunde 84:319–321, 1981.

38. Brooks, A.L.; Henning, G.D. Injury to the proximal clavicular epiphysis. J Bone Joint Surg Am 54:1347–1348, 1972.

39. Brown, J.E. Anterior sternoclavicular dislocation—a method of repair. Am J Orthop 31:184–189, 1961.

40. Burman, M.; Grossman, S.; Rosenak, M. The migration of a fracture-transfixing pin from the humerus into the mediastinum. AJR Am J Roentgenol 76:1061, 1956.

41. Burri, C.; Neugebauer, R. Carbon fiber replacement of the ligaments of the shoulder girdle and the treatment of lateral instability of the ankle joint. Clin Orthop 196:112–117, 1985.

42. Burrows, H.J. Tenodesis of subclavius in the treatment of recurrent dislocation of the sterno-clavicular joint. J Bone Joint Surg Br 33:240–243, 1951.

43. Caldwell, G.D. Treatment of complete permanent acromioclavicular dislocation by surgical arthrodesis. J Bone Joint Surg 25:368–374, 1943.

44. Campbell, E.; Howard, W.P.; Burkland, C.W. Clinical notes, suggestions and new instruments. JAMA 139:91–92, 1949.

45. Capicotto, P.N.; Heiple, K.G.; Wilber, J.H. Midshaft clavicle nonunions treated with intramedullary Steinmann pin fixation and onlay bone graft. J Orthop Trauma 8:88–93, 1994.

46. Caspi, I.; Ezra, E; Oliver, S; et al. Treatment of avulsed clavicle and recurrent subluxations of the ipsilateral shoulder by dynamic fixation. J Trauma 27:94–95, 1986.

47. Cayford, E.H.; Tees, F.J. Traumatic aneurysm of the subclavian artery as a late complication of fractured clavicle. Can Med Assoc J 25:450–452, 1931.

48. Chan, K.Y.; Jupiter, J.B.; Leffert, R.D.; Marti, R. Clavicle malunion. J Shoulder Elbow Surg 8:287–290, 1999.

49. Clark, R.L.; Milgram, J.W.; Yawn, D.H. Fatal aortic perforation and cardiac tamponade due to a Kirschner wire migrating from the right sternoclavicular joint. South Med J 67:316–318, 1974.

50. Codman, E.A. The Shoulder: Rupture of the Supraspinatus Tendon and Other Lesions in or about the Subacromial Bursa. Boston, Thomas Todd, 1989.

51. Connolly, J.F. Electrical treatment of nonunions: Its use and abuse in 100 consecutive fractures. Orthop Clin North Am 15:89–106, 1984.

52. Connolly, J.F.; Dehne, R. Nonunion of the clavicle and thoracic outlet syndrome. J Trauma 29:1127–1133, 1989.

53. Conwell, H.E. Fractures of the clavicle: A simple fixation dressing with a summary of the treatment and results attained in ninety-two cases. JAMA 90.838–839, 1928.

54. Cook, T.W. Reduction and external fixation of fracture of the clavicle in recumbency. J Bone Joint Surg Am 36:878–879, 1954.

55. Copeland, S.M. Total resection of the clavicle. Am J Surg 72:280–281, 1946.

56. Costa, M.C.; Robbs, J.V. Nonpenetrating subclavian artery trauma. J Vasc Surg 8:72–75, 1988.

57. Craig, E.V. Fractures of the clavicle. In: Rockwood CA, Jr.; Matsen, F.A., III, eds. The Shoulder, Vol. 1. Philadelphia, W.B. Saunders, 1990, pp. 367–412.

58. Dahl, E. Follow-up after coracoclavicular ligament prosthesis for acromioclavicular joint dislocation. Acta Chir Scand Suppl 506:96, 1981.

59. Dameron, T.B. Letter to the editor. J Bone Joint Surg Am 71:1272, 1989.

60. Dash, U.N.; Handler, D. A case of compression of subclavian vessels by a fractured clavicle treated by excision of the first rib. J Bone Joint Surg Am 42:798–799, 1960.

61. Daskalakis, E.; Bouhoutsos, A. A subclavian and axillary vein compression of musculoskeletal origin. Br J Surg 67:573–576, 1980.

62. Davids, P.H.P.; Luitse, J.S.K.; Strating, P.; Vanderhart, C.P. Operative treatment for delayed union and nonunion of midshaft clavicular fractures: AO reconstruction plate fixation and early mobilization. J Trauma 40:985–986, 1996.

63. Day, L. Electrical stimulation in the treatment of ununited fractures. Clin Orthop 161:54–57, 1981.

64. DeBakey, M.E.; Beall, A.C., Jr.; Wukasch, D.C. Recent developments in vascular surgery with particular reference to orthopedics. Am J Surg 109:134–142, 1965.

65. Denham, R.H.; Dingley, A.F. Epiphyseal separation of the medial end of the clavicle. J Bone Joint Surg Am 49:1179–1183, 1967.

66. DePalma, A.F. Surgery of the Shoulder, 3rd ed. Philadelphia. J.B. Lippincott, 1983.

67. Deshmukh, A.; Wilson, D.; Zilberfarb, J.; Perlmutter, G. The biomechanics of acromioclavicular instability. Harvard Orthop J 1:115–118, 1999.

68. Dickson, J.W. Death following fractured clavicle. BMJ 2:266, 1952.

69. Dugdale, T.W.; Fulkerson, J.P. Pneumothorax complicating a closed fracture of the clavicle. A case report. Clin Orthop 221:212–214, 1987.

70. Dupuytren, G. Fracture de la clavicule en plusieurs fragments par cause indirecte. Gaz Hopitaux 4:315, 1831.

71. Dupuytren, G. On injuries and disease of bone. Selections from the collected edition of the clinical lectures of Baron Dupuytren, 1847.

72. Dvir, Z.; Berme, N. The shoulder complex in elevation of the arm: A mechanism approach. J Biomech 11:219–225, 1978.

73. Ebraheim, N.A.; Pearlstein, S.R.; Savolaine, E.R.; et al. Scapulothoracic dissociation (closed avulsion of the scapula, subclavian artery, and brachial plexus: A newly recognized variant, a new classification, and a review of the literature and treatment options. J Orthop Trauma 1:18–23, 1987.

74. Ebraheim, N.A.; An, H.S.; Jackson, W.T.; et al. Scapulothoracic dissociation. J Bone Joint Surg Am 70:428–432, 1988.

75. Ebraheim, N.A.; Mekhail, A.O.; Darwich, M. Open reduction and internal fixation with bone grafting of clavicular nonunion. J Trauma 42:701–704, 1997.

76. Edeland, H.G.; Zachrisson, H.E. Fracture of the scapular notch associated with lesion of the suprascapular nerve. Acta Orthop Scand 46:758, 1975.

77. Edvardsen, P.; Odegard, O. Treatment of posttraumatic clavicular pseudoarthrosis. Acta Orthop Scand 48:456–457, 1977.

78. Edwards, D.J.; Kavanagh, T.G.; Flannery, M.C. Fractures of the distal clavicle: A case for fixation. Injury 23:44–46, 1992.

79. Elkin, D.C.; Cooper, F.W. Resection of the clavicle in vascular surgery. J Bone Joint Surg Am 28:117–119, 1946.

80. Elliot, A.C. Tripartite injury of the clavicle: A case report. S Afr Med J 70:115, 1986.

81. Elting, J.J. Retrosternal dislocation of the clavicle. Arch Surg 104:35–37, 1972.

82. Enker, S.H.; Murthy, K.K. Brachial plexus compression by excessive callus formation secondary to a fractured clavicle: A case report. Mt Sinai J Med 37:678–682, 1972.

83. Enneking, T.J.M.Q.; Hartlief, M.T.; Fontijne, W.P.J. Rushpin fixation for midshaft clavicular nonunions. Good results in 13/14 cases. Acta Orthop Scand 70:514–516, 1999.

84. Erichsen, J. Clinical lecture on a case of comminuted fracture of the clavicle with compression of the subclavian vein by one of the fragments. BMJ 1:637–638, 1873.

85. Eskola, A.; Vainionpaa, S.; Patiala, H.; Rokkanen, P. Outcome of operative treatment in fresh lateral clavicular fracture. Ann Chir Gynaecol 76:167–169, 1987.

86. Eskola, A.; Vainionpaa, S.; Myllynen, P.; et al. Outcome of clavicular fracture in 89 patients. Arch Orthop Trauma Surg 105:337–338, 1986.

87. Eskola, A.; Vainionpaa, S.; Myllynen, P.; et al. Surgery for ununited clavicular fracture. Acta Orthop Scand 57:366–367, 1986.

88. Fairbank, H.A. Cranio-cleido-dysostosis. J Bone Joint Surg Br 31:608–617, 1949.

89. Falconer, M.A.; Weddell, G. Costoclavicular compression of the subclavian artery and vein: Relation to the scalenus anticus syndrome. Lancet 1:539–543, 1943.

90. Falstie-Jensen, S.; Mikkelsen, P. Pseudodislocation of the acromioclavicular joint. J Bone Joint Surg Br 64:368–369, 1982.

91. Flatow, E.L. Arthroscopic resection of the outer end of the clavicle from a superior approach: A critical quantitative radiographic assessment of bone removal. Arthroscopy 8:55–64, 1992.

92. Flatow, E.L. The biomechanics of the acromioclavicular, sternoclavicular and scapulothoracic joints. Instr Course Lect 42:237–245, 1993.

93. Fowler, A.W. Fracture of the clavicle. J Bone Joint Surg Br 44:440, 1962.

94. Fowler, A.W. Treatment of the fractured clavicle. Lancet 1:46, 1968.

95. Freeland, A. Unstable adult midclavicular fracture. Orthopedics 13:1279–1281, 1990.

96. Fukuda, K.; Craig, E.V.; An, K.; et al. Biomechanical study of the ligamentous system of the acromioclavicular joint. J Bone Joint Surg Am 68:434–440, 1986.

97. Fullerton, L.R. Recurrent third degree acromioclavicular joint separation after failure of a Dacron ligament prosthesis. A case report. Am J Sports Med 18:106–107, 1990.

98. Gearen, P.F.; Petty, W. Panclavicular dislocation. Report of a case. J Bone Joint Surg Am 64:454–455, 1982.

99. Ghormley, R.K.; Black, J.R.; Cherry, J.H. Ununited fracture of the clavicle. Am J Surg 51:343–349, 1941.

100. Goldberg, J.; Bruce, W.J.M.; Sonnabend, D.H.; Walsh, W.R. Type 2 fractures of the distal clavicle: A new surgical approach. J Shoulder Elbow Surg 6:380–382, 1997.

101. Goss, T.P. Fractures of the glenoid cavity: Current concepts review. J Bone Joint Surg Am 74:299–305, 1992.

102. Goss, T.P. Double disruptions of the superior shoulder suspensory complex. J Orthop Trauma 7:99–106, 1993.

103. Goss, T.P. Fractures of the scapula: Diagnosis and treatment. In: Iannotti, J.P.; Williams, G.R., eds. Disorders of the Shoulder: Diagnosis and Management. Philadelphia, Lippincott Williams & Wilkins, 1999, pp. 597–637.

104. Gryska, P.F. Major vascular injuries: Principles of management in selected cases of arterial and venous injury. N Engl J Med 266:381–385, 1962.

105. Guilfoil, P.H.; Christiansen, T. An unusual vascular complication of a fractured clavicle. JAMA 200:72–73, 1967.

106. Guillemin, A. Dechirure de la veine sous-claviere par fracture fermee de la clavicule. Bull Mem Soc Nat Chir 56:302–304, 1930.

107. Gurd, F.B. The treatment of complete dislocation of the outer end of the clavicle: A hitherto undescribed operation. Ann Surg 113:1094–1097, 1941.

108. Gurd, F.B. Surplus parts of the skeleton: A recommendation for the excision of certain portions as a means of shortening the period of disability following trauma. Am J Surg 74:705–720, 1947.

109. Hansky, B.; Murray, E.; Minami, K.; Korfer, R. Delayed brachial plexus paralysis due to subclavian pseudoaneurysm after clavicle fracture. Eur J Cardiothorac Surg 7:497–498, 1993.

110. Hardegger, F.H.; Simspon, L.A.; Weber, B.G. The operative treatment of scapular fractures. J Bone Joint Surg Br 66:725, 1984.

111. Haug, W. Retention einer seltenen Sternoclavicular-Luxationsfractur Mittls modifizierter Y-Platte der AO. Aktuelle Traumatol 16:39–40, 1986.

112. Hawley, G.W. A method of treating fracture of the clavicle. J Bone Joint Surg Br 19:232, 1937.

113. Heim, U.; Pfeiffer, K.M. Internal Fixation of Small Fractures: Technique Recommended by the AO-ASIF Group, 3rd ed. New York, Springer-Verlag, 1987.

114. Heinig, C.F. Retrosternal dislocation of the clavicle: Early recognition, x-ray diagnosis, and management. J Bone Joint Surg Am 50:830, 1968.

115. Heppenstall, R.B. Fractures and dislocations of the distal clavicle. Orthop Clin North Am 6:477–486, 1975.

116. Herscovici, D., Jr.; Fiennes, A.G.T.W.; Allgower, M.; Ruedi, T. The floating shoulder: Ipsilateral clavicle and scapular neck fractures. J Bone Joint Surg Br 74:362–364, 1992.

117. Herscovici, D., Jr.; Sanders, R.; Dipasquale, T.; Gregory, P. Injuries of the shoulder girdle. Clin Orthop 318:54–60, 1995.

118. Hessman, M.; Kirschner, R.; Baumgaertel, F.; et al. Treatment of unstable distal clavicular fractures with and without lesions of the acromioclavicular joint. Injury 27:47–52, 1996.

119. Hill, J.M.; McGuire, M.H.; Crosby, L.A. Closed treatment of displaced middle-third fractures of the clavicle gives poor results. J Bone Joint Surg Br 79:537–539, 1997.

120. Howard, F.M.; Shafer, S.J. Injuries to the clavicle with neurovascular complications: A study of 14 cases. J Bone Joint Surg Am 67:1335–1346, 1965.

121. Ideberg, R.; Grevsten, S.; Larsson, S. Epidemiology of scapular fractures: Incidence and classification of 338 fractures. Acta Orthop Scand 66:395–397, 1995.

122. Inman, V.T.; Saunders, J.B.; De, C.M. Observations of the function of the shoulder joint. J Bone Joint Surg Am 26:1–30, 1944.

123. Inman, V.T.; Saunders, J.B. Observations on the function of the clavicle. Calif Med 65:158–166, 1946.

124. Iqbal, O. Axillary artery thrombosis associated with fracture of the clavicle. Med J Malaya 26:68–70, 1971.

125. Jablon, M.; Sutker, A; Post, M. Irreducible fracture of the middle third of the clavicle: Report of a case. J Bone Joint Surg Am 61:296–298, 1979.

126. Jacobs, B.; Wade, P.A. Acromioclavicular joint injury: An end-result study. J Bone Joint Surg 46:475–486, 1966.

127. Javid, H. Vascular injuries of the neck. Clin Orthop 28:70–78, 1963.

128. Jit, I.; Kulkarni, M. Times of appearance and fusion of epiphysis at the medial end of the clavicle. Indian J Med Res 64:773–781, 1976.

129. Johnson, E.W.; Collins, H.R. Nonunion of the clavicle. Arch Surg 87:963–966, 1963.

130. Joukainen, J.; Karaharju, E. Pseudoarthrosis of the clavicle. Acta Orthop Scand 48:550–551, 1977.

131. Jupiter, J.B.; Leffert, R.D. Non-union of the clavicle. Associated complications and surgical management. J Bone Joint Surg Am 69:753–760, 1987.

132. Kanoksikarin, S.; Wearne, W.M. Fracture and retrosternal dislocation of the clavicle. Aust N Z J Surg 48:95–96, 1978.

133. Kappakas, G.S.; McMaster, J.H. Repair of acromioclavicular separation using a Dacron prosthesis graft. Clin Orthop 131:247–251, 1978.

134. Karaharju, E.; Joukainen, J.; Peltonen, J. Treatment of pseudarthrosis of the clavicle. Injury 13:400–403, 1981.

135. Katz, R.; Landman, J.; Dulitzky, F.; Bar-Ziv, J. Fracture of the clavicle in the newborn: An ultrasound diagnosis. J Ultrasound Med 7:21–23, 1988.

136. Katznelson, A.; Nerubay, J.; Oliver, S. Dynamic fixation of the avulsed clavicle. J Trauma 16:841–844, 1976.

137. Kay, S.P.; Eckardt, J.J. Brachial plexus palsy secondary to clavicular nonunion: Case report and literature survey. Clin Orthop 206:219–222, 1986.

138. Kennedy, J.C. Complete dislocation of the acromioclavicular joint: 14 years later. J Trauma 8:311–318, 1968.

139. Kennedy, J.C.; Cameron, H. Complete dislocation of the acromioclavicular joint. J Bone Joint Surg Br 36:202–208, 1954.

140. Key, J.A.; Conwell, W.H. The Management of Fractures, Dislocations, and Sprains, 5th ed. St. Louis, C.V. Mosby, 1961.

141. Ali Khan, M.A.; Lucas, H.K. Plating of fractures of the middle third of the clavicle. Injury 9:263–267, 1977.

142. Kini, M.G. A simple method of ambulatory treatment of fracture of the clavicle. J Bone Joint Surg Br 23:795–798, 1941.

143. Koelliker, F. Behandlungsergebnisse der Clavicula-pseudarthrose. Unfallchirurg 92:164–168, 1989.

144. Kona, J.; Bosse, M.J.; Staeheli, J.W.; Rosseau, R.L. Type II distal clavicle fractures: A retrospective review of surgical treatment. J Orthop Trauma 4:115–120, 1990.

145. Koss, S.D.; Goitz, H.T.; Redler, M.R.; Whitehill, R. Nonunion of a midshaft clavicle fracture associated with subclavian vein compression: A case report. Orthop Rev 28:431–434, 1989.

146. Kreisinger, V. Sur le traitement des fractures de la clavicule. Rev Chir 46:376, 1927.

147. Kremens, V.; Glauser, F. Unusual sequela following pinning of medial clavicular fracture. AJR Am J Roentgenol 76:1066–1069, 1956.

148. Kuner, E.H.; Schlickewei, W.; Mydla, F. Operative Therapie der Claviculafrakturen, Indikation, Technik, Ergebnisse. Hefte Unfallheilkunde 160:76–77, 1982.

149. Lancet. Sir Robert Peel's death [editorial]. Lancet 2:19, 1850.

150. Lancourt, J.E. Acromioclavicular dislocation with adjacent clavicular fracture in a horseback rider. Am J Sports Med 18:321–322, 1990.

151. Lange, R.H.; Noel, S.H. Traumatic lateral scapular displacement: An expanded spectrum of associated neurovascular injury. J Orthop Trauma 7:361–366, 1993.

152. Lee, H.G. Treatment of fracture of the clavicle by internal nail fixation. N Engl J Med 234:222–224, 1946.

153. Leese, G.B.; J.J.F.; Rickhos, P.; Nimmo, M. Post-traumatic axillary artery thrombosis dissolution with low-dose intra-arterial streptokinase. Injury 24:212–213, 1993.

154. Leffert, R.D.S.; H.J. Infraclavicular brachial plexus injuries. J Bone Joint Surg Br 47:9–22, 1965.

155. Lemire, L.; Rosman, M. Sternoclavicular epiphyseal separation with adjacent clavicular fracture. J Pediatr Orthop 4:118–128, 1984.

156. Lengua, F.; Nuss, J.M.; Lechner, R.; et al. Traitement des fractures de la clavicule par embrochage a foyer ferme de dedans en dehors sans va-et-vient. Rev Chir Orthop Reparatrice Appar Mot 73:377–380, 1987.

157. Leonard, J.W.; Gifford, R.W., Jr. Migration of a Kirschner wire from the clavicle into the pulmonary artery. Am J Cardiol 16:598–600, 1965.

158. Lester, C.W. The treatment of fractures of the clavicle. Ann Surg 89:600–606, 1929.

159. Leung, K.S.; Lam, T.P. Open reduction and internal fixation of ipsilateral fractures of the scapular neck and clavicle. J Bone Joint Surg Am 75:1015–1018, 1993.

160. Le Vay, D. Treatment of midclavicular fractures. Lancet 1:723, 1967.

161. Lewonowski, K.; Bassett, G.S. Complete posterior sternoclavicular epiphysial separation: A case report and review of the literature. Clin Orthop 281:84–88, 1992.

162. Lim, E.V.A.; Day, L.J. Subclavian vein thrombosis following fracture of the clavicle: A case report. Orthopedics 10:349–351, 1987.

163. Lipton, H.A.; Jupiter, J.B. Nonunion of clavicular fractures: Characteristics and surgical management. Surg Rounds Orthop July:17–25, 1988.

164. Ljunggren, A.E. Clavicular function. Acta Orthop Scand 50:261–268, 1979.

165. Lowman, C.L. Operative correction of old sternoclavicular dislocation. J Bone Joint Surg 10:740–741, 1928.

166. Lunseth, P.A.; Chapman, K.W.; Frankel, V.H. Surgical treatment of chronic dislocation of the sternoclavicular joint. J Bone Joint Surg Br 57:193–196, 1975.

167. Lusskin, R.; Weiss, C.A.; Winer, J. The role of the subclavius muscle in the subclavian vein syndrome (costoclavicular syndrome) following fracture of the clavicle. A case report with a review of the pathophysiology of the costoclavicular space. Clin Orthop 54:75–83, 1967.

168. Lyons, F.A.; Rockwood, C.A. Migration of pins used in operations on the shoulder. J Bone Joint Surg Am 72:1262–1267, 1990.

169. MacDonald, P.B.; Alexander, M.J.; Frejuk, J.; Johnson, G.E. Comprehensive functional analysis of shoulders following complete acromioclavicular separation. Am J Sports Med 16:475–480, 1988.

170. Madsen, B. Osteolysis of the acromial end of the clavicle following trauma. Br J Radiol 36:822–828, 1963.

171. Maguire, W.B. Safe and simple method of repair of recurrent dislocation of the sternoclavicular joint. J Bone Joint Surg Br 68:332, 1986.

172. Malcolm, B.W.; Ameli, F.M.; Simmons, E.H. Pneumothorax complicating a fracture of the clavicle. Can J Surg 22:84, 1979.

173. Malgaigne, J.F. A Treatise of Fractures. Philadelphia, J.B. Lippincott, 1859.

174. Manske, D.J.; Szabo, R.M. The operative treatment of mid-shaft clavicular non-unions. J Bone Joint Surg Am 67:1367–1371, 1985.

175. Marie, P.; Sainton, P. The classic: On hereditary cleido-cranial dysostosis. Clin Orthop 58:5–7, 1968.

176. Marsh, H.O.; Hazarian, E. Pseudarthrosis of the clavicle. J Bone Joint Surg Br 52:793, 1970.

177. Matry, C. Fracture de la clavicule gauche au tiers interne: Blessure de la veine sous-clav iere. Osteosynthese Bull Mem Soc Nat Chir 58:75–78, 1932.

178. Matz, S.O.; Welliver, P.S.; Welliver, D.I. Brachial plexus neuropraxia complicating a comminuted clavicle fracture in a college football player: Case report and review of the literature. Am J Sports Med 17:581–583, 1989.

179. Maunoury, G. Fracture de la clavicule compliquee de dechireure de la veine sousclav iere: Operation. Mort par hemorrhagie et entree de l'air dans les veines. Prog Med Paris 10:302, 1881.

180. Mazet, R., Jr. Migration of a Kirschner wire from the shoulder region into the lung: Report of two cases. J Bone Joint Surg Am 25:477–483, 1943.

181. McCandless, D.N.; Mobray, M.A.S. Treatment of displaced fractures of the clavicle. Sling versus figure-of-eight bandage. Practitioner 223:266–267, 1979.

182. McCaughan, J.S., Jr.; Miller, P.R. Migration of Steinmann pin from shoulder to lung. JAMA 207:1917, 1969.

183. McLaughlin, H. Trauma. Philadelphia, W.B. Saunders, 1959.

184. Meeks, R.J.; Riebel, G.D. Isolated clavicle fracture with associated pneumothorax: A case report. Am J Emerg Med 9:555–556, 1991.

185. Mehta, J.C.; Sachdev, A.; Collins, J.J. Retrosternal dislocation of the clavicle. Injury 79–83, 1973.

186. Milch, H. The rhomboid ligament in surgery of the sternoclavicular joint. J Int Coll Surg 17:41–51, 1952.

187. Miller, D.S.; Boswick, J.A., Jr. Lesions of the brachial plexus associated with fractures of the clavicle. Clin Orthop 64:144–149, 1969.

188. Miller, M.R.; Ada, J.R. Injuries to the shoulder girdle. In: Browner, B.D.; Jupiter, J.B.; Levine, A.M.; Trafton, P.G., eds. Skeletal Trauma, 1st ed. Philadelphia, W.B. Saunders, 1991, pp. 1291–1310.

189. Mital, M.A.; Aufranc, O.E. Venous occlusion following greenstick fracture of clavicle. JAMA 206:1301–1302, 1968.

190. Moore, T.O. Internal pin fixation for fracture of clavicle. Am Surg 17:580–583, 1951.

191. Moseley, H.F. The clavicle: Its anatomy and function. Clin Orthop 58:17–27, 1968.

192. Mulder, D.S.; Greenwood, F.A.H.; Brooks, C.E. Posttraumatic thoracic outlet syndrome. J Trauma 13:706–715, 1973.

193. Muller, M.E.; Thomas, R.J. Treatment of non-union in fractures of long bones. Clin Orthop 138:141–152, 1979.

194. Mullick, S. Treatment of mid-clavicular fractures. Lancet 1:499, 1967.

195. Murray, G. A method of fixation for fracture of the clavicle. J Bone Joint Surg Am 22:616–620, 1940.

196. Naidoo, P. Migration of a Kirschner wire from the clavicle into the abdominal aorta. Arch Emerg Med 8:292–295, 1991.

197. Natali, J.; Maraval, M.; Kieffer, E.; Petrovic, P. Fractures of the clavicle and injuries of the subclavian artery: Report of 10 cases. J Cardiovasc Surg (Torino) 16:541–547, 1975.

198. Neer, C.S. Nonunion of the clavicle. JAMA 172:1006–1011, 1960.

199. Neer, C.S. Fracture of the distal clavicle with detachment of the coracoclavicular ligaments in adults. J Trauma 3:99–110, 1963.

200. Neer, C.S. Fractures of the distal third of the clavicle. Clin Orthop 58:43–50, 1968.

201. Neer, C.S. Fractures about the shoulder. In: Rockwood, C.A., Jr.; Green, D.P., eds. Philadelphia, J.B. Lippincott, 1984, pp. 707–713.

202. Nelson, C.L. Repair of acromioclavicular separations with knitted Dacron graft. Clin Orthop 143:289, 1979.

203. Nettles, J.L.; Linscheid, R. Sternoclavicular dislocations. J Trauma 8:158–164, 1968.

204. Neviaser, J.S. The treatment of fractures of the clavicle. Surg Clin North Am 43:1555, 1963.

205. Neviaser, J.S. Injuries of the clavicle and its articulations. Orthop Clin North Am 11:233–237, 1980.

206. Neviaser, R.J. Injuries to the clavicle and acromioclavicular joint. Orthop Clin North Am 18:433–438, 1987.

207. Neviaser, R.J.; Neviaser, J.S.; Neviaser, T.J.; Neviaser, J.S. A simple technique for internal fixation of the clavicle: A long-term evaluation. Clin Orthop 109:103–107, 1975.

208. Ngarmukos, C.; Parkpian, V.; Patradul, A. Fixation of fractures of the midshaft of the clavicle with Kirschner wires. Results in 108 patients. J Bone Joint Surg Br 80:106–108, 1998.

209. Nicoll, E.A. Miners and mannequins. J Bone Joint Surg Br 36:171–172, 1954.

210. Nordback, I.; Markkula, H. Migration of Kirschner wire from clavicle into ascending aorta. Acta Chir Scand 151:177–179, 1985.

211. Nordqvist, A.; Petersson, C. Fracture of the body, neck or spine of the scapula. Clin Orthop 283:139, 1992.

212. Nordqvist, A.; Petersson, C.J. Shoulder injuries common in alcoholics. An analysis of 413 injuries. Acta Orthop Scand 67:364–366, 1996.

213. Nordqvist, A.; Petersson, C.J.; Redlund-Johnell, I. Mid-clavicle fractures in adults: End result study after conservative treatment. J Orthop Trauma 12:572–576, 1998.

214. Nordqvist, A.; Redlund-Johnell, I.; von Scheele, A.; Peetersson, C.J. Shortening of clavicle after fracture. Incidence and clinical significance, a 5-year follow-up of 85 patients. Acta Orthop Scand 68:349–351, 1997.

215. Nordqvist, A.; Petersson, C.; Redlund-Johnell, I. The natural course of lateral clavicle fracture: 15 (11–21) year follow-up of 110 cases. Acta Orthop Scand 64:87–91, 1993.

216. Nordqvist, A.; Petersson, C. The incidence of fractures of the clavicle. Clin Orthop 300:127–132, 1994.

217. Norrell H., Jr.; Llewellyn, R.C. Migration of a threaded Steinmann pin from an acromioclavicular joint into the spinal canal. J Bone Joint Surg Am 47:1024–1026, 1965.

218. Nowak, J.; Mallmin, H.; Larsson, S. The aetiology and epidemiology of clavicular fractures. A prospective study during a two-year period in Uppsala, Sweden. Injury 31:353–358, 2000.

219. Nuber, G.W.; Bowen, M.K. Injuries of the acromioclavicular joint and fractures of the distal clavicle. J Am Acad Orthop Surg 5:11–18, 1997.

220. Nuber, G.W.; Bowen, M.K. Disorders of the acromioclavicular joint: Pathophysiology, diagnosis, and management. In: Iannotti, J.P.; Williams, G.R., eds. Disorders of the Shoulder: Diagnosis and Management. Philadelphia, Lippincott, Williams & Wilkins, 1999, pp. 739–762.

221. Ogden, J.A. Distal clavicular physeal injury. Clin Orthop 188:68–73, 1984.

222. Ogden, J.A.; Conlogue, G.J.; Bronson, M.L. Radiology of postnatal skeletal development III. The clavicle. Skeletal Radiol 4:196, 1979.

223. Olsen, B.S.; Vaesel, M.T.; Sojbjerg, J.O. Treatment of midshaft clavicular nonunion with plate fixation and autologous bone grafting. J Shoulder Elbow Surg 4:337–344, 1995.

224. Omer, G.E. Osteotomy of the clavicle in surgical reduction of anterior sternoclavicular dislocation. J Trauma 7:584–590, 1967.

225. Oppenheim, W.L.; Davis, A.; Growdon, W.A.; et al. Clavicle fractures in the newborn. Clin Orthop 250:176–180, 1990.

226. Oreck, S.L.; Burgess, A; Levine, A. Traumatic lateral displacement of the scapula: A radiographic sign of neurovascular disruption. J Bone Joint Surg Am 66:758–763, 1984.

227. Oroko, P.K.; Buchan, M.; Winkler, A.; Kelly, I.G. Does shortening matter after clavicular fractures? Bull Hosp Jt Dis 58:6–8, 1999.

228. O'Rourke, I.C.; Middleton, R.W.D. The place and management of operative management of fractured clavicle. Injury 6:236–240, 1974.

229. Oxnard, C.E. The functional morphology of the primate shoulder as revealed by comparative anatomical, osteometric and discrimination function techniques. Am J Phys Anthropol 26:219–240, 1967.

230. Oxnard, C.E. The architecture of the shoulder in some mammals. J Morphol 126:249–290, 1968.

231. Packer, B.D. Conservative treatment of fracture of the clavicle. J Bone Joint Surg Br 26:770–774, 1944.

232. Pannier, R.; Daems, J. A propos d'un cas de corps etranger intrapulmonaire apres osteosynthese de la clavicule. Acta Tuberc Belg 40:360–362, 1949.

233. Parkes, J.C.; Deland, J.T. A three-part distal clavicle fracture. J Trauma 23:437–438, 1983.

234. Pate, J.W.; Wilhite, J.L. Migration of a foreign body from the sternoclavicular joint to the heart: A case report. Am Surg 35:448–449, 1969.

235. Penn, I. The vascular complications of fractures of the clavicle. J Trauma 4:819, 1964.

236. Perry, B.F. An improved clavicle pin. Am J Surg 112:143–144, 1966.

237. Peters, G.; Bosch, U.; Tscherne, H. Die Verlangerungsosteotomie bei fehlverheilter Kalvikulafractur. Unfallchirurg 100:270–273, 1997.

238. Pipkin, G. Tardy shoulder hand syndrome following united fracture of the clavicle. J Missouri State Med Assoc 48:643–646, 1951.

239. Piterman, L. The fractured clavicle. Aust Fam Physician 11:614, 1982.

240. Poigenfurst, J.; Rappold, G.; Fischer, W. Plating of fresh clavicular fractures: Results of 122 operations. Injury 23:237–241, 1992.

241. Post, M. Current concepts in the treatment of fractures of the clavicle. Clin Orthop 245:89–101, 1989.

242. Pridie, K. Dislocation of acromio-clavicular and sterno-clavicular joints. J Bone Joint Surg Br 41:429, 1959.

243. Prime, H.T.; Doig, S.G.; Hooper, J.C. Retrosternal dislocation of the clavicle. A case report. Am J Sports Med 19:92–93, 1991.

244. Pyper, J.B. Non-union of fractures of the clavicle. Injury 9:268–270, 1977.

245. Quesada, F. Technique for the roentgen diagnosis of fractures of the clavicle. Surg Gynecol Obstet 42:424–428, 1926.

246. Quigley, T.B. The management of simple fractures of the clavicle. N Engl J Med 243:286–290, 1950.

247. Quinn, S.F.; Glass, T.A. Posttraumatic osteolysis of the clavicle. South Med J 76:307–308, 1983.

248. Redmond, A.D. Letter to the editor. Injury 13:352, 1982.

249. Reichenbacher, D.; Siebler, G. [Early post-traumatic plexus lesions: A rare complication after clavicle fractures.] Unfallchirurg 13:91–92, 1987.

250. Reid, J.; Kennedy, J. Direct fracture of clavicle with symptoms simulating cervical rib. BMJ 2:608–609, 1925.

251. Reimer, B.L.; Butterfield, S.L.; Daffner, R.H.; O'Keeffe, R.M., Jr. The abduction lordotic view of the clavicle: A new technique for radiographic visualization. J Orthop Trauma 5:392–394, 1991.

252. Rey-Baltar, E.; Errazu, D. Unusual outcome of Steinmann wire: Case of fractured clavicle. Arch Surg 89:1024–1025, 1964.

253. Rikli, D.; Regazzoni, P.; Renner, N. The unstable shoulder girdle: Early functional treatment utilizing open reduction and internal fixation. J Orthop Trauma 9:93–97, 1995.

254. Ring, D.; Barrick, W.T.; Jupiter, J.B. Recalcitrant nonunion. Clin Orthop 340:181–189, 1997.

255. Ring, D.; Jupiter, J.B. Ununited fractures of the clavicle: Treatment with a sculptured corticocancellous iliac crest autogenous bone graft and plate fixation. Techn Hand Upper Extremity Surg 2000 (in press).

256. Robinson, C.M. Fractures of the clavicle in the adult. J Bone Joint Surg Br 80:476–484, 1998.

257. Rockwood, C.A., Jr. Fractures of the outer clavicle in children and adults. J Bone Joint Surg Br 64:642, 1982.

258. Rockwood, C.A. Fractures and dislocations of the ends of the clavicle, scapula, and glenohumeral joint. In: Rockwood, C.A.; Wilkins, K.E.; King, R.E., eds. Fractures in Children. Philadelphia, J.B. Lippincott, 1984, pp. 624–681.

259. Rockwood, C.A. Disorders of the acromioclavicular joint. In: Rockwood, C.A.; Matsen, F.A., eds. The Shoulder. Philadelphia, W.B. Saunders, 1985, pp. 413–476.

260. Roper, B.A.; Levack, B. The surgical treatment of acromioclavicular dislocations. J Bone Joint Surg Br 64:597–599, 1982.

261. Rowe, C.R. An atlas of anatomy and treatment of midclavicular fractures. Clin Orthop 58:29–42, 1968.

262. Rubenstein, J.D.; Ebraheim, N.A.; Kellam, J.F. Traumatic scapu-lothoracic dissociation. Radiology 157:297–298, 1985.

263. Rumball, K.M.; Da Silva, V.F.; Preston, D.N.; Carruthers, C.C. Brachial-plexus injury after clavicular fracture: Case report and literature review. Can J Surg 34:264–266, 1991.

264. Rush, L.V.; Rush, H.L. Technique of longitudinal pin fixation in fractures of the clavicle and jaw. Miss Doctor 27:332–336, 1949.

265. Sadiq, S.; Doyle, J. Double plating technique for clavicle fractures, non-union/malunion. Injury 30:559, 1999.

266. Sakellarides, H. Pseudarthrosis of the clavicle: A report of twenty cases. J Bone Joint Surg Am 43:130–138, 1961.

267. Salter, E.G.; Nasca, R.J.; Shelley, B.S. Anatomical observations on the acromioclavicular joint and supporting ligaments. Am J Sports Med 15.199–206, 1987.

268. Sankarankutty, M.T.; B.W. Fractures of the clavicle. Injury 7:101–106, 1975.

269. Sayre, L.A. A simple dressing for fracture of the clavicle. Am Pract 4:1, 1871.

270. Scarpa, F.J.; Levy, R.M. Pulmonary embolism complicating clavicle fracture. Conn Med 43:771–773, 1979.

271. Schuind, F.; Pay-Pay, E.; Andrianne, Y.; et al. External fixation of the clavicle for fracture or non-union in adults. J Bone Joint Surg Am 70:692–695, 1988.

272. Schwarz, N.; Hocker, K. Osteosynthesis of irreducible fractures of the clavicle with 2.7-mm ASIF plates. J Trauma 33:179–183, 1992.

273. Seddon, H.J. Nerve lesions complicating certain closed bone injuries. JAMA 135:691–694, 1947.

274. Shen, W.J.; Liu, T.J.; Shen, Y.S. Plate fixation of fresh displaced midshaft clavicle fractures. Injury 30:497–500, 1999.

275. Shih, J.-S.; Chao, E.-K.; Chang, C.-H. Subclavian pseudoaneurysm after clavicle fracture—a case report. Taiwan Yi Xue Hui Za Zhi 82:332–335, 1983.

276. Siffre, A. Thrombose post-traumatique de l'artere sous-claviere gauche. Lyon Chir 51:479–481, 1956.

277. Silloway, K.A.; McLaughlin, R.E.; Edlich, R.C.; Edlich, R.F. Clavicular fractures and acromioclavicular joint injuries in lacrosse: Preventable injuries. J Emerg Med 3:117–121, 1985.

278. Simpson, N.S.; Jupiter, J.B. Clavicular nonunion and malunion: Evaluation and surgical management. J Am Acad Orthop Surg 4:1–8, 1996.

279. Solheim, L.F.; Roaas, A. Compression of the suprascapular nerve after fracture of the scapular notch. Acta Orthop Scand 49:338, 1978.

280. Spar, I. Total claviculectomy for pathological fractures. Clin Orthop 129:236–237, 1977.

281. Speed, K. A Textbook of Fractures and Dislocations, 4th ed. Philadelphia, Lea & Febiger, 1942.

282. Stanley, D.; Norris, S.H. Recovery following fractures of the clavicle treated conservatively. Injury 19.162–164, 1988.

283. Steinberg, I. Subclavian vein thrombosis associated with fractures of the clavicle: Report of two cases. N Engl J Med 264:686–688, 1961.

284. Stone, P.W.; Lord, J.W., Jr. The clavicle and its relation to trauma to the subclavian artery and vein. Am J Surg 89:834–839, 1955.

285. Storen, H. Old clavicular pseudarthrosis with late appearing neuralgias and vasomotoric disturbances cured by operation. Acta Chir Scand 94:187, 1946.

286. Sturm, J.T.; Strate, R.G.; Mowlem, A.; et al. Blunt trauma to the subclavian artery. Surg Gynecol Obstet 138:915–918, 1974.

287. Taft, T.N.; Wilson, F.C.; Oglesby, J.W. Dislocation of the acromio-clavicular joint: An end-result study. J Bone Joint Surg Am 69:1045–1051, 1987.

288. Taylor, A.R. Some observations on fractures of the clavicle. Proc R Soc Med 62:33–34, 1969.

289. Taylor, A.R. Non-union of fractures of the clavicle: A review of thirty-one cases. J Bone Joint Surg Br 51:568–569, 1974.

290. Taylor, W. Traumatic aneurysm of the left subclavian artery produced by fracture of the clavicle. Ann Surg 38:638–651, 1903.

291. Telford, E.D. Pressure at the cervico-brachial junction: An operative and anatomical study. J Bone Joint Surg Br 30:249–265, 1948.

292. Thomas, C.B., Jr.; Friedman, R.J. Ipsilateral sternoclavicular dislocation and clavicular fracture. J Orthop Trauma 3:355–357, 1989.

293. Thompson, A.G.; Butten, R.L. The application of rigid internal fixation to the treatment of non-union and delayed union using the AO technique. Injury 8:188–198, 1976.

294. Tibone, J.; Sellers, R.; Tonino, P. Strength testing after third degree acromioclavicular dislocations. Am J Sports Med 20:328–331, 1992.

295. Todd, T.W.; D'Errico, J., Jr. The clavicular epiphysis. Am J Anat 41:25–50, 1928.

296. Tossy, J.D.; Mead, N.C.; Sigmond, H.M. Acromioclavicular separa-tions: Useful and practical classification for treatment. Clin Orthop 28:111–119, 1963.

297. Tregonning, G.; Macnab, I. Post-traumatic pseudarthrosis of the clavicle. J Bone Joint Surg Br 58:264, 1976.

298. Tristan, T.A.; Daughtridge, T.G. Migration of a metallic pin from the humerus into the lung. N Engl J Med 270:987, 1964.

299. Trynin, A.H. The Bohler clavicular splint in the treatment of clavicular injuries. J Bone Joint Surg 19:417–423, 1937.

300. Tse, D.H.W.; Slabaugh, P.B.; Carlson, P.A. Injury to the axillary artery by a closed fracture of the clavicle. A case report. J Bone Joint Surg Am 62.1372–1374, 1980.

301. Urist, M.R. Complete dislocations of the acromioclavicular joint: The nature of the traumatic lesion and effective methods of treatment with an analysis of forty-one cases. J Bone Joint Surg 28:813–837, 1946.

302. Van Vlack, H.G. Comminuted fracture of the clavicle with pressure on brachial plexus. J Bone Joint Surg 22:446–447, 1940.

303. Walsh, W.M.; Peterson, D.A.; Shelton, G.; Newman, R.D. Shoulder strength following acromioclavicular injury. Am J Sports Med 13:153–158, 1985.

304. Waskowitz, W.J. Disruption of the sternoclavicular joint: An analysis and review. Am J Orthop 3:176–179, 1961.

305. Weaver, J.K.; Dunn, H.K. Treatment of acromioclavicular injuries, especially complete acromioclavicular separation. J Bone Joint Surg Am 54:1187–1194, 1972.

306. Webber, M.C.B.; Haines, J.F. The treatment of lateral clavicle fractures. Injury 31:175–179, 2000.

307. Weinberg, B.; Seife, B.; Alonso, P. The apical oblique view of the clavicle: Its usefulness in neonatal and childhood trauma. Skeletal Radiol 20:201–203, 1991.

308. Weiner, D.S.; O'Dell, H.W. Fractures of the first rib associated with injuries to the clavicle. J Trauma 9:412–422, 1989.

309. White, R.R.A.; P.S.; Kristiansen, T. Adult clavicle fractures: Rela-tionship between mechanism of injury and healing. Orthop Trans 13:514–515, 1989.

310. Wilkins, R.M.; Johnston, R.M. Ununited fractures of the clavicle. J Bone Joint Surg Am 65:774–778, 1983.

311. Wood, V.E. The results of total claviculectomy. Clin Orthop 207:186–190, 1986.

312. Wu, C.C.; Shih, C.H.; Chen, W.J.; Tai, C.L. Treatment of clavicular aseptic nonunion: Comparison of plating and intramedullary nailing techniques. J Trauma 45:512–516, 1998.

313. Wurtz, L.D.; Lyons, F.A.; Rockwood, C.A., Jr. Fracture of the middle third of the clavicle and dislocation of the acromioclavicular joint: A report of four cases. J Bone Joint Surg Am 74:133–137, 1992.

314. Yates, A.G. Complications of fractures of the clavicle. Injury 7:189–193, 1976.

315. Yates, A.G.; Guest, D. Cerebral embolism due to an ununited fracture of the clavicle and subclavian thrombosis. Lancet 2:225, 1928.

316. Zaslav, K.R.; Ray, S.; Neer, C.S., 2nd. Conservative management of a displaced medial clavicular physeal injury in an adolescent male. A case report and literature review. Am J Sports Med 17:833–836, 1989.

317. Zdravkovic, D.; Damholt, V.V. Comminuted and severely displaced fractures of the scapula. Acta Orthop Scand 45:60, 1974.

318. Zenni, E.J., Jr.; Krieg, J.K.; Rosen, M.J. Open reduction and internal fixation of clavicular fractures. J Bone Joint Surg Am 63:147–151, 1981.

# Lower Extremity

SECTION EDITOR

**Peter G. Trafton, M.D.**

# CHAPTER 46

# Hip Dislocations

James A. Goulet, M.D.
Paul E. Levin, M.D.

Dislocations of the hip encompass a spectrum of injuries with considerable potential for long-term disability and rapidly progressive joint degeneration. Dislocation of the hip requires massive force. Associated hip region injuries are common, and must be sought. In addition to the evident femoral head dislocation, associated injuries may include fractures of the femoral head, the femoral neck, the acetabulum, or a combination of these. Small cartilaginous or osseous fragments may remain in the joint space, preventing a congruous reduction. In addition, the vascular supply to the femoral head may be irreversibly damaged at the time of the injury. These associated injuries greatly compromise the likelihood of re-attaining a normally functioning hip joint. Sciatic nerve injuries and knee or other lower extremity trauma also affect management and outcome of patients with hip dislocations

Reports of patients with hip dislocations first appeared in the medical literature in the second half of the 19th century, prior to Roentgen's discovery of x-rays. Subsequent cadaveric studies defined the various anatomic injuries associated with hip dislocations.[1, 9, 10, 175] The first large clinical series of patients with hip dislocations was published in 1938 by Funsten and co-workers, who noted that most of the reported dislocations were sustained by front seat occupants' striking their knees against the dashboard.[55] Following this initial report, Thompson and Epstein,[181] Stewart and Milford,[174] Brav,[15] Epstein,[43] and Stewart[172] all described mechanisms, treatments, and complications related to hip dislocations. These reports documented the numerous complications and long-term disability associated with hip dislocations.

The guarded prognosis of hip dislocations has been well-recognized.[186, 188, 192] Although pure dislocations fare better than fracture-dislocations, recent reports have indicated that unsatisfactory long-term results are common even with pure dislocations, and may be anticipated in up to one-half of this better-prognosis group.[36, 198] Delayed treatment and failure to recognize and treat associated injuries may contribute to poor results. The treatment of hip dislocations is directed toward avoidance of complications.

This chapter reviews the use of current methods of evaluating and treating hip dislocations. The treatment of associated fractures of the acetabulum and femoral head is reserved for those chapters addressing those injuries (see Chapters 37 and 48).

## PATHOLOGY

### Relevant Anatomy

The hip is an intrinsically stable joint. More than 400 N of force (90 lb) is required simply to distract the femoral head from the acetabulum.[48] Hip stability is directly related to the bony and labral anatomy of the acetabulum and femoral head. The thick fibrous capsule with ligamentous condensations and the local muscular anatomy substantially augment the inherent stability afforded by the ball and socket configuration of the hip.

Inherent bony stability is achieved through the size and relationship of the femoral head and femoral neck to the acetabular socket, which is deepened by an osteocartilaginous labrum.[71] The femoral head forms approximately two thirds of a sphere and is situated on a femoral neck approximately three quarters the diameter of the femoral head. This relationship in size between the femoral head and the femoral neck allows the femoral head to be deeply seated within its acetabular socket without compromising either stability or range of motion.

The acetabulum is formed from the convergence of the ischium, ilium, and pubis at the triradiate cartilage. Biomechanical testing of newborn cadavers found the joints to be extremely stable at birth, although some debate exists as to the actual stabilizing structures.[25, 53] It is unclear whether the acetabulum deepens with development, but anatomic studies reveal in adult hips that approximately 40% of the femoral head is covered by the bony acetabulum at any position of hip motion.[79] The articular surface of the acetabulum is horseshoe shaped, with articular cartilage covering the posterior, superior, and anterior portions of the acetabular cavity. The cartilaginous labrum is attached to the perimeter of the portion of acetabulum covered by articular cartilage. The acetabular notch or cotyloid fossa lies in the mid-inferior portion of the acetabulum. The transverse acetabular ligament crosses the most inferior portion of the acetabular notch, extending from the posteroinferior end of the labrum to its anteroinferior limit. The ligamentum teres originates from the acetabular notch (Fig. 46–1).

The labrum deepens the acetabulum and increases the stability of the joint. The labrum ensures that at least 50% of the femoral head is covered by the osteocartilaginous labral-acetabular complex in any position of hip motion. These motions include extension (from a prone position) of 20° to 30°, flexion of 120° to 135°, abduction of 45° to 50°, adduction of 20° to 30°, and internal (medial) and external (lateral) rotation of 45° each. Individual variability is seen, and rotational measurements will differ if the rotation is tested in hip extension or hip flexion.[13, 80, 126, 153]

A capsule that extends posteriorly from the acetabular rim to the midfemoral neck and anteriorly from the acetabular rim to the intertrochanteric ridge surrounds the hip joint. The primary capsular fibers run longitudinally and are supplemented by much stronger ligamentous condensations that run in a circular and spiral fashion. The iliofemoral ligament courses inferiorly from the iliac body and anterior inferior iliac spine in two distinct directions. One band continues directly inferiorly to insert on the intertrochanteric line just anterior to the lesser trochanter. The second band courses obliquely in a spiral fashion to insert on the intertrochanteric line overlying the greater trochanter. An additional anterior ligamentous condensation extends from the anterior border of the superior pubic ramus to the intertrochanteric line and is called the pubofemoral ligament. This ligament is believed to be a checkrein against pathologic extension of the hip. Posteriorly, the ischiofemoral ligament is a broad and less dense condensation extending in an oblique and horizontal fashion from the ischial border of the acetabulum to the superior base of the femoral neck and the region of the trochanteric fossa (Fig. 46–2).[79, 117]

The femoral neck is normally anteverted in its relationship to the transcondylar axis of the femur. Cadaveric studies have demonstrated a significant variability in average anteversion, and in range of anteversion based on gender, and genetic background.[77] White males, for example, were found to have an average of 7° of anteversion with a range of 2° of retroversion to 35° of anteversion. White females had an average anteversion of 10° with a range of 2° of retroversion to 25° of anteversion. In contrast, Hong Kong Chinese males averaged 14° of anteversion with a range of −4° to 36°, and

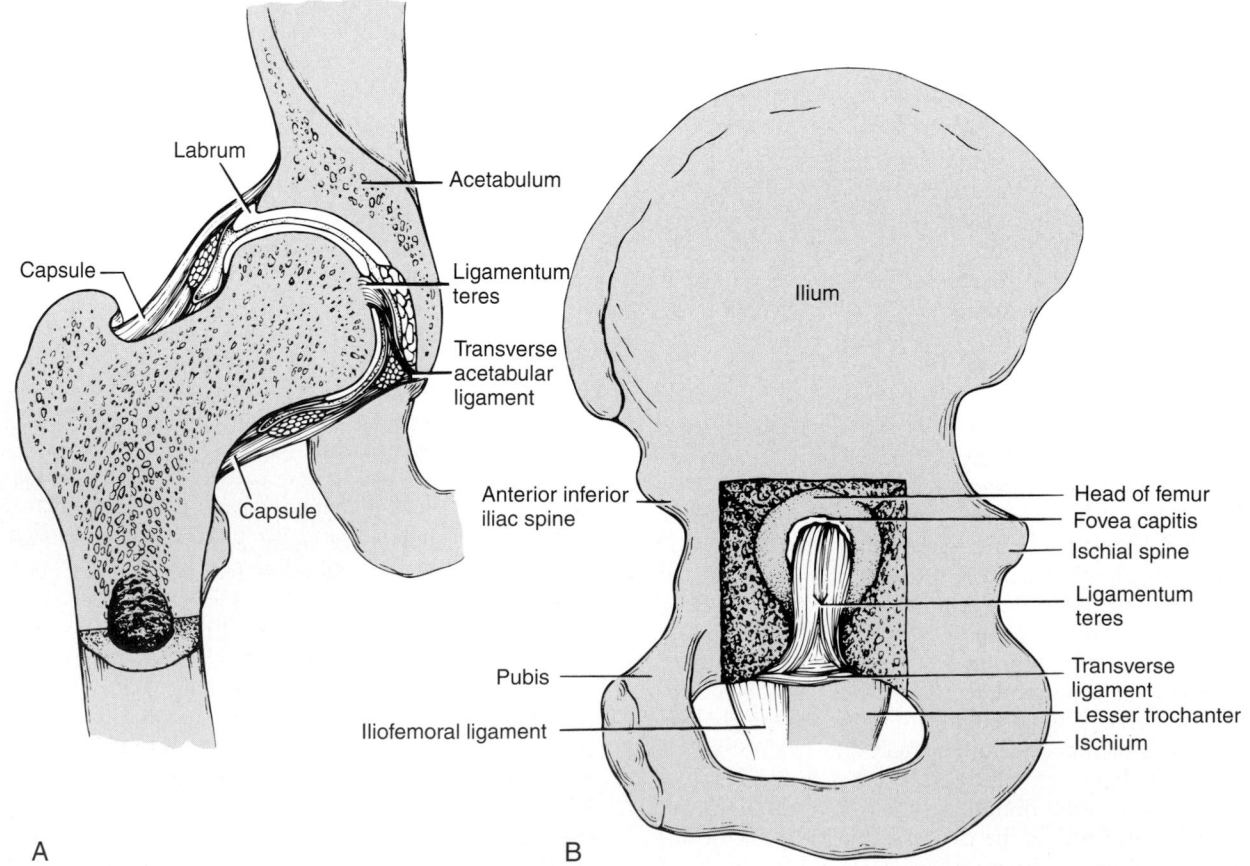

**FIGURE 46–1.** *A, B,* Schematic representation of the relationship of the femoral head, labrum, and acetabulum. The labrum extends beyond the equator of the femoral head, producing excellent joint stability.

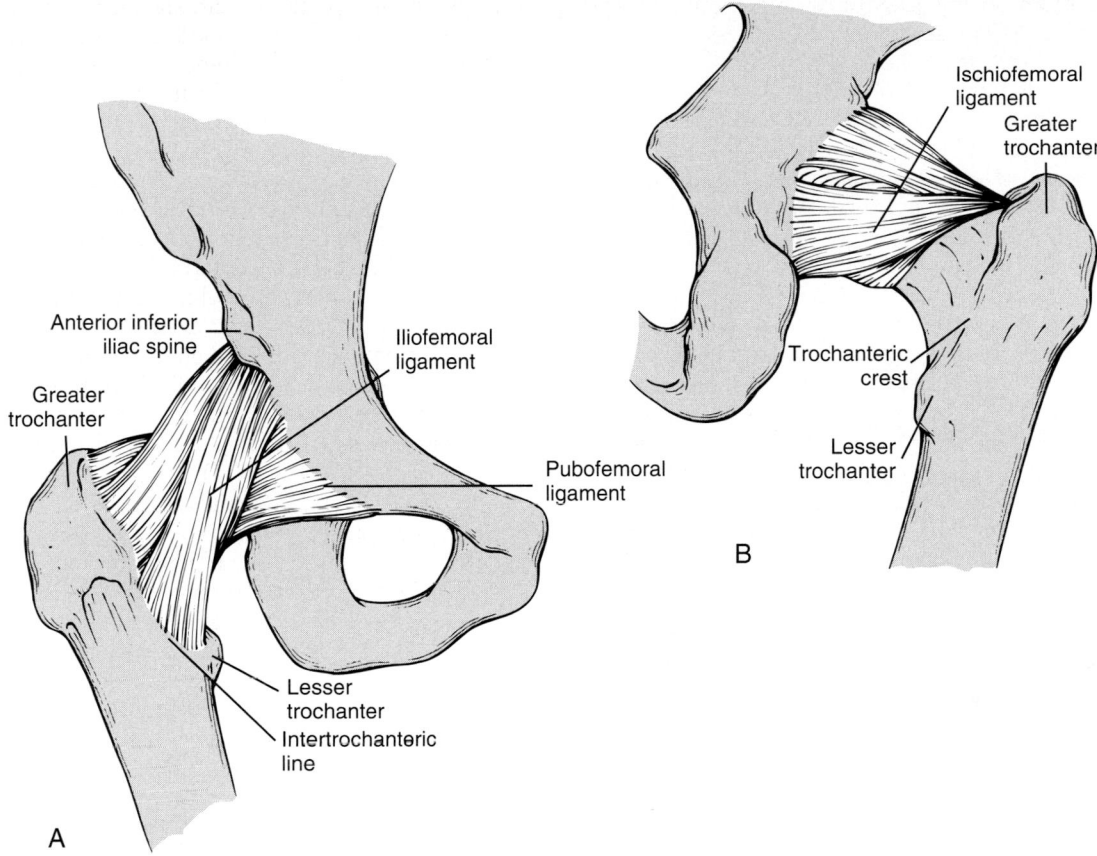

**FIGURE 46–2.** *A, B,* Ligamentous condensation about the hip capsule supplements hip stability and blocks pathologic motion.

Hong Kong Chinese females averaged 16° of anteversion with a range of only 7° to 28°.

Ultrasonographic measurements performed by Upadhyay and colleagues on a series of patients who had sustained a posterior hip dislocation demonstrated significantly less anteversion on both the injured and the uninjured sides when compared with a control group.[187] Diminished anteversion may therefore be a predisposing factor to hip dislocations. Further discussion of this possibility is included in the section of this chapter on mechanisms of injury.

The arterial supply of the femoral head has been widely studied, and a definite change in vascular patterns from infancy to adulthood has been identified. The main arterial supply of the adult femoral head originates from the medial and lateral femoral circumflex arteries, which are branches of either the femoral artery or the deep femoral artery. The obturator artery and the inferior and superior gluteal arteries have also been demonstrated to contribute blood supply to the hip joint.[185]

An extracapsular vascular ring is formed at the base of the femoral neck. This vascular ring is fed posteriorly by a branch at the medial circumflex artery and anteriorly by a branch of the lateral circumflex artery. Multiple ascending cervical branches arise from this arterial ring and pierce the hip joint at the level of the capsular insertion. From this point, they ascend either along the femoral neck or laterally to supply the trochanter. Once these ascending cervical branches have entered the hip joint, they continue along the synovial reflections on the femoral neck and enter the bone just inferior to the articular cartilage of the femoral head (Fig. 46–3).[26, 71, 79]

A high degree of variability exists in the vascular contribution of the artery of the ligamentum teres,[194] which contributes to the blood supply of the epiphyseal region of the femoral head when it is present.

The sciatic nerve is formed from nerve roots from L4 to S3. As these nerve roots converge, an immediate division develops within the pelvis of the peroneal nerve and tibial nerve. These nerves exit the pelvis at the greater sciatic notch in a common sheath. A certain degree of variability exists in the relationship of the sciatic nerve with the piriformis muscle and short external rotators of the hip, which under some circumstances may protect the sciatic nerve from injury (Fig. 46–4). Beaton and Anson demonstrated through anatomic dissections that in 85% of individuals, the sciatic nerve exits the pelvis deep (anterior) to the muscle belly of the piriformis.[7] In 11% of individuals, the common peroneal nerve and tibial nerve are split by a portion of the piriformis muscle, with the peroneal nerve exiting through the substance of the muscle belly. In an additional 3% of individuals, the common peroneal nerve emerges superficial (posterior) to the piriformis, whereas the tibial nerve emerges deep (anterior) to the muscle belly. These anatomic variations are especially important considerations in extensile approaches to the posterior hip region.

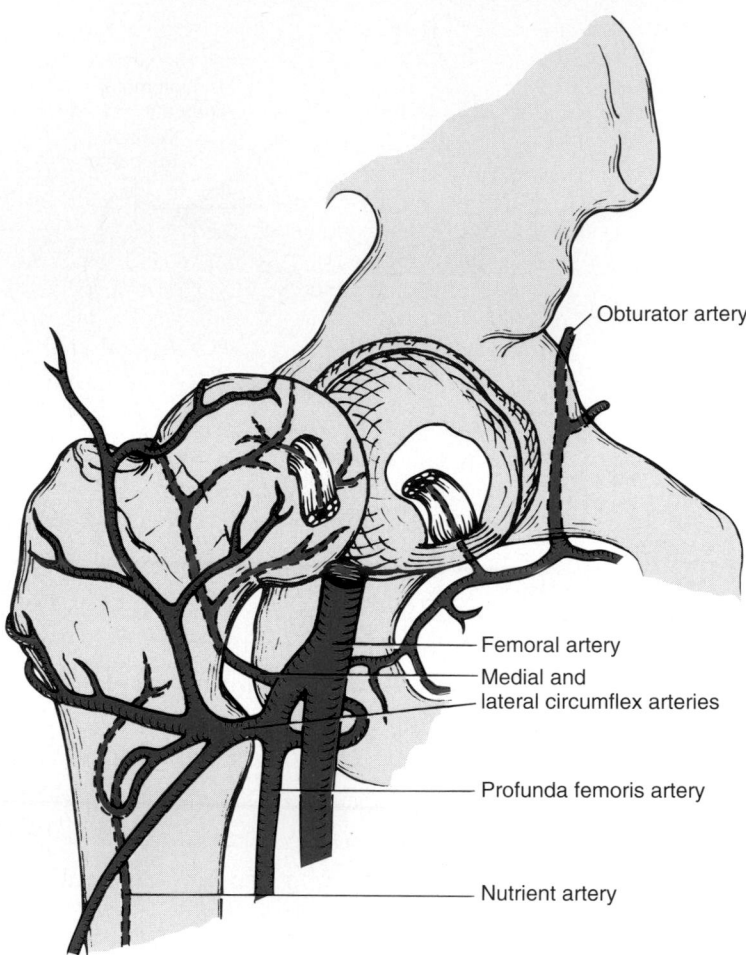

**Figure 46–3.** Vascular supply of the proximal femur.

Obturator artery

Femoral artery

Medial and
lateral circumflex arteries

Profunda femoris artery

Nutrient artery

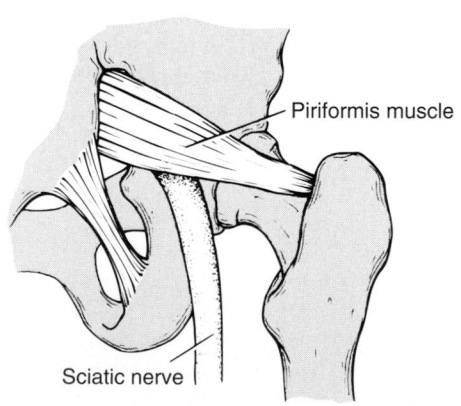

Piriformis muscle

Sciatic nerve

A          84.2%

**Figure 46–4.** *A–D,* Schematic representation
of the most common relationships between
the sciatic nerve and the piriformis muscle.

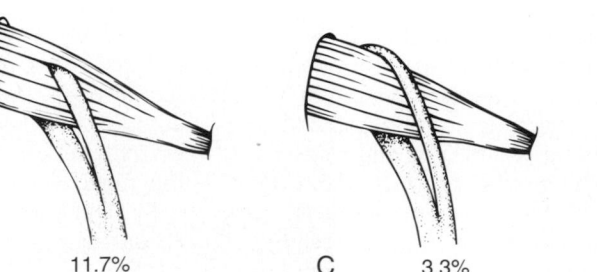

B          11.7%          C          3.3%          D          0.8%

## Mechanisms of Injury

The anatomic configuration of the hip joint provides a high degree of inherent stability. As a result, hip dislocations are almost always due to high-energy trauma. Motor vehicle crashes account for more than two-thirds of hip dislocations reported in the literature.[15, 16, 43, 44, 89, 102, 103, 139, 146, 173] Advances in vehicle restraints should theoretically reduce the morbidity and mortality of patients who do sustain hip dislocations resulting from motor vehicle collisions, but recent reports have unfortunately been unable to substantiate this anticipated benefit of passenger restraints.[68] Automobile-pedestrian accidents, falls from heights, industrial injuries, and athletic trauma account for the other reported mechanisms of injury.[44, 53, 174, 178, 181]

Pathologic forces transmitted to the hip joint in all hip dislocations result from one of three common sources: the anterior surface of the flexed knee striking an object; the sole of the foot, with the ipsilateral knee extended; and the greater trochanter. Less frequently, the dislocating force may be applied to the posterior pelvis, with the ipsilateral foot or knee acting as the counterforce.[41, 43, 101, 174]

The type of hip injury sustained depends on the amount and direction of applied force, the quality of bone at both the proximal femur and the acetabulum, and the position of the hip. Letournel demonstrated through vector analysis the relationship of the position of the leg and pelvis to the injury sustained, explaining why an individual sustains an anterior dislocation, posterior dislocation, or fracture-dislocation of the hip.[100, 101] In the classic dislocation seen in unrestrained automobile drivers, the left hip tends to dislocate posteriorly, whereas the right hip develops either a posterior fracture-dislocation or an anterior dislocation. At the time of the rapid deceleration of the automobile, the right foot is positioned either on the brake pedal or on the accelerator pedal. The body pivots forward on this fixed foot, and the left knee strikes the dashboard with the hip and knee both flexed to 90°. This force delivered in this position tends to force the femoral head out posteriorly, usually without a fracture. With less flexion of the hip at the time of impact, the femoral head

strikes either the posterior or the postero-superior aspect of the acetabulum, leading to a fracture-dislocation. Similarly, if the right foot is firmly pressed against the brake pedal at the moment of impact, the femoral head strikes the posterior or postero-superior acetabulum. If an unsuspecting driver is involved in a collision, the right leg may be in a relaxed position on the gas pedal, with the hip externally rotated and abducted. In this position, the inner aspect of the knee strikes the dashboard, resulting in accentuation of both abduction and external rotation. This extreme position results in anterior dislocation (Fig. 46–5).

The degree of internal or external rotation of the hip dramatically affects the position of the head within the acetabulum and therefore the resulting injury complex. Another factor potentially affecting hip dislocation pathology, noted previously, is femoral neck anteversion. In one series of patients studied with ultrasound, significantly less anteversion was found in patients who sustained posterior hip dislocations.[187] Individuals with posterior fracture-dislocations had less anteversion than the control population but more than the pure dislocation group (Table 46–1). These findings strongly imply that femoral head position, based on an instantaneous position secondary to hip rotation and on the anatomic structure of the hip, determines the type of injury.

Pringle demonstrated that extreme abduction with external rotation of the leg can produce anterior dislocations in cadaver specimens.[145] In a flexed hip position, extreme abduction and external rotation led to anterior obturator dislocation. With the hip extended, these pathologic forces result in a superoanterior (pubic) dislocation. Epstein and Harvey also proposed that anterior dislocations are secondary to hyperabduction of the hip,[15] and suggested that either the greater trochanter or the femoral neck impinges on the lateral ilium, which then acts as a lever to push the femoral head out of the acetabulum.

Femoral head fractures, impactions, and osteochondral injuries occur as the femoral head exits the acetabulum. Actual shearing of the superior, anterosuperior, or posterosuperior femoral head can occur as the femoral head strikes the anterior or posterior acetabular

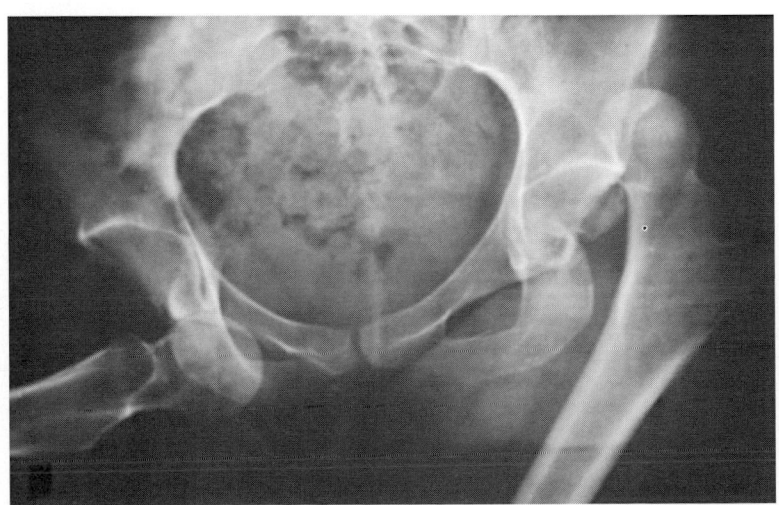

**FIGURE 46–5.** Bilateral hip dislocations were sustained by an unrestrained intoxicated driver. The right hip was dislocated anteriorly and the left hip posteriorly.

## Table 46–1

Mean Femoral Anteversion as Measured by Ultrasonographic Techniques

|  | Right Hip Mean Anteversion (°) | Left Hip Mean Anteversion (°) |
|---|---|---|
| Normal subjects | 15.4 | 16.3 |
| Type I dislocation, right hip | 1.1 | 10.4 |
| Type I dislocation, left hip | 4.4 | −3.2 |
| Posterior fracture-dislocation, right hip | 3.2 | −5.5 |
| Posterior fracture-dislocation, left hip | 5.0 | −6.1 |

*Source:* Adapted from Upadhyay, S.S.; et al. J Bone Joint Surg Br 67:232–236, 1985.

lip.[24, 32, 37, 46, 140] Ligamentum teres avulsion fractures from the femoral head are frequently seen. These fragments can range in size from small cartilaginous avulsion fragments to major osteocartilaginous fragments of the femoral head (Fig. 46–6). Such loose fragments can become incarcerated between the femoral head and the acetabular articular surface following reduction of the dislocation. Failure to remove these incarcerated fragments could possibly lead to symptoms of a loose body and articular cartilage erosion.

Femoral neck fractures associated with femoral head dislocations may result from two different mechanisms. Several case reports describing these associated injuries propose that the injury forces that first dislocate the femoral head, then force the head against the pelvis. If the energy that produced the dislocation has not been fully dissipated, the continued application of force to the leg while the femoral head abuts the pelvis will fracture the femoral neck or the femoral shaft.[35, 51, 90, 116, 141, 160]

The second proposed mechanism of femoral neck fracture is "iatrogenic" and occurs at the time of manipulative reduction.[140, 157, 172] Most reported cases of so-called iatrogenic neck fractures also report an associated femoral head fracture. This may imply that the femoral neck absorbed a significant amount of energy and developed a nondisplaced fracture that was not radiographically visible prior to the manipulation. Obviously, extreme care must be taken in reviewing the films prior to the reduction to ensure that a nondisplaced fracture is not present. In addition, reduction techniques must be gentle and well controlled; lever-type manipulations must be avoided.

## Consequences of Injury

### POST-TRAUMATIC ARTHRITIS

Normal articular cartilage is a highly resilient material that withstands both monotonic and cyclical loading.[148, 152] Despite this resilience, Repo and Finley demonstrated a threshold deformity resulting in chondrocyte death.[152] Cartilage strain levels as low as 20% to 30% have been demonstrated to lead to chondrocyte death. The initial energy absorbed by the articular cartilage of the femoral head and acetabulum likely far exceed this critical threshold for chondrocyte death. This high initial energy could also be one possible explanation for the high incidence of traumatic arthritis reported following simple hip dislocations and progressively higher rates of traumatic arthritis in more extensive fracture-dislocations.[44, 186, 188]

Displacement of posterior wall fragments or surgical excision of femoral head fragments may also have significant biomechanical implications. Brown and Ferguson investigated the alteration in femoral head stress patterns in response to narrowing of the superior articular cartilage of the femoral head.[17] This loss of superior cartilage thickness created abnormally large transverse compressive stresses and increased stress concentration about the periphery of the femoral head. Brown and Ferguson proposed that this change in femoral head stress patterns secondary to loss of articular cartilage height was a predisposing factor to the development of osteoarthritis.[17]

Bernard and associates similarly studied the changes in femoral head stress patterns in relationship to varying thickness of the articular cartilage.[8] They theorize that a built-in "incongruence" of the hip joint secondary to varying cartilage thickness is physiologically well tolerated and probably necessary for round joint mechanics. However, when cartilage thickness between the acetabulum and the femoral head decreased to less than 1 mm total or 0.5 mm each (28% of normal), a dramatic increase in contact stresses was demonstrated. Genda and co-workers reported on a computer simulation of joint reaction forces in normal hips and dysplastic hips.[59] They found that normal hips maintained even and relatively low joint reaction forces. In contrast, dysplastic hips had a dramatically increased concentration of joint forces.

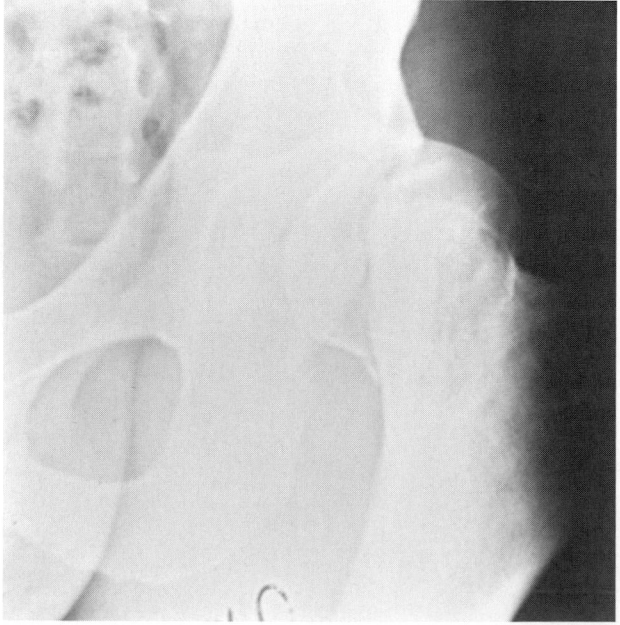

**Figure 46–6.** Large femoral head fracture associated with a posterior hip dislocation (a Pipkin type II or comprehensive classification type V). Compare with Figures 46–9 and 46–10.

Although none of these investigations specifically addresses the question of loss of cartilage and bone secondary to trauma, the situations seem to be analogous. Any significant loss of normal articular congruence or articular contact secondary to femoral head depressions or defects would also seem to predispose to similar changes in contact stresses and the development of early traumatic arthritis.

Studies on the ability of articular cartilage to heal defects and on the nature of the repair tissue also demonstrate the potential problems created by cartilaginous defects.[19, 34, 78, 109, 120, 162, 179] Abnormalities secondary to the loss of articular cartilage and alterations in contact stress seem likely to predispose to the development of traumatic arthritis.

## AVASCULAR NECROSIS

Avascular necrosis (AVN) of the femoral head secondary to vascular compromise is the second most significant consequence of hip dislocation. However, the incidence of AVN is controversial; some investigators suggest that previous radiologic diagnoses of AVN may in fact have been advanced traumatic arthritis.[43, 154] Estimates of AVN vary in the literature from 1% to 2% to 15% to 17%.[93, 114, 118, 136, 146, 155, 174]

The specific anatomic lesion or lesions responsible for the development of AVN have never been identified. Numerous authors have demonstrated a strong correlation between the incidence of AVN and the length of time the hip remains dislocated. The time threshold within which the hip should be reduced to prevent AVN is reported to be in the range of 6 to 24 hours.[43, 75, 83, 139, 173, 183, 189] Stewart and Milford reported good results in 88% of hips reduced within 12 hours of dislocation.[174] Similarly, Brav reported that reduction more than 12 hours following injury increased the percentage of unsatisfactory results from 22% to 52%.[15] Among patients in Morton's series, excellent results were found only in patients whose hips were reduced within 12 hours.[125] Similarly, Hougaard and Thomsen found higher rates of AVN and arthritis if the time to reduction exceeded 6 hours.[83] Reigstad reported no instances of AVN or arthritis when simple dislocations were reduced within 6 hours.[150]

The association between AVN and the period of time in which the hip remains dislocated suggests three mechanisms that may contribute to the development of AVN. The first mechanism is immediate complete disruption of blood supply to the femoral head occurring at the time of a violent dislocation. The second proposed mechanism is a slower process in which, due to prolonged abnormal stretching of the arterial supply, the arteries develop vascular spasm or thrombosis. The third proposed mechanism invokes a venous phenomenon in which mechanically compromised drainage leads to venous occlusion, back pressure, and arterial obstruction. These second two mechanisms would seem to be favorably affected through early reduction.

Yue and colleagues conducted a human cadaveric angiographic study offering support for these theories.[199] Vessels filled with a radiopaque latex liquid polymer were examined under cinefluoroscopy in cadaver hips that had

been forcefully dislocated posteriorly, and were compared to the contralateral normal hips. Significant changes in the extraosseous hip vasculature were demonstrated, with defects most common in the common femoral and circumflex vessels. The authors hypothesized that consistent changes in intraosseous blood flow were not demonstrable might be due to collateral circulation, and that early reduction of a dislocated hip might allow reversal of these findings.

Other factors that have been proposed as causes of AVN have not been proved. Early weight bearing following successful reduction of a hip dislocation had previously been proposed as a cause of AVN,[30, 39, 85] but this theory has been disproved by numerous investigators, and no association has been demonstrated.[15, 44, 136, 167, 173] Similarly, Epstein and colleagues proposed that an anterior surgical approach to treat a posteriorly dislocated hip might place the patient at high risk for AVN.[43, 46] This theory has also not been proved clinically. Recent clinical experience of treatment of femoral head fractures through a variety of anterior surgical approaches have not demonstrated an increased incidence of AVN.[20, 21, 164, 182]

The long-term significance of traumatic osteonecrosis is extremely variable. Glimcher and Kenzora described significant pathologic and histologic differences among idiopathic and metabolic osteonecrosis and avascular osteonecrosis.[61–63] Unlike idiopathic varieties, not all hips affected with avascular osteonecrosis progress to collapse and joint degeneration. At times, only a segment of the femoral head will be affected with AVN, and only this portion may undergo a segmental collapse (Fig. 46–7). This must be remembered prior to undertaking prophy-

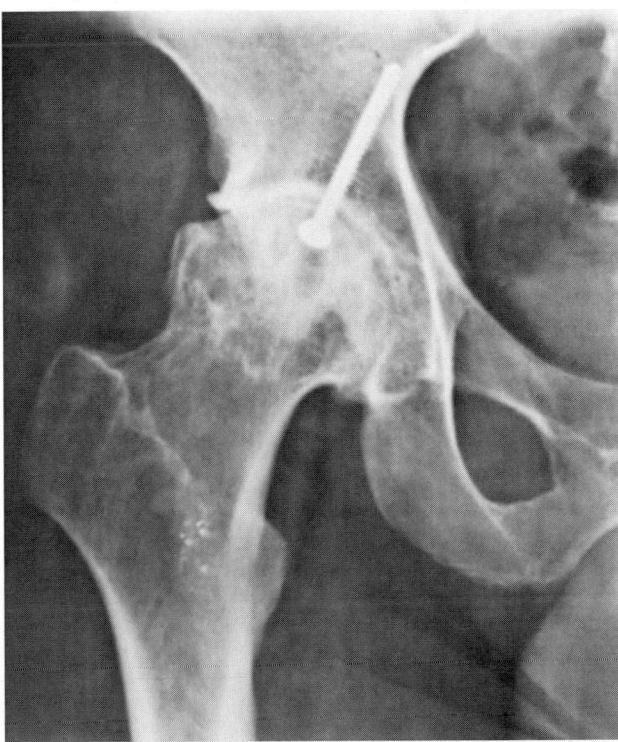

**FIGURE 46–7.** Segmental avascular necrosis of the femoral head after a posterior fracture-dislocation of the hip.

lactic or salvage procedures that may be appropriate for idiopathic AVN but not for post-traumatic AVN.

## Commonly Associated Injuries

Hip dislocations are usually caused by high energy trauma and as a result are often associated with other significant injuries. Attendant neurologic injuries, musculoskeletal injuries, and intraabdominal and chest injuries have all been widely reported.[134, 178]

A large variety of knee injuries are associated with hip dislocations. Gillespie reported on a series of 35 associated knee injuries; 25 were attributed to direct trauma to the knee region, and 10 were associated with pathologic stresses applied to the knee ligaments.[60] Among the reported injuries were osteochondral fractures of the patella, tibia, and femur; posterior cruciate injuries; collateral ligament injuries; and traumatic patellofemoral chondrosis. A delay in the diagnosis of these injuries frequently occurred (2 days to 6 months). Tabuenca and Truan reported that 46 of 187 patients (25%) with fracture or fracture/dislocation of the hip had an ipsilateral knee injury.[180] The diagnosis of knee injury was delayed in 7 of the 46 patients, prolonging overall recovery in these patients.

Sciatic nerve injuries have been documented in association with hip dislocations in 8% to 19% of patients.[16, 42, 44, 65, 79, 84, 97, 173, 174] The mechanism of injury is presumed to be stretching of the nerve over the posteriorly dislocated, internally rotated femoral head.[46] Large posterior wall acetabular fragments can also stretch the nerve or even pierce or partially lacerate it. Intraoperatively, the nerve may appear normal or nearly so, in spite of a functional deficit. No cases of sciatic nerve injury have been reported secondary to anterior dislocations.

A complete disruption of the sciatic nerve is unusual. Most commonly, the peroneal portion of the nerve is significantly involved, with little or no evident tibial nerve dysfunction. The peroneal component of the sciatic nerve lies more posterior than the tibial component, so that proximity of this portion of the nerve to the dislocated femoral head may alone account for the higher incidence of peroneal nerve injury whereas the tibial nerve is usually spared. Gregory proposed that the unusual association of the peroneal portion of the nerve with the piriformis muscle may further place this portion of the nerve at risk.[65]

Nerve function should be carefully assessed prior to a manipulative reduction. Obviously, if the patient has sustained a head injury or is unconscious or uncooperative, neurologic examination will be incomplete. This should be noted on the patient's medical record.

All dislocated hips must be reduced as soon as possible. This is especially the case when nerve palsy is present, to relieve stretching of the nerve. Surgical exploration is not indicated for associated neurologic injury, except when initially normal neurologic function is lost secondary to the reduction.[31] In this situation, the surgeon must ascertain whether the nerve has become incarcerated either in fracture fragments or in the hip joint. Some investigators

recommend immediate surgical repair of displaced posterior wall fragments that are associated with sciatic nerve injuries. This may protect the nerve from further injury by the fracture fragments.[146] The implications of sciatic nerve injury are addressed later in this chapter.

Ipsilateral femur fractures have also been frequently reported with hip dislocations.[39, 52, 73, 168] Unfortunately, in some of these reported cases, the diagnosis of hip dislocation was not initially made accurately. Because a femoral fracture masks the typical physical findings of a hip dislocation, routine adherence to a policy of radiographic examination of the joint above and below the fracture should minimize missing this combination of injuries.

## CLASSIFICATION OF HIP DISLOCATIONS

### Evolution

Hip dislocations are subdivided into either anterior or posterior dislocations based on the location of the femoral head.[64] A "central dislocation" is in fact a medial displacement of the femoral head secondary to a displaced acetabular fracture.[97, 101, 159, 174] This poorly descriptive term, *central dislocation,* is an outdated phrase and is no longer relevant in modern classification systems.

Thompson and Epstein and, later, Stewart and Milford devised similar classification systems for posterior hip dislocations.[174, 181] Both systems were based on the severity of the associated acetabular fracture as well as the presence of a femoral head fracture. A Thompson-Epstein type I dislocation is a pure dislocation with at most an insignificant posterior wall fragment. A type II dislocation is associated with a single large posterior wall fragment. A type III dislocation has a comminuted posterior wall fracture, and a type IV has an "acetabular floor" (more than posterior wall) fracture. Finally, a type V dislocation is associated with a femoral head fracture (Fig. 46–8).

Stewart and Milford's system was based on the stability of the hip joint and the condition of the femoral head.[174] Type I dislocations have either no fracture or an insignificant acetabular rim fracture. A type II dislocation is associated with either a single or a comminuted posterior wall fracture, but the hip remains stable. Type III injuries are fracture-dislocations with gross instability of the hip joint secondary to loss of structural support, and a type IV dislocation is associated with a femoral head fracture.

Pipkin classified posterior hip dislocations associated with femoral head fractures based on the location of the femoral head fracture.[140] A Pipkin type I injury has a femoral head fracture inferior to the fovea centralis; a type II injury has a fracture line extending superior to the fovea centralis (and usually including the fovea); a type III injury is any femoral head fracture in association with a femoral neck fracture; and a type IV injury is any femoral head fracture associated with an acetabular fracture (Fig. 46–9).

A classification system for posterior dislocations that

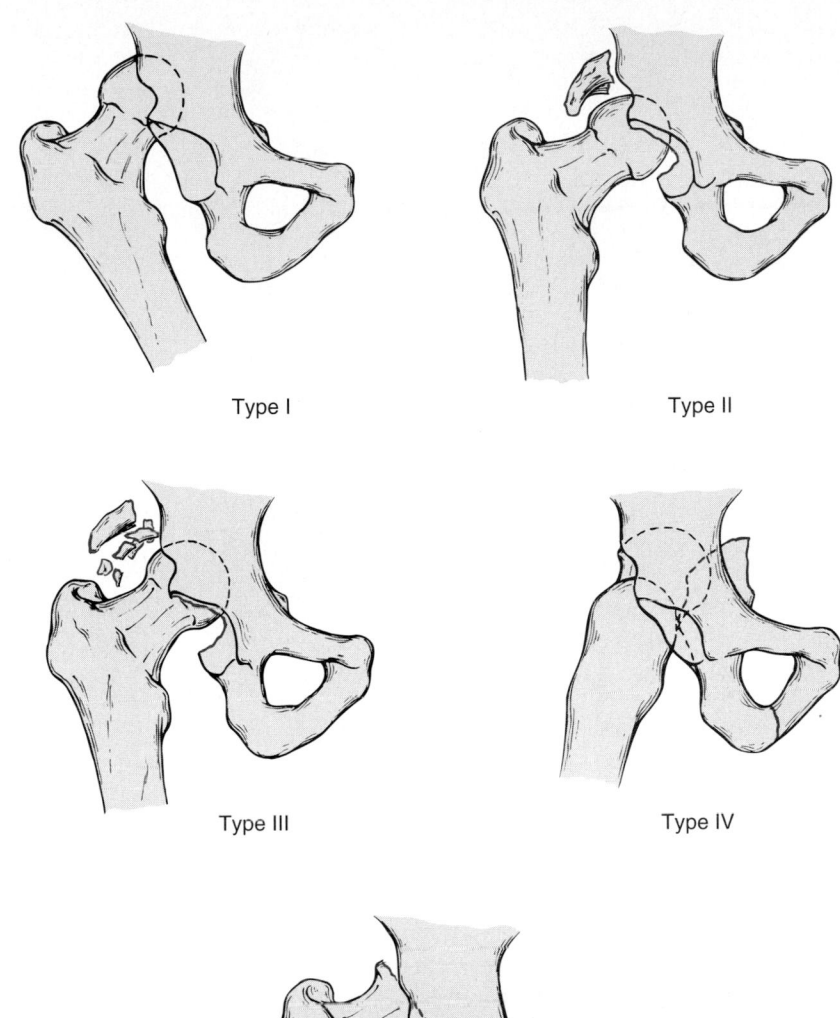

Type I

Type II

Type III

Type IV

**FIGURE 46–8.** Thompson-Epstein classification of posterior hip dislocations. (Adapted from DeLee, J.C. In: Rockwood, C.A., Jr.; Green, D.P., eds. Fractures, 2nd ed., Vol. 2. Philadelphia, J.B. Lippincott, 1985.)

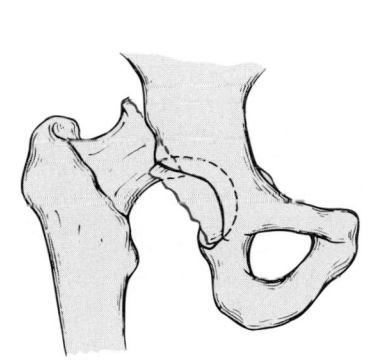

Type V

combines elements of earlier classification systems was proposed by Levin and is presented in Table 46–2 and Figure 46–10. A Levin type I posterior dislocation either is a pure dislocation or is associated with an insignificant posterior wall fracture. The post-reduction CT scan demonstrates a concentric reduction, no widening of the joint, no incarcerated fragments between articular surfaces, and no femoral head or posterior wall impaction fractures. Occasionally, a post-reduction CT image demonstrates a small bone fragment within the acetabular fossa secondary to a ligamentum teres avulsion. This fragment is of no clinical significance as long as it is not incarcerated between the articular surfaces of the femoral head and the acetabulum.

Levin type II posterior dislocations are pure dislocations without associated femoral head or acetabular fractures in which the femoral head is irreducible by closed manipulation. A hip will be presumed to be irreducible only if a closed reduction under general anesthesia fails to bring the femoral head back into the acetabulum.

A Levin type III posterior dislocation is one in which the post-reduction clinical examination reveals an unstable hip or one in which the post-reduction imaging studies reveal a widened joint space or an incarcerated cartilaginous or osseous fragment. The instability can be secondary to failure to fully seat the femoral head due to an incarcerated fragment, an extensive labral detachment, or massive capsular and ligamentous disruption.

A Levin type IV posterior dislocation is associated with a significant acetabular fracture requiring reconstruction. Surgery in these patients is indicated to restore joint stability or joint congruity, or both. These fracture-

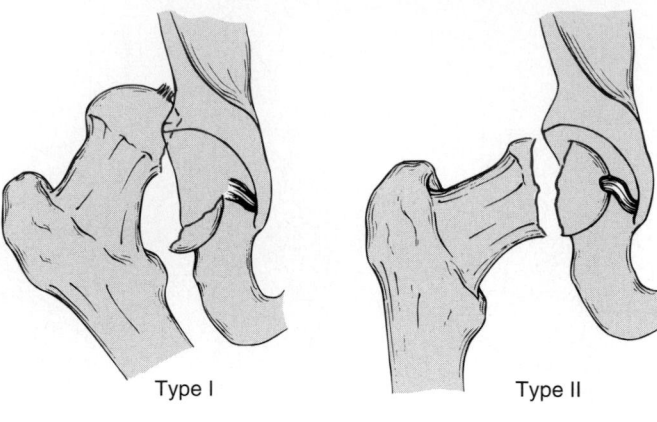

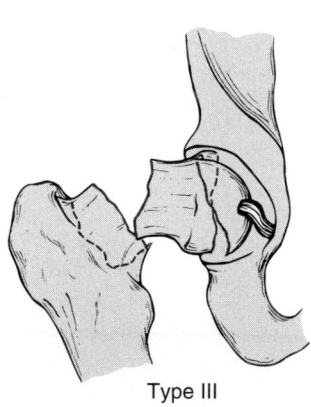

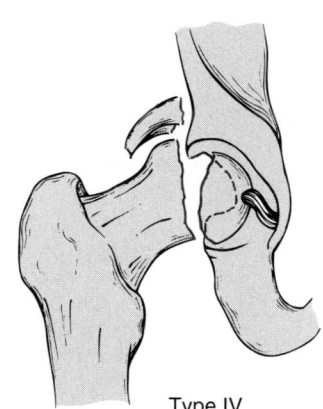

**FIGURE 46–9.** Pipkin classification system of posterior hip dislocations associated with femoral head fractures.

dislocations of the hip are more appropriately classified according to their acetabular fracture pattern.

Levin type V posterior dislocations are associated with femoral head or femoral neck injuries. The femoral head injuries may be indentations, depressions, or cleavage fractures. These injuries are classified further based on the femoral head fracture classification system.

## Anterior Hip Dislocations

Anterior hip dislocations occur much less frequently than do posterior hip dislocations. Thompson and Epstein classified these injuries based on their anterior location

(superior or inferior) as well as on the presence of associated acetabular fractures.[181] Recent long term evaluations of these injuries have revealed a much less favorable prognosis than was previously believed.[32, 45] A significant portion of the poor results may be related to associated femoral head injuries.

Although both classification systems divided anterior dislocations into subgroups of superior and inferior types and then simply subdivided these into groups based on associated fractures, the treatment plan is not altered by the subdivision of inferior or superior dislocation. Levin proposed a system for classifying anterior dislocations that follows his scheme for posterior dislocations but includes the suffix *anterior* following the subtype (e.g., type I anterior dislocation) (Fig. 46–11 and Table 46–3).

## DIAGNOSIS

### History

Patients presenting with dislocations and fracture-dislocations of the hip are in severe discomfort. They complain of inability to move their lower extremity and may also complain of numbness distally. Typically, they have been involved in high-energy trauma such as motor vehicle accidents, industrial accidents, or falls from heights.

Individuals suffering multiple injuries often experience

**TABLE 46–2**

Levin Classification of Posterior Hip Dislocations

| | |
|---|---|
| Type I | No significant associated fractures; no clinical instability after concentric reduction |
| Type II | Irreducible dislocation without significant femoral head or acetabular fractures (reduction must be attempted under general anesthesia) |
| Type III | Unstable hip after reduction or incarcerated fragments of cartilage, labrum, or bone |
| Type IV | Associated acetabular fracture requiring reconstruction to restore hip stability or joint congruity |
| Type V | Associated femoral head or femoral neck injury (fractures or impactions) |

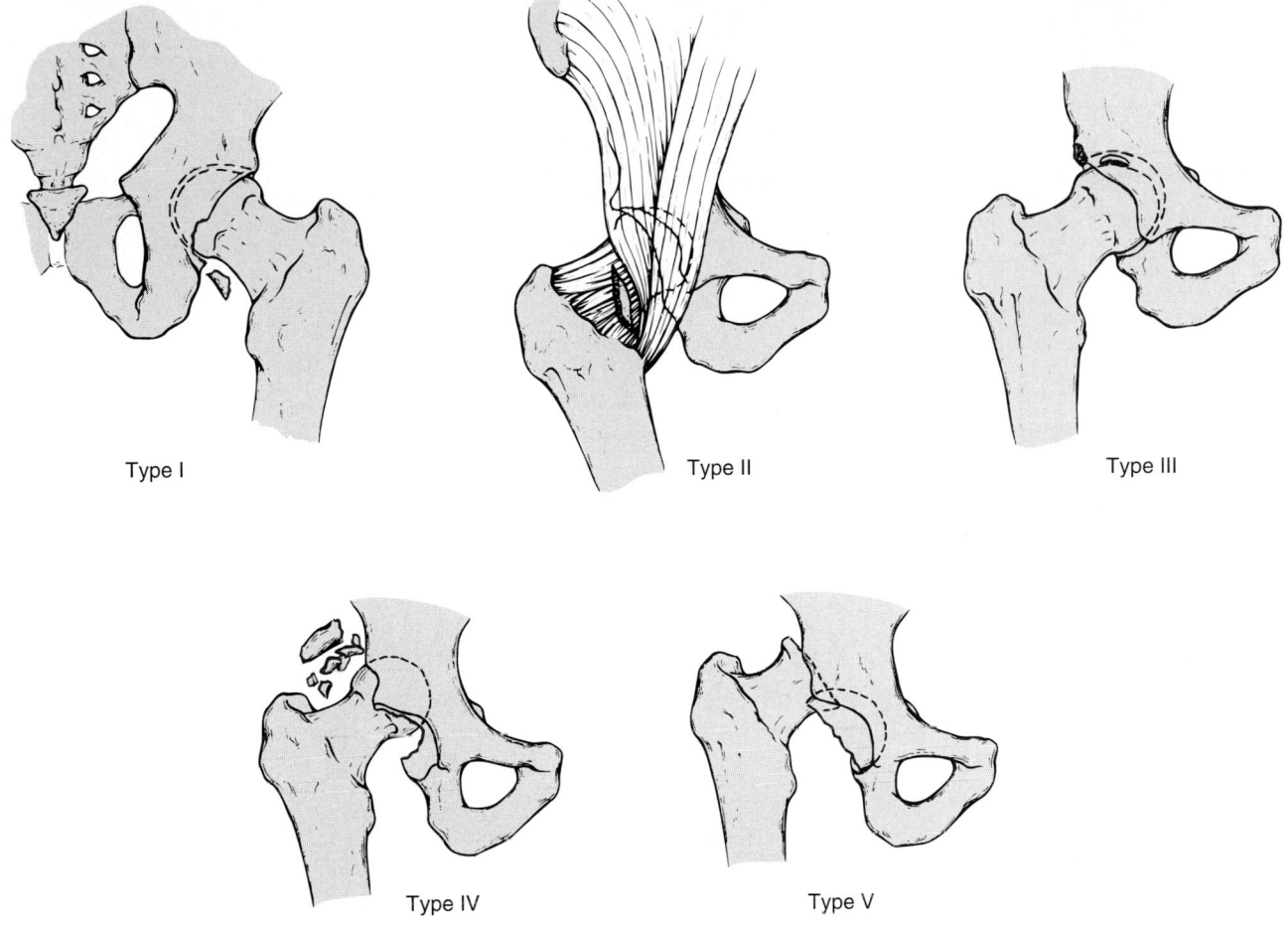

Type I    Type II    Type III

Type IV    Type V

**Figure 46–10.** Comprehensive classification of posterior hip dislocations. (see Table 46–2.)

pain at numerous sites and as a result may not be able to localize specific injuries. Associated injuries to the chest, abdomen, spine, and extremities all compromise the ability of the patients to isolate and differentiate their symptoms. A high percentage of patients with hip dislocations will be obtunded or unconscious when they arrive in the emergency department and as a result will be unable to assist the physician in their initial evaluation.

## Physical Examination

The classic appearance of an individual with an isolated posterior hip dislocation is a patient in severe pain with the hip fixed in a position of flexion, internal rotation, and adduction (Fig. 46–12). Patients with an isolated anterior dislocation hold their hip in marked external rotation with mild flexion and abduction (Fig. 46–13). Despite these classic descriptions, the appearance and alignment of the extremity can be dramatically altered by ipsilateral extremity injuries.

The initial physical examination must include an evaluation of the entire involved limb. Care must be taken to check for the presence of a partial or complete sciatic nerve injury. Sciatic nerve injuries are frequently seen, and an accurate diagnosis should be made prior to any closed or open manipulation of the hip.[16, 44, 84, 97, 173, 174] Lum-

bosacral plexus injuries are associated with major pelvic trauma, but a careful neurologic examination in a cooperative patient may be required to demonstrate their presence, and injury may not be evident until sufficient patient comfort is attained.[40]

Abrasions overlying the patella or proximal anterior tibia are often evidence of the site of application of the injury force.[39, 52, 65] These findings should alert the physician to the possibility of occult knee ligament injuries, patella fractures, or osteochondral fractures of the distal femur.[60] Pelvic ring injuries and spine injuries may also be associated with hip dislocations, and these areas must be carefully assessed.

## Imaging Studies

The association of hip dislocations with high-energy trauma and multiple injuries should maintain the physician's high index of suspicion for such injuries. All blunt trauma patients with an altered mental state, or local signs or symptoms, must have a screening anteroposterior (AP) radiograph of the pelvis. Similarly, all patients with significant lower extremity injuries, spine fractures, or abdominal or chest injuries should also have an AP pelvic radiograph. Alert and fully cooperative injured patients may not need pelvic radiographs if they are hemodynam-

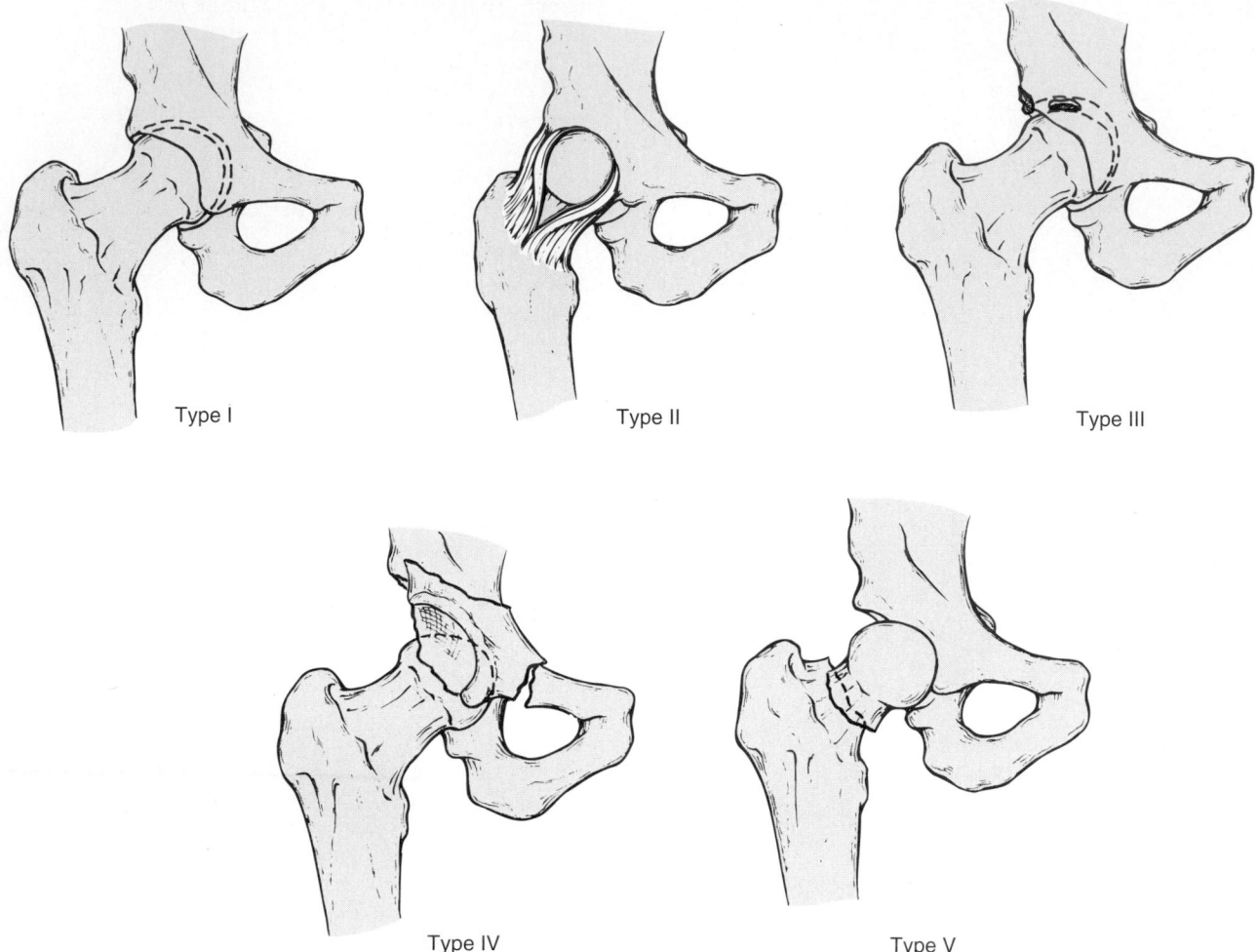

Type I

Type II

Type III

Type IV

Type V

**Figure 46–11.** Comprehensive classification of anterior hip dislocations. (see Table 46–3.)

ically stable and no symptoms or signs suggest an occult pelvic fracture or hip region injury.

The review of the initial screening AP pelvic radiograph must be done carefully and systematically. The femoral heads should appear symmetric in size, and the joint spaces should be symmetric throughout the arc of the acetabulum as well as when comparing left with right. In the presence of a posterior hip dislocation, the femoral head will appear smaller on the AP radiograph. In an anterior dislocation, the femoral head will appear slightly larger than that in the normal hip. Shenton's line should be smooth and continuous. The relative appearance of the greater and lesser trochanters may indicate pathologic internal or external rotation of the hip. An adducted or abducted position of the femoral shaft should also be noted. Finally, careful evaluation of the femoral neck must rule out the presence of a femoral neck fracture prior to any manipulative reduction. A true AP view of the proximal femur may be required to evaluate this region prior to attempted closed reduction maneuvers.

Following the diagnosis of a hip dislocation, additional imaging studies are required prior to definitive surgical treatment. Most often, these additional studies are obtained after a closed reduction has been achieved.

## PLAIN FILM ANALYSIS

Once the diagnosis of a hip dislocation is made, additional radiographs are obtained prior to any open surgical intervention. Usually, these films are obtained following a successful closed reduction, but on occasion, they are obtained prior to an open reduction of an irreducible femoral head. Additional films usually include a post-

**TABLE 46–3**

Levin Classification of Anterior Hip Dislocations

| | |
|---|---|
| Type I | No significant associated fractures; no clinical instability after concentric reduction |
| Type II | Irreducible dislocation without significant femoral head or acetabular fractures (reduction must be attempted under general anesthesia) |
| Type III | Unstable hip after reduction or incarcerated fragments of cartilage, labrum, or bone |
| Type IV | Associated acetabular fracture requiring reconstruction to restore hip stability or joint congruity |
| Type V | Associated femoral head or femoral neck injury (fractures or impactions) |

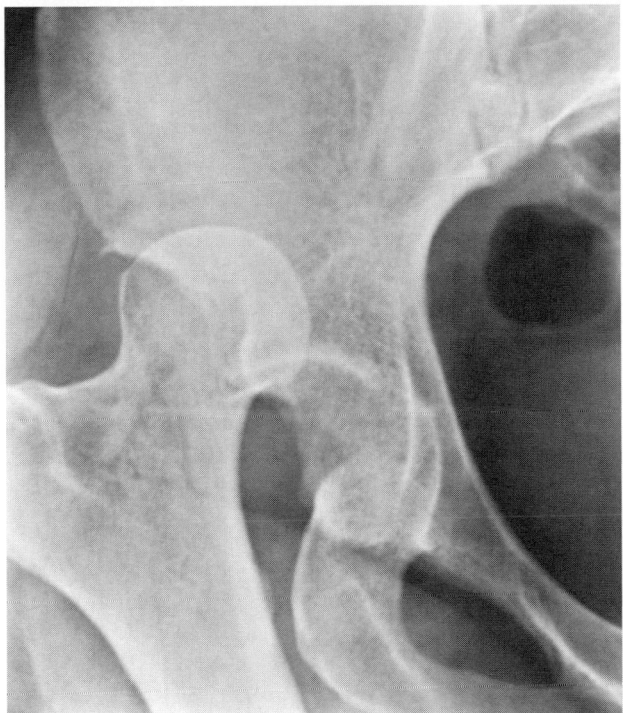

**FIGURE 46–12.** Type I posterior dislocation, with the classic position of the leg in adduction and internal rotation.

reduction AP view of the hip and a CT scan, but may also include additional plain films.

Plain film analysis should include an AP radiograph centered on the affected hip. Internal and external oblique views (Judet views) at 45° centered on the affected hip are obtained if a CT scan is not available, and may be desirable in some cases even with CT availability. These views are always obtained if a significant acetabular fracture is present. The AP radiograph should be carefully reviewed to determine the presence of incarcerated osteochondral fragments and asymmetry of the joint space. The iliac oblique (with the opposite side anterior) view brings the beam perpendicular to the posterior column and is best for evaluation of the integrity of the posterior column and the anterior wall. The obturator oblique (lateral anterior oblique) view brings the anterior column into profile and is the best view for evaluating the integrity of the anterior column and posterior wall (Figs. 46–14 and 46–15).[101]

In addition, each oblique view will present a different profile of the femoral head. Femoral head depressions and fractures should be noted. Precise interpretation of these initial films is most critical if open surgery will be required prior to obtaining CT analysis. Proper choice of surgical approach may depend on correct preoperative identification of associated acetabular or femoral head fractures. If necessary, they can be obtained in the operating room after induction of anesthesia.

## COMPUTED TOMOGRAPHY

CT should be routinely obtained following successful closed reduction of a dislocated hip. If a successful closed reduction is not possible and an open reduction is planned, a CT scan should be obtained if no undue delay is required. Emergency CT scanning is readily available in most hospitals and has demonstrated accuracy in the evaluation of the traumatized abdomen.[17, 137] A specific request for multiple 3 mm cuts through the hips and additional cuts through the sacroiliac joints may be required to ensure that CT scans done for evaluating the abdomen also include these regions.

The value of CT scanning is its ability to assess the femoral head, to demonstrate the presence of small intra-

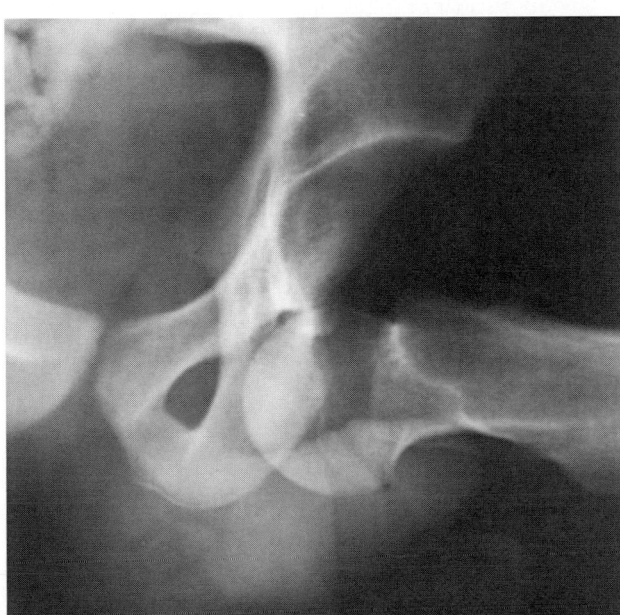

**FIGURE 46–13.** Anterior dislocation of the hip. Notice that the leg is widely abducted and externally rotated.

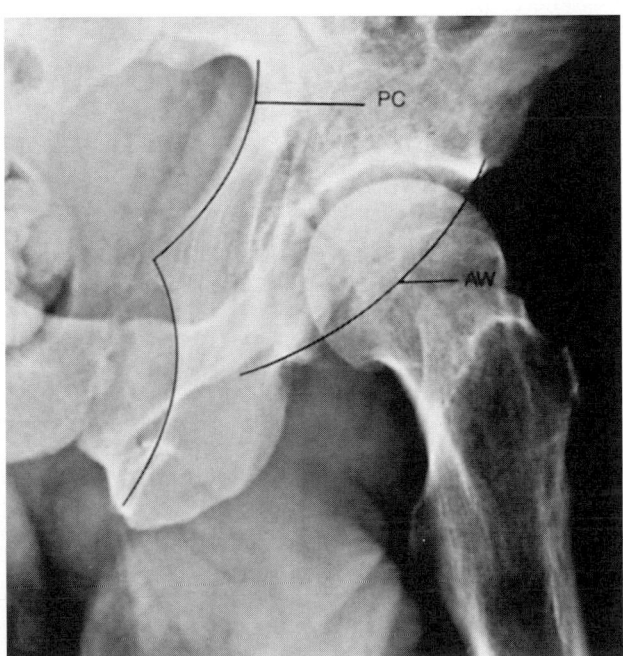

**FIGURE 46–14.** The iliac oblique radiograph brings the posterior column (PC) and anterior wall (AW) of the acetabulum into profile.

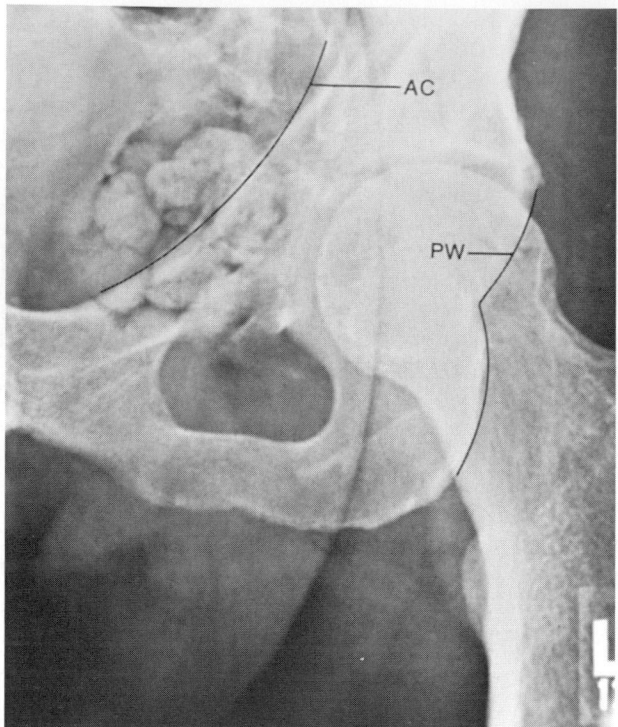

**Figure 46–15.** The obturator oblique radiograph brings the anterior column (AC) and posterior wall (PW) of the acetabulum into profile.

articular fragments, and to assess the congruence of the femoral head and acetabulum.[4, 70, 82, 107, 165, 171, 191, 196] Baird and colleagues placed 2 and 4mm methyl methacrylate spacers in cadaver hip joints and then performed plain radiographs and CT scans on these specimens.[4] The CT scans routinely revealed the 2mm spacers, whereas the plain radiographs failed to demonstrate their presence. Figure 46–16 demonstrates an incarcerated osteochondral fragment not visualized on post-reduction plain radiographs.

CT imaging better visualizes the size, location, and displacement of acetabular wall fractures.

Ebraheim and associates described the use of soft tissue windows with enhancement techniques of CT images in an attempt to improve the visualization of intraarticular fragments.[38] Fairbairn and co-workers described the presence of gas bubbles in the hip joint seen on CT scan.[50] This finding in a hip not having a documented dislocation could reflect a hip that was subluxed and spontaneously reduced. Calkins and colleagues devised a scale that attempts to correlate the percentage of displaced acetabular wall as measured on CT scan with hip stability.[22] Although some basic parameters can be developed from this study, a significant degree of variability exists, making precise correlations impossible (Figs. 46–17 and 46–18). CT scanning has also proved to be valuable in demonstrating displaced impaction injuries of the acetabular articular surface (Fig. 46–19).

The value of CT scanning in demonstrating femoral head injury has been reported by a number of investigators.[107, 133, 171, 196] Occult impactions, indentations, and other fractures have all been clearly visualized on CT scanning. The severity of displacement of fractures is accurately assessed by CT scanning.

## MAGNETIC RESONANCE IMAGING

A critical role for MRI following traumatic hip dislocation has not been well established. Numerous investigations have reported the diagnosis of labral disruptions, femoral head contusions and microfractures, sciatic nerve injury, intra-articular fragments, and pelvic vein thrombophlebitis.[96, 98, 143, 144, 176] In the acute setting, MRI might become most valuable in evaluating a widened hip joint in the presence of a normal CT scan (to image interposed soft tissues and incarcerated fragments). In addition, a diagnosis of a labral disruption may be documented in a hip that is unstable despite normal CT analysis (Fig.46–20). Magnetic resonance phlebography can assess the pelvic veins for occult thrombophlebitis.[124] MRI has been

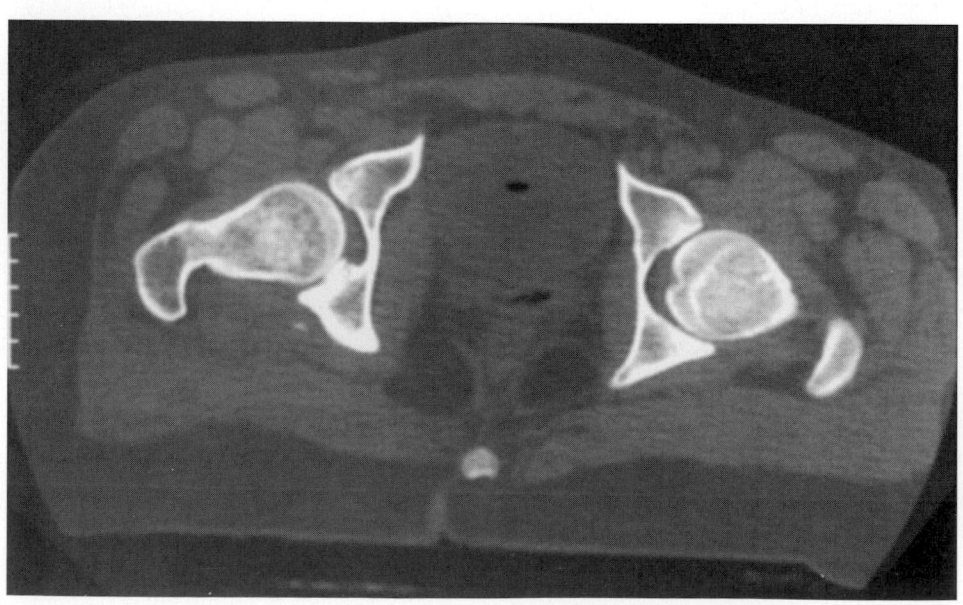

**Figure 46–16.** After reduction of a right posterior hip dislocation, a computed tomography scan demonstrates an incarcerated osteochondral fragment. This fragment (comprehensive classification, type III) requires removal.

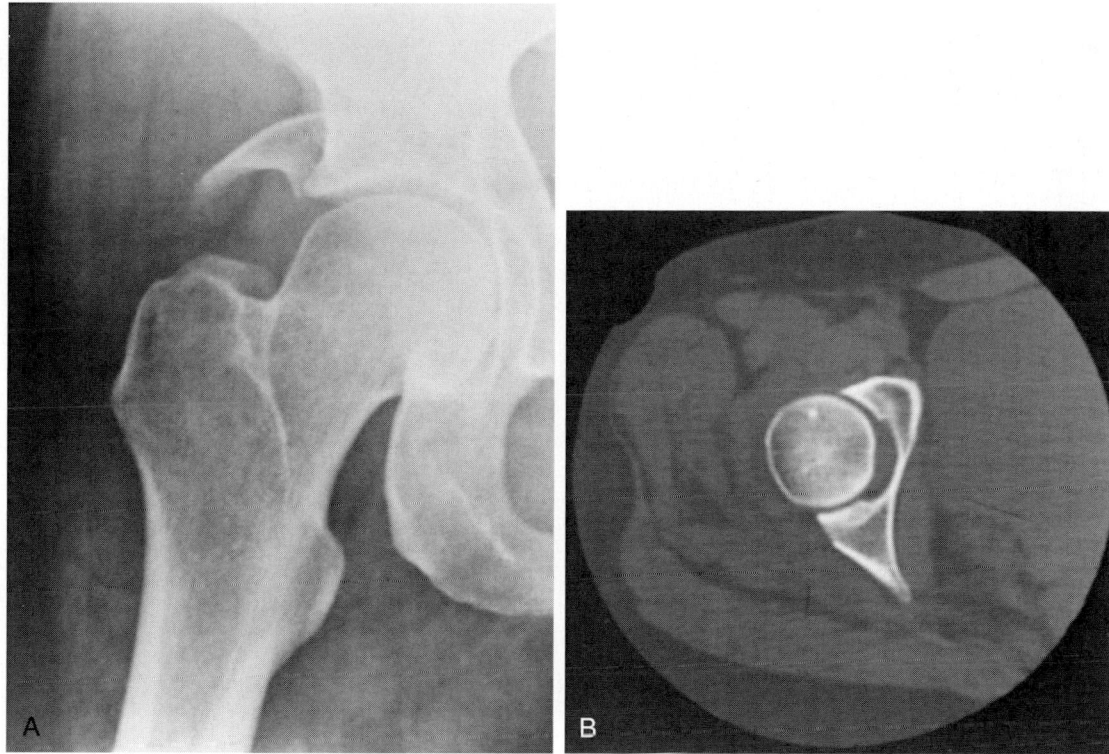

**FIGURE 46–17.** A displaced posterior wall fragment appears relatively large on a postreduction film (*A*), but the computed tomography scan (*B*) demonstrates that only a minimal portion of the posterior articular surface is involved.

proposed to monitor for the development of osteonecrosis at the femoral head, but early investigations have not supported this use.[96, 142]

## ISOTOPE IMAGING

Isotope imaging with either technetium-labeled phosphate compounds or technetium 99m-sulfur colloid is not indicated in the post-injury imaging of hip dislocations. Meyers and co-workers suggested using technetium 99m-sulfur colloid to predict femoral head viability following hip dislocation.[118] The value of such studies has not, however, been demonstrated.

## MANAGEMENT

The management of a patient with a hip dislocation is divided into an initial phase of achieving rapid reduction of the dislocation followed by a secondary phase of

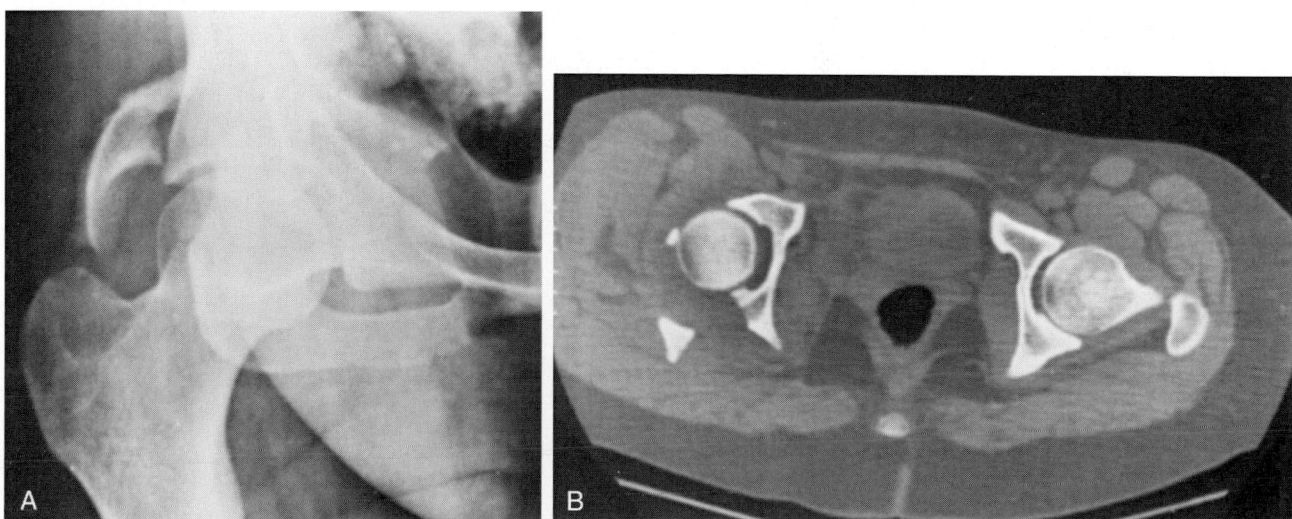

**FIGURE 46–18.** The displaced posterior wall fragment (*A*) is demonstrated on the computed tomography (CT) scan (*B*) to encompass a major portion of the posterior articular surface. Comparison of the contours of the normal and the injured hips on the CT scan elucidates the extent of the fracture.

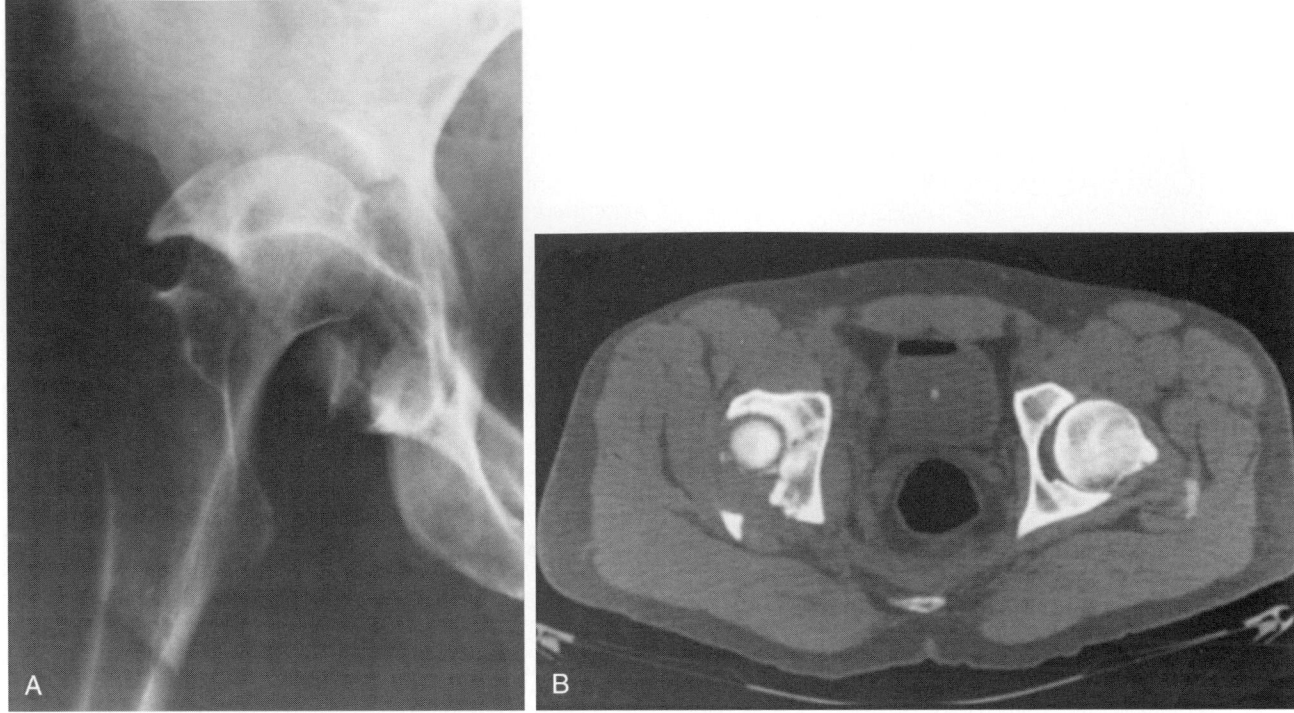

**FIGURE 46–19.** *A,* The injury film demonstrates a displaced posterior wall fragment with some possible comminution. *B,* The computed tomography scan demonstrates extensive involvement of the posterior articular surface, with major joint depression extending to the acetabular fossa.

planning and performing definitive care.[197] This division into phases is necessary because of the initial urgency of reducing the hip to decrease the risk of long-term complications. Numerous investigators reported a strong correlation of AVN of the femoral head with the amount of time during which the hip remains dislocated.[15, 83, 174, 181, 183] After the femoral head has been reduced, urgency is diminished. The appropriate diagnostic workup, including CT analysis of the hip, can then be

completed. Surgical intervention, if necessary, can be undertaken when the patient has become physiologically stable and higher priority injuries have been addressed.

## Initial Management

Although it is generally agreed that dislocated hips should be reduced rapidly, some debate exists in older literature as

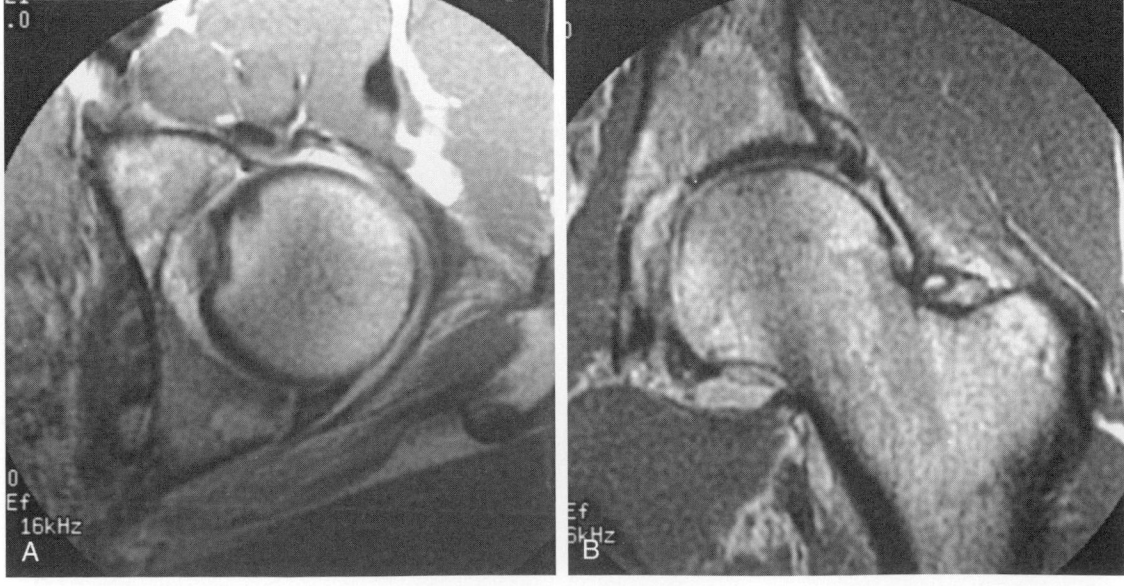

**FIGURE 46–20.** Magnetic resonance imaging scans of a hip after acute fracture-dislocation. *A,* The axial view demonstrates a posterior wall fracture. *B,* The sagittal image demonstrates a superior labral tear. (*A, B,* Courtesy of Dr. Hollis G. Potter, Dept. of Radiology, Hospital for Special Surgery, New York, NY.)

to whether this should be by closed or open methods. Most investigators recommend an immediate attempt at a closed reduction.[15, 83, 84, 94, 95, 101, 146, 173, 183] Epstein[42] and DeLee[31] recommended that closed reduction be reserved for simple dislocations not associated with any fractures. They urged that all fracture-dislocations should be treated by immediate open surgery to remove loose fragments from the joint and to reconstruct fractures. Thompson and Epstein demonstrated improved long-term results in a retrospective comparison of open treatment with closed treatment.[44, 181] It is probable that the improved results of immediate open reduction were related to the ability to visually clear the acetabulum of all loose fragments, which at the time of Epstein's work[43] could not be radiographically demonstrated. The introduction of CT scanning and its routine use in post-reduction evaluation obviate this benefit of routine immediate open reduction.

## SPECIAL CONSIDERATIONS IN THE MULTIPLE-INJURED PATIENT

Hip dislocations are frequently encountered in patients with multiple injuries. The initial return of the femoral head to the acetabulum remains of utmost importance, whereas associated acetabular or femoral head fractures can be treated during the subacute phase of patient management.

Any patient requiring an immediate general anesthetic for surgical treatment of a head, abdominal, or thoracic injury can have a rapid closed reduction of the hip dislocation. A patient who requires intubation in the emergency department might also benefit from a rapid closed reduction during pharmacologic paralysis for intubation.

A hip that is stable following reduction does not require traction. An unstable hip secondary to an acetabular fracture should be placed in skeletal traction, with care being taken to keep the leg slightly externally rotated and abducted when posterior instability is present and in neutral to mild internal rotation for anterior instability. The timing of surgery is discussed in Chapter 37 on acetabular fractures. It is often helpful to treat patients requiring traction in specially cushioned beds while they await acetabular surgery.

## ALGORITHM FOR INITIAL MANAGEMENT

Prompt reduction of the femoral head is the goal of initial management. Regardless of the direction (anterior or posterior) of the dislocation, the reduction can be attempted with inline traction with the patient lying supine. The preferred approach is to perform a closed reduction under conscious sedation, or possibly under general anesthesia if an anesthesiologist is readily available. An operating room is not required, because reductions can be performed in a properly equipped emergency department with the benefit of sufficient, adequately monitored, anesthesia.

If it is not feasible to place the patient under general anesthesia immediately, then an attempt at a closed reduction in the emergency department is performed using conscious sedation. It is crucial that no attempt at reduction be performed until the patient is appropriately sedated. Intermittent attempts at reduction followed by incremental administration of medication are much less fruitful and usually fail.

If closed reduction is unsuccessful using conscious sedation, the patient should be transported to the operating room, where closed reduction should be attempted with the patient under general anesthesia, including adequate muscle paralysis. If a closed reduction cannot be achieved in this setting, then an immediate open reduction is indicated.

It is incumbent on the orthopaedic surgeon to stress the urgency of the situation to the trauma team, anesthesiologist, and operating room personnel. It must be made clear that the prevention of long-term complications demands urgent treatment in the operating room. The urgency of reducing a hip dislocation is at least as great as that of treating an open fracture.

Historically, the two most popular methods of achieving closed reduction have been the supine method of Allis and the prone, gravity-assisted method of Stimson.[1, 175] Both maneuvers are applicable to all types of hip dislocations, with the exception of subspinous and pubic dislocations, which must be reduced with the Allis method.[27] The forceful rotational technique of Bigelow[9] should be avoided, because it risks an iatrogenic femoral neck fracture.

The Allis method of reduction relies primarily on traction applied in line with the deformity. The patient remains supine. The surgeon must be able to achieve a mechanical advantage by either standing on the stretcher or placing the patient on the floor. No attempt should be made to reduce the hip while the patient is lying on the stretcher and the surgeon is standing on the floor. Initially, the surgeon should apply inline traction while the assistant applies countertraction manually by stabilizing the patient's pelvis. As in the reduction of any joint dislocation, a slow progressive increase in the traction force is much more effective than a rapid abrupt pull. While increasing the traction force, the surgeon should slowly increase the degree of flexion to approximately 60° to 90°. Gentle rotational motions of the hip as well as slight adduction will often help the femoral head clear the lip of the acetabulum. Some authors recommend application of a lateral force to the proximal thigh to assist in the reduction. The successful closed reduction is usually indicated by an audible "clunk" as well as return of the leg to a neutral alignment. An awake patient usually has an immediate improvement in symptoms (Fig. 46–21).

The Stimson gravity technique of reduction has historically been preferred by some surgeons because of the ease of reduction (from the surgeon's perspective) and therefore the theoretical benefit of decreasing the risk of damage to the femoral head articular cartilage.[31, 174, 175] The patient is placed prone on the stretcher with the affected leg hanging off the side of the stretcher. This brings the extremity into a position of hip flexion and knee flexion at 90° each. In this position, the surgeon can easily apply an anteriorly directed force on the proximal calf. In actuality, the Allis and Stimson maneuvers are precisely the same, with the ultimate reduction force being applied to the hip in a flexed position. The apparent benefit lies in the surgeon's position (Fig. 46–22). Despite the similarity of

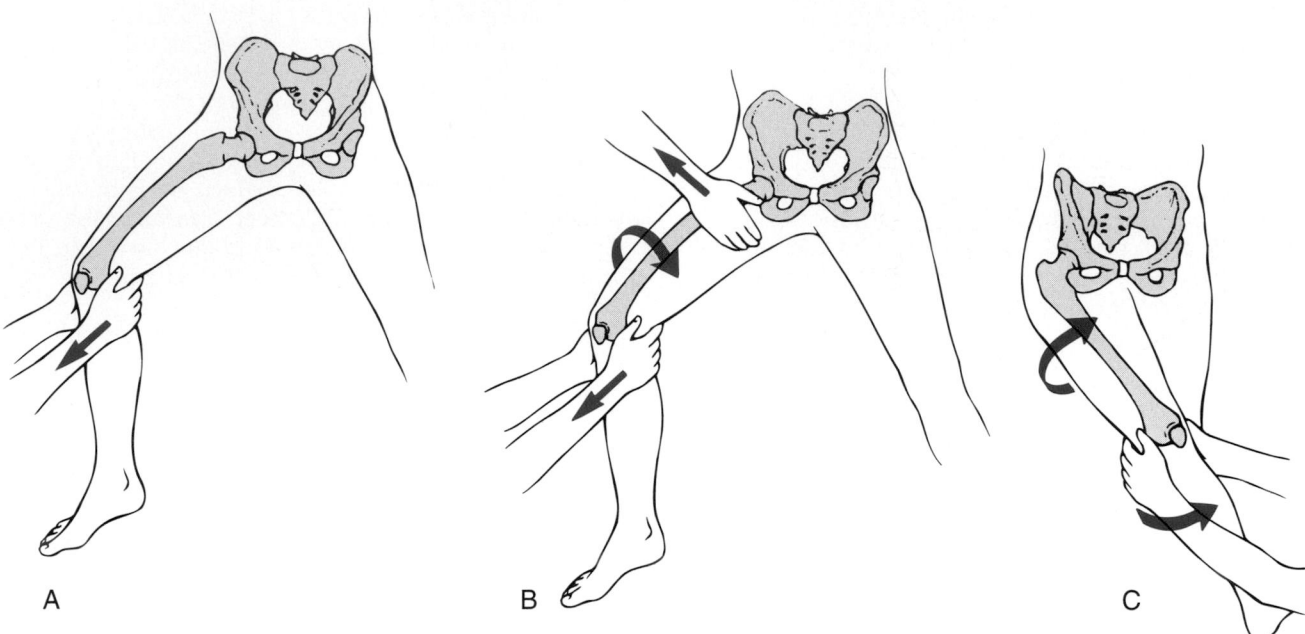

**FIGURE 46–21.** Allis technique for reduction of a hip dislocation. The surgeon's position must provide a mechanical advantage for the application of traction. *A*, Internal and external rotation is gently alternated, perhaps with lateral traction on the proximal thigh by an assistant. *B*, Inline traction with hip flexes. *C*, Adduction is often a helpful adjunct to inline traction. (*A–C*, Adapted from DeLee, J.C. In: Rockwood, C.A., Jr.; Green, D.P. Fractures, 2nd ed., Vol. 2. Philadelphia, J.B. Lippincott, 1985.)

the two maneuvers, the Stimson maneuver is seldom used today because a large percentage of these patients have multiple injuries, and placing them in the prone position may risk additional complications.

In addition to the classic reduction techniques of Allis and Stimson, numerous other techniques have been devised that generate sufficient force to reduce a dislocated hip without creating large torsional forces that could lead to iatrogenic femoral neck fractures. One simple widely used technique is the lateral traction method, a modification of the Allis technique in which a longitudinal distraction force is applied to the affected hip of a supine patient. A sheet through which an assistant applies lateral

traction is wrapped around the patient's upper thigh (Fig. 46–23).[130] A similar traction-counter-traction maneuver in which the hip is reduced with the patient turned on the stretcher to a lateral position has been proposed by Dahners and Hundley.[28] This allows easy application of traction to the adducted and flexed hip, which is also internally rotated so the femoral head clears the posterior acetabular wall (Fig. 46–24).

Several authors have described techniques that use a fulcrum formed by the knee or forearm of the examiner or the examiner's assistant as a useful adjunct to reduction with the patient in a supine position. All of these techniques minimize the effort required by the examiner,

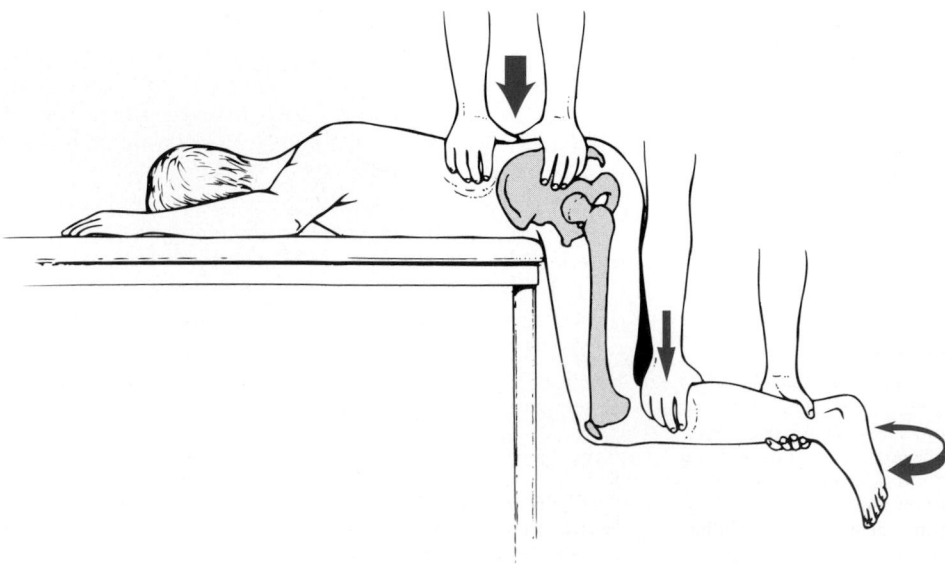

**FIGURE 46–22.** Stimson gravity reduction technique. This method has limited application in patients with multiple injuries. (Adapted from DeLee, J.C. In: Rockwood, C.A., Jr.; Green, D.P. Fractures, 2nd ed., Vol. 2. Philadelphia, J.B. Lippincott, 1985.)

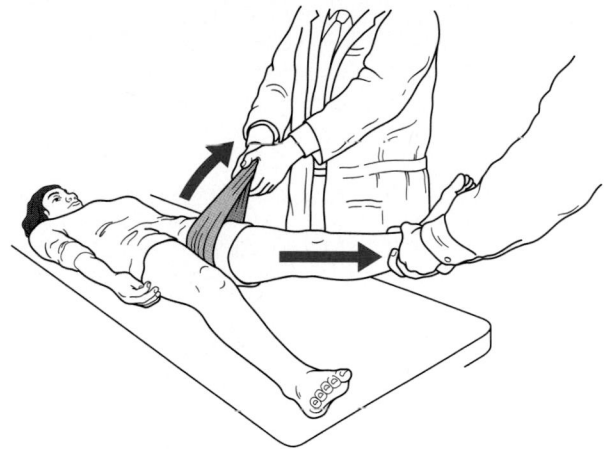

**FIGURE 46–23.** Lateral traction method of reduction. A longitudinal distraction force is applied to the affected hip of a supine patient. An assistant applies lateral traction through a sheet, which is wrapped around the patient's upper thigh.

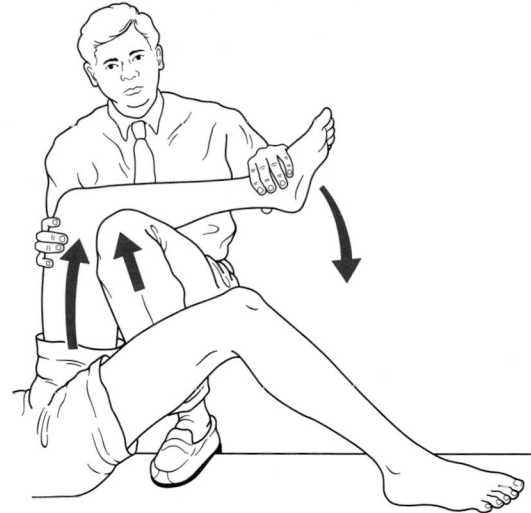

**FIGURE 46–25.** Reduction technique described by Lefkowitz, 1993. The flexed leg of the examiner is placed on the table, and the examiner's knee is used as a fulcrum. The patient's tibia is levered against the fulcrum as an anterior distraction force is applied to the hip.

allowing greater control while creating and sustaining substantial traction force. Each of these maneuvers places stress on the patient's knee, and relies on reasonable integrity of the knee, the femur, and the proximal tibia. The number of assistants required varies among these techniques. Lefkowitz[99] described a reduction technique in which the flexed leg of the examiner is placed on the table and the examiner's knee is used as a fulcrum. The patient's tibia is levered against the fulcrum as an anterior distraction force is applied to the hip (Fig. 46–25). Marya and Samuel[113] described a "piggyback method" with the patient supine at the end of a table with the hip flexed. In this method, the examiner's shoulder is used as a fulcrum. The patient's tibia is levered against the shoulder fulcrum and the limb is adducted as an anterior distraction force is applied to the hip (Fig. 46–26). Nordt[130] described a

technique in which the examiner's hand is placed on the patient's contralateral knee. The involved knee is flexed over the examiner's forearm, creating a fulcrum against which the distal tibia can be levered downward. This maneuver distracts the femoral head anteriorly and distally, allowing the femoral head to clear the posteroinferior rim of the acetabulum as simultaneous gentle internal rotation of the hip is performed (Fig. 46–27).

Schafer and Anglen[166] described the East Baltimore lift, a technique popular among house officers at Johns Hopkins Hospital, in which the forearms of an examiner and assistant are used together to create a fulcrum for reduction. The examiner stands on the side of the dislocation at the level of the pelvis, with the assistant facing across the table. Both begin the maneuver with knees bent approximately 45°. The examiner places

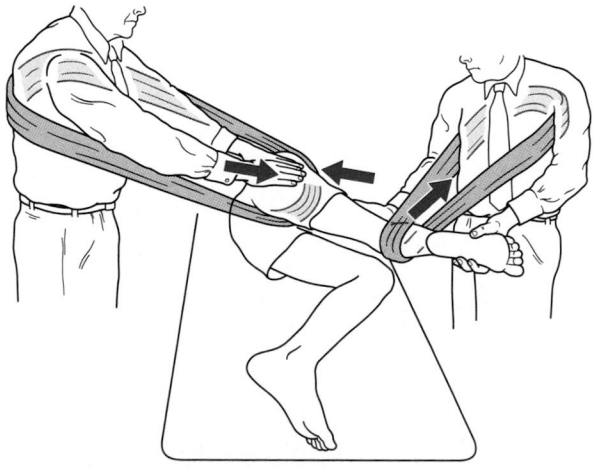

**FIGURE 46–24.** Lateral decubitus reduction technique described by Dahners and Hundley.[28] The patient's affected hip is adducted, flexed significantly, and internally rotated. Traction is applied through looped bed sheets, the surgeon's just distal to the patient's flexed knee and the assistant's around the patient's groin on the dislocated side. Wrapped around their waists, these loops allow traction forces to be exerted by surgeon and assistant leaning backward against them, rather than lifting the patient's leg or climbing up on the stretcher.

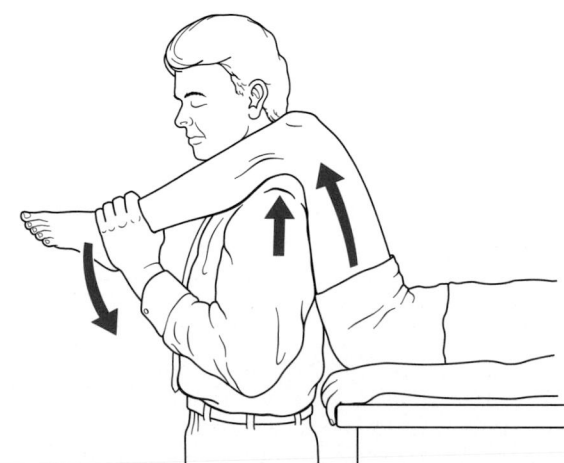

**FIGURE 46–26.** "Piggyback" reduction technique described by Marya and Samuel.[113] With the patient supine at the end of a table and with the hip flexed, the examiner's shoulder is used as a fulcrum. The patient's tibia is levered against the shoulder fulcrum, and the limb is adducted while an anterior distraction force is applied to the hip.

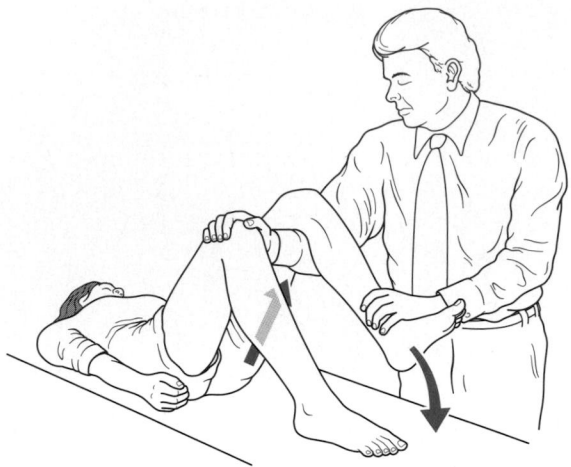

**FIGURE 46–27.** Reduction technique described by Nordt, 1999. The examiner's hand is placed on the patient's contralateral knee, and the involved knee is flexed over the examiner's forearm, creating a fulcrum against which the distal tibia can be levered downward. This maneuver distracts the femoral head anteriorly and distally, allowing the femoral head to clear the posteroinferior rim of the acetabulum. Simultaneous gentle internal rotation of the hip is performed.

one arm under the proximal calf of the patient, with his hand resting on the shoulder of the assistant standing across the table. The assistant's arm passes under the proximal calf of the patient in a similar fashion, with the assistant's hand resting on the shoulder of the examiner. The examiner's free hand stabilizes the patient's ankle, while the assistant's free hand is used to hold down the ipsilateral iliac crest. The examiner and assistant apply traction to the femur by slowly standing up, using their arms to create controlled, gentle traction on the patient's leg (Fig. 46–28).

If the hip cannot be reduced by closed manipulation under general anesthesia, an immediate open reduction must be performed. Prior to open reduction, either a CT scan or Judet views of the hip should be obtained. It is preferable to obtain a CT scan prior to undertaking an open surgical procedure. A CT scan provides valuable preoperative information concerning intraarticular fragments or a femoral head injury that was not appreciated on plain films. These findings may help determine which surgical exposure is used. Under some circumstances, a CT scan may be unavailable, or an anesthetized patient may be unable to be transported to the CT suite. Judet views are useful substitutes if CT is not available. These two oblique radiographs also allow assessment of the acetabulum and permit accurate surgical planning. In general, anterior acetabular fractures or femoral head injuries will require an anterior exposure of the hip joint regardless of the direction of the hip dislocation. Posterior acetabular fractures require repair through a posterior hip exposure, which is not adequate for open reduction and internal fixation of most femoral head fractures.

## Management after Reduction

Postreduction management of hip dislocations has historically been controversial. Recommendations have run the spectrum from short periods of simple bedrest to hip spica cast immobilization or various durations of skeletal traction.[3, 16, 181, 182] Although some previous authors suggested that early weight bearing predisposes the patient to AVN, this correlation could not be established in more recent series.[15, 31, 41, 44, 136, 167, 173, 183]

## ALGORITHM FOR POSTREDUCTION MANAGEMENT

Management following successful closed reduction will depend on the postreduction physical examination and imaging studies. The direction of the dislocation is not a factor in determining postreduction management. The grading of the injury, the presence and location of femoral head or acetabular fractures, and the presence and direction of instability must be considered in planning the next step of treatment. For example, a hip that demonstrates posterior instability without fracture following posterior dislocation will most probably require a posterior soft tissue repair. A hip that demonstrates anterior instability without fracture following an anterior dislocation may instead require an anterior exploration and repair.

Immediately following closed reduction, AP and lateral radiographs of the involved hip as well as an AP radiograph of the pelvis should be obtained. Systematic analysis of the radiographs should be carried out to verify that the hip has been concentrically reduced (e.g., by looking for subtle widening of the joint). If there are significant acetabular fractures (fractures other than small avulsion fractures), Judet views should also be obtained (Fig. 46–29).

Once radiographic verification of reduction has been obtained, an examination for hip stability is performed.

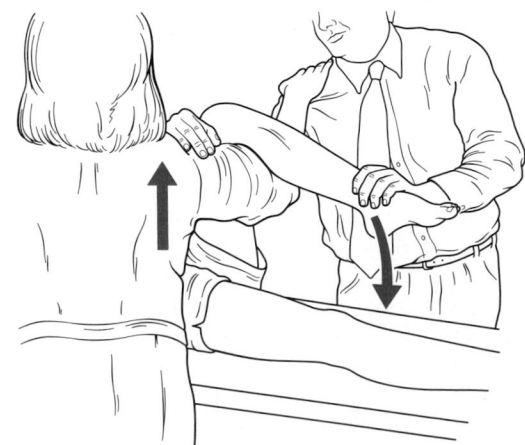

**FIGURE 46–28.** East Baltimore lift. The examiner stands on the side of the dislocation at the level of the patient's pelvis. The assistant faces across the table. Each begins the maneuver with knees bent approximately 45°. The examiner places one arm under the proximal calf of the patient, with a hand resting on the shoulder of the assistant, who is standing across the table. The assistant's arm passes under the proximal calf of the patient in a similar fashion, with the assistant's hand resting on the shoulder of the examiner. The examiner's free hand stabilizes the patient's ankle, while the assistant's free hand is used to hold down the ipsilateral iliac crest. The examiner and assistant apply traction to the femur by slowly standing up, using their arms as a fulcrum that creates controlled, gentle traction on the patient's leg.

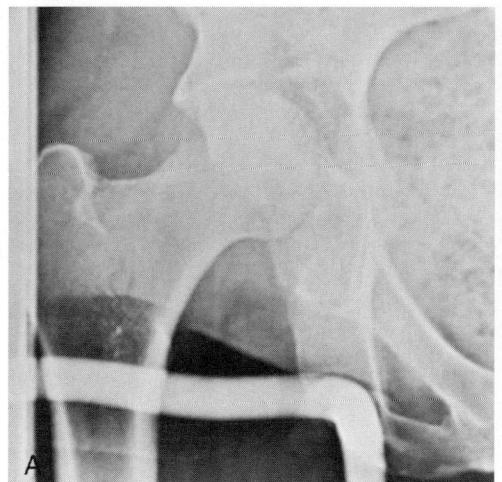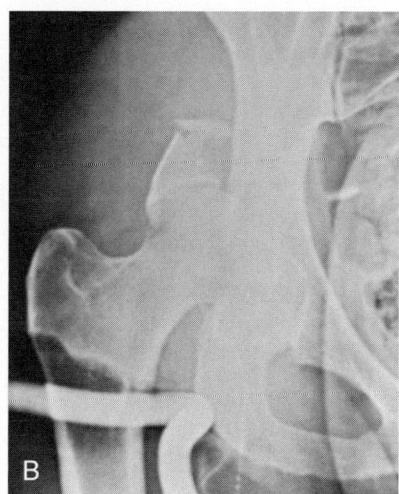

FIGURE 46–29. *A,* Careful assessment of postreduction films must be undertaken to avoid errors. This anteroposterior radiograph was initially misinterpreted because of the apparent congruence of the femoral head with the displaced acetabular fragment. Notice the abnormal appearance of Shenton's line. *B,* The obturator oblique view clearly shows the persistent posterior dislocation with comminuted posterior wall fracture (comprehensive classification type IV).

The examination is done while the patient remains sedated or under anesthesia, depending on the method used for the initial closed reduction. If there is an obvious large, displaced posterior or postero-superior acetabular wall fracture, the stability examination is not performed. The examination is also deferred in the presence of displaced acetabular column fractures, or other surgical indications.

The capsule and supporting ligamentous condensations of the hip supply secondary stabilization, and a portion of these structures is likely damaged at the time of dislocation. Despite this relative loss of stability, the combined bony acetabulum and cartilaginous labrum should leave the hip relatively stable. Following verification of reduction, the hip is flexed to between 90° and 95° in neutral abduction/adduction and neutral rotation. A strong posteriorly directed force is then applied.[65] If any sensation of subluxation is detected, the patient will require additional diagnostic studies and possibly surgical exploration. If the patient is awake during this examination, she or he may be able to assist the surgeon in detecting instability. Larson retrospectively reviewed a series of hip dislocations and found that 17 hips treated in traction had obvious radiographic signs of instability or incongruity.[97] Each one of these patients developed traumatic arthritis, attesting to the importance of surgical exploration and repair in the setting of instability.

A CT scan should be obtained, the femoral head should be carefully analyzed for the presence of fractures or depressions, and the acetabulum should be examined for impaction fractures.

Although CT scans did not alter patient treatment in one small series of patients with simple hip dislocations,[54] obtaining a CT scan to evaluate for posterior wall or femoral head impactions remains an essential part of the treatment algorithm for most surgeons treating hip dislocations. Early treatment of these injuries can dramatically improve long-term results. The CT should be obtained with three millimeter sections through the entire acetabulum and processed for both bone and soft tissue windows.[38] The presence of incarcerated osteochondral fragments between the acetabular articular cartilage and the femoral articular cartilage should be noted (see Fig. 46–16).

MRI scanning is uncommonly indicated, but may play a role in the analysis of an unstable hip in which CT scanning has not demonstrated an intraarticular fragment and in which no acetabular wall fracture exists. Rashleigh-Belcher reported on a case of recurrent hip dislocation following an initial traumatic dislocation in which surgical exploration revealed a labral detachment.[149] MRI scanning does visualize the acetabular labrum and therefore may demonstrate such a detachment (see Fig. 46–20).[11, 96] A second indication for MRI exists when both plain radiographs and CT images demonstrate unexplained joint widening. MRI scanning may demonstrate incarcerated fragments or interposed soft tissues.[96, 143] Canale and Manugian,[23] Dameron,[30] and Paterson[135] all reported cases in which the acetabular labrum either blocked reduction or became incarcerated in the joint. MRI scanning is well suited for analyzing unexplained widening, as it differentiates between labral incarcerations, pure articular cartilage incarcerations, and simple hematomas. MRI is indicated only in an unstable or widened hip with no other obvious cause (e.g., fractures or intraarticular fragments).

Definitive management is based on the classification of the dislocation. The direction of the dislocation (anterior or posterior) may or may not determine the actual surgical approach. The final decisions regarding surgical exploration and specific surgical approach must be determined by the pathology. The classification of dislocation as well as the location of the fractures and the direction of the instability determines the optimal treatment. It is therefore unnecessary to separately discuss the treatment of anterior and posterior dislocations.

## Management of Specific Types of Hip Dislocations

The type of dislocation and the detailed pathology determines the treatment of each type of hip dislocation. As discussed previously, the surgical approach chosen must not be determined by the direction of the dislocation. Epstein and colleagues raised concerns over using an anterior approach following posterior dislocation, believing that this would lead to complete vascular disruption.[46] This belief is not supported either by a careful analysis of the vascular supply of the femoral head or by a review of the recent literature. Injury should not occur to the lateral femoral circumflex artery or its branches if the dissection avoids removal of the capsule from the femoral neck and trochanters. Evidence supporting this recommendation can be found in the works of Butler[20] and Thorpe and associates.[182] The following sections address the treatment of each type of hip dislocation, following the proposed classification that de-emphasizes the initial position of the dislocated femoral head.

## LEVIN TYPE I: CLOSED REDUCTION SUCCESSFUL

Type I injuries are essentially pure dislocations with either no associated fractures or small acetabular rim fractures. The physical examination verifies inherent stability, and no surgical stabilization is indicated. These individuals are begun as soon as comfort permits, on an active and passive range of motion protocol. Flexion beyond 90° and internal rotation beyond 10° are not permitted for 6 weeks. Traction is not clearly indicated, but may be used until the majority of the hip irritability resolves. The patient is instructed in ambulation with weight bearing as tolerated and is advised to use crutches until near-normal hip muscle strength and a normal gait are restored, usually within 6 weeks. Followup radiographs are obtained only if the patient's symptoms are not resolving as expected.

A small bone fragment noted to be in the acetabular fossa on CT scanning but not incarcerated between the articular surfaces of the femoral head and the acetabulum is believed to not be significant. This is a nonarticular region of the hip joint, and a bone fragment in this location should not create any more symptoms than a fragment in the lateral gutter of the knee. If the patient later develops symptoms of a loose intraarticular fragment (e.g., catching, locking, pain, or the hip giving way), consideration should be given to possible removal of the fragment.

## LEVIN TYPE II: CLOSED REDUCTION UNSUCCESSFUL

The type II dislocation is one in which a successful closed reduction cannot be achieved. If the femoral head has been returned to the confines of the acetabulum but the joint space is widened, the ultimate grading of the dislocation will be type III, IV, or V, depending on the cause of the widening.

A hip that is irreducible purely for reasons of soft tissue interposition (e.g., capsular, tendinous, or muscular) will be definitely diagnosed during open reduction of the dislocation. In this instance, the grading will remain type II.

Proctor reported a case in which the piriformis tendon became wrapped around the femoral neck, preventing reduction.[146] Epstein described a case in which the iliopsoas tendon prevented reduction of an anterior dislocation.[44]

Bucholz and Wheeless reported a series of six irreducible posterior hip fracture-dislocations.[18] Surgical explora-tion of these six hips and cadaveric dissection and analysis revealed that a portion of the broad base of the iliofemoral ligament remained tethered between the displaced wall fragment and the postero-superior ilium just proximal to the acetabulum. This tethering effect left the displaced posterior wall fragment caught between the femoral head and the acetabulum, preventing reduction (Fig. 46–30).

No matter what the cause for the type II dislocation, immediate open surgical reduction must be performed. Preoperative radiographs (Judet views) should be obtained to determine the surgical approach. If logistically possible without excessive delay in treatment, it is also desirable to obtain a CT scan prior to the surgical procedure.

If there are no associated acetabular or femoral head fractures, the surgical approach should expose the hip joint on the side of the dislocation. In the event of an irreducible posterior dislocation, a standard Kocher-Langenbeck approach is performed. An irreducible anterior dislocation is exposed through a surgical approach that visualizes the anterior hip capsule (e.g., Watson-Jones or Hardinge).[69, 81] It may be advisable to avoid an anterior exposure such as the Smith-Petersen approach in order to reduce the risk of damaging the taut and displaced femoral nerve, artery, and vein.

Prior to reducing the femoral head, the hip joint should be examined. Femoral head and acetabular depressions should be elevated and grafted if of appropriate size. The joint should be thoroughly irrigated to remove all loose fragments and debris. The status of the articular cartilage of the femoral head and acetabulum should be noted. Gentle manipulation of the hip with appropriate traction on the leg may then be performed. A bone hook on the greater trochanter will help the femoral head gain

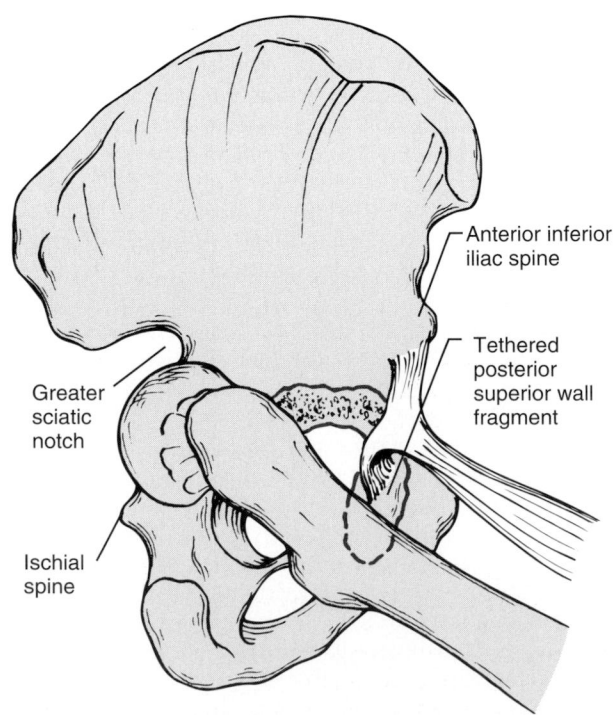

**FIGURE 46–30.** Tethering of the displaced posterior wall fragment by the iliofemoral ligament is blocking reduction of the hip dislocation.

clearance over the acetabular margin. Manual pressure on the femoral head when guiding it into the acetabulum will diminish the need for aggressive traction and torsion to the leg.

Following successful open reduction, a stability examination is performed. If the hip is stable at 90° of flexion with a strong posteriorly applied force, the postoperative regimen is the same as for the type I dislocation. The patient is instructed in the use of crutches for weightbearing-as-tolerated ambulation. Initially restricted range of motion and progressive strengthening exercises are begun, and crutches are used until a normal gait is established.

If the intraoperative post-reduction examination reveals instability, additional surgical exploration is essential to uncover the cause. Extensive capsular tears or labral disruptions should be repaired. Intraoperative radiographs should be obtained to evaluate for a widened hip joint secondary to incarcerated fragments. These are the most common causes of failure to achieve stability.

If the irreducible hip dislocation is associated with a femoral head or acetabular fracture, the fracture pattern must be fully understood prior to performing open reduction. In this situation, the surgical approach used must be appropriate in order to achieve reduction of the associated fractures. The reader is referred to Chapter 37 for more detailed information on surgical approaches and treatment of acetabular fractures.

When faced with an extensive acetabular fracture and an irreducible hip, the surgeon should be confident that open reduction and internal fixation of the acetabular fracture can be achieved at the same time. If anatomic reduction of the acetabulum cannot be achieved on an emergent basis, such patients may benefit from immediate referral to an experienced acetabular surgeon.

Treatment of an irreducible dislocation associated with a femoral head fracture requires precise localization of the femoral head injury. The femoral head injury associated with posterior hip dislocations is almost always located anteriorly, and therefore an anterior exposure of the hip joint will be necessary. In this situation, the hip can be approached through either a direct lateral or anterolateral approach. An extended Kocher-Langenbeck approach in which the greater trochanter and the entire abductor mechanism are osteotomized and released from the proximal femur may also provide adequate exposure with acceptable morbidity. These approaches will allow posterior hip exposure through the same skin incision, which may be necessary to release soft tissues that are incarcerating the femoral head. Chapter 48 provides a more detailed discussion of the treatment of femoral head injury.

The final situation in which the femoral head will be irreducible by closed manipulation occurs in the setting of an ipsilateral displaced femoral neck fracture. In this situation, open reduction and internal fixation of the femoral neck fracture is required. This is usually best accomplished through a direct lateral approach to the hip, with the patient on a fracture table to allow for fluoroscopic control of femoral neck fracture fixation.

A patient noted to have a nondisplaced femoral neck fracture is best treated as if the hip is irreducible by closed means. Although it is possible to achieve a reduction by closed manipulation under general anesthesia, the risks of displacing the fracture and dramatically affecting the prognosis mandate fixation of the femoral neck fracture prior to reduction of the dislocation. In this situation, the patient is placed on a fracture table, and a direct lateral approach to the hip is performed. At least one screw should be placed across the fracture prior to manipulative reduction. Following provisional fixation of the femoral neck fracture, the proximal femur is held with a bone-holding forceps while gentle reduction of the dislocation is performed. Additional parallel screws are placed to complete the fixation of the femoral neck fracture.

## LEVIN TYPE III: REDUCTION UNSUCCESSFUL OR NOT CONCENTRIC

In type III dislocations, either the post-reduction physical examination demonstrates an unstable hip with no associated fractures or the post-reduction imaging studies (CT or MRI) demonstrate an osteochondral or purely cartilaginous fragment or displaced labrum incarcerated between the articular surfaces of the femoral head and the acetabulum.

In the circumstance of an unstable hip dislocation with no associated fractures and no incarcerated fragment preventing full seating of the femoral head, MRI is recommended. The surgeon will be faced with several treatment options. If imaging studies reveal detachment of the acetabular labrum, surgical repair is considered.[105, 149] Minor labral detachments, labral tears, or ligamentous and capsular disruptions may sometimes be treated with a brace that limits the hip to its stable arc of motion. If the hip remains unstable following 6 weeks of bracing, surgical exploration and repair are indicated.

Intraarticular fragments prevent complete reduction of the femoral head and also act as an abrasive, damaging the articular surfaces. Such fragments must be removed if they are too small to be surgically replaced. Surgical removal is best planned through a surgical approach that will bring the surgeon most directly to the fragment (see Fig. 46–16).

When opening the hip, capsulotomy must be performed on the acetabular side of the joint so as to preserve the blood supply to the femoral head. This maneuver may be assisted by a distractor placed from the iliac crest to proximal femur, or by placing the patient on a surgical table that is used for acetabular fracture surgery and which permits the application of traction. All the fragments visualized on the CT scan should be removed. Small forceps, curved hemostats, and pituitary rongeurs are excellent aids for this task. Rarely, dislocation of the hip must be performed to allow for removal of the fragments. Forceful pulsatile lavage may also help flush out fine debris. An intraoperative radiograph should be obtained to verify that the reduction is concentric and symmetric to the unaffected hip joint. A stability examination should be performed following reduction to determine the stable arc of hip motion. Although bracing might be considered postoperatively to maintain the hip in a stable arc of motion, this is seldom necessary. The patient is instructed in use of crutches with a weightbearing-as-tolerated protocol and begun on aggressive rehabilitation of all hip muscle groups. Crutches may be discontinued once good hip strength has been regained.

Arthroscopic surgery of the hip has been proposed as a potential means for removal of loose fragments.[88] In this procedure, a distracting force is required, again through the use of either a fracture table or a well-applied distractor. Fluoroscopic guidance is used for the safe placement of the arthroscope and instruments.[86, 131, 195] Bartlett and associates have reported cardiac arrest as a result of intraabdominal extravasation of fluid during arthroscopic removal of a loose body from the hip joint of a patient with an acetabular fracture.[5] As a consequence, hip arthroscopy cannot be advocated for the treatment of acute or healing acetabular fractures.

## LEVIN TYPE IV: SIGNIFICANT ASSOCIATED ACETABULAR FRACTURES REQUIRING RECONSTRUCTION

Type IV dislocations are associated with significant acetabular fractures that require reconstruction. Surgical stabilization may be warranted to restore the anterior or posterior wall to correct instability (Fig. 46–31).[2, 84, 112, 115] The precise indications and surgical techniques for acetabular fracture reconstruction are discussed in Chapter 37.

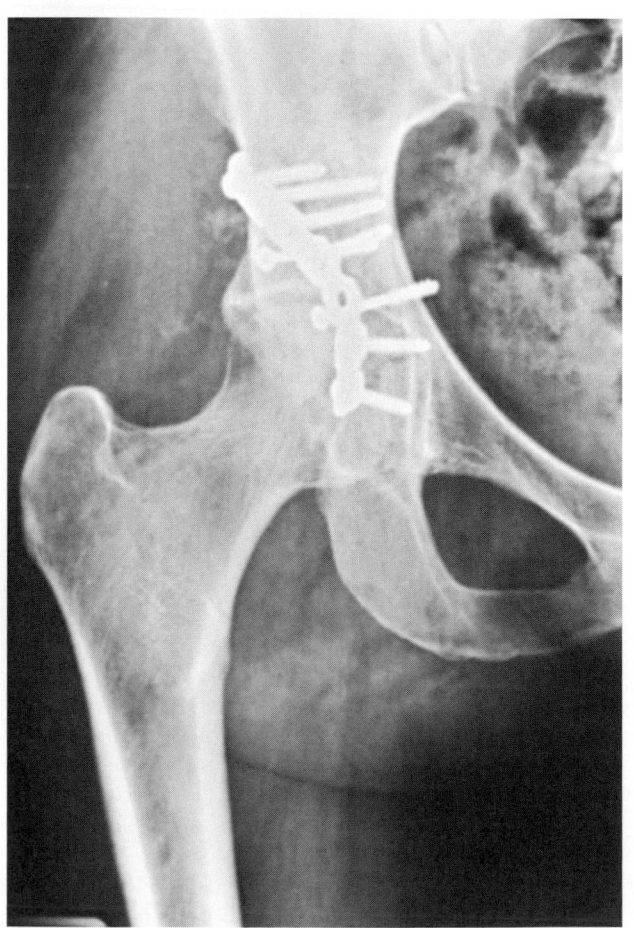

**FIGURE 46–31.** Comminuted posterosuperior acetabular wall fracture reconstructed with a lag screw in each main fracture fragment and buttressed with a 3.5-mm pelvic reconstruction plate. The injury films can be seen in Figure 46–18.

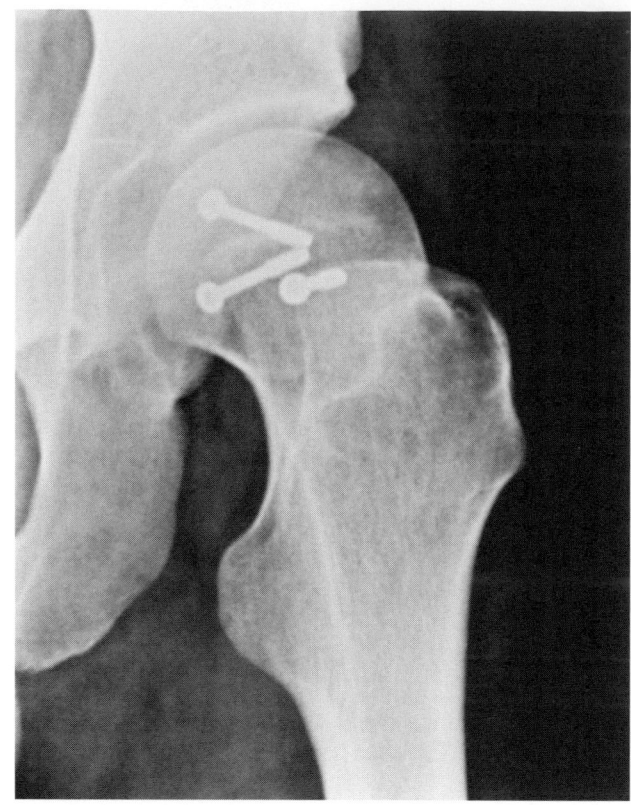

**FIGURE 46–32.** The femoral head fracture demonstrated in Figure 46–6 was repaired through a direct lateral approach.

## LEVIN TYPE V: ASSOCIATED FEMORAL HEAD OR NECK INJURY

Femoral head injuries associated with hip dislocations, as occur in type V dislocations, can dramatically affect the long-term prognosis. Some investigators have recommended excision of femoral head fragments, but the results are generally poor.[46] Butler developed a prospective protocol for treatment of displaced femoral head fractures.[20] Fragments that were not anatomically reduced by closed reduction were treated by internal fixation. Nine of 10 patients ultimately had excellent results (Fig. 46–32). Stannard[170] reported less favorable results in a larger, more recent series of femoral head fractures treated with open reduction and internal fixation, with only 11 of 22 fractures achieving a good or excellent result.

Mast described a technique for elevation of femoral head impaction injuries.[111] The depressed fragment is elevated, and cancellous bone is packed deep to the subchondral bone. No internal fixation is required.

## Surgical Approaches to the Hip

### POSTERIOR APPROACH

The standard posterior approach to the hip joint is the Kocher-Langenbeck approach. My preference is to perform the procedure as described by Letournel and Judet, who recommended prone positioning with a femoral traction pin.[100, 101] Such positioning, with the hip fully extended and the knee flexed, allows maximal relaxation and protection of the sciatic nerve. After splitting the gluteus maximus muscle, the sciatic nerve must be identified. The nerve should be examined for contusion, hemorrhage, and partial or complete laceration. Care must be taken not to split the gluteus maximus too proximally, as this can lead to denervation secondary to injury of the inferior gluteal nerve. After identifying the sciatic nerve, the tendinous insertions of the piriformis muscle and obturator internus are identified and tagged with a heavy absorbable suture. If not torn, they are detached and retracted posteriorly. The piriformis muscle is usually posterior to the nerve and does not protect it when reflected. The obturator internus and other short external rotators lie anterior to the sciatic nerve and protect it when retracted. The need for further surgical dissection and capsulotomy is determined by injury to acetabular wall, labrum, and hip capsule. Care is taken to avoid injury to the labrum when performing capsulotomies. Capsulotomy, if not already created by the injury, is always performed by releasing the capsule from its *acetabular* attachment to prevent injury to the vascular supply to the femoral head at the base of the femoral neck (Fig. 46–33). Depending on the procedure, the hip joint may require distraction by an assistant's traction, by a bone distractor (from iliac crest to proximal femur), or by traction with a fracture table. Rarely, the hip may actually require dislocation for a successful surgical exploration.[87]

Intraoperative radiographs are obtained to verify concentric hip reduction without widening. The capsule is closed with heavy absorbable sutures, and the piriformis and obturator internus tendons are reattached. The rehabilitative regimen varies depending on the surgical procedure performed.

## ANTERIOR APPROACH

The surgical approach utilized to expose the hip joint anteriorly will be determined by the injury complex. Thorpe and associates recommend the Smith-Petersen approach for fixation of isolated femoral head fractures.[182] A Watson-Jones incision may be better if there is a combined fracture of both femoral head and neck.

The direct lateral approach of Hardinge and the anterolateral approach of Watson-Jones provide good access to femoral head fractures following an anterior capsulotomy and anterior dislocation or subluxation of the hip.[69, 81] When performed with the patient in the lateral decubitus position, additional exposure of the posterior hip can be achieved through the same skin incision. The main advantage of the anterior approach of Smith-Petersen is that it allows more direct visualization of the anterior femoral head, and as a result, reduction and screw insertion may be somewhat easier. Extensive stripping of the abductors from the lateral ilium may increase the risk of heterotopic bone. Prophylaxis with indomethacin and/or radiation therapy should be considered.

## DIRECT LATERAL AND ANTEROLATERAL APPROACH

The patient is placed in either the lateral decubitus position or the semilateral position with a sandbag under the affected side. If the surgeon feels that posterior exposure may be necessary, the lateral position is mandatory. The affected leg is draped free.

A straight lateral incision is made extending from the iliac crest to 4 to 6 cm distal to the tip of the greater trochanter. The fascia lata is incised longitudinally, with care being taken to remain just posterior to the palpable muscle belly of the tensor fasciae muscle. If an anterolateral approach is used, the anterior third of the gluteus medius muscle is subperiosteally freed off the trochanter, and the gluteus minimus tendon is incised. If a direct lateral approach is used, the tendon of the gluteus medius is longitudinally split for 3 to 4 cm proximal to the tip of the trochanter. The fascia of the vastus lateralis is split longitudinally for approximately 4 cm distal to the vastus ridge, and the anterior vastus insertion is subperiosteally dissected off the base of the trochanter. The proximal and distal incisions are then connected (medius tendon to vastus lateralis), cutting sharply down to the greater trochanter. A large, curved osteotome can be used to remove an anterior sliver of bone, ensuring that the soft tissues of the anterior gluteus medius and anterior vastus lateralis remain as a continuous sleeve.

A Hohmann retractor is placed anteromedially over the femoral neck superficial to the capsule, and a second retractor is placed in the trochanteric fossa lateral to the neck. If necessary, the capsule can be divided near its acetabular attachment, leaving a cuff of tissue for repair. An assistant with a bone hook can distract the joint manually, or a distractor can be used. If necessary, the hip can be dislocated anteriorly following a wide capsulotomy.

At the completion of the procedure, the wound is irrigated. The capsule is closed with heavy sutures, and a deep suction drain may be placed in the wound. The gluteus medius is reattached with interrupted sutures, and the anterior trochanteric bone sliver, if created, is reattached through drill holes with a heavy nonabsorbable suture. The fascia of the tensor is closed with heavy interrupted sutures. The rehabilitative regimen varies depending on the procedure performed.

## Assessment of Results

Functional outcomes following hip dislocation ranges from an essentially normal hip, both clinically and radiographically, to a severely painful degenerative joint. Both insufficient followup and small patient populations compromise data from numerous published series. Even those series that report all good and excellent results following type I dislocations have a high percentage of good rather than excellent results (i.e., abnormal hips).

Most series utilize the criteria established by Stewart and Milford to analyze results.[174] A determination of excellent is reserved for those hips with no symptoms, normal physical examination, and normal radiographs. A good result is considered to be a hip with minimal stiffness after sitting, slight pain after a long day of work, no more than 25% loss of motion, and minimal arthritic changes. Fair results had mild to moderate pain, slight limp, 25% to

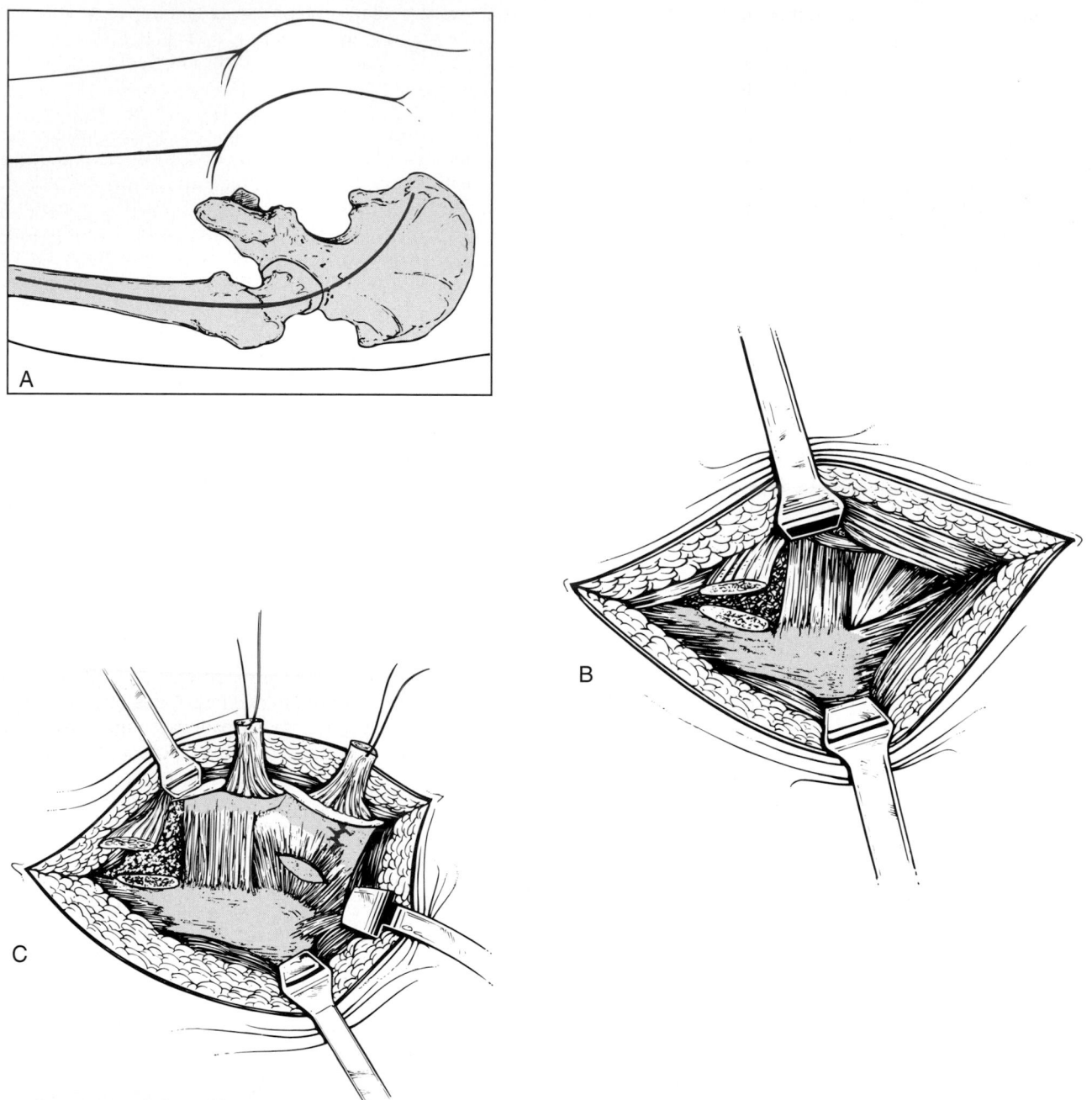

**FIGURE 46–33.** Kocher Langenbeck posterior approach to the hip. *A,* The lateral thigh skin incision curves toward the posterosuperior iliac spine proximal to the greater trochanter. *B,* The fascia lata is incised just posterior to the tensor fascia lata, extending proximally over the gluteus medius. The osseous insertion of the gluteus maximus is divided, at least partially, adjacent to the femur. *C,* Care is taken in developing the incision, because the sciatic nerve may be displaced into the field by the dislocated hip. The vascular supply to the proximal femur is protected by avoiding dissection around the base of the femoral neck and leaving the quadratus femoris and obturator externus intact. After identification and protection of the sciatic nerve, with the hip extended and the knee flexed, the piriformis can be released from the proximal femur, and the other short extensor rotators are reflected posteriorly over the sciatic nerve. The surgeon should protect the hip capsule, reflecting muscles off it and identifying its detachment or disruption without making additional incisions in it unless necessary. Capsular repair may improve hip stability.

50% loss of motion, and moderate degenerative changes. A poor result had persistent pain and limp, marked limitation of motion, and severe joint degeneration.

Based on these guidelines, a review of the literature will highlight the difficulties encountered in treating simple type I (Thompson-Epstein type I) dislocations. Upadhyay and co-workers retrospectively reviewed 74 cases of simple posterior dislocations with an average 12 year followup.[188] They found a 16% incidence of osteoarthritis

and an 8% incidence of AVN. Manual laborers were at nearly twice the risk of developing traumatic arthritis when compared with sedentary workers. In general, most large retrospective series report a 70% to 80% good or excellent outcome in simple posterior dislocations.[44, 95, 111, 136, 173] Other series by Hunter,[84] Kristensen and Stougaard,[94] and Reigstad[150] also report good and excellent results in retrospective analyses of type I dislocations. However, in these studies, the length of followup varied, and the total number of patients reviewed was small (Table 46–4).

When posterior dislocations are associated with femoral head fractures or acetabular fractures, the associated fractures generally determine the outcome. Epstein reported no excellent results in his extensive review of fracture-dislocations of the hip (type II-type V, Thompson-Epstein classification).[41, 43, 44, 158, 181]

Anterior dislocations of the hip have been noted to have a high incidence of associated femoral head injuries. DeLee and colleagues reported a series of 15 anterior dislocations, 13 of which were noted to have femoral head injuries.[32] The only patients with excellent results in these series were those without femoral head injuries. Ten of 15 patients developed traumatic arthritis. Among the 5 with radiographically normal hips were 2 without fractures, 2 with indentations less than 4 mm, and 1 with a 6 mm indentation. Epstein and Harvey[45] and, later, Epstein[44] reported a series of anterior hip dislocations and noted only 70% good and excellent results. There were 8 associated femoral head fractures in this series.

## COMPLICATIONS

### Avascular Necrosis

AVN of the femoral head following hip dislocations has been reported to occur in 1% to 2% to 15% to 17% of injuries.[114, 118, 136, 146, 174] Numerous investigators reported that the risk of AVN increases when the hip remains dislocated for a period of time. This threshold time has been reported to be from 6 to 24 hours.[43, 75, 83, 128, 139, 173, 183] More recent investigators suggest that the incidence of AVN is less than previously reported and may, in fact, result from the initial injury and not from a prolonged dislocation.[101, 114, 188] However, no well-controlled studies support this hypothesis, and prompt reduction is still considered vital. Avoiding this complication is paramount and may make the difference between a normal, functioning hip and a severely painful and degenerating hip.

Treatment for post-traumatic avascular necrosis is not based on strong evidence. As Rodríguez-Marchán points

out, post-traumatic osteonecrosis is often focal and may not always carry as dire a prognosis as that due to other etiologies.[156] Treatment should reasonably be based on the severity of symptoms and the location and size of the involved area in the femoral head. He lists a variety of options: conservative treatment with limited weightbearing and/or magnetic or capacitance coupled electrical stimulation, or operative treatment including core decompression, bone grafting of several varieties, osteotomy, arthrodesis, and total joint arthroplasty. Unfortunately, reports of these treatments rarely include more than a small number of patients with post-traumatic osteonecrosis, and provide limited information about their outcome. It appears that the exact role of conservative surgical treatment (core decompression with or without bone grafting, or osteotomy) for post-traumatic osteonecrosis remains to be determined, although such procedures might be considered for a localized, or radiographically early, area of involvement. For more severe pathology, the patient with intractable symptoms must choose between arthrodesis or hip replacement (see Chapter 50).

### Traumatic Arthritis

Traumatic arthritis is the most frequent long-term complication of hip dislocations. The symptoms can vary greatly. Those individuals most severely affected may ultimately be unable to remain gainfully employed; this often occurs at an early, productive age. Upadhyay and co-workers reported a 14 year follow-up of 74 cases of apparently uncomplicated hip dislocations with no associated fractures.[188] Surprisingly, 16% developed traumatic arthritis, and an additional 8% developed arthritis secondary to AVN. Manual laborers were nearly twice as likely as sedentary workers to develop traumatic arthritis.

The incidence of traumatic arthritis becomes dramatically higher when dislocations with associated acetabular fractures are reviewed (Fig. 46–34). Upadhyay and Moulton report the incidence of traumatic arthritis to be as high as 88% in those dislocations associated with severe acetabular fractures.[186] Epstein also reported much higher rates of traumatic arthritis in this group of injuries (Table 46–5).[44]

Several authors,[100, 112, 115] have reported large series of

**TABLE 46–4**

Long-Term Results, Complications, and Average Follow-Up for Simple Posterior Hip Dislocations

| Investigator* | Total No. Cases | Good or Excellent Results | Osteoarthritis | Avascular Necrosis |
|---|---|---|---|---|
| Upadhyay et al., 1983[188] | 74 | 56 | 16 | 8 |
| Upadhyay and Moulton, 1981[186] | 53 | 40 | 13 | — |
| Epstein, 1980[44] | 134 | 87 | 9 | 1 |
| Reigstad, 1980[150] | 20 | 20 | 6 | 6 |
| Kristensen and Stougaard, 1974[94] | 11 | 7 | — | — |
| Lamke, 1970[95] | 34 | 24 | — | — |
| Yang et al., 1991[198] | 31 | 27 | — | — |

*Referenced articles used similar classification systems and based results on both clinical and radiographic findings.
*Note:* Most articles did not provide specific rates of osteoarthritis and avascular necrosis for patients with simple posterior hip dislocations.

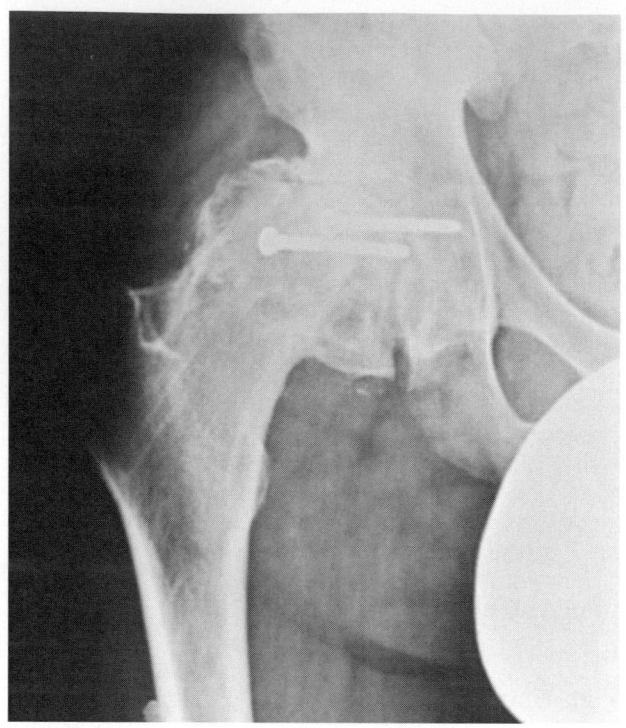

**Figure 46–34.** Traumatic arthritis after a posterior fracture-dislocation of the hip.

acetabular fractures treated by open reduction and internal fixation. In each series, good to excellent results were reported when anatomic reduction was obtained.

When significantly symptomatic hip arthritis develops, occasionally trochanteric osteotomy can reposition relatively intact cartilage into a weightbearing zone, but, as with osteonecrosis, the choice often comes down to arthrodesis or hip replacement arthroplasty (see Chapter 50).

## Recurrent Dislocation

Recurrent dislocation of the hip is rare. The literature related to this subject is limited to simple case reports, with approximately half involving children and half involving adults.* The cases reported include only pure dislocations, without associated femoral head or acetabular fractures. Many of the initial injuries described in these reports are secondary to relatively minor low-energy injuries such as sporting injuries, simple falls, and falls off tricycles.† Lieberman and associates described a patient with recurrent dislocations of the hip following surgical removal of incarcerated bony fragments.[105]

*See references 29, 58, 67, 72, 78, 92, 105, 106, 127, 147, 149, 153, 161, 169, 177, 184.

†See references 58, 67, 78, 92, 104, 106, 139, 149, 169, 177.

**TABLE 46–5**

Long-Term Results for Posterior Hip Dislocations Associated with Acetabular Fractures or Femoral Head Fractures

| Investigation | Total No. Cases* | Results | | |
|---|---|---|---|---|
| | | Excellent | Good | Fair |
| Upadhyay and Moulton, 1981[186] | 28 | 5 | 4 | 4 |
| Epstein, 1980[44] | | | | |
|   Closed reduction | | | | |
|     Dislocation with acetabular fracture | 102 | 0 | 13 | 33 |
|     Dislocation with femoral head fracture | 14 | 0 | 0 | 6 |
|   Closed followed by open reduction | | | | |
|     Dislocation with acetabular fracture | 78 | 0 | 34 | 15 |
|     Dislocation with femoral head fracture | 15 | 0 | 5 | 3 |
|   Primary open reduction | | | | |
|     Dislocation with acetabular fracture | 66 | 0 | 42 | 12 |
|     Dislocation with femoral head fracture | 17 | 0 | 8 | 2 |
| Reigstad, 1980[150] | | | | |
|   Mixed treatment | | | | |
|     Dislocation with acetabular fracture | 22 | 16 | — | 6 |
|     Dislocation with femoral head fracture | 5 | 2 | — | 3 |
| Kristensen and Stougaard, 1974[94] | | | | |
|   Closed reduction, skeletal traction | | | | |
|     Dislocation with acetabular fracture | 29 | 8 | 15 | 4 |
|     Dislocation with femoral head fracture | 5 | 1 | 1 | 1 |
| Yang et al., 1991[198] | | | | |
|   Closed reduction, skeletal traction | | | | |
|     Dislocation with acetabular fracture | 28 | 13 | 5 | 5 |
|     Dislocation with femoral head fracture | 23 | 2 | 3 | 7 |
| Stannard et al., 2000[170] | | | | |
|   Open reduction, internal fixation | 22 | 7 | 4 | 3 |
|   Dislocation with femoral head fracture | | | | |
| Moed et al., 2000[123] | | | | |
|   Open reduction, internal fixation | | | | |
|   Dislocation with posterior wall fracture | 94 | 34 | 49 | 2 |

*The dislocations associated with acetabular fractures have been grouped together, regardless of the fracture pattern, in an effort to compare the reported results in various series.

Arthrograms and CT arthrograms have been successful diagnostic modalities in demonstrating capsular defects and large saccular expansions of the capsule.[67, 92, 106, 154] CT arthrography has an additional benefit of demonstrating cartilaginous fragments not visualized on plain CT. MRI may augment these modalities because of its ability to detect cartilaginous fragments, fluid-filled regions, and soft tissue injuries.

Upadhyay and colleagues demonstrated a correlation of decreased femoral anteversion in patients who suffered posterior dislocations when compared with a control group.[187] They proposed that people are prone to posterior hip dislocation secondary to their relative retroversion. This anatomic variation could also be a predisposing factor in recurrent hip dislocations. Dall and colleagues reported the case of an adult with recurrent anterior hip dislocation.[29] Operative exploration revealed "moderate" anteversion that was treated by a derotation osteotomy. This report suggests that osseous anatomic variations could predispose to acute and recurrent dislocations.

Surgical exploration usually reveals a capsular defect with a large synovial sac. Capsular defects and synovial evaginations have been found at different muscular intervals between the short rotators of the hip, through which the femoral head could dislocate. Rashleigh-Belcher and Cannon[149] and Nelson[127] reported a Bankart-type lesion in a patient with recurrent dislocation. The intraoperative findings noted a posterosuperior labral detachment. Lieberman and associates described a Bankart-type repair of a large, labral detachment associated with symptomatic hip instability.[105]

Various surgical reconstructive procedures have been described to treat recurrent dislocations. Most authors describe imbrication procedures at the site of capsular tear and redundancy. The piriformis tendon has been reattached in the area of the defect to support the repair. Lutter[106] and Rashleigh-Belcher and Cannon[149] described the use of a bone block to buttress the area with the capsular or labral deficiency. Marti and Kloen[110] described successful use of a bone block acetabuloplasty with supplemental intertrochanteric rotational osteotomy.

Although the operative findings in these numerous case reports are surprisingly similar, the surgeon should search for predisposing osseous abnormalities. This recommendation is supported by Upadhyay and colleagues' sonographic studies as well as by the fact that the majority of individuals reported had relatively minor accidents leading to the first episode of dislocation.[187] In addition, all patients suffering hip dislocations are presumed to suffer capsular tears at the time of the initial dislocation. Possibly, patients with less than average anteversion place abnormal stresses on the healing capsule, resulting in capsular redundancy and laxity.

Preoperative evaluation should include MRI to search for intraarticular chondral fragments, labral detachments, and capsular outpockets filled with synovial fluid. Femoral anteversion should be measured by one of the described radiographic techniques.[76, 138, 151] CT scanning may demonstrate deficiency of the anterior or posterior acetabular wall. The acetabular stress patterns described by Bombelli must be carefully examined; abnormalities may be representative of acetabular dysplasia.[12] If no obvious osseous abnormality is uncovered, repair of a labral detachment, capsular plication, or placement of a posterior bone block may be performed, as described in various case reports. Concurrent rotational intertrochanteric osteotomy may provide benefit in some cases in which rotational instability is noted.[110] Each report claims no recurrence of a dislocation, but follow-up time is not sufficient, and none of the series are large enough to recommend a specific procedure.[106, 127, 149]

## Missed and Delayed Diagnoses

Failure to obtain adequate routine radiographs of the pelvis in the multiple injured patient may delay diagnosis of hip dislocation. This delays treatment and places the patient at increased risk for developing AVN, sciatic nerve injury, joint stiffness, and traumatic arthritis.[43, 44, 173, 174]

Nixon described the treatment of three patients following delayed diagnosis of 4 to 13 weeks. These three patients were treated with open reduction, and all achieved excellent clinical results.[129]

Gupta and Shravat described the treatment of seven hip dislocations in which the diagnosis was delayed for 26 to 75 days.[66] This group of patients was treated with skeletal traction until length was achieved, and then the legs were brought into abduction. One hip associated with extensive pelvic fracture failed to reduce by this method. Oni and associates[132] and Sarkar[163] described a similar technique using 3 weeks of traction followed by open reduction if closed reduction is not accomplished.

Garrett and colleagues reported far less encouraging results in a group of 39 dislocations that had not been treated for a period ranging from 3 days to 9 years after injury.[57] Eleven of 18 patients who had successful closed or open reduction developed AVN within 1 year. Six hips that were left dislocated all had poor results. The best results occurred in the group of patients who underwent primary reconstructive procedures.[52] Malkin and Tauber reported two cases that were treated with primary total hip arthroplasty using the femoral head to reconstruct the deficient posterior acetabulum.[108]

Despite the guarded prognosis resulting from a delay in treatment of hip dislocations, an aggressive attempt should be made to salvage the hip in a young patient. Use of skeletal traction has been successful in a number of patients and seems to be a prudent approach. Arthrodesis or prosthetic arthroplasty, if necessary, can be performed at a future time.

Obviously, optimal treatment for the delayed diagnosis of hip dislocation is to prevent it by maintaining a high level of suspicion to avoid missing the diagnosis. All unconscious and multiple injured patients must have an AP pelvic radiograph. Any radiographic uncertainty or abnormality should be immediately followed up with a CT scan.

## Sciatic Nerve Injury

Sciatic nerve injuries occur in 8% to 19% of hip dislocations. As previously mentioned, this is usually caused by stretching of the nerve from a posteriorly dislocated femoral head or from a displaced fracture fragment.

The prognosis for nerve recovery is extremely variable and unpredictable. Epstein[44] reported a 43% incidence of recovery, whereas Gregory[65] reported a 40% full recovery and a 30% partial recovery. Fassler and co-workers reported on a series of 14 patients with sciatic nerve injuries following acetabular fracture.[49] With a mean followup of 27 months, 13 patients had a fair or better functional outcome but 11 did have residual neurologic findings.

Patients with significant neurologic injury must have meticulous nursing care to prevent skin breakdown in the areas with sensory compromise. The patient should be placed in a well-padded neutral ankle splint to prevent the rapid onset of a fixed equinus deformity. Electromyography (EMG) and nerve conduction studies are indicated at 3 to 4 weeks for baseline information and prognostic guidance. In addition, the precise level of the neurologic injury, including possible lumbosacral plexus injury, can be determined.

Because of the variability of nerve recovery, no definitive surgical procedure addressing the disability should be considered for at least 1 year. Patients tolerate a lightweight ankle-foot orthosis (AFO) well with only slight disability. Follow-up electromyographs can be obtained at 3 months to evaluate for electrical evidence of repair. If no clinical or electrical improvement is seen by 1 year, tendon transfers may be considered.[14] Often patients would rather continue with the AFO rather than undergo an additional surgical procedure that requires immobilization and extensive rehabilitation. Such transfers are less successful if there is significant weakness of the transferred muscles from injury to the tibial portion of the sciatic nerve.

## Surgical Complications

### INFECTION

Postoperative infection rates are relatively low after operative treatment of simple dislocations or minor posterior wall fractures. More extensive fractures requiring large surgical exposures and prolonged operative time have an increased prevalence of infection. Prophylactic antibiotics are recommended.

If an infection is suspected, or if persistent wound drainage is noted, immediate surgical exploration is recommended. This permits thorough evaluation of the wound including Gram stains and multiple cultures. If a hematoma rather than an obvious infection is encountered, it is evacuated and the wound closed, with appropriate antibiotic coverage until negative cultures are confirmed. If an infection is encountered, treatment usually requires repeated débridements, culture-specific antibiotics, and delayed wound closure.

### SCIATIC NERVE INJURY

Sciatic nerve injury in extensive posterior approaches to the hip is reported to occur in approximately 11% of cases.[101] This is usually a temporary neurapraxia, and the treatment should be the same as outlined for immediate sciatic nerve injuries. Intraoperative measures should be undertaken to limit the occurrence. The knee should remain flexed throughout the procedure, and whenever possible, the hip should be extended. When using a retractor behind the posterior column, care must be taken to maintain the retractor parallel to the nerve. As the retractor rotates, its edge will press against the nerve and may injure it. Baumgaertner and associates,[6] Helfet and co-workers,[74] and Vrahas and colleagues[190] reported on the use of somatosensory evoked potentials to detect evidence of intraoperative nerve trauma. Middlebrooks and colleagues, however, reported only a 1% incidence of sciatic nerve injury when current surgical techniques without somatosensory monitoring are used, and concluded that routine somatosensory monitoring is unnecessary on a routine basis.[119] At the present time, this technique is not routinely used at most trauma centers.

### LATE SCIATIC NERVE PALSY

Several cases of delayed sciatic neurapraxia have been reported. These are thought to be secondary to hematoma, scar formation, or heterotopic ossification.[33, 91, 101] Any significant neurologic deficit might best be treated with nerve exploration and decompression. The few cases reported with delayed exploration had no significant return of nerve function.

### HETEROTOPIC OSSIFICATION

Heterotopic ossification is primarily associated with acetabular fractures and not with simple dislocations. The exception to this rule is the patient with a head injury.[56] The most commonly reported prophylactic measures are low-dose radiation and indomethacin. Moed and Karges reported excellent results in limiting heterotopic ossification with the use of indomethacin 25 mg tid for 6 weeks postoperatively.[121] Early radiation may be equally effective, and the two may be synergistic.[122]

### THROMBOEMBOLISM

No completely effective method for preventing thromboembolic disease (deep venous thrombosis and pulmonary embolism) has been convincingly established for trauma patients.[193] Low-dose warfarin, low molecular weight heparin compounds, and mechanical compression are all currently popular methods of prophylaxis against deep venous thrombosis (DVT) and pulmonary embolism following total joint arthroplasty. If possible, patients with hip dislocations should be up in a chair on the first post-reduction day if the hip is stable or on the first postoperative day if surgery was required. In the event of a pulmonary embolism, the patients are appropriately treated with anticoagulants. Vena caval filters may on occasion have to be considered in the immediate preoperative period or to control continued showering of emboli. Helfet and co-workers reported on the routine use of magnetic resonance venography scanning of the pelvis to diagnose pelvic vein thrombosis.[124, 144]

# REFERENCES

1. Allis, O.H. An Inquiry Into the Difficulties Encountered in the Reduction of Dislocations of the Hip. Philadelphia, Dornan Printer, 1986.
2. Alonzo, J.E.; Volgas, D.A.; Giordano, V.; Stannard, J.P. A review of the treatment of hip dislocations associated with acetabular fractures. Clin Orthop 377:32–43, 2000.
3. Armstrong, J.R. Traumatic dislocation of the hip joint. Review of one hundred and one disorders. J Bone Joint Surg Br 30:430–445, 1948.
4. Baird, R.A.; Schobert, W.E.; Pais, M.J.; et al. Radiographic identification of loose bodies in the traumatized hip joint. Radiology 145:661–665, 1982.
5. Bartlett, C.S.; DiFelice, G.S.; Buly, R.L.; et al. Cardiac arrest as a result of intraabdominal extravasation of fluid during arthroscopic removal of a loose body from the hip joint of a patient with an acetabular fracture. J Orthop Trauma 12:294–299, 1998.
6. Baumgaertner, M.R.; Wegner, D.; Brooke, J. SSEP monitoring during pelvic and acetabular surgery. J Orthop Trauma 8:127–133, 1994.
7. Beaton, L.E.; Anson, B.J. The relation of the sciatic nerve and of its subdivisions to the piriformis muscle. Anat Rec 70:1–5, 1937.
8. Bernard, R.F.; Christel, R.S.; Meearier, A.; et al. Role of articular incongruence and cartilage thickness in hip joint stresses distribution: A biphasic and two dimensional photoelastic study Acta Orthop Belg 48:335–344, 1982.
9. Bigelow, H.J. Luxations of the hip joint. Boston Med Surg J 5:1–3, 1870.
10. Birkett, J. Description of a dislocation of the head of the femur complicated with its fractures. Trans Med Chir Soc 52:133, 1869.
11. Bisese, J.H. MRI: A Teaching File Approach. New York, McGraw-Hill, 1988, pp. 203–305.
12. Bombelli, R. Osteoarthritis of the Hip. New York, Springer-Verlag, 1983, pp. 13–31.
13. Bosce, A.R. The range of active abduction and lateral rotation of the hip joint of men. J Bone Joint Surg 14:325–331, 1932.
14. Brand, P.W. The insensitive foot (including leprosy). In: Jahss, M.H., ed. Disorders of the Foot. Philadelphia, W.B. Saunders, 1982, pp. 1281–1282.
15. Brav, E.A. Traumatic dislocation of the hip. Army experience and results over a twelve year period. J Bone Joint Surg Am 44:1115–1134, 1962.
16. Bromberg, E.; Weiss, A.B. Posterior fracture-dislocation of the hip. South Med J 70:8–11, 1977.
17. Brown, T.D.; Ferguson, A.B. The effect of hip contact aberrations on stress patterns within the human femoral head. Ann Biomed Eng 8:75–92, 1980.
18. Bucholz, R.W.; Wheeless, G. Irreducible posterior fracture-dislocations of the hip. The role of the iliofemoral ligament and the rectus femoris muscle. Clin Orthop 167:118–122, 1982.
19. Buckwalter, J.A. Articular cartilage. Instr Course Lect 32:349–370, 1983.
20. Butler, J.E. Pipkin type II fractures of the femoral head. J Bone Joint Surg Am 63:1292–1296, 1981.
21. Butler, J.E. Personal communication, Houston, Texas, 1986.
22. Calkins, M.S.; Zych, G.; Latta, L.; et al. Computed tomography evaluation of stability: Posterior fracture-dislocation of the hip. Clin Orthop 227:152–163, 1988.
23. Canale, S.T.; Manugian, A.H. Irreducible traumatic dislocations of the hip. J Bone Joint Surg Am 61:7–14, 1979.
24. Chakraborti, S.; Miller, I.M. Dislocation of the hip associated with fracture of the femoral head. Injury 7:134–142, 1975.
25. Crelin, E.S. An experimental study of hip stability in human newborn cadavers. Yale Biol Med 49:109–121, 1976.
26. Crock, H.V. An atlas of the arterial supply of the head and neck of the femur in man. Clin Orthop 152:17–27, 1980.
27. Cornwall, R.; Radomisli, T.E. Nerve injury in traumatic dislocation of the hip. Clin Orthop 377:84–91, 2000.
28. Dahners, L.E.; Hundley, J.D. Reduction of posterior hip dislocations in the lateral position using traction-countertraction: Safer for the surgeon? J Orthop Trauma 13:373–374, 1999.
29. Dall, D.; MacNab, I.; Gross, A. Recurrent anterior dislocations of the hip. J Bone Joint Surg Am 52:574–576, 1970.
30. Dameron, T.B. Bucket handle tear of acetabular labrum accompanying posterior dislocation of the hip. J Bone Joint Surg Am 41:131, 134, 1959.
31. DeLee, J.C. Dislocations and fracture-dislocations of the hip. In: Rockwood, C.A.; Green, D.P., eds. Fractures and Dislocations, 2nd ed. Philadelphia, J.B. Lippincott, 1984, pp. 1287–1327.
32. DeLee, J.C.; Evans, J.A.; Thomas, J. Anterior dislocation of the hip and associated femoral head fractures. J Bone Joint Surg Am 62:960–964, 1980.
33. Derian, P.S.; Bibighaus, A.J. Sciatic nerve entrapment by ectopic bone after posterior fracture-dislocation of the hip. South Med J 67:209–210, 1974.
34. Donohue, J.M.; Buss, D.; Oegema, T.R.; Thompson, R.C. The effects of indirect blunt trauma on adult canine articular cartilage. J Bone Joint Surg Am 65:948–957, 1983.
35. Dowd, G.S.E.; Johnson, R. Successful conservative treatment of a fracture-dislocation of the femoral head. A case report. J Bone Joint Surg Am 61:1244–1246, 1979.
36. Dreinhofer, K.E.; Schwarzkopf, S.R.; Haas, N.P.; et al. Isolated traumatic dislocation of the hip: Long-term results in 50 patients. J Bone Joint Surg Br 76:6–12, 1994.
37. Dussault, R.G.; Beauregard, G.; Fauteaux, P.; et al. Femoral head defect following anterior hip dislocation. Radiology 135:627–629, 1980.
38. Ebraheim, N.A.; Savolaine, E.R.; Skie, M.C.; Hoeflinger, M.J. Soft tissue window to enhance visualization of entrapped osteocartilaginous fragments in the hip joint. Orthop Rev 22:1017–1021, 1993.
39. Ehtisham, S.M.A. Traumatic dislocation of the hip joint with fracture of shaft of femur on the same side. J Trauma 16:196–205, 1976.
40. Eisenberg, K.S.; Sheft, D.J.; Murray, W.R. Posterior dislocation of the hip producing lumbosacral nerve root avulsion. A case report. J Bone Joint Surg Am 54:1083–1086, 1972.
41. Epstein, H.C. Traumatic dislocations of the hip. Clin Orthop 92:116–142, 1973.
42. Epstein, H.C. Traumatic anterior and simple posterior dislocations of the hip in adults and children. Instr Course Lect 22:115–145, 1973.
43. Epstein, H.C. Posterior fracture-dislocations of the hip: Long-term follow-up. J Bone Joint Surg Am 56:1103–1127, 1974.
44. Epstein, H.C. Traumatic Dislocation of the Hip. Baltimore, Williams & Wilkins, 1980.
45. Epstein, H.C.; Harvey, J.P. Traumatic anterior dislocations of the hip. Management and results. An analysis of fifty-five cases. J Bone Joint Surg Am 54:1561–1562, 1972.
46. Epstein, H.C.; Wiss, D.A.; Coze, L. Posterior fracture-dislocation of the hip with fractures of the femoral head. Clin Orthop 201:9–17, 1985.
47. Fabian, T.C.; Mangiante, E.C.; White, T.J.; et al. A prospective study of 91 patients undergoing both computed tomography and peritoneal lavage following blunt abdominal trauma. J Trauma 26:602–608, 1986.
48. Fairbairn, K.J.; Mulligan, M.E.; Murphey, M.D.; et al. Gas bubbles in the hip joint on CT: An indication of recent dislocation. AJR Am J Roentgenol 164:931–934, 1995.
49. Fassler, P.R.; Swiotkowski, M.F.; Kilroy, A.W.; Routt, M.L. Injury to the sciatic nerve associated with acetabular fractures. J Bone Joint Surg Am 75:1157–1166, 1993.
50. Fairbairn, K.J.; Mulligan, M.E.; Murphey, M.D.; Resnik, C.S. Gas bubbles in the hip joint on CT: An indication of recent dislocation. AJR Am J Roentgenol 164:931–934, 1995.
51. Fernandes, A. Traumatic posterior dislocation of hip joint with a fracture of the head and neck of the femur on the same side: A case report. Injury 12:487–490, 1981.
52. Fina, C.P.; Kelly, P.J. Dislocations of the hip with fractures of the proximal femur. J Trauma 10:77–87, 1970.
53. Frankel, V.H.; Pugh, J.W. Biomechanics of the hip. In: Tronzo, R.G., ed. Surgery of the Hip Joint. Philadelphia, Lea & Febiger, 1973, pp. 115–131.
54. Frick, S.L.; Sims, S.H. Is computed tomography useful after simple posterior hip dislocation? J Orthop Trauma 9:388–391, 1995.
55. Funsten, R.V.; Kinser, P.; Frankel, C.J. Dashboard dislocation of the hip: A report of twenty cases of traumatic dislocations. J Bone Joint Surg 20:124–132, 1938.
56. Garland, D.E.; Miller, G. Fractures and dislocations about the hip in head injured adults. Clin Orthop 186:154–158, 1984.
57. Garrett, J.C.; Epstein, H.C.; Harris, W.H.; et al. Treatment of unreduced traumatic posterior dislocations of the hip. J Bone Joint Surg Am 61:2–6, 1979.

58. Gaul, R.W. Recurrent traumatic dislocation of the hip in children. Clin Orthop 90:107–109, 1977.

59. Genda, E.; Kovski, N.; Haseggua, Y.; Miura, T. A complete simulation study of normal and abnormal joint contact pressure. Arch Orthop Trauma Surg 114:202–206, 1995.

60. Gillespie, W.J. The incidence and pattern of knee injury associated with dislocation of the hip. J Bone Joint Surg Br 57:376–378, 1975.

61. Glimcher, M.J.; Kenzora, J.E. The biology of osteonecrosis of the human femoral head and its clinical implications. I. Tissue biology. Clin Orthop 138:284–309, 1979.

62. Glimcher, M.J.; Kenzora, J.E. The biology of osteonecrosis of the human femoral head and its clinical implications. II. The pathologic changes in the femoral head as an organ and in the hip joint. Clin Orthop 139:283–312, 1979.

63. Glimcher, M.J.; Kenzora, J.E. The biology of osteonecrosis of the human femoral head and its clinical implications. III. Discussion of the etiology and genesis of the pathologic sequelae; comments on treatment. Clin Orthop 140:273–312, 1979.

64. Goddard, N.J. Classification of traumatic hip dislocation. Clin Orthop 377:11–14, 2000.

65. Gregory, C.F. Early complications of dislocation and fracture-dislocations of the hip joint. Instr Course Lect 22:105–114, 1973.

66. Gupta, R.C.; Shravat, B.P. Reduction of neglected traumatic dislocation of the hip by heavy traction. J Bone Joint Surg Am 59:249–251, 1977.

67. Guyer, B.; Lainsohn, E.M. Recurrent anterior dislocation of the hip: Case report with arthrographic findings. Skeletal Radiol 10:262–264, 1983.

68. Hak, D.J.; Goulet, J.A. Severity of injuries associated with traumatic hip dislocation as a result of motor vehicle collisions. J Trauma 47:60–63, 1999.

69. Hardinge, K. The direct lateral approach to the hip. J Bone Joint Surg Br 64:17–19, 1982.

70. Harley, J.C.; Mack, L.A.; Winquist, R.A. CT of acetabular fractures: Comparison with conventional radiography. AJR Am J Roentgenol 138:413–417, 1982.

71. Harty, M. The anatomy of the hip joint. In: Tronzo, R.G., ed. Surgery of the Hip Joint, 2nd ed. New York, Springer-Verlag, 1984, pp. 45–74.

72. Heikkinen, E.S.; Sulamaa, R. Recurrent dislocation of the hip: Report of two children. Acta Orthop Scand 42:58–62, 1971.

73. Helal, B.; Skevis, X. Unrecognized dislocation of the hip in fractures of the femoral shaft. J Bone Joint Surg Br 49:293–300, 1967.

74. Helfet, D.L.; Hissa, E.A.; Sergay, S.; Mast, J.W. Somatosensory evoked potential monitoring in the surgical management of acute acetabular fractures. J Orthop Trauma 5:161–166, 1991.

75. Herndon, J.H.; Aufranc, O.E. Avascular necrosis of the femoral head in the adult. A review of its incidence in a variety of conditions. Clin Orthop 86:43–62, 1977.

76. Herrlin, K.; Ekelund, L. Radiographic measurements of the femoral neck anteversion. Comparison of two simplified procedures. Acta Orthop Scand 54:141–147, 1983.

77. Hoaglund, F.T.; Low, W.D. Anatomy of the femoral neck and head with comparative data from Caucasians and Hong Kong Chinese. Clin Orthop 152:10–16, 1980.

78. Hollingdale, J.P.; Aichroth, P.M. Recurrent posttraumatic dislocation of the hip in children. J R Soc Med 74:545–546, 1981.

79. Hollingshead, W.H. Anatomy for Surgeons, 3rd ed., Vol. 3. Philadelphia, Harper & Row, 1982, pp. 563–732.

80. Hoppenfeld, S. Physical Examination of the Extremities. New York, Appleton-Century-Crofts, 1976, pp. 155–159.

81. Hoppenfeld, S.; deBoer, P. Surgical Exposures in Orthopaedics. Philadelphia, J.B. Lippincott, 1984, pp. 301–356.

82. Hougaard, K.; Lindequist, S.; Nielsen, L.B. Computerized tomography after posterior dislocation of the hip. J Bone Joint Surg Br 69:556–557, 1987.

83. Hougaard, K.; Thomsen, P.B. Traumatic posterior dislocation of the hip—Prognostic factors influencing the incidence of avascular necrosis of the femoral head. Arch Orthop Trauma Surg 106:32–35, 1986.

84. Hunter, G.A. Posterior dislocation and fracture-dislocations of the hip. A review of fifty-seven patients. J Bone Joint Surg Br 51:38–44, 1969.

85. Johnson, K.D.; Cadambi, A.; Seibert, B. Incidence of adult respiratory distress syndrome in patients with multiple musculoskeletal injuries. Effect of early operative stabilization of fractures. J Trauma 25:375–383, 1985.

86. Johnson, L.L. Arthroscopic Surgery: Principles and Practice. St. Louis, C.V. Mosby, 1986, pp. 1491–1516.

87. Judet, R.; Judet, J.; LeTournel, E. Fractures of the acetabulum: Classification and surgical approaches for open reduction. J Bone Joint Surg Am 46:1615–1646, 1964.

88. Keene, A.S.; Villar, R.N. Arthroscopic loose body retrieval following traumatic hip dislocation. Injury 25:507–510, 1994.

89. Kelly, R.P.; Yarbrough, S.H. Posterior fracture-dislocation of the femoral head with retained medial head fragment. J Trauma 11:97–108, 1971.

90. Klasen, H.J.; Binnendijk, B. Fracture of the neck of the femur associated with posterior dislocation of the hip. J Bone Joint Surg Br 66:45–48, 1984.

91. Kleiman, S.G.; Stevens, J.; Kolb, L.; Pankovich, A. Late sciatic nerve palsy following posterior fracture-dislocation of the hip. J Bone Joint Surg Am 53:781–782, 1971.

92. Klein, A.; Sumner, T.E.; Volberg, F.M.; Orbon, R.J. Combined CT arthrography in recurrent traumatic hip dislocation. AJR Am J Roentgenol 138:963–964, 1982.

93. Kleinberg, S. Aseptic necrosis of the femoral head following traumatic dislocation. Arch Surg 39:637–646, 1939.

94. Kristensen, O.; Stougaard, J. Traumatic dislocation of the hip: Results of conservative treatment. Acta Orthop Scand 45:206–212, 1974.

95. Lamke, L. Traumatic dislocations of the hip: Follow-up on cases from Stockholm area. Acta Orthop Scand 41:188–198, 1970.

96. Laorr, A.; Greenspan, A.; Anderson, M.W.; et al. Traumatic hip dislocation: Early MRI findings. Skeletal Radiol 24:239–245, 1995.

97. Larson, C.B. Fracture-dislocations of the hip. Clin Orthop 92:147–154, 1973.

98. Lawson, T.L.; Middleton, W.D. The hip. In: Middleton, W.D.; Lawson, T.L., eds. Anatomy and MRI of the Joints. A Multiplanar Atlas. New York, Raven Press, 1989, pp. 153–204.

99. Lefkowitz M: A new method for reduction for traumatic dislocations. Orthop Rev 2:253–256, 1993.

100. Letournel, E. Fractures of the Acetabulum and Pelvis. Fourth Course and Workshop. Paris, 1986.

101. Letournel, E.; Judet, R. Fractures of the Acetabulum. New York, Springer-Verlag, 1981.

102. Levin, P. Femoral head fracture associated with a posterior hip dislocation in a restrained passenger. Case report. Unpublished data.

103. Levin, P. Posterior fracture-dislocation of hip in a restrained passenger. Case report. Unpublished data.

104. Liebenberg, F.; Dommisse, G.F. Recurrent posttraumatic dislocation of the hip. J Bone Joint Surg Br 51:632–637, 1969.

105. Lieberman, J.R.; Altcheck, D.W.; Salvati, E.A. Recurrent dislocation of a hip with a labral lesion: Treatment with a modified Bankart-type repair. J Bone Joint Surg Am 75:1524–1527, 1993.

106. Lutter, L.D. Posttraumatic hip redislocation. J Bone Joint Surg Am 55:391–399, 1977.

107. Mack, L.A.; Harvey, J.D.; Winquist, R.A. CT of acetabular fractures: Analysis of fracture patterns. AJR Am J Roentgenol 138:407–412, 1982.

108. Malkin, C.; Tauber, C. Total hip arthroplasty and acetabular bone grafting for unreduced fracture-dislocation of the hip. Clin Orthop 201:57–59, 1985.

109. Mankin, H.J. The response of articular cartilage to mechanical injury. J Bone Joint Surg Am 64:460–466, 1982.

110. Marti, R.K.; Kloen, P. Chronic recurrent posterior dislocation of the hip after a Pipkin fracture treated with intertrochanteric osteotomy and acetabuloplasty: A case report. J Bone Joint Surg Am 82:867–872, 2000.

111. Mast, J. Fractures of the Acetabulum and Pelvis. Fourth Course and Workshop. Paris, 1986.

112. Matta, J.M. Fractures of the Acetabulum and Pelvis. Fourth Course and Workshop. Paris, 1986.

113. Mayra, S.K.S.; Samuel, A.W. Piggyback technique for relocation of posterior dislocation of the hip. Injury 25:483–484, 1994.

114. Mears, D.C. Personal communication, 1986.
115. Mears, D.C. Fractures of the Acetabulum and Pelvis. Fourth Course and Workshop. Paris, 1986.
116. Meller, Y.; Tennenbaum, Y.; Torok, G. Subcapital fracture of neck of femur with complete posterior dislocation of the hip. J Trauma 22:327–329, 1982.
117. Meyers, M.H. Anatomy of the hip. In: Meyers, M.H., ed. Fractures of the Hip. Chicago, Year Book Medical, 1985, pp. 12–22.
118. Meyers, M.H.; Telfer, N.; Moore, T.M. Determination of the vascularity of the femoral head with technetium 99 mm-sulfur colloid: Diagnostic and prognostic significance. J Bone Joint Surg Am 59:658–664, 1977.
119. Middlebrooks, E.S.; Sims, S.H.; Kellam, J.F.; Bosse, M.J. Incidence of sciatic nerve injury in operatively treated acetabular fractures without somatosensory monitoring. J Orthop Trauma 11:327–329, 1997.
120. Mitchell, N.; Shepard, N. Healing of articular cartilage in intraarticular fractures in rabbits. J Bone Joint Surg Am 62:628–634, 1980.
121. Moed, B.R.; Karges, D.E. Prophylactic indomethacin for the prevention of heterotopic ossification after acetabular fracture surgery in high-risk patients. J Orthop Trauma 8:34–39, 1994.
122. Moed B.R.; Letournel, E. Low-dose irradiation and indomethacin prevent heterotopic ossification after acetabular fracture surgery. J Bone Joint Surg Br 76:895–900, 1994.
123. Moed, B.R.; Willson Carr, S.E.; Watson, J.T.; Open reduction and internal fixation of posterior wall fractures of the acetabulum. Clin Orthop 377:57–67, 2000.
124. Montgomery, K.D.; Potter, H.G.; Helfet, D.L. Magnetic resonance venography to evaluate the deep venous system of the pelvis in patients who have an acetabular fracture. J Bone Joint Surg Am 77:1639–1649, 1995.
125. Morton, K.S. Traumatic dislocation of the hip: A follow-up study. Can J Surg 3:67–74, 1959.
126. Mundale, M.O.; Hislop, H.J.; Rabidean, R.J.; Kottke, F.J. Evaluation of extension at hip. Arch Phys Med 37:75–80, 1956.
127. Nelson, C.L. Traumatic recurrent dislocation of the hip: Report of a case. J Bone Joint Surg Am 52:128–130, 1970.
128. Nicoll, E.A. Proceedings and reports of councils and associations: Traumatic dislocation of the hip joint. J Bone Joint Surg Br 34:503–505, 1952.
129. Nixon, J.R. Late open reduction of traumatic dislocation of the hip: Report of three cases. J Bone Joint Surg Br 58:41–43, 1976.
130. Nordt, W.E. Maneuvers for reducing dislocated hips. A new technique and a literature review. Clin Orthop 360:260–264, 1999.
131. Nordt, W.; Giangarra, C.E.; Levy, I.M.J.; Habermann, E.T. Arthroscopic retrieval of entrapped debris following dislocation of a total hip arthroplasty. Arthroscopy 3:196–198, 1987.
132. Oni, O.O.A.; Orhewee, F.A.; Keswani, H. The treatment of old unreduced traumatic dislocations of the hip. Injury 15:219–223, 1984.
133. Ordway, C.B.; Xeller, C.F. Transverse computerized axial tomography of patients with posterior dislocation of the hip. J Trauma 24:76–79, 1989.
134. Pape, H.-C.; Rice, J; Wolfram, K.; et al. Hip dislocation in patients with multiple injuries. Clin Orthop 377:99–105, 2000.
135. Paterson, I. The torn acetabular labrum. A block to reduction of a dislocated hip. J Bone Joint Surg Br 39:306–309, 1957.
136. Paus, B. Traumatic dislocation of the hip. Late results in 76 cases. Acta Orthop Scand 21:99–112, 1951.
137. Peitzman, A.B.; Makaroon, M.S.; Slasky, B.S.; Ritter, P. Prospective study of computed tomography in initial management of blunt abdominal trauma. J Trauma 26:585–592, 1986.
138. Peterson, H.A.; Krassen, R.A.; McLeod, R.A.; Hoffman, A.D. The use of computerized tomography in dislocation of the hip and femoral neck anteversion in children. J Bone Joint Surg Br 63:198–208, 1981.
139. Pietratesa, C.A.; Hoffman, J.R. Traumatic dislocation of the hip. JAMA 249:3342–3346, 1983.
140. Pipkin, G. Treatment of grade IV fracture-dislocation of the hip. J Bone Joint Surg Am 39:1027–1042, 1957.
141. Polesky, R.E., Polesky, F.A. Intrapelvic dislocation of the femoral head following anterior dislocation of the hip. J Bone Joint Surg Am 54:1097–1098, 1972.

142. Poggi, J.J.; Callaghan, J.J.; Spritzer, C.E.; et al. Changes in magnetic resonance images after traumatic hip dislocation. Clin Orthop 319:249–259, 1995.
143. Potter, H.G.; Montgomery, K.D.; Heise, C.W.; Helfet, D.L. MR imaging of acetabular fractures: Value in detecting femoral head injury, intraarticular fragments and sciatic nerve injury. AJR Am J Roentgenol 163:881–886, 1994.
144. Potter, H.G.; Montgomery, K.D.; Padgett, D.E.; et al. Magnetic resonance imaging of the pelvis. New orthopaedic applications. Clin Orthop 319:223–231, 1995.
145. Pringle, J.H. Traumatic dislocation of the hip joint. An experimental study on the cadaver. Glasgow Med J 21:25–40, 1943.
146. Proctor, H. Dislocations of the hip joint (excluding central dislocations) and their complications. Injury 5:1–12, 1973.
147. Provenzano, M.P.; Holmes, P.F.; Tullos, H.S. Atraumatic recurrent dislocation of the hip: A case report. J Bone Joint Surg Am 69:938–940, 1987.
148. Radin, E.L.; Ehrlich, M.G.; Chernack, R.; et al. Effect of repetitive impulsive loading on the knee joints of rabbits. Clin Orthop 131:288–293, 1978.
149. Rashleigh Belcher, H.J.C.; Cannon, S.R. Recurrent dislocation of the hip with a "Bankart-type" lesion. J Bone Joint Surg Br 68:398–399, 1986.
150. Reigstad, A. Traumatic dislocation of the hip. J Trauma 20:603–606, 1980.
151. Reikeras, O.; Bjerkreim, I.; Kolbenstuedt, A. Anteversion of the acetabulum in patients with idiopathic increased anteversion of the femoral neck. Acta Orthop Scand 53:847–852, 1982.
152. Repo, R.V.; Finley, J.B. Survival of articular cartilage after controlled impact. J Bone Joint Surg Am 59:1068–1076, 1977.
153. Roberts, W. The locking mechanism at the hip joint. Anat Rec 147:321–324, 1963.
154. Roberts, J.M.; Taylor, J.; Burke, S. Recurrent dislocation of the hip in congenital indifference to pain. J Bone Joint Surg Am 62:829–831, 1980.
155. Rodríguez-Merchán, E.C. Osteonecrosis of the femoral head after traumatic hip dislocation in the adult. Clin Orthop 377:68–77, 2000.
156. Rodríguez-Merchán, E.C. Coxarthrosis after traumatic hip dislocation in the adult. Clin Orthop 377:92–98, 2000.
157. Roeder, L.F.; DeLee, J.C. Femoral head fractures associated with posterior hip dislocations. Clin Orthop 147:121–130, 1980.
158. Rosenthal, R.E.; Coker, W.L. Posterior fracture-dislocation of the hip. J Trauma 19:572–581, 1979.
159. Rowe, C.R.; Lowell, J.D. Prognosis of fractures of the acetabulum. J Bone Joint Surg Am 43:30–59, 1961.
160. Sadler, A.H.; Distefano, M. Anterior dislocation of the hip with ipsilateral basicervical fracture. J Bone Joint Surg Am 67:326–329, 1985.
161. Salisbury, R.D.; Eastwood, D.M. Traumatic dislocation of the hip in children. Clin Orthop 377:106–111, 2000.
162. Salter, R.B.; Simmonds, D.F.; Malcolm, B.W.; et al. The biologic effects of continuous passive motion on the healing of full thickness defects in articular cartilage. An experimental investigation in the rabbit. J Bone Joint Surg Am 62:1232–1251, 1980.
163. Sarkar, S.D. Delayed open reduction of traumatic dislocation of the hip: A case report and historical review. Clin Orthop 186:38–41, 1989.
164. Sarmiento, A.; Laird, C.A. Posterior fracture-dislocation of the femoral head. Clin Orthop 92:143–146, 1973.
165. Sauser, D.B.; Billimoria, P.E.; Rouse, G.A.; Mudge, K. CT evaluation of hip trauma. AJR Am J Roentgenol 135:269–274, 1980.
166. Schafer, S.J.; Anglen, J.O. The East Baltimore lift: A simple and effective method for reduction of posterior hip dislocations. J Orthop Trauma 13:56–57, 1999.
167. Schlickewei, W.; Elsasser, B.; Mullaji, A.S.; Kuner, E.H. Hip dislocation without fracture: Traction or mobilization after reduction? Injury 24:27–31, 1993.
168. Schoenecker, P.L.; Manske, P.R.; Sertl, G.O. Traumatic hip dislocation with ipsilateral femoral shaft fractures. Clin Orthop 130:233–238, 1978.
169. Scudese, V.A. Traumatic anterior hip redislocation. A case report. Clin Orthop 88:60–63, 1972.

170. Stannard, J.P.; Harris, H.W.; Volgas, D.A.; Alonzo, J.E. Functional outcome of patients with femoral head fractures associated with hip dislocations. Clin Orthop 377:44–56, 2000.

171. Stein, H. Computerized tomography for ascertaining osteocartilaginous intraarticular (slice) fractures of the femoral head. Isr J Med Sci 19:180–184, 1983.

172. Stewart, M.J. Management of fractures of the head of the femur complicated by dislocation of the hip. Orthop Clin North Am 5:793–798, 1974.

173. Stewart, M.J.; McCarroll, H.R.; Mulhollan, J.S. Fracture-dislocation of the hip. Acta Orthop Scand 46:507–525, 1975.

174. Stewart, M.J.; Milford, L.W. Fracture-dislocation of the hip. J Bone Joint Surg Am 36:315–342, 1954.

175. Stimson, L.A. A Treatise on Fractures. Philadelphia, H.C. Leas Son, 1883.

176. Stoller, D.W. Personal communication, Los Angeles, 1989.

177. Sullivan, C.R.; Bickel, W.H.; Lipscomb, P.R. Recurrent dislocation of the hip. J Bone Joint Surg Am 37:1266–1270, 1955.

178. Suraci, A.J. Distribution and severity of injuries associated with hip dislocations secondary to motor vehicle accidents. J Trauma 26:458–460, 1986.

179. Suzuki, Y. Studies on repair tissue of injured articular cartilage: Biochemical and biomechanical properties. Nippon Seikeigeka Gakkai Zasshi 57:741–752, 1983.

180. Tabuenca, J.; Truan, J.R. Knee injuries in traumatic hip dislocation. Clin Orthop 377:78–83, 2000.

181. Thompson, V.P.; Epstein, H.C. Traumatic dislocation of the hip. J Bone Joint Surg Am 33:746–778, 1951.

182. Thorpe, M.; Swiontkowski, M.F.; Seiler, J.; Hansen, S.T. Operative management of femoral head fractures. Orthop Trans 13:51, 1989.

183. Toni, A.; Gulino, G.; Baldini, N.; Gulino, F. Clinical and radiographic long-term results of acetabular fractures associated with dislocations of the hip. Ital J Orthop Traumatol 11:443–454, 1985.

184. Townsend, R.G.; Edwards, G.E.; Bazant, F.J. Posttraumatic recurrent dislocation of the hip without fracture. J Bone Joint Surg Br 51:194, 1969.

185. Trueta, J.; Harrison, M.H.M. The normal vascular anatomy of the femoral head in adult man. J Bone Joint Surg Br 35:442–461, 1953.

186. Upadhyay, S.S.; Moulton, A. The long-term results of traumatic posterior dislocation of the hip. J Bone Joint Surg Br 63:548–551, 1981.

187. Upadhyay, S.S.; Moulton, A.; Burwell, R.G. Biological factors predisposing to traumatic posterior dislocation of the hip. J Bone Joint Surg Br 67:232–236, 1985.

188. Upadhyay, S.S.; Moulton, A.; Srikrishnamurthy, K. An analysis of the late effects of traumatic posterior dislocation of the hip without fractures. J Bone Joint Surg Br 65:150–157, 1983.

189. Urist, M.R. Fracture-dislocation of the hip joint: The nature of the traumatic lesion, treatment, late complications, and end results. J Bone Joint Surg Am 30:699–727, 1948.

190. Vrahas, M; Gordon, R.G.; Mears, D.C.; et al. Intraoperative somatosensory evoked potential monitoring of pelvic and acetabular fractures. J Orthop Trauma 6:50–58, 1992.

191. Walker, R.H.; Burton, D.S. Computerized tomography in assessment of acetabular fractures. J Trauma 22:227–234, 1982.

192. Watson-Jones, R. Fractures and Joint Injuries, 5th ed. New York, Churchill Livingstone, 1976, pp. 885–926.

193. Webb, L.X.; Rush, P.T.; Fuller S.B.; Meredith, J.W. Greenfield filter prophylaxis of pulmonary embolism in patients undergoing surgery for acetabular fracture. J Orthop Trauma 6:139–145, 1992.

194. Wertheimer, L.G.; Lopes, S.D.F. Arterial supply of the femoral head. A combined angiographic and histological study. J Bone Joint Surg aM 53:545–555, 1971.

195. Witwity, T.; Uhlmann, R.D.; Fisher, J. Arthroscopic management of chondromatosis of the hip: A case report. Arthroscopy 4:55–56, 1988.

196. Yandown, D.R.; Austin, C.W. Femoral defect after anterior dislocation. J Comput Assist Tomogr 7:1112–1113, 1983.

197. Yang, E.C.; Cornwall, R. Initial treatment of traumatic hip dislocations in the adult. Clin Orthop 377:24–31, 2000.

198. Yang RS, Tsuang YH, Hang YS; et al. Traumatic dislocation of the hip. Clin Orthop 265:218–227, 1991.

199. Yue, J.J.; Wilber, J.H.; Lipuma, J.P.; et al. Posterior hip dislocations: A cadaveric angiographic study. J Orthop Trauma 10:447–454, 1996.

# CHAPTER 47

# Medical Management of the Patient with Hip Fracture

Victor A. Morris, M.D.
Michael R. Baumgaertner, M.D.
Leo M. Cooney, Jr., M.D.

The outcome of a patient with hip fracture is only partially related to the successful management of the fracture. Many elderly patients have multiple, significant concomitant illnesses. These co-morbidities as well as perioperative complications significantly affect the patient's ultimate outcome. This chapter provides a brief synopsis of outcome variables and reviews the evaluation and management of common coexisting medical conditions, perioperative considerations, and postoperative complications.

## OUTCOME VARIABLES

### Mortality

Although hip fracture increases the mortality rate for older patients by 10% to 20% in the first year following the fracture, most of this impact occurs in the first 6 months after the fracture. After the first 12 months, survival curves are equal to those of age-matched controls without a fracture. Because of the importance of prefracture level of function and mental status as predictors of outcome (see following section), the mortality for patients admitted from nursing homes is much higher than the mortality for those admitted from the community. It is important to note the site of residence of patients when comparing the results of different studies.

The overwhelming important predictors of mortality for patients with hip fractures are related to the underlying mental, medical, and functional status of the patient, not the site, nature, or operative treatment of the fracture (Table 47–1). Although patients with intertrochanteric fracture have a higher mortality than do patients with femoral neck fractures, the actual site of injury does not predict mortality. A recent study confirmed that the population with intertrochanteric fractures is older and sicker on admission.[18] These differences account for the increased mortality. Dementia has the strongest adverse predictive effect on mortality Morrison and Siu confirmed the results of many previous studies, which indicated an approximately 50% mortality in patients with hip fracture and dementia in the 6 months to 1 year following the fracture.[43]

Prefracture physical and social function is also a strong predictor of outcome. Immobility before the fracture, poor social function (proportional to the amount of care patients required before their fracture), and decreased frequency of going out of one's home before the fracture are all associated with significantly higher mortality.[37, 44] In addition to dementia and poor prefracture physical function, congestive heart failure, male gender, deep wound infections, postoperative chest infections, and delirium at hospital admission have all been associated with a higher mortality in these patients.[10]

### Functional Outcome

Patients with hip fractures very often have a significantly reduced physical function. Marottoli and associates demonstrated that this decline was closely associated with prefracture physical function.[36] Young and colleagues found that unsteady gait before fracture predicted a poor outcome.[57] Multiple studies revealed that patients with a better baseline functional status, such as being able to shop independently and having frequent social contacts outside the home, have a better functional outcome with more complete recovery of their prefracture level of function.[6, 11, 12]

## PREOPERATIVE ASSESSMENT

A preoperative examination and assessment are required to determine the patient's baseline medical condition, identify

**TABLE 47-1** · · · · · · · · · · · · · · · · · · · · · · · · · · · · · · · · · · ·

Predictors of Mortality

---

Dementia
Prefracture physical function
Prefracture social function
Delirium upon admission
Congestive heart failure
Deep wound infections
Postoperative chest infections

· · · · · · · · · · · · · · · · · · · · · · · · · · · · · · · · · · · · · · · · · ·

decompensated or previously unrecognized conditions, and assess the perioperative risk for a cardiac event. The vast majority of patients with hip fractures are older than 70 years. The surgeon should be aware of a number of special problems commonly encountered in the older patient undergoing surgery. In the first instance, there are a number of physiologic changes that occur with aging. The older individual has a decreased ability to adapt to change. In addition to this decreased physiologic reserve, there is a predictable decline with age in pulmonary vital capacity, cardiac output, renal blood flow, glomerular filtration rate, grip strength, and neuromuscular reaction time. There is also a marked increase in the prevalence of diseases with aging. Ninety percent of patients older than 70 years have at least one co-morbid condition. In the second instance, one third of older patients have at least three or more co-morbid conditions. It is the presence of these diseases, more than the changes with age, that increases the risk of surgery for older individuals. As a result of these changes, the older individual loses a good deal of his or her ability to react to stress. This diminished reserve of the older patient may be less apparent on history and physical examination because of decreased activity due to joint disease, vascular insufficiency, or other limiting factors.

The two organ systems that are associated with the greatest number of perioperative problems are the pulmonary and cardiovascular systems. Identifying disorders in these two systems, as well as others, and optimizing their management, even if this delays surgery for a day or two, reduces the chance that complications will mar a successful outcome.[32, 51]

## Cardiovascular Assessment

A number of studies have evaluated factors that increase the risk of cardiovascular events in patients undergoing noncardiac surgery.[13, 25] The stress of surgery causes increased cardiac output. In addition, anesthetic agents can depress the myocardium, cause peripheral vasodilatation, and induce arrhythmias. A recent guideline by the American Heart Association and the American College of Cardiology on the evaluation of patients undergoing noncardiac surgery categorized the cardiac risk factors into major, intermediate, and minor predictors of perioperative cardiac events (myocardial infarction, congestive heart failure, and death)[14] (Table 47-2). Major predictors require acute investigation and management and may require delay or cancellation of the surgery. Intermediate

predictors require careful perioperative assessment. Minor predictors have not been shown to affect perioperative cardiac risk. Patients with a recent myocardial infarction or unstable angina should be evaluated further before surgery. To determine the severity of these risk factors, the surgeon must evaluate how often the patient stresses his or her cardiovascular system in normal activities. Patients with good exercise tolerance, such as the ability to walk a city block or ascend a flight of stairs without significant difficulty, do well with surgery.[14] In addition, patients who have had coronary artery revascularization, with either coronary artery bypass grafts or percutaneous transluminal coronary angioplasty or stent within the previous 5 years and have done well since the procedure and are ambulatory, do not have increased cardiac risk and can proceed to surgery without further cardiac evaluation.[14]

Patients at risk for or with coronary artery disease should receive a beta-blocker preoperatively and postoperatively. Mangano and co-workers[34] showed an 11% absolute reduction in mortality (21% placebo, 10% atenolol) after 2 years for those randomized to receive atenolol during hospitalization for noncardiac surgery. Patients who should receive beta-blocker therapy include those with known coronary artery disease or those at risk for coronary artery disease with at least two of the following characteristics: active smoker, diabetes mellitus, hypertension, elevated cholesterol, age older than 65, and no contraindications. Beta-blocker therapy should be continued for those taking a beta-blocker before hospitalization. For patients not previously taking a beta-blocker, initial administration should be given intravenously preoperatively, again postoperatively, and then orally while hospitalized (Table 47-3).

Congestive heart failure is a major determinant of perioperative complications.[13, 25] Patients with compen-

**TABLE 47-2** · · · · · · · · · · · · · · · · · · · · · · · · · · · · · · · · · · · · ·

Clinical Predictors of Increased Perioperative
Cardiovascular Risk

---

| **MAJOR** | Unstable coronary syndromes |
| | Recent MI (greater than 7 days but less than 1 month) |
| | Canadian class III (limitation of ordinary activity) or IV (angina with any physical activity or rest) angina pectoris |
| | Decompensated congestive heart failure |
| | Severe valvular disease |
| | Significant arrhythmias |
| **INTERMEDIATE** | Mild angina pectoris (Canadian class I or II) |
| | Prior myocardial infarction |
| | Compensated or history of congestive heart failure |
| | Diabetes mellitus |
| **MINOR** | Advanced age |
| | Abnormal electrocardiogram |
| | Rhythm other than sinus |
| | Low functional capacity (inability to climb one flight of stairs with a bag of groceries) |
| | History of stroke |
| | Uncontrolled systemic hypertension |

· · · · · · · · · · · · · · · · · · · · · · · · · · · · · · · · · · · · · · · · · · · ·

*Source:* Adapted from Eagle, K.A.; Brundage, B.H.; Chairman, B.R.; et al. J Am Coll Cardiol 27:910–948, 1996.

| TABLE 47–3 | |
|---|---|
| **Perioperative Beta Antagonists** | |

| | |
|---|---|
| **INDICATIONS** | Known coronary artery disease |
| | History suggestive of coronary artery disease |
| | Two or more of the following risk factors for coronary artery disease |
| |    Age ≥65 |
| |    Diabetes mellitus |
| |    Cholesterol ≥240 |
| |    Smoker |
| |    Hypertension |
| **CONTRAINDICATIONS** | Heart rate <55 |
| | Hypotension |
| | Congestive heart failure |
| | Second degree heart block or greater |
| | Active wheezing |
| | History of adverse reaction to beta antagonists |
| **DOSAGE** | Preoperative |
| |   If on beta blocker, continue IV or PO |
| |   If not previously on beta blocker: |
| |     heart rate ≥55, systolic blood pressure ≥100 mm Hg: atenolol 5 mg IV over 5 min; repeat × 1 if heart rate ≥55, and systolic blood pressure ≥100 |
| |     repeat above immediately postoperatively |
| | Postoperative |
| |   Atenolol 50 mg po qd; increase to 100 mg po qd if heart rate ≥55 and systolic blood pressure ≥100 |
| |   Continue duration of hospitalization or 7 days |

sated left ventricular dysfunction who are asymptomatic and have moderate exercise tolerance and normal results on cardiovascular examination have an increased risk of perioperative pulmonary edema but not of myocardial infarction.[1] Patients should be maintained on their outpatient medications and monitored for signs and symptoms of pulmonary edema. Appropriate electrolyte and drug levels should be confirmed and corrected as needed.

Patients who have symptomatic congestive heart failure or findings on examination of elevated jugular venous distention, pulmonary crackles, or an $S_3$ gallop have an increased risk of pulmonary edema and cardiac death. Transthoracic echocardiography does not add to the clinical evaluation and does not have a routine role in preoperative assessment.[27, 38] Having the transthoracic echocardiogram data did not improve the prognostic information already obtained with the known risk factors from the preoperative evaluation.[27] The cause of the patient's congestive heart failure should be investigated, and treatment should be optimized before surgery. The introduction of digitalis preparations in the perioperative stage should be avoided because digitalis increases the risk of bradyarrhythmias.[26] Diuretics must be used with caution because overdiuresis leads to intravascular volume depletion and intraoperative hypotension and may lead to hypokalemia, with a resultant increased risk for dysrhythmias.

Significant aortic stenosis increases perioperative car-

diac risk.[13, 25] Patients with known aortic stenosis, or a history and examination consistent with significant aortic stenosis, however, can be operated on safely, provided they do not have congestive heart failure.[56] Intraoperative hypotension often develops, which requires an intra-arterial catheter and possibly pulmonary artery catheterization for prompt recognition and management.

Patients with known mitral regurgitation or aortic insufficiency who are asymptomatic with no evidence of decompensation require no further evaluation. Patients on maintenance diuretics, afterload reduction, and other cardiac medications should have their dosages continued. As with congestive heart failure, patients with evidence of decompensation should be treated aggressively before surgery.

Hypertension is a common problem in the elderly. Patients with well-controlled blood pressure have wider fluctuations in both systolic and diastolic pressures intraoperatively but do not experience more cardiac complications as the result of the hypertension.[74] Antihypertensive therapy should be continued orally or intravenously. Patients whose blood pressure is not well controlled (those with a diastolic blood pressure greater than 110 mm Hg) may be at increased risk for intraoperative and postoperative cardiac complications.[14, 24] Treatment with intravenous antihypertensive medications is warranted, and blood pressure should be controlled before surgery. Labetolol, atenolol, lopressor, hydralazine, and enalaprilat are all effective perioperative agents.

## Pulmonary Assessment

Pulmonary complications are another source of significant postoperative morbidity and mortality. Elderly patients have decreased pulmonary reserve, leading to increased risk of pulmonary complications. Causes of declining lung function include decreased elasticity, increased functional residual capacity, decreased chest wall compliance, and decreased respiratory muscle strength. The elderly also have decreased cough reflex and mucociliary clearance. The supine position mandated by a hip fracture plus the use of general anesthesia predispose the elderly to atelectasis.

Several other risk factors have been identified. Patients with a greater than 20 pack-year history of smoking are at increased risk, even if asymptomatic.[7] Pulmonary complications develop in 27% of patients with chronic obstructive pulmonary disease who are not undergoing cardiac or major abdominal procedures; 1% of them die.[33] Poorly controlled asthma, as evidenced by cough, shortness of breath, reduced peak flow rate, or wheezing, leads to increased risk.[23] Patients with well-controlled asthma are not at increased risk for pulmonary complications. While previous studies noted obesity as a risk factor, a recent review found that obesity is not a significant risk factor for pulmonary complications.[52] An arterial blood gas level should be obtained in patients with a history of significant pulmonary disease or evidence of decompensation on history or examination. An $Sao_2$ is not sufficient because alterations in $Pco_2$ are not measured.

Patients with shortness of breath, active wheezing, or other evidence of decompensation such as low peak flow rates should be treated aggressively with beta-agonists, ipratropium (an inhaled anticholinergic, Atrovent), and intravenous steroids preoperatively; these should be continued postoperatively. A short course of steroids does not lead to increased postoperative complications.[29] Steroids should, however, be tapered rapidly, as allowed by the symptoms and examination, to prevent complications with infection, wound healing, and diabetes mellitus.

Antibiotics, such as a second-generation cephalosporin, should be considered preoperatively and continued for 7 to 10 days in patients with exacerbation of chronic obstructive pulmonary disease. Incentive spirometry, as well as instruction in cough and deep breathing, should begin preoperatively and continue postoperatively.

## Renal Assessment

Because renal function declines with age and fluid shifts may occur perioperatively, a preoperative assessment of renal function is essential. Factors leading to renal function decline include decreased renal blood flow, loss of nephrons, and decreased ability to dilute or concentrate the urine.[31] These changes result in decreased clearance of renally excreted medications; decreased ability to conserve water, leading to hypovolemia; and decreased ability to excrete free water, leading to volume overload. In addition, the serum creatinine level may be within reference range, because many elderly patients often have decreased muscle mass. Creatinine clearance can be estimated by the formula:

$$\text{Creatinine clearance} = (140 - \text{age}) \times \text{weight (kg)}/72 \times \text{creatinine} (\times 0.85 \text{ for women}).$$

Several perioperative factors can exacerbate these limitations of apparent normal renal function in the elderly population. Elderly patients have decreased thirst.[48] This, coupled with the inability to concentrate urine, leads to asymptomatic hypovolemia, which increases the risk for intraoperative hypotension, decreases renal blood flow, and increases the risk for acute renal failure. By inhibiting prostaglandins, nonsteroidal anti-inflammatory drugs (NSAIDs), including cyclooxygenase-2 (COX-2) inhibitors, must be used cautiously because they decrease renal blood flow and can cause acute renal failure. Patients with a glomerular filtration rate (GFR) of less than 70 mL/min (correlating to approximately a creatinine of 1.0 in a 70-year-old 70-kg man) have a further reduction in GFR with NSAID use.[45] Declining renal function with NSAID use can develop in patients with a GFR greater than 70 (creatinine approximately 1.0) but with other risk factors for NSAID-induced renal insufficiency, such as congestive heart failure, cirrhosis, diuretic use, hypovolemia, and sodium-restricted diet. Patients on NSAIDs should undergo regular testing for blood urea nitrogen and creatinine levels. Similar precautions should be adhered to with aminoglycoside therapy, with the addition of monitoring and adjusting serum peak and trough levels. Gentamicin should be given in a daily dose rather than every 8 hours. Daily dosing results in higher peak concentrations for better bactericidal activity and lower troughs, resulting in less renal toxicity.

Pain, opiates, and anesthesia all enhance release of antidiuretic hormone. Patients given large volume of fluids may have difficulty excreting free water, leading to volume overload and hyponatremia. In the first 1 to 2 postoperative days, intravenous diuretics may be needed to assist in the elimination of perioperatively administered fluid as it mobilizes from the exravascular to intravascular space. Symptoms and signs of early intravascular volume overload include increased weight, dyspnea, jugular venous distention, pulmonary crackles, and dependent edema. Patients with congestive heart failure may require up to 5 days to completely eliminate excess fluids.

## Liver Assessment

Patients with decreased hepatic function must be evaluated closely by the anesthesiologist. The selection of the anesthetic agent is important because these agents, both general and regional, reduce hepatic blood flow, may increase liver damage, and may be metabolized and excreted by the liver. Patients with hepatic failure must be monitored closely for disorders of coagulation, namely, with the prothrombin time, gastrointestinal hemorrhage by testing stools for occult blood and serial complete blood cell counts, and portosystemic encephalopathy by testing for orientation, asterixis, and serum ammonia levels.

Patients with jaundice are at increased risk for postoperative renal failure, with an incidence of 8.4% and a mortality rate of 64.1%.[31] Risk is proportionate to the serum bilirubin level. Jaundiced patients are more likely to become hypotensive perioperatively owing to an increased sensitivity to hypovolemia from decreased peripheral vascular resistance. In addition, bilirubin, when combined with perioperative hypotension, may potentiate renal ischemia. Finally, jaundiced patients have fewer bile salts in the intestinal lumen, resulting in enhanced absorption of endotoxin, and have decreased degradation of endotoxin owing to depression of the reticuloendothelial system. Elevated endotoxin levels can decrease renal perfusion and cause disseminated intravascular coagulation, acute tubular necrosis, and thrombotic glomerulopathy.

## Assessment for Diabetes Mellitus

Diabetes mellitus has a prevalence of 7% to 9% in individuals older than 65 years. Poorly controlled glucose levels can lead to dehydration, electrolyte abnormalities, poor wound healing, and increased incidence of infections. By limiting the negative impact hyperglycemia has on wound healing, neutrophil chemotaxis and bactericidal activity, tight perioperative glycemic control (150–200 mg/dl) may improve the outcome. Many clinicians allow the glucose levels to increase owing to concern for hypoglycemia, but frequent monitoring of serum glucose levels allows corrections to be made and hypoglycemia to be avoided.

Hospitalization leads to unpredictable glucose levels. Increased stress, anesthetics, inactivity, infection, use of steroids, and other factors can lead to elevated levels. Rigid diet, nothing-by-mouth status, and compliance with medications may lead to decreased glucose levels. Therefore, all patients should undergo frequent fingerstick glucose checks, as frequent as every 1 to 2 hours perioperatively and no less than four times daily later. If possible, procedures should be scheduled for early in the day. Finally, clinicians should not rely only on a "sliding scale" of regular insulin, as this can lead to very poor control with wide swings in the serum glucose.

Patients with type 1 diabetes mellitus—insulin-dependent diabetes mellitus—must have insulin at all times, even when they are taking nothing by mouth. Patients with type 1 diabetes mellitus can become ketotic in as little as 12 hours without insulin. An infusate containing glucose, along with subcutaneous or intravenous insulin, must be given at all times the patient is taking nothing by mouth. Table 47–4 provides a regimen for perioperative management of type 1 diabetes mellitus. Once the patient is stable and tolerating oral food, resumption of the patient's outpatient regimen, with a 10% to 25% reduction in insulin owing to improved diet, can be resumed.

Patients with type 2 diabetes mellitus, or non–insulin-dependent diabetes, on oral agents or insulin are not prone to ketoacidosis but may have glucose levels more difficult to control closely. If renal function is or becomes impaired, metformin (Glucophage), a relatively new oral agent, should be withheld because of the risk that it may cause lactic acidosis. As stated earlier, elderly patients are more prone to hypovolemia and acute renal failure. Poorly controlled blood glucose leads to an osmotic diuresis, further exacerbating hypovolemia. Table 47–5 provides recommended options for perioperative management. As with patients with type 1 diabetes, patients with type 2 diabetes may resume the outpatient regimen once they are stable and can tolerate oral foods.

## Glucocorticoid Replacement Therapy Assessment

Many elderly persons suffer from acute and chronic diseases, such as polymyalgia rheumatica, that require

**TABLE 47–4** ......................................

Perioperative Management Type 1 Diabetes Mellitus

| | |
|---|---|
| **INSULIN DRIP** | Place on insulin drip at 1 to 2 U/hr<br>Give a 5% dextrose containing fluid at 50–100 cc/hr<br>Finger stick glucose q 1–2 hr<br>Adjust to maintain serum glucose at 150–200 mg/dL<br>OR |
| **SUBCUTANEOUS INSULIN** | ½ to ⅔ maintenance morning NPH or Lente dose<br>Give a 5% dextrose containing fluid at 50–100 cc/hr<br>Finger stick q 2 hr<br>Small doses, <4 U, regular insulin subcutaneously to maintain serum glucose at 150–200 mg/dl |

**TABLE 47–5** ......................................

Perioperative Management Type 2 Diabetes

| | |
|---|---|
| **IF ON ORAL AGENT** | Hold medication day of surgery<br>Finger stick glucoses q 4 hr<br>Small doses regular insulin subcutaneously to maintain serum glucose at 150–200 mg/dl |
| **IF ON INSULIN** | ½ Maintenance morning NPH or a Lente subcutaneously<br>Give a 5% dextrose containing fluid at 50–100 cc/hr<br>Finger sticks q 4 hr<br>Small doses of regular insulin subcutaneously for finger stick glucose >200 mg/dl<br>OR<br>Insulin drip at 1–2 U/hr<br>Give a 5% dextrose containing fluid at 50–100 cc/hr<br>Finger stick glucose q 1–2 hr; adjust to maintain serum glucose at 150–200 mg/dl |

........................................................

glucocorticoid therapy. Treatment with as little as 5 mg of prednisone, or the equivalent, for 2 weeks can suppress the hypothalamic-pituitary-adrenal (HPA) axis. Similar doses for as little as a month within the previous year can result in persistent HPA axis suppression. The suppressed HPA axis may not respond normally to the stress of a fracture, trauma, surgery, infection, and the like. Symptoms including weakness, fatigue, abdominal pain, nausea, vomiting, fever, altered mental status, hypoglycemia, and hypotension may appear gradually or suddenly. Patients who are on chronic glucocorticoid treatment or who received prednisone within the previous year should receive full stress dose glucocorticoid replacement. A common regimen is hydrocortisone succinate 100 mg IV every 8 hours, beginning on admission and continuing for at least 2 days postoperatively. Once stable on postoperative day 2, or later, stress dose glucocorticoids can be discontinued and the chronic dose resumed. No tapering is needed unless large doses were given for 7 or more days.

## Mental and Functional Status Assessment

A careful assessment of a patient's mental and physical function before the fracture is an essential component of the preoperative workup of a patient with a hip fracture. As reviewed below, prefracture functional status is an important predictor of both rehabilitative outcome and mortality following a hip fracture. The clinician should ask about the patient's ability to get on and off a chair; walk short distances; climb stairs; and perform such daily living activities as dressing, bathing, toileting, and grooming. In addition, the clinician should ask how often an individual gets out of the house or apartment and how active he or she is with occupational, social, and recreational activities. This functional history not only predicts the outcome of the patient, but also identifies potential physical problems that might be important in the subsequent treatment.

An assessment of a patient's mental status is crucial to the treatment of a patient with a hip fracture. Altered mental status is the most important prognostic indicator of mortality and recovery of function. Dementia is also the most important risk factor for the development of delirium, a complication that can adversely affect the patient's course. A baseline of a patient's mental status should include assessment of memory because memory loss is the earliest feature of dementia. One quick screen of mental status is to ask the patient to remember three words in 2 minutes. This is a much more sensitive test of dementia than is orientation to time and place. The best formal screening test for altered mental status is the Folstein Mini Mental Status examination, which can be performed easily within 5 minutes.[16]

If a patient demonstrates any evidence of memory loss or altered mental status, a clinician should be careful to avoid any actions that could lead to delirium. The class of drugs most frequently associated with delirium are those with potent anticholinergic actions, such as tricyclic antidepressants, antihistamines, phenothiazines, phenobarbital, and antipsychotics. Meperidine is also associated with delirium.[35] These drugs should be avoided whenever possible. In addition, hypnotic and sedating drugs such as benzodiazapines often precipitate delirium. The use of physical restraints can also lead to this complication.

The clinician should be aware that, in patients with altered mental status, acute confusion or delirium is often the presenting feature of a medical illness or a drug complication. Common postoperative causes include pain, bladder distention, medications, infection, hypoxia, electrolyte abnormalities, hypoglycemia or hyperglycemia, congestive heart failure, myocardial ischemia, and stroke. Each of these should be investigated and treated as appropriate. Finally, patients often do not or cannot complain of pain and request analgesic medication. Therefore, pain medication should be scheduled on a regular basis rather than given only if requested.

## Laboratory Assessment

Preoperative laboratory assessment aids the evaluation. Some controversy exists over the extent of routine testing. Owing to the increased incidence of co-morbid conditions in the elderly and the inability to obtain a history in some patients, a complete blood cell count, platelet count, serum electrolyte levels, blood urea nitrogen (BUN), glucose, chest radiograph, and electrocardiogram should be obtained. Prothrombin time (PT) and partial thromboplastin time (PTT) should be reserved for patients who are unable to give a history or whose history—either personal or family—or examination may include a bleeding diathesis. Routine testing of PT/PTT has not been shown to be of benefit in low-risk patients.[54] Further testing can be scheduled based on the findings of the history and physical examination.

An evaluation of nutritional status should be done and a serum albumin level obtained in all patients. Malnutrition is common in hospitalized patients and is often unrecognized by physicians[50]; it may be found in up to 20% of patients with hip fracture[2] and is associated with increased morbidity and mortality.[47] Albumin levels below 3.0 g/dl predict increased mortality at 1 year.[17] Multiple studies have demonstrated the benefit of oral protein supplementation postoperatively.[42] Patients who received

supplementation had better 6-month outcomes, improved albumin levels, and shorter length of stays. Evidence strongly suggests that patients with evidence of malnutrition should receive postoperative oral protein supplements.

## Wound Infection Prophylaxis

Nosocomial infections produce significant postoperative morbidity and mortality in patients with hip fracture. The most common organism found in wound infections is *Staphylococcus aureus*. Multiple studies have demonstrated the benefit of antimicrobial prophylaxis in decreasing the incidence of superficial and deep wound infections.[4, 5, 19, 21, 22] Perioperative prophylactic antibiotics are indicated for all patients with hip fracture. Although most studies evaluated intravenous antibiotics, one study found equivalence of oral and intravenous administration.[46]

Antibiotics should be administered in the 2 hours before surgery.[9] Delivery more than 2 hours before the procedure allows for tissue levels to fall below the minimal inhibitory concentration. If given at the time of the incision or postoperatively, arterial spasm at the incision prevents adequate tissue levels. Patients receiving antibiotics more than 2 hours before the incision had a surgical wound infection rate of 3.8%. Those receiving the antibiotics within 2 hours before the incision had an infection rate of 0.6%. Patients who received the medication within 3 hours after the incision had a rate of 1.4%, whereas patients who received antibiotics more than 3 hours after the incision had a wound infection rate of 3.3%.

Although controversy exists surrounding the number of doses required, antibiotic levels should exceed the minimum inhibitory concentration levels for 12 hours.[22] A single preoperative dose of a cephalosporin with a long half-life proved to be equivalent to multiple doses of a shorter-acting cephalosporin.[5, 19] A single preoperative dose of a short-acting cephalosporin, however, was not as effective as multiple doses.[20] Intraoperative doses may be needed for prolonged procedures or when extensive blood loss occurs.

Table 47–6 lists recommended antimicrobial prophylaxis regimens.

## Deep Vein Thrombosis Prophylaxis

Without prophylaxis, 40% to 80% of patients with hip fracture will develop deep vein thrombosis, 10% to 30%

| **Table 47–6** |||
| :--- | :--- | :--- |
| Prophylactic Antibiotics |||
| **Antibiotic** | **Preoperative** | **Postoperative** |
| Cefazolin | 1 g IV | 1 g IV q 8 hr × 2 doses |
| Vancomycin* | 1 g IV | 1 g IV |

*For patients allergic to penicillins or cephalosporins, or, when infection with methicillin-resistant *Staphylococcus aureus* or *Staphylococcus epidermidis* is suspected.

proximal vein thrombosis, and 1% to 10% a fatal pulmonary embolism.[55] In addition to leg trauma, the perioperative state exacerbates the three risk factors for venous thrombosis: stasis, vascular damage, and hypercoagulable state.[41] Immobilization and patient positioning increase venous stasis. Anesthesia causes vasodilatation, increasing venous pooling, and intimal injury. Finally, impaired venous flow decreases clearance of activated clot factors and levels of endogenous anticoagulants.

A number of studies have shown the benefits of multiple medications and devices at decreasing the risk of deep vein thrombosis and pulmonary embolism. A recent review discusses in detail the effectiveness of low-molecular-weight heparin, low-dose unfractionated heparin, aspirin, low-dose warfarin, dextran, and external pneumatic compression devices.[42] Controversy exists over which agent is most effective. Low-dose unfractionated heparin and low-molecular-weight heparin are likely the agents of choice. Low-molecular-weight heparin is slightly more effective but also more costly. Low-dose warfarin is also effective but requires monitoring of the international normalized ratio (INR). External pneumatic compression stockings should be added to any medical regimen while the patient is hospitalized. Aspirin can be used if anticoagulation is contraindicated.

Some patients require a delay in surgery. Zahn and associates found that of the patients with a delay to operation of more than 48 hours, 62% were diagnosed with a deep vein thrombosis preoperatively.[58] Patients with a delay in surgery should begin thromboembolic prophylaxis early in the admission.

One study found a significant benefit with the addition of 160 mg aspirin a day to any form of thromboembolic prophylaxis.[49] Patients with a hip fracture who received aspirin and other prophylaxis had a 43% reduction in pulmonary embolism and a 29% reduction in symptomatic deep vein thrombosis. Furthermore, aspirin can be continued after discharge.

Therefore, unless contraindicated, patients should receive low-dose aspirin, external pneumatic compression stockings, and either low-molecular-weight heparin or low-dose heparin, beginning on admission to the hospital and continued until discharge. Aspirin can be continued on an outpatient basis.

Table 47–7 lists common medications used for thromboembolic prophylaxis.

## POSTOPERATIVE MANAGEMENT

### Bladder Management

Many older patients are at risk for the onset of difficulty with voiding and urinary tract infection after hip fracture surgery.[53] Large volumes of undrained urine in the bladder can stretch the detrusor muscle and aggravate voiding difficulties. As noted previously, bladder distention can also precipitate delirium. Although an indwelling Foley catheter is a reasonable approach for the first 24 to 48 hours after surgery, more prolonged use of this device has an unacceptable infection rate. Scheduled intermittent

| TABLE 47–7 | |
|---|---|
| **Thromboembolic Prophylaxis** | |
| Enoxaparin: | 30 mg subcutaneously every 12 hr or 40 mg subcutaneously daily (a low-molecular-weight heparin) |
| Heparin: | 5000 U subcutaneously every 8–12 hr |
| Aspirin: | 162–325 mg po daily |
| Warfarin: | adjust for INR 1.2–1.6 |

straight catheterization is a preferred method for bladder drainage after the first 24 hours. To avoid detrusor muscle injury, the patient should not be left without voiding for more than 8 hours. If the patient voids small amounts, the postvoid urine residual should be checked. This test can now be done noninvasively with a bladder scanner.

## Osteoporosis: Diagnosis and Management Options

Osteoporosis is common in both elderly men and women. Not enough attention is given to men, especially those on long-term glucocorticoids. Beginning at age 30, bone mass begins a continuous decline in men and women, at a rate of approximately 0.3% to 0.5% per year. Women have an accelerated decline in bone mass of 3% to 5% per year in the 5 to 7 years after menopause before returning to the normal rate of decline. Furthermore, women do not attain the same peak level of bone mineral density. With the increasing life span, osteoporosis and resultant increase in hip fractures, especially intertrochanteric fractures, become even more important medical problems for both surgeons and primary care providers. Treating osteoporosis, preventing falls, and decreasing the impact of falls are essential.

The best method to diagnose osteoporosis is bone densitometry.[40] Because most patients with a hip fracture have decreased bone density, testing may have little impact on treatment but can be used to monitor the efficacy of treatment. In younger, more active patients with hip fracture, bone densitometry should be performed to rule out osteoporosis.

Modifiable risk factors should be investigated in all patients. Patients should be advised to stop smoking and to decrease alcohol consumption. Glucocorticoids should be tapered to the lowest effective dose or discontinued. Patients and families should be educated about the risks of falling and the need for physical activity. Further education should be delivered on the identification and modification in the home environment of potential objects that may precipitate falls, such as carpets, wires, and furniture. Hyperthyroidism, hyperparathyroidism, and hypogonadism are all reversible causes of osteoporosis that should be investigated in appropriate patients, particularly younger patients. All three disorders can be asymptomatic. A thyroid-stimulating hormone assay is sufficient to evaluate both hyperthyroidism and hypothyroidism. A full panel of thyroid function tests is unnecessary unless an abnormality is found in the thyroid stimulating hormone assay. Hyperparathyroidism can be diagnosed with an inappropriately low serum intact parathyroid hormone level in relation to the serum calcium level. Hypogonadism in men can be diagnosed by a low morning serum testosterone level.

Hip protectors decrease the incidence of hip fractures and possibly pelvic fractures. A recent study revealed that patients assigned to the hip protector group had a hip fracture rate (per 1000 person years) of 21.3, with a rate of 46.0 in the control group.[30] Furthermore, nine of the fractures in the hip protector group occurred in falls while the subject was not wearing the device. If the hip protector was worn, fracture risk decreased 80%. Subjects in the intervention group also suffered fewer pelvic fractures (2 versus 12), but that difference was not statistically significant.

All patients should receive vitamin D and calcium supplements. Vitamin D is required for optimal calcium absorption. One study revealed a 43% reduction in hip fractures in those receiving 800 IU of vitamin $D_3$ and 1.2 g of calcium daily compared with those receiving a placebo.[8]

Estrogen replacement therapy has been shown to increase bone mass, but no randomized study has revealed a reduction in hip fractures. Retrospective studies have found a decreased incidence of spine and hip fractures.[39] Progesterone must be added for women with a uterus to decrease the risk of uterine cancer.

Calcitonin decreases osteoclast activity, inhibits bone resorption, and has been shown to decrease vertebral fractures but has not been shown to affect bone loss elsewhere. Both nasal spray and subcutaneous formulations are available.

Raloxifene is a selective estrogen receptor agonist with estrogen-like effects on bone and cardiac tissue but antagonistic activity on breast and uterine tissue. A large randomized trial of women with osteoporosis revealed an increase in spine and femoral neck density but no decrease in hip fracture.[15] Side effects include hot flashes, leg cramps, and an increased risk of thromboembolic events. Raloxifene is given as 60 mg a day.

Bisphosphonates, most notably alendronate (Fosamax) and risedronate (Actonel), are potent inhibitors of osteoclast function. Alendronate has been shown to increase bone mass in the lumbar spine and hip and to decrease hip fractures by 51% in women with osteoporosis and previous spinal fracture.[3] Risedronate has also been shown to decrease vertebral and nonvertebral fractures, including hip fractures, in women with osteoporosis.[28] Alendronate is dosed 5 mg a day for prevention and 10 mg a day for treatment of osteoporosis. Risedronate is dosed 5 mg a day for both prevention and treatment. Treatment with either medication should be held or not begun until the patient can remain upright for at least 30 minutes after taking the medication. Severe esophageal irritation can occur from gastroesophageal reflux while in the recumbent position.

## SUMMARY

This chapter has attempted to demonstrate that, in addition to the management of the fracture, close attention to assessment and appropriate treatment of cardiac, respiratory, and other organ system co-morbidities in the preoperative and postoperative setting can minimize complications and improve outcome for patients who sustain a hip fracture.

## REFERENCES

1. Adler, J.S.; Goldman, L. Preoperative evaluation. In: Tierney, L.M.; McPhee, S.J.; Papadakis, M.A., eds. Current Medical Diagnosis and Treatment 2000, 39th ed. Stamford, CT, Appleton & Lange, 2000, pp. 35–46.
2. Bastow, M.; Rawlings, J.; Allison, S.P. Undernutrition, hypothermia, and injury in elderly women with fractured femur: An injury response to altered metabolism? Lancet 1:143–146, 1983.
3. Black, D.M.; Cummings, S.R.; Karpf, D.B.; et al. Randomized trial of alendronate on risk of fracture in women with existing vertebral fractures. Lancet 348:1535–1541, 1996.
4. Bodoky, A. Antibiotic prophylaxis with two doses of cephalosporin in patients managed with internal fixation for a fracture of the hip. J Bone Joint Surg Am 75:61–65, 1993.
5. Boxma, H.; Broekhuizen, T.; Patka, P.; Oosting, H. Randomised controlled trial of single-dose antibiotic prophylaxis in surgical treatment of closed fractures: The Dutch Trauma Trial. Lancet 347:1133–1137, 1996.
6. Ceder, L.; Thorngren, K.G.; Wallden, B. Prognostic indicators and early home rehabilitation in elderly patients with hip fractures. Clin Orthop 152:173–184, 1980.
7. Chalon, J.; Tayae, M.A.; Ramanathan, S. Cytology of respiratory epithelium as a predictor of respiratory complications after operation. Chest 67:32–35, 1975.
8. Chapuy, M.C.; Arlot, M.E.; Doboeuf, F.; et al. Vitamin $D_3$ and calcium to prevent hip fractures in elderly women. N Engl J Med 327:1637–1642, 1992.
9. Classen, D.C.; Evans, R.S.; Pestotnik, S.L.; et al. The timing of prophylactic administration of antibiotics and the risk of surgical wound infection. N Engl J Med 326:281–286, 1992.
10. Clayer, M.T.; Bauze, R.J. Morbidity and mortality following fractures of the femoral neck and trochanteric region: Analysis of risk factors. J Trauma 29:1673–1678, 1989.
11. Cobey, J.C.; Cobey, J.H.; Conant, L.; et al. Indicators of recovery from fractures of the hip. Clin Orthop 117:258–262, 1976.
12. Cummings, S.R.; Phillips, S.L.; Wheat, M.E.; et al. Recovery of function after hip fracture. The role of social supports. J Am Geriatr Soc 36:801–806, 1988.
13. Detsky, A.S.; Abrams, H.B.; McLaughlin, J.R.; et al. Predicting cardiac complications in patients undergoing non-cardiac surgery. J Gen Intern Med 1:211–219, 1986.
14. Eagle, K.A.; Brundage, B.H.; Chairman, B.R.; et al. Guidelines for perioperative cardiovascular evaluation for noncardiac surgery. Report of the American College of Cardiology/American Heart Association Task Force on Practice Guidelines (Committee on Perioperative Cardiovascular Evaluation for Noncardiac Surgery). J Am Coll Cardiol 27:910–948, 1996.
15. Ettinger, B.; Black, D.M.; Mitlak, B.H.; et al. Reduction of vertebral fracture risk in postmenopausal women with osteoporosis treated with raloxifene: Results from a 3-year randomized clinical trial. Multiple Outcomes of Raloxifene Evaluation (MORE) Investigators. JAMA 282:637–645, 1999.
16. Folstein, M.F.; Folstein, S.E.; McHugh, P.R. Mini-mental state: A practical method for grading the cognitive state of patients for the clinician. J Psychiatr Res 12:189–198, 1975.
17. Foster, M.R.; Heppenstall, R.B. A prospective assessment of nutritional status and complications in patients with fractures of the hip. J Orthop Trauma 4:49–57, 1997.
18. Fox, K.M.; Magaziner, J.; Hebel, J.R.; et al. Intertrochanteric versus femoral neck hip fractures: Differential characteristics, treatment, and sequelae. J Gerontol A Biol Sci Med Sci 54:M635–M640, 1999.
19. Garcia, S.; Lozano, M.L.; Gatell, J.M.; et al. Prophylaxis against infection. J Bone Joint Surg Am 73:1044–1048, 1991.
20. Gatell, J.M.; Garcia, S.; Lozano, L.; et al. Perioperative cefamandole prophylaxis against infections. J Bone Joint Surg Am 69:1189–1193, 1987.
21. Gatell, J.M.; Riba, J.; Lozano, M.L.; et al. Prophylactic cefamandole in orthopaedic surgery. J Bone Joint Surg Am 66:1219–1222, 1984.

22. Gillespie, W.J.; Walenkamp, G. Antibiotic prophylaxis for surgery for proximal femoral and other closed long bone fractures (Cochrane Review). In: The Cochrane Library, Issue 2, 2000. Oxford: Update Software.

23. Gold, M.I.; Helrich, M. A study of the complications related to anesthesia in asthmatic patients. Anesth Analg 42:283–293, 1963.

24. Goldman, L.; Caldera, D.L. Risks of general anesthesia and elective operation in the hypertensive patient. Anesthesiology 50:285–292, 1979.

25. Goldman, L.; Caldera, D.L.; Nussbaum, S.R.; et al. Multifactorial index of cardiac risk in noncardiac surgical procedures. N Engl J Med 297:845–850, 1977.

26. Goldman, L.; Caldera, D.L.; Southwick, F.S.; et al. Cardiac risk factors and complications in non-cardiac surgery. Medicine 57:357–370, 1978.

27. Halm, E.A.; Browner, W.S.; Tubau, J.F.; et al. Echocardiography for preoperative assessment of cardiac risk in noncardiac surgery. Ann Intern Med 125:433–441, 1996.

28. Harris, S.T.; Watts, N.B.; Genant, H.K.; et al. Effects of risedronate treatment on vertebral and nonvertebral fractures in women with postmenopausal osteoporosis: A randomized controlled trial. JAMA 282:1344–1353, 1999.

29. Kabalin, C.S.; Yarnold, P.R.; Grammer, L.C. Low complication rate of corticosteroid-treated asthmatics undergoing surgical procedures. Arch Intern Med 155:1379–1384, 1995.

30. Kannus, P.; Parkari, J.; Niemi, S.; et al. Prevention of hip fracture in elderly people with use of a hip protector. N Engl J Med 343:1506–1513, 2000.

31. Kellerman, P.S. Perioperative care of the renal patient. Arch Intern Med 154:1674–1688, 1994.

32. Kenzora, J.E.; McCarthy, R.E.; Lowell, J.D.; et al. Hip fracture mortality: Relation to age, treatment, preoperative illness, time of surgery, and complications. Clin Orthop 186:45–56, 1984.

33. Kroenke, K.; Lawrence, V.A.; Theroux, J.F.; et al. Operative risk in patients with severe obstructive pulmonary disease. Arch Intern Med 152:967–971, 1992.

34. Mangano, D.T.; Layug, E.L.; Wallace, A.; et al. Effect of atenolol on mortality and cardiovascular morbidity after noncardiac surgery. N Engl J Med 335:1713–1720, 1996.

35. Marcantonia, E.R.; Juarez, G.; Goldman, L.; et al. The relationship of postoperative delirium with psychoactive medications. JAMA 272:1518–1522, 1994.

36. Marottoli, R.A.; Berkman, L.F.; Cooney, L.M. Decline in physical function following hip fracture. J Am Geriatr Soc 40:861–866, 1992.

37. Marottoli, R.A.; Berkman, L.F.; Leo-Summers, L.; Cooney, L.M. Predictors of mortality and institutionalization after hip fracture: The New Haven EPESE Cohort. Am J Pub Health 84:1807–1812, 1994.

38. McCann, R.L.; Wolfe, W.G. Resection of abdominal aortic aneurysm in patients with low ejection fractions. J Vasc Surg 10:240–244, 1989.

39. Drugs for prevention and treatment of postmenopausal osteoporosis. Med Lett 42:97–100, 2000.

40. Melton, L.J.; Wahner, H.W.; Richelson, L.S.; et al. Osteoporosis and the risk of hip fracture. Am J Epidemiol 124:154, 1986.

41. Merli, G.J. Deep vein thrombosis and pulmonary embolism prophylaxis in orthopedic surgery. Med Clin North Am 77:397–411, 1993.

42. Morrison, R.S.; Chassin, M.R.; Siu, A.L. The medical consultant's role in caring for patients with hip fracture. Ann Intern Med 128:1010–1020, 1998.

43. Morrison, R.S.; Siu, A.L. Survival in end-stage dementia following acute illness. JAMA 284:47–52, 2000.

44. Mullen, J.O.; Mullen, N.L. Hip fracture mortality. Clin Orthop Relat Res 280:214–222, 1992.

45. Murray, M.D.; Black, P.K.; Kuzmik, D.D.; et al. Acute and chronic effects of non-steroidal anti-inflammatory drugs on glomerular filtration rate in elderly patients. Am J Med Sci 310:188–197, 1995.

46. Nungu, K.S.; Larsson, S.; et al. Prophylaxis with oral cephadril versus intravenous cefuroxime in trochanteric fracture surgery. Acta Orthop Trauma Surg 114:303–307, 1995.

47. Patterson, B.M.; Cornell, C.N.; Carbone, B.; et al. Protein depletion and metabolic stress in elderly patients who have a fracture of the hip. J Bone Joint Surg Am 74:251–260, 1992.

48. Phillips, P.A.; Rolls, B.J.; Ledingham, J.G.; et al. Reduced thirst after water deprivation in healthy elderly men. N Engl J Med 311:753–759, 1984.

49. Pulmonary Embolism Prevention (PEP) Trial Collaborative Group. Prevention of pulmonary embolism and deep vein thrombosis with low dose aspirin: Pulmonary Embolism Prevention (PEP) trial. Lancet 355:1295–1302, 2000.

50. Roubenoff, R.; Roubenoff, R.A.; et al. Malnutrition among hospitalized patients: A problem of physician awareness. Arch Intern Med 147:1462–1465, 1987.

51. Sexon, S.B.; Lehne, J.T. Factors affecting hip fracture mortality. J Orthop Trauma 1:298–305, 1987.

52. Smetana, G.W. Preoperative pulmonary evaluation. N Engl J Med 340:937–944, 1999.

53. Smith, N.K.; Albazzaz, M.K. A prospective study of urinary retention and risk of death after proximal femoral fracture. Age Ageing 25:150–154, 1995.

54. Suchman, A.L.; Griner, P.F. Diagnostic uses of the activated partial thromboplastin time and prothrombin time. Ann Intern Med 104:810–816, 1986.

55. Thromboembolic Risk Factors Consensus Group (THRIFT). Risk of and prophylaxis for venous thromboembolism in hospital patients. BMJ 305:567–574, 1992.

56. Torsher, L.C.; Shub, C.; Rettke, S.R.; et al. Risk of patients with severe aortic stenosis undergoing noncardiac surgery. Am J Cardiol 81:448–452, 1998.

57. Young, Y.; Brant, L.; German, P.; et al. A longitudinal examination of functional recovery among older people with subcapital hip fractures. J Am Geriatr Soc 45:288–294, 1997.

58. Zahn, H.R.; Skinner, J.A.; Porteous, M.J. The preoperative prevalence of deep vein thrombosis in patients with femoral neck fractures and delayed operation. Injury 30:605–607, 1999.

# CHAPTER 48

# Intracapsular Hip Fractures

Marc F. Swiontkowski, M.D.

## FEMORAL HEAD FRACTURES

### Relevant Anatomy

Because femoral head fractures nearly exclusively occur as a result of hip dislocations or fracture-dislocations, the anatomy of the proximal end of the femur, particularly the vascular anatomy, plays a critical role in determining outcome. The end results of fracture healing, fragment resorption, or femoral head necrosis are determined by the traumatic effect of the hip dislocation on the vascular anatomy, and these results are influenced to some degree by management of the injury.[16] Similarly, the effects of traumatic dislocation on femoral and acetabular articular cartilage could lead to arthrosis, which may be functionally limiting. Arthrosis, too, can be affected to some extent by management of the injury. Finally, damage to the hip capsule and hip musculature may lead to periarticular fibrosis and heterotopic ossification, which can produce functional limitations.[38]

The femoral head is supplied by three terminal arterial sources: the artery of the ligamentum teres; a terminal branch of the lateral femoral circumflex artery; and the terminal branch of the medial femoral circumflex artery, the lateral epiphyseal artery[68] (Fig. 48–1). The last source is the critical blood supply to most of the weight-bearing superior portions of the femoral head. In most cases in which hip dislocation is associated with a femoral head fracture, the direction of the dislocation is posterior.[5] The medial femoral circumflex artery is stretched, and the lateral epiphyseal artery may be occluded because of pressure from the edge of the disrupted posterior hip capsule.[16] Intracapsular hematoma does not result because of loss of capsular integrity. The anteroinferior femoral head fragment generally remains within the acetabulum attached to the ligamentum teres. The intact blood supply to this fragment and the artery of the ligamentum teres from the obturator artery allow fracture healing to occur. The plane of the fracture, especially in posterior hip dislocation, most likely disrupts the osseous branches of

the terminal divisions of the lateral femoral circumflex artery. The tension or occlusive pressure on the lateral epiphyseal artery makes it critical to promptly reduce the femoral head back into the acetabulum. As noted in Chapter 46, avascular necrosis of the femoral head increases in frequency with the number of hours that the hip remains dislocated.[18, 19, 32, 70] This temporal effect is also true when the dislocation is associated with fracture of the femoral head.

### ARTICULAR CARTILAGE

Articular cartilage covers the proximal femoral epiphysis, which roughly involves the weight-bearing hemisphere.[7, 28] The cartilage reaches a maximal thickness of 4 mm in the superior-most region and tapers as it approaches the equator of the hemisphere. It thins in the region of the insertion of the ligamentum teres. At the periphery of the cartilage the retinaculum vessels penetrate the bone. Approximately 70% of the entire articular surface of the femoral head is involved in load transfer.[28] Damage to this surface, such as that produced by fracture of the femoral head, decreases the total surface of the femoral head available for load transfer. Accompanying increases in peak compressive forces may lead to breakdown of the articular cartilage matrix, loss of the articular seal, and the development of post-traumatic osteoarthritis.[49] Femoral head indentation fractures, which are associated with acetabular fractures and anterior hip dislocations, produce focal crushing of cartilage matrix, as well as loss of total contact area, effects that have the same result.[14, 56]

### OSSEOUS ANATOMY

The adult human femoral head ranges in diameter from 40 to 60 mm and is not a perfect sphere. Out-of-round estimates are in the 1- to 1.5-mm range.[7] This subtle asphericity is reflected on the acetabular side and was previously thought to be an important factor in prosthetic design.[7] Accurate reduction of femoral head fragments

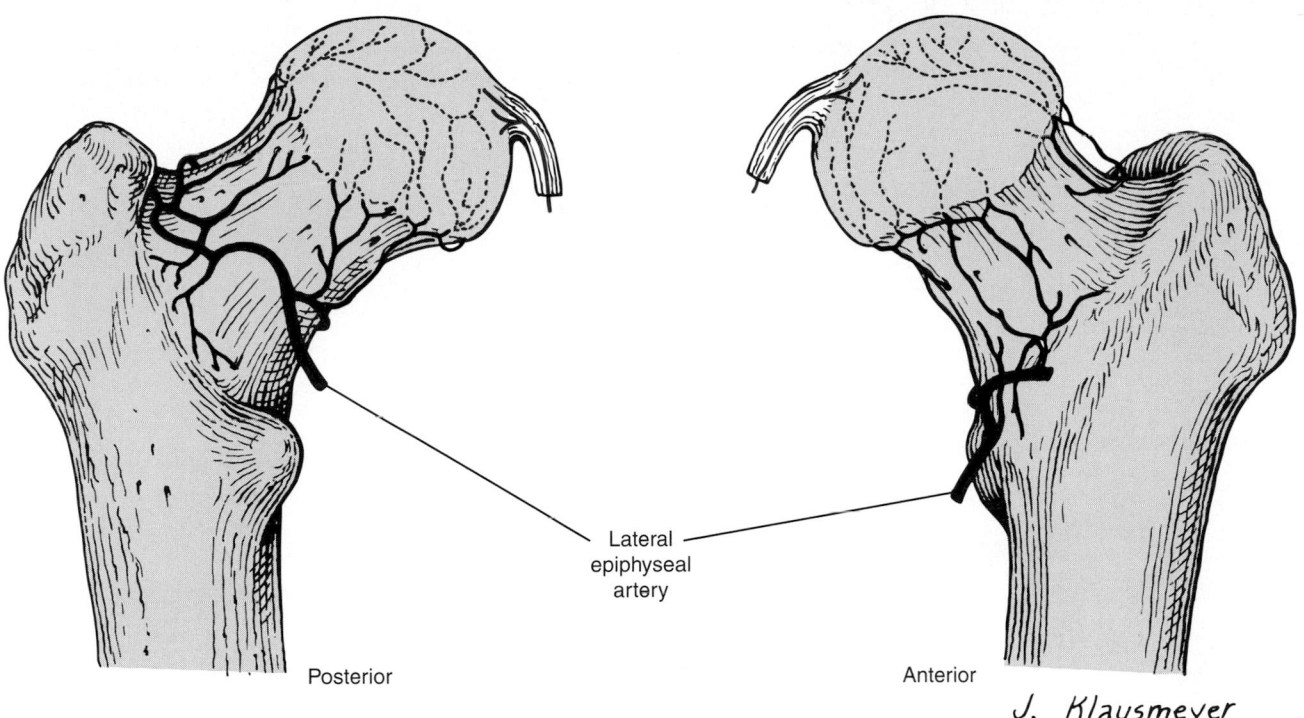

Lateral
epiphyseal
artery

Posterior                                                    Anterior

J. Klausmeyer

FIGURE 48–1. Arterial blood supply to the proximal end of the femur in an adult. The lateral epiphyseal artery supplies most of the weight-bearing surface of the femoral head in more than 90% of adults. Note the lack of significant arterial supply from the region of insertion of the anterior capsule.

that involve the articular cartilage is necessary to maximize contact between the femoral head and acetabulum and minimize peak stresses across the articular cartilage.

Maintenance of optimal femoral head–acetabular contact requires the entire femoral head. Loss of a significant piece of the femoral head will allow radial-lateral, noncongruent motion. How large the anteroinferior fragment has to be to allow the loss of this "shim" effect is not known. The short-term clinical results of resection of small fragments have been satisfactory in some series and poor in others.[5, 45, 63]

## Incidence

Femoral head fractures occur in association with hip dislocations.[3] Of the 238 published cases identified by Brumback and co-workers,[5] only 24 (10%) were associated with anterior hip dislocations. In a series of reported anterior hip dislocations, 15 of 22 (68%) had associated femoral head fractures.[14] Because anterior dislocations occur infrequently, additional data on the association of femoral head fractures are inadequate. However, indentation fracture of the femoral head seems to be commonly associated.[14, 17, 20, 56, 64] The anatomic variations of a shallow acetabulum and femoral neck retroversion may play a role in predisposing patients to traumatic hip dislocation.[70]

Eighty-five percent to 90% of hip dislocations are posterior. In the largest series of posterior hip dislocations, the incidence of associated femoral head fracture was

7%.[19, 21] In much of the published literature on femoral head fractures, no attempt is made to identify the type of hip dislocations that produce these fractures. Most of the 265 published cases of femoral head fracture are of the shear, or cleavage, type.[5, 19] The phenomenon of indentation or crush fracture has been recognized,[5] and the results in this group of patients seem to be worse than those in the cleavage group. These injuries have been reported to be commonly associated with anterior hip dislocation but are now frequently being recognized in association with acetabular fractures.

## Mechanism

The vast majority of the 265 reported cases of femoral head fracture are secondary to motor vehicle crashes.[10, 62] The mechanism in most cases associated with posterior hip dislocation is similar to that believed to produce femoral neck, shaft, or combination fractures.[23, 25] The thigh is axially loaded on impact with the dashboard, and if the femoral shaft does not fracture, a hip injury will result if sufficient force is present. If the thigh is abducted, a femoral neck fracture may result, and if neutral or adducted, posterior hip dislocation with or without a concomitant femoral head or acetabular posterior wall fracture may result (Fig. 48–2). Femoral head fractures may be the result of avulsion by the ligamentum teres or cleavage over the posterior margin of the acetabulum. Especially in anterior dislocations, impacted femoral head fractures may result from a direct blow by the edge of the acetabulum.[17, 64]

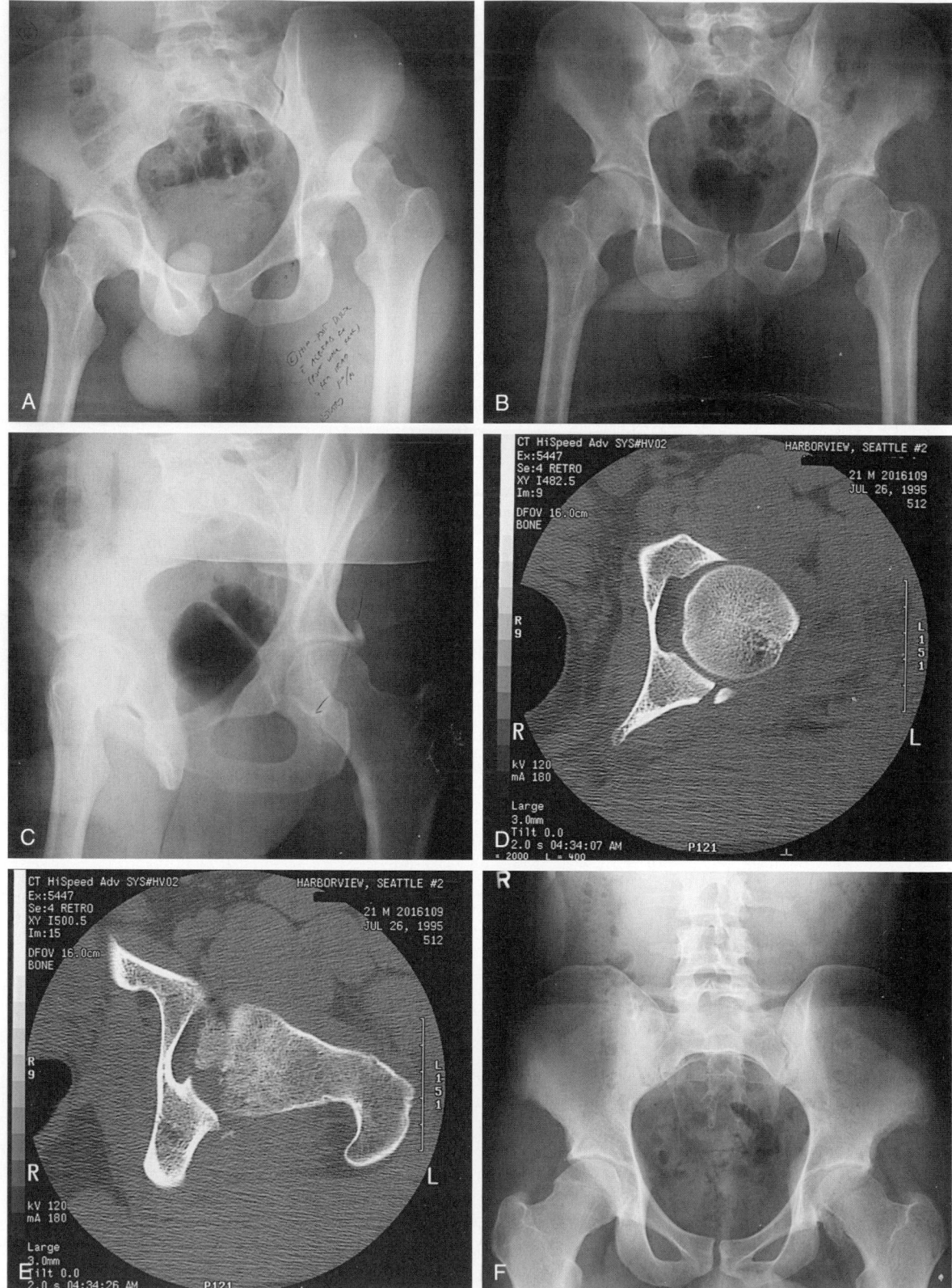

**FIGURE 48–2.** A 22-year-old man was an unrestrained driver involved in a motor vehicle accident. He had a shortened, adducted, and internally rotated left lower extremity. Closed reduction was attempted in the emergency department but was unsuccessful. *A,* Closed reduction was performed under general anesthesia in the operating room. *B,* A follow-up Judet radiograph and computed tomographic (CT) scan revealed no articular debris, a malrotated inferior head fragment, and a small posterior wall acetabular fracture. *C–E,* After discussing the options with the patient, nonoperative management was chosen. *F,* At 9 months after injury, his only detectable clinical deficiency is loss of 20° of internal rotation of the hip. He has rare hip discomfort that is not limiting.

# Consequences of Injury

## DEGENERATIVE JOINT DISEASE

Hip dislocations occur as a result of high-velocity injury. Significant force is required to disrupt the posterior hip capsule, and more may be required to add a shearing injury and produce a femoral head fracture as the head is impaled on the posterior rim of the acetabulum. Crushed, indented, or fragmented articular cartilage results in loss of function of this critical material.[17, 64] If the injury is associated with poor reduction, loss of bone stock, or excision, the mechanical environment for the remaining articular cartilage is negatively affected, thereby adding further impetus to the breakdown of cartilage matrix.[49] If significant posterior wall bone loss is also seen, posterior hip instability adds to the deterioration in hip function.[12, 26] In the same manner, loss of the medial "shim" effect produces a poor environment for survival of the remaining intact femoral head cartilage. The end result of the trauma and subsequent inferior conditions for articular cartilage is degenerative arthritis of the hip and poor hip function.[38, 58, 59, 63, 68] Because most of these injuries occur in young adults, subsequent reconstruction becomes problematic. Total-hip replacement has not been successful in the long term for this patient population.[9] Hip arthrodesis, though effective in limiting pain and optimizing function, is not an attractive option for most patients.

## AVASCULAR NECROSIS

Avascular necrosis is frequently reported in association with posterior hip dislocation.[38] It accompanies 13% of posterior hip dislocations and is seen in 18% of such dislocations associated with femoral head fracture.[19, 21, 38] The higher incidence may be a result of the greater amount of force required to produce the accompanying fracture, which also produces more soft tissue disruption. In addition, delay in closed reduction may occur because of the fracture surfaces or interposed fragments; such delay has been associated with higher rates of avascular necrosis after hip dislocation with fracture of the femoral head.[32, 70] Optimal management of hip dislocation is required to minimize the risk of avascular necrosis because in a young adult, this complication is a devastating problem without good options for treatment. Avascular necrosis appears to be more commonly associated with posterior surgical approaches to treatment than with anterior surgical approaches.[58]

## LIMITED MOTION

Poor functional results frequently occur after dislocation of the hip complicated by femoral head fracture. In addition to joint arthrosis and avascular necrosis of the femoral head, femoral head fracture is often associated with heterotopic ossification.[32, 38, 63] Such ossification results from disruption of the joint capsule and contusion, tearing, and avulsion of the abductor musculature. Heterotopic ossification can also be associated with surgical exposure.

---

**TABLE 48-1**

Thompson and Epstein's Classification of Posterior Hip Dislocations

| Type | Description |
|------|-------------|
| II | With a large single fracture off the posterior acetabular rim |
| III | With comminuted fractures of the acetabular rim (with or without a major fragment) |
| IV | With fracture of the acetabular rim and floor |
| V | With fracture of the femoral head |

*Source:* Thompson, V.P.; Epstein, H.C. J Bone Joint Surg Am 33:746, 1951.

---

# Associated Injuries

The association of femoral head fracture with hip dislocation is strong.[13, 69] It is difficult to conceive how a shearing fracture of the femoral head could be produced without dislocation.[8] Indentation fractures frequently accompany acetabular fractures and result from "central dislocation" with impaction of the head of the femur on the acetabular fragments. Management of hip dislocation can have an impact on the incidence of sciatic nerve palsy because delayed reduction of the hip dislocation results in an increasing incidence and severity of sciatic neurapraxia. The axial loading mechanism described previously explains the not infrequent association of knee ligament injury, patella fracture, and femoral shaft fracture. The knee and femur must be carefully examined in patients with femoral head fractures because the force is usually transmitted through these structures. Radiographic examination is mandatory for the ipsilateral limb.

Because these injuries are a result of high-energy trauma, injury to other body systems is frequent. An early report on these fractures revealed a 47% mortality rate overall.[12] Critical evaluation of the whole patient by the trauma team must be performed as outlined in Chapter 5.

# Classification

The first recognition of femoral head fracture as a unique entity was published in 1869 by Birkett.[2] Thompson and Epstein's classification of posterior hip dislocations, published in 1951,[66] included the classification of femoral head fracture as a separate entity (Table 48-1). This classification did not include anterior hip dislocation, nor did it include fractures of both the acetabulum and femoral head.

Stewart and Milford's classification, published in 1954,[60] did include the distinction between anterior and posterior hip dislocations. The associated fractures were classified as shown in Table 48-2. Again, the system was limited by the inability to include fractures of the acetabulum with femoral head fractures. Additionally, classification of the acetabular component was lacking in detail. Because more conditions are clearly included, the Thompson-Epstein classification was used in most publications of the 1950s and 1960s.

Pipkin's landmark article on femoral head fractures included his classification system[46] (Fig. 48–3). This article has remained the most significant contribution to the subject more than 45 years after its publication. The Pipkin classification is shown in Table 48–3. The major deficiencies of this classification are the lack of differentiation of anterior hip dislocation and insufficient expansion of the acetabular fracture categorization. The last point is minor, and the need for the first was not apparent to Pipkin because the cases on which this classification was based were collected from his Kansas City associates and were probably all associated with posterior hip dislocations.

The association of femoral head fracture with anterior hip dislocation has become more apparent in recent years, and Brumback and co-workers[5] have published the most complete classification (Table 48–4).

Although most authors have used Pipkin's classification since its publication, Brumback and co-workers' classification is more complete and includes fractures of the femoral head reorganized with associated fractures. Though somewhat cumbersome, its precision warrants the use of this system in future publications.

Another classification of femoral head fractures has been proposed by Müller and colleagues[44] and adopted by the Orthopaedic Trauma Association. Its alphanumeric categories separate and subcategorize split and depression injuries, as well as those associated with femoral neck fracture.

## Diagnosis

### HISTORY

Most femoral head fractures occur as a result of high-velocity motor vehicle accidents. Although the mechanism of posterior dislocation is believed to be axial loading of a flexed and adducted hip and that of anterior dislocation to be abduction, flexion, and external rotation, most patients are unable to give such detailed descriptions. Bilateral hip dislocations with femoral head fracture have been reported.[35, 41] Especially when multiple trauma is involved, the type and direction of the force are difficult to ascertain and are not germane to the problems at hand.

### PHYSICAL EXAMINATION

The associated hip dislocation, if it remains unreduced, determines the findings of the examination on admission. Posterior dislocation leaves the limb shortened, slightly flexed, adducted, and internally rotated. The anterior obturator type of dislocation results in the injured limb being flexed, abducted, and externally rotated. The position of the limb should be noted, and then rapid assessment of circulatory status should be performed, including pulses, capillary refill, and skin temperature. This examination must be followed by a thorough assessment of sciatic and femoral nerve function. The ability or lack thereof to dorsiflex and plantar flex the ankle, invert and evert the foot, and flex and extend the knee should be evaluated by palpating the muscle bellies as the indicated motion is attempted, followed by a careful sensory examination involving light touch and pinprick. No reduction of the hip joint should be attempted until this examination is complete.

### RADIOGRAPHIC IMAGING

An anteroposterior (AP) pelvic radiograph is a routine part of the evaluation of a multiply injured patient (see Chapter 5). In any case of suspected hip dislocation, proximal femoral fracture, or pelvic fracture, an AP radiograph must be obtained because the findings on this critical radiograph determine which other radiographic studies are needed. In the case of posterior hip dislocation, the radiograph must be scrutinized with regard to femoral head fragments remaining in the acetabular fossa. The femoral head defect is not obvious unless the angle of the beam catches the plane of the femoral head fracture in profile. To avoid displacement of an undisplaced femoral neck component of a Pipkin type III fracture, the femoral neck should be carefully scrutinized before any decision is made to reduce the hip. If the radiograph clearly demonstrates a hip dislocation with or without a concomitant femoral head fracture, the surgeon should proceed with a closed reduction maneuver. If the dislocation is associated with disruption of the anterior or posterior pelvic ring, the prereduction evaluation should also include pelvic inlet and outlet views. Similarly, if an associated acetabular fracture is suspected either on the contralateral side or as in a Pipkin type IV fracture, the prereduction radiographic evaluation should include the 45° oblique views described by Judet and Letournel.

After obtaining the best possible plain radiographs, an attempt is usually made at closed reduction, which may be done in the emergency department with analgesia and sedation or in the operating room with general anesthesia and complete muscle relaxation. Although the latter is probably less traumatic, it may not be an available option without excessive delay. Thus, it is often appropriate to attempt gentle closed reduction in the emergency department. If such reduction is unsuccessful and if further studies do not delay general anesthesia, computed tomography (CT) through the acetabulum and femoral head at 1- to 3-mm cut intervals should be rapidly performed. If open reduction becomes necessary, CT will assist the

---

**TABLE 48–2** ......................................

Stewart and Milford's Classification of Fracture-Dislocation of the Hip

| Grade | Description |
|-------|-------------|
| I | No acetabular fracture or only a minor chip |
| II | Posterior rim fracture, but stable after reduction |
| III | Posterior rim fracture with hip instability after reduction |
| IV | Dislocation accompanied by fracture of the femoral head or neck |

................................................

*Source:* Stewart, M.J.; Milford, L.W. J Bone Joint Surg Am 36:315, 1954.

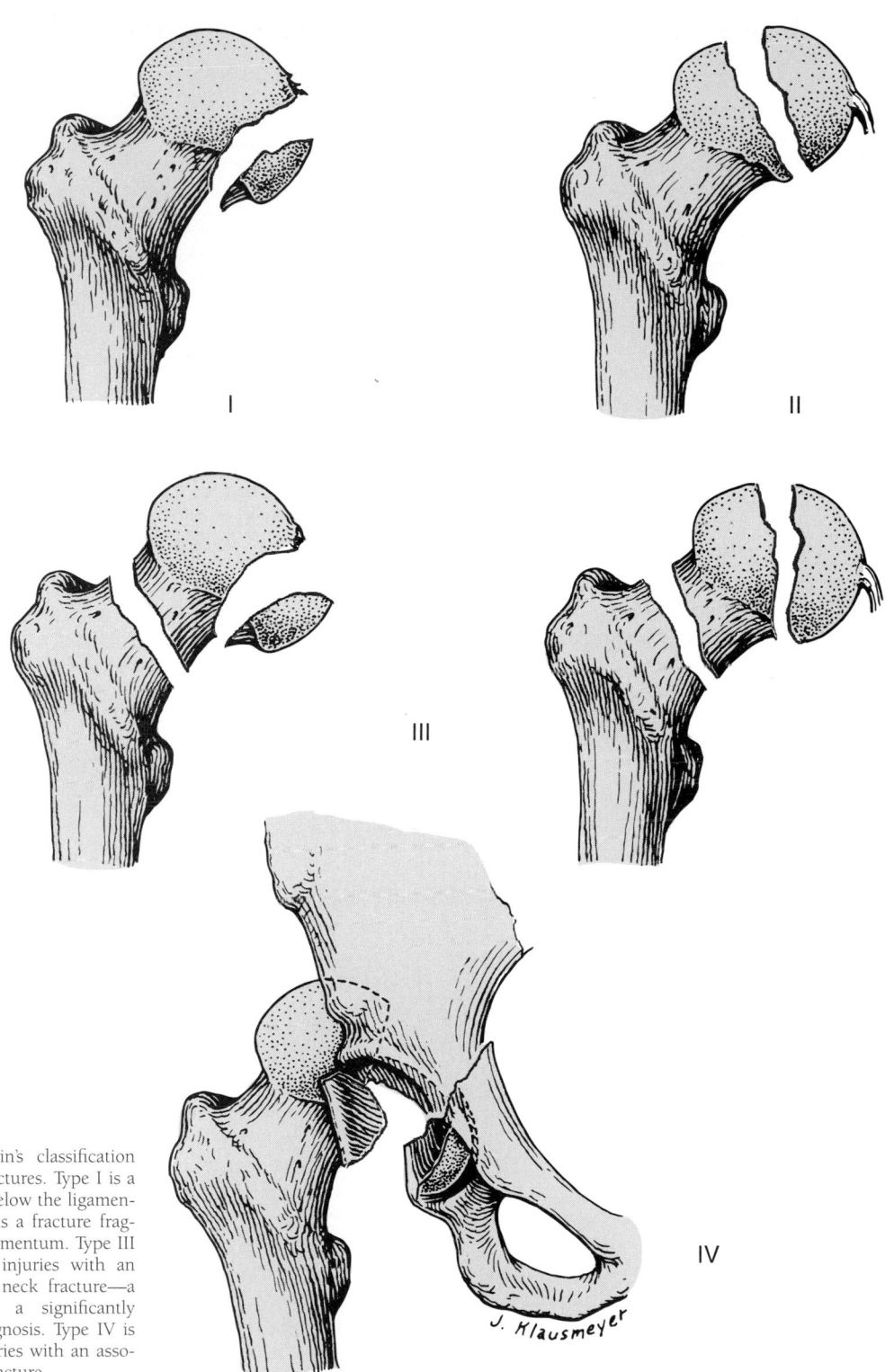

**FIGURE 48–3.** Pipkin's classification of femoral head fractures. Type I is a fracture fragment below the ligamentum teres; type II is a fracture fragment above the ligamentum. Type III is either of these injuries with an associated femoral neck fracture—a combination with a significantly poorer patient prognosis. Type IV is either of these injuries with an associated acetabular fracture.

surgeon in searching for loose bodies and interposed soft tissue[11] or in performing open reduction and internal fixation (ORIF) of an associated femoral head or acetabular fracture.* It additionally serves as a valuable source of information for the surgeon regarding the choice of

surgical approach. A CT-directed pelvic oblique radiograph can also be of assistance in accurately determining the size of the fragment, as well as any displacement.[42]

If closed reduction is successful in either setting, it must be confirmed by a follow-up AP pelvic radiograph. Follow-up studies should also include pelvic CT with 1.5-mm cuts through the acetabulum to search for loose

*See references 1, 18, 19, 21, 30, 39, 47, 48, 50, 52.

bodies, check for acetabular integrity, and evaluate the reduction status of associated femoral head fractures.

## OTHER STUDIES

In certain settings, electromyography, contrast venography, cystography and urethrography, bone scans, and magnetic resonance imaging (MRI) may be useful as part of the prereduction or postreduction evaluation. Hip dislocations (especially those that remain dislocated for long periods) may have associated sciatic nerve palsies. Electromyography can play an important role in determining the specific areas of the nerve that are involved and the degree of involvement. This information is helpful in relating the prognosis for recovery to the patient, especially if electromyograms are repeated serially. The initial study should not be obtained until 3 weeks after injury to allow accurate diagnosis. Duplex ultrasonography is a convenient and reliable test for deep venous thrombosis in the thigh and popliteal fossa, but contrast venography remains the confirmatory "gold standard."[24] Urethrography and cystography are seldom indicated in pure hip dislocation with an associated femoral head fracture but may be indicated in cases with an associated anterior pelvic ring fracture and significant displacement (see Chapter 36). Technetium bone scanning can offer some predictive information regarding the chance of later avascular necrosis.[22, 61] If femoral head uptake is significantly lower than that of the contralateral normal hip as measured by quantitative scintimetry, the risk of later avascular necrosis may be as high as 80% to 90% but is dependent on multiple factors. Finally, MRI may offer some prognostic information in regard to the risk of femoral head avascular necrosis. The exact clinical implications of an abnormal femoral head MRI signal are yet to be clearly defined, but MRI can explicitly identify bone contusion, sciatic nerve contusion, osteochondral fracture, and fractures of the acetabular rim or femoral head; however, its routine use cannot be recommended until clear cost-benefit advantages are apparent.[37] The accuracy of MRI in identifying intra-articular fragments seems to be much lower than that of CT.[46]

## Management

Two significant problems are evident when attempting to analyze the published series of femoral head fractures: (1)

**TABLE 48–3**

Pipkin's Classification of Hip Fractures

| Type | Description |
|------|-------------|
| I | Hip dislocation with fracture of the femoral head caudad to the fovea capitis femoris |
| II | Hip dislocation with fracture of the femoral head cephalad to the fovea capitis femoris |
| III | Type 1 or type 2 injury associated with fracture of the femoral neck |
| IV | Type 1 or type 2 injury associated with fracture of the acetabular rim |

*Source:* Pipkin, G.J. J Bone Joint Surg Am 39:1027, 1957.

**TABLE 48–4**

Brumback and Colleagues' Classification of Hip Dislocations

| Type | Description |
|------|-------------|
| 1 | Posterior hip dislocation with femoral head fracture involving the inferomedial, non–weight-bearing portion of the femoral head |
| 1A | With minimal or no fracture of the acetabular rim and a stable hip joint after reduction |
| 1B | With significant acetabular fracture and hip joint instability |
| 2 | Posterior hip dislocation with femoral head fracture involving the superomedial, weight-bearing portion of the femoral head |
| 2A | With minimal or no fracture of the acetabular rim and a stable hip joint after reduction |
| 2B | With significant acetabular fracture and hip joint instability |
| 3 | Dislocation of the hip (unspecified direction) with associated femoral neck fracture |
| 3A | Without fracture of the femoral head |
| 3B | With fracture of the femoral head |
| 4 | Anterior dislocation of the hip with fracture of the femoral head |
| 4A | Indentation type; depression of the superolateral, weight-bearing surface of the femoral head |
| 4B | Transchondral type; osteocartilaginous shear fracture of the weight-bearing surface of the femoral head |
| 5 | Central fracture-dislocation of the hip with fracture of the femoral head |

*Source:* Brumback, R.J.; et al. Proceedings of the Hip Society, 1986. St. Louis, C.V. Mosby, 1987, pp. 181–206.

inadequate follow-up both in the percentage of patients within the series and in duration and (2) lack of a uniform classification. Since Pipkin's important article of 1957, most authors, including us, have attempted to use his classification. Brumback's classification is more expansive and complete but has only recently been applied to a series of published patients.[58] This classification should be used in future publications.

Of the 265 published cases of hip dislocation with associated femoral head fracture, 170 can be classified by the Pipkin scheme.* Femoral head fractures associated with anterior hip dislocation are not included because they do not fall into Pipkin's categories. Of the 170 cases in the literature, 37 (22%) are type I, 72 (42%) are type II, 25 (15%) are type III, and 36 (21%) are type IV femoral head fractures. Multiple treatment regimens were used for each classification and are discussed independently. Although Pipkin categorized results as excellent, good, serviceable, and poor, the criteria were not clearly defined. Other authors have used a similar softly defined classification of results, which makes comparison of series difficult. Evaluation of these series is made more complex by the fact that many treating surgeons were involved in all series. Limitation of follow-up is a more serious qualifying factor. Because of these problems, conclusions regarding treatment remain uncertain.

Of the 26 Pipkin type I femoral head fractures reported

---

*See references 2, 5, 6, 8, 15, 24, 26, 27, 29, 33, 51, 53, 55, 60.

with adequate follow-up, 18 were treated by closed reduction and traction. Of these, 13 showed excellent or good results, 2 were fair, and 1 was poor; 2 patients were lost to follow-up. The length of traction varied but was generally 4 to 6 weeks. Eight patients were treated by fragment excision because of a noncongruent reduction, fragmentation, or other intra-articular fragments. Two of these fractures had excellent or good results, three were fair, and two were poor; one patient was lost to follow-up. No patient in any published series has been treated with ORIF. Of the 36 Pipkin type II fracture cases published with follow-up, 13 were treated by closed reduction and traction. Of these, eight had excellent or good results, three were fair, and two were poor. Six were treated by closed reduction and excision of the fragment. Four had excellent or good results, and two were fair, with no poor results. Of 17 fractures treated by ORIF, 10 had excellent or good results, 3 had fair results, and 4 had poor results. The large size of the fragment would seem to lend itself to internal fixation.[6, 43, 63] Surgical sectioning of the ligamentum teres facilitates reduction and has not resulted in an increase in poor results.[5, 63] The loss of uniform contact of the femoral head with the acetabulum (the "shim effect") that occurs with fragment excision adds motivation to attempt ORIF, especially when the position of the fragment on CT reveals a nonanatomic reduction.

The segmental femoral head fracture classified as Pipkin type III has been reported in 17 patients with adequate follow-up.[34] Three patients received primary arthroplasty because of the anticipated high risk of complications.[32] Another three underwent closed reduction and traction, all with poor results, and one underwent closed reduction and excision with a poor result. Of the 10 treated by ORIF, 5 had excellent or good results, in 2 the results were fair, and 3 had poor results. In this situation, long-term (minimum of 3 to 5 years) follow-up is necessary because of the anticipated complication of avascular necrosis, but this information was not available in a significant number of these cases. Of interest is the fact that 5 of 17 cases were situations in which the femoral neck fracture was produced by the closed reduction. Although these cases may have been simply displacement of nondisplaced neck fractures, the consequences of displacement are significant and the prereduction radiographs should be reviewed carefully to search for a femoral neck fracture. If the attempt at closed reduction requires significant force, the surgeon should proceed with open reduction to maneuver interposed soft tissue out of the way.[11, 19, 21]

Pipkin's type IV category introduces the variable of acetabular fracture. Management of the femoral head fracture must be included in the overall decision making for management of an acetabular fracture. Of the 28 type IV femoral neck fractures with associated acetabular fractures and adequate follow-up, 12 were treated with closed reduction and traction; 6 had excellent or good results, the result in 1 was fair, and in 3 it was poor, with 2 patients lost to follow-up. Eight fractures were treated by closed reduction and excision, with no good results, three fair results, and three poor results; two patients were lost to follow-up. Eight fractures were treated with ORIF, with two excellent or good results, one fair result, and four poor results; two patients had no follow-up. The difficulty in evaluating these results is that details regarding classification of the acetabular fracture are lacking but are of extreme importance in the final outcome. This fracture type similarly suffers from unclear reporting of the final results in relation to the treatment used.

Swiontkowski and associates[63] reported 37 cases of femoral head fracture: 17 fractures were Pipkin type I, 9 were type II, 8 were type IV, and 3 were unclassifiable fractures. All but five patients were treated with ORIF, and one patient with a bilateral type IV fracture died. In evaluating anterior versus posterior approaches for internal fixation of type I and type II fractures (12 in each group), the authors concluded that the anterior approach provided superior visualization and a better opportunity to internally fix the femoral head fragment while offering no increase in the risk of femoral head avascular necrosis (2 cases of avascular necrosis occurred with posterior approaches, none with anterior approaches). The incidence of functionally significant heterotopic ossification in Pipkin type I and II fractures treated with the anterior approach was 2 of 12 versus 0 of 12 posteriorly. The cause of the heterotopic bone is stripping of the gluteal muscles off the outer aspect of the iliac wing; the surgical approach now recommended involves the distal half of the Smith-Petersen approach, with the gluteal muscles left intact. These results have recently been confirmed in a subsequent patient cohort.[58] The two cases treated by closed reduction and traction had excellent results in this series.

Anterior dislocation of the hip associated with a superior indentation or shear fracture is a more recently reported occurrence and is not included in Pipkin's classification. It is becoming an increasingly recognized phenomenon with acetabular fractures as well. The association of superior femoral head fracture with anterior hip dislocation was initially reported by Funsten and colleagues[25] and subsequently delineated by DeLee and co-workers.[14] The indentation of the superior weight-bearing portion of the femoral head occurs as it levers off the anterior wall of the acetabulum or possibly as it impacts against the superior margin of the obturator ring. Similarly, shear fractures occur as the superior aspect of the femoral head impacts the anterior acetabular rim and is cleaved off. Of the 10 published cases of impaction-type femoral head fractures associated with anterior hip dislocation, 7 had evidence of significant post-traumatic arthritis at follow-up. Of the four cleavage, or shear, fractures, all had significant joint space narrowing at follow-up. It is fortunate that anterior hip dislocations with their associated femoral head fractures are rare because such patients have a high risk of post-traumatic arthritis.

## ALGORITHM FOR MANAGEMENT OF FEMORAL HEAD FRACTURES

After adequate physical examination, review of the AP pelvic radiograph for location of the femoral head fracture, and evaluation of the femoral neck and acetabulum, urgent gentle closed reduction is recommended, as outlined in Chapter 46. If closed reduction is unsuccessful, open reduction is indicated. A preoperative CT scan (if it can be obtained without a delay of more than 45 to 60 minutes) is helpful in evaluating the acetabulum and femoral neck and checking for the size of the femoral head fragment and for loose bodies. If closed reduction is successful, a postreduction CT scan is indicated. The scan is then reviewed for reduction of the fragment, status of the femoral neck and acetabulum, and loose bodies. Treatment recommendations are then based on the classification, reduction of the fracture, and general considerations.

For isolated Pipkin type I fractures with excellent (less than 1-mm step-off) reduction, closed treatment is recommended. One to 4 weeks of light traction (Buck's skin traction or skeletal traction) followed by touch-down weight bearing on crutches for 4 weeks has produced good results in most patients.[5, 38] If the reduction is not adequate, ORIF with small cancellous[63] or Herbert[36, 45] screws inserted in an anterior approach is recommended. Herbert screws provide less compressive force across large cancellous surface areas than do standard small-fragment screws.[36] In polytrauma, ORIF may also be indicated, even when the reduction is good, to allow mobilization of younger patients. The same recommendations apply to type II fractures, but because of involvement of the superior femoral head, only an anatomic reduction on repeated radiographic evaluations should be accepted for conservative care. For cleavage femoral head fractures associated with a femoral neck fracture (Pipkin type III), the prognosis is poor (Fig. 48–4). The prognosis for the injury in regard to post-traumatic avascular necrosis of the femoral head is related to the degree of displacement of the femoral neck fracture. For this reason, care must be taken during closed reduction to prevent displacement of a recognized or unrecognized femoral neck fracture. In a younger, more active patient, emergency ORIF of a type I or II femoral head fracture through an anterior Smith-Petersen approach is recommended, along with screw fixation of the femoral neck fracture. The decision to proceed in this manner should be weighted toward treating those who are active, are physiologically young, and have minimally displaced or nondisplaced femoral neck fractures. In patients who do not fulfill these criteria, a bipolar endoprosthesis or total-hip arthroplasty should be inserted.[35, 41]

Pipkin type IV fractures must be treated in tandem with their associated acetabular fractures. The acetabular fracture should dictate the surgical approach, and the femoral head fracture, even if it is nondisplaced, should be internally fixed to allow early motion of the hip joint. Management of the associated acetabular fracture is covered in Chapter 37.

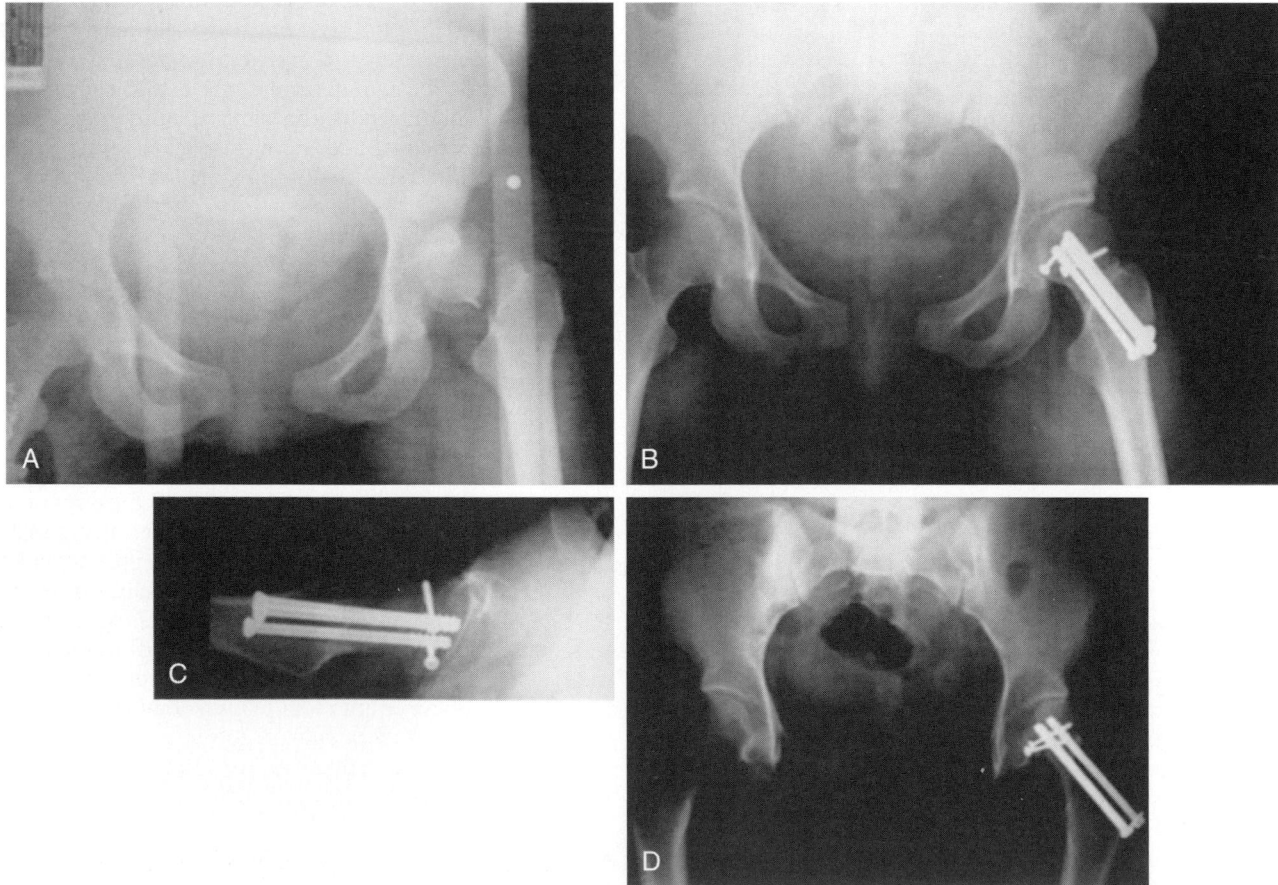

**Figure 48–4.** Combined fractures of the femoral head and neck. *A,* This 22-year-old woman, 20 weeks pregnant, was involved in a motor vehicle accident and sustained a Pipkin type III fracture-dislocation of the femoral neck and femoral head. *B, C,* After being cleared for anesthesia by the obstetrics department, the patient was taken for emergency open reduction and internal fixation (ORIF), which was performed through an anterior approach. The major femoral head fragment was trapped within the subgluteal fascial space and was devoid of all soft tissue attachments. The anteroinferior femoral head fragment was reduced and fixed to the major head fragment, which was then stabilized to the neck with multiple cannulated screws. Anatomic reduction was achieved. *D,* At 1½ years' follow-up, the patient had some groin pain and changes consistent with osteonecrosis of the proximal end of the femur, a complication that was not unexpected. She underwent hip arthroplasty in the third year after injury.

Femoral head fractures associated with anterior hip dislocations are very difficult to manage. Elevation of the indentation fragment has been advocated by Mears,[40] but the long-term results of this technique are not known. The prognosis is poor because of the risk of post-traumatic arthritis, and the patient should be so informed. Cleavage fractures, if they are large and noncomminuted, may be internally fixed. The repair should be performed from an anterior approach if the CT scan indicates that the major portion of the fragment is anterior and from a posterior approach if the fragment involves the posterior, weight-bearing portion of the femoral head. No results with this treatment have been published.

## SPECIAL CONSIDERATIONS FOR PATIENTS WITH POLYTRAUMA

An unreduced hip dislocation is a musculoskeletal emergency because of the consequences of post-traumatic femoral head necrosis, which increases in incidence with increasing duration of the dislocation. An AP pelvic radiograph is part of the initial evaluation of a patient with multiple injuries and will reveal the hip dislocation plus the femoral head fracture. If the patient is going to the operating room for head, abdominal, or chest procedures, closed reduction of the hip dislocation can be expedited by the orthopaedist's presence during induction of anesthesia. As soon as muscle relaxation has been achieved and the airway secured, closed reduction of the hip is performed as described in Chapter 46. If unsuccessful, open reduction should be performed as soon as other lifesaving procedures are completed. If closed reduction is successful, the same algorithm of postreduction CT followed by ORIF of a poorly reduced fracture, débridement of loose bodies, or ORIF of the femoral neck or acetabulum is used. In the case of an associated unrecognized femoral neck fracture or loose bodies, an open procedure should follow as soon as the patient can tolerate a second anesthetic. This open procedure is performed to avoid damage to the articular surfaces in the case of small loose fragments of bone or cartilage and to lower the risk of avascular necrosis of the femoral head in the case of the femoral neck fracture. Skeletal traction should be initiated in the interim when loose fragments are identified to minimize damage to the articular cartilage.

In patients with well-reduced femoral head fractures of the Pipkin type I or II classification, it may be advisable to perform ORIF of the femoral head fragment to allow the patient to be mobilized. Traction, in general, should be avoided in patients with serious thoracic trauma or pulmonary dysfunction. The ability to mobilize patients with multiple injuries has been shown to have the positive benefit of reducing the incidence of pulmonary failure and sepsis.[57]

## Treatment

### CLOSED REDUCTION

Urgent closed reduction of the hip is indicated in *all* hip dislocations regardless of whether an associated femoral head fracture is present.[18] Techniques for closed reduction are outlined in Chapter 46. Delay must be avoided to minimize the risk of post-traumatic avascular necrosis of the femoral head. If a femoral neck fracture is identified, it is probably better to forego any attempt at closed reduction and proceed with open surgery after an urgent preoperative CT scan, if possible. Such an approach may decrease the risk of displacement of the femoral neck fracture with further injury to the vascular supply of the femoral head.

### OPEN REDUCTION ALONE

The indication for open reduction of a dislocated hip is failure of closed reduction. A preoperative CT scan, whenever possible, helps alert the surgeon to intra-articular fragments, acetabular or femoral neck fractures, and the size of the femoral head fragment. A delay of more than an hour to allow completion of a CT scan should be avoided. In general, posterior dislocations should be reduced through a posterior approach. The external rotators and buttonholed capsule are the usual structures blocking reduction. Intra-articular fragments can be removed with this approach, and posterior wall acetabular fractures can be operatively reduced under direct vision. Internal fixation of the femoral neck and head, as well as reduction of these fractures, is difficult with this approach.[63] The patient should be placed in the lateral decubitus position to allow access to the anterior aspect of the pelvis should a simultaneous approach be necessary to reduce and internally fix the femoral head fragment. A femoral distractor applied from the iliac crest to the proximal femoral shaft helps gain distraction of the hip joint to improve visualization of the reduction. If the surgeon chooses to leave the femoral head fragment unfixed, the patient should be treated by skin or light skeletal traction for 4 to 6 weeks (Fig. 48–5).

### FRAGMENT EXCISION

In combination with closed or open reduction, the indications for fragment excision are severe comminution and interposition of a small femoral head fragment between the femoral head and acetabulum. Excision of the fragment can be accomplished through the same surgical approach used for open reduction. If done subsequent to reviewing the CT scan after closed reduction, the approach is dictated by the location of the fragments. Anterior and inferior fragments should be approached through the Smith-Petersen interval. In the case of interposed fragments, excision is urgent and the procedure must be done quickly to avoid further damage to the articular surfaces. General or spinal anesthesia is used for excision of the fragment regardless of the approach used.

### OPEN REDUCTION AND INTERNAL FIXATION

ORIF is indicated for all fractures with residual displacement of 1 mm or more, for fractures associated with femoral neck or acetabular fractures, and for fractures with large femoral head fragments that require open reduction of the associated hip dislocation. For most Pipkin type I and II fractures, ORIF should be performed through an

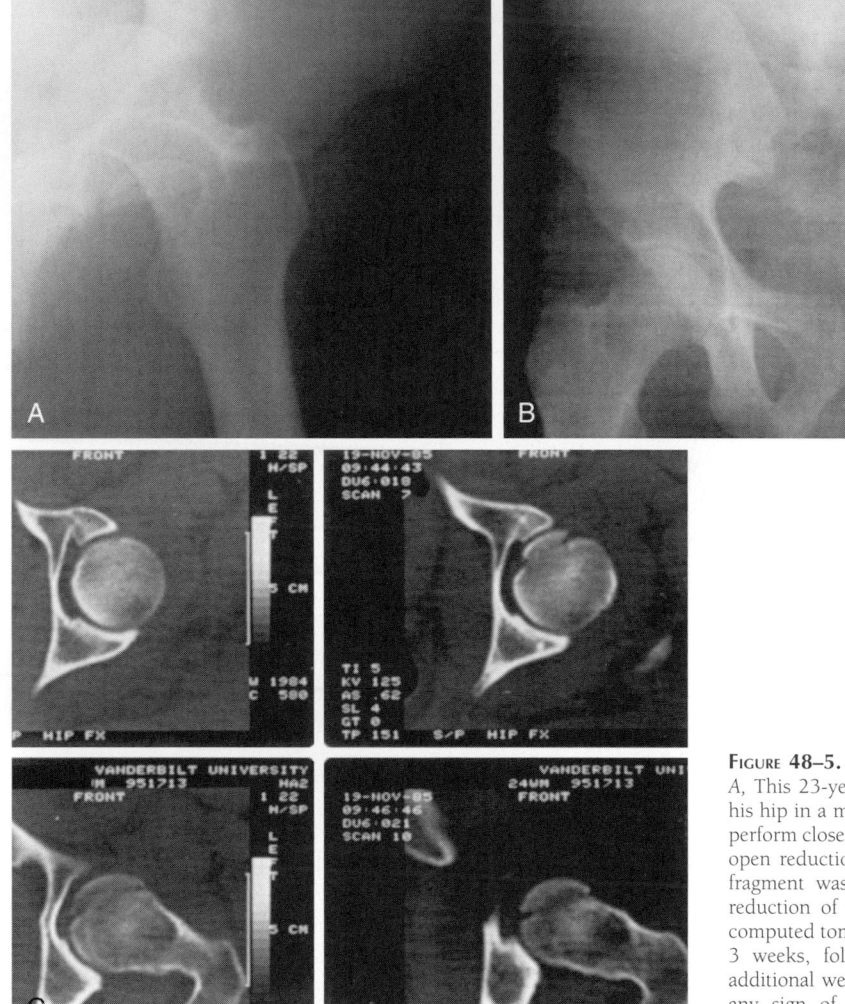

**FIGURE 48–5.** Traction treatment of a femoral head fracture. *A,* This 23-year-old man sustained a posterior dislocation of his hip in a motor vehicle accident. Because of an inability to perform closed reduction of the hip dislocation, he underwent open reduction under general anesthesia. The femoral head fragment was not visualized. *B, C,* The ensuing anatomic reduction of the femoral head fragment was confirmed by computed tomography. The patient was treated by traction for 3 weeks, followed by touch-down weight bearing for 3 additional weeks, and has excellent range of motion without any sign of osteonecrosis or degenerative hip disease at long-term follow-up.

anterior Smith-Petersen approach[63] (Fig. 48–6). The surgery is performed with the patient in the "semilateral" position and a large pad underneath the affected hip. These procedures can be performed within several days after closed reduction and the postreduction CT scan. In the case of a posterior approach, fragments off the anterior aspect of the femoral head are difficult to visualize, are harder to reduce, and can be nearly impossible to fix internally. This approach was recommended by Epstein because of fear of damage to the blood supply to the femoral head from the anterior capsule.[21] The blood supply to the femoral head from this source is negligible, and because of these operative difficulties, the anterior approach is favored.[63, 67] The patient may be treated in a continuous passive-motion machine postoperatively,[54] along with 8 weeks of touch-down weight bearing and avoidance of extreme hip flexion (>70°) for 4 to 6 weeks. The anterior approach may be accompanied by heterotopic ossification of functional significance.[61] Such ossification can be avoided by minimizing stripping of the tensor fasciae latae and abductor musculature. Indomethacin (Indocin), 25 mg orally three times a day for 6 weeks, or low-dose irradiation may also have a favorable influence, but diphosphonates are probably of limited therapeutic value[4, 51, 65] (Fig. 48–7).

## PROSTHETIC REPLACEMENT

Prosthetic replacement is indicated in a Pipkin type III fracture when the patient is physiologically elderly or the femoral neck fracture is markedly displaced in patients older than 50 or 60 years.[5, 33] Primary femoral head replacement is otherwise contraindicated and should be performed only after a trial of conservative care when the end result of internal fixation is joint incongruity or degenerative arthritis. Should such problems develop, total-hip replacement is indicated. Details regarding the procedure of endoprosthetic replacement are discussed under Femoral Neck Fractures (Fig. 48–8).

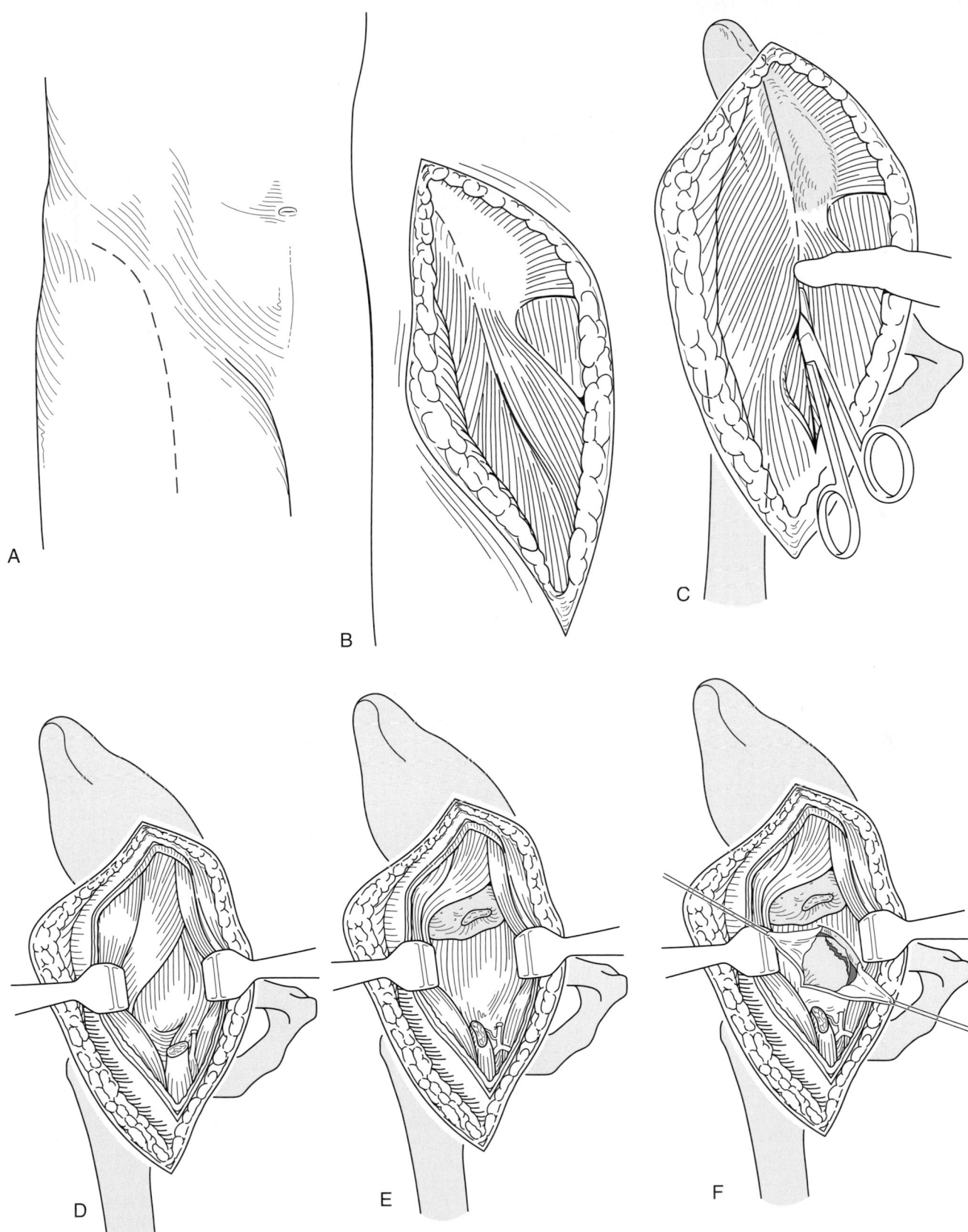

**FIGURE 48–6.** Anterior (Smith-Petersen) approach for open reduction and internal fixation of a femoral head fracture. *A,* Skin incision. The leg is draped free for manipulation. *B,* Exposure of the deep fascia and release of the abductors from the iliac crest. *C,* Development of the interval between the sartorius and the tensor fasciae latae, which is usually palpable with a finger. *D,* Identification, division, and ligation of ascending branches of the lateral femoral circumflex vessels in the distal portion of the wound and release and suture tag of the direct and reflected heads of the rectus femoris to define the hip capsule. *E,* Elevation and reflection of the rectus femoris to expose the anterior hip capsule in its entirety. *F,* By releasing the hip capsule from its trochanteric attachment and incising longitudinally along the anterior of the femoral neck, arthrotomy reveals the femoral head fracture. Sutures placed at the edges of the capsulotomy are useful for retraction to enhance exposure. By flexing and maximally externally rotating the limb, the reduction can be assessed and adjusted. This exposure permits fixation with small lag screws recessed below the articular surface.

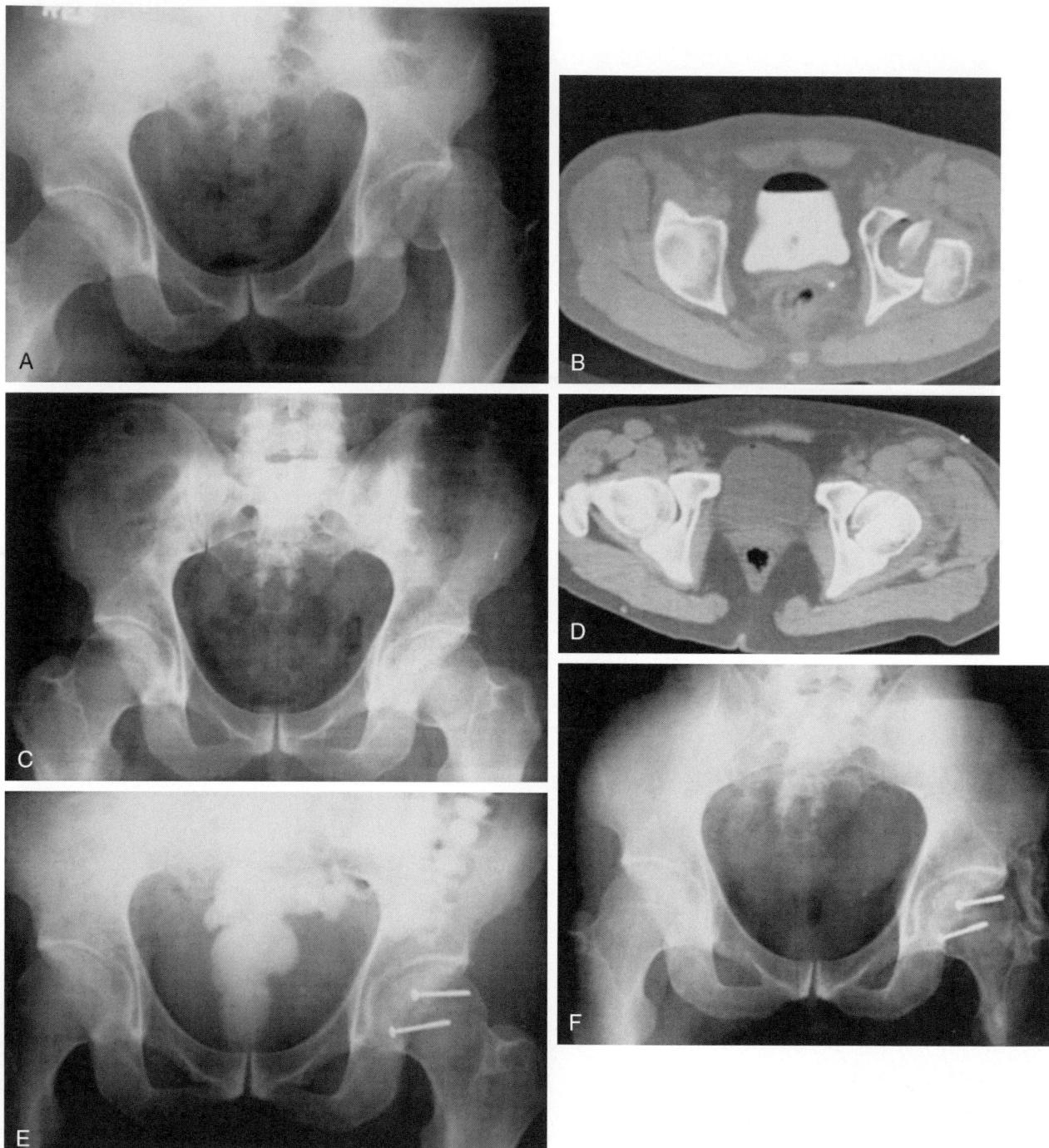

**FIGURE 48–7.** Internal fixation of a femoral head fracture from an anterior approach. *A, B,* This 44-year-old man was involved in a high-speed motor vehicle accident in which he sustained an open mandibular fracture, multiple rib fractures, pneumothorax, and this posterior hip dislocation with a Pipkin type II femoral head fracture. On admission, he was taken emergently to the CT scanner for an intra-abdominal scan before reduction of the hip. *C, D,* Closed reduction of the hip dislocation was successful. *E,* Because of his pulmonary injuries, which required ventilation, it was thought that open reduction and internal fixation (ORIF) was indicated to mobilize the patient. Therefore, he underwent ORIF through an anterior Smith-Petersen approach on the day of admission. *F,* The patient was mobilized postoperatively, extubated on the fourth postoperative day, and limited to touch-down weight bearing for 12 weeks. At 3 years' follow-up, flexion was limited to 80° because of heterotopic ossification. The patient has no pain and does not desire to have the heterotopic ossification resected. Heterotopic ossification has been related to stripping of the abductor muscles off the lateral aspect of the ilium; such stripping is no longer recommended.

## OPEN REDUCTION AND INTERNAL FIXATION OF ASSOCIATED ACETABULAR FRACTURES

ORIF of the acetabular fracture in a Pipkin type IV injury is indicated when the fracture is displaced or the hip reduction is unstable. The femoral head fragment should also be internally fixed to gain the benefits of early, relatively unrestricted joint motion. Whereas the main component of the acetabular fracture dictates the surgical approach, the femoral head fracture may require a separate anterior approach to accomplish the reduction and fixation. The details of operative management of an acetabular fracture are described in Chapter 37.

## EARLY MOBILIZATION

Disregard of femoral head fracture reduction with prompt mobilization of the patient should be performed only when the patient is extremely debilitated and unable to undergo surgery. In an elderly patient, this approach may be reasonable if post-traumatic arthritis develops because secondary replacement can be performed after optimization of the patient's general medical condition. Hip flexion precautions should be followed for 6 to 8 weeks, as recommended for hip dislocations (see Chapter 46).

## Follow-up Care and Rehabilitation

In the situation in which treatment by closed reduction and traction is selected, the 4 to 6 weeks of skin or light skeletal traction should be followed by an additional 4 to 6 weeks of crutch ambulation with touch-down weight bearing. In general, hip flexion of more than 70° should be

avoided for the same period. At 3 months, supervised active and passive range-of-motion exercises, as well as abduction strengthening, can be initiated.

For ORIF of femoral head fractures, the patient should be immediately mobilized and treated with 6 to 8 weeks of touch-down weight bearing and crutch ambulation, followed by motion exercises and strengthening as previously noted. Continuous passive motion can be used in the early postoperative period.[54]

In the case of fragment excision, the patient should be asked to limit hip flexion to 60° to 70° for 8 to 12 weeks and should be treated with crutch ambulation during this period, followed by strengthening and motion exercises.

When femoral head fractures are internally fixed in connection with femoral neck or acetabular fractures, early range-of-motion exercises are indicated. The patient should also be treated with touch-down weight bearing and crutches for 8 to 12 weeks.

Postoperative care in patients who have undergone prosthetic replacement is covered later in this chapter (see Femoral Neck Fractures).

## Assessment of Results

A standardized system for evaluating end results is necessary to facilitate communication regarding treatment and results. Such a system is especially necessary for femoral head fractures because very few surgeons treat more than four or five of these fractures in a career. The system developed by Brumback and co-workers[5] is the most comprehensive system used in the literature, and it is not overly complex (Table 48–5). Because of the associa

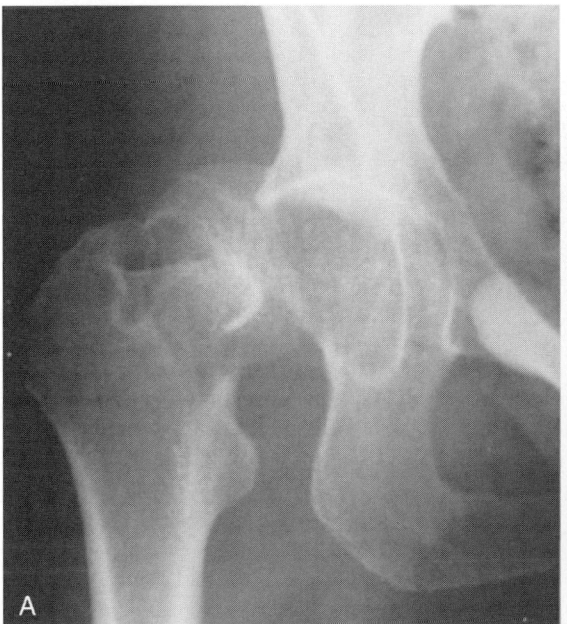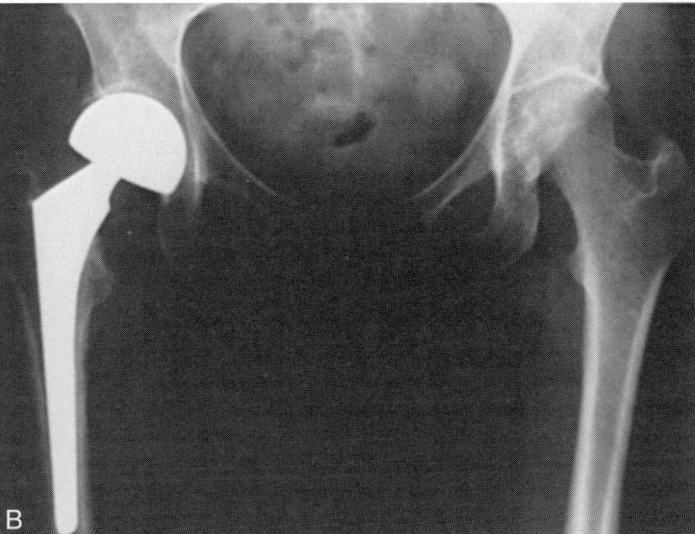

**FIGURE 48–8.** Prosthetic replacement for femoral head and neck fracture. *A,* This 55-year-old woman was involved in a rollover motor vehicle accident and sustained a fracture of the femoral neck with an inferior femoral head fragment and dislocation of the major femoral head fragment. This lesion is not, strictly speaking, a Pipkin type III injury because of the dislocation of the femoral head. *B,* Because of the age of the patient, an uncemented bipolar prosthesis was selected as the treatment of choice. The patient had done reasonably well at 3 years' follow-up; she has occasional groin pain, but the prosthesis has not been revised to a total-hip replacement.

**Table 48–5**

Assessment of Results of Treatment of Femoral Head Fractures

| Result | Description |
|---|---|
| Excellent | Normal hip motion, no pain, no significant radiographic changes |
| Good | Seventy-five percent of normal hip motion, no pain, minimal degenerative changes of the hip joint on radiographic evaluation |
| Fair/poor | Painful hip with moderate or severe restriction of hip motion, moderate or severe radiographic joint incongruity, or degenerative joint disease |

*Source:* Brumback, R.J.; et al. Proceedings of the Hip Society, 1986. St. Louis, C.V. Mosby, 1987, pp. 181–206.

tion with hip dislocation, optimal follow-up should be a minimum of 3 to 5 years to rule out post-traumatic osteonecrosis of the femoral head.

## Complications

### CHRONIC INSTABILITY

Chronic instability is most likely to occur in the setting of fragment excision, especially when accompanied by an unreduced or excised acetabular posterior wall fragment. This complication is best avoided by internal fixation of the femoral head and acetabular fragments when they are of adequate size. When instability is recognized early, placement of a posterior wall bone graft with a tricortical iliac crest bone graft can be attempted. Chronic subluxation may result in degenerative arthritis with joint space narrowing, which requires hip arthroplasty or arthrodesis.

### WOUND INFECTION

Wound infection can result from any operative procedure and, in general, should occur in no more than 1% of patients in whom open reduction of femoral head fragments is performed. Postoperative hip infections are usually occult, so a high index of suspicion is required. Joint aspiration is necessary for early diagnosis. Treatment of deep wound infection is prompt and thorough surgical débridement of necrotic tissue and systemic administration of appropriate antibiotics (see Chapter 18 for more details).

### HETEROTOPIC OSSIFICATION

Heterotopic ossification may follow use of either the anterior or the posterior approach for reduction and internal fixation of femoral head fractures. In Pipkin type IV fractures in which extended surgical exposure is required to reduce and internally fix the acetabular fracture, the incidence of heterotopic ossification may be significant and is related to the approach used (see Chapter 37). For Pipkin type I and II fractures, the incidence of functionally significant heterotopic ossification is higher with anterior approaches.[63] Resection of the heterotopic

mass 18 to 24 months after injury, when alkaline phosphatase levels are declining toward normal and bone scan activity is decreasing, generally yields improvement in hip motion. Although diphosphonates play no role in prophylaxis against this complication, indomethacin, 25 mg orally three times a day, or low-dose radiation prophylaxis may be helpful.[4, 51, 65] Irradiation should probably be avoided in young patients until some long-term follow-up data regarding its use are available.

### SCIATIC NERVE PALSY

Sciatic nerve palsy occurs in 10% or more of posterior hip dislocations and may thus be associated with femoral head fractures. It may be more common when reduction is delayed, thus adding another reason for prompt reduction. Not infrequently, patients with sciatic nerve palsy have significant dysesthesias during the early recovery period. Should such symptoms develop, they may be helped with gabapentin, amitriptyline, carbamazepine, or a combination of these drugs. Serial electromyograms can yield prognostic information regarding return of function. Ankle dorsiflexion is generally the last function to return, and therefore a posterior splint or plastic ankle-foot orthosis must be used. A dense sciatic nerve palsy that follows a hip fracture-dislocation generally carries a poor prognosis.

### AVASCULAR NECROSIS

The incidence of avascular necrosis increases with the length of time that the hip remains unreduced. It is also slightly more frequent when hip dislocation is associated with femoral head fracture, probably indicative of the greater degree of trauma required to fracture the femoral head. Treatment is difficult. If the area of subchondral resorption and subsequent fracture is limited, flexion osteotomy may play a role in avoiding hip arthroplasty or arthrodesis in younger patients.

### DEGENERATIVE ARTHRITIS

Degenerative arthritis occurs in the vast majority of cases associated with anterior hip dislocation. Similarly, it occurred in about half of the Pipkin type II, most of the Pipkin type III, and about half of the Pipkin type IV injuries reported.[31] Treatment of this complication is weight control, walking aids, and anti-inflammatory medications. In physiologically older patients, treatment of severe symptoms is total-hip replacement. In younger patients with manual labor professions, hip arthrodesis should be considered. In general, total-hip arthroplasty should be delayed as long as possible.

## FEMORAL NECK FRACTURES

### Relevant Anatomy

#### OSSEOUS ANATOMY

The upper femoral epiphysis is generally closed by the age of 16 years, thus establishing the adult proximal femoral anatomy.[201, 452] The neck shaft angle in adults does not seem to vary significantly between the sexes and is approximately $130° ± 7°$.[378] The femoral neck is normally anteverted with respect to the femoral shaft and has been measured at $10.4° ± 6.7°$ in normal specimens, again with no difference between the sexes.[377–379] Proximal femoral anteversion does not change after skeletal maturity. The femoral head diameter varies according to the size of the individual and ranges from 40 to 60 mm.

Hoaglund and Low[247] measured the articular cartilage covering the femoral head and found that it averages 4 mm at the superior portion and tapers to 3 mm at the periphery. A substantial synovial membrane covers the entire anterior of the femoral neck, but only the most proximal half posteriorly.[460] The femoral neck has wide variability in length and shape. The greater trochanter has a large posterior overhang, which locates the femoral neck in the anterior half of the proximal end of the femur when viewed from the lateral orientation, a fact that must be recognized for accurate placement of internal fixation devices. The calcar femorale is a condensed, vertically oriented plate of bone within the proximal part of the femur. It originates in the posteromedial portion of the femoral shaft, radiates superiorly toward the greater trochanter, and fuses with the cortex at the posterior of the femoral neck.[235] This structure has been frequently misunderstood and mislabeled in the hip arthroplasty literature. As pointed out by Harty[235] and later by Griffin,[220] it plays a central role in the development of upper femoral fracture patterns.

It is generally agreed that bone density in the upper part of the femur declines with age.[73, 278] Certainly, chronic disease, surgical or biologic menopause, and medications (i.e., corticosteroids, barbiturates, calcium- or magnesium-binding agents, seizure control medications, and hormonal therapy) have an adverse effect on bone metabolism and may affect the mechanical properties of the proximal end of the femur. Freeman and associates[196] identified trabecular fatigue fractures in the femoral head and at the head-neck junction in cadavers and in specimens removed at surgery (arthroplasty) for femoral neck fracture. Only 1 necropsy specimen (from a 20-year-old patient) did not have any recognizable trabecular fatigue fracture in the upper part of the femur, whereas all 10 of the surgically removed specimens had them. The highest concentration of fatigue fractures (56%) was at the head-neck junction. The threshold density value below which fatigue fractures were observed was 0.5 g/mL. Femoral neck fractures have been similarly associated with declining bone density by Singh and associates[407] and by Sugimoto and colleagues,[432] but more than just simple aging trends seem to be responsible for this phenomenon.

## VASCULAR ANATOMY AND PHYSIOLOGY

Trueta and Harrison[453] expanded on the work of Howe and co-workers[261] and used injection techniques to study the vascular anatomy of the proximal end of the femur. The lateral epiphyseal artery, which is the terminal branch of the medial femoral circumflex artery of the profunda femoris circulation, supplies most of the femoral head (see Fig. 48–1). In 15 of Trueta and Harrison's high-quality injection studies (barium suspensions examined in 15-μm-thick sections by light microscopy), the lateral epiphyseal artery supplied four fifths of the femoral head in seven cases, two thirds in another seven, and slightly more than half in one case. The inferior metaphyseal artery is the terminal branch of the ascending portion of the lateral femoral circumflex artery, and it pierces the midportion of the anterior hip capsule. This vessel supplies the more distal metaphyseal bone anteriorly and inferiorly in two thirds of the cases studied. The third major blood supply of the femoral head is the medial epiphyseal artery of the ligamentum teres from the obturator arterial system. This vessel generally connects with the lateral epiphyseal artery system. This anastomotic system formed by the two minor vessels may play a role in revascularization of the femoral head after femoral neck fracture. There seems to be no evidence in multiple other injection studies to support the concept that the metaphyseal vessels extending proximally from the nutrient artery system play a role in supply of nutrition to the proximal part of the femoral neck or the femoral head. The distribution of the minor arterioles from the lateral epiphyseal artery system is preferentially toward the subchondral bone of the femoral head articular surface. Many authors have noted that the important vessels supplying most of the femoral head (the lateral epiphyseal system) are contained within the retinacular reflection at the superior aspect of the femoral neck (the retinacular arteries of Weitbrecht).[117, 133, 140, 151, 152, 234, 280, 402, 454]

### Effect of Femoral Neck Fracture on Vascular Supply

A femoral neck fracture produces a devastating effect on the blood supply to the femoral head.[85, 86, 419, 422, 440] Displacement generally correlates with the severity of damage to the major blood supply, which is the lateral epiphyseal artery system.[129, 443] In Sevitt's series of 25 patients who died after femoral neck fracture, only four femoral heads had a normal vascular pattern when studied with standard injection techniques.[401] Several authors have noted that after a femoral neck fracture compromises the retinacular vessels, the ligamentum teres system provides a source of blood for revascularization of the femoral head by creeping substitution. Focal mechanical failure of the femoral head during this process accounts for the development of segmental collapse in avascular necrosis.

Catto[129] examined 188 femoral heads removed at necropsy or at surgery for femoral neck fracture and compared them with 50 control femoral heads. The study was primarily a histologic analysis and confirmed that the control specimens had no evidence of marrow cellular changes or osteocyte death. In all 109 femoral heads removed more than 16 days after femoral neck fracture, some damage to the vascular supply was revealed by histologic changes. The cellular changes are detectable from 48 hours on, but it is generally agreed that osteocyte loss proceeds slowly after ischemia and that the cellular changes become irreversible after 12 hours. That cellular death proceeds slowly was confirmed by the fact that osteocyte "dropout" was not complete in uncrushed trabeculae proximal to the femoral neck fracture until the third week after fracture. By using dynamic blood flow studies, it has been documented in adult miniature swine that a femoral neck fracture displaced 5 to 7 mm with an osteotome and then reduced anatomically produces a 60% decrease in blood flow to the femoral head.[439]

Although the adverse effect of femoral neck fracture on femoral head blood flow has been documented with certainty, some elements of the situation remain under the surgeon's control. Optimal reduction of the femoral neck fracture has been shown in numerous studies to be associated with a lower incidence of femoral head avascular necrosis.[96, 171, 202, 203, 413] This decreased incidence may be a result of the fact that all of the vessels of the lateral epiphyseal artery system may not be torn and that reduction may "unkink" some vessels or, when performed beyond the acute phase, may allow for rapid arterial recanalization. Claffey[140] has shown that a complete, displaced femoral neck fracture can occur without disruption of this critical vascular supply. Similarly, stabilization of the fracture with internal fixation allows revascularization to proceed in an optimal mechanical environment. Although further vascular damage to the femoral head is unlikely with standard techniques of fixation, Brodetti[117] has demonstrated that the posterior and superior femoral head quadrant should be avoided.

Marked displacement of a femoral neck fracture can potentially disrupt the posterior hip capsule.[167] Such disruption is especially likely when high energy is imparted to the femoral neck to produce the fracture, such as in young patients with normal bone density. In cases in which the displacement is not greater than half the diameter of the neck, the hip capsule may remain intact. Intracapsular hematoma may produce an elevation in pressure significant enough to occlude the venous drainage system within the capsule or actually limit arteriolar flow in the retinacular reflection of the superior portion of the femoral neck. Using different techniques to measure blood flow in the femoral head, several authors have shown that increased intracapsular pressure has an adverse effect on femoral head blood flow and may produce cellular death.[439, 440, 458] Increased intracapsular pressure has been documented by numerous authors in clinical studies and in patients with femoral neck fracture.[151, 222, 230, 253, 267, 324, 417, 472] Reduction of femoral head blood flow in association with elevated intracapsular pressure has been confirmed clinically with technetium bone scanning by Stromqvist and co-workers.[431] Most authors have confirmed that extension and internal rotation of the hip elevate intracapsular pressure to a significant degree by limiting capsular volume. This position should be avoided in the preoperative phase of treatment, and the position of flexion and external rotation should be encouraged. Because pressure that exceeds local arteriolar pressure has frequently been documented by multiple authors, anterior capsulotomy may play a positive role in minimizing femoral head ischemia.[441, 442] Aspiration of the hematoma has been shown to lower intraosseous pressure within the femoral head after femoral neck fracture (an indirect assessment of venous drainage of the head); however, a hematoma will reaccumulate rapidly, and aspiration must be repeated.[230] Therefore, most

authors recommend capsulotomy as the definitive solution, with aspiration used as a temporizing measure. This surgical maneuver, along with rapid and accurate reduction, remains within the surgeon's control, and to the extent that they may limit the risk of necrosis of the femoral head after acute ischemia resulting from femoral neck fracture, these maneuvers are encouraged. Additionally, fixation with triflanged nails has been demonstrated to increase intracapsular pressure and should be avoided.[222]

## Incidence

Femoral neck fracture is primarily a disease of individuals older than 50 years.[76, 244, 477] Published reports in the early 1980s indicated that patients younger than 50 accounted for 2% to 3% of all femoral neck fractures.[477] The incidence of hip fracture in patients younger than 50 years was 3% of the total 3147 patients with hip fractures treated over a 5-year interval in Edinburgh, Scotland, between 1987 and 1991.[383] It is the impression of many individuals working in trauma centers in the United States that the incidence of femoral neck fracture is increasing in younger, active adults involved in vehicular trauma. Some have pointed to the increased incidence of femoral neck fracture associated with femoral shaft fracture as evidence. It has also been suggested that smaller automobiles with lower dashboards increase the risk of forces being applied to the distal end of the femur in a way that causes fracture of the femoral neck.

The rates of cervical, trochanteric, and subtrochanteric fracture and the overall rate of fracture at all three levels increase with age, are greater for women than men, and are higher in the southern part of the United States.[244, 245] Femoral neck fractures occur more frequently in females.[245, 477] Zetterberg and colleagues found the female-to-male ratio for femoral neck fracture over the 43-year period from 1940 through 1983 to be 3.4:1.[477] The incidence of femoral neck fracture has been seen to be greater than can be explained by aging trends in the population in multiple studies.[156, 193, 360, 388, 477] Aging of the population explains some of the increase because the mean age of patients sustaining femoral neck fractures has increased from 71.7 to 74.3 years for males and from 72.6 to 79 years for females from 1965 to 1981.[258] The annual incidence of femoral neck fracture for 1000 persons in 1981 was 7.4 for females and 3.6 for males. The increase in annual incidence has been higher in urban (6%) than in rural (3%) populations[188, 316] and has been confirmed in Great Britain, Korea, and Italy.[156, 360, 388] Most of the literature published on femoral neck fracture is based on population studies done in Scandinavia. Because osteoporosis is associated with fair skin and northern, female smokers, these studies may not be strictly applicable to North American populations. Rates of femoral neck fracture seem to be higher in whites than in African or Japanese populations, and at least a portion of the increased risk can be explained by upper femoral geometry.[181, 221, 340] Although Melton and co-workers did not identify an increasing incidence of femoral neck fracture in the U.S. population, the incidence of the fracture in the late 1970s (9.2 per 1000 persons per year) is not dissimilar.[327] Left-sided fractures may be more common than right-sided fractures for unclear reasons not related to hand dominance.[236, 391] Patients with a femoral neck fracture are at risk for a second fracture. Schroder and colleagues[398] found that 68% of second hip fractures were the same type as the first; the mean interval between fractures was 3.3 years, and no male/female differences in risk were noted. The risk for a first fracture was 1.6 per 1000 men per year and 3.6 per 1000 women per year, and for the second fracture it was 15 per 1000 men per year and 22 per 1000 women per year.

## Mechanism of Injury and Prevention

The less common femoral neck fracture associated with vehicular trauma or falls from significant heights is believed to be caused by axial loading of the thigh (by the dashboard in an automobile) with the hip positioned in abduction.[442] This "high-energy" loading will fracture a femoral neck of normal density. If the hip were adducted, the most likely injury would be a hip dislocation, with or without an associated posterior acetabular wall or femoral head fracture.

The most common (in excess of 90%) type of trauma associated with femoral neck fractures is a fall from a standing position.[139] This "low-energy" type of injury will not generally produce a fracture in a femoral neck of normal density.[148] The issue of whether the fracture precedes the fall or the fall causes the fracture has been raised. Sloan and Holloway identified 13 of 54 patients (24%) who complained of increasing groin pain before their leg "gave way."[408] Freeman and associates[196] found numerous fatigue fractures in control specimens, with the highest concentration in the subcapital region. Although fatigue fractures of the femoral neck do occur and fairly frequently become displaced, most authors believe that the trauma of the fall plays a role in creating the fracture in most cases. Because the number of fatigue fractures of trabeculae in the femoral neck increases with decreasing bone density, fractures occurring before falling or without falling occur most often in the setting of severe osteoporosis.

Neuromuscular conditions exclusive of Parkinson's disease[146, 424] are more frequently associated with intertrochanteric than femoral neck fractures.[139, 168] Balance problems related to falling while rising from a seated position are very common and are related to strength and conditioning.[268] Rashiq and Logan[373] investigated the role of drugs as a cause of femoral neck fracture in 102 patients and 204 age-matched controls. One hypothesis that has been advanced is that hypnotic or sedating drugs impair postural control and result in falls. Although the association between femoral neck fracture and sedative/benzodiazepine use has not been consistent, emerging evidence suggests that it plays a role.[155, 374, 464] The risk of hip fracture in women may be minimized by maintaining body weight, walking for exercise, performing high-intensity resistive exercises, avoiding long-acting benzodiazepines, minimizing caffeine intake, ceasing smoking, and treating impaired visual function.[154, 184, 331, 343, 369] A history of stroke and current use of walking aids are associated with an increased risk of hip fracture.[223, 323, 325] Functional dependence on others is related to the risk of falling.[449] Multinutrient supplementation alone does not appear to affect weakness or frailty.[184] Postmenopausal estrogen replacement protects against hip fracture in women younger than 75 years.[183, 223] The bisphosphonates offer promise as a means of increasing bone density and lowering the risk of hip and other nonvertebral fractures,[304] as do calcium and vitamin D supplementation and growth hormone therapy.[115, 251, 390, 479] Recently, the cholesterol-lowering class of drugs known as the statins have been shown to increase bone mineral density.[131, 153, 172] Coordinated programs of medication review and adjustment, instruction/education, and exercise programs have been demonstrated to be efficacious in preventing falls in the elderly.[82, 448] Hip protective devices have been shown to decrease the incidence of hip fracture in nursing home patients.[296, 479]

The incidence, mechanism, and prevention of hip fractures are also discussed in Chapter 49.

## Bone Density

Singh and colleagues[407] developed a classification scheme for the severity of osteoporosis that involves changes in trabecular patterns as seen on radiographs of the intact proximal end of the femur (Fig. 48–9). The radiographic changes were compared with graded iliac crest biopsy specimens and correlation identified. A Singh grade IV or lower represents some degree of osteoporosis. The three-dimensional relationship of primary and secondary compression and tensile trabeculae has been demonstrated from CT data.[176] The radiographic Singh index has been shown to be related to bone mineral density as determined by dual-energy x-ray absorptiometry (DEXA).[319] Ultrasonography has also been shown to correlate with bone mineral density as determined by DEXA.[396] The Singh index had fair reproducibility in the same study, with an intraobserver and interobserver $\kappa$ statistic of 0.6.[319] Associations have been identified between osteoporosis as defined by this method and femoral neck fracture displacement,[158, 259, 394] and strong correlations between osteoporosis as determined by DEXA and the incidence and risk of femoral neck fracture have generally been confirmed.[136, 154, 181, 190, 277, 293, 432] DEXA can be affected by hip rotation, but the rotation has to be in the range of 10° to 15° to have any significant effect on evaluation.[208]

In one prospective cohort of perimenopausal women,[293] patients in the lowest quartile of bone density had a 2.9 times greater risk of fracture in some region of the skeleton; in another cohort, a 2.7-fold increased risk was observed.[154, 181] Wilton and co-workers[471] sought to identify osteomalacia as being associated with femoral neck fracture by performing iliac crest biopsies on nearly 1000 patients with a femoral neck fracture. They found an incidence of 2%. In an aged-matched population of acutely ill patients, the incidence was 3.7%. The lack of a strong association was also found by Hoikka and colleagues[250] and by Lund and associates.[311] It does seem apparent that iliac crest bone morphology and bioactivity may not necessarily reflect the morphology and function within the

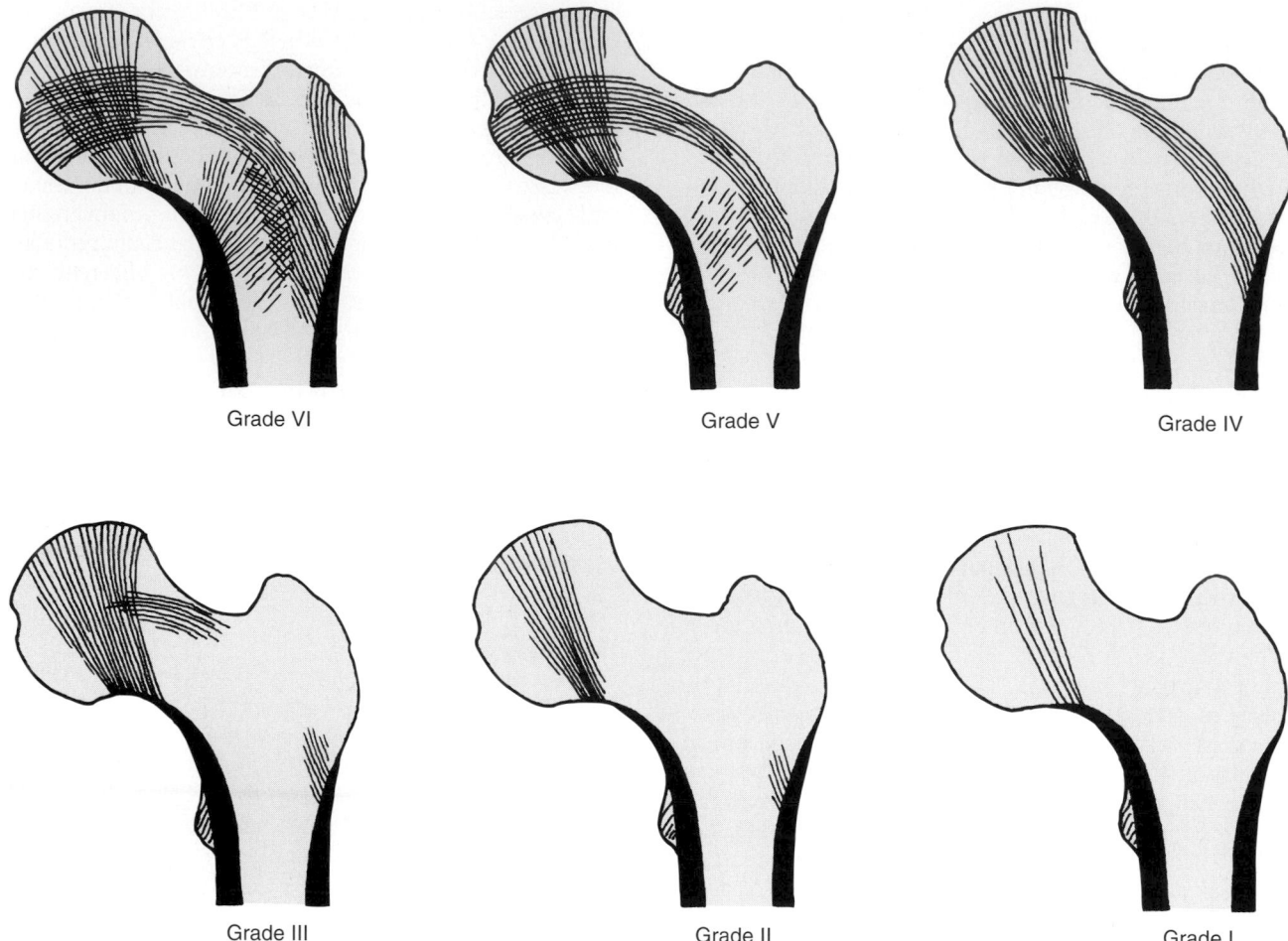

Grade VI          Grade V          Grade IV

Grade III          Grade II          Grade I

**FIGURE 48–9.** The Singh index of proximal femoral osteopenia. Progression is from normal grade VI with well-defined primary and secondary tension and compression trabeculae to severely osteopenic grade I with only a few residual primary compression trabeculae. Although this scheme is extremely useful in determining suitability for reduction and internal fixation, it has limited application as a research tool because of interobserver variability and difficulty in interpreting many radiographs.

femoral neck; femoral neck biopsy specimens have shown greater degrees of cancellous bone atrophy and lower concentrations of osteoblasts and osteoclasts than have corresponding iliac crest biopsy specimens in the same patients.[178] Medial femoral neck histologic specimens in patients with femoral neck fracture have shown haversian canals of greater diameter than in aged-matched controls.[98] Occult vitamin D deficiency in serum in patients with femoral neck fracture has been confirmed, and vitamin D concentrations within bone in patients with femoral neck fracture have been documented to be significantly lower.[301, 305] Alcohol has been shown to have a negative impact on bone density, possibly through the vitamin D mechanism, as well as through effects on calcium absorption from the gut.[361] Additionally, smoking and high intake of antioxidant vitamins (E and C), as well as vitamin A, have been demonstrated to decrease bone density and increase the risk of hip fracture.[325, 326]

Bone loss is progressive throughout life and continues to occur in the hip region after 65 years of age,[136, 148, 214] with ultimate strength and load to failure both decreasing with advancing age.[148] Bone density as determined by quantitative CT and dual-photon absorptiometry was 15%

lower than in matched controls in one series of women with hip fractures.[414] In addition, the rate of bone loss in the femoral neck increases with increasing age.[278] Bone loss may preferentially occur in the femoral neck region in patients who sustain femoral neck fractures.[76]

Aitken[73] used metacarpal morphometry to study bone density in a population of 195 women who had sustained a hip fracture in a minor fall; these women were compared with a control population who had similar bone mass measurements. Only 16% were *not* osteoporotic by this method. Femoral neck fractures were more common than trochanteric injuries in patients who were not osteoporotic. Trochanteric bone mineral density has been shown to be 13% lower in female and 11% lower in male patients with intertrochanteric fracture than in those with femoral neck fracture.[215] Aitken[73] thought that osteoporosis, as determined by metacarpal morphometry, was not a significant cause of hip fracture, even though it might influence the fracture type. Firooznia and colleagues[190] used CT to investigate spinal bone mineral content in a series of 74 women with vertebral fractures, 83 with hip fractures, and 28 with both. Only 4% of patients had spinal bone mineral content below that of their age-matched peers. Osteoporosis has been shown to involve all skeletal sites in patients who are found to have a single vertebral fracture.[94] Although osteoporosis plays a significant role in the severity of fracture displacement and the ability to obtain stable internal fixation, it seems safe to conclude that by itself, osteoporosis is not sufficient to cause femoral neck fractures. Although the level of physical activity before fracture has been proved to have a role (i.e., greater activity leads to a lower incidence) and may well be related to bone density and the quality of trabecular organization, falls are the initial factor in the production of femoral neck fracture.[93, 148, 215, 216, 237, 268, 406] Impact forces after falls exceed the strength of the proximal part of the femur by 50% in older individuals and are approximately 20% less than the strength of the femur in younger individuals.[148]

The progression of bone loss from osteoporosis is treatable by hormone replacement therapy[183, 241]; by the use of calcium and vitamin D, bisphosphonate, and statin drugs; and by high-intensity strength training.[135, 153, 342] In addition, endurance, resistance, flexibility, and balance platform training have been demonstrated to significantly decrease the risk of falling in the elderly population (aged 60 to 75 years).[368]

Black males have been shown to have greater bone density at multiple skeletal sites that is not related to body size, mass, or hip axis length.[241] However, some of the explanation for the lower risk of femoral neck fracture in the Japanese can be explained by upper femoral geometry.[340] Geometric factors that may increase the risk of femoral neck fracture include thickness of the femoral shaft cortex, thickness of the femoral neck cortex, reduction in the index of tensile trabeculae, and a wider trochanteric region.[212] Femoral neck length has been shown to be increasing over time and may be related to femoral neck bone mineral density and generalized osteoporosis.[375] Females have an age-related loss in the femoral neck cross-sectional moment of inertia that is compensated by an increase in femoral neck girth in males.[103] An assessment of hip axis length can be included in a routine DEXA evaluation and has been shown to be related to the risk of hip fracture.[181] Smoking and alcohol intake have a negative influence on bone density.[341, 361] In one analysis of risk, decreased bone density increased the risk of hip fracture 2.7-fold, whereas an increase in hip axis length increased the risk 2-fold.[154, 181]

Patients with osteoarthritis of the hip have a lower rate of age-related decline in proximal femoral bone density.[462] In comparing patients with femoral neck fracture and those with intertrochanteric/subtrochanteric fracture, patients with femoral neck fracture tend to be younger and more mobile, are less likely to use walking aids, and more often live independently.[356] When in-hospital clinical outcomes were compared, these patients had shorter lengths of stay.[356]

## Consequences of Injury

### NONUNION

The problem of nonunion is rare after a nondisplaced or impacted fracture. The incidence of nonunion after a displaced fracture is in the range of 50% to 60% with traction or cast treatment[145, 146, 467, 468] and 4% to 33% after internal fixation.[91, 96, 110, 194, 202] Several studies have shown that nonunion is a rare problem in patients with normal bone density and in whom stable fixation is achieved and that it is most closely associated with increasing age and fracture displacement.[91, 249, 442, 478] In the vast majority of cases, femoral neck nonunion is associated with moderate to severe groin or proximal thigh pain and related limping, typically a Trendelenburg gait. Because of these symptoms, most patients will require a reconstructive procedure.

### AVASCULAR NECROSIS

The ischemic event of a femoral neck fracture that leads to revascularization with subsequent trabecular thinning and collapse has been called post-traumatic osteonecrosis, aseptic necrosis of the femoral head, late segmental collapse, and avascular necrosis.[74, 97, 109, 211] It occurs in 10% to 15% of patients with impacted or nondisplaced fractures and in 30% to 35% of patients with displaced fractures.[91, 96, 313] Fracture displacement with damage to the arteriolar supply, as well as intracapsular tamponade, plays a causative role.[230] Some reports indicate that patients with normal bone density are at greater risk for this complication.[112] This observation implies that a greater amount of force is involved in causing the fracture and that the displacement and soft tissue injury are therefore greater.[246] Certainly, the incidence of avascular necrosis has been reported to be higher in younger adults with high-energy injuries.[155, 213, 367, 442, 454] Older individuals with lower functional demands will have symptoms of groin and proximal thigh pain severe enough to warrant a reconstructive procedure in 35% to 50% of cases.[96] Most agree that the higher the functional demands, the more likely that the patient will require a secondary procedure. Nearly all patients younger than 50 years in whom this complication develops require a reconstructive procedure.[367]

### PAIN

Pain after a femoral neck fracture is minimized by stable internal fixation. Preoperative traction does not favorably limit pain.[78] Groin or buttock pain that develops in the recovery period is generally associated with impending nonunion (with loss of stability) or avascular necrosis. However, with modern fixation techniques, the incidence of nonunion is well below 10%, and thus the latter is more likely.[249, 477] The pain is probably caused by revascularization of the femoral head with resorption of dead trabeculae and associated microfractures in the subchondral region, which leads to segmental collapse.[101] An acute increase in pain not related to a traumatic event is frequently associated with final collapse of the segment. Pain can rarely be associated with postsurgical sepsis or injury to the sciatic nerve. In the late stages, pain can be caused by the development of post-traumatic degenerative arthritis, which is most frequently related to avascular necrosis and resultant loss of femoral head sphericity.[110, 217, 382]

## LIMITED MOTION

Limited motion is commonly associated with pain because the position of maximal hip extension is avoided. This position decreases capsular volume and raises intra-articular pressure while placing maximal stress across the femoral neck. This symptom is therefore generally associated with nonunion or avascular necrosis. In the remote phase, true loss of motion caused by capsular fibrosis and osteophyte formation is a result of post-traumatic degenerative hip arthritis.

## IMPAIRED MOBILITY

After hip fractures, half or more of patients fail to regain their preoperative level of mobility.[271, 332, 345] In some patients, it may result from complications of the fracture; in others, it may be from deterioration of their overall mental or physical condition. In many cases, the impaired mobility that results from a femoral neck fracture will result in the loss of independent living for an older patient.[457] Holmberg and colleagues[254] reviewed 3053 consecutive patients from Stockholm with femoral neck fractures. A relatively large percentage (79%) were living in their own homes, 16% were in chronic care hospitals, and 5% were in homes for the elderly. Mortality was lowest in patients admitted from home: 9% at 4 months, 16% at 1 year, and 22% at 2 years as compared with 16%, 22%, and 30%, respectively, for the entire series, thus illustrating the greater impact of the injury on institutionalized patients. By 4 months, 69% of those living at home when injured had returned there, 20% were in chronic care hospitals, and 2% were in acute care institutions. Most of the patients initially discharged to convalescent facilities returned home after 2 months. Concomitant illness rather than the hip fracture itself was the reason for long-term institutionalization.[255] The biggest predictive factors for return to independent living after hip fracture are preinjury function in activities of daily living, absence of medical conditions that limit rehabilitation, and cognitive function.[433] Women have lower mortality after hip fracture than men do from the first year throughout the first decade after hip fracture.[397]

It may be assumed that differences among societies and medical care systems will influence the course and site of rehabilitation after femoral neck fracture. No convincing data have been published that demonstrate the superiority of any given form of treatment of femoral neck fracture with regard to outcome measured by the ability to walk or by the rate of institutionalization. Rehabilitation strategies to improve hip fracture outcomes have been identified as a research priority.[238] Patients with senile dementia have worse functional outcomes and higher mortality rates.[457, 475]

## MEDICAL COMPLICATIONS

Medical complications associated with femoral neck fractures increase in incidence with increasing age and severity of medical co-morbidities of the patient at injury. One prospective review demonstrated that major medical complications occurred in 9% of patients who were healthy before the fracture and in 21% of patients with medical co-morbidities (64% of these patients died).[338] Potential complications include urinary tract infection, wound infection, ileus (occasionally with a risk of cecal rupture), mental status changes, stroke, myocardial infarction, pneumonia, deep venous thrombosis, pulmonary embolism, and death.[224] For older patients with hip fractures, a full medical evaluation must be performed and treatment instituted to deal with dehydration, electrolyte imbalance, and pulmonary dysfunction. The risk of medical complications is favorably influenced by early surgery and mobilization.[403] However, the findings of Kenzora and co-workers[288] and Eiskjaer and Ostgard[175] of a higher rate of mortality in patients undergoing surgery the first day after injury emphasize the need for adequate medical evaluation and preoperative treatment of correctable medical conditions. Treatment protocols have been developed that use physiologic status scores[384] to select patients with better physiologic status for internal fixation.

Deep venous thrombosis is not uncommon after hip fracture, with one series reporting a rate of 23% in patients treated with standard means of prophylaxis (aspirin or warfarin).[209] The vast majority of investigators have identified prophylaxis as a favorable influence on the rate of deep venous thrombosis.[128, 226, 228, 232, 280, 365] Dextran, warfarin, subcutaneous heparin therapy, phenindione, aspirin, dihydroergotamine, low-molecular-weight heparin, and intermittent compression boots have all been reported to decrease the incidence of deep venous thrombosis.[479] Limb elevation and early patient mobilization also favorably influence the rate of thrombosis.[233, 288] Some form of prophylaxis against deep venous thrombosis and pulmonary embolism should be instituted in the preoperative or early postoperative period. Ultrasonographic scanning is the diagnostic technique of choice for the diagnosis of lower extremity deep venous thrombosis because of its very high sensitivity and specificity.[198, 209]

A low serum albumin level is associated with a higher risk of mortality in older patients.[137] Nutritional supplements have been shown to play an important role in aiding recovery and minimizing wound-healing complications.[99, 100, 422, 459] Medical consultation should be sought preoperatively and again with any sign of postoperative complication to minimize the effect of these problems.

## MORTALITY

An increased mortality rate over that of the general population after femoral neck fracture has been confirmed in numerous studies. Higher rates of mortality are apparent for patients with medical co-morbidities and for males.[229, 366, 397] In the large series of Barnes,[97] the mortality rate in the first month after surgery was 13.3% in men and 7.4% in women. The mortality rate increased significantly when the surgery was delayed beyond 72 hours. Similarly, in a large Norwegian series published by Dahl,[157] the figures were 17.1% for males and 9.8% for females in the first month after fracture. When compared with an age-matched population, the mortality rate was 15 times greater in the first month and 7 times greater in the second month and thereafter followed the population trends. Kenzora and colleagues[288] found a mortality rate of

13% at 1 year in the femoral neck fracture population versus 9% for age-matched controls. Eiskjaer and Ostgard[175] identified the following factors (in order of decreasing importance) as influencing mortality in a series of 204 patients treated with cemented bipolar hemiarthroplasty: cardiac factors, status as a nursing home patient, chronic pulmonary disease, serum creatinine value greater than 1.7 mg/dL, pneumonia, previous myocardial infarction, duration of surgery, and gender. These medical co-morbidities do not completely explain the increase in hospital mortality risk in patients with femoral neck fracture.[81] The finding of higher mortality in nursing home patients has been confirmed in the North Sydney "fractured neck of femur" outcomes project.[317] The following factors had no influence on mortality: age, time delay from admission to surgery, mode of anesthesia, and cerebrovascular disease. The overall mortality rate in their series was 20% at 6 months and 28% at 1 year. Holmberg and co-workers[252] confirmed the clinical suspicion that patients who sustain their femoral neck fractures in institutions have higher mortality (three times) than do those who are injured at home. Similarly, patients with senile dementia have a mortality rate 21% higher than controls who do not have dementia.[457] Patients who sustain a second femoral neck fracture have a higher mortality rate than do those with a single fracture. This finding was confirmed by Boston,[112] who found a 3-month mortality rate of 30% after the second fracture versus 13% for a single such injury. Several studies have suggested that the mortality rate is higher after prosthetic replacement than after internal fixation.[264, 266, 385] In addition, Chan and Hoskinson[132] found a higher mortality rate after a posterior approach for prosthetic replacement (20.6%) than after an anterior approach (6.5%). Despite the high mortality rate after femoral neck fracture, 1-year mortality rates have been shown to be higher with intertrochanteric fractures than with intracapsular fractures (29% versus 38%).[286] Because deaths after hip fracture are frequently attributable to thromboemboli and nutritional and pulmonary dysfunction, prophylaxis against deep venous thrombosis, supplemental nutrition, and early mobilization of the patient are warranted.[342]

## Commonly Associated Injuries

In the "high-energy" femoral neck fracture population, associated injuries are common. Most series involving patients younger than 50 years with nonpathologic femoral neck fractures report an incidence of head, chest, abdominal, or extremity fractures or dislocations in the range of 50% to 60%.[83, 161, 366, 442, 450] Closed head injury, cervical or thoracic spine fractures, pneumothorax or hemopneumothorax, and splenic or bowel injury occur commonly in association with a high-energy femoral neck fracture. Because of the axial loading mechanism, the most frequent musculoskeletal injury associations are ipsilateral tibial or femoral fractures, patellar fracture or knee ligament injury, and ipsilateral pelvic or acetabular fracture or hip dislocation.[197]

In the more common "low-energy" femoral neck fractures, which are related to falls from a standing position, associated injuries are less common. Head injury, including subdural and epidural hematoma, may occur occasionally. Ipsilateral injury to the upper extremity (commonly the distal end of the radius or the proximal part of the humerus), which occurs in an attempt to break the fall, is seen in 1% to 2% of cases. Far more common is the situation in which a medical problem such as a cerebrovascular accident or myocardial infarction is responsible for the fall.

## Evolution of Classification Systems

When Senn in 1889 became the first to advocate immediate reduction and internal fixation, a need was created for a classification system with which to compare and report results.[400] Speed advocated the formation of groups to study this fracture and noted that "in comparison to practically all other [fractures] this fracture remains unsolved."[418] Pauwels' classification system, reported in 1928, classified femoral neck fractures in reference to the inclination of the fracture relative to the horizontal axis of the hip joint.[359] His type I was a horizontal fracture that because of the forces of impaction, had the lowest risk of nonunion. Pauwels' type II has an intermediate inclination, and his type III fracture is a more vertical fracture that produces a high risk of nonunion. Because the more horizontal fractures tended to be impacted fractures and the more vertically oriented fractures were generally associated with higher energy and displacement, the classification system was somewhat prognostic. Pauwels' concepts have been incorporated into the proximal femoral section of the AO comprehensive classification of fractures, which has been adopted by the Orthopaedic Trauma Association.[339] Its alphanumeric categories separate and subcategorize undisplaced transcervical and displaced subcapital proximal femoral fractures, as well as those associated with femoral head fractures.

Garden's classification was an attempt to classify fractures according to their prognosis and incidence of complications.[96] His grade I is an incomplete fracture impacted in a valgus position, grade II is a nondisplaced fracture, grade III is a fracture displaced in a varus position, and grade IV is a completely displaced fracture in which the bony trabeculae within the head have realigned themselves with the trabecular system within the acetabulum (Fig. 48–10). It is probable that many, if not most grade I injuries are actually complete fractures impacted in a valgus position. Nondisplaced, nonimpacted fractures are only occasionally seen. Because of their high risk of displacement, these grade II fractures deserve to remain a separate category. The difference between Garden's grade III and grade IV in displaced fractures is frequently difficult to delineate on radiographic review. Furthermore, the large clinical series of Barnes and co-workers[96] failed to demonstrate a significant difference in the risk of nonunion and avascular necrosis between these two groups. In terms of the results and incidence of complications when using the Garden classification in this large series, grades I and II (nondisplaced) and grades III and IV (displaced) fell together with little confirmation of any need to distinguish between them. This finding has subsequently been

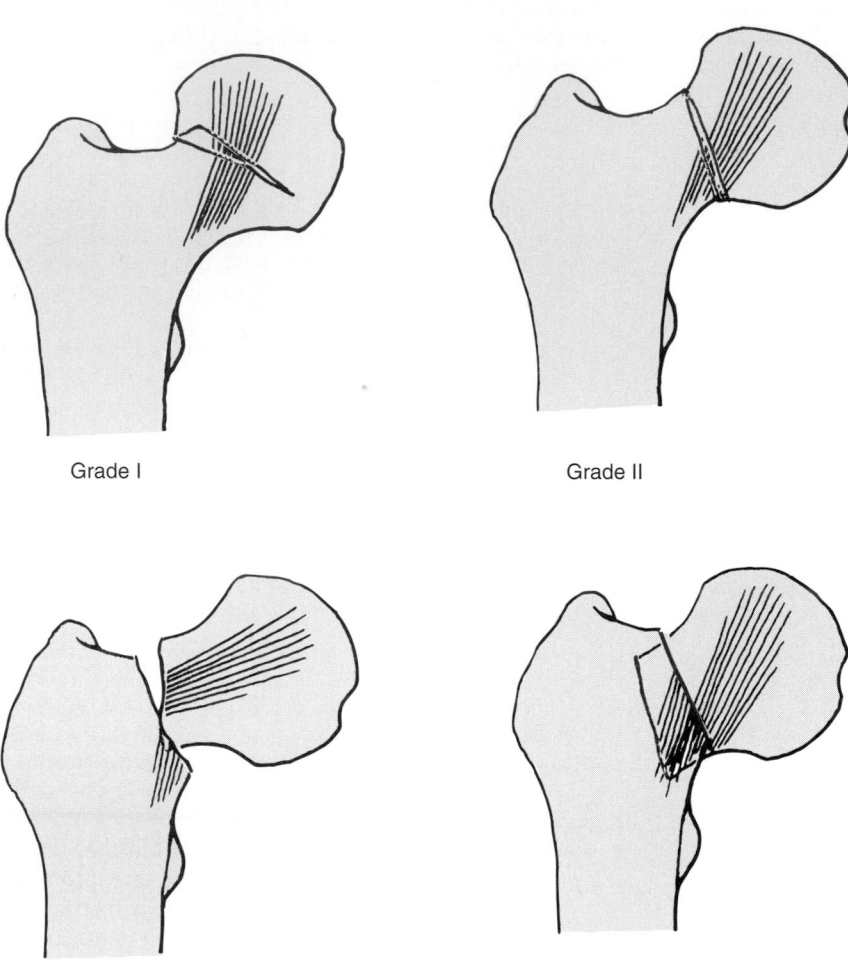

Grade I

Grade II

Grade III

Grade IV

**FIGURE 48–10.** The Garden classification of femoral neck fractures. Grade I is an incomplete, impacted fracture in valgus malalignment (generally stable). Grade II is a nondisplaced fracture. Grade III is an incompletely displaced fracture in varus malalignment. Grade IV is a completely displaced fracture with no engagement of the two fragments. The compression trabeculae in the femoral head line up with the trabeculae on the acetabular side. Displacement is generally more evident on the lateral view in grade IV. For prognostic purposes, these groupings can be lumped into nondisplaced/impacted (grades I and II) and displaced (grades III and IV) because the risk of nonunion and aseptic necrosis is similar within these grouped stages.

confirmed by Parker.[351] The AO/Orthopaedic Trauma Association "31" section of the comprehensive classification of fractures incorporates these concepts as well as those of Pauwels. It has been proposed that this system can be used to select appropriate methods of management; however, this application has not been validated in a series of patients.[344]

Femoral neck fractures with associated femoral shaft, femoral head, or acetabular fractures need to be classified separately. In the case of ipsilateral femoral shaft/femoral neck fracture, the risk of avascular necrosis is 5%, far lower than without the associated shaft fracture.[434] Casey and Chapman[126] have offered the hypothesis that much of the energy producing the fractures is dissipated through the femoral shaft, which frequently makes a femoral neck injury a lower-energy, minimally displaced fracture. Femoral neck fractures associated with femoral head fractures carry a very poor overall prognosis in terms of their high risk of avascular necrosis and joint degeneration and are therefore included in the classification of femoral head fractures. Finally, the outcome of a femoral neck fracture associated with an acetabular fracture is as dependent on the pattern of the acetabular fracture (perhaps more so) as it is on the outcome of the femoral neck injury and should therefore be classified with the acetabular injury (see Chapter 37).

## Current Classification

### NONDISPLACED FEMORAL NECK FRACTURES

Nondisplaced fractures include both a truly nondisplaced fracture and an impacted valgus femoral neck fracture. The lack of displacement places this fracture type in a much better prognostic situation in terms of nonunion or avascular necrosis.[92] Biologically, this better prognosis results from the fact that the main arterial supply to the femoral head is seldom (if ever) disrupted with these fracture patterns. Similarly, because of the lower amount of energy involved in producing the fracture and the resultant lack of displacement, intracapsular tamponade may play a more central role in producing avascular necrosis when it occurs.[435]

### DISPLACED FEMORAL NECK FRACTURES

Displaced fractures include all femoral neck fractures with any detectable displacement. In the strictest sense, such displacement refers to any alignment offset between the distal intertrochanteric fragment and the proximal femoral head fragment. Important prognostic factors are associated with this designation because with the fracture offset, the major arterial supply to the femoral head may be disrupted, which has implications with regard to both avascular necrosis and nonunion. Additionally, when fracture management is delayed, synovial fluid may bathe the fracture surfaces and negatively influence the rate of union. The higher risk of both complication categories plays a major role in determining fracture treatment, especially in an older, more sedentary patient.

## FATIGUE FRACTURES OF THE FEMORAL NECK

Fatigue fractures result from repetitive loading in pathologic (rheumatoid arthritis, osteoporosis) and nonpathologic (military recruits) bone.[87, 107, 173, 177, 242, 270, 451] Devas subclassified stress, or fatigue, fractures into two subgroups, transverse (tension) and compression, based on prognostic factors.[164] It is important to recognize that fatigue fractures occur more often in patients with osteoporosis than in those with normal bone density.[258, 282] An association between stress fractures of the femoral neck and recent total-knee replacement has been repeatedly identified.[189, 303, 321, 347]

**Transverse (Tension) Fractures.** Transverse fractures start as a crack at the superior part of the neck, apparent on an internally rotated AP pelvic radiograph, and become complete over days to weeks. If left untreated, patients in this fracture subgroup have a significant risk of displacement.[95, 149, 349] These fractures are distinct from nondisplaced acute fractures in that they are not associated with a single traumatic event.[166]

**Compression Fractures.** Compression fractures are seen radiographically as a haze of internal callus at the inferior part of the neck. They have essentially no risk of displacement without additional trauma, so most authors agree that these fractures should be treated by partial weight bearing with crutch ambulation.[164, 173]

## PATHOLOGIC FEMORAL NECK FRACTURE

Treatment of pathologic fractures, including those of the femoral neck, is covered in Chapter 16.

## FEMORAL NECK FRACTURES IN YOUNG ADULTS

Treatment of fractures of the femoral neck in patients with open proximal femoral physes is beyond the scope of this text. In adolescents and adults younger than 50 years, femoral neck fractures do occur as a result of high-velocity trauma in persons with normal bone density.[89] The same classification applies as noted previously, but the prognosis is worse in these younger patients.[367] In these individuals, extreme trauma is required to produce displacement of the fracture fragments, which explains the increased incidence of avascular necrosis and nonunion in series of young patients. Smith[409] documented loads of 900 to 2000 lb to produce femoral neck fractures in cadavers. Based on the supposition that the articulated hips in his study were probably from older individuals, one can extrapolate that

even higher forces are needed to produce femoral neck fractures in young adults.

## SPECIAL CASES

Certain conditions of abnormal bone metabolism can make the diagnosis and treatment recommendations quite different. For these reasons, the standard classification can be applied, but with modifications as noted in the following two sections.

**Rheumatoid Arthritis.** Because of the severe hip synovitis that can occur with rheumatoid arthritis, bone density is generally poor and chronic hip symptoms can mask acute femoral neck fractures.[431] Williams and associates[469] reported that four of five patients with rheumatoid arthritis and a femoral neck fracture had not fallen, which implies that fatigue fractures through severely osteoporotic bone are a common occurrence in this setting. Femoral neck fracture can also occasionally be seen in an osteoarthritic hip, although patients with coxarthrosis have been shown to be at lower risk of osteoporosis and femoral neck fracture.[462, 465] Treatment in both situations, because of the underlying articular disease, should generally be total-hip arthroplasty.[88, 142, 162, 405, 406, 444] Prefracture ambulatory status in patients with rheumatoid arthritis can be reliably restored with total-hip arthroplasty.[88]

**Renal Failure.** Patients undergoing chronic renal dialysis have metabolic bone disease and are prone to femoral neck fatigue fractures as outlined previously. Patients with end-stage renal disease may not have higher mortality rates than age- and sex-matched controls; however, a hip fracture in a patient with end-stage renal disease results in a higher rate of mortality.[447] When the fractures are displaced, treatment is generally total-hip arthroplasty. Internal fixation of displaced fractures in the setting of severe osteoporosis will be mechanically suboptimal.[438] Biologic factors may interfere with healing as well.

## BASILAR NECK FRACTURE

The low femoral neck/high intertrochanteric hip fracture occurs through an area of transition. Though generally true, it cannot be universally stated that these fractures are extracapsular and carry a better prognosis. A severely displaced low femoral neck fracture can still result in disruption of the lateral epiphyseal artery complex. From laboratory studies, Claffey[140] determined this degree of displacement to be half the diameter of the femoral head superiorly (distal fragment relative to the femoral head). Because the fracture is not frequently viewed radiographically at the extreme of displacement that occurs at the time of the injury, arterial disruption is a distinct possibility in the case of a basilar neck fracture. Although most surgeons may favor an internal fixation construct that would be selected for an intertrochanteric hip fracture,[106, 141, 346] the fracture should be viewed biologically as a femoral neck fracture (with its attendant risk of avascular necrosis of the femoral head) and treated as such with urgent fixation and capsulotomy.

# Diagnosis

## CLINICAL SUSPICION

In the most common setting of low-velocity femoral neck fractures resulting from falls, clinical suspicion is based on the history, the complaint, and the results of physical examination. In the case of a high-velocity femoral neck fracture, suspicion is often based on the history alone inasmuch as the complaint and the results of physical examination may be unavailable because of central nervous system injury or may be masked by other musculoskeletal injuries. When high-quality plain radiographs in two planes fail to demonstrate the fracture, a high index of suspicion mandates further evaluation. In a low-energy case, tomography or CT can be used to evaluate the femoral neck region. If results are still inconclusive, the patient should be treated by bedrest and evaluated with a technetium bone scan 48 to 72 hours after injury.[180] If the scan is negative, the patient can be safely treated symptomatically, but false negatives may be present for several days in the elderly population. Alternatively, MRI may be used for a quicker answer.[90, 225]

In the case of a high-energy injury, clinical suspicion should be high in those with an associated patellar fracture or knee ligament (especially posterior cruciate) injury, midshaft femoral shaft fracture, or an ipsilateral calcaneus, distal tibia, or tibial or femoral shaft fracture resulting from vehicular trauma or a jump or fall from a significant height.[434] If high-quality films do not reveal the fracture and the associated injuries require urgent care, the physician should proceed. Whenever procedures are done on the femur (i.e., intramedullary nailing), the femoral neck should be quickly reevaluated with the image intensifier. When treatment of other injuries is not pressing, the surgeon can proceed with tomography, CT, or bone scanning as outlined previously.

## HISTORY

In the case of a young patient involved in a high-velocity accident, information about the event is helpful in directing the clinical and radiographic evaluation. The physical and radiographic examinations, however, are usually more valuable than the history for directing evaluation and treatment. An accurate history is more important in the more common situation, a low-energy femoral neck fracture that usually occurs in older individuals. For these elderly, occasionally demented patients, it is essential to obtain a reliable description of the activity level before injury. Did the patient ambulate independently? Was the patient able to assist with transfers from bed to chair and so forth? This information can help the physician in making a choice between internal fixation of the fracture and prosthetic replacement. The prognosis is influenced by the patient's preinjury functional level, preexisting medical problems, and especially, mental status.

In addition, in an older patient, it is critical to seek information about the potential for the fracture to be associated with significant osteoporosis. Information concerning medications, medical conditions, and activity level is helpful in this regard. Finally, investigating whether the patient had pain in the groin or proximal part of the thigh before the fracture may suggest the presence of some type of pathologic fracture.

## PHYSICAL EXAMINATION

Evaluation of a patient involved in high-energy trauma is covered in Chapter 5. In the case of a femoral neck fracture associated with a minor fall, the examination can be conducted in a more methodic manner. The presence of a femoral neck fracture may be apparent from the attitude of the affected leg, such as obvious shortening, external rotation, and reluctance to move the limb. Alternatively, usually with an undisplaced fracture, the injury may be occult and suggested only by the patient's complaints of groin, thigh, or (rarely) lateral hip pain. Tenderness in the hip region produced by percussion on the sole of the foot with the fist or pain at the extremes of hip motion, particularly rotation, may be the only local physical findings to suggest such an occult hip fracture.

After evaluating vital signs and mental status, the head and neck examination should focus on areas of tenderness, evidence of contusions or abrasions, and decreased cervical range of motion. If any of these findings are present, a hard cervical collar should be applied until the cervical spine can be cleared radiographically. The chest should be palpated for signs of rib fracture and auscultated to rule out pneumothorax. A screening examination of the upper and lower extremities should follow, with palpation and with the patient, if alert, putting the joints through a range of motion. The examination should then focus on the affected lower extremity. The trochanteric region should be evaluated for contusions and for traumatic or nontraumatic skin conditions that might influence surgical management. The knee should be examined for tenderness, effusion, and instability. If such evaluation is not possible because of thigh pain, the knee examination must be repeated before the surgical procedure but after initiation of anesthesia. The thigh and leg should be palpated and the foot and ankle examined for signs of trauma. The circulatory status of both limbs should be assessed as a baseline for follow-up evaluations and the status of the pulses carefully recorded. Finally, a complete sensory and motor examination of the limb should be performed and the findings on physical examination detailed in the medical record.

When the patient's complaints and history suggest a femoral neck fracture but physical findings are lacking, the patient should be evaluated with MRI or a technetium bone scan, as outlined earlier.

## IMAGING

### Plain Films

For patients involved in high-energy injuries, an AP radiograph of the pelvis is routinely obtained as part of the early trauma series of radiographs. The area of the femoral neck should always be carefully scrutinized. When possible, the legs should be taped in internal rotation before obtaining this film. Physical or radiographic findings of ipsilateral trauma in the leg or the presence of hip pain is also an indication for a routine AP pelvic radiograph.

In the low-energy setting, an AP pelvic radiograph, with the legs gently internally rotated, should be obtained and carefully inspected for a femoral neck fracture. If a hip fracture is suggested from the history and physical findings but is not evident on this initial radiograph, it is important to obtain an AP radiograph of the symptomatic hip with the femur sufficiently internally rotated to show a maximal profile of the anteverted femoral neck region because this projection will be the most likely to demonstrate an occult fracture. Nonpathologic high subcapital fractures can simulate a pathologic fracture in 17% of cases on plain radiographic evaluation.[399]

An estimate of osteoporosis should be made with the Singh index because it has some predictive value regarding the degree of osteoporosis and the potential for obtaining stable internal fixation.[407] If a fracture is evident or suspected on clinical grounds, a cross-table lateral radiograph of the affected limb is also required. This radiograph is made with the affected limb remaining on the stretcher while the good limb is flexed up and out of the x-ray beam. The lateral view should be scrutinized for posterior femoral neck comminution because this view likewise affects the prognosis for obtaining stable internal fixation.

### Computed Tomography

CT and earlier tomographic techniques are helpful in identifying a nondisplaced femoral neck fracture when it is not radiographically apparent but is suspected on clinical grounds (e.g., history, complaint, or pain on rotation of the hip). Tomography can also provide critical information with regard to typing fatigue fractures for treatment purposes. Detailed, high-quality images should be obtained in planes parallel to the femoral neck. Occult and pathologic fractures of the upper part of the femur can be detected with this technique. CT may be particularly useful in a patient with a high-energy fracture who is undergoing an examination for abdominal, pelvic, or spine trauma. This technique is also of use in differentiating pathologic (nonosteoporotic) femoral neck fractures from nonpathologic fractures. Although good studies have confirmed that stability of the postfixation construct is most dependent on bone density, as yet, no clinical data derived from CT-measured density can be used to determine the potential for stability of internally fixed femoral neck fractures.[438]

### Radionuclide Studies

Radionuclide uptake has been studied for more than 50 years in the hope that such techniques will detect avascular necrosis at an early stage. Historically, radioactive calcium, phosphorus, and iodine were injected and Geiger counter systems used to obtain data that could be assessed in terms of femoral head blood flow.[113, 115, 257] These studies, although they showed some early promise, were not consistently reliable and involved high radiation burdens for the patient.

The two techniques that remain in use for assessment of femoral neck fractures are sulfur colloid scans and technetium 99m diphosphonate scans.[329, 428] The former is a compound that demonstrates bone marrow viability and has been used with good success as a predictor of avascular necrosis. Unfortunately, a large series of patients have not been monitored after the use of this technique. It has been considered to be accurate, and the data obtained have been used to decide whether to perform prosthetic replacement.[330] It has the drawbacks of a significantly higher radiation burden, less detailed images, and a longer delay after injection before the images are obtained.

Tc 99m diphosphonate scanning is the method of choice for obtaining predictive data in regard to the risk of nonunion and avascular necrosis.[101, 218, 219, 297, 310] Stromqvist and co-workers[426–428, 430] published results from 468 patients who underwent serial bone scans after femoral neck fractures. They determined that visual evaluation of pictorial images (scintigrams) is neither reproducible nor reliable. Quantitative scans (scintimetry) allow side-to-side comparison based on carefully defined regions of interest. Preoperative bone scans were not helpful as predictors of avascular necrosis or nonunion because internal fixation procedures could be monitored by either deterioration of perfusion with avascular necrosis or recovery of an apparently unperfused femoral head. They also reported that screw-type implants have a much more favorable influence on femoral head circulation than do triflanged nails hammered into the bone.[430] Data on femoral head uptake are expressed as a ratio relative to the intact side. The best prediction of results after internal fixation of a femoral neck fracture is provided by scintimetry performed between 2 and 3 weeks after injury and fixation. If the ratio of the injured to the uninjured region of interest is less than 0.9, patients had an 84% chance of nonunion, avascular necrosis, or both. For patients with an abnormal contralateral hip, the uptake ratio of the femoral head to the ipsilateral femoral shaft can be measured. If this ratio is at least 1.4, uneventful healing is likely. By 4 weeks after injury, those in whom nonunion or avascular necrosis eventually develops have equal or higher femoral head uptake that lasts up to 24 months after injury. These findings have been duplicated in animal models.[391] These data integrate well with the hypothesis that revascularization follows an avascular episode and produces trabecular resorption and weakening, which allows mechanical failure in the subchondral plate and femoral head collapse.[211]

Scintigraphic images produced by nuclear medicine scanning can be helpful for diagnosing occult problems of the proximal end of the femur. When plain radiographs are normal, osteoblastic activity in the region of the femoral neck, as demonstrated by a technetium-labeled phosphate scan, may indicate a nondisplaced or fatigue fracture of the femoral neck.[180] These changes may take up to 72 hours after fracture to be apparent. In this setting, visual inspection of scintigrams, rather than scintimetric data, is most helpful, as it is in searching for additional occult metastases of a primary lesion when planning treatment of a pathologic fracture. Thus, scintigraphic bone scans can be valuable for localizing and identifying lesions, but unlike scintimetric data, they have not proved helpful in the effort to preoperatively establish the prognosis for uneventful healing of a given femoral neck fracture (Fig. 48–11).

### Dual-Photon Absorptiometry

Dual-photon absorptiometry has been shown to provide an accurate determination of spinal osteoporosis. However, some published reports indicate that spinal bone density is not directly related to femoral neck bone density.[190] The technique is being adapted to more accurately determine femoral neck bone density, and data regarding the bone density necessary to achieve stable internal fixation may be forthcoming.[215] Incorporation of hip axis length as an additional predictor of hip fracture risk is feasible.[181]

### Magnetic Resonance Imaging

MRI has been shown to be a sensitive indicator of avascular change within the femoral head in nontraumatic forms of avascular necrosis. The ability of MRI to detect acute femoral head vascular changes has been noted to be somewhat limited in clinical as well as in vivo laboratory studies.[90, 294, 392] Severe distortion of the images is produced by proximal femoral internal fixation devices. Pure titanium or nearly pure titanium fixation devices must be used to study femoral head signals after internal fixation; dark shadows remain on the images, but distortion is minimized. This technique may ultimately allow a greater understanding of the pathologic processes of post-traumatic avascular necrosis; however, it remains a tool that is unable to predict the patients in whom femoral head collapse will develop from post-traumatic osteonecrosis.[90, 419, 420] It is the method of choice for detecting nondisplaced femoral neck fractures in patients with symptoms and normal radiographs because of the delay (up to 72 hours) in radionuclide uptake in fresh fractures and the suboptimal uptake of technetium-labeled phosphate compounds in the most elderly patients.[225, 470]

### Ultrasonographic Venography

High-resolution, real-time ultrasonography has attracted interest as a simple, repeatable, noninvasive means of diagnosing deep venous thrombosis.[209] A variety of criteria have been proposed for the ultrasonographic diagnosis of venous thrombosis. In a prospective study of 40 patients with hip fractures, Froehlich and co-workers[198] used a single test: noncompressibility of the vein lumen. This test was applied from the calf veins to the common femoral artery and validated by venography. Five patients (12.5%) had major thrombi; all were asymptomatic. Compression ultrasonography had an accuracy of 97%, a sensitivity of 100%, and a specificity of 97%. It is well tolerated and is significantly less expensive than venography, but it requires a well-trained technologist.

## NUTRITIONAL ASSESSMENT

Malnutrition is more common than what might be expected in elderly patients with hip fractures, even in those with adequate resources.[99, 100, 205, 358, 422] Improved outcome after hip fracture has been demonstrated when dietary supplements are provided. Screening studies that may be used to evaluate nutritional status are the absolute lymphocyte count, serum albumin, transferrin, and skin fold thickness.[99, 100, 138, 410]

## ESSENTIAL STUDIES

Diagnostic algorithms for patients with multiple injuries are presented in Chapter 5. To prevent missing a femoral neck fracture (which occurs most frequently in midshaft femoral neck fractures), the femoral neck must be carefully scrutinized, as outlined previously. Spine and extremity radiographs are obtained in accordance with

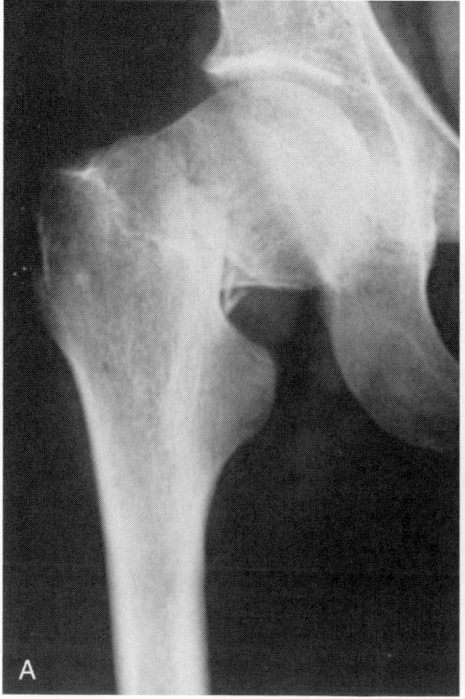
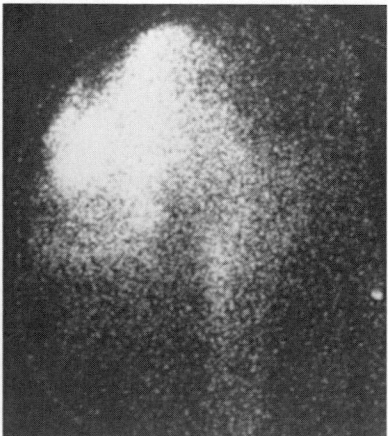

**FIGURE 48–11.** Scintigraphy after femoral neck fracture. *A,* A 23-year-old man fell off a bunk bed and sustained a displaced Garden grade III femoral neck fracture. *B,* The patient underwent a preoperative bone scan 8 hours after injury, with the right side showing lower femoral head uptake than the left.

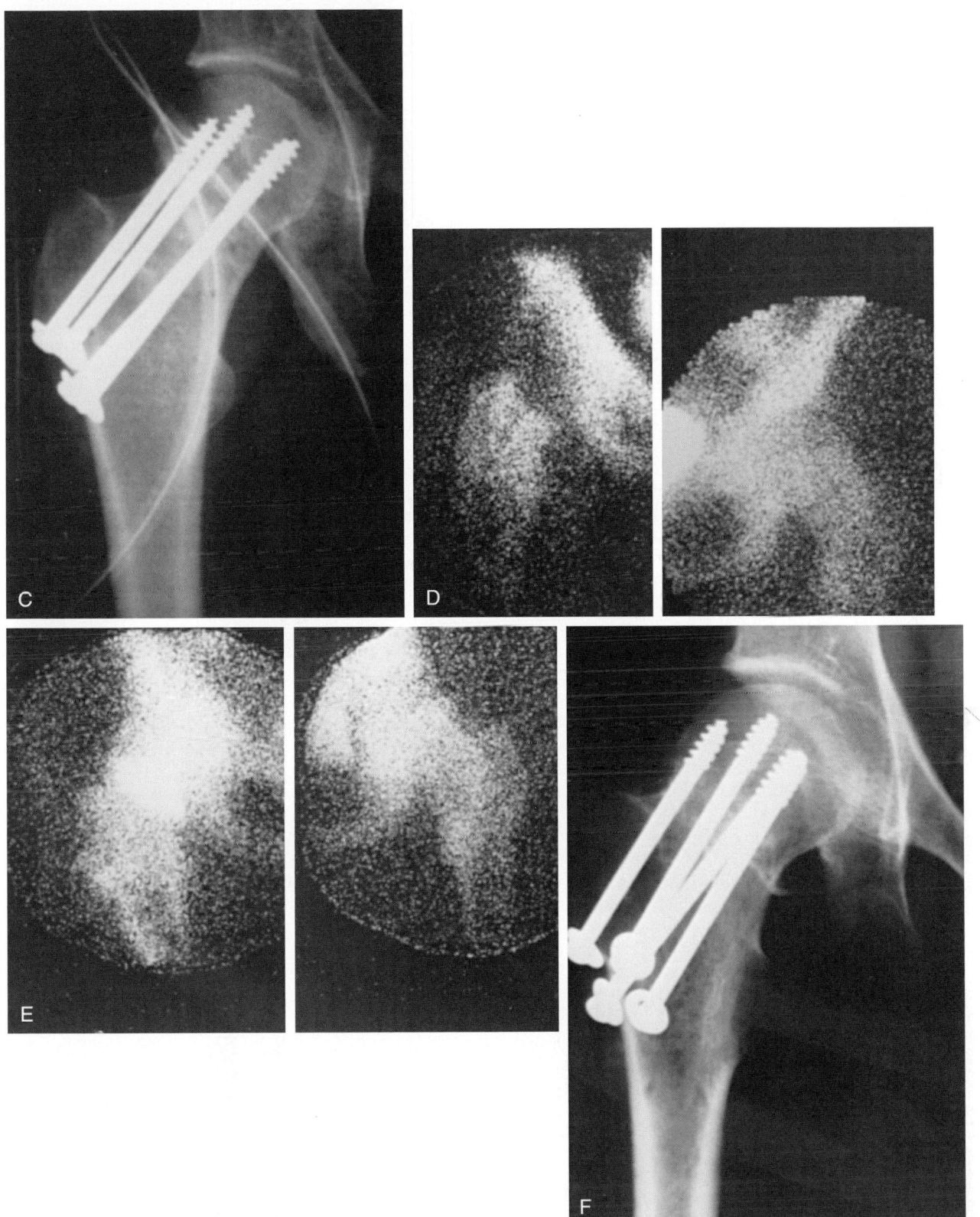

**FIGURE 48–11** *Continued.  C,* He underwent emergency open reduction using the Watson-Jones approach, with evacuation of intracapsulary hematoma and screw fixation with four cancellous screws. *D,* A bone scan obtained the day after surgery shows an even lower amount of femoral head uptake than previously when compared with the normal side. *E,* At 3 weeks, a bone scan showed a high degree of uptake, greater than on the intact side. *F,* An 18-month follow-up radiograph showed the fracture to be united with no evidence of osteonecrosis. This result was confirmed at 10 years.

findings from the initial assessment, which includes a history of the injury and physical examination. A preoperative electrocardiogram, chest radiograph, complete blood cell count, urinalysis, and serum electrolyte, creatinine, and serum albumin studies should be obtained in all patients older than 40 years. See under Patient Assessment in Chapter 49.

## Differential Diagnosis

The differential diagnosis for a femoral neck fracture in a high-energy trauma patient must include pelvic fracture, acetabular fracture, hip dislocation, intertrochanteric or subtrochanteric femoral fracture, isolated trochanteric fracture, and a contusion or muscle avulsion without fracture. The differential diagnosis of a patient with a low-energy femoral neck fracture should include intertrochanteric or subtrochanteric femoral fracture, pelvic fracture, acetabular fracture, isolated trochanteric fracture, and hip contusion/traumatic trochanteric bursitis. Both the history and the results of physical examination must be used to evaluate the potential for pathologic lesions, nondisplaced fractures, fatigue fracture of the proximal part of the femur or pelvis, and hip arthritis.

## Management

### EVOLUTION OF TREATMENT

Nonunion and avascular necrosis of the femoral head have long been recognized to be the major problems associated with a femoral neck fracture. In 1901, Senn stated, "We are not only justified but warranted in assessing that the only cause for nonunion in the case of an intracapsular fracture is to be found in our inability to maintain coaptation and immobilization of the fragments during the time required for bony union to take place."[400] He had previously advocated immediate reduction and internal fixation of these fractures in 1889 and had published animal data to support the concept that these fractures would heal with internal fixation.[400] Whitman in 1902 and 1933 and Cotton in 1927 and 1934 advocated closed reduction and impaction followed by placement into a spica cast in internal rotation as the method of choice for the management of femoral neck fractures.[145, 146, 467, 468] Leadbetter further detailed the method of closed reduction and stated that "plaster fixation cannot be expected to yield good results consistently and logically in more than 65 or 75 percent of these [femoral neck fracture] cases."[300] Phemister outlined the pathophysiology of "creeping substitution" as it pertains to avascular necrosis of the femoral head after femoral neck fracture.[362]

The first widely accepted method of internal fixation was reported by Smith-Petersen and colleagues in 1931.[412] Use of this device was reported in many publications until the mid-1970s. The most highly documented series was that of Fielding and associates,[187] published in 1962, which revealed a nonunion rate of 18% and an avascular necrosis rate of 29% in a series of 284 displaced and nondisplaced femoral neck fractures. Moore[334] published

a report on the first implant with multiple pins (adjustable nails) in 1937. He thought that the advantage of this type of implant was that no special tools were necessary for insertion. A 96% rate of union was reported. Several designs of implants with multiple pins followed shortly thereafter. Moore then developed a prosthetic replacement for the femoral head and reported on its use in 33 cases in 1952. The Thompson prosthesis was developed shortly thereafter, and the current debate of whether to fix the femoral neck fracture or replace the femoral head began.[445] Sliding devices such as the Pugh nail (1955)[186, 218, 370] and the Richards screw (1964)[112] were developed for controlled impaction of femoral neck fractures. More designs with multiple pins and screws were added to the already numerous devices in the late 1960s and 1970s.[84, 91] The debate rages on regarding replacement of the femoral head versus internal fixation and the indications for both.[114] In Europe, use of 130° blade plates has enjoyed fairly widespread acceptance.[169] When internal fixation is warranted, however, most surgeons now use some type of multiple pins or screws, including a compression hip screw with an added screw or pin to prevent rotation of the femoral head.[91, 111, 213] That quality of reduction is a key factor in achieving union has been reconfirmed repeatedly; placement of implants with multiple screws to within 3 mm of the inferior femoral neck cortex has also been shown to be important in achieving fracture union.[202, 306, 333]

Judet developed a method of placing a viable bone graft across the posterior aspect of a femoral neck fracture and into the femoral head to decrease the incidence of avascular necrosis and nonunion.[281] This quadratus femoris muscle pedicle graft was advocated by Meyers and colleagues, who reported an 8% incidence of posttraumatic avascular necrosis and an 11% incidence of nonunion.[329] Subsequent reports have not confirmed these results, however[276] (Fig. 48–12).

### CURRENT ALGORITHM FOR TREATMENT OF FEMORAL NECK FRACTURE

#### Initial Treatment

During initial evaluation and care of a patient with a femoral neck fracture, it is important to splint the injured limb to protect it from additional damage, as well as minimize the patient's discomfort. Moderate flexion and external rotation increase the volume of the hip capsule and may thus decrease intracapsular pressure, with potential improvement in femoral head perfusion. A pillow under the knee will provide this effect. It is important that the leg be elevated enough from the mattress to protect the heel from pressure and subsequent skin breakdown.

#### Undisplaced Femoral Neck Fractures

As defined previously, undisplaced femoral neck fractures include both valgus impacted (Garden grade I) and complete (Garden grade II) femoral neck fractures because of the similar prognosis of both fracture types. Their treatment is the same. *Internal fixation is indicated for most undisplaced acute femoral neck fractures.* It has clearly been shown that mobilization of the patient results in a lower

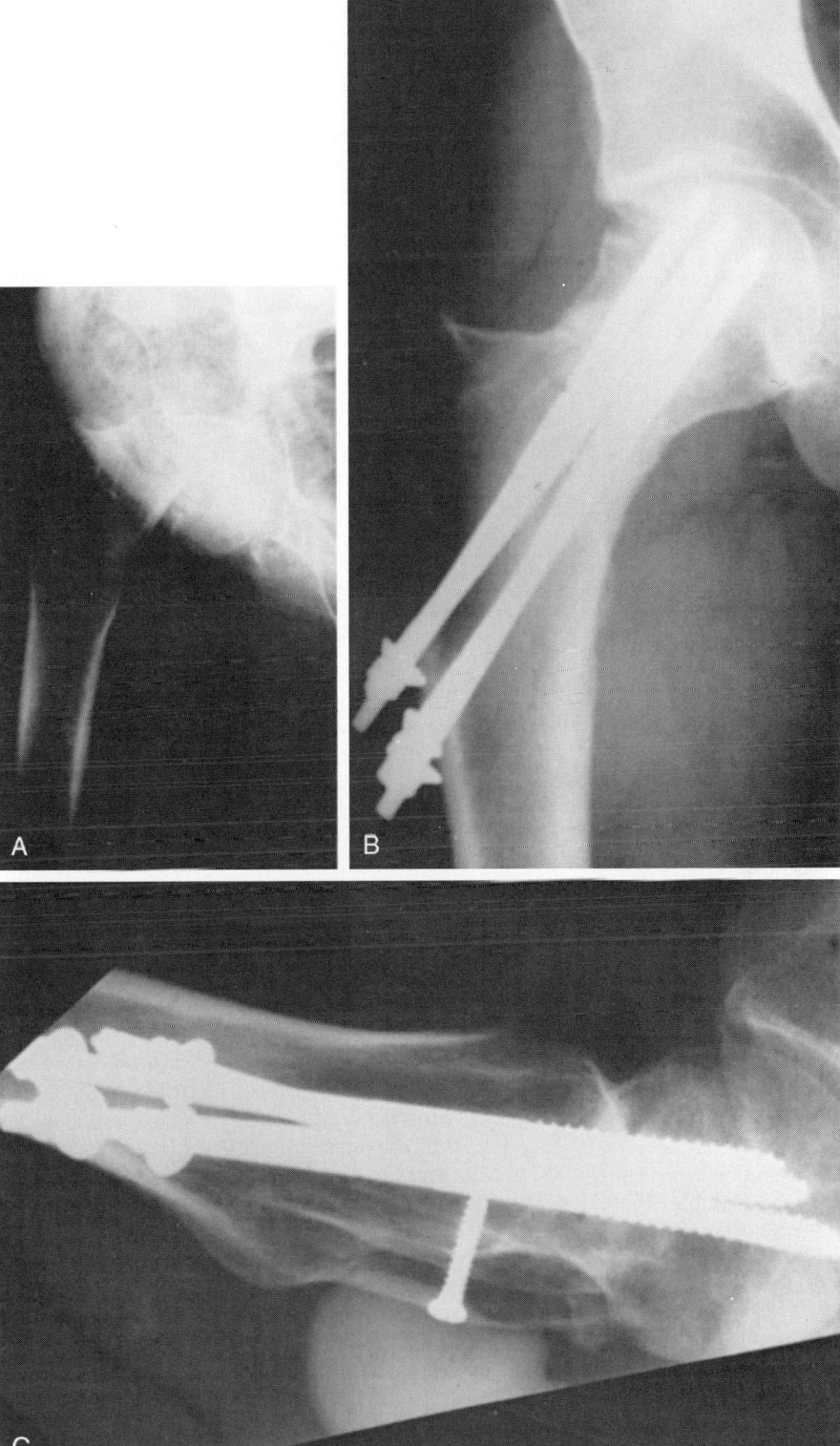

**FIGURE 48–12.** Quadratus femoris muscle pedicle graft for femoral neck fracture. *A,* A 63-year-old man was treated for a Garden grade III femoral neck fracture with a Judet quadratus femoris muscle pedicle graft. The patient was treated on a fracture table in the prone position with multiple modified Hagie pins. The quadratus femoris graft was placed posteriorly and fixed with a single screw. *B, C,* The result at 2½ years. The patient is ambulatory with a cane and is not complaining of hip symptoms.

mortality rate.[403] Internal fixation allows mobilization of the patient without loss of fracture reduction in most cases (osteoporotic femoral heads are infrequently an exception). With conservative treatment (recumbent position for 7 weeks), the displacement rate or disimpaction rate has been shown to be 10% to 27% by Bentley,[104] Hilleboe and colleagues,[242] and Jensen and Hogh.[272] Bentley reported that rates of avascular necrosis after a nondisplaced femoral neck fracture were 14% for conservative treatment and 18% for internal fixation.[104] If displacement occurs, the rates more than double, and prosthetic replacement may become the treatment of choice for an older patient. Therefore, internal fixation with multiple pins or screws and an implant of the surgeon's choice seems justified. No difference in clinical results is apparent with cannulated screws or Knowles pins.[256, 269] One retrospective review suggests that the reoperation rate for nondisplaced or impacted femoral neck fractures in patients older than 80 years who are treated by internal fixation may warrant consideration of hemiarthroplasty.[263] Because insertion of a nail-type device might displace the fracture, nails should *not* be used. Several laboratory and clinical publications support the concept of performing a capsulotomy to release excessive pressure caused by fracture bleeding into the hip joint capsule.[253, 267]

### Displaced Femoral Neck Fracture

As previously discussed, treatment of displaced femoral neck fractures is aimed at restoring hip function. Rapid mobilization of the patient is thought to reduce the risk of medical complications and improve the ultimate functional outcome. Additionally, it decreases the costly length of stay in an acute care hospital.[353] Failure of fracture fixation, nonunion, and avascular necrosis with symptomatic late segmental collapse have long been recognized as serious complications that compromise the results of treatment of femoral neck fractures. In striving to provide mobilization while avoiding these and other complications, the treatment scheme has evolved from closed reduction and casting, to internal fixation, to prosthetic replacement, and presently to selective use of prosthetic replacement or internal fixation. The currently offered algorithm for displaced femoral neck fractures recommends internal fixation, after closed or open reduction, for most patients with adequate bone density. Prosthetic replacement is reserved for physiologically older patients in whom internal fixation is unlikely to succeed—those with marked osteopenia, fracture comminution, or both. In general, such patients are physiologically elderly, with low functional demands. Their ambulation is at best restricted to their domicile, they may be unable to assist with their own care, and their life expectancy is often limited. They are thus less at risk of having late complications that might require revision of an arthroplasty. Although different types of prosthetic replacement for the proximal part of the femur have relative advantages and disadvantages, none can provide as durable and functional a hip as that regained by satisfactory bone healing. Furthermore, failure after internal fixation of a femoral neck fracture can be satisfactorily salvaged by total-hip arthroplasty, which has a low rate of complications.[227] Failed hemiarthroplasties require a similar procedure, though a more difficult one with possibly poorer results.[179]

**Indications.** Surgical treatment is warranted for all but the most medically fragile and bed-bound patients with displaced femoral neck fractures. Operative management has been shown to achieve significant functional benefit in cost-benefit analyses.[192, 320, 353] The basic choice of treatment is between internal fixation and arthroplasty. This controversy is discussed in further detail later. It is recommended that several factors be considered when choosing treatment for patients with displaced femoral neck fractures.

Age alone is a poor predictor of activity level, bone quality, physiologic status, and life expectancy, all of which should also be considered when deciding between reduction/fixation and replacement arthroplasty.[383] If successful, reduction (either closed or open) and internal fixation provide the best and most durable result after displaced femoral neck fractures. Failure of reduction and fixation is caused by early loss of fixation, by nonunion, and by symptomatic segmental collapse from avascular necrosis. Though not always predictable, fixation problems are most common in patients with osteopenic bone and comminution. Prosthetic replacement of the proximal part of the femur avoids the problems of nonunion and avascular necrosis but may be associated with higher perioperative morbidity than seen with internal fixation.[264] In addition, it poses late problems of loosening and acetabular erosion, either of which may require revision surgery. Results after revision of failed hemiarthroplasties are not as good as those after primary total-hip arthroplasty, and the procedure may be quite difficult.[179] Therefore, initial treatment of a displaced femoral neck fracture should seek to minimize the likelihood of needing to revise a failed arthroplasty in the future. In general, avoidance of revision arthroplasties is best accomplished by restricting hemiarthroplasties to low-demand users with limited life spans. Variations in arthroplasty implants and technique may increase their durability and ease of revision, although the data to support this assertion are not yet conclusive.

Factors that suggest the advisability of prosthetic replacement include pathologic bone, severe chronic illness (especially rheumatoid arthritis[469] and chronic renal failure), and a significantly limited life span. Advanced chronologic age alone is a questionable indication for hemiarthroplasty.[263] The average life expectancy for 75-year-olds is more than 10 years.[79] Therefore, many orthopaedists would extend the indications for internal fixation into the early and mid 70s for active individuals with good bone density and no chronic illness. Inactive, osteoporotic elderly patients with a limited life span are candidates for simple unipolar hemiarthroplasties. Those with displaced femoral neck fractures who can ambulate functionally outside their homes (community ambulators) and whose likelihood of success with internal fixation is low should receive modern bipolar hemiarthroplasties, with the awareness that revision may be required in the future because of loosening of the femoral component or acetabular degenerative changes, including protrusion. These problems are greater in younger and more active patients. It is thought that a bipolar hemiarthroplasty may survive longer in more active patients and that a Morse taper modular design might make revision easier without removal of a securely fixed femoral component.[226] Primary total-hip arthroplasty may be an alternative for such individuals.[142, 162, 405, 406, 444] This option is discussed further in Chapter 61.

**Controversy.** The debate regarding prosthetic replacement versus internal fixation for femoral neck fractures in older patients is widespread.[200, 371, 404, 416] Hunter[265, 266] reviewed the subject in detail. The literature on prosthetic replacement reveals the rate of clinically poor results to be 28%, with dislocation rates of 0.3% to 11%, infection rates of 2% to 42%, and a 6-month mortality of 14% to 39%, all of which are significantly higher than the corresponding rates for internal fixation[266] (Tables 48–6 and 48–7). However, Sikorski and Barrington[404] found that anterior-approach hemiarthroplasty had a lower 6-month mortality than did internal fixation. Holmberg and co-workers[254] found complication rates to be lower after prosthetic replacement (15%) than after internal fixation (37%). In a retrospective nonrandomized study, Johnson and Crothers[275] found the incidence of unsatisfactory results to be lower after prosthetic replacement. Rodriguez and colleagues[385] reviewed multiple factors and concentrated on morbidity and mortality. They found internal fixation to be the most innocuous method of treatment. Other reports of hemiarthroplasty suggest that perioperative complications might be less frequent than reported in earlier series[108, 173, 380, 393, 404, 416] (see Tables 48–6 and 48–7).

Insistence on adequate reduction and proper use of fixation with multiple screws or pins has decreased the rate of fixation failure and nonunion to 10% or less in most recent series. Although avascular necrosis occurs in 10% to 30% of united, initially displaced femoral neck fractures, it may not become symptomatic enough to require treatment, especially in low demand users. If it does occur, salvage with total-hip arthroplasty is safe and successful.[226]

When the cost and potential complications of modern hip prostheses are considered, it appears wise to limit the use of bicentric and total-hip arthroplasties to patients who are most likely to benefit from them. In fact, many patients will not survive long enough after their hip fracture to justify procedures with higher risk and higher cost. Wathne and co-workers[463] could not identify any improvement in functional outcome after femoral neck fracture in a prospective series of patients treated with a cemented modular unipolar versus a cemented modular bipolar prosthesis. White and colleagues[466] reported that increased mortality occurs during the first year after hip fracture. This effect is greater for those with more severe preoperative medical problems and senile dementia.[175, 457] For 75-year-old patients, they found an approximately 6.5-fold increase in mortality during the first year after hip fracture. By applying this figure to the U.S. population with mortality rates identified in 1986,[80] it can be calculated that only 10% of patients with hip fractures at age 75 will still be alive 10 years later. A therapeutic strategy that advocates routine bipolar or total-hip arthroplasty for 75-year-olds with femoral neck fractures will result in many patients receiving operations that they do not need to obtain comfortable function for the rest of their lives. However, more recent noncontrolled studies suggest that such arthroplasties may offer a better functional outcome with less variation and better survival of the prosthesis.[118, 174, 313]

Bauer and his group from the University of Lund, Sweden,[101] demonstrated the efficacy and safety of a therapeutic strategy that relies on initial internal fixation of all femoral neck fractures. From their department, Stromqvist and co-workers[429] reported 215 displaced femoral neck fractures treated by internal fixation. At a 2-year follow-up, 63 patients (29%) had died. Of the survivors, 53 had fracture-healing complications: redisplacement or nonunion in 39 (18% of the original group) and avascular necrosis with segmental collapse in 14 (6.5% of the original group). These complications led to reoperations in 36 (17%) of the original group: 28 total-hip arthroplasties and 4 hardware removal procedures in the redisplacement/nonunion category and 3 total-hip arthroplasties and 1 osteotomy in those with segmental collapse. The authors point out that if they had chosen routine arthroplasty for the displaced femoral neck fractures, the procedure would have been done unnecessarily for the 83% of patients who did not require revision operations. The end result in these patients was uneventful healing, death from other problems, or complications with tolerable symptoms. It is tempting to speculate that the 17% incidence of reoperations, mostly caused by loss of fixation and nonunion, could have been further decreased if those markedly

**TABLE 48–7** ••••••••••••••••••••••••••••••••••••••••••

Reported Incidence of Infection after Prosthetic Arthroplasty

| Investigator | Percent |
|---|---|
| Garcia et al. (1961)[200] | 6 |
| Hinchey and Day (1964)[243] | 2 |
| Glass (1965)[210] | 10 |
| Niemann and Mankin (1968)[345] | 42 |
| Hunter (1969)[264] | 8 |
| Lunt (1971)[312] | 19 |
| Riska (1971)[380] | 5 |
| Wrighton and Woodyard (1971)[476] | 9 |
| Chan and Hoskinson (1975)[132] | 2 |
| Raine (1973)[371] | 6 |
| Arnold et al. (1974)[84] | 16 |
| Fielding et al. (1974)[186] | 8 |
| Hunter (1974)[265] | 8 |
| Kavlie and Sundal (1974)[284] | 3 |
| Salvati et al. (1977)[393] | 17 |
| Long and Knight (1980)[308] | 0.5 |
| Franklin and Gallannaugh (1983)[195] | 0 |
| Staeheli et al. (1988)[423] | 0 |

••••••••••••••••••••••••••••••••••••••••••••••••••••••

**TABLE 48–6** ••••••••••••••••••••••••••••••••••••••••

Reported Incidence of Dislocation of the Prosthesis after Primary Prosthetic Implantation

| Investigator | Percent |
|---|---|
| Hinchey and Day (1964)[243] | 0.3 |
| Glass (1965)[210] | 5 |
| Hunter (1969)[264] | 3 |
| Lunt (1971)[312] | 10 |
| Wrighton and Woodyard (1971)[476] | 3 |
| Raine (1973)[371] | 8 |
| Hunter (1974)[265] | 7 |
| Chan and Hoskinson (1975)[132] | 8 |
| D'Arcy and Devas (1976)[159] | 2 |
| Hunter (1980)[266] | 11 |
| Long and Knight (1980)[308] | 2.6 |
| Franklin and Gallannaugh (1983)[195] | 0 |
| Staeheli et al. (1988)[423] | 2 |

••••••••••••••••••••••••••••••••••••••••••••••••••••••

osteopenic individuals with the greatest risk of such fixation problems had been treated instead with primary hemiarthroplasty. Note, however, that such individuals are a small proportion of the whole group, whose average age was only 78 years.

Orthopaedists who take the middle ground seem to agree that patients are best off with a healed femoral neck fracture, their own femoral head, and no avascular necrosis. When factors such as limited life span, chronic disease, and poor bone quality intervene, most North American surgeons would recommend prosthetic replacement.

**Timing of Surgery.** Numerous laboratory and clinical studies indicate that reduction of a displaced femoral neck fracture improves femoral head blood flow, probably because of "unkinking" of the lateral epiphyseal artery complex in patients in whom it remains intact. Claffey[140] showed that superior displacement of the femoral head of up to half the femoral neck diameter can occur without disruption of these vessels. These data all indicate the need for urgent, if not emergency reduction of femoral neck fractures. In one series of patients younger than 50 years with displaced femoral neck fractures, the rate of nonunion was 0% and that of avascular necrosis was 20% when the femoral neck fractures were reduced and internally fixed with compression within 8 hours; in addition, in other studies with control groups, urgent ORIF provided better outcomes in terms of lowering the rate of osteonecrosis.[111, 116, 442]

Intracapsular tamponade has similarly been found to have a negative influence on femoral head blood flow in numerous laboratory and clinical studies.[253] Although some authors disagree, the current recommendation is to extend the standard lateral approach into the Watson-Jones interval between the tensor fasciae latae and gluteus medius and perform an anterior capsulotomy under direct vision (see Fig. 48–14). Although possibly only 5% to 10% of fractures are seen in which the hip capsule is not disrupted and sufficient intracapsular pressure has accumulated to impede venous drainage or arteriolar supply of the femoral head, these fractures can be effectively treated by this simple maneuver. Capsulotomy adds 5 to 10 minutes to the dissection and exposes the patient to no further risk. Furthermore, anatomic reduction can then be achieved under direct vision. Many older patients with femoral neck fractures have significant medical problems. Correcting these problems preoperatively may greatly reduce the risk of complications.[175, 288] Therefore, extreme care should be taken to optimize the patient's condition for surgery. The time required for such correction is well spent. Medical consultation should be obtained and the patient's fluid status evaluated. Cardiac and pulmonary status should be optimized and any indicated drug or respiratory therapy instituted as soon as possible. However, Zuckerman and colleagues[481] showed increased mortality in patients with two or fewer co-morbidities in whom surgery had been delayed for more than 2 calendar days. Parker and Pryor[355] confirmed the increased morbidity in patients who have no co-morbidities but in whom surgery is delayed. Similarly, Rogers and associates[386] documented a significant increase in mortality in physio-

logically stable elderly patients with isolated proximal femoral fractures and a delay of more than 24 hours before surgery. Therefore, delay longer than it takes to stabilize patients medically is not advised.

Nutritional factors should also be assessed so that they can be addressed early in the postoperative period. Bastow and co-workers[99, 100] and Patterson and associates[358] emphasized that mortality after hip fracture is increased in thin and very thin patients and that nutritional supplements can reduce both the length of hospitalization and mortality. As soon as the patient is optimally prepared, surgery should be performed. If internal fixation has been chosen, early surgery may be especially beneficial because as noted previously, evidence indicates that early reduction of a displaced femoral neck fracture can improve the circulation of the femoral head.[442] This benefit may be of greatest value in minimizing the risk of symptomatic avascular necrosis in young patients with femoral neck fractures. However, the large series of Barnes and co-workers[96] did not demonstrate a time-related difference in the complication rate (avascular necrosis, nonunion) for fractures that underwent fixation within the first 72 hours.[96]

If arthroplasty has been selected as the treatment of choice, early surgery after optimal patient evaluation and preparation is also beneficial because of the medical deterioration that is likely to occur as a result of immobility and pain in a bed-bound patient.

**Treatment by Patient Status.** Considerations for treatment of displaced femoral neck fractures by patient status are given in Table 48–8.

### Fatigue Fractures

Devas[164] classified fatigue fractures as compression or transverse fractures (Table 48–9). The latter appear as a crack at the superior aspect of the femoral neck and have a significant risk (10% to 15%) of displacement and a secondarily increased risk of avascular necrosis. A compression fracture starts at the inferior aspect of the femoral neck and gradually over many weeks appears as a haze of internal callus. These fractures are much more common in osteoporotic elderly women and are less likely to become displaced.[258]

### Pathologic Femoral Neck Fractures

The reader is referred to Chapter 16 for details of the diagnosis and treatment of pathologic fracture of the femoral neck. If surgery is indicated, some form of arthroplasty is necessary.

## PATIENTS WITH MULTIPLE INJURIES

Nearly all femoral neck fractures in young patients with normal bone are secondary to high-velocity trauma. Fifty percent to 70% of patients younger than 50 years with a nonfatigue, displaced femoral neck fracture will have other organ system injuries.[366, 442] A young patient with a displaced femoral neck fracture should be assumed to have other injuries until proven otherwise.

**TABLE 48–8** . . . . . . . . . . . . . . . . . . . . . . . . . . . . . .

Treatment of Displaced Femoral Neck Fractures by Patient Status

| Patient Group | Treatment |
|---|---|
| Young patients with normal bone and high-energy injuries | Urgent closed or open reduction and internal fixation with multiple pins or screws and with simultaneous capsulotomy[111, 182, 437] |
| Older patients with high functional demands and good bone density | Rapid medical evaluation followed promptly by closed or open reduction and internal fixation with multiple pins or screws and with simultaneous capsulotomy[182] |
| Older patients with normal or intermediate longevity, poor bone density, chronic illness, and lower functional demands | Bipolar hemiarthroplasty, cemented, or total-hip arthroplasty |
| Elderly, low-demand users with poor bone density | Unipolar hemiarthroplasty |
| Bed-bound, nonambulatory patients | Trial of nonoperative treatment with consideration of early surgery (internal fixation, unipolar hemiarthroplasty, or excisional arthroplasty) if sufficient comfort for routine nursing care is not regained within a few days |

. . . . . . . . . . . . . . . . . . . . . . . . . . . . . . . . . . . . . . . . .

### Timing of Femoral Neck Fracture Management

Because of the significant risk of avascular necrosis with segmental collapse and the limited therapeutic alternatives for managing this complication, reduction plus fixation of displaced femoral neck fractures is a matter of great urgency for young individuals.[314, 315] Therefore, in the orthopaedic management of a patient with multiple injuries, treatment of a femoral neck fracture should be superseded only by stabilization of a pelvic ring injury associated with serious bleeding by débridement (not stabilization) of contaminated open fracture wounds and by reduction of cervical spine subluxations or dislocations. A displaced femoral neck fracture in a young patient is a true orthopaedic emergency.

### Protocols for Associated Injuries

**Femoral Shaft Fractures.** Ipsilateral femoral neck fractures occur in approximately 2.5% of femoral shaft fractures. Generally, femoral neck fracture displacement is minimal, but it can be severe. Most often, the hip injury is associated with a fracture within the middle third of the femoral shaft (more than 80% of reported cases).[434] The femoral neck fracture was missed on initial evaluation in 34% of published cases.[434] The initial radiographs of a patient with a femoral shaft fracture must include high-quality AP and lateral views of the femoral neck. A

femoral neck fracture must take precedence over a femoral shaft fracture because of the poor results of treatment of post-traumatic avascular necrosis in young patients. Optimal surgical management must be carried out to minimize the risk of avascular necrosis. As outlined previously, the femoral neck should be treated by emergency reduction, capsulotomy, and internal fixation with multiple pins or screws. In no case should an antegrade femoral nail be inserted adjacent to the femoral neck fracture without initially stabilizing the femoral neck because of the high risk of displacing it. After the femoral neck is fixed, the femoral shaft may be fixed with a plate and screws, flexible retrograde intramedullary nails, or a retrograde interlocking nail[126, 434, 437] (Fig. 48–13). If the femoral neck can be stabilized with screws or pins anterior to the standard intramedullary starting portal, an antegrade standard or interlocking nail can be introduced, but this technique has been associated with extremely high rates of nonunion (18%) and subsequent osteonecrosis.[474] Cephalomedullary nails with proximal locking screws directed into the femoral head have also been advocated for the fixation of ipsilateral neck and shaft fractures of the femur.[143, 207, 239, 372] Displacement of the neck fracture is a risk during insertion of such a nail, and location of the entry portal is critical. Initial reduction and provisional wire or pin fixation of the neck fracture should precede preparation of the femur for insertion of the cephalomedullary device. Adequate biomechanical properties have been confirmed by Ramser and colleagues.[372]

**Femoral Neck and Head Fractures.** The reader is referred to the previous section on femoral head fractures for management of this rare injury combination.[321] The first priority is urgent reduction of the hip dislocation. Fixation of the femoral head fracture concomitant with fixation of the femoral neck should be seriously considered in such a patient with multiple injuries. In older patients, prosthetic replacement may be advisable for more severe femoral head fractures (Pipkin grades 2 and 3).

**Femoral Neck/Acetabular Fractures.** The treatment principles for the femoral neck fracture remain the same. The femoral neck fracture should be treated urgently with operative stabilization; the acetabular fracture can be managed at a later time if indications for open reduction are present. Operative management of both fractures by an experienced surgeon is usually important for optimal results. See Chapter 37 for details regarding management of the acetabular portion of this fracture combination.

**TABLE 48–9** . . . . . . . . . . . . . . . . . . . . . . . . . . . . . .

Treatment of Fatigue Fractures of the Femoral Neck by Type of Fracture

| Type of Fracture | Treatment |
|---|---|
| Transverse type | Urgent internal fixation with multiple pins |
| Compression type | Mobilization with limited weight bearing on crutches or a walker |

. . . . . . . . . . . . . . . . . . . . . . . . . . . . . . . . . . . . . . . . .

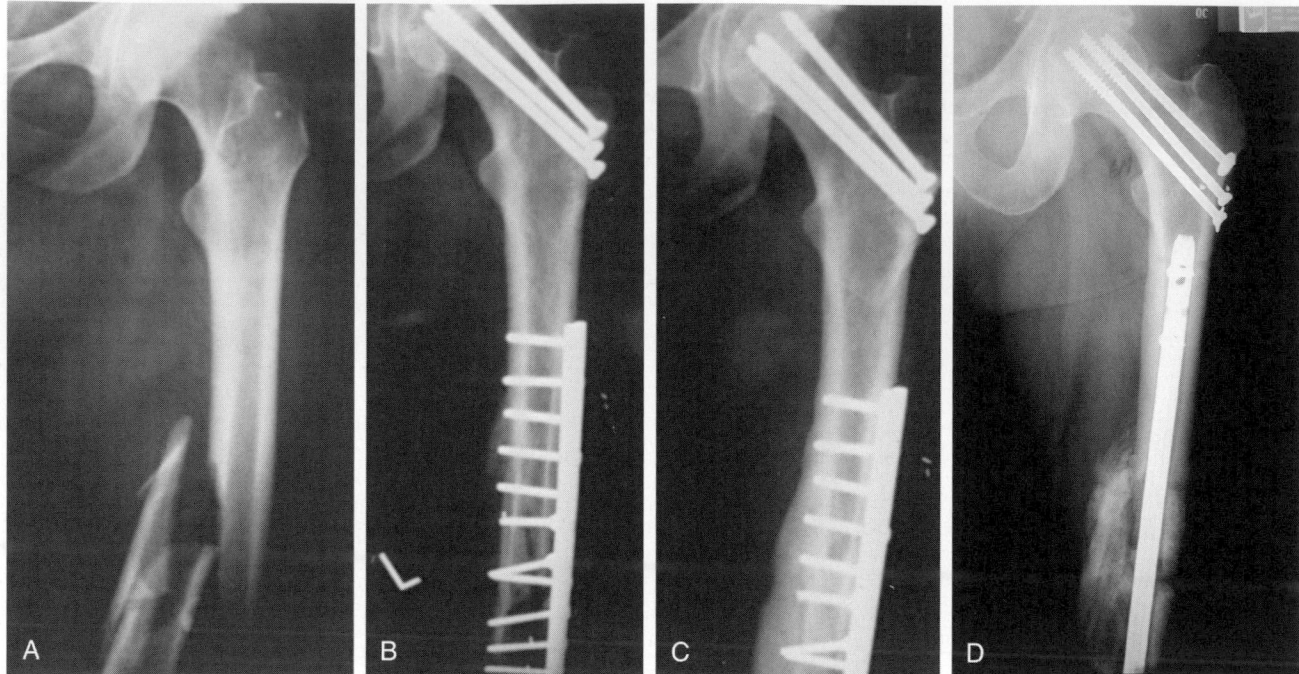

**FIGURE 48–13.** Associated femoral neck and shaft fractures. *A,* A 24-year-old woman sustained this highly comminuted femoral shaft fracture with an ipsilateral vertical femoral neck fracture. She had an intra-articular distal femoral fracture on the opposite side and a ruptured spleen. *B,* After resuscitative laparotomy, she underwent open reduction and internal fixation of her femoral neck fracture with fixation by cannulated screws, followed by plating of her femoral shaft. *C,* A radiograph at 8 months shows complete healing of both fractures. At 4.5 years, she had no signs of post-traumatic osteonecrosis. To diminish the risk of osteonecrosis, the femoral neck fracture should receive priority regardless of the treatment selected for the femoral shaft fracture in this injury combination. *D,* Ipsilateral femoral neck and shaft fracture fixed in another patient with initial urgent closed reduction and cannulated screw fixation for the neck fracture and retrograde locked intramedullary nail fixation for the femoral shaft.

## INDIVIDUAL TREATMENT PROCEDURES

### Nonoperative Management

The indications for nonoperative treatment are limited primarily to the compression type of fatigue fracture. The risk of displacement with its attendant higher risk of avascular necrosis is great enough that nonoperative treatment should not be considered for impacted acute or transverse fatigue fractures of the femoral neck. Nonoperative treatment of fatigue fractures consists of limiting activity to a pain-free level, often with crutches and partial weight bearing initially. Risky activities should also be avoided. Once symptoms have resolved and sufficient time (6 to 12 weeks) has elapsed for mechanically secure healing, progressive resumption of normal activity is begun.

Occasionally, nonoperative treatment may be indicated for debilitated, usually demented, nonambulatory bedridden patients, possibly including those who may be able to transfer to a chair with significant assistance.[473] Although it is relatively easy to forgo surgery for such patients if they have severe cardiopulmonary illness and a very limited life span, some do not appear to be on the verge of death. For these individuals, it is hard to justify surgical treatment in view of the limited benefit it offers and its high risks. A good test for the adequacy of nonoperative treatment in such patients is the achievement of comfort sufficient to tolerate routine nursing care. A few days with analgesia and careful logrolling will often suffice and may permit the patient to remain in a chronic care setting. In other circumstances, the patient may be transferred to a hospital emergency department, where the treating surgeon is faced with deciding between admitting or sending the patient back to the chronic care facility. Good communication and collaboration between the surgeon and the patient's caretakers are essential. If the patient appears quite uncomfortable, hospitalization for a few days may be best, often with a special low-pressure bed so that frequent turning is not necessary to avoid skin breakdown. With small doses of narcotics initially, the patient will usually become comfortable enough to tolerate routine nursing and may then return to the previous situation. Occasionally, this type of treatment is not well tolerated, and consideration should be given to unipolar hemiarthroplasty, excisional arthroplasty, or possibly closed reduction and fixation with multiple pins. A drawback of internal fixation in such patients, especially if flexion contractures restrict them to a lateral decubitus position, is the risk of skin breakdown over prominent hardware, but it may offer the least invasive form of treatment.

### In Situ Fixation

**Indications.** Indications for in situ fixation include nondisplaced femoral neck fractures, fatigue fractures, and impacted femoral neck fractures.

**Timing of Surgery.** Stabilization should be done as soon as the patient's medical status has stabilized. Zuckerman and co-workers showed an increase in the overall mortality of patients with two or fewer co-morbidities when surgery was delayed more than 48 hours.[481] Because some evidence indicates that intracapsular hematoma can be involved in the pathophysiology of avascular necrosis after this fracture, the need for internal fixation combined with a decompressive anterior capsulotomy is urgent.[111, 116, 441] A limited amount of clinical data confirm a lower rate of post-traumatic osteonecrosis in patients managed with reduction and internal fixation within 6 hours.[314, 315]

**Preoperative Planning and Preparation.** Radiographs of the fracture must be carefully evaluated in both planes to be sure that no reduction is indicated. Implants, multiple screws (cannulated or noncannulated) or pins, must be available in several lengths. Equipment must be on hand for screw or pin insertion (e.g., guides, depth-measuring systems). A C-arm image-intensifier fluoroscope is required. Perioperative systemic antistaphylococcal antibiotics (e.g., cefazolin, 1 g given intravenously every 8 hours for 24 hours or less) should be administered to reduce the frequency of postoperative infection.[138]

**Anesthesia and Positioning.** The patient should be positioned supine on the fracture table with the well leg in the lithotomy position or abducted in gentle traction. Radiographic control in the AP and lateral planes must be confirmed before starting the procedure. If not absolutely clear on the fluoroscope monitor, permanent films should be made with the appropriate attachment on the C-arm. These actual radiographs, rather than digital copies of the fluoroscopic image, provide the best detail. Either spinal or general anesthesia is equally appropriate.[105, 144, 160, 455, 466]

**Surgical Technique.** Percutaneous fixation can be achieved through small stab incisions, but such fixation is not recommended, especially in younger patients in whom an anterior capsulotomy is indicated.[260, 289] A straight lateral incision is made from the top of the trochanter to a point 1 cm distal to the lesser trochanter. The fascia lata is incised longitudinally, and the vastus lateralis is either split or reflected anteriorly. The capsular attachments at the trochanteric ridge/vastus tubercle can be exposed by anterior retraction and the capsule incised in line with the neck of the femur and released proximally and distally from the intertrochanteric ridge to produce a T-shaped capsulotomy, which allows release of the hematoma and palpation of the fracture if indicated. Extending this lateral incision into a femoral Watson-Jones approach through the interval between the tensor fasciae latae and the gluteus medius aids in visualization of the fracture (Fig. 48–14).

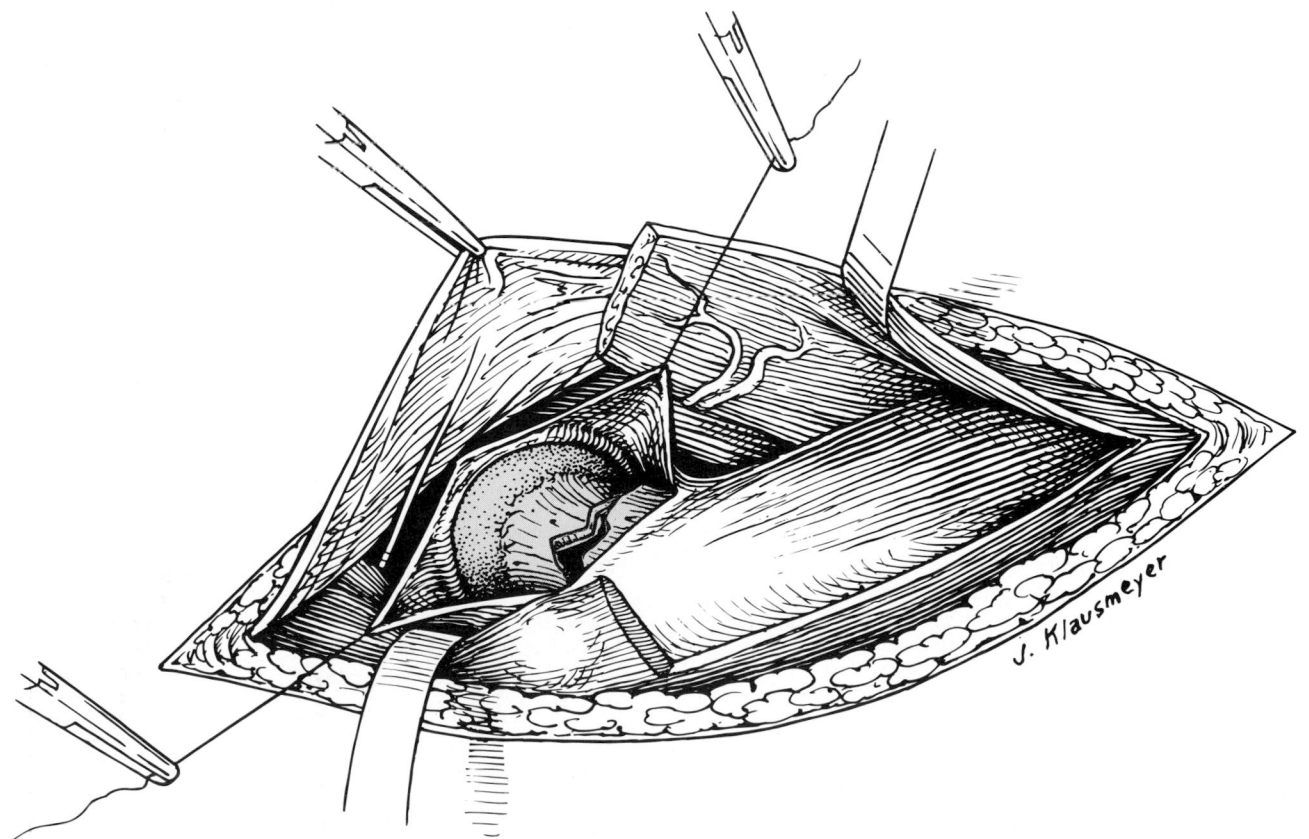

**FIGURE 48–14.** The Watson-Jones anterolateral exposure to the hip for open reduction of femoral neck fractures. The interval between the tensor fasciae latae and the abductors is bluntly developed, and the vastus lateralis is elevated off the intertrochanteric ridge. The capsule is divided anteriorly along the axis of the neck of the femur and transversely released from its insertion into the proximal part of the femur. With sutures as retracting aids, the fracture can be visualized. A bone hook can be used to disimpact the fracture by applying a laterally directed force, and a blunt instrument can be inserted to improve the reduction (i.e., lift the proximal fragment anteriorly). The insertion area for internal fixation devices on the lateral aspect of the proximal end of the femur is easily exposed.

A guide pin is placed centrally in the neck under fluoroscopic control in two planes with the aid of a similar wire placed by hand along the anterior surface of the femoral neck. A multiholed guide can then be placed over the guide pin and used to predrill and insert three parallel screws (Fig. 48–15). Insignificant mechanical advantage is gained by adding more implants.[240, 256, 421, 438, 456] Sliding hip screws, telescoping nails, and crossed screws are not recommended for routine use in femoral neck fractures. However, these devices are advocated for osteoporotic patients[182, 354] and basilar neck fractures.[106, 119] Implant position must be verified by permanent AP and lateral radiographs, which are readily made with the C-arm fluoroscope, as well as by careful fluoroscopy in different positions of hip rotation.

### Intraoperative Complications

*Displacement of the Fracture.* Fracture displacement can be avoided by gentle handling of the patient in positioning. If the fracture does become displaced, it is suggested that reduction and internal fixation be performed in active patients with good bone stock. If displacement is recognized before the procedure is initiated and the patient is not a candidate for internal fixation, the patient should be moved to a regular operating table and prepared for insertion of a prosthesis instead.

*Intra-articular Pin Placement.* Placement of pins or screws into the hip joint may easily go unrecognized because a two-dimensional monitoring technique is used for a three-dimensional problem.[461] Thus, the tips of intra-articular pins can appear to be inside the shadow of the femoral head. This fact should remind the surgeon to beware of subchondral pin positioning, especially in the periphery of the femoral head. Visualizing the joint in different rotational positions helps identify intra-articular pins. If recognized, replacement rather than partial withdrawal is best to avoid repenetration of the joint should the femoral neck shorten by impaction during fracture healing.

**Aftercare.** The patient should be out of bed in a chair two to three times daily beginning on the first postoperative day. Physical therapy generally starts on the second or third postoperative day, and the patient is instructed in touch-down weight bearing with a walker (for most elderly patients) or crutches (for younger patients). The use of ketorolac should be limited in elderly patients because of the increased risk of gastrointestinal and operative site bleeding.[425] Walking aids should be used for 8 to 12 weeks after injury. Many older patients are unable to comply with restricted weight bearing, and this restriction appears to be of limited additional benefit, especially after internal fixation of undisplaced fractures. Most patients can be mobilized safely, with weight bearing as tolerated, by using external support for the first 4 to 6 weeks after fixation. Long-term follow-up is advisable because of the risk of avascular necrosis, which may not be manifested for 2 or even 3 years.

**Hardware Removal.** Hardware removal is not generally indicated for elderly patients. If 1 year has elapsed and the patient is unable to lie on the injured side because of pain over prominent hardware, the implants may be removed if fracture healing has been clinically and radiographically confirmed.

### Reduction of Displaced Fractures

**Closed Reduction.** Closed reduction of displaced femoral neck fractures has been described by numerous authors, including Speed, Smith-Petersen, Cotton, Leadbetter, and Deyerle, with minor differences in technique.[145, 146, 165, 300, 411, 418] A good technique is to flex the externally rotated hip to 45° in slight abduction, extend it while gently increasing traction, and then internally rotate to 30° to 45° in full extension. Alternatively, traction can be applied with the hip in extension, slight abduction, and external rotation. After length is appropriately restored, the leg is internally rotated until the neck axis is properly aligned with the femoral head. If the neck is too anterior, external rotation "unlocks" the reduction, and internal rotation is repeated with posteriorly directed pressure applied manually to the front of the upper part of the thigh (Fig. 48–16).

A number of criteria have been advanced for satisfactory reduction. Although restoration of normal anatomy is desirable, posterior comminution and osteoporosis can make such a reduction less stable than a slightly valgus, over-reduced alignment (i.e., what Brunner and Weber[120] called a *hat hook* reduction). Excessive valgus can increase the risk of avascular necrosis; AP and lateral radiographs should be inspected carefully. The AP view should be examined to ensure that length has been restored and that the femoral neck is in anatomic or slight valgus alignment. Garden has emphasized the crucial nature of the reduction on the lateral view. It should demonstrate neither anterior (the usual) nor posterior displacement of the femoral neck relative to the head. Especially important is correction of the angulation seen on the lateral radiograph. Garden[203] demonstrated that absence of angulation produced the best results and that angulation of more than 20° produced a high incidence of failure (Fig. 48–17). Parker and colleagues[354] have demonstrated that clinical outcome is highly dependent on the quality of the reduction.

If the reduction maneuver, which should rely primarily on extension and internal rotation, is not producing satisfactory alignment, rather than repeating closed manipulation with greater force (which could potentially damage the blood supply to the femoral head), the surgeon should proceed to open reduction.[287] Although many authors believe that reduction of a femoral neck fracture should routinely be performed by open means, some clinicians have reported better results with closed reduction.[213, 435]

**Open Reduction.** The Watson-Jones incision, recommended for open reduction of a femoral neck fracture, was illustrated earlier in Figure 48–13. The full technique is shown in Figure 48–18. The initial lateral incision is extended proximally in the interval between the tensor fasciae and the gluteus medius muscles. This interval is split bluntly down to the anterior hip capsule. The origin of the vastus lateralis is elevated off the intertrochanteric ridge. The hip capsule is split onto the femoral neck anteriorly and then dissected off the intertrochanteric ridge 1 cm inferiorly and 1 cm superiorly. By inserting a small pointed (Hohmann) retractor intracapsularly onto the anterior acetabular rim, the fracture can be easily visualized.

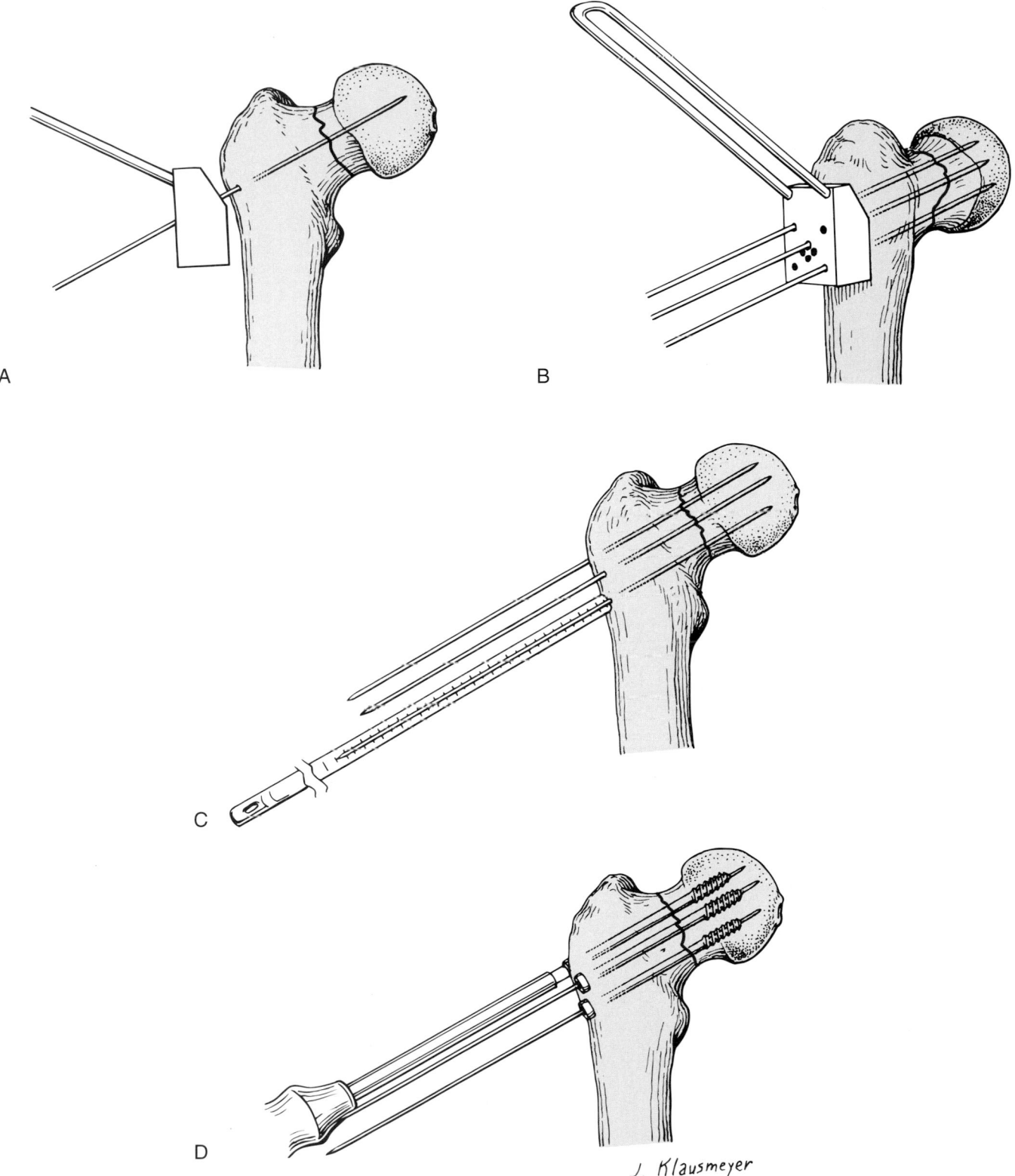

J. Klausmeyer

**FIGURE 48–15.** Internal fixation of a femoral neck fracture with a cannulated screw system. *A,* After satisfactory reduction is confirmed, the lateral aspect of the proximal end of the femur is exposed and a control guide wire is inserted. The guide is placed over the initial guide wire, and adjustments are made with the multiple holes available to allow placement of all screws within the femoral neck. *B,* The remaining guide wires are inserted through the guide; drilling at high revolutions per minute with light hand pressure will allow optimal control of the wires. *C,* Once three satisfactory parallel guide wires have been inserted under fluoroscopic control, the length of the wires is determined. A cannulated drill bit may be used and should be inserted to 10 mm less than the total length of the wire to prevent the wire from being removed. *D,* A cannulated tap can be used in dense cancellous bone, and screws of appropriate length are inserted over guide wires to the preselected depth.

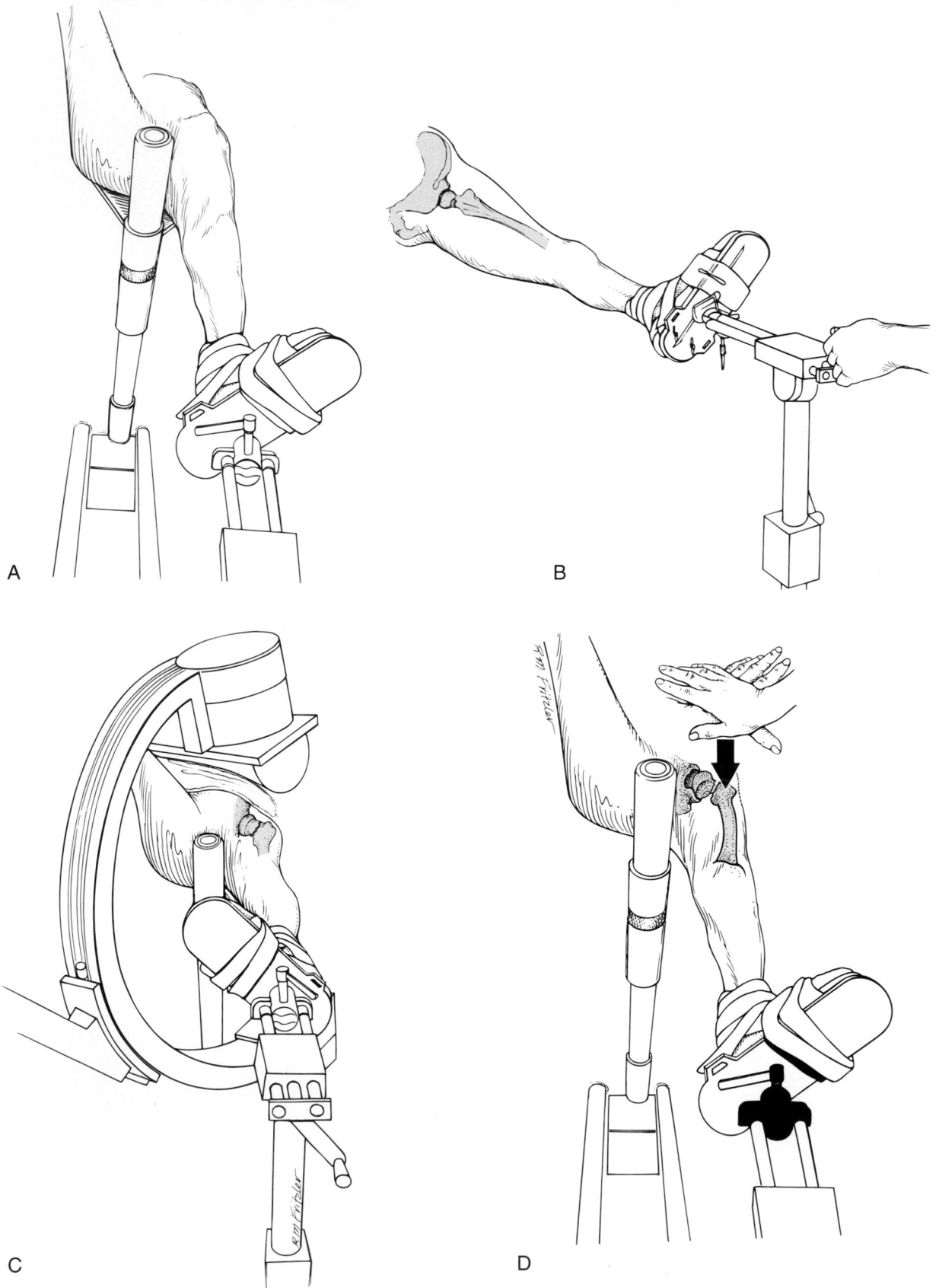

**FIGURE 48–16.** Closed reduction of a femoral neck fracture. *A,* The patient is positioned supine on a fracture table with the uninjured leg in a lithotomy position to allow access of the C-arm image intensifier to the injured hip in anteroposterior (AP) and lateral projections. The injured leg is attached to the foot piece securely, but with adequate padding. The leg is slightly abducted and flexed and externally rotated with minimal traction initially. *B,* Traction is increased to correct length and varus deformity at the fracture site, as revealed by the drawing of the AP fluoroscopic view. *C,* The leg is internally rotated and adducted to a neutral position to correct anterior angulation of the apex and to oppose the fracture surfaces. *D,* If the distal fragment is too anterior, the leg is externally rotated again, and pressure is firmly applied to the proximal part of the thigh while the leg is rotated internally.

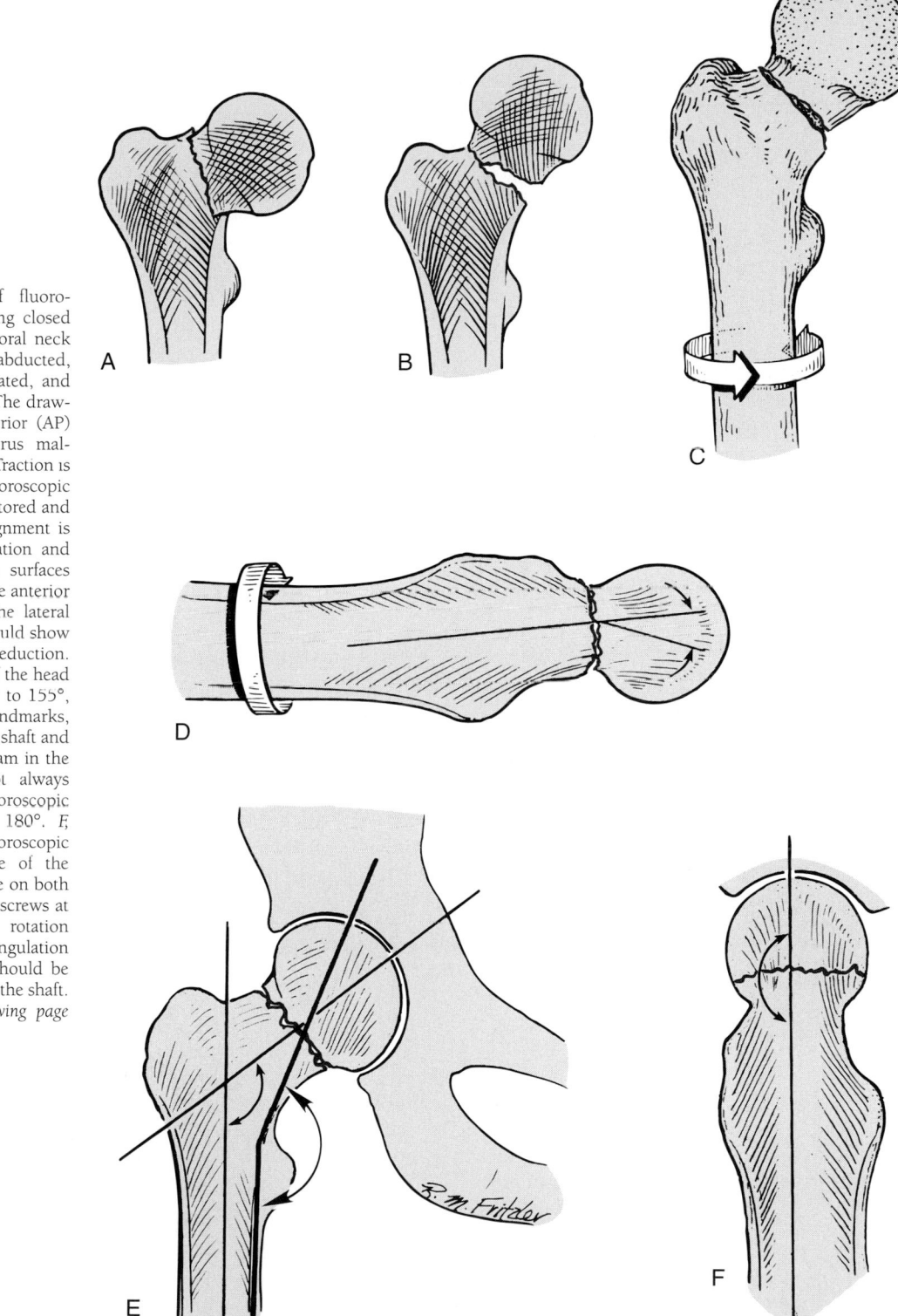

**FIGURE 48–17.** Drawings of fluoroscopic images obtained during closed reduction of a displaced femoral neck fracture. *A,* The hip is slightly abducted, slightly flexed, externally rotated, and initially in minimal traction. The drawing of the initial anteroposterior (AP) fluoroscopic view shows varus malalignment and shortening. *B,* Traction is applied with intermittent fluoroscopic views taken until length is restored and anatomic or slight valgus alignment is achieved. *C, D,* Internal rotation and adduction bring the fracture surfaces into opposition and correct the anterior angulation of the apex on the lateral view. *E,* The final AP view should show anatomic or slight valgus reduction. The angle between the axes of the head and the shaft should be 150° to 155°, or with the use of Garden's landmarks, the angle between the femoral shaft and the axis of the trabecular stream in the femoral head (which is not always visible, especially on the fluoroscopic image) should be 160° to 180°. *F,* Drawing of the final lateral fluoroscopic view. The subchondral bone of the femoral head should be visible on both views to permit placement of screws at the proper depth. Internal rotation should correct the anterior angulation of the apex. No angulation should be present between the head and the shaft. *Illustration continued on following page*

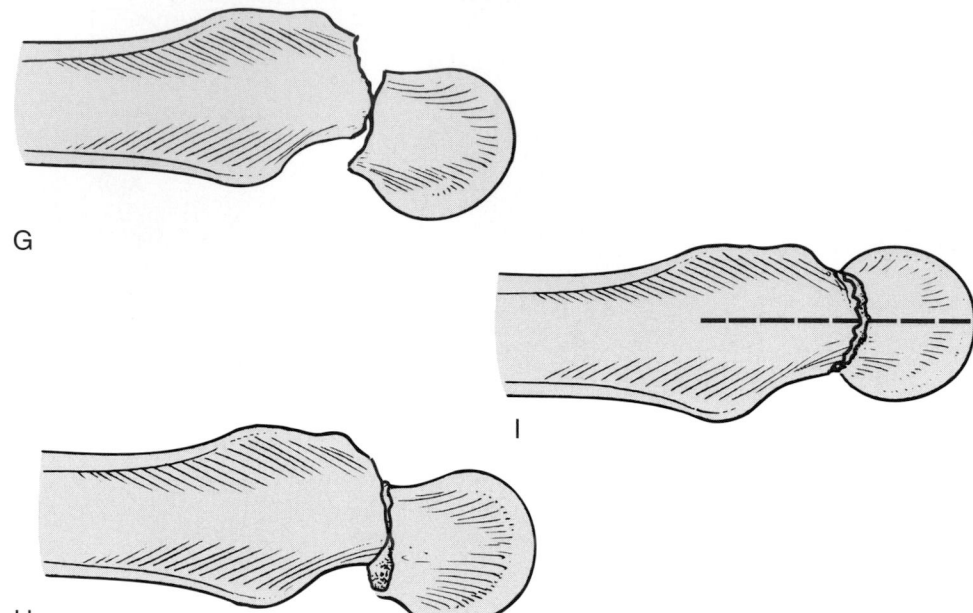

G

H

I

Figure **48–17** Continued. G, Adjustment may be required to eliminate angulation between the neck and the shaft. H, Anterior displacement of the distal portion of the neck relative to the head is not uncommon and also requires correction to maximize contact of the fracture surfaces. Both anterior and posterior neck profiles should appear concave on the lateral radiograph. To correct anterior displacement, the distal end of the femur is first externally rotated, and posteriorly directed pressure is then applied to the subtrochanteric region of the thigh. The fracture surfaces are reapproximated by restoring internal rotation. I, Finally, the AP image is rechecked to ensure that the reduction has remained satisfactory during correction of the displacement while using the lateral view.

For reduction, a bone hook is placed onto the greater trochanter, or a Schantz screw in a Thandle chuck is inserted into the proximal end of the femur. The hip is brought into external rotation by adjusting the fracture table. With lateral traction applied with a bone hook or Schantz screw, the fracture is disimpacted. The femoral neck (distal fragment) is usually found anterior to the femoral head (proximal fragment). This displacement is corrected with leverage from a blunt, curved instrument placed between the fracture surfaces as the lateral traction is released, and the limb is returned into maximal internal rotation. The reduction is provisionally held by a 2.0-mm Kirschner wire placed centrally in the neck in both planes (see Fig. 48–18). The reduction should then be confirmed visually, by palpation, and by radiography in both planes.

*Fixation of Femoral Neck Fractures*

More than 100 different internal fixation devices have been used for stabilizing femoral neck fractures. Triflanged nails, either with or without femoral shaft side plates, should not be used to internally fix femoral neck fractures. The distraction produced when using these devices has been shown to have an adverse effect on femoral head blood flow.[222, 427, 430] The device chosen should have a mechanism for producing compression across the fracture site.

In general, large hip compression screws such as those recommended for intertrochanteric hip fractures should not be routinely used. They sacrifice large amounts of central bone in the femoral neck, which can make reconstruction of an eventual nonunion very difficult. Furthermore, Brodetti[117] has shown that these large implants, if placed suboptimally in the posterior or superior aspect of the femoral head, can damage the blood supply to the femoral head. However, Ort and Lamont[347] have reported results with compression screws that are equal to those of other techniques, and Bonnaire and associates[111] reported that their results (in terms of osteonecrosis) were better with sliding hip screws. If this device is selected, a second pin or screw should be inserted superior to the centrally placed guide wire for the large compression screw to control rotation of the femoral head fragment during insertion of the screw. Because the hip compression screw by itself controls rotation poorly when compared with implants with multiple screws or pins, this superior screw should remain as part of the definitive fixation.[182, 438] Hernefalk and Messner[240] demonstrated increased stiffness of implants with side plates; however, this finding has not been universally repeated. Malposition of the screw within the femoral head in patients with a femoral neck fracture has been shown to be more common in patients with left hip fractures when the surgeon is right hand dominant.[333]

*Recommended Fixation Technique*

The recommended implant for internal fixation of a femoral neck fracture is an implant with multiple pins (e.g., Knowles, Gouffon) or some type of cannulated or noncannulated cancellous screw (e.g., Ace, AO/Association for the Study of Internal Fixation [ASIF], Asnis, Richards).[182, 438] Screw cannulation allows the use of guide wires, thereby enabling the use of more sophisticated guide systems with which to ensure parallel placement of the implants.[91] In general, the amount of compression generated across the fracture is proportional to the thread area of the screw. The critical element in fracture stability is the density of the bone. The use of more than three implants does not seem to provide any increased mechanical advantage.[421, 438, 456] The general technique for inserting multiple screws was depicted earlier in Figure 48–15. The drill guide device is placed over the centrally positioned guide wire. Three parallel drill or screw guide wires are then inserted and the length measured for insertion of the screws. The location of one or more implants within 3 mm of the inferior femoral neck cortex may be critical in promoting optimal stability in

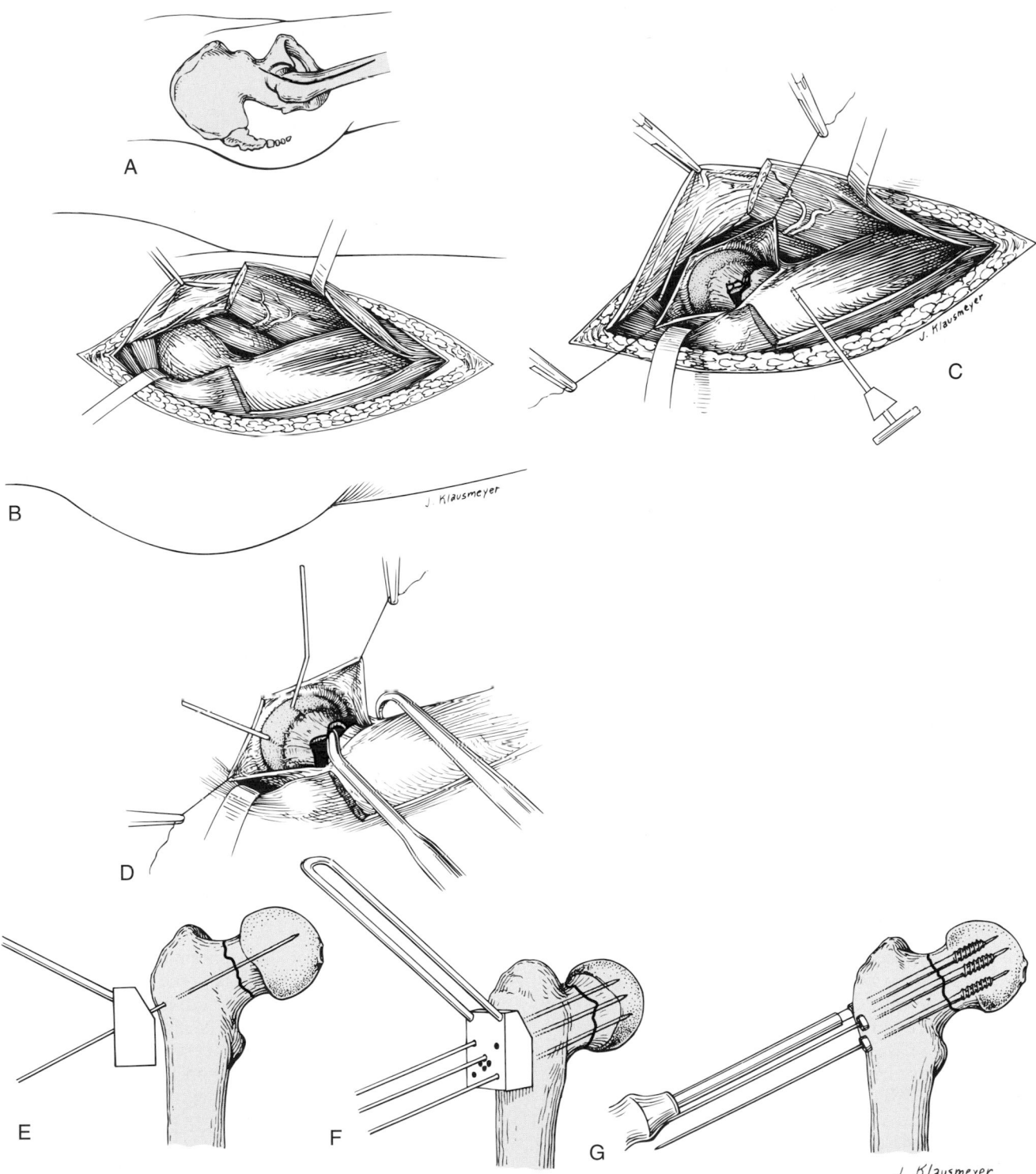

**FIGURE 48–18.** Open reduction of a femoral neck fracture. *A,* Watson-Jones skin incision. *B,* Blunt dissection to develop the interval between the tensor fasciae latae muscle and the abductors. The vastus lateralis is dissected from the intertrochanteric ridge. *C,* The capsule is divided in line with the femoral neck and transected off its insertion at the base of the femoral neck. Sutures function as retractors. *D,* A blunt, curved instrument can be inserted into the joint to lift the proximal femoral head fragment as the fracture is disimpacted by lateral traction applied either with a Schanz pin inserted distal to the planned starting location for a fixation device (*C*) or with a bone hook in the greater trochanter. *E,* A guide wire for a cannulated screw is inserted up the femoral neck across the fracture line under fluoroscopic control to stabilize the fracture. *F,* Additional wires are inserted in a parallel fashion with use of the drill guide, as in Figure 48–15. *G,* The screws are inserted one at a time; tapping may be necessary in dense bone. The fluoroscope is used to confirm that each screw is within the femoral head. Correct placement is confirmed by checking the anteroposterior and lateral views with the hip at both extremes of rotation.

patients with suboptimal bone density.[307] If appropriate for the selected implant system, a cannulated drill is then placed over each pin one at a time, and drilling is carried out to a depth of 8 to 10 mm short of the tip of the pin to keep the guide wire from coming out. In very dense bone, a tap may be required for the femoral head, but it is generally only necessary to tap the lateral cortex. The screws are then inserted sequentially and retightened after any traction that has been placed on the limb has been released. The guide wire should be removed after a screw has passed across the fracture to prevent advancement of the guide wire into the hip joint. Reinsertion of such a guide wire permits easy exchange of the screw if its length is inappropriate. Care should be exercised to avoid stripping the screw threads through osteopenic cancellous bone and also to avoid penetration into the joint space. When the bone is very dense, impaction of the fracture can be performed after the traction is released by applying mallet blows to a broad bone tamp placed on the lateral surface of the proximal end of the femur adjacent to the screws. After such impaction, the screws should be retightened in the hope of maintaining interfragmentary compression. Fracture reduction and implant location are confirmed with multiple-plane fluoroscopy and with permanent radiographs. After removal of the central guide wire and all screw guide wires, the wound is closed in layers over a drain with the hip capsule left open.

With the exception of fracture reduction, the essential considerations in internal fixation procedures for displaced femoral neck fractures are similar to those for internal fixation of undisplaced fractures as discussed previously. Urgent reduction and decompressive capsulotomy may be valuable in reducing the risk of avascular necrosis and are thus especially important in younger patients.[111, 435] Proper general preoperative assessment and patient preparation are also essential, particularly for older patients. Preoperative planning must include the possible need for prosthetic arthroplasty. In general, this decision should be made preoperatively because of the logistic problems posed by the different operating table, position, and surgical instruments and implants. Failure to gain satisfactory reduction by closed manipulation should be an indication for open reduction rather than arthroplasty. The details of fixation have been discussed previously.

Postoperative management is also similar to that for undisplaced injuries, but the potential for increased fracture instability raises additional concern about weight bearing after fixation of displaced femoral neck fractures. A limited weight-bearing regimen until fracture healing has progressed significantly (8 to 12 weeks) is preferable if the patient is able to cooperate. If the patient is unable to comply with limited weight-bearing ambulation, the surgeon must decide among restricting the patient to bed and chair activity, ambulation only under supervision, or acceptance of a greater or lesser amount of weight bearing. Various reports have indicated that weight bearing can be permitted for most patients after satisfactory reduction and fixation of femoral neck fractures.[83, 130] Furthermore, the forces applied to the hip during bedrest are essentially the same as those with protected ambulation[248] (Fig. 48–19).

Displaced fractures, especially in elderly patients, may heal more slowly than undisplaced fractures. This differ-ence in the length of time needed for healing must be appreciated if premature removal of symptomatic hardware is to be avoided.

## HEMIARTHROPLASTY

### Indications and Implant Choice

As noted previously, prosthetic replacement is selected for management of a femoral neck fracture when the patient has preexisting hip joint pathology, a medical condition that precludes fracture healing, or poor bone stock and is physiologically older with low functional demands. This consideration is based on an estimate of the patient's physiologic, not chronologic age. Prophylactic antibiotics are effective and indicated.[138]

Although prostheses eliminate concern about fixation failure, nonunion, and avascular necrosis, they also introduce problems related to prosthetic loosening, acetabular erosion, dislocation, infection, and the potential perioperative consequences of a more extensive surgical procedure. These difficulties were recognized by Moore, Thompson, and others soon after introduction of the first generation of well-accepted endoprostheses.[159, 210, 231, 335, 445] The most frequent problems were loosening and protrusion with late pain, primarily in younger and more active patients, who provided significant challenges to the durability of hip prostheses. Continuing efforts have led to improvements in prosthetic design and technique. Beginning in 1974, prostheses with internal ball-and-socket bearings were developed.[163, 170, 195, 295, 298, 312, 395] These prostheses consisted of a femoral component with a smaller head onto which was placed a plastic socket with a rounded external metal shell available in several graduated sizes to fit the acetabulum. The anticipated advantages of such so-called bipolar or bicentric devices were reduced frictional wear between the prosthesis and the acetabular articular cartilage, as well as possibly improved cushioning of weight-bearing forces by the plastic insert between the metal stem and cup.[363] Analysis of retrospective series has confirmed continued motion between the head components and decreased acetabular wear,[313] and prospective randomized trials have demonstrated functional advantages of the bipolar designs for patients aged 65 to 79 years.[123] One prospective analysis could not identify any improvement in functional outcome for patients receiving cemented modular unipolar versus segmented modular bipolar prostheses.[463] Because outcomes are similar with both types of prostheses and the cost of a bipolar head is usually much higher, a modular unipolar prosthesis is favored by many surgeons when hemiarthroplasty is chosen to treat a femoral neck fracture. Reaming of the acetabulum before insertion of the bipolar components has been suggested as a means of preserving greater in-bearing motion; however, this technique is not widely used.[121] It has also been claimed that the two articulating surfaces provide more resistance to postoperative dislocation than do other types of prostheses.

Improvements in bipolar implants have included the development of locking head components to increase stability and prevent dislocation of the prosthetic head from the femur.[206] Additionally, the head component has

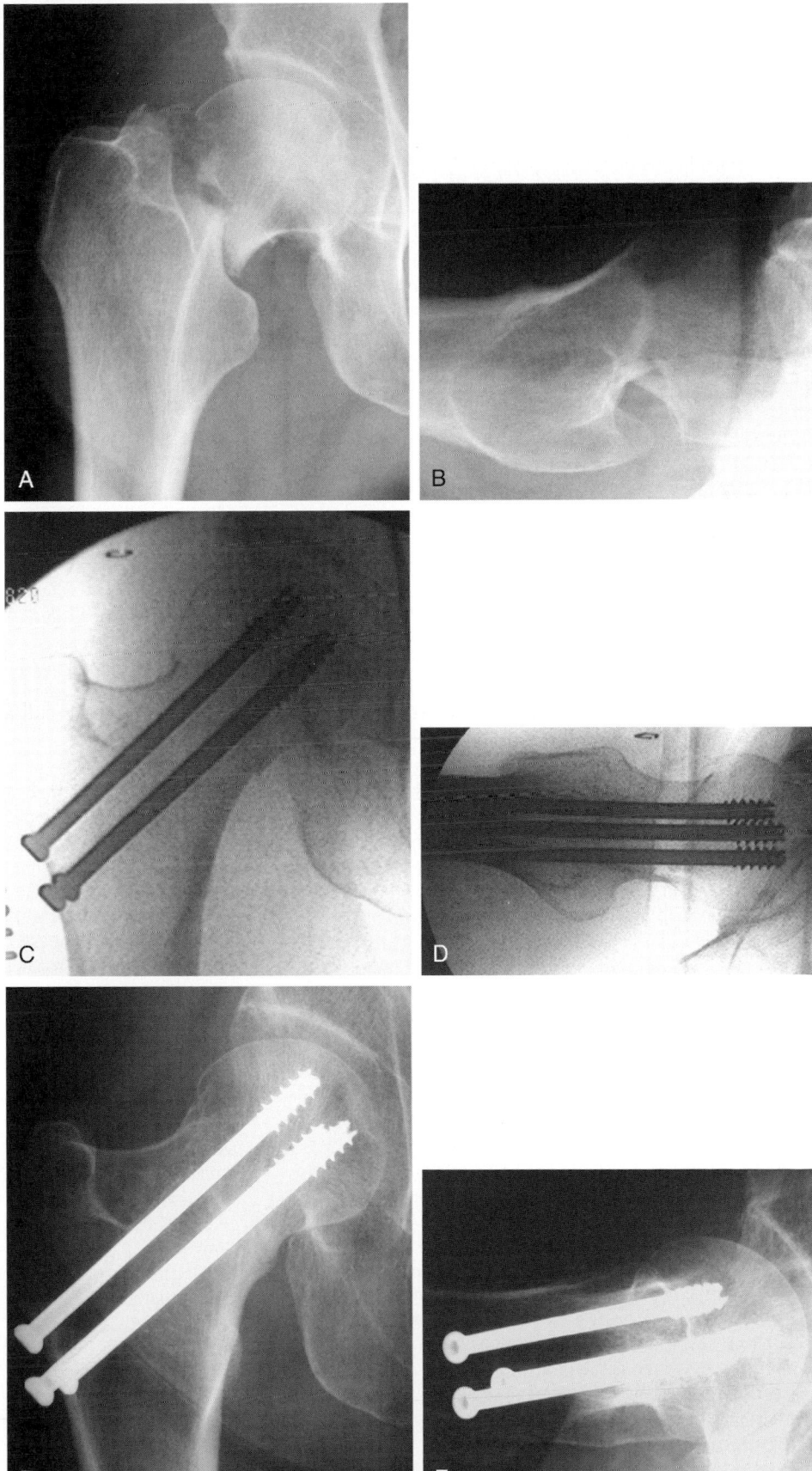

**FIGURE 48–19.** Closed reduction and internal fixation of a displaced femoral neck fracture. *A, B,* This 55-year-old woman slipped and fell in a parking lot and sustained the fracture illustrated by these anteroposterior (AP) and lateral views. *C, D,* Her injury was treated by urgent closed reduction, internal fixation, and capsulotomy. *E, F,* A year after her injury, AP and lateral radiographs show nearly anatomic fracture union with as yet no sign of avascular necrosis.

been modified so that its axis of rotation around the femoral implant is medial to the center of the external acetabular cup to provide better stability. This modification avoids an abduction moment, which tends to make the cup impinge on the medial side of the femoral neck, and instead tends to position the cup concentrically about the femoral implant's head. Hemiarthroplasty design has also benefited from the evolution of total-hip replacement. Changes have focused on improving the stability of the prosthesis in the proximal part of the femur. Three different modes of stem fixation have emerged: press fit, polymethyl methacrylate (PMMA) cement, and bony ingrowth. The Austin-Moore original endoprosthetic design incorporated a window in the stem in the hope that bone would fill it and provide an anchor to the proximal end of the femur. It was advocated that this window be filled with bone graft (from the femoral head) when the prosthesis was inserted. The first generation of femoral endoprostheses relied on interference fit between the stem and the medullary canal, which was enlarged by removal of cancellous bone to accommodate the chosen stem. Some osteoporotic individuals have such large medullary diameters, however, that a snug press fit cannot be achieved. With adoption of PMMA bone cement for fixation of total-hip prostheses, it soon became common to fix nonfenestrated endoprostheses in place with cement. This technique is of obvious value in maintaining satisfactory alignment of a prosthesis that does not fill the medullary canal. It has been documented to increase patient comfort and improve early results in controlled trials when the same prosthesis (Bateman) was used but without cement.[307] However, in active patients with unipolar prostheses, cementing has been associated with progressive acetabular wear, painful arthropathy, and protrusio acetabuli, all of which may require revision surgery.[362]

Recent femoral stem designs offer an evolving collection of prostheses that may be considered in the treatment of displaced femoral neck fractures in suitable individuals. Larger, anatomically shaped stems better match the medullary cavity and may improve on results achieved with early press-fit prostheses; in addition, they are better suited to cement fixation.

The third approach to implant fixation, in addition to press fit and PMMA cement, is fabrication of endoprosthetic femoral stems with a microporous surface. Bony ingrowth into the pores of such implants can provide secure fixation of a prosthesis without the use of PMMA cement. Given the known durability of cemented prostheses and their acknowledged success rate, it is hard to justify using a bony ingrowth prosthesis for a femoral neck fracture, except in the most unusual circumstances.[284, 307]

It is not known whether elderly, low-demand ambulators gain sufficient benefit to justify the use of modern modular press-fit femoral stems, which are often costly and require more complex femoral canal preparation than needed with the first-generation endoprostheses. Furthermore, it has not been proved that they are more successful than cemented implants in slightly younger, moderate-demand ambulators, who are the usual recipients of bipolar hemiarthroplasties for displaced femoral neck fractures.

An ever-changing array of modern hip prostheses have been developed and produced by a number of different manufacturers. The following design features have become well accepted:

1. A specific system of instruments provided to prepare the femoral canal to the size and shape of the prosthesis.
2. Modular components with Morse taper junctions that permit custom adjustment of prosthetic neck length and head size, thus reducing the inventory required to achieve optimal fit and also providing the possibility for later revision of a stable femoral component to a total-hip arthroplasty should acetabular problems occur after the hemiarthroplasty. Both unipolar and bipolar prosthetic femoral head components are available for many modern hemiarthroplasty systems.
3. Use of high-performance alloys with great strength and fatigue life.

In addition to improvements in prosthetic design, newer cementing techniques probably offer more durable fixation than that first achieved with PMMA, which was initially manually packed into the proximal part of the femur in a doughy consistency. Modern techniques of cement application include (1) preliminary canal shaping to a uniformly larger size than the stem, (2) thorough cleansing to remove blood and fat, (3) use of a distal plug to contain the cement, (4) injection and pressurization of semiliquid cement to fill bony interstices and increase fixation, (5) use of PMMA or other spacers to maintain uniform thickness of the cement mantle, and (6) improved mixing techniques to avoid air bubbles and lack of homogeneity. In summary, at present, two major categories of hemiarthroplasty can be considered for femoral neck fractures: first-generation implants such as the Austin-Moore and current-generation implants with femoral stems designed for cement fixation (or possibly press-fit insertion). Although many authors have reported superior results with bipolar designs than with unipolar historical prostheses, such superiority has not been proved conclusively.[108, 127, 195, 298] Even with the improved stem design and newer cementing techniques, radiolucent lines around the cement mantle have been reported in up to 80% of cases. Long-term follow-up information is lacking. Most dislocations of bipolar prostheses, though less frequent than with unipolar designs, have to be treated by open reduction because of the inner and outer components.[170] Revision to total-hip arthroplasty has not been as easy as anticipated.[179]

Despite these uncertainties, the recommendation at this time is for cemented bipolar prosthetic replacement for displaced femoral neck fractures in elderly, but moderately active patients.[123, 127] For younger patients in whom symptomatic avascular necrosis develops, many surgeons would consider modern uncemented stem designs in anticipation of better long-term function. For debilitated elderly patients with limited activity and life expectancy, a unipolar implant should be considered. The physician should be aware of the higher reported difficulty with revision of older stem designs.[179] The use of cement has not been associated with higher mortality or complication rates.[302]

Finally, it must be noted that some authors are now recommending total hip replacement for selected active older patients with displaced femoral neck fractures and preexisting hip disorders, such as significant osteoarthritis, rheumatoid arthritis, and Paget's disease.[112, 162, 405, 406, 461] In such patients, hemiarthroplasty is less likely to provide a satisfactory result. Long-term outcome and more detailed indications for total-hip replacement as primary treatment of femoral neck fractures remain areas for further study.[340] This topic is discussed further in Chapter 61.

### Surgical Approach

Hemiarthroplasty for a femoral neck fracture can be performed through any of a variety of posterior or anterior surgical approaches. In anterior approaches, including the so-called direct lateral approach, an anterior capsulotomy is performed, and the proximal part of the femur is delivered through the capsulotomy by externally rotating the thigh, which may be done with the hip extended or flexed. In posterior approaches, flexion and internal rotation are used to expose the proximal end of the femur through a posterior capsulotomy. The surgeon's previous experience appears to be the most common reason for choosing one approach over the other. However, some have reported lower rates of serious complications after anterior approaches for prosthetic replacement,[132, 313] possibly because such approaches spare the posterior capsule so that the hip is more stable postoperatively in the flexed, sitting position, thus diminishing the chance of dislocation.

The posterolateral modified Gibson approach, for which the patient is placed in the lateral decubitus position, is illustrated in Figure 48–20. The important elements of this approach include (1) a lateral skin incision, the proximal portion of which may be directed somewhat posteriorly; (2) longitudinal, lateral division of the fascia lata beginning distally and extending proximally posterior to the tensor fasciae latae; (3) deepening of the proximal part of the wound by splitting the muscle fibers of the gluteus maximus; (4) going posterior to the gluteus medius and dividing the tendons of the short external rotators; (5) performing a T-shaped posterior hip capsulotomy; and (6) delivering the distal fragment through the capsulotomy by flexing and internally rotating the thigh. After completion of the procedure, the posterior capsulotomy is repaired with stout sutures. This technique may not be a significant preventive measure against posterior dislocation because of the tenuous reattachment of the capsule to the femur.

As mentioned previously, anterior approaches leave the capsule intact posteriorly. Examples are the approach of Smith-Petersen through the interval between the sartorius and the tensor fasciae latae (Fig. 48–21); that of Watson-Jones between the tensor and the gluteus medius (see Fig. 48–13); and the "direct lateral" approach of Hardinge, which proximally passes between the anterior and posterior halves of the gluteus medius (Fig. 48–22). In each of these approaches, an anterior capsulotomy provides access to the hip for removal of the femoral head and insertion of the prosthesis. Each can be done with the patient supine. Burwell and Scott modified Watson-Jones's technique by

placing the patient on the side, angling the proximal part of the skin incision posteriorly to improve access to the proximal end of the femur through the wound, and delivering it through the anterior capsulotomy by externally rotating the flexed hip and knee, with good muscle relaxation. The direct lateral approach is also well suited to the lateral decubitus position; in this approach, an anteriorly placed sterile envelope receives the leg when the knee is flexed to a right angle and the moderately flexed hip is externally rotated. Familiarity with the chosen approach greatly facilitates positioning, placement of retractors, and minor variations in the extent and location of dissection, all of which aid in gaining atraumatic exposure.

### Procedure

**Indications and Contraindications.** As discussed earlier, hemiarthroplasty is recommended for ambulatory (generally elderly) individuals who because of osteopenia or preexisting hip disease may have problems with internal fixation.

**Timing of Surgery.** In the case of prosthetic replacement, surgery should be performed within 24 to 48 hours of admission whenever possible. Such timing should allow for medical clearance and optimization of hydration, cardiorespiratory status, and electrolyte and hematologic balance.

**Preoperative Planning.** High-quality radiographs, perhaps with a magnification marker, should be available for every patient undergoing prosthetic replacement. Templates for the chosen stem system should be matched to the radiograph to guide in selecting stem, neck, and outer bearing size. Preoperative selection of implant type and size is essential for current-generation systems, whose femoral stems are designed to fit within close tolerance. With first-generation implants, radiographic templates are not usually available, and they have only one stem size. It is still valuable to preoperatively determine whether problems will arise with the femoral anatomy or fracture level, either of which might require a different choice of implant. A blood sample should be obtained and typed and crossmatched for 2 U of blood. A perioperative antibiotic should be chosen and made available for administration when anesthesia is induced.[138]

**Anesthesia and Positioning.** The patient is positioned laterally with the pelvis perpendicular to the floor and held there with an inflatable beanbag, kidney rests, or hip positioner. Alternatively, with anterior approaches the surgeon may choose a supine position with the affected buttock just over the edge of the table to allow the soft tissues to hang posteriorly. The hindquarter and leg are draped free. Spinal and general anesthesia are equally appropriate.

### Surgical Technique

**First-Generation Endoprostheses.** Insertion of a first-generation Austin-Moore endoprosthesis is depicted in Figure 48–23. In this example, a posterolateral incision is illustrated. After splitting the fascia lata and gluteus maximus, the external rotators are tagged and divided. A T-shaped incision is made in the hip capsule in line with the femoral neck and across its base and retracted with

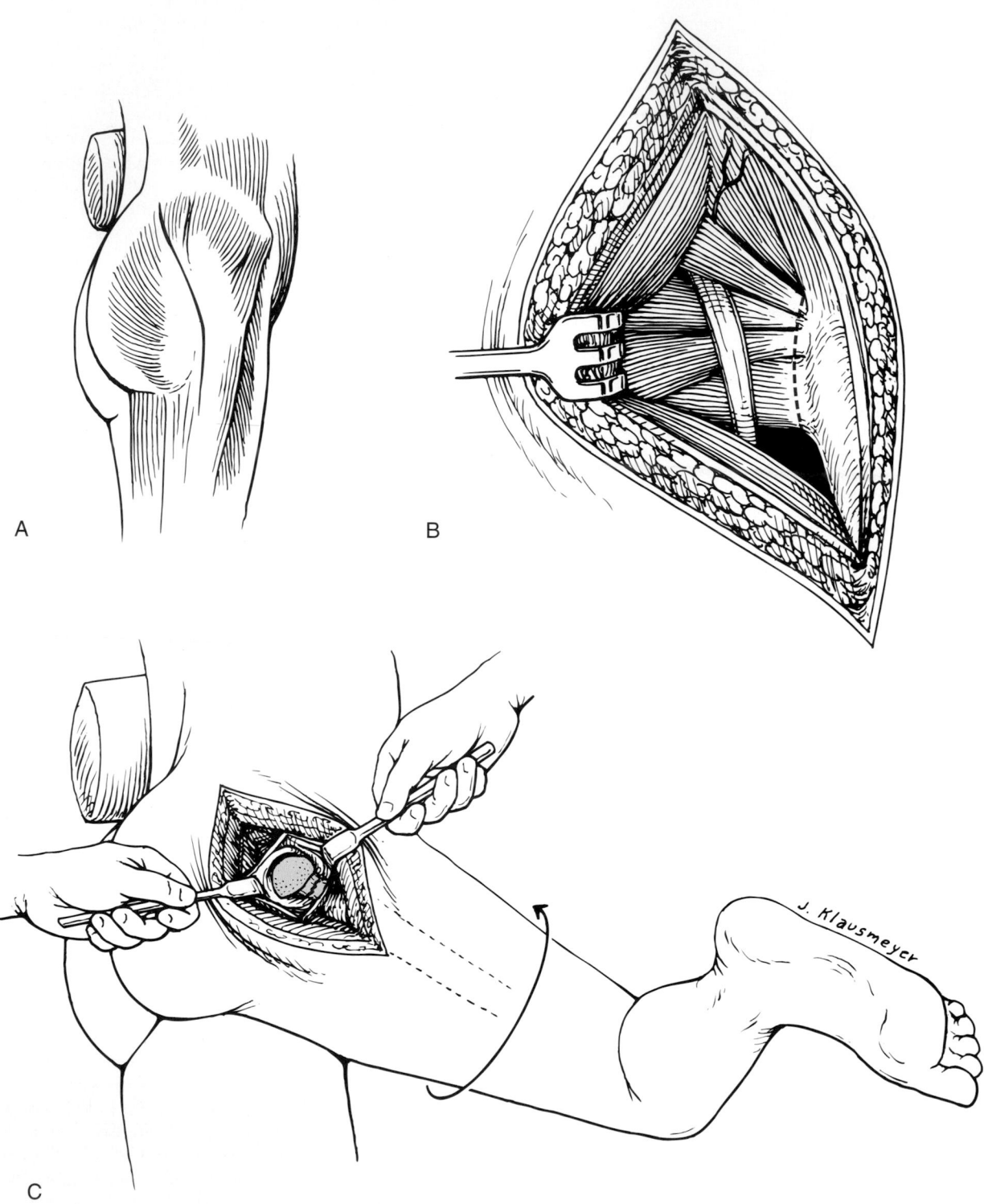

**FIGURE 48–20.** Posterolateral (Kocher-Gibson) approach to the hip. The frequently chosen posterolateral approach to the hip has been modified by so many authors that eponyms poorly denote the exact procedure. *A,* The lateral decubitus position is used. Typical skin and fascial incisions are made over the proximal end of the femur for 15 cm to the tip of the greater trochanter and then angled slightly posteriorly toward the posterior superior iliac spine for another 10 cm. The fascial incision is made first through the fascia lata directly over the proximal femoral shaft. The thinnest part of the superficial muscular cover is palpated between the index finger (inserted proximally through the fasciotomy) and the thumb (placed outside the fascia). Such palpation locates a spot anterior to the bulk of the gluteus maximus and posterior to the tensor fasciae latae. The overlying fascia is incised, and the muscle fibers are spread bluntly while watching for crossing vessels that may need to be divided and coagulated. *B,* The gluteal bursa is reflected posteriorly or excised to reveal the trochanteric attachments of the short external rotators. The sciatic nerve is illustrated here but is not usually exposed at surgery. Note that the piriformis is typically superficial to the nerve, so only the more distal muscles protect it when it is reflected posteriorly. *C,* The hip capsule is exposed by reflecting the short external rotators; for hemiarthroplasty, it is usually incised in a manner suitable for subsequent closure. The proximal end of the femur is delivered through the capsulotomy by flexing, adducting, and internally rotating the hip. Closure involves capsular repair, reattachment of the short rotators, and suture of the fascia and skin. Suction drains are optional.

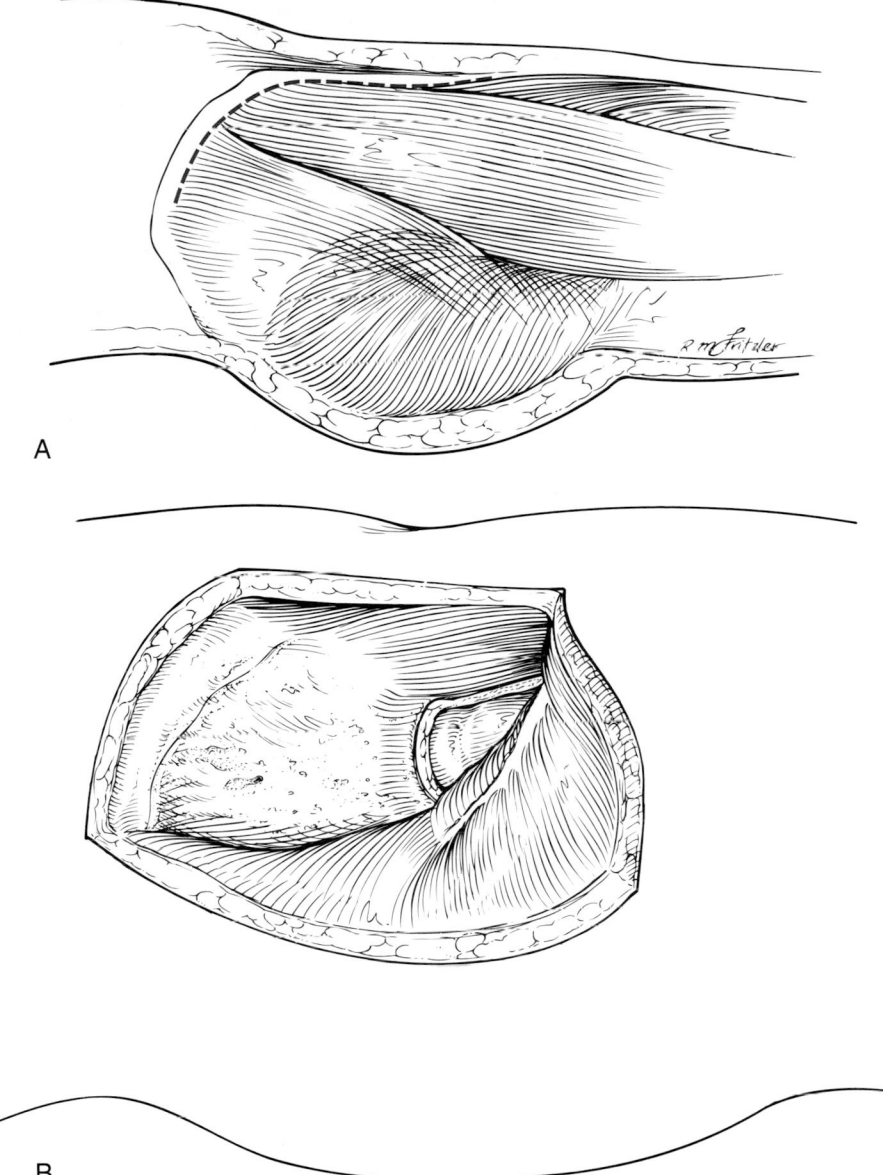

**FIGURE 48–21.** Anterior (Smith-Petersen) approach to the hip. This approach uses the interval between the sartorius and the tensor fasciae latae. *A,* The patient is supine. This skin incision overlies that in the fascia and follows the iliac crest from its highest point to the anterior superior spine and then directly distal approximately 15 cm. *B,* The abductors are released and reflected as shown from the lateral surface of the ilium, but only as much as necessary to minimize the risk of heterotopic bone formation. The anterior edge of the tensor fasciae latae is followed distally. Branches of the lateral femoral circumflex artery crossing the interval between the tensor and the sartorius must be identified and controlled. The capsule is incised longitudinally and released along its acetabular margin, with sparing of the labrum, to permit retraction and visualization of the hip joint. Closure involves repair of the capsulotomy, reattachment of the abductors to the iliac crest, and closure of the anterior fascia. Suction drains are used.

sutures. The labrum must be preserved. The femoral head is removed intact if possible with a "corkscrew," and its outside diameter is measured as a guide in choosing the properly sized prosthesis. The femoral neck is delivered with a bone hook, cleared of soft tissue, and inspected. Sufficient neck length (at least 0.5 inch) is required for an Austin-Moore prosthesis. If the fracture is lower, another implant (e.g., Thompson) may provide a better fit. With the prosthesis as a guide, the neck is tailored appropriately with rongeurs or a power saw to fit the flange of the prosthesis and to support it with an appropriate degree of anteversion. After any necessary neck osteotomy, access to the acetabulum is easier, and it can be inspected for degenerative changes. The ligamentum teres, if especially large, can be resected, and a trial or definitive prosthesis can be checked for fit. The head size should be neither too loose nor too tight. Its fit in the acetabulum, rather than suction produced by the labrum, should be assessed. Next, a box chisel is used to start the medullary

preparation by excising adequate bone extending from the medial neck (calcar) into the substance of the greater trochanter. An awl or straight curette inserted in line with the femoral shaft aids in entering the diaphyseal medullary canal. The appropriate broach or rasp is used to enlarge the canal. Its rotational alignment will determine the ultimate anteversion of the prosthesis. It should be directed 10° to 15° anteriorly relative to the plane in which the axis of the knee joint lies. By using the rasp, curettes, and other tools as needed, enough medullary bone is removed to allow the prosthesis to be inserted with a snug, but not overly tight press fit. The prosthesis should not be forced into the femur, which can be fractured by such a maneuver. Once the flange of the prosthesis is seated on the calcar, the implant's position, including version, and stability are checked and the prosthetic femoral head carefully and gently inserted into the acetabulum. Forcing the head in or out of the acetabulum, especially using the femur as a lever, may

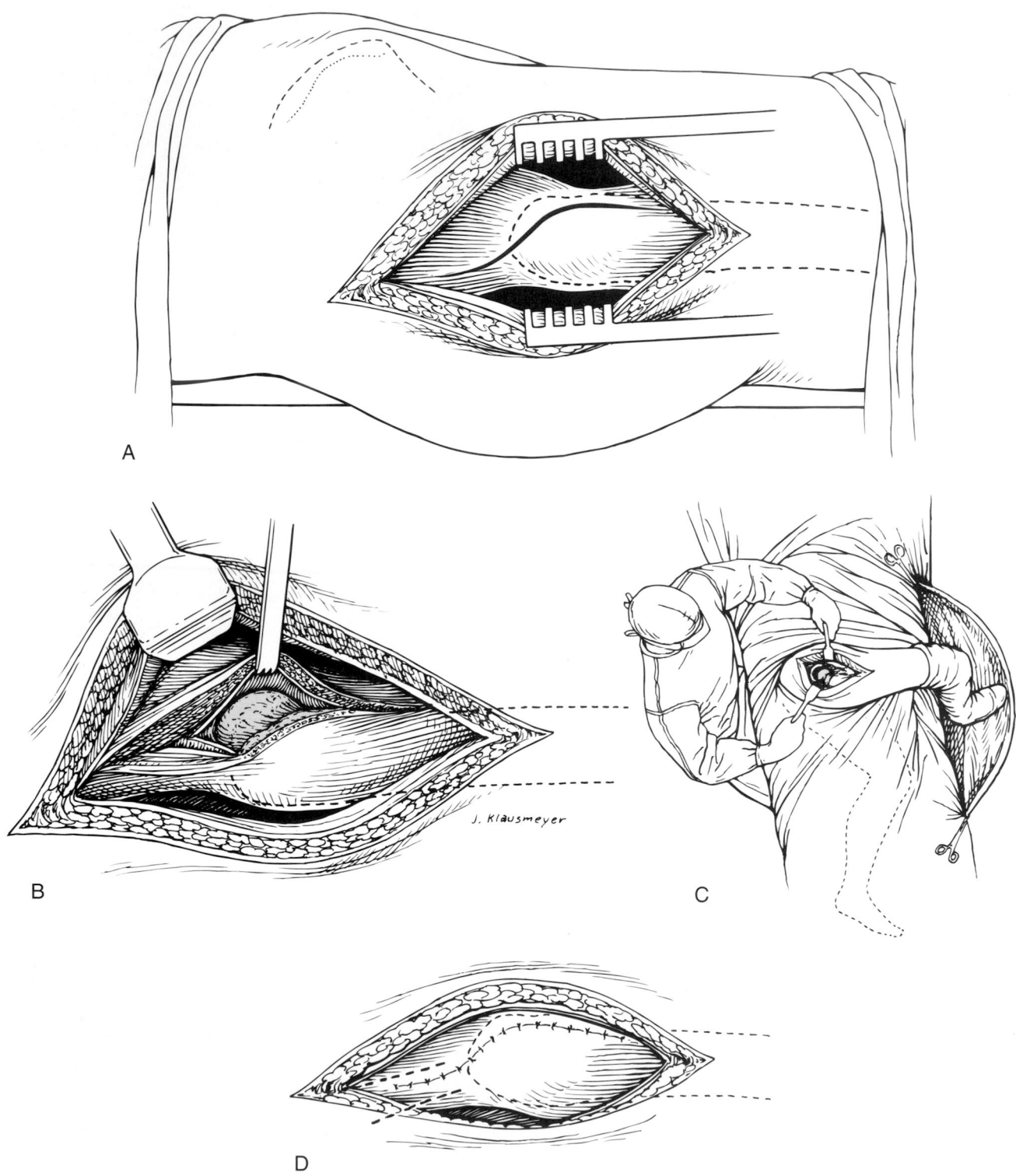

J. Klausmeyer

**Figure 48–22.**  Direct lateral (Hardinge) approach to the hip. This approach gains access to the anterior hip capsule through a longitudinal incision along the anterior edge of the greater trochanter that releases the anterior bulk of the gluteus medius in continuity with the vastus lateralis fascia. *A,* A straight lateral skin incision is deepened through the fascia lata and extended proximally to split the anterior fibers of the gluteus maximus. The incision in the gluteus medius, through tendon anterior and just proximal to the greater trochanter, is shown. Its proximal extent is limited by the superior gluteal neurovascular structures. *B,* The incision is deepened, and with retraction an anterior capsulotomy is performed. *C,* The proximal end of the femur is delivered by externally rotating the flexed, adducted hip. *D,* The abductor repair is effected by closure of the tenotomy, including direct reattachment to the trochanter if soft tissues are tenuous. Stout nonabsorbable sutures are used.

fracture the proximal femoral shaft. Little force is needed to produce such a fracture in an osteopenic elderly patient. If a fenestrated prosthesis such as the Austin-Moore is used, the holes in the stem may be filled with bone to aid in maintaining fixation. Stability and range of motion are documented. One must confirm that full extension is possible, flexion is at least 90°, and the joint has no tendency to dislocate in the functional positions of rotation and adduction. Length should be adequate to maintain tension on the soft tissues that cross the hip. Preexisting contractures may benefit from release of the iliopsoas or adductor tendons. The capsule is repaired, the external rotators are reattached, and the wound is closed in layers. Suction drains may be used if desired (Figs. 48–23 and 48–24).

**Current-Generation Endoprostheses.** Insertion of a modern modular prosthesis is shown in Figure 48–25. Because implants and instrumentation systems continue to evolve, reference must be made to the appropriate product literature, and the surgeon should have hands-on familiarity with the chosen system before using it clinically. A direct lateral approach is illustrated with the patient in the lateral decubitus position (see also Fig. 48–22). After anterior capsulotomy, the femoral head is removed with a corkscrew extractor and its diameter is measured. An osteotomy of the femoral neck is performed with the aid of

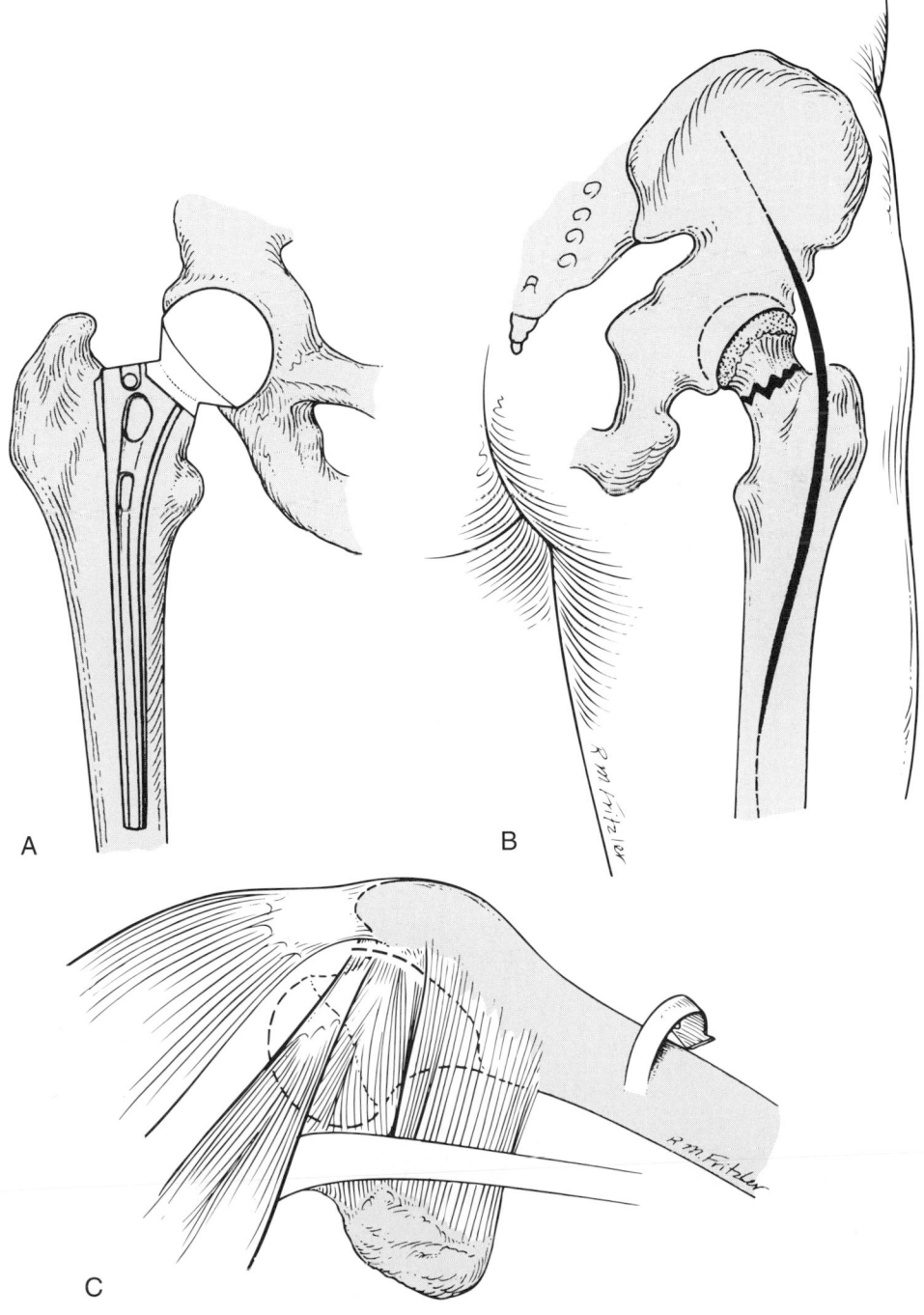

**FIGURE 48–23.** Insertion of an Austin-Moore prosthesis from a posterolateral approach. *A,* The prosthesis in place. *B,* Skin incision for the posterolateral approach. The patient is in the lateral decubitus position with the affected side up and the leg draped free. This procedure can also be done with other suitable hip incisions, depending on the surgeon's preference (see text). The fascia lata is divided in line with the skin, and the incision is extended proximally through the gluteus maximus, the fibers of which must be spread bluntly. The inferior gluteal neurovascular bundle defines the proximal extent of the split. *C,* The gluteal bursa is reflected or excised, and the short external rotators are released from the greater trochanter and reflected posteriorly to protect the sciatic nerve, which usually lies ventral to the piriformis and dorsal to the more distal rotators. This maneuver is aided by internal rotation of the thigh while being careful to not injure the osteopenic limb.

*Illustration continued on following page*

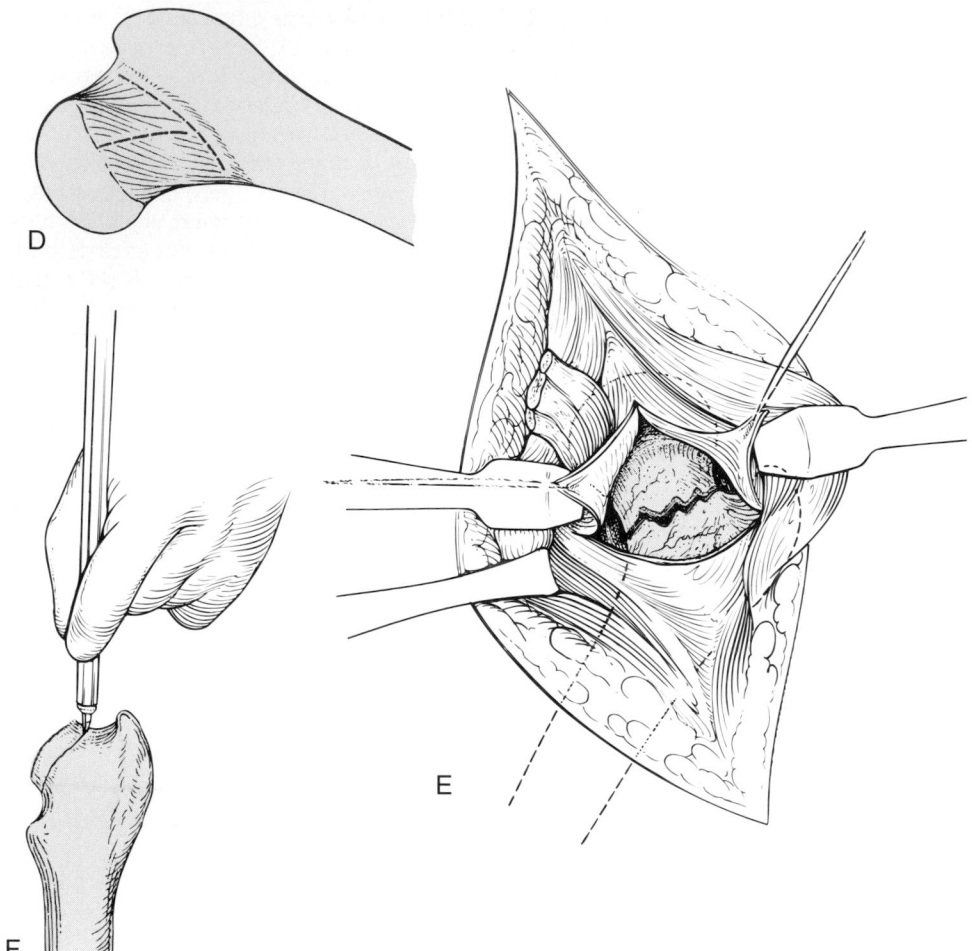

**FIGURE 48–23** *Continued.* *D, E,* The posterior hip capsule, thus exposed, is incised in a manner suitable for later repair. Such exposure reveals the fractured femoral neck. *F,* The femoral neck is then delivered into the wound by internal rotation of the thigh with the knee flexed. It is marked and osteotomized (most easily with a power saw) about 1.0 to 1.5 cm proximal to the lesser trochanter's flare, on a line suitable for the flange of the prosthesis, and positioned with its stem down the femoral canal. The plane of the osteotomy should be inclined anteriorly, or anteverted, so that the flange of the prosthesis receives bony support in this position.

the appropriate guide. A box chisel and tapered Charnley awl are used to begin preparation of the femoral canal. Depending on the system used and the size of the proximal end of the femur, reaming of the medullary canal may be required. A rasp or broach of a size chosen according to preoperative radiographs and templates is used to complete preparation of the canal. Care is taken to avoid fracturing the proximal part of the femur during insertion of the rasp with a mallet. For a press-fit application, the rasp should be essentially the same size as the implant stem and should fit snugly within the femur. Its alignment and rotational stability must be confirmed. In some systems, the rasp handle is removable and the rasp doubles as a trial prosthesis, with proximal attachments of varying lengths and diameters. Such a rasp may also be provided with an attachment for final planing of the femoral neck osteotomy to gain optimal contact with the flange of the prosthesis. In any event, an effort should be made to ensure appropriate contact between the calcar and the flange of the prosthesis.

Once the bone is prepared, the trial rasp combination or a separate trial prosthesis is used to check neck length and stem alignment, as well as fit into the acetabulum. Range of motion, stability, and length are assessed. If the fit is satisfactory, the definitive prosthesis is inserted directly into the femur, if press fit, or with cement if this option is

selected. Although the relative indications for press-fit versus cemented endoprostheses for femoral neck fractures remain debatable, if a stable press fit cannot be achieved, the use of cement is advisable. The prosthetic stem is inserted after or before the chosen head-neck component is driven onto its Morse taper. The appropriate-diameter femoral head component is applied over the neck component, and the hip is reduced after lavaging the acetabulum to remove any debris.

**Cement Insertion.** A solid rather than fenestrated stem should be used with cement. Some prostheses are provided with obturators that effectively convert a windowed stem to a solid one. Modern cement application techniques have been developed in an effort to decrease the risk of mechanical loosening of the cement–bone interface. The manufacturer's recommendations should be reviewed and followed for a given cement and cement insertion system. General principles include (1) preparation of the canal to a uniformly larger size than the prosthetic stem to accommodate the cement mantle; (2) insertion of a canal plug several centimeters distal to the intended location of the stem tip; (3) cleansing and drying the medullary canal with a pulsating lavage system, a bone brush, and dry sponges; (4) preparation of the cement in ways that avoid bubbles and other discontinuities; and (5) pressurized application of semiliquid, viscous cement and filling the canal with a syringe from the bottom up so that the cement mantle interdigitates with the porous structure of residual cancellous bone and completely fills the canal. When compared with earlier techniques using doughy cement, a larger volume of PMMA is often needed, and insertion of the prosthesis is more difficult and requires final impaction with a mallet and inserter. During insertion of the prosthesis, it is important that access to the proximal end of the femur be free and adequate so that appropriate alignment can be achieved and evaluated before the cement has hardened. Cement extruded around the prosthesis is removed with a curette. A small sponge in the acetabulum helps collect the extra cement. After the cement has set, all excess PMMA, both free fragments and overhanging pieces that might fracture later, must be removed to avoid potential loose bodies that might cause acetabular erosion. The head-neck assembly is then placed on the Morse taper and the outer bearing snapped on. The hip is reduced after irrigating and recovering any fragments. Motion and stability are confirmed, and if satisfactory, the wound is closed, over suction drains if desired. Secure repair of the capsulotomy helps decrease the risk of early dislocation. Reattachment of the gluteus medius tendon, which was released from the femur anteriorly in

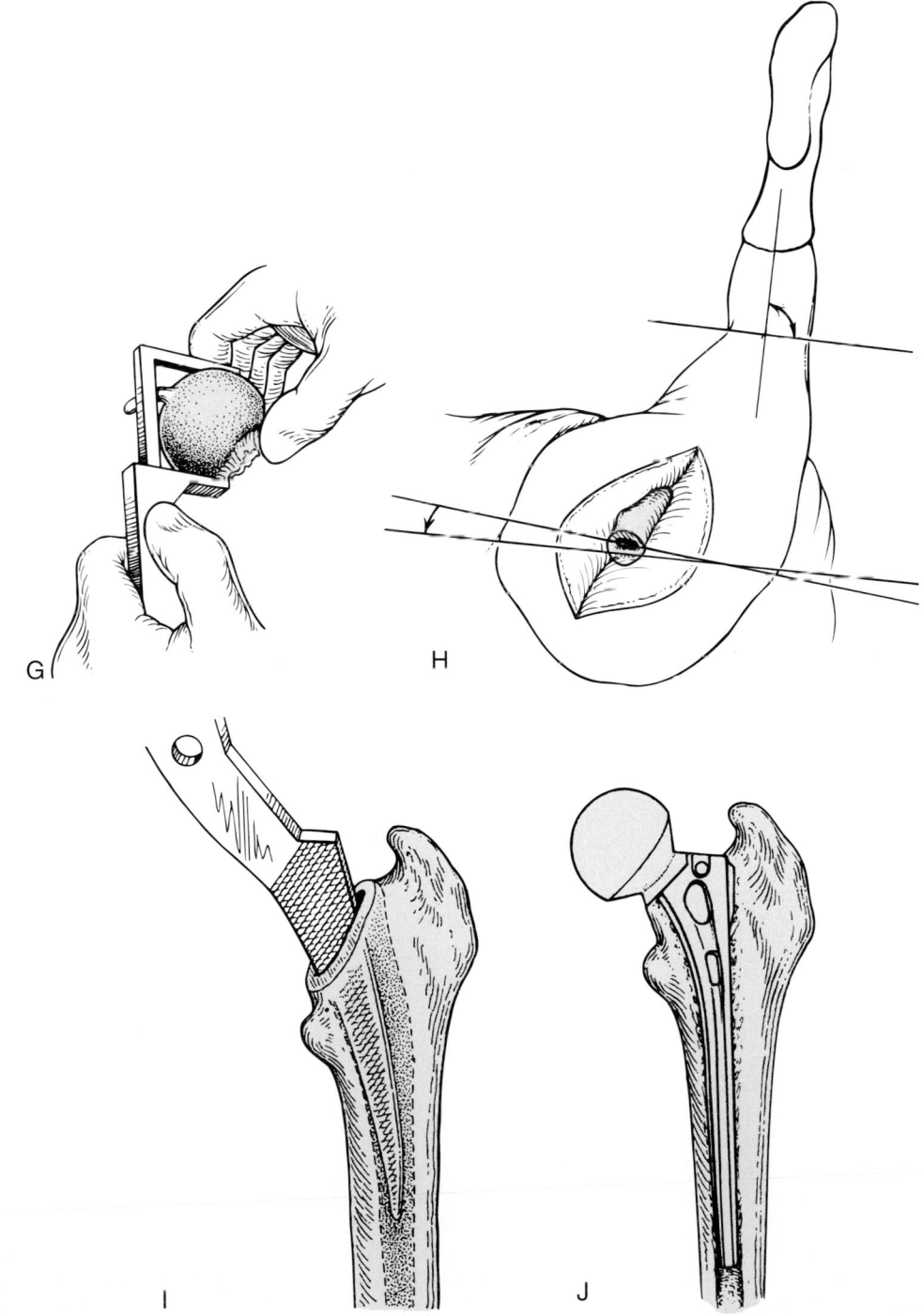

**FIGURE 48–23** *Continued. G,* Shortening of the neck provides more room for removal of the femoral head fragment from the acetabulum with a "corkscrew." It may be necessary to transect the ligamentum teres. The head diameter must then be measured to choose the size of the prosthesis. *H,* The femur is held internally rotated with a retractor under the base of the neck, and the medullary canal of the proximal femoral shaft is entered with an awl or straight curette. Next, a box chisel and Austin-Moore rasp are used to prepare the medullary canal. The flexed leg can be used to guide rotational alignment of these instruments so that version remains appropriate (10° to 15° anteverted). The prosthetic stem is placed centrally in the medullary canal. Gentleness is required to avoid damaging the proximal end of the femur, especially if the osteoporosis is profound. *I,* The entry site is centralized by ensuring that the rasp works adequately against the medial border of the greater trochanter. *J,* If desired, the fenestrations of the prosthetic stem are filled with morcellized cancellous graft prepared from the patient's femoral head, and the prosthesis is securely impacted into the proximal part of the femur. Its rotational stability as well as alignment must be assessed. Problems with either may require further tailoring of the proximal end of the femur or the use of bone cement or another prosthesis. The prosthetic head is gently guided into the acetabulum while the capsule is retracted and after all debris has been irrigated and removed with suction. Range of motion and stability are assessed, and if satisfactory, the capsule is closed, the short rotators are reattached to the base of the trochanter if desired, and the deep fascia, subcutaneous tissue, and skin are closed, with suction drains left posteriorly in the region of the hip capsule.

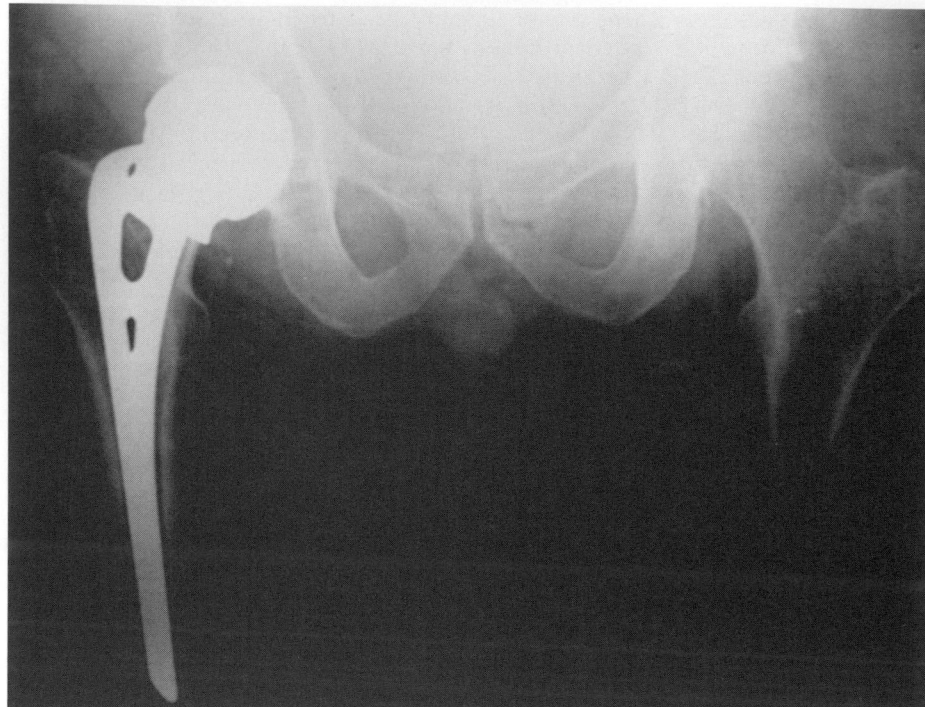

**FIGURE 48–24.** Anteroposterior radiograph of an Austin-Moore unipolar femoral head and neck prosthesis inserted for a displaced femoral neck fracture in an elderly patient with limited ambulation outside the home.

the direct lateral approach, should be secure enough to permit immediate mobilization of the patient (Fig. 48–26).

### Intraoperative Complications

**Femoral Shaft Fracture.** Femoral shaft fracture is avoided by obtaining a well-lateralized starting point for broaching the femur, by correctly estimating the size of the stem, and by being cautious with broaching, component insertion, and relocation-dislocation maneuvers. If a shaft fracture occurs, it should be treated by cerclage wire or cable fixation if it is the usual longitudinal pattern. If it occurs before cementing, a longer stem should be considered in addition to cerclage wiring.

**Incorrect Sizing of the Outer Bearing.** Incorrect sizing may lead to acetabular erosion but can be prevented by careful preoperative and intraoperative measurement. Most authorities agree that it is better for long-term hip function for the bearing to be 1 mm larger rather than 1 mm smaller than the measured size.

**Poor Implant Position.** Errors in insertion can result in a malaligned femoral prosthesis. Often, such malalignment occurs because of inappropriate version (malrotation about the long axis of the femur). Most prostheses are designed to be anteverted 10° to 20° relative to the coronal plane of the femur. Insertion in a varus position with a femoral neck cut that is too proximal or too distal will result in a higher failure rate.[364] Penetration of the femoral cortex may also occur with extreme malposition of the stem. Attention to prosthetic alignment during preparation of the femur, trial insertion, and definitive prosthesis insertion should identify such problems. When any question arises, intraoperative radiographs are recommended. Inappropriate prosthetic alignment usually requires removal and reinsertion of the device, often with cement if it was not initially used.

### Aftercare

Intraoperative assessment of stability helps in selecting any restrictions that may be advisable to prevent dislocation. After a posterior approach, flexion greater than 70°, particularly with adduction, should be avoided for 6 weeks. Low chairs and toilets must be avoided, as well as crossing the legs. The patient may sit in an elevated chair. An abduction pillow, Buck's traction, a knee immobilizer that blocks hip flexion by preventing knee flexion, and pillow suspension have all been advocated for postoperative management. If stability is adequate, no external support is required. It is essential to protect the patient's heel from pressure on the bed by supporting the weight of the leg with a pillow under the calf. After an anterior approach, hip stability in flexion is less of a concern, and mobilization may be facilitated. Such a patient should, however, be cautioned against abducting and externally rotating the extended hip during the first few weeks. It has recently been shown that the rate of complications, as well as the length of stay, is related to the annual volume for individual surgeons.[299]

Beginning on the second postoperative day, progressive weight bearing as tolerated is encouraged with the help of the physical therapy team. Prophylactic anticoagulation is generally indicated until the patient resumes more normal activity. Intermittent venous compression devices and elastic stockings are frequently added.

### TOTAL-HIP ARTHROPLASTY

As previously noted, because of acetabular erosion, some surgeons are recommending total-hip arthroplasty for acute femoral neck fractures,[118] and the functional results may be most predictable with this treatment.[204, 313] The dislocation rate is higher in such cases than when the arthroplasty is done for some form of arthritis because the native hip, before the fracture, had a normal range of motion.[162, 313, 405, 406] Certainly, when the femoral neck fracture occurs in the setting of previous hip disease, rheumatoid arthritis, osteoarthritis, or Paget's disease, total-hip arthroplasty is indicated. For the vast majority of patients receiving a total-hip replacement for a femoral neck fracture, it is best to use a cemented stem technique

because of its demonstrated long-term results. Total-hip arthroplasty is best reserved for the healthiest group of patients with the greatest possibility for claiming the benefits of the prosthesis.[204] Many surgeons recommend an uncemented acetabular component because of its improved fixation. For details regarding the surgical technique for total-hip arthroplasty, the reader is referred to standard texts.[111, 122, 336, 387, 422]

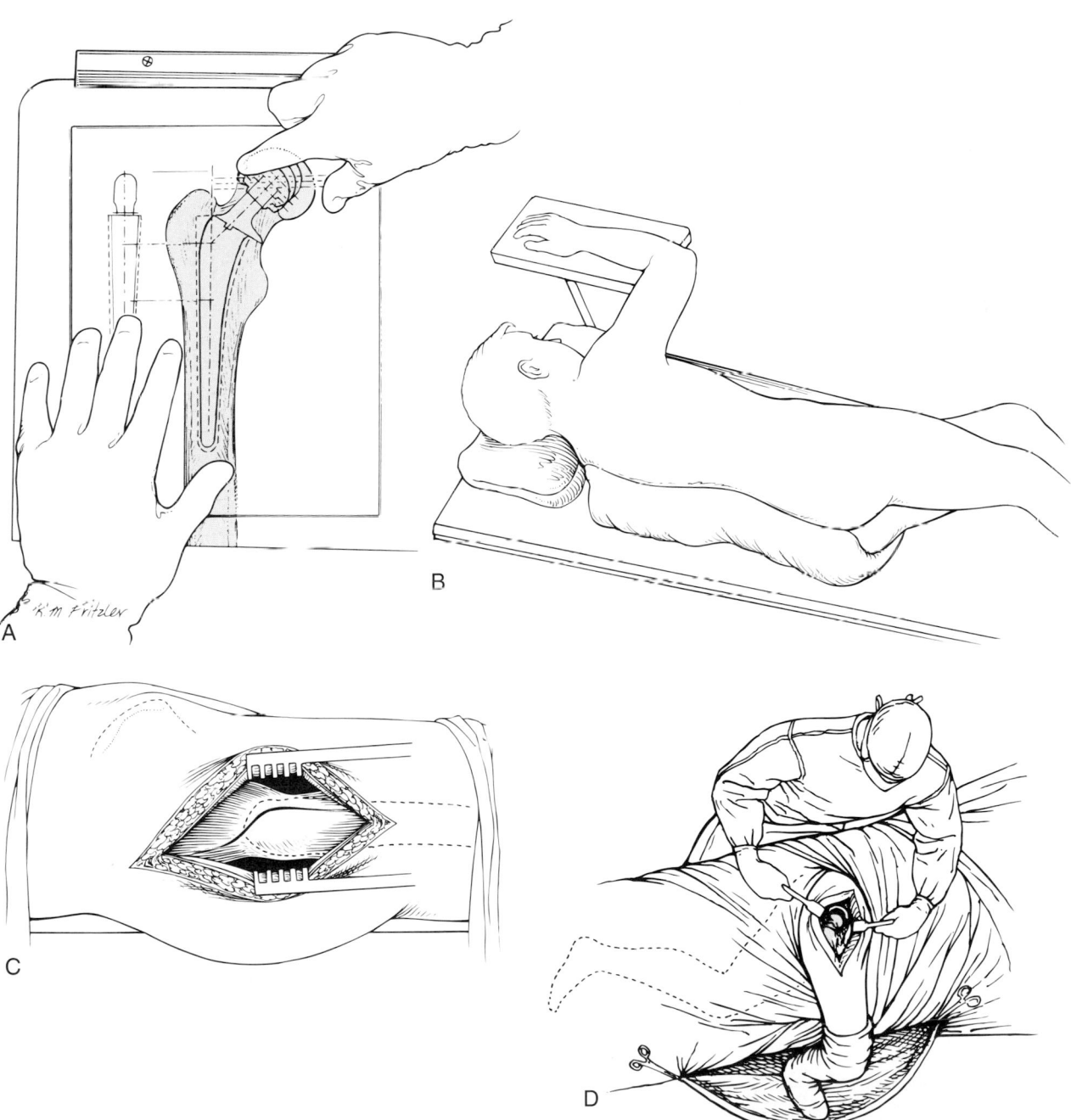

**FIGURE 48–25.** Insertion of a modular prosthesis through a direct lateral approach with cement fixation. *A,* Preoperative planning using radiographs and outline drawings of proposed implants allows a provisional choice of the prosthesis, stem size, and neck length, as well as the appropriate site and orientation of the femoral neck osteotomy. Availability of the necessary implants and instruments is thus confirmed before surgery. *B,* The patient is placed in the lateral decubitus position. The affected limb is prepared and draped free. *C,* The skin incision is made as shown. Details of the incision are presented in Figure 48–22. *D,* Anterior dislocation in external rotation permits ready access to the proximal end of the femur, the rotational orientation of which is demonstrated by the flexed knee with the leg perpendicular to the frontal plane.

*Illustration continued on following page*

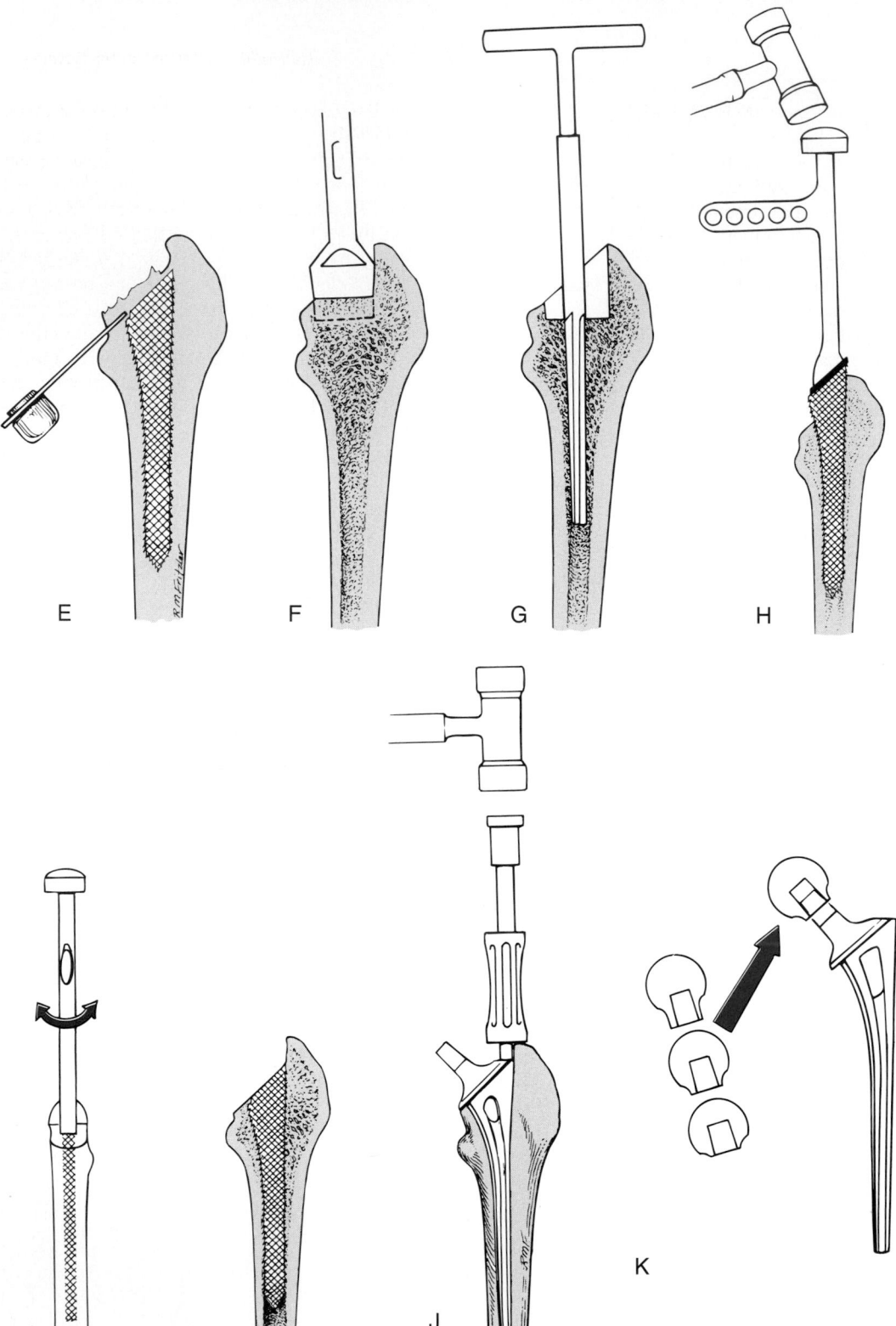

**FIGURE 48–25** *Continued.* *E,* The rasp or trial prosthesis is used to orient the femoral neck osteotomy at the level determined by preoperative planning. The plane of the osteotomy should be anteverted 10° to 15° from the plane of the knee axis. The femoral head is removed and its diameter measured to estimate the appropriate size for the prosthetic head. A trial head is selected and attached to its handle. It should fit the acetabulum closely, turn freely, but not permit "sloppy" sideways mobility. *F, G,* The femoral canal is opened with a box chisel centered over the axis of the femoral shaft. This step requires encroaching on the medial wall of the greater trochanter. Additionally, anteversion should be appropriately adjusted. The canal is defined and deepened with a straight awl. *H,* The handle is attached to a rasp of appropriate size for the prosthesis chosen preoperatively. The rasp is inserted into the medullary canal while maintaining 10° to 15° anteversion and proceeding slowly and cautiously to not fracture the proximal end of the femur. If the rasp is too large, a smaller one should be selected. If it is too loose, a larger size and a correspondingly larger prosthesis will be needed to obtain a secure fit. Advancing and withdrawing the rasp intermittently aid in removal of bone debris. *I,* The rasp is confirmed to fit snugly enough to provide rotational control, and it is verified that the femoral neck is trimmed to the level of the top of the rasp. Some rasps have provision for a femoral neck planing attachment to facilitate final preparation of the neck osteotomy. A precise fit of the flange of the prosthesis against the top of the femur may enhance its stability. *J, K,* An appropriate trial prosthesis is inserted next. At this point, the surgeon makes a final choice between cement and press-fit fixation. A snug fit must be maintained if cement is not to be used. Use of cement usually requires a rasp one size larger than the prosthesis. Neck length is provisionally chosen by mounting a trial head of appropriate height.

## Follow-up Care and Rehabilitation

The comments in this section will, when necessary, differentiate between patients who have had internal fixation of femoral neck fractures and those who have undergone bipolar replacement for such injuries.

**Immobilization.** Neither the patient nor the injured extremity should be immobilized after a femoral neck fracture. Surgery is performed to allow mobilization of the patient. Any positioning aids or other devices used in bed should promote patient mobilization with comfort and safety. After either internal fixation or arthroplasty, a patient should be out of bed and in a chair on the first postoperative day. Hip flexion beyond 70° is to be avoided initially after prosthetic replacement from a posterior approach.

**Mobilization.** As noted previously, the patient should be mobilized with assistance from the nursing staff on the first postoperative day. A totally assisted transfer or mechanical lift may be required for debilitated or uncooperative patients. Patients treated with internal fixation should pivot off the nonoperated limb, as should patients treated with prosthetic replacement; however, it is not as critical in

the latter group. Full weight bearing can be tolerated as rapidly as the patient can progress after the usual prosthetic replacement. Touch-down weight bearing may be wiser for 8 to 12 weeks after internal fixation of a displaced femoral neck fracture, but it can be liberalized to 6 to 8 weeks or less for impacted or nondisplaced fractures.[71] Some surgeons have reported results that suggest that little if anything is lost by allowing weight bearing as tolerated for most patients after either displaced or undisplaced injuries.[80, 130, 415] Because ambulatory function tends to decrease after hip fracture, unless fixation is especially tenuous, it may be best to avoid placing restrictions that cannot be followed on elderly, uncooperative patients.[291] Younger individuals, who have more to lose from loss of fixation and who usually have much more ability to cooperate, are candidates for ambulation with limited weight bearing until fracture healing is confirmed.

**Physical Therapy.** The role of physical therapy during the acute phase after surgery for a femoral neck fracture is to assist with gait training, provide reminders of flexion restriction in the case of prosthetic replacement, and identify the need for and instruct in the use of aids for ambulation and activities of daily living. As

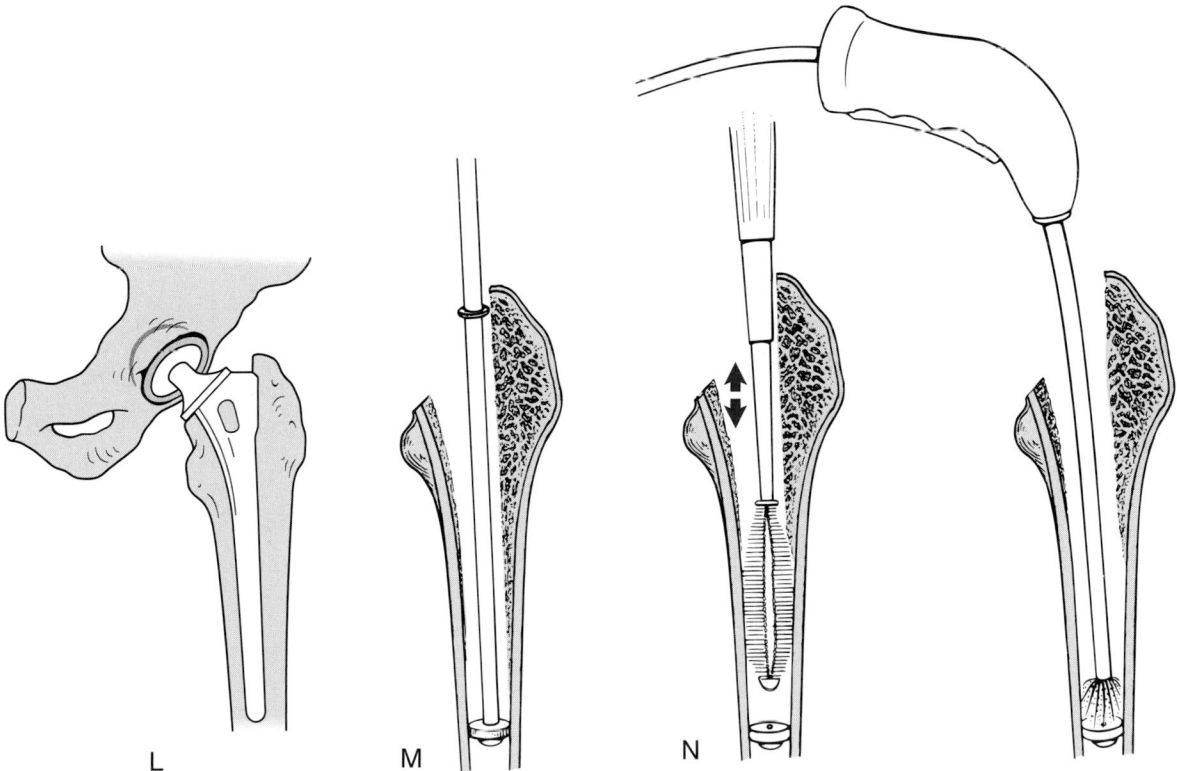

**FIGURE 48–25** *Continued.* *L,* The prosthetic "cup" presently in the acetabulum is part of a two-part ("bipolar") hemiarthroplasty femoral head. The cup should be removed from the normal-appearing acetabulum and placed on the femoral stem component so that it is just outside the acetabulum. It should look something like this. Next, the surgeon assesses range of motion, stability, and leg length and makes adjustments in the prosthesis or its orientation if needed. The hip should have nearly normal range of motion and no tendency to dislocate, especially in flexion, adduction, and external rotation. Length is assessed by soft tissue tension, by the ability to "shuck" the prosthesis distally from the acetabulum with manual traction on the limb, and by the relative position of the tip of the trochanter and the top of the femoral head. At the conclusion of this step, the surgeon chooses the definitive prosthesis. *M,* Assuming that cement fixation is chosen, an appropriately sized cement restrictor is inserted into the femoral canal 1 cm distal to the point at which the tip of the prosthetic stem will rest. *N,* The canal is prepared with a brush and pulsatile lavage spray to remove fat and blood.

*Illustration continued on following page*

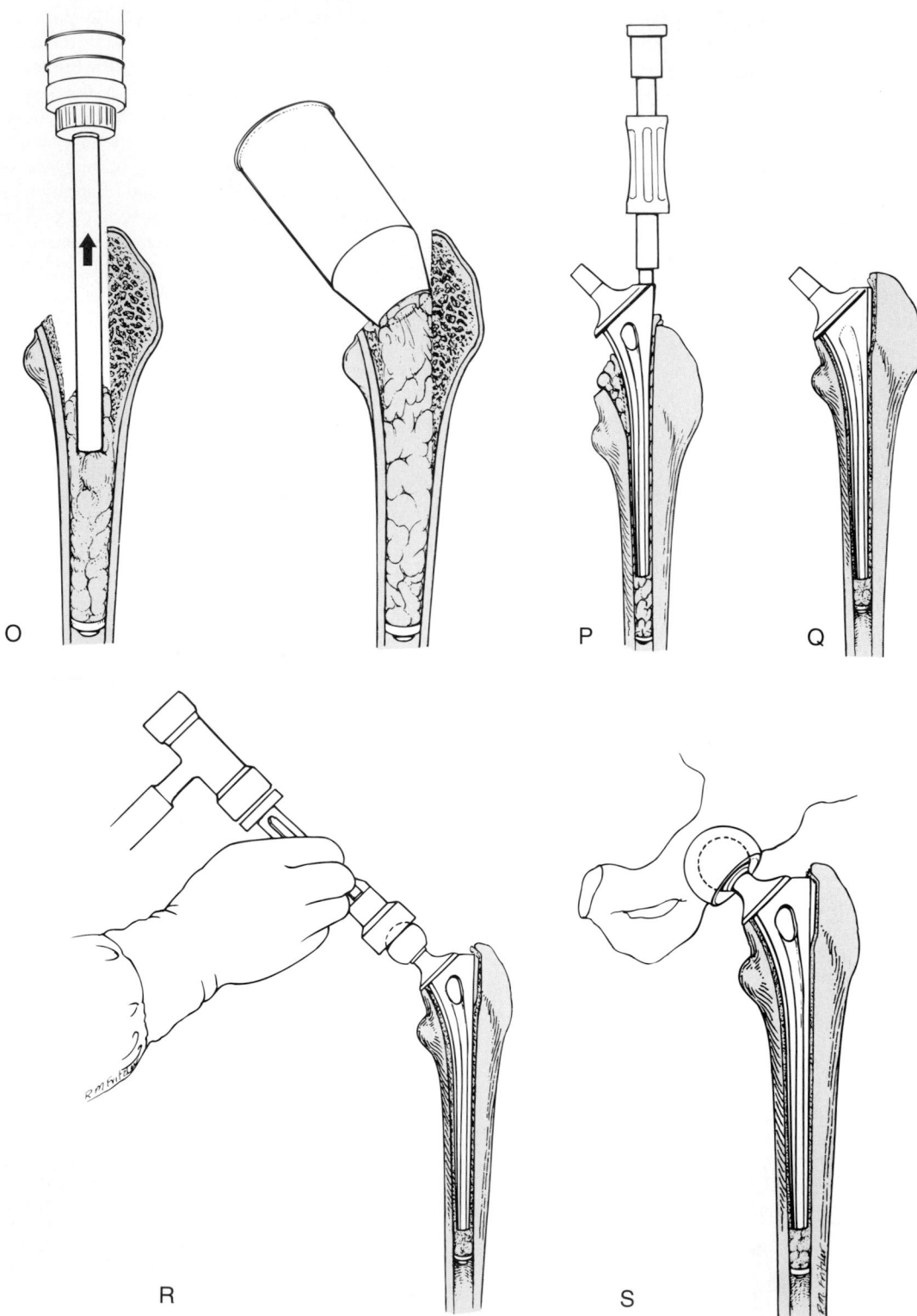

**FIGURE 48–25** *Continued.* *O,* Viscous liquid cement is inserted into the femoral canal, starting at the distal end, with a long-tipped cement delivery syringe. Once the canal is full of cement, a pressurizing nozzle may be used to gain further penetration of the cement into the bony interstices to improve fixation and stability of the cement envelope relative to the femur. *P, Q,* The prosthesis is next inserted into the proximal part of the femur while ensuring that its rotational alignment provides the desired 10° to 15° of anteversion and that it is driven into the prepared channel so that its collar rests squarely on the osteotomized proximal part of the femur. It is held in place until the cement hardens. A nonfenestrated, or plugged, stem is used with cement. All excess cement is removed from the acetabulum and adjacent wound. *R,* Based on the selected trial components, the appropriate prosthetic modular head is placed onto the Morse taper fitting of the stem and impacted lightly but firmly with the appropriate instrument. *S,* The prosthetic femoral head is then reduced into the acetabulum. The surgeon once again confirms leg length, stability, and range of motion. It is important to check for excess cement, interposed soft tissue, and prominent osteophytes that might affect mobility and stability. Once satisfactory joint alignment and mechanics are confirmed, the wound is closed over a suction drain, with the anterior abductors reattached to the proximal end of the femur as shown in Figure 48–22.

the fracture heals, the therapist should progress with muscle-strengthening and gait-training regimens. Similarly, abductor/adductor strengthening and gait-training rehabilitation are progressively indicated after prosthetic replacement.

**Rehabilitation Units.** Discharging patients from acute care facilities to rehabilitation units after surgery for proximal femoral fractures is a practice under active study. One hospital practice comparison study confirmed improved rates of patient independence and mobility for those treated in rehabilitation units; however, the differences had disappeared 1 year after hip fracture.[262] Another follow-up study of a randomized trial confirmed lasting benefit for patients treated in special rehabilitation units.[376] Jensen and Bagger,[271] in a follow-up study 2½ years after hip fracture, found deterioration in social function in 31% of patients discharged home, in 45% of those discharged to a nursing home, and in 55% of patients discharged to a rehabilitation center; however, this series was not controlled (for premorbid state). For the most part, this practice should be reserved for patients with the greatest potential for recovery of independent functional status and is dependent on the wishes of the patient and family, as well as the availability of facilities and funding. Programs to optimize the match of patient rehabilitation potential with discharge destination are being developed.[416]

**Duration and Extent of Disability.** Function is the most relevant outcome of the management of hip frac-

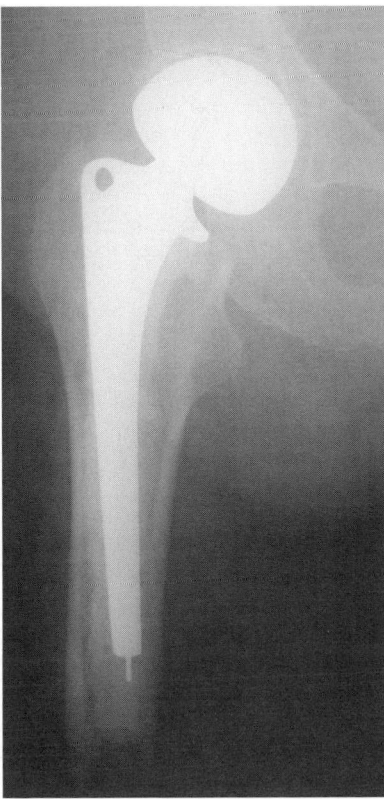

**FIGURE 48-26.** Cemented unipolar modular hemiarthroplasty for a displaced femoral neck fracture in an elderly, osteopenic household ambulator. These implants are as effective as bipolar hemiarthroplasties in this population and have a significantly lower cost.

ture,[72] but unfortunately, loss of function is very common. Miller[332] showed that only 51% of patients in his region returned to the ambulatory status that they possessed before injury. Jette and colleagues[274] prospectively studied a group of 75 patients with hip fracture, 71% of whom survived a year after fracture. Only 33% of the survivors returned to their preinjury function in five basic activities of daily living: indoor walking, bed-to-chair transfers, donning shoes and socks, and getting on and off a toilet. Only 21% returned to their previous level of instrumental activities of daily living: climbing stairs, outdoor walking, getting in and out of the bathtub, preparing meals, washing dishes, and doing light housework. As expected, these disabilities resulted in a significant disturbance in social role function, which was recovered by only 26% of survivors. Recovery is not clearly related to the type of fracture or to fracture treatment.[292] Rather, it depends on the age of the patient, the patient's mental status, preexisting medical problems, and the number of close social contacts.[135, 332] Barring complications, a healthy patient in the age range of 50 to 60 years will generally return to nearly full function by 6 to 8 months after a displaced fracture and in half that time after undisplaced injuries. Initial recovery may be more rapid in displaced fractures treated with prosthetic replacement, although abductor weakness may cause a limp for several months.

**Assistance/Living Arrangements.** In the case of an older patient suffering a femoral neck fracture, advent of the diagnosis-related grouping payment program for Medicare in the United States has resulted in less in-hospital therapy, earlier discharge, and poorer function at discharge.[191, 381] Assistance with discharge planning must be requested on the day of admission for essentially all patients with femoral neck fractures.

Such assistance involves specification of when and to what location and level of care the patient will be discharged, the type of assistance needed, the equipment needed, and a schedule for follow-up appointments. Care protocols collaboratively developed by medical and nursing staff have been demonstrated to be effective in decreasing length of stay and cost of care.[346] Early involvement of family and friends, regardless of the type of surgery performed for a femoral neck fracture, will optimize outcome. Interdisciplinary in-hospital geriatric fracture teams have been shown to reduce the length of stay and improve early functional and clinical outcomes.[480] However, in a randomized trial studying in-hospital comprehensive geriatric assessment teams for broader geriatric diagnoses, no benefit was observed in terms of 1-year survival or health status at 3 or 12 months.[389]

**Assessment of Results.** Functional ratings that are of importance include hip motion, the presence of pain or limp, and walking, sitting, and stair-climbing functions.

The radiographic ratings are different for internal fixation (neck shaft angle, fracture healing, avascular necrosis) than for prosthetic replacement (stem loosening, acetabular wear). A hip-rating scale such as that developed by Harris is suggested for functional rating (Table 48-10).

Impacted or nondisplaced femoral neck fractures will heal uneventfully in most cases, although functional impairment is common. Avascular necrosis occurs in 5%

**Table 48–10** ......................................

Harris Hip Rating Scale

| Index | Rating |
|---|---|
| I. Pain (44 possible) | |
|   A. None or ignores it | 44 |
|   B. Slight or occasional; no compromise in activities | 40 |
|   C. Mild pain, no effect on average activities; rarely, moderate pain with unusual activity, may take aspirin | 30 |
|   D. Moderate pain, tolerable but makes concessions to pain; some limitation of ordinary activity or work; may require occasional pain medicine stronger than aspirin | 20 |
|   E. Marked pain, serious limitation of activities | 10 |
|   F. Totally disabled, crippled, pain in bed, bedridden | 0 |
| II. Function (47 possible) | |
|   A. Gait (33 possible) | |
|     1. Limp | |
|       a. None | 11 |
|       b. Slight | 8 |
|       c. Moderate | 5 |
|       d. Severe | 0 |
|     2. Support | |
|       a. None | 11 |
|       b. Cane for long walks | 7 |
|       c. Cane most of the time | 5 |
|       d. One crutch | 3 |
|       e. Two canes | 2 |
|       f. Two crutches | 0 |
|       g. Not able to walk (specify reason) | 0 |
|   B. Activities (14 possible) | |
|     1. Stairs | |
|       a. Normally without using a railing | 4 |
|       b. Normally while using a railing | 2 |
|       c. In any manner | 1 |
|       d. Unable to climb stairs | 0 |
|     2. Shoes and socks | |
|       a. With ease | 4 |
|       b. With difficulty | 2 |
|       c. Unable | 0 |
|     3. Sitting | |
|       a. Comfortable in an ordinary chair for 1 hr | 5 |
|       b. Comfortable in a high chair for 30 min | 3 |
|       c. Unable to sit comfortably in any chair | 0 |
|     4. Enter public transportation | 1 |
| III. Absence of deformity; points (4) are given if the patient demonstrates the following: | |
|   A. Less than 30° fixed flexion contracture | |
|   B. Less than 10° fixed adduction | |
|   C. Less than 10° fixed internal rotation in extension | |
|   D. Limb length discrepancy less than 3.2 cm | |
| IV. Range of motion; index values are determined by multiplying the degrees of motion possible in each arc by the appropriate index | |
|   A. Flexion | |
|     0°–45° × 1.0 | |
|     45°–90° × 0.6 | |
|     90°–110° × 0.3 | |
|   B. Abduction | |
|     0°–15° × 0.8 | |
|     15°–20° × 0.3 | |
|     >20° × 0 | |
|   C. External rotation in extension | |
|     0°–15° × 0.4 | |
|     >15° × 0 | |
|   D. Internal rotation in extension | |
|     Any amount × 0 | |
|   E. Adduction | |
|     0°–15° × 0.2 | |

......................................

To determine the overall rating for range of motion, multiply the sum of the index values by 0.05. Record the Trendelenburg test as positive, level, or neutral.

*Source:* Data from Harris, W.H. J Bone Joint Surg Am 51:737–755, 1969.

to 15% of these fractures and nonunion in 2% to 5%. After reduction and internal fixation of displaced femoral neck fractures, nonunion has been reported to occur in 4% to 33% of cases[91, 96, 110, 194, 202] and avascular necrosis in 30% to 35%.[91, 96, 313]

Results depend on multiple factors, including but not limited to surgical complications, which vary in frequency and severity. For example, prosthetic replacement for femoral neck fracture has a wide range of reported complications. Rates of dislocation and infection are listed in Tables 48–6 and 48–7.

## Complications: Identification and Treatment

### AVASCULAR NECROSIS

Most patients in whom avascular necrosis of the femoral head eventually develops have groin, buttock, or proximal thigh pain. This pain may not be functionally significant.[96] It is generally true that the higher the functional demands on the hip, the more significant the symptoms. For example, most patients younger than 50 years in whom post-traumatic femoral head osteonecrosis develops are symptomatic enough to require a reconstructive procedure.[367] Only one third of older patients in the extensive series of Barnes and co-workers[96] had symptoms severe enough to warrant a second surgical procedure.

The risk of avascular necrosis generally corresponds to the degree of displacement of the femoral neck fracture on the initial radiographs.[171] Patients with normal bone stock have a higher risk of avascular necrosis because higher energy must be imparted to produce a hip fracture that is accompanied by greater soft tissue damage. Although some estimation of the risk of this complication can be made from radiographs, more detailed information can be obtained from technetium bone scans. Stromqvist[426] was able to document the risk of avascular necrosis or nonunion based on quantitative bone scans obtained 1 to 2 weeks after injury. A femoral head uptake ratio of 90% or less on the intact side was found to carry an 84% risk of avascular necrosis or nonunion.

Tomograms or CT can show, with higher resolution, the bony appearance of stippled areas of bone sclerosis, trabecular resorption, microfracture, and subchondral collapse at an earlier stage than plain radiographs can. MRI may offer the potential for very early diagnosis of the condition, but ferrous metals and other materials distort the images. Prospective data on the use of these scans for predictive purposes have not yet been reported.

Once the diagnosis is established, the problem of post-traumatic avascular necrosis is extremely difficult to treat. Core decompression as a means of treating non-traumatic avascular necrosis has provided mixed results.[124, 185] Natural history data on nontreated avascular necrosis are insufficient. Most authors doubt that core decompression has any favorable influence on post-traumatic avascular necrosis, but adequate data are unavailable. In older patients, in whom radiographic findings may not correlate with function, observation is probably indicated, with arthroplasty as a backup. In younger patients, no good option is available. If the area of collapse is found to involve less than 50% of the femoral head based on tomograms, CT, or plain radiographs in various degrees of flexion and abduction, flexion osteotomy may provide acceptable improvement in function.[199] Hip arthrodesis is an option in a younger patient with high functional demands but is made more difficult by the presence of avascular bone. Many authors have advocated bipolar endoprosthetic replacement for this complication, but long-term functional results are lacking. Because of the difficulty with acetabular wear, total-hip arthroplasty may be the procedure of choice for elderly patients with displaced femoral neck fractures and perhaps even in patients younger than 50 years[118, 313] (see Chapter 61). In the past, this procedure has produced a high incidence of early failure in younger patients, but data are unavailable for newer, uncemented techniques. All things considered, with the lack of reliable reconstructive options, every reasonable effort at prevention seems appropriate.

## FIXATION FAILURE

Failure of fixation is suspected from the results of clinical examination in the early postoperative period. A patient with unstable fixation will generally have symptoms of groin or buttock pain.[436] The suspicion is verified by plain radiographic studies or tomograms that confirm displacement or angulation of the fracture, usually inferiorly and posteriorly; by radiolucency around the implants; or by backing out of the implants. The last finding can, however, occur with settling of the fracture as healing progresses and is encouraged by parallel insertion of multiple implants. Some degree of fracture settling is often associated with otherwise uneventful healing. Of the factors that predict failure of fixation, patient age and preoperative fracture displacement have been found to have the greatest predictive value.[352] Fixation failure early in the postoperative period is related to comminution of the femoral neck.[75]

Because loss of fixation is probably related to failure of osteoporotic bone around the implants, it may perhaps best be seen as a problem of patient selection. In the future, bone density studies may aid in assigning patients to internal fixation or prosthetic replacement. Technical problems such as malreduction or the use of implants that are too short, have threads that cross the fracture line, or are widely divergent and prevent fracture settling play a role in fixation failure. Similarly, implants that do not provide adequate stability of the fragments may play a role. This problem is best avoided by selecting a pin or screw that provides adequate fracture stabilization[421, 438] (Fig. 48–27). Dedicating a surgical team to the management of hip fractures has been shown to reduce the incidence of these complications.[101, 357]

Post-traumatic arthritis can also result from fixation problems. Implant penetration into the joint can occur with femoral neck fixation.[134, 436] This problem has been most clearly defined in reference to pin fixation of a slipped capital femoral epiphysis, but it has also been reported in reference to fixation of femoral neck fractures.[461] The risk increases as the number of implants increases; thus, no more than three implants should be used. The screw tips must be carefully observed radio-

graphically at surgery. The safe-zone concept of Walters and Simon, with the central axis being the area where screws can be the closest to the joint, applies to femoral neck fixation as well.[461] If screws are intraoperatively recognized to penetrate the femoral head, they should be exchanged for a shorter screw inserted through a new tract. If the old tract is used and fracture settling begins to develop, the screw, rather than backing out of the lateral cortex, may repenetrate the hip joint.[165] Screw penetration recognized in the early postoperative period should be managed in the same way. If it is recognized late, after post-traumatic degenerative arthritis has developed, the surgeon may elect to remove the implant and treat the arthritis conservatively or with arthroplasty if symptoms warrant.

With loss of reduction caused by fixation failure, the choice of procedure is again related to patient age, functional demand, medical condition, and bone density.[309] When these factors are favorable in an active individual with good bone quality, the surgeon should elect to rereduce and internally fix the fracture (Fig. 48–28). When the failure occurs in association with nonunion, valgus osteotomy may be indicated.[316, 318] When these factors involve an older patient with poor bone density and lower functional demands, bipolar or total-hip arthroplasty becomes the procedure of choice.[309] Failure of fixation leading to reoperation has been associated with worse functional outcomes; however, Keating and colleagues have demonstrated that reoperation for problems associated with hemiarthroplasty lead to similarly poor outcomes.[285]

## NONUNION

The diagnosis of nonunion is initially suspected on a clinical basis. The symptoms of groin or buttock pain, pain on hip extension, and pain with weight bearing all suggest this complication. In comparison to avascular necrosis, the symptoms of nonunion occur earlier and are more severe. Radiographs suggest a lucent zone, and tomography will confirm the lack of healing. If bone scanning is performed, increased uptake is usually seen in the area of nonunion. Increasing patient age and fracture displacement are correlated with an increased risk of nonunion.[352]

As with fixation failure, the decision regarding how to proceed is based on consideration of the patient's age, function, medical history, and bone density. In a younger patient, if adequate bone remains in the femoral head, refixation with cancellous or muscle pedicle bone grafting is indicated.[281, 328, 337] Many have advocated valgus osteotomy to improve the mechanical loading of the nonunion, with good results[318] (Figs. 48–29 and 48–30). If the physiologic neck-shaft axis remains intact, however, refixation with bone grafting but without osteotomy has similarly produced good radiographic and clinical results (Fig 48–31). When a short limb is involved, valgus osteotomy is the procedure of choice.

In the case of an older, osteoporotic patient or in a situation in which instability has produced loss of bone in the femoral head, hip arthroplasty is the procedure of choice. Good to excellent functional results in this setting have been reported.[227, 318] Again, prevention is the best method of treatment. Conservative treatment of undis-

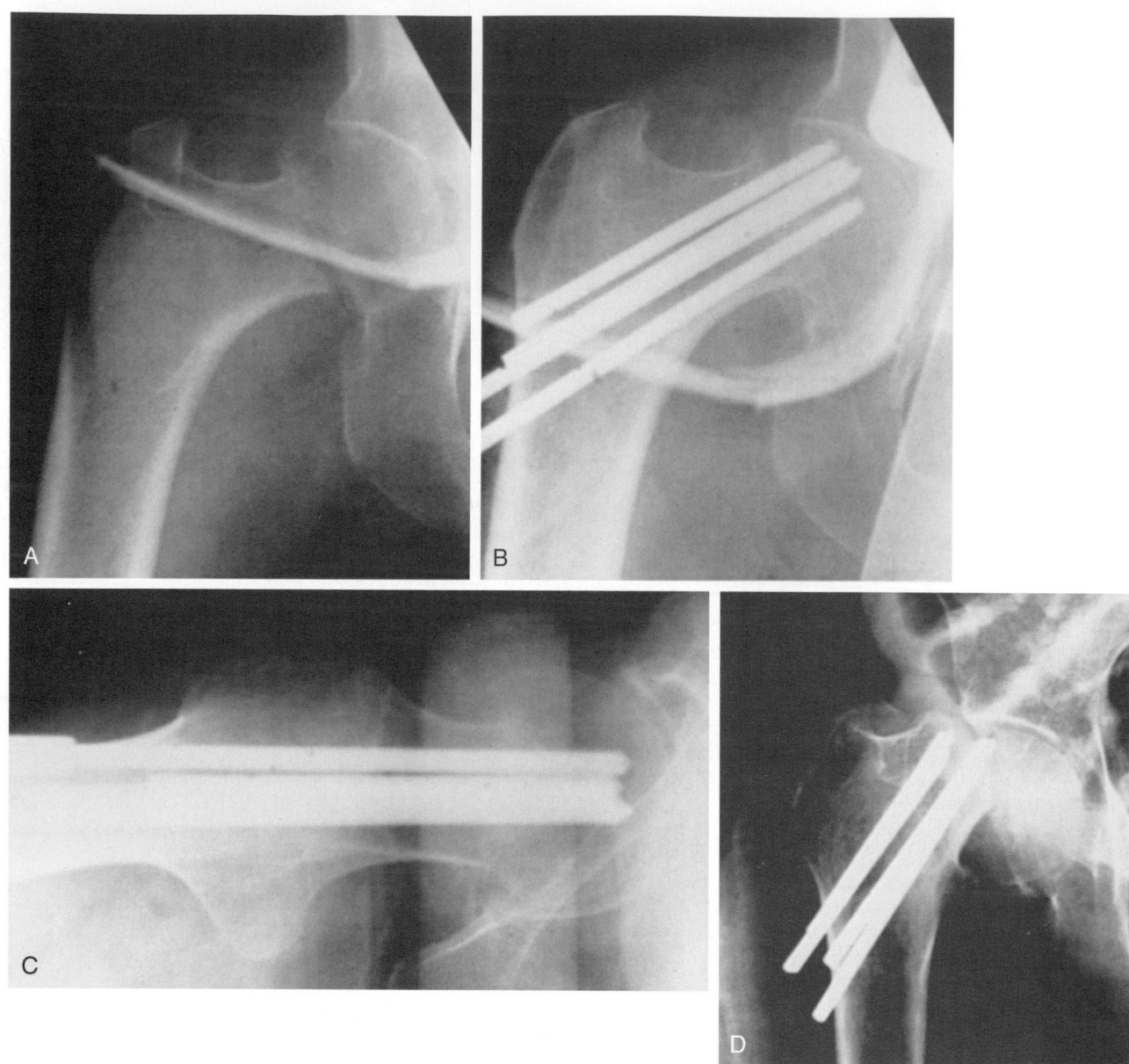

**Figure 48–27.** Loss of fixation of a femoral neck fracture. *A*, This 78-year-old woman sustained a displaced Garden grade IV femoral neck fracture in a low-energy fall. *B, C,* She underwent Neufeld pinning with four pins. Good reduction was apparent on the lateral view, but the anteroposterior (AP) view revealed a varus malreduction. *D,* By 10 days postoperatively she was complaining of pain while ambulating with a walker, and the femoral head had fallen off the femoral neck. This example illustrates the importance of good reduction in the AP view, something that is especially critical in osteoporotic individuals.

placed fractures should be avoided. Internal fixation with multiple implants having adequate threads or with a sliding hip screw and a second cancellous screw for rotation control should provide stability for fracture union in at least 90% of displaced fractures with adequate bone stock. Internal fixation is relatively contraindicated in osteopenic patients.

## FAILED ARTHROPLASTY

Failure of primary prosthetic replacement for femoral neck fractures has been reported to be caused by infection, acetabular wear (protrusio), stem loosening, and dislocation.[163, 290]

Infection after prosthetic replacement has been noted in 0% to 10% or more of cases[266] (see Table 48–7). It is less frequent after fracture fixation. Superficial infection is best managed by antibiotic treatment, local débridement, and appropriate wound care. Septic arthritis may develop after either arthroplasty or fracture fixation; diagnosis requires aspiration of the joint. Early deep infection (i.e., in the first 1 to 2 weeks) in a relatively healthy patient may be managed by deep débridement, closure over suction drains, and prolonged intravenous antibiotic treatment. If this regimen fails or sepsis develops, the prosthesis and all cement must be removed, followed by débridement, closure of the wound over drains, and prolonged antibiotic treatment. In a younger, healthy patient, reimplantation of

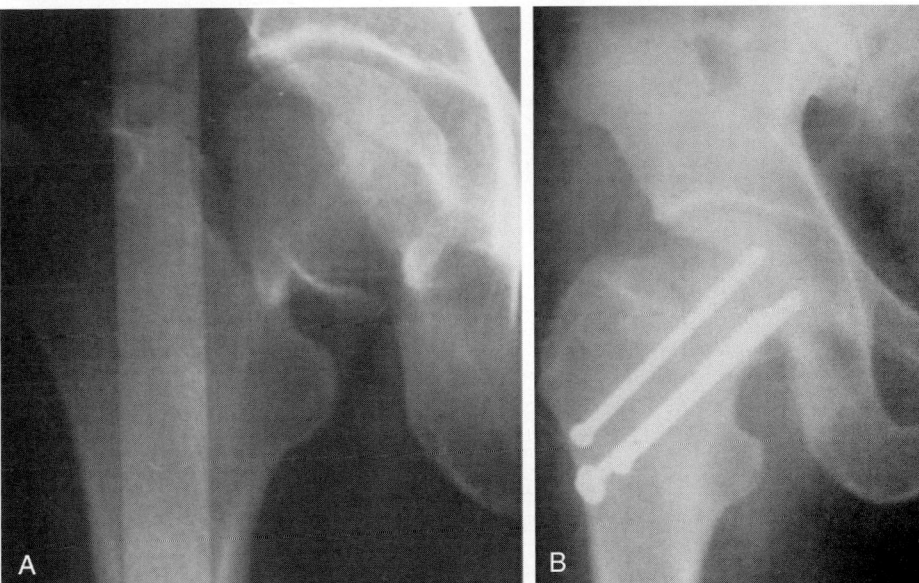

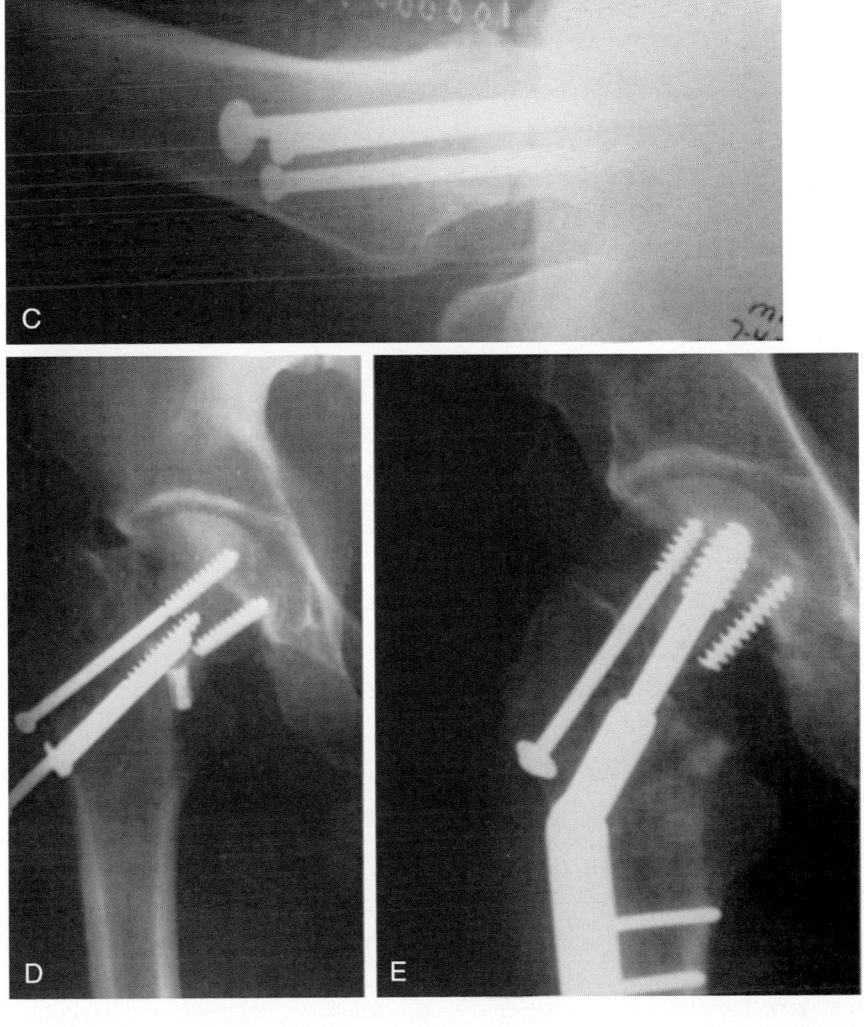

**FIGURE 48–28.** Loss of fixation of a femoral neck fracture. *A,* This 44-year-old man fell off a roof and sustained a displaced Garden grade II femoral neck fracture with an associated intra-articular distal radial fracture. *B, C,* He was treated by anterior capsulotomy through a Watson-Jones approach, with the findings of a hematoma under pressure. The fracture was fixed with three cancellous screws. *D,* The patient began immediate full weight bearing against advice and was doing lumbar hyperextension exercises at 3 weeks when he felt a snap in his groin. *E,* Salvage with a compression hip screw. Post traumatic osteonecrosis with collapse developed at 9 months. He is symptomatic but has not undergone revision surgery. This case emphasizes the importance of a careful postoperative plan and touch-down weight bearing until fracture union occurs.

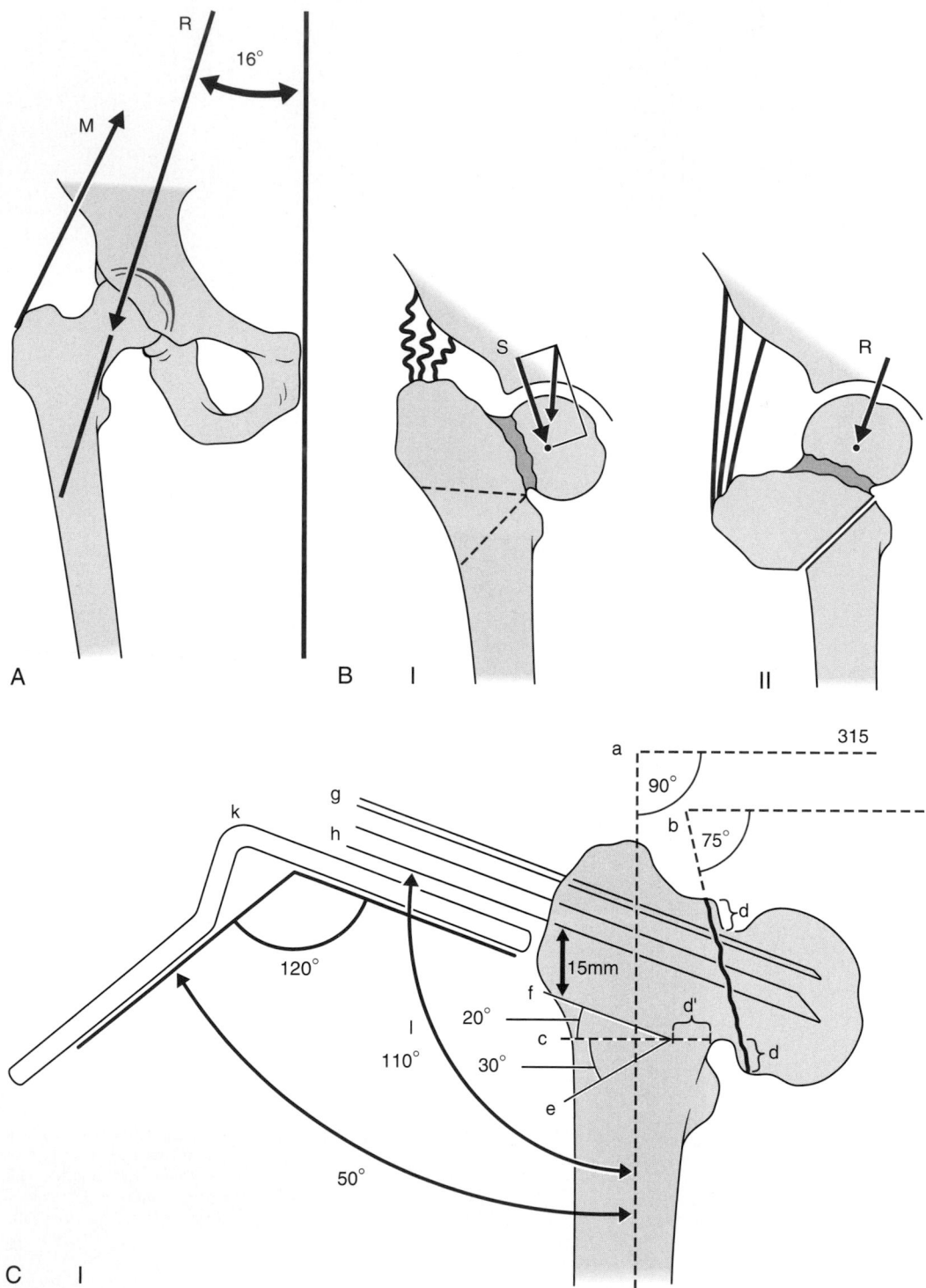

**FIGURE 48–29.** Valgus osteotomy for ununited femoral neck fracture. *A,* Pauwels (1976) pointed out that the resultant force (R) through the center of the hip joint was due to the force of gravity on the body supported by the hip and the muscular force (M) of the abductors. He showed that this force was directed approximately 16° from the vertical plane. *B,* Pauwels suggested and demonstrated the success of a valgus intertrochanteric osteotomy with resection of a laterally based wedge of bone to reorient the ununited femoral neck fracture so that its plane is nearly perpendicular to the force across the hip joint. Converting a shearing force parallel to the nonunion to a compressive one stabilizes the nonunion and promotes healing. It also improves adductor mechanics by restoring length and tension. *C,* Müller and associates expanded the techniques of repositioning osteotomy for ununited femoral neck fractures to improve correction of complex deformities. A viable femoral head without segmental collapse or sclerosis is an essential prerequisite for repositioning osteotomy in an adult. It may be indicated for teenagers in the event of avascular necrosis. *I,* Preoperative planning.

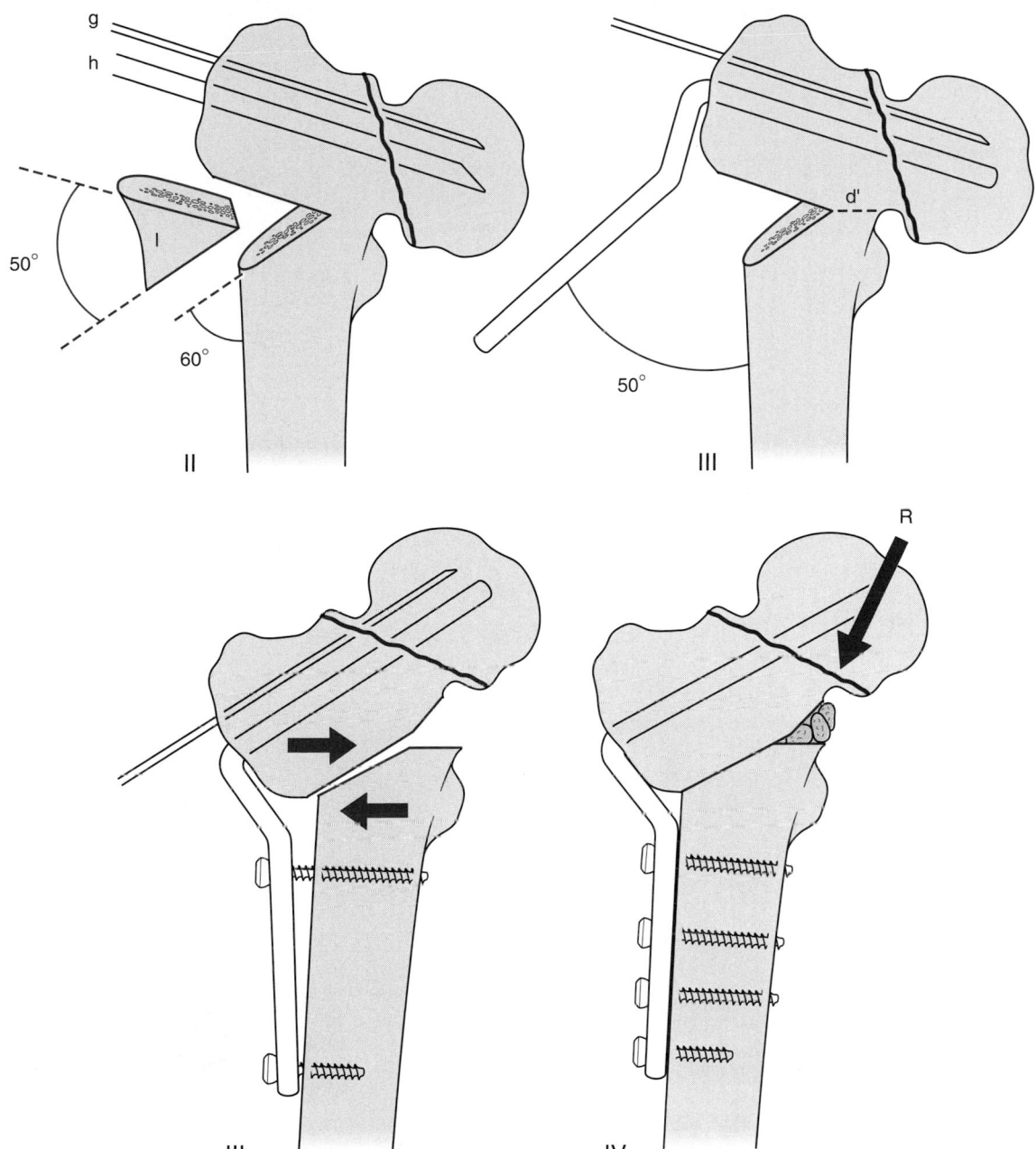

**FIGURE 48–29** *Continued. II* and *III,* Execution of the plan: insertion of a guide wire and seating chisel, resection of a wedge of bone, and then completion of the osteotomy to the inferomedial side of the femoral neck. *IV* and *V,* Fixation is next carried out as preplanned with a 120° angled blade plate. The joint reaction force is now perpendicular to the union. (*A,* Modified from Müller, M.E. In: Hierholzer,E.; Müller, M.E., eds. Osteotomies. p. 67. *B,* From Pauwels, F. Biomechanics of the Normal and Diseased Hip. New York, Springer-Verlag, 1976, p. 83. *C,* From Müller, M.E.; et al. Manual of Internal Fixation. Techniques Recommended by the AO-Group, 2nd ed. Berlin, Springer-Verlag, 1979, pp. 363, 365.)

a prosthesis with antibiotic-impregnated cement may be considered at a later date. Such treatment is most frequently chosen in the setting of a gram-positive infection. An excellent review of the management of infected hip prostheses has been published by Canner and colleagues.[125] Infection after an internally fixed femoral neck fracture may respond to treatment as described with retention of fixation. If fixation fails, however, removal of the implants and the head-neck segment is usually required.

Failure of older unipolar prosthetic designs (Austin-

Moore, Thompson) as a result of acetabular wear was a major impetus in developing bipolar designs. This radiographic complication has been reported to be as common as 20%.[78] Symptomatic acetabular erosion occurs in 6% to 8% of patients with Thompson or Austin-Moore prostheses, but it has been reported to be as high as 37%.[163] Although bipolar designs, because of their inner bearing motion, theoretically decrease acetabular wear, such wear has not been documented in a large series with long-term follow-up; the functional results of both unipolar and bipolar designs are similar.[308] Short-term improvement in acetabular wear in 161 cases was reported by Devas and Hinves.[163] The belief that this complication is unaltered by bipolar endoprosthetic design has led some surgeons to recommend total-hip arthroplasty for displaced femoral neck fractures in selected patients. When acetabular erosion occurs and is symptomatic, conversion to a total-hip arthroplasty is indicated. If no concomitant stem loosening has occurred and the prosthesis is bipolar, the femoral component can be retained and an acetabular component placed. Some debate has arisen over the issue of using cemented versus noncemented acetabular components in this setting. There is good evidence that revision of a unipolar Thompson or Austin-Moore prosthesis to a total-hip arthroplasty is difficult and has a high incidence of both later loosening of the new femoral component and shaft fracture on insertion. Consequently, some authors have condemned the use of these components in patients with a life expectancy in excess of 1 to 2 years.

Failure of prosthetic replacement can also occur from stem loosening. Loosening is generally present on radiographic examination before the development of clinical symptoms. Sinking or subsidence of the prosthesis,

radiolucent lines around the cement mantle, and scalloping around the cement or prosthesis are radiographic signs of loosening of the prostheses. It may be more frequent with bipolar prostheses. In Long and Knight's study, some radiolucency around the cement was present in 81% of 156 Bateman prostheses with a minimum of 1-year follow-up.[308] In the series reported by Lausten and co-workers,[298] these lines exceeded 2 mm in 15% of 77 cases. When this radiographic picture is present and the patient has a complaint of thigh or buttock pain, revision is generally indicated. In general, revision should be to a total-hip prosthesis. In the event that component loosening is identified concomitantly with a proximal femoral fracture, revision should be to a long-stem femoral component[283] (see Chapter 61).

## SUBTROCHANTERIC FRACTURE BELOW SCREWS

Subtrochanteric fracture below screws is readily apparent from the history and symptoms of a patient with a subtrochanteric femoral fracture. Usually, it is the result of a minor fall or twisting with unprotected, full weight

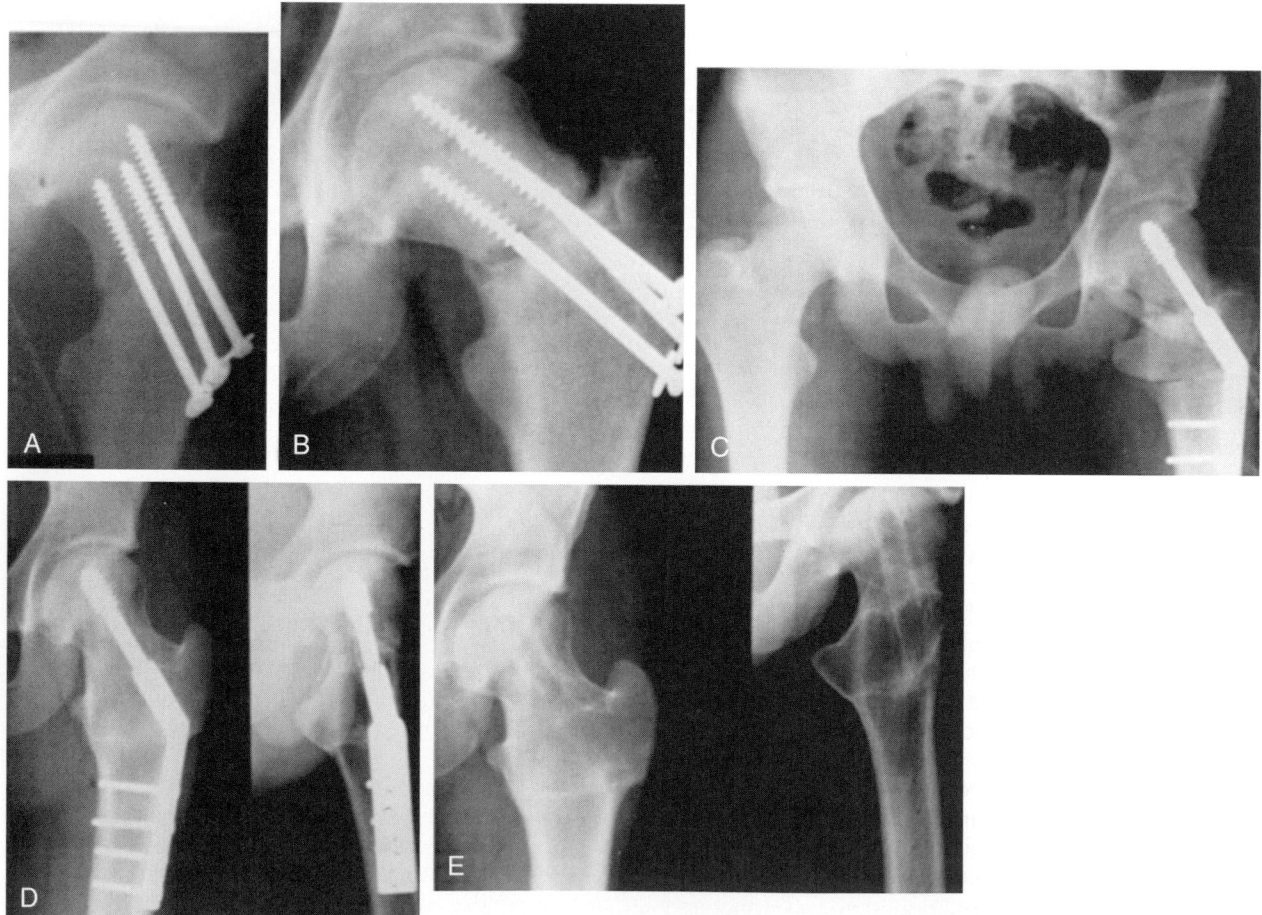

**FIGURE 48–30.** Nonunion of a femoral neck fracture. *A,* This 26-year-old man underwent open reduction and internal fixation of a displaced femoral neck fracture, with subsequent poor reduction. *B,* This reduction showed excessive valgus malalignment, and with touch-down weight bearing and active motion of the hip, followed by progressive weight bearing beginning at 12 weeks, a varus deformity with nonunion developed at 6 months. *C,* This problem was salvaged by performing a valgus intertrochanteric/subtrochanteric osteotomy and hip screw fixation. *D,* Union of the osteotomy and the femoral neck fracture. *E,* At 22 months' follow-up, the patient had no evidence of osteonecrosis.

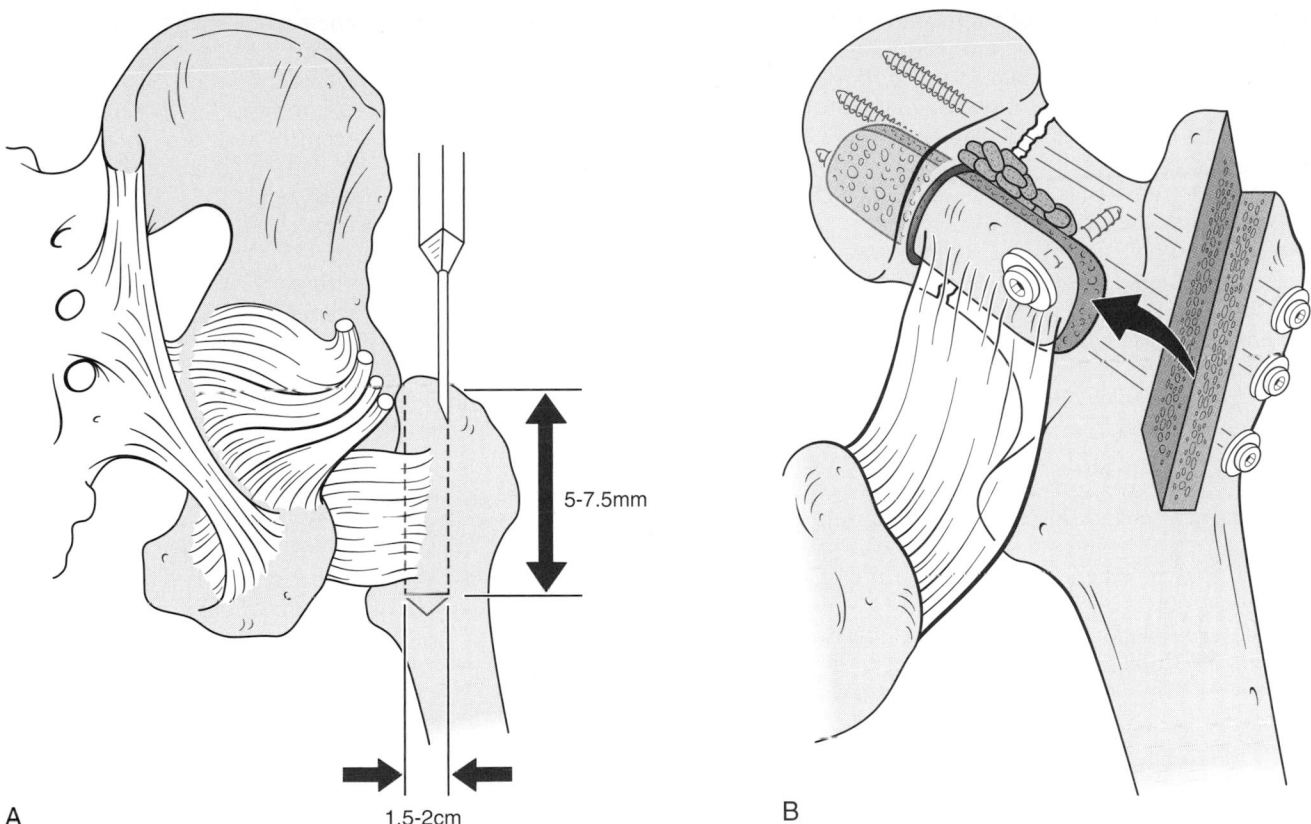

**FIGURE 48–31.** Refixation and muscle pedicle bone graft for well-aligned nonunion. *A, B,* An alternative to consider for satisfactorily aligned, ununited femoral neck fractures in younger adults is to refix the fracture, together with a muscle pedicle bone graft as described by Judet and Meyers (see earlier). (From Chapman, M.W. Operative Orthopaedics. Philadelphia, J.B. Lippincott, 1988, p. 561.)

bearing after fixation of a femoral neck fracture. The diagnosis is confirmed by plain radiographs. Factors believed to play a role in this phenomenon are unfilled drill holes (from attempted screw or pin placement) in the subtrochanteric region and pins inserted from too distal a location. Very low-angle implants that start in the region of the proximal part of the femur where the cortical bone is thick (distal to the point opposite the middle of the lesser trochanter) pass through bone that is in an area of high stress during weight bearing. If the pin holes have not been predrilled, radial cracks may develop during insertion. Small cracks, unfilled holes, or the implants themselves concentrate the stresses in this region and may lead to propagation of a subtrochanteric fracture. The factors mentioned are generally visible on radiographs or at inspection of the fracture site during reoperation.

When this complication occurs in the early postoperative phase (which it generally does), treatment consists of reoperation. Conservative treatment of minimally displaced or nondisplaced fractures usually results in fracture displacement, so operative stabilization is therefore recommended. The implant selected must allow continued stabilization of the femoral neck fracture while extending fixation to the subtrochanteric fracture. This objective is best accomplished by leaving one or two of the screws or pins in place and fixing the subtrochanteric fracture by inserting a compression hip screw with a side plate long enough to provide good purchase of four screws distal to

the fracture or an equivalent angled blade plate. Lag screws should be added to stabilize the subtrochanteric femoral fracture wherever possible. Primary autogenous bone grafting of the subtrochanteric injury is mandatory, especially with any gapping of the medial cortex. In general, changing to an intramedullary device is to be avoided unless the main portion of the neck fixation can be left during insertion of the device. Although large series of patients treated for this complication have not been published, successful healing of a subtrochanteric fracture usually occurs when the preceding principles are followed.

## PRESSURE SORES

Pressure sores still occur too frequently in patients with femoral neck fractures. Occasionally, they are the result of a debilitated patient lying unassisted on the floor for a prolonged period after a fall. More often, they develop in the hospital before, during, or after surgery for hip fracture and should thus be preventable. Jensen and Junker[273] reported a 30% incidence of pressure sores after hip fracture. They are most common in elderly women, appear within a week of surgery, increase the hospital stay, and are associated with higher mortality. Pressure sores occur most frequently on the sacrum or posterior of the heel, especially on the injured limb. Most of these lesions can be prevented by turning the patient at least every 2 hours and by supporting the legs with pillows placed longitudinally under the calves so that the heels do not contact the mattress. Rarely, a special bed with a flotation or air cushion mattress may be required. Close monitoring for the persisting erythema of a low-grade pressure sore, with prompt, complete relief of pressure on affected areas, can significantly decrease the severity and cost of these troublesome problems.[457]

## REFERENCES

### Femoral Head Fractures

1. Albrechtsen, J.; Hede, J.; Jurik, A.G. Pelvic fractures: Assessment by conventional radiography and CT. Acta Radiol 35:420–425, 1994.
2. Birkett, J. Traumatic dislocation of the head of the femur complicated with its fracture. Med Chir Trans 52:133, 1869.
3. Blankenstein, J.D.; Loris, C.A.; Van der Werken, C. Traumatic dislocation of the hip with fracture of the femoral head. Neth J Surg 38:121–124, 1986.
4. Bosse, M.J.; Poka, A.; Reinert, C.M.; et al. Heterotopic ossification as a complication of acetabular fracture. J Bone Joint Surg Am 70:1231–1237, 1988.
5. Brumback, R.J.; Kenzora, J.E.; Levitt, L.E.; et al. Proceedings of the Hip Society, 1986, St. Louis, C.V. Mosby, 1987, pp. 181–206.
6. Butler, J.E. Pipkin type II fractures of the femoral head. J Bone Joint Surg Am 63:1292, 1981.
7. Cathcart, R.F. The shape of the femoral head and preliminary results of clinical use of a nonspherical hip prosthesis. J Bone Joint Surg Am 53:397, 1971.
8. Chakraborti, S.; Miller, I.M. Dislocation of the hip associated with fracture of the femoral head. Injury 7:134–142, 1975.
9. Chandler, H.P.; Reineck, F.T.; Wixson, R.L.; McCarthy, J.C. Total hip replacement in patients younger than thirty years old: A five year follow up study. J Bone Joint Surg Am 63:1426–1434, 1981.
10. Christopher, F. Fractures of the head of the femur. Arch Surg 12:1049, 1926.
11. Connolly, J.F. Acetabular labrum entrapment associated with a femoral-head fracture-dislocation. A case report. J Bone Joint Surg Am 56:1735–1737, 1974.
12. Coventry, M.B. The treatment of fracture-dislocation of the hip by total hip arthroplasty. J Bone Joint Surg Am 56:1128–1134, 1974.
13. David, J.B. Simultaneous femoral head fracture and traumatic hip dislocation. Am J Surg 80:893, 1950.
14. DeLee, J.C.; Evans, J.A.; Thomas, J. Anterior dislocation of the hip and associated femoral head fractures. J Bone Joint Surg Am 62:960–964, 1980.
15. Dowd, G.S.E.; Johnson, R. Successful conservative treatment of a fracture dislocation of the femoral head. A case report. J Bone Joint Surg Am 61:1244–1246, 1979.
16. Duncan, C.P.; Shim, S.S. Blood supply of the head of the femur in traumatic hip dislocation. Surg Gynecol Obstet 144:185–191, 1977.
17. Dussault, R.G.; Beauregard, G.; Fauteaux, P; et al. Femoral head defect following anterior hip dislocation. Radiology 135:627–629, 1980.
18. Epstein, H.C. Posterior fracture dislocation of the femoral head: A case report. J Bone Joint Surg Am 43:1079, 1961.
19. Epstein, H.C. Posterior fracture dislocation of the hip; long term follow-up. J Bone Joint Surg Am 56:1103–1127, 1974.
20. Epstein, H.C.; Harvey, J.P., Jr. Traumatic anterior dislocation of the hip [abstract]. J Bone Joint Surg Am 56:1103, 1974.
21. Epstein, H.C.; Wiss, D.A.; Cozen, L. Posterior fracture dislocation of the hip with fractures of the femoral head. Clin Orthop 201:9–17, 1985.
22. Faulkner, K.G.; McClung, M.; Cummings, S.R. Automated evaluation of hip axis length for predicting hip fracture. J Bone Miner Res 9:1065–1070, 1994.
23. Fina, C.P.; Kelly, P.J. Dislocations of the hip with fractures of the proximal femur. J Trauma 10:77–87, 1970.
24. Froehlich, J.A.; Dorfman, G.S.; Cronan, J.J.; et al. Compression ultrasonography for detection of deep venous thrombosis in patients who have a fracture of the hip. J Bone Joint Surg Am 71:249–256, 1989.
25. Funsten, R.V.; Kinser, P.; Frankel, C.H. Dashboard dislocation of the hip: A report of twenty cases of traumatic dislocation. J Bone Joint Surg 20:124, 1938.
26. Garrett, J.C.; Epstein, H.C.; Harris, W.H.; et al. Treatment of unreduced traumatic posterior dislocations of the hip. J Bone Joint Surg Am 61:91:2–6, 1979.
27. Gordon, E.J.; Freiberg, J.A. Posterior dislocation of the hip with fracture of the head of the femur. J Bone Joint Surg Am 31:869, 1949.
28. Greenwald, A.S.; Haynes, D.W. Weight-bearing areas in the human hip joint. J Bone Joint Surg Br 54:157–163, 1972.
29. Johnstone, G. Posterior dislocation of the hip with fracture of the femoral head. East Afr Med J 42:429–437, 1965.
30. Hougaard, K.; Lindequist, S.; Nielsen, L.B. Computerised tomography after posterior dislocation of the hip. J Bone Joint Surg Br 69:556–557, 1987.
31. Hougaard, K.; Thomsen, P.B. Coxarthrosis following traumatic posterior dislocation of the hip. J Bone Joint Surg Am 69:679–683, 1987.
32. Hougaard, K.; Thomsen, P.B. Traumatic posterior fracture-dislocation of the hip with fracture of the femoral head or neck, or both. J Bone Joint Surg Am 70:233–239, 1988.
33. Kelly, P.J.; Lipscomb, P.R. Primary Vitallium mold arthroplasty for posterior dislocation of the hip with fracture of the femoral head. J Bone Joint Surg Am 40:675, 1958.
34. Klasen, H.J.; Binnendjik, B. Fracture of the neck of the femur associated with posterior dislocation of the hip. J Bone Joint Surg Br 66:45–48, 1984.
35. Kozin, S.H.; Kolessar, D.J.; Guanche, C.A.; Marmar, E.C. Bilateral femoral head fracture with posterior hip dislocation. Orthop Rev Suppl:20–24, 1994.
36. Lange, R.H.; Engber, W.D.; Clancy, W.G. Expanding application for the Herbert scaphoid screw. Orthopedics 9:1393–1397, 1986.
37. Laorr, A.; Greenspan, A.; Anderson, M.W.; et al. Traumatic hip dislocation: Early MRI findings. Skeletal Radiol 24:239–245, 1995.
38. Leenen, L.P.H.; Van der Werken, C. Traumatic posterior luxation of the hip. Neth J Surg 42:136–139, 1990.
39. Mack, L.A.; Harley, J.D.; Winquist, R.A. CT of acetabular fractures: Analysis of fracture patterns. AJR Am J Roentgenol 138:407–412, 1982.
40. Mears, D.C. Personal communication, 1988.
41. Meislin, R.J.; Zuckerman, J.D. Case report: Bilateral posterior hip dislocations with femoral head fractures. J Orthop Trauma 3:353–361, 1989.
42. Moed B.R.; Maxey J.W. Evaluation of the femoral head using the CT-directed pelvic oblique radiograph. Clin Orthop 296:161–167, 1993.
43. Mowery, C.; Gershuni, D.H. Fracture dislocation of the femoral head treated by open reduction and internal fixation. J Trauma 26:1041–1044, 1989.
44. Mumlautuller, M.E.; Nazarian, S.; Koch, P.; Schatzker, J. The Comprehensive Classification of Fractures of Long Bones. Berlin, Springer-Verlag, 1990.
45. Murry, P.; McGee, H.M.; Mulvihill, N. Fixation of femoral head fractures using the Herbert screw. Injury 19:220–221, 1988.
46. Pipkin, G. Treatment of grade IV fracture dislocation of the hip: A review. J Bone Joint Surg Am 39:1027, 1957.
47. Potter, H.G.; Montgomery, K.D.; Heise, C.W.; Helfet, D.L. MR imaging of acetabular fractures: Value in detecting femoral head injury, intraarticular fragments and sciatic nerve injury. AJR Am J Roentgenol 163:881–886, 1993.
48. Rafii, M.; Firooznia, H.; Golimbu, C.; et al. The impact of CT in clinical management of pelvic and acetabular fractures. Clin Orthop 178:228–235, 1983.
49. Repo, R.U.; Finlay, J.B. Survival of articular cartilage after controlled impact. J Bone Joint Surg Am 59:1068–1076, 1977.
50. Richardson, P.; Young, J.W.R.; Porter, D. CT detection of cortical fracture of the femoral head associated with posterior hip dislocation. AJR Am J Roentgenol 155:93–94, 1990.
51. Ritter, M.A.; Gioe, T.J. The effect of indomethacin on para-articular ectopic ossification following total hip arthroplasty. Clin Orthop 167:113–117, 1982.
52. Rizzo, P.F.; Gould, E.S.; Lyden, J.P.; Asnis, S.E. Diagnosis of occult fractures about the hip. J Bone Joint Surg Am 75:395–401, 1993.

53. Roeder, L.F., Jr.; DeLee, J.C. Femoral head fractures associated with posterior hip dislocations. Clin Orthop 147:121–130, 1980.

54. Salter, R.B.; Simmonds, D.F.; Malcolm, B.W.; et al. The biologic effect of continuous passive motion on the healing of full thickness defects in articular cartilage. An experimental investigation in the rabbit. J Bone Joint Surg Am 62:1232–1257, 1980.

55. Sarmiento, A.; Laird, C.A. Posterior fracture-dislocation of the femoral head. Report of a case. Clin Orthop 92:143–146, 1973.

56. Scham, S.M.; Fry, L.R. Traumatic anterior dislocation of the hip with fracture of the femoral head: A case report. Clin Orthop 62:133–135, 1969.

57. Seibel, R.; LaDuca, J.; Hassett, J.M.; et al. Blunt multiple trauma (ISS 36), femur traction, and the pulmonary failure septic state. Ann Surg 202:283–295, 1985.

58. Stannard, J.P.; Harris, H.W.; Volgas, D.A.; Alonso, J.E. Functional outcome of patients with femoral head fractures associated with hip dislocations. Clin Orthop 377:44–56, 2000.

59. Stewart, M.J. Management of the fractures of the head of the femur complicated by dislocation of the hip. Orthop Clin North Am 5:793–798, 1974.

60. Stewart, M.J.; Milford, L.W. Fracture dislocation of the hip: An end result study. J Bone Joint Surg Am 36:315, 1954.

61. Stromqvist, B. Femoral head vitality after intracapsular hip fracture; 490 cases studied by intravital tetracycline labeling and TCMDP radionuclide imaging. Acta Orthop Scand 54(Suppl 200):5–71, 1983.

62. Swiontkowski, M.F. Femoral head fractures. Curr Orthop 5:99–105, 1991.

63. Swiontkowski, M.F.; Thorpe, M.; Seiler, J.G.; Hansen, S.T. Operative management of femoral head fractures. Orthop Trans 13:51, 1989.

64. Tehranzadeh, J.; Vanarthros, W.; Pais, M.J. Osteochondral impaction of the femoral head associated with hip dislocation: CT study in 35 patients. AJR Am J Roentgenol 155:1049–1052, 1990.

65. Thomas, B.J.; Amstutz, H.C. Results of the administration of diphosphonate for the prevention of heterotopic ossification after total hip arthroplasty. J Bone Joint Surg Am 67:400–403, 1984.

66. Thompson, V.P.; Epstein, H.C. Traumatic dislocation of the hip: A survey of 204 cases covering a period of 21 years. J Bone Joint Surg Am 33:746, 1951.

67. Trueta, J.; Harrison, M.H.M. The normal vascular anatomy of the femoral head in adult man. J Bone Joint Surg Br 35:442–461, 1953.

68. Upadhyay, S.S.; Moulton, A. The long-term results of traumatic posterior dislocation of the hip. J Bone Joint Surg Br 63:548–551, 1981.

69. Upadhyay, S.S.; Moulton, A.; Burwell, R.G.; Biological factors predisposing to traumatic posterior dislocation of the hip. J Bone Joint Surg Br 67:232–236, 1985.

70. Weigand, H.; Schweikert, C.H.; Strube, H.D. Die traumatische Huftluxation mit huftkopfkalottenfraktur. Unfallheilkunde 81:377–389, 1978.

## Femoral Neck Fractures

71. Abrami, G.; Stevens J. Early weight bearing after internal fixation of transcervical fracture of the femur; preliminary report of a clinical trial. J Bone Joint Surg Br 46:204–205, 1965.

72. Ahmad, L.A.; Eckhoff, D.G.; Kramer, A.M. Outcome studies of hip fractures—a functional viewpoint. Orthop Rev 23:19–24, 1994.

73. Aitken, J.M. Relevance of osteoporosis in women with fracture of the femoral neck. BMJ 288:597–601, 1984.

74. Alberts, K.A.; Dahlborn, M.; Glas, J.E.; et al. Radionuclide scintigraphy of femoral head specimens removed at arthroplasty for failed femoral neck fractures. Clin Orthop 205:222–229, 1986.

75. Alho, A.; Benterud, J.G.; Muller, C.; Husby, T. Prediction of fixation failure in femoral neck fractures: Comminution and avascularity studied in 40 patients. Acta Orthop Scand 64:408–410, 1993.

76. Aloia, J.F.; Vaswani, A.; McGowan, D.; Ross, P. Preferential osteopenia in women with osteoporotic fractures. Bone Miner 18:51–63, 1992.

77. Anderson, G.H.; Harper, W.M.; Connolly, C.D.; et al. Preoperative skin traction for fractures of the proximal femur. J Bone Joint Surg Br 75:794–796, 1993.

78. Anderson, L.D.; Hamsa, W.R.; Waring, T.L. Femoral-head prosthesis; A review of three hundred and fifty-six operations and their results. J Bone Joint Surg Am 46:1049–1065, 1964.

79. Andersson, G. Hip assessment: A comparison of nine different methods. J Bone Joint Surg Br 54:621, 1972.

80. Anonymous: Life expectancy remains at record level. Stat Bull 70:26–30, 1989.

81. Antonelli-Incalzi, R.; Capparella, O.; Gemma, A.; et al. Predicting in-hospital mortality after hip fracture in elderly patients. J Trauma 36:79–82, 1994.

82. Apple, D.F.; Hayes, W.C., eds. Prevention of Falls and Hip Fractures in the Elderly. Rosemont, IL, American Academy of Orthopaedic Surgeons, 1994.

83. Arnold, W.D. The effect of early weight-bearing on the stability of femoral neck fractures treated with Knowles pins. J Bone Joint Surg Am 66:847–852, 1984.

84. Arnold, W.D.; Lynden, J.P.; Minkoff, J. Treatment of intracapsular fractures of the femoral neck. J Bone Joint Surg Am 56:254, 1974.

85. Arnoldi, C.C.; Lemperg, R.K. Fracture of the femoral neck: II. Relative importance of primary vascular damage and surgical procedure for the development of necrosis of the femoral head. Clin Orthop 129:217–222, 1977.

86. Arnoldi, C.C.; Linderholm, H. Fracture of the femoral neck: I. Vascular disturbances in different types of fractures, assessed by measurements of intraosseous pressure. Clin Orthop 84:116–127, 1972.

87. Aro, H.; Dahlstrom, S. Conservative management of distraction-type stress fractures of the femoral neck. J Bone Joint Surg Br 68:65–67, 1986.

88. Asai, T.; Nagaya, I.; Miyake, N.; et al. The treatment of intracapsular hip fractures with total hip arthroplasty in rheumatoid arthritis. Bull Hosp Jt Dis 53:29–33, 1993.

89. Askin, S.R.; Bryan, R.S. Femoral neck fractures in young adults. Clin Orthop 114:259–264, 1976.

90. Asnis, S.E.; Gould, E.S.; Bansal, M.; et al. Magnetic resonance imaging of the hip after displaced femoral neck fractures. Clin Orthop 298:191–198, 1994.

91. Asnis, S.E.; Wanek-Sgaglione, L. Intracapsular fractures of the femoral neck: Results of cannulated screw fixation. J Bone Joint Surg Am 76:1793–1803, 1994.

92. Asser Hansen, B.; Solgaard, S. Impacted fractures of the femoral neck treated by early mobilization and weight-bearing. Acta Orthop Scand 49:180–185, 1978.

93. Astrom, J.; Ahnqvist, S.; Beertema, J.; Jonsson, B. Physical activity in women sustaining fracture of the neck of the femur. J Bone Joint Surg Br 69:381–383, 1987.

94. Bagur, A.; Vega, E.; Mautalen, C. Discrimination of total body bone mineral density measured by DEXA in vertebral osteoporosis. Calcif Tissue Int 56:263–267, 1995.

95. Bargren, J.H.; Tilson, D.H.; Bridgeford, O.E. Prevention of displaced fatigue fractures of the femur. J Bone Joint Surg Am 53:1115–1117, 1971.

96. Barnes, J.T.; Brown, J.T.; Garden, R.S.; Nicoll, E.A. Subcapital fractures of the femur: A prospective review. J Bone Joint Surg Br 58:2–24, 1976.

97. Barnes, R. The diagnosis of ischaemia of the capital fragment in femoral neck fractures. J Bone Joint Surg Br 44:760–761, 1962.

98. Barth, R.W.; Williams, J.L.; Kaplan, F.S. Osteon morphometry in females with femoral neck fractures. Clin Orthop 283:178–186, 1992.

99. Bastow, M.D.; Rawlings, J.; Allison, S.P. Benefits of supplemental tube feeding after fractured neck of femur: A randomized controlled trial. BMJ 287:1589–1592, 1983.

100. Bastow, M.D.; Rawlings, J.; Allison, S.P. Undernutrition, hypothermia, and injury in elderly women with fractured femur: An injury response to altered metabolism? Lancet 1:143–146, 1983.

101. Bauer, G.; Weber, D.A.; Ceder, L.; et al. Dynamics of technetium-99m methylenediphosphonate imaging of the femoral head after femoral neck fracture. Clin Orthop 152:85–92, 1982.

102. Bayliss, A.P.; Davidson, J.K. Traumatic osteonecrosis of the femoral head following intracapsular fracture: Incidence and earliest radiological features. Clin Radiol 28:407–414, 1977.

103. Beck, T.J.; Ruff, C.B.; Scott, W.W., Jr.; et al. Sex differences in geometry of the femoral neck with aging: A structural analysis of bone-mineral data. Calcif Tissue Int 50:24–29, 1992.

104. Bentley, G. Impacted fractures of the neck of the femur. J Bone Joint Surg Br 50:551–561, 1968.

105. Bigler, D.; Adelhoj, B.; Petring, O.U.; et al. Mental function and morbidity after acute hip surgery during spinal and general anesthesia. Anesthesia 40:672–676, 1985.

106. Blair, B.; Koval, K.J.; Kummer, F.; Zuckerman, J.D. Basicervical fractures of the proximal femur: A biomechanical study of 3 internal fixation techniques. Clin Orthop 306:256–263, 1994.

107. Blickenstaff, L.D.; Morris, J.M. Fatigue fracture of the femoral neck. J Bone Joint Surg Am 48:1031–1047, 1966.

108. Bochner, R.M.; Pellici, P.M.; Lyden, J.P. Bipolar hemiarthroplasty for fracture of the femoral neck. J Bone Joint Surg Am 70:1001–1010, 1988.

109. Bohr, H.; Larsen, E.H. On necrosis of the femoral head after fracture of the neck of the femur—a microradiographic and histologic study. J Bone Joint Surg Br 47:330–338, 1965.

110. Bonfiglio, M.; Voke, E.M. Aseptic necrosis of the femoral head and nonunion of the femoral neck: Effect of treatment of drilling and bone-grafting (Phemister technique). J Bone Joint Surg Am 50:48–66, 1968.

111. Bonnaire, F.; Kuner, E.H.; Lorz, W. Schenkelhalsfrakturen beim Erwachsenen: Gelenkerhaltende Operationen II. Die Bedeutung des Operationspunkts und des Implantats fur die Genese der aseptis-chen Huftkopfnekrose. Unfallchirurg 98:259–264, 1995.

112. Boston, D.A. Bilateral fractures of the femoral neck. Injury 14:207–210, 1982.

113. Boyd, H.B.; Calandruccio, R.A. Further observations on the use of radioactive phosphorous (P32) to determine the viability of the head of the femur: Correlation of clinical and experimental data in 130 patients with fractures of the femoral neck. J Bone Joint Surg Am 45:445–460, 1963.

114. Boyd, H.B.; Salvatore, J.E. Acute fracture of the femoral neck: Internal fixation or prosthesis? J Bone Joint Surg Am 46:1066–1068, 1964.

115. Boyd, H.B.; Zilversmit, D.B.; Calandruccio, R.A. The use of radioactive phosphorous (P32) to determine the viability of the head of the femur. J Bone Joint Surg Am 37:260–269, 1960.

116. Braun, W.; Ruter, A.; Wiederman, M.; Kissing, F. Kopferhaltende Therapie bei medialen Shenkelhalsfrakturen. Eine klinische Studie zum Einfluss des Behandlungsregimes auf das Heilungsergebenis. Unfallchirurg 94:325–330, 1991.

117. Brodetti, A. The blood supply of the femoral neck and head in relation to the damaging effects of nails and screws. J Bone Joint Surg Br 42:794–801, 1960.

118. Broos, P.L. Hip fractures in elderly people: The surgical treatment in Leuven, Belgium. Acta Chir Belg 3:130–135, 1994.

119. Brown, T.I.S.; Court-Brown, C. Failure of sliding nail-plate fixation in subcapital fractures of the femoral neck. J Bone Joint Surg Br 61:342–346, 1979.

120. Brunner, C.F.; Weber, B.G. Special Techniques in Internal Fixation. Berlin, Springer-Verlag, 1982, p. 34.

121. Burton, P.; Prieskorn, D.; Smith, R.; et al. Component motion in bipolar hip arthroplasty: An evaluation of reamed and nonreamed acetabula. Orthopedics 17:319–324, 1994.

122. Calandruccio, R.A. Arthroplasty of the hip. In: Crenshaw, A.H., ed. Campbell's Operative Orthopaedics, 7th ed. St. Louis, C.V. Mosby, 1987.

123. Calder, S.J.; Anderson, G.H.; Harper, W.M.; et al. A subjective health indicator for follow-up: A randomized trial after treatment of displaced intracapsular hip fractures. J Bone Joint Surg Br 77:494–496, 1995.

124. Camp, J.F.; Colwell, C.E. Core decompression of the femoral head for osteonecrosis. J Bone Joint Surg Am 68:1313–1319, 1986.

125. Canner, G.C.; Steinberg, M.E.; Heppenstall, R.B.; Balderston, R. The infected hip after total hip arthroplasty. J Bone Joint Surg Am 66:1393–1399, 1984.

126. Casey, M.J.; Chapman, M.W. Ipsilateral concomitant fractures of the hip and femoral shaft. J Bone Joint Surg Am 61:503–509, 1979.

127. Casserly, H.B.; Healy, B. The Monk hardtop prosthesis for displaced intracapsular fractures of the femoral neck. Ir J Med Sci 160:5–7, 1991.

128. Castle, M.E.; Orinion, E.A. Prophylactic anticoagulation in fractures. J Bone Joint Surg Am 52:521–528, 1970.

129. Catto, M. A histological study of avascular necrosis of the femoral head after transcervical fracture. J Bone Joint Surg Br 47:749–776, 1965.

130. Ceder, L.; Stromqvist, B.; Hansson, L.I. Effects of strategy changes in the treatment of femoral neck fractures during a 17-year period. Clin Orthop 218:53–57, 1987.

131. Chan, K.A.; Andrade, S.E.; Boles, M.; et al. Inhibitors of hydroxymethylglutaryl–coenzyme A reductase and risk of fracture among older women. Lancet 355:2185–2188, 2000.

132. Chan, R.N.W.; Hoskinson, J. Thompson prosthesis for fractures of the neck of the femur: A comparison of surgical approaches. J Bone Joint Surg Br 57:437–443, 1975.

133. Chandler, S.B.; Kreuscher, P.H. A study of the blood supply of the ligamentum teres and its relation to the circulation of the head of the femur. J Bone Joint Surg 14:834–846, 1932.

134. Chapman, M.W.; Stehr, J.H.; Eberle, C.F.; et al. Treatment of intracapsular hip fractures by the Deyerle method: A comparative review of 119 cases. J Bone Joint Surg Am 57:735–744, 1975.

135. Chapuy, M.C.; Arlot, M.E.; Duboeuf, F.; et al. Vitamin $D_3$ and calcium prevent hip fractures in elderly women. N Engl J Med 327:1637–1642, 1992.

136. Chevalley, T.; Rizzoli, R.; Nydegger, V.; et al. Preferential low bone mineral density of the femoral neck in patients with a recent fracture of the proximal femur. Osteoporos Int 1:147–154, 1991.

137. Chiara-Corti, M.; Guralnik, J.M.; Salive, M.E.; Sorkin, J.D. Serum albumin level and physical disability as predictors of mortality in older persons. JAMA 272:1036–1042, 1994.

138. Chiu, K.Y.; Ng, K.H.; Lau, S.K.; et al. Antibiotic prophylaxis for hip fracture operations: A prospective study comparing four different regimes. Int J Orthop Trauma 3:174–177, 1993.

139. Christodoulou, N.A.; Dretakis, E.K. Significance of muscular disturbances in the localization of fractures of the proximal femur. Clin Orthop 187:215–217, 1984.

140. Claffey, T.J. Avascular necrosis of the femoral head: An anatomical study. J Bone Joint Surg Br 42:802–809, 1960.

141. Clawson, D.K. Intracapsular fractures of the femur treated by the sliding screw plate fixation method. J Trauma 4:753–756, 1964.

142. Coates, R.L.; Armour, P. Treatment of subcapital femoral fractures by primary total hip replacement. Injury 11:132–135, 1979.

143. Cole, J.D.; Browner, B.D.; Cotler, H.B.; et al. Initial experience with a second generation locking nail. Orthop Trans 14:269, 1990.

144. Coleman, S.A.; Boyce, W.J.; Cosh, P.H.; McKenzie, P.J. Outcome after general anesthesia for repair of fractured neck of femur—a randomized trial of spontaneous v. controlled ventilation. Br J Anaesth 60:43–47, 1988.

145. Cotton, F.J. Artificial impaction in hip fractures. Surg Gynecol Obstet 45:307–319, 1927.

146. Cotton, F.J. Intracapsular hip fracture. J Bone Joint Surg 16:105–109, 1934.

147. Coughlin, L.; Templeton, J. Hip fractures in patients with Parkinson's disease. Clin Orthop 148:192–195, 1980.

148. Courtney, A.C.; Wachtel, E.F.; Myers, E.R.; Hayes, W.C. Age related reductions in the strength of the femur tested in a fall-loading configuration. J Bone Joint Surg Am 77:387–395, 1995.

149. Crawford, H.B. Conservative treatment of impacted fractures of the femoral neck: A report of fifty cases. J Bone Joint Surg Am 42:471–479, 1960.

150. Crawfurd, E.J.P.; Emery, R.J.H.; Hansell, D.M.; et al. Capsular distension and intracapsular pressure in subcapital fractures of the femur. J Bone Joint Surg Br 70:195–198, 1988.

151. Crock, H.V. A revision of the anatomy of the arteries supplying the upper end of the human femur. J Anat 99:77–88, 1965.

152. Crock, H.V. An atlas of the arterial supply of the head and neck of the femur in man. Clin Orthop 152:17–27, 1980.

153. Cummings, S.R.; Bauer, D.C.; Do statins prevent both cardiovascular disease and fracture? JAMA 283:3255–3257, 2000.

154. Cummings, S.R.; Marcus, R.; Palermo, L.; et al. Does estimating volumetric bone density of the femoral neck improve the prediction of hip fracture? A prospective study: Study of osteoporotic fractures research group. J Bone Miner Res 9:1429–1432, 1994.

155. Cummings, S.R.; Phillips, S.L.; Wheat, M.E.; et al. Recovery of function after hip fracture: The role of social supports. J Am Geriatr Soc 36:801–806, 1988.

156. Currie, A.L.; Reid, D.M.; Brown, N.; Nuki, G. An epidemiological study of fracture of the neck of the femur. Health Bull 44:143–148, 1986.

157. Dahl, E. Mortality and life expectancy after hip fractures. Acta Orthop Scand 51:163–170, 1980.

158. Dalen, N.; Jacobsson, B. Rarefied femoral neck trabecular patterns, fracture displacement, and femoral head vitality in femoral neck fractures. Clin Orthop 205:97–98, 1986.

159. D'Arcy, L.; Devas, M. Treatment of fractures of the femoral neck by replacement with the Thompson prosthesis. J Bone Joint Surg Br 58:279–286, 1976.

160. Davis, F.M.; Woolner, D.F.; Frampton, C.; et al. Prospective, multicenter trial of mortality following general or spinal anesthesia for hip fracture surgery in the elderly. Br J Anaesth 59:1080–1088, 1987.

161. Dedrick, D.K.; Mackenzie, J.R.; Burney, R.E. Complications of femoral neck fractures in young adults. J Trauma 26:932–937, 1986.

162. Delamarter, R.; Moreland, J.R. Treatment of acute femoral neck fractures with total hip arthroplasty. Clin Orthop 218:68–74, 1987.

163. Devas, M.; Hinves, B. Prevention of acetabular erosion after hemiarthroplasty for fractured neck of femur. J Bone Joint Surg Br 65:548–551, 1983.

164. Devas, M.B. Stress fractures of the femoral neck. J Bone Joint Surg Br 47:728–738, 1965.

165. Deyerle, W.M. Impacted fixation over resilient multiple pins. Clin Orthop 152:102–122, 1980.

166. Dorne, H.L.; Lander, P.H. Spontaneous stress fractures of the femoral neck. Am J Radiol 144:343–347, 1984.

167. Drake, J.K.; Meyers, M.H. Intracapsular pressure and hemarthrosis following femoral neck fracture. Clin Orthop 182:172–176, 1984.

168. Dretakis, E.K.; Christodoulou, N.A. Significance of endogenic factors in the location of fractures of the proximal femur. Acta Orthop Scand 54:198–203, 1983.

169. Driesen, R.; Nijs, S.; Broos, P.L.; Fabry, G. Unstable femoral neck fractures treated with a 130 degree blade plate. Acta Orthop Belg 60:322–327, 1994.

170. Drinker, H.; Murray, W.R. The universal proximal femoral endoprosthesis: A short term comparison with conventional hemiarthroplasty. J Bone Joint Surg Am 61:1167–1174, 1979.

171. Edholm, P.; Lindblom, K.; Maurseth, K. Angulations in the fractures of the femoral neck with and without subsequent necrosis of the head. Acta Radiol Scand 6:329–336, 1967.

172. Edwards, C.J.; Hart, D.J.; Spector, T.D. Oral statins and increased bone mineral density in postmenopausal women. Lancet 355: 2218–2219, 2000.

173. Eiskjaer, S.; Gelineck, J.; Soballe, K. Fractures of the femoral neck treated with cemented bipolar hemiarthroplasty. Orthopedics 12:1545–1550, 1989.

174. Eiskjaer, S.; Ostgard, S.E. Survivorship analysis of hemiarthroplasties. Clin Orthop 286:206–211, 1993.

175. Eiskjaer, S.; Ostgard, S.E. Risk factors influencing mortality after bipolar hemiarthroplasty in the treatment of fracture of the femoral neck. Clin Orthop 270:295–300, 1991.

176. Elke, R.P.E.; Cheal, E.J.; Simmons, C.; Poss, R. Three-dimensional anatomy of the cancellous structures within the proximal femur from computed tomography data. J Orthop Res 13:513–523, 1995.

177. Ernst, J. Stress fractures of the neck of the femur. J Trauma 4:71–83, 1964.

178. Eventov, I.; Frisch, B.; Cohen, Z.; Hammel, I. Osteopenia, hematopoiesis, and bone remodelling after iliac crest and femoral biopsies: A prospective study of 102 cases of femoral neck fractures. Bone 12:1–6, 1991.

179. Ewald, F.C.; Christie, M.J.; Thomas, W.H.; et al. Total hip arthroplasty for failed hemiarthroplasty. Paper presented at the 52nd Annual Meeting of the American Academy of Orthopaedic Surgeons, Las Vegas, Nevada, January 28, 1985.

180. Fairclough, J.; Colhoun, E.; Johnston, D.; Williams, L.A. Bone scanning for suspected hip fractures—a prospective study in elderly patients. J Bone Joint Surg Br 69:251–253, 1987.

181. Faulkner, K.G.; Cummings, S.R.; Black, D.; et al. Simple measurement of femoral geometry predicts hip fracture: The study of osteoporotic fractures. J Bone Miner Res 8:1211–1217, 1993.

182. Fehr, H.R.; Steiner, W.; Noesberger, B. Osteosynthese bei der dislozierten Schenkelhalsfraktur (Garden 3 and 4): Langzeitresultate und Behandlungskonzept. Helv Chir Acta 59:539–542, 1993.

183. Felson, D.T.; Zhang, Y.; Hannan, M.T.; et al. The effect of postmenopausal estrogen therapy in bone density in elderly women. N Engl J Med 329:1141–1146, 1993.

184. Fiatatore, M.A.; O'Neill, E.F.; Doyle-Ryan, N.; et al. Exercise training and nutritional supplementation for physical frailty in very elderly people. N Engl J Med 330:1769–1775, 1994.

185. Ficat, R.P. Idiopathic bone necrosis of the femoral head: Early diagnosis and treatment. J Bone Joint Surg Br 67:3–9, 1985.

186. Fielding, J.W.; Wilson, S.A.; Ratzaw, S. A continuing end-result study of displaced intracapsular fractures of the neck of the femur treated with the Pugh nail. J Bone Joint Surg Am 56:1464, 1974.

187. Fielding, J.W.; Wilson, H.J.; Zickel, R.E. A continuing end-result study of intracapsular fracture of the neck of the femur. J Bone Joint Surg Am 44:965–974, 1962.

188. Finsen, V.; Benum, P. Changing incidence of hip fractures in rural and urban areas of central Norway. Clin Orthop 218:104–110, 1987.

189. Fipp, G. Stress fracture of the femoral neck following TKA. J Arthroplasty 3:347–351, 1988.

190. Firooznia, H.; Rafii, M.; Golimbu, C.; et al. Trabecular mineral content of the spine in women with hip fracture: CT measurement. Radiology 159:737–740, 1986.

191. Fitzgerald, J.F.; Fagan, L.F.; Tierny, W.M.; Dittus, R.S. Changing patterns of hip fracture care before and after implementation of the prospective payment system. JAMA 258:218–221, 1987.

192. Fordham, R. Hip fractures and QALYS [letter]. J Bone Joint Surg Br 75:163–164, 1993.

193. Frandsen, P.A.; Kruse, T. Hip fractures in the county of Funen, Denmark; implications of demographic aging and changes in incidence rates. Acta Orthop Scand 54:681–686, 1983.

194. Frangakis, E.K. Intracapsular fractures of the neck of the femur—factors influencing nonunion and ischaemic necrosis. J Bone Joint Surg Br 48:17–30, 1966.

195. Franklin, A.; Gallannaugh, S.C. The biarticular hip prosthesis for fractures of the femoral neck—a preliminary report. Injury 15:159–162, 1983.

196. Freeman, M.A.R.; Todd, R.C.; Pirie, C.J. The role of fatigue in the pathogenesis of senile femoral neck fractures. J Bone Joint Surg Br 56:698–702, 1974.

197. Friedman, R.J.; Wyman, F.T. Ipsilateral hip and femoral shaft fractures. Clin Orthop 208:188–194, 1986.

198. Froehlich, J.A.; Dorfman, G.S.; Cronan, J.J.; et al. Compression ultrasonography for detection of deep venous thrombosis in patients who have a fracture of the hip. J Bone Joint Surg Am 71:249–256, 1989.

199. Ganz, R.; Bumlautuchler. U. Overview of attempts to revitalize the dead head in aseptic necrosis of the femoral head—osteotomy and revascularization. In: Proceedings of the Eleventh Hip Society. St. Louis, C.V. Mosby, 1983, pp. 296–305.

200. Garcia, A.; Meer, E.S.; Ambrose, G.B. Displaced intracapsular fractures of the neck of the femur. J Trauma 1:128, 1961.

201. Garden, R.S. The structure and function of the proximal end of the femur. J Bone Joint Surg Br 43:576–589, 1961.

202. Garden, R.S. Stability and union in subcapital fractures of the femur. J Bone Joint Surg Br 46:630–647, 1964.

203. Garden, R.S. Malreduction and avascular necrosis in subcapital fractures of the femur. J Bone Joint Surg Br 53:183–197, 1971.

204. Gebhard, J.S.; Amstutz, H.C.; Zinar, D.M.; Dorey, F.J. A comparison of total hip arthroplasty and hemiarthroplasty for treatment of acute fractures of the femoral neck. Clin Orthop 282:123–131, 1992.

205. Gegerle, P.; Bengoa, J.M.; Delmi, M.; et al. Enquête alimentaire après fracture du col du femur: Effect d'un supplement diététique sur les apports nutritionels. Schweiz Rundsch Med Prax 75:933–935, 1986.

206. Gilberty, R.P. Hemiarthroplasty of the hip using a low friction bipolar endoprosthesis. Clin Orthop 175:86–92, 1983.

207. Giordani, M.; Sarmiento, A.; Wiss, D.A.; et al. Complex fractures of the hip treated with a second generation locking nail. Orthop Trans 14:269, 1990.

208. Girard, M.S.; Sartoris, D.J.; Moscona, A.A.; Ramos, E. Measured femoral density by dual-energy X-ray absorptiometry as a function of rotation. Orthop Rev 23:38–40, 1994.

209. Girasole, G.J.; Cuomo, F.; Denton, J.R.; et al. Diagnosis of deep vein thrombosis in elderly hip fracture patients by using duplex scanning technique. Orthop Rev 23:411–416, 1994.

210. Glass, K.E. Moore arthroplasty operations. J Bone Joint Surg Br 47:598, 1965.

211. Glimcher, M.J.; Kenzora, J.E. The biology of osteonecrosis of the human femoral head and its clinical implications: III. Discussion of the etiology and genesis of the pathological sequelae: Comments on treatment. Clin Orthop 140:273–312, 1979.

212. Gluer, C.C.; Cummings, S.R.; Pressman, A.; et al. Prediction of hip fractures from pelvic radiographics: The study of osteoporotic fractures. J Bone Miner Res 9:671–677, 1994.

213. Gray, A.J.; Parker, M.J. Intracapsular fractures of the neck of the femur in young patients. Injury 25:667–669, 1994.

214. Greenspan, S.L.; Maitland, L.A.; Myers, E.R.; et al. Femoral bone loss progresses with age: A longitudinal study in women over age 65. J Bone Miner Res 9:1959–1965, 1994.

215. Greenspan, S.L.; Meyers, F.R.; Maitland, I.A.; et al. Trochanteric bone mineral density is associated with type of hip fracture in the elderly. J Bone Miner Res 9:1889–1894, 1994.

216. Greenspan, S.L.; Meyers, E.R.; Maitland, L.A.; et al. Fall severity and bone mineral density as risk factors for hip fracture in ambulatory elderly. JAMA 271:128–133, 1994.

217. Greenwald, A.S.; Haynes, D.W. Weightbearing areas in the human hip joint. J Bone Joint Surg Br 54:157–163, 1972.

218. Grieff, J. Determination of the vitality of the femoral head with $^{99m}$Tc-Sn-pyrophosphate scintigraphy. Acta Orthop Scand 51:109–117, 1980.

219. Greiff, J.; Lanng, S.; Hoilund-Carlsen, P.F.; et al. Early detection by $^{99m}$Tc-Sn-pyrophosphate scintigraphy of femoral head necrosis following medial femoral neck fractures. Acta Orthop Scand 51:119–125, 1980.

220. Griffin, J.B. The calcar femorale redefined. Clin Orthop 164:211–214, 1982.

221. Griffin, M.R.; Ray, W.A.; Fought, R.L.; Melton, J.L., III. Black white differences in fracture rates. Am J Epidemiol 136:1378–1385, 1992.

222. Grispigni, C.; Lazzerini, A. Reduction and osteosynthesis of subcapital fractures of the femoral neck: Possible repercussions on postfracture hemarthrosis of the hip. Ital J Orthop Traumatol 18:539–542, 1992.

223. Grisso, J.A.; Kelsey, J.L.; Strom, B.L.; et al. Risk factors for hip fracture in black women. N Engl J Med 330:1555–1559, 1994.

224. Gruber, U.F. Prevention of fatal pulmonary embolism in patients with fractures of the neck of the femur. Surg Gynecol Obstet 161:37–42, 1985.

225. Guanache, C.A.; Kozin, S.H.; Levy, A.S.; Brody, L.A. The use of MRI in the diagnosis of occult hip fracture in the elderly: A preliminary report. Orthopedics 17:327–330, 1994.

226. Gustke, K. The treatment of intracapsular hip fractures. Techn Orthop 4:19–29, 1989.

227. Hagglund, G.; Nordstrom, B.; Lidgren, L. Total hip replacement after nailing failure in femoral neck fractures. Arch Orthop Trauma Surg 103:125–127, 1984.

228. Hamilton, H.W.; Crawford, J.S.; Gardiner, J.H.; Wiley, A.M. Venous thrombosis in patients with fracture of the upper end of the femur: A phlebographic study of the effect of prophylactic anticoagulation. J Bone Joint Surg Br 52:268–289, 1970.

229. Hannan, E.L.; Mendeloff, J.; Szypulski-Farrell, L.; et al. Multivariate models for predicting survival of patients with trauma from low falls: The impact of gender and preexisting conditions. J Trauma 38:697–704, 1995.

230. Harper, W.M.; Barnes, M.R.; Gregg, P.J. Femoral head blood flow in femoral neck fractures: An analysis using intraosseous pressure measurement. J Bone Joint Surg Br 73:73–75, 1991.

231. Harris, W.H. Traumatic arthritis of the hip after dislocation and acetabular fractures: Treatment by mold arthroplasty. J Bone Joint Surg Am 51:737–755, 1969.

232. Harris, W.H.; Athanasoulis, C.A.; Waltman, A.C.; Salzman, E.W. High and low dose aspirin prophylaxis against venous thromboembolic disease in total hip replacement. J Bone Joint Surg Am 64:63–66, 1982.

233. Hartman, J.T.; Altner, P.C.; Freeark, R.J. The effect of limb elevation in preventing venous thrombosis; A venographic study. J Bone Joint Surg Am 52:1618–1622, 1970.

234. Harty, M. Blood supply of the femoral head. BMJ 7:1236–1237, 1953.

235. Harty, M. The calcar femorale and the femoral neck. J Bone Joint Surg Am 39:625–630, 1957.

236. Has, B.; Has-Schon, E.; Veber, B.; Mijatovic, Z. [Hip fracture analysis according to age, sex, side, and fracture.] Lijec Vjesn 110:147–151, 1988.

237. Hayes, W.C.; Myers, E.R.; Morris, J.N.; et al. Impact near the hip dominates fracture risk in elderly nursing home residents who fall. Calcif Tissue Int 52:192–198, 1993.

238. Heithoff, K.A.; Lohr, K.N., eds: Hip Fracture: Setting Priorities for Effectiveness Research. Institute of Medicine Report, National Academy Press, 1990.

239. Henry, S.L.; Seligson, D. Ipsilateral femoral neck-shaft fractures: A comparison of therapeutic devices. Orthop Trans 14:269, 1990.

240. Hernefalk, L.; Messner, K. Femoral stiffness after osteosynthesis of a subcapital osteotomy in osteoporotic bone: An in-vitro comparison of nine fixation methods. J Orthop Trauma 9:464–469, 1995.

241. Hillard, T.C.; Whitcroft, S.J.; Marsh, M.S.; et al. Long-term effects of transdermal and oral hormone replacement therapy on postmenopausal bone loss. Osteoporos Int 4:341–348, 1994.

242. Hilleboe, J.W.; Staple, T.W.; Lansche, E.W.; Reynolds, F.C. The nonoperative treatment of impacted fractures of the femoral neck. South Med J 63:1103–1109, 1970.

243. Hinchey, J.J.; Day, P.L. Primary prosthetic replacement in fresh femoral neck fractures. J Bone Joint Surg Am 46:223–240, 1964.

244. Hindou, R.Y.; Lennox, D.W.; Ebert, F.R.; et al. Relative rates of fracture of the hip in the United States. J Bone Joint Surg Am 77:695–702, 1995.

245. Hinton, R.Y.; Smith, G.S. The association of age, race and sex with the location of proximal femoral fractures in the elderly. J Bone Joint Surg Am 75:752–759, 1993.

246. Hirsch, C.; Frankel, V.H. Analysis of forces producing fractures of the proximal end of the femur. J Bone Joint Surg Br 42:633–640, 1960.

247. Hoaglund, F.T.; Low, W.D. Anatomy of the femoral neck and head, with comparative data from Caucasians and Hong Kong Chinese. Clin Orthop 152:10–16, 1980.

248. Hodge, W.A.; Carlson, K.L.; Fijan, R.S.; et al. Contact pressures from an instrumented hip endoprosthesis. J Bone Joint Surg Am 71:1378–1386, 1989.

249. Hogh, J.; Jensen, J.; Lauritzen, J. Dislocated femoral neck fractures: A follow-up study of 98 cases treated by multiple AO (ASIF) cancellous bone screws. Acta Orthop Scand 53:245–249, 1982.

250. Hoikka, V.; Alhava, E.M.; Savolainen, K.; Parviainen, M. Osteomalacia in fractures of the proximal femur. Acta Orthop Scand 53:255–260, 1982.

251. Holbrook, T.; Barrett-Connor, E.; Wingard, D.L. Dietary calcium and risk of hip fracture: Fourteen year prospective population study. Lancet 2:1046–1049, 1988.

252. Holmberg, S.; Conradi, P.; Kalen, R.; Thorngren, K.G. Mortality after cervical hip fracture: 3002 patients followed for 6 years. Acta Orthop Scand 57:8–11, 1986.

253. Holmberg, S.; Dalen, N. Intracapsular pressure and caput circulation in nondisplaced femoral neck fractures. Clin Orthop 219:124–126, 1987.

254. Holmberg, S.; Kalen, R.; Thorngren, K.G. Treatment and outcome of femoral neck fractures—an analysis of 2418 patients admitted from their own homes. Clin Orthop 218:42–52, 1987.

255. Holmberg, S.; Thorngren, K.G. Rehabilitation after femoral neck fracture. Acta Orthop Scand 56:305–308, 1985.

256. Holmes, C.A.; Edwards, W.T.; Myers, E.R.; et al. Biomechanics of pin and screw fixation of femoral neck fractures. J Orthop Trauma 7:242–247, 1993.

257. Holmquist, B.; Alffram, P.A. Prediction of avascular necrosis following cervical fracture of the femur based on clearance of radioactive iodine from the head of the femur. Acta Orthop Scand 36:62–69, 1965.

258. Horiuchi, T.; Igarashi, M.; Karube, S.; et al. Spontaneous fractures of the hip in the elderly. Orthopedics 11:1277–1280, 1988.

259. Horsman, A.H.; Nordin, B.E.; Simpson, M.; Speed, R. Cortical and trabecular bone status in elderly women with femoral neck fracture. Clin Orthop 166:143–151, 1982.

260. Howard, C.B.; Mackie, I.G.; Fairclough, J. Femoral neck surgery using a local anesthetic technique. Anesthesia 38:993–994, 1983.

261. Howe, W.W.; Lacey, T.; Schwartz, R.P. A study of the gross anatomy of the arteries supplying the proximal portion of the femur and acetabulum. J Bone Joint Surg Am 32:856–866, 1950.

262. Hubble, M.J.; Little, C.P.; Barrowclough, H.K.; et al. Rehabilitation after proximal femoral fracture: A two hospital comparison. Int J Orthop Trauma 4:123–125, 1994.

263. Hui, A.C.; Anderson, G.H.; Choudry, R.; et al. Internal fixation or hemiarthroplasty for undisplaced fractures of the femoral neck in octogenarians. J Bone Joint Surg Br 76:891–894, 1994.

264. Hunter, G.A. A comparison of the use of internal fixation and prosthetic replacement for fresh fractures of the neck of the femur. Br J Surg 56:229–232, 1969.

265. Hunter, G.A. A further comparison of the use of internal fixation and prosthetic replacement for fresh fractures of the femur. Br J Surg 61:382, 1974.

266. Hunter, G.A. Should we abandon primary prosthetic replacement for fresh displaced fractures of the neck of the femur? Clin Orthop 152:158–161, 1980.

267. Jacobsson, B.; Dalen, N.; Jonsson, B.; Ackerman, P. Intraarticular pressure during operation of cervical hip fractures. Acta Orthop Scand 59:16–18, 1988.

268. Jarnlo, G.B.; Thorngren, K.G. Background factors to hip fractures. Clin Orthop 287:41–49, 1993.

269. Jarolem, K.L.; Koval, K.J.; Zuckerman, J.D.; Aharnoff, G. A comparison of modified Knowles pins and cannulated cancellous screws for the treatment of nondisplaced or impacted femoral neck fractures. Bull Hosp Jt Dis 53:11–14, 1993.

270. Jeffery, C.C. Spontaneous fractures of the femoral neck. J Bone Joint Surg Br 44:543–549, 1962.

271. Jensen, J.S.; Bagger, J. Long-term social prognosis after hip fractures. Acta Orthop Scand 53:97–101, 1982.

272. Jensen, J.; Hogh, J. Fractures of the femoral neck: A follow-up study after nonoperative treatment of Garden's stage 1 and 2 fractures. Injury 14:339–342, 1982.

273. Jensen, T.T.; Junker, Y. Pressure sores common after hip operations. Acta Orthop Scand 58:209–211, 1987.

274. Jette, A.M.; Harris, B.A.; Cleary, P.D.; Campion, E.W. Functional recovery after hip fracture. Arch Phys Med Rehabil 68:735–740, 1987.

275. Johnson, J.T.H.; Crothers, O. Nailing versus prosthesis for femoral neck fractures: A critical review of long-term results in two hundred and thirty-nine consecutive private patients. J Bone Joint Surg Am 57:686–692, 1975.

276. Johnson, K.D.; Brock, G. A review of reduction and internal fixation of adult femoral neck fractures in a county hospital. J Orthop Trauma 2:83–96, 1989.

277. Johnston, C.C., Jr.; Slemenda, C.W. Risk assessment: Theoretic considerations. Am J Med 95(Suppl):2–5, 1993.

278. Jones, G.; Nguyen, T.; Sambrook, P.; et al. Progressive loss of bone in the femoral neck in elderly people: Longitudinal findings from the Dubbo osteoporosis epidemiology study. BMJ 309:691–695, 1994.

279. Jorgensen, P.S.; Knudsen, J.B.; Broeng, L.; et al. The thromboprophylactic effect of a low molecular weight heparin (Fragmin) in hip fracture surgery: A placebo-controlled study. Clin Orthop 278:95–100, 1992.

280. Judet, J.; Judet, R.; Langrange, J.; Dunoyer, J. A study of the arterial vascularization of the femoral neck in the adult. J Bone Joint Surg Am 37:663–680, 1955.

281. Judet, R. Traitment des fractures du col du femur par greffe pediculée. Acta Orthop Scand 23:421–427, 1952.

282. Kaltsas, D.K. Stress fractures of the femoral neck in young adults; a report of seven cases. J Bone Joint Surg Br 63:33–37, 1981.

283. Kavanaugh, B.F.; Fitzgerald, R.H. Multiple revisions for failed total hip arthroplasty not associated with infection. J Bone Joint Surg Am 69:1144–1149, 1987.

284. Kavlie, H.; Sundal, B. Primary arthroplasty in femoral neck fractures. A review of 269 consecutive cases treated with the Christiansen prosthesis. Acta Orthop Scand 45:579–590, 1974.

285. Keating, J.F.; Robinson, C.M.; Court-Brown, C.M.; et al. The effect of complications after hip fracture on rehabilitation. J Bone Joint Surg Br 75:976, 1993.

286. Keene, G.S.; Parker, M.J.; Pryor, G.A. Mortality and morbidity after hip fractures. BMJ 307:1248–1250, 1993.

287. Keller, C.S.; Laros, G.S. Indications for open reduction of femoral neck fractures. Clin Orthop 152:131–137, 1980.

288. Kenzora, J.E.; McCarthy, R.E.; Lowell, J.D.; Sledge, C.B. Hip fracture mortality—relation to age, treatment, preoperative illness, time of surgery, and complications. Clin Orthop 186:45–56, 1984.

289. Kofoed, H.; Alberts, A. Femoral neck fractures; 165 cases treated by multiple percutaneous pinning. Acta Orthop Scand 51:127–136, 1980.

290. Kofoed, H.; Kofod, J. Moore prosthesis in the treatment of fresh femoral neck fractures—a critical review with special attention to secondary acetabular degeneration. Injury 14:531–540, 1981.

291. Koval, K.J.; Skovron, M.L.; Aharonoff, G.B.; et al. Ambulatory ability after hip fracture: A prospective study in geriatric patients. Clin Orthop 310:150–159, 1995.

292. Koval, K.J.; Zuckerman, J.D. Functional recovery after fracture of the hip. J Bone Joint Surg Am 76:751–758, 1994.

293. Kroger, H.; Huopio, J.; Honkanen, R., et al. Prediction of fracture risk using axial bone mineral density in a perimenopausal population: A prospective study. J Bone Miner Res 10:302–306, 1995.

294. Lang, P.; Jergensen, H.E.; Genant, H.K.; et al. Magnetic resonance imaging of the ischemic femoral head in pigs. Dependency of signal intensities and relaxation times on elapsed time. Clin Orthop 244:272–280, 1989.

295. Langan, P. The Gilberty bipolar prosthesis: A clinical and radiographical review. Clin Orthop 141:169–175, 1979.

296. Lauritzen, J.B.; Petersen, M.M.; Lund, B. Effect of external hip protectors on hip fractures. Lancet 341:11–13, 1993.

297. Lausten, G.S.; Hesse, B.; Thygesen, V.; Fogh, J. Knogleskintigrafi til vurdering af risiko for komplikationer efter medial collum femoris fraktur. Ugeskr Laeger 14:1864–1867, 1993.

298. Lausten, G.S.; Vedel, P.; Nielsen, P.M. Fractures of the femoral neck treated with a bipolar endoprosthesis. Clin Orthop 218:63–67, 1987.

299. Lavernia, C.J. Hemiarthroplasty in hip fracture care—effects of surgical volume on short-term outcome. J Arthroplasty 13:774–778, 1998.

300. Leadbetter, G.W. Closed reduction of fractures of the neck of the femur. J Bone Joint Surg 20:108–113, 1938.

301. LeBoff, M.S.; Kohlmeier, L.; Hurwitz, S.; et al. Occult vitamin D deficiency in postmenopausal US women with acute hip fracture. JAMA 281:1505–1511, 1999.

302. Lennox, I.A.; McLauchlan, J. Comparing the mortality and morbidity of cemented and uncemented hemiarthroplasties. Injury 24:185–186, 1993.

303. Lesniewski, PJ.; Testa, N.N. Stress fracture of the hip as a complication of total knee replacement. J Bone Joint Surg Am 64:304–306, 1982.

304. Liberman, U.A.; Weiss, S.R.; Broll, J.; et al. Effect of oral alendronate on bone mineral density and the incidence of fractures in postmenopausal osteoporosis. N Engl J Med 333:1437–1443, 1995.

305. Lidor, C.; Sagiv, P.; Amdur, B.; et al. Decrease in bone levels of 1,25 dihydroxyvitamin D in women with subcapital fracture of the femur. Calcif Tissue Int 52:146–148, 1993.

306. Lindequist, S.; Tornkvist, H. Quality of reduction and cortical screw support in femoral neck fractures—an analysis of 72 fractures with a new computerized measuring method. J Orthop Trauma 9:215–221, 1995.

307. Lo, W.H.; Chen, W.M.; Huang, C.K.; et al. Bateman bipolar hemiarthroplasty for displaced intracapsular femoral neck fractures: Uncemented versus cemented. Clin Orthop 302:75–82, 1994.

308. Long, J.W.; Knight, W. Bateman UPF prosthesis in fractures of the femoral neck. Clin Orthop 152:198–201, 1980.

309. Lozano-Requena JA, Bas-Hermida T, Perez-Belmonte C, et al. Breakage of Knowles pins used for femoral neck fractures. Int J Orthop 17:365–366, 1993.

310. Lucie, R.S.; Fuller, S.; Burdick, D.C.; Johnston, R.M. Early prediction of avascular necrosis of the femoral head following femoral neck fractures. Clin Orthop 161:207–214, 1981.

311. Lund, B.; Sorensen, O.H.; Melsen, F.; Mosekilde, L. Vitamin D metabolism and osteomalacia in patients with fractures of the proximal femur. Acta Orthop Scand 53:251–254, 1982.

312. Lunt, H.R. The use of prosthetic replacement of the head of the femur as primary treatment for subcapital fractures. Injury 3:107, 1971.

313. Lu-Yao, G.L.; Keller, R.B.; Littenberg, B.; Wennberg, J.E. Outcomes after displaced fractures of the femoral neck: A meta-analysis of one

hundred and six published reports. J Bone Joint Surg Am 76:15–25, 1994.

314. Manninger, J.; Kazar, G.; Fekete, G.; et al. Significance of urgent (within 6h) internal fixation in the management of fractures of the neck of the femur. Injury 20:101–105, 1989.

315. Manninger, J.; Kazar, G.; Fekete, G.; et al. Avoidance of avascular necrosis of the femoral head, following fractures of the femoral neck, by early reduction and internal fixation. Injury 16:437–448, 1985.

316. Mannius, S.; Mellstrom, D.; Oden, A.; et al. Incidence of hip fracture in Western Sweden 1974–1982—comparison of rural and urban populations. Acta Orthop Scand 58:38–42, 1987.

317. March, L.; Chamberlain, A.; Cameron, I.; et al. Report of the Northern Sydney Area Fractured Neck of Femur Health Outcomes Project. State Health Publication PHD 950112, Sydney Australia, 1996.

318. Marti, R.K.; Schuller, H.M.; Raaymakers, E.L. Intertrochanteric osteotomy for nonunion of the femoral neck. J Bone Joint Surg Br 71:782–787, 1989.

319. Masud, T.; Jawed, S.; Doyle, D.V.; Spector, T.D. A population study of the screening potential of assessment of trabecular pattern of the femoral neck (Singh index): The Chingford study. Br J Radiol 68:389–393, 1995.

320. May, P.C.; Mahendran, V.; Habib, K. Are costs per QALY a useful orthopaedic tool? J Bone Joint Surg Br 73(Suppl 1):70, 1991.

321. McElwaine, J.P.; Sheehan, J.M. Spontaneous fractures of the femoral neck after total replacement of the knee. J Bone Joint Surg Br 64:323–325, 1982.

322. Mehara, A.K.; Ramchandani, G.D.; Sharma, C.S.; et al. Unusual posterior dislocation with ipsilateral fractures of the femoral neck and head. J Trauma 38:658–659, 1995.

323. Meier, D.E.; Luckey, M.M.; Wallenstein, S.; et al. Racial differences in pre and postmenopausal bone homeostasis: Association with bone density. J Bone Miner Res 7:1181–1189, 1992.

324. Melberg, P.E.; Korner, L.; Lansinger, O. Hip joint pressure after femoral neck fracture. Acta Orthop Scand 57:501–504, 1986.

325. Melhaus, H.; Michaelsson, K.; Holmberg, L.; et al. Smoking, antioxidant vitamins, and the risk of hip fracture. J Bone Miner Res 14:129–135,1999.

326. Melhaus, H.; Michaelsson, K.; Kindmark, A.; et al. Excessive dietary intake of vitamin A is associated with reduced bone mineral density and increased risk for hip fracture. Ann Intern Med 129:770–778, 1998.

327. Melton, J.L.; Ilstrup, D.M.; Riggs, B.L.; Beckenbaugh, R.D. Fifty-year trend in hip fracture incidence. Clin Orthop 162:144–149, 1982.

328. Meyers, M.H.; Harvery, J.P., Jr.; Moore, T.M. Delayed treatment of subcapital and transcervical fractures of the neck of the femur with internal fixation and a muscle-pedicle bone graft. Orthop Clin North Am 5:743–756, 1974.

329. Meyers, M.H.; Harvery, J.P., Jr.; Moore, T.M. Treatment of displaced subcapital and transcervical fractures of the femoral neck by muscle-pedicle-bone grafts and internal fixation. A preliminary report on one hundred and fifty cases. J Bone Joint Surg Am 55:257–274, 1973.

330. Meyers, M.H.; Telfer, N.; Moore, T.M. Determination of the vascularity of the femoral head with technetium 99m-sulfur-colloid: Diagnostic and prognostic significance. J Bone Joint Surg Am 59:658–664, 1977.

331. Michel, B.A.; Bloch, D.A.; Fries, J.F. Physical activity and fractures over the age of fifty years. Int Orthop 16:87–91, 1992.

332. Miller, C.W. Survival and ambulation following hip fracture. J Bone Joint Surg Am 60:930–934, 1978.

333. Moloney, D.; Bishay, M.; Ivory, J.; Pozo, J. Failure of the sliding hip screw in the treatment of femoral neck fractures: Left-handed surgeons for left sided hips. Injury 25(Suppl 2):B9–B13, 1994.

334. Moore, A.T. Fracture of the hip joint: Treatment by extraarticular fixation with adjustable nails. Surg Gynecol Obstet 64:420–436, 1937.

335. Moore, A.T. Metal hip joint: A new self-locking Vitallium prosthesis. South Med J 45:1015–1018, 1952.

336. Moreland, J.R. Primary total hip arthroplasty. In: Chapman, M.W., ed. Operative Orthopaedics. Philadelphia, J.B. Lippincott, 1988.

337. Morwessel, R.; Evarts, C.M. The use of quadratus femoris muscle pedicle bone graft for the treatment of displaced femoral neck fractures. Orthopedics 8:972–976, 1985.

338. Mullen, J.O.; Mullen, N.L. Hip fracture mortality—a prospective, multifactorial study to predict and minimize death risk. Clin Orthop 280:214–222, 1992.

339. Müller, M.E.; Nazarian, S.; Koch, P.; Schatzker, J. The Comprehensive Classification of Fractures of Long Bones. Berlin, Springer-Verlag, 1990.

340. Nakamura, T.; Turner, C.H.; Yoshikawa, T.; et al. Do variations in hip geometry explain differences in hip fracture risk between Japanese and white Americans? J Bone Miner Res 9:1071–1076, 1994.

341. Nelson, D.A.; Jacobsen, G.; Barondess, D.A.; Parfitt, A.M. Ethnic differences in regional bone density, hip axis length, and lifestyle variables among healthy black and white men. J Bone Miner Res 10:782–787, 1995.

342. Nelson, K.M.; Richards, E.W.; Long, C.L.; et al. Protein and energy balance following femoral neck fracture in geriatric patients. Metabolism 44:59–66, 1995.

343. Nelson, M.E.; Fiatarone, M.A.; Morganti, C.M.; et al. Effects of high-intensity strength training on multiple risk factors for osteoporotic fractures—a randomized controlled trial. JAMA 272:1909–1914, 1994.

344. Newman, K.J.H. Femoral neck fractures: AO screws, DHS or hemiarthroplasty? Using the AO classification to rationalise treatment. Int J Orthop Trauma 4:100–108, 1994.

345. Niemann, K.M.W.; Mankin, H. Fractures about the hip in an institutionalized patient population: II. Survival and ability to walk again. J Bone Joint Surg Am 50:1327–1340, 1968.

346. Ogilvie-Harris, D.J.; Botsford, D.J.; Worder-Hawker, R. Elderly patients with hip fractures: Improved outcome with the use of care maps with high-quality medical and nursing protocols. J Orthop Trauma 7:428–437, 1993.

347. Ort, P.J.; Lamont, J. Treatment of femoral neck fractures with a sliding hip screw and two Knowles pins. Clin Orthop 190:158–162, 1984.

348. Palanca-Martin, D.; Albareda, J.; Seral, F. Subcapital stress fracture of the femoral neck after total knee arthroplasty. Int Orthop 18:308–309, 1994.

349. Pankovich, A.M. Primary internal fixation of femoral neck fractures. Arch Surg 110:20–26, 1975.

350. Papandrea, R.F.; Froimson, M.I. Total hip arthroplasty after acute displaced femoral neck fractures. Am J Orthop 25:85–88, 1996.

351. Parker, M.J. Garden grading of intracapsular fractures: Meaningful or misleading? Injury 24:241–242, 1993.

352. Parker, M.J. Prediction of fracture union after internal fixation of intracapsular femoral neck fractures. Injury 25(Suppl 2):B3–B6, 1994.

353. Parker, M.J.; Myles, J.W.; Anand, J.K.; Drewett, R. Cost benefit analysis of hip fracture treatment. J Bone Joint Surg Br 74:261–264, 1992.

354. Parker, M.J.; Porter, K.M.; Eastwood, D.M.; et al. Intracapsular fractures of the neck of the femur. Parallel or crossed Garden screws? J Bone Joint Surg Br 73:826–827, 1991.

355. Parker, M.J.; Pryor, G.A. The timing of surgery for proximal femoral fractures. J Bone Joint Surg Br 74:203–205, 1992.

356. Parker, M.J.; Pryor, G.A.; Anand, J.K.; et al. A comparison of presenting characteristics of patients with intracapsular and extracapsular proximal femur fractures. J R Soc Med 85:152–155, 1992.

357. Parker, M.J.; Pryor, G.A.; Myles, J.W. The value of a special surgical team in preventing complications in the treatment of hip fractures. Int Orthop 18:184–188, 1994.

358. Patterson, B.M.; Cornell, C.N.; Carbone, B.; et al. Protein depletion and metabolic stress in elderly patients who have a fracture of the hip. J Bone Joint Surg Am 74:251–260, 1992.

359. Pauwels, F. Biomechanics of the Normal and Diseased Hip. New York, Springer-Verlag, 1976, p. 83.

360. Pedrazzoni, M.; Alfano, F.S.; Gatti, C.; et al. Indagine epidemiologica sulle fratture del collo del femore nella provincia di Parma (1980–1992). Minerva Med 85:379–386, 1994.

361. Peris, P.; Pares, A.; Guanabens, N.; et al. Reduced spinal and femoral bone mass and deranged bone mineral metabolism in chronic alcoholics. Alcohol 27:619–625, 1992.

362. Phemister, D.B. Fractures of neck of femur, dislocations of hip, and obscure vascular disturbances producing aseptic necrosis of head of femur. Surg Gynecol Obstet 59:415–440, 1934.

363. Phillips, T.W. Thompson hemiarthroplasty and acetabula erosion. J Bone Joint Surg Am 71:913–917, 1989.

364. Pike, J.; Patterson, M. Hemiarthroplasty: Can failure be predicted? Int J Orthop Trauma 3:168–170, 1993.

365. Pini, M.; Spadini, E.; Carluccio, L.; et al. Dextran/aspirin versus heparin/dihydroergotamine in preventing thrombosis after hip fractures. J Bone Joint Surg Br 67:305–309, 1985.

366. Poo'r, G.; Atkinson, E.J.; O'Fallon, W.M.; Melton, J.L., III. Determinants of reduced survival following hip fractures in men. Clin Orthop 319:260–265, 1995.

367. Protzman, R.F.; Burkhalter, W.E. Femoral neck fractures in young adults. J Bone Joint Surg Am 58:689–695, 1976.

368. Province, M.A.; Hadley, E.C.; Hornbrook, M.C.; et al. The effects of exercise on falls in elderly patients—a preplanned meta-analysis of the FICSIT trials. JAMA 273:1341–1347, 1995.

369. Pruzansky, M.E.; Turano, M.; Luckey, M.; Seine, R. Low body weight as a risk factor for hip fracture in both black and white women. J Orthop Res 7:192–197, 1989.

370. Pugh, W.L. A self adjusting nail-plate for fractures about the hip joint. J Bone Joint Surg Am 37:1085–1093, 1955.

371. Raine, G.E. A comparison of internal fixation and prosthetic replacement for recent displaced subcapital fractures of the neck of the femur. Injury 5:25–30, 1973.

372. Ramser, J.R., Jr.; Mihalko, W.M.; Carr, J.R.; et al. A comparison of femoral neck fixation with the reconstruction nail versus cancellous screws in anatomic specimens. Clin Orthop 290:189–196, 1993.

373. Rashiq, S.; Logan, R.F.A. Role of drugs in fractures of the femoral neck. BMJ 292:861–863, 1986.

374. Ray, W.A.; Griffin, M.R.; Downey, W. Benzodiazepines of long and short elimination half-life and the risk of hip fracture. JAMA 262:3303–3307, 1989.

375. Reid, I.R.; Chin, K.; Evans, M.C.; Jones, J.G. Relation between increase in length of hip axis in older women between 1950s and 1990s and increase in age specific rates of hip fractures. BMJ 309:508–509, 1994.

376. Reid, J.; Kennie, D.C. Geriatric rehabilitative care after fractures of the proximal femur: One year follow up of a randomized clinical trial. BMJ 299:25–26, 1989.

377. Reikeras, O.; Hoiseth, A. Femoral neck angles in osteoarthritis of the hip. Acta Orthop Scand 53:781–784, 1982.

378. Reikeras, O.; Bjerkreim, I.; Kolbenstvedt, A. Anteversion of the acetabulum and femoral neck in normals and in patients with osteoarthritis of the hip. Acta Orthop Scand 54:18–23, 1983.

379. Reikeras, O.; Hoiseth, A.; Reigstad, A.; Fonstein, E. Femoral neck angles: A specimen study with special regard to bilateral differences. Acta Orthop Scand 53:775–779, 1982.

380. Riska, E.B. Prosthetic replacement in the treatment of subcapital fractures of the femur. Acta Orthop Scand 42:281–290, 1971.

381. Robbins, J.A.; Donaldson, L.J. Analyzing stages of care in hospital stay for fractured neck of femur. Lancet 239:1028–1029, 1984.

382. Roberts, S.; Weightman, B.; Urban, J.; Chappell, D. Mechanical and biochemical properties of human articular cartilage from the femoral head after subcapital fracture. J Bone Joint Surg Br 68:418–422, 1986.

383. Robinson, C.M.; Court-Brown, C.M.; McQueen, M.M.; Christie, J. Hip fracture in adults younger than 50 years of age—epidemiology and results. Clin Orthop 312:238–246, 1995.

384. Robinson, C.M.; Saran, D.; Annan, I.H. Intracapsular hip fractures: Results of management adopting a treatment protocol. Clin Orthop 302:83–91, 1994.

385. Rodriguez, J.; Herrara, A.; Canales, V.; Serrano, S. Epidemiologic factors, morbidity and mortality after femoral neck fractures in the elderly—a comparative study: Internal fixation vs. hemiarthroplasty. Acta Orthop Belg 53:472–479, 1987.

386. Rogers, F.B.; Shackford, S.R.; Keller, M.S. Early fixation reduces morbidity and mortality in elderly patients with hip fractures from low impact falls. J Trauma 39:261–265, 1995.

387. Rothman, R.H. Total Hip Arthroplasty. Philadelphia, W.B. Saunders, 1987.

388. Rowe, S.M.; Yoon, T.R.; Ryang, D.H. An epidemiological study of hip fracture in Honam, Korea. Int J Orthop 17:139–143, 1993.

389. Ruben, D.B.; Borok, G.M.; Wolde-Tsadik, G.; A randomized trial of comprehensive geriatric assessment in the care of hospitalized patients. N Engl J Med 332:1345–1350, 1995.

390. Rudman, D.; Feller, A.G.; Nagraj, H.S.; et al. Effects of human growth hormone in men over 60 years old. N Engl J Med 323:1–6, 1990.

391. Rudolph, V. Predominance of left sided fractures of the proximal femur in a geriatric population. Orthopedics 17:601–603, 1994.

392. Ruland, L.J.; Wang, G.J.; Teates, C.D.; et al. A comparison of magnetic resonance imaging to bone scintigraphy in early traumatic ischemia of the femoral head. Clin Orthop 285:30–34, 1992.

393. Salvati, E.A.; Artz, T.; Aglietti, P.; Asnis, S.E. Endoprostheses in the treatment of femoral neck fractures. Orthop Clin North Am 5:757–777, 1977.

394. Sastry, N.V.; Sridhar, G.R.; Reddy, G.N.; et al. Evaluation of osteoporosis in patients with fracture neck of femur using conventional radiography. J Assoc Physicians India 42:209–211, 1994.

395. Scales, J.T. Prosthetic replacement of the femoral head for femoral neck fractures: Which design? J Bone Joint Surg Br 65:530–531, 1983.

396. Schott, A.M.; Weill-Engerer, S.; Hans, D.; et al. Ultrasound discriminates patients with hip fracture equally well as dual energy x-ray absorptiometry and independently of bone mineral density. J Bone Miner Res 10:243–249, 1995.

397. Schroder, H.M.; Erlandsen, M. Age and sex as determinants of mortality after hip fracture: 3895 patients followed for 2.5–18.5 years. J Orthop Trauma 7:525–531, 1993.

398. Schroder, H.M.; Peterson, K.K.; Erlandsen, M. Occurrence and incidence of the second hip fracture. Clin Orthop 289:166–169, 1993.

399. Schwappach, J.R.; Murphey, M.D.; Kokmeyer, S.F.; et al. Subcapital fractures of the femoral neck: Prevalence and cause of radiographic appearance simulating pathologic fracture. AJR Am J Roentgenol 162:651–654, 1994.

400. Senn, N. The treatment of fractures of the neck of the femur by immediate reduction and permanent fixation. JAMA 13:150, 1889.

401. Sevitt, S. Avascular necrosis and revascularization of the femoral head after intracapsular fractures: A combined arteriographic and histological necropsy study. J Bone Joint Surg Br 46:270–296, 1964.

402. Sevitt, S.; Thompson, R.G. The distribution and anastomoses of arteries supplying the head and neck of the femur. J Bone Joint Surg Br 47:560–573, 1965.

403. Sherk, H.H.; Snape, W.J.; Loprette, F.L. Internal fixation versus nontreatment of hip fractures in senile patients. Clin Orthop 141:196–198, 1979.

404. Sikorski, J.M.; Barrington, R. Internal fixation versus hemiarthroplasty for the displaced subcapital fracture of the femur: A prospective randomized study. J Bone Joint Surg Br 63:357–361, 1981.

405. Sim, F.H.; Sigmond, E.R. Acute fractures of the femoral neck, managed by total hip replacement. Orthopedics 9:35–38, 1986.

406. Sim, F.H.; Stauffer, R.N. Management of hip fractures by total hip arthroplasty. Clin Orthop 152:191–197, 1980.

407. Singh, M.; Nagrath, A.R.; Maini, P.S. Changes in trabecular pattern of the upper end of the femur as an index of osteoporosis. J Bone Joint Surg Am 52:457–467, 1970.

408. Sloan, J.; Holloway, G. Fractured neck of the femur: The cause of the fall? Injury 113:230–232, 1982.

409. Smith, L.D. Hip fractures: The role of muscle contraction or intrinsic forces in the causation of fractures of the femoral neck. J Bone Joint Surg Am 35:367–383, 1953.

410. Smith, T.K. Prevention of complications in orthopedic surgery secondary to nutritional depletion. Clin Orthop 222:91–97, 1987.

411. Smith-Petersen, M.N. Treatment of fractures of the neck of the femur by internal fixation. Surg Gynecol Obstet 64:287–295, 1937.

412. Smith-Petersen, M.N.; Cave, E.F.; Vangorder, G.W. Intracapsular fractures of the neck of the femur—treatment by internal fixation. Arch Surg 23:715–759, 1931.

413. Smyth, E.H.J.; Shah, V.M. The significance of good reduction and fixation in displaced subcapital fractures of the femur. Injury 5:197–209, 1974.

414. Soghikian, G.W.; Boden, S.A.; Labropoulos, P.A. Bone mineral content of the spine and proximal femur in female patients with hip fracture. Orthopedics 17:917–921, 1994.

415. Soreide, O.; Molster, A.; Raugstad, T.S. Immediate weight-bearing after internal fixation of femoral neck fractures using Von Bahr screws. Preliminary report of a prospective clinical trial. Act Orthop Scand 48:659–664, 1977.

416. Soreide, O.; Molster, A.; Raugstad, T.S. Internal fixation versus primary prosthetic replacement in acute femoral neck fractures: A prospective, randomized clinical study. Br J Surg 66:56–60, 1979.

417. Soto-Hall, R.; Johnson, L.H.; Johnson, R.A. Variations in the intraarticular pressure of the hip joint in injury and disease: A probable factor in avascular necrosis. J Bone Joint Surg Am 46:509–516, 1964.

418. Speed, D. The unsolved fracture. Surg Gynecol Obstet 60:341–351, 1935.

419. Speer, K.P.; Quarles, L.D.; Harrelson, J.M.; Nunley, J.A. Tetracycline labeling of the femoral head following acute intracapsular fracture of the femoral neck. Clin Orthop 267:224–227, 1991.

420. Speer, K.P.; Spritzer, C.E.; Harrelson, J.M.; Nunley, J.A. Magnetic resonance imaging of the femoral head after intracapsular fracture of the femoral neck. J Bone Joint Surg Am 72:98–103, 1990.

421. Springer, E.R.; Lachiewicz, P.F.; Gilbert, J.A. Internal fixation of femoral neck fractures: A comparative biomechanical study of Knowles pins and 6.5 mm cancellous screws. Clin Orthop 267:85–92, 1991.

422. Stableforth, P.G. Supplement feeds and nitrogen and calorie balance following femoral neck fracture. Br J Surg 73:651–655, 1986.

423. Staeheli, J.W.; Frassica, F.J.; Sim, F.H. Prosthetic replacement of the femoral head for fracture of the femoral neck in patients who have Parkinson's disease. J Bone Joint Surg Am 70:565–568, 1988.

424. Stillwell, W.T. The Art of Total Hip Arthroplasty. Orlando, FL, Grune & Stratton, 1987.

425. Strom, B.L.; Berlin, J.A.; Kinman, J.L.; et al. Parenteral ketorolac and risk of gastrointestinal and operative site bleeding. JAMA 275:376–382, 1996.

426. Stromqvist, B. Femoral head vitality after intracapsular hip fracture; 490 cases studied by intravital tetracycline labeling and Tc-MDP radionuclide imaging. Acta Orthop Scand 54(Suppl 200):5–71, 1983.

427. Stromqvist, B.; Hansson, L.I. Avascular necrosis associated with nailing of femoral neck fracture—two cases examined pre and postoperatively by tetracycline and radionuclide tracer techniques. Acta Orthop Scand 54:687–694, 1983.

428. Stromqvist, B.; Hansson, L.I.; Ljung, P.; et al. Preoperative and postoperative scintimetry after femoral neck fracture. J Bone Joint Surg Br 66:49–54, 1984.

429. Stromqvist, B.; Hansson, L.I.; Nilsson, L.T.; Thorngren, K.G. Hookpin fixation in femoral neck fractures: A two-year follow-up study of 300 cases. Clin Orthop 218:58–62, 1987.

430. Stromqvist, B.; Hansson, L.T.; Palmer, J.; et al. Scintimetric evaluation of nailed femoral neck fractures with special reference to type of osteosynthesis. Acta Orthop Scand 54:340–347, 1983.

431. Stromqvist, B.; Kelly, I.; Lidgren, L. Treatment of hip fractures in rheumatoid arthritis. Clin Orthop 28:75–78, 1988.

432. Sugimoto, T.; Kanbara, Y.; Shiraishi, H.; et al. Femoral and spinal bone mineral density in Japanese osteoporotics with hip fracture. Osteoporos Int 4:144–148, 1994.

433. Svensson, O.; Stromberg, L.; Ohlen, G.; Lidgren, U. Prediction of the outcome after hip fracture in elderly patients. J Bone Joint Surg Br 78:115–118, 1996.

434. Swiontkowski, M.F. Ipsilateral femoral shaft and hip fractures. Orthop Clin North Am 18:73–84, 1987.

435. Swiontkowski, M.F. Intracapsular fractures of the hip. J Bone Joint Surg Am 76:129–136, 199.

436. Swiontkowski, M.F.; Hansen, S.T. The Deyerle device for fixation of femoral neck fractures: A review of one hundred twenty-five consecutive cases. Clin Orthop 206:248–252, 1986.

437. Swiontkowski, M.F.; Hansen, S.T.; Kellam, J. Ipsilateral fractures of the femoral neck and shaft: A treatment protocol. J Bone Joint Surg Am 66:260–268, 1984.

438. Swiontkowski, M.F.; Harrington, R.N.; Keller, T.S.; Van Patten, P.K. Torsion and bending analysis of internal fixation techniques for femoral neck fractures: The role of implant design and bone density. J Orthop Res 5:433–444, 1987.

439. Swiontkowski, M.F.; Tepic, S.; Perren, S.M.; et al. Laser Doppler flowmetry for bone blood flow measurement: Correlation with microsphere estimates and evaluation of the effect of intracapsular

440. Swiontkowski, M.F.; Tepic, S.; Rahn, B.A.; Perren, S.M. The effect of femoral neck fracture on femoral head blood flow. Orthop Trans 11:344–345, 1987.

441. Swiontkowski, M.F.; Winquist, R.A. Displaced hip fractures in children and adolescents. J Trauma 26:384–388, 1986.

442. Swiontkowski, M.F.; Winquist, R.A.; Hansen, S.T. Fractures of the femoral neck in patients between the ages of twelve and forty-nine years. J Bone Joint Surg Am 66:837–846, 1984.

443. Takeuchi, T.; Shidou, T. Impairment of blood supply to the head of the femur after fracture of the neck. Int Orthop 17:325–329, 1993.

444. Taine, W.H.; Armour, P.C. Primary total hip replacement for displaced subcapital fractures of the femur. J Bone Joint Surg Br 67:214–217, 1985.

445. Thompson, F.R. Two and a half years' experience with a Vitallium intramedullary hip prosthesis. J Bone Joint Surg Am 36:489–502, 1954.

446. Thorngren, K.G.; Ceder, L.; Svensson, K. Predicting results of rehabilitation after hip fracture—a ten year follow-up study. Clin Orthop 287:76–81, 1993.

447. Tierney, G.S.; Goulet, J.A.; Greenfield, M.L.; Port, F.K. Mortality after fracture of the hip in patients who have end stage renal disease. J Bone Joint Surg Am 76:709–712, 1994.

448. Tinetti, M.E.; Baker, D.I.; McAvay, G.; et al. A multifactorial intervention to reduce the risk of falling among elderly people living in the community. N Engl J Med 331:821–827, 1994.

449. Tinetti, M.E.; Inouye, S.K.; Gill, T.M.; Doucette, J.T. Shared risk factors for falls, incontinence, and functional dependence. JAMA 273:1348–1353, 1995.

450. Tooke, S.M.; Favero, K.J. Femoral neck fractures in skeletally mature patients, fifty years old or less. J Bone Joint Surg Am 67:1255–1260, 1985.

451. Tountas, A.A.; Wadell, J.P. Stress fractures of the femoral neck: A report of seven cases. Clin Orthop 210:160–165, 1986.

452. Trueta, J. The normal vascular anatomy of the human femoral head during growth. J Bone Joint Surg Br 39:358–393, 1957.

453. Trueta, J.; Harrison, M.H.M. The normal vascular anatomy of the femoral head in adult man. J Bone Joint Surg Br 35:442–461, 1953.

454. Tucker, F.R. Arterial supply to the femoral head and its clinical importance. J Bone Joint Surg Br 31:82–93, 1949.

455. Valentin, N.; Lomholt, B.; Jensen, J.S.; et al. Spinal or general anesthesia for surgery of the fractured hip? A prospective study of mortality in 578 patients. Br J Anaesth 58:284–291, 1986.

456. Van Audekercke, R.; Martens, M.; Mulier, J.C.; Stuyck, J. Experimental study on the internal fixation of femoral neck fractures. Clin Orthop 141:203–212, 1979.

457. Van Dortmont, L.M.; Oner, F.C.; Wereldsma, J.C.; Mulder, P.G. Effect of mental state on mortality after hemiarthroplasty for fracture of the femoral neck. Eur J Surg 160:203–208, 1994.

458. Vegter, J.; Klopper, P.J. Effect of intracapsular hyperpressure on femoral head blood flow—laser Doppler flowmetry in dogs. Acta Orthop Scand 62:337–341, 1991.

459. Versluysen, M. Pressure sores in elderly patients: The epidemiology related to hip operations. J Bone Joint Surg Br 67:10–13, 1985.

460. Walmsley, M.B. A note on the retinacula of Weitbrecht. J Anat 51:61–64, 1917.

461. Walters, R.; Simon, S. Joint destruction: A sequel of unrecognized pin penetration in patients with slipped capital femoral epiphysis. In: Proceedings of the Hip Society. St. Louis, C.V. Mosby, 1980.

462. Wand, J.S.; Hill, I.D.; Reeve, J. Coxarthrosis and femoral neck fracture. Clin Orthop 278:88–94, 1992.

463. Wathne, R.A.; Koval, K.J.; Aharonoff, G.B.; et al. Modular unipolar versus bipolar prosthesis: A prospective evaluation of functional outcome after femoral neck fracture. J Orthop Trauma 9:298–302, 1995.

464. Weintraub, M.; Handy, B.M. Benzodiazepines and hip fracture: The New York state experience. Clin Pharmacol Ther 54:252–256, 1993.

465. Weintraub, S.; Papo, J.; Ashkenazi, R.; et al. Osteorthritis of the hip and fractures of the proximal end of the femur. Acta Orthop Scand 53:261–264, 1982.

466. White, B.L.; Fisher, W.D.; Laurin, C.A. Rate of mortality for elderly patients after fracture of the hip in the 1980s. J Bone Joint Surg Am 69:1335–1340, 1987.

467. Whitman, R. A new method of treatment for fracture of the neck of the femur, together with remarks on coxa vara. Ann Surg 36:746–761, 1902.

468. Whitman, R. The abduction method: Considered as the exponent of a treatment for all forms of fracture at the hip in accord with surgical principles. Am J Surg 21:335–344, 1933.

469. Williams, P.L.; Amin, N.K.; Young, A. Unsuspected fractures of the femoral neck in patients with chronic hip pain due to rheumatoid arthritis. BMJ 292:1125–1126, 1986.

470. Wilson, M.A. The effect of age on the quality of bone scans using technetium-99m pyrophosphate. Radiology 139:703–705, 1981.

471. Wilton, T.J.; Hosking, D.J.; Pawley, E.; et al. Osteomalacia and femoral neck fractures in the elderly patient. J Bone Joint Surg Br 69:388–390, 1987.

472. Wingstrand, H.; Stromqvist, B.; Egund, N.; et al. Hemarthrosis in undisplaced cervical fractures: Tamponade may cause reversible femoral head ischemia. Acta Orthop Scand 57:305–308, 1986.

473. Winter, W.G. Nonoperative treatment of proximal femoral fractures in the demented nonambulatory patient. Clin Orthop 218:97–103, 1987.

474. Wiss, D.A.; Sima, W.; Brien, W.W. Ipsilateral fractures of the femoral neck and shaft. J Orthop Trauma 6:159–166, 1992.

475. Wood, D.J.; Ions, G.K.; Quinby, J.M.; et al. Factors which influence mortality after subcapital hip fracture. J Bone Joint Surg Br 74:199–202, 1992.

476. Wrighton, L.D.; Woodyard, J.E. Prosthetic replacement for subcapital fractures of the femur: A comparative study. Injury 2:287–293, 1971.

477. Zetterberg, C.; Elmerson, S.; Andersson, G.B.J. Epidemiology of hip fractures in Goteborg, Sweden, 1940–1983. Clin Orthop 191:43–52, 1984.

478. Zetterberg, C.H.; Irstram, L.; Andersson, G.B. Femoral neck fractures in young adults. Acta Orthop Scand 53:427–435, 1982.

479. Zohman, G.L.; Lieberman, J.R. Perioperative aspects of hip fracture: Guidelines for intervention that will impact prevalence and outcome. Am J Orthop 1:666–671, 1995.

480. Zuckerman, J.D.; Sakales, S.R.; Fabian, D.R.; Frankel, V.H. Hip fractures in geriatric patients: Results of an interdisciplinary hospital care program. Clin Orthop 274:213–225, 1992.

481. Zuckerman, J.D.; Skovron, M.L.; Koval, K.J.; et al. Postoperative complications and mortality associated with operative delay in older patients who have a fracture of the hip. J Bone Joint Surg Am 77:1551–1556, 1995.

# CHAPTER 49

# Intertrochanteric Hip Fractures

Michael R. Baumgaertner, M.D.

When an elderly patient sustains an intertrochanteric hip fracture, bone continuity is disrupted, and frequently there is a severe insult to the medical health, mental vigor, and potential for independent living of that person as well. Together with femoral neck fractures, intertrochanteric hip injuries represent perhaps the most important public health problem facing the orthopaedic surgeon today. In an era when health care resources are being limited, we must ensure that the treatment offered is the most efficient and effective available. To this end, the orthopaedist must work with the internist or gerontologist, the anesthesiologist, the rehabilitation specialist, and social support networks to achieve a successful outcome for the fracture and the patient and for the health care system.[150]

The success of surgical treatment for these difficult injuries depends to a large part on the stability of the fixed fracture. As summarized by Kaufer,[72] the stability of the fracture-implant assembly depends on five factors: the quality of the bone, the fracture pattern, the reduction achieved, the design of the implant selected, and the position of the implant within the bone. The surgeon can influence only the last three but must appreciate the first two factors to plan appropriate treatment. Each of these variables is addressed in this chapter.

The intertrochanteric area of the hip is defined as the region from the extracapsular femoral neck to the area just distal to the lesser trochanter. This chapter discusses fractures in this area, including the so-called reverse-oblique fracture and the intertrochanteric fracture with subtrochanteric extension.

## INCIDENCE AND ETIOLOGY

The incidence of intertrochanteric fractures is increasing. Currently, it is estimated that 250,000 hip fractures occur annually in the United States. Investigators predict the incidence to approach 500,000 by the year 2040.[32] Almost 9 of 10 hip fractures occur in patients older than 65 years, and almost 3 of 4 fractures occur in women (Fig. 49–1). It is estimated that one third of all women (and one sixth of all men) reaching the age of 90 years will have sustained at least one hip fracture.[29] Approximately half will be intertrochanteric fractures.

Intertrochanteric fractures occur in a more aged population than do femoral neck fractures. Older people are more seriously affected by osteoporosis and medical conditions in general, and they are poorer ambulators.[77] The incidence of the more unstable, comminuted fractures is increasing, paralleling the increased longevity of the world's population. Data can be derived from studies performed in the United States, England, and the Scandinavian nations.[44, 94, 140] Areas of agreement include the increasing incidence of intertrochanteric fracture, especially the more unstable types. These occur at a rate of 16.6 per 100 person-years in women with a bone density of 0.6 g/cm or less and rarely occur in women with a bone density of 1.0 g/cm or more. This relation of osteopenia to age is independent of gender and of the menopause. Zain Elabdien and colleagues[149] noted a continuous decrease in bone quantity with age and a direct relation between bone quality and the severity of intertrochanteric fracture patterns. They suggested that with the increasing age of the population and the longer survival of the aged, more unstable, comminuted intertrochanteric fractures will be seen.

Estimates of the cost of treatment of all U.S. hip fractures range up to $10 billion, with the cost predicted to double by the year 2040.[32, 103] The increasing cost of hip fracture treatment is compounded by the costs of care after the acute hospitalization. Although the in-hospital costs may decrease if the acute hospital stay becomes shorter, expenses for rehabilitation facilities and part-time or even full-time nursing care are becoming more common and burden the health care system as well.

Falls in the elderly have many causes. Postural and gait disturbances, decreased visual and hearing acuity, and the use of potentially disorienting medications increase with age and may cause elderly persons to fall more frequently. For the fall to cause a hip fracture, Cummmings and Nevitt argue that four conditions must be met.[30] First, the

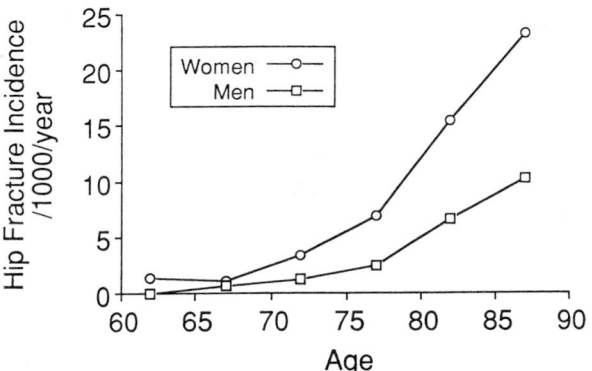

**FIGURE 49–1.** The incidence of hip fractures as related to age and gender, 1987–1988 data. (Redrawn from Apple, D.F., Jr.; Hayes, W.C., eds. Prevention of Falls and Hip Fractures in the Elderly. Rosemont, IL, American Academy of Orthopaedic Surgeons, 1993.)

orientation of the faller should lead to an impact at or near the trochanter. Second, the protective responses of the patient, such as grabbing for a supportive object or extending the arms to reduce the energy of the fall, are inadequate. Third, local soft tissues around the hip are unable to dissipate energy adequately, and fourth, the bone strength is less than that necessary to withstand the residual energy imparted. As people age, walking speed decreases. Forward inertia may cause a 65 year old who trips to fall forward, landing on the hands and knees (the patient may sustain a wrist or shoulder fracture in an attempt to break the fall). In contrast, an 85 year old will be moving much slower. If balance is lost, she or he will tend to collapse to the side, which affects the hip directly.[30] Appreciation of this mechanism helps explain why the risk of hip fracture increases dramatically faster than the rate of falling or the worsening of osteoporosis as patients age.

Most fractures occur at home, but studies demonstrate that hospitalized patients have 11 times the frequency of fracture of age-matched control subjects living at home.[49, 58, 116] This is perhaps reflective of the role that medical infirmity plays in the incidence of hip fractures. In one case-control study, the risk of hip fracture was increased fivefold in patients with chronic illness.[20] Although most elderly patients with intertrochanteric femur fractures do not suffer other injuries, 7% to 15% have associated fractures. Commonly affected bones include those most susceptible to osteopenia: the distal radius, proximal humerus, ribs, pubis, and spine. It is not rare to see patients with significant osteoporosis present after a fall to the side with multiple fractures on one side of the body.

When an intertrochanteric fracture occurs in a young person or is the result of a fall from a height or a motor vehicle collision, management must proceed as with any patient sustaining high-energy trauma. The possibility of one or more occult associated injuries must be assumed until it can be effectively excluded. Occasionally, the intertrochanteric fracture itself can be occult. Barquet and others reported that 15% of such injuries associated with ipsilateral femoral shaft fractures were missed during initial assessment of the patient.[5, 46] A routine trauma evaluation protocol must be initiated, and injuries identi-

fied should be managed accordingly (see Chapter 5). Young patients suffering trauma significant enough to cause an intertrochanteric fracture frequently present with fractures with gross displacement and fracture patterns demonstrating reverse obliquity or subtrochanteric extension. These high-energy injuries pose special problems for fixation and must be differentiated from the lower energy fractures commonly seen in elderly persons.

## RELEVANT ANATOMY

### Osseous Anatomy

The hip is a ball-and-socket joint that composes the acetabulum and the head of the femur. Linking the femoral head to the shaft of the femur is the femoral neck. The angle that the femoral neck subtends with the long axis of the femur is the angle of inclination. In the adult population, this angle is usually between 120° and 135°. Anthropometric studies by Noble and associates[112] showed a gradual decrease in the neck-shaft angle with age; the average angle is slightly less than 125° for those older than 75 years (Fig. 49–2). In addition to its angle in the frontal plane relative to the vertical axis, the femoral neck is slightly anteverted, on average 10° to 15° in relation to the position of the femoral condyles in the horizontal or transverse plane.

Supporting the femoral head and neck is an internal scaffolding system of trabecular bone. This trabecular pattern was originally described by Ward in 1838.[143] Fanning out under the superior dome of the femoral head and concentrating at the medial femoral neck are the primary compressive trabeculae. This is the most dense cancellous bone of the proximal femur and transmits the weight of the body to the lower extremity. Arching from the area of the fovea to the lateral femoral cortex just distal to the greater trochanter is the primary tensile group. Secondary compressive and tensile trabecular groups, as well as a greater trochanteric group, are oriented along stress lines in the lateral femoral neck, with a relative paucity of trabecular scaffolding in the central area known as Ward's triangle (Fig. 49–3).[50]

It is the presence or absence of these primary and secondary trabecular groups that Singh and colleagues[135] and Obrant[114] used as an index of osteopenia. In the former study, radiographs of the hip and histologic examination of iliac crest biopsy specimens were evaluated in 35 patients. Eighteen patients in the study group had femoral neck fractures, and the remaining 17 were admitted for other reasons, usually a fracture of another bone. From these evaluations, Singh developed a six-level classification system for grading of osteoporosis based on the anteroposterior (AP) radiograph of the uninjured hip. Singh graded the femoral neck cancellous bone pattern from VI to I. Grade VI is normal bone with all five trabecular groups present; grade I is severe osteopenia with evident loss of all trabecular groups, including a portion of the primary compressive group.[135] This radiologic rating system was then compared with the histologic analysis of the iliac crest specimens, and correlation between them

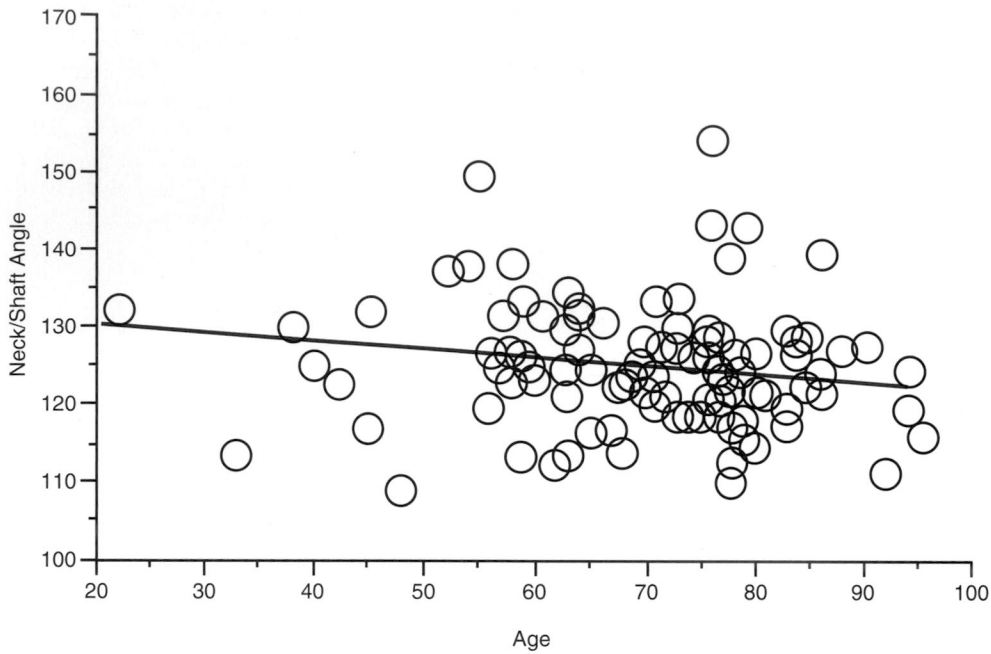

**FIGURE 49-2.** There is a slight but progressive diminution of the neck-shaft angle with age.

was found to be highly significant (r = 0.812, P < 0.001). Later investigators demonstrated a relation between low Singh grades and increased incidence of mechanical failure of fracture stabilization.[87] Others noted the limitations of this subjective classification, especially with regard to observer error.[74] It must be recalled that the entire six-tier classification was based on the study of fewer than three dozen AP radiographs with no attempt to control for interobserver or intraobserver error. Despite its limitations as a research tool, the Singh grading system is often used as a way to generally characterize the degree of osteoporosis affecting a particular patient. Furthermore, it allows an appreciation of the variations in density and strength of the cancellous bone throughout the femoral head and neck of the osteoporotic patient. This is critical information to consider when choosing appropriate implants and implant position for the stabilization of intertrochanteric fractures.

## Muscular Anatomy

In addition to the direct forces acting on the hip to produce the intertrochanteric fracture pattern, indirect muscle forces also contribute.[72] The magnitude of force applied, the direction of force, and the degree of osteoporosis all contribute to the variations in fracture pattern that may be encountered.[37] The iliopsoas muscle pulls on its insertion at the lesser trochanter, and the abductors and short rotator muscles act through their attachments on the greater trochanter. Simple biomechanical forces lead to the shortened and externally rotated lower extremity seen with most displaced intertrochanteric fractures. In the presence of an intertrochanteric fracture and any hip joint reaction force at all, given the neck-shaft inclination angle, a varus deformity of the hip and shortening of the limb must occur. The increased external

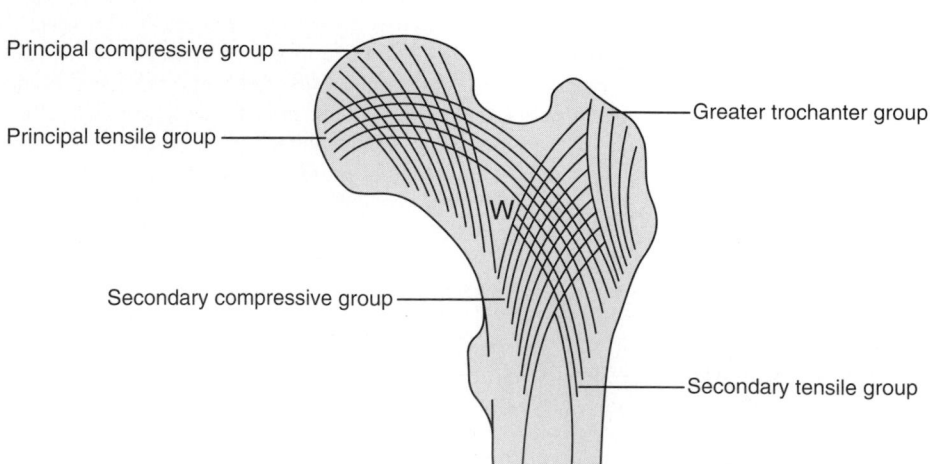

**FIGURE 49-3.** Diagram of an anteroposterior (AP) radiographic projection of a normal hip. Note the five trabecular groups and Ward's triangle (W). (Redrawn from Rockwood, C.A., Jr.; Green, D.A.; Bucholz, R.W., eds. Rockwood and Green's Fractures in Adults, 4th ed. Philadelphia, J.B. Lippincott, 1996.)

rotation of the limb is as easily explained. The person who has just fallen and suffered a hip fracture minimizes motion and further muscular activity to avoid any further pain. Even in an uninjured person lying supine, the foot falls naturally into some degree of external rotation as muscular forces subside with rest. Gravity externally rotates the lower limb until the foot rests on its lateral aspect.

The iliopsoas, which originates from the iliac fossa and the transverse processes of the lumbar vertebrae, inserts on the lesser trochanter and acts primarily to flex and externally rotate the hip joint. As with all of the muscles acting across the hip, the iliopsoas acts to shorten the limb in the presence of a simple intertrochanteric fracture. With comminution, the psoas tends to displace proximally and anteromedially the lesser trochanter and a varying size of neighboring posteromedial cortex. The pectineus, a hip flexor, adductor, and external rotator, arises from the pectineal line of the pubis and inserts on the pectineal line of the femur. The sartorius and the rectus femoris are also hip flexors.

The major abductors of the hip joint (the gluteus medius, the gluteus minimus, and the tensor fasciae latae) further shorten the extremity and exacerbate varus deformity. The gluteus muscles insert on the greater trochanter and are responsible for the proximal medial migration of the trochanter when the trochanter itself is involved. The tensor fasciae latae arises from the anterolateral ileum and inserts into the iliotibial band. The lateral approach to the proximal femur can avoid the tensor if it is made just posterior to its muscle belly.

The adductors of the hip joint (the adductor longus, the adductor brevis, the posterior portion of adductor magnus, and the gracilis) all originate on the pubic or ischial rami and insert well distal to the fracture zone. Because neither the origin nor the insertion is disrupted after intertrochanteric fracture, this muscle group always invites a varus and external rotation deformity at the fracture. In addition, preexisting adductor contractures can complicate fracture reduction and can interfere with adequate abduction of the well leg for C-arm imaging on a fracture table.

The external rotators of the hip joint include the gluteus maximus and the short external rotators (the piriformis, the superior gemellus, the inferior gemellus, the obturator internus, the obturator externus, and the quadratus femoris). Although the gluteus maximus inserts into the femoral shaft and the iliotibial band, most of the other external rotators insert on the medial aspect of the trochanter. In certain fractures, their insertions remain intact and unopposed on the proximal fragment, maintaining it in external rotation despite manipulations of the distal fragment. This deformity must be suspected and appreciated to avoid malreduction.

The hip extensors (hamstrings and gluteus maximus) are never detached by an intertrochanteric fracture, so they act only to shorten the extremity after fracture. Although not a hip motor, the vastus lateralis muscle, with its tough fibrous origin anteriorly and along the vastus ridge, plays an important role in some comminuted fractures by limiting the displacement of bony fragments.

The numerous muscular origins and insertions within the intertrochanteric area bring with them a rich and redundant blood supply to the intertrochanteric fracture, making an environment very conducive to fracture healing unless iatrogenic compromised by excessive surgical dissection. This is in sharp contrast to the limited vascularity of the intracapsular femoral neck, where healing complications are common.

## RADIOGRAPHIC ASSESSMENT

An AP view of the pelvis and a cross-table lateral of the affected hip are necessary to assess the fracture pattern adequately and to allow inspection of the unaffected hip joint. Ideally, the AP view should be performed while gentle traction and internal rotation are applied to the affected extremity. This ensures a true AP image of at least the distal fragment and allows a better comparison to the uninjured side. The AP view demonstrates the fracture obliquity, its location, and the presence or absence of a medial fragmentation. The surgeon can also inspect the opposite hip to measure the prefracture neck-shaft angle and the degree of osteoporosis, as Singh grading is exceedingly difficult, if not impossible, to do on the affected, distorted side. Bilateral injury and other pathologic processes that may influence treatment must also be ruled out. The lateral view is most helpful in delineating the posterior fracture fragments and the amount of posterior displacement (sag) at the fracture line. In most cases, these films confirm the diagnosis of trochanteric hip fracture and demonstrate the fracture pattern. Rarely, computed tomography (CT) may be indicated to more clearly delineate the multiple fracture planes and fragments of a complex fracture pattern that is not fully visualized on standard films. Rather than subject the patient to the pain of numerous repeat or oblique radiographic studies, or both, a single transfer to the CT scanner allows fracture analysis in all planes and in the third dimension, given modern image reconstruction techniques.

On occasion, intertrochanteric fractures may not be apparent on initial radiographs. If the patient's history and physical examination are consistent with a hip fracture but radiographs fail to confirm the diagnosis, further diagnostic imaging is indicated. Until recently, technetium 99m bone scanning had been the mainstay of occult fracture detection. However, its accuracy in delineating the occult fracture is not perfect, especially in the first 24 to 48 hours after injury. In patients in whom a hip fracture is strongly suspected despite initial negative radiographs, a technetium bone scan should be obtained at 48 to 72 hours after injury. If the initial bone scan results are negative and pain persists, the bone scan is repeated 7 to 10 days later. In patients older than 65 years, approximately 80% of technetium bone scan results are positive 1 day after fracture; 95% are positive in patients younger than 65 years. Some investigators believe that to exclude a fracture it is necessary to document a negative bone scan result at 3 days after presentation, when almost 100% of scan results are positive.[54]

Advances in magnetic resonancy imaging (MRI) have enabled the detection of occult fractures of the hip to take place in a more timely fashion, and this now appears to be the study of choice to exclude a fracture.[43] Work by Rizzo and associates[125] showed that MRI is superior to bone scanning in the detection of occult hip fractures. In their investigation, MRI was more effective than bone scintigraphy in detecting occult fracture around the hip within 24 hours of presentation. In some cases of occult fracture, repeat bone scanning was necessary up to 6 days after presentation to detect the fracture. These patients required hospital admission and bedrest for about a week before definitive diagnosis and the initiation of appropriate treatment. Similarly, Quinn and McCarthy[121] demonstrated that a limited MRI study used to evaluate the hip for fracture could be competitively priced when compared with bone scanning, laminar tomography, or CT. The higher cost of MRI compared with scintigraphy was more than offset by the prompt initiation of appropriate treatment in these cases. In cases without evidence of fracture, lengthy hospital stays and the complications associated with forced recumbency while awaiting repeat bone scans were avoided. When a suspected fracture was confirmed, the prompt initiation of treatment also decreased length of stay and lessened the likelihood of fracture displacement and the need for more complex management. MRI was also able to detect other pathologic lesions, including avascular necrosis or metastatic lesions, in addition to or in the absence of a fracture. In summary, MRI allows the definitive diagnosis to be made in short order in most cases.

## CLASSIFICATION OF INTERTROCHANTERIC FRACTURES

The ideal fracture classification system should be easy to apply and communicate, guide treatment, predict outcome, be reproducible among different observers, and be consistent with a generalized classification scheme for all skeletal injuries. No such system yet exists for intertrochanteric fractures.

In 1949, Evans published a classification system based on the general direction of the fracture line and the ability to obtain and maintain a reduction with closed manipulation and skeletal traction.[41] He emphasized the importance of reestablishing posteromedial contact in achieving a stable reduction. The Evans classification was modified by Jensen and Michaelsen in 1975.[65] Their version describes decreasing stability as the number of associated lesser and greater trochanteric fractures increases (Fig. 49–4A to C). Type IA (nondisplaced) and type IB (displaced) fractures are simple two-part fractures. Type I fractures were considered stable because they could be reduced into anatomic position (no fracture gap >4 mm in either plane) in 94% of patients and were followed by loss of position in only 9% of patients. The type IIA fracture pattern is a three-part fracture with a separate greater trochanteric fragment. Jensen felt that these fractures tended to "sag" with reduction maneuvers, leaving the fracture malpositioned in the sagittal plane (Fig. 49–5). Type IIB fractures are three-part fractures involving the lesser trochanter. Type IIB fractures could be anatomically reduced in only 21% of all patients, with displacement occurring in 61%. The problem primarily resulted from an inability to reduce and reestablish the medial cortical buttress (Fig. 49–6). The type III pattern is a four-part fracture. Only 8% of these very comminuted fractures could be reduced, and in 78% displacement occurred later. Jensen retrospectively applied five different classification schemes, using the fracture reduction initially achieved and the possibility of later loss of reduction as measures to evaluate the validity and reliability of various classifications. Their modified Evans classification system proved to be significantly more informative than all other classifications in Jensen's 1980 review of 234 fractures.[67, 68]

Before the introduction of modular devices designed to

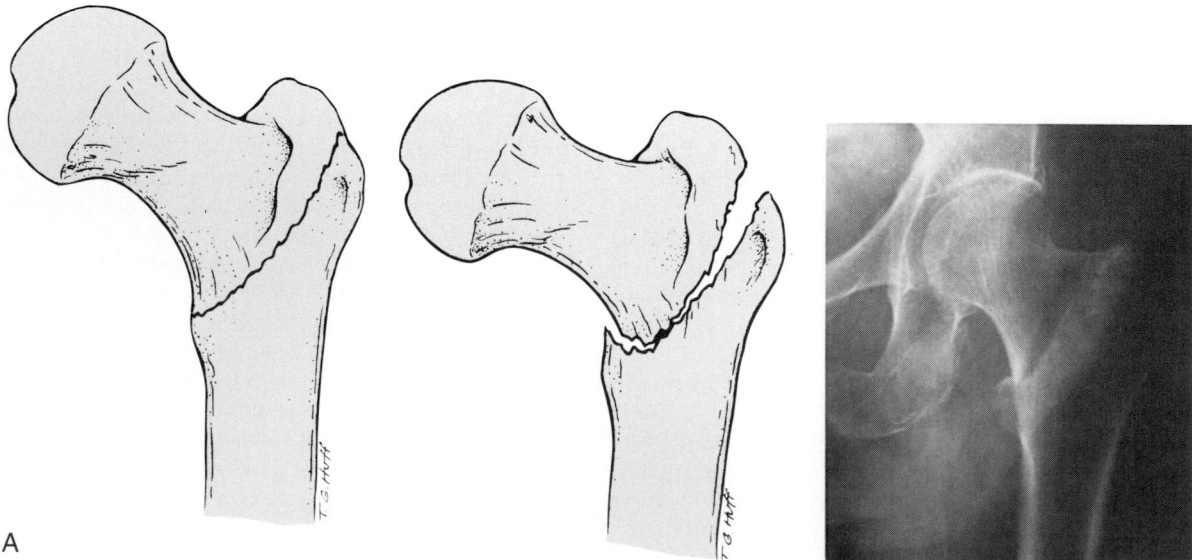

A

**FIGURE 49–4.** *A,* Diagrams of a nondisplaced and displaced, stable, two-part intertrochanteric fracture (Evans-Jensen Type 1; AO/OTA 31-A1.1) The radiograph depicts a typical two-part fracture (AO/OTA 31-A1.1)

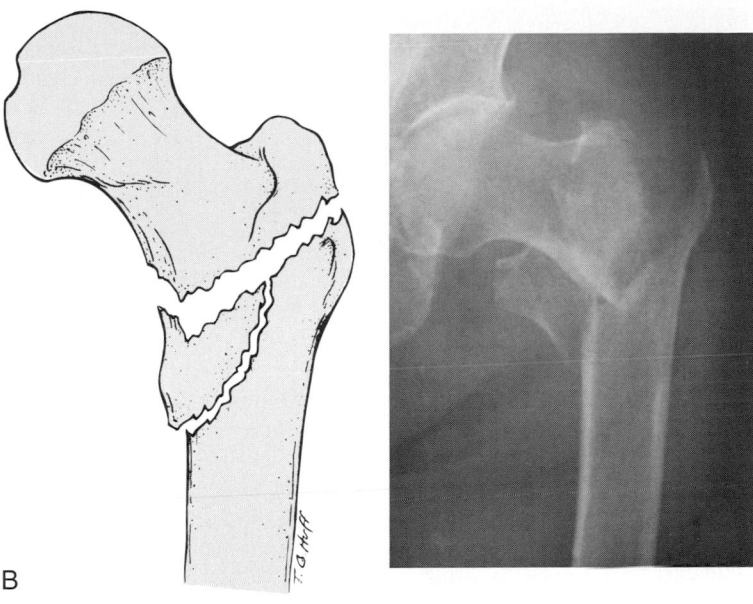

B

**FIGURE 49–4** *Continued. B,* Diagram and AP radiograph of an unstable three part fracture (Evans-Jensen IIB, AO/OTA 31-A2.1). *C,* Diagram and AP radiograph of unstable four part fracture (Evans-Jensen III, AO/OTA 31-A2.2)

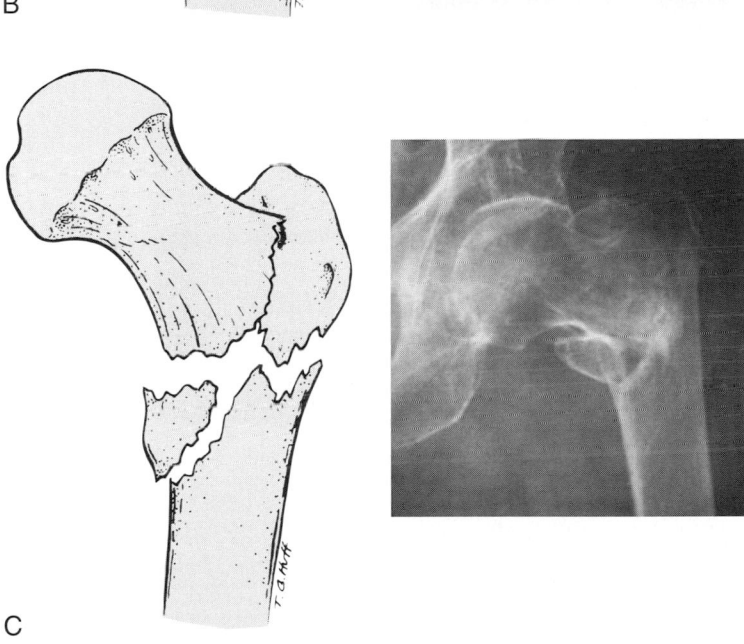

C

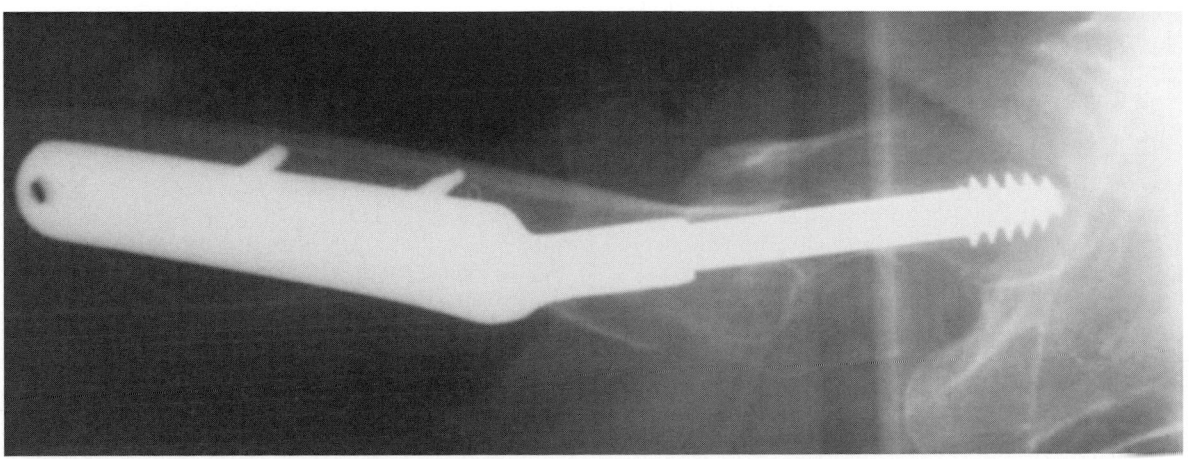

**FIGURE 49–5.** Three-part fracture involving the greater trochanter (Evans-Jensen type IIA) with unsatisfactory reduction of translation as seen on lateral radiograph after fixation with sliding screw and side plate.

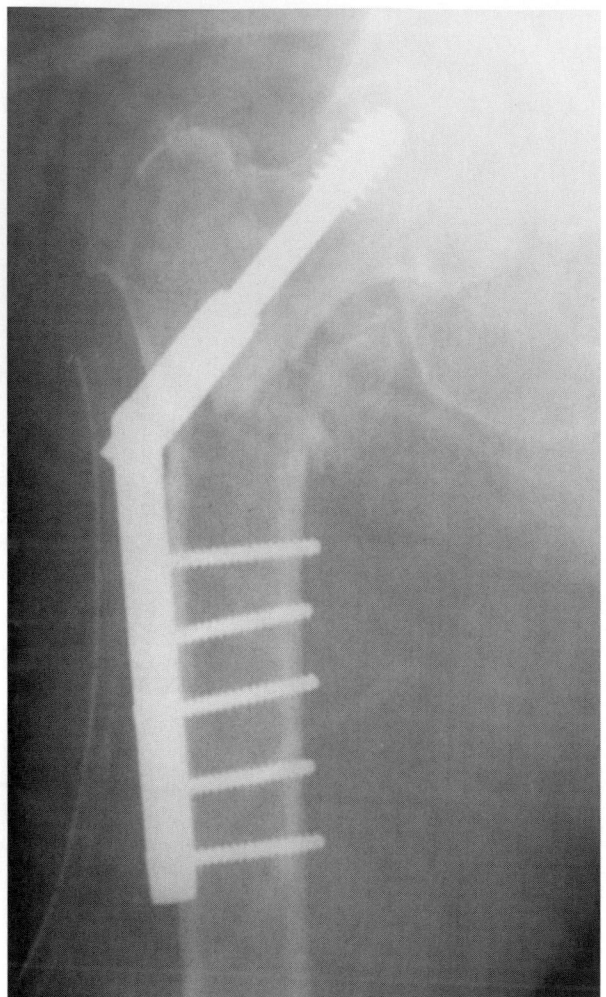

**FIGURE 49–6.** Four-part unstable fracture (Evans-Jensen type III, AO/OTA 31-A2.2) demonstrating varus angulatory malreduction and malpositioning of the implant.

allow controlled fracture impaction during the postoperative period, any shift of fragments after treatment with a fixed length angled plate (generally termed *secondary displacement*) was often poorly tolerated. With present techniques, slight settling of the fragments along the axis of the implant allows the fractured bone to "unload" the collapsing implant without risk of penetration of the head by the implant. Usually, slight shortening of the extremity is the only consequence of this shifting of the fragments after surgery. Very few of the older studies regarding intertrochanteric fractures differentiate this secondary displacement from the angulatory shifts that frequently lead to rapid and complete fracture collapse and technical failure. Therefore, the reader must be cautious in applying conclusions from these studies to current fracture management.

In *The Comprehensive Classification of Fractures of the Long Bones,* Müller and colleagues[110] coded proximal hip fractures as part of an attempt to offer a uniform alphanumeric fracture classification that incorporates prognosis and suggests treatment for the entire skeleton. In this system, advocated by the AO/ASIF, and adopted by The Orthopaedic Trauma Association in their Fracture Compendium,[115] type 31A fractures involve the trochanteric area of the proximal femur. These fractures are divided into three groups, and each group is further divided into three subgroups (Fig. 49–7). Group 1 fractures are simple (two part) fractures with a single extension into the medial cortex; the lateral cortex of the greater trochanter remains intact. The subgrouping further defines the geometry of the fracture line. All group 1 fractures are inherently stable. Group 2 fractures are multifragmentary by definition. The fracture line begins anywhere on the greater trochanter and extends medially in two or more places. This creates a third fracture fragment that includes the lesser trochanter. The lateral cortex remains intact. With the exception of a trivial lesser trochanteric fragment, fractures in this group are unstable. The subgrouping for group 2 fractures defines the number and geometry of the fragments. Group 3 fractures are those with both medial and lateral cortices of the proximal femur fractured; the subgroups describe fracture direction and comminution. Generally, the Evans-Jensen type I fracture is represented by the 31-A1 group. Evans-Jensen type II fractures are in the 31-A2 group. The so-called reverse obliquity intertrochanteric fracture is in group 31-A3. Although there is documented inconsistent interobserver reliability at the subgroup level of the AO/OTA classification system for intracapsular proximal femur fractures,[14] and it is likely the same liability exists for extracapular fractures, its alphanumeric and standardized format make the system useful, particularly for research and documentation.

The reader should realize that the common bond among all of the classification systems is the concept of stability. A stable fracture is one in which the posteromedial cortex is fractured in only one place and can, after anatomic reduction and fixation, withstand compressive loads without redisplacement. A fracture is considered unstable when, due to a large posteromedial fragment, multiple fragments, or a reverse oblique fracture line, despite realignment and fixation, it remains incompetent and the fracture tends to collapse on axial loading. This intuitive, simple, and reproducible description of stable versus unstable helps guide treatment and suggests prognosis. A majority of clinicians, and some respected researchers[76] prefer this binary description.

## PATIENT ASSESSMENT

### History

Most patients report a slip and fall at home involving only moderate trauma. A history of dizziness or temporary loss of consciousness should be specifically sought. Preexisting pain may indicate a pathologic lesion or symptomatic arthritis. In addition, the patient should be questioned regarding pain in other extremities or in the axial skeleton, because fractures of the humeral head, distal radius, ipsilateral femoral shaft, knee, or ankle can occur concurrently with the hip fracture.

An important part of the patient's history is the documentation of preexisting medical problems. Collaboration with the patient's primary physician and others, if appropriate, may be crucial for obtaining the complete history, including allergies and drug sensitivities, medications and dosages, and results of previous laboratory studies. The number of significant preexisting medical conditions is related to patient mortality after hip fracture surgery, particularly those affecting the cardiopulmonary system. The reader is referred to Chapter 47 for a focussed discussion on the medical workup and management of the elderly patient with a hip fracture.

It is important to determine the patient's level of function before the hip fracture occurred. Under the best circumstances, this level is the most the patient can expect to achieve on recovery. After recovery from a hip fracture, the ambulatory status of most patients has deteriorated to some degree. For example, a community ambulator may become limited to household ambulation after recovering from the injury. Moreover, many patients require or choose to use a cane, crutches, or a walker to ambulate efficiently or with confidence. To best facilitate the maximal physical and emotional recovery of the patient, these possibilities should be communicated to the patient and family early in the course of treatment.

The patient's social function before injury has great significance. Miller[105] documented that a patient's preinjury socioenvironmental level not only determined the level achievable after hip fracture surgery but also had great impact on the mortality rate after surgery. Recovery is also related to the number of close social contacts that a patient has before hip fracture, with patients having a greater number of social supports tending to have a more complete recovery of their prefracture level of function.[31] Campion and co-workers[23] showed that preinjury functional impairments in elderly patients with trochanteric hip fractures are common. Before their hip fractures, his patients had problems with community ambulation (49%), using a bathtub (40%), walking outdoors (26%), and climbing stairs (18%). These preinjury functional impairments were reliable predictors of length of hospital stay.

In addition to assessment of medical and function issues, consultation with social service or other discharge

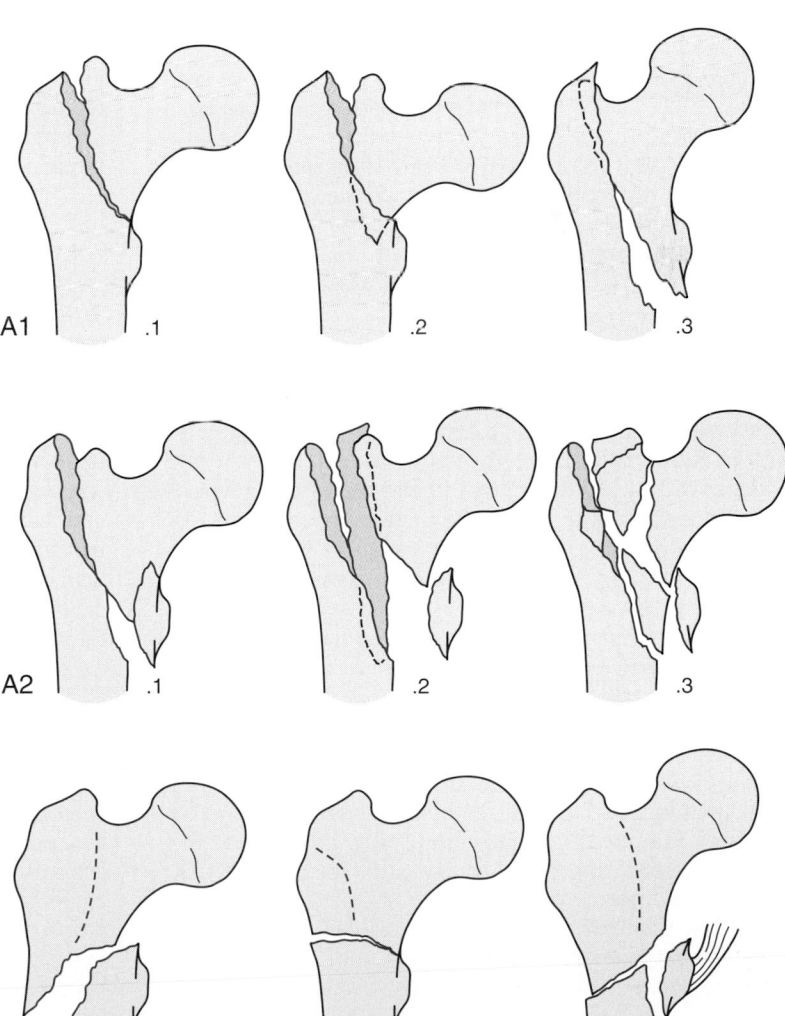

**FIGURE 49–7.** The comprehensive long bone classification of peritrochanteric femur fractures. To accurately classify the fracture subgroups, the full text should be consulted. (Redrawn from Müller, M.E.; Nazarian, S.; Koch, P.; Schatzker, J. The Comprehensive Classification of Fractures of Long Bones. Berlin, Heidelberg, New York, Springer Verlag, 1994.)

planning personnel should occur as soon as possible after hospitalization. In many patients without significant co-morbid disease, hospital stays can be quite short if appropriate postoperative support is available. To best facilitate appropriate rehabilitational placement, the necessary inquiries about rehabilitation needs and available resources should begin early.

## Physical Examination

Typically, the affected lower extremity appears relatively short and externally rotated. Depending on the time since injury, local ecchymosis from the fracture hematoma may be observed. This is usually found at the posterolateral aspect of the trochanteric area. Local skin conditions and pressure point areas such as the sacrum, buttocks, and heels should be inspected for evidence of breakdown. These pressure sores can cause significant postoperative morbidity, dramatically complicating the patient's hospital course.

One should quickly but conscientiously palpate and take through a range of motion the three other extremities, looking for occult injury in these apparently unaffected limbs. Particular attention must be paid to the range of motion of the contralateral hip; if restricted, it could complicate surgical positioning. On palpation of the affected hip, local tenderness should be noted over the trochanteric area but not over the femoral shaft or the pelvis. Crepitus of mobile fracture fragments may be present to palpation or on motion of the hip, but both stimuli should be minimized to avoid further pain and trauma to the patient.

## MANAGEMENT

The goal of treatment for patients with intertrochanteric hip fractures should be the early mobilization of the patient, with a prompt return to the prefracture level of functioning. This approach minimizes patient morbidity as well as the impact on health care resources. For displaced fractures, this goal is rarely, if ever, achieved without surgical intervention.

Closed treatment of intertrochanteric hip fractures has historically been associated with high mortality rates, and it has been suggested that nonoperative treatment has a significantly higher morbidity and mortality than operative treatment. In Evans' study, the result of 101 hip fractures treated by closed methods was compared with those of 110 fractures treated by operative stabilization. The mortality rate for the former group was 15% during the average 3.5-month hospital course, compared with 10.9% in the open treatment group over a 20-week period.[42] Although the early patient mobilization that surgical management offers is a major factor in improved outcome, many advances in medical care also contribute to reducing mortality.

A prospective trial of skeletal traction versus sliding hip screw fixation by Hornby and associates[61] demonstrated low complications with both methods of treatment.

Mortality at 6 months, pain, leg swelling, and nonhealed pressure sores occurred at similar rates after either treatment. The demonstrated advantages of surgical fixation in comparison with traction were shorter hospitalization, better restoration of normal anatomy, and better preservation of the ability to live independently after treatment.

Historically, straight nails, fixed nail plates, intramedullary devices, and osteotomies have been used to treat intertrochanteric fractures. Unfortunately, because of design and material weaknesses of these fixed length implants, most patients required some amount of external protection or activity restriction to prevent implant failure, thus diluting the major benefit of fixation. In the early 1970s, sliding nail and screw devices were introduced. Their purpose was to maintain anatomic axial alignment of the fracture as it impacted into a stable configuration (Fig. 49–8). These devices are strong enough to control bending and rotation without external protection in almost all situations and have sufficient fatigue life to last until the intertrochanteric fracture is healed. Fracture fixation depends on the durability of a composite made from the fixation device and bone. Because of the use of modern sliding hip screws, unlike the devices they replaced, it is the patient's bone and not the metallic implant that is the weakest factor in the construct. The well-documented clinical success of the sliding hip screw has made surgical management with this device the standard by which to compare all other methods of care for patients with intertrochanteric fractures.[40]

## Nonoperative Treatment

There are certain relative indications for nonoperative treatment of intertrochanteric fractures. These include the nonambulatory or demented patient with little evidence of pain, the septic patient, and the patient with significant skin breakdown over proposed surgical sites.[133, 146] Patients who are in the end stages of terminal illness, patients with unstable medical problems that are not correctable, and patients with old, less symptomatic fractures may reasonably be treated nonoperatively. Lyon and Nevins[95] believed that if the patient was nonambulatory or had little chance to walk again, a nonsurgical treatment regimen in the nursing home was safer, more humane, and less expensive than hospitalization with surgical treatment.

Closed fracture treatment falls into one of two regimens: early mobilization with no attempt to preserve normal anatomy (disregarding the fracture) or stabilization of the fracture with traction in an attempt to achieve near anatomic union. In the first method of treatment, which is generally reserved for patients with no hope of walking again, the patient is allowed up in bed, and transfers to chairs are allowed as soon as they are tolerated. For the first few days after injury, a special pressure-reducing bed may be helpful to avoid skin problems and minimize the need for uncomfortable repositioning. Pain is controlled with analgesics. In patients who have the potential for ambulation, skeletal traction through use of a proximal tibial Steinmann pin is commonly used. Approximately 15% of body weight is used to maintain traction on the

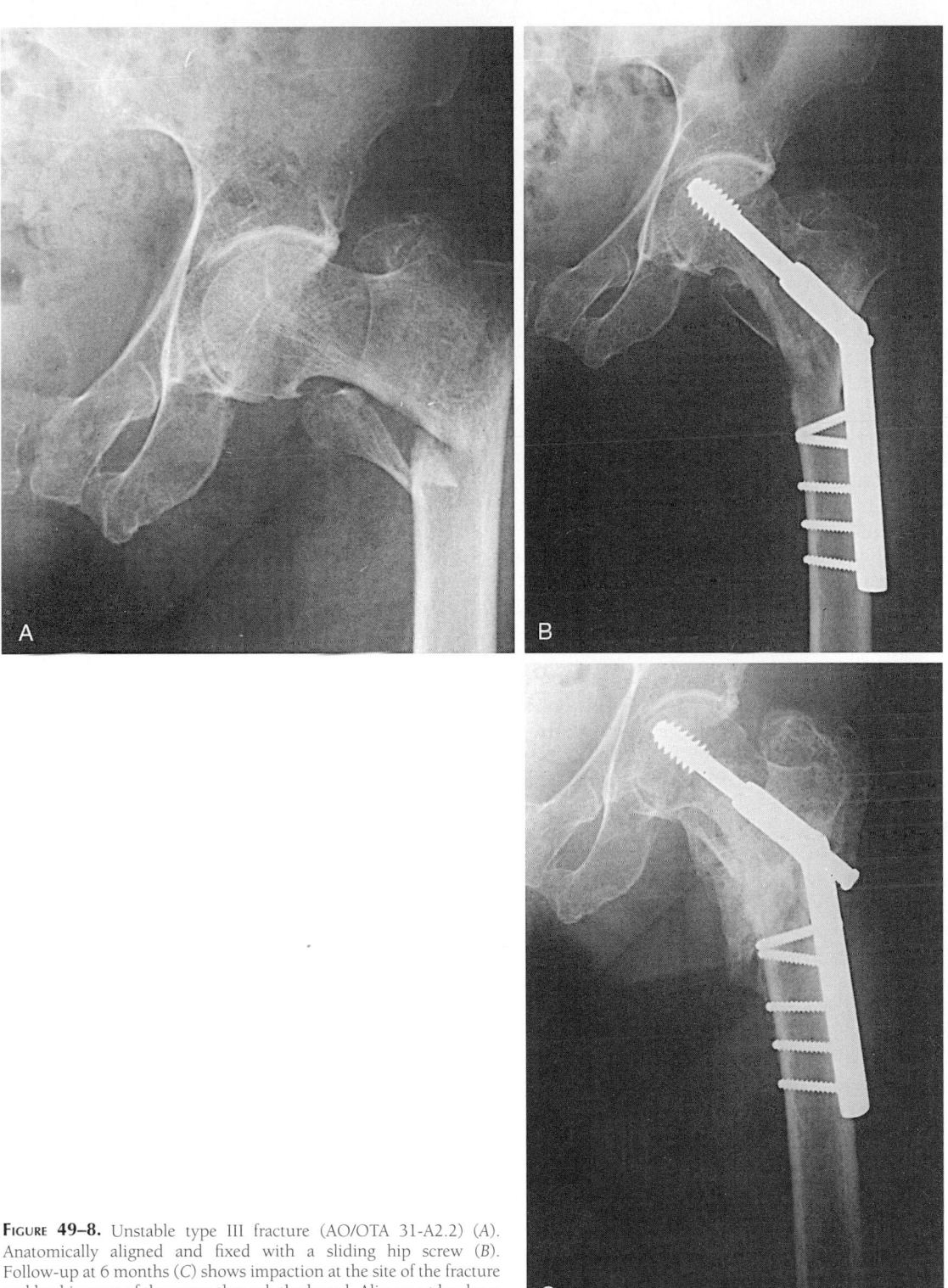

**FIGURE 49–8.** Unstable type III fracture (AO/OTA 31-A2.2) (*A*). Anatomically aligned and fixed with a sliding hip screw (*B*). Follow-up at 6 months (*C*) shows impaction at the site of the fracture and backing out of the screw through the barrel. Alignment has been maintained and the fracture has healed.

hip. The leg is placed in balanced suspension with minimal abduction. The traction maintains alignment and prevents varus angulation or shortening with external rotation. Serial radiographs are obtained to check position. Traction is maintained for 8 to 12 weeks, at which time mobilization to partial weight bearing is allowed until full union occurs. Special low-pressure or air suspension beds may be used to prevent skin breakdown and decubitus

ulcer formation. An aggressive physical therapy program for the bedbound patient can aid in maximizing recovery.

## Operative Treatment

The goal of surgical treatment of an intertrochanteric hip fracture is to obtain stable reduction of the fragments and internally fix them with a well-placed, mechanically strong implant. Surgical intervention should permit immediate transfers and early ambulation. This rapid return to function is critical to the recovery of the aged and very aged patients who form a large proportion of this fracture population.

## TIMING OF SURGERY

The relative urgency of surgical stabilization for these fractures has been debated extensively. In an often cited retrospective study, Kenzora and colleagues[73] noted increased mortality at 1 year in patients surgically stabilized within 24 hours of admission. They recommended a thorough medical evaluation and optimizing of the patient's condition over the initial 12 to 24 hours before proceeding with surgery. There is consensus agreement that surgery should proceed within 48 hours unless there are strong medical contraindications.[45, 127, 132, 151] Zuckerman and colleagues reported that the 1-year mortality rate doubled when surgical repair did not occur in the first 2 days after admission in 367 prospectively evaluated community dwelling cognitively intact ambulators who sustained a proximal femur fracture.[151] There seems to be no advantage to rushing the geriatric hip fracture patient from the emergency department directly to the operating suite without adequate medical evaluation, particularly late at night. Instead, up to 12 or 24 hours spent optimizing intravascular volume and oxygen transport and correcting electrolyte imbalances and nontherapeutic drug levels seems to be a reasonable approach. The patient should then proceed with stabilization by a well-prepared surgical and anesthetic team. The institution of prompt, appropriate medical and subsequent surgical management facilitates a quick recovery and reduces the risk of complications. While awaiting surgery, the patient is placed on bedrest with decubitus precautions. The affected lower extremity is carefully supported with pillows. Two recent randomized, prospective clinical trials showed no difference in pain level or complications between patients treated with or without skin traction.[3, 69]

## FRACTURE REDUCTION

Of the five factors that affect the strength of the fixed fracture (bone quality, fracture pattern, fracture reduction, implant design, and implant placement), the first one that the surgeon can control is fracture reduction, and its importance cannot be overstated. No internal fixation device, regardless of design, can improve the result of a poorly reduced fracture. Although the sliding hip screw allows for progressive impaction of fracture surfaces and closure of gaps between fragments that remained at surgery, it cannot convert a poor reduction into a good one. A good result is best obtained by applying fixation only after satisfactory reduction of the fracture.

### Stable Fractures

In fracture patterns without posteromedial comminution (type I stable intertrochanteric fractures), anatomic fracture reduction restores the ability of the bone to transmit compressive loads across the medial cortex. Anatomic

reduction of the fracture fragments can usually be achieved. Reduction simply requires adequate longitudinal traction to overcome shortening caused from unopposed muscle action and bleeding into the proximal thigh, mild abduction to correct any residual varus, and slight internal rotation to "screw home" the distal fragment. Because of the inherent stability of the fracture, any device that can hold the fragments aligned during healing should be successful. In fact, type I fractures respond well to a variety of well-executed fixation techniques. Kyle,[85] Levy,[92] and Steinberg[137] and their associates all obtained similar superior results in stable fracture patterns employing different surgical techniques. MacEachern and Heyse-Moore[96] did note that postoperative impaction occurred in approximately one fourth of injuries considered stable at the time of surgery. However, the small amount of impaction that may occur after adequate fixation of stable intertrochanteric fractures is rarely of consequence to the patient.

### Unstable Fractures

Although there is almost universal agreement that anatomic reduction is best for stable fractures, there have been numerous opinions regarding the preferred reduction for unstable fractures. A considerable amount of clinical and some laboratory data exist to aid in decision making, but some conflicting conclusions remain evident. Most investigators recommend attempted anatomic reduction of the unstable intertrochanteric fracture. In practice, because it is rare for the posteromedial lesser trochanter fragment and the lateral greater trochanter fragment to reduce spontaneously and formal exposure and fixation of these fragments exact too much of a biologic cost to be beneficial, absolute anatomic reconstruction is rarely attempted. In fact, the likelihood of residual gaps greater than 4 mm between fragments after reduction was part of the basis for the Evans-Jensen classification into stable (type I), unstable (type II), and very unstable (type III) fractures. Instead, the goal is to reestablish an anatomic relation between the head and neck fragment and the shaft fragment, both axially and translationally, in the AP and lateral planes. Fixation of these fragments with a fatigue resistant sliding hip screw allows for a controlled impaction of the fracture surfaces without loss of axial or translational alignment as the fracture is loaded during the postoperative period. Clinical support for this method of reduction exists in various reports, such as those of Clawson,[28] Kyle,[83] Heyse-Moore and co-workers,[59] and Rao and associates.[124] Laboratory evidence, reported by Chang and colleagues,[26] indicates that anatomic reduction of a four-part fracture model prepared from cadaver bone consistently provided higher compression forces across the medial cortical bone area and lower tensile stresses on the sliding hip screw than reduction by medial displacement osteotomy, even if the posteromedial lesser trochanter fragment was discarded rather than reduced. Of the 162 unstable fractures treated by anatomic reduction and sliding screw fixation reported by Rao and associates,[124] only 2% retained the anatomic reduction; 90% were reported to have moved to a medial displacement position and 8% to a lateral displacement position. Nonetheless, the clinical success rate was still high.

Valgus reduction with high-angled fixation (140° to 150°) is a reasonable alternative to anatomic reduction in unstable fracture patterns. The valgus reduction of the fracture decreases the bending forces on the implant by decreasing the neck-shaft offset, and the more vertical orientation of the neck tends to offset some of the shortening expected with unstable fractures. Finally, positioning of the fragments into valgus reorients the fracture plane so that it is more perpendicular to the weight-bearing load vector and thus more favorably positioned for interfragmentary compression (Fig. 49–9). Experimentally, a high-angled device has a greater tendency to slide because the barrel is more closely aligned to the direction of the joint reaction force than that of a 130° device during single leg stance.[85] Good results have been reported with this technique.[128, 129] One in vitro study by Meislin and co-workers[102] confirmed increased sliding for high-angled devices but noted that none of the expected benefits of increased loading of the medial cortex or reduction of implant strain occurred. These findings call into question the assumption that the high-angled implant is in itself advantageous. Clinically, a causal relation between high-angled fixation and increased tendency to slide has not been shown.[148] The complex and variable hip joint reaction forces and torsional strains that affect the fracture of a patient in the immediate postoperative period during log rolls, chair transfers, four-point gait, and so on may not relate well to the ideal laboratory setting of static uniplanar axial loading. Although valgus reduction supported by high-angle fixation is an attractive alternative to anatomic reduction, there is no reason to use a high-angled device in an anatomically aligned fracture, because the implant will be forced into the superolateral aspect of the femoral head, where the bone is known to be weaker (Fig. 49–10).

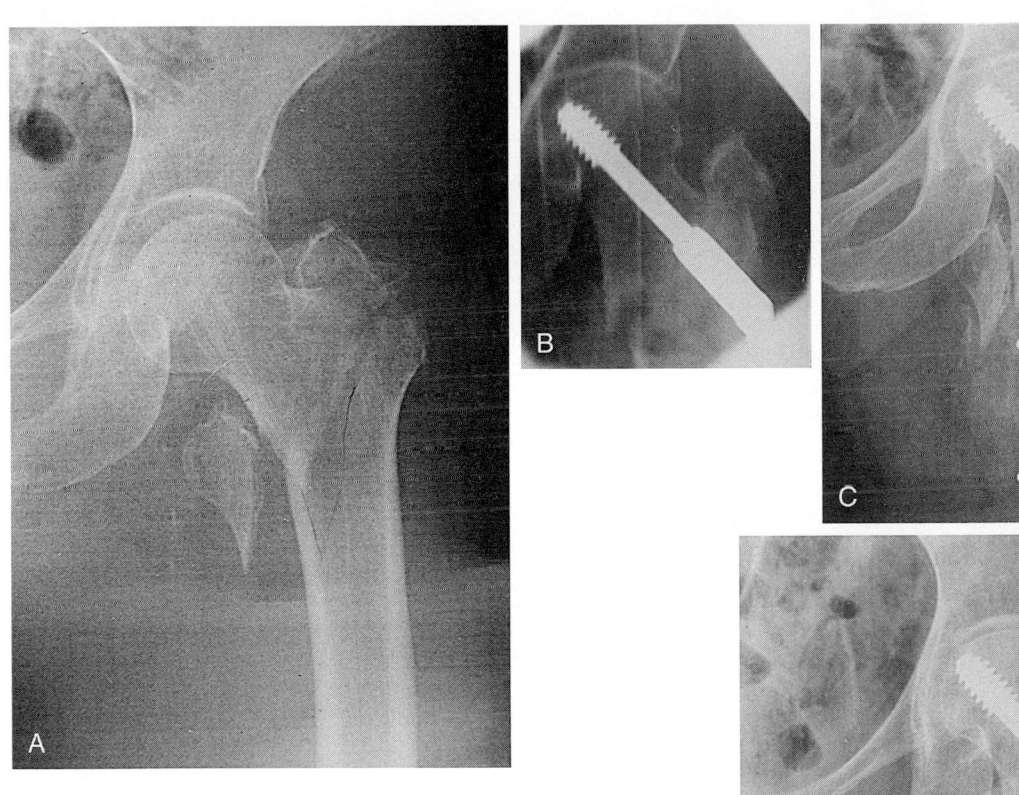

**FIGURE 49–9.** *A,* Four-part, unstable intertrochanteric fracture (AO/OTA 31-A2.3). *B,* Postoperative radiograph shows valgus reduction and fixation with a 135° sliding hip screw. Note the slight gap at the medial cortex. *C, D,* Follow-up demonstrates impaction and uneventful union. Valgus alignment has decreased the bending force on the implant and offset the tendency for limb shortening despite fracture settling.

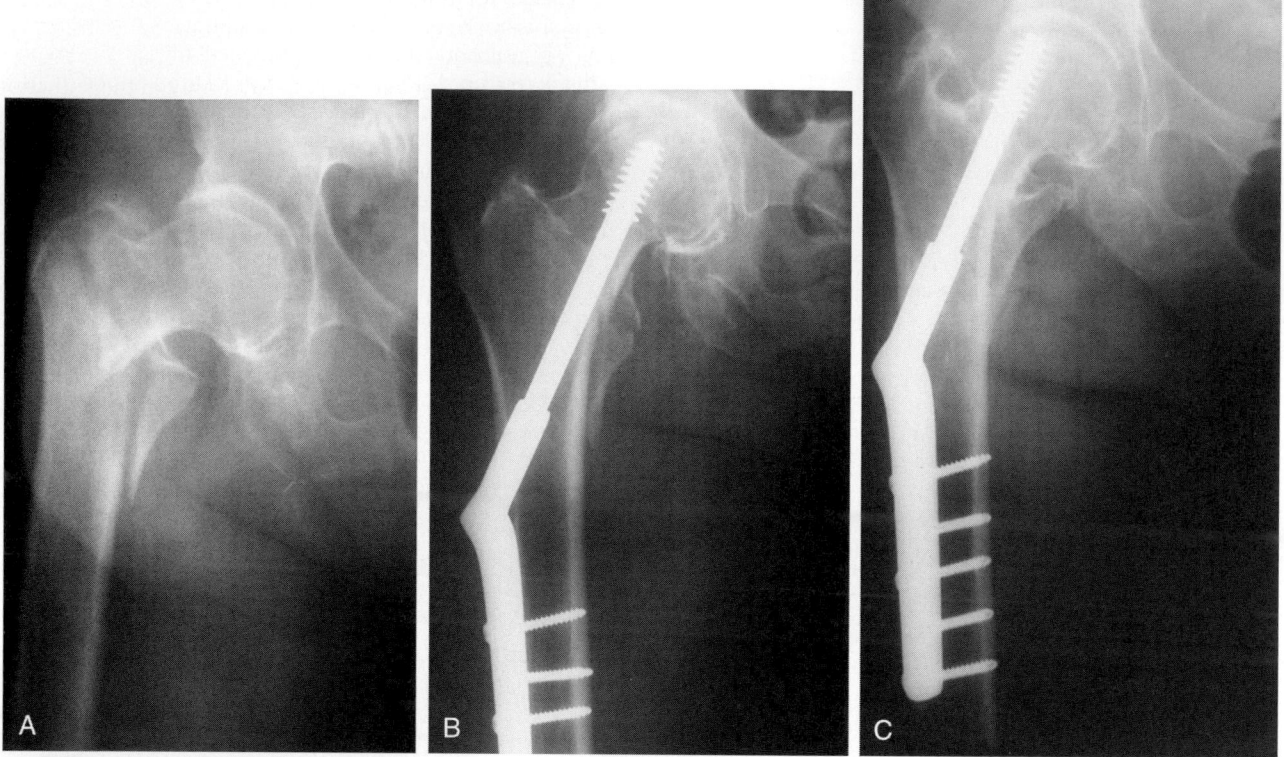

**FIGURE 49–10.** Unstable, three-part fracture (*A*) is reduced to anatomic alignment and fixed with a 150° angled plate, forcing the sliding hip screw along the medial cortex of the neck but into the superolateral periphery of the head (*B*). The implant collapses minimally before cutting out of the femoral head (*C*). Either a valgus reduction or an appropriately positioned 135° angled plate may have avoided this complication.

## OSTEOTOMIES

Before the development of devices that could collapse during postoperative fracture settling, surgeons had to achieve complete fracture stability during the operation. Lacking this, the incidence of fatigue failure of the implant or joint perforation (if the fracture collapsed on a fixed-length implant) was high. Methods to achieve stable medial cortical opposition include nonanatomic neck-shaft valgus alignment and high-angled fixation, with or without osteotomy.

Historically, a medial displacement osteotomy was advocated to convert the unstable fracture into one that was stable but nonanatomically reduced. Dimon and Hughston reported improved results with Jewett nail fixation of unstable intertrochanteric fractures by displacement of the distal shaft fragment medially and insertion of the medial spike of the major proximal fragment into the medullary canal of the distal fragment.[38, 39] If the fragments are firmly impacted proximal into distal, then a stable position can be obtained from a previously unstable fracture pattern. To the extent that the proximal fragment is impacted into the distal, femoral shortening occurs. This can be at least partially counteracted by a valgus positioning of the proximal fragment. However, such a valgus alignment at the hip may adversely affect the function and appearance of the knee. Despite the reduced rate of fixation failure after Jewett nailing, medial displacement osteotomy has found limited acceptance because of

its technical difficulties, poorer functional results, and greater alteration of normal anatomy when compared with anatomic sliding hip screw fixation.[71] Roberts and colleagues[126] found higher rates of shortening and external rotation deformity, as well as impaired gait. Other clinical reviews confirm that medial displacement osteotomy is of no value unless a stable reduction is actually achieved in the process. Currently, the indications for medial displacement osteotomy for acute fractures are extremely limited.

Sarmiento[130] recommended improving stability by removing a wedge of bone, with the base lateral and apex medial, so that the plane of the fracture becomes more transverse (Fig. 49–11), but his good results have rarely been reproduced elsewhere. Possible problems include excessive valgus of the proximal fragment causing a subjective perception of instability at the hip, excessive shortening, and external rotation deformity of the limb.[62]

Two clinical trials compared osteotomy techniques (both medial displacement and valgus) with anatomic reduction in randomized, prospective protocols using sliding hip screws. Osteotomy procedures were associated with significantly longer surgery and greater blood loss but no clinical benefit.[36, 47] In the study by Gargan and colleagues,[47] the mechanical failure rate was 2.5 times greater in the osteotomy group than in the group for whom anatomic reduction was attempted.

The development of the sliding hip screw appears to have made these relatively aggressive osteotomies obsolete for most acute intertrochanteric fractures. However, knowledge of these techniques and an appreciation of the principles behind them may be of value in managing fixation failure and nonunions of fractures in this region.

## Surgical Techniques

### COMPRESSION HIP SCREW AND SIDE PLATE

Surgery is carried out as soon as the patient's medical status is optimized, adequate radiographs have been acquired and understood, and the appropriate instrument and implant inventory is confirmed to be available. After the successful induction of general or spinal anesthesia, the patient is transferred onto the operating table. Although any radiolucent table is acceptable, the use of a fracture table is strongly recommended. Not only can the reduction usually be obtained and maintained indefinitely by indirect means, obviating the need for tissue stripping and cumbersome bone clamps, but biplanar fluoroscopy can be achieved repeatedly without having to move the fractured extremity.

The patient should be carefully transferred from the bed to the table and placed in a supine position. A safety belt should be applied immediately, particularly in patients

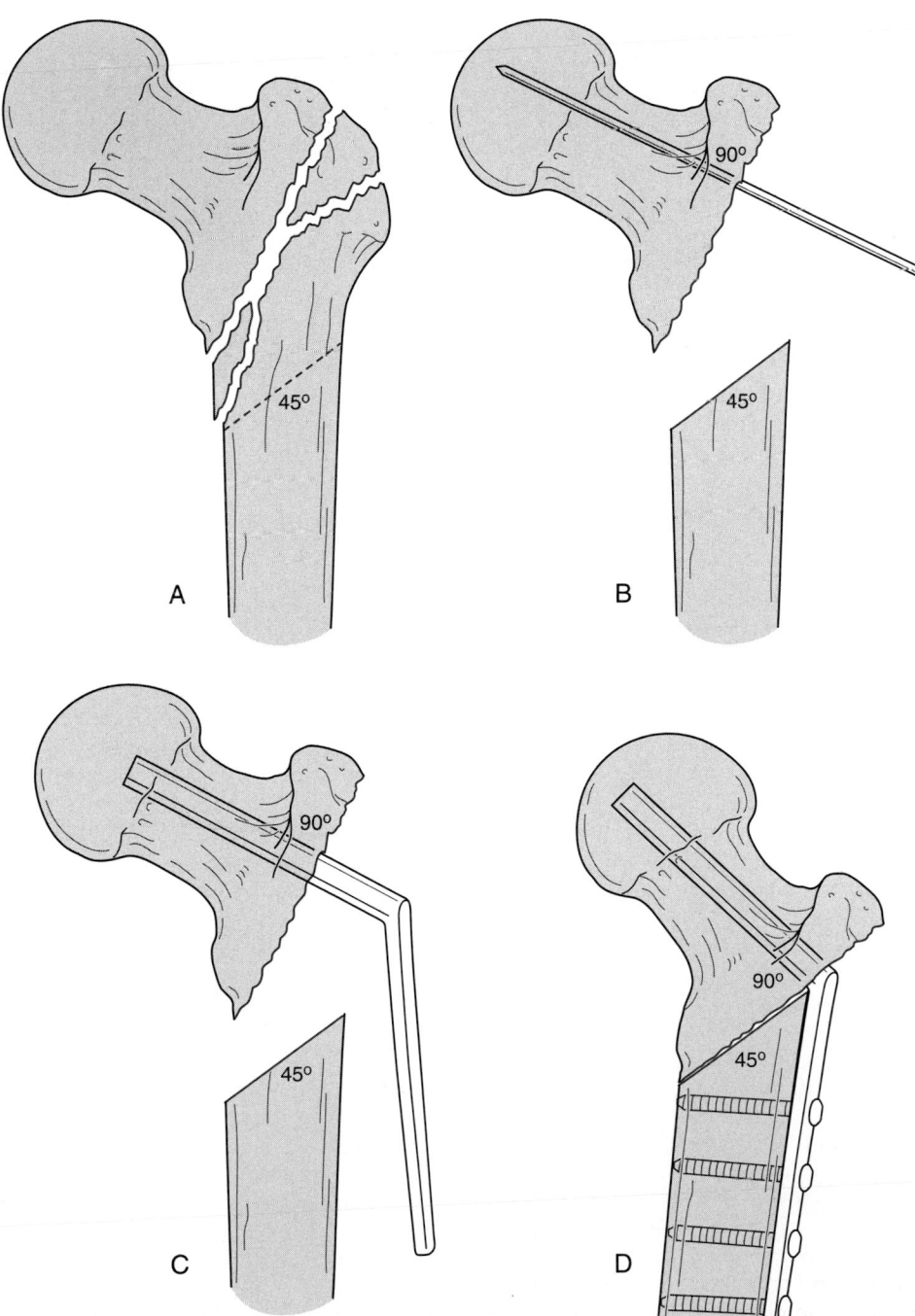

**FIGURE 49–11.** *A–D,* A valgus osteotomy of the proximal femoral shaft increases stability by orienting the fracture plate perpendicular to the deforming forces of the hip muscles and weight bearing. A sliding screw device can be used instead of the one-piece, fixed-angle implant shown here to decrease the risk of joint penetration.

under spinal anesthesia, in whom upper extremity and torso motions can result in falls. The physician should ascertain the normal position of slight external rotation that characterizes the uninjured hip and note the range of motion available under anesthesia. A well-padded perineal post for countertraction is attached to the table, and the patient is positioned against it. The affected extremity is carefully padded and firmly secured to the foot holder. Some fracture tables have pneumatic, padded foot holders that can be applied rapidly, but they often are problematic and afford poor control of the foot when applying firm traction or rotation. It is preferable to pad the heel and circumferentially tape the foot to the heel rest, leaving the posteromedial neurovascular bundle completely uncompromised. When the padded metatarsal bar is raised, it dorsiflexes the ankle and stabilizes the transverse tarsal joint, locking the foot into a position that can transmit strong longitudinal traction and rotational forces to the fracture (Fig. 49–12).

If there is an adequate range of motion of the unaffected extremity, the hip is flexed, abducted, and internally rotated. This position allows free positioning of the fractured extremity and interferes least with fluoroscopic visualization of the fracture, but the pelvis can tilt and rotate if strong traction is applied, because no countertraction is applied to the well leg. Alternative positions for the unaffected extremity include wide abduction or extension of the uninjured side (heel to toe). These positions have the potential advantage of maintaining a stable pelvis, because countertraction can be applied to the unaffected limb. However, the critically important lateral plane fluoroscopic imaging can be compromised. Most acute intertrochanteric fractures do not require much traction, so the flexed and abducted hip position generally is preferred because of the superior imaging it offers.

Many fracture tables provide improved access to the fractured hip by allowing a portion of the table under the affected hip to be shifted down or toward the other side. This allows the buttock to sag and prevents a bulging of compressed tissue in the posterior aspect of the wound. When this posteriorly positioned buttress is removed, the pelvis can tilt, and in the case of a significantly unstable fracture the fracture itself can sag into an unacceptable position. This feature should be used with some caution.

### Fluoroscopic Imaging

After positioning of the patient and provisional closed reduction but before preparation and draping of the field, the surgeon should supervise the positioning of the C-arm fluoroscope. Both AP and lateral images of the affected hip are scrutinized, particularly the lateral view. The surgeon must be able to visualize the proximal shaft, the fracture zone, the femoral neck, and the complete circumference of the femoral head on the AP and lateral fluoroscopic images. Only when the images are judged adequate should further fracture reduction and subsequent fixation proceed.

### Fracture Reduction

Undisplaced fractures require no reduction maneuver. Slight internal rotation to place the femoral neck parallel to

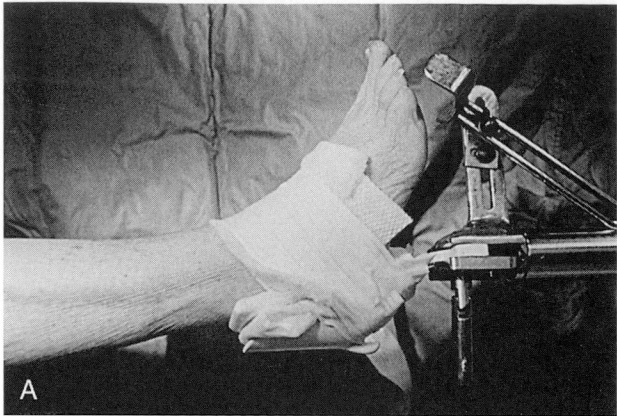
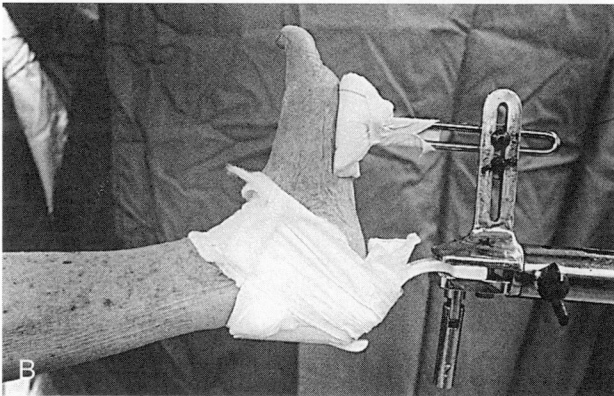

**FIGURE 49–12.** After the well-padded foot is secured to the holder (*A*, lateral view of foot), the metatarsal support bar is raised to dorsiflex the ankle and stabilize the transverse tarsal joint (*B*, medial view of foot). Strong traction and rotation can now be applied.

the floor on the lateral view simplifies placement of the central guide pin.

Displaced fractures that are stable usually reduce well with traction. Mild abduction can help correct varus and facilitates restoration of an anatomic neck-shaft axis. Gentle internal rotation frequently completes the reduction of a stable fracture, and facilitates placement of a guide pin parallel to the neck by placing the neck horizontally. One must be certain that the proximal fragment rotates with the distal one; otherwise, internal rotation of the limb can cause a malreduction of the fracture. The lateral fluoroscopic view, together with the clinical assessment of thigh rotation (judged by the plane of the patella), aids in assessing the rotational reduction.

Unstable fractures can often be well reduced by the technique previously discussed. Occasionally, however, the proximal fragment remains externally rotated and the limb must be rotated to match this resting position. The posterior translational sag of the shaft fragment or apex posterior angulation at the fracture may be corrected by placing a crutch between limb and floor under the drapes, or simply by elevating the ipsilateral buttocks support. Frequently, raising the foot holder to allow for mild hip flexion improves the reduction in the lateral plane, particularly in the setting of a preexisting hip flexion contracture (typically seen in nonambulators). Rarely, the fracture leaves the gluteus medius and minimus attached to the proximal fragment, with all opposing muscles distal to the fracture. The resulting abduction, internal rotation, and flexion of the proximal fragment make closed reduction very difficult.

The quality of the reduction is evaluated with regard to fracture displacement, neck-shaft angle, anteversion, and femoral shaft "sag." Anatomic rotational alignment is assessed clinically. The closed reduction is then accepted, modified, or set aside in favor of a formal open reduction. If a closed reduction cannot be achieved after one or two attempts, further manipulations should be deferred until the wound is opened and the fracture can be palpated and openly reduced, if necessary. Although a hip screw and side plate can often be placed accurately without exposure of the fracture itself, the surgeon should take advantage of the open nature of this technique and control the fracture fragments directly when necessary for accurate reduction and fixation.

### Lateral Approach to the Proximal Femur

After appropriate skin preparation, the wound is surgically draped. Preferably, a sterile, transparent plastic curtain is suspended vertically from the fracture table to separate the surgical field from the image intensifier. A straight incision paralleling the shaft of the femur should begin proximally at the palpable vastus lateralis ridge on the greater trochanter and proceed distally. The length should be adequate to allow insertion of the side plate to be used.

The incision should continue through the subcutaneous tissue and to the longitudinal thick fibers of the fascia lata. The fascia lata is incised distally, directly over the femoral shaft, to avoid cutting the tensor muscle and the significant bleeders within it. The tensor can then be palpated within the fascia between thumb and index finger, and the fascial incision extended proximally, posterior to the palpable muscle. Beneath the fascia lata, a variably sized hematoma is usually present. This is evacuated and the posterior junction of the fascia lata and the vastus lateralis muscle is visualized. The vastus is pulled anteriorly with a retractor, and its fascia is incised 2 to 3 cm anterior to the linea aspera attachment, leaving adequate tissue to hold a suture at the time of closure. The muscular incision then goes through a thin part of the vastus muscle, allowing control of the perforating vessels with less risk of their posterior retraction. The underlying muscle is split longitudinally. Proximally, the vastus origin is released sharply from the vastus ridge to facilitate atraumatic anterior retraction of the muscle to expose the lateral shaft.

The surgeon who is gentle and conservative with exposure and retraction for fracture fixation is repaid with reduced complications of wound and fracture healing. Although adequate visualization is necessary for assessment, reduction, and fixation of the fracture, nonessential trauma to soft tissue should be avoided. This can best be achieved by adequate preoperative assessment of the fracture pattern. The surgeon should know which fracture line and which fragments need to be controlled and which ones can be left within their nourishing muscular and fascial envelopes. Indirect reduction techniques using the fracture table or a bone distractor along with fluoroscopic control help to minimize the unavoidable trauma of fracture fixation procedures.

### Fracture Assessment

If there is any question regarding the fracture pattern or the adequacy of the manipulative reduction as seen fluoroscopically, the assessment is confirmed with visual and digital examination of the fracture site. The reduction can easily be assessed by running a fingertip along the intertrochanteric line from greater to lesser trochanter to determine whether the main fragments are aligned. Medial palpation can be used to determine whether the lesser trochanter is intact, displaced, or displaced with a major posteromedial fragment. Posterior palpation behind the greater trochanter can reveal whether there is a large displaced posterolateral fragment.

If a stable reduction is present, the surgeon proceeds to guide pin insertion. If an adequate reduction is not present, the fracture alignment can usually be improved by manipulation of the limb by an unscrubbed assistant combined with direct fragment control. The value of rotating the limb externally should be considered if a large posterior gap is present. Increased traction may be required. Alternatively, temporary release of all traction and a manipulation may allow disengagement of a buttonholed fragment. If the fracture sags posteriorly, reduction can be improved by placing a broad elevator, a Bennett retractor, or a hip skid under the trochanter and lifting the fracture. Provisional fixation with one or more small Steinmann pins (e.g., extra guide pins) placed so as not to interfere with insertion of the fixation device often aids reduction and fixation of difficult intertrochanteric fractures. They offer the added benefit of maintaining reduction if the guide pin is inadvertently withdrawn after reaming. Rarely, stabilization of the proximal fragment to the acetabulum with a pin may greatly facilitate achievement of anatomic alignment and translation at the fracture site. If comminution and instability are so severe that an acceptable open reduction cannot be achieved, then consideration must be given to osteotomy or prosthetic replacement. Fixation should not be attempted for a fracture that has not been reduced.

### Guide Pin Insertion

For a 135° angled plate, an entry point about 2 cm below the vastus lateralis ridge is selected. Two landmarks assist in locating this level: it is directly opposite the lesser trochanter, and it is at the same level as the most proximal fibers of the gluteus maximus tendon's posterior osseous insertion on the femoral shaft. If a higher angle side plate is used, the entrance site is moved 5 mm distally for each 5° increase in barrel angle.

Although some surgeons prefer to insert the guide pin freely, after overdrilling the proposed entrance site on the lateral cortex, primary use of the pin and angled guide is recommended. The angled guide is positioned at the proper level, midway between anterior and posterior cortices on the femoral shaft. To assist in directing the guide pin properly in the transverse plane, a free guide pin may be advanced along the anterior surface of the femoral neck, paralleling the intended angle of the implant, and inserted into the anterior hip capsule or impacted gently into the femoral head (Fig. 49–13). This pin provides a visual guide to the anteversion of the proximal fragment, subject to radiographic validation on the lateral fluoroscopic view. Appropriate caution should be used to stay on the neck, because anterior misdirection can place the femoral vessels at risk. Before drilling the guide pin, fluoroscopic confirmation should be obtained to ensure that the angle guide lies flush on the lateral cortex of the femoral shaft.

The guide pin is directed to the apex of the femoral head: the point at which a line parallel to and in the center of the femoral neck intersects the subchondral bone. Peripheral placement in any direction should be avoided, because only with the pin directed centrally in both views can the screw be advanced safely to within 5 mm of the joint line without risking joint penetration. Central and deep placement allows screw purchase in the best bone available and allows maximal telescoping of the screw into the barrel of the side plate before the threads are stopped by the barrel. These factors greatly reduce the risk of mechanical failure of fixation.[9] The C-arm images are carefully assessed to confirm the position of the guide pin relative to the apex of the femoral head on both views. Peripheral or shallow position on either view should not be accepted. Rather, the reduction should be reassessed and the guide pin redirected. If difficulty is encountered in centering the guide pin, the surgeon should make certain that the real problem is not an unreduced fracture. One of the major advantages of the fluoroscopically guided cannulated compression hip screw system is that the final position of the implant may be established with the guide pin, before any irreversible bone removal by the reamer has occurred. Precise guide pin placement must be verified at this point before the procedure is carried any further. Adequate fluoroscopic visualization is critical to appropriate implant placement and a successful clinical outcome. To maintain the position of the guide pin in the bone during reaming, advance the tip into the subchondral bone. An appropriate correction must then be made when measuring the hip screw length.

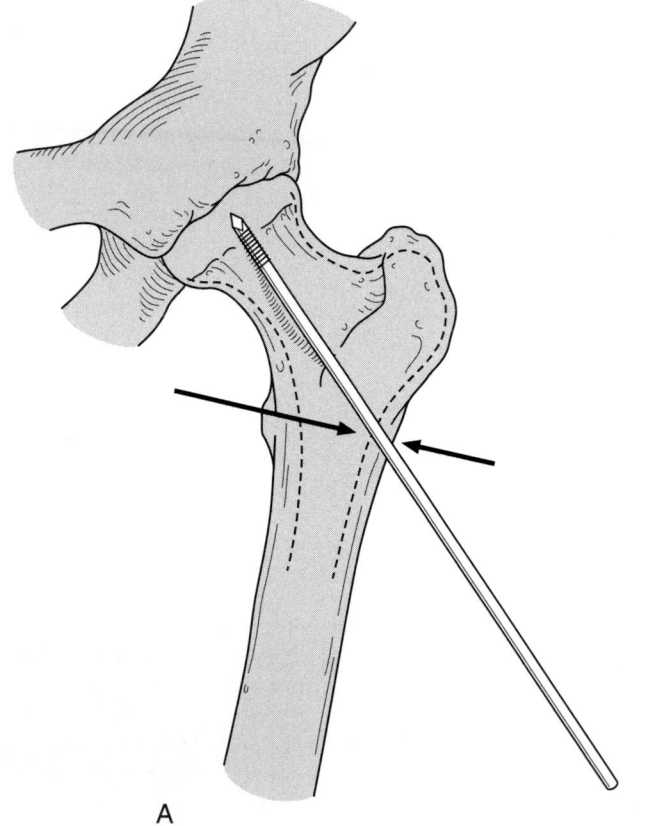

A

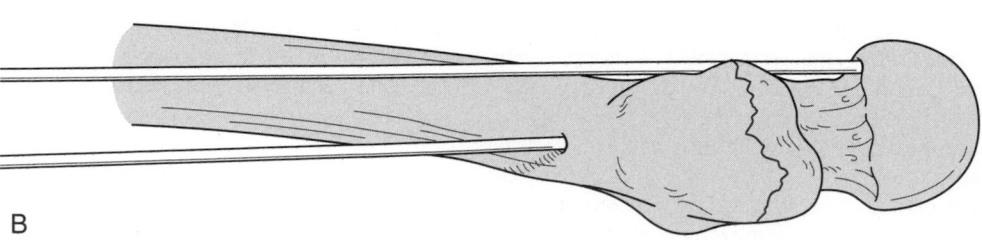

B

**FIGURE 49–13.** *A,* Starting at the level of the lesser trochanter, a guide pin is inserted by hand through the anterior hip capsule and is advanced along and in line with the femoral neck until it encounters the head of the femur. This serves as a radiographic marker for positioning the definitive guide wire on the AP view. *B,* Demonstration of the version of the femoral neck in this way is also a visual aid to orientation on the lateral view.

## Lag Screw Length Selection and Preparation

Most contemporary systems provide for a direct reading of the intraosseous length of the guide pin with the use of a special ruler. It is important that the surgeon be familiar with the chosen system, because some rulers have built-in correction factors for the threaded tip, the compressing screw, and so on. Another simple measurement method is to place an identical pin on the lateral cortex alongside the protruding portion of the guide pin and measure the length extending beyond the inserted guide pin. This is the length of pin in the bone.

The appropriate length of the hip lag screw is determined from the guide pin measurement. The distance that the tip of the pin extends beyond the desired screw position and the estimated amount of immediate telescoping of the screw within the side plate barrel that will occur after intraoperative traction is released must be taken into account. Unstable fractures and fractures requiring stronger traction to maintain anatomic alignment tend to have more acute collapse than stable fractures. The goal is to leave the operating room with the fracture reduced and impacted and with at least 80% to 90% of the screw shaft engaged within the barrel but not protruding laterally. As described previously, the screw tip should be exactly central in both planes and no more than 5 mm away from the joint surface.

Preparation of the channel for the lag screw should not be undertaken until the surgeon is completely satisfied with the reduction and position of the guide pin in the head-neck fragment. It may also be wise to reconfirm by fluoroscopy the angle the guide wire makes with the lateral femoral cortex, using an appropriate tool, because fixation with a device of a different angle changes the relation of proximal and distal fragments. After this angle has been confirmed, the angle of the side plate may be chosen.

Most contemporary hip screw systems use a so-called triple reamer, which drills a hole in the femoral head for the lag screw, increases its diameter laterally for the barrel of the side plate, and chamfers the lateral femoral cortex to accommodate the barrel-plate junction (Fig. 49–14). The triple reamer is adjusted by setting the length of the central drill so that it penetrates as deeply as desired for final screw placement. This depth should be 5 mm less than the inserted guide pin to minimize the chance of inadvertent guide pin withdrawal after reaming. It is important to realize that the triple reamer must accomplish three not necessarily related tasks and that its length setting is not always reliable. Fluoroscopy should be used to ensure that the drill tip penetrates just to the chosen depth. Direct inspection laterally is required to ensure that the second and third stages of the reamer prepare the lateral femur satisfactorily. Adjustment of the triple reamer may be required during this procedure. Even if a threaded tip guide pin is used and is inserted into the subchondral bone, it may bind and be removed inadvertently on withdrawal of the reamer. Should this occur, the pin must be reinserted carefully and concentrically. Routine use of a supplemental pin transfixing the fracture helps maintain the reduction. Assuming there has been no loss of reduction, guide pin replacement can be done by nesting suitable instruments from the insertion set or by placing

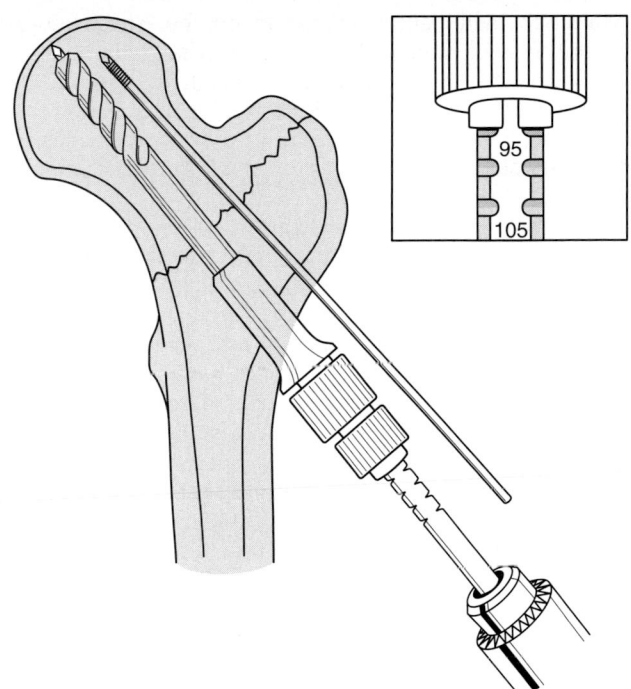

**FIGURE 49–14.** The compression screw triple reamer is adjusted appropriately, based on guide pin depth and fracture (see text). It is then advanced over the previously placed guide pin, under fluoroscopic and visual control, (1) to create a channel of appropriate (but not excessive) length for the lag screw; (2) to prepare a shorter, wider channel for the barrel of the side plate; and (3) to bevel, or chamfer, the inferior edge of the hole in the lateral femoral cortex to improve apposition of the side plate to the bone. Intermittent fluoroscopy monitors the depth of the central reamer and confirms that the guide pin has not become incarcerated in the drill. A proximal stabilizing pin is used to resist torque during reaming and screw insertion and to maintain reduction if the guide pin is inadvertently removed.

the barrel of a side plate into the prepared hole and placing the shaft of a lag screw backward through the barrel. The guide pin is reinserted concentrically by sliding it through the cannulated screw, and then the implants used to realign the guide pin are removed.

Although tapping is unnecessary in osteopenic bone, it may be necessary to cut the lag screw threads into the bone in physiologically younger patients with dense cancellous bone. Like the triple reamer and the lag screw itself, the tap is inserted over the guide pin.

## Implant Insertion and Fixation

Traditionally, most intertrochanteric fractures have been fixed with side plates of four or five holes. Longer plates with more screws do not improve proximal purchase, nor do they alter the inherent stability of the fracture or the quality of the reduction achieved. They do, however, require more dissection to apply, and they complicate any subsequent surgery in the area (Fig. 49–15). The surgeon must justify use of longer plates. Recently, plates with fewer holes have been used in an attempt to minimize operative time and surgical dissection. Bolhofner reported a consecutive series of 70 intertrochanteric fractures treated with a two-hole plate. Although there were three technical failures (two cutouts and one screw barrel dissociation), no loss of shaft fixation occurred.[17] In laboratory analysis, Yian found that a third screw was helpful in reducing tensile forces on the proximal two screws but that further fixation offered little additional protection.[147] Another cadaver study demonstrated no significant difference in performance between two- and four-hole plates for three-part unstable intertrochanteric fractures under failure testing.[100]

Whereas some sliding screw devices permit free rotation of the screw within the side plate barrel, others block this rotation with a keyed cross section or occasionally an optional mechanical clip. If a locked (e.g., Synthes, DHS) or lockable (e.g., Richards, Ambi) device is chosen, the screw must be inserted so that its rotational alignment allows the side plate to seat parallel to the femoral shaft. The theoretical advantage of a keyed system is improved rotational control of the fracture; however, very little prevents the fracture from rotating on the screw itself. Furthermore, the interdigitated and impacted fracture line should offer adequate resistance to torque for the well-centered hip screw. The advantage of the keyless system is a slightly simpler surgical technique. The surgeon should be familiar with the selected implant and its instrumentation to facilitate proper insertion of the device. A trial run with the system on a plastic bone model in a motor skills

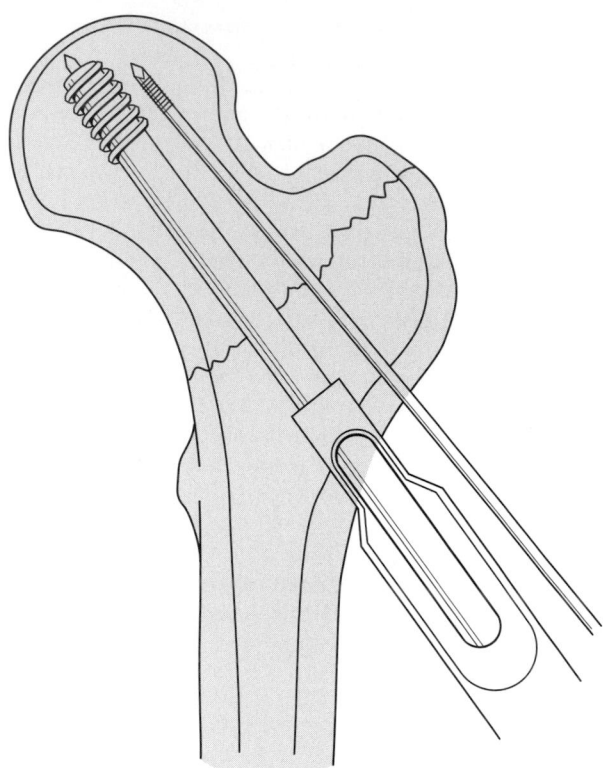

**Figure 49–16.** The lag screw is inserted over the guide pin with a centering sleeve to a depth of 5 to 10 mm from the subchondral bone and centrally in the femoral head on both anteroposterior and lateral radiographs. Proper guide pin placement is essential to this step. This must be confirmed first on both views. In dense bone, threads for the lag screw should be tapped.

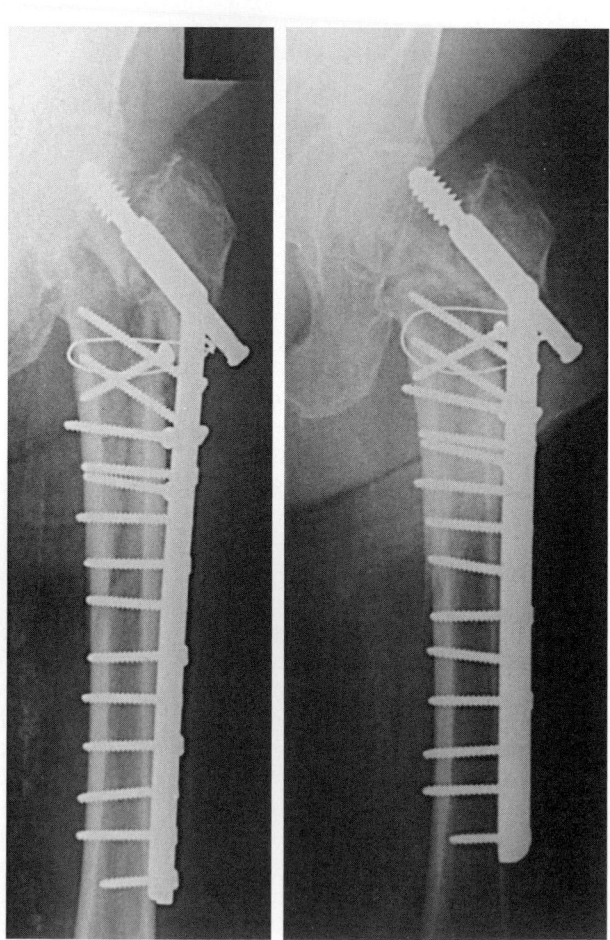

**Figure 49–15.** Early failure of proximal fixation of a reverse obliquity intertrochanteric fracture with subtrochanteric extension. An excessive number of shaft screws does not improve the proximal fixation achieved by a poorly positioned single lag screw.

laboratory or at an instructional course is an appropriate way to gain familiarity with a new hip fixation system.

With the guide pin's position confirmed by biplanar fluoroscopy, the cannulated lag screw is inserted using a centering sleeve (Fig. 49–16). A palpating finger over the femoral neck ensures that the proximal fragment does not become malrotated as the screw is torqued home. If extreme resistance is met, tapping may be required. Intermittent fluoroscopy verifies proper insertion and ensures that the guide pin is not bent or jammed and advancing ahead of the screw. After the screw position is judged satisfactory, the depth of the screw relative to the lateral cortex is confirmed, and the barrel is slid over the screw so that the plate is approximated to the lateral cortex of the femoral shaft. Then the guide pin is removed.

Once the assembly is properly positioned, it should be checked to ensure that the screw shaft engages the barrel sufficiently. If a locking clip is to be used, it should be placed at this time, before fixation of the plate to the shaft. Alignment may be improved by clamping the plate to the femoral shaft before attaching it with screws. Usually at this point traction is released, and in unstable fracture patterns the distal femur is slid proximally very slightly to allow optimal impaction of the fracture without excessive immediate collapse of the implant. The angled plate acts as an aid to reduction, controlling alignment during this impaction process, which occurs in two ways. Initial fracture impaction is by intraoperative proximal displacement of the femoral shaft along the plate before screw insertion. The cortical screws are inserted through the plate into the shaft in routine fashion. Subsequent impaction occurs postoperatively as the lag screw collapses into the barrel of the sideplate. This can be initiated intraoperatively by manually impacting the proximal femur in line with the screw axis, by impacting an instrument that engages the barrel of the side plate, or by using the separate compressing screw that is inserted through the end of the barrel into the shaft of the lag screw (Fig. 49–17). Routine use of this screw also prevents the rare but severe complication of postoperative hip screw–barrel disengagement. These two modes of impaction of the fracture site represent the completion of reduction maneuvers and should gain stable impaction of the proximal against the distal fragment while maintaining biplanar anatomic alignment (Fig. 49–18).

### Wound Closure

The wound should be débrided of any devitalized tissue and thoroughly irrigated. The use of closed suction drains is at the surgeon's discretion. The muscular, fascial,

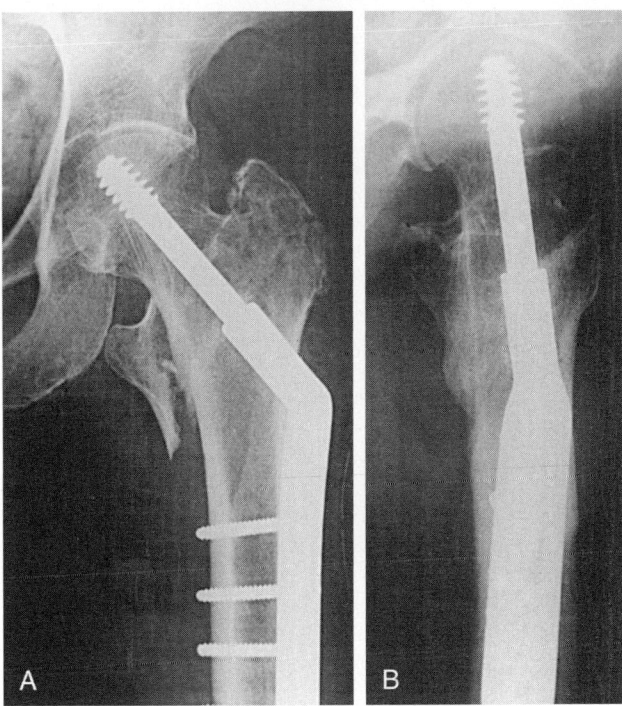

**FIGURE 49–18.** Postoperative radiographs demonstrating appropriate fracture reduction and implant position on anteroposterior (A) and lateral (B) views.

subcutaneous, and skin layers are closed separately. An elastic bandage spica dressing may protect the wound from a disoriented patient's exploring fingers. All bony prominences are rechecked on transfer of the patient off the fracture table, and precautions against postoperative skin breakdown are taken.

### Adjuncts for Plate Fixation

Although it is usually preferred to neglect lesser trochanteric fragments, occasionally they are so large that stabilization is indicated. It is exceedingly important not to devitalize the medial fracture zone in an overzealous attempt to achieve anatomic reduction. If nondisplaced, a soft tissue–sparing pointed reduction clamp can be applied, and a countersunk screw directed from anterolateral to posteromedial can be inserted before plate application. For displaced fragments, a carefully placed cerclage can effectively reduce a large posteromedial fragment into a position in which it can support the head-neck fragment (Fig. 49–19).

Occasionally the greater trochanter is completely displaced and retracted proximally. A wire can be passed along the tendonous insertion of the abductors and positioned to lie just distal to the insertion site for the barrel of the sideplate to function as a tension band. With the side plate in position but not fully seated and the extremity abducted, the wire is tightened to fully reduce the trochanter.

The trochanteric stabilizing plate is a supplemental plate that can be used for very unstable fractures to prevent excessive collapse of the screw and medial translation of the shaft. The device is sandwiched between a standard sideplate and the shaft screws and projects proximally to

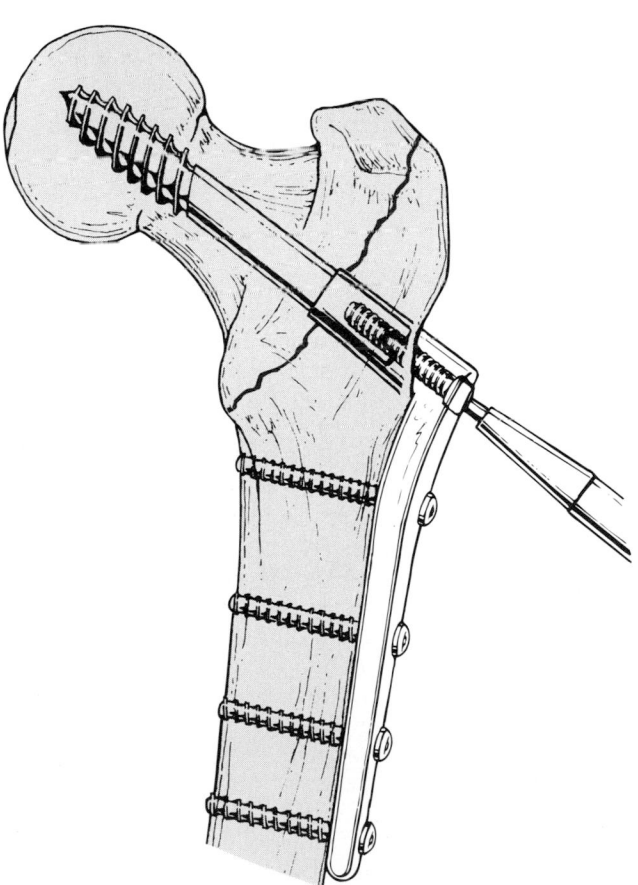

**FIGURE 49–17.** Advancing the compressing screw into the lag screw shaft effectively compresses the fracture by pulling the lag screw and attached head and neck laterally back into the barrel. Although some tightening initiates sliding and minimizes the risk of the screw jamming within the barrel, excessive tightening can potentially strip the lag screw from the femoral head. Some surgeons prefer to use the lag screw but remove it before closing to prevent lateral prominence if there is further postoperative collapse. Others maintain it in place to avoid any possibility of screw-barrel disassembly.

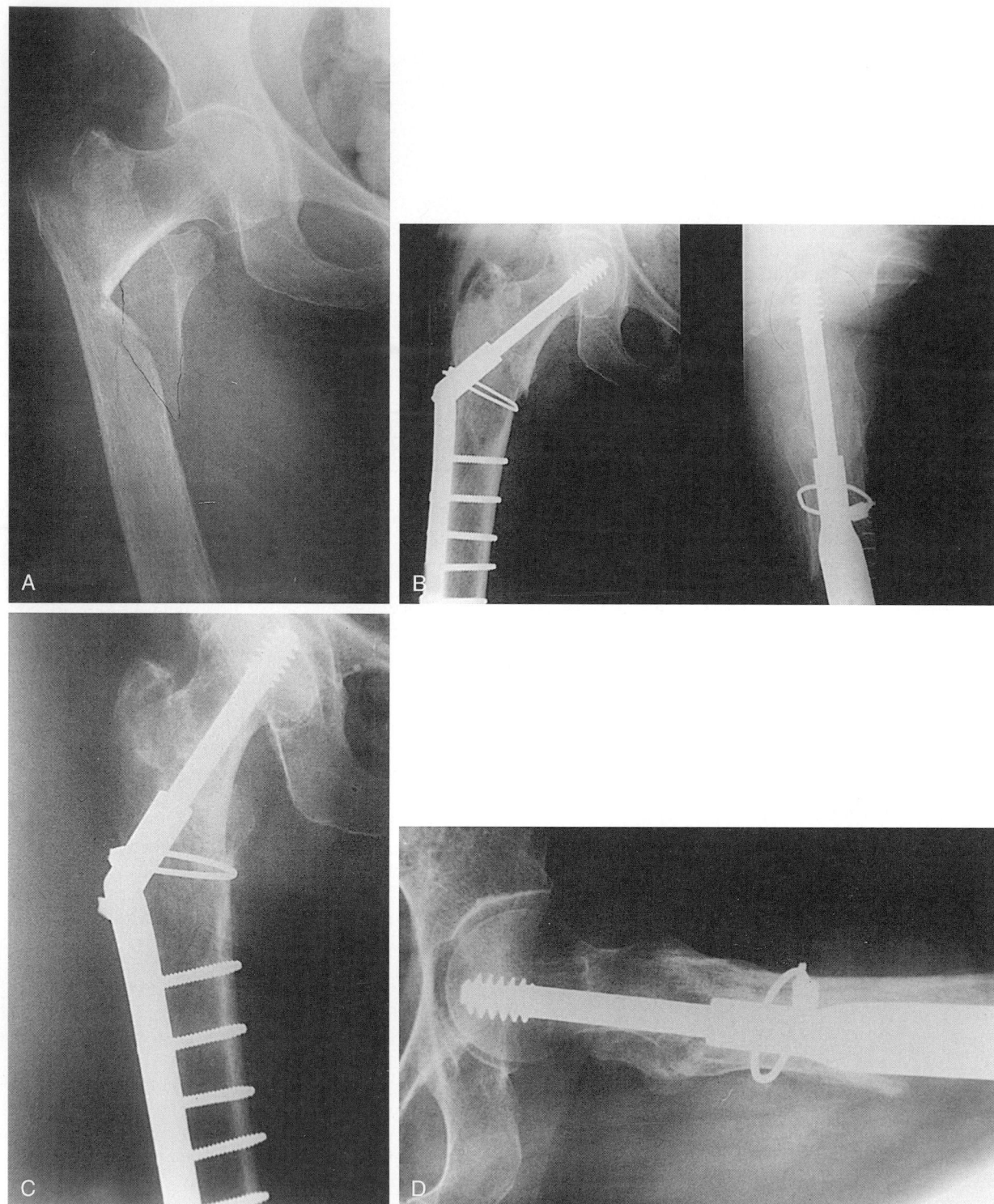

**Figure 49–19.** *A,* Unstable, four-part intertrochanteric fracture with a very large posteromedial fragment. *B,* Immediate postoperative radiographs show a deeply seated lag screw and the posteromedial fragment reduced and secured with a cerclage cable. *C, D,* At 6 weeks, there is minimal collapse and healing is progressing.

buttress the greater trochanter. It has holes to allow the compression screw to slide through and to insert additional screws into the head. Although surgical time and blood loss are necessarily greater by the increased dissection and exposure, two reports have shown that the trochanteric stabilizing plate is effective in limiting collapse and subsequent limb shortening.[4, 97]

## AXIAL DYNAMIC COMPRESSION PLATING

A sliding hip screw with a modular side plate has been introduced that allows controlled impaction not only in the axis of the hip compression screw (as with all sliding hip screws) but also in the axis of the femoral shaft, making it potentially useful for severely unstable fractures and fractures with subtrochanteric extension (Fig. 49–20).

The surgical technique for so-called axial compression plating is very similar to that for insertion of standard compression hip screws. The lag screw is inserted into the femoral head in the same fashion as for a standard sliding hip screw, but it is critical that it is well centered on the lateral aspect of the femoral shaft so that the concavity of the undersurface of the plate conforms to the convexity of the lateral femoral cortex. Because the bone screw holes lie

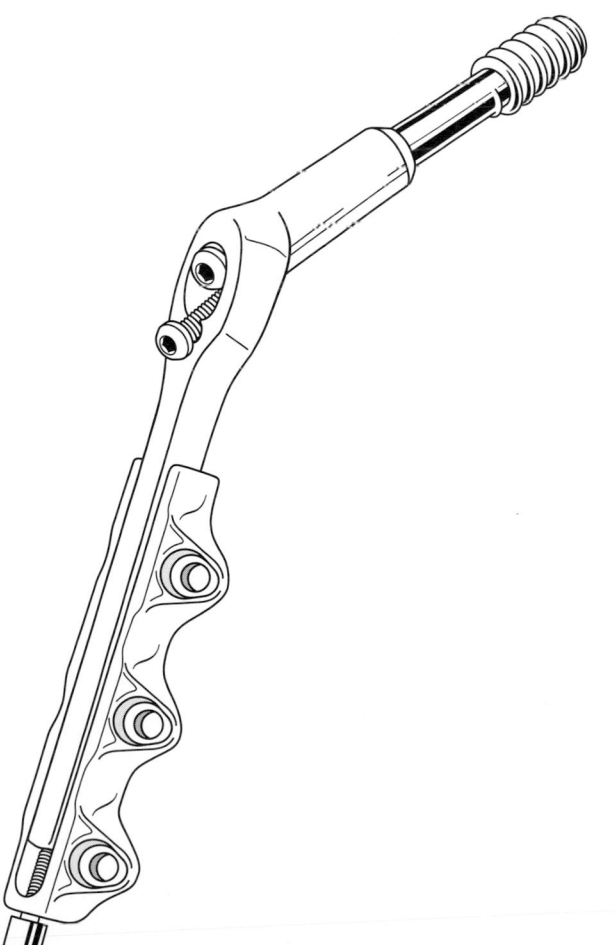

**FIGURE 49–20.** The biaxial dynamic compression plate designed by Medoff. (Redrawn from The Medoff Sliding Plate, Product Information. Arlington, TN, Wright Medical Technology, 1995.)

on either side of the plate, and a compressing screw is located distally, greater exposure of the femoral shaft is required. In addition, in fractures in which the barrel traverses the intact lateral cortex (AO/OTA 31-A1 and 31-A2 fractures), a slot the width of the barrel and 1 to 2 cm long must be made in the lateral cortex distal to the site of the barrel insertion to allow for axial collapse. The modular compression slide and the side plate are applied and adjusted so that 1.5 to 2.0 cm of the compression slide protrudes from the proximal end of the plate. The side plate is secured to the femoral shaft by anterior and posteriorly positioned bone screws. Like standard compression hip screws, the fracture can be compressed by tightening the proximal compression screw. Optionally, a locking set screw may be placed and tightened after sufficient impaction is obtained. This prevents any further lateral settling of the lag screw and proximal fragment if compression along this axis is undesirable. By tightening the distal compression screw with the angled Allen wrench, load can be applied along the axis of the femur.

Dynamic impaction in the axis of the femoral shaft offers significant potential advantages in the treatment of unstable intertrochanteric fractures and those with subtrochanteric extension particularly those with a reverse oblique fracture geometry, where excessive medial translation can be limited by locking the sliding hip screw. Medoff[101] reported good results and no failures with the first 25 unstable fractures treated with this device. Lunsjo reported similar results.[93] In 1998, Watson and colleagues published their results of a randomized, prospective comparison of the Medoff device to a compression hip screw in the treatment of 160 stable and unstable intertrochanteric fractures. They found no advantages when treating stable fractures, but they reduced their failure rate from 14% to 3% ($p$ – 0.01) in the treatment of unstable fractures when the Medoff device was used. They did note that the Medoff procedures were associated with a longer operative time and with greater blood loss.[144] This device appears to combine a known surgical technique with improved potential for controlled axial collapse to unload the implant and add stress to the healing bone. Whether these benefits outweigh the liabilities of the greater surgical exposure and increased femoral shortening has not yet been satisfactorily answered.

## INTRAMEDULLARY SLIDING HIP SCREWS

The advantages of a sliding hip screw are combined with intramedullary shaft stabilization in the so-called intramedullary hip screws used for the stabilization of intertrochanteric fractures. These devices offer the biologic advantage of a potentially closed technique with periosteal disruption limited to that caused by the fracture itself. The operative insult is reduced, potentially leading to fewer complications and faster rehabilitation. In addition, proponents note that these implants offer the mechanical advantage of decreased implant bending strain, because the shaft fixation is moved from the lateral cortex to the intramedullary canal, decreasing the lever arm on the implant. Probably more importantly, the device acts as a robust intramedullary buttress, limiting excessive shaft medialization in unstable and reverse oblique fractures,

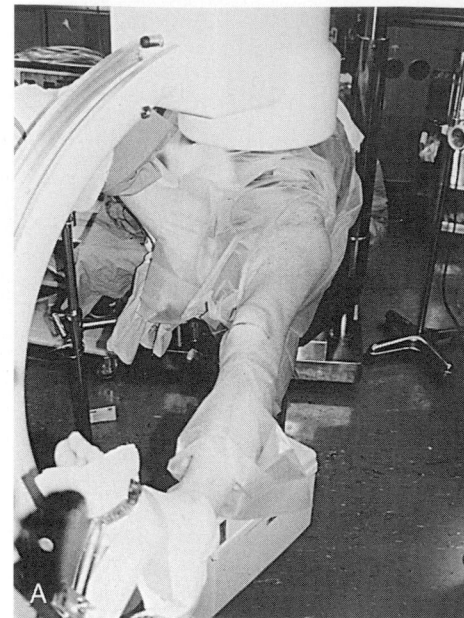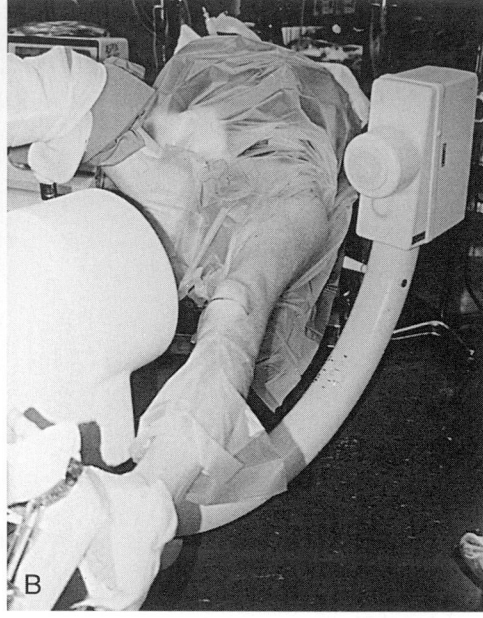

FIGURE **49–21.** Patient positioned with operative extremity adducted for intramedullary nailing. Position should allow uncompromised anteroposterior (*A*) and lateral (*B*) fluoroscopic imaging.

and, depending on distal interlocking options, it can allow impaction in the axis of the shaft. Thus, the purported advantages offered by the Trochanteric Stabilizing Plate (prevention of excessive shaft medialization) and the Medoff plate (collapse along the shaft axis) are both available with an intramedullary hip screw but without the need of a surgical exposure. All of the current implants have a slight valgus configuration to allow introduction of the nail through the tip of the greater trochanter. Typically, such short intramedullary nails, without a sagittal bow, can be used on either the left or the right side. Longer versions (indicated for fractures with significant subtrochanteric extension) must match the anterior bow of the femoral shaft. Distal interlocking of these longer nails requires a freehand technique.

The Gamma nail (Howmedica), introduced in North America in the late 1980s, has a 12-mm hip screw with a grooved shank that articulates with the intramedullary nail. A set screw prevents rotation of the screw but allows it to back out through the nail, as in the Zickel nail design. The Gamma nail has 6-mm distal interlocking screws and comes in several angles and sizes. The IMHS (Smith + Nephew), introduced in 1990, uses the same lag screw used with sliding hip screw side plates. A keyed sleeve of similar proportion to the barrel of a side plate is inserted between the screw shaft and nail, and it is locked to the nail with a set screw. The screw can slide but not rotate within the sleeve, and a compressing screw can be used, as with side plates, to initially impact the fracture and later to prevent implant disassembly. The 4.5-mm distal interlocking screws are also the same as those used to attach a side plate device. Dedicated soft tissue protectors and an entrance site reamer in the IMHS system allow for truly percutaneous fixation of fractures provided that an anatomic closed reduction can be achieved. Other intramedullary hip screw designs employ two proximal screws of smaller diameter to gain purchase and prevent rotation of the proximal fragment.[63, 134]

The surgical technique for insertion of an intramedullary hip screw is different from that for a hip screw and side plate. Just as in supine femoral intramedullary nailing, the hip must be adducted slightly and the torso shifted toward the opposite side to allow unobstructed access to the femoral medullary canal. This position increases varus deformity at the fracture unless adequate traction is applied. It is critical that the extremity be attached to the traction apparatus in such a way that strong traction can safely be applied (see Fig. 49–11). If the procedure is to be done percutaneously, it is an absolute prerequisite that an acceptable closed reduction be obtained and confirmed fluoroscopically (Fig. 49–21).

With the fracture reduced, a guide pin for the cannulated entrance reamer is inserted percutaneously approximately 3 cm proximal to the greater trochanter, in line with the shaft, and advanced to the tip of the trochanter. Usually with manual force it can be passed through the fracture zone and into the intramedullary canal, until it deflects off the medial endosteum of the subtrochanteric femur (Fig. 49–22). After confirming that the pin is in the plane of the femoral neck on the lateral fluoroscopic view, a scalpel is used to make a 2- to 4-cm cutdown along the guide pin through the deep fascia and to the trochanter. The entrance site and proximal 9 cm of medullary canal are then reamed with a special one-step graduated reamer to accommodate the nail, which has an enlarged proximal diameter of 17 mm (Fig. 49–23). It is important to ensure that the reamer cuts a channel for the implant rather than simply displacing the fragments as it passes; otherwise the nail will displace the fracture when inserted. Medially directed pressure applied to the trochanter during reaming ensures that an adequate channel is cut. It is better to err on the side of too much rather than too little entrance site reaming. In elderly patients with wide intramedullary diameters, it is rarely necessary to ream the isthmus of the canal, so there is no need for routine use of additional flexible reamers. A nail of

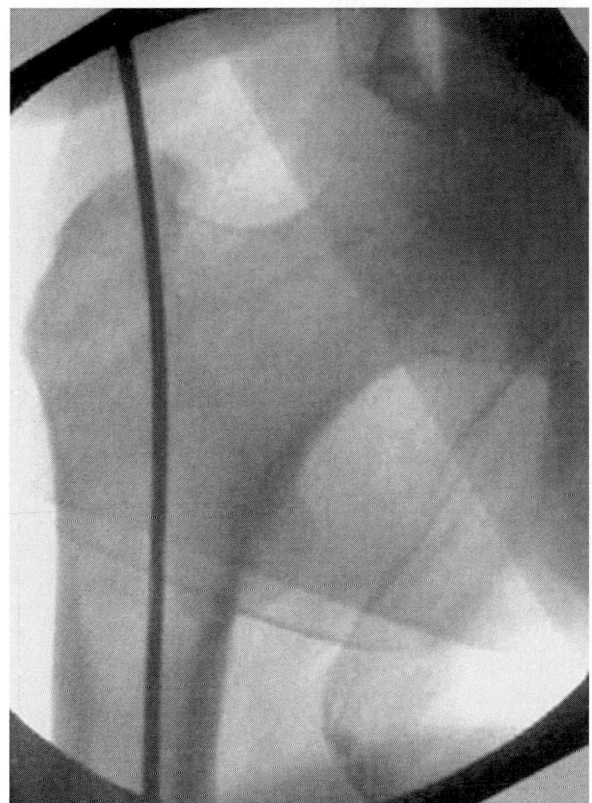

**FIGURE 49–22.** The correct entrance site for the nail portion of the intramedullary hip screw is at the tip of the trochanter on the anteroposterior image and in line with the femoral neck on the lateral view.

jig and readvancing the nail or, if necessary, eccentrically enlarging the entrance site anteriorly. As a final alternative, a smaller nail diameter can be selected.

Once the nail has been inserted fully into the canal, the limb can be brought out of adduction (possibly with additional traction) to correct any residual varus deformity at the fracture. The sleeves for the sliding screw guide pin are then attached to the nail insertion jig and the guide pin is drilled through the nail, across the fracture, and into the femoral head. As with all compression screws, the goal for placement is absolute central position within 5 mm of subchondral bone. By advancing the nail distally or retracting it proximally, varying traction, abducting or adducting the extremity, as well as rotating the jig internally or externally, the surgeon can precisely control the direction of the guide pin relative to the femoral head. Posterior sag of the fracture can be counteracted by having an assistant lift the jig anteriorly. The attached intramedullary nail translates the femur anteriorly, correcting the sag before placement of the guide pin.

Reaming, lag screw insertion, and blocking of rotation with the set screw are carried out in accordance with the design of the particular device being used. At this point, traction is released and rotational and length stability are assessed. Essentially all stable fractures and many unstable fracture patterns move as a unit after the insertion of an intramedullary hip screw, so distal interlocking is rarely required. If there is rotational instability, or if the potential for it exists (e.g., a fractured but nondisplaced large posteromedial fragment), a single distal interlocking screw

appropriate distal diameter (usually 12 mm, occasionally 10) is attached to the insertion jig and introduced into the canal with manual force only. Gentle rotational motions facilitate advancement of the nail; mallet blows risk intraoperative fracture propagation and should be avoided. If the nail does not advance, the surgeon must determine the cause of the obstruction. The tip of the straight nail may impinge on the anterior cortex of the bowed femoral shaft, particularly if the entrance site is too posterior. This can be appreciated only if the lateral fluoroscopic view is examined (Fig. 49–24). Treatment involves elevating the

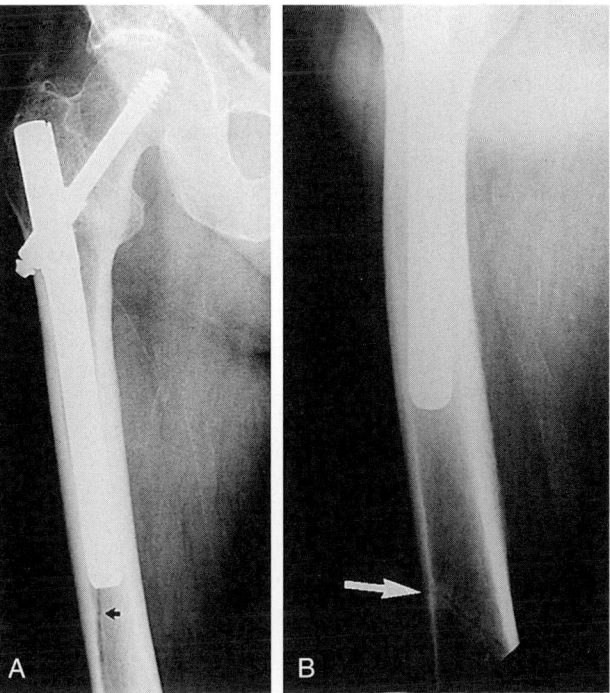

**FIGURE 49–24.** Femoral shaft fracture (arrows) that occurred during intramedullary hip screw insertion. *A,* This excessively large, canal-filling intramedullary nail appears well aligned on the anteroposterior view. *B,* The lateral view demonstrates the anterior cortical impingement and the cause of the intraoperative fracture. A smaller diameter nail, a more anterior entrance site, or less aggressive malleting would have avoided this complication, which fortunately did not influence outcome.

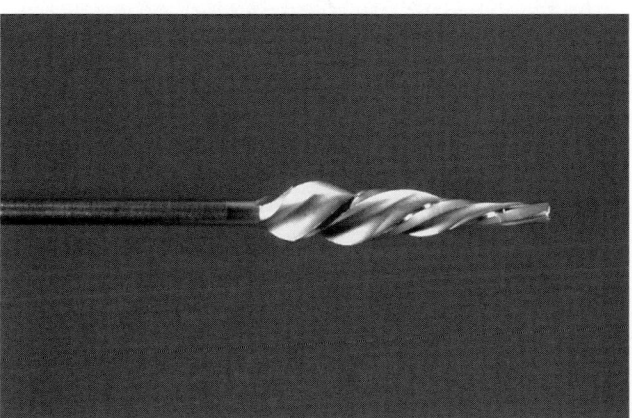

**FIGURE 49–23.** This one step entrance reamer prepares the channel for the nail and usually obviates the need for flexible intramedullary reamers.

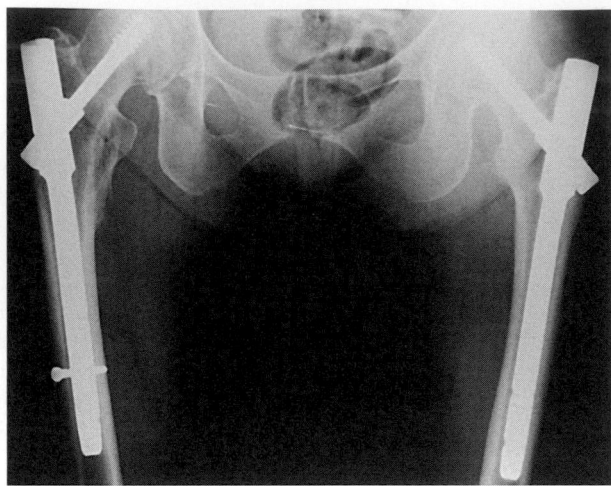

**FIGURE 49–25.** Uneventful union of a stable left intertrochanteric fracture and an unstable right intertrochanteric fracture treated with intramedullary hip screws. Distal locking was probably not necessary for either fracture.

is adequate (Fig. 49–25). If significant comminution exists and shortening of the fracture is possible, insertion of both screws is warranted. Screw insertion is similar to proximal interlocking on conventional interlocking nails. A drill guide is attached to the jig, and the hole is drilled carefully, guarding against wandering of the drill away from the intended hole in the intramedullary nail. The screw length can be read from the calibrated drill, and the screw is inserted percutaneously through the outer drill sleeve. A lateral fluoroscopic image confirms that the screw has engaged the nail.

Many investigators reported their early experience with the Gamma nail.[19, 53, 122] Most reports noted some differences but no major improvement compared with the compression hip screw to encourage the widespread use of the new technique. Shaft fracture, both intraoperatively and during rehabilitation, was a frequently reported complication. In a meta-analysis of 10 randomized, prospective studies comparing the use of the Gamma nail with that of the compression hip screw, Parker and Pryor documented a significantly increased relative risk of femur fracture (8.8 relative risk, $p < 0.001$) and reoperation (1.9 relative risk, $p < 0.005$) when the Gamma nail was used. They cautioned that the device was unforgiving and should be considered only for very unstable fractures and those with reverse obliquity.[118]

More recent reports of intramedullary hip screws have consistently shown a significantly reduced incidence or an absence of femoral shaft fractures and results equal to or better than those achieved with compression hip screws.[12, 55, 63, 91, 123, 134, 142] The reasons for this improvement appear multifactorial. The original design of the Gamma nail has been modified, and all subsequent intramedullary hip screw designs have reduced valgus bends and smaller distal interlocking screws, as well as smaller nail diameter options. Perhaps more importantly, improvements in surgical technique as well as more limited indications for distal interlocking have occurred. The IMHS has compared favorably with the compression

hip screw in terms of blood loss and surgical time, particularly for unstable fracture patterns, in randomized, prospective clinical trials.[8] Hardy and co-workers noted more rapid return of mobility and reduced implant collapse and subsequent limb length discrepancy in patients receiving intramedullary fixation in their randomized clinical trial.[55]

The ultimate role that intramedullary fixation will have for the treatment of intertrochanteric fractures remains unclear. The original Gamma nail was met with enthusiasm that was quickly followed by near abandonment as poor results, difficult procedures, and unacceptable complication rates were reported. Since then there has been increasing evidence that intramedullary devices will have at least a niche in our treatment armamentarium. Although it may be difficult to improve significantly on the results achieved with a well-reduced stable intertrochanteric fracture fixed with a compression hip screw, certain unstable fractures, such as those with subtrochanteric extension or reverse obliquity, have been problematic when treated with sideplates and appear to be more effectively managed with an intramedullary hip screw (see below, under Special Situations).

## FLEXIBLE INTRAMEDULLARY PINNING

Flexible intramedullary devices for the fixation of hip fractures enjoyed popularity in the early 1970s, just before the widespread acceptance of sliding hip screws. Dissatisfied with the complications of malunion, nonunion, joint penetration, implant breakage, and deep infection encountered with the fixed-length angled plate, surgeons looked for alternative solutions. Like current intramedullary nails, the theoretical advantages of flexible intramedullary devices were shortened operation time, decreased infection rates (because the operative site is far removed from the fracture site), and a lower bending moment on the implant than that on laterally applied plates and screws.[33] Ender flexible pins rarely break, but complications relating to retrograde migration of the pins have been reported by Levy and co-workers, Kuderna and associates, and others.[25, 81, 92] Because the pins are a fixed length, any postoperative fracture impaction must be associated with either proximal penetration or pin protrusion distally. This may result in soft tissue impingement and knee pain. Not surprisingly, the best results with this method are obtained in stable intertrochanteric fractures, in which little postsurgical impaction occurs.[66]

The most commonly used intramedullary devices were the multiple curved pins described by Ender and the single, more rigid, condylocephalic nails originally introduced by Kuntscher and later modified by Harris.[56, 57] Both single and multiple devices are inserted through a portal in the medial femoral condyle and driven up toward the femoral head. The increased flexibility and stacking potential of the Ender pins allow for easier insertion and more stable fixation than with the single nail device. Multiple pin fixation can be augmented by inserting some of the pins from a lateral distal femoral portal as well.

In the surgical technique for flexible nailing, the patient is placed in a supine position on the fracture table. The feet are both fastened to traction devices, and the legs are placed in sufficient abduction to allow room for the surgeon and for C-arm positioning. A valgus reduction facilitates nail insertion, especially when the patient has a narrow medullary canal, which tends to remove the proximal curve from the implants. A 7-cm longitudinal skin incision is made just anterior to the medial femoral epicondyle. The fascia is incised, and the vastus medialis is retracted anteriorly. Care is taken to avoid entering the knee joint. The medial femoral cortex is exposed just proximal to the condyle, where the superior medial geniculate artery is frequently seen, and a 6-mm drill hole is made at the midportion of the femoral shaft in the coronal plane and is enlarged with the use of the curved awl. An Ender nail of appropriate length is placed over the draped thigh. The distal end of the nail should extend 1 cm beyond the pilot hole, and the proximal tip should be at the level of the hip joint, as confirmed by fluoroscopy. Additional bending of the nail may be necessary to facilitate accurate nail placement. A nail 1 cm longer than the original estimate is used if the curvature of the pin must be increased. Bending should follow a gradual sloping curve, using the provided bending instruments and avoiding sharp bends.

The first nail is inserted into the hole and driven proximally. The nail deflects off the lateral femoral cortex and passes medially into the femoral head. The final seating of each nail should be delayed until several nails are in place. This keeps the first nail from being carried across the hip joint or disappearing into the medullary canal as subsequent nails are passed. The ends of the Ender nails should fan out into the femoral head and neck fragment (Fig. 49–26). Usually, four pins are sufficient to

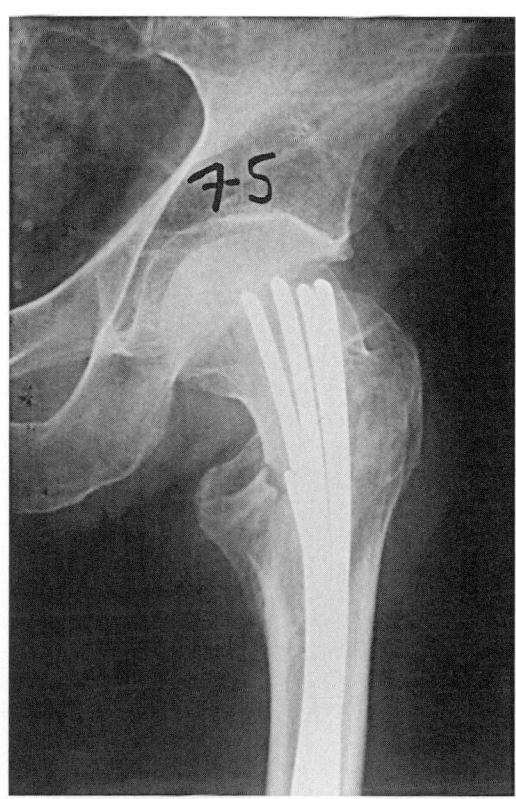

**Figure 49–26.** Intertrochanteric fracture stabilized with Ender nails.

fill the medullary canal and adequately control fracture alignment.

Overall, the results from using flexible intramedullary nails to fix intertrochanteric hip fractures were disappointing. In Sherk and Foster's review of condylocephalic devices, 51% of the patients lost fixation.[133] In addition, when comparing the use of condylocephalic rods with that of compression screw systems, none of the proposed advantages of condylocephalic rods was observed. Harris[57] suggested that condylocephalic nailing should be reserved for debilitated patients with stable intertrochanteric fractures. Similarly, Ender's method of multiple pin fixation has met with mixed success, at best. Levy and co-workers[92] reported on a series of 200 hip fractures fixed with Ender pins. There was a 50% incidence of distal pin migration; 76% of patients experienced knee pain, and 36% developed significant external malrotation. In addition, failure of fixation occurred in all of the basicervical-type fractures. Knee pain, loss of knee motion, external malrotation, and pin migration seem to be prevalent in most reported series. The reoperation rate in three separate series varied from 12% to 31%.[82, 92, 99] Kuokkanen and associates, after reviewing their complications, categorized intramedullary fixation as a semiconservative method that should be reserved for elderly people with systemic illnesses or poor general health that precluded other surgery.[82]

## BONE CEMENT AUGMENTATION

Polymethyl methacrylate (PMMA) bone cement has been used adjunctively in the treatment of intertrochanteric fractures to stabilize internal fixation devices within osteoporotic bone and to replace deficient medial cortical support. As reported by Schatzker and colleagues,[131] individual screw purchase can be improved by injection of liquid cement into the hole of a loose cortical screw, which is then replaced and (after the cement has hardened) tightened. Bartucci and co-workers[7] reported on Laros' technique[86] of excavating osteopenic cancellous bone from the head and neck fragment, injecting liquid PMMA under fluoroscopic control, and then replacing the previously prepared sliding hip screw. Failure occurred in only 1 of 29 cases in which PMMA was added and in 10 of 17 in which it was not. The remarkably high failure rate of the control patients makes this study difficult to interpret. This technique can be simplified with some hip fixation implants (e.g., Alta hip bolt, Howmedica) that are designed to permit injection of liquid PMMA through special ports in the lag screw.[27]

Calcium phosphate cement is a biocompatible crystal with mechanical properties similar to those of bone that can be incorporated and ultimately remodeled. This injectable material cures euthermically at a neutral pH and has been demonstrated to restore pullout strength to stripped cancellous screw holes.[104] Industry-supported research has demonstrated a measurable increase in strength of fixation when the material is injected into the reamed channel before insertion of the hip screw, and initial clinical experimentation demonstrated no significant complications with the use of calcium phosphate cement.[48, 109] This material may replace polymethylmethacrylate in the salvage of a complicated or revision fixation to improve screw purchase, but its value in the primary management of acute osteoporotic hip fractures remains unproven.

## PROSTHETIC REPLACEMENT

Prosthetic replacement has been proposed as an alternative to internal fixation of severely comminuted, markedly osteopenic, intertrochanteric fractures.[24, 120, 141] An intertrochanteric fracture occurring in a patient with rheumatoid arthritis (even if not involving the hip) is another indication for consideration of replacement rather than attempted repair. Bogoch reported a fixation failure rate of 24% and marked increases in nonunion and infection in his review of intertrochanteric fractures occurring in patients with rheumatoid arthritis.[16]

Early mobilization and weight bearing are usually achieved with joint replacement, minimizing medical complications. The surgical complication rate is necessarily increased, owing to the complexity of the fractures selected for this procedure and the scope of the operative intervention. Green and colleagues reported on 20 comminuted intertrochanteric fractures treated with cemented bipolar prostheses.[49] Full unrestricted weight bearing occurred at an average of 5 days after surgery. By use of the greater trochanter as a landmark, correct limb length was easily achieved. Using Leinbach prosthetic replacements, Stern and Angerman also found early unrestricted weight bearing and markedly shortened hospital stays.[138] In selecting a prosthetic component for this purpose, it is important to ensure sufficient prosthetic stem length for long-term stability. The stem tip must extend beyond the most distal point of apparent stress concentration by a distance equal to at least two to three times the diameter of the canal. If a large posteromedial defect exists, an intermediate or long-stem component may be required. Current systems employ modular components to facilitate restoration of anatomic length and offset as well as to secure comminuted fragments (Fig. 49–27). Haentjens and associates[51] compared the results in 37 patients with unstable comminuted intertrochanteric fractures treated with a primary bipolar prosthesis with those in a control group of 42 patients with similar fractures treated with a fixed-length angled plate. They found rehabilitation to be easier and faster and the rates of pressure sores and pulmonary complications to be significantly reduced in the prosthesis group, and good functional outcome to occur in 75% of their patients. Nonetheless, most surgeons reserve prosthetic replacement for salvage of a failed reconstruction or for pathologic proximal femoral fractures.

## Special Situations

### REVERSE OBLIQUE FRACTURES AND FRACTURES WITH SUBTROCHANTERIC EXTENSION

The reverse oblique intertrochanteric fracture pattern and certain intertrochanteric fractures with subtrochanteric extension (most AO/OTA 33-A3 fractures) are unique in that the sliding screw portion of the conventional hip

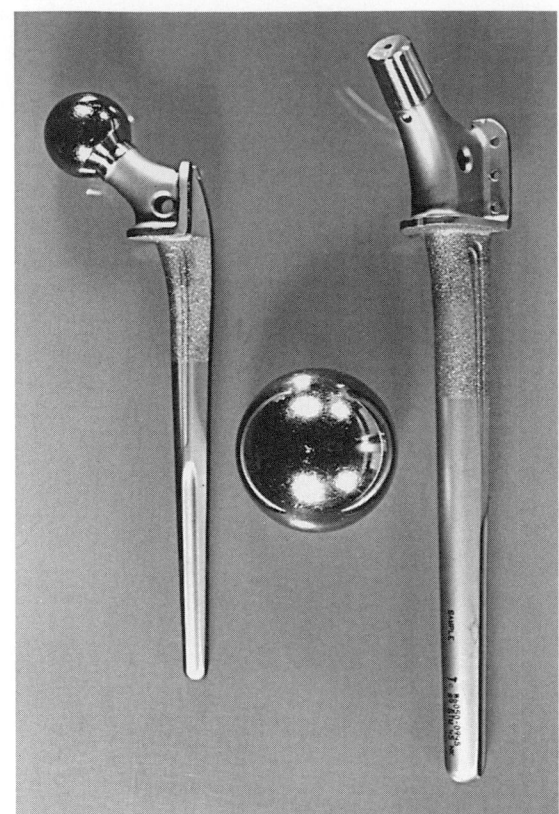

**Figure 49–27.** Modular prostheses for proximal femoral replacement offer varying sizes and are designed to facilitate reattachment of the trochanters.

screw does not cross the primary fracture line. A less than perfect reduction or a gap from fracture line resorption is not compensated by collapsing of the hip screw. In fact, for reverse oblique fractures, the sliding screw implant can promote fracture separation rather than impaction (Fig. 49–28). This leads to an unacceptably high failure rate when a conventional sliding hip screw is used to treat this fracture pattern (Fig. 49–29). In Haidukowych's review of 49 reverse oblique fractures, the worst results were associated with the use of compression hip screws, of which 56% failed.[52]

An excellent treatment option for these fractures is an intramedullary hip screw, because its medullary location provides a buttress against significant medial displacement of the shaft and decreases the bending strain on the implant (Fig. 49–30). In a cadaveric reverse-oblique fracture (with interfragmentary gap) model, the specimens fixed with an IMHS demonstrated improved stiffness and greater ultimate strength than those instrumented with 95° or 135° sliding screw plates. The ability to place the device percutaneously (or with a limited open technique) minimizes the biologic insult to the fracture zone and is another attractive feature of this technique. Barquet and co-workers achieved a 100% union rate in 43 intertrochanteric-subtrochanteric fractures treated with a long intramedullary hip screw.[6] There were no infections, and the only mechanical complication reported was fatigue of the distal interlocking bolts in one fracture. They emphasized the difficulty in reducing these fractures and

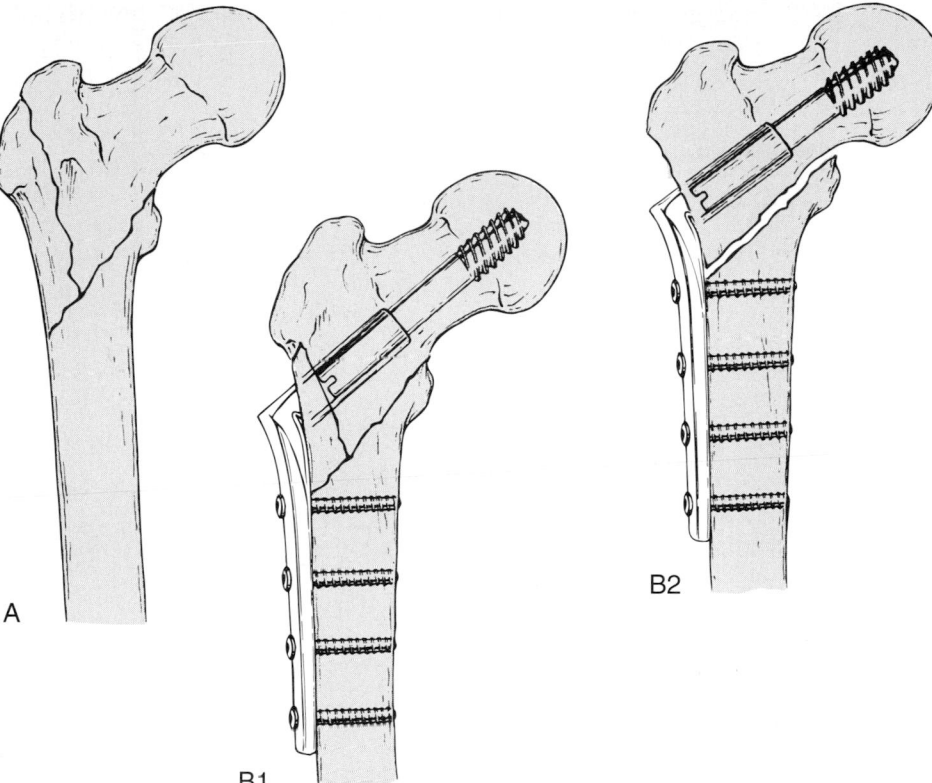

**FIGURE 49–28.** *A,* Reverse oblique intertrochanteric fracture. A fracture line into the greater trochanter is very common. *B1, B2,* Telescoping of the sliding hip screw does not promote interfragmentary compression because of the orientation of the fracture plane. Stability requires secure impaction of the fracture, with either osteotomy of the distal piece to provide mechanical engagement or an implant that resists progressive medial displacement of the shaft.

described the adjunctive, percutaneous techniques that they employed to achieve reduction (such as use of a Schanz screw or a ball-spiked pusher).

For surgeons who prefer open plating techniques, the 95°-angled blade plate and the condylar compression screw are appropriate devices for these fractures. Compared with a 135° hip screw, such devices provide stable control of the proximal fragment and reduce the potential for rotational or translational instability. Depending on the obliquity and fragmentation of the fracture, screws lagging together the two major fragments may be placed through the plate (Fig. 49–31). The blade plate, which must be

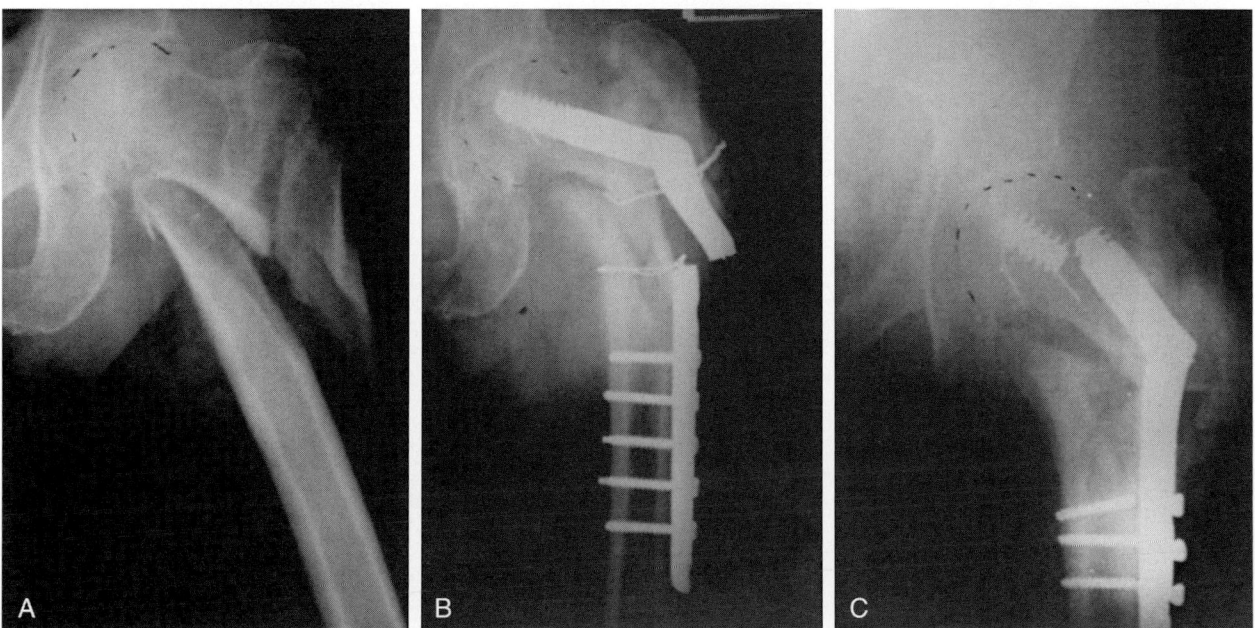

**FIGURE 49–29.** *A,* Reverse oblique intertrochanteric fracture (AO/OTA 31-A3.1) in an elderly woman. *B,* Medial displacement, nonunion, and fixation failure after complete telescoping of the sliding hip screw. *C,* Several months after revision with a similar sliding hip screw, medial displacement and nonunion persist, and fixation has failed again.

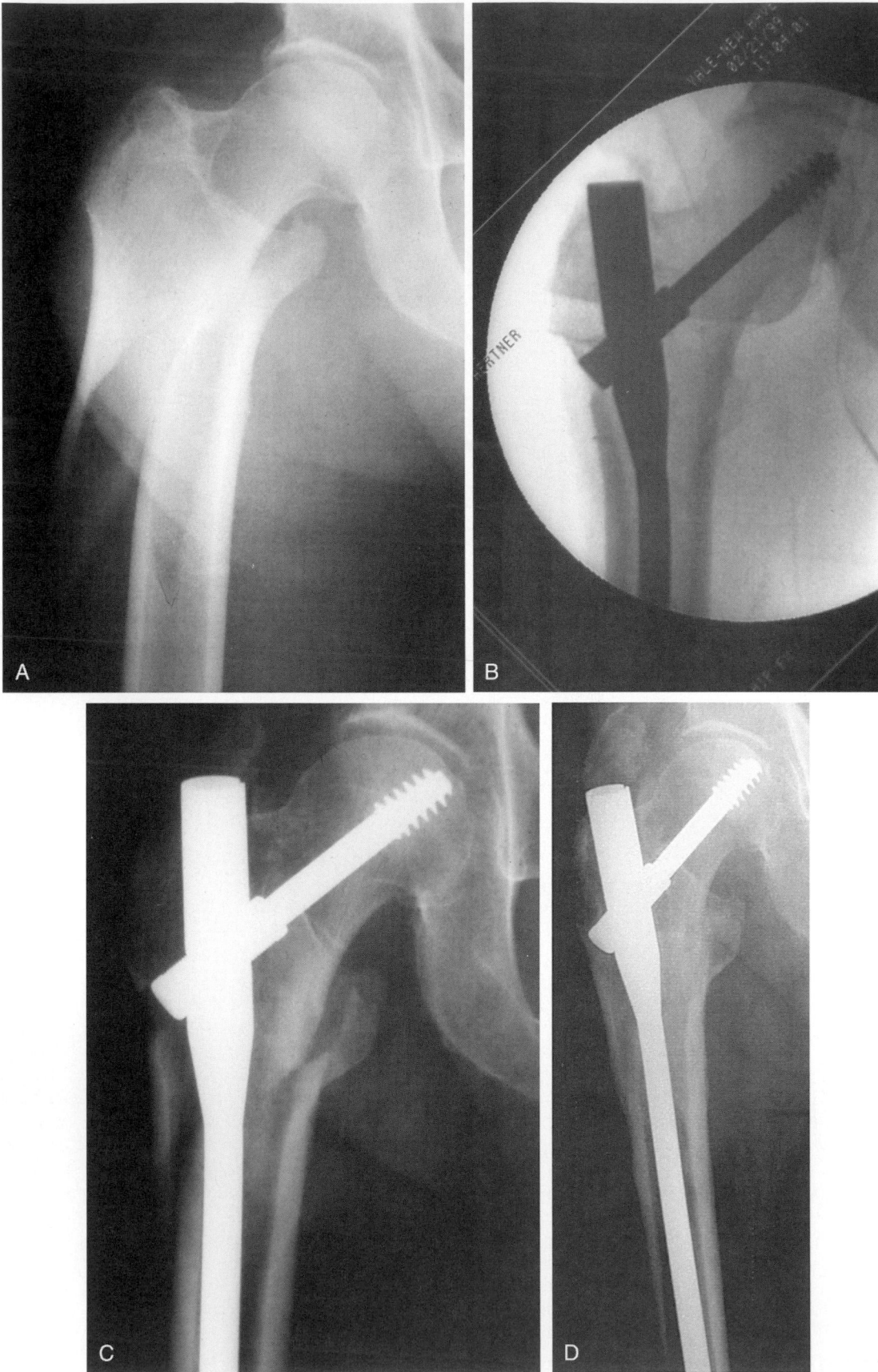

**Figure 49–30.** Reverse oblique intertrochanteric fracture treated with an intramedullary hip screw. The lesser trochanter remains attached to the shaft fragment (*A*). Anatomic reduction is achieved intraoperatively and a deeply seated intramedullary hip screw is placed (*B*). Early postoperative control radiograph shows that significant shaft medialization is limited by the intramedullary position of the implant (*C*). Healing is uneventful since the fracture zone was not violated (*D*).

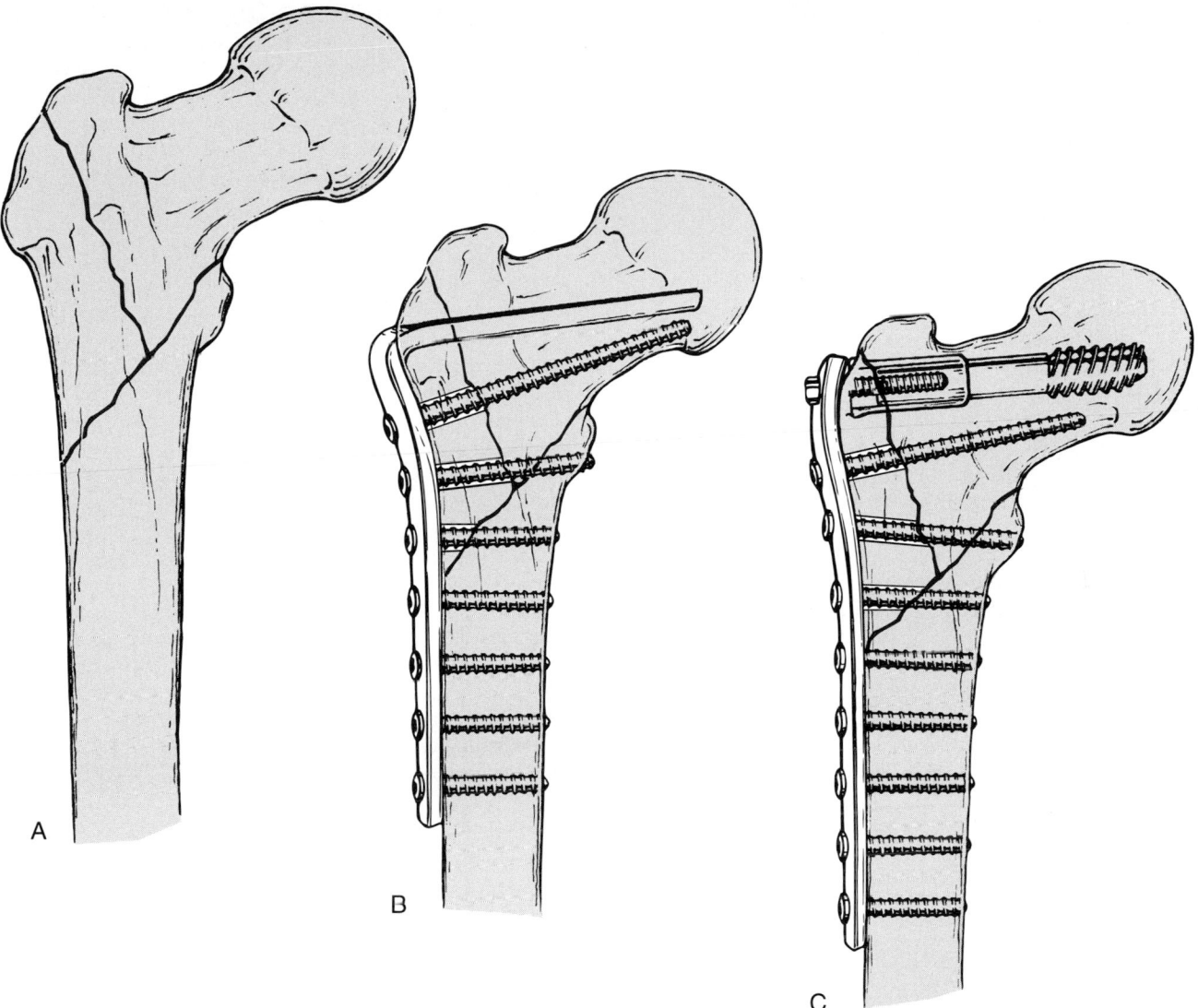

**FIGURE 49–31.** *A,* Reverse oblique intertrochanteric fracture, illustrating typical lateral comminution. *B,* Anatomic reduction and fixation with a 95° angled blade plate. *C,* Anatomic reduction and fixation with a 95° angled condylar compression screw.

inserted while controlling the reduction in all three planes, has the advantage of offering much more rotational stability than the condylar screw, and it can be placed without removing any significant amount of bone from the femoral head. However, many prefer the 95°-angled condylar screw because it can be placed over a guide pin, and reduction in the sagittal plane can be done after the implant is seated, simply by rotating the screw.

The table setup, patient positioning, and surgical approach for fixation with a 95°-angled device (either the blade plate or the condylar screw and side plate) are similar to those described for the compression hip screw with the exception that the vastus lateralis origin must be formally released anteriorly to give exposure to the femoral neck and hip joint. Instead of a fracture table, many surgeons prefer to drape the extremity freely, using a standard fluoroscopically compatible operating table in conjunction with a femoral distractor. Preoperative planning is essential for proper use of these implants. The surgeon must identify the major fragments and fracture

planes, the bony landmarks, and particularly the exact location and direction of the blade plate entrance site (or guide pin if the condylar screw is to be used) that will reestablish anatomic alignment. As with any fixed angle plate, the quality of the reduction is determined by the correct positioning of the implant. Generally, a template overlay is used with a properly oriented radiograph of the contralateral proximal femur to determine the length and placement of the implant. This technique permits placement of the angled blade into the proximal fragment before fracture reduction, which may be especially helpful in fractures with significant comminution.

Kirschner wires are placed to mark the anteversion of the neck and an angle of 95° from the shaft of the femur. The location and direction of these wires are based on proximal femoral landmarks (the center of the femoral head, the superior cortex of the neck, or the vastus ridge of the greater trochanter) and fluoroscopy, because the fracture has not yet been reduced. These wires define the direction of the blade. Next, the location of the blade plate entry site is determined from visible landmarks and the preoperative plan, and a cortical entry site is prepared. The correct placement of this entry window is at the junction of the anterior and middle thirds of the greater trochanter, because the neck is anterior to the midline of trochanter and femoral shaft. The entry site for the 95° blade plate should be placed so that the seating chisel enters the neck 1 cm distal to the superior cortex of the neck. This allows the tip of the blade to seat in the dense cancellous bone of the inferomedial femoral head. The entry site must be perpendicular to the long axis of the greater trochanter to prevent flexing or extending of the fracture. If the window is made too far superiorly, the neck may not accommodate the width of the blade and the blade will be deflected inferiorly. If the window is made too far inferiorly, the blade may strike the internal aspect of the inferior cortex of the femoral neck. This can lead to further fracture comminution or at the least force the use of a shorter blade plate with less purchase. In addition, low placement of the plate interferes with the insertion of the required additional screw in the proximal fragment.

After the entry site has been marked and prepared, typically with three 4.5-mm drill holes connected with a router bit and enlarged with an osteotome, the seating chisel is inserted according to the orientation and depth determined by the preoperative plan. With the path for the blade cut, the chisel is removed and the angled blade of appropriate length is inserted until the plate sits flush against the lateral cortex of the greater trochanter. Once in place, the blade is further secured to the proximal fragment by insertion of a 4.5-mm cortical lag screw through the plate and into the medial cortex (Fig. 49–32).

The fracture is then reduced by aligning the plate and the attached proximal fragment to the shaft of the femur and temporarily securing it with a Verbrugge bone clamp. There is no need to expose the fracture area by stripping

soft tissues from the bone fragments. If the device was placed according to the preoperative plan, reduction of the plate to the shaft should anatomically align the fracture in the coronal and sagittal planes. Anatomic rotational alignment must be confirmed clinically. Next, a femoral distractor or the compressor-distractor plate outrigger can be applied to fine tune the reduction before definitive fixation of the fracture. Screw insertion and closure are the same as with a standard hip screw.

Because the major compressive and shearing stresses occur on the medial side of the femur, any comminution that creates bony discontinuity at that location will lead to significant cyclical loading, which tends to bend the laterally applied implant. This may result in fatigue failure of the fixation before fracture union. Traditionally, when significant comminution is present, autologous bone grafting is recommended to facilitate rapid restoration of the medial cortical buttress. The graft should be inserted through the fracture site and placed along its medial side before reduction and application of internal fixation. This prevents additional dissection and injury to the local blood supply.

Current fracture stabilization techniques emphasize indirect reduction technique that avoid any dissection of the fracture zone. The comminuted fragments themselves act as a vascularized bone graft, obviating the need for additional grafting. An important report by Kinast compared formal open reduction and autologous bone grafting with indirect reduction without grafting in a series of subtrochanteric fractures treated with a blade plate.[75] Delayed or nonunion occurred in 17% of the openly reduced fractures and in none of those without fracture zone dissection or bone grafting.

## PATIENTS WITH MULTIPLE INJURIES

It is well documented that early stabilization (within 24 hours of injury) of femur fractures lessens the morbidity and mortality of victims of multiple (blunt) trauma. Because of the high energy transfer required to cause this injury in a younger patient, the surgeon should expect more soft tissue injury, bleeding, and fracture instability than is typically associated with radiographically similar injuries in osteopenic persons. Nonetheless, if the only bony injury is an intertrochanteric fracture, treatment is much like that described for the older patient with an isolated injury.

If the hip is fractured along with other long bones in the same or contralateral lower extremity, priority should be given to fixation of the hip fracture. Ipsilateral femoral shaft and intertrochanteric hip fractures occur less frequently than do concomitant shaft and femoral neck fractures.[139] The choice of fixation for combined hip and shaft fractures depends on the fracture pattern as well as on the patient considerations and the surgeon's preference. If the hip and shaft fractures are in proximity, a sliding hip screw with a long side plate may suffice. This is probably the simplest means of stabilizing closely related fractures. The surgeon should strive to reestablish anatomic alignment of the limb, but it is not necessary to expose and reduce each fragment. As the distance between the intertrochanteric fracture and the shaft fracture increases,

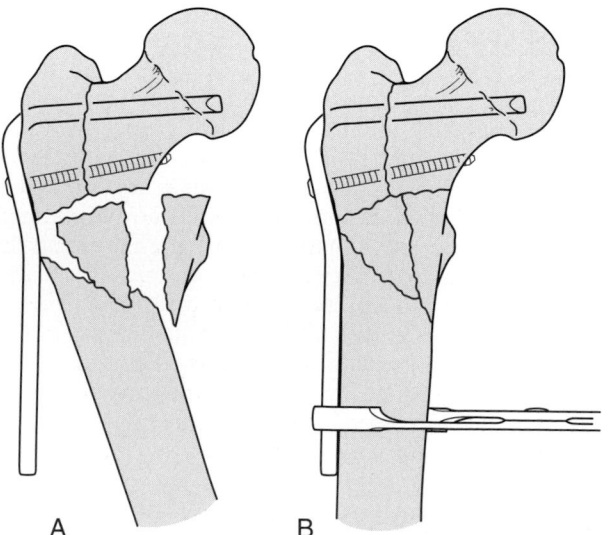

**Figure 49–32.** *A,* Preoperative planning and fluoroscopic control allow placement of a 95°-angled device according to known landmarks before fracture reduction. *B,* If the blade is correctly inserted, reducing the plate to the shaft reestablishes axial alignment and version. (*A, B,* Redrawn from Mast, J.; et al. Planning and Reduction Technique in Fracture Surgery. New York, Springer Verlag, 1988, p. 120.)

fixation techniques become more complicated, but the hip fracture should retain priority. Multiple stacked pins (Ender pins) usually require supplementary cerclage wiring. These pins may improve fracture alignment but usually offer insufficient stability for unprotected early mobility. Currently, there are few indications for their use in the adult population. Reconstruction nails, with screws anchored in the femoral head and neck, offer excellent stability, but the entrance site anatomy is grossly distorted as a result of the intertrochanteric fracture, and nail placement is fraught with difficulties. Long-stem intramedullary hip screws are a reasonable option for the surgeon with experience in their use, but their large proximal cross-sectional diameters (17 to 18 mm) may require very aggressive reaming in younger patients with normal bone, and there are no data available concerning potential difficulties in removing these slightly angled nails. Retrograde insertion of a femoral intramedullary nail can control the shaft fracture, leaving the proximal shaft available for compression screw and side plate fixation.[106] On the other hand, a separate dynamic compression plate, although biomechanically not ideal, may provide a solution for fixation of a femoral shaft fracture significantly distal to an intertrochanteric fracture. At the least, the complications stemming from plate fixation of shaft fractures are relatively easy to treat, especially if the anatomically aligned intertrochanteric fracture has healed uneventfully.

## PATHOLOGIC AND IMPENDING FRACTURES

Pathologic fractures usually occur only with trivial trauma. Most are caused by metastatic malignancy. Typically, the patient reports that pain at rest and with weight bearing was locally present for some time before fracture. Every patient presenting with a hip fracture should be questioned about such symptoms. The specific workup of a pathologic lesion is addressed comprehensively in Chapter 16. Radiographic examination may demonstrate striking findings that make diagnosis obvious or may reveal only localized bone lysis or, occasionally, sclerosis. If pathologic fracture is the result of metastatic disease, the patient may have other destructive lesions in the affected femur, and therefore preoperative radiographs of the entire bone are required. Metastases may also exist elsewhere in the skeleton; all such lesions should be evaluated preoperatively. Bone scanning frequently reveals additional metastatic sites, which can then be radiographically assessed for the need for prophylactic fixation.

Because of the unacceptably high complication rate, poor pain control, and low union rate with nonoperative treatment, operative stabilization has long been the standard of care for treatment of pathologic fractures of the long bones. Some basic criteria should be met before fixation is undertaken in these patients. The patient's medical status should be stable enough to tolerate anesthesia, and the life expectancy of the patient should be long enough to allow adequate recuperation from the operation to appreciate the benefits of pain relief and mobilization that stabilization offers.

With the evaluation complete, fixation of the fracture and of any impending lesions can proceed at the same operation. Prophylactic fixation provides a better prognosis and avoids significant morbidity when compared with treatment after fracture. Fracture treatment must be individualized, but important principles include the operative goal of achieving adequate stability to reduce pain and to allow immediate mobilization of the patient and creation of a fixation construct that has an adequate fatigue life to remain intact for the remainder of the patient's life, even if the fracture does not heal. In addition, the surgeon must assume that lesions or deterioration will occur elsewhere on the same bone. Preferably, the construct should support the entire bone, or, if this is not practical, it should not add an obvious stress riser or unnecessarily complicate further surgery on the limb. In other words, the surgeon's plan should take into account the progressive nature of the disease.

For an isolated intertrochanteric fracture from a discrete lesion, a standard hip screw and side plate are frequently adequate. With more extended involvement, intramedullary fixation using long-stem intramedullary hip screws or so-called reconstruction interlocking nails is usually preferred. These strong load-sharing devices are fatigue resistant, can be placed through percutaneous incisions well away from the fracture, and can support any lesion from the femoral neck to near the physeal scar at the knee.

Open treatment with PMMA augmentation may be of some benefit in cases of significant bony destruction in patients with limited life expectancy, in which ultimate bone union is not a priority. If the lesion has extended into the femoral neck and head, cemented prosthetic replacement is usually indicated. If there is diaphyseal involvement as well, a long-stem component is required. A bipolar prosthesis is appropriate, unless acetabular involvement is present. Postoperative radiation therapy is usually indicated for the entire operative field. The presence of metal or cement, or both, does not interfere with the radiation effect, nor does radiation mechanically weaken the implant-cement system. Radiation does, however, slow fracture repair, and therefore its effects should be taken into account when deciding between fracture fixation and prosthetic replacement.

A decision to prophylactically fix a pathologic lesion in the femur, before it fractures, is made after assessment of several variables. Lytic lesions of the femur that exceed 2.5 cm in diameter, involve 50% of the cortical diameter, or cause pain unresponsive to radiation therapy should be prophylactically fixed. Estimation of lesion size requires two views of the hip that are perpendicular to each other. Fixation is indicated for any lesion that has a maximal diameter of 2.5 cm on either view or involves 50% of the cortex when both views are assessed.[11] Permeative lesions of the bone are more difficult to assess, and in such cases other factors should be evaluated. Pain on weight bearing facilitates the decision to fix prophylactically, particularly if the underlying process is not responsive to radiation.

## ISOLATED LESSER AND GREATER TROCHANTERIC FRACTURES

In the past, perhaps the most challenging aspect of managing a patient presenting with an apparent isolated fracture of a trochanter was excluding a nondisplaced intertrochanteric fracture. With the widespread availability of MRI, this is now easily done. In elderly patients, an isolated lesser trochanteric avulsion fracture must raise the possibility of an occult malignancy.[13, 119] Again, MRI has greatly aided in this diagnostic workup. If no associated process is identified, treatment is invariably conservative. Short-term crutch support and stretching exercises to avoid joint contractures are indicated.

An isolated but completely displaced greater trochanteric fracture should probably be operatively repaired, particularly in physiologically younger patients. Use of a cable or a strong wire through the abductor insertion and anchored into the cortex distally to act as a tension band is an effective construct. Often times, only a part of the trochanter is involved, and displacement is limited. Treatment with a walker or crutches and subsequently a cane is usually adequate. The minimal loss of power is probably preferred to the risks of operative intervention and the irritation caused by trochanteric implants.

## Postoperative Management and Discharge Planning

Postoperative medical treatment of patients with hip fractures is discussed in Chapter 47. Patients should be mobilized as soon as their cardiopulmonary status allows. If fracture fixation is stable and co-morbidities permit, ambulation with a walker or crutches is begun on the second postoperative day. Non–weight bearing on the fractured hip should not be ordered, because older patients rarely have the concentration, strength, or coordination to remain non–weight bearing during transfers and ambulation, and such orders may force caregivers to keep the patient in bed. In addition, joint reaction forces produced across the hip during bed activities and while maintaining the limb in a non–weight-bearing state are equal to or higher than those seen with partial weight bearing.[113] No study has demonstrated early weight bearing to cause an increased rate of mechanical failure, and many surgeons do allow immediate unrestricted weight bearing. Koval and co-workers have presented convincing evidence supporting their practice of allowing patients to bear weight to their own tolerance.[78] In a prospective study of 208 cognitively intact, previously ambulating patients who sustained intertrochanteric fractures that were fixed and allowed immediate unrestricted weight bearing, they noted a 2.9% rate of surgical revision at an average follow-up of nearly 3 years (1 year minimum). These results compare very favorably to other reports where postoperative restrictions were employed. In another important study from Koval's laboratoy, gait analysis using a transducer mounted in the shoe was used to measure the load applied to the operative extremity in patients who were allowed to bear weight to their own tolerance.[79] The data showed that patients effectively "autoregulate" the force across their hip fracture. More stable fracture patterns and longer follow-up were associated with increased weight bearing. Patients with unstable fractures placed no more than 25% of their weight on the fractured extremity immediately postoperatively, but by 6 weeks they elected to fully bear weight. There seems to be very little reason to complicate the postoperative manage-

ment of cognitively intact previous ambulators with arbitrary restrictions on their activities. Patients who are incapable of following any restrictions or have altered pain perception (because of mental or physical impairments) are probably best managed by unrestricted weight bearing for transfers from bed to chair to bathroom but limiting ambulation to these specific activities for the first few weeks.

Pressures to shorten acute care hospital stays have led to the rapid expansion of short-term rehabilitation centers. Patients who are medically stable but not yet capable of being managed safely at home are candidates for these centers, which are intermediate steps between hospitalization and the patient's return home. Hospital stays of as little as 72 hours are possible when such resources are available. If a rehabilitation center is not needed or is unavailable, physical therapy should be provided in the home. Jarnlo and associates[64] found that most patients receiving at home physical therapy regained their preoperative level of function within 4 months. The cost of therapy at home was found to be one tenth that of therapy in a nursing home facility. Others have similarly demonstrated the efficacy of outpatient rehabilitation after hip fractures and have emphasized the value of an organized, team management approach for such patients.[18, 22] The patients should be seen at 2 weeks after surgery to confirm uneventful healing of the wound. Clinical and radiographic evaluations at 6 and 12 weeks are indicated to exclude mechanical complications and to assess fracture union.

## COMPLICATIONS

### Loss of Proximal Fixation

The most common mode of fixation failure of the sliding hip screw continues to be varus collapse of the proximal fragment with cutout of the compression screw from the femoral head (Fig. 49–33). This mode of failure occurs in up to 20% of some fracture patterns and rarely in less than 4%. Cutouts usually occur within 4 months of fixation. The patient's age and level of osteoporosis, the fracture pattern, the quality of the reduction, and the position of the lag screw within the femoral head have all been related to implant cutout, but there has been no clear consensus as to the interrelations or relative importance of each factor.[35, 84, 85, 88–90, 107]

Most investigators have recognized the critical importance of central and deep placement of the screw, but the methods used to describe screw position have had little predictive value or have been cumbersome to use. Baumgaertner and colleagues[9] demonstrated the value of the tip-apex distance (TAD) for assessment of hip screw position. This measurement technique generates a single number (in millimeters) to describe the screw position by summing the distance from the tip of the screw to the apex of the femoral head on both AP and lateral radiographic images after controlling for radiographic magnification (Fig. 49–34). Peripheral malposition of the screw is not specifically differentiated from shallow positioning; only

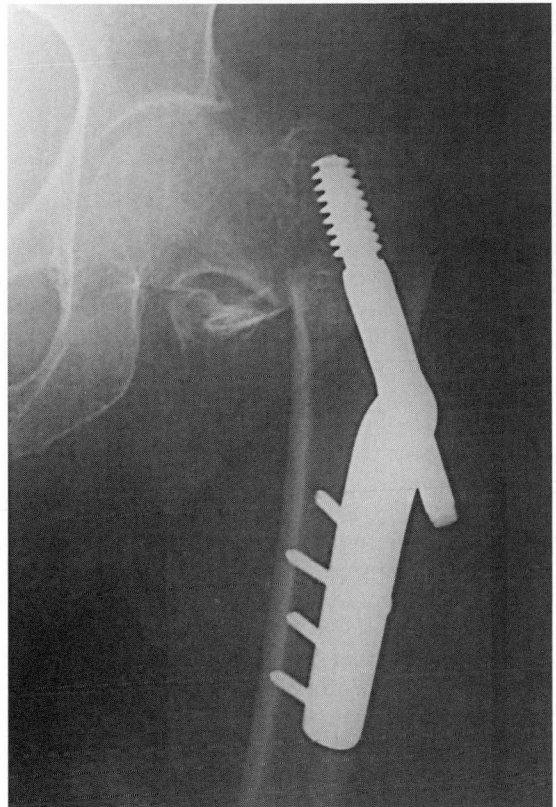

**FIGURE 49–33.** Loss of proximal fixation by cutout of the lag screw from the femoral head is by far the most common form of mechanical failure of fixation of intertrochanteric fractures.

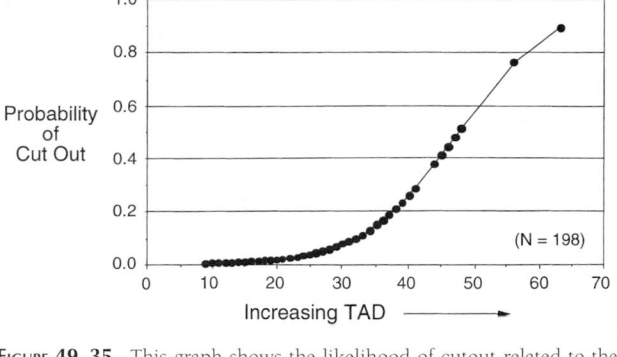

**FIGURE 49–35.** This graph shows the likelihood of cutout related to the tip-apex distance of 198 fractures. (Redrawn from Baumgaertner, M.R.; Curtin, S.L.; Lindskog, D.M.; et al. J Bone Joint Surg Am 77:1058–1064, 1995.)

the actual distance from the tip of the screw to the apex of the femoral head is considered. The researchers monitored 198 intertrochanteric fractures to union and identified 16 sliding screws that cut out. Regardless of the age of the patient, the stability of the fracture, the quality of reduction achieved, or the type or angle of implant used, no cutouts occurred in any of the 128 fixed fractures in which the TAD was 27 mm or less. Conversely, the cutout rate increased to 60% as the TAD increased to more than

45 mm. Using multivariate logistic regression statistical techniques, the investigators demonstrated that screw position, as measured by the TAD, was the strongest but not the only independent predictor of cutout ($P = 0.0001$). Unstable fractures ($P = 0.02$) and increasing patient age ($P = 0.02$) were also predictive for hip screw cutout. Bivariate logistic regression was employed to define the risk of cutout for a given TAD (Fig. 49–35). The investigators encouraged routine intraoperative estimation of the TAD (Fig. 49–36). If the guide pin location suggests a TAD of greater than 25 mm, they recommended both reassessment of the reduction and repositioning of the guide pin.

To test the value of this technique as an intraoperative guide, Baumgaertner compared treatment results in the 198 intertrochanteric fractures treated before and the 118 treated after the introduction of the tip-apex distance at the authors' institution.[10] The average TAD decreased from 25 to 20 mm, and the failure rate due to cut out fell from 8% to zero.

The quality of an intertrochanteric fracture's reduction has repeatedly been shown to be inversely related to the risk of cutout.[89, 117] Although multivariate analysis failed to identify poor reduction as a statistically significant

**FIGURE 49–34.** Measurement of the tip-apex distance (TAD) generates a single number, in millimeters, to describe the position of the screw. Note that it does not specifically distinguish between peripheral malpositioning and shallow placement of the screw. (If desired, magnification can be controlled by comparing the diameter of the projected screw shaft against its known size.) (Redrawn from Baumgaertner, M.R.; Curtin, S.L.; Lindskog, D.M.; et al. J Bone Joint Surg Am 77:1058–1064, 1995.)

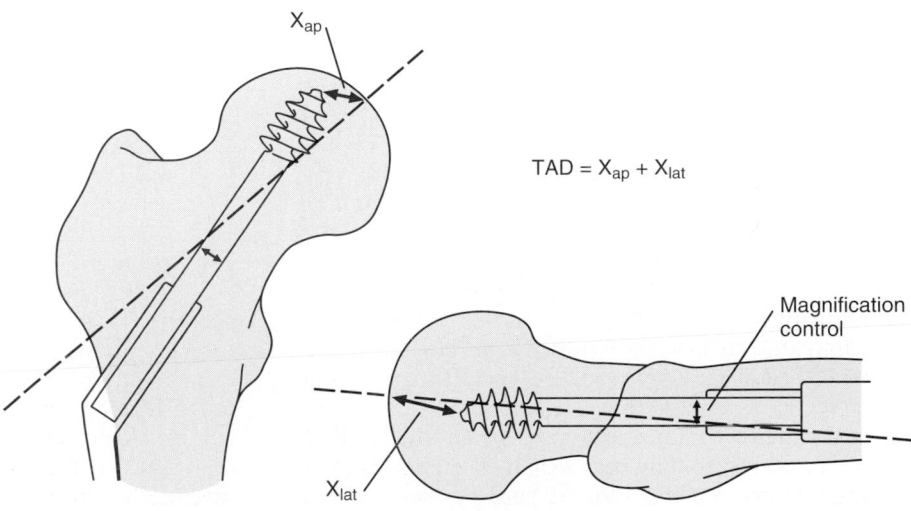

$$TAD = X_{ap} + X_{lat}$$

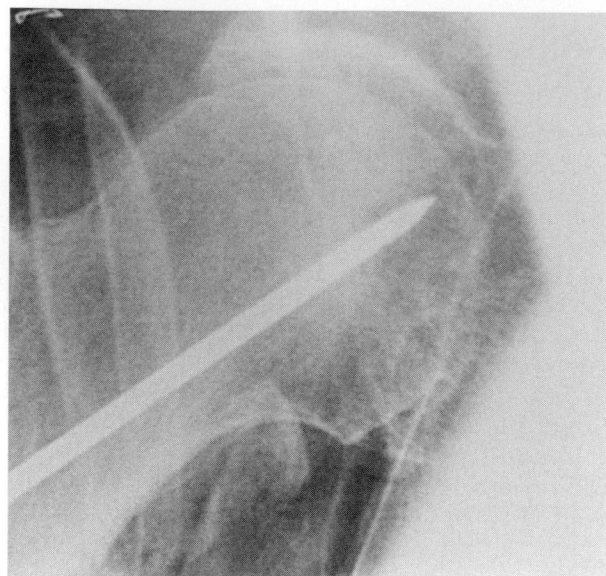

**FIGURE 49–36.** The tip of the guide pin should be within 10 mm of the apex of the femoral head on both fluoroscopic views before reaming.

independent risk factor (*P* = 0.06) in Baumgaertner's study (probably because poor reductions tended to be associated with increased TAD measurements), fractures with poor reductions were more than three times as likely to progress to cutout than fractures with good reductions (Fig. 49–37).

Implant designs have been modified in an attempt to further lessen the chance of cutout. For example, most current devices avoid excessively sharp edges on the hip screw threads in favor of more rounded edges to decrease the tendency of the implant to slice through osteoporotic bone. An expanding bolt completely replaces a threaded screw in one unique design (Alta, Howmedica), but the significantly greater amount of bone that must be reamed

away to insert this implant has to be weighed against any theoretical advantage of improved purchase. This device also allows insertion of PMMA into the bolt, if necessary, to further support the implant-bone interface. Short-threaded screws and short-barreled side plates are available and offer more potential for telescoping before thread-barrel impingement occurs.

In summary, several factors can be implicated that increase the risk of hip screw cutout. The surgeon must be aware that the patient's age, fracture pattern, and bone quality influence the rate of failure, but these factors cannot be controlled. On the other hand, the surgeon does control the reduction and the choice and placement of the implant. Of all factors, it appears that correct central and deep positioning of the implant (TAD < 25 mm) is most important for ensuring successful stabilization of intertrochanteric fractures with sliding hip screws. By directing the screw along the center axis of the femoral neck and head on both radiographic views, torsional forces around the screw are minimized and the surgeon can confidently advance the screw into the dense subchondral bone to within millimeters of the articular cartilage without the risk of inadvertent penetration that exists with off-center positioning. Not only is the best quality bone located in this central and subchondral area but the added depth of penetration allows the sliding screw to telescope that much farther to achieve stability before the screw's threads impinge on the barrel of the side plate.

Occasionally, failure of the sliding hip screw occurs because of postoperative disassembly of the lag screw from the barrel of the side plate (Fig. 49–38). This can occur only when the compressing screw is not used or is used and removed (to avoid excessive and potentially painful lateral prominence when the screw shaft collapses through the side plate). If the compressing screw is omitted, there is no mechanical block to disassembly. To prevent implant disassembly with associated loss of fracture reduction, it is important to ensure that there is ample engagement of the

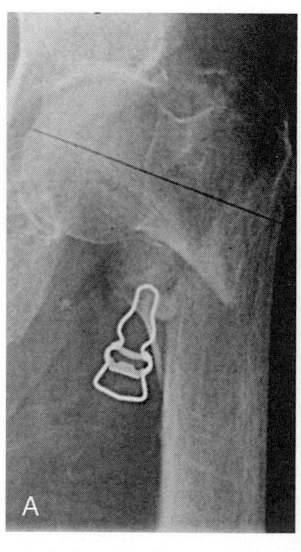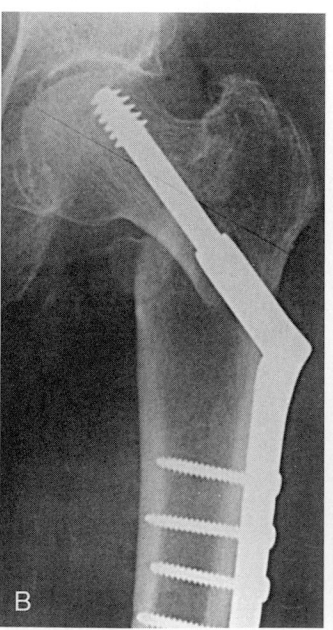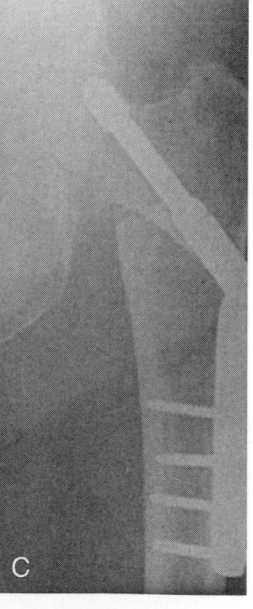

**FIGURE 49–37.** Loss of proximal fixation and cutout in a three part unstable fracture (AO/OTA 31-A2.1) that was not reduced before being fixed.

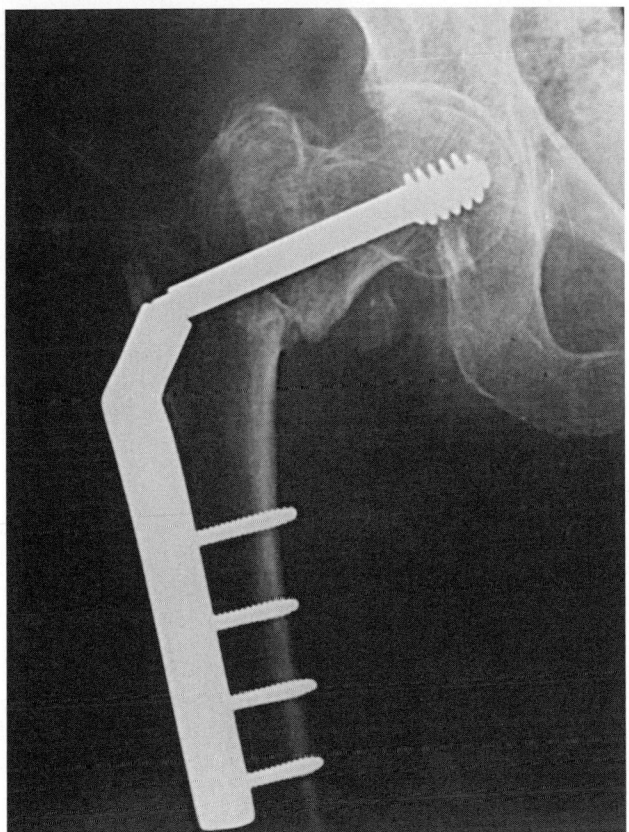

**FIGURE 49–38.** Disassembly of the sliding hip screw from the barrel. Although not indicated, a short barreled side plate was used, and the compressing screw was omitted. (From Rokito, A.S.; Koval, K.J.; Zuckerman, J.D. Technical pitfalls in the use of the sliding hip screw for fixation of intertrochanteric hip fractures. Contemp Orthop 26:354, 1993.)

screw shaft within the barrel of the implant. In addition, the compressing screw should be left in place to prevent disassembly in the setting of neuromuscular disorders (particularly with unstable fracture patterns), fractures requiring osteotomy, or any time the short-barreled implant is used.

## Nonunion

Nonunion of intertrochanteric fractures is reported to occur in 1% to 2% of patients regardless of the initial treatment.[2] Nonunions are uncommon because these fractures occur through cancellous bone, which has an abundant blood supply. However, nonunion rates may approach 10% when complex fixation schemes of comminuted fractures disturb bone nutrition. Mariani and Rand[98] found that 19 of their 20 nonunions occurred in patients who had unstable fractures with loss of medial calcar continuity. Most reported nonunions follow unsuccessful attempts at operative stabilization of fractures, with subsequent collapse into the varus position. This collapse leads to implant cutout through the femoral head and neck or, on occasion (in hip screws that are well positioned), implant fatigue failure. Ample clinical experience has shown that fatigue failure of the angled barrel-plate

portion of the implant assembly is quite rare. Rather, the screws break or pull out of the femoral shaft, or the lag screw breaks at the thread or barrel junction (Fig. 49–39).

A diagnosis of nonunion is made if the patient has pain in the hip and radiographs reveal a persistent radiolucent defect at the fracture site 4 to 7 months after fracture fixation. Progressive loss of alignment strongly suggests nonunion, although healing may occur after an initial change in alignment, particularly if it improves fragment contact. Fixation failure is often associated with nonunion, either as a cause or as an effect. Because abundant callus and marked sclerosis may be present, the diagnosis often is not obvious. Laminar tomography in the plane of the barrel and screws may help to confirm the diagnosis; otherwise, the diagnosis may have to be made during surgical exploration. As with any nonunion, the possibility of an occult infection must be considered and excluded.

The surgical treatment of an intertrochanteric nonunion that has collapsed into varus involves identification and management of any occult infection together with a valgus osteotomy, refixation, and bone grafting. If implant cutout has damaged the hip joint itself, arthroplasty is indicated. In addition to the nonunion, the retained hardware and the marked anatomic disorganization of the proximal femur make for a challenging reconstruction that frequently requires a calcar-replacing prosthesis. Patients with stable alignment and tolerable symptoms despite nonunion may be managed expectantly.

## Wound Problems and Infection

Wound hematomas may cause persisting hip wound drainage during the first several days after fixation of an intertrochanteric fracture, particularly in obese, medically unstable, or nutritionally compromised patients. With reduced motion at the site and sterile pressure dressings, such drainage often resolves uneventfully. However, persistent drainage is best treated actively. If it is copious or increasing or does not resolve within 7 to 10 days, reoperation is advisable. This involves formal wound exploration, often best done with the patient in the lateral decubitus position and the leg draped free. Deep cultures and gram-stained slides of the exudate are obtained. Appropriate antibiotics are then begun intraoperatively, and after thorough débridement and irrigation the wound is closed over suction drains. Antibiotics are soon discontinued if the final intraoperative culture results are negative. However, if bacterial organisms are recovered, the adjunctive antibiotic treatment may need modification according to sensitivity tests and should be continued for several weeks.

The reported incidence of postoperative wound infections has varied from 0.15% to 15%. The lowest figures were obtained in studies that used perioperative prophylactic antibiotics.[15, 136] Burnett and associates demonstrated in a double-blind, prospective study the value of prophylactic antibiotics in reducing wound infections.[21] The value of perioperative antibiotics in operations for hip fracture is now generally accepted.[1, 60] Less clear is the optimal duration of prophylaxis. A single day's treatment may be sufficient.[111] Because most infecting organisms are

*Staphylococcus aureus* or other gram-positive cocci, a first-generation cephalosporin is commonly used, with an initial preoperative dose followed by doses for 24 to 48 hours postoperatively.

Infections are usually divided into superficial and deep varieties. Superficial wound infections occur early in the postoperative period and are characterized by wound swelling, erythema, and discharge with or without persistent fever. These infections should be treated with appropriate antibiotics, prompt débridement as needed, and open drainage, followed by secondary closure. If deep infection cannot be ruled out, it is much better to assume

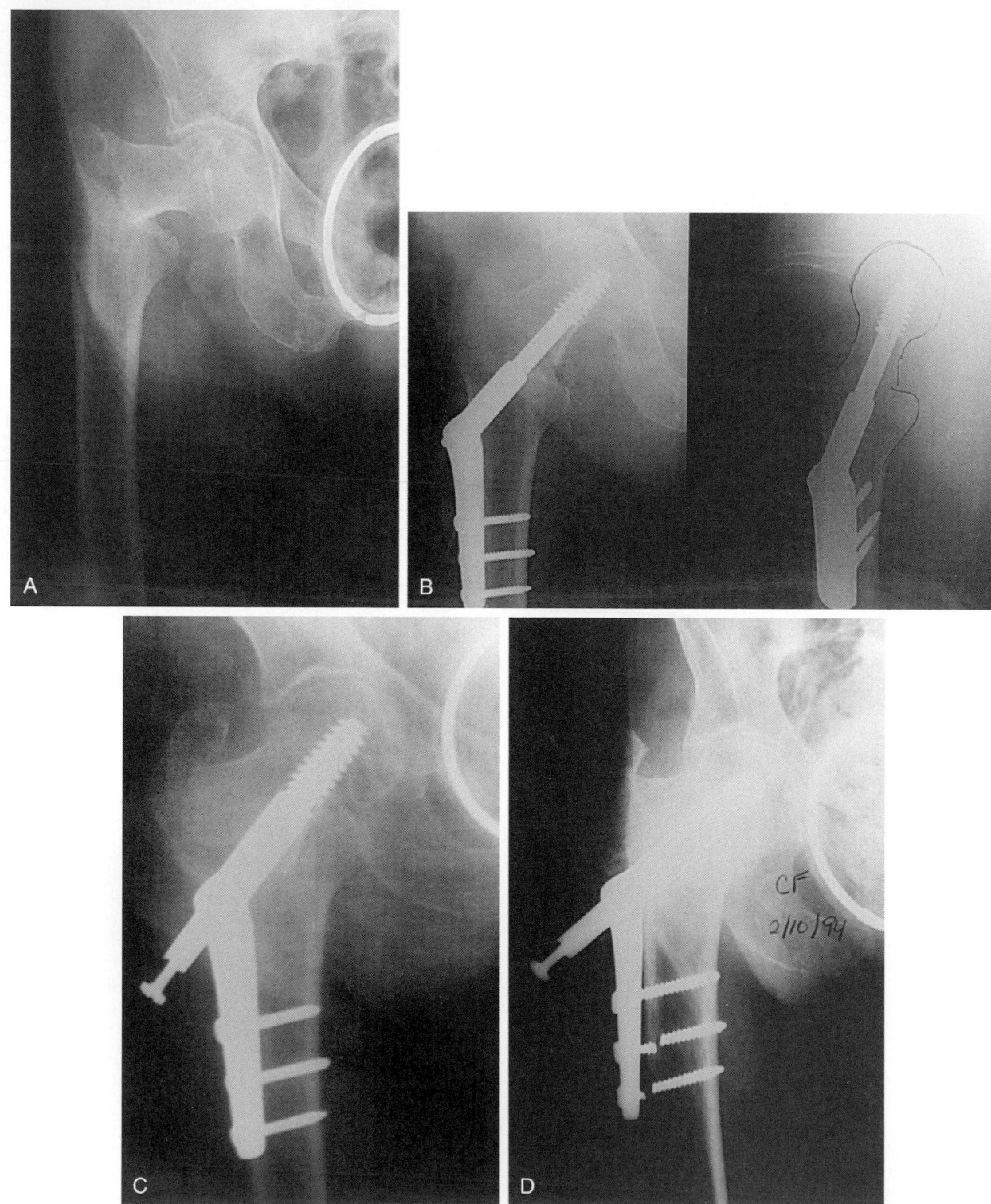

**Figure 49–39.** *A,* Apparently stable, two-part fracture (AO/OTA31-A1.1) in a 90-year-old woman. *B,* Immediate postoperative radiographs demonstrate acceptable reduction and implant position. *C,* Early complete collapse of the sliding hip screw without loss of fixation. *D,* Fatigue failure of the shaft screws, varus collapse, and union at the eighth postoperative month.

involvement and to treat empirically than to watch and wait for signs of chronic low-grade infection (e.g., nonunion, osteomyelitis) before initiating treatment.

Deep infections may arise before or after fracture healing, even several years after the initial surgery, and they have a high morbidity. It can be difficult to diagnose late deep infection. Symptoms include unexplained pain in the hip, decreased range of motion, and an increased sedimentation rate. An increased leukocyte count and fever are frequently absent. These infections require surgical débridement and antibiotics. If the fracture is not yet healed and fixation is stable, the implant should not be removed.[84, 108] If there is hip joint involvement, removal of the internal fixation device and débridement to produce an excisional arthroplasty may be necessary.

## PATIENT OUTCOME

We attempted to relate fracture outcome to the five independent variables of bone quality, fracture geometry, reduction achieved, implant selected, and position of implant. We documented successful fracture outcomes in up to 98% of cases and reviewed the common causes of failure. Patient outcome is a much more complex concept, in terms of both its definition and its evaluation. There are considerably more variables to take into account, many of which are subjective and therefore difficult to quantify. The endpoint is much less clear than, for example, a "healed fracture capable of withstanding physiologic loads."

Traditionally, orthopaedists have looked at endpoints such as mortality, ambulation, and ability to return home to describe patient outcome. Mortality rates reported for patients with hip fractures range from 7% to 27% within 3 months of injury.[34, 145] Mortality risk after hip fracture is increased over that of the age-matched control population for as long as 1 year in various reports. In our own experience, intertrochanteric fracture mortality is approximately 20% at 1 year.[8] In a well-documented study, Kenzora and colleagues[73] noted a 15% mortality rate after intertrochanteric hip fractures, compared with 9% for the age-matched population group. He noted mortality to be related to the number of preoperative significant medical problems as well as to postoperative significant medical complications. Mortality rates tend to vary with the source of hip fracture patient referral. Miller noted a 20% mortality rate to be related more to preinjury functional status than to age.[105] Return of preinjury function has been subject to many interpretations and has been measured by varying means, ranging from satisfactory completion of scored tasks to the ability to live alone. In an evaluation of the contribution of intensive rehabilitation efforts, Jette and co-workers[70] observed that only 33% of patients recovered preinjury function. This contrasts with a 69% good or excellent hip function noted by Miller[105] and an optimistic report of Jarnlo and associates[64] that most of their patients regained preinjury function within 4 months. The individual elderly patient is unlikely to regain full preinjury function. Only 41% will walk as well as they did before injury, according to Koval and colleagues' prospective evaluation of 336 community-dwelling ambu-

lators who sustained hip fractures and were monitored prospectively for at least 1 year.[80] In that study, another 40% had increased dependency but were still able to remain ambulatory, 12% became household ambulators, and 8% became nonambulators. As many as two thirds to three fourths of patients ultimately return to their own homes, but most do not do so directly. Of those who do return home, at least 50% are more dependent than before.

## SUMMARY

In summary, the geriatric hip fracture epidemic is a major health care problem in which the orthopaedic surgeon plays a pivotal but not isolated role. Although others certainly contribute to advances in preventive therapies and in the medical management of patients who fracture their hips, it is the orthopaedist who must efficiently and effectively fix the fracture to allow mobilization of the patient and initiation of rehabilitation. Fortunately, the intertrochanteric fracture responds very well to surgical intervention in terms of fracture healing and return of limb function. For most of these fractures (the exceptions have already been discussed), success is highly probable if a sliding hip screw can be placed accurately into a well-reduced fracture. Failures of fixation are almost exclusively caused by technical shortcomings at the time of surgical repair. The conscientious orthopaedist who adopts an attitude of zero tolerance for inadequate fracture reduction and peripheral implant position will be doing his or her part to provide high-quality yet cost effective care for the geriatric patient with an intertrochanteric hip fracture.

### REFERENCES

1. Aagaard, H.; Noer, H.H.; Scavenius, M.; et al. Computer registration of infections used to measure the effect of prophylactic antibiotics on postoperative infections following osteosynthesis in hip fractures. J Hosp Infect 27:257–262, 1994.
2. Altner, P.C. Reasons for failure in treatment of intertrochanteric fractures. Orthop Rev 11:117, 1982.
3. Anderson, G.H.; Harper, W.M.; Connolly, C.D.; et al. Preoperative skin traction for fractures of the proximal femur. A randomised prospective trial. J Bone Joint Surg Br 75:794–796, 1993.
4. Babst, R.; Renner, N.; Biedermann, M.; et al. Clinical results using the trochanter stabilizing plate (TSP): The modular extension of the dynamic hip screw (DHS) for internal fixation of selected unstable intertrochanteric fractures. J Orthop Trauma 12:392–399, 1998.
5. Barquet, A.; Fernandez, A.; Leon, H. Simultaneous ipsilateral trochanteric and femoral shaft fracture. Acta Orthop Scand 56:36–39, 1985.
6. Barquet, A.; Francescoli, L.; Rienzi, D.; et al. Intertrochanteric-subtrochanteric fractures: Treatment with the long Gamma nail. J Orthop Trauma 14:324–328, 2000.
7. Bartucci, E.J.; Gonzalez, M.H.; Cooperman, D.R.; et al. The effect of adjunctive methylmethacrylate on failures of fixation and function in patients with intertrochanteric fractures and osteoporosis. J Bone Joint Surg Am 67:1094–1107, 1985.
8. Baumgaertner, M.R.; Curtin, S.L.; Lindskog, D.M. Intramedullary versus extramedullary fixation for the treatment of intertrochanteric hip fractures. Clin Orthop 348:87–94, 1998.
9. Baumgaertner, M.R.; Curtin, S.L.; Lindskog, D.M.; et al. The value of the tip-apex distance in predicting failure of fixation of peritrochanteric fractures of the hip. J Bone Joint Surg Am 77:1058–1064, 1995.

10. Baumgaertner, M.R.; Solberg, B.D. Awareness of tip-apex distance reduces failure of fixation of trochanteric fractures of the hip. J Bone Joint Surg Am 79:969–971, 1997.

11. Beals, R.K.; Lawton, G.D.; Snell, W.E. Prophylactic internal fixation of the femur in metastatic breast cancer. Cancer 28:1350–1354, 1971.

12. Bellabarba, C.; Herscovici, D., Jr.; Ricci, W.M. Percutaneous treatment of peritrochanteric fractures using the Gamma nail. Clin Orthop 375:30–42, 2000.

13. Bertin, K.C.; Horstman, J.; Coleman, S.S. Isolated fracture of the lesser trochanter in adults: An initial manifestation of metastatic malignant disease. J Bone Joint Surg Am 66:770–773, 1984.

14. Blundell, C.M.; Parker, M.J.; Pryor, G.A.; et al. Assessment of the AO classification of intracapsular fractures of the proximal femur. J Bone Joint Surg Br 80:679–683, 1998.

15. Bodoky, A.; Neff, U.; Heberer, M.; et al. Antibiotic prophylaxis with two doses of cephalosporin in patients managed with internal fixation for a fracture of the hip. J Bone Joint Surg Am 75:61–65, 1993.

16. Bogoch, E.R.; Ouellette, G.; Hastings, D.E. Intertrochanteric fractures of the femur in rheumatoid arthritis patients. Clin Orthop 294:181–186, 1993.

17. Bolhofner, B.R.; Russo, P.R.; Carmen, B. Results of intertrochanteric femur fractures treated with a 135-degree sliding screw with a two-hole side plate. J Orthop Trauma 13:5–8, 1999.

18. Borgquist, L.; Lindelow, G.; Thorngren, K.G. Costs of hip fracture. Rehabilitation of 180 patients in primary health care. Acta Orthop Scan 62:39–48, 1991.

19. Bridle, S.H.; Patel, A.D.; Bircher, M.; et al. Fixation of intertrochanteric fractures of the femur. A randomised prospective comparison of the gamma nail and the dynamic hip screw. J Bone Joint Surg Br 73:330–334, 1991.

20. Buchner, D.M.; Koepsell, T.D.; Abrass, I.B.; et al. Chronic illness as a risk factor for hip fracture: Results of a case-control study and review of the literature. In: Apple, J.D.; Wilson, C., eds. Prevention of Falls and Hip Fractures in the Elderly. Rosemont, IL, American Academy of Orthopaedic Surgeons, 1994.

21. Burnett, J.W.; Gustilo, R.B.; Williams, D.N. Prophylactic antibiotics in hip fractures. A double-blind, prospective study. J Bone Joint Surg Am 62:457–462, 1980.

22. Cameron, I.D.; Lyle, D.M.; Quine, S. Cost effectiveness of accelerated rehabilitation after proximal femoral fracture. J Clin Epidemiol 47:1307–1313, 1994.

23. Campion, E.W.; Jette, A.M.; Cleary, P.D.; et al. Hip fracture: A prospective study of hospital course, complications, and costs. J Gen Intern Med 2:78–82, 1987.

24. Chan, K.C.; Gill, G.S. Cemented hemiarthroplasties for elderly patients with intertrochanteric fractures. Clin Orthop 371:206–215, 2000.

25. Chan, K.M.; Tse, P.Y. Late subcapital fracture of the neck of the femur—A rare complication of Ender nailing. J Trauma 26:196–198, 1986.

26. Chang, W.S.; Zuckerman, J.D.; Kummer, F.J.; et al. Biomechanical evaluation of anatomic reduction versus medial displacement osteotomy in unstable intertrochanteric fractures. Clin Orthop 225:141–146, 1987.

27. Choueka, J.; Koval, K.J.; Kummer, F.J.; et al. Cement augmentation of intertrochanteric fracture fixation: A cadaver comparison of 2 techniques. Acta Orthop Scand 67:153–157, 1996.

28. Clawson, D.K. Trochanteric fractures treated by the sliding screw plate fixation method. J Trauma 4:753, 1964.

29. Cummings, S.R.; Kelsey, J.L.; Nevitt, M.C.; et al. Epidemiology of osteoporosis and osteoporotic fractures. Epidemiol Rev 7:178–208, 1985.

30. Cummings, S.R.; Nevitt, M.C. A hypothesis: The cause of hip fractures. J Gerontol 44:M107–111, 1989.

31. Cummings, S.R.; Phillips, S.L.; Wheat, M.E.; et al. Recovery of function after hip fracture. The role of social supports. J Am Geriatr Soc 36:801–806, 1988.

32. Cummings, S.R.; Rubin, S.M.; Black, D. The future of hip fractures in the United States: Numbers, costs, and potential effects of postmenopausal estrogen. Clin Orthop 252:163–166, 1990.

33. Dalen, N.; Jacobsson, B.; Eriksson, P.A. A comparison of nail-plate fixation and Ender's nailing in pertrochanteric fractures. J Trauma 28:405–412, 1988.

34. Davidson, T.I.; Bodey, W.N. Factors influencing survival following fractures of the upper end of the femur. Injury 17:12–14, 1986.

35. Davis, T.R.; Sher, J.L.; Horsman, A.; et al. Intertrochanteric femoral fractures. Mechanical failure after internal fixation. J Bone Joint Surg Br 72:26–31, 1990.

36. Desjardins, A.L.; Roy, A.; Paiement, G.; et al. Unstable intertrochanteric fracture of the femur. A prospective randomised study comparing anatomical reduction and medial displacement osteotomy. J Bone Joint Surg Br 75:445–447, 1993.

37. Dias, J.J.; Robbins, J.A.; Steingold, R.F.; et al. Subcapital vs intertrochanteric fracture of the neck of the femur: Are there two distinct subpopulations? J R Coll Surg Edinb 32:303–305, 1987.

38. Dimon, J.H.; Hughston, J.C. Unstable intertrochanteric fractures of the hip. J Bone Joint Surg Am 49:440–450, 1967.

39. Dimon, J.H. III. The unstable intertrochanteric fracture. Clin Orthop 92:100–107, 1973.

40. Doppelt, S.H. The sliding compression screw—Today's best answer for stabilization of intertrochanteric hip fractures. Orthop Clin North Am 11:507–523, 1980.

41. Evans, E.M. The treatment of trochanteric fractures of the femur. J Bone Joint Surg Br 31:190–203, 1949.

42. Evans, E.M. Trochanteric fractures. J Bone Joint Surg Br 33:192–204, 1951.

43. Evans, P.D.; Wilson, C.; Lyons, K. Comparison of MRI with bone scanning for suspected hip fracture in elderly patients. J Bone Joint Surg Br 76:158–159, 1994.

44. Finsen, V.; Benum, P. The second hip fracture. An epidemiologic study. Acta Orthop Scand 57:431–433, 1986.

45. Fox, H.J.; Pooler, J.; Prothero, D.; et al. Factors affecting the outcome after proximal femoral fractures. Injury 25:297–300, 1994.

46. Friedman, R.J.; Wyman, E.T. Ipsilateral hip and femoral shaft fractures. Clin Orthop 208:188, 1986.

47. Gargan, M.F.; Gundle, R.; Simpson, A.H. How effective are osteotomies for unstable intertrochanteric fractures? J Bone Joint Surg Br 76:789–792, 1994.

48. Goodman, S.B.; Bauer, T.W.; Carter, D.; et al. Norian SRS cement augmentation in hip fracture treatment. Laboratory and initial clinical results. Clin Orthop 348:42–50, 1998.

49. Green, S.; Moore, T.; Proano, F. Bipolar prosthetic replacement for the management of unstable intertrochanteric hip fractures in the elderly. Clin Orthop 224:169–177, 1987.

50. Griffin, J.B. The calcar femorale redefined. Clin Orthop 164:211–214, 1982.

51. Haentjens, P.; Casteleyn, P.P.; De Boeck, H.; et al. Treatment of unstable intertrochanteric and subtrochanteric fractures in elderly patients. Primary bipolar arthroplasty compared with internal fixation. J Bone Joint Surg Am 71:1214–1225, 1989.

52. Haidukewych, G.; Israel, T.; Berry, D. Reverse obliquity fractures of the proximal femur. Presented at the 15th annual meeting of the Orthopaedic Trauma Association, Charlotte, NC, 1999.

53. Halder, S.C. The Gamma nail for peritrochanteric fractures. J Bone Joint Surg Br 74:340–344, 1992.

54. Haramati, N.; Staron, R.B.; Barax, C.; et al. Magnetic resonance imaging of occult fractures of the proximal femur. Skeletal Radiol 23:19–22, 1994.

55. Hardy, D.C.; Descamps, P.Y.; Krallis, P.; et al. Use of an intramedullary hip-screw compared with a compression hip-screw with a plate for intertrochanteric femoral fractures. A prospective, randomized study of one hundred patients. J Bone Joint Surg Am 80:618–630, 1998.

56. Harris, L.J. Closed retrograde nailing of peritrochanteric fractures of the femur with a new nail. J Bone Joint Surg Am 62:1185–1193, 1980.

57. Harris, L.J. Condylocephalic nailing of proximal femur fractures. Instr Course Lect 32:292–303, 1983.

58. Hedlund, R.; Lindgren, U.; Ahlbom, A. Age- and sex-specific incidence of femoral neck and trochanteric fractures. An analysis based on 20,538 fractures in Stockholm County, Sweden, 1972–1981. Clin Orthop 222:132–139, 1987.

59. Heyse-Moore, G.H.; MacEachern, A.G.; Evans, D.C.J. Treatment of intertrochanteric fractures of the femur. J Bone Joint Surg Br 65:262–267, 1983.

60. Hjortrup, A.; Sorensen, C.; Mejdahl, S. Antibiotic prophylaxis in surgery for hip fractures. Acta Orthop Scand 61:152–153, 1990.

61. Hornby, R.; Evans, J.G.; Vardon, V. Operative or conservative treatment for trochanteric fractures of the femur. A randomised epidemiological trial in elderly patients. J Bone Joint Surg Br 71:619–623, 1989.

62. Hubbard, M.J.; Burke, F.D.; Houghton, G.R.; et al. A prospective controlled trial of valgus osteotomy in the fixation of unstable pertrochanteric fractures of the femur. Injury 11:228–232, 1980.

63. Ingman, A.M. Percutaneous intramedullary fixation of trochanteric fractures of the femur. Clinical trial of a new hip nail. Injury 31:483–487, 2000.

64. Jarnlo, G.B.; Ceder, L.; Thorngren, K.G. Early rehabilitation at home of elderly patients with hip fractures and consumption of resources in primary care. Scand J Prim Health Care 2:105–112, 1984.

65. Jensen, J.S.; Michaelsen, M. Trochanteric femoral fractures treated with McLaughlin osteosynthesis. Acta Orthop Scand 46:795–803, 1975.

66. Jensen, J.S.; Sonne-Holm, S. Critical analysis of Ender nailing in the treatment of trochanteric fractures. Acta Orthop Scand 51:817–825, 1980.

67. Jensen, J.S.; Sonne-Holm, S.; Tondevold, E. Unstable trochanteric fractures. A comparative analysis of four methods of internal fixation. Acta Orthop Scand 51:949–962, 1980.

68. Jensen, J.S.; Tondevold, F.; Sonne-Holm, S. Stable trochanteric fractures. A comparable analysis of four methods of internal fixation. Acta Orthop Scand 51:811–816, 1980.

69. Jerre, R.; Doshe, A.; Karlsson, J. Preoperative skin traction in patients with hip fractures is not useful. Clin Orthop 378:169–173, 2000.

70. Jette, A.M.; Harris, B.A.; Cleary, P.D.; et al. Functional recovery after hip fracture. Arch Phys Med Rehab 68:735–740, 1987.

71. Jewett, E.L. One piece angle nail for trochanteric fractures. J Bone Joint Surg 23:803, 1941.

72. Kaufer, H. Mechanics of the treatment of hip injuries. Clin Orthop 146:53–61, 1980.

73. Kenzora, J.E.; McCarthy, R.E.; Lowell, J.D.; et al. Hip fracture mortality. Relation to age, treatment, preoperative illness, time of surgery, and complications. Clin Orthop 186:45–56, 1984.

74. Khairi, M.R.A.; Cronin, J.H.; Robb, J.A.; et al. Femoral trabecular pattern index and bone mineral content measurment by photon absorption in senile osteoporosis. J Bone Joint Surg Am 58:221, 1976.

75. Kinast, C.; Bolhofner, B.R.; Mast, J.W.; et al. Subtrochanteric fractures of the femur. Results of treatment with the 95 degrees condylar blade-plate [see comments]. Clin Orthop 238:122 130, 1989.

76. Koval, K.; Zuckerman, J. Intertrochanteric fractures. In: Rockwood, C.A.; Bucholz, R.W.; Heckman, J., eds. Rockwood & Greens' Fractures in Adults. Philadelphia, Lippincott Williams & Wilkins, 2001.

77. Koval, K.J.; Aharonoff, G.B.; Rokito, A.S.; et al. Patients with femoral neck and intertrochanteric fractures. Are they the same? Clin Orthop 330:166–172, 1996.

78. Koval, K.J.; Friend, K.D.; Aharonoff, G.B.; et al. Weight bearing after hip fracture: A prospective series of 596 geriatric hip fracture patients. J Orthop Trauma 10:526–530, 1996.

79. Koval, K.J.; Sala, D.A.; Kummer, F.J.; et al. Postoperative weight-bearing after a fracture of the femoral neck or an intertrochanteric fracture. J Bone Joint Surg Am 80:352–356, 1998.

80. Koval, K.J.; Skovron, M.L.; Aharonoff, G.B.; et al. Ambulatory ability after hip fracture. A prospective study in geriatric patients. Clin Orthop 310:150–159, 1995.

81. Kuderna, H.; Bohler, N.; Collon D.J. Treatment of intertrochanteric and subtrochanteric fractures of the hip by the Ender method. J Bone Joint Surg Am 58:604–611, 1976.

82. Kuokkanen, H.; Korkala, O.; Lautamus, L. Ender nailing of trochanteric fracture. A review of 73 cases. Arch Orthop Trauma Surg 105:46–48, 1986.

83. Kyle, R.F. Fixation of intertrochanteric hip fractures with sliding devices. Instr Course Lect 197–203, 1984.

84. Kyle, R.F.; Gustilo, R.B.; Premer, R.F. Analysis of six hundred and twenty-two intertrochanteric hip fractures. J Bone Joint Surg Am 61:216–221, 1979.

85. Kyle, R.F.; Wright, T.M.; Burstein, A.H. Biomechanical analysis of the sliding characteristics of compression hip screws. J Bone Joint Surg Am 62:1308–1314, 1980.

86. Laros, G.S. Intertrochanteric fractures. In: Evarts, C.M., ed. Surgery of the Musculoskeletal System, 2nd ed. New York, Churchill-Livingstone, 1990, p. 2613.

87. Laros, G.S. The role of osteoporosis in intertrochanteric fractures. Orthop Clin North Am 11:525–537, 1980.

88. Laros, G.S.; Moore, J.F. Complications of fixation in intertrochanteric fractures. Clin Orthop 101:110–119, 1974.

89. Larsson, S.; Friberg, S.; Hansson, L. Trochanteric fractures: Influence of reduction and implant position on impaction and complications. Clin Orthop 259:130–139, 1990.

90. Larsson, S.; Friberg, S.; Hansson, Ll. Trochanteric fractures. Mobility, complications, and mortality in 607 cases treated with the sliding-screw technique. Clin Orthop 260:232–241, 1990.

91. Leung, K.S.; So, W.S.; Shen, W.Y.; et al. Gamma nails and dynamic hip screws for peritrochanteric fractures. A randomised prospective study in elderly patients. J Bone Joint Surg Br 74:345–351, 1992.

92. Levy, R.N.; Siegel, M.; Sedlin, E.D.; et al. Complications of Ender pin fixation in basicervical, intertrochanteric, and subtrochanteric fractures of the hip. J Bone Joint Surg Am 65:66–69, 1983.

93. Lunsjo, K.; Ceder, L.; Stigsson, L.; et al. One-way compression along the femoral shaft with the Medoff sliding plate. The first European experience of 104 intertrochanteric fractures with a 1-year follow-up. Acta Orthop Scand 66:343–346, 1995.

94. Luthje, P. Incidence of hip fracture in Finland. A forecast for 1990. Acta Orthop Scand 56:223–225, 1985.

95. Lyon, L.J.; Nevins, M.A. Nontreatment of hip fractures in senile patients. JAMA 238:1175–1176, 1977.

96. MacEachern, A.G.; Heyse-Moore, G.H. Stable intertrochanteric femoral fractures: A misnomer? J Bone Joint Surg Br 65:582–583, 1983.

97. Madsen, J.E.; Naess, L.; Aune, A.K.; et al. Dynamic hip screw with trochanteric stabilizing plate in the treatment of unstable proximal femoral fractures: A comparative study with the Gamma nail and compression hip screw. J Orthop Trauma 12:241–248, 1998.

98. Mariani, E.M.; Rand, J.A. Nonunion of intertrochanteric fractures of the femur following open reduction and internal fixation. Results of second attempts to gain union. Clin Orthop 218:81–89, 1987.

99. Marsh, C.H. Use of Ender's nails in unstable intertrochanteric femoral fractures. J R Soc Med 76:550, 1983.

100. McLoughlin, S.; Wheeler, D.; Rider, J.; et al. Biomechanical evaluation of the dynamic hip screw with two- and four-hole sideplates. J Orthop Trauma 14:318–323, 2000.

101. Medoff, R.J.; Maes, K. A new device for the fixation of unstable peritrochanteric fractures of the hip. J Bone Joint Surg Am 73:1192–1199, 1991.

102. Meislin, R.J.; Zuckerman, J.D.; Kummer, F.J.; et al. A biomechanical analysis of the sliding hip screw: The question of plate angle. J Orthop Trauma 4:130–136, 1990.

103. Melton, L.J. Hip fractures: A worldwide problem today and tomorrow. Bone 14(Suppl 1):S1–8, 1993.

104. Mermelstein, L.E.; Chow, L.C.; Friedman, C.; et al. The reinforcement of cancellous bone screws with calcium phosphate cement. J Orthop Trauma 10:15–20, 1996.

105. Miller, C.W. Survival and ambulation following hip fracture. J Bone Joint Surg Am 60:930–934, 1978.

106. Moed, B.R.; Watson, J.T. Retrograde intramedullary nailing without reaming of fractures of the femoral shft in multiply injured patients. J Bone Joint Surg Am 77:1520–1527, 1995.

107. Moller, B.N.; Lucht, U.; Grymer, F.; Bartholdy, N.J. Instability of trochanteric hip fractures following internal fixation. Acta Orthop Scand 55:517–520, 1984.

108. Moller, B.N.; Lucht, U.; Grymer, F.; et al. Early rehabilitation following osteosynthesis with the sliding hip screw for trochanteric fractures. Scand J Rehab Med 17:39, 1985.

109. Moore, D.C.; Frankenburg, E.P.; Goulet, J.A.; et al. Hip screw augmentation with an in situ-setting calcium phosphate cement: An in vitro biomechanical analysis. J Orthop Trauma 11:577–583, 1997.

110. Müller, M.E.; Nazarian, S.; Koch, P.; et al. The Comprehensive Classification of Fractures of Long Bones. New York, Springer-Verlag, 1990, p. 118.

111. Nelson, C.L.; Green, T.G.; Porter, R.A. One day versus seven days of preventive antibiotic therapy in orthopaedic surgery. Clin Orthop 176:258–263, 1983.

112. Noble, P.C.; Alexander, J.W.; Lindahl, L.J. The anatomic basis of femoral component design. Clin Orthop 235:148, 1988.

113. Nordin, M.; Frankel, V. Biomechanic of bone. In: Nordin, M.; Frankel, V., eds. Basic Biomechanics of the Musculoskeletal System. Philadelphia, Lea & Febiger, 1989, pp. 3–29.

114. Obrant, K.J. Trabecular bone changes in the greater trochanter after fracture of the femoral neck. Acta Orthop Scand 55:78, 1984.

115. Orthopaedic Trauma Association Committee for Coding: Fracture and dislocation compendium. J Orthop Trauma 10(Suppl 1):32–35, 1996.

116. Owen, R.A.; Melton, L.J.; Gallagher, J.C.; et al. The national cost of acute care of hip fractures associated with osteoporosis. Clin Orthop 150:172–176, 1980.

117. Parker, M.J. Cutting-out of the dynamic hip screw related to its position. J Bone Joint Surg Br 74:625, 1992.

118. Parker, M.J.; Pryor, G.A. Gamma versus DHS nailing for extracapsular femoral fractures. Meta-analysis of ten randomised trials. Int Orthop 20:163–168, 1996.

119. Phillips, C.D.; Pope, T.L., Jr.; Jones, J.E.; et al. Nontraumatic avulsion of the lesser trochanter: A pathognomonic sign of metastatic disease? Skel Radiol 17:106–110, 1988.

120. Pho, R.W.; Nather, A.; Tong, G.O.; et al. Endoprosthetic replacement of unstable, comminuted intertrochanteric fracture of the femur in the elderly, osteoporotic patient. J Trauma 21:792–797, 1981.

121. Quinn, S.F.; McCarthy, J.L. Prospective evaluation of patients with suspected hip fracture and indeterminate radiographs: Use of T1-weighted MR images. Radiology 187:469–471, 1993.

122. Radford, P.J.; Needoff, M.; Webb, J.K. A prospective randomised comparison of the dynamic hip screw and the gamma locking nail. J Bone Joint Surg Br 75:789–793, 1993.

123. Rantanen, J.; Aro, H.T. Intramedullary fixation of high subtrochanteric femoral fractures: A study comparing two implant designs, the Gamma nail and the intramedullary hip screw. J Orthop Trauma 12:249–252, 1998.

124. Rao, J.P.; Banzon, M.T.; Weiss, A.B.; et al. Treatment of unstable intertrochanteric fractures with anatomic reduction and compression hip screw fixation. Clin Orthop 175:65–71, 1983.

125. Rizzo, P.F.; Gould, E.S.; Lyden, J.P.; et al. Diagnosis of occult fractures about the hip. Magnetic resonance imaging compared with bone-scanning [see comments]. J Bone Joint Surg Am 75:395–401, 1993.

126. Roberts, A.; Rooney, T.; Loone J. A comparison of the functional results of anatomic and medial displacement valgus nailing of intertrochanteric fractures of the femur. J Trauma 12:341, 1972.

127. Rogers, F.B.; Shackford, S.R.; Keller, M.S. Early fixation reduces morbidity and mortality in elderly patients with hip fractures from low-impact falls. J Trauma 39:261–265, 1995.

128. Sarmiento, A. Avoidance of complication of internal fixation of intertrochanteric fractures: Experience with 250 consecutive cases. Clin Orthop 53:47, 1967.

129. Sarmiento, A. Intertrochanteric fractures of the femur: 150-degree-angle nail-plate fixation and early rehabilitation: A preliminary report of 100 cases. J Bone Joint Surg Am 45:706, 1963.

130. Sarmiento, A. Valgus osteotomy technique for unstable intertrochanteric fractures. In: The Hip. St. Louis, Mosby–Year Book, 1975.

131. Schatzker, J.; Ha'eri, G.B.; Chapman, M. Methylmethacrylate as an adjunct in the internal fixation of intertrochanteric fractures of the femur. J Trauma 18:732–735, 1978.

132. Sexson, S.B.; Lehner, J.T. Factors affecting hip fracture mortality. J Orthop Trauma 1:298–305, 1987.

133. Sherk, H.H.; Foster, M.D. Hip fractures: Condylocephalic rod versus compression screw. Clin Orthop 192:255–259, 1985.

134. Simmermacher, R.K.; Bosch, A.M.; Van der Werken, C. The AO/ASIF-proximal femoral nail (PFN): A new device for the treatment of unstable proximal femoral fractures. Injury 30:327–332, 1999.

135. Singh, M.; Nagrath, A.R.; Maini P.S. Changes in trabecular pattern of the upper end of the femur as an index of osteoporosis. J Bone Joint Surg Am 52:457–467, 1970.

136. Sorensen, T.S.; Colding, H.; Schroeder, E.; et al. The penetration of cefazolin, erythromycin and methicillin into human bone tissue. Acta Orthop Scand 49:549–553, 1978.

137. Steinberg, G.G.; Desai, S.S.; Kornwitz, N.A.; et al. The intertrochanteric hip fracture. A retrospective analysis. Orthopedics 11:265–273, 1988.

138. Stern, M.B.; Angerman, A. Comminuted intertrochanteric fractures treated with a Leinbach prosthesis. Clin Orthop 218:75–80, 1987.

139. Swiontkowski, M.F. Ipsilateral femoral shaft and hip fractures. Orthop Clin North Am 18:73–84, 1987.

140. Uden, G.; Nilsson, B. Hip fracture frequent in hospital. Acta Orthop Scand 57:428–430, 1986.

141. Vahl, A.C.; Dunki Jacobs, P.B.; Patka, P.; et al. Hemiarthroplasty in elderly, debilitated patients with an unstable femoral fracture in the trochanteric region. Acta Orthop Belg 60:274–279, 1994.

142. Wahl, C.; Baumgaertner, M. Intramedullary fixation: A more efficient technique for pertrochanteric fractures of the hip? Presented at the 15th Annual Meeting of the Orthopaedic Trauma Association, Charlotte, NC, 1999.

143. Ward, F.O. Human Anatomy. London, Renshaw, 1838.

144. Watson, J.T.; Moed, B.R.; Cramer, K.E.; et al. Comparison of the compression hip screw with the Medoff sliding plate for intertrochanteric fractures. Clin Orthop 348:79–86, 1998.

145. White, B.L.; Fisher, W.D.; Laurin, C.A. Rate of mortality for elderly patients after fracture of the hip in the 1980s. J Bone Joint Surg Am 69:1335–1340, 1987.

146. Winter, W.G. Nonoperative treatment of proximal femoral fractures in the demented, nonambulatory patient. Clin Orthop 218:97–103, 1987.

147. Yian, E.H.; Banerji, I.; Matthews, L.S. Optimal side plate fixation for unstable intertrochanteric hip fractures. J Orthop Trauma 11:254–259, 1997.

148. Yoshimine, F.; Latta, L.L.; Milne, E.L. Sliding characteristics of compression hip screws in the intertrochanteric fracture: A clinical study. J Orthop Trauma 7:348–353, 1993.

149. Zain Elabdien B.S.; Olerud, S.; Karlstrom, G. The influence of age on the morphology of trochanteric fracture. Arch Orthop Trauma Surg 103:156–161, 1984.

150. Zuckerman, J.D.; Sakales, S.R.; Fabian, D.R.; et al. Hip fractures in geriatric patients. Results of an interdisciplinary hospital care program. Clin Orthop 274:213–225, 1992.

151. Zuckerman, J.D.; Skovron, M.L.; Koval, K.J.; et al. Postoperative complications and mortality associated with operative delay in older patients who have a fracture of the hip. J Bone Joint Surg Am 77:1551–1556, 1995.

# 50

## Reconstructive Total Hip Replacement after Proximal Femoral Injuries

Dana C. Mears, M.D., Ph.D.
Sridhar M. Durbhakula, M.D.
John H. Velyvis, M.D.

In the aftermath of trauma to the proximal femur, a patient may present for an evaluation of one or more complaints that merit consideration for treatment with a total hip arthroplasty (THA).[8, 20, 30, 38, 51] Similar to a patient who presents with degenerative arthritis, the most frequent complaint of a post-traumatic patient is a painful hip or a corresponding referred pain. Occasionally the pain is due to a complicating factor such as an occult infection of the primary traumatized site, a nonunion, neurogenic pain, or the presence of scar tissue. Additional complaints may include stiffness of the hip, the presence of a fixed deformity, or a limb-length discrepancy. The presence of one or more complicating factors such as a wound infection, massive heterotopic bone, a femoral nonunion or malunion, or a neuromuscular weakness may render the surgical reconstruction immeasurably more difficult than a conventional primary THA. This chapter reviews the preoperative assessment of the patient, the indications for the surgical reconstruction, the optimal timing, and various technical considerations.

## PERTINENT HISTORY AND PHYSICAL EXAMINATION

At the time of the patient's presentation, a detailed evaluation of the nature and timing of the initial injury is necessary. The site or sites of the injury, the magnitude of the provocative blow, the presence of abnormalities of the wound, and the types of the initial conservative or operative treatment are characterized. Any complicating event is documented, such as a superficial, deep, or intra-articular wound infection; a traumatic or iatrogenic sciatic nerve palsy; the presence of heterotopic bone; or a thromboembolic event. Also, late complications are assessed, including a femoral nonunion, malunion, post-traumatic arthrosis of the hip, or avascular necrosis of the

femoral head. The general health of the patient and the presence of significant co-morbidities such as ischemic heart disease, immune suppression, or a central neurologic impairment with dementia, involuntary movements, or posturing of the lower extremities are evaluated. Behavioral status, including a history of substance abuse, is assessed, along with vocational background and sporting or recreational interests. Overall, many patients who present with post-traumatic arthrosis of the hip after a proximal femoral fracture are young adult men with a history of drug or alcohol abuse, a heavy laboring vocation, and an interest in motorcycling or other self-destructive activity. This type of patient is unlikely to have a long-term satisfactory outcome after a THA. The orthopaedist has to balance the short-term goals of the patient, such as the relief of incapacitating hip pain, with the surgical complexities that would accompany a periprosthetic fracture or an extensive area of lysis around a loose and failed component. Therapeutic alternatives to a THA merit consideration, including appropriate alterations in the lifestyle of the patient.

Although complications following high-energy trauma account for most of the clinical presentations, a rapidly growing subgroup is the elderly population who present following minor trauma. In this instance, the presence of preexisting degenerative arthrosis of the hip along with impaired healing and remodeling of fragile, osteopenic bone may account for a femoral nonunion or malunion and apparent post-traumatic arthrosis.[17, 25, 30] An elderly patient with significant medical co-morbidities may be unable to withstand an arduous reconstructive procedure with significant intraoperative blood loss. If operative treatment is selected for an elderly osteopenic patient, both the objectives of the late reconstruction, such as the restoration of limb length, and the surgical methods, such as the use of a cemented femoral component, are carefully assessed and prioritized. In an attempt to limit the magnitude of the surgical procedure, the THA may be undertaken to alleviate hip pain without an effort to correct a limb length discrepancy (LLD).

On physical examination of the patient, the appearance of the hip is assessed for the appearance of post-traumatic or surgical scars, muscular atrophy, a femoral deformity, a limb-length discrepancy, or a sign of a chronic infection such as a draining sinus. The range of motion of the hip is recorded, along with the presence of a fixed contracture. The strength of the hip abductors and of the other principal hip muscles is assessed. If the hip is totally stiff, a visible or palpable volitional contraction of the hip abductors may be the only available confirmation that the muscle units are intact. Both knees and the contralateral hip along with the lumbosacral spine are carefully assessed for their mobility, stability, and neurologic integrity. The pattern of gait is evaluated for the presence of an antalgic or short-leg gait, a stiff-hip pattern, or a gluteus medius lurch. Alternative causes of a limp are considered, including problematic neighboring or contralateral joints, the lumbosacral spine, or the presence of a generalized neuromuscular disorder.

## RADIOGRAPHIC EVALUATION

High-quality radiographs of the hip, pelvis, and femur of known magnification are needed along with suitable templates of the proposed implants. Supplementary images such as inlet, outlet, obturator, and iliac oblique views may be necessary to examine a concomitant deformity of the pelvis and acetabulum or the presence of heterotopic bone around the hip.[45] Either a conventional or preferably a computed tomography (CT) scan can be used to evaluate a limb-length deformity. In the presence of a marked distortion of the hip and femur, a three-dimensional CT scan may be helpful to appreciate the complex rotational element of the problem.[42] Although it is costly, for an exceptionally complex deformity, possibly secondary to a lengthy comminuted or a segmental fracture, a life-sized plastic model can be prepared from the data that is used to assemble a three-dimensional CT scan. In this way, the surgeon can actually rehearse the preoperative plan with respect to the sites for an osteotomy and the optimal technique for a correction of the deformity. If a significant femoral bow is present, multiple lateral radiographic projections taken at slightly differing degrees of rotation facilitate an assessment for the optimal configuration and alignment of the femoral stem.

## INDICATIONS FOR SURGERY

The principal indication for a THA after trauma to the hip and proximal femur is disabling pain secondary to the presence of post-traumatic degenerative arthritis or avascular necrosis of the hip. In many of the patients, however, the presence of secondary complicating features of the problem may contribute to the indications for reconstructive surgery. The presence of heterotopic bone and secondary stiffness of the hip, a proximal femoral non-union or malunion, or an associated limb-length discrepancy are examples of concomitant factors that may be addressed at the time of a THA.

Occasionally, a painful hip is a minor factor; the principal complaint is the presence of a florid proximal femoral deformity, stiffness of the hip, or another factor. Because the relevant secondary factor may be a legitimate indication for the reconstructive procedure, the need for the associated THA merits careful inspection. In one case, possibly with marked heterotopic bone and the presence of a proximal femoral deformity, removal of the heterotopic ossification (HO) and performance of a femoral osteotomy may be appropriate procedures. In an alternative situation, with a painless and stiff hip secondary to the combination of proliferative HO and marked post-traumatic degenerative arthritis, removal of the HO along with a THA may be necessary to achieve a favorable outcome. Nevertheless, whenever the patient does not experience preoperative pain, he or she needs to be aware that the surgeon cannot guarantee that the postoperative outcome will be free of residual pain. Before a reconstructive procedure, this concern has to be emphasized to the patient.

## CONTRAINDICATIONS FOR SURGERY

In common with other reconstructive procedures, the presence of a co-morbidity that jeopardizes the life of the patient during or after the operation is a contraindication. Most of these factors are temporary and subject to an adequate correction after the application of appropriate medical management. The presence of a neurologic disorder that jeopardizes the stability of the hip or renders the patient vulnerable to frequent falls and premature failure of the arthroplasty is a contraindication. Rarely, the traumatic loss of abductor muscle function limits the feasibility of the procedure. For the trauma victim in whom behavioral problems or the use of excessive alcohol and drugs heavily compromises the likelihood of prolonged function of the arthroplasty, an alternative method of treatment may be in the patient's best interest.

In a younger patient with mild or minimal post-traumatic arthrosis and a nonunion or malunion of the proximal femur that is secondary to a failure of the initial treatment, an attempt is made to salvage the native femoral head and neck and the integrity of the hip joint. In either of these situations, an open reduction and internal fixation of the proximal femur is recommended. For an elderly patient with osteopenic bone and a large "windshield wiper" hole around a failed hip screw, salvage of the femoral head may not have a great likelihood for a successful outcome. Likewise, in a young adult in whom an attempt to manage a nonunion of the femoral neck has failed and available bone stock is extraordinarily limited, a hemiarthroplasty or a THA may be indicated. In a young adult, however, every realistic attempt is made to preserve viable bone stock and the native hip joint. This objective follows the potential long-term complications of an arthroplasty, notably, aseptic loosening and premature failure.

Before a THA, an active infection involving the hip or

**Figure 50–1.** This 24-year-old man underwent a cementless total hip arthroplasty (THA) for post-traumatic arthrosis of the left hip, along with a hardware removal and a resection of grade III heterotopic ossification (HO) around the hip. Previously, he was involved in an motor vehicle accident and sustained a closed head injury, a T-type acetabular fracture, and an ipsilateral femoral shaft fracture. An extended iliofemoral incision had been used to undertake an open reduction with internal fixation of the acetabulum and an intramedullary nailing of the femur. After the THA, the patient developed a recurrence of grade IV HO that resulted in an effective fusion of the left hip and knee, despite the administration of prophylactic irradiation therapy. One year later, the heterotopic bone was removed in an extensive procedure. Afterward, the patient achieved 0° to 80° of hip motion and 0° to 60° of knee motion. *A*, Nine months after the THA, an anteroposterior (AP) view of the hip displays an effective hip fusion, with grade IV HO. *B*, An accompanying AP view of the distal femur displays the extent of the HO.

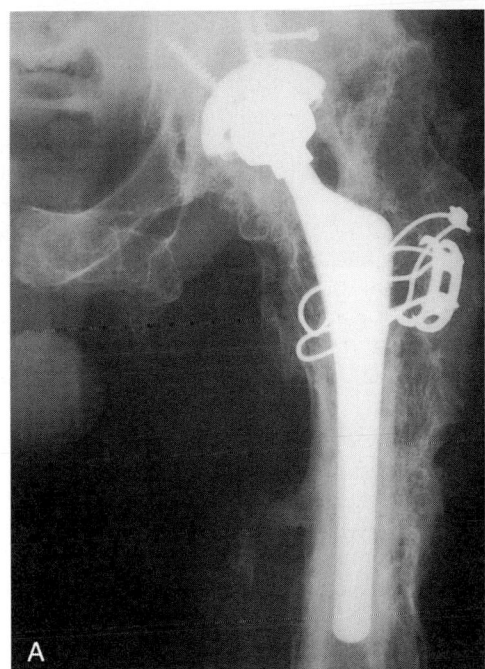
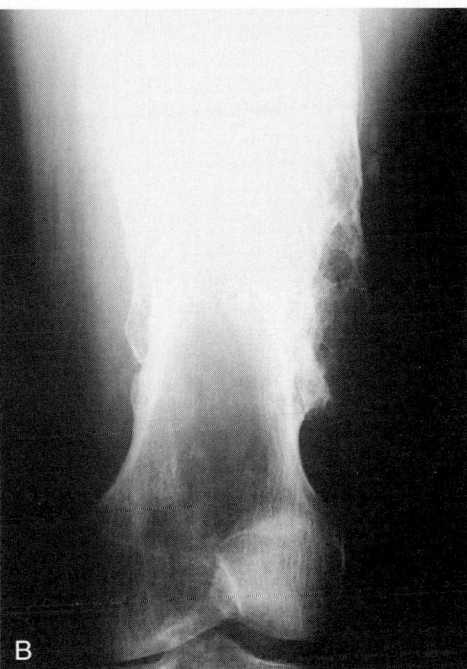

proximal femur has to be eradicated by taking appropriate measures, including the potential removal of retained hardware and débridement of the hip along with an individualized regimen of intravenous or oral antibiotics.[16] Consultation with an infectious disease specialist is highly recommended.

## TIMING OF SURGERY

Most patients present many months after the initial traumatic event, when their general condition has stabilized and the long-term fate of the hip and proximal femur is clearly evident. For such a case, usually the timing of the procedure is a matter of convenience for the patient and the medical staff. In the presence of post-traumatic arthritis of the hip that is not symptomatic to the point of disabling pain, an initial delay in the reconstructive procedure may be prudent. A smaller number of patients present soon after the initial injury. Following the initial course of conservative or operative management, a patient may present with a marked malalignment, a collapse of the femoral head, heterotopic bone, or a wound infection. Particularly in the face of a wound infection, prompt initiation of treatment, including surgical débridement and administration of antibiotic therapy, is indicated. When a surgical or post-traumatic wound is incompletely healed or possesses a persistent eschar, the reconstructive procedure is delayed until complete healing is evident. When an unacceptable malalignment of the femur accompanies the post-traumatic arthrosis of the hip, we prefer to address both aspects of the problem in a single procedure. Not

only does this strategy minimize the overall duration of the recovery period but the concomitant correction of an unacceptable axial deformity optimizes the likelihood of an uneventful healing of a delayed union or nonunion.

A more controversial situation is the presence of massive Brooker grade III or IV HO around the hip.[10] The typical patient is a young adult obese man with a history of a closed head injury. We prefer to wait 1 year after the initial injury before the excision of HO and supplementary reconstructive surgery. This deferral seems to lessen the risk for a recurrence, although it certainly does not guarantee a favorable outcome (Fig. 50–1). On the day after the excision of HO, irradiation therapy with 700 cGy is used to decrease the likelihood for recurrent HO.[3] Also, indomethicin, 75 mg per day, may be given for 6 weeks, although variable results of this treatment have been reported.[35] Another situation that favors a deferral of a secondary arthroplasty for 6 months or more is that of a comatose or an intubated patient with multiple trauma who was treated for an extended period in an intensive care unit. Generally, such a patient undergoes marked weight loss with the onset of malnutrition, which requires many months to resolve. During this period, a secondary reconstructive procedure predisposes the patient to a postoperative wound infection or a dehiscence of the surgical incision. In addition, such a patient may not be psychologically able to cope with the recovery period to participate in an intensive course of physical therapy. Before undertaking the arthroplasty, these parameters should be optimized.

For a patient who has had a recent thromboembolic event, a secondary procedure is delayed for several months whenever possible. Following a confirmation of the event, the patient is treated with a therapeutic level of anticoagulation.[2, 48] At surgery, the anticoagulation is briefly terminated and is resumed afterward. Following a thromboembolic event, if an urgent indication for surgery arises, an inferior vena cava filter may be inserted.[15]

## PREOPERATIVE EVALUATION AND DECISION MAKING

Two principal considerations dictate the general features of the surgical strategy: the anatomic site and the type of tissue involved in the reconstructive problem. The proximal femur is subcategorized into the femoral head and neck, the intertrochanteric and subtrochanteric regions, and the femoral shaft. The site of a nonunion, HO, or retained hardware dictates the options for the surgical incision and the nature of the reconstructive procedure, including the type of femoral stem to be used. In Table 50–1, the most common problems for specific regions of the femur and the general principles of reconstruction are listed, including the selection of the femoral stem, the potential complicating factors, and

special considerations including the use of bone graft and fixation devices.

The second consideration is the type of tissue involved in the reconstruction. A compromised resiliency and vascularity of the skin around a traumatized hip may be manifest by the presence of a persistent open wound, a surgical scar, or a split-thickness skin graft. Heavy blunt trauma damages the cutaneous envelope so that it is predisposed to ischemic damage from a surgical incision. When the surgical field involves a large area of compromised skin, an alteration in the surgical approach is advisable to minimize the risk of a postoperative sloughing of the wound.[11] In a more limited case, the incision can be displaced by a few centimeters outside the border of the scarified zone. To compensate for this repositioning, usually an increase in the length of the incision is necessary. When a large area of compromised skin is centrally located at the site for a posterior incision to the hip, one option is to perform an anterior approach. If the entire lateral aspect of the hip has compromised skin, a Smith-Peterson or extended iliofemoral approach, with a preservation of the greater trochanter and gluteal insertion, can be performed through the neighboring normal soft tissues. If an extensile incision is selected, postoperative prophylaxis against HO merits consideration.

---

**TABLE 50–1**

### Guidelines for Performing a Total Hip Replacement after a Prior Proximal Femoral Fracture

| Site of Femoral Fracture | Potential Complicating Factors | Selection of the Components | Additional Considerations | Bone Grafting | Fixational Devices |
|---|---|---|---|---|---|
| Femoral head | Associated acetabular fracture<br>Heterotopic ossification<br>Retained hardware | Standard components<br>Cemented stem in osteoporotic bone | Removal of heterotopic bone (+/−)<br>Restoration of weakened abductor lever arm<br>Correction of femoral offset<br>Removal of hardware (+/−) | None | None |
| Femoral neck | Avascular necrosis<br>Heterotopic ossification<br>Nonunion/malunion<br>Retained hardware | Standard components<br>Cemented stem in osteoporotic bone | Removal of heterotopic bone (+/−)<br>Restoration of weakened abductor lever arm<br>Correction of femoral offset<br>Removal of hardware (+/−) | None | None |
| Intertrochanteric region | Limb-length discrepancy<br>Structural deformity<br>Nonunion/malunion<br>Retained hardware | Standard components<br>Proximal femoral replacement stem<br>Collarless, polished stem for impaction grafting | Correction of deformity<br>Correction of shortening<br>Approximation of displaced fragments<br>Hardware removal (+/−) | Femoral head autograft<br>Impaction grafting with morselized cancellous allograft | Cables<br>Mesh |
| Subtrochanteric region and proximal femoral shaft | Osteolysis<br>Limb-length discrepancy<br>Structural deformity<br>Nonunion/malunion<br>Retained hardware | Cemented or cementless prosthesis with long stem<br>Segmental replacement stem for osteolysis | Quadricepsplasty<br>Correction of deformity<br>Correction of shortening<br>Approximation of displaced fragments<br>Hardware removal (+/−) | Femoral head autograft<br>Impaction grafting with morselized cancellous allograft<br>Strut allograft<br>Segmental femoral replacement allograft | Cables<br>Mesh<br>Special plates |

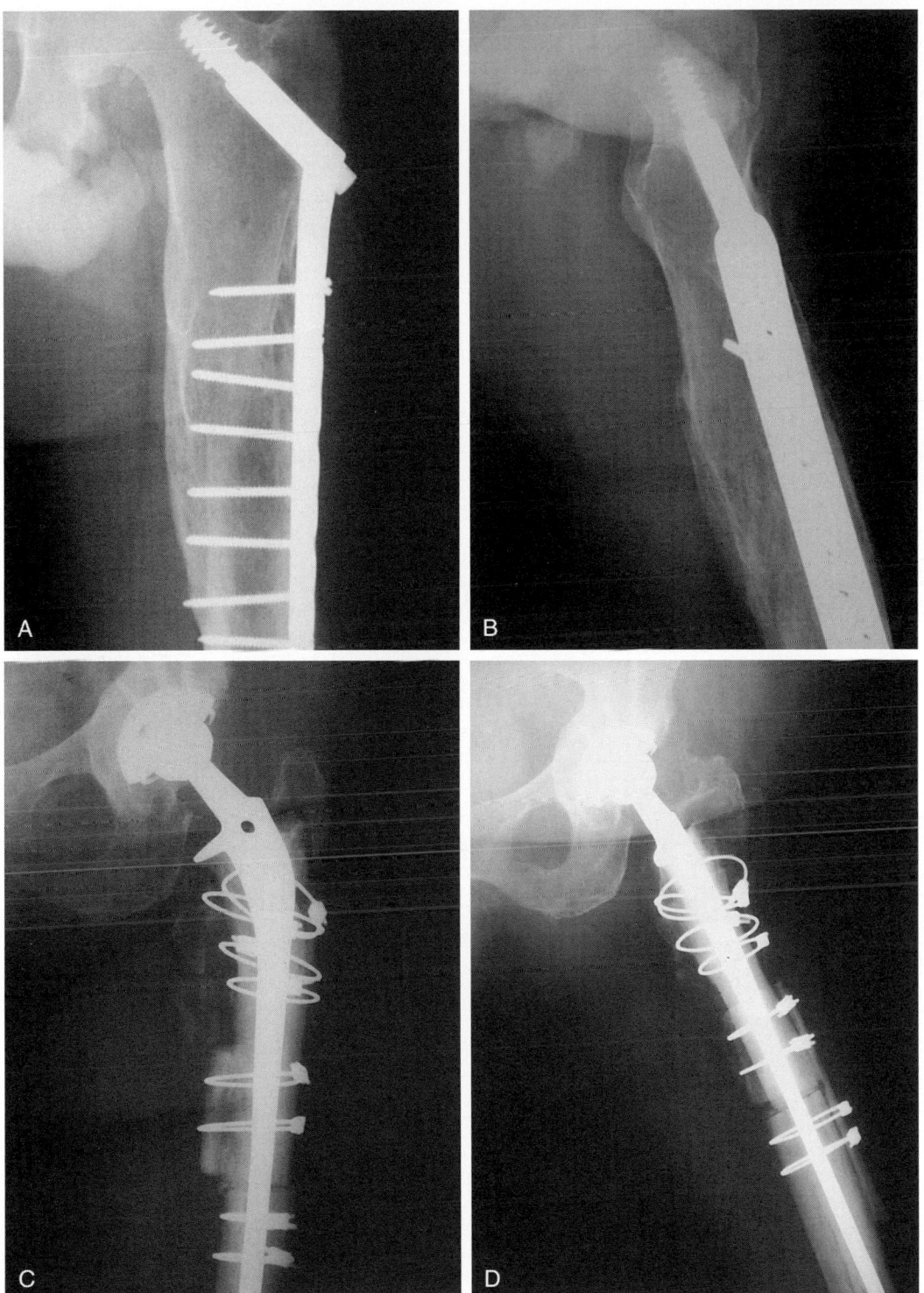

**FIGURE 50–2.** This 33-year-old man sustained a proximal femoral shaft fracture, for which a hip screw with a lengthy side plate was used. An anatomic reduction was not attained, although the fracture had healed uneventfully. Six years later, he presented with a painful arthritic hip. A hybrid total hip arthroplasty was performed, accompanied by a femoral osteotomy and use of a long femoral stem, strut allografts, and cable fixation. The cables were used proximally and distally in a prophylactic manner, in view of the compromised strength of the osteopenic bone and the presence of empty screw holes. *A,* Preoperative anteroposterior (AP) view to display the proximal femoral malunion. *B,* Preoperative lateral view. *C,* Postoperative AP view. *D,* Postoperative lateral view.

A more complicated problem is the presence of a large soft tissue defect in the lateral aspect of the hip, secondary to the traumatic loss of the skin and part of the gluteal musculature, and typically treated with a split-thickness skin graft. A preoperative consultation with a plastic surgeon is advisable to plan the soft tissue reconstruction that may include the use of a local muscle flap or a free vascularized musculocutaneous flap (Fig. 50–2). If the latter solution is used, then the plastic procedure is performed as a preliminary stage. Once the soft tissues have completely healed, the orthopaedic reconstruction is undertaken. During the orthopaedic approach, the presence of the plastic surgeon is advisable to minimize the risk of damaging the vessels that nourish the flap.

For a case with prior radiation therapy to the hip, usually the patient presents with a pathologic fracture and possibly with avascular necrosis of the hip.[7] The extent of radiation necrosis to the proximal femur and the acetabulum may be difficult to fully appreciate with standard radiographs. With the subtle nature of the radiographic changes, a strong degree of suspicion by the orthopaedist is necessary. Although the management of this problem is beyond the scope of this chapter, a case with extensive radiation of the hip may be a contraindication for a THA, especially in a younger adult.

## Heterotopic Bone

Following a traumatic injury to the hip, and especially in a young adult man who also sustains a closed head injury, a highly variable extent of HO formation may arise in the periacetabular muscles and adjacent soft tissues. In the most extensive case, an enormous area of involvement may extend from the iliac crest to the distal insertion of the quadriceps muscle at the knee (see Fig. 50–1). If extensive HO is documented in the plain radiographs of the hip, supplementary iliac and obturator oblique views are needed to visualize the anterior and posterior aspects of the hip.[45] A CT scan permits the delineation of soft tissue planes between the deep muscles around the hip and the capsule. The most sinister type of HO permeates the capsule and deep muscles so that all of the normal mobile interfaces are lost. In the presence of grade III or IV HO, usually a CT scan is necessary to determine the severity of post-traumatic arthrosis of the hip. In a questionable case, an arthrotomy of the hip, undertaken as part of the removal of HO, may be needed to confirm the degree of intra-articular damage and whether a THA is necessary.

When the anterior and posterior aspects of the hip are involved in the HO, both anterior and posterior exposures are necessary to complete the excision. We prefer to use a triradiate incision with a preservation of the greater trochanter.[41] During removal of the HO, great care is needed to ensure that the normal bony architecture is not excised. Intraoperative image intensification is recommended to inspect the standard bony landmarks such as the acetabular rim and the base of the greater trochanter. If an acetabular plate is identified, it is left in situ as a marker of the intact posterior column. If, subsequently, further HO regenerates, and another surgical procedure on the hip is necessary, the plate is a valuable landmark for the normal pelvic surface.

## Contracture of the Hip and Post-traumatic Fusion

When a prior proximal femoral fracture with an accompanying dislocation of the hip or an acetabular fracture was managed surgically, a secondary reconstruction may be hampered by dense scar tissue, and, not infrequently, an effective hip fusion. The surgical plan is designed to cope with this anticipated problem.[40] A somewhat enlarged incision is needed to facilitate the surgical release of the capsular adhesions, the short external rotators, and potentially the hip flexors and adductors. If the hip is exceedingly stiff, following the initial deep exposure, the femoral neck is provisionally osteotomized in its mid portion. With external rotation of the lower extremity, the femoral neck guide is applied to the conventional site on the intertrochanteric region and the standard osteotomy of the base of the femoral neck is made. Subsequently, the femoral head is dislocated or, if necessary, morselized to assist in its removal.

## Weakness of the Gluteal Musculature

If the gluteus medius and gluteus minimus are markedly weakened by a traumatically or an iatrogenically induced gluteal nerve palsy, lumbosacral plexopathy, or other mechanism, the stability of a THA is markedly compromised. If the gluteal muscles are not functional, then the arthroplastic hip is highly vulnerable to recurrent dislocations.[7, 20] When the hip is highly mobile, the preoperative assessment of the gluteal strength is straightforward. In the presence of exuberant HO, or of an effective hip fusion, the assessment of the gluteal function is immeasurably more difficult. Although a clinical evaluation of the muscular function is preferred, the use of electromyelographic studies is a suitable alternative.

For a patient with an exceedingly stiff hip or effectively fused hip and with marked weakness of the hip abductors, a THA may have an unpredictable impact on the patient's gait.[13, 40] A patient who could walk without a walking aid before the surgery may require the use of a cane or a crutch. After the arthroplasty, an instability of the hip and an inability to stand on one leg may develop. The degree to which these problems resolve is uncertain. Before a reconstructive procedure, a detailed discussion with the patient about these possible postoperative problems is necessary.

## Quadriceps Contracture

In the presence of extensive HO or fixed flexion contracture of the hip or knee, the quadriceps muscle may become secondarily contracted. Although this problem may be suspected preoperatively, it is confirmed at the time of the THA after a mobilization of the hip joint from its sources of intrinsic contracture. Once the problem is identified, a quadriceps release is performed. If the muscular contribution to the contracture is not corrected, the hip retains the fixed flexion contracture. In the early postoperative period, the healing capsule and other periarticular tissues all become involved in the process to further compromise the situation. For the quadriceps plasty, Dr. Mears prefers the technique proposed by Judet,[44] whereby the quadriceps muscle is released from its contracted bony origins and the affected segment of the femoral shaft. A considerable lengthening of the standard incision is necessary to visualize from the anterior-inferior iliac spine to at least the midportion of the femoral shaft. The principal complication of the method is a deep wound infection. If that scenario ensues, usually an extensive infection occurs. Despite a timely débridement and the use of appropriate antibiotic therapy, a marked contracture of the hip generally recurs. After the use of a quadriceps plasty, extensive physical therapy, with active and gentle passive range-of-motion exercises of the hip and knee, is essential, along with progressive resistance exercises for the quadriceps.

## Femoral Deformity

Post-traumatic deformities that are distal to the base of the femoral neck are the principal concern for a conversion hip replacement, as a more proximal deformity is excised as part of the THA.[30, 50, 51] One type of minor deformity occurs when a portion of the intertrochanteric region or the proximal femoral shaft possesses a single large displaced fragment while the remainder of that segment is properly aligned.[5, 53] In this instance, the displaced segment is mobilized and anatomically reduced. The fixation can be achieved with a combination of cerclage wires, cables, and strut allograft along with the use of a femoral stem that traverses the region to obtain effective distal anchorage in the intact bone.[58] In the presence of a minor displacement in the intertrochanteric region, a special configuration of stem may be identified radiographically that can be inserted into the deformed bone without a correction of the deformity. Similarly, if a mild deformity with adequate preservation of the axial alignment is located near the anticipated tip of the femoral stem, one possibility is to use a somewhat shorter model of stem. At the level of the lesser trochanter and distal to it, usually the deformity has to be corrected, either before or at the time of the THA (see Fig. 50–2). Generally, a combined procedure is preferred to achieve the most rapid recovery. For up to a year after the initial trauma, generally, at the time of the reconstruction, the original fracture line is readily disassembled by a careful removal of the callus that is distinctly softer than normal bone. This technique affords the greatest likelihood of accurately restoring the original configuration of the bone. If the bony deformity has been present for a year or more, usually an osteotomy through the healed and remodeled bone is necessary, which is a more complicated task. The healed callus contributes to the deformity and obscures the anatomic contour of the bone. Intraoperative image intensification is useful to assess the restoration of axial alignment. With the small field size of some models of image intensifier, the use of standard radiographic views may be necessary. To immobilize an osteotomy in the upper femoral shaft, the use of a long-stemmed component that extends at least 8 to 10 cm beyond the osteotomy site is preferred. For a more distal deformity, which is located at the distal tip of a standard stem, an alternative technique is to stabilize the osteotomy with a plate. Special models are available that permit the use of cables to anchor the proximal segment adjacent to the femoral stem. For an osteotomy that is accompanied by a bone defect, the excised femoral head is available as a morselized or a structural bone graft.

Another option is to use femoral strut allografts that are immobilized with cerclage cables and possibly a supplementary plate.

## Femoral Nonunion or an Extensive Osseous Defect

From the intertrochanteric region to the midfemoral shaft, the presence of a nonunion or the traumatic loss of bone influences the type of reconstruction.[38] Occasionally, an apparent osseous defect actually represents a large, markedly displaced and nonunited fragment. In this instance, the fragment can be repositioned and stabilized. If the bone is absent, markedly comminuted, or otherwise unsuitable for use, the corresponding defect may be obliterated with autograft from the excised femoral head. For an exceptionally large defect, alternative methods of reconstruction are available.[21–23, 27] Particularly for a young adult, the restoration of bone substance is desirable, with a view toward an anticipated revision arthroplasty.[34] The application of impaction grafting, with the use of autograft, or, if necessary, morselized bone allograft, is a highly satisfactory technique (Fig. 50–3).[18, 19] The defective region is buttressed with the use of heavy stainless steel mesh that is wrapped around the defective femoral segment and supported with cerclage cables. We prefer the use of a cemented, collarless, polished stem, as first described by Ling and associates.[36] As an alternative method, when a circumferential bone loss is encountered, the use of a structural allograft is another viable technique.[4] For an older patient or for one with a shorter life expectancy, and especially to cope with a defect in the intertrochanteric or subtrochanteric region, another method is to use a special replacement stem as a cementless or a cemented model.[37, 49] This latter technique is less involved than the use of impaction grafting. For a younger patient and one with a proximal defect, the use of a fully coated, porous, cementless stem is preferred (Fig. 50–4). If the osseous defect extends distal to the femoral isthmus, or in the presence of an elderly and osteopenic patient, the use of cement can be anticipated to achieve stability of the stem. In either case, one of the modular designs is useful to permit the selection of the optimal length of implant during the procedure. The previous generation of custom stems is excessively costly and fails to provide this intraoperative flexibility.

## Limb Length Discrepancy

When an LLD of more than 2.5 cm accompanies post-traumatic arthrosis of the hip, a reconstructive arthroplasty affords the opportunity to decrease or eliminate this deformity.[1, 26] A careful evaluation is necessary to identify the presence of a fixed flexion contracture of the hip that creates an apparent LLD. The site and the magnitude of the LLD are determined from preoperative CT.[9, 31] It is prudent to emphasize to the patient that the precise degree of correction of the LLD cannot be guaranteed. Intraoperatively, the presence of soft tissue contractures may hamper the restoration of limb length.

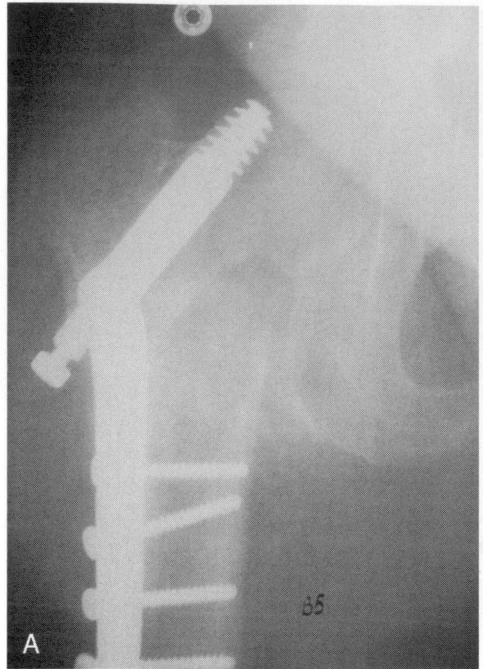
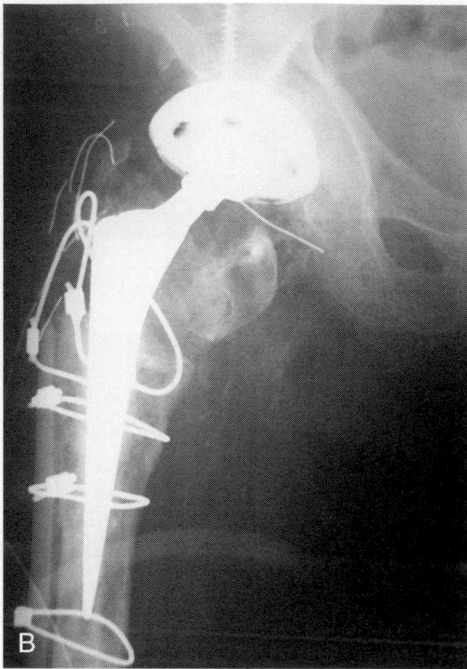

**Figure 50–3.** This 79-year-old osteoporotic woman experienced a nonunion of a peritrochanteric fracture that had occurred 9 months earlier. A hybrid total hip arthroplasty was performed, along with an impaction grafting and buttressing of the proximal femur with two strut femoral allografts and cable fixation. A femoral head autograft was used to restore the calcar region. *A,* Preoperative anteroposterior (AP) view. *B,* Postoperative AP view.

Especially when a traumatically induced injury to the sciatic nerve or the lumbosacral plexus occurred, the limb lengthening is vulnerable to provoke a recurrence or a deterioration of the nerve palsy. At the time of the initial trauma, a transient or subtle injury to the sciatic nerve may not be detected. For post-traumatic lengthening of more than 2.5 cm, the use of intraoperative neurologic monitoring with continuous electromyelographic studies or somatosensory-evoked potential monitoring is recommended.[28, 29] The former method provides a more accu-

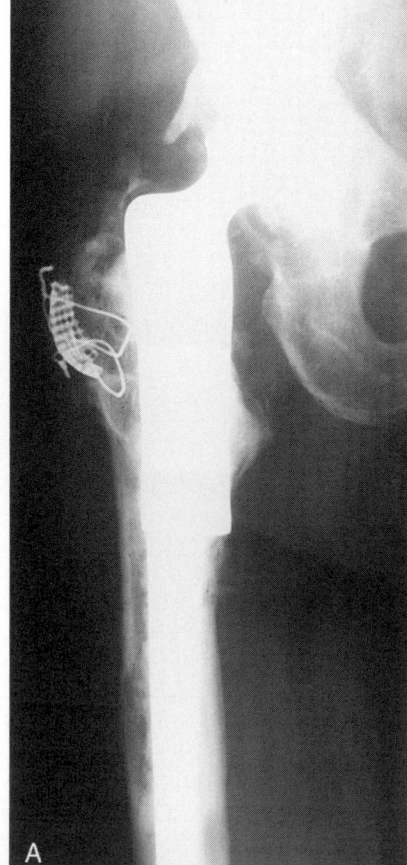
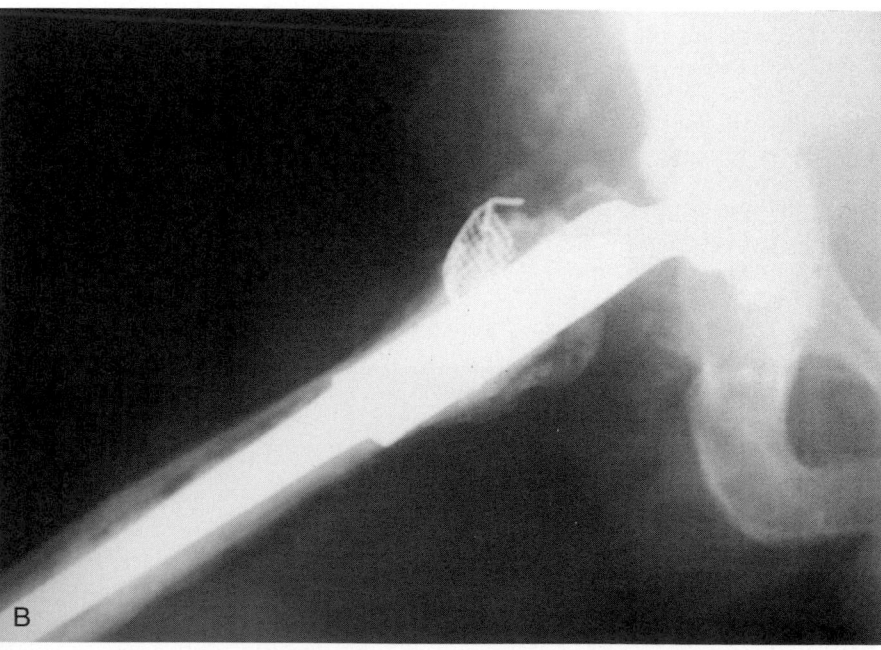

**Figure 50–4.** A 54-year-old man sustained an open proximal femoral shaft fracture and an ipsilateral femoral neck fracture, for which a débridement and an insertion of a hip screw were performed. The proximal femoral fragments were not accurately reduced and underwent a partial resorption. The femoral head developed avascular necrosis, and secondary degenerative arthritic changes ensued. A cementless total hip arthroplasty (THA) with a proximal femoral replacement was inserted, along with the use of mesh and wires to attach the greater trochanter. *A,* Anteroposterior view obtained 10 years after the THA. *B,* Accompanying lateral view.

rate and rapid indication of neurologic injury than the latter. Once the limb lengthening exceeds 4 cm, the incidence of a postoperative neurologic complication increases rapidly.[13]

At the site of the lengthening, the resultant bone defect can be obliterated by an open reduction of displaced bone fragments, or a segmental replacement type of stem can be used. In either case, the knee is kept in a flexed position, greater than 90°, while the hip is extended as much as possible. This position affords the maximal relaxation for the sciatic nerve. Immediately after the procedure, the knee is maintained in a flexed position until the patient is sufficiently alert to undertake the initial provocative straight leg test.

## Retained Hardware

When a removal of retained hardware is necessary, a full complement of removal tools is organized to ensure the availability of the proper devices to permit the efficient removal of broken implants. If the hardware has been retained for a period of years, it may be covered with HO that requires a preliminary excision before a disassembly of the device. Occasionally, the bone deep to the device is highly defective so that the plate has become the effective sidewall of the bone. This problem is difficult to detect even with a close scrutiny of the preoperative radiographs (Fig. 50–5). To cope with this problem, following the removal of the screws, the plate can be retained to buttress the femur and anchored with cerclage cables. An impaction grafting permits the restoration of bone to surround the cemented type of femoral stem. If the plate is removed, one technique for the restoration of the bone employs a structural allograft, and another option utilizes impaction grafting with supportive mesh and cerclage cables. As an alternative, a lengthy stem can be used to bridge the defective region.

Once the screws are removed, during the insertion of a broach or a cementless stem, the femoral segment is vulnerable to fracture through the empty screw holes. A prophylactic application of a cerclage cable or wire to the affected segment affords a considerable protection. If the segment is further weakened by an accompanying muscle atrophy or bony defect, the application of one or two strut allografts, along with a plate or mesh and cerclage cables, provides a greater degree of support. When the use of a cemented stem is planned, occlusion of the empty screw holes during the cementation can be achieved by a temporary reinsertion of the screws into the lateral cortex. Admittedly, this maneuver does not inhibit extrusion of cement through the medial screw holes during the pressurization of the cement and insertion of the stem. Another effective method to occlude a variety of defects such as empty screw holes is impaction grafting. For a larger hole that follows a removal of a hip screw, obliteration with a structural autograft from the femoral head is preferred.

When a proximal femoral side plate is removed at the time of a reconstructive arthroplasty that is complicated by the presence of a proximal femoral nonunion or a malunion, the area of bone around the plate may be distorted by heterotopic bone. Also the intramedullary

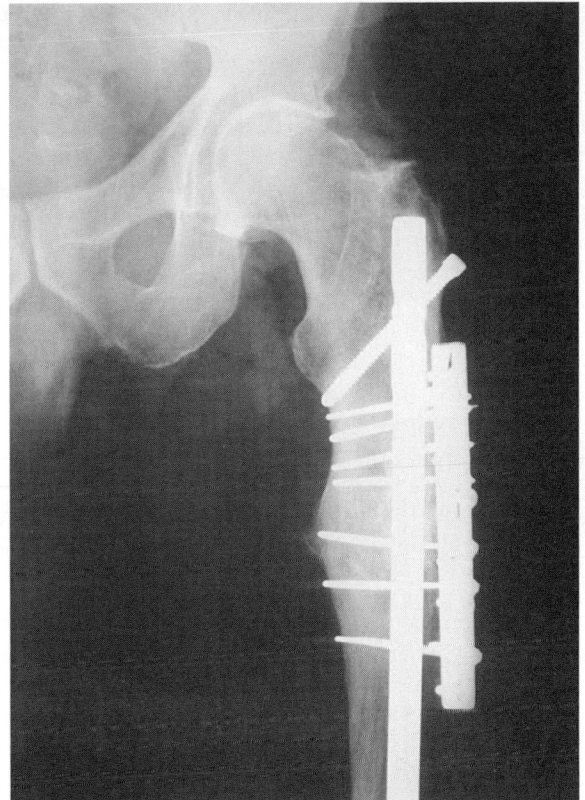

**FIGURE 50–5.** This 46-year-old man sustained a comminuted femoral shaft fracture and underwent combined fixation with a plate and a statically locked intramedullary nail. Eight years later, the patient presented with painful degenerative arthrosis of the ipsilateral hip. From this preoperative anteroposterior view it is impossible to determine whether the lateral femoral cortex is defective deep to the plate. The surgical plan included strategies to replace either a limited or a large segmental defect. At the time of the reconstruction, the completely defective side wall of the femur was replaced with the use of a segmental allograft along with the use of a lengthy cemented stem and cerclage cables.

canal of the adjacent segment of femur may be partly or completely occluded by additional bone. The use of intraoperative image intensification is helpful to confirm the axial realignment of the femur and the restoration of the intramedullary canal.

## Frank or Occult Infection

When a patient presents with a painful hip, especially after internal fixation of a proximal femoral fracture or an open fracture, the potential for a deep wound infection is evaluated.[16] The diagnosis may be readily apparent when features of sepsis are visible, such as a draining sinus or a large abscess. In this instance, a formal surgical débridement of the wound and necrotic tissue is performed, along with a removal of failed hardware and the administration of appropriate antibiotic therapy. More typically, no clinical or radiographic manifestations of sepsis are evident, and the results of conventional laboratory tests are normal. Although an aspiration of the hip or a trephine biopsy of the proximal femur should be attempted, the presence of dense scar tissue or of heterotopic bone may thwart a successful effort. Aspiration of the hip is considered to be positive in the setting of a positive culture, or a white blood cell count of greater than 25,000, with greater than 75% neutrophils present.[16] A technetium or an indium bone scan can be undertaken, but generally we have not found it to be helpful. At arthroplasty, samples of joint fluid are sent for analysis, including the use of a Gram stain, white blood cell count, and culture. The presence of 5 to 10 white blood cells per high-power field is presumptive evidence of an infection.[16] If the hip is infected, our preferred method of treatment is to débride the hip thoroughly and to remove the degenerative femoral head and neck. Following pulsatile jet lavage with a copious amount of saline solution and antibiotic irrigation, a cement block spacer impregnated with an antibiotic, such as tobramycin powder, is inserted into the acetabulum and the proximal femoral defect. The wound is closed in layers over a suction drain. Postoperatively, after the identification of the pathogen, appropriate intravenous antibiotic therapy, with bactericidal titers of 1:8, is given for at least 6 weeks.[26] On cessation of the antibiotics, a trephine biopsy of the hip under image intensification is performed. If the specimen is sterile, insertion of the arthroplasty is arranged (Fig. 50–6). If the specimen confirms the persistence of the infection, another débridement with the insertion of a new cement spacer is followed by a repeat course of appropriate antibiotic therapy. If results of a repeat biopsy are sterile, then the THA is performed. In view of the arduous demands of a suitable reconstructive procedure that usually involves the application of costly implants and bone graft, we prefer to use this protracted method that provides a great probability for an uncomplicated postoperative course without a recurrence of the infection.

## REHABILITATION

On the day after surgery, the patient is mobilized with transfers from the bed to a chair, and physical therapy is started with a partial weight-bearing gait. Active flexion of the hip is encouraged to 90° or more, depending on the type of surgical approach and the intraoperative stability of the hip. A partial weight-bearing gait with the use of a walker or crutches is used for 6 weeks, when typically after radiographic confirmation of appropriate healing, weight bearing to tolerance is encouraged. From the second postoperative day, progressive resistance exercises of the hip muscles are initiated, with a focus on the hip abductors. Four weeks afterward, the use of a stationary

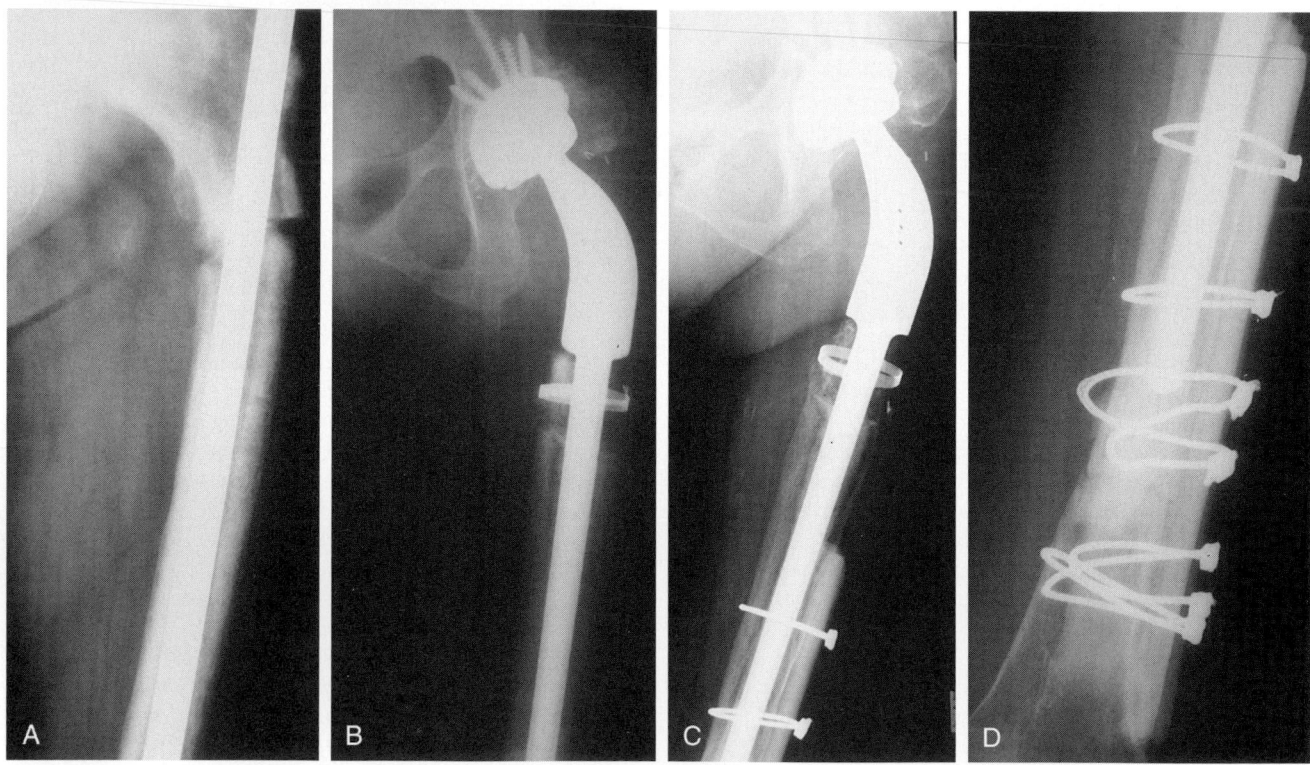

**Figure 50–6.** This 22-year-old woman sustained a proximal femoral shaft fracture and underwent an intramedullary nailing. During the subsequent months, the nail disengaged from the proximal fragment, which became infected. Ten years later, the patient presented with a large draining sinus in the vicinity of the greater trochanter, a 12-cm soft tissue defect, a septic hip, and extensive osteomyelitis of the proximal femur. Initially, the wound was débrided, and the proximal femoral fragment and the hardware were removed. Then, a cement spacer was inserted and appropriate culture-specific intravenous antibiotics were administered. A few days later, a plastic surgeon used a free, vascularized latissimus dorsi flap to obliterate the soft tissue defect. Three months later, with an apparent eradication of the infection, a hybrid total hip arthroplasty with a segmental replacement femoral stem was inserted. The patient did well for 9 years until she sustained a distal periprosthetic fracture in a motor vehicle accident. She underwent an open reduction with internal fixation with the application of strut allografts and cable fixation. *A*, Presenting anteroposterior (AP) view with an infected intramedullary nail. *B*, Postoperative AP view taken 9 years later. *C*, AP view taken 2 years after the treatment of a periprosthetic fracture of the distal femur with strut allografts and cerclage cable fixation. *D*, Accompanying AP view of the distal femur.

bicycle, swimming, and weight machines is encouraged. The patient is advised to continue with a weight-training and strengthening program for at least a year.

## A SURVEY OF THE RELEVANT LITERATURE

There are few reports of the results of THA after proximal femoral injuries.* Most of these represent small series of heterogenous groups of patients with respect to the initial type of proximal femoral fracture and the type of surgical reconstruction. Nevertheless, a few of the series provide insight into the outcome for a THA that follows a failure of primary treatment after certain types of fracture, notably ones that involves the femoral neck or the intertrochanteric region.

The largest reported experience pertains to patients who develop either a failure of internal fixation after a femoral neck fracture or secondary avascular necrosis of the femoral head (AVN) and subsequently progress to a THA.

Franzen and co-workers[17] reported the results for 84 patients who underwent a THA after a failure of internal fixation for a femoral neck fracture. Each of the cases was reviewed after a period of 5 to 12 years. Of the patients who were followed for a minimum of 5 years, there were 5.9% dislocations, 2.4% deep infections, and 18.2% loosenings of the stem. The risk of prosthetic failure was 2.5 times greater than for an age- and sex-matched group of primary THA for osteoarthritis, although this increased risk applied only to patients older than 70 years of age. Nine of the cases required a surgical revision in less than 5 years: four for recurrent dislocation, two for infection, two for stem loosening, and one for a failed cup. Of the patients who were followed for a minimum period of 5 years, there were 5.9% dislocations, 2.4% deep infections, and 18.2% loosenings of the femoral stem. The risk of prosthetic failure was 2.5 times greater than for an age- and sex-matched group of patients who underwent a primary THA for osteoarthritis, although this increased risk of failure pertained solely to the patients older than 70 years.

Likewise, Turner and Wroblewski[56] reported the results of 205 patients who were treated with a THA after a failure of fixation of a femoral neck fracture. In nearly 90% of the patients, the authors documented a satisfactory relief of pain, mobility of the hip, and ambulation, and this despite the use of an early technique of cementation and an outmoded implant design. Their major complications were a superficial wound infection in 7.8%, a deep wound infection in 3.9%, and aseptic loosening in 3.4%. Using a transtrochanteric surgical approach, the dislocation rate was 0.5%.

Stambough and associates[54] reported the results of 27 patients who underwent a THA after a failure of internal fixation of a femoral neck fracture. At a mean follow-up period of 6.3 years, most of the outcomes were satisfactory.

The major complications included a nonunion or a malunion of the trochanteric osteotomy in 26% and a malposition of the stem in 26%. Symptomatic aseptic loosening occurred in 3.7%, with radiographic loosening of the cups in 33% and of the stems in 22%. Neither deep infections nor dislocations were reported.

Neander and co-workers[46] undertook a review of 16 patients who had undergone a THA to manage avascular necrosis of the femoral head that followed a displaced femoral neck fracture for which the primary treatment was an open reduction and internal fixation. The objective of the study was to determine whether the disuse atrophy of the bone and muscle was reversible following the THA. There was a mean 12% relative loss of bone mineral density and 23% loss of muscle volume in the midfemur on the fractured side compared with that on the uninjured side. In the distal femur and proximal tibia of the fractured side, there was a relative loss of bone mineral density of 14% and 21%, respectively. Six months after the THA, there was no change in bone mineral density at any location on either side, whereas the thigh muscles increased by 20% in volume on the fractured side without a change on the uninjured side. Following the THA, no restoration of bone mineral was found despite the improved levels of activities by the patients. The results of this study indicate that osteopenic bone does not adapt to a patient's improved mobility after a reoperation, at least for the study period of 18 months.

Still another somewhat related problem is that of a patient who sustains a femoral neck fracture and is treated with a hemiarthroplasty that fails prematurely and is converted to a THA. In a report on the results of 15 of these patients by Bilgen and associates,[6] after the THA, the average Harris hip score improved from 36.4 (28–42) to 85.9 (69–98). Before the THA, all of the cases possessed more than 2 mm of radiolucency around the endoprosthetic stem, 5 cases displayed acetabular protrusion, and 13 other cases possessed cartilaginous erosion. At the latest assessment, performed at an average period of 32 months after the THA, no radiolucency was documented around any of the arthroplastic components. A comparison group of patients who underwent a primary THA for a femoral neck fracture achieved better results than the patients who initially underwent a hemiarthroplasty.

Warwick and co-workers[57] observed 56 patients who, likewise, underwent a conversion of a hemiarthroplasty to a THA after an initial femoral neck fracture. The modes of hemiarthroplastic failure included femoral loosening in 21 patients, acetabular erosion in 26 patients, and both problems in 5 patients. The median time to the onset of symptoms was 12 months and to a surgical revision was 33 months. After the THA, there were 38 major intraoperative or postoperative complications in 27 patients (48%).

Another problem pertains to the group of patients who initially sustained an intertrochanteric fracture that progressed to a failure of the internal fixation and a conversion to a THA. In a report on the results of 16 such patients, Kligman and Roffman[33] observed a high incidence of intraoperative and postoperative complications, including a periprosthetic femoral fracture, a wound infection, and aseptic loosening. When compared with a matched series of patients who underwent a primary THA for osteoarthri-

---

*See references 6, 17, 24, 25, 33, 43, 46, 47, 50, 52, and 54–57.

tis, the fracture patients who progressed to a THA achieved many more unsatisfactory results.

Mehlhoff and co-workers[43] compared the results of patients who underwent a cemented THA after a failure of internal fixation of a femoral neck fracture with those who underwent a THA after a failure of internal fixation of an intertrochanteric fracture. For the 13 patients who initially sustained a femoral neck fracture, the arthroplastic results were comparable to those of another control group of patients who underwent a primary arthroplasty to manage a femoral neck fracture. For the 14 patients who initially sustained an intertrochanteric fracture, the arthroplastic results were inferior and the incidence of postoperative complications was higher. The investigators attributed the problems after the intertrochanteric fractures to the uncorrected medial displacement of the fractures and the presence of disuse osteoporosis. For a patient who undergoes a THA after a failure of internal fixation for an intertrochanteric fracture, the investigators concluded that bone graft should be used for the arthroplasty.

Tabsh and colleagues[55] compared the results of 53 patients who were treated with a THA for various complications that arose after the primary treatment of previous proximal femoral fracture with those of matched controls who underwent a primary THA for osteoarthritis. Both the intraoperative surgical complexities and the postoperative complications were encountered more frequently in the patients who sustained some type of proximal femoral fracture than in the patients in the control group. However, at a period of more than 2 years after the THA, there was no statistical difference in the functional outcome of the fracture group and the control group. The researchers concluded that THA complications included a nonunion or malunion of the trochanteric osteotomy in 26% and a malpositioning of the stem in 26%. Symptomatic aseptic loosening was observed in 3.7% of the patients, with radiographic loosening in 33% of the cups and 22% of the stems. There were no cases of a deep infection or a dislocation, despite the presence of several nonunions or migrations of the greater trochanter. The investigators concluded that a THA was a viable salvage procedure to address the failed treatment of a previous proximal femoral fracture.

Haentjens and associates[24] reported their results for nine elderly patients who were treated with THA to salvage a failed internal fixation of an intertrochanteric or a subtrochanteric fracture. At a mean follow-up period of 41 months, the clinical results were fair to excellent in all of the patients. The mean time between the initial fracture fixation and the THA was 7 months. The investigators stressed that following the THA, an early functional restoration with full weight-bearing ambulation was essential to achieve a reproducibly good result.

As a summary of these and other somewhat similar reports on the results of failed primary surgical treatment of various patterns of proximal femoral fractures, THA holds the potential to achieve a favorable outcome for the patient, although the procedure may be technically challenging and the potential for postoperative complications is greater than those for a THA performed for osteoarthritis.

# POSTOPERATIVE COMPLICATIONS

## Intraoperative and Postoperative Hemorrhage

The incidence and types of complications that follow a THA performed after a proximal femoral fracture involving the femoral head or neck that initially was treated nonoperatively are similar to those that follow a primary total hip replacement for osteoarthrosis.[7, 14, 35, 39] If the arthroplasty follows an initial fracture of the subtrochanteric region or the proximal portion of the femoral shaft, many of the cases are at an increased risk of culminating in one or more postoperative complications. The contributing factors include a surgical approach through scar tissue or traumatized tissue, a technically demanding correction of a bony deformity, a removal of retained hardware, or an excision of heterotopic bone. A wide variety of these complicating features contribute to the typical prolongation of the operative times and the corresponding increase in the intraoperative blood loss.[26] The use of a surgical drain that allows a reinfusion of the collected blood products may be indicated. Before the surgery, if sufficient time permits, the use of autologous blood donation, iron supplementation, and recombinant erythropoetin may be considered. In certain situations, the postoperative blood loss may be substantial. An elderly patient and others with multiple medical co-morbidities or a patient with a large intraoperative blood loss resulting in the dilution and consumption of coagulation factors also is vulnerable to considerable postoperative blood loss. Diligent postoperative care with fluid resuscitation and the administration of suitable blood products are necessary, along with the potential for initial management in an intensive care unit. The nutritional state of the patient has to be managed appropriately to optimize the healing of the wound.

## Sciatic Nerve Injury

Following a proximal femoral injury, especially one that initially was managed operatively, the sciatic nerve may become scarified to a highly variable extent. The most sinister scenario is when supplementary heterotopic bone surrounds the nerve. For a THA, we prefer to use an anterolateral or a lateral approach to minimize the need for a posterior dissection. In many of these cases, some degree of contusion of the sciatic nerve accompanies the initial traumatic injury. At the time of the arthroplasty, the sciatic nerve is particularly vulnerable to a secondary injury as a manifestation of the "double crush syndrome," merely by a seemingly trivial retraction.[28, 29] To minimize the tension on the nerve, the knee is maintained in a flexed position beyond 90°, apart from the brief period when the hip joint is reduced.

In an attempt to monitor the function of the sciatic nerve during a surgical procedure, a wake-up test along with somatosensory-evoked potentials and continuous electromyelographic measurements have been used.[13, 28, 29] With somatosensory-evoked potentials, there is a small incidence of both false-positive and false-negative results as well as a significant latent period. In contrast, electromyelographic motor monitoring documents virtually instantaneous changes in nerve function. Also, the electromyelographic studies are technically less demanding to obtain and are performed with the use of less sophisticated and costly instrumentation.

## Wound Infection

The risk of a wound infection increases after a more extensive surgical reconstruction with a correspondingly longer operative time, following an incision through compromised soft tissue, and after a patient has had a history of sepsis in and around the hip joint.[48] Other potential risk factors include an immunocompromised patient, a history of diabetes mellitus, a prolonged drainage of a wound, a failure of the standard aseptic surgical technique, and an improper use of perioperative antibiotics. The routine postoperative assessments for the symptoms and signs of a wound infection are performed, including a review for fever and chills, incisional erythema, drainage, warmth, swelling, and pain at the surgical site. An aspiration of the hip or other studies may be indicated, as well as a consultation with an infectious disease specialist. If the presence of a wound infection is confirmed, prompt surgical débridement and administration of appropriate antibiotic therapy are indicated.

## Thromboembolic Events

Prophylactic measures against deep venous thrombosis and pulmonary embolism include an early mobilization of the patient, as well as the use of elastic stockings, sequential compression devices or foot pumps, and anticoagulation with warfarin or a low-molecular-weight heparin.[12, 48] For a patient who cannot tolerate the use of therapeutic anticoagulation, and especially for one who possesses risk factors for deep venous thrombosis or pulmonary embolism, the use of an inferior vena cana filter may be indicated. Either as a routine form of assessment or particularly for a patient who develops the symptoms and signs of a possible deep venous thrombosis, various screening techniques may be used, including the use of ultrasound, magnetic resonance imaging, and venography.[48]

## Heterotopic Ossification

Although routine prophylaxis against the formation of heterotopic bone does not appear to be indicated, a patient who possesses one or more risk factors for HO merits special consideration.[35] Examples include an obese young adult man with a history of a closed head injury or one who previously was treated operatively for his or her femoral injury with an extensile lateral approach to the hip that was followed by HO formation. Suitable prophylaxis includes the use radiation therapy with a single dose of 700 cGy. For a fertile young female patient in whom the use of radiation therapy is discouraged, indomethacin,

75 mg per day, may be used for 6 weeks. When indomethacin and anticoagulation with a low-molecular-weight heparin or warfarin are used concomitantly, appropriate medical supervision is needed to minimize the risk of a coagulopathy.

## Dislocation

A patient with an uncorrected proximal femoral deformity may be at an increased risk for a dislocation of the hip due to impingement of the femur against the pelvis or the presence of a malaligned component.[39] Factors such as increased age of the patient, dementia, neuromuscular imbalance, and weakness of the abductor muscles amplify the risk for a postoperative dislocation, along with the conventional risk factors such as the malalignment of a component. After a single dislocation that is successfully reduced by a closed reduction, a period of immobilization can be attempted as a definitive treatment. If two or more dislocations occur and when a component is malaligned, a surgical revision is generally necessary to eliminate the recurrent dislocations.

## Persistent Nonunion

A common complication after a malunion or nonunion of a proximal femoral fracture is a persistent nonunion after a THA. The source of such a nonunion can be attributable to an intraoperative periprosthetic fracture.[32] Also, the risk of a nonunion after an osteotomy to correct a deformity is increased if the axial malalignment persists. To achieve a high likelihood of a successful outcome, an anatomic realignment of the femur and the presence of stable internal fixation are crucial, along with the preservation of the blood supply to the principal bone fragments. In the presence of a large bone defect, the secondary THA is accompanied by the use of a suitable bone graft, preferably of an autogenous material.

## Premature Failure of the Total Hip Arthroplasty

The results of THA for a proximal femoral deformity below the intertrochanteric line are poorer than those for a primary THA that is performed for osteoarthritis. A persistent axial malalignment, inadequate internal fixation, and the presence of structurally deficient bone in an osteopenic elderly patient all may contribute to a premature failure of the arthroplasty.[11, 14] In a high-risk case, after the surgical procedure, a careful maintenance of protected weight bearing is recommended.

## Fracture and Perforation of the Femoral Canal

In the presence of a femoral deformity, during the preparation of the canal, the most frequent complications are a femoral fracture and a femoral perforation.[7, 32]

During the preoperative planning with the use of radiographs and templates of the implants, the magnitude of a proximal femoral deformity is assessed to determine whether the use of a specialized stem or of a corrective osteotomy is preferred. If the surgeon elects to attempt to use a specialized stem, all of the necessary resources to undertake the osteotomy are obtained, in case the specialized stem cannot be inserted into the deformed bone. At surgery, if a weakened segment of bone or a stress riser such as an empty screw hole is encountered, a prophylactic fixation with the use of cerclage cables, or possibly supplementary strut allografts, is performed to minimize the risk of a fracture during the broaching of the femur or the insertion of the stem.

## GUIDANCE AND EDUCATION OF THE PATIENT

During the first preoperative assessment, after a thorough clinical and radiographic evaluation, the orthopaedist is advised to discuss the complexities of the case and the indications for reconstruction with the patient. Providing a realistic analysis of the likelihood that surgery can correct the principal complaints is crucial. In the presence of major deformity, marked scar formation, deep wound infection, or massive heterotopic bone, the ultimate outcome of an arthroplasty is unlikely to be equivalent to that achieved after a conventional THA for degenerative arthrosis, with respect to pain relief, mobility of the hip, and muscle strength. A realistic expectation by the patient is essential for his or her ultimate satisfaction with the clinical outcome. When the patient's expectations about the outcome remain unrealistic, a deferral of a reconstructive procedure is advisable.

After an arthroplasty on a young adult, the need to limit activities that provide an excessive predilection for premature loosening, excessive wear, or a periprosthetic fracture is emphasized. The orthopaedist is advised to maintain a special vigilance for the typically younger, adult male trauma victim who may continue to use drugs and alcohol with a lifestyle that is not consistent with a high likelihood of a prolonged function of an arthroplastic hip. Strong encouragement by the physician to the patient may be necessary to guide the individual toward more appropriate treatment until or unless he modifies his lifestyle.

### REFERENCES

1. Abraham, W.D.; Dimon, J.H. Leg length discrepancy in total hip arthroplasty. Orthop Clin North Am 23:201–209, 1992.
2. Amstutz, H.C.; Friscia, D.A.; Dorey, F.; et al. Warfarin prophylaxis to prevent mortality from pulmonary embolism after total hip replacement. J Bone Joint Surg Am 71:321–326, 1989.
3. Ayers, D.C.; Evarts, C.M.; Parkinson, J.R. The prevention of heterotopic ossification in high-risk patients by low-dose radiation therapy after total hip arthroplasty. J Bone Joint Surg Am 68:1423–1430, 1986.
4. Barrack, R.L.; Wolfe, M.W.; Michas, P.; Frentz, B. Distal femoral allograft for massive proximal femoral deficiency. Acta Orthop Scand 71:90–94, 2000.
5. Berry, D.J. Total hip arthroplasty in patients with proximal femoral deformity. Clin Orthop 369:262–272, 1999.
6. Bilgen, O.; Karaeminogullari, O.; Kulecioglu, A. Results of conversion total hip prosthesis performed following painful hemiarthroplasty. J Int Med Res 28:307–312, 2000.
7. Blackley, H.R.L.; Howell, G.E.D.; Rorabeck, C.H. Planning and management of the difficult primary total hip replacement. Instr Course Lect 49:3–11, 2000.
8. Boardman, K.P.; Charnley, J. Low-friction arthroplasty after fracture-dislocations of the hip. J Bone Joint Surg Br 60:495, 1978.
9. Bose, W.J. Accurate limb-length equalization during total hip arthroplasty. Orthopaedics 23:433–436, 2000.
10. Brooker, A.F.; Bowerman, J.W.; Robinson, R.A.; et al. Ectopic ossification following total hip replacement. Incidence and a method of classification. J Bone Joint Surg Am 55:1629–1632, 1973.
11. Callaghan, J.J. Difficult primary total hip arthroplasty: Selected surgical exposures. Instr Course Lect 49:13–21, 2000.
12. Della Valle, C.J.; Steiger, D.J.; Di Cesare, P.E. Thromboembolism after hip and knee arthroplasty. J Am Acad Orthop Surg 6:327–336, 1998.
13. DeHart, M.M.; Riley, L.H., Jr. Nerve injuries in total hip arthroplasty. J Am Acad Orthop Surg 7:101–111, 1999.
14. Dunbar, M.J.; Blackley, H.R.L.; Bourne, R.B. Osteolysis of the femur: Principles of management. Instr Course Lect 50:197–209, 2001.
15. Emerson, R.H.; Cross, R.; Head, W.C. Prophylactic and early therapeutic use of the Greenfield filter in hip and knee joint arthroplasty. J Arthroplasty 6:129–135, 1991.
16. Fitzgerald, R.H., Jr. Infected total hip arthroplasty: Diagnosis and treatment. J Am Acad Orthop Surg 3:249–262, 1995.
17. Franzen, H.; Nilsson, L.T.; Stromqvist, B.; et al. Secondary total hip replacement after fractures of the femoral neck. J Bone Joint Surg Br 72:784–787, 1990.
18. Gie, G.A.; Linder, L.; Ling, R.S.M.; et al. Contained morselized allograft in revision total hip arthroplasty: Surgical technique. Orthop Clin North Am 24:717–725, 1993.
19. Gie, G.A.; Linder, L.; Ling, R.S.M.; et al. Impacted cancellous allografts and cement for revision total hip arthroplasty. J Bone Joint Surg Br 75:14–21, 1993.
20. Glassman, A.H. Complex primary femoral replacement. In: Callaghan, J.J.; Rosenberg, A.G.; Rubash, H.E., eds. The Adult Hip. Philadelphia, Lippincott-Raven, 1998, pp. 1201–1220.
21. Haddad, F.S.; Garbuz, D.S.; Masri, B.A.; et al. Structural proximal femoral allografts for failed total hip replacements: A minimum review of five years. J Bone Joint Surg Br 82:830–836, 2000.
22. Haddad, F.S.; Garbuz, D.S.; Masri, B.A.; et al. Femoral bone loss in patients managed with revision hip replacement: Results of circumferential allograft replacement. Instr Course Lect 49:147–162, 2000.
23. Haddad, F.S.; Masri, B.A.; Garbuz, D.S.; et al. Femoral bone loss in total hip arthroplasty: Classification and preoperative planning. Instr Course Lect 49:83–96, 2000.
24. Haentjens, P.; Castelyn, P.P.; Opdecam, P. Hip arthroplasty for failed internal fixation of intertrochanteric and subtrochanteric fractures in the elderly patient. Arch Orthop Trauma Surg 113:222–227, 1994.
25. Hagglund, G.; Nordstrom, B.; Lidgren, L. Total hip replacement after nailing failure in femoral neck fractures. Arch Orthop Trauma Surg 103:125–127, 1984.
26. Harkess, J.W. Arthroplasty of hip. In: Crenshaw, A.H., ed. Campbell's Operative Orthopaedics, 9th ed. St. Louis, Mosby–Year Book, 1998, pp. 296–472.
27. Head, W.C.; Emerson, R.H.; Malinin, T.I. Structural bone grafting for femoral reconstruction. Clin Orthop 369:223–229, 1999.
28. Helfet, D.L.; Anand, N.; Malkani A.L.; et al. Intraoperative monitoring of motor pathways during operative fixation of acute acetabular fractures. J Orthop Trauma 11:2–6, 1997.
29. Helfet, D.L.; Schmeling, G.J. Somatosensory evoked potential monitoring in the surgical treatment of acute, displaced acetabular fractures. Results of a prospective study. Clin Orthop 301:213–220, 1994.
30. Huo, M.H.; Carbone, J.J. Conversion total hip replacement. In: Callaghan, J.J.; Rosenberg, A.G.; Rubash, H.E., eds. The Adult Hip. Philadelphia, Lippincott-Raven, 1998, pp. 1555–1570.
31. Johnson, E.E. Acute lengthening of shortened lower extremities after malunion or non-union of a fracture. J Bone Joint Surg Am 76:379–389, 1994.
32. Kelly, S.S. Periprosthetic femoral fractures. J Am Acad Orthop Surg 2:164–172, 1994.

33. Kligman, M.; Roffman, M. Conversion total hip replacement after failed internal fixation of intertrochanteric fracture. Harefuah 134:690–692, 1998.

34. Leopold, S.S.; Rosenberg, A.G. Current status of impaction allografting for revision of a femoral component. Instr Course Lect 49:111–118, 2000.

35. Lewallen, D.G. Heterotopic ossification following total hip arthroplasty. Instr Course Lect 44:187–198, 1995.

36. Ling, R.S.M.; Timperley, A.J.; Linder, L. History of cancellous impaction grafting in the femur, J Bone Joint Surg Br 75:693–696, 1993.

37. Malkani, A.L.; Paiso, J.M.; Sim, F.H. Proximal femoral replacement with megaprosthesis. Instr Course Lect 49:141–146, 2000.

38. McCarthy, J.C.; Bono, J.V.; Lee, J.A. The difficult femur. Instr Course Lect 49:63–69, 2000.

39. McCollum, D.E.; Gray, W.J. Dislocation after total hip arthroplasty. Causes and prevention. Clin Orthop 261:159–170, 1990.

40. Mears, D.C.; Durbhakula, S.M.; Slowik, G. Total hip replacement in special circumstances. In: Northmore-Ball, M.D.; Bannister, G., eds. Clinical Challenges in Orthopaedics: The Hip. Oxford, Isis Medical Media Limited, 2001, pp. 89–121.

41. Mears, D.C.; MacLeod, M.D. Surgical approaches: Triradiate and modified triradiate. In: Wiss, D., ed. Masters Techniques in Orthopaedic Surgery: Fractures. Philadelphia, Lippincott Raven Press, 1997, pp. 701–728.

42. Mears, D.C.; Ward, A.J.; Wright, M.S. The radiological assessment of pelvic and acetabular fractures using three-dimensional comuted tomography. Int J Orthop Trauma 2:196–209, 1992.

43. Mehlhoff, T.; Landon, G.C.; Tullos, H.S. Total hip arthroplasty following failed internal fixation of hip fractures. Clin Orthop 269:32–37, 1991.

44. Merchan, E.C.; Myong, C. Quadricepsplasty: The Judet technique and results of 21 post-traumatic cases. Orthopedics 15:1081–1085, 1992.

45. Moed, B.R.; Smith, S.T. Three-view radiographic assessment of heterotopic ossification after acetabular fracture surgery. J Orthop Trauma 10:93–98, 1996.

46. Neander, G.; von Sivers, K.; Adolphson, P.; et al. An evaluation of bone loss after total hip arthroplasty for femoral head necrosis after femoral neck fracture: A quantitative CT study in 16 patients. J Arthroplasty 14:64–70, 1999.

47. Nilsson, L.T.; Jalovaara, P.; Franzen, H.; et al. Function after primary hemiarthroplasty and secondary total hip arthroplasty in femoral neck fracture. J Arthroplasty 9:369–374, 1994.

48. Paiement, G.D. Prevention and treatment of venous thromboembolic disease and complications in primary hip arthroplasty patients. Instr Course Lect 47:331–335, 1998.

49. Paprosky, W.G.; Aribindi, R. Hip replacement: Treatment of femoral bone loss using distal bypass fixation. Instr Course Lect 49:119–130, 2000.

50. Patterson, B.M.; Salvati, E.A.; Huo, M.H. Total hip arthroplasty for complications of intertrochanteric fracture. A technical note. J Bone Joint Surg Am 72:776–777, 1990.

51. Poss, R. Complex primary total hip arthroplasty: The difficult femur. Instr Coures Lect 44:281–286, 1995.

52. Skeide, B.I.; Lie, S.A ; Havelin, L.I.; et al. Total hip arthroplasty after femoral neck fractures. Results from the national registry on joint prostheses. Tidsskr Nor Laegeforen 116:1440–1451, 1996.

53. Soballe, K.; Boll, K.L.; Kofod, S.; et al. Total hip replacement after medial-displacement osteotomy of the proximal part of the femur. J Bone Joint Surg Am 71:692–697, 1989.

54. Stambough, J.L.; Balderston, R.A.; Booth, R.E., Jr.; et al. Conversion total hip replacement. Review of 140 hips with greater than 6-year follow-up study. J Arthroplasty 1:261–269, 1986.

55. Tabsh, I.; Waddell, J.P.; Morton, J. Total hip arthroplasty for complications of proximal femoral fractures. J Orthop Trauma 11:166–169, 1997.

56. Turner, A.; Wroblewski, B.M. Charnley low-friction arthroplasty for the treatment of hips with late complications of femoral neck fractures. Clin Orthop 185:126–130, 1984.

57. Warwick, D.; Hubbie, M.; Sarris, I.; et al. Revision of failed hemiarthroplasty for fractures at the hip. Int Orthop 22:165–168, 1998.

58. Wong, P.; Gross, A.E. The use of structural allografts for treating periprosthetic fractures about the hip and knee. Orthop Clin North Am 30:259–264, 1999.

# CHAPTER 51

# Subtrochanteric Fractures of the Femur

Thomas A. Russell, M.D.

A better understanding of fracture biomechanics and the development of better implants and new surgical techniques have led to improved treatment of subtrochanteric fractures, which have historically been difficult to treat.[8, 16, 29, 65, 110] Closed interlocking nailing and open indirect reduction techniques emphasizing preservation of the blood supply to the fracture fragments have decreased the incidence of nonunion and permitted earlier functional return to our patients. Improved engineering and manufacturing techniques have yielded implants of greater strength and longer fatigue life. With a thorough understanding of the variants of subtrochanteric fractures and their treatment options, the optimal treatment can be selected for each patient.

## PATHOLOGY

### Anatomy and Biomechanics

In a detailed morphometric analysis of the femur, Yoshioka and colleagues[137] found significant interspecimen variation in linear and angular measurements. The plane of the femoral head and neck is anteverted $13° ± 7°$ to the plane of the femoral shaft in most adults. In Asian populations, anteversion may approach $30°$. The average neck-shaft angle in women is $133° ± 6.6°$, and it is $129° ± 7.3°$ in men.[134] The plane of the femoral neck and head is also anteriorly positioned 1 to 1.5 cm in relation to the center axis of the femoral shaft. If the centerline of the femoral shaft is continued through the intertrochanteric region, it emerges from the femur in the region of the piriformis fossa. On an anteroposterior (AP) radiographic projection, this line appears to transect the femur at the medial wall of the greater trochanter. On the lateral projection, the line crosses the piriformis fossa. The lesser trochanter is a posteromedial prominence at the termination of the intertrochanteric ridge and serves as the prominent insertion point of the iliacus and psoas tendons. Its prominence in the AP radiographic projection helps in

assessing anteversion of the proximal fragment in fractures with an intact lesser trochanter. This portion of the medial femoral cortex involving the lesser trochanter and an area just anterior to it is important in obtaining stable fixation with proximal locking screws when using interlocking nailing techniques. Inclusion of the region of the lesser trochanter in the fracture usually precludes the use of standard interlocking femoral nails; instead, cephalomedullary nails (nails with proximal locking devices that can be inserted up into the femoral head) or specialized plate-and-screw–type devices are required. The femoral shaft is bowed primarily anteriorly, but also slightly laterally. The plane of the bow is situated approximately $15°$ lateral to the pure AP plane. During nailing of an impending pathologic fracture of the femoral shaft, the intramedullary (IM) nail tends to align itself along this plane in a slightly lateral rather than a purely AP plane.

In the subtrochanteric and shaft regions, the femur is covered circumferentially by well-vascularized muscle groups (Fig. 51–1). Direct surgical exposure of the subtrochanteric shaft region involves either splitting the vastus lateralis muscle or reflecting it anteriorly from the lateral intermuscular septum. Profuse bleeding from the perforating branches of the profundus femoris artery can complicate this exposure (Fig. 51–2). The attachments of the hip muscles (iliacus and psoas, gluteus medius and minimus, gluteus maximus and adductors) all contribute to the powerful forces that act on the individual fragments of subtrochanteric fractures.

Controversy has always existed regarding the significance of damage to the proximal femoral anatomy and vascular supply of the femoral head with closed nailing techniques. Although the piriformis fossa portal has been favored in North America since a study by Johnson and colleagues[62] on potential bursting forces of the proximal anatomy with Küntscher nail insertion, new dissection studies by Dora and associates[36] have documented less potential for damage to the vascular and musculotendinous units about the proximal end of the femur from nail insertion with a trochanteric entry portal. New implant designs incorporating trochanteric entry portal capability

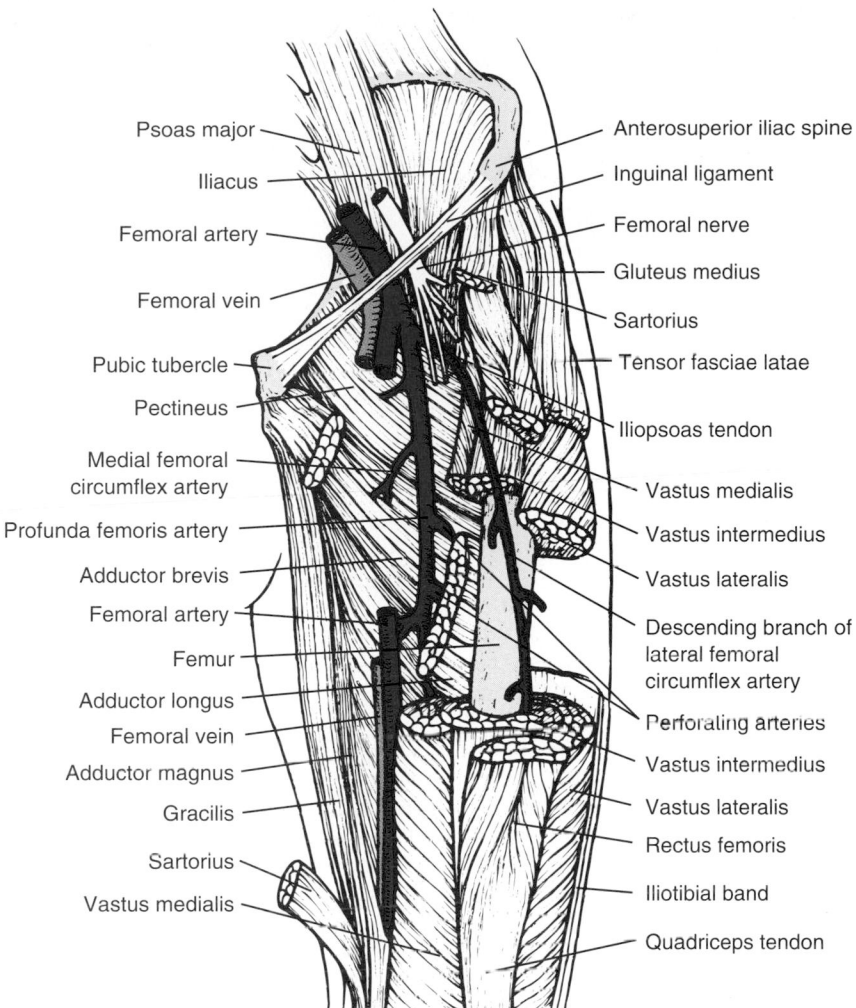

**Psoas major**
**Iliacus**
**Femoral artery**
**Femoral vein**
**Pubic tubercle**
**Pectineus**
**Medial femoral circumflex artery**
**Profunda femoris artery**
**Adductor brevis**
**Femoral artery**
**Femur**
**Adductor longus**
**Femoral vein**
**Adductor magnus**
**Gracilis**
**Sartorius**
**Vastus medialis**

**Anterosuperior iliac spine**
**Inguinal ligament**
**Femoral nerve**
**Gluteus medius**
**Sartorius**
**Tensor fasciae latae**
**Iliopsoas tendon**
**Vastus medialis**
**Vastus intermedius**
**Vastus lateralis**
**Descending branch of lateral femoral circumflex artery**
**Perforating arteries**
**Vastus intermedius**
**Vastus lateralis**
**Rectus femoris**
**Iliotibial band**
**Quadriceps tendon**

**FIGURE 51–1.** Anterior anatomy of the hip and subtrochanteric area. (Modified from Hoppenfeld, S.; de Boer, P. Surgical Exposures in Orthopaedics. Philadelphia, J.B. Lippincott, 1984.)

without excessive bursting effects on the proximal end of the femur are now clinically available and may return the surgical technique to a trochanteric entry portal as originally described by Küntscher with his first nail designs in the 1940s. Even though vascular complications from traditional antegrade femoral nailing are exceedingly rare with a piriformis portal in adults, a trochanteric portal is definitely advisable in children with open physeal plates to minimize the risk of avascular necrosis of the femoral head.

The major regional nerves are the sciatic posteriorly and the femoral anteriorly. They are rarely involved in closed injuries (Fig. 51–3). Because of the transition from cancellous bone in the intertrochanteric region to thick cortical bone in the diaphysis, the subtrochanteric region has a thinner cortex than the rest of the femur does.[37]

In the early 20th century Koch[69] was one of the first to analyze mechanical stress on the femur during weight bearing. He showed that up to 1200 lb/inch$^2$ of force could be generated in a 200-lb man. Compression stress exceeds 1200 lb/inch$^2$ in the medial subtrochanteric area 1 to 3 inches distal to the level of the lesser trochanter. Lateral

tensile stresses are approximately 20% less. Koch's analysis did not, however, take into account the additional effects of muscle forces.[99] Frankel and Burstein[43] demonstrated significant force on the hip and proximal part of the femur from flexion and extension of the hip in bed, thus indicating continuous stress on a proximal femoral fixation device even with the patient at bedrest. Fielding and co-workers,[39] in an analysis of the biomechanics of subtrochanteric fractures, showed that a medial cortical buttress was required to minimize local stress. They noted that nonunion inevitably results in fatigue failure of a fixation device and that nonunion is in fact the cause of implant failure. Higher bending force is borne by an implant applied laterally (e.g., a plate-and-screw device) than by a centromedullary device, which is closer to the line of joint reaction force.[98] Froimson's description of muscle forces aids our understanding of subtrochanteric fracture displacement and also suggests how such fractures may be reduced[46] (Fig. 51–4). The proximal fragment, including the greater trochanteric attachment, is abducted by the gluteus medius and minimus muscles. The iliopsoas flexes and externally rotates the proximal fragment if the lesser trochanter is attached. The adductors and hamstrings cause shortening and adduction of the distal fragment, thereby resulting in relative varus of the hip. All three forces must be neutralized for successful immobilization of the fracture. In 1969, Toridis[122] noted the torsional effects of stress in the subtrochanteric region, an important development in regard to the current concepts of static interlocking techniques to reduce the rotational shear force that may lead to implant failure from cyclical loading.

Tencer and associates[120] in 1984 presented a detailed evaluation of implant devices used for subtrochanteric fractures at that time. They studied Ender pins, the Klemm-Shelman nail, the Zickel nail, the Grosse-Kempf interlocking nail, the Brooker-Wills nail, a hip compression screw, and a blade plate device. These investigators used transverse osteotomy and segmental defect models to evaluate bending stress, torsional stress, and load to axial failure in cadavers with simulated subtrochanteric femoral fractures. Their results were reported in relation to the femoral bending stiffness of the cadaver femur. They found that in transverse osteotomies, interlocking nails and Zickel nails approached 75% to 80% of the bone's intact bending stiffness and Ender pins, less than 50% of bending stiffness. In segmental defects, the compression hip screw, which permitted free rotation of the screw shaft inside the side plate barrel, resulted in a marked diminution in stiffness because of rotation of the femoral head. With torsional testing, all the slotted, open-section nails and Ender nails restored less than 5% of normal femoral torsional stiffness. The plate-and-screw devices restored approximately 40% of femoral torsional stiffness. When tested in a single load to failure, the Grosse-Kempf and Klemm-Shelman devices failed at loads of 350% to 400% of body weight. Plate-and-screw devices failed at approximately 200% of body weight, and the Ender system, blade plate, and Brooker-Wills nail failed at less than 150% of body weight.

To reduce implant failure and maximize torsional stability, Russell and Taylor in 1984 developed a closed-section, cloverleaf, interlocking centromedullary nail and subsequently a closed-section, interlocking cephalomedullary nail known as the *reconstruction nail*. The design goals were to improve fatigue performance and decrease shear at the fracture site by eliminating the longitudinal slot and by adjusting implant wall thickness to approximate the stiffness of an intact femur. In a subsequent study by Tencer and colleagues[119] in which the Russell-Taylor femoral nail was tested in the same manner as previous implants, the 15-mm Russell-Taylor femoral nail approached the stiffness of the intact femur, with 106% of its bending stiffness. Because of the closed-section design,

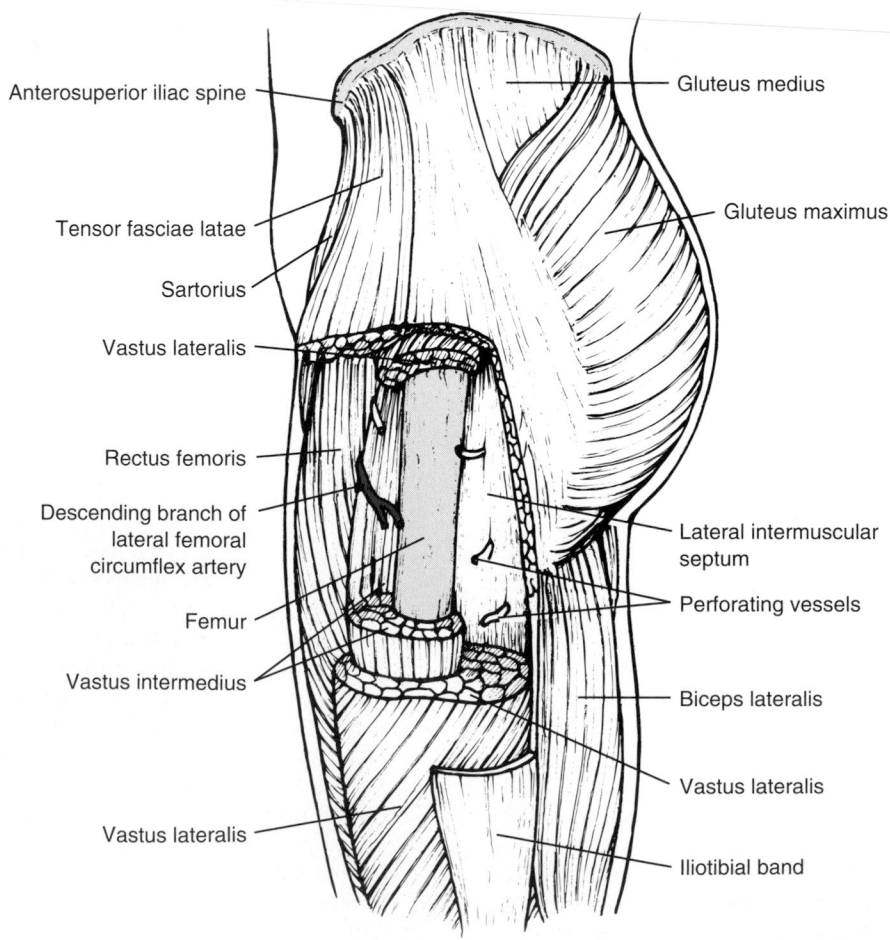

**Figure 51–2.** Lateral anatomy of the hip and subtrochanteric area. (Modified from Hoppenfeld, S.; de Boer, P. Surgical Exposures in Orthopaedics. Philadelphia, J.B. Lippincott, 1984.)

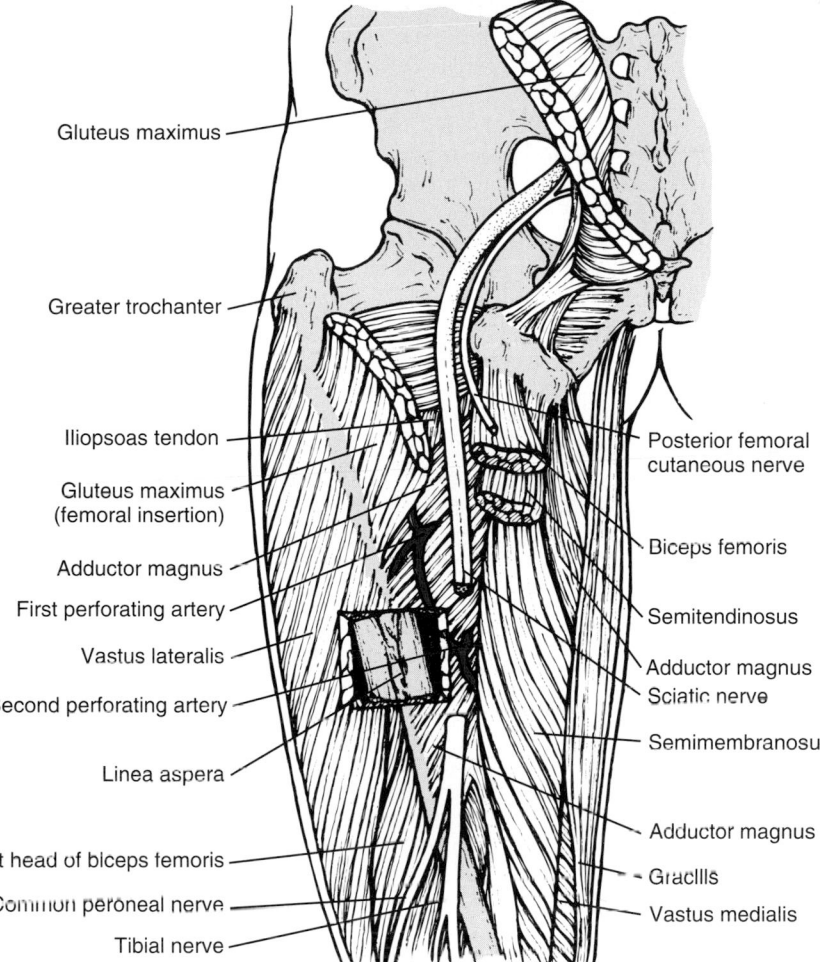

**Figure 51–3.** Posterior anatomy of the hip and subtrochanteric area. (Modified from Hoppenfeld, S.; de Boer, P. Surgical Exposures in Orthopaedics. Philadelphia, J.B. Lippincott, 1984.)

Labels in figure:
- Gluteus maximus
- Greater trochanter
- Iliopsoas tendon
- Gluteus maximus (femoral insertion)
- Adductor magnus
- First perforating artery
- Vastus lateralis
- Second perforating artery
- Linea aspera
- Short head of biceps femoris
- Common peroneal nerve
- Tibial nerve
- Posterior femoral cutaneous nerve
- Biceps femoris
- Semitendinosus
- Adductor magnus
- Sciatic nerve
- Semimembranosus
- Adductor magnus
- Gracilis
- Vastus medialis

58% of the intact torsional stiffness of the cadaver femurs was restored, a 10-fold increase over the torsional stiffness of open-section interlocking nails. When tested for axial load to failure, the Russell-Taylor closed-section femoral nail was the strongest implant tested; it failed at 450% of body weight. The 13-mm Russell-Taylor reconstruction nail was tested in a similar fashion. Because of its greater wall thickness, it restored approximately 96% of the bending stiffness of cadaver femurs. Torsional stiffness was the same as for the closed-section, standard Russell-Taylor nail (58% of the intact femur), and axial load to failure was 500% of body weight (Fig. 51–5).

Most hip compression screws marketed in the United States have sufficient strength and fatigue life for manufacturers to approve their use for subtrochanteric fractures. Only hip compression screws and side plates indicated for subtrochanteric fractures should be used for these fractures because all are not the same with respect to bending strength and fatigue life.

Though used primarily for intertrochanteric fractures, the original IM hip screws such as the Gamma nail (Howmedica) and intramedullary hip screw (IMHS; Smith-Nephew) have also been adopted for more proximal subtrochanteric fractures. Although torsional and bending forces are dissipated along the full length of a standard or reconstruction interlocking nail, these same forces are concentrated at the distal tip of the short Gamma nail, which ends above the femoral isthmus of the IM stem. Locking screws for these short nails are placed in the isthmus rather than the distal metaphysis, thus presenting additional stress risers to an already highly stressed region. More popular now are the longer versions of these implants, which, in addition to changing the proximal angulation to 4° to 5° instead of 10°, have resulted in fewer implant complications and are preferred for subtrochanteric fractures.

Curtis and co-workers[26] showed that an IM device provides stronger and more rigid fixation for subtrochanteric fractures than do 135° or 95° screw-plate devices.

Shaw and Wilson[109] analyzed the mechanical behavior of an IMHS in simulated intertrochanteric and subtrochanteric fractures. Fracture motion was greater with the Gamma locking nail because the proximal fragments pivoted about the distal screws. The potential for generation of iatrogenic fractures appeared to be greater with the Gamma locking nail. No mechanical advantage of the short Gamma nail versus the Omega compression screw was observed.

Wheeler and colleagues[132] used a subtrochanteric femoral fracture cadaver model to test three commercially available cephalomedullary implants for subtrochanteric fractures and related the failure of the implant to the stiffness of the intact femur. They found that the more flexible device with a stiffness approximating 17% of the intact femur and the open-section device failed by bending whereas the closed-section design with a relative stiffness of 40% of the intact femur allowed stable fixation for postoperative fatigue loading. In a cadaveric load-to-failure model, Kraemer and associates[70] found that the closed-section Russell-Taylor reconstruction nail was able to withstand higher stress than the IMHS was (Russell-Taylor reconstruction nail, 2869-N failure by screw cutout of femoral head; short IMHS, 2330-N failure by screw cutout of femoral head; short IMHS, 2330-N failure by fracture of the femoral shaft at the tip of the nail in the mid-diaphysis; and long IMHS, 2181-N failure by implant bending).

Biomechanical studies such as these are for the first time setting relative values in implant design for subtrochanteric hip fractures because these implant designs can be related to known clinical results.

## Incidence

Subtrochanteric fractures have been variously defined, but most authors limit the term to fractures occurring between the lesser trochanter and the isthmus of the diaphysis of the femoral shaft. Such fractures account for approximately 10% to 34% of all hip fractures. In their review of 300 hip fractures, Boyd and Griffin[12] classified 26.7% as subtrochanteric. Retrospective reviews have noted a bi-

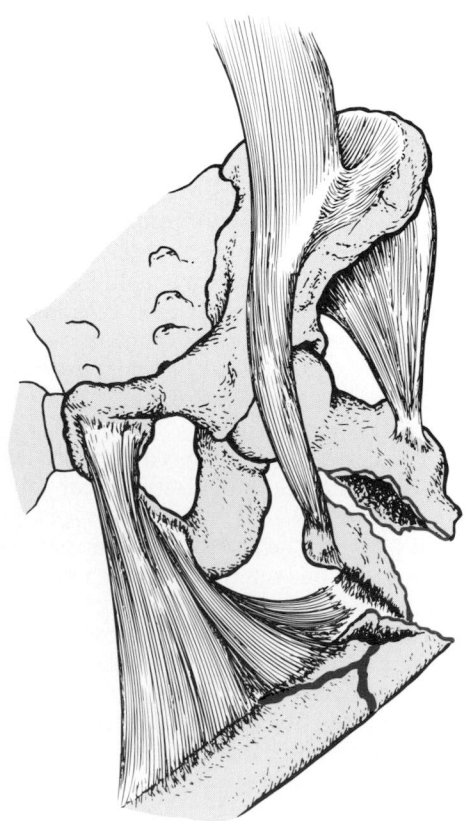

FIGURE 51–4. Pathologic anatomy: additional deforming forces on a subtrochanteric fracture. (Modified from Froimson, A.L. Surg Gynecol Obstet 131:465–472, 1970.)

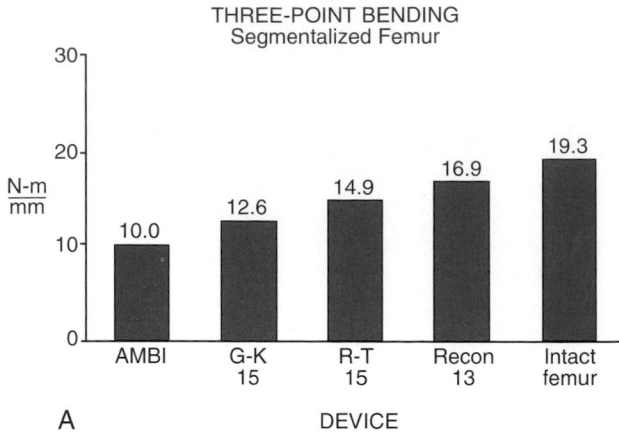

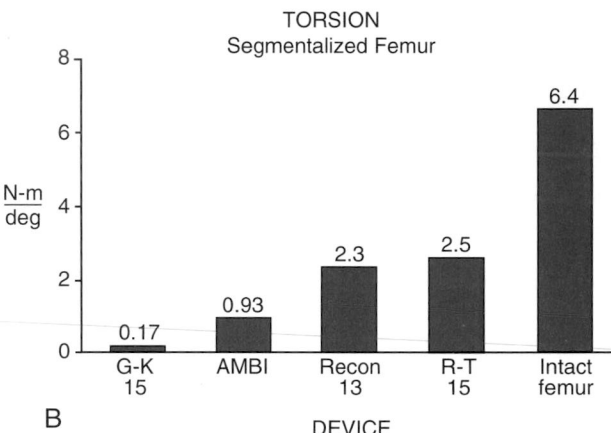

FIGURE 51–5. *A,* Three-point bend testing of devices indicated for use in subtrochanteric fractures in relation to the stiffness of an intact cadaver femur. *B,* The results of testing various implants denote poor resistance to torsional stress in open-section intramedullary devices. *Abbreviations:* G-K, Grosse-Kempf; Recon, reconstruction; R-T, Russell-Taylor. (*A, B,* Modified from Tencer, A.F.; et al. Orthop Biomech Lab Report #002. Memphis, Richards Medical Co., 1985.)

modal age distribution for these fractures.[7, 94, 127, 129] In a study of subtrochanteric fractures, Velasco and Comfort[127] found that 63% of subtrochanteric fractures occurred in patients 51 to older than 70 years and 24% in patients between 17 and 50 years old. Waddell[129] found a 33% incidence of subtrochanteric fractures in patients 20 to 49 years old and a 67% incidence in patients between 50 and 100 years old in their review of proximal femoral fractures. Michelson and associates[85] reported that 14% of hip fractures in patients older than 50 years were subtrochanteric fractures.

The mechanism of injury varies with age. In younger patients, the fracture is more commonly caused by high-energy trauma, such as motor vehicle accidents, vehicle-pedestrian accidents, falls from significant heights, and penetrating injuries, although occasional sports-related subtrochanteric fractures occur.[51] In the older age group, fractures occur with low-energy trauma, as in a simple fall. Bergman and colleagues,[7] in a review of subtrochanteric fractures at a Level I trauma center, noted an average age of 40 years in the high-energy trauma group and 76 years in the low-energy trauma group. A review of our patients at the Presley Trauma Center in Memphis, Tennessee, from 1984 to 1985 revealed that 17% to 44% of femoral fractures were subtrochanteric, depending on the classification system used. As the population of the United States ages over the next 2 decades, a significant increase in the number of low-energy subtrochanteric fractures is anticipated.[53]

This chapter does not include a discussion of patients whose subtrochanteric fractures occur as a result of pathologic states of the bone (tumors, metastatic bone disease, primary neoplastic processes, or metabolic bone disease). The reader is referred to Chapter 16 for more information on the specifics of treatment of pathologic proximal femoral fractures, which are nonetheless mechanically similar to acute fractures.

## Mechanisms of Injury

Fractures from low-energy trauma usually involve minimal comminution, and spiral fractures are relatively common. Frequently, these fractures occur in more osteopenic bone with widened medullary canals and thinner cortices. Subtrochanteric fractures from high-energy trauma are often associated with comminution involving large areas of the proximal end of the femur, with the potential for significant soft tissue damage even in closed injuries, and with compromise of the vascularity of the fracture fragments. In the United States, gunshot wounds are a common source of high-energy trauma in the subtrochanteric region. In our series, approximately 10% of high-energy subtrochanteric fractures were caused by gunshot or shotgun wounds. Excluding penetrating trauma, most subtrochanteric fractures are caused either by direct lateral force to the proximal part of the thigh (as in side impacts from motor vehicle accidents or falls from a height) or by axial loading failure in the subtrochanteric region. Low-energy trauma usually results in transverse, short, oblique or spiral fractures. As with femoral shaft fractures, hemorrhage into soft tissues may be significant. The physician should be attentive to the possible complications of hemorrhage and compartment syndrome.

## Anatomic and Functional Consequences of Injury

A subtrochanteric fracture results in shortening of the affected extremity and varus positioning of the femoral head and neck, effectively creating a functionally weakened abductor muscle group. If not corrected, this deformity causes a significant limp (abductor lurch) because of the shortened working length of the abductor muscles. Therefore, the goals of subtrochanteric fracture management are restoration of normal length and rotation and correction of the femoral head and neck angulation to restore adequate tension to the abductor muscles. The most common error is reduction of the hip in a varus position, which is most undesirable because of the increased stress placed on the implant and the diminished effectiveness of the hip abductors.

## Commonly Associated Injuries

Major associated injuries are unusual in patients with low-energy trauma. Contusions and abrasions are most common, but cranial or vertebral injury must be considered. Older patients are frequently taking medications that affect their mentation and coordination and may impair their ability to call attention to significant trauma in the cranial or vertebral area. When a subtrochanteric fracture is caused by high-energy trauma, total-system examination is required, as with all polytrauma patients. Bergman and colleagues[7] noted that 16 of 31 patients had other injuries to the long bones, pelvis, spine, or viscus. Waddell's retrospective review of eight different hospitals over a 6-year period found associated injuries of the cranium, thorax, and abdomen that required surgical treatment in 27 of 130 patients.[129] Twenty of these 27 patients had more than one additional injury. We have noted a high incidence of ipsilateral patellar and tibial fractures associated with high-energy subtrochanteric fractures. These injuries are particularly serious because they may compromise knee flexion and ankle motion, which, together with possible loss of hip function, may severely limit the patient's functional ability.

## Classification

Boyd and Griffin[12, 13] originally called attention to subtrochanteric fractures as a variant of pertrochanteric fractures and noted a higher incidence of unsatisfactory results after operative treatment. They also first proposed open reduction and two-plane fixation of complex subtrochanteric injuries with sagittal fracture planes in addition to the transverse fracture components.

Classification systems are useful if they alert the surgeon to potential complications, if they recommend specific treatment options, and if they demonstrate interobserver reproducibility. A review of classification schemes gives insight into the evolution of treatment options for subtrochanteric fractures. Fielding and Magliato[40] devised a three-part classification in 1966, with type I fractures at the level of the lesser trochanter, type II fractures within 1 inch below the lesser trochanter, and type III fractures within 1 to 2 inches of the lesser trochanter. This classification did not take into account extension over a large area or comminution. The AO/ASIF group, in their *Manual of Internal Fixation*,[86] also recommended a three-part classification: simple transverse and oblique fractures; fractures with three major fragments, one fragment being either a medial or lateral butterfly fragment; and fractures with marked comminution. This classification also did not consider trochanteric extension. Zickel[139] in 1976 reported a six-part classification system that added long spiral fractures and trochanteric extension. He used his classification to indicate the need for adjunctive fixation to prevent rotational and length deformity with his cephalomedullary nail. Seinsheimer[107] presented a rather complex but concise classification in 1978 involving eight subgroups: type I, nondisplaced fractures; type II, fractures with three subgroups (transverse and oblique medially or laterally); type III, fractures with two subgroups (medial or lateral butterfly); type IV, fractures with bicortical comminution; and type V, fractures involving bicortical comminution with extension into the trochanteric mass. The significance of Seinsheimer's classification is that it identified fractures with loss of medial cortical stability, which would be expected to have a higher rate of implant failure. Unfortunately, interobserver reproducibility is poor with this classification.

Waddell[129] in 1979 presented yet another classification with three major subgroups: transverse or short oblique fractures, long oblique fractures, and comminuted fractures with extension into the trochanteric mass. In 1988, Johnson[61] revived attention to the importance of regional involvement—specifically, involvement of the greater trochanteric area, the lesser trochanteric area, and the area immediately below the lesser trochanter. Johnson recommended IM fixation of fractures involving the lesser trochanteric area and below and hip screw fixation of fractures with proximal extension into the greater trochanteric region.

De Boeck[29] noted that most surgeons prefer simple anatomic identification of subtrochanteric fractures. They believe that classification is necessary for research but do not agree on a particular system, and they have shown great interobserver variation when applying the AO classification. The Orthopaedic Trauma Association (OTA)/AO classification does not list a specific grouping for subtrochanteric fractures, and thus the classification borrows from pertrochanteric and femoral diaphyseal variations.[104]

Russell and Taylor proposed the following classification in the first edition of this textbook, which was based primarily on guidance toward the type of internal fixation that allows the best biomechanical construct with the least vascular damage. This classification was based on techniques and principles of closed IM nailing and interlocking techniques popularized in the 1980s. It emphasizes the biologic imperatives of preserving vascularity to the fracture fragments, optimal implant selection whether intramedullary or extramedullary, and, if appropriate, augmentation of the fracture repair with bone grafting, an approach that was initially recommended by Stewart[113] and supported by Kyle and associates.[74] Because intramedullary techniques bridge the proximal to the distal metaphysis and modern indirect reduction techniques preserve vascularity better than previous open reduction techniques do, this classification does not need to consider such comminution. The important variables are continuity of the lesser trochanter and extension of the fracture, with involvement of the greater trochanter and posterior involvement of the piriformis fossa—specifically, the possible entry sites for an IM nail. This region is critical because lack of integrity in this area makes it difficult to create a stable nail entry portal.

This classification system divides subtrochanteric fractures into two major groups, each of which has two subgroups. Group I fractures do not involve the piriformis fossa, so conventional antegrade IM nailing techniques are relatively straightforward from a piriformis fossa approach. In type IA fractures, comminution and fracture lines extend from below the lesser trochanter to the femoral isthmus; any degree of comminution may be involved in

this area, including bicortical comminution (Fig. 51–6A). Type IB fractures have fracture lines and comminution involving the area of the lesser trochanter to the isthmus (see Fig. 51–6B). Because the lesser trochanter is not intact and is out of continuity with the proximal fragment, conventional proximal femoral interlocking screws cannot gain effective bicortical fixation, and a cephalomedullary interlocking nail technique is required. In both types IA and IB, however, closed IM nailing techniques have the biologic advantage of minimizing vascular compromise of the fracture fragments. The so-called reverse-obliquity intertrochanteric hip fracture may be included in group IB fractures because it behaves more as a subtrochanteric fracture than a conventional intertrochanteric hip fracture.[53] Extension into the greater trochanter not involving the piriformis fossa does not affect the use of closed interlocking nailing through the piriformis portal, but extreme care must be used during reaming to avoid connecting the piriformis portal with the trochanteric extension, which will inevitably result in varus reduction of the hip during nail insertion and possible loss of

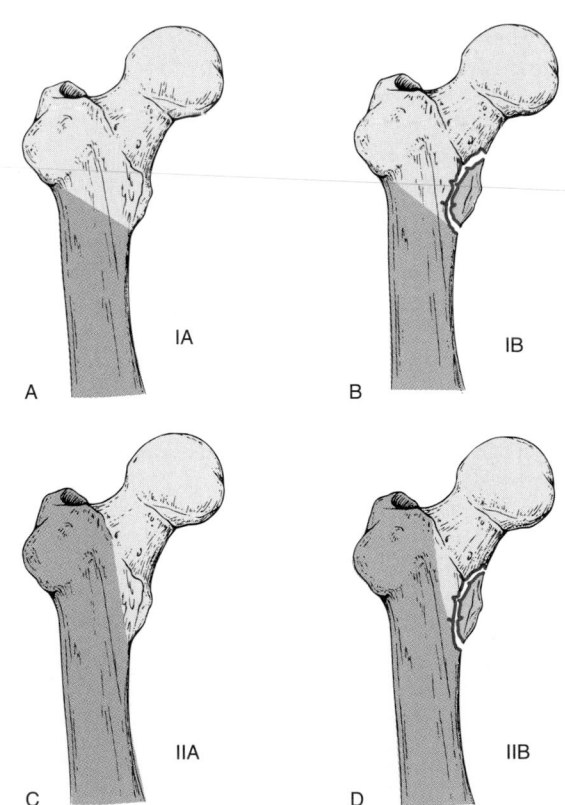

**Figure 51–6.** Russell-Taylor classification of subtrochanteric fractures. Fracture lines may lie anywhere within red zones. In type I fractures, the piriformis fossa remains intact. Involvement of the piriformis fossa IM nail entry site is the hallmark of type II fractures. Subtype A fractures do not involve the lesser trochanter, but in subtype B, the lesser trochanter is a separate fragment. *A,* Type IA subtrochanteric fracture, which can be fixed with a centromedullary nail using an oblique proximal locking screw from greater to lesser trochanter. *B,* Type IB subtrochanteric fracture, which requires a cephalomedullary nail that controls the proximal fragment with locking screws placed into the femoral head. *C,* Type IIA subtrochanteric fracture. The entry site is involved, but the lesser trochanter is intact, so that medial bone contact adds stability. *D,* Type IIB subtrochanteric fracture, with instability due to medial cortical comminution. See text. (Modified from Tencer, A.F.; et al. Orthop Biomech Lab Report #002, Memphis, Richards Medical Co. 1985.)

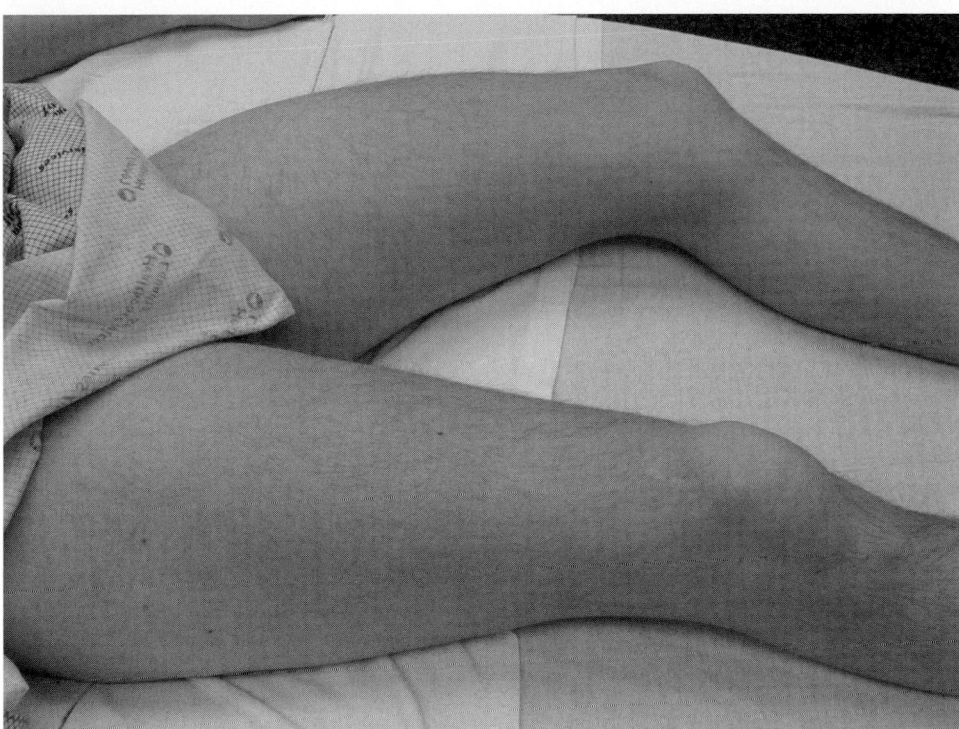

**FIGURE 51–7.** Clinical appearance of a patient with a closed subtrochanteric femoral fracture. Note the shortening, external rotation, and swelling of the thigh.

containment of the nail in the proximal end of the femur. IM nails work best when kept within the medullary canal of both the proximal and distal fragments.

Group II fractures extend proximally into the greater trochanter and involve the piriformis fossa entry site, as detected on a lateral radiograph of the hip. Such involvement of the greater trochanter complicates closed nailing techniques, which depend on the piriformis fossa portal. Group II fractures are more easily secured with indirect reduction techniques using closed interlocking nails through greater trochanteric portals (trochanteric antegrade nails [TANs]), such as the Gamma nail, IMHS nail, and TriGen trochanteric nails, or with plate-and-screw devices such as the 95° blade plate, dynamic compression plate–and-screw systems, and the Medoff biaxial compression hip screw system. Type IIA fractures begin in the trochanteric region and extend distally. They involve the piriformis fossa nail entry site, but the lesser trochanteric region remains intact (see Fig. 51–6C). Type IIB fractures involve the entire trochanteric region, including both the piriformis fossa and the lesser trochanter, with only the femoral head and neck left intact (see Fig. 51–6D).

## DIAGNOSIS

### History

The patient's history is most significant in determining whether the fracture occurred from high- or low-energy trauma. Patients who report minimal trauma or no trauma associated with their subtrochanteric fracture should be extensively evaluated to rule out preexisting pathologic bone disease. Almost universal is an inability to bear weight on the affected extremity. Most patients require transport to the hospital by ambulance after appropriate splinting because of pain with any attempted movement of the extremity.

### Physical Examination

The patient is usually apprehensive and in pain from the injury. Examination most often reveals a shortened extremity with a swollen thigh. Internal or external rotation of the foot results from loss of continuity at the fracture site (Fig. 51–7). Patients are unable to flex their hip actively or move it through a range of motion. Neurologic and vascular deficits are unusual with these fractures unless they are the result of a penetrating injury. On palpation, prominence of the proximal fragment as a result of flexion, abduction, and external rotation of the hip is common.

### Radiographic Imaging

Radiographic evaluation consists of full-length views of the femur from the hip to the knee in both the AP and lateral views, together with an AP radiograph of the pelvis. Both the pelvis and knee must be inspected carefully because of the frequency of associated injuries. We obtain a cross-table lateral radiograph of the affected hip to detect any trochanteric extension that may exit anteriorly or posteriorly into the piriformis fossa. Because of treatment ramifications, attention should be paid to the inner and outer diameter of the medullary canal, the curvature of the femoral shaft, the neck-shaft angle of the unaffected side, and any preexisting deformities or implants of the femur.

Additional radiographic views are usually unnecessary, except to rule out associated injuries. In patients with neurologic deficits, further evaluation is indicated to rule out intraspinal or lumbosacral plexus injury; sciatic nerve injury is rare in patients with subtrochanteric fractures. In severely comminuted fractures, we use an intraoperative scanogram ruler on the normal side to measure length and then use a traction table or femoral distractor to obtain proper length of the affected extremity. In penetrating trauma, arteriograms may be advisable if the Doppler arterial pressure at the ankle is less than 90% of that at the wrist.

## Differential Diagnosis

The differential diagnosis of subtrochanteric fractures essentially requires discrimination only between purely traumatic lesions and those with underlying pathology. If the patient gives a history of preinjury pain or limp or metastatic disease, the surgeon should always consider biopsy of the proximal end of the femur during surgical repair. In a series of 99 older patients with subtrochanteric, shaft, or supracondylar fractures, Boyd and Wilber[11] found that the development of a new medical problem after injury was the most significant factor leading to a poor result and death. They stressed the importance of aggressive medical management in elderly patients.

## MANAGEMENT

As with any complex fracture, subtrochanteric femoral fractures require that surgeons assess their own abilities when choosing operative instead of nonoperative treatment. At issue is how best to obtain adequate fracture stability without devascularizing the fracture site and thus interfering with bone healing. Because mechanical stress is high in the proximal third of the femur, fatigue life of the selected implant is a real concern. Nonoperative treatment (traction and bracing) was previously advocated to avoid the complications of implant failure and infection. It still has a role in mass casualty situations and when surgical treatment cannot be performed safely. Current surgical treatments are usually successful and have lower complication rates than those initially encountered. Therefore, operative treatment is the first choice for subtrochanteric fractures, unless specifically contraindicated.[56]

## Evolution of Treatment

In 1891, Allis[2] analyzed the deforming forces acting on subtrochanteric fractures and advised surgical treatment after noting the difficulty of obtaining satisfactory reduction with longitudinal traction alone. In 1902, Hibbs[58] suggested that traction reduction could be improved by bringing the distal fragment into alignment with the deviated proximal end of the femur. When traction treatment is used, the 90-90 position is required because straight longitudinal traction will not align the fracture.

Waddell[129] retrospectively reviewed traction treatment of nondisplaced fractures and displaced fractures in patients unsuited for surgical treatment. He noted that although nondisplaced fractures did well with traction treatment, only 4 of 11 patients with displaced fractures obtained satisfactory results with Thomas splint traction. Of four patients treated with 90-90 skeletal traction (skeletal traction through a distal femoral pin with an overhead frame and pulley so that both the hip and knee are supported in 90° of flexion), three had satisfactory results. Velasco and Comfort[127] reported that half of 22 adults with subtrochanteric fractures treated by traction had unsatisfactory results, including significant shortening, varus or valgus deformity, or persistent peroneal palsy. In the late 1960s and early 1970s, femoral cast bracing was popularized by Sarmiento,[101] but most reports indicated frequent poor results with this method in proximal femoral fractures.[84] Moreover, Sarmiento stated that primary cast bracing was not indicated for fractures of the proximal third of the femur. DeLee and co-workers[30] reported on 15 subtrochanteric fractures treated by 90-90 traction followed by fracture bracing with a hinged-knee, single hip spica cast. All fractures united, and no patients had refractures. They recommended this treatment protocol for patients with inoperable or open fractures. Despite a 21% complication rate with primary treatment of patients younger than 50 years and a 17% rate of secondary revision, in 1995 Robinson and colleagues[95] recommended early, accurate fracture reduction and internal fixation of hip fractures in young adults. No additional closed treatment studies have been conducted since then in North America, primarily because of the superior results of surgical treatment options.

Nikolic and associates[87] reported on the use of nonoperative fracture stabilization in combat victims sustaining open subtrochanteric fractures from explosions, mines, and high-velocity missile injuries. They compared the results of initial débridement and irrigation followed by either traction and later casting or external fixation. The traction/cast group had a complication rate of 87% as compared with a complication rate of 52% for external fixation; the major complications were nonunion (10%) and osteomyelitis (15%), with most nonunions being associated with external fixation and contractures being the most problematic in the group treated by casting. These authors favored external fixation over casting for high-energy open subtrochanteric fractures. As a reflection of the severity of these injuries, 27% of patients in the study sustained significant neurovascular injuries as a result of the initial trauma.

External fixation of subtrochanteric fractures is used by Dahl and Singh,[31] who described their experience in treating 51 subtrochanteric fractures by external fixation over a 9-year period. They reported a union rate of 94%, refracture after external fixation in one case, and significant leg length discrepancy in two cases. This technique is most applicable to Russell-Taylor class IA fractures that have sufficient bone stock for multiplanar half-pin fixation in the proximal fragment. Our experience with this technique has been for provisional fixation of severely contaminated open fractures not amenable to initial definitive internal fixation, provisional treatment of infected failed internal fixation until the wound can be definitively stabilized after decontamination, and bilateral pathologic femoral fractures in which sequential nailing is performed to prevent fatal pulmonary events during reaming of both femurs with a simultaneous nailing technique.

Operative treatment of subtrochanteric femoral fractures initially began with the surgical treatment of intertrochanteric fractures with the Jewett nail. Boyd and Griffin[12] identified subtrochanteric fractures as having the highest incidence of loss of reduction and migration of the distal fragment medially, as well as a high incidence of coxa vara deformity after healing. They reported good preliminary results with use of the Jewett nail.[60] From the 1940s to the 1960s, the Jewett nail was probably the most frequently used device for fixation of subtrochanteric femoral fractures. Concern about fatigue failure led Jewett to design a nail specifically for subtrochanteric fractures that consisted of two plates welded together for anterior and lateral fixation; however, this nail did not gain widespread acceptance. Reports documented failure rates of approximately 20% to 30% with the Jewett nail, and in 1976, in a study of 155 subtrochanteric fractures, Teitge[117] recommended that the Jewett nail not be used for subtrochanteric femoral fractures.

In 1978, Hanson and Tullos[54] reported an 87.5% rate of union in 42 fractures treated with a nail-plate device and prolonged non–weight bearing. The AO blade plate became popular during the late 1970s, and reported success rates with the device varied from 65% to 85%, with most authors recommending the AO plate for transverse subtrochanteric fractures.[21, 131] Asher and associates[1] advocated that it be used as primary treatment for noncomminuted fractures and stressed the importance of interfragmentary compression, anatomic reduction, and placement of the blade under tension. A high rate (32%) of postoperative complications, including mechanical failure in 13%, led Schlemminger and colleagues[105] to change from condylar plating to the use of dynamic hip screws for intertrochanteric and subtrochanteric fractures.

In 1989, Kinast and associates[67] reported union in all fractures treated with the AO plate when (1) extensive preoperative planning was done, (2) the AO blade plate and femoral distractor were used without dissection of the medial comminution, and (3) prophylactic antibiotics were administered. Of the cases in which anatomic reduction required dissection of the fracture, delayed union or nonunion occurred in 16.6%. These authors also stressed the importance of obtaining a stable construct with interfragmentary compression and tensioning of the AO plate. van Meeteren and co-workers obtained good results with the AO indirect technique and the condylar blade plate: a 97% union rate and a 10% deep infection rate.[126]

Popularization of the sliding hip screw in the early 1970s improved results because of the impaction at the fracture site provided by this implant. Waddell[129] reported a 10% rate of failure or nonunion in 21 fractures treated with the hip compression screw and noted that it functioned as an IM nail in the femoral neck. Wile and co-workers[133] and Berman and associates[8] reported no implant failures after use of the compression hip screw in

25 and 38 subtrochanteric fractures, respectively. Berman's group added bone grafting in all fractures and lag screw fixation when possible. Ruff and Lubbers[97] obtained union in 95% of their series of subtrochanteric fractures, most of which were comminuted. They recommended valgus reduction, medial displacement of the shaft, and insertion of only the lag screw into the proximal fragment to promote impaction of the fracture.

Medoff and Maes[83] reported good results with an axially dynamic side plate and sliding hip screw, primarily for intertrochanteric fractures but also for some high subtrochanteric fractures. Axial impaction was generally less than 1 cm. Subsequent studies of the Medoff sliding plate have validated the design for the treatment of subtrochanteric fractures, with reported union rates of 97% or higher and implant failure rates lower than that noted with other sliding screw systems.[23, 79] Ceder[22] and others have used the plate with uniaxial sliding along the shaft of the femur and biaxial sliding through the sliding lag screw in addition to the plate-sliding feature. They have proved that axial sliding with uniaxial dynamization minimizes medialization of the shaft, but at the risk of lag screw penetration into the femoral head in unstable fractures. Biaxial dynamization minimizes the risk of penetration of the femoral head, but at the risk of medialization of the shaft and greater leg length discrepancy. New plate-and-screw devices for minimally invasive surgery are now under study and may be the next advance in extramedullary fixation for subtrochanteric fractures.[71]

IM nails can be categorized as centromedullary, condylocephalic, or cephalomedullary. *Centromedullary* nails are contained within the medullary canal and are usually inserted from the piriformis fossa; if of interlocking design, the screws are inserted into the metaphyseal-diaphyseal area proximally and distally. *Condylocephalic* nails (e.g., Ender nails) are inserted into the femoral condyle and extend into the femoral head and neck. *Cephalomedullary* nails are derived from the first-generation Küntscher Y nail and Zickel nails and are now represented by interlocking centromedullary nails with screw or nail devices that can be inserted cephalad into the femoral head and neck, such as the Russell-Taylor reconstruction nail (Smith-Nephew), spiral blade nail (Synthes), and similar devices inserted through a piriformis portal. Trochanteric nails are represented by devices such as the Gamma nail, IMHS devices using a single large sliding lag screw into the femoral head, and the TriGen trochanteric nails using two smaller sliding lag screws into the femoral head. Retrograde femoral nailing is rarely, if ever, indicated for subtrochanteric fractures.[32]

Anecdotal descriptions of IM nailing techniques were presented as early as 1918, when Hey-Groves[57] reported centromedullary nailing of a subtrochanteric fracture resulting from a gunshot wound. Küntscher[73] first reported IM nailing of subtrochanteric fractures in 1939. Aronoff and colleagues[3] reported good results with centromedullary nails, particularly in reoperations for nonunion of subtrochanteric fractures. Interest in these techniques was revived in the late 1960s and early 1970s, particularly for the Zickel and Ender nails. The Zickel device, introduced in 1967,[138] consisted of a strong, solid, rectangular rod with a cross bolt engaging the femoral head. Küntscher had designed a Y nail with similar biomechanical principles but without the strength of Zickel's device.[27] In 1976, Zickel[139] described 9 years' experience with his cephalomedullary interlocking nail and reported union in 75 of 76 fractures, 26 of which required accessory fixation for either obliquity or comminution. During the late 1970s and early 1980s, the Zickel device became the treatment of choice for pathologic subtrochanteric fractures.[28, 118, 121] In 1987, Bergman and colleagues[7] classified 154 subtrochanteric fractures treated with the Zickel device as involving high-energy trauma, pathologic fractures, low-energy trauma, or failure of previous internal fixation. Union was obtained in approximately 90% in each group. They recommended the Zickel device for low-energy trauma but preferred other forms of fixation for high-energy trauma because of frequent comminution. For such injuries, they suggested the use of interlocking nail techniques that control shortening and rotation. Because of difficulty with Zickel nails in controlling length and rotation and in refracture after removal, Ovadia and Chess,[88] Shifflett and Bray,[111] Garbarino and colleagues,[48] and other authors[17, 19, 20, 80, 102, 108, 123, 136] recommend interlocking IM nail fixation as the treatment of choice for subtrochanteric fractures in which the lesser trochanter is intact.

Proponents of the Ender technique suggested that it resulted in lower morbidity and less blood loss than the open technique did. However, some reports suggested a high incidence of knee pain, rotational deformity, and instability.[76] Those familiar with the Ender technique obtained good results if certain criteria were met.[38, 90] Common factors in most reports of successful use of the Ender technique included low-energy fractures, minimal comminution, and elderly patients. The larger medullary canals in these patients allowed entry into the canal with four or five Ender pins from both the medial and lateral portals. The use of Ender nails for subtrochanteric fractures essentially ended with the introduction of interlocking nails.

Other IM nailing techniques of historical significance include that of Heiple and co-workers,[55] who modified the Sampson nail by expanding it proximally in an attempt to control rotation. Scherfel[103] reported good results in 16 fractures treated with a special nail with fins in the proximal portion to control rotation. These implants, along with the Zickel nail, became obsolete because of the advantages of static interlocking nails.

The biomechanical advantages of centromedullary, condylocephalic, and cephalomedullary implants were well recognized, as were their shortcomings in controlling rotation and shortening.[66, 72, 78] In three large series[14, 48, 111] of subtrochanteric fractures presented at the 1987 meeting of the American Academy of Orthopaedic Surgeons, the addition of interlocking capability to IM nails achieved the highest rates of union ever reported in cases of high-energy trauma. Use of these nails was limited, however, by the requirement for an intact entry portal in the greater trochanter in relation to the piriformis fossa and an intact lesser trochanter for proximal fixation. Brien and associates[14] reported a single nonunion in 66 subtrochanteric fractures, 75% of which were caused by high-energy trauma. Subsequently, Wiss and Brien,[134] after reviewing 95 subtrochanteric fractures treated with locked IM nails,

showed that essentially all nonpathologic, subtrochanteric femoral fractures can be stabilized by interlocking nailing, regardless of the fracture pattern or degree of comminution. They concluded that closed locked nailing is the treatment of choice for subtrochanteric fractures.

The Russell-Taylor reconstruction interlocking nail was introduced in 1986 as a subtrochanteric fracture fixation device that combined cephalomedullary interlocking with section modulus modifications to maximize its strength in the proximal end of the nail while avoiding excessive stiffness in the diaphyseal region of the femur.[10] As with earlier implants, preoperative planning includes evaluation for fracture extension into the greater trochanter and particularly into the piriformis fossa, which is the entry portal for this device. Because of two-screw fixation in the femoral head, rotation is well maintained, and the lesser trochanter does not have to be intact. In our series of almost 200 subtrochanteric fractures, 100% have united without nail failure.[116] Fifty complex subtrochanteric fractures with comminution of the lesser trochanteric region have been treated with the reconstruction nail; 28% of these fractures were open, usually because of motor vehicle accidents or gunshot wounds. At a 3-year followup, all fractures were united. One patient required a reoperation to correct an external rotation deformity. Browner[16] also reported excellent results with the reconstruction nail in the treatment of 16 subtrochanteric fractures and nonunions. At follow-up ranging from 6 months to 2 years, the rate of union was 100%, and all patients had excellent hip and knee motion. French and Tornetta reported similar results with the Russell-Taylor reconstruction nail in 45 Russell-Taylor type IB subtrochanteric fractures: 100% union rate at an average of 13.5 weeks; the most frequent complication was varus reduction of the hip because of lateralization of the starting portal into the greater trochanter.[44] Taylor and colleagues reported excellent results in high-energy trauma with the reconstruction nail for military parachuting injuries.[115]

IM nails such as the Gamma nail, the IMHS, and the TriGen TAN, which are inserted through an entry portal in the tip of the greater trochanter instead of the more medially located piriformis fossa entry site, have revived interest in the trochanteric entry portal.* Nails designed for this entry site, with a slight valgus bend at the metadiaphyseal junction, offer advantages discussed later, especially for Russell-Taylor group II fracture patterns. They can be used in either the centromedullary or cephalomedullary modes (Fig. 51–8).

## Current Algorithm

The choice of treatment for subtrochanteric fractures depends on several factors (Fig. 51–9). Balanced (90°-90°) traction, possibly followed by a hinged-knee hip spica cast brace as advocated by DeLee and co-workers,[30] remains an option, although it does not provide for early mobilization of a multiply injured patient. Closed treatment is appropriate, at least as provisional management, in mass casualty situations. In elderly patients, nonoperative treatment of

---

*See references 5, 6, 9, 25, 33, 42, 45, 82, 92, 96, 125.

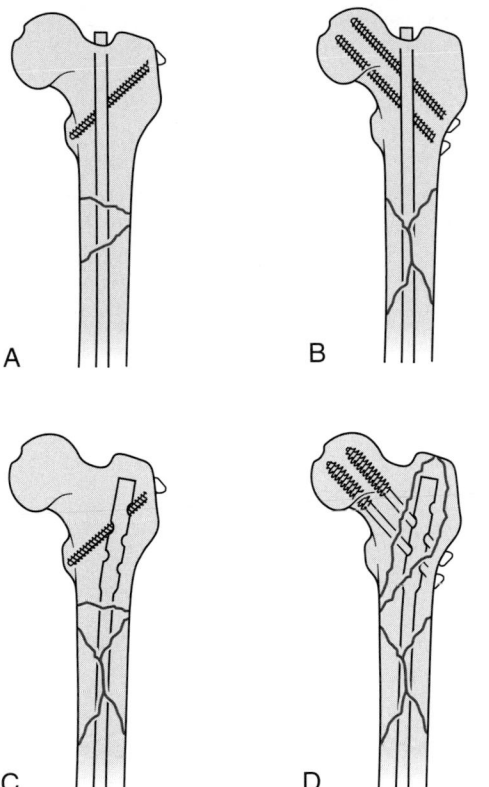

**FIGURE 51–8.** Different nail design for different entry sites. Nails intended for the piriformis fossa entry site are straight. *A,* Centromedullary. *B,* Cephalomedullary locking screws. Those for trochanteric insertion site are slightly angled. *C,* Centromedullary. *D,* Cephalomedullary locking screws

subtrochanteric fractures should generally be limited to situations in which the patient's medical situation makes the risks of surgery excessive or in which bone quality is so poor that there is no hope of secure fixation. Unfortunately, geriatric patients who are too ill for surgical treatment rarely regain their previous ambulatory status and have a higher mortality rate after their injury.

Fixation for subtrochanteric fractures depends on the fracture configuration. Russell-Taylor type IA fractures with intact trochanters are most effectively managed by closed insertion of a conventional interlocked centromedullary nail in a static locked mode (Fig. 51–10). In type IB subtrochanteric fractures with extension into the lesser trochanter, a cephalomedullary interlocking nail is indicated (Fig. 51–11).

For Russell-Taylor type IIA and IIB fractures with comminution of the greater trochanter, including the piriformis fossa, modern hip compression screws offer reliable fixation, as do cephalomedullary IM nails. A hip compression screw with a locking barrel should be used to limit rotation of the femoral head (Fig. 51–12). If the hip compression screw is to function as a dynamically interlocked device, placement of the screws through the plate and into the proximal fragment must be avoided because in this position they could maintain distraction of the fracture. The Medoff plate, with its bimodal dynamization capabilities, may be a more satisfactory alternative for selected subtrochanteric fractures than the

95° angled plates and conventional compression hip screws (see Fig. 51–20).

After more than a decade of experience with the reconstruction nail and Gamma-type trochanteric nail devices, we and others realize that type IIA and IIB fractures—those with fracture lines extending into the entry site—can be successfully treated with cephalomedullary nails.[112, 127, 135] Admittedly, these fractures are more technically demanding because of comminution involving the piriformis fossa and intertrochanteric region. However, other advantages have become apparent. A locked nail, in contrast to the compression hip screw and side plate, can span the entire femur, thus making the extent of shaft comminution relatively unimportant. The use of longer nails to bridge the femur from metaphysis to metaphysis also effectively prevents subsequent fractures proximal or distal to the nail.[37] The shaft of the IM nail blocks lateral migration of the neck-head fragment and thereby avoids shaft medialization, in contrast to the compression hip screw, which does not control such displacement and related shortening. The results of reconstruction nailing of subtrochanteric fractures are usually more anatomic in spite of intertrochanteric comminution or reverse-obliquity patterns. Design differences among cephalomedullary nails that facilitate the trochanteric entry site and more closely fit the anatomy of the femoral medullary canal may help avoid fractures around the implant[93] (Fig. 51–13).

Similar to closed IM nailing, plating with an indirect reduction technique that preserves soft tissue integrity around the fracture has reduced implant failure rates and the need for bone grafting. Kinast and associates[67] achieved a 100% success rate when a blade plate was used with the indirect reduction technique without autogenous bone graft. Sanders and co-workers[100] were less successful when this technique was used with a 95° condylar screw device, but Pai reported good results in Russell-Taylor type IIB fractures with the 95° condylar screw to avoid the difficulty encountered with greater trochanteric comminution.[89]

Plate-and-screw fixation of subtrochanteric fractures is probably best indicated for fractures associated with preexisting deformities of the proximal end of the femur or previous implants (e.g., hip arthrodesis or arthroplasty). External fixation is reserved for open fractures with severe contamination, for provisional stabilization in the acute injury period, or for intermediate treatment of complications from previous failed internal fixation. Pathologic fractures of the subtrochanteric area (see Chapter 16) are best treated with cephalomedullary implants that allow prophylactic stabilization of the entire femur from the knee to the femoral head, such as a reconstruction nail in a static locked mode. Cephalomedullary nails might also be chosen to avoid the risk of femoral neck insufficiency fractures in patients with poor bone stock.[68]

## Indications for Bone Grafting

The use of autogenous bone grafting in subtrochanteric fractures has been suggested by numerous authors since the 1960s, especially for revision of failed internal fixation. Stewart,[113] in a discussion of the presentation of Watson and colleagues[130] in 1964, advocated acute autogenous iliac bone grafting of traumatic subtrochanteric fractures in young patients. Autogenous bone grafting is indicated during true open reduction of fractures with significant comminution of the medial wall. No prospective studies using allograft techniques are available. Closed nailing and indirect reduction techniques obviate the need for bone grafting, possibly because the fracture fragments are not devascularized as much as with a traditional open reduction.[74] The role of newer bone graft substitutes is currently unknown.

## Open Subtrochanteric Fractures

Open subtrochanteric fractures are rare and almost always associated with either penetrating injury or high-energy trauma from motor vehicle accidents or falls from heights. The same principles that apply to all open fractures apply as well to subtrochanteric fractures: immediate surgical débridement and, after conversion to a clean contaminated wound, stabilization to help resist infection (Fig. 51–14). The objective is to use the minimal fixation necessary to adequately stabilize the subtrochanteric fracture. In the past, this goal presented problems because most fixation methods for subtrochanteric fractures involved further tissue dissection and contamination of tissue planes, which prompted DeLee and co-workers[30] to recommend 90-90 traction and cast bracing for open subtrochanteric fractures. Johnson[61] recommended IM fixation of subtrochanteric fractures after adequate débridement and conversion to a clean contaminated wound, either acutely or 10 to 21 days later, after delayed primary closure.

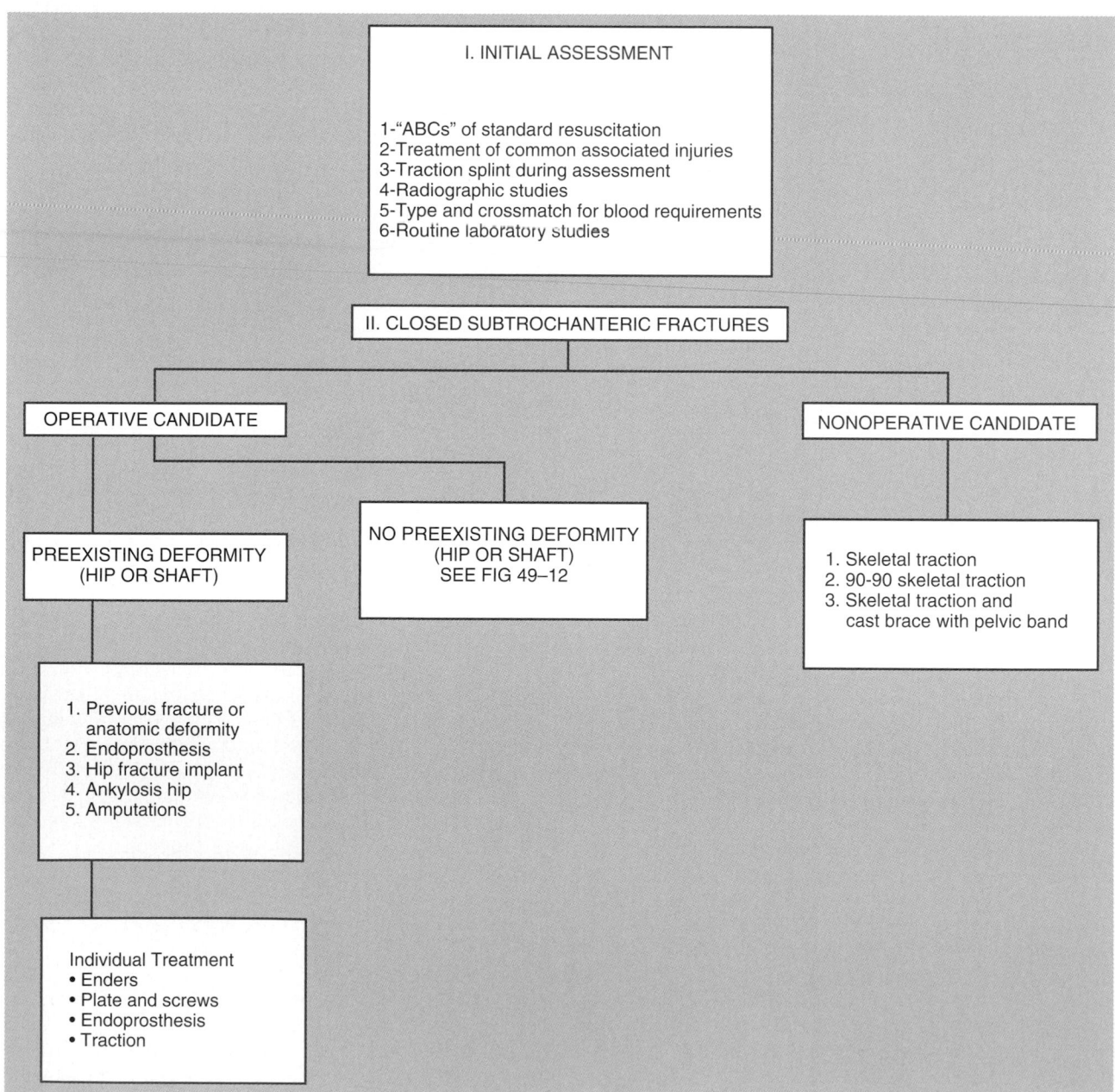

**I. INITIAL ASSESSMENT**

1-"ABCs" of standard resuscitation
2-Treatment of common associated injuries
3-Traction splint during assessment
4-Radiographic studies
5-Type and crossmatch for blood requirements
6-Routine laboratory studies

**II. CLOSED SUBTROCHANTERIC FRACTURES**

OPERATIVE CANDIDATE

NONOPERATIVE CANDIDATE

PREEXISTING DEFORMITY
(HIP OR SHAFT)

NO PREEXISTING DEFORMITY
(HIP OR SHAFT)
SEE FIG 49–12

1. Skeletal traction
2. 90-90 skeletal traction
3. Skeletal traction and
   cast brace with pelvic band

1. Previous fracture or
   anatomic deformity
2. Endoprosthesis
3. Hip fracture implant
4. Ankylosis hip
5. Amputations

Individual Treatment
• Enders
• Plate and screws
• Endoprosthesis
• Traction

FIGURE 51–9. Algorithm for the treatment of closed subtrochanteric fractures.

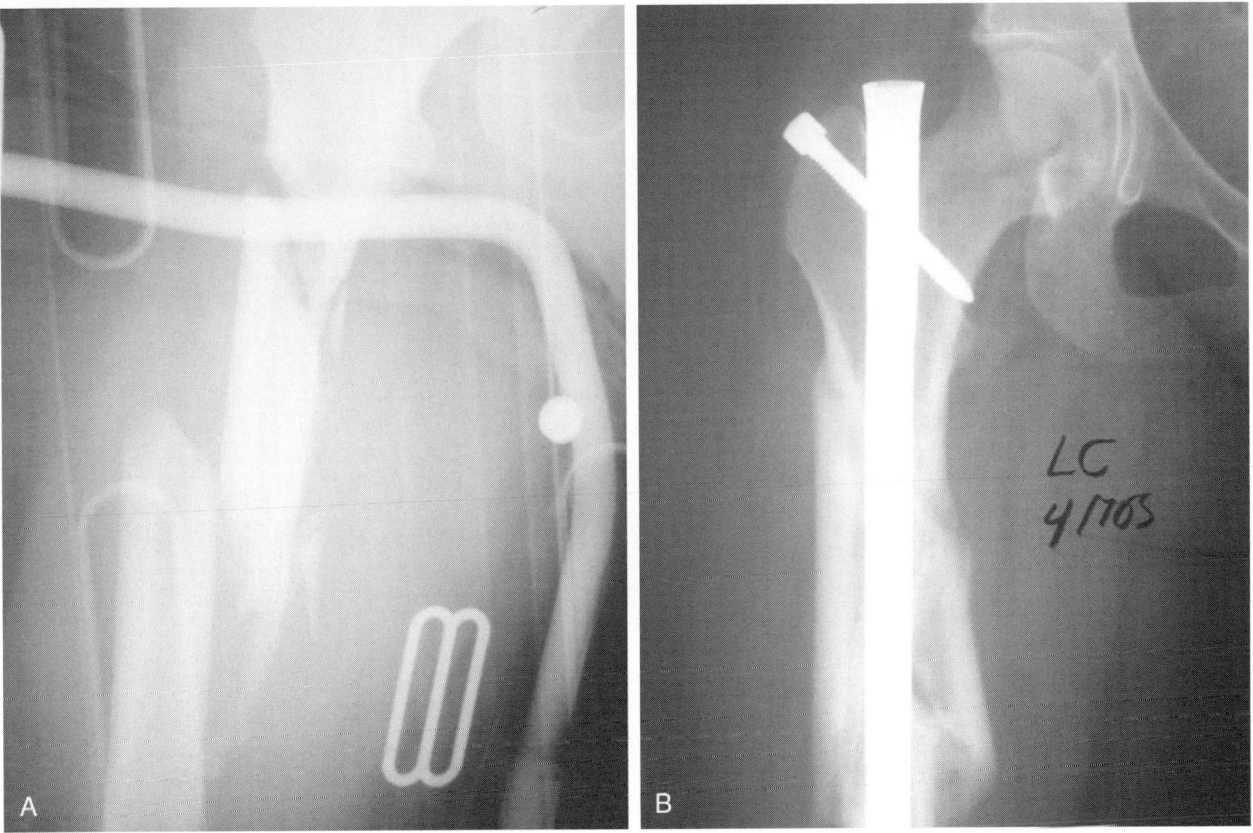

FIGURE 51–10. *A,* Segmental type IA subtrochanteric fracture in a young woman. *B,* Healed 4 months after closed intramedullary nailing.

FIGURE 51–11. Russell-Taylor type IB fracture in a 39-year-old man that was sustained while parachuting. *A,* Preoperative radiographs. *B,* Postoperative radiographs after immediate fixation with a Russell-Taylor reconstruction nail in the static locking mode.

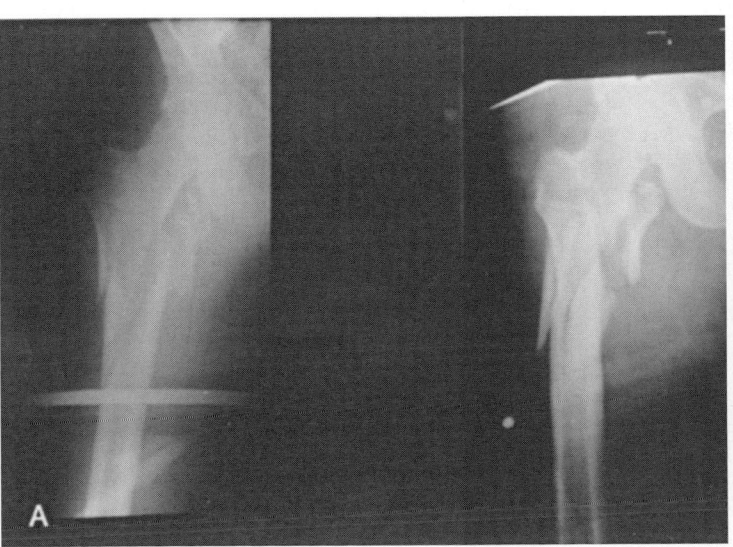

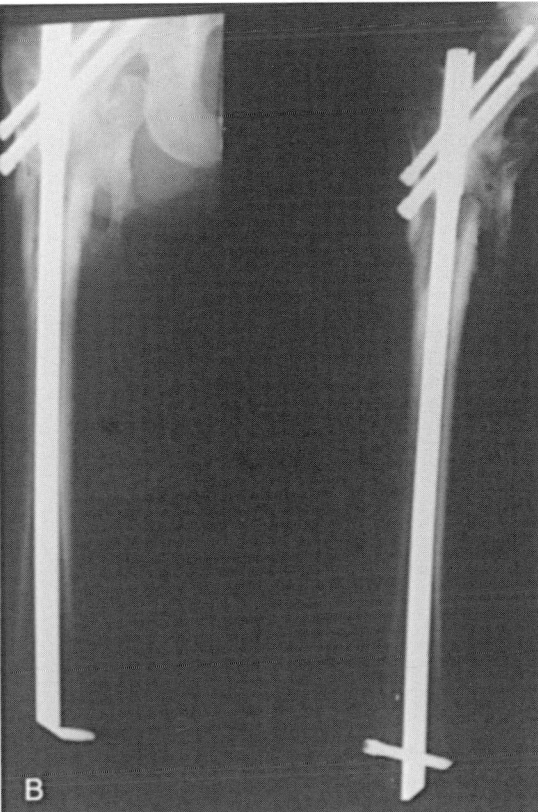

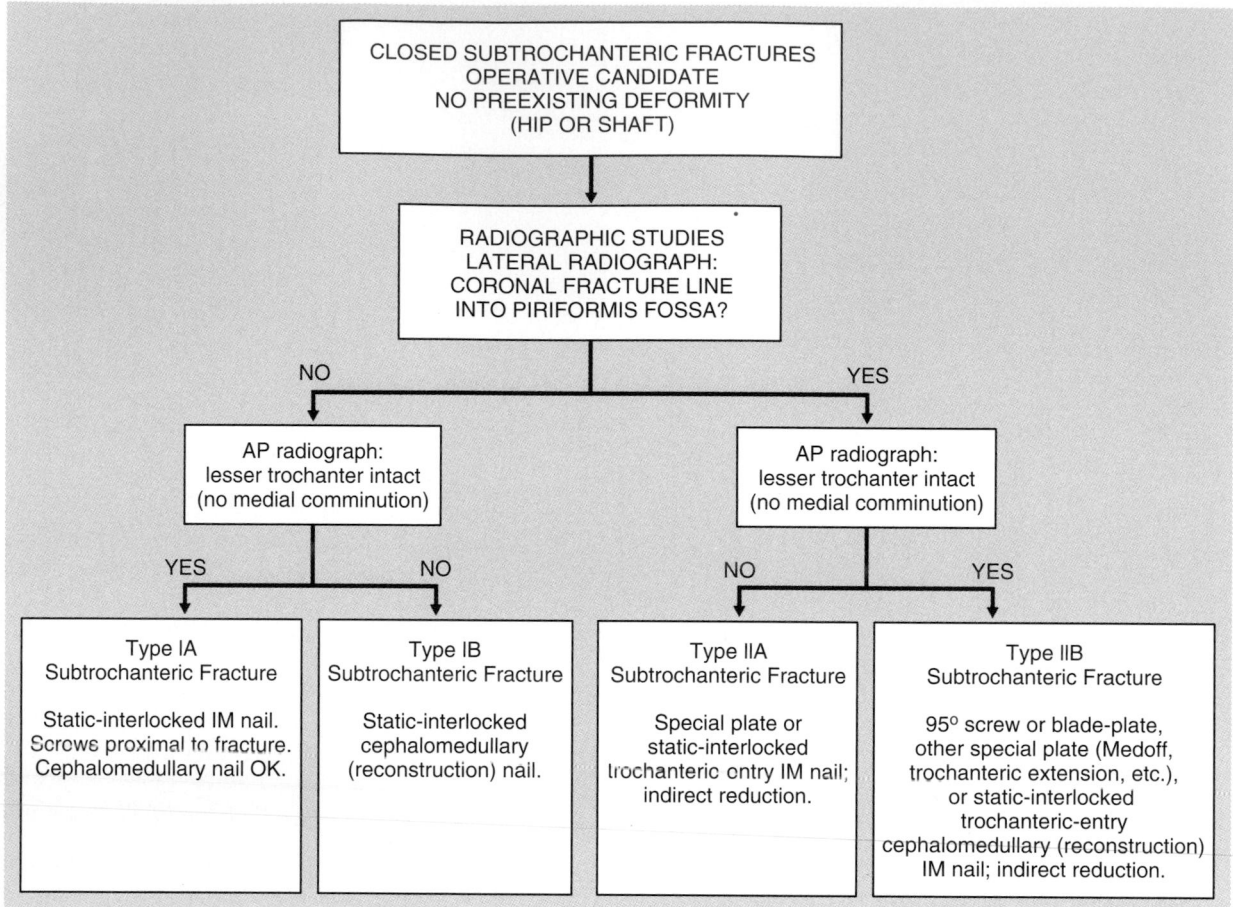

**Figure 51–12.** Algorithm for the operative treatment of closed subtrochanteric fractures according to the Russell-Taylor classification.

I prefer immediate internal fixation of type I though type IIIA open subtrochanteric fractures (Gustilo[50] classification) after adequate débridement, in addition to combined cephalosporin and aminoglycoside antibiotic coverage. I believe that all wounds should be left open, except for extensions, and repeat débridement performed 24 to 48 hours later and as often as necessary until either delayed primary closure or plastic surgical wound coverage is obtained. I suggest external fixation for type IIIB or IIIC subtrochanteric fractures when the proximal fragment is large enough to insert pins in a delta configuration or when the fracture is accompanied by vascular injury requiring repair and the wound cannot be converted to a clean contaminated wound with the initial débridement and irrigation. Minimal reaming should be the goal in open subtrochanteric femoral fractures, but sufficient medullary canal fill by the nail in the diaphysis is required for translational stability of the nail. The option of interlocking nail insertion without reaming for the treatment of open type IIIB subtrochanteric fractures may be beneficial, but studies as of yet are indeterminate. Nail techniques should not be used acutely in severely contaminated subtrochanteric fractures or in wounds with treatment delayed more than 12 hours. IM nailing of an open subtrochanteric fracture requires direct visualization of the proximal and distal medullary canals to ensure that no foreign bodies are left in the medullary canal before canal preparation and nailing. We do not remove all fragments from gunshot wounds, but wadding must be found and removed from shotgun blast injuries (Fig. 51–15).

## Special Considerations for Polytrauma Patients

Both retrospective and prospective studies provide justification for prompt (within the first 24 hours) stabilization of long bone injuries in polytrauma patients.[34, 77] A subtrochanteric fracture is certainly an injury requiring early stabilization to obtain the benefits of early mobilization and avoid "traction syndrome" in a polytrauma patient. Maximal effort should be made to obtain stabilization, either internally or externally, because of the susceptibility of these patients to pulmonary failure and sepsis.[18] If other injuries involve the ipsilateral extremity, we first attempt to stabilize the injury that will keep the patient in bed. If the patient's condition deteriorates (intraoperatively) and surgery cannot be continued, only closed methods are used until the patient is stable enough for surgical fixation. In a severely injured patient, provisional external fixation should always be considered as an acute option during the resuscitation phase of treatment if the patient's general medical condition precludes acute nailing.

## Description of Individual Procedures

### TRACTION

The technique of DeLee and co-workers[30] is recommended for subtrochanteric fractures that must be treated by traction. Skeletal traction is applied with a femoral pin, if possible, to avoid pulling through the knee; however, tibial traction has been used successfully. The limb is suspended with both the hip and knee flexed to 90°. The leg and foot are placed in a well-padded short leg cast with the foot plantigrade. Casting may be performed with local or general anesthesia. For the average adult, initial traction is 30 to 40 lb (13.6 to 18.2 kg). Appropriate adjustments are made, with radiographic monitoring, until satisfactory reduction is achieved in both the AP and lateral views: less than 5° of varus or valgus angulation and at least 25% apposition of the fracture fragments on both views. Shortening of more than 1 cm is avoided. After approximately 3 to 4 weeks, as the patient's symptoms subside, the leg may gradually be lowered to a less flexed position, with abduction as necessary to prevent varus angulation. When clinical consolidation has been achieved, as indicated by

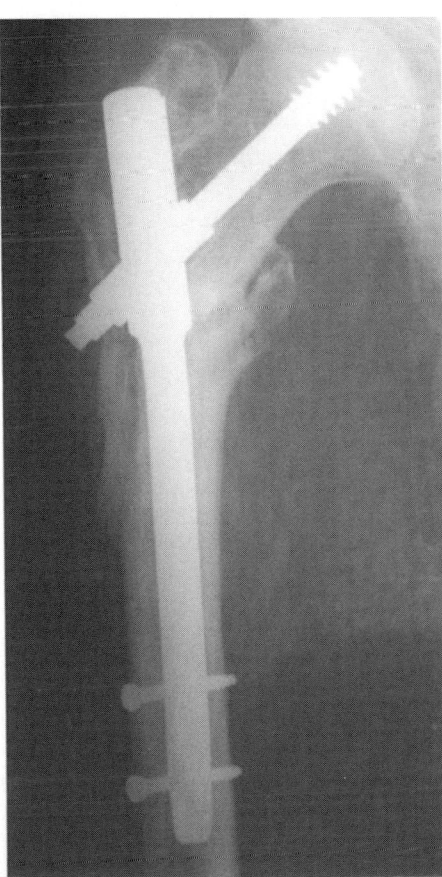

**FIGURE 51–13.** Russell-Taylor type IIB subtrochanteric fracture healed with an intramedullary hip screw (IMHS) static locking cephalomedullary nail (Courtesy of Smith and Nephew, Richards Co., Memphis, TN.)

restoration of some mechanical continuity (e.g., rotation of the distal portion of the thigh yielding rotation of the greater trochanter) and early callus formation on radiographs, the patient may be placed in a cast brace with a pelvic band and a proximal quadrilateral mold. We usually incorporate the traction pin in the cast. The patient is then taught transfers out of bed, and touch-down weight bearing ambulation is allowed with a built-up shoe on the contralateral leg. Radiographs should be taken weekly, and if signs of lost reduction occur, manipulation or conversion to internal fixation should be performed as necessary.

### SLIDING HIP SCREW

For open reduction and internal fixation of fractures with type IIA and IIB patterns, biomechanical and clinical studies indicate the use of a hip compression screw system that is approved for subtrochanteric fractures of the femur.[59, 75, 81, 128] Current compression hip screws have improved fatigue characteristics. Fixation failure usually results from cutout of the screw from the femoral head rather than from fracture of the plate, as with earlier implants.[63, 64] The general technique of insertion of a compression screw is described in Chapter 49; only specific references to subtrochanteric fractures are included here.

As noted previously, hip compression screws are most often indicated for open reduction and internal fixation of Russell-Taylor type IIA or IIB injuries (Fig. 51–16). Contraindications to open reduction and internal fixation, other than general medical contraindications, are related to potential problems in obtaining stability. If the patient has osteoporosis to such a degree that internal fixation will not hold, the fracture should be considered pathologic. Adjunctive use of methyl methacrylate may permit secure fixation of such injuries. Surgery should be performed within 24 hours of injury if possible; if not, the patient should be placed in skeletal traction. Although Finsen and associates[41] found no benefit in preoperative skin or skeletal traction for pertrochanteric fractures, the hydraulic force generated from bleeding of the subtrochanteric fracture into the surrounding muscle groups may make intraoperative restoration of length quite difficult unless it is maintained with preoperative skeletal traction.

Hip screw fixation of subtrochanteric fractures is difficult and often results in increased operative time and blood loss. Detailed preoperative planning is mandatory, including measurement of the head-neck angle for selection of the hip screw device and the correct side plate length. Lag screw fixation of major fragments is now generally avoided in favor of indirect reduction techniques in which the fracture fragments are aligned with traction and bypassed by the plate.

The patient, usually under general anesthesia, is placed supine on a fracture table. The iliac crest is draped in the operative field to allow procurement of autogenous iliac bone graft if necessary. It is important to avoid internal rotation when securing the foot on the fracture table. We use the image intensifier to determine the correct position of the femoral head and match the rotation of the lower extremity; however, during reduction of the proximal end of the femur, adjustments to the fracture table may be

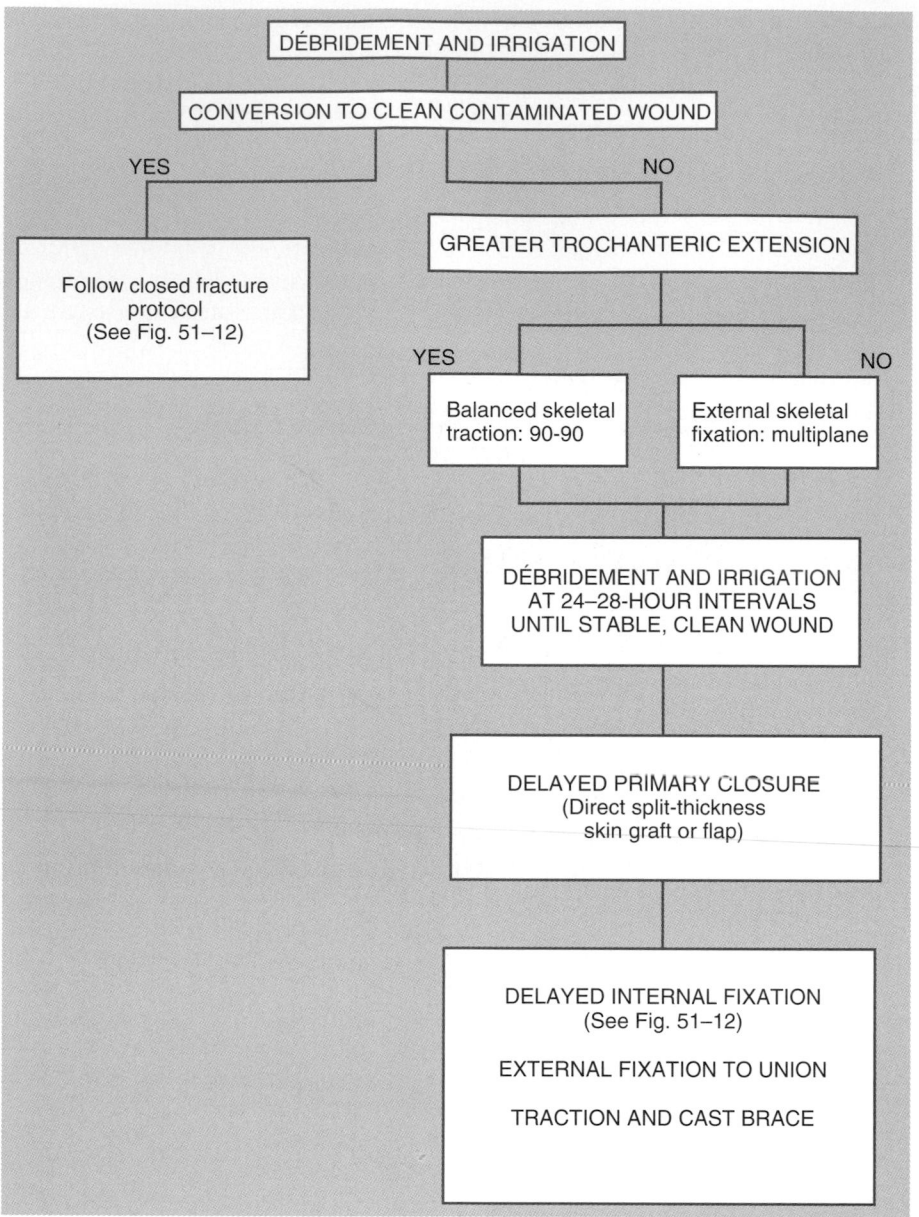

**FIGURE 51–14.** Algorithm for the treatment of open subtrochanteric fractures.

required before definitive fixation. A straight lateral incision is made over the hip. Rather than a muscle-splitting approach, we prefer to incise the fascia of the vastus lateralis and reflect the muscle from the intermuscular septum while attempting to identify and individually ligate each perforating vessel. These vessels should not be cauterized because they frequently retract and resume bleeding, which may be difficult to control. The relationship of the linea aspera should be noted as a further check of the correct rotational alignment of the fracture reduction. We prefer the AO femoral distractor and the technique of indirect reduction advocated by Kinast and associates[67] for open reduction and internal fixation of subtrochanteric fractures (Fig. 51–17). Avoiding dissection medially helps preserve the vascularity of the fracture fragments. The femoral distractor is usually positioned anterior to the incision with Schanz screws proximally in the greater trochanteric area and

distally in the shaft. Gradual distraction can then be carried out. This technique is especially useful in very muscular patients and in fractures not repaired in the first 24 hours.

After provisional reduction is obtained and held with K-wires, the hip compression screw is inserted in the standard manner. It is important to attach the plate to the distal fragment with at least four screws engaging a minimum of eight cortices.[106] Lag screws may be used through the plate, but it is preferable to avoid fixing the plate to the proximal fragment because such fixation prevents the compression screw from telescoping and thus interferes with impaction of the fracture (Fig. 51–18). We believe that it is imperative to use a hip compression screw device that prevents rotation of the lag screw in the barrel. If medial dissection is necessary, autogenous iliac bone grafting should be considered. Obtaining good-quality radiographic control during internal fixation of the fracture can prevent most problems of implant fixation. After débridement of any devitalized tissue, the wounds should be closed in layers, with suction drains used if necessary (Figs. 51–19 and 51–20).

The patient is allowed to sit in a chair the day after surgery and encouraged to begin ambulation with a partial weight-bearing, heel-to-toe gait and a walker or crutches. We do not routinely remove hip compression screws in elderly patients. In young patients involved in competitive sports or heavy manual labor, we offer implant removal 1 to 2 years after surgery if solid union is confirmed

radiographically. The patient is cautioned to use crutches with weight bearing to tolerance for 6 weeks after removal of the implant and to avoid all contact sports for 3 months. This time frame may be overly cautious, but with this protocol we have not experienced refracture of the subtrochanteric region.

## CONDYLOCEPHALIC NAIL

In our experience, indications for condylocephalic (Ender) nailing of subtrochanteric fractures are few. It might be

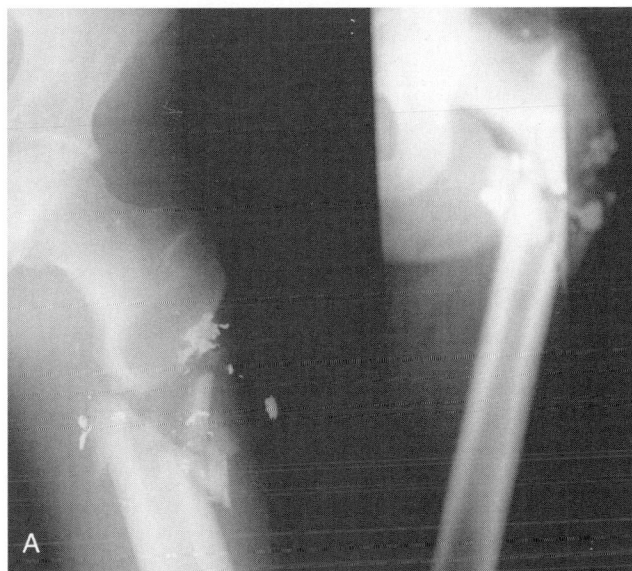

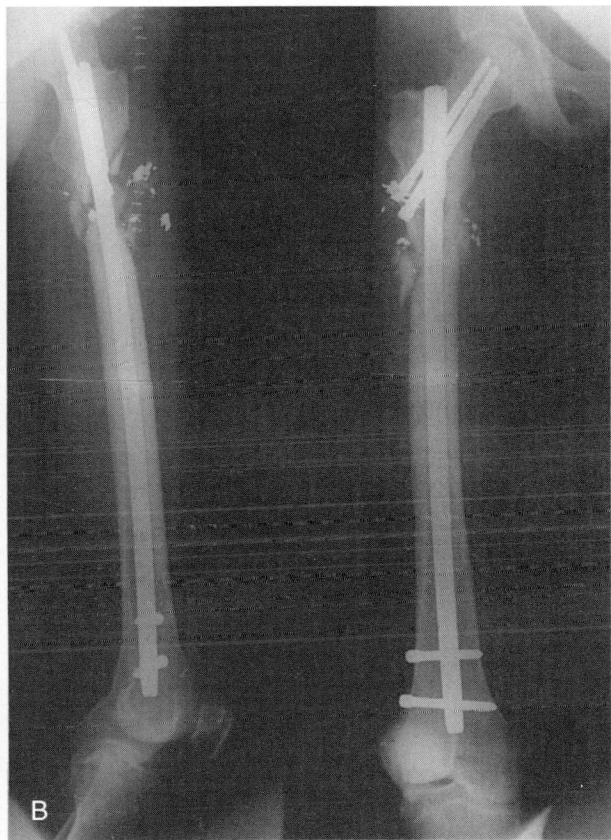

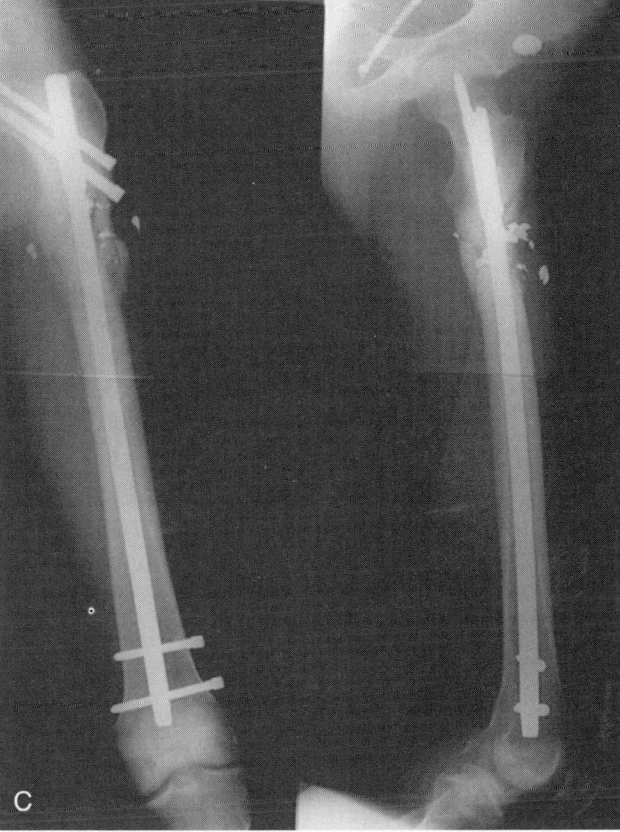

**FIGURE 51–15.** *A*, A 40-year-old man with a point-blank 357-magnum gunshot wound to the proximal end of the femur. *B*, The patient was treated by emergency débridement, irrigation, and stabilization with a regular reconstruction nail. Note the significant bone loss. *C*, Six months after surgery, the fracture has healed radiographically and clinically without a bone graft.

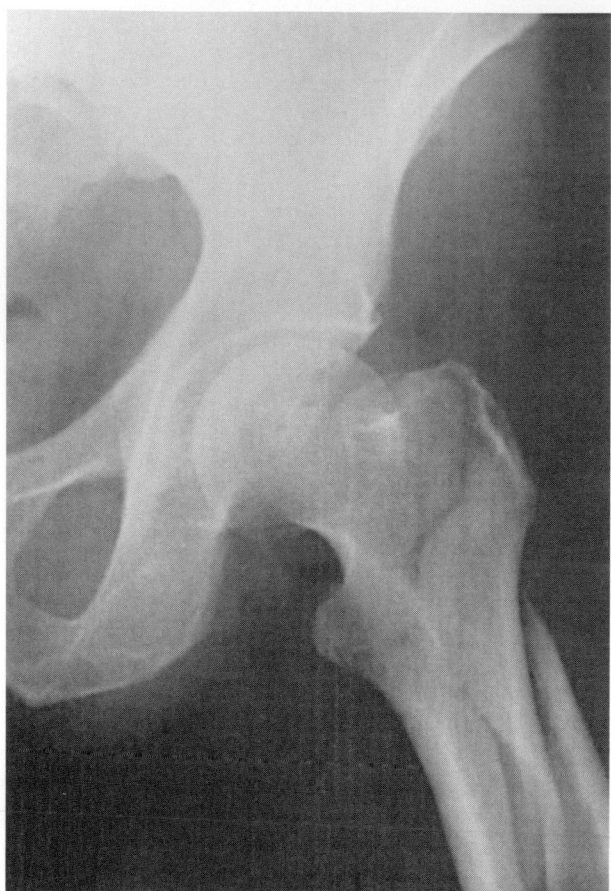

**FIGURE 51–16.** Russell-Taylor type IIA subtrochanteric fracture with fracture extension into the piriformis fossa. The medial cortex was stable after reduction.

considered for patients who have traumatized skin over the proximal hip area that makes incisions for either hip compression screws or closed nailing procedures undesirable, but it should not be used if more stable fixation techniques are possible. As with other techniques, condylocephalic nailing should be performed within the first 24 hours, if possible, or as soon as the patient can be stabilized medically. In accordance with the recommendations of Dobozi and colleagues,[35] both medial and lateral entry portals should be used, and the patient should be placed supine on a fracture table with image control. A Lowman clamp about the femur just proximal to both entry portals may help avoid their extension into a supracondylar fracture. Transverse or short oblique fractures with minimal comminution are the most suitable for this type of fixation; if adjunctive fixation is required, an interlocking nail or hip compression screw would be preferable. Postoperative care may range from several weeks of traction to mobilization as described for hip compression screws. A common difficulty is obtaining full knee motion postoperatively, especially if pins are inserted too anteriorly or are allowed to protrude into the supracondylar region. Loss of fixation is also a frequent complication of Ender nail fixation of the proximal end of the femur.

## INTERLOCKED INTRAMEDULLARY NAIL (FIRST-, SECOND-, AND THIRD-GENERATION TECHNIQUES)

First-generation femoral interlocking nail systems allow centromedullary fixation of most femoral fractures, including those with severe or segmental comminution between the distal fifth of the femur and a point just distal to the lesser trochanter (see Fig. 51–8A). Grosse and associates[49] originally established guidelines for IM nailing of femoral fractures: stable fractures of the isthmus (transverse, short oblique, spiral, or mildly comminuted fractures of the lateral cortex) are treated with an unlocked nail; fractures proximal to the isthmus, with proximal locking; and more distal fractures, with one or two distal locking screws. Although excellent results have been reported when these guidelines are followed, most large series include some patients with postoperative shortening because of unrecognized nondisplaced cracks in the cortex or overestimation of fracture stability. In our experience and that of others, union can be achieved in almost all fractures with static interlocking because rotation and length can be better controlled. Therefore, we currently recommend static locking of all femoral IM nails. Dynamization (removal of the distal screws) is seldom required for fracture healing.[1, 16] The technique for standard femoral antegrade nailing with an entry portal through the piriformis fossa is described in Chapter 52.

### Intramedullary Nail Preoperative Planning

Preoperative radiographs of the uninjured femur are used to estimate the proper nail diameter, the expected amount of reaming, and the final nail length. Proper length of the extremity should be obtained with traction before closed antegrade IM nailing, except in acute cases. Nail length should permit the proximal end of the nail to lie flush to 10 mm below the tip of the greater trochanter and the distal end to lie between the proximal pole of the patella and the distal femoral physeal scar. This position is also dependent on the individual nail design. Subtrochanteric fractures should be stabilized immediately if the patient's general condition is stable. I recommend perioperative administration of a first-generation cephalosporin antibiotic for 24 to 48 hours, with an alternative drug chosen if the patient has an allergy. For open fractures, tobramycin is usually added and the antibiotics continued for 3 days, pending the results of operative culture, and continued for 24 to 48 hours after delayed wound closure.

Patient positioning options include the use of fracture tables in either the supine or lateral decubitus position and nontraction fluoroscopic tables with manual traction. The goals of positioning are to allow access to the correct portal and reduction and fixation in correct alignment, rotation, and length. The use of a fracture table is advised in most community hospitals because more assistants are required for manual traction techniques. I have found the lateral position most helpful in Russell-Taylor type IIB fractures and in revision nailing for nonunion and previous implant failures.

General anesthesia is most commonly used, but spinal or epidural anesthesia is also acceptable. Usually, the patient is anesthetized in bed or a stretcher and then

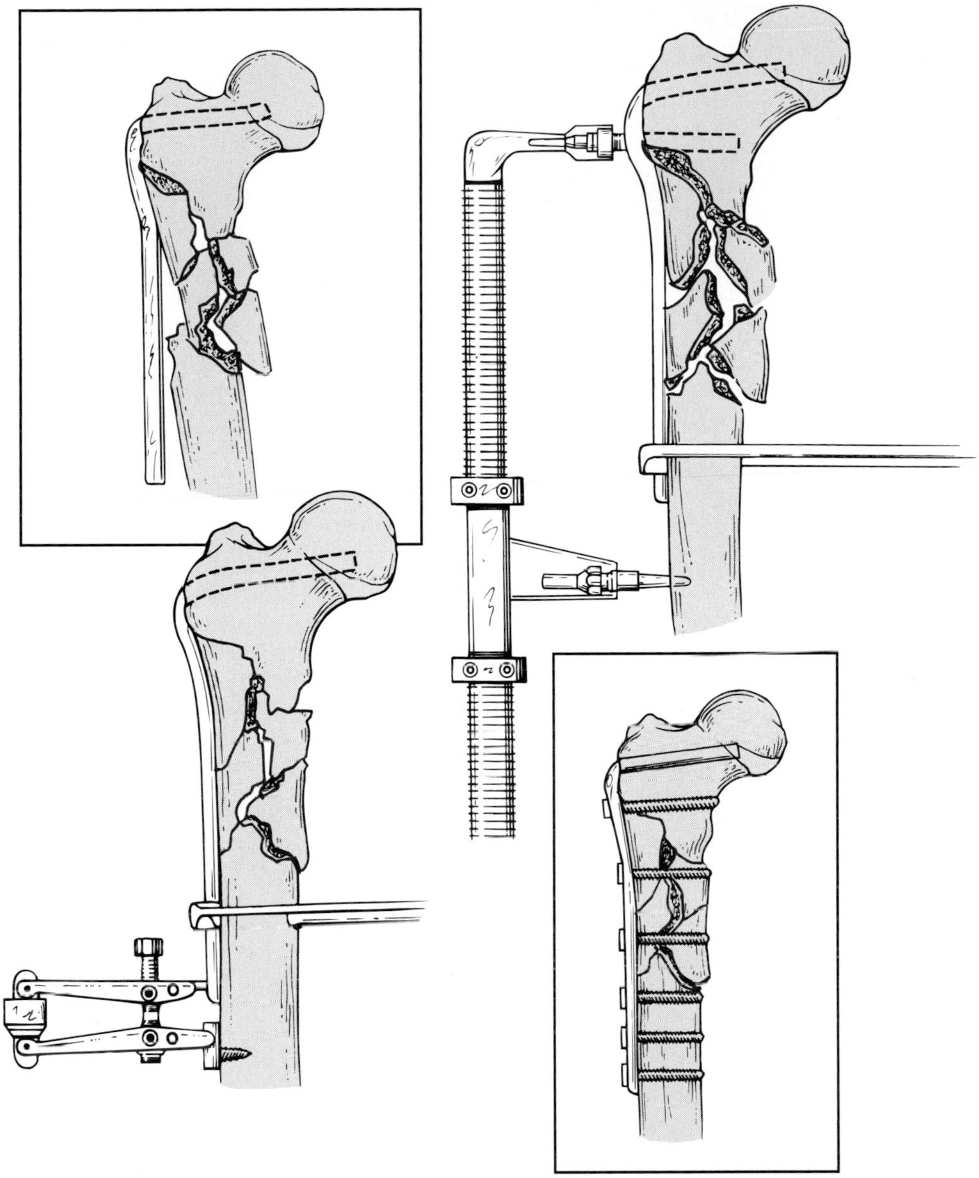

**FIGURE 51–17.** The indirect reduction technique using the AO femoral distractor described by Kinast and associates allows satisfactory reduction of the fracture without devascularization of the major fragments. (Redrawn from Kinast, C.; et al. Clin Orthop 238:122–130, 1989.)

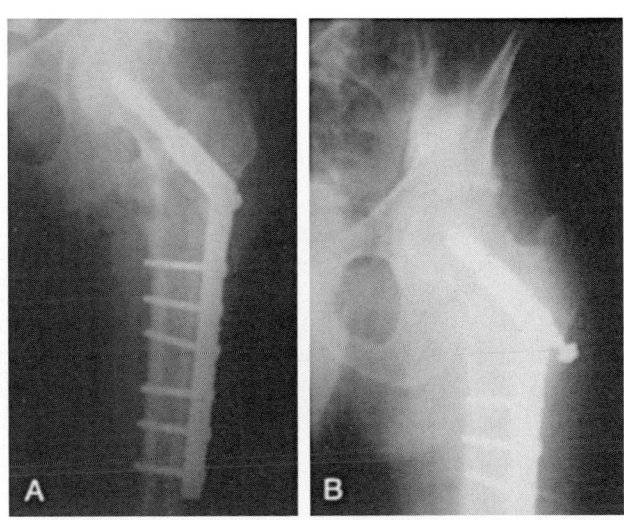

**FIGURE 51–18.** Russell-Taylor type IIA fracture. *A*, Postoperative stabilization with a compression hip screw. *B*, Impaction of the fracture fragments without loss of the correct neck-shaft angle.

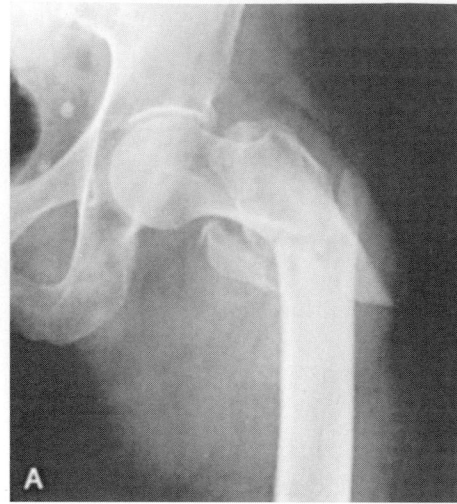
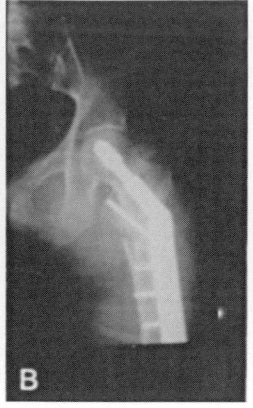
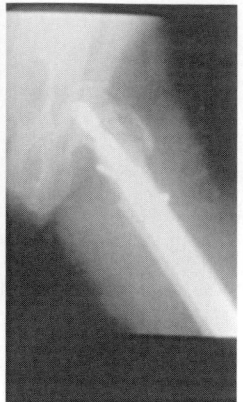

**FIGURE 51–19.** Russell-Taylor type IIB subtrochanteric fracture in a 50-year-old woman. *A,* Compression hip screw fixation 2 days after injury. *B,* Anteroposterior and lateral postoperative radiographs.

moved by several assistants onto the fracture table. The table should permit easy access to the patient, with complete exposure of the femur on both the AP and lateral radiographic projections. Buttock supports are used for most patients with subtrochanteric fractures to provide gentle internal rotation, thus offering a more usual AP view rather than the common externally rotated view (Fig. 51–21). If the standard centromedullary interlocking nail is used for a fracture distal to the lesser trochanter, either the supine or the lateral position is possible, but we

strongly recommend the supine position because it is easier for the anesthesiologist, is more familiar to radiographic technicians, and allows for rapid preparation of patients with bilateral injuries.

With the patient supine, the affected extremity is adducted and the trunk is bent laterally toward the opposite side. The affected hip is flexed approximately 10° to 15° and traction applied through a skeletal pin or the foot (Fig. 51–22). Correct rotational alignment with respect to the normal anteversion of the hip is determined

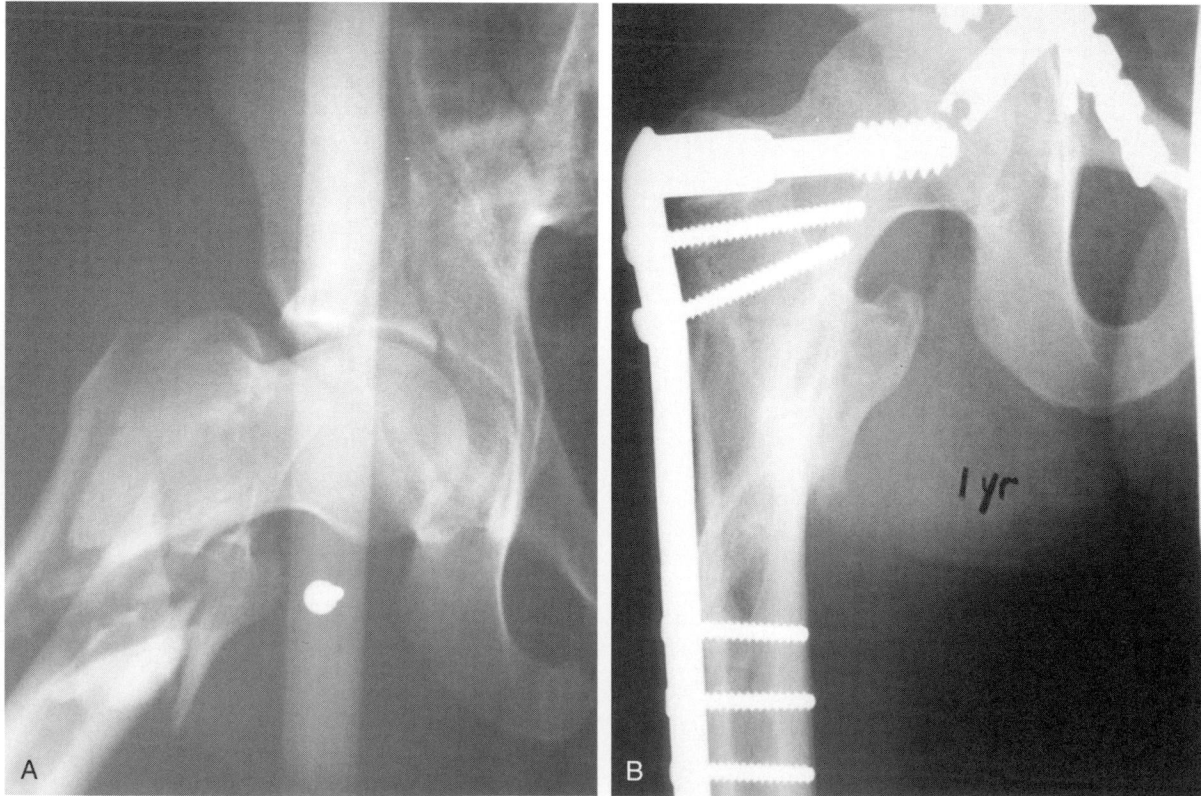

**FIGURE 51–20.** Young man with a comminuted displaced subtrochanteric fracture sustained in a high-speed motor vehicle crash. Note the associated acetabular fracture. *A,* Initial postinjury anteroposterior radiograph. *B,* Twelve months after indirect reduction and bridge plating with a 95° condylar compression screw. No bone graft was used, but the integrity of the medial soft tissues was strictly maintained.

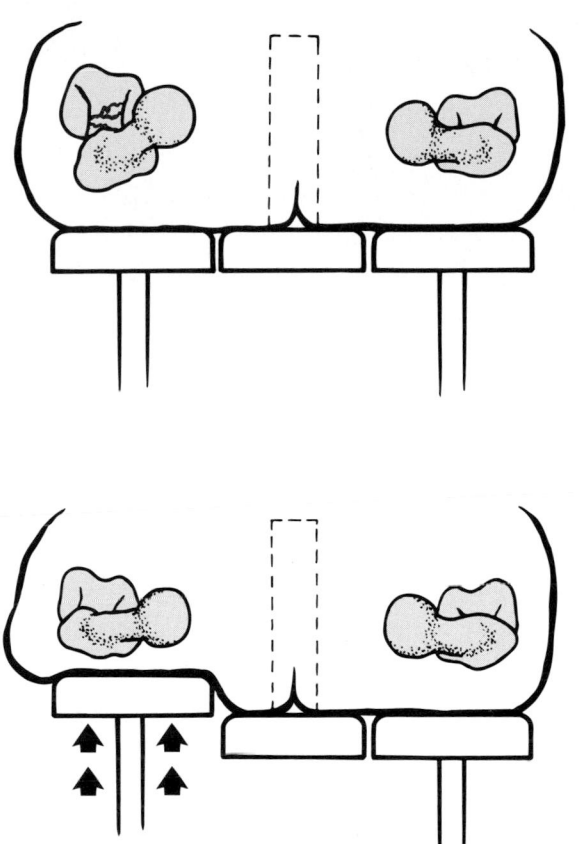

**FIGURE 51–21.** Buttock support used to internally rotate the proximal fragment. (Courtesy of Campbell Clinic, Memphis, TN.)

with the use of image intensification. With a normal anteversion of 15° to 20°, the plane of motion of the knee is in the sagittal plane (Fig. 51–23A). The second ray of the foot is usually pointed vertically. When the patient is initially placed on the fracture table, the proximal fracture fragment may be externally rotated as much as 45° to 50° (see Fig. 51–23B), and the plane of the femoral neck will not match that of the femoral condyles, so the foot must be turned out to match this external rotation (see Fig. 51–23C). The buttock support or a percutaneous pin can be used to internally rotate the proximal fragment, thus helping to correct rotational alignment. Another method of estimating rotation or anteversion of the proximal fragment is to place a small guide wire along the anterior femoral neck (Fig. 51–24). In addition, rotation can be verified by internally and externally rotating the leg until it can be determined that the skin tension lines are in their most relaxed position. The normal hip should be in neutral to very slight flexion. The entire femur from knee to hip should be examined on both AP and lateral image intensifier projections. The projected axis of the shaft is 1 to 1.5 cm posterior to the center of the femoral neck. The entry site for the guide wire must be placed in line with the shaft axis, or where it will be after reduction (Fig. 51–25).

The affected extremity is scrubbed and prepared from several centimeters below the tibial tubercle to the peroneal post and from the midline to the fracture table as far proximally as the lower ribs. The operative field is draped from the level of the umbilicus proximally to the tibial tubercle distally and from approximately the mid-sagittal posterior and anterior lines of the extremity. A vertical isolation drape may be used or the image intensifier covered with a sterile drape. The standard technique is as described in Chapter 52 for femoral shaft fractures.

### Cephalomedullary Techniques with Second-Generation Interlocking Nails

Second-generation cephalomedullary nails use the piriformis fossa for the entry site. This "traditional" reconstruction nail technique will be discussed first, followed by minimally invasive trochanteric nailing and a consideration of IM nail fixation for proximally comminuted Russell-Taylor type II fractures. The reader is referred to the hip fracture section for discussion of the single–lag screw cephalomedullary fixation technique (e.g., Gamma nail or IMHS).

## RECONSTRUCTION NAIL (RUSSELL-TAYLOR SYSTEM)

The technique for insertion of a reconstruction (cephalomedullary) nail differs from that for the standard nail only at the proximal end (see Fig. 51–8B). The proximal 8-cm section of the standard reconstruction nail is 15 mm in diameter; shaft diameters are 12, 13, and 14 mm. The femoral shaft must be reamed 1 mm larger than the diameter of the intended nail, and the proximal 8 cm must be reamed to a diameter of 15 mm. Because of its additional 8° of anteversion to facilitate screw fixation in the femoral head, separate reconstruction nails are required for right and left femurs. An additional 1-cm offset

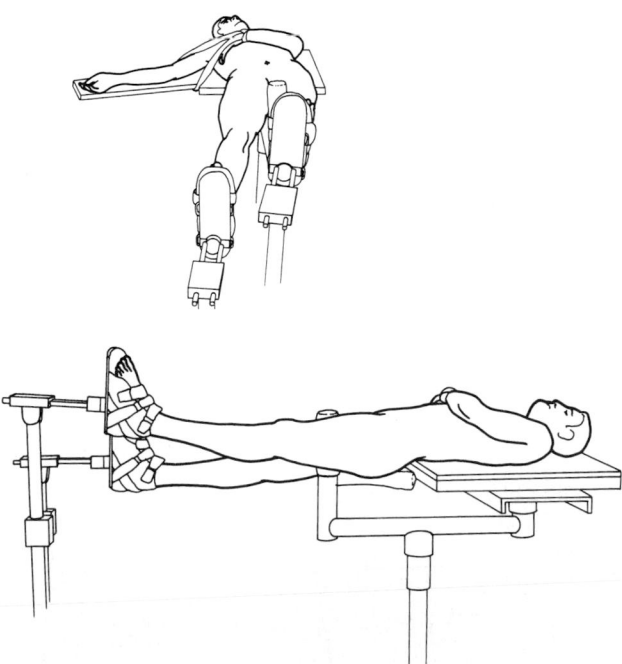

**FIGURE 51–22.** Patient in the supine position with the trunk and lower extremities adducted and the affected hip flexed approximately 15°. (Courtesy of Smith and Nephew, Richards Co., Memphis, TN.)

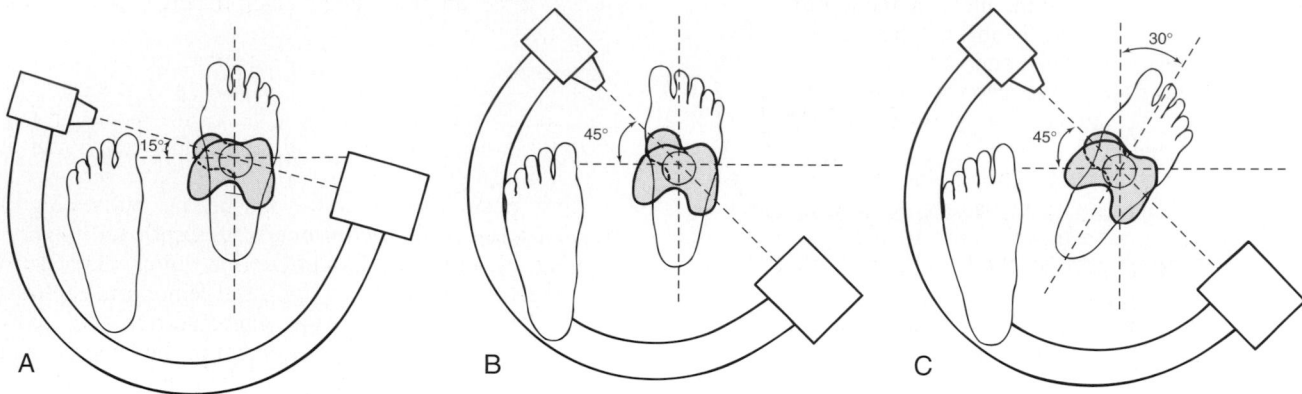

**Figure 51–23.** *A,* Normal radiographic anatomy with the foot and knee aligned in the midsagittal plane and the femoral head and neck anteverted 15°. *B,* Typical radiographic anatomy of a subtrochanteric fracture. The proximal fragment is externally rotated an additional 30°. *C,* With additional external rotation of the proximal fragment, the foot and knee must be externally rotated to match. (*A–C,* Courtesy of Campbell Clinic, Memphis, TN.)

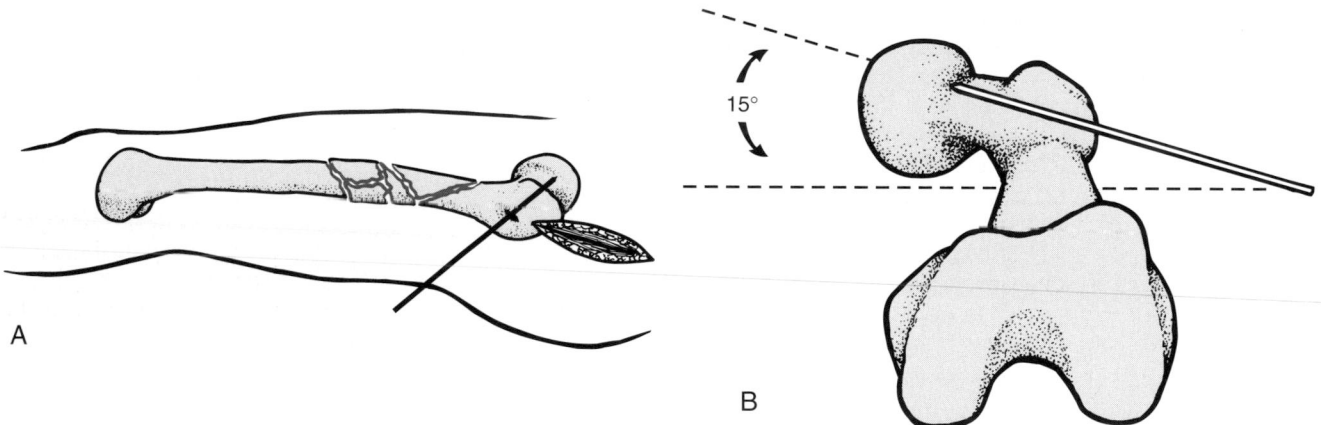

**Figure 51–24.** *A, B,* Use of a guide pin to determine anteversion of the femoral neck. (*A, B,* Courtesy of Campbell Clinic, Memphis, TN.)

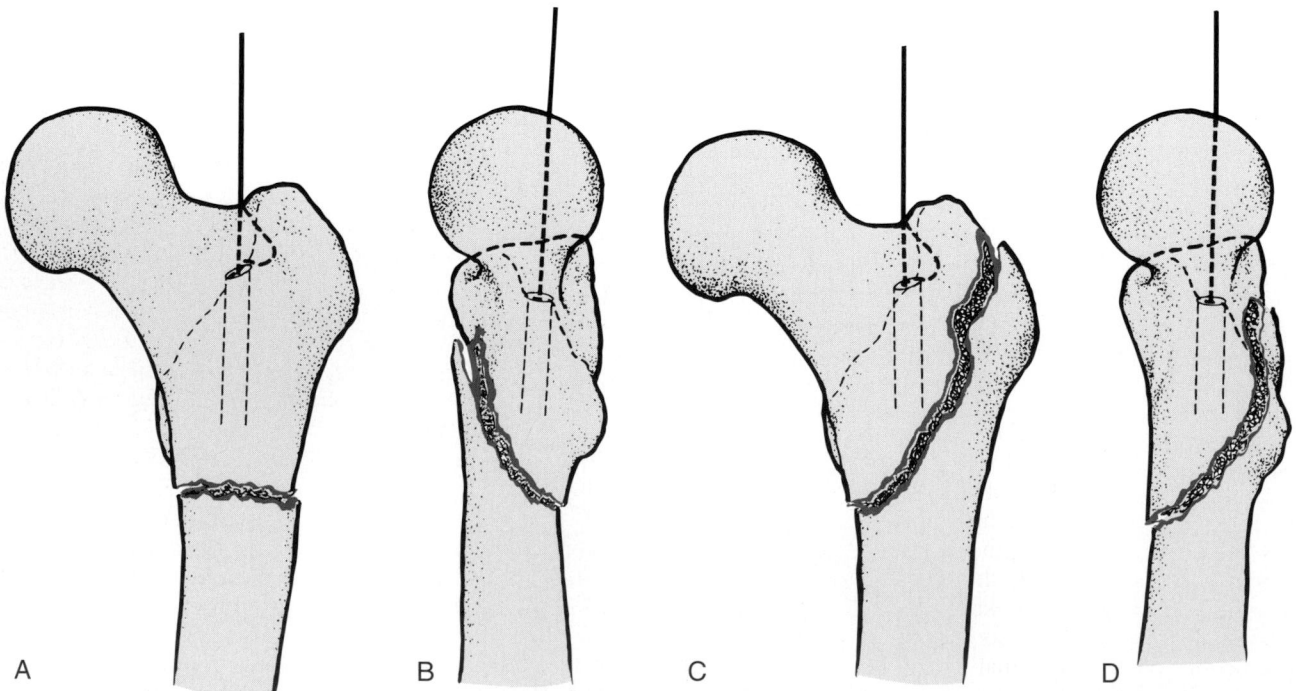

**Figure 51–25.** The guide wire is centered on the anteroposterior and lateral views of Russell-Taylor type IA (*A, B*) and type IIA (*C, D*) subtrochanteric fractures. (*A–D,* Courtesy of Campbell Clinic, Memphis, TN.)

on the proximal drill guide allows some adjustability for the proximal screws: the 8-mm bolt can be placed low in the femoral neck and head and thus provide room for the second 6.4-mm screw. We recommend two-screw fixation into the femoral head for better rotational control of the proximal fragment.

**Patient Positioning.** The supine position is recommended for reconstruction nailing because it is usually more familiar to the surgical team and allows adequate AP and lateral visualization of the femoral head; these factors are critical to successful implantation of the device. However, the lateral decubitus position is helpful with revision nailing, especially in failed nailing with incorrect entry portals, because it allows better visualization of the entry portal than can be obtained with supine nailing. Newer fracture table designs that allow visualization of the subtrochanteric fracture region and femoral head have revived interest in the lateral decubitus position.

With the patient supine, the unaffected limb is abducted while the trunk and affected extremity are adducted. The affected hip is flexed 15° to 30° with the "heel-to-toe" relationship maintained (see Fig. 51–22). Traction is applied through the foot holder attached to the fracture table or through a skeletal pin in the distal end of the femur or proximal portion of the tibia. Rotational alignment of the proximal fragment is determined with the use of the image intensifier, and the distal fragment is rotated to match it. It should be remembered that femoral neck anteversion in adults averages 15° in most white persons but may be up to 30° in Asian populations. In the supine position, correct rotation of the leg usually places the foot in 0° to 15° of external rotation. The uninvolved hip should always be checked for rotational range of motion. The more restricted hip motion is preoperatively, the more critical correct rotational alignment will be in the postoperative rehabilitation phase.

**Technique.** After preparation, draping, and administration of prophylactic antibiotics, the skin is incised from the tip of the trochanter proximally and slightly posteriorly for 6 to 8 cm (Fig. 51–26A). The guide wire from a cannulated hip screw reamer set is inserted and centered in the piriformis fossa on both the AP and lateral projections (see Fig. 51–26B). A cannulated 8-mm reamer is used to ream over the guide wire (see Fig. 51–26C). The anterior offset of the center of the head and neck, as opposed to the shaft, must be kept in mind (see Fig. 51–26D). With the reconstruction nail it is imperative to verify that the guide wire and reamer are centered on the true lateral projection of the proximal end of the femur (see Fig. 51–26E). The guide wire is then advanced to the level of the fracture (see Fig. 51–26F), and the proximal fragment is reamed to approximately 11 mm. The internal fracture alignment device is used to reduce the fracture, and the guide is advanced to the level of the physeal scar (see Fig. 51–26G). A second guide wire or a nail length gauge is used to determine proper nail length. Any remaining isthmus is reamed to 1 mm larger than the selected nail shaft size (see Fig. 51–26H), and the proximal 8 cm of the femur is reamed to 15 mm. Care should be exercised to avoid destruction of the proximal entry portal by reaming eccentrically laterally. Such reaming usually occurs during insertion of the reamer and during extraction. A slotted hammer or other instrument should be used to direct a

medial force on the reamer shaft during insertion and extraction to avoid this complication.

The nail is driven over the reamer guide (see Fig. 51–26I); with these closed-section nails, it is not necessary to exchange the reamer guide wire for the 4-mm driving wire. Rotational alignment of the nail must match that of the proximal fragment so that the cephalic screws are properly positioned in the femoral head. Final seating of the nail must be adjusted properly for depth and rotation (see Fig. 51–26J to L). Proper depth requires reference to both the femoral head and the distal femoral metaphysis (with the aid of AP image intensification) to allow centralized proximal screw placement in the femoral head and adequate length of fixation of the diaphyseal fracture extension. External extrapolation for final nail insertion and screw centralization can be initially performed with the nail length gauge and a radiopaque ruler or guide; its outline is drawn with a skin marker over the femoral head and neck. After the nail is partially inserted, the inferior drill sleeves are placed into the proximal drill guide to extrapolate the eventual location of the inferior screw. When two proximal screws are used, the nail is inserted to a level allowing the inferior screw to be placed just superior to the calcar, approximately 5 mm from the medial femoral neck cortex. After positioning of the C-arm to obtain a true lateral view of the femoral head and neck, the proximal targeting guide attached to the nail is aligned with the C-arm axis by rotating the proximal drill guide in the transverse plane. If the proximal targeting guide is radiopaque, the guide is centralized with respect to the femoral head and bisects the femoral head in the coronal plane on the true lateral C-arm view. The posterior and anterior portion of the femoral head must be seen in relation to the proximal drill guide to confirm that the screws will be contained in the optimal position in the femoral head. Further verification of containment of the proximal locking screws may be obtained with oblique C-arm views. A horizontal line is drawn with a skin marker on the lateral aspect of the thigh as a reference to correct rotation of the proximal drill guide. Traction is released, final seating of the nail is completed, and the driving guide wire is removed.

With the percutaneous knife, the skin and fascia are incised through the inferior hole in the proximal drill guide, and the stacked drill sleeves are inserted with all four sheaths (9.5-mm silver, 8.0-mm green, 4.8-mm blue, and 3.2-mm red) through this hole. The drill sleeve is pushed to the bone, and the 3.2-mm tip-threaded guide pin is inserted through the red drill sleeve and advanced into the femoral head just superior to the calcar to a level approximately 5 mm from subchondral bone (see Fig. 51–26M). The position of the guide pin within the femoral head is confirmed on AP, oblique, and lateral views (see Fig. 51–26N and O). Even if only a single 8-mm screw is to be used, a second 3.2-mm tip-threaded guide pin is inserted into the superior hole to prevent movement of the proximal fragment when the lower screw is inserted. The skin and fascia are incised through the superior hole of the proximal drill guide, and the stacked drill sleeves (green, blue, and red) are inserted through the superior hole. The drill sleeves are pushed to bone, and the 3.2-mm tip-threaded guide pin is inserted through the drill sleeve and advanced to the femoral head (see Fig. 51–26P).

Confirmation that the second guide pin is contained within the femoral head is obtained on AP, oblique, and lateral views (see Fig. 51–26Q and R). The inferior guide pin and red drill sleeve are removed, and a pilot hole is left in which to center the 4.8-mm twist drill. The twist drill is centered through the blue drill sleeve into the femoral head within 5 mm of subchondral bone while making sure that the drill sleeves are against the bone (see Fig. 51–26S). Screw length is measured with the drill calibrations, and the depth is read against the top of the blue drill sleeve. The 4.8-mm twist drill and the blue drill sleeve are then

removed. The large cortical reamer is used to ream the lateral cortex through the green drill sleeve until the blunt nose is within 5 mm of subchondral bone (see Fig. 51–26T). If the bone is especially dense, it may be helpful to use the 6.5-mm cortical reamer first, followed by the 8.0-mm cortical reamer. Because of its sharp cutting flutes, the cortical reamer should always be pushed rather than advanced with power when it is within the nail. In very dense bone, tapping may be required; the large tap is used through the silver drill sleeve (see Fig. 51–26U). The selected 8.0-mm lag screw is inserted into the femoral

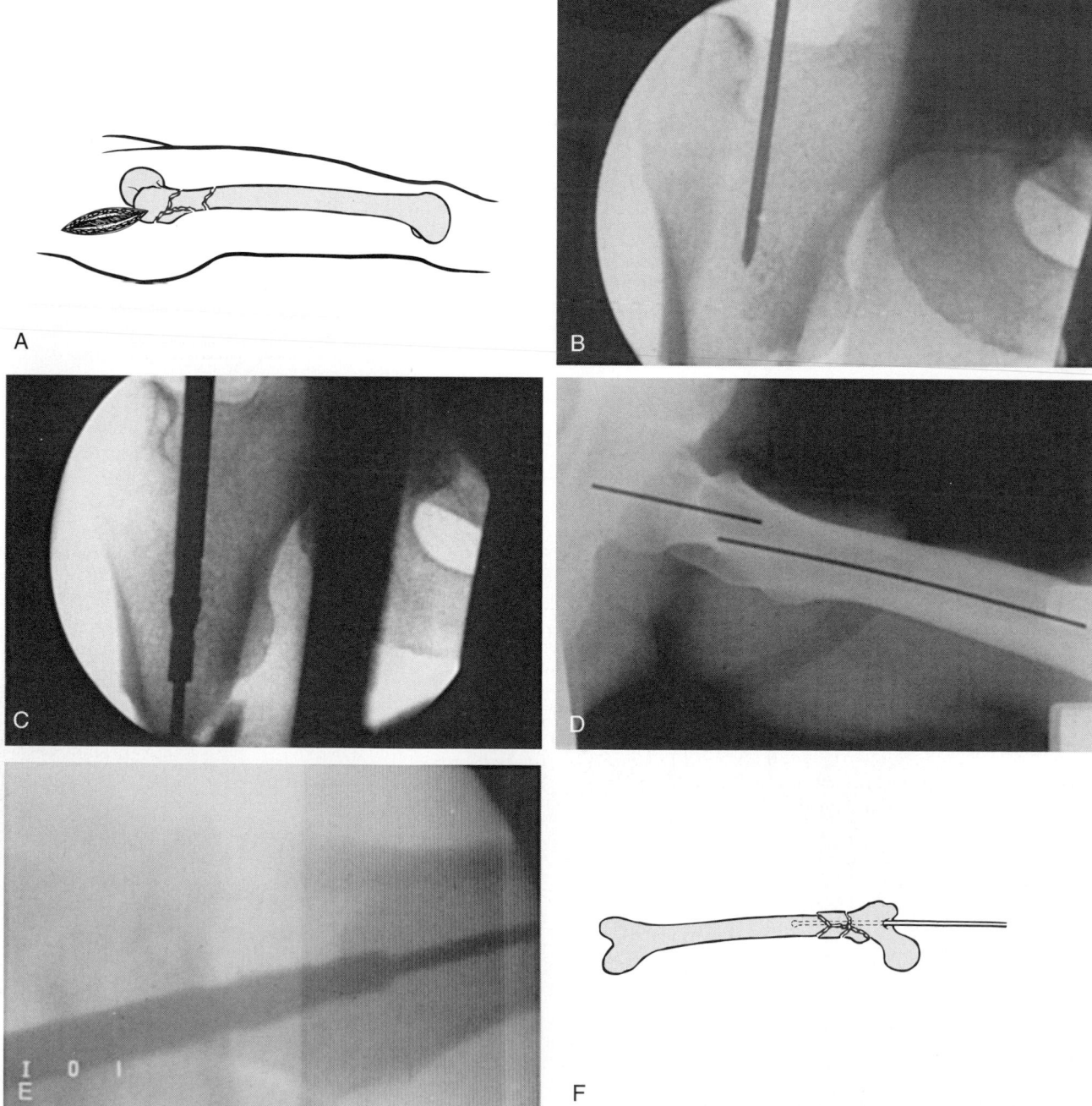

**FIGURE 51–26.** Technique for insertion of a Russell-Taylor reconstruction nail. *A,* Skin incision. *B,* The guide pin is centered on the anteroposterior view. *C,* An 8-mm cannulated reamer is used to enlarge the starting portal. *D,* Center lines of the femoral neck and head and the femoral shaft; note the offset of approximately 1 cm. *E,* An 8-mm reamer positioned over the guide wire in the lateral projection. *F,* The reamer guide wire is advanced to the fracture.

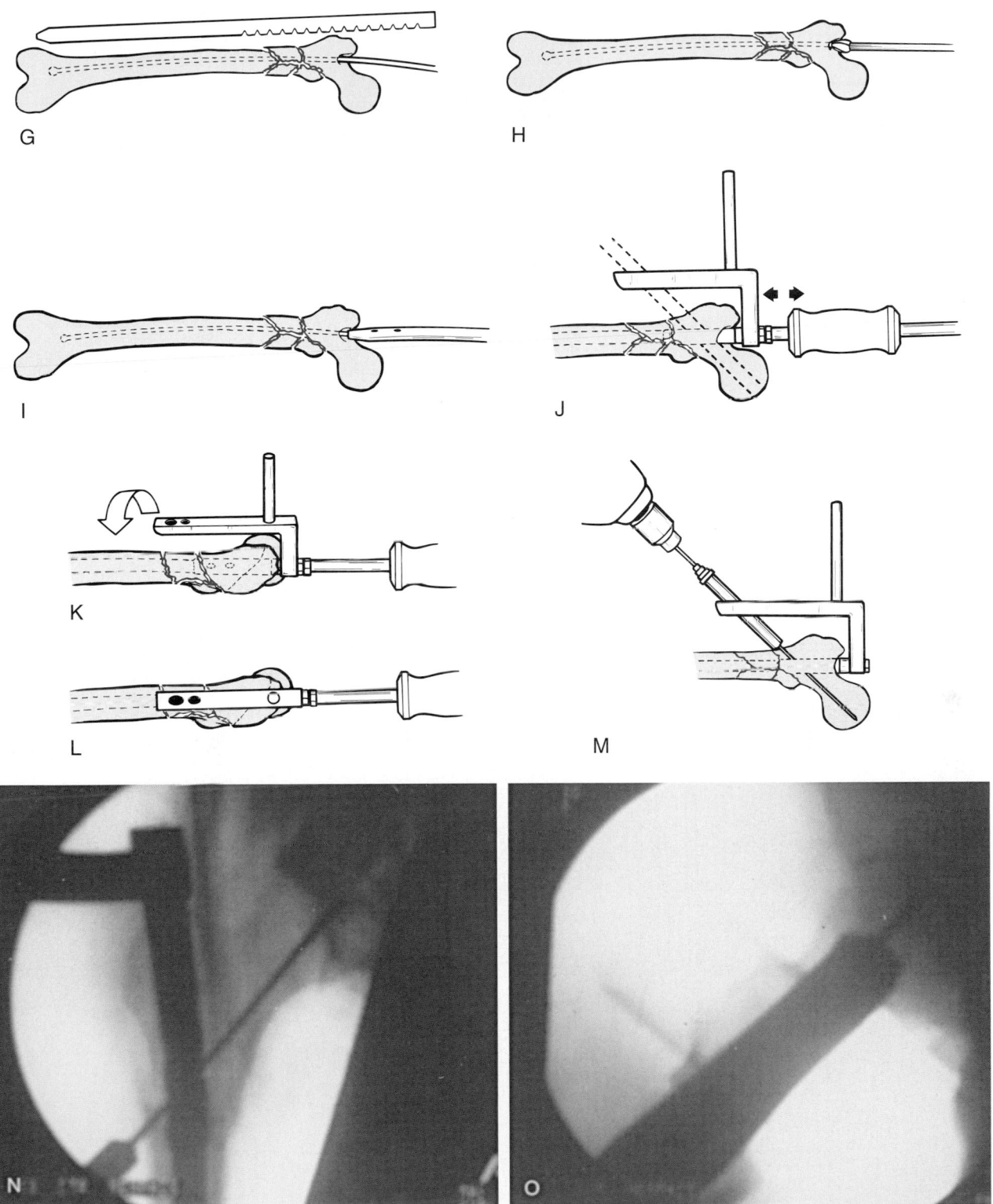

**FIGURE 51–26** *Continued. G,* The reamer guide wire is advanced to the physeal scar. *H,* The remaining isthmus is reamed. *I,* The nail is driven over the reamer guide. *J,* Final seating of the nail. Note the 1.5-cm adjustability with proximal seating to allow the large 8-mm screw to lie on the calcar. *K,* The proximal screw insertion jig is brought to lie in the true lateral plane of the proximal end of the femur. *L,* The proximal jig is aligned with the true lateral plane of the proximal end of the femur. *M,* The guide wire for the 8-mm screw is inserted. *N,* Anteroposterior (AP) view of the first guide wire. *O,* Lateral view of the first guide wire. Note the guide wire positioned safely within the femoral head and neck.

*Illustration continued on following page*

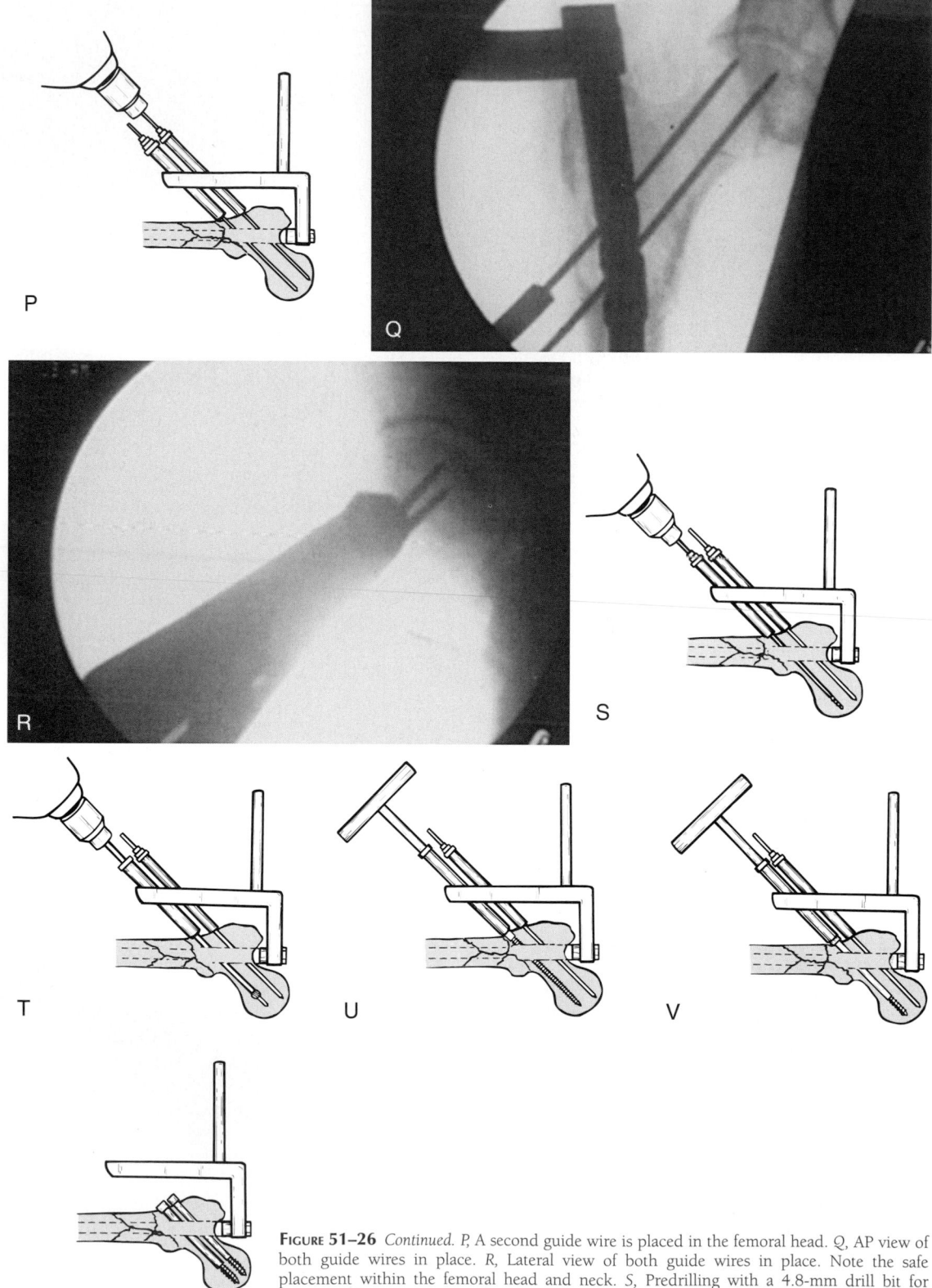

**Figure 51–26** *Continued. P,* A second guide wire is placed in the femoral head. *Q,* AP view of both guide wires in place. *R,* Lateral view of both guide wires in place. Note the safe placement within the femoral head and neck. *S,* Predrilling with a 4.8-mm drill bit for insertion of an 8-mm screw. *T,* Lateral cortical reaming for an 8-mm screw. *U,* Tapping for an 8-mm screw. *V,* Insertion of an 8-mm screw. *W,* Final seating of both proximal screws.

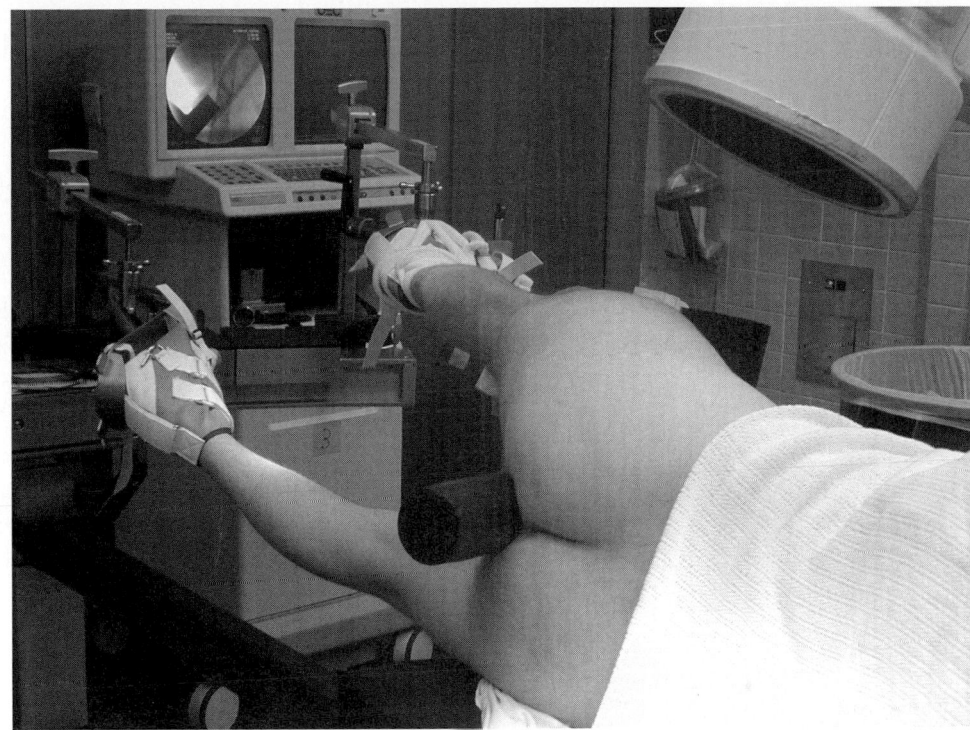

**FIGURE 51–27.** Patient on a fracture table in the lateral decubitus position with the involved hip flexed forward and the unaffected leg kept in extension.

head through the silver drill sleeve (see Fig. 51–26V), which is then removed.

If they are not already in place, the red, blue, and green drill sleeves are inserted through the superior hole of the proximal drill guide. The 3.2-mm tip-threaded guide pin is advanced to within 5 mm of subchondral bone. The guide pin and red drill sleeve are removed, and the 4.8-mm twist drill is inserted through the blue drill sleeve into the femoral head within 5 mm of subchondral bone while verifying that the drill sleeves are against bone. Screw length is measured with the drill calibrations, and the depth is read against the top of the blue drill sleeve. The 4.8-mm twist drill and the blue drill sleeve are then removed. The small cortical reamer is used to ream the lateral cortex through the green drill sleeve until the blunt nose is within 5 mm of subchondral bone. In very dense bone, tapping may be required with the small tap through the green drill sleeve. After the reamer is removed, the selected 6.4-mm lag screw is inserted into the femoral head (see Fig. 51–26W). Containment of both screws within the femoral head is confirmed on AP and lateral views.

Proximal locking is now complete. Note that the screws for proximal locking of the reconstruction nail have only a 2-cm threaded portion, with a smooth shank to allow impaction if needed. Distal interlocking is then performed, usually with a freehand technique.

### Minimally Invasive Insertion Technique with Third-Generation Nails

Percutaneous nailing technique allows for less soft tissue dissection and a less obvious scar. Pepper, Russell, and Sanders[91] have developed a third-generation nail insertion technique that facilitates either piriformis or trochanteric entry portal selection and allows faster fracture reduction

with less chance of damage to the proximal femoral bone stock with a closed reaming system.

### TROCHANTERIC ANTEGRADE NAIL TECHNIQUE

The following is the recommended technique for use of the TriGen TAN system (see Fig. 51–8B and C). This device uses special entry site instrumentation to prepare the trochanteric portal under image intensifier control.

**Patient Positioning and Incision.** The patient is placed supine or lateral with the unaffected limb extending below the affected limb and trunk (see Fig 51–22). The affected limb is adducted and the affected hip flexed 15° to 30°. Traction is applied through a skeletal pin or to the foot with the fracture table foot holder. The affected limb is adjusted for length and rotation by comparison with the unaffected limb. Rotation is further checked by rotating the C-arm to align the femoral neck anteversion and then making the appropriate correction by the foot, usually in 0° to 15° of external rotation. Lateral decubitus positioning may also be used with the fracture table in this situation because of the change in position of the femoral head; the leg is usually internally rotated 10° to 15° (Fig. 51–27). This position is best checked by visualizing the femoral anteversion proximally and matching it with correct rotation at the knee. The greater trochanter is palpated. It should be confirmed that fracture reduction is possible before skin incision and that the C-arm views are of good quality (Fig. 51–28A, i and ii). A 2.5-cm incision is made 3 cm proximal to the greater trochanter in line with the femoral shaft, and the incision is carried through the fascia.

**Entry Portal Preparation.** The entry tool and honeycomb insert are assembled, oriented so that the superior side of the bevel is medial (*Note:* The entry tool indicator must be set to "R" for a left nail and to "L" for a right nail, which is opposite the standard femoral antegrade nail technique), and advanced until the assembly rests against the lateral aspect of the greater trochanter (see Fig. 51–28B). Suction is attached to the entry tool to assist in blood evacuation and minimize aerosolization of blood to the operative team. The 3.2-mm tip-threaded guide wire is inserted through the honeycomb and the wire advanced 1 cm into the cortex at the tip of the greater trochanter on the AP view and in line with the center of the femoral canal on the lateral view. Under image guidance, a second guide wire may be placed through an alternative hole in the honeycomb to optimize the entry portal location. Once proper placement of the guide wire has been established, the honeycomb insert should be removed. (see Fig. 51–28C, *i* to *iv*). The entry reamer connector is tightened

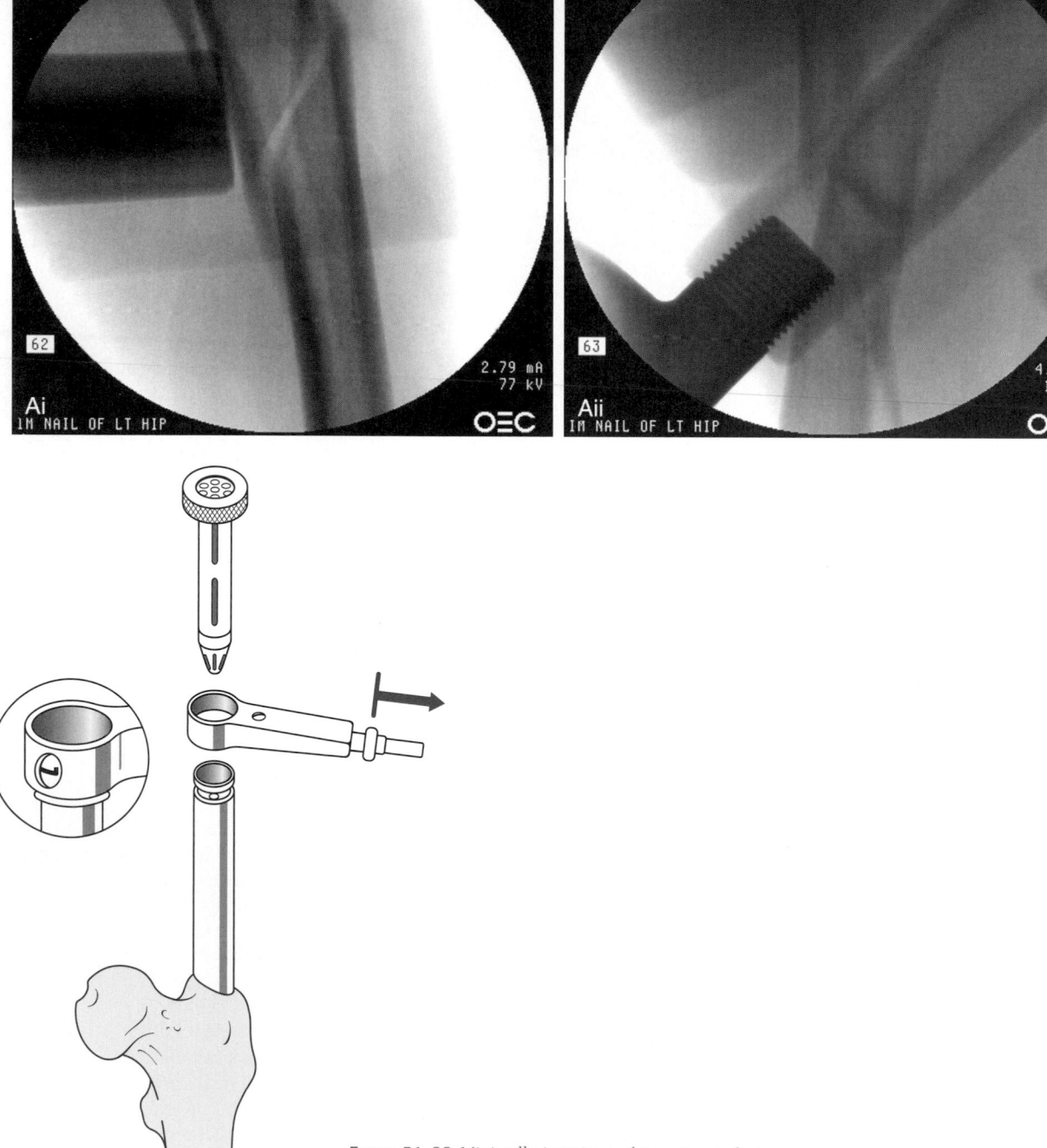

**FIGURE 51–28** Minimally invasive nail insertion technique.
*A*, Lateral-position C-arm views with traction.
    *i*, Anteroposterior (AP).
    *ii*, Lateral.
*B*, Entry portal tool assembly.

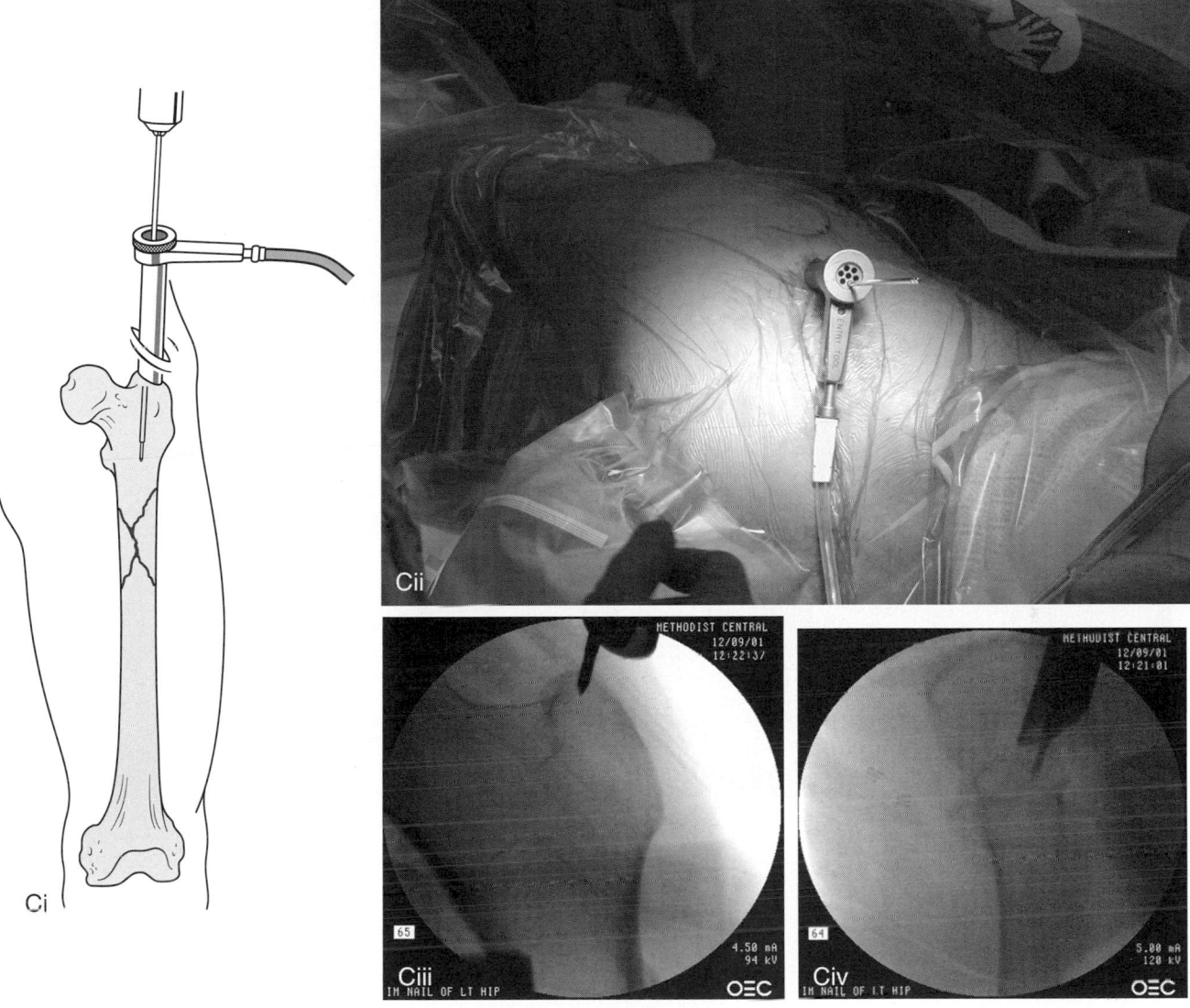

**FIGURE 51–28** *Continued.*
C, Guide wire insertion through the entry portal tool.
  i, A guide wire is drilled into the trochanteric starting point through the percutaneous entry tool.
  ii, Surgeon's view of a properly inserted entry tool.
  iii, Radiographic control, AP view.
  iv, Radiographic control, lateral view.

*Illustration continued on following page*

onto the 14-mm channel reamer, and the 12.5-mm entry reamer is inserted until it "clicks" into the assembly. The 12.5-mm entry reamer is attached to power to ream the proximal section of the femur through the entry tool. The channel reamer assembly is introduced over the tip-threaded guide wire and advanced 1 to 2 cm into bone (see Fig. 51–28D, i to iv). The reamer assembly is then manipulated under image guidance until the shaft axis and intended path of the reamer form an angle of approximately 5° in the AP view and are in line in the lateral view. The tip of the reamer should be directed to a point just inferior to the normal location of the lesser trochanter on the AP view. Once the correct orientation is obtained, the reamer assembly is advanced full depth to the point at which it contacts the proximal end of the entry portal tool. This reamer assembly enlarges the proximal end of the

femur 1.0 mm over the diameter of the head of the nail to 14 mm. The 12.5-mm entry reamer and guide wire are removed, with the entry tool and 14-mm channel reamer kept in place.

**Fracture Reduction Technique.** The T handle is snapped onto the reducer and the reducer is placed through the entry tool and 14-mm channel reamer to reduce the fracture (see Fig. 51–28E, i and ii). The reducer is advanced down the medullary canal to the fracture site, and the proximal fragment is then manipulated with the entry portal tool and reducer until it is aligned with the medullary canal of the distal fragment. The tip of the reducer is inserted into the distal end of the medullary canal to capture the distal fragment. The 3.0-mm ball-tipped guide rod is inserted through the reducer into the distal end of the femur in the region of the old physeal scar. The reducer is then rotated to center the guide wire distally in the femur on the AP and lateral views.

**Medullary Canal Preparation.** Canal preparation is selected by the surgeon in accordance with patient and injury requirements. If reaming is planned, progressively larger reamers are used through the entry tool. Unreamed nails may be used as per preoperative planning, but they should be of sufficient size to fill the medullary canal completely and thus correct translational displacement. Once the guide rod is in place, the reducer is removed but the 14-mm channel reamer is left in place. The femoral shaft is sequentially reamed to 1.0 mm or more above the chosen nail diameter through the 14-mm channel reamer. For more curved femoral shafts, 1.5 to 2.0 mm of reaming beyond the diameter of the nail may be required to avoid nail incarceration. In patients with long femurs, the flex reamer extender may be added to extend the shaft of the flexible reamer for very distal fractures or nails longer than 42 cm. *Note:* For 13-mm nails, the 14-mm channel reamer must be removed before reaming with the 13.5- and 14-mm reamers.

**Nail Selection.** Nail diameter is determined from the image intensifier or templating. A nail should never be inserted that has a larger diameter than the last reamer used. With the distal tip of the guide rod at the desired level of the distal end of the femur, nail length is measured by positioning the open end of the cannulated ruler over the exposed end of the guide rod and pushing the end down to the level of bone through the 14-mm channel reamer. The position of the ruler is confirmed on the image intensifier. The tip of the ruler should line up with the final position of the proximal end of the nail. This position may be predetermined by preoperative templating. Generally, 10 to 20 mm of countersinking below the tip of the greater

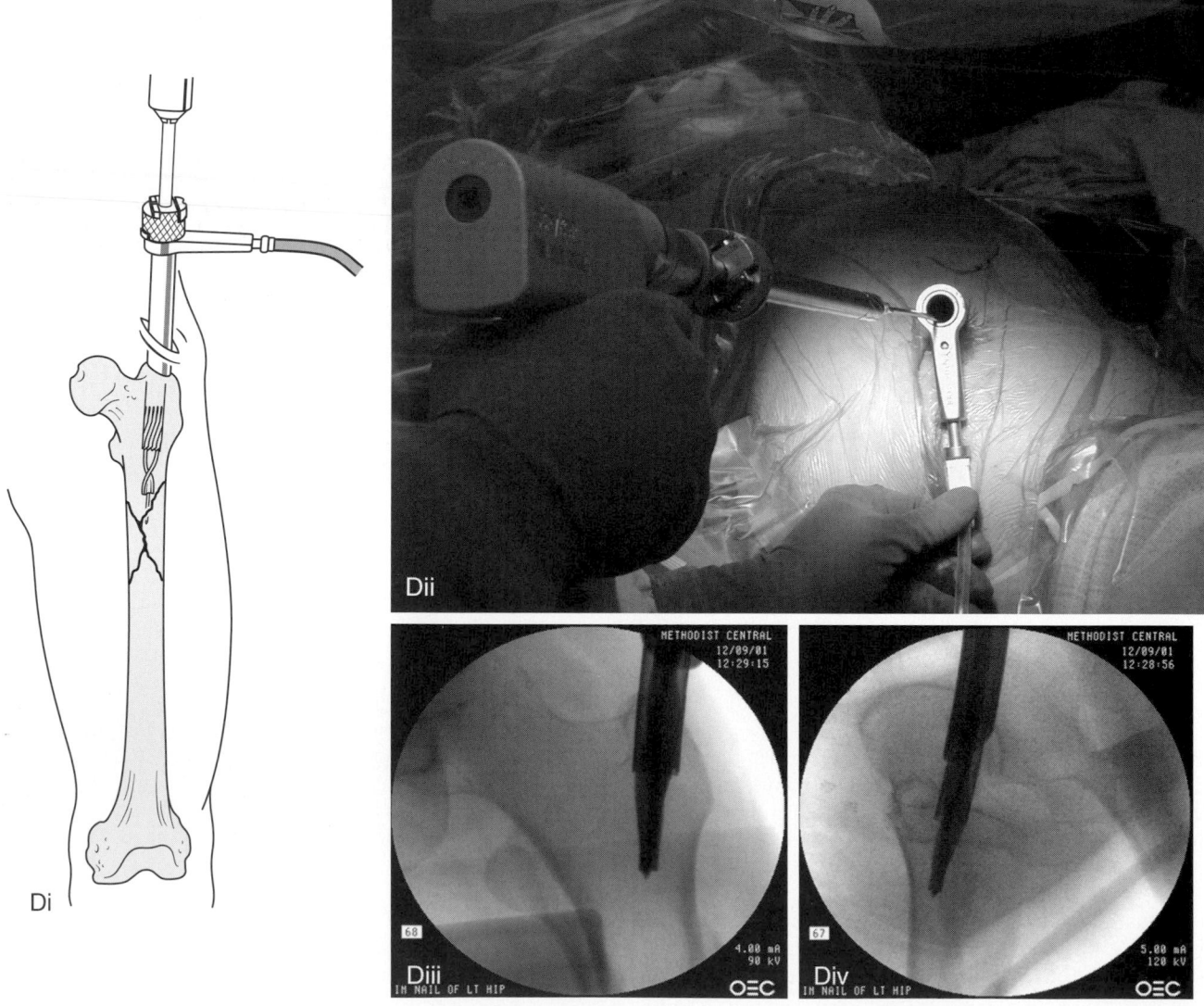

**Figure 51–28** *Continued.*
*D,* Insertion of the channel reamer.
    *i,* Insertion of the channel reamer over a guide wire.
    *ii,* Surgeon's view.
    *iii,* Radiograph AP view.
    *iv,* Radiographic lateral view.

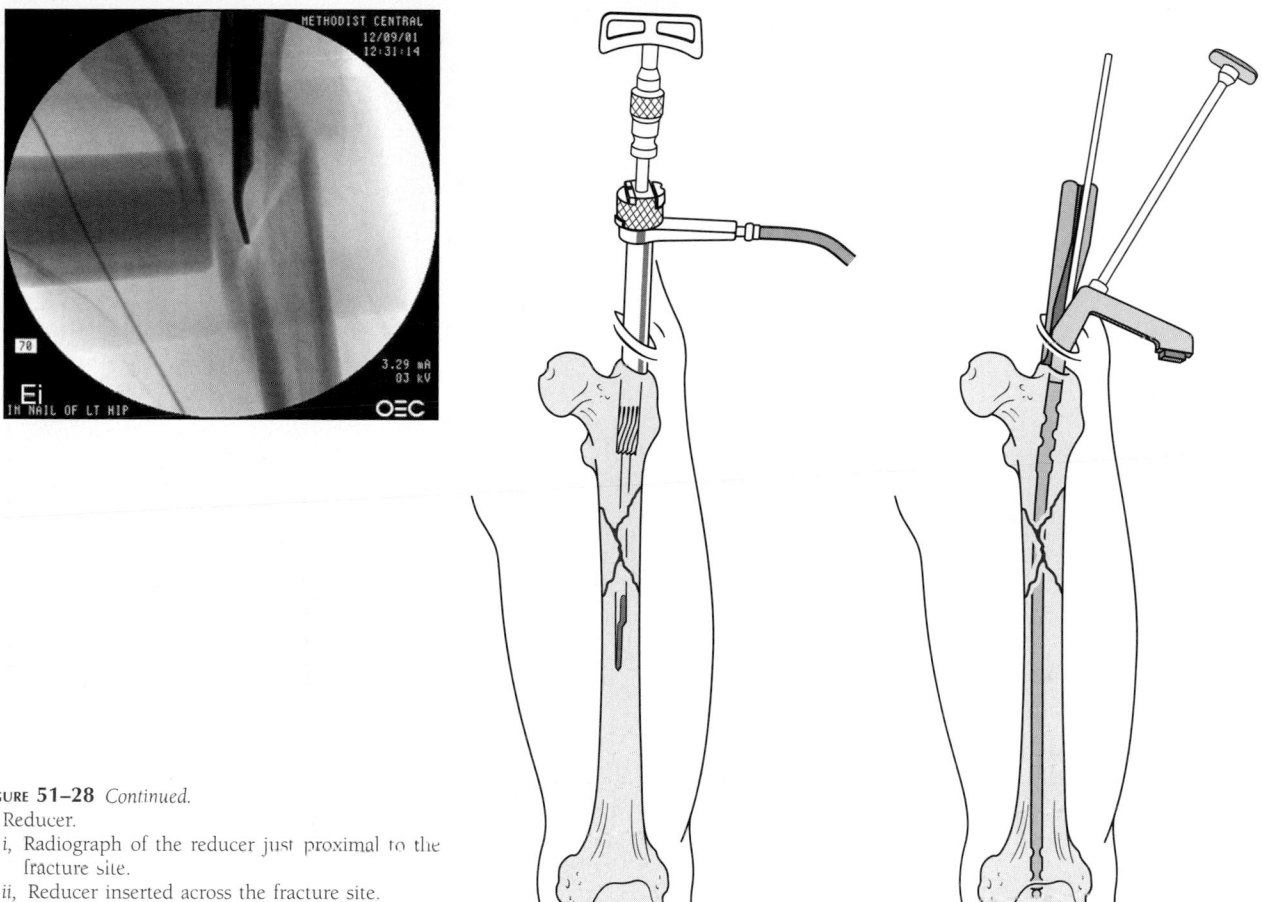

Figure 51–28 Continued.
E, Reducer.
  i, Radiograph of the reducer just proximal to the fracture site.
  ii, Reducer inserted across the fracture site.
F, Nail insertion with instrumentation.
Illustration continued on following page

trochanter allows optimal screw positioning. Nail length is read from the calibrations exposed at the other end of the ruler. The guide rod is left in place for placement of the nail. Exchange of the ball-tipped guide rod is not necessary.

**Drill Guide Assembly.** The guide bolt is inserted into the drill guide, and the guide bolt wrench is used to secure the bolt to the nail. The impactor is screwed onto the top of the drill guide to drive the nail into the medullary canal (see Fig. 51–28F). The skin protector is inserted into the incision parallel to the entry reamer tool. The entry reamer tool and 14-mm channel reamer are then removed. The skin protector will assist in maintaining control of the surrounding tissue and provide continued access to the bone. The nail is advanced over the guide rod with the nail rotated 90° and the proximal guide aimed anteriorly, and the nail is carefully inserted past the fracture; the nail is rotated into correct rotational alignment after it is approximately 50% inserted. This insertion technique minimizes the insertion forces required for inserting the nail from the trochanteric portal. The guide rod is removed after the nail is inserted to within 2 cm of the nail tip's final position and before inserting the locking screws.

**Proximal Interlocking for the Standard (Oblique) Mode.** Proximal interlocking allows placement of a 5.0-mm screw at a 45° angle from the greater to the lesser trochanter for Russell-Taylor type IA fracture patterns. A 6-mm stab incision is made at the entry hole, and the gold outer drill sleeve with the silver inner drill sleeve is pushed through the drill guide hole until it is touching the lateral cortex. The long pilot drill is attached to power with the miniconnector. Length measurements are taken from calibrations on the drill in relation to the end of the silver inner drill sleeve. Alternatively, a standard depth gauge technique may be used through the gold sleeve. The appropriate-length 5.0-mm screw (gold) is selected and attached to the screwdriver. These 5.0-mm (gold) screws are used to lock the 10-, 11.5-, and 13-mm-diameter TAN implants proximally in the femoral mode. The drill and silver inner drill sleeve are removed, and the screw is inserted through the gold outer drill sleeve. The screwdriver is connected to power, or a manual T handle is used to insert the screw. It is recommended that final tightening of the 5.0-mm screw always be under manual control with the T handle.

**Proximal Interlocking for the Reconstruction Mode.** For cephalomedullary (reconstruction-type) proximal locking, only one additional instrument is attached to the nail as a drill guide (see Fig. 51–28G, i). It may be added after the nail is inserted or beforehand if a cephalomedullary configuration is planned. Screws (blue) 6.4 mm in diameter are used to lock the 10-, 11.5-, and 13-mm-diameter TAN implants proximally in the cephalomedullary mode. The guide bolt is inserted into the drill guide,

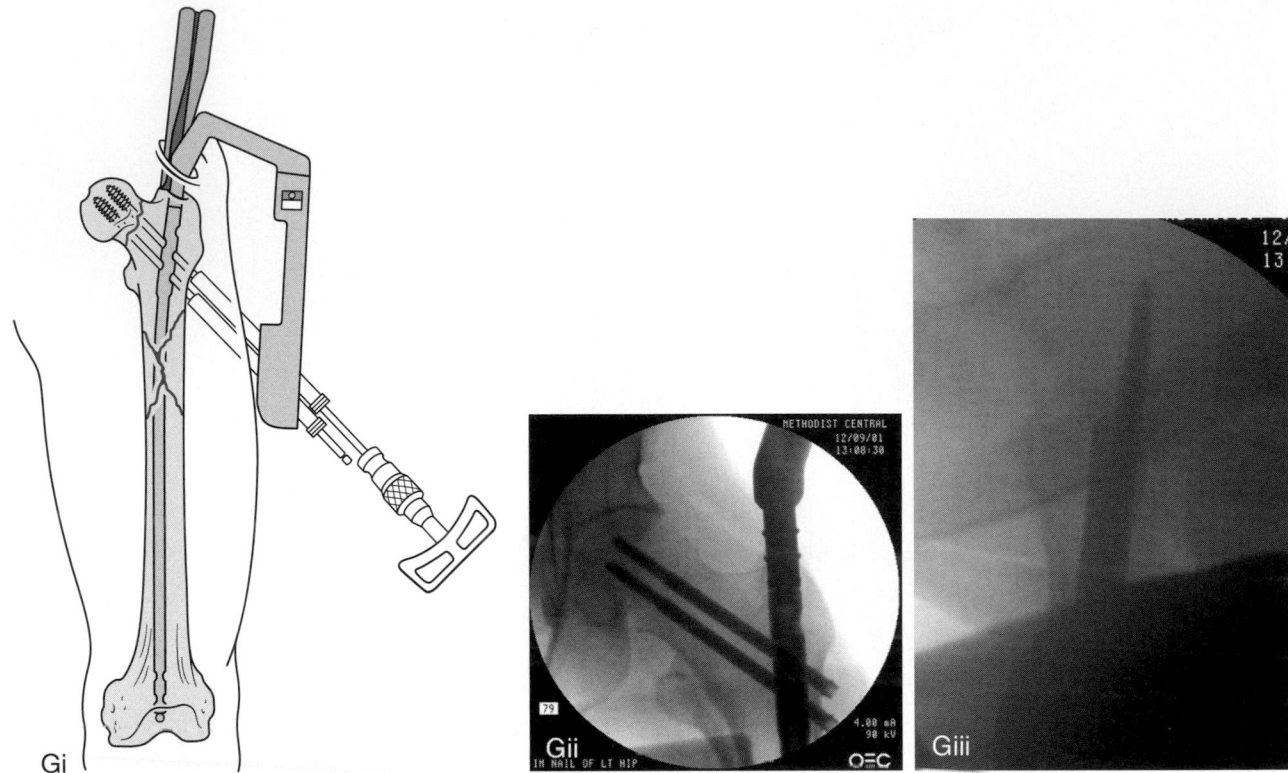

**FIGURE 51–28** *Continued.*
*G,* Proximal locking in the cephalomedullary mode.
　*i,* Nail assembly.
　*ii,* AP radiograph showing proximal screw placement.
　*iii,* Lateral radiograph showing proximal screw containment.

and the guide bolt wrench is used to secure the bolt to the nail. Alignment of the guide to the screw holes is checked by passing the medium screwdriver through the gold outer drill sleeve up into the holes of the nail. The impactor is screwed onto the top of the drill guide to drive the nail into the medullary canal. The skin protector is placed in the incision parallel to the entry reamer tool, and the entry reamer tool and channel reamer are removed. The skin protector will assist in maintaining control of the surrounding tissue and provide continued access to the bone. The nail is advanced over the guide rod and carefully past the fracture. The guide rod is removed after the nail is inserted and before inserting the locking screws.

Two aspects of screw placement into the femoral head must be noted before drilling into the femoral head: alignment of anteversion and the depth of nail insertion. To begin, the C-arm is rotated proximally until a true lateral of the hip is visualized because this view gives the correct axis of alignment for anteversion. The handle of the nail guide is rotated until it bisects the femoral head in the lateral view. In this position the nail and guide are overlaid on the center of the femoral head such that femoral head is visualized anteriorly and posteriorly. This position is marked with a skin marker on the leg parallel to the driving handle. Next, the C-arm is rotated into an AP view by using the calibrated notches on the proximal attachment of the nail, which is visualized radiographically. Preoperative planning with template overlays will aid in determining what depth of nail insertion will center

both screws within the femoral head. The insertion guide has radiographically visible marks to aid in placing the top of the nail in the preplanned position. Usually, the nail will be countersunk 10 to 20 mm below the tip of the greater trochanter. As a rule, the inferior screw is placed first. These screws are angled 135° relative to the shaft. If both screws will not seat within the femoral head, it is probable that too much varus positioning of the proximal fragment has occurred or the proximal nail entry portal is too lateral. An incision is made at the entry holes of the proximal screw sleeves, and then the two puncture wounds are connected for an approximately 2.5-cm incision that will accommodate the insertion of both screws. The silver inner drill sleeve is inserted into the gold outer drill sleeve, and they are pushed to bone. The 4.0-mm drill bit in inserted into the silver inner drill sleeve and the drill connected to power with the miniconnector. The femoral neck and head are drilled to the desired depth and position. The femoral neck is drilled with the 6.4-mm step drill to slightly less than the depth desired. Alignment is again verified in the AP and 15° lateral views before removing the 6.4-mm drill. The 6.4-mm tap is used in very dense bone. The depth of the screw is measured from the calibrations on the drill or tap with respect to the gold outer drill sleeve. The appropriate-length 6.4-mm screw is attached to the medium screwdriver. The screwdriver T handle is attached and the captured screw inserted into the inferior proximal hole. Once the first screw is inserted, the screwdriver should not be disassembled. The procedure is

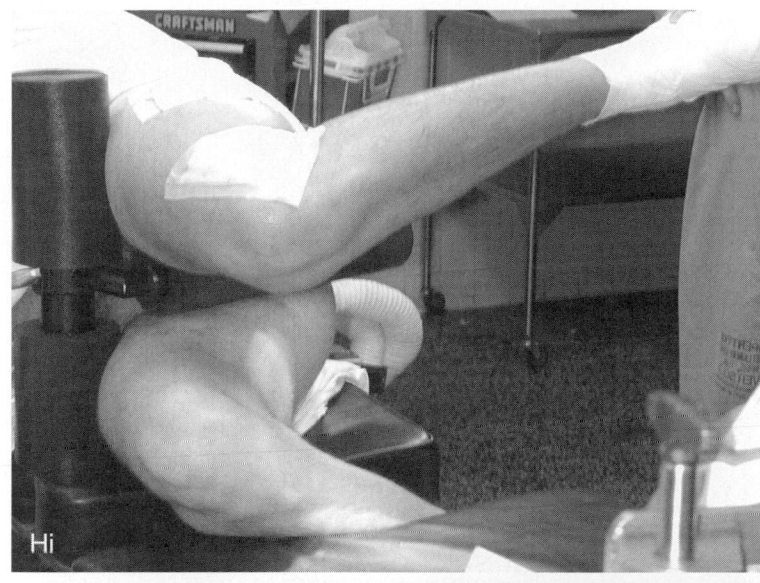

FIGURE **51–28** *Continued.*
*H,* Final reduction check.
  *i,* Internal rotation.
  *ii,* External rotation.
  *iii,* Length assessment.

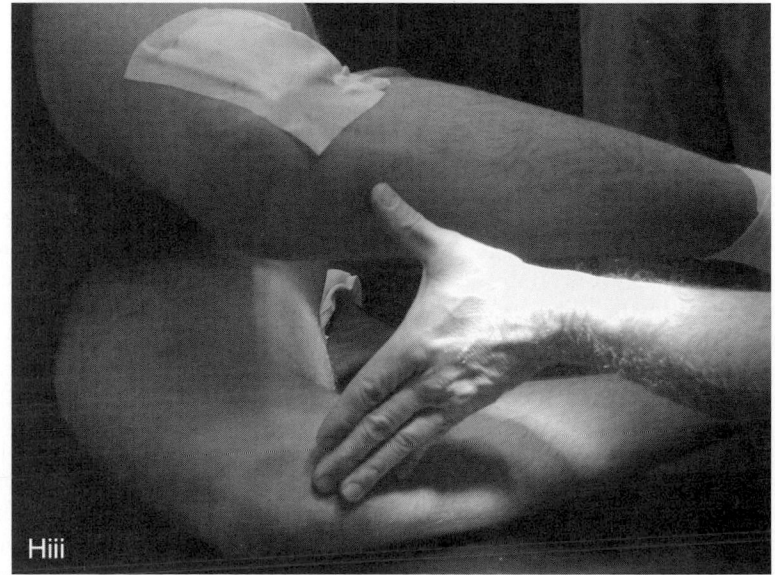

repeated for the most proximal screw with the long screwdriver. Final tightening of the proximal screws is performed, the screwdriver is detached from the screws, and proximal locking is complete (see Fig. 51–28G, ii and iii). Distal locking is performed in standard freehand technique. Two distal locking screws are preferred for very comminuted fractures and for long spiral fracture components into the diaphysis. The freehand technique is used with the C-arm placed medial to the patient to permit proper imaging of the femur. Screws 5.0 mm in diameter (gold) are used to distally lock the 10-, 11.5-, and 13-mm-diameter TAN implants.

**Wound Closure.** Once implant insertion is complete, the proximal guide is removed with the guide bolt wrench, and the wounds are irrigated and closed in standard fashion. Verification of rotation and a final check of length are performed before the patient is awakened and transferred from the operating table (see Fig. 51–28H, i to iii)

## Follow-up Care and Rehabilitation

Postoperative care depends on the stability achieved at surgery, which is determined by the strength of the implant and the quality of the bone (in particular, the quality of the medial femoral cortex). Because the forces of muscle contraction are essentially equal to those encountered with partial weight bearing, we recommend ambulation with a heel-to-toe gait on crutches or a walker and partial weight bearing to patient tolerance.

In the absence of other complicating injuries, patients with reconstruction nails and either a trochanteric portal or piriformis portal are mobilized on the first postoperative day with bed-to-chair transfers and ambulation with a walker or crutches. Weight bearing is restricted to 10 to 15 kg on the affected extremity in comminuted cases. If bone-to-bone contact is achieved and good bone quality was present at the time of surgery, weight bearing is permitted as tolerated with crutches or a walker. Range-of-motion exercises and straight leg lifts are started during the first few days. Patients are usually discharged home according to the usual surgical guidelines (e.g., no fever or wound drainage) and after the patient demonstrates lower extremity control sufficient for household ambulation with ambulatory assist devices. Follow-up visits occur at 3- to 4-week intervals, with radiographs taken at that time. As callus is detected, usually at 4 to 8 weeks, progressive weight bearing is allowed. Between 6 and 12 weeks, standing abductor exercises are begun bilaterally to resolve the limp commonly seen in these patients. Patients must demonstrate full weight bearing on the affected leg for 60 seconds before the use of crutches is discontinued. A progressive resistance exercise program is prescribed, and swimming or stationary bicycling is recommended.

Implant removal is not considered until mature radiographic callus is seen bridging the bone on both AP and lateral radiographs. For implant removal, a general anesthetic is required, as well as 24-hour hospitalization in most cases. We place patients on crutches after implant removal until their gait returns to preremoval status. After removal of the implant, contact sports should be avoided for 3 months.

Most patients with isolated fractures attain community ambulation status within 6 to 8 weeks with crutches, begin driving motor vehicles at 8 to 16 weeks, and achieve full weight bearing by 3 to 5 months after injury. Patients can expect functional recovery sufficient to return to their previous occupations in most cases. The rate of union with reconstruction nails averages 95% to 100% in acute subtrochanteric fractures uncomplicated by other injuries (Fig. 51–29).

If the patient is not fully weight bearing and walking without assistive devices by 6 months after fracture, the possibility of nonunion should be considered. If evidence of nonunion is present, autogenous iliac bone grafting, perhaps with renailing and a larger implant, should be considered within 9 to 12 months. We have not used immobilization postoperatively for subtrochanteric fractures.

## Entry Site Comminution: Special Surgical Considerations

As previously stated, even the more difficult type IIA and IIB subtrochanteric fractures, which involve the proximal end of the femur, including the greater trochanter and piriformis fossa, can be treated effectively with the Gamma-type and reconstruction-type nails. With these fracture patterns, the surgeon must expect more technical difficulties and should have a lower threshold for open reduction to ensure that reduction and proximal fixation are satisfactory. Furthermore, when comminution is severe, the surgeon should consider eliminating some of the normal anterior displacement of the neck-head fragment and reducing the shaft almost directly lateral to the neck to increase apposition. A minimally comminuted fracture line through the piriformis fossa tends to become displaced when drills or reamers are passed (Fig. 51–30). The fragments must be held clamped during reaming, or a side-biting rongeur must be used to prepare a proximal portal correctly positioned and large enough to prevent fragment displacement as the nail is passed through the entry. Generally, subtrochanteric fractures with significant intertrochanteric comminution are more easily treated with trochanteric entry portal nails or extramedullary plate-and-screw devices.

The surgeon must be careful to keep the guide wires reduced as the reamers and finally the nail are passed; otherwise, the nail will end up in a subluxated position, too posterior to allow proximal screw insertion. Once the nail is inserted, it must be maintained in proper alignment with the neck as the proximal screws are inserted. Failure to address these issues is the most common technical error in nailing type IIA and IIB fractures.

Entry portal selection for the reconstruction nail in the supine position is significantly more difficult than for a standard femoral nail. Subtrochanteric fractures frequently become displaced with external rotation and varus positioning of the proximal fragment, thus making it very difficult to visualize the entry portal on conventional views. This challenge may be solved either by manually pushing the proximal femoral segment into internal

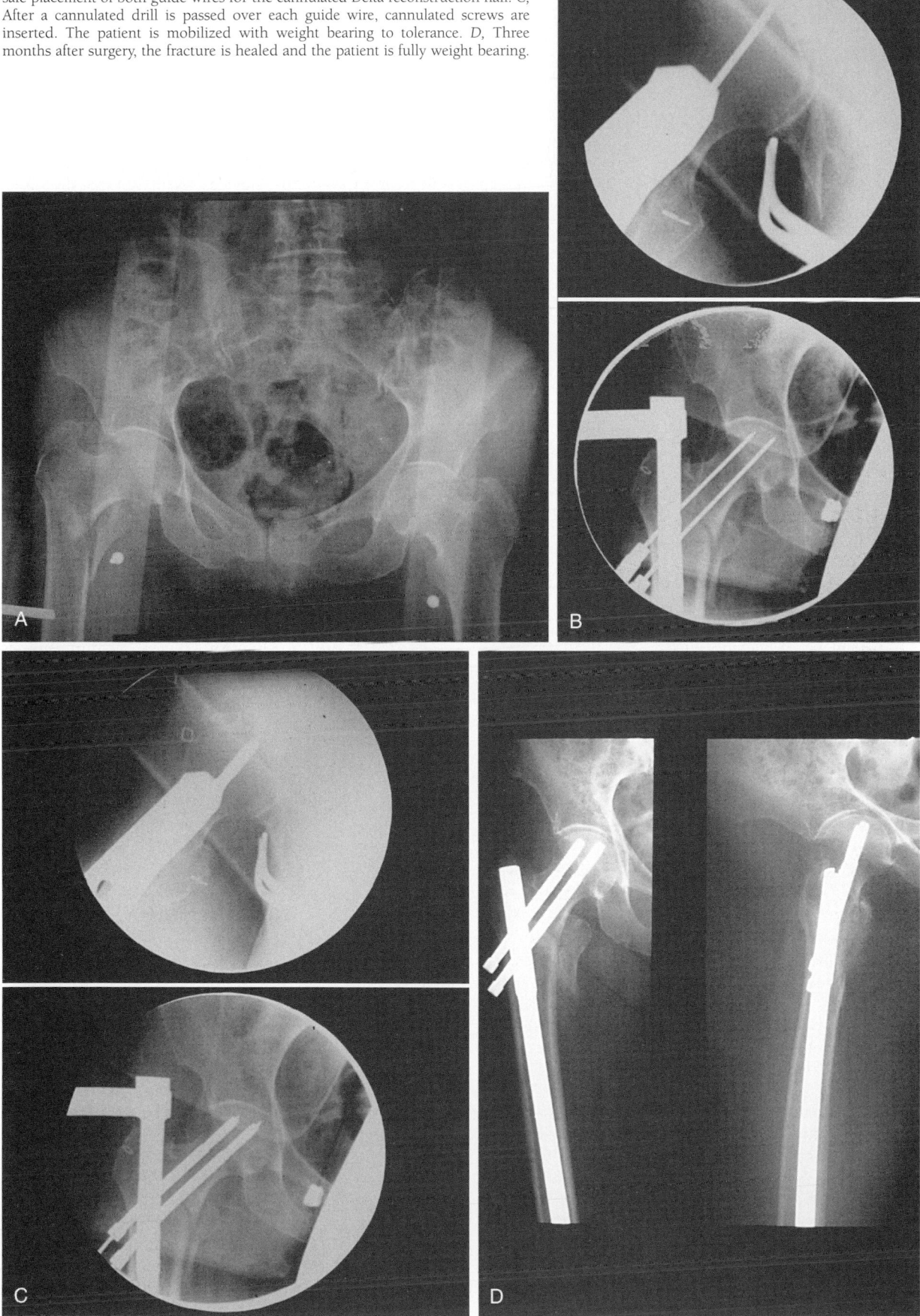

**FIGURE 51–29.** *A,* An 80-year-old woman with a comminuted intertrochanteric fracture and subtrochanteric extension. *B,* Intraoperative C-arm radiographs show safe placement of both guide wires for the cannulated Delta reconstruction nail. *C,* After a cannulated drill is passed over each guide wire, cannulated screws are inserted. The patient is mobilized with weight bearing to tolerance. *D,* Three months after surgery, the fracture is healed and the patient is fully weight bearing.

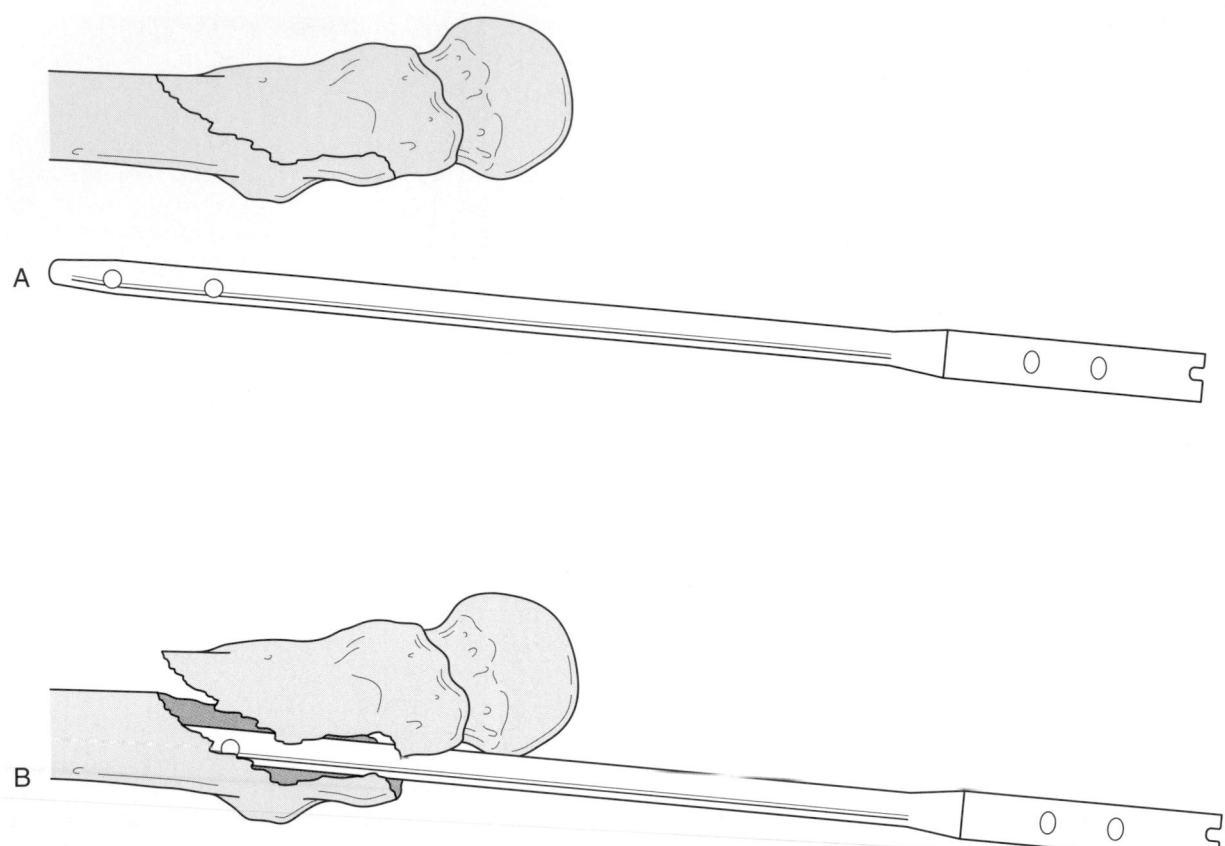

**Figure 51-30.** *A,* With subtrochanteric fractures involving the piriformis fossa, care must be taken to prepare the point of the nail insertion portal correctly in both the proximal and distal fragments. *B,* Without a correct nail entry point, the proximal fragment is displaced as the nail is inserted and malreduction results, along with difficulty inserting the proximal locking screws.

rotation or by inserting a Schanz pin percutaneously into the trochanteric mass and using it as a "joystick" to rotate the proximal end of the femur into a more anatomically recognizable position. In obese patients, a straight nail driver tends to offset the nail laterally and force the hip into varus if fracture extension or comminution is present medially. This varus angulation is caused by pressure of the driver on the lateral aspect of the ilium. A larger incision may be helpful. The surgeon may use an offset driver and apply pressure medially through the driver after the nail is inserted to the correct depth to restore normal hip alignment. These complications are generally avoided by using lateral decubitus positioning, a trochanteric entry portal, or both.

Proper nail depth in reference to the proximal part of the femur and proper rotation of the nail to maximize centering of the screw in the femoral head are also problematic. Preoperative templating is very helpful in determining the diameter of the femoral neck and aids in selection of the proper implant.

Radiographic visualization of the proximal end of the femur may be difficult and disorienting at first with reconstruction nailing. The C-arm must be rotated until a true lateral projection of the femoral head and neck is seen, which is facilitated by rotating the proximal guide anteriorly. Once a true lateral projection of the femoral neck can be visualized and reduction confirmed, the handle is rotated posteriorly until the opaque guide bisects the femoral head. This position allows visualization of the

femoral head anterior and posterior to the locking guide. If the femoral head is seen both anterior and posterior to the proximal guide handle, the screws are contained in the center of the femoral head. The tendency should be toward central or slightly anterior positioning of the screws in the femoral head.

In most cases when the supine position is used, the femoral head is anterior to the shaft of the femur, thereby requiring the proximal drill guide to be rotated no more than 10° below horizontal to prevent proximal screw placement posterior to the femoral head. Note that the anteversion in the nail is designed to compensate for the anterior offset of the femoral head and neck from the center of the medullary canal (the point known as the trochanteric or piriformis fossa) and to optimize distal interlocking so that distal screw insertion is not too posterior at the knee. The proximal drill guide should point toward the femoral head and neck. The tendency during insertion is for retroversion of the proximal locking screws. Even though 8° to 15° of anteversion is built into reconstruction nails relative to the distal locking holes, the proximal drill guide should be positioned slightly below the horizontal axis of the limb; rotational alignment and centralization of the proximal drill guide are then confirmed by noting bisection of the femoral head by the guide on the lateral radiographic view.

In some patients, it is difficult to place two screws within the femoral head because of three possible reasons: (1) varus malreduction, (2) a smaller than normal proximal femoral segment, and (3) preexisting coxa vara. Correct proximal femoral alignment should be the first consideration. If the screw seems to go in a more inferior-to-superior tract into the femoral head during insertion or if it is the surgeon's perspective that only one screw can be inserted, the fracture should be reevaluated for varus reduction. Reduction of the femoral neck-shaft axis must be achieved and maintained during nail insertion. Generally, a correct neck-shaft angle results in the center of the femoral head being at the same level as the tip of the greater trochanter. Because the screws are oriented at an angle of 125° to 135°, it is frequently a clue that the hip may be reduced into varus when only one screw can be inserted. Varus malreduction encountered during nail insertion may be corrected more easily with trochanteric nails than piriformis nails. With trochanteric portal nails, adducting the leg and applying more traction may correct the neck-shaft angle. If not, a lateral-to-medial force on the proximal drill guide may reduce the hip, and this reduction is maintained until the inferior drill guide is inserted correctly into the femoral head. Piriformis nails that have eroded laterally into the trochanter can rarely be corrected. If such displacement has occurred with a neck-shaft angle of 130° or less, consideration should be given to exchanging the nail for a trochanteric portal nail or plate-and-screw device.

In addition to proper neck-shaft reduction, placing two screws in the femoral neck requires that the nail be inserted to the proper depth, which is facilitated by preoperative planning, typically using the outline of the intact opposite femur as a guide. The goal is to place the inferior lag screw just above the medial femoral cortex. If the nail is inserted too deep, it will be difficult to insert the screw, or the screw will penetrate the cortex. At least 4 to 5 mm should be allowed for spacing of the guide wire proximal to the medial femoral neck. Use of the initial guide wire through the sheaths helps ensure that this portal is the correct one. Alternatively, a K-wire may be inserted percutaneously, anteriorly over the femoral neck into the desired position, which is confirmed fluoroscopically. The nail is then inserted with the K-wire used as a reference point.

Not infrequently during insertion of the proximal locking screw, the screw seems to spin and not advance past the nail into the femoral neck. This lack of screw advancement is due to the fact that the threads of the screw are contained within the proximal part of the nail and thus cannot pull the nail into the bone. The surgeon can hammer the screw through the nail and into intact bone proximal to the relatively osteopenic Ward triangle. Turning the screw will then advance it into the desired location. The proximal screws must provide immediately stable fixation. If they do not have good purchase because of severe osteoporosis or pathologic lesions, augmentation of the proximal screw fixation with nonpressurized methyl methacrylate is advisable.

## Assessment of Results

Successful treatment of a subtrochanteric fracture restores the patient to preinjury ambulatory status. Attainment of such status requires union and restoration of the normal neck-shaft angle and correct length and rotation of the limb. Even with the best treatment, some loss of motion about the hip can be expected. Most patients recover a functional range of motion, although some may have prolonged difficulty with squatting. Frequently, high-energy trauma injuries result in some type of liability or disability compensation. The most widely used source for evaluation of permanent impairment from these injuries is the *Guide to the Evaluation of Permanent Physical Impairment,* published by the American Medical Association (AMA).[25a] This guide focuses primarily on range of motion but also considers residual weakness and limb length inequality. Sanders and co-workers[100] recommended a modification of the Hospital for Special Surgery Hip Grading Score, which, unlike the AMA guide, takes into account pain and walking capability and relates preinjury to postinjury status. It also considers the ability to perform such tasks as putting on shoes and socks and negotiating stairs and incorporates radiographic criteria for success. We believe that this rating scale has much to offer in comparative studies (Fig. 51–31). Further discussion of outcome assessment can be found in Chapter 24.

## COMPLICATIONS

Failure of subtrochanteric fracture treatment can be grouped into five areas: loss of fixation, implant failure, nonunion, malunion, and sepsis.[124]

### Loss of Fixation and Implant Failure

With the hip compression screws in current use, implant failure most commonly occurs in osteopenic bone when the screw cuts out of the femoral head, or in younger patients, failure may occur with screw and plate breakage. It is important to obtain sufficient screw fixation of the plate to the shaft, but fixation of more than eight cortices distally is rarely necessary. Failure of fixation is manifested as progressive deformity and shortening of the leg or as an acute episode of snapping or popping followed by pain and an inability to bear weight (Fig. 51–32). Loss of fixation with IM devices is related to not using a static interlocking construct, not evaluating the entry portal for comminution into the piriformis fossa (resulting in nail cutout proximally), using implants without sufficient strength to stabilize the fracture for sufficient cycles of loading, or failure of the fracture repair mechanism because of malnutrition, devascularization of the fracture zone during the initial injury, metabolic deficiencies, or toxins such as smoking.[15, 114]

After failure of plate-and-screw fixation, union has usually been achieved by repeat open reduction and reapplication of internal fixation, coupled with autogenous iliac bone grafting. Frequently, compression hip screw devices will damage the bone stock within the femoral head and thus necessitate 95° devices or bone grafting of the femoral head. Blade plates can be helpful in dealing with bone loss caused by larger screw devices. Cortical allograft inserts may improve the purchase of fixation devices when the femoral head has defects related to bone

| TRAUMATIC HIP RATING SCALE | | | |
|---|---|---|---|
| **No. of points** | **Criteria** | **No. of points** | **Criteria** |

**I. PAIN**

| Points | Criteria |
|---|---|
| 0 | Constant; unbearable; uses strong medication frequently |
| 2 | Constant but bearable; uses strong medication occasionally |
| 4 | Little or none at rest; with activities; uses salicylates frequently |
| 6 | When starting, then better, or after a certain activity; uses salicylates occasionally |
| 8 | Occasional and slight |
| 10 | None |

**II. WALKING**

| (GAIT) | Points | Criteria |
|---|---|---|
| | 0 | Bedridden |
| | 2 | Uses a wheelchair; transfer activities with walker |
| | | Uses no support, housebound |
| (Markedly restricted) | 4 | Uses one support, less than one block |
| | | Uses bilateral support, short distances |
| (Moderately restricted) | 6 | Uses no support, less than one block |
| | | Uses one support, up to five blocks |
| | | Uses bilateral support, unrestricted |
| (Mildly restricted) | 8 | Uses no support, limp |
| | | Uses one support, no limp |
| (Unrestricted) | 10 | Uses no support, no appreciable limp |

**III. FUNCTION**

| A. Retired Preinjury | Points | Criteria |
|---|---|---|
| | 0 | Completely dependent and confined |
| | 2 | Partially dependent |
| | 4 | Independent; can do limited housework, limited shopping |
| | 6 | Can do most housework; shops freely; can do desk-type work |
| | 8 | Very little restriction; can work on feet |
| | 10 | Normal activities |

| B. Employed Preinjury | Points | Criteria |
|---|---|---|
| | 0 | Unemployed/retired secondary to injury |
| | 2 | Part-time/light duty |
| | 4 | Changed jobs secondary to injury |
| | 6 | Altered job description somewhat |
| | 8 | Returned to work with some disability |
| | 10 | Returned to full work |

**IV. MOTION-MUSCLE POWER**

| Points | Criteria |
|---|---|
| 0 | Ankylosis with deformity |
| 2 | Ankylosis with good functional position |
| 4 | Muscle power poor to fair; arc of flexion <60°; restricted lateral and rotary movement |
| 6 | Muscle power fair to good; arc of flexion as much as 90°; restricted lateral/rotary motion |
| 8 | Muscle power good or normal; arc of flexion >90°; fair lateral and rotary movement |
| 10 | Muscle power normal; motion normal or almost normal |

**V. DAILY ACTIVITIES**

| A. Shoes & socks | Points | Criteria |
|---|---|---|
| | 0 | Unable |
| | 3 | With difficulty |
| | 5 | With ease |

| B. Stairs | Points | Criteria |
|---|---|---|
| | 0 | Unable |
| | 2 | One at a time |
| | 4 | With railing |
| | 5 | Normal |

**VI. RADIOGRAPHIC EVALUATION**

| Points | Criteria |
|---|---|
| 0 | Nonunion/plate failure/arthritis |
| 2 | Delayed union |
| 4 | Varus >10°, shortening >2.5 cm |
| 6 | Varus >5° but <10°, shortening >1 cm but <2.5 cm |
| 8 | Varus <5°, shortening <1 cm |
| 10 | Anatomic reduction |

| TOTAL SCORE | RESULT |
|---|---|
| 55–60 | Excellent |
| 45–54 | Good |
| 35–44 | Poor |
| <35 | Failure |

**FIGURE 51–31.** Traumatic hip rating score proposed by Sanders and co-workers. (Courtesy of R. Sanders, M.D.)

resorption around the initial fixation device (Fig. 51–33). Aronoff and colleagues[3] recommended IM nailing for failed plates and screws because the trochanteric extension that may occur with type II subtrochanteric fractures usually heals, with only a single subtrochanteric nonunion defect. This approach is generally ill-advised unless the initial procedure has restored normal proximal femoral anatomy so that an appropriately configured medullary canal is available for IM nailing.[24] Haentjens and co-workers[52] reported a small series with fair to good to results in which endoprostheses were used for salvage after failed open reduction and internal fixation. Prosthetic replacement of the proximal part of the femur is primarily an end-stage salvage procedure indicated for geriatric patients.

## Nonunion

Nonunion of a subtrochanteric fracture is generally indicated by an inability to resume full weight bearing in the usual 3- to 6-month period. Continued pain and warmth about the proximal part of the thigh and pain with attempted weight bearing are clinical indicators of delayed union and nonunion and should be confirmed with radiographs and tomograms as necessary. Nonunion usually persists in the shaft portion of the fracture and actually converts the fracture to a Russell-Taylor type IA pattern, which is best treated with an IM device in a static locking fashion. If open reduction is required, autogenous iliac bone grafting is indicated, preferably applied medially. Nails may fail by implant failure, and removal of the nail

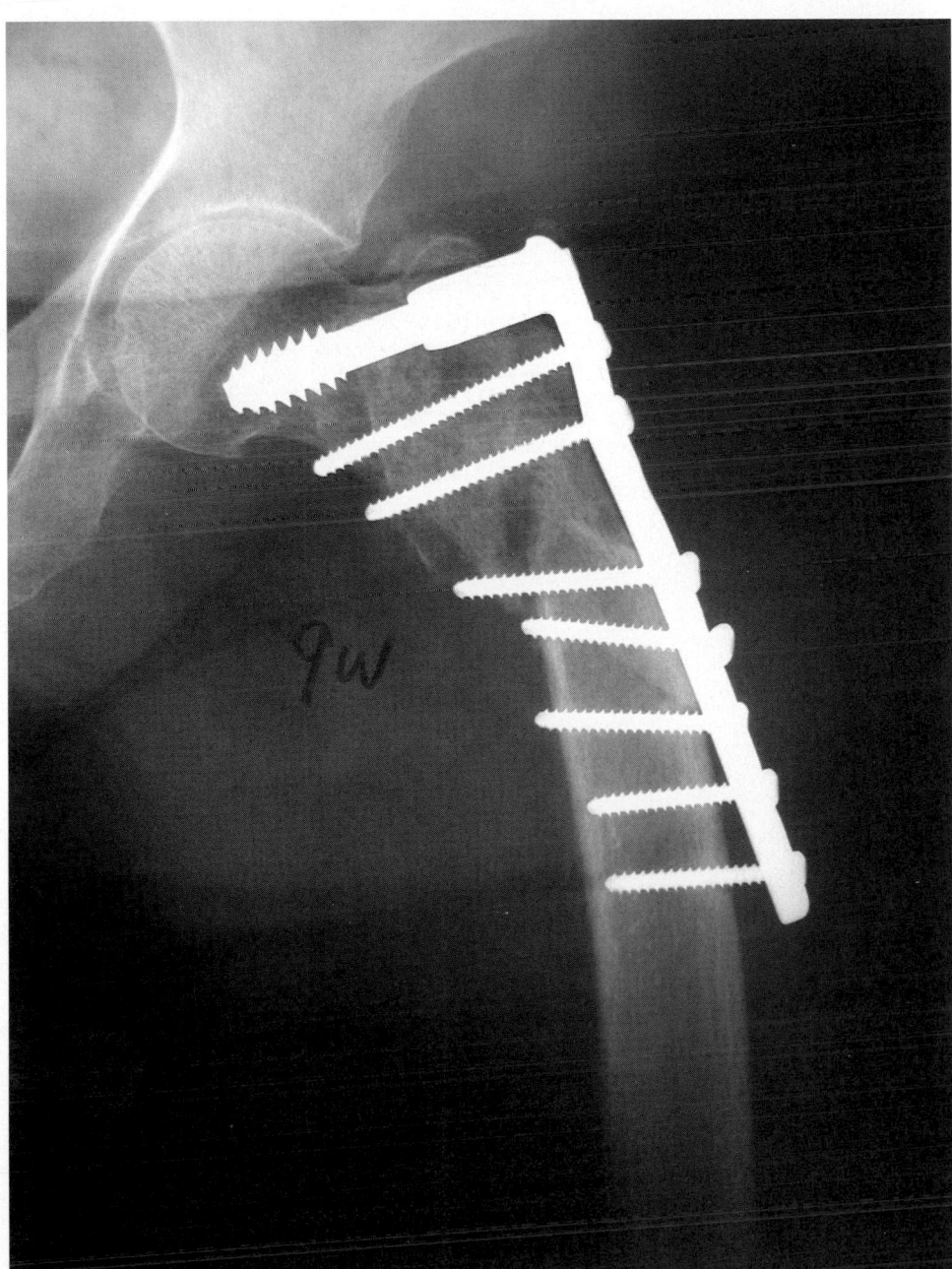

**FIGURE 51–32.** Elderly woman with a sudden onset of hip pain, deformity, and difficulty walking 9 weeks after fixation of a subtrochanteric fracture with a 95° condylar compression screw.

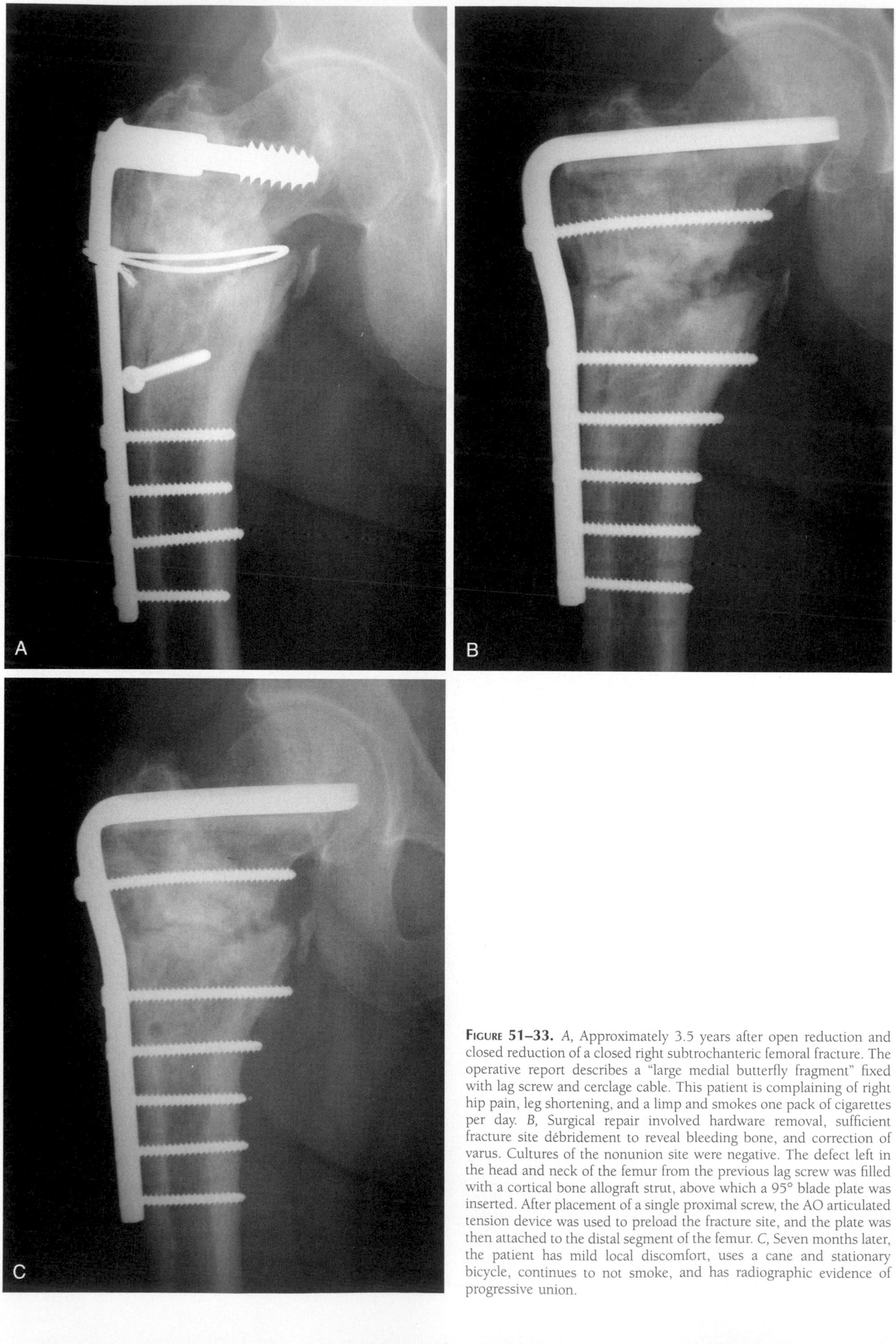

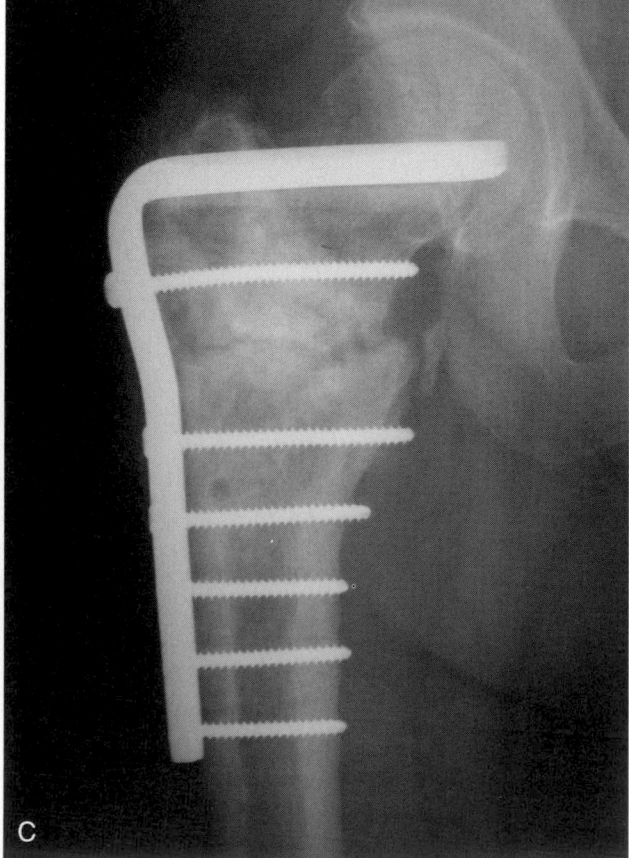

**Figure 51–33.** *A,* Approximately 3.5 years after open reduction and closed reduction of a closed right subtrochanteric femoral fracture. The operative report describes a "large medial butterfly fragment" fixed with lag screw and cerclage cable. This patient is complaining of right hip pain, leg shortening, and a limp and smokes one pack of cigarettes per day. *B,* Surgical repair involved hardware removal, sufficient fracture site débridement to reveal bleeding bone, and correction of varus. Cultures of the nonunion site were negative. The defect left in the head and neck of the femur from the previous lag screw was filled with a cortical bone allograft strut, above which a 95° blade plate was inserted. After placement of a single proximal screw, the AO articulated tension device was used to preload the fracture site, and the plate was then attached to the distal segment of the femur. *C,* Seven months later, the patient has mild local discomfort, uses a cane and stationary bicycle, continues to not smoke, and has radiographic evidence of progressive union.

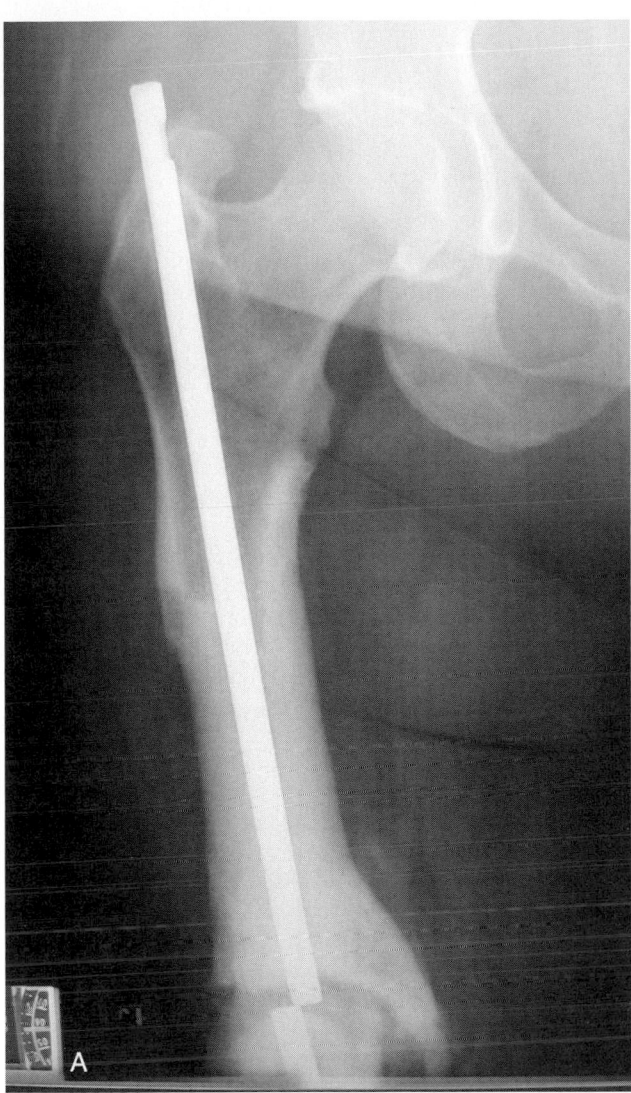

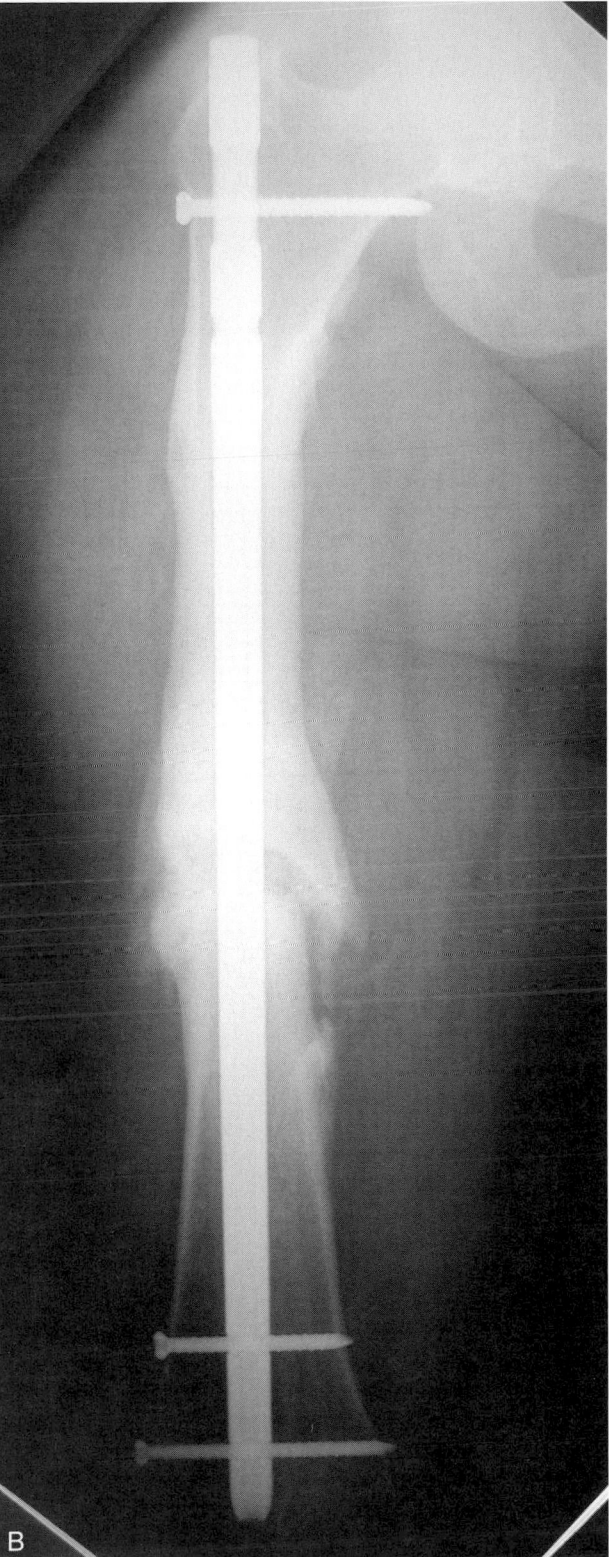

**FIGURE 51–34.** *A,* Three years after first-generation, nonlocked intramedullary (IM) fixation of a subtrochanteric femoral fracture in a mentally retarded, middle-aged woman. She is complaining of persisting deformity and trouble walking. *B,* Four months after nail removal and refixation with a static locked IM nail and an iliac crest bone graft, healing was uneventful, with resolution of all complaints.

plus repeat reaming and nailing with a larger implant yields a high success rate if the failure was due to a small-diameter nail or unlocked nail (Fig. 51–34). With exchange nailing, closed manipulation of the nonunion is advisable after nail removal to reactivate the fracture repair mechanism. The question is whether the fracture should

then be treated with dynamic locking or static locking. Static locking is preferable to resist rotational shear forces, which contribute to mechanical instability at the site of nonunion. As in all nonunions, culturing the fracture site (or medullary reaming debris) is advisable to identify the occasional occult infection, which if found is usually an indication for several weeks of culture-specific intravenous antibiotics.

Plate fixation is an alternative to IM nailing as treatment of ununited subtrochanteric fractures. Hypertrophic, mechanically compressible nonunion often responds to a tension band plate loaded with an external tension device. If the nonunion is truly hypertrophic and stable, bone grafting may not be required. If a defect or atrophic nonunion is present, the so-called wave plate configuration should be considered.

Cessation of smoking is an essential recommendation. Avoidance of nonsteroidal anti-inflammatory medications seems wise as well. Healing adjuncts (magnetic or ultrasound stimulation) may increase the likelihood of healing. Although initially protected weight bearing may need to be limited, most patients with subtrochanteric nonunion fixed with IM nails can soon be allowed progressive, even vigorous weight bearing. Plated nonunion, however, needs mechanical protection until bone healing is sufficient to reduce the risk of failure in a cyclically loaded plate.

## Malunion

Patients with malunion usually complain of a limp, shortness of the leg, or rotational deformity. The affected leg should be compared with the opposite side for evaluation of these deformities. Varus deformity may occur if a standard IM nail is used and the entry portal is too far lateral into the tip of the trochanter. However, such varus deformity is usually less than 5°, is frequently well tolerated by the patient, and does not require reoperation. Malunion potentially involves three aspects of fracture reduction: angulation, leg length, and rotation.

**Angulation.** It is imperative that the neck-shaft angle be restored, as shown by the AP radiograph. If it is not, the patient typically has a Trendelenburg gait with abductor weakness from shortening of the muscle group. In plated fractures, a valgus osteotomy plus repeat internal fixation with bone grafting is the treatment of choice. The same can be done to revise deformity after an IM nail—either plate fixation or another nail (Fig. 51–35).

**Leg Length.** Leg length discrepancy is a complex problem and is most likely to occur after a trochanteric fracture with extensive shaft comminution and extension into the diaphysis treated with a dynamic rather than a static locking nail construct. It may also be due to angular deformity or bone loss from an open fracture or infection. Leg length inequality, if not satisfactorily managed with a shoe lift, can be treated by lengthening or shortening. Shortening of the opposite leg might be considered for an occasional patient. Because femoral lengthening procedures in adults are slow and prone to complications, avoidance is the best treatment of this problem. Careful attention must be paid preoperatively and intraoperatively to restore acceptable length. Occasionally with locked IM nailing, the injured limb is distracted and heals with excessive length. This problem typically occurs when length is not carefully equalized in comminuted fractures. If severe enough, this deformity is best corrected by closed IM shortening, which can be performed by open

means if a plate needs to be removed, but IM fixation is generally best.

**Rotation.** Malrotation may occur with either plating or IM fixation if the surgeon is not alert to this potential complication. Adherence to guidelines for reduction and confirmation, including radiographic verification and matching of the linea aspera, helps prevent this complication. It is essential to compare leg lengths and also to confirm rotational alignment by comparing range of internal and external rotation before awakening the patient after IM nailing. Such comparison permits early correction of malalignment. If significant internal or external rotational deformities are detected late, reoperation with derotation osteotomy may be indicated. After IM nailing, closed derotation osteotomy with a static interlocking nail is the treatment of choice.

## Wound Infection

Infections are generally evident between the 4th and 10th postoperative days because of increasing pain and the usual signs of inflammation. Sterile aspiration of the operative site may be carried out to confirm infection, but false-negative results are frequent. Bone scanning is rarely helpful for the diagnosis of acute infection. Late infections are usually manifested as nonunion, and the sepsis is frequently occult. Gallium scanning has been of limited use in diagnosing septic nonunion, and it is best to rely on biopsy results. When evaluating a nonunion, biopsy of the site for anaerobic and aerobic cultures during revision surgery is recommended. If the culture is positive, prolonged intravenous antibiotics for 6 weeks plus conversion to oral antibiotics for an indefinite period is indicated, depending on the patient's immune and nutritional status and the type of infecting organism. When any surgical revision is required for subtrochanteric complications, intraoperative specimens for culture, both anaerobic and aerobic, should be taken. Sepsis in subtrochanteric fractures most commonly follows open reduction and internal fixation; with closed IM nailing techniques, the risk of infection is significantly less. The use of prophylactic antibiotics also significantly decreases the possibility of postoperative sepsis.

Particularly in older and obese patients, persisting serous wound drainage may occur if a larger incision was required. Unless this drainage resolves within 7 to 10 days, during which time reduced activity is advisable, return to the operating room is advisable for evacuation of any residual wound hematoma, the typical cause of such drainage. Cultures and Gram stain are obtained. Antibiotic coverage is continued from the time that the samples are taken until culture is negative or the infection has been treated adequately. Unless an obvious infection is discovered, such a wound can usually be closed immediately over a suction drain or drains, or it can be left open with a tobramycin-loaded bead pouch dressing at the surgeon's discretion.

Acute postoperative infection is best managed by immediate surgery for drainage and débridement of all necrotic material. The wound should be left open for repeat débridement or closed over antibiotic beads. If the fixation is stable, the implant should be retained until the fracture has healed. If the implant is unstable, it should be removed and either traction (usually temporary) or external fixation used during treatment of the infection (Fig. 51–36). Once the active infection is under control and all necrotic and infected bone has been débrided, internal fixation can be reinserted. Internal fixation is generally better tolerated than an external fixator, but external fixation is required if infection recurs after refixation with adequate suppressive antibiotics. Delayed bone grafting will usually be needed to fill any residual defect and to promote union, which is typically delayed after infection. Prolonged antibiotic therapy, typically for 6 weeks followed by long-term oral antibiotics in susceptible microbial cases, may be necessary in these difficult problems. Removal of implants is usually recommended after fracture healing in patients with sepsis because of the latent possibility of reactivation of the infection in the future. Specimens for culture are taken during implant removal, and prophylactic antibiotics of a broad-spectrum type are used until final cultures are sterile. When significant bone loss is present and sometimes to ensure adequate stability, Ilizarov external fixation and bone transport techniques should be considered. See Chapter 21.

## Functional Loss

Functional loss is almost always secondary to complications about the hip or knee.[124] Heterotopic ossification is a frequent radiographic finding but is rarely symptomatic. Associated lesions of the patella, periarticular knee fractures, and soft tissue injuries can result in primary

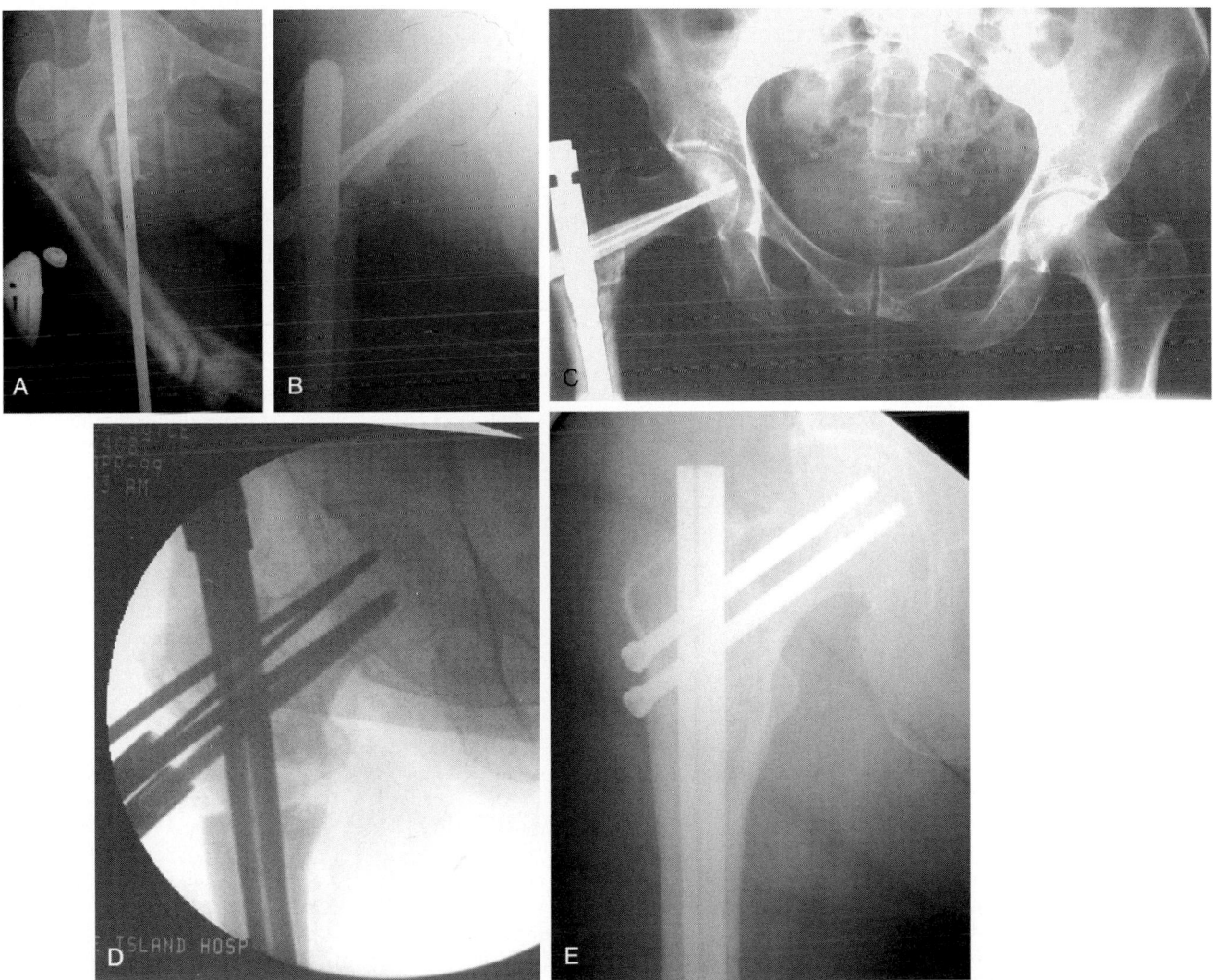

**FIGURE 51–35.** *A,* Subtrochanteric femoral fracture (segmental) sustained in a motor vehicle crash by a healthy 52-year-old woman. *B,* Fixation with an AO spiral blade, static locked cephalomedullary nail. *C,* Union was delayed. Failure of fixation and progressive varus collapse developed over the next several months, during which time the fracture healed. This radiograph was taken 13 months after injury. *D,* Treatment involved nail removal, negative cultures, and subtrochanteric osteotomy with external fixator–assisted cephalomedullary nailing. The proximal external fixator pins are placed into the femoral head-neck segment anterior to the planned path of the nail and locking screws. The distal pins are similarly outside the path of the nail. The fixator is adjusted to achieve satisfactory alignment, after which the nail is inserted as described in the text and locked statically before the external fixator is removed. *E,* Healed osteotomy with fixation maintained 18 months later.

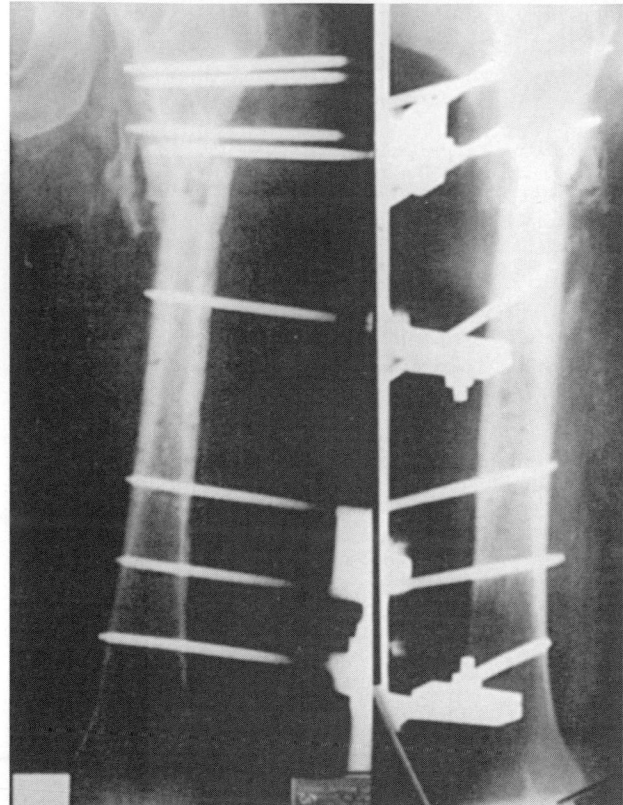

**Figure 51-36.** Deep sepsis and loss of fixation after fixation with a blade plate device. Septic nonunion was treated by débridement, irrigation, and stabilization with external fixation.

functional loss in a subtrochanteric fracture. Neurologic injuries associated with a subtrochanteric fracture are rare but must be evaluated carefully before nailing is performed. Sciatic and pudendal nerve injuries observed postoperatively are usually caused by the excessive traction required for reduction or by compartment syndrome; these injuries do not always resolve with time and can result in significant morbidity.

## REFERENCES

1. Alho, A.; Ekeland, A.; Stromsoe, K.N. Subtrochanteric femoral fractures treated with locked intramedullary nails: Experience from 31 cases. Acta Orthop Scand 62:573–576, 1992.
2. Allis, O.H. Fracture in the upper third of the femur exclusive of the neck. Med News 59:585–589, 1891.
3. Aronoff, P.M.; Davis, P.M., Jr.; Wickstrom, J.K. Intramedullary nail fixation treatment of subtrochanteric fractures of the femur. J Trauma 11:637–650, 1971.
4. Asher, M.A.; Tipper, J.W.; Rockwood, C.A.; Zilber, S. Compression fixation of subtrochanteric fractures. Clin Orthop 117:202–208, 1976.
5. Aune, A.K.; Ekeland, A.; Odegaard, B.; et al. Gamma nail vs compression screw for trochanteric femoral fractures: 15 reoperations in a prospective, randomized study of 378 patients. Acta Orthop Scand 65:127–130, 1994.
6. Barquet, A.; Francescoli, L.; Rienzi, D. Intertrochanteric-subtrochanteric fractures: Treatment with the long Gamma nail. J Orthop Trauma 14:324–328, 2000.
7. Bergman, G.D.; Winquist, R.A.; Mayo, K.A.; Hansen, S.T., Jr. Subtrochanteric fracture of the femur: Fixation using the Zickel nail. J Bone Joint Surg Am 69:1032–1040, 1987.
8. Berman, A.T.; Metzger, P.C.; Bosacco, S.J.; et al. Treatment of the subtrochanteric fracture with the compression hip nail: A review of 138 consecutive cases. Abstract. Orthop Trans 3:225–256, 1979.
9. Boriani, S.; De Iure, F.; Bettelli, G.; et al. The results of a multicenter Italian study on the use of the Gamma nail for the treatment of pertrochanteric and subtrochanteric fractures: A review of 1181 cases. Chir Organi Mov 79:193–203, 1994.
10. Bose, W.J.; Corces, A.; Anderson, L.D. A preliminary experience with the Russell-Taylor reconstruction nail for complex femoral fractures. J Trauma 32:71–76, 1992.
11. Boyd, A.D., Jr.; Wilber, J.H. Patterns and complications of femur fractures below the hip in patients over 65 years of age. J Orthop Trauma 6:167–174, 1992.
12. Boyd, H.B.; Griffin, L.L. Classification and treatment of trochanteric fractures. Arch Surg 58:853–866, 1949.
13. Boyd, H.B.; Lipiniski, S.W. Nonunion of trochanteric and subtrochanteric fractures. Surg Gynecol Obstet 104:463–470, 1957.
14. Brien, W.; Wiss, D.A.; Peter, K.; Merrett, P.O. Subtrochanteric fractures of the femur: Treatment with locked medullary nails. Paper presented at the 54th Annual Meeting of the American Academy of Orthopaedic Surgeons, San Francisco, January 25, 1987.
15. Broos, P.L.; Reynders, P.; Vanderspeeten, K. Mechanical complications associated with the use of the unreamed AO femoral intramedullary nail with spiral blade: First experiences with thirty-five consecutive cases. J Orthop Trauma 12:186–189, 1998.
16. Browner, B. Personal communication, June 1989.
17. Brumback, R.J.; Lakatos, R.P.; Garbarino, J.L.; et al. Closed interlocking intramedullary nailing of subtrochanteric fractures. Abstract. Orthop Trans 11:478, 1987.
18. Brumback, R.J.; Lakatos, R.P.; Poka, A.; Burgess, A.R. Risks of infection with reamed intramedullary femoral fixation in multiple trauma. Abstract. Orthop Trans 11:490, 1987.
19. Brumback, R.J.; Reilly, J.P.; Poka, A.; et al. Intramedullary nailing of femoral shaft fractures: Part I. Decision-making errors with interlocking fixation. J Bone Joint Surg Am 70:1441–1452, 1988.
20. Brumback, R.J.; Uwagie-Ero, S.; Lakatos, R.P.; et al. Intramedullary nailing of femoral shaft fractures: Part II. Fracture healing with static interlocking fixation. J Bone Joint Surg Am 70:1453–1462, 1988.
21. Cech, H.; Sosna, A. Principles of the surgical treatment of subtrochanteric fractures. Orthop Clin North Am 5:651–662, 1974.
22. Ceder, L.; Lunsjo, K.; Olsson, O.; et al. Different ways to treat subtrochanteric fractures with the Medoff sliding plate. Clin Orthop 348:101–106, 1998.
23. Ceder, L.; Tidermark, J.; Hamberg, P.; et al. Extramedullary fixation of 107 subtrochanteric fractures: A randomized multicenter trial of the Medoff sliding plate versus 3 other screw-plate systems. Acta Orthop Scand 70:459–466, 1999.
24. Charnley, G.J.; Ward, A.J. Reconstruction femoral nailing for nonunion of subtrochanteric fracture: A revision technique following dynamic condylar screw failure. Int Orthop 20:55–57, 1996.
25. Chevalley, F.; Gamba, D. Gamma nailing of pertrochanteric and subtrochanteric fractures: Clinical results of a series of 63 consecutive cases. J Orthop Trauma 11:412–415, 1997.
25a Cocchiarella, L.; Andersson, G.B.J. Guides to the Evaluation of Permanent Impairment, 5th ed. Chicago: AMA Press, 2000.
26. Curtis, M.J.; Jinnah, R.H.; Wilson, V., et al. Proximal femoral fractures: A biomechanical study to compare intramedullary and extramedullary fixation. Injury 25:99–104, 1994.
27. Cuthbert, H.I.; Howat, T.W. The use of the Küntscher Y nail in the treatment of intertrochanteric and subtrochanteric fractures of the femur. Injury 8:135–142, 1974.
28. Davis, A.D.; Meyer, R.D.; Miller, M.E.; Killian, J.T. Closed Zickel nailing. Clin Orthop 201:138–146, 1985.
29. De Boeck, H. Classification of hip fractures. Acta Orthop Belg 60(Suppl 1):106–109, 1994.
30. DeLee, J.C.; Clanton, T.O.; Rockwood, C.A., Jr. Closed treatment of subtrochanteric fractures of the femur in a modified cast-brace. J Bone Joint Surg Am 63:773–779, 1982.
31. Dhal, A.; Singh, S.S. Biological fixation of subtrochanteric fractures by external fixation. Injury 27:723–731, 1996.
32. DiCicco, J.D., 3rd; Jenkins, M.; Ostrum, R.F. Retrograde nailing for subtrochanteric femur fractures. Am J Orthop 29(9 Suppl): 4–8, 2000.
33. Di Puccio, G.; Lunati, P.; Franceschi, G.; et al. The long gamma nail: Indications and results. Chir Organi Mov 82:49–52, 1997.

34. DiStefano, V.J.; Nixon, J.E.; Klein, K.S. Stable fixation of the difficult subtrochanteric fracture. J Trauma 12:1066–1070, 1972.

35. Dobozi, W.R.; Larson, B.J.; Zindrick, M.; et al. Flexible intramedullary nailing of subtrochanteric fractures of the femur. Clin Orthop 212:66–78, 1986.

36. Dora, C.; Leunig, M.; Beck, M.; et al. Entry point soft tissue damage in antegrade femoral nailing: A cadaver study. J Orthop Trauma 15:488–493, 2001.

37. Edwards, S.A.; Pandit, H.G.; Clarke, H.J. The long gamma nail: A DGH experience. Injury 31:701–709, 2000.

38. Elabdien, B.S.Z.; Olerud, S.; Karlstrom, G. Subtrochanteric fractures: Classification and results of Ender nailing. Arch Orthop Trauma Surg 103:241–250, 1984.

39. Fielding, J.W.; Cochran, G.V.B.; Zickel, R.E. Biomechanical characteristics and surgical management of subtrochanteric fractures. Orthop Clin North Am 5:629–650, 1974.

40. Fielding, J.W.; Magliato, H.J. Subtrochanteric fractures. Surg Gynecol Obstet 122:555–560, 1966.

41. Finsen, V.; Borset, M.; Buvik, G.E.; et al. Preoperative traction in patients with hip fractures. Injury 23:242–244, 1992.

42. Forthomme, J.P.; Costenoble, V.; Soete, P.; et al. Traitement des fractures trochanteriennes du femur par le clou gamma (a propos d'une serie de 92 cas). Acta Orthop Belg 59:22–29, 1993.

43. Frankel, V.H.; Burstein, A.H. Orthopaedic Biomechanics. Philadelphia, Lea & Febiger, 1970.

44. French, B.G.; Tornetta, P., 3rd. Use of an interlocked cephalomedullary nail for subtrochanteric fracture stabilization. Clin Orthop 348:95–100, 1998.

45. Friedl, W.; Colombo-Benkmann, M.; Dockter, S.; et al. Gammanagel-Osteosynthese per und subtrochanterer Femurfrakturen. 4-Jahres Erfahrungen und ihre Konsequenzen für die weitere Implantatentwicklung. Chirurg 65:953–963, 1994.

46. Froimson, A.L. Treatment of comminuted subtrochanteric fractures. Surg Gynecol Obstet 131:465–472, 1970.

47. Frost, H.M. The Laws of Bone Structure. Springfield, IL, Charles C. Thomas, 1964.

48. Garbarino, J.L.; Brumback, R.J.; Poka, A.; Burgess, A.R. Closed interlocking intramedullary nailing of subtrochanteric fractures. Paper presented at the 54th Annual Meeting of the American Academy of Orthopaedic Surgeons, San Francisco, January 25, 1987.

49. Grosse, A.; Kempf, I.; Lafforgue, D. Le traitement des fracas, perte de substance osseuse et pseudoarthroses due femur et du tibia par l'enclouage verrouille (a propos de 40 cas). Rev Chir Orthop 64(Suppl 2):33, 1978.

50. Gustilo, R.B. Management of Open Fractures and Their Complications. Philadelphia, W.B. Saunders, 1982.

51. Habernek, H.; Schmid, L.; Frauenschuh, E. Sport related proximal femoral fractures; a retrospective review of 31 cases treated in an eight year period. Br J Sports Med 34:54–58, 2000.

52. Haentjens, P.; De Neve, W.; Opdecam, P. Remplacement prothetique pour fracture pathologique de l'extremite superieure du femur: Prothese totale ou prothese intermediaire? Rev Chir Orthop Reparatrice Appar Mot 80:493–502, 1994.

53. Haidukewych, G.J.; Israel, T.A.; Berry, D.J. Reverse obliquity fractures of the intertrochanteric region of the femur. J Bone Joint Surg Am 83:643–650, 2001.

54. Hanson, G.W.; Tullos, H.S. Subtrochanteric fractures of the femur treated with nail plate devices: A retrospective study. Clin Orthop 131:191–194, 1978.

55. Heiple, K.G.; Brooks, D.B.; Sampson, B.L.; Burstein, A.H. A fluted intramedullary rod for subtrochanteric fractures: Biomechanical considerations and preliminary clinical results. J Bone Joint Surg Am 61:730–737, 1979.

56. Herscovici, D., Jr.; Pistel, W.L.; Sanders, R.W. Evaluation and treatment of high subtrochanteric femur fractures. Am J Orthop 29(9 Suppl):27–33, 2000.

57. Hey-Groves, E.W. Ununited fractures, with special reference to gunshot injuries and the use of bone grafting. Br J Surg 6:203, 1918.

58. Hibbs, R.A. The management of the tendency of the upper fragment to tilt forward in fractures of the upper third of the femur. N Y Med J 75:177–179, 1902.

59. Hogh, J. Sliding screw in the treatment of trochanteric fractures. Injury 14:141–145, 1982.

60. Jewett, E.L. New approach for subtrochanteric and upper femoral shaft fractures using a dual flange nail plate: Preliminary report. Am J Surg 81:186–188, 1951.

61. Johnson, K.D. Current techniques in the treatment of subtrochanteric fractures. Tech Orthop 3:14–24, 1988.

62. Johnson, K.D.; Tencer, A.F.; Sherman, M.C. Biomechanical factors affecting fracture stability and femoral bursting in closed intramedullary nailing of femoral shaft fractures, with illustrative case presentations. J Orthop Trauma 14:1–11, 1987.

63. Jones, J.B. Screw fixation of the lesser trochanteric fragment. Clin Orthop 123:107, 1977.

64. Karr, R.K.; Schwab, J.P. Subtrochanteric fracture as a complication of proximal femoral pinning. Clin Orthop 194:214–217, 1985.

65. Keenan, M.A. Subtrochanteric fracture of the femur. Abstract. Orthop Trans 4:359, 1980.

66. Kempf, I.; Grosse, A.; Beck, G. Closed locked intramedullary nailing. J Bone Joint Surg Am 67:709–720, 1985.

67. Kinast, C.; Bolhofner, B.R.; Mast, J.W.; Ganz, R. Subtrochanteric fractures of the femur: Results of treatment with the 95-degree condylar blade plate. Clin Orthop 238:122–130, 1989.

68. Kitajima, I.; Tachibana, S.; Mikami, Y.; et al. Insufficiency fracture of the femoral neck after intramedullary nailing. Orthop Sci 4:304–306, 1999.

69. Koch, J.C. The laws of bone architecture. Am J Anat 21:177–298, 1917.

70. Kraemer, W.J.; Hearn, T.C.; Powell, J.N.; et al. Fixation of segmental subtrochanteric fractures. A biomechanical study. Clin Orthop 331:71–79, 1996.

71. Krettek, C.; Schandelmaier, P.; Miclau, T.; et al: Minimally invasive percutaneous plate osteosynthesis (MIPPO) using the DCS in proximal and distal femoral fractures. Injury 28(Suppl 1):A20–A30, 1997.

72. Kummer, F.J.; Olsson, O.; Pearlman, C.A.; et al. Intramedullary versus extramedullary fixation of subtrochanteric fractures. A biomechanical study. Acta Orthop Scand 69:580–584, 1998.

73. Küntscher, G. Dauerbruch und Umbauzone. Bruns Beitrage Klin Chir 169:558, 1939.

74. Kyle, R.F.; Cabanela, M.E.; Russell, T.A.; et al. Fractures of the proximal part of the femur. Review. Instr Course Lect 44:227–253, 1995.

75. Kyle, R.F.; Wright, T.M.; Burstein, A.H. Biomechanical analysis of the sliding characteristics of compression hip screws. J Bone Joint Surg Am 62:1308–1314, 1980.

76. Levy, R.N.; Siegel, M.; Sedlin, E.D.; Siffert, R.S. Complications of Ender-pin fixation in basicervical, intertrochanteric, and subtrochanteric fractures of the hip. J Bone Joint Surg Am 65:66–69, 1983.

77. Lhowe, D.W.; Hansen, S.T. Immediate nailing of open fractures of the femoral shaft. J Bone Joint Surg Am 70:812–820, 1988.

78. Loch, D.A.; Kyle, R.F.; Bechtold, J.E.; et al. Forces required to initiate sliding in second-generation intramedullary nails. J Bone Joint Surg Am 80:1626–1631, 1998.

79. Lunsjo, K.; Ceder, L.; Stigsson, L.; et al. Two-way compression along the shaft and the neck of the femur with the Medoff sliding plate: One-year follow-up of 108 intertrochanteric fractures. J Bone Joint Surg Br 78:387–390, 1996.

80. Maatz, R.; Lentz, W.; Arens, W.; Beck, H., eds. Intramedullary Nailing and Other Intramedullary Osteosyntheses. Philadelphia, W.B. Saunders, 1986.

81. MacEachern, A.G.; Heyse-Moore, G.H.; Jones, R.N. Subtrochanteric fractures of the femur through the track of the lower Garden screw: Treatment with a Richards sliding screw. Injury 15:337–340, 1984.

82. Mahomed, N.; Harrington, I.; Kellam, J.; et al. Biomechanical analysis of the Gamma nail and sliding hip screw. Clin Orthop 304:280–288, 1994.

83. Medoff, R.J.; Maes, K. A new device for the fixation of unstable pertrochanteric fractures of the hip. J Bone Joint Surg Am 73:1192–1199, 1991.

84. Meggitt, B.F.; Juett, D.A.; Smith, J.D. Cast-bracing for fractures of the femoral shaft. J Bone Joint Surg Br 63:12–23, 1981.

85. Michelson, J.D.; Myers, A.; Jinnah, R.; et al. Epidemiology of hip fractures among the elderly: Risk factors for fracture type. Clin Orthop 311:129–135, 1995.

86. Müller, M.E.; Allgöwer, M.; Schneider, R.; et al. Manual of Internal Fixation, 2nd ed. Berlin, Springer-Verlag, 1979.

87. Nikolic, D.; Jovanovic, Z.; Turkovic, G.; et al. Subtrochanteric missile fractures of the femur. Injury 29:743–749, 1998.

88. Ovadia, D.N.; Chess, J.L. Intraoperative and postoperative subtrochanteric fracture of the femur associated with removal of the Zickel nail. J Bone Joint Surg Am 70:239–243, 1988.

89. Pai, C.H. Dynamic condylar screw for subtrochanteric femur fractures with greater trochanteric extension. J Orthop Trauma 10:317–322, 1996.

90. Pankovich, A.M.; Tarabishy, I.E. Ender nailing of intertrochanteric and subtrochanteric fractures of the femur. J Bone Joint Surg Am 62:635–645, 1980.

91. Pepper, J.; Russell, T.; Sanders, R.; et al. Minimally invasive intramedullary nail insertion instruments and method. US Patent 5,951,561. Sept 14, 1999.

92. Rantanen, J.; Aro, H.T. Intramedullary fixation of high subtrochanteric femoral fractures: A study comparing two implant designs, the Gamma nail and the intramedullary hip screw. J Orthop Trauma 12:249–252, 1998.

93. Rantanen, J.; Aro, H. Mechanical failure of the intramedullary hip screw in a subtrochanteric femoral fracture. J Orthop Trauma 10:348–359, 1996.

94. Robey, L.R. Intertrochanteric and subtrochanteric fractures of the femur in the Negro. J Bone Joint Surg Am 38:1301–1312, 1956.

95. Robinson, C.M.; Court-Brown, C.M.; McQueen, M.M.; et al. Hip fractures in adults younger than 50 years of age: Epidemiology and results. Clin Orthop 312:238–246, 1995.

96. Rodriguez Alverez, J.; Casteleiro Gonzolez, C.; Laguna Aranda, R.; et al. Indications for use of the long Gamma nail. Clin Orthop 350:62–66, 1998.

97. Ruff, M.E.; Lubbers, L.M. Treatment of subtrochanteric fractures with a sliding screw-plate device. J Trauma 26:75–80, 1986.

98. Rybicki, E.F.; Simonen, F.A.; Weis, E.B., Jr. On the mathematical analysis of stress in the human femur. J Biomech 5:203–215, 1972.

99. Rydell, N.W. Forces acting on the femoral head prosthesis: A study on strain gauge supplied prostheses in living persons. Acta Orthop Scand Suppl 88:1–132, 1972.

100. Sanders, R.; Regazzoni, P.; Routt, M.L., Jr. The treatment of subtrochanteric fractures of the femur using the dynamic condylar screw. Paper presented at American Academy of Orthopaedic Surgeons Annual Meeting, Atlanta, February 4–9, 1988.

101. Sarmiento, A. Functional bracing of tibial and femoral shaft fractures. Clin Orthop 82:2–13, 1972.

102. Schatzker, J. Subtrochanteric fractures of the femur. In: Schatzker, J.; Tile, M., eds. The Rationale of Operative Fracture Care. Berlin, Springer-Verlag, 1987.

103. Scherfel, T. A new type of intramedullary nail for the internal fixation of subtrochanteric fractures of the femur. Int Orthop 8:255–261, 1985.

104. Schipper, I.B.; Steyerberg, E.W.; Castelein, R.M.; et al. Reliability of the AO/ASIF classification for pertrochanteric femoral fractures. Acta Orthop Scand 72:36–41, 2000.

105. Schlemminger, R.; Kniess, T.; Schleef, J.; et al. Ergebnisse nach Winkelplattenosteosynthese der per und subtrochantaren Bruche beim alten Menschen. Akt Traumatol 22:149–156, 1992.

106. Seinsheimer, F. Concerning the proper length of femoral side plates. J Trauma 21:42–45, 1981.

107. Seinsheimer, F. Subtrochanteric fractures of the femur. J Bone Joint Surg Am 60:300–306, 1978.

108. Seligson, D. Concepts in Intramedullary Nailing. Orlando, FL, Grune & Stratton, 1985.

109. Shaw, J.A.; Wilson, S. Internal fixation of proximal femur fractures: A biomechanical comparison of the Gamma locking nail and the Omega compression hip screw. Orthop Rev 22:61–68, 1993.

110. Shelton, M.L. Subtrochanteric fractures of the femur. Arch Surg 110:41–48, 1975.

111. Shifflett, M.W.; Bray, T.J. Subtrochanteric femur fractures treated by Zickel and Grosse-Kempf nailing. Paper presented at the 54th Annual Meeting of the American Academy of Orthopaedic Surgeons, San Francisco, January 25, 1987.

112. Smith, J.T.; Goodman, S.B.; Tischenko, G. Treatment of comminuted femoral subtrochanteric fractures using the Russell-Taylor reconstruction intramedullary nail. Orthopedics 14:125–129, 1991.

113. Stewart, M.J. Discussion of paper, "Classification, treatment and complications of the adult subtrochanteric fracture." J Trauma 4:481, 1964.

114. Stover, M.D.; Lin, I.; Bosse, M.J. Removal of a broken Synthes proximal spiral blade. J Orthop Trauma 12:190–191, 1998.

115. Taylor, D.C.; Erpelding, J.M.; Whitman, C.S.; Kragh, J.F., Jr. Treatment of comminuted subtrochanteric femoral fractures in a young population with a reconstruction nail. Mil Med 161:735–738, 1996.

116. Taylor, J.C.; Russell, T.A.; LaVelle, D.G.; Calandruccio, R.A. Clinical results of 100 femoral shaft fractures treated with the Russell-Taylor interlocking nail system. Abstract. Orthop Trans 11:491, 1987.

117. Teitge, R.A. Subtrochanteric fracture of the femur. J Bone Joint Surg Am 58:282, 1976.

118. Templeton, T.; Saunders, E.A. A review of fractures in the proximal femur treated with the Zickel nail. Clin Orthop 141:213–216, 1979.

119. Tencer, A.F.; Calhoun, J.; Miller, B.B. Stiffness of subtrochanteric fracture of the femur stabilized using a Richards interlocking intramedullary rod or Richards AMBI. Orthop Biomech Lab Report #002. Memphis, Richards Medical Co., 1985.

120. Tencer, A.F.; Johnson, K.D.; Johnston, D.W.C.; Gill, K. A biomechanical comparison of various methods of stabilization of subtrochanteric fractures of the femur. J Orthop Res 2:297–305, 1984.

121. Thomas, W.G.; Villar, R.N. Subtrochanteric fractures: Zickel nail or nail plate? J Bone Joint Surg Br 68:255–259, 1986.

122. Toridis, T.G. Stress analysis of the femur. J Biomech 2:163–174, 1969.

123. Trafton, P.G. Subtrochanteric-intertrochanteric femoral fractures. Orthop Clin North Am 18:59–71, 1987.

124. Vanderschot, P.; Vanderspeeten, K.; Verheyen, L.; et al. A review on 161 subtrochanteric fractures—risk factors influencing outcome: Age, fracture pattern and fracture level. Unfallchirurg 98:265–271, 1995.

125. van Doorn, R.; Stapert, J.W. The long gamma nail in the treatment of 329 subtrochanteric fractures with major extension into the femoral shaft. Eur J Surg 166:240–246, 2000.

126. van Meeteren, M.C.; van Rief, Y.E.; Roukema, J.A.; et al. Condylar plate fixation of subtrochanteric femoral fractures. Injury 27:715–717, 1996.

127. Velasco, R.U.; Comfort, T. Analysis of treatment problems in subtrochanteric fractures of the femur. J Trauma 18:513–522, 1978.

128. Waddell, J.P. Sliding screw fixation for proximal femoral fractures. Orthop Clin North Am 11:607–622, 1980.

129. Waddell, J.P. Subtrochanteric fractures of the femur: A review of 130 patients. J Trauma 19:585–592, 1979.

130. Watson, H.K.; Campbell, R.D.; Wade, P.A. Classification, treatment and complications of the adult subtrochanteric fracture. J Trauma 4:457–480, 1964.

131. Whatley, J.R.; Garland, D.E.; Whitecloud, T.; Wickstrom, J. Subtrochanteric fractures of the femur: Treatment with ASIF blade plate fixation. South Med J 17:1372–1375, 1978.

132. Wheeler, D.L.; Croy, T.J.; Woll, T.S.; et al. Comparison of reconstruction nails for high subtrochanteric femur fracture fixation. Clin Orthop 338:231–239, 1997.

133. Wile, P.B.; Panjabi, M.M.; Southwick, W.O. Treatment of subtrochanteric fractures with a high-angle compression hip screw. Clin Orthop 175:72–78, 1983.

134. Wiss, D.A.; Brien, W.W. Subtrochanteric fractures of the femur: Results of treatment by interlocking nailing. Clin Orthop 283:231–236, 1992.

135. Wu, C.C.; Shih, C.H.; Lee, Z.L. Subtrochanteric fractures treated with interlocking nailing. J Trauma 31:326–333, 1991.

136. Yelton, C.; Low, W. Iatrogenic subtrochanteric fracture: A complication of Zickel nails. J Bone Joint Surg Am 68:1237–1240, 1986.

137. Yoshioka, Y.; Siu, D.; Cooke, D.V. The anatomy and functional axes of the femur. J Bone Joint Surg Am 69:873–880, 1987.

138. Zickel, R.E. A new fixation device for subtrochanteric fractures of the femur: Preliminary report. Clin Orthop 54:115–123, 1967.

139. Zickel, R.E. An intramedullary fixation device for the proximal part of the femur. J Bone Joint Surg Am 58:866–872, 1976.

CHAPTER 52

# Femoral Diaphyseal Fractures

Charles M. Court-Brown, M.D.

Management of femoral fractures has always interested orthopaedic surgeons. The size of the bone and the frequent association of femoral fractures with other injuries have often complicated treatment. Until relatively recently, management of femoral diaphyseal fractures was nonambulatory, which made it particularly difficult to treat any coexisting injuries. The evolution of internal fixation techniques has changed the treatment of femoral fractures, and in the last 30 years, considerable interest has been shown in the early operative management of femoral fractures, particularly in the context of a multiply injured patient. The management of femoral fractures and their treatment has, however, continued to change. Improvements in road safety legislation in many countries, coupled with an increase in the number of elderly individuals in the population, have changed the epidemiology of femoral fractures. In many countries, fewer young people are now sustaining high-velocity femoral fractures, and increasing numbers of elderly patients are being seen with low-velocity femoral fractures. The increasing number of periprosthetic fractures associated with hip arthroplasty has likewise contributed to this state of affairs.

Recent interest has also been shown in fixation methods for femoral fractures. Retrograde femoral nailing has become popular for certain fractures, particularly in the management of multiply injured patients. Suggestions that reamed intramedullary nailing may cause pulmonary complications in severely injured patients led surgeons to reexamine their treatment of multiply injured patients and to institute research into the association between adult respiratory distress syndrome (ARDS) and femoral reaming and nailing. In addition, awareness of complications such as compartment syndrome has increased, as well as interest in the potential osteogenic effect of intramedullary reaming. Femoral bone loss, nonunion, and malunion are now frequently treated by distraction osteogenesis, but the role of this technique and the indications for its use are still being debated.

## HISTORY

It is salutary to remember that early forms of the surgical techniques we now take for granted in the management of femoral diaphyseal fractures started to be used only about 100 years ago. Before that, all femoral fractures had to be treated by some form of bandaging, with the bandages being stiffened to support the fracture, or by traction, a method that is still in widespread use today. Hippocrates is credited with introducing the concept of managing fractures by bandages, although the ancient Chinese, Indian, and Egyptian civilizations were all familiar with the use of splints tied around the thigh to maintain femoral alignment until union occurred. All these cultures advocated that the knee be splinted in extension, but Albucasis, the great Arabic surgeon, suggested that patients with femoral diaphyseal fractures be managed with the knee flexed. He was also innovative in other ways and did not change the supportive dressings as frequently as had been advocated by Hippocrates a millennium earlier. Albucasis believed that the supportive dressings should remain undisturbed for a long period.

## Traction

Peltier,[193] in his iconography of fracture treatment, states that Malgaigne, the celebrated Parisian surgeon of the 19th century, credited Guy de Chauliac, who died in 1368, with the innovation of continuous isotonic traction. Variations of this technique have been in use for about 650 years and are still used in parts of the world today. The basic traction setup remains unchanged. The leg is placed on a splint with traction applied to the foot and countertraction achieved either by pressure of the splint in the groin or by placing the patient head-down and relying on gravity to maintain alignment. This type of traction is in widespread use today, with the Thomas splint frequently being used to support the leg and apply countertraction. The earliest type of traction was relatively straightforward. The traction was static in that a piece of cloth was tied around the ankle and foot, which was then pulled distally with the cloth being tied to the splint.[192] Unfortunately, the results of this type of management were poor. Hamilton, the foremost American expert in fracture management in the 19th century, published the results of treatment of femoral diaphyseal fractures with this type of rudimentary traction.[103, 192] He estimated that the results were perfect in only 9 of the 83 fractures that he assessed. The problems that he encountered were shortening and angular and rotational deformities.

The evolution of traction management continued, with surgeons developing balanced traction to which longitudinal traction could be applied. John T. Hodgen of St. Louis is credited with devising a splint that became popular in the United States and the United Kingdom.[192] It was used widely in the American Civil War and saw service in World War I. Although the introduction of skin traction with adhesive materials improved traction, the next major advance occurred when skin traction was connected to a weight hanging over the end of the bed. This technique was pioneered by Buck in the United States and became popular in both North America and Europe.[35] It was a relatively short step to using a single weight to support the leg, flex the knee, and apply longitudinal traction. This improvement was devised by Hamilton Russell,[207] and the technique remains in widespread use today, particularly if traction is required for a short period.

The evolution of traction into the technique that would be recognizable today was completed by the introduction of skeletal traction by Steinmann in 1907.[231] Balanced skeletal traction quickly became the method of choice for the management of femoral diaphyseal fractures. As understanding grew about the intricacies of management by traction, surgeons adopted different techniques of traction for different fractures. This specialized use of traction is well illustrated by the work of George Perkins,[194] who used three different traction systems, depending on whether the fracture was located proximally, in the midshaft, or in the supracondylar area of the femur. These systems are illustrated in Figure 52–1.

## Intramedullary Nailing

Treatment of diaphyseal femoral fractures with an intramedullary device started toward the end of the 19th century. Surgeons such as Bardenheuer[6] and Bircher[17] used ivory pegs for nonunion and displaced fresh fractures. These short pegs were inserted across the fracture in an open technique. Hey Groves in England was a keen proponent of intramedullary pegs and thought that the technique was straightforward, involved minimal periosteal damage, and allowed interfragmentary movement, which facilitated rapid union and rendered external splintage unnecessary. However, Hey Groves's major contribution was that he started to use both solid and fenestrated metal rods to stabilize femurs at the end of the First World War.[110] Intramedullary nailing with metal nails became standard treatment, and two schools of thought quickly

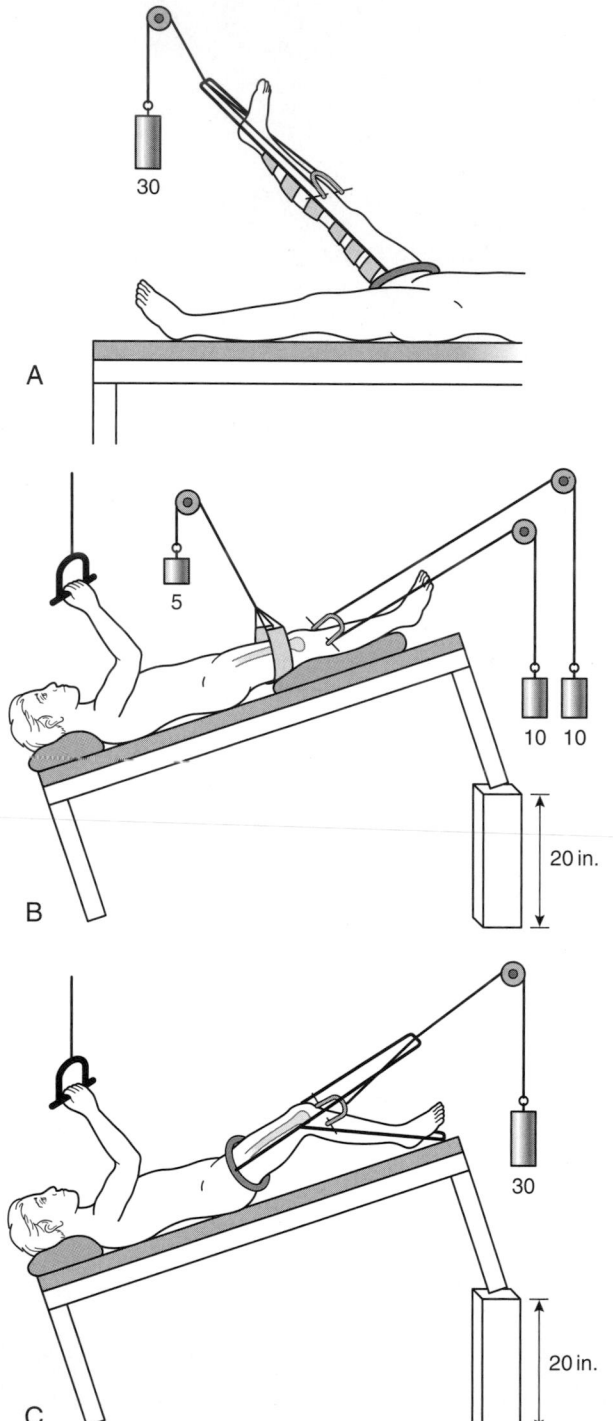

**FIGURE 52–1.** Basic traction systems for proximal *(A),* midshaft *(B),* and distal femoral *(C)* fractures. (Diagrams from Perkins, G. Fractures. London, Oxford University Press, 1940.)

developed. Gerhard Küntscher from Germany[142] used the same method as Hey Groves and continued to implant large-diameter metal nails. In the United States, the Rush brothers popularized the use of small-diameter unreamed metal nails. They published a manual of their techniques[206] and pioneered the use of closed nailing with the aid of fluoroscopy.

It was Küntscher, however, who was the main force behind intramedullary nailing, and his clinical research is responsible for the current popularity of intramedullary nailing throughout the world.[142] Küntscher not only developed the classic cloverleaf nail with his engineer Pohl (Fig. 52–2), but he also devised the first reconstruction nail in which a sidearm could be placed through the nail into the femoral neck. In addition, he used multiple small flexible intramedullary nails and developed the first intramedullary saw.

Initially, Küntscher was wary about reaming because he believed that it would damage the endosteal surface of the bone and might cause fat embolism. However, he was clearly a pragmatist and quickly realized the advantages of the technique. He subsequently produced the first set of intramedullary reamers. Küntscher's last invention was the detensornagel, a locked intramedullary nail. He designed this nail close to the end of his life, but the device made a considerable impression on Klaus Klemm, who together with Schellmann devised an interlocking nail.[135] At the same time, a similar nail was introduced by Ivan Kempf and Arsene Grosse in Strasbourg, France.[129] These nails were to revolutionize the management of both femoral and tibial diaphyseal fractures.

## Plating

Femoral plating was popularized by three orthopaedic surgeons. Albin Lambotte in Belgium, William Arbuthnott Lane in England, and William Shermann in the United States not only developed plating systems but also undertook clinical research to improve patient management.[193] Lane, in particular, was disenchanted with nonoperative management, and having undertaken a number of postmortem examinations that highlighted the problem of malunion after nonoperative management of femoral frac-

tures, he advocated the use of plates. However, the major advance in plate design followed the work of Robert Danis in Brussels, whose philosophy guided the AO group. He believed in early rigid fracture fixation to allow immediate active mobilization of the adjacent joints and muscles. Danis also believed in the restoration of normal osseous anatomy and in primary bone healing without callus formation. He invented a "coapteur," or compression plate, that achieved sufficient rigidity to fulfill his criteria for successful fracture management. Danis was clearly a visionary, but it might reasonably be suggested that his main contribution was to influence Maurice Müller, who together with Hans Willenegger, Robert Schneider, and Martin Allgöwer, formed the Arbeitgemeinschaft für Osteosynthesefragen (AO). This group has been responsible for all of the advances in plating.[173]

## External Skeletal Fixation

External fixation of the femur was initially popularized by Albin Lambotte in Belgium.[143] He devised a unilateral frame that was mechanically adequate and did not require supplementary cast fixation. The technique was not used widely during World War I but became popular again after the war, with a number of frames being fashioned to facilitate fracture management. Raoul Hoffmann in Geneva,[114] Switzerland, created the best-known external fixation device. He constructed a multiplanar frame that could be applied in a variety of configurations, depending on the morphology of the fracture and the surgeon's wish to have more or less rigid fixation. In the United States, external fixation was popular before World War II but fell out of favor after the war. After World War II, the Hoffman device remained in widespread

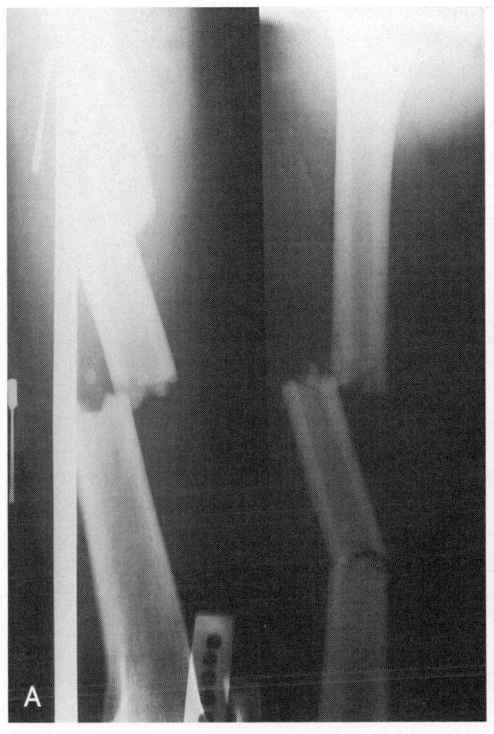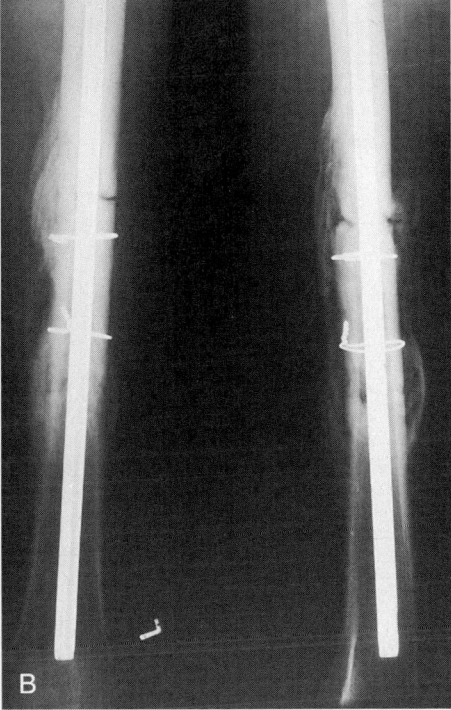

**FIGURE 52–2.** *A,* AO/OTA C2.1 femoral diaphyseal fracture. *B,* It has been treated by open Küntscher nailing with supplementary cerclage wiring. A good result was obtained.

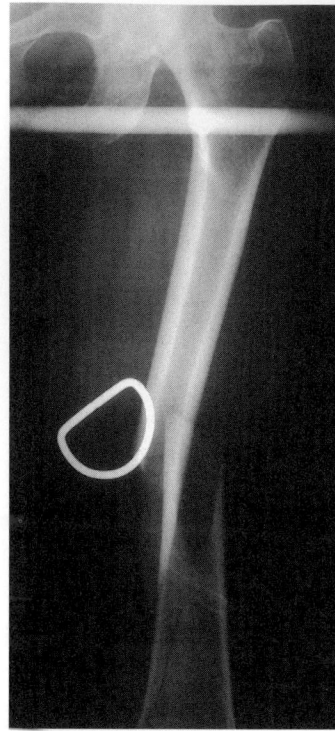 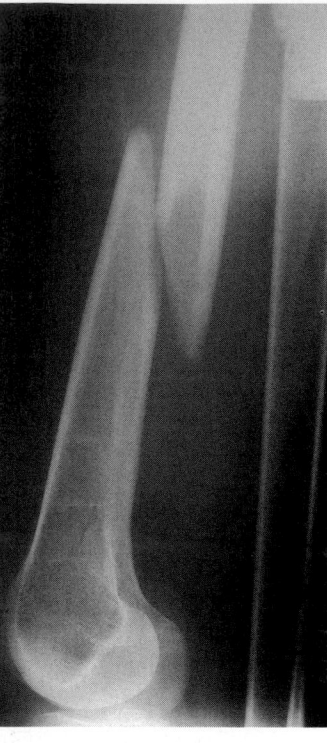

**Figure 52–3.** AO/OTA A1.2 femoral diaphyseal fracture in a 67-year-old woman. It was treated with a locked intramedullary nail (see Fig. 52–25).

use in Europe.[193, 259] External fixation became popular in the management of tibial fractures. Some proponents advocate its use for femoral diaphyseal fractures, but the indications for its application are few (see Figs. 52–10 and 52–17).

## CLASSIFICATION

Femoral fractures are commonly classified according to their morphology and degree of comminution and the extent and severity of any associated soft tissue injury. The best-known morphologic classification is the AO classification,[172] which was later adopted by the Orthopaedic Trauma Association (OTA). The degree of comminution is classified according to the Winquist-Hansen classification,[268] and soft tissue injury is best classified with the Gustilo classification.[98, 99]

The AO/OTA morphologic classification is based on the location and type of fracture. As with all AO classifications, femoral fractures are divided in 27 different subgroups with a number of added qualifications. The classification is based on the initial anteroposterior and lateral radiographs. Type A fractures (Fig. 52–3) are simple fractures and include spiral fractures (A1), oblique fractures (A2), and transverse fractures (A3). Type B fractures (Fig. 52–4) are wedge fractures and include spiral wedges (B1), bending wedges (B2), and fragmented wedges (B3). Type C fractures are complex fractures (Fig. 52–5), with the C1 group containing all complex spiral fractures. The C2 group contains segmental fractures, and the C3 group, comminuted fractures. In type A and B fractures, the suffix .1 represents a fracture in the subtrochanteric zone, with .2 being used for the middle zone and .3 for the

distal zone. In type C fractures, the suffixes .1 through .3 represent increasing bone damage. The full classification is explained in Table 52–1 and illustrated in Figure 52–6.

The Winquist-Hansen classification of comminution[268] is based on the degree of cortical continuity after fracture (Fig. 52–7). Type 1 fractures have only a small separate piece of bone. In type 2 fractures, the butterfly fragment is larger, but the cortex is at least 50% intact, thus permitting control of rotation and length. Type 3 fractures have a larger butterfly fragment precluding control of rotation and length, and type 4 fractures are characterized by severe comminution with no cortical abutment. The Gustilo classification of open fractures[98, 99] is shown in Table 52–2. The classification is based on the size of the skin wound, the degree of soft tissue contamination, and the amount of soft tissue damage. Type III injuries are classified into subtypes reflecting the amount of periosteal damage and the requirement for vascular surgery.

Surgeons should be aware that there is little evidence that the AO/OTA, Winquist-Hansen, and Gustilo classification systems are more than descriptive. The ideal classification would be prognostic as well as descriptive, but beyond a crude correlation between outcome and fracture type, modern classifications are not predictive of outcome. Indeed, the more complex the classification, the less predictive it is liable to be. Unfortunately, virtually no information can be found regarding the prognostic value of classification systems for femoral diaphyseal fractures. Most of the information about long bone classifications comes from studies of tibial diaphyseal fractures, but there is no logical reason why the results for the tibia and femur should be different. Gaston and colleagues[89] examined 100 tibial diaphyseal fractures with regard to all the currently available classifications. They were unable to show a significant correlation with outcome and concluded that an experienced orthopaedic surgeon could predict outcome as well as the modern classification systems. Swiontkowski and associates[234] examined the AO/OTA fracture classification and concluded that it does not predict 6- and 12-month functional outcome in patients with isolated unilateral lower extremity fractures. Classifications are essentially descriptive, but as such are important.

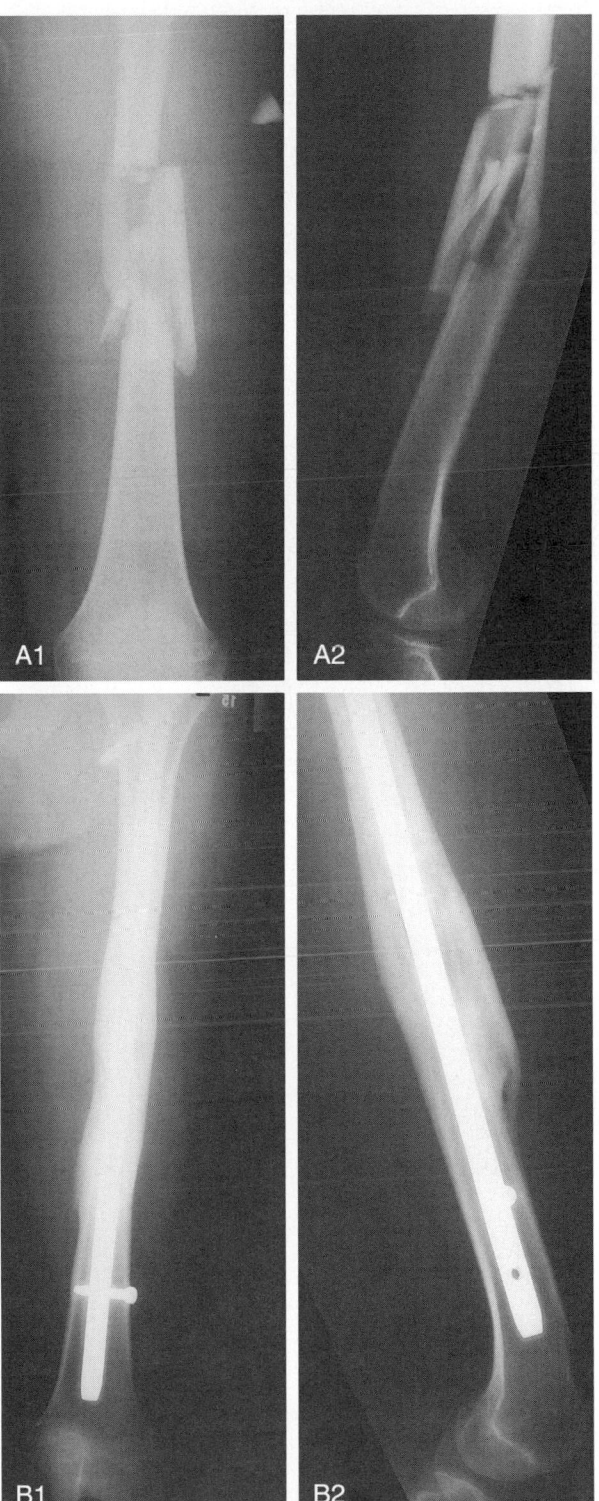

**FIGURE 52–5.** *A,* AO/OTA C3.3 fracture in a 15-year-old girl who had multiple injuries, including a severe head injury, an L1 flexion-distraction fracture, and a type C distal humeral fracture. *B,* The fracture was treated by locked intramedullary nailing, with good radiologic union and good function 6 months later.

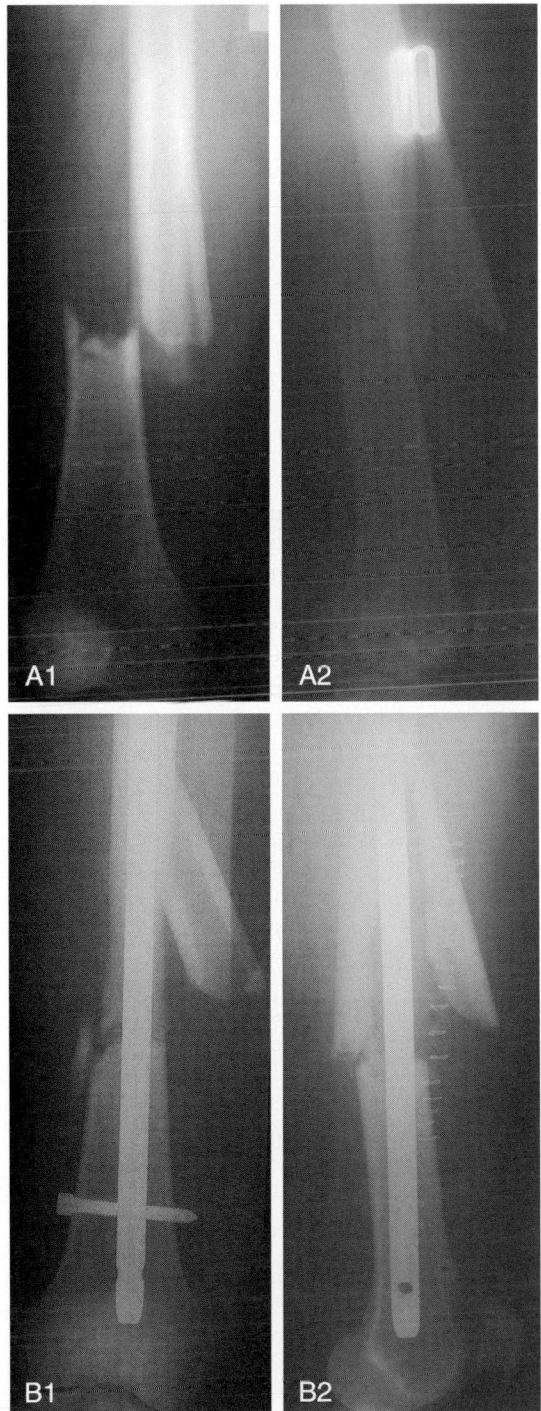

**FIGURE 52–4.** *A,* AO/OTA B2.2 femoral diaphyseal fracture. *B,* After treatment by locked intramedullary nailing, displacement of a large bone fragment is evident. See Figure 52–47 for continuation of the clinical history.

**TABLE 52–1**

AO/OTA Classification of Femoral Diaphyseal Fractures

**Type A—Simple Fractures**

Group A1: Spiral fractures
| | |
|---|---|
| A1.1 | Subtrochanteric zone |
| A1.2 | Middle zone |
| A1.3 | Distal zone |

Group A2: Oblique fractures
| | |
|---|---|
| A2.1 | Subtrochanteric zone |
| A2.2 | Middle zone |
| A2.3 | Distal zone |

Group A3: Transverse fractures
| | |
|---|---|
| A3.1 | Subtrochanteric zone |
| A3.2 | Middle zone |
| A3.3 | Distal zone |

**Type B—Wedge Fractures**

Group B1: Spiral wedge
| | |
|---|---|
| B1.1 | Subtrochanteric zone |
| B1.2 | Middle zone |
| B1.3 | Distal zone |

Group B2: Bending wedge
| | |
|---|---|
| B2.1 | Subtrochanteric zone |
| B2.2 | Middle zone |
| B2.3 | Distal zone |

Group B3: Fragmental wedge
| | |
|---|---|
| B3.1 | Subtrochanteric zone |
| B3.2 | Middle zone |
| B3.3 | Distal zone |

**Group C—Complex Fractures**

Group C1: Spiral fractures
| | |
|---|---|
| C1.1 | Two intermediate fragments |
| C1.2 | Three intermediate fragments |
| C1.3 | More than three intermediate fragments |

Group C2: Segmental fractures
| | |
|---|---|
| C2.1 | One intermediate segmental fragment |
| C2.2 | One intermediate segment and wedge fragment(s) |
| C2.3 | Two intermediate segmental fragments |

Group C3: Comminuted fractures
| | |
|---|---|
| C3.1 | Two or three intermediate fragments |
| C3.2 | Limited comminution (<5 cm) |
| C3.3 | Extreme comminution (>5 cm) |

# EPIDEMIOLOGY

*Charles M. Court-Brown, M.D.,*
*and C. M. Robinson, M.D., F.R.C.S.*

Given the importance of femoral diaphyseal fractures, it is perhaps surprising that little has been documented about their epidemiology. This lack of epidemiologic data is probably due to the fact that few hospitals admit all the patients who sustain femoral diaphyseal fractures in their area. Many younger patients, who are often involved in motor vehicle accidents, are taken to major trauma centers, whereas an elderly patient who sustains an osteopenic femoral diaphyseal fracture will usually be admitted to a peripheral or private institution, depending on the medical system of the country. Because very few large hospitals admit all femoral fractures from a particular community, data from the Royal Infirmary of Edinburgh, Scotland, have

been used to illustrate the epidemiology of femoral diaphyseal fractures. This institution admits all adult femoral diaphyseal fractures from a population of about 700,000, and its results reflect the overall epidemiology of femoral fractures in many parts of the world.

The data from Edinburgh were collected retrospectively from 1988 to 1994; all nonpathologic femoral fractures in the population are included, but periprosthetic fractures are excluded. During this period, 312 femoral fractures were observed, for an incidence of $7.1/10^5$/yr. In 295 patients, 190 (65%) patients were male, for an incidence of $9.5/10^5$/yr. The remaining 105 (35%) patients were female, an incidence of $4.8/10^5$/yr. The average age of the whole group was 38 years, with an average of 31 years for males and 49 years for females. Figure 52–8 shows that femoral fractures have the typical bimodal distribution associated with an average age in the fourth decade. The fracture is relatively common in young males between 15 and 19 years old, with an incidence of $26/10^5$/yr, and in elderly women between 85 and 89 years of age, in whom the incidence is $28/10^5$/yr. The highest incidence was actually seen in patients older than 90 years, although the proportion of such patients in the population is relatively small. It is interesting to note the particularly high incidence of femoral diaphyseal fractures in men older than 90 years, an observation illustrating the increasing importance of osteopenic fractures in this population.

An analysis of the morphology of femoral diaphyseal fractures is shown in Table 52–3. The fractures are broken down into their AO/OTA groups (see Fig. 52–6), with 51.8% of the fractures being AO/OTA type A (see Fig. 52–3), 26.4% being type B (Fig. 52–4), and 21.7% being type C (see Fig. 52–5). The average age of patients with type A fractures was 40 years, with 33 years of age being recorded for both type B and type C fractures. The most common fracture encountered in the 7-year study was an A3.2 transverse fracture in the middle third of the bone (see Fig. 52–34), which occurred in 24.3% of all the fractures. The next most common fracture was an A2.2 oblique fracture in the middle third of the bone (11.9%), followed by a B2.2 bending wedge fracture (see Fig. 52–4) in the middle third of the femur (11.4%), a B3.2 fragmented wedge fracture in the middle third (8.8%), and an A3.3 simple transverse fracture in the distal third of the femur (5.2%). A C3.1 complex fracture with two or three intermediate fragments occurred in 5.2% of cases, and C2.2 complex segmental fractures and C3.3 extensively comminuted fractures (see Fig. 52–5) were both seen in 4.7% of patients. Analysis of soft tissue damage showed that 249 (79.8%) of the fractures were closed. Ten (3.2%) of the fractures were Gustilo type I, 13 (4.2%) were type II, and 40 (12.8%) were type III fractures. Of the type III fractures, 17 (42.5%) were Gustilo type IIIa, 15 (37.5%) were type IIIb, and 8 (20%) were type IIIc fractures with significant vascular damage. Thus, 5.4% of the overall fracture group had Gustilo type IIIa fractures, 4.8% had type IIIb fractures, and 2.6% had type IIIc fractures.

## Causes of Femoral Fracture

The main causes of femoral diaphyseal fractures are simple falls, falls from heights, motor vehicle accidents, and

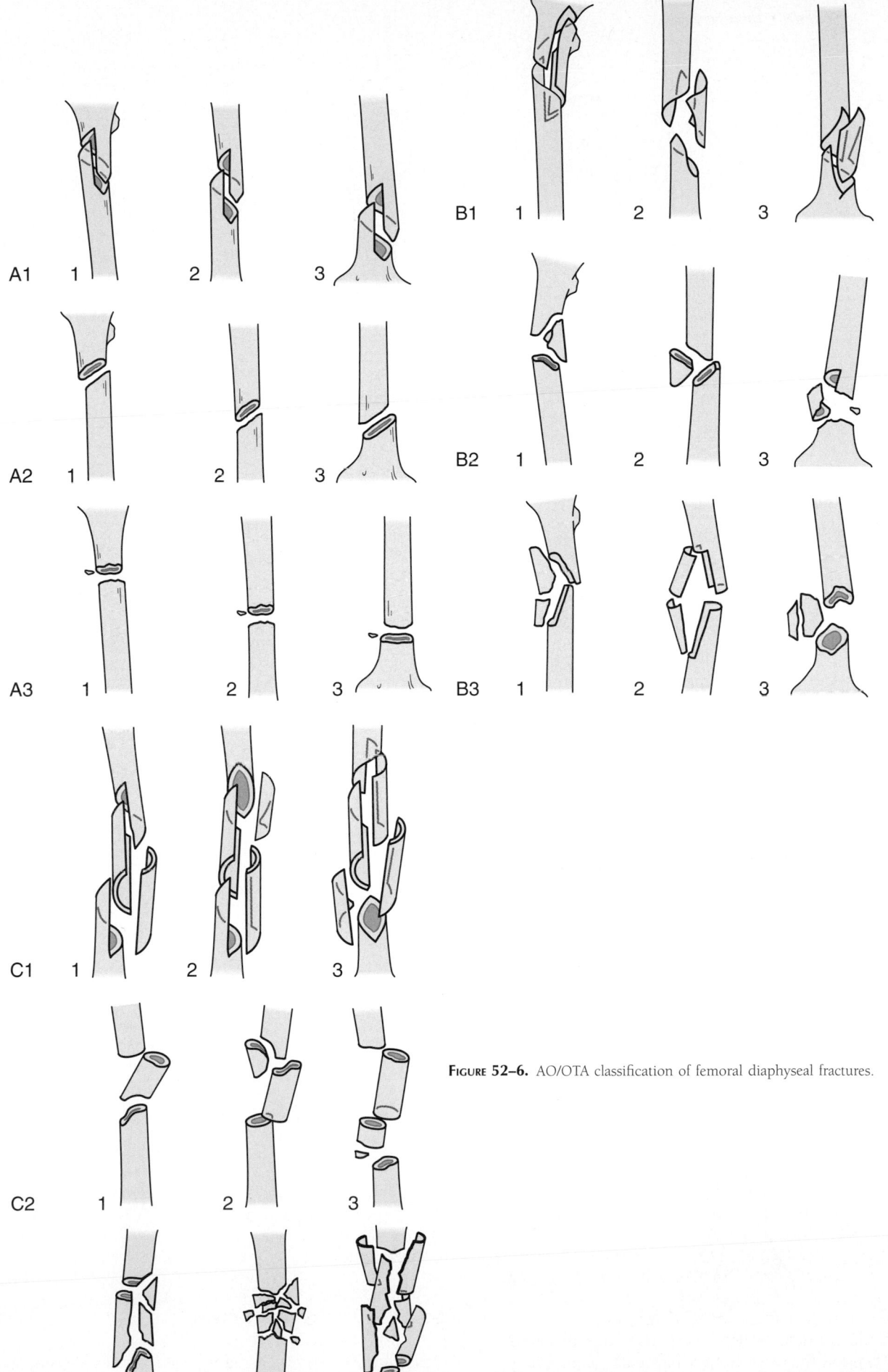

**FIGURE 52–6.** AO/OTA classification of femoral diaphyseal fractures.

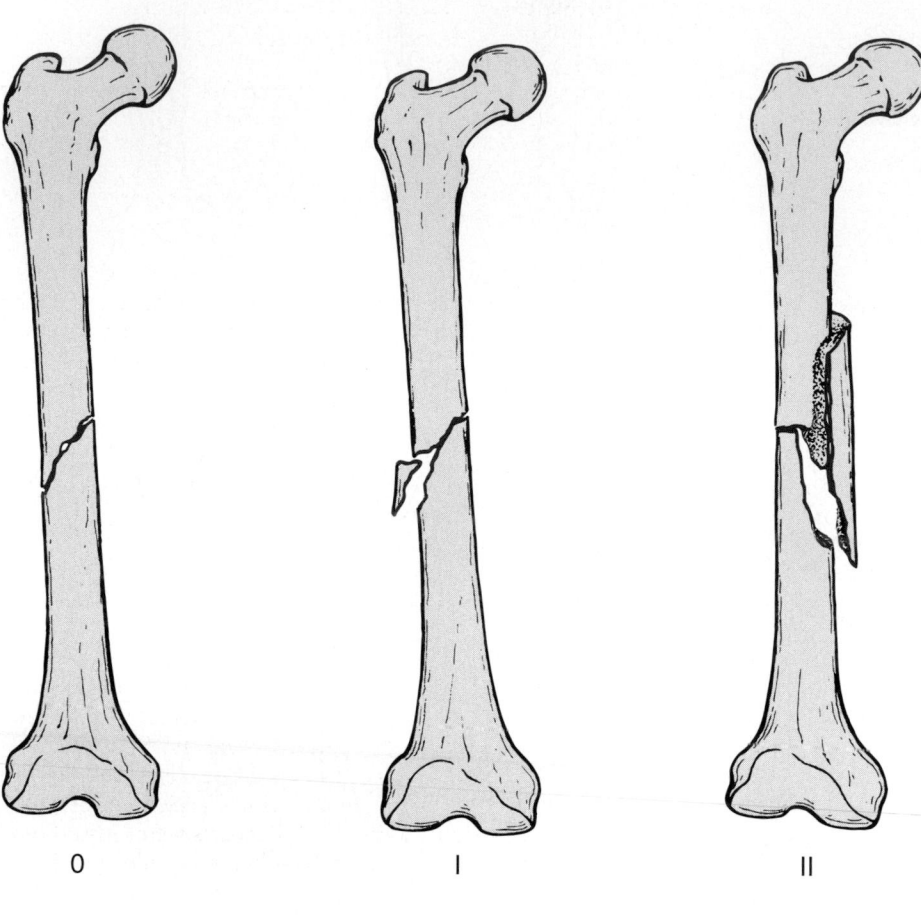

0       I       II

III      IV

**FIGURE 52–7.** Winquist-Hansen classification of diaphyseal comminution. See text for an explanation.

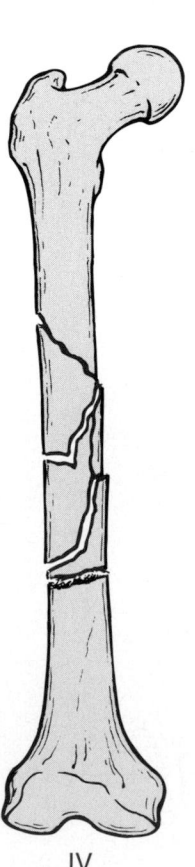

**TABLE 52–2** ...........................................................

Gustilo Classification of Open Femoral Fractures

| | |
|---|---|
| Type I | Clean wound less than 1 cm in length |
| Type II | Wound larger than 1 cm in length without extensive soft tissue damage |
| Type III | Wound associated with extensive soft tissue damage; usually longer than 5 cm |
| | Open segmental fracture |
| | Traumatic amputation |
| | Gunshot injuries |
| | Farmyard injuries |
| | Fractures associated with vascular repair |
| | Fractures more than 8 hours old |
| IIIa | Adequate periosteal cover |
| IIIb | Presence of significant periosteal stripping |
| IIIc | Vascular repair required to revascularize leg |

**TABLE 52–3** ...........................................................

Morphology of Femoral Diaphyseal Fractures (AO/OTA Classification)

| A1 | 8.8% | B1 | 3.1% | C1 | 0.5% |
|---|---|---|---|---|---|
| A2 | 13.5% | B2 | 13.5% | C2 | 8.8% |
| A3 | 29.5% | B3 | 9.8% | C3 | 12.4% |

Table 52–4. It can be seen that most femoral diaphyseal fractures are caused by motor vehicle accidents, with the average age of this group being 29 years. Open fractures tend to occur after motor vehicle accidents and falls from a height. Not unexpectedly, many type C fractures are caused by motor vehicle accidents. It is striking that the average age of individuals who fracture their femoral diaphysis after a simple fall is 80 years, with most of these patients having type A fractures.

## Open Fractures

Sixty-three (20.2%) of the fractures were open (Fig. 52–9). The average age of the open fracture group was 32 years, as compared with 39 years for patients with closed fractures. Thirty-seven percent were type C fractures versus 15% in the closed fracture group. All open fractures were caused by either motor vehicle accidents (89%) or falls from a height (11%). Most fractures were Gustilo type III in severity (63%), with 16% being Gustilo type I and 21% being type II fractures. Further analysis of the type III fractures showed that 42% were Gustilo type IIIa, 38% were type IIIb, and the remaining 20% were type IIIc fractures. Thirty percent of the fractures had an AO/OTA type A pattern, 33% were type B, and 37% showed a type C morphology.

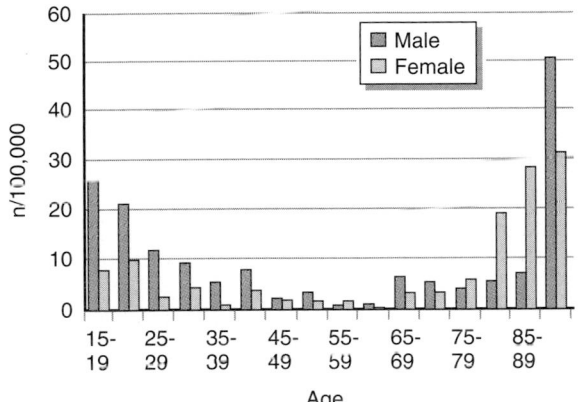

**FIGURE 52–8.** Age- and sex-adjusted incidence of femoral diaphyseal fractures. The figures are presented in 5-year bands.

## Association with Age

Table 52–5 illustrates the relationship of epidemiology to age. It shows that type A fractures tend to occur in the younger and older age groups, presumably because the former group has better bone quality and the latter group tends to be injured in simple falls. The elderly population usually sustains closed femoral fractures after a simple fall. Few are involved in motor vehicle accidents, and very few have severe open fractures. The average Injury Severity

gunshot injuries. Less frequent causes are sports injuries and direct assaults or blows. Occasionally, stress fractures occur (see Figs. 52–51 and 52–52), but they are less common and are discussed later in this chapter. No stress fractures were recorded in Edinburgh in the 7-year study period, although there can be little doubt that some of the fractures that occurred in the elderly, apparently as a result of simple falls, were insufficiency fractures. The Edinburgh data contain no gunshot injuries, but the distribution of other causes of femoral diaphyseal fractures is shown in

**TABLE 52–4** ...........................................................

Epidemiology of Femoral Diaphyseal Fractures of Different Causes

| | % | Average Age (yr) | Open Fracture (%) | AO/OTA Type A (%) | AO/OTA Type B (%) | AO/OTA Type C (%) |
|---|---|---|---|---|---|---|
| Fall | 15.1 | 80 | 0 | 79.3 | 17.2 | 3.4 |
| Fall from a height | 10.9 | 42 | 20.6 | 55.5 | 33.3 | 11.1 |
| Motor vehicle accident | 71.8 | 29 | 25.0 | 44.3 | 28.8 | 26.8 |
| Sports | 1.3 | 23 | 0 | — | — | — |
| Assault | 1.0 | 44 | 0 | — | — | — |

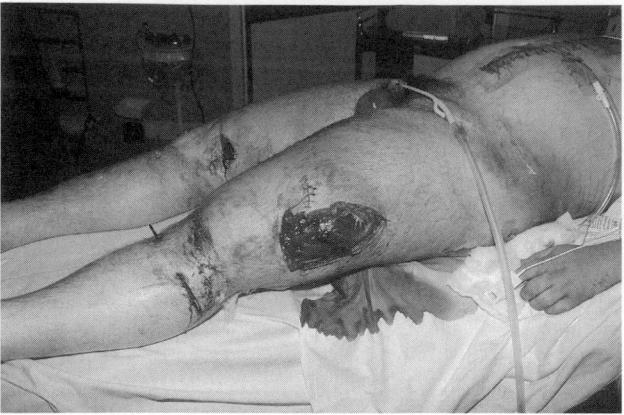

**Figure 52–9.** Gustilo type III open femoral fracture in a multiply injured patient.

Score (ISS) for this group was only 12, and only 12% had an ISS of 16 or more on initial examination. The most severely injured was the 25- to 69-year-old group, where a third of the patients were multiply injured and had an ISS of at least 16. This group had a higher incidence of type C comminuted or segmental fractures, and almost a fifth of the fractures were Gustilo type III in severity. It is interesting to note that whereas more of the group younger than 25 years sustained their femoral fracture in a motor vehicle accident, fewer of this age group had a type C fracture or a Gustilo type III open fracture. They tended to be less severely injured than the 25- to 69-year-old group. Further analysis of the data showed that 55% of the group younger than 25 years had other musculoskeletal injuries as compared with 59% of the 25- to 69-year-old group and 45% of the elderly group.

## Associated Injuries

One hundred ninety-two (61.5%) of the femoral diaphyseal fractures were isolated, with the remaining 120 (38.5%) having additional injuries. Seventy-nine (25.3%) fractures occurred in patients who had an ISS greater than 15. Of these patients, 59.5% had a coexisting head injury, 16.4% had a facial injury, 62% had a thoracic injury, 35.4% had an abdominal injury, and 93.7% had other musculoskeletal injuries.

Seventeen (5.4%) of the patients had bilateral open femoral fractures. The comparative epidemiology of the patients with bilateral and unilateral fractures is presented in Table 52–6. This group of patients was more severely injured and had an average ISS of 23. The bilateral fracture group was also younger, with an average age of 27 years. Fifty-four percent of the fractures had an AO/OTA type A morphology, with 22% being type B fractures and 25% being type C fractures. Thus, the fracture morphology of the bilateral and unilateral fractures was very similar. Forty-four percent of the bilateral fractures were open, with 71% of these open fractures being Gustilo type III in severity. These figures indicate that the soft tissue injury associated with bilateral fractures tends to be worse than that after unilateral fractures. Bilateral femoral fractures are discussed in greater detail later in the chapter.

Very little in the literature can be found on the incidence of femoral diaphyseal fractures, but it seems reasonable to suggest that the incidence must vary between countries and probably between different areas of the same country. Because most fractures are caused by road traffic accidents, with some caused by gunshot injuries, it is obvious that laws governing driving, especially those concerning alcohol intake, and laws governing gun ownership are going to influence the number of femoral fractures in the population. These laws may account for differences in the age- and sex-adjusted incidence of femoral fractures in different populations. Salminen and coauthors[212] from Finland have reported figures very similar to those obtained in Edinburgh. They recorded 9.9 femoral fractures per $10^5$ population per year, whereas Arneson and colleagues[3] found an incidence of 18.9 fractures per $10^5$ per year in Rochester, Minnesota. Their age-adjusted incidence in men was 26/$10^5$/yr versus 11.2/$10^5$/yr for females. The authors studied femoral fractures between 1965 and 1984, and it may be that the incidence of high-energy fractures in their area has declined since the mid-1980s, as it has in other areas. This possible decline in incidence is supported by the epidemiologic analysis of diaphyseal fractures in children living in Maryland between 1990 and 1996.[111] Because adolescents were included in this study, some comparisons can be

### Table 52–5

Age-Related Epidemiologic Differences in Femoral Diaphyseal Fractures

|  | <25 yr | 25–69 yr | ≥70 yr |
|---|---|---|---|
| Percentage | 42.3 | 42.6 | 16.0 |
| ISS >15 (%) | 27.3 | 33.3 | 12.0 |
| Average ISS | 15 | 18 | 12 |
| OTA type A (%) | 55.1 | 37.8 | 77.4 |
| OTA type B (%) | 30.3 | 25.6 | 19.3 |
| OTA type C (%) | 14.6 | 36.6 | 3.2 |
| Closed (%) | 81.8 | 73.6 | 90.0 |
| Gustilo III (%) | 10.6 | 18.6 | 4.0 |
| Simple fall (%) | 6.1 | 7.7 | 74.0 |
| MVA (%) | 90.9 | 75.2 | 14.0 |

*Abbreviations:* ISS, Injury Severity Score; MVA, motor vehicle accident.

### Table 52–6

Data Comparing Unilateral and Bilateral Femoral Fractures

|  | Unilateral | Bilateral |
|---|---|---|
| Age (yr) | 39 | 27 |
| Average ISS | 15 | 23 |
| OTA type A (%) | 51.1 | 54.2 |
| OTA type B (%) | 27.5 | 20.8 |
| OTA type C (%) | 21.3 | 25.0 |
| Closed (%) | 82.4 | 58.8 |
| Gustilo IIIa (%) | 4.0 | 17.6 |
| Gustilo IIIb (%) | 5.0 | 2.9 |
| Gustilo IIIc (%) | 1.8 | 8.8 |
| MVA (%) | 70.5 | 82.4 |

*Abbreviations:* ISS, Injury Severity Score; MVA, motor vehicle accident.

made with the Edinburgh data. Hinton and associates[111] found an annual femoral diaphyseal fracture rate of 21.7/10⁵/yr for patients between 14 and 17 years of age. This figure compares with 17.9/10⁵/yr for both males and females between 15 and 19 years of age in Edinburgh, Scotland, and 35.3/10⁵/yr in Minnesota.[3] This lower rate would seem to suggest that the incidence of femoral fractures is declining in some parts of the world. Hinton and co-workers[111] undertook an in-depth analysis of the sociodemographic risk factors associated with adolescent femoral fractures and showed a positive correlation between an increased incidence of femoral diaphyseal fractures and low household income.

The Finnish study[212] produced results remarkably similar to the Edinburgh figures. The highest age- and sex-specific incidence was seen in males 15 to 24 years old and in women older than 75 years. Their fracture morphology was almost identical, with 48% AO/OTA type A fractures, 39% type B fractures, and 13% type C fractures. They had relatively few open fractures (12.4%), 24% of which were Gustilo type III in severity. All these fractures were Gustilo type IIIa, and they encountered no type IIIb or type IIIc fractures in the 10-year period that they studied. Because Scandinavia tends to have much more stringent road traffic and drinking and driving laws, a correlation is suggested between legislation and the severity of femoral fractures. However, 65.2% of the Finnish femoral fractures were still caused by road traffic accidents. The authors also pointed out the importance of low-energy fractures in the elderly, with 24.9% of the fractures being caused by low-energy injuries.

Arneson and coauthors[3] also recorded a high incidence of femoral diaphyseal fractures in women older than 65 years, and it is indisputable that osteopenic femoral diaphyseal fractures are increasing in incidence. Bengnér and associates[12] compared the incidence of femoral fractures in Malmö, Sweden, in 1950 to 1957 with those seen in 1979 to 1983. A similar number of fractures per year were noted in the two time periods, but between 1979 and 1983, significantly more women older than 50 years sustained femoral fractures. This increase was balanced by a lower incidence of high-energy fractures in young males.

## Fractures after Falls

Because femoral fractures are becoming more common after simple falls, it is worthwhile to analyze their epidemiology and outcome. Many surgeons believe that these fractures are relatively straightforward to treat and that a good prognosis can be expected. However, the advanced age of patients who sustain low-energy femoral fractures after a fall means that they will frequently be medically unfit. Osteopenic bone is more difficult to treat, and elderly patients often have a higher incidence of infection. In the Edinburgh series, 47 patients sustained a femoral diaphyseal fracture after a simple fall. Table 52–4 shows that the average age was 80 years, and the average age was very similar for men (76 years) and women (81 years). The average ISS was 9, and 79.3% had AO/OTA type A fractures.

Salminen and colleagues[211] analyzed 50 patients who sustained acute femoral diaphyseal fractures after a low-energy injury, which was defined as a fall from ground level or from a height less than 1 m. They did not include periprosthetic fractures in their series. The average age was 65 years, with an average of 73 years for females and 52 years for males. The most common fracture type was an A1.2 fracture (26%), followed by A3.2 fractures (14%). Thirty-six (72%) of the fractures had no comminution or only Winquist-Hansen type I comminution. Four (8%) showed type II comminution, and 10 (20%) had type III comminution. It was possible to monitor 40 patients to union, and a high complication rate was documented. Postoperative mortality was 10%, and only 11 (27.5%) of the fractures united uneventfully. The infection rate was 10%, with a 14% incidence of nonunion. In addition, 26% of the patients had a malunion, although they generally exhibited only mild symptoms and no corrective surgery was required. However, it is clear from this study and from the observation of Patton and colleagues[191] that elderly patients have a high incidence of late proximal femoral fractures after reamed intramedullary nailing and that low-energy femoral fractures after falls are associated with high morbidity and mortality. As with other osteopenic fractures, surgeons must be aware of the problems inherent in operating on elderly patients if good results are to be obtained.

## Gunshot Fractures

In view of the apparent relative frequency of gunshot fractures of the femur (Fig. 52–10) in some countries, it is surprising that very little epidemiologic information is available. Clearly, the type and severity of femoral fractures will vary with the muscle velocity of the gun. Tornetta and Tiburzi[242] documented 38 patients, 34 (89.5%) of whom were male. The average age was 28 years, and 33 (86.8%) had Winquist-Hansen grade 3 or 4 comminution. Wiss and co-workers[271] examined 56 patients with an average age of 29 years. The distribution of comminution as measured by the Winquist-Hansen classification was virtually identical to that of Tornetta and Tiburzi.[242] Gunshot femoral fractures are discussed in depth later in the chapter.

## Sports Fractures

Table 52–4 shows that sports-related femoral diaphyseal fractures are extremely rare. However, certain sports do cause high-velocity injuries, and fractures associated with alpine skiing have been documented by Sterett and Krissoff.[232] It is interesting to note that in skiing, fractures have a sex-related variation with age. The authors recorded 19 fractures in skiers younger than 18 years, 2 (10.5%) of which were in girls. In the 27 diaphyseal fractures that occurred in skiers between 18 and 45 years of age, 11 (40.7%) were in women, and in the 5 fractures seen in skiers older than 45 years, 4 (80%) occurred in female skiers. A positive correlation was also found between increasing age and increasing comminution, with 26.3%

of the group younger than 18 years presenting with Winquist-Hansen type III or IV comminution. This figure compared with 55.5% in the group 18 to 45 years old and 80% in the group older than 45 years. The authors pointed out that skiing-related injuries in the group younger than 18 tended to occur while skiing fast. In the group 18 to 45 years old, the fractures occurred in advanced skiers skiing on difficult terrain in firm snow conditions. Fractures were often sustained after a collision with a tree or a rock. In the group older than 45 years, most fractures occurred in icy or firm machine-groomed conditions.

## Motor Vehicle Accidents

Very little information is available about the epidemiology of femoral diaphyseal fractures that occur in motor vehicle accidents despite the fact that it is generally agreed that

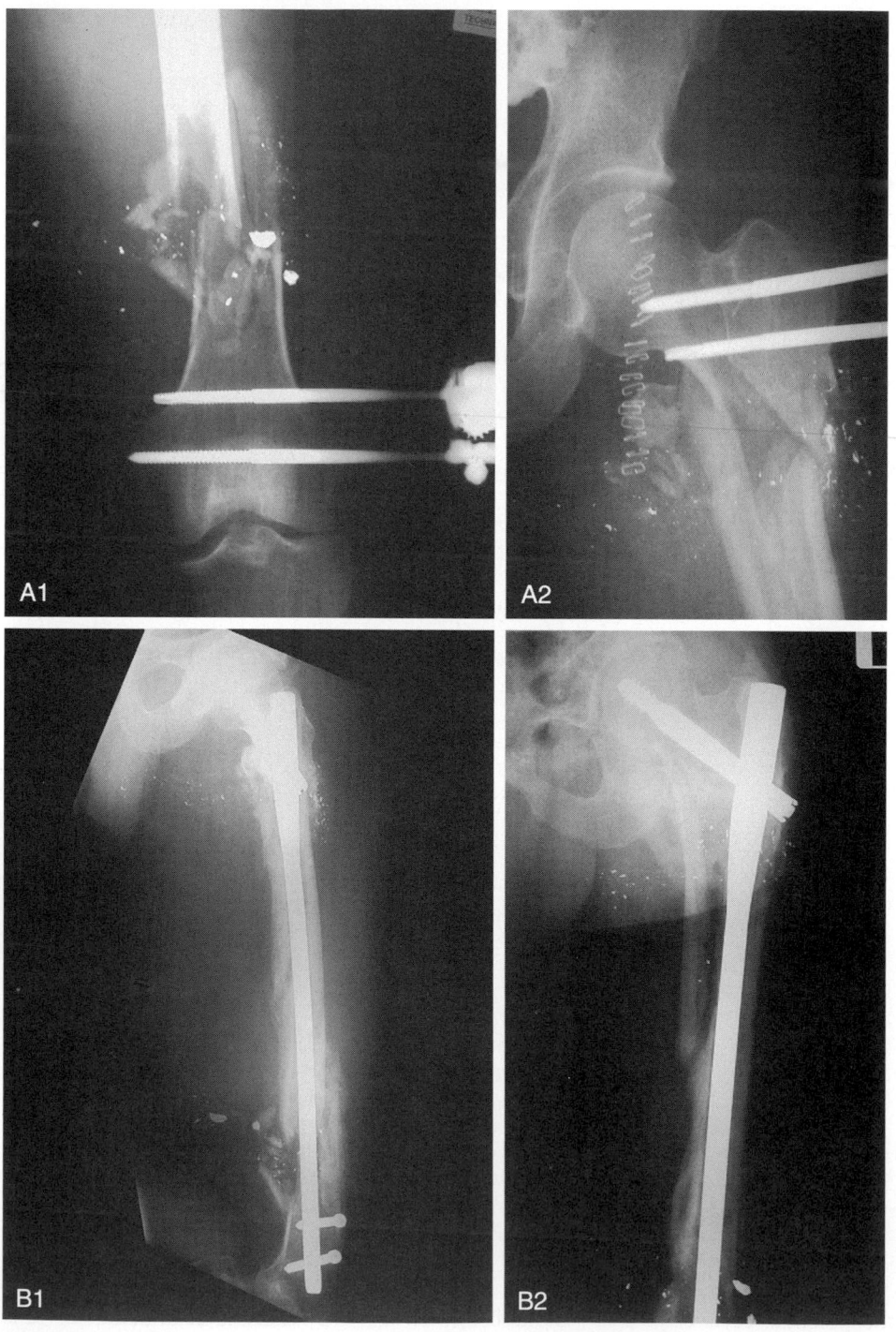

**Figure 52–10.** *A,* Anteroposterior radiographs of an AO/OTA type C gunshot femoral fracture. The vascularity of the limb was of concern, so a temporary external fixator was used. *B,* Secondary intramedullary nailing was performed with a cephalomedullary reconstruction nail. A good result was obtained. (Courtesy of P. Tornetta, M.D.)

| TABLE 52–7 | | | | | |
|---|---|---|---|---|---|

**Epidemiologic Differences in Patients Involved in Motor Vehicle Accidents**

| | Age (yr) | ISS | Gustilo III (%) | Gustillo IIIb* (%) | AO/OTA Type C (%) |
|---|---|---|---|---|---|
| Passenger | 35 | 31 | 71.4 | 80 | 42.8 |
| Driver | 33 | 30 | 24.6 | 66.6 | 54.5 |
| Pedestrian | 40 | 34 | 46.1 | 50 | 18.1 |
| Motorcyclist | 23 | 22 | 92.8 | 76.9 | 41.6 |

*Gustilo IIIb fractures are expressed as a percentage of Gustilo grade III fractures.
*Abbreviation:* ISS, Injury Severity Score.

they cause most femoral fractures. The Edinburgh data indicate that most femoral fractures caused by motor vehicle accidents occur in younger patients, with 77.2% being younger than 35 years. Only 6.7% of patients were older than 50 years. Twenty-five percent of the fractures were open, and 26.8% were AO/OTA type C. Clearly, patients involved in motor vehicle accidents are usually vehicle drivers or passengers, motorcyclists, or pedestrians. Little is known about the differences between the four groups. However, Court-Brown and co-workers[63] examined the epidemiology of open long bone fractures, and by extrapolating their data, it is possible to analyze the open femoral fractures sustained in these four groups of motor vehicle accident victims. Differences between the four groups are shown in Table 52–7. Motorcyclists tend to be the least seriously injured and have the lowest ISS, but they tend to have the most severely injured femurs, with over 90% sustaining a Gustilo type III open fracture. Vehicle drivers had a lower incidence of Gustilo type III fractures, but 66% of the type III fractures were type IIIb in severity.

## CLINICAL FEATURES OF FEMORAL FRACTURES

### Signs and Symptoms

Fractures of the femoral diaphysis are rarely missed, particularly in a conscious patient. Pain and deformity are usually obvious, and the surgeon will note soft tissue swelling at a very early stage. In an unconscious patient, femoral fractures will also be accompanied by local deformity and swelling. These findings are usually obvious, but the possibility of femoral diaphyseal fracture must be considered in all unconscious patients, particularly if they have been involved in a motor vehicle accident or a fall from a height. Femurs should be carefully examined in a routine systematic examination that must be used for all unconscious patients.

It is important to take a complete history from the patient if conscious or from a companion if the patient is unconscious, uncooperative, or unable to communicate. The main purpose of the history in a young patient is to determine the cause of injury and thereby whether any associated injuries may be present. The cause of injury will also provide information about the potential severity of any soft tissue injury associated with the fracture. In older patients, the history is even more important. Figure 52–8 shows that patients with femoral diaphyseal fractures may be very old and therefore have a number of co-morbid conditions that may have resulted in the fracture in the first place. Their overall health, function, and degree of independence may affect their management and determine whether the patient can return home or will require a period of rehabilitation or convalescence. Sartoretti and colleagues[214] retrospectively analyzed a group of 102 patients with femoral fractures who had an average age of 81 years. They also analyzed an age-matched control group consisting of patients with proximal humeral fractures. These authors showed that elderly patients with femoral diaphyseal fractures had a significantly higher rate of co-morbidity. Eighty percent of the femoral fracture group had cardiovascular disease, 41% had pulmonary disease, 67% had gastrointestinal disease, and 81% had coexisting neurologic diseases. In addition, 55% had neurologic symptoms, 75% had other musculoskeletal complaints, and 61% had psychiatric disorders. Analysis of their drug regimens showed that 90% were taking various medications. This work illustrates the importance of an adequate history in older patients with femoral fractures.

It is vital to undertake a complete physical examination according to advanced trauma life support (ATLS) guidelines. The Edinburgh data detailed in the Epidemiology section of this chapter indicate that 25.3% of patients have an ISS of at least 16. Multiple injuries are common in younger patients, but even in patients older than 70 years treated by the Edinburgh Trauma Unit, 12% had an ISS of more than 15. In the large trauma centers of the United States, Germany, and other countries, the incidence of multiple injuries in patients who have femoral fractures is higher.[21, 105, 123, 130, 187] Thus, it can be seen that a thorough systematic physical examination of all patients with femoral fractures is essential.

The fractured limb should also be assessed very carefully. The skin should be examined to look for open wounds and to check for the state of the soft tissues. Any open wound should be carefully documented. It is usually fairly obvious if a femoral fracture is open, but such may not always be the case, and any skin abrasions and apparently minor wounds should be examined to try to establish whether they communicate with the fracture. When possible, photographs of the open wound should be taken to minimize the need for later surgeons to inspect the wound before formal débridement is undertaken. It is important to try to establish whether the injury had a crushing component. Motor vehicle accidents can cause the front compartment of the vehicle to collapse and the engine to be propelled backward to crush the lower limbs. Prolonged crushing may cause myonecrosis and necessitate muscle resection or amputation. The myoglobinuria associated with myonecrosis may also cause renal failure. In addition, muscle crushing may occur in drug addicts, alcoholics, and elderly individuals when they lie on the floor or the ground for a prolonged period after a fracture.[224] Extensive bleeding into the muscles may also occur and may be exacerbated by anticoagulant medication. Thigh compartment syndrome is rare[159, 218, 235] but can certainly occur. If multiple injuries are present or the patient has bled significantly into the soft tissues around the femur, transfusion may well be required, and again, ATLS guidelines should be followed regarding resuscitation and the establishment of adequate venous access.

A thorough examination of the neurovascular status of the affected limb must be undertaken. Femoral nerve damage is very unusual after a femoral diaphyseal fracture, but sciatic nerve damage can occur,[29, 48, 269] although its incidence is low. If sciatic nerve damage is suspected, the surgeon should always examine the hip joint in case a posterior fracture-dislocation has been sustained. The neurologic status of the limb should be recorded before operative treatment is initiated, while bearing in mind that it is of course possible that other nerves may be damaged by other musculoskeletal injuries in the same limb. The vascular status of the limb must also be noted. Vascular injury may be assessed by palpation of distal pulses and examination of capillary return in the limb. However, if the patient is hypovolemic, it may well be difficult to accurately assess the vascular status of the limb. Clearly, the presence of an open wound, particularly if it has been caused by a gunshot injury, may well indicate a penetrating injury to the femoral artery, so the surgeon should look for an expanding hematoma or bleeding. However, blunt injuries can also cause vascular damage, which may be more difficult to assess. Normal pulses do not exclude vascular injury, and Kluger and associates[138] documented normal pulses in 5 of 31 (16.1%) patients who had major vascular damage associated with a mid-diaphyseal femoral fracture. They found that in four of the patients, the pulses eventually disappeared, thus emphasizing the need for repeated clinical examinations. Other indications of a possible vascular injury associated with blunt trauma are deformity, a large hematoma, altered limb color or temperature, or reduced sensation. However, none of these signs is diagnostic of a vascular injury. Doppler pulse pressures and possibly arteriography should be undertaken in patients with any suggestion of vascular damage (Fig. 52–11).

## Associated Injuries

The surgeon should be aware that a number of other musculoskeletal injuries may be associated with femoral fractures. Clearly, any other bone or joint may be involved, but the surgeon should carefully examine the rest of the affected leg and specifically look for hip and knee damage.

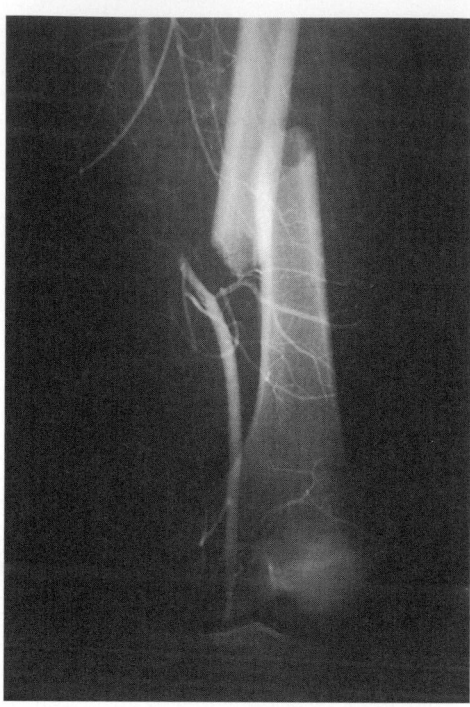

**FIGURE 52–11.** An arteriogram performed after a road traffic accident illustrates arterial damage and shows that this fracture is a Gustilo type IIIc.

The most common associated injury around the hip is a femoral neck fracture (see Fig. 52–38). These injuries have been stated to occur in 2.3% of femoral diaphyseal fractures.[233] Wu and coauthors[275] described 16 cases of femoral diaphyseal fracture complicated by hip dislocation and stated that the incidence was 1.1%. Acetabular and pelvic ring fractures likewise occur in association with femoral diaphyseal fractures,[171] and the pelvis should also be carefully examined clinically and radiologically to check for any coexisting pelvic or acetabular fracture. Mosheiff and associates[170] described an injury triad consisting of a femoral diaphyseal fracture, ipsilateral hip joint injury, and disruption of the knee extensor mechanism that occurred as a result of a dashboard injury in motor vehicle accidents.

Distal femoral fractures may also be seen in association with a diaphyseal fracture. Butler and colleagues[38] described 23 patients who had a combination of a diaphyseal fracture with either a supracondylar or an intercondylar femoral fracture. They analyzed 684 fractures and found an incidence of 3.4%. The association of knee ligament injuries with femoral fractures is well known, and the incidence has been stated to be between 17% and 48%.[254] Vangsness and co-workers[254] examined 47 patients with closed femoral diaphyseal fractures after femoral nailing to determine the incidence of meniscal lesions. They found 12 medial meniscal injuries and 13 lateral injuries. Of the 25 injuries, 13 were meniscal tears and 10 were in the posterior third of the meniscus. In a later study,[66] the same group showed that 55% of the patients who sustained femoral fractures in high-energy trauma had significant arthroscopic findings. Surgeons should also be aware of the association of femoral and tibial diaphyseal fractures, the "floating knee" (see Fig. 52–38). This association has been described by a number of surgeons.[68, 83, 182, 257] These patients tend to be very seriously injured and may well have other ipsilateral lower limb injuries. Veith and associates[257] documented that 29.8% of patients with a "floating knee" had other significant musculoskeletal injuries in the same limb.

## Radiographic Studies

Anteroposterior and lateral radiographs should be all that is required to diagnose a femoral diaphyseal fracture. It is important to radiograph the whole femur, and it is mandatory that the hip and knee be included in the radiographic series because of the possibility or injuries in or adjacent to the proximal and distal ends of the femur. Standardization of radiographs in the acute situation is virtually impossible, but inadequate radiography should not be accepted. Computed axial tomographic (CAT) scans or magnetic resonance imaging (MRI) is not necessary to diagnose a femoral diaphyseal fracture, although technetium-labeled bone scans or MRI may be useful to diagnose the infrequent femoral diaphyseal stress or insufficiency fractures. Further imaging may be helpful for diagnosing injuries associated with femoral diaphyseal fractures. An example is shown in Figure 52–38, in which a CAT scan was used to confirm the presence of a femoral neck fracture.

The surgeon should look for a number of features on the anteroposterior and lateral radiographs:

1. The location and morphology of the fracture.
2. The presence of secondary fracture lines that might become displaced during operative treatment.
3. The presence of comminution or an intact femoral segment suggestive of a high-energy injury.
4. The distance that bone fragments have traveled from their normal location. Widely displaced fragments suggest that the soft tissue attachments have been damaged and the fragments are probably avascular.
5. Bone defects suggesting missing bone.
6. Proximal or distal fractures or fracture-dislocations involving the hip or knee joints.
7. The state of the bone. Does the patient have evidence of osteopenia, metastases, metabolic bone disease, or a previous fracture?
8. Osteoarthritis or the presence of a hip and knee prosthesis. These conditions may change the treatment method selected by the surgeon.
9. Gas in the tissues. This finding points to the fact that the fracture is open, but it may also signify the presence of gas gangrene, necrotizing fasciitis, or other anaerobic infections.

## Surgical Anatomy

The femur is the largest and strongest bone in the human body. The proximal end of the femur consists of the head of the femur, the neck of the femur, and the greater and lesser trochanters. The distal part of the femur consists of the lateral medial condyle separated by the intercondylar notch. Proximally, the two condyles join to form the supracondylar portion of the femur.

The femoral shaft or diaphysis is cylindrical proximally but compressed in the anteroposterior plane distally. It has a gradual but definite anteroposterior bow. The rounded lateral border may be traced from the greater trochanter to the lateral side of the articular surface of the patella. The medial border extends from beneath the lesser tuberosity near the midpoint of the spiral line to the medial condyle. The posterior border, or the linea aspera, is found in the middle third of the bone, where it acts as a buttress to strengthen the concavity of the diaphysis. Proximally, the linea aspera divides into two ridges. The lateral ridge extends to the base of the greater trochanter, and the medial ridge winds around the proximal diaphysis as the spiral line. Distally, the linea aspera divides into the lateral and medial supracondylar lines. The muscle attachments to the femur are shown in Figure 52–12. This figure illustrates that the hip abductors are attached proximally to the greater trochanter and that the principal hip flexor iliopsoas is attached to the lesser trochanter and to the bone below it. The abductors are mainly attached to the posterior surface of the femur throughout the length of the femoral diaphysis. The vastus intermedius arises from much of the anterior and lateral borders of the femur, but the bulk of the vastus intermedius is covered by the vastus lateralis, which arises from the lateral and posterior aspects of the bone (Fig. 52–13). The vastus medialis arises from the medial and posterior aspects of the femur.

The position of the muscles around the femur is important to the orthopaedic trauma surgeon for two reasons. First, the surgeon must understand the position of the muscles to facilitate surgery, and second, the relative forces imparted by the different muscles in the thigh will cause deformity of the femur after fracture. Clearly, the muscle pull is balanced if the femur is intact, but after fracture, the differential pull of the muscles can cause malalignment. The classic deformities are illustrated in Figure 52–14. In proximal diaphyseal fractures, the unbalanced pull of the gluteal muscles and iliopsoas will tend to flex the proximal fragment, which can give rise to difficulty when nailing proximal fractures. Figure 52–14 also demonstrates the characteristic deformities associated with mid-diaphyseal and distal fractures. In distal fractures, the unopposed action of the gastrocnemius can cause the distal fragment to flex.

The major arteries in the thigh are shown in Figure 52–15. The femoral artery enters the thigh within the femoral triangle. It gives off the profunda femoris branch, which leaves the femoral triangle behind the adductor longus close to the femur. The lateral and medial circumflex branches arise from the profunda femoris near its origin. The lateral circumflex leaves the femoral triangle behind the sartorius and the medial circumflex artery and passes through the floor of the femoral triangle between the psoas and pectineus. The profunda femoris artery continues distally and gives off three perforating arteries close to the femur. It ends as the fourth perforating artery. These arteries are at risk during femoral plating, or they may occasionally be damaged by external fixation pins.

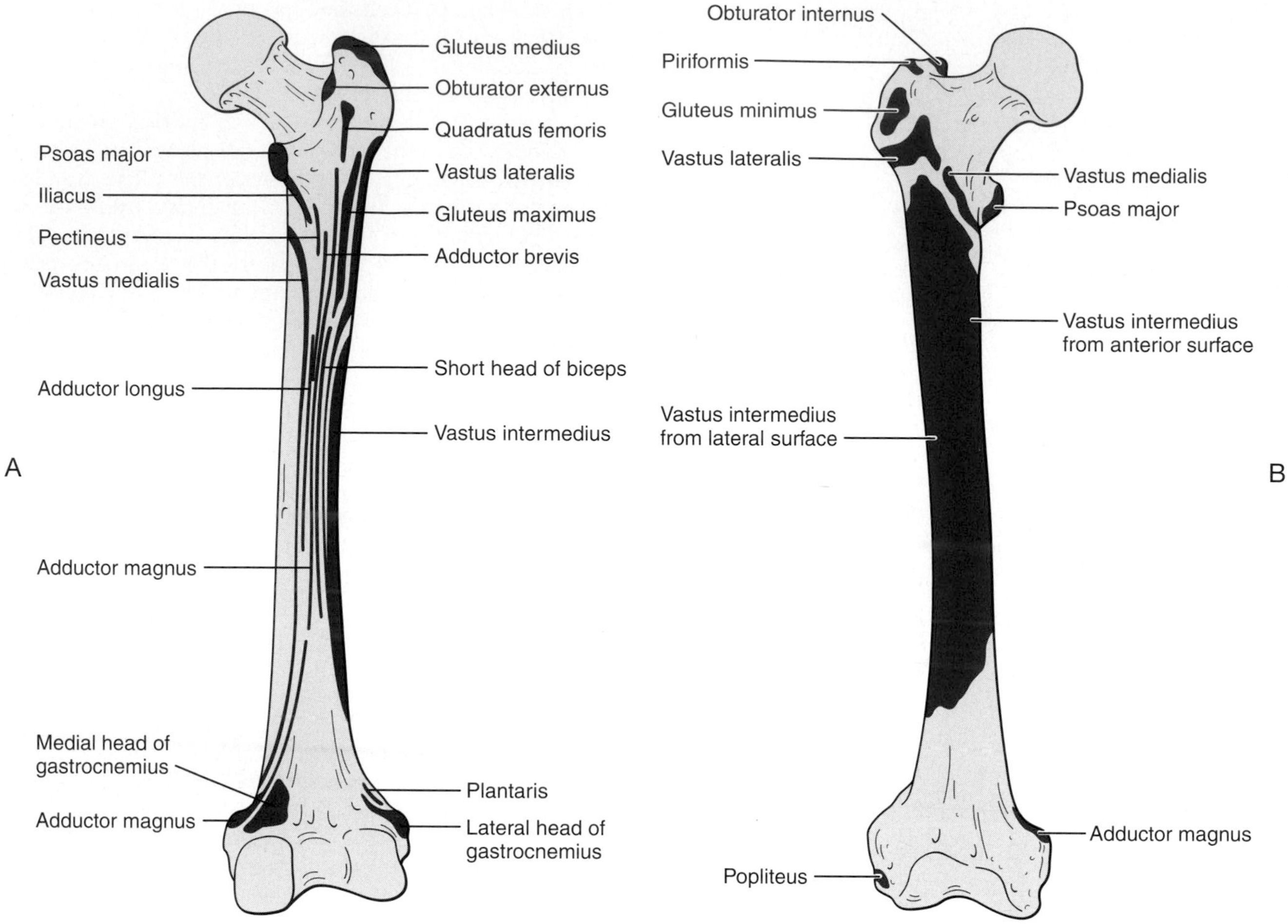

Gluteus medius
Obturator externus
Quadratus femoris
Vastus lateralis
Gluteus maximus
Adductor brevis

Psoas major
Iliacus
Pectineus
Vastus medialis

Adductor longus

Short head of biceps

Vastus intermedius

A

Adductor magnus

Medial head of
gastrocnemius

Adductor magnus

Plantaris

Lateral head of
gastrocnemius

Obturator internus
Piriformis
Gluteus minimus
Vastus lateralis

Vastus medialis
Psoas major

Vastus intermedius
from anterior surface

Vastus intermedius
from lateral surface

B

Adductor magnus

Popliteus

**FIGURE 52–12.** *A,* Muscle attachments to the anterior aspect of the femur. *B,* Muscle attachments to the posterior aspect of the femur.

The femoral artery continues as the superficial femoral artery after giving off the profunda femoris. After it leaves the femoral triangle, it enters the adductor canal and lies against the posteromedial aspect of the femur. It then passes through the hiatus in the adductor magnus and enters the posterior compartment of the thigh, where it runs into the popliteal fossa. The superficial femoral artery should not be at risk from any of the operations used to treat femoral fractures. The obturator artery enters the thigh through the obturator foramen, but it soon divides into its two terminal branches and is of no importance in the treatment of femoral diaphyseal fractures.

The sciatic and femoral nerves are the two major nerves of the thigh. The femoral nerve enters the thigh under the inguinal ligament and lateral to the femoral artery. It ends about 2 cm below the inguinal ligament, where it divides into a number of muscular and cutaneous nerves. The sciatic nerve enters the thigh through the greater sciatic foramen and descends into the thigh under the long head of the biceps femoris on the posterior surface of the adductor magnus. It ends at a variable point above the popliteal fossa by dividing into the common peroneal and tibial nerves.

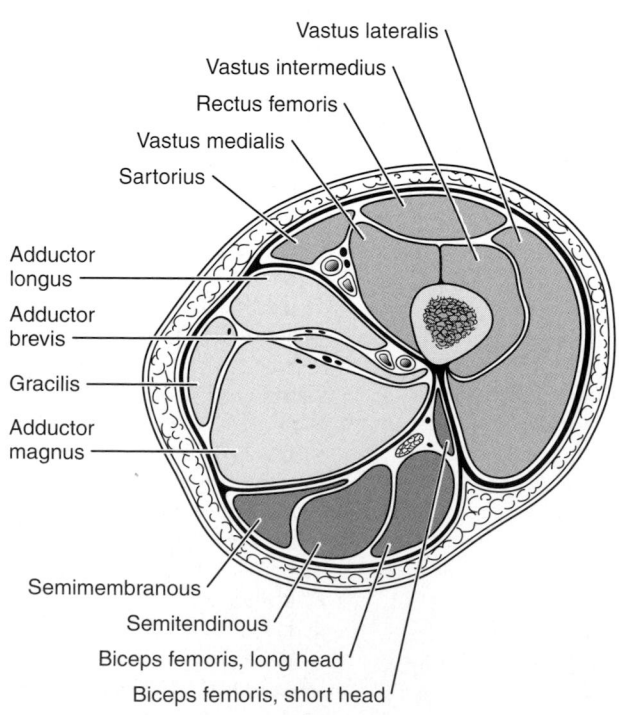

Vastus lateralis
Vastus intermedius
Rectus femoris
Vastus medialis
Sartorius

Adductor
longus

Adductor
brevis

Gracilis

Adductor
magnus

Semimembranous
Semitendinous
Biceps femoris, long head
Biceps femoris, short head

**FIGURE 52–13.** Cross section of the middle third of the thigh showing the relative positions of the neurovascular structures, bones, and muscles. Different shading indicates the different compartments in the thigh.

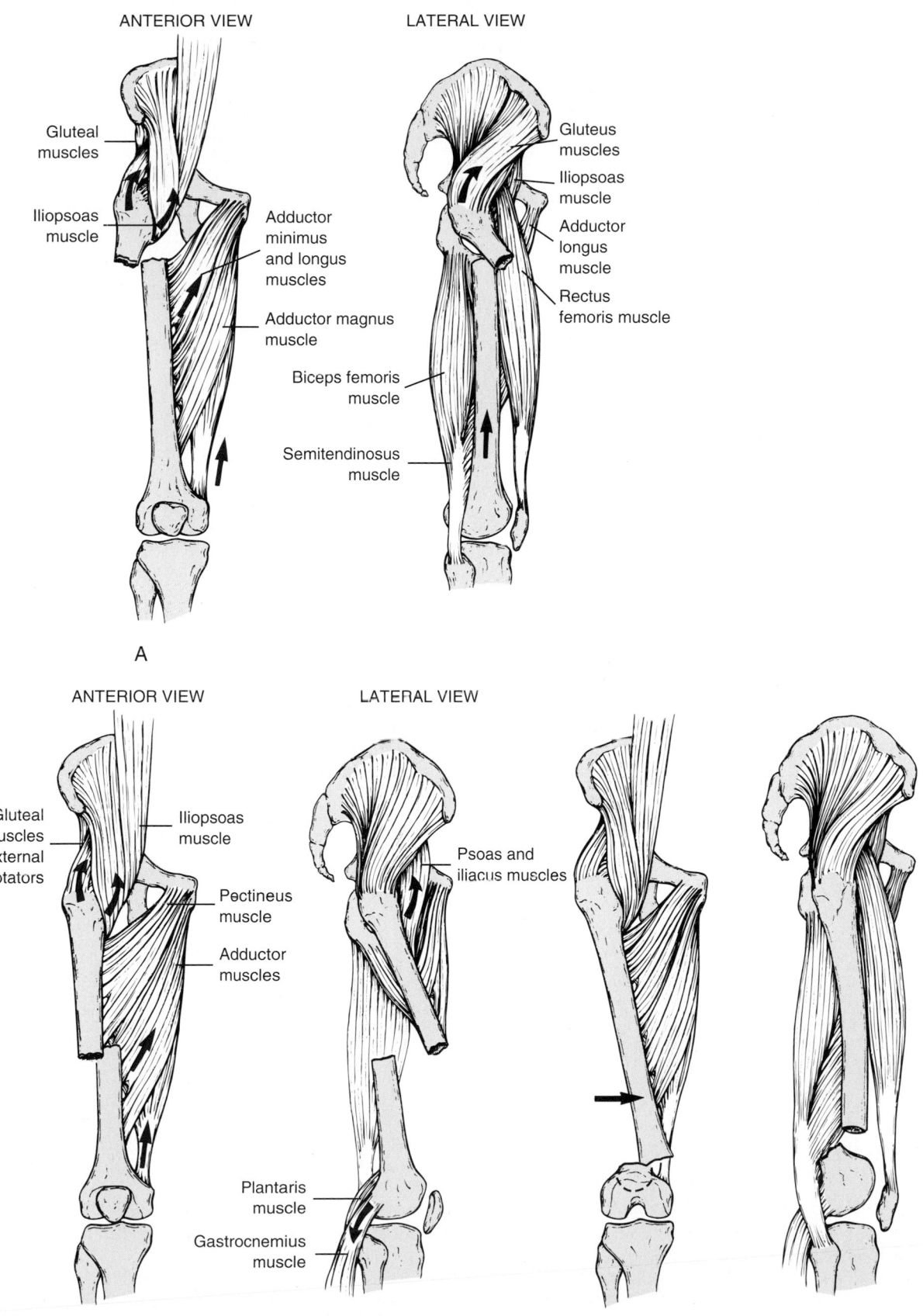

**FIGURE 52–14.** Characteristic bone deformities associated with proximal (*A*), midshaft (*B*), and distal (*C*) fractures. The deformities are the result of unbalanced muscle action.

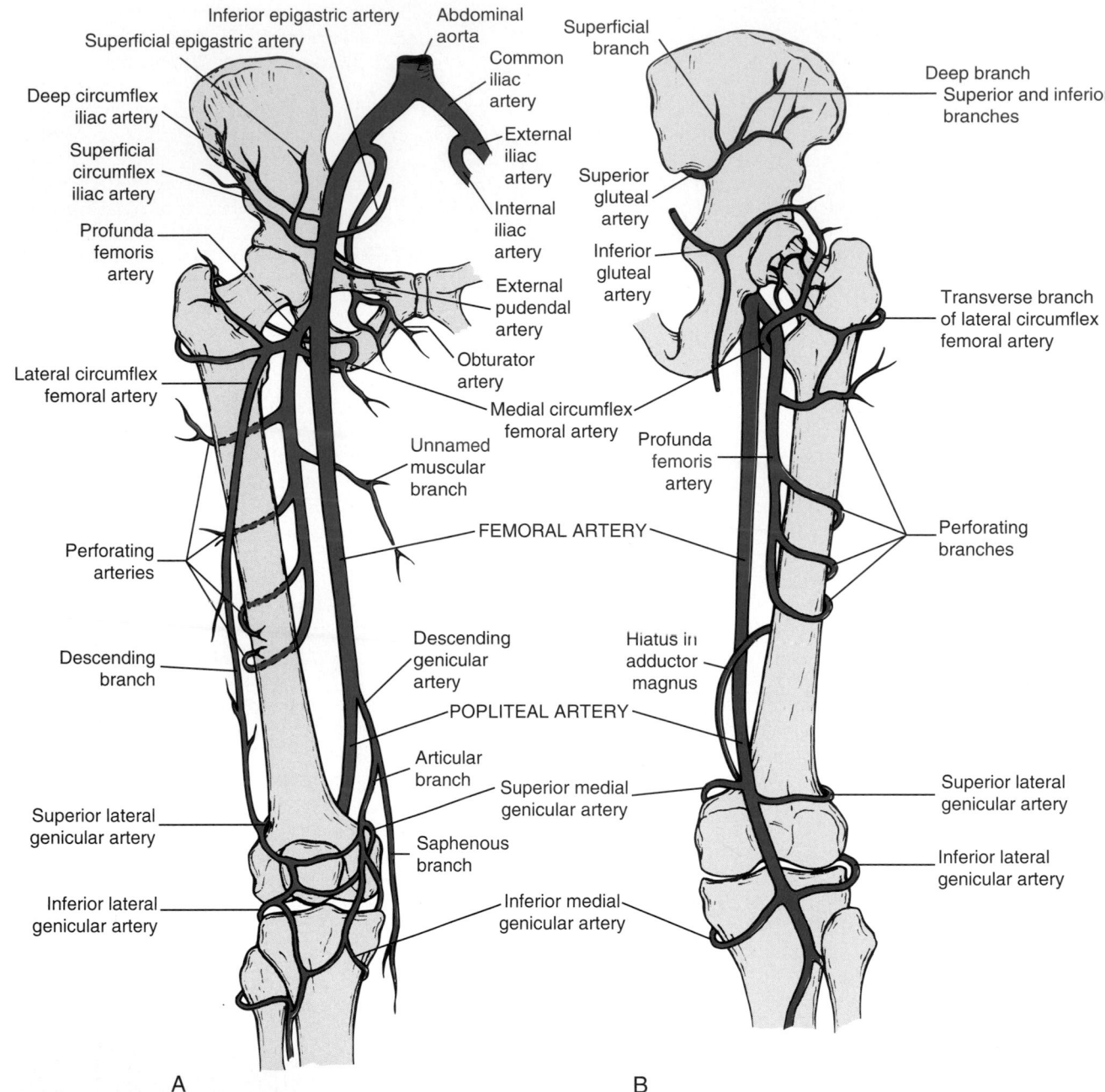

**FIGURE 52–15.** Anatomy of the major arteries of the thigh. *A,* Anterior view; *B,* posterior view.

## METHODS OF TREATMENT

Femoral diaphyseal fractures, like other long bone fractures, can be treated by four basic methods: nonoperative management involving traction and cast bracing, external skeletal fixation, plating, and intramedullary nailing. Nowadays, few surgeons who have access to interlocking intramedullary nails use the other techniques, but external skeletal fixation and plating do have some indications. When resources or equipment to internally or externally

fix fractures is unavailable, surgeons will have to use nonoperative management.

### Nonoperative Management

Few surgeons have to resort to treating patients exclusively with traction. If nonoperative management is initiated, traction is generally applied for 4 to 8 weeks, after which a cast brace is used to allow the patient to mobilize. The traction system in use is essentially that developed by

Steinmann[231] and refined by Böhler.[20] The basic traction types for different fracture locations are illustrated in Figure 52–1. If traction is planned to last more than a few days, it should be skeletal. A pin is passed through the proximal end of the tibia just posterior to the tibial tuberosity. The leg is placed on a balanced suspension as illustrated in Figure 52–16. Traction is then applied by attaching weight with a rope and pulley system to a Steinmann pin traction bow. Placing an appropriately sized pad on the sling under the femoral fracture prevents an antecurvatum deformity of the femoral diaphysis.

Radiographs are used to check the position of the fracture over the first 2 to 3 weeks. Once the surgeon believes that the fracture is "sticky" and is beginning to stabilize, knee flexion can be increased. As the fracture starts to unite, a number of alternatives are open to the surgeon.

A split-bed traction technique can be used. In this method, the patient sits on a bed with the thigh supported and the knee placed over the end of the bed. Traction is maintained, but knee flexion is allowed and indeed encouraged. Alternatively, the balanced traction can be maintained until the fracture is sufficiently united to allow the patient to mobilize. However, at least 12 to 16 weeks may be needed, and refractures after early mobilization are not uncommon. Refracture is a disastrous complication for the patient, who is then faced with another prolonged period of bedrest. The third technique is to immobilize the patient, usually after 4 to 8 weeks in some form of cast. This technique has been in widespread use since the end of the 19th century, and the only major change in recent decades has been the substitution of a cast brace of the type developed by Mooney[167] for the spica cast used in earlier decades. Kaufer[127] analyzed the use of a hip spica cast after a period in traction. Its relative usefulness is highlighted by the fact that of 207 patients treated in a 3-year period, only 66 (31.9%) were considered appropriate for a "walking spica" regimen. Of the 60 patients who

were eventually treated with early mobilization in a spica, the average hospitalization was 29 days, and the average time to full weight bearing without support was 175 days. By applying modern outcome criteria, 14.9% had significant angular malunion and 40% of the femurs were significantly short. Knee flexion of 90° was considered good!

The cast brace introduced by Mooney[167] used medial and lateral knee hinges to facilitate knee movement and allow early weight bearing. Connolly and colleagues[54] treated 143 fractures. Fifty seven (39.9%) had shortening of more than 1 cm, and 9 (6.3%) patients had angulation of more than 15°. Only 5.4% of the patients had knee flexion less than 90°. The authors graded 130 patients for overall function and classed 107 (82.3%) as having a good result. Hardy[106] undertook a prospective study of 106 patients with 108 femoral fractures. He applied the cast brace at an average of 16 days after the fracture and noted malalignment in 69 (63.9%) femurs, with the average shortening being 10.9 mm. Only four patients had less than 100° of knee flexion, and most patients returned to full-time occupations or studies within 30 weeks.

Studies analyzing the use of primary traction and secondary bracing have all found comminuted and distal femoral diaphyseal fractures particularly difficult to treat. It must be remembered that most of the literature dealing with this method of management was written over 30 years ago, and although the surgeons undoubtedly achieved results that were acceptable at the time, their outcome criteria would not be considered adequate today. The method was time consuming, expensive, and associated with prolonged hospitalization, shortening, angular malunion, and knee stiffness.[47] It clearly still has a place in areas where operative facilities are lacking, but nonoperative management has no role nowadays if resources are adequate to permit internal fixation, especially in multiply injured patients, in whom nonoperative

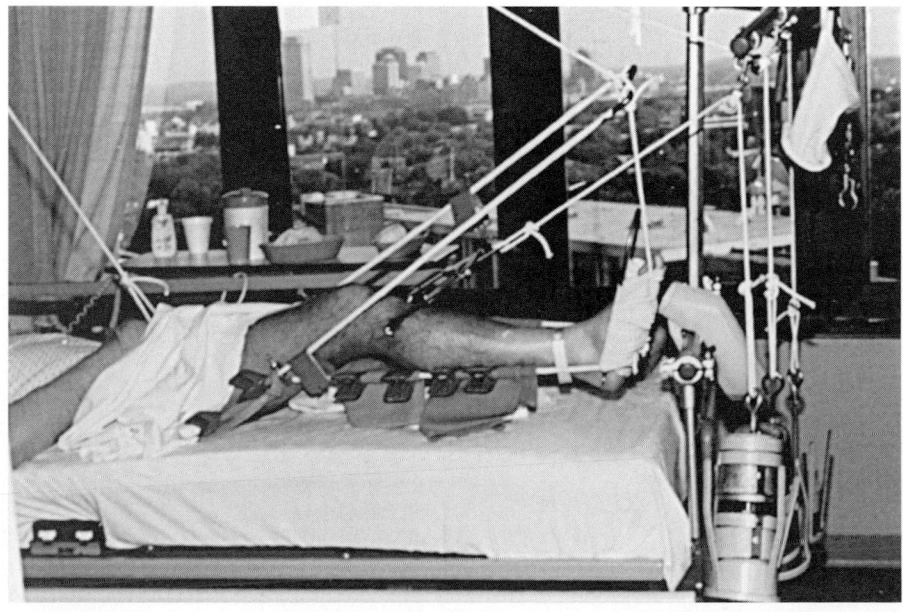

FIGURE 52–16. Balanced skeletal traction. Note the weight suspending the leg and the second weight applying traction to the fracture through a proximal tibial transfixion pin. The knee is slightly flexed, and both the thigh and leg are supported.

management is associated with significant morbidity and mortality.[69, 93, 123, 202, 220, 247]

## External Skeletal Fixation

External skeletal fixation remains popular in the management of tibial diaphyseal fractures, but it has few indications in the management of femoral fractures. The prob-

lems are self-evident. Unlike the tibia, the fracture is surrounded by muscles, and therefore soft tissue tethering is inevitable if external fixation is used. Because closed intramedullary nailing produces such good results in the management of both closed and open femoral diaphyseal fractures, it is not logical to compromise limb function by using an external fixator. The main exception is when severely injured patients are being treated. Friedl and colleagues[84] emphasized the advantage of primary external

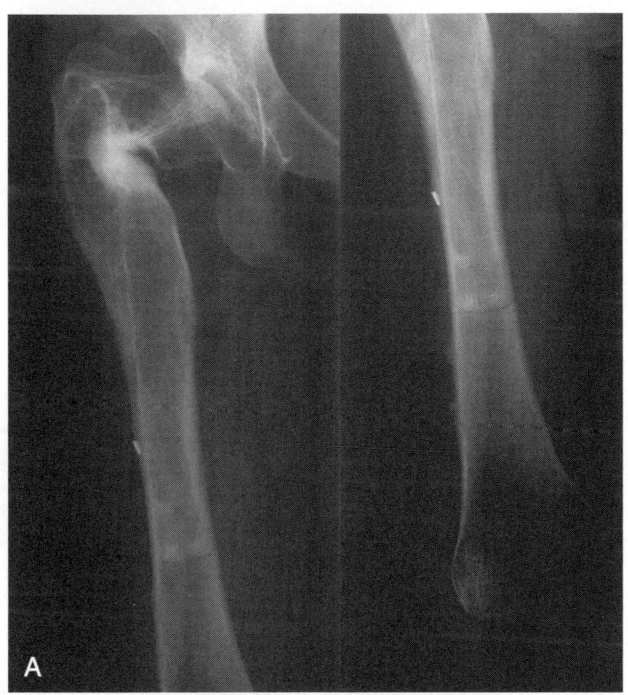

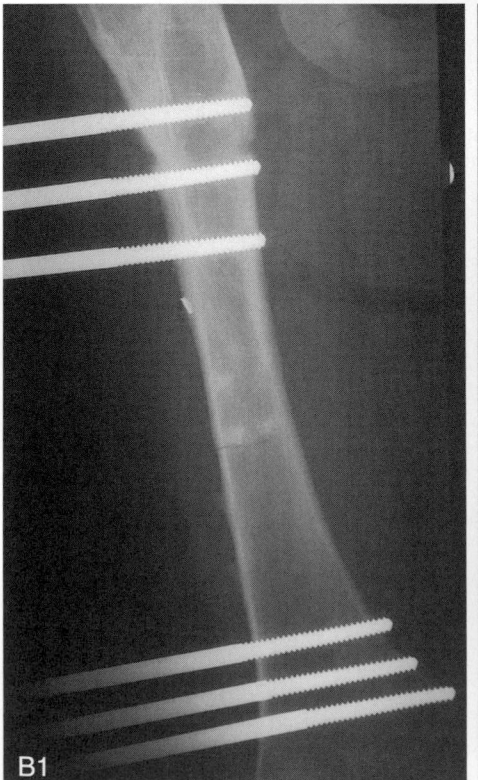

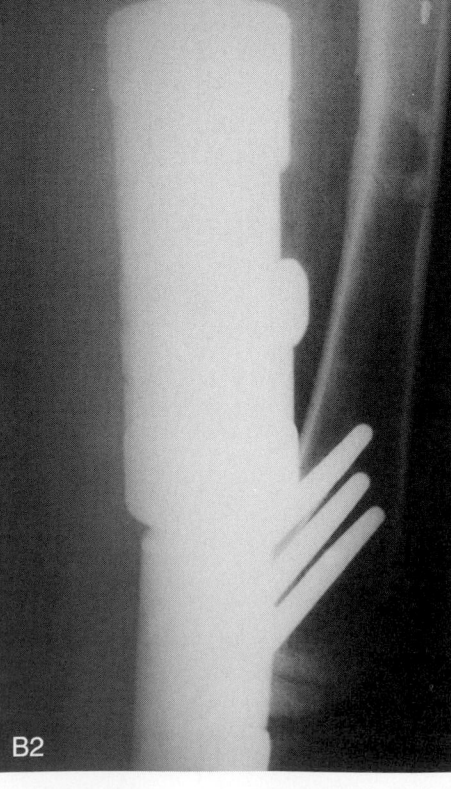

**Figure 52–17.** *A,* Anteroposterior and lateral radiographs of the femur of a 22-year-old woman with a proximal femoral focal deficiency. An insufficiency fracture has occurred through regenerate bone from previous leg lengthening. The abnormal proximal femoral anatomy and a stiff knee precluded femoral intramedullary nailing. *B,* A unilateral external fixator has been used to treat the fracture. The frame was maintained for 4 months and union occurred.

fixation and secondary intramedullary nailing in patients who have an ISS of more than 40. Under these circumstances, external fixation is quick and relatively straightforward. The patient can be returned to the operating room for secondary intramedullary nailing after the patient's status has improved.

Nowotarski and co-workers[177] examined the problems of converting from primary external fixation to secondary intramedullary nailing. They examined 54 multiply injured patients with 59 fractures of the femoral diaphysis. The mean ISS on initial evaluation was 29. Forty-four (81.5%) of the patients had additional musculoskeletal injuries. All fractures were stabilized with a unilateral external fixator, the average time taken to apply the fixator being 30 minutes. The duration of external fixation averaged 7 days, and the authors undertook one-stage conversion to intramedullary nailing in 55 fractures, with the remaining 4 fractures having a period of skeletal traction to allow discharging pin sites to settle. The overall infection rate was 1.7%, and the average range of final knee motion was 107°. Given the severity of the injuries that they were treating and the fact that 32.2% of the fractures were open, these results are excellent and compare well with those of primary nailing (see Tables 52–9, 52–10, and 52–13).

Table 52–11 shows the results of the use of locked intramedullary nailing for open fractures. These results indicate that no advantage is gained by using external fixation for open fractures. Mohr and colleagues[164] examined the use of external fixation in Gustilo type II and III open fractures and demonstrated that osteomyelitis developed in 11% and that 20% had restricted knee function. They also found that 27% had at least 10° of angular malunion. External fixation does not produce better results than intramedullary nailing does in the management of open femoral diaphyseal fractures and will inevitably restrict access for plastic surgery and cause muscle tethering. Its routine use for definitive management of open femoral fractures cannot be recommended.

Occasionally, relative indications will of course be seen for external fixation of the femur. Figure 52–17 shows the femur of a 22-year-old woman with a proximal femoral focal deficiency after three previous femoral lengthening procedures. She had an insufficiency fracture of her femur that occurred through regenerate bone. The morphology of her hip precluded antegrade nailing, and her knee was already stiff, which made retrograde nailing very difficult. Given the uncomplicated nature of the fracture, external fixation was chosen and was successful. However, the author believes that notwithstanding unusual cases, the only indication for external fixation in the management of femoral fractures is as a temporary measure in severely injured patients or when it is suspected that the vascular injury is reconstructible (see Fig. 52–10).[250]

## Plating

Modern plating methods were introduced by the AO group in the early 1960s. The initial principle that governed treatment was that rigid fixation with meticulous fracture reduction be achieved. Interfragmentary screws were used to fix the bone fragments, and a plate was then

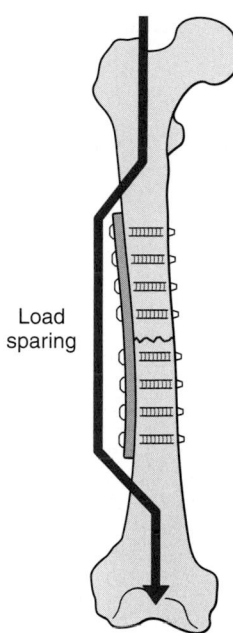

**FIGURE 52–18.** Diagrammatic representation of traditional femoral plating of the femur. The phenomenon of load sparing or stress shielding is also illustrated.

applied to the lateral cortex of the femur[173] (Fig. 52–18; see Fig. 52–20). In general, it was agreed that eight cortices should be secured above and below the fracture site.[149] (One bicortical screw in the diaphysis captures "two cortices.") The dynamic compression plate (DCP) was also introduced to facilitate fracture compression (Fig. 52–18). Use of the AO principles and implants allowed surgeons to rigidly fix bone and therefore permit early joint movement and facilitate patient mobilization, although the rigidity of the implant tended to lead to stress shielding of the bone and a degree of localized osteopenia. However, the introduction of locked intramedullary nailing in the 1970s and its widespread acceptance in the 1980s and 1990s forced the proponents of rigid plating to evaluate their original ideas and introduce the concepts of indirect reduction and biologic plating. Proponents of these ideas suggested that less soft tissue dissection during plating was desirable and that it was no longer necessary to reduce and fix every bone fragment. Plates were introduced to span the comminuted areas of bone, and surgeons came to favor longer plates with fewer screws[204] (Fig. 52–19).

In recent years it has been realized that the standard DCP deleteriously affects bone vasculature. As a result, the AO group developed the low-contact dynamic compression (LCDC) plate, which allowed the plate to stand off the periosteum, thereby preserving more of the periosteal blood supply. However, both the DCP and the LCDC plates required open surgery to insert the plate onto the bone, and recently, interest has been shown in percutaneous plating methods in which a plate is placed onto the bone through a small incision after the fracture has been reduced indirectly by the use of traction or a femoral distractor.[264] Fluoroscopy is used to position the plate and to percutaneously introduce the appropriate number of screws. Unfortunately, virtually all the published studies

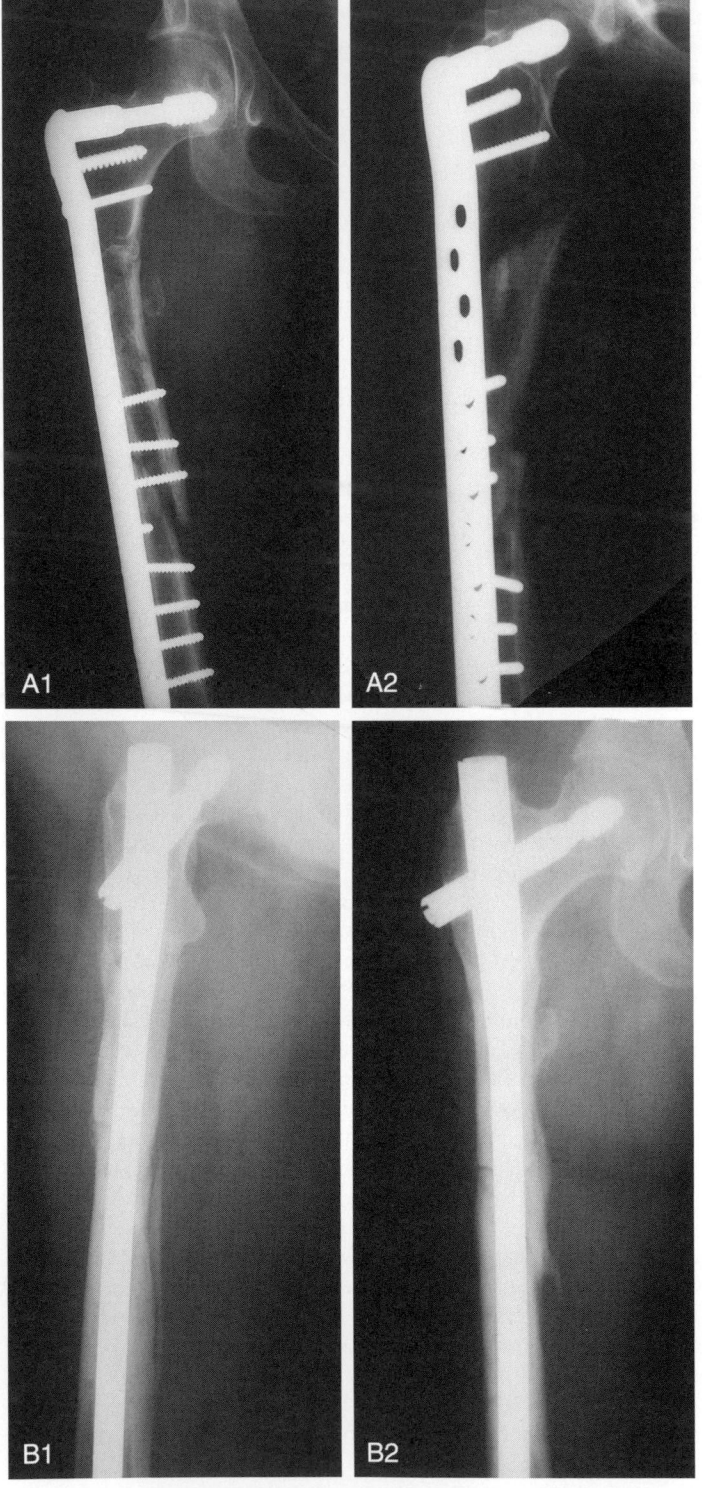

**FIGURE 52–19.** *A,* Biologic plating of a complex fracture of the upper diaphyseal and subtrochanteric area of the femur of a 24-year-old woman involved in a motor vehicle accident. Note that the comminuted fracture has been left undisturbed and screws have been placed proximally and distally. A 95° screw-plate system has been used to maximize proximal bone fixation. *B,* Union did not occur, so a cephalomedullary reconstruction nail was used to stabilize the fracture. Union occurred and a good result was obtained.

on the use of plates in the management of femoral fractures have involved the use of a DCP or interfragmentary screws and a laterally located neutralization plate. Despite interest in more modern plating techniques, few studies have investigated their application in clinical situations. The results of a number of studies examining the use of femoral plating are shown in Table 52–8.

Rüedi and Lüscher[205] undertook femoral plating of 290 fractures in Basel, Switzerland. They analyzed 131 comminuted and segmental fractures, and the results of their study are shown in Table 52–8. They analyzed patient function and considered a very good result to be restitution of normal anatomy and the patient's professional and social activities. This goal was attained in 42% of their patients. Another 54.6% of their patients had good results, which was defined as good function but some limitation in hip or knee movement. Thus, 96.6% of their patients had a very good or good result. They pointed out the relatively high incidence of plate failure and stressed the need for bone grafting of the medial cortex to achieve good results.

In the same year, Magerl and coauthors[151] published their results from St. Gallen, Switzerland. They were able to monitor 67 patients stabilized with either standard diaphyseal plates or condylar plates if the fractures were more proximal or distal (see Table 52–8). They graded their final results slightly differently from Rüedi and Lüscher and took pain into account. They found that 67.2% of patients had excellent and 25.4% had good results. When they analyzed individual outcome criteria, 59.8% of patients had some pain in the thigh, and 14.9% had minimal loss of hip rotation, with only 7.5% losing more than 10°. No loss of hip flexion or extension was noted. Only four patients lost any knee movement, with no patient who had an isolated femoral fracture reporting loss of knee function. They also stressed the need for bone grafting, particularly for secondary bone grafting, which, they said, should be performed early if union was not proceeding. Loomer and colleagues[150] in Vancouver, Canada, had similar results. They assessed final function and stated that 80% of the patients who were assessed had excellent or good results. They pointed out that 53% of their fractures united without bone grafting and agreed with Magerl and associates that bone grafting should be performed in patients with cortical defects, unstable fracture fixation, or devascularized bone fragments. Cheng and coauthors[45] stated that 90.6% of their patients had excellent or good results after plating. Screw loosening and refracture occurred in two elderly patients, and the problems of using plates in osteoporotic femurs was also discussed by Thompson and co-workers,[240] who recorded complications in 38% of their patients who were older than 60 years. They found that 37.5% of this elderly group had poor functional results. These authors recommended screw fixation in a minimum of 10 cortices in each main fragment. They also suggested that acrylic cement might be used to supplement screw fixation if osteoporotic fractures were being treated.

Van Niekerit and Schoots[255] retrospectively reviewed 20 plated femurs and compared them with 19 femoral fractures treated with an interlocking nail. The results for the plated group are shown in Table 52–8. The two groups of patients had similar demographic characteristics, most of the patients being young men injured in motor vehicle accidents. The interlocking nail group had no infections or union problems, and cancellous bone grafting was not needed, although it was required in 35% of the plated group. Final function appears to have been similar in both groups. Rozbruch and associates[204] analyzed the evolution of femoral plating and compared the results of the technique in one hospital in Bern, Switzerland, in three time periods: 1972–1973, 1982, and 1993–1994. They made the point that femoral plating in their hospital had changed over the study period. In 1972–1973 and in 1982 they mainly used DCPs. Use of the 95° condylar blade plate increased with time, and in 1993–1994, it was used for all proximal and distal diaphyseal fractures. The LCDC plate was used only in 1993–1994. Primary bone grafting was used frequently in 1982 but in only 4% of cases in 1993–1994. The authors noted that over time they tended to use longer plates but fewer screws and that the use of interfragmentary screws decreased significantly as they moved away from the original philosophy of meticulous reduction and rigid stabilization to indirect reduction with preservation of more of the soft tissues. The nonunion rate fell from 9.5% in 1972–1973 to 4.3% in 1993–1994, but the infection rate stayed unchanged at about 4%. The union time improved from 4.9 months in 1972–1973 to 3.4 months in 1993–1994.

This study is of interest because it presents the best results associated with femoral plating. The authors state that intramedullary nailing is the standard treatment of femoral fractures, but they believe that plates are useful under certain circumstances. They correctly emphasize that plating is technique dependent, and they stress the importance of careful tissue dissection, extraperiosteal bone exposure, indirect fracture reduction, and bridge plating of comminuted fragments with preservation of the vascular supply of the fracture fragments.

A comparison of Table 52–8 with Tables 52–9, 52–10, and 52–13, which present the results of antegrade and retrograde reamed and unreamed femoral nailing, unquestionably indicates that plating is associated with a higher incidence of infection than reamed and unreamed nailing is. The incidence of nonunion after plating is similar to that of unreamed nailing, with reamed nailing being associated with better results. Implant failure, implant loosening, and refracture are rarely encountered after intramedullary nailing, with nail breakage occurring only if a nonunion remains untreated. Screw breakage is obviously more frequent in intramedullary nailing, but it is rarely a significant problem. The other disadvantage of plating is the much higher requirement for bone grafting, although the study by Rozbruch and colleagues[204] shows that with

---

**TABLE 52–8**

Data from Studies of the Use of Plating in the Treatment of Femoral Diaphyseal Fractures

| | N | Age (yr) | Open Fracture (%) | Infection (%) | Implant Failure/ Loosening (%) | Nonunion (%) | Refracture (%) |
|---|---|---|---|---|---|---|---|
| Rüedi and Lüscher[205] | 131 | 40.8 | 21.4 | 6.3 | 7.1 | 7.1 | 1.6 |
| Magerl et al.[151] | 67 | 31.4 | 13.4 | 3.0 | 10.4 | 7.5 | 3.0 |
| Loomer et al.[150] | 46 | ? | 15.2 | 6.5 | 13 | 2.2 | 8.7 |
| Cheng et al.[45] | 32 | 36 | 6.2 | 0 | 6.2 | 3.1 | 3.1 |
| Thompson et al.[240] | 86 | 32 | 11.6 | 0 | 10.8 | 5.4 | 2.7 |
| Van Niekerit and Schoots[255] | 20 | 27 | 5 | 10 | ? | 15 | ? |
| Rozbruch et al.[204] | 80 | 35.7 | 26.2 | 4 | 5 | 5 | ? |

care, the requirement for grafting can be reduced to more acceptable levels.

Rozbruch and co-workers[204] included six LCDC plates in the 1993–1994 patient group. However, it was not possible to isolate information about this plate. Riemer and colleagues[200] presented their experience with the LCDC plate, although no results were given. They believed that LCDC plates had greater flexibility than the DCP, but noted that they failed with greater frequency. Their flexibility encouraged the formation of callus, and they thought that the requirement for bone grafting with this device might be less than with conventional plates.

The most recent innovation in plating has been the introduction of percutaneous plating, which involves insertion of a plate of the correct length through a short longitudinal incision made over the trochanteric area. The plate is passed under the vastus lateralis, and fluoroscopy is used to aid in screw insertion. Wenda and associates[264] documented the use of this technique in 17 femurs, but data about their patients are sparse. Thirteen (76.5%) of the patients healed without complications, but 3 of these 13 (23.1%) required bone grafting and 1 patient needed corrective osteotomy to correct rotational malalignment. An extension of this technique has been described by Van Reit and coauthors.[236] They placed femoral plates under the fascia lata and, under fluoroscopic control, inserted screws through the vastus lateralis into the femur. This technique was thought to represent an internal fixator and was intended to take advantage of biologic fixation. However, even the authors believed that it had few indications!

It does not seem that there is any logical reason to use submuscular or subfascial plating. If surgeons wish to use closed techniques to treat a femoral diaphyseal fracture, it is abundantly clear that intramedullary nailing is much easier and more likely to produce better results. The early results of Wenda and colleagues[264] are not encouraging, and it would seem that closed plating techniques merely increase the difficulty of the operation without conferring any obvious benefit. This technique cannot be recommended at this time, and indeed, it is difficult to see why any plating method should be used for the primary management of diaphyseal femoral fractures if interlocking intramedullary nailing is available. The arguments are better for using plating techniques in proximal and distal fractures, but these indications are discussed elsewhere.

## INDICATIONS FOR FEMORAL DIAPHYSEAL PLATING

Plating is the second best method after interlocking intramedullary nailing for treating femoral diaphyseal fractures, and one obvious indication for its use is if the equipment necessary to use interlocking intramedullary nailing is unavailable. If plates are to be used to stabilize femoral diaphyseal fractures, surgeons should adhere to the modern principles described by Rozbruch and colleagues.[204] If AO type A fractures are being treated, the traditional use of a lagged interfragmentary screw and a neutralization plate or a DCP is perfectly adequate, but if AO type B and C fractures are being treated, it is advisable to maintain the soft tissue attachments to the intermediate bone fragments and use a bridge-plating technique. A longer plate with fewer screws should be used, with the area of comminution being spanned by the plate (see Fig. 52–19).

Two other circumstances in which femoral diaphyseal plating is useful are in the management of periprosthetic fractures (see Fig. 52–49) and when primary nailing has resulted in fracture malalignment (Fig. 52–20). Peripros-

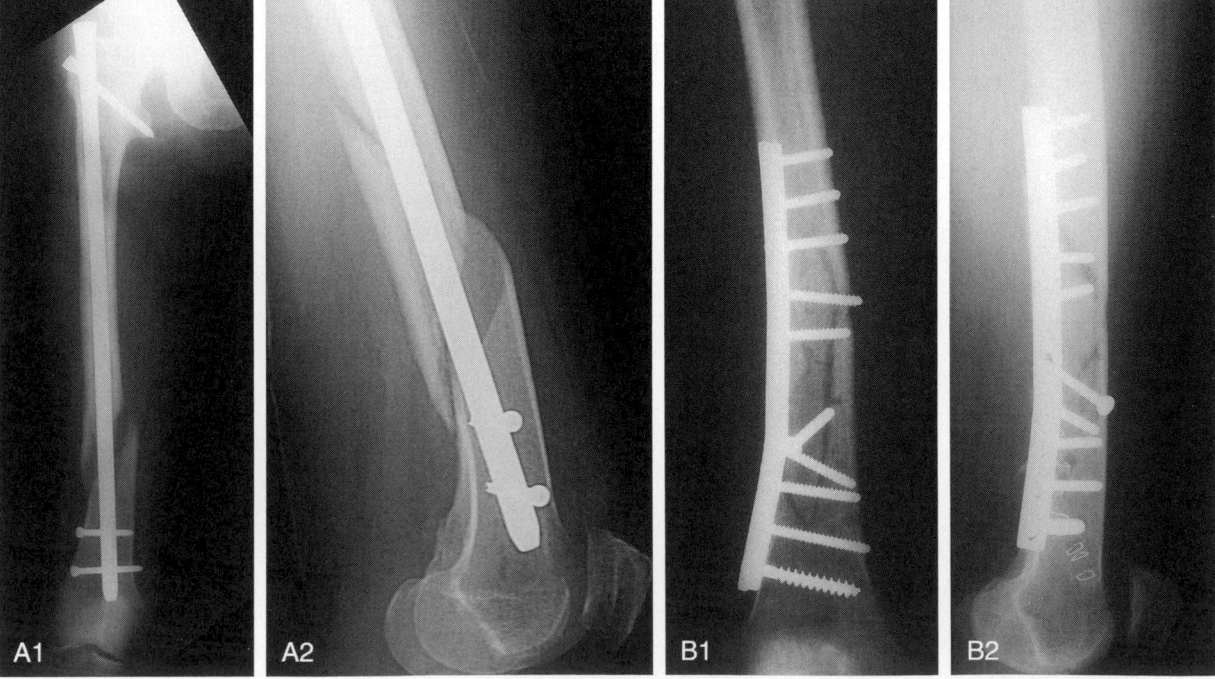

**FIGURE 52–20.** *A,* Intramedullary nailing of a femoral fracture in a middle-aged woman. This fracture was caused by a high-energy injury, and the muscle interposition was not noticed. The fracture has not been reduced. *B,* It proved impossible to create a new tract in the intramedullary canal and nail the femur in a better position. Accordingly, a dynamic compression plate was used to plate the fracture, which united.

thetic fractures and their management are described later in the chapter, but it is useful to highlight the use of plates in the management of failed intramedullary nailing. One of the problems of intramedullary nailing is that it may be difficult to reposition the nail if the initial nailing procedure results in a valgus or varus malposition of a distal femoral fracture. In these circumstances, the author has sometimes found revision nailing to be difficult because the guide wire, reamers, and second nail tend to follow the original nail tract. Plating can be useful in these circumstances, as illustrated in Figure 52–20.

## TECHNIQUE OF FEMORAL PLATING

Femoral plating is undertaken through a midlateral approach with the patient placed in the lateral position. A femoral distractor or external fixator aids in reduction and stabilization. After incision of the skin and subcutaneous tissue, the fascia lata is incised and the vastus lateralis exposed. This muscle is mobilized forward off the underlying fascia to expose the femur. In well-muscled males with fractures in the proximal third of the femur, it may be difficult to expose the fracture adequately, and under these circumstances, the surgeon will have to incise the muscle to expose the femur. The plate is placed on the lateral aspect of the femur according to the principles documented by the AO group,[173] although in AO/OTA type B and type C fractures, surgeons should use indirect reduction techniques with longer plates and fewer screws.

## Intramedullary Nailing

The change from nonoperative management to intramedullary nailing started in the 1950s and 1960s, but intramedullary nailing did not assume its current popularity until the late 1970s and 1980s after the introduction of interlocking nails. Until then, surgeons had used unlocked femoral nails, which proved to be very successful for many fractures but required considerable expertise if they were to be used for comminuted or distal femoral fractures (see Fig. 52–2). However, these fractures were the same ones that the proponents of cast management had found difficult to treat, and these surgeons pointed out that the increased risk of sepsis associated with intramedullary nailing rendered the technique of intramedullary nailing unacceptable. Dencker[70] analyzed all femoral fractures in Sweden between 1952 and 1954. Even then, 43% were treated by a Küntscher nail, with 32% being treated by closed means. He found technical errors in 14% of the fractures treated by intramedullary nailing but reported no difference in the incidence of nonunion or infection between the two methods. The percentage of excellent and good results at final follow-up was also about the same.

Other surgeons found considerable benefit from the use of intramedullary nails. Rascher and co-workers[197] treated 42 patients with Küntscher nailing. They had one successfully treated infection with no nonunions, pulmonary emboli, or fat emboli. Patients were discharged 10 to 14 days after surgery. Hansen and Winquist[105] analyzed 300 femoral fractures monitored for at least 3 years. They reported a 6.3% incidence of malunion with a 0.7% rate of infection and a 0.3% rate of nonunion. In their later report

of 520 cases of closed intramedullary nailing of femoral fractures, they noted that the union rate was 99.1% and that the range of motion of the knee at follow-up averaged 130°.[268] The infection rate was 0.9%, and only 2% of patients showed more than 2 cm of shortening. A further 2.3% of patients had malrotation of more than 20°.

Initially, surgeons used Küntscher nailing for transverse or short oblique fractures near the isthmus and relied on reaming to widen the intramedullary canal and achieve an interference fit between the nail and the endosteal surface of the intramedullary canal. However, they soon discovered that butterfly fragments and spiral fractures could be treated with supplementary cerclage wiring (see Fig. 52–2), and Winquist and colleagues[268] reported the use of cerclage wiring in 23 of their 520 cases. Surgeons soon found that with care, the technique of closed Küntscher nailing could be used for a range of femoral fractures. It is also possible to combine Küntscher nailing with cast bracing, and this technique was documented by Sharma and co-workers.[223] They analyzed 81 comminuted femoral fractures treated by unlocked nailing and supplementary cast bracing. The average hospitalization was 28 days, and the mean time to union was 14 weeks. Two (2.5%) patients had shortening of more than 2 cm, with no angular deformity. They also reported no infections or nonunions, and 68 (83.9%) of the patients had full hip and knee function at final review. Hooper and Lyon[115] analyzed 50 patients treated by unlocked femoral nailing. They had no infections or nonunions, and satisfactory results were achieved in 76%. However, they stressed that although the technique was useful for Winquist-Hansen grade 2 fractures, they had problems with shortening when treating Winquist-Hansen grade 3 and 4 fractures. Unlike Sharma and colleagues,[223] they found that the shortening could not be controlled with the use of a supplementary cast brace.

If interlocking nailing is available, there is no logical reason to use unlocked nails at all. If, on the other hand, the surgeon has access to only unlocked nails, good results can still be achieved, particularly if the technique is combined with cast bracing or cerclage wiring. However, great care must be exercised when treating Winquist-Hansen type III and type IV fractures because stable reduction is not always possible. If fluoroscopy is not available, the surgeon can use an open nailing technique. This technique is performed by placing the patient in the lateral position, making a midlateral approach to the femur, and either passing the nail retrogradely up the proximal femoral fragment and then down the distal fragment after fracture reduction or inserting the nail through the piriformis fossa in the usual way after reduction. It is of interest that Rokkanen and associates[203] noted only slight overall benefit with closed nailing versus open nailing. They found that 86% of patients treated by closed nailing had good results as compared with 79% treated by open nailing and 56% treated by nonoperative management.

### FLEXIBLE INTRAMEDULLARY NAILING

An alternative to the use of a large-diameter unlocked nail was the use of two or more flexible small-diameter nails such as Rush pins (Fig. 52–21) or Ender nails (Fig. 52–22). These pins rely either on three-point fixation (see

Fig. 52–21), with appropriate pin bending, or stacking of the pins so that fracture stability is maintained (see Fig. 52–22). Pankovich and co-workers[186] investigated the use of Ender nails in 52 femoral fractures. Two nails were introduced through the posteromedial and posterolateral aspects of the femoral cortex at a level 2 to 3 cm proximal to the superior pole of the patella. Under fluoroscopy, they were passed proximally simultaneously so that their tips were proximal to the lesser trochanter. They reported no nonunions, and the average time to union was 13.2 weeks. The major complications were that 7 (13.5%) patients had to use a cast brace because of instability and 29 (55.8%) patients needed to have the nails removed because of discomfort or restriction of knee movement. The authors pointed out that supplementary fixation such as cerclage wires or cast bracing was required for long oblique fractures or for fractures with bicortical comminution. Eriksson and Hovelius[76] used a similar technique but used up to four Ender nails, with some fractures being treated by nails inserted only through the medial femoral condyle. All 16 fractures healed, but fracture shortening was a problem, as was backing out of the nails. Walters and colleagues[260] used Ender nails to treat 106 fractures, but they inserted the nails through the greater trochanter. With the patient on a nailing table, they used a bone awl to broach the trochanter near its tip and inserted up to four Ender nails. They reported union in 96.6% and one case of infection. Malunion occurred in 9 (8.5%) patients, and 21 (19.8%) complained of trochanteric discomfort, although only 8 of these patients required treatment.

Ender nailing is a relatively straightforward technique and can produce good results in stable fracture configurations. However, it does not have any advantages over

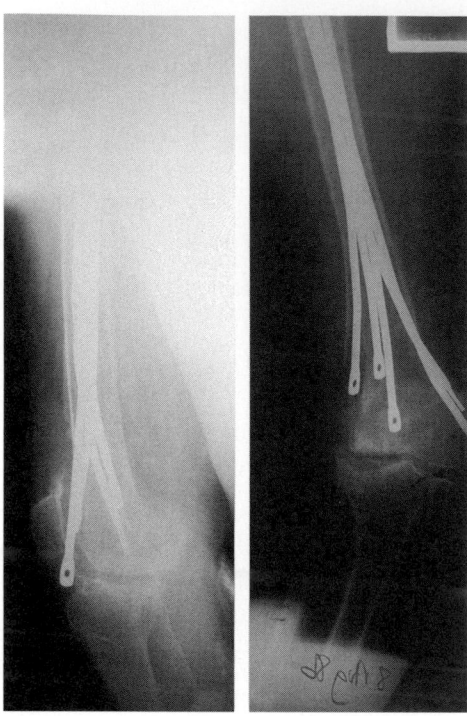

**FIGURE 52–22.** The use of stacked Ender nails to treat a femoral fracture in an elderly woman.

conventional locked nailing, and it has very few indications if locked nailing is available. Figure 52–21 shows a case in which flexible nailing was used successfully in an elderly lady who had a femoral fracture distal to a malunion of an old nonoperatively managed femoral fracture. Conventional nailing and plating would have been impossible without taking the fracture down, and Rush nails were successfully used.

## INTERLOCKING INTRAMEDULLARY NAILING

Such is the dominance of interlocking intramedullary nailing in the management of femoral diaphyseal fractures that it is unlikely that any other fracture enjoys such a strong consensus for one method of management. Most interlocking nailing is carried out with an antegrade technique, with the nail being inserted from the proximal end of the femur and passed distally (see Figs. 52–4 and 52–5). In recent years, however, increased interest has been shown in retrograde intramedullary nailing (see Fig. 52–36), and both techniques will be discussed.

## ANTEGRADE NAILING

Antegrade nailing was introduced in the 1970s, and the first results of its use were published in the 1980s. Initially, virtually all surgeons used reamed intramedullary nailing, and the results of a number of studies of reamed antegrade femoral nailing are given in Table 52–9. Johnson and colleagues[123] compared the results of traction, conventional unlocked intramedullary nailing plus cerclage wires, and interlocking intramedullary nailing. They used reamed intramedullary nails 13 to 16 mm in diameter, which are somewhat larger than most surgeons would routinely use

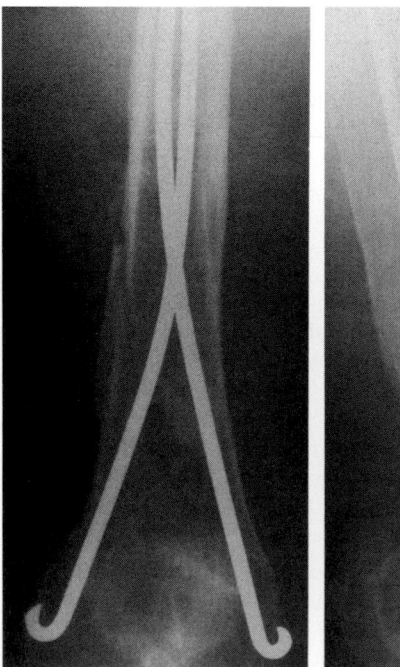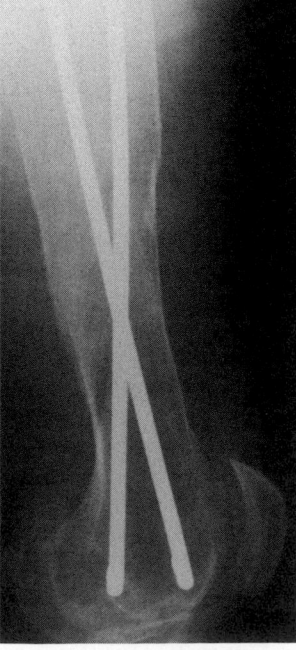

**FIGURE 52–21.** The use of two appropriately contoured Rush pins to stabilize a femoral fracture in an elderly patient. She had a previously sustained a fracture that had been treated nonoperatively and resulted in a malunion that precluded conventional nailing.

**TABLE 52–9** ................................................................................................................

Results from Series of Closed and Open Femoral Fractures Treated by Reamed Antegrade Intramedullary Nailing

| | N | Open (%) | Age (yr) | Union (wk) | Secondary Surgery* (%) | Malunion (%) | Infection (%) |
|---|---|---|---|---|---|---|---|
| Johnson et al.[123] | 24 | 16.7 | 27.6 | 13.8 | 4.2 | 12.5 | 0 |
| Klemm and Börner[137] | 293 | 16 | ? | ? | 2.4 | ? | 2.4 |
| Wiss et al.[269] | 112 | 28.5 | 28 | ? | 1.8 | 9.5 | 0 |
| Kempf et al.[130] | 52 | 36.5 | ? | 19.5 | 9.6 | 1.7 | 2.1 |
| Christie et al.[48] | 120 | 20 | 33 | 17 | 1.7 | 2.5 | 0 |
| Brumback et al.[30] | 87 | 23 | 29 | 19 | 2.3 | 0 | 1.1 |
| Søjbjerg et al.[229] | 40 | 27.5 | 31 | 12 | 0 | 15 | 0 |
| Alho et al.[1] | 123 | 12.2 | 27 | 13 | 0 | 8.1 | 0.8 |
| Wiss et al.[270] | 33 | 21.2 | 31 | 32 | 3.3 | 6.1 | 0 |
| Bråten et al.[27] | 120 | 10 | 29 | ? | 0.8 | 13.3 | 0.8 |
| Clatworthy et al.[51] | 22 | 14 | 33.7 | 28.6 | 14 | ? | 0 |
| Reynder and Broos[199] | 54 | ? | 30.7 | 19.6 | 5.6 | 0 | 0 |
| Giannoudis et al.[91] | 15 | ? | 29.5 | 20.5 | 6.7 | 0 | 0 |
| Tornetta and Tiburzi[244] | 83 | 51.8 | ? | 11.4 | 0 | 2.4 | 0 |

.........................................................................................................................

*Operations used to achieve fracture union.

nowadays. The study was retrospective but showed that locked intramedullary nailing conferred significant advantages. They defined failure of management to have occurred if a change in treatment was necessary and an unplanned reoperation was performed, femoral shortening exceeded 2.5 cm, angulation was more than 15°, nonunion or deep infection occurred during treatment, less than 70° of knee flexion was achieved, or a refracture occurred. With these criteria, the frequency of failure after traction was 66%, with failure usually being due to malalignment and shortening. A 38% failure rate was noted after the use of conventional intramedullary nailing supplemented by cerclage wiring, mainly as a result of unplanned surgery, nonunion, shortening, and infection. Interlocking intramedullary nailing was associated with only a 4% failure rate, most of the failures being due to shortening. It is obvious that the results with locked intramedullary nailing were much better than those with older techniques, and the improvement was maintained in the other studies illustrated in Table 52–9. Klemm and Börner[137] published the results of treatment of 293 femoral fractures in 1986. Table 52–9 shows that the incidence of infection and secondary surgery was low. They defined their functional results as excellent, good, or fair, depending on the degree of hip and knee movement, the presence of muscle atrophy, and radiographic alignment. Their results showed that 79.3% of patients had full joint function, no muscle atrophy, and normal femoral alignment. A further 17.7% had slight loss of function, and only 3% had significant functional impairment, muscle atrophy, or angular deformity.

Further early reports on the use of interlocking intramedullary nailing in femoral diaphyseal fractures came from Kempf and colleagues[130] in France and from Wiss and associates[269] in the United States. Kempf and co-workers[130] examined 52 patients who had femoral fractures and significant comminution or bone loss. These fractures were associated with severe soft tissue damage, which probably accounts for the relatively high incidence of secondary surgery to treat delayed union or nonunion

(see Table 52–9). They defined a number of complications associated with the technique. All their patients had quadriceps and gluteal atrophy after surgery, but the quadriceps atrophy had resolved by 6 to 12 months. Four patients had a perineal hematoma from excessive traction on the fracture table, and two patients had increased fracture comminution caused by passage of the nail down the intramedullary canal.

Wiss and colleagues[269] also examined the use of reamed interlocking antegrade intramedullary nails in comminuted femoral fractures. Seventy-nine percent of their fractures were segmental or had Winquist-Hansen type III or IV comminution. Nonunion developed in only two (1.8%) patients, with one being successfully treated by bone grafting and the other by exchange nailing. They noted that failure to achieve dynamization of statically locked intramedullary nailing did not prolong the union time. Wiss and co-workers reported a relatively high incidence of malunion, but most of the deformity was slight, although an external rotation deformity of 10° to 30° was noted in eight patients. They reported that knee flexion after treatment averaged 125°.

Christie and associates[48] examined a mixed group of patients that included 13 with pathologic fractures. They also reported excellent results (see Table 52–9) with no infection and only minor problems with malunion. Final knee flexion averaged 130°. The authors did comment on some of the complications associated with the technique. They encountered comminution of the proximal fragment in six (5%) of the fractures and believed that it was secondary to too lateral a starting point. They also reported three femoral neck fractures that did not appear to have been present before nailing was undertaken.[49] All three occurred in women with relatively small medullary canals, and all healed after treatment with cancellous screws. They encountered one significant external rotation deformity and three cases of pudendal neurapraxia.

Brumback and co-workers[30] prospectively examined 100 fractures treated by statically locked intramedullary nailing. They set out to examine whether routine conversion from static to dynamic locking was required to facilitate fracture union. They were able to monitor 87 fractures to union and noted that 98% of the fractures healed without any need for dynamization. In two patients dynamization was achieved, but both fractures were severe, one being a comminuted closed fracture and the other a Gustilo type III open fracture. Both healed after dynamization, but it is of course quite possible that this healing was coincidental and that the apparent delay to union was associated with the severe soft tissue injury. They concluded that routine dynamization of statically locked intramedullary femoral nails was not required.[30, 33]

Søjbjerg and associates[229] reported on the treatment of 40 comminuted or unstable femoral fractures with reamed intramedullary nails. As with the study of Brumback and colleagues,[30] they used only statically locked nails, and they reported no cases of nonunion with a median time to union of 12 weeks. They also thought that dynamization was unnecessary. Alho and co-workers[1] dealt with complications of the technique in detail. They encountered complications such as fracture comminution, femoral nail fracture, superficial infection, and screw loosening in 15.4% of patients, but they graded their final results as excellent in 63.4%, good in 19.5%, fair in 15.5%, and poor in only two patients (1.6%).

Wiss and colleagues[270] undertook a second study of intramedullary nailing of femoral fractures, although on this occasion they investigated the use of interlocking nailing in the management of segmental femoral fractures. They examined 33 such fractures and found that 32 (97%) united without secondary surgery. Time to union was prolonged when compared with the other series quoted in Table 52–9, but 87.5% of the fractures were caused by high-energy injuries, and it is likely that the prolonged union time merely indicates the extent of the associated soft tissue damage. Again, Wiss and co-workers[270] examined the role of dynamization and demonstrated that dynamization of femoral fractures was not necessary to secure union. They also discussed the likelihood of a femoral segment spinning during reaming. They stressed that the soft tissues attached to the linea aspera tended to prevent this complication, and it was their opinion that spinning of a femoral segment occurred only when the segment was less than 10 cm in length.

Bråten and colleagues[27] focused on the problems associated with femoral nailing. Table 52–9 shows that they had a higher incidence of malunion than seen in other series, but this higher incidence refers mainly to the presence of an external rotation deformity after nailing. Few surgeons have assessed the degree of postoperative external femoral rotation as carefully as Bråten and colleagues, and therefore the actual incidence of external rotation deformity in other series may well be higher. Bråten and co-workers[27] reported that only 39.1% of the patients with an external rotation deformity of more than 15° were actually symptomatic. They reported that 26% of their patients had hip pain and 20% had knee pain, with many patients becoming pain free after nail removal.

The remaining four studies detailed in Table 52–9 compared reamed and unreamed femoral diaphyseal nailing. The results of treatment of reamed fractures are shown in Table 52–9 and those of unreamed fractures in Table 52–10. Giannoudis and colleagues[91] undertook a retrospective study but stressed that the two study groups had no significant differences in demographic parameters. They found that time to union was 20.5 weeks in the reamed group versus 26.9 weeks in the unreamed group, the difference being statistically significant. No difference was observed in the incidence of nonunion. Similar findings were published by Clatworthy and coauthors.[51] They undertook a prospective randomized trial of reamed and unreamed nailing with a titanium nail. Comparison of the two groups showed that the unreamed group had a significantly higher ISS and that patients in the reamed group were significantly older. Fractures treated with an unreamed nail took significantly longer to unite, with the difference being more obvious in closed fractures. Court-Brown and co-workers[60] showed the same results in tibial fractures, and they theorized that any advantage of reaming was negated by the influence of the severe injury in open fractures. Clatworthy and colleagues have confirmed the same results in the femur.[51] They also showed that 39% of the unreamed group required secondary procedures to gain union as compared with 14% of the reamed group. Their trial was stopped early because of an unacceptably high incidence of implant failure, with 13 nails either bending or breaking. They found no correlation between nail failure and a mismatch between intramedullary canal and nail diameter. Tornetta and Tiburzi[244] also undertook a prospective randomized study and found no statistical difference in operative time or transfusion requirements between reamed and unreamed nailing, but the time to union in the reamed group was statistically shorter. This advantage was most obvious in fractures located in the distal end of the

---

**TABLE 52–10**

Results from Series of Closed and Open Femoral Fractures Treated by Unreamed Antegrade Femoral Nailing

| | N | Open (%) | Age (yr) | Union (wk) | Secondary Surgery* (%) | Malunion (%) | Infection (%) |
|---|---|---|---|---|---|---|---|
| Clatworthy et al.[51] | 23 | 26 | 24.8 | 39.4 | 39 | ? | 0 |
| Kröpfl et al.[140] | 81 | 9.9 | 36 | 16.5 | 0 | 2.5 | 0 |
| Giannoudis et al.[91] | 13 | ? | 33.8 | 26.9 | 7.7 | 0 | 0 |
| Hammacher et al.[104] | 129 | 25.6 | 35 | ? | 6.6 | 0.8 | 2.9 |
| Reynder and Broos[199] | 53 | ? | 34.4 | 19.2 | 7.6 | 0 | 0 |
| Tornetta and Tiburzi[244] | 89 | 52.8 | ? | 15.6 | 0 | 4.5 | 0 |

*Operations used to achieve fracture union.

femur, where the average time to union after reamed nailing was 11.4 weeks versus 22.6 weeks after unreamed nailing. They also reported more technical complications and delayed union in the unreamed group. A contrary view was expressed by Reynders and Broos.[199] They undertook a nonrandomized prospective study and found no difference between reamed and unreamed nailing.

### Unreamed Nailing

The role of reaming has been debated since the technique was introduced. Danckwardt-Lilliström[64] showed that reaming damaged the intramedullary blood supply of rabbit diaphyses. He demonstrated that significant periosteal reaction occurred after reaming and that revascularization in the rabbit diaphysis was maximal at about 8 weeks. More recently, Klein and colleagues[134] showed that reaming of the canine tibia resulted in damage to the blood supply of 70% of the cortex as compared with only 31% of the cortex if an unreamed nail was used. Schemitsch and co-workers[215] created a standard spiral fracture in sheep tibias and showed that when an unreamed nail was used to stabilize the tibia, it took 6 weeks for the cortex to revascularize as compared with 12 weeks if a reamed nail was used. In a later experiment,[216] the same sheep model was used to investigate cortical porosity and new bone formation. In this experiment, no difference in new bone formation could be demonstrated after treatment with reamed and unreamed nails.

Utvåg and colleagues[249] examined the effect of different degrees of reaming on the healing of segmental fractures in rats, with particular reference to the biomechanical properties of the bone. They found no evidence that the degree of reaming significantly affected the healing pattern. Reichert and associates[198] reamed intact sheep tibias and showed no overall reduction in cortical blood flow, but they did demonstrate a sixfold increase in periosteal blood flow 30 minutes after reaming and theorized that this increase compensated for any intramedullary vascular damage caused by reaming. It has also been demonstrated that the periosteal and endosteal systems are connected by anastomoses in the middle layers of the cortex and that blood can flow centrifugally or centripetally, depending on the prevailing physiologic conditions. The basic research dealing with bone blood flow after reaming or nailing is complicated by the fact that researchers have tended to study only one aspect of bone blood flow and its potential effect on fracture union. The results have then often been overextrapolated and unjustified assumptions made about the clinical effect of vascular impairment. Clearly, comparative clinical studies are required to investigate the role of reaming in bone union.

Table 52–10 shows the results of two European studies of the use of unreamed femoral nails in addition to the results of the unreamed fractures in four comparative studies. Kröpfl and colleagues[140] investigated their use in 81 femoral fractures, 9.9% of which were open. They reported an average time to union of 16.5 weeks with no requirement for secondary surgery to gain union and no infection. Hammacher and associates[104] documented the use of unreamed nails in 129 femoral fractures, 25.6% of which were open. They reported a 5.1% incidence of nonunion with a 2.9% rate of infection and a 0.8% rate

of malunion. Unlike Tornetta and Tiburzi,[244] they did not report any difference in nonunion rates based on the location of the fracture within the femur.

Tables 52–9 and 52–10 suggest that reamed nailing is more effective than unreamed nailing. Overall, the incidence of secondary surgery for nonunion in the 1178 fractures reported in Table 52–9 is 2.4%, and the incidence of infection is 0.4%. Table 52–10 shows the results for a total of 388 fractures treated with unreamed nails. The incidence of secondary surgery for nonunion is 5.9%, with a 0.8% rate of infection. Clearly, these tables are not a proper meta-analysis of the results, but a systematic meta-analysis of the results of reamed and unreamed nailing has been undertaken by Bhandari and co-workers.[16] They examined 10 studies dealing with both femoral and tibial fractures and showed that all studies favored reamed nailing. They reported that the use of reamed nails was associated with a lower incidence of nonunion and implant failure. Reaming did not increase the incidence of malunion, infection, pulmonary emboli, or compartment syndrome. The authors believe that antegrade reamed nailing is the treatment of choice in most femoral fractures and that no good evidence supports the use of unreamed femoral nails.

### Technique of Antegrade Femoral Nailing

The technique of antegrade femoral nailing is shown in Figure 52–23. The procedure can be undertaken with the patient on a fracture table lying either in the supine position (see Fig. 52–23) or in the lateral position (Fig. 52–24). Alternatively, the operation can be performed on a normal table with the use of manual traction[126] or a femoral distractor. As with all surgical techniques, each method of femoral nailing is associated with advantages and disadvantages, and surgeons must decide which method is best in their hands.

The use of a nailing table means that the patient is static and the position of the fracture is maintained by traction, which can be altered to facilitate reduction. The lateral position (see Fig. 52–24) is favored by a number of surgeons. The fact that the hip is flexed provides easy access to the greater trochanter. Hip flexion also facilitates nailing of femoral fractures in the elderly, who may have a fixed flexion contraction secondary to osteoarthritis. It may also be advantageous in nailing proximal femoral diaphyseal fractures when the proximal femoral fragment is flexed. Potential disadvantages of the lateral position include poor visualization of the proximal end of the femur with fluoroscopy and difficulty controlling the position of a distal femoral fracture because the distal fragment may drift into valgus. In addition, some surgeons find it easier to insert distal cross screws with the patient in the supine position. The author has always preferred to place the patient supine on a fracture table when nailing femurs, and it is the supine position that will be described. However, the basic technique is the same for both the lateral and supine positions.

The patient is placed on the fracture table with sufficient traction being applied to reduce the fracture (see Fig. 52–23A). Closed nailing should never be undertaken if the surgeon cannot preoperatively demonstrate that the fracture can be reduced. It is not necessary to be able to maintain the reduced position because muscle pull and

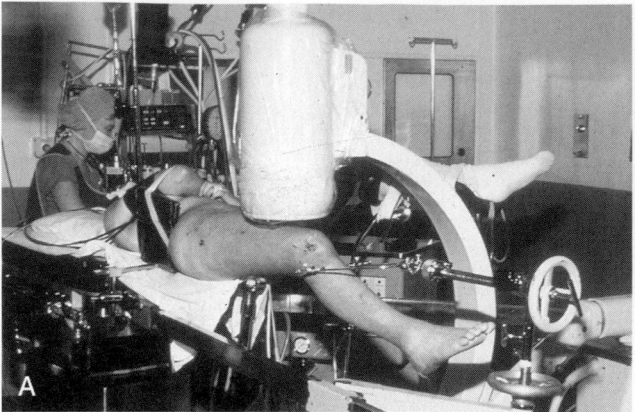
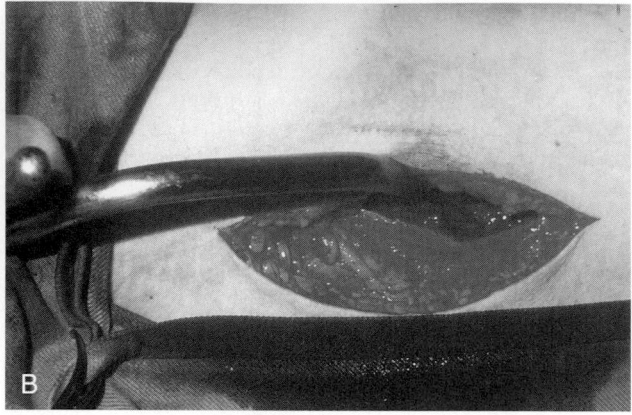

**FIGURE 52–23.** *A,* Supine position for antegrade intramedullary nailing. The fractured limb is in varus, with traction being applied through a proximal tibial pin. The contralateral hip is abducted and the hip and knee flexed. The fluoroscope has access to the full length of the thigh. *B,* The incision should pass upward from the greater trochanter. A bone awl has been placed on the greater trochanter.    *Figure continued on following page*

gravity may displace the bone fragments, but if a reduced position cannot be obtained at all, it may be that soft tissue is interposed and open reduction will be required. This complication, however, is rare. In the supine position, the contralateral hip is flexed and abducted and the contralateral knee is flexed. The leg is then placed on a well-padded support and secured carefully. The fractured leg is pulled straight, with traction being applied through a boot attached to the table or through a distal femoral or proximal tibial transfixion pin. If a distal femoral pin is used, care must be taken to place it so that it does not interfere with passage of the nail, and if a proximal tibial pin is used, the pin must be inserted such that the common peroneal nerve at the neck of the fibula is not damaged. To facilitate access to the greater trochanter, the fractured leg should be adducted, and in obese patients, the abdomen can be pushed medially with a pad placed in the ipsilateral loin. The fluoroscope should have access to the whole length of the femur.

One of the most common mistakes made by inexperienced surgeons is to center the skin incision on the greater trochanter. Such an incision does not allow sufficient space to insert the instruments proximally. The incision should start at the greater trochanter and be extended proximally for about 10 cm, although the exact length of the incision will vary between patients, depending on their size (see Fig. 52–23B). The subcutaneous fat, fascia, and abductor muscles are then divided, with the incision in the abductors kept as small as needed to insert the instruments. Digital palpation will then be used to feel the piriformis fossa on the medial side of the greater trochanter. Most surgeons agree that this starting point is ideal because it is located in line with the intramedullary canal in normal femurs. Formerly, surgeons often used the greater trochanter as the starting point, but if modern stiffer nails are used, the medial cortex and femoral neck may be damaged from too lateral a starting point. Thus, most surgeons use the piriformis fossa as their starting point except with nails designed for trochanteric insertion (Fig. 52–23C).

It is worth taking a little time to locate the starting point in the piriformis fossa because an eccentric starting point can make the rest of the operative procedure more difficult and may well damage the femur (see Fig. 52–29). The

initial starting point in the bone can be made with a bone awl or with a guide pin, over which a reamer can be placed to penetrate the proximal part of the femur. Once the entry point is made, a hand reamer should be used to penetrate the proximal femoral metaphysis, which may be hard in young bone (see Fig. 52–23D). Again, care must be taken to ensure that the hand reamer passes into the intramedullary canal and is not driven medially to penetrate the medial cortex.

A guide wire can then be placed into the canal. If the femoral fracture is undisplaced or minimally displaced, a guide wire with an olive tip at the distal end can be used. It should be placed down the femoral canal as far as the distal metaphysis (see Fig. 52–23E). If fracture reduction is required, an olive-tipped guide wire with a bend distal to the olive can be used. The distal bend can be used to "locate" the distal fragment. To facilitate fracture reduction, it is important to have an assistant to reduce the fracture or to push the guide wire distally. Once the guide wire is across the fracture, it should be pushed distally so that it is centrally located in the anteroposterior and lateral fluoroscope views. If the guide wire is placed close to the medial or lateral supracondylar cortices, the reamers and nail will be similarly placed and thus ensure a valgus or varus deformity (Fig. 52–25).

Once the guide wire is in position, the intramedullary canal can be reamed (see Fig. 52–23F). The size of the starting reamer will vary, but it usually measures 9 mm in diameter. The initial reamer is end-cutting, and subsequent reamers are side-cutting. Reaming should always be undertaken in 0.5-mm increments. If 1-mm increments are used, the chance of the reamer becoming stuck is much higher. Reaming should be undertaken until cortical chatter between the endosteal surface of the cortex and the reamer is heard. Generally, a 12-mm nail is used, with the surgeon having reamed to 13 or 13.5 mm. The length of the nail can be determined by preoperative measurement on radiographs, by direct measurement from a graduated guide wire, or by placement of a second guide wire outside the leg and visualization of both guide wires on the image intensifier. The appropriate nail length can be selected and the nail introduced (see Fig. 52–23G).

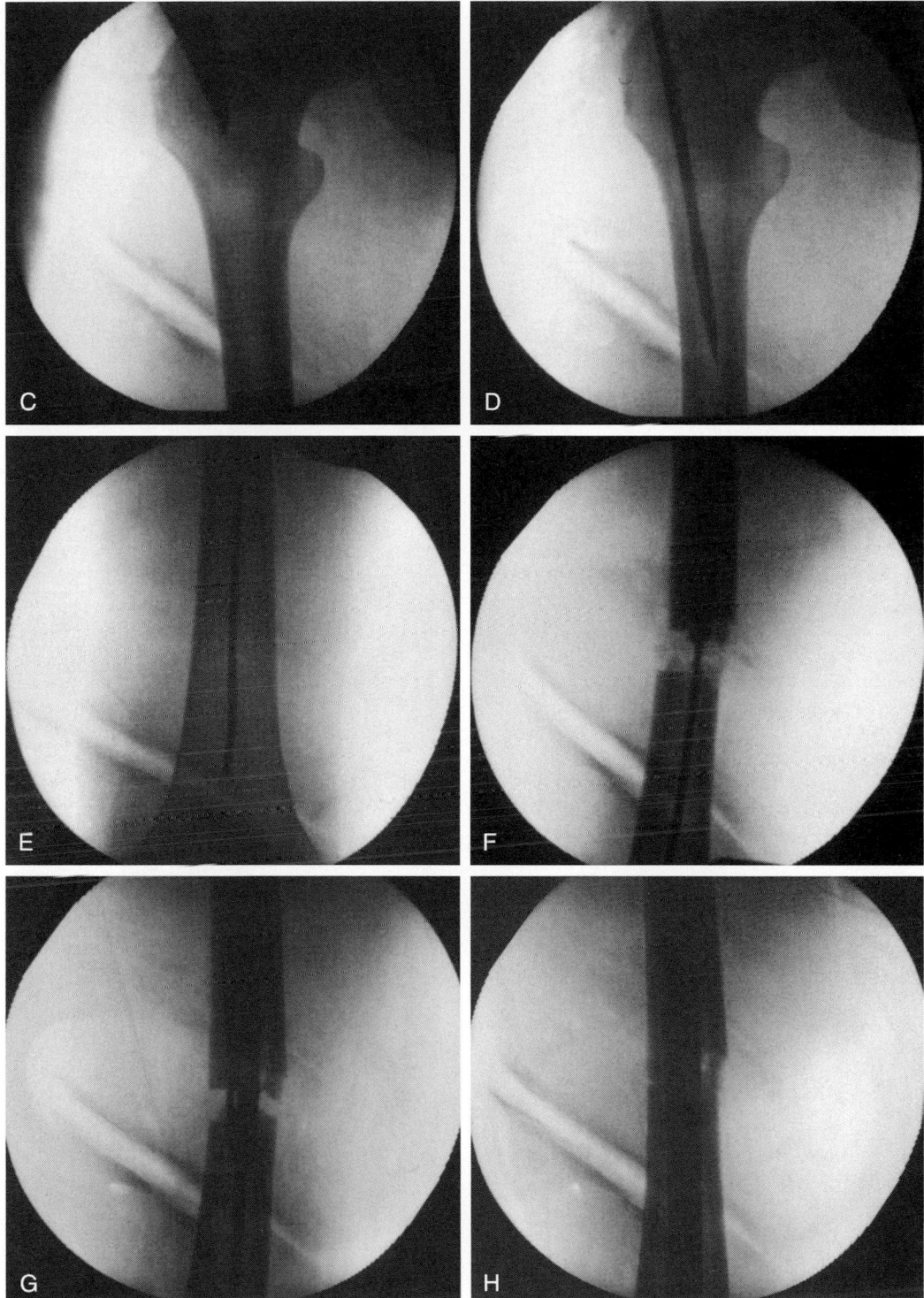

**FIGURE 52–23** *Continued. C,* The bone awl is placed in the piriformis fossa and the bone entered. An alternative to the use of a bone awl is to place a guide wire into the fossa and then drill over it. Either way, a hole of about 12 mm is required. *D,* A hand reamer is useful to penetrate the proximal femoral metaphysis. *E,* A guide wire is placed down the femur so that it is located centrally on both anteroposterior and lateral fluoroscopic views. If the wire is placed alongside the medial or lateral supracondylar ridges, malunion may result (see Fig. 52–25). *F,* The intramedullary canal is reamed. In this case, the fracture is distracted, which does not matter during reaming, but the gap must be closed during nailing. *G,* The nail has been passed over the fracture site. Traction is then discontinued. *H,* As the nail is hammered down the canal, the fracture gap closes and the fracture is stabilized.

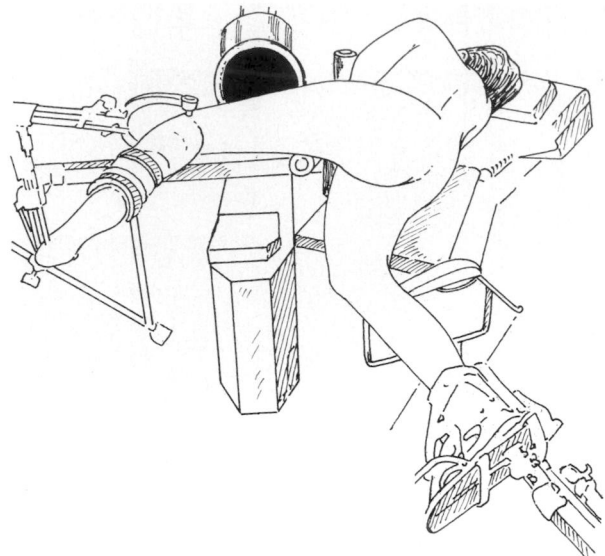

**FIGURE 52–24.** Diagrammatic representation of the lateral nailing position.

The surgeon should always reduce the fracture as the nail is passed across it to minimize cortical damage. The nail should be passed distally as far as the metaphysis. The surgeon should ensure on the anteroposterior and lateral fluoroscopic views that the nail is definitely within the femur and that malalignment or increased bone comminution has not occurred. The proximal screw or screws can be inserted with a jig, but the distal screw or screws are usually inserted freehand.

Freehand insertion of screws is straightforward (Fig. 52–26). The fluoroscope beam is placed 90° to the long axis of the femur in the midlateral plane. If the nail has rotated as it passed down the canal, the table and the patient may need to be rotated appropriately to compensate. Once the holes in the nail appear as perfect circles in the fluoroscope beam, the distal screws can be introduced (see Fig. 52–26A). A bone awl or Steinmann pin can be placed on the skin so that the point is seen in the center of the screw holes (see Fig. 52–26B). As this step is done, the surgeon should take care to keep hands out of the fluoroscope beam! A skin incision about 1.5 cm long is made, and dissecting scissors are used to open the muscle down to bone. A pointed instrument is then placed on the lateral cortex of the femur so that the tip is once again central in the screw hole as visualized in the fluoroscope beam (see Fig. 52–26B). The awl, Steinmann pin, or pointed drill bit is then used to make a divot in the femoral cortex, and a drill bit is used to penetrate the bone cortices and the nail. An appropriately sized screw is inserted. To check that the screw is passing through the nail, the screwdriver is removed, and partial insertion of the screw should obliterate the screw hole (see Fig. 52–26C). Surgeons frequently debate about whether one or two distal cross screws should be used. The author believes that one is sufficient unless the distal fragment is small enough to rotate around the distal screw or the bone is very osteoporotic. Hajek and colleagues[101] undertook a study of the use of one or two distal cross screws and concluded that one distal cross screw provides adequate distal fixation for femoral diaphyseal fractures.

Figure 52–14 indicates that in proximal diaphyseal femoral fractures, the proximal fragment tends to flex because of the unopposed action of the hip flexors. Traction may well not reduce the fracture. Use of the lateral

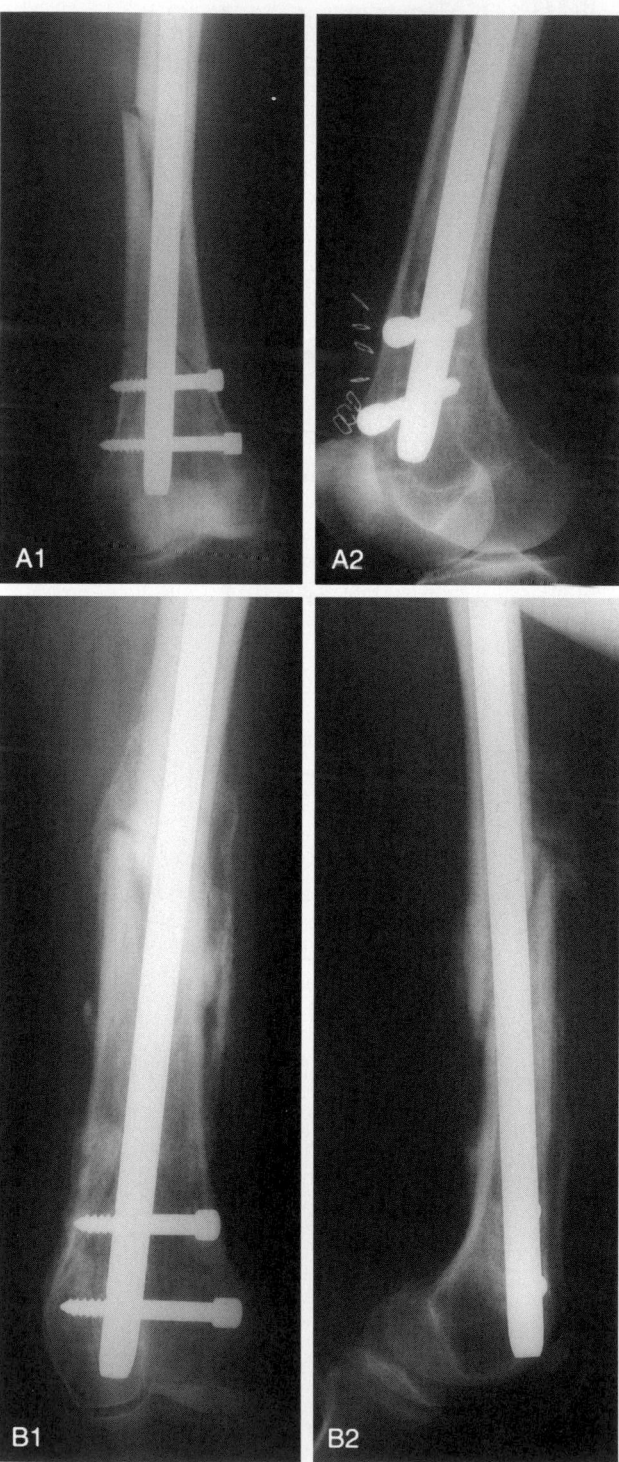

**FIGURE 52–25.** *A,* The fracture has been nailed with a valgus deformity because of inappropriate positioning of the guide wire in the distal end of the femur before reaming and nailing. *B,* The fracture is uniting. Reconstructive surgery was not undertaken because the patient was asymptomatic.

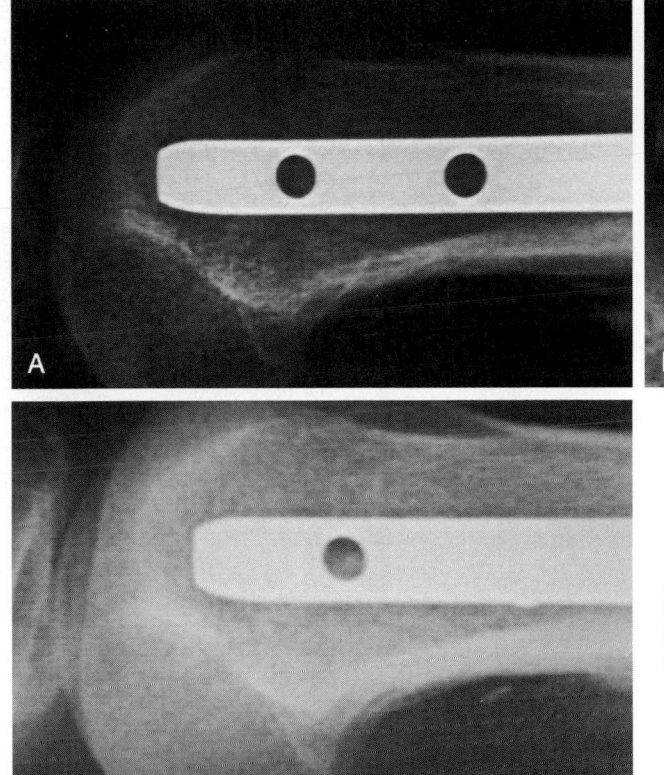

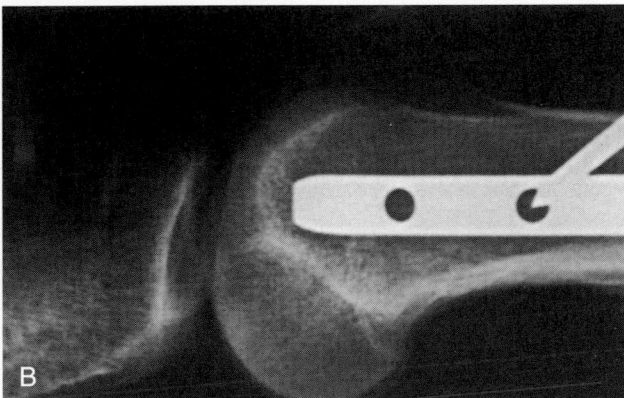

**FIGURE 52–26.** *A,* The fluoroscope beam is positioned so that the screw holes appear as perfect circles. *B,* A pointed awl, Steinmann pin, or drill bit is centered in the beam and a mark made on the cortex. *C,* The screw is inserted.

position means that the distal end of the femur can be placed so that a nail can be inserted, but this technique is not possible if the supine position is used. To reduce the proximal femoral fragment in the supine position, it is suggested that a short straight nail be introduced into the fragment through the conventional entry point in the piriformis fossa (Fig. 52–27). A short Küntscher nail is ideal. The nail can be used as a lever to reduce the proximal fragment, and a guide wire can be placed through the short nail and down the intramedullary canal. Obviously, the femur will then flex around the guide wire, but the

definitive nail can be used as a lever to reduce the fracture during nailing. The nail can then be passed down the canal in the usual manner.

If unreamed nails are used, the surgical technique is similar. The diameter of the nail should be calculated from the preoperative radiographs and the nails passed down the femoral canal. It is not unusual for an unreamed nail to distract the fracture site if the fracture is at or near the isthmus of the femur. If the fracture does become distracted as the nail is passed across it, the distal screw or screws should be inserted and the nail retracted by an

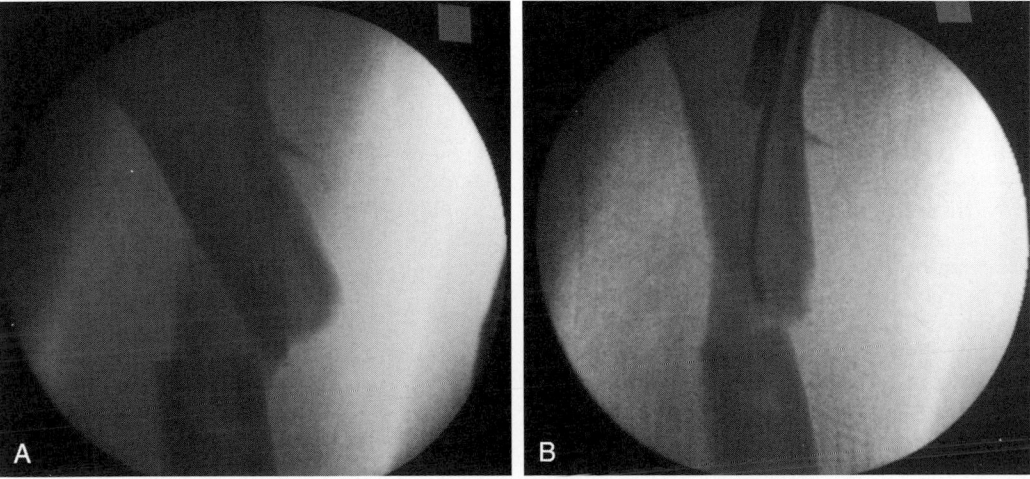

**FIGURE 52–27.** *A,* Proximal femoral diaphyseal fracture. Note the flexion of the proximal fragment. *B,* A short Küntscher nail has been used to reduce the proximal fragment, and the guide wire can now be passed over the fracture.

appropriate amount with the extraction equipment. This technique will close the fracture gap. The proximal screws can then be inserted.

An alternative to using a traction table for reamed or unreamed femoral nailing is the use of a femoral distractor.[9] This device has no specific advantages apart from allowing greater access in a multiply injured patient. The femur is distracted between two 5-mm Schanz screws inserted into the proximal and distal fragments. A proximal Schanz pin is inserted into the lesser trochanter, and the second Schanz screw is inserted 90° to the long axis of the femur just proximal to the condyles. Clearly, it is important that the Schanz screws not impede progress of the nail down the femur. Once reduction is achieved, the distractor is tightened and nailing undertaken in a conventional manner.

It is also possible to nail femoral fractures without a table or femoral distractor.[126, 228] Proponents of this technique point to the fact that traction on a fracture table can cause nerve palsies and may also make treatment of a polytrauma patient more difficult. A radiolucent operating table is required, and the patient is placed supine with the ipsilateral hip raised 30° to 45°. A standard proximal incision is made, and manual traction is used to reduce the fracture. The femur is then nailed in a conventional way. Good results have been reported.[228] All techniques of femoral nailing have advantages and disadvantages, and no individual method is superior to the others.

Postoperative management of femoral fractures is straightforward but clearly depends on the extent and severity of other injuries and whether the fracture is open. The author treats isolated closed fractures by immediate weight bearing, as tolerated by the patient, and physical therapy. The more severe the soft tissue injury, the greater the delay before weight bearing can be undertaken. Weight bearing is particularly important in elderly patients, who find it difficult to mobilize with non–weight bearing. Routine follow-up consists of monthly radiographs until union, with follow-up usually being undertaken until full function is achieved.

## INTRAMEDULLARY NAILING OF ADOLESCENT FEMORAL DIAPHYSEAL FRACTURES

In recent years, interest has increased in the use of interlocking intramedullary nailing in the management of femoral diaphyseal fractures in adolescents. Many of these patients are of adult size but still have open physes. The traditional method for management of pediatric femoral fractures has been nonoperative, but a number of papers in the 1980s advocated the use of intramedullary techniques.[107, 133, 279] Timmerman and Rab[241] reviewed 20 patients with 22 femoral fractures treated by intramedullary nails in a 6-year period. The average age of the patients was 13.8 years, and all had open physes. All the fractures united, and all patients with nailed femoral fractures were mobilizing by the second postoperative day. The authors found no evidence of premature closure of the proximal femoral, distal femoral, or trochanteric epiphyses. No nail-related infections, malunions, or leg length discrepancies occurred. Buford and colleagues[36] treated 60 patients with interlocking intramedullary nails. The aver-

age age was 12 years. Again, the results were good, with all fractures uniting in a mean time of 6 weeks. No infections, nerve palsies, or gait disturbances were observed. Two patients had subclinical avascular necrosis of the femoral head diagnosed by MRI, but neither patient was symptomatic.

Although intramedullary nailing of adolescent femoral fractures produces good results, avascular necrosis of the femoral head is undoubtedly the main complication and has been detailed by a number of authors.[4, 160, 239] The cause of the problem is not entirely understood, but it seems likely that avascular necrosis is due to damage to the medial circumflex artery near the piriformis fossa, which vascularizes much of the femoral head. Surgeons must balance the risk of avascular necrosis against the obvious benefits of intramedullary nailing when treating adolescent femoral fractures.

## INTRAMEDULLARY NAILING IN ELDERLY PATIENTS

The increasing number of femoral diaphyseal fractures in the elderly population detailed in the Epidemiology section of this chapter raises the problem of how to treat relatively large numbers of elderly patients. It is well understood that elderly patients do not tolerate prolonged bedrest and that plate fixation in osteopenic bone is problematic. Thus, intramedullary nailing provides the best solution to the problem. Bouchard and co-workers[25] thought that intramedullary nailing was probably advantageous for the elderly because it allowed early weight bearing. However, in an analysis of 138 patients older than 65 years, they could not demonstrate an advantage for any particular treatment method. They stressed the high complication rate (46%) and pointed out that 20% of patients died within 6 months. Age and mental status were the important determinants of survival.

Moran and colleagues[168] examined the problems of intramedullary nailing in elderly patients by analyzing a series of 24 fractures in patients with an average age of 77 years. They also had a high mortality (17%) and complication rate (54%). The authors pointed out the difficulties of operating on osteoporotic bone or below an osteoarthritic hip. They used cement augmentation in some osteoporotic fractures and in some cases had to operate from below the patient to compensate for a fixed flexion deformity. More practical alternatives are use of the lateral position or retrograde nailing, provided that the knee can be adequately flexed. Despite the difficulty of nailing osteoporotic femurs in the elderly population, it is the best method of management for fractures in this patient group.

## INTRAMEDULLARY NAILING IN THE MORBIDLY OBESE

McKee and Waddell[156] investigated the role of intramedullary nailing in the management of morbidly obese patients with a femoral fracture. They pointed out that 5 million Americans are morbidly obese and that orthopaedic surgeons in the United States might therefore be called on to treat these patients. They reported on seven patients with an average age of 41.8 years and an average weight of 300 lb. Four fractures were diaphyseal, two were subtrochanteric, and one patient had fractures in both the femoral neck and femoral diaphysis. All surgery was undertaken with the patient in the supine position. The average surgical time was 3.8 hours, and the mean blood loss exceeded 1 L.

The authors drew attention to the considerable difficulty in establishing the correct insertion point for the nail. This difficulty resulted in a fracture of the greater trochanter in two patients. They believed that this complication might have been avoided by use of the lateral position. The most common complications were deep venous thrombosis and pulmonary embolism. Deep venous thrombosis developed in four patients, and two had a pulmonary embolus, one being fatal. The authors highlighted the difficulties involved in nailing fractures in obese patients and suggested that close attention to surgical technique was required to produce a favorable outcome.

## INTRAMEDULLARY NAILING IN THE MULTIPLY INJURED

It has been accepted for 15 to 20 years that optimal treatment of multiply injured patients includes primary fixation of long bone fractures.[93, 123, 202, 220] Johnson and co-workers[124] reported a significant decrease in the incidence of ARDS in multiply injured patients whose major fractures were stabilized primarily. They also showed that the benefit was greatest in the most severely injured patients. It is self-evident that if early fracture stabilization is important, the femur must be key to the success of this philosophy. Delayed femoral stabilization or nonoperative management dooms the patient to a period of traction with the increased pulmonary and other complications associated with this method of management. Bone and colleagues[21] undertook a prospective randomized study to specifically examine the effect of early stabilization of femoral fractures. They looked at 178 patients younger than 65 years who had femoral fractures. They excluded hip fractures. Two groups of patients had isolated femoral fractures, and two groups were multiply injured, which was defined as an ISS higher than 18. One group of patients with isolated femoral fractures and one multiply injured group were treated with primary fracture fixation. All patients who had early fracture fixation fared better than those whose fixation was delayed, regardless of whether the femoral fracture was isolated or the patient was multiply injured. In the isolated fracture group, the differences were less apparent clinically, with more patients having abnormal blood gas results in the delayed group. However, in the multiply injured patients, delay in femoral fracture treatment increased the incidence of significant pulmonary complications and led to an increased number of days in the intensive care unit and hospital. Behrman and associates[11] carried out a similar study but divided the patients according to the degree of injury as assessed by the ISS. They had three categories of patients: an ISS of 0 to 15, 16 to 35, and above 35. All categories benefited from early femoral fracture fixation, with particular benefit being noted in the more severely injured groups and in older patients.

It is fair to say that in the late 1980s and the early 1990s,

many surgeons regarded the management of femoral fractures in multiply injured patients as straightforward. Research had shown that early fracture fixation was important, and the literature suggested that intramedullary nailing was the best technique. However, research from Hannover, Germany, challenged this view. Pape and co-workers[187] retrospectively examined 766 multiply injured patients. One hundred six had an ISS higher than 18, a midshaft femoral fracture, primary admission or early referral within 8 hours, and no death from head injury or hemorrhage. These patients were divided into four groups depending on whether they had a severe chest injury and whether femoral stabilization was undertaken within 24 hours. In patients with severe chest trauma, they found a higher incidence of post-traumatic ARDS and mortality in the group treated by early femoral intramedullary nailing. The same research group[188] also investigated the effect of reamed and unreamed nailing on lung function and pulmonary hemodynamics in multiply injured patients. They found that lung function was stable in patients treated with a small-diameter unreamed femoral nail but deteriorated if a reamed femoral nail was used, only to improve after 48 hours. They also found that pulmonary artery pressure did not change during unreamed femoral nailing but, in the reamed group, showed a statistically significant increase and took an hour to return to normal. They postulated that this increase in pressure could trigger ARDS in patients who might already be at risk for the complication, and they theorized that unreamed nailing might allow early fracture stabilization without any deleterious effect on lung function. A third study from the same group[189] compared different reamer types to see whether the physical characteristics of the reamer head affected pulmonary function. They used a sheep model and compared three different types of reamers. As in their previous studies, they found that intramedullary nailing caused a significant increase in pulmonary artery pressure but showed that the effect on pulmonary function varied with the design of the reamer.

These studies from Hannover undoubtedly caused considerable interest, and a number of animal and clinical studies were undertaken to investigate the role of intramedullary fixation in multiply injured patients. Wozasek and colleagues[273] used a sheep model and treated four groups of sheep in different ways. In group 1, they undertook closed nailing of the intact femur and tibia. In group 2, the animals sustained hypovolemic shock and reperfusion before closed nailing. In group 3, the sheep were treated in the same way as group 2 animals but were infused with *Escherichia coli* endotoxin 24 and 48 hours after surgery. Group 4 animals were merely exposed to endotoxin without any surgical procedure. The authors concluded that although intramedullary nailing causes a moderate increase in pulmonary artery pressure, it does not lead to increased lung permeability and that it is the hypovolemic shock, despite adequate resuscitation, that leads to postoperative lung disturbance. A later study from the same group[174] compared reamed nailing, unreamed nailing, and plate fixation in a sheep model. These authors analyzed femoral intramedullary pressure, fat embolization, and pulmonary response. They showed that the highest intramedullary pressure was caused by reamed nailing and occurred when the initial 9-mm reamer was passed. Similar average pressures were seen during the insertion of an unreamed 9-mm nail, but low pressure was noted during femoral plating. Embolization was associated with use of the bone awl, 9-mm reamer, or the unreamed 9-mm nail, and pulmonary arterial pressure did not vary significantly between the three groups. They concluded that differences in pulmonary hemodynamic response were only minimal, even in the presence of thoracic trauma.

Wolinsky and colleagues[272] used a sheep model and created an ARDS-like state by intravenous infusion of *Perilla* ketone before reamed nailing of a femoral osteotomy. The results were compared with those of sheep that had no pulmonary dysfunction. They found no evidence that reamed intramedullary nailing in an appropriately resuscitated sheep had a clinically significant effect on pulmonary dysfunction. Willis and associates[267] undertook a study in rats and showed that femoral fracture with intramedullary fixation causes lung capillary leakage that is not increased by femoral reaming. Fracture by itself did not cause pulmonary dysfunction, and they thought that pulmonary complications after femoral fractures were probably the result of prolonged immobilization, massive blood transfusion, fluid overload, underlying illness, aspiration of gastric contents, or activation of the systemic inflammatory response. They stated that the clinical advantages of reaming outweighed any particular disadvantages associated with the use of intramedullary nails.

## CLINICAL STUDIES

Charash and colleagues[42] retrospectively reviewed patients by using the same criteria as Pape and co-workers[187]; the ISS was greater than 18, the femoral fracture was in the midshaft and was treated by reamed intramedullary nailing, and the patients did not die of head injury or hemorrhagic shock. They used the same four surgical groups, which differed in the time of surgery and the presence of a severe chest injury. These investigators stressed that the four groups had no significant demographic differences. However, contrary to Pape and colleagues' findings, they found significantly more pulmonary complications associated with delayed nailing. Further studies have shown exactly the same results.[26, 39, 251] The methodology used in all these studies was similar to that of Pape and colleagues[187] and Charash and associates,[42] although Carlson and co-workers[39] examined the effects of reamed and unreamed femoral fixation in addition to comparing nailing results in patients with and without chest injuries. Boulanger and co-workers[26] used the same methodology as Charash and colleagues[42] and arrived at the same conclusions. Van den Made and associates[251] compared three groups consisting of patients with thoracic injury and femoral fracture, patients with thoracic injury but no fracture, and those with a femoral fracture but no thoracic trauma. They found no significant different in the incidence of ARDS in patients with nailed femoral fractures regardless of whether they had thoracic trauma. Carlson and co-workers retrospectively examined four groups of patients.[39] In addition to patients with chest trauma but no fracture and patients without chest trauma but with femoral fractures treated by reamed intramedullary nailing, they also examined two groups that had chest injury and

were treated by reamed nailing or unreamed methods, including Rush nails, plates, or external fixation. The conclusion from this paper was that patients treated with reamed nailing fared better than those treated with unreamed methods. An obvious concern about this study is that intramedullary nailing is a superior technique for managing femoral fractures, and perhaps the poor results in the unreamed group could actually be attributable to the use of less effective fixation methods. Bone and colleagues[22] also undertook a retrospective comparative study of patients who had their femoral fractures treated by reamed nails or plates. Their results showed that the lowest incidence of pulmonary complications followed reamed femoral nailing, and their conclusion was that the thoracic trauma, not the femoral fracture, governed the development of late pulmonary complications.

A large retrospective study using a similar methodology was undertaken in two U.S. Level I trauma centers.[24] Multiply injured patients with a thoracic injury were compared in a center that routinely used reamed intramedullary nailing and one that treated femoral fractures by plating. The patient population and the protocols for patient management were similar in the two centers. The overall incidence of ARDS in patients with femoral fracture was 2% in both centers, as compared with 6% and 8% in patients with thoracic trauma but no fracture. No difference was noted in the incidence of ARDS, pneumonia, pulmonary embolism, multiple organ failure, or mortality in the patients who had the femoral fracture nailed or plated.

Christie[50] performed transesophageal echocardiography in a large number of patients to investigate the embolic events associated with medullary instrumentation. In a report of 160 patients, he showed that 92% had fat and marrow embolization during intramedullary procedures that included reamed nailing of femoral and tibial fractures, nailing of metastatic deposits or fractures, and cemented and uncemented hemiarthroplasty. He showed that severe embolic events occurred mainly in patients with pathologic deposits or in patients undergoing cemented hemiarthroplasty, these being elderly patients being treated for proximal femoral fractures. The author noted significant embolic showers in the right atrium of 10% of the patients who had femoral reaming, but he failed to correlate these findings with clinical problems. Friedl and colleagues[84] retrospectively compared primary nailing in multiply injured patients with those who had primary external fixation and secondary nailing at least 5 days after the injury. The early-nailing group had an ISS averaging 21.4, a 12.5% mortality rate, and a 25% incidence of ARDS. The delayed-nailing group had no ARDS or deaths, and the authors recommended that primary intramedullary nailing was safe in patients with an ISS below 25 and should be delayed for at least 5 days if the ISS was above 40. This work raises the possibility that the extent of injury is important and patients with very severe injuries may be at risk from primary nailing.

The conclusion to be drawn from these studies is that primary reamed intramedullary nailing seems to be perfectly safe in most patients. Pulmonary complications are largely dictated by the initial parenchymal or thoracic damage and by the degree of hypovolemia. Some evidence indicates that even if resuscitation is adequate, pulmonary complications follow hypovolemia. It is indisputable that reamed intramedullary nailing is superior to other methods in treating isolated femoral fractures, and in patients with thoracic injury, it seems to give better results than plating, flexible nails, and external fixation. No good studies have directly compared unreamed and reamed nailing, but there seems to be little clinical evidence that raised intramedullary pressure is associated with clinical pulmonary dysfunction.

It is important to remember, however, that surgeons should not insist on using intramedullary nailing in severely injured patients whose clinical condition gives rise to concern. If it is thought that surgery should be expeditiously performed, a primary femoral external fixator followed by secondary nailing will give good results.[84, 177] These very severely injured patients are very likely to have preoperative pulmonary dysfunction and head injury, and it has been shown that the time taken to nail a difficult femoral fracture increases the risk of secondary brain injury.[246] The majority of patients treated by most orthopaedic surgeons will be suitable for primary reamed femoral nailing, but if secondary injury is a concern, delayed nailing can produce excellent results.

## INTRAMEDULLARY NAILING OF OPEN FRACTURES

When a new technique is introduced, surgeons are understandably apprehensive about extending the indications for its use to progressively more severe fractures. In the mid-1980s, surgeons were fairly happy about treating Gustilo type I and II open fractures with primary intramedullary nailing but still thought that external fixation was preferable for type III fractures[11] (see Fig. 52–9). This view was first challenged by Lhowe and Hansen,[148] who undertook intramedullary nailing in 42 selected patients with open femoral fractures, 8 (19%) of which were Gustilo type III in severity. Their results and those of later studies are given in Table 52–11. They had no nonunions and a 4.8% incidence of infection. They believed that their results were comparable to those associated with the management of closed fractures and that the technique allowed immediate control of the fracture and the soft tissues, easier access to the open wound, and rapid mobilization of the patient.

Brumback and colleagues[31] undertook a retrospective study of acute femoral fractures treated by a Level I trauma center after blunt trauma. They also reported on a selected series of patients that excluded Gustilo type IIIc fractures and patients who had severe contamination or extensive multiple injuries. Their results were good, with no nonunions and a 3.4% incidence of infection (see Table 52–11). These authors pointed out that 58.7% of their Gustilo type III fractures were IIIb in severity and that all three of their infections occurred in this group, for an infection rate in Gustilo type IIIb fractures of 11.1%. This group of patients tended to be treated by delayed intramedullary nailing, but the authors pointed out that two of the infections occurred after delayed nailing, which raises the possibility that the delay was unnecessary.

O'Brien and co-workers[178] documented a series of 63 open femoral fractures treated by reamed intramedullary nailing. These fractures were unselected, the surgeons having elected to nail all open femoral fractures. Table 52–11 shows that most of the fractures followed motor vehicle accidents and, in fact, only 6% were gunshot injuries. The results were comparable with those of the earlier unselected series. They documented an aseptic nonunion rate of 4.8% and an infection rate of 4.8%, but stated that they only had one (1.6%) case of osteomyelitis and no septic nonunions. Grosse and coauthors[96] reported on a large series of unselected fractures from Edinburgh, Scotland, and Strasbourg, France. They had a very high incidence of multiply injured patients, with most of their patients being injured in motor vehicle accidents. Only three (2.6%) had gunshot injuries. The authors reported good results (see Table 52–11) but noted two transient sciatic nerve palsies and a femoral neck fracture. They examined joint motion in some detail and showed that the patients did not have any hip stiffness. The average knee flexion after treatment was 135°, with all but three patients achieving more than 120° of flexion. They recommended reamed intramedullary nailing for all open femoral fractures regardless of the severity of the soft tissue injury. Rütter and colleagues[208] reported results similar to those of Grosse and co-workers in a study from Utrecht, Holland. They used reamed nails to treat 28 patients. These authors examined fracture morphology and predictably showed that nine (32.1%) were AO/OTA type C, with eight of these injuries being C3 fractures associated with considerable comminution. Table 52–11 shows that 82.1% of the patients were multiply injured, and they noted that 57.1% of the patients had at least four fractures. Williams and co-workers[266] looked at 42 patients with

---

**TABLE 52–11**

Results of Studies of the Role of Intramedullary Nailing in the Treatment of Open Femoral Fractures

| | N | Age (yr) | Multiply Injured (%) | MVA (%) | GIII* (%) | GIIIb* (%) | Union (wk) | Infection (%) | Nonunion (%) |
|---|---|---|---|---|---|---|---|---|---|
| Lhowe and Hansen[148] | 42 | 21.8 | 66.6 | 78.6 | 19.0 | ? | ? | 4.8 | 0 |
| Brumback et al.[31] | 89 | 29.1 | ? | 87.6 | 51.7 | 58.7 | 22.5 | 3.4 | 0 |
| O'Brien et al.[178] | 63 | 28 | 83 | 83 | 23.8 | ? | ? | 4.8 | 4.8 |
| Grosse et al.[96] | 115 | 25 | 92.5 | 84.3 | 32.2 | 32.4 | 22.3 | 2.6 | 3.5 |
| Rütter et al.[208] | 28 | 28 | 82.1 | 75 | 32.1 | 55.5 | ? | 7.1 | 0 |
| Williams et al.[266] | 42 | 36.1 | 60 | 71 | 33.3 | 35.7 | 16.5 | 2.4 | 2.4 |

*G refers to the Gustilo fracture grade. The incidence of Gustilo IIIb fractures is expressed as a percentage of Gustilo grade III fractures.
*Abbreviation:* MVA, motor vehicle accident.

open femoral fractures. Only one (2.4%) patient had a gunshot injury, with most patients being injured in motor vehicle accidents. They reported good results.

Table 52–11 shows that the results of treatment of open femoral fractures with reamed intramedullary nails are remarkably good. Analysis of all the data in the six studies detailed in Table 52–11 shows an overall infection rate of 3.7% with a 2.4% incidence of nonunion. All the infections seem to have occurred in Gustilo type II and type IIIb fractures. Without doubt, intramedullary nailing of open fractures confers considerable advantages over other techniques. Flexible nailing does not stabilize comminuted, segmental, or spiral fractures adequately, and external fixation is associated with pin tract sepsis, nonunion, and joint stiffness.

Optimal results in the management of any open fracture are related more to the skill with which the soft tissues are treated than to the type of implant used. Unlike the tibia, no studies have compared different types of fixation in the management of open femoral fractures, but as with open tibial fractures, it is the skill of the initial débridement and later handling of the soft tissue defect that will govern the long-term prognosis. Thus, the good results shown in Table 52–11 can be attributed in part to the fact that the studies came from major trauma centers staffed by experienced orthopaedic trauma surgeons.

The importance of débridement is often understated, with surgeons concentrating on different types of fixation rather than the soft tissues. Court-Brown and Zych[61] detailed the operation of débridement, which consists of thorough exploration of all affected tissues and excision of all devitalized or dubious tissue. It is mandatory that all open wounds associated with femoral fractures be surgically explored. The surgeon should look for areas of degloving, although degloving of the thigh is less frequent than in the leg. If any skin has been degloved, it should be resected until adequate dermal bleeding is encountered.

All affected tissue planes must be opened and explored for retained debris or damaged soft tissue. To do so, the open wound will have to be extended proximally and distally. The wound should be digitally examined to allow assessment of where the damaged soft tissues are. All affected soft tissue must then be explored and all devitalized soft tissue removed. Skin is very resistant to direct damage, and usually only the skin edges need to be resected. The obvious exception is degloving, which is more commonly seen in elderly patients. All devitalized fat must be removed. The extent of fat necrosis may well be greater than was apparent preoperatively, and the surgeon may have to resect more overlying skin in patients with significant devitalization of subcutaneous fat. Damaged muscle provides the most significant problem for the surgeon. Failure to remove damaged muscle increases the risk of infection significantly, and failure to exposure damaged muscle may leave retained material that can cause an anaerobic infection.

It can be difficult to assess muscle viability, particularly if the patient is hypotensive. The classic signs of muscle viability are color, consistency, contractility to mechanical stimuli, and bleeding. If the patient is peripherally shut down, muscles can be difficult to assess properly. The best sign is muscle contractility, but it is important that the

surgeon be guided by the appearance and consistency of the muscle as well. Muscle that is shredded or disintegrates on touch should be excised. The surgeon should not hesitate to excise a considerable quantity of muscle if required. At the end of a successful débridement procedure, only viable muscle tissue should remain. Bone resection is also important in the débridement of open fractures. This topic always excites debate among orthopaedic surgeons because of the relative difficulty in reconstructing the bone. However, with modern bone grafting and bone transport techniques, surgeons should not be afraid to remove all devitalized bone. This problem will arise mainly in AO/OTA C3 fractures with significant comminution. In the Epidemiology section of this chapter, it was reported that 22.2% of open femoral fractures in Edinburgh were C3 fractures. This figure compares with the 32% reported by Rütter and colleagues.[208] Segmental (C2) fractures rarely require significant bone resection because the bone segment virtually always has a good vascular supply. The longer the segment, the less the potential vascular problem. It is important to reexplore the open wound about 48 hours after the initial débridement. It is not always possible to know whether the surgeon has been successful in removing all dead and devitalized tissue, so a second-look procedure should be undertaken. Other factors such as the administration of antibiotics and wound lavage are dealt with in Chapter 13.

## PLASTIC SURGERY

Very little is known about the requirement for plastic surgery after open femoral fracture. In the six studies detailed in Table 52–11, only Rütter and colleagues did not document how the soft tissue defects were treated. All the other studies did, and no patients required flap cover. Court-Brown and Quaba[62] examined the relationship between plastic surgery and orthopaedic trauma surgery and documented the frequency of plastic surgical intervention in different open fractures. They found that the greatest requirement for plastic surgery follows open fractures of the ankle, tibial diaphysis, and tibial plafond, with 55% of these patients needing plastic surgery to close the soft tissues. They found that 29% of patients with open femoral fractures required plastic surgery but that all the soft tissue defects were closed with split-skin grafting. They showed that 16.6% of Gustilo type 1 fractures required split-skin grafting as compared with 42.8% of type II, 66.8% of type IIIa, and 45% of type IIIb fractures. The high incidence of split-skin grafting in Gustilo type IIIa fractures reflects the increased incidence of degloving in this group of fractures.

## INTRAMEDULLARY NAILING OF GUNSHOT INJURIES

A specific type of open fracture is the gunshot femoral fracture (see Fig. 52–10). This problem is of obvious interest, particularly in the United States, where many of the large trauma centers have to deal with gunshot fractures. However, it is not a significant problem in civilian practice outside the United States, and even within the United States, it is mainly confined to certain areas. Table

52–4 shows that most open femoral fractures occur in motor vehicle accidents and that the number of open femoral fractures caused by gunshots is relatively small. It is, however, an important topic because of certain major differences between gunshot femoral fractures and those caused by a motor vehicle accident. The fracture morphology and soft tissue damage caused by gunshots to the femur vary with the muscle velocity of the weapon. Low-velocity injuries associated with a muzzle velocity of less than 2000 ft/sec are commonly seen in civilian practice, with high-velocity injuries being associated mainly with military weapons.

### Low-Velocity Gunshot Fractures

Treatment of low-velocity gunshot femoral fractures has been documented in a number of studies.[14, 175, 176, 242, 271, 274] The results of these studies are shown in Table 52–12. Just as surgeons were slow in adopting the technique of nailing Gustilo type III open fractures, they were also slow in adopting immediate nailing of low-velocity gunshot femoral fractures. Wiss and colleagues[271] adhered to the conventional view at the time that isolated low-velocity gunshot femoral fractures should be treated by delayed nailing. They used immediate nailing only if the victim had limb-threatening injuries. Table 52–12 shows that their results were good, with no infections or nonunions. The other studies detailed in Table 52–12 all used immediate nailing with good results. It can be seen that the age of the patients was similar in all studies and that the degree of comminution as measured by the Winquist-Hansen system was also similar. Wright and co-workers[274] reported a higher number of nonunions, but unlike the other series, they discussed the management of patients with bone loss. They had two patients who were both successfully treated by bone grafting. The authors demonstrated that immediate intramedullary fixation of low-velocity femoral fractures resulted in a shorter hospital stay than required with other techniques. This conclusion was supported by Levy and associates,[146] who showed that the average hospital stay was 7 days and that the hospital saved up to $9000 when compared with delayed nailing.

The results of the studies detailed in Table 52–12 are very similar, and analysis of the table indicates that the prognosis for low-velocity gunshot femoral fractures is good. Overall, the infection rate for the six series was 0.4% and the incidence of nonunion was 2.2%. A comparison with Table 52–11, which shows the results of open fractures mainly caused by motor vehicle accidents, indicates that the prognosis after low-velocity gunshot injuries is better. Table 52–12 also shows the incidence of Gustilo type IIIc fractures in the studies dealing with low-velocity gunshot injuries. The overall incidence of type IIIc fractures in these studies is 5.2%. All were treated by vein grafts, and only one patient subsequently required an amputation.[175] Undeniably, immediate intramedullary nailing is the treatment of choice for low-velocity gunshot femoral fractures, with reconstruction of the femoral artery undertaken in Gustilo type IIIc fractures. Figure 52–10 illustrates the use of primary external fixation to achieve rapid femoral stabilization to allow investigation and treatment of arterial damage.

Tejan and Lind[237] published a good overview of the management of gunshot injuries of the femur and summarized the overall treatment of these injuries. The assessment and initial management of low-velocity gunshot injuries is the same as for injuries that follow other causes. Standard anteroposterior and lateral radiographs are essential to delineate the extent and severity of the fracture. A thorough history and examination are required, and it is mandatory that the neurovascular status of the limb be assessed. In the studies detailed in Table 52–12, the six sciatic and five peroneal nerve palsies reported indicate that 6.7% of patients had a significant nerve lesion. If evidence of major vascular damage is apparent, immediate angiography is essential. Any arterial damage should be treated by interpositional vein grafting. However, most patients will not have evidence of vascular damage, and the question of how to treat the soft tissue injuries must be considered. Unlike open femoral fractures after blunt trauma, it is accepted that low-velocity gunshot fractures do not require full débridement. Local wound care plus irrigation with or without an antiseptic solution is usually adequate, but antibiotic prophylaxis is required for up to 24 hours.[237] A second-generation cephalosporin is generally used, but it may be combined with an aminoglycoside.

### High-Velocity Gunshot Fractures

Management of high-velocity gunshot femoral fractures is very different from that of low-velocity injuries, and in fact, it is the same as for open fractures caused by blunt injuries. Accordingly, extensive initial débridement must be performed initially, with further débridement after 48 hours and later wound closure. Antibiotic administration

---

**TABLE 52–12**  ·················································································

Data from Studies of Gunshot Femoral Fractures

| | N | Age (yr) | GIIIc* (%) | WH3 and 4* (%) | Union (wk) | Nonunion (%) | Infection (%) |
|---|---|---|---|---|---|---|---|
| Wiss et al.[271] | 56 | 29 | 9 | 93 | 23 | 0 | 0 |
| Wright et al.[274] | 18 | 30 | 5.6 | 83.3 | ? | 16.7 | 0 |
| Bergman et al.[14] | 65 | 24 | 1.5 | 98.5 | 18 | 0 | 0 |
| Nowotarski and Brumback[176] | 39 | 26 | 5.1 | 76.9 | 14 | 5.1 | 2.6 |
| Nicholas and McCoy[175] | 14 | 26.6 | 21.4 | 100 | 23.8 | 7.1 | 0 |
| Tornetta and Tiburzi[242] | 38 | 28 | 0 | 86.8 | 8.6 | 0 | 0 |

·································································································

*G refers to the Gustilo grade and WH refers to the Winquist-Hansen fracture grade.

is mandatory. It is difficult to detail the optimal method of fracture fixation because most of these injuries occur in wartime and definitive treatment often has to be delayed. Most military surgeons use external fixation for primary management of these injuries and then evacuate the patient to a secondary hospital where definitive management can be undertaken.

In recent wars such as the war in old Yugoslavia, about 45% of open wounds were in the soldiers' lower limbs.[113] Hodalic and colleagues[113] documented a relatively high incidence of traumatic amputations because 90% of the injuries in Croatia were caused by a blast. They stated that 156 leg amputations were performed in 1211 patients during the 1991–1992 Serbian offensive. Islinger and associates[117] examined the casualties from three recent conflicts involving U.S. personnel. It is interesting to note that the rate of amputation associated with extremity trauma has not declined significantly since the Vietnam War.[117]

### Gustilo Type IIIc Fractures

Table 52–12 shows that the reported incidence of Gustilo type IIIc fractures associated with low-velocity gunshot femoral fractures varies between 0% and 21% and averages 5.2%. The prognosis is clearly very good if adequate vascular surgery facilities are available. However, such is certainly not the case for high-velocity or blast injuries, and it does not appear to be the case for blunt trauma after motor vehicle accidents. DiChristina and coauthors[72] stated that the literature reported a 20% to 50% amputation rate in type IIIc femoral fractures caused by blunt trauma. Court-Brown and Quaba[62] commented that all seven of the Gustilo type IIIc fractures in the 62 open femoral fractures in their series eventually necessitated amputation despite a number of successful primary vein

grafts. It is impossible to set adequate criteria to predict the success of limb salvage in Gustilo type IIIc fractures, although it has been attempted with the Mangled Extremity Severity Score.[119] However, this score is designed to predict the need for acute amputation. The real problem is predicting the need for amputation based on the medium- and long-term outcome, which remains very difficult. Unquestionably, vascular injuries associated with femoral fractures caused by blunt trauma have a poor prognosis.

## INTRAMEDULLARY NAILING OF METASTATIC FRACTURES

Management of pathologic fractures is discussed in detail in Chapter 16. However, some important points about intramedullary nailing of impending or actual femoral metastatic fractures should be made (Fig. 52–28). This technique has become established as the best method of treating metastatic fractures of the femur, with methyl methacrylate sometimes being used to fill large bone defects. Patients with femoral metastases are often in poor physical condition and have a poor prognosis. Intramedullary nailing is a good option in these patients because they can mobilize to full weight bearing after treatment and the stability of fixation is superior to that achieved by plating or external fixation. The use of cephalomedullary, or reconstruction, nails has extended the indications for intramedullary femoral nailing in metastatic fractures in that the fixation gained by inserting the proximal screw into the femoral head and neck means that subtrochanteric and intertrochanteric metastases can be treated with intramedullary nails. Van Doorn and Stapert[253] described the use of a long cephalomedullary nail in the treatment of 101 patients with femoral metastases. They reported that 92% of their patients were mobile postoperatively and that

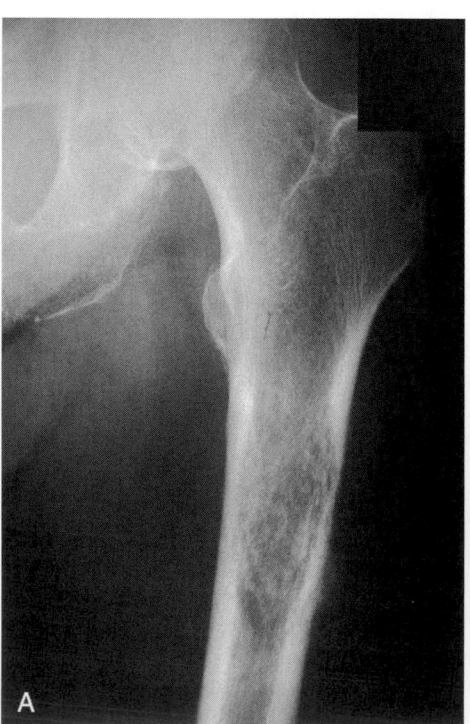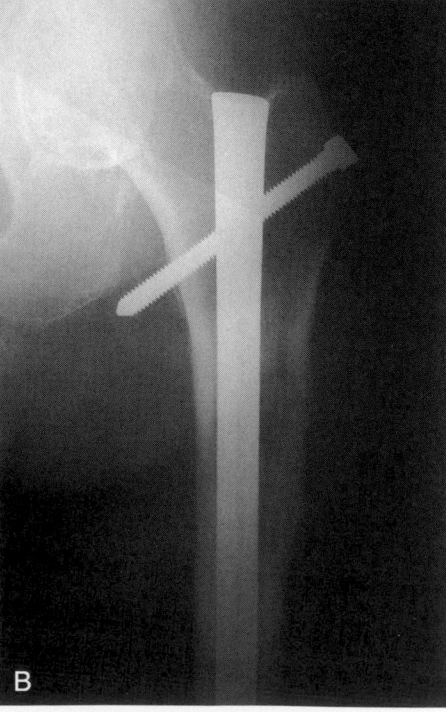

**Figure 52–28.** *A*, Anteroposterior radiograph of the proximal end of a femur showing a metastatic tumor deposit. Evidence of cortical damage is apparent, and the patient had been complaining of thigh pain for 2 weeks. *B*, The femur has been stabilized with a intramedullary nail.

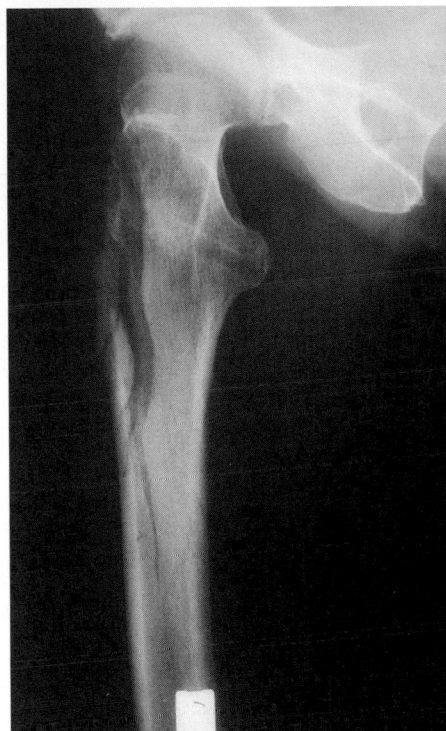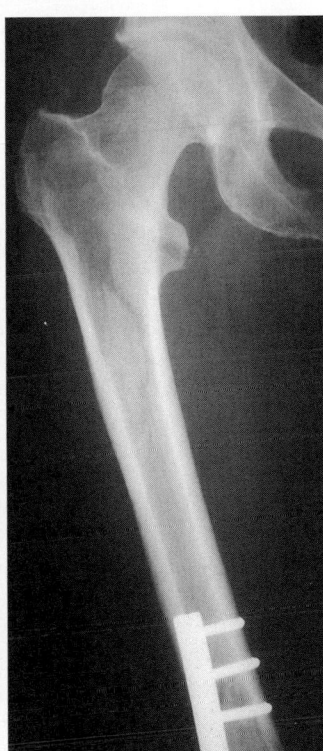

**FIGURE 52–29.** Anteroposterior and lateral radiographs demonstrating the potential problem of an eccentric starting point. In this case, a posterior starting point has been used and the proximal femoral damage is obvious. This patient is the same one as in Figure 52–20.

pain was absent or acceptable in 93%. They suspected fat embolism in three patients. However, other surgeons have reported a higher incidence of acute pulmonary dysfunction after intramedullary nailing of femoral metastases.[8, 50] Barwood and colleagues[8] reviewed 45 intramedullary nailing operations for femoral metastatic fractures and showed that acute oxygen desaturation and hypotension occurred in 11 patients and 3 died. Christie[50] reported a 10% mortality rate after nailing femoral metastatic fractures.

Cole and associates[53] compared the use of reamed and unreamed nails in the management of femoral metastatic fractures. They recorded two perioperative deaths, both from fat embolism. One death followed reamed nailing and the other occurred after unreamed nailing. They documented no difference in the results of reamed and unreamed nailing. Currently, intramedullary nailing is the best method of treating impending or actual metastatic femoral fractures. However, these patients are frequently debilitated, and perioperative mortality of up to 10% has been reported.[50]

## COMPLICATIONS OF ANTEGRADE INTRAMEDULLARY NAILING

A number of complications such as nonunion, infection, and compartment syndrome are not specific to any particular method of management, although the incidence of these complications will vary with the method of management. All operative techniques, however, are associated with specific complications, and antegrade intramedullary nailing of the femur is no exception. Surgeons have documented a number of different complications specific to this technique.

### Proximal Femoral Comminution

Failure to select the correct starting point means that an intramedullary nail can be placed eccentrically within the intramedullary canal of the femur. A common error is to place the starting point too lateral and insert the nail lateral to the greater trochanter. If this mistake is made, the nail may be passed medially and damage the medial femoral cortex. A similar problem can occur if the starting point is too anterior or posterior (Fig. 52–29). Clearly, if too medial a point is chosen, the surgeon may damage the base of the neck of the femur and cause a fracture, but this complication is so obvious that its incidence is low.

Surgeons who use more flexible slotted intramedullary nails will have a greater margin of error when inserting a nail because the nail will tend to curve once it makes contact with the medial wall of the proximal intramedullary canal. However, in recent years, surgeons have favored stiffer unslotted nails, and insertion of these nails demands greater attention to detail regarding the nail entry point.[90] Proximal comminution is rarely a problem provided that the complication is recognized and a statically locked intramedullary nail is used. If, however, the comminution extends proximal to the lesser trochanter, the surgeon should substitute a reconstruction nail, which will gain fixation in the femoral head and neck, for the conventional interlocking nail. This problem is rare, and usually a statically locked nail is all that is required to treat increased proximal comminution.

### Fracture Propagation

In the same way that an intramedullary nail can cause proximal femoral comminution, it can also cause increased comminution at the fracture site, particularly if unrecognized undisplaced fractures are already present. Under most circumstances, such comminution should not be a problem provided that the nail is statically locked. However, it is possible to displace an undisplaced intra-articular fracture running distally from a low femoral diaphyseal fracture. This fracture pattern is more common in fractures in the elderly population, and not infrequently the periosteum is actually intact around the fracture extension. However, if the surgeon is concerned about displacing such a fracture, interfragmentary screws should be placed across the fracture before nailing.

### Heterotopic Ossification

Heterotopic ossification in the hip abductors after intramedullary nailing is common and has been reported in up to 68% of cases.[154] It may take the form of a small ossified area just proximal to the end of the nail (Fig. 52–30), but occasionally, the area of ossification may be much more extensive and cause restriction of hip abduction and even ankylosis of the hip joint. The most common symptom related to heterotopic ossification is pain, with the pain being felt over the area of the greater trochanter and proximal part of the thigh.

Dodenhoff and colleagues[73] analyzed 80 patients in an attempt to assess the incidence and causes of persistent proximal thigh pain. Thirty-three (41.2%) patients complained of pain severe enough to interfere with their lifestyle or mobility. The pain was situated in the trochanteric area in 22 patients and in the proximal part of the thigh in a further 9 patients. One patient complained of pain in the operative scar. Statistical analysis showed no correlation between pain and age or nail prominence above the proximal end of the femur. However, significantly more males complained of pain than females, and a significant association was noted between pain and the presence of heterotopic ossification. The more extensive the heterotopic ossification, the more severe the pain. The authors found that prominent proximal screws and nail fracture caused proximal pain in some patients. Nail removal resulted in relief of pain in 64.7% of the patients.

Brumback and co-workers[32] undertook an extensive analysis of heterotopic ossification after femoral nailing and derived a scoring system that has been used by other authors. They divided patients into four categories based on the size of the ossific area. Grade 1 patients had an ossific focus of less than 1 cm. Grade 2 patients had ossific foci between 1 and 2 cm, with grade 3 patients having foci more than 2 cm in length. Grade 4 patients had severe heterotopic ossification with evidence of nearly complete or complete hip ankylosis. In a group of 80 patients, they showed that 40% had no heterotopic ossification, 23% had grade 1 changes, 11% had grade 2 changes, and 15% had grade 3 heterotopic ossification. The remaining 11% had severe grade 4 heterotopic ossification. They found no correlation with age, sex, severity of the femoral fracture, presence of an open wound, the type of interlocking fixation, or whether the nailing procedure was delayed for more than 24 hours after surgery. They also found no association between heterotopic ossification and the ISS or the Glasgow Coma Scale on admission. The use of pulsed lavage did not decrease the incidence of heterotopic ossification. Similar results were achieved by Steinberg and Hubbard,[230] who reported that heterotopic ossification developed in 55% of their patients They found an association between heterotopic ossification and male gender and increased delay before surgery. However, the average delay was 3.75 days, which is longer than in the study by Brumback and colleagues.[32]

Furlong and co-workers[86] examined heterotopic ossification after both reamed and unreamed nailing. They found a 35.7% incidence of heterotopic ossification after reamed nailing and 9.4% after unreamed nailing. The use of reamed nails was associated with Brumback grade 1 (10.7%), grade 2 (17.9%), and grade 3 (7.1%) heterotopic ossification, but all of the heterotopic ossification associated with unreamed nailing was grade 1. The authors suggested that the difference demonstrated the osteogenic potential of reaming debris. These studies indicate that heterotopic ossification is usually a relatively minor problem that may cause thigh pain. It may well be more common in males and if surgery is delayed for a prolonged period. Some evidence has shown that it is caused by reaming debris, although it is highly unlikely that such debris is the only cause because heterotopic ossification around the hip can occur with other injuries and surgical procedures.

### Femoral Neck Fracture

Femoral neck fracture is a rare, but potentially serious complication of antegrade intramedullary femoral nailing. Christie and Court-Brown[49] described four cases of femoral neck fracture in patients who they were sure had not had femoral neck fractures preoperatively (Fig. 52–31). They thought that the starting point had been too lateral in all cases. Proximal comminution occurred in three patients, a finding that seemed to vindicate this belief. All fractures were treated with cancellous screws placed posterior to the nail, and all healed. Simonian and colleagues[226] described four cases of femoral neck fracture in

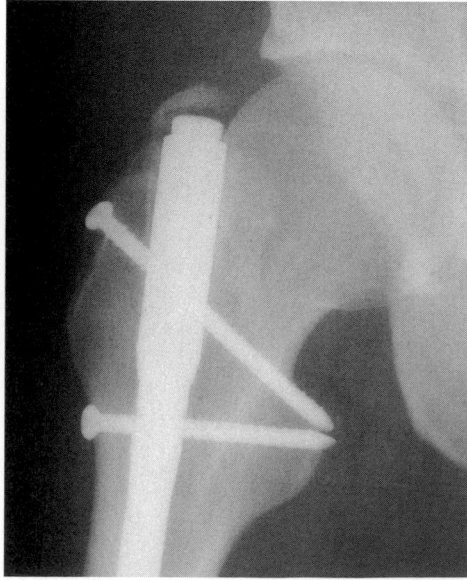

**FIGURE 52–30.** Grade 2 heterotopic ossification in a 23-year-old man with buttock discomfort.

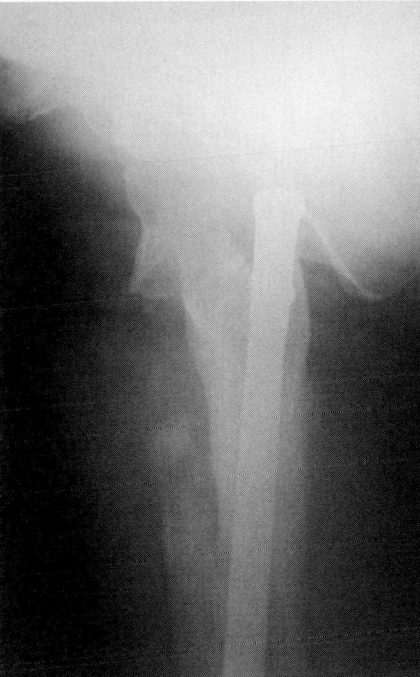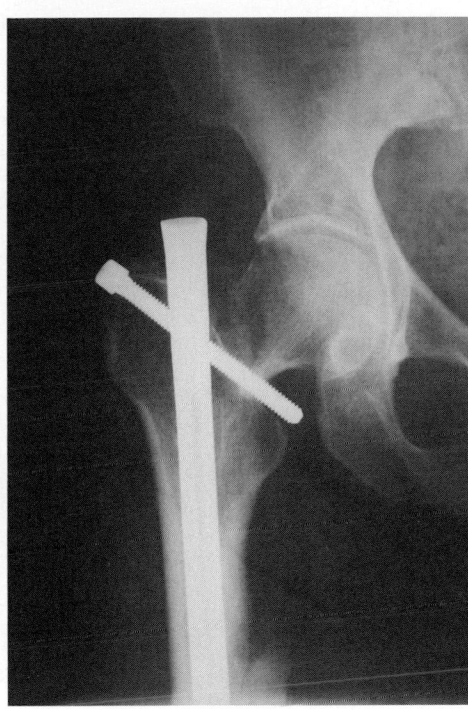

**Figure 52–31.** Anteroposterior and lateral radiographs of the proximal end of the femur of a 23-year-old woman after intramedullary nailing. A femoral neck fracture is apparent. Preoperative radiographs showed no evidence of the fracture.

315 nailed femurs. They pointed out that all the patients with fractured femoral necks had neck shaft angles of more than 135°. All were successfully treated.

Yang and associates[278] identified 14 fractures of the ipsilateral femoral neck in 152 closed antegrade femoral nailing procedures. They obtained preoperative and postoperative computed tomographic (CT) scans in addition to standard radiographs. In three patients, they were unsure about the timing of the femoral neck fracture. A further three had definite radiologic evidence of a fracture before nailing. Of the eight patients who had formal preoperative radiographs and both preoperative and postoperative CT scans, six had evidence of a preoperative femoral neck fracture. Thus, it seems likely that most femoral neck fractures will probably have occurred before nailing. However, iatrogenic femoral neck fracture during nailing undoubtedly occurs and must be looked for. If it does occur, it should be treated. The options are cancellous screws placed posterior to the proximal nail[49] or removal of the locking nail and insertion of a reconstruction nail. The former would seem to be associated with a lower potential morbidity and is the recommended treatment when a femoral neck fracture is discovered after insertion of an intramedullary nail. Should a fracture of the femoral neck be discovered before nailing, its reduction and fixation take priority, after which plating or retrograde nailing can be used for the shaft fracture (see Ipsilateral Femoral Diaphyseal and Hip Fractures).

Patton and colleagues[191] emphasized that older patients are at risk of a late proximal femoral fracture after intramedullary nailing of a femoral diaphyseal fracture. They reported 13 patients who had femoral neck fractures out of a total of 498 patients who had a femoral diaphyseal fracture treated by reamed intramedullary nailing. The proximal femoral fracture was not apparent on the preoperative or postoperative radiographs. Indeed, in most patients it was not apparent until 3 months after the diaphyseal fracture. Multivariate analysis showed that late fracture was associated with the femoral fracture being in the proximal third of the diaphysis, a low-energy injury, and the presence of radiographic osteopenia. The average age of the patients was 80 years, and the incidence of late proximal femoral fracture in patients older than 60 years was 6.9%. Two patients had late intertrochanteric fractures, but the rest had subcapital fractures and were treated by prosthetic replacement. Five patients died within 2 years of the initial fracture. The authors suggested that the surgeons should consider using reconstruction nails rather than conventional locking nails in femoral diaphyseal fractures in the elderly because of the incidence of late proximal femoral fracture.

### External Rotation Deformity

Femoral rotation is usually assessed preoperatively by rotating the thigh such that the patella is facing directly upward if the supine position is used or is parallel to the floor if nailing in the lateral position. However, the degree of femoral rotation also depends on the degree of femoral neck anteversion, which has been reported to vary from −4° to +36°.[112] Tornetta and co-workers[243] assessed 22 patients treated by static intramedullary nailing and showed that the average malrotation was 16°. Twelve patients were placed in more than 10° of malrotation, and 10 of them were in external rotation (Fig. 52–32). No difference could be found between the results of nailing in the supine position and in the lateral position. Physical examination showed an average loss of 9° of rotational arc on the fractured side. Analysis of gait suggested that the patients compensated by rotating their pelvis, but interestingly, only one patient accepted the offer of a derotation osteotomy and then failed to show up for surgery! This study undoubtedly shows that external rotation of more

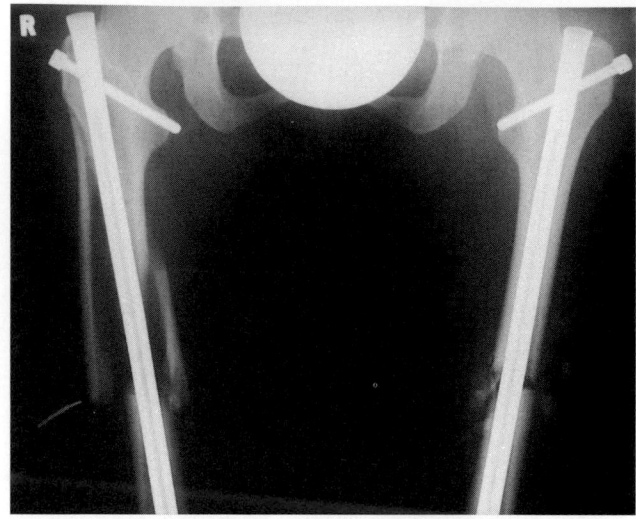

**Figure 52–32.** External rotation deformity after bilateral femoral nailing. The left femur was externally rotated. Note the difference in the diameter of the cortices.

than 10° is relatively easy to achieve, but it is likely that only gross external rotation will be associated with clinical symptoms. Both Tornetta[243] and Bråten[28] and their colleagues have described the use of a fluoroscope to accurately assess femoral rotation during nailing. However, clinical evidence suggests that such assessment is a counsel of perfection, and unless the rotational deformity is considerable, clinical problems are few and derotation osteotomy is very rarely required. Krettek and co-workers[139] pointed out that if a derotation osteotomy is performed, small-diameter femoral nails may not be sufficiently stiff to hold the osteotomy, and late recurrence of the deformity may occur.

### Neurologic Damage

Damage to the peroneal, pudendal, and sciatic nerves has been reported after intramedullary nailing. Winquist and colleagues[268] documented four cases of peroneal nerve palsy that they attributed to strong perioperative traction. Peroneal nerve palsy has also been reported by other surgeons.[1, 137, 221] The literature suggests that most patients who acquire a peroneal nerve palsy after nailing recover fully, although some patients are left with residual disability. It seems likely that peroneal nerve palsy is usually caused by traction, but it could also occur after incorrect insertion of a traction pin in the proximal end of the tibia. Sciatic nerve palsy has likewise been described.[29, 48, 270] This palsy is also generally caused by traction and will recover in time, but trapping of the sciatic nerve in the fracture site has been documented in a patient.[29]

Pudendal nerve palsy is the most common neurologic problem associated with femoral nailing. It has been mentioned in a number of studies,[48, 221, 244, 270] but more detailed reports of its etiology and features are available. France and Aurori[81] estimated its incidence to be 1.9% in a retrospective study and 2.8% in a subsequent prospective study. They stressed the relationship of pudendal nerve palsy to time on the fracture table, and they emphasized the need to place the perineal post of the table

in the contralateral side of the groin. Brumback and associates[34] showed a correlation with the magnitude of intraoperative traction and stressed the need for lower traction forces. Pudendal nerve palsies are characterized by numbness of the penis and scrotum with erectile dysfunction in males and genitoperoneal dysesthesia in females. As with peroneal nerve palsy, it tends to be self-limiting, but it is very worrying for the patient, who should be reassured that the neurapraxia almost always resolves within a few months.

### Broken Intramedullary Nails and Cross Screws

Broken nails usually occur in association with nonunion, and if a nonunion is not treated, the surgeon should expect any nail to break eventually (Fig. 52–33). Obviously, the elapsed time before nail breakage will depend on the size of the nail and the activity of the patient, with small unreamed nails tending to break more quickly than larger reamed nails. Most nails will break at the site of the nonunion, but some slotted nails may break at the junction of the slotted and unslotted portions of the nail (see Fig. 52–33). Alternatively, any nail may fracture through one of the screw holes. Franklin and colleagues[82] analyzed 60 broken intramedullary nails and commented that the incidence in the literature varied from 1% to 3.3%. However, this study is a historical series, and it is unlikely that the current incidence is as high. Nail removal is usually straightforward if the nail is cannulated and the two parts of the nail are in alignment. Under these circumstances, the proximal fragment is usually easy to retrieve with standard removal equipment. To remove the distal fragment, the cross screws should be removed and a long hook used to catch and remove the distal nail fragment. If the nonunion has become displaced and cannot be reduced, open surgery may be required to remove the distal nail fragment. The recent interest in solid nails has given surgeons more problems when nail breakage occurs. It may be possible to over-ream the proximal fragment after the proximal part of the nail has been removed. Such over-reaming may allow the insertion of grasping forceps to remove the distal part of the nail. However, the nonunion site will generally need to be opened to extract the distal nail fragment.

Broken cross screws are encountered fairly frequently, particularly if small-diameter unreamed nails are used. If the fracture site is distracted or comminuted, the distal cross screws in particular may break (see Fig. 52–42). Such breakage is rarely a clinical problem because the screws usually remain intact long enough for the fracture to become stable. However, if the cross screws break before the fracture is stable, the surgeon should be aware that fracture alignment might be lost. It is important that the surgeon be aware of the location of the break in the cross screw. Generally, the screw breaks either centrally within the nail or close to one of the screw holes in the nail. One screw fragment is often longer than the other (see Fig. 52–42), and one or both fragments may catch within the nail as extraction is attempted. If the surgeon persists with nail extraction without removing both screw fragments, considerable cortical damage may be inflicted. Removal of the proximal screw fragment is straightforward, but removal of the distal fragment is more difficult. It is best achieved by using a thin Steinmann pin or similar

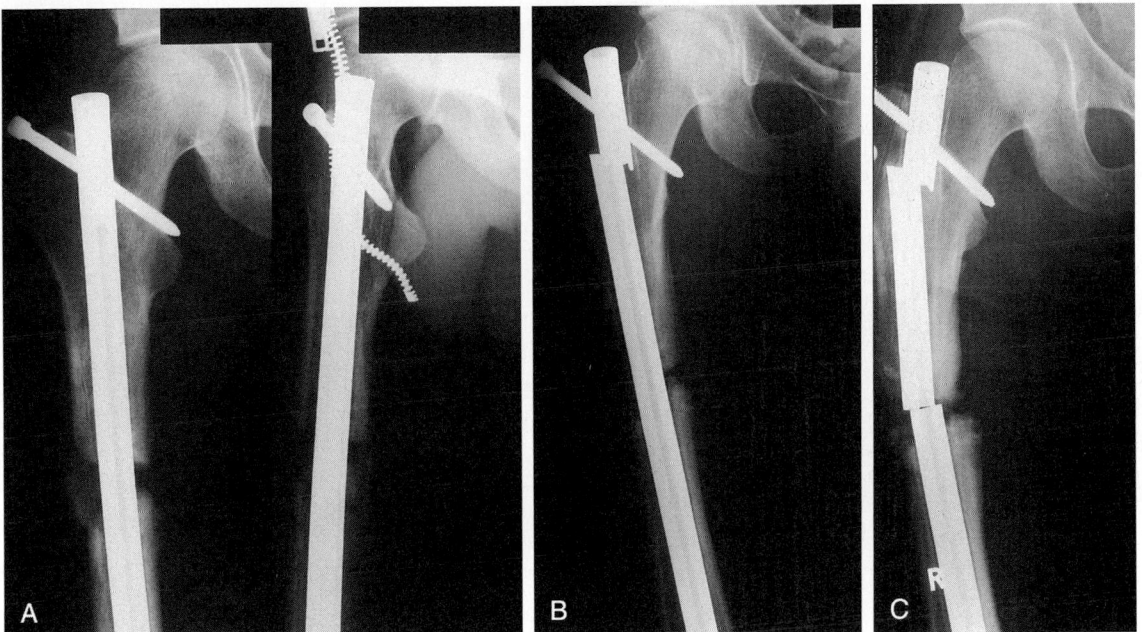

**FIGURE 52–33.** *A,* A statically locked nail has been used to treat a femoral fracture. The fracture is slightly distracted. *B,* The nail fractured at the junction of its slotted and nonslotted portions. The surgeon thought that the stability was still adequate and left the nail in situ. *C,* The nonunion persisted, and the nail fractured again at the level of the nonunion. Note the slight varus angulation permitted by the first nail fracture.

instrument to push the distal screw fragment out of the bone (Fig. 52–34). The Steinmann pin is applied to the proximal end of the distal screw fragment and tapped with a hammer to facilitate removal. It can then be retrieved from the soft tissues if necessary. Sometimes, a distal cross screw will have broken because the surgeon has distracted the fracture during the initial nailing. As the fracture distraction closes, the screw will break and angulate with the apex of the broken screw being pushed distally by a few millimeters. The screw can be straightened by inserting the nail extraction bolt and tapping the nail out a few millimeters. This maneuver will cause the screw fragments to straighten, and the proximal and distal fragments can then be removed by the technique already described.

### Bent Intramedullary Nails

Nowadays it is unusual for intramedullary nails to bend, but surgeons may still encounter bent intramedullary nails. These bent nails are generally thin unreamed Küntscher nails inserted many years ago. An example is shown in Figure 52–35. The nails may break, but if union proceeds, the femur and nail may be permanently deformed. These nails are usually impossible to extract unless the femur and nail are cut. When possible, bent nails in healed femurs should be left in situ.

### Muscle Weakness

One obvious potential problem with closed nailing is that the hip abductors must be incised to permit the operation to be undertaken. Danckwardt-Lilliström and Sjögren[65] examined muscle weakness and its recovery in 23 patients who underwent intramedullary femoral nailing after a fracture. However, 21 patients were treated by open nailing

and 7 patients had other serious injuries, including fractures of the ipsilateral tibia. Interestingly, they found no significant difference in hip abduction power between the fractured side and the normal side, but they did demonstrate weakness in knee flexion and extension when compared with the normal side. The authors stratified their

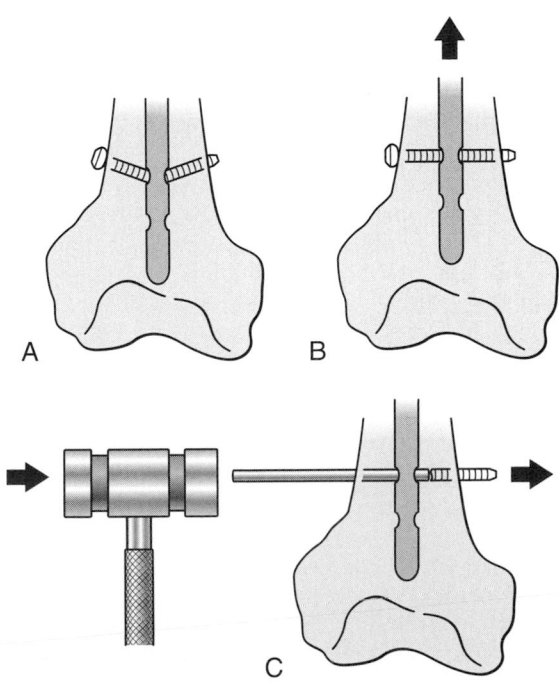

**FIGURE 52–34.** *A,* A broken cross screw frequently angulates. *B,* The nail should be backed out until the cross screw is straight. The proximal fragment can be removed easily. *C,* A thin Steinmann pin or similar instrument can then be passed into the nail and the distal screw fragment knocked out. It can then be removed.

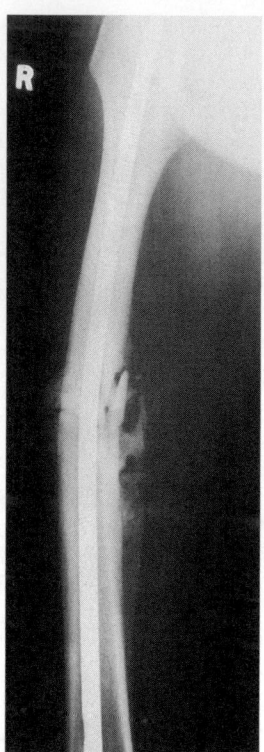

FIGURE 52–35. A bent unreamed Küntscher nail in a healing femur.

patients according to age and showed that in patients younger than 50 years who were monitored for 1 to 2 years, no difference in hip abductor power could be seen between the affected and unaffected legs. They also compared power in the hip abductors, quadriceps, and hamstrings with an age-matched control group. This comparison showed that hip abduction in both the fractured and nonfractured legs was weak after intramedullary nailing of a femoral fracture. They concluded that it was the reciprocal muscles controlling the knee joint that were most affected by the fracture and the subsequent nailing and that muscle recovery might take up to 5 years. Bain and co-workers[5] also compared abduction power in nailed femurs and the uninjured contralateral side. No significant difference was found in mean abductor power, although the abductor power was weaker than in an uninjured control group. They did not examine quadriceps and hamstring power. Finsen and associates[79] investigated muscle function in 26 patients, 14 of whom had their femoral fractures treated by intramedullary nailing. The remaining 12 had been treated by AO plating. Muscle power was compared with that on the normal side. They found that quadriceps function was restored in patients treated by nailing but that patients treated by plating had persistent weakness in quadriceps power.

These studies suggest that bilateral abductor weakness occurs after unilateral femoral fracture. However, no evidence has been presented that closed intramedullary nailing significantly affects the abductor muscles of the fractured side, and presumably, it is the effect of the fracture and the ensuing disability that results in quadriceps and hamstring weakness. It would seem that the improvement in quadriceps function is better after nailing than after plating.

## Other Complications

Surgeons should remember that the major blood vessels in the thigh can be damaged by overzealous drilling or very rarely by inserting too long a cross screw. However, significant vascular damage is very rare, and the author has not seen a case after femoral nailing. De Casas and coauthors[67] reported an arteriovenous fistula of the femoral vessels caused by a long distal cross screw. It was successfully treated by excising the affected arterial segment and interposing a vein graft. Johnson and Wiss[121] reported a fragment of cortical bone being caught on the tip of the nail and then driven into the knee joint during nailing of the femur. An arthrotomy was required to remove the bone fragment. This complication is clearly very rare, but it is not uncommon for the guide wire to be passed into the knee joint if the bone is osteopenic. Care should be taken to monitor the end of the guide wire, particularly when nailing distal femoral fractures in elderly osteopenic bone or in patients with metabolic bone disease. The guide wire may be placed in the canal initially but later be found to have been driven into the knee joint during reaming. Care must also be taken to ensure that reamers are not passed distally into the knee joint under these circumstances.

Thermal necrosis has not been reported in femoral nailing, but there is no reason why it should not occur. It was described by Leunig and Hertel[115] in reference to tibial reaming. The subcutaneous nature of the tibia means that the thermal injury to bone and the overlying soft tissues is more obvious. However, overzealous reaming will increase the cortical temperature in the femur as well, and it has been shown that temperatures over 47°C may damage bone.[77] It is therefore important to ensure that the reamers are sharp, not fouled with bone chips, and used in a controlled manner. It is certainly possible that some femoral nonunions are associated with thermal injury to bone during reaming.

# RETROGRADE NAILING

*Charles M. Court-Brown, M.D.,*
*and P. Tornetta, M.D.*

Retrograde femoral diaphyseal nailing has become more popular in the last 10 years (Fig. 52–36). Originally, retrograde nailing was undertaken to treat trochanteric fractures, with flexible small-diameter nails being inserted through the medial femoral condyle and passed proximally.[147] Swiontkowski and colleagues[233] adopted this technique to treat femoral diaphyseal fractures. They inserted reamed femoral nails through the medial condyle in 15 patients with combined femoral neck and diaphyseal fractures. The subcapital fracture was fixed with cancellous screws, and a retrograde femoral nail was used to stabilize the diaphyseal fracture. They used 12- or 13-mm cloverleaf nails and stressed that the nails had to be flexible to permit use of the medial femoral condyle as the insertion point.

Retrograde nailing was also performed by Sanders and co-workers,[213] who analyzed the use of this technique in 29 femoral diaphyseal fractures. They suggested that the indications for retrograde femoral nailing should be

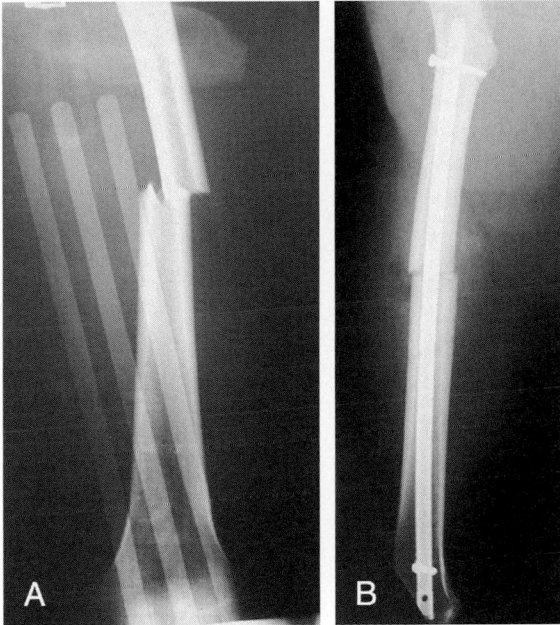

FIGURE **52–36.** *A,* Anteroposterior radiograph of an AO/OTA A3.2 femoral diaphyseal fracture. *B,* The fracture has been treated by retrograde nailing. (Courtesy of P. Tornetta, M.D.)

extended to include pregnancy to minimize radiation exposure and ipsilateral pelvic or acetabular fractures and polytrauma to allow a number of surgical teams to perform simultaneous procedures. The results of this and other studies of retrograde femoral nailing are shown in Table 52–13. The researchers documented a 16% incidence of malunion and an 8% incidence of nonunion or delayed union. No cases of infection were recorded. They initially used a femoral nail to stabilize the fractures but changed their technique to the use of a tibial nail. The tibial nail was found to parallel the flare of the medial femoral condyle more closely and minimized the tendency to valgus malreduction that they had noticed with the use of a femoral nail.

The same group of surgeons extended their use of retrograde nailing further and specifically examined use of the technique in cases of "floating knee," a condition characterized by ipsilateral fractures of the femur and tibia.[95] They examined 24 patients whose 26 femur/tibia fractures were treated by retrograde insertion of a femoral nail and antegrade insertion of an unreamed tibial nail. During the time of the study, the surgeons changed from the medial condylar approach to an intercondylar approach that permitted the insertion of femoral nails without the valgus malalignment that they had noted previously. The authors used both reamed and unreamed femoral nails, with 14 fractures being treated through the medial condylar approach and 12 with the intercondylar starting point. Of the 20 patients available for follow-up, 13 (65%) had good or excellent results. Fifteen percent (3/20) of the femoral fractures required secondary surgery for nonunion. Of particular interest is the fact that the patients reported no more than occasional knee discomfort. No septic arthritis was reported, and the average knee flexion after treatment was 120°.

A third publication by the same group[108] documented the results of unreamed retrograde femoral nailing through an intercondylar approach. These results are shown in Table 52–13. In this paper, the authors examined 45 fractures treated by retrograde nailing with an intercondylar insertion site (see Fig. 52–36). Forty-three fractures healed without secondary surgery, and no postoperative infections occurred. They encountered two broken nails and one case of femoral malrotation. Thirteen patients (28.9%) reported knee pain, although the pain was generally mild.

Moed and Watson[162] prospectively investigated the use of retrograde femoral nailing through an intercondylar approach for 22 fractures in 20 multiply injured patients. They used unreamed nails. Table 52–13 shows their results. Given the severity of injury to their patients, they obtained good results, with a 13.6% incidence of nonunion and a 4.5% incidence of malunion. They reported that six (30%) of their patients complained of some knee pain, but in three of these patients the femur did not unite primarily. Overall, the effects of knee pain were slight.

The role of retrograde femoral nailing in the treatment of very severely injured patients was also examined by Patterson and co-workers.[190] They retrospectively reviewed the use of a reamed intramedullary nail in 17

**TABLE 52–13** ● ● ● ● ● ● ● ● ● ● ● ● ● ● ● ● ● ● ● ● ● ● ● ● ● ● ● ● ● ● ● ● ● ● ● ● ● ● ● ● ● ● ● ● ● ● ● ● ● ● ● ● ● ●

Data from Studies of Retrograde Nailing

| | N | Open Fractures (%) | Union Time (wk) | Nonunion (%) | Malunion (%) | Infection (%) |
|---|---|---|---|---|---|---|
| **REAMED NAILS** | | | | | | |
| Sanders et al.[213] | 29 | 17.2 | ? | 8 | 13.8 | 0 |
| Patterson et al.[190] | 17 | 64.7 | ? | 29.4 | 5.9 | 5.9 |
| Ostrum et al.[181] | 61 | 23.5 | 12.6 | 4.9 | 1.7 | 0 |
| Tornetta and Tiburzi[245] | 31 | 40.6 | 13.1 | 0 | 33 | 0 |
| Ostrum et al.[183] | 47 | 25.9 | 18.1 | 4.2 | ? | ? |
| **UNREAMED NAILS** | | | | | | |
| Moed and Watson[162] | 22 | 31.8 | 15 | 13.6 | 4.5 | 0 |
| Herscovici and Whiteman[108] | 45 | 17 | ? | 4.5 | 2.2 | 0 |
| Moed et al.[163] | 35 | 31.4 | 12.6 | 6 | 0 | 0 |
| Herscovici et al.[109] | 56 | 23.3 | 19.9 | 10.7 | ? | 0 |

● ● ● ● ● ● ● ● ● ● ● ● ● ● ● ● ● ● ● ● ● ● ● ● ● ● ● ● ● ● ● ● ● ● ● ● ● ● ● ● ● ● ● ● ● ● ● ● ● ● ● ● ● ● ● ● ● ● ● ● ● ● ● ● ●

The studies of Sanders et al.[213] and Patterson et al.[190] used the medial femoral approach for some or all fractures. The other studies used the intercondylar approach.

femoral fractures that occurred in 16 very severely injured patients. The severity of injury can be seen in Table 52–13, and it should be noted that 64.7% of the fractures were open. The severity of injury accounts for the 29.4% nonunion rate. Five of the patients had ipsilateral knee dislocations, but despite this additional injury, the final range of knee flexion was 3° to 110°.

The relative success of retrograde femoral nailing caused surgeons to extend the indications for its use to isolated femoral fractures, and Ostrum and colleagues[181] undertook a prospective evaluation of 61 femoral fractures, 14 of which were isolated. However, the average ISS of the group was only 15.6, and clearly, the patients were not as badly injured as in previous studies. The nails were inserted after reaming, but canal filling was not attempted because all patients were treated with a 10-mm nail. Only 85% of the fractures healed after the primary procedure, but the authors were rigorous in their definition of nonunion, and a number of patients healed after dynamization. The fractures in only three patients (5%) did not unite and required exchange nailing. Septic arthritis of the knee developed in one patient and was successfully treated, and all patients in whom complications did not develop achieved good knee function within 3 months. However, they did report that four patients had symptomatic chondromalacia patellae.

Moed and colleagues[163] also extended their indications for retrograde nailing and documented their results in 35 fractures, 16 of which were isolated. They adopted a protocol in which all statically locked nails underwent dynamization at 6 to 12 weeks if minimal signs of union were noted. Table 52–13 shows that they had a relatively high incidence of open fractures, but they reported a 95% union rate with no infection or malunion. They used a knee score and showed that all patients who had a healed fracture and follow-up of at least 6 months were graded excellent for pain, and all but one patient were graded excellent for knee function.

The use of unreamed antegrade nails and unreamed retrograde nails was compared by Herscovici and co-workers[109] (see Table 52–13). They examined 121 patients with 125 fractures and used the AO/OTA classification. Overall, 93% of the fractures healed primarily, with the mean time to union being 3.8 months for type A fractures, 4.8 months for type B fractures, and 6.2 months for type C fractures. Sixty-nine fractures were treated by antegrade nailing and 56 by retrograde nailing. Nine (7.2%) nonunions occurred, three (4.3%) of which followed antegrade nailing and six (10.7%) followed retrograde nailing. Antegrade unreamed nailing resulted in a significantly shorter union time than retrograde nailing did in type A fractures but not in type B or type C fractures. It should be remembered that the AO/OTA classification is only loosely associated with soft tissue injury and that the difference in union time may well relate to the degree of soft tissue damage, which was not documented by the authors. In addition, more distal fractures were treated with the unreamed technique. This point is important because it has been demonstrated that distal femoral fractures treated with an unreamed nail have a prolonged union time.[245]

Tornetta and Tiburzi[245] published the results of a prospective randomized trial of antegrade and retrograde femoral nailing. They compared 38 femoral diaphyseal fractures treated by reamed antegrade nailing with 31 treated by reamed retrograde nailing (see Table 52–13). They found that antegrade nailing was associated with a significantly shorter operating time, but when the setup time was considered, the overall operating time was similar. CAT scanning was used to assess malrotation, and the authors demonstrated a greater incidence of malrotation of more than 10° in the retrograde group (33% versus 17%) in patients with unstable fracture patterns. This difference may well relate to the fact that a fracture table was used for the antegrade nailing and manual traction for the retrograde nailing. Analysis showed no difference in the time to union or in the final range of hip or knee motion. Postoperative knee pain was predictably higher in the retrograde group, but no difference was noted in knee pain by the time that the fracture had united. Three patients in the retrograde group required aspiration of a knee hemarthrosis, and heterotopic ossification developed in three patients in the antegrade group. No heterotopic ossification was seen in the retrograde group.

Ostrum and co-workers[183] also undertook a prospective study comparing reamed antegrade and retrograde femoral nailing. Although this study was prospective, most distal fractures were treated with retrograde nails, with more proximal fractures being treated with antegrade nails. Thus, the study did not compare retrograde and antegrade nailing in equivalent fracture patterns. As in their previous paper,[181] they used a 10-mm reamed titanium nail for all cases regardless of the diameter of the intramedullary canal. The results for the retrograde nails are shown in Table 52–13. Eight (17%) of the fractures treated by a retrograde nail were dynamized for delayed union, but only two (4.2%) required secondary surgery for nonunion. Detailed analysis showed no difference in operative time or blood loss. The antegrade group regained knee motion more quickly than the retrograde group did, but no difference was found in eventual knee function between the groups. The investigators also detected no difference in the incidence of knee pain. They did show that 38% of patients with retrograde nails complained of painful distal cross screws and 22% of patients treated with an antegrade nail complained of proximal femoral discomfort. It is interesting to note that the average time to union for fractures treated by retrograde nailing was 18.1 weeks versus 14.4 weeks for the fractures treated by antegrade nailing. The difference was just statistically significant, but the authors attributed the difference in union times to mismatch between the size of the nail and the diameter of the intramedullary canal and to differences in fracture morphology between the two groups. It is likely that these factors may well account for the difference in union times because it seems illogical to suppose that the entry point of the nail would be the sole determinant of the speed of union given the fact that both groups were similarly treated with a reamed intramedullary 10-mm nail.

The results of retrograde femoral nailing suggest that the technique is useful. Most surgeons will continue to use antegrade nailing for isolated femoral diaphyseal fractures, and it should be pointed out that despite an increasing tendency to undertake retrograde nailing in patients with isolated fractures, most patients who have been documented in the papers quoted in this chapter have actually been multiply injured or have had combinations of fractures that were particularly suited to retrograde nailing. Retrograde nailing is clearly a good option for the management of pregnant and multiply injured patients, in addition to those who have coexisting femoral neck, acetabular, and pelvic fractures, ipsilateral hip pathology, obesity, wounds near the hip, or unstable spinal fractures. It is also an excellent technique in patients with a "floating knee" secondary to ipsilateral femoral and tibial diaphyseal fractures. The use of a single percutaneous approach to the problem of a "floating knee" (see Fig. 52–38) has been examined by Ostrum.[182] He looked at the results of retrograde femoral nailing and antegrade tibial nailing in 17 patients who had a "floating knee"; 88% of the patients had good or excellent results, and no patients had limitation of knee movement or knee pain.

Two other indications for retrograde femoral nailing have been reported. It has been shown to be a useful technique in patients with a diaphyseal fracture at or below a hip prosthesis. Ponzer and coauthors[195] described the use of a retrograde femoral nail for the treatment of seven femoral fractures that occurred below uncemented Moore hemiarthroplasties. They used a 16-mm femoral nail with the end cut off. They reamed the canal to 17 mm, and the end of the intramedullary nail was inserted over the stem of the hemiarthroplasty prosthesis. They reported good results, but this technique should be considered only for the treatment of periprosthetic fractures in some elderly patients with suitable uncemented endoprostheses.

Chin and colleagues[46] reported that retrograde femoral nailing is also useful in the management of nonambulatory patients with myelopathy. They treated 10 patients who had either a femoral diaphyseal or femoral supracondylar fracture. The average age of the group was 60.7 years. The authors reported that the operation was a safe alternative to nonoperative management in nonambulatory patients. They had no nonunions, malunions, significant shortening, implant failure, or wound infection.

## Complications of Retrograde Nailing

Retrograde nailing has been popularized only recently, and therefore little has been published about specific complications associated with its use. Logically, a number of the complications associated with antegrade nailing, such as increased fracture comminution, neurovascular damage, and broken hardware, will also occur in retrograde nailing. However, the particular complication that has concerned orthopaedic surgeons relates to the potential knee damage caused by the insertion of a retrograde femoral nail through the intercondylar notch of the femur. Knee pain has been reported in up to 30% of cases, although prospective randomized series comparing antegrade and retrograde nailing have not demonstrated significantly more pain after retrograde nailing than after antegrade nailing and the knee pain that has been reported is mild. Septic arthritis has been reported,[181] and heterotopic ossification in the knee has also occurred.[116] Elmaraghy and co-workers[75] examined the effect of retrograde

femoral reaming on blood flow in the distal end of the femur and the cruciate ligaments in dogs. They confirmed that reaming doubled the blood flow of the distal part of the femur, but they found that blood flow to the anterior cruciate decreased by 52% and blood flow to the posterior cruciate decreased by 49%. They emphasized that a direct extrapolation to reaming in humans could not be made, and no clinical data suggest that retrograde nailing is harmful to the cruciate ligaments. Overall, the knee problems after retrograde nailing appear to not be severe. However, it is obvious that as yet, surgeons do not have any knowledge of the long-term effects of retrograde femoral nailing. The position of the insertion point for retrograde nailing is clearly important, and Morgan and colleagues[169] have undertaken a study of the effects of retrograde femoral intramedullary nailing on the patellofemoral articulation. They showed that it was important that the nail not protrude beyond the subchondral bone. They suggested that placement of the retrograde nail was critical and that proper placement should not significantly influence the biomechanics of the patellofemoral joint.

In the absence of a study comparing reamed and unreamed retrograde femoral nailing, it is necessary to examine the results of individual studies of the two techniques to see whether the advantages of reaming that have been demonstrated for antegrade nailing also occur with the retrograde approach. It is not logical that the position of the entry point should alter the effect of reaming, and Table 52–13 suggests that such is the case. If the study by Patterson and associates[190] is ignored because it deals with a much higher proportion of seriously injured patients than the other studies, the average incidence of nonunion after reamed retrograde femoral nailing was 3.8% as compared with 8.2% for unreamed retrograde femoral nailing. Based on the studies that have been undertaken, a reamed canal-filling technique has the highest union rate and should be used for retrograde femoral nailing.

## Technique of Retrograde Nailing

The technique of retrograde nailing is relatively straightforward, but like all procedures, certain pitfalls must be avoided to obtain good results. One advantage of the technique is that a fracture table is not required. However, the table must be radiolucent from the patient's hip to the knee, and fluoroscopy is essential. The patient is placed supine on the operating table. Before draping, a trial reduction is performed manually under fluoroscopic control to determine whether the fracture can be reduced and length restored. In young patients with transverse fractures and significant shortening it may be difficult to restore length. If appropriate length cannot be maintained easily by manual traction, a femoral distractor will be necessary during the procedure. The surgeon should also check that the knee can flex to at least 40° because a stiff knee is a contraindication to retrograde nailing. The extremity should be draped free to allow access from the anterior superior iliac spine to the midtibial level (Fig. 52–37A). If a distractor is required, the pins should be placed in the trochanter and the proximal end of the tibia. The distal end

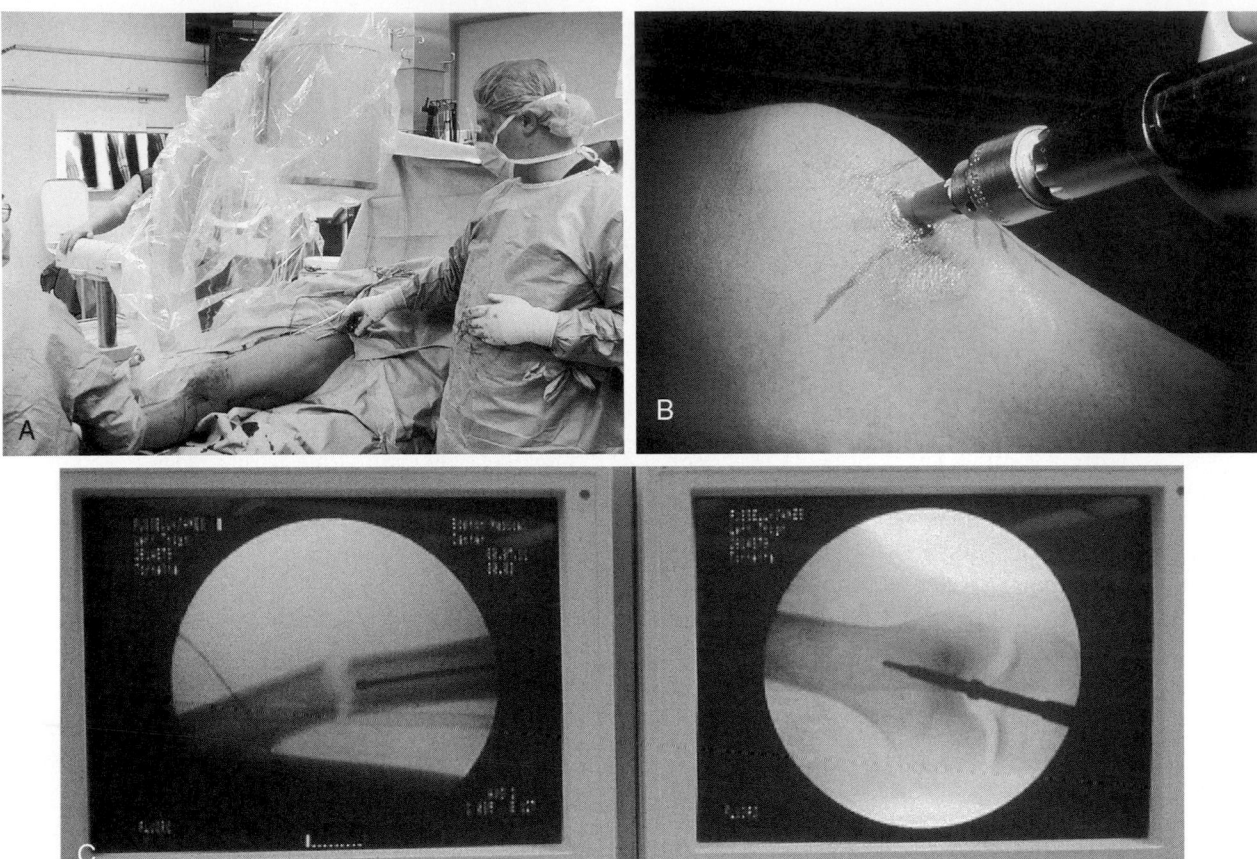

**Figure 52–37.** *A,* The extremity is prepared free to allow access from the anterior-superior iliac spine to the midportion of the tibia. *B,* A defect in the intercondylar notch is made through a 15-mm skin incision under fluoroscopic control. *C,* Care must be taken to drill the distal part of the femur in the long axis of the diaphysis and make sure that the fracture is reduced.   *Illustration continued on following page*

of the femur can be used for the distal distractor pin, but the pin must be placed outside the path of the nail.

Unless the fracture has an intra-articular extension that requires direct exposure for reduction and internal fixation, the retrograde nailing procedure is percutaneous and is undertaken through a 15-mm incision. Only a small arc of safety is available when passing the reamers if damage to the proximal part of the tibia or patella is to be avoided. The proximal end of the tibia tends to be damaged if the knee is placed in too little flexion, and the patella is damaged if the knee is in too much flexion. About 40° of knee flexion is appropriate. A perfect lateral radiograph is essential to confirm the correct amount of flexion and the appropriate nail entry portal. A sterile bolster is placed under the knee, and the fluoroscope is adjusted so that a perfect lateral image is available. With this view, a radiopaque object is used to identify the correct level of skin incision, specifically, in line with the long axis of the femur. The skin incision is 15 mm in length and placed in the midline or slightly medial to it (see Fig. 52–37*B*). Subcutaneous dissection is used to create a medial flap from the distal part of the patella to the proximal end of the tibia, and the skin is then retracted medially. Cautery is used to make a medial paratendinous arthrotomy 2.5 cm in length. Many techniques have been described for creating the entry portal, including a guide wire followed by a straight reamer, a straight awl, or a step drill with a sharp tip. As

with any nailing procedure, the location of the entry portal is very important. On the lateral radiograph it is situated at the junction of the shadow of the trochlear groove and Blumensat's line, and on the anteroposterior radiograph it is centered on the convexity of the trochlear groove between the condyles (see Fig. 52–37*C*). In both views, the entry portal must be drilled in line with the femoral shaft. This technique is relatively straightforward on the lateral view, but the anteroposterior view can be difficult to interpret because the image intensifier displays only a small field. Surgeons have a natural tendency to introduce the drill or awl perpendicular to the condyles. If such drilling is done, the normal valgus of the distal end of the femur will create a varus deformity. The image field should be moved as proximal as possible to allow the drill to be inserted into the middle of the shaft to take into account the valgus of the distal end of the femur (see Fig. 52–37*C*).

Once the starting portal is created in the appropriate place and direction, the procedure is similar to antegrade femoral nailing. If a reamed nail is to be used, an olive-tipped guide wire is introduced and passed across the fracture site (see Fig. 52–37*D*). The guide wire should be advanced to just below the level of the piriformis fossa (see Fig. 52–37*E*). The reduction must be maintained during the reaming process, so if length is difficult to hold or an assistant is not available, the femoral distractor is used as previously described. Reaming is performed slowly

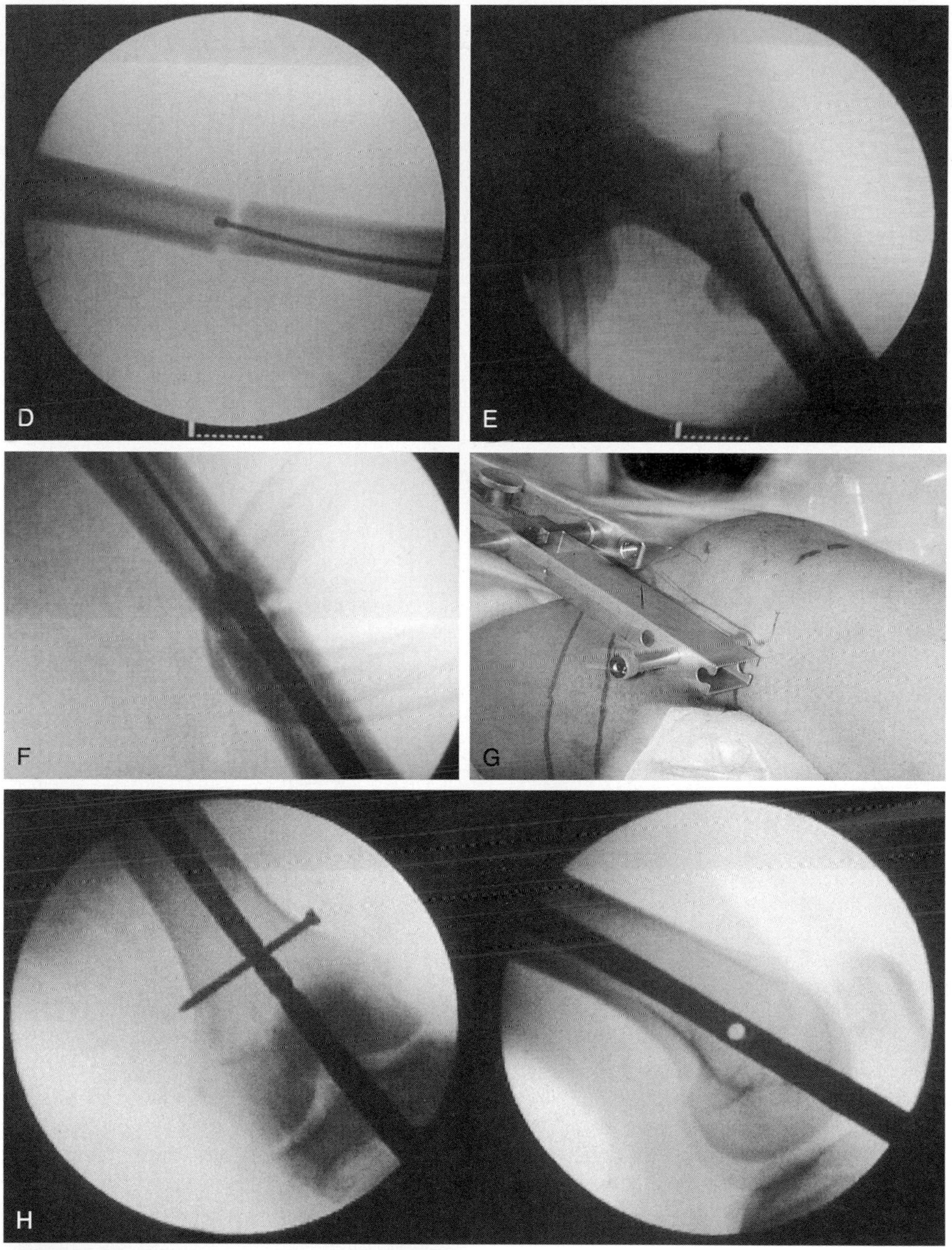

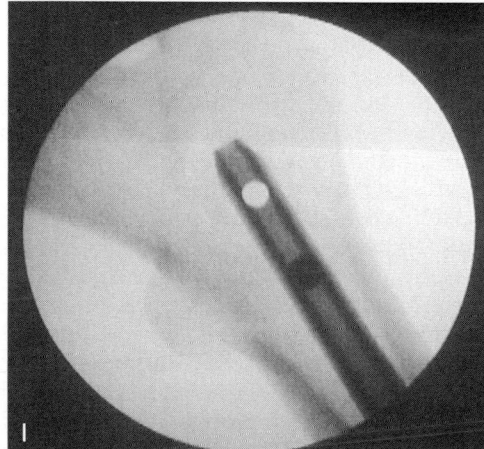

FIGURE 52–37 *Continued. D,* A guide wire is then passed proximally while ensuring that the fracture is reduced. *E,* The guide wire is passed up to the area of the piriformis fossa. *F,* The intramedullary canal is reamed in the same manner as for antegrade nailing. *G,* The nail is attached to the appropriate jig and passed up the femur. *H,* Distal locking is achieved by using the appropriate jig. Care should be taken to make sure that the distal end of the nail is not within the knee. *I,* Proximal locking is achieved in the same way as for distal locking in antegrade nailing. The proximal holes are visualized as full circles and one or two cross screws inserted. (Courtesy of P. Tornetta, M.D.)

and in 0.5-mm increments to avoid thermal necrosis and the reamer becoming stuck in the intramedullary canal (see Fig. 52–37F). The canal is reamed to 1.5 mm beyond the first sign of cortical chatter, and a nail 1 or 1.5 mm smaller than the reamer is chosen. As with antegrade nailing, many methods of assessing nail length have been described. The recommended method is to introduce a guide wire of the same length deep to the subchondral bone on the lateral radiograph of the knee to prevent any chance of the nail being long. The portion distal to the guide wire in place represents the amount of olive-tipped guide wire in the canal. The goal is to have the nail long enough to lock at or above the level of the lesser trochanter to avoid neurologic and vascular injury[244] but remain seated proximal to the subchondral bone at the level of the knee. It is imperative that the surgeon recognize that the piriformis shadow on the anteroposterior radiograph is the most proximal level that the nail can reach without broaching the posterior cortex.

After exchanging the olive-tipped guide wire for a straight guide wire, the nail is introduced. Gentle tapping is all that should be required, and if the nail cannot be advanced easily, careful fluoroscopic assessment of reduction of the fracture and the position of the nail in both planes should be undertaken (see Fig. 52–36G). Final impaction of the nail may be up to 1.5 cm deep to subchondral bone at the level of the knee, depending on the nail system chosen, to allow proximal locking at the lesser trochanter. Most nail systems have end-caps that can be used to add to the length of the nail in this situation.

In very distal fractures, the surgeon may choose to lock proximally in a more distal position to be sure that the locking screws at the knee are in the distal fragment. It is also important that the femur be held out to length and in the proper rotation until statically locked as locking at the knee is performed first. If the manual traction is released after distal locking in an unstable fracture pattern, shortening or malrotation may occur. Locking screw configurations are the same as those used in antegrade nailing. For diaphyseal fractures, only one proximal and one distal screw are needed, and they should be placed in the hole closest to the fracture. In proximal fractures, two proximal screws are used, and in distal fractures, two distal screws are used. Distal locking is performed with a jig attached to the nail to orient the drill sleeves (see Fig. 52–36H). Proximal locking is performed freehand with the leg flat on the table after the distal jig is removed. The technique is the same as for distal locking in antegrade nailing (see Fig. 52–26). To facilitate proximal locking, the image intensifier is raised as high as possible and angled slightly in a proximal-to-distal direction to take account of the curve of the nail. Maximal magnification and a perfect circle technique are used (see Fig. 52–36I). A 10- to 15-mm incision is made in the proximal aspect of the thigh anteriorly, and careful blunt dissection exposes the anterior of the femur. Unlike distal freehand locking in the metaphysis during antegrade nailing, the anterior of the femur is hard cortical bone, and a standard drill bit will easily slip medially or laterally. For this reason, a sharp bone awl or a pointed drill bit is used to begin the hole. The femoral artery lies 1 cm medial to the femur at the level of the lesser trochanter, so any error in direction should be directed laterally. It is important to not advance the drill too far through the posterior cortex because the sciatic nerve is located beneath the femur proximally. Once the hole is drilled, the appropriate screw is inserted. A locking screwdriver should be used to avoid losing the screw in the thick soft tissue of the rectus muscle. To make retrieval easier, some surgeons have recommended tying a suture around the head of the screw to retrieve it if necessary.

After the nail is statically locked, the wounds are closed in layers. The knee wound should not be forcefully irrigated because the bony fragments in the fat pad region will be naturally resorbed. If forceful irrigation is used, the fragments may be driven into the joint and require arthroscopic or even open removal. Rehabilitation is the same as for antegrade nailing, except that a higher percentage of early knee pain can be expected.

## IPSILATERAL FEMORAL DIAPHYSEAL AND HIP FRACTURES

Surgeons have been interested in the management of ipsilateral femoral hip and diaphyseal fractures (Fig. 52–38) since they were first described in 1953 by Delaney and Street.[68] This particular fracture combination is actually fairly uncommon; nonetheless, a considerable number of studies have been undertaken, probably because of the difficulty that this combination of fractures has given orthopaedic surgeons over the years. In the days when most diaphyseal fractures were treated nonoperatively, the combination of diaphyseal and hip fractures was difficult to manage, but with modern fixation techniques, the results are better. However, authorities still have no uniformity of opinion about how this fracture combination should be treated.

The details of a number of the studies undertaken since 1979 are shown in Table 52–14. These studies indicate that the fracture combination generally occurs in younger people as a result of high-energy trauma. Most of the patients sustain this injury pattern in motor vehicle accidents. The injury is associated with ipsilateral knee injuries and particularly with fractures of the patella. Studies have shown that over 25% of patients have injuries to the ipsilateral knee,[40, 85] and Bennett and associates[13] recorded a 39% incidence of injuries in the ipsilateral knee, with 21% of patients presenting with a patellar fracture. It is thought that the mechanism of injury that accounts for this particular distribution of fractures involves the femur being longitudinally loaded with the knee in flexion and the hip in neutral abduction/adduction. The femoral fracture is usually located in the middle third of the bone.

Table 52–14 shows the distribution of different proximal femoral fracture types. The incidence of extracapsular, basal cervical, and subcapital fractures varies considerably between different series. In series that have distinguished between displaced and undisplaced subcapital fractures, considerable variation is also seen, although in most series

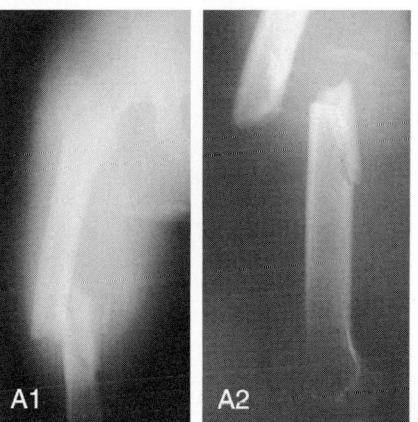

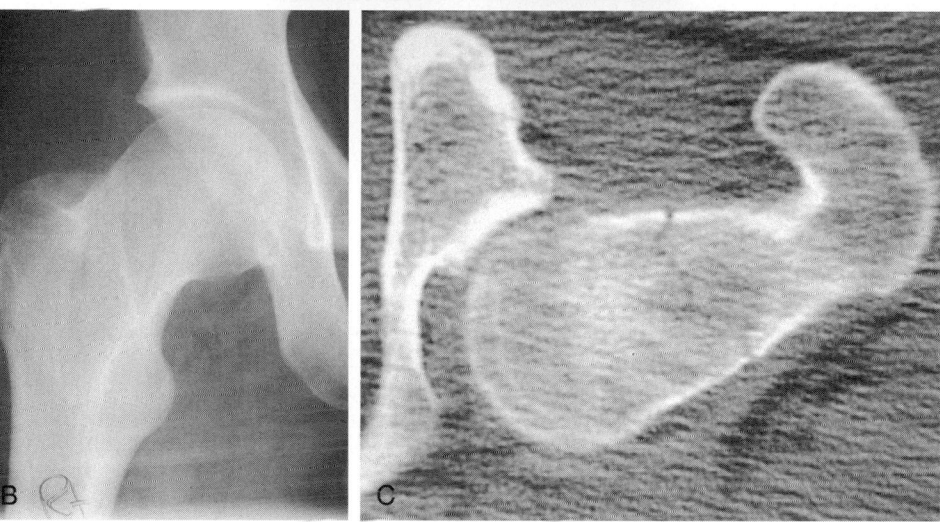

**FIGURE 52–38.** *A,* Patient with ipsilateral femoral diaphyseal and neck fractures. Radiographs show the diaphyseal fracture. *B,* Radiograph of the proximal end of the femur showing the neck fracture. *C,* Computed axial tomographic scan confirming a neck fracture.

*Figure continued on following page*

the majority of the proximal femoral fractures are displaced. The spectrum of proximal femoral fractures was investigated by Shuler and colleagues,[225] who examined 52 patients from three different U.S. Level I trauma centers. They used the AO/OTA classification and found three distinct proximal femoral fracture patterns. They reported that 55% of the patients had AO/OTA B2.1 basal cervical fractures. A further 35% had B2.3 intracapsular midcervical shear fractures, and the remaining 10% were A1.2 intertrochanteric fractures with a fracture through the greater trochanter. They also pointed out that 21% of the femoral neck fractures were missed initially. Initial failure to diagnose a femoral neck fracture varies in different studies, but the incidence has been quoted to be between 6% and 39%.[13, 40, 144, 233] Shuler and co-workers[225] found that 80% of the diaphyseal fractures were located in the middle or distal thirds of the femur. Two fractures were segmental, and of the remaining 50 fractures, 66% had Winquist-Hansen type 3 or 4 comminution.

Management of combined hip and femoral shaft fractures has changed considerably in the last 25 years. Casey and Chapman[40] reported on the treatment of 21 fractures. Eight patients were treated in traction, with some being supplemented by a spica cast, two were treated by fixing the femoral neck and using traction to treat the diaphyseal fracture, five had femoral neck fixa-

tion and diaphyseal plate fixation, one had femoral neck fixation and a Küntscher intramedullary nail, and the remaining five were treated by flexible Ender nails, which were used to stabilize both fractures. This study is important in that it concluded that fixation of femoral neck fractures was mandatory and fixation of femoral diaphyseal fractures strongly advised. Subsequent treatment has consisted of a gradual refinement of the internal fixation techniques. Nowadays, four basic methods may be used to fix combined neck shaft fractures. These methods are shown in Figure 52–39. Swiontkowski and colleagues[233] developed a protocol of using cancellous screw fixation for the femoral neck fracture and retrograde nailing for the shaft fracture. They treated the femoral neck fracture first in the hope of minimizing avascular necrosis. Their retrograde nailing technique involved placing the reamed nail through the medial femoral condyle above the articular surface. This technique is no longer used, but as yet, no reports have described the use of cancellous screw fixation and retrograde nailing from the intercondylar approach. There is, however, no good reason why this technique should not work well, and it may well prove easier to use than antegrade nailing and cancellous screw fixation.

In the study of Bennett and co-workers,[13] only three patients were treated in traction. Twenty-one (15%) of their fractures were treated with an antegrade femoral nail, with

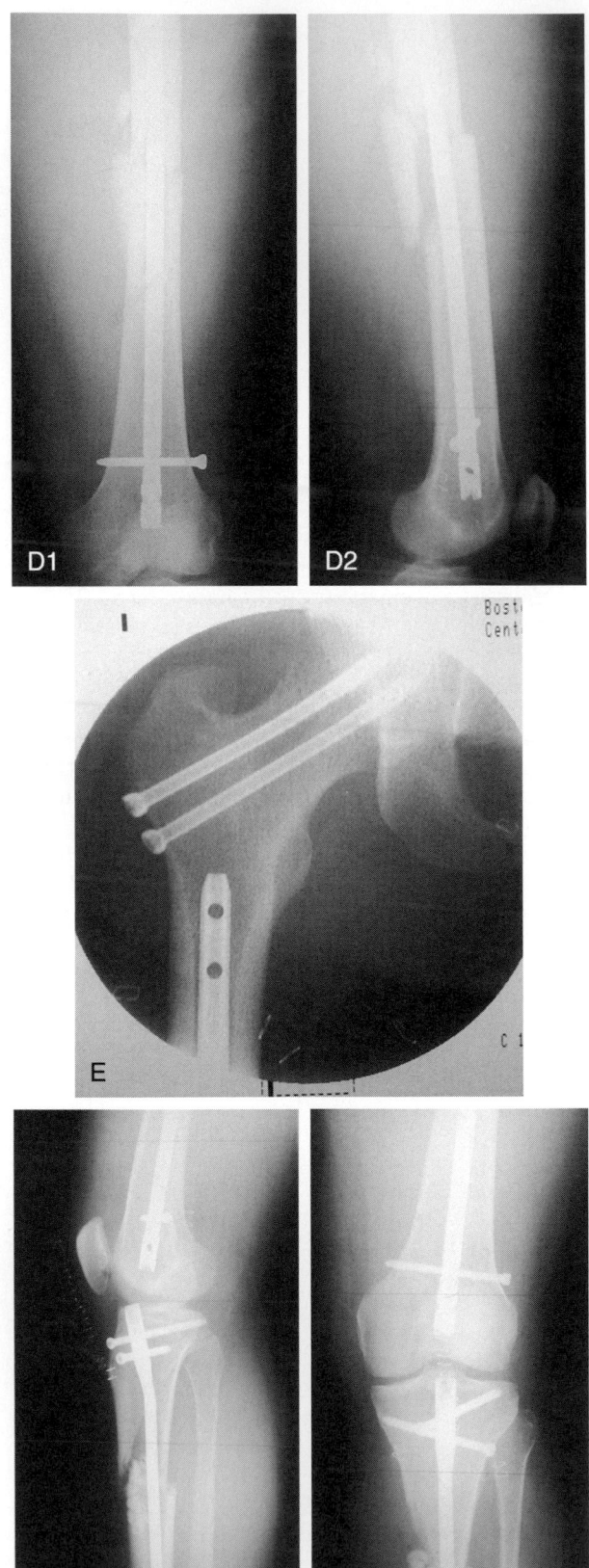

multiple pins or screws being used for the neck fracture. In this study, six patients were treated with reconstruction nails so that, as with flexible Ender nails, one implant could be used to treat both fractures. Unlike Ender nails, reconstruction nails can be used to treat all diaphyseal fractures regardless of comminution. Leung and colleagues[144] treated all 16 fractures with antegrade reamed nailing and cancellous screws for the femoral neck fracture. Chen and associates[44] used this technique for 2 of their 18 fractures, but the remaining 16 diaphyseal fractures were treated with plates, and the neck fracture was treated with cancellous screws or a hip screw system. They treated two hip fractures with bipolar arthroplasty. Alho and co-workers[2] examined the use of cephalomedullary reconstruction nails in the management of complex femoral fracture patterns (see Figs. 52–10 and 52–19). They defined four fracture types: fractures below a previously inserted proximal femoral hip screw system, complex intertrochanteric/subtrochanteric fractures, ipsilateral trochanteric and diaphyseal fractures, and ipsilateral subcapital and diaphyseal fractures. Overall, their results were good, but they emphasized the need for experience in intramedullary nailing techniques if cephalomedullary reconstruction nails are to be used.

Given the severity of this fracture combination, the outcome is usually good. Table 52–14 shows that in most series, the femoral neck fractures all united without late avascular necrosis. This outcome is interesting given the high incidence of displaced neck fractures in some series. Presumably, the good results relate to the relative youth of the patients. The femoral diaphyseal fractures had a nonunion rate of 0% to 29.2%. Most nonunions were treated by bone grafting, although exchange nailing is appropriate for some of these fractures. Friedman and Wyman[85] reported that 65% of their patients had good results, and patients with extracapsular and intracapsular proximal fractures had equivalent results. Leung and colleagues[144] used the same scoring system and rated 87.5% of the patients to have good results.

Femoral neck and shaft fractures are fairly rare, and a significant proportion of them are missed primarily. Surgeons should always bear this combination of fractures in mind when examining a patient with a femoral fracture, particularly if the fracture has resulted from a motor vehicle accident. If a proximal fracture is suspected, MRI or CAT scans can be used to confirm the diagnosis for fractures not readily apparent on standard radiographs (see Fig. 52–38C). A number of treatment methods can be used. Priority goes to reduction and fixation of the femoral neck fracture. Most fractures have been treated by antegrade femoral nailing and cancellous screws. If this technique is used, the nail must be inserted first in case the cancellous screws block its passage down the intramedullary canal. The technique gives good results, but the options of cephalomedullary reconstruction nailing or retrograde femoral nailing and cancellous screws (see Fig. 52–38) exist and may well prove to be better techniques. If a surgeon is not familiar with intramedullary nailing techniques, the use of cancellous screws and a diaphyseal plate has been shown to give good results. If a complex intertrochanteric fracture is associated with a diaphyseal

**Figure 52–38** *Continued. D,* The diaphyseal fracture was treated by retrograde nailing. *E,* The femoral neck fracture was treated with cancellous screws. *F,* The patient also had a floating knee that was treated by intramedullary nailing. (Courtesy of P. Tornetta, M.D.)

**TABLE 52–14**

Data from Studies of Ipsilateral Femoral Diaphyseal and Proximal Femoral Fractures

| | N | Age (yr) | MVA (%) | Extracapsular (%) | Subcapital* U | Subcapital* D | Basal Cervical (%) | Femoral Shaft Nonunion (%) | Proximal Femoral Nonunion (%) | AVN (%) |
|---|---|---|---|---|---|---|---|---|---|---|
| Casey and Chapman[40] | 21 | 37 | 71.4 | 42.9 | 14.3 | 23.8 | 19.0 | 4.8 | 0 | 0 |
| Swiontkowski et al.[233] | 15 | 32 | 100 | 0 | 20 | 80 | 0 | 0 | 0 | 13.3 |
| Friedman and Wyman[85] | 24 | 37.4 | 75 | 58 | 42 | | 0 | 29.2 | 0 | 0 |
| Chaturvedi and Sahu[43] | 17 | 28 | 88.2 | 0 | 58.8 | 41.2 | 0 | 11.8 | 5.9 | 0 |
| Bennett et al.[13] | 42 | 31 | 88.1 | 11.9 | 88.1 | | 0 | 4.8 | 7.1 | 0 |
| Leung et al.[144] | 16 | 29.8 | 56.2 | 25 | 18.7 | 12.5 | 43.7 | 0 | 6.2 | 0 |
| Chen et al.[44] | 18 | 40 | 83 | 0 | 33.3 | 44.4 | 22.2 | 5.5 | 0 | 0 |

*U and D refer to undisplaced and displaced subcapital fractures.
*Abbreviations:* AVN, avascular necrosis; MVA, motor vehicle accident.

fracture, either a reconstruction nail or a proximal hip screw and a diaphyseal plate is recommended.

## BILATERAL FRACTURES

The Epidemiology section of this chapter shows that in Edinburgh, Scotland, 5.8% of patients with femoral fractures had bilateral fractures. Because this unit admits all patients with femoral fractures from a defined population, the incidence would seem to be accurate. However, the incidence of bilateral femoral fractures will vary between hospitals, depending on the type of patients admitted to the institutions. For example, Shock Trauma in Baltimore admits more seriously injured patients, and their incidence of bilateral femoral fractures was higher at 9.6%.[56]

It is generally agreed that patients with bilateral femoral fractures are more severely injured than those with a unilateral fracture. The descriptive indices for both unilateral and bilateral femoral fractures in Edinburgh, Scotland, are shown in Table 52–6. Bilateral fracture patients tended to be younger and have a higher ISS. The morphology of the fractures was similar between the two groups, but the soft tissue injuries, as graded by the Gustilo classification, were worse in the bilateral group. This detail is borne out by the fact that 24% of the bilateral group had other more serious musculoskeletal injuries, such as pelvic fractures, as compared with 5% in the unilateral group.

Copeland and colleagues[56] have shown similar findings in Baltimore, although the patients all tended to be more seriously injured. They found no age difference between bilateral and unilateral fracture groups, but the respective ISSs were 30.2 and 24.5. A 25.9% mortality rate was observed in the bilateral group as compared with 11.7% in the unilateral group, but multivariate analysis showed that it was factors other than bilaterality that accounted for the

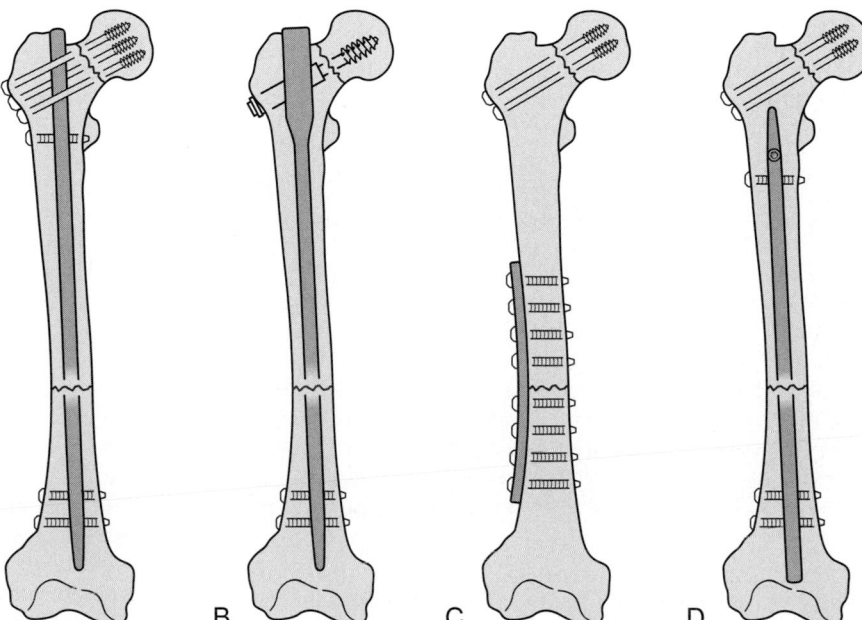

**FIGURE 52–39.** Different treatment methods for the combination of femoral diaphyseal and hip fractures.

increased mortality. They also found that the bilateral group had a significantly greater incidence of head injuries, abdominal injuries, and pelvic fractures.

Treatment of bilateral femoral fracture is the same as for unilateral fractures (see Fig. 52–32). Virtually all surgeons would use intramedullary nailing. Concern has been expressed about the use of simultaneous intramedullary nailing for bilateral fractures[23] because of the potential problems with fat embolism. This problem is discussed in depth elsewhere in this chapter, but clinical evidence of problems related to bilateral femoral nailing is sparse. Bonnevialle and co-workers[23] examined 40 simultaneous nailing procedures retrospectively. They looked at pulmonary function preoperatively, intraoperatively, and postoperatively and showed no evidence that the risks of bilateral simultaneous femoral nailing were greater than those of unilateral nailing. This conclusion was confirmed by Christie[50] with transesophageal echocardiography.

## COMPLICATIONS OF FEMORAL FRACTURES

### Nonunion

#### ASEPTIC NONUNION

Femoral nonunion is relatively uncommon. Nowadays, most surgeons use intramedullary nails to treat both closed and open femoral fractures, and Tables 52–9 and 52–11 show that nonunion is rare after reamed nailing. It is a little more common after unreamed nailing, but the incidence is still only about 5%. However, femoral nonunion does occur, and surgeons should be aware of the methods of treatment.

Nonunion is conventionally classified as aseptic or infected, with the former being more common. It is also classified according to whether the bone has shown any healing response. If it has, the nonunion is termed hypertrophic or oligotrophic, depending on the extent of the response. Failure to mount a healing response at all results in an atrophic nonunion. The classification commonly used for nonunion is that of Weber and Cech,[262] as shown in Figure 52–40.

Aseptic nonunion usually manifests as persistent pain at the site of the fracture, along with radiologic failure of progression of union (Fig. 52–41). The definition of what actually constitutes a nonunion can be difficult to pinpoint because union varies with the degree of soft tissue damage associated with the fracture. Because such damage is difficult to measure reliably, it is impossible to be specific about when a particular fracture will unite. It has been suggested that a nonunion is present when a minimum of 9 months has elapsed since surgery and the fracture has shown no visible progressive signs of healing for 3 months.[236] This time frame is reasonable in that few closed or Gustilo type I, II, or IIIa fractures will take 6 months to unite and the type IIIb or IIIc fractures that do take longer should show signs of progression of union. However, it is unreasonable to wait 9 months to treat every nonunion, so secondary surgery to stimulate union should

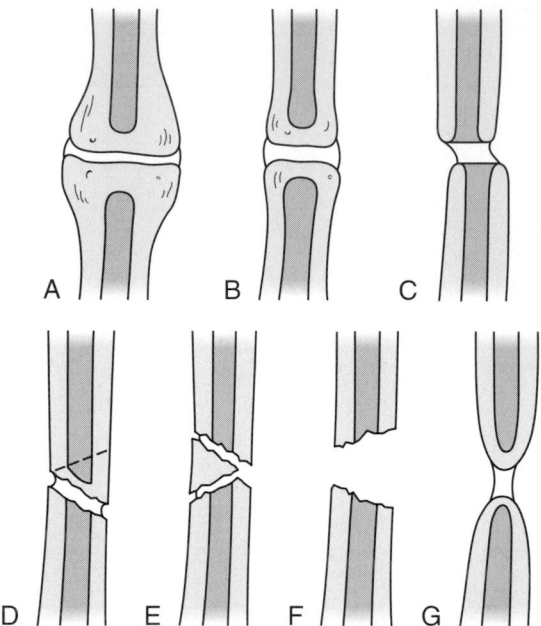

**Figure 52–40.** Classification of nonunion described by Weber and Cech (1976). The *top line* represents nonunions capable of a biologic reaction (hypertrophic or oligotrophic). *A,* Elephant's foot; *B,* horse's foot; *C,* oligotrophic nonunion. The *bottom line* represents nonunions incapable of a biologic reaction (atrophic). *D,* Dystrophic (torsional) wedge fracture; *E,* necrotic nonunion (avascular segment), *F,* bone defect; *G,* atrophic nonunion.

be offered to the patient whenever it is clear that union is not progressing satisfactorily.

The use of intramedullary nailing has complicated the problem of diagnosing nonunion further. Movement at the fracture site or pain on stressing a fracture was always used as a method of detecting nonunion, but these clinical signs are not applicable if a nail or plate has been used to treat the fracture. A particular problem of intramedullary nailing is that the fracture may partially unite such that the bone across the fracture is rigid but circumferential union is deficient (Fig. 52–42). Technically, this condition is not a nonunion, but it may be necessary to graft the femur to get circumferential union at the fracture site if the surgeon considers that the existing bone bridge is inadequate or is considering nail removal. Unfortunately, no guidelines have been proposed for when this type of bone defect should be grafted, and the surgeon will have to rely on judgment and experience. However, bone grafting is advised if the strength of the bone bridge at the fracture site is at all in doubt.

Because most femoral fractures will be nailed, the surgeon will have to rely on the patient's subjective symptoms and the radiologic appearance. The radiologic appearance of aseptic nonunion may be obvious, but not in all cases. It is always tempting for the surgeon to believe that successive radiographs are showing improved union, but it must be remembered that outpatient radiographs are not standardized and that radiographs taken at different angles may appear to show different results. Thus the surgeon must be careful when interpreting radiographs. The surgeon may resort to conventional tomography, CAT scans, or radioisotope bone scans to confirm the presence of a nonunion, but even after extensive investigation, neither the radiologist nor the surgeon may be sure about the diagnosis; under these circumstances, the surgeon must rely on experience, and the decision regarding whether treatment is required is often based on the history and clinical signs.

Nonunions are caused by a number of factors. The most common causes are infection, soft tissue damage resulting in impaired bone vascularity, excessive fracture site mobility, bone loss, distraction, and soft tissue interposi-

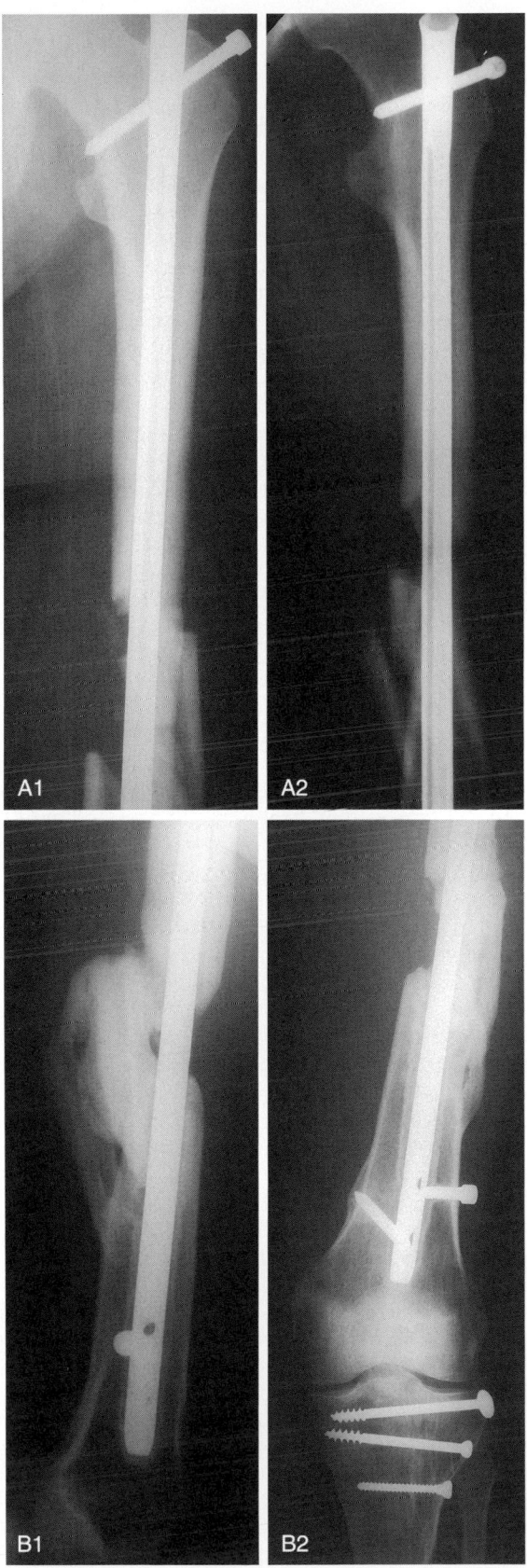

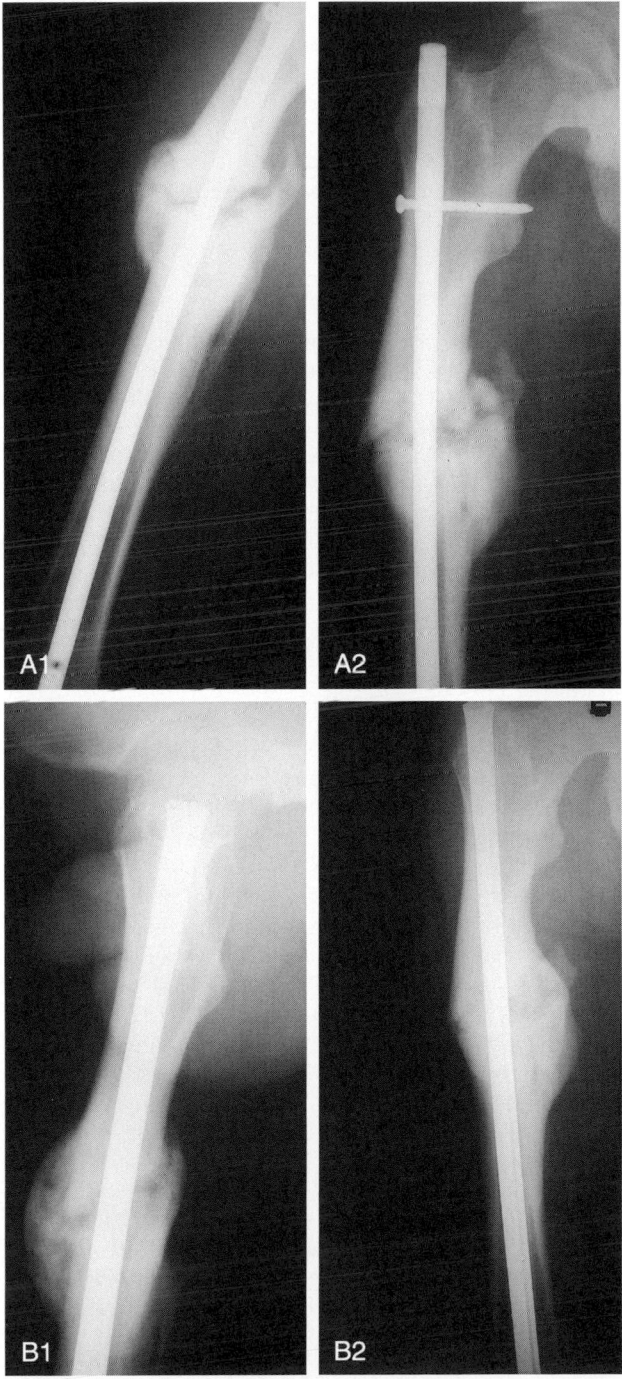

**FIGURE 52–41.** *A,* A Hypertrophic nonunion in a young adult man 6 months after primary intramedullary nailing. *B,* Exchange nailing induced bone union.

**FIGURE 52–42.** *A,* AO/OTA type C femoral fracture in a 35-year-old man. Note the displacement of the comminuted fragments after nailing. *B,* Union occurred but was deficient anteromedially, although a good posterolateral bone buttress was present. The patient was asymptomatic, but the nail was not removed. Note that the single distal cross screw has broken and the fracture has shortened. The medial end of the broken screw is caught in the nail and has angulated.

tion. Other causes are compartment syndrome[57] and the use of nonsteroidal anti-inflammatory drugs.[92] Any factor that causes impaired tissue vascularity will increase the incidence of diaphyseal nonunion. Common causes of impaired vascularity are smoking, diabetes, and peripheral vascular disease. Nonunion is also associated with certain neurologic diseases and diseases that affect bone turnover and bone union, such as hyperparathyroidism and Paget's disease.

### Treatment of Aseptic Aligned Nonunion

Most nonunions will be aseptic nonunions that have occurred after the use of an intramedullary nail. The usual methods that surgeons consider when treating such a nonunion are dynamization, exchange nailing, and bone grafting. Dynamization refers to the conversion of a statically locked intramedullary nail to a dynamically locked nail by removal of either the proximal or distal cross screws. It is perhaps surprising that it has become popular because the evidence that it actually works is anecdotal. Indeed, good evidence from the literature has shown that dynamization has little effect on fracture union.[30, 229, 269, 270] Wu[276] examined 28 statically locked femurs and used dynamization at an average of 6 months after fracture. Radiographs of all the femurs suggested either an oligotrophic or atrophic nonunion. He found that 58% of the fractures went on to union. Wu and Chen[277] also examined 56 segmental femoral fractures treated by statically locked nailing. They reported that 44 (78.6%) united without further treatment. In the remaining 12 cases, the fracture was dynamized at 6 months, and five fractures then united. They recommended the use of early cancellous bone grafting for nonunions.

Studies of dynamization of the femur are bedeviled by a lack of definition of nonunion and when dynamization should be undertaken. It is difficult to see why dynamization should work 6 months after the fracture was initially treated. Presumably, fibrous union has occurred by this time, and it is not easy to know how much fracture site movement is engendered by dynamization. With such a high rate of union, it would be difficult to undertake a prospective study, but all the papers that have examined dynamization have suggested that it has little value in the treatment of femoral nonunion.

**Exchange Nailing.** Exchange nailing refers to the practice of removing an intramedullary nail, reaming the intramedullary canal, and inserting a larger nail (see Fig. 52–41). It has been shown to be particularly useful in the management of tibial nonunion after primary nailing.[59, 238] Webb and colleagues[261] examined the treatment of femoral diaphyseal nonunion by reamed intramedullary nailing. They reported on 105 nonunions but stressed that only 55 fractures had initially been treated by intramedullary nailing. Bone grafting was required in only 7 cases, and in the 101 patients whom they were able to monitor, 98 (97%) achieved union in an average of 20 weeks. The remaining fractures healed after repeat exchange nailing, and the authors stressed that 2 mm of additional reaming is necessary to stimulate the healing response. Furlong and co-workers[87] analyzed 25 patients who had exchange nailing carried out for aseptic femoral nonunion. They stated that the average time to establish a definitive diagnosis of femoral nonunion was 54.7 weeks, and they emphasized the need for early diagnosis and treatment to permit patients to return to normal activities as soon as possible. All patients were treated by exchange nailing, but 48% of the patients had open autologous bone grafting performed at the same time. Only one patient's fracture did not unite, and the mean time to union for the exchange nailing group was 36.2 weeks, with 24.6 weeks being reported for the group that had both exchange nailing and bone grafting. The difference was not significant. They showed no correlation between union time and smoking habits or nail type.

Weresh and associates[265] also undertook a retrospective review of aseptic femoral nonunion treated by exchange nailing. Their results were not as good as those of Furlong and co-workers. They analyzed 19 patients and reamed all the femurs by at least 2 mm before inserting the second nail. The investigators reported that 53% of the fractures healed but the remaining patients had to have a third procedure involving further bone stabilization and grafting. They found no correlation between the type of nonunion, the location of the diaphyseal fracture, the use of static or dynamic locking, or the use of tobacco products and the need for additional surgical procedures after exchange nailing.

Hak and colleagues[102] studied 23 patients whose femoral fracture failed to show progression of union 4 months after primary treatment with a reamed nail. The exchange nailing procedure involved reaming between 1 and 3 mm, although most femurs were reamed an extra 2 mm. Unlike the previous two papers, this study showed an association between smoking and fracture union. All the nonsmokers' fractures united after exchange nailing, but only 66.7% of the smokers' fractures healed after exchange nailing. Overall, their success rate was 78.3%, and the authors thought that it was the treatment of choice for most femoral diaphyseal nonunions.

Surgeons may well encounter aligned aseptic nonunions in fractures that have been previously plated. Optimal treatment of these fractures is reamed intramedullary nailing, particularly if they are oligotrophic or hypertrophic. Kempf and co-workers[131] examined the use of reamed intramedullary nailing in the management of 27 aseptic femoral nonunions. Eighteen (66.7%) of their patients had been treated primarily with a plate. The authors removed the plate, closed the wound, and undertook closed nailing of the nonunion. They reported excellent results, with a 92.6% overall union rate and no requirement for further surgery.

Ring and colleagues[201] described the use of a wave plate to treat complex femoral nonunions. Wave plates are regular plates with a contour bent into the plate so that it stands away from the bone in the area of the nonunion. This design is said to reduce damage to the local vascular supply of the bone, and the ability to place bone graft laterally under the "wave" in the plate is said to have a biomechanical advantage.[19] Ring and co-workers treated 42 femoral nonunions.[201] This series was a mixed group of segmental defects, previous infections, and pathologic fractures. A review of the paper suggests that 90.5% of the fractures united. They recommend the use of wave plates, but it is in fact difficult to see the advantages of this technique over a reamed interlocking nail, which allows early weight bearing and is associated with less soft tissue stripping to insert the implant. Biomechanical arguments regarding the use of lateral grafting are also fallacious because an intramedullary nail provides more advantageous biomechanical conditions for fracture union. Using plates over nails seems to have little advantage in this situation.

### Treatment of Malaligned Aseptic Fractures

Malaligned nonunions will usually follow nonoperative management or primary external fixation of the femoral fracture. External fixation is rarely used, but if surgeons have to treat a nonunion after external skeletal fixation, it is important to be aware of the problems associated with pin tract sepsis. It is likely that a malaligned aseptic nonunion in an externally fixed femoral fracture will be treated by open reduction and reamed intramedullary nailing. Little information is available about the late consequences of reamed nailing after primary external fixation in femurs, but based on the tibial literature, surgeons should not nail if draining pin tracts are present. Nowotarski and co-workers[176] followed this principle when they treated multiply injured patients with primary external fixation and secondary reamed nailing, and they reported good results. If the pin tracts are draining, they should undergo curettage or be overdrilled and local treatment instituted. Nailing should be delayed until no evidence of pin tract sepsis can be found.

One of the major problems associated with nonoperative management of femoral fractures is malunion, and if nonunion occurs in a femoral fracture originally treated by traction or cast management, it is highly unlikely that surgeons will be able to treat the nonunion by closed intramedullary nailing. The best treatment for nonunion under these circumstances is open correction of the deformity and reamed intramedullary nailing. Okhotsky and Souvalyan[179] treated 197 nonunions with unlocked nails, 51 of which were femoral. They reported 76.2% good results and 20.6% satisfactory results. If a surgeon is faced with nailing a femur in which the primary treatment was not an intramedullary nail, it should be realized that a fibro-osseous callous plug will be present at the nonunion site. This material is extremely difficult to penetrate, and under no circumstance should a nail be hammered through it without previous reaming. Power reamers will not penetrate the fibrous plug, so hand reamers of increasing size must be used to break the fibrous tissue down to allow passage of a nail. If the operation is open, it is usually easier to mobilize the nonunion and remove the endosteal plug by reaming proximally and distally from the nonunion site. The fracture can then be reduced and nailed in the usual way. Bone graft is frequently required to fill any defects that are left after reduction of the nonunion.

## INFECTED NONUNION

Infected femoral nonunion is extremely rare and will usually follow inadequately treated open femoral fractures, although an operatively treated closed fracture can become infected. Patients will usually have thigh pain and a pyogenic collection or a discharging sinus. If the infection is detected at an early stage, evidence of a pyogenic collection may not be found, but the patient may complain of increasing pain associated with systemic symptoms. The erythrocyte sedimentation rate and C-reactive protein levels may be elevated, and the patient may complain of pyrexia, shivering, fatigue, or other symptoms of infection. If the infection is detected early without evidence of a pyogenic collection on clinical examination or ultrasound, the infection can be treated by high-dose antibiotics with every expectation of success.[58] However, early diagnosis is uncommon, and patients will usually have a pyogenic collection related to the fracture or a discharging sinus. Under these circumstances, basic surgical principles should be followed. The femur should be explored, with all infected or devitalized material removed. It is often difficult to judge whether bone is infected, and a surgeon may have to assess the extent of the devitalized bone from preoperative radiographs and intraoperative clinical examination. If the femur has previously been nailed, exchange nailing should be undertaken to remove the infected membrane from the intramedullary canal. Indeed, reaming of the intramedullary canal is useful no matter what method of bone fixation was used primarily because infected material will usually be found within the intramedullary canal. The femur should then be stabilized and the soft tissues closed. Klemm[136] suggested that the femur be stabilized with an intramedullary nail and that an irrigation-drainage system be established for about 4 weeks. Many surgeons would find such management difficult, but an irrigation system for a shorter period can be used to facilitate wound cleansing after surgical débridement of all infected tissues. Nowadays, many surgeons would place antibiotic-impregnated beads into the femoral defect. This practice may well be beneficial in delivering antibiotics to the infected area, but a second benefit of using antibiotic-impregnated beads is that they preserve the space between the bone ends from encroachment by the surrounding soft tissues, thereby facilitating later bone grafting. The use of antibiotic-impregnated beads should not replace adequate excision of all infected or avascular tissue.

Once all infected or devitalized tissue has been removed, the nonunion site should be stabilized. As with primary fracture management, the surgeon can choose among locked intramedullary nailing, external fixation, or plating. Each stabilization method has its proponents, and few studies are available in the literature to help the surgeon decide among them. External fixation was advocated by Barquet and colleagues.[7] They presented 13 cases of infected femoral nonunion and used a multiplanar fixator in their treatment protocol. Gentamicin-impregnated beads were implanted and systemic antibiotics administered for 4 to 6 weeks after débridement. After this period, they grafted the nonunions with corticocancellous autograft. These authors succeeded in controlling the infection in 11 (84.6%) patients and achieved union in 12 (92.3%). Their major problem was clearly knee movement, which was described as "useful" in 7 (53.8%) patients. Ueng and associates[248] documented the use of a two-stage procedure to treat 15 infected femoral nonunions. They used the same basic protocol as Barquet and co-workers[7]:

débridement, antibiotic beads, and external skeletal fixation. The resulting bone defects measured between 0.5 and 15 cm. The authors performed the second operation 2 to 6 weeks after the initial débridement, and they used autogenous iliac crest grafts in 11 patients and microvascular osteoseptocutaneous fibular grafts in 4. They achieved union in all patients, the fixator being in position for an average of 9 months. Again, the main complication was knee stiffness, with three (20%) patients requiring quadricepsplasty and arthrolysis to improve knee mobility. The study by Ring and colleagues[201] detailing use of the wave plate has already been described. They ascribed considerable advantages to this plate and achieved a high rate of union given the complexity of some of the fractures that were treated. Thirty-one (73.8%) patients regained full knee movement.

Klemm[136] analyzed 37 patients who had infected nonunion of the femur after both primary plate and intramedullary nail treatment. All 37 patients were treated in a similar manner: removal of the implant, thorough débridement, insertion of an intramedullary nail, and establishment of an irrigation system. Antibiotics were given for 2 to 3 weeks after surgery, and in some patients, gentamicin-impregnated beads were used. Of the 21 patients who were originally treated by plate osteosynthesis, union was achieved in 18 (85.7%), and all 16 of the fractures originally treated with an intramedullary nail united.

The author favors the use of intramedullary nails for stabilizing infected femoral nonunions after complete excision of all infected and devitalized material. The advantage of intramedullary nailing is that less dissection is involved than with plating, the biomechanics of intramedullary nailing are superior, and earlier weight bearing is possible. Plating offers some advantages over external fixation, which is inevitably associated with joint stiffness when used on the femur for a prolonged period.

## Bone Loss

Treatment of primary bone loss depends mainly on the amount of bone that has to be replaced. Up to 5 cm of bone loss can be replaced by corticocancellous autograft, but in longer bone defects, the surgeon should consider other methods of management. In many respects, management of bone loss after a fracture is much the same as after resection of infected or dead bone in an infected nonunion. Bone loss has been classified by the OTA (Fig. 52–43) into three types. Type 1 occurs when the missing segment includes less than 50% of the bone diameter, such as when caused by the loss of a small butterfly fragment. In type 2 bone loss, the deficit involves more than 50% of the bone circumference, and in type 3, a bone segment is missing. In the acute situation, all type 1 and most type 2 degrees of bone loss can be treated by reamed intramedullary nailing, although bone grafting will be required if the surgeon favors plating or external fixation. Very few femoral defects will be OTA type 3, but the treatment is essentially the same no matter whether the bone loss is primary (i.e., after the fracture) or secondary, such as after treatment of an infected nonunion. The options for treating a type 3 bone defect are autogenous bone grafts,

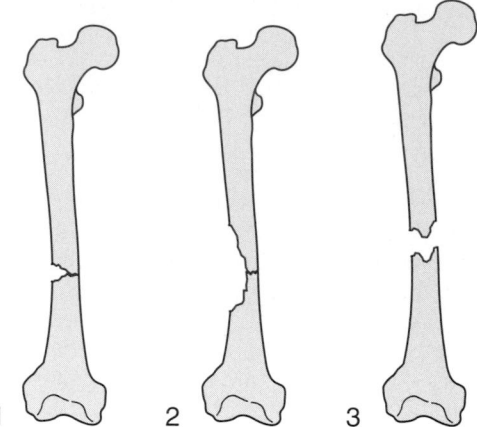

**FIGURE 52–43.** OTA classification of bone loss. See text for an explanation.

vascularized bone grafts, bone shortening and lengthening, or bone transport. Very little information in the literature is available to suggest which is the best technique. Autogenous bone grafting can be used to fill defects larger than 5 cm, but it is a time-consuming treatment method, and frequently more than one bone graft may be required. The author has used autogenous bone graft to treat a 12-cm defect stabilized with a reamed intramedullary nail (Fig. 52–44). During the healing process, the patient walked on the nail, which broke and had to be replaced, but eventually she healed well with normal hip and knee movement. Wei and coauthors[263] described the use of vascularized free fibula osteoseptocu-

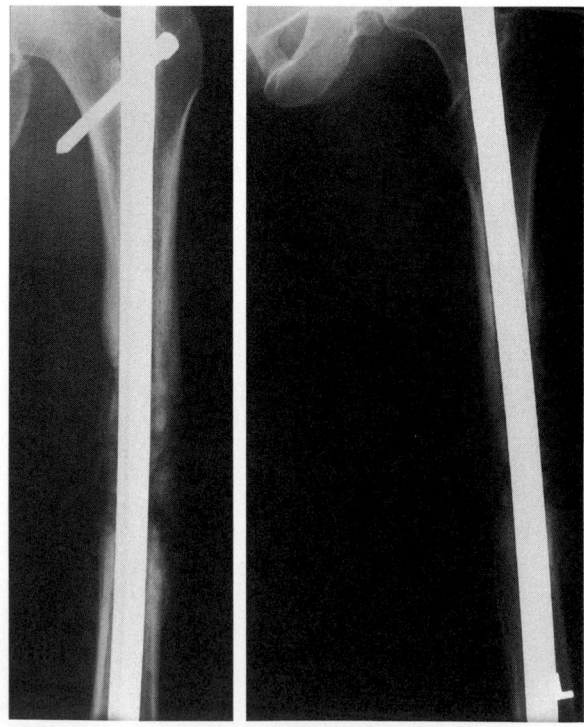

**FIGURE 52–44.** Anteroposterior and lateral radiographs showing bone grafting of a bone defect resulting from the treatment of infection. Two grafts were required, but excellent long-term function was achieved.

taneous grafts for the reconstruction of segmental femoral defects. In an 8-year period they undertook 17 such operations in patients with bone defects that averaged 10 cm. The bone was stabilized with an external fixator, and the average time to radiologic union was 8 months, with the average time to weight bearing being 14 months. Secondary bone grafting was required in five (29.4%) cases. The major problem was loss of knee mobility, and four patients (23.5%) required quadricepsplasty. The other common problem with diaphyseal external fixation is malunion, and five of their patients (29.4%) had a varus deformity averaging 30°.

External fixation can be used to treat complex nonunions and correct shortening and angular deformity simultaneously. More information is available about the tibia than the femur, but Saleh and Royston[210] documented use of the technique in four femoral nonunions. They used distraction osteogenesis and gained union in all cases. The duration of treatment averaged 9.5 months, but the authors did not comment on limb function. Maini and colleagues[152] used the Ilizarov fixator to treat six infected femoral nonunions. All the femurs united, but five of the patients had a stiff knee and walked with a limp. Saleh and Rees[209] compared bone transport with primary compression and secondary distraction in long bone fractures. Most of the fractures were tibial, but they did treat five femoral nonunions. They favored compression distraction but presented no functional results and stressed the need for such surgery to be performed in specialist centers.

It is difficult to be prescriptive about the best method of treating OTA type 3 bone defects. Small wire external fixators are currently popular, and union can undoubtedly be achieved with good correction of deformity and length. However, virtually no information has been presented regarding function, and the overwhelming impression in the literature dealing with external fixation of the femur is that knee stiffness is a considerable problem. Stiffness may not matter if the alternative is amputation, but more studies are required before the technique can be recommended for widespread use in femoral nonunions or for bone loss in patients with normal limb function. Currently, the author favors bone grafting and intramedullary nailing for all OTA type 1, 2, and smaller type 3 defects because function is more likely to be maintained.

## Malunion

No adequate definition of what constitutes femoral malunion after treatment of a femoral diaphyseal fracture has been presented, and virtually no investigation of the effect of femoral malunion on function has been conducted (Fig. 52–45). Most of the studies of lower limb malunion have been undertaken in the tibia, and it has been shown that tibial malunion is associated with late knee and ankle osteoarthritis.[95, 252] No equivalent studies, however, have examined the effect of femoral malunion on ipsilateral hip or knee function or have investigated whether malunited femurs cause hip or knee osteoarthritis. In the absence of any good data, it is reasonable to suggest that a definition of femoral malunion should be based on that of tibial malunion. Unfortunately, authorities have shown

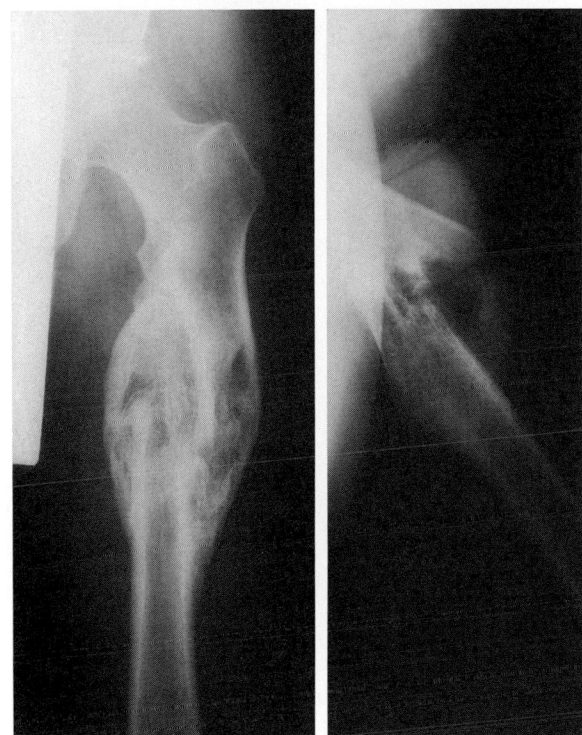

**FIGURE 52–45.** Malunion of a nonoperatively managed proximal diaphyseal fracture. Note the flexed position of the proximal fragment. This position affected the patient's hip function, so an osteotomy was undertaken.

little uniformity of opinion about the definition of what constitutes tibial malunion, although many surgeons will accept up to 5° of rotational or angular deformity and up to 1 cm of shortening.

Logically, it seems reasonable to return the femur to its normal length and alignment after fracture, and presumably, any significant deviation from normal will have some long-term effects, although they may be minimal. However, the definition of what constitutes an acceptable deviation from the normal femur will always be difficult to define because it depends on the patient's tolerance of long-term symptoms, which will depend on age, general health, and a number of other factors. Many younger patients may also have other coexisting injuries, including knee damage, and these injuries may mask the effects of femoral malunion. The author believes it reasonable to strive for anatomic femoral alignment but to accept up to 5° of angular or rotational malalignment and up to 1 cm of shortening. However, I accept that many patients with greater degrees of deformity will refuse reconstructive surgery because they have little or no symptoms, and no evidence has shown that all deformities greater than 5° cause significant clinical symptoms.

Nowadays, most malunions are related to previous femoral intramedullary nailing. Figure 52–25 shows an angular malunion that resulted from a poorly performed femoral nailing procedure. The patient was middle aged and asymptomatic, and corrective surgery was not desired or undertaken. Figure 52–32 shows bilateral closed femoral fractures treated by bilateral interlocking nailing. The left femur was nailed in 40° of external rotation. The

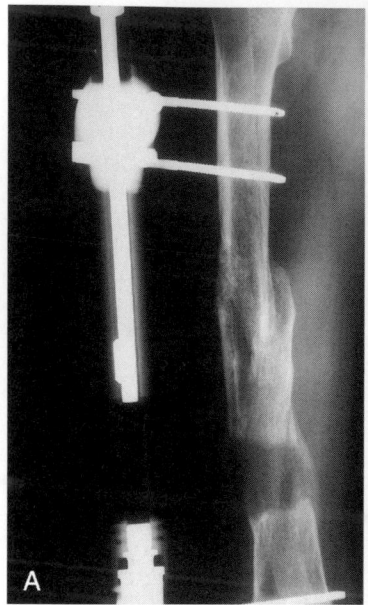
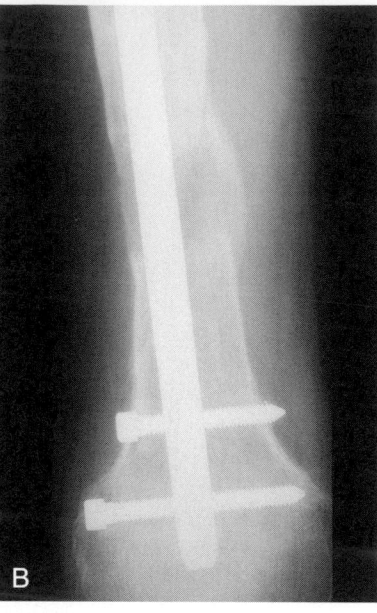

**FIGURE 52–46.** *A,* A femoral fracture in a 45-year-old man treated by dynamically locked nailing despite an unstable fracture pattern. Five centimeters of shortening occurred at the nonunion site. The nonunion was successfully treated by exchange nailing, and 4 cm of lengthening was regained by distraction osteogenesis with a unilateral fixator. *B,* After sufficient length had been regained, a statically locked nail was used to stabilize the regenerate bone.

radiologic sign that a rotational deformity is present is an alteration in width of the cortices above and below the fracture. A third problem encountered after intramedullary femoral nailing is shortening (Fig. 52–46). Shortening usually occurs after inappropriate dynamic nailing of an unstable fracture pattern. If this situation is not rectified before femoral shortening occurs, the femur may well unite short and later lengthening may be required.

If methods other than intramedullary nailing are used to treat diaphyseal femoral fractures, malunion may well follow. It is associated with external fixation and nonoperative management, and although the former method is rarely used for femoral fracture management, many surgeons around the world still rely on nonoperative management in the form of traction or functional bracing. If malunion occurs under these circumstances, it is likely that the femoral intramedullary canal will be malaligned and significant angular or rotational deformity may well be present, in addition to shortening of the femur.

## TREATMENT

If an intramedullary nail has been used to treat the original fracture and an external rotation deformity has ensued, it is relatively easy to correct the malrotation. If the surgeon has access to an intramedullary saw and experience with its use, the best method of derotating the femur is to remove the intramedullary nail, use the intramedullary saw to osteotomize the femur, and then derotate the bone by an appropriate amount. It can then be renailed with the nail being statically locked. Bühren[37] has illustrated the use of a compression nail for such procedures. A proximal screw in the long axis of the nail can be screwed down onto a conventional lateral-to-medial proximal locking screw that lies in a proximal slot. This technique facilitates compression at the osteotomy site. The use of an intramedullary bone saw and a compression nail allows the osteotomy to be undertaken in closed fashion and compression to be applied. If an intramedullary saw is not available, a

conventional open derotation femoral osteotomy is undertaken, with the femur being renailed in the usual way. This osteotomy can be performed with a small incision and the use of multiple drill holes and a small osteotome to minimize bone devascularization.

If varus or valgus malunion has occurred after the intramedullary nailing of a distal diaphyseal fracture (see Fig. 52–25), the surgeon can osteotomize the femur at or close to the fracture site and attempt to renail the femur with the fracture in the reduced position. However, it is often difficult to find a new tract for the guide wires and the nail, and not infrequently, the nail ends up in the original tract and malreduction persists. If this problem occurs, plating can be a very useful alternative procedure to permit femoral straightening (see Fig. 52–20).

Treatment of femoral shortening depends on the degree of shortening present. One hopes that the shortening will be only between 1 and 3 cm, although it is of course quite possible that more than 3 cm of shortening may be present. Shortening of up to 3 cm may be treated effectively by a shoe lift, and in many cases, a lift will be sufficient to treat the patient's symptoms. If, however, the patient remains symptomatic or the shortening is too much to be treated by a shoe lift, surgery will be required. The options are to undertake a gradual lengthening or to attempt to regain femoral length in one operation. The latter procedure has been performed by Kempf and co-workers[132] with intramedullary nailing and by Johnson[122] with both intramedullary nails and plates.

Kempf and colleagues[132] emphasized that the surgical technique of one-stage femoral lengthening is very demanding and requires careful preoperative planning and surgical technique. The patient is placed on a fracture table and a Steinmann pin inserted through the distal end of the femur. The knee is flexed 90° to protect the sciatic nerve, and the hip is flexed slightly to release tension on the femoral nerve. The medullary canal is then over-reamed by at least 2 mm to allow the femur to slide with respect to the intramedullary nail. A Z-shaped osteotomy is then created in the femur, with a second incision made if the osteotomy is placed in the middle or distal thirds of the bone. The length of the vertical axis of the osteotomy should be twice the desired correction. Once the femur is osteotomized, gradual lengthening is undertaken with a transcondylar pin supplemented by a femoral distractor. As the femur lengthens, transverse incisions are made through the tight aponeuroses, fascia, and intermuscular septa. Once the desired length has been achieved, the nail is statically locked and the defect at the osteotomy site is corrected with a bone graft. Kempf and co-workers emphasized the importance of postoperative care to minimize the risk of sciatic or femoral nerve palsies. They stated that up to 4 cm of femoral length could be regained by one-stage lengthening, but they encountered a number of complications. They reported that deep infection developed in 3 of 17 patients (17.6%). Four (23.5%) patients had a femoral nerve palsy, with one patient being left with residual neurologic symptoms. Secondary loss of up to 5 mm in length occurred in seven patients, with four more experiencing secondary shortening of 8 to 10 mm. The authors recommended gradual femoral lengthening if the defect exceeded 4 cm.

Johnson[122] described one-stage lengthening in 19 femoral malunions and nonunions. He used a femoral distractor and an intramedullary nail in 8 femurs and a 95° fixed angled blade plate in the remaining 11 femurs. He grafted 17 of the lengthened femurs with either allograft or autograft. Johnson obtained between 2 and 5 cm of lengthening in the femur, the average length being 3.2 cm. Seven of the femurs failed to unite after the lengthening procedure and required further surgery. He did not encounter neurologic damage after one-stage lengthening of up to 5 cm. Farquharson-Roberts[78] described a fairly simple technique for correcting combined shortening and rotational malunion of the femur after intramedullary nailing. He pointed out that rotation of an oblique osteotomy in a large bone about the axis of an intramedullary nail will cause lengthening as the fragments move on the inclined plane between them. The amount of lengthening in relation to the amount of rotation will depend on the obliquity of the osteotomy. He published a formula to calculate the appropriate angle for an osteotomy that would produce the desired correction in length. Again, the osseous defect left after derotation and lengthening was filled by autograft. Only one case was reported in which 3.5 cm of length and 30° of external rotation were regained. He believed that the maximal safe correction for this technique was 4 cm.

If the malunion is malaligned as a result of the initial use of nonoperative management, the surgeon has little option but to undertake an open procedure and use as many osteotomies as required to straighten the femur so that an intramedullary nail can be introduced. Defects will require bone grafting, and if the procedure is combined with the use of traction or a femoral distractor, up to 4 to 5 cm of lengthening can be achieved.

If the femoral shortening exceeds 4 cm, gradual femoral lengthening should be performed (see Fig. 52–46). In recent years, distraction osteogenesis performed with the Ilizarov device has become popular for lengthening bone, and good results have been obtained with this device in the management of malunion and nonunion of the femur.[184]

However, like all techniques, distraction osteogenesis has its problems, including the long period of external fixation, pin tract sepsis, malalignment, joint stiffness, and late fracture of the regenerate bone[227] (see Fig. 52–17). In an attempt to minimize these complications, surgeons have investigated the combination of intramedullary nailing and external fixation in leg lengthening.

Paley and coauthors[185] reported on 29 patients who had femoral lengthening performed over an intramedullary nail. The nail and external fixator were applied at the time of the osteotomy, which was then distracted by 1 mm/day. The nail was locked when the required length was reached. The results were compared with those of 31 patients who had had femoral lengthening performed with a standard Ilizarov frame. They found that lengthening over the intramedullary nail reduced the average duration of external fixation by about 50%. The radiographic consolidation index (the number of months needed for radiographic consolidation for each centimeter of lengthening) for the limbs lengthened over an intramedullary nail was significantly reduced, and knee motion returned to normal 2.2 times faster in the patients treated with intramedullary nails. The complications in the intramedullary nail group were much less severe than in the age-matched Ilizarov control group, and it was quite clear that lengthening over an intramedullary nail is advantageous. This work was confirmed by Simpson and associates,[227] who presented 20 cases of lengthening over an intramedullary nail. The mean gain in length was 4.7 cm, and they concluded that the method permitted early rehabilitation with rapid return of knee movement. They also reported a lower rate of complications than with the use of an external fixator on its own, but they did raise the particular problem of sepsis because they had three cases of infection, although two followed open fractures. It is clear from the literature that femoral malunion can be treated. However, no matter which method is used, treatment is time consuming, difficult, and associated with a relatively high complication rate. It is obvious that malunion is best avoided, and prevention of malunion is accomplished by adherence to the correct surgical technique when treating the femoral fracture primarily.

## Compartment Syndrome

Thigh compartment syndrome is less common than compartment syndrome of the leg, but it certainly occurs and has a definite association with femoral fracture. In a review of 164 compartment syndromes treated by the Trauma Unit in Edinburgh, Scotland, McQueen and colleagues[159] noted that 5 followed femoral fractures. In the 8-year period of this study, 360 femoral fractures were treated, for a 1.4% incidence of thigh compartment syndrome. This figure is in broad agreement with research from the Shock Trauma Unit in Baltimore.[218] They did not publish a true incidence of compartment syndrome in femoral fractures, but they did establish an incidence of about 1% after closed intramedullary nailing of femoral fractures.

It seems likely that thigh compartment syndrome is underdiagnosed. Schwartz and co-workers[218] noted that only 17 cases had been documented up to 1987, and only one other publication had documented more than 2 cases.[235] It must be emphasized that thigh compartment syndrome is associated with a number of conditions other than fracture. The use of military antishock trousers can cause compartment syndrome, as can crushing from other causes. In addition, coagulopathy, vascular injury, or a direct blow to the thigh may also cause compartment syndrome. Schwartz and colleagues[218] described 21 thigh compartment syndromes, 11 (52.4%) of which were not associated with fracture.

Diagnosis in a conscious patient is usually based on the clinical criteria of increasing pain, with pain on passive muscle stretching being particularly important. If a surgeon waits for dysesthesia or absent pulses, valuable time will be lost and the incidence of myonecrosis will rise. In an unconscious patient, the surgeon will have to rely on clinical suspicion and the presence of a tense swollen thigh. Compartment monitoring is an indispensable aid to diagnosis in these circumstances and has been used successfully by Tarlow and associates[235] and Schwartz and co-workers.[218] The conventional accepted pressure level is either 30 or 40 mm Hg, and in all studies dealing with thigh compartment syndrome, a specific pressure has been used. McQueen and Court-Brown[158] showed the importance of measuring the difference between diastolic blood pressure and intracompartment pressure in tibial fractures. This difference in pressure has not been measured in the thigh, but there is no logical reason why the results should differ from those in the leg. Regardless of the method of compartment monitoring used by the surgeon, direct pressure measuring is a helpful tool and should be used in any patient in whom a thigh compartment syndrome is suspected.

The thigh is divided into three compartments by fascia: the anterior compartment, which contains the vasti, sartorius, and rectus femoris; the medial compartment, which contains the adductors; and the posterior compartment, which contains the hamstrings (see Fig. 52–13). Schwartz and colleagues[218] showed that the anterior compartment was involved in all cases. The medial component had a pressure higher than 30 mm Hg in 8 of 9 cases, and the posterior compartment had a similar pressure in 10 of 11 cases. The importance of early diagnosis is emphasized in the study of Tarlow and co-workers.[235] They used pressure monitoring, but the diagnosis and treatment were delayed. Two of the patients had significant sequelae, including persistent paresthesia, muscle weakness, and fracture nonunion. These observations mirror the situation in the leg, where McQueen and associates[158] have shown significant morbidity related to the late diagnosis of compartment syndrome as compared with early diagnosis facilitated by monitoring. Court-Brown and McQueen[57] also showed that late diagnosis and treatment of compartment syndrome were associated with nonunion.

Treatment of thigh compartment syndrome is by fasciotomy. Schwartz and colleagues[218] suggested decompressing the anterior and posterior compartments through one incision and then measuring the pressure in the medial compartment. If the pressure remained elevated, they decompressed the medial compartment through a separate incision. If monitoring is not used, a three-compartment fasciotomy is mandatory. The approach to the anterior and posterior compartments was described by Tarlow and coauthors.[235] They advocated a midlateral incision from the intertrochanteric line to the lateral condyle. The anterior compartment is then decompressed, and the vastus lateralis is retracted medially to expose the lateral intermuscular septum, which is then incised to expose the musculature of the posterior compartment.

Schwartz and colleagues[218] analyzed the incidence of compartment syndrome after femoral nailing in particular, but in the decade since they completed their study, it has become clear that the act of reaming or nailing a long bone does not increase the incidence of compartment syndrome. Compartment pressure certainly rises during reduction of the fracture as the muscles are stretched, and fracture distraction may significantly raise intracompartment pressure. Open fractures do not protect the patient against compartment syndrome. A number of the fractures documented in the Baltimore series were open, three being Gustilo type III in severity. It seems likely that thigh compartment syndrome is more common than was previously thought. More pressure studies are required, but it is possible that some of the knee stiffness and fracture-healing problems that follow treatment of femoral fractures are related to subclinical or undiagnosed compartment syndrome.

## Knee Stiffness

The incidence of knee stiffness after a femoral diaphyseal fracture depends on a number of factors, such as the severity of the injury, the willingness of the patient to move the knee postoperatively, the state of the knee before injury, and whether a coexisting knee injury is present.[66, 204] It is also obvious that the method of management affects knee stiffness, with nonoperative management[54, 106, 127] and external skeletal fixation[7, 164, 248] resulting in a higher incidence of knee stiffness. Plating and intramedullary nailing are associated with a lower incidence of knee stiffness, but the requirement for muscle mobilization in plating tends to produce more postoperative knee stiffness, although this stiffness will respond to physiotherapy.

Intramedullary nailing can be associated with knee stiffness if a large bone fragment is malaligned in an AO/OTA type B or C fracture (Fig. 52–47). If such malalignment occurs, considerable adhesions may develop between the bone and the overlying muscle, or the bone fragment may actually block muscle action and therefore knee movement. It may be necessary to remove the fragment to regain knee movement. If knee stiffness cannot be treated by physical therapy, surgery to free the adhesions around the fracture may be required. Usually, limited soft tissue release is sufficient, but occasionally, quadricepsplasty will be necessary. Postoperative continuous passive movement is often useful after soft tissue release.

## Periprosthetic Femoral Diaphyseal Fractures

Periprosthetic femoral diaphyseal fractures (Figs. 52–48 and 52–49; see also Chapter 63) provide a challenge to both orthopaedic trauma surgeons and reconstructive

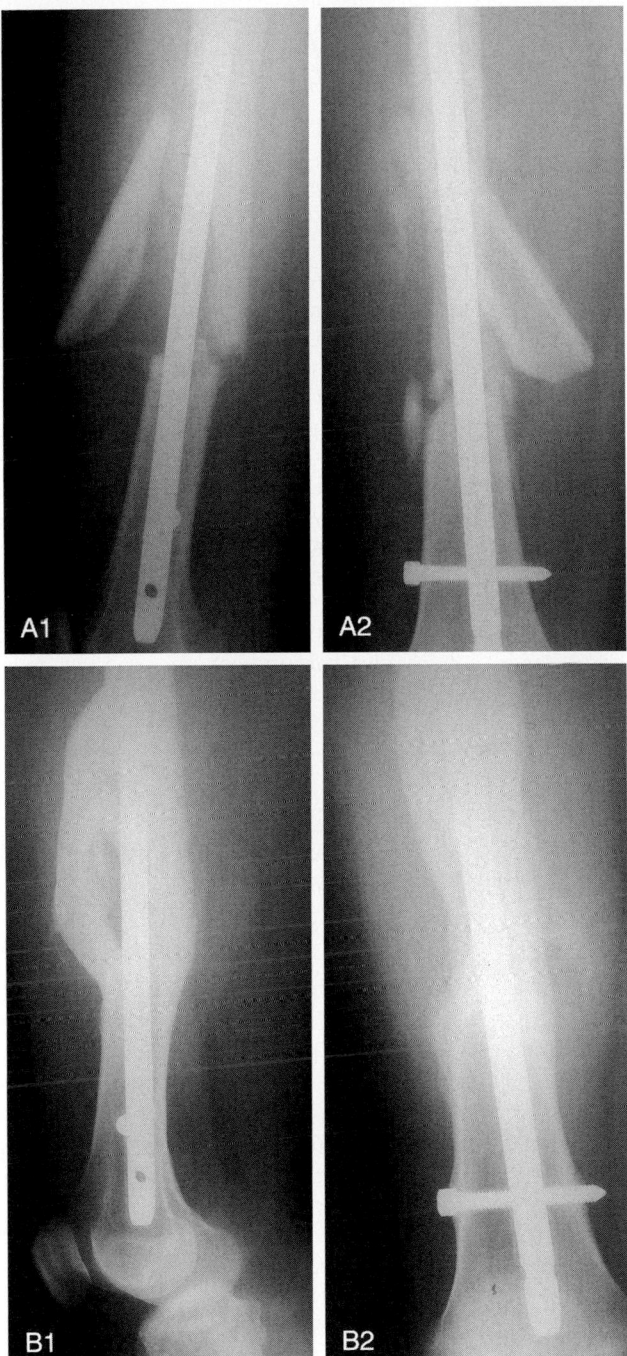

**FIGURE 52–47.** *A,* A displaced anterior bone fragment restricted knee movement and was removed. *B,* The resulting bone defect healed without bone grafting. The patient had a further quadricepsplasty but regained full knee movement.

surgeons. They usually occur in elderly patients, who often have a number of medical co-morbidities and may well have restricted mobility because of arthritis in other joints. Their bone is osteopenic, the implant may be loose, and they may have very little diaphysis that is not already filled with metallic implant. It is inevitable that the incidence of periprosthetic fractures will rise markedly over the next few decades as a result of the increasing number of elderly patients who have had hip arthroplasties. These patients will be older and more medically fit than the elderly

patients of today, and because of their advanced age, it is likely that their bone will become progressively more osteopenic and be subject to an increased incidence of fracture. Surgeons are most aware of the periprosthetic fractures that occur around hip prostheses. However, femoral diaphyseal fractures associated with implants used to internally fix proximal femoral fractures are also recognized.

The operation of hip arthroplasty increases the risk of periprosthetic fracture by increasing local stress and altering the biomechanical characteristics of femurs that are already osteopenic.[15, 74, 120, 128] In cemented arthroplasty, the incidence of intraoperative periprosthetic fractures has been reported to be less than 1%,[10, 219] although this figure can rise to 6.3% in revision hip replacement.[47] The need for a tight fit when using an uncemented femoral stem increases the incidence of intraoperative fracture, which has been reported to be 3.5% by Fitzgerald and coauthors.[80] This group also reported a 17.5% incidence of intraoperative fracture in uncemented revision arthroplasties. The incidence of periprosthetic fracture is increased in patients who have femoral deformity, a narrow intramedullary canal, or previous femoral osteotomy. Table 52–15 gives a list of the main conditions associated with periprosthetic fracture.

An intraoperative femoral fracture may be overlooked during the operation and be detected only on postoperative radiographs. It may also become apparent after a minor crack has expanded to become a displaced fracture. This situation is particularly relevant after revision arthroplasty, where the bone is weakened by bone defects and instrumentation. In a series from Helsinki,[125] 23% of postoperative fractures were caused by minimal trauma to weakened bone. In these fractures, it was found that 54% of the prostheses were loose as compared with 32% of the prostheses in fractures caused by trauma to normal bone. Prosthetic loosening is an important factor in postoperative fractures in that loosening is always associated with bone resorption. Granulomatosis caused by wear debris may result in large defects, which increases the risk of fracture. In the series of periprosthetic fractures reported by Jensen and colleagues,[118] 35% of the prostheses were loose, with no difference in incidence noted between uncemented and cemented prostheses. Similar figures were reported by Blatter and co-workers.[18] In the Helsinki study, the prosthesis was loose in 48 of 95 (50.5%) postoperative fractures.[125]

## CLASSIFICATION

A number of classifications of periprosthetic fractures associated with hip arthroplasty have been devised. They have become more complex over the years, but the early classifications remain useful for descriptive purposes, although later classifications have more therapeutic value. Johansson and colleagues[120] divided periprosthetic proximal femoral fractures into three types. Type 1 fractures were proximal to the tip of the prosthesis, whereas type 2 fractures started proximal to the tip of the femoral stem, but finished distal to the tip. In type 3 fractures, the fracture was entirely distal to the tip of the femoral prosthesis. The Vancouver classification[74] is an example of a more modern classification that considers factors influ-

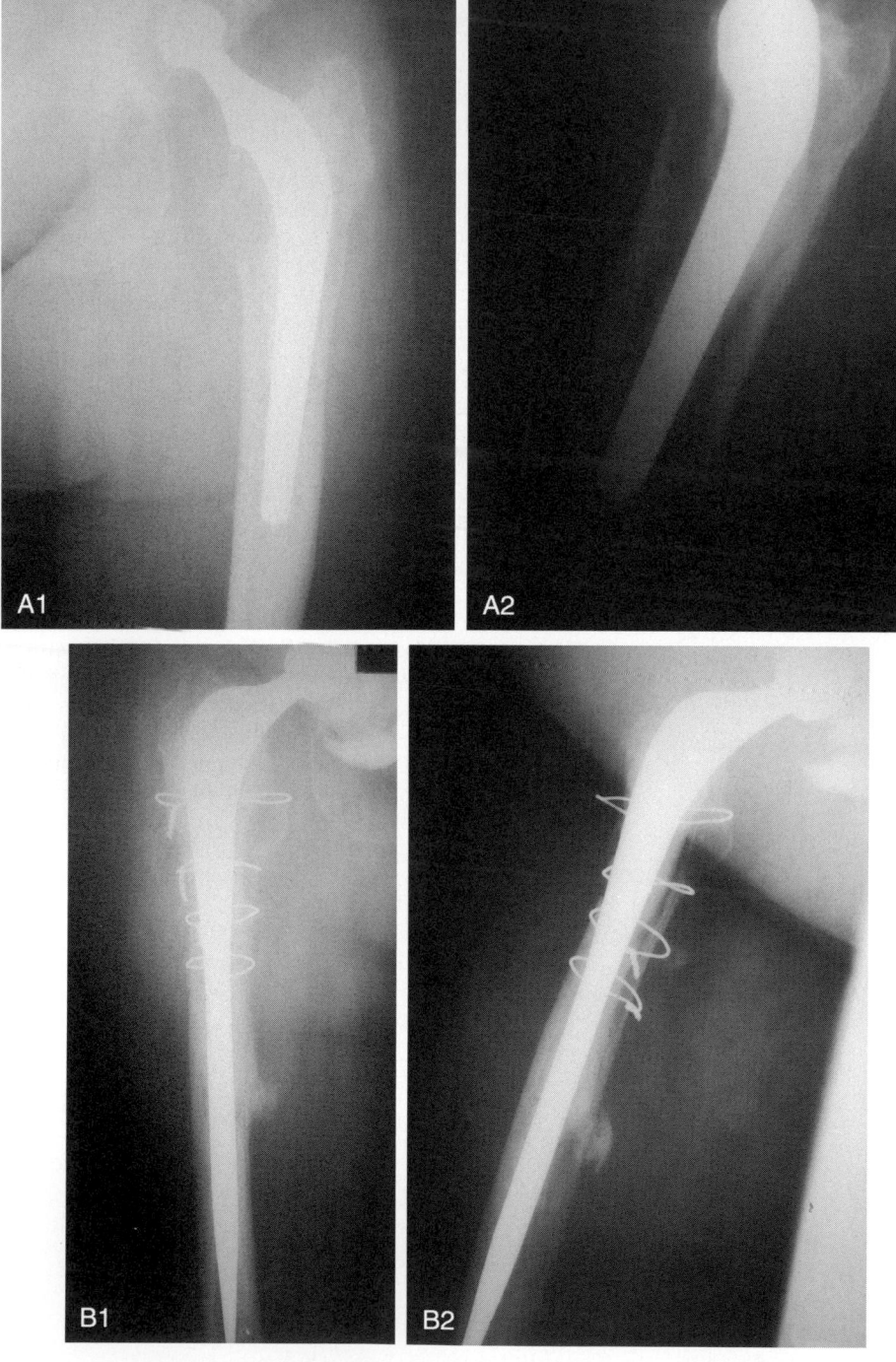

**FIGURE 52–48.** *A,* Anteroposterior and lateral radiograph of a Johansson type 2, Vancouver B2 periprosthetic fracture in an 86-year-old man. The prosthesis had been inserted 12 years earlier. *B,* A cemented long-stem prosthesis has been used. Note the use of cerclage wires to stabilize the fracture before insertion of the implant.

encing treatment. It is shown in Figure 52–50. Not only is the location of the fracture taken into account, but the state of the bone stock and the fixation of the femoral implant are also considered. The Vancouver classification divides femoral periprosthetic fractures into three basic types, depending on the location of the fracture. Type A fractures have either a greater trochanteric ($A_G$) or a lesser trochanteric ($A_L$) fracture. In type B fractures, the fracture is located around or just below the prosthetic stem, but three subtypes are differentiated, depending on the adequacy of femoral stem fixation and the condition of the

bone stock. In $B_1$ fractures, the stem is well fixed, whereas in $B_2$ fractures, the prosthetic stem is loose. In the $B_3$ fracture subgroup, the bone stock around the stem is poor. Type C fractures occur well below the stem and, like Johansson type 3 fractures, are unlikely to be related to the presence of the implant, although treatment will be affected by the presence of the femoral prosthesis.

Duncan and Masri[74] reviewed 75 consecutive periprosthetic femoral diaphyseal fractures treated in Vancouver, Canada, over a 10-year period. They found that 4% were Vancouver type A, 86.7% were type B, and the remaining

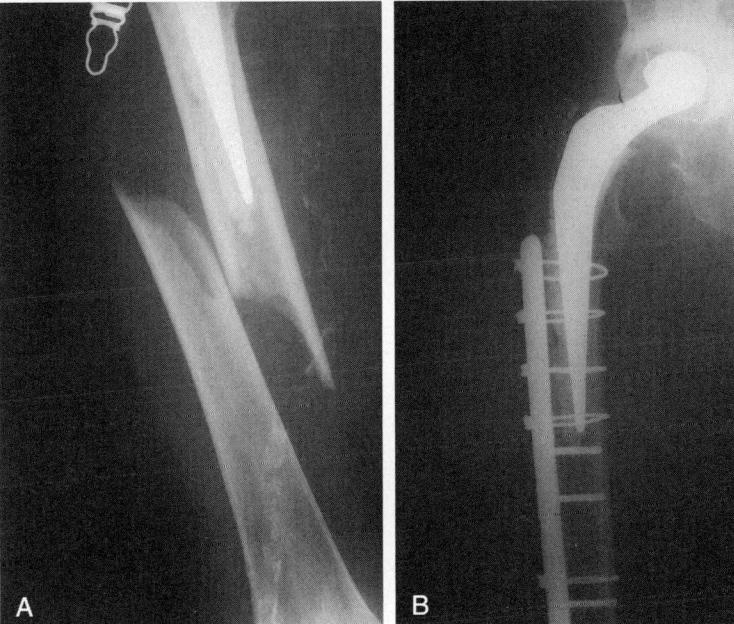

**FIGURE 52–49.** *A,* Anteroposterior radiograph of a Johansson type 2, Vancouver B$_1$ periprosthetic fracture in a 74-year-old man. The prosthesis had been inserted 8 years earlier and was secure. *B,* Plating was successfully performed. Note the use of screws distal to the prosthesis and cables proximally.

9.3% were type C fractures. Analysis of type B fractures showed that 18.5% were B$_1$ fractures, 44.6% were B$_2$ fractures, and 36.9% were B$_3$ fractures. Therefore, 71% of all femoral diaphyseal periprosthetic fractures will occur around or slightly below the femoral stem and be associated with stem loosening or poor bone stock. This classification illustrates the complexity of many of these fractures.

## TREATMENT

Four basic treatment methods can be used to treat periprosthetic femoral fractures: nonoperative management, wiring or cables, plating, and revision hip arthroplasty, usually with a long stem implant. The three goals of treatment are to heal the fracture, achieve early patient mobilization, and provide a stable construct that will

| TABLE 52–15 |
| --- |

Principal Causes of Periprosthetic Fracture

Femoral deformity
Narrow intramedullary canal
Previous femoral osteotomy
Previous femoral diaphyseal fracture
Previous proximal femoral fracture
Rheumatoid arthritis
Metabolic bone disease
Increasing age

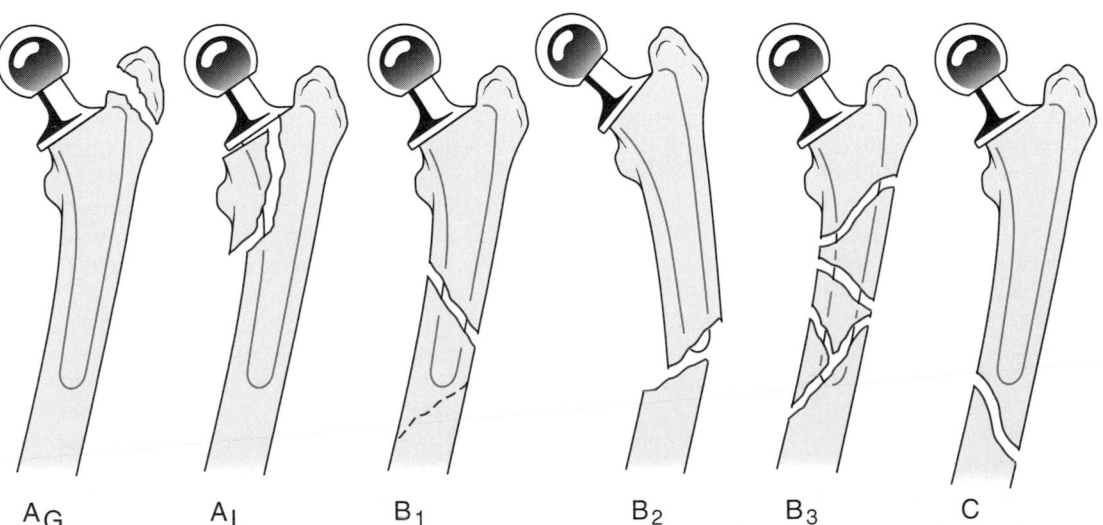

$A_G$ $\quad$ $A_L$ $\quad$ $B_1$ $\quad$ $B_2$ $\quad$ $B_3$ $\quad$ C

**FIGURE 52–50.** The Vancouver classification of periprosthetic fractures. See text for an explanation.

ensure maximal longevity of the implant. As with treatment of post-traumatic femoral diaphyseal fractures, treatment of periprosthetic fractures has altered markedly over the last 30 years, with decreasing emphasis on nonoperative management. To illustrate the alteration in fracture management, it is worth noting that Bethea and co-workers[15] analyzed the treatment of 31 periprosthetic fractures in 1982 and concluded that only fractures now classified as Vancouver $B_3$ fractures actually required surgical management. In recent years, surgeons have moved toward a more surgical approach.

### Nonoperative Management

Because early mobilization of the patient is one of the major goals of treatment of any femoral periprosthetic fracture, traction or the use of a plaster cast is seldom advisable. Bracing may be used in $A_L$ fractures or in the rare stable undisplaced or minimally displaced very proximal $B_1$ fracture, although careful follow-up is required to ensure that late fracture displacement does not occur. Garcia-Cimbrelo and colleagues[88] reported poor results in 5 of 12 periprosthetic proximal femoral fractures treated by functional bracing. Traction will not maintain alignment in most cases and is associated with a number of well-documented medical and surgical problems. Mont and Maar[165] reviewed the experience of 487 fractures in 26 reports and came to the conclusion that closed, nonoperative treatment was inappropriate for most periprosthetic proximal femoral fractures. They suggested that the only situation in which traction and long stem revision replacement were about equally successful was when the fracture was distal to the tip of the prosthesis. In essence, traction and brace treatment should be reserved only for patients who are deemed to be medically unfit for surgery. However, the prognosis for nonoperative management in these patients is also poor.

### Wires or Cables

Cerclage wires have frequently been used to treat minor intraoperative proximal femoral longitudinal fractures, often in association with the introduction of an uncemented hemiarthroplasty. They may also be used to reduce and stabilize separate bone fragments around a femoral prosthesis (see Fig. 52–48). In addition, they can be used to attach a greater trochanteric fragment after an $A_G$ fracture, and they have been used to fix spiral $B_1$ fractures, although the fixation is poor and the use of isolated wires, cables, and plastic bands cannot be advocated in this situation. However, they can be successfully used to stabilize a spiral $B_2$ fracture before insertion of a long stem femoral prosthesis (see Fig. 52–48). Recently, cable systems have been introduced that supplement or replace screw fixation when used with specially designed plates (see Fig. 52–49), and these systems have proved very useful as screw fixation in elderly osteopenic bone, which is frequently suboptimal.

### Intramedullary Devices

The usefulness of intramedullary fixation of femoral fractures is well documented. In clinical studies, revision arthroplasties (see Fig. 52–48) have yielded better results in the management of diaphyseal periprosthetic fractures than plates have.[165] However, the usefulness of bone cement in revision arthroplasty is debated. Comparative studies of cemented and cementless revision stems in fracture treatment have not yet been carried out, but Jensen and co-workers[118] found that cement had no adverse effect on fracture healing, whereas Serocki and colleagues[222] reported an unsatisfactorily high number of nonunions. Later studies have favored the use of uncemented stems.[10, 125] However, given the degree of complexity inherent in a number of these operations, surgeons should be prepared to use both cemented and uncemented prostheses as the clinical situation requires.

The femoral stem should adequately stabilize the main proximal and distal fragments. Therefore, a long femoral stem will be used in most instances. If a cemented arthroplasty is used, the surgeon will rely on the cement for proximal and distal fixation. However, if an uncemented arthroplasty is used, it may be difficult to achieve good distal fixation. Implants are now available that combine a femoral prosthetic head with a distal interlocking nail, and it may be necessary to use such an implant in a difficult fracture.

### Plate Fixation

If the prosthesis is stable, the surgeon may elect to use a plate.[18, 71, 157, 166, 280] (see Fig. 52–49). For optimal fixation, the fracture reduction should be exact, and the principles of compression osteosynthesis involving lag screws should be followed. The surgeon should bear in mind that the bone will be osteopenic and that optimal fixation can be achieved only by using long plates. Screw fixation of at least eight cortices (four screws with bicortical purchase) should be performed on both sides of the fracture, and it is not contraindicated to use five or six screws on each side of the fracture to improve fixation. In distal type C fractures, good fixation can often be obtained by using a 95° condylar plate. In mid-diaphyseal fractures, it is often necessary to use adjunctive fixation in the form of cables or bands placed around the plate, but the rotational stability afforded solely by the use of wires or cables without a plate may not be adequate.[217] Plates fixed with screws, cerclage wires, or cables have yielded more than 90% satisfactory results in many series.[18, 71, 166, 280]

### Revision Arthroplasty or Plate Fixation?

In their meta-analysis, Mont and Maar[165] found that treatment with long revision stems yielded better results than did plate fixation in all types of fracture. In Helsinki, Jukkala-Partio and colleagues[125] treated 40 femoral periprosthetic fractures by revision arthroplasty and 35 by compression plate fixation. Autologous bone grafting was used in 15 revision arthroplasties and in 20 plate fixations. Five nonunions in the revision arthroplasty group and nine nonunions in the plated group were treated by further revision and bone grafts. A total of 20 secondary operations were needed after prosthetic stem revision and 27 after plate fixation. The level of fracture did not affect the requirement for secondary surgery. It was concluded that in general, the results of stem revision were better than those of plate fixation. However, the potential benefits of long stem replacement must be balanced against the problems associated with cement removal in stable $B_1$ fractures.

*Suggested Treatment Methods*

**Type A Fractures.** Displaced fractures of the greater trochanter should usually be fixed. They are associated with diminished abductor strength and may have a deleterious effect on patient mobility. Fixation should be achieved with a cable system or a hook plate.

**Type B Fractures.** Type $B_1$ fractures associated with a stable, well-cemented femoral prosthesis are best treated with a plate that can be fixed with both screws and cables. $B_2$ and $B_3$ fractures should be treated with long stem femoral implants, with bone graft being used to supplement the deficient bone stock encountered in $B_3$ fractures.

**Type C Fractures.** Type C fractures should be treated by the appropriate method, with the location and morphology of the fracture taken into account. The appropriate method will usually be plating or retrograde supracondylar nailing.

## "Periprosthetic" Fractures after Proximal Femoral Fracture Fixation

It would seem obvious that patients who have proximal femoral fractures are at risk for a subsequent femoral diaphyseal fracture because of their age. These patients tend to be elderly, they are osteopenic and may be osteoporotic, and they have a number of medical comorbidities. They are also subject to recurrent falls and reinjury. However, remarkably little is known about the epidemiology of late femoral fracture after proximal femoral fracture surgery.

The problem has been investigated in detail in the Edinburgh Orthopaedic Trauma Unit by analyzing 6230 patients with 6696 hip fractures. All patients were admitted to the Edinburgh Orthopaedic Trauma Unit in the 10-year period between January 1988 and December 1997. Extracapsular fractures were stabilized with either a compression hip screw or a gamma nail. Most undisplaced intracapsular fractures were treated by internal fixation with either three cannulated screws or a compression hip screw. In most frail elderly patients, displaced intracapsular fractures were treated with an uncemented Austin-Moore hemiarthroplasty prosthesis. Primary reduction and internal fixation, cemented bipolar arthroplasty, or total-hip arthroplasty was used for the treatment of younger, ambulant patients with displaced intracapsular fractures. Revision to secondary cemented bipolar or total-hip arthroplasty was required in 210 patients for complications or failure of primary treatment. This group was considered separately from the primarily cemented arthroplasty group in subsequent analysis. All femoral fractures were classified according to the classification of Johansson and colleagues.[120]

Overall, 141 (2.1%) of the 6696 fractures were associated with late fracture of the ipsilateral femur. The rate of femoral fracture on survivorship analysis of the hip fracture population was 2.9% after 5 years and increased to 5.1% after 10 years. The average age of patients with late femoral fractures was 82 years, identical to that of the hip fracture population. The incidence of late femoral fracture in-

creased with age, and the incidence was consistently higher in postmenopausal women than men. In hip fracture patients, the risk of later femoral fracture was increased by a factor of 40 when compared with the risk of femoral fracture in the general population.

Analysis of femoral fractures by the type of implant used to treat the earlier proximal femoral fracture revealed considerable differences in both the incidence and configuration of the fractures. Table 52–16 shows the incidence of late femoral fracture after primary proximal femoral fracture fixation with different implants. It can be seen that the lowest incidence of fracture is associated with the use of three cancellous screws or a compression hip screw. The highest incidence of diaphyseal fracture after primary proximal femoral fracture fixation is associated with the use of an uncemented hemiarthroplasty or a gamma nail. The incidence of late ipsilateral femoral fracture after secondary cemented hemiarthroplasty for failure of primary proximal femoral fracture fixation is high at 7.6%. The most common diaphyseal fracture was the Johansson type II fracture, which accounted for 66.7% of all fractures. Type I proximal fractures were associated with the use of uncemented hemiarthroplasties, and distal type III fractures tended to occur in association with a compression hip screw or after a primary cemented arthroplasty.

Multivariate logistic regression analysis showed that the type of implant and severe osteopenia were significant independent predictors of late femoral failure. Use of the short gamma nail to treat an extracapsular fracture increased the risk of femoral fracture by almost threefold, and revision to a cemented arthroplasty after failed primary treatment of an intracapsular fracture increased the risk of late femoral fracture by fourfold. This study highlights the importance of secondary late femoral fracture after initial proximal femoral fracture surgery. The spectrum of femoral fracture is different from that after elective hip replacement, but with increasing numbers of hip fracture patients, it is likely that surgeons will have to treat increasingly larger numbers of late ipsilateral femoral fractures after primary femoral fracture fixation.

**TABLE 52–16**

Data Relating to Late Femoral Diaphyseal Fracture after Proximal Femoral Fracture Fixation with Different Implants

| | N | Fracture | % | Median Time to Fracture (wk) |
|---|---|---|---|---|
| Compression hip screw | 2734 | 34 | 1.2 | 78 |
| Gamma nail | 254 | 10 | 3.9 | 30 |
| Cancellous screws | 939 | 15 | 1.6 | 4 |
| Uncemented hemiarthroplasty | 1953 | 54 | 2.8 | 9 |
| Primary cemented arthroplasty | 600 | 12 | 2.0 | 84 |
| Secondary cemented arthroplasty | 210 | 16 | 7.6 | 9 |
| Others | 6 | 0 | 0 | — |
| Total | 6696 | 141 | | |

## Stress Fractures

Stress fractures occur as a result of overuse, usually in patients who give no history of specific trauma to account for the fracture. They are divided into two types: fatigue fractures resulting from excessive repetitive stress on normal bone (Fig. 52–51) and insufficiency fractures (Fig. 52–52) resulting from normal muscular activity on abnormally weak bone. The former tend to occur in military recruits and athletes, and the latter are seen in the elderly population and in patients who have conditions such as Paget's disease or osteoporosis. A list of the conditions associated with insufficiency fractures is presented in Table 52–17. It is likely that stress fractures arise as a result of an imbalance between bone injury and bone repair and remodeling. It is theorized that stress fractures can occur when the surrounding muscles are fatigued and less able to protect bone. Alternatively, it may be that excessive muscular force may produce the fracture.

The true incidence of stress fractures is unknown, although studies have been undertaken to investigate the incidence in at-risk groups in the population, particularly young soldiers and athletes. It is likely, however, that the incidence of stress fractures is higher than was formerly thought. Increasingly sophisticated detection techniques have shown a higher incidence of stress fractures in the population. When surgeons had to rely on radiographs for detection, it is probable that a relatively large number of stress fractures were missed, with surgeons attributing pain to soft tissue damage. The techniques of technetium-labeled bone scanning and CAT scanning have increased the detection rate of stress fractures, but the comparatively recent introduction of MRI has allowed surgeons to investigate painful areas in the body that were formerly

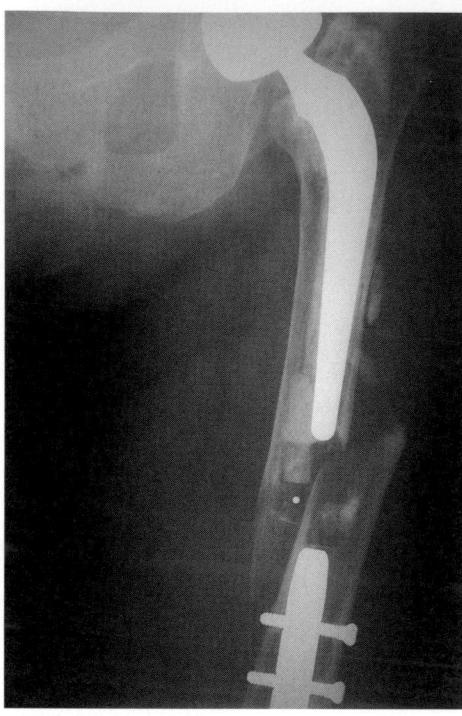

**Figure 52–52.** Insufficiency fracture in an 82-year-old woman. It occurred between a bipolar arthroplasty and a supracondylar nail.

negative on plain radiographs but show clear signs of fracture on MRI.

Femoral stress fractures probably account for between 7% and 12% of all stress fractures in athletes.[100, 155] However, the incidence may well be higher in military recruits. Milgrom and colleagues[161] showed that 33.6% of stress fractures in male Israeli military recruits occurred in the femur, with 33.8% occurring in the femoral neck, 27.4% in the mid-diaphysis, 27.4% in the distal diaphysis, and 11.4% in the medial femoral condyle. The most common site for stress fractures in Milgrom and colleagues' series was the tibial diaphysis, with 40.8% of all stress fractures occurring at this site. A total of 51.2% of the stress fractures occurred in the tibia.

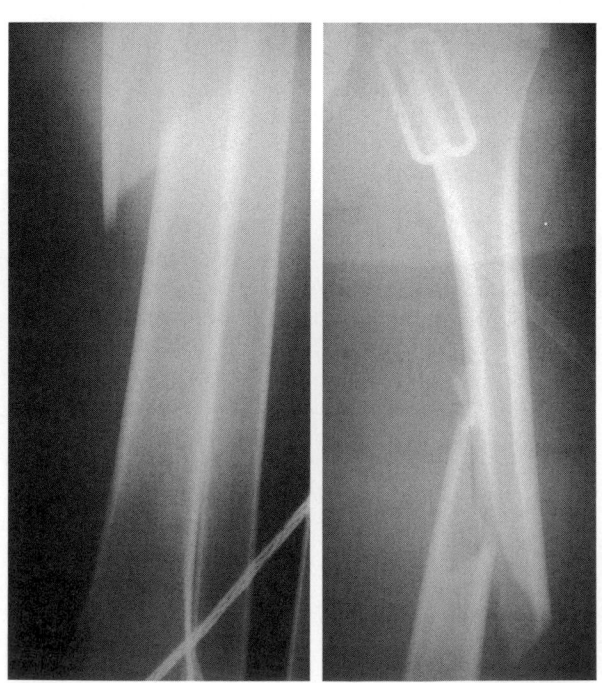

**Figure 52–51.** Anteroposterior and lateral radiographs of a 17-year-old new military recruit who sustained a fatigue fracture of his femur during marching.

| TABLE 52–17 |
| --- |

Causes of Stress Fracture

Osteoporosis
Rheumatoid arthritis
Osteomalacia or rickets
Diabetes mellitus
Fibrous dysplasia
Paget's disease
Pyrophosphate arthropathy
Osteogenesis imperfecta
Osteopetrosis
Hyperparathyroidism
Scurvy
Irradiation
Drugs, e.g., corticosteroids, diphosphonates
Previous arthroplasty and other limb surgery
Previous fractures

Stress fractures in athletes are also most commonly seen in the tibia. Matheson and associates[155] analyzed a group of 320 athletes with bone scan–positive stress fractures. They showed that 49.1% of the stress fractures occurred in the tibia, with the femur being the fourth most common bone involved (7.2%). Tarsal stress fractures accounted for 25.3% and metatarsal fractures for 8.8% of the group. Ha and associates[100] monitored 169 patients with stress fractures over a period of 6 years. They found that 31.5% of the fractures occurred in the tibia and 12.5% in the femur. Unlike the series of military recruits reported by Milgrom and co-workers,[161] they found that most of the femoral stress fractures (57.1%) occurred in the distal diaphysis, with 23.7% being seen in the femoral neck. A further 9.6% were located in the mid-diaphysis and 9.6% were seen in the distal end of the femur. Clement and colleagues[52] examined 71 athletes with 74 exercise-induced stress injuries of the femur detected by technetium bone scanning. They showed that most of the stress injuries (52.7%) occurred in the femoral diaphysis, with the remaining 47.3% being located in the proximal part of the femur.

Patients who sustain fatigue-type stress fractures are obviously young, with the average age usually between 20 and 22 years.[100, 180] In their analysis of 131 stress fractures, Ha and co-workers[100] showed that 64 (48.9%) occurred between the ages of 10 and 19 years, 56 (42.7%) occurred between 20 and 29 years of age, 4 (3.1%) occurred between 30 and 39 years of age, and the remaining 7 (5.3%) occurred after the age of 40 years. The highest incidence that they encountered was in teenage girls, with 25.5% of this group having a stress fracture. In their series dealing solely with femoral stress fractures, Clement and associates[52] noted that the patients were slightly older, with an overall mean age of 29 years. The mean age of the females was 26.6 years, with 31.2 years being recorded for the males. The tendency for these injuries to occur in women has been demonstrated by other authors. Protzman and Griffis[196] demonstrated a 12:1 female-to-male ratio in army recruits training in the U.S. Military Academy. Clement and colleagues[52] showed that 61.4% of the femoral stress injuries occurred in women.

It is interesting to examine the timing of the onset of symptoms in military recruits and the type of sporting activity in athletes that commonly gives rise to stress fractures. Protzman and Griffis[196] could not demonstrate any correlation between the time of onset of symptoms and any particular type of military activity. They found that a constant number of recruits sustained stress fractures between 2 and 8 weeks after the start of basic training. No recruit presented in the first week after the commencement of training. Milgrom and co-workers[161] compared the time of the onset of symptoms in patients with femoral and tibial stress fractures. They also showed that no patient with a femoral stress fracture presented within 1 week of training but that stress fractures occurred at a steady rate in soldiers between weeks 2 and 13. They also found that 69% of the femoral stress fractures detected by bone scanning were in fact asymptomatic.

Analysis of the type of sport and its association with stress fractures shows that different sports predominate,

depending on the nationality of the patients who are studied. However, running activities are undoubtedly the most common cause of stress fractures.[52, 100, 155] Ha and colleagues[100] reported that in a Korean population, volleyball accounted for 25.1% of all stress fractures, with running causing 18.3% of such fractures. Orava and associates[180] demonstrated that track and field activities, jogging, and skiing accounted for all of the femoral stress fractures, and Clement and colleagues[52] also showed that running was most often associated with femoral stress fractures. They found that recreational running was associated with 44% of the total injuries, marathon running caused 27%, and competitive running was responsible for 17% of the fractures. Triathlon training accounted for 5% of the femoral stress fractures, and only 7% of the femoral stress fractures were not associated with running.

Many of the athletes affected by stress fractures are running prodigious distances. In their study of femoral stress injuries, Clement and co-workers[52] documented that recreational runners were averaging 56.9 km/wk; marathon runners, 73.2 km; and competitive runners, 114.4 km. Over 30% of the runners had increased their training distance within 1 to 2 weeks of the onset of their first symptoms. In the group studied by Orava and associates,[180] the average distance run by the athletes was 110 km/wk, and most stress fractures occurred in April, although the highest incidence in females was in the autumn.

## INITIAL SYMPTOMS

Patients usually have a history of gradually increasing pain in the hip or thigh. The exact location of the pain may depend on the location of the stress fracture in the femur, but not infrequently the surgeon will have to rely on radiologic imaging to identify the exact position. The pain is exacerbated by exercise and relieved by rest. Older patients with insufficiency fractures may, of course, not give a history of excessive physical exercise, but even in this group of patients, it is not unusual for such patients to have undertaken more exercise than they are used to. Female athletes may have a history of menstrual irregularity. Marcus and colleagues[153] studied 17 female distance runners and showed that 11 had secondary amenorrhea for 1 to 7 years. Running-related fractures were found to be more common in amenorrheic women. Oligomenorrheic runners have been shown to have significantly lower bone mineral density than their eumenorrheic counterparts.[55] The physical history may also reveal that the athlete is consuming a diet low in energy with inadequate calcium intake. Most amenorrheic or oligomenorrheic female runners will sustain stress fractures of the femoral neck rather than the diaphysis.

Physical examination may indicate the site of the femoral stress fracture, but locating the point of maximal tenderness is often difficult; however, if gentle rotation of the femur causes groin pain, it is likely that the stress fracture is in the femoral neck. Initial imaging is with plain radiographs, which may show the fracture (see Fig. 52–2). Supplementary information may be gained from technetium bone scanning, CAT scanning, or MRI, with the latter having revealed many more insufficiency fractures than were previously suspected from the history and clinical examination.

Stress fractures of the femoral diaphysis can be either fatigue or insufficiency fractures. With an increasingly aging population, most femoral stress fractures seen by orthopaedic surgeons will be insufficiency fractures, and it seems logical to predict that the incidence of these fractures will rise over the next few decades, even if medical treatment of osteoporosis becomes widespread. Increasing leisure activities may also increase the incidence of fatigue stress fractures of the femoral diaphysis.

Figure 52–51 shows the anteroposterior and lateral radiographs of a 17-year-old military recruit who had been in the army for 3 weeks and undergoing rigorous marching and drilling. He was fit, with no previous history of significance. A dull ache developed in his thigh, and 2 days later he collapsed as he was walking at normal speed across a sports field. Radiographs showed a spiral stress fracture of the femoral diaphysis. It was treated with a reamed intramedullary nail.

Insufficiency fractures are more common and can occur after certain medical conditions or as a result of irradiation or the administration of a number of drugs such as corticosteroids. They have also been reported to occur at the site of previous screw holes[258] or after knee arthroplasty[141] (see Table 52–17).

The most common types of insufficiency fractures of the femoral diaphysis encountered by orthopaedic surgeons are those associated with osteopenia or osteoporosis. With an aging population, these fractures are becoming more common and often present surgeons with a considerable challenge. With the increased use of both internal fixation for fracture management and hip arthroplasty for the management of fractures or arthritis, an increase has been noted in the number of stress fractures that occur between a hip prosthesis and a lower femoral plate, nail, or prosthesis (see Fig. 52–52). These fractures may be very difficult to treat in that lateral plating may be complicated by the difficulty of placing screws around the intramedullary implants. Surgeons may have to use plates and cables or cemented arthroplasty with a long femoral stem.

Treatment of displaced femoral diaphyseal stress fractures such as the one illustrated in Figure 52–51 is usually straightforward. A reamed intramedullary nail should be used to stabilize the fracture, and a high success rate can be expected. If the femoral fracture is undisplaced, the surgeon will have to take the age and general health of the patient into account. In undisplaced fatigue stress fractures in young adults, it is recommended that intramedullary nailing be used because nonoperative management is time consuming and painful and may well be unsuccessful. In undisplaced insufficiency fractures, nailing is recommended when possible to facilitate patient mobilization. In patients with advanced metabolic disease, the shape of the bone may preclude nailing, and the surgeon may need to undertake one or more diaphyseal osteotomies to straighten the femur before nailing can be undertaken.

## PAGET'S DISEASE

The classic metabolic bone disease in which stress fractures commonly occur is Paget's disease (Fig. 52–53). Stress fractures are the most common complication of

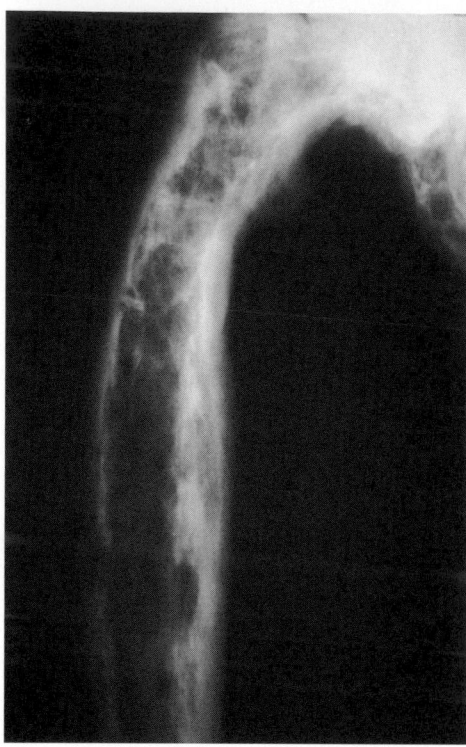

**FIGURE 52–53.** Pagetic femur showing the characteristic deformity.

Paget's disease and frequently occur in the femur. Despite the fact that Paget's disease is more common in men, the incidence of stress fractures is higher in women, possibly because of their smaller bone mass and their increased susceptibility to osteoporosis. Unlike other types of stress fracture, pagetic fractures are about twice as common in the femur as in the tibia. Grundy[97] detailed the site of involvement in 63 femoral fractures and showed that the most common site was the subtrochanteric region (28.6%), followed by the upper third of the diaphysis (20.6%) and the femoral neck (17.5%). The middle third of the diaphysis accounted for 19% of the fractures and the lower third for 11.1%. He found that 3.2% of the fractures occurred in the trochanteric area. Pagetic fractures are often related to the deformity that occurs in pagetic bone. They usually begin as transverse "pseudofractures" in the tension side of a bowed long bone. These pseudofractures may heal or extend to become a complete fracture. Treatment may be symptomatic, depending on the age, health, and functional status of the patient, but complete fractures are usually treated by intramedullary nailing, with one or more femoral osteotomies being undertaken if the rest of the femur is significantly bowed.

## REFERENCES

1. Alho, A.; Strømsøe, K.; Ekeland, A. Locked intramedullary nailing of femoral shaft fractures. J Trauma 31:49–59, 1991.
2. Alho, A.; Ekeland, A.; Grøgaard, B.; Dokke, J.R. A locked hip screw–intramedullary nail (cephalomedullary nail) for the treatment of fractures of the proximal part of the femur combined with fractures of the femoral shaft. J Trauma 40:10–16, 1996.
3. Arneson, T.J.; Melton, L.J.; Lewallen, D.G.; O'Fallon, W.M. Epidemiology of diaphyseal and distal femoral fractures in Rochester, Minnesota, 1965–1984. Clin Orthop 234:188–194, 1988.

4. Astion, D.J.; Wilber, J.H.; Scoles, P.V. Avascular necrosis of the capital femoral epiphysis after intramedullary nailing for a fracture of the femoral shaft. J Bone Joint Surg Am 77:1092–1094, 1995.

5. Bain, G.I.; Zacest, A.C.; Paterson, D.C.; et al. Abduction strength following intramedullary nailing of the femur. J Orthop Trauma 11:93–97, 1997.

6. Bardenheuer, B. De behandlung der intra- und juxtaarticulären Fracturen mittles Extension und orthopädischen Massnahmen während der eigentlichen Fracturheilung. Z Orthop Chir 12:107, 1904.

7. Barquet, A.; Silva, R.; Massaferro, J.; Dubra, A. The AO tubular external fixator in the treatment of open fractures and infected non-unions of the shaft of the femur. Injury 19:415–420, 1988.

8. Barwood, S.A.; Wilson, J.L.; Molnar, R.R.; Choong, P.F. The incidence of acute cardiorespiratory and vascular dysfunction following intramedullary nail fixation of femoral metastasis. Acta Orthop Scand 71:147–152, 2000.

9. Baumgaertel, F.; Dahlen, C.; Stiletto, R.; Gotzen, L. Technique of using the AO-femoral distractor for femoral intramedullary nailing. J Orthop Trauma 8:315–321, 1994.

10. Beals, R.K.; Tower, S.S. Periprosthetic fractures of the femur. An analysis of 93 fractures. Clin Orthop 327:238–246, 1996.

11. Behrman, S.W.; Fabian, T.C.; Kudsk, K.A.; Taylor, J.C. Improved outcome with femur fractures: Early vs. delayed fixation. J Trauma 30:792–798, 1990.

12. Bengnér, R.U.; Ekbom, T.; Johnell, O.; Nilsson, B.E. Incidence of femoral and tibial shaft fractures. Epidemiology 1950–1983 in Malmö, Sweden. Acta Orthop Scand 61:251–254, 1990.

13. Bennett, F.S.; Zinar, D.M.; Kilgus, D.J. Ipsilateral hip and femoral shaft fractures. Clin Orthop 296:168–177, 1993.

14. Bergman, M.; Tornetta, P.; Kerina, M.; et al. Femur fractures caused by gunshots: Treatment by immediate reamed intramedullary nailing. J Trauma 34:783–785, 1993.

15. Bethea, J.S.; De Andrade, J.R.; Fleming, L.L.; et al. Proximal femoral fractures following total hip arthroplasty. Clin Orthop 170:95–106, 1982.

16. Bhandari, M.; Guyatt, G.H.; Tong, D.; et al. Reamed versus non-reamed intramedullary nailing of lower extremity long bone fractures: A systematic overview and meta-analysis. J Orthop Trauma 14:2–9, 2000.

17. Bircher, H. Eine neue Methode un mittelbarer Retention bei Fracturen der Röhrenknochen. Arch Clin Chir 34:410–422, 1887.

18. Blatter, G.; Fiechter, T.; Magerl, F. Periprothetische Frakturen bein hüfttotalendoprothesen Orthopäde. 18:545–551, 1989.

19. Blatter, G.; Weber, B.G. Wave plate osteosynthesis as a salvage procedure. Arch Orthop Trauma Surg 109:330–333, 1990.

20. Böhler, L. Technik der Knochenbruchbehandlungen. Wien, Wilhelm Maudrich, 1929.

21. Bone, L.B.; Johnson, K.D.; Weigelt, J.; Scheinberg, R. Early versus delayed stabilization of femoral fractures. J Bone Joint Surg Am 71:336–340, 1989.

22. Bone.L.B.; Babikian, G.; Stegemann, P.M. Femoral canal reaming in the polytrauma patient with chest injury. Clin Orthop 318:91–94, 1995.

23. Bonnevialle, P.; Cauhepe, C.; Alqoh, F.; et al. Risks and results after simultaneous intramedullary nailing in bilateral femoral fractures: A retrospective study of 40 cases. Rev Chir Orthop Reparatrice Appar Mot 86:598–607, 2000.

24. Bosse, M.J.; MacKenzie, E.J.; Riemer, B.L.; et al. Adult respiratory distress syndrome, pneumonia, and mortality following thoracic injury and a femoral fracture treated either with intramedullary nailing with reaming or with a plate. J Bone Joint Surg Am 79:799–809, 1997.

25. Bouchard, J.A.; Barei, D.; Cayer, D.; O'Neil, J. Outcome of femoral shaft fractures in the elderly. Clin Orthop 332:105–109, 1996.

26. Boulanger, B.R.; Stephen, D.; Brenneman, F.D. Thoracic trauma and early intramedullary nailing of femur fractures: Are we doing harm? J Trauma 40:24–28, 1997.

27. Bråten, M.; Terjesen, T.; Rossvoll, I. Femoral shaft fractures treated by intramedullary nailing. A follow-up study focusing on problems related to the method. Injury 26:379–383, 1995.

28. Bråten, M.; Tveit, K.; Junk, S.; et al. The role of fluoroscopy in avoiding rotational deformity of treated femoral shaft fractures: An anatomical and clinical study. Injury 31:311–315, 2000.

29. Britton, J.M.; Dunkerley, D.R. Closed nailing of a femoral fracture followed by sciatic nerve palsy. J Bone Joint Surg Br 72:318, 1990.

30. Brumback, R.J.; Uwagie-Ero, S.; Lakatos, R.P.; et al. Intramedullary nailing of femoral shaft fractures. Part II: Fracture-healing with static interlocking fixation. J Bone Joint Surg Am 70:1453–1462, 1988.

31. Brumback, R.J.; Ellison, T.S., Jr.; Poka, A.; et al. Intramedullary nailing of open fractures of the femoral shaft. J Bone Joint Surg Am 71:1324–1330, 1989.

32. Brumback, R.J.; Wells, J.D.; Lakatos, R.; et al. Heterotopic ossification about the hip after intramedullary nailing for fractures of the femur. J Bone Joint Surg Am 72:1067–1073, 1990.

33. Brumback, R.J.; Ellison, T.S.; Poka, A.; et al. Intramedullary nailing of femoral shaft fractures. Part III: Long-term effects of static interlocking fixation. J Bone Joint Surg Am 74:106–112, 1992.

34. Brumback, R.J.; Ellison, T.S.; Molligan, H.; et al. Pudendal nerve palsy complicating intramedullary nailing of the femur. J Bone Joint Surg Am 74:1450–1455, 1992.

35. Buck, G. An improved method of treating fractures of the thigh illustrated by cases and a drawing. Trans N Y Acad Med 2:232–250, 1861.

36. Buford, D.; Christensen, K.; Weatherall, P. Intramedullary nailing of femoral fractures in adolescents. Clin Orthop 350:85–89, 1998.

37. Bühren, V. Kompressionsmarknagelung langer Röhrenknochen. Unfallchirurg 103:708–721, 2000.

38. Butler, M.S.; Brumback, R.J.; Ellison, T.S.; et al. Interlocking intramedullary nailing for ipsilateral fractures of the femoral shaft and distal part of the femur. J Bone Joint Surg Am 73:1492–1502, 1991.

39. Carlson, D.A.; Rodman, G.H.; Kaehr, D.; et al. Femur fractures in chest-injured patients: Is reaming contraindicated? J Orthop Trauma 12:164–168, 1998.

40. Casey, M.J.; Chapman, M.W. Ipsilateral concomitant fractures of the hip and femoral shaft. J Bone Joint Surg Am 61:503–509, 1979.

41. Chapman, M.W. The role of intramedullary fixation in open fractures. Clin Orthop 212:26–34, 1986.

42. Charash, W.E.; Fabian, T.C.; Croce, M.A. Delayed surgical fixation of femur fractures is a risk factor for pulmonary failure independent of thoracic trauma. J Trauma 37:667–672, 1994.

43. Chaturvedi, S.; Sahu, S.C. Ipsilateral concomitant fractures of the femoral neck and shaft. Injury 24:243–246, 1993.

44. Chen, C.H.; Chen, T.B.; Cheng, Y.M.; et al. Ipsilateral fractures of the femoral neck and shaft. Injury 31:719–722, 2000.

45. Cheng, J.C.Y.; Tse, P.Y.T.; Chow, Y.Y.N. The place of the dynamic compression plate in femoral shaft fractures. Injury 16:519–534, 1985.

46. Chin, K.R.; Altman, D.T.; Altman, G.T.; et al. Retrograde nailing of femur fractures in patients with myelopathy and who are nonambulatory. Clin Orthop 373:218–226, 2000.

47. Christensen, C.M.; Seger, B.M.; Schultz, R.B. Management of intraoperative femur fractures associated with revision total hip arthroplasty. Clin Orthop 248:177–180, 1989.

48. Christie, J.; Court-Brown, C.; Kinninmonth, A.W.G.; Howie, C.R. Intramedullary locking nails in the management of femoral shaft fractures. J Bone Joint Surg Br 70:206–210, 1988.

49. Christie, J.; Court-Brown, C. Femoral neck fracture during closed medullary nailing: Brief report. J Bone Joint Surg Br 70:670, 1988.

50. Christie, J. The coagulative effects of fat embolisation during intramedullary manipulative procedures. Techn Orthop 11:14–17, 1996.

51. Clatworthy, M.G.; Clark, D.I.; Gray, D.H.; Hardy, A.E. Reamed versus unreamed femoral nails. J Bone Joint Surg Br 80:485–489, 1998.

52. Clement, D.B.; Ammann, W.; Taunton, J.E.; et al. Exercise-induced stress fractures to the femur. Int J Sports Med 14:347–352, 1993.

53. Cole, A.S.; Hill, G.A.; Theologis, T.N.; et al. Femoral nailing for metastatic disease of the femur: A comparison of reamed and unreamed femoral nailing. Injury 31:25–31, 2000.

54. Connolly, J.F.; Dehne, E.; Lafollette, B. Closed reduction and early cast-brace ambulation in the treatment of femoral fractures. Part II: Results in one hundred and forty-three fractures. J Bone Joint Surg Am 55:1581–1599, 1973.

55. Cook, S.D.; Harding, A.F.; Thomas, K.A.; et al. Trabecular bone density and menstrual function in women runners. Am J Sports Med 15:503–507, 1987.

56. Copeland, C.E.; Mitchell, K.A.; Brumback, R.J.; et al. Mortality in patients with bilateral femoral fractures. J Orthop Trauma 12.315–319, 1998.

57. Court-Brown, C.; McQueen, M. Compartment syndrome delays tibial union. Acta Orthop Scand 58:249–252, 1987.

58. Court-Brown, C.M.; Keating, J.F.; McQueen, M.M. Infection after intramedullary nailing of the tibia. Incidence and protocol for management. J Bone Joint Surg Br 74:770–774, 1992.

59. Court-Brown, C.M.; Keating, J.F.; Christie, J.; McQueen, M.M. Exchange intramedullary nailing. J Bone Joint Surg Br 77:407–411, 1995.

60. Court-Brown, C.M.; Will, E.; Christie, J.; McQueen, M.M. Reamed or unreamed nailing for closed tibial fractures. A prospective study in Tscherne C1 fractures. J Bone Joint Surg Br 78:580–583, 1996.

61. Court-Brown, C.M.; Zych, G.A. Pre- and peri-operative wound assessment and management. In: Court-Brown, C.M.; McQueen, M.M.; Quaba, A.A., eds. Management of Open Fractures. London, Martin Dunitz, 1996, pp. 43–54.

62. Court-Brown, C.M.; Quaba, A.A. The relationship between plastic surgery and orthopaedic trauma surgery. In: Court-Brown, C.M.; McQueen, M.M.; Quaba, A.A., eds. Management of Open Fractures. London, Martin Dunitz, 1996, pp. 157–164.

63. Court-Brown, C.M.; Rimmer, S.; Prakash, U.; McQueen, M.M. The epidemiology of open long bone fractures. Injury 29:529–534, 1998.

64. Danckwardt-Lilliström, G. Reaming of the medullary cavity and its effect on diaphyseal bone. Acta Orthop Scand Suppl 128:1–53, 1969.

65. Danckwardt-Lilliström, G.; Sjögren, S. Postoperative restoration of muscle strength after intramedullary nailing of fractures of the femoral shaft. Acta Orthop Scand 47:101–107, 1976.

66. DeCampos, J.; Vangsness, T.; Merritt, P.O.; Sher, J. Ipsilateral knee injury with femoral fracture. Clin Orthop 300:178–182, 1994.

67. De Casas, R.; Lázaro, F.J.G.; García-Rayo, M.R.; Arias, J. Arteriovenous fistula after interlocking nailing of the femur: A case report. J Trauma 38:303–304, 1995.

68. Delaney, W.M.; Street, D.M. Fracture of femoral shaft with fracture of neck of same femur. Treatment with medullary nail for shaft and Knowles pins for neck. J Int Coll Surg 19:303–312, 1953.

69. DeLee, J.C. Ipsilateral fracture of the femur and tibia treated in a quadrilateral cast. Clin Orthop 142:115–122, 1979.

70. Dencker, H. Shaft fractures of the femur. A comparative study of the results of various methods of treatment in 1,003 cases. Acta Chir Scand 130:173–184, 1965.

71. De Ridder, V.A.; de Lange, S.; Koomen, A.R.; Heatley, F.W. Partridge osteosynthesis: A prospective clinical study on the use of nylon cerclage bands and plates in the treatment of periprosthetic femoral shaft fractures. J Orthop Trauma 15:61–65, 2001.

72. DiChristina, D.G.; Riemer, B.L.; Butterfield, S.L.; et al. Femur fractures with femoral or popliteal artery injuries in blunt trauma. J Orthop Trauma 8:494–503, 1994.

73. Dodenhoff, R.M.; Dainton, J.N.; Hutchins, P.M. Proximal thigh pain after femoral nailing. J Bone Joint Surg Br 79:738–741, 1997.

74. Duncan, C.P.; Masri, B.A. Fractures of the femur after hip replacement. Instr Course Lect 44:293–304, 1995.

75. Elmaraghy, A.W.; Schemitsch, E.H.; Richards, R.R. Femoral and cruciate blood flow after retrograde femoral reaming: A canine study using laser Doppler flowmetry. J Orthop Trauma 12:253–258, 1998.

76. Eriksson, E.; Hovelius, L. Ender nailing in fractures of the diaphysis of the femur. J Bone Joint Surg Am 61:1175–1181, 1979.

77. Eriksson, A.R.; Albrektsson, T. Temperature threshold levels for heat-induced bone tissue injury: A vital-microscopic study in a rabbit. J Prosthet Dent 50:101–107, 1983.

78. Farquharson-Roberts, M.A. Corrective osteotomy for combined shortening and rotational malunion of the femur. J Bone Joint Surg Br 77:979–980, 1995.

79. Finsen, V.; Harnes, O.B.; Nesse, O.; Benum, P. Muscle function after plated and nailed femoral shaft fractures. Injury 24:531–534, 1993.

80. Fitzgerald, R.H.; Brindley, G.W.; Kavanagh, B.F. The uncemented total hip arthroplasty: Intraoperative femoral fractures. Clin Orthop 235:61–66, 1988.

81. France, M.P.; Aurori, B.F. Pudendal nerve palsy following fracture table traction. Clin Orthop 276:272–276, 1992.

82. Franklin, J.L.; Winquist, R.A.; Benirschke, S.K.; Hansen, S.T. Broken intramedullary nails. J Bone Joint Surg Am 70:1463–1471, 1998.

83. Fraser, R.D.; Hunter, G.A.; Waddell, J.P. Ipsilateral fracture of the femur and tibia. J Bone Joint Surg Br 60:510–515, 1978.

84. Friedl, H.P.; Stocker, R.; Czermak, B.; et al. Primary fixation and delayed nailing of long bone fractures in severe trauma. Techn Orthop 11:59–66, 1996.

85. Friedman, R.J.; Wyman, E.T. Ipsilateral hip and femoral shaft fractures. Clin Orthop 208:188–194, 1986.

86. Furlong, A.J.; Giannoudis, P.V.; Smith, R.M. Heterotopic ossification: A comparison between reamed and unreamed femoral nailing. Injury 28:9–14, 1997.

87. Furlong, A.J.; Giannoudis, P.V.; De Boer, P.; et al. Exchange nailing for femoral shaft aseptic non-union. Injury 30:245–249, 1999.

88. Garcia-Cimbrelo, E.; Munuera, L.; Gil-Garay, E. Femoral shaft fractures after cemented total hip arthroplasty. Int Orthop 16:97–100, 1992.

89. Gaston, P.; Will, E.; Elton, R.A.; et al. Fractures of the tibia. Can their outcome be predicted? J Bone Joint Surg Br 81:71–76, 1999.

90. Georgiadis, G.M.; Olexa, T.A.; Ebraheim, N.A. Entry sites for antegrade femoral nailing. Clin Orthop 330:281–287, 1996.

91. Giannoudis, P.V.; Furlong, A.J.; MacDonald, D.A.; Smith, R.M. Reamed against unreamed nailing of the femoral diaphysis: A retrospective study of healing time. Injury 28:15–18, 1997.

92. Giannoudis, P.V.; MacDonald, D.A.; Matthews, S.J.; et al. Nonunion of the femoral diaphysis. The influence of reaming and non-steroidal anti-inflammatory drugs. J Bone Joint Surg Br 82:655–658, 2000.

93. Goris, R.J.A.; Gimbrère, J.S.F.; Van Niekerk, J.L.M.; et al. Early osteosynthesis and prophylactic mechanical ventilation in the multitrauma patient. J Trauma 22:895–903, 1982.

94. Greenwood, D.C.; Muir, K.R.; Doherty, M.; et al. Conservatively managed tibial shaft fractures in Nottingham, UK: Are pain, osteoarthritis, and disability long-tern complications? J Epidemiol Community Health 51:701–704, 1997.

95. Gregory, P.; DiCicco, J.; Karpik, K.; et al. Ipsilateral fractures of the femur and tibia: Treatment with retrograde femoral nailing and unreamed tibial nailing. J Orthop Trauma 10:309–316, 1996.

96. Grosse, A.; Christie, J.; Taglang, G.; et al. Open adult femoral shaft fracture treated by early intramedullary nailing. J Bone Joint Surg Br 75:562–565, 1993.

97. Grundy, M. Fractures of femur in Paget's disease of bone. Their aetiology and treatment. J Bone Joint Surg Br 52:252–263, 1970.

98. Gustilo, R.B.; Anderson, J.T. Prevention of infection in the treatment of 1025 open fractures of long bones: Retrospective and prospective analysis. J Bone Joint Surg Am 58:453–458, 1976.

99. Gustilo, R.B.; Mendoza, R.M.; Williams, D.N. Problems in the management of type III (severe) open fractures: A new classification of type III open fractures. J Trauma 24:742–746, 1984.

100. Ha, K.I.; Hahn, S.H.; Chung, M.Y.; et al. A clinical study of stress fractures in sports activities. Orthopedics 14:1089–1095, 1991.

101. Hajek, P.D.; Bicknell, H.R.; Bronson, W.E.; et al. The use of one compared with two distal screws in the treatment of femoral shaft fractures with interlocking intramedullary nailing. J Bone Joint Surg Am 75:519–525, 1993.

102. Hak, D.G.; Lee, S.S.; Goulet, J.A. Success of exchange reamed intramedullary nailing for femoral shaft non-union or delayed union. J Orthop Trauma 14:178–182, 2000.

103. Hamilton, F.H. Deformities after fractures. Trans Am Med Assoc 8:347–444, 1855.

104. Hammacher, E.R.; van Meeteren, M.C.; van der Werken, C. Improved results in the treatment of femoral shaft fractures with the unreamed femoral nail? A multi-centre experience. J Trauma 45:517–521, 1998.

105. Hansen, S.T.; Winquist, R.A. Closed intramedullary nailing of the femur. Küntscher technique with reaming. Clin Orthop 138:56–61, 1979.

106. Hardy, A.E. The treatment of femoral fractures by cast-brace application and early ambulation. A prospective review of one hundred and six patients. J Bone Joint Surg Am 65:56–65, 1983.

107. Herndon, W.A.; Mahnken, R.F.; Yngve, D.A.; Sullivan, J.A. Management of femoral shaft fractures in the adolescent. J Pediatr Orthop 9:29–32, 1989.

108. Herscovici, D.; Whiteman, K.W. Retrograde nailing of the femur using an intercondylar approach. Clin Orthop 332:98–104, 1996.

109. Herscovici, D.; Ricci, W.M.; McAndrews, P.; et al. Treatment of femoral shaft fracture using unreamed interlocked nails. J Orthop Trauma 14:10–24, 2000.

110. Hey Groves, E.W. On Modern Methods of Treating Fractures, 2nd ed. Bristol, England, John Wright, 1921.

111. Hinton, R.Y.; Lincoln, A.; Crockett, M.M.; et al. Fractures of the femoral shaft in children. Incidence, mechanisms and sociodemographic risk factors. J Bone Joint Surg Am 81:500–509, 1999.

112. Hoaglund, F.T.; Low, W.D. Anatomy of the femoral neck and head, with comparative data from Caucasians and Hong Kong Chinese. Clin Orthop 152:10–16, 1980.

113. Hodalic, Z.; Svagelj, M.; Sebalj, I.; Sebalj, D. Surgical treatment of 1,211 patients at the Vinkovci General Hospital, Vinkovci, Croatia during the 1991–1992 Serbian Offensive in East Slavonia. Mil Med 164:803–808, 1999.

114. Hoffmann, R. Rotules à os pour la réduction dirigée, non sanglante des fractures ("ostéotaxis"). Helv Med Acta 5:844–850, 1938.

115. Hooper, G.J.; Lyon, D.W. Closed unlocked nailing for comminuted femoral fractures. J Bone Joint Surg Br 70:619–621, 1988.

116. Horne, L.T.; Blue, B.A. Intraarticular heterotopic ossification in the knee following intramedullary nailing of the fractured femur using a retrograde method. J Orthop Trauma 13:385–388, 1999.

117. Islinger, R.B.; Kuklo, T.R.; McHale, K.A. A review of orthopedic injuries in three recent US military conflicts. Mil Med 165:463–465, 2000.

118. Jensen, T.T.; Overgaard, S.; Mossing, N.B. Partridge Cerclene system for femoral fractures in osteoporotic bones with ipsilateral hemi/total arthroplasty. J Arthroplasty 5:123–126, 1990.

119. Johansen, K.; Daines, M.; Howey, T.; et al. Objective criteria accurately predict amputation following lower extremity trauma. J Trauma 30:568–572, 1990.

120. Johansson, J.E.; McBroom, R.; Barrington, T.W.; Hunter, O.A. Fracture of the ipsilateral femur in patients with total hip replacement. J Bone Joint Surg Am 63:1435–1442, 1981.

121. Johnson, D.L.; Wiss, D.A. Intra-articular penetration of the knee joint by a fragment of cortical bone during intramedullary nailing of the femur. J Bone Joint Surg Am 78:1092–1095, 1996.

122. Johnson, E.E. Acute lengthening of shortened lower extremities after malunion or non-union of a fracture. J Bone Joint Surg Am 76:379–389, 1994.

123. Johnson, K.D.; Johnson, D.W.C.; Parker, B. Comminuted femoral-shaft fractures: Treatment by roller traction, cerclage wires and an intramedullary nail, or an interlocking intramedullary nail. J Bone Joint Surg Am 66:1222–1235, 1984.

124. Johnson, K.D.; Cadambi, A.; Seibert, G.B. Incidence of adult respiratory distress syndrome in patients with multiple musculo-skeletal injuries: Effect of early operative stabilisation of fractures. J Trauma 25:375–384, 1985.

125. Jukkala-Partio, K.; Partio, E.K.; Solovieva, S.; et al. Treatment of periprosthetic hip fractures in association with total hip arthroplasty—a retrospective comparison between revision stem and plate fixation. Ann Chir Gynaecol 87:229–235, 1998.

126. Karpos, P.A.G.; McFerran, M.A.; Johnson, K.D. Intramedullary nailing of acute femoral shaft fractures using manual traction without a fracture table. J Orthop Trauma 9:57–62, 1995.

127. Kaufer, H. Non-operative ambulatory treatment for fracture of the shaft of the femur. Clin Orthop 87:192–199, 1972.

128. Kavanagh, B.F. Femoral fractures associated with total hip arthroplasty. Orthop Clin North Am 23:249–257, 1992.

129. Kempf, I.; Grosse, A.; Lafforgue, D. L'apport du verrouillage dans l'enclouage centro-médullaire des os longs. Rev Chir Orthop 64:635–651, 1978.

130. Kempf, I.; Grosse, A.; Beck, G. Closed locked intramedullary nailing. Its application to comminuted fractures of the femur. J Bone Joint Surg Am 67:709–720, 1985.

131. Kempf, I.; Grosse, A.; Rigaut, P. The treatment of noninfected pseudarthrosis of the femur and tibia with locked intramedullary nailing. Clin Orthop 212:142–154, 1986.

132. Kempf, I.; Grosse, A.; Abalo, C. Locked intramedullary nailing. Its application to femoral and tibial axial, rotational, lengthening and shortening osteotomies. Clin Orthop 212:165–173, 1986.

133. Kirby, R.M.; Winquist, R.A.; Hansen, S.T. Femoral shaft fractures in adolescents: A comparison between traction plus cast treatment and closed intramedullary nailing. J Pediatr Orthop 1:193–197, 1981.

134. Klein, M.P.; Rahn, B.A.; Frigg, R.; et al. Reaming versus non-reaming in medullary nailing: Interference with cortical circulation of the canine tibia. Arch Orthop Trauma Surg 109:314–316, 1990.

135. Klemm, K.; Schellman, W.D. Dynamische und statische Verriege-lung des Markangels. Monatsschr Unfallheilkunde 75:568–575, 1972.

136. Klemm, K.W. Treatment of infected pseudarthrosis of the femur and tibia with interlocking nail. Clin Orthop 212:174–181, 1986.

137. Klemm, K.W.; Börner, M. Interlocking nailing of complex fractures of the femur and tibia. Clin Orthop 212:89–100, 1986.

138. Kluger, Y.; Gonze, M.D.; Paul, D.B.; et al. Blunt vascular injury associated with closed mid-shaft femur fracture: A plea for concern. J Trauma 36:222–225, 1994.

139. Krettek, C.; Miclau, T.; Blauth, M.; et al. Recurrent rotational deformity of the femur after static locking of intramedullary nails. J Bone Joint Surg Br 79:4–8, 1997.

140. Kröpfl, A.; Naglik, H.; Primavesi, C.; Hertz, H. Unreamed intramedullary nailing of femoral fractures. J Trauma 38:717–726, 1995.

141. Kumm, D.A.; Rack, C.; Rutt, J. Subtrochanteric stress fracture of the femur following total knee arthroplasty. J Arthroplasty 12:580–583, 1997.

142. Küntscher, G. Praxis der Marknagelung. Stuttgart, Germany, F.K. Schattaur Verlag, 1961.

143. Lambotte, A. L'Intervention Opératoire dans les Fractures Récents et Anciennes Envisagée Paticulièrement au Point de Vue de l'Osté-synthèse. Brussels, Lamertin, 1907.

144. Leung, K.S.; So, W.S.; Lam, T.P.; Leung, P.C. Treatment of ipsilat-eral femoral shaft fractures and hip fractures. Injury 24:41–45, 1993.

145. Leunig, M.; Hertel, R. Thermal necrosis after tibial reaming for intramedullary nail fixation. A report of three cases. J Bone Joint Surg Br 78:584–587, 1996.

146. Levy, A.S.; Wetzler, M.J.; Guttman, G.; et al. Treating gunshot femoral fractures with immediate reamed intramedullary nailing. Orthop Rev 22:805–809, 1993.

147. Lezius, A. Intramedullary nailing of intertrochanteric and subtro-chanteric fractures with curved nail. J Int Coll Surg 13:569–572, 1950.

148. Thowe, D.W.; Hansen, S.T. Immediate nailing of open fractures of the femoral shaft. J Bone Joint Surg Am 70:812–820, 1988.

149. Lindahl, O. The rigidity of fracture immobilisation with plates. Acta Orthop Scand 38:101–114, 1967.

150. Loomer, R.L.; Meek, R.; De Sommer, F. Plating of femoral shaft fractures: The Vancouver experience. J Trauma 20:1038–1042, 1980.

151. Magerl, F.; Wyss, A.; Brunner, C.; Binder, W. Plate osteosynthesis of femoral shaft fractures in adults. Clin Orthop 138:62–73, 1979.

152. Maini, L.; Chadha, M.; Vishwanath, J.; et al. The Ilizarov method in infected non-union of fractures. Injury 31:509–517, 2000.

153. Marcus, R.; Cann, C.; Madvig, P.; et al. Menstrual function and bone mass in elite women distance runners. Endocrine and metabolic features. Ann Intern Med 102:158–163, 1985.

154. Marks, P.H.; Paley, D.; Kellam, J.F. Heterotopic ossification around the hip with intramedullary nailing of the femur. J Trauma 28:1207–1213, 1988.

155. Matheson, G.O.; Clement, D.B.; McKenzie, D.C.; et al. Stress fractures in athletes. A study of 320 cases. Am J Sports Med 15:46–58, 1987.

156. McKee, M.D.; Waddell, J.P. Intramedullary nailing of femoral fractures in morbidly obese patients. J Trauma 36:208–210, 1994.

157. McLauchlan, G.J.; Robinson, C.M.; Singer, B.R.; Christie, J. Results of an operative policy in the treatment of periprosthetic femoral fracture. J Orthop Trauma 11:170–179, 1997.

158. McQueen, M.M.; Court-Brown, C.M. Compartment monitoring in tibial fractures. J Bone Joint Surg Br 78:99–104, 1996.

159. McQueen, M.M.; Gaston, P.; Court-Brown, C.M. Acute compart-ment syndrome. Who is at risk? J Bone Joint Surg Br 82:200–203, 2000.

160. Mileski, R.A.; Garvin, K.L.; Crosby, L.A. Avascular necrosis of the femoral head in an adolescent following intramedullary nailing of the femur. A case report. J Bone Joint Surg Am 76:1706–1708, 1994.

161. Milgrom, C.; Giladi, M.; Stein, M.; et al. Stress fractures in military recruits. A prospective study showing an unusually high incidence. J Bone Joint Surg Br 67:732–735, 1985.

162. Moed, B.R.; Watson, J.T. Retrograde intramedullary nailing, without reaming, of fractures of the femoral shaft in multiply injured patients. J Bone Joint Surg Am 77:1520–1527, 1995.

163. Moed, B.R.; Watson, J.T.; Cramer, K.E.; et al. Unreamed retrograde intramedullary nailing of the femoral shaft. J Orthop Trauma 12:334–342, 1998.

164. Mohr, V.D.; Eickhoff, U.; Haaker, R.; Klammer, H.L. External fixation of open femoral shaft fractures. J Trauma 38:648–652, 1995.

165. Mont, M.A.; Maar, D.C. Fractures of the ipsilateral femur after hip arthroplasty. A statistical analysis of outcome based on 487 patients. J Arthroplasty 9:511–519, 1994.

166. Montijo, H.; Ebert, F.R.; Lennox, D.A. Treatment of proximal femoral fractures associated with total hip arthroplasty. J Arthroplasty 4:115–123, 1989.

167. Mooney, V.; Nickel, V.L.; Harvey, J.P.; Snelson, R. Cast-brace treatment for fractures of the distal part of the femur. A prospective controlled study of one hundred and fifty patients. J Bone Joint Surg Am 52:1563–1578, 1970.

168. Moran, C.J.; Gibson, M.J.; Cross, A.T. Intramedullary locking nails for femoral shaft fractures in elderly patients. J Bone Joint Surg Br 72:19–22, 1990.

169. Morgan, E.; Ostrum, R.F.; DiCicco, J.; et al. Effects of retrograde femoral intramedullary nailing on the patellofemoral articulation. J Orthop Trauma 13:13–16, 1999.

170. Mosheiff, R.; Segal, D.; Wollstein, R.; et al. Midshaft femoral fracture, concomitant ipsilateral hip joint injury, and disruption of the knee extensor mechanism: A unique triad of dashboard injury. Am J Orthop 27:465–473, 1998.

171. Muller, E.J.; Siebenrock, K.; Ekkernkamp, A.; et al. Ipsilateral fractures of the pelvis and the femur—floating hip? A retrospective analysis of 42 cases. Arch Orthop Trauma Surg 119:179–182, 1999.

172. Müller, M.E.; Nazarian, S.; Koch, P.; Schatzker, J. A Comprehensive Classification of Fractures of Long Bones. Berlin, Springer-Verlag, 1990.

173. Müller, M.E.; Allgöwer, M.; Schneider, R.; Willenegger, H. Manual of Internal Fixation, 3rd ed. Berlin, Springer-Verlag, 1990.

174. Neudeck, F.; Wozasek, G.E.; Obertacke, U.; et al. Nailing versus plating in thoracic trauma: An experimental study in sheep. J Trauma 40:980–984, 1996.

175. Nicholas, R.M.; McCoy, G.F. Immediate intramedullary nailing of femoral shaft fractures due to gunshots. Injury 26:257–259, 1995.

176. Nowotarski, P.; Brumback, R.J. Immediate interlocking nailing of fractures of the femur caused by low- to mid-velocity gunshots. J Orthop Trauma 8:134–141, 1994.

177. Nowotarski, P.J.; Turen, C.H.; Brumback, R.J.; Scarboro, J.M. Conversion of external fixation to intramedullary nailing for fractures of the shaft of the femur in multiply injured patients. J Bone Joint Surg Am 82:781–788, 2000.

178. O'Brien, P.J.; Meek, R.N.; Powell, J.N.; Blachut, P.A. Primary intramedullary nailing of open femoral shaft fractures. J Trauma 31:113–116, 1991.

179. Okhotsky, V.P.; Souvalyan, A.G. The treatment of non-union and pseudarthrosis of the long bones with thick nails. Injury 10:92–98, 1978.

180. Orava, S.; Puranen, J.; Ala-Ketola, L. Stress fractures caused by physical exercise. Acta Orthop Scand 49:19–27, 1978.

181. Ostrum, R.F.; DiCicco, J.; Lakatos, R.; Poka, A. Retrograde intramedullary nailing of femoral diaphyseal fractures. J Orthop Trauma 12:464–468, 1998.

182. Ostrum, R.F. Treatment of floating knee injuries through a single percutaneous approach. Clin Orthop 375:43–50, 2000.

183. Ostrum, R.F.; Agarwal, A.; Lakatos, R.; Poka, A. Prospective comparison of retrograde and antegrade femoral intramedullary nailing. J Orthop Trauma 14:496–501, 2000.

184. Paley, D.; Chaudray, M.; Pirone, A.M.; et al. Treatment of malunions and mal-nonunions of the femur and tibia by detailed preoperative planning and the Ilizarov techniques. Orthop Clin North Am 21:667–691, 1990.

185. Paley, D.; Herzenberg, J.E.; Paremain, G.; Bhave, A. Femoral lengthening over an intramedullary nail. A matched-case comparison with Ilizarov femoral lengthening. J Bone Joint Surg Am 79:1464–1480, 1997.

186. Pankovich, A.M.; Goldflies, M.L.; Pearson, R.L. Closed Ender nailing of femoral-shaft fractures. J Bone Joint Surg Am 61:222–232, 1979.

187. Pape, H.C.; Auf'm'Kolk, M.; Paffrath, T.; et al. Primary intramedullary femur fixation in multiple trauma patients with associated lung contusion—a cause of post-traumatic ARDS? J Trauma 34:540–548, 1993.

188. Pape, H.C.; Regel, G.; Dwenger, A.; et al. Influences of different methods of intramedullary femoral nailing on lung function in patients with multiple trauma. J Trauma 35:709–716, 1993.

189. Pape, H.C.; Dwenger, A.; Grotz, M.; et al. Does the reamer type influence the degree of lung dysfunction after femoral nailing following severe trauma? An animal study. J Orthop Trauma 8:300–309, 1994.

190. Patterson, B.M.; Routt, M.L.; Benirschke, S.K.; Hansen, S.T. Retrograde nailing of femoral shaft fractures. J Trauma 38:38–43, 1995.

191. Patton, J.T.; Cook, R.E.; Adams, C.I.; Robinson, C.M. Late fracture of the hip after reamed intramedullary nailing of the femur. J Bone Joint Surg Br 82:967–971, 2000.

192. Peltier, L.F. A brief history of traction. J Bone Joint Surg Am 50:1603–1617, 1968.

193. Peltier, L.F. Fractures. A History and Iconography of Their Treatment. San Francisco, Norman, 1990.

194. Perkins, G. Fractures. London, Oxford University Press, 1940.

195. Ponzer, S.; Tidermark, J.; Törnkvist, H. Retrograde nailing of femoral fractures distal to a Moore prosthesis. J Orthop Trauma 12:588–591, 1998.

196. Protzman, R.R.; Griffis, C.G. Stress fractures in men and women undergoing military training. J Bone Joint Surg Am 59:825, 1977.

197. Rascher, J.J.; Nahigian, S.H.; Macys, J.R.; Brown, J.E. Closed nailing of femoral-shaft fractures. J Bone Joint Surg Am 54:534–544, 1972.

198. Reichert, I.L.H.; McCarthy, I.D.; Hughes, S.P.F. The acute vascular response to intramedullary nailing. J Bone Joint Surg Br 77:490–493, 1995.

199. Reynders, P.A.; Broos, P.L.O. Healing of closed femoral shaft fractures treated with the AO unreamed femoral nail. A comparative study with the AO reamed femoral nail. Injury 31:367–371, 2000.

200. Riemer, B.L.; Foglesong, M.E.; Miranda, M.A. Femoral plating. Orthop Clin North Am 25:625–634, 1994.

201. Ring, D.; Jupiter, J.B.; Sanders, R.A.; et al. Complex nonunion of fractures of the femoral shaft treated by wave-plate osteosynthesis. J Bone Joint Surg Br 79:289–294, 1997.

202. Riska, E.B.; von Bonsdorff, H.; Hakkinen, S.; et al. Primary operative fixation of long bone fractures in patients with multiple injuries. J Trauma 17:111–121, 1977.

203. Rokkanen, P.; Slätis, P.; Vankka, E. Closed or open intramedullary nailing of femoral shaft fractures? J Bone Joint Surg Br 51:313–323, 1969.

204. Rozbruch, S.R.; Müller, U.; Gautier, E.; Ganz, R. The evolution of femoral shaft plating technique. Clin Orthop 354:195–208, 1998.

205. Rüedi, T.P.; Lüscher, N. Results after internal fixation of comminuted fractures of the femoral shaft with DC plates. Clin Orthop 138:74–76, 1979.

206. Rush, L.V. Atlas of Rush Pin Techniques. Meridian, MS, Beviron, 1955.

207. Russell, R.H. Fracture of the femur: A clinical study. Br J Surg 11:491–502, 1924.

208. Rütter, J.E.; de Vries, L.S.; van der Werken, C. Intramedullary nailing of open femoral shaft fractures. Injury 25:419–422, 1994.

209. Saleh, M.; Rees, A. Bifocal surgery for deformity and bone loss after lower-limb fractures. Compression of bone-transport and compression-distraction methods. J Bone Joint Surg Br 77:429–434, 1995.

210. Saleh, M.; Royston, S. Management of nonunion of fractures by distraction with correction of angulation and shortening. J Bone Joint Surg Br 78:105–109, 1996.

211. Salminen, S.T.; Pihlajamäki, H.; Avikainen, V.; et al. Specific features associated with femoral shaft fractures caused by low-energy trauma. J Trauma 43:117–122, 1997.

212. Salminen, S.T.; Pihlajamäki, H.; Avikainen, V.J.; Böstman, O. Population based epidemiologic and morphologic study of femoral shaft fractures. Clin Orthop 372:241–249, 2000.

213. Sanders, R.; Koval, K.J.; DiPasquale, T.; et al. Retrograde reamed femoral nailing. J Orthop Trauma 7:293–302, 1993.

214. Sartoretti, C.; Sartoretti-Schefer, S.; Ruckert, R.; Buchmann, P. Comorbid conditions in old patients with femur fractures. J Trauma 43:570–577, 1997.

215. Schemitsch, E.H.; Kowalski, M.J.; Swiontkowski, M.F.; Senft, D. Cortical bone blood flow in reamed and unreamed locked intramedullary nailing. A fractured tibial model in sheep. J Orthop Trauma 8:373–382, 1994.

216. Schemitsch, E.H.; Turchin, D.C.; Kowalski, M.J.; Swiontkowski, M.F. Quantitative assessment of bone injury and repair after reamed and unreamed locked intramedullary nailing. J Trauma 45:250–255, 1998.

217. Schmotzer, H.; Tchejeyan, G.H.; Dall, D.M. Surgical management of intra- and postoperative fractures of the femur about the tip of the stem in total hip arthroplasty. J Arthroplasty 11:709–717, 1996.

218. Schwartz, J.T.; Brumback, R.J.; Lakatos, R.; et al. Acute compartment syndrome of the thigh. J Bone Joint Surg Am 71:392–400, 1989.

219. Scott, R.D.; Turner, R.H.; Leitzes, S.M.; Aufranc, O.E. Femoral fractures in conjunction with total hip replacement. J Bone Joint Surg Am 57:494–501, 1975.

220. Seibel, R.; La Duca, J.; Hassett, J.M.; et al. Blunt multiple trauma (ISS 36), femur traction, and the pulmonary failure-septic state. Ann Surg 202:283–295, 1985.

221. Seiler, J.G.; Swiontkowski, M.F. Prospective evaluation of the AO/ASIF universal femoral nail in the treatment of traumatic and reconstructive problems of the femur. J Trauma 31:121–126, 1991.

222. Serocki, J.H.; Chandler, R.W.; Dorr, L.D. Treatment of fractures about hip prostheses with compression plating. J Arthroplasty 7:129–135, 1992.

223. Sharma, J.C.; Gupta, S.P.; Mathur, N.C.; et al. Comminuted femoral shaft fractures treated by closed intramedullary nailing and functional cast bracing. J Trauma 34:786–791, 1993.

224. Shaw, A.D.; Sjolin, S.U.; McQueen, M.M. Crush syndrome following unconsciousness: Need for urgent orthopaedic referral. BMJ 309:857–859, 1994.

225. Shuler, T.E.; Gruen, G.S.; DiTano, O.; Riemer, B.I. Ipsilateral proximal shaft fractures: Spectrum of injury involving the femoral neck. Injury 28:293–297, 1997.

226. Simonian, P.T.; Chapman, J.R.; Selznick, H.S.; et al. Iatrogenic fractures of the femoral neck during closed nailing of the femoral shaft. J Bone Joint Surg Br 76:293–296, 1994.

227. Simpson, A.H.R.W.; Cole, A.S.; Kenwright, J. Leg lengthening over an intramedullary nail. J Bone Joint Surg Br 81:1041–1045, 1999.

228. Sirkin, M.S.; Behrens, F.; McCracken, K.; et al. Femoral nailing without a fracture table. Clin Orthop 332:119–225, 1996.

229. Søjbjerg, J.O.; Eiskjaer, S.; Møller-Larsen, F. Locked nailing of comminuted and unstable fractures of the femur. J Bone Joint Surg Br 72:23–25, 1990.

230. Steinberg, G.G.; Hubbard, C. Heterotopic ossification after femoral intramedullary rodding. J Orthop Trauma 7:536–542, 1993.

231. Steinmann, F. Eine neu extensions Methode in der Frakturenbehandlung. Zentralbl Chir 34:938–942, 1907.

232. Sterett, W.I.; Krissoff, W.B. Femur fractures in alpine skiing: Classification and mechanisms of injury in 85 cases. J Orthop Trauma 8:310–314, 1994.

233. Swiontkowski, M.F.; Hansen, S.T.; Kellam, J. Ipsilateral fractures of the femoral neck and shaft. J Bone Joint Surg Am 66:260–268, 1984.

234. Swiontkowski, M.F.; Agel, J.; McAndrew, M.P.; et al. Outcome validation of the AO/OTA fracture classification system. J Orthop Trauma 14:534–541, 2000.

235. Tarlow, S.D.; Achterman, C.A.; Hayhurst, J.; Ovadia, D.N. Acute compartment syndrome in the thigh complicating fracture of the femur. A report of three cases. J Bone Joint Surg Am 68:1439–1443, 1986.

236. Taylor, J.C. Delayed union and non-union of fractures. In: Crenshaw, A.H., ed. Campbell's Operative Orthopaedics, 8th ed., Vol. 2. St. Louis, C.V. Mosby, 1992, p. 1287.

237. Tejan, J.; Lindsey, R.W. Management of civilian gunshot injury to the femur. A review of the literature. Injury 29(Suppl 1):SA18–SA22, 1998.

238. Templeman, D.; Thomas, M.; Varecka, T.; Kyle, R. Exchange reamed intramedullary nailing for delayed union and non-union of the tibia. Clin Orthop 315:169–175, 1995.

239. Thometz, J.G.; Lamdan, R. Osteonecrosis of the femoral head after intramedullary nailing of a fracture of the femoral shaft in an adolescent. J Bone Joint Surg Am 77:1423–1426, 1995.

240. Thompson, F.; O'Beirne, J.; Gallagher, J.; et al. Fractures of the femoral shaft treated by plating. Injury 16:535–538, 1985.

241. Timmerman, L.A.; Rab, G.T. Intramedullary nailing of femoral shaft fractures in adolescents. J Orthop Trauma 7:331–337, 1993.

242. Tornetta, P.; Tiburzi, D. Anterograde interlocked nailing of distal femoral fractures after gunshot wounds. J Orthop Trauma 8:220–227, 1994.

243. Tornetta, P.; Ritz, G.; Kantor, A. Femoral torsion after interlocked nailing of unstable femoral fractures. J Trauma 38:213–219, 1995.

244. Tornetta, P.; Tiburzi, D. Reamed versus nonreamed anterograde femoral nailing. J Orthop Trauma 14:15–19, 2000.

245. Tornetta, P.; Tiburzi, D. Antegrade or retrograde reamed femoral nailing. J Bone Joint Surg Br 82:652–654, 2000.

246. Townsend, R.N.; Lheureau, T.; Protetch, J.; et al. Timing fracture repair in patients with severe brain injury. J Trauma 44:977–982, 1998.

247. Tylman, D.; Siwek, W. Long-term results of functional treatment in intra-articular knee fractures and multi-fragment fracture of the shaft of the femurs. Clin Orthop 272:114–121, 1991.

248. Ueng, S.W.N.; Wei, F.C.; Shih, C.H. Management of femoral diaphyseal infected nonunion with antibiotic beads, local therapy, external skeletal fixation, and staged bone grafting. J Trauma 46:97–103, 1999.

249. Utvåg, S.E.; Grundnes, O.; Reikerås, O. Effects of degrees of reaming on healing of segmental fractures in rats. J Orthop Trauma 12:192–199, 1998.

250. Van den Bossche, M.R.P.; Broos, P.L.; Rommens, P.M. Open fractures of the femoral shaft, treated with osteosynthesis or temporary external fixation. Injury 26:323–325, 1995.

251. Van den Made, W.J.; Smit, E.J.M.; van Luyt, P.A.; van Vugt, A.B. Intramedullary femoral osteosynthesis: An additional cause of ARDS in multiply injured patients? Injury 27:391–393, 1996.

252. Van der Schoot, D.K.E.; Den Outer, H.A.; Bode, P.J.; et al. Degenerative changes at the knee and ankle related to malunion of tibial fractures. J Bone Joint Surg Br 78:722–725, 1996.

253. Van Doorn, R.; Stapert, J.W. Treatment of impending and actual pathological femoral fractures with the long Gamma nail in The Netherlands. Eur J Surg 166:247–254, 2000.

254. Vangsness, C.T., Jr.; DeCampos, J.; Merritt, P.O.; Wiss, D.A. Meniscal injury associated with femoral shaft fractures. An arthroscopic evaluation of incidence. J Bone Joint Surg Br 75:207–209, 1993.

255. Van Niekerk, K.J.L.M.; Schoots, F.J. Femoral shaft fractures treated with plate fixation and interlocked nailing: A comparative retrospective study. Injury 23:219–222, 1992.

256. Van Reit, Y.E.A.; van der Werken, C.; Marti, R.K. Sub-fascial plate fixation of comminuted diaphyseal femoral fractures: A report of three cases utilising biological osteosynthesis. J Orthop Trauma 11:57–60, 1997.

257. Veith, R.G.; Winquist, R.A.; Hansen, S.T. Ipsilateral fractures of the femur and tibia. A report of fifty-seven consecutive cases. J Bone Joint Surg Am 66:991–1002, 1984.

258. Velkes, S.; Nerubay, J.; Lokiec, F. Stress fracture of the proximal femur after screw removal. Arch Orthop Trauma Surg 115:61–62, 1996.

259. Vidal, J.; Rabischong, P.; Boneel, F. Étude bioméchanique du fixateur externe d'Hoffmann dans les fractures de jambe. Soc Chir Montpellier Séance Jan:43–52, 1970.

260. Walters, J.; Shepherd-Wilson, W.; Lyons, T. Femoral shaft fractures treated by Ender nails using a trochanteric approach. J Bone Joint Surg Br 72:14–18, 1990.

261. Webb, L.X.; Winquist, R.A.; Hansen, S.T. Intramedullary nailing and reaming for delayed union or nonunion of the femoral shaft: A report of 105 consecutive cases. Clin Orthop 212:133–141, 1986.

262. Weber, B.G.; Cech, O. Pseudarthrosis. Berne, Huber, 1976.

263. Wei, F.C.; El-Gammal, T.A.; Lin, C.H.; Ueng, W.N. Free fibular osteoseptocutaneous graft for reconstruction of segmental femoral shaft defects. J Trauma 43:784–792, 1997.

264. Wenda, K.; Runkel, M.; Degreif, J.; Rudig, L. Minimally invasive plate fixation in femoral shaft fractures. Injury 28(Suppl 1):SA13–SA19, 1997.

265. Weresh, M.J.; Hakanson, R.; Stover, M.D.; et al. Failure of exchange reamed intramedullary nails for ununited femoral shaft fractures. J Orthop Trauma 14:335–338, 2000.

266. Williams, M.M.; Askins, V.; Hinkes, E.W.; Zych, G.A. Primary reamed intramedullary nailing of open femoral shaft fractures. Clin Orthop 318:182–190, 1995.

267. Willis, B.H.; Carden, D.L.; Sadasivan, K.K. Effect of femoral fracture and intramedullary fixation on lung capillary leak. J Trauma 46:687–692, 1999.

268. Winquist, R.A.; Hansen, S.T.; Clawson, D.K. Closed intramedullary nailing of femoral fractures. A report of five hundred and twenty cases. J Bone Joint Surg Am 66:529–539, 1984.

269. Wiss, D.A.; Fleming, C.H.; Matta, J.M.; Clark, D. Comminuted and rotationally unstable fractures of the femur treated with an interlocking nail. Clin Orthop 212:35–47, 1986.

270. Wiss, D.A.; Brien, W.W.; Stetson, W.B. Interlocked nailing for treatment of segmental fractures of the femur. J Bone Joint Surg Am 72:724–728, 1990.

271. Wiss, D.A.; Brien, W.W.; Becker, V. Interlocking nailing for the treatment of femoral fractures due to gunshot wounds. J Bone Joint Surg Am 73:598–606, 1991.

272. Wolinsky, P.R.; Banit, D.; Parker, R.E.; et al. Reamed intramedullary femoral nailing after induction of an "ARDS-like" state in sheep: Effect on clinically applicable markers of pulmonary function. J Orthop Trauma 12:169–176, 1998.

273. Wozasek, G.E.; Thurnher, M.; Redl, H.; Schlag, G. Pulmonary reaction during intramedullary fracture management in traumatic shock. An experimental study. J Trauma 37:249–254, 1994.

274. Wright, D.G.; Levin, J.S.; Esterhai, J.L.; Heppenstall, R.B. Immediate internal fixation of low-velocity gunshot related femoral fractures. J Trauma 35:678–682, 1993.

275. Wu, C.C.; Shih, C.H.; Chen, N.H. Femoral shaft fractures complicated by fracture-dislocations of the ipsilateral hip. J Trauma 34:70–75, 1993.

276. Wu, C.C. The effect of dynamisation on slowing the healing of femur shaft fractures after interlocking nailing. J Trauma 43:263–267, 1997.

277. Wu, C.C.; Chen, W.J. Healing of 56 segmental femoral shaft fractures after locked nailing. Poor results of dynamisation. Acta Orthop Scand 68:537–540, 1997.

278. Yang, K.H.; Han, D.Y.; Park, H.W.; et al. Fracture of the ipsilateral neck of the femur in shaft nailing. The role of CT in diagnosis. J Bone Joint Surg Br 80:673–678, 1998.

279. Ziv, I.; Blackburn, N.; Rang, M. Femoral intramedullary nailing in the growing child. J Trauma 24:432–434, 1984.

280. Zuber, K.; Kock, P.; Lustenberger, A.; Ganz, R. Femurfraktur nach Hüfttotalprotese. Unfallchirurg 93:467–472, 1990.

# CHAPTER 53

# Fractures of the Distal Femur

Christian Krettek, M.D.
David L. Helfet, M.D.

## PATHOLOGY

### Relevant Anatomy

The distal end of the femur traditionally encompasses the lower third of this bone. This zone varies greatly in the literature, from the distal 7.6 cm to the distal 15 cm of the femur. This chapter deals only with fractures that involve the supracondylar (metaphyseal) or intercondylar (epiphyseal) areas of the distal end of the femur. Distal femoral fractures that are purely diaphyseal are discussed in Chapter 52.

### BONE

The supracondylar (metaphyseal) area of the distal portion of the femur is the transition zone between the distal diaphysis and the femoral articular condyles (Fig. 53–1A). At the diaphyseal-metaphyseal junction, the metaphysis flares, especially on the medial side, to provide a platform for the broad condylar weight-bearing surface of the knee joint. Anteriorly between these two condyles is a smooth articular depression for the patella, the trochlear groove. Posteriorly between the two condyles is the intercondyloid notch. Medially, a readily identifiable landmark is the adductor tubercle at the maximal point of flare of the metaphysis. Both condyles have epicondyles on their outer surfaces.

Of surgical importance, the shaft of the femur in the sagittal view is aligned with the anterior half of the condyles, whereas the posterior half of both condyles is in a posterior position relative to the proximal femoral shaft. In addition, the condyles are wider posteriorly than anteriorly. A transverse cut through the condyles shows a trapezoid with a 25° posterior-to-anterior decrease in width on the medial side.

### MUSCLE

Anteriorly, the extensor compartment contains the quadriceps femoris, the single largest muscle in the body. It consists of four heads: the rectus femoris more superficially and, in the deeper layer from lateral to medial, the vastus lateralis, vastus intermedius, and vastus medialis. The anterior extensor compartment is separated from the posterior compartment by the lateral and medial intermuscular septa. These partitions provide important landmarks for both the lateral and medial approaches to the knee joint. Of major significance on the medial side is the superficial femoral artery, which runs down the thigh between the extensor and adductor compartments. The artery passes into the popliteal fossa approximately 10 cm above the knee joint by passing through the adductor magnus muscle. It obviously must be identified and avoided in medial approaches to the distal end of the femur.

The powerful muscles of the distal part of the thigh produce characteristic bony deformities with fractures. The muscle pull of the quadriceps and posterior hamstrings produces shortening of the femur. As the shaft overrides anteriorly and the gastrocnemius muscles pull posteriorly, the condyles are displaced and angulated posteriorly (see Fig. 53–1B). When the condyles are separated by a fracture, rotational malalignment is common because of the unrestrained pull of the gastrocnemius muscles and the anterior overriding of the shaft.

### ALIGNMENT

The anatomic axis of the shaft of the femur is different from the weight-bearing, or mechanical, axis (Fig. 53–2). The latter passes through the head of the femur and the middle of the knee joint. Generally, the weight-bearing femoral axis subtends an angle of 3° from the vertical. The anatomic femoral axis has a valgus angulation of 7°

1957

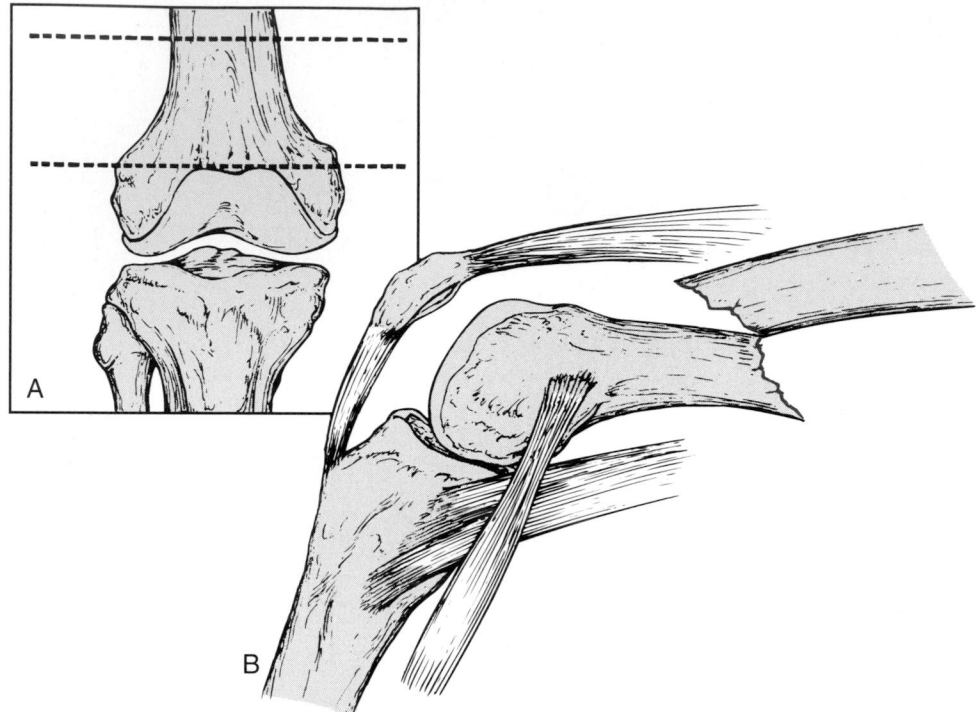

**FIGURE 53–1.** Anatomic representation of the distal end of the femur. *A,* Sketch of an anteroposterior radiograph of the metaphysis. The segment between the *dashed lines* is the supracondylar zone. *B,* Sketch of a lateral radiograph demonstrating muscle attachments and bone displacement.

(average, 9°) relative to the vertical axis. Normally, the knee joint axis is parallel to the ground, and the anatomic femoral axis subtends an 81° lateral distal femoral angle relative to the knee joint axis. For each patient it is important to confirm this angle from the opposite femur. Then, at the time of surgical reconstruction, the correct femoral valgus angulation (anatomic axis) can be re-created and the knee joint kept parallel to the ground.

## Incidence

Distal femoral fractures have been reported to account for between 4%[57] and 7%[95] of all femoral fractures, which in Sweden corresponds to an annual incidence of 51 per million inhabitants older than 16 years.[57] If fractures of the hip are excluded, 31% of femoral fractures involve the distal end.[1] With the modern trends of high-energy lifestyles combined with increased longevity, this incidence is probably increasing.

Distal femoral fractures occur predominantly in two patient populations: young persons, especially young men, after high-energy trauma, and elderly persons, especially elderly women, after low-energy injuries. In one series from Sweden, up to 84% of distal femoral fractures occurred in patients older than 50 years.[57] In a Rochester, Minnesota, study of patients aged 65 years or older, 84% of the femoral fractures occurred in women. The conclusion of this epidemiologic study was that the "incidence rates for distal femoral fractures do indeed rise exponentially with age and are greater among elderly women than men."[1]

In the older group, most of the injuries occur after moderate trauma, such as a fall on a flexed knee. Two thirds of the fractures caused by moderate trauma were "preceded by prior age-related fractures (hip, proximal humerus, distal forearm, pelvis or vertebra) or with roentgenographic evidence of generalized osteopenia."[1]

In the younger group, distal femoral fractures occur after high-energy trauma. These fractures are often open, comminuted, and most probably the result of direct application of load to a flexed knee. Most are caused by vehicular accidents, including motorcycle accidents, but they can also result from industrial accidents or falls from heights. Most of these patients are younger than 35 years, with a definite male preponderance.

Surprisingly, the degree of comminution in the supracondylar region is often equivalent in both these groups. However, younger patients experiencing high-energy trauma have a greater incidence of additional intra-articular disruption or segmental or more proximal shaft comminution.[104]

## Anatomic and Functional Consequences of the Injury

Fractures in the supracondylar area characteristically deform with femoral shortening and posterior angulation and displacement of the distal fragment. In more severe fractures with intercondylar involvement, one often sees rotational malalignment of the condyles relative to each other in the frontal plane, a result of their muscle attachments.

Even with significant supracondylar comminution and displacement of the distal fragment, axial alignment can often be regained with traction, but the alignment is hard to maintain. Conversely, with intercondylar involvement and malrotation of the condyles, reduction is almost impossible by traction alone and is often difficult even with surgery. The aims of treatment must be restoration of length, rotation, and axial alignment and anatomic reconstitution of articular surface to avoid long-term morbidity. Length and rotation can usually be restored by traction alone, but restoration of axial alignment of the knee joint relative to the femoral anatomic axis often requires additional measures, including surgical intervention. Disruption of the articular surface also requires anatomic reduction and usually mandates an operative procedure.

# Commonly Associated Injuries

High-energy distal femoral fractures, especially in young patients, are often only one of several injuries sustained by the individual. The whole patient must be carefully evaluated by a multidisciplinary team approach (see Chapter 5). This section addresses only commonly associated injuries in the involved lower extremity.

The most common mechanism of distal femoral fracture is direct trauma to a flexed knee, typically impact against the dashboard of a moving vehicle. The position of the leg at the time of the injury determines the presence and type of injury. Care must be taken to exclude

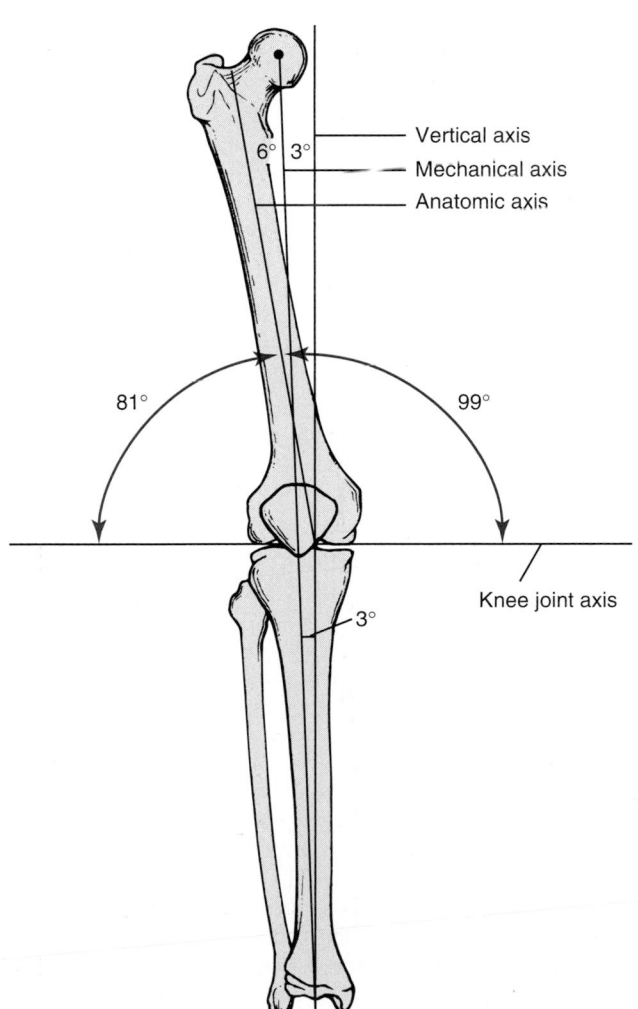

**FIGURE 53–2.** Lower extremity axes.

concomitant acetabular fractures, hip dislocations, femoral neck fractures, and associated femoral shaft fractures.

## SOFT TISSUE INJURIES

Significant soft tissue injuries of the knee are often associated with distal femoral fractures. Associated ligamentous disruptions of the knee joint have been reported in approximately 20% of these fractures.[125] They are hard to diagnose until the distal part of the femur has been stabilized because both clinical examination and stress radiographs require stability above the knee.

In a polytraumatized patient, distal femoral fractures commonly occur with associated injuries to the tibia. Associated tibial plateau fractures occur after a predominantly varus or valgus force. Careful evaluation of the plateau is needed and often requires tomograms. Associated tibial shaft fractures, often comminuted or open, mandate aggressive treatment of both injuries to avoid the morbidity associated with the "floating knee" syndrome.

## VASCULAR INJURIES

The femoral artery in the adductor canal is in close proximity to the medial cortex of the distal end of the femur as it passes through to the posterior compartment only 10 cm above the knee joint. With high-energy or open distal femoral injuries, the artery is at significant risk of injury. With associated ligament disruptions of the knee (especially a posterior dislocation), the popliteal artery is at great risk of injury—up to 40% in some series.[32, 54, 79, 113] Arterial injuries must be aggressively sought. Arteriography or immediate surgical exploration is mandatory in patients with evidence of ischemia or diminished pulse pressure. In these instances, the information gained must justify the time needed to perform the angiography in an angiography suite. For example, in cases in which surgical exploration of the vascular bundle is needed anyway or in patients in whom amputation is being planned, an "on-table angiogram" is another option to be considered. In delayed cases, deep venous thrombosis should be considered.

## COMPLEX TRAUMA OF THE KNEE

For severe accompanying local injuries around the knee, the term "complex trauma of the knee" has been defined and includes (1) a distal supracondylar or intercondylar femoral fracture combined with a proximal tibial fracture ("floating knee"), (2) a supracondylar or intercondylar femoral fracture with a second- or third-degree closed or open soft tissue injury, and (3) complete knee joint dislocation. The thin soft tissue coverage on the anterior aspect of the distal end of the femur is a frequent problem. Neurovascular injuries are mostly observed in the type 3 "distal femur complex trauma." Because of the need for interdisciplinary management (vascular surgery, plastic surgery), the high technical demands (joint reconstruction, alignment, ligamentous instability, soft tissue coverage), and the risk of complications (nonunion, infection, malalignment), we recommend that "complex knee trauma"

**TABLE 53-1** ••••••••••••••••••••••••••••••••••••••••••

Definition of "Complex Knee Trauma"

| Complex Knee Trauma | Soft Tissue Injury | Fracture Pattern |
| --- | --- | --- |
| Type 1 | | Supracondylar-intercondylar fracture of distal end of femur **and** proximal end of tibia (floating knee) |
| Type 2 | 2nd- or 3rd-degree closed or open soft tissue damage | Supracondylar-intercondylar fracture of distal end of femur **or** proximal end of tibia |
| Type 3 | Complete knee dislocation | |

••••••••••••••••••••••••••••••••••••••••••

*Source:* Krettek, C.; Tscherne, H. In: Fu, F.H.; et al., eds. Knee Surgery. Baltimore, Williams & Wilkins, 1994, pp. 1027–1035.

be treated in trauma centers with a high case load and extended experience (Table 53–1).

## Classification

One of the original and simpler classification schemes of supracondylar-intracondylar femoral fractures was that of Neer and associates.[89] They subdivided intracondylar fractures into the following categories: minimal displacement (grade I); displacement of the condyles (grade II), including medial (A) and lateral (B) displacement; and concomitant supracondylar and shaft fractures (grade III). This classification system is very basic and does not provide the surgeon with much clinical and prognostic information.

Seinsheimer[106] classified fractures of the distal 3.5 inches of the femur into four basic types: nondisplaced fractures—any fracture with less than 2-mm displacement of the fractured fragments (grade I); fractures involving only the distal metaphysis, without extension into the intracondylar region (type IIA: two-part fractures; type IIB: comminuted fractures); fractures involving the intercondylar notch in which one or both condyles are separate fragments (type IIIA to IIIC); and fractures extending through the articular surface of the femoral condyles (type IVA or IVB: a fracture through the medial [A] or lateral [B] condyle, with two parts comminuted; type IVC: more complex and comminuted fractures involving one femoral condyle and the intercondylar notch, both femoral condyles, or all three; it usually involves a comminuted fracture across the metaphysis as well). Seinsheimer[106] found that patients with type I nondisplaced fractures and type II simple, two-part supracondylar fractures all had preexisting pathologic osteoporosis before their injury. At the other end of the spectrum, patients with type IV fractures involving the articular surface were the youngest patients, and all fractures resulted from high-energy trauma.

The "Schweizer Arbeitsgemeinschaft für Osteosynthesesfragen" (SWISS AO) Group, through the AO Documen-

tation Center in Davos, has collated its vast experience and has documentation on thousands of these fractures. Müller and colleagues,[86] in an updated AO classification system for distal femoral fractures, separated these fractures into three main groups[87] (Fig. 53–3): type A (extra-articular), type B (unicondylar), and type C (bicondylar). The three groups are each further divided into three subgroups. Type A (extra-articular) fractures are divided into simple, two-part supracondylar fractures (type A1), metaphyseal wedge fractures (type A2), and comminuted supracondylar fractures (type A3). Type B (unicondylar) fractures are divided into lateral condyle sagittal fractures (type B1), medial condyle sagittal fractures (type B2), and coronal fractures (type B3). Type C (bicondylar) fractures are divided into noncomminuted supracondylar (T or Y) fractures (type C1), supracondylar comminuted fractures (type C2), and supracondylar or intercondylar comminuted fractures (type C3). In progressing from A to C, the severity of the fracture increases, whereas the prognosis for a good result decreases. This relationship is also true for the progression from 1 to 3 within each group.

For a classification system to have clinical significance, it must be able to do the following: (1) allow for adequate documentation of all fractures so that a common language is possible when discussing these injuries, (2) be simple enough that it is "user friendly," (3) help the surgeon in clinical decision making so that the correct treatment option can be selected for a particular fracture, and (4) provide prognostic information detailing the results that can be expected for a particular fracture, depending on the treatment option selected. The Müller updated classification system meets these criteria and is used for classifying and describing fractures in the remainder of this chapter.

## DIAGNOSIS

### History and Physical Examination

A careful evaluation of the whole patient as well as the involved lower extremity is mandatory, especially in a polytraumatized patient. Assessment must include careful scrutiny of the hip joint above the fracture and the knee and leg below it. If vascularity to the lower extremity is a concern, Doppler pulse pressure readings can be obtained. If vascularity is still a concern after these procedures, an urgent arteriogram may be indicated. Rarely, if tense swelling of the thigh is noted, a thigh compartment syndrome must also be ruled out by examination and possibly compartment pressure monitoring.

Grossly open and contaminated wounds are easily identifiable. However, when the injury results from direct trauma, skin abrasions are frequently present and must be differentiated from open fracture wounds of the soft tissues. The examination usually reveals swelling of the knee and supracondylar area, often obvious deformity, and marked tenderness on palpation. Manipulation of the extremity, if tolerated by the patient, demonstrates motion and crepitance at the fracture site. However, such manipulation is cruel and unnecessary if immediate radiographs are available.

## Radiographic Evaluation

Routine anteroposterior (AP) and lateral radiographs of the knee and supracondylar region are standard. When fractures are comminuted or displaced, an exact classification of the fracture is often difficult to make. AP and lateral radiographs, both with manual traction applied to the lower extremity, frequently demonstrate the fracture morphology more clearly. These studies can be performed in the emergency department or operating room. In patients with intracondylar involvement, 45° oblique radiographs also help delineate the extent of the injury,

especially if comminution or additional tibial plateau injuries are present. Stress radiographs to identify ligamentous disruptions of the knee or associated tibial plateau fractures are not usually indicated until the distal femoral injury is stabilized. If in doubt about intra-articular involvement, computed tomography (CT) scans help in planning the surgical approach, especially in minimally invasive techniques. CT scans may also be useful for isolated chondral or osteochondral lesions or for the identification of impression zones.

As with all orthopaedic injuries, it is necessary to rule out additional injuries to the joint above and the joint

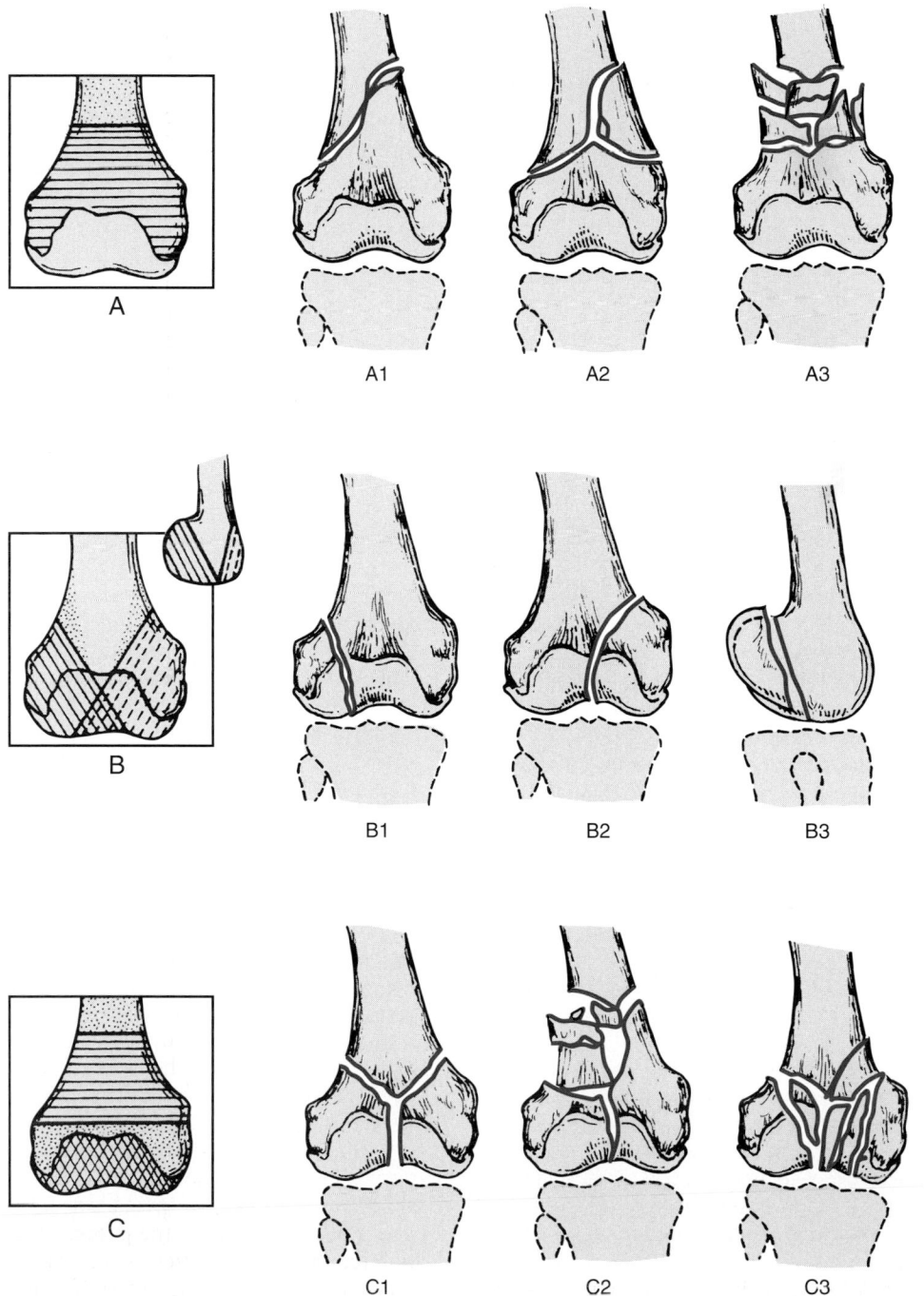

**FIGURE 53–3.** The Müller classification.

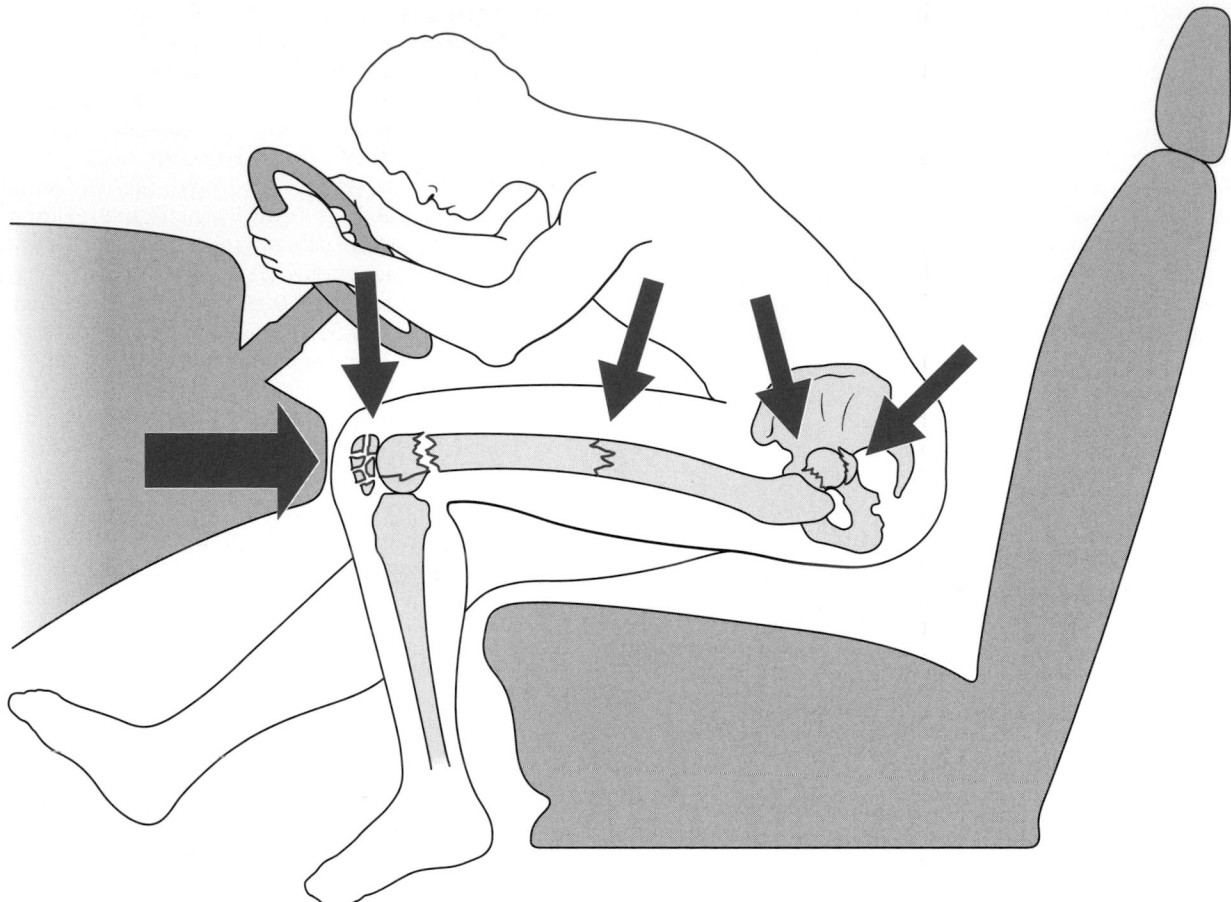

**FIGURE 53–4.** Transmission of energy results in typical concomitant injury patterns.

below because of a significant incidence of ipsilateral fractures of the femur (shaft, neck), patella, and acetabulum, especially after high-energy vehicular trauma (Fig. 53–4). An adequate AP view of the pelvis and AP and lateral views of the hip and whole femur are indicated for all these fractures.

Unless a frank dislocation of the knee joint is associated with the distal femoral fracture, radiographic evaluation of the knee joint has not proved to be as reliable as a careful examination in assessing the extent of ligamentous and soft tissue injury. If such lesions are clinically suspected, magnetic resonance imaging may be effective preoperatively to confirm injuries to the knee joint ligamentous or meniscal tissue.

Comparison radiographs of the normal or uninvolved opposite extremity help the surgeon with preoperative planning. Radiographs should include an AP view of the whole femur to determine valgus alignment and AP and lateral views of the distal end of the femur to allow superimposition of the fracture fragments on the normal template (see the section on preoperative planning).

Unless a thorough vascular examination (pulses, Doppler pulse pressure, sensation, and motor strength) is normal and unless frequent, skillful repeat examinations are feasible, arteriography is indicated in patients with an associated frank dislocation of the knee joint because of the 40% incidence of arterial injuries reported with knee dislocations.[32, 54, 79, 113] An absent or diminished pulse

(determined clinically or by Doppler pressure measurement) compared with that of the normal lower extremity is also an indication for immediate arteriography or vascular exploration if the limb is frankly ischemic. Arteriography is contraindicated if it will delay surgical treatment of limb-threatening ischemia.

## MANAGEMENT

### Objectives

It is essential to appreciate the following goals of operative management of periarticular fractures: (1) anatomic reconstitution of the articular surface; (2) reduction of the metaphyseal component of the fracture to the diaphysis and restoration of normal axial alignment, length, and rotation; (3) stable internal fixation; (4) undisturbed fracture healing; and (5) early motion and functional rehabilitation of the limb.

### Conservative and Operative Treatment

Previously, the treatment of choice for management of femoral fractures, including supracondylar fractures, was traction and subsequent mobilization in cast braces. The traction technique used was either a single pin in the proximal end of the tibia[56, 73, 115] or a two-pin system with an additional pin through the supracondylar fragment.[34, 82, 127]

Neer and associates[89] in 1967 reported on 110 supracondylar fractures treated at New York Orthopaedic Hospital over a 24-year period. They proposed a three-part classification system as well as a rating system for evaluation based on a functional and anatomic assessment. Ninety percent of those treated by closed methods had satisfactory results versus only 52% of those treated by open procedures. However, they considered patients to be "satisfied" in this rating system as long as they had strong extensor power and could flex the knee 70°! These criteria are no longer acceptable. In their summary, Neer and associates stated that "no category of fracture at this level seemed well suited for internal fixation, and sufficient fixation to eliminate the need for external support or to shorten convalescence was rarely attained." In fact, almost all their surgically treated patients had prolonged postoperative immobilization because of the inadequacy of the fixation techniques used at that time. In conclusion, these authors believed that operative intervention should be limited to débridement of open fractures or internal fixation of a fracture with an associated problem such as an arterial injury.

Such papers definitely prejudiced the North American orthopaedic community against internal fixation during the 1960s and 1970s. As a result, more advanced techniques of closed treatment were proposed in the early 1970s by Connolly and Dehne[16] and by Mooney.[84] To shorten traction time and allow earlier ambulation and knee motion, they recommended the use of early cast bracing for femoral shaft and supracondylar fractures.

In 1958 the Swiss AO Group was formed, thus commencing a new era in fracture care. Their desire was to restore full function to the limb and the patient and to avoid the so-called fracture disease associated with prolonged immobilization.[86] They recommended the principles of anatomic reduction of the fracture fragments, preservation of the blood supply, stable internal fixation, and early, active, pain-free mobilization. It was not until 1970 that the AO published its first results on the treatment of supracondylar femoral fractures according to these principles. Wenzl and colleagues[126] reported on 112 patients, 73.5% of whom had good or excellent results. For open reduction, these results were far superior to the 52% satisfactory results reported by Neer and associates, even though the criteria used by Wenzl and colleagues were much more stringent.

Schatzker and co-workers[102] reported on 71 distal femoral fractures, 32 of which were treated by open reduction and internal fixation (ORIF). They were able to achieve good or excellent results in 75% of fractures treated with the AO method as compared with only 32% in the conservatively treated group. They concluded that "if normal function or near normal function is to be achieved, . . . then unquestionably, if correctly employed, open reduction internal fixation ensures a very high rate of success." However, they did emphasize that ORIF is not appropriate for all patients. For fractures that are not displaced or are easily reduced, especially in elderly persons, immediate mobilization in weight-bearing func-

tional braces is the treatment of choice. They also cautioned against internal fixation in severely osteoporotic patients. In 1979, Schatzker and Lambert reviewed an additional 35 patients with supracondylar distal femoral fractures treated by ORIF; only 49% had good or excellent results.[103] When they analyzed the 17 cases treated in accordance with the principles of rigid internal fixation as promoted by the AO Group, 71% had good to excellent results. Among the 18 patients treated with AO implants but not AO technique, only 21% had a good to excellent outcome. Critical review of these 18 patients revealed that most were elderly with severely comminuted fractures; however, surgical technical error was the common denominator contributing to the poor results. The most common errors included (1) incomplete reduction, (2) failure to achieve interfragmentary compression with lag screws, (3) failure to use autogenous cancellous bone graft to fill defects or comminution, (4) ineffective use of acrylic cement to supplement screw fixation in osteoporotic bone, and (5) use of blade plates that were either too long or too far from the joint.

Schatzker and co-workers recommended that elderly patients with thin, osteoporotic bone and comminuted fractures "are better treated by such methods as closed reduction and early cast bracing, than an attempt at operative reduction."[102] In such patients, the only clear indication for ORIF is an intra-articular fracture in which adequate joint congruity cannot be restored by manipulation. In conclusion, these authors stated:

*"Rigid fixation is difficult to achieve with osteoporotic bone because of the degree of comminution and the poor holding power of the bone. The mere use of the appropriate implant does not assure rigid fixation. Failure to meticulously observe all the details of the method of rigid fixation resulted in a high complication rate with failures. These factors must be considered in evaluating criteria for surgical treatment."*

Slatis and associates[114] in 1971 reported on 21 "severe" fractures of the lower end of the femur that were treated by open reduction according to the AO method. Among the 16 patients available for follow-up longer than 1 year, 83% had good to excellent results. These authors recommended the technique as "reliable" but stated that it "should be restricted to fractures of considerable severity and to selected cases among patients with multiple injuries." Olerud,[91] in 1972, reviewed 15 patients with complex articular fractures of the distal end of the femur. He reported 92% good to excellent results with use of the angled blade plate but concluded that satisfactory osteosynthesis of fractures of this type is a difficult procedure and should not be attempted without experience with the technique.

In 1974, Chiron and Casey[13] reviewed 137 patients with distal femoral fractures who underwent stable internal fixation with the 95° condylar blade plate (CBP). Seventy-two percent of patients fulfilled their criteria for good to excellent results (i.e., 135° of motion and only mild swelling on prolonged weight bearing). In 1982, Mize and colleagues[81] reported on 30 supracondylar and intracondylar fractures of the femur that were reduced and stabilized with the AO technique. They reported good to excellent results in 80% of patients and also recommended the use of an extensile surgical exposure with elevation of the tibial tuberosity to facilitate exposure of the condyles in more complex fractures with intra-articular comminution. Healy and Brooker[36] in 1983 reviewed 98 distal femoral fractures to compare open and closed treatment methods; 38 of the 47 fractures treated by open methods but only 18 of 51 treated by closed methods had good functional results. Of significance in this review was that age, with an increasing degree of osteoporosis, did not adversely affect the operative results. The authors concluded that fractures of the distal part of the femur, except in more simple cases, are best managed by open methods.

From all recent reports, it would appear that better functional results can be obtained with ORIF in all but the most simple fracture types.[107] However, the superior outcome seems to depend on the use of improved fixation devices, meticulous surgical technique, and adherence to principles of the AO Group: anatomic reduction, stable internal fixation, preservation of tissue vascularity, and early mobilization.

Although AO techniques initially relied on plates and screws, intramedullary (IM) nailing has also found an important and enlarging role in the treatment of distal femoral fractures, particularly extra-articular type A and, increasingly, total articular (type C) injuries. Given the appropriate fracture patterns, Leung and co-workers[71] and Butler and associates[10] demonstrated that antegrade interlocking IM nailing is an acceptable treatment of supracondylar and intercondylar femoral fractures. Leung and co-workers included in their study only fractures 9 cm or less from the knee and found the technique of antegrade femoral nailing applicable to ASIF (Association for the Study of Internal Fixation) type A fractures and to selected type C (C1 and C2) fractures. Variables that determined the applicability of distal femoral fractures for closed nailing were the pattern and reducibility of the intercondylar fracture and the extent of metaphyseal and condylar comminution. The condylar fragment had to be reducible by closed traction and manipulation, and it had to be sufficiently large to permit stable fixation with supplementary percutaneously inserted lag screws placed under fluoroscopic guidance. The authors found that type B and type C3 fractures were not amenable to this form of treatment. Given these limitations, they had 95% good to excellent results, and normal healing was achieved in all but 1 of their 37 cases.[71] Butler and associates used a similar method to specifically treat ipsilateral femoral shaft and supracondylar-intercondylar distal femoral fractures. Fractures of the femoral condyle in the coronal plane (type B3) and type C3 injuries were relative contraindications to this technique. In their series, no patients had loss of fixation or alignment or implant failure. The authors warned, however, that the rigidity of fixation of distal femoral fractures achieved with interlocking nails must be regarded with caution, and weight bearing must be restricted.[10] The advantage of treating ipsilateral femoral shaft and supracondylar femoral fractures with this method of antegrade interlocking femoral nailing is the ability to treat both fractures with one device.[8]

Several recent series have investigated the treatment of supracondylar-intercondylar distal femoral fractures with the GSH supracondylar IM nail (Smith and Nephew, Richards, Memphis, TN). Henry and associates reported in 1991 that "by virtue of the intramedullary position, the GSH nail has a biomechanical advantage over the laterally placed conventional devices. The intramedullary position decreases the lever arm, reducing varus/valgus angulation."[39] In 1995, Firoozbakhsh and colleagues[28] mechanically tested the retrograde IM nail and the 95° angled screw and side plate in composite bone with an intercondylar split and a medial segmental shaft defect. They found that the bending stiffness of both constructs was not significantly different in varus compression and in flexion. The plate-and-screw device was three times stiffer in lateral bending and 1.6 times stiffer with torsion than the retrograde supracondylar nail. Clinically, medial comminution or a defect with varus collapse is the most common cause of failure of implant fixation in a supracondylar femoral fracture. The authors concluded that the supracondylar nail has biomechanical rigidity comparable to that of the screw and side plate with varus loading, thus making it a reasonable alternative to plate fixation for the treatment of these fractures.

Lucas and co-workers[72] in 1993 reported follow-up on 25 AO type A and type C distal femoral fractures treated with the GSH nail. All the fractures healed, but 4 of the 19 type C fractures eventually required a bone graft. Danziger and associates[18] in 1995 found similar success with the GSH nail: 15 of 16 patients with supracondylar-intercondylar distal femoral fractures had union with good to excellent results. They also found that postoperative alignment was maintained in this group.

Not all investigators have had similar success with the GSH nail, however. Iannacone and colleagues[45] in 1994 reported on 41 complex distal femoral fractures treated with the GSH nail; they had 4 nonunions, 5 delayed unions (2 of which required revision of the fixation), and 4 fatigue fractures. The authors stated that fatigue fractures occurred only with the 11- and 12-mm nails and 6.4-mm interlocking screws. They had no nail failures when the rod system was modified to use 12- and 13-mm-diameter nails with 5.0-mm interlocking screws. Aside from the theoretical biomechanical advantage of this IM locked nail over plating techniques, both Lucas and co-workers[72] and Danziger and associates[18] reported that treatment of complex distal femoral fractures with this system was also associated with decreased blood loss, operative time, and periosteal stripping and allowed the IM reaming debris to be used as bone graft. In addition, use of the median parapatellar approach for surgical exposure and nail insertion permitted direct visualization of the articular surface, thus facilitating anatomic reduction.

Giles and associates[30] reported in 1982 on the use of a supracondylar lag screw and side plate for fixation of 26 supracondylar-intercondylar fractures of the distal end of the femur. They stated that "the advantages of this device over others are that the lag screw supplies not only interfragmentary compression across the intracondylar fractured surfaces, but also better purchase in osteopenic bone," thereby allowing earlier aggressive restoration of knee motion and muscle power. In their series, they did not have any nonunions or infections, and the average postoperative range of motion was 120°, which compares very favorably with other reported series of similar fractures. These authors concluded that "meticulous open reduction and stable internal fixation of supracondylar fractures with supracondylar plate and lag screw, combined with autogenous bone grafting in patients with severe comminution, provide an excellent opportunity to secure bone union and restore limb alignment, joint congruity and range of motion." Similar excellent results with the use of this device have been reported by Hall,[33] Pritchett,[94] Regazzoni and colleagues,[95] Sanders and associates,[99] and Shewring and Meggitt.[110]

Brown and D'Arcy[7] reported on the use of a nail plate with an additional adapted medial compression plate to provide stable fixation on both sides of the femoral condyles. They recommended this technique to obtain better fixation in elderly, osteoporotic patients; in their series, all but one patient obtained knee flexion better than 55°, and the average time to walking was only 4 weeks.

The use of bone cement as an adjunct to stable internal fixation for supracondylar fractures in osteoporotic femurs was advocated by Benum in 1977.[3] He reviewed 14 patients with an average age of 75 years. Eighty-six percent (12 patients) healed uneventfully despite early mobilization. The two failures were the result of technical error in application of the plate and not loosening of the screw from the bone cement. Although all fractures in this study were extra-articular, Struhl and colleagues[117] in 1990 reviewed 17 supracondylar femoral fractures in osteoporotic patients, 8 of which were of the T-intercondylar type. Using a modification of Benum's bone cement technique, they achieved bony union in all cases and overall 79% satisfactory to excellent results. They concluded that the use of bone cement for adjunctive fixation was effective in restoring patient and joint mobility while avoiding the complication of implant failure in osteoporotic patients.

Sanders and co-workers[100] reported on the use of double-plate fixation for complicated, comminuted, intra-articular fractures of the distal part of the femur; union was obtained in all patients.

## Assessment for Surgery

In assessing any patient for surgery, it is important to evaluate not only the "personality" of the fracture but also the personality of the patient.

Patient factors to consider in deciding between operative and nonoperative treatment must include age, activity level, medical condition, hemodynamic status, the presence of infection, the presence of implants, ipsilateral or contralateral injuries, the cause of the injury (high- or low-velocity trauma), and the personality of the distal femoral fracture itself. However, deciding that both the patient and the fracture are candidates for surgery is not sufficient. It is important that potential surgeons honestly assess their own expertise in the management of these difficult problems, including a clear understanding of the pathomechanics and morphology of the fracture, and have the necessary practical experience, equipment, and knowledgeable operating personnel and assistants.

Schatzker and Lambert[103] showed that the mere use of an optimal implant alone is not sufficient to guarantee a good result with these difficult fractures. If the preceding objectives cannot be achieved by surgical intervention,

either because of the complexity of the fracture or because of the lack of equipment or skill of the surgical team, conservative treatment is preferable to the complications of poor surgery followed by prolonged immobilization.

## Indications for Surgery

### DISPLACED INTRA-ARTICULAR FRACTURES

In displaced intra-articular fractures, joint congruity cannot be restored by closed methods. These fractures include unicondylar and bicondylar fractures.

**Unicondylar Fractures (Type B).** Because of the pull of the gastrocnemius muscle, most unicondylar fractures are displaced by posterior rotation of the condyle relative to the knee joint axis. As a result, joint incongruity occurs, and anatomic reduction is mandatory to prevent long-term axial malalignment and post-traumatic arthritis. These fractures almost always require open reduction to achieve anatomic reconstitution. Of particular importance is a B3 or coronal fracture (the so-called Hoffa fracture), in which the only soft tissue attachment is the posterior capsule. Such a fracture behaves like a large loose fragment in the joint. Traction and closed means do not reduce this fracture. Internal fixation is required to maintain stability, and surgical intervention is thus necessary. Impression zones are often present, and the shape of the condylar fragments makes judgment of anatomic reduction difficult. Recently, a significant frequency of bicondylar involvement with coronal-plane type B distal femoral fractures has been recognized. A CT scan is helpful to clarify this pathology

**Bicondylar Fractures (Type C).** The predominant deforming force on the condyles is the gastrocnemius muscle, whose medial and lateral origins cause posterior angulation and rotation. This deformity is compounded by shortening and anterior displacement of the shaft by unrestrained pull of the quadriceps and hamstring muscles. Traction, if applied early, usually corrects the shortening but rarely affects the rotational displacement of the condyles in relation to each other. If joint congruity cannot be restored by closed means, surgery is required to gain anatomic reduction of the articular surface.

### OPEN FRACTURES

All open fractures require aggressive surgical débridement. Most would agree that joint congruity should be restored immediately, which can be accomplished in most cases by limited internal fixation of the condyles. Whether stable internal fixation of the condyles to the shaft should be performed primarily, however, is still questioned by some surgeons. Experimental and clinical evidence suggests that the rate of sepsis can be decreased by stabilizing the bony skeleton and hence the surrounding soft tissues.[75] Experience and clinical judgment are required because each of these fractures must be individually evaluated by assessing the whole patient, any associated injuries, the energy and type of fracture involved, the degree of contamination of the soft tissue injury, the adequacy of débridement, and the ability of the surgery to stabilize the bony skeleton without further devascularization of the already compromised bone and soft tissue.

In grade I and most grade II soft tissue injuries, after adequate débridement of all contaminated and devitalized bone and soft tissue, stabilization of the reduced condyles to the shaft can be performed in standard fashion. However, it is essential to leave the injury wound open and return the patient to the operating room within 48 hours for reassessment and repeat débridement until the soft tissues can be safely closed. The most difficult problems are grade III fractures, which are often associated with high-energy bone and soft tissue injury and significant contamination. Absolute and aggressive débridement of all contaminated and devitalized soft tissue and bone is mandatory. Copious irrigation should be performed with 9 to 12 L of irrigating solution, followed by repair of the articular condyles with minimal internal fixation. At this stage, the treating surgeon has two options: (1) stable internal fixation of the condyles to the shaft or (2) stabilization of the bony skeleton and soft tissues by the application of an external fixator across the knee joint (probably the safer option). The latter choice allows immediate stabilization of bone and soft tissue and permits adequate access for débridement and care of the wounds. Eventual control of the soft tissues is obtained by either delayed primary closure of the wound or tissue transfer for wound coverage. Once adequate soft tissue control has been achieved, delayed internal fixation with reattachment of the condyles to the shaft can be performed.

## ASSOCIATED VASCULAR COMPROMISE

Injury to the superficial femoral artery in the adductor canal or to the popliteal artery in the popliteal fossa associated with a distal femoral fracture is a limb-threatening emergency. If reinstitution of blood flow to the distal end of the extremity is not accomplished within 6 hours of injury, the chance for successful limb salvage decreases exponentially with greater delay. The timing of vascular repair in relation to stable fixation of the fracture is critical. Optimally, the wound should be débrided, if open, and rapid but stable skeletal fixation should be performed before the vascular repair. If the vascular repair is done before bony stabilization is accomplished, length is hard to determine and manipulation may disrupt the repair. If débridement and skeletal stabilization require a delay of more than 6 hours after injury, Johansen and colleagues[50] recommended the use of a temporary arterial shunt to restore flow. They reported an average time of only 35 minutes to shunt and restore arterial blood flow to an ischemic limb. This technique allows sufficient time for adequate débridement and skeletal stabilization without compromising salvage of the extremity.

## IPSILATERAL FRACTURES OF THE TIBIAL SHAFT

An ipsilateral fracture of the tibia associated with a femoral fracture is a well-described injury complex: the floating knee. The best method of restoring knee motion and function in these severe injuries is by surgical fixation of both sides of the knee joint. Such fixation may be done definitively in the initial procedure (often by intramedullary fixation of both fractures with a retrograde femoral and an antegrade tibial nail through the same anterior knee incision). However, patients with this injury complex are frequently severely injured, so complex extremity surgery should be deferred. Depending on the patient's condition, both the distal femoral and tibial fracture sites may be temporarily spanned by external fixation ("orthopaedic damage control surgery"). Alternatively, definitive fixation might be carried out for one bone while the other is externally fixed, or otherwise immobilized, and definitive repair deferred until after the acute period.

## IPSILATERAL FRACTURES OF THE TIBIAL PLATEAU

Ipsilateral fractures of the tibial plateau in association with a distal femoral fracture should be addressed like any complex intra-articular fracture (i.e., anatomic reduction of the articular surface, stable internal fixation, and early functional mobilization).

## BILATERAL FEMORAL FRACTURES

Patients with bilateral femoral fractures do not tolerate traction well. Nursing care is extremely difficult, and functional rehabilitation is decidedly impaired. As a result, ORIF is indicated to allow patient mobilization, as well as for reasons enumerated later. If the patient is not a candidate for immediate internal fixation, temporary external fixation is a very good alternative because these patients are usually severely injured and need adequate fracture immobilization even if definitive repair must be delayed.

## POLYTRAUMATIZED PATIENTS

A severely injured patient with multisystem involvement and an associated femoral fracture has a significant risk of mortality and prolonged morbidity. Bone[6] demonstrated the value of femoral shaft fixation within the first 24 hours. The incidence of multisystem organ failure and adult respiratory distress syndrome, the number of respirator and intensive care unit days, and the incidence of sepsis were all decreased by immediate stabilization of the femoral shaft fracture. Conversely, traction and prolonged bedrest in patients with high Injury Severity Scores and multisystem trauma had a significant detrimental effect on mortality rate and long-term morbidity. In a polytraumatized patient, the same indications for early stabilization of femoral shaft fractures and patient mobilization also apply to distal femoral fractures.

Patients with distal femoral fractures and associated head injuries represent a group of the polytrauma patient population with complex management issues. Impaired consciousness, often with associated spasticity, makes reduction difficult to maintain by traction or closed means. In addition, avoidance of skin breakdown and joint contractures is particularly difficult. Early ORIF facilitates nursing care and allows easier maintenance of skeletal alignment.

Patients with significant burns in addition to their

femoral fractures require skilled nursing, frequent immersion in tubs, and multiple dressing changes. Treatment by closed methods and traction severely compromises the management of burns that are potentially life-threatening. Operative stabilization before burn colonization is the treatment of choice.

## PATHOLOGIC FRACTURES

In pathologic fractures, especially with bone loss, healing cannot be expected to occur with treatment by closed means and prolonged immobilization. Surgical options depend not only on the type of tumor (primary or metastatic) but also on many patient factors, including medical status, life expectancy, and functional demands. Decision making must be individualized. ORIF of pathologic distal femoral fractures is technically demanding and often requires multiple forms of internal fixation and additional stabilization with methyl methacrylate. Healy and Lane[35] in 1990 reviewed 14 patients with pathologic supracondylar fractures treated by Zickel nailing and augmented with bone cement. In 11 of the 14 patients, their goals of pain relief and functional restoration were achieved. They concluded that intramedullary fracture fixation was the method of choice in treating pathologic fractures of the distal end of the femur because of the presence of bone defects and the rarity of bone healing. However, the authors cautioned that in patients with massive bone destruction of the femoral condyles, an IM device is not indicated; in such cases, they recommended distal femoral knee arthroplasty.

## ASSOCIATED LIGAMENTOUS DISRUPTION OF THE KNEE JOINT

Distal femoral fractures with associated knee ligament disruption require a stable distal femoral platform, not only for repair or augmentation of ligaments but also to allow functional aftercare and rehabilitation. This goal can be accomplished only by initial ORIF of the distal femoral fracture.

## EXTRA-ARTICULAR FRACTURES IN WHICH REDUCTION CANNOT BE OBTAINED OR MAINTAINED

Supracondylar extra-articular fractures that are displaced or markedly comminuted and in which axial alignment length or rotation cannot be restored or maintained by closed means require surgical reduction and fixation.

## RELATIVE INDICATIONS

Patients in whom axial alignment, rotation, and length can be obtained or maintained by closed means are considered relative candidates for operative stabilization if they prefer to avoid the prolonged immobilization associated with closed treatment methods. However, the patient must be made aware of the risks and benefits of all treatment options.

Recent reports also indicate that elderly patients are candidates for operative intervention in the management of distal femoral fractures.[11, 36, 90, 95, 99, 100, 103, 108, 132] However, the decision regarding operative versus closed treatment must be based on the personality of both the patient and the fracture, as discussed previously. Stable fixation can often be obtained, especially if the surgeon is skilled in all available techniques in the armamentarium, including the use of newer implants and methyl methacrylate. Careful assessment of the degree of osteopenia and the amount of comminution is necessary to avoid operative intervention that is inadequate and necessitates prolonged traction or immobilization postoperatively. However, if stable fixation is achieved, the adverse effects of prolonged immobilization, especially in the elderly, can be avoided.

## ORTHOPAEDIC DAMAGE CONTROL—STAGED STABILIZATION

"Orthopaedic damage control" refers to provisional skeletal fixation when immediate definitive surgery is contraindicated. The high force required to produce a distal femoral fracture contributes to a high incidence of local and distant associated injuries. In polytraumatized patients, treatment planning must be guided first by the patient's overall clinical status. Orthopaedic "tunnel vision" must be avoided. Consultation with the general surgery team leader is necessary to ensure optimal care of not only the orthopaedic injury but also the patient as a whole. If the patient is hemodynamically labile, acidotic, hypothermic, hypoxic, coagulopathic, or septic or has severely contaminated soft tissues that cannot be débrided or are inadequately débrided, definitive surgical stabilization of the orthopaedic injury is contraindicated until these problems can be resolved. Instead, temporary stabilization with bridging external fixation should be performed. In undisplaced fractures, temporary treatment with a cast is an option. Only patients in a metabolically stable condition should have definitive osteosynthesis in the primary period after admission.

Especially in elderly patients, medical conditions in which the anesthetic and operative risks are potentially life-threatening (e.g., associated myocardial infarction) are obvious contraindications to surgical intervention for return of function to a limb.

Massive comminution of the fracture or very severe osteopenia (e.g., paralyzed limb) should not be considered contraindications but should be addressed by careful selection of the method of treatment and aftertreatment.

It is mandatory that surgeons evaluate the complexity of the injury and make an honest appraisal of their experience, the ability of the team to deal with such technically demanding fractures, and the facilities available. If any of these factors is found to be lacking, the patient is best served by closed treatment or referral.

## Principles of Surgical Treatment

Principles of surgical treatment include the following:

1. Careful handling of soft tissues and careful planning of the surgical approach

2. Direct and anatomic reduction of the articular surface

3. Treatment of multifragmentary metaphyseal fractures by indirect reduction techniques to preserve as much of the vascular supply to the fracture fragments as possible

4. Restoration of limb axial alignment, rotation, and length

5. Stable internal fixation

6. Early and active functional rehabilitation of the patient and the limb

## PREOPERATIVE PLANNING

Preoperative planning is essential to help the surgeon anticipate the potential problems associated with operative fixation of all fractures, especially the more complex periarticular fractures. It also allows the surgeon to consider the extent of the definitive surgical fixation procedure and to determine the optimal timing for the procedure (discussed further later). Our suggested planning technique is relatively simple and can usually be accomplished within 10 minutes. Tracings of the uninvolved or opposite femur are made on tracing paper in both the AP and the lateral planes. These tracings are then turned over to form templates for the involved extremity. Tracings are made of all the fracture fragments on the involved side, in both the AP and lateral planes. These fragments are individually reduced and drawn in different colors on the tracing of the normal femur to demonstrate the amount of comminution and whether bone defects are present. However, this planning does not reflect the three-dimensional properties of the broken bone, and this technique therefore does not always give satisfying results.

At this stage, the planned internal fixation can be drawn from transparent templates that can be obtained from Synthes, USA (Paoli, PA). With use of the templates, one can determine the need for and position of temporary fixation with K-wires, the optimal locations and angles for lag screws, the types and sizes of any plates required, the angles of the screws in the plates (to avoid fracture lines on the opposite side), the need for bone graft based on comminution or the size of the defect, and the need for adjunctive fixation (e.g., methyl methacrylate). On the final drawing showing the reduction of the fracture lines and the composite fixation, a surgical tactic that lists the steps of the procedure should also be developed.

The advantages of careful preoperative planning cannot be sufficiently stressed. It allows the surgeon to study the fracture more carefully and understand its particular morphology and what will be required to achieve reduction. It ensures that all equipment and implants required for the procedure are available in the operating room, thereby avoiding possible compromise of the fixation. It decreases the delays imposed by intraoperative indecision and waiting for instruments and implants (which often prolongs open wound time) and therefore decreases the infection rate. By comparing the postoperative result with the preoperative plan, the surgeon has a readily available method to assess results and to help with quality control.

### Preoperative Planning in the Presence of Preexisting Deformity

In normally aligned knees, 95° implants such as the 95° CBP and the dynamic condylar screw (DCS) are planned for insertion parallel to the distal femoral joint line (Fig. 53–5). In the presence of shaft deformities or a malaligned distal femoral joint line, implant placement parallel to the joint line will lead to malalignment in either varus or valgus or require bending of the plate component (Fig. 53–6). The problem can be solved by separate radiographs of the femur and tibia, including the hip, knee, and ankle joints. These radiographs are transferred to transparent paper: the tibia with the ankle and knee joint (paper 1) and the femoral condyles with the proximal end of the tibia (paper 2). The proximal end of the femur with the shaft and hip joint is transferred to a third paper (paper 3). Papers 1 and 2 are then put together in a way that shows the contours of the proximal end of the tibia of both radiographs to be congruent. Onto these two papers, paper 3 is added in a way that shows the mechanical axis (a line through the center of the femoral head and through the center of the talus) in the middle of the knee joint. The 95° template is now aligned to the lateral side of the drawing of the femoral shaft and taped in that position. If shaft deformities or a malaligned distal femoral joint line (or both) are present, the implant will not be parallel to the distal femoral joint line despite the fact that the mechanical axis is in the middle of the knee joint. This angle between the intraosseous implant and the joint line should be measured and considered when placing the chisel (95° CBP) or guide wire (DCS) (see Fig. 53–6).

## TIMING OF SURGERY

Distal femoral fractures, particularly if caused by high-energy forces, are often associated with multiple injuries, systemic decompensation, severe local soft tissue contusions, or any combination of these problems. In elderly, osteoporotic patients with isolated, low-energy injuries, fracture fixation may be challenging, and the patient's underlying medical status may include conditions that should be corrected to reduce the risk of surgery. In either case, definitive surgery should be postponed until it is safest and has the best possible chance of success. It is not usually advisable to carry out definitive osteosynthesis acutely. Primary treatment should consist of closed reduction, wound débridement or fasciotomy (if necessary) only, and temporary transarticular external fixation.

The timing of surgery is dependent on the general condition of the patient, additional injuries, the condition of the soft tissues, and the neurovascular status of the limb. Additional important factors are the infrastructure of the hospital and the technical skills of the treating surgeon and surgical team. The extent of surgical intervention is also influenced by several factors: it may range from initial soft tissue débridement and temporary external fixation up to complete definitive osteosynthesis. No hard data have indicated that these fractures need immediate definitive fixation. The situation is similar to that for other intra-articular fractures such as acetabular fractures, proximal tibial fractures, tibial pilon fractures, or calcaneus

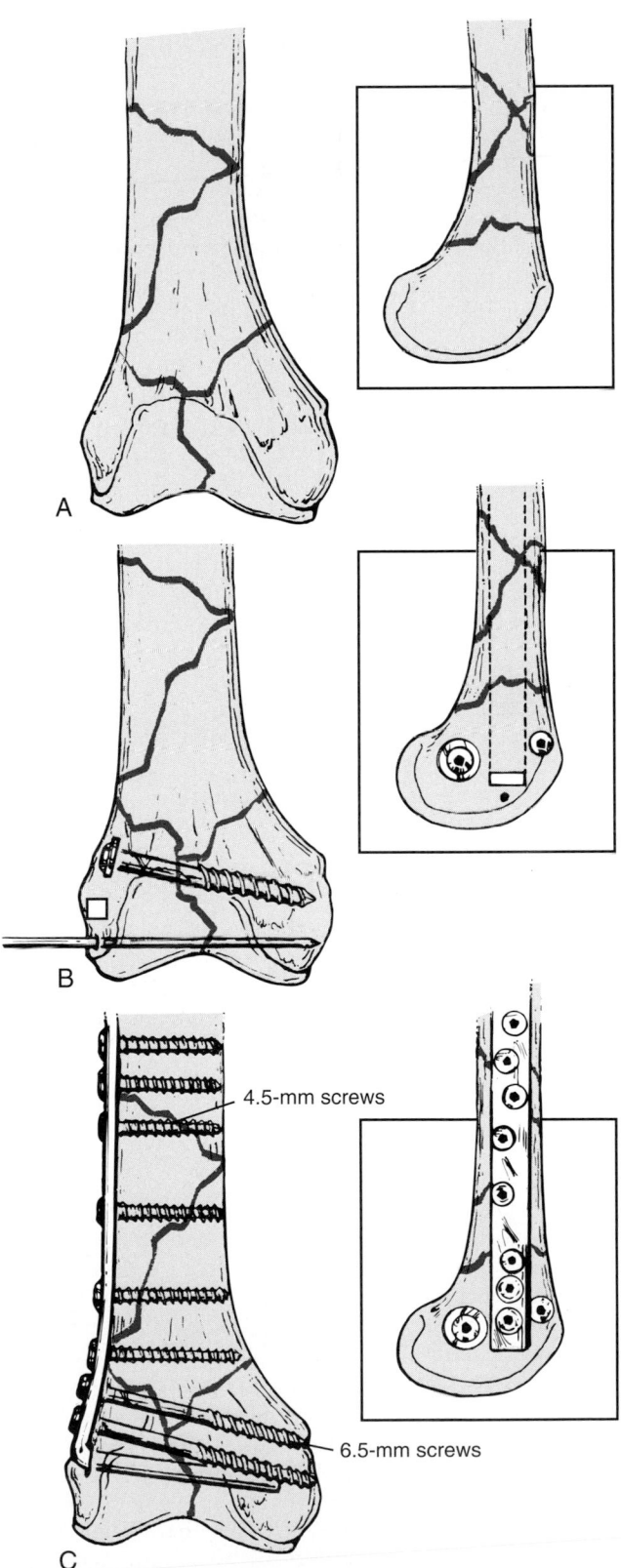

**FIGURE 53–5.** Preoperative planning. *A,* The fracture lines are reduced. *B,* Position for insertion of lag screws, summation K-wire, and the 95° angled condylar blade. *C,* Final plan with the fracture reduced and positioning and fixation of all hardware.

4.5-mm screws

6.5-mm screws

fractures, which are all difficult to treat. Temporary external fixation with later, well-prepared, and properly planned elective and definitive fixation by an experienced team is much more preferable. Definitive surgery should not be undertaken without adequate preoperative evaluation and the availability of all necessary resources. In certain situations, however, immediate emergency surgery is indicated; examples include open fractures and fractures with vascular impairment. For such injuries, discretion is necessary regarding fixation. Only completely stable patients in perfect circumstances should have definitive osteosynthesis in the primary period after admission. Unstable patients and those with questionable soft tissue should have delayed treatment. Their primary treatment should consist of closed reduction, wound débridement or fasciotomy (if necessary) only, and then temporary trans-articular external fixation. Definitive ORIF, as well as complex soft tissue reconstruction, free flaps, or extensive bone grafting in large defects, is performed at the second operation after stabilization of the patient and soft tissue.

In the case of open fractures, discretion is necessary regarding the type of fixation indicated at the time of initial débridement.

Successful management of the soft tissue envelope is the key to avoiding the major complications associated with surgical intervention and internal fixation. Decision making regarding the timing of definitive internal fixation and optimal management of the soft tissue injury is one of the hardest aspects to learn. Surgeons must use their own experience and judgment, in consultation with others if necessary, to choose the best time for surgery. Delay of definitive stabilization for 3 weeks or longer makes the surgery much more difficult. The limb often remains malreduced and shortened, early callus forms, and the fracture lines lose their clear demarcation, especially in cancellous bone. These factors make exposure and reduction technically more demanding.

If surgery is to be delayed more than a few hours, the limb should be stabilized with an external fixator. If not possible, skeletal traction offers a less satisfactory alternative: traction is applied through a tibial pin inserted at least 10 cm inferior to the tibial tubercle to avoid the potential operative field. The patient is then placed in balanced suspension in a Thomas splint with a Pearson attachment flexed at approximately 20° (Fig. 53–7). The weight of the traction should be sufficient to correct length (usually between 15 and 30 lb). Such management stabilizes the fracture and greatly facilitates future manipulation of the fracture fragments at the time of surgical reduction so that indirect techniques with less exposure and soft tissue stripping can be used at the time of stable internal fixation.

## CONSERVATIVE TREATMENT

### Traction

Traction can be used for the treatment of Müller type A2 and A3 supracondylar femoral fractures as long as it is possible to restore limb axial alignment, rotation, and length. Commonly, such treatment involves skeletal traction with one pin placed 10 cm below the tibial tubercle and the leg maintained in a Thomas splint with a Pearson attachment at the level of the fracture and flexed about

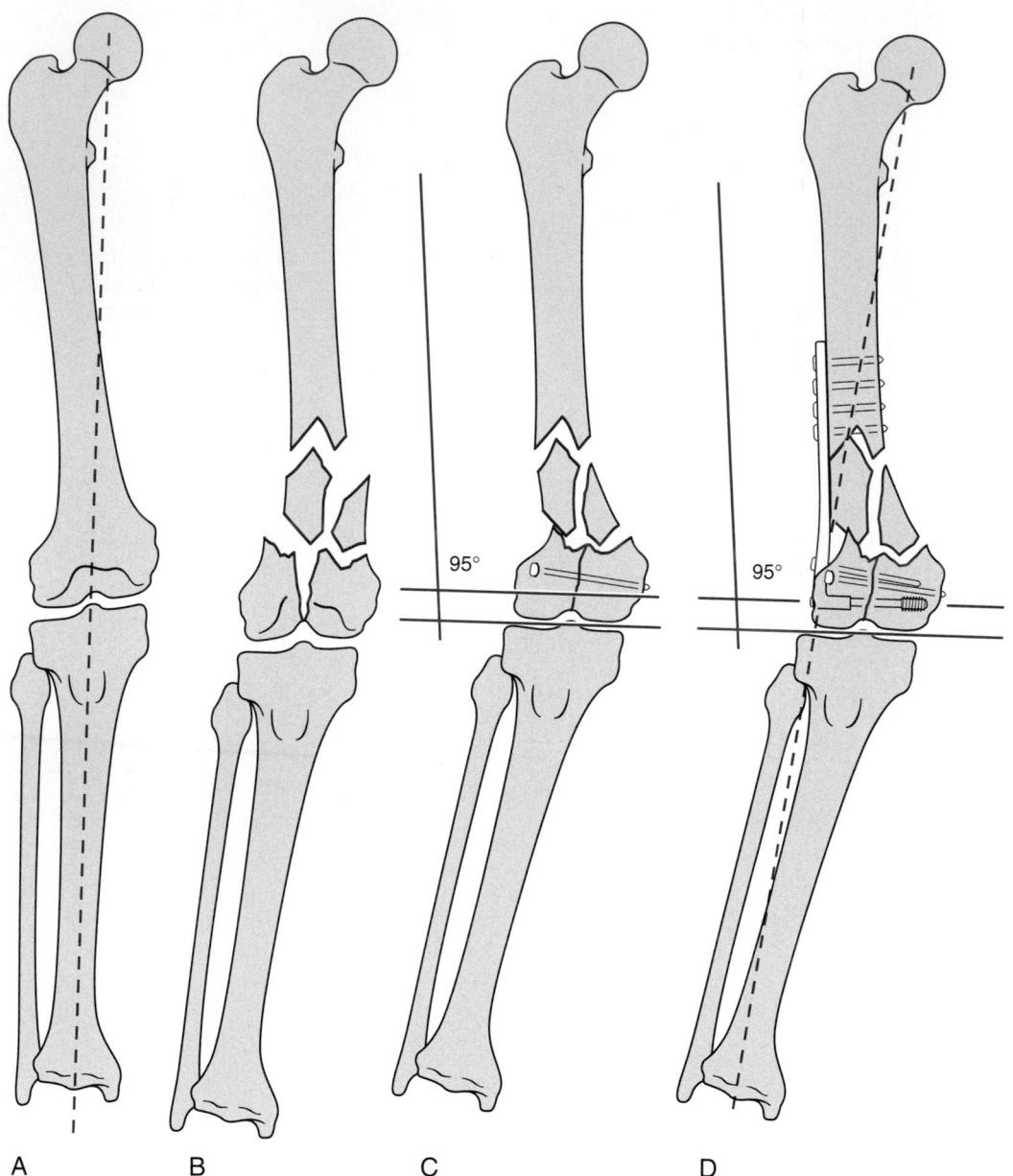

**Figure 53–6.** Preoperative planning (preexisting deformity). See text.

20°. The patient must remain bed bound with maintenance of traction for 2 to 12 weeks, depending on the fracture. Manipulation can be performed under anesthesia to obtain reduction if traction alone is not successful. In the present era of managed care, low-risk anesthesia, and better surgical implants and techniques, most surgeons would opt for surgical stabilization and early active mobilization. However, medical complications, the age and functional demands of the patient, and local factors such as excessive comminution or an inability to manage the soft tissues adequately may make the option of traction more favorable. Rarely, the use of two-pin traction, with the second pin through the femoral condyles, may provide better reduction.[115] However, this technique adds significant risk to traction treatment (i.e., the potential for vascular impairment from pin insertion and also intra-articular and fracture sepsis if a pin tract infection develops around the condylar pin).

Prolonged joint immobilization with traction results in intra-articular adhesions and fibrosis and scarring of the quadriceps musculature. Therefore, active flexion and extension of the knee, even in traction, must be encouraged as soon as pain tolerance allows. Excessive or prolonged traction is detrimental to functional rehabilitation of the patient and the extremity. Connolly,[15] Mooney,[84] and others[83, 97] have advocated the use of early cast bracing for the management of femoral and supracondylar fractures. In most cases, traction can be converted to cast brace treatment 3 to 8 weeks after fracture consolidation, but before radiographic evidence of significant callus.

### Early Fracture Bracing or Cast Bracing

Impacted supracondylar fractures that do not have intracondylar extension can, in most cases, be reliably stabilized immediately in a knee immobilizer, which is replaced with a fracture brace or cast brace once the pain and swelling have decreased. Care must be taken to monitor progress until union occurs because the powerful muscles of the thigh can easily cause angulation or displacement. It may be wiser to start treatment with the patient in skeletal traction to allow the swelling and pain to decrease and the fracture to become "sticky" before the application of a cast or brace.

### Delayed Cast Bracing

The main indication for cast bracing is at a subsequent stage of treatment. After the patient is treated by traction, traditionally for 6 to 12 weeks, and after sufficient signs of early healing have appeared, a cast brace is applied. Connolly,[15] Mooney,[84] and others have reported that earlier progression from traction to cast bracing (i.e., at 2 to 3 weeks) prevents the sequelae of prolonged traction immobilization and gives good results. Such management requires experience and not only an understanding of the pathomechanics of the fracture but also knowledge of the technique of successful cast brace application. Optimally, patients should be given a general anesthetic or an intravenous sedative. When the cast brace is being applied, the patient's knee should be extended with 20° of external rotation and slight valgus angulation of the leg. Knee extension counteracts the posterior displacement and angulation of the condyles. The external rotation and valgus force counteract the varus deformity commonly seen after prolonged traction. The stability of the cast brace is greatly enhanced by careful molding around the femoral condyles distally and by sufficient proximal control above the fracture site. A longer thigh and a more slender habitus improve the control provided by a long leg fracture brace. Modern fiberglass casting material has become as easy to mold as plaster and is significantly lighter.

## OPERATIVE TREATMENT

### Temporary External Fixation

An external fixator is used in the management of distal femoral fractures not to treat the bony injury but rather to treat the soft tissues and avoid shortening and gross malalignment. In patients with severe open wounds and in those who are septic or whose medical condition precludes definitive distal femoral fracture fixation, the use of a temporary external fixator across the knee joint allows for adequate access and management of the soft tissues. It also reduces pain and facilitates nursing care and patient mobilization.

Proximally, two 4.5-mm half pins are placed anteriorly (or laterally) in the femoral shaft. A connecting rod is clamped to them. Distally, two shorter 4.5-mm half pins are placed anteromedially in the tibial shaft. Care must be taken to ensure that the pins are sufficiently proximal and distal so that even if they become infected, they will not compromise later open fixation of the distal end of the femur. A similar rod joins the two tibial pins. A third connecting rod, attached with adjustable clamps, links the femoral and tibial rods and permits adjustment of limb alignment in all planes.

This simple fixator provides adequate temporary stabilization of the supracondylar component and the knee joint. However, articular condyle displacement is not reduced and stabilized with such a construct. In cases in which a long time interval between initial temporary and definitive fixation cannot be excluded, gross reduction of the femoral condyles and temporary fixation with two crossed K-wires prevents shortening of the gastrocnemius and makes definitive reduction much easier (Fig. 53–8).

If the condyles are readily exposed through an open fracture wound, they may be fixed immediately after

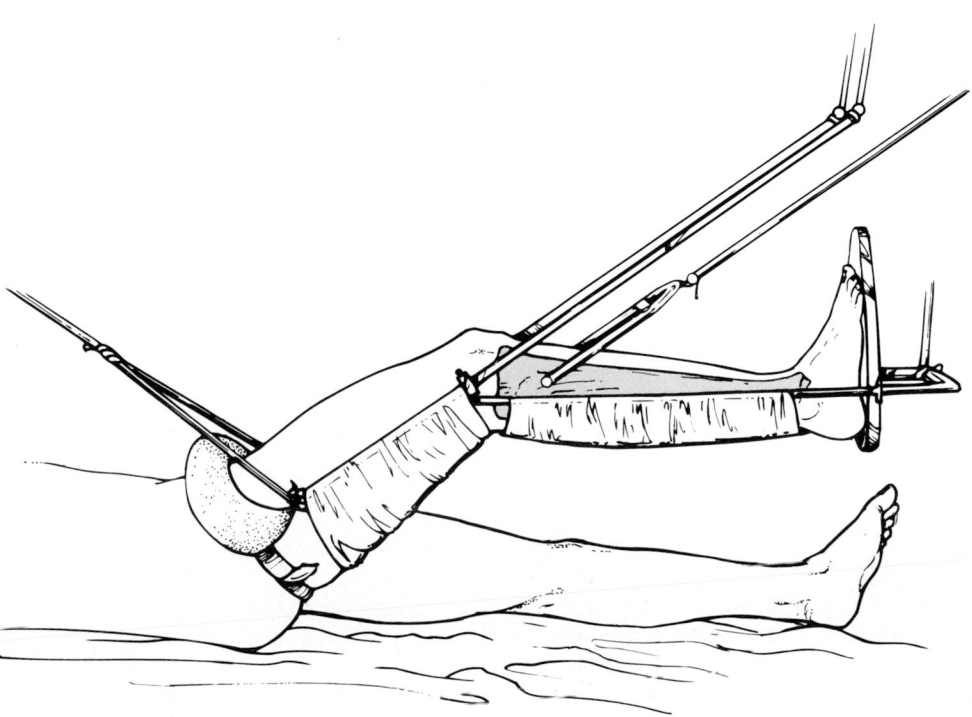

**FIGURE 53–7.** Single-pin proximal tibial skeletal traction.

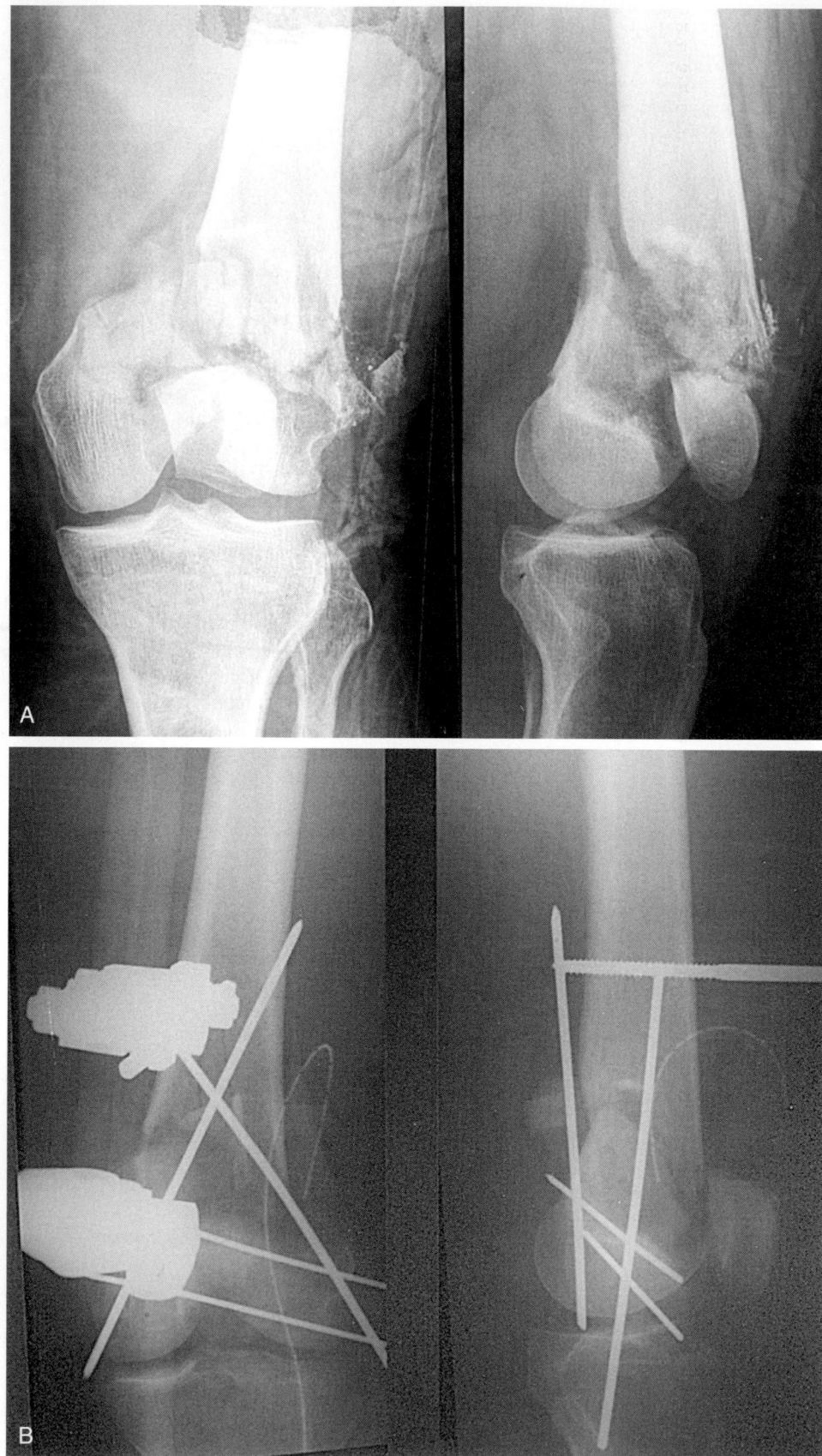

**Figure 53–8.** Temporary external fixation and provisional K-wire fixation.

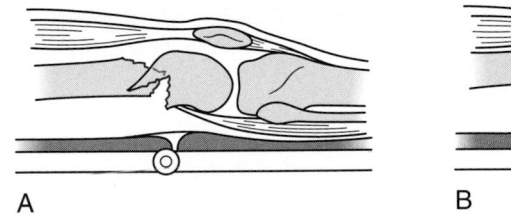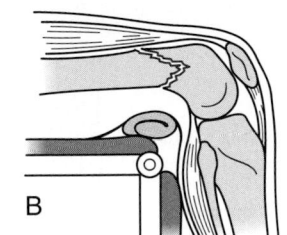

**FIGURE 53–9.** Positioning for distal femoral fractures. Patients are placed on a standard radiolucent table with the knee joint line of the injured knee slightly distal to the mechanical hinge of the table to reduce the pull from the gastrocnemius muscles. Gravity on the lower part of the leg results in gross rotational alignment. (From Krettek, C.; et al. Tech Orthop 14:247–256, 1999.)

A                    B

adequate débridement, and the next step of fixing the condyles to the shaft can be delayed.

In the event of undisplaced C1 or C2 intra-articular fractures, percutaneous screw fixation secures the position until definitive fracture fixation. Later, exact anatomic reduction should be checked by CT because it has consequences for the approach when minimally invasive techniques are used: anatomic intra-articular reduction will allow a small lateral approach without joint exposure. A nonanatomic position will require joint reconstruction and therefore preferably a lateral parapatellar approach.

Screws for articular fixation should be placed in such a way that they will not interfere with future definitive internal fixation.

## SURGICAL EXPOSURE

### Positioning

The patient is placed supine on a fluoroscopy table, and a tourniquet is not usually applied to the proximal part of the thigh. If necessary, a sterile tourniquet may be used. The ipsilateral iliac crest and the whole lower extremity are prepared in sterile fashion, but the foot can remain unsterile and is draped in a boot-type bag (Fig. 53–9).

### Conventional Lateral Approach

Many distal femoral fractures can be approached through a single lateral incision (Fig. 53–10). The incision is made directly laterally in the thigh and through the midpoint of the lateral condyle distally while staying anterior to the proximal insertion of the lateral collateral ligament.[44] Proximally, the incision is extended as necessary for diaphyseal involvement of the supracondylar fracture. The distal incision can be extended so that it gently curves from the knee joint axis anteriorly to the lateral border of the tibial tubercle when the fracture involves the articular condyles. The fascia lata is incised in line with the skin incision, and its fibers are split. Distally, it is often necessary to incise the anterior fibers of the iliotibial tract, and the incision is then carried down through the capsule and synovium on the lateral aspect of the lateral femoral condyle. Care must be taken to identify the superior lateral geniculate artery, which must often be ligated, and to avoid damage distally to the lateral meniscus. To expose the articular surface, a blunt Hohmann retractor is placed across the joint and over the medial femoral condyle. Visualization of the articular surfaces of the lateral condyle is usually adequate. The medial condyle, especially its posteromedial aspect, is difficult to visualize. The more comminuted the metaphysis, the easier the visualization. In extra-articular type A supracondylar femoral fractures,

joint visualization is not necessary because the extraosseous guide wires can be inserted under fluoroscopic control. To expose the distal femoral shaft, the vastus lateralis muscle must be reflected off the lateral intermuscular septum. Care must be taken to identify and ligate the perforating vessels. It is only necessary to expose enough of the lateral cortex to apply the plate. Any additional unnecessary soft tissue stripping or the careless insertion of anterior or posterior retractors should be avoided.

### Tibial Tubercle Osteotomy

Occasionally in type C3 distal femoral fractures, if intercondylar comminution is present, more extensive dissection is necessary to increase intra-articular exposure. Mize and colleagues[81] recommended that such exposure be accomplished with a tibial tubercle osteotomy. The distal incision is extended inferiorly and medially to expose the tibial tuberosity. A 3.2-mm hole is drilled in the middle of the tibial tuberosity from the anterior to the posterior tibial cortex. The depth is measured, and the near cortex is tapped with a 6.5-mm tap. The tibial tuberosity is osteotomized with a fine oscillating saw to release a piece of bone approximately 2 cm long and at least 0.5 cm thick. Because the tibial tuberosity bone block and infrapatellar tendon are reflected proximally, it is necessary to detach the fat pad from the tibia to provide exposure to the whole articular distal end of the femur. If further medial exposure is necessary, the supracondylar synovium can be incised, and then the whole quadriceps mechanism can be reflected proximally and medially. This technique is one way to provide enough exposure if additional medial plating was indicated. However, it may devascularize the distal end of the femur because a large part of the metaphyseal blood flow comes through the reflected tissues. At closure, the tibial tubercle bone block is replaced in its bed and fixed with a 6.5-mm cancellous screw of appropriate length.

### Infrapatellar Tenotomy

An alternative method for extensive exposure of the distal femoral articular surface is a Z infrapatellar tenotomy. This technique requires not only repair of the infrapatellar tendon but also protection of the repair with an anterior wire tension band from the patella to the tibial tubercle.

### Medial Approach

Occasionally, medial exposure to the distal end of the femur is indicated, primarily for ORIF of type B2 unicondylar medial femoral fractures. However, it is also used in conjunction with lateral exposure when double plating of the distal end of the femur is indicated for severe supracondylar comminution or for bone defects requiring additional medial stabilization and in patients with complex combined supracondylar and intracondylar type C3 distal femoral fractures. The incision is straight medial just anterior to the adductor tubercle and midmedial in the thigh. The deep fascia is incised in the same line as the skin

incision. The vastus medialis is reflected anteriorly off the adductor magnus to expose the distal medial shaft of the femur. Care must be taken to identify the superior medial geniculate artery, which must often be ligated. The incision must remain anterior to the proximal insertion of the superficial medial collateral ligament on the adductor

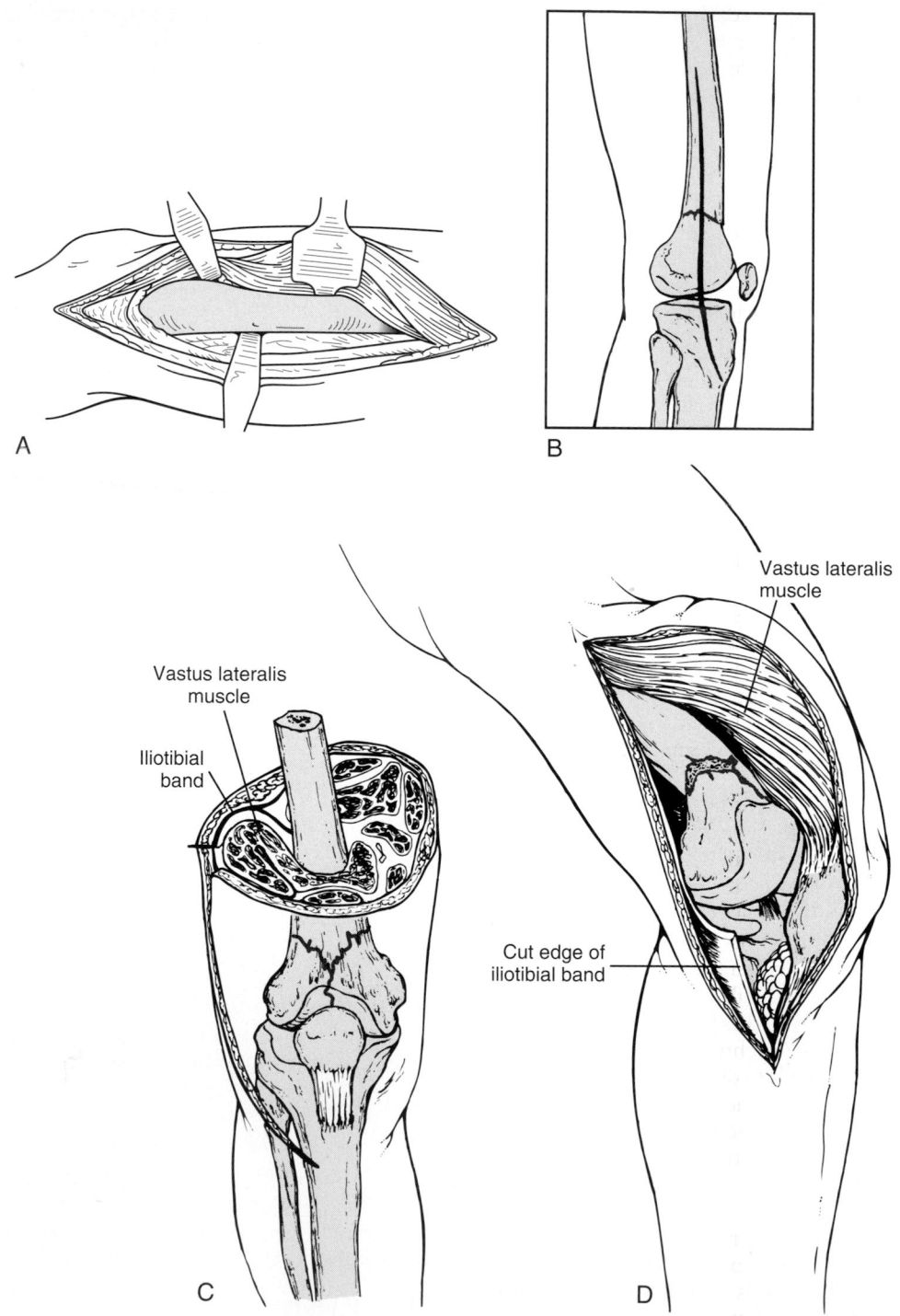

**Figure 53–10.** Conventional lateral approach. *A,* The standard lateral approach to the distal end of the femur with the typical use of a broad retractor. The retractor is placed medially, and muscles are forcefully reflected at the level of the fracture site with soft tissue and periosteal stripping. An additional disturbance of the blood supply to the fracture site is caused by ligation of the perforator vessels. (From Hoppenfeld, S.; deBoer, P.I. Surgical Exposures in Orthopaedics. The Anatomic Approach. Philadelphia, J.B. Lippincott, 1984, pp. 357–387.) *B,* Lateral skin incision. *C,* Demonstration of the lateral incision for femoral exposure posterior to the vastus lateralis and anterior to the intermuscular septum. *D,* Extensive exposure is possible, but care must be taken to not strip the soft tissues unnecessarily.

tubercle. For complete exposure of the medial femoral condyle, the medial patellar retinaculum and capsule are incised, with care taken to avoid damage to the medial meniscus. The major risk with medial exposure is damage to the femoral artery and vein as they pierce the adductor magnus 1 handbreadth above the knee joint and enter the popliteal space.

Of the three extensile exposures available and just described, the most widely used has probably been the tibial tubercle osteotomy. However, a review by Sanders and co-workers[100] recommended an additional medial incision, which is associated with lower morbidity and requires the least additional soft tissue dissection and stripping.

### Minimally Invasive Techniques

Treatment of displaced supracondylar femoral fractures by ORIF has traditionally resulted in 70% to 90% good and excellent results.* However, the use of bone grafts is frequently recommended if medial comminution or bone loss is present, particularly in intercondylar type C2 and C3 fractures.[30, 52, 81, 88, 99, 103, 112, 129] Without the use of bone grafts, many series report an increased incidence of delayed union, pseudarthrosis, loss of reduction, and implant failure.[36, 91, 103, 128] The traditional surgical approach for severe intra-articular distal femoral fractures is through a lateral incision with elevation of the vastus lateralis muscle and ligation of the perforating vessels.[86] This approach allows for good visualization and reduction of the shaft fracture (see Fig. 53–10). Reconstruction of complex intra-articular fractures through a lateral exposure, however, may be difficult. Medially placed retractors are often necessary to visualize the articular fragments, and soft tissue is consequently stripped from the metaphyseal bone. As a result, fracture healing may be delayed with increased rates of secondary revision and primary or secondary bone grafting.[36, 81, 99, 101, 103, 128] The following two approaches are suggested as alternatives.

**Transarticular Approach and Retrograde Plate Osteosynthesis with a Lateral Parapatellar Arthrotomy (TARPO).** Indirect reduction techniques have been developed to avoid the potential complications associated with soft tissue stripping.[74] These techniques have been used successfully in the treatment of proximal and distal femoral fractures and have resulted in improved rates of union in comparison to the "classic" AO technique.[55, 93] With an indirect reduction technique, Ostrum and Geel obtained fracture union in 29 of 30 cases after internal fixation without autogenous bone grafting.[93] Although the authors avoided placing retractors in the medial supracondylar region, the reconstruction required exposure of the anterior and lateral aspect of the distal end of the femur.[93]

Because anatomic articular reconstruction remains a primary goal in these complex fractures and because complete joint visualization is difficult with a lateral approach (particularly one that attempts to avoid soft tissue stripping),[70] the authors developed a new minimally invasive approach.[62, 68, 69] This technique uses a lateral

*See references 14, 30, 33, 52, 81, 91, 94, 99, 103, 109, 110, 112, 119, 121, 123, 129.

parapatellar arthrotomy for direct reduction of the joint surface and indirect plate fixation to secure the articular block with the femoral shaft (Fig. 53–11). The skin incision is placed above the lateral third of the patella, approximately 15 to 20 cm long. The lateral parapatellar approach extends proximally between the rectus femoris and vastus lateralis muscles along the course of their fibers in the tendinous intersection. Extension underneath the skin is important to get enough retraction of the patella. After retracting the patella medially, excellent access to both femoral condyles is achieved. This exposure facilitates direct anatomic joint reconstruction, even in the posteromedial aspect. After blunt dissection of the iliotibial tract and the muscle fibers with scissors, retrograde insertion of the plate beneath the vastus lateralis muscle is performed.

**Approach for Minimally Invasive Percutaneous Plate Osteosynthesis (MIPPO).** This approach is designed for only extra-articular or undisplaced fractures because it does not allow adequate joint reduction (Fig. 53–12). The approach was developed for the DCS and later adapted to the less invasive stabilization system for the distal end of the femur (LISS-DF).[65] The DCS was introduced as an alternative to the 95° CBP,[51, 81, 91] with the screw replacing the blade portion of the plate. Although the CBP requires three-plane alignment, the DCS has the advantage of requiring only two-plane alignment. Sagittal-plane alignment with the DCS can be accomplished by rotating the plate-screw construct after insertion.

In the treatment of distal femoral fractures, the DCS is commonly inserted through a standard lateral approach with elevation of the vastus lateralis muscle.[86] The approach provides for wide exposure of the femoral shaft and direct ORIF of the fracture. However, to directly visualize the fracture, the soft tissues are stripped, the perforating arteries are ligated, the nutrient artery may be placed at risk, and local periosteal and medullary perfusion is decreased.[24–26] This soft tissue disruption may lead to a decrease in the rate of union and an increased need for primary and secondary bone grafting in both subtrochanteric and supracondylar femoral fractures.[55, 93]

To limit the amount of soft tissue elevation at the fracture site, indirect reduction techniques have been developed to treat proximal[55] and distal[5, 51, 64, 65, 93] femoral fractures. Each of these techniques limits the approach to a lateral exposure and avoids medial dissection. The reported results of these indirect techniques demonstrate rates of union at least as rapid as those achieved with the "classic" technique, but without the need for a bone graft.[5, 51, 55, 93]

Current indirect reduction techniques limit the amount of medial dissection. Farouk and associates demonstrated that lateral dissection may also decrease the periosteal and medullary circulation by disrupting the femoral perforators and nutrient vessels.[24–26] To preserve the local blood supply, the MIPPO method limits lateral as well as medial dissection.[65]

**Approach for Retrograde Nailing.** Whereas displaced intra-articular fractures require an arthrotomy for anatomic, open fracture reduction, retrograde nailing of extra-articular fractures can be performed through stab

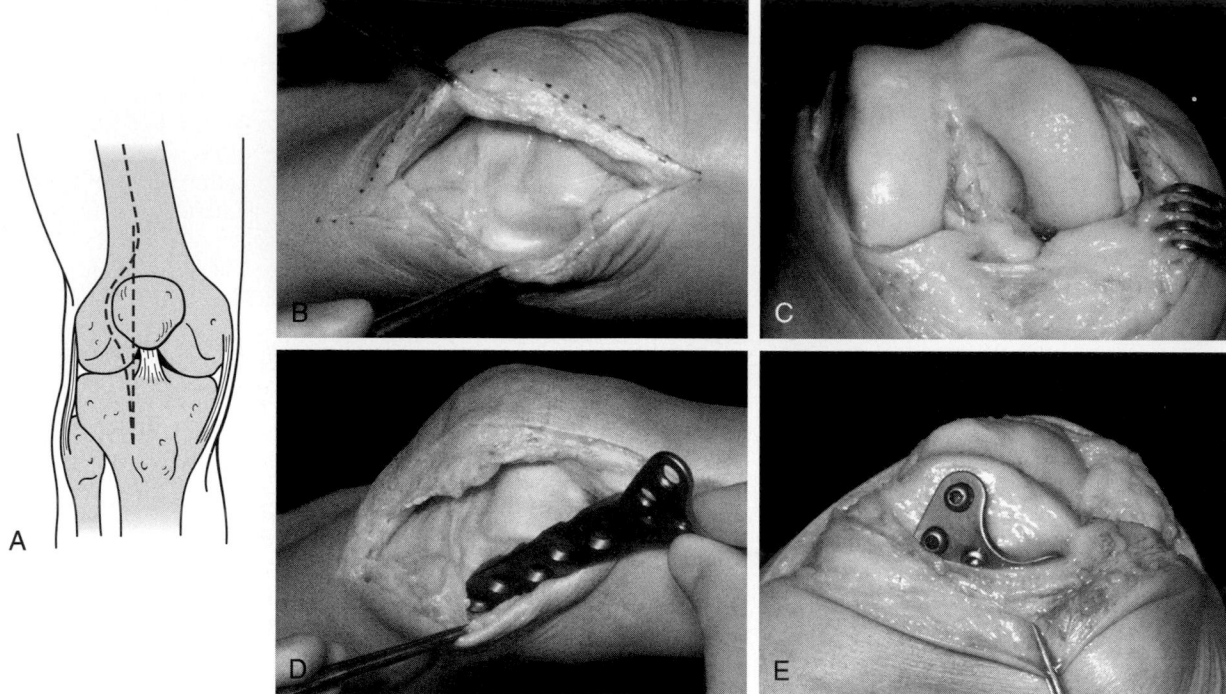

**Figure 53–11.** TARPO: transarticular approach and retrograde plate osteosynthesis with a lateral parapatellar arthrotomy (Krettek et al., 1997) for intra-articular B and C type fractures. *A,* A skin incision is placed above the lateral third of the patella approximately 15 to 20 cm in length. *B,* The lateral parapatellar approach extends proximally beneath the rectus and vastus lateralis muscle along the course of its fibers in the tendinous intersection. *C,* After retracting the patella medially, excellent access to both femoral condyles is achieved. This exposure facilitates direct anatomic joint reconstruction, even in the posteromedial aspects. *D,* After blunt dissection of the iliotibial tract and the muscle with scissors, the plate is inserted retrogradely beneath the vastus lateralis muscle. *E,* After completion of plate fixation.

incisions under image intensifier control. The patient is positioned supine on a radiolucent table to allow fluoroscopy from the hip joints to the knees. The optimal knee position for the approach is approximately 30° to 40° of flexion (Fig. 53–13). Too much knee flexion pulls the patella down and prevents an easy approach. If the position of the knee is too extended, the anterior crest of the proximal end of the tibia limits access to the intercondylar notch. Accurate placement of the skin incision and the starting hole in the bone is verified by visualization on an image intensifier in two planes. The correct entry site is where the anatomic axis of the femoral shaft passes through in extension to the center of the femoral shaft. On the lateral view, this site usually corresponds to a point slightly anterior to the anterior-distal end of Blumensaat's line (Fig. 53–13). On the AP view, the optimal entry site can be determined by projecting the anatomic axis of the femoral shaft through the articular surface.

## FRACTURE REDUCTION AND STABILIZATION

Because of the diversity of fracture types encountered in the distal end of the femur, it is necessary to first discuss the basic techniques available for reduction and stabilization and then specific applications for each fracture type.[67]

### Conventional Plate Fixation

**95° Condylar Blade Plate.** For illustrative purposes, the fracture type C1 is selected (T or Y supracondylar fracture with intercondylar extension). The incision is the standard lateral incision as described. The initial step must be anatomic reduction of the condyles, both the distal articular surface and the patellar femoral groove. The reduction is provisionally secured with temporary 2.0-mm K-wire fixation in a lateral-to-medial direction.

The next step is to plan insertion of the 95° condylar blade plate (Fig. 53–14) before placing the intercondylar lag screws. The length of the blade and side plate are determined through preoperative planning, as described previously. The position for insertion of the blade plate is 1.5 to 2 cm from the inferior articular surface and in the middle third of the anterior half of the sagittal diameter of the condyles at their widest point (Fig. 53–15). This position can be determined by palpating the posterior edge of the lateral femoral condyle while visualizing the anterior margin. At its broadest point, the distance is divided in two. The anterior half of this distance is then divided in three; the middle third is the location for insertion of the blade and should be marked with the cautery. This position must be determined exactly because the fixation device is used to realign the condyles and articular surface with the femoral shaft. The blade must be inserted in line with the longest sagittal diameter so that the plate, which is perpendicular, correctly restores the relationship between the condyles and shaft and lies along the shaft, on the lateral view, rather than with its proximal end too far anterior or posterior.

The next step is lag screw fixation of the condyles to each other, usually with 6.5-mm cancellous screws, one

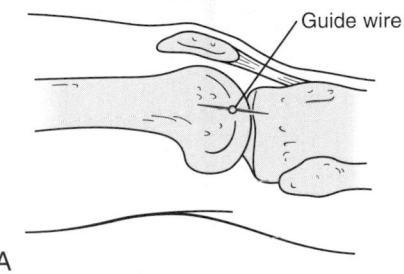

A

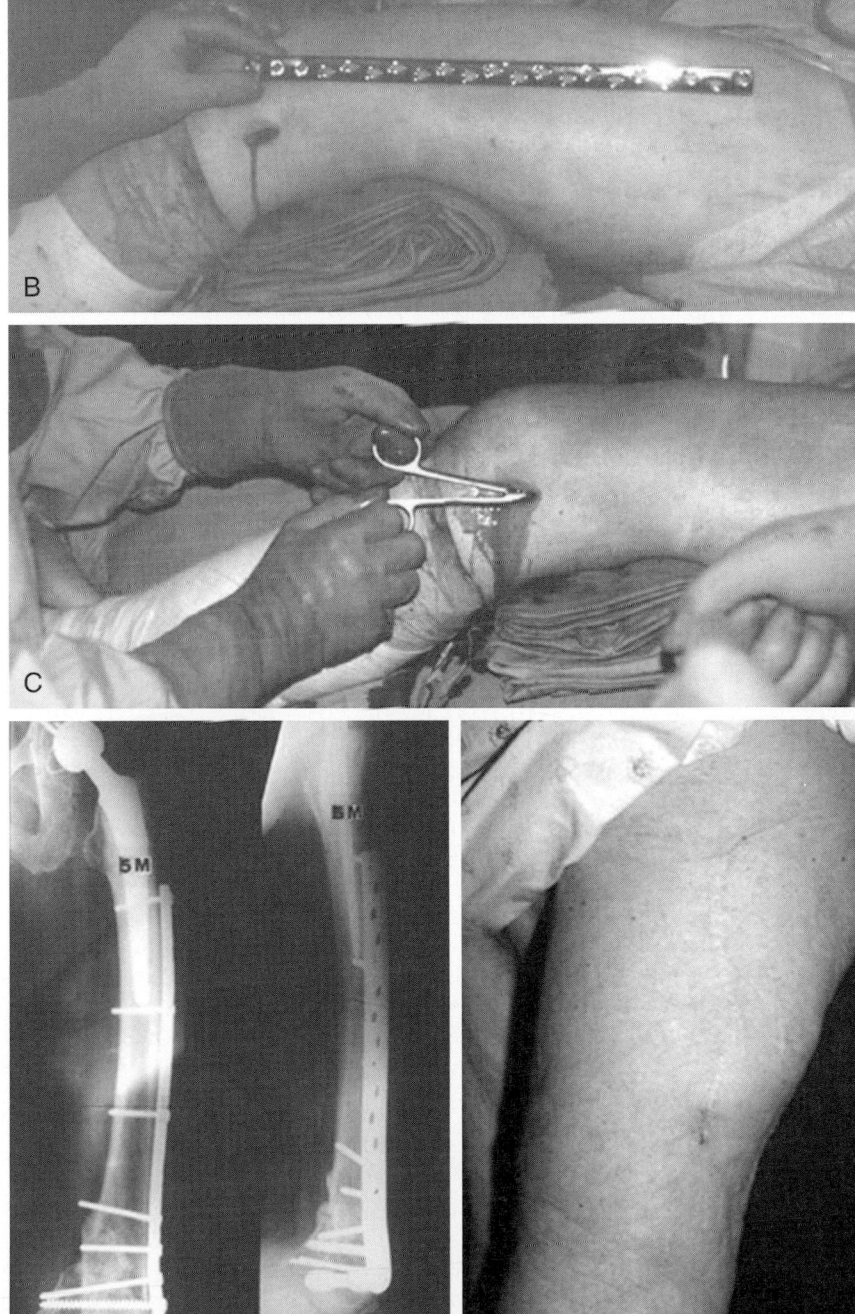

**FIGURE 53–12.** MIPPO: minimally invasive percutaneous plate osteosynthesis (Krettek et al., 1997) for extra-articular type A fractures. *A,* After adequate placement of the threaded guide wire, a longitudinal 4-cm skin incision centered on the guide pin is made and carried through the iliotibial band. The condylar screw is inserted percutaneously according to the principles of dynamic condylar screw (DCS) application. *B,* The DCS plate length is selected with fluoroscopy. *C,* The iliotibial band is spread for an additional 2 to 3 cm longitudinally to facilitate insertion of the plate. The DCS plate is then inserted through the skin and iliotibial tract incision beneath the lateral vastus muscle. After reinsertion of the guide wire through both the plate and the condylar screw, a T handle (cannulated) is introduced over the guide wire. The T handle is fixed to the condylar screw with a cannulated connecting screw, and the plate is slipped onto the condylar screw by using the modified T handle as a guide. The three or four plate screws are then inserted through a 4-cm percutaneous/transmuscular incision. The screws are placed divergently to increase screw pull-out strength and decrease the length of incision needed for their insertion. *D,* Radiographs 9 months after a supracondylar fracture caused by a fall in an 82-year-old woman with a loosened porous-coated anatomic total-hip endoprosthesis. Insertion of a short plate or a retrograde nail would have created an inherent risk for fatigue fracture between these two implants. Insertion of a long angled blade plate by standard technique would have necessitated a long incision, extended the soft tissue disruption, and increased blood loss. Therefore, MIPPO with a long DCS was chosen. It overlaps the femoral stem, and two screws are inserted in the cement anterior and posterior to the stem. *E,* Soft tissue status 6 weeks after surgery.

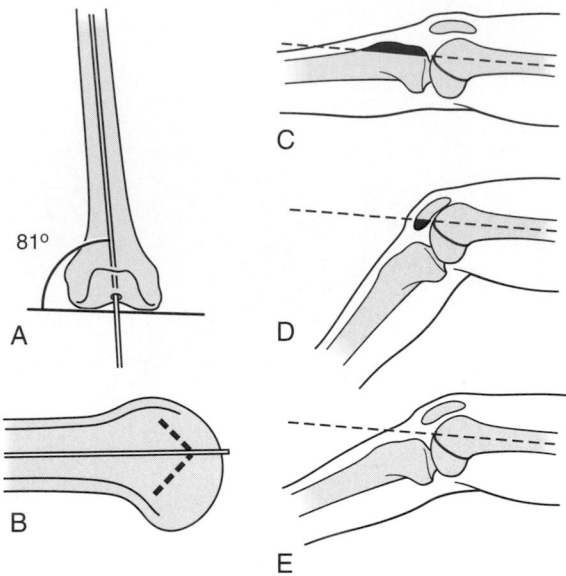

**FIGURE 53–13.** Positioning and approach for retrograde femoral nailing. *A,* In the anteroposterior view, the entry site is where the femoral anatomic axis crosses the plane of the joint surface. For correct frontal plane alignment, the direction of the nail should duplicate that of the anatomic axis, which intersects the joint plane at a valgus angle of approximately 81°. *B,* On the lateral view, the entry site is just anterior to the distal end of Blumensaat's line. Fluoroscopically, this is usually visible as a line of dense bone, often intersecting an anterior linear density. The apex of this apparent angle points toward the usual entry site. Knee flexion of 30° to 40° is required to gain appropriate access. *C,* The tibia blocks nail insertion if the knee is too extended. *D,* The patella is in the way with too much flexion. *E,* Correct knee flexion of 30° to 40° provides an adequate window for percutaneous nail insertion.

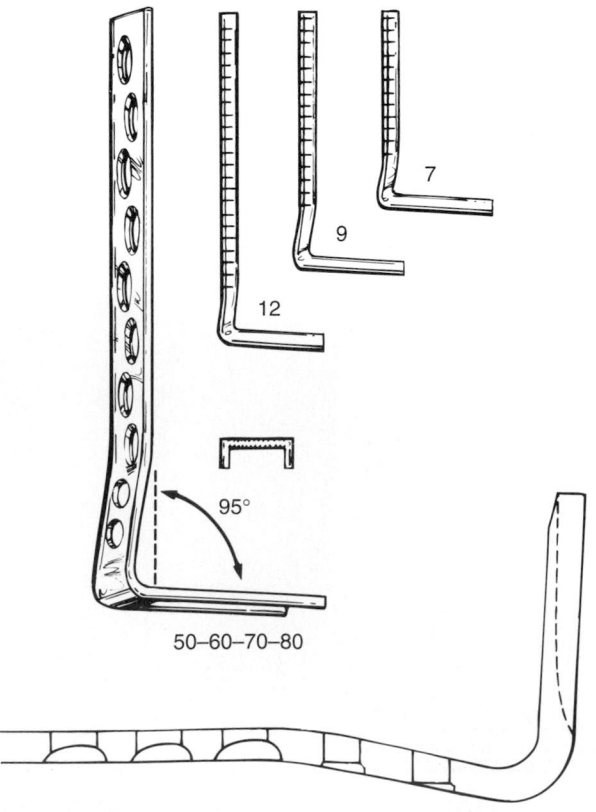

**FIGURE 53–14.** The 95° condylar buttress plate. Blade lengths range from 50 to 80 mm; plate lengths, from 92 mm (5 holes) to 299 mm (18 holes).

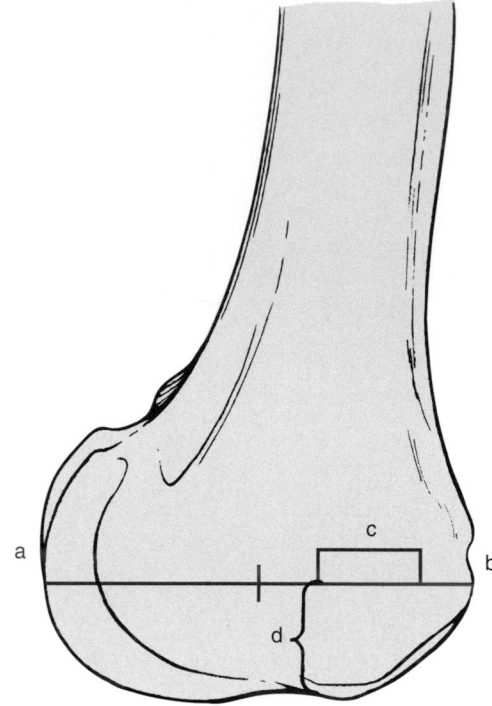

**FIGURE 53–15.** Position for insertion of the 95° condylar buttress plate in the lateral cortex of the distal end of the femur. *A, B,* Longest sagittal diameter on the lateral femoral condyle. *C,* Middle third of the anterior half. *D,* Distance 1.5 to 2 cm proximal to the articular surface.

placed anteriorly and one posteriorly. Only by first marking the insertion site and path of the seating chisel can these lag screws be placed outside the path of the blade plate. Both 6.5-mm cancellous screws should be inserted slightly proximal to the level of insertion of the blade plate (Fig. 53–16). The anterior screw is inserted in a slightly anterior-to-posterior direction, from lateral to medial, just inferior and lateral to the most anterior aspect of the patellar femoral groove. This anterior 6.5-mm cancellous screw should be inserted without a washer to ensure that it does not interfere with the patellofemoral mechanism. The posterior screw is also inserted slightly proximal to the insertion of the blade and just anterior to the proximal insertion of the lateral collateral ligament. It should be inserted in a slightly posterior-to-anterior direction to avoid penetration of the intracondylar notch and should be inserted with a washer. It is important that both screws act as lag screws (i.e., all their threads must be on the far side of the fracture and neither should penetrate the medial cortex) because long-term pain and disability can result from interference with medial structures during knee movement.

Once the condyles are anatomically reduced and internally fixed, the distal portion of the femur must be properly aligned and attached to the femoral shaft, which is accomplished by inserting the blade plate correctly into the condyles and then using it to reduce and stabilize the fracture. Two temporary K-wires are placed as guides for insertion of the seating chisel of the 95° CBP (see Fig. 53–16). K-wire 1 is inserted across the knee joint parallel to the inferior aspect of the medial and lateral condyles (i.e., the knee joint axis). K-wire 2 is inserted anteriorly across the patellofemoral joint; it slopes in an anterior-to-

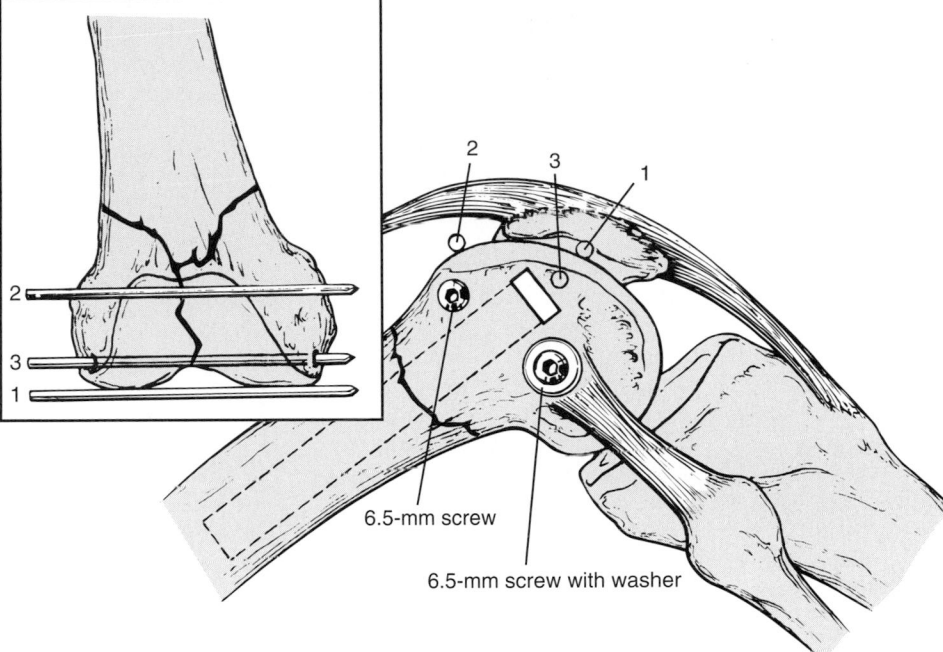

**FIGURE 53–16.** Position for insertion of alignment and summation K-wires: K-wire 1, inferiorly along the femoral condyles; K-wire 2, anteriorly along the femoral condyles; and K-wire 3 (summation), parallel to both wires 1 and 2 and inferior to the window for blade plate insertion.

6.5-mm screw

6.5-mm screw with washer

posterior direction and is kept parallel to the condyles in the coronal plane (Fig. 53–17). As originally described, the blade should be inserted parallel to the plane determined by the medial and lateral prominences of the patellofemoral articular surfaces (demonstrated by wire 2). However, such insertion may result in too little purchase in the narrow anterior portion of the distal end of the femur. It is better to consider wire 2 as a boundary limit and insert the summation wire (No. 3), seating chisel, and fixation device blade or screw in a relatively more posterior direction, perpendicular to the cortical surface at the insertion site. The definitive K-wire 3 is inserted approximately 1 cm proximal to the inferior aspect of the knee joint, just inferior to the area marked out on the lateral condyle for insertion of the seating chisel (see Fig. 53–16). K-wire 3, which "summates" the information of wires 1 and 2, represents the definitive guide for insertion of the 95° CBP.

It must therefore be parallel to wire 1 in the frontal plane (Fig. 53–16) and to wire 2 in the coronal plane (see Fig. 53–17). If the surgeon is inexperienced with this technique, it is a good idea to fluoroscopically verify that wire 3 is parallel to the knee joint axis in the frontal plane. In fractures without supracondylar comminution, the position of summation wire 3 can also be checked with the condylar guide, which is a mirror image of the condylar plate (Fig. 53–18). Provisional guide wires 1 and 2 are removed before the seating chisel is used. The main principle of 95° distal femoral fracture fixation implants is derived from the fact that on the frontal (AP) projection,

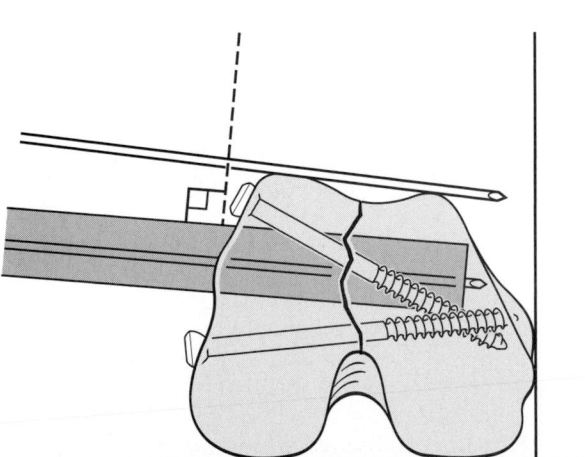

**FIGURE 53–17.** A coronal view of the distal end of the femur demonstrates the trapezoidal shape, the angle for the lag screws, and the position for insertion of the chisel.

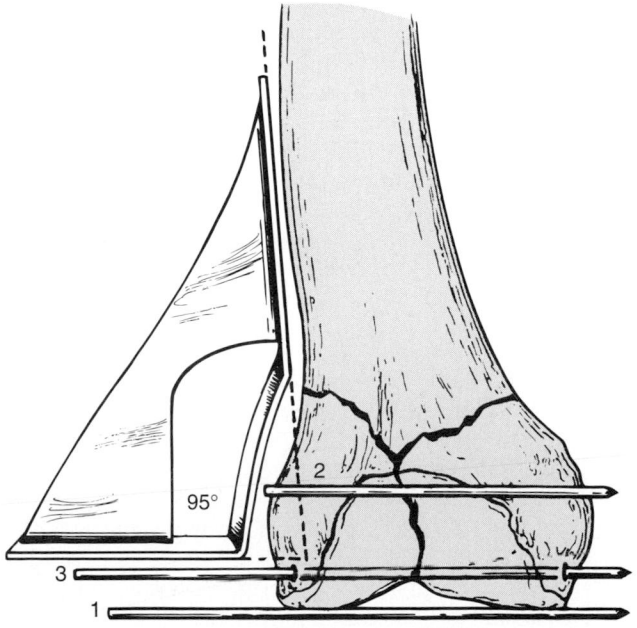

**FIGURE 53–18.** Use of the condylar guide for checking the position of summation K-wire 3.

the articular surface lies at an angle of 95° to the lateral femoral shaft. A properly inserted blade, parallel to the articular surface (wire 1), reduces the fracture without varus or valgus malalignment when its plate portion is attached to the femoral shaft. Wire 2 defines the anterior surface of the distal end of the femur, which the blade should diverge from to avoid protrusion through the medial condyle's sloping anterior surface and to ensure adequate distal fixation.

In young patients with dense trabecular cancellous bone, it is necessary to predrill the condylar path tract for the seating chisel. If predrilling is not done, impaction of the seating chisel into the condyles can require tremendous force and, as a result, may disrupt the lag screw fixation of the condyles. Predrilling is easily accomplished with the use of a 4.5-mm drill bit and the appropriate three-hole guide. This guide is applied to the lateral condyle parallel to summation K-wire 3. Three 4.5-mm channels can be drilled out in a lateral-to-medial direction in the previously marked window for insertion of the chisel. If any uncertainty remains, the result can be checked by fluoroscopy. The window in the lateral cortex is then expanded by using the router in the three drill holes. To seat the condylar plate flush with the lateral cortex in young patients, it is helpful to bevel the proximal lip of the lateral window with an osteotome and remove approximately 0.5 cm of bone.

The seating chisel is assembled with the seating chisel guide. The guide allows assessment of rotation (i.e., flexion and extension) in the sagittal plane as the chisel is inserted into the condyles. The seating chisel is then inserted into the condylar fragment while maintaining it parallel to K-wire 3 in both the frontal and coronal planes and ensuring correct rotation in the sagittal plane. The blade must remain parallel to the longest sagittal diameter of the condyles because rotation angulates the fracture on the lateral view. In young patients with good bone, it is helpful to insert the chisel approximately 1 cm at a time and then back it out a few millimeters before continuing. This technique greatly facilitates the ability to subsequently remove the seating chisel after full insertion. Again, if the surgeon is inexperienced with this technique, the use of fluoroscopy provides reassurance of correct position for the seating chisel. The seating chisel is inserted to the predetermined depth. It should be appreciated that the distal part of the femur is a trapezoid, with a 25° angle on the medial side from posterior to anterior (see Fig. 53–17); care must be taken to not penetrate the medial condylar cortex with the seating chisel, which on radiography looks "too short" in relation to the wide posterior cortical shadow. The 95° CBP is then inserted along the prepared tract in the femoral condyles and impacted to lie flush with the lateral cortex.

Before reduction of the fracture, it is necessary to stabilize the fixation of the condylar plate within the condyles by inserting one or two 6.5-mm cancellous lag screws through the distal plate holes into the condylar fragment. These screws not only enhance the rotational stability of the condylar fragment but also prevent lateral excursion of the blade with the application of axial compression. The reconstituted distal portion of the femur, with blade plate securely attached, is then reduced to the femoral shaft and provisionally held there with a Verbrugge clamp around the side plate and shaft. After the comminuted fragments, if any, are reduced, axial compression can be achieved by use of the tension device. (Occasionally, with no bony defect and an anatomic reduction, compression can be accomplished with the use of loaded screws in the dynamic compression plate.) If at all possible, a lag screw should be inserted across the supracondylar fracture through the plate. This screw will greatly enhance the stability of the fixation. If a bone defect or lack of cortical contact is observed after fracture reduction, axial compression cannot be achieved without causing shortening, so the fixation mode must be bridge plating rather than compression plating.

The 95° CBP requires purchase in the distal condyles to be efficacious. Distal fixation is achieved by (1) contact of the broad surface of the blade and (2) addition of distal cancellous lag screws through the plate into the condyles. In very low transcondylar fractures, especially in elderly patients, distal fixation with the CBP will be inadequate, and alternative methods may be indicated. If the lateral condyle or the intercondylar area is markedly comminuted, adequate fixation is achieved with a locking condylar plate or LISS (see later)

**Condylar Compression Screw and Side Plate (DCS), Standard Technique.** The condylar compression screw system has a design analogous to that of the 95° CBP, but the blade is replaced with a cannulated compression screw (Fig. 53–19). Technically, this device may be easier to use because most surgeons are familiar with cannulated compression screw systems for the fixation of intertrochanteric hip fractures. The condylar compression screw is

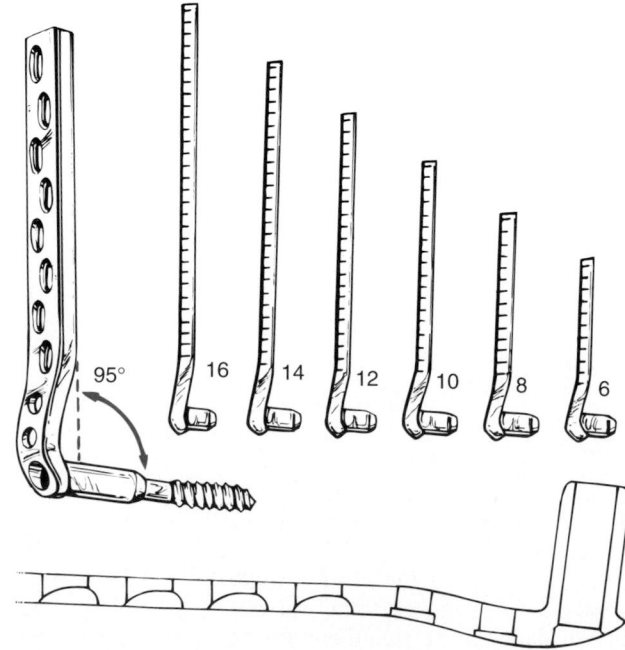

FIGURE 53–19. The condylar compression screw system. The 95° side plate slides over a cannulated lag screw. Lag screw lengths range from 50 to 75 mm; side plates (6 to 16 holes), from 113.5 to 273.5 mm.

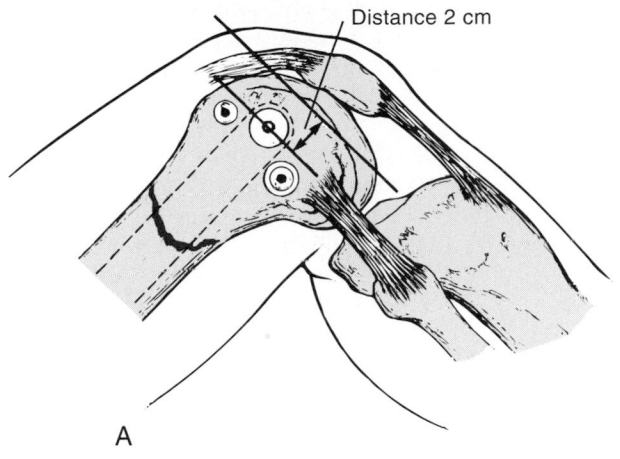

Distance 2 cm

A

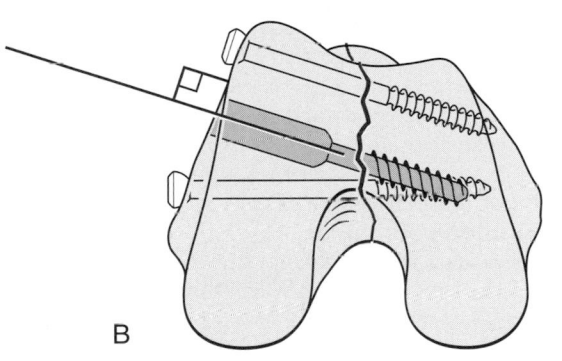

B

**FIGURE 53–20.** Position for insertion of the condylar compression screw. *A*, Lateral view: junction of the anterior and middle thirds, 2 cm from the articular surface. *B*, Coronal view.

easier to insert into the condyles than the 95° blade plate is for the following reasons:

1. It is a cannulated screw system inserted over a guide wire.

2. By using a power-driven triple reamer, which allows precutting of the path of the condylar screw, the system eliminates the problems encountered in hammering the chisel into the condyles.

3. The system eliminates the necessity to control flexion and extension in the sagittal plane when inserting the condylar screw because it can be corrected by rotation of the screw and side plate.

The operative technique for insertion of the DCS differs from that for the 95° blade plate only in the technique for insertion of the condylar screw. Again, three guide wires are inserted. Wire 1 is inserted parallel to the knee joint axis, and wire 2 is inserted parallel to the anterior patellofemoral articulation. The location on the lateral femoral condyle for insertion of the DCS is slightly more proximal and posterior than that of the 95° blade plate, approximately 2 cm from the inferior articular surface and at the junction of the anterior and middle thirds of the longest sagittal diameter of the lateral femoral condyle (Fig. 53–20). This point is just proximal to the posterior edge of the window for insertion of the 95° blade plate (see

Fig. 53–15). The third guide wire becomes the definitive guide for the cannulated screw system. This 230-mm guide wire with a threaded tip is inserted into the premarked area on the lateral cortex parallel to wire 1 and diverging posteriorly from wire 2, as discussed earlier regarding the blade plate (Fig. 53–21). The condylar compression screw angle guide may be helpful in patients without supracondylar comminution. This angle guide is a mirror image of the side plate and is held against the lateral cortex with a T handle. Again, guide wire 3 is the definitive guide for the cannulated condylar screw system and must be inserted parallel to wire 1 and diverge posteriorly from wire 2, perpendicular to the entry site cortex. This process is greatly facilitated, as in hip fracture surgery, by the use of fluoroscopy. The threaded guide wire should be inserted until the tip is felt to just penetrate the medial cortex; fluoroscopy may be deceiving here because the posterior femoral condyles are broader than the anterior ones, especially on the medial side (Fig. 53–22). A reverse-calibrated measuring device is placed over the guide wire to allow direct measurement of length. The triple-cannulated reamer is set for the desired length, which should be 10 mm less than the measurement to prevent penetration of the medial cortex. The channel is power reamed over the guide wire; again, the result can be checked with fluoroscopy. In young patients with firm trabecular cancellous bone, a cannulated tap with a short centering sleeve is used. A cannulated compression screw of the correct length is connected to the T handle and wrench and inserted over the guide wire with the long centering sleeve (Fig. 53–23). It is inserted until the zero mark on the wrench is seen to be flush with the lateral cortex and the handle of the inserter is parallel with the reduced femoral shaft. In elderly patients with osteoporotic bone, the condylar screw can be inserted an extra 5 mm beyond the prereamed channel to obtain better fixation. The appropriate side plate is then slid over the condylar screw and keyed to align with the proximal part of the femur in the sagittal plane. The remainder of the technique is similar to that described for the 95° blade plate.

**Condylar Buttress Plate, Standard Technique.** The condylar buttress plate was designed to allow multiple lag screw fixation of complex condylar fractures. It consists of a broad compression side plate and a bifurcated, precontoured distal portion to fit the lateral surface of the femoral condyle (Fig. 53–24). The posterior projection is broader and longer than the anterior projection to fit the larger posterior aspect of the femoral condyle, so different plates must be used for the right and the left. It allows insertion of up to six interfragmentary lag screws through the distal portion of the plate for fixation of the condyles. However, this plate is not a fixed-angle device and therefore does not maintain correct axial alignment of the joint axis. It should be used only when the fracture morphology does not allow the use of either the 95° blade plate or the condylar screw. Its primary indications are (1) low transcondylar fractures or comminuted fractures of the lateral or medial condyles in which stable fixation with a fixed-angle device is not possible and (2) coronal or very comminuted articular fractures in which screw fixation of the condyles precludes insertion of a fixed-angle device (Fig. 53–25).

The condylar buttress plate should be part of the armamentarium available for fixation of all distal femoral fractures, even the most simple, in the event that intraoperative complications preclude the use of one of the fixed-angle devices. However, the advent of similar plates with locking screws, to be discussed later, may result in their obsolescence in the near future. It is easy to make errors in alignment and fixation with the condylar buttress plate. The most common mistake is to lag the condyles to the condylar buttress plate in a valgus position. The position should be carefully checked intraoperatively by fluoroscopy with use of the cable technique discussed later (see Fig. 53–32).

Because the condylar buttress plate is not a fixed-angle device, it cannot guarantee axial alignment, especially in the frontal plane. This shortcoming is especially problematic with comminution in the supracondylar region (Fig. 53–26). One of the major long-term deforming forces after fixation of distal femoral fractures is the tendency for the condyles to drift into varus angulation. Such angulation is also a problem with the condylar buttress

plate because the individual lag screws are not fixed to the plate and can shift their angulation relative to it (Fig. 53–27). Varus angulation is much more likely to happen in those with supracondylar comminution or bone loss. To avoid the tendency of the fracture to drift into varus in these cases, the use of a medial buttressing plate applied to the medial side of the distal end of the femur, with a bone graft for long-term medial support, has been described.[100] This procedure can readily be accomplished after the lateral fixation through a separate, small medial incision.

### Minimally Invasive Plate Osteosynthesis

**Positioning of the Patient.** Positioning is similar to that for standard procedures; however, a couple of issues must be considered. Patients are placed on a standard radiolucent table with the knee joint line of the injured knee slightly distal to the mechanical hinge of the table. Except for bilateral fractures, the contralateral extremity may be placed on an obstetric leg holder[63, 64] (see Fig. 53–9).

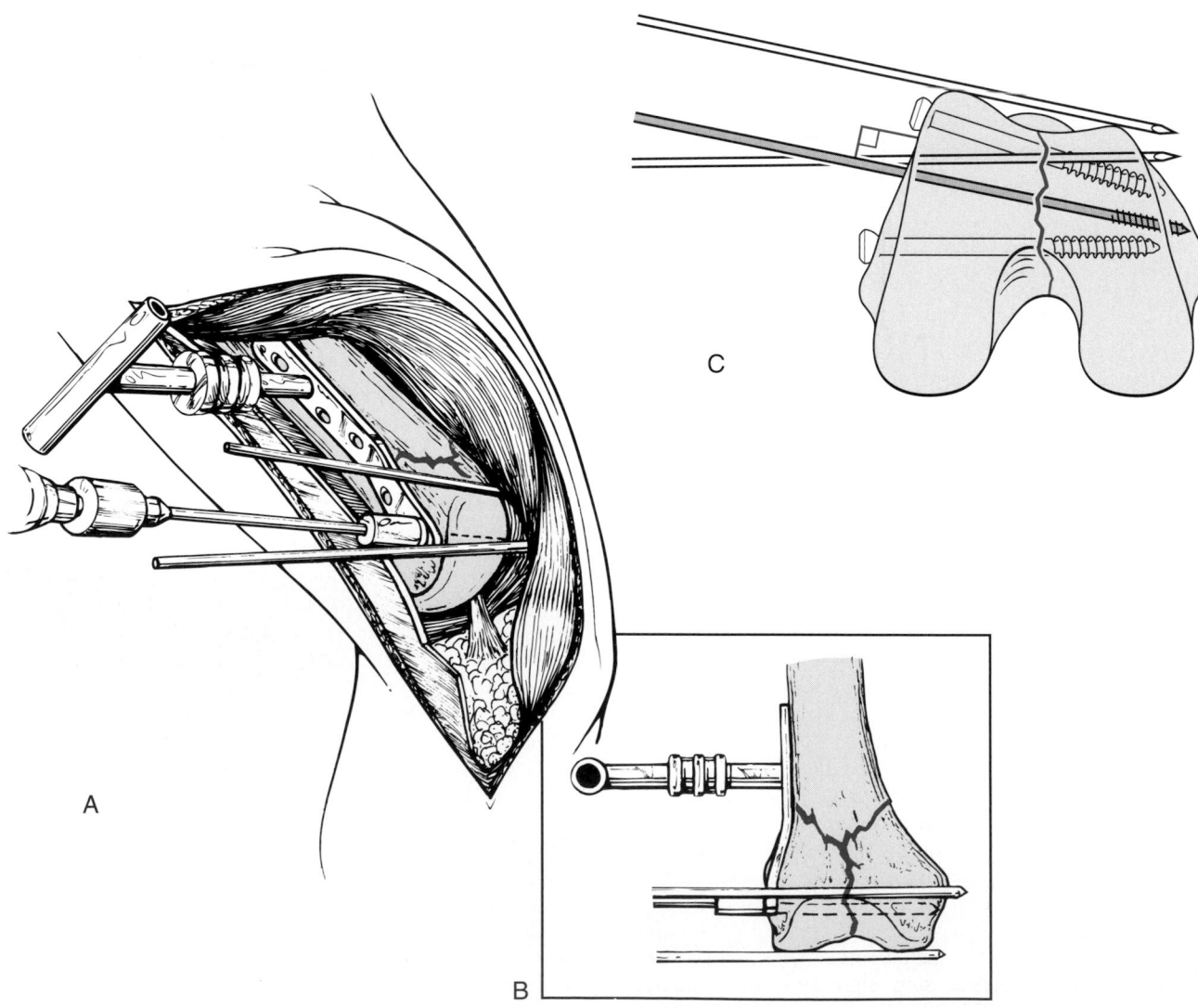

**FIGURE 53–21.** Technique for insertion of a threaded summation guide wire for placement of a condylar screw. *A,* Position for the condylar compression screw guide. *B,* Anteroposterior view. *C,* Coronal view.

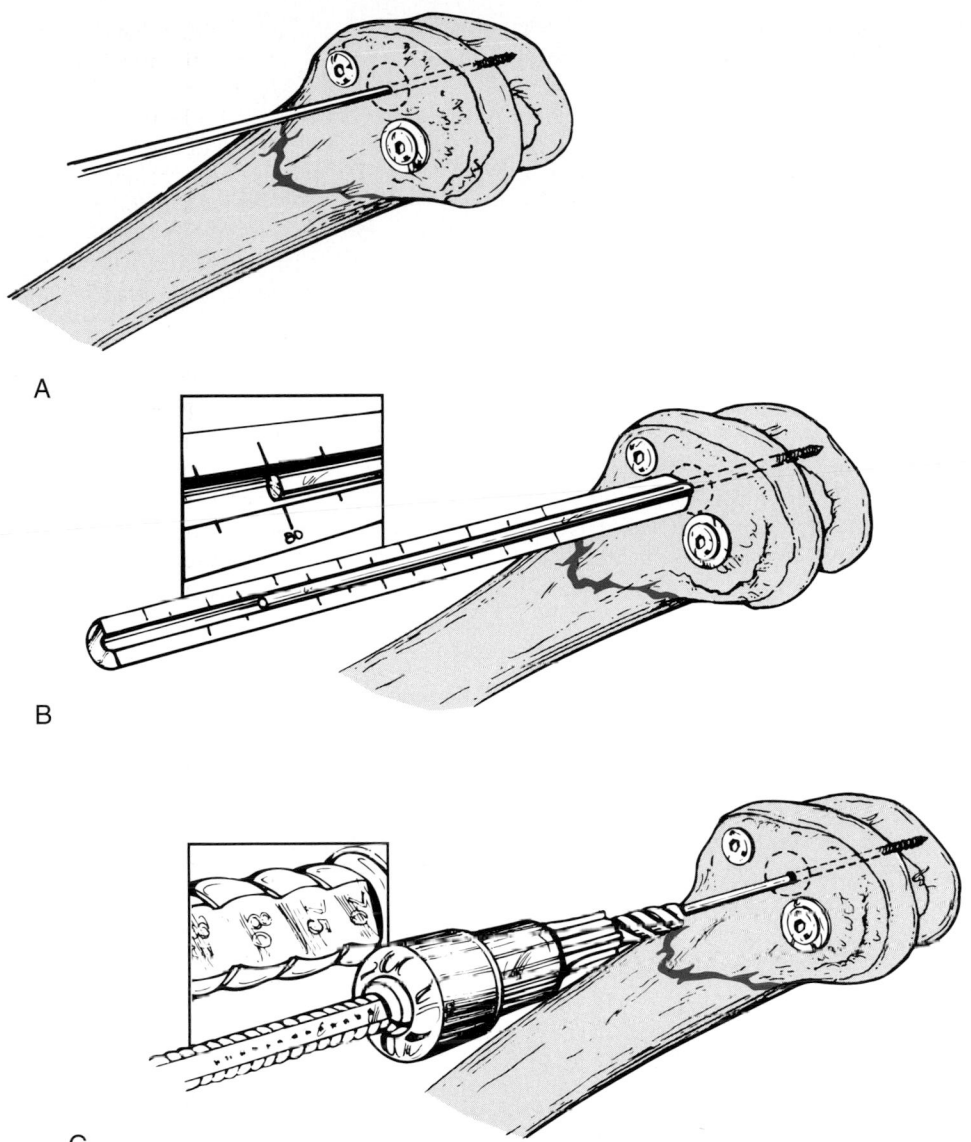

**FIGURE 53–22.** Technique for measurement of condylar screw length and cannulated reaming. *A,* Final position of the threaded summation guide wire. *B,* Measurement of length. *C,* Use of the triple-cannulated reamer.

**Alignment Control.** Minimally invasive, indirect fracture fixation techniques have a higher risk of malalignment than open techniques do. We have therefore developed techniques that help control alignment in minimally invasive, indirect fracture fixation techniques[64] (Figs. 53–28 to 53–35).

Before the procedure, the range of rotation of the uninjured hip joint is measured with the hip and knee in flexion or with the hip extended and the knee flexed (Fig. 53–28). The patient's position is checked to verify that the pelvis is not vertically or sagittally rotated. In addition, the shape of the lesser trochanter is stored for later use in the image intensifier with the patella directed anterior or the medial foot edge in a vertical position (Fig. 53–29). During surgery, hints for major rotational malalignment are the so-called cortical step sign and the diameter difference sign (Fig. 53–30). In the case of complex fracture types, the distance between the top of the femoral

head and the distal end of the lateral condyle is measured by image intensification and a meter stick (Fig. 53–31). The imaged structures are centered on the screen with the x-ray beam perpendicular to the longitudinal axis. The "cable method" is an easy, flexible, and reproducible technique for analysis of frontal-plane deformity (Fig. 53–32). Several clinical and radiographic techniques are available for assessment of sagittal-plane deformities (Figs. 53–33 to 53–35).

### Minimally Invasive Percutaneous Plate Osteosynthesis

In the treatment of proximal and distal femoral fractures, the DCS is commonly inserted through a standard lateral approach with elevation of the vastus lateralis muscle.[86] This approach provides wide exposure of the femoral shaft and facilitates direct ORIF of the fracture. However, to directly visualize the fracture, the soft tissues are stripped, the perforating arteries are ligated, the nutrient artery may be placed at risk, and local periosteal and medullary perfusion are decreased.[24–26] This soft tissue disruption may lead to a decrease in the rate of union and an increased need for primary and secondary bone grafting in both subtrochanteric and supracondylar femoral fractures.[55, 93]

To limit the amount of soft tissue elevation at the fracture site, indirect reduction techniques have been developed to treat proximal[55] and distal[5, 51, 64, 65, 93] femoral fractures. Each of these techniques limits the approach to a lateral exposure and avoids medial dissection. The reported results of these indirect techniques demonstrate rates of union at least as rapid as those with the "classic" technique, but without the need for bone grafting.[5, 51, 55, 93]

Therefore, a method has been developed that limits the amount of both medial and lateral dissection. This

technique, MIPPO,[65] was developed for the treatment of extra-articular proximal and distal femoral fractures. It takes advantage of the two-part properties and two-plane alignment requirement of the DCS, which is inserted in percutaneous, submuscular fashion.

**Condylar Screw Placement, Surgical Approach, and Plate Fixation.** The implant is inserted percutaneously according to the standard principles of DCS application with following modifications (Fig. 53–36). First, a threaded guide wire is placed in the proper frontal and horizontal plane under fluoroscopic guidance. After adequate placement of the threaded guide wire, a longitudinal 4-cm skin incision centered on the guide pin is made and carried through the iliotibial band. With adequate soft tissue protection, the condylar screw hole is drilled and taped and the condylar screw inserted as measured. In supracondylar fractures, the guide wire is temporarily

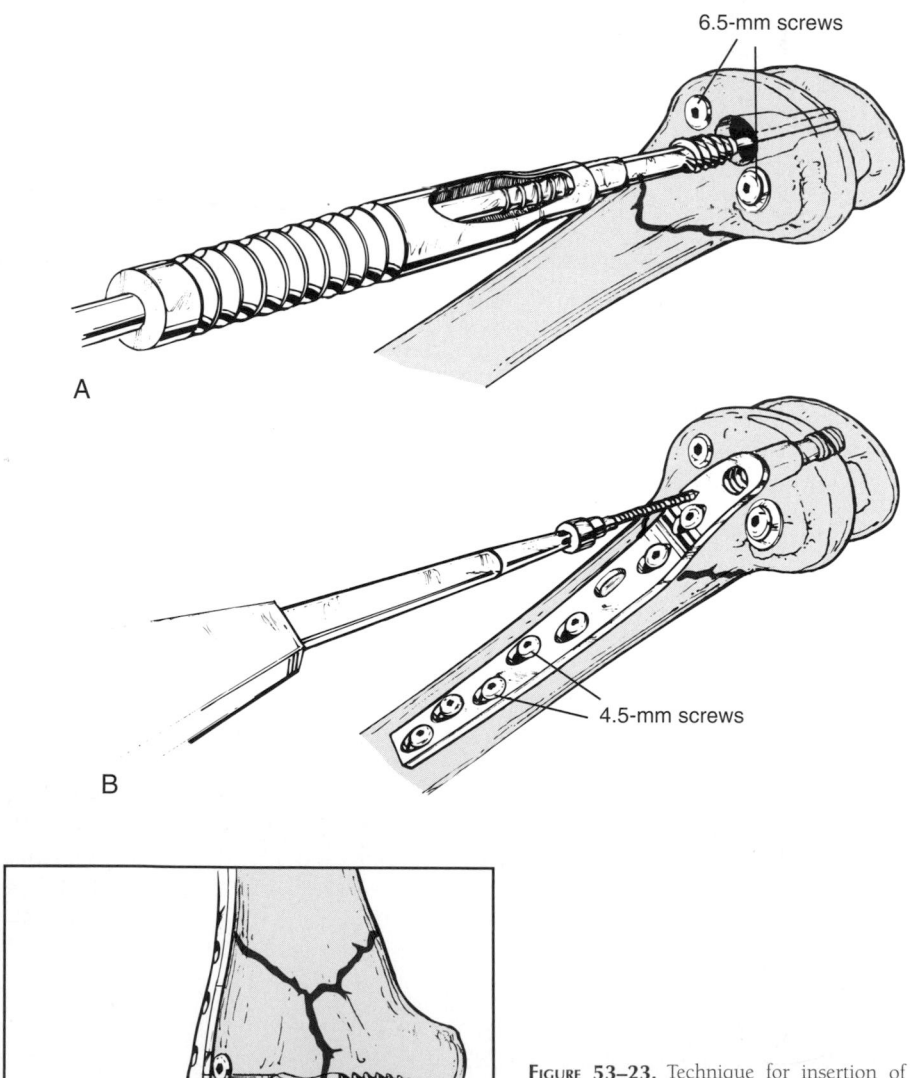

**FIGURE 53–23.** Technique for insertion of the condylar lag screw and side plate. *A,* Insertion of the condylar lag screw to the desired depth. *B,* Insertion of the set screw after side plate fixation. *C,* Anteroposterior view showing condylar screw threads engaging the medial fragment to ensure that it compresses the fracture in lag fashion.

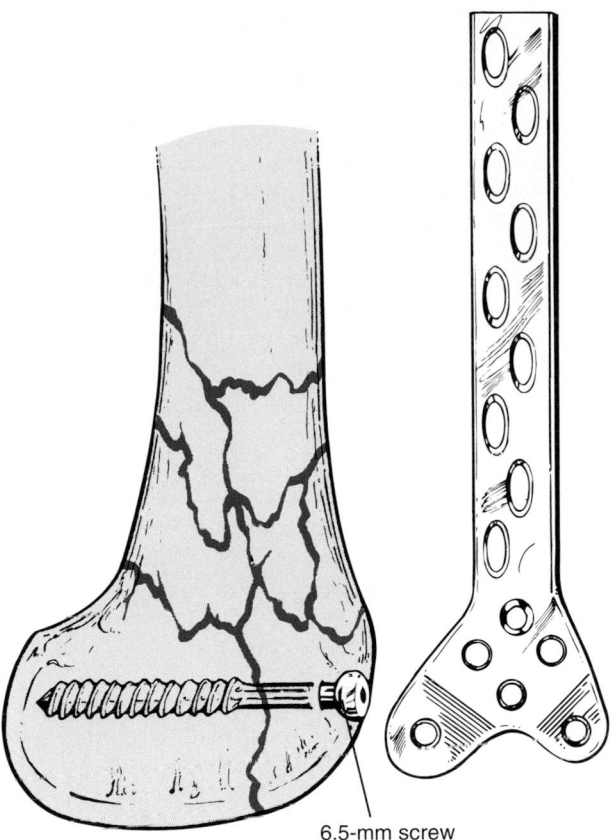

6.5-mm screw

**FIGURE 53–24.** The condylar buttress plate must often be used when sagittally directed lag screws are required to fix coronal fracture planes.

pushed through the medial condyle, and the iliotibial band is spread for an additional 2 to 3 cm longitudinally to facilitate plate insertion. The DCS plate is inserted through the skin and iliotibial tract incision beneath the lateral

vastus muscle. After reinsertion of the guide wire through both the plate and the condylar screw, a modified cannulated T handle (Stratec Waldenburg, Switzerland) is introduced over the guide wire. The T handle is fixed to the condylar screw with the cannulated long coupling screw, and the plate is slipped onto the condylar screw by using the modified T handle as a guide.

The condylar screw and its attached proximal or distal joint fragment are fixed to the shaft fragment indirectly and nonanatomically. The position of the plate can still be adjusted in the sagittal plane with the T handle mounted to the joint fragment to allow corrections in the sagittal plane. Once adequate alignment is achieved, a small custom-made transmuscular clamp can be used for temporary fixation. Limb axes, length, and rotation are then confirmed with the previously described clinical and image intensification techniques.[62, 63, 66, 68] The three or four plate screws are then inserted through a 4-cm percutaneous/transmuscular incision. The screws are placed divergently to increase screw pull-out strength and decrease the length of the incision needed for their insertion (see Fig. 53–12). The distractor is not routinely used, nor is bone graft or bone cement. Suction drains are not generally used.

*Transarticular Approach and Retrograde Plate Osteosynthesis*

Because anatomic articular reconstruction remains a primary goal in these complex fractures and complete joint visualization is difficult with a lateral approach (particularly with one that attempts to avoid soft tissue stripping), a new minimally invasive approach, TARPO, has recently been developed.[62, 68, 69] This technique uses a lateral parapatellar arthrotomy for direct reduction of the joint surface and an indirect plate fixation technique to secure the articular block to the femoral shaft.

The joint is approached through a lateral parapatellar

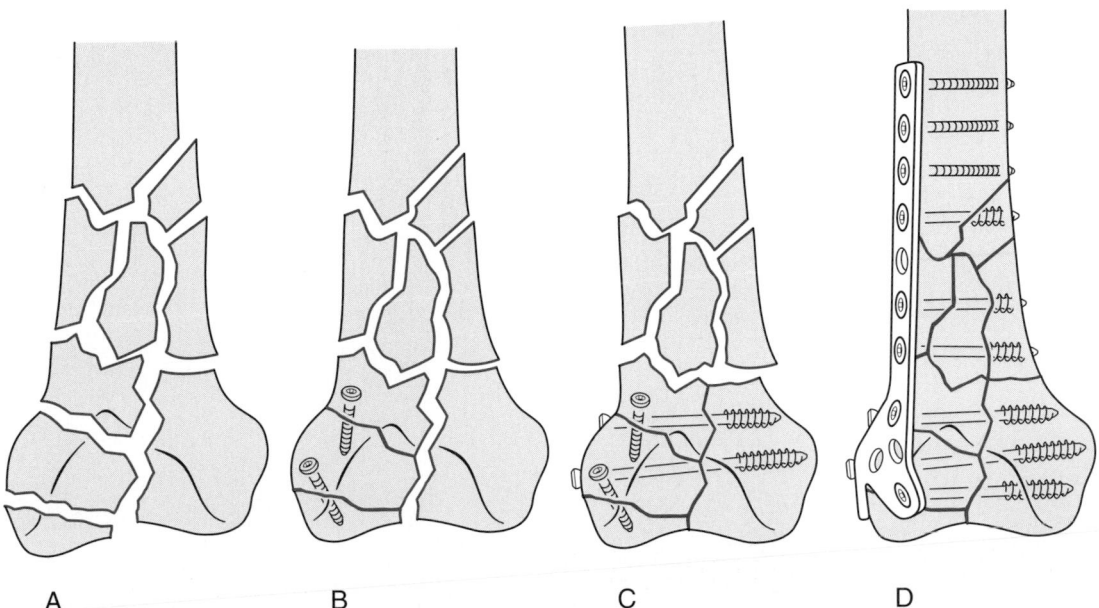

| A | B | C | D |
|---|---|---|---|

**FIGURE 53–25.** Stepwise reconstruction of 33C3 distal femoral fractures with the condylar buttress plate (Krettek and Tscherne, 1996). *A,* Fracture pattern 33C3. *B,* Reconstruction of the medial and lateral condyle (3.5 mm small-fragment screws). *C,* Fixation of both condyles (6.5-mm cancellous screws). *D,* Reduction of the reconstructed joint block with the femoral shaft and fixation with a condylar buttress plate.

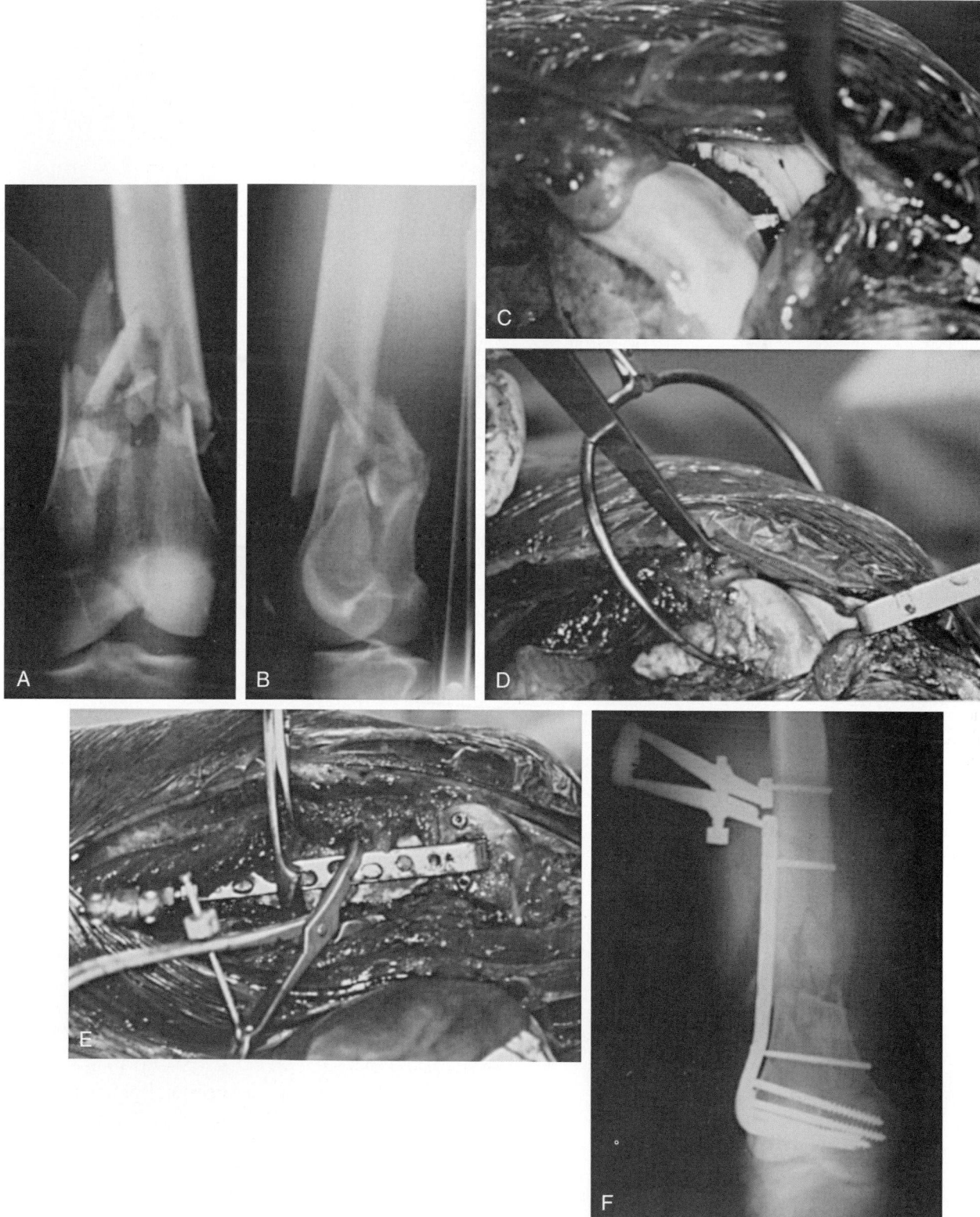

**Figure 53–26.** Closed supracondylar comminuted C2 fracture of the distal end of the right femur in a 23-year-old man. Anteroposterior (AP) (A) and lateral (B) radiographs. C, Intraoperative clinical picture showing the intracondylar fracture. D, The intracondylar fracture is reduced with a clamp and stabilized with two 6.5-mm cancellous screws. E, Restoration of the condyles to the shaft with a 95° condylar blade device and reduction of the fracture with bone clamps (no anteromedial supracondylar soft tissue stripping). F, AP radiograph after axial compression of the indirectly reduced supracondylar comminuted fractures with the eccentric compression device.

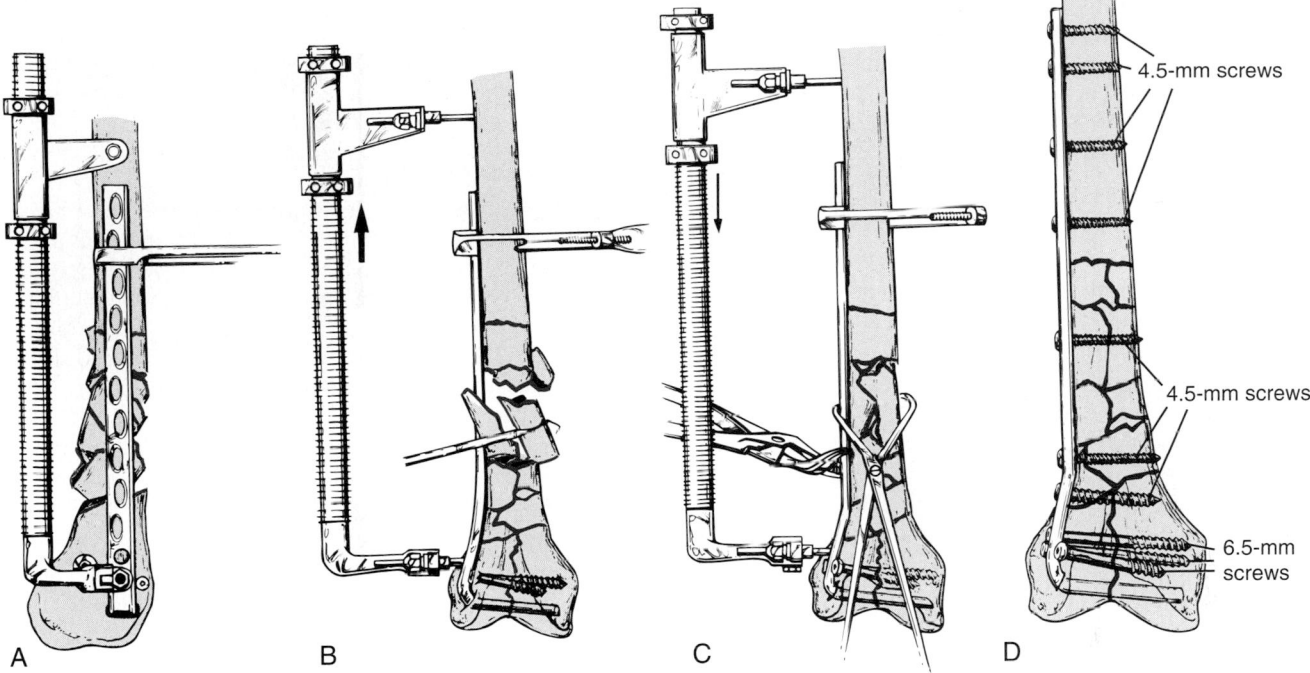

**FIGURE 53–27.** Technique for use of the femoral distractor for indirect fracture reduction after plate fixation distally. *A,* Insertion of Schanz screws proximally and distally (the latter through the plate). *B,* Distraction applied for fracture reduction. The fracture fragments are teased into place with a dental pick while avoiding unnecessary soft tissue stripping. *C,* Compression with the femoral distractor to provide axial loading when the fracture has sufficient bony support with the use of bone reduction clamps as indicated. *D,* Final construct after indirect fracture reduction, screw stabilization of the plate proximally, and judicious lag screw fixation of the fracture as indicated.

arthrotomy approximately 15 to 20 cm long (see Fig. 53–11). A proximal deep incision is developed between the rectus and the vastus lateralis muscles along the course of the muscle fibers. The incision is carried distally to the tibial tuberosity. The patella is retracted medially to provide extensive exposure to both femoral condyles. Direct anatomic joint reconstruction is performed with K-wires, screws, and reabsorbable pins.

**Fixation of the Joint to the Proximal Shaft.** Fixation of the reconstructed condylar block to the proximal shaft fragment is performed indirectly and nonanatomically.

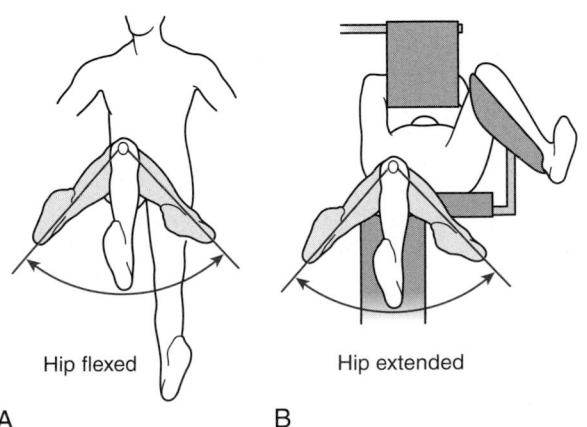

**FIGURE 53–28.** Clinical techniques for analysis of femoral rotation (Krettek et al., 1997). *A,* Drawing shows a patient with the hip and the knee flexed. Range of rotation is assessed before draping on the unaffected side, to be duplicated by fixation of the fractured femur. *B,* This can also be done with the hip extended and the table bent to allow knee flexion.

Either a dynamic compression plate (DCS), a condylar buttress plate, or an LISS-DF is placed beneath the vastus lateralis muscle in a distal-to-proximal direction. If a condylar buttress plate is used, the plate is fixed first to the condylar block to optimize plate position and fixation. The plate is fixed percutaneously and transmuscularly with an oscillating drill and self-tapping screws. Temporary plate fixation for stabilization during alignment control is achieved with the help of a specially designed MIPPO clamp (see Fig. 53–8). Three or four diverging plate screws, often sufficient for proximal plate fixation, are placed through a 3-cm incision. Limb length, rotation, and axes are determined with clinical and fluoroscopic techniques.[62, 66, 68] The distractor is not used routinely, nor is bone grafting or cementing performed routinely. Suction drains are used when necessary.

*Less Invasive Stabilization System*

Apart from biologic problems in distal femoral fractures, mechanical problems at the bone–implant interface related to mechanical instability (loss of frontal-plane alignment and movement of screws in this plane similar to that of windshield wiper blades) have been well described[19, 47, 59, 60] (Fig. 53–37). Studies have shown that the fixed-angle mechanical advantage of angular stability between the plate and screws increases stability.[23, 43, 59] The two key concepts of the LISS are (1) an anatomically precontoured condylar "buttress" plate to which the screws interlock and (2) the use of self-drilling, self-tapping monocortical screws (Fig. 53–38). The LISS combines some properties of a condylar buttress plate with the fixed-angle concept of a DCS. For insertion, the plate is attached to an insertion guide, which allows positioning of the plate and provides holes for the drill sleeves. The LISS acts mechanically as an internal fixator. Monocortical self-drilling screws are locked in the anatomically pre-shaped plate to provide angular stability and fix the bone fragments after indirect reduction has been performed. Furthermore, an aiming guide allows insertion of the plate and subsequent percutaneous placement of screws in the femoral shaft. The stability of the bone–implant construct is based on the angular stability of the plate–screw interface and not on friction between the plate and bone resulting from tightly applied screws.

**Implant Concept.** Fixed-angle devices have been tested mechanically and clinically and compared with implants without a fixed angle.[58, 61, 80, 105] A mechanical evaluation of the LISS in a paired human cadaver model used randomly selected femurs instrumented with a five-hole LISS in the distal end.[23] In the first series of paired femurs, the LISS was compared with a six-hole DCS, and in the second series it was compared with a seven-hole 95° CBP. A 1-cm gap was cut to mimic a group A3 fracture. The load was applied proximally through the "head of the femur" and distally through the lateral condyle. The applied cyclical load was increased in four stages ($F_{min}$ = 100 N; $F_{max}$ = 1000 N, 1400 N, 1800 N, 2200 N) for 10 cycles each.

Three different systems fixed on paired cadaver human femurs, LISS versus CBP and LISS versus DCS, were compared with respect to their potential to withstand applied load. During the loading cycles, the construct underwent reversible as well as permanent deformation. The total irreversible deformation for LISS was 51% lower than DCS and 62% lower than the CBP system. Ten of 12 paired tests showed more subsidence in the conventional bicortical fixation technique.

Bicortical fixation seems unnecessary with these plates because the plate itself mimics the second cortex. Without any need to penetrate the far cortex, self-drilling screws are possible[118] and facilitate percutaneous fixation. Drilling, length measurement, tapping, and screw insertion are all combined into a single screw insertion procedure. A correct insertion angle of the screw into the plate is necessary to allow interlocking of the screw to the plate, which can be ascertained with the LISS aiming guide. Distal fixation is designed to respect the anatomy of the distal end of the femur. The angles between the screws and the LISS are chosen to prevent screw penetration into the intercondylar notch or the knee. The LISS allows placement of seven long screws into the condyles.

The surgical technique differs from that for conventional open reduction.[120] The approach closely matched the technique used for plate placement as described for intra-articular[64] and extra-articular fractures.[65]

**Preoperative Planning.** A preoperative radiograph of the whole femur with good exposure of the knee joint, preferably including the hip joint, is necessary. Radio-

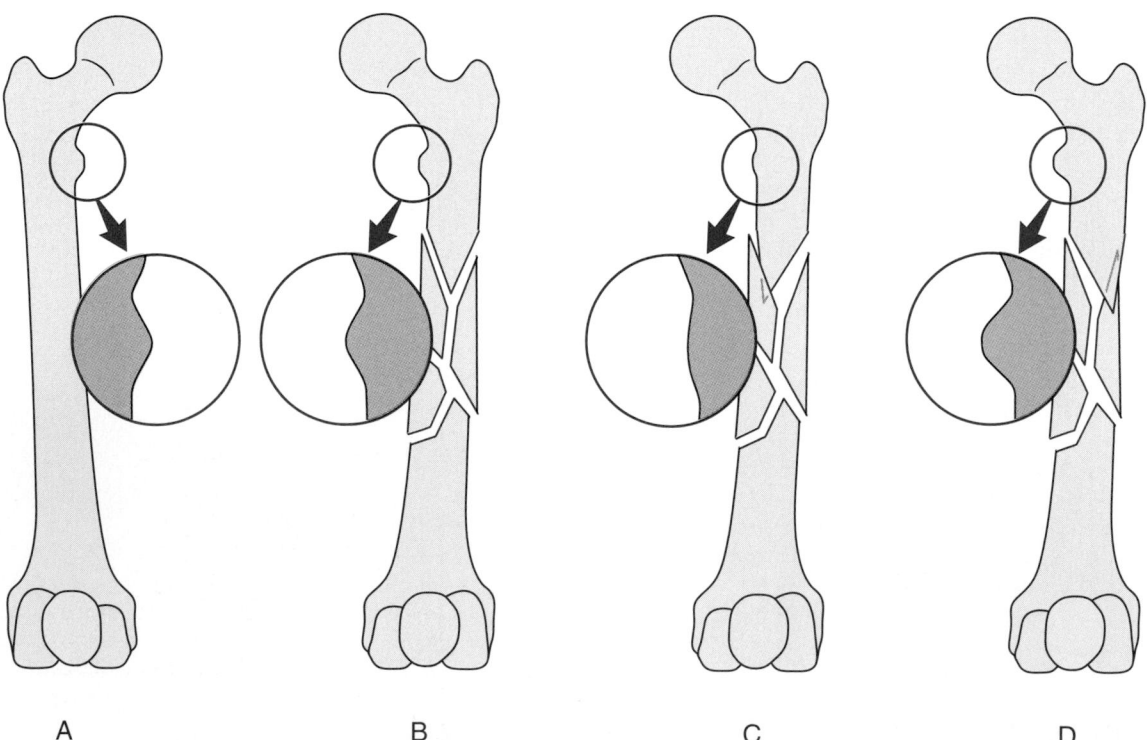

A          B          C          D

**FIGURE 53–29.** Lesser trochanter shape sign (Krettek et al., 1997). Radiologic determination of rotation intraoperatively by comparison of the shape of the lesser trochanter on the ipsilateral and contralateral sides. *A,* Preoperatively, before positioning the patient, the shape of the lesser trochanter on the contralateral side is stored in the image intensifier's memory, whereas the position of the patella is controlled and oriented strictly in an anterior direction. *B,* Before locking the second main fragment, the patella is oriented in a strictly anterior direction, whereas the proximal fragment is rotated until the shape of the lesser trochanter on the ipsilateral side matches the contralateral shape. *C,* In the event of an external rotation deformity, the shape of the lesser trochanter is diminished. With the patella pointing in a strictly anterior direction, the lesser trochanter is partially hidden by the proximal femoral shaft. *D,* In the case of an internal rotation deformity, the shape of the lesser trochanter is enlarged. With the patella pointing in a strictly anterior direction, the lesser trochanter is less hidden by the proximal femoral shaft.

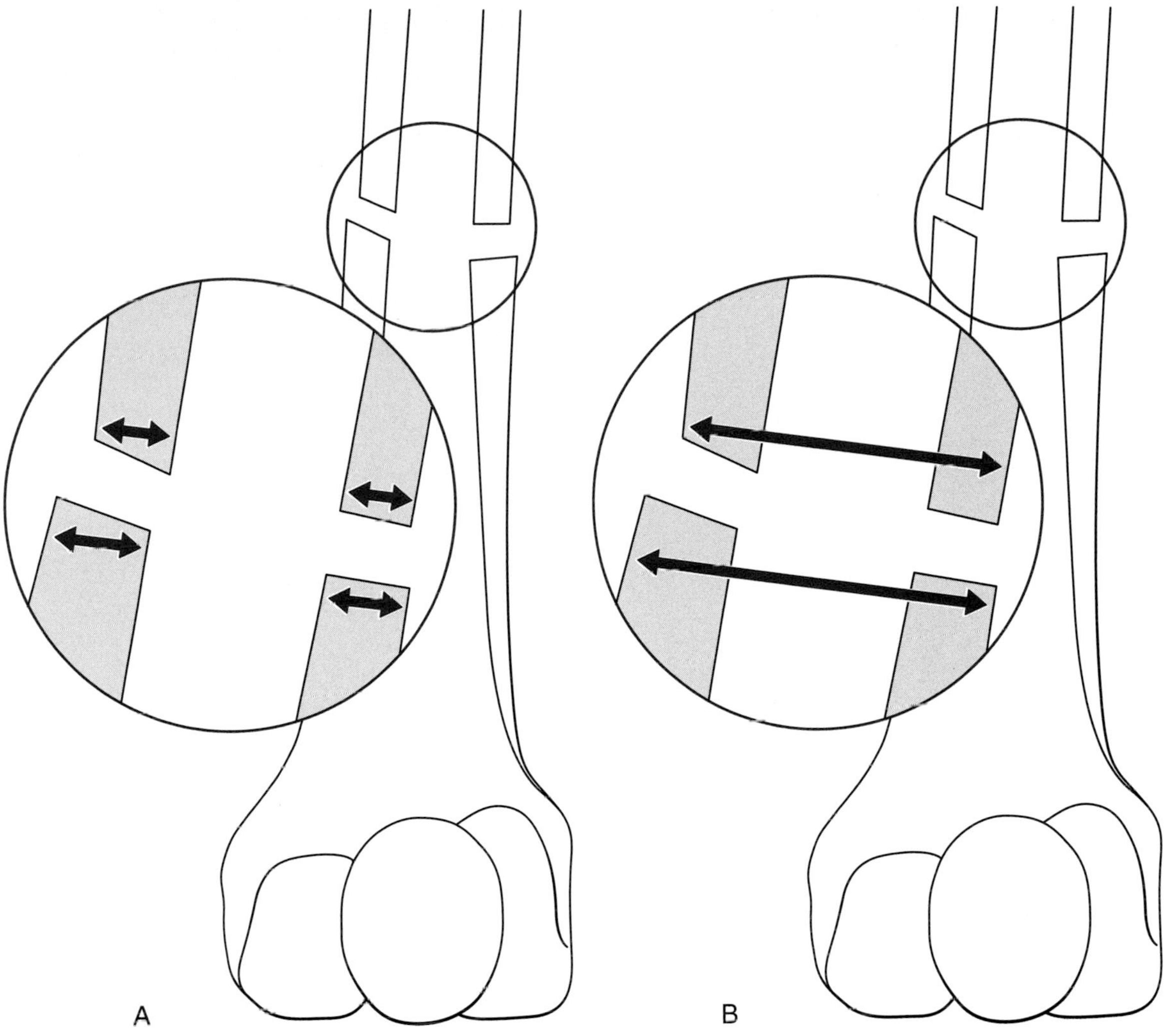

**FIGURE 53–30.** Radiologic determination of rotation intraoperatively by the cortical step sign and the diameter difference sign (Krettek et al., 1997). *A,* Cortical step sign. In the presence of rotational deformity, the cortical structures of the proximal and distal main fragments can be projected in different thicknesses. *B,* Diameter difference sign This sign is positive at levels at which the diameter is oval rather than round. In these cases, the transverse diameters of the proximal and distal main fragments can be projected as different diameters.

graphic preoperative selection of screw length is possible with an AP radiograph of the knee and the LISS radiographic calibrator placed medial or lateral at the height of the femoral condyles. The length of the calibrator on the film is measured, as well as the width of the femoral condyles. By tracing both measurements on the screw length table, one of four groups of screw lengths is chosen. The length of the plate should be long enough to ensure possible placement of at least four screws in the proximal fragment. To choose the correct approach, the fracture is classified according to the AO classification.[88] Group A fractures are best fixed from a short lateral approach. Group B and C fractures with intra-articular displacement are fixed through an anterior transarticular approach with a lateral parapatellar arthrotomy.

**Approach.** Type A distal femoral fractures and group C2 fractures without intra-articular displacement are stabilized with the previously described percutaneous approach (MIPPO)[64] (Fig. 53–39). The skin incision is guided by an orthograde femoral condyle projection (medial and lateral condyle shadows superimposed) in an

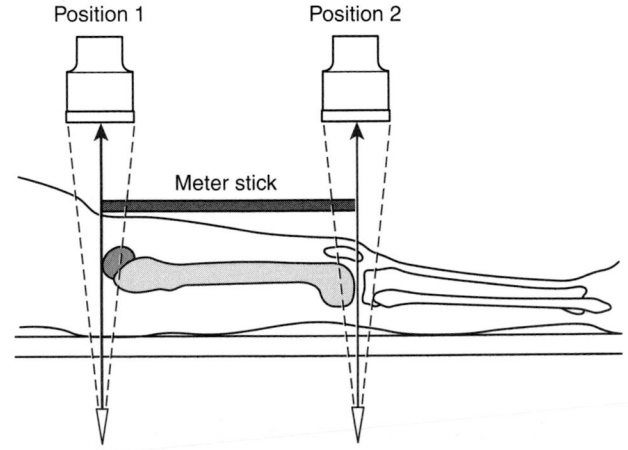

**FIGURE 53–31.** Technique for analysis of femoral length in a drawing depicting the arrangement of the patient, image intensifier, and meter stick for analysis of femoral length discrepancies (Krettek et al., 1997). Correct measurement requires orthograde projection of both the meter stick and bone. The point of measurement must be in the center of the image display, with the central ray perpendicular to the long axes of both the femur and meter stick.

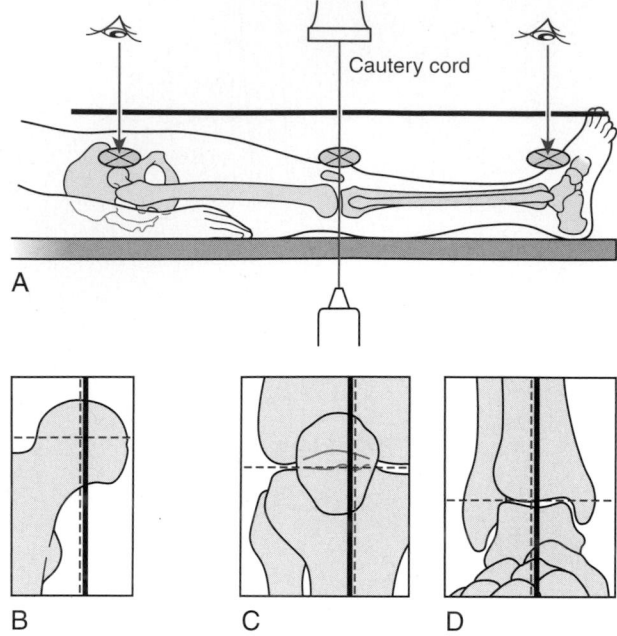

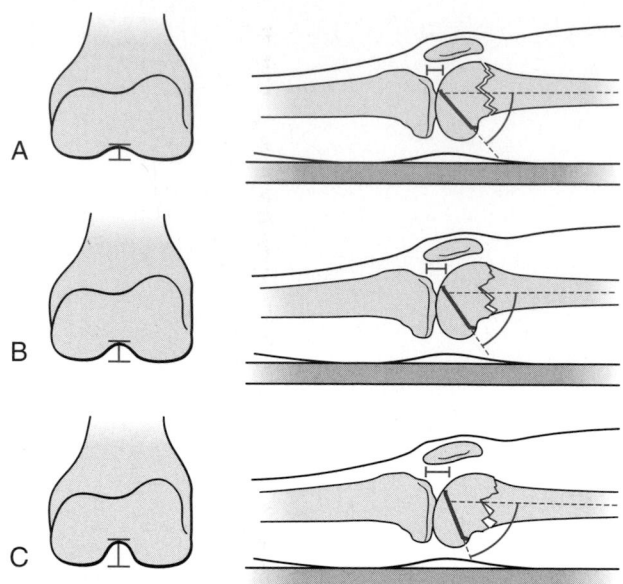

**FIGURE 53–32.** Cable method for analysis of frontal-plane deformity. To assess frontal-plane alignment, the electrocautery cable is stretched from a position over the center of the femoral head to the center of the tibiotalar joint to radiographically display the mechanical axis of the lower extremity. With the knee in extension and rotated so that the patella is in the midline, the image over the knee joint demonstrates where this axis crosses the knee joint. This view permits quantitative assessment of alignment and comparison with the opposite leg. Normally, the mechanical axis is 10 ± 7 mm medial to the midline of the knee (see Chapter 62).

**FIGURE 53–34.** Recurvatum deformity in the distal end of the femur (Krettek et al., 1997). *A,* Normal appearance of the intercondylar notch with the knee centered in the x-ray beam. *B, C,* The increasing recurvatum deformity is difficult to detect if only the shape of the condyles is analyzed. However, the increased height of the intercondylar notch on the anteroposterior view and the increased Blumensaat line-shaft angle in the lateral view help detect and quantify the recurvatum deformity

intensified view of the lateral image. The incision is made in line with the axis of the femoral shaft starting at the joint line and going proximally. This approach is not adequate for C3 fractures and type B fractures or for group C2 fractures with intra-articular displacement. For such injuries, we use TARPO[65] (Fig. 53–40). The incision for TARPO is enlarged proximally along the interval between the rectus and vastus lateralis muscles and splits the fibers of the quadriceps tendon. It is carried distally to the tibial tubercle. With displacement of the patella medially, the femoral condyles are fully exposed without disrupting the

soft tissues from the bone. Direct anatomic joint reconstruction can be performed with K-wires, screws, and resorbable pins. Placement of lag screws between the femoral condyles must be planned to avoid the LISS and its screws.

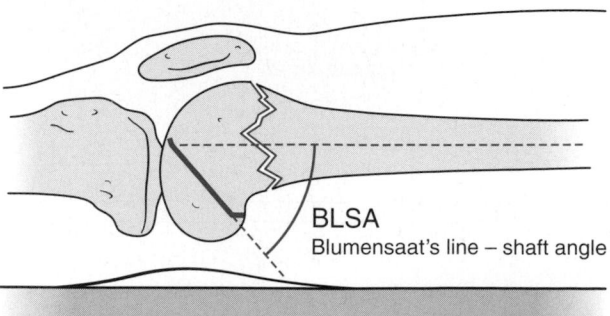

**FIGURE 53–33.** Blumensaat's line-shaft angle (BLSA) as an intraoperative guideline for correct alignment in the sagittal plane (Krettek et al., 1997). With the knee flexed 30°, this line is reported to intersect the lower pole of the patella. However, during reconstruction, we recommend that BLSA be adjusted so that it is equal to that of the opposite femur.

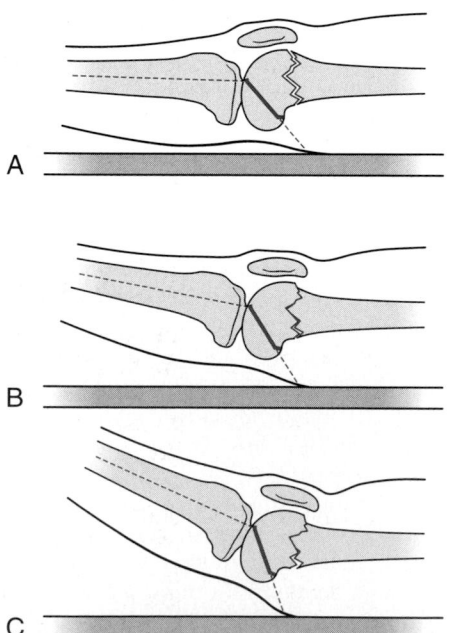

**FIGURE 53–35.** Hyperextension test for recurvatum (Krettek et al., 1997): schematic representation of the effects of recurvatum deformity. *A,* Extension within normal limits (slight overextension between 5° and 10°). *B* and *C,* Recurvatum deformity results in pathologic overextension, depending on the amount of recurvatum deformity.

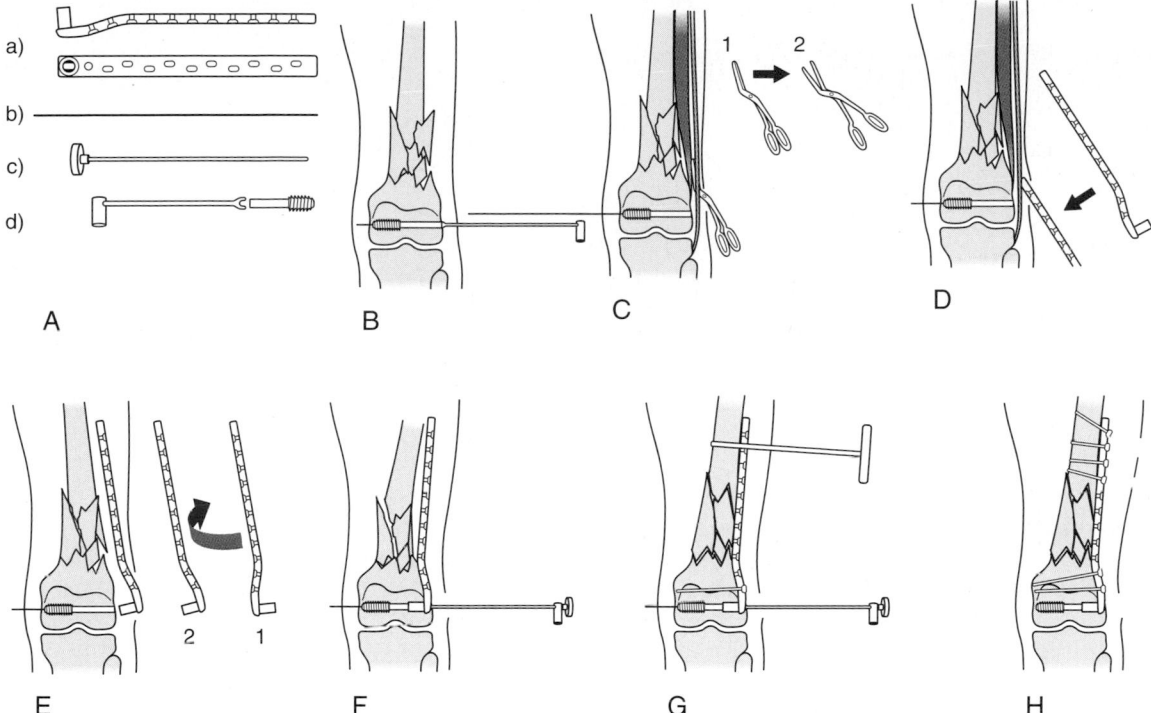

**FIGURE 53–36.** Instruments and step-by-step procedure for minimally invasive percutaneous plate osteosynthesis (MIPPO). *A,* Modified dynamic condylar screw (DCS) instruments. *B,* Screw insertion. *C,* Splitting of the iliotibial tract. *D,* Insertion of the DCS side plate. *E,* Side plate rotation and preparation for assembly. *F,* Side plate sliding on the DCS screw. *G,* Fixation of the plate to the shaft. *H,* Completion of MIPPO.

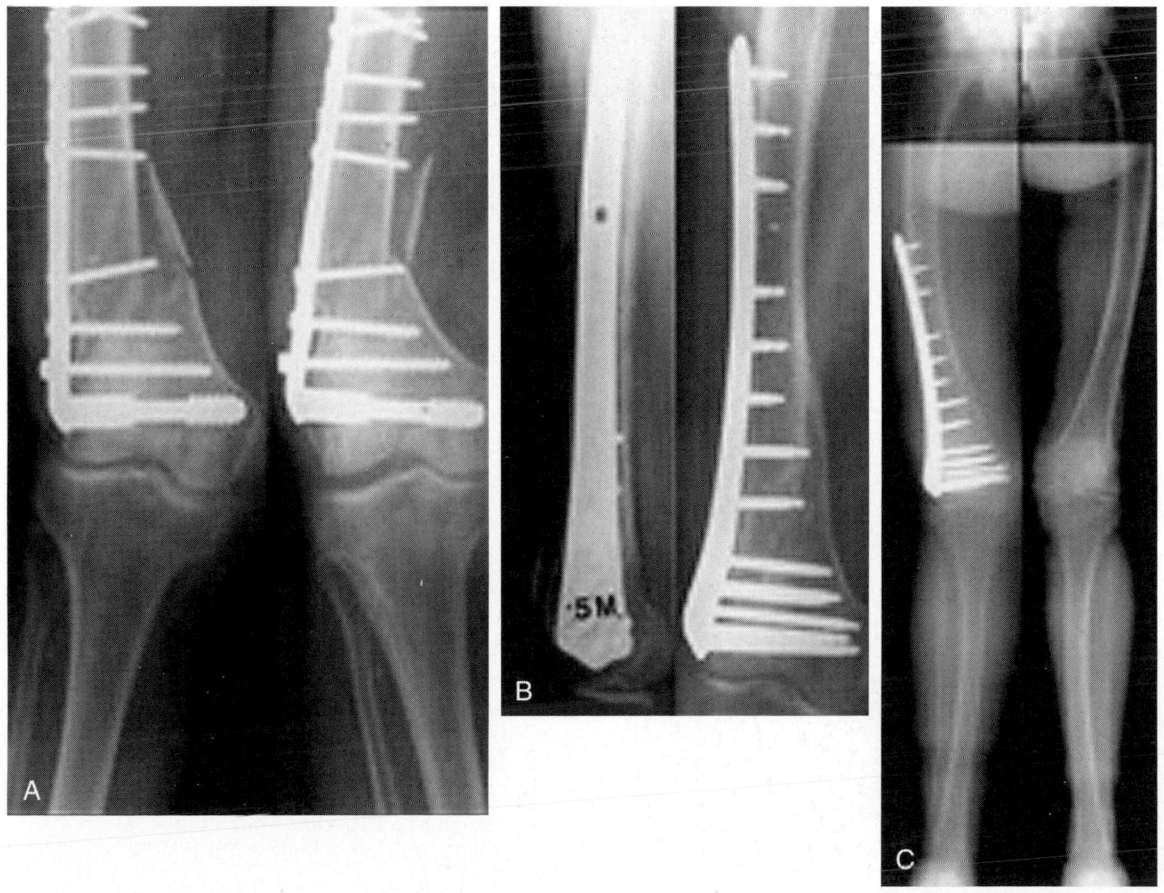

**FIGURE 53–37.** Treatment of instability 1 week after dynamic condylar screw (DCS) fixation in an 86-year-old woman. *A,* Radiographs showing the degree of instability with a "windshield wiper effect." *B,* Healed fracture after 5 months. *C,* Long leg standing views.

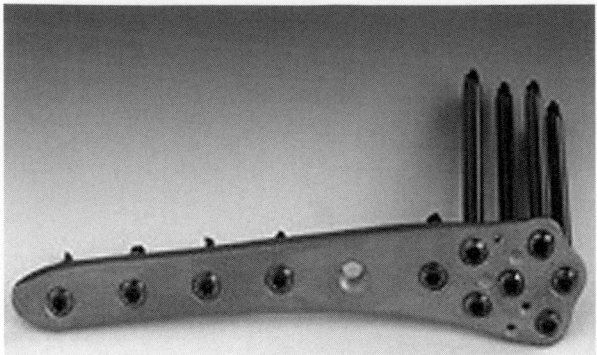
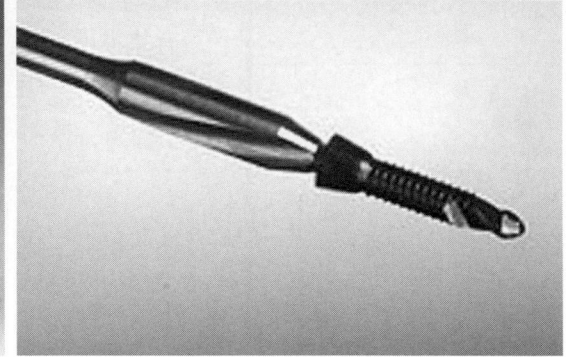

**FIGURE 53–38.** Less invasive stabilization system (LISS) with monocortical, self-drilling, and self-tapping screws and screwdriver.

**Reduction Aids.** After reconstruction of the condylar block, reduction of the block to the proximal fragment is performed with indirect reduction techniques. It is important to realize that this reduction needs to be accomplished before the LISS is definitively fixed to the femur. If manual traction is insufficient, a distractor or a temporary external fixator is useful. In extra-articular fractures, Schanz screws are inserted into either the distal and proximal main fragment or the proximal end of the tibia or medial condyle.

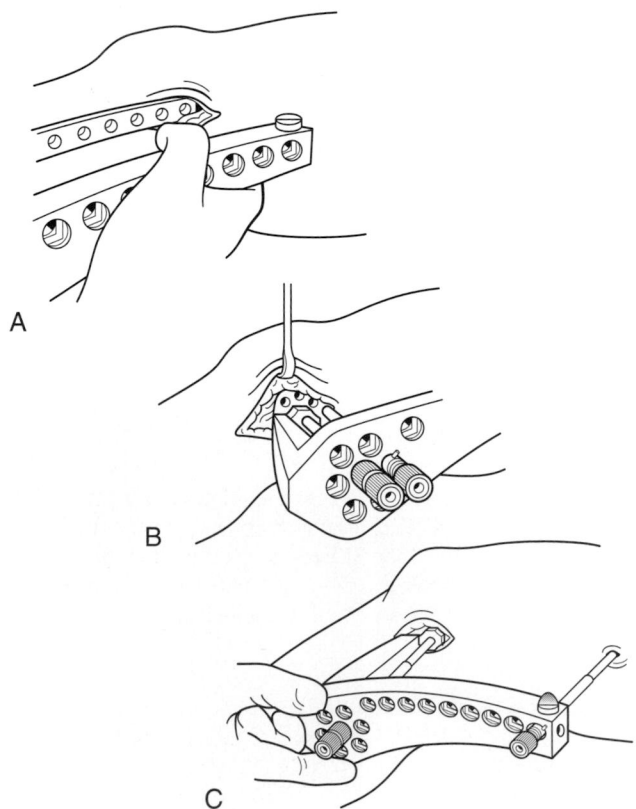

**FIGURE 53–39.** Insertion of the less invasive stabilization system (LISS) through the minimally invasive percutaneous plate osteosynthesis (MIPPO) approach. *A,* Sliding the LISS along the lateral cortex. *B,* Positioning of the end of the LISS on the lateral condyle. *C,* The stabilization bolt is inserted into the most proximal hole.

**Instruments.** The LISS set consists of different insertion guides for the left and right sides, a torque-limited (4.0 Nm) screwdriver, stabilization and fixation bolts for the aiming arm, an aiming device for K-wires, and a tensioning device. The LISS is connected to the insertion guide with a fixation bolt, which has to be inserted into the central distal hole (hole A). The fixation bolt is fixed into the LISS and tightened. For better stabilization during insertion, a stabilization bolt is inserted into hole B, the next proximal hole to hole A. After insertion of the LISS underneath the vastus lateralis muscle, the second stabilization bolt is changed from hole B to the most proximal hole to enhance the stability of the LISS–insertion guide construct (see Fig. 53–39).

**Implant Insertion.** The LISS with its insertion guide is introduced between the iliotibial tract and the periosteum under the vastus lateralis muscle while feeling the tip of the LISS slide along the bone. The LISS is moved proximally and then back distally toward the knee until it has good contact with the lateral femoral condyle. Care is taken to keep the insertion guide at angle of approximately 15° to the sagittal plane to fit to the condyles. Were it oriented strictly in the sagittal plane, a gap between the anterior distal part of the LISS and the lateral femoral condyles would result. This gap might restrict knee motion because of anterior hardware prominence and could direct the distal femoral screws too anteriorly.

**Fixation of the LISS.** In any intracondylar fracture, the condyles are fixed first through an anterior transarticular approach with a lateral parapatellar arthrotomy and carefully placed lag screws, K-wires, or both, followed by determination of the correct position of the femoral condyles. The distal end of the LISS is positioned approximately 1 to 1.5 cm proximal to the joint line. Because of the weight of the insertion guide, the LISS has a tendency to move toward external rotation and create a gap between the condyles and the LISS. Careful biplanar fluoroscopy is recommended to ensure the right position of the LISS at the condyles to avoid a position that is too far anterior. The condylar block usually has a tendency to rotate into a recurvatum position because of pull of the gastrocnemius muscle. This complication can be prevented by putting a pillow under the distal end of the femur and flexing the knee.

When correct alignment has been achieved, the LISS is preliminarily fixed to the condylar block with K-wires in

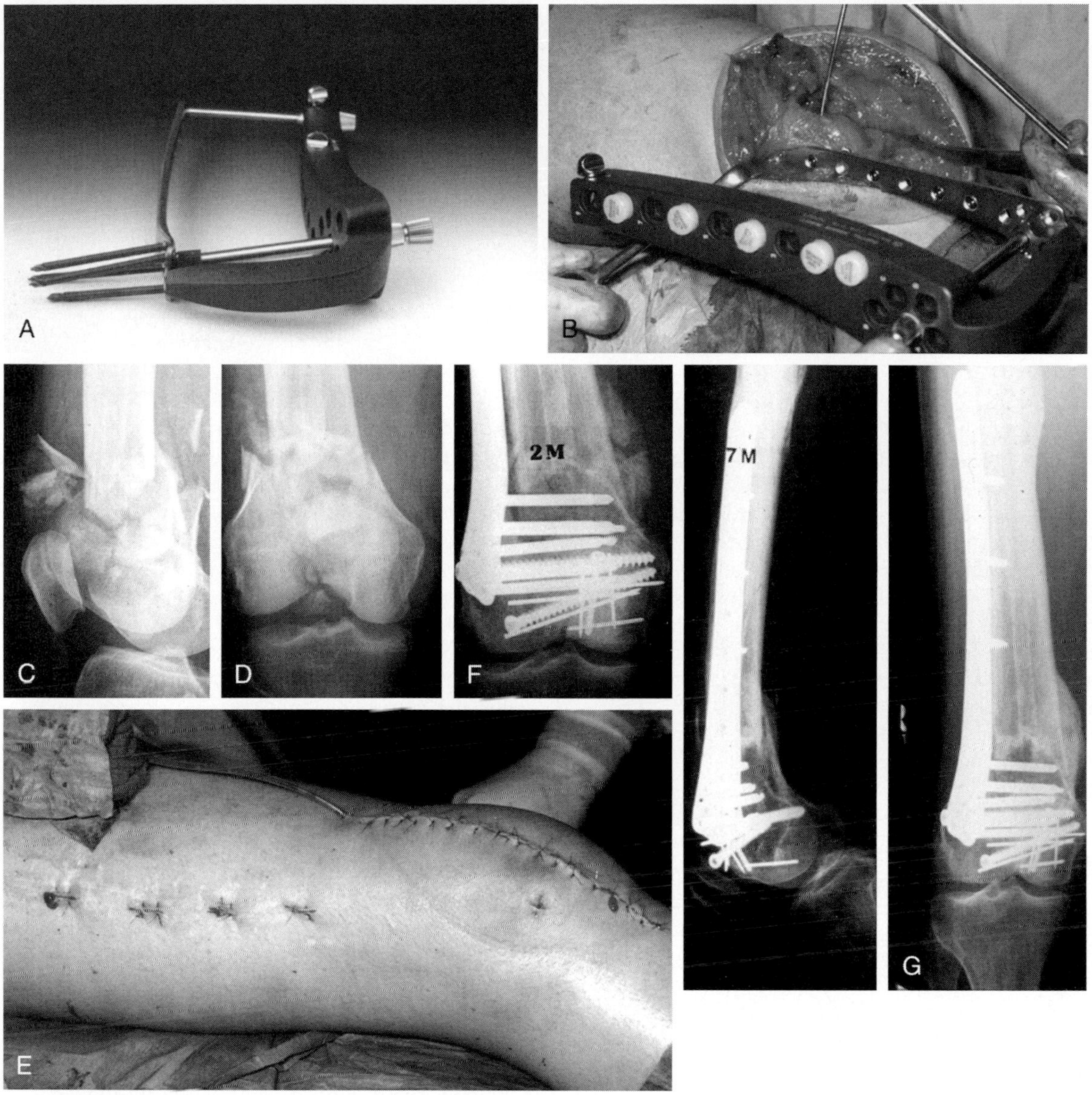

**FIGURE 53–40.** Transarticular approach and retrograde plate osteosynthesis (TARPO) for an intra-articular fracture stabilized with a less invasive stabilization system (LISS). *A,* LISS plate with distal locked screws and insertion guide with distal and proximal stabilizing bolts in place. *B,* Insertion of the LISS through the TARPO approach after reconstruction of the comminuted articular portion of a C3 fracture. *C,* Lateral preoperative radiograph. *D,* Anteroposterior (AP) preoperative radiograph. *E,* Appearance of the leg immediately after wound closure. *F,* AP radiograph 2 months after fixation. *G,* Lateral and AP radiographs of the healed fracture 7 months after injury.

hole A and additional K-wire holes. The direction of the K-wires is checked with the image intensifier to verify that they are running parallel to the distal edge of the femoral condyles. If not done preoperatively, the screws for distal fixation are chosen by a single direct fluoroscopic measurement of condylar width with a ruler.

The position of the LISS on the femoral shaft must also be verified because of the tendency for the proximal end of the LISS to be placed too far anterior on the femoral shaft. Such placement can cause the screw to be inserted at a tangent and result in insufficient holding strength (Fig. 53–41). Good purchase of monocortical screws requires a true lateral position of the LISS on the femoral shaft.

Preliminary fixation to the femoral shaft is done with a K-wire through the proximal fixation bolt, and the tension device is inserted into the second hole to further ensure

fixation and contact between the LISS and bone (Figs. 53–42 and 53–43) so that alignment can be checked. Additional screws are then seated in the proximal and distal fragments. An irrigated drilling guide is used to reduce the heat generated by insertion of the self-drilling screws.

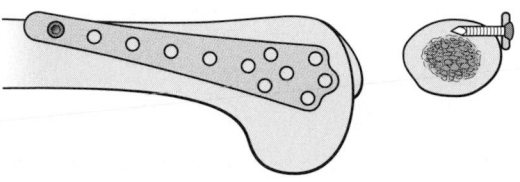

**FIGURE 53–41.** Placement of the proximal end of the less invasive stabilization system (LISS) too far anterior causes tangential placement of screws and dangerously reduces holding strength.

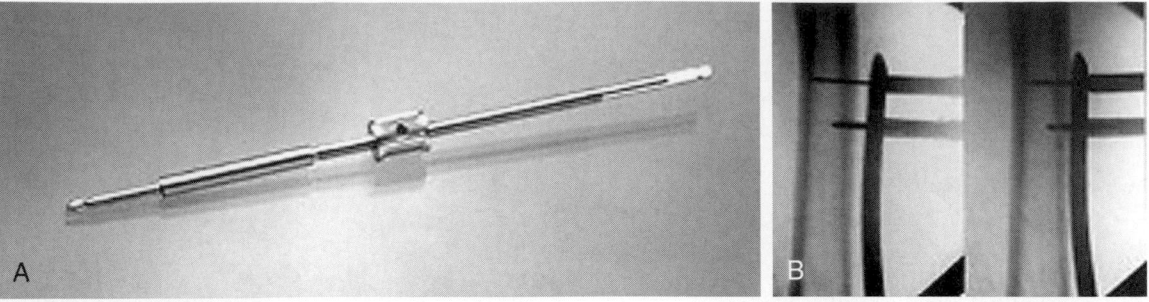

**FIGURE 53–42.** *A,* Tensioning instrument. *B,* Reduction with the tensioning instrument to push the less invasive stabilization system (LISS) onto the femur.

Insertion of the first screw can displace the femoral shaft away from the LISS and cause loss of reduction. Because the screws are locked into the LISS regardless of whether they have any grip in the bone, care is needed to ensure adequate resistance during the drilling phase.

At least four screws should be used in the proximal as well as the distal main fragment. A "stopper" for insertion guide holes can be used to mark screws as they are inserted.

**Tips and Tricks for Reduction.** The first screw in each main fragment determines length and rotation. Because the screw head is threaded and locks into the plate, it is impossible to pull the plate and bone together as it is with traditional unthreaded screw heads. Thus, the LISS instruments include a plate-seating device ("tensioning instrument") consisting of a monocortical self-drilling 4.0-mm screw with a long-threaded shaft. A nut on this shaft is turned to pull the femoral shaft and LISS together (see Fig. 53–42).

When the LISS is used, preliminary reduction must be accomplished first. The stability of the osteosynthesis is not dependent on contact and friction between the plate and the bone. The LISS acts like an internal fixator. Some space between LISS and bone can be tolerated, and to improve alignment, it is sometimes necessary to vary the distance from the bone to the LISS. The plate-seating device can be used to push the plate onto the bone. The 4.0-mm screw gets good purchase in the lateral femoral cortex, and the plate and bone can be approximated. In the metaphyseal area, this plate-seating device usually pulls out of the thin cortex, so additional help is needed. In this region, a large gap between the LISS and the femur disturbs knee motion. To avoid impairment of knee motion, a pointed forceps or a pointed hook retractor can be used to hold the LISS in place until it is securely fixed.

Small frontal-plane deformities can be compensated by loosening the distal screw with a few turns. After reduction under fluoroscopic control (cable technique), the screw can be retightened and the position fixed. With a slight deviation in angle between the LISS and screw, angled interlocking is possible, although major angular changes (>5°) require complete screw removal. Reduction is performed while the LISS is fixed to the bone with K-wires. A change in length and rotation cannot be done without taking all the screws out either proximally or distally.

**Postoperative Treatment.** Postoperative care is the same for conventional and minimally invasive approaches. Patients are initially exercised on continuous passive-motion machines. They are allowed partial weight bearing (15 to 20 kg) and are advanced to full weight bearing when their postoperative radiographs demonstrate callus. In multiply injured patients, the postoperative treatment is adapted to treat the other associated injuries. Casts and splints are not used. Implant removal is facilitated by the use of a specifically designed MIPPO plate remover.

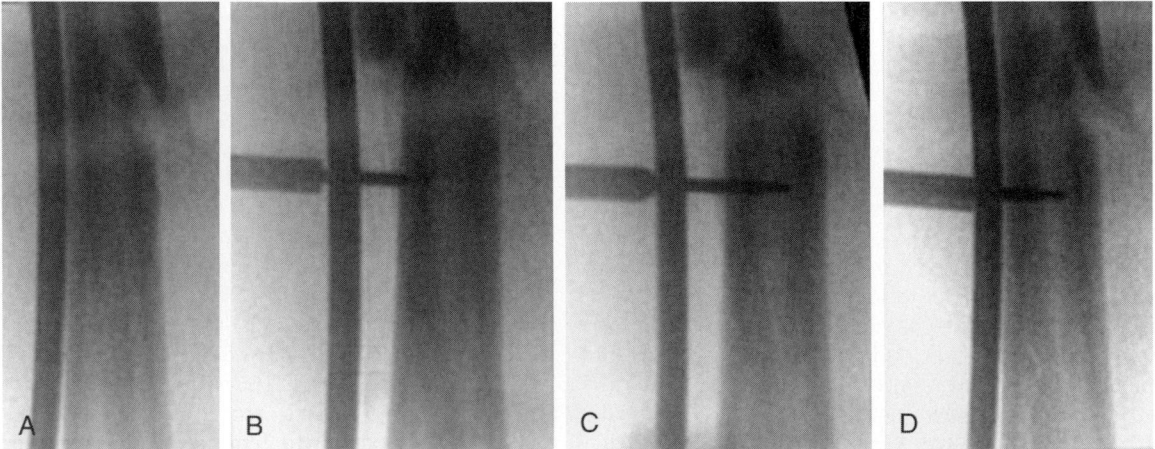

**FIGURE 53–43.** *A,* Reduction before insertion of the tensioning instrument. *B,* Loss of reduction. *C,* Tensioning instrument driven into place. *D,* Use of the tensioning instrument.

*Intramedullary Nail Fixation*

**Antegrade Interlocking Intramedullary Reamed Nail.** It is possible to stabilize supracondylar femoral fractures with an antegrade reamed IM locked nail. Previously, most authors recommended that the fracture be at least 10 cm from the joint line; however, Leung and co-workers[71] in 1991 treated all ASIF type A, type C1, and type C2 fractures within 9 cm of the knee joint. Butler and associates,[10] also in 1991, treated similar patterns of supracondylar-intercondylar femoral fractures associated with ipsilateral femoral shaft fractures with an antegrade interlocked IM rod. The criterion for the distal fracture was that it be within 5 cm of the epiphyseal scar. In both series, intra-articular fracture components were anatomically aligned and preliminarily stabilized before insertion of the locked nail. Dominguez and colleagues have also confirmed satisfactory use of antegrade nailing for distal femoral fractures.[21]

If the intercondylar component was displaced, Butler and associates advocated supine nailing on a radiolucent operating room table, without traction, to allow visualization of the articular cartilage through a parapatellar arthrotomy. Two lag screws were routinely used for fixation of the intracondylar fracture to ensure screw placement in the anterior and posterior portions of the femoral condyles and thereby prevent the screws from impeding subsequent passage of the nail. The arthrotomy was then closed, the patient reprepared, and closed antegrade IM rodding performed. This procedure is much more technically demanding than standard femoral shaft IM nailing and requires a great deal of experience with IM nailing of femoral fractures. Intraoperatively, attention must be directed to maintaining axial alignment, length, and rotation, especially when the procedure is done on a fracture table with the patient in the lateral decubitus position, because the tendency is to then fix the distal fragment in an externally rotated and valgus position. If at all possible, the supine position with use of a distal femoral traction pin is preferable for distal femoral fractures, and specific attention must be paid to maintaining alignment during nail insertion.

Because correct placement of the locking screws necessitates very distal nail insertion, the choice of nail length is extremely important. Leung and co-workers[71] cut the distal 15 mm from the rod to shorten it to just below the distal screw hole. The tip of the nail was then driven as close to subchondral bone as possible. Bucholz and colleagues[9] reported on nail breakage in distal femoral fractures, especially through the distal interlocking screw holes. Most occurred within 5 cm of the fracture after IM nailing with distal interlocking, and these authors cautioned about its use for fractures with significant comminution or for very low fractures. Given these concerns, Butler and associates[10] recommended restricted weight bearing and had no implant failures in their series.

**Retrograde Intramedullary Nailing for Distal Femoral Fractures.** Retrograde IM nailing from an intra-articular, intercondylar approach was introduced during the late 1980s and continues to increase in popularity for more proximal femoral fractures, as well as the distal ones for which such nails were first introduced.[37, 38] Like antegrade IM nailing, this technique offers indirect reduction with less soft tissue exposure and theoretically less interference with fracture healing than occurs with plate fixation through the conventional lateral approach. Proximal and distal locking screws help maintain reduction. However, direct exposure and adequate reduction with supplementary internal fixation are still required for intra-articular fractures, nail insertion does not restore alignment of metaphyseal fractures as it does in the diaphysis, and theoretical concerns about knee joint damage have not been answered with long-term follow-up studies, although problems have not been obvious. Furthermore, initial clinical series have shown some problems with delayed union. However, as experience increases, it appears that for properly selected type A and C fractures and with carefully planned, well-executed procedures, retrograde IM nailing offers a valuable addition to our armamentarium, particularly for floating knees,[31, 92] significant soft tissue injuries, and obese patients and after suitable knee replacement arthroplasties. Retrograde nailing is an advantageous and attractive option for patients with ipsilateral hip fractures. Although extensive intercondylar comminution involving the nail entry site makes retrograde nailing challenging and may contraindicate it, many C1 and some carefully chosen C3 fractures can be treated with retrograde IM nails after adequate articular segment reduction and fixation.

The GSH nail, a short retrograde nail with multiple locking screws and a small sagittal-plane bend several centimeters above its distal end, was the first extensively used retrograde IM nail. It is cannulated for insertion over a guide wire and has an insertion guide for placement of proximal and distal locking screws. Like other short IM nails, it has had some problems with fractures adjacent to its tip, often related to difficulty inserting diaphyseal locking screws. Such problems can be avoided with longer nails that extend to the lesser trochanter. Shorter nails can be valuable when an intramedullary implant such as a hip prosthesis is already present, although subsequent fracture between the two IM devices remains a hazard. Several manufacturers have now developed locking IM nails for retrograde use in the femur, and efforts to improve their design and instrumentation continue. Several issues are common to all of them.

Retrograde IM nailing for distal femoral fractures has certain challenges: (1) the surgeon must reduce the fracture because the nail does not do it automatically. (2) A correct entry site is essential. For an intra-articular fracture (type C1, C2, or C3), the intra-articular components must be reduced anatomically and fixed securely, usually with independent lag screws, in a way that will not interfere with insertion of the nail and that is stable enough so that insertion does not disrupt or destabilize the reduction. (3) The nail must not protrude into the joint. (4) Intraoperative confirmation of alignment (frontal, sagittal), rotation, and length is necessary. (5) Proximal locking is required.

These challenges can be met by careful preoperative planning and meticulous technique.

*Planning.* Preoperatively, with an AP radiograph of the intact knee positioned so that the patella is in the midline, the anatomic axis of the femoral diaphysis is drawn. This line is extended across the knee joint to show the location of the proper nail entry site on an AP radiograph. The joint line is drawn, and the angle laterally between it and the mechanical axis is measured. This anatomic lateral distal femoral angle is normally 81° ± 2°, and duplication of the angle by fracture reduction during nail insertion and distal locking will provide symmetric varus/valgus alignment. Attention must be paid to femoral rotation and to sagittal-plane angulation at the fracture site because they can affect this measurement. Preoperative assessment of the intact lateral radiograph of the distal end of the femur, with the anatomic axis of the femoral shaft drawn in, permits confirmation of the entry site on the lateral view, where it is also the intersection of the mechanical axis and the knee joint surface. Sagittal-plane alignment of the distal femoral fracture may be difficult to determine by inspection of the cortical surfaces, but it can be quantitated well by using the angle made by Blumensaat's line and the anatomic axis (see Fig. 53–33). Similarly, the alignment assessment tools presented earlier (see Figs. 53–28 to 53–35) should be used to ensure that adequate alignment is achieved during retrograde IM nailing. Thus, preoperatively it is important to assess the length of the intact side (see Fig. 53–31), particularly if fracture comminution makes it hard to determine and if there are rotational clues such as the radiographic appearance of the trochanteric region with the knee axis horizontal (see Fig. 53–29) and the arcs of internal and external rotation of the hip (see Fig. 53–28). The internal diameter of the femoral shaft is measured on AP and lateral views to estimate the probable diameter of the nail after reaming has been carried out, usually to a size 1 to 2 mm greater than the diameter of the nail.

*Technique.* The patient is positioned supine on a radiolucent table. The fluoroscope can be on either side of the table but must permit unobstructed view of both entire femurs in the AP, lateral, and oblique planes. The entire involved limb is prepared from the lower part of the abdomen and iliac crest to well below the knee and sterilely draped to permit free manipulation. A percutaneous "stab" incision as described earlier can be used if the fracture does not involve the articular surface. If it does, exposure must be adequate to reduce and fix the condyles and assess the entry site during insertion of the nail. Either a medial or a lateral parapatellar incision, similar to the TARPO approach, will serve. The entry site and direction of its proximal prolongation must be fluoroscopically confirmed on AP and lateral views, which can be done by inserting a guide wire and, once it is properly positioned, passing a cannulated drill over this wire. Correct knee flexion, over a bump of variable size, is essential (see Fig. 53–13).

Once a proper entry site is prepared, a reaming guide wire is inserted across the fracture and proximally into the intertrochanteric region. Reduction can be aided with a Schanz screw in the proximal segment (Fig. 53–44), perhaps one placed for initial temporary external fixation. Femoral alignment during reaming and nailing can be aided by the use of a properly positioned and adjusted external fixator or femoral distractor. Nail length is chosen to allow proximal locking in the metaphyseal bone with its thinner cortex, unless proximal femoral hardware must be accommodated. Reaming through the isthmus and sufficiently proximally to accommodate the diameter of the nail is carried out incrementally with cannulated reamers over the guide wire, and debris is carefully removed from the knee. Enough reaming to permit easy nail insertion is essential because too tight a fit might require excessive force and threaten reduction or associated injuries. Nail insertion must be done precisely, with maintenance of alignment of the nail in the distal segment, which is difficult when the medullary diameter at the fracture site is typically several times larger than the diameter of the nail. Precise insertion is aided by leg positioning and the use of external fixation or manipulating pins or clamps on the distal segment. The nail must be inserted to a proper depth, 1 mm or more below the articular cartilage.[85] Once there, the position of the nail in the distal end of the femur can be stabilized by insertion of its locking screws, aided if required by "Poller" (positioning) screws (Fig. 53–45).

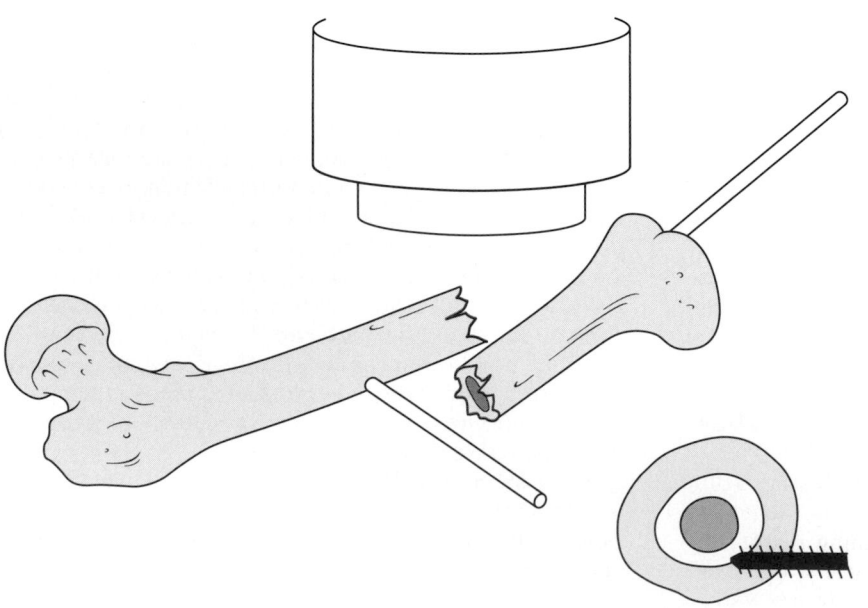

**FIGURE 53–44.** Reduction technique in retrograde nailing. Reduction is facilitated by the use of Schanz screws in the proximal main fragment.

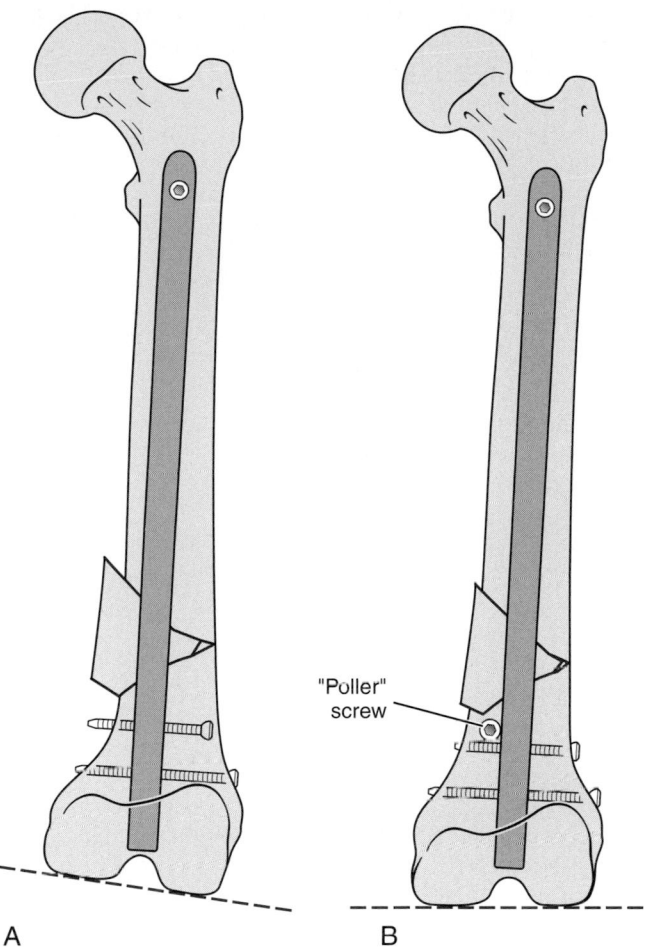

"Poller" screw

**FIGURE 53–45.** Poller screw principle in retrograde nailing. Poller screws help prevent malalignment and increase the stability of the bone-implant complex.

A         B

After insertion of the nail to an appropriate depth and during distal locking of the nail, it is essential to confirm satisfactory alignment with the techniques described earlier (see Figs. 53–28 to 53–35). Definitive AP alignment is done with the mechanical axis–"cable" technique. Sagittal-plane alignment is quickly checked with the hyperextension test (see Fig. 53–35) and more precisely with Blumensaat's line-shaft angle (see Fig. 51–33). Once the angulation is correct, length and rotation are adjusted as needed, and proximal locking is carried out, typically "freehand" in the AP or lateral directions under fluoroscopic guidance, in accordance with the design of the chosen nail. Depending on contact stability of the fracture fragments, either "static" (round hole) or the easier "dynamic" (oval hole) locking may be selected. Locking through the ample soft tissues of the proximal part of the thigh requires care to avoid neurovascular structures, which are theoretically outside the screw tract, and also attention to maintain control of the screw (a suture around it facilitates retrieval if necessary).[96] After locking, alignment should be reconfirmed. If still satisfactory, the knee is thoroughly irrigated to remove any reaming debris, the subchondral position of the nail, including any "end-cap," is confirmed, and the wound is closed in layers, with a

drain used only if bleeding is significant. Although range of motion can and should begin as soon as possible, weight bearing should be protected until fracture healing is sufficient at both the articular and more proximal sites.

Several series have reported on the use of supracondylar IM nails as an alternative to standard AO internal fixation methods in the treatment of some supracondylar-intercondylar distal femoral fractures.[18, 39, 45, 72, 131] Clinical results now appear to be fairly similar. It is important to remember that retrograde IM nails do not provide as much stability as fixed-angle 95° implants,[60, 78] which may compromise the care of some injuries, but the optimal fixation stiffness for distal femoral fractures remains unknown.

## SPECIFIC CONSIDERATIONS AND RECOMMENDATIONS

Because of the tremendous diversity of fractures encountered in the distal end of the femur, specific techniques are required for their stabilization. Fracture types are discussed according to the Müller classification. The fixations described are those recommended and used by us.

### Type A Fractures

Extra-articular distal femoral fractures are subdivided into type A1 (noncomminuted), type A2 (metaphyseal wedge), and type A3 (comminuted) fractures. They are best stabilized with a fixed-angle device, either the 95° CBP or the DCS. In type A1 fractures, temporary reduction of the supracondylar component can be obtained with the use of crossed K-wires. In type A2 and A3 fractures, it is important to preserve the vascularity of all fracture fragments. To accomplish supracondylar reduction and fixation without unnecessary devascularization, the indirect techniques proposed by Mast and co-workers should be used.[74] The condylar fragment is stabilized, and the 95° blade plate or condylar screw is inserted as previously described. Additional lag screws are required in the distal plate holes to stabilize the implant to the condylar fragment. With only a small malreduction or limited comminution in the supracondylar region, distraction for fracture reduction can be achieved by using the AO/ASIF articulated tension device in the reversed mode. The tension device is fixed to the femoral shaft with a 4.5-mm cortical screw, just proximal to the proximal tip of the side plate. The hook on the tension device is reversed and inserted under the proximal end of the side plate in a notch designed for this purpose. Spreading the tension device distracts the fracture by pushing the fixed-angle plate with the attached condyles distally. Distraction and reduction can be checked by fluoroscopy. If necessary, individual large fragments can be teased into reduction on the medial side with the use of a dental pick or small instrument. Again, care must be taken to avoid unnecessary soft tissue stripping. Once reduction has been accomplished, lag screw fixation of these fragments can be achieved through the plate. The tension device is then reversed, the hook is placed in the proximal hole of the side plate, and axial compression is applied across the fracture before insertion of the proximal plate screws (see Fig. 53–26).

With more significant comminution, as in a severe type A3 supracondylar fracture, the reversed tension device may not provide enough distraction to allow atraumatic reduction of the fragments. The AO femoral distractor is an excellent device for this purpose and should be used because of the tremendous mechanical advantage that it allows, not only for distraction but also for maintenance of axial alignment and rotational control of the distal fragment; moreover, use of the AO distractor precludes the necessity of exposing the multiple supracondylar fragments to achieve reduction (see Fig. 53–27). First, the blade plate or condylar compression screw is inserted into the distal end of the femur as described previously. Precise orientation of the blade or screw, as preoperatively planned from a radiograph of the normal side, is essential. One of the distractor bolts or a 5-mm Schanz screw is then inserted into one of the distal two holes of the plate. A second bolt or Schanz screw is inserted into the femur well proximal to the plate. Before insertion of these two bolts, the surgeon should correct rotational alignment. The bolts or Schanz screws for the distractor must be inserted parallel to each other in the frontal plane to maintain axial alignment. By turning the adjusting nut on the femoral distractor, the supracondylar fracture can be distracted to restore axial length and alignment. Fracture reduction is facilitated by overdistraction and by visualizing the fracture on the fluoroscope. Commonly, the fracture fragments are reduced according to the principle of "ligamentotaxis" through the application of tension on the soft tissue attachments. As with the reversed tension device, a dental pick can be used to gently tease in major fragments on the medial side and avoid unnecessary soft tissue stripping. Atraumatic bone clamps are applied if necessary, followed by lag screw fixation of the larger comminuted fragments to each other or to the plate.

If cortical contact has occurred, the distraction can be released, axial compression can be applied proximally with the tension device, and the proximal plate can be fixed to the shaft with 4.5-mm cortical screws. However, if comminution is severe or a bone defect is noted in the supracondylar region, after distraction of the fracture and restoration of axial alignment, rotation, and length, the proximal plate should be held to the femoral shaft with a Verbrugge clamp and fixed with 4.5-mm cortical screws without addressing the comminuted supracondylar area. The surgeon then must assess medial stability. Lack of medial cortical contact as a result of severe comminution or a bone defect may cause the fixed-angle device to fail through cyclical loading. If medial cortical contact is not present or delayed healing is likely, additional medial support with a T plate through a limited medial exposure is indicated. (Adjunctive medial bone grafting is also indicated; see later discussion.) IM nailing, either antegrade or retrograde, is another option for type A distal femoral fractures. Restoration and maintenance of normal alignment are essential.

### Type B (Unicondylar) Fractures

**Type B1 and B2 Fractures.** A type B1 or B2 distal femoral fracture is a unicondylar fracture of either the lateral or medial condyle. The fracture is exposed through a small medial or lateral incision. The condyle must be anatomically reduced and held temporarily with K-wires. In young patients with firm cancellous bone, stable fixation can be achieved with the use of 6.5-mm cancellous screws (32-mm threads) and washers. However, in elderly patients with osteoporotic bone, additional fixation is required. The use of a buttress plate that allows cancellous screw fixation through the distal holes is preferred. Similarly, to counteract the potential for sheer and proximal fracture migration, an antiglide or buttress plate is indicated if the condylar fracture line extends into the proximal metadiaphyseal area. A well-contoured T buttress plate with 6.5-mm cancellous lag screws distally, 4.5-mm cortical screws proximally, and lag screws across the fracture line is recommended.

**Type B3 Fractures.** A type B3 unicondylar distal femoral fracture is a coronal fracture through the femoral condyle (Hoffa fracture). The possibility of both condyles being involved should be remembered. Preoperative CT scanning may be very helpful. As with B1 and B2 injuries, a medial or lateral incision is necessary to expose the articular condyle. Anatomic reduction of the articular surface is mandatory; the reduction is temporarily stabilized with K-wires. Permanent stable fixation is accomplished with lag screws inserted in the AP direction at a right angle to the plane of the fracture. The screws should be inserted as far laterally or medially as possible to avoid the articular cartilage. The size of the fragments determines the size of the screw. For larger fragments, 6.5-mm cancellous screws with 16-mm threads should be used, whereas 4-mm cancellous screws are used for smaller fragments. If it is necessary to insert the screws through articular cartilage because of the particular fracture morphology, the screw heads should be countersunk. Occasionally, screws are best inserted posteriorly, directly across the condylar fracture.

**Osteochondral Fractures.** Osteochondral fractures of the femoral condyles are not uncommon. Sometimes it is difficult to differentiate fractures caused by osteochondritis dissecans from those caused by an acute traumatic episode. If the fracture occurs in the patellofemoral articulation or in the weight-bearing region of the femoral condyles or if it is large enough, it should be anatomically reduced and stabilized with small screws, countersunk as required, or absorbable pins.

### Type C Fractures

Type C fractures are bicondylar supracondylar femoral fractures that separate both condyles from each other and from the femoral shaft.

**Type C1 and C2 Fractures.** Type C1 and C2 fractures are bicondylar supracondylar fractures without intercondylar comminution. Type C2 is complicated by additional supracondylar comminution. The implant of choice is a fixed-angle device, either the 95° blade plate or the condylar compression screw. Of prime importance is anatomic reconstruction of the vertical component of the intercondylar fracture and thus reconstruction of the articular surface, which is accomplished temporarily with provisional K-wire fixation and then definitively with the use of 6.5-mm lag screws, as described in the section on use of the 95° blade plate (see Fig. 53–26). Once the condyles are reconstituted to one fragment, the fracture pattern is converted to type A2 or A3, depending on the presence of supracondylar comminution. The technique for stabilization of the condyles to the shaft is then identical to that previously described for type A2 or A3 supracondylar fractures. If intramedullary fixation is chosen, it is essential that the articular condyles first be reduced anatomically and securely fixed with lag screws. Great care should then be taken to maintain this reduction and ensure anatomically normal alignment during insertion and locking of the nail.

**Type C3 Fractures.** The most complex and difficult of all the distal femoral fractures is a type C3 fracture, which has both supracondylar and intercondylar comminution. This lesion often necessitates a more extensile approach involving bilateral approaches or an osteotomy of the tibial tubercle to ensure an adequate view of the femoral condyles from below. The first step is anatomic reconstruction of the articular surface, which is not always possible because of articular damage, impaction, or severe comminution. However, if possible, it should be accomplished provisionally with the use of K-wires. Definitive fixation of the articular fragments is then accomplished with lag screws. Optimally, they should be inserted through the nonarticular portions of the joint. If not possible, every attempt should be made to avoid inserting the screws through the weight-bearing area of the joint surface, and the screw heads should be countersunk below the level of the articular cartilage. Special types of screws such as Herbert and Acutrak screws should be considered, as should absorbable fixation pins.

If significant comminution is present between the condyles, it is important to not narrow the intercondylar distance and hence the femoral articulation with either the tibia or the patella. In this situation, intercondylar screws across the area of the comminution should be inserted as position screws and not as lag screws. A corticocancellous iliac crest bone graft can also be fashioned to fill the defect and allow increased stability and possibly lag screw fixation across the condyles. The use of a 95° blade plate or a condylar compression screw is optimal. If correctly inserted, they not only restore axial alignment but also, by virtue of the fixed angle, provide better long-term stability. However, in low supracondylar fractures and those with significant intercondylar comminution or condylar bone loss, it may not be possible to obtain stability of the blade or the condylar screw. Additionally, in fractures with significant comminution, especially in the coronal plane, condylar lag screw fixation may preclude the ability to insert a fixed-angle device. In these instances, the implant of choice has been the condylar buttress plate, which allows multiple lag screw fixation in the condyles (see Fig. 53–24). Although the condylar buttress plate is an excellent salvage device for more complicated fractures, it poses significant inherent problems, as discussed earlier. Axial alignment is more difficult to obtain, and fixation failure may occur with repeated cyclical loading. Intraoperative fluoroscopy or radiography is necessary to confirm the alignment; often, additional medial support to prevent long-term varus malalignment is indicated. Plates with locking screws (LISS, locking condylar plate) may therefore be better choices for these complex distal femoral fractures. Once

the articular portion of the distal end of the femur is reconstructed, the condylar block is reattached to the shaft as previously described for type A3 comminuted supracondylar fractures.

### Frontal-Plane Fractures

Fracture lines in the frontal (coronal) plane are found in type B3 and C3 distal femoral fractures (Fig. 53–46A). They produce fragments that are largely, if not totally, articular without extra-articular sites for screw fixation. Frontal-plane fracture fragments are often quite thin. Finding a place to put screws that provide good fixation but do not encroach on the joint is often quite challenging. Helpful techniques for dealing with these injuries— cortical bone "washers" and threaded screw washers—are illustrated in Figure 53–49B to D. K-wires and absorbable pins offer supplementary assistance.

### Temporary Shortening–Secondary Lengthening

In the presence of soft tissue and bone defects, temporary shortening plus secondary lengthening is a good option in situations without sufficient soft tissue coverage in the original length. Later, the soft tissue can be covered in either a single step with a flap in combination with bone reconstruction or continuously.

### Definitive Shortening

Definitive shortening is a simple and safe option in patients with bilateral metaphyseal comminution or contralateral amputation.

### Periprosthetic Fractures above Total Knee Arthroplasty

Supracondylar femoral fractures after total knee replacement are complex injuries that present numerous potential complications. They can significantly alter the integrity of the total knee implant. This increasingly prevalent injury is common enough to be encountered by many surgeons. However, it is still sufficiently rare that few have significant experience with this injury. DiGioia and Rubash[20] defined fractures after total knee arthroplasty as being in the supracondylar region if they were within 15 cm of the knee joint. In addition, fractures occurring within 5 cm of the most proximal extent of the IM stem of a knee prosthesis should be included in this definition. Predisposing factors for fracture after total knee arthroplasty include notching of the anterior femoral cortex, preexisting neurologic disorders, osteopenia, conditions that induce osteopenia (e.g., rheumatoid arthritis, steroid use), and revision arthroplasty with distal femoral bone loss.[17, 20] A wide variety of treatment options have been used in treating distal femoral fractures after total knee arthroplasty, including skeletal traction, brace immobilization and casting, rigid plate-and-screw fixation, IM rodding, and full revision arthroplasty with an IM stem to fix the fracture. The most appropriate management of these injuries has not been clearly defined.

The first reports of periprosthetic distal femoral fractures appeared in the literature in the early 1980s. Hirsch and colleagues,[41] Merkel and Johnson,[77] and Figgie and associates[27] concluded that initial treatment of supracondylar femoral fractures after total knee arthroplasty

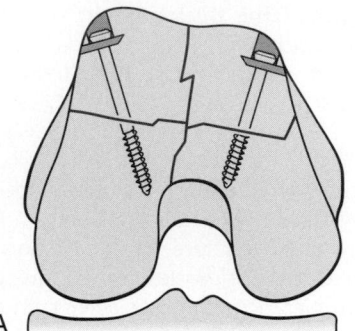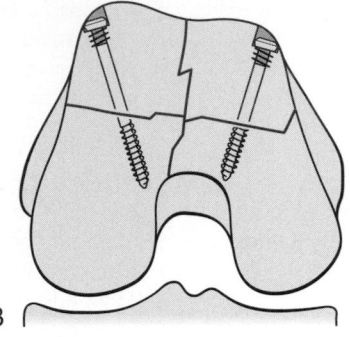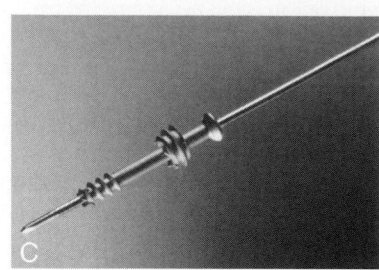

**FIGURE 53–46.** Problems and solutions for frontal-plane fractures. Fixation of a frontal-plane fracture components with 4.0-mm screws. The subchondral bone is usually mechanically strong. However, insertion and countersinking of the screw results in an articular cartilage defect. Placing the screw obliquely, from outside the articular cartilage, results in weak screw fixation. *A,* Schematic drawing of a solution involving a "biologic washer" made out of a piece of cortical bone from the supracondylar zone. It is inserted from the lateral direction, outside the cartilage, to reinforce the screw head's anchorage. The bony washer increases the contact surface and holding power of the screw. An additional screw should be placed more proximally in the articular fragment to stabilize its fixation. *B,* Schematic drawing of a similar fracture repaired with small screw-threaded washers to augment screw fixation. *C,* Photograph of a threaded washer, which is screwed into the bone to lie flush with its surface (Synthes).

should be nonoperative, with closed reduction, traction, and cast bracing. When satisfactory alignment cannot be maintained with such conservative treatment, open reduction with rigid internal fixation is indicated, provided that the bone stock is adequate.[27, 77]

In contrast, Culp and co-workers[17] found that the best treatment of all fractures was early open reduction followed by early motion. Bogoch and associates[4] supported early treatment with ORIF after having significant difficulty maintaining fracture reduction by closed means. Garnavos and colleagues[29] treated seven patients with displaced fractures above a knee prosthesis by traction. Four of these patients later required a surgical procedure to treat malunion or nonunion. However, five of six patients with similar injuries treated operatively returned to their pre-fracture activities. Garnavos and colleagues concluded that displaced fractures above a knee prosthesis should be treated by immediate stable internal fixation and early mobilization and that nonoperative treatment was satisfactory only for undisplaced fractures. Figgie and associates[27] suggested that in the event of implant loosening at the time of fracture, a Neer grade III fracture, or a grade I or II fracture without adequate bone stock, immediate revision arthroplasty with a custom prosthesis and distal femoral allograft is indicated to minimize prolonged immobilization.

Chen and colleagues,[12] in a multicenter review in 1994, incorporated the experience of many investigators to examine the success of operative and nonoperative procedures. They found an 83% rate of satisfactory results in Neer grade I fractures treated conservatively. In contrast, only a 64% rate of satisfactory results was achieved in displaced fractures, and no statistical difference was found between the operative and nonoperative groups. Based on an operative complication rate of 7.4% for deep infection,

a 1.2% perioperative death rate, a nonunion rate of 7.4%, and a malunion rate of 3%, they suggest that conservative treatment is a better initial option, especially in elderly patients with underlying osteoporosis and medical problems. If nonoperative treatment fails to achieve a satisfactory outcome, secondary surgical intervention is advocated. The authors found that the results of a salvage operation are not compromised by the initial trial of nonoperative treatment. In fact, revision arthroplasty was found to have a success rate of 91%, and they concluded that in the treatment of Neer grade II periprosthetic fractures, revision arthroplasty is superior to ORIF.[12] Based on these findings, we recommend the following treatment algorithm for supracondylar femoral fractures after total-knee replacement:

**Type I (Nondisplaced Fractures).** Use nonoperative methods first; if the fracture becomes displaced, go to type II treatment.

**Type II (Displaced/Comminuted Fractures).** If the prosthesis is loose, revise.

Choose ORIF if

1. The patient is unable to tolerate prolonged bedrest.
2. Bone is of sufficient quality to hold screws.
3. The patient has multiple or bilateral fractures.

Choose traction if

1. The patient can tolerate bedrest.
2. Acceptable alignment is achieved.
3. Bone is of poor stock, thus precluding ORIF.
4. The patient has a high risk of infection.

A very similar treatment protocol has been proposed by Digioa and Rubash.[20]

The advent of the GSH and other supracondylar femoral nails provided another option for the treatment of supracondylar femoral fractures above a total knee prosthesis. Rolston and co-workers[98] reported results equal to those achieved with revision arthroplasty. Functional outcome also seemed better in patients managed with the GSH nail versus ORIF with a plate-and-screw implant. Jabczenski and Crawford,[48] in a preliminary small study of retrograde nailing for the treatment of four supracondylar femoral fractures above total knee implants, reported that all fractures had healed and were fully weight bearing at 4 months. However, McLaren and associates[76] warned that the GSH nail is not indicated in any fracture in which the femoral component is loose.

Because of their good fixation even in osteoporotic bone, the LISS and locking condylar plate are excellent options for suitable periprosthetic fractures in which the prosthesis is secure and the fracture configuration permits satisfactory application of these devices (Fig. 53–47).

Supracondylar femoral fractures above a total knee implant are difficult fractures to treat optimally.[111] A wide variety of treatment options are available to the orthopaedic surgeon, including brace immobilization, skeletal traction, open reduction with plate-and-screw fixation, retrograde IM rodding, and revision arthroplasty with a long-stem prosthesis. Although many authors recommend conservative treatment for this injury, the trend is toward operative stabilization to ensure anatomic realignment and early mobilization of the knee joint.[20]

When confronted with a supracondylar fracture above a total knee arthroplasty, the surgeon's first obligation is to assess the integrity of the bone–prosthesis interface. Accurate evaluation is often impossible until the prosthesis is seen in place during surgery. Therefore, the surgeon should be prepared for both femoral and tibial revision with a more constrained prosthetic design. Revision arthroplasty with intramedullary stabilization is indicated for patients whose knee arthroplasties have failed because of instability, stiffness, loosening, or component failure and for patients who have extremely distal or comminuted fractures complicated by femoral metaphyseal osteoporosis.[40]

Technically, when performing revision procedures, femoral bone stock should be preserved and every attempt made to maintain intercondylar continuity. Reconstruction is easier if the two condyles are maintained as one unit. If comminution is present along with loss of ligamentous stability, a more constrained prosthesis with an IM stem is indicated. Often, even with tight-fitting stems, it is difficult to maintain femoral length because of comminution and osteopenia of supracondylar bone stock. Bone allograft consisting of a femoral head or the entire distal end of the femur may be needed.[29] The tendency toward proximal migration of the joint line should be avoided because it retards flexion and transmits increased stress to the femoral components. The patellofemoral articulation can serve as a guide to joint placement.[40]

Internal fixation is recommended for fractures in which the prosthesis has a stable interface with the condyles,

provided that adequate bone stock is available distally to permit fixation. Modern plating techniques, though very successful in younger patients with supracondylar distal femoral fractures, have met with limited success in the treatment of fractures above an implant because of the paucity of distal bone stock and the poor quality of bone available for fixation. The GSH supracondylar femoral nail has the advantage of allowing internal fixation without opening the fracture site, thus facilitating early rehabilitation. When applied to periprosthetic fractures above total knee arthroplasties, the nail is placed through the intercondylar notch of the femoral component. The nail is available in 12- and 13-mm diameters and fits through many standard implants. However, a preoperative sunrise radiograph should be obtained to measure intercondylar distance before surgery. The GSH nail can be used only when the prosthesis is one that provides access to the femoral medullary canal through the intercondylar entry site.[48] Although preliminary results are encouraging,[48, 98] this device is in investigational stages and requires further study. As mentioned earlier, distal femoral fixation plates with fixed-angle locking screws are another alternative to consider.

### Bone Grafting

All patients undergoing ORIF of distal femoral fractures should have the ipsilateral iliac crest prepared sterilely in case adjunctive bone grafting is necessary. For comminuted supracondylar fractures (either in elderly patients or in younger patients after high-energy trauma) and for fractures in which adequate medial stability cannot be achieved at the time of fracture reduction and stabilization, primary medial autogenous cancellous bone grafting is indicated. For fractures with significant bone devascularization, such as high-energy or open fractures, bone grafting is also indicated. However, the timing of grafting depends on the condition and control of the soft tissues. If at all in doubt, bone grafting should be delayed after severe soft tissue injuries. In fractures necessitating additional medial plating (i.e., when significant instability or a bone defect is present), bone grafting is also indicated. The liberal use of autogenous cancellous bone graft in supracondylar femoral fractures with bone loss, severe comminution, or bony devascularization helps preserve the integrity of the implant until bone healing can occur.

The intercondylar portion of the distal end of the femur is well vascularized, and nonunion is very rare. The only indication for intercondylar bone grafting is for significant comminution or bone defects, especially between the condyles. By fashioning a well-contoured corticocancellous graft, the defect can be spanned to permit compression fixation between the condyles and increase the stability of the construct.

Most investigators recommend the use of autologous bone graft when medial comminution or bone loss is present.[30, 81, 99, 103] Recently, however, Ostrum and Geel[93] prospectively investigated the use of indirect reduction techniques, as described by Mast and co-workers,[74] without supplementary bone graft for the treatment of

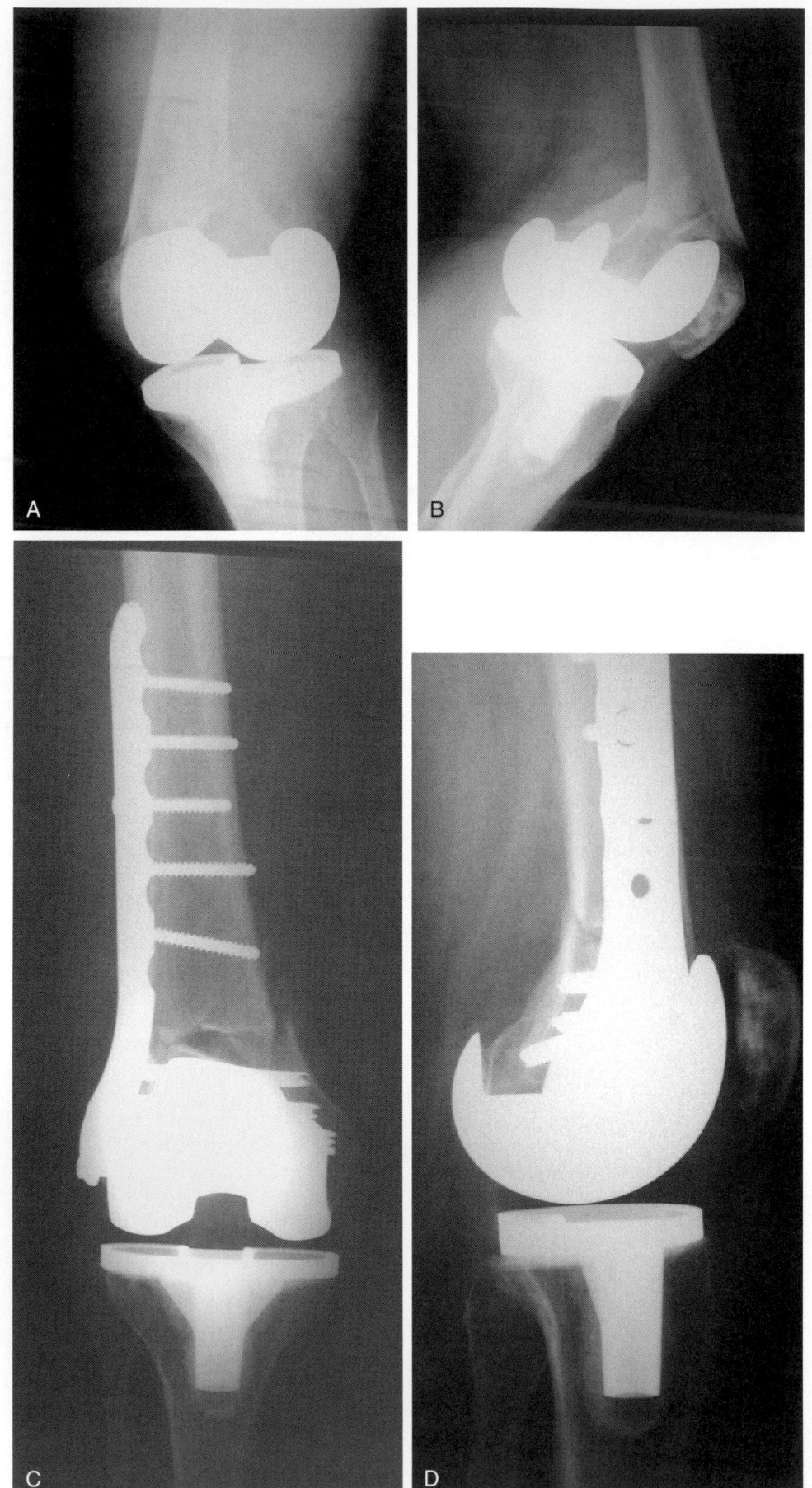

**Figure 53–47.** Fixation of a periprosthetic supracondylar fracture with a locking plate. *A, B,* Preoperative anteroposterior and lateral radiographs. *C, D,* Healing fracture with anatomic alignment 10 weeks after repair. (Case of John Froehlich, M.D., Brown University, Providence, RI.)

supracondylar-intercondylar fractures of the femur. The obvious advantages include not only avoidance of the need for additional bone graft surgery but also preservation of medial bony and soft tissue vascularity. These authors reported excellent to satisfactory results in 86.6% of patients treated with this technique. Most of the failures, they believed, resulted not from the indirect reduction techniques but rather from the extent of the bony injuries. They suggested that this technique may not be suitable for severe open fractures or when marked osteoporosis is present; for such cases, they recommended standard bone graft techniques. Similar good results were reported by Bolhofner and associates.[5] Bone loss, wide displacement, or injury-related soft tissue stripping may require a medial bone graft. Rather than going around the fixed fracture and causing additional devascularization, the graft can be inserted through the fracture site before it is fixed or, alternatively, through a small medial incision. Also through a medial incision, formation of an adequate bony medial buttress can be encouraged by fixation of a corticocancellous graft, as illustrated in Figure 53–48.

### Adjunctive Fixation Techniques

**Bone Cement (Liquid Injection).** In elderly patients with severe osteoporosis, the holding power of screws is often inadequate to provide stable fixation. Screw fixation can be greatly enhanced with the use of methyl methacrylate. It is advisable to keep both the methyl methacrylate powder and the liquid methyl methacrylate refrigerated before use to slow the polymerization process down. Questionable screws are removed, and the precooled methyl methacrylate is mixed and (while liquid) poured into a 30-mm plastic syringe. It is then injected into the screw holes under pressure. (To facilitate this process, it is useful to widen the tip of the syringe with a 3.5-mm drill

bit.) The screws are then inserted into their respective holes but are not fully tightened. Once the cement hardens, the screws are tightened the final few turns. This technique greatly enhances the stability of the screw–bone interface and provides more stable fixation. Care must be taken to avoid extravasation of the methyl methacrylate into the fracture site because in this location it may interfere with fracture healing. In addition, if the distal cortex of a screw hole is intra-articular, the insertion of methyl methacrylate under pressure is contraindicated to avoid extravasation of cement into the joint.

**Bone Cement (Dough Insertion Technique).** Struhl and colleagues[117] described a different technique for methyl methacrylate enhancement of screw fixation in osteoporotic patients with supracondylar-intercondylar femoral fractures. The proximal end of the distal fragment is cleaned of all cancellous bone by curette and saved as bone graft. A dynamic compression screw is then placed in the distal fragment. Methyl methacrylate in its doughy state is finger-packed to fill the distal fragment and surround the screws. Care is taken to exclude cement from the fracture site. The proximal fracture fragment is then approached by removal of cancellous bone from the medullary canal. A cement restrictor is placed in the proximal femoral canal above the proposed level of the plate. The canal is then filled with relatively liquid cement. Again, cement is kept from the fracture site. The cement is allowed to harden, and reduction is accomplished. The dynamic compression screw–side plate construct is rotated into place along the proximal shaft, and the AO tensioning device is used to give maximal compression. The proximal screw holes are then filled after drilling and tapping through the hardened intramedullary cement. Bone graft is packed around the fracture site. The authors stated that this technique provides sufficient fixation in osteoporotic patients to allow early motion and partial weight bearing.

**Cerclage Wires.** The use of adjunctive cerclage wire fixation may be indicated in elderly patients with osteoporotic bone. To avoid devascularization of the fracture, its use should not be indiscriminate, but one or two cerclage wires in the supracondylar area may occasionally help restore reasonable fragment alignment and thereby provide greater stability.

## FOLLOW-UP CARE AND REHABILITATION

Postoperatively, the area from the groin to the toes is covered by a soft, bulky dressing. Müller and colleagues[86] recommended immobilization of the knee at 90° of flexion on a Böhler-Braun frame for 3 to 4 days. Following the work by Driscoll and co-workers,[22] it became apparent that immediate continuous passive motion not only enhances cartilage healing but also helps prevent quadriceps contractures, decreases swelling, and enhances early knee motion. Use of the continuous passive-motion machine immediately after surgery is tolerated better by the patient if the joint is injected before wound closure with 20 mL of 0.5% bupivacaine with epinephrine (1:200,000). Continuous passive motion is maintained full-time until ambulation is commenced on the third to

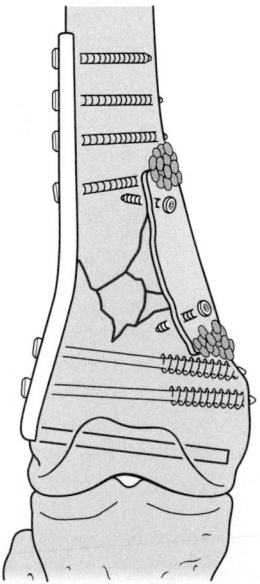

**FIGURE 53–48.** Bone grafting technique in the presence of large medial defects (Krettek and Tscherne, 1994). To avoid additional soft tissue disruption, the corticocancellous graft is inserted through a separate medial approach and fixed with small-fragment screws.

fourth postoperative day and thereafter used only inter-mittently while the patient is in bed. In conjunction with this treatment, the patient initiates active exercises of the quadriceps and hamstring musculature on postoperative day 2. Gait training on days 3 to 5 progresses from use of the parallel bars to a walker or crutches, with weight bearing as determined by intraoperative stability of the fixation. If stable fixation has been achieved, the patient can begin immediate minimal weight bearing (20- to 30-lb loading). Active physical therapy and limited weight bearing with crutches or a walker are continued until clinical and radiographic evidence of fracture healing. At this point (usually 2 to 3 months after surgery), the patient progressively increases weight bearing and resistance exercises until solid union is achieved at about 4 to 6 months.

The necessity for additional support is determined by the presence of additional or associated injuries, the type of reduction, and the stability of fixation obtained at the time of surgery. In patients who have associated ligamentous disruptions of the knee, functional bracing or cast bracing is indicated to control motion in the allowable range and yet allow early active mobilization of the knee. However, the primary indication for additional external support is tenuous internal fixation. Only the surgeon, at the end of the procedure, can determine the efficacy of the fixation. If any suspicion remains regarding the adequacy of fixation, the holding power of the bone, or the stability of the construct, external protection must be used to avoid loss of fixation, malunion, or nonunion before bone healing. However, as with all periarticular fractures, early active motion must be encouraged to promote restoration of joint motion and function. The judicious use of functional or cast braces lends external support while still allowing active rehabil-itation. In patients with markedly unstable fixation, postoperative skeletal traction provides the best control and stability for fracture healing. The patient should be encouraged, even in traction, to start early and active (though limited) functional rehabilitation of the knee. Intermittent, brief removal of traction for active-assisted range-of-motion exercises can often be done until sufficient fracture healing allows discontinuation of skeletal traction.

# COMPLICATIONS

## Infection

The major complication of operative intervention in the management of distal femoral fractures is infection. In the older literature, especially that of the 1960s, the postop-erative infection rate was approximately 20%.[89, 116] In more recent literature, the infection rate from operative stabilization of these demanding fractures has ranged from zero to approximately 7%.[13, 30, 36, 53, 81, 99, 103] Factors that predispose to infection include (1) high-energy injuries, especially when extensive bony devascularization has occurred; (2) open fractures; (3) extensive surgical dissection that further compromises bony vascularity; (4)

an inexperienced operating team with prolonged open wound time; and (5) inadequate fixation. Acceptable rates of postoperative infection can be obtained with meticulous surgical technique, gentle handling and preservation of soft tissues, the use of prophylactic antibiotics, and adequate, rigid bony stabilization with external or internal fixation. Optimal timing of surgery is essential, especially with open wounds or major soft tissue injuries. Addition-ally, open wounds should not be primarily closed but should be treated by serial débridement in the operating room until delayed primary closure or additional soft tissue procedures can be safely performed. By strict adherence to these principles, the benefits of stable internal fixation and early mobilization will produce better functional results and outweigh the risks of infection (a 1% to 2% incidence is acceptable).

The presence of a postoperative infection mandates aggressive management. The patient must be immediately returned to the operating room for irrigation and débride-ment. As long as the internal fixation is sound and adequate, it should not be removed. If a large soft tissue defect is present, antibiotic-impregnated cement beads serve not only to leach antibiotic locally into the hematoma but also as a soft tissue spacer. Repeated irrigation plus débridement is performed until bone cultures indicate that the infection is controlled. Antibiotic coverage is recommended for 6 weeks or longer if a deep wound infection involves the knee or fracture site.

## Nonunion

Nonunion of fractures of the distal third of the femur have been reported to occur regardless of the treatment modality used. The incidence varies greatly in the literature, but some of the early larger series reported a rate of nonunion after ORIF of more than 10%.[89] More recent series indicate a nonunion rate of zero to 4% with ORIF.* The nonunion invariably occurs in the supra-condylar rather than the intercondylar region. Factors predisposing to nonunion include (1) bone loss or defect; (2) high-energy injuries, especially fractures that are open or comminuted with extensive soft tissue stripping and loss of bony vascularity; (3) inability of the surgical team to obtain adequate bony fixation; (4) failure to augment healing in comminuted fractures with autogenous bone graft; and (5) the presence of a wound infection.

Nonunion of the distal end of the femur is an extremely difficult management problem, and the best treatment is prophylaxis. In long-standing nonunion, the knee joint becomes stiff, and most of the motion that is present occurs through pseudarthrosis. Successful management requires that both stable fixation of the nonunion and restoration of knee movement be regained in one stage. Early postoperative mobilization increases the vascularity to the area and decreases the lever arm on the fixation of the nonunion. Nonunion fixation in the supracondylar region, if the fractures are high supracondylar ones, can be

---

*See references 13, 30, 36, 53, 81, 95, 99, 103, 122, 130.

accomplished with a locked IM nail. However, most cases of supracondylar nonunion are not amenable to this form of treatment and require internal fixation with a fixed-angle device and side plate. The addition of lag screws significantly increases the stability across the nonunion site. If the nonunion is hypertrophic, stable fixation with subsequent restoration of mechanical stability is all that is required. If the nonunion is atrophic, in addition to mechanical stability, the biologic potential of the bone to heal must be restored by decortication and bone grafting in all such injuries (Fig. 53–49). If a bone defect is present or the distal fragment is small and osteopenic, adequate fixation with a fixed-angle device may not be possible. In that case, both medial and lateral buttress plating may be indicated. If distal femoral fixation cannot be achieved, Beall and colleagues[2] recommended the use of an IM rod driven across the knee joint as a salvage procedure (Fig. 53–50).

## Malunion or Malalignment

Malunion after treatment of distal femoral fractures is more common with conservative than with operative treatment. The major problems are malrotation, shortening, and axial malalignment. If conservative treatment with traction or bracing cannot maintain length, rotation, or axial alignment, ORIF should be considered.

Even if anatomic reduction is obtained by ORIF, the distal femoral fixation has a tendency to fail and produce a varus malunion if significant supracondylar comminution is present.[100] To avoid this complication, supplementary medial bone grafting or plating is indicated. An additional problem with ORIF is fixation of the distal fragment in either too much extension or too much flexion. This mistake can occur when the distal fragment is small and it is difficult to determine the correct flexion or extension alignment at the time of surgical reconstruction. Varus or valgus deformities can result from the use of fixed-angle devices from the lateral side of the distal end of the femur, unless these devices are absolutely parallel to the knee joint AP axis. To avoid these potential malalignment problems with internal fixation, adequate preoperative planning is essential. Determining normal anatomy from the opposite, uninvolved side, choosing the exact location for the fixation device, and obtaining adequate intraoperative radiographs to ensure that the preoperative plan is followed all help avoid the problem of malalignment. (See also Alignment Control, p. 1983.)

When IM nails are used for distal femoral and

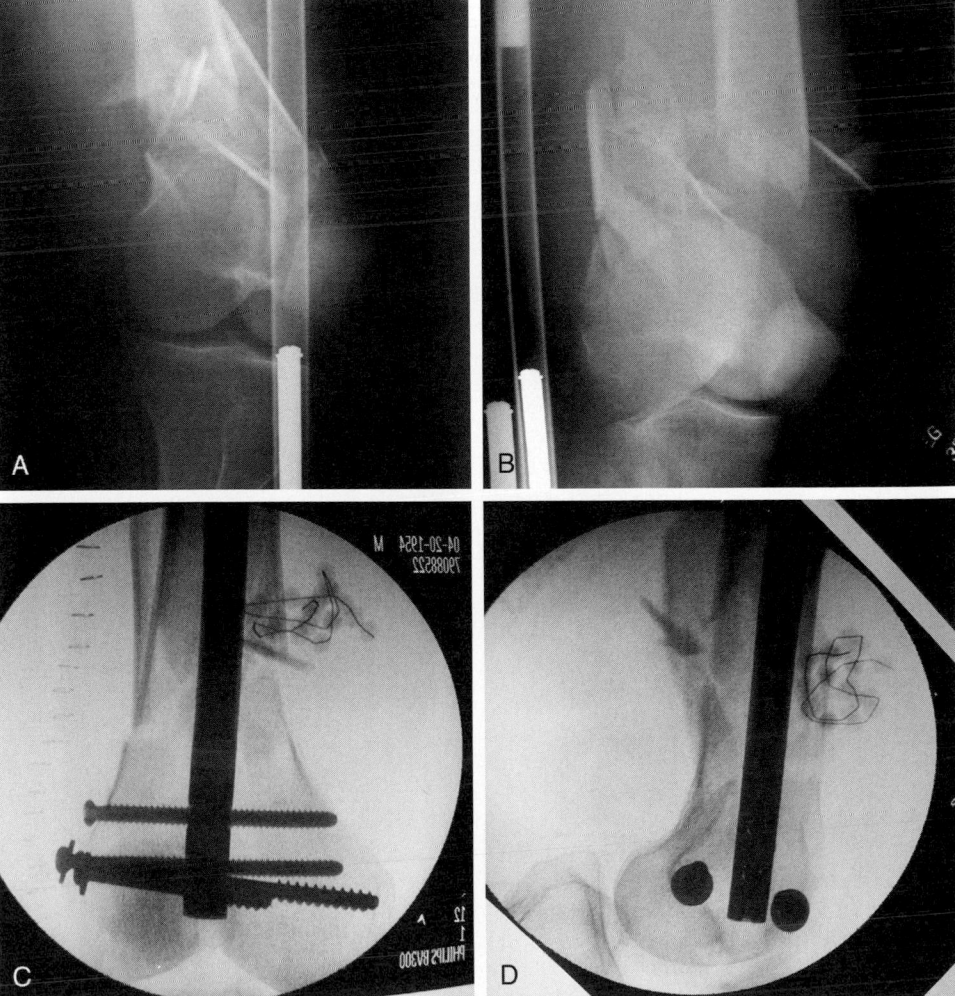

**FIGURE 53–49.** Atrophic nonunion of a supracondylar femoral fracture. Successful treatment with a blade plate after initial retrograde intramedullary (IM) nailing. *A, B,* Preoperative radiographs of a type 3A open femoral fracture after a 10-m fall. *C, D,* Anteroposterior (AP) and lateral radiographs after débridement and open reduction plus internal fixation with intercondylar lag screws and a retrograde IM nail.
*Illustration continued on following page*

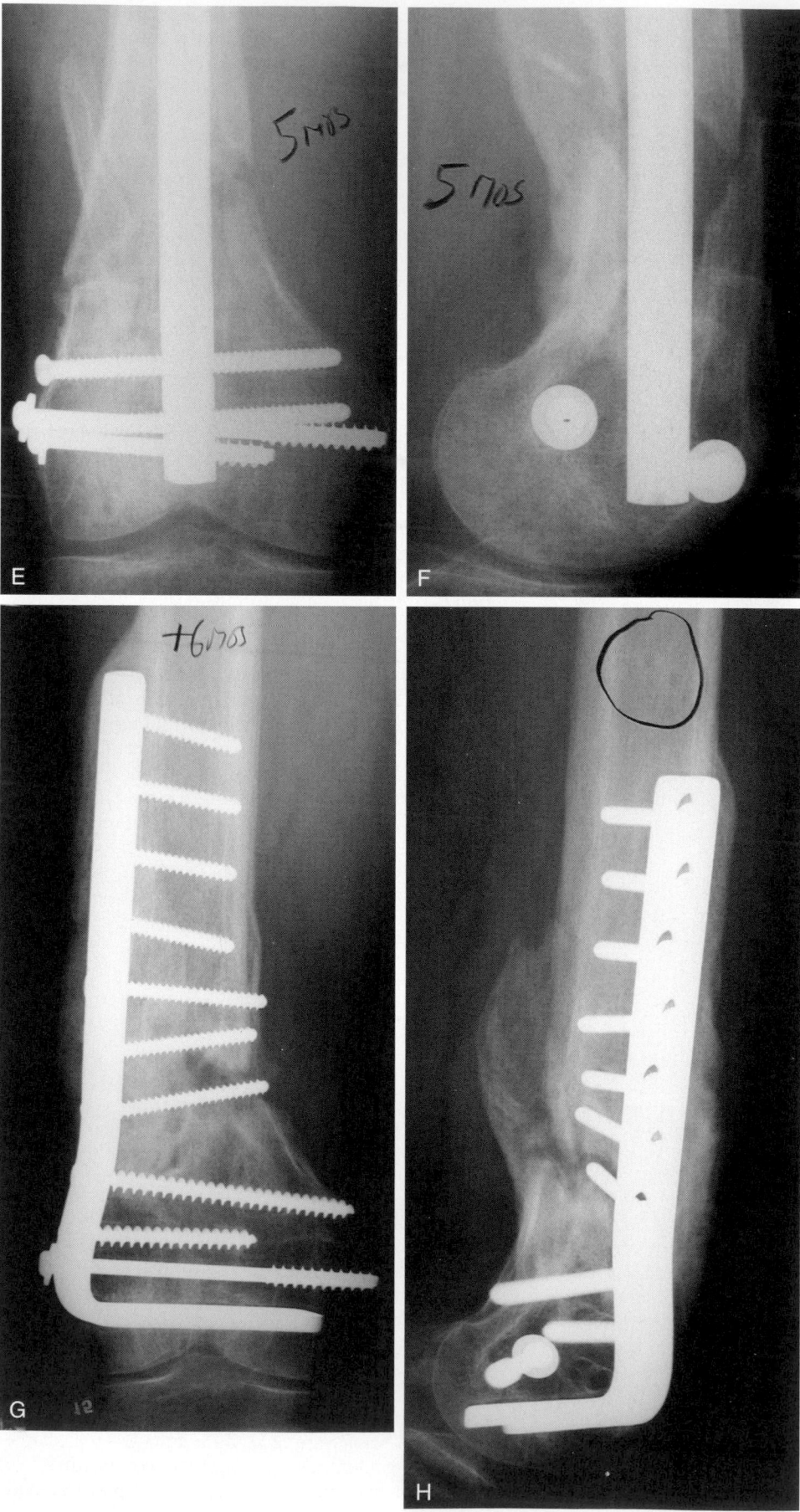

**Figure 53–49** *Continued. E, F,* AP and lateral radiographs 5 months later. The patient had persistent pain, hardware loosening, and no callus bridging the metadiaphyseal nonunion, although the articular fracture is healed. Tissue taken for culture at exploration proved negative. *G, H,* AP and lateral radiographs 6 months after repair. A 95° blade plate was applied with an external tension device (*circled* screw hole on the lateral view), and an iliac crest bone graft was used to stimulate healing in atrophic nonunion.

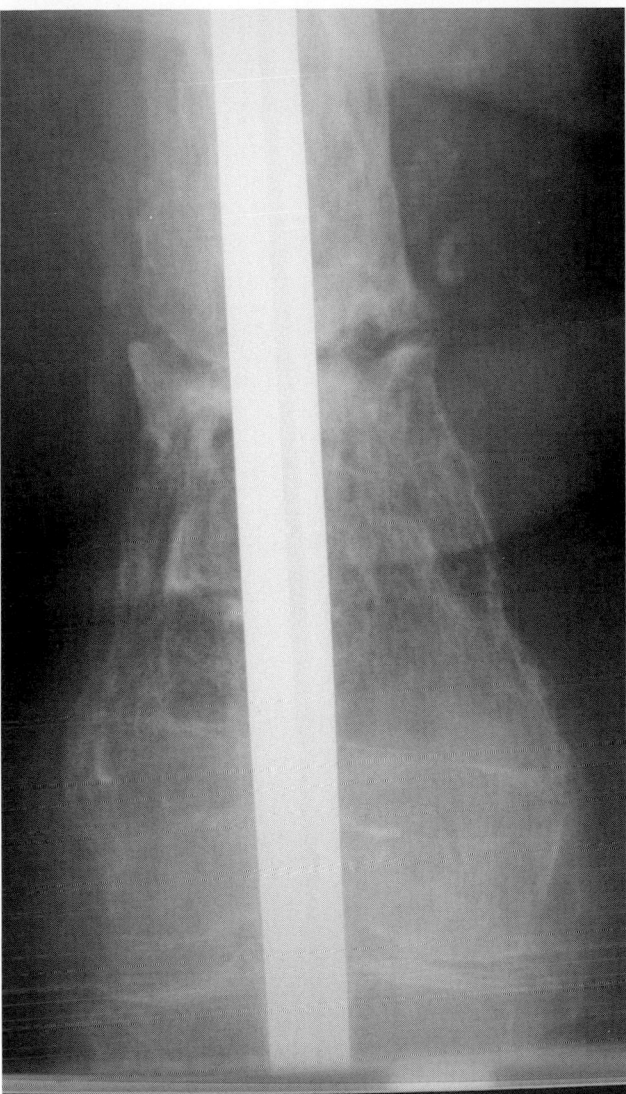

**FIGURE 53–50.** Atrophic aseptic nonunion 20 years after radiation therapy for soft tissue sarcoma. After failure of fixation with a 95° blade plate, an antegrade intramedullary nail across the knee joint permitted pain-free ambulation for 6 years until the nail broke at the nonunion. Its replacement with a larger closed-section nail was again successful.

supracondylar fractures, especially with the patient on a fracture table in the lateral decubitus position, there is a tendency to nail the distal fragment in valgus angulation with excessive malrotation. Appreciation and avoidance of this potential problem are essential at the time of nailing.

Once distal femoral malunion is established, the degree and planes of deformity must be exactly determined, which requires adequate AP and lateral radiographs of the involved and the contralateral side and appreciation of both displacement and angulation in all planes. Shortening must also be ascertained, and scanograms may thus be indicated. Rotational malalignment is best determined clinically or, if necessary, with CT scanning. Correction of malunion is accomplished with a supracondylar osteotomy. The type of osteotomy is determined by the deformity present (Fig. 53–51).

Rarely, an intercondylar malunion is associated with deformity of the articular surface. Tomograms or a CT scan may be required to establish the exact degree of the deformity. This problem significantly complicates treatment because an intra-articular osteotomy is required to correct the additional deformity.

## Loss of Fixation

One of the major complications after ORIF of the distal end of the femur is loss of bony fixation. Factors predisposing to loss of fixation include (1) increased comminution, (2) increased age and osteopenia, (3) low transcondylar and comminuted intercondylar fractures in which distal fixation is hard to achieve, (4) poor patient compliance with loading and weight bearing before healing, and (5) infection. Optimally, early mobilization is preferred after ORIF, initially with continuous passive motion and subsequently with active and active-assisted physical therapy. However, the surgeon must determine at the time of surgery the degree of bony fixation achieved. If the quality of the bone or the fracture type prevents stable or adequate fixation, mobilization should be delayed, and supplementary procedures such as bone grafting or double plating are required. Once evidence of progressive loss of fixation is noted, the surgeon must decide whether union can still be achieved, by decreasing mobilization or weight bearing, without loss of function. If not, repeat open reduction and stabilization are indicated. The addition of a biologic stimulator such as a bone graft is also useful in this scenario to speed union before fixation is lost.

Whenever loss of fixation occurs, infection must be definitely excluded as a cause. Careful clinical evaluation, a leukocyte count with differential, a sedimentation rate, and aspiration under fluoroscopy are all probably indicated. In addition, a nutritional consultation may be advisable. In a nutritionally depleted patient, some form of hyperalimentation should be considered before further reconstructive procedures are undertaken[49] (see Fig. 53–49).

## Contractures and Decreased Knee Motion

After treatment of distal femoral fractures, it is common to have some loss of motion. However, it is important to obtain functional range of motion (i.e., full extension and at least 110° of flexion). Moore and co-workers[84a] found that patients with decreased range of motion were usually young patients who had sustained high-energy trauma. The extent of their soft tissue injuries often necessitated immobilization of the knee joint. To prevent this complication, we advocate early motion of the knee joint, particularly in patients with an intra-articular fracture component.

If range of motion is limited, the cause must be determined. Possibilities include (1) malreduction of the articular surface, either patellofemoral or tibiofemoral; (2) intra-articular hardware; (3) intra-articular joint adhesions; (4) ligamentous or capsular contractures; (5) quadriceps or hamstring scarring; and (6) post-traumatic arthritis.

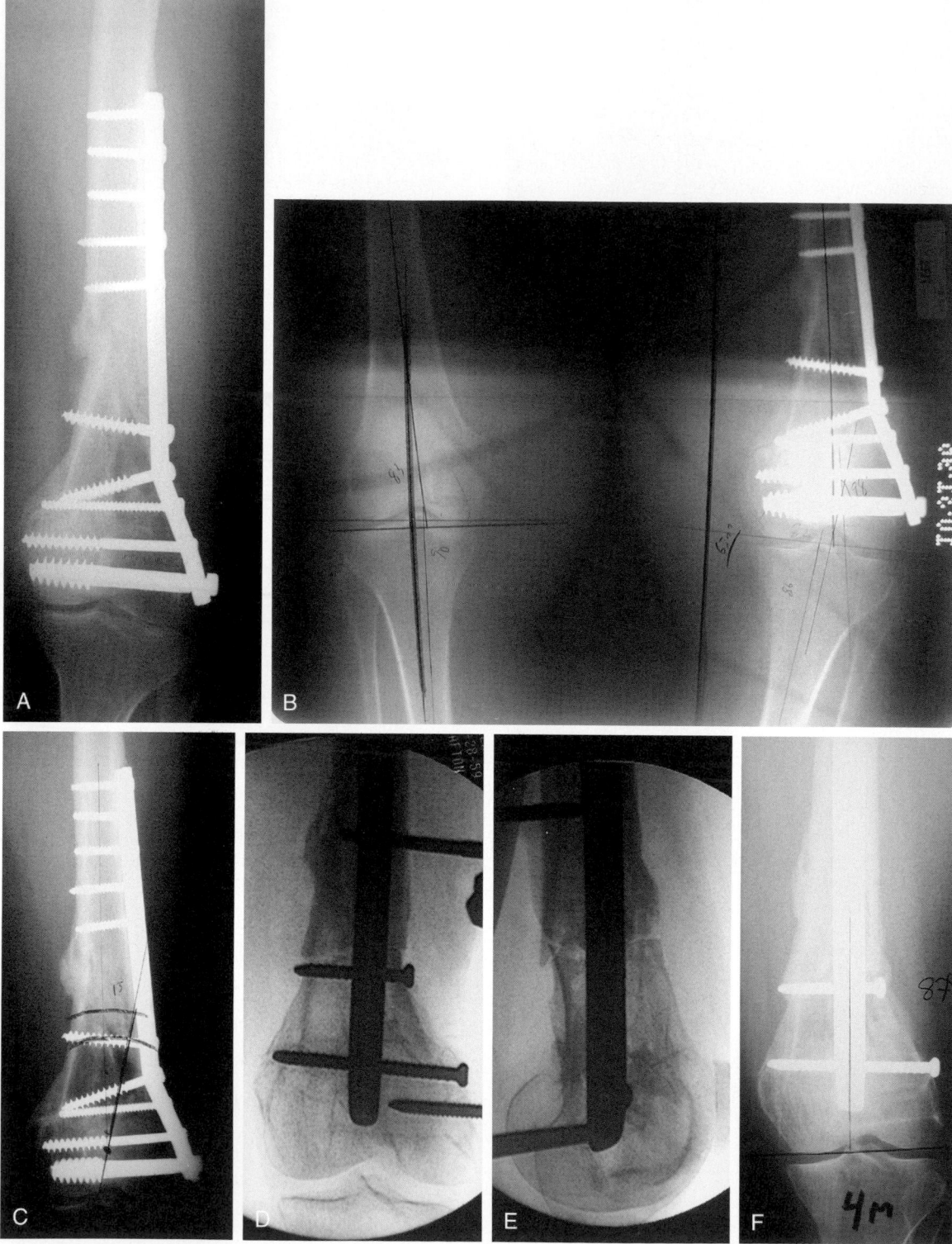

**FIGURE 53–51.** Malunion after a technically unsatisfactory fixation repaired with a focal dome osteotomy and fixator-assisted antegrade intramedullary (IM) nailing. The patient was hemiplegic on the opposite side because of a previous head injury. IM nailing was chosen to facilitate mobility with earlier weight bearing. *A,* Anteroposterior (AP) radiograph of unconventional fixation with a dynamic compression plate attached to a malpositioned dynamic condylar lag screw distally. *B,* Standing AP radiograph showing a varus deformity. The mechanical axis of the left lower extremity is 6.5 cm medial to the position of that on the right. *C,* Proposed focal dome osteotomy with two possible locations drawn (see Chapter 62). *D,* Intraoperative AP radiograph after osteotomy and insertion of the nail with the temporary external fixator still in place. *E,* Lateral intraoperative radiograph. *F,* Four-month postoperative AP radiograph showing healing in correct alignment, the pain relieved, and the patient fully weight bearing for 2 months.

After the cause is determined, a decision can be made regarding whether an option for improvement exists. If malreduction of the articular surface or intra-articular hardware is present, the only chance of restoring function is repeat surgery to correct the deformity or remove the hardware. Intra-articular adhesions and periarticular and muscular contractures should be initially treated with aggressive physical therapy. If this measure fails, manipulation under anesthesia, arthrotomy and lysis of adhesions, and progressive capsular, ligamentous, and muscular release may be indicated. Severe quadriceps contractures are particularly vexing problems to treat, especially if the muscle is scarred to the supracondylar region of the distal part of the femur. If the limitation in motion is significant, quadriceps release from the underlying bone may be indicated. In patients with intramuscular quadriceps contracture and scarring, some form of quadriceps release or lengthening may be indicated. For rehabilitation after any of these procedures, we recommend immediate postoperative continuous passive motion, followed by an aggressive range-of-motion and strengthening program.

If significant post-traumatic arthrosis or arthritis develops in the joint with pain and limitation of motion, it should be treated initially with anti-inflammatory agents and physical therapy procedures to decrease the inflammation and increase motion. If these measures prove unsuccessful, arthroscopic evaluation of the articular surface may be indicated. If significant long-term pain, decreased function, and disability ensue, salvage procedures such as arthrodesis or arthroplasty may be indicated.[46]

## REFERENCES

1. Arneson, T.J.; Melton, L.J., III; Lewallen, D.G.; O'Fallon, W.M. Epidemiology of diaphyseal and distal femoral fractures in Rochester, Minnesota, 1965–1984. Clin Orthop 234:188–194, 1988.
2. Beall, M.S.; Nebel, E.; Bailey, R. Transarticular fixation in the treatment of nonunion of supracondylar fractures of the femur: A salvage procedure. Am J Bone Joint Surg 61:1018–1023, 1979.
3. Benum, P. The use of bone cement as an adjunct to internal fixation of supracondylar fractures of osteoporotic femurs. Acta Orthop Scand 48:52–56, 1977.
4. Bogoch, E.; Hastings, D.; Gross, A.; Gschwend, N. Supracondylar fractures of the femur adjacent to resurfacing and MacIntosh arthroplasties of the knee in patients with rheumatoid arthritis. Clin Orthop 229:213–220, 1988.
5. Bolhofner, B.R.; Carmen, B.; Clifford, P. The results of open reduction and internal fixation of distal femur fractures using a biologic (indirect) reduction technique. J Orthop Trauma 10:372–377, 1996.
6. Bone, L.T. The management of fractures in the patient with multiple trauma. J Bone Joint Surg Am 68:945–949, 1986.
7. Brown, A.; D'Arcy, J.C. Internal fixation for supracondylar fractures of the femur in the elderly patient. J Bone Joint Surg Br 53:420–424, 1971.
8. Browner, B.D.; Burgess, A.R.; Robertson, R.J.; et al. Immediate closed antegrade Ender nailing of femoral fractures in polytrauma patients. J Trauma 24:921–927, 1984.
9. Bucholz, R.W.; Ross, S.E.; Lawrence, K.L. Fatigue fracture of the interlocking nail in the treatment of fractures of the distal part of the femoral shaft. J Bone Joint Surg Am 69:1391–1399, 1987.
10. Butler, M.S.; Brumback, R.J.; Ellison, T.S.; et al. Interlocking intramedullary nailing for ipsilateral fractures of the femoral shaft and distal part of the femur. J Bone Joint Surg Am 73:1492–1502, 1991.
11. Butt, M.S.; Krikler, S.R.; Ali, M.S. Displaced fractures of the distal femur in elderly patients. J Bone Joint Surg Br 77:110–114, 1995.
12. Chen, F.; Mont, M.A.; Bachner, B.S. Management of ipsilateral supracondylar femur fractures following total knee arthroplasty. J Arthroplasty 9:521–526, 1994.
13. Chiron, H.S.; Casey, P. Fractures of the distal third of the femur treated by internal fixation. Clin Orthop 100:160–170, 1974.
14. Chiron, H.S.; Tremoulet, J.; Casey, P.; Muller, M. Fractures of the distal third of the femur treated by internal fixation. Clin Orthop 100:160–170, 1974.
15. Connolly, J.F. Closed management of distal femoral fractures. Instr Course Lect 36:428–437, 1987.
16. Connolly, J.F.; Dehne, E. Closed reduction and early cast-brace ambulation in the treatment of femoral fractures. J Bone Joint Surg Am 55:1581–1599, 1973.
17. Culp, R.W.; Schmidt, R.D.; Hands, G.; et al. Supracondylar fracture of the femur following prosthetic knee arthroplasty. Clin Orthop 222:212–222, 1987.
18. Danziger, M.; Caucci, D.; Zechner, B.; et al. Treatment of intercondylar and supracondylar distal femur fractures using the GSH supracondylar nail. Am J Orthop 8:684–690, 1995.
19. David, S.M.; Harrow, M.E.; Peindl, R.D.; et al. Comparative biomechanical analysis of supracondylar femur fracture fixation: Locked intramedullary nail versus 95-degree angled plate. J Orthop Trauma 11:344–350, 1997.
20. DiGioia, A.M., III; Rubash, H.E. Periprosthetic fractures of the femur after total knee arthroplasty: A literature review and treatment algorithm. Clin Orthop 271:135–142, 1991.
21. Dominguez, I.; Moro Rodriguez, E.; De Pedro Moro, J.A.; et al. Antegrade nailing for fractures of the distal femur. Clin Orthop 350:74–79, 1998.
22. Driscoll, S.W.; Keeley, F.W.; Salter, R.B. The chondrogenic potential of free autogenous periosteal grafts for biological resurfacing of major full-thickness defects in joint surfaces under the influence of continuous passive motion. J Bone Joint Surg Am 68:1017–1034, 1986.
23. Fankhauser, C.; Frenk, A.; Marti, A. A comparative biomechanical evaluation of three systems for the internal fixation of distal fractures of the femur. Abstract CD. Paper presented at the 24th Annual Meeting of the Orthopaedic Research Society, Anaheim, California, 1999, p. 498.
24. Farouk, O.; Krettek, C.; Miclau, T.; et al. Effects of percutaneous and conventional plating techniques on the blood supply to the femur. Arch Orthop Trauma Surg 117:438–441, 1998.
25. Farouk, O.; Krettek, C.; Miclau, T.; et al. Minimally invasive plate osteosynthesis and vascularity: Preliminary results of a cadaver injection study. Injury 28(Suppl 1):7–12, 1997.
26. Farouk, O.; Krettek, C.; Miclau, T.; et al. The minimal invasive plate osteosynthesis: Is percutaneous plating biologically superior to the traditional technique? J Orthop Trauma 13:401–406, 1999.
27. Figgie, M.P.; Goldberg, V.M.; Figgie, H.E., III; Sobel, M. The results of treatment of supracondylar fracture above total knee arthroplasty. J Arthroplasty 5:267–276, 1990.
28. Firoozbakhsh, K.; Behzadi, K.; Decoster, T.A.; et al. Mechanics of retrograde nail versus plate fixation for supracondylar femur fractures. J Orthop Trauma 9:152–157, 1995.
29. Garnavos, C.; Rafiq, M.; Henry, A.P. Treatment of femoral fracture above a knee prosthesis: 18 cases followed 0.5.14 years. Acta Orthop Scand 65:610–614, 1994.
30. Giles, J.B.; DeLee, J.C.; Heckman, J.D.; Keever, J.E. Supracondylar-intercondylar fractures of the femur treated with a supracondylar plate and lag screw. J Bone Joint Surg Am 64:864–870, 1982.
31. Gregory, P.; DiCicco, J.; Karpik, K.; et al. Ipsilateral fractures of the femur and tibia: Treatment with retrograde femoral nailing and unreamed tibial nailing. J Orthop Trauma 10:309–316, 1996.
32. Green, N.E.; Allen, B.L. Vascular injuries associated with dislocation of the knee. J Bone and Joint Surg Am 59:236–239, 1977.
33. Hall, M.F. Two-plane fixation of acute supracondylar and intracondylar fractures of the femur. South Med J 71:1474–1479, 1978.
34. Hampton, O.P. Wounds of the Extremities in Military Surgery. St. Louis, C.V. Mosby, 1951.
35. Healy, J.H.; Lane, J.M. Treatment of pathologic fractures of the distal femur with the Zickel supracondylar nail. Clin Orthop 250:216–220, 1990.
36. Healy, W.L.; Brooker, A.F. Distal femoral fractures. Comparison of open and closed methods of treatment. Clin Orthop 166–171, 1983.

37. Helfet, D.L.; Lorich, D.G. Retrograde intramedullary nailing of supracondylar femoral fractures. Clin Orthop 350:80–84, 1998.

38. Henry, S.L. Supracondylar femur fractures treated percutaneously. Clin Orthop 375:51–59, 2000.

39. Henry, S.; Trager, S.; Green, S.; Seligson, D. Management of supracondylar fractures of the femur with the GSH supracondylar nail. Contemp Orthop 22:631–640, 1991.

40. Henry, S.L.; Booth, R.E. Management of supracondylar fractures above total knee prosthesis. Tech Orthop 9:243–252, 1994.

41. Hirsch, D.M.; Bhalla, S.; Roffman, M. Supracondylar fracture of the femur following total knee replacement. J Bone Joint Surg Am 63:162–163, 1981.

42. No reference cited.

43. Hopf, T.; Osthege, S.(1987) Die interfragmentaere Kompression des ZESPOL-Osteosynthese-Systems. Experimentelle biomechanische Untersuchung. [Interfragmental compression of the Zespol osteosynthesis system. Experimental biomechanical studies.] Z Orthop Ihre Grenzgeb 125:546–552, 1987.

44. Hoppenfeld, S.; deBoer, P. The femur. In: Surgical Exposures in Orthopaedics. The Anatomic Approach. Philadelphia, J.B. Lippincott, 1984, pp. 357–387.

45. Iannacone, W.M.; Bennett, F.S.; DeLong, W.G., Jr.; et al. Initial experience with the treatment of supracondylar femoral fractures using the supracondylar intramedullary nail: A preliminary report. J Orthop Trauma 8:322–327, 1994.

46. Insall, J.N. Surgery of the Knee. New York, Churchill Livingstone, 1984.

47. Ito, K.; Grass, R.; Zwipp, H. Internal fixation of supracondylar femoral fractures: Comparative biomechanical performance of the 95-degree blade plate and two retrograde nails. J Orthop Trauma 12:259–266, 1998.

48. Jabczenski, F.F.; Crawford, M. Retrograde intramedullary nailing of supracondylar femur fractures above total knee arthroplasty. J Arthroplasty 10:95–101, 1995.

49. Jenson, J.E.; Jenson, T.G.; Smith, T.K. Nutrition in orthopaedic surgery. J Bone Joint Surg Am 64:1263–1271, 1982.

50. Johansen, K.; Bandyk, D.; Thiele, B.; Hansen, S.T. Temporary intraluminal shunts: Resolution of a management dilemma in complex vascular injuries. J Trauma 22:395–402, 1982.

51. Johnson, E.E. Combined direct and indirect reduction of comminuted four-part intraarticular T-type fractures of the distal femur. Clin Orthop 231:154–162, 1988.

52. Johnson, K.D. Internal fixation of distal femoral fractures. Instr Course Lect 36:437–448, 1987.

53. Johnson, K.D.; Hicken, G. Distal femoral fractures. Orthop Clin North Am 18:115–131, 1987.

54. Kennedy, J.C. Complete dislocation of the knee joint. J Bone Joint Surg Am 45:889–904, 1963.

55. Kinast, C.; Bolhofner, B.R.; Mast, J.W.; Ganz, R. Subtrochanteric fractures of the femur. Clin Orthop 238:122–130, 1989.

56. Kirschner, M. Ueber Nagelextension. Beitr Klin Chir 64:266–279, 1909.

57. Kolmert, L.; Wulff, K. Epidemiology and treatment of distal femoral fractures in adults. Acta Orthop Scand 53:957–962, 1982.

58. Kolodziej, P.; Lee, F.S.; Patel, A.; et al. Biomechanical evaluation of the Schuhli nut. Clin Orthop 347:79–85, 1998.

59. Koval, K.J.; Hoehl, J.J.; Kummer, F.J.; Simon, J.A. Distal femoral fixation: A biomechanical comparison of the standard condylar buttress plate, a locked buttress plate, and the 95-degree blade plate. J Orthop Trauma 11:521–524, 1991.

60. Koval, K.J.; Kummer, F.J.; Bharam, S.; et al. Distal femoral fixation: A laboratory comparison of the 95 degrees plate, antegrade and retrograde inserted reamed intramedullary nails. J Orthop Trauma 10:378–382, 1996.

61. Kowalski, M.J.; Schemitsch, E.H.; Harrington, R.M.; et al. A comparative biomechanical evaluation of a noncontacting plate and currently used devices for tibial fixation. J Trauma 40:5–9, 1996.

62. Krettek, C. Komplextrauma des Kniegelenkes—Diagnostik, Management und Therapieprinzipien. Handout D3. Zentraleuropäischer Unfallkongress Budapest 4.-7.5., Tscherne, H., Hrsg. Budapest, 1994, pp. 1–5.

63. Krettek, C.; Miclau, T.; Grün, O.; et al. Techniques for assessing limb alignment during closed reduction and internal fixation of lower extremity fractures. Tech Orthop 14:247–256, 1999.

64. Krettek, C.; Schandelmaier, P.; Miclau, T.; et al. Transarticular joint reconstruction and indirect plate osteosynthesis for complex distal supracondylar femoral fractures. Injury 28(Suppl 1):A31–A41, 1997.

65. Krettek, C.; Schandelmaier, P.; Miclau, T.; Tscherne, S. Minimally invasive percutaneous plate osteosynthesis (MIPPO) using the DCS in proximal and distal femoral fractures. Injury 28(Suppl 1): A31–A41.

66. Krettek, C.; Schandelmaier, P.; Miclau, T.; et al. Intraoperative control of axes, rotation and length in femoral and tibial fractures—technical note. Injury 29(Suppl 3):C29–C39, 1998.

67. Krettek, C.; Schandelmaier, P.; Stephan, C.; Tscherne, H. Kondylenplatten- und Kondylenschraubenosteosynthese (DCS)—Indikation, technische Hinweise und Ergebnisse. OP J 13:294–304, 1997.

68. Krettek, C.; Schandelmaier, P.; Tscherne, H. Distale Femurfrakturen: Transartikuläre Rekonstruktion, perkutane Plattenosteosynthese und retrograde Nagelung. Unfallchirurg 99:2–10, 1996.

69. Krettek, C.; Tscherne, H. Distal femoral fractures. In: Fu, F.H.; Harner, C.D.; Vince, K.G., eds. Knee Surgery. Baltimore, Williams & Wilkins, 1994, pp. 1027–1035.

70. Lee, T.T.; Gravel, C.J.; Chapman, M.W. (1994) Operative management of the supracondylar fracture of the femur: Comparison of the anterolateral approach to other surgical approaches. Poster. Presented at the annual meeting of the Orthopaedic Trauma Association, 1994, p. 166.

71. Leung, K.S.; Shen, W.Y.; So, W.S.; et al. Interlocking intramedullary nailing for supracondylar and intercondylar fractures for the distal part of the femur. J Bone Joint Surg Am 73:332–340, 1991.

72. Lucas, S.E.; Seligson, D.; Henry, S.L. Intramedullary supracondylar nailing of femoral fractures: A preliminary report of the GSH supracondylar nail. Clin Orthop 296:200–206, 1993.

73. Mahorner, H.R.; Bradburn, M. (1933) Fractures of the femur. Report of 308 cases. Surg Gynecol Obstet 56:1066–1979, 1933.

74. Mast, J.; Jakob, R.; Ganz, R. Planning and Reduction Technique in Fracture Surgery. New York, Springer-Verlag, 1989.

75. Matter, P.; Rittman, W. The Open Fracture. Huber, Bern, Switzerland, 1978.

76. McLaren, A.C.; Dupont, J.A.; Chroeber, D.C. Open reduction internal fixation of supracondylar femur fractures above total knee arthroplasties using the intramedullary supracondylar rod. Clin Orthop 302:194–198, 1992.

77. Merkel, K.D.; Johnson, E.W. Supracondylar fracture of the femur after total knee arthroplasty. J Bone Joint Surg Am 68:29–43, 1986.

78. Meyer, R.W.; Plaxton, N.A.; Postak, P.D.; et al. Mechanical comparison of a distal femoral side plate and a retrograde intramedullary nail. J Orthop Trauma 14:398–404, 2000.

79. Meyers, M.H.; Moore, T.M.; Harvey, J.P. Traumatic dislocation of the knee joint. J Bone Joint Surg Am 57:430–433, 1975.

80. Miclau, T.; Remiger, A.; Tepic, S.; et al. A mechanical comparison of the dynamic compression plate, limited contact–dynamic compression plate, and point contact fixator. J Orthop Trauma 9:17–22, 1995.

81. Mize, R.D.; Bucholz, R.W.; Grogan, D.P. Surgical treatment of displaced, comminuted fractures of the distal end of the femur. J Bone Joint Surg Am 64:871–878, 1982.

82. Modlin, J. Double skeletal traction in battle fractures of the lower femur. Band 4:19–129, 1945.

83. Moll, J. The cast brace walking treatment of open and closed femur fractures. South Med J 66:345–352, 1973.

84. Mooney, V. Fractures of the distal femur. Instr Course Lect 36:427, 1987.

84a. Moore, T.J.; Watson, T.; Green, S.A.; et al. Complications of surgically treated supracondylar fractures of the femur. J Trauma 27:402–406, 1987.

85. Morgan, E.; Ostrum, R.F.; DiCicco, J.; et al. Effects of retrograde femoral intramedullary nailing on the patellofemoral articulation. J Orthop Trauma 13:13–16, 1999.

86. Müller, M.E.; Allgöwer, M.; Schneider, R.; Willenegger, H. Manual of Internal Fixation, 3rd ed. New York, Springer-Verlag, 1991.

87. Müller, M.E.; Nazarian, S.; Koch, P. 1987. Classification AO des Fractures. Springer-Verlag New York,

88. Müller, M.E.; Nazarian, S.; Koch, P.; Schatzker, J. The Comprehensive Classification of Fractures of Long Bones. New York, Springer-Verlag, 1990.

89. Neer, C.S.; Grantham, S.A.; Shelton, M.L. Supracondylar fracture of the adult femur. A study of one hundred and ten cases. J Bone Joint Surg Am 49:591–613, 1967.

90. Nielsen, B.F.; Petersen, V.S.; Varmarken, J.E. Fracture of the femur after knee arthroplasty. Acta Orthop Scand 59:155–157, 1988.

91. Olerud, S. Operative treatment of supracondylar-condylar fractures of the femur: Technique and results in fifteen cases. J Bone and Joint Surg Am 54:1015–1032, 1972.

92. Ostrum, R.F. Treatment of floating knee injuries through a single percutaneous approach. Clin Orthop 375:43–50, 2000.

93. Ostrum, R.; Geel, C. Indirect reduction and internal fixation of supracondylar femur fractures without bone graft. J Orthop Trauma 9:278–284, 1995.

94. Pritchett, J.W. Supracondylar fractures of the femur. Clin Orthop 184:173–177, 1984.

95. Regazzoni, P.; Leutenegger, A.; Ruedi, T.; Staehelin, F. Erste Erfahrungen mit der dynamischen Kondylenschraube (dcs) bei distalen Femurfrakturen. Helv Chir Acta 53:61–64, 1986.

96. Riina, J.; Tornetta, P.; Ritter, C.; et al. Neurologic and vascular structures at risk during anterior-posterior locking of retrograde femoral nails. J Orthop Trauma 12:379–381, 1998.

97. Rockwood, C.A., Jr.; Ryan, V.L.; Richards, J.A. Experience with quadrilateral cast brace. Abstract. J Bone Joint Surg Am 55:421, 1973.

98. Rolston, L.R.; Christ, D.J.; Halpern, A.; et al. Treatment of supracondylar fractures of the femur proximal to a total knee arthroplasty. J Bone Joint Surg Am 77:924–931, 1995.

99. Sanders, R.; Regazzoni, P.; Ruedi, T. Treatment of supracondylar-intraarticular fractures of the femur using the dynamic condylar screw. J Orthop Trauma 3:214–222, 1989.

100. Sanders, R.W.; Swiontkowski, M.; Rosen, H.; Helfet, D. Complex fractures and malunions of the distal femur: Results of treatment with double plates. J Bone Joint Surg Am 73:341–346, 1991.

101. Sanders, R.; Swiontkowski, M.F.; Rosen, H.; Helfet, D. Double plating of comminuted, unstable fractures of the distal part of the femur. J Bone Joint Surg Am 73:341–346, 1991.

102. Schatzker, J.; Horne, G.; Waddell, J. The Toronto experience with the supracondylar fracture of the femur, 1966–72. Injury 6:113–128, 1974.

103. Schatzker, J.; Lambert, D.C. Supracondylar fractures of the femur. Clin Orthop 138:77–83, 1979.

104. Schatzker, J.; Tile, M. The Rationale of Operative Fracture Care. New York, Springer-Verlag, 1987.

105. Seide, K.; Zierold, W.; Wolter, D.; et al. The effect of an angle-stable plate-screw connection and various screw diameters on the stability of plate osteosynthesis. An FE model study. Unfallchirurg 93:552–558, 1990.

106. Seinsheimer, F. Fractures of the distal femur. Clin Orthop 153:169–179, 1980.

107. Shahcheraghi, G.H.; Doroodchi, H.R. Supracondylar fracture of the femur: Closed or open reduction? J Trauma 34:499–502, 1993.

108. Shelbourne, K.D.; Brueckmann, F.R. Rush pin fixation of supra-condylar and intercondylar fractures of the femur. J Bone Joint Surg Am 64:161–169, 1982.

109. Shelton, M.L.; Grantham, S.A.; Neer, C.S.; Singh, M. A new fixation device for supracondylar and low femoral shaft fractures. J Trauma 14:821–835, 1974.

110. Shewring, D.J.; Meggitt, B.F. Fractures of the distal femur treated with the AO dynamic condylar screw. J Bone Joint Surg Br 74:122–125, 1992.

111. Short, W.H.; Hootnick, D.R.; Murry, D.G. Ipsilateral supracondylar femur fractures following total knee arthroplasty. Clin Orthop 158:111–116, 1981.

112. Siliski, J.M.; Mahring, M.; Hofer, H.P. Supracondylar-intercondylar fractures of the femur. Treatment by internal fixation. J Bone Joint Surg Am 71:95–104, 1989.

113. Sisto, D.J.; Warren, R.F. Complete knee dislocation. A follow-up study of operative treatment. Clin Orthop 198:94–101, 1985.

114. Slatis, P.; Ryoppy, S.; Huttinen, V. AO osteosynthesis of fractures of the distal third of the femur. Acta Orthop Scand 42:162–172, 1971.

115. Steinman, F.R. Eine neue Extensionsmethode in der Frakturenbe-handlung. Zentralbl Chir 34:398–442, 1907.

116. Stewart, M.J.; Sisk, T.D.; Walace, S.L. Fractures of distal third of the femur. J Bone Joint Surg Am 48:784–807, 1966.

117. Struhl, S.; Szporn, M.N.; Cobelli, N.J.; Sadler, A.H. Cemented internal fixation for supracondylar femur fractures in osteoporotic patients. J Orthop Trauma 4:151–157, 1990.

118. Tepic, S.; Remiger, A.R.; Morikawa, K.; et al. Strength recovery in fractured sheep tibia treated with a plate or an internal fixator: An experimental study with a two-year follow-up. J Orthop Trauma 11:14–23, 1997.

119. Trentz, O.; Tscherne, H.; Oestern, H.J. Operationstechnik und Ergebnisse bei distalen Femurfrakturen. Unfallheilkde 80:441–448, 1977.

120. Tscherne H. Femoral shaft and distal femur. In: Müller, M.E.; Allgöwer, M.; Schneider, R., Willenegger, H., eds. Manual of Internal Fixation. Berlin, Springer-Verlag, 1991, pp. 535–552.

121. Tscherne, H.; Oestern, H.J.; Trentz, O. Spätergebnisse der distalen Femurfraktur und ihre besonderen Probleme. Zentrabl Chir 102:897–904, 1977.

122. Tscherne, H.; Trentz, O. [Recent injuries of the femoral condyles.] Langenbecks Arch Chir 345:396–401, 1977.

123. van der Werken, C.; Marti, R.K.; Raaymakers, E.L. Distal femoral fractures, results of operative treatment. Neth J Surg 33:230–236, 1981.

124. No reference cited.

125. Walling, A.K.; Seradge, H.; Spiegel, P.G. Injuries to the knee ligaments with fractures of the femur. J Bone Joint Surg Am 64:1324–1327, 1982.

126. Wenzel, H.; Casey, P.A.; Herbert, P.; Belin, J. Die operative Behandlung der distalen Femurfraktur. AO Bull 1970.

127. Wiggins, H.E. Vertical traction in open fractures of the femur. US Armed Forces Med J 4:1633–1636, 1953.

128. Yang, R.S.; Liu, H.C.; Liu, T.K. Supracondylar fractures of the femur. J Trauma 30:315–319, 1990.

129. Zehntner, M.K.; Marchesi, D.G.; Burch, H.; Ganz, R. Alignment of supracondylar/intercondylar fractures of the femur after internal fixation by AO/ASIF technique. J Orthop Trauma 6:318–326, 1992.

130. Zickel, R.E. Nonunions of fractures of the proximal and distal thirds of the shaft of the femur. Instr Course Lect 37:173–179, 1988.

131. Zickel, R.E.; Fietti, V.G., Jr.; Lawsing, J.F., III; Cochran, G.V. A new intramedullary fixation device for the distal third of the femur. Clin Orthop 125:185–191, 1977.

132. Zickel, R.E.; Hobeika, P.; Robbins, D.S. Zickel supracondylar nails for fractures of the distal end of the femur. Clin Orthop 212:79–88, 1986.

# CHAPTER 54

# Patella Fractures and Extensor Mechanism Injuries

Michael T. Archdeacon, M.D.
Roy W. Sanders, M.D.

## HISTORICAL BACKGROUND

Before the beginning of the 20th century, treatment of patella fractures was extremely controversial. Nonoperative methods, usually extension splinting and rest, were most commonly used. Results were poor, bony union was rare, and permanent disability was expected.[31] As improvements in surgical asepsis occurred, two operative solutions to the problem emerged: arthrotomy with open wiring and patellectomy. Heineck reviewed 1100 patella fractures and advised operative treatment over extension splinting for the following reasons: improved fracture reduction, maintenance of reduction until union, reestablishment of soft tissue continuity, and restoration of the functional integrity of the knee joint.[48] Open reduction and wire fixation subsequently became the treatment of choice for patella fractures.

Although reduction of simple transverse fractures was made possible by an open procedure, stable fixation remained difficult. Various materials were tried, including silver, aluminum, and copper wire; chromic suture; kangaroo tendon; cancellous bone pegs; Achilles tendon; and fascial strips.[50] In 1936, Blodgett and Fairchild reported 35 patella fractures treated with open reduction and wire suture; less than 50% had good results.[10] They then reported on the use of partial or, in certain cases, total excision of the patella for fractures and described excellent clinical results.[10] A year earlier, Thompson also recommended partial excision of the patella.[100] In the same year as Blodgett and Fairchild's study, Brooke published a revolutionary paper on the treatment of patella fractures by total excision.[16] Quoting embryologic data to support the vestigial nature of the patella, his functional studies showed that postpatellectomy limbs were stronger than their normal counterparts. Based on these studies, patellectomy gained significant popularity.[31, 40, 44, 45, 50]

This initial enthusiasm was tempered by many experimental and long-term clinical studies that disproved the benefits of patellectomy as routine treatment of fractures of this bone.* Cohn[27] and Bruce and Walmsley[18] studied patellectomized rabbits and found degenerative changes on the femoral condyles. They suggested that this complication could occur in humans as well. Haxton and others presented biomechanical evidence that the patella served a necessary purpose in the extensor mechanism.[30, 47, 58, 67, 105, 109] In long-term clinical studies evaluating patients after total patellectomy, variable results were also found.[30, 35, 56, 70, 76, 99, 110, 112] These studies revealed poor patient satisfaction, decreased quadriceps power, prolonged recovery time, and significant changes in activities of daily living.[35, 89, 99, 112]

Treatment of patella fractures with the anterior tension band principle was first reported in the 1950s.[79] This technique was subsequently advocated by the Arbeitsgemeinschaft für Osteosynthesefragen/Association for the Study of Internal Fixation (AO/ASIF) group as the treatment of choice for transverse patellar fractures.[79] Weber and colleagues compared the tension band principle with cerclage and interosseous wire suture in cadavers and found that modified anterior tension band wiring with retinacular repair gave the most stable fixation of a transversely fractured patella.[108] Additionally, this construct was the only one that allowed early active range of motion of the knee.[108] Other authors subsequently confirmed this fact clinically.[11, 12, 54, 64]

At present, three forms of operative treatment survive: various types of fixation, usually with tension band wiring; partial patellectomy; and total patellectomy. Definitive indications for each procedure are related to the type of

*See references 18, 27, 30, 35, 47, 56, 58, 67, 70, 76, 89, 99, 105, 109, 110, 112.

fracture encountered, and good results can be expected with proper treatment.

## ANATOMY

### Skeletal Anatomy

The patella lies deep to the fascia lata and the tendinous fibers of the rectus femoris (Fig. 54–1A). It is flat and roughly ovoid and comes to a rounded point, known as the apex, on its anteroinferior margin. Its proximal part is called the basis (see Fig. 54–1B).

Wiberg classified patellas into three types based on the size of the medial and lateral facets.[111] In type I, the medial and lateral facets are approximately equal, whereas in types II and III, the medial facets are progressively smaller than the lateral. Baumgartl described a fourth type, the "Jägerhut patella," in which the medial facet is lacking altogether.[5] These facets have importance with respect to the functional anatomy of the patellofemoral joint (see the section Extensor Apparatus Biomechanics).

### Soft Tissue Anatomy

#### QUADRICEPS MECHANISM

The quadriceps muscle complex is composed of four separate muscles: the rectus femoris, vastus medialis, vastus lateralis, and vastus intermedius (Fig. 54–2). Classically, the quadriceps tendon is described as trilaminar in structure; it inserts onto the patella with the rectus femoris superficial, the vastus medialis and lateralis in the middle, and the vastus intermedius deep.[67] The actual arrangement is more complex because of blending of the tendons as they insert on the patella.[86]

The rectus femoris is a long fusiform muscle that assumes the central and superficial position in the quadriceps structure.[86] The fibers angle 7° to 10° medially in the frontal plane relative to the shaft of the femur.[67]

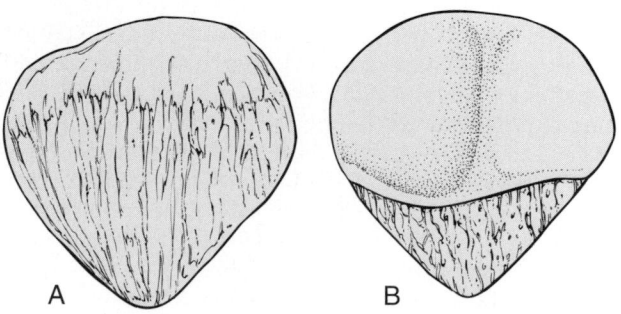

**FIGURE 54–1.** *A,* Superficial aspect of the patella, with extensive soft tissue attachments indicated by roughened surface. *B,* Articular surface of the patella (see text). Note the extra-articular distal pole occupying a significant portion of the bone's length. The articular surface is divided into seven facets by several ridges (see Fig. 54–1A). A major vertical ridge separates the medial from the lateral facets, and a second vertical ridge near the medial border isolates a narrow strip known as the odd facet. In addition, two transverse ridges create superior, intermediate, and inferior facets (Boström, 1972; Reider et al., 1981).

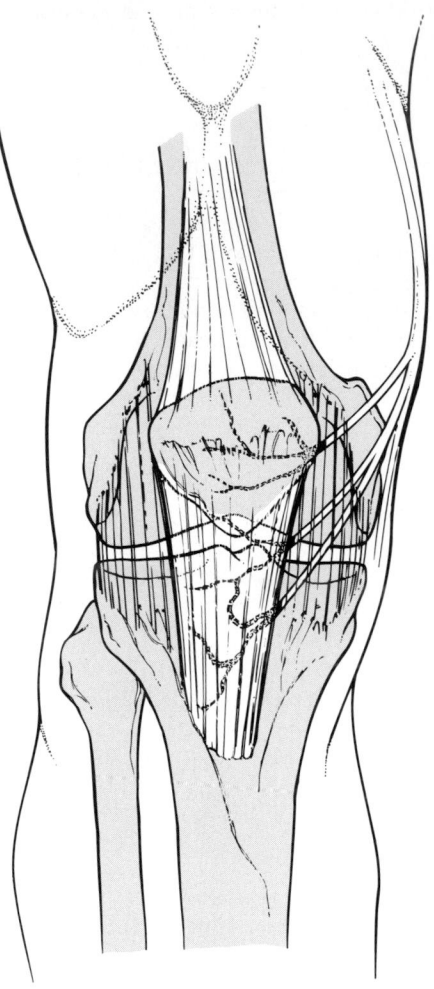

**FIGURE 54–2.** Soft tissue attachments of the patella. Major components of the extensor mechanism include the quadriceps tendon proximally and the patellar ligament (tendon) distally. The medial and lateral retinacula help position the patella and can provide active knee extension if they remain intact after a patella fracture without significant displacement.

The vastus medialis divides into two parts. The more proximal fibers are known as the vastus medialis longus and enter the patella at an angle of 15° to 18°. The more distal fibers, the vastus medialis obliquus, enter the patella at an angle of 50° to 55°.[67] The fibers of each group are divided by fascia into separate fascicles. Innervation of the vastus medialis obliquus is by a separate branch of the femoral nerve.[67, 86]

The fibers of the vastus lateralis approach the patella at an angle of approximately 30° and terminate more proximally than do the fibers of the vastus medialis. The most medial fibers insert into the supralateral edge of the patella, with the more lateral fibers traveling laterally past the patella. These fibers contribute to the lateral retinaculum and, at their lateral extreme, fuse with the iliotibial tract.

The vastus intermedius lies in a plane deep to the other three elements of the quadriceps. Most of the fibers insert directly into the superior aspect of the patella. Deep to the major components of the quadriceps lies the articularis genus. This muscle is highly variable in occurrence and arises from the anterior aspect of the supracondylar portion of the femur. It inserts on the joint capsule at the suprapatellar pouch.

## PATELLAR RETINACULUM

The deep investing fascial layer of the thigh is known as the fascia lata. As it spreads over the anterior surface of the knee, its medial and lateral extensions combine with aponeurotic fibers from both the vastus medialis and the vastus lateralis to form the patellar retinaculum, which inserts directly into the proximal part of the tibia (see Fig. 52–2). The patellofemoral ligaments—deep transverse fibers that are palpable thickenings of the joint capsule connecting the patella with the femoral epicondyles—complete the retinaculum.[13, 86] In addition, the lateral aspect of the vastus lateralis and the iliotibial tract both contribute to the thicker lateral patellar retinaculum. Together, the patellar retinaculum and the iliotibial band serve as "the auxiliary extensors of the knee."[13]

## PATELLAR TENDON

Derived primarily from fibers of the rectus femoris, the patellar tendon is flat and strong and inserts onto the tibial tubercle. Its average length is slightly less than 5 cm. The fascial expansions of the iliotibial tract and the patellar retinaculum blend into the patellar tendon as it inserts onto the anterior surface of the tibia.

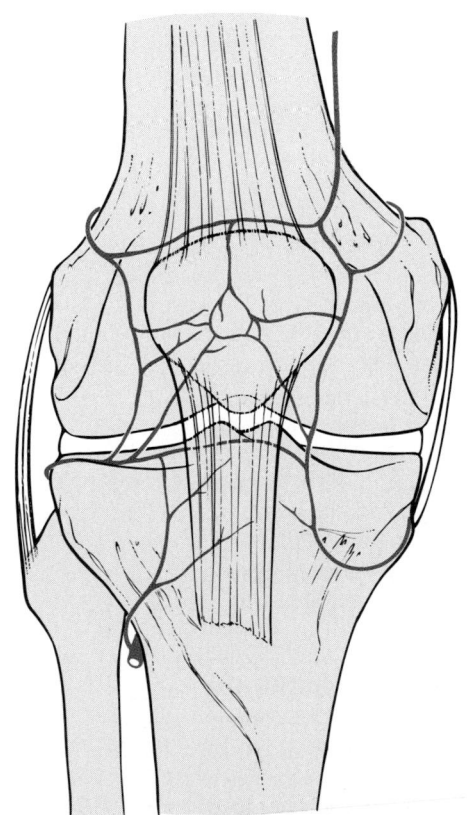

**FIGURE 54–3.** Blood supply of the patella. Note the extraosseous arterial anastomotic ring, which receives inflow from branches of each of the genicular arteries. (From Scapinelli, R. J Bone Joint Surg Br 49:563–570, 1967.)

## ARTERIAL BLOOD SUPPLY

The anterior surface of the patella is covered with an extraosseous arterial ring derived mainly from branches of the geniculate arteries[28] (Fig. 54–3). The intraosseous blood supply of the patella is supplied by two systems of vessels, both derived from this extraosseous vascular ring: the midpatellar vessels, which penetrate the middle third of the anterior surface of the patella, and the polar vessels, which enter the patella at its apex.[3, 87]

The patellar tendon receives its blood supply from two sources. The infrapatellar fat pad supplies the deep surface of the patellar tendon with contributions from the inferior medial and inferior lateral geniculate arteries. The anterior or superficial surface of the tendon is supplied by the retinaculum, which receives its supply from the inferior medial geniculate artery and the recurrent tibial artery.[3]

## EXTENSOR APPARATUS BIOMECHANICS

The principal function of the extensor mechanism of the knee in humans is to maintain the erect position. Ambulation, rising from a chair, and ascending or descending stairs are examples of this ability to overcome gravity. The biomechanical principles necessary for these actions should be understood to treat extensor mechanism injuries rationally.

A moment is a force that produces rotation about an axis. It is equal to the product of a force and the perpendicular distance from the line of action of that force to the axis of rotation. This perpendicular distance is the moment arm.[91] The force necessary for knee extension (torque) is directly dependent on the perpendicular distance between the patellar tendon and the knee flexion axis (moment arm)[58] (Fig. 54–4A).

Twice as much torque is needed to extend the knee the final 15° as to bring it from a fully flexed position to 15°.[67] To do so, the knee requires a moment arm that increases during extension so that it can maintain a constant level of torque. The patella provides this mechanical advantage by two separate mechanisms: linking and displacement.[58]

As the knee begins extension from the fully flexed position, the patella functions primarily as a link between the quadriceps and the patellar tendon. This linking function allows for generation of torque from the quadriceps muscle to the tibia.[58] Maximal forces across the quadriceps tendon have been recorded at 3200 N, whereas those across the patellar tendon are 2800 N.[52] These values are between four and five times the standard body weight of 700 N. For young, physically trained men, these forces can reach up to 6000 N.[52]

Typically, the linking function occurs in the more flexed positions. At 135° of flexion, the patella slips into the intercondylar notch. The patellar facets of the femur have an extensive contact area with both the patella and the broad posterior surface of the quadriceps tendon. Load bearing shifts to a combination of the patellofemoral and the tendofemoral areas, with the latter being the greater of the two after 90° of flexion.[41] Without patellofemoral

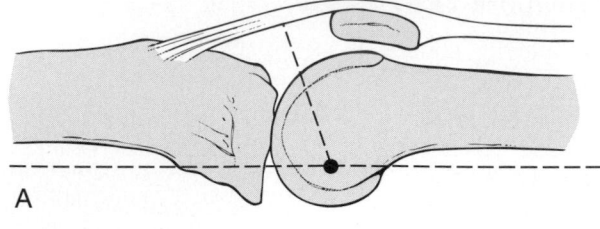

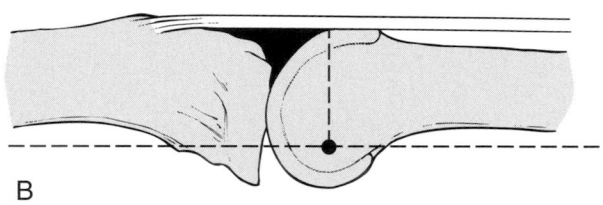

**FIGURE 54–4.** Mechanical role of the patella. *A,* The patella increases the moment arm of the extensor mechanism (i.e., the distance between the vector of applied force and the knee's instant center of rotation). *B,* After patellectomy, this moment is decreased, and thus extensor force is effectively diminished. (*A, B,* Redrawn from Kaufer, H. J Bone Joint Surg Am 53:1551–1560, 1971.)

contact, the moment arm is small[41] (see Fig. 54–4*B*). From 135° to 45° of flexion, the odd facet engages the femur. It is the only part of the patella that fails to meet the true patellar facets of the femur and the only part to articulate with the true tibial surface of the medial femoral condyle of the femur.[41]

From 45° of flexion to full extension, the patella is the only component of the extensor mechanism that contacts the femur. It acts to displace the quadriceps tendon–patellar tendon linkage away from the axis of knee rotation. This action increases the effective moment arm of the quadriceps mechanism and contributes the additional 60% of torque that is needed to gain the last 15° of knee extension.[67] This second action therefore creates a mechanical advantage analogous to that of a pulley.[58, 109]

By displacing the tendon away from the axis of rotation, greater excursion of the quadriceps is needed for a given range of motion.[109] Theoretically, when performing a patellectomy, a quadriceps-shortening or tubercle-elevating procedure may be performed to take this requirement into account.

## DIAGNOSIS

### History and Physical Examination

Fractures of the patella are diagnosed by obtaining a history of the injury, performing a thorough physical examination, and acquiring the appropriate radiographic studies. Completion of these investigations should result in a final diagnosis that includes the fracture type, the presence or absence of retinacular disruption, a description

of the wound, if any, and the presence of any associated injuries.

The history usually describes a fall from a height, a near fall, a direct blow to the patella, or a combination of these mechanisms. Correlation with the mechanism of injury allows the physician to anticipate the fracture pattern. If the patient has an open wound, the history should include questions regarding the location of the accident (e.g., at home, in the water, on a farm).

The physical examination should include an evaluation of the skin to look for contusions, abrasions, blisters (if treatment has been delayed), and the presence of an open fracture or an open-joint injury. In patients with a displaced patella fracture, physical examination will reveal a visible or palpable defect between the fragments. Significant hemarthrosis usually develops secondary to the fracture. If a palpable bony defect is present with little or no effusion, a large retinacular tear should be expected.

Knee extension is then evaluated. A tense hemarthrosis will make this part of the examination extremely painful for the patient. Arthrocentesis with injection of lidocaine or bupivacaine into the joint is often helpful. The patient's ability to extend the knee does not rule out a patella fracture and may simply mean that the patellar retinaculum is intact. An inability to extend the knee, however, suggests a discontinuity in the extensor mechanism. With a patellar fracture, such inability implies a tear of both the medial and the lateral quadriceps expansion.[13, 73, 92]

Occasionally, a laceration may be noted in proximity to a patella fracture. It may represent an open fracture or an open-joint injury. Because both are surgical emergencies, it is imperative to diagnose these injuries early. A simple means of evaluation is the saline load test. A large-bore needle (18 gauge or higher) and a 50-mL syringe are used to perform joint aspiration. A significant amount of bloody fluid may be removed, usually resulting in relief of pain. The needle is left in place while the syringe is removed and filled with saline solution, which is then injected into the knee joint. Any communication between the fracture or joint and the outside environment will become obvious if the saline solution exits the wound.

After the history and physical examination, radiographic evaluation is performed. Once a diagnosis is made, the knee is splinted in a position of comfort (usually slight flexion), iced, and elevated. If the patient requires immediate transfer to the operating room or intensive care unit, portable radiographs will suffice.

### Radiographic Evaluation

Radiographic evaluation of the patella includes standard and specialized radiographic techniques, tomography, computed tomography (CT), bone scanning, and magnetic resonance imaging (MRI). When time permits, standard radiographic evaluation of the uninvolved knee should be obtained. Such imaging affords the physician a comparison view for evaluation and assists in any preoperative planning that might be necessary.

## STANDARD VIEWS

### Anteroposterior

The normal anteroposterior (AP) radiograph is taken with the patient standing, but this position is impossible for a patient with an acute fracture. Instead, the film must be taken with the cassette underneath the knee of a supine patient. The extremity should be aligned so that the patella points straight up. Such alignment is especially important in a patient with an ipsilateral femoral shaft fracture. If the patient has a large hemarthrosis creating moderate knee flexion, the x-ray beam must be angled accordingly. Because of the possibility of concomitant occult ipsilateral leg

injuries, the largest cassette possible (14 × 17 inches) should be used.

Evaluation of the AP radiograph requires analysis of several factors. Patella position should be assessed; the patella should lie in the midline of the femoral sulcus. In addition, patellar height should be examined; the inferior pole of the patella is normally located just above a line drawn across the distal profile of the femoral condyles (Fig. 54–5A).

At times mistaken for a patellar fracture, a bipartite or tripartite patella is a developmental residuum from a variation in which the patella arises from two or more ossification centers that fail to fuse (Fig. 54–6). It is usually a bilateral finding. The most common type is a bipartite patella, in which a bony mass is located in the upper outer quadrant of the patella. It is separated from the main patellar mass by opposing smooth bony surfaces. The

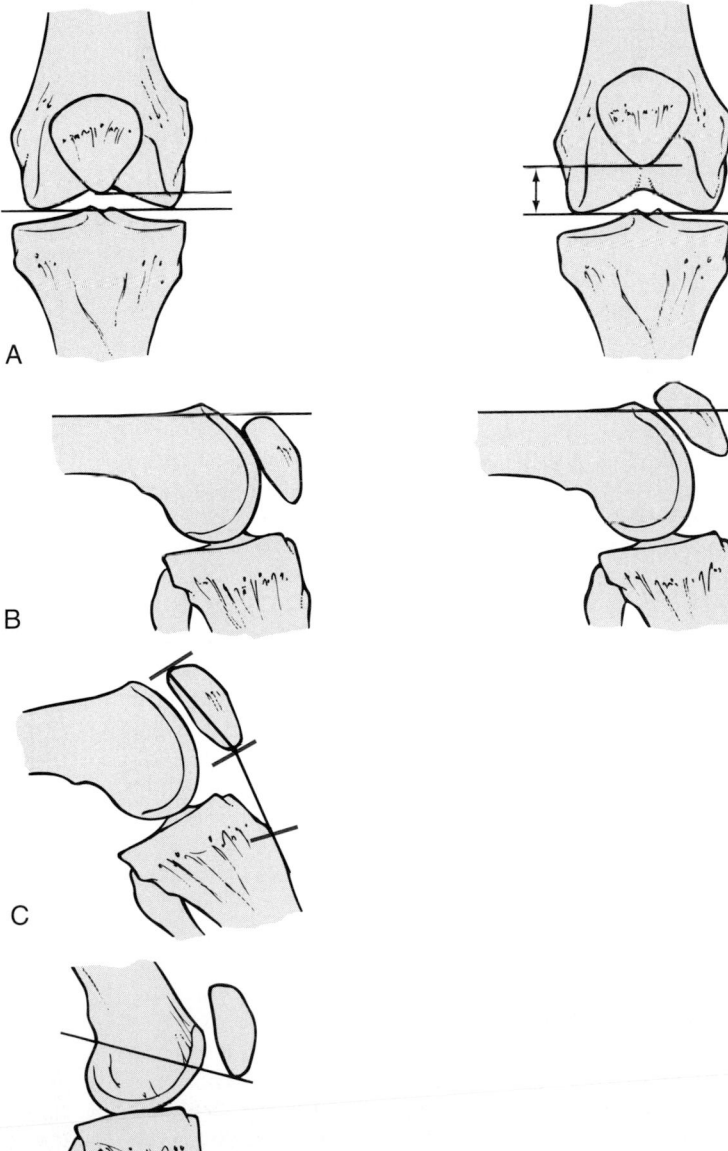

**FIGURE 54–5.** Radiographic indicators of an abnormal patellotibial relationship. An excessive distance between the distal pole of the patella and the tibial tubercle may represent disruption of the patellar ligament or chronic patella alta. *A,* On the anteroposterior view, the distal pole of the patella lies no more than 20 mm above the plane of the femoral condyles. *B,* When the knee is flexed 90°, a lateral radiograph should show that the proximal pole of the patella lies posterior to the anterior surface of the femoral shaft. *C,* On a lateral radiograph, the length of the patellar ligament (from the distal pole of the patella to the tibial tubercle) approximates that of the patella. If the patella-to-patellar ligament ratio is less than 0.8, the patella is excessively high. *D,* Blumensaat's line, the plane of the residual distal femoral physeal scar, normally projects near the distal pole of the patella (see Fig. 54–7). *(A–D,* Redrawn from Resnick, D.; Niwayama, G. Diagnosis of Bone and Joint Disorders, 2nd ed. Philadelphia, W.B. Saunders, 1988.)

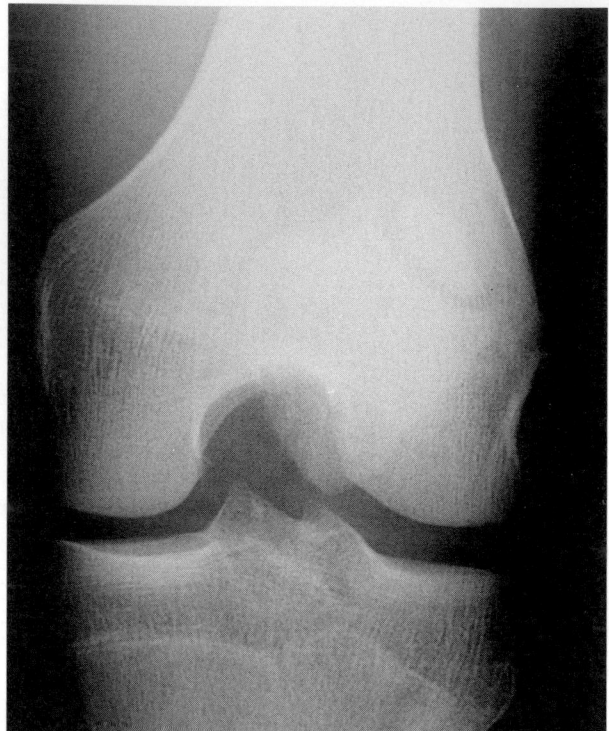

FIGURE 54–6. Radiograph of a bipartite patella demonstrating the characteristic proximal lateral ossification center with a curved, well-demarcated lucent zone of separation.

condition is generally asymptomatic and requires no treatment, but it can cause confusion when treating patients with a history of injury to the knee area.[73] In such cases, a radiograph of the opposite patella should be obtained. Invariably, a similar pattern will be found, thus making the diagnosis. A true unilateral bipartite patella is very rare and may represent an old marginal patella fracture.[32]

### Lateral

Although a lateral radiograph is easy to obtain, attention to detail is necessary because rotation of the limb will negate the benefits of this view. The proximal end of the tibia must be seen so that rupture or avulsion of the patellar ligament can be excluded (Fig. 54–7). This view of the knee will portray a transverse or comminuted patellar fracture rather dramatically. Unfortunately, however, it may prevent discovery of more subtle findings.

With the knee flexed 90°, the proximal patellar pole normally lies posterior to the anterior surface of the femur; with a ruptured patellar tendon, the proximal part of the patella rests anterior to the anterior surface of the femoral shaft (see Fig. 54–5B). The most reliable means of assessing patellar height is the method of Insall and co-workers,[21, 55] which involves determination of the ratio of the greatest diagonal patella length to patellar tendon length. In a normal subject, this ratio is 1.0. A ratio less than 1.0 suggests a high-riding patella (patella alta) or rupture of the patellar tendon. Up to 20% variance is normal (see Fig. 54–5C). Blumensaat's line, the plane of the residual distal femoral physeal scar, normally projects near the distal pole of the patella (see Fig. 54–5D).

### Tangential

Tangential or axial (sunrise, sunset, or skyline) views of the patella are primarily used in the analysis of patellofemoral disorders (Fig. 54–8). In fractures of the patella, these studies aid the surgeon in diagnosis of longitudinal (i.e., marginal or vertical) fractures and osteochondral defects.

The three most common views are those of Hughston, Laurin, and Merchant.[21, 74] Although all give approximately the same information with respect to patellofemoral congruence, the views of Hughston and Laurin are impractical in a trauma setting. The former requires that the patient be prone, whereas the latter requires patient participation.

Merchant and associates in 1974 described a method of obtaining an axial view of the patella[74] (see Fig. 54–8A). The patient is placed supine on the x-ray table with the knees flexed 45° over the end. The knees are elevated slightly to keep the femurs horizontal and parallel with the table surface. An x-ray beam is angled 30° from the horizontal. The cassette is then placed about 1 ft below the knees and perpendicular to the x-ray beam. This method is simple, easily reproducible by x-ray technicians, and able to obtain accurate radiographs in a patient with a painful, partially flexed knee secondary to hemarthrosis (see Fig. 54–8B).

## TOMOGRAPHY

The principal use of tomography in the evaluation of bony injuries about the knee is in the detection of occult fractures. Apple and associates recommended tomography over bone scanning in these cases, especially for stress fractures and in elderly patients with osteopenia and hemarthrosis.[2] In their series, routine radiographs were negative in all cases; 71% of the fractures were identified

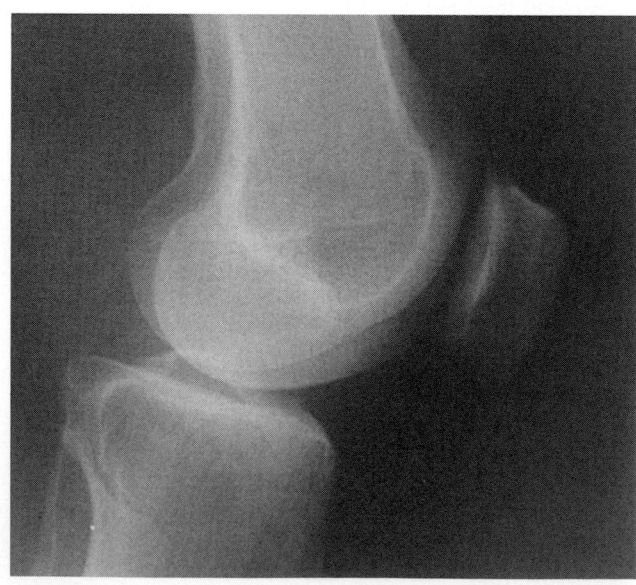

FIGURE 54–7. Lateral radiograph of a normal patella. (From Resnick, D.; Niwayama, G. Diagnosis of Bone and Joint Disorders, 2nd ed. Philadelphia, W.B. Saunders, 1988.)

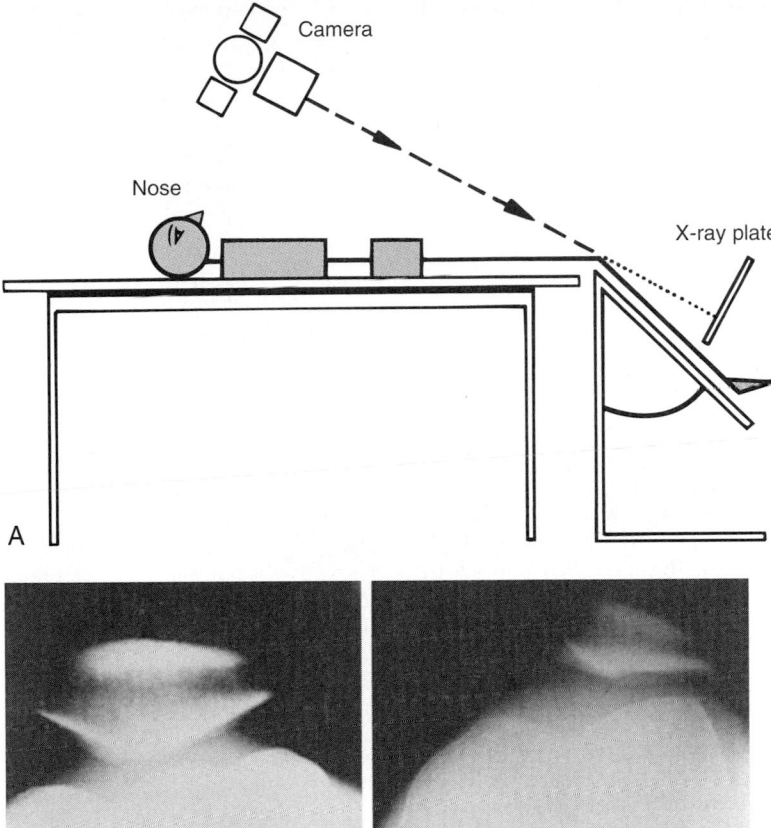

**FIGURE 54–8.** *A,* A Merchant tangential view of the patella is made with the knee flexed 45° and the radiograph exposed as shown (see text). *B,* A skyline radiograph exposed in this fashion demonstrates the patellofemoral relationship, which may be made incongruent by quadriceps contraction The image on the *left* is normal; that on the *right* shows lateral subluxation. (*B,* From Resnick, D.; Niwayama, G. Diagnosis of Bone and Joint Disorders, 2nd ed. Philadelphia, W.B. Saunders, 1988.)

with tomography versus only 30% with bone scans.[2] Tomography may also be of benefit in the evaluation of patellar nonunion or malunion.[107]

Although theoretically of benefit to the diagnostician, CT scanning is rarely used for evaluation of an isolated patella fracture. It is generally performed as an incidental study during the evaluation of distal femoral or proximal tibial fractures. The information presented rarely adds to that obtained with more conventional techniques. CT may aid the surgeon in evaluation of articular incongruity in cases of nonunion, malunion, and patellofemoral alignment disorders (Fig. 54–9).

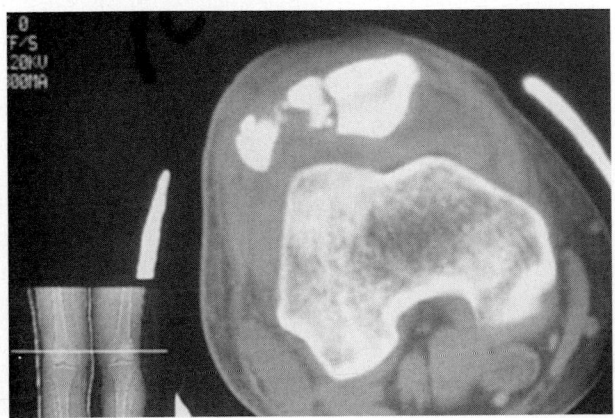

**FIGURE 54–9.** Computed tomographic scan of a fractured patella. Note the extent of comminution, as well as the secondary sagittal fracture and the resulting articular incongruity.

## BONE SCANNING

Scintigraphic examinations with technetium-labeled phosphate compounds are helpful in the diagnosis of stress fractures, although our preference would be to obtain plain tomograms. A bone scan may also be useful with indium-labeled leukocytes or gallium scanning for the assessment of patellar osteomyelitis.

## MAGNETIC RESONANCE IMAGING

MRI has become increasingly useful in the early diagnosis of extensor mechanism injuries. A normal quadriceps tendon has a laminated appearance on MRI studies, whereas the patellar tendon has a homogeneous low signal intensity. The normal patella has the signal intensity of cancellous and cortical bone.[115]

Injuries of all types can produce hemorrhage and edema, which cause increased signal intensity on T2-weighted images. Patella fractures and avulsions of the tibial tubercle do not generally require MRI evaluation but will result in changes in marrow signal intensity.[115]

Complete rupture of the quadriceps tendon is well demonstrated by MRI, and transection of all layers of the tendon is diagnostic of a complete rupture. In the more unusual patellar tendon ruptures, MRI evaluation shows absence of distinct margins and increased signal intensity within the patellar tendon.[115]

Dislocation of the patella produces a characteristic pattern of change on MRI that allows diagnosis of this injury even if the patient is initially seen after relocation of the patella.[104] These findings include contusion of the lateral femoral condyle (manifested as low signal intensity on T1-weighted images), tear of the medial retinaculum, and joint effusion.

## FRACTURE CLASSIFICATION

The three major categories of patella fractures are transverse, stellate, and vertical. Transverse fractures that are proximal (basal) or distal (apical) are termed polar. Because

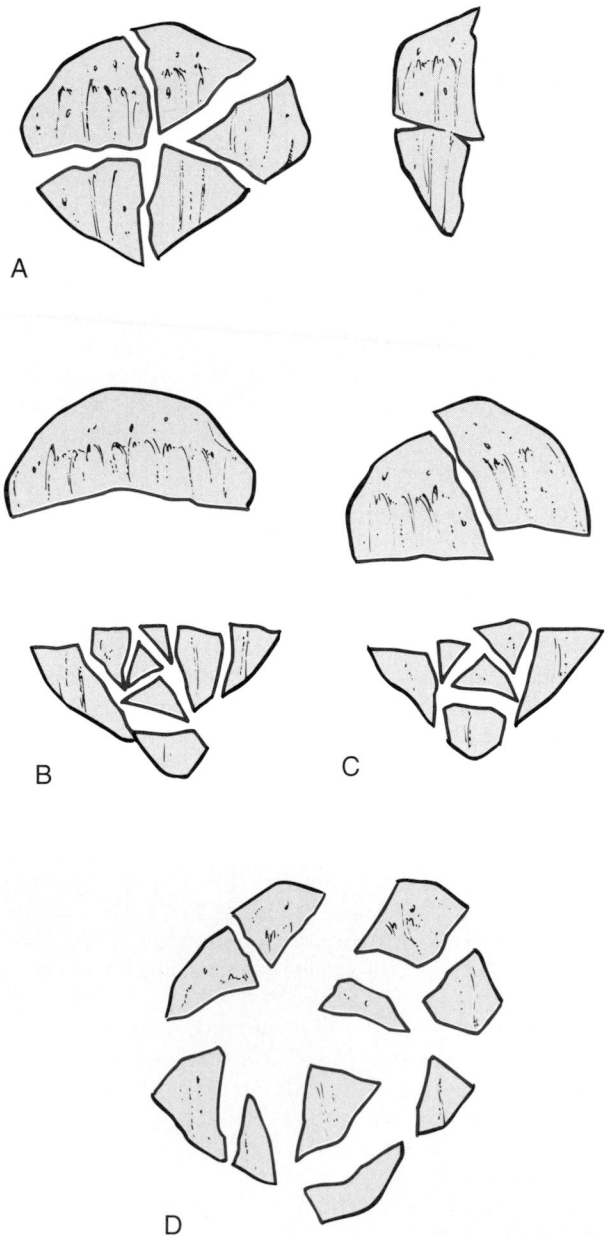

**Figure 54–10.** Examples of patellar fractures. *A,* Undisplaced fractures may have any degree of comminution, but fragments are displaced no more than 3 mm. The articular surface as seen on the lateral view should have a step-off of no more than 2 mm. *B,* Displaced transverse fracture with comminution of the apical pole. *C,* Displaced transverse fracture with comminution of both the apical and basilar poles. *D,* Highly comminuted, highly displaced fracture.

| **Table 54–1** |
|---|
| Fracture Classification |

A. Nondisplaced fractures
   1. Stellate
   2. Transverse
   3. Vertical
B. Displaced fractures
   1. Noncomminuted
      a. Transverse (central)
      b. Polar
         1. Apical
         2. Basal
   2. Comminuted
      a. Stellate
      b. Transverse
      c. Polar
      d. Highly comminuted, highly displaced
C. Fractures associated with bone–patellar tendon–bone autograft
   1. Longitudinal
   2. Transverse

these usually extra-articular disruptions of the quadriceps pose different therapeutic challenges, they are classified separately[13, 68] (Fig. 54–10). Wide variations within each fracture pattern have prevented the creation of a useful classification scheme.[11, 13, 92] Because of this difficulty, most authors have reviewed long term results according to treatment rather than fracture type.[11, 13, 14, 25, 68, 82, 92, 100]

For the purposes of this chapter, existing classification schemes were combined for better understanding[11, 13, 68, 100] (Table 54–1). Although the terms stellate and comminuted are interchangeable in much of the published literature, we recommend distinguishing comminuted transverse fractures, which often have retinacular disruption, from stellate patellar fractures, which are associated with an intact retinaculum.

## Nondisplaced Fractures

### STELLATE

Stellate fractures of the patella are the result of a direct compressive blow that forces the bone against the femoral condyles. Damage to the articular cartilage of the femoral condyles and the creation of osteochondral fragments may occur and must be ruled out.[19] Typically, well over half (65%) of these fractures are nondisplaced. In these fractures, the blow is insufficient to tear the patellar retinaculum, and active extension of the knee is therefore possible. Displacement between fragments is, by definition, less than 3 mm, and displacement between the articular surfaces, less than 2 mm. Unless an osteochondral fragment is present and requires arthrotomy or arthroscopy, nonoperative therapy is indicated (Fig. 54–11).

### TRANSVERSE

Transverse fractures of the patella are the result of a tensile stress applied to the extensor mechanism. Typically, 35% or more of all transverse patellar fractures are nondisplaced.[1, 13] Damage to both the femoral and the patellar articular surface is minimal,[89] and the force is usually insufficient to tear the medial and lateral patellar retinaculum.[13, 42, 73, 89, 92] As a result, the patient retains the ability to extend the knee. In addition, the intact soft tissue envelope maintains patellar alignment; typically, less than 3 mm of fragment diastasis and 2 mm of articular incongruity exist. If these conditions are met, nonoperative treatment is suggested (see Fig. 54–10).

## VERTICAL

Vertical fractures (marginal or longitudinal fractures), contrary to earlier reports, are a common type of patellar fracture, with a combined incidence of 22% (384/1707) in several large series.[9, 14, 32] The fracture may be caused by different mechanisms. Dowd stated that direct compression of the patella in a slightly hyperflexed knee creates this fracture.[32] In Boström's series, lateral avulsions accounted for more than 75% of all vertical fractures.[14] Bony separation is most commonly found at the junction of the middle and lateral thirds of the patella; less commonly, a medial pole avulsion may occur.

Clinically, the patient has a somewhat painful knee and a mild effusion. Full extension of the joint is possible because the patellar retinaculum is intact.[9, 14, 32] A diastasis of greater than 3 mm is most unusual.[13, 14] The fracture may be missed on standard radiographs, and therefore axial views are usually necessary to make the diagnosis.[9, 14] If the defect is seen on the AP radiograph, it may easily be mistaken for a bipartite patella, so radiographs of the opposite limb should be obtained. Because the fracture fragments are minimally displaced and the patellar retinaculum remains intact, these fractures are best treated nonoperatively.

## Displaced Fractures

### NONCOMMINUTED

#### Transverse/Midpatellar

Displaced fractures account for slightly more than half (52%) of all noncomminuted transverse fractures of the patella. The diagnosis is made in a patient with loss of active extension of the knee (after aspiration), more than 3-mm separation between fracture fragments, or an articular step greater than 2 mm.[8–10, 73, 92] These findings suggest retinacular disruption and joint incongruity. Either finding warrants operative repair (Fig. 54–12).

Some patients may have a gap of 4 to 5 mm between fracture fragments but can extend their leg actively. McMaster warned of nonunion in these patients when treated conservatively.[73] Boström, in reviewing the results of his and other large published series, however, concluded that active extension implied retinacular continuity and that these patients could heal satisfactorily without surgery.[13] We concur with his advice.

### Polar

Polar fractures of the patella are transverse fractures occurring either proximal or distal to the patella equator and taking varying amounts of bone. Proximal, or basal pole, fractures imply avulsion of the quadriceps mechanism from the patella. The amount of accompanying retinacular rupture determines the patient's ability to extend the leg. Displacement is extremely rare and was seen in less than 4% of patients in several large series.[13, 92]

Distal, or apical, fractures are bony avulsions of the proximal patellar tendon (Fig. 54–13). These fractures, which occur toward the distal margin of the retinaculum, are almost invariably associated with loss of knee extension. As a result, displacement in apical fractures is almost three times as common (11.5%) as in basal injuries.

### COMMINUTED

#### Stellate

A result of direct compression, comminuted stellate fractures usually exhibit displacement with varying degrees of comminution.[19] Although the patellar retinaculum is intact, operative intervention is indicated because of existing articular incongruity (Fig. 54–14).

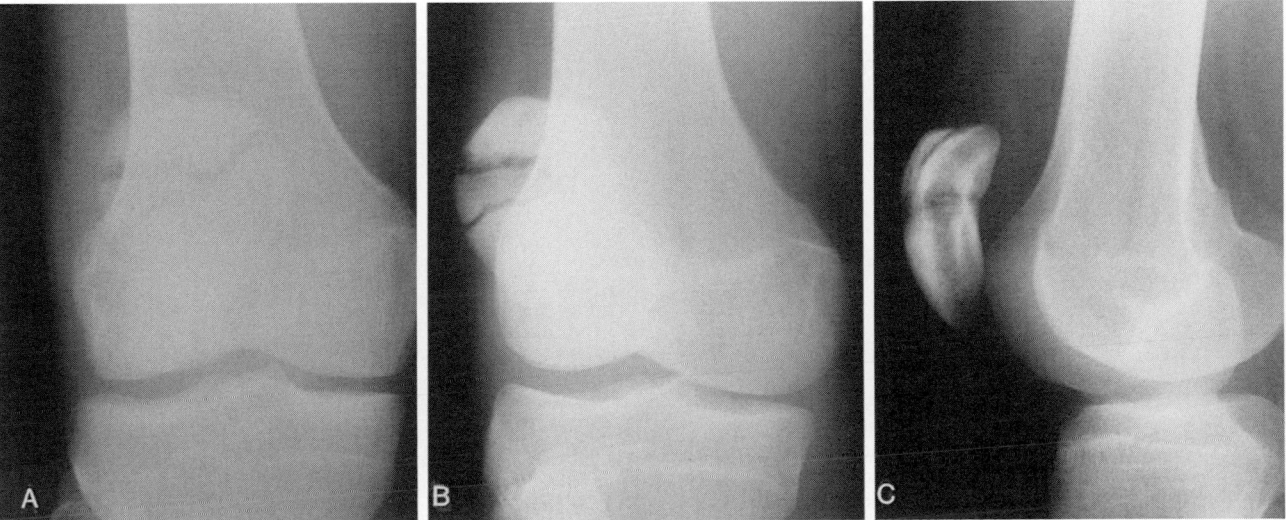

**FIGURE 54–11.** Nondisplaced stellate fracture of the patella. Radiographic projections are anteroposterior *(A)*, oblique *(B)*, and lateral *(C)*.

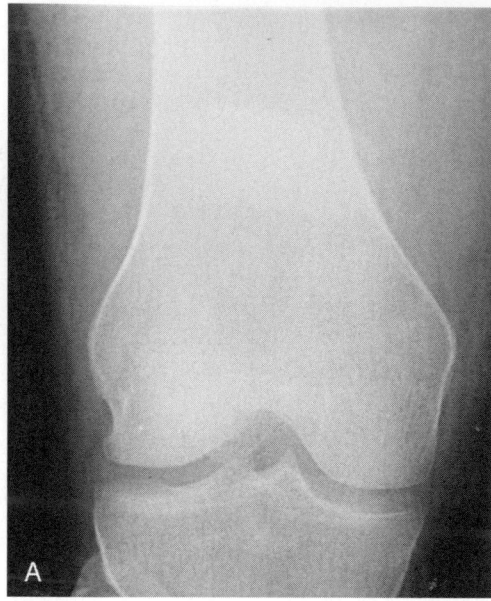
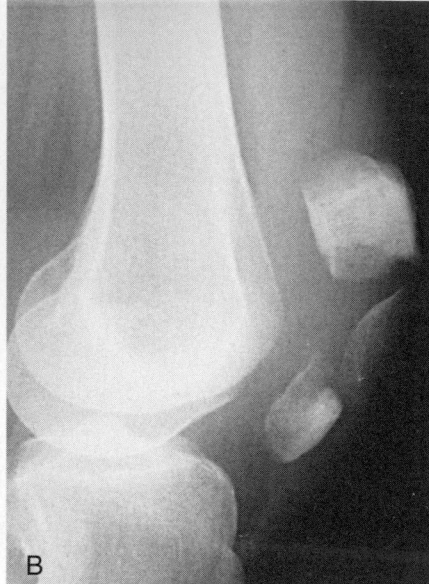

**FIGURE 54–12.** Displaced transverse fracture of the patella. *A*, Anteroposterior radiograph. *B*, Lateral radiograph.

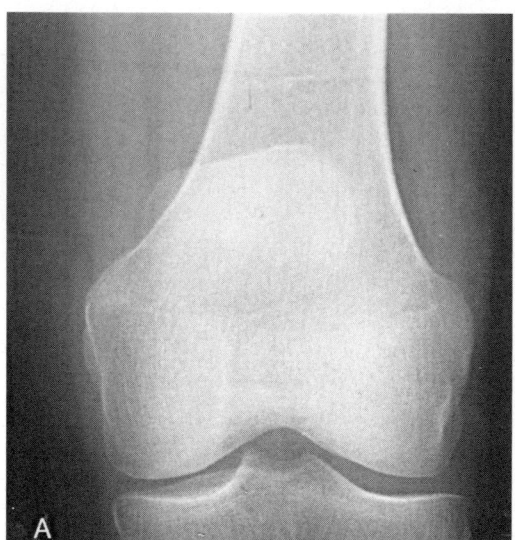
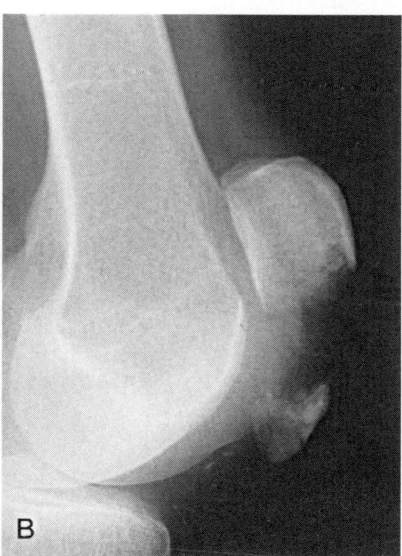

**FIGURE 54–13.** Displaced distal polar fracture of the patella. *A*, Anteroposterior radiograph. *B*, Lateral radiograph.

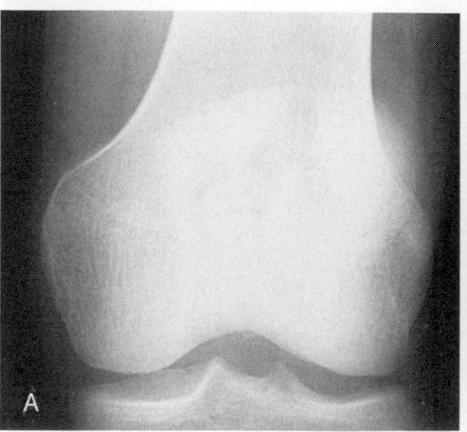
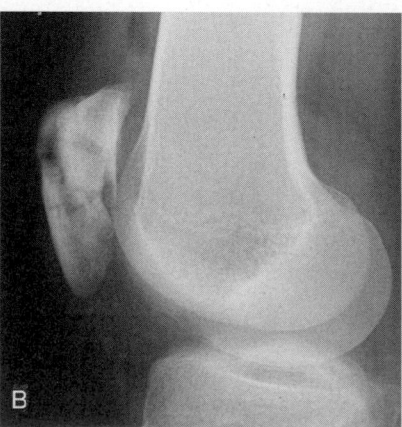
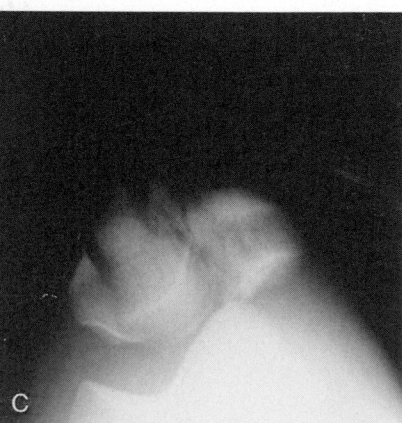

**FIGURE 54–14.** Displaced stellate fracture of the patella. *A*, Anteroposterior view. The fracture is difficult to see. *B*, Lateral view. The fracture is apparent, but displacement appears to be only moderate. *C*, A skyline radiograph clearly indicates displacement and incongruity of the articular surfaces.

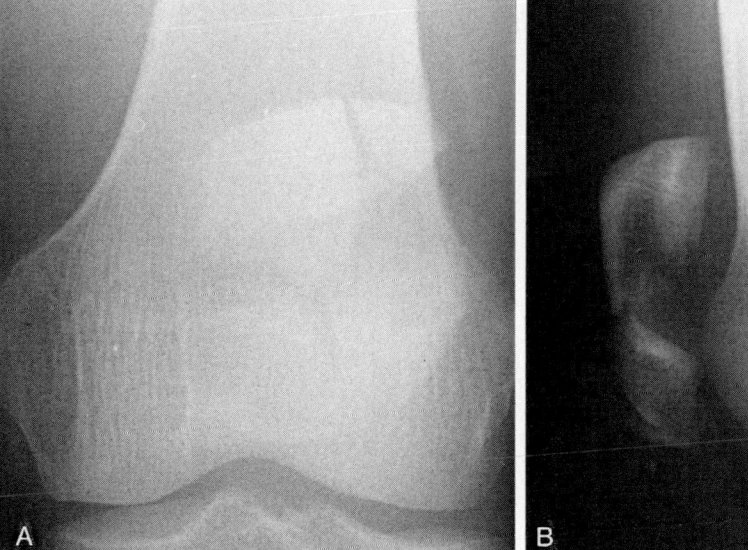

**FIGURE 54–15.** Comminuted transverse fracture of the patella. *A,* Anteroposterior view. The details of the fracture's configuration are hard to see. The main displaced transverse component and secondary vertical fracture lines are evident. *B,* Lateral view. Displacement is more obvious, but comminution is less apparent.

### Transverse/Polar

These comminuted fractures exhibit varying degrees of comminution of one major patellar fragment. Upper fragment comminution is usually accompanied by one or two additional fracture lines that are minimally displaced. Lower fragment comminution is generally more severe and may be accompanied by upper pole comminution.[11, 13] Comminution is much more prevalent in the lower pole than the upper pole.

### Highly Comminuted, Highly Displaced

Highly comminuted and displaced fractures consist of either transverse fractures with massive comminution secondary to compression or stellate fractures with massive diastasis secondary to a violent quadriceps contraction (Fig. 54–15). All major fragments are separated by more than 6 mm, and sagittal splits are often present as well. These fractures frequently occur as open injuries and can be accompanied by supracondylar femur fractures.

### Fractures Associated with Bone–Patellar Tendon–Bone Autograft

A subset of patella fractures has been reported in patients who have had a bone–patellar tendon–bone autograft for reconstruction of the anterior cruciate ligament.[6, 17, 75, 103] An incidence of approximately 0.2% has been reported in one study involving 1320 anterior cruciate reconstructions.[103] The etiology of these fractures is most often related to a traumatic fall or injury, but it has been hypothesized that an "accelerated" rehabilitation protocol may put patients at higher risk than the traditional rehabilitation protocol.[17] These fractures occur in two patterns. A transverse fracture is the most common and is generally treated with traditional tension band wiring or screw fixation techniques.[6] Vertical, or "fissure," fractures have been noted as well. These injuries are thought to occur from a stress riser created by a rectangular bone plug in the patella or as a nondisplaced fracture created by the

osteotome at the time of graft harvest.[7, 75] These fractures are treated by neutralization with screws directed in the coronal plane. The screws are not placed in a lag fashion because of the potential to create a distracting force at the articular surface secondary to the defect from harvesting of a graft.[6] The rehabilitation protocol need not be modified if the fractures are rigidly fixed, and rehabilitation should be aggressively pursued.

## TREATMENT

Management of patella fractures is based on the morphology of the injury. Options include nonoperative treatment, tension band wiring, lag screw fixation, partial patellectomy, partial patellectomy combined with tension band wiring, and total patellectomy. These techniques are performed with careful reconstruction of the extensor mechanism and the patellar joint surface whenever possible. Figure 54–16 outlines this chapter's proposed algorithm for the management of patella fractures. Specific details of fixation may need to be modified to accommodate a given fracture pattern.

### Biomechanics of Patellar Fracture Fixation

Carpenter and colleagues compared three internal fixation constructs for transverse patella fractures in a cadaver model.[20] The three constructs included a modified tension band (AO technique), two parallel 4.5-mm interfragmentary lag screws, and a 4.0-mm cannulated lag screw technique with a tension band through the cannulated screws[20] (Fig. 54–17). A significant difference in displacement was noted between the modified tension band construct and the lag screw techniques. The highest load to failure occurred with the cannulated lag screw and tension band construct. They concluded that the cannulated lag

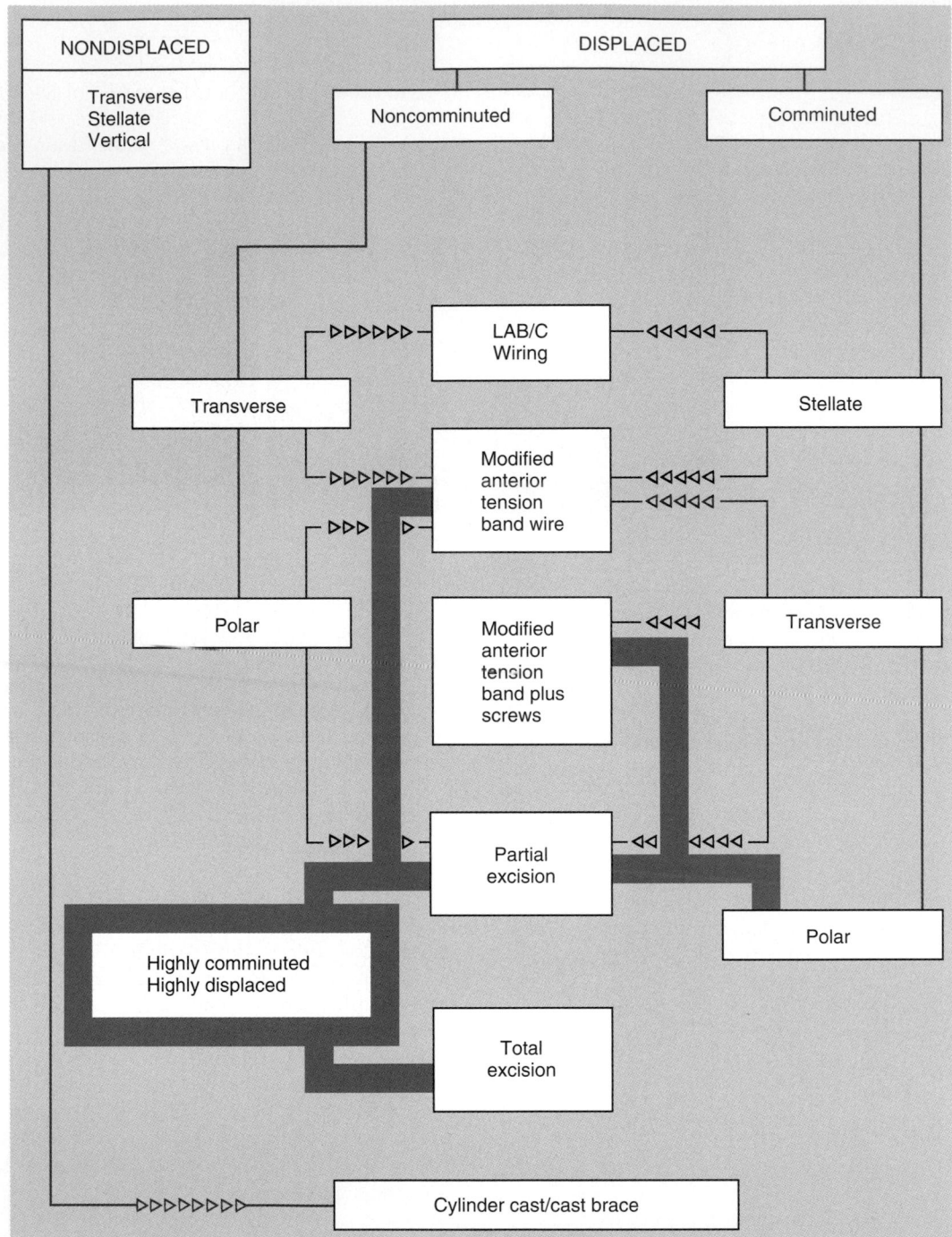

**Figure 54–16.** Displacement and the fracture pattern both guide the choice of treatment with which to obtain the two primary goals of quadriceps mechanism continuity and stable anatomic reduction of the patellar articular surface. Nondisplaced fractures are managed nonoperatively. Displaced articular fractures are repaired, if possible, by using tension band wiring techniques with or without screws or interosseous wiring. Polar avulsion fractures may be excised, but secure reattachment of the quadriceps or patellar tendon is required. If comminution prevents satisfactory repair, total patellectomy may be the only option to restore the quadriceps. *Abbreviation:* LAB/C, longitudinal anterior band plus cerclage.

screw and tension band technique provided improved stability in the fixation of transverse fractures of the patella.

Scilaris and associates compared tension band techniques with a monofilament wire versus a braided cable in a transverse patella fracture cadaver model.[88] The braided cable construct allowed significantly less fracture displacement in cyclic loading than did the monofilament construct. They concluded that the braided cable plus tension band construct was superior to the monofilament technique and was more predictable in cyclic loading.

## Open Fractures

Open patellar fractures are surgical emergencies, and surgeons must be aware of the possibility of osteomyelitis and septic arthritis. Irrigation, débridement, and stable fixation remain the principles of treatment. Devitalized fragments should not be saved, and heroic efforts at salvage are not indicated. Fixation should be performed with a minimum of soft tissue stripping and must be stable. Subsequent repeat débridement will be necessary, and closure may require skin grafts, muscle flaps, or free tissue transfer.

Catalano and co-workers retrospectively reported on a series of 79 open patella fractures with an average of 21 months of follow-up.[22] Open fractures were classified as grade I (15%), grade II (53%), and grade III (32%) injuries. Additionally, most open patella fractures were displaced, with 22% being transverse fractures and 39% being comminuted fractures. Approximately 80% of the patients sustained multiple injuries. Treatment consisted of operative débridement and irrigation with appropriate antibiotics, followed by open reduction and internal fixation in 57% and partial patellectomy in 32%. Eleven percent were treated with débridement only, and no patients had a primary total patellectomy. They reported no deep infections, and only one patient required repeat open reduction and internal fixation. Seventy-six percent of the patients were available for follow-up, and they had an average of 112° of knee motion.[22]

## Nonoperative Treatment

Indications for nonoperative management include transverse, stellate, and vertical nondisplaced closed patellar fractures. Treatment consists of extension splinting for 4 to 6 weeks.[13, 42, 73, 89, 92] If plaster is used, care should be taken to extend the cast from a few centimeters above the malleoli to the groin (not the middle of the thigh). If the patient is elderly or has varicose veins, an Unna boot is applied to the foot and ankle before casting to minimize swelling.[92]

Immediate weight bearing as tolerated is permitted. Isometric quadriceps exercises and straight leg raises are encouraged within several days.[13, 42, 73] After radiographic evidence of consolidation, usually at 4 weeks, the plaster may be removed, and progressive active (not passive) flexion and strengthening exercises are begun.

In reliable patients, we prefer the use of an off-the-shelf hinged knee brace. These braces are lightweight and easily adjustable and permit controlled motion of the knee joint. The knee hinge is locked in extension during ambulation but may be opened to permit controlled motion during the convalescent period. This type of brace may be advantageous for elderly patients. A simple knee immobilizer of adequate length is a similar alternative.

## Operative Treatment

### PREOPERATIVE PLANNING

Before embarking on surgical repair of the patella, an operative plan should be firmly established. Formulation of the plan requires radiographic evaluation of the normal opposite patella. On tracing paper or clear x-ray film, the normal patella is outlined. The fracture fragments are then

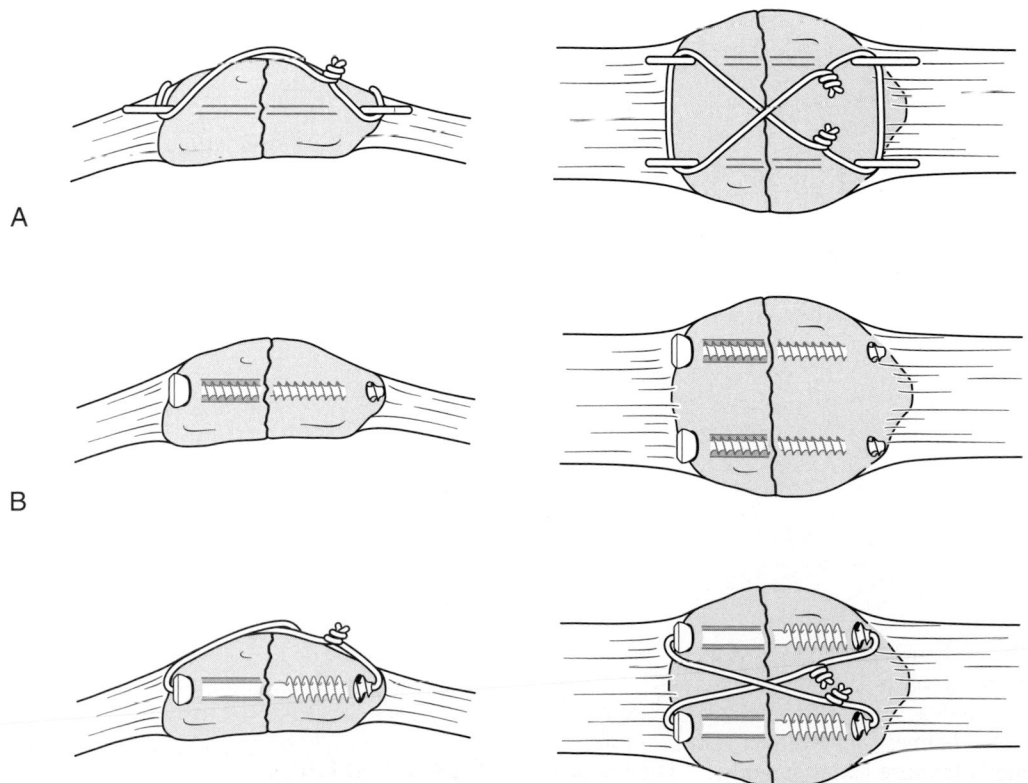

A

B

C

**FIGURE 54–17.** Comparison of constructs for internal fixation of patella fractures. *A,* AO modified tension band construct. *B,* AO compression screws, 4.5 mm. *C,* Cannulated 4.0-mm screws combined with a tension band. (From Carpenter, J.E.; et al. J Orthop Trauma 11:351–356, 1997.)

superimposed onto this outline in both the AP and the lateral planes. In effect, such superimposition "reduces" the fracture. Attention is then turned to fixation, be it wires, screws, partial excision, or a combination of methods. These elements should be drawn onto the plan and numbered in sequence. Finally, contingency plans, as well as the necessary equipment, should be listed. The surgeon should be aware that superimposition of the patella on the femur makes this exercise difficult at times. It therefore requires optimal radiographic technique and an awareness that unanticipated comminution may be encountered.

Preoperative planning allows the surgeon to think through the operative procedure and become acquainted with the personality of the fracture. In addition, equipment requirements will be known beforehand, thus promoting a smoother operation without unnecessary delays. When this plan is followed, the postoperative film will appear remarkably similar to the preoperative plan.

## EQUIPMENT

A wire set incorporating Kirschner wires (K-wires), 1.2-mm (18-gauge) and 1-mm (19-gauge) wire on spools, wire holders, wire tighteners, wire pliers, and a wire passer is necessary, along with a power drill and a wire driver (Fig. 54–18). A small-fragment instrument and implant set and Weber (large, pointed) bone reduction forceps are also useful. A special patella clamp is an invaluable device because the Weber clamps may rotate. Angiocatheters (14 or 16 gauge) are helpful for passing wire. A

large-fragment set should always be available. Large osteochondral fragments will require minifragment screws or Herbert screws, and for small fragments, absorbable polyglactin 910 (Vicryl) pins (Ethipins) should be on hand.

## SETUP

The patient is placed in the supine position, and a tourniquet is applied high on the thigh, if desired. Trapping of the quadriceps may cause difficulty in repositioning the patella when the tourniquet is inflated. This complication may be prevented by flexing the knee carefully beyond 90° to bring the quadriceps and proximal patella fragment down before inflating the tourniquet. In patients with complete retinacular disruption and a high-riding proximal patellar fragment, a sterile tourniquet can be inflated, if necessary, after the patella has been brought down with an Esmarch bandage wrapped in a proximal-to-distal direction.[23]

## INCISIONS

Although any anterior knee incision can be used, a transverse, midline longitudinal, or lateral parapatellar incision is preferred (Fig. 54–19). In patients with severe retinacular disruption, a transverse incision should parallel this disruption to minimize the development of flaps.[68, 79] In more comminuted fractures, a midline longitudinal or lateral parapatellar incision is necessary, especially if concomitant injuries suggest the possibility of joint replace-

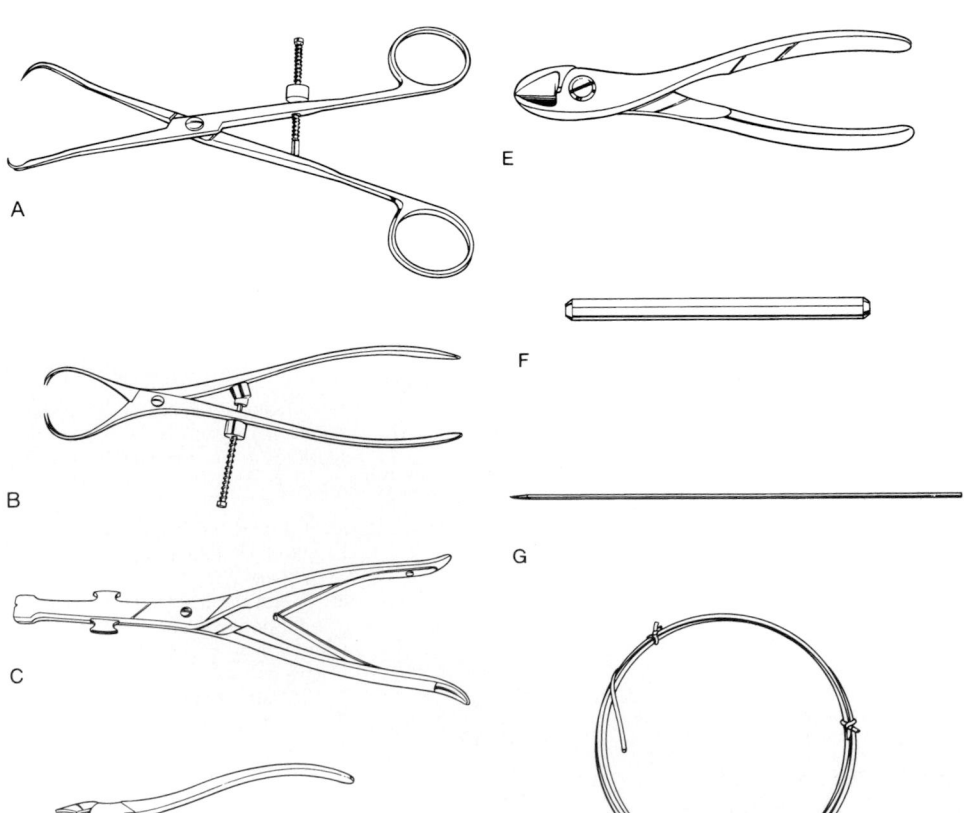

**FIGURE 54–18.** Instruments and implants helpful for fixation of patella fractures include pointed reduction forceps for large bones (*A*), patella forceps (*B*), wire tightener (*C*), wire-bending pliers (*D*), wire cutter (*E*) for Kirschner wires, wire bender/impactor (*F*), Kirschner wire (*G*), and malleable wire at least 1 mm in diameter (*H*).

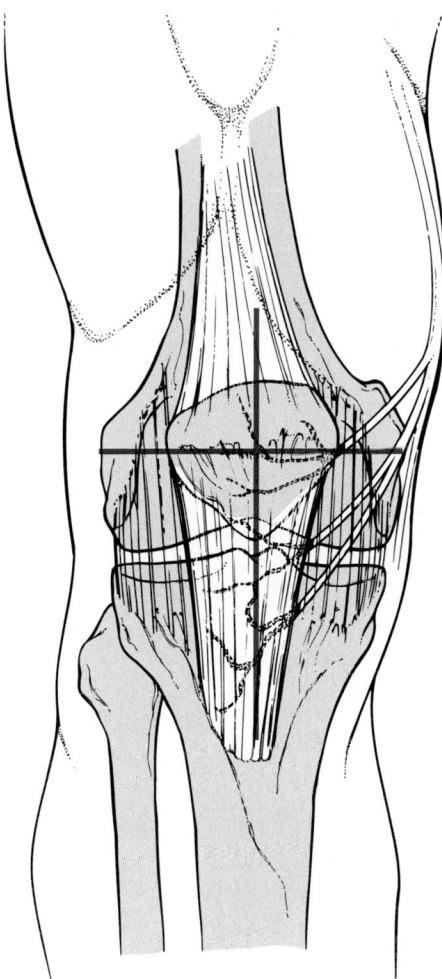

**FIGURE 54–19.** Incisions for exposure and treatment of patellar fractures. Either a longitudinal or a transverse approach may be used. Sufficient exposure to see and effectively repair medial and lateral retinacular tears is important. Superficial dissection should be avoided to preserve thickness and viability of the skin flaps.

ment in the future. These latter incisions also avoid damage to the saphenous branch of the femoral nerve medially. A percutaneous fixation technique for patella fractures has been described. This method might be considered with severely compromised skin.[69] Berg has described an extensile exposure for comminuted fractures of the patella that involves osteotomy of a tibial tubercle for retropatellar exposure and fracture fixation.[7] This technique facilitates exposure and reconstruction of the patella and maintenance of bone stock without any morbidity associated with the tibial tubercle osteotomy. Additionally, ablative salvage procedures can be avoided and thus further improve joint reconstruction options in the future.

## OPERATIVE TECHNIQUES

All displaced fractures of the patella require operative intervention. As previously mentioned, the techniques used are based on the fracture pattern and concomitant injuries (Table 54–2).

### Tension Band Wiring

**Modified Anterior Tension Band Wiring.** For displaced noncomminuted two-part transverse patellar fractures, open reduction and internal fixation using the modified anterior tension band technique is the treatment of choice (Fig. 54–20).

A midline longitudinal incision is made through the skin and overlying bursa. The fracture edges are exposed and completely cleaned of debris and clot, with care taken to not devitalize the fragments. The knee joint is then irrigated to remove any loose fragments.

A preliminary reduction is performed to evaluate the proper position of the fragments. The reduction is then taken down, and the proximal fragment is flexed 90°. A hole is drilled through the proximal fragment in a retrograde manner with a 2-mm drill bit. This hole should start within the fracture line, approximately 5 mm from the anterior surface of the patella and at the junction of a line separating the patella into thirds. The drill bit is then exchanged for a 1.6-mm K-wire that is pushed proximally until it is flush with the fracture edge. A second hole (parallel to the first and at the junction of a line separating the patella into thirds) is drilled. The drill bit is exchanged with a K-wire in a similar manner. The fracture is then reduced and held with Weber or patellar reduction forceps. The wires are sequentially removed and the holes drilled distally with a 2.0-mm drill bit up to, but not through, the distal cortex. A prebent 1.6-mm K-wire is inserted into the drill hole and hammered through the far cortex. Next, a 1.2-mm (18-gauge) wire is placed underneath the upper hooks and the lower protruding pin tips. The wire is loosely tightened with a wire tightener. The reduction is

**TABLE 54–2** ·····························

Treatment of Patella Fractures

| Patella Fracture Type | Treatment |
|---|---|
| A. Nondisplaced fractures | Cylinder cast |
|   1. Transverse | |
|   2. Stellate | |
|   3. Vertical | |
| B. Displaced fractures | |
|   1. Noncomminuted | |
|     a. Transverse | Modified anterior tension band wiring |
|     b. Polar | Partial patellectomy |
|       1. Apical | Modified anterior tension band wiring |
|       2. Basal | |
|   2. Comminuted | |
|     a. Stellate | Modified anterior tension band wiring |
|  | Longitudinal anterior tension band plus cerclage |
|     b. Transverse | Independent lag screws plus modified anterior tension band wiring |
|  | Longitudinal anterior tension band wiring |
|  | Partial patellectomy |
|     c. Polar | Partial patellectomy |
|     d. Highly comminuted, highly displaced | Modified anterior tension band wiring |
|  | Longitudinal anterior tension band wiring |
|  | Partial patellectomy |
|  | Total patellectomy |

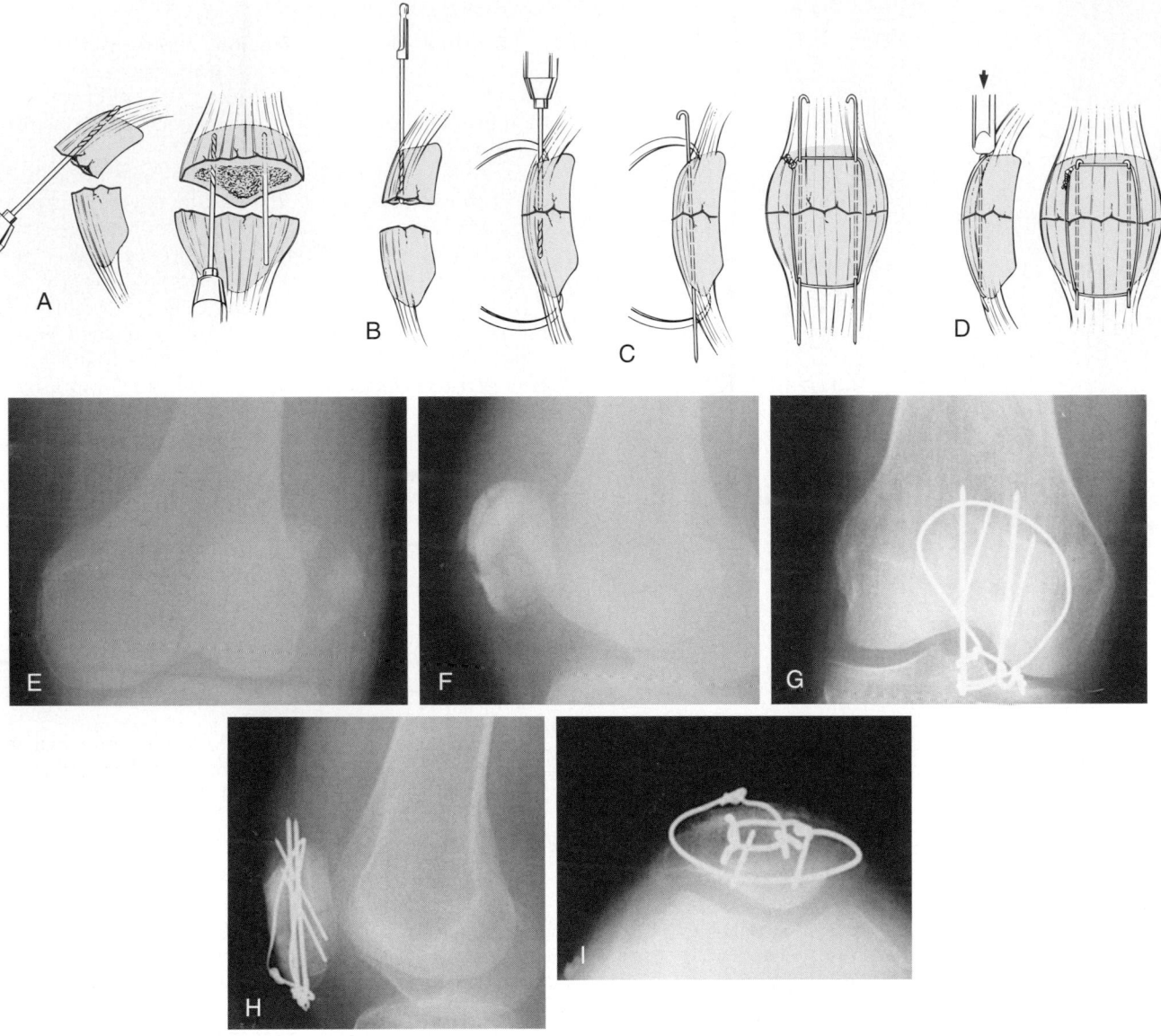

**FIGURE 54–20.** Modified AO tension band technique for patella fracture fixation (see text). *A,* Retrograde drilling of the proximal fragment. Kirschner wires mark the proximal ends of the holes during reduction. *B,* Reduction, clamping, and antegrade partial drilling of the distal fragment. K-wires with prebent proximal ends are then hammered through the remaining bone of the distal pole. *C,* With a large-bore needle, the 1.2-mm tension band wire is placed deep to the proximal and distal ends of the K-wires immediately adjacent to the patella through the stout soft tissue attachments of the quadriceps tendon and patellar ligament. Medially and laterally, the tension band wire lies anterior to the patella and is not usually crossed. It is tightened and twisted securely, and the "pigtail" end is bent flush with the bone surface. A twist or a square knot is reliable. The AO bent-wire fastening technique is not secure enough for definitive fixation. *D,* The prebent proximal ends of the K-wires are driven into the proximal pole, and the distal ends are trimmed if necessary. *E, F,* Anteroposterior (AP) and lateral radiographs show a displaced comminuted patellar fracture. *G,* AP radiograph after fixation. Note the modifications in technique for fixation of comminuted fragments: supplementary K-wires, distal-to-proximal K-wire insertion, and a distally crossed tension band wire, which was tightened with medial and lateral twists to equalize tension. *H, I,* Lateral and skyline views show anatomic reduction and anterior placement of the tension band wire.

checked by extending the knee and palpating the undersurface of the patella with a finger. If a finger cannot be easily inserted through the retinacular tear (or if none exists), the retinaculum should be longitudinally incised to permit insertion. If articular congruity is satisfactory, the wire should be twisted tightly with a wire tightener and buried. The K-wires are twisted so that the bend is facing backward and then buried in the patella. The excess distal ends of the K-wires are cut off distally.

Although certain authors recommend crossing the tension band wire, in our experience, crossing reduces the area of patella that can be compressed and often leads to an unstable osteosynthesis. A prefabricated cerclage loop (AO type) is also not recommended for use as a tension band wire because it can come undone with early motion. Finally, the retinaculum is sutured closed with figure-of-eight 0 Vicryl interrupted sutures, and the wound is closed in layers over a drain.

**Modified Anterior Tension Band Wiring through Cannulated Compression Screws.** When failure of the standard tension band technique is a concern in an elderly patient with osteopenic bone, an alternative is a modified

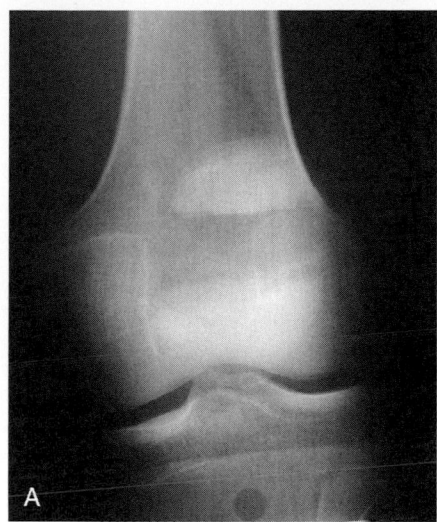 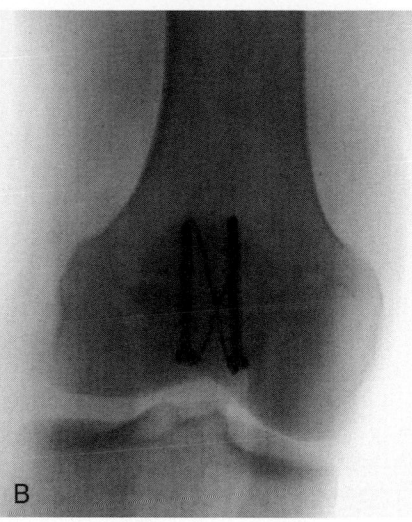 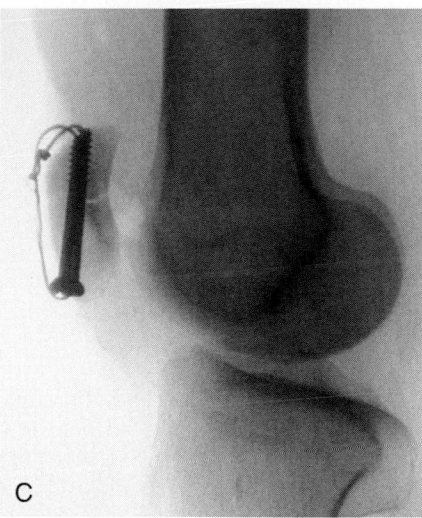

**FIGURE 54–21.** Tension band technique through cannulated compression screws. *A,* Transverse patella fracture. *B,* Anteroposterior view of 4.5-mm cannulated compression screw fixation with a tension band wire. *C,* Lateral view demonstrating the tension band construct through cannulated compression screws.

anterior tension band through cannulated compression screws.[8] Berg described this technique in which two parallel cannulated cancellous screws are placed longitudinally over guide wires with lagged interfragmentary compression. An 18-gauge AO wire is then passed in a figure-of-eight fashion through the cannulated screws and tightened with a Kirschner traction bow. The remainder of the fixation technique remains the same as for the standard anterior tension band construct (Fig. 54–21).

**Longitudinal Anterior Band plus Cerclage Wiring.** Minimally displaced stellate fractures requiring operative intervention may not have a single fragment large enough to permit a modified anterior tension band technique. In these cases, either the K-wire should be angled appropriately or the longitudinal anterior band plus cerclage (LAB/C) wiring technique of Lotke and Ecker may be used[68] (Fig. 54–22).

The patella is approached, and the fragments are cleaned as described in the section Modified Anterior

Tension Band Wiring. Two parallel Beath-Steinmann pins (with holes in the distal tip) are drilled 1 cm from the patellar edges through the aligned patella fragments in an antegrade manner. A 22-gauge wire is then inserted into both drill holes, and both pins are removed proximally. The distal loop is brought anteriorly, and one free proximal end is passed through this anterior loop. It is then tied to the other proximal end and tightened. This technique results in a strong and secure combination of anterior band and interosseous wiring techniques. Heavier-gauge wire may be safer for fixation—for example, 18-gauge wire passed with the aid of a large angiocatheter placed over the K-wire and held in place when it is withdrawn.

If marked comminution is present, a cerclage wire should first be placed around the circumference of the patella, which can easily be done with a wire passer or a 16- or 14-gauge angiocatheter inserted immediately next to the patella. The LAB/C wiring is then performed. The retinaculum is sutured closed with figure-of-eight 0 Vicryl

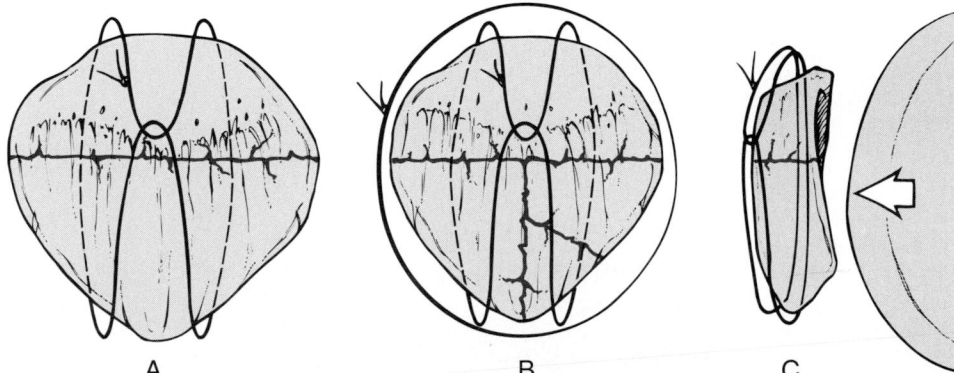

**FIGURE 54–22.** Longitudinal anterior band plus cerclage technique for interfragmentary wire loop fixation of patella fractures. *A,* For transverse fractures, the two ends of a wire loop are passed through longitudinal drill holes in the patella. One of these wire ends is then passed through the loop made by the middle of the wire distally. Next, the ends are pulled tight and twisted to provide a taut anterior tension band. *B,* Lateral view. *C,* In fractures with significant comminution, fixation is aided by first placing a cerclage wire around the patella to trap the comminuted fragments and then drilling and applying the longitudinal anterior band wire as in *A.* (*A–C,* Redrawn from Lotke, P.A.; Ecker, M.L. Clin Orthop 158:180–184, 1981.)

interrupted sutures, and the wound is closed in layers over a drain.

**Independent Lag Screws plus Modified Anterior Tension Band Wiring.** Transverse fractures may have one or two additional fracture lines in the main fragments that separate the main fragments into halves or thirds. These secondary fracture lines are not usually displaced, but they may become so after operative intervention is attempted. The general principles of internal fixation of fractures should be followed (i.e., to make many fragments into two main fragments and then unite these two into one). Such fixation can usually be accomplished with independent lag screws placed in a horizontal direction, followed by a modified anterior tension band wiring technique. The size of the screw should fit the size of the bone (e.g., 3.5-mm cortical screws will usually suffice, except in large adult men, in whom 4.5-mm screws should be used) (Fig. 54–23). If the fragment is comminuted at the point of screw entry, a washer is used. Frequently, a fragment has or acquires a sagittal split during insertion of the lag screw; the split separates the anterior cortex from the main chondral surface of that fragment. If this fragment cannot

be salvaged by repositioning the screw, LAB/C wiring or excision of the fragment should be considered.

### Partial Patellectomy

Not infrequently, patellar fractures exhibit significant comminution of one pole, and the fragments may involve a smaller or larger portion of the patella. At times, indirect reduction with a modified anterior tension band or LAB/C wiring technique will be effective. If these techniques are not possible, the time-honored method of partial patellectomy should be performed[1, 25, 79, 101] (Fig. 54–24).

The patella is approached and the fracture exposed as previously described. All large, stable, distal fragments should be retained, and all small, comminuted fragments should be excised. All loose strands of the torn quadriceps expansion are removed. If one large distal fragment is present, it may be lagged into position with screws after reduction has been secured. Care must be taken to not angle this fragment or patellofemoral arthritis will develop (see Fig. 54–24C). This procedure can be simplified by placing a bolster underneath the ankle to extend the knee.

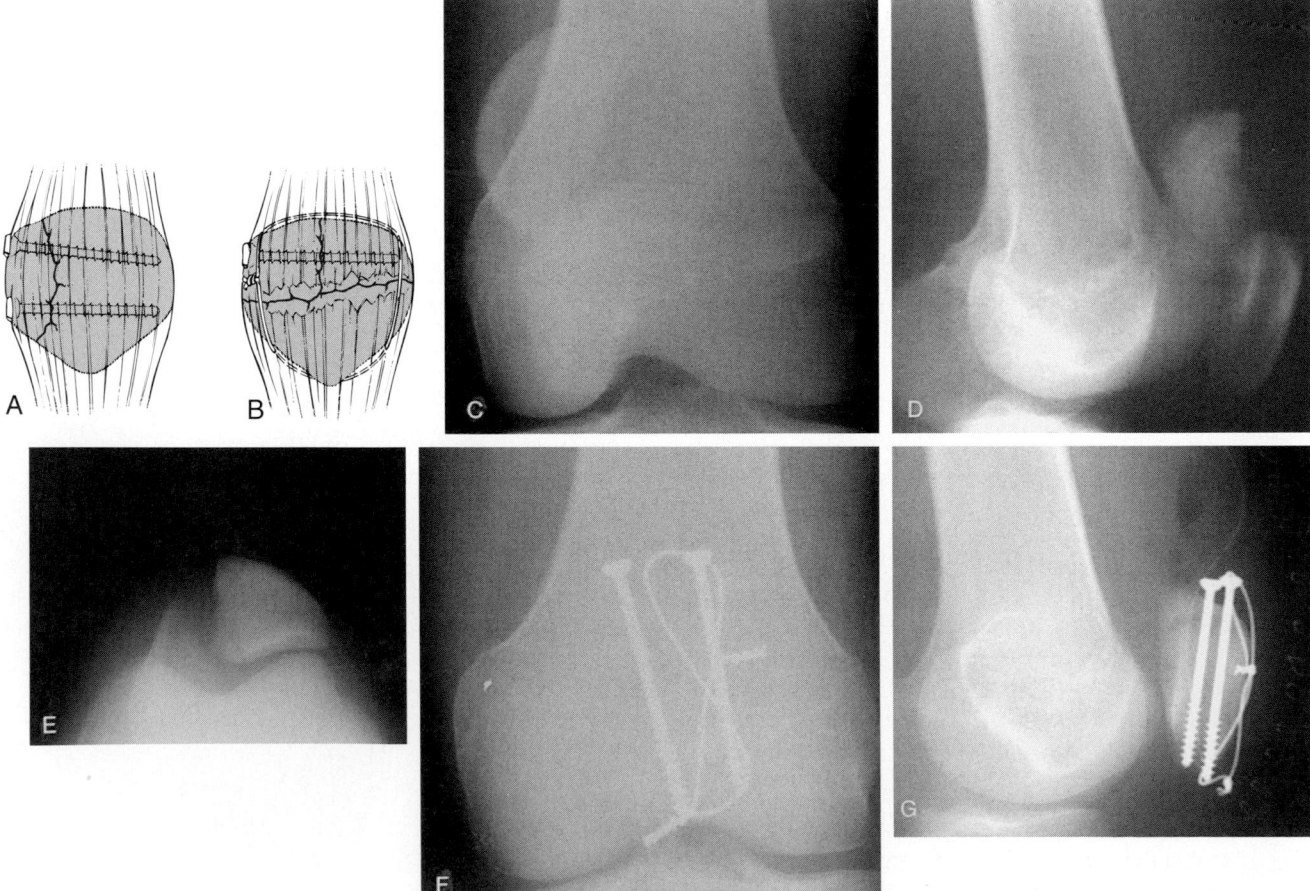

**FIGURE 54–23.** AO lag screw plus tension band technique. *A,* Small-fragment screws can be used alone to fix vertical components or comminuted portions of the patella. *B,* These screws should be supplemented with a tension band wire for fixation of displaced transverse fractures because screws alone may not withstand the significant forces developed by the quadriceps mechanism. Anteroposterior (AP) *(C),* lateral *(D),* and skyline *(E)* radiographs show a displaced oblique (functionally transverse) patellar fracture. Postoperative AP *(F)* and lateral *(G)* radiographs show the use of 4.0-mm cancellous lag screws supplemented by an anterior tension band wire. The wire is crossed in this case to maintain its position anterior to the fracture.

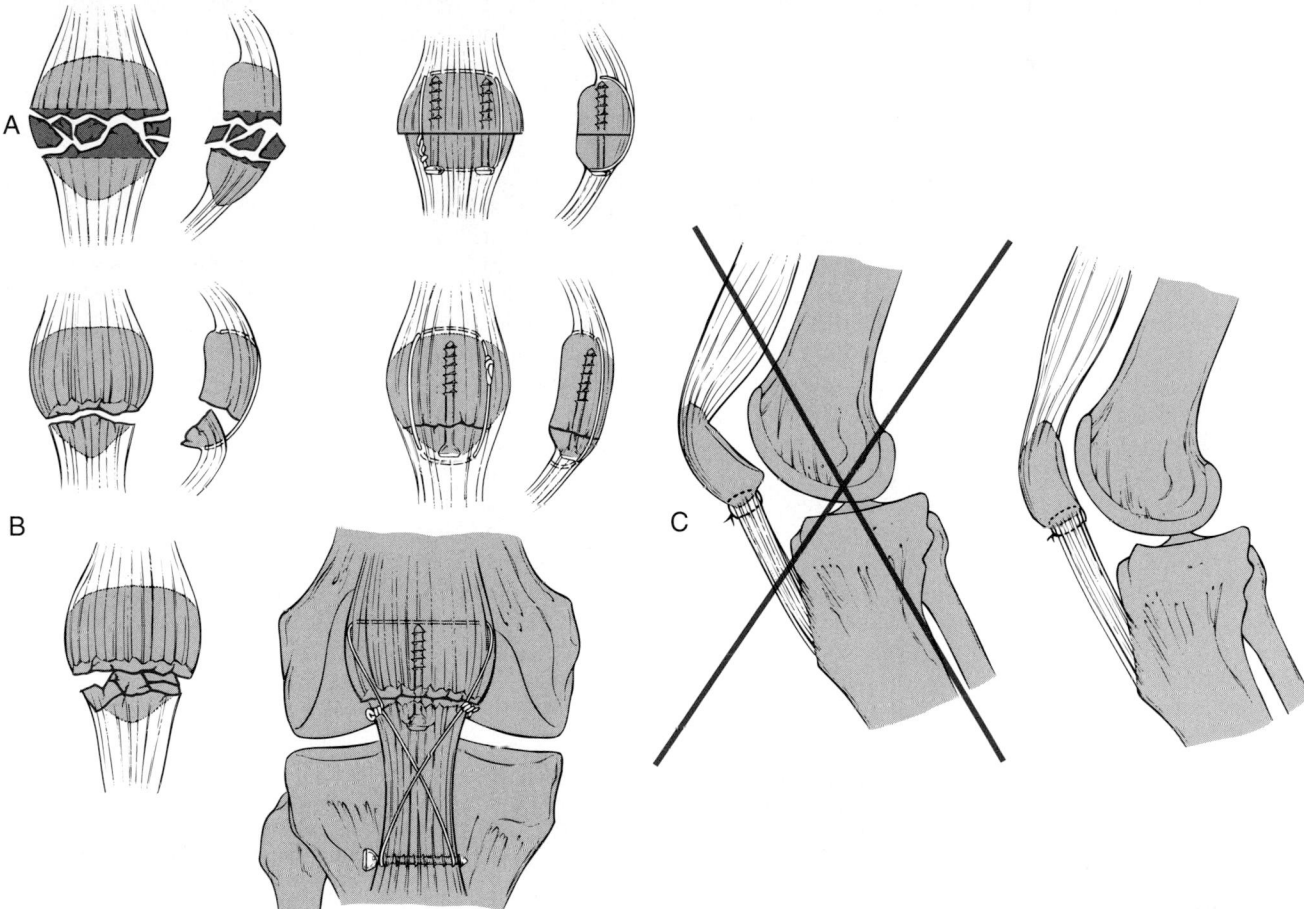

**FIGURE 54–24.** Techniques of partial patellectomy. *A,* Extensive comminution of the central portion may be excised, with fixation of the proximal-to-distal poles with screws or K-wires and a tension band. The results of this technique are not well documented. *B,* A small (usually extra-articular) bony fragment may aid in reattachment of the patellar ligament distally. Screws, K-wires, or sutures may be used, but they should always be protected with a tension band, either limited to the patella if the distal pole fragment is sufficient or from the patella to the tibial tubercle if it is not sufficient. *C,* When suturing the patellar ligament into a defect in the distal pole of the patella, it is essential to not attach it too anteriorly because such positioning will result in malalignment of the patella *(left),* the distal articular surface being forced too far posteriorly. The example on the *right* shows proper reattachment of the patellar ligament. A tension band from the patella to the tibia should protect this repair.

Because of the powerful tension developed in the quadriceps mechanism, significant stress is placed on its repairs, which must be protected. This goal can be accomplished by using a crossed tension band through either the quadriceps insertion or the proximal part of the patella and through the proximal end of the tibia by a variety of means (Fig. 54–25). We prefer wire passed directly through the bone because it is less bulky and easier to remove. Mersilene tape or fascia may also be used.

If only small fragments remain distally, the following technique is used. The anterior periosteum is reflected on the proximal fragment approximately 5 mm, and with a rongeur, a transverse groove is made in the proximal fragment within the fracture line itself. Three holes are drilled so that they are equally spaced from the fracture line and exit the superior aspect of the patella. Next, with a heavy, braided, nonabsorbable suture and an atraumatic needle, the suture is passed distally in a running, locking stitch along one edge of the tendon and then returned in the midline of the tendon. A second suture is passed in a similar manner along the opposite side of the tendon and

back along the midline. The suture ends are passed through the appropriate drill holes in the patella, with two sutures through the central hole. A straight, free needle can be used to pass the sutures. Each suture is tied to its opposite end. This step should be done while the knee is hyperextended and should bring the tendon end into close approximation with the trough in the distal aspect of the proximal part of the patella. A tension band should be added to neutralize stress on the repair. The retinaculum is then sutured closed with figure-of-eight 0 Vicryl interrupted sutures, and the wound is closed in layers, over a drain if desired.

### Total Patellectomy

For highly displaced, highly comminuted fractures, an attempt at reconstruction should be made before total patellectomy is performed. Several authors have stressed the retention of even one fragment to maintain a lever arm.[33, 92, 100, 101] A combination of partial patellectomy and modified anterior tension band or LAB/C wiring is usually tried before total excision is performed. Although many techniques exist, those presented in the

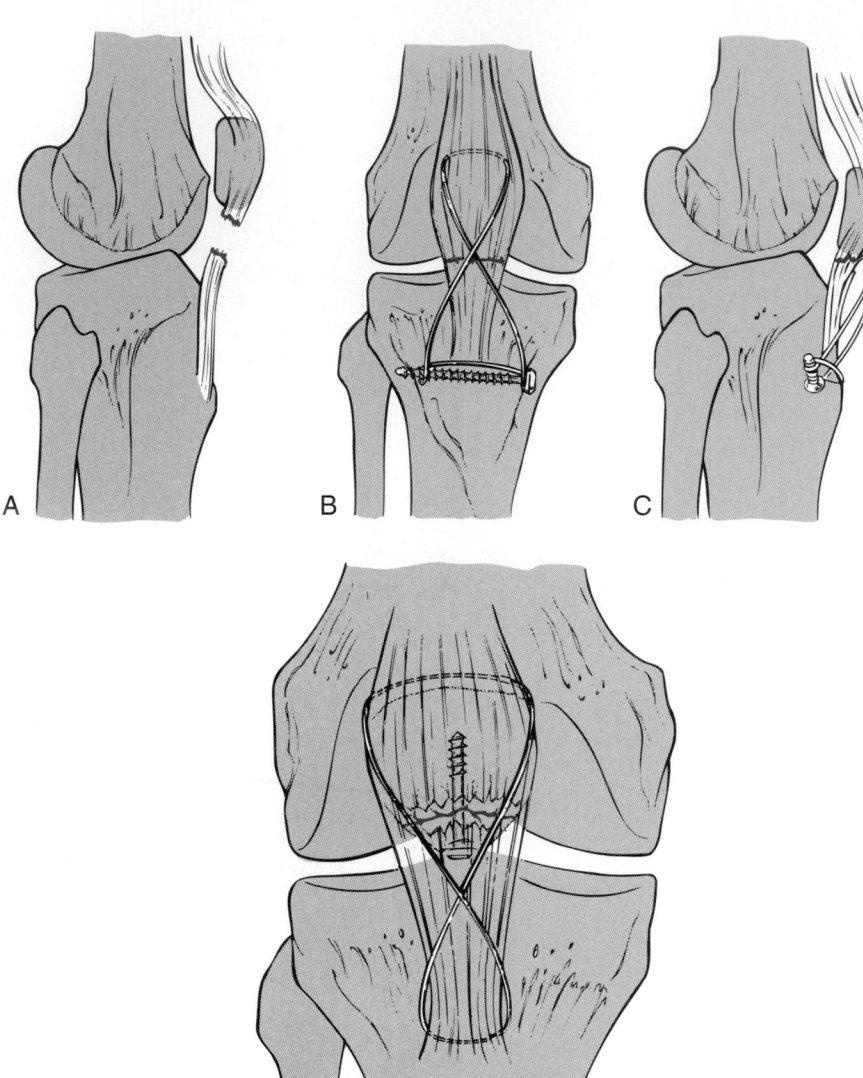

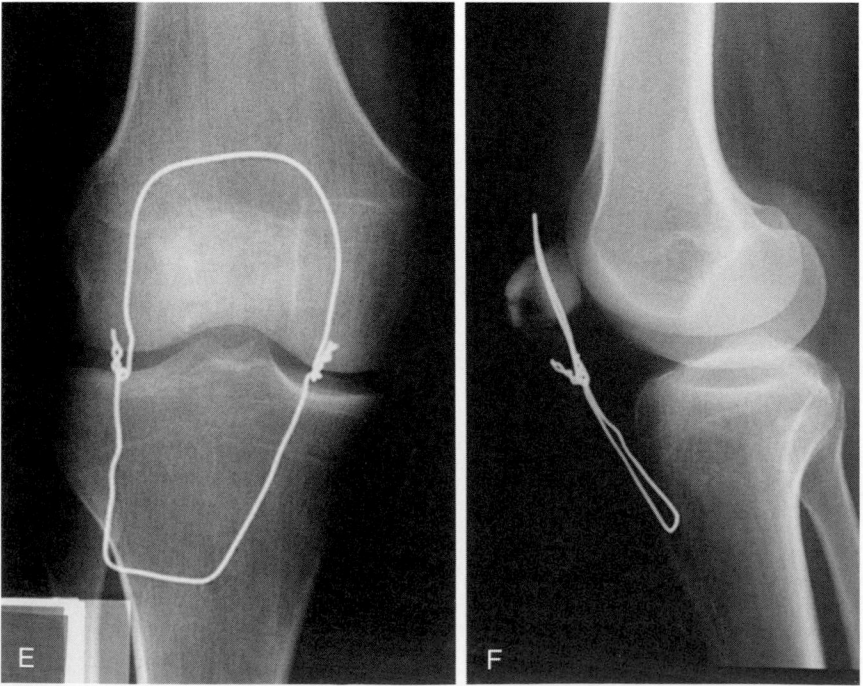

**FIGURE 54–25.** A tension band wire technique should be used to protect the patellar ligament reattachment after distal pole fracture fixation, partial patellectomy, or repair of a ruptured patellar ligament (*A*). *B, C,* The 1.0- or 1.2-mm wire can be attached to a screw through the tibial tubercle. *D,* It can be placed through the quadriceps tendon just proximal to the patella or through a drill hole in the patella and through a drill hole distally. Anteroposterior (*E*) and lateral (*F*) radiographs show the tension band wire protecting the reattached patellar ligament after distal partial patellectomy.

following paragraphs are the most favorably reviewed in the literature.

Because total patellectomy is often a salvage procedure, the surgeon may find various skin incisions and retinacular remnants. Once a decision for total extirpation has been made, all fragments of bone and shredded tendon are removed sharply, but as much tendinous expansion as possible is left. The critical feature of a total patellectomy is the tendinous repair. Because the quadriceps tendon is effectively lengthened by the removal of bone, this slack should be taken up by imbrication (i.e., in a pursestring repair), or an extensor lag will result.

If insufficient tendon exists for primary repair, several options are available. These options can be separated into two categories: quadriceps turndown procedures and fascial or tendinous weaving. The former technique is used when prepatellar soft tissue is absent, whereas the latter is reserved for injuries with destroyed quadriceps tendon as well.

The most common quadriceps turndown technique is the inverted V-plasty of Shorbe and Dobson.[93] After the patella has been excised, the quadriceps tendon is exposed for approximately 3 inches (Fig. 54–26). A full-thickness incision is made into the quadriceps tendon in the shape of a V, with the apex located 2.5 inches proximal to the former proximal patellar edge. The limbs of the incisions extend distally for 2 inches such that ¼ to ½ inch of tendon is continuous with the retinaculum. The corners may be reinforced with suture if necessary. The apex is subsequently folded down, inserted through the proximal portion of the patellar tendon, and sutured down. The quadriceps tendon should then be closed and all edges repaired. This repair is simple to perform, yet has the advantage of being strong enough to allow early motion.

Should a large defect involving the quadriceps tendon be present, a free fascial or tendinous strip is woven into the tendinous remnants after the method of Gallie and Lemesurier.[39] First, all excess tendinous shreds are removed from the wound. The knee is extended with padding under the ankle and the defect measured. This length should be doubled and 2 inches added to obtain the ideal length of a fascial graft. A separate lateral incision is made or the wound is extended, and a strip of fascia lata or an iliotibial band of the appropriate length and 1 to 1.5 cm in width is obtained. The strip of fascia is rolled into a cylinder along its long axis and sutured to itself. It is then woven through the remaining quadriceps tendon or muscle, sewn to itself, passed through the patellar tendon, and tacked down after the slack is taken out. The graft should be of sufficient length to sew one end down to the other. Finally, all edges are firmly sutured down. If the defect requires an exceptionally long strip, plantaris tendon can be used.

## POSTOPERATIVE MANAGEMENT

With a stable osteosynthesis, the patient may begin using a continuous passive motion machine to tolerance immediately postoperatively. In our experience, use of this device decreases pain and stiffness. On the first postoperative day, the patient can be out of bed with the leg elevated, and quadriceps isometric exercises are begun. Drains, if used, are generally removed after 48 hours. The patient is then placed in a removable knee brace and permitted to ambulate with weight bearing as tolerated and the knee locked in extension. The hinges may be loosened for active range-of-motion exercises. These exercises should not be performed until the wound is well healed, usually at 3 weeks. Active extension and straight leg raising exer-

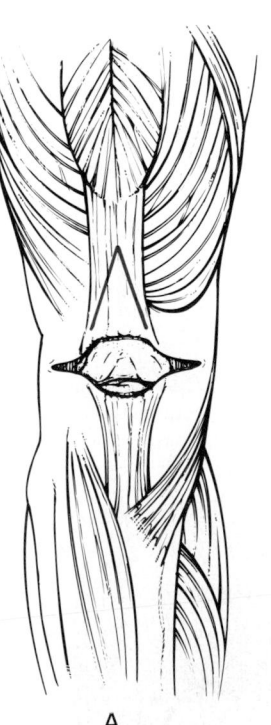 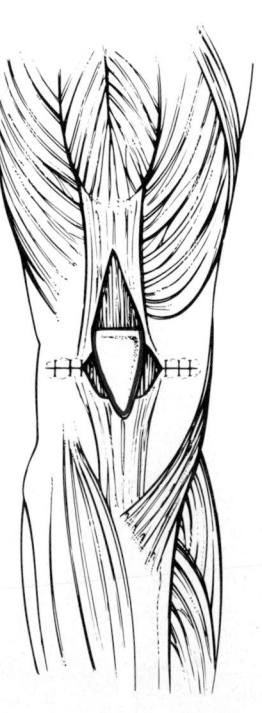 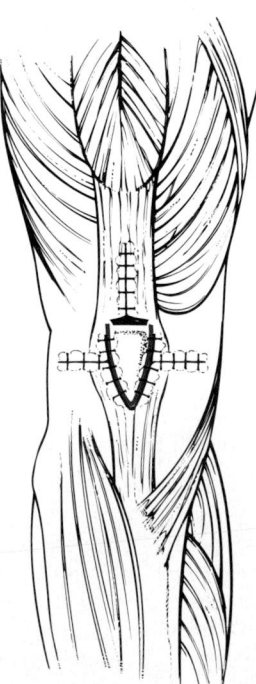

**FIGURE 54–26.** Inverted V-plasty technique of Shorbe and Dobson for repair of a patellectomy defect. *A,* The patella is resected, with a transverse defect left in the quadriceps mechanism. The retinacular rents are repaired first. *B,* If a defect remains centrally, an inverted, distally based, V-shaped flap of quadriceps tendon is turned distally as shown. *C,* The flap is sutured in place to cover and reinforce the defect.

A       B       C

cises may be initiated as early as 1 week postoperatively. Progressive resistance exercises are performed after radiographic evidence of healing, usually at 6 weeks. The patient is then weaned from the brace and, by 3 months postoperatively, usually has a healed fracture and strong quadriceps. Sports and vigorous work may be resumed after rehabilitation is complete, usually in 4 to 6 months.

For an unstable osteosynthesis, the repair must be protected. Ideally, a knee brace with locking hinges will permit controlled motion. The hinges are set to allow full extension. Flexion to the degree possible during intraoperative assessment of the repair is permitted, primarily for cartilage nutrition. The brace should be worn at all times, and active flexion exercises should not begin until the fracture has healed. Isometric quadriceps extension exercises should be initiated at 2 weeks. Weight bearing in full extension can usually be allowed once comfort permits. Weight bearing on the flexed knee should be avoided until fracture healing is secure. The patient should be made aware of possible knee stiffness. When the fracture has healed radiographically and is clinically stable, attempts at rehabilitation are begun to improve flexion range and strength of all muscle groups.

Implant removal should be delayed until fracture union is mature, which usually requires a minimum of 6 months. K-wires may be extracted if they are painful and protruding, but loss of fixation with fracture displacement generally requires revision surgery. Asymptomatic implants may be retained indefinitely. Wires used to protect tendon repairs should be left in place for a minimum of 3 to 6 months.

## Results

No generally accepted outcome assessment system is available for patellar fractures. Most authors base outcome on subjective complaints of pain, limitation in activities of daily living, change in job status, and ambulation.[14, 35, 92] Böstman and colleagues developed the most complete evaluation of clinical results to date[11] (Table 54–3). However, this table, like most reports in the literature, does not evaluate radiographic findings. Radiographic criteria would include osteoarthritis, fibrous union or nonunion, the presence of osteochondral fragments, and the degree of articular step-off on the radiograph.[11, 19, 92] The lack of a uniform assessment scale allows only broad generalizations to be made about the results of treatment of these injuries (Table 54–4).

### NONOPERATIVE TREATMENT

Nonoperative treatment of nondisplaced fractures nearly always has a uniformly good outcome,[13, 73, 89, 96] which implies full range of motion and no arthrosis, weakness, or pain (see Table 54–3). In Boström's series of 422 patellar fractures, 219 were treated nonoperatively and were available for follow-up.[13] All cases initially had less than 4 mm of articular incongruity; 54% (118/219) had excellent results, and 44% (97/219) had good results. Only two failures occurred. His results agree with the findings of

**TABLE 54–3**

Clinical Grading Scale

| Clinical Grading Scale/Variable | Score |
|---|---|
| Range of motion (ROM) | |
| Full extension, ROM >120° | 6 |
| Full extension, ROM 90°–120° | 3 |
| Loss of full extension, ROM <90° | 0 |
| Pain | |
| None or minimal on exertion | 6 |
| Moderate on exertion | 3 |
| In daily activities | 0 |
| Work | |
| Original job | 4 |
| Different job | 2 |
| Cannot work | 0 |
| Atrophy (10 cm, proximal part of patella) | |
| <12 mm | 4 |
| 12–25 mm | 2 |
| >25 mm | 0 |
| Aids | |
| None | 4 |
| Cane part-time | 2 |
| Cane full-time | 0 |
| Effusion | |
| None | 2 |
| Reported to be present | 1 |
| Present | 0 |
| Giving way | |
| No | 2 |
| Sometimes | 1 |
| All the time | 0 |
| Stair climbing | |
| Normal | 2 |
| Difficult | 1 |
| Disabling | 0 |

Excellent, 30 to 28 points; good, 20 to 27 points; failure, <20 points.
*Source:* Modified from Böstman, O.; et al. Injury 13:196–202, 1981.

other large series in that the failure rate from nonoperatively treated, nondisplaced patellar fractures was 5%.

### OPERATIVE TREATMENT

Results of operative repair are based on the type of fracture and the technique used (Table 54–5). Modified anterior tension band wiring has given the best results in the literature to date, with 57% excellent and 29% good results[11, 12, 54, 64, 108] (Table 54–6). Unfortunately, many studies are vague in reporting results, and studies

**TABLE 54–4**

Combined Results of Various Forms of Operative Treatment in the Literature

| Treatment | Results | | | Total No. |
| | Excellent | Good | Fair | |
|---|---|---|---|---|
| ORIF | 135 (37%) | 129 (36%) | 97 (27%) | 361 |
| Partial excision | 32 (23%) | 67 (49%) | 39 (28%) | 138 |
| Total excision | 62 (28%) | 96 (44%) | 61 (28%) | 219 |
| Totals | 229 | 292 | 197 | 718 |

*Abbreviation:* ORIF, open reduction and internal fixation.

Table 54–5 ••••••••••••••••••••••••••••••••

### Results of Operative Repair in Patellar Fractures

| Author, Year | No. Patients | Excellent | Good | Fair |
|---|---|---|---|---|
| **Open Reduction, Internal Fixation** | | | | |
| Seligo,[92] 1971 | 35 | 10 | 18 | 7 |
| Nummi,[82] 1971 | 66 | 3 | 18 | 45 |
| Boström,[13] 1972 | 75 | 19 | 42 | 14 |
| Böstman et al.,[12] 1983 | 48 | 17 | 21 | 10 |
| Ma et al.,[69] 1984 | 107 | 77 | 20 | 10 |
| Levack et al.,[64] 1985 | 30 | 9 | 10 | 11 |
| Totals | 361 | 135 (37%) | 129 (36%) | 97 (27%) |
| **Partial Excision** | | | | |
| Seligo,[92] 1971 | 3 | 0 | 1 | 2 |
| Nummi,[82] 1971 | 68 | 14 | 28 | 26 |
| Boström,[13] 1972 | 28 | 8 | 15 | 5 |
| Mishra,[76] 1972 | 4 | 2 | 1 | 1 |
| Böstman et al.,[12] 1983 | 35 | 8 | 22 | 5 |
| Totals | 138 | 32 (23%) | 67 (49%) | 39 (28%) |
| **Total Excision** | | | | |
| Seligo,[92] 1971 | 44 | 14 | 25 | 5 |
| Nummi,[82] 1971 | 13 | 0 | 5 | 8 |
| Boström,[13] 1972 | 5 | 0 | 1 | 4 |
| Mishra,[76] 1972 | 26 | 3 | 15 | 8 |
| Einola et al.,[35] 1976 | 28 | 6 | 18 | 4 |
| Wilkinson,[112] 1977 | 31 | 7 | 12 | 12 |
| Böstman et al.,[12] 1983 | 10 | 0 | 3 | 7 |
| Levack et al.,[64] 1985 | 34 | 20 | 7 | 7 |
| Jakobsen et al.,[56] 1985 | 28 | 12 | 10 | 6 |
| Totals | 219 | 62 (28%) | 96 (44%) | 61 (28%) |

reporting this technique are few. Analysis of combined data shows tension band wiring to be superior to simple cerclage wiring clinically. In addition, Weber and colleagues showed the superiority of tension band wiring biomechanically[108] (see Table 52–6). Modified wiring techniques can also be effective. In Lotke and Ecker's report on LAB/C wiring, 16 cases were presented; 13 (81%) had excellent results.[68]

## Partial Patellectomy

Partial patellectomy may give functional results comparable to those of open reduction and internal fixation, but comparison is difficult because the fracture patterns treated by these techniques are different.[12, 13, 64, 68, 101] Sutton and co-workers showed that the only deficit with partial excision of at least one third of the patella is an 18° loss of motion.[99] In studies by Böstman and associates, Boström, Mishra, Nummi, and Seligo, a nearly normal outcome occurred when large fragments of patella were retained and articular congruity was maintained.[12, 13, 76, 82, 92] Small fragments without soft tissue, sagittally split fragments, and those missing cartilage were excised. These authors found that saving these fragments did not improve function and even compromised it. Retention of one or two large fragments, however, improved quadriceps function.[12, 13, 41, 58, 64, 101, 109] Hung and colleagues reported the results of a 25-month follow-up in a retrospective series of patients in which radiographic changes consistent with post-traumatic arthritis developed in 55% after partial patellectomy and tension band repair.[53] However, most of these patients were asymptomatic within that time frame.

## Total Patellectomy

Total patellectomy has yielded varying degrees of success. Before the 1970s, poor reconstructive results justified total patellectomy.[16, 31, 40, 44, 45, 50] Investigators compared operative repair with a single cerclage wire and total excision. Although many stated that good clinical results were expected, more recent studies have questioned this conclusion[11, 13, 64, 89] (see Table 54–5).

Sutton and co-workers evaluated quadriceps strength, activities of daily living, and functional ability in patients who had undergone either partial or total patellectomy.[99] The opposite normal knee was the control. Both groups had an average loss of 18° range of motion. A 49% reduction in strength of the extensor mechanism was present in the total-excision group. This reduction in strength was the result of loss of the lever arm produced by loss of the patella. Instability was greater in this group, with the patellectomized knee losing almost 50% of excursion in stance-phase flexion. This loss was a result of the patellar tendon sinking into the intercondylar notch. Clinically, this

Table 54–6 ••••••••••••••••••••••••••••••••••••••••••••••••••••

### Comparison of Anterior Tension Band vs. Cerclage Wiring

| Author | No. Patients | Results of Anterior Tension Band | | | Results of Cerclage Wiring | | |
|---|---|---|---|---|---|---|---|
| | | Excellent | Good | Poor | Excellent | Good | Poor |
| Böstman et al.[12] | 29 | 9 | 3 | 2 | 6 | 6 | 3 |
| Boström[13] | 75 | — | — | — | 19 | 42 | 14 |
| Levack et al.[64] | 30 | 7 | 5 | 2 | 2 | 5 | 9 |
| Seligo[92] | 31 | — | — | — | 10 | 14 | 7 |
| Ma et al.[69] | 81 | — | — | — | 59 | 15 | 7 |
| Nummi[82] | 66 | — | — | — | 3 | 18 | 45 |
| Totals | 312 | 16 (57%) | 8 (29%) | 4 (14%) | 99 (35%) | 100 (35%) | 85 (30%) |

instability was manifested as insufficiency and inability to support the loaded knee in stair climbing. Biomechanical studies on cadaver knees performed by Watkins and associates, Wendt and Johnson, and others all showed that total patellectomy resulted in loss of tibial torque and, therefore, strength.[42, 58, 105, 109]

Srensen noted that the quadriceps did not improve in strength after patellectomy.[96] All patients complained of frequent giving way and difficulty running and walking down stairs. He concluded that none of his operative reconstructions would have fared better with total excision of the patella and thus justified attempts at salvage. Wilkinson evaluated 31 patients 4.5 to 13 years after total excision.[112] In this study, less than a fourth of the patients had an excellent result. He also noted that maximal recovery took up to 3 years. Einola and colleagues were able to monitor 28 patients for an average of 7.5 years after total excision.[35] Good results were seen in only six patients. The predominant complaint was weakness and pain on movement and exertion. The most common finding was quadriceps atrophy. Quadriceps power was within 75% of the normal knee in only seven cases. He concluded that saving as much patella as possible was advisable. Scott reported that only 6% (4/71) of patients were happy with their long-term outcome after patellectomy.[89] Ninety percent had aching in the joint, and 60% complained of weakness. Quadriceps wasting was a constant finding.

The present recommendations are to therefore retain as much patella as possible.[11–13, 33, 54, 64, 79, 100, 101] Total patellectomy is reserved for fractures that are so comminuted that repair is futile. This plan will offer the patient the best possible knee function for the longest period. How much patella should be saved? No definitive answer exists. It is our opinion that as little as 25% of the patella (i.e., one quadrant) may be retained with a subsequently good outcome. We have never found a patella so comminuted that one fragment could not be salvaged with repair. If no articular congruity exists, however, excision is the only option.

## COMPLICATIONS

### Infection

Superficial wound infections should be treated by standard protocol based on the degree of soft tissue involvement. Osteomyelitis is aggressively treated with resection of all sequestra and dead tissue. Irrigation and débridement of the knee must be repeated every 48 to 72 hours until the joint is free of necrotic tissue to prevent septic arthritis. Daily bedside aspiration is not indicated. The patient should receive 6 weeks of culture-specific intravenous antibiotics. Once the deep bone infection is under control, an attempt should be made to salvage any remaining patella by individualized and modified wiring techniques. If salvage is not possible, total patellectomy may be required.

### Breakage of Wires, Loss of Fixation, and Refracture

After osteosynthesis, especially with early motion, the tension band may break, but it is unusual for such breakage to occur before healing of the patella. If the fracture is healed, the wire, pins, or screws may be removed if they cause symptoms.

Loss of fixation during the healing phase will require revision if the fragments separate more than 3 to 4 mm or if the articular surface has an incongruity greater than 3 mm. Before returning to the operating room, a radiograph should be obtained in full extension. If reduction has improved, the patient may benefit from 6 weeks of extension splinting. Usually, however, isometric exercises will continue to separate the fragments, and unless the patient refuses, revision should be undertaken.

Refracture should be treated as a fresh fracture according to the principles previously described (i.e., nondisplaced fractures are treated nonoperatively and displaced fractures are treated operatively).

### Delayed Union and Malunion

Delayed union, once a routine result, is extremely uncommon. If identified, a period of decreased motion is begun because the fracture will often spontaneously unite. Weber and Cech could find only three cases of patellar pseudarthrosis in their large series of nonunions.[107] All healed after revision surgery performed with established fracture fixation methods. If it is an old nonunion with 4 to 5 inches of separation, reconstruction should be attempted. Quadriceps shortening will make this repair difficult, and formal quadricepsplasty may be required. Care must be taken to obtain the correct length or disability will continue. If chondromalacia exists, consideration should be given to performing a total patellectomy and fascial reconstruction according to the method of Gallie and Lemesurier.[39]

### Loss of Knee Motion

The advent of tension band wiring has permitted early range of motion, and functional range of motion can be expected in most cases. If flexion is still decreased several months postoperatively, intensive physiotherapy is begun. If such physiotherapy does not suffice, manipulation under anesthesia should be contemplated. Care must be exercised in patients requiring manipulation who have had patellectomies because rupture of the repair may occur. A report has been published of a "boutonnière deformity" after manipulation of a longitudinally repaired extensor retinaculum.[81] If gentle manipulation is unsuccessful, consideration is given to arthroscopic lysis of intra-articular adhesions. Quadricepsplasty is performed only in exceptional cases, usually when no improvement is seen after 9 to 12 months. This situation is most often the case after concomitant injury to the distal end of the femur has resulted in binding down of the quadriceps mechanism.

Occasionally after total patellectomy, the extensor mechanism is too long, which may result in loss of full extension. The patient has a sensation of instability and giving way.[96] In this rare situation, consideration is given to a Maquet procedure to bring the patellar tendon forward and increase its mechanical advantage. This technique has been described by Kaufer in excellent biomechanical studies.[58] Reports of clinical results of the Maquet procedure for this purpose are nonexistent. We would caution against using too large a bone block because of subsequent skin breakdown and pain. Other authors suggest reefing the extensor mechanism, but this maneuver runs the risk of rerupture.[93]

## Osteoarthritis and Patellar Enlargement

Although Bruce and Walmsley[18] and Cohn[27] showed that osteoarthritis occurred in rabbits after patellectomy, this complication has never been borne out in long-term studies of postpatellectomy human knees.[1, 13, 19, 35, 56, 76, 99, 112] In addition, articular incongruity causing osteoarthritis has not been reported in long-term studies.[13, 96]

Two situations have been demonstrated to increase the incidence of osteoarthritis. Patellar enlargement, a result of exuberant bone formation during the healing of comminuted fractures, has been unequivocally shown to cause patellofemoral arthritis. Total patellectomy should be entertained if such enlargement has developed.

The second situation that will cause osteoarthritis is posterior rotation of the distal pole of the patella after reattachment of the patellar ligament in too anterior a position in distal pole patellectomy.[33, 92] Care must be taken during repair to avoid such reattachment (see the section Partial Patellectomy and Fig. 52–24C).

## Tendon Rupture after Total Patellectomy

Rarely, the extensor mechanism will rupture after total patellectomy, usually at the proximal edge of the patellar tendon.[36] This rupture should be repaired by the variety of techniques suggested in the following section.

## EXTENSOR MECHANISM INJURIES

A patient with post-traumatic loss of knee extension and negative results on radiographs should be suspected of having a quadriceps or a patellar tendon rupture. Rupture of the extensor mechanism appears to be age specific. Most quadriceps ruptures occur in patients older than 40 years, and most patellar tendon ruptures occur in patients younger than 40.[94] The tendon may rupture from a tension tear, direct sharp or blunt trauma, metabolic abnormalities, collagen disease, repeated microtrauma, or repeated adrenocorticoid injections.[77] In elderly patients, fatty degeneration and tendon scarring are the predisposing causes.[90]

## Quadriceps Rupture

Rupture of the quadriceps occurs primarily in the rectus tendon, usually 0 to 2 cm from the superior pole of the patella.[90, 95] The diagnosis is often missed if the patient has little pain or effusion.[84] Physical examination will reveal a palpable defect proximal to the superior pole of the patella.[84] In addition, extension against gravity must be assessed. If the quadriceps tendon has a palpable defect but active, full extension is maintained, the tear is incomplete. Such a partial tear does not require operative repair.[90]

If the ability to extend the knee is completely lost, both the tendon and the retinaculum are torn. The patient will have difficulty climbing stairs, and the knee will buckle with ambulation.[84] Operative repair is required.[95] Furthermore, if a complete quadriceps rupture is not treated acutely, the quadriceps may ride as far as 5 cm proximally on the femur and then bind down.[90] For this reason, repair should be done as quickly as possible.

### ACUTE RUPTURES

Most authors agree that an end-to-end repair produces excellent results in acute quadriceps tendon ruptures.[62, 77, 94, 95, 102] In Miskew and co-workers' series, 90% of their patients had an excellent outcome.[77] Similarly, Larsen and Lund considered their results in 15 of 18 cases (83%) to be excellent,[62] and Vainionpää and associates had only 1 failure in 12 cases.[102] The largest series in the literature is that of Siwek and Rao, who reported 36 cases of rupture. They found that all 30 patients with an immediate end-to-end repair had excellent or good results with knee range of motion of 0° to 120°.[94] Complicating primary end-to-end repairs is the difficulty in neutralizing forces across the repair. A review of the literature revealed only five cases in which a stress-relieving wire was used to protect this repair.[62, 94, 97, 102] Several authors reported on the use of a 5-mm Dacron graft to protect the primary repair.[66, 77] Levy and colleagues used this technique and permitted early motion without the use of a cast postoperatively, but weight bearing was delayed for 6 weeks.[66] Most published series used a local reinforcement flap as suggested by Scuderi, followed by 6 weeks in an extension cast.[62, 84, 90, 94, 95, 102]

### Scuderi Repair

In the Scuderi repair (Fig. 54–27), the edges of the torn quadriceps are freshened and then pulled together so that a slightly overlapping repair is performed. A distally based, partial-thickness triangular flap of quadriceps tendon is then turned down over the suture line to protect the repair. This flap is an isosceles triangle, 3 inches along each side and 2 inches at the base. Alternatively, a variation involving the middle third of the patellar tendon may be used.[24] In this case, the tendon is freed distally, folded proximally, and sewn down. After such repairs, immobilization in a cylinder cast for 6 weeks is advised.

Haas and Callaway described a technique for repair of a ruptured quadriceps tendon.[43] A midline incision is made, with dissection carried down to the level of the patella and

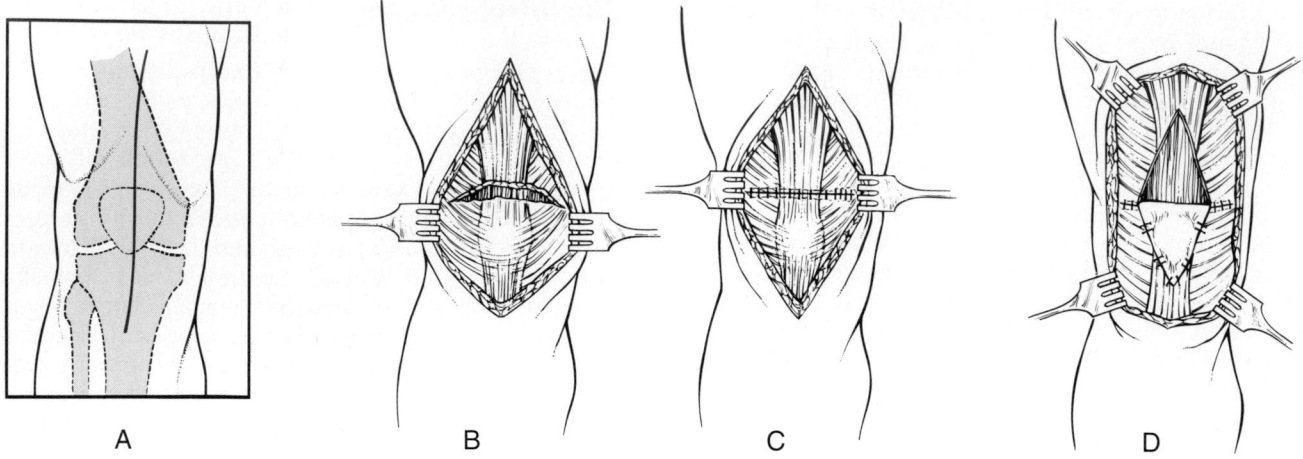

**FIGURE 54–27.** Scuderi repair of a ruptured quadriceps tendon. *A,* The defect is exposed through a midline longitudinal incision. *B,* Fasciocutaneous flaps are developed to reveal the defect. *C,* Interrupted nonabsorbable stout mattress sutures repair the tendon. These sutures may be directed to the patella centrally. *D,* An inverted, partial-thickness, distally based, V-shaped flap is used to reinforce the repair. (*A–D,* Redrawn from Scuderi, C. Am J Surg 95:626–635, 1958.)

tendon. Hematoma and fibrous debris are excised without removing an excessive amount of tendon. Three heavy nonabsorbable sutures are passed through the proximal tendon remnant in a Kessler-type stitch. A transverse trough is created in the proximal pole of the patella with a bur. Care must be taken to prevent placing the trough too

anterior to avoid subsequent tilting of the patella. Three longitudinal holes are drilled in the patella, and the sutures are passed through these tunnels and tied distally at the inferior pole of the patella. The retinaculum is repaired primarily with absorbable suture, and the leg is immobilized in full extension for 6 weeks (Fig. 54–28).[43]

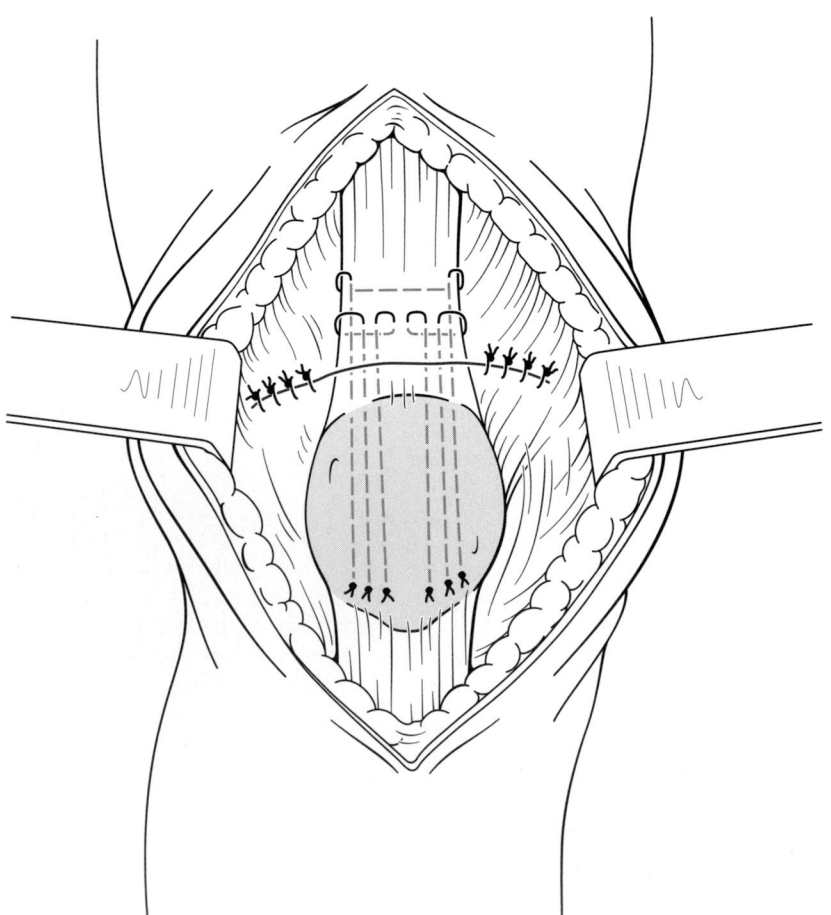

**FIGURE 54–28.** Three heavy nonabsorbable sutures are passed through the proximal tendon remnant in a Kessler-type stitch. Three longitudinal drill holes are created in the patella, and the sutures are passed through these tunnels and tied distally at the inferior pole of the patella. (From Haas, S.B.; Callaway, H. Orthop Clin North Am 23:687–695, 1992.)

## CHRONIC RUPTURES

In patients with quadriceps ruptures older than 2 weeks, muscle retraction of as much as 5 cm with adherence of the quadriceps muscle to the femur is common.[90, 94] The delay in treatment may require quadriceps lengthening, tendon or muscle transfers, or a combination of these methods as discussed in the sections that follow.[24, 49, 83, 90, 94]

### *Codivilla V-Y Lengthening*

For a Codivilla V-Y lengthening procedure (Fig. 54–29), a standard midline or lateral incision is made, and all soft tissue adhesions are freed from the quadriceps tendon and muscle. The quadriceps muscle is then freed from the femur, with elevators used if necessary to break all scars. The knee should be in extension with a roll under the heel. The old tear is located, and the ends are freshened. The gap is then measured. A full-thickness, distally based, V-shaped incision is made in the quadriceps tendon. Partial-thickness incisions in the vasti may be necessary to aid in stretching. The original quadriceps defect is then repaired. The V may be turned distally to reinforce the repair as in the method of Scuderi. The proximal defect in the quadriceps tendon is then repaired in a side-to-side manner. A cylinder cast is worn for 6 weeks.

### *Myoplasties and Tendon Transfers*

When quadriceps retraction and adhesions make standard techniques impossible (as in neglected tears), neither the Scuderi technique nor Codivilla V-Y lengthening may be sufficient. In these complex, long-standing cases, an aponeurotic vastus lateralis strip 2 to 5 cm thick may be used. This strip is left proximally based and swung medially. The remaining vastus lateralis and medialis are then closed around it. The patient is kept in a cylinder cast for 6 weeks.[83]

In cases in which large defects occur, as in major wounds of the anterior aspect of the knee, no quadriceps, patella, or patellar ligament may exist. The sartorius can be used as a rotational flap to cover the area.[49] The tendon is freed distally and inserted into the tibial tubercle region.

The advantage of this transfer over a semitendinosus transfer is muscle bulk. Postoperatively, the patient is placed in a cylinder cast for 6 weeks.

## POSTOPERATIVE REHABILITATION

In all cases, the patient is able to walk in a cylinder cast during the first several weeks postoperatively. Isometric quadriceps-setting exercises are not begun until after the cast is removed (6 weeks). Controlled motion to 45°, isometric exercises, and straight leg raises are then begun. One month later, range of motion may be increased to 115°, and strengthening exercises are begun. The third month should be spent returning the limb to its preinjury status. The patient should expect that recovery will require at least 6 months.

## Patellar Tendon Ruptures

### ACUTE RUPTURES

Patellar tendon rupture occurs most frequently in athletic patients younger than 40 years; however, it can be observed in patients with systemic illness in which the collagen structure is weakened.[71] This condition is commonly seen in patients with systemic lupus erythematosus, rheumatoid arthritis, chronic renal failure, diabetes mellitus, and long-term corticosteroid therapy.[106] In a younger, athletic patient, the injury is thought to result from cumulative microtrauma because the patella more often fractures when a healthy tendon undergoes acute overload.[60] This theory is supported pathologically. Kannus and Jozsa reported that 97% of 53 patellar tendon ruptures demonstrated degenerative changes, including hypoxic tendinopathy, mucoid degeneration, tendolipomatosis, and calcifying tendinopathy.[57]

The patellar tendon ruptures most frequently at its proximal insertion site rather than midsubstance. This tendency has been hypothesized to result from a relative decrease in collagen fiber stiffness observed at the insertion sites of the tendon and from the greater tensile strain

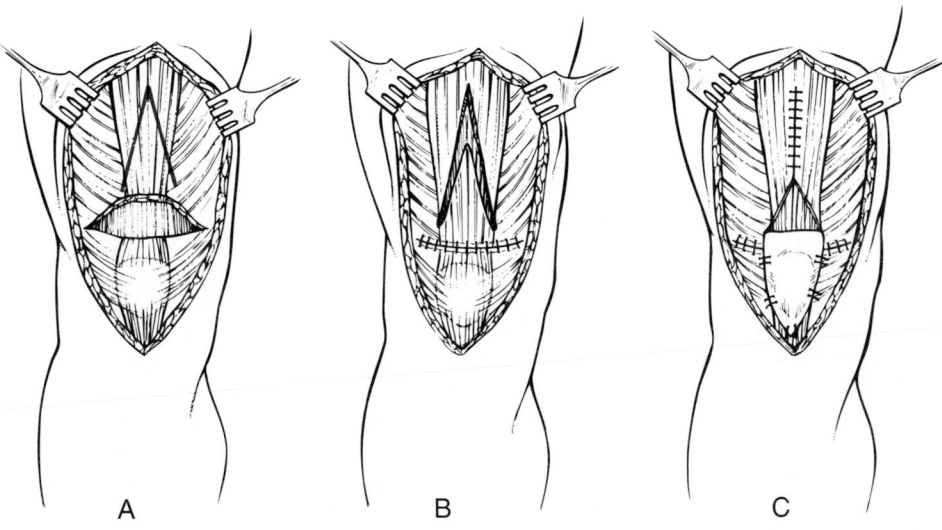

**FIGURE 54–29.** The Codivilla V-Y–plasty repair for neglected ruptures of the quadriceps tendon. *A,* A distally based V of quadriceps tendon is developed proximal to the defect. *B,* As much of the defect as possible is closed with nonabsorbable stout mattress sutures medially and laterally in the retinacula. *C,* The flap is turned distally and sutured in place over the defect in the quadriceps tendon to restore central continuity. As much as possible of the defect left by the V is closed in a proximal-to-distal direction.

A          B          C

occurring in the insertion fibers than in the midsubstance fibers.[114]

The history of the injury almost always consists of an eccentric quadriceps contraction against the full body weight. Physical examination of an acute rupture reveals a hemarthrosis with an inability to extend the knee actively or maintain a passively extended knee against gravity. A palpable defect in the tendon itself may be appreciated. In the case of an isolated tendon rupture with an intact retinaculum, active extension may be possible, but an extension lag will be present.[71] Over time, a neglected tear will permit knee extension with subsequent contracture of the quadriceps tendon and patella.

Radiographically, patella alta will be apparent on a plain radiograph. Ultrasonography and MRI have been successful in identifying acute and chronic rupture of the patellar tendon.[29, 115]

Immediate repair, combined with a wire to relieve stress from the suture line, is standard treatment of these injuries.[62, 72, 79, 94, 106] Although many authors place their patients in a cylinder cast for 6 weeks postoperatively, the original purpose of the pull-out wire as described by McLaughlin and Francis[72] was to allow early knee motion.[79, 106]

### Repair

For repair of acute ruptures, a toe-to-groin Esmarch bandage is applied and then the proximal end is pulled down. This technique will help bring the patella down. The tourniquet is inflated and the bandage is removed to prevent the quadriceps from getting stuck under the tourniquet.[23] A standard midline longitudinal incision is made. The tendon ends are freshened, and if bony avulsion has occurred, several holes should be drilled in bone to allow for strong fixation. Care should be taken when determining the length of the repair because studies have shown patellofemoral incongruence to occur when the length is incorrect.[62]

An 18-gauge wire should be placed closely along the medial, superior, and lateral borders of the patella. It may be attached to the tibia (posterior and slightly distal to the tubercle) through a drill hole or with a bolt or a screw (see Fig. 54–25). In the latter two cases, a pull-out wire may be added for removal of the 18-gauge wire in the office. After the wire has been tightened, an end-to-end repair with heavy suture is performed. The tendon may be repaired through three bony tunnels in the patella with a modified Bunnell-type suture in the tendinous portion. This construct should be reinforced by transosseous cerclage as well.[71] The torn retinaculum should also be repaired. The repair is then tested in flexion in the operating room, and any loose sutures are tightened. Standard closure over a suction drain is then performed.

Several authors have used fabric material (e.g., Dacron graft or Mersilene tape) for repair, reinforcement, or both.[38, 62, 65, 66, 77] Levin presented a case with a 5-cm gap.[65] Holes were drilled in the patella and tibia, and Dacron vascular graft was used to reconstruct the tendon, with the graft pulled tight for tension. At 15 months, the repair was still good. Levy and colleagues used Dacron in place of wire with good results, thus obviating the need for subsequent wire removal.[66] Miskew and co-workers used 5-mm Mersilene tape as suture to augment the primary repair.[77] If the tendon was avulsed from the proximal part of the patella, holes were drilled into the distal aspect. If the tendon was avulsed distally, holes were drilled into the tibia. They reported 10 cases with good results.

Postoperatively, isometric hamstring and quadriceps exercises are begun immediately, as is toe-touch weight bearing. At 2 to 3 weeks, active flexion and passive extension are initiated, with active extension started at 3 to 4 weeks. At 6 weeks, the patient should be at full weight bearing. Resistance exercises are introduced at 6 to 8 weeks. Competitive sports should be delayed for 4 to 6 months until 90% of isokinetic strength has been regained.[71]

## CHRONIC RUPTURES

Reconstructions months and years later prove unsatisfactory because of difficulty overcoming contracture and adhesions. Similar to repair of the quadriceps mechanism, reconstruction of tendon ruptures can be separated into quadriceps lengthening, tendon transfers, the use of fascial or synthetic grafts, or a combination of these techniques.

### Tendon Transfers

For late repairs with large patellar tendon defects, the quadriceps may need to be released from the femur to translate the patella distally (Fig. 54–30). For severe long-standing patella alta, extensor mechanism traction is applied with a Steinmann pin or K-wire placed transversely through the patella and 5 lb of skeletal traction for several days to several weeks. Passive range-of-motion exercises are done during the traction phase to improve postoperative knee motion.[94] When lateral radiographs demonstrate the patella to be correctly positioned, the reconstruction can be accomplished surgically. Two holes are drilled into the patella and one oblique hole in the tibia. The semitendinosus and gracilis tendons are released proximally. The tendons are routed through the tibial hole; then each tendon is passed into the patella from opposite sides. A pull-out wire is cerclaged around the proximal part of the patella or through a transverse bony tunnel and passed through the tibial tubercle region, the primary repair is completed, and the wire is tightened. A cylinder cast is worn for 6 weeks. Isometric exercises are initiated immediately and active range-of-motion and resistance exercises 6 weeks after cast removal.[34, 59]

A second newly described method for reconstruction of the extensor mechanism involves the use of a rotational medial or lateral gastrocnemius flap.[63] The muscle belly can be used for soft tissue coverage, and the tendon can be used to replace the patellar tendon or even larger portions of the extensor mechanism that may have been lost. The proximal portion of the Achilles tendon is sutured to the patellar or quadriceps tendon remnant, and the distal portion is sutured to the patellar tendon remnant. A bony block can even be harvested from the Achilles insertion for patients with massive loss of the extensor mechanism. A split-thickness skin graft is used to cover the muscle flap.

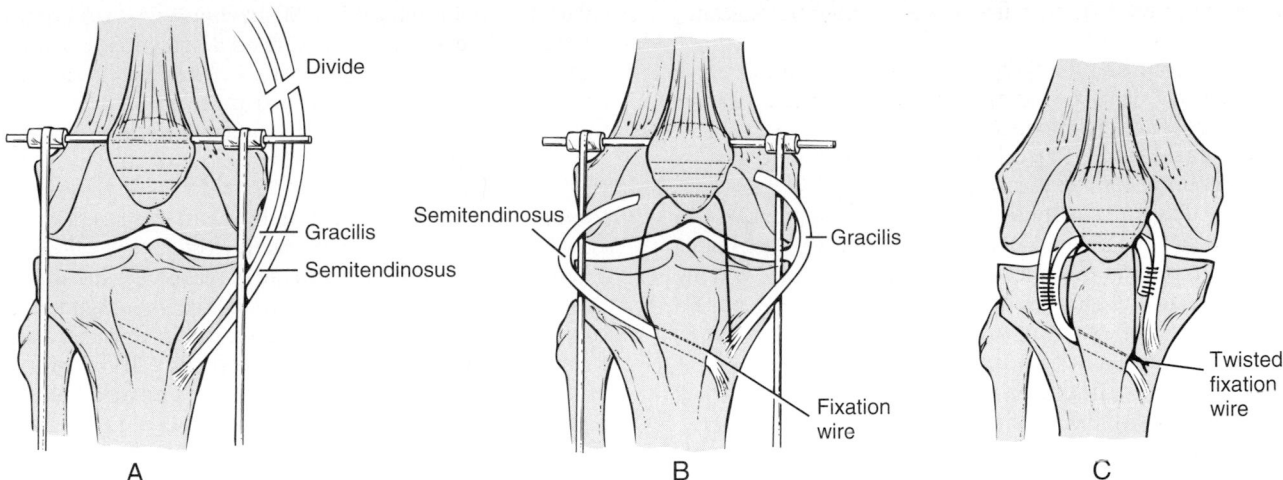

**FIGURE 54–30.** Late reconstruction of the patellar ligament with the semitendinosus and gracilis tendons (after the method of Ecker). *A,* The patella is brought down with traction, and the semitendinosus and gracilis tendons are cut as far proximally as possible. *B,* These tendons are routed as shown through drill holes in the patella. Also note the use of a tension band wire through both the patella and tibia. *C,* The tendons are sutured distally, and the wire is secured with appropriate tension. (*A–C,* Modified from Ecker, M.L.; et al. J Bone Joint Surg Am 61:884–886, 1979.)

### *Synthetic Grafts*

Mersilene tape, Dacron graft, and carbon fiber materials have been advocated in the severe situation in which local tissues are not available or are of inadequate quality for substantial repair. More commonly, these materials have been used to augment primary repair or tendon transfers.[36, 47, 94]

### OUTCOMES

Clinical outcome appears to correlate with the interval between injury and repair. Siwek and Rao reported 80% excellent and 16% good outcomes in patients treated with primary repair within 7 days of injury. The results declined in patients treated 2 weeks or more after injury. This group had only 33% excellent and 50% good results.[94] Larsen and Lund reported 70% excellent and good results in 10 patients treated acutely for patellar tendon rupture.[62] The results of Hsu and colleagues were encouraging as well.[51] Fifty-seven percent and 29% of their 35 patients treated acutely were rated as excellent and good, respectively.[51] Overall, the literature supports acute primary repair supplemented with a stress-relieving wire or nonabsorbable suture as the treatment of choice for rupture of the patellar tendon.

## Tibial Tubercle Avulsions

Repair of tibial tubercle avulsions, a variant of patellar tendon avulsions, should incorporate bony reconstruction with 3.5- or 4.5-mm lag screws and a stress-relieving wire, if possible, to guarantee accurate tendon length and patellar tracking. Anchorage may be improved with a small plate (Fig. 54–31). If the tubercle is comminuted and the fragments are too small for screw fixation, holes should be drilled distal and posterior to the avulsion site in the tibia. Fixation should then proceed as with tendon avulsions.

## Acute Patellar Dislocations

Although recurrent patellar subluxations are a common cause of knee injury, an acute traumatic patellar dislocation is a relatively rare event. These injuries are most commonly manifested as lateral dislocations, but intra-articular and superior dislocations may occasionally occur.

### LATERAL DISLOCATIONS

The mechanism of lateral patellar dislocation is forced internal rotation of the femur on an externally rotated and planted tibia with the knee flexed. Tension in the quadriceps pulls the patella laterally. If the medial retinaculum tears, the patella dislocates over the edge of the lateral

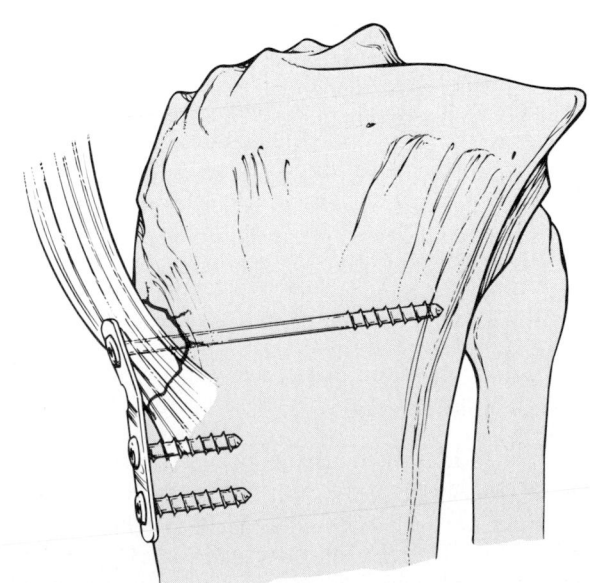

**FIGURE 54–31.** Repair of an avulsion fracture of the tibial tubercle can be made more secure with a small plate. The plate acts as a tension band to stabilize the head of a lag screw through the avulsed fragment.

femoral condyle. Such dislocation results in shearing between the medial inferior edge of the patella and the lateral femoral condyle.[78] Osteochondral fractures in these areas strongly suggest a lateral patellar dislocation, with the former having an incidence of 5%.[78, 85]

### Diagnosis

A patient with an unreduced lateral patellar dislocation will have a large lateral mass, hemarthrosis, medial retinacular pain, and an inability to flex the knee. An attempt should be made to reduce the patella on evaluation to decrease the patient's discomfort. Standard radiographs are then taken, including a tangential view to rule out osteochondral fractures.[78] If the bony portion of the osteochondral fragment is small, the lesion may be missed on radiographs. For this reason, as well as for comfort, arthrocentesis is performed. If blood from the hemarthrosis contains fat globules on aspiration, an osteochondral fracture should be considered.[4, 78, 85]

If the patella is already reduced, diagnosis of an acute traumatic dislocation will be made more difficult inasmuch as medial joint pain and an effusion may be the only findings. This diagnosis is important to make because osteochondral fractures must be ruled out. Common symptoms associated with osteochondral fragments include blocking, locking, giving way, and tenderness to palpation on the medial side of the knee that is not meniscal or ligamentous in origin.[78]

### Treatment

Treatment of an acute lateral patellar dislocation consists of reduction and extension casting for 3 to 6 weeks. Cofield and Bryan evaluated 50 patients treated conservatively in extension casts with a follow-up period of 5 years or until operative reconstruction was needed. Patient age, sex, the mechanism of injury, and the length of time spent in a cast had no effect on outcome.[26] Although a third of their patients were considered treatment failures, they concluded that initial surgery for acute patellar dislocations was not warranted except in cases with displaced intra-articular fractures exclusive of the medial border.[26] We agree with these recommendations.

Larsen and Lauridsen studied the incidence of redislocation after conservative treatment of 79 acute patellar dislocations.[61] Treatment included a cylinder cast in 22 patients and an elastic wrap in 57 patients. The clinical results and the tendency to redislocate were independent of the treatment method. The risk of redislocation was statistically significantly less in patients older than 20 years at the time of the first episode of dislocation. The authors stressed initial conservative treatment and quadriceps-strengthening exercises, with realignment procedures considered only if the dislocation recurred.

In Morscher's series of 34 osteochondral fractures of the knee, the fracture was caused by an acute lateral dislocation of the patella in 21 of the 34 fractures (62%).[78] Sixteen were found on the medial edge of the patella, 1 on the lateral femoral condyle, and 4 on both surfaces. Operative treatment was chosen in all cases.

Currently, we recommend conservative treatment with a cast or brace in extension for ambulation for 3 weeks. Flexion can then be progressively increased as the patient's comfort permits, usually over another 3 weeks. If an osteochondral fragment is suspected, diagnostic arthroscopy is recommended, and if a fragment is present, operative repair or excision is warranted.

## INTRA-ARTICULAR DISLOCATIONS

Though rare, intra-articular or horizontal dislocations of the patella usually occur in adolescent boys.[80] In these dislocations, the patella is violently ripped off the quadriceps tendon and rotated around its horizontal axis such that the proximal part of the patella becomes stuck within the intercondylar notch. The knee is slightly flexed, and the quadriceps tendon is intact.[15, 37, 80, 98] Treatment consists of closed manipulation under anesthesia and extension casting for 6 weeks with quadriceps exercises. Healing is usually uneventful.[15, 37, 80, 98, 113]

## SUPERIOR DISLOCATIONS

Four cases of superior patella dislocation exist in the literature.[46, 113] The injury occurs in an older population and results from hyperextension of the knee with the patella locked on a femoral osteophyte. Gentle manipulation in the emergency room is all that is usually required.[46, 113]

### REFERENCES

1. Andrews, J.R.; Hughston, J.C. Treatment of patellar fractures by partial patellectomy. South Med J 70:809–813, 1977.
2. Apple, J.S.; Martinez, S.; Allen, N.B.; et al. Occult fractures of the knee: Tomographic evaluation. Radiology 148:383–387, 1983.
3. Arnoczky, S.P. Blood supply to the anterior cruciate ligament and supporting structures. Orthop Clin North Am 16:15–28, 1985.
4. Ashby, M.E.; Shields, C.L.; Karmy, J.R. Diagnosis of osteochondral fractures in acute traumatic patellar-dislocations using air arthrography. J Trauma 15:1032–1033, 1975.
5. Baumgartl, F. Das Kniegelenk. Berlin, Springer-Verlag, 1964.
6. Berg, E.E. Management of patella fractures associated with central third bone–patella tendon–bone autograft ACL reconstructions. Arthroscopy 12:756–759, 1996.
7. Berg, E.E.B. Extensile exposure of comminuted patella fractures using a tibial tubercle osteotomy: Results of a new technique. J Orthop Trauma 12:351–355, 1998.
8. Berg, E.E.B. Open reduction internal fixation of displaced transverse patella fractures with figure-eight wiring through parallel cannulated compression screws. J Orthop Trauma 11:573–576, 1997.
9. Black, J.K.; Conners, J.J. Vertical fractures of the patella. South Med J 62:76–77, 1969.
10. Blodgett, W.E.; Fairchild, R.D. Fractures of the patella. JAMA 20:2121–2125, 1936.
11. Böstman, O.; Kiviluoto, O.; Nirhamo, J. Comminuted displaced fractures of the patella. Injury 13:196–202, 1981.
12. Böstman, O.; Kiviluoto, O.; Santavirta, S.; et al. Fractures of the patella treated by operation. Arch Orthop Trauma Surg 102:78–81, 1983.
13. Boström, A. Fracture of the patella. Acta Orthop Scand Suppl 143:1–80, 1972.
14. Boström, A. Longitudinal fractures of the patella. Reconstr Surg Traumatol 14:136–146, 1974.
15. Brady, T.A.; Russell, D. Interarticular horizontal dislocation of the patella. J Bone Joint Surg Am 47:1393–1396, 1965.
16. Brooke, R. The treatment of fractured patella by excision. A study of morphology and function. Br J Surg 24:733–747, 1936.
17. Brownstein, B.; Bronner, S. Patella fractures associated with accelerated ACL rehabilitation in patients with autogenous patella tendon reconstructions. J Orthop Sports Phys Ther 26:168–172, 1997.

18. Bruce, J.; Walmsley, R. Excision of the patella. J Bone Joint Surg 24:311–325, 1942.

19. Cargill, A.O. The long-term effect on the tibiofemoral compartment of the knee joint of comminuted fractures of the patella. Injury 6:309–312, 1975.

20. Carpenter, J.E.; Kasman, R.A.; Patel, N.; et al. Biomechanical evaluation of current patella fracture fixation techniques. J Orthop Trauma 11:351–356, 1997.

21. Carson, W.G.; James, S.L.; Larson, R.L.; et al. Patellofemoral disorders: Physical and radiographic evaluation, part II: Radiographic examination. Clin Orthop 185:178–186, 1984.

22. Catalano, J.B.; Iannacone, W.M.; Marczyk, S.; et al. Open fractures of the patella: Long-term functional outcome. J Trauma 39:439–444, 1995.

23. Chari, P.R.; Kishore, R.G.; Satyanarayana, M.V. Repair of the quadriceps apparatus following patellectomy in recent fractures of the patella: A new technique with results. Aust N Z J Surg 48:99–103, 1978.

24. Chekofsky, K.M.; Spero, C.R.; Scott, W.N. A method of repair of late quadriceps rupture. Clin Orthop 147:190-191, 1980.

25. Chiroff, R.T. A new technique for the treatment of comminuted, transverse fractures of the patella. Surg Gynecol Obstet 145:909–912, 1977.

26. Cofield, R.H.; Bryan, R.S. Acute dislocation of the patella: Results of conservative treatment. J Trauma 17:526–531, 1977.

27. Cohn, B.N.E. Total and partial patellectomy. Surg Gynecol Obstet 79:526–536, 1944.

28. Crock, H.V. The arterial supply and venous drainage of the bones of the human knee joint. Anat Rec 144:199–218, 1962.

29. Davies, S.G.; Baudouin, C.J.; King, J.D.; et al. Ultrasound, computed tomography and magnetic resonance imaging in patellar tendinitis. Clin Radiol 43:52–56, 1991

30. Depalma, A.F.; Flynn, J.J. Joint changes following experimental partial and total patellectomy. J Bone Joint Surg Am 40.395–413, 1958.

31. Dobbie, R.P.; Ryerson, S. The treatment of fractured patella by excision. Am J Surg 55:339–373, 1942.

32. Dowd, G.S.E. Marginal fractures of the patella. Injury 14:287–291, 1982.

33. Duthie, H.L.; Hutchinson, J.R. The results of partial and total excision of the patella. J Bone Joint Surg Br 40:75–81, 1958.

34. Ecker, M.L.; Lotke, P.A.; Glazer, R.M. Late reconstruction of the patellar tendon. J Bone Joint Surg Am 61:884–886, 1979.

35. Einola, S.; Aho, A.J.; Kallio, P. Patellectomy after fracture. Acta Orthop Scand 47:441–447, 1976.

36. Evans, P.D.; Pritchard, G.A.; Jenkins, D.H.R. Carbon fibre used in the late reconstruction of rupture of the extensor mechanism of the knee. Injury 18:57–60, 1987.

37. Feneley, R.C.L. Intra-articular dislocation of the patella. J Bone Joint Surg Br 50:653–655, 1968.

38. Frazier, C.H.; Clark, E.M. Major tendon repairs with Dacron vascular graft suture. Orthopedics 3:323–325, 1980.

39. Gallie, W.E.; Lemesurier, A.B. The late repair of fractures of the patella and of rupture of the ligamentum patellae and quadriceps tendon. J Bone Joint Surg 9:48–54, 1927.

40. Geckler, E.O.; Queranta, A.V. Patellectomy for degenerative arthritis of the knee—late results. J Bone Joint Surg Am 44:1109, 1962.

41. Goodfellow, J.; Hungerford, D.S.; Zindel, M. Patello-femoral joint mechanics and pathology: 1. Functional anatomy of the patello-femoral joint. J Bone Joint Surg Br 58:287–299, 1976.

42. Griswold, A.S. Fractures of the patella. Clin Orthop 4:44–56, 1954.

43. Haas, S.B.; Callaway, H. Disruptions of the extensor mechanism. Orthop Clin North Am 23:687–695, 1992.

44. Haggart, G.E. Surgical treatment of degenerative arthritis of the knee joint. J Bone Joint Surg 22:717, 1940.

45. Halliburton, R.A.; Sullivan, C.R. The patella in degenerative joint diseases. Arch Surg 77:677–683, 1958.

46. Hanspal, R.S. Superior dislocation of the patella. Injury 16:487–488, 1985.

47. Haxton, H. The function of the patella and the effects of its excision. Surg Gynecol Obstet 80:389–395, 1945.

48. Heineck, A.P. The modern operative treatment of fractures of the patella. Surg Gynecol Obstet 9:177–248, 1909.

49. Hess, P.; Reinders, J. Transposition of the sartorius muscle for reconstruction of the extensor apparatus of the knee. J Trauma 26:90–91, 1986.

50. Horwitz, T.; Lambert, R.C. Patellectomy in the military service. A report of 19 cases. Surg Gynecol Obstet 82:423–426, 1946.

51. Hsu, K.Y.; Wand, K.C.; Ho, W.P.; et al. Traumatic patellar tendon ruptures: A follow-up study of primary repair and a neutralization wire. J Trauma 36:658–660, 1994.

52. Huberti, H.H.; Hayes, W.C.; Stone, J.L.; Shybut, G.T. Force ratios in the quadriceps tendon and the ligamentum patellae. J Orthop Res 2:49–54, 1984.

53. Hung, L.K.; Lee, S.Y.; Leung, K.S.; et al. Partial patellectomy for patellar fracture: Tension band wiring and early mobilization. J Orthop Trauma 7:252–260, 1993.

54. Hung, L.K.; Chan, K.M.; Chow, Y.N.; Leung, P.C. Fractured patella: Operative treatment using the tension band principle. Injury 16:343–347, 1985.

55. Insall, J.; Goldberg, V.; Salvati, E. Recurrent dislocation and the high riding patella. Clin Orthop 88:67–69, 1972.

56. Jakobsen, J.; Christensen, K.S.; Rasmussen, O.S. Patellectomy— a 20-year follow-up. Acta Orthop Scand 56:430–432, 1985.

57. Kannus, P.; Jozsa, L. Histopathological changes preceding spontaneous rupture of a tendon. A controlled study of 891 patients. J Bone Joint Surg Am 73:1507–1525, 1991.

58. Kaufer, H. Mechanical function of the patella. J Bone Joint Surg Am 53:1551–1560, 1971.

59. Kelikian, H.; Riashi, E.; Gleason, J. Restoration of quadriceps function in neglected tears of the patellar tendon. Surg Gynecol Obstet 104:200–204, 1957.

60. Kelly, D.W.; Carter, V.S.; Jobe, F.W.; et al. Patellar and quadriceps tendon ruptures: Jumper's knee. Am J Sports Med 12:375–380, 1984.

61. Larsen, E.; Lauridsen, F. Conservative treatment of patellar dislocations. Clin Orthop 171:131–136, 1982.

62. Larsen, E.; Lund, P.M. Ruptures of the extensor mechanism of the knee joint. Clin Orthop 213:150–153, 1986.

63. Leung, K.S.; Yip, K.M.H.; Shen, W.Y.; Leung, P.C. Reconstruction of extensor mechanism after trauma and infection by transposition of the Achilles tendon: Report of technique and four cases. J Orthop Trauma 8:40–44, 1994.

64. Levack, B.; Flannagan, J.P.; Hobbs, S. Results of surgical treatment of patellar fractures. J Bone Joint Surg Br 67:416–419, 1985.

65. Levin, P. Reconstruction of the patellar tendon using a Dacron graft. Clin Orthop 118:70–72, 1976.

66. Levy, M.; Goldstein, J.; Rosner, M. A method of repair for quadriceps tendon or patellar ligament ruptures without cast immobilization. Clin Orthop 218:297–301, 1987.

67. Lieb, F.J.; Perry, J. Quadriceps function. J Bone Joint Surg Am 50:1535–1548, 1968.

68. Lotke, P.A.; Ecker, M.L. Transverse fractures of the patella. Clin Orthop 158:180–184, 1981.

69. Ma, Y.Z.; Zheng, Y.F.; Qu, K.F.; et al. Treatment of fractures of the patella with percutaneous suture. Clin Orthop 191:235–241, 1984.

70. Macausland, W.R. Total excision of the patella for fracture. Am J Surg 72:510–516, 1946.

71. Matava, M.J. Patellar tendon ruptures. J Am Acad Orthop Surg 4:287–296, 1996.

72. McLaughlin, H.L.; Francis, K.C. Operative repair of injuries to the quadriceps extensor mechanism. Am J Surg 91:651–653, 1956.

73. McMaster, P.E. Fractures of the patella. Clin Orthop 4:24–43, 1954.

74. Merchant, A.C.; Mercer, R.L.; Jacobsen, R.H.; Cool, R.T. Roentgenographic analysis of patellofemoral congruence. J Bone Joint Surg Am 56:1391–1396, 1974.

75. Miller, M.D.; Nichols, T.; Butler, C.A. Patella fracture and proximal patellar tendon rupture following arthroscopic anterior cruciate ligament reconstruction. Arthroscopy 15:640–643, 1999.

76. Mishra, U.S. Late results of patellectomy in fractured patella. Acta Orthop Scand 43:256–263, 1972.

77. Miskew, D.B.W.; Pearson, R.L.; Pankovich, A.M. Mersilene strip suture in repair of disruptions of the quadriceps and patellar tendons. J Trauma 20:867–872, 1980.

78. Morscher, E. Cartilage-bone lesions of the knee joint following injury. Reconstr Surg Traumatol 12:2–26, 1971.

79. Müller, M.E.; Allgöwer, M.; Schneider, R.; Willinegger, H. Manual of Internal Fixation. Techniques Recommended by the AO Group. Berlin, Springer-Verlag, 1979, pp. 248–253.

80. Murakami, Y. Intra-articular dislocation of the patella. Clin Orthop 171:137–139, 1982.

81. Noble, H.B.; Hajek, M.R. Boutonnière-type deformity of the knee following patellectomy and manipulations. J Bone Joint Surg Am 66:137–138, 1984.

82. Nummi, J. Operative treatment of patella fractures. Acta Orthop Scand 42:437–438, 1971.

83. Oni, O.O.A.; Ahmad, S.H. The vastus lateralis derived flap for repair of neglected rupture of the quadriceps femoris tendon. Surg Gynecol Obstet 161:385–387, 1985.

84. Ramsey, R.H.; Muller, G.E. Quadriceps tendon rupture: A diagnostic trap. Clin Orthop 70:161–164, 1970.

85. Rees, D.; Thompson, S.K. Osteochondral fractures of the patella. J R Coll Surg Edinb 30:88–90, 1985.

86. Reider, B.; Marshall, J.L.; Koslin, B.; et al. The anterior aspect of the knee joint. J Bone Joint Surg Am 63:351–356, 1981.

87. Scapinelli, R. Blood supply of the human patella. J Bone Joint Surg Br 49:563–570, 1967.

88. Scilaris, T.A.; Grantham, J.L.; Prayson, M.J.; et al. Biomechanical comparison of fixation methods in transverse patella fractures. J Orthop Trauma 12:356–359, 1998.

89. Scott, J.C. Fractures of the patella. J Bone Joint Surg Br 31:76–81, 1949.

90. Scuderi, C. Ruptures of the quadriceps tendon. Am J Surg 95:626–635, 1958.

91. Sears, F.W.; Zemansky, M.W. University Physics. Reading, MA, Addison-Wesley, 1970, pp. 30–31.

92. Seligo, W. Fractures of the patella. Reconstr Surg Traumatol 12:84–102, 1971.

93. Shorbe, H.B.; Dobson, C.H. Patellectomy. J Bone Joint Surg Am 40:1281–1284, 1958.

94. Siwek, C.W.; Rao, J.P. Ruptures of the extensor mechanism of the knee joint. J Bone Joint Surg Am 63:932–937, 1981.

95. Siwek, K.W.; Rao, J.P. Bilateral simultaneous rupture of the quadriceps tendon. Clin Orthop 131:252–254, 1978.

96. Srensen, K.H. The late prognosis after fracture of the patella. Acta Orthop Scand 34:198–212, 1964.

97. Stern, R.E.; Harwin, S.F. Spontaneous and simultaneous rupture of both quadriceps tendons. Clin Orthop 147:188–189, 1980.

98. Stover, C.N. Interarticular dislocation of the patella. JAMA 200:966, 1967.

99. Sutton, F.S.; Thompson, C.H.; Lipke, J.; Kettlekamp, D.B. The effect of patellectomy on knee function. J Bone Joint Surg Am 58:537–540, 1976.

100. Thompson, J.E.M. Comminuted fractures of the patella. J Bone Joint Surg Am 17:431–434, 1935.

101. Thompson, J.E.M. Fracture of the patella treated by removal of the loose fragments and plastic repair of the tendon. Surg Gynecol Obstet 74:860–866, 1942.

102. Vainionpää, S.; Böstman, O.; Pätiälä, H.; Rokkanen, P. Rupture of the quadriceps tendon. Acta Orthop Scand 56:433–435, 1985.

103. Viola, R.; Vianello, R. Three cases of patella fracture in 1,320 anterior cruciate ligament reconstructions with bone–patellar tendon–bone autograft. Arthroscopy 15:93–97, 1999.

104. Virolainen, H.; Visuri, T.; Kuusela, T. Acute dislocation of the patella: MR findings. Radiology 189:243–246, 1993.

105. Watkins, M.P.; Harris, B.A.; Wender, S.; et al. Effect of patellectomy on the function of the quadriceps and hamstrings. J Bone Joint Surg Am 65:390–395, 1983.

106. Webb, L.X.; Toby, E.B. Bilateral rupture of the patella tendon in an otherwise healthy male patient following minor trauma. J Trauma 26:1045–1048, 1986.

107. Weber, B.G.; Cech, O. Pseudarthrosis. New York, Grune & Stratton, 1976, pp. 224–225.

108. Weber, M.J.; Janecki, C.J.; McLeod, P.; et al. Efficacy of various forms of fixation of transverse fractures of the patella. J Bone Joint Surg Am 62:215–220, 1980.

109. Wendt, P.P.; Johnson, R.P. A study of quadriceps excursion, torque, and the effect of patellectomy on cadaver knees. J Bone Joint Surg Am 67:726–732, 1985.

110. West, F.E. End results of patellectomy. J Bone Joint Surg Am 44:1089–1108, 1962.

111. Wiberg, G. Roentgenographic and anatomic studies on the patellofemoral joint. Acta Orthop Scand 12:319–410, 1941.

112. Wilkinson, J. Fracture of the patella treated by total excision. J Bone Joint Surg Br 59:352–354, 1977.

113. Wimsatt, M.H.; Carey, E.J. Superior dislocation of the patella. J Trauma 17:77–80, 1977.

114. Woo, S.; Maynard, J.; Butler, D.; et al. Ligament, tendon, and joint capsule insertions to bone. In: Woo, S.L.Y.; Buckwalter, J.A., eds. Injury and Repair of the Musculoskeletal Soft Tissues. Park Ridge, IL, American Academy of Orthopaedic Surgeons, 1988, pp. 133–166.

115. Yu, J.S.; Petersilge, C.; Sartoris, D.J.; et al. MR imaging of injuries of the extensor mechanism of the knee. Radiographics 14:541–551, 1994.

# Dislocations and Soft Tissue Injuries of the Knee

John M. Siliski, M.D.

The knee is the largest and arguably the most complex joint in the body. Its bony geometry and dissimilar surfaces offer little inherent stability. The components of the soft tissue envelope of the knee, including the static capsuloligamentous and meniscal restraints and the dynamic musculotendinous units, work in concert to stabilize the knee and allow multidirectional motion. Not simply a hinge joint, the knee has six degrees of freedom: flexion-extension, internal-external rotation, and abduction-adduction.

Injury to the knee is common and can result from varying levels of energy. Knee injury is the most frequent cause of disability related to sports activity. In the polytrauma setting, knee injury is often occult and unrecognized and may cause prolonged morbidity. Unlike assessment of fractures, an acutely injured knee often lacks radiographic clues to diagnosis, so a premium is placed on knowledge of functional anatomy, hands-on examination, diagnostic acumen, and appropriate ancillary tests. A correct diagnosis allows the implementation of appropriate treatment according to the nature of the injury, patient-related variables, and the capabilities of the medical team.

Knee injuries can be divided into broad diagnostic categories, including fractures and injuries to the extensor mechanism, ligamentous structures, menisci, articular surfaces, and musculotendinous structures. This chapter introduces an approach to the acutely injured knee with a discussion of the examination and recognition of symptom complexes, the use of appropriate ancillary diagnostic tests, and a treatment philosophy for soft tissue injury. Emphasis is placed on diagnosis and conceptual treatment algorithms. Paralleling the advances in functional treatment of fractures has been a welcome and aggressive trend toward early, stable soft tissue repair in acute knee injury that minimizes joint immobility and promotes early return of function.

## DIAGNOSTIC APPROACH TO THE INJURED KNEE

### History

The type of knee injury can often be inferred from a proper history. The diagnostic approach (Fig. 55–1) should begin by establishing the magnitude and direction of forces applied to the knee (Fig. 55–2). Such forces may vary from high-velocity vehicular accidents to noncontact sports injuries. Application of the force can be direct, such as contact of the anterior of the knee with the dashboard in a motor vehicle accident, or indirect, such as rotational forces applied through the leg with dissipation of these forces through the knee ligaments.[15] A combination of forces can also occur, as exemplified by a valgus rotational injury sustained by a football player struck from the outside on his planted leg. Accurate knowledge of the magnitude and direction of forces applied and the position of the knee at impact, coupled with an understanding of anatomy, often leads to a suspected diagnosis or pattern of injury before physical examination. In polytraumatized patients, particularly those with long bone lower extremity fractures, the possibility of traumatic soft tissue injury to the knee must be expected rather than excluded.

In isolated injury to the knee, important factors to determine in the history are the ability to ambulate after injury, the rapidity of onset of swelling, whether tearing or popping was perceived, and whether an initial deformity reduced spontaneously or in response to manipulation.

The presence of acute hemarthrosis after knee injury has been shown conclusively to be an indicator of significant intra-articular injury.[2, 5, 16] In 75% to 80% of cases, such injury means a tear of the anterior cruciate ligament. Other causes of hemarthrosis are intra-articular fractures, tears of menisci in the vascular zone, and patellar

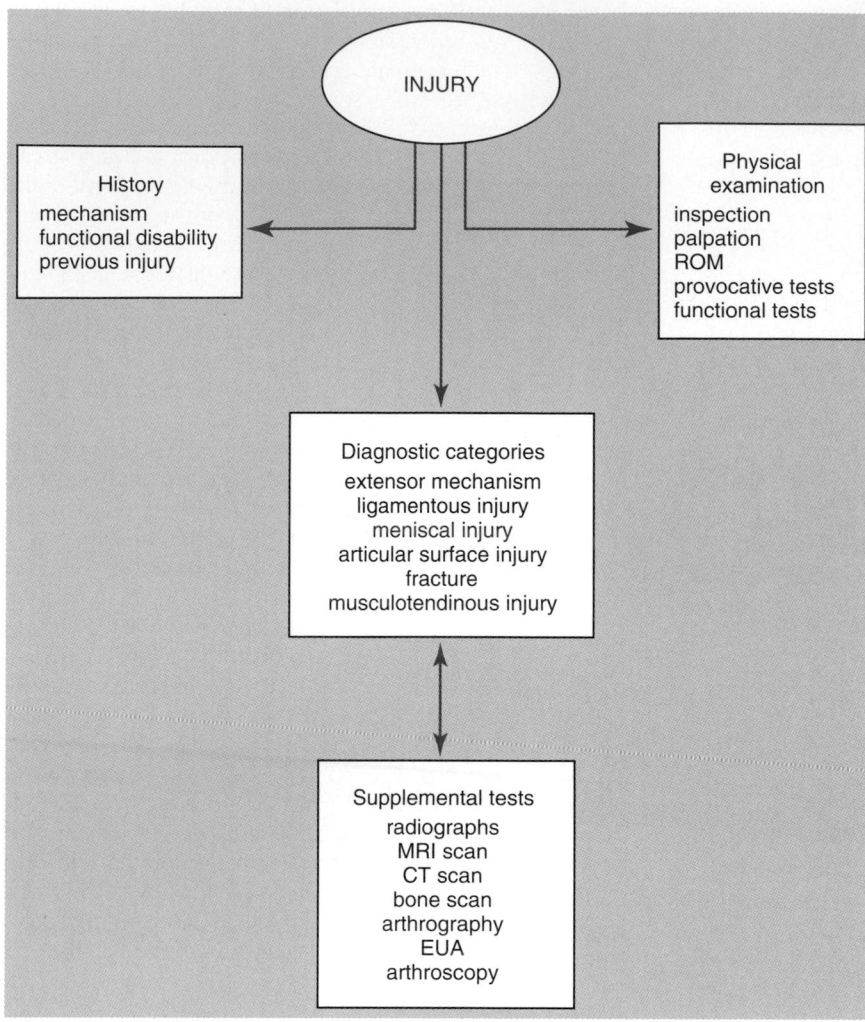

**Figure 55–1.** Diagnostic algorithm for an injured knee. *Abbreviations:* CT, computed tomography; EUA, examination under anesthesia; MRI, magnetic resonance imaging; ROM, range of motion.

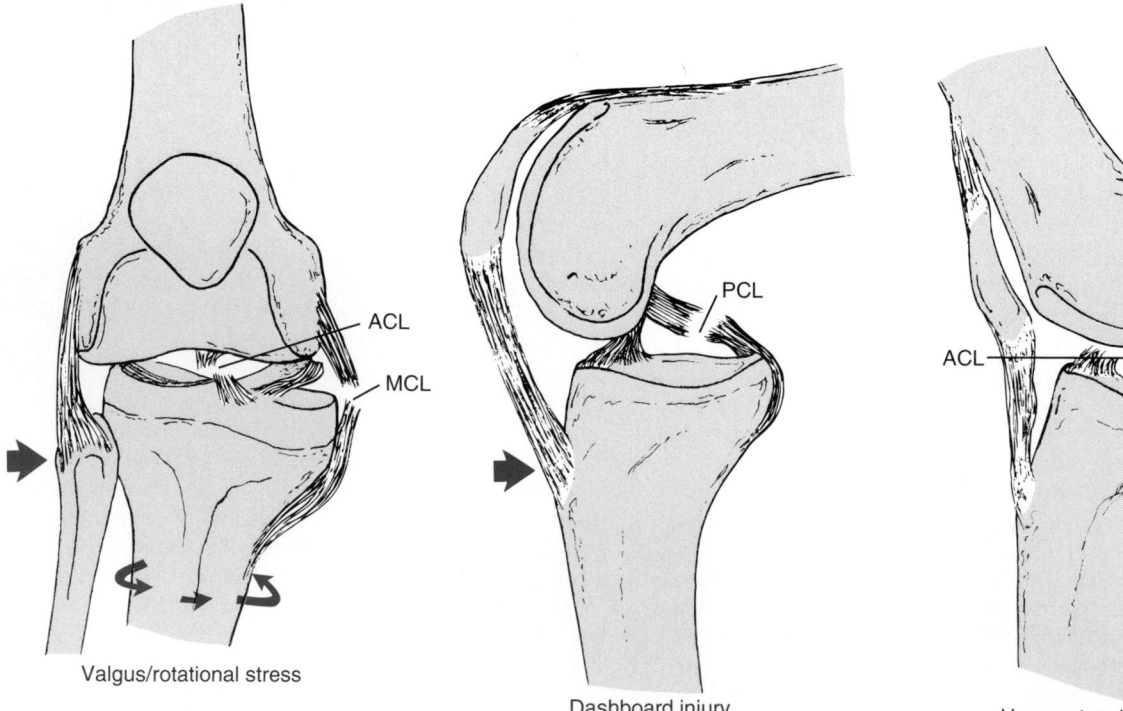

**Figure 55–2.** Common mechanisms of knee injuries. *Abbreviations:* ACL, anterior cruciate ligament; MCL, medial collateral ligament; PCL, posterior cruciate ligament.

dislocation. Hemarthrosis is a sign, not a diagnosis. When hemarthrosis is present, a systematic approach must be taken to arrive at a pathoanatomic diagnosis and should include careful clinical examination and radiographs. On occasion, supplemental studies include stress radiographs, tomograms, and magnetic resonance imaging (MRI) scans.

## Physical Examination

The clinical examination should be performed in a relaxed setting. For unilateral knee injuries, it is wise to examine the uninvolved knee for range of motion and stability. Such assessment gives the examiner a baseline for comparison and often allays patient apprehension. Inspection may identify areas of ecchymosis or swelling. Anatomic structures are palpated with emphasis on the collateral ligaments, joint lines, and the extensor mechanism. Active range of motion should be noted and compared with passive measurements. Discrepancies in active and passive motion are usually secondary to pain but may reflect disruption of the extensor mechanism. Restriction of passive motion may be due to muscle spasm, effusion, or internal derangement.

Hemarthrosis usually incites protective muscle spasms and makes adequate ligament examination difficult. Aspiration of the hemarthrosis and instillation of 10 to 15 mL of a local anesthetic into the joint may decrease pain and improve diagnostic accuracy. The sensitivity of clinical examination for isolated anterior cruciate ligament tears, however, has been shown to be unsatisfactory.[16] An accurate diagnosis may be determined by several methods, including MRI, examination under anesthesia, arthroscopy, or reexamination after acute hemarthrosis has resolved.

### LIGAMENT LAXITY EXAMINATION

Examination for ligament laxity should include anterior and posterior translational tests for the cruciate ligaments, fixed-fulcrum varus and valgus tests for the collateral ligaments, and special tests for combined or rotational instability.[6, 17, 21]

For the *anterior cruciate ligament,* the Lachman test (Fig. 55–3) is performed with the knee in approximately 20° of flexion, the distal end of the femur stabilized by the examiner's upper hand, and an anterior force applied to the posterior aspect of the upper part of the tibia by the lower hand. Anterior translation of the tibia on the femur is estimated in millimeters, and the status of the end-point is noted. The Lachman test is more sensitive than the classic anterior drawer test performed at 90° of flexion and is certainly more comfortable for the patient in the acute setting.[12] The status of the *posterior cruciate ligament* can also be ascertained in moderate flexion with reversal of the direction of tibial force. Posterior sag of the proximal part of the tibia with the hip and knee flexed at 90° is pathognomonic for posterior cruciate ligament instability.

Varus and valgus stress tests for the *lateral and medial collateral ligaments,* respectively, are performed in full extension and at 20° to 30° of flexion. Again, estimates are made in terms of millimeters of laxity and end-point. Ligament tears are conventionally graded from I to III. A grade I injury is indicated by a painful stress examination with at most minimal instability. A grade II injury is a more significant incomplete ligament tear with obvious laxity, but with a definite end-point. A grade III injury is a complete tear with no apparent end-point. Instability in extension implies a complete (grade III) tear of the collateral ligament and its associated posterior quadrant capsular mechanism and a probable posterior cruciate ligament sprain to a variable degree. Stability in extension generally excludes significant capsular and posterior cruciate injury.[9, 10] Rotational instability of the knee signifies abnormal excursion of the tibial condyle in relation to the femur and can theoretically occur in four quadrants: anteromedial, anterolateral, posteromedial, and posterolateral. Combined rotational instabilities can also exist. As its name implies, *rotational instability* involves a shift in the center of rotation (cruciate ligament injury) and loss of secondary capsular restraint. Anteromedial instability is documented by excessive displacement during an anterior drawer test with the leg in internal rotation. Tests for anterolateral laxity (pivot shift, Slocum, jerk, Losee, and flexion-rotation drawer) have as a common denominator a valgus load with extension or flexion, either to produce or to reduce tibial subluxation.[14, 20] Posterolateral instability can be detected by a reverse pivot shift or external rotation recurvatum test performed by lifting the leg by the great toe.[3] Quantification of rotational instability is highly subjective and best determined by comparing the injured with the uninjured knee.

The use of ligament arthrometers is increasing.[4] These instruments are in large part educational and research tools to supply objective data to supplement clinical laxity

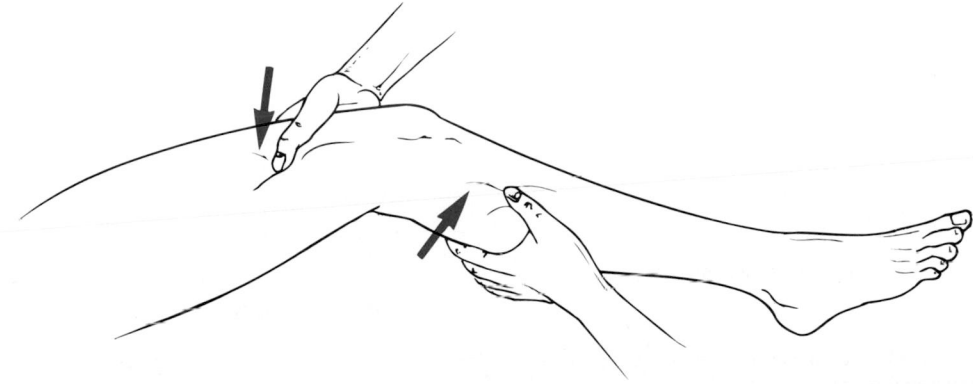

**FIGURE 55–3.** Lachman test for anterior drawer instability. The test is done at 20° to 30° of flexion. The femur is stabilized with one hand, and the tibia is drawn anteriorly with the other hand.

examinations for anterior or posterior instability. However, no arthrometer is universally accepted, nor have results with different devices been standardized. Their use is most valuable when making side-to-side comparisons and in longitudinal evaluations after injury and treatment. The use of arthrometers in acute injury is limited by pain, guarding, and restricted motion, as is the clinical examination. It should be remembered that the loads applied in clinical laxity tests are nonphysiologic and must be correlated with functional evaluation of the patient.

## Imaging Studies

### RADIOGRAPHS

Radiographs should be obtained for all acute knee injuries. The standard knee trauma series includes anteroposterior, lateral, oblique, and patellar tangential views. Alignment, soft tissue detail, and the presence or absence of bony injury should be discerned. Ligament injury may be associated with avulsion fractures. The lateral capsular sign, a small avulsion fracture of the lateral tibial plateau, is associated with injuries to the anterior cruciate ligament. Avulsion fractures may be seen at the origin and insertion sites of the collateral and cruciate ligaments. Osteochondral fractures may also be apparent. Patellar dislocations may be accompanied by a fracture fragment of the medial aspect of the patella or the lateral edge of the trochlear groove. All radiographic clues are valuable in making a diagnosis and planning appropriate treatment.

### Stress Radiographs

Stress radiographs have not been shown to increase diagnostic accuracy over examination under anesthesia and arthroscopy. Their use may aid in grading isolated collateral ligament injuries, in assessing the stability of nondisplaced avulsion fractures, and in differentiating skeletal and ligament instability in skeletally immature patients.

### TOMOGRAMS AND COMPUTED TOMOGRAPHY

Tomograms and computed tomography (CT) of an acutely injured knee are largely reserved for evaluation of intra-articular fractures involving the weight-bearing surfaces and for localization of the origin of osteochondral fractures when not evident on plain films.

### MAGNETIC RESONANCE IMAGING

The use of MRI in the evaluation of acute knee injuries is evolving.[1, 7, 11, 18, 19] The sensitivity and specificity of MRI for the menisci and cruciate ligaments are greater than 90% when correlated with findings at the time of arthrotomy or arthroscopy[8, 13] (Fig. 55–4). Because MRI is also noninvasive and eliminates exposure to ionizing radiation, it has largely replaced knee arthrography. However, MRI should not be used indiscriminately in place of careful clinical examination and plain radiographs. Its benefit in an acute knee injury may lie in

excluding meniscal tears in isolated ligament injuries, particularly of the collateral ligaments, which can otherwise be treated successfully by nonoperative means. Conventional MRI poorly delineates cartilaginous defects, chondromalacia, and loose bodies other than osteochondral bodies. MRI can also be used to refine a preoperative plan regarding the likelihood of meniscal repair versus excision.

With meniscal tears, changes in signal intensity vary from focal intrameniscal degeneration (grade I) (Fig. 55–5) to clear-cut linear communication with an articular surface (grade III). The former condition is generally treated nonoperatively and the latter by surgical excision or repair. MRI should certainly be considered a valuable adjunct in the diagnostic armamentarium, but it should be used in a thoughtful and purposeful manner.

### ARTHROGRAPHY

Indications for arthrography in acute knee injury are limited, and MRI is a superior study without patient risk. In suspected penetrating knee injury, however, arthrography or a saline load test may confirm extravasation. The latter is a sterile injection to distend the joint while examining for leakage through the open wound.

### ARTERIOGRAMS

Arteriograms are indicated in suspected vascular injury or insufficiency after knee trauma. When vascular injury is clinically present, arteriography should not delay operative restoration of flow for more than 6 hours after its interruption by injury.

## KNEE INJURY IN POLYTRAUMA PATIENTS

Knee injury should be suspected in any patient with lower extremity long bone fracture, polytrauma, or head injury.[23, 27] The acute management of a knee injury in these circumstances is a low priority (unless associated with vascular injury). If unrecognized, however, a knee injury may become the source of long-term functional disability. For polytrauma patients, resuscitation and skeletal stabilization allow patient mobilization. Knee injury can be addressed when optimal patient conditions allow, preferably within 10 days of injury but often satisfactorily as late as 3 weeks after trauma. Pending surgical repair, the injured knee can be immobilized in appropriate splints or braces without disrupting mobilization.

With a long bone fracture, an ipsilateral knee injury should be suspected in the presence of ecchymosis, tenderness, or swelling about the knee.[22] Radiographs should include the knee when a femoral or tibial fracture is present. With osseous instability, it is often impossible to perform an adequate examination of the knee and its ligaments. If skeletal stabilization of the long bone fracture is undertaken, examination of the knee under anesthesia should immediately follow.[24] Ligament injury may be

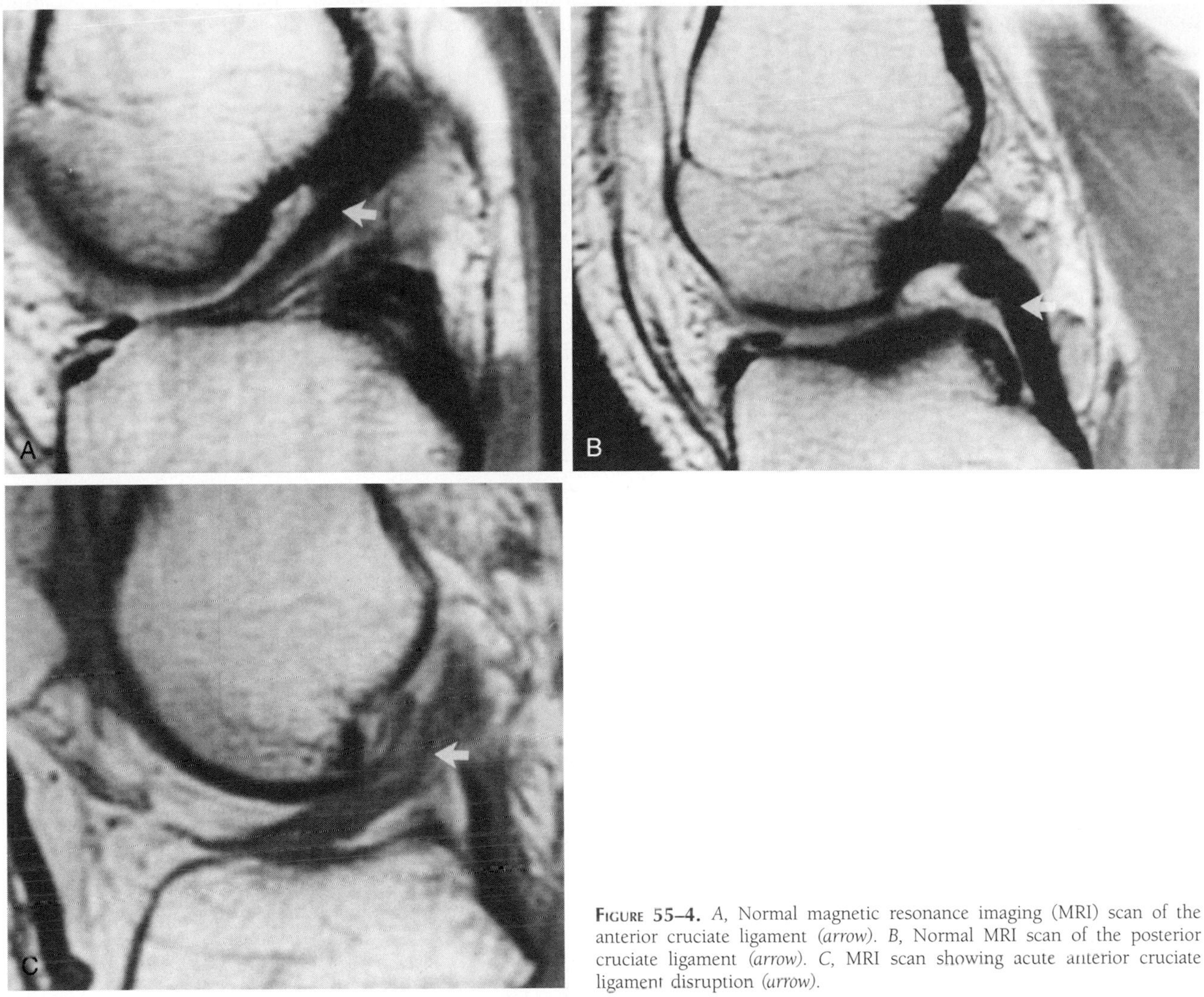

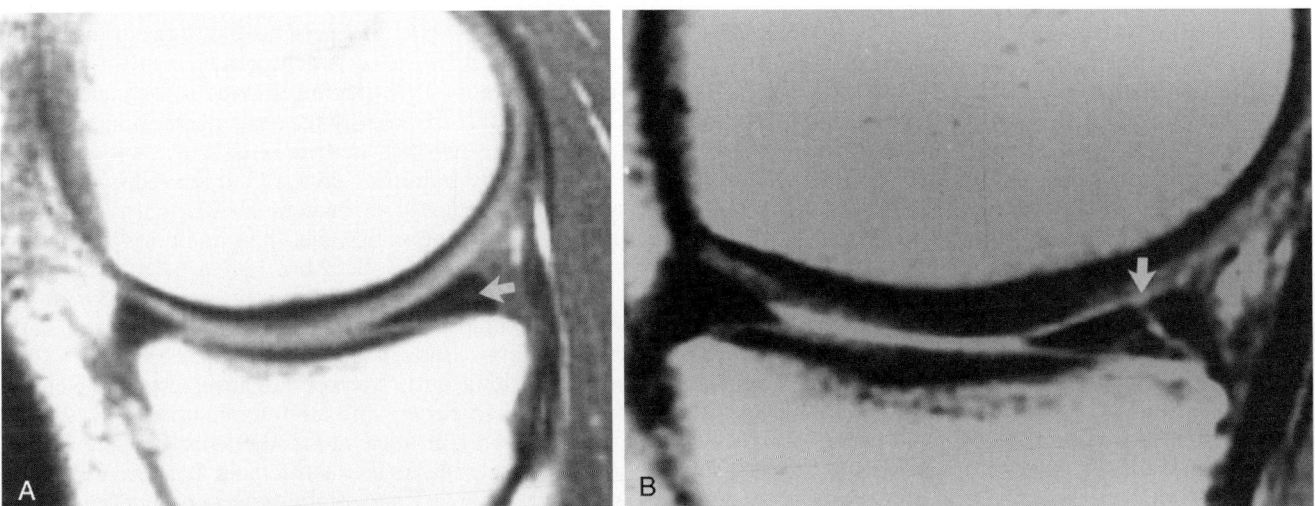

**FIGURE 55–4.** *A,* Normal magnetic resonance imaging (MRI) scan of the anterior cruciate ligament *(arrow). B,* Normal MRI scan of the posterior cruciate ligament *(arrow). C,* MRI scan showing acute anterior cruciate ligament disruption *(arrow).*

**FIGURE 55–5.** *A,* Magnetic resonance imaging scan showing intrameniscal degeneration (within the posterior horn of the meniscus) *(arrow). B,* Meniscal tear extending to the articular surface *(arrow).*

treated primarily or by delayed repair, depending on the overall condition of the patient. If gross knee ligament disruption is suspected, traction across the knee through a tibial pin should be avoided. In patients with a floating knee and ipsilateral femoral and tibial fractures, rigid skeletal fixation of at least the femur should be performed, followed by examination of the knee under anesthesia.[26]

Management of vascular injuries about the knee is urgent and should immediately follow resuscitation of the patient if limb-threatening ischemia is present. If the popliteal artery is occluded, rapid restoration of perfusion is crucial to avoid amputation. The timing and technique of skeletal stabilization must be determined by close consultation between vascular and orthopaedic surgeons. A temporary arterial shunt or the rapid application of an external fixator may facilitate limb salvage. In the absence of ischemia, preliminary fracture stabilization may simplify arterial repair.

Neurologic injury is generally an axonotmesis, except in cases of penetrating trauma. Acute repair is not generally indicated, and exploration is deferred unless it is part of a planned surgical approach.

In soft tissue injuries the principles of débridement apply, with removal of devitalized tissue, irrigation, capsular closure to prevent cartilage desiccation, and appropriate soft tissue coverage.

Appropriate suspicion must be maintained to rule out knee ligament injury adjacent to a fracture of the femur or tibia. Prospective studies of presumably isolated femoral and tibial shaft fractures have shown the incidence of associated knee ligament injury to be 33%[28] and 22%,[25] respectively, although many of these injuries are relatively mild.

## OPEN KNEE INJURIES

The knee is the joint that most often incurs penetrating or open injury (Fig. 55–6). Joint penetration can be directed from without, such as gunshot or stab wounds, or from extension into the knee through open periarticular fractures. Knee dislocations are open in 20% to 30% of cases. Proper recognition plus treatment of periarticular soft tissue injury, associated capsuloligamentous damage, and intra-articular pathology is necessary to restore joint function.

## Classification

Patzakis and co-workers classified open joint injuries into those with fractures, those without fractures, and gunshot wounds.[30] In their review of 140 cases, however, the parameter most closely correlating with poor outcome and wound infection was the degree of soft tissue injury about the open joint. Collins and Temple proposed a grading system based principally on the periarticular soft tissue injury.[29] Class I injury is a singular laceration without extensive soft tissue injury. Class II includes single or multiple lacerations with extensive soft tissue injury or

loss. Class III includes open joints from extension of open periarticular fractures. Each class is subdivided according to the degree of articular injury and meniscoligamentous disruption. Class IV injuries are open dislocations with nerve or vascular injury requiring repair. This classification system is useful because it includes grading of injury to both the soft tissue component, which influences the early outcome, and the articular surface, which bears long-term prognostic significance.

## Diagnosis

Open knee injuries range from visible communication with the joint to a quite imperceptible puncture wound. Particularly with penetrating trauma to the anterior of the knee in a position of flexion, the skin and joint capsule wounds may not be superimposed when the knee is examined in extension. Passive flexion of the knee will often elucidate the staggered nature of the wound and may produce a characteristic sucking sound. Radiographs should be obtained for all suspected open knee injuries; the presence of air in the joint confirms the diagnosis. A saline load test can be performed in selected cases to demonstrate extravasation. It is helpful when skin and capsular disruptions are at different levels. Under sterile conditions, 30 to 50 mL of sterile saline solution can be injected intra-articularly through nontraumatized skin while any drainage through open wounds is noted. Other imaging techniques such as arthrography, CT, and MRI help identify foreign bodies or air, but they can delay expeditious surgical treatment. Probing a wound should be discouraged because probing is an unreliable test, may introduce additional contaminated material into the joint, and is often painful to the patient.

## Treatment

The mainstays of treatment of open knee injuries are antibiotics, thorough wound débridement and irrigation, and capsular closure. In the emergency department, the wound should be inspected, accessible foreign material removed, and a sterile dressing applied. Antibiotic administration should be considered therapeutic and not prophylactic because the wound is contaminated. Tetanus prophylaxis should be given if indicated. A broad-spectrum cephalosporin or equivalent should be started intravenously. Antibiotics are continued for 48 to 72 hours.

Débridement of devitalized soft tissue followed by gentle pulsatile lavage of the joint is carried out next. Primary skin closure is appropriate for clean lacerations, regardless of length; however, delayed primary closure, split-thickness skin grafts, soft tissue rotation flaps, or other measures may be required, depending on wound severity. If extensive soft tissue loss has occurred, the knee should be packed open, with repeat débridement and coverage performed as rapidly as clinically acceptable to avoid desiccation of articular cartilage. Treatment of an articular surface injury should generally proceed as if it were a closed joint injury. Such treatment includes

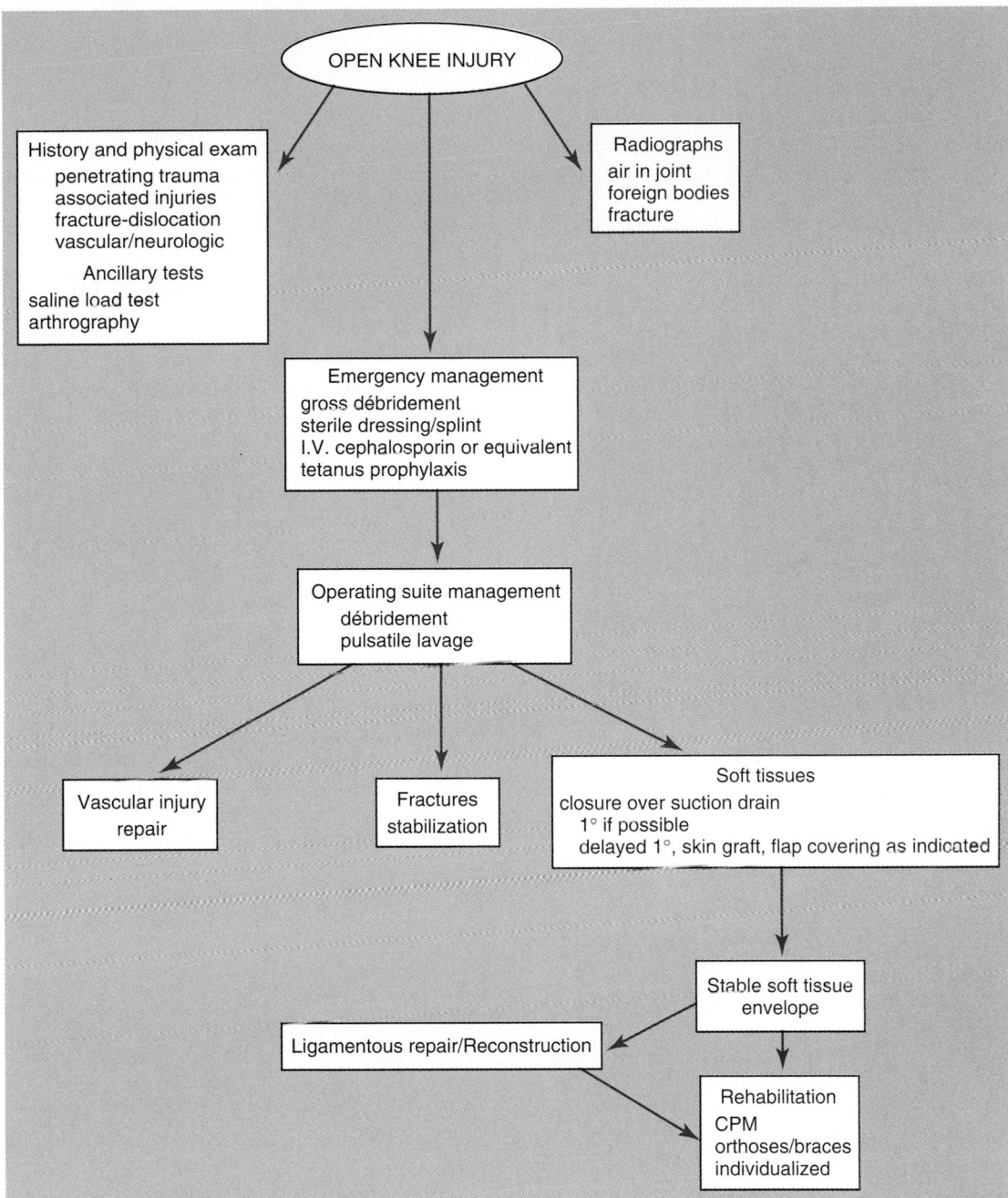

**FIGURE 55–6.** Treatment algorithm for an open knee injury. *Abbreviation:* CPM, continuous passive motion.

operative fixation of periarticular and intra-articular fractures. Management of an associated ligament injury is probably best deferred in most cases until the risk of infection has passed and the soft tissues are favorable for further surgery. This strategy limits further acute insult to the knee from the soft tissue dissection or from the secondary incisions often necessary for ligament repair. Exceptions are isolated ligament injuries in open wounds resulting from direct laceration and ligaments avulsed in continuity with their bony attachment.

If possible, capsular closure should be performed over suction tubes. The use of suction-irrigation systems was questioned by Patzakis and co-workers as a possible source of iatrogenic joint contamination.[30] The benefit of mechanical fluid lavage is unknown but probably negligible. The risks inherent in using closed irrigation systems are infection and disturbance of the cartilage matrix by prolonged exposure to irrigating fluids. The validity of a positive effluent culture must also be questioned. It is suggested that suction tubes be removed after 24 to 48 hours.

The role of arthroscopy in open knee injuries is limited, but it is valuable in selected cases. It is of primary benefit in detecting perforation by a foreign body, such as gunshot or pellet injuries, when the soft tissue injury is small (often the size of a normal arthroscopic portal) and fluid extravasation is limited. Arthroscopic débridement, irrigation, removal of loose and foreign bodies, and documentation and treatment of articular surface injury can be accomplished. The arthroscope can also be used in a "dry" fashion through an open injury or accessory portal to visualize areas in the knee not readily accessible from the primary wound, thus perhaps limiting the need for extension of surgical incisions.

The ease of an arthroscopic procedure should not be allowed to cloud judgment. If adequate débridement has not been or will not be performed arthroscopically, open arthrotomy should be carried out. The difference in short-term morbidity is indeed secondary to the ultimate outcome.

A special consideration in open knee injuries is vascular disruption. The vascular injury and its ramifications assume first priority, followed by treatment of the joint injury according to the aforementioned guidelines.

Rehabilitation after an open knee injury is in large part dictated by the soft tissue injury. After successful closure and removal of drains, controlled passive and active motion can be instituted. Early passive motion is helpful in preventing arthrofibrosis and has a beneficial effect on cartilage metabolism. The rapidity and intensity of exercise and therapeutic measures are based on articular and capsuloligamentous integrity.

## TRAUMATIC DISLOCATION OF THE KNEE

Traumatic dislocation of the knee (Fig. 55–7) is relatively uncommon but is limb threatening because of the possibility of vascular disruption in the popliteal fossa. It is therefore considered an orthopaedic emergency.

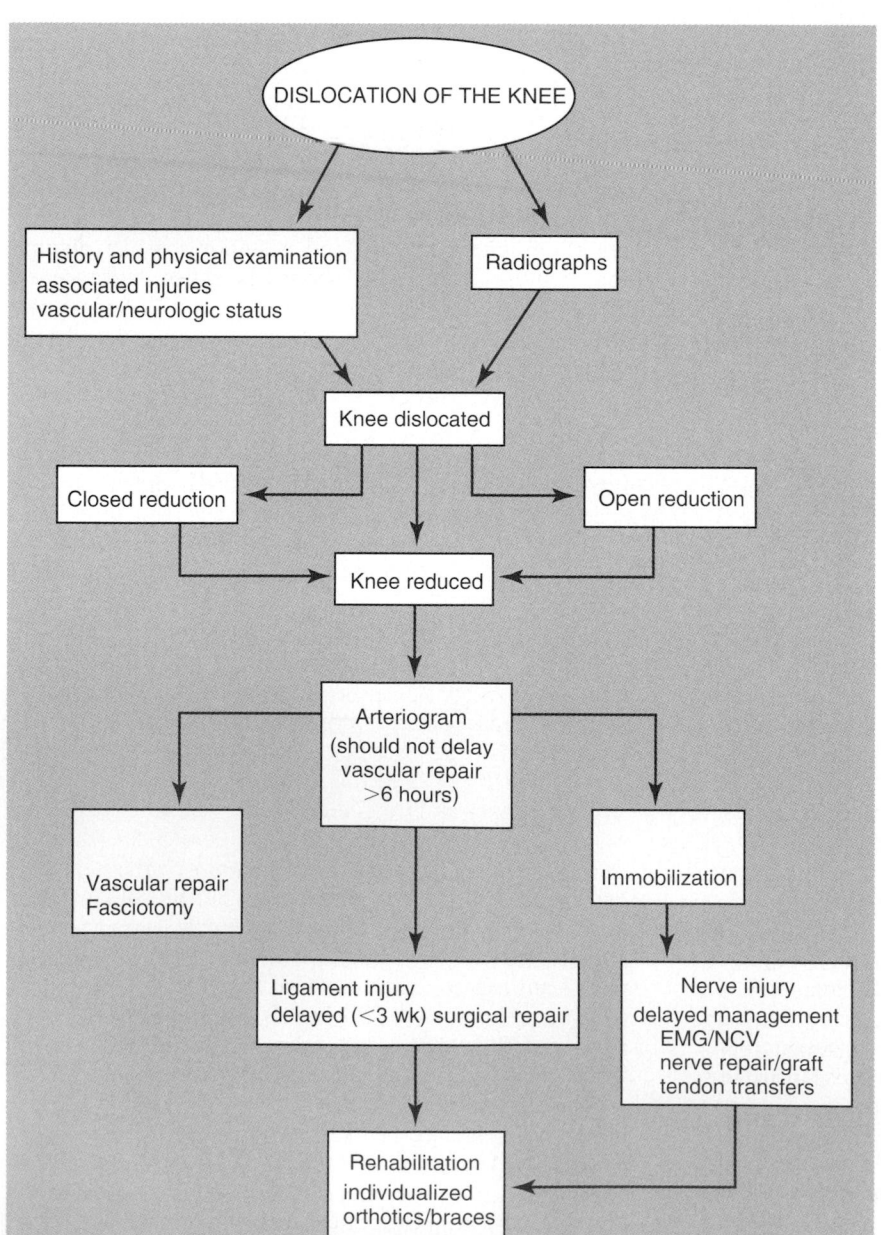

**FIGURE 55–7.** Treatment algorithm for dislocation of the knee. *Abbreviation:* EMG/NCV, electromyelography/nerve conduction velocity.

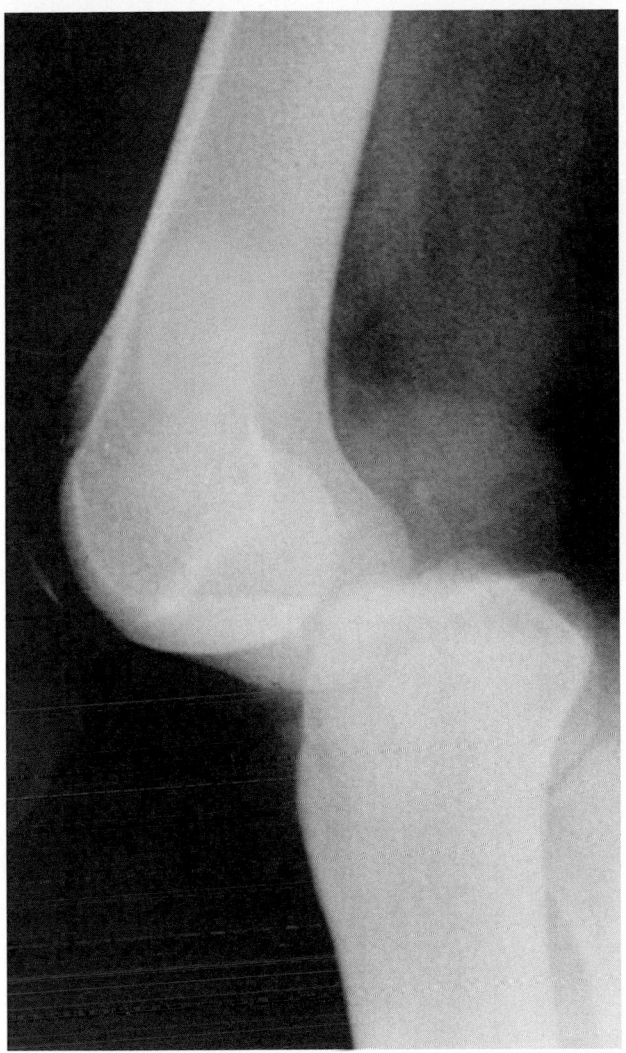

**FIGURE 55–8.** Posterior dislocation of the knee from a dashboard injury.

## Classification

Vehicular accidents are the most common cause of dislocation of the knee and typically produce high-energy trauma. Dislocation of the knee has also occurred from falls and during sports, but these mechanisms usually produce a lower-energy injury.[53]

Knee dislocations may be classified according to the relationship of the tibia to the femur in response to the forces incurred. Anterior dislocation occurs most often from a posteriorly directed force on the anterior aspect of the thigh with the foot planted; such a force causes hyperextension and, as shown by Kennedy, sequential disruption of the posterior capsule and the posterior cruciate and anterior cruciate ligaments.[75] In cadaver specimens, tearing of the popliteal artery occurred, on average, at 50° of hyperextension. Posterior dislocation typically results from a "dashboard injury" in which the flexed knee has a posteriorly directed force applied to the anterior of the tibia (Fig. 55–8). Lateral dislocation (Fig. 55–9) occurs from a valgus stress with the tibia fixed and the thigh adducted. Medial dislocation of the knee can result from a varus force to the thigh, but it often has a

rotational component. Rotational dislocations can occur in any quadrant of the knee, with the posterolateral quadrant being the most common. Anterior and posterior dislocations account for 50% to 75% of all dislocations. As a result of high-energy trauma, 20% to 30% of dislocations are open injuries.[43–45, 51, 54, 55] Knee dislocations may also have associated intra-articular fractures of the tibial plateau or femoral condyles.

Dislocations may also be classified by the capsuloligamentous structures disrupted. Almost all cases have disruption of both cruciate ligaments. In addition, neither, one, or both collateral ligament complexes may be disrupted.

## Diagnosis

Dislocation of the knee is probably underdiagnosed for several reasons. Reduction and realignment of the limb may occur at the scene of the accident. Because of the extreme capsular disruption, tense hemarthrosis is generally absent, and overt signs of knee injury may be absent as well, particularly in a patient with associated skeletal instability or multiple trauma. A clue to the presence of a reduced knee dislocation is coexistent varus or valgus instability in full extension, a finding that indicates tears of both the anterior cruciate and posterior cruciate ligaments. Exaggerated hyperextension or recurvatum is also indicative of combined cruciate and posterior capsular disruption. Diffuse tenderness about the knee, absence of hemarthrosis, and the presence of popliteal ecchymosis may also be initial signs. Vascular insufficiency after closed knee injury suggests severe instability. An associated peroneal nerve deficit is likewise suggestive of knee dislocation.

The principal test for instability is adequate examination of the ligaments, which may require examination after skeletal stabilization in patients with ipsilateral long bone fractures.[57] It should be possible by examination to identify the combination of ligament complexes disrupted in a dislocation. The examination, in combination with imaging studies, should be sufficient to define the pathology of the injury and to plan the surgical approach, repairs, and reconstructions. Rarely is arthroscopy necessary as a diagnostic tool. Moreover, arthroscopy with fluid runs the risk of excessive extravasation into muscle compartments in the setting of capsular disruption.

Plain radiographs of the knee should be obtained to look for possible avulsion fractures, which are clues to ligament injury (Fig. 55–10). Injuries associated with knee dislocation include fractures of the patella, tibial spine, tibial plateau, fibular head, and femoral condyles. In patients with avulsion fractures or tibial plateau fractures, stress films can be used if necessary to differentiate skeletal and ligament instability. MRI can be used preoperatively to identify associated meniscal injury and define the nature of the ligament injury (midsubstance versus avulsion tears).[40]

## Reduction

When faced with a dislocated knee, documentation of the neurovascular status of the limb is mandatory. Closed

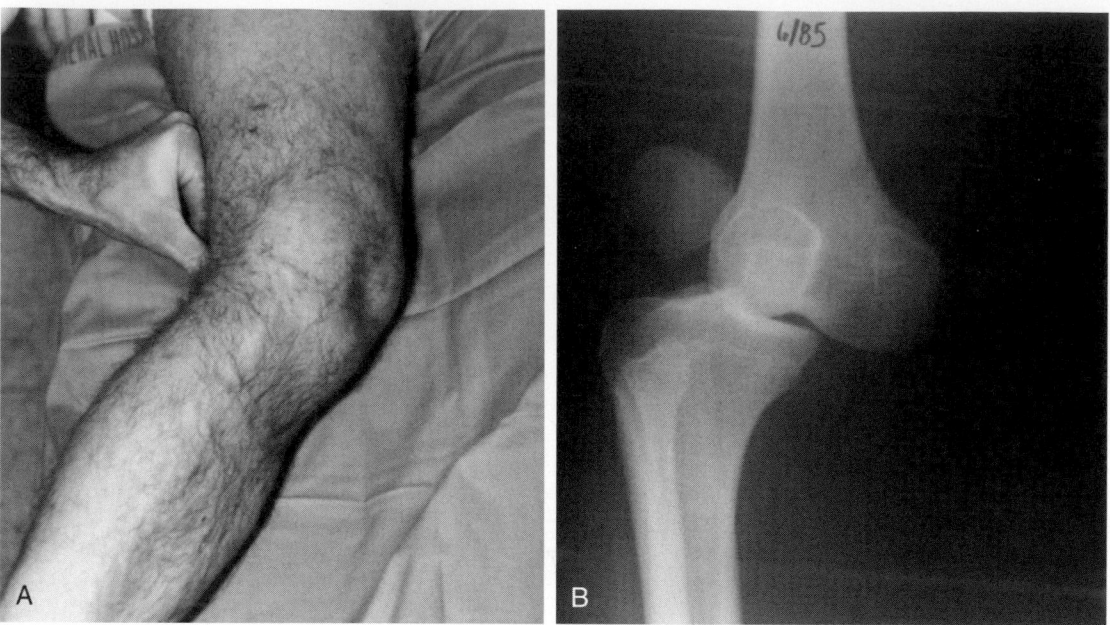

**FIGURE 55–9.** *A, B,* Lateral dislocation of the knee after a valgus stress resulted in disrupted cruciate ligaments and medial structures. (*A, B,* From Siliski, J.M., ed. Traumatic Disorders of the Knee. New York, Springer-Verlag, 1994.)

reduction of a dislocated knee can generally be accomplished in the emergency department with appropriate analgesia. For anterior dislocation, reduction is carried out with traction of the limb and elevation of the distal end of the femur. Posterior dislocation is reduced with traction on the tibia coupled with extension and lifting of the proximal part of the tibia in an anterior direction. An important

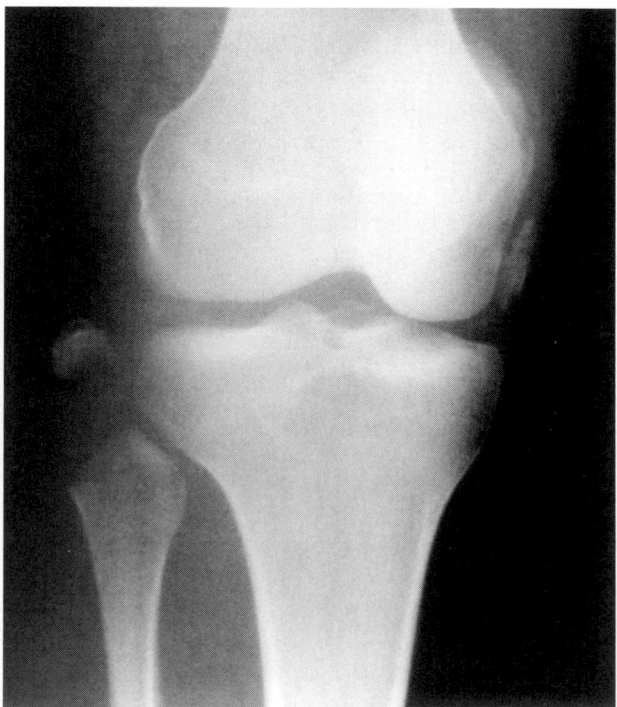

**FIGURE 55–10.** Avulsion fragments from the fibula, medial femoral condyle, and the tibial eminence suggested disruption of the collateral and cruciate ligaments. (From Siliski, J.M., ed. Traumatic Disorders of the Knee. New York, Springer-Verlag, 1994.)

principle is to avoid directing any force against the popliteal fossa when compromised vascularity may be present. Medial and lateral dislocations are reduced by longitudinal traction and appropriate translation of the femur and tibia. Rotational injuries are reduced by traction and appropriate derotation of the tibia. Posterolateral dislocations have been called *irreducible dislocations.* With this type of injury, a "dimple sign" will often be noted clinically on the medial joint line as a result of medial capsular and collateral ligament invagination with button-holing of the medial femoral condyle through the soft tissue rent.[49] For a dislocation that is irreducible by the preceding means, emergency reduction attempted under general anesthesia is necessary. On rare occasion, open reduction may be required. It is important to document the patient's neurologic and vascular status before and after any attempt at reduction. After reduction, the knee should be immobilized in 20° to 30° of flexion pending further evaluation. No circular plaster or constricting dressing should be applied.

## Vascular Injury

The sinister reputation of knee dislocation comes from the possible presence of vascular injury. Injury to the popliteal artery has been reported in 5% to 30% of dislocations[34, 44, 50, 56] and is most common in anterior and posterior dislocations because of tethering of the popliteal artery at its entrance to the fossa at the adductor hiatus and at its exit by the soleal arch. With significant tibial displacement, the artery is at risk because of this proximal and distal fixation. Important tenets in regard to vascular injury at this level are that (1) the collateral circulation about the knee is inadequate to maintain limb viability if popliteal artery disruption is present and (2) the presence of pedal pulses does not exclude vascular injury. Most patients with vascular deficiency before reduction will continue to have ischemia after reduction. Green and Allen reported restoration of only 5 of 56 absent pulses after closed reduction of a knee dislocation.[37] Thus, any evidence of vascular insufficiency distal to a knee dislocation implies that an arterial injury is present until proved otherwise. Diminished pulses must not be ascribed to "vascular spasm."

Time is critical in the salvage of an avascular limb after knee dislocation.[58] Amputation rates as high as 86% have been reported. Additional studies show a dramatic increase in the amputation rate if the limb is not revascularized within 6 to 8 hours.

Indications for arteriography after knee dislocation or an equivalent injury are somewhat controversial (Fig. 53–11). Prompt recognition of diminished or absent pulses is absolutely essential for timely treatment of amputation threatening popliteal artery injuries associated with knee dislocation. Careful physical examination during the early stages of care identifies almost all patients with serious arterial injuries. Failure to recognize an ischemic limb and treat it immediately is a far more common cause of disaster than is omission of arteriography for well-perfused limbs because performing such studies solely almost never reveals significant injuries. Nonocclusive intimal tears rarely if ever cause late thrombosis.

Routine monitoring of Doppler-assisted ankle/brachial indices (ABIs) is a highly effective method to exclude limb-threatening arterial injury. The ABI is the ratio of ankle (posterior tibial or dorsalis pedis) systolic blood pressure to that of the brachial artery at the elbow. Unless the ABI is less than 0.9, the likelihood of arteriography revealing an injury that requires treatment is so low that many trauma and vascular surgeons now argue that routine arteriography is not required after knee dislocation.[31–33, 39, 41] Others and perhaps most orthopaedic surgeons aware of the dire consequences of missing an occluded or disrupted popliteal artery continue to urge that arteriography be performed in all patients with knee dislocations or gross instability from fracture-dislocations or combined ligament disruptions.[36, 41, 43, 47] Noninvasive arterial imaging techniques (e.g., ultrasonography or magnetic resonance angiography) may prove to be helpful alternatives for these patients.

If distal ischemia persists after reduction of the dislocated knee, surgical exploration and restoration of flow are urgent and should not be delayed to obtain an arteriogram. If necessary, arteriography can be performed in the surgical suite before exploration. However, time is of the essence, and because of the high probability of popliteal fossa localization, arteriography adds little to confirmation of injury or surgical planning in an isolated knee dislocation with vascular injury. After repair of the occluded popliteal artery, a complete four-compartment fasciotomy is advisable to protect against reperfusion swelling and compartment syndrome.

Arteriography, if initially omitted, probably adds little or nothing to the evaluation of a knee dislocation if the study is performed several days after injury. The risk of an intimal tear progressing to thrombosis becomes very low after 5 to 7 days. Our protocol for treatment of dislocations with intimal lesions but no vascular insufficiency is anticoagulation for 1 week and to then proceed with ligament repair.

## Neurologic Injury

The incidence of peroneal nerve injury associated with knee dislocation has been reported to range from 14% to 35%.[50] This injury is usually an axonotmesis over a broad area of injury and carries with it a poor prognosis. Primary exploration with repair or grafting has not been effective and is not recommended. Secondary exploration at 3 months for complete injury along with nerve grafting has also produced poor functional results. The resultant muscular deficiencies usually require bracing or tendon transfers to improve foot position and gait.

## Treatment

Treatment of ligament injuries resulting from knee dislocation has been the subject of some debate.[34, 44, 45, 51, 53–55]

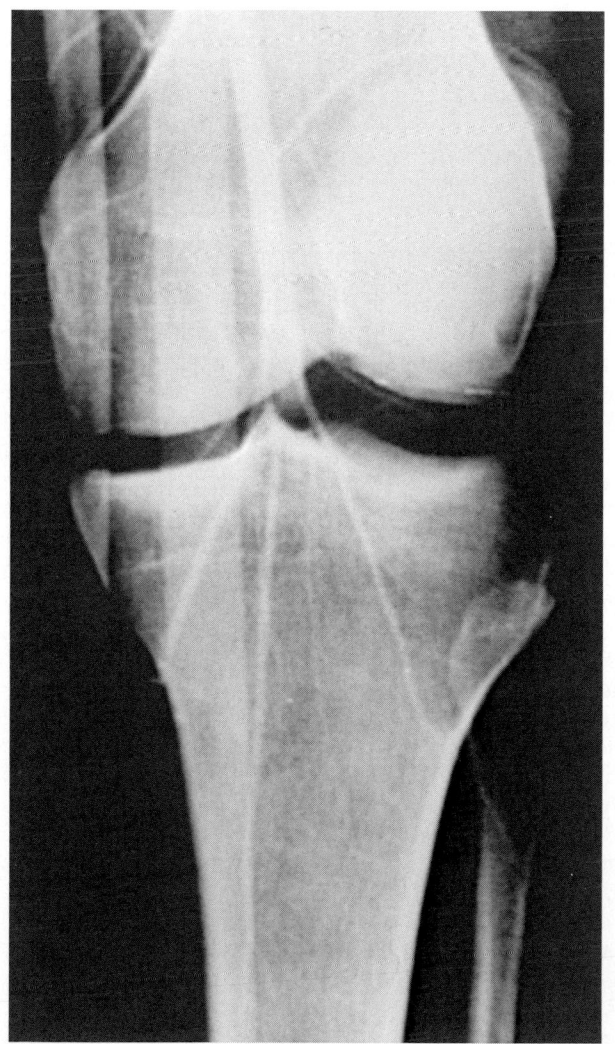

**FIGURE 55–11.** Arteriogram demonstrating a popliteal artery injury with disruption of flow after knee dislocation.

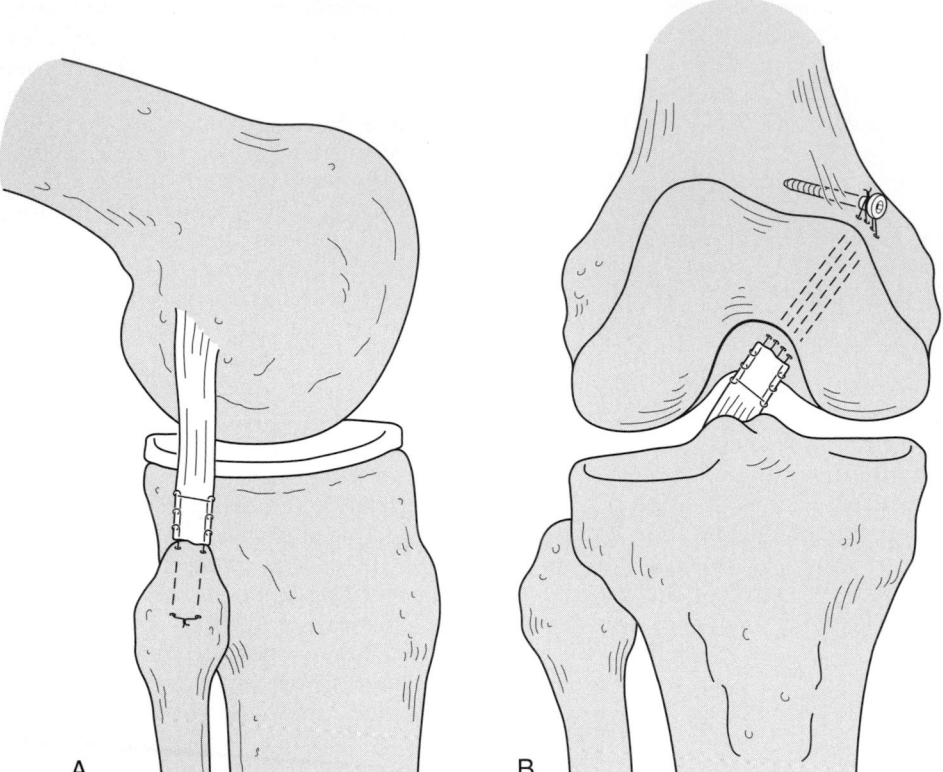

**FIGURE 55–12.** Ligament fixation to bone. *A,* An avulsed lateral collateral ligament is reattached to the fibula with sutures placed through drill holes. *B,* An avulsed posterior cruciate ligament is reattached to the femur with sutures passed through drill holes and tied over a screw.

Most authors currently favor operative repair of all ligament injuries, followed by early mobilization and functional bracing to promote optimal results.[39, 46, 48, 52] In dislocation, most knees will have combined anterior and posterior cruciate ligament disruption associated with variable collateral ligament, capsular, and meniscal tears. The timing of ligament repair is dependent on the condition of both the patient and limb. The priority of surgical interventions is vascular repair, skeletal stabilization, and finally, ligament repair. If vascular repair is undertaken, ligament repair can be delayed for up to 2 to 3 weeks until vascular stabilization and early soft tissue healing have occurred.

The surgical approach should be based on an accurate examination of the ligaments and the instability pattern. A vertical anteromedial incision permits exposure of the cruciate ligaments, medial meniscus, and medial capsuloligamentous complex. If the posterolateral corner is also disrupted, a second vertical incision can be made over the lateral collateral ligament. Because of the significant capsular and ligament disruption, exposure is not generally a problem and often makes primary repair easier than when undertaken for an isolated ligament injury. Sequential repair/reconstruction of meniscus and cruciate and collateral ligament tears is undertaken.

A general strategy is to first reattach or reconstruct the cruciate ligaments without performing the final fixation. Quite commonly, the posterior cruciate ligament is avulsed from the femur and can be reattached by using Marshall's technique (Fig. 55–12). The anterior cruciate ligament usually requires reconstruction with an autograft or allograft. Once the cruciate ligament repairs are in place, they should not be secured until the other injured structures are addressed. The general approach is to identify and tag all disrupted structures and first repair the deep and posterior structures and then the superficial and anterior structures. Meniscal detachments are sutured, and unrepairable menisci are excised. Posteromedial and posterolateral capsular tears are either sutured if torn in the midsubstance or reattached to the tibia with anchor sutures if avulsed from bone (Fig. 55–13). The collateral ligaments are likewise either sutured or reattached to bone (Fig. 55–14; see also Fig. 55–12). The iliotibial band, biceps femoris tendon, and patellar tendon should be checked for partial or complete tears and appropriately repaired.

With stable soft tissue repair, it is generally unnecessary to maintain reduction with transarticular pins. A hinged postoperative brace affords initial immobilization, wound access, and early controlled range of motion. The rapidity of graduated mobilization depends on the adequacy of repair, but it is desirable to regain full passive motion 6 to 8 weeks after surgery. Protected weight bearing can begin at approximately 4 to 6 weeks.

## ANTERIOR CRUCIATE LIGAMENT INJURY

The importance of the anterior cruciate ligament in the overall kinematics and stability of the knee is not in

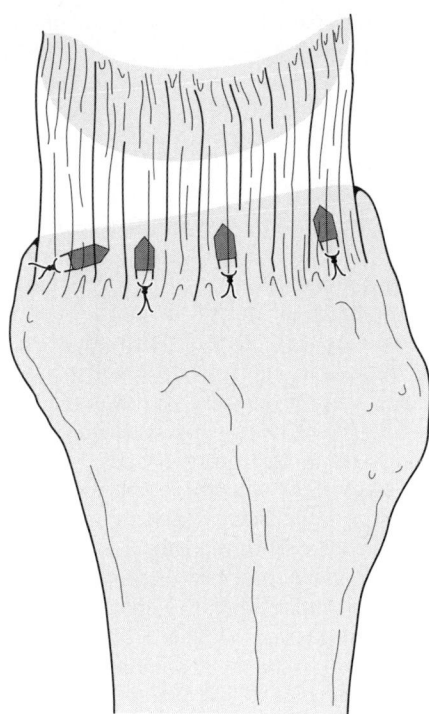

**FIGURE 55–13.** Reattachment of the capsule with anchor sutures.

doubt.[60, 62, 65, 68, 75] Authorities do, however, disagree about appropriate treatment of an injury to the anterior cruciate ligament.[61, 72, 73, 85] One would certainly like to offer the best possible treatment for any given injury to restore function. The difficulty in decision making with anterior cruciate ligament injury lies in the many variables that influence the degree of functional loss and in the variable expression of this functional loss from individual to individual. The two main subgroups of variables are those related to the pathoanatomy of the injury and patient-related variables. Anterior cruciate ligament sprain can be an incomplete or complete lesion, isolated or associated with other ligament or meniscal injury, and acute or chronic in nature. Patient-related variables include the age, activity level, and phenotype of the individual.[65] Anterior cruciate ligament injury has variable expressivity, and the decision whether to treat an individual by nonoperative or operative measures must include an analysis of these variables to make an appropriate treatment decision. Knowledge of these variables and how they affect operative and nonoperative treatment is important.

An accurate diagnosis is the foundation for treatment of any injury. The classic history of an anterior cruciate ligament sprain is a decelerating, hyperextension, or twisting injury to the knee, often associated with a pop, immediate functional loss, rapid onset of swelling, and pain.

If acute swelling and muscle spasm preclude an accurate physical diagnosis, aspiration of the knee and instillation of local anesthetic may facilitate examination. Plain radiographs of the knee should be taken in all cases of acute injury to inspect for bony avulsions or fractures. In the acute setting, when a diagnosis is suspected but not

confirmed, examination under anesthesia may be warranted.[6] Such examination allows for complete muscle relaxation and evaluation of knee stability in all planes and comparison with the opposite knee. The degree of instability is quite subjective, varies according to the experience of the examiner, and should always be compared with that of the opposite knee. Instrumented knee ligament testing devices are more objective in quantifying anterior instability and may be useful. The presence of rotational instability (pivot shift) correlates highly with functional disability in a "high-demand" knee.[81, 82] The role of arthroscopy in the diagnosis and management of acute knee injuries is well documented. The type of anterior cruciate ligament injury can be determined by inspection and probing. The status of the menisci and chondral surfaces can also be ascertained, and their status may directly affect the choice of treatment. Again, the key to appropriate management is an exact diagnosis.

Once the pathoanatomy is known, other variables can be considered. Patient variables also play a significant role in planning treatment. A young, athletically active patient involved in a high-demand sport would be a more likely candidate for arthroscopy and subsequent surgical intervention than would be an older, recreationally active individual involved in low-demand activities.[64, 79] In terms of knee function, high-demand sports include contact sports and those involving jumping, twisting, and deceleration forces (e.g., football, soccer, basketball, and wrestling). Less demanding sports include golfing and running. The

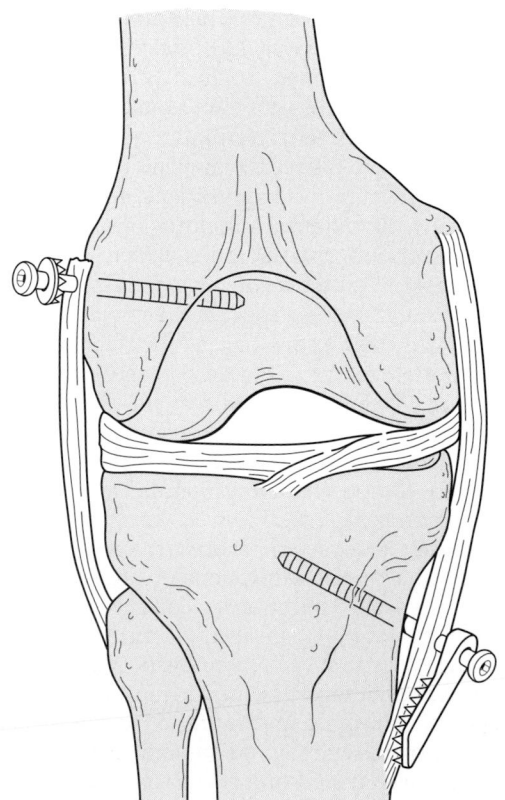

**FIGURE 55–14.** Ligament fixation to bone with a spiked washer and a spiked soft tissue plate.

level of athletic competition is also a significant factor.[81] The physician might suggest a change from a high-demand to a low-demand sport for a recreational athlete, but such a proposal would not be acceptable to an elite athlete or professional.[70, 82] Expected time lost from work is also important when considering various treatment options with the patient. As a result of financial concerns, a patient may not wish to undergo an operative procedure that would limit employability. An individual may not want the "best knee possible" if it is going to require significant time lost from work, but an active, competitive athlete who wishes to maintain that performance level without compromise will probably request and deserve surgical intervention. In cases treated nonoperatively, it has been shown that with rehabilitative exercise, functional bracing, and modification of activity, patients have a reasonable chance to achieve a successful outcome in terms of functional stability.[82, 83] Such an outcome is particularly likely with isolated partial injuries of the anterior cruciate ligament.[74] In some less active individuals, associated intra-articular injury might be treated arthroscopically with a similar pathway of rehabilitation, bracing, and activity modification followed.[66] In competitive athletes or laborers, treatment of any existing intra-articular injury is desirable, as well as surgical treatment of the anterior cruciate ligament to restore anatomic function.[64, 67, 69, 79, 80] Isolated primary repair of the anterior cruciate ligament has been shown to be less effective than repair with augmentation.[63, 77, 78] Acute, intra-articular reconstruction has become the most commonly used method of reconstruction because of technical improvements in isometric placement and fixation of ligament grafts.[59, 62, 84, 86] Of paramount importance in a surgical approach are a successful rehabilitation program and utmost patient compliance.[83]

It must be remembered that isolated injury to the anterior cruciate ligament is not a static injury. The syndrome of an anterior cruciate–insufficient knee is well documented.[60, 65, 69, 76] Recurrent episodes of giving way place intact menisci at risk of tearing, and the strain on secondary restraints also increases and may worsen the functional disability.[82] In cases of anterior cruciate ligament injury and associated reparable meniscal lesions, repair of the menisci alone in the face of cruciate instability often leads to failure. If meniscal repair is undertaken, it is recommended that the anterior cruciate ligament also be addressed surgically for joint stabilization. If the patient does not wish to undertake this option, the meniscal lesion should be treated accordingly with appropriate resection.

In terms of therapy, appropriate muscle reeducation and strengthening should generally include all muscle groups that act about the knee. Emphasis is placed on rehabilitation of the hamstrings, which are anterior cruciate ligament agonists. One must not, however, forget maximal strengthening in the quadriceps musculature and gastrocnemius complex. Institution of rehabilitation generally follows restoration of motion and absence of pain in both nonoperatively and operatively treated patients. Full range of motion should be the goal. Flexion contracture produces excessive patellofemoral compression and is a primary source of pain in those who do not regain full extension. Evidence suggests that an older, less physically active individual can respond to this program favorably. Patient understanding and compliance are key factors in the success or failure of such a program. It must also be understood that rehabilitation must be followed by maintenance exercise.

The use of functional knee braces in an anterior cruciate–deficient knee is an ongoing topic of discussion and research, but such braces are generally used to increase the margin of safety in both operatively and conservatively managed patients. They are more helpful in controlling one-plane anterior instability than rotational instability. It is important to let the patient know that a brace is not a substitute for vigorous and conscientious muscle strengthening and proprioceptive training.

In certain individuals, operative treatment is recognized as the treatment of choice. Anterior cruciate ligament disruptions associated with recognizable injury to secondary restraints or other complete ligament injuries are best treated with appropriate operative intervention and stabilization. Knees with combined acute ligament injuries and multiplane instability have poor functional outcome if treated nonoperatively. These knees have limited functional reserve when treated conservatively. In addition, injuries associated with displaced bony avulsion fractures are best stabilized surgically and, when treated in this fashion, will often yield the best results because of bone-to-bone healing and a structurally intact ligament.

In summary, the treatment options offered to a patient are predicated on an accurate anatomic diagnosis of both the type of anterior cruciate ligament injury and the associated intra-articular and other ligament injuries. Once these injuries are defined, a treatment plan can be offered, with attendant risks and benefits based on the patient's age, employment, level and type of sports participation, and ability and willingness to adapt this participation according to functional impairment, if present.

## POSTERIOR CRUCIATE LIGAMENT INJURY

The primary function of the posterior cruciate ligament is to prevent posterior translation of the tibia on the femur. It also plays a role as a central axis in controlling and imparting rotational stability to the knee.[93, 95] The posterior cruciate ligament is less commonly injured, and injury more often passes unrecognized than does injury to its counterpart, the anterior cruciate ligament.

Injury most often occurs from trauma to the anterior aspect of the proximal end of the tibia with the knee flexed, as in a fall or dashboard injury. It can also be torn during extreme hypertension or rotational or varus/valgus stress. Posterior cruciate ligament injury may be isolated or associated with other capsuloligamentous injury.[88, 91] In the acute setting, pain may significantly decrease the accuracy of examination of the ligament, and evaluation under anesthesia may be necessary.

## Isolated Posterior Cruciate Ligament Injuries

The clinical findings with an isolated injury may be subtle because of its posterior position, frequent lack of swelling or ecchymosis, and uncommon history of a pop or tearing sensation. This injury will frequently be diagnosed as a nonspecific sprain and treated symptomatically. It is not uncommon to detect posterior instability on routine screening of athletes in whom no functional deficit has been present. In one-plane posterior instability, secondary restraints at the posterior corners prevent rotational instability.[92] Diagnostic tests for isolated posterior cruciate ligament instability are the posterior sag and posterior drawer signs. A decrease in posterior drawer with the tibia in internal rotation implies some functional restraint in the posterior cruciate (a grade I or II tear) or integrity of the posterior meniscofemoral ligaments.[87]

Radiographs of the knee should be obtained in an acute injury to rule out avulsion fracture. An avulsion fracture most commonly occurs at the tibial insertion and is more frequent than an avulsion fracture of the anterior cruciate ligament, particularly in skeletally mature patients. Biomechanically, such a fracture may be a result of the posterior cruciate ligament's larger size, broader area of bony insertion, and lack of bony impingement from the intercondylar notch. Grade III instability (grossly positive posterior sag or drawer sign) with an avulsion fracture of the posterior cruciate ligament is an indication for primary repair because bone-to-bone fixation can be achieved and an excellent result can be expected.

Literature reviews generally support nonoperative treatment of an isolated posterior cruciate ligament tear.[89, 90, 96, 97] Individuals who maximize strength of the quadriceps, the agonist of the posterior cruciate ligament, experience the best outcome. It has been shown in a case study of a professional athlete that a conditioned quadriceps contracts earlier in the gait cycle, thereby dynamically limiting posterior tibial translation.[87] Subsequent medial compartment degenerative changes have not been statistically associated with an isolated posterior cruciate–deficient knee.

## Combined Posterior Cruciate Ligament Injuries

A key point in evaluating posterior cruciate ligament injury is to search for and identify associated capsuloligamentous injury. Combined posterior cruciate ligament and collateral or capsular tears impart multiplane and rotational instability, lead to functional disability, and do have a positive correlation with medial compartment arthrosis.[87] Combined injury also jeopardizes the popliteal vessels more frequently, and as a result, vascular evaluation is mandatory.

Clinical laxity tests for combined injuries attempt to detect one-plane collateral and associated rotational instabilities. Collateral instability in extension is suggestive of complete tear of the primary collateral restraint and

associated capsular structures and probable cruciate injury. With loss of posterior cruciate ligament function, additional laxity of the posterolateral corner increases external tibial rotation and rollback, as demonstrated by the reverse pivot shift[94] and external rotation recurvatum tests.[93] Primary surgical repair or augmentation is recommended for combined posterior cruciate and associated ligament injuries. Medial arthrosis has been reported in 48% of functionally unstable posterior cruciate–deficient knees and increases with the chronicity of injury.

## MEDIAL COLLATERAL LIGAMENT INJURY

The medial (tibial) collateral ligament is the primary medial stabilizer of the knee and is generally depicted as having a superficial fan-shaped component and a deep capsular complex consisting of the meniscofemoral and meniscotibial ligaments.[108, 109] The fan-shaped superficial ligament has, by design, anterior fibers that are most taut in flexion and posterior fibers that are most taut in extension. The superficial medial collateral ligament is the most important medial stabilizer; secondary static restraints to valgus stress include the cruciate ligaments. Injury to the medial collateral ligament is most often caused by a valgus stress produced by a force applied to the lateral aspect of the knee while the foot is planted. Sprain of the medial collateral ligament is the most common of the knee ligament injuries, and such sprains are recognized by the presence of an appropriate history, tenderness along the course of the ligament, medial swelling, and medial ecchymosis (variable). Valgus stress testing in extension and at 30° of flexion should be performed and compared with results in the opposite knee. Instability in extension indicates complete injury to the medial collateral ligament, as well as the posterior and medial capsule and possibly the posterior cruciate ligament. Medial stability in extension does not exclude third-degree or complete rupture. At 20° to 30° of flexion, the restraining effect of an intact capsular complex is eliminated, and isolated collateral laxity can be determined.

## Isolated Medial Collateral Ligament Injuries

The recommended treatment for isolated medial collateral ligament injuries is symptomatic and functional and involves the use of hinged bracing to prevent valgus stress.[98] When to begin motion is dictated largely by patient comfort. For complete grade III injuries, fixed hinges at 30° to 45° of flexion for 2 to 4 weeks can be used to allow for decreases in swelling and pain; motion is then begun. Once satisfactory, painless range of motion has been restored, appropriate muscle rehabilitation and proprioceptive training can begin. The results of nonoperative treatment of isolated medial collateral ligament injuries are quite good.[99–104, 106] With complete injuries, clinical laxity is often seen on examination but little functional loss. The use of prophylactic knee bracing to prevent knee ligament injury has been the subject of a number of reviews, with mixed conclusions regarding their efficacy. Reasons for failure of laterally hinged braces include failure to match the knee axis of rotation, preload in tension of the medial collateral ligament, and improper fit. However, in a controlled prospective study, the incidence, but not the severity of medial collateral ligament injury was reduced by bracing.[108]

## Combined Medial Collateral Ligament Injuries

Combined ligament injury, particularly injury to the medial collateral–anterior cruciate ligament complex, generally warrants surgical intervention because of the presence of multiplane instability.[103, 107] Such management is particularly appropriate in a young, active, athletic individual. In combined injuries as well as complete grade III medial collateral disruptions, the presence of meniscal injury must be excluded. MRI or arthroscopy is suitable for this purpose. The most common current treatment of combined anterior cruciate–medial collateral ligament injuries is to use a leg brace for up to 6 weeks to prevent valgus deformation and permit healing of the medial structures while motion is recovered. Reconstruction of the anterior cruciate ligament may then be performed. Any mild residual medial collateral ligament laxity is usually well tolerated once anterior cruciate ligament stability is restored.

## LATERAL COLLATERAL LIGAMENT INJURY

The lateral (fibular) collateral ligament is a cordlike structure running from the fibular head to the lateral femoral condyle.[116] It is readily palpable with the knee placed in a "figure-of-four" position. The function of the lateral collateral ligament is to resist tensile stress when varus force is applied to the knee, and it is aided on the lateral side, particularly in extension, by the iliotibial tract. Other secondary restraints include the arcuate ligament and popliteus muscle, which combine with the lateral collateral ligament to form the arcuate complex at the posterolateral corner of the knee.[114, 117] Isolated injury to the lateral collateral ligament is unusual, but it may be seen with high-energy trauma. An example is a windswept or sideswipe knee injury with contralateral injury to the medial structures of the opposite knee. With lateral collateral ligament injury, peroneal nerve function should be checked during the physical examination. Testing for varus instability should be performed in full extension and at relaxed flexion, with similar implications of capsular and possible cruciate disruption if instability is present in extension.[113, 114] Isolated grade III injury to the lateral collateral ligament (varus laxity without an end-point in full extension) is unusual and more often associated with

combined cruciate and secondary restraint tears.[111] Avulsion fractures (lateral capsular sign) are indicators of significant lateral soft tissue injury.[118]

Isolated injury to the posterolateral corner (arcuate complex) results from trauma to the anterior medial aspect of the extended knee, noted clinically by varus instability at 30° of flexion and a positive posterolateral drawer sign.[110] The cruciate ligaments are generally spared. Isolated injury to the lateral collateral ligament, particularly incomplete lesions, can be treated nonoperatively with limited bracing and rehabilitation, but grade III injuries warrant primary surgical intervention.[112] Functional problems in laterally unstable knees may be more common than with isolated medial collateral injury as a result of the normal varus thrust and tensile forces on the lateral side of the knee with ambulation. Chronic lateral collateral ligament insufficiency is more apt to require late surgical intervention because of this functional deficit.[115]

## PRINCIPLES OF LIGAMENT SURGERY

The general function of ligaments is to resist tensile or joint distraction forces. The goal in the treatment of injury to the ligaments of the knee is to restore functional stability and normal kinematics. The biology of ligament injury and repair must be considered in the decision-making process. At the cellular level, ligaments undergo a continuum of events in response to injury. The stages of inflammation (injury to 48 hours), proliferation (48 hours to 6 weeks), remodeling, and maturation (up to 12 months or more) can be altered favorably or unfavorably by surgical intervention,[119] the type and length of immobilization, and rehabilitation.

Nonsurgical treatment is generally indicated for grade I and grade II collateral ligament injuries and isolated grade III injuries to these same structures. Isolated injuries to the anterior or posterior cruciate ligaments are variable in their manifestations and instability pattern. Variables involved in the treatment of these injuries have been discussed previously. Operative repair is indicated in ligament avulsion fractures and combined collateral, cruciate, and capsular ligament tears.

Repair of ligament injury involves one of three scenarios: (1) end-to-end ligament anastomosis; (2) ligament-to-bone fixation; and (3) bone-to-bone fixation.

End-to-end ligament anastomosis is probably unnecessary for midsubstance isolated tears of the collateral ligaments. Proponents of repair cite realignment of the soft tissues with gap closure and reduction of scars during the proliferative phase as yielding better ultimate tensile strength.[121, 123] However, in medial collateral ligament injury models treated *nonoperatively*, ultimate tensile strength was improved over that in ligaments treated by operative repair, and the additional morbidity of surgical exposure was avoided.[125] Clinical experience substantiates this approach. In combined injuries and, in particular, knee dislocations, repair of the collateral ligaments and their associated structures may add substantially to overall knee stability.[105]

End-to-end suture fixation can be used in primary

cruciate repairs when supplemented by intra-articular augmentation. Multiple loop sutures,[120, 125] Bunnell sutures, and a locked-loop suture technique have been used to coapt ligament ends.[120] A heavy, nonabsorbable suture is recommended. When brought out through drill holes, sutures should not be tied over a bone bridge because they are at risk of cutting through the bone and thereby decreasing knot tension. An effective way to anchor sutures through bone is to secure the knot around the smooth proximal shank of a bone screw. The screw acts as a fixation post, and tension can be increased by angling the screw away from the direction of the suture line and securing the knot before final seating of the screw. However, reconstruction with an intra-articular tissue graft is initially more secure and more successful in the long run than intrasubstance ligament suturing.

Ligament-to-bone fixation preserves the original ligament and works well for the collateral and posterior cruciate ligaments. Soft tissue fixation techniques have been studied by Robertson and colleagues.[124] The use of staples was inadequate in terms of pull-out strength and the amount of tissue necrosis beneath the implant. The best results were obtained with the use of a screw with a spiked plastic washer or with a spiked ligament plate (see Fig. 55–14). The spiked design allows microcirculation beneath the washer or plate and multiple fixation sites. Strength was improved by placing the screw through the tissue rather than in an adjacent position where only partial capture may occur. Posterior cruciate ligament avulsions commonly occur off the femoral side. Sutures in the end of the ligament can be passed through bone and tied over the medial femoral condyle to pull the ligament against its attachment site, which is abraded down to bleeding bone (see Fig. 55–12B).

Bone-to-bone fixation in ligamentous avulsion fractures can be secured, depending on size, with lag screws or suturing techniques. The cruciate and collateral ligaments may be avulsed with bone from either end. Large bone fragments may accept lag screw fixation. Smaller bone fragments may be secured with suturing techniques, either as a tension band or by passing the sutures through bone. Secure bone-to-bone fixation allows early motion and is the ideal scenario for ligament repair.

The purpose of secure soft tissue fixation is to allow controlled passive motion after repair. The effects of immobilization[122] (loss of collagen fiber orientation, increased stiffness, and subchondral resorption at the ligament–bone interface) can be countered by mobilization and application of graduated tensile stress to the repaired ligament.

## MENISCAL INJURY

The menisci of the knee are vital to knee function and longevity. Although the menisci were once considered vestigial structures, their preservation is now believed to be of paramount importance.[137] They transmit up to 50% of the force across the knee, aid in shock absorption, and provide joint stability, particularly in ligament-deficient knees.[136, 142] Absence of the menisci has been shown to lead to degenerative joint changes inasmuch as loss of the load-sharing and shock absorption functions effectively increases load per unit area on the articular surfaces.[132, 135, 144]

Meniscal tears (Fig. 55–15) are generally caused by a combination of axial loading and rotational forces that shear the meniscus between the femoral and tibial condyles. Traumatic tears are usually associated with a known insult to the knee and may be isolated or associated with ligament or articular surface injury. Traumatic tears generally occur in younger, active individuals. Degenerative tears reflect cumulative stress and correlate with the presence of associated chondromalacia. Symptoms produced by a meniscal tear are usually mechanical in nature and include locking, catching, grinding, and giving way. The frequency and severity of the symptoms vary according to the size and mobility of the meniscal tear. Pain and swelling are also variable. The body of the meniscus is aneural, and pain is generally produced by abnormal traction on the meniscocapsular junction or meniscofemoral ligaments (which are enervated), by the abnormal stress distribution created, or by localized inflammation.[130]

Clinical diagnosis is aided by provocative meniscal impingement tests (e.g., McMurray, Apley, and Steinmann) that attempt to produce pain or a mechanical event, such as a click or pop, by the application of an axial load and rotational stress to the knee. An excellent functional test is requesting the patient to "duck walk," which can only be done apprehensively or with pain in those with unstable tears, particularly tears involving the posterior horn. As part of the physical examination, specific joint line tenderness should be assessed. Active or passive motion may be restricted because of displaced meniscal fragments. No single test is pathognomonic for the presence of a meniscal tear. However, a composite historical and clinical picture generally yields a presumptive diagnosis.[134] A comprehensive ligament examination should also be performed to establish the presence or absence of associated instability. An unstable knee may be the underlying cause of a meniscal tear, and the presence of instability may alter treatment of the meniscal lesion.

Plain radiographs should be considered in all suspected cases of a meniscal tear because mechanical symptoms can also be produced by other joint abnormalities such as loose bodies, osteochondritis dissecans, osteoarthritis, occult fracture, and tumors. MRI has supplanted arthrography as a diagnostic tool in the detection of meniscal lesions. It is noninvasive and both highly sensitive and specific.[129] In acute knee injuries, particularly isolated injuries to the anterior cruciate ligament, clinical examination often fails to elucidate the presence of meniscal injury. MRI is helpful in this situation if the physician plans to treat the ligament injury nonoperatively. The presence of an associated meniscal tear may warrant arthroscopic evaluation and treatment apart from the planned management of the ligament injury.

No classification of meniscal tears is universally accepted. Causal mechanisms are categorized broadly as traumatic or degenerative. Tears are generally classified in descriptive terms denoting location and configuration. Location in terms of circumference can be in the posterior, middle, or anterior third of the meniscus (Fig. 55–16A).

With regard to the cross section of the meniscus, tears can be located in the inner, middle, or peripheral third or cross more than one zone (Fig. 55–16*B*). A cross-sectional location has implications for healing, which is possible in the more vascular peripheral third but is unlikely in the inner two thirds. Peripheral detachment can also occur at the meniscocapsular junction. By configuration, meniscal tears are categorized as vertical or horizontal in their cleavage planes (Fig. 55–17). Vertical tears may be longitudinal (i.e., bucket-handle), radial, or oblique (flap or parrot-beaked) (Fig. 55–18). Complex tears denote primary and secondary tears and multiple cleavage planes. The most common vertical longitudinal tear involves the posterior third of the medial meniscus (Fig. 55–19). An isolated radial tear is most common in the middle third of the lateral meniscus. In operative reports, one should describe meniscal tears accurately with regard to location and configuration.

Symptomatic meniscal injury warrants arthroscopic treatment, and meniscal preservation should be the goal. The vascular supply to the meniscus is derived from the perimeniscal capillary plexus and penetrates the peripheral 10% to 30% of the medial meniscus and the peripheral 10% to 25% of the lateral meniscus.[128] Tears located within this vascular meniscal zone have excellent healing potential. Asymptomatic, stable, vertical longitudinal tears in the vascularized portion of the meniscus may be treated by "skillful neglect" with good results.[134, 143] Contributing factors in the decision-making process regarding meniscal repair versus excision include associated ligament injury and the age, occupation, and sports and activity level of the patient. Meniscal repair in the presence of ligament

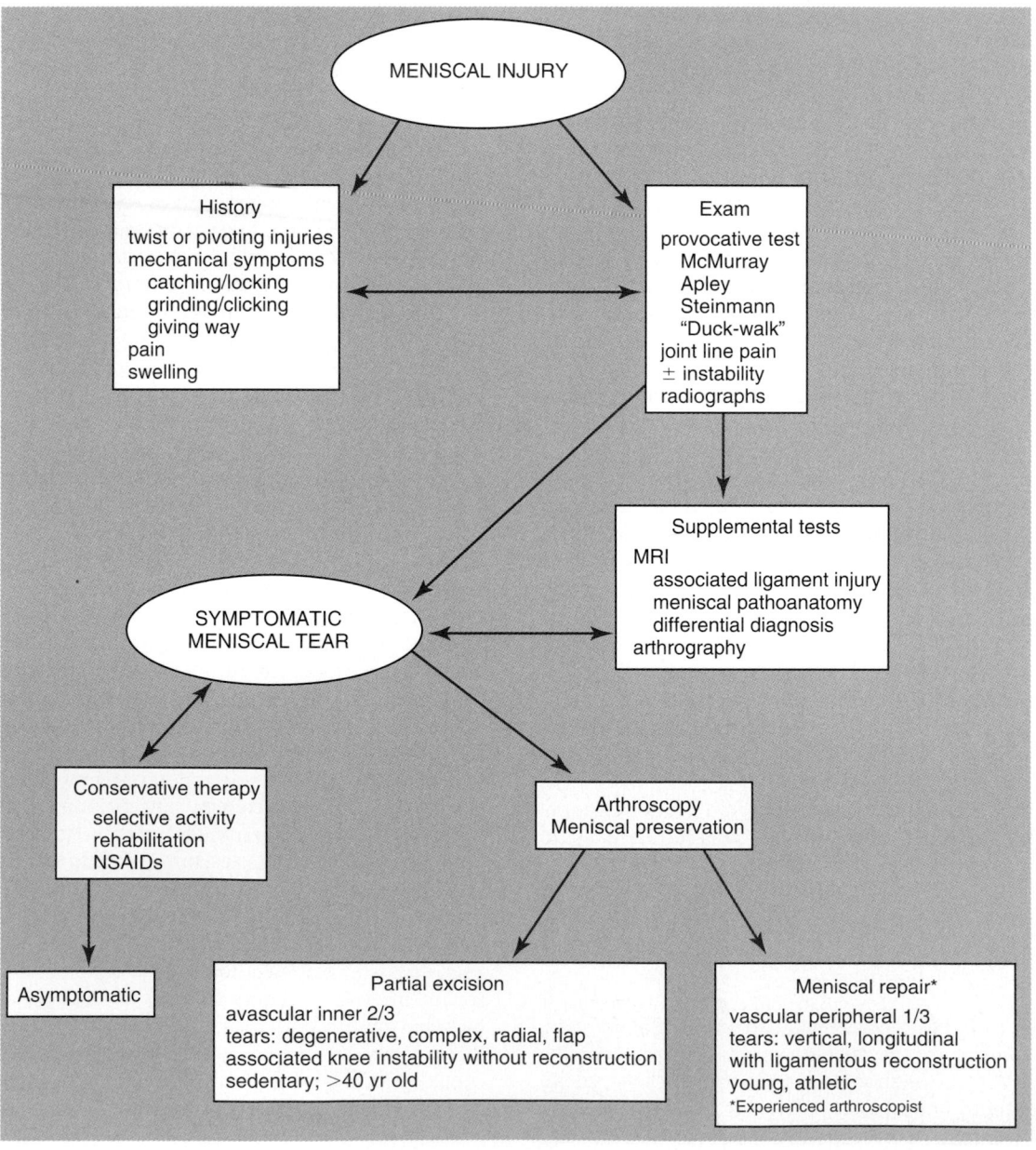

**FIGURE 55–15.** Treatment algorithm for meniscal injuries. *Abbreviations:* MRI, magnetic resonance imaging; NSAIDs, nonsteroidal anti-inflammatory drugs.

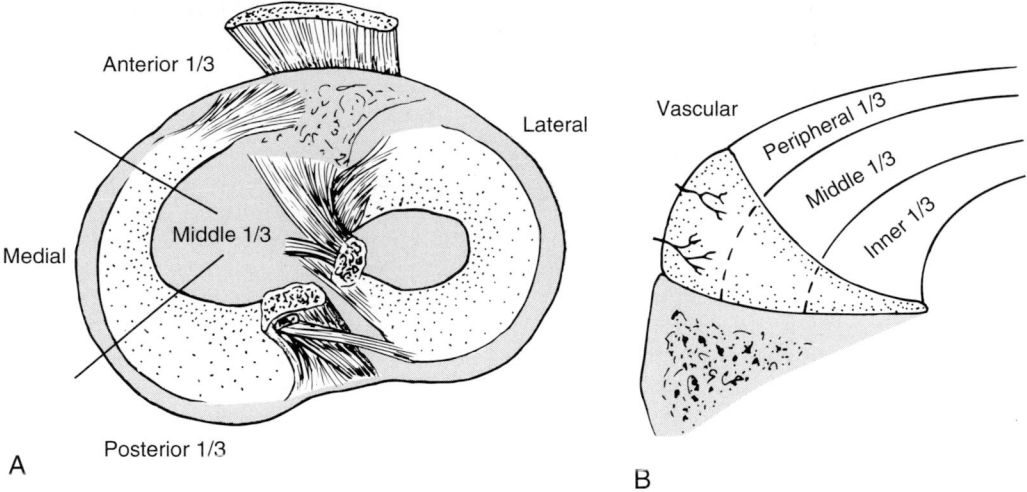

**FIGURE 55–16.** A, Meniscal tear location by position within the meniscus in an anterior-to-posterior direction B, Meniscal tear sites in relation to diameter of the radius.

instability in a patient older than 40 years yields unsatisfactory results. Arthroscopic or arthroscopically assisted meniscal repair is a technically demanding procedure. Complications such as peripheral nerve and vascular injury, infection, and arthrofibrosis are more common than in simple arthroscopic partial meniscectomy.[132, 140] In general, for tears located in the avascular inner two thirds of the meniscus and for flap tears, radial tears, and complex tears, partial arthroscopic excision with balancing of the meniscal rim is recommended. Reparable meniscal tears are ideally those located in the vascular outer third of the body or at the meniscocapsular junction, tears greater than 1 cm in length, and tears that are vertical in cleavage pattern[126, 131] (Fig. 55–20). The chronicity of the tear does not adversely affect healing potential. The benefits of partial meniscectomy versus meniscal repair are less morbidity and a quicker return to activity. Meniscal

preservation truly restores optimal knee function and should prevent degenerative changes.

General principles of meniscal repair include excision of loose or frayed fibrocartilage, preparation of the meniscal surfaces by débridement and abrasion to promote vascular proliferation, and meniscal repair with sutures or absorbable darts. Healing potential has also been shown to be enhanced by the addition of fibrin clot to the repaired surface. Specific techniques of meniscal repair include arthroscopic, arthroscopically assisted, and open procedures.[131, 138, 139] The arthroscopically assisted procedure is probably the most commonly used and safest because it does not require tying sutures on the outside of the capsule. The success of meniscal repair is increased by concomitant reconstruction of associated ligament instability, usually involving the anterior cruciate ligament.[141]

Rehabilitation after isolated meniscal repair generally includes controlled motion bracing with avoidance of full flexion and limited weight bearing for 4 to 8 weeks, followed by progression to full weight bearing and an exercise program. No cutting, squatting, or jumping activity is allowed for up to 6 months after repair. In meniscal repairs associated with ligament reconstruction, rehabilitation is dictated by the reconstructive procedure. Excellent results can be anticipated with partial meniscectomy of isolated vertical, longitudinal, or flap tears. Poorer results can be expected with associated chondromalacia, degenerative or complex tears, and ligament instability.[124, 133] In properly selected patients for meniscal repair and ligament reconstruction, results are comparable to those of partial excision. The goal of meniscal preservation has prompted research to improve vascular access to the meniscus and investigation into allograft replacement.[127]

## SURGICAL APPROACHES TO AN ACUTELY INJURED KNEE

The surgical approach used in an acutely injured knee should follow the principles of utility and extensibility of

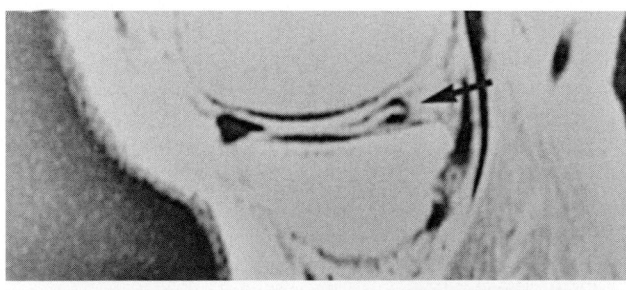
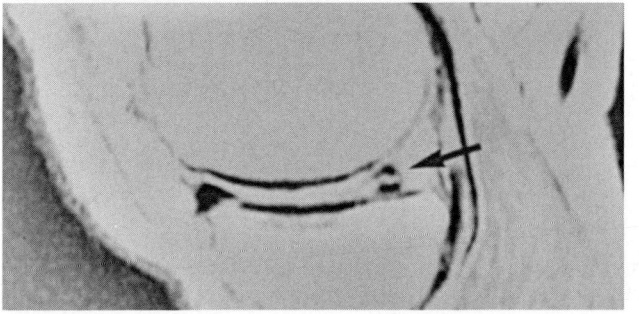

**FIGURE 55–17.** Magnetic resonance imaging scan showing a horizontal cleavage tear (*arrows*) of the posterior horn of the medial meniscus.

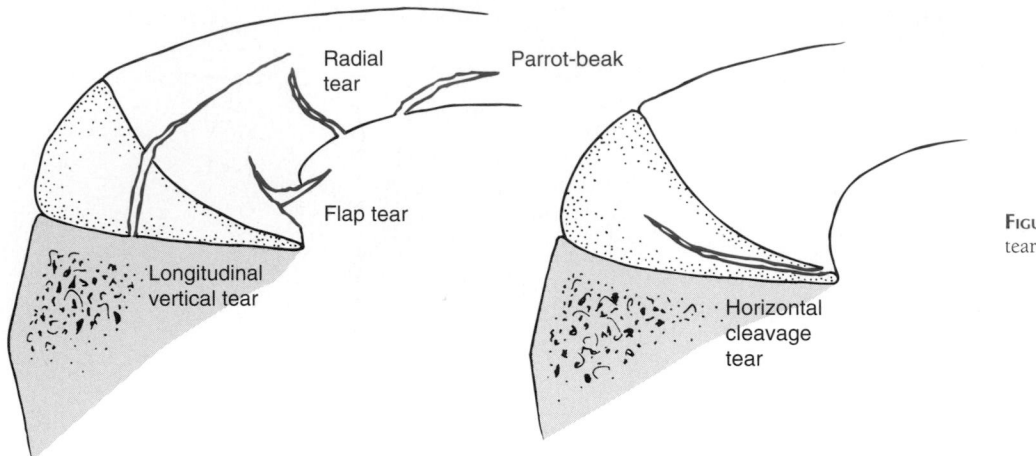

Radial tear

Parrot-beak

Flap tear

Longitudinal vertical tear

Horizontal cleavage tear

**FIGURE 55–18.** Types of meniscal tears.

incisions.[145–147] In addition, the incisions used for an acute injury should not compromise future reconstructive procedures such as knee replacement, which is most easily performed through an anterior or anteromedial vertical incision. The most difficult preexisting incisions to deal with during joint replacement are long anterolateral vertical scars and long oblique anteromedial scars. In general, incisions for acute injuries should be straight or gently curved, with transverse and oblique placement avoided. Secondary incisions to expose deep capsuloligamentous structures should be parallel to these structures (i.e., avoidance of transverse capsular or ligamentous incisions, which may result in operative injury in addition to primary ligament disruption). An exception is a gross third-degree rupture in a transverse or oblique fashion that allows direct visualization and repair. Four basic incisions allow treatment of most acute soft tissue knee injuries: anterior, medial, lateral, and posterior.[145, 147] The surgeon should be cautious about making extensive incisions through contused tissues during the first days after injury. Significant skin flap necrosis may result.

## Anterior Incision

An anterior midline incision (Fig. 55–21) is most often used for the treatment of extensor mechanism disruption in acute knee injury. It can be used to harvest a patellar tendon autograft for reconstruction of the anterior cruciate ligament. An anterior skin incision must be elevated and retracted a long distance to reach the posteromedial corner. For extensive repair of both cruciate ligaments and the medial collateral complex in a knee dislocation, a vertical anteromedial skin incision is better located (see Medial Incision). This incision is still acceptable for future reconstructive surgery such as a knee replacement.

## Medial Incision

A medial incision is used to approach the medial collateral ligament, associated capsular structures, and the cruciate

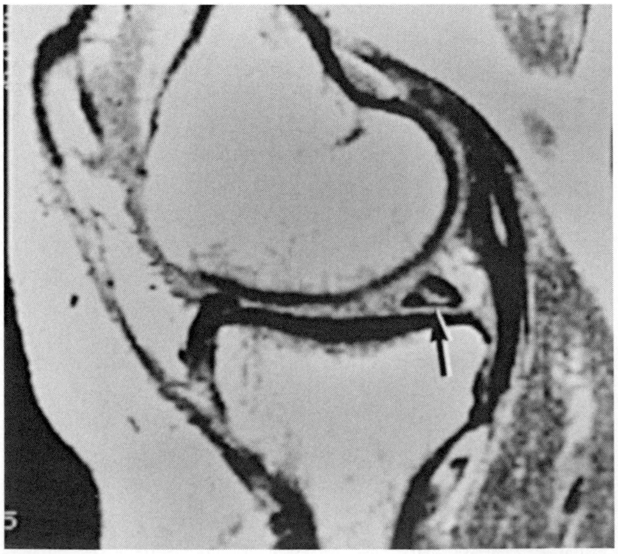

**FIGURE 55–19.** Magnetic resonance imaging scan showing a nondisplaced vertical tear (*arrow*) of the posterior horn of the medial meniscus.

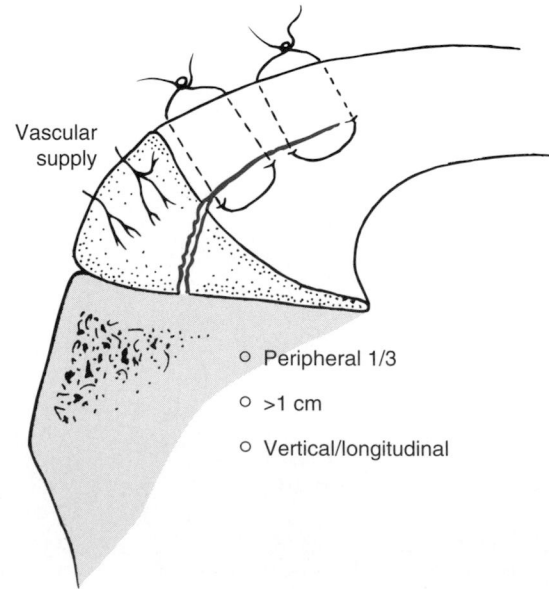

Vascular supply

o  Peripheral 1/3

o  >1 cm

o  Vertical/longitudinal

**FIGURE 55–20.** Meniscal repair illustrated for an ideal injury type and location.

**FIGURE 55–21.** Anterior approach to the knee. An anterior vertical skin incision is made. The joint can be entered through one of three arthrotomy incisions. *Abbreviations:* ACL, anterior cruciate ligament; LCL, lateral collateral ligament; PCL, posterior cruciate ligament. *A,* Lateral parapatellar incision for the lateral meniscus and articular surfaces. *B,* Transpatellar tendon approach through a patellar tendon defect after harvesting a graft for ligament reconstruction. The fat pad is divided and retracted to provide exposure of the anterior cruciate ligament. *C,* Medial parapatellar arthrotomy for the medial meniscus, articular surfaces, and cruciate ligaments.

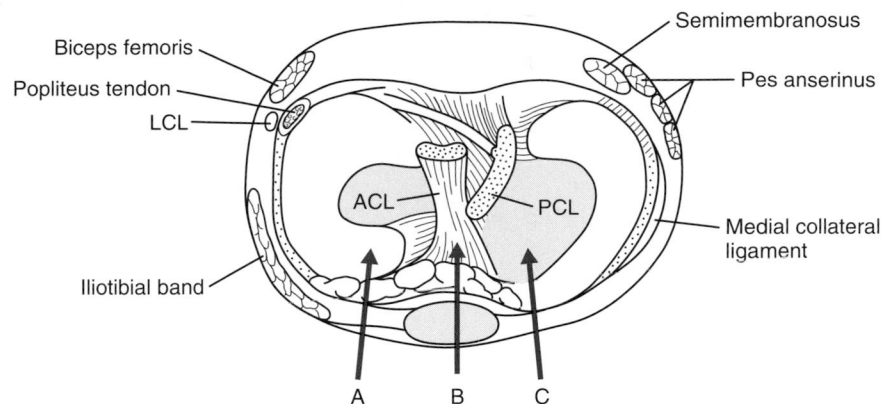

ligaments (Fig. 55–22). The incision is gently curved or straight; it starts just anterior to the adductor tubercle of the medial femoral condyle and extends distally in a parapatellar fashion to the medial border of the tibial tuberosity. With full-thickness anterior and posterior skin flaps, a medial parapatellar arthrotomy incision can be used to expose the posteromedial corner. Exposure of the medial collateral ligament can be facilitated by raising a proximally based retinacular flap. Posteromedial exposure for meniscal, capsular, or posterior cruciate repair is through a vertically oriented incision posterior to the medial collateral ligament, superior to the semimembranosus, and anterior to the medial head of the gastrocnemius.

## Lateral Incision

A lateral incision is used to approach the fibular collateral ligament and associated capsular structures, including the arcuate complex (Fig. 55–23). The lateral incision is centered over the midportion of the lateral femoral condyle and carried in a curved or straight fashion to Gerdy's tubercle by staying just anterior to the lateral collateral ligament. A lateral parapatellar arthrotomy and access to the posterolateral corner are possible with the development of full-thickness skin and subcutaneous flaps. The approach to the posterolateral corner is made through a vertical incision posterior and parallel to the fibular collateral ligament. If greater exposure is necessary, detachment of Gerdy's tubercle with bone and proximal retraction expose the lateral capsuloligamentous structures. The iliotibial band can likewise be split and retracted without distal detachment. Care must be taken to identify and preserve the common peroneal nerve just beneath the biceps femoris.

The lateral approach can be combined with the medial approach if access is required to the posterolateral corner in addition to the cruciate ligaments and medial structures. The two skin incisions should be on opposite sides of the knee with a wide skin bridge left anteriorly.

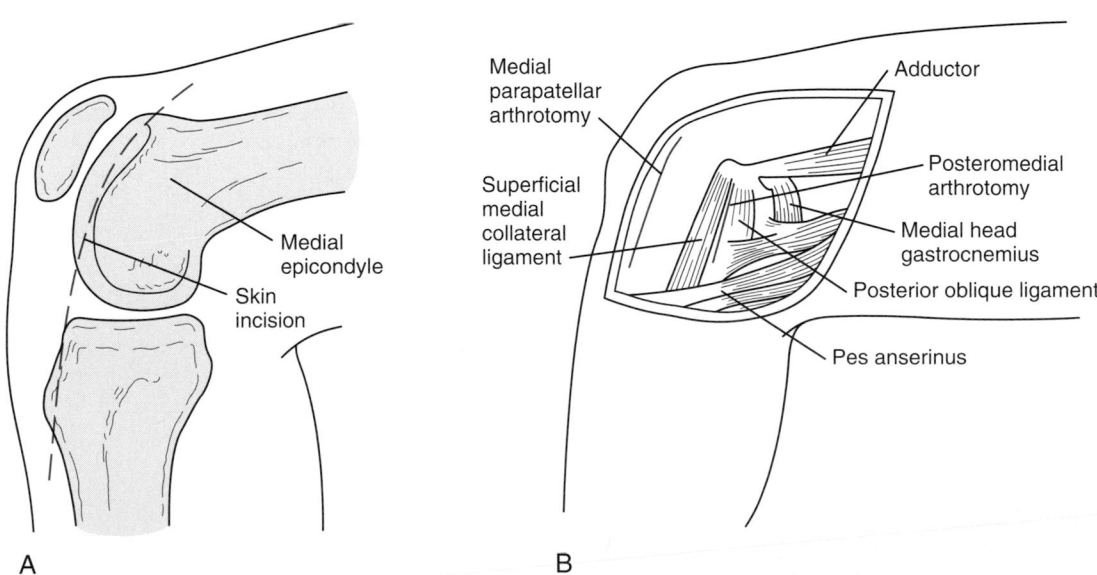

**FIGURE 55–22.** Medial approach to the knee. *A,* A skin incision placed vertically over the anteromedial surface of the knee permits skin flaps to be raised. *B,* A medial parapatellar arthrotomy may be performed for an approach to the cruciate ligaments, articular surfaces of the medial compartment, and medial meniscus. The superficial medial collateral ligament (MCL) and posterior oblique ligament can be exposed and repaired if disrupted. An incision through an intact capsule posterior to the superficial MCL permits exposure of the posterior portion of the medial compartment.

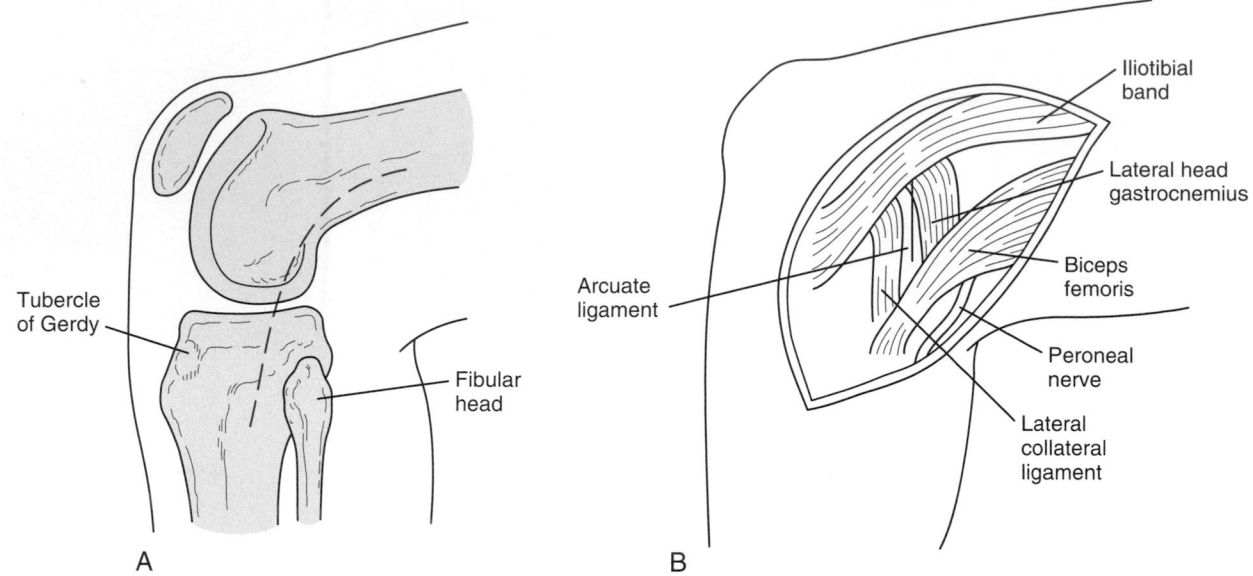

**FIGURE 55–23.** Lateral approach to the knee. Most commonly, this approach is used to reach the posterolateral structures, in combination with a second incision to reach the anteromedial side of the knee. *A,* Skin incision passing vertically between Gerdy's tubercle and the fibular head. *B,* The iliotibial band, lateral collateral ligament, arcuate ligament, and biceps femoris are easily exposed. The peroneal nerve is posterior to the biceps femoris and passes laterally over the fibular neck. If the capsule is intact and the posterior portion of the lateral compartment requires exposure, such as for open meniscal repair, the incision can be performed posterior to the lateral collateral ligament through the arcuate ligament.

## Posterior Incision

In acute knee injuries, a posterior incision is rarely used except in penetrating trauma to the posterior aspect of the knee and in isolated posterior cruciate ligament avulsion fractures in which a direct approach for bone-to-bone surgical stabilization is necessary. Best done with the patient prone, this incision involves identification of the sural nerve and short saphenous vein in the midline of the fascia of the proximal part of the calf. These structures are followed to the popliteal neurovascular structures, and the gastrocnemius muscle heads are separated, medial from lateral. The vessels can be retracted medially or laterally after the tethering geniculate branches are divided. Either gastrocnemius head can be detached proximally to gain access to the posteromedial or posterolateral corner of the knee.[145, 147]

## RECONSTRUCTION FOR POST-TRAUMATIC ARTHRITIS OF THE KNEE

Post-traumatic arthritis of the knee may occur as a result of meniscectomy, isolated or combined ligament insufficiency, and intra- and extra-articular fractures. The typical patient with post-traumatic arthritis of the knee has had a few previous surgical procedures, which often include major open surgeries for fracture fixation or ligament reconstruction. Pathologic processes that result in arthritic changes include increased loading of the joint surfaces (because of loss of meniscal load-bearing surfaces or malalignment of the limb), direct damage to the joint surface from the original trauma (because of intra-articular fracture or chondral injury), or chronic sheer forces resulting from ligament instability (because of cruciate ligament insufficiency with or without associated collateral insufficiency). A knee with post-traumatic arthritis may, depending on the original injury, have a number of anatomic abnormalities, including extra-articular malalignment, intra-articular osteochondral deficits, ligament instability, and stiffness. In addition, retained hardware, patella baja, and preexisting scars from previous surgical exposure may be encountered. In the worst-case scenario, the surgeon may be faced with multiple factors that make any reconstruction more difficult and risky than in cases of primary knee replacement for osteoarthritis. Every aspect of the knee must be considered during the preoperative planning process so that the best procedure is selected and each step of that procedure is planned carefully.

Reconstructive options include extra-articular osteotomy, intra-articular osteotomy, osteochondral allografting, unicompartmental replacement, and total-knee replacement (TKR).

Osteotomies may be chosen for patients with correctable malalignment in the setting of unicompartmental arthritis, good knee motion, and good ligament stability. Examples of conditions that may be amenable to osteotomy are mild to moderate medial compartment arthritis after varus malunion of an extra-articular distal femoral fracture and after an intra-articular medial tibial plateau fracture.

Osteochondral allografts, either fresh or frozen, are an option for reconstruction of significant osteochondral damage to a femoral condyle or tibial plateau before secondary degenerative changes occur on the opposing joint surface. The knee should have retained good motion and ligament stability.

Joint replacement can be performed as either a unicompartmental or total-knee arthroplasty.[148] Unicompartmental replacement can be performed for medial or lateral compartment post-traumatic arthritis, usually secondary to a tibial plateau fracture. The varus or valgus deformity should be relatively small and joint motion and ligament stability relatively good because correction of alignment, improvement in motion, and ligament balancing are all limited with unicompartmental replacement.

TKR may be the best option when none of the aforementioned procedures are ideal. TKR offers the greatest flexibility in management of ligament instability. Soft tissue balancing can be performed during the arthroplasty, and implants can be chosen that make up for deficits in ligament stability. Moreover, TKR offers options regarding management of bone loss. Metal augmentations can be used to fill in defects adjacent to the joint surfaces, and metal stems can be used to bridge defects and osteoporotic areas in the metaphysis. TKR for post-traumatic arthritis does, however, have its difficulties. Preexisting surgical scars must either be reused, completely avoided, or partially incorporated into the ap-

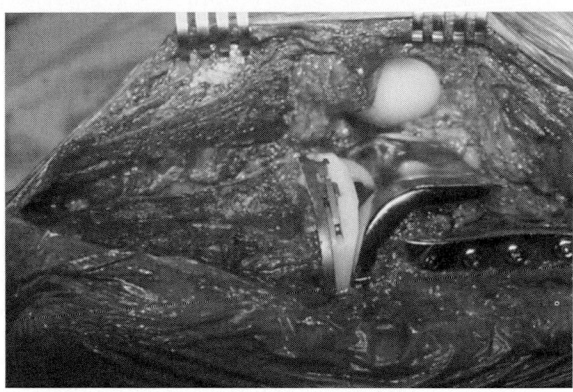

**FIGURE 55–25.** Tibial tubercle osteotomy from a lateral subvastus approach has been performed to gain extensile exposure for total-knee replacement after a previous distal femoral fracture.

proach for the replacement surgery (Fig. 55–24). If arthrofibrosis and poor motion are noted, an extensile exposure such as tibial tubercle osteotomy or quadriceps release may be required (Fig. 55–25).

Old hardware may need to be partially or completely removed. In some situations, it may be best to remove the hardware in a staged operation. Ligament balancing may be difficult to achieve. If the medial or lateral collateral ligament is completely incompetent, soft tissue reconstruction or a highly constrained implant may be required. If the flexion and extension gaps are grossly unequal, it is usually because a significant flexion contracture has developed with good flexion retained. To restore full extension and maintain stability in flexion, several technical steps can be used. More extensive distal femoral resection and posterior capsular release may improve extension. To improve stability in flexion, a femoral implant with a larger anterior-posterior dimension than the original femur can be used to fill the flexion gap. In extreme cases, a constrained implant with a tall tibial post in the femoral recess may be necessary (Fig. 55–26).

Periarticular malunion, either in the distal end of the femur or the proximal part of the tibia, can present an additional challenge when performing TKR. If the malunion is relatively minor, correction of overall limb alignment can be achieved by somewhat asymmetric cuts for the knee replacement. If the malunion is more severe, 10° or more, corrective osteotomy can be performed to restore normal limb alignment and permit the use of standard cuts and implants for the TKR.[149] The osteotomy can be performed as a separate staged procedure or at the time of the TKR (Fig. 55–27).

Because of the complex nature of TKR for post-traumatic arthritis, the complication rate and the number of poor and fair results are greater than with primary TKR for osteoarthritis. The outcomes of TKR for post-traumatic arthritis are similar to those for series of revision TKR. The surgeon and the patient should appreciate and accept this fact before undertaking TKR for this diagnosis.

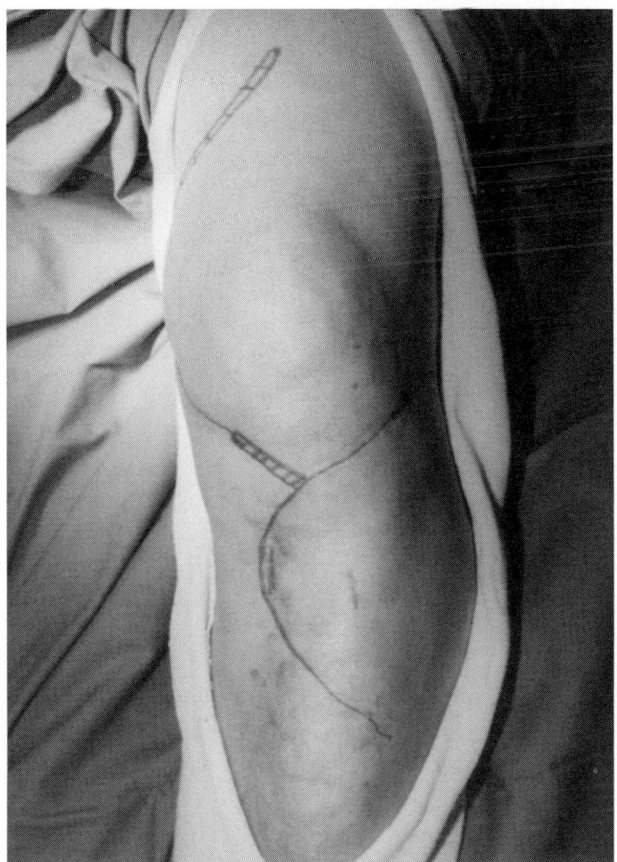

**FIGURE 55–24.** Preexisting surgical scars that are not ideal for total-knee replacement. In this case, the old scars were incorporated into an anteromedial irregular incision with new segments indicated by cross-hatched double lines.

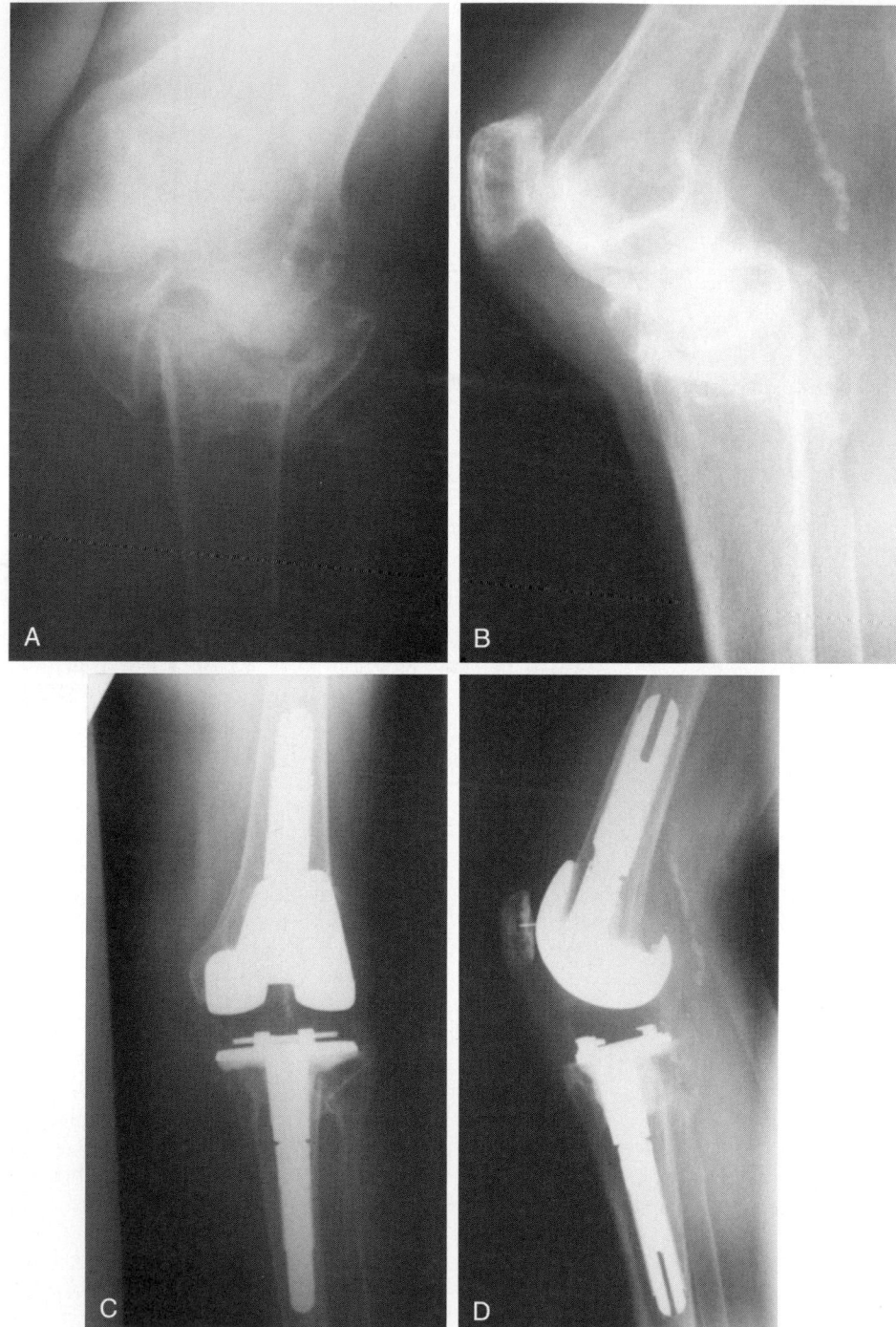

**FIGURE 55–26.** A constrained condylar implant has been used for post-traumatic arthritis after a proximal tibial fracture. Preoperatively, the patient had a 45° flexion contracture. At the time of surgery, a tight extension gap and wide flexion gap were noted. *A,* Preoperative anteroposterior (AP) radiograph. *B,* Preoperative lateral radiograph. *C,* Postoperative AP radiograph. *D,* Postoperative lateral radiograph.

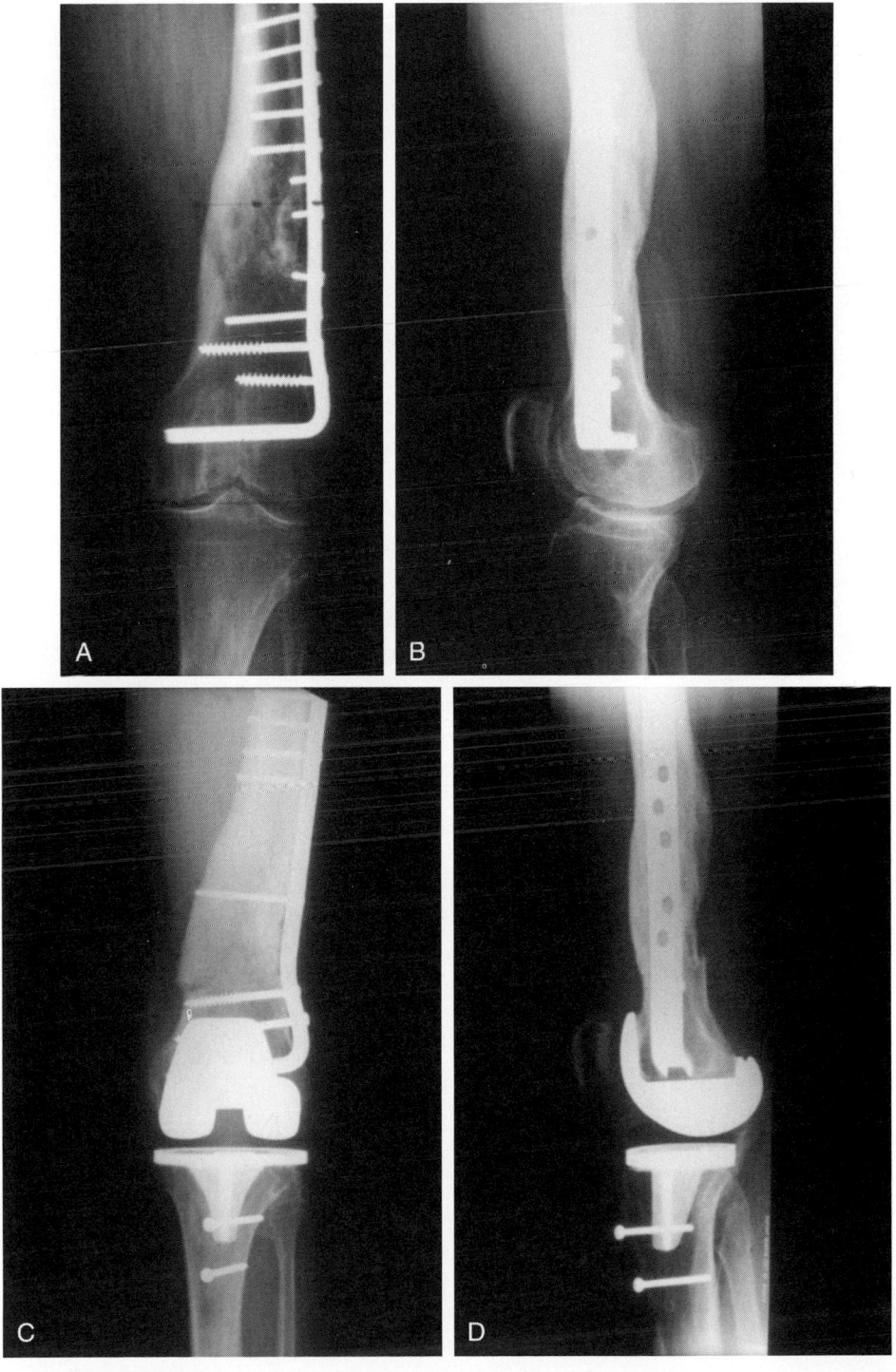

**FIGURE 55–27.** Combined simultaneous femoral osteotomy and total-knee arthroplasty. *A,* Preoperative anteroposterior (AP) radiograph. *B,* Preoperative lateral radiograph. Note varus deformity. *C,* Postoperative AP radiograph. *D,* Postoperative lateral radiograph.

## REFERENCES

### Diagnostic Approach to the Injured Knee

1. Alioto, R.J.; Browne, J.E.; Barnthouse, C.D.; Scott, A.R. The influence of MRI on treatment decisions regarding knee injuries. Am J Knee Surg 12:91–97, 1999.
2. Butler, J.C.; Andrews, J.R. The role of arthroscopic surgery in evaluation of acute traumatic hemarthrosis of the knee. Clin Orthop 228:150–152, 1988.
3. Chen, F.S.; Rokito, A.S.; Pitman, M.I. Acute and chronic posterolateral rotatory instability of the knee. J Am Acad Orthop Surg 8:97–110, 2000.
4. Daniel, D.M.; Stone M.L. Instrumented measurement of knee motion. In: Daniel, D.M.; Akeson, W.H.; O'Connor, J.J., eds. Knee Ligaments: Structure, Function, Injury, and Repair. New York, Raven, 1990, pp. 421–426.
5. DeHaven, K.E. Diagnosis of acute knee injuries with hemarthrosis. Am J Sports Med 8:9–14, 1980.
6. Donaldson, W.F.; Warren, R.F.; Wickiewicz T. A comparison of acute anterior cruciate ligament examinations. Initial versus examination under anesthesia. Am J Sports Med 13:5–10, 1985.
7. Farooki, S.; Seeger, L.L. Magnetic resonance imaging in the evaluation of ligament injuries. Skeletal Radiol 28:61–74, 1999.
8. Fischer, S.P.; Fox, J.M.; Del Pizzo, W.; et al. Accuracy of diagnosis from magnetic resonance imaging of the knee. J Bone Joint Surg Am 73:2–10, 1991.
9. Hughston, J.C.; Andrews, J.R.; Cross, M.J.; Moschi, A. Classification of knee ligament instabilities. Part I. The medial compartment and cruciate ligaments. J Bone Joint Surg Am 58:159–172, 1976.
10. Hughston, J.C.; Andrews, J.R.; Cross, M.J.; Moschi, A. Classification of knee ligament instabilities. Part II. The lateral compartment. J Bone Joint Surg Am 58:173–179, 1976.
11. Jackson, D.W.; Jennings, L.D.; Maywood, R.M.; Berger, P.E. Magnetic resonance imaging of the knee. Am J Sports Med 16:29–38, 1988.
12. Katz, J.W.; Fingeroth, R.J. The diagnostic accuracy of ruptures of the anterior cruciate ligament comparing the Lachman test, the anterior drawer sign, and the pivot shift test in acute and chronic knee injuries. Am J Sports Med 14:88–91, 1986.
13. Lee, J.K.; Yao, L.; Phelps, C.T.; et al. Anterior cruciate ligament tears: MR imaging compared with arthroscopy and clinical tests. Radiology 166:861–864, 1988.
14. Losee, R.E.; Johnson, T.R.; Southwick, W.O. Anterior subluxation of the lateral tibial plateau. A diagnostic test and operative repair. J Bone Joint Surg Am 50:211–242, 1968.
15. Nagel, D.A.; Burton, D.S.; Manning, J. The dashboard knee injury. Clin Orthop 126:203–208, 1977.
16. Noyes, F.R.; Bassett, R.W.; Grood, E.S.; Butler, D.L. Arthroscopy in acute traumatic hemarthrosis of the knee. Incidence of anterior cruciate tears and other injuries. J Bone Joint Surg Am 62:687–695, 1980.
17. Noyes, F.R.; Grood, E.S. Diagnosis of knee ligament injuries: Clinical concepts. In: Feagin, J.A., ed. The Crucial Ligaments. New York, Churchill Livingstone, 1988, pp. 261–285.
18. Polly, D.W.; Callaghan, J.J.; Sikes, R.A.; et al. The accuracy of selective magnetic resonance imaging compared with the findings of arthroscopy of the knee. J Bone Joint Surg Am 70:192–198, 1988.
19. Rangger, C.; Klestil, T.; Kathrein, A.; et al. Influence of magnetic resonance imaging on indications for arthroscopy of the knee. Clin Orthop 330:133–142, 1996.
20. Slocum, D.B.; Larson, R.L., Rotatory instability of the knee. Its pathogenesis and a clinical test to demonstrate its presence. J Bone Joint Surg Am 50:211–242, 1968.
21. Strobel, M.; Stedtfeld, H.W. Evaluation of the ligaments. In: Diagnostic Evaluations of the Knee. New York, Springer-Verlag, 1990, p. 118.

### Knee Injury in Polytrauma Patients

22. Gillespie, W.J. The incidence and pattern of knee injury associated with dislocation of the hip. J Bone Joint Surg Br 57:376–387, 1975.
23. McAndrew, M.P.; Lantz, B.A. Initial care of massively traumatized lower extremities. Clin Orthop 243:20–29, 1989.
24. Moore, J.M.; Patzakis, M.J.; Harvey, J.P. Ipsilateral diaphyseal femur fractures and knee ligament injuries. Clin Orthop 232:182–189, 1988.
25. Templeman, D.C.; Marder, R.A. Injuries of the knee associated with fractures of the tibial shaft. Detection by examination under anesthesia: A prospective study. J Bone Joint Surg Am 71:1392–1395, 1989.
26. Veith, R.G.; Winquist, R.A.; Hansen, S.T. Ipsilateral fractures of the femur and tibia. A report of fifty-seven consecutive cases. J Bone Joint Surg Am 66:991–1002, 1984.
27. Walker, D.M.; Kennedy, J.C. Occult knee ligament injuries associated with femoral shaft fractures. Am J Sports Med 8:172–174, 1980.
28. Walling, A.K.; Seradge, H.; Spiegel, P.G. Injuries to the knee ligaments with fractures of the femur. J Bone Joint Surg Am 64:1324–1327, 1982.

### Open Knee Injuries

29. Collins, D.N.; Temple, S.D. Open joint injuries. Classification and treatment. Clin Orthop 243:48–56, 1988.
30. Patzakis, M.J.; Dorr, L.D.; Ivler, D.; et al. The early management of open joint injuries. A prospective study of one hundred and forty patients. J Bone Joint Surg Am 57:1065–1071, 1975.

### Traumatic Dislocation of the Knee

31. Applebaum, R.R.; Yellin, A.E.; Weaver, F.A.; et al. Role of routine arteriography in blunt lower extremity trauma. Am J Surg 160:221–225, 1990.
32. Bunt, T.J.; Malone, J.M.; Moody, M.; et al. Frequency of vascular injury with blunt trauma–induced extremity injury. Am J Surg 160:226–228, 1990.
33. Dennis, J.W.; Jagger, C.; Butcher, J.L.; et al. Reassessing the role of arteriograms in the management of posterior knee dislocations. J Trauma 35:692–695, 1993.
34. Frassica, F.J.; Sim, F.H.; Staeheli, J.W.; Pairolero, P.C. Dislocation of the knee. Clin Orthop 263:200–205, 1992.
35. Frykberg, E.R.; Crump, J.M.; Vines, F.S.; et al. A reassessment of the role of arteriography in penetrating proximity extremity trauma: A prospective study. J Trauma 29:1041–1051, 1989.
36. Gable, D.R.; Allen, J.W.; Richardson, J.D. Blunt popliteal artery injury: Is physical examination alone enough for examination? J Trauma 43:541–544, 1997.
37. Green, N.E.; Allen, B.L. Vascular injuries associated with dislocation of the knee. J Bone Joint Surg Am 59:236–239, 1977.
38. Ibrahim, S.A. Primary repair of the cruciate and collateral ligaments after traumatic dislocation of the knee. J Bone Joint Surg Br 81:987–990, 1999.
39. Kendall, R.W.; Taylor, D.C.; Salvian, A.J.; O'Brien, P.J. The role of arteriography in assessing vascular injuries associated with dislocations of the knee. J Trauma 35:875–878, 1993.
40. Lonner, J.H.; Dupuy, D.E.; Siliski, J.M. Comparison of magnetic resonance imaging with operative findings in acute traumatic dislocations of the adult knee. J Orthop Trauma 14:183–186, 2000.
41. Martinez, D.; Sweatman, K.; Thompson, E.C. Popliteal artery injury associated with knee dislocation. Am Surg 67:165–167, 2001.
42. McCoy, G.F.; Hannon, D.G.; Barr, R.J.; Templeton, J. Vascular injury associated with low-velocity dislocations of the knee. J Bone Joint Surg Br 69:285–287, 1987.
43. McCutchan, J.D.; Gillham, N.R. Injury to the popliteal artery associated with dislocation of the knee: Palpable distal pulses do not negate the requirement for arteriography. Injury 20:307–310, 1989.
44. Meyers, M.H.; Harvey, J.P. Traumatic dislocation of the knee joint. J Bone Joint Surg Am 53:16–29, 1971.
45. Meyers, M.H.; Moore, T.M.; Harvey, J.P. Traumatic dislocation of the knee joint. Followup notes on articles previously published in the journal. J Bone Joint Surg Am 57:430–433, 1975.
46. Noyes, F.R.; Barber-Westin, S.D. Reconstruction of the anterior and posterior cruciate ligaments after knee dislocation. Use of early protected postoperative motion to decrease arthrofibrosis. Am J Sports Med 25:769–778, 1997.

47. O'Donnell, T.F.; Brewster, D.D.; Darling, B.C.; et al. Arterial injuries associated with fractures and/or dislocations of the knee. J Trauma 17:775–784, 1977.

48. Plancher, K.; Siliski, J.M. Dislocation of the knee. In: Siliski, J.M., ed. Traumatic Disorders of the Knee. New York, Springer-Verlag, 1994, pp. 315–332.

49. Quinlan, A.G.; Sharrard, W.J.W. Posterolateral dislocation of the knee with capsular interposition. J Bone Joint Surg Br 40:660–663, 1958.

50. Reckling, F.W.; Peltier, L.F. Acute knee dislocations and their complications. J Trauma 9:181–191, 1969.

51. Roman, P.D.; Hopson, C.N.; Zenni, E.J. Traumatic dislocation of the knee: A report of 30 cases and literature review. Orthop Rev 16:33–40, 1987.

52. Shapiro, M.S.; Freedman, E.L. Allograft reconstruction of the anterior and posterior cruciate ligaments after traumatic knee dislocation. Am J Sports Med 23:580–587, 1995.

53. Shelbourne, K.D.; Porter, D.A.; Clingman, J.A.; et al. Low velocity knee dislocations. Orthop Rev 20:995–1004, 1991.

54. Sisto, J.D.; Warren, R.F. Complete knee dislocation. A followup study of operative treatment. Clin Orthop 198:94–101, 1985.

55. Taylor, A.R.; Arden, G.P.; Rainey, H.A. Traumatic dislocation of the knee. A report of forty-three cases with special reference to conservative treatment. J Bone Joint Surg Br 54:96–102, 1972.

56. Varnell, R.M.; Coldwell, D.M.; Sangeorzan, R.J.; Johansen, K.H. Arterial injury complicating knee disruption. Am Surg 55:699–704, 1989.

57. Wascher, D.C.; Dvirnak, P.C.; DeCoster, T.A. Knee dislocation: Initial assessment and implications for treatment. J Orthop Trauma 11:525–529, 1997.

58. Wolma, F.J.; Larrieu, A.J.; Alsop, G.C. Arterial injuries of the legs associated with fractures and dislocations. Am J Surg 140:806–809, 1980.

## Anterior Cruciate Ligament Injury

59. Aglietti, P.; Buzzi, R.; Menchetti, P.M.; Giron, F. Arthroscopically assisted semitendinosus and gracilis tendon graft in reconstruction for acute anterior cruciate ligament injuries in athletes. Am J Sports Med 24:726–731, 1996.

60. Arnold, J.A.; Coker, T.P.; Heaton, L.M.; et al. Natural history of anterior cruciate tears. Am J Sports Med 7:305–313, 1979.

61. Barrack, R.L.; Bruckner, J.D.; Inman, W.S.; Alexander, A.H. The outcomes of nonoperatively treated complete tears of the anterior cruciate ligament in active young adults. Clin Orthop 259:192–198, 1990.

62. Brown, C. Anterior cruciate ligament injuries. In: Siliski, J.M., ed. Traumatic Disorders of the Knee. New York, Springer-Verlag, 1994.

63. Cabaud, H.E.; Feagin, J.A. Experimental studies of acute anterior cruciate ligament injury and repair. Am J Sports Med 7:18–22, 1979.

64. Chick, R.R.; Jackson, D.W. Tears of the anterior cruciate ligament in young athletes. J Bone Joint Surg Am 60:970–973, 1978.

65. Fetto, J.F.; Marshall, J.L. The natural history and diagnosis of anterior cruciate insufficiency. Clin Orthop 147:29–37, 1980.

66. Fowler, P.J.; Reagan, W.D. The patient with symptomatic chronic anterior cruciate ligament insufficiency. Results of minimal arthroscopic surgery and rehabilitation. Am J Sports Med 15:321–325, 1987.

67. Giove, T.P.; Miller, S.J; Kent, B.E.; et al. Nonoperative treatment of the torn anterior cruciate ligament. J Bone Joint Surg Am 65:184–192, 1983.

68. Girgis, F.G.; Marshall, J.L.; Monajem, A.R.S. The cruciate ligaments of the knee joint. Anatomical functional and experimental analysis. Clin Orthop 106:216–231, 1975.

69. Hawkins, R.J.; Misamore, G.W.; Merritt, T.R. Followup of the acute nonoperated isolated anterior cruciate ligament tear. Am J Sports Med 14:205–210, 1986.

70. Higgins, R.W.; Steadman, J.R. Anterior cruciate ligament repairs in world class skiers. Am J Sports Med 15:439–447, 1987.

71. Holden, D.L.; Jackson, D.W. Treatment selection in acute anterior cruciate ligament tears. Orthop Clin North Am 16:99–108, 1985.

72. Johnson, R.J. The anterior cruciate: A dilemma in sports medicine. Int J Sports Med 3:71–79, 1982.

73. Johnson, R.J.; Beynnon, B.D.; Nichols, C.E; Restrom, P.A. The treatment of injuries of the anterior cruciate ligament. J Bone Joint Surg Am 74:140–151, 1992.

74. Kannus, P.; Jarvinen, M. Long-term prognosis of nonoperatively treated acute knee distortions having primary hemarthrosis without clinical instability. Am J Sports Med 15:138–143, 1987.

75. Kennedy, J.C.; Weinberg, H.W.; Wilson, A.S. The anatomy and function of the anterior cruciate ligament. J Bone Joint Surg Am 56:223–235, 1974.

76. Lipscomb, A.B.; Johnston, R.K.; Snyder, R.B.; Brothers, R.C. Secondary reconstruction of anterior cruciate ligament in athletes using the semitendinosus tendon. Am J Sports Med 7:81–84, 1979.

77. Marshall, J.L.; Warren, R.F.; Wickiewicz, T.L. Primary surgical treatment of anterior cruciate lesions. Am J Sports Med 10:103–107, 1982.

78. Marshall, J.L.; Warren, R.F.; Wickiewicz, T.L.; Reider, B. The anterior cruciate ligament: A technique of repair and reconstruction. Clin Orthop 143:97–106, 1979.

79. McCarroll, J.R.; Rettig, R.C.; Shelbourne, K.D. Anterior cruciate ligament injuries in the young athlete with open physes. Am J Sports Med 16:44–47, 1988.

80. McDaniel, W.J.; Dameron, T.B. Untreated ruptures of the anterior cruciate ligament. J Bone Joint Surg Am 62:696–704, 1980.

81. Noyes, F.R.; Barber, S.D.; Mooar, L.A. A rationale for assessing sports activity levels and limitations in knee disorders. Clin Orthop 246:238–249, 1989.

82. Noyes, F.R.; Mooar, P.A.; Mathews, D.S.; Butler, D.L. The symptomatic anterior cruciate–deficient knee. Part I: The long-term functional disability in athletically active individuals. J Bone Joint Surg Am 65:154–162, 1983.

83. Noyes, F.R.; Matthews, D.S.; Mooar, P.A.; Grood, E.S. The symptomatic anterior cruciate–deficient knee. Part II: The results of rehabilitation, activity modification, and counseling on functional disability. J Bone Joint Surg Am 65:163–174, 1983.

84. O'Brien, S.J.; Warren, R.F.; Wickiewicz, T.L.; et al. Reconstruction of the chronically insufficient anterior cruciate ligament using the central third of the patellar ligament. J Bone Joint Surg Am 73:278–285, 1991.

85. Odensten, M.; Hamberg, P.; Nordin, M.; et al. Surgical or conservative treatment of the acutely torn anterior cruciate ligament. A randomized study with short-term follow-up observations. Clin Orthop 198:87–93, 1985.

86. O'Neill, D.B. Arthroscopically assisted reconstruction of the anterior cruciate ligament. A prospective randomized analysis of three techniques. J Bone Joint Surg Am 78:803–813, 1996.

## Posterior Cruciate Ligament Injury

87. Clancy, W.G.; Shelbourne, K.D.; Zoellan, G.B.; et al. Treatment of knee joint instability secondary to rupture of the posterior cruciate ligament. J Bone Joint Surg Am 65:310–322, 1983.

88. Cooper, D.E.; Warren, R.F.; Warren J.J. The posterior cruciate ligament and posterolateral structures of the knee: Anatomy, function, and patterns of injury. Instr Course Lect 40:249–270, 1991.

89. Cross, M.J.; Powell J.F. Long-term followup of posterior cruciate ligament rupture: A study of 116 cases. Am J Sports Med 12:292–300, 1984.

90. Dandy, D.J.; Pusey, R.J. The long-term results of unrepaired tears of the posterior cruciate ligament. J Bone Joint Surg Br 64:92–98, 1982.

91. Foster, T.E.; Zarins, B. Posterior cruciate ligament injuries. In: Siliski, J.M., ed. Traumatic Disorders of the Knee. New York, Springer-Verlag, 1994, pp. 285–300.

92. Gollehon, D.L.; Torzilli, P.A.; Warren, R.F. The role of the posterolateral and cruciate ligaments in the stability of the human knee. J Bone Joint Surg Am 69:233–242, 1987.

93. Hughston, J.C.; Bowden, J.A.; Andrews, J.R., Norwood, A.A. Acute tears of the posterior cruciate ligament. J Bone Joint Surg Am 62:438–450, 1980.

94. Jakob, R.P.; Hassler, H.; Staeubli, H.U. Observations on rotatory instability of the lateral compartment of the knee. Experimental

studies on the functional anatomy and the pathomechanism of the true and the reversed pivot shift sign. Acta Orthop Scand Suppl 191:1–32, 1981.

95. Janousek, A.T.; Jones, D.G.; Clatworthy, M.; et al. Posterior cruciate ligament injuries of the knee joint. Sports Med 28:429–441, 1999.

96. Loos, W.C.; Fox, J.M.; Blazina, M.E.; et al. Acute posterior cruciate ligament injuries. Am J Sports Med 9:86–92, 1981.

97. Parolie, J.M.; Bergfeld, J.A. Long-term results of nonoperative treatment of isolated posterior cruciate ligament injuries in the athlete. Am J Sports Med 14:35–38, 1986.

### Medial Collateral Ligament Injury

98. Arnozcky, S.P. Physiologic principles of ligament injuries and healing. In: Scott, W.N., ed. Ligament and Extensor Mechanism Injuries of the Knee: Diagnosis and Treatment. St. Louis, Mosby–Year Book, 1991, pp. 67–81.

99. Fetto, J.F.; Marshall, J.L. Medial collateral ligament injuries of the knee: A rationale for treatment. Clin Orthop 132:206–218, 1978.

100. Frank, C.B.; Schachar, N.; Dittrick, D. Natural history of healing in the repaired medial collateral ligament. J Orthop Res 1:179–188, 1983.

101. Gomez, M.A.; Woo, S.L.Y.; Amiel, D.; et al. Medial collateral ligament healing subsequent to different treatment regimens. J Appl Physiol 66:245–252, 1989.

102. Holden, D.L.; Ebbert, A.W.; Butler, J.E. Nonoperative treatment of grade I and grade II medial collateral ligament injuries to the knee. Am J Sports Med 11:340–344, 1983.

103. Hughston, J.C.; Andrews, J.R., Cross, M.J.; Moschi, A. Classification of knee ligament injuries. I. The medial compartment and cruciate ligaments. J Bone Joint Surg Am 58:159–172, 1976.

104. Indelicato, P.A. Nonoperative treatment of complete tears of the medial collateral ligament of the knee. J Bone Joint Surg Am 65:323–329, 1983.

105. Jacobson, K.E. Technical pitfalls of collateral ligament surgery. Clin Sports Med 18:847–882, 1999.

106. Kannus, P. Long-term results of conservatively treated medial collateral ligament injuries of the knee joint. Clin Orthop 226:103–112, 1988.

107. McMahon, M.S.; Boland, A.L. Collateral ligament injuries. In: Siliski, J.M., ed. Traumatic Disorders of the Knee. New York, Springer-Verlag, 1994, pp. 301–314.

108. Sitler, M.; Ryan, J.; Hopkinson, W.; et al. The efficacy of a prophylactic knee brace to reduce knee injuries in football. A prospective, randomized study at West Point. Am J Sports Med 18:310–315, 1990.

109. Warren, L.F.; Marshall, J.L. The supporting structures and layers of the medial side of the knee. An anatomical analysis. J Bone Joint Surg Am 61:56–62, 1979.

### Lateral Collateral Ligament Injury

110. DeLee, J.C.; Riley, M.B.; Rockwood, C.A. Acute posterolateral rotatory instability of the knee. Am J Sports Med 11:199–207, 1983.

111. DeLee, J.C.; Riley, M.B.; Rockwood, C.A. Acute straight lateral instability of the knee. Am J Sports Med 11:404–411, 1983.

112. Grana, W.A.; Janssen, T. Lateral ligament injury of the knee. Orthopedics 10:1039–1044, 1987.

113. Hughston, J.C.; Andrews, J.R.; Cross, M.D.; Moschi, A. Classification of knee ligament instabilities. Part II. The lateral compartment. J Bone Joint Surg Am 58:173–179, 1976.

114. Hughston, J.C.; Norwood, L.R. The posterolateral drawer test and external rotational recurvatum test for posterolateral rotatory instability of the knee. Clin Orthop 147:82–87, 1980.

115. Hughston, J.C.; Jacobson, K.E. Chronic posterolateral rotatory instability of the knee. J Bone Joint Surg Am 67:351–359, 1985.

116. Johnson, L.L. Lateral capsular ligament complex. Anatomical and surgical considerations. Am J Sports Med 7:156–160, 1979.

117. Seebacher, J.R.; Inglis, A.E.; Marshall, J.L; Warren, R.F. The structure of the posterolateral aspect of the knee. J Bone Joint Surg Am 64:536–541, 1982.

118. Woods, W.G.; Stanley, R.F; Tullos, H.S. Lateral capsular sign: X-ray clue to a significant knee instability. Am J Sports Med 7:27–33, 1979.

### Principles of Ligament Surgery

119. Daniel, D.M. Principles of knee ligament surgery, In: Daniel, D.M.; Akeson, W.H.; O'Connor, J.M., eds. Knee Ligaments: Structure, Function, Injury, and Repair. New York, Raven, 1990, pp. 11–29.

120. Krackow, J.A.; Thomas, S.C.; Jones, C.C. A new stitch for ligament tendon fixation. J Bone Joint Surg Am 68:764–765, 1986.

121. Miller, W. The Knee. Form, Function, and Ligament Reconstruction. New York, Springer-Verlag, 1983.

122. Noyes, F.R. Functional properties of knee ligaments and alterations induced by immobilization. A correlative biomechanical and histologic study in primates. Clin Orthop 123:210–242, 1977.

123. O'Donoghue, D.H. An analysis of end results of surgical treatment of major injuries to the ligaments of the knee. J Bone Joint Surg Am 37:1–12, 1955.

124. Robertson, D.B.; Daniel, D.M.; Biden, E. Soft tissue fixation to bone. Am J Sports Med 14:398–403, 1986.

125. Woo, S.L.Y.; Inoue, M.; McGurk-Burleson, E. Treatment of the medial collateral ligament injury: Structure and function of canine knees in response to differing treatment regimens. Am J Sports Med 15:22–29, 1987.

### Meniscal Injury

126. Arnoczky, S.P.; Dodds, J., Cooper, D.E. Meniscal repair and replacement. In: Siliski, J.M., ed. Traumatic Disorders of the Knee. New York, Springer-Verlag, 1994, pp. 333–346.

127. Arnoczky, S.P.; Milachowski, K.A. Meniscal allografts: Where do we stand? In: Ewing, J.W., ed. Articular Cartilage and Knee Joint Function: Basic Science and Arthroscopy. New York, Raven, 1992, pp. 129–136.

128. Arnoczky, S.P.; Warren, R.F. Microvasculature of the human meniscus Am J Sports Med 10:90–95, 1982.

129. Barronian, A.D.; Zoltan J.D.; Bucon, K.A Magnetic resonance imaging of the knee: Correlation with arthroscopy. Arthroscopy 5:187–191, 1989.

130. Day, B.; Mackenzie, W.G.; Shim, S.S.; Leung, G. The vascular and nerve supply of the human meniscus. Arthroscopy 1:58–62, 1985.

131. Dehaven, K.E.; Black, K.P.; Griffiths, H.J. Open meniscus repair. Technique and two to nine year results. Am J Sports Med 17:788–795, 1989.

132. Fairbank, T.J. Knee joint changes after meniscectomy. J Bone Joint Surg Br 30:664–670, 1948.

133. Ferkel, R.D.; Davis, J.R.; Friedman, M.J.; et al. Arthroscopic partial medial meniscectomy: An analysis of unsatisfactory results. Arthroscopy 1:44–52, 1985.

134. Fowler, P.J.; Lubliner, J.A., The predictive value of five clinical signs in the evaluation of meniscal pathology. Arthroscopy 5:184–186, 1989.

135. Krause, M.S.; Pope, M.H. Mechanical changes in the knee after meniscectomy. J Bone Joint Surg Am 58:599–604, 1976.

136. Levy, I.M.; Torzilli, P.A.; Warren, R.F. The effect of medial meniscectomy on anterior-posterior motion of the knee. J Bone Joint Surg Am 64:883–888, 1982.

137. Mow, V.C; Arnoczky, S.P.; Jackson, D.W. Knee Meniscus: Basic and Clinical Foundations. New York, Raven, 1992.

138. Rosenberg, T.; Scott, S.; Paulos, L. Arthroscopic surgery: Repair of peripheral detachment of the meniscus. Contemp Orthop 10:43–50, 1985.

139. Scott, G.A.; Jolly, B.L.; Henning, C.E. Combined posterior incision and arthroscopic intraarticular repair of the meniscus. An examination of factors affecting healing. J Bone Joint Surg Am 68:847–861, 1986.

140. Small, N.C. Complications in meniscal repair. Comp Orthop 2:109–112, 1987.

141. Sommerlath, K. Prognosis of repaired and intact menisci in unstable knees: A comparative study. Arthroscopy 4:93–95, 1988.

142. Walker, P.S.; Erkman, M.J. The role of the menisci in force transmission across the knee. Clin Orthop 109:184–192, 1975.

143. Weiss, C.B.; Lundberg, M.; Hambert, P.; et al. Nonoperative treatment of meniscal tears. J Bone Joint Surg Am 71:811–822, 1989.

144. Yocum, L.A.; Kerlan, R.K.; Jobe, F.W.; et al. Isolated lateral meniscectomy. A study of twenty-six patients with isolated tears. J Bone Joint Surg Am 61:338–342, 1979.

**Surgical Approaches to the Acutely Injured Knee**

145. Austin, K.S.; Siliski, J.M. Extensile exposure of the knee. In: Siliski, J.M., ed. Traumatic Disorders of the Knee. New York, Springer-Verlag, 1994, pp. 69–82.

146. Henry, A.K. Extensile Exposure, 2nd ed. Baltimore, Williams & Wilkins, 1970.

147. Hoppenfield, S.; deBoer, P. Surgical Exposures in Orthopaedics. Philadelphia, J.B. Lippincott, 1984.

**Reconstruction for Post-traumatic Arthritis of the Knee**

148. Lonner, J.H.; Pedlow, F.X.; Siliski, J.M. Total knee arthroplasty for post-traumatic arthrosis. J Arthroplasty 14:969–975, 1999.

149. Lonner, J.H.; Siliski, J.M.; Lotke, P.A. Simultaneous femoral osteotomy and total knee arthroplasty for treatment of osteoarthritis associated with severe extra-articular deformity. J. Bone Joint Surg Am 82:342–348, 2000.

# CHAPTER 56

# Tibial Plateau Fractures

J. Tracy Watson, M.D.
Joseph Schatzker, M.D.

## RELEVANT ANATOMY

The medial and lateral tibial plateaus are the articular surfaces of the medial and lateral tibial condyles; they articulate with the medial and lateral femoral condyles, respectively. The medial plateau is the larger of the two and is concave from front to back as well as from side to side. The lateral plateau is smaller and higher than the medial and is convex from front to back as well as from side to side.

The fact that the lateral plateau is higher than the medial must be remembered during internal fixation so that a screw inserted from lateral to medial does not enter the medial articulation. Likewise, the articular surfaces of the tibia slope approximately 10 degrees from anterior to posterior, and placement of subchondral screws from front to back should avoid penetrating the posterior aspects of the joint.

The convexity of the lateral plateau helps the surgeon to identify it on a lateral radiograph of the proximal tibia. The two plateaus are separated by the intercondyloid eminence with its prominent medial and lateral tubercles ("tibial spines"). This region is nonarticular. The tibial attachment of the anterior cruciate ligament is just anterior to the medial intercondylar tubercle. The posterior cruciate ligament's attachment is in the posterior intercondylar area, extending onto the posterior surface of the metaphysis.

Bony landmarks in the subcondylar region function as sites of attachment for tendinous structures that are important to identify when considering operative approaches to the tibial plateau. The tibial tubercle is located on the anterior tibial crest 2 to 3 cm below the anterior joint line and provides attachment for the patellar tendon. In some individuals this insertion may be very broad whereas in others it is limited. The iliotibial band inserts along the lateral tibial flare into a prominence known as Gerdy's tubercle. The fibular head is prominent along the posterolateral aspect of the tibial condyle. It serves as a site of attachment for the fibular collateral ligament and biceps tendon. The proximal tibiofibular joint is a true synovial joint and in some individuals it communicates with the knee joint proper. It is important to remember that the fibula buttresses the lateral tibial condyle and may be used for this function as an in situ buttress plate in certain constructs when using plating and hybrid external fixation techniques[132] (Fig. 56–1).

The outer portion of each plateau is covered by a semilunar fibrocartilaginous meniscus. The meniscotibial ligaments attach these structures to the tibia. These structures should be identified and incised horizontally to gain visualization of the joint through a submeniscal exposure.

These structures are often torn; if not repaired, these injuries may lead to a peripheral meniscal tear. The lateral meniscus covers a much larger portion of the articular surface than the medial. The medial articular surface and its supporting medial condyle are stronger than their lateral counterparts. As a result, fractures of the lateral plateau are more common and occur as a result of a lower energy mechanism of injury. When fractures of the medial plateau occur, they are invariably associated with more violent injuries and more commonly have associated soft tissue injuries, such as disruptions of the lateral collateral ligament complex, lesions of the peroneal nerve, or damage to the popliteal vessels.

## MECHANISM OF INJURY

Injuries to the plateaus occur as a result of (1) a force directed either medially (valgus deformity, the classic "bumper fracture") or laterally (varus deformity), (2) an axial compressive force, or (3) both an axial force and a force from the side. The respective femoral condyle in this mechanism of injury exerts both shearing and compressive forces on the underlying tibial plateau. The resulting fracture is therefore most commonly a split fracture or a depression fracture, or both.

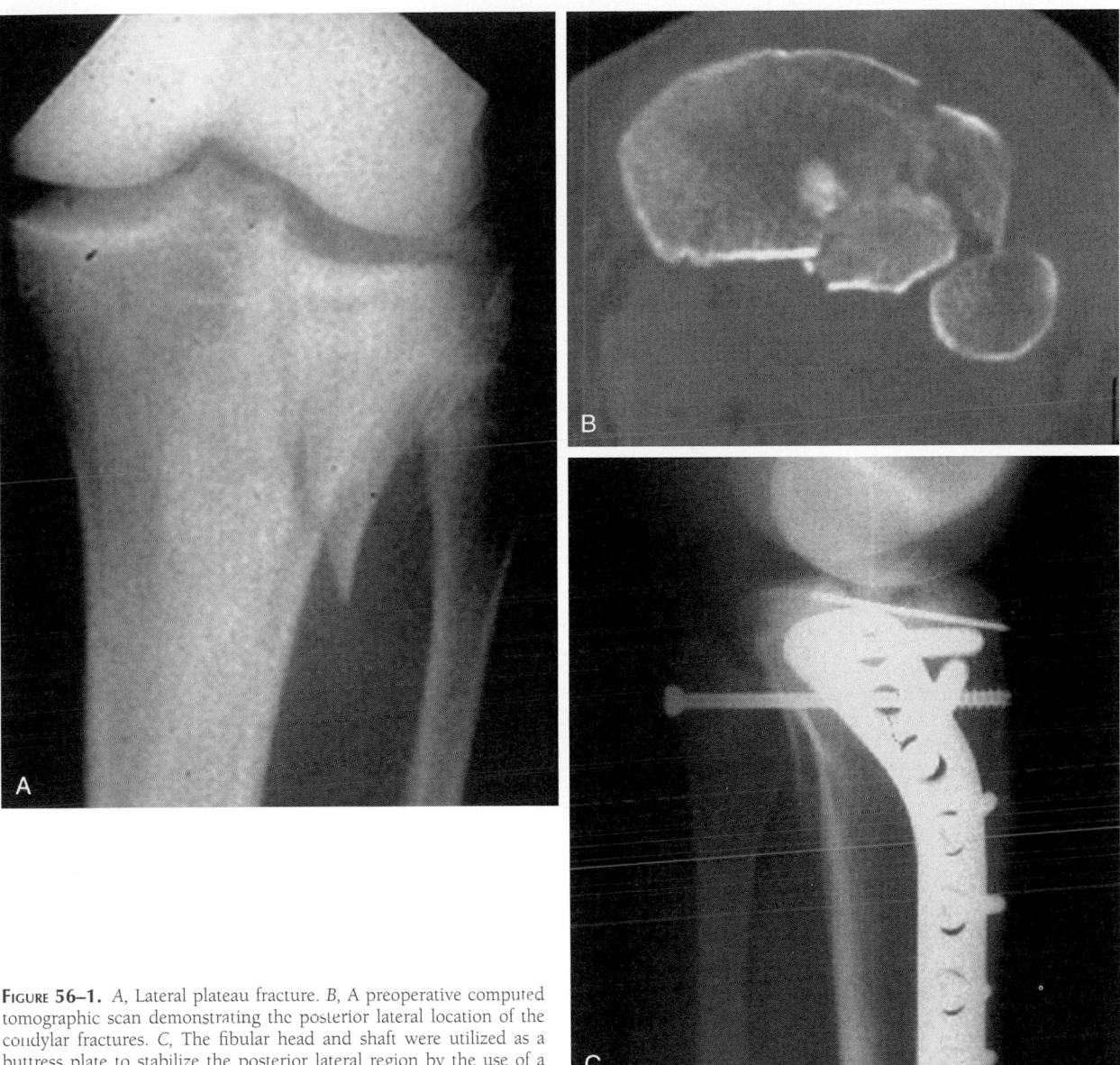

**FIGURE 56–1.** *A,* Lateral plateau fracture. *B,* A preoperative computed tomographic scan demonstrating the posterior lateral location of the condylar fractures. *C,* The fibular head and shaft were utilized as a buttress plate to stabilize the posterior lateral region by the use of a fibular head lag screw into the tibial metaphysis.

Pure split fractures are more common in younger patients, in whom the strong subchondral bone of the tibial condyle is able to withstand the compressive force of the overlying femoral condyle but the shear component of the load produces a split in the condyle. With age, the dense cancellous bone of the young tibial condyle becomes osteopenic, with diminished physical properties; it is no longer able to withstand compressive forces as well. As a result, split depression fractures become common in patients after the fifth decade of life. These fractures typically result from low-energy injuries, usually simple slip and fall accidents[13, 96] (Fig. 56–2).

However, as just noted, fracture patterns also reflect the forces involved. Kennedy and Bailey[83] were able to produce many of the commonly observed plateau fracture patterns by subjecting cadaver knees to valgus or varus forces combined with axial loads in the range of 1600 to 8000 pounds. Valgus loads in the range of 2250 to 3750

inch pounds produced mixed fractures with large variations in the amount and degree of joint impaction and condylar separation. These forces were thought to be comparable to those seen in the classic bumper fracture. This is a fracture of the lateral plateau, the result of a lateral blow to the leg that creates a valgus deforming force and a loading of the lateral plateau by the overlying femoral condyle. In high-energy injuries, the forces may be so great that the plateau explodes into numerous fracture fragments (Fig. 56–3). When axial loading exceeded 8000 pounds, severely comminuted fractures were produced in biomechanical studies. This mechanism is seen typically after a fall from a height or after a motor vehicle accident occurring with an axial load delivered to an extended knee.

The magnitude of the force determines not only the degree of fragmentation but also the degree of displacement. In addition to the fracture, there may be associated soft tissue lesions—for example, a tear of the medial collateral ligament or a tear of the anterior cruciate ligament in association with a lateral plateau fracture. Some investigators believe that an intact collateral ligament on one side of the knee is necessary for a fracture to occur on the contralateral side. The lateral collateral ligament acts in a similar way, with varus forces causing medial plateau fractures with an associated tear of the lateral collateral ligament complex, the posterior cruciate, and the peroneal nerve or a lesion of the popliteal vessels associated with a medial plateau fracture. With the increased use of magnetic resonance imaging (MRI) for these fractures, recognition of associated ligamentous injuries has increased.[9, 34, 65] The surgeon must also differentiate split fractures that are the result of a shearing force from rim avulsion fractures that are associated with knee dislocations and point to an unstable injury.[110, 111]

## CONSEQUENCES OF INJURY

Tibial plateau fractures pose major threats to the structure and function of the knee joint. Immobilization alone in a plaster cast, if prolonged for more than 2 to 3 weeks, may result in an unacceptable degree of stiffness that does not respond to physiotherapy.[20, 62, 63] Traction with early motion preserves movement but does not ensure reduction because impacted articular fragments, which are driven into the underlying cancellous bone of the metaphysis and do not have any soft tissue attachment, are not reduced.[43, 47, 61, 64, 134, 135] The joint depression together

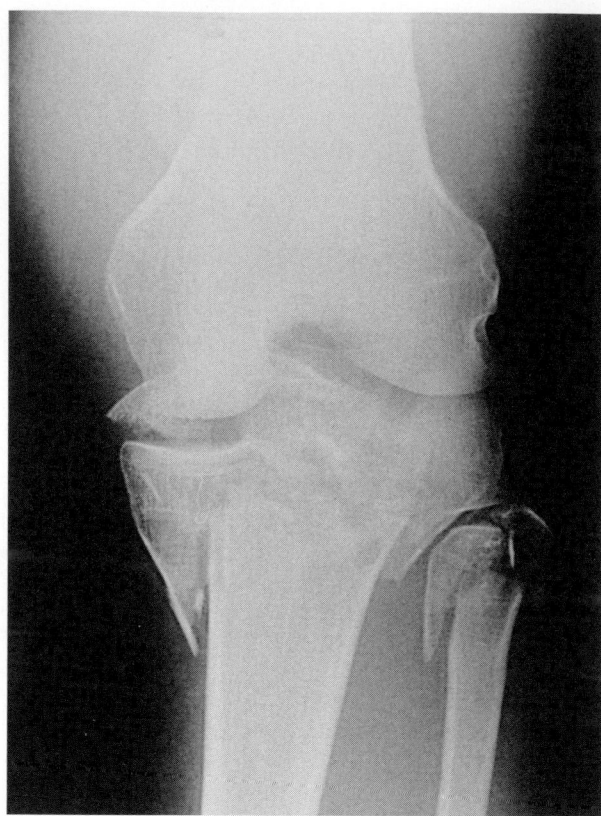

**FIGURE 56–3.** Fracture pattern consistent with a high-energy impact. Note the multiple condylar fracture lines as well as the articular comminution and impaction.

with metaphyseal fragmentation may also result in an angular deformity, leading to a major degree of joint overload.

Unless the joint is reduced anatomically, the alignment of the limb preserved, and motion instituted early (which can be achieved only with an early open reduction and internal fixation [ORIF]), major complications can be anticipated. Delayed mobilization results in permanent stiffness. Failure to restore bone anatomy and ligament function may result in permanent instability, which alone or when coupled with joint incongruity leads to post-traumatic arthritis. Even with the most successful form of treatment, post-traumatic arthritis can develop, depending on the degree of initial joint fragmentation and damage to the articular cartilage.

Tibial plateau fractures can be associated with serious soft tissue damage. Tears of the menisci, particularly peripheral detachments, occur, as do tears of the collateral and cruciate ligaments. Avulsion of the infrapatellar tendon together with the tibial tubercle occurs but is rare. However, high-energy fracture patterns often demonstrate a fracture through the tibial tubercle with associated posterior cortex comminution, which would prevent typical lag screw fixation of this fragment.[66, 67, 155]

Fractures of the lateral plateau are rarely associated with arterial or nerve lesions. However, fractures of the medial plateau, because they are invariably associated with much greater violence and often represent a knee dislocation that has been realigned, are frequently associated with lesions

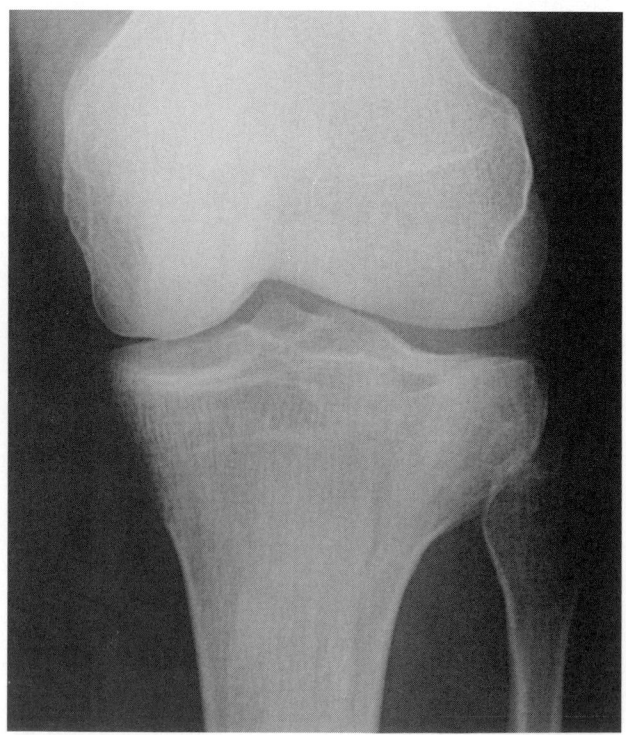

**FIGURE 56–2.** Fracture pattern consistent with a low-energy mechanism of injury. These fractures are typically a combination of condylar split and joint depression.

of the peroneal nerve or the popliteal vessels. The arterial lesions are rarely seen as hemorrhage. They are commonly seen either as an acute obstruction (because of a complete tear in the vessel or an acute thrombosis) or as a delayed thrombosis or a thrombosis seemingly initiated by the reparative surgery. The reason is that the injury to the artery is typically a small intimal tear, which may enlarge or initiate clotting, or both.

Tibial plateau fractures, particularly if they extend into the diaphysis, may be associated with acute compartment syndromes because of hemorrhage and edema of the involved compartments.[2] Another important mechanism of compartment syndrome development is reperfusion swelling after successful correction of ischemia.

The proximal tibia is subcutaneous except posteriorly. Anteriorly, it is covered only by the skin and subcutaneous tissues that overlie the few tendons and ligaments that cross the joint. The bone, together with the tendons and ligaments, is at risk of necrosis if skin coverage is lost. Severe contusions of this skin envelope occur particularly with high-energy injuries to the area. Therefore, even in the absence of open fractures, the contused soft tissue envelope may be in jeopardy because of instability of the underlying fractures; severe swelling associated with the injury; or any injudicious, traumatizing, or poorly timed surgical procedure. Fractures of the proximal tibia may become complicated by wound sloughs, infections, and osteomyelitis.

# CLASSIFICATION

Development of an appropriate treatment plan is essential and depends on proper assessment of injury severity. Numerous authors have reported satisfactory results using both operative and nonoperative management tactics for the treatment of low-energy tibial plateau fractures, particularly in elderly patients.* However, the high-energy fractures that occur in a younger age group usually preclude nonoperative management. Nonoperative treatment of complex fractures has historically been unsatisfactory.[16, 37, 42, 135, 152]

Plateau fractures cannot be viewed collectively because they differ not only in the mechanism of injury and energy expenditure but also in the patterns of fracture displacement, in the required treatment protocols, and ultimately in the overall prognosis after treatment. A classification scheme is necessary to group fractures that are similar in their mechanism of injury and fracture pattern and as such require a similar approach in their treatment and have a similar prognosis.

Unfortunately, most anatomic fracture pattern classifications do not completely address other associated conditions that routinely influence the treatment or outcome of these injuries. These factors play a dynamic role in determining the "personality" of the fracture. The factors include (1) amount of fracture displacement, (2) degree of

comminution, (3) extent of soft tissue injury, (4) associated neurovascular injuries, (5) magnitude of articular surface involvement, (6) bone quality (e.g., osteopenic), (7) presence of other injuries, and (8) associated ipsilateral injuries (e.g., floating knee, segmental tibial involvement).

## Fracture Classifications: AO and Schatzker

The *Comprehensive Classification of Fractures of Long Bones* is a unique classification system because it applies to all long bones rather than being a regionally based classification.[112] It classifies fractures in such a way that they are organized in ascending order of severity. Therefore, a type A fracture is generally easier to treat than a type B, and a type C fracture has a worse prognosis and is more difficult to manage than a type A or B. In this classification, *extra-articular* metaphyseal and epiphyseal fractures are type A. *Partial articular* fractures are type B; in these injures, part of the articular surface retains its continuity with the diaphysis. *Complete articular* fractures—type C—are those in which the articular surface has lost all connection to the diaphysis (Fig. 56–4). It is important to recognize that a fracture may be intracapsular and yet extra-articular. An articular fracture must involve the articular surface. In the AO classification, an initial numerical term specifies the injury location. The first digit indicates the involved bone, and the second indicates the involved portion. Therefore, the designations for all tibial plateau fractures begin with *41,* which specifies the tibia's proximal segment. The AO classification divides the fractures not only into types but also into groups and subgroups. Considering only the partial and complete articular fractures (excluding the type A metaphyseal fractures), there are 18 fracture types classified into six groups.

The most widely used and accepted classification of tibial plateau fractures in North America is that proposed by Schatzker.[134, 135] Schatzker's scheme addresses with greater precision the regional idiosyncrasies of tibial plateau fractures. In general, the six fracture categories indicate increasing severity, reflecting not only an increased energy expenditure with regard to the mechanism of injury but also a worse prognosis. It is possible to relate a Schatzker classification to subgroups of the AO classification. The AO type 41B (partial articular) fractures correspond to Schatzker types I, II, III, and IV (Fig. 56–5). The type C (complete articular) fractures correspond to Schatzker types V and VI. Specifically, AO group 41C1 corresponds to Schatzker type V. These fractures (Fig. 56–6), including subgroups 41C1.1, 41C1.2, and 41C1.3, are all extra-articular as long as they do not involve articular cartilage, and therefore they have a better prognosis than some of the AO type 41B fractures. Note also that the medial plateau fracture, type IV in the Schatzker classification, is evident in the AO classification only as subgroups 41B1.2 and 41B1.3, 41B2.3, and 41B3.2 and 41B3.3. As discussed later, fractures of the medial tibial plateau are very serious lesions and deserve more prominent recognition as a separate group rather

---

*See references 3, 4, 13, 16, 20, 35, 37, 38, 42, 43, 62, 63, 64, 79, 80, 89, 94, 134, 138, 140.

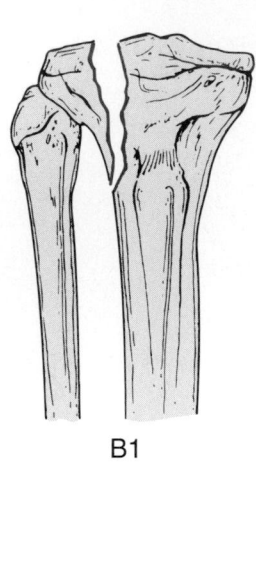
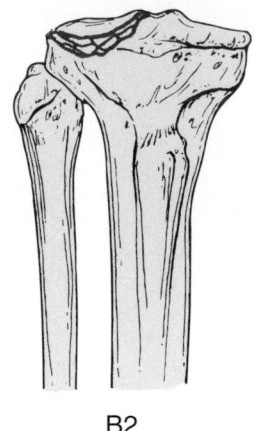
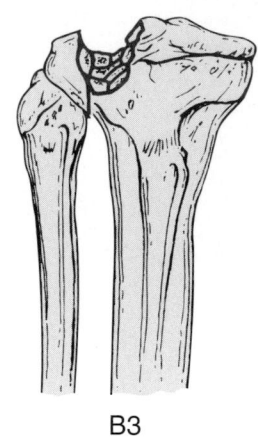

B1    B2    B3

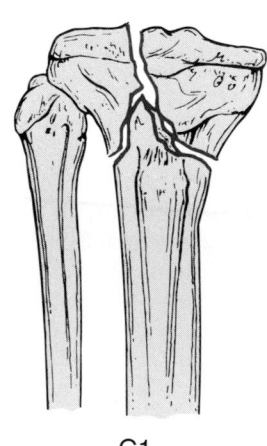
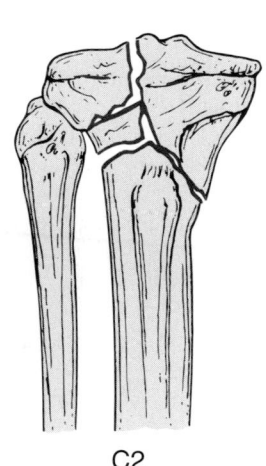
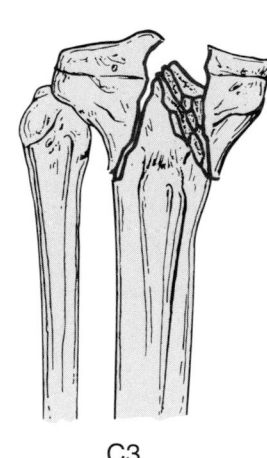

C1    C2    C3

**FIGURE 56–4.** The AO classification of fractures of long bones, tibia-fibula, proximal segment. B1, Partial articular fracture, pure split. B2, Partial articular fracture, pure depression. B3, Partial articular fracture, split depression. C1, Complete articular fracture, articular simple, metaphyseal simple. C2, Complete articular fracture, articular simple, metaphyseal multifragmentary. C3, Complete articular fracture, multifragmentary. (Redrawn from Mueller, M.E.; Nazarian, S.; Koch, P.; et al. The Comprehensive Classification of Fractures of Long Bones. Berlin, Springer-Verlag, 1990, p. 151.)

than as a subgroup. Because of these slight variations between the two systems, Schatzker's classification is used to discuss these injuries.

## TYPE I

Type I is a *"pure" wedge* or *split fracture* of the lateral plateau (Fig. 56–7), the result of bending and axial forces.[83] It occurs in young people in whom the strong cancellous bone of the plateau resists depression; therefore, there is no associated articular depression. If displaced, this fracture is frequently associated with a peripheral tear of the lateral meniscus, with the meniscus caught in the fracture. It is a partial articular fracture and corresponds to the 41B1 fracture group of the AO classification.

## TYPE II

Type II is a *split-depression fracture* of the lateral plateau (Fig. 56–8). The mechanism of injury is similar to that of type I, a lateral bending force with combined axial loading. It usually occurs in patients in their fourth decade of life or later. The cancellous bone is usually weaker because of some osteoporosis and does not resist depression as it does

in the younger population. In this age group, because of the weakened subchondral bone, impaction of the articular surface occurs in addition to the split or wedge. This is also a partial articular fracture and corresponds to the 41B3.1 subgroup of the AO classification.

## TYPE III

Type III is a *pure depression fracture* of the lateral plateau (Fig. 56–9). Like type II, it is a common fracture pattern in patients in their fourth or fifth decade. The depression may involve any portion of the articular surface but is usually located centrally or laterally. Depending on its location, size, degree of depression, and coverage by the lateral meniscus, this lesion may be stable or unstable. If the depression is central, the joint is usually stable because the depression is usually covered by the large lateral meniscus. However, if enough of the joint surface is depressed centrally, axial instability can result. The depression of the articular surface may also be peripheral. Lateral and posterior peripheral depressions are usually associated with a greater incidence of joint instability than the central depressions. This type corresponds to subgroups 41B2.1 and 41B2.2 of the AO classification.

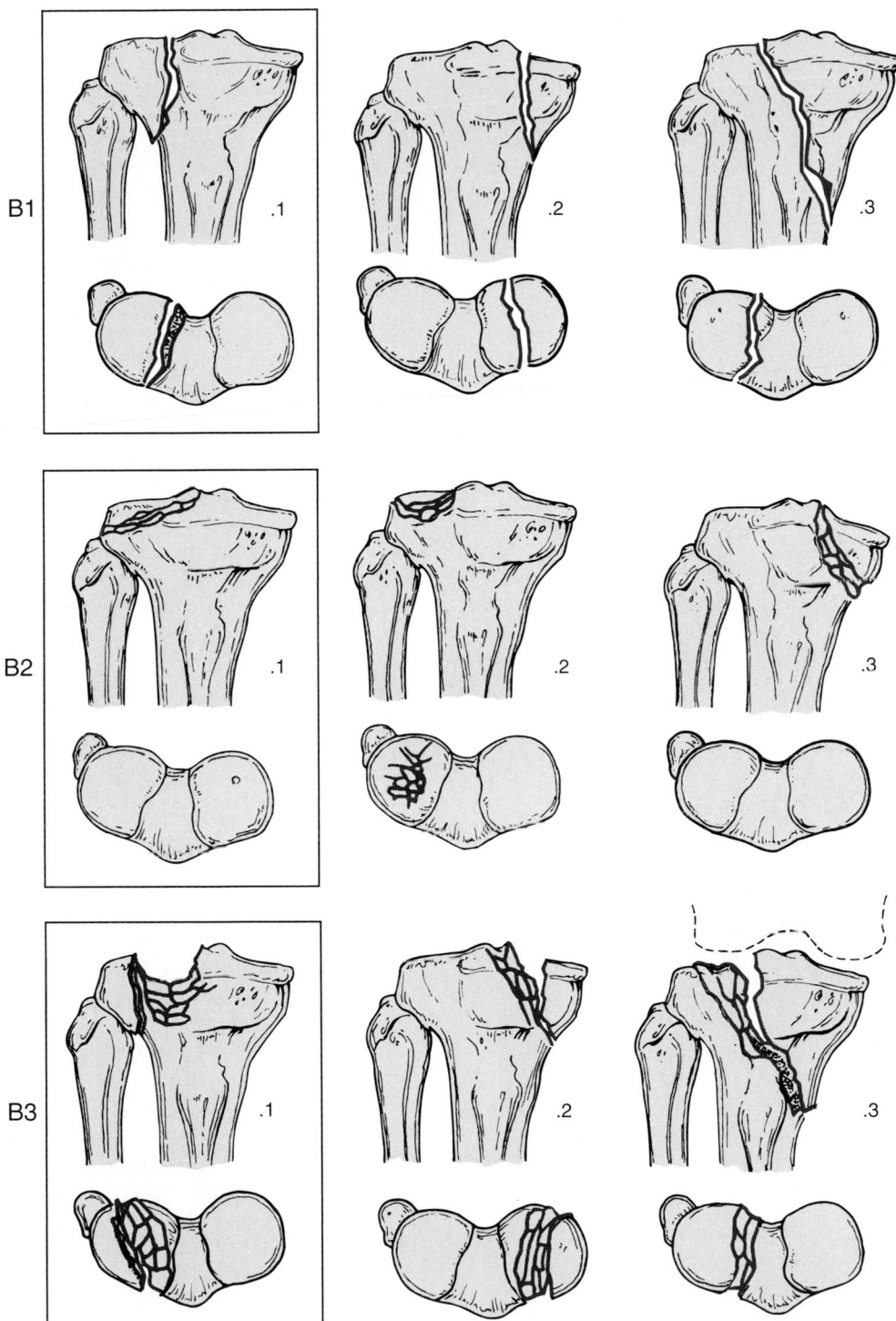

**FIGURE 56–5.** Group B fractures. B1, Partial articular fracture, pure split. The subgroups are .1, lateral plateau (marginal, sagittal, frontal anterior, or frontal posterior); .2, medial plateau (marginal, sagittal, frontal anterior, or frontal posterior); and .3, oblique, involving the tibial spines and one of the surfaces (lateral or medial). B2, Partial articular fracture, pure depression. The subgroups are .1, lateral total (one-piece depression, mosaic-like depression); .2, lateral limited (peripheral, central, anterior, or posterior); and .3, medial (peripheral, central, anterior, posterior, or total). B3, Partial articular fracture, split depression. These include anterior lateral depression, posterior lateral depression, anterior medial depression, and posterior medial depression fractures. The subgroups are .1, lateral; .2, medial; and .3, oblique, involving the tibial spines and one of the surfaces (lateral or medial). Schatzer types I, II, III, and IV correspond to these type B fractures. Note that the Schatzker type IV pattern corresponds to the B1.2, B1.3, B2.3, B3.2, and B3.3 groupings in the AO classification. (Redrawn from Mueller, M.E.; Nazarian, S.; Koch, P.; et al. The Comprehensive Classification of Fractures of Long Bones. Berlin, Springer-Verlag, 1990, p. 75.)

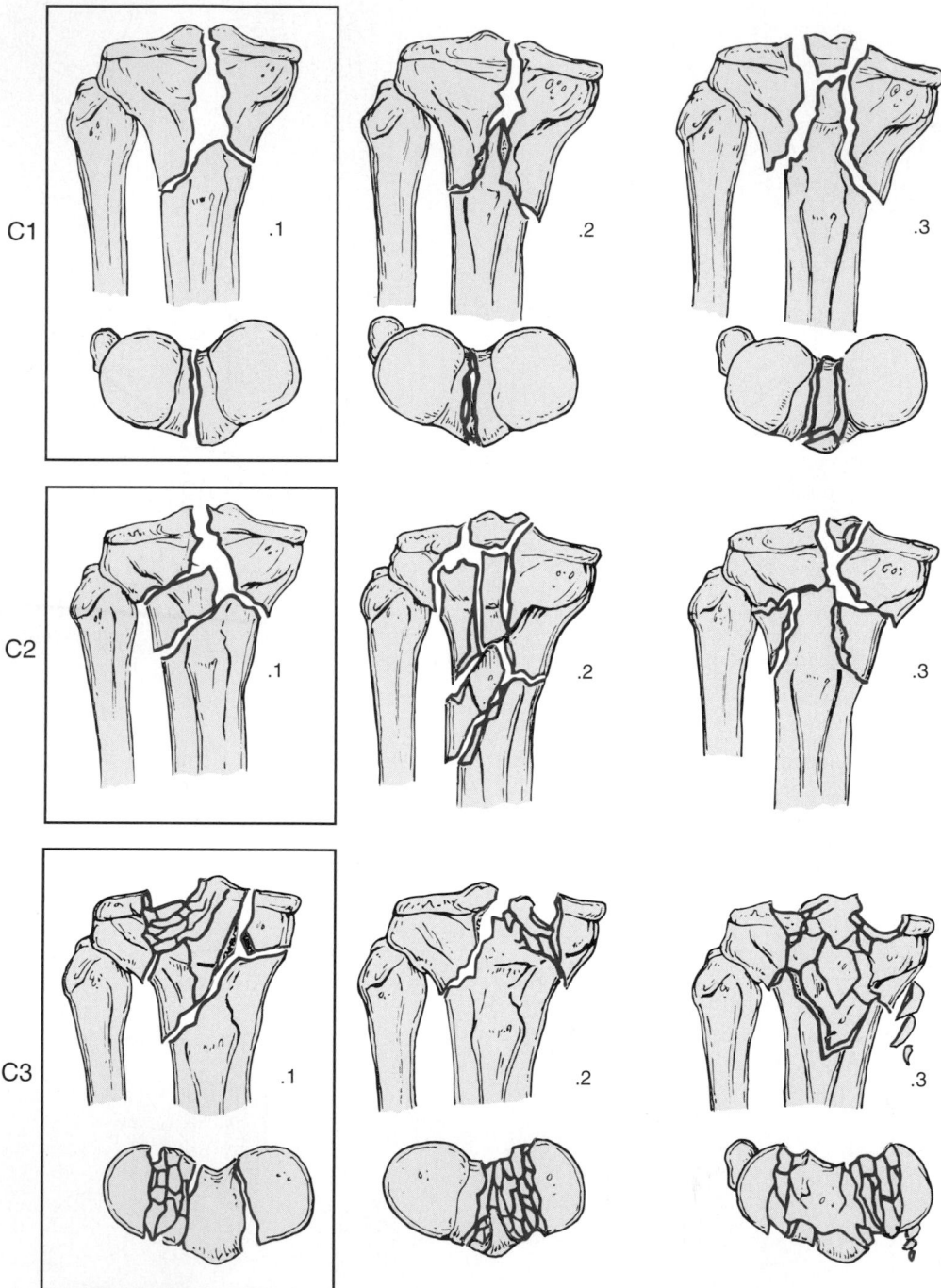

**FIGURE 56–6.** Group C fractures. C1, Complete articular fracture, articular simple, metaphyseal simple. This includes fractures with an intact anterior tibial tubercle and intercondylar eminence, fractures involving the anterior tibial tubercle, and fractures involving the intracondylar eminence. The subgroups are .1, slight displacement; .2, one condyle displaced; and .3, both condyles displaced. C2, Complete articular fracture, articular simple, metaphyseal multifragmentary. The subgroups are .1, intact wedge (lateral and medial); .2, fragmented wedge (lateral and medial); and .3, complex. C3, Complete articular fracture, multifragmentary. This includes metaphyseal simple, metaphyseal lateral wedge, metaphyseal medial wedge, metaphyseal complex, and metaphyseal-diaphyseal complex fractures. The subgroups are .1, lateral; .2, medial; and .3, lateral and medial. Schatzker types V and VI correspond to the AO type C1 fractures. Subgroups C1.1, C1.2, and C1.3 correspond to the Schatzker type V. (Redrawn from Mueller, M.E.; Nazarian, S.; Koch, P.; et al. The Comprehensive Classification of Fractures of Long Bones. Berlin, Springer-Verlag, 1990, p. 157.)

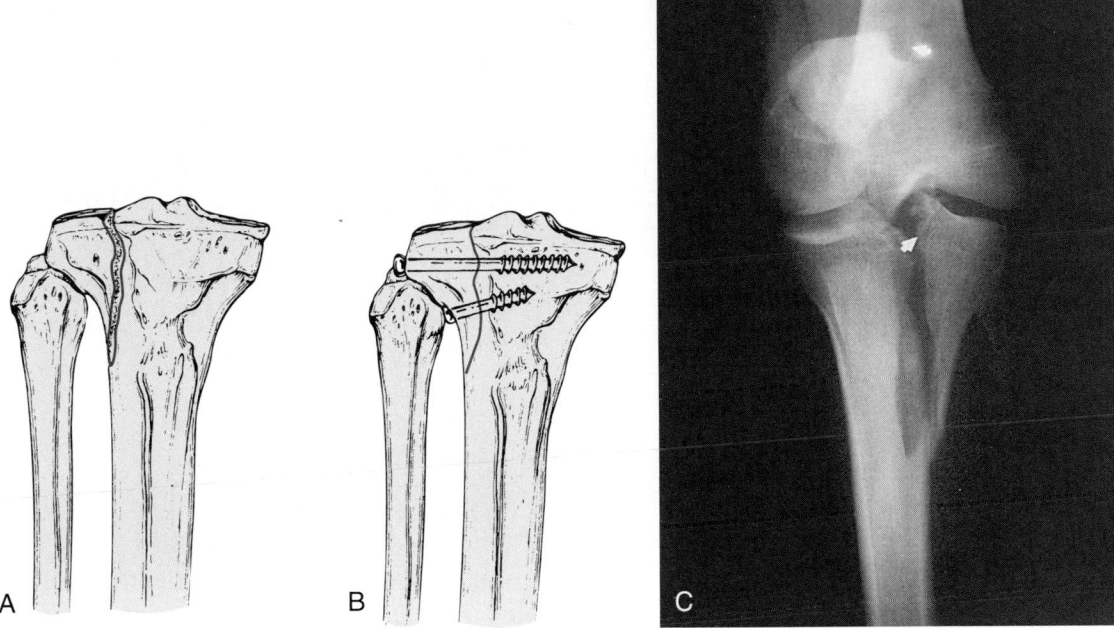

**FIGURE 56–7.** *A,* A type I fracture involves a split-wedge fracture of the lateral plateau without any joint depression or impaction. Lateral meniscal pathology may be present that may preclude closed manipulation and percutaneous treatment. *B,* Type I fractures can usually be fixed with lag screws (often with washers) if the bone is of good quality. Those that involve a large condylar split or have comminution of the fracture line necessitate fixation with lag screws and a buttress plate. *C,* Radiographic appearance of a type I injury with a large condylar fragment *(arrow).* This condition would necessitate buttress plating rather than lag screw fixation only. *(A, B,* Redrawn from Schatzker, J. In: Chapman, M.W., ed. Operative Orthopaedics. Philadelphia, J.B. Lippincott, 1988, Fig. 35–1, p. 422.)

Typically, the appearance of the condylar fracture patterns on x-ray films has been the basis for the classification of plateau injuries. The Schatzker type I, II, and III fractures are classically the result of a lower energy mechanism of injury. The fractures that result from a

![Figure 56-8 illustration]

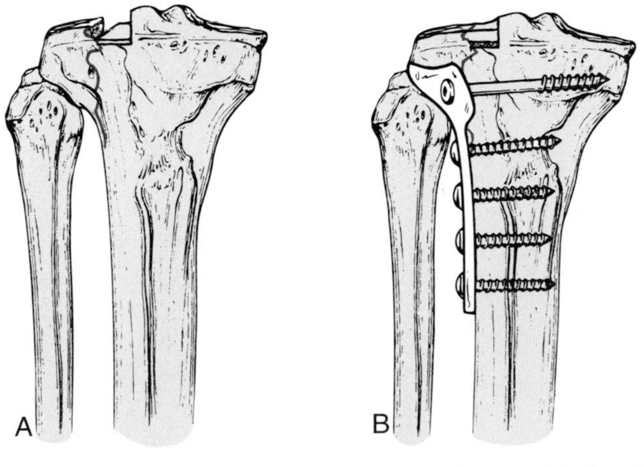

**FIGURE 56–8.** *A,* A type II fracture involves a split fracture of the lateral condyle with associated impaction and depression of the lateral articular surface. The depressed fragment is often comminuted. *B,* Visualization of the lateral plateau is accomplished utilizing a submeniscal exposure with subsequent elevation of the depressed articular fragments. Buttress plate fixation is necessary because of the lateral condylar comminution and typical cortical fragility. The radiographic appearance of a typical split-depression fracture is illustrated in Figure 56–1. *(A, B,* Redrawn from Schatzker, J. In: Chapman, M.W., ed. Operative Orthopaedics. Philadelphia, J.B. Lippincott, 1988, Fig. 35–3A, p. 423.)

higher energy mechanism are more complex and can often be described as Schatzker type IV, V, or VI injuries.[154]

## TYPE IV

Type IV is a *fracture of the medial tibial plateau* (Fig. 56–10) and may be a split or a split-depression fracture. The injury results from varus and axial loading forces and is much less common than lateral plateau injuries. The medial plateau resists fracture more than the lateral; therefore, its fractures are usually the result of a much greater force.

Medial plateau injuries are most frequently associated with an avulsion of the intercondylar eminence, which may signify rupture of one or both cruciate ligaments.[10] The fracture line most commonly exits the articular surface *lateral* to the intercondylar eminence and is often associated with impaction of the lateral plateau. In addition, the varus force frequently results in a rupture of the lateral collateral ligamentous complex. If the displacement at the time of injury is sufficient to cause subluxation or dislocation of the knee, the fracture may also be associated with a traction lesion of the peroneal nerve or a lesion of the popliteal artery. Thus, type IV fractures actually represent a dislocation of the knee that has typically been realigned before the radiograph is exposed.[135, 152] It is not the fracture of the medial plateau that gives this injury its bad prognosis but the associated soft tissue injuries, such as those involving the peroneal nerve, the popliteal artery, and the cruciate and lateral collateral ligaments.

Because of the likelihood of associated popliteal artery

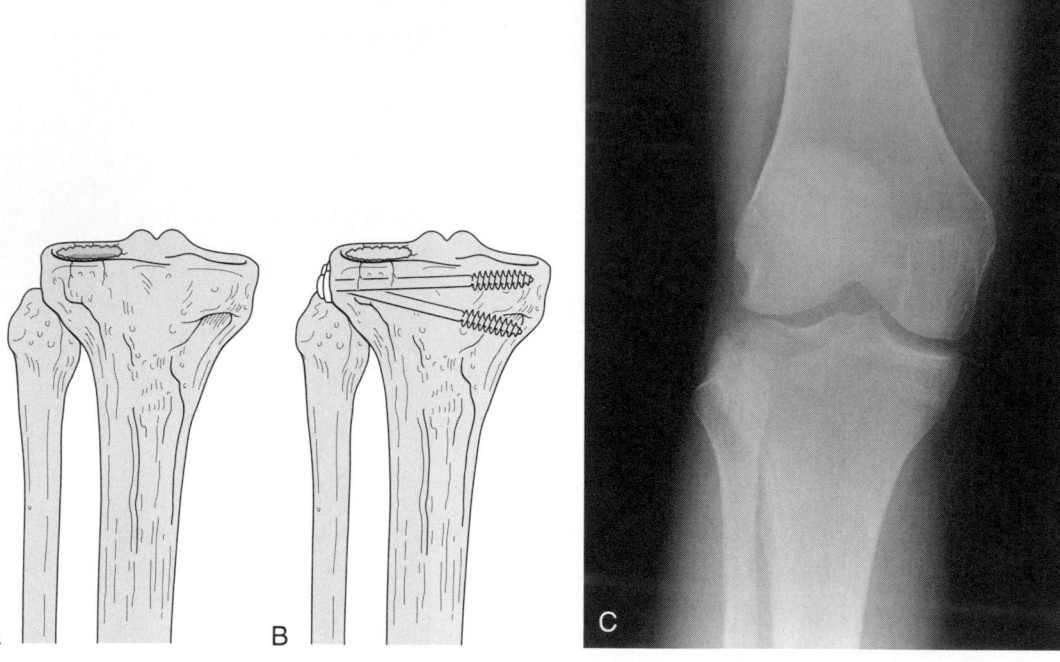

**FIGURE 56–9.** A, A type III fracture involves a pure depression of the lateral articular surface only. There is no associated metaphyseal condylar fracture line. Instability may not be present when the depressed area is small or centrally located. Examination under anesthesia may be required to assess stability of the knee with a type III fracture. B, If a central or peripheral depression results in joint instability, the depressed portion of the plateau is elevated through a submetaphyseal cortical window. Bone graft is packed into the defect, thus elevating the articular surface. The bone graft is stabilized either with cancellous lag screws or, in cases in which a larger cortical window is required or the bone is fragile, with a buttress plate and associated condylar screws to prevent extension to a condylar split fracture. Arthroscopy may be used instead of arthrotomy to visualize the articular surface directly. C, Radiographic appearance showing the centrally depressed articular surface. (A, Redrawn from Schatzker, J. In: Chapman, M.W., ed. Operative Orthopaedics. Philadelphia, J.B. Lippincott, 1988, Fig. 35–3A, p. 423.)

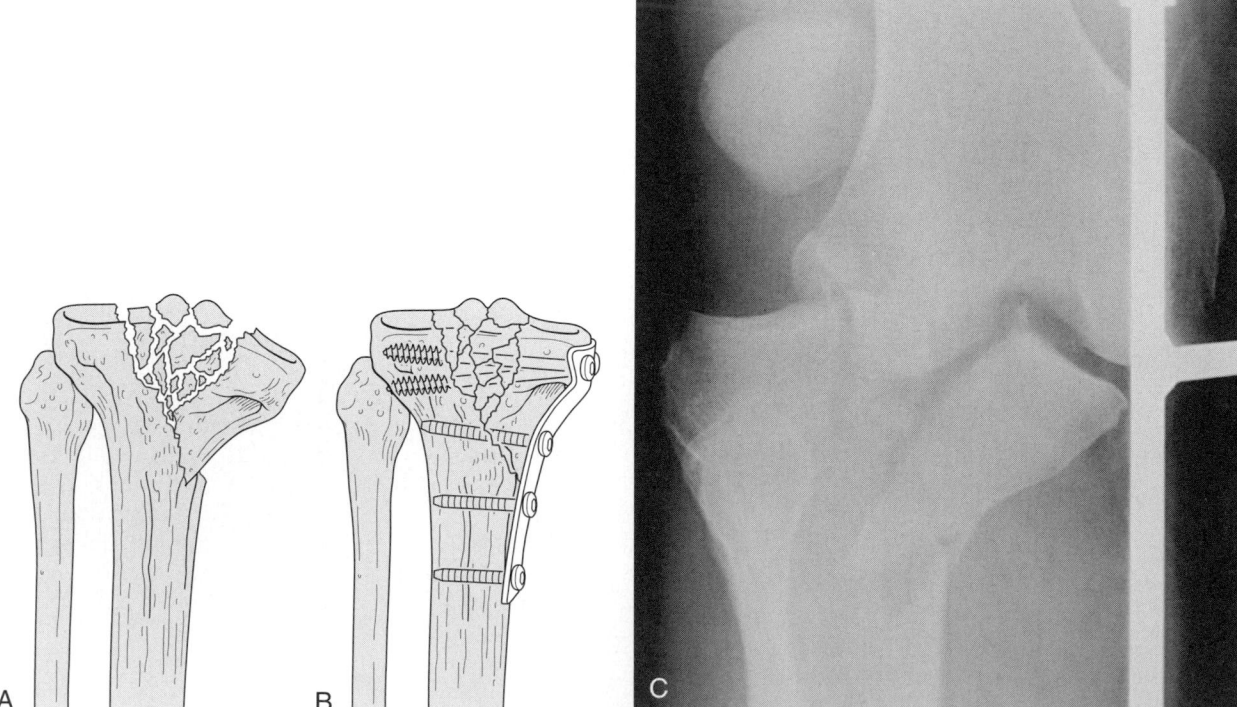

**FIGURE 56–10.** A, A type IV fracture involves a split fracture of the medial plateau with associated comminution of the intracondylar eminence or medial plateau articular surface. B, The associated comminution usually precludes the use of solitary condylar lag screws. Definitive fixation usually requires a medial buttress plate to support this very unstable fragment. Lag screws or wire suture may be needed to anchor the intercondylar eminence fracture fragments. C, This fracture pattern is often the result of a high-energy mechanism of injury. It is often associated with neurovascular or other significant soft tissue injury. In this instance, the radiograph reveals essentially a knee dislocation. Note the location of the patella, as this injury also had an associated avulsion of the patellar tendon as well as rupture of all associated knee ligaments. (A, B, Redrawn from Schatzker, J. In: Chapman, M.W., ed. Operative Orthopaedics. Philadelphia, J.B. Lippincott, 1988, Fig. 35–4A, p. 424.)

injuries, which may be nonocclusive intimal tears, frequent neurovascular checks, Doppler arterial pressure determinations, and perhaps arteriography, should be done to evaluate arterial integrity and thus to promptly identify limb-threatening popliteal artery thrombosis. Some of these fractures may involve a posterior split of the medial plateau, which causes the femoral condyle to subluxate posteriorly and greatly increases the instability of the joint. These fractures correspond to groups 41B1, 41B2, and 41B3 in the AO classification. However, a percentage of these fractures do not fit clinically into the Schatzker or AO fracture subgroups, especially the fractures that have the primary fracture line in the coronal plane. These fractures are usually not amenable to a standard anterior operative approach.

This pattern was recognized by Moore, who sought to include these unusual fracture types in his classification scheme denoted as true fracture-dislocations because of their instability.[110, 111] These fracture-dislocations as described by Moore account for approximately 10% of all articular fractures of the proximal tibia and encompass the vast majority of fractures with associated injuries to the popliteal artery, peroneal nerve, and cruciate ligaments (Fig. 56–11).

## TYPE V

Type V is a *bicondylar fracture that involves a split of the lateral and medial plateaus* (Fig. 56–12) and is usually the result of a pure axial load applied to the extended knee. It may also involve varying degrees of articular depression and displacement of the condyles. A common pattern is a fracture of the medial condyle in association with a depressed or split-depressed lateral tibial plateau fracture.

The prognosis depends on whether the fracture line involves the articular surfaces or begins in the intercondylar area and skirts the articular surfaces as it exits in the metaphysis medially and laterally. If the articular surfaces are not involved, the patient's prognosis is correspondingly better. However, evaluation of the neurovascular status is important, especially because these injuries are usually the result of a high-energy mechanism. These fractures correspond to the 41C1 fracture group of the AO classification.

## TYPE VI

Type VI injuries combine articular surface fractures with a metaphyseal fracture that separates the tibial condylar components from the diaphysis, so-called diaphyseal-metaphyseal dissociation (Figs. 56–13 and 56–14). Often, the patient presents with considerable joint disruption, comminution, and depression with condylar displacement. Many of these fractures are associated with depression and impaction of one or both articular surfaces. In addition, because of the high-energy mechanism of energy, these fractures are frequently associated with compromise of the soft tissue envelope around the knee. Compartment syndrome and neurovascular compromise are often associated with these injuries. These fractures correspond to the 41C2 and 41C3 groups of the AO classification.

Avulsion fractures of the spine and intercondylar eminence are often associated with the high-energy plateau fractures, particularly the Schatzker IV, V, and VI patterns. When these fracture patterns are treated surgically, the intercondylar eminence fragment should also be repaired. If the eminence fragment is large and noncomminuted,

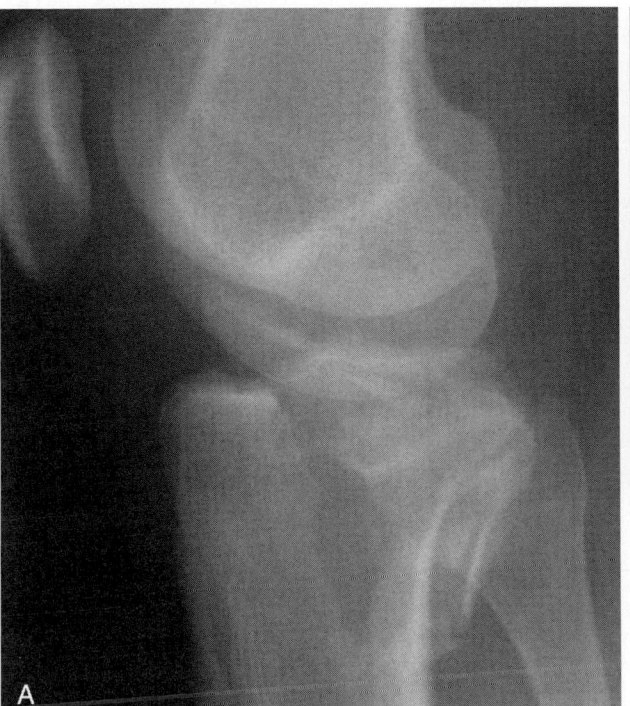

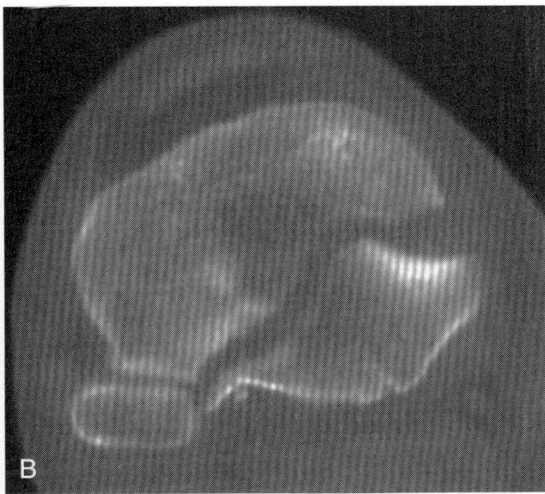

**FIGURE 56–11.** *A,* Plateau fracture demonstrating subluxation of the distal femur in association with a coronal plane fracture. *B,* Computed tomographic scan demonstrating the posterior one half of the tibial condylar involvement, which requires a direct posterior approach for fixation to prevent further subluxation.

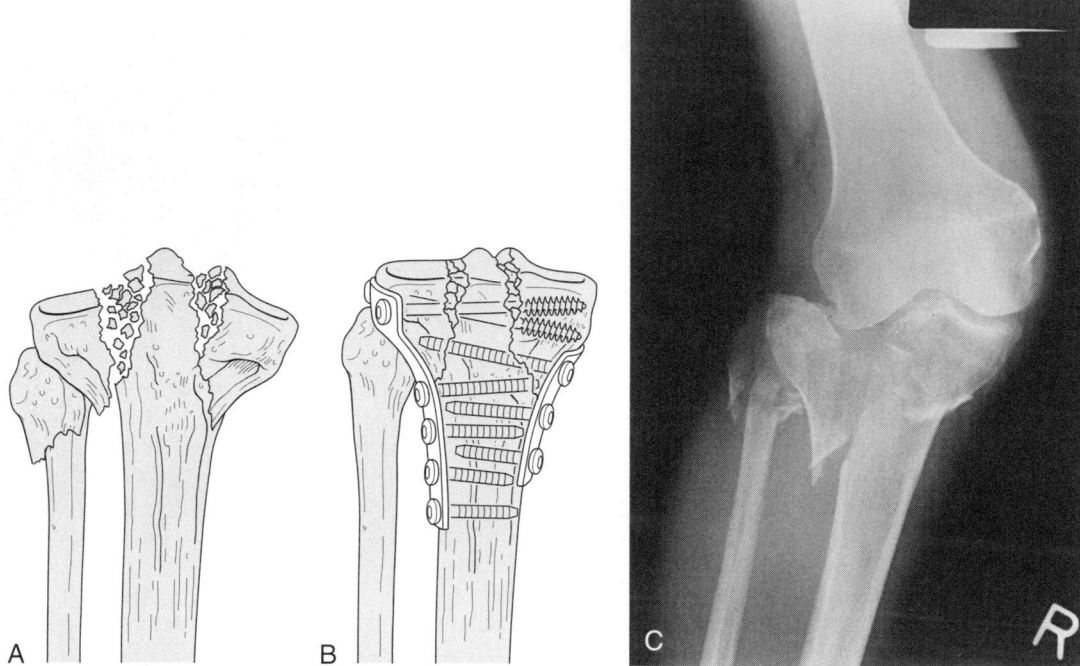

**FIGURE 56–12.** *A,* A type V fracture is a bicondylar fracture that may involve both condylar articular surfaces. The fracture lines may resemble an inverted **Y**. The hallmark of these injuries is that at least a small part of the metaphysis remains in continuity with the joint. *B,* Fixation requires attention to both tibial condyles, a lateral buttress plate with lag screws, and a posteromedially placed antiglide plate. *C,* A high-energy type V fracture. The bicondylar nature of the injury is apparent, as are impaction and depression of the lateral articular surface. It is important to address stabilization of the medial condyle in some fashion with either a buttress plate or an external fixator in order to prevent its collapse. (*A, B,* Redrawn from Schatzker, J. In: Chapman, M.W., ed. Operative Orthopaedics. Philadelphia, J.B. Lippincott, 1988, Fig. 35–5*A,* p. 424.)

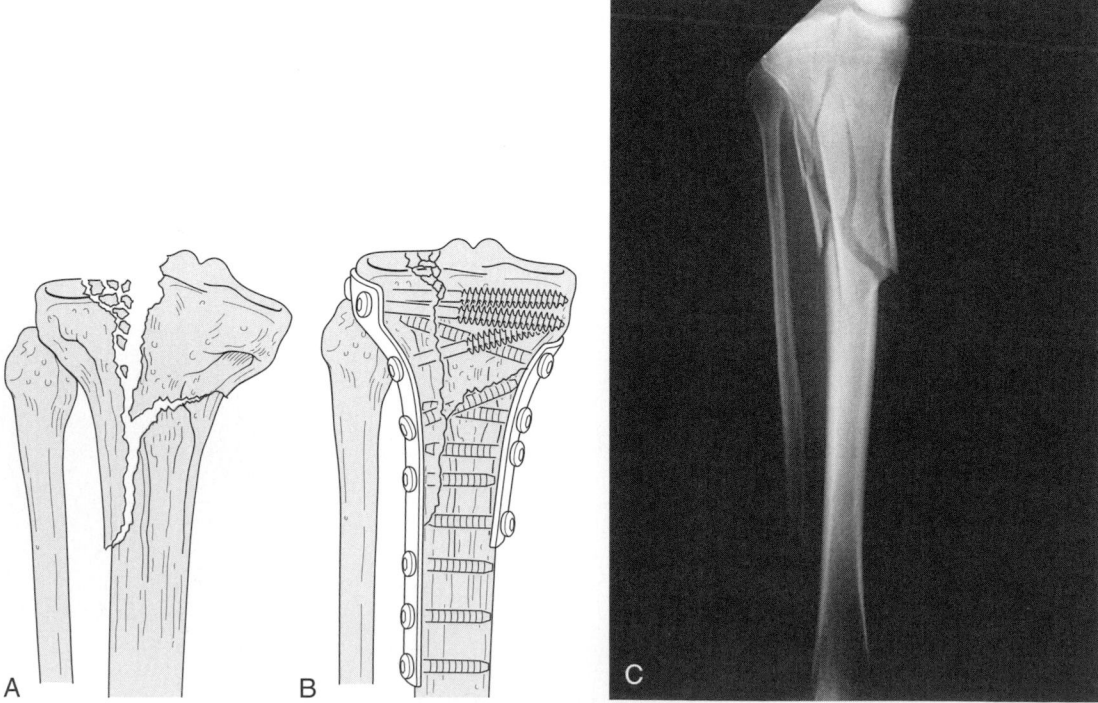

**FIGURE 56–13.** *A,* A type VI plateau fracture is distinguished by the complete dissociation of the metaphysis from the diaphyseal region. Frequently, along with the bicondylar nature of the injury there is joint impaction. *B,* Optimal fixation requires a long rigid buttress plate connecting the metaphysis to the diaphyseal region. In addition, fixation must buttress the medial condylar component. Often the diaphyseal-metaphyseal junction requires bone grafting. *C,* A type VI fracture with comminution at the diaphyseal-metaphyseal junction. These fractures are often accompanied by significant soft tissue compromise. (*A, B,* Redrawn from Schatzker, J. In: Chapman, M.W., ed. Operative Orthopaedics. Philadelphia, J.B. Lippincott, 1988, Fig. 35–6*A,* p. 435.)

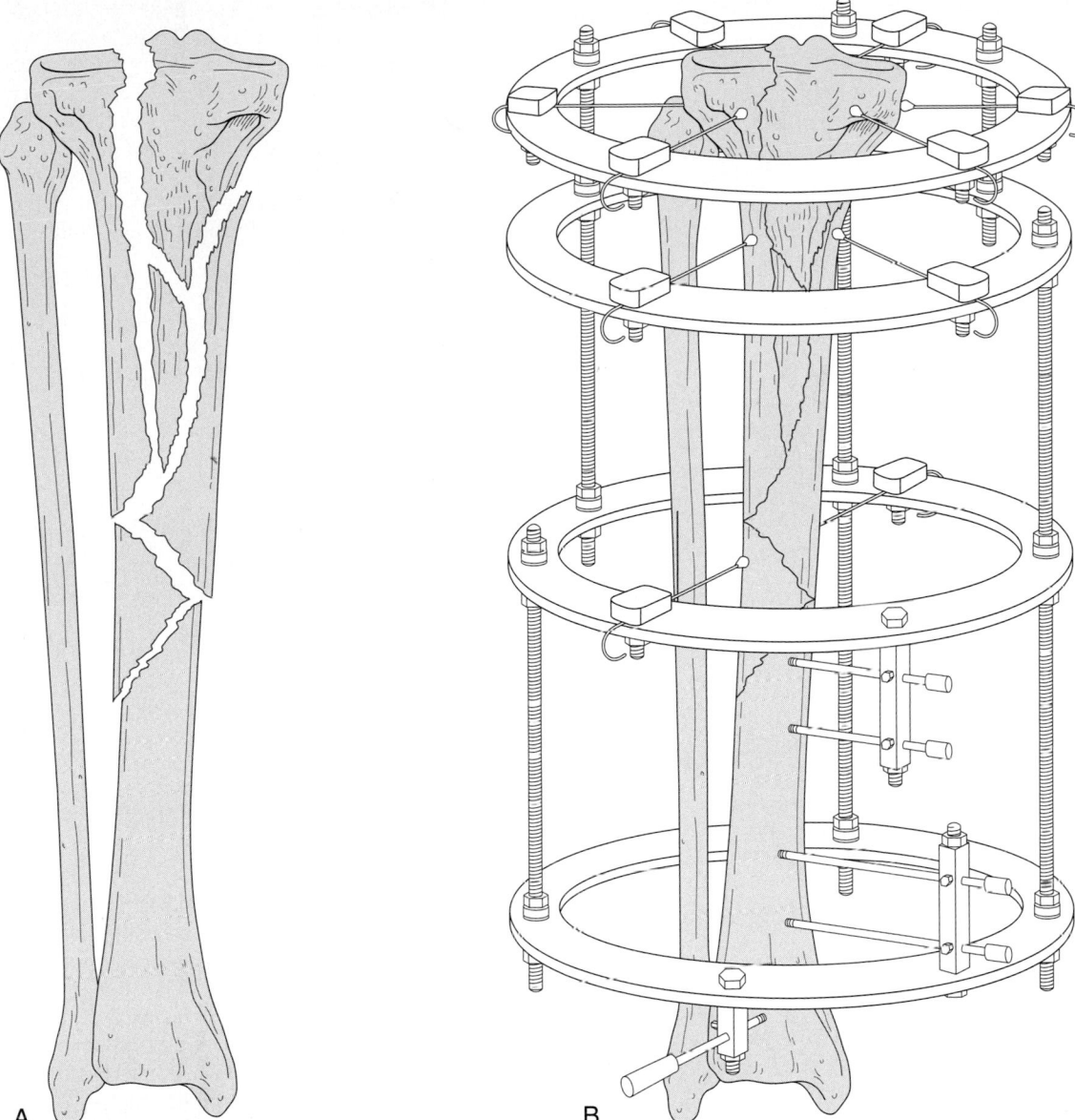

**A**    **B**

**FIGURE 56–14.** *A,* Type VI fracture with extensive shaft comminution. The complex extent of the skeletal injury and compromised soft tissue often preclude traditional internal fixation techniques. *B,* External fixators with small, tensioned wires or hybrid fixators are required in these instances to span the wide zone of injury and provide excellent skeletal fixation.

small cancellous screws may provide better fixation than is obtained with isolated Kirschner wires (K-wires) or sutures. With smaller or comminuted fragments, suture fixation through drill holes in the proximal tibia is the usual mechanism of fixation.

## Fractures of the Intercondylar Eminence

Isolated fractures of the intercondylar eminence represent avulsion of the anterior cruciate ligament and therefore are not included under fractures of the tibial plateau. Occasionally, when the fragment is large, it may encroach on the articular surface of the medial tibial plateau. In the AO classification, these lesions are assigned to the 41A1 group.

## DIAGNOSIS

### History

The patient is rarely able to relate the exact mechanism of injury, but the history is nevertheless very useful because it may permit the physician to determine the direction of the force, the deformity produced, and whether the injury was caused by a high- or a low-velocity force. This information has an important bearing on the associated soft tissue injuries, such as fracture blisters, arterial injury, and compartment syndrome, each of which may require several hours to develop, as well as neurologic and ligament injuries.

## Physical Examination

The physical examination is an extremely important aspect of the evaluation because it gives invaluable information not available from most laboratory investigations. Physical examination is the most accurate method by which to evaluate the soft tissue envelope and its injuries, whether they are closed or open. The examination should focus on the continuity of the soft tissue envelope and the presence of blisters or superficial abrasions. Deep contusions, hemorrhagic blisters, and lack of skin wrinkles all indicate an internal degloving injury. The presence of some or all of these findings would preclude the use of emergent extensile exposures, and in some circumstances surgery should be delayed or temporized until the soft tissue envelope has recovered sufficiently to allow surgical intervention.

Physical examination is also the most accurate means of evaluating the neurologic status of the extremity and the most rapid means of assessing the vascular status and the presence or absence of a major tear of a collateral ligament. Fullness or tenseness of any compartment in the leg and severe pain on passive stretch of the muscles in the specific compartment are fairly accurate indications of increased compartment pressure and the possibility of a compartment syndrome. Pedal pulses must be assessed early and repeatedly, and quantitative assessment of the ankle-brachial index, a ratio of Doppler-aided systolic pressure measurements, is strongly urged. An abnormal pulse or ankle-brachial index is grounds for arteriography or vascular surgery consultation.

## Imaging

### STANDARD RADIOGRAPHIC VIEWS

Radiography is the only way to assess accurately the fracture pattern and its severity. The standard anteroposterior (AP) and lateral views are inadequate and must be supplemented with two oblique projections taken with the leg in internal and external rotation (Fig. 56–15). The internal oblique view projects to advantage the lateral plateau, and the external oblique, the medial. The oblique views frequently give information that is completely missed on a standard AP projection. If plain x-ray films reveal a medial plateau or bicondylar plateau fracture pattern, the physician should be alerted to the fact that an associated injury may be present and a thorough review of the physical examination is indicated.

If surgical intervention is contemplated, traction radiographs are an additional tool to be used in determining the efficacy of distraction techniques. Traction films reveal whether a ligamentotaxis reduction is possible and also aid in planning surgical incisions (Fig. 56–16).[154, 157] Preoperative planning on the basis of initial injury films is often inaccurate because of overlapping fragments and malalignment of any shaft extension.

### TOMOGRAPHY

Whenever there is any uncertainty about the degree of fragmentation or depression of the articular surface, the physician can consider AP and lateral tomographs. These frequently reveal the extent and position of important fracture lines, the number and size of fragments, and the degree of depression (Fig. 56–17). In many hospitals tomography is no longer available, having been replaced by computed tomography.

### COMPUTED TOMOGRAPHY SCANNING

Computed tomography (CT) with axial, coronal, and sagittal reconstructions has essentially replaced linear tomography in most trauma centers in North America. The CT scan provides the surgeon with the cross-sectional anatomy of the fracture and the potential for sagittal or coronal reconstruction at any desired depth (Fig. 56–18). Contemporary surgical techniques utilize indirect methods of reduction and fixation and require precise knowledge of the three-dimensional anatomy. We find that CT scanning is an extremely helpful, almost essential, form of imaging for these fractures. It allows the surgeon to formulate a three-dimensional concept of the fracture and is useful in delineating the extent and location of condylar fracture lines as well as the location and depth of articular comminution and impaction.[104, 121, 122] The degree of articular depression is often underappreciated on plain films.[15, 28, 41, 46, 97, 108] Additional information is gained by using CT scan data compared with plain film data, especially with the higher grade Schatzker type VI, V, and VI fracture patterns.[156] However, CT scans are usually unnecessary for treating the simpler fracture patterns.

Traction CT scanning is preferable as it gives the surgeon a much better indication of the effectiveness of distraction techniques. Properly interpreted, CT scans can influence the choice of surgical approach and determine the effectiveness of less invasive techniques such as use of percutaneous cannulated screws or thin wire hybrid external fixation (Fig. 56–19).

### MAGNETIC RESONANCE IMAGING

MRI is becoming more widely used in the preoperative evaluation of plateau fractures because of the high incidence of soft tissue lesions accompanying these injuries.[6, 9, 18.] MRI has been shown to be superior for assessment of associated soft tissue injuries such as meniscal and ligamentous disruptions. The incidence of soft tissue injury as diagnosed by MRI is higher than

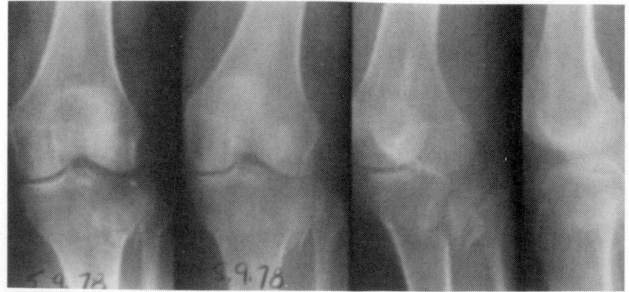

**Figure 56–15.** Oblique projections provide additional fracture information.

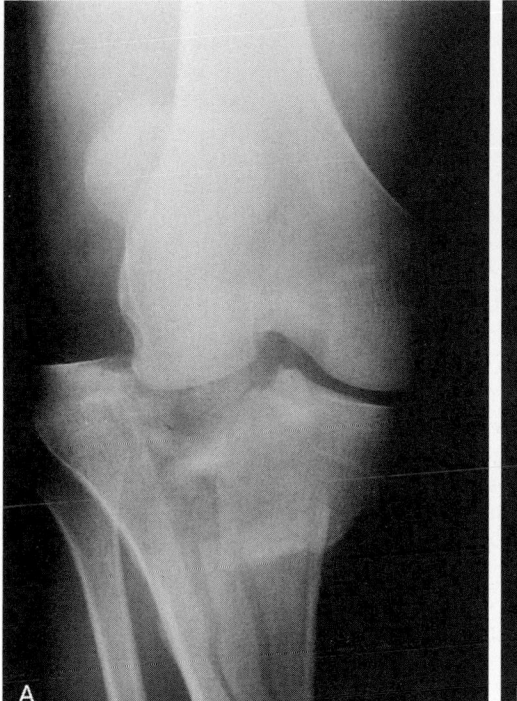
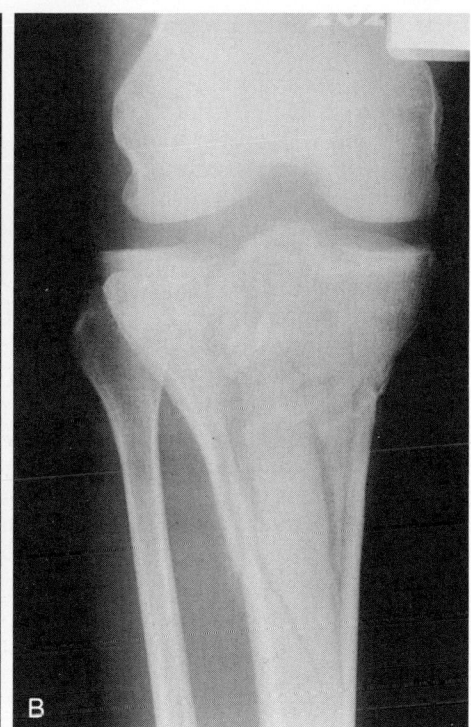

**FIGURE 56–16.** *A,* Injury film reveals a complex Schatzker type V injury with shaft dissociation and lateral articular surface impaction. *B,* Traction radiograph reveals generalized reduction of the condylar and shaft components. Note the residual impaction and depression of the lateral articular surface. This information can be used preoperatively in determining the location and extent of incisions and fixation hardware.

previously reported when this modality was not utilized. Studies have reported the incidence of "internal derangement" indicated by MRI results ranging between 47% to 97% per plateau fracture.[34, 65] One should be cautioned, however, not to overread these findings because many of these soft tissue injuries do not need immediate surgical attention. MRI does identify the occult fracture line better than linear tomography[65, 87]; however, it does not demonstrate visualized fractures as well as CT, and it may not be widely available on an acute basis in most institutions.

Much less is known about its efficacy in total assessment of complex injuries.

Bennett and Browner[9] evaluated the frequency of soft tissue injuries of the collateral and cruciate ligaments, menisci, and surrounding nerves and arteries that may occur in association with plateau fractures. Schatzker type II and IV fractures were associated with the highest frequency of soft tissue injuries. They determined that medial collateral ligament injuries were most commonly associated with Schatzker type II fracture patterns. Menisci were most commonly injured with the type IV fracture patterns.[9]

## ARTERIOGRAPHY

An arteriogram should be considered whenever there is serious concern about the possibility of an arterial lesion. An intimal tear may be present without a clinically detectable deficit. During fracture surgery, such a lesion may lead to an occlusive thrombosis that jeopardizes the extremity. The fracture pattern most commonly associated with an arterial injury is the Schatzker type IV, the fracture of the medial plateau. The knee is very unstable and may have been dislocated at the time of injury. However, the presence of any high-energy tibial plateau fractures, including Schatzker types V and VI, should lower the surgeon's threshold for obtaining an arteriogram as part of the preoperative evaluation.[135, 154]

## OVERVIEW OF FRACTURE MANAGEMENT

**FIGURE 56–17.** Tomography reveals a central depression of the articular surface as well as the split in the lateral tibial condyle, thus defining the nature of a type II fracture.

In the past, major intra-articular fractures remained an unsolved problem, and disability in varying degrees after a major intra-articular fracture was considered unavoidable. Charnley[31] recognized in 1961 that anatomic reduction and early motion were desirable in the treatment of intra-articular injuries, but the techniques of surgery and internal fixation available at the time made these objectives of treatment unattainable. Attempts at early motion after internal fixation frequently resulted in pain because of instability, with resultant loss of fixation and varying degrees of malunion or nonunion. Surgery combined with plaster immobilization resulted in even greater stiffness than plaster immobilization alone. The pathophysiology of joint stiffness was poorly understood, and stiffness after surgery was blamed on the added trauma of surgery and the periarticular location of the fixation device.[64, 93, 152] Therefore, surgery was considered the last resort, and nonoperative techniques were generally favored for treatment of articular injuries. The phases of treatment were evaluation, reduction, immobilization, and rehabilitation; rehabilitation followed fracture union, resulting invariably in joint stiffness. Apley[3, 4] pioneered early joint rehabilitation and developed successful methods of traction that permitted early motion of joints while providing sufficient immobilization for the fracture to unite. He applied these techniques to the treatment of tibial plateau fractures and reported what he considered to be satisfactory results, compared with the results of surgery.

The difficulty in evaluating the preceding studies is that the authors reported the results of treatment collectively without analyzing the types of tibial plateau fractures that had satisfactory outcomes. Classification categories such as undisplaced, slightly displaced, and severely displaced, amplified by such terms as vertical or oblique fracture line or split or comminuted, are unable to separate fracture types with intrinsically different prognoses. Furthermore, these authors compared the results of the best nonoperative treatment with those of surgical treatment methods that would be considered unacceptable by current standards.

The development by the AO group of atraumatic techniques of open reduction and stable fixation; of new techniques and principles of internal fixation that permitted absolute stability of fixation and early motion without fear of displacement, malunion, or nonunion; and of new implants and instruments that facilitated the attainment of the new goals of ORIF brought about a revolution in fracture surgery.[133–135, 152] However, as the severity of the skeletal injury increases, so does the concomitant injury to the soft tissue envelope. As surgical treatment became increasingly popular, high-energy fracture types (Schatzker IV, V, and VI) were often managed with large extensile approaches and internal fixation hardware. The usually lengthy operation and surgical approach through a tenu-

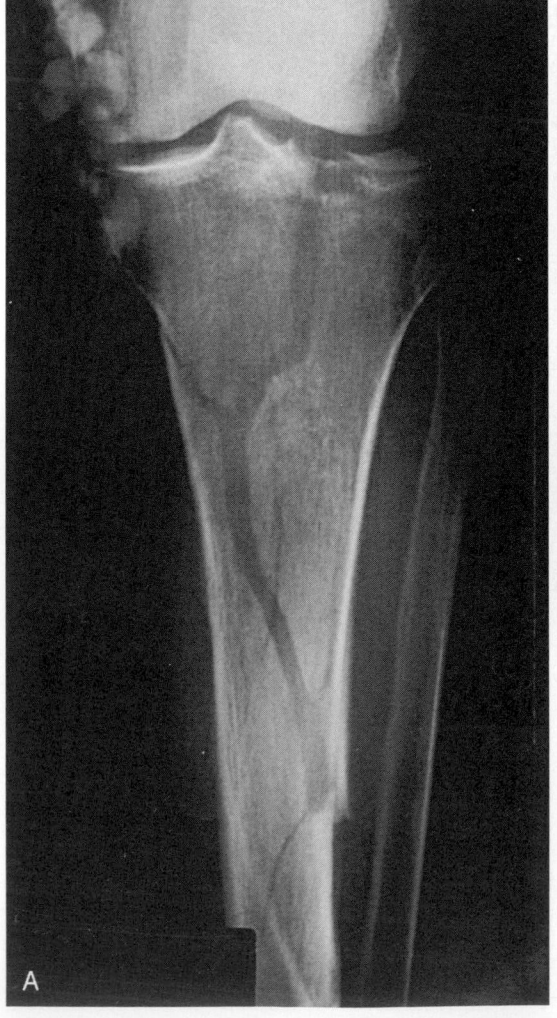

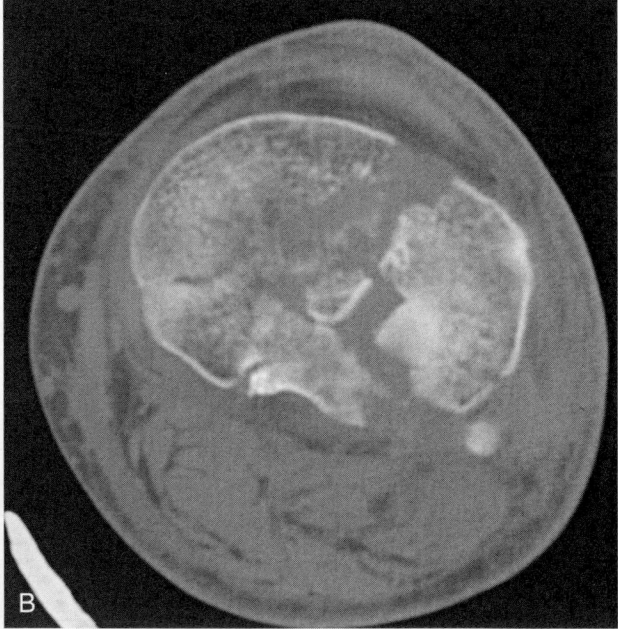

**FIGURE 56–18.** *A,* Schatzker type V injury. *B,* Computed tomographic scan reveals the cross-sectional anatomy of this complex articular injury.

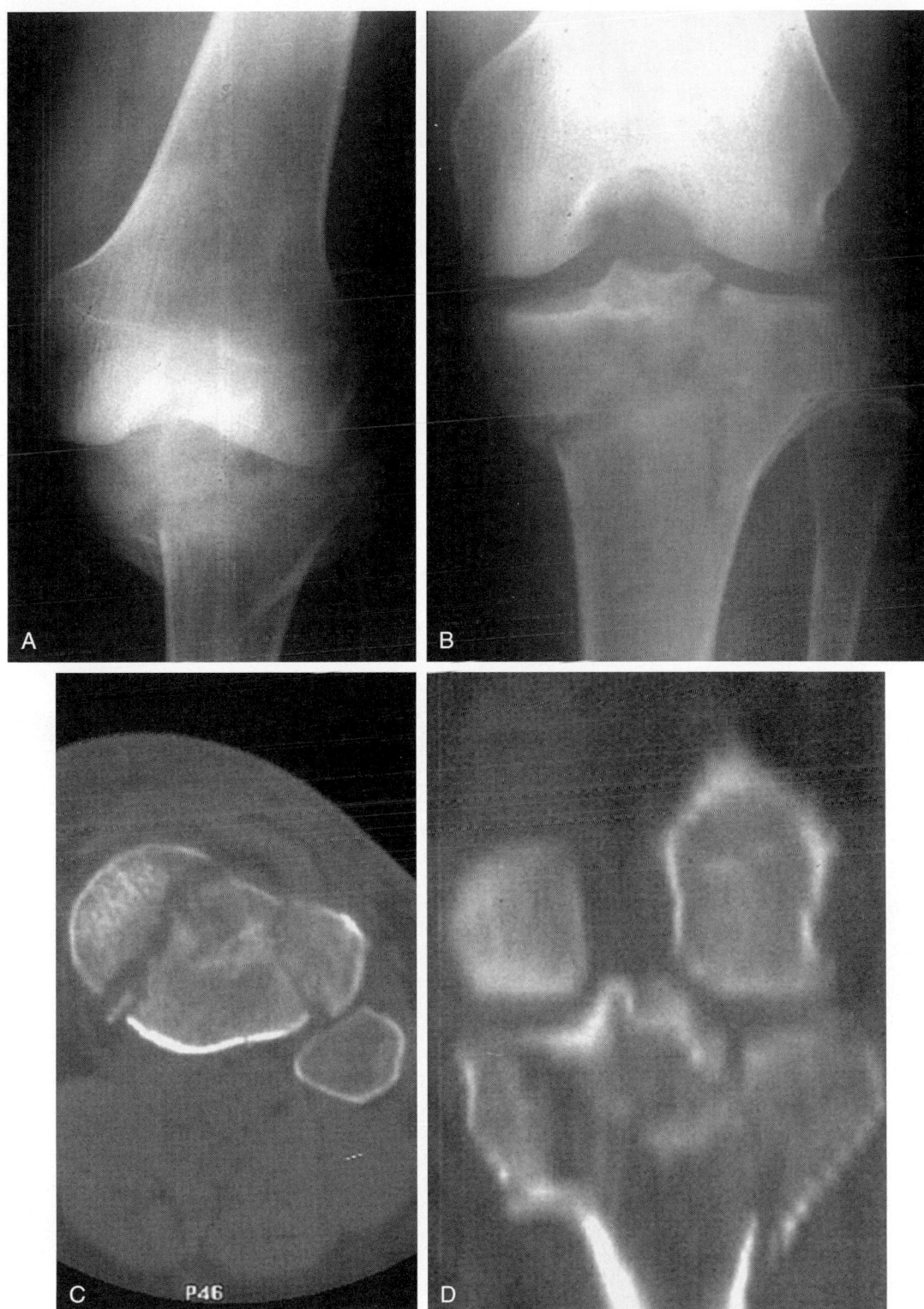

**FIGURE 56–19.** Injury film (*A*) and distraction film (*B*) documenting the excellent reduction achieved with an early ligamentotaxis force. *C, D,* Transverse and coronal computed tomographic studies performed in traction, showing near-anatomic reduction for preoperative planning purposes.

ous soft tissue envelope, combined with the use of multiple implants, led to complication rates as high as 50% in some studies.[111, 120, 133, 134, 146, 152, 160]

For these more complex injuries, contemporary surgical techniques have evolved to include concepts such as indirect reduction, antiglide fixation, and composite fixation, as advocated by Mast and colleagues.[102] Newer devices such as cannulated screws, monolateral external fixators, anatomic periarticular plates, and hybrid external fixation techniques based on circular Ilizarov-type fixators with tensioned small wires have been used in concert with limited surgical approaches (guided by CT scans and careful preoperative planning) to achieve excellent results with minimal surgical complications.[58, 84, 89, 98, 142, 154]

The concept of staged fixation has now gained favor. When the soft tissues are significantly compromised, immediate exposure for internal stable fixation is risky. Overall limb realignment and stabilization, important for soft tissue healing, can be achieved with an external fixator that initially spans the zone of injury. For tibial plateau fractures, these typically extend from the femoral shaft to the tibial shaft. If the plateau fracture is open, the wound may provide adequate access for anatomic reduction and secure fixation of the articular surface. However, further exposure for internal fixation may increase the risk of wound slough unacceptably, especially if done during the first days after injury. If the initial fracture is not open, it may be safest to delay the entire open reduction and fixation procedure until the soft tissue envelope has recovered enough to tolerate exposure adequate for articular reduction and the chosen means of fixation. During this period of soft tissue recovery, external fixation is available to splint the fracture and its surrounding soft tissues as well as maintain a general ligamentotaxis reduction of the major metaphyseal and diaphyseal fracture components (Fig. 56–20).[14, 23, 44, 45, 47, 149, 155] When the soft tissues have recovered sufficiently to allow a secondary procedure, delayed fixation can be accom-

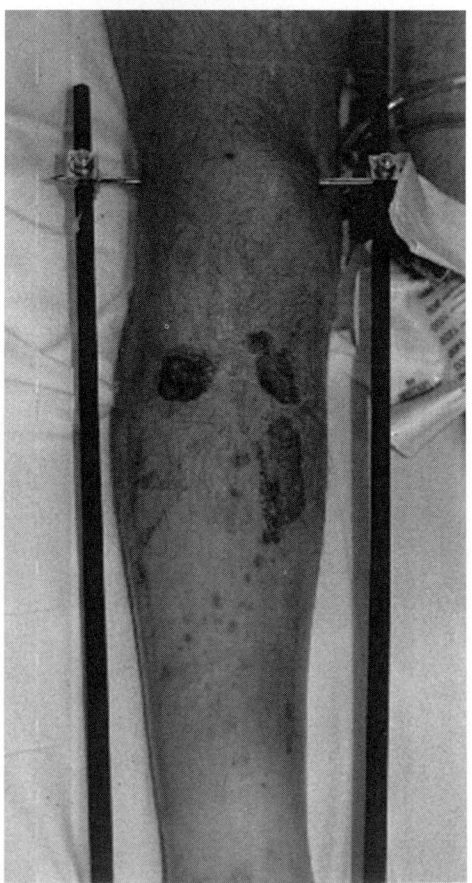

**Figure 56–20.** Temporary two-pin external fixator allowing temporary stabilization while the soft tissues recover prior to definitive stabilization.

plished through a safe operative corridor of healthy soft tissues.

## Indications for Treatment: Closed versus Open

The goals of treatment for any intra-articular fracture are to preserve joint mobility, joint stability, articular surface congruence, and axial alignment; to provide freedom from pain; and to prevent post-traumatic osteoarthritis.

Most investigators would agree that four primary factors can ultimately determine the prognosis of proximal plateau injuries: (1) the degree of articular depression, (2) the extent and separation of the condylar fracture lines, (3) the degree of diaphyseal-metaphyseal comminution and dissociation,[2, 25, 37, 68, 79, 93, 99, 111] and (4) the integrity of the soft tissue envelope.[25, 47, 148, 149] When considering operative treatment, all four of these factors must be evaluated to determine the best course of treatment.

A distinction should be made between the degree of osseous depression of the articular joint surface (i.e., true joint depression) and the translational or axial displacement of an entire fractured condyle, as may be seen with a severely displaced lateral condyle. This displacement may occur without any joint impaction or compression. Joint instability can result from articular depression, condylar displacement, or rupture of collateral and cruciate ligaments. There is no universal agreement on the amount of articular depression that can be accepted; ranges from 4 to 10 mm have been described as tolerable.* Long-term studies (>20 years' follow-up) have indicated a lack of correlation between residual osseous depression of the joint surface and the development of arthrosis.[69, 94, 124] However, joint deformity or depression that is significant enough to produce joint instability or dynamic alteration of the mechanical axis is predictive of a poor result.[78, 83, 94, 111, 134, 155] It is well accepted that a depressed portion of intra-articular surface cannot be reduced by traction alone; these surfaces must be surgically elevated and supported with bone graft.

Pauwels[118] demonstrated that if the degree of stress (force per unit area) that results from weight bearing exceeds the ability of articular cartilage to regenerate or repair itself, articular cartilage degeneration ensues, leading to post-traumatic osteoarthritis. Displacement of articular fragments results in a decrease of the available surface area of contact and therefore in increased stress, even in the presence of a normal load and normal direction of load application. There are, however, no accurate data on the amount (area) of articular displacement and depression that leads to degenerative joint disease.

Mechanical studies have indicated that statistically significant elevation of contact pressures occurs in a joint when the articular step-off or incongruence is greater than 3 mm.[20] An incongruence of less than 1.5 mm appears to result in no significant increase in contact pressures. Therefore, there may be some ability of the joint to compensate for a limited degree of joint depression.

*See references 3, 28, 37, 63, 67, 68, 93, 94, 111, 124, 135, 140, 143.

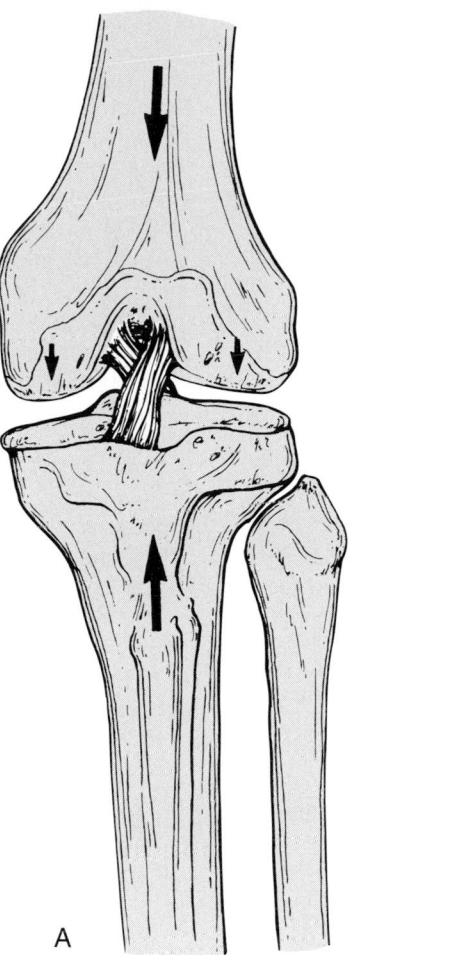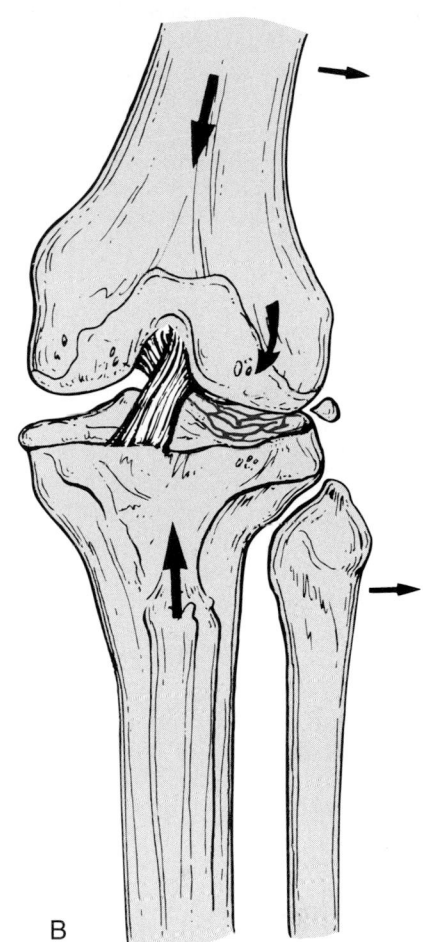

FIGURE 56–21. *A,* In a normal knee, the articular surfaces are congruous and, when weight bearing, the medial and lateral compartments share the load almost equally, with the medial taking slightly more than the lateral. *B,* When fractured and partially depressed, the articular surface becomes incongruous, and a smaller portion of the joint carries the full load. Pathologic loading can be further increased by axial malalignment.

A

B

However, if there is an associated axial malalignment (the result of joint depression or a metaphyseal fracture), the rise in stress is more significant (Fig. 56–21).

Mitchell and Shepard,[106] in their studies of the effects of articular malreduction and unstable fixation on the outcome of articular fractures, showed that accurate reduction and stable fixation of intra-articular fragments are necessary for articular cartilage regeneration and that malreduction and instability result in rapid articular cartilage degeneration. These findings not only support the need for an anatomic reduction of the joint but also emphasize the need for stable fixation to enhance articular cartilage regeneration.[131] Stable fixation also facilitates early motion by relieving pain, which is often the result of instability and motion at the fracture site.

A factor in the long-term prognosis for these injuries is the ability to maintain the normal relations of the femoral condyles on the plateau surfaces.[37, 94] It is crucial not to develop a contact pressure overload on either of the condyles. Rasmussen[124] showed a high correlation between post-traumatic osteoarthrosis and residual condylar widening or discontinuity between the tibial plateau surfaces and the femoral condyles. Lansinger and colleagues[94] later reviewed the same cohort of patients and found good to excellent results in 90% of the patients with stable knees at 20 years follow-up. The investigators concluded that knee stability rather than residual displace-ment was the main indication for surgery and a good long-term result. Thus, with certain high-energy fracture patterns, anatomic joint reconstruction may be impossible to achieve, but this does not necessarily preclude a reasonable functional outcome provided the metaphyseal and diaphyseal components that are still under the surgeon's control are maintained in such a way as to maintain the overall mechanical axis. This concept is the basis for a less invasive approach when treating some selected high-energy fracture patterns where the joint surface is severely traumatized or in cases in which the patient cannot undergo a significant surgical procedure.

Large fracture gaps may also contribute to knee instability resulting from a malreduced and longitudinally displaced condyle. Malalignment of the condyles in relation to the tibial shaft with subsequent shift of the mechanical axis is another prominent factor in the outcome for these patients. The radiographic appearance of osteoarthrosis and degenerative joint disease does not always correlate with the clinical picture[69]; however, Kettlekamp and co-workers[85] suggested that the maintenance of the correct mechanical axis at the knee is a major factor in determining the functional outcome and in the prevention of osteoarthrosis. Two factors, a decrease in joint surface area and a rise in stress resulting from the deformity and the increase in axial loading, may lead to post-traumatic osteoarthrosis. The likelihood of osteoarthrosis is greatly increased if these two factors are coupled with instability, which can result from either joint depression and incongruity or an associated ligament rupture.[39, 72, 109] See Chapter 62 for a discussion of mechanical axis.

We can conclude that in treating intra-articular fractures we must strive to achieve joint congruity and to maintain the maximal amount of surface area of contact. This goal can be achieved only by an anatomic reduction of the joint surface. We must also strive to prevent compartment overload by correcting any coexistent axial malalignment. In certain complex fractures, such as the Schatzker type VI injury, the zone of comminution at the diaphyseal-metaphyseal junction may hinder the surgeon's ability to reconstruct the appropriate mechanical axis.[8, 14, 154] Internal fixation must span this area, and additional bone grafts may be required. Such fractures typically have significant associated soft tissue injury, and internal fixation may not be safe to apply initially, as discussed previously.

Newer techniques for reconstructive procedures (i.e., fresh allograft plateau transplantation, resurfacing hemiarthroplasty, and total-knee replacement) all depend on correct maintenance of the mechanical axis. Because of this, the initial fracture treatment[135] should restore and maintain alignment so as not to compromise secondary reconstruction.

Schatzker and McBroom's review[135] of tibial plateau fractures has allowed the formulation of additional principles of treatment. Treatment of tibial plateau fractures nonoperatively in a plaster cast for 1 month or longer produced marked stiffness of the knee. Patients with similar fractures treated with ORIF, followed by postoperative plaster immobilization, experienced much greater stiffness of the involved knee.[51] We conclude that intra-articular fractures, regardless of treatment, must be mobilized early. However, only open reduction and stable fixation permit early motion without loss of articular fragment reduction and consequent malunion or nonunion. Therefore, if surgery is inadvisable or not possible, the joint with an intra-articular fracture should be treated with skeletal traction and early motion to preserve mobility, even if such treatment may result in joint incongruity or instability.[64, 101, 138] As long as joint mobility is preserved, secondary reconstructive joint salvage procedures such as intra-articular osteotomies are possible. These procedures are usually much less successful in the presence of joint stiffness.

Fractures that were initially treated nonoperatively (i.e., by manipulation and traction) often showed persistent displacement of some articular fragments. If these fractures were then operated on early, the unreduced fragments were always found to be impacted in the metaphysis and required considerable force to be disimpacted and reduced. Therefore, any displaced articular fragments that are not reduced after suitable closed manipulation and traction can be considered impacted. Their reduction can be achieved only by open means. Furthermore, joint depression and articular defects resulting from impacted articular fragments remain as permanent joint defects. These defects, when examined at the time of late articular reconstructions, have never been found to be filled with

fibrocartilage, which would have restored stability. Therefore, any joint that is unstable as a result of joint depression or displacement remains unstable unless the depression or displacement is corrected surgically. Articular reduction is best done in the acute setting. Late intra-articular osteotomy is a complex procedure with many potential complications, especially when performed in the presence of significant joint stiffness.

From these observations, we have formulated the following principles of treatment of tibial plateau fractures:

1. Any tibial plateau fracture that results in joint instability requires ORIF.
2. Maximal joint congruity can be restored only by open reduction.
3. Stable fixation of articular fragments and anatomic reduction are necessary for articular cartilage regeneration.
4. If an open reduction is indicated but is inadvisable because of patient-related or injury factors or because the complexity of the injury exceeds the ability of the treating team, the fracture must be treated with skeletal traction and early motion. Alternatively, if formal fixation is contraindicated, early fixation of the articular portion of the injury is recommended if possible. Once injury factors have been resolved, delayed metaphyseal reconstruction is possible.

These principles of treatment are general. When treating a particular patient, the surgeon must be governed not only by joint congruity, joint stability, and axial alignment but also by what we call the personality of the fracture, which is a synthesis of patient-related factors, injury factors, ability of the treating team, and suitability of the hospital environment, as discussed in the next section.

The absolute indications for surgery are (1) an open tibial plateau fracture and (2) a tibial plateau fracture combined with an acute compartment syndrome or an acute vascular lesion. The relative indications include (1) most displaced bicondylar fractures, (2) displaced medial condylar fractures, (3) lateral plateau fractures that result in joint instability, and (4) plateau fractures in the context of a multiply injured patient.[5, 15, 29, 45, 89] The biggest contraindication to immediate formal ORIF is a compromised soft tissue envelope with either an open or a closed fracture.

## Personality of the Injury

If the fracture is displaced and unstable, joint congruity, axial alignment, and stability are most likely restorable only by ORIF or external fixation. Whether such a course is to be pursued has to be worked out carefully, however. The decision is best made by defining the personality of the injury. This concept includes, first, the patient-related factors: age, history of past health, concurrent health problems, occupation and leisure activities, and expectations of treatment results. For example, the goals of treatment are quite different for an osteoporotic octogenarian than for a healthy young athlete.

Second are the injury factors. Here the surgeon must define carefully the injury to the soft tissue envelope, taking into consideration the location of the fracture and the condition of the skin in and around the proposed surgical exposure if surgery is contemplated. The open or closed nature of the fracture, the associated soft tissue and bone injuries, and the possibility of a concomitant neurologic or vascular deficit or an acute compartment syndrome must be determined. Next, the characteristics of the fracture itself must be defined with great care in order to classify it. Information regarding the depth of articular impaction, degree of condylar displacement, and amount of fracture line extension from the metaphysis into the diaphyseal region must be obtained from the plain radiographs, traction radiographs, and traction CT scans. The degree of osteoporosis must be determined because the quality of bone is of paramount importance in judging the operability of the fracture. With this insight, the surgeon is able to formulate a preoperative surgical plan that helps define the surgical tactic and outlines the expected difficulties of treatment. Ultimately, the same information suggests the patient's prognosis.

Third, in defining the personality of the injury, the surgeon must evaluate the treatment team and the treatment environment. For many complex tibial plateau fractures, the surgical treatment is difficult and complex. Such injuries are best managed by persons experienced in the management of complex intra-articular injuries. This area may be the most difficult to assess, for it forces the surgeon to evaluate objectively his or her own skills and those of the surgical assistants as well as the adequacy of the treatment environment. For complex injuries, complete sets of large and small plates and screws including anatomic periarticular plates, large articular reduction forceps, femoral distractors, and in some circumstances various external fixation devices should be available. In addition, the treatment team should include skilled nursing and physiotherapy staff with experience in the treatment of these patients.

## Nonoperative Treatment

Nonoperative treatment is indicated for many tibial plateau fractures. Fractures that occur after a low-energy injury are usually incomplete or nondisplaced. Other injuries that may be treated successfully in a nonoperative fashion include a displaced lateral plateau fracture without articular instability and some unstable lateral plateau fractures in osteoporotic patients. Another relative indication for nonoperative treatment is the presence of significant cardiovascular, pulmonary, neurologic, or metabolic compromise (e.g., severe diabetes with occlusive vascular disease or significant venous stasis ulceration). Nonoperative treatment of these injuries does require early motion and subsequent prevention of displacement.[3, 51] In most instances, fracture displacement is prevented by instituting controlled motion with the knee placed in a hinged knee fracture brace.[35, 37, 38, 43, 51, 61, 138] Weight bearing is also prohibited. Depending on fracture stability, the knee may be locked in full extension for 1 to 2 weeks, after which the hinges are adjusted to begin a gradual increase in range of motion. Frequent clinical and radiographic follow-up is required early in the course of treatment to guard against unrecognized loss of metaphyseal reduction. The goal is to achieve at least 90 degrees of flexion by 4 weeks after injury. Unlimited motion may be encouraged from the outset for stable fractures. Weight bearing is delayed until there is radiographic appearance of early fracture line consolidation. Usually, by 6 to 8 weeks the patient has progressed to 50% partial weight bearing and by 12 weeks the patient is allowed to ambulate with full weight bearing. For partially or totally displaced condylar fractures for which nonoperative treatment is being considered, the stability of the knee should be determined.

A fracture is considered stable if it does not exhibit, on varus or valgus stressing, any more than 10 degrees of instability at any point in the arc of motion, from full extension to 90 degrees of flexion. The degree of instability that one is prepared to accept within this range must also be viewed in terms of the personality of the injury. In evaluating a partial articular fracture for stability, it must be remembered that a peripheral wedge fragment, if it involves the posterior part of the plateau, does not contribute to instability in the frontal plane, and the joint may appear to be perfectly stable on varus and valgus stressing. However, the fragment does create instability in the sagittal plane and is an absolute indication for surgical reduction and stabilization. Because small degrees of malalignment and instability may have adverse long-term effects on the knee joint, no more than 10 degrees of instability in the frontal plane should be accepted. If more than 10 degrees of instability is noted on stressing, the fracture is deemed unstable[37] (Fig. 56–22).

If the fracture is unstable but is not suited for ORIF because of excessive comminution, advanced osteoporosis, or other patient-related factors or if it is decided that the fracture should be treated openly but the treatment must be delayed, the patient must be treated with skeletal traction and early motion. When skeletal traction is employed for comminuted or unstable fractures, a distal supramalleolar tibial pin should be inserted. Ten to 15 pounds of traction usually reduces the condylar fragments by ligamentotaxis. As stated previously, however, impacted articular fragments are not reduced with manipulation or traction alone because there are no soft tissue attachments with which to pull them upward. If skeletal traction has been employed, a Thomas splint and Pierson knee attachment can often be used to initiate early active knee flexion.[42, 64, 101, 138] A radiograph should be obtained with the leg out of traction at 4 to 6 weeks after injury to see whether there is any subsequent displacement. If the fracture shows early signs of union or reveals no further displacement, the traction pin can be removed and a fracture brace or hinged knee brace should be placed at this time. With this method of treatment, the patient should remain strictly without weight bearing for at least 12 weeks, after which progressive weight bearing is allowed as healing is determined radiographically.

A compromise between traction management and a full surgical approach to these injuries is to utilize simple external fixation treatment[80] (Fig. 56–23). This treatment involves the application of a simple "traveling traction" external frame that is stable enough to maintain a traction ligamentotaxis reduction force across the knee. It enables

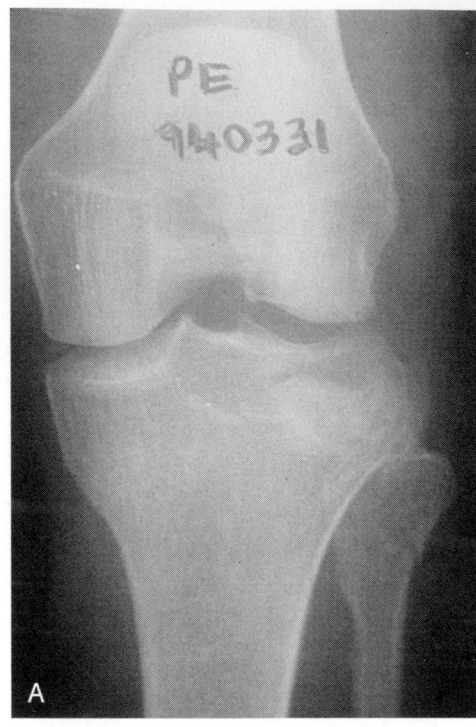 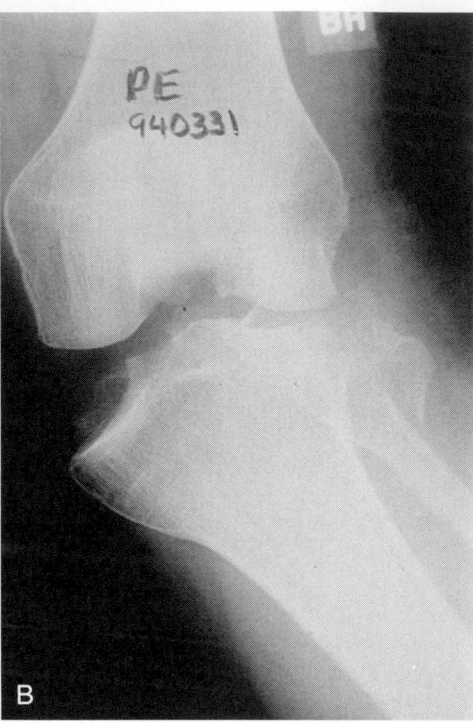

FIGURE 56–22. The decision to operate or to proceed with nonoperative management is sometimes aided by the use of stress radiographs. Instability with greater than 7 to 10 degrees of motion in the coronal plane is usually managed with surgery. A, Anteroposterior (AP) radiograph of a lateral tibial plateau fracture. B, AP stress radiograph of same knee.

the patient to be treated in a more ambulatory fashion and avoids the prolonged bedrest, hospital stay, and complications associated with traditional skeletal traction, noted by Moore and colleagues[111] to be as high as 8%.

These frames are augmented with a simple posterior mold applied from foot to midthigh. As long as the external pins are in good condition, the frames are maintained for 6 to 8 weeks until the metaphyseal and diaphyseal components of the injury show evidence of consolidation. These frames can then be removed, the limb placed in a hinged knee brace, and rehabilitation initiated. This treatment may still require a brief anesthetic to apply the simple knee-spanning external fixator and thus may be contraindicated for the infirm patient.

Many investigators have identified the most common fracture pattern in the elderly population as the split depression (Schatzker type II). In general, these and other low-energy fracture patterns maintain their overall reduction[13, 19, 38, 80, 101, 111, 138] when treated with a short period of traction followed by fracture brace application. The

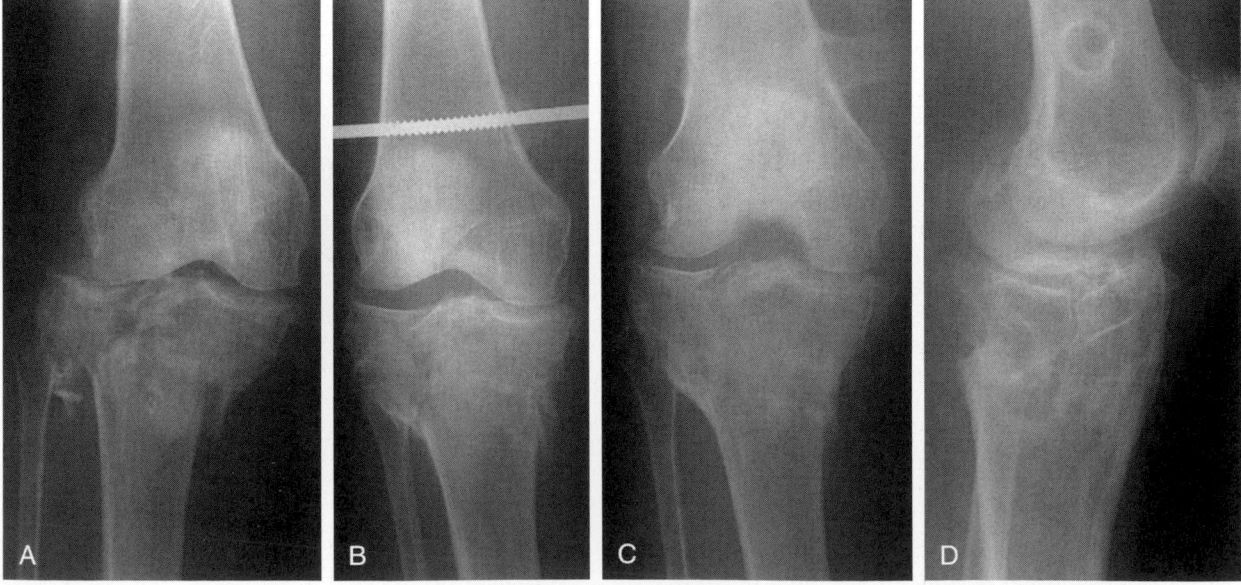

FIGURE 56–23. A, Injury film demonstrating a bicondylar fracture in an elderly patient with significant medical problems that prohibit extensive surgical management. B, Two-pin fixator demonstrating reasonable reduction with a minimally invasive procedure. C, D, Fixation time was approximately 10 weeks, with maintenance of alignment and healing of the bicondylar fracture.

fracture patterns that have been shown to lose their reduction when treated in a conservative fashion include fractures with a medial condylar component and those with diaphyseal dissociation.[38]

The results of the treatment of tibial plateau fractures in the elderly population in general are mediocre regardless of the methodology used. Many studies demonstrate little correlation between the final radiographic reduction and overall clinical function. However, the later conversion to total knee arthroplasty treatment is low regardless of whether the patient had surgical intervention or conservative management. This observation may demonstrate more about the elderly population as a treatment group than about the advisability of either type of management for these injuries.[13, 96, 111, 137]

## Surgical Treatment

### TIMING OF SURGERY

All authors agree that an open fracture should be operated on immediately, as should a fracture associated with an acute compartment syndrome or arterial occlusion. All other tibial plateau fractures should be evaluated individually. Fractures that occur in conjunction with multiple injuries as a result of blunt trauma should be stabilized as soon as the patient's overall condition permits. In polytrauma patients[148, 154] and in those with soft tissue compromise, reduction of the joint is advocated as soon as possible. The reduction may be done through percutaneous or limited incision approaches. In this fashion, the articular surface is reduced within the acute period. This approach is combined with temporary spanning external fixation across the joint, which allows mobilization of the polytrauma patient. This tactic is also useful for patients who are critically ill or who have severe soft tissue compromise that precludes a complex operative approach. External fixation or traction provides better initial restoration of length and alignment and gives better access to the soft tissues for wound care or further compartment monitoring.

The isolated complex tibial plateau fracture is not a life-threatening injury, and adequate time should be taken to evaluate the lesion thoroughly. The evaluation often involves additional radiographic as well as CT or MRI scans. The timing of surgery for these injuries depends primarily on the soft tissue conditions. If the condition of the patient allows and the fracture is well defined, it is best to deal with it immediately; however, a complex fracture may require 3 to 4 hours of surgery, and a delay of 24 to 48 hours does not compromise the treatment. Another consideration is the patient for whom delay is indicated because of severe swelling or contusion of the soft tissues. With high-energy plateau fractures, there is often rapid massive limb swelling secondary to fracture hematoma and delayed soft tissue necrosis.

For patients who have sustained a typical bumper injury, the contusion to the anterior proximal tibia often compromises the pretibial soft tissues. Sometimes the soft tissues have undergone a closed degloving-type injury that may not be apparent for several days.[148] If a delay of more than 1 or 2 days is necessary, the leg should be immobilized in plaster or in another type of splint. This type of immobilization is useful only for the low-energy fracture types (Schatzker I, II, and III) and injuries involving slight displacement. It does not prevent shortening and collapse of the fracture and therefore makes subsequent reduction much more difficult. For those more complex, high-energy fractures, it is best to place the leg in skeletal traction or external fixation, as previously described, until the soft tissues have recovered and the operative procedure can be safely carried out.

### PREOPERATIVE PLANNING

The surgical procedure must be planned carefully, especially for high-energy fractures (Schatzker IV, V, and VI).[154, 156, 157] The planning involves consideration of the surgical approach, which must be atraumatic and must expose all the component parts of the injury without sacrificing any important structures. Often, traction radiographs help determine the surgical tactic by indicating which fragments may be reduced by a ligamentotaxis approach, thereby helping to limit the overall extent of the incision. In addition, they identify the components of the fracture that cannot be reduced by ligamentotaxis alone and therefore require a direct operative "hands on" approach. It is helpful to obtain radiographs of the opposite knee, which can serve as a template.

It is possible through the use of preoperative drawings to make a detailed plan of all the steps in the surgical tactic. Surgery is performed on paper before being carried out in the operating room. The plan must include an indication of the exact position of every screw and its function as well as the position and length of each plate. Multiple surgical tactics are often necessary to arrive at the optimal fixation construct involving the least amount of soft tissue dissection. In addition to preparing the surgeon to execute the surgical tactic properly, such planning ensures the availability of supplemental bone grafts, special implants, and ancillary personnel such as radiography and fluoroscopy technicians.

### POSITIONING OF THE PATIENT

The patient is placed supine on a radiolucent operating table. The table should provide the capability to flex the knee to 90 degrees. Alternatively, a large sterile bolster or a beanbag positioner can be used to elevate the operative extremity so that it can be flexed to 90 degrees intraoperatively. Knee flexion allows the iliotibial band to slip posteriorly off the lateral condyle of the femur, which permits the surgeon to make an incision in the capsule at its attachment to the upper tibia without having to cut through the iliotibial band.

The ability of the knee to flex not only facilitates exposure but also greatly aids visualization of the joint. The table should be tilted slightly into the Trendelenburg position so that the patient does not slide forward. The dependent position of the leg applies traction through its weight and frees an assistant from holding the leg; it allows the surgeon to apply a varus or valgus force simply by pushing on the foot in the desired direction. The

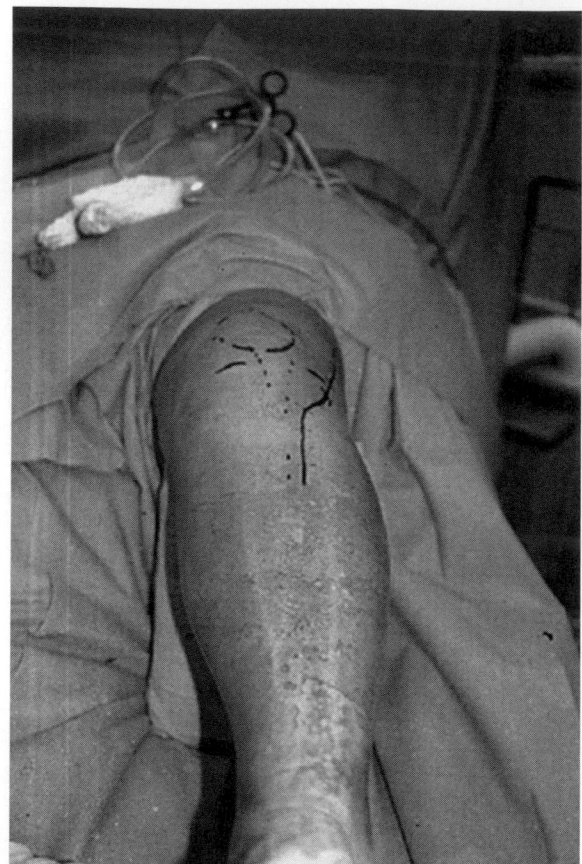

**FIGURE 56–24.** Surgical positioning of the limb should be able to accommodate flexion of the joint. The end of the table can be lowered or sterile bumps used to achieve this positioning.

dependent position of the leg also applies a distraction force and helps the surgeon visualize the intra-articular nature of the fracture component (Fig. 56–24).

If desired, a **C**-arm fluoroscope should be available to be brought in from the opposite side of the operating table. Before preparation and draping of the patient, trial images should be obtained to ensure that accurate AP and lateral fluoroscopic images are easily visualized, including a true AP view of the patella centered in the midportion of the joint. This orientation is useful to note fluoroscopically when utilizing percutaneous techniques, especially those that have been determined by CT preoperative planning. Fluoroscopic visualization from femoral head to ankle allows assessment of the mechanical axis, using an electrocautery cord held tightly between these points. Normally, with the patella centered, this line lies 1 to 15 mm medial to the joint center.

The entire extremity is then prepared and draped. If an iliac crest bone graft is to be used, the ipsilateral crest is also included in the initial preparation, and a sterile tourniquet is used.

## SURGICAL APPROACHES

We recommend either a straight midline incision or a medial or lateral parapatellar incision, depending on the location of the primary condylar fracture line[135, 143] (Fig.

56–25). The lazy-**S** incision, the **L**-shaped incision, and the "Mercedes star" incision are contraindicated. For many of the complex, high-energy fracture patterns, straight longitudinal incisions are best because they interfere least with the blood supply to the skin flaps and do not interfere with any future reconstructive procedures. The skin incisions should be planned in such a way that they are not positioned directly over an implant. The flaps that are raised must be full thickness, consisting of the subcutaneous fat down to the fascia. Using full-thickness flaps is important to prevent wound edge necrosis. In addition, prolonged forceful retraction and direct grasping of the wound edges with heavy forceps should be avoided.

The meniscus must be preserved and should never be excised to facilitate exposure. Submeniscal arthrotomy should be performed to gain visualization of the articular component of the fracture.[55, 120] The capsule (i.e., meniscotibial) ligament should be incised horizontally below the meniscus, whether the approach is from the lateral or the medial side of the joint (Fig. 56–26). The horizontal

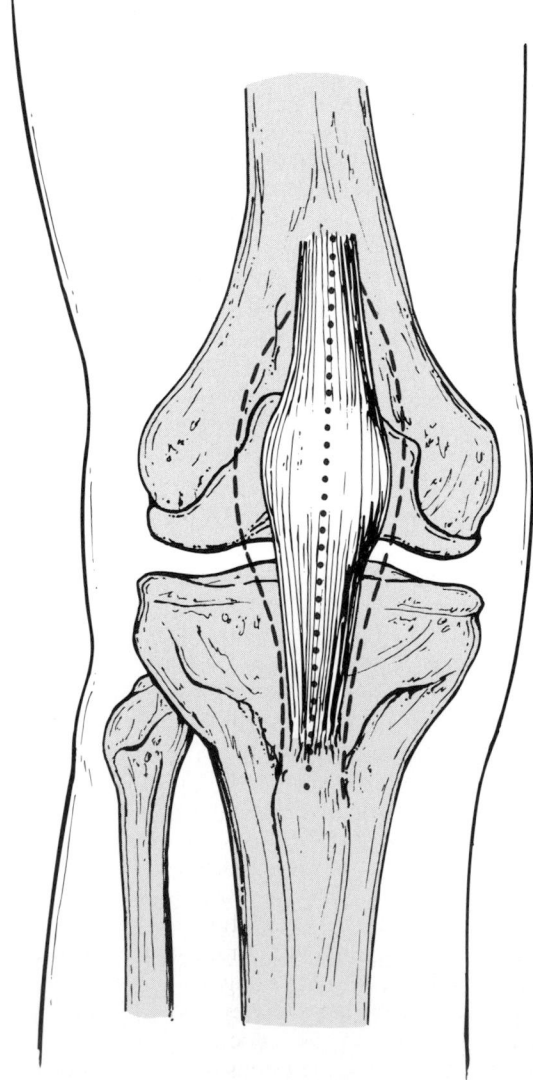

**FIGURE 56–25.** The incision should be straight, and an increase in exposure is gained by extension of the incision proximally and distally.

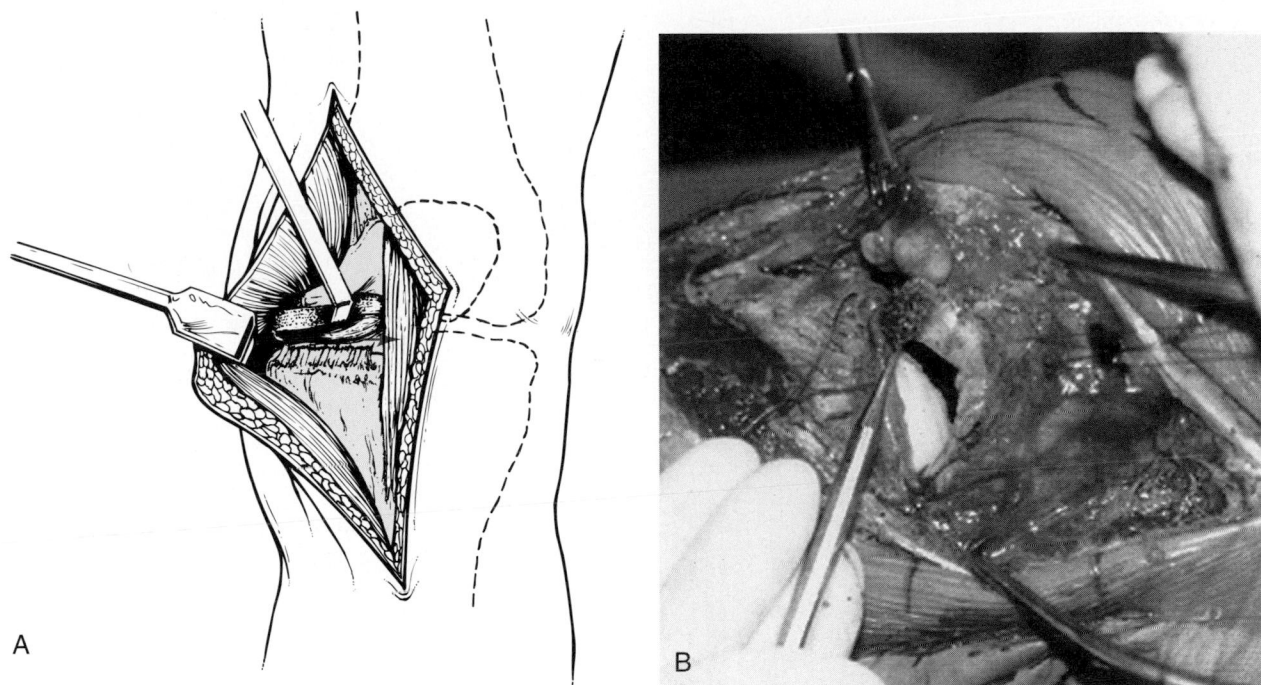

**FIGURE 56–26.** *A*, The arthrotomy should be made by incising the capsule transversely below the meniscus. *B*, The meniscal tibial ligament has been incised (probe) with retraction of the capsule to reveal the articular surfaces.

incision allows the surgeon to pull up on the meniscus and the attached capsule with a heavy suture or small rake retractor to gain an unobstructed view of the articular surface. Alternatively, if a peripheral lateral meniscal tear is encountered during the exposure, the anterior horn of the lateral meniscus can be divided at the transverse ligament, leaving a stump for repair. The meniscus is then elevated with its meniscotibial ligament in a subperiosteal fashion and retracted laterally. In this way, the meniscus can be elevated all the way to the popliteus recess to give excellent visualization of the entire lateral plateau.[116] At closure, the meniscal tibial ligament is then repaired as is the anterior horn, if complete retraction is required. If there is a tear into the body of the meniscus, it should also be repaired at the end of the procedure. The advent of modern bone anchors has facilitated the reattachment of the meniscotibial ligament to the tibial surface.

With all transmeniscal or submeniscal approaches, every effort should be made to repair and preserve the meniscus.[153] The meniscus shares in load transmission and distributes the body weight over a broad surface area. This cushioning effect protects the damaged and repaired articular cartilage, prevents redisplacement of the elevated articular fragments, and enhances cartilage healing.

To gain exposure of the depressed articular fragments, the surgeon should make use of the fracture. For example, if there is a peripheral wedge fragment, regardless of its size, it should be hinged back on its soft tissue attachment like the cover of a book.[120] Hinging it back allows perfect visualization of the joint depression, and the soft tissue attachment preserves the blood supply to the wedge fragment. However, some extension or enlargement of the initial surgical exposure may be required, which may not be advantageous in injuries with significant soft tissue

compromise. Alternatively, this area can be manipulated with the use of K-wires and the large wedge fragment tentatively held reduced by percutaneous reduction forceps. The depressed area can be approached from below through a window made in the cortex of the respective tibial condyle. The articular surface can then be elevated and visualized indirectly through the peripheral detachment of the meniscus, using the standard submeniscal articular exposure. This approach avoids excessive soft tissue stripping, which may be produced if one tries to wedge the fracture open like a book.

The surgeon should also be aware of the posterior split or wedge fracture, which may occur medially or laterally with any fracture pattern, although it is most commonly associated with a Schatzker type IV fracture of the medial tibial plateau (Fig. 56–27). Such a posterior wedge cannot be adequately exposed or reduced and fixed from the front; it must be approached directly through a posteromedial or posterolateral direction.

For a few selected posterior fractures, a direct posterior approach may be necessary, especially if the apex of the fragment is directly posterior on the shaft. This approach is accomplished with the patient in a prone position. An **S**- or **L**-shaped incision is directed across the popliteal fossa and extended down the posterior-medial aspect of the tibial shaft. The medial head of the gastrocnemius tendon is identified and may be either retracted laterally or partially divided close to its attachment to bone in the tendinous region. The medial head of the muscle is then retracted laterally after incision of the fascia, and the entire posterior aspect of the proximal tibia can be visualized and is available for fixation. This approach does *not* specifically expose the neurovascular bundle as it is retracted laterally along with the gastrocnemius musculature. By incising the

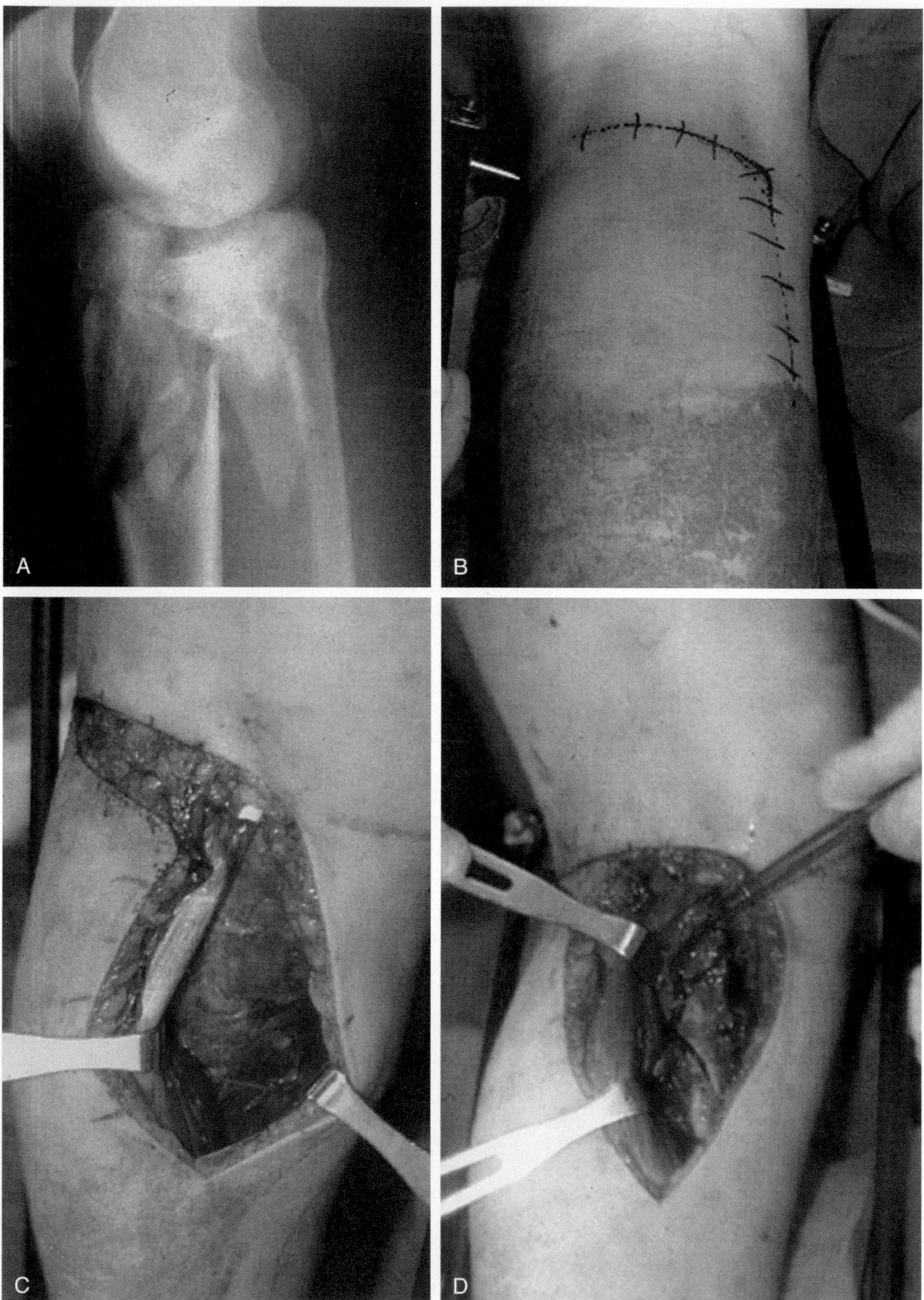

**FIGURE 56–27.** *A,* Injury film showing extensive coronal plane fracture lines with posterior displacement, which can be stabilized only through a direct posterior approach. *B,* Direct posterior incision directed at the popliteal crease and extended medially. *C,* The medial gastrocnemius is identified and medial fascia incised and retracted laterally to expose the entire posterior aspect of the joint if necessary (*D*).

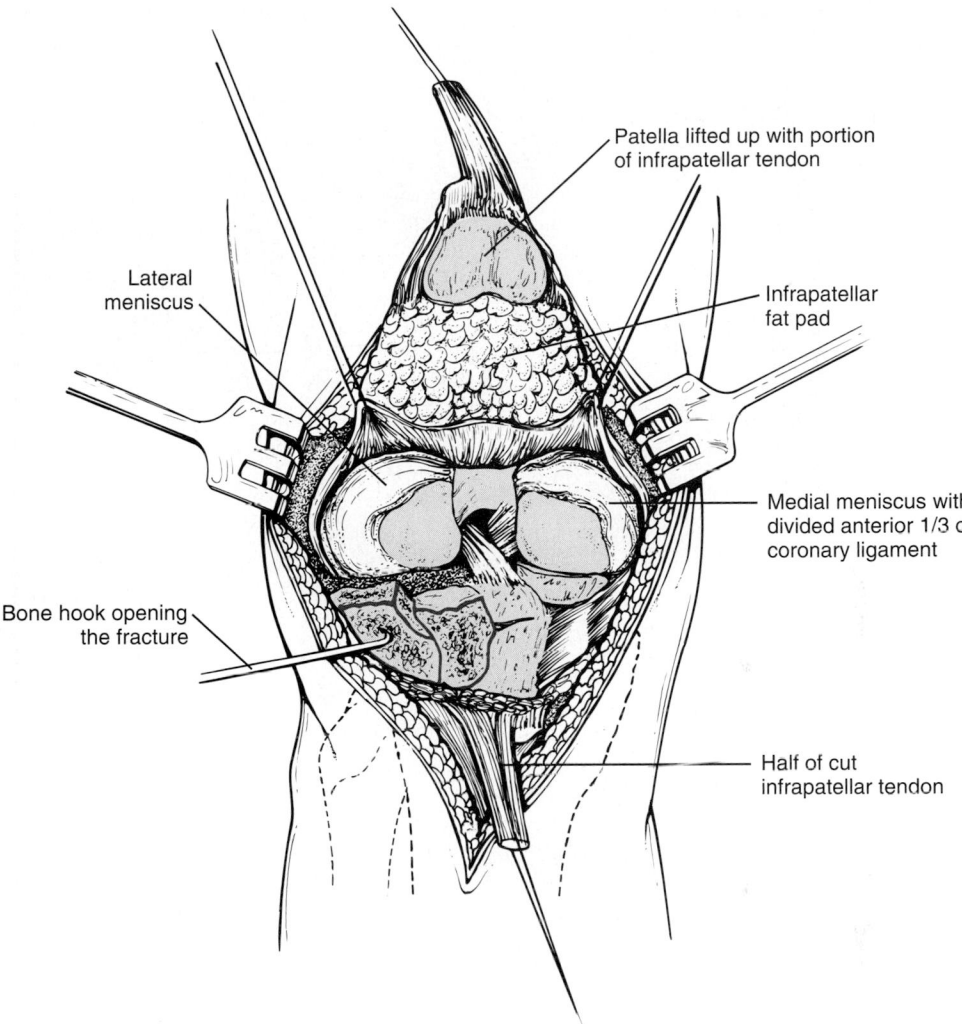

Patella lifted up with portion
of infrapatellar tendon

Lateral
meniscus

Infrapatellar
fat pad

Medial meniscus with
divided anterior 1/3 of
coronary ligament

Bone hook opening
the fracture

Half of cut
infrapatellar tendon

FIGURE 56–28. The best exposure of the depressed fragments is gained by opening the fracture. The lateral wedge is pulled to the side, much like opening the cover of a book. To achieve exposure of bilateral tibial plateau fracture lines, it is best to divide the infrapatellar tendon in a Z fashion and divide across the medial and lateral capsule below the menisci. The capsule, the attached menisci, and the patella are then lifted up to give unlimited exposure of the entire proximal tibia. Osteotomy of the tibial tubercle could enter the main fracture lines and make subsequent fixation difficult. (Redrawn from Schatzker, J.; Tile, M. Rationale of Fracture Management Care. New York, Springer-Verlag, 1987, p. 289.)

posterior capsule in a horizontal fashion, the articular surface of the posterior tibial plateau can be visualized[24, 36, 147] (see Fig. 56–27).

Occasionally, with very severe fractures that involve both tibial plateaus, it is necessary to gain simultaneous or bicondylar exposure. This can be accomplished only after the entire quadriceps mechanism has been reflected upward so that both sides of the joint are simultaneously exposed.[47] This type of exposure should not be combined with an osteotomy of the tibial tubercle. In these severe fractures, the tibial tubercle and adjacent bone may be the only intact anterior cortex. If the tubercle is osteotomized, reduction of highly comminuted fractures may be made more difficult because of greater fracture instability. It may be impossible to reattach the tubercle, particularly if the posterior cortex is also comminuted. If the posterior cortex is also fractured, the tibial tubercle and anterior cortex may be the only available bone in which to anchor fixation hardware directed from anterior to posterior. Exposure with a tubercle osteotomy has inherent dangers in that if the wound should break down over this area, the osteotomized tubercle could easily become an infected sequestrum because its only blood supply would be through the tendon. When an extensile exposure is

necessary, we advocate cutting the infrapatellar tendon in a Z-type fashion[134, 135] (Fig. 56–28). This facilitates reflection of the entire quadriceps mechanism proximally. Great care must be taken at this point not to devitalize the fracture fragments further by performing additional subperiosteal exposure both laterally and medially. The fracture line should be identified by gentle extraperiosteal exposure only or by indirect reduction and visualization through the use of distraction and fluoroscopic imaging techniques.

After completion of the surgical procedure, the cut tendon is resutured together with the incised capsule and the quadriceps retinaculum. The repair is then protected with a figure-of-eight tension band wire (1.0 or 1.2 mm), cable, or heavy suture. The surgeon must make sure not to overtighten the tension band, or patella baja may result. The tension band's only function is to protect the tendon repair. The patient should be told that such a wire usually breaks at about the third month after surgery.

In some instances, with acute fractures, the tibial tubercle is fractured as a separate fragment in conjunction with posterior cortical comminution. The fixation of this tubercle fragment is then accomplished with an anterior hook plate (Fig. 56–29). This allows rigid fixation of the

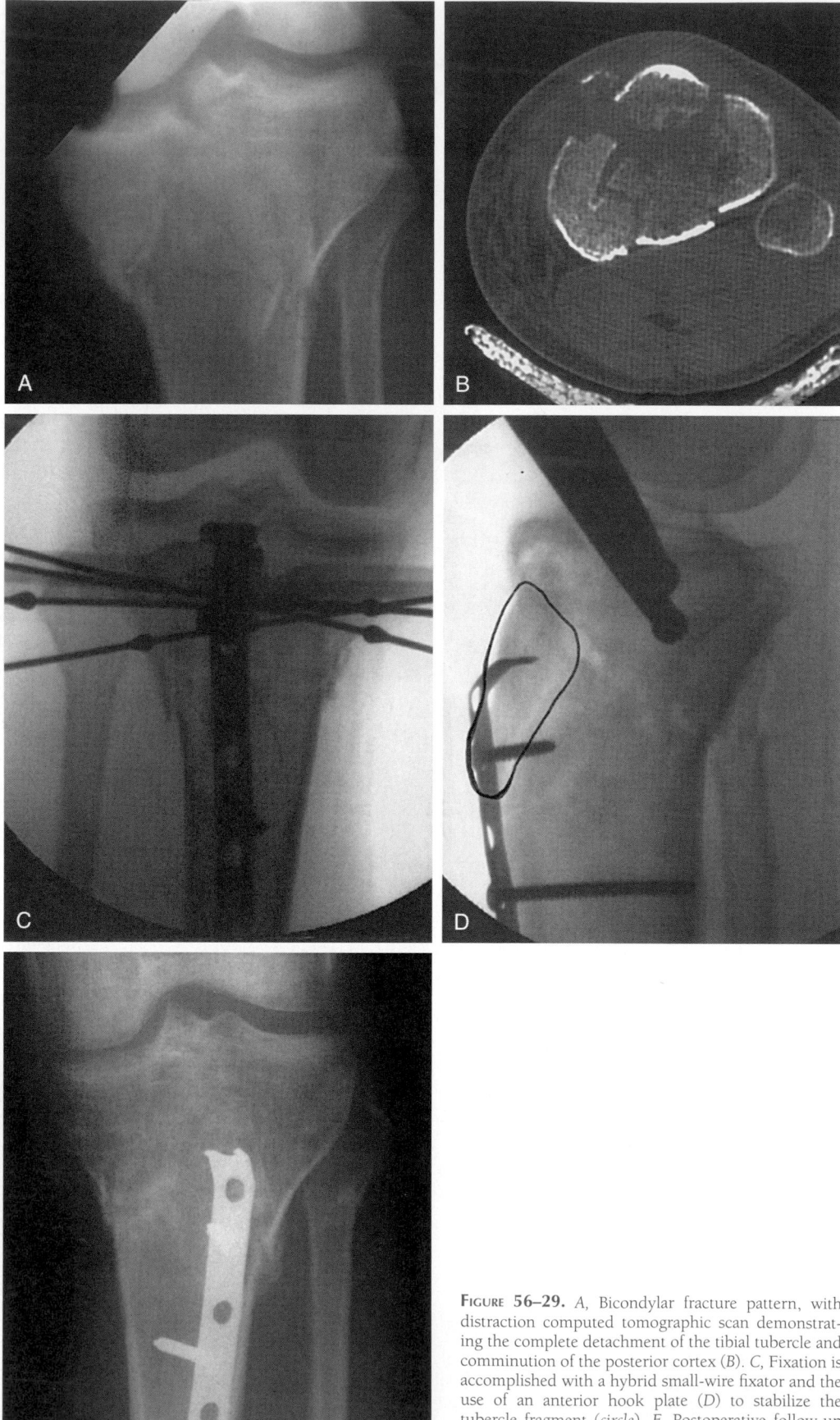

**Figure 56–29.** *A,* Bicondylar fracture pattern, with distraction computed tomographic scan demonstrating the complete detachment of the tibial tubercle and comminution of the posterior cortex (*B*). *C,* Fixation is accomplished with a hybrid small-wire fixator and the use of an anterior hook plate (*D*) to stabilize the tubercle fragment (*circle*). *E,* Postoperative follow-up demonstrates a healed fracture with intact tubercle fragment, allowing active rehabilitation without displacement of the patellar tendon.

tubercle fragment with distally directed screws that are able to purchase intact posterior cortex at a site distal to the tubercle fragment.[155]

For the high-energy type IV, V, and VI fractures, damage to the surrounding soft tissue envelope is often severe even in closed fractures. The extensive surgical exposure required for application of bilateral buttress plates to such a displaced bicondylar fracture pattern may provoke a wound slough and secondary infection. In these types of situations, newer surgical techniques have been developed in an effort to avoid complete exposure of both condyles by use of percutaneous lag screws or external fixators opposite a plate to buttress the less unstable plateau.

When dealing with a severe fracture pattern involving both plateaus, reconstruction should always begin with evaluation of the simpler condyle fracture, usually the medial one.

In the more complex fracture pattern, it is advantageous to rely on indirect reduction techniques to realign the leg and bring about partial reduction of the injury. This is best done by bridging the flexed knee with one or two femoral distractors applied on each side of the knee (Fig. 56–30). As traction is applied through the distractors, ligamentotaxis is able to reduce a considerable portion of the fracture.[102] Final adjustments to reduction can be done through a limited midline incision without further devitalization of the fracture fragments. This indirect technique aids not only in achieving reduction in difficult situations but also in achieving rapid union because it facilitates preservation of the blood supply to the bone fragments.

Alternatively, for bicondylar fractures with minor soft tissue compromise, in some instances a second incision can safely be undertaken. Because most bicondylar plateau fractures involve primarily the lateral plateau, a straight lateral parapatellar incision is first used. This incision can be extended proximally and distally if a more extensive exposure is needed. After reduction of the lateral plateau, a medial or posteromedial approach as described by

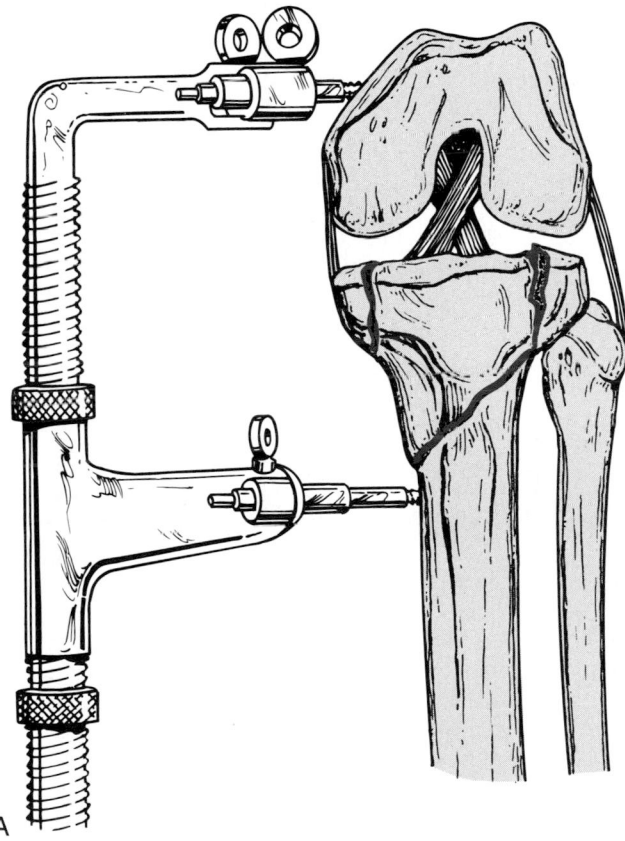
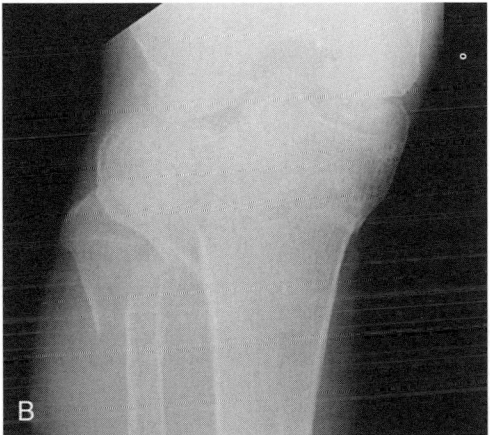
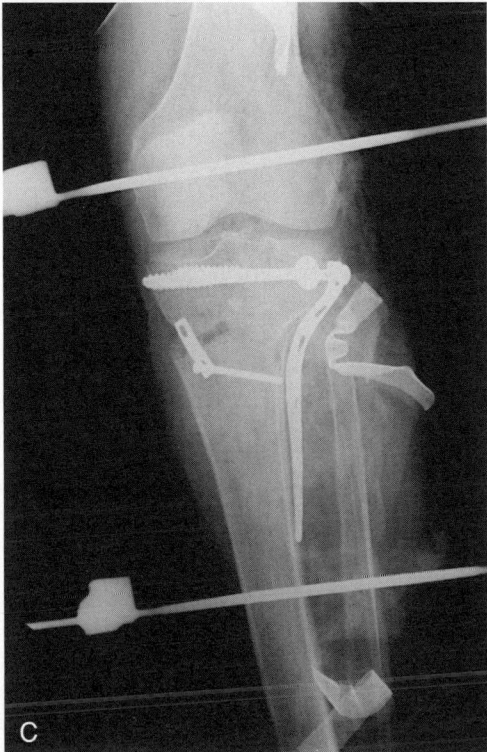

**FIGURE 56–30.** *A,* One limb of the AO distractor is inserted into the medial femoral condyle while the other is inserted into the subcutaneous anterior medial surface of the tibia. Five-millimeter Schanz screws should be used to anchor the distractor to bone. *B,* Schatzker type V fracture prior to application of a distractor for reduction. *C,* The AO tubular external fixator is utilized in place of two femoral distractors. An intraoperative radiograph reveals excellent overall condylar reduction, and distraction facilitates the precontouring of fixation plates before screw placement. (*A,* Redrawn from Schatzker, J. In: Chapman, M.W., ed. Operative Orthopaedics. Philadelphia, J.B. Lippincott, 1988, Fig. 35–8, p. 427.)

Georgiadis[53] can also be used when treating the specific fracture pattern.[25, 152] It is advisable, however, that an extraperiosteal dissection be done for this second medial or posteromedial incision. This incision should be directed to the apex of the fracture as determined by the preoperative CT scan. This helps to limit the extent of this secondary exposure.

## Articular Reduction and Bone Graft

To treat a depressed articular fracture, the articular fragments that have been driven into the supporting cancellous bone of the metaphysis must be disimpacted. The reduction of such a fracture should never begin by an attempt to elevate the fragments through the joint but instead should be accomplished by elevating the fragments en masse from below. Once elevated, the fragments tend to fall back into the hole left behind in the metaphysis, so bone graft is used in the metaphysis to support the articular surface. Autogenous bone graft options include the use of cortical slabs to hold up the elevated fragments or pure cancellous bone autografts, obtained from the iliac crest or the greater trochanter. The cancellous bone adapts better to the shape of the metaphyseal defect and, when firmly compacted with the bone punch, provides excellent support for the articular fragments.[139]

Theoretically, K-wires or screws should not be inserted immediately deep to the subchondral bone plate to maintain elevation of the articular fragments because this may stiffen the subchondral bone plate and could lead to osteoarthritic articular cartilage degeneration. However, Beris and colleagues[11] and Ishiguro and co-workers[75] showed that a subchondral cluster of K-wires does protect the articular cartilage from the loss of reduction resulting from the forces applied to the knee during non–weight-bearing motion.[11] Utilizing this concept, newer plate designs have incorporated a lower profile, with an anatomically precontoured lateral metaphyseal flare, and have small periarticular holes that allow multiple screws to be placed in the subchondral region of the plate. It is thought that these subchondral screws function similarly to the K-wires but are much stronger. In addition, the concept of "raft" fixation specifies that these subchondral screws should capture the far (opposite) cortex as well as engage the plate, which acts as a cortical substitution. The force is thus transmitted across the joint to these multiple screws (rafters), which are supported by intact medial and lateral cortices (walls) (Fig. 56–31).

Alternatives to autologous bone graft have been used to fill metaphyseal defects and add stability to articular surface reductions of tibial plateau fractures. Coralline hydroxyapatite (Pro-Osteon, Interpore Orthopaedics, Irvine, CA), an osteoconductive porous ceramic bone graft substitute, is relatively brittle until sufficient bone in-growth has occurred, although it does sustain compressive loading fairly well. It is effective as a space-filling graft for tibial plateau fractures but requires concomitant stable internal fixation.[22, 76, 77, 95] OsteoSet (Wright Medical Technology, Arlington, TN) is a calcium sulfate material that is supplied in pellet and putty forms. This material offers structural stability and is not as brittle as the hydroxyapatite materials. It appears to osteointegrate more rapidly than the hydroxyapatite material, with complete resorption occurring by 4 months[82, 107, 158] (Fig. 56–32). Demineralized and irradiated cancellous allograft "croutons" can also be used.[92, 141, 151] They are first reconstituted in an antibiotic solution, morselized, and used in much the same fashion as autogenous cancellous bone.

Another commercially available graft substitute from a number of manufacturers is a freeze-dried human demineralized bone matrix available as a powder, putty, crushed granules, chips, or gel. It offers little structural strength until replaced with host bone and must be augmented with internal fixation devices.[158] Collagraft (Zimmer, Warsaw, IN, and Collagen Corp., Palo Alto, CA) is a composite of specially prepared bovine fibrillar collagen and porous calcium phosphate (65% hydroxyapatite and 35% tricalcium phosphate). It is intended to be mixed with autogenous iliac crest bone marrow. Available as a paste or soft strips, it too has little intrinsic strength until replaced by host bone. Unquestionably, other bone graft substitutes will be developed that have improved mechanical properties and osteoconductivity, osteoinductivity, and perhaps osteogenic cells as well. The surgeon must stay abreast of this rapidly developing field, which offers important adjuncts for treatment of tibial plateau fractures.[52]

## General Treatment Principles for Specific Fracture Types

### TYPE I

A wedge or split fracture of the lateral plateau, if displaced, represents an unstable joint and is an absolute indication for ORIF. In some circumstances, however, a preoperative MRI scan is helpful to determine whether the lateral meniscus is intact. In many instances, we have found the lateral meniscus to be trapped in the fracture line even in the setting of relatively minor displacement. For fractures in which the lateral meniscus is intact and joint impaction is minimal, reduction is achieved by applying a varus force manually or by using a laterally based femoral distractor. Reduction is maintained and the fracture line is compressed with the use of a large, pointed reduction forceps placed percutaneously through small stab wounds. Larger pelvic reduction or specifically designed periarticular reduction forceps may be helpful. A useful maneuver to achieve reduction involves eccentric placement of the reduction forceps followed by a twist or torque of the forceps to improve the reduction.

Fixation is accomplished with two or three 6.5- or 7.0-mm cannulated screws inserted over guide wires through small stab incisions. Washers may be added if desired. The location of these screws should be planned preoperatively on the basis of CT or MRI studies. The screws should be perpendicular to the major lateral condylar fracture line.[89–91, 123]

If a preoperative MRI study shows a peripheral meniscal tear or incarceration of the meniscus within the fracture lines or if closed reduction fails (less than 1 mm) to

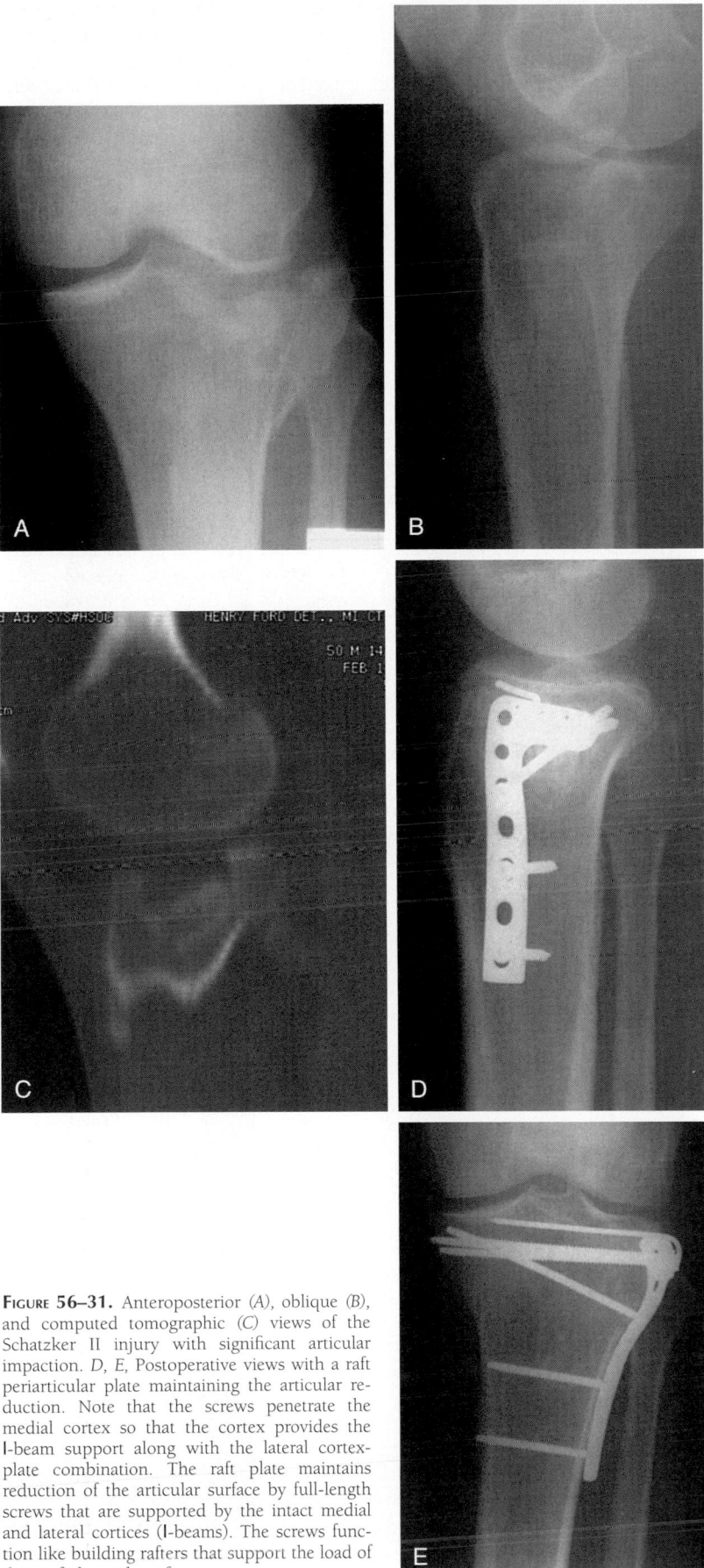

**FIGURE 56–31.** Anteroposterior (*A*), oblique (*B*), and computed tomographic (*C*) views of the Schatzker II injury with significant articular impaction. *D, E,* Postoperative views with a raft periarticular plate maintaining the articular reduction. Note that the screws penetrate the medial cortex so that the cortex provides the I-beam support along with the lateral cortex-plate combination. The raft plate maintains reduction of the articular surface by full-length screws that are supported by the intact medial and lateral cortices (I-beams). The screws function like building rafters that support the load of the roof above the rafters.

compress the fracture line adequately, ORIF is recommended.

Biomechanical studies evaluating the fixation of noncomminuted or type I fractures have demonstrated the superiority of two solitary lag screws compared with three lag screws or two lag screws and a single antiglide screw.[90, 117] Koval and colleagues[90] demonstrated that the use of an antiglide screw or buttress plate does not offer an advantage over solitary lag screw fixation alone for a similar noncomminuted fracture model. However, if the

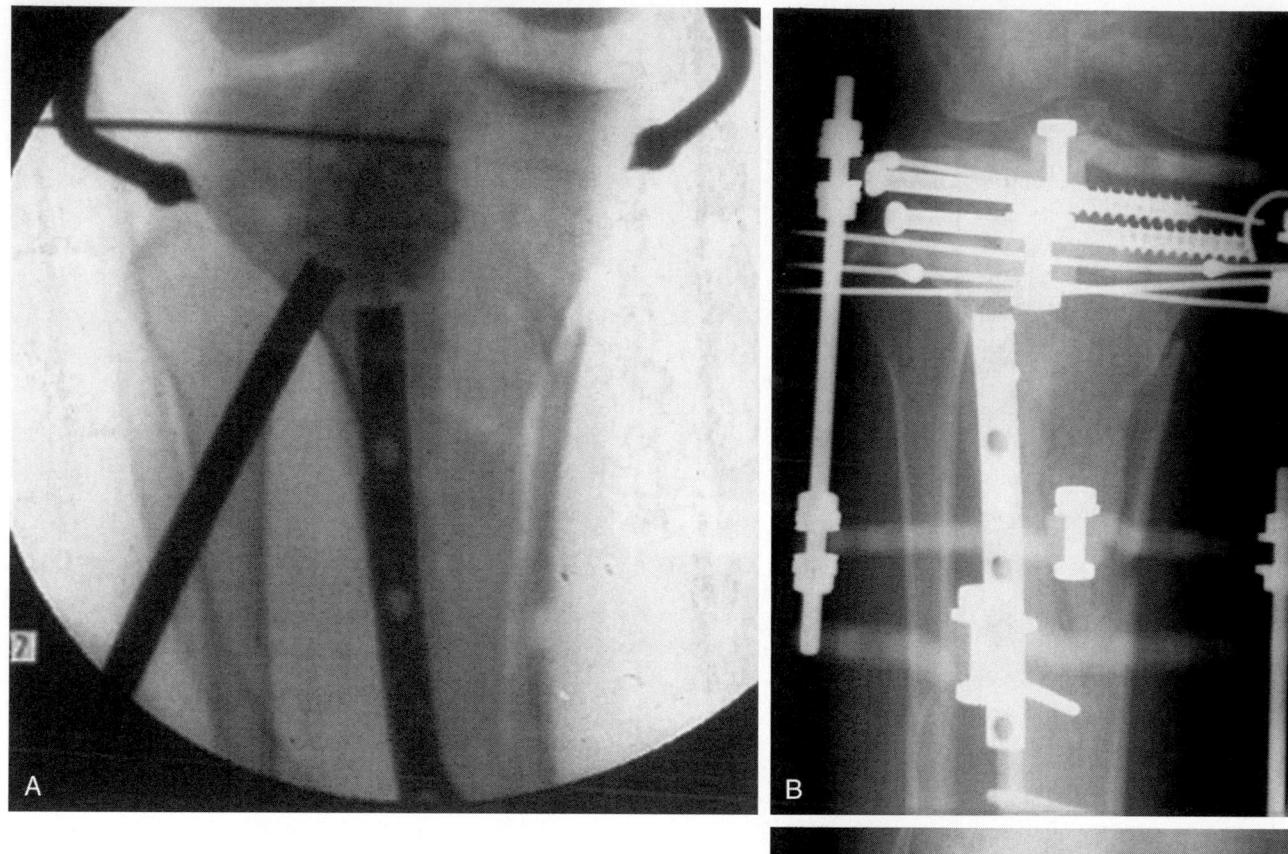

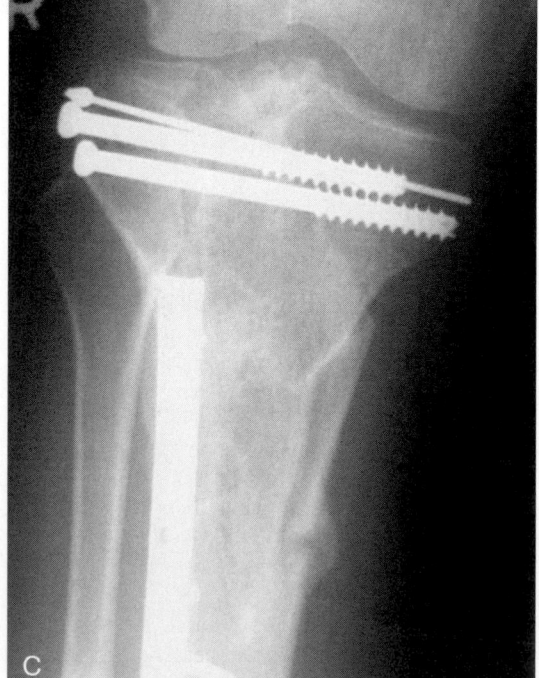

**FIGURE 56–32.** *A,* Intraoperative view demonstrating a cannula placing the bone graft substitute (OsteoSet) under the elevated articular surface. *B,* Fixation construct consisting of an anterior hook plate, hybrid fixator, and graft substitute. *C,* Postoperative radiograph shows complete incorporation of the graft and healing of the defect.

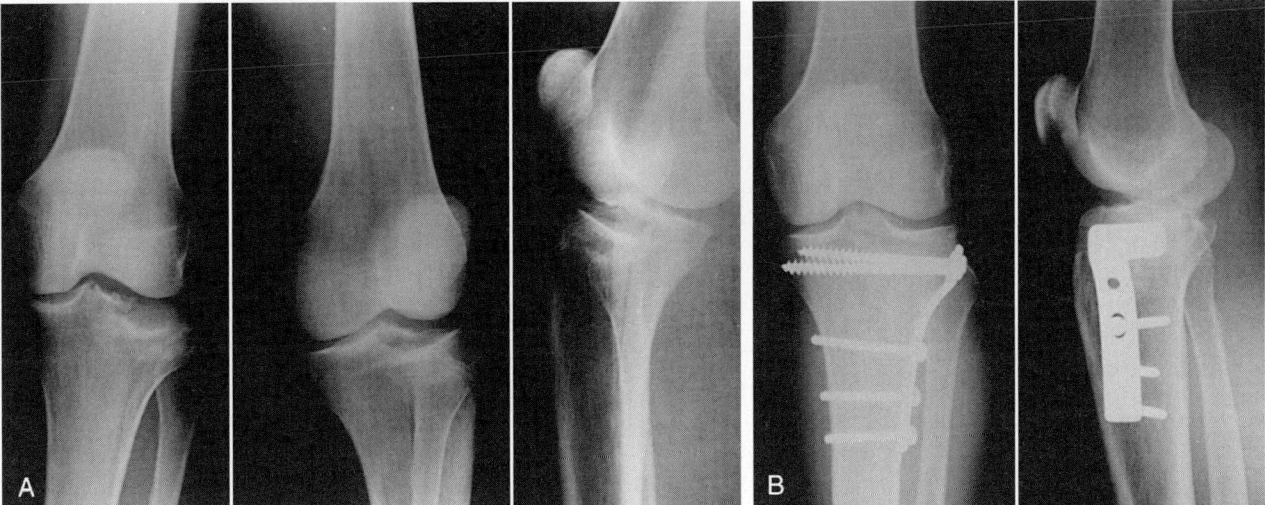

**FIGURE 56–33.** *A,* A type I fracture with an incarcerated lateral meniscal fragment. This condition precluded percutaneous reduction and fixation. *B,* An open procedure was required to reduce the condylar split and repair the meniscus. The large condylar fragment was stabilized with a buttress plate.

fracture fragment is unusually large or comminuted at its metaphyseal base or if significant osteoporosis is present, a laterally based buttress or antiglide plate should be used instead of solitary lag screws (Fig. 56–33).

In injuries with slight displacement and those in which a closed reduction is contemplated, the quality of reduction can be assessed either arthroscopically or with an image intensifier, or both. Arthroscopy is preferred to rule out any meniscal lesion.[26, 84, 98, 142, 150] If there is a peripheral detachment of the meniscus or if this is combined with trapping of the meniscus in the minimally displaced fracture line, the surgeon must proceed to an open reduction. If the meniscus is sound, however, the displaced fragments may be manipulated into place with large reduction forceps and the reduction confirmed arthroscopically. Definitive fixation is then carried out with the use of percutaneous cannulated screws.

## TYPE II

Type II injuries involve the combination of a lateral condyle fracture with depression of the lateral articular surface. Preoperative imaging studies are crucial to determine the extent and location of the impacted articular surface, and the surgical treatment must address the impacted fragments if joint instability results. Poor results after open or closed treatment may be related to residual joint depression, incongruity, or instability.

Both closed manipulative reduction combined with traction and traction alone have been associated with varying degrees of success. The displaced lateral wedge reduces surprisingly well with traction, but the impacted joint depression cannot be dislodged by traction or manipulation alone.

In most instances, a straight lateral parapatellar approach is used, and the lateral joint line is visualized through a submeniscal approach. The lateral meniscal tibial ligament is incised transversely, and the meniscus is elevated with the use of numerous stay sutures or small

sharp-toothed retractors. The condylar fracture line is visualized at the joint level through the submeniscal approach and distally along the lateral aspect of the shaft. The anterior compartment muscles are elevated extraperiosteally from the proximal tibia. In addition, before the fractured lateral condyle is exposed, a femoral distractor should be applied to achieve a ligamentotaxis-type reduction and to widen the joint space to improve visualization. With this technique, one may be able to limit the extent of the skin incision and to reflect less of the anterior compartment musculature.

At this point, the knee is flexed to 90 degrees. Flexing the knee also facilitates visualization of the joint surface by displacing the femoral contact area posteriorly and allowing the weight of the freely hanging leg to distract the joint, in concert with the bone femoral distractor.

The impacted fragments can be approached in two different fashions. If the condylar fracture line is visualized directly in line with the surgical exposure or with minor reflection of the anterior compartment musculature, the condylar fracture line can be wedged open slightly like a book. The depressed articular surface is evaluated by direct vision, and an impactor is manipulated from below to disimpact and elevate the fracture fragments. Reduction of such an articular injury should never begin with an attempt to elevate the fragment through the joint; instead, this should be accomplished by elevation of the fragments from below. Lifting the fragments up through the joint usually results in a number of devitalized, loose articular fragments that cannot be put back and fitted together.

To reduce a joint depression properly, a curved bone tamp is inserted deep into the compact metaphysis, and reduction is initiated with upward pressure (Fig. 56–34). Bone graft material must be used to support the articular fragment. One should not attempt to elevate the articular fragment directly with the impactor. The impacted fragments may be elevated by continuing to place graft material underneath the fragments. In this fashion, the solitary pressure head of the impactor is distributed over a larger surface area. As graft is packed in and around the articular fragment, the large volume of graft material acts as a plunger and begins to disimpact the joint segments. With continued insertion of graft into this area, the articular surface is elevated without fragmentation en masse. The fragments should be slightly overreduced. A dental pick or similar instrument is occasionally required if the depressed fragment is also malrotated. If the articular surface is severely comminuted with chondral substance loss, replacement utilizing the proximal fibular or tibial chondral surface is recommended.[129]

In some circumstances, the condylar fracture line extends beyond the surgical exposure. To avoid excessive stripping of the anterior compartment musculature, the major condylar fracture line should be reduced first and held with a large reduction forceps. Through the submeniscal exposure, the articular surface can be visualized and the adequacy of the major condylar articular fracture lines assessed. In most circumstances, the articular depression remains in an impacted state. A small cortical window is then developed at the base of the condylar fracture line. Multiple small (2-mm) drill holes are then placed in a 1-cm oval. These drill holes are then connected with the

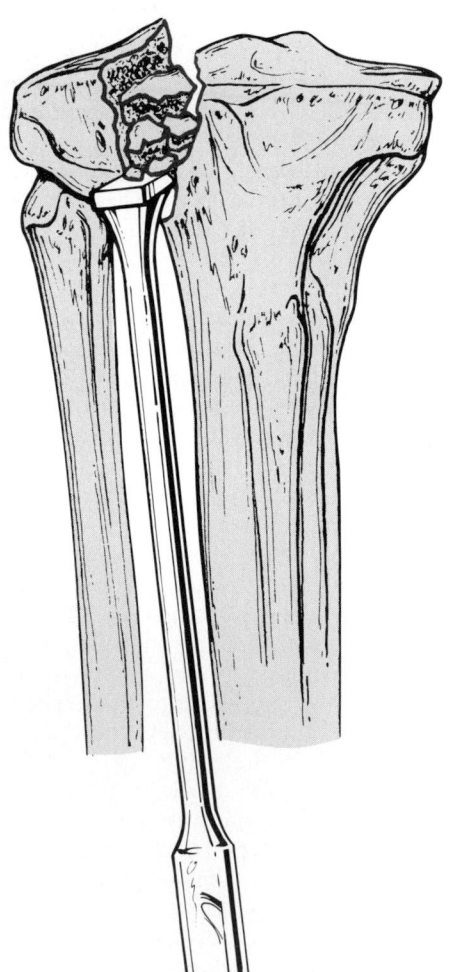

**FIGURE 56–34.** Technique for en masse elevation of fragments consists of insertion of a bone punch deep into the depressed fragments. Upward blows on the punch effect the reduction. (Redrawn from Schatzker, J. In: Chapman, M.W., ed. Operative Orthopaedics. Philadelphia, J.B. Lippincott, 1988, Fig. 35–9, p. 428.)

use of a small osteotome to develop a cortical window. The small cortical window is impacted directly into the metaphysis with the use of a small curved impactor. Bone graft is then incrementally placed through the cortical window into the metaphyseal defect and packed under the fragment, gradually elevating it. The adequacy of reduction is visualized through the submeniscal exposure and also with the image intensifier. This technique minimizes excessive subperiosteal stripping of the condylar fracture line and proximal tibia.

After joint elevation, if the open-book technique has been used, the split condyle is reduced and held with a large reduction forceps. Fixation of the condyle is then achieved with a buttress plate or periarticular raft plate. In some circumstances, if the condylar fracture line is minimally comminuted and bone quality is exceptionally good, solitary lag screws with or without an antiglide plate can be used to stabilize this condylar fragment (Fig. 56–35).

## TYPE III

The type III fracture is a pure depression fracture of the lateral plateau. This injury usually occurs in older patients with osteoporotic bone after a trivial valgus stress. If the depression is slight, the joint remains stable and excellent function without joint instability is the usual outcome. It is important when determining the efficacy of surgery to examine the joint, with the patient under anesthesia if necessary, testing it from full extension to 90 degrees of flexion. If no valgus instability with greater than 5 to 8 degrees of motion is found, it is safe to treat the joint with early motion without weight bearing. However, if instability results, surgical management should be undertaken. CT or MRI scanning is extremely helpful to determine the location, depth, and orientation of articular depression. This information is crucial when contemplating the location of the subcondylar window through which to elevate the impacted articular surface (Fig. 56–36). Occasionally, a *medially* tilted *lateral* articular surface may be approached through a *medially* based subcondylar window.

Treatment of this injury has evolved to a less invasive form. Historically, a standard laterally based submeniscal exposure was necessary to visualize and elevate the impacted fragments. This fracture can now be treated with the use of an image intensifier to evaluate the adequacy of reduction; however, this approach may be inadequate. Direct visualization with the aid of an arthroscope is our preferred method for confirming articular reduction* (Fig. 56–37).

### Arthroscopy and Fracture Management

After direct visualization of the joint by arthroscopy, a 2- to 3-cm portion of the standard lateral surgical exposure is developed over the lateral metaphyseal region of the fracture. Exposure is needed only for access to the subcondylar flare in order to develop a small metaphyseal cortical window. It is accomplished by using an anterior cruciate ligament reconstruction drill guide or equivalent

---

*See references 12, 26, 48, 56, 78, 91, 103, 113, 115, 119, 136, 150.

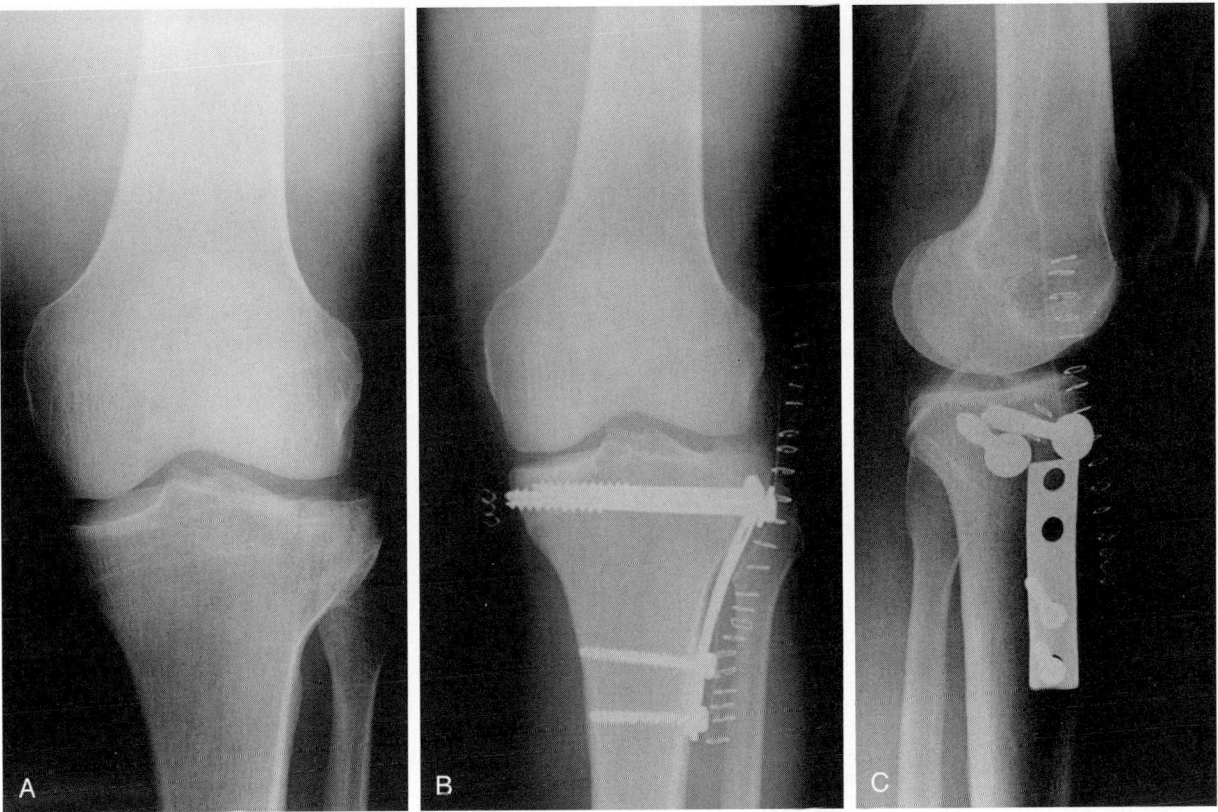

**FIGURE 56–35.** *A,* A type II fracture condylar split and joint impaction. *B,* Fixation is accomplished by open reduction followed by elevation of the articular surface and bone grafting. The condylar fragment and bone graft are supported by cancellous lag screws and an antiglide plate. Note: The antiglide plate is undercontoured to provide a significant "spring" buttress effect to the condylar fragment *C,* Screws through the proximal portion of an antiglide plate are not necessary.

device. A small guide wire is passed through this metaphyseal region directly to the area of joint impaction, as confirmed with arthroscopy.

After placement of the guide wire, a small cannulated drill is used to develop the metaphyseal cortical window and also to drill the impacted metaphyseal bone to the level of the impacted articular surface. The resulting tunnel must be of sufficient size to allow grafting and elevation of the fragment from below. Using a curved bone impactor and bone graft material, the depressed segment is elevated in the same fashion as previously discussed for type II injuries. After the articular surface of the joint has been restored as confirmed by arthroscopy, the graft can be stabilized by percutaneous placement of cannulated screws located under the subchondral compact bone[66, 76–78, 113] (Fig. 56–38).

Many patients with this fracture type are severely osteoporotic. The metaphyseal cortex is usually very thin and is further weakened by the development of a cortical window. To prevent its fracture under axial load with a resultant deformity, a buttress plate is often advisable in addition to the lag screws. Usually, a small plate can be placed through the lateral incision extraperiosteally to avoid excessive stripping of the lateral condyle.

Additional advantages of arthroscopy-assisted fixation include treatment of meniscal lesions and obtaining valuable diagnostic information regarding the cruciate ligaments and adjacent articular surfaces.[12, 21, 119] Adverse

outcomes have been reported and include infection, deep vein thrombosis, pulmonary embolism, peroneal nerve palsy, and fluid extravasation into the soft tissues leading to compartment syndrome.[7] To decrease this potential complication, irrigation under pressure must be avoided.

Less well defined is which plateau fractures are amenable to arthroscopy-assisted reduction and fixation. Studies suggest that arthroscopy may be a useful adjunct in the management of Schatzker type I and III plateau fractures,[12, 103, 115, 119] primarily low-energy injuries. Previously, most of the published series on the arthroscopic management of plateau fractures have come from sports medicine and arthroscopic specialists treating these low-energy fracture patterns. Experience is now evolving in the use of these techniques in managing higher energy fractures.

Buchko and Johnson[21] and Scheerlinck and colleagues[136] have both reported on the use of arthroscopy to assist in the treatment of the more complex C-type and Schatzker VI injuries. These less invasive techniques involve the use of a ligamentotaxis force to achieve a metaphyseal reduction, followed by an arthroscopically assisted articular surface reduction and stabilization. Limited ORIF or external fixation of the metaphyseal-diaphyseal dissociation is then carried out under fluoroscopic guidance. This technique has been shown to be safe but is also quite demanding with regard to the extensive equipment necessary to treat these complex injuries in this fashion.

## TYPE IV

Fractures of the medial plateau are usually caused by high-energy trauma. Their potential for soft tissue injuries is often overlooked. They are poorly described by the term *isolated medial plateau fracture*. Medial plateau fractures usually occur as a relatively simple wedge, similar to the split-wedge fracture of the lateral plateau. However, there is typically a fracture of the intercondylar eminence and the adjacent bone with its attached cruciate ligaments. Furthermore, there is frequently a disruption of the lateral collateral ligament complex, which may be either a tear through the substance of the ligament or an avulsion of the fibular head. The severity spectrum extends to fracture-dislocations with neurovascular injuries. The poor prognosis of medial plateau fractures is the result not of the fracture but of the associated soft tissue injuries.

Nonoperative management of these injuries has been associated with a high incidence of varus malunion.[3, 38, 42] We recommend nonoperative treatment only for rare, totally nondisplaced fractures. These must be managed with strict non–weight bearing for at least 3 months.

For fractures with little or no comminution, caused by a lower energy mechanism, closed reduction can be attempted and held with large, percutaneously placed reduction forceps. A valgus force is usually successful in reducing these injuries because of intact capsular attachments; fixation is then maintained with multiple cannulated screws. In most cases, these fractures result from high-energy forces and are grossly unstable, with comminution extending into the region of the intercondylar eminence. Often the anterior cruciate ligament is avulsed with a small piece of bone in this region. There is also gross displacement of the knee joint proper with disruption of the lateral collateral ligament complex or fibular head. This significant displacement may result in traction lesions to the peroneal nerve or popliteal vessels (Fig. 56–39). Such fracture patterns preclude percutaneous treatment. Adequate fixation requires a buttress plate because the large forces placed on the medial plateau cause displacement, especially if the apex of the fracture is comminuted or there is bone loss that would preclude intact cortex-on-cortex apposition. Buttress plating is also advised if there is an associated posterior split-wedge fracture of the medial plateau.

For these cases, a medial parapatellar exposure is carried out and direct reduction of the fragments is achieved. Fixation of the comminuted condyle is achieved with a buttress plate. In order to place this correctly, the entire pes anserinus should be elevated in continuity with the superficial portion of the medial collateral ligament. The elevation should be done in an extraperiosteal fashion to avoid any further stripping of the large condylar fragment. In this way, the plate makes direct contact with the entire medial metaphyseal surface and provides a significant buttress effect to the fragment. The intercondylar comminution should also be repaired and the avulsed ligament fixed with a small screw if the fragment of bone permits. Alternatively, one can use a suture placed through drill holes in the anterior tibial cortex (Fig. 56–40).

Lesions with a large posterior wedge fragment should be buttressed posteromedially. In order to reach this posterior wedge fragment, it is best to make a second incision posteromedially.[53] This incision can be used alone if the articular displacement is greatest posteromedially.

## TYPES V AND VI

These complex injuries are usually associated with severely compromised soft tissues. They comprise a wide variety of injuries but are characterized by involvement of both the medial and lateral plateaus. What distinguishes the type V fracture from the type VI is the degree of metaphyseal-diaphyseal dissociation. The type V fracture has a portion of the metaphysis intact proximally up to the joint surface, which Schatzker describes as an "inverted **Y**." In a type VI fracture, the entire metaphysis is completely dissociated from the diaphyseal region of the tibial shaft.

The type V bicondylar fracture may be either extra-articular or intra-articular, depending on whether the fracture lines involve the articular surfaces. Fractures involving both condyles are frequently comminuted and have areas of articular depression. The type V injury more commonly occurs as a split fracture involving a substantial portion of the medial tibial condyle with an associated depressed lateral plateau fracture.

Nonoperative management is seldom used as primary treatment for these injuries. The extra-articular portion of

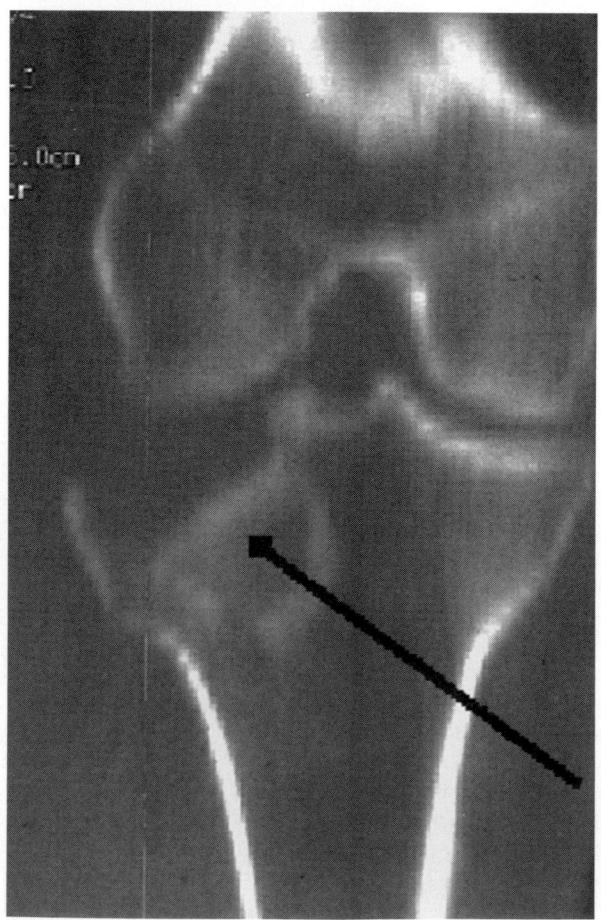

**FIGURE 56–36.** Computed tomographic scan shows the orientation of the impacted articular surface. This is best approached through a *medially* directed subcondylar window *(arrow)*.

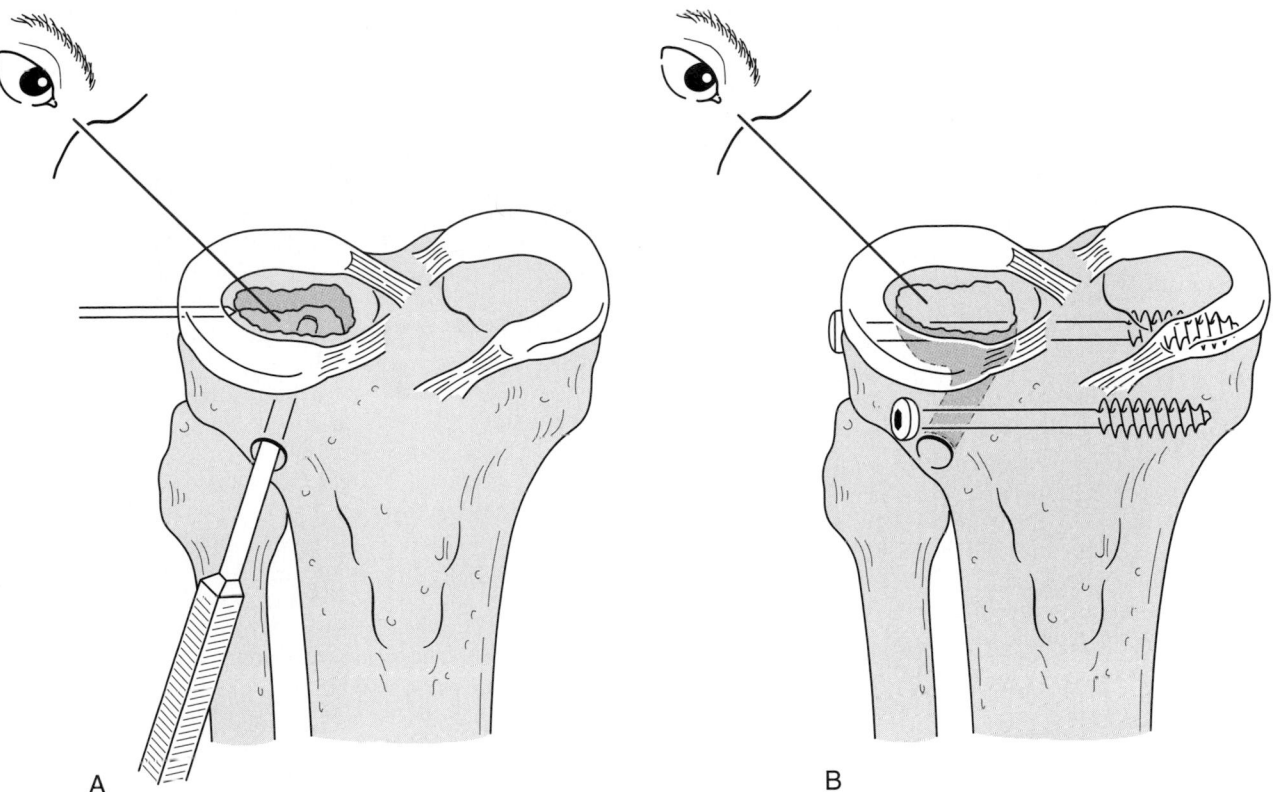

**FIGURE 56–37.** *A,* The arthroscope provides direct visualization of the articular surface. Reduction of the joint is accomplished through a submetaphyseal cortical window with subsequent elevation of the depressed segment utilizing bone graft material. *B,* The reduction is confirmed arthroscopically, and cannulated screws are placed to support the bone graft.

the fracture may initially be managed successfully in skeletal traction and subsequently in a fracture brace. However, some axial collapse is inevitable despite traction. This event results in varus or valgus instability and is usually symptomatic, especially in young persons. Therefore, unless surgery is contraindicated, operative fixation is the treatment of choice for these injuries.

The surgical tactic previously involved the use of extensile exposures and stabilization with dual plates and other large implants. ORIF in the presence of severe soft tissue compromise has been shown to be fraught with many complications, including wound dehiscence, infection, articular collapse, nonunion, and mechanical axis malalignment.[16, 85, 100, 112, 123, 143, 152]

Therefore, in addition to dealing with the significant skeletal injury, a primary concern in surgical management of these injuries should be preservation of the tenuous soft tissue envelope. Indirect reduction techniques, using one or two femoral distractors, are recommended. Distraction usually improves the alignment of the condyles through the principle of ligamentotaxis. If necessary, K-wire "joysticks" and large percutaneous reduction clamps can be applied to manipulate major condylar fracture fragments in accordance with the preoperative CT data.

After reduction, cannulated screw guide wires are inserted percutaneously across the major condylar fracture fragments for temporary fixation. The value of preoperative imaging studies (CT and MRI) to localize any joint impaction is realized here. Depending on the location of the joint depression or fracture comminution, the proxi-

mal tibia can be approached through a limited midline, lateral, or medial parapatellar incision.[154–156] Any articular impaction is elevated from below through the anterior portion of the split condyle or the use of a submetaphyseal cortical window placed either medially or laterally in the subcondylar region (Fig. 56–41).

The cannulated screws are used to secure the condylar reduction, and the condyles must then be attached to the shaft component. In most of these cases, the lateral condylar fragment is more comminuted than the medial condyle, and in most cases, joint depression is also laterally based. Therefore, a laterally based plate is used to buttress the more comminuted of the two condyles. Following condylar reduction, an extension of the lateral parapatellar incision in an extraperiosteal fashion exposes the lateral submetaphyseal and shaft region. An extraperiosteal buttress plate or stronger tibial condylar plate along the lateral aspect of the tibial shaft accomplishes the fixation of the condyle to the shaft. Likewise, if the more comminuted condylar fragment is the medial condyle, a medially placed buttress plate to fix the condyle to the shaft is indicated. The stronger tibial condylar plates should be used for the type VI fracture to bridge the bone defect that is often found at the metaphyseal-diaphyseal junction. It is crucial in these injuries to restore the correct mechanical axis (Fig. 56–42).

If the condylar fracture fragments are minimally comminuted and the fracture line is well opposed, it is occasionally possible to control the medial condyle with only a lateral plate and screws, assuming that cortical

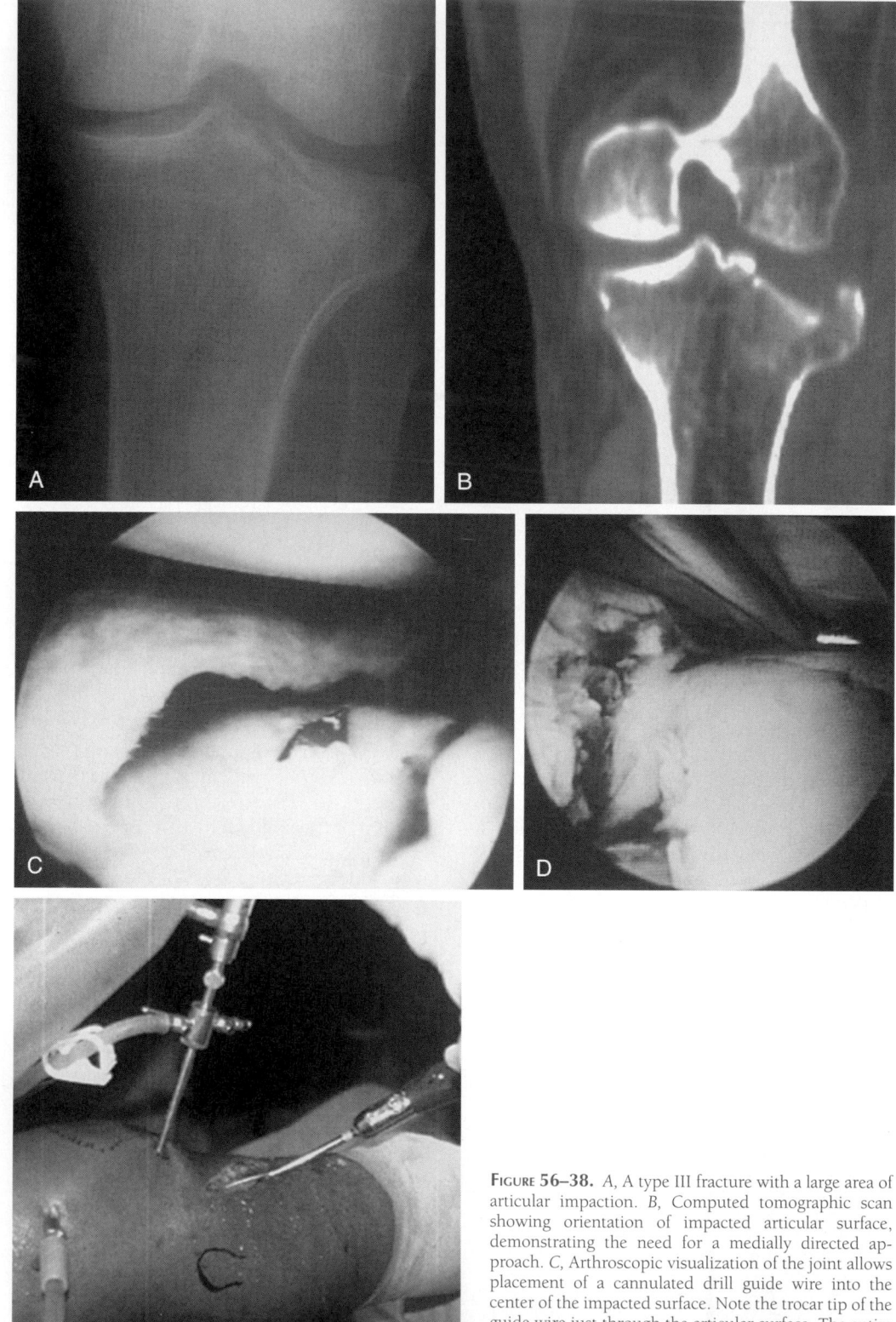

**FIGURE 56–38.** *A,* A type III fracture with a large area of articular impaction. *B,* Computed tomographic scan showing orientation of impacted articular surface, demonstrating the need for a medially directed approach. *C,* Arthroscopic visualization of the joint allows placement of a cannulated drill guide wire into the center of the impacted surface. Note the trocar tip of the guide wire just through the articular surface. The entire aspect of the impacted area is visualized arthroscopically. *D,* A probe is used to check the stability of the lateral meniscus. The articular step-off is easily visualized arthroscopically. *E,* A small incision exposes the medial submetaphyseal tibial cortex.

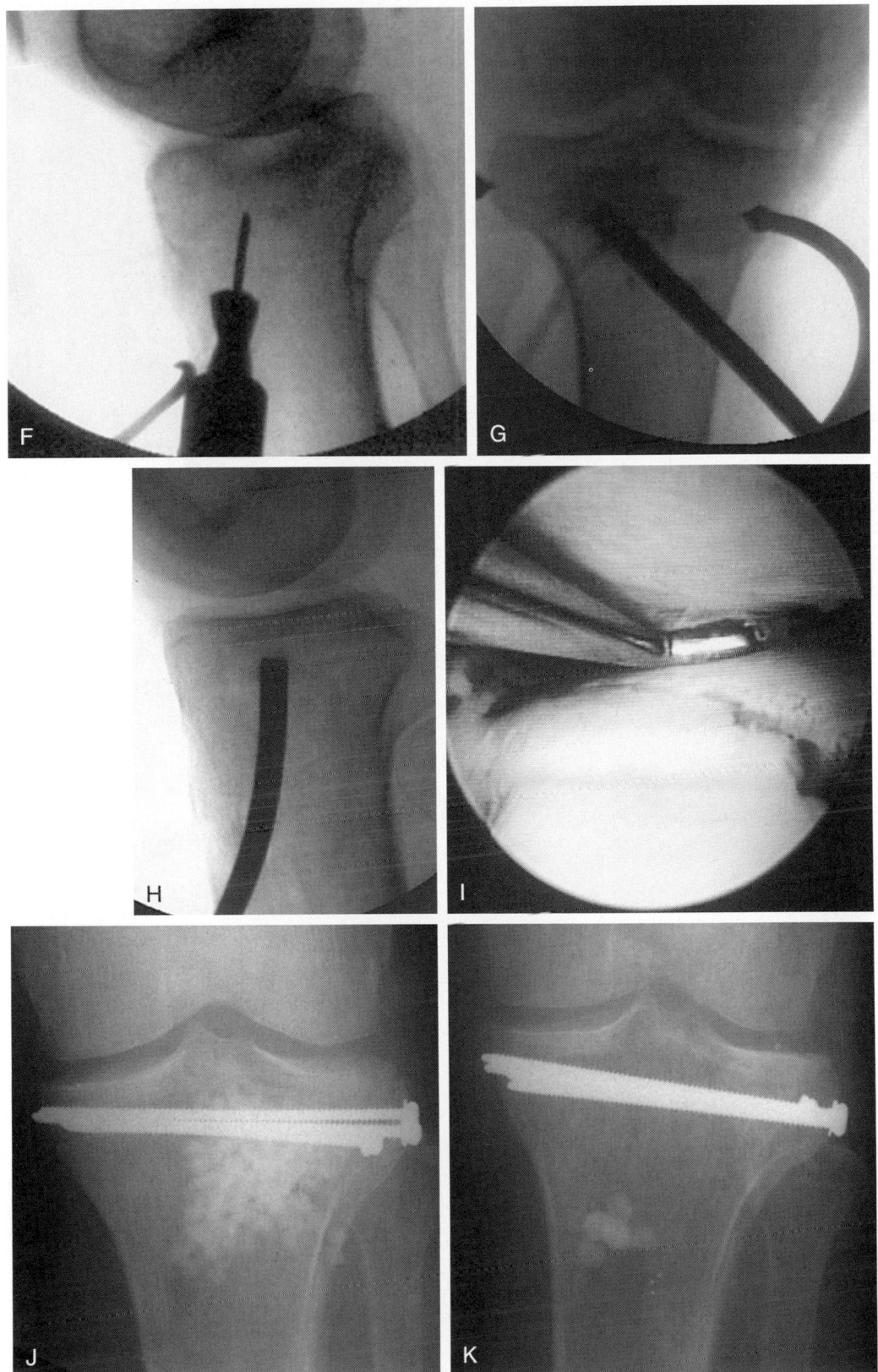

**FIGURE 56–38** *Continued. F,* A cannulated drill is then used to drill a submetaphyseal cortical window for direct disimpaction (*G*) and subsequent elevation of the joint surface using bone graft material (*H*). *I,* Arthroscopic confirmation of the articular reduction. *J,* Following articular reduction, the placement of percutaneous raft screws facilitates support of the articular surface and bone graft material. *K,* One-year follow-up film showing complete incorporation of graft material and healing of articular surface impaction.

contact is reestablished at the base of the medial condyle. In most circumstances, however, the medial condyle is highly comminuted and requires support to prevent late varus collapse. This buttress support can be accomplished with a small one-third tubular or 3.5-mm dynamic compression plate.[8, 57, 61, 99, 134, 135, 149, 152] On the basis

of preoperative CT scan information, a medial incision is performed and the plate is placed extraperiosteally. The usual location is on the posterior medial or direct medial tibial surface at the *apex* of the medial metaphyseal fracture line. Care should be taken to limit this second incision and to avoid large subperiosteal flaps. Additional percutaneous

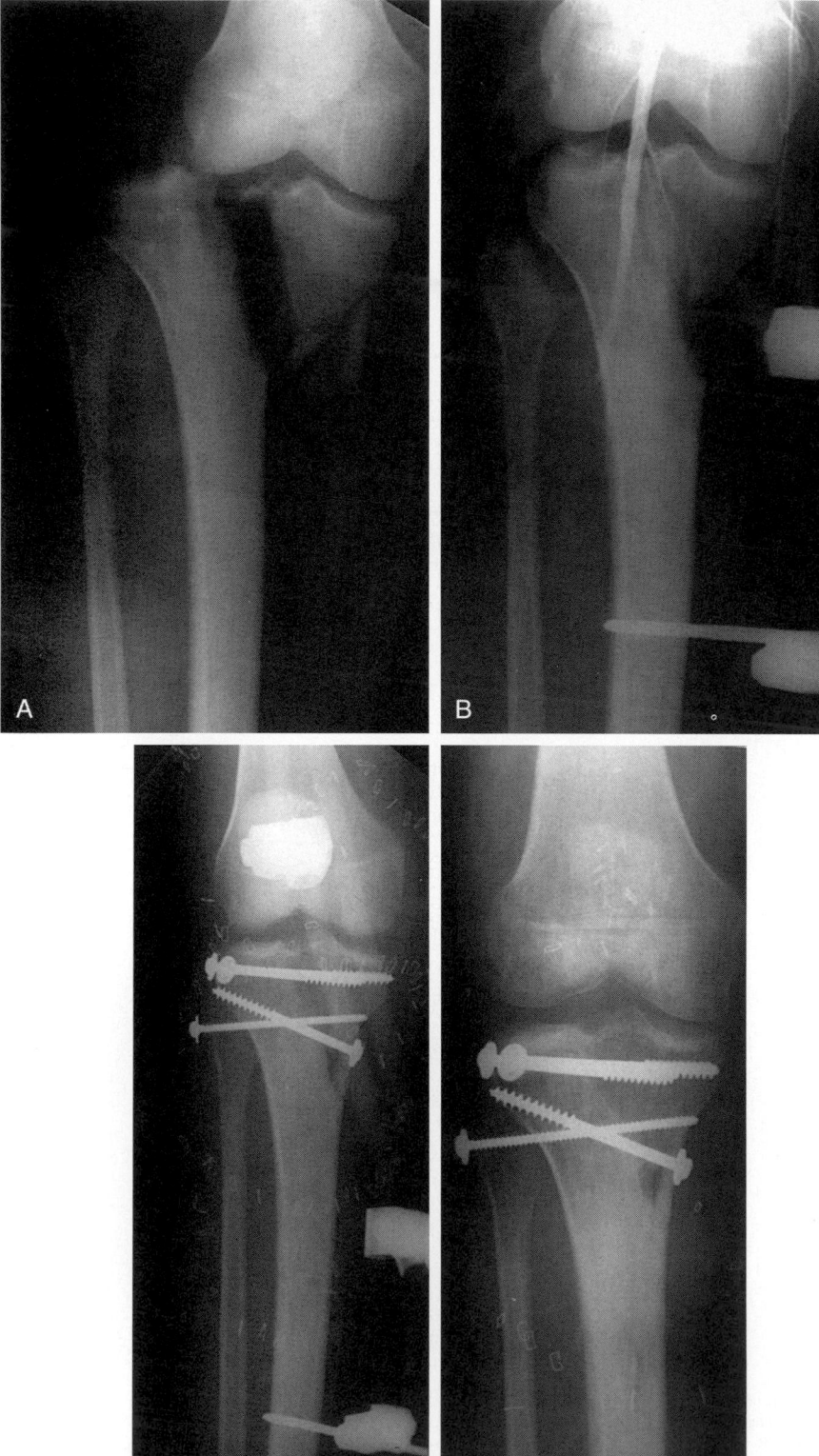

**FIGURE 56–39.** *A,* Open Schatzker IV fracture with subluxation of the knee. *B,* Immediate spanning external fixator was applied, and intraoperative angiogram reveals occlusion at the trifurcation. *C,* Following arterial repair, the condylar surface was reconstructed with lag screws and the fixator left in place for wound management. *D,* Follow-up after fixator removal demonstrates healing of the condylar surfaces and maintenance of the joint space.

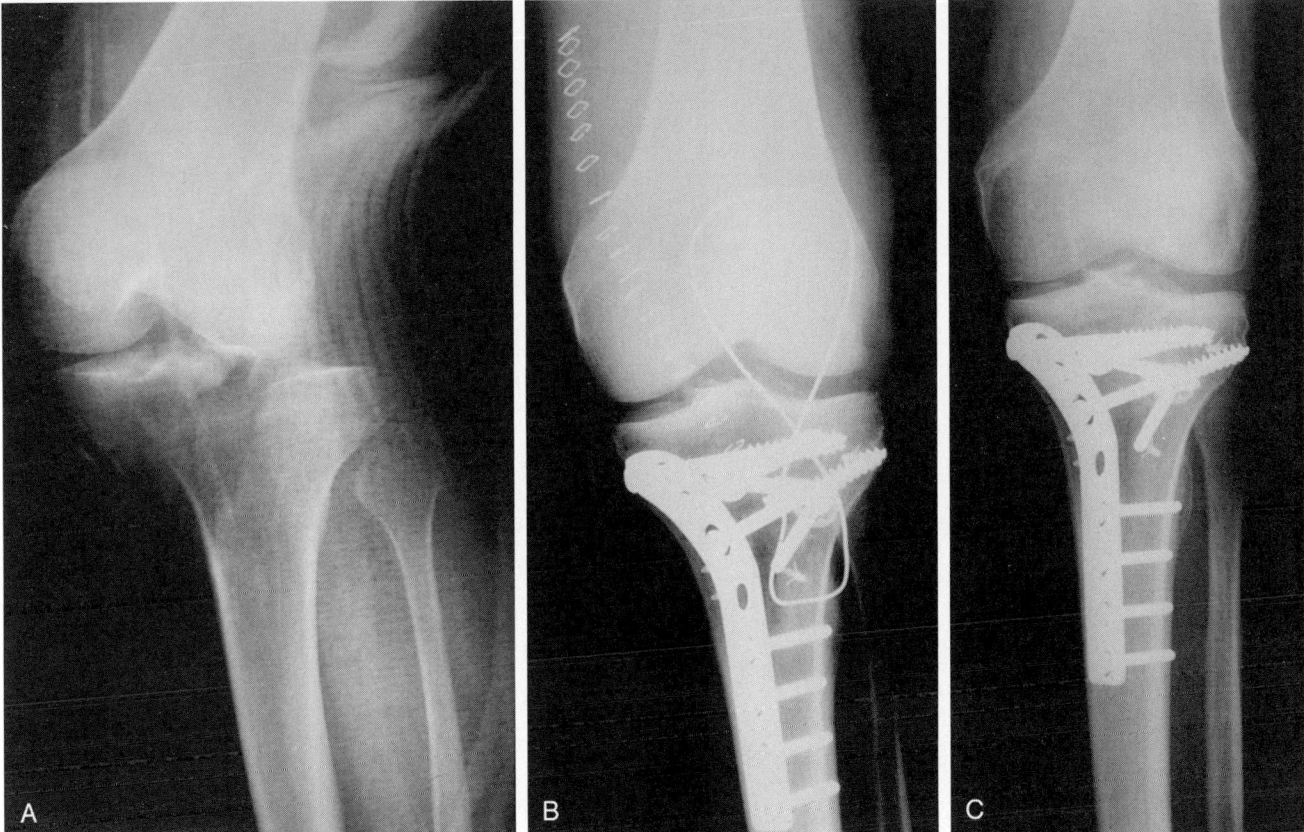

**FIGURE 56–40.** *A,* A type IV injury with an associated peroneal nerve injury as well as partial avulsion of the patellar tendon. *B,* Immediate postoperative fixation utilizing a medially based buttress plate and direct screw fixation of the patellar tendon with a screw and ligament washer. The repair was protected using a figure-of-eight tension band wire. *C,* One-year follow-up film after removal of the tension band wire shows complete healing of the fracture.

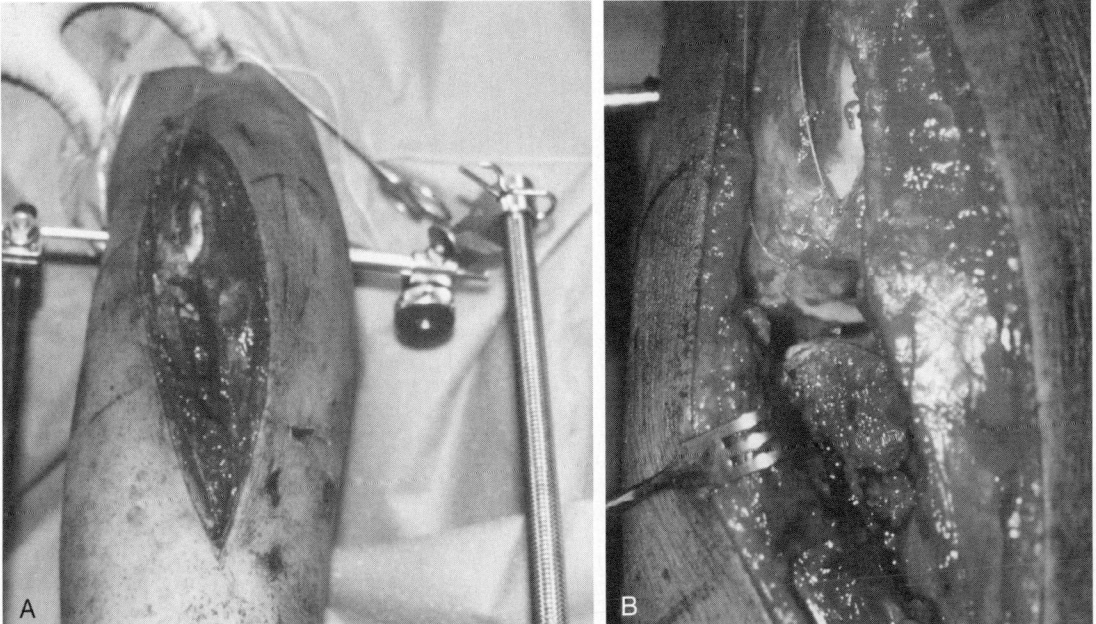

**FIGURE 56–41.** *A,* Ligamentotaxis reduction is achieved using femoral distractors or components of the AO tubular fixator. A medial distractor is combined with a tubular fixator to provide symmetric distraction across the fracture lines. Straight incisions are utilized to gain exposure, as seen here. *B,* A submeniscal exposure is accomplished and, using sutures to elevate the meniscus, the joint is directly visualized. The rake retractor is used to wedge open the lateral condylar split, thus exposing the impacted articular surface, which has been partially elevated in this case.

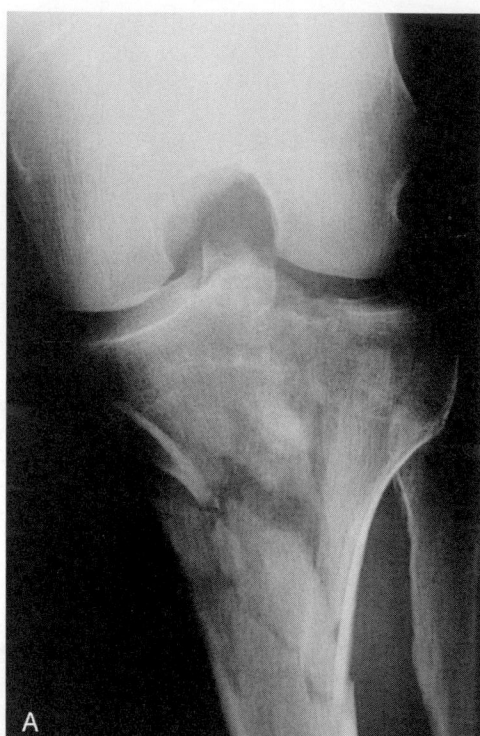

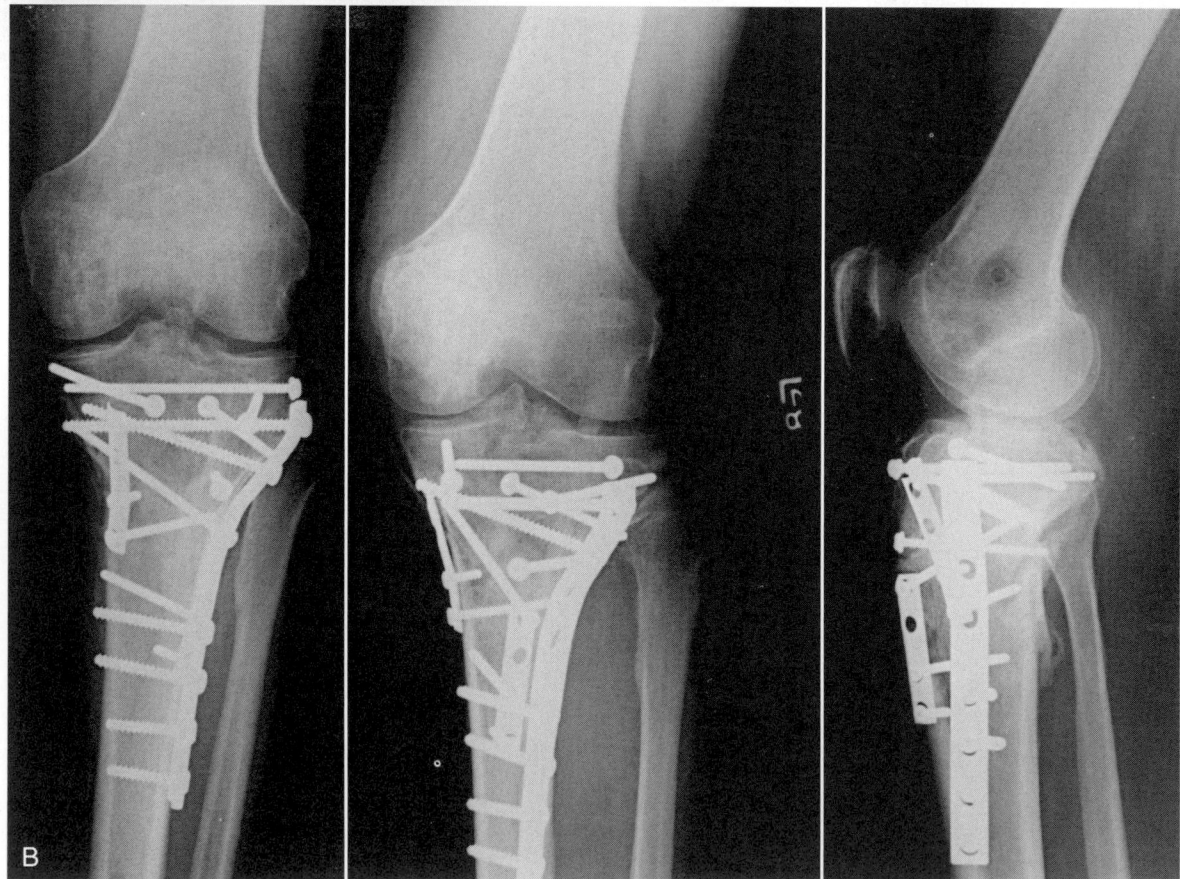

**Figure 56–42.** *A,* A Schatzker type VI injury with a bicondylar component as well as metaphyseal shaft dissociation. *B,* A stronger dynamic compression plate is used to "bridge" the diaphyseal-metaphyseal defect. In addition, a smaller medial antiglide plate is located at the apex of the medial fragment.

lag screws through this plate can be added through small stab wounds. This second incision should be just large enough to allow placement of the plate. Such an incision should never be used for fracture manipulations with the large subperiosteal reduction forceps (Fig. 56–43).

Biomechanical analysis of plating constructs has demonstrated no significant measurable difference between a dual buttress plate construct and a lateral buttress plate–medial antiglide plate construct. However, a solitary lateral buttress plate provided significantly less stability across a bicondylar plateau fracture model. A lateral buttress plate with an adjunctive posteromedial antiglide plate may therefore provide fixation as effective as that obtained with a dual buttress plating technique in managing complex tibial plateau fractures. This less invasive technique may also have biologic advantages because it does not require soft tissue stripping, as does medial antiglide plate application.[71]

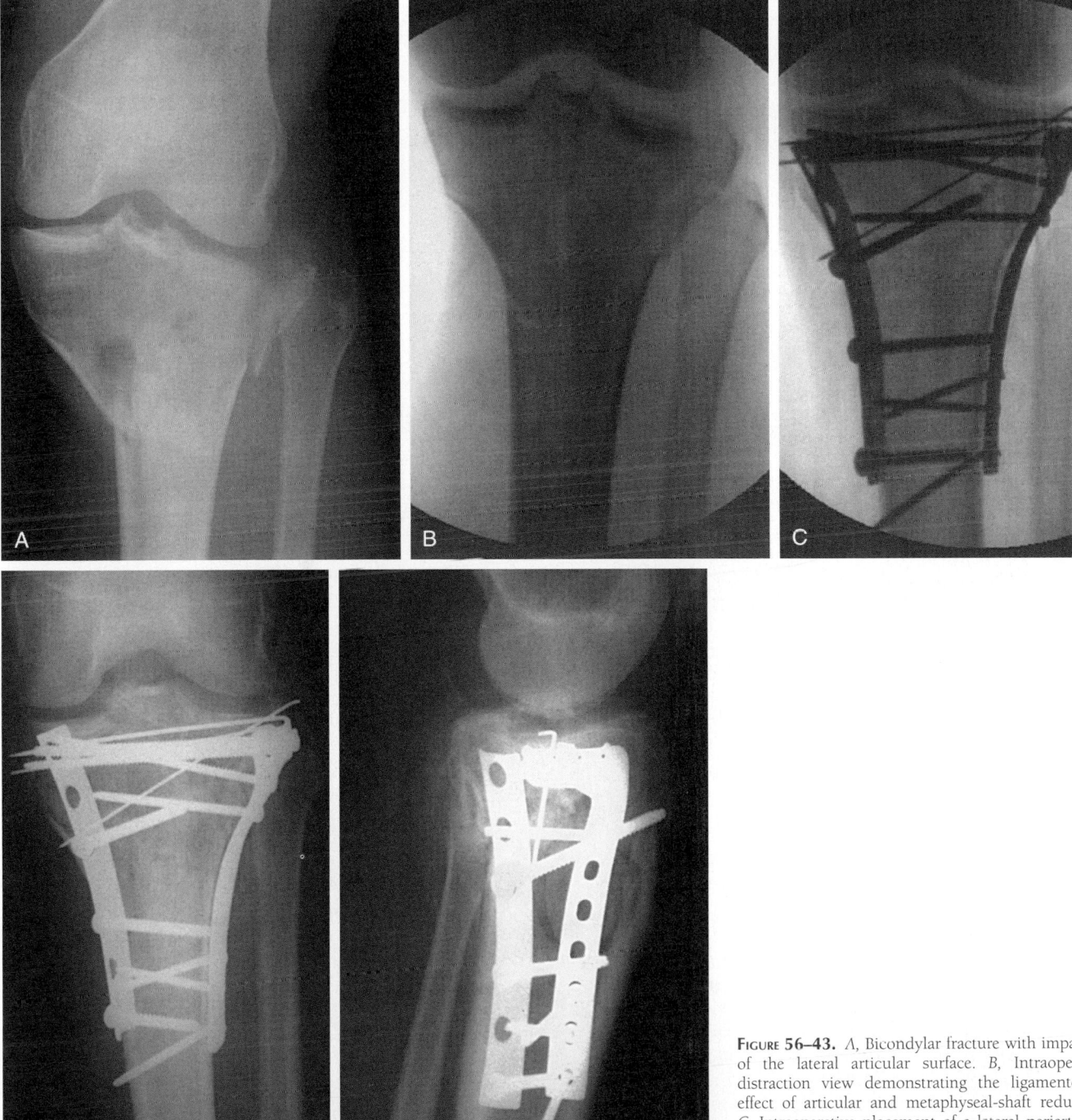

**FIGURE 56–43.** *A*, Bicondylar fracture with impaction of the lateral articular surface. *B*, Intraoperative distraction view demonstrating the ligamentotaxis effect of articular and metaphyseal-shaft reduction. *C*, Intraoperative placement of a lateral periarticular 4.5-mm dynamic compression plate and a posteromedial antiglide plate. *D, E*, Postoperative radiographs at 2-year follow-up with healing of all fracture components.

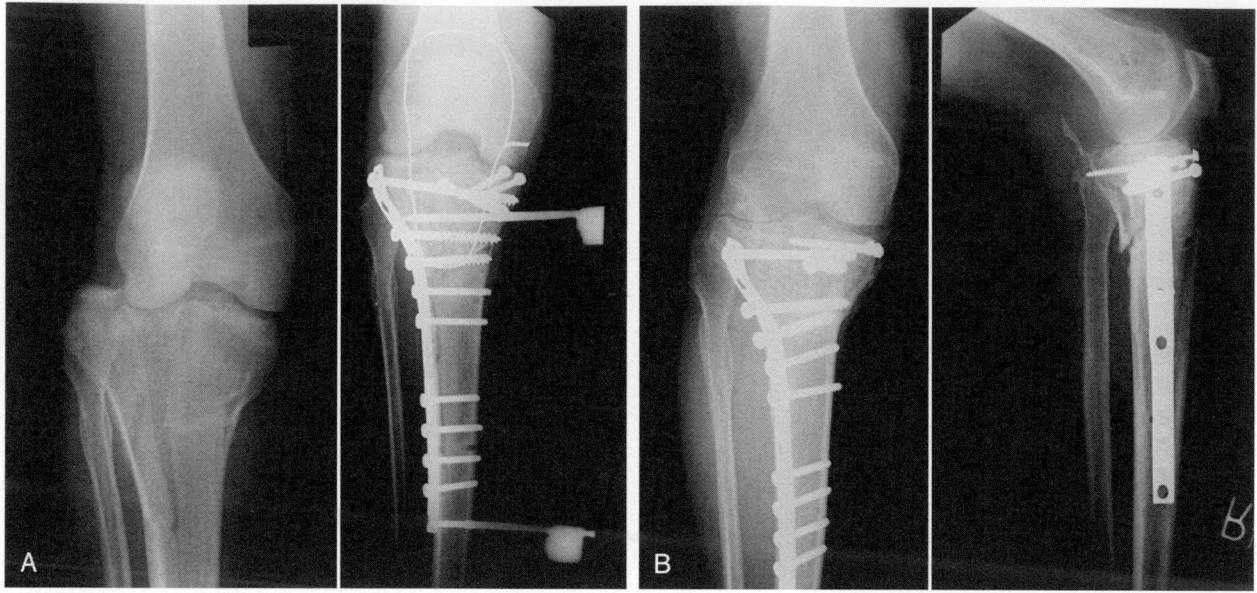

**FIGURE 56–44.** *A,* A Schatzker type VI injury requiring a lateral buttress plate and simple monolateral fixator to support fracture of the medial condyle. *B,* Two-year follow-up radiograph. Note the erosions of the lateral articular surface as well as slight collapse of the medial condyle. However, the overall mechanical axis has been maintained.

As fracture comminution and soft tissue injury increase, the pros and cons of a second medial incision should be carefully weighed. With the increased soft tissue dissection necessary to apply the plate, the risk of wound problems and infection also increases. However, the medial condylar fragments still need to be stabilized. In this circumstance, the supplementary medial plate may be abandoned in favor of a simple half-pin external fixator (Fig. 56–44). One or two Schanz screws are placed percutaneously, parallel to the articular surface of the medial condyle.[17, 32, 127] These pins are then connected to one or two distally applied Schanz screws along the anterior medial shaft of the tibia. By distraction across these pin groups with a simple monolateral frame, the medial condyle is prevented from displacing distally. This technique has been employed by many investigators with success; the majority of complications resulted from the use of the large Schanz pins in the proximal metaphyseal regions.[54]

In some circumstances, the lateral condylar buttress plate and cannulated lag screws may prevent Schanz screws from being placed into the medial condyle. In this situation, small tensioned wires applied to an external fixator can be used to support the medial condylar fragment.[144] Two or three percutaneously placed 1.8-mm olive wires can easily be passed across the condylar fracture fragments and attached to a proximal circular ring. A second ring is positioned with the use of two or three distally placed Schanz pins along the shaft. The two rings are connected together, producing a simple two-ring Ilizarov fixator to support the medial condyle. Likewise, the two distally based Schanz pins can be connected to a solitary bar connected to the proximal ring, producing the typical hybrid-type fixator. In both circumstances, the medial condyle is supported by small-diameter tensioned transfixation wires (Fig. 56–45).

Whether a monolateral, hybrid, or full circular external fixator is used, fixation should be maintained for 6 to 10 weeks until there is radiographic evidence of bridging of the medial condylar fracture lines.

We evaluate a number of clinical signs to determine whether a limited open approach can be used for these injuries. The absence of fracture blisters, the ability to palpate all bony landmarks about the knee, the presence of skin wrinkles, and the absence of extensive subcutaneous hemorrhage and bruising (indicative of a direct blow) all favor a limited open approach.[148, 154]

However, as the severity of the soft tissue injury increases, many of the factors that would preclude even a limited lateral exposure and plating are present. Some authors have recommended the use of monolateral large-pin external fixation in combination with percutaneous metaphyseal screws. Bal and colleagues[5] utilized an anterior T-frame half-pin external fixator with percutaneous internal fixation for the treatment of these complex injuries. The proximal half-pin configuration consists of AP-directed Schanz pins into the medial and lateral condylar fragments as well as an oblique pin placed from anteroinferior to posterosuperior in the proximal tibial metaphysis, thus achieving a triangulation effect to stabilize the periarticular metaphyseal segment in three planes[5] (Fig. 56–46).

Marsh and associates[100] treated 21 fractures in 22 patients with closed reduction, interfragmental screw fixation, and application of a large unilateral half-pin external fixator. They reported good results in patients who had maintained their mechanical axis. Complications in both of these studies were attributable to the use of proximal metaphyseal half pins. Pin tract infection and knee sepsis were reported; however, the major advantage of this technique was the avoidance of severe soft tissue complications.[5, 100]

The advantages of using a circular, tensioned *small*-wire

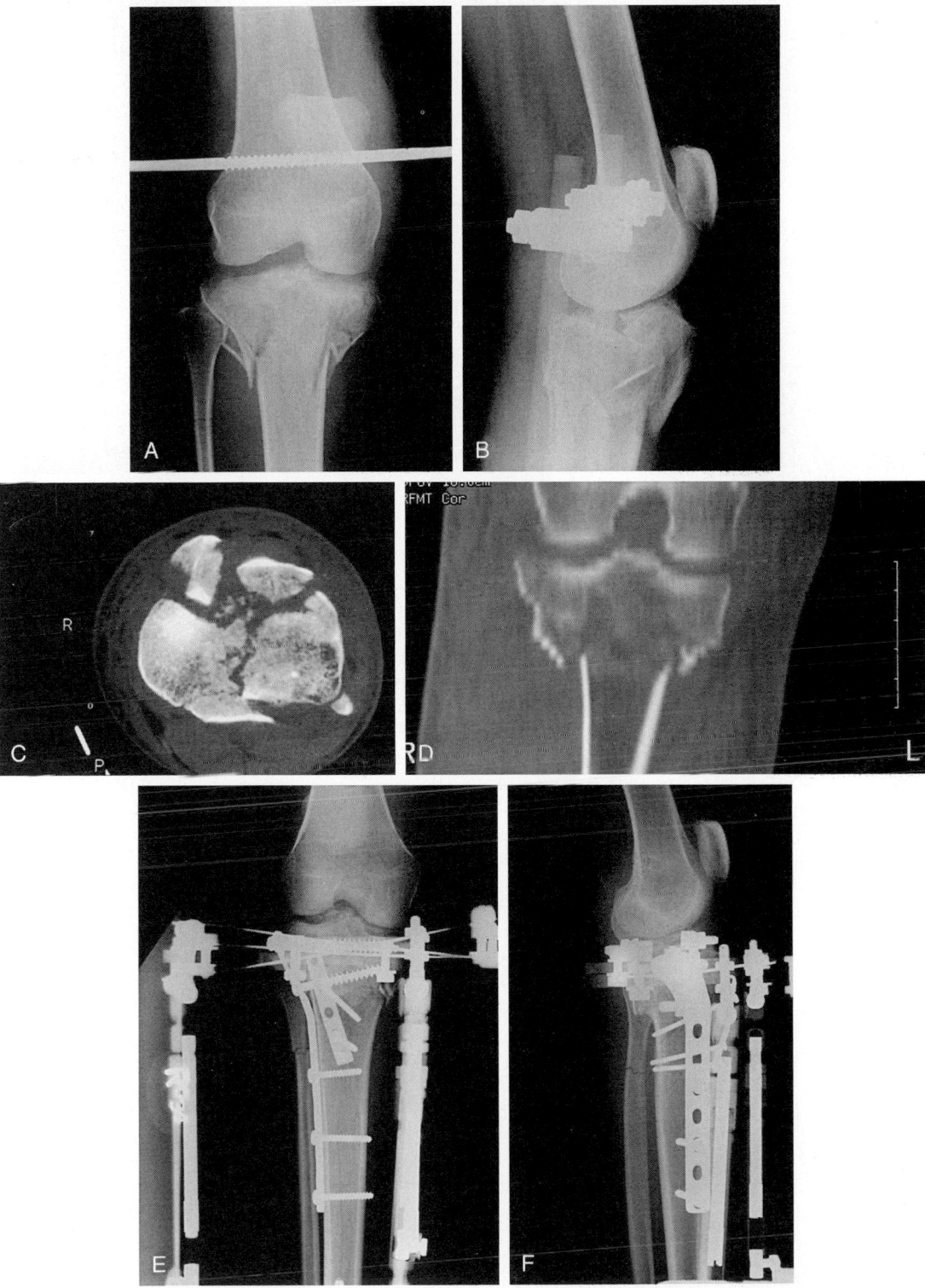

**FIGURE 56–45.** *A, B,* A Schatzker type V injury in a polytrauma patient. In order to stabilize the injury temporarily with ligamentotaxis, a "traveling traction" external fixator was applied. This fixator facilitates the overall management of the patient and at the same time provides some reasonable immobilization of the injury. Definitive reduction and fixation can be undertaken when the overall condition of the patient and the soft tissues allows. *C, D,* Preoperative computed tomographic scans with coronal reconstruction reveal the complex nature of the injury and aid in the preoperative planning of the surgical procedure. Such reconstructions can be done in various planes. *E, F,* Composite fixation was utilized in this complex skeletal injury with associated soft tissue compromise. A lateral tibial condylar plate was used to attach the condylar components to the shaft region. A 3.5-mm semitubular plate was used to stabilize the avulsed tibial tubercle, and a hybrid fixator was placed to support the comminuted small medial condylar component. Only a lateral incision was necessary for this fixation.

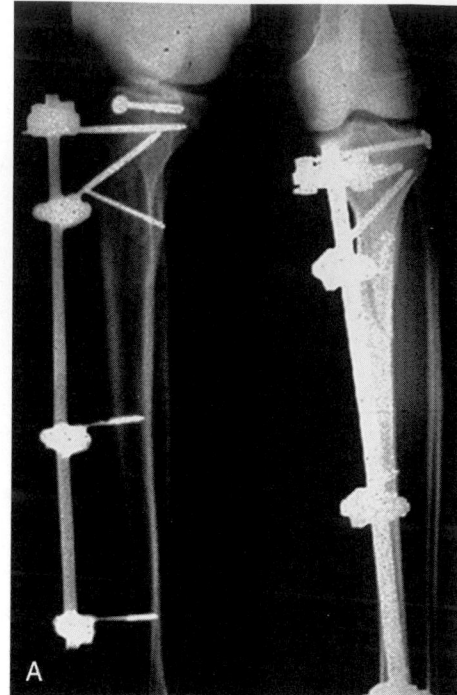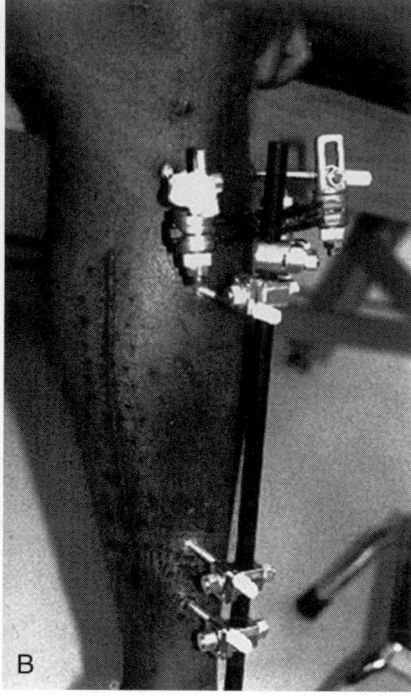

**FIGURE 56–46.** *A*, Radiograph with monofixator and articular lag screw fixation. *B*, Clinical view of monofixator for plateau stabilization.

external fixator in these situations are numerous.* The articular wires are placed percutaneously with minimal additional devitalization of the bone and its periosteal and endosteal blood supplies. Small tensioned wires allow capture of very small metaphyseal segments. Therefore, this type of fixation is especially useful in comminuted periarticular injuries. For Schatzker IV and V fractures, olive wires can compress the condylar fracture lines, much as lag screws are used.

A circular or hybrid fixator can span the fracture gap in cases of comminution or minimal bone loss, functioning much as does an internal neutralization plate. Compression can be directed across the site of bone loss or fracture gap that occurs in type VI injuries when comminution is found at the diaphyseal-metaphyseal region. The fixator can be used to compress fracture gaps to achieve bone-to-bone contact without additional bone grafting. The maintenance of the mechanical axis can be continually modified by patients' self-adjustment of the frame. Rotational as well as translational deformities can also be corrected as consolidation progresses. In addition, small tensioned wire fixators allow early partial weight bearing and range of motion of the knee.

## Surgical Technique for External Fixation of Plateau Fractures

The technique of hybrid application relies heavily on the principles of ligamentotaxis to achieve a metaphyseal reduction. These techniques usually do not reduce the impacted articular surfaces. Simply "pulling on it" is not indicated when there are large areas of articular de-

pression and comminution. These defects must be addressed through limited incisions utilizing fluoroscopic or arthroscopic guidance to reestablish congruent articular surfaces.

Application of a circular or hybrid external fixator may involve positioning the patient on a fracture or radiolucent table with calcaneal pin or distal tibial pin traction. Alternatively, femoral distractors can be used to obtain ligamentotaxis and reduction. Additional closed reduction of the condylar components is achieved by use of large, percutaneously placed reduction forceps. Percutaneous K-wires can also function as joysticks and aid in the manipulation of these large condylar fragments.

After reduction of the condyles, olive wires (1.8-mm K-wires with a 4-mm bead located eccentrically on the wire) are used to achieve interfragmentary compression of the condylar articular surface. If necessary, limited incisions are used to elevate depressed fragments and bone graft defects through submetaphyseal cortical windows. Careful preoperative planning utilizing CT scan data is of inestimable value. The ability to maintain the condylar reduction depends on the presence of compressive forces on either side of the fracture lines; this is accomplished by placing counteropposed olive wires through the fragments coming from opposite sides of the major condylar fracture line. One can also substitute cannulated screws for olive wires if the metaphyseal fragments are large enough and not extensively comminuted.

Placement and direction of periarticular olive wires and cannulated screws are achieved with the aid of fluoroscopy, following the surgical plan as determined by the preoperative CT scan. Three to four olive wires are usually required for stabilization of the condylar and metaphyseal fragments. These wires should be applied in such a way that they cross perpendicular to the major fracture lines, much as a lag screw would be placed. This orientation is

*See references 14, 23, 27, 40, 49, 50, 73, 99, 105, 114, 153–155, 157, 161.

used in order to achieve maximal condylar compression. If this wire orientation cannot be used to achieve interfragmentary compression because of anatomic constraints (as with front-to-back transfixion wires), cannulated screws accomplish this without risk of neurovascular compromise. Great care should be taken to avoid the proximal tibial capsular reflection. Olive wires should not transfix this region in order to avoid secondary seeding of the joint with resulting joint sepsis. To avoid articular penetration, the wires should be placed at least 14 mm from the subchondral line of the joint.[126]

After articular reduction, a preassembled frame consisting of three or four appropriately sized rings is placed around the limb. The proximal ring is temporarily placed at the level of the fibular head, and the wires are attached and tensioned to the proximal ring. The distal aspect of the frame is attached to the bone using 5-mm half pins or, in some cases of extensive shaft comminution, transfixion wires. The proximal and distal rings are connected to each other with fully adjustable components to allow the appropriate correction and alignment of the overall mechanical axis (Fig. 56–47).

As this technique has developed, many authors have found it necessary to utilize additional small plates for fixation of heavily comminuted metaphyseal fragments (cortical substitution) or for fracture patterns that preclude small-wire fixation because of anatomic constraints and wire corridors that orient wires in a front-to-back fashion[40, 155] (Fig. 56–48).

Utilizing these techniques, many investigators have obtained improved clinical results, with average knee scores (Knee Society rating system)[74] for most patients ranging from 85 to 90. More important, these studies continue to demonstrate reductions in the rates of major wound complications or residual osteomyelitis, which had been seen previously with traditional ORIF techniques, in spite of the fact that these series included approximately one third open injuries[7, 100, 154, 157] (see Fig. 56–48).

## OPEN TIBIAL PLATEAU FRACTURE

Patients who present with open injuries should be carefully evaluated for the location and severity of the open wound. An open fracture of the tibial plateau is a surgical emergency presenting special problems in management. It must be thoroughly débrided and stabilized to prevent infection. Adjunctive intravenous antibiotics and appropriate tetanus prophylaxis are required. The decision about how best to provide the desired stability usually presents the most difficult problem in decision making.

Even in cases of a severe open wound, we believe the primary goal should be reduction and stabilization of the intra-articular portion of the fracture (if the fracture configuration allows it). However, this should be done with the least possible additional dissection and soft tissue trauma. If the open wound coincides with the planned location of fixation hardware, then, after thorough irrigation and débridement, fixation of the articular portion of the fracture should be carried out at the time of presentation.[8, 30, 45, 128] The smallest amount of hardware consistent with stable fracture fixation should be chosen. Usually, it can be limited to lag screws and K-wires.

Immediate internal fixation for open fractures is not indicated for all open tibial plateau fractures. The risk-to-benefit ratio must be carefully assessed when contemplating primary internal fixation. Internal fixation for open fractures has been shown to be beneficial in patients with multiple injuries, massive or mutilating limb injuries, open fractures with vascular injuries, and open intra-articular fractures.[8, 17, 30, 33, 44, 45, 57, 59]

If additional fasciotomy incisions are required or if the surgical incision would create large underlying flaps in conjunction with the open wound, a staged procedure is indicated. In the situation of a very severe open fracture, once the joint has been reduced and stabilized, an attempt should be made to close the joint and further stabilize the metaphyseal fracture component with an external fixator. For staged procedures it is advisable that all wounds and incisions including fasciotomy incisions be closed and without drainage prior to initiating subsequent internal fixation or limited surgical approaches (Fig. 56–49).

An external fixator that spans the knee joint provides immediate temporary stability.[8, 45, 143, 154, 155] Thorough irrigation plus débridement of the fracture and traumatic wounds remains the single most important step in the prevention of infection. Repeated débridement may be necessary. Especially for severe injuries, reassessment of the wound in the operating room is advisable within 48 hours of the initial débridement. Although administration of perioperative antibiotics is routine for each such débridement procedure, the duration of coverage remains debatable. Brief use of systemic antibiotics, perhaps supplemented with local depot delivery systems such as the tobramycin–polymethyl methacrylate bead pouch dressing described by Seligson and colleagues,[60] reduces the risk of superinfection.[81]

Rotational or free flap coverage of the joint and soft tissue defect should be undertaken as soon as a healthy wound is achieved. An appropriate goal is to obtain soft tissue coverage within the first 5 to 7 days.

When the soft tissue envelope has healed sufficiently and the wound appears free of infection, reconstruction of the metaphyseal-diaphyseal bone defect may be addressed. For patients who have had rotational or free vascularized flap procedures, this reconstruction should typically be delayed 3 to 4 weeks after definitive wound coverage. At that time, the flap can usually be elevated in a manner that avoids or protects its vascular pedicle, and plate fixation can be applied, with simultaneous bone grafting for bone defects in these selected fractures.

For more severe injuries, one may choose to avoid internal plate fixation and maintain alignment and a generalized ligamentotaxis reduction with a knee-spanning external fixator until preliminary bone union has been achieved. Following soft tissue healing, conversion of the knee-spanning fixator to a typical hybrid fixator using tensioned articular wires and diaphyseal half pins can then be carried out within 3 to 6 weeks to allow knee motion to begin. Bone grafting should still be considered in cases of diaphyseal-metaphyseal bone loss in order to promote union within the expected life span of the external fixator.

For the less severe open fracture, if immediate ORIF is performed, the surgical extension of the open wound can be closed, but the open fracture wound itself should be left open.[8] The amount of exposed hardware should be minimized. The major risk of immediate internal fixation in open plateau fractures is the risk of infection as a consequence of further stripping of the soft tissues and subsequent devascularization of the fracture fragments.

However, with the use of contemporary surgical techniques, such as indirect reduction by femoral distractors, antiglide plates that require limited surgical extension, and the additional adjunctive measures of monolateral or hybrid external fixation, immediate skeletal stability

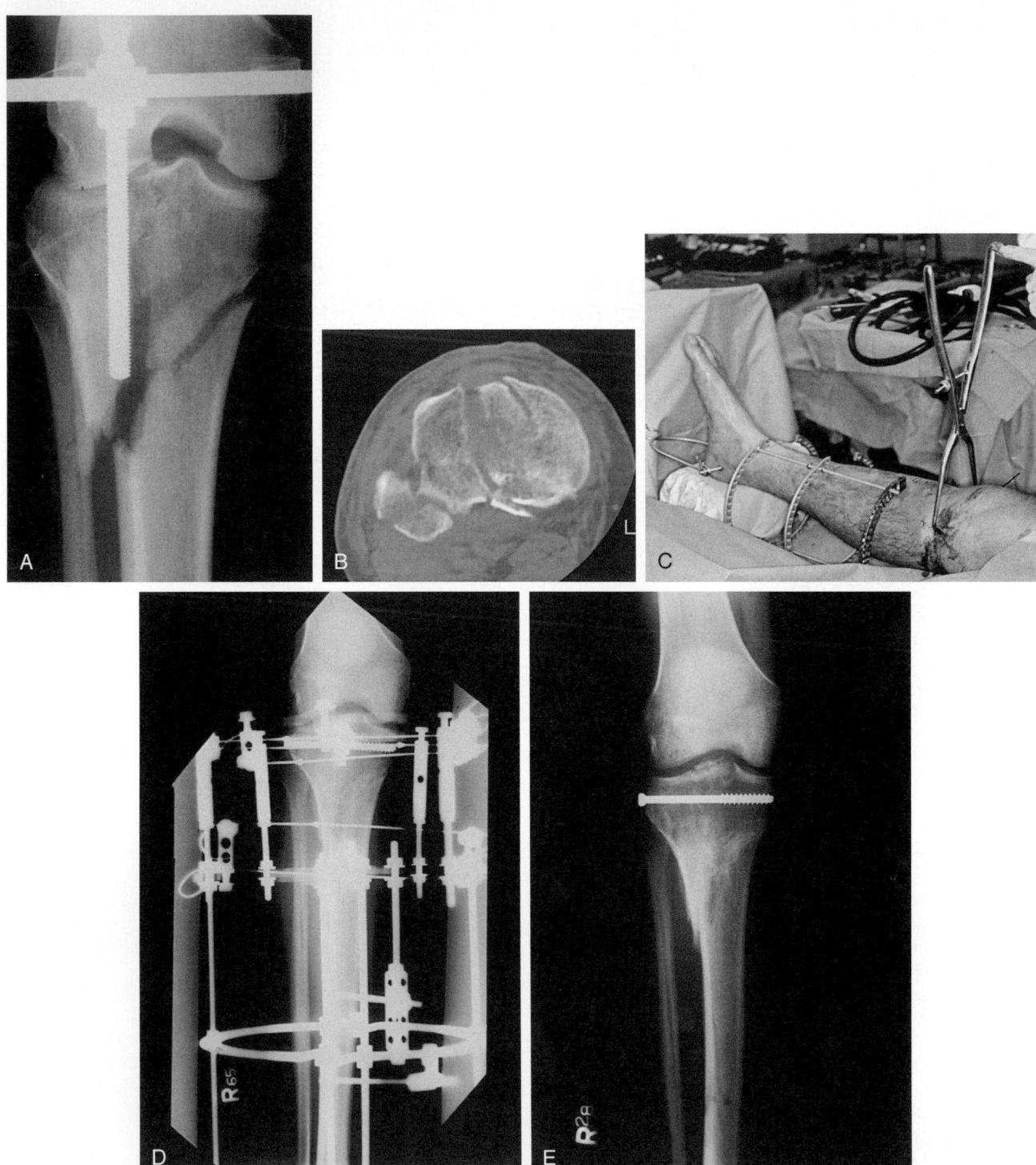

**Figure 56–47.** *A, B,* A Schatzker type VI injury with a computed tomography (CT) scan showing the bicondylar nature of the injury. *C,* A ligamentotaxis reduction is achieved intraoperatively using a portable traction unit attached to the end of the radiolucent operating table. Condylar manipulation is achieved in a closed fashion using large percutaneous reduction forceps. Intra-articular reduction is held using a cannulated screw. *D,* A four-ring circular frame is used to stabilize the fracture construct. Olive wires are placed as planned from the CT scan to achieve interfragmentary compression as well as reduction of the metaphysis-shaft dissociation. Half pins are used in a hybrid fashion for attaching the frame to the diaphysis distally. *E,* Two-year follow-up radiograph shows the overall maintenance of the mechanical axis and complete healing of the fracture.

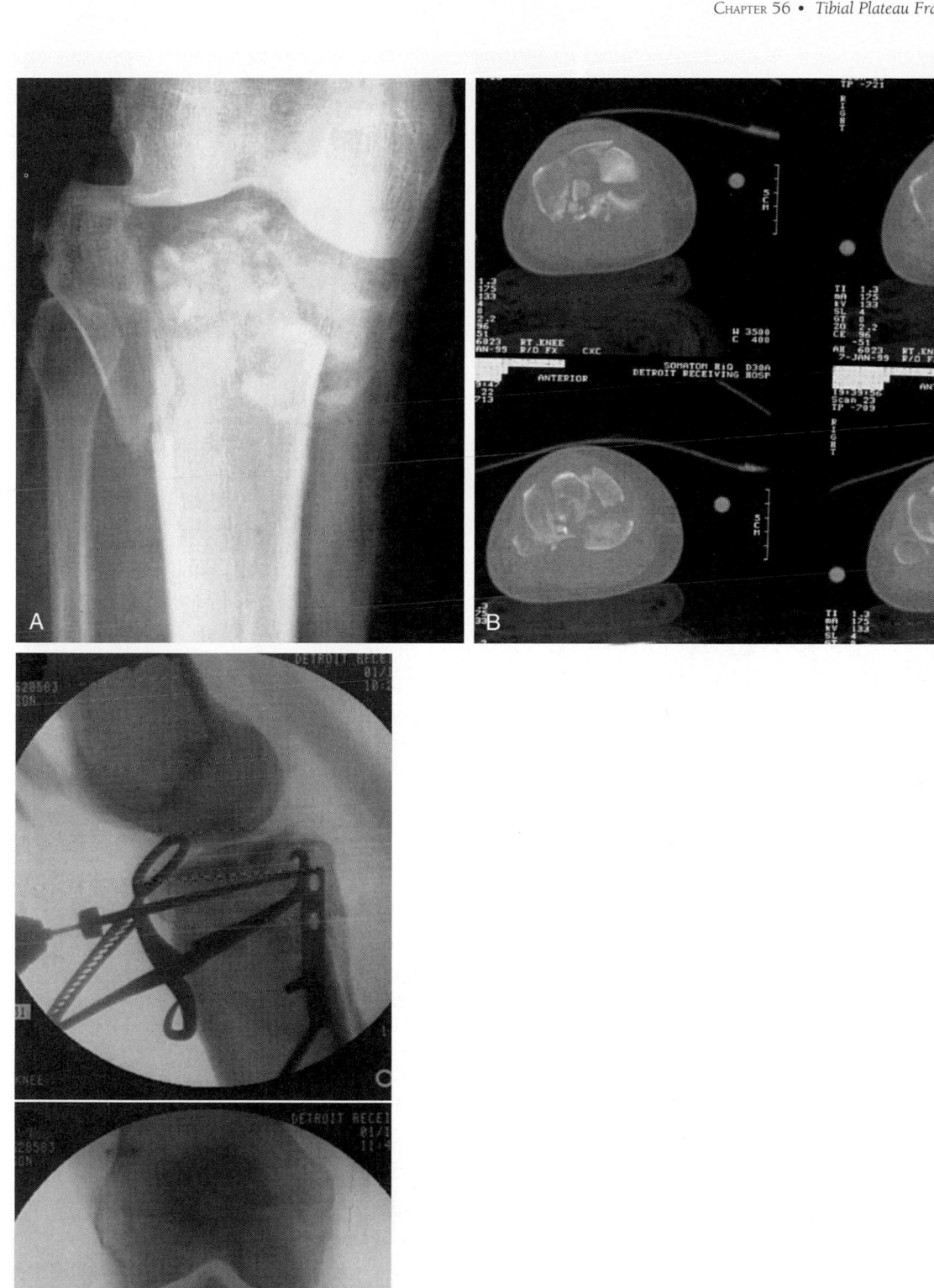

**FIGURE 56–48.** *A,* Bicondylar fracture with severe comminution and soft tissue compromise. *B,* Computed tomography documents coronal fracture through the medial condylar fragment with posterior displacement. *C,* Intraoperative views showing posterior condylar buttress plate application and anterior-to-posterior lag screw fixation.

*Illustration continued on following page*

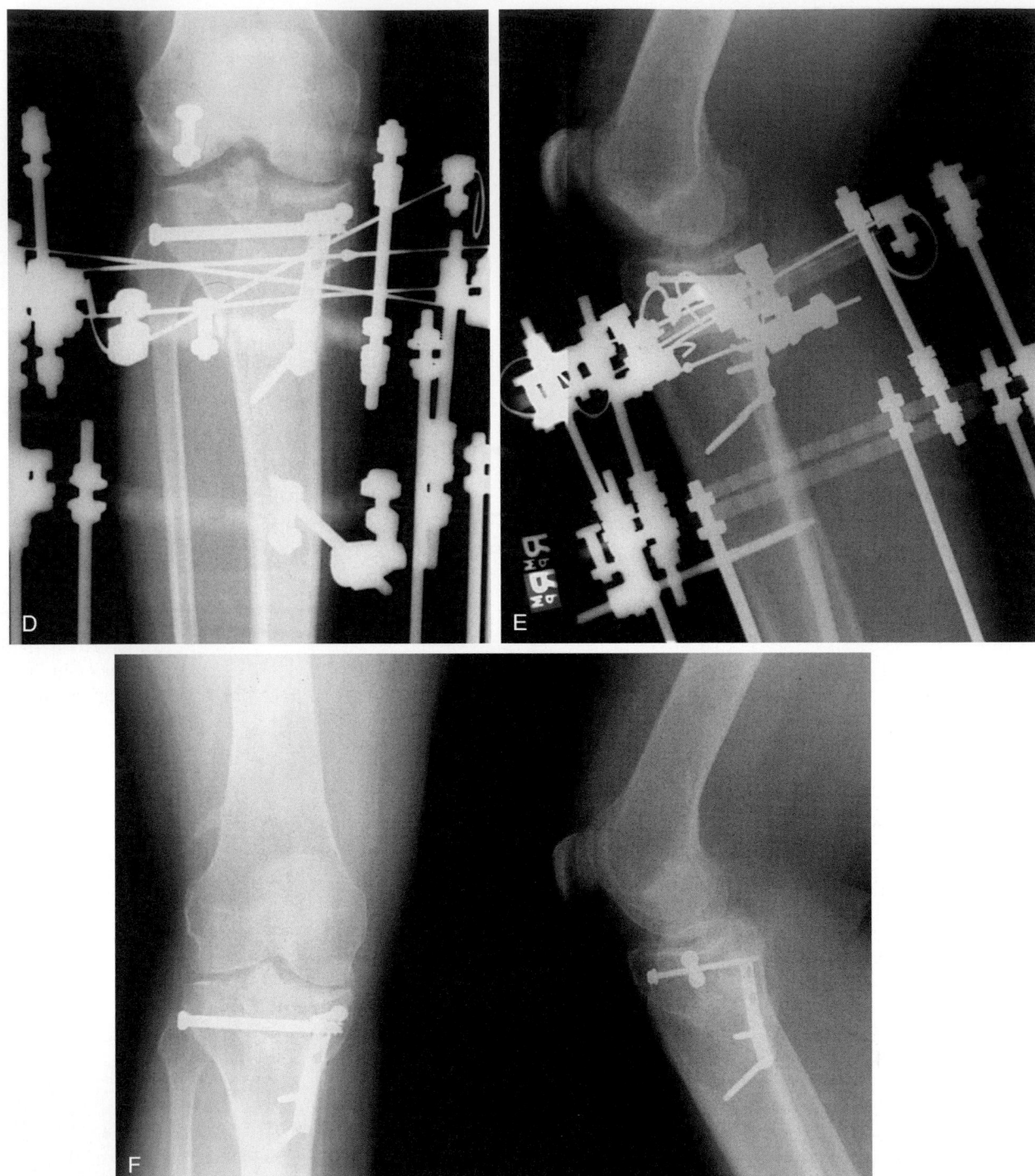

**FIGURE 56–48** *Continued. D, E,* Fixation completed with a small-wire external fixator with four periarticular wires providing articular stabilization. *F,* Postoperative views at 2-year follow-up.

may be obtained with a minimum of additional devascularization.

After immediate stable internal fixation, the patient should be returned to surgery within 48 hours for a second assessment of the wound and débridement as needed. When a healthy wound has been established, delayed primary closure, or other procedures if required, should accomplish wound closure within 5 to 7 days. At the time of initial stabilization, immediate metaphyseal bone grafting under a depressed articular segment is recom-

mended if joint closure can be obtained at the initial procedure. However, we recommend that metaphyseal or diametaphyseal bone grafting be performed on a delayed basis after complete wound healing has been achieved.[7, 57, 134, 155]

## MANAGEMENT IN THE POLYTRAUMA PATIENT

Tibial plateau fractures are not emergencies unless they are open or associated with a compartment syndrome or

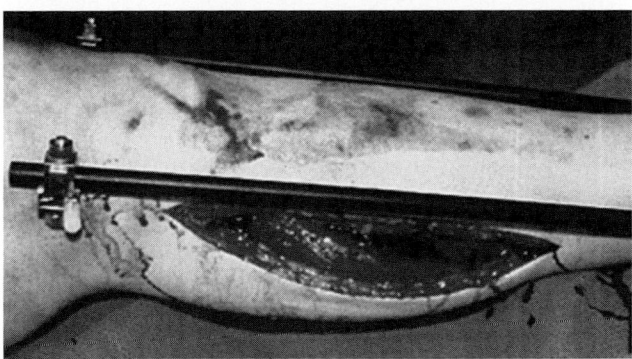

**FIGURE 56–49.** Complex plateau fracture in association with a compartment syndrome and severe soft tissue contusion, temporarily spanned with a fixator to allow soft tissue management.

vascular lesion. However, we have found, as have others, that the anatomy is more easily restored if surgery is performed early. The principles and techniques of ligamentotaxis are much more easily accomplished in the acute setting. This promptness also helps to minimize the extent of any open surgical approach. If surgical reduction is delayed, it is mandatory that the fracture be maintained in a reduced or distracted position; this is a basic principle when treating these injuries in the multiply injured patient.

Although skeletal traction can maintain proximal tibial fracture alignment, it is an unacceptable form of treatment for the polytrauma patient because it enforces a recumbent position, interfering with pulmonary and gastrointestinal function. Too often, the multiply injured patient develops problems that delay definitive fixation and result in a longer than anticipated period of bedrest in skeletal traction. To reduce the risk of complications related to recumbency during temporary stabilization and distraction of the tibial plateau fracture, we favor a bridging external fixator that spans the knee.

Alternatives include a quadrilateral external fixation frame with 6-mm, centrally threaded transfixation pins through the distal femoral condyles and calcaneal tuberosity. The knee joint is spanned by extra-long carbon fiber rods (see Fig. 56–20). Alternatively, a simple monolateral frame placed along the anterolateral aspect of the femur and anteromedial tibia, with two Schanz pins in the femur and two in the tibia, allows temporary bridging of the knee joint (Fig. 56–50). This type of bridging fixation should be applied early. An articular reduction, effected through limited incisions or in a percutaneous fashion, can be performed as well. After the overall condition of the patient has improved, the bridging fixator can, at a second surgery, be converted to a standard internal fixation construct for metaphyseal reconstruction. In some instances, severe soft tissue compromise forever precludes the use of internal fixation techniques. In these circumstances, we favor early conversion to a hybrid-type external fixator, as discussed previously. Alternatively, some authors have used a unilateral half-pin frame in combination with metaphyseal interfragmentary screw fixation.[100]

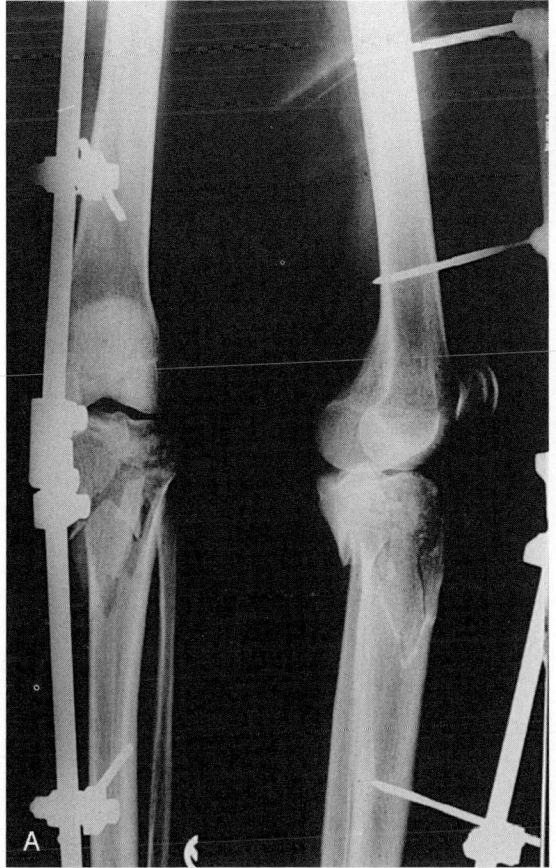

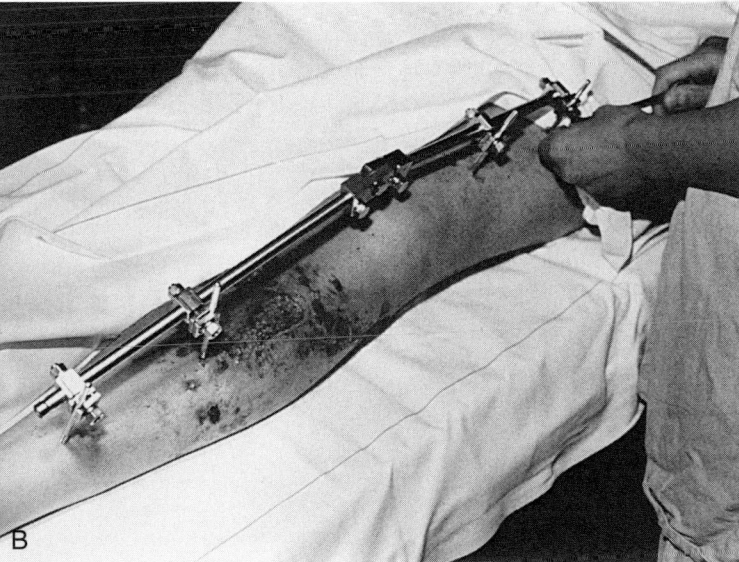

**FIGURE 56–50.** *A, B,* An open type VI injury in a polytrauma patient. A simple four-pin spanning external fixator was utilized to allow the soft tissue envelope to heal. Delayed fixation and metaphyseal reconstruction were undertaken after this had occurred.

For the multiply injured patient in whom the proximal plateau fracture is typically severe, the risk of popliteal vascular injury is present. The exact incidence of this injury pattern is unknown. It appears rarely after low-energy injuries such as the isolated type II lateral plateau fracture.

However, high-energy displaced Schatzker type IV, V, and VI fractures place the popliteal artery and the trifurcation at risk. Such trauma patients often require angiograms for evaluation of other vascular structures (e.g., the aortic arch). Especially if pedal pulses or Doppler-assisted pressure measurements are abnormal, a lower extremity angiogram should be considered to exclude an occult vascular injury. However, excessive administration of a contrast agent poses risks to the multiply injured patient's kidneys.

If an arterial repair is required, a bridging external fixator should first be applied rapidly to restore length and stability, thereby aiding the vascular surgeon. One of the most common and preventable mistakes is to repair the vessel with the fracture in a displaced position. Subsequent restitution of fracture length can disrupt the anastomosis. An anterior monolateral frame with Schanz screws and an articulated connection is usually best in this situation. Alternatively, a femoral distractor can be used to bring the fracture out to length and provide enough stability to facilitate temporary shunting or definitive arterial repair. Limited articular fixation may then be achieved after arterial repair.

Because most vascular surgeons use a rather extensive posteromedial exposure, we do not recommend further metaphyseal reconstruction until the vascular access wound has healed. In many circumstances, fasciotomies should accompany the vascular repair. Calf fasciotomies should be done whenever the warm ischemia time exceeds 6 hours or other factors suggest risk of reperfusion-related compartment syndrome. Metaphyseal reconstruction should also be delayed in these cases until the fasciotomy wounds have healed without signs of infection.

## ASSOCIATED LIGAMENTOUS INJURIES

Traditionally, ligament injury associated with plateau fractures has been diagnosed indirectly, with stress radiographs and physical examination. With increasing use of more sensitive MRI and arthroscopy, associated ligament and meniscus injuries have been found in one third to two thirds of plateau injuries. These soft tissue injuries consist primarily of medial collateral ligament lesions, meniscal injuries, and anterior cruciate ligament disruptions.[9] However, studies addressing associated soft tissue injuries all agree that neither the type of plateau fracture nor the presence or absence of ligament injury correlates with the incidence of meniscal tears.[9, 150]

Whether a midsubstance ligament tear associated with a plateau fracture should be repaired is controversial.[9, 38, 39, 48, 56, 88, 159] There is no convincing evidence that the results are better if these injuries are repaired acutely. However, there is widespread agreement that ligament injuries involving bone avulsion fractures should be repaired at the time of initial surgical management. Midsubstance tears of cruciate ligaments should be initially managed without repair. Protected motion in a hinged knee brace, proceeding to vigorous rehabilitation, may obviate the need for late reconstruction in some patients. Primary repairs, ligament augmentation, and formal reconstruction are made more complex by the presence of an acute fracture and the associated internal and external fixation devices necessary to repair the skeletal injury. In patients with persistent functional instability, a late ligament reconstruction can be carried out after the fracture has healed and fixation hardware has been removed.

## POSTOPERATIVE MANAGEMENT

Postoperative care of fractures of the tibial plateau is governed by the findings at surgery and the degree of stability achieved by fixation. Initially, a well-padded compression dressing is applied from toes to groin. Appropriate antibiotics are continued briefly after surgery, and closed suction drainage is maintained for at least 24 hours or until drainage is minimal.

Mainstays of lower extremity articular injury treatment are early motion and protected weight bearing. If the soft tissue envelope was not significantly damaged at the time of injury and wound closure was accomplished without undue tension, continuous passive motion can be started immediately. The physician should consider limiting the arc of motion to avoid excessive stress on the operative wound as well as any meniscal repair. If significant swelling or tension on the suture line is present, continuous passive motion is delayed for 48 to 72 hours after surgery until the swelling has subsided. Then the bulky dressing is removed, and the limb is placed into a hinged brace that allows gradual increase in range of motion.[138, 145] Although rapid mobilization of the knee may be painful initially, its benefits are definite. By the end of 1 week it is usually possible to cease continuous passive motion and encourage the patient to carry on with rehabilitation using active or gently assisted motion.

Physical therapy is initiated immediately for transfer and gait training, range of motion, and maintenance of proximal muscle strength. Discharged patients are seen within 2 weeks for suture removal and at monthly intervals thereafter. Radiographic studies are obtained, and weight bearing is advanced as articular healing progresses. Strict non–weight bearing is maintained for at least 6 to 8 weeks for all fracture patterns to prevent subsidence of the articular surface.[130] When early wound healing is secure, active and active-assisted range-of-motion exercises can progress more vigorously. It is important to achieve 90 degrees of knee flexion by at least 4 weeks postoperatively.

Fifty percent partial weight bearing is usually begun at 6 to 8 weeks, depending on radiographic evidence of articular consolidation.[140] In the higher energy type V and VI injuries, significant partial weight bearing may need to be delayed for 10 to 12 weeks. For most injury types, patients can begin full weight bearing by 12 to 14 weeks. Quadriceps and hamstring strengthening is continued and advanced as activity demands. Long-term follow-up of plateau fractures has shown that residual quadriceps strength loss correlates directly with decreased functional results and therefore rehabilitation efforts should be directed at the quadriceps mechanism.[70]

Type V and VI injuries may have some comminution or bone loss at the metaphyseal shaft junction, especially in fractures that were initially open. Fracture healing in this region may be delayed. If union is not progressing, bone grafting should be encouraged early, before increasing weight bearing. Autogenous bone grafting can be done as soon as the soft tissues are adequately healed. Delayed healing can often be recognized as early as 8 to 10 weeks after injury.

For patients treated with hybrid or circular small-wire external fixation, it is important to initiate early active range of motion as soon as possible. In many circumstances, a fibular transfixion wire and a medial tibial face wire are present and impinge on local soft tissues. These wires in particular may be painful and inhibit the patient's active flexion and extension. Great care should be taken to ensure that soft tissue tension around these wires is released early. In this way local tissue necrosis and subsequent pin tract infection are avoided; furthermore, early range of motion is facilitated because it is less painful.[155] Serial radiographs should be observed for any deviation of the mechanical axis while the limb is in the external fixator. If needed, adjustments may be made gradually to realign the extremity and to add compression to small areas of bone comminution. This maneuver allows one to gain bone-on-bone contact and thus a more stable fracture configuration. As fracture consolidation progresses, these frames allow full, unrestricted weight bearing. After consolidation is complete, the connections between the proximal and distal rings are loosened (frame dynamization) so that the pin-bone stresses are decreased and the weight-bearing forces are transmitted by the bone instead of the external fixator.

Before frame removal, we allow the patient unrestricted activity for approximately 10 days after frame dynamization in the hope of preventing late deformity. If the patient has an increase in pain or subtle changes are visualized on x-ray films after the frame is dynamized, it can be assumed that fracture healing is incomplete. If so, the frame is retightened to allow further consolidation before its removal, and bone grafting is considered.

## COMPLICATIONS

On the basis of the concepts that we have discussed, the results of treatment of plateau fractures have improved. Newer concepts of preoperative planning, less traumatic methods of exposure and implant placement, and less invasive surgical techniques (e.g., arthroscopy-aided reconstruction, use of small tension wire hybrid fixators) have all reduced the prevalence of complications and improved the functional outcome of these injuries. However, recognition of complications and their appropriate treatment remain as important as any of the previously discussed concepts. In spite of the many improvements in diagnosis and treatment of these injuries, complications still occur.[2, 125, 160]

Poorly timed surgical incisions through traumatized soft tissue with extensive dissection often contribute to wound breakdown and infection.[146, 157, 160] Risk of wound slough can be reduced by carefully evaluating the soft tissue envelope, delaying the surgery, limiting the extent of skin flaps, using extraperiosteal dissection of fracture fragments, and minimizing soft tissue stripping at the fracture site. Preoperative CT scan information can help to guide subsequent surgical incisions directly to the fracture site. Indirect reduction techniques employing an external fixator or femoral distractor, large percutaneous reduction forceps, and percutaneously inserted cannulated screws also help to decrease additional surgical trauma to the soft tissue envelope.

Should wound breakdown occur, even if it seems superficial, immediate surgical intervention is indicated. Irrigation and débridement of all devitalized skin, muscle, and bone are mandatory. Only if the wound can be closed without tension can immediate closure over suction drains be considered.

If a deep abscess is encountered, the wound should be packed open and subsequent irrigation and débridement procedures undertaken within 48 hours. If a culture-negative wound has been confirmed, secondary wound closure should be accomplished. In most cases, this requires a lateral or medial gastrocnemius-soleus rotational flap. Rarely, for large areas of wound breakdown and soft tissue necrosis, a vascularized free flap is necessary.

Fixation that provides fracture stability should be maintained. If hardware is obviously loose or provides inadequate fixation, it should be removed and the limb stabilized with a spanning external fixator. Fixation failure with wound breakdown and infection is often a disastrous complication that may ultimately lead to a secondary knee arthrodesis. Intra-articular sepsis combined with instability results in rapid chondrolysis and destruction of the joint.

Aseptic nonunion can occur, especially in the higher energy type V and VI fractures, at the junction of the metaphysis and diaphysis.[8, 14, 154, 157] As previously mentioned, these lesions should be bone grafted as soon as they become apparent. In some circumstances, fixation may need to be revised. If a loss of articular reduction occurs because a major articular fragment displaces, revision should be considered as soon as possible, particularly if the displacement causes joint instability, because a late revision is extremely difficult. Malunion or nonunion can occur with late articular collapse or deformation of the metaphysis-shaft junction.[86] If the mechanical axis is affected, an osteotomy to restore the normal mechanical axis is indicated. If an articular surface malunion occurs in an older patient, a total-knee arthroplasty may be the best salvage procedure (Figs. 56–51 and 56–52).

Arthrofibrosis can occur after severe fractures or if early range of motion was not instituted in the immediate postoperative period. To reduce the risk of an extension contracture, patients for whom continuous passive motion is unavailable, and whose wound can tolerate such a position, can be immobilized in 60 to 90 degrees of flexion for the first 2 or 3 days after surgery. After splint removal, active motion is encouraged if wound healing is progressing satisfactorily. Mobilization in flexion greatly accelerates and facilitates postoperative mobilization of the knee in these circumstances. Arthroscopic lysis of adhesions combined with gentle manipulation under anesthesia is indicated for patients who do not achieve 90 degrees of flexion within the first 4 weeks after surgery (Fig. 56–53).

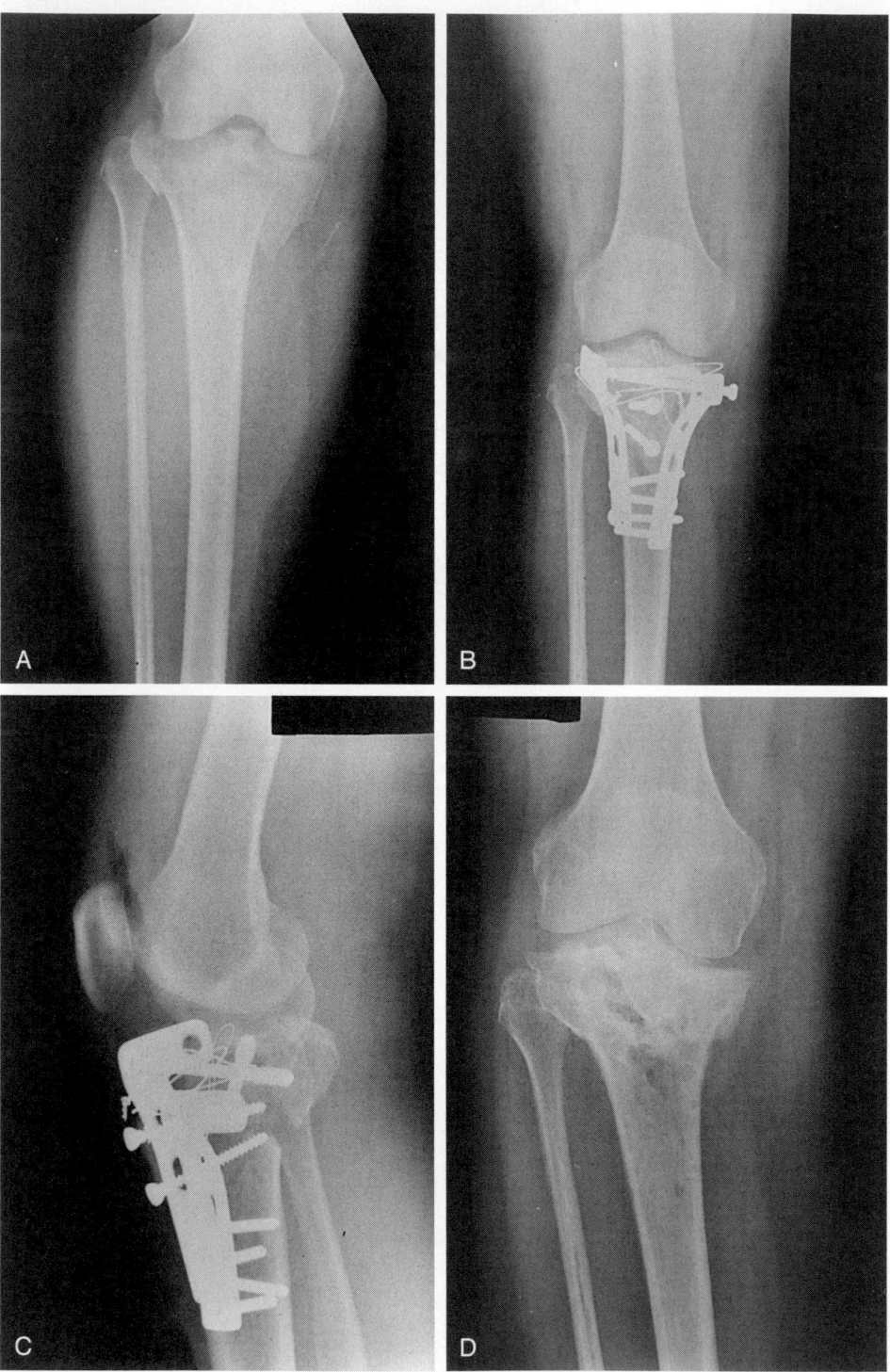

**FIGURE 56–51.** *A,* A type V fracture that requires stabilization of both tibial condyles. *B, C,* The fixation construct consists of dual plating and cerclage wires. This nonrecommended technique involves extensive stripping of the soft tissues. Note the malreduction of the posterior condyle. *D,* With such extensive soft tissue dissection and malreduction, this fracture went on to late collapse and severe varus deformity. Salvage required a total-knee arthroplasty.

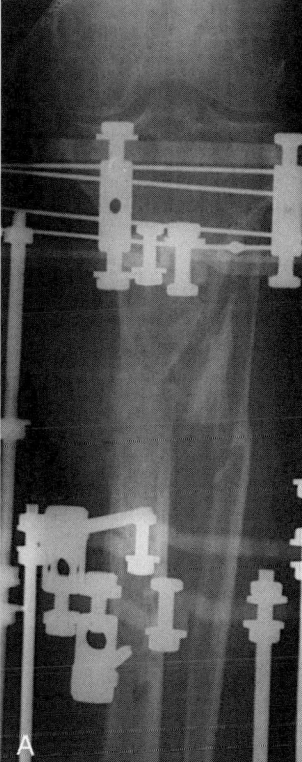
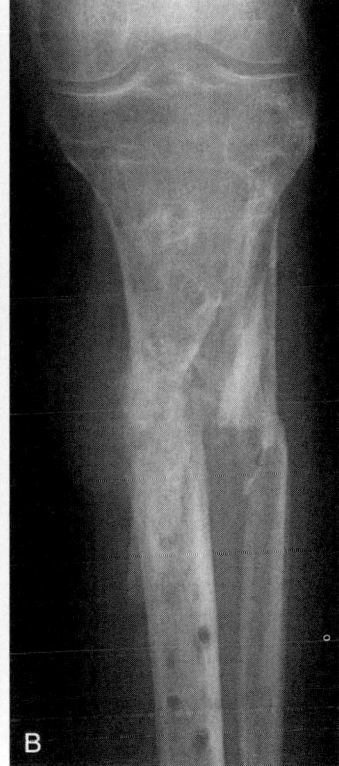
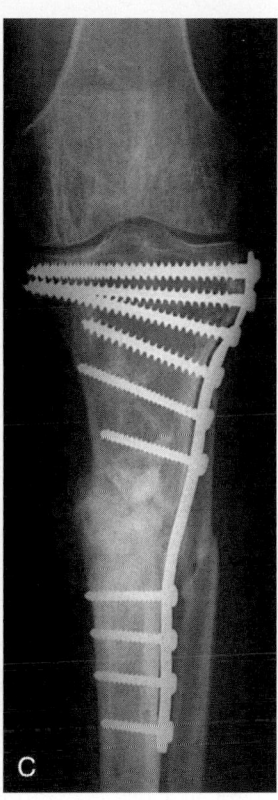

**FIGURE 56–52.** *A,* Severe plateau fracture treated with hybrid external fixation. Note extensive diaphyseal-metaphyseal comminution (location of most complications). *B,* This region progressed to nonunion with development of mild deformity. *C,* After healing of all pin tract sites, revision osteosynthesis with bone grafting resulted in complete healing and resolution of deformity.

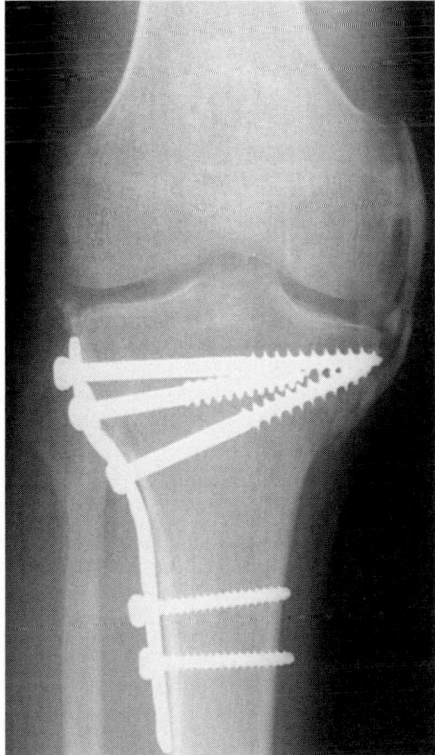

**FIGURE 56–53.** Postoperative complication with development of heterotopic ossification resulting in complete loss of motion and near-ankylosis of the knee. This complication required extensive open bone resection and intra-articular lysis of adhesions in an effort to restore a satisfactory range of motion.

During the postoperative period prior to full unrestricted weight bearing, the operative limb may experience periods of significant swelling, especially when placed in a dependent position. Swelling occurs more frequently with higher energy fracture patterns and is expected. However, if the swelling continues even after periods of recumbency, ultrasonographic or venographic surveillance for deep venous thrombosis should be carried out.

## SUMMARY

Fractures of the tibial plateau involve a major weight-bearing joint. To preserve normal knee function, the surgeon must strive to restore joint congruity, maintain the normal mechanical axis, ensure joint stability, and restore a full range of motion. If the fracture is undisplaced or the joint is stable, closed treatment with early protected joint mobilization usually yields satisfactory results. Plaster immobilization of even undisplaced fractures often leads to significant knee stiffness. Joint instability and significant incongruity are clear indications for surgical treatment. Moderate osteoporosis is not an argument against open reduction techniques.[13, 96, 135]

With more complex fractures, it is essential to consider not only the bone injury but also the associated soft tissue damage. Use of limited open approaches in conjunction with ligamentotaxis, indirect reduction aids, wire-guided cannulated screws, and minimally invasive plating techniques allows the surgeon to treat higher energy injuries effectively with internal fixation. If extensive comminution and soft tissue conditions are not favorable for ORIF, hybrid and circular small-wire external fixators offer a safer means for early fracture reduction and stabilization. Treatment based on the general principles and techniques we have described usually results in a functionally satisfactory outcome.

## REFERENCES

1. Abbott, L.C.; Carpenter, W.F. Surgical approaches to the knee joint. J Bone Joint Surg Am 27:277, 1945.
2. Andrews, J.R.; Tedder, J.L.; Godbout, B.P. Bicondylar tibial plateau fracture complicated by compartment syndrome. Orthop Rev 21:317, 1992.
3. Apley, A.G. Fractures of the lateral tibial condyle treated by skeletal traction and early mobilization. J Bone Joint Surg Br 38:699, 1956.
4. Apley, A.G. Fractures of the tibial plateau. Orthop Clin North Am 10:61, 1979.
5. Bal, G.K.; Kuo, R.S.; Chapman, J.R.; et al. The anterior T-frame external fixator for high-energy proximal tibial fractures. Clin Orthop 380:234, 2000.
6. Barrow, B.A.; Fajman, W.A.; Parker, L.M.; et al. Tibial plateau fractures: Evaluation with MR imaging. Radiographics 14:553, 1994.
7. Belanger, M.; Fadale, P. Compartment syndrome of the leg after arthroscopic examination of a tibial plateau fracture: Case report and review of the literature. Arthroscopy 13:646, 1997.
8. Benirschke, S.K.; Agner, S.G.; Mayo, K.A.; et al. Open reduction internal fixation of complex proximal tibial fractures. J Orthop Trauma 5:236, 1991.
9. Bennett, W.F.; Browner, B. Tibial plateau fractures: A study of associated soft tissue injuries. J Orthop Trauma 8:183, 1994.
10. Berg, E.E. Comminuted tibial eminence anterior cruciate ligament avulsion fractures: Failure of arthroscopic treatment. Arthroscopy 9:446, 1993.
11. Beris, A.E.; Soucacos, P.N.; Glisson, R.R.; et al. Load tolerance of tibial plateau depressions reinforced with a cluster of K-wires. Bull Hosp Jt Dis 55:12, 1996.
12. Bernfeld, B.; Kligman, M.; Roffman, M. Arthroscopic assistance for unselected tibial plateau fractures. Arthroscopy 12:598, 1996.
13. Biyani, A.; Reddy, N.S.; Chaudhury, J.; et al. The results of surgical management of displaced tibial plateau fractures in the elderly. Injury 26:291, 1995.
14. Blake, R.; Watson, J.T.; Morandi, M.; et al. Treatment of complex tibial plateau fractures with the Ilizarov external fixator. J Orthop Trauma 7:167, 1993.
15. Blaser, P.F.; Wicky, S.; Husmann, O.; et al. Value of 3D CT in diagnosis and treatment of fractures of the tibial plateau. Swiss Surg 4:180, 1998.
16. Blokker, C.P.; Rorabeck, C.H.; Bourne, R.B. Tibial plateau fractures and analysis of treatment in 60 patients. Clin Orthop 182:193, 1984.
17. Bolhofner, B.R. Indirect reduction and composite fixation of extra-articular proximal tibial fractures. Clin Orthop 315:75, 1995.
18. Brophy, D.P.; O'Malley, M.; Li, D.; et al. MR imaging of tibial plateau fractures. Clin Radiol 51:873, 1996.
19. Brown, G.A.; Sprague, B.L. Cast brace treatment of plateau and bicondylar fractures of the proximal tibia. Clin Orthop 119:184, 1976.
20. Brown, T.D.; Anderson, D.D.; Nepola, J.V.; et al. Contact stress aberrations following imprecise reduction of simple tibial plateau fractures. J Orthop Res 6:851, 1988.
21. Buchko, G.M.; Johnson, D.H. Arthroscopy assisted operative management of tibial plateau fractures. Clin Orthop 332:29, 1996.
22. Bucholz, R.W.; Carlton, A.; Holmes, R. Interporous hydroxyapatite as a bone graft substitute in tibial plateau fractures. Clin Orthop 240:53, 1989.
23. Buckle, R.; Blake, R.; Watson, J.T.; et al. Treatment of complex tibial plateau fractures with the Ilizarov external fixator. J Orthop Trauma 7:167, 1993.
24. Burks, R.T.; Schaffer, J.J. A simplified approach to the tibial attachment of the posterior cruciate ligament. Clin Orthop 254:216, 1990.
25. Burri, C.; Bartzke, G.; Coldeway, J.; et al. Fractures of the tibial plateau. Clin Orthop 138:84, 1979.
26. Caspari, R.B.; Hutton, P.M.; Whipple, T.L.; et al. The role of arthroscopy in the management of tibial plateau fractures. Arthroscopy 1:76, 1985.
27. Catagni, M. Fractures of the leg (tibia). In: Maiocchi, A.B.; Aronson, J., eds. Operative Principles of Ilizarov. Baltimore, Williams & Wilkins, 1991, p. 91.
28. Chan, P.S.; Klimkiewicz, J.J.; Luchetti, W.T.; et al. Impact of CT scan on treatment plan and fracture classification of tibial plateau fractures. J Orthop Trauma 11:484, 1997.
29. Chapman, M.W. The use of internal fixation in open fractures. Orthop Clin North Am 11:579, 1980.
30. Chapman, M.W.; Mahoney, M. The role of internal fixation in the management of open fractures. Clin Orthop 138:120, 1979.
31. Charnley, J. The Closed Treatment of Common Fractures, 3rd ed. Baltimore, Williams & Wilkins, 1961.
32. Christensen, K.; Powell, J.; Bucholz, R. Early results of a new technique for treatment of high grade tibial plateau fractures. J Orthop Trauma 4:226, 1990.
33. Clancey, G.J.; Hanson, S.T. Open fractures of the tibia. J Bone Joint Surg Am 60:118, 1978.
34. Colletti, P.; Greenberg, H.; Terk, M.R. MR findings in patients with acute tibial plateau fractures. Comput Med Imaging Graph 20:389, 1996.
35. Daniel, D.; Rice, T. Valgus-varus stability in a hinged cast used for controlled mobilization of the knee. J Bone Joint Surg Am 61:135, 1979.
36. DeBoeck, H.; Opdecam, P. Posteromedial tibial plateau fractures: Operative treatment by posterior approach. Clin Orthop 320:125, 1995.
37. DeCoster, T.A.; Nepola, J.V. Cast brace treatment of proximal tibial plateau fractures: Ten year follow-up study. Clin Orthop 231:196, 1988.
38. Delamarter, R.; Hohl, M. The cast brace and tibial plateau fractures. Clin Orthop 242:26, 1989.
39. Delamarter, R.; Hohl, M.; Hopp, E. Ligament injuries associated with tibial plateau fractures. Clin Orthop 250:226, 1990.
40. Dendrinos, G.K.; Kontos, S.; Katsenis, D.; Dalas, A. Treatment of high-energy tibial plateau fractures by the Ilizarov circular fixator. J Bone Joint Surg Br 78:710, 1996.
41. Dias, J.J.; Stirling, A.M.; Finlay, D.B.; Gregg, R.J. Computerised axial tomography for tibial plateau fractures. J Bone Joint Surg Br 69:84, 1987.
42. Drennan, D.B.; Locker, F.G.; Maylahn, D. Fractures of the tibial plateau: Treatment by closed reduction and spica cast. J Bone Joint Surg Am 61:989, 1979.
43. Duwelius, P.T.; Connolly, F.T. Closed reduction of tibial plateau fractures: A comparison of functional and radiographic results. Clin Orthop 230:116, 1988.
44. Edwards, C.C. Staged reconstruction of complex open tibial fractures using Hoffmann external fixation. Clin Orthop 178:130, 1983.
45. Edwards, C.C.; Browner, B.D. Early management of open periarticular fractures using the Hoffmann external fixator. Int Orthop 5:4, 1982.
46. Elstrom, J.; Pankovich, A.M.; Sassoon, H.; Rodriguez, J. The use of tomography in the assessment of fractures of the tibial plateau. J Bone Joint Surg Am 58:551, 1976.
47. Fernandez, D.L. Anterior approach to the knee with osteotomy of the tibial tubercle for bicondylar tibial plateau fractures. J Bone Joint Surg Am 70:208, 1988.
48. Fowble, C.D.; Zimmer, J.W.; Schepsis, A.A. The role of arthroscopy in the assessment and treatment of tibial plateau fractures. Arthroscopy 9:584, 1993.
49. Frankel, V.H.; Green, S.A.; Paley, D.; et al. Symposium: Current applications for the Ilizarov technique. Contemp Orthop 28:51, 1994.
50. Gaudinez, R.F.; Mallik, A.R.; Szporn, M. Hybrid external fixation of comminuted tibial plateau fractures. Clin Orthop 328:203, 1996.
51. Gausewitz, S.; Hohl, M. The significance of early motion in the treatment of tibial plateau fractures. Clin Orthop 202:135, 1986.
52. Gazdag, A.R.; Lane, J.M.; Glaser, D.; Foster, R.A. Alternatives to autogenous bone graft: Efficacy and indications. J Am Acad Orthop Surg 3:1, 1995.

53. Georgiadis, G.M. Combined anterior and posterior approaches for complex tibial plateau fractures. J Bone Joint Surg Br 76:285, 1994.

54. Gerber, A.; Ganz, R. Combined internal and external osteosynthesis: A biological approach to the treatment of complex fractures of the proximal tibia. Injury 29:C22.

55. Gossling, H.R.; Peterson, C.A. A new surgical approach in the treatment of depressed lateral condylar fractures of the tibia. Clin Orthop 140:96, 1979.

56. Guanche, C.A.; Markman, A.W. Arthroscopic management of tibial plateau fractures. Arthroscopy 9:467, 1993.

57. Gustilo, R.B. Fractures of the tibial plateau. In: Gustilo, R.B.; Kyle, R.; Templeman, D., eds. Fractures and Dislocations. St. Louis, C.V. Mosby, 1993, p. 945.

58. Harper, M.C.; Henstorf, J.E.; Vessely, M.B.; et al. Closed reduction and percutaneous stabilization of tibial plateau fractures. Orthopaedics 18:623, 1995.

59. Helpenstell, T.; Hansen, S.T., Jr. The treatment of open distal femur fractures with immediate open reduction and internal fixation. J Orthop Trauma 5:235, 1991.

60. Henry, S.L.; Ostermann, P.A.W.; Seligson, D. The antibiotic bead pouch technique: The management of severe compound fractures. Clin Orthop 295:54, 1993.

61. Hohl, M. Part I fractures of the proximal tibia and fibula. In: Rockwood, C.A.; Green, D.; Bucholz, R., eds. Fractures in Adults, 3rd ed. Philadelphia, J.B. Lippincott, 1991, p. 1725.

62. Hohl, M. Tibial condylar fractures. Instr Course Lect 33:206, 1963.

63. Hohl, M. Tibial condyle fractures. J Bone Joint Surg Am 49:1455, 1967.

64. Hohl, M.; Luck, V. Fractures of the tibial condyle. J Bone Joint Surg Am 38:1001, 1956.

65. Holt, M.D.; Williams, L.A.; Dent, C.M. MRI in the management of tibial plateau fractures. Injury 26:595, 1995.

66. Holzach, P.; Matter, P.; Minter, J. Arthroscopically assisted treatment of lateral tibial plateau fractures in skiers: Use of a cannulated reduction system. J Orthop Trauma 8:273, 1994.

67. Honkonen, S.E. Indications for surgical treatment of tibial condyle fractures. Clin Orthop 302:199, 1994.

68. Honkonen, S.E.; Järvinen, M.J. Classification of fractures of the tibial condyles. J Bone Joint Surg Br 74:840, 1992.

69. Honkonen, S.E. Degenerative arthritis after tibial plateau fractures. J Orthop Trauma 9:273, 1995.

70. Honkonen, S.E.; Kannus, P.; Natri, A.; et al. Isokinetic performance of the thigh muscles after tibial plateau fractures. Int Orthop 21:323, 1997.

71. Horwitz, D.S.; Bachus, K.N.; Craig, M.A.; Peters, C.L. A biomechanical analysis of internal fixation of complex tibial plateau fractures. J Orthop. Trauma 13:545, 1999.

72. Houben, P.F.; van der Linden, E.S.; van den Wildenberg, F.A.; Stapert, J.W. Functional and radiological outcome after intra-articular tibial plateau fractures. Injury 28:459, 1997.

73. Ilizarov, G.A. The treatment of fractures: Theoretical considerations, experimental studies and clinical application of the apparatus. In: Ilizarov, G.A.; Green, S.A., eds. Transosseous Osteosynthesis: Theoretical and Clinical Aspects of the Regeneration and Growth of Tissue. Berlin, Springer-Verlag, 1992, p. 369.

74. Insall, J.N.; Door, L.D.; Scott, R.D.; Scott, W.N. Rationale of the Knee Society clinical rating system. Clin Orthop 248:13, 1989.

75. Ishiguro, T.; Imai, N.; Tomatsu, T.; et al. A new method of closed reduction using the spring action of Kirschner wires for fractures of the tibial plateau: A preliminary report. Nippon Seikeigeka Gakkai Zasshi 60:227, 1986.

76. Itokazu, M.; Matsunaga, T.; Ishii, M.; et al. Use of arthroscopy and interporous hydroxyapatite as a bone graft substitute in tibial plateau fractures. Arch Orthop Trauma Surg 115:45, 1996.

77. Itokazu, M.; Matsunaga, T. Arthroscopic restoration of depressed tibial plateau fractures using bone and hydroxyapatite grafts. Arthroscopy 9:103, 1993.

78. Jennings, J.E. Arthroscopic management of tibial plateau fractures. Arthroscopy 1:160, 1985.

79. Jensen, D.B.; Rude, C.; Duus, B.; Bjerg-Nielsen, A. Tibial plateau fractures: A comparison of conservative and surgical treatment. J Bone Joint Surg Br 72:49, 1990.

80. Keating, J.F. Tibial plateau fractures in the older patient. Bull Hosp Jt Dis 58:19, 1999.

81. Keating, J.F.; Blachut, P.A.; O'Brien, P.J.; et al. Reamed nailing of open tibial fractures: Does the antibiotic bead pouch reduce the deep infection rate? J Orthop Trauma 10:298, 1996.

82. Kelly, C.M.; Wilkins, R.M.; Gitelis, S.; et al. The use of a surgical grade calcium sulfate as a bone graft substitute. Clin Orthop 382:42, 2001.

83. Kennedy, J.C.; Bailey, W.H. Experimental tibial plateau fractures. J Bone Joint Surg Am 50:1522, 1969.

84. Keogh, P.; Kelly, C.; Cashman, W.F.; et al. Percutaneous screw fixation of tibial plateau fractures. Injury 23:387, 1992.

85. Kettlekamp, D.B.; Hillberry, B.M.; Murrish, D.E.; Heck, D.A. Degenerative arthritis of the knee secondary to fracture malunion. Clin Orthop 234:159, 1988.

86. King, G.J.; Schatzker, J. Nonunion of a complex tibial plateau fracture. J Orthop Trauma 5:209, 1991.

87. Kode, L.; Lieberman, J.M.; Motta, A.O.; et al. Evaluation of tibial plateau fractures: Efficacy of MR imaging compared with CT. AJR 163:141, 1994.

88. Koechlin, P.; Nael, J.F.; Bonnet, J.C.; et al. Ligamentous lesions associated with fractures of the tibial plateau. Acta Orthop Belg 49:751, 1983.

89. Koval, K.J.; Helfet, D.L. Tibial plateau fractures: Evaluation and treatment. J Am Acad Orthop Surg 3:86, 1995.

90. Koval, K.J.; Polatsch, D.; Kummer, F.J.; et al. Split fractures of the lateral tibial plateau: Evaluation of three fixation methods. J Orthop Trauma 10:304, 1996.

91. Koval, K.T.; Sanders, R.; Borrelli, J.; et al. Indirect reduction and percutaneous screw fixation of displaced tibial plateau fractures. J Orthop Trauma 6:340, 1992.

92. Kwiatkowski, K.; Cejmer, W.; Sowinski, T. Frozen allogenic spongy bone grafts in filling the defects caused by fractures of proximal tibia. Ann Transplant 4(3–4):49, 1999.

93. Lachiewicz, P.F.; Funcik, I. Factors influencing the results of open reduction and internal fixation of tibial plateau fractures. Clin Orthop 259:210, 1990.

94. Lansinger, O.; Bergman, B.; Courmner, L.; et al. Tibial condylar fractures: A 20 year followup. J Bone Joint Surg Am 68:13, 1986.

95. Leutenegger, A. Integration and resorption of calcium phosphate ceramics in defect filling of fractures of the tibial head: Radiologic long-term results. Helv Chir Acta 60:1061, 1994

96. Levy, O.; Salai, M.; Ganel, A.; et al. The operative results of tibial plateau fractures in older patients: A long-term followup and review. Bull Hosp Jt Dis 53:15, 1993.

97. Liow, R.Y.; Birdsall, P.D.; Mucci, B; Greiss, M.E. Spiral computed tomography with two- and three-dimensional reconstruction in the management of tibial plateau fractures. Orthopedics 22:929, 1999.

98. Lobenhoffer, P.; Schulze, M.; Gerich, T.; et al. Closed reduction/percutaneous fixation of tibial plateau fractures: Arthroscopic versus fluoroscopic control of reduction. J. Orthop Trauma 13:426, 1999.

99. Mallik, A.R.; Coval, D.J.; Whitelaw, G.P. Internal versus external fixation of bicondylar tibial plateau fractures. Orthop Rev 21:1433, 1992.

100. Marsh, J.L.; Smith, S.T.; Do, T.T. External fixation and limited internal fixation for complex fractures of the tibial plateau. J Bone Joint Surg Am 77:661, 1995.

101. Marwah, V.; Gadegone, W.M.; Magarkar, D.S. The treatment of fractures of the tibial plateau by skeletal traction and early mobilisation. Int Orthop 9:217, 1985.

102. Mast, J.; Ganz, R.; Jacob, R. Planning and Reduction Techniques in Fracture Surgery. Berlin, Springer-Verlag, 1989.

103. Mazoue, C.G.; Guanche, C.A.; Vrahas, M.S. Arthroscopic management of tibial plateau fractures: An unselected series. Am J Orthop 28:508, 1999.

104. McEnery, K.W.; Wilson, A.J.; Pilgram, T.K.; et al. Fractures of the tibial plateau: Value of spiral CT coronal plane reconstruction for detecting displacement in vitro. AJR 163:1177, 1994.

105. Mikulak, S.A.; Gold, S.M.; Zinar, D.M. Small wire external fixation of high energy tibial plateau fractures. Clin Orthop 356:230, 1998.

106. Mitchell, N.; Shepard, N. Healing of articular cartilage in intra-articular fractures in rabbits. J Bone Joint Surg Am 62:628, 1980.

107. Moed, B.R.; Carr, S.E.W.; Craig, J.G.; Watson, J.T. Open reduction and internal fixation of posterior wall fractures of the acetabulum. Clin Orthop 377:57, 2000.

108. Moore, T.M.; Harvey, J.P., Jr. Roentgenographic measurement of tibial-plateau depression due to fracture. J Bone Joint Surg Am 56:155, 1974.

109. Moore, T.M.; Meyers, M.H.; Harvey, J.P., Jr. Collateral ligament laxity of the knee: Long-term comparison between plateau fractures and normal. J Bone Joint Surg Am 58:594, 1976.

110. Moore, T.M. Fracture dislocation of the knee. Clin Orthop 156:128, 1981.

111. Moore, T.M.; Patzakis, M.G.; Harvey, J.B. Tibial plateau fractures: Definition, demographics, treatment rationale, and long term results of closed traction management or operative reduction. J Orthop Trauma 1:97, 1987.

112. Mueller, M.E.; Nazarian, S.; Koch, P.; et al. Comprehensive Classification of Fractures of Long Bones. Berlin, Springer-Verlag, 1990.

113. Muezzinoglu, U.S.; Guner, G.; Gurfidan, E. Arthroscopically assisted tibial plateau fracture management: A modified method. Arthroscopy 11:506, 1995.

114. Murphy, C.P.; D'Ambrosia, R.; Dabezies, E.T. The small pin circular fixator for proximal tibial fractures with soft tissue compromise. Orthopedics 14:273, 1991.

115. O'Dwyer, K.J.; Bobic, V.R. Arthroscopic management of tibial plateau fractures. Injury 23:261, 1992.

116. Padanilam, T.G.; Ebraheim, N.A.; Frogameni, A. Meniscal detachment to approach lateral tibial plateau fractures. Clin Orthop 314:192, 1995.

117. Parker, P.J.; Tepper, K.B.; Brumback, R.J.; et al. Biomechanical comparison of fixation of type-I fractures of the lateral tibial plateau. Is the antiglide screw effective? J Bone Joint Surg Br 81:478, 1999.

118. Pauwels, F. Neue Richtlinien fuer die operative Behandlung der Coxarthrose. Verh Dtsch Orthop Ges 48:332, 1932.

119. Perez Carro, L. Arthroscopic management of tibial plateau fractures: Special techniques. Arthroscopy 13:265, 1997.

120. Perry, C.R.; Evans, G.; Rice, S.; et al. New surgical approach to fractures of the lateral tibial plateau. J Bone Joint Surg Am 66:1236, 1984.

121. Rafi, M.; Firooznia, H.; Golimba, C.; et al. Computed tomography of tibial plateau fractures. AJR 142:1181, 1984.

122. Rafi, M.; Lamont, J.G.; Firooznia, H. Tibial plateau fractures: CT evaluation and classification. Crit Rev Diagn Imaging 27:91, 1987.

123. Rangitsch, M.R.; Duwelius, P.J.; Colville, M.R. Limited internal fixation of tibial plateau fractures. J Orthop Trauma 7:168, 1993.

124. Rasmussen, P. Tibial condylar fractures, impairment of knee joint stability as an indicator for surgical treatment. J Bone Joint Surg Am 55:1331, 1973.

125. Rawes, M.L.; Harper, W.H.; Oni, O.O. A serious vascular complication of internal fixation of a tibial plateau fracture: A cautionary tale from which several lessons can be learned. J Trauma 40:323, 1996.

126. Reid, J.S.; Vanslyke, M.; Moulton, M.J.R.; Mann, T.A. Safe placement of proximal tibial transfixation wires with respect to intracapsular penetration. Orthopaedic Transactions, Orthopaedic Trauma Association meeting, Tampa, Fla, Sept 29–Oct 1, 1995.

127. Ries, M.D.; Meinhard, B.P. Medial external fixation with lateral plateau internal fixation in metaphyseal tibia fractures: A report of eight cases associated with severe soft-tissue injury. Clin Orthop 256:215, 1990.

128. Rittmann, W.W.; Schibli, M.; Matter, P.; Allgower, M. Open fractures: Long-term results in 200 consecutive cases. Clin Orthop 138:132, 1979.

129. Russell, T.A.; Kumar, A.; Davidson, R.L.; et al. Fibular head autograft. A salvage technique for severely comminuted lateral fractures of the tibial plateau: Report of five cases. Am J Orthop 25:766, 1996.

130. Ryd, L.; Toksvig-Larsen, S. Stability of the elevated fragment in tibial plateau fractures: A radiographic stereophotogrammetric study of postoperative healing. Int Orthop 18:131, 1994.

131. Salter, R.; Simmonds, D.F.; Malcolm, B.W.; et al. The biological effects of continuous passive motion on the healing of full thickness defects in articular cartilage: An experimental investigation in the rabbit. J Bone Joint Surg Am 62:1232, 1980.

132. Sarmiento, A.; Kinnman, P.B.; Latta, L.L. Fractures of the proximal tibia and tibial condyle: A clinical and laboratory comparative study. Clin Orthop 145:136, 1979.

133. Savoie, F.H.; Vander Griend, R.A.; Ward, E.F.; Hughes, J.L. Tibial plateau fractures: A review of operative treatment using AO technique. Orthopedics 10:745, 1987.

134. Schatzker, J. Fractures of the tibial plateau. In: Schatzker, J.; Tile, M., eds. Rationale of Operative Fracture Care. Berlin, Springer-Verlag, 1988, p. 279.

135. Schatzker, J.; McBroom, R. Tibial plateau fractures: The Toronto experience 1968–1975. Clin Orthop 138:94, 1979.

136. Scheerlinck, T.; Ng, C.S.; Handelberg, F.; Casteleyn, P.P. Medium-term results of percutaneous, arthroscopically-assisted osteosynthesis of fractures of the tibial plateau. J Bone Joint Surg Br 80:959, 1998.

137. Schwartsman, R.; Brinker, M.R.; Beaver, R.; Cox, D.D. Patient self-assessment of tibial plateau fractures in 40 older adults. Am J Orthop 27:512, 1998.

138. Scotland, T.; Wardlaw, D. The use of cast bracing as treatment for fractures of the tibial plateau. J Bone Joint Surg Br 63:575, 1991.

139. Segal, D.; Franchi, A.V.; Campanile, J. Iliac autograft for reconstruction of severely depressed fracture of a lateral tibial plateau: Brief note. J Bone Joint Surg Am 67:1270, 1985.

140. Segal, D.; Mallik, A.R.; Wetzler, M.J.; et al. Early weight bearing of lateral tibial plateau fractures. Clin Orthop 294:232, 1993.

141. Segur, J.M.; Torner, P.; Garcia, S.; et al. Use of bone allograft in tibial plateau fractures. Arch Orthop Trauma Surg 117:357, 1998.

142. Sirkin, M.S.; Bono, C.M.; Reilly, M.C.; Behrens, F.F. Percutaneous methods of tibial plateau fixation. Clin Orthop 375:60, 2000.

143. Spiegel, P.G.; Shybut, G.T. Tibial plateau fractures. Editorial. Clin Orthop 183:12, 1979.

144. Stamer, D.T.; Schenk, R.; Staggers, B.; et al. Bicondylar tibial plateau fractures treated with a hybrid ring external fixator: A preliminary study. J Orthop Trauma 8:455, 1994.

145. Stills, M.; Christensen, K.; Powell, J.; Bucholz, R. Cast bracing of bicondylar tibial plateau fractures after combined internal and external fixation. J Prosthet Orthot 3:106, 1991.

146. Stokel, E.A.; Sadesivan, K.K. Tibial plateau fractures: Standardized evaluation of operative results. Orthopedics 14:263, 1991.

147. Trickey, E.L. Rupture of the posterior cruciate ligament of the knee. J Bone Joint Surg Br 50:334, 1968.

148. Tscherne, H.; Gotzen, L. Fractures With Soft Tissue Injuries. Berlin, Springer-Verlag, 1984.

149. Tscherne, H.; Lobenhoffer, P. Tibial plateau fractures: Management and expected results. Clin Orthop 292:87, 1993.

150. Vangsness, C.T., Jr.; Ghaderi, B.; Hohl, M.; et al. Arthroscopy of meniscal injuries with tibial plateau fractures. J Bone Joint Surg Br 76:488, 1994.

151. Villas, C.; Mora, G.; Arriola, F.J. Use of bone allografts in the surgical repair of tibial plateau fractures. Rev Med Univ Navarra 40(3):13, 1996.

152. Waddell, A.P.; Johnston, D.W.C.; Neidre, A. Fractures of the tibial plateau: A review of 95 patients and comparison of treatment methods. J Trauma 21:376, 1981.

153. Walker, S.; Erkman, M.J. The role of the menisci in force transmission across the knee. Clin Orthop 109:184, 1975.

154. Watson, J.T. High energy fractures of the tibial plateau. Orthop Clin North Am 25:728, 1994.

155. Watson, J.T.; Coufal, C. Treatment of complex lateral plateau fractures using Ilizarov techniques. Clin Orthop 353:97, 1998.

156. Watson, J.T.; Karges, D.; Moed, B.R. The value of CT scanning for preoperative evaluation of tibial plateau fractures. Abstract. Programs and Abstracts of the 9th Annual Meeting of the Orthopaedic Trauma Association, New Orleans, 1993, p. 76.

157. Weiner, L.S.; Kelley, M.; Yang, E.; et al. The use of combination internal fixation and hybrid external fixation in severe proximal tibia fractures. J Orthop Trauma 9:244, 1995.

158. Wilkins, R. Bioassayed demineralized bone matrix and calcium sulfate: Use in bone graft procedures. Paper presented at the 10th Annual Meeting of the International Society of Limb Salvage, Cairns, Australia, Apr 11–14, 1999.

159. Wilppula, E.; Bakalim, G. Ligamentous tear concomitant with tibial condylar fracture. Acta Orthop Scand 43:292, 1972.

160. Young, M.J.; Barrack, R.L. Complications of internal fixation of tibial plateau fractures. Orthop Rev 23:149, 1994.

161. Zecher, S.B.; Danziger, M.B.; Segal, D.; et al. Treatment of high-energy proximal tibial fractures using the Monticelli-Spinelli external fixator: A preliminary report. Am J Orthop 25:49, 1996.

# 57

# Tibial Shaft Fractures

Peter G. Trafton, M.D.

Fractures of the tibia are among the most common of serious skeletal injuries. They are slow to heal and frequently cause permanent sequelae. Complications related to both injury and treatment will occur, especially after more severe injuries. It is often difficult to separate problems related to the injury from those associated with therapy. In treating tibial fractures, the surgeon not so much avoids the risk of complications as exchanges one risk for another. For example, nonreamed intramedullary (IM) nailing reduces the frequency of reoperation, nonunion, and infection in comparison to external fixation.[47] However, in the proximal end of the tibia, IM nailing carries a significant risk of malunion.[179, 326] For better alignment, some surgeons advocate the use of plates, which have a higher risk of wound complications, including infection.[602] Using preliminary external fixation, delayed plate insertion, and less invasive indirect reduction techniques may help avoid the complications of plating while gaining the advantages of a more appropriate form of fixation for the metadiaphyseal region of the tibia.

Because tibial fractures vary greatly in severity, general prescriptions for treatment are not applicable to each patient. The spectrum of injury extends from trivial enough to be ignored to so severe that amputation is the best treatment. Tibial fractures tax a surgeon's judgment and skill. After carefully evaluating all aspects of the patient, the injury, and the available options, the surgeon must select and manage an effective treatment regimen. This aspect of fracture management remains true even as our knowledge about these injuries and their treatment improves. Differences of opinion about management of tibial shaft fractures have been well documented.[47, 300] In spite of strong evidence that nonreamed IM nailing is associated with fewer complications than external fixation for open tibial fractures is, many surgeons have been slow to adopt IM nailing, particularly for more severe open fractures.[47] Reamed IM nailing has a reduced incidence of nonunion and hardware breakage in comparison to nonreamed nailing. Few studies have directly compared reamed nailing with nonreamed nailing for open fractures. Such studies suggest that the two procedures have similar rates of infection, but they do not establish equivalency. Many thus believe that it is premature to conclude that reamed nailing is preferable for open tibial fractures, much less those that are severely contaminated or infected and ununited.[46] However, a randomized prospective trial has shown that reamed nailing is better for lower energy closed tibial shaft fractures.[125] It is still true that much has yet to be learned about tibial shaft fractures.[342] At long last, improved clinical studies are providing helpful evidence for surgeons who treat these common injuries. Nonetheless, there remains a glaring absence of current information regarding the grading of injury severity and factors that determine whether to operate on a tibial shaft fracture. Proponents of nonoperative treatment present their opinions zealously and can show numerous good and excellent results after functional fracture bracing of clearly less severe injuries.[509] However, the available comparative studies suggest that unless one is skilled at selecting patients for nonoperative care, surgery, particularly closed IM nailing, provides more predictable results with fewer complications.[9, 112, 147, 252, 280, 281, 575, 602] How we assess the outcome of injury and treatment can also influence our judgment about management preferences. When comparing different treatments of tibial fractures, no convincing yardstick such as acute mortality or 5-year survival rate can be used. Newer patient-oriented functional outcome scales are invaluable tools,[557] but present outcome studies do not yet answer, for a given patient, whether the risk of knee pain after IM nailing or the risk of ankle stiffness after cast treatment should be accepted.

It has been suggested that strong evidence has established the superiority of one approach (nonreamed IM nailing versus external fixation) for open tibial shaft fractures.[46, 47] However, the surgeon must still decide, based on an evaluation of the patient and the entire clinical situation, whether IM nailing is feasible and, indeed, optimal for this patient at this time. In many, if not most situations, it may well be that no single "best" treatment exists. If done well and with careful follow-up that identifies and appropriately addresses the inevitable complications, one might make a reasonable case for nailing, for plating, or for external fixation, depending on which complications will have a greater impact on the patient and which can be corrected more easily or more effectively.

Judgment is developed through clinical experience, and thus the wisdom of a consultant who treats many such injuries may be helpful. Because several variables are involved, a protocol that mandates one treatment for a certain type of tibial fracture may not be optimal in a particular clinical situation. Fracture location, morphology, soft tissue envelope, and bacterial contamination all help in suggesting the fixation method, should fixation be indicated.

In this chapter, the spectrum of injuries and the available options for treatment of tibial shaft fractures are reviewed. Each recommendation must be considered in the light of a clinical situation. Much of the controversy associated with the treatment of tibial fractures is the result of proponents of a given therapy failing to clearly specify the characteristics of the patients for whom they use it. Indeed, some surgeons may not recognize the selection biases affecting the populations that they treat. They may thus conclude that a treatment that is successful in their hands will be similarly well suited to all patients with tibial fractures. Physicians who wish to avoid such errors are warned to pay as much attention to the injury and its evaluation as is paid to its treatment.

Complications from tibial shaft fractures are inevitable. Their management will be discussed in detail after review of acute care. An astute surgeon will realize that initial diagnosis plus treatment of tibial fractures offers an excellent opportunity for damage control that minimizes the consequences and hastens recovery from infection, nonunion, and loss of alignment or fixation.

After discussion of tibial shaft fractures, brief sections are included on isolated fractures of the fibular shaft, injuries to the proximal tibiofibular joint, and fatigue fractures of both bones.

# PATHOLOGY

## Relevant Anatomy

The lower part of the leg, from the knee to the ankle, participates in the structure and function of these important joints. It serves as a weight-bearing support for the body and is also a conduit for the neurovascular supply of the foot, as well as the location of its important extrinsic myotendinous units.

The tibia, with its asymmetric surrounding soft tissues, determines the shape of the lower part of the leg. Its roughly triangular external cross section has an anteriorly directed apex. Its anteromedial subcutaneous surface has no muscular or ligamentous attachments from the pes anserinus tendons and tibial collateral ligament of the knee to the deltoid ligament of the ankle. This readily palpable surface is concave medially as it approaches the medial malleolus. Its anterolateral surface forms the medial wall of the anterior muscular compartment of the leg, with the tibialis anterior and, more distally, the neurovascular bundle and extensor hallucis longus muscles adjacent to it.

The tibia's posterior surface, buried under superficial and deep muscle compartments, has attachments, in a proximal-to-distal direction, for the semimembranosus, popliteus, soleus, tibialis posterior, and flexor digitorum longus muscles. The posterior tibial vessels, the tibial nerve, and the flexor hallucis longus muscle approach it distally by curving around the medial malleolus behind the tibialis posterior and flexor digitorum longus.

The adult tibia ranges from less than 30 cm to more than 47 cm in length. In today's heterogenic world, the entire spectrum of tibial dimensions may be encountered by a trauma surgeon in nearly any location. The tibia varies not only in length but also in minimal diameter of the medullary canal, which may be less than 8 mm to more than 15 mm. Length and internal diameter have significant implications for the size of implants required for IM fixation. Most of the tibia is diaphyseal (Fig. 57–1). Its enlarged proximal and distal ends are composed of cancellous bone, which varies in density according to both location and the individual's age and metabolic bone status. The cortex surrounding the metaphyseal spongiosa becomes quite thin as distance increases from the diaphysis. Screw purchase in the tibial metaphysis is thus provided by the threads engaging cancellous rather than cortical bone. The transition zone, readily apparent on radiographs, is important to consider. It may be thick enough to require drilling to the outside diameter of the thick shank of a cancellous lag screw, but it might also be so thin that neither drilling nor tapping of threads is necessary.

The proximal tibial metaphysis, with its medial and lateral tibial plateaus, is much larger in diameter than the shaft but is similarly triangular in cross section. Laterally, it overhangs the interosseous membrane and articulates posterolaterally with the head of the fibula. Its anterior apex forms the tibial tubercle with the attached patellar ligament. Also apparent is the apex-anterior angulation of the proximal end of the tibia, which averages 15°. The backward-sloping, but variably shaped anterior surface of the tibial metaphysis offers a more or less obvious surface for inserting an IM nail. The cancellous bone of the proximal metaphysis can be perforated fairly easily to gain access to the medullary canal. However, the shape of the proximal end of the tibia, its posterior overhang, and its thin, flat posterior wall make it possible to err and perforate the posterior cortex.

The medullary canal becomes distinctly tubular 5 or 10 cm distal to the tibial tubercle and has thick walls, especially anteriorly, where the prominent crest of the tibia occupies nearly a third of the diameter of the entire bone. This dense cortical bone is difficult to pierce with anything but the sharpest bit and is dense enough to generate significant heat during penetration. When placing screws or pins across the tibial diaphysis, it is essential to remember the thickness of the anterior crest and aim posteriorly enough to bisect the internal rather than the external diameter and thus obtain true bicortical purchase (Fig. 57–2).

Distally, the shaft flares and becomes more rounded as it undergoes a transition from diaphysis to metaphysis. The cortex thins, and the fatty medullary contents are replaced with cancellous bone that is surprisingly dense,

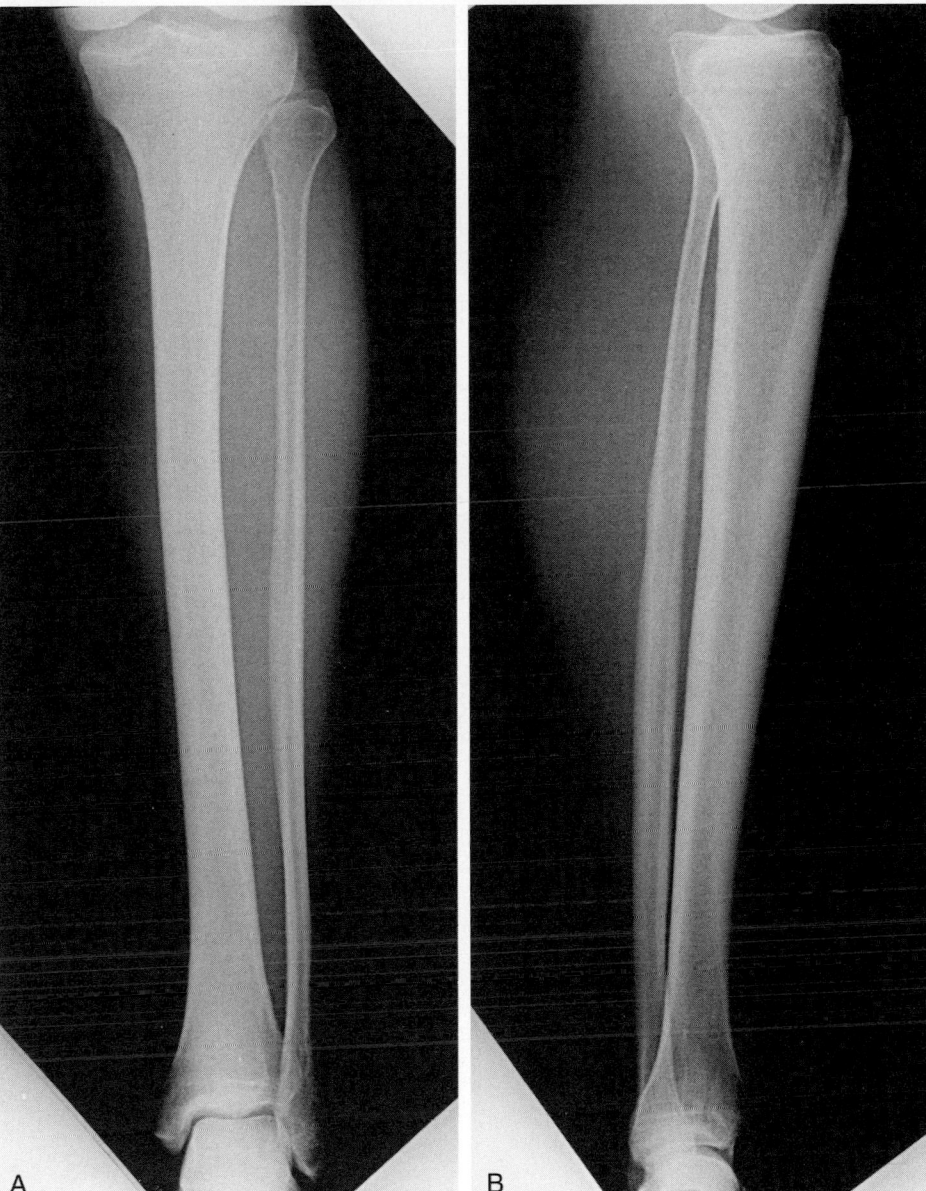

**FIGURE 57–1.** Anteroposterior (A) and lateral (B) radiographs of a normal adult male tibia and fibula. Note the variable thickness of the cortex and typical surface curvature.

especially in the young and active, in the 5 cm or so above the subchondral bone of the transverse tibial plafond, the "ceiling" of the ankle joint. This cancellous bone provides secure purchase for screws and is often compact enough to resist penetration by an IM nail.

The contour of the distal end of the tibia is notable for a somewhat pronounced concavity on its anteromedial surface—enough to suggest a varus deformity if one looks at the subcutaneous outline rather than the central axis of the bone. Restoring this distal medial concavity is an essential part of closed reduction of distal tibial shaft fractures. If a cast applied to such an injury is straight along its medial side rather than concave over the distal third, a valgus malalignment is produced. Mast and co-workers[356] point out that the shape of the tibia's medial surface is fairly constant from patient to patient. The radius of the supramalleolar curvature is approximately 20 cm. As the triangular diaphyseal cross section rounds gently into

the pilon, or distal tibial metaphysis, the anteromedial surface, oriented about 45° to the sagittal plane, turns medially so that its most distal extent lies nearly in a sagittal plane. According to Mast and colleagues, the relative constancy of this surface shape permits precontouring of a plate that can be used to reduce a fracture without complete exposure of all its fragments.

The tibia's medullary canal extends from the cancellous bone of the proximal metaphysis to that of the distal metaphysis. If the canal were extended proximally along its axis, it would enter the lateral plateau because of the relatively greater medial overhang. The largest sagittal dimension of the proximal end of the tibia is also laterally located. Buehler and associates pointed out that for both these reasons, a lateral entry site for an IM nail, anterior to the lateral intercondylar eminence, is least likely to deform a proximal fracture.[84] The diaphyseal canal is significantly more round in cross section than the external appearance

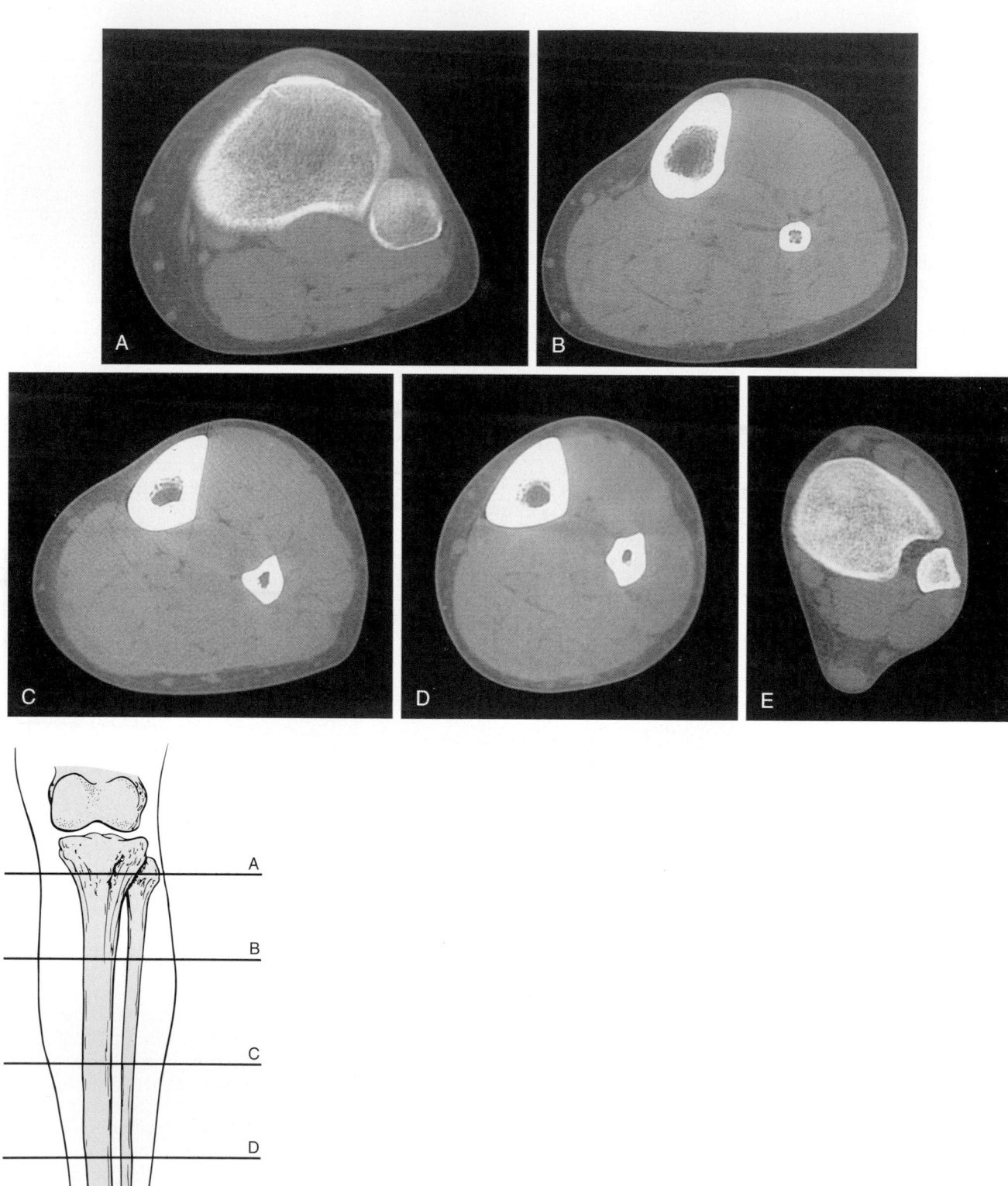

**FIGURE 57–2.** *A–E,* Transverse computed tomographic scans of a normal adult male tibia at the levels indicated on the drawing. Note the relatively round diaphyseal medullary canal with a diameter measuring approximately 10 mm. The anterior cortex is especially thick, and the external surface shape is roughly triangular. The asymmetric soft tissue coverage is readily apparent.

of the tibia would suggest. Unlike the femur, it is more hourglass shaped than tubular, with a variably pronounced isthmus. Even after IM reaming, a snug fit for an IM nail can be obtained only in the middle few centimeters of the tibia. This limitation adversely affects the stability of proximal and distal fractures fixed with a nail. In the young, the medullary canal tends to be narrow. With aging and osteoporosis, the cortex becomes thinner, the metaphyseal cancellous bone becomes less dense, and the internal diameter of the medullary canal increases.

The diaphyseal blood supply typically reaches the tibia by way of a single nutrient artery, a proximal branch of the posterior tibial artery.[465] After passing through the most proximal portion of the tibialis posterior, it obliquely enters the tibial shaft on its posterior surface in the proximal portion of the middle third of the bone. It is easily injured by displacement of a fracture through its long cortical foramen. Within the medullary canal, it courses proximally and distally and anastomoses with the metaphyseal endosteal vessels (Fig. 57–3). A displaced fracture of the diaphysis is thus likely to devascularize the shaft downstream from the nutrient artery. If peripheral soft tissues are also significantly stripped, the entire vascular supply can be lost over a distance of several centimeters. Combined loss of the medullary and periosteal blood supply interferes with fracture healing and places the tibia at risk for post-traumatic osteomyelitis.

Through its intraosseous distribution, the medullary arterial system of the tibia provides nourishment to most of the uninjured diaphysis. Only the peripheral fourth to third of the diaphyseal cortex is supplied by anastomosing periosteal vessels.[466] This fact is of special significance after reaming for an IM nail because the combined devascularization caused by both the fracture and reaming produces a layer of necrotic bone through much of the diaphysis.[466] The medullary arterial circulation regenerates in a few weeks in the space that exists around a medullary nail. This arterial regeneration permits revascularization of the inner cortical bone, which is also supported by recruitment of periosteal collateral circulation if the surrounding soft tissues are healthy enough. However, until revascularization has occurred, the dead cortical bone is not able to participate in the healing process or resist infection.

After a fracture, the tibial blood supply changes dramatically. Peripheral vessels are recruited to take over much of the arterial supply of the cortex and revascularize necrotic areas, as well as provide nourishment for the metabolically active peripheral callus.[21, 467, 468, 551] This process requires healthy surrounding tissue and is most effective in areas with muscles closely applied to the tibia. Surfaces that are covered only with periosteum, subcutaneous tissue, and skin are less able to benefit from this temporary extraosseous blood supply. Viable attached

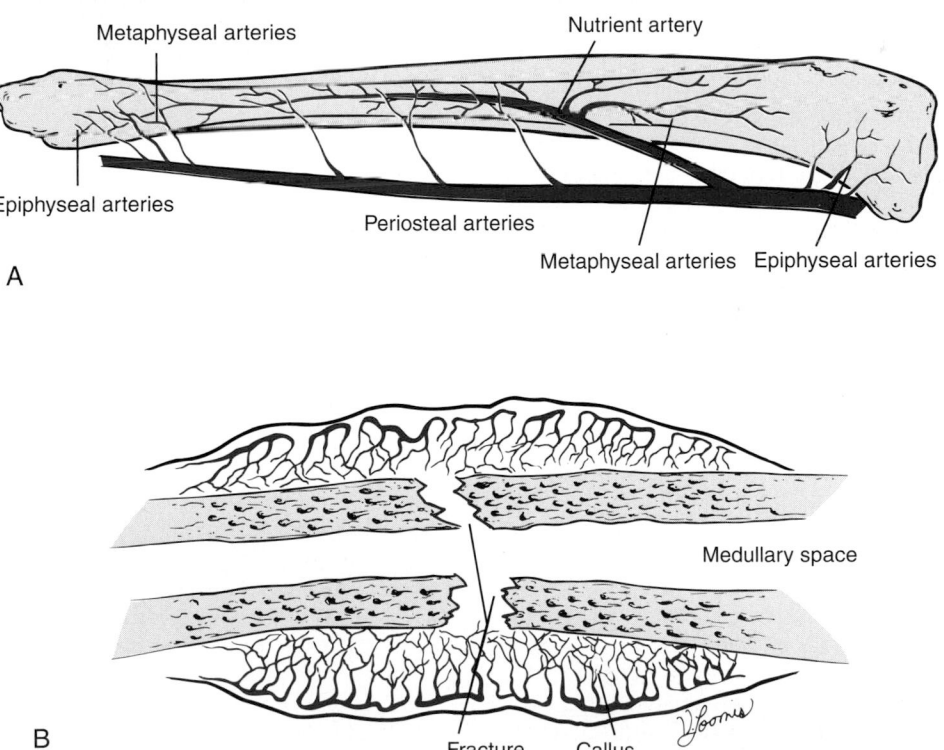

**FIGURE 57–3.** *A,* The arterial blood supply of an intact human tibia arrives primarily by way of a single nutrient artery, a branch of the posterior tibial artery. It enters through an oblique, fairly long, and distally angled foramen that is usually located in the upper part of the middle third of the tibia. Where the external surface of the tibia is covered only by periosteum, the nutrient artery supplies nearly the full cortical thickness. Where muscles and ligaments are firmly attached, periosteal arterioles supply as much as the outer third of the cortex. A comparatively rich system of metaphyseal arteries is present proximally and distally. These arteries anastomose with the medullary branches of the nutrient artery and provide collateral flow and regenerative potential after injury to this system. *B,* The blood supply changes significantly after a fracture. Peripheral callus is nourished primarily by a rich vascular plexus derived from the surrounding musculature. The greater the soft tissue injury, the less potential for recruiting this blood supply.

muscular pedicles are thus crucial for segments of a fractured tibia and should be preserved during surgical exposure for débridement or fixation.

A most important feature of the anatomy of the lower extremity is the relationship between the tibia and the obviously smaller fibula, which is situated posterolaterally and has more muscle surrounding it than its larger neighbor does. The fibula is farther from the tibia in the proximal half of the leg and approaches it quite closely in the distal half until it lies within a shallow articular facet on the posterolateral surface of the distal tibial metaphysis. Securely attached to each other, these parallel bones articulate proximally at the superior tibiofibular joint and distally at the inferior one.

The subcutaneous fibular head anchors the lateral collateral ligament of the knee and the biceps femoris tendon. The common peroneal nerve wraps superficially around its neck from an initially posterior location and divides into superficial and deep portions. As it rounds the fibula, the peroneal nerve is at risk of injury from a direct blow, from the stretching that occurs with widely displaced fractures or dislocations, and importantly, from the pressure of casts, splints, and even firm mattresses.

Although the fibula does bear a small portion of body weight, its function is only slightly affected by absence of its diaphysis or proximal extent.[331] Removal of a portion of the fibula decreases, but does not abolish tension strain on the tibia's anterior surfaces.[569] The fibular shaft is a significant site of muscle origin. Closely accompanied by the peroneal artery, it can be surgically transferred with this artery as a free or pedicle graft to treat distant or local bone defects.

The distal end of the fibula, or the lateral malleolus, has a major role in the structural integrity of the ankle joint. It is securely attached to the distal end of the tibia through the ligaments of the ankle syndesmosis—the anterior and posterior distal tibiofibular ligaments, the inferior transverse ligament, and the interosseous ligament—as well as through the distal interosseous membrane. Disruption of these ligaments, with resultant loss of fibular support for the talus, may occur in association with tibial shaft fractures; therefore, the integrity of the ankle joint should always be assessed in patients with tibial fractures.

A thick interosseous membrane connects the lateral crest of the tibia to the anteromedial border of the fibula. Its major fibers run downward and laterally. This membrane is often largely intact after indirect torsional fractures of the tibia, and according to Sarmiento, Latta, and others, it is the major constraint to shortening of such injuries.[504, 507, 543, 569]

Over the top of the interosseous membrane beneath the proximal tibiofibular joint, the anterior tibial artery and its accompanying veins enter the anterior compartment of the leg. Injury to these structures may be associated with proximal tibial fractures and tibiofibular joint dislocations. The terminal peroneal artery passes anteriorly under the distal edge of the interosseous membrane to join the vascular anastomoses about the ankle.

The tibia and fibula are surrounded by soft tissues that are most important in any consideration of injuries to this region.[240, 572, 588] In fact, surgeons who pay more attention to the bones than to these soft tissues may commit irretrievable errors in evaluating and treating fractures of the tibia and fibula. The soft tissue envelope of the leg is injured to a greater or lesser extent whenever a fracture occurs. Open wounds are usually obvious, although they may be small and may under-represent the extent of damage within. Subcutaneous degloving may soon result in extensive skin necrosis. Initially, however, such a wound can appear quite benign. Swelling within the fascial compartments of the leg may gradually lead to tissue pressure high enough to occlude capillary blood flow, thus producing a compartment syndrome with loss of nerve and muscle tissue. Direct or indirect injuries may occur to the nerves and blood vessels of the leg. Clearly, each anatomic element of the leg must be considered together with injuries to its bones and joints.

The skin receives significant blood supply from the underlying fascia by way of small perforating arteries. These arteries are disrupted by subcutaneous dissection or by degloving injuries that separate the subcutaneous fat from the underlying fascia. Therefore, dissection should proceed beneath, rather than superficial to the deep fascia to decrease the risk of skin necrosis and take advantage of the subfascial arterial plexus, which is raised off the underlying muscle with the fascia. The dermal plexus is the terminal vascular bed of the skin. Its patency and perfusion are clearly demonstrated by punctate bleeding after tangential excision of a split-thickness layer of skin. This technique has been used by Ziv and associates to assess the viability of degloved skin.[643] A significant advance has been the development of fasciocutaneous flaps nourished by local vessels, often those accompanying superficial sensory nerves.[117] Awareness of superficial vascular anatomy is the key to success with these nonrandom flaps.

Superficial veins in the subcutaneous tissue of the leg include the saphenous on the medial side and the short saphenous on the lateral side. The small saphenous nerve branches that run with the former, as well as the sural nerve near the latter, may become entrapped in a scar or suture and result in a painful neuroma. Because the deep venous system may be damaged at the time of injury or may subsequently be occluded by venous thrombosis, it is important to preserve the major superficial veins when operating on a tibial fracture. Note that the saphenous vein, which is anterior to the medial malleolus, crosses the subcutaneous surface of the tibia in its lower third to lie posterior to the bone on its course proximally to the medial aspect of the thigh.

The deep fascia of the leg envelops it circumferentially and is adherent to the tibia along its anteromedial surface, as well as proximally and distally, except for narrow passages for tendons and neurovascular structures. The cylinder thus formed is subdivided into four well-defined longitudinal compartments by septa that attach along the fibula. An anterolateral septum divides the lateral compartment from the anterior one. A posterolateral septum lies between the lateral and superficial posterior compartments. Finally, a posterior septum intervenes between the deep and superficial posterior compartments. More proximally, this septum attaches to the medial aspect of the tibia. Beyond the midshaft, it attaches to the medial surface of the deep investing fascia so that only a small part of the medial surface of the deep posterior compartment is subcutaneous, that behind the posteromedial border of the distal half of the tibia.

Familiarity with the cross-sectional anatomy of the leg is essential for fracture surgeons.[332a] Such knowledge aids in the physical examination, facilitates surgical approaches, and helps avoid injury to neurovascular and tendinous structures during insertion of percutaneous pins and wires (Fig. 57–4).

## COMPARTMENTAL ANATOMY

The *anterior compartment* contains the dorsiflexors of the ankle and toes: the tibialis anterior, the extensor hallucis longus (in its distal half), and the extensor digitorum communis along with the accompanying peroneus tertius. Its neurovascular bundle consists of the anterior tibial artery and veins, joined in the proximal part of the compartment by the deep peroneal nerve. The artery is assessed distally by the dorsalis pedis pulse. However, flow may be retrograde from the deep plantar arch and may thus be present in spite of loss of the anterior tibial artery. The deep peroneal nerve supplies an autonomous sensory zone dorsally on the foot between the bases of the first and second toes. It provides motor control for the anterior compartment muscles, as well as the short toe extensors. During most of its course through the anterior compartment, the neurovascular bundle lies deep on the interosseous membrane lateral to the tibialis anterior. However, as this muscle becomes tendinous and thinner in the proximal third of the distal quarter, the neurovascular bundle advances anteriorly across the lateral surface of the tibia, where it may be harmed by pins inserted through the bone. A little more distally, it lies anteriorly on the tibia

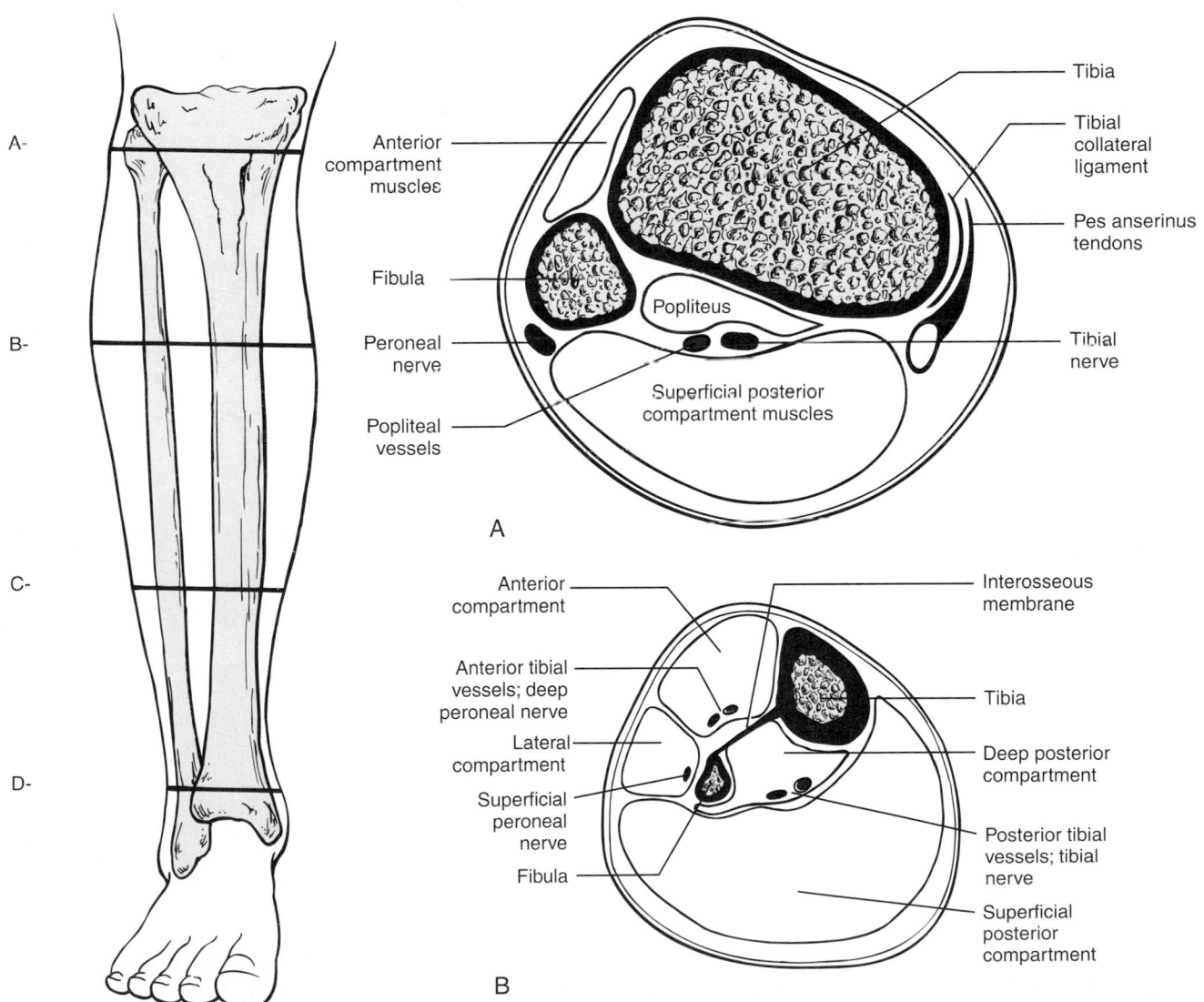

**FIGURE 57–4.** *A–D,* Cross-sectional drawings at the levels indicated demonstrate the location of the major nerves and arteries of the leg. Note that the anteromedial surface of the entire tibia, though through a variable arc, is accessible immediately below the skin and subcutaneous tissue. The distal popliteal artery and tibial nerve are in the midline posterior to the proximal end of the tibia. The close proximity of both the anterior tibial artery and the accompanying deep peroneal nerve is an important aspect of the anterolateral tibial surface near the junction of the third and fourth quarters. The posterior tibial artery and tibial nerve are close behind the posteromedial surface of the distal quarter of the tibia.

*Illustration continued on following page*

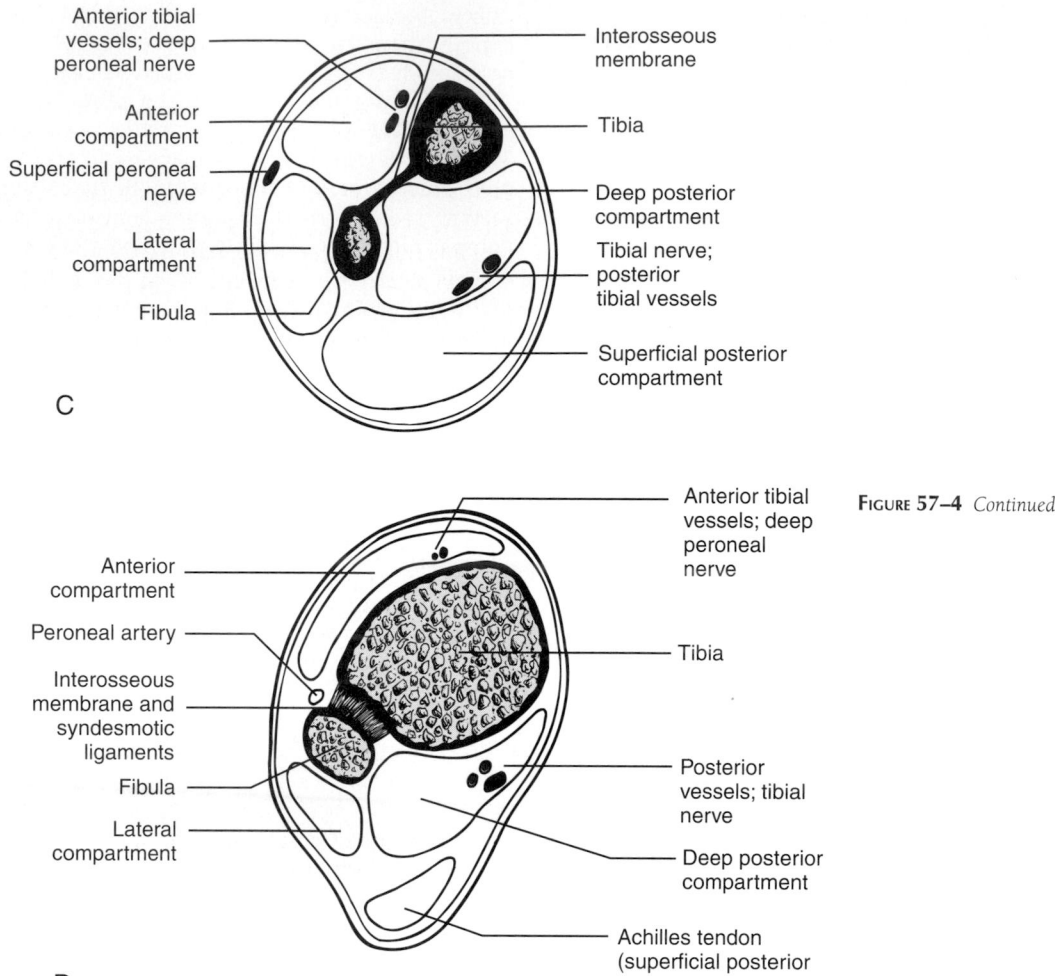

Anterior tibial vessels; deep peroneal nerve

Anterior compartment

Superficial peroneal nerve

Lateral compartment

Fibula

Interosseous membrane

Tibia

Deep posterior compartment

Tibial nerve; posterior tibial vessels

Superficial posterior compartment

C

Anterior compartment

Peroneal artery

Interosseous membrane and syndesmotic ligaments

Fibula

Lateral compartment

Anterior tibial vessels; deep peroneal nerve

Tibia

Posterior vessels; tibial nerve

Deep posterior compartment

Achilles tendon (superficial posterior compartment)

D

**FIGURE 57–4** *Continued.*

between the tendons of the tibialis anterior and extensor hallucis muscles.

The *lateral compartment,* superficial to the fibula, contains the peroneus brevis and longus muscles, the evertors of the foot. The peroneus longus begins proximally on the lateral aspect of the fibular head. The common peroneal nerve passes under this muscle at the point where it covers the neck of the fibula. Proximally, the peroneus brevis is deep to the peroneus longus, whereas distally, it becomes anterior. Thus, behind the lateral malleolus, the brevis is the more anterior of the two tendons. The superficial peroneal nerve, which provides sensory input from the remainder of the dorsum of the foot and motor function to the peroneus muscles, lies within the lateral compartment, but no major vascular structures are present.

The *superficial posterior compartment* contains the triceps surae, or the primary ankle flexors consisting of the gastrocnemius, soleus, and plantaris muscles. The sural nerve lies between layers of the posterior fascia of this compartment and provides sensation to the lateral aspect of the heel. No major artery lies within this compartment, which is the most distensible and least likely to have elevated pressure after injury.

The *deep posterior compartment* lies underneath (anterior to) the superficial compartment and distal to the popliteal line, with its muscles applied to the posterior surfaces of the tibia, the interosseous membrane, and the fibula. Within it lie the posterior tibial vessels and the tibial nerve, which provides motor function to the compartmental and plantar intrinsic muscles and sensory input from the sole of the foot. Also present are the peroneal vessels. The muscles in the deep posterior compartment are the flexor digitorum longus medially, the flexor hallucis longus laterally, and deep to these muscles, the tibialis posterior. In a proximal-to-distal direction, the tibial neurovascular bundle first lies posterior to the popliteus and then posterior to the medial border of the tibialis posterior. The tibial nutrient artery leaves the posterior tibial artery shortly after it is formed and reaches the bone through the proximal part of the tibialis posterior. The tendon of the tibialis posterior passes across the tibia and under the flexor digitorum longus to lie anterior to it and establish the well-known relationship of the deep posterior compartment structures behind the medial malleolus: the tibialis posterior, flexor digitorum longus, posterior tibial artery and tibial nerve, and flexor hallucis longus—"Tom, Dick, ANd Harry" (Table 57–1).

# Incidence

The tibial shaft is the most common location for a diaphyseal fracture of a long bone. Such fractures occur approximately twice a year per 1000 population in Malmö, Sweden[42]; the rate is similar in the United States. From 1993 to 1995 in the United States, an average of 61,000 hospitalizations for fractures of the tibia and fibula occurred annually in patients older than 18 years.[449] Court-Brown and McBirnie have provided epidemiologic data for tibial shaft fractures in Edinburgh, Scotland, from 1988 through 1990, where the entire 750,000 population receives inpatient and outpatient treatment of tibial shaft fractures at their institution.[122] In patients older than 12 years, they found an incidence of 174 diaphyseal fractures per year, approximately 2 per 10,000. Nearly one third were sports injuries, 80% of which were due to soccer, a less likely cause in regions where this sport is less popular. Road traffic injuries were most common, with falls not far behind. Assaults accounted for less than 5%. Gunshot wound fractures, so common in parts of the United States, were very rare. Seventy-six percent of the tibial shaft fractures were closed. Of the 24% that were open, 21% were Gustilo type I, 19% were type II, 17% were type IIIA, 36% were type IIIB, and 5% were type IIIC. These authors noted that only 24% of their tibial fractures were severe, as indicated by Müller fracture type C, Tscherne soft tissue injury grade C3, or Gustilo type III. The worst injuries were sustained by motorcyclists and by pedestrians struck by motor vehicles. The frequency of tibial fractures appears to be increasing in the osteoporotic elderly in some populations.[163]

# Mechanisms of Injury

Tibial fractures have many causes ranging from simple falls with a twisting force to severe injuries (e.g., being crushed between two automobile bumpers). Severity may be graded in several ways, and it is essential to distinguish between high- and low-energy injuries. Indirect fractures, which are produced by a torsional force acting at a distance, have a typical spiral pattern and usually cause little soft tissue injury unless they are quite comminuted. The history of the injury, findings on physical examination, and radiographs all corroborate the relatively less forceful nature of this indirectly produced fracture. Even indirect injuries, however, have a spectrum of severity. Much more kinetic energy ($\frac{1}{2}MV^2$) may result from a skiing injury than from a simple slip and fall. The amount of comminution of a spiral fracture is proportional to the amount of energy involved in its production. Comminuted fragments dispersed at high velocity can act as missiles and may cause significant injury to the soft tissues surrounding the fracture. It is thus important to recognize that some indirect tibial fractures are high-energy injuries.[270]

Direct injury mechanisms include bending, as in a skier's "boot top" fracture, in which the top of the boot acts as a fulcrum over which the tibia is broken. Naturally, such direct application of force results in a greater or lesser amount (depending on the amount of force) of direct local soft tissue injury. When a great amount of force is involved, as may occur when a pedestrian is struck by an automobile, the extent of injury is correspondingly more severe. Not surprisingly, the prognosis for such injuries is worse.[86] The application of direct force is often revealed by the history or appearance of the limb, as well as by a fracture pattern that is transverse or has a transverse component on the tension side and a wedge-shaped butterfly fragment on the opposite side that is compressed during a bending mechanism of injury.[33, 156]

The most severe tibial fractures are those caused by crushing injuries. They typically have complex, highly comminuted or segmental patterns with extensive damage to the surrounding soft tissue. Often, however, the skin is minimally burst, a finding suggesting a so-called type I open fracture. However, *by definition,* type I injuries consist of laceration of the skin envelope by a spike of bone produced in an indirect, torsional injury. The term should not be used for injuries caused by direct trauma mechanisms. It is important to not underestimate the severity and consequences of tibial fractures caused by crushing.

Patients with spinal cord injuries may have high-energy tibial fractures associated with their original injury. They behave as typical high-energy injuries, but management must involve consideration of the patient's neurologic status. Patients with chronic spinal cord injuries and marked osteopenia from disuse can sustain tibial fractures from either low- or high-energy mechanisms.[184]

Some tibial fractures are caused by repeated loading with ultimate failure in a fatigue mode. These fractures, known as fatigue or "stress" fractures, are discussed at the end of this chapter. Low levels of force can cause a pathologic fracture (see Chapter 16) of the tibia when it is weakened by any of a variety of processes. Conditions that weaken the tibia sufficiently for a fracture to occur under normally applied loads include secondary and primary malignancies, benign neoplasms, dysplasias, infection, and injuries, including surgery.

An additional injury that remains all too common in the United States is a fracture caused by a gunshot wound. These injuries are reviewed in Chapter 15.

**TABLE 57-1** ● ● ● ● ● ● ● ● ● ● ● ● ● ● ● ● ● ● ● ● ● ● ● ● ● ● ● ● ● ● ● ●

Tests for Assessment of Peripheral Nerves and Compartments of the Leg*

| Nerve | Compartment | Motor Function | Sensory Function |
|---|---|---|---|
| Deep peroneal | Anterior | Toe dorsiflexion | Dorsal I–II web space |
| Superficial peroneal | Lateral | Foot eversion | Lateral dorsum of foot |
| Tibial | Deep posterior | Toe plantar flexion | Sole of foot |
| Sural | Superficial posterior | Gastro-soleus | Lateral heel |

*By testing each nerve and associated muscle group, it is possible to assess the status of myoneural tissue within each compartment.

## Consequences of Injury

Fractures of the tibial shaft prevent weight bearing and ambulation, at least initially, and cause pain and instability. If the fracture is open, serious infection may threaten life and limb. These fractures may be associated with immediate or delayed neurovascular deficits that also threaten survival and function of the limb. Although the average tibial fracture heals in approximately 17 weeks, with more time required for complete rehabilitation, some patients are disabled for a year or more.[161] Even then, recovery is rarely complete. Gaston and colleagues found that the power of knee extensors and flexors averaged 15% to 25% less than that on the opposite side a year after treatment of isolated tibial fractures with IM nails.[186] Long-term functional impairment from tibial fractures is typical,[130, 253, 441, 453] and healing may not occur without additional treatment of nonunion. Deformity may result from either fracture malalignment or contractures of the joints and soft tissues of the ankle and foot. Tibial fractures themselves are rarely lethal injuries, but their prolonged recovery period and their potential for permanent disability are of great significance for the injured person.[253, 345, 574]

Considerable concern exists that malalignment of a healed tibial shaft fracture may result in post-traumatic arthritis of the ankle or knee. However, this possibility has not been irrefutably established,[320, 379, 455, 456, 573, 610] but it is well discussed by Tetsworth and Paley.[566] Assuming that axial deformity does result in joint damage over time, it is not clear what degree of deformity is significant. The location of the malunion is important, with distal deformities more likely to be symptomatic. It may also be that the amount of acceptable deformity varies from patient to patient, as well as with the demands placed on the healed limb. Separating the consequences of deformity from those of associated injuries proves difficult, so the surgeon typically must decide whether to accept a given reduction in the absence of data allowing a reliable prediction of results.

## Commonly Associated Injuries

As many as 30% of tibial fractures occur in patients with multiple injuries. Therefore, because additional injuries could be present, complete assessment of the patient is mandatory and should be repeated 24 to 48 hours after injury, when the tibial fracture becomes less painful and the patient is better able to identify other sites of discomfort. Injuries to other parts are possible even with low-energy slips and falls; they are not restricted to obvious polytrauma patients. Particular attention must be paid to upper extremities injuries, which might interfere with weight bearing for transfers or for walkers and crutches. Injuries involving the opposite leg also pose significant obstacles to early mobilization. Treatment modifications may be required for some or all of the injuries if the patient is to resume ambulation as rapidly as possible.

The most frequent injury associated with a fractured tibia is fracture of the ipsilateral fibula, which occurs in approximately 80% of most series, though less often with lower energy mechanisms.[122, 416] This smaller and weaker bone is often disrupted by indirect or direct forces sufficient to fracture the tibia, and injury may occur at the same or at a distant level and may occasionally be segmental. The commonly associated fibular injury is often ignored because rarely is any specific treatment required for the fibula. Some believe that the presence of an intact fibula makes an isolated tibial fracture more prone to complications such as delayed union and nonunion or varus deformity from maintenance of length on the lateral side, but delayed healing does not appear to be caused by an intact fibula.[415, 416, 561] A fibular fracture, once fixed or healed, may stabilize and aid in the reconstruction of a severe tibial shaft fracture. It may be used as the basis for bypassing a segmental defect in the tibia and also guides restoration of tibial alignment. In addition to a complete fibular fracture, this bone can be plastically deformed or angulated by a "greenstick" fracture and thus interfere with reduction of a tibial deformity.[196]

Usually, the fibula itself fails when forces are sufficient to fracture the tibia. However, as in Monteggia and Galeazzi fractures of the forearm, the proximal or distal tibiofibular joints may occasionally be disrupted so that the tibial fragments override and shorten in spite of an apparently intact fibula. If such injuries are not recognized, deformity or dysfunction of the ankle joint may result. Proximal dislocation of the proximal tibiofibular joint may be associated with serious neurovascular injury.

Tibial shaft fractures may themselves be segmental, with one or more additional diaphyseal disruptions. Occasionally, the second level of injury may be metaphyseal, with intra-articular or extra-articular fractures that threaten the knee or ankle.[68, 343, 605] These fractures vary in their degree of displacement and instability. Such combined injuries often require modification of the usual treatment of the diaphyseal injury; therefore, it is important that they be identified initially. Generally, their treatment takes precedence, according to guidelines described in Chapters 56, 58, and 59. Management of the tibial shaft fracture may require modification. (For example, an injury that would ordinarily be treated nonoperatively might be fixed internally to permit early motion of an associated tibial plateau fracture.) More common than fractures at multiple levels, a single transitional fracture may extend from the diaphysis through the metaphysis and into the articular surface.[572] Identification and appropriate management of the articular involvement are crucial to obtaining an optimal result.

Injuries to the supporting ligaments of the knee joint are fairly commonly associated with tibial shaft fractures, especially those caused by higher levels of energy.[568] In addition to purely ligamentous injuries, fracture-dislocations of the knee may occur, often with associated vascular or neural trauma (Fig. 57–5). Because knee stability is difficult to assess when the tibial shaft is fractured and because arterial occlusion may be delayed, it is vital to not underestimate the significance of marginal avulsion and displaced wedge fractures of the tibial plateau. They may be the only sign of gross knee instability. Arteriography should be considered for such

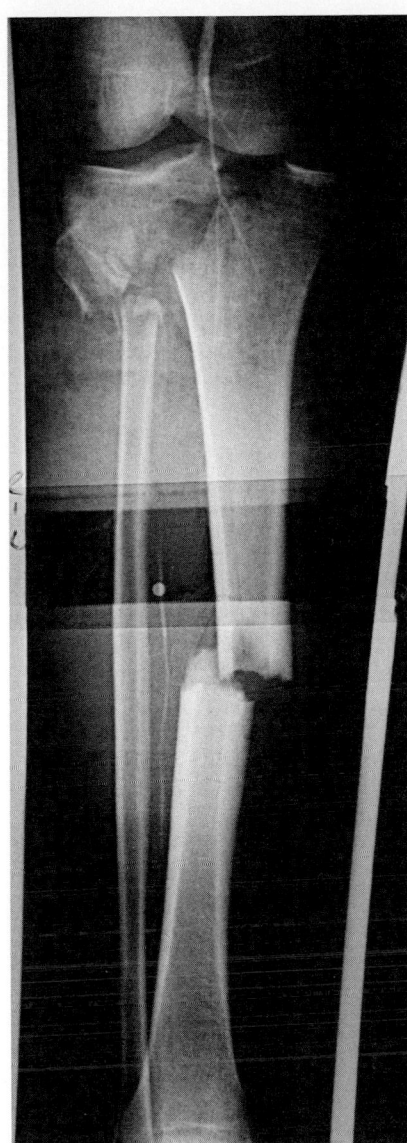

**FIGURE 57–5.** Popliteal artery occlusion is demonstrated by this arteriogram, which was obtained to identify the site of arterial compromise in an ischemic leg with two levels of severe skeletal injury. (Treatment is shown in Figure 57–13.)

limbs, in spite of apparently adequate perfusion, to permit identification and repair of an intimal injury before it thromboses. If the arterial perfusion index (API) is less than 0.9 (Doppler-assisted arterial pressure at the ankle versus that at the wrist), a significant arterial injury must be suspected.[267, 268]

Especially in patients with high-energy injuries, tibial fractures may be associated with fractures of the ipsilateral femur—the so-called floating knee injury.[428] These injuries often involve the knee ligaments as well. Type I floating knees are those with purely diaphyseal fractures of the femur and tibia. Type II floating knees are variations on this theme with involvement of the hip, knee, or ankle joints. Adamson and associates have shown the poor prognosis of these injuries when fractures extend into the knee.[4] Fractures and dislocations distal to a tibial fracture are also not unusual, so careful assessment of the foot and

ankle is required (Fig. 57–6). Because these areas are covered and splinted in the course of treating the tibial fracture, adequate initial physical examination and radiographs are essential if the surgeon is to avoid failing to identify and treat such injuries, which typically involve the tarsometatarsal joints, the metatarsals, or the toes.

Involvement of adjacent arteries, veins, and nerves is common with tibial fractures. These structures may have an immediately apparent injury, or detection of the injury may be delayed. Because of their profound significance for preservation of limb and function, the neurovascular structures of the leg require repeated assessment during care of a patient with a tibial fracture. Arterial injuries may be occult because of the three arterial conduits distal to the popliteal "trifurcation." The limb may survive with flow in only a single artery. Another reason that an arterial injury may be inapparent initially is the previously mentioned phenomenon of an intimal tear that may thrombose several hours or days after fracture. Arterial flow may also be compromised by kinking of the vessels in the zone of injury. This problem may be corrected by reduction of the fracture, but an arteriogram may still be advisable to ensure that this temporary mechanism is the only cause of the ischemia, unless realignment restores a normal API. Venous injury is often occult unless a laceration produces copious bleeding from an open fracture wound. Multiple pathways for venous return exist in both the deep and superficial systems. Venous injuries may accompany injuries to the arterial side of the circulation. They may also be manifested as deep vein thrombosis, which occurs in as many as two thirds of tibial fractures according to Nylander and Semb.[411] Although deep venous thrombosis is commonly associated with tibial shaft fractures, it is not perceived as frequently progressing to more proximal thrombosis or as causing clinically evident pulmonary embolism. However, the risk may be higher than thought, and better data are needed.[1, 306] Late venous insufficiency remains a hazard.[6, 452, 630]

## Development of Classification

Since ancient Egyptian times, many have emphasized that tibial fractures are not all alike and that the prognosis varies with the severity of injury. The importance of an open wound extending to the fracture site was recorded in the Edwin Smith Papyrus. Hamilton emphasized the prognostic significance of comminution.[224] Not until the end of the 19th century, when radiography was applied to the diagnosis and treatment of fractures, could fracture configuration and displacement be used for classifying fracture severity.[440] Ellis, in 1958, used displacement, comminution, and wound severity to assign tibial shaft fractures to one of three grades: minor, moderate, and major.[160, 161] His "minor" tibial fractures were undisplaced or had only angular deformity; an open wound, if present, was small, and comminution was either absent or minimal. He defined "moderate" fractures as those with complete displacement but with no more than a minor wound or minor comminution. His "major" tibial fractures included those with significant comminution or a major open wound. He reviewed 343 conservatively treated tibial fractures and found that average healing times were 10 weeks for minor injuries, 15 weeks for moderate injuries, and 23 weeks for major injuries. Delayed union (20 weeks) occurred in 2% of minor, 11% of moderate, and 60% of major fractures. The importance of injury severity

was made clear by Ellis' work, yet too frequently authors fail to stratify their cases by severity. Instead, they group all such injuries together for analysis and report an "average healing time" for a given treatment without specifying severity. Notable exceptions include Nicoll, who also

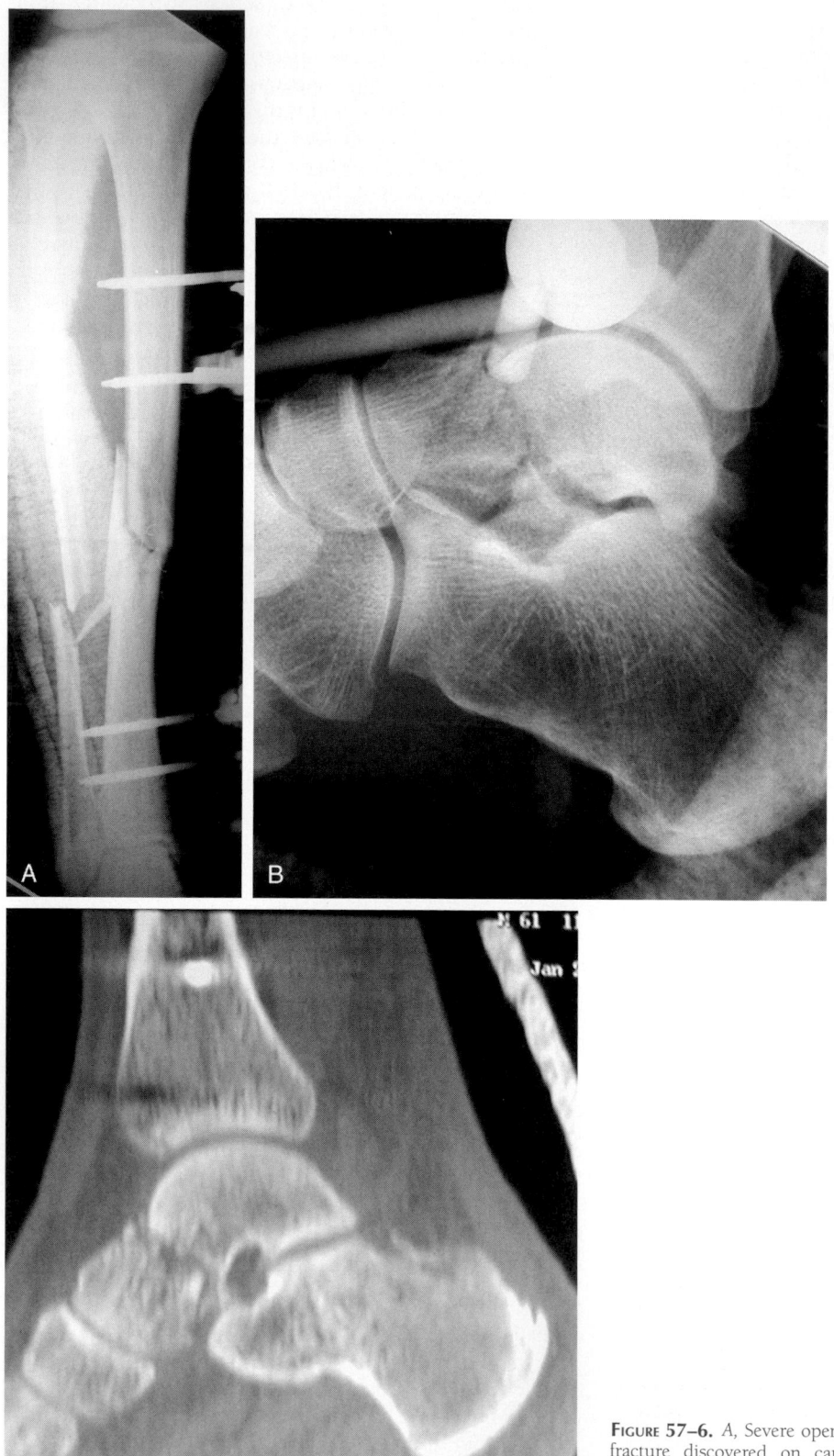

**Figure 57–6.** *A,* Severe open tibia-fibula fracture with associated talar neck fracture discovered on careful follow-up radiographs after emergency external fixation. *B,* Lateral radiograph. *C,* Computed tomographic reconstruction.

demonstrated the significance of displacement, comminution, and wound severity.[406] He further identified segmental bone loss of a centimeter or more and infection as other factors that delayed healing. In 1971, Burwell used Ellis' classification system in his report of plate fixation for tibial shaft fractures, the only author to do so before Austin's meta-analysis was published in 1977.[25, 90] Bauer and colleagues and Edwards noted that the type of trauma (direct or high energy versus indirect or low energy) had a significant effect on outcome and related it to the extent of soft tissue damage.[33, 156] They suggested that the prognosis in fractures of the shaft of the tibia was related more to the severity of soft tissue damage than to the bone injury. This concept is a most important one for the fracture surgeon. There is a close relationship between wound severity and complications such as infection, problems with union, and rate of amputation. Early open-wound classification systems focused on the size of the skin wound. However, it has become clear that the extent of muscle necrosis, microvascular and macrovascular damage, and periosteal stripping is of greater significance. Gustilo and colleagues developed the classification system that is used by most North American orthopaedic surgeons. Initially, it had three categories, but they have been expanded to five and their specifications refined to emphasize the importance of the entire wound.[564] Gustilo's type I open fracture has a wound smaller than 1 cm, "usually a moderately clean puncture through which a spike of bone has pierced the skin." No crushing is involved, and the soft tissue injury is minor. A type II open fracture has a larger wound but no extensive avulsion or crushing of soft tissue and only slight or moderate crushing. All open fractures with severe soft tissue injury and serious contamination are grouped in type III. Because type III itself represents a considerable spectrum of severity, it was necessary to divide these injuries into three very different subtypes. After adequate débridement, type IIIA injuries have sufficient soft tissue coverage of the fractured bone remaining that delayed closure is possible without local or free muscle flaps. Type IIIB open fractures, with more extensive soft tissue injury, leave the bone exposed and require muscle flap coverage. Type IIIC injuries include all open fractures associated with an arterial injury that must be repaired for limb salvage. This system is highly predictive of the risk of wound infection, which with adequate management ranges up to 2% for type I, up to 7% for types II and IIIA, 10% to 50% for type IIIB, and 25% to 50% for type IIIC. Gustilo and colleagues specified that open fractures resulting from high-energy or high-velocity trauma, segmental fractures, and those with severe comminution should be classified as type III injuries regardless of the size of the wound. However, this system permits categorization of open tibial fractures with transverse patterns and some comminution into type I. Edwards has shown that the transverse fracture pattern, which is caused by a direct rather than an indirect mechanism, carries a higher risk of problems.[156] It may therefore be more appropriate to limit the lowest grade open-fracture category to spiral tibial fractures produced by indirect injuries.

Interobserver agreement in grading open tibial fractures according to Gustilo and colleagues' classification was investigated by Brumback and Jones.[82] They found approximately 60% agreement in the grading of individual fractures from videotapes of the initial débridement and radiographs. However, consensus was better regarding the most severe or most minor extremes. This variation in grading should be kept in mind by surgeons who wish to compare results of different series, particularly from different institutions.

Tscherne's grading system for open fractures similarly uses wound size, contamination, and fracture pattern to grade open fractures.[418] In this system, grade I open fractures have a small puncture wound without skin contusion, negligible bacterial contamination, and a low-energy fracture pattern. Grade II open injuries have small skin and soft tissue contusions, moderate contamination, and variable fracture patterns. Grade III open fractures have heavy contamination, extensive soft tissue damage, and often, associated arterial or neural injuries. Grade IV open fractures are incomplete or complete amputations. Obviously, the location and character of such injuries are also important. A cleanly amputated finger has a much better prognosis for replantation than does a crushed or avulsed amputation through the midportion of the tibia.

An important conceptual contribution is Tscherne's emphasis on grading the severity of soft tissue damage in *closed* as well as open injuries. He has proposed a system for doing so, with four grades of severity for soft tissue injury in closed fractures.[418] Grade 0 injuries result from indirect forces and have negligible soft tissue damage. Grade I closed fractures, which are caused by low- or moderate-energy mechanisms, have superficial abrasions or contusions of the soft tissues overlying the fracture. Grade II closed fractures have significant muscle contusion and may have deep contaminated skin abrasions. Fractures caused by direct violence, such as a "bumper" fracture, and moderate to severe bone injury patterns qualify for this category. These injuries carry a significant risk of compartment syndrome. Grade III closed fractures have extensive crushing, subcutaneous "degloving" or avulsion, and perhaps arterial disruption or an established compartment syndrome. Clearly, Tscherne's classification spans a wide spectrum of injury. Proper assessment of the degree of soft tissue injury is crucial for determining prognosis and choosing treatment of tibial shaft fractures, yet it is likely that interobserver variability would be a problem in the application of this classification. In discussing the possibility of predicting the outcome of tibial fractures, Gaston and associates stated that the judgment of "an experienced surgeon is at least as prognostic as any classification system in present use."[185] However, they considered only fractures treated by IM nailing and thus did not assess the possibility that the classification systems might be helpful in predicting behavior after nonoperative or other treatment. The bony pattern of tibial fractures is evident radiographically. In addition to the fracture's location and displacement, its shape and comminution should be noted. The pattern may be spiral, oblique, transverse, or segmental. Comminution ranges from none to total circumferential involvement. The extent of comminution has been graded by Winquist and Hansen, initially for femoral fractures.[625] Their emphasis on the amount of contact between the two major fracture fragments is

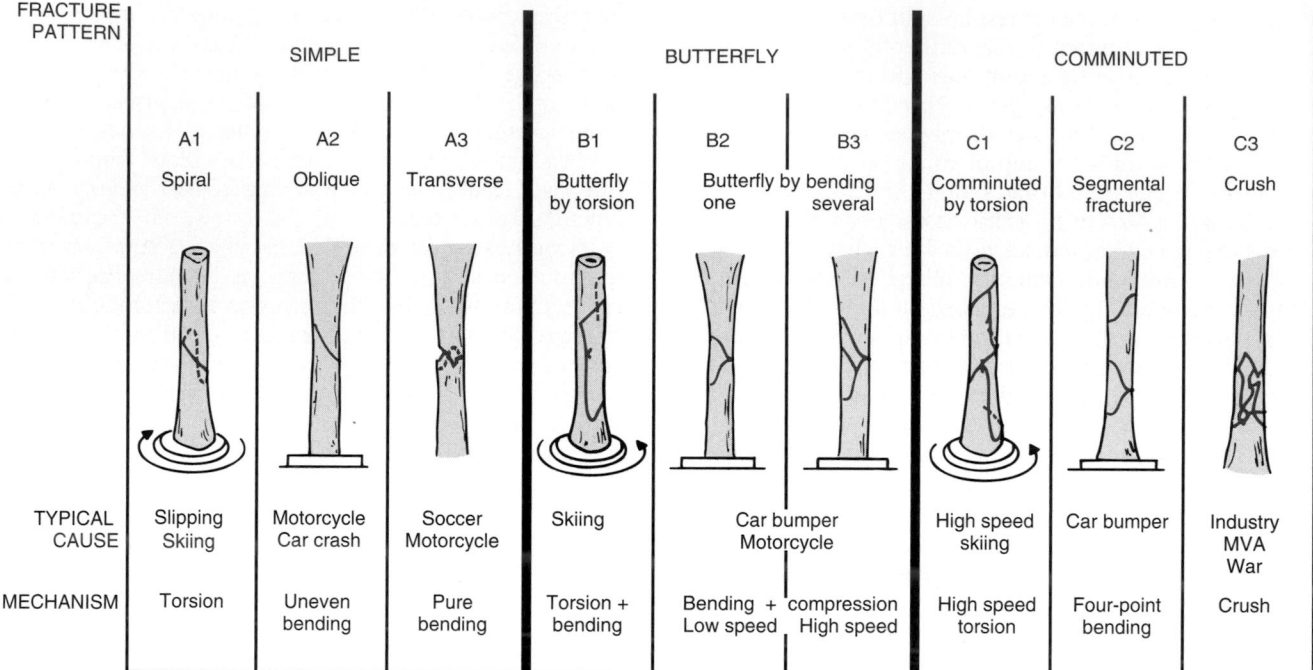

**Figure 57–7.** Johner and Wruhs' classification system for tibial shaft fractures. Note that neither displacement nor soft tissue wound severity is considered in this system. *Abbreviation:* MVA, motor vehicle accident. (Redrawn from Johner, R.; Wruhs, O. Clin Orthop 178:7–25, 1983.) The AO/OTA classification of tibia shaft fractures is an expansion of that of Johner and Wruhs (Orthopaedic Trauma Association Committee for Coding and Classification, 1996). The prefix 42 implies the tibial diaphysis. Nine alphanumeric groups (A to C, 1 to 3) are illustrated in this figure. Each group can be separated into 3 subgroups, each of which may have three qualifications. The subgroups are the same for each of the A and B groups: 1 = fibula intact, 2 = fibula fracture at a different level, and 3 = fibula fracture at the same level. The qualifications are also the same for all the A and B groups: (1) = proximal, (2) = middle, and (3) = distal. The subgroups within group C1 are .1, two intermediate fragments; .2, three intermediate fragments; and .3, more than three intermediate fragments. The C1 qualifications are (1) pure diaphyseal, (2) proximal metadiaphyseal, and (3) distal metadiaphyseal. The C2 subgroups are .1, single intermediate segmental fragment; .2, intermediate segmental and wedge fragments; and .3, two intermediate segmental fragments. For C2.1, the qualifications are (1) pure diaphyseal, (2) proximal metadiaphyseal, (3) distal metadiaphyseal, (4) oblique lines, and (5) transverse and oblique lines. For C2.2, the qualifications are (1) pure diaphyseal, (2) proximal metadiaphyseal, (3) distal metadiaphyseal, (4) distal wedge, and (5) three wedges, proximal and distal. For C2.3, the qualifications are (1) pure diaphyseal, (2) proximal metadiaphyseal, and (3) distal metadiaphyseal. For group C3, the subgroups are .1, two or three intermediate fragments; .2, limited shattering (<4 cm); and .3, extensive shattering (>4 cm). Qualifications for C3.1 are (1) two intermediate fragments and (2) three intermediate fragments. For C3.2 and C3.3, qualifications are (1) pure diaphyseal, (2) proximal metadiaphyseal, and (3) distal metadiaphyseal. See also Müller and colleagues (1990) for details.

meaningful with regard to the stability of traditional IM nailing, but with a locked nail, a plate, or an external fixator, these distinctions may be less important, although they reflect energy absorbed and potential problems with restoration of length.[185]

Johner and Wruhs used fracture morphology to classify tibial shaft fractures treated with AO/ASIF techniques.[270] This classification has been adopted by Müller and associates[401] and the AO/ASIF group in their comprehensive classification of long bone fractures and subsequently by the Orthopaedic Trauma Association.[426] It is now the accepted classification system for scientific studies of tibia shaft fractures. Details regarding subcategories are provided in the legend of Figure 57–7. Johner and Wruhs recognized the relationship between fracture pattern and injury mechanism: a spiral pattern caused by torsion; an oblique or transverse pattern caused by various modes of bending, often with direct injury; and a segmental or transverse, highly comminuted pattern caused by crushing. They also used the extent of comminution, which correlates with absorbed energy, as an indicator of severity. Their resulting classification has three major categories: A, simple, noncomminuted patterns; B, patterns with butterfly or "wedge" fragments; and C, comminuted, including segmental fractures (see Fig. 57–7). Though somewhat

cumbersome to use with 27 separate categories in its final form,[401] this classification is demonstrably well suited for assessing results after internal fixation of closed tibial shaft fractures. It is not a comprehensive tibial fracture classification because it does not include the severity of soft tissue injury, although the authors clearly emphasize the important influence that such injury has on results. Fracture displacement is also not considered, perhaps because it has little effect on the outcome of fractures treated by expert internal fixation. However, it may be quite significant if nonoperative treatment or an ill-conceived operation is chosen. Also excluded from Johner and Wruhs' classification is the location of the fracture. Proximal and distal fractures, which can encroach on the knee or ankle and preclude the use of IM nailing, may deserve recognition as separate categories of injury. From Johner and Wruhs' reported results, it is evident that spiral and oblique fractures have the best prognosis after internal fixation. Their A1, A2, B1, and C1 fractures had 91% to 100% good or excellent outcomes. Transverse fractures had intermediate results, with A3 and B2 fractures having 80% to 92% good or excellent outcomes. Comminuted or crushing injuries had significantly worse results, with good or excellent outcomes noted in 75% of B3, 68% of C2, and 50% of C3 tibial fractures.[270] A fracture classification system ought to predict results and guide treatment. Because injuries respond differently to different treatments, the choice of treatment may affect the validity of a grading system. For example, Johner and Wruhs found faster recovery in transverse, higher energy fractures treated with IM nails and reported higher infection (17%) and implant failure (5%) rates after plate fixation of type B3 injuries that might have had lower rates of complications if treated with closed locked IM nailing.

Another important limitation of the proposed classification systems for tibial fractures is that they have typically been validated with end-points such as average time to union, risk of nonunion, or risk of infection rather than ultimate function, risk of deformity, and response to a given treatment.

## Recommended Classification

Although many parameters affect the outcome and choice of treatment of tibial shaft fractures, a matrix of all or even a moderate number of selected factors produces a system that is too complex for clinical use. Thus, a classification such as Ellis' becomes attractive as a rough guide to prognosis and management.[25, 160, 161] Until a better system is validated, the Ellis system may be used, as it was by Austin in a prospective study of patellar tendon–bearing (PTB) cast treatment.[26] Note that Ellis' three categories are not the same as those of the AO/ASIF classification of Johner and Wruhs described previously. The Ellis' system emphasizes the benign nature of minimally displaced, low-energy fractures and their suitability for nonoperative treatment, and it correlates the extent of injury with healing time, if not with functional outcome.[130] Ellis originally put undisplaced fractures in the minor category and totally displaced ones in the moderate category, thus leaving some question about how to classify partial displacement. Assigning fractures with up to 50% displacement to the minor category is justified by Böstman's demonstration that more than 50% displacement of spiral fractures is associated with more soft tissue disruption and greater difficulty maintaining alignment.[70] More recently, however, Toivanen has demonstrated that displacement of 30% or more increased the risk that cast immobilization would fail to control alignment.[577]

When grading fracture severity, it is necessary to recognize the preeminence of soft tissue damage, regardless of whether an open wound is present.[481] In Tscherne's classification, minor tibial fractures are classified as grade 0 closed or grade I open wounds. Moderate fractures are grade I closed or grade II open injuries. Major-severity injuries are grade II or grade III closed injuries or grade II (with a more severe fracture pattern) or grade III or IV open wounds. In Gustilo and colleagues' open fracture grading system, type I injuries are minor, type II are moderate, and type III (A, B, or C) are major. When wound severity cannot be judged, as in closed treatment or before adequate surgical exploration, the mechanism of injury provides the best guide. The mechanism may be indicated by the history but can also be inferred from the fracture pattern and displacement. Indirect, low-energy (spiral) fractures are minor. Transverse fractures with no comminution or a single butterfly fragment are moderate. High-energy, multiply comminuted or segmental, and crush fractures are major, despite a small external wound (Table 57–2; Fig. 57–8).

## Diagnosis

An acute tibial shaft fracture is usually apparent from the patient's localized pain after injury and the typical physical findings of deformity, tenderness, instability, swelling, and possibly an open wound. The surgeon's diagnostic efforts primarily involve acquiring the necessary data to plan treatment, as well as exclude other injuries and co-morbid conditions. Occasionally, undisplaced or incomplete acute injuries or more chronic processes such as fatigue and pathologic fractures can be difficult to identify, and special studies may be required.

### HISTORY

Conscious patients can localize injuries by describing where they feel pain and its character. Severe, unremitting pain may indicate muscle ischemia. Absence of sensation can be caused by nerve injury, progressive ischemia, or both.

The time, the place, and the events of the injury should be determined as precisely as possible. Elapsed time is especially important for vascular injuries, compartment syndromes, and open wounds. Certain locales (e.g., barnyards and swamps) are notorious for the presence of virulent microorganisms. The amount of energy involved in causing the injury is the major determinant of its severity. The mechanism (i.e., the cause) of injury, if known, is a most helpful indicator of the force involved.[336]

---

**TABLE 57–2**

Tibial Fracture Classification*

| Fracture Characteristic | Minor | Moderate | Major |
|---|---|---|---|
| Displacement | 0%–50% diameter | 51%–100% | 100% |
| Comminution | 0–minimal | 0 or 1 butterfly fragments | ≥2 free fragments or segmental |
| Wound | Open grade I, closed to grade 0 | Open grade II, closed grade I | Open grades III–V, closed grades II–III |
| Available energy (history) | Low | Moderate | High, crushing |
| Mechanism (fracture pattern) | Spiral | Oblique/transverse | Transverse/fragmented |

*After Ellis[160] and Edwards,[156] with Leach's modification.[330] This system incorporates soft tissue wound grading, after Gustilo[564] and Tscherne,[418] and is proposed as a general means for clinically grading tibial shaft fractures. Use the factor of greatest severity to grade the fracture.

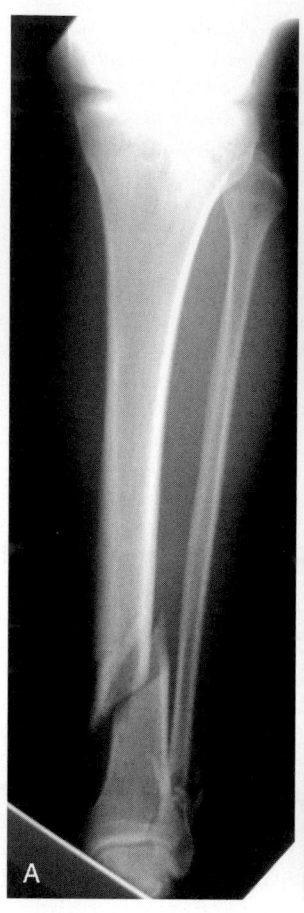
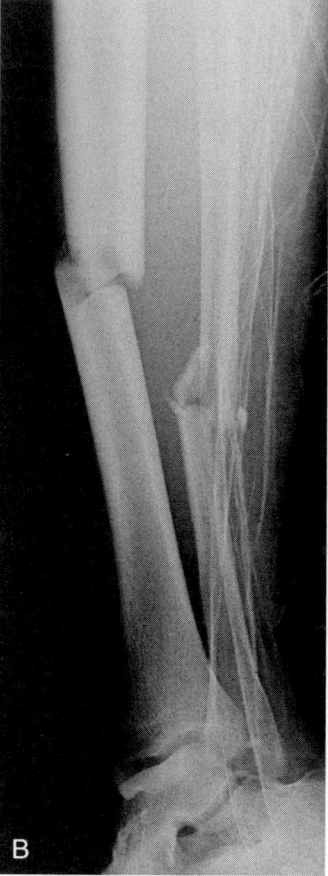
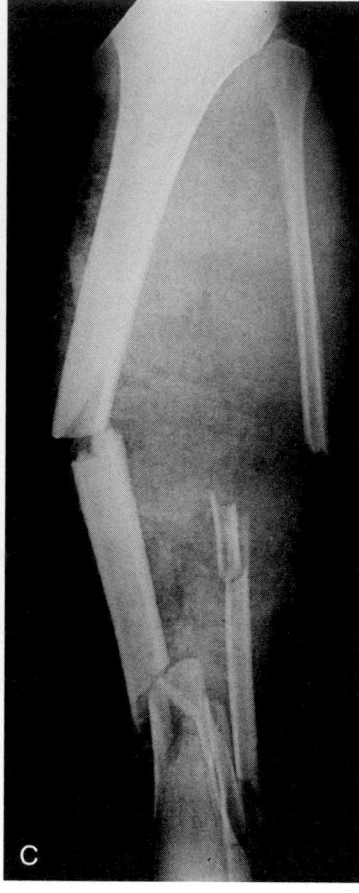

**Figure 57–8.** Radiographic examples of the three grades of tibial fracture severity. *A, Minor severity:* spiral fracture caused by a simple slip and fall. *B, Moderate severity:* fracture in a pedestrian struck by a slowly moving vehicle. *C, Major severity:* fracture caused by a high-velocity motorcycle crash.

Did the patient trip on a curb, or was the patient struck by a car or run over and crushed by its wheel? Reports of bystanders may be helpful. Emergency medical personnel may have detailed knowledge of the injury mechanism, the initial deformity, the presence of wounds and exposed bone, and the neurovascular status of the limb.

Baseline medical information should not be neglected. Previous injuries to the part and any related disability should be documented. Exercise tolerance helps identify preexisting peripheral vascular disease. The patient's activity level, both recreational and occupational, may help set functional goals or suggest an injury resulting from overuse. Evaluation of the patient's general medical status must include identification of any allergies to medications, the current or recent use of any medications, known medical problems and previous operations, personal or family history of bleeding disorders, and problems with anesthesia or with frequent or poorly healing fractures. Diabetes mellitus may be associated with peripheral neuropathy, vascular disease, and an increased risk of infection. Human immunodeficiency virus infection increases the risk of infectious complications from open tibial fractures.[413] Smoking, drinking, and drug use should be determined. Fracture and wound-healing problems are more frequent in smokers.[3, 210, 445, 458, 514] A thorough systems review is a helpful screening device. If the patient is unable to provide some or all of this information initially, family and friends can be questioned, and once the patient has recovered sufficiently, the history should be updated as needed.

## PHYSICAL EXAMINATION

The strong possibility of multiple injuries, often occult, makes thorough systematic evaluation of the whole patient essential. The principles and practice of initial evaluation and treatment of trauma patients are taught in the Advanced Trauma Life Support (ATLS) course of the American College of Surgeons and are reviewed in Chapter 5.

The injured limb itself must be thoroughly assessed and adequately splinted. If a splint is already in place, it should remain in place during the patient's primary survey and may appropriately be left in place during the secondary survey as well if a reliably described wound will need urgent surgical care and if distal neurovascular examination is not obscured (see later). Distal perfusion is assessed primarily by pulses, but also by skin color, warmth, and capillary filling. If the adequacy of perfusion is at all in question, Doppler-assisted pulse pressure measurement is a rapid, valuable adjunct. Motor and sensory function in the foot is assessed. If an open fracture has been identified in the field and satisfactorily dressed and splinted by a reliable emergency medical team, little is to be gained by reexposing the wound in the emergency department. Tscherne and Gotzen have shown that reexposure increases the risk of infection and is better deferred until the patient is in the operating room.[588]

Examination of the injured limb includes inspection, palpation, and manipulation and should be goal directed. The surgeon must identify and assess the fracture, establish the presence and severity of soft tissue wounds, and determine the neurologic and vascular status of the injured limb. Furthermore, a search must also be made for associated injuries of the limb above and below the tibia.

A fractured tibia may have a variable amount of deformity consisting of angulation, shortening, malrotation, or other asymmetry relative to the opposite limb (which may itself be injured). Swelling may be localized or diffuse and may be less evident in an early examination, particularly if the patient is in shock. An open wound exposing bone fragments leaves no doubt about the presence of a tibial fracture. Palpation localizes any tenderness, if the patient can cooperate. It may also demonstrate bony irregularity or crepitus. Palpation may reveal soft boggy swelling typical of a subcutaneous hematoma or degloved area. Alternatively, the swelling may be quite tense and suggestive of increased compartmental pressure. Passive manipulation may produce pain and demonstrate instability.

Soft tissue injuries are either open or closed, depending on the integrity of the skin. It is essential to promptly distinguish between the two because of the well-accepted principle that all open fractures require formal surgical débridement and irrigation, as well as tetanus toxoid and appropriate antibiotics, begun as soon as possible. Complete circumferential inspection of the limb is essential to avoid missing a small wound. If even a small opening extends through the dermis, it should be presumed to communicate with a nearby fracture. In addition to the character and amount of drainage, the wound should be briefly inspected for foreign material, as well as identifiable exposed anatomic structures. The physician should resist the temptation to probe or explore potential open fracture wounds in the emergency department. Instead, it should be assumed that the fracture is open, and the physician should dress the wound, splint the leg, and proceed to the operating room for formal exploration under optimal conditions. The true severity of the soft tissue injury associated with an open fracture is easily underestimated before adequate surgical exploration. Extensively crushed muscle may be present under a small skin laceration. In addition to potential open fracture wounds, it is important to note any lacerations or abrasions in areas that might be required for surgical approaches to a closed tibial fracture. Such surgery may best be performed immediately or delayed until after a contaminated wound has healed.

Impaired perfusion of the injured limb is revealed by skin pallor, coolness, an absence of venous and capillary filling, and above all, the absence or significant diminution of palpable pulses. After a tibial fracture, both the dorsalis pedis and posterior tibial pulses should be assessed promptly, recorded, and monitored closely. As shown by Johansen and associates, the API is a reliable means of identifying arterial injuries.[268] A blood pressure cuff is inflated around the calf or upper part of the arm, and a Doppler probe is used to determine blood pressure at the ankle and brachial arteries. An ankle-brachial systolic pressure ratio (API) below 0.9 indicates a high probability of arterial injury.[344]

Paralysis and loss of sensation may be due to ischemia, which must always be specifically excluded whenever neurologic abnormalities are found in association with a tibial fracture. Swelling may indicate soft tissue edema or venous obstruction, or if rapidly developing, it may be the result of arterial hemorrhage. A thrill or bruit suggests an arteriovenous fistula.

Compartment syndromes are initially characterized by pain, swelling, and loss of neuromuscular function, with pulses and skin perfusion usually unaffected until late in the course. In an unconscious or insensate patient, the physician must recognize the special significance of swelling and induration and promptly assess tissue pressure in the compartments at risk. When a compartment syndrome is developing in a conscious patient, pain can be produced by passively stretching ischemic muscles in the involved compartments (e.g., anterior compartment pain is produced by passively plantar flexing the patient's toes, and deep posterior compartment pain is assessed by passive toe dorsiflexion).

Neurologic function is assessed by specific tests for movement and sensation served by the nerves of the lower part of the leg (see Table 57–1). Because these nerves lie within different deep fascial compartments, the tests are valuable for identifying compartment syndromes. Sensation is assessed by light touch or pain (e.g., a pinprick). Motor function should be tested with formal manual motor tests requiring the patient to demonstrate maximal power against the examiner's hand. Strength is then graded from 0 to 5. The deep peroneal nerve lies in the anterior compartment. Its sensory area is the dorsal webspace between the first and second toes, and its motor test is toe dorsiflexion. The superficial peroneal nerve, located in the lateral compartment, provides sensation to the rest of the dorsum of the foot and motor function for the foot evertors. The tibial nerve provides sensation to the sole of the foot and motor activity to the toe plantar flexors; it travels through the deep posterior compartment. The sural nerve lies within the superficial posterior compartment and provides sensation to the lateral aspect of the heel but no motor activity. An adequate neurologic examination in a limb with a tibial fracture involves testing and recording the response in each of the aforementioned nerves. If the examination results are initially normal, a splint or cast may be applied that interferes with assessment of pedal pulses, as well as motor and sensory reevaluation of all but the patient's toes. However, in limbs with questionable neurologic status, access to the foot must be preserved so that a complete examination can be repeated periodically. Reexamination can be accomplished by removing the cast or splint from the dorsum of the foot and trimming or windowing over the posteromedial aspect to palpate the posterior tibial pulse as well.

Finally, examination of the injured limb must exclude, as well as possible, any coexisting injuries above or below the tibial fracture. Although pain and instability of the tibia make it difficult to perform a complete examination of the pelvis, thigh, knee, ankle, and foot, it is essential that these regions not be ignored. Alert patients should be specifically questioned about pain and tenderness. Deformity, wound, and swelling may be present. The pelvis should be palpated to exclude tenderness and instability. Similarly, the femur, patella, and knee should be assessed for tenderness, deformity, crepitus, and effusion. The patellar ligament and tibial tubercle should also be specifically palpated. Assessment of knee joint stability must usually wait until the patient is under anesthesia and the tibia has been securely fixed. Ankle swelling, tenderness, and crepitus may alert the surgeon to an injury to this joint. The foot must also be assessed carefully because external deformity and even swelling may be subtle with an injury to the hindfoot or midfoot.

## IMAGING

### Radiographs

Adequate plain radiographs are an essential diagnostic supplement to the history and physical examination and usually provide definitive diagnosis of a tibial shaft fracture. They offer detailed documentation of a fracture's configuration, but because they are not similarly informative about radiolucent structures, radiographs tend to divert the surgeon's attention from the all-important soft tissues. For this reason, examination of the patient takes precedence over radiographs, and they should be correlated with information from the history and physical examination.

Radiographs of the tibia must be obtained whenever significant localized tenderness, pain, or deformity involves the bone. An obvious unstable fracture should be aligned and splinted before obtaining radiographs. However, many splinting materials compromise the detail available with current radiographic techniques. Most tibias can be displayed from top to bottom diagonally on a standard 14 × 17-inch film, but the knee and ankle regions receive an oblique beam and deserve their own centered views with any question of injury to these regions. It is essential to obtain two perpendicular views, conventionally in the frontal (anteroposterior [AP]) and sagittal (lateral) planes (see Fig. 57–1). It may be difficult to position the injured limb precisely. Certainly, the leg should be rotated as a unit and not twisted through the fracture site. Occasionally, an undisplaced spiral fracture may not be apparent on standard films. In this situation and when one wishes to assess healing, complex deformity, or the placement of hardware or bone grafts, 45° oblique radiographs are valuable supplements (Fig. 57–9). In any questionable situation, directing the central x-ray beam at the area of interest rather than at the middle of the tibia may give more informative results. Fluoroscopically guided spot films can be most helpful in searching for a nonunion cleft or occult injury because they permit precise alignment of the area of interest with the central beam of the x-ray source. Correct rotational alignment is also essential if one wishes to demonstrate the true angle of deformity because angulation appears less if its plane is not parallel with the film. True length measurements must be obtained with scanographic techniques, but length can be estimated quite well with a special ruler placed at the level of the tibia (Fig. 57–10). Comparison views of the opposite tibia, if intact, can be invaluable for determining correct length when severe comminution or bone loss is present and for defining the shape of the metaphyseal and articular regions of the tibia for preoperative planning. A C-arm fluoroscope can be used to calculate torsional alignment of the tibia, which is poorly demonstrated by routine radiographs. In fact, it is essential to remember this limitation of conventional radiography and make an independent assessment of rotational alignment by physical examination for all tibial fractures.

### Descriptive Terminology

The radiographic appearance of a tibial shaft fracture is described by its location, pattern, degree of comminution, extent and direction of displacement, and alignment. The physician should also look for soft tissue abnormalities such as swelling, loss of fat shadows, and the presence of gas or other foreign material.

### Other Imaging Techniques

In addition to standard radiographs, other imaging techniques can provide helpful information. Occult problems such as fatigue fractures and pathologic lesions may be localized with technetium phosphate bone scanning. Detailed views of both tibias should be requested. Abnormal early uptake of Tc 99m methylene diphosphonate (MDP) may be related to delayed fracture union; however, the usefulness of nuclear medicine studies for predicting fracture healing has not been confirmed.[212] Indium-labeled white blood cell scans are probably the best technique for finding an occult infection, but such scanning may still yield false-negative or false-positive results.[517] Computed tomography (CT) is most helpful for demonstrating transverse images of metaphyseal fractures. This information can be invaluable in preoperative planning. Computer reprocessing can also provide AP and lateral reconstructions that rival standard tomographic techniques, but very thin or overlapping cuts are required. CT scanning offers a precise assessment of rotational alignment and reduction of spiral fractures, should such information be needed. The preliminary digital radiograph (scout view) can be used for measuring tibial length. CT scan assessment of healing, based on the volume and density of callus, may be helpful.[515] However, it is my opinion that radiologists often have difficulty assessing fracture healing with CT scans, which may lag behind clinical and plain radiographic signs of union. Magnetic resonance imaging (MRI) may be used to demonstrate bone contusions, occult infractions, and fatigue fractures when other studies are negative, but rarely is MRI helpful for the care of patients with tibial shaft fractures, except to investigate associated knee ligament injuries.

Arteriography is rarely needed for patients whose physical examinations show obvious arterial occlusion, except perhaps when several possible sites of injury exist. Direct exploration, perhaps guided by an intraoperative arteriogram, avoids time-consuming studies in the radiology suite and may permit revascularization before irreversible tissue necrosis occurs (see Chapter 11).

Venography remains the gold standard for assessment of venous circulation. Ultrasonography, which is technologist dependent, is also effective but similarly obstructed by a cast or splint. Ultrasound imaging has been proposed as a way to assess fracture callus volume in patients with nonreamed IM nails; such patients might need bone grafting if healing is deficient.[392]

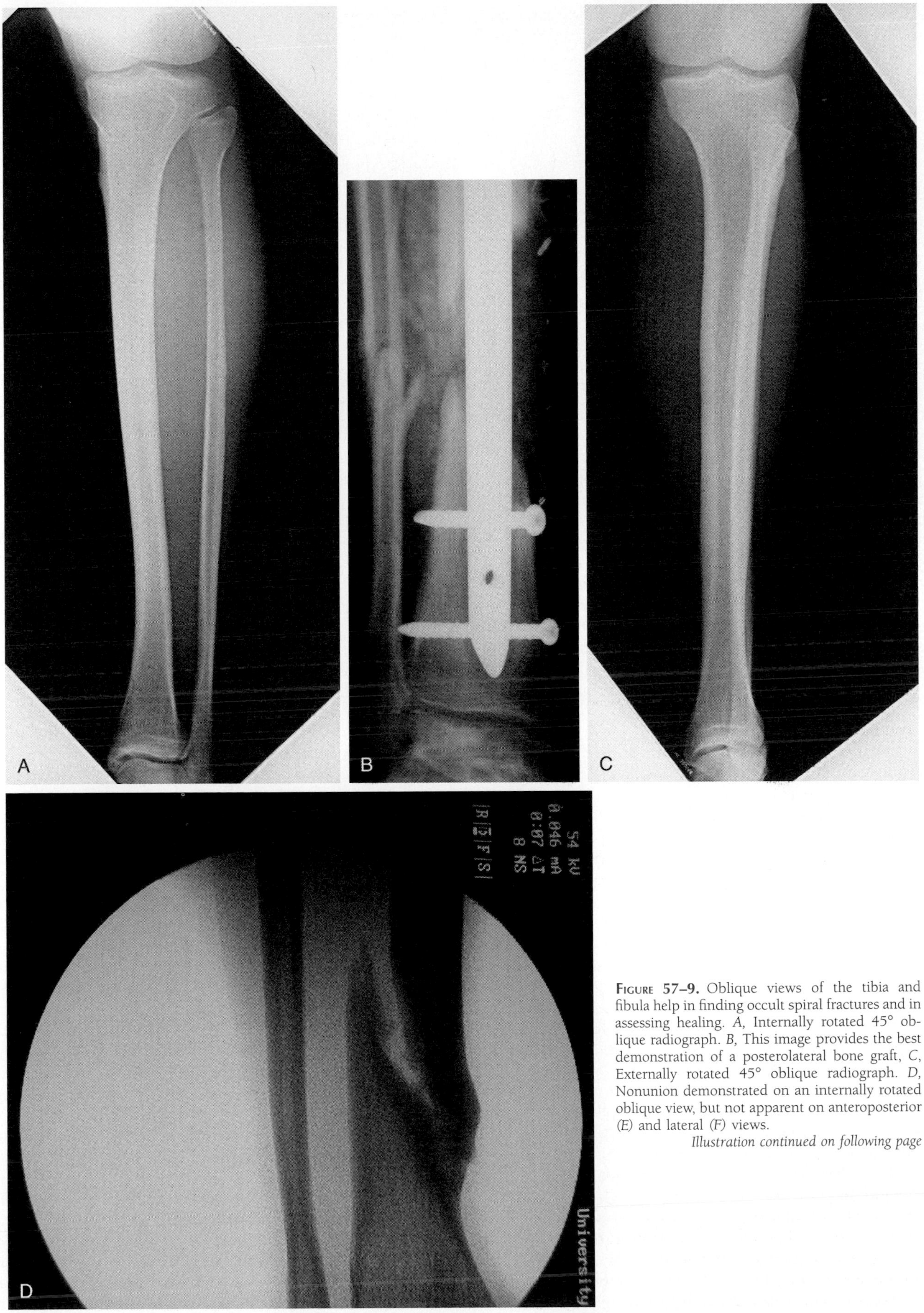

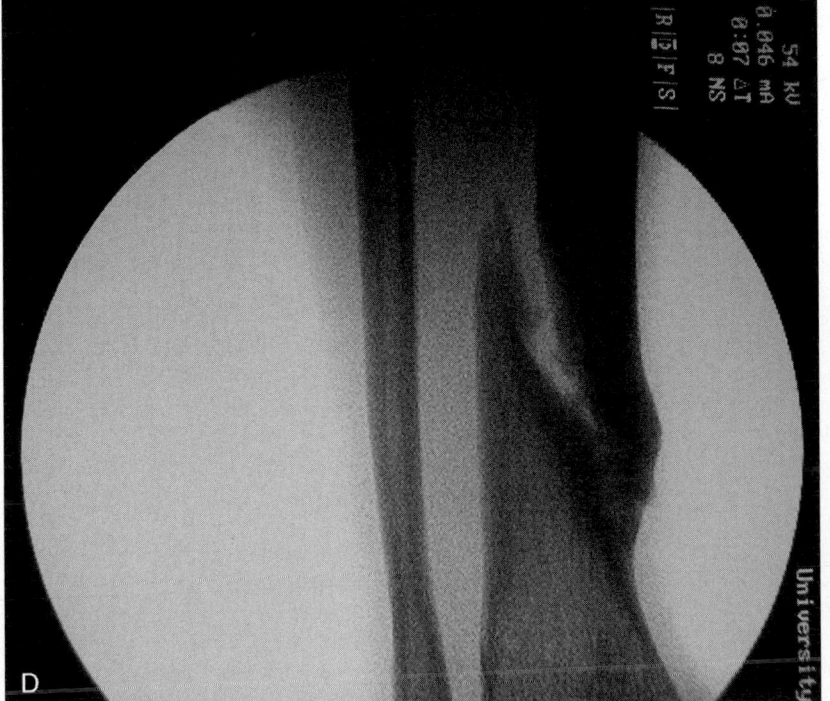

FIGURE 57–9. Oblique views of the tibia and fibula help in finding occult spiral fractures and in assessing healing. *A,* Internally rotated 45° oblique radiograph. *B,* This image provides the best demonstration of a posterolateral bone graft, *C,* Externally rotated 45° oblique radiograph. *D,* Nonunion demonstrated on an internally rotated oblique view, but not apparent on anteroposterior *(E)* and lateral *(F)* views.

*Illustration continued on following page*

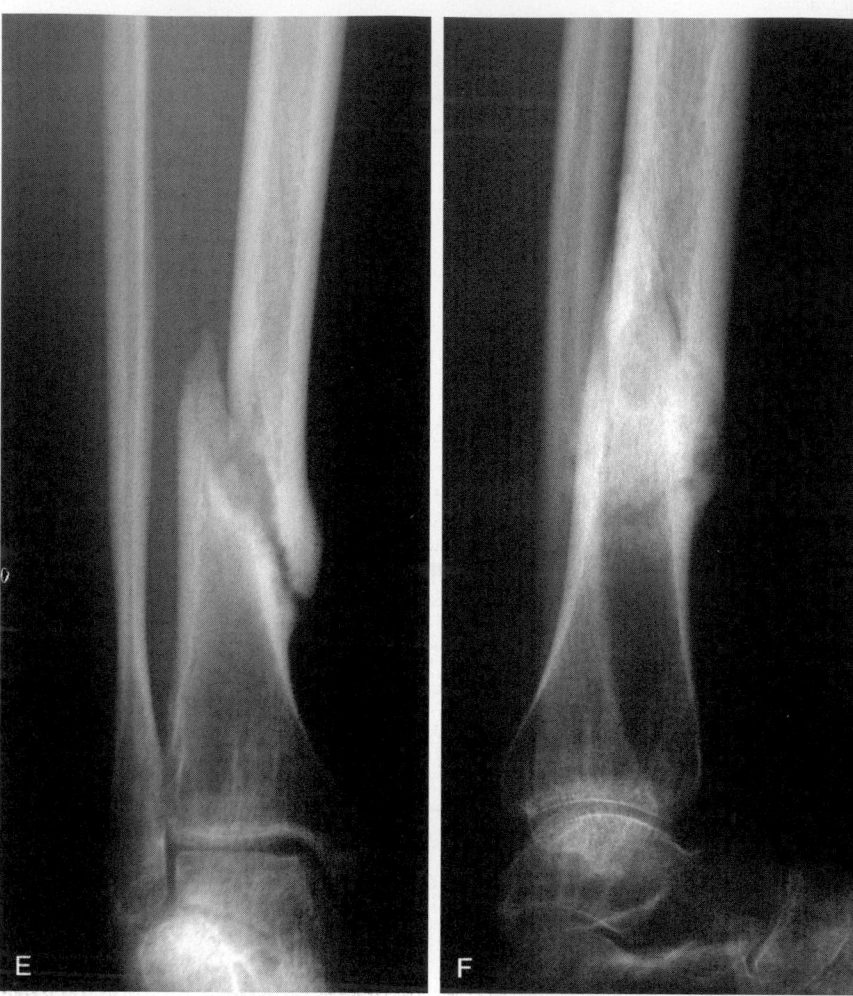

FIGURE 57–9 *Continued.*

## OTHER STUDIES

Routine culture and sensitivity studies are no longer recommended for open tibial fractures because they provide minimal useful information in proportion to their cost.[332] However, Gram stain and microbial culture and sensitivity studies are of value whenever an infection is suspected and, perhaps, if débridement is exceptionally delayed. An urgent Gram stain may be diagnostic of clostridial myonecrosis and should be promptly performed whenever this dreaded complication is a possibility or a wound appears to be infected.

Ancillary vascular studies may be helpful in assessing patients with a tibial fracture. Doppler devices may indicate pulsatile arterial flow but can be dangerously deceiving if relied on as indicators of adequate perfusion. Instead, as described by Johansen and colleagues[268] and discussed earlier, Doppler should be used with a sphygmomanometer cuff about the calf to measure arterial pressure in the dorsalis pedis and posterior tibial arteries. As mentioned, this test is a sensitive and specific indicator of significant arterial injuries. Demonstrating an incompletely occlusive intimal flap tear may require formal biplanar arteriography. The increasing availability of equipment for instantaneous measurement of oxygen saturation in skin capillary beds permits assessment and monitoring of skin perfusion.[477] Laser Doppler flowmetry has been proposed as another means of evaluating perfusion and can be used intraoperatively to assess blood flow in muscle and bone.[554] In practice, the presence of punctate capillary bleeding from cut tissues, including bone, and observation of capillary flush after release of an arterial tourniquet are both valuable tools for assessment of tissue microperfusion. Temporary split-thickness skin excision is a rapid way of assessing the viability of a degloved flap.[643] Bleeding of the dermal surface after graft harvesting indicates perfusion; the graft is then replaced on such surfaces. Nonbleeding portions of dermal flaps are excised, with the application of a split-thickness graft to the underlying muscle and fascia instead.

Physical examination is the best early test of peripheral nerve function, but electrodiagnostic studies may be helpful, particularly nerve conduction velocities, which are immediately affected by neural pathology and do not require a period of delay until the classic electromyographic changes of denervation have occurred.

Tissue pressure measurement techniques are discussed in Chapter 12. Instant-reading, hand-held digital devices are particularly valuable because of their ease of use and ability to obtain multiple measurements quickly. After tibial fractures, pressure is most elevated in the region of the bony injury and is not as high in more remote regions of the same compartment.[235] One or more of the four leg compartments can be involved, with or without open wounds, and the dynamic nature of compartment pressure elevation is such that interpretation of a single pressure measurement must be correlated with the clinical situation. Pressure measurements are helpful to (1) avoid fasciotomy in a swollen limb with normal pressure, (2) assess compartment pressure in unconscious patients or insensate limbs, (3) differentiate between involved and uninvolved compartments, and (4) confirm the adequacy of fasciotomy.

The extent of the soft tissue injury associated with tibial fractures correlates with serum creatinine phosphokinase activity.[421]

Fracture healing has been investigationally assessed by

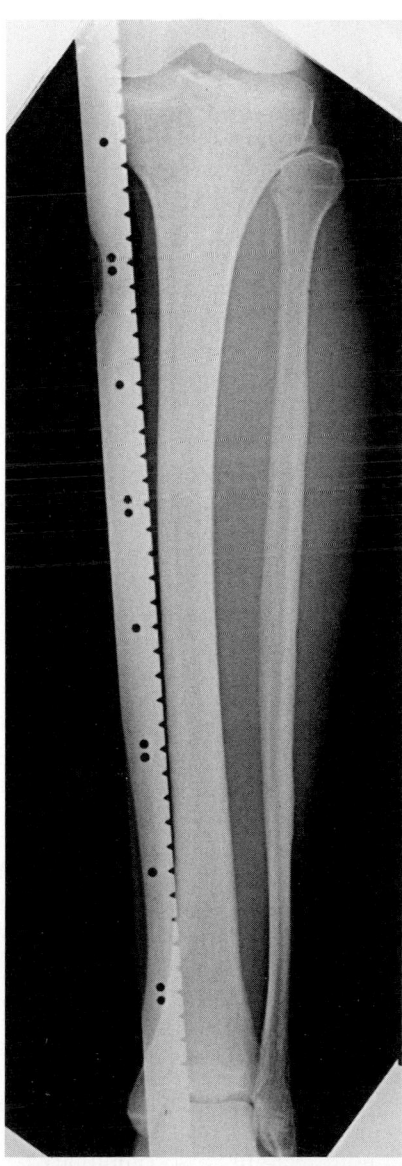

**FIGURE 57–10.** A radiographic ruler, as demonstrated, permits a reliable estimation of tibial length for choosing an appropriate intramedullary nail. Length can be measured more precisely if a scanogram technique is used with separate exposure made over the proximal and distal ends of the bone and the central ray perpendicular to the bone at the point of measurement. The film, leg, and ruler are not moved between exposures.

several types of mechanical tests, although these tests have not yet found clinical acceptance. Fracture stiffness can be assessed with transducers attached to an external fixator or by measuring radiographic displacement in response to a known force.[127, 226, 470] Ultrasound imaging can demonstrate developing fracture callus and may predict healing in fractures treated with nonreamed IM nails.[388, 392]

## ESSENTIAL STUDIES TO EXCLUDE OTHER INJURIES

A careful history and physical examination, with appropriate radiographic views, should be adequate to exclude other injuries associated with an acute tibial fracture. A high index of suspicion is required regarding both distant and local associated injuries. The risk of circulatory compromise and nerve injury and problems with the knee and ankle should in particular be kept in mind. Follow-up assessment with repeated examinations and radiographs, guided by any new patient complaints, is the key to early discovery and treatment of any injuries missed initially, as well as any complications from previously identified injuries.

## DIFFERENTIAL DIAGNOSIS

A pure soft tissue injury may be present in a patient who appears to have a tibial fracture. Isolated fibular fractures or injuries proximal or distal to the tibial shaft may also become apparent with adequate radiographs, as may the presence of more extensive comminution. The diagnosis of an acute injury does not usually cause much confusion. However, patients with little, if any, trauma may have a fatigue fracture, osteomyelitis, a tumor, or pain of neurogenic or vascular origin.

## MANAGEMENT OF TIBIAL FRACTURES

### Evolution of Treatment

Fractures have been treated since antiquity by bone setters in the folk medicine tradition and by surgeons who have recorded their results in learned treatises, the previously mentioned Smith Papyrus being the earliest of which we have record. The history of management of severe wounds has in large part been the history of open tibial fracture care.[434] Peltier has reviewed the history of fracture treatment,[440] and interested readers are referred to his text for details, as well as Colton's review in Chapter 1. Watson-Jones, the British surgeon and teacher, had an overwhelming influence on fracture treatment throughout the English-speaking world during the latter half of the 20th century. He and his associate Coltart believed that "nonunion is never inevitable and that every fracture will unite if it is immobilized long enough."[614] They recommended immediate anatomic reduction and absolute immobilization in a long leg, non–weight-bearing plaster cast until union was secure. They further believed that open reduction and internal fixation, if properly performed and protected postoperatively with plaster, led to healing as rapid as with any other treatment. They thus emphasized reduction and rest until bone union, followed by rehabilitation.

Since the 1960s, fracture treatment can be briefly characterized as a reaction to Watson-Jones' theories. During this period, functional weight-bearing treatment has been emphasized, with or without surgery, with care taken to restrict weight bearing only if it threatens the stability of the chosen fixation (plates or less secure external fixators, for example). In the absence of weight bearing, early joint motion received emphasis, all to avoid the joint stiffness and disuse atrophy produced by prolonged immobilization in a non–weight-bearing cast. Appreciation of the benefits of both varieties of functional fracture treatment was solidified by Sarmiento's 1974 symposium in *Clinical Orthopaedics and Related Research,* and an interesting perspective on progress in the treatment of tibial shaft fractures is provided by contrasting this symposium with another in the same journal by Wiss 21 years later.[506, 626]

More recent approaches for treating tibial shaft fractures borrow freely from earlier work and emphasize (1) categorization according to severity, (2) nonoperative management of less severe injuries, (3) adequate débridement of necrotic and contaminated tissue in open fractures, (4) early fixation with an IM nail or external fixator and early soft tissue repair for severe open injuries, (5) minimally traumatic but mechanically sound internal fixation for unstable fractures, and (6) early bone grafting of severe injuries with a high risk of healing problems.[*]

Wiss' June 1995 *Clinical Orthopaedics* symposium revealed a remarkable expansion of interest in IM nail fixation of tibial shaft fractures.[626] Mechanical problems with nonreamed nails were evident. IM nail fixation of *proximal* tibial fractures was shown to be difficult and frequently associated with malalignment,[180, 326] so alternative fixation techniques were suggested.[59, 326] However, complications occur with every management protocol.[437, 563, 592, 613, 645] The chronic debilitating nature of an infected nonunion of the tibia remains a major concern in spite of apparently successful protocols for gaining union and control of infection.[574]

Efforts to reduce the frequency of infection are a major part of the history of tibial fracture treatment. Potential for further reducing the infection rate of open tibial fractures may be found in antibacterial coatings for IM nails,[129] as well as in more expert application of the established techniques of wound care and fracture fixation.[88, 242, 288, 393, 445, 554, 564, 593]

Historically, concern about high infection rates after surgical fixation of tibial fractures led to strong recommendations against plating and then (with much more limited supporting evidence) against IM nailing. The advent of modern external fixation and the demonstration that it offered significantly reduced rates of infection resulted in a period in the late 1970s and early 1980s when this approach was accepted as the standard treatment of open tibial fractures.[27, 94] However, with external fixation, surgeons exchanged fracture site infections for problems with fracture union, maintenance of alignment, and pin

sepsis and loosening. It was not long before comparative studies demonstrated that a "less invasive" form of IM nailing, without IM reaming, had an infection rate no higher than that of external fixation while avoiding many of its problems and complications. This technique was first adopted for lower grade open fractures.[8, 18, 47, 62, 213, 499, 548] Evidence continues to accumulate that it is at least as good as external fixation for open fractures of high severity, as long as bone structure and fracture configuration allow stable IM fixation.[137, 240, 581] Currently, the presumed advantages of nonreamed IM nailing are being reassessed.[217, 599] Smaller nails and locking screws are less durable and thus subject to fatigue failure. Comparisons suggest that in spite of theoretical objections and the so recently accepted "conventional wisdom," reamed IM nailing may have no greater risk of infection, so its advantages can be obtained with higher as well as lower grade open fractures.[17, 125, 288, 293] An apparent advantage of IM nail fixation for tibial shaft fractures is the opportunity that it provides for the treatment of impaired healing with the frequently successful and less invasive technique of IM nail "exchange"— removing an initially placed nail, reaming the medullary canal, and inserting a larger nail. This option is one that is often more attractive than others for symptomatic tibial shaft nonunion.

Reviews of prospective studies comparing alternative treatments of open tibial fractures have demonstrated extremely limited potential for meta-analysis and generally weak evidence for choosing one treatment over another. Such disheartening conclusions must be kept in mind by surgeons who treat these common injuries. Also to be remembered are the spectrum of injury severity, the abundance of other factors that affect results, and the different implications that a given outcome will have for any individual patient.

## Current Treatment Algorithm

The first priority in treating a patient with a tibial shaft fracture is a thorough, systematic search for other injuries, as described in Chapter 5. Emergency care of life-threatening injuries necessarily takes precedence. In a similar manner, the surgeon must identify and treat limb-threatening injuries—arterial trauma, compartment syndrome, and open fractures (which are potentially life-threatening as well). Frequent reassessment, just as taught by the ATLS program for the patient as a whole, is important to avoid missing a delayed neurovascular catastrophe. Then, considering the tibial shaft fracture itself, the surgeon must evaluate the injury, anticipate any problems that might develop, and from several alternatives, choose an appropriate plan of management that will be simultaneously safe and effective. The goal is a healed functional limb with minimal pain and deformity and without an unduly long period of disability.

Although everyone hopes for a complete recovery and some patients with tibial shaft fractures approach this result, most have at least some residual symptoms and functional deficits, even years after their injury.[130, 203, 253, 441, 453, 512, 528] The surgeon and patient

---

*See references 38, 46, 94, 190, 206, 387, 479, 509, 586, 612, 628.

should discuss the injury and expected outcome and determine an explicit plan of treatment through rehabilitation, including potential complications and how to address them should they occur.[167]

As mentioned earlier, initial evaluation of a tibial fracture must identify the need for urgent limb-saving treatment. Inadequate arterial inflow requires diagnosis and speedy correction; otherwise, myoneural necrosis and often amputation result. An elevation in compartment pressure can produce similar complications and similarly requires urgent treatment. These two conditions typically have different features. Acute arterial insufficiency is usually present when the patient is first encountered, although its onset may be delayed. Compartment syndromes, on the other hand, generally develop some hours after injury, although exceptionally they may be found during a patient's initial evaluation. Each condition requires emergency treatment, and therefore both must be kept in mind during the early care of a tibial fracture.

Arterial insufficiency requires that the fractured tibia immediately be provisionally reduced and splinted and then reassessed for palpable pulses. While maintaining alignment, it may be possible to measure arterial pressure at the ankle with Doppler ultrasonography. If perfusion is restored by such a reduction, caution remains advisable because an arterial injury with the potential for delayed occlusion may still exist. An arteriogram should be considered and vascular surgical consultation obtained. If reduction and splinting do not immediately restore adequate blood flow, vascular surgery is required if the leg is to be saved. The fracture surgeon must obtain an immediate vascular consultation. Consideration of arteriography is often raised. In some cases, such a study might be helpful if it can be finished without excessive delay. Usually, however, the patient should be taken directly to the operating room for exploration and arterial repair or amputation if satisfactory reconstruction is impossible or contraindicated. Some tibial fractures with arterial injuries, particularly open fractures and those involving long treatment delays or in compromised patients, are best managed by primary amputation.[228, 233] Treatment of vascular injuries with tibial fractures is discussed later in this chapter and in Chapter 11.

If the injured limb is severely painful or swollen or demonstrates impaired neuromuscular function, an acute compartment syndrome may have developed. If persuasive clinical findings are present, the patient needs immediate fasciotomies and fracture stabilization. Tissue pressure measurements can aid in making this decision but are not required. Compartment syndromes are discussed in Chapter 12, and their management with tibial fractures is discussed later in this chapter.

Severe peripheral nerve deficits should also be identified as early as possible. Although they rarely require primary treatment, their effect on the prognosis and management of the entire injury complex may be considerable, they may obscure identification of a vascular injury or compartment syndrome, and their prompt identification establishes an important baseline that may indicate the need for urgent surgical treatment of a progressing arterial occlusion or compartmental syndrome.

In addition to limb or compartment ischemia, any open

fracture wound must be promptly identified because such injuries also require emergency surgical treatment. Skin wounds in the field of a potential surgical incision are an indication for relatively immediate surgery, as might be exceptionally severe closed soft tissue injuries with impending compartment syndromes or such severe soft tissue damage that skeletal stabilization, usually with a provisional external fixator, provides the best setting for recovery. If an open fracture is present, a sterile dressing is placed on the wound, with the application of pressure if needed to control bleeding. An appropriately padded splint is applied. Tetanus prophylaxis and parenteral antibiotics are administered, and the patient is taken to the operating room as soon as practical. Treatment of open tibial shaft fractures is discussed later and also in Chapters 13 and 14.

Unless acute arterial insufficiency, compartmental ischemia, or an open wound is present, definitive reduction and stabilization of a closed tibial shaft fracture are not urgent. What is important is restoration of overall alignment and the application of a well-padded splint or cast, followed by *moderate* elevation and rest for the injured limb. Repeated manipulation, cast changes, or wedging and the use of prolonged anesthetics while striving for an optimal reduction should not be part of the early care of patients with a tibial fracture because such maneuvers may add soft tissue injury, are painful, interfere with the detection of developing ischemia, are often followed by a need to loosen or remove a laboriously adjusted cast, and must usually be done at an inconvenient time with insufficient assistance. A much better policy is thus prompt and gentle realignment of the injured limb, followed by the application of a well-padded cast. The quality of the reduction achieved by a single good attempt is then a guide for subsequent therapy. Unless an indication for immediate surgery develops, the next phase of treatment may be deferred until the patient's swelling is resolving and the necessary assistance and equipment are available. In contrast to fractures of the femur or pelvis, such a cast supports tibial fractures well enough for early mobilization of the patient to a sitting position. A long leg cast could insignificantly interfere with the care of a patient with multiple injuries, which is not to say that early fixation of a tibial fracture cannot be carried out safely.[375] However, no prospective study has convincingly established that patients benefit from this approach. Bhandari's retrospective review, however, did indicate an association of longer hospitalization, more complications, and increased cost with delayed fixation (>12 hours).[45] Although studies have shown that traction to regain the length of an acute tibial shaft fracture elevates compartmental pressure, it is quite rare for compartment syndromes to occur after closed nailing of these injuries.[361, 374, 389] They may also follow repeated attempts at closed reduction and have been missed because the patient was anesthetized during the initial period of painful ischemia.[260] The risk of precipitating or missing a compartment syndrome is, based on the infrequency of such complications, a fairly weak argument against immediate surgical fixation of the tibia.

Definitive treatment of tibial shaft fractures is discussed later and is based on the severity of the injury according to the modified Ellis classification (see Recommended Classification, earlier). In general, closed minor-severity injuries are well treated by closed functional means consisting of casts and fracture braces.[509] Only exceptionally should an open (grade I: indirect, "inside-out") minor fracture be similarly managed. Almost all moderate- and all major-severity tibial fractures benefit from well-executed surgical fracture stabilization. IM nailing is the technique of choice whenever the fracture is neither too proximal nor too distal, the medullary canal permits this technique, and the technology is available.[9, 252] Reamed IM nailing appears to be better for all closed fractures, usually with both proximal and distal interlocking bolts.[125] Although non-reamed IM nailing has been shown to be successful in treating open tibial shaft fractures, there is little clinical evidence that reaming adds significant risk to these injuries. As mentioned earlier, most reports demonstrating the relative benefits of IM nailing (versus external fixation) for open tibial shaft fractures have involved nonreamed nails.[8, 137, 240, 499, 540] Some authors have demonstrated equally good results for open tibial fractures treated with reamed IM nails.[17, 137, 288, 293] It does appear that whenever the fracture configuration permits, IM nailing offers the best means of stabilizing tibial shaft fractures. Although reaming may expand our ability to nail these fractures, the current trend is still to avoid reaming with higher grade open fractures or to limit reaming to the least amount required for insertion of an adequate nail.[513, 599] External fixation with one of several well-documented systems is usually the best way of acutely stabilizing a tibial fracture that is too proximal or distal to fix with a nail or if other contraindications to IM fixation exist. The adaptability of external fixation makes it a workhorse for the care of complex, severe tibial shaft fractures. It can be used temporarily, either to span or to fix directly to the tibia, and it can be used for definitive or staged treatment.[16, 19, 110, 513, 531, 599] Externally fixed tibial shaft fractures are, however, at risk for malunion and nonunion unless fracture healing is achieved before the fixator is removed. Therefore, sequential procedures are worth considering in patients with externally fixed tibial shaft fractures. Plate fixation of tibial shaft fractures, somewhat out of favor because of its relatively high risk of wound healing complications, offers excellent control of fractures extending into the metaphyses.[59] Greater appreciation for evaluation and management of soft tissue injuries, improved surgical techniques for exposure and indirect fracture reduction, and convincing evidence of the long-term satisfactory outcome of plated tibial fractures have secured a place for plate fixation in the primary and especially the secondary stabilization of tibial fractures.[50, 236, 627] Loss of tibial bone stock can be managed with various reconstructive techniques that emphasize early restoration of the surrounding soft tissues, fixation at normal length, and reconstruction with bone grafting, bone transport, or alternatively, acute shortening, which may create soft tissue problems if more than 2.5 cm, although repair of 8- to 10-cm defects has been reported with this approach. Such shortening can then be corrected by subsequent traction histogenesis, as developed and taught by Ilizarov.[613] When reconstructive techniques will not yield a functional leg with safety or without excessively

prolonged treatment, primary amputation remains the best choice for many patients with severe tibial shaft fractures, particularly open fractures with ischemia-producing arterial injuries below the popliteal trifurcation, although the decision may be controversial and good results are occasionally achieved through limb salvage instead of amputation.[190, 248]

## Special Considerations for Polytrauma Patients

Patients with multiple injuries are more likely to have more severe tibial fractures and are thus more likely to require operative treatment. These fractures may be open, ischemic, or associated with ipsilateral femoral fractures (floating knees) or contralateral lower extremity injuries. Regardless of whether the tibial fracture itself requires surgery, the *patient* usually does for other reasons. Therefore, primary management of the tibial fracture takes place in the operating room. If the tibial injury requires surgical care for any indication listed previously, the major issue becomes one of where its treatment falls in the sequence of procedures that must be carried out. Lifesaving treatment, limb-saving wound management, and fracture stabilization procedures are generally carried out in that order, with some variations possible if multiple teams make simultaneous procedures possible or if transfer from one operating table to another can be eliminated safely. Although a fracture table may be desired for IM fixation of the femur, it provides a poor surface for exposure of a tibial fracture, especially if extensive débridement or vascular repair becomes necessary. Therefore, with an ipsilateral femoral fracture, it may be best to splint the tibia, nail the femur, and then move the patient to a regular or radiolucent operating table for treatment of the tibial injury, unless arterial or compartmental pressure problems are present and require treatment first. Combining retrograde femoral IM nailing with antegrade nailing of the tibial shaft fracture through a single knee incision offers an elegant, less invasive means of stabilizing appropriate floating-knee fractures.[205, 258, 428] Patients with multiple lower extremity injuries are best placed on a radiolucent operating table or extension, where all fractures can be dealt with. Open fractures are first débrided, a sterile field is reestablished, and then the diaphyseal fractures are reduced and fixed, typically with IM nails inserted by manual traction, a temporary external fixator, or an AO distractor instead of a fracture table. This situation is similarly conducive to comprehensive management of a multiply injured patient by several operating teams. The patient's physiologic status or logistic reasons might contraindicate definitive internal fixation of some or all of the lower extremity skeletal injuries. In such situations, provisional external fixation can be applied rapidly with minimal additional threat, thus providing the benefits of skeletal stabilization without the time, blood loss, and open wounds required for internal fixation. Once the patient is stabilized and preparations for internal fixation are complete and before significant bacterial colonization of the pin sites, external fixators applied for resuscitation can be replaced with definitive internal fixation devices.

Severe, limb-threatening tibial fractures in a polytrauma patient deserve serious consideration of amputation. This expedient débridement of crushed tissue may be in the patient's overall best interests, even if the leg is potentially salvageable. If a polytrauma patient's tibial fracture is a less serious one and nonoperative management of it does not compromise the overall care of the patient or the injured limb, primary immobilization as described later is appropriate. If closed nailing is the optimal treatment of the tibial fracture, delaying the nailing may prove safer, as mentioned previously. Deferral of tibial fixation must, however, be weighed against the possibility of unexpectedly prolonged delays. Early fixation of an associated tibial fracture, particularly in the case of an ipsilateral femoral fracture, may expedite the diagnosis and treatment of an associated knee injury. Pinless external fixators offer provisional reduction and stabilization while avoiding contamination of the medullary canal and may be beneficial for staged treatment of diaphyseal tibial fractures.[190, 248, 516, 555, 624]

Sterett and co-workers demonstrated a higher risk of chronic osteomyelitis and other complications in trauma patients requiring splenectomy.[549] Awareness of this risk factor for tibial fractures treated with locked IM nails adds support to efforts to avoid splenectomy in a polytrauma patient and should guide the fracture surgeon toward minimizing the risk of infection during the treatment of patients who have had splenectomies.

## The Decision for Operative Treatment

Limb-threatening tibial fractures require urgent surgery. Such fractures include those with associated arterial injuries, fractures with compartment syndromes, and open fractures. In addition to correction of the primary problem by vascular repair, fasciotomy, or irrigation and débridement of the open wound, some form of operative fracture fixation is usually advisable.

With the exception of such limb-threatening conditions, the indications for surgical stabilization of a tibial fracture are relative and require good judgment by the surgeon. Because most low-energy tibial fractures respond well to functional fracture bracing techniques, such injuries require specific indications for fracture fixation. These indications are usually present in more severe injuries and are outlined in Figure 57–11, the recommended algorithm for tibial fracture management.

Unless urgent surgery is required, the tibial fracture is provisionally reduced by gravity manipulation and immobilized in a long leg cast as described in Figure 57–15. If alignment is satisfactory and other indications for surgery are and remain absent, functional bracing becomes the definitive treatment. Major- and moderate-severity injuries, those with unsatisfactory reduction, and others with specific indications deserve elective surgical fixation at an appropriate time, usually within the next few days. No good study has defined the optimal time for fixation of tibial shaft fractures without limb-threatening problems. Fat embolism syndrome is rare after isolated tibial fractures. Timing thus remains a matter of surgical judgment. Concern about the cost of hospitalization and the desire of the patient and family for prompt treatment must be balanced against the rather small risk of compartment syndrome and the inconvenience and possibly increased technical complication rate of surgical fixation during "off hours." It must be remembered that a delay of more than a few days may render fracture reduction more difficult, particularly if length must be regained.

Specific indications for fixation of tibial fractures include displaced fractures involving the knee or ankle, segmental fractures, ipsilateral femoral fractures (floating knees), patients with contralateral lower extremity injuries, and most patients with multiple injuries, particularly if fixation of the tibial fracture will significantly aid in management or provide earlier ambulation.[290] Closed tibial fractures of moderate and major severity heal slowly, and some fail to heal without surgery. Their alignment is not reliably maintained with a cast or brace. Once lost, satisfactory reduction is difficult to regain without extensive surgery. Functional impairment is more common with nonoperatively treated tibial fractures of moderate and major severity. For these reasons, my preference is to use surgical fixation for all but minor-severity acute tibial shaft fractures. Reamed IM nailing is my choice for definitive fixation of all fractures that can be nailed. If a tibia's anatomy is not suited for nailing, the choice is between external fixation and plating, selection of which is best individualized. External fixation is safer for fractures with significant soft tissue injury. Such fixation can "jump" from the distal end of the femur to the distal end of the tibia, beyond the zone of injury, and can often be replaced with a plate once the soft tissue envelope has sufficiently recovered. Because of the difficulty in nailing proximal tibial fractures, surgeons should be prepared to use either external fixation, provisionally or definitively, or plate fixation, depending on circumstances. Figure 55–12 shows examples of fixation options for each of the three grades of tibial fracture severity. The details of these options are discussed in the following sections.

## Tibial Fractures Requiring Immediate Surgery

### TIBIAL FRACTURES WITH VASCULAR INJURIES

The dire prognosis of open tibial fractures plus associated arterial injuries has been emphasized by many authors.[79, 199, 211, 228, 233, 255, 328, 611] If tissue ischemia is present, only prompt successful vascular repair will permit limb salvage. The extent of associated injuries may be such that the salvaged limb is less functional than a prosthesis in spite of lengthy, elaborate, and potentially dangerous reconstructive procedures. Therefore, it is essential to carefully balance the risks and probable functional outcome of salvage attempts against the expectations after primary amputation. Early amputation is often a safer, surer, swifter, and less costly means of restoring function than attempts at limb salvage are. It must be carefully considered for patients with severe tibial fractures, espe-

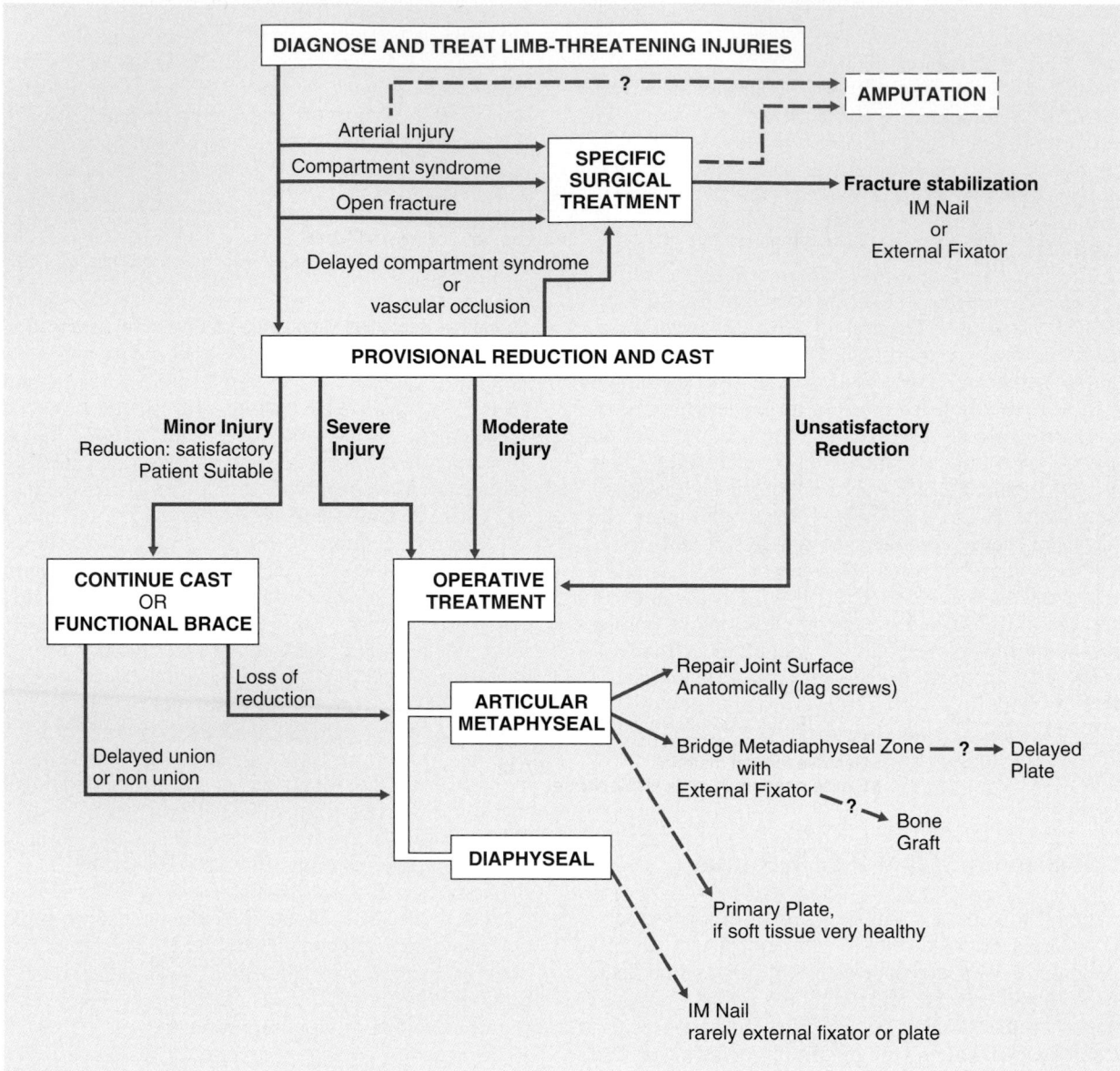

**FIGURE 57–11.** Algorithm for the management of tibial shaft fractures. The first step is to identify and treat limb-threatening conditions. Next, a provisional gravity reduction is performed in the emergency treatment area, and a long leg cast is applied. Such management provides satisfactory immobilization. Following Ellis' classification, a fracture of minor severity with satisfactory reduction can be managed definitively with a cast and fracture brace. Injuries of moderate and major severity should usually be treated with intramedullary nails. For fractures too proximal or distal and those without nailable medullary canals, external fixation or plating should be considered. Patients with significant soft tissue injuries may be more safely treated with initial "bridging" external fixation, followed by delayed plate fixation.

cially those with arterial compromise.[448, 593] However, when the situation permits, vascular repair can be followed by wound and fracture healing and restoration of normal function (Fig. 57–13). Thus, respect for the travails and frequently poor functional results of attempted limb salvage must be tempered by an awareness that such salvage attempts may be appropriate.[190, 248, 457] A patient with a tibial fracture and an arterial injury that is causing limb-threatening ischemia is a candidate for arterial reconstruction if flow can be restored within 6 to 8 hours after injury; if anatomic loss of the tibial nerve, which provides sensation to the sole of the foot, has not occurred; and if salvage of a useful limb is possible without compromising the patient's overall condition.[327] Prompt

diagnosis is established as described previously. Immediate surgery with the participation and collaboration of both vascular and orthopaedic surgeons is indicated. Experience, prearranged protocols, and flexibility of both teams help achieve optimal results. A vascular injury that does not immediately threaten death of the tissue is a less urgent situation than one with established muscle ischemia. In the former situation, skeletal stabilization may be accomplished first, followed by vascular repair. In the latter, perfusion must be reestablished as rapidly as possible, followed by wound and fracture care. In such situations, the use of a temporary arterial shunt permits rapid reperfusion, followed by fracture stabilization and then definitive vascular repair. This is no time for elaborate early fracture repair. A simple external fixator can be applied as a splint across the tibial fracture site if sufficient bone stock or otherwise is available across the knee or ankle. Lag screw fixation of an open articular surface fracture is of high priority but should not delay urgent arterial repair.

Musculoskeletal structures should be respected during exposure of the injured vessels.

An effective collaborative approach is as follows: both legs are prepared and draped. Both vascular and orthopaedic teams work together to rapidly assess the injured leg.

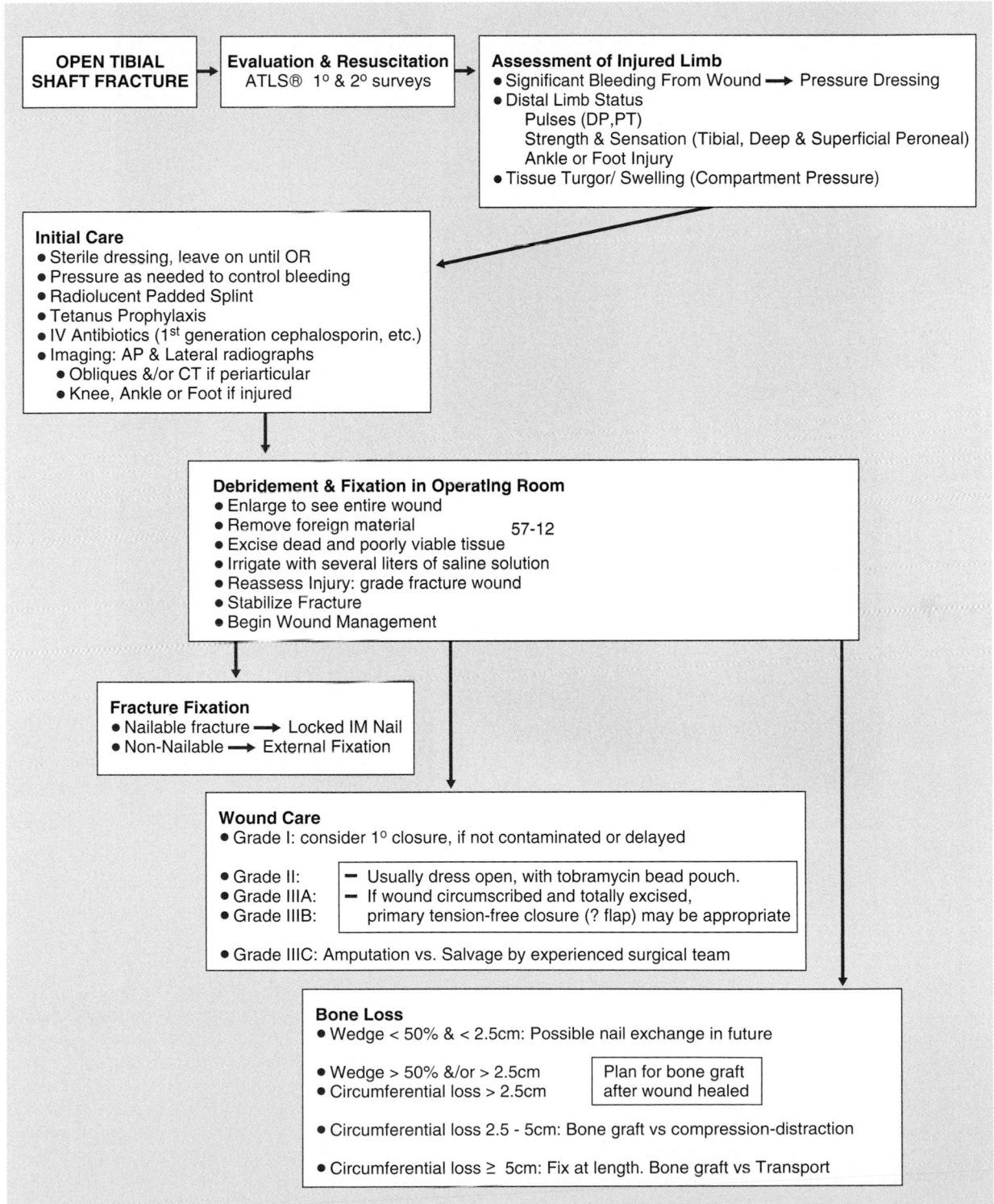

**FIGURE 57–12.** Algorithm for the management of open tibial fractures. After débridement, decisions must be made about fixation, wound closure, and bone loss, if any. If the fracture permits, intramedullary nailing is preferred. External fixation is an appropriate option for provisional or definitive stabilization for non-nailable open fractures. If a plate is used, it should usually follow initial external fixation and be deferred until the wound has healed. Wound closure depends on severity and defect size. Delayed bone grafting or bone transport may be needed, depending on the volume of bone loss.

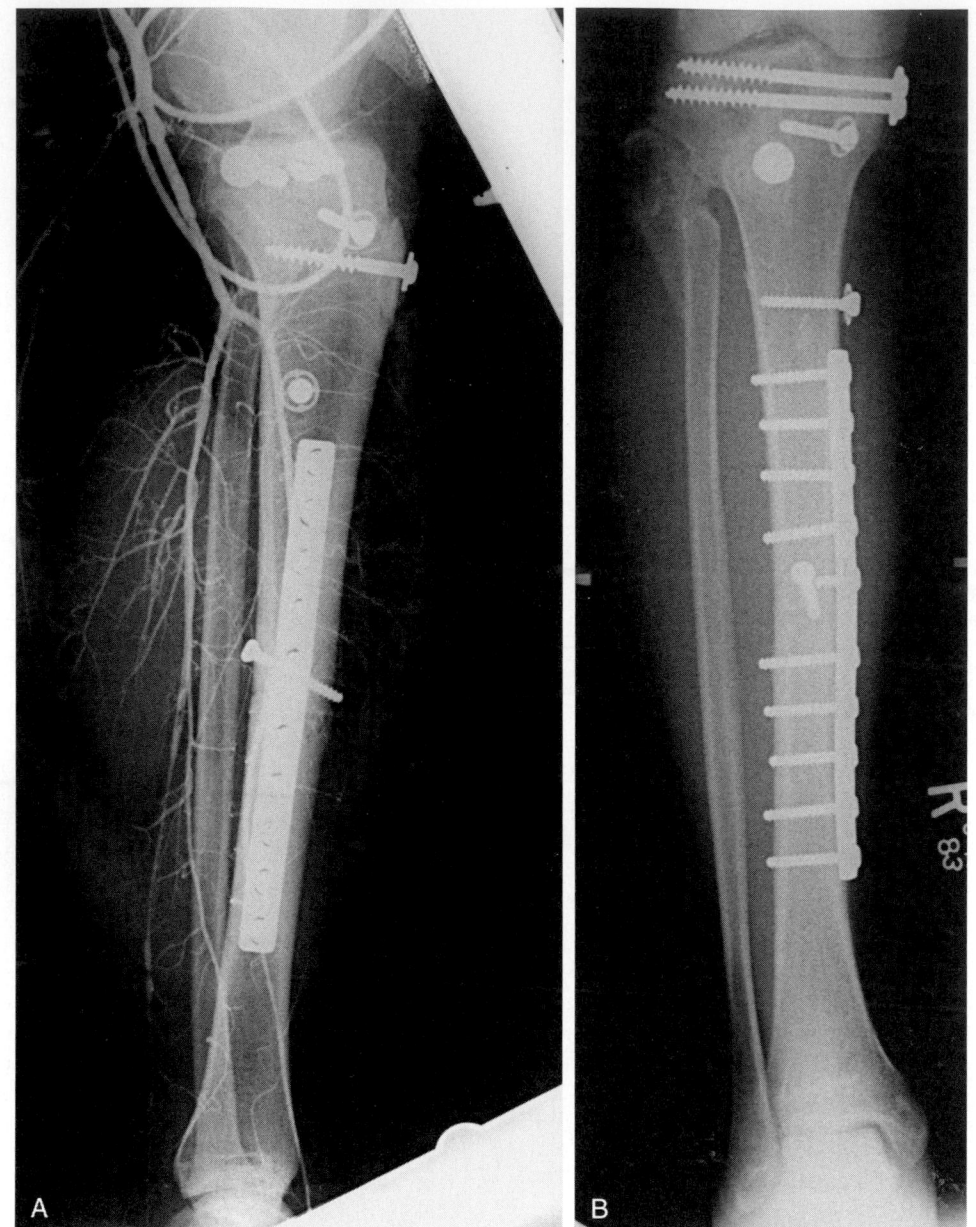

**Figure 57–13.** *A,* This completion arteriogram demonstrates satisfactory perfusion after arterial repair and fracture fixation in a patient with a grade IIIC open fracture of the proximal end of the tibia with an associated fracture-dislocation of the knee (see Fig. 57–5 for preoperative appearance). *B,* Fracture healing with essentially normal function 6 months later. Although many tibia fractures with arterial injuries have a poor prognosis, limb salvage may occasionally be rewarding. It remains difficult to distinguish between patients who are best treated by amputation and those for whom reconstruction of a severely injured limb should be attempted.

The decision to revascularize instead of amputate is crucial. Generally, this choice involves exploration of the injured vessels. If revascularization is chosen, it must be accomplished as rapidly as possible, perhaps with a temporary vascular shunt. If blood flow is restored, the vascular team can harvest a vein graft from the opposite leg while the orthopaedic team rapidly applies an external fixator to stabilize the reduced fracture and provide an optimal field for vascular repair. Complete wound débridement must usually be delayed for ischemic limbs until revascularization has been accomplished, but significant débridement can be accomplished after a temporary shunt has been established. If resulting loss of muscles or

tendons significantly compromises the ultimate functional outcome of the leg, amputation should be chosen over "salvage" of a dysfunctional lower extremity. Because severe crushing injuries of the lower two thirds or so of the tibia cause so much myotendinous damage in association with arterial injury at this level, restoration of arterial flow does not necessarily salvage a functional extremity. Revascularization is more likely to be of benefit when the level of injury is in the upper calf or popliteal region.

It is essential to remember how important wound débridement and subsequent management are for all open fractures, especially severe open tibial fractures. Although wound toilette must not delay revascularization, the high risk of infection must be acknowledged.[110, 197, 564] Thorough débridement is required, even though its completion may need to await vascular repair. Pulsatile wound lavage can usually be started without delaying the vascular anastomosis. Lavage plus antibiotic irrigation may reduce the risk of bacterial contamination spreading throughout the wound. At the completion of arterial and any necessary venous repair, attention is once again turned to the adequacy of wound débridement. Four-compartment fasciotomies are routine after arterial repair because of "reperfusion" capillary leakage after blood flow is restored to ischemic tissue.[172] All necrotic tissue, as well as foreign contamination, must be removed. Fracture fixation must be adequate without adding to the soft tissue injury. External fixation with inclusion of the foot or, perhaps exceptionally, a locked IM nail may be considered. An intraoperative arteriogram is advisable to confirm adequate blood flow after arterial repair and fracture stabilization. Possibly because limb-threatening arterial injuries accompany tibial fractures relatively rarely, optimal management remains controversial and in need of better clinical evidence.[80, 255, 519]

Wounds should be managed by open means, as described for open fractures, but exposed blood vessels, especially when repaired, should be covered to prevent delayed anastomotic rupture. The antibiotic bead pouch technique seems helpful.[288, 393] Early return to the operating room for wound assessment and care should be routine and should involve both surgical teams.

## TIBIAL FRACTURES WITH COMPARTMENT SYNDROMES

Whenever it develops, on initial evaluation or during the subsequent course of a tibial fracture, a compartment syndrome requires emergency management.[189, 374, 377, 592] The diagnosis of compartment syndrome has been discussed previously, and the reader is also referred to Chapter 12. A compartment syndrome may develop after *any* tibial fracture, whatever the apparent severity or mechanism and whether open or closed.[56] Vigilance is necessary during the first several days after every tibial fracture. Risk factors are proximal fractures, especially if very displaced, and segmental fractures. Young muscular men are more commonly involved. Compartment syndrome may occasionally develop soon after IM nailing. More common is transiently elevated tissue pressure, which resolves.[55, 361, 389, 394]

At the first suggestion of increasing severe pain or neurovascular compromise, it is essential to loosen any cast or splint by cutting or spreading it to leave a wide, trough-like support for the injured limb. If this technique fails to provide complete relief, the surgeon must consider whether the patient has an established or developing compartment syndrome, whether arterial inflow is obstructed, or whether a nerve injury is mimicking the motor and sensory changes of a compartment syndrome and may also be preventing awareness of ischemic pain.

Increasing pain, swelling, and progressive motor and sensory deficits are diagnostic of a compartment syndrome, for which emergency fasciotomies are indicated. Absence of peripheral pulses raises serious concern about arterial occlusion, although diminished or absent pulses can also be found in well-established compartment syndromes. The best course is to perform immediate fasciotomies, followed by an intraoperative arteriogram if pulses do not return when normal compartment pressures are restored.

### Compartment Pressure Measurement

Rather than an absolute tissue pressure measurement, it is important to consider the difference ($\Delta P$) between tissue pressure and mean arterial pressure because this difference is a better indicator of the risk of tissue ischemia.[243] McQueen and Court-Brown have recommended using the more obtainable difference between diastolic arterial pressure and tissue pressure. If this "differential pressure" falls to 30 mm Hg or less, they recommend fasciotomies. A number of their continuously monitored patients had compartmental pressures in the 40s and 50s, without symptoms but with differential pressures over 30 mm Hg. Only 1 of their 116 tibial fracture patients had a lower differential pressure and required fasciotomy.[376] Continued vigilance and repeated measurements or continuous monitoring are needed if the patient's neurologic status prevents using the usual clinical symptoms and signs for detection of compartment syndrome.[230, 260]

Rapid measurement of intracompartmental pressure can be helpful for identifying patients with some of the signs and symptoms of compartment syndrome but without elevated tissue pressure; these patients will not benefit from fasciotomy and should be checked carefully for external pressure over a superficial nerve, especially the peroneal nerve at the proximal end of the fibula. Although low absolute compartmental pressures (less than 30 to 35 mm Hg) might dissuade the surgeon from fasciotomy, it is important to remember that the pressure may still be rising. In patients who are hypotensive, compartment syndromes may develop with lower absolute pressure. Patients with more direct muscle injury may also have a lower tolerance for elevated pressure, the duration of which must likewise be considered.[243] Because pressure is highest in the region of the tibial fracture, it should be measured in this area.[235]

## FASCIOTOMY

Adequate fasciotomy allows unfettered swelling of injured muscles without elevation of interstitial fluid pressure, and local capillary blood flow is preserved. Such management permits survival of nerve and muscle tissues that are sensitive to ischemia. A wide, truly decompressive fasciotomy is needed if intracompartmental pressure is or may become dangerously elevated. Unlike fasciotomies for exercise-related compartment syndromes, those required after tibial fractures are extensive. It is safest and most appropriate to treat any such leg as though all four compartments are involved. Therefore, all four compartments are released to ensure decompression. Two incisions, medial and lateral, are recommended by many traumatologists. They should be placed on the midmedial and midlateral sides of the limb, over muscle to facilitate split-thickness skin coverage if necessary. The fascia must be divided the entire length of each compartment (Fig.

57–14) (see Chapter 12). A four-compartment fasciotomy performed with a single lateral incision that is directed both anterior and posterior to the fibula has also been proposed. This approach has two drawbacks: it is less likely to provide adequate decompression than the two-incision technique is, and it adds significant soft tissue damage by requiring circumferential fibular dissection. Although fibulectomy may theoretically decompress all four compartments, it is never appropriate in the setting of a tibial fracture because loss of the fibula may compromise reconstruction of the injured leg.

## SKELETAL STABILIZATION

After fasciotomy, adequate skeletal stabilization is required for wound management and to maintain fracture alignment. External fixation, as advocated by Tscherne and Gotzen, is a safe initial choice unless another technique has already been applied.[588] However, IM nailing, if the fracture location permits, offers acknowledged advantages.[189, 221] The suggested benefits of a nonreamed nail in this setting have yet to be proved. For some metaphyseal fractures, plate fixation may be helpful, either acutely or secondarily applied after external fixation. Turen and colleagues showed no significant difference between IM nailing and external fixation.[592] A cast is not recommended because it may constrict the swollen limb, provides less adequate stability, and interferes with the management of fasciotomy wounds. To splint soft tissues well and to control the position of the foot and ankle, the external fixator should extend to the forefoot. Alterna-

tively, a footplate or plaster splint may be used, but caution and ample padding are required if any sensory impairment has occurred.

Continuing management of a tibial fracture with compartment syndrome includes delayed wound closure, often with a meshed split-thickness skin graft or with elastic loops, progressive suture tightening, or mechanical wound-stretching devices.[145, 231] Depending on fracture severity, delayed bone grafting may be advisable, especially if external fixation is used.

## OPEN TIBIAL FRACTURES

Because the tibial shaft is the most common site of significant open fractures (reviewed in detail in Chapter 13), the important features of its management are discussed here. Like closed tibial fractures, the spectrum of severity is wide, with several factors affecting outcome. Therefore, although general principles hold true, allowances must be made for the specific features of an individual patient's injury.[564, 593]

Gunshot wounds produce tibial fractures that are technically open. However, if they are due to low-energy missiles, débridement is rarely required and management is similar to that for closed fractures with similar comminution and displacement.[77, 173] More severe gunshot wound fractures require standard open fracture care. This topic is reviewed in Chapter 15.

The initial evaluation is carried out as described previously. The wound is covered with a sterile dressing, a splint is applied to the leg, and periodic neurovascular monitoring is instituted. Appropriate tetanus prophylaxis is provided: tetanus toxoid (0.5 mL) if more than 5 years has elapsed since the last tetanus toxoid injection or if this time is unknown. If previous immunization is unknown or incomplete, tetanus immune globulin (250 U) should be administered. Separately, active immunization is then completed with a tetanus toxoid series. Intravenous antibiotics are begun. Unless allergies indicate an alternative choice, a first- or second-generation cephalosporin is routinely administered, with an aminoglycoside added for more severe wounds and high-dose penicillin if clostridial contamination is likely.[564] An alternative to a first-generation cephalosporin and an aminoglycoside is the use of a third-generation cephalosporin alone (e.g., cefotaxime).

### Débridement

Every patient with an open tibial fracture must be taken promptly to an operating room for thorough débridement and irrigation. The priority for open fracture débridement is immediately after lifesaving and limb-saving care. The delay between injury and débridement should be kept under 6 hours if at all possible.[37, 303]

The actual severity of a wound becomes apparent during exposure and débridement. Experience improves the ability to grade and treat an open fracture—good results are less likely when the initial operative care is relegated to junior staff. The wound should be graded by the senior surgeon during débridement, as discussed previously and in Chapter 13, and documented in the patient's operative report. Severity is related not just to

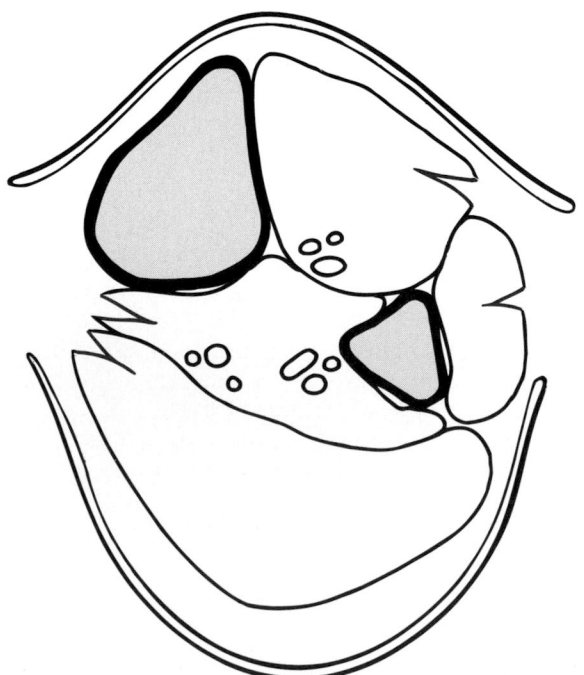

**FIGURE 57–14.** A double-incision fasciotomy permits reliable decompression of the fascial compartments of the leg. To ensure that an adequate bridge of anterior skin is left, it is important to place the incisions on the midmedial and midlateral sides of the leg. Sufficient length of fasciotomy incisions and release of internal fascial envelopes, such as that around the tibialis posterior, are also important.

wound size but to its other characteristics as well, including the degree of contamination; the amount of soft tissue necrosis, ischemia, and crushing; the extent that periosteum is stripped from bone; evidence of comminution and bone loss; injury to neurovascular structures; and the amount of energy absorbed. A significant delay between wounding and débridement may also increase the likelihood of wound problems. Careful determination of wound severity guides both wound care and fracture fixation and establishes the patient's prognosis. By the end of débridement, there should be little doubt about the severity of an open tibial fracture, which can then be graded appropriately.

It is easiest to carry out the initial surgical treatment of an open tibial fracture with the patient supine on a radiolucent operating table so that C-arm fluoroscopy can be used if needed to aid in fixation. A tourniquet is placed around the upper part of the thigh for potential use in controlling excessive bleeding, improving visualization, or producing a postischemic capillary flush that can be used to help determine tissue viability. Waterproof sterile drapes, instruments and supplies for débridement and irrigation, and sufficient assistance are essential. It may be possible to hold the leg manually or with a support during skin preparation, but débridement can be difficult if the limb is unstable. An alternative is to carry out the preparation with the leg on waterproof sterile drapes, which are sequentially replaced as the preparation progresses. With dressings covering the wounds, gross dirt is removed from the skin, often best accomplished with a surgical scrub brush. Hair immediately adjacent to a wound is trimmed or shaved. Degreasing solvents may be required. These solvents, soaps, and alcohols should be kept out of open wounds. Very contaminated wounds often benefit from pulsatile lavage at this stage, but lavage is usually reserved until after a sterile field has been established. After all soap has been rinsed away and the limb dried, the skin is prepared with a povidone-iodine solution, which need not be excluded from the wound surfaces. The prepared area extends from the toes to the tourniquet. Sterile drapes are applied so that circumferential access to the entire limb is possible. A sterile glove or small adhesive drape can cover the toes.

Skin incisions for débridement require careful planning. Unless the initial wound is unquestionably adequate, the surgeon must choose between enlarging it or bypassing it with a standard incision. It is essential to obtain adequate access for wound débridement while preserving thick viable tissue flaps (preferably including the deep fascia) that will at least cover bone, tendons, and neurovascular structures. All these tissues are harmed by desiccation and are poorly covered by split-thickness skin grafts. Incisions over muscle, in contrast, can readily be managed with such skin grafts if delayed suture closure proves impossible.

Because a significant component of skin blood flow is carried at the level of the deep fascia, all surgically created flaps should be fasciocutaneous (i.e., they should include skin, subcutaneous fat, and underlying deep fascia, which is dissected as required from the underlying muscle). This technique preserves local blood flow and improves flap survival. As much as possible, the boundaries of cutaneous angiosomes should be respected.[560] During exposure of open tibial fractures, the physician should look for degloved flaps of skin and subcutaneous tissue separated from underlying fascia by shearing forces produced by crushing and rollover mechanisms. If viability is at all in doubt, the technique of split-thickness skin excision can be used to identify the viable portion of the flap, which is preserved while the avascular part is excised down to healthy muscle.[643] It is essential to explore the wound thoroughly because the fractured end of the tibia can temporarily protrude through a small surface wound and then retract inside and carry with it a surprising amount of dirt and debris. In addition to foreign material, all necrotic muscle, unattached bone fragments, tags of subcutaneous fat, and exposed fascia should be excised. Necrotic muscle is identified primarily by its lack of bleeding, contractility, and normal elastic consistency. Nerves, superficial and deep veins, arteries, and tendons of functional muscles should be retained, as should the periosteum with blood supply and the paratenon, which protects its tendon from desiccation and necrosis. Complete removal of dead bone reduces the risk of infection.[554] The physician must remember the possibility of a compartment syndrome developing in an open fracture, for these wounds do not reliably decompress even a single compartment.[55] For severe injuries, fasciotomies should be a routine part of the débridement procedure. Copious irrigation, conventionally with warmed lactated Ringer's or normal saline solution, is best delivered with a pulsatile lavage system. Conventionally, 6 or more L of irrigation is used. The surgeon should be aware that forceful irrigation can carry contamination into the medullary canal.[44] Excessive irrigation pressure, which may be more effective at removing bacteria, especially if lavage is delayed several hours, may also be more injurious to the exposed tissue.[49] Irrigation is aided by supporting the leg on an irrigating pan that collects the fluid after it has run through the wound. New gowns, gloves, sterile waterproof drapes, and new sterile instruments are used by many surgeons for the fracture fixation phase of the initial operation for open tibial fractures.

A definitive management plan is developed in accordance with the characteristics of the wound, the configuration of the fracture, the patient's overall status, and the resources available. Any incisions should be planned to accommodate the likely choice of fixation. However, the needs of the wound rather than the surgeon's favorite stabilization should ultimately determine all choices made during débridement of an open fracture.

Occasionally, a very severe open tibial fracture, especially in a patient with multiple injuries or one with preexisting medical problems, is better treated by amputation than salvage. (Amputation is discussed later in this chapter.)

### Fixation for Open Fractures

Fractures that have an appropriate bone configuration should be stabilized with an IM nail. Although many have advocated nonreamed nailing for open tibial fractures, such nailing has not been proved to decrease problems with infection or nonunion.[118, 124, 137, 141, 240, 290] Proximal and distal open tibial fractures are usually best stabilized with external fixation, as are others unsuitable for IM nail fixation. If the fracture extends into the articular surface of the knee or ankle, anatomic reduction and lag screw fixation should generally be performed as soon as possible after injury, especially if the wound is severe and coverage problems are anticipated.

The next decision after reconstructing the joint surface is more difficult. The entire tibial injury may be stabilized by external fixation, either from the metaphyseal fragment to the diaphysis or by ligamentotaxis, with the fixator anchored beyond the tibia to the femur proximally or the calcaneus distally. Although a buttress plate can be used to internally fix these fractures, the risk of infection is high enough with plating of open fractures that it is safer to initially use external fixation, with plating delayed until after the wound has healed. Rarely, with low-energy wounds and stable fracture configurations, nonoperative fracture fixation (also discussed later) may be considered as a means of maintaining alignment of an open tibial fracture, but it does not provide enough stability of bone and soft tissue to produce the optimal environment for early wound healing and resistance to infection. Especially for more distal fractures, the ankle should be splinted to minimize soft tissue motion in the wound area. Ultimately, the choice of fixation for an open tibial fracture is a compromise between that required for the fracture and that required for the soft tissue, with the latter taking precedence.

### Wound Care for Open Fractures

Whatever fixation is chosen, it is conventionally advised that an open fracture wound not be closed primarily but instead be left open to avoid tension on the soft tissue and resulting microvascular embarrassment. An additional benefit is the opportunity to reassess the adequacy of débridement and soft tissue viability early in the postinjury course. The time-honored practice of delayed wound closure has been supported by the experimental studies of Edlich and co-workers[154] and the clinical studies of Russell and associates.[490] However, interest in primary closure of properly selected and managed wounds is increasing in experienced trauma surgeons.[133] Several technical aspects of open wound care are important. Desiccation of exposed tissue must be prevented. Continuous wet dressings can be used, but they typically dry and may increase the risk of wound contamination. An immediate split-thickness skin graft, allograft or xenograft skin, or artificial skin substitutes (e.g., Epigard, Biobrane) should be considered. Particularly helpful is the "bead pouch" technique described by Ostermann, Seligson, and co-workers.[242, 427, 520] Keating and colleagues confirmed that this technique of open wound management significantly reduces the risk of infection in severe open tibial fractures treated with reamed IM nails.[288] At the completion of débridement, tobramycin-loaded polymethyl methacrylate (PMMA) beads are placed in the wound, which is then sealed with a transparent, adhesive film dressing (e.g., Opsite, Tegaderm). This dressing is then covered with a bulky absorbent dressing, which can be changed in case of leakage, but the bead pouch itself is left intact until the wound is reexplored under sterile conditions in the operating room. Although tobramycin beads can be made by the surgical team in the operating room, advance

preparation by hospital pharmacy staff allows them to be delivered in sterile peel-wrap packages for immediate use. (The typical concentration is 2.4 g of tobramycin powder in one full "mix" of methacrylate cement.[288])

Continuing management of an open fracture wound depends on its severity. Type I and many type II wounds can be left covered with sterile dressings and then closed 5 to 7 days after injury either with sutures or by the application of a meshed split-thickness skin graft if the wound edges are not easily brought together. All patients with type III wounds or any questionable type II wound should be returned to the operating room, usually in 24 to 48 hours, for thorough reassessment under adequate anesthesia. This procedure involves gently irrigating out all clot, carefully looking for and removing any necrotic tissue, reassessing fracture reduction and stability, and then resuming open wound management in a manner that prevents desiccation, as just described. At this time it is too early to proceed with delayed primary closure, although if the wound is clean and viable, application of a meshed split-thickness skin graft may be considered.

During this first return to the operating room, which should be repeated as many times and as frequently as needed to obtain a clean wound containing only viable tissue, plans for definitive wound closure are formulated and carried out as soon as appropriate.[110, 141, 387, 628] During dressing change and débridement under anesthesia in the operating room, consulting physicians can inspect the wound together with the primary fracture surgeon and collaborate on decision making. Type IIIA wounds can usually be closed by suture or a meshed split-thickness skin graft. Type IIIB wounds, on the other hand, usually require muscle flap coverage with either a healthy local muscle or a microvascular free flap. (Many surgeons use this scenario as a working definition of type IIIB wounds.) The timing of such closure should be as prompt as possible once adequate débridement is ensured. Published support is growing for very early or even immediate closure of such wounds after radical débridement.[197, 246, 539, 586] However, application of a muscle flap makes subsequent wound evaluation more difficult. When retained nonviable tissue is a significant possibility, less hasty coverage is advisable.[387] One should not delay once it is clear that the wound is free of necrotic tissue. Failure to achieve adequate débridement and gain wound coverage within the first 1 or 2 weeks after injury is associated with a higher risk of problems after flap coverage. The greatest difficulty comes with severe wounds in which it is difficult to determine tissue viability until after several débridement sessions. It is not entirely clear whether the delay, the more severe wound, or both are responsible for the acknowledged higher rate of wound complications.

Attempts to gain coverage with local tissues by using "relaxing incisions" or local rotational flaps may be unwise, especially when the amount of soft tissue damage is more severe.[144, 445] Such coverage attempts can result in loss of additional soft tissue. Preservation of injured local skin is best achieved by avoiding incisions that create superficial, narrow, or distally based flaps, by taking pains to place incisions over muscle, and by using tension-free closure with split-thickness skin over viable muscle or, if not possible, by transposing healthy muscle into the wound as a pedicle or free flap, depending on the location and available tissue. A recently reported technique—vacuum-assisted closure—appears to offer significant help in the noninvasive management of severe lower extremity wounds by reduction of edema and promotion of granulation tissue overgrowth, thus permitting split-thickness skin coverage of wounds that might otherwise require significant flaps.[132, 204]

## BONE DEFECTS AND NEED FOR GRAFTING

Loss of bone may occur at the time of the fracture or during necessary débridement. Absence of either an intercalary segment or a substantial paraxial portion requires restoration of bone substance to obtain fracture union or to prevent pathologic fracture through a seriously weakened area. Soft tissue defects are frequently present and may need to be repaired before bone grafting.[30, 105, 360, 584, 628, 645]

Occasional reports have described replacement of extruded fragments of the tibia after sterilization.[93, 223] Although this technique may work, the risk of infection and delayed reincorporation of the bone increases the attractiveness of other alternatives: primarily autogenous cancellous bone graft. Allografts (if no infection is present), fibular transfer on its vascular pedicle,[247] free vascularized autografts,[608] nailing with delayed bone grafting,[476, 608] and Ilizarov traction osteogenesis[107, 430, 431, 491, 591] are other possibilities, as is shortening in bilateral injuries (see Chapters 14, 20, and 21). Watson and associates' review is a helpful summary.[613] Small amounts of missing bone can be ignored. The surgeon must remember that in spite of bone loss, particularly in a youthful patient with some spared periosteum, some patients will fill in or bridge over a defect so that bone grafting is not required. Radiographs should thus always be checked before delayed grafting to ensure that the procedure is still needed.

Healing of severe open tibial fractures often benefits from a cancellous bone graft, and grafting may be essential if a bone defect is present. Healing of open tibial fractures is delayed by severe soft tissue damage. Bone autografts can promote the healing of such injuries and thus help prevent prolonged disability, as well as fixation failure and loss of alignment. The benefit of grafting is particularly relevant when external fixation is used to stabilize the fracture because the fixator may not last long enough for secure fracture healing unless bone grafts are used or the pins are replaced.[155] Bone grafts offer similar protection with plate fixation as well, particularly if bone has been lost at the fracture site. Bone grafting is less important when IM nail fixation is used, unless an injury or débridement has created a critically sized defect. Robinson and colleagues suggest that for fractures fixed with IM nails, this critical defect size is longer than 2.5 cm or involves a "wedge" of more than 50% of the circumference.[476]

Bone grafts should be placed under healthy, well-vascularized tissue, such as the muscles of the deep posterior compartment or a muscle pedicle flap. It is generally wise to delay bone grafting until secure wound healing is present. However, the advisability of this procedure should be considered early in the care of a severe open fracture because it may affect the location of incisions, as well as the technique of wound closure. For example, if a graft will be required under a muscle flap, one should place antibiotic-laden methacrylate beads under the flap to save room for the cancellous bone graft several weeks later.[105]

When faced with larger bone defects, the surgeon must choose between bone grafting and traction histogenesis (Ilizarov) solutions to the problem.[107, 339, 463, 546, 613] Early in the management of a patient with acute tibial bone loss, it is important to make plans for its reconstruction. The choice of fixation will be affected by how the defect will be addressed. Small defects are perhaps easiest to manage with IM nail fixation, with later bone grafting if Robinson's 2.5-cm, greater than 50% circumference, or both thresholds are exceeded.[476] With larger defects, as mentioned, either more extensive bone grafting or bone transport should be considered. Acute shortening with subsequent distractive restoration of length may help gain earlier wound closure.[24, 700] This procedure is often aided by Z-plasty of the original wound.[536] It is not appropriate for defects over 5 cm or so because of neurovascular compromise. Longer defects, if appropriate for limb salvage, are best dealt with by applying an external fixator, often a provisional one, to maintain length. Subsequently, once adequate planning and patient counseling have been completed, conversion to a fixator suitable for bone transport is accomplished. No convincing evidence has indicated that one of these approaches is better than another.[108, 352] It is best to choose an individualized plan based on the patient and the injury, as well as the experience and resources available to the treating physicians. Collaboration between orthopaedic surgeons and plastic surgeons is important with regard to flap coverage in combination with traction histogenesis techniques.[5, 435] (Tibial defects that develop later in the course of care are discussed in a subsequent section.)

## Initial Care if Immediate Surgery Is Not Planned

### PRIMARY (PROVISIONAL) FRACTURE IMMOBILIZATION WITH A CAST

Unless an indication for immediate surgery is identified, the following approach is recommended. Most low-energy closed tibial fractures can be aligned quite well by closed reduction in a dependent position and application of a long leg cast.[504, 507, 572] Such a cast usually provides better immobilization than do splints made of plaster or fiberglass slabs or those that are available commercially. The technique is presented in the next section.

Radiographs of the fracture are then obtained, rotational alignment is reconfirmed by visual comparison, and unless a *major* problem with malalignment is noted, the reduction is accepted, at least temporarily. The patient is usually hospitalized with the leg elevated slightly above heart level and observed for comfort and neurovascular status. Outpatient care is possible if comfort, monitoring, and gait training can be ensured. If the cast becomes too tight or the surgeon has serious concern about impending circulatory compromise, the plaster is loosened and the cast padding divided. If these measures do not maintain or restore satisfactory neurovascular status, arterial perfusion and compartmental pressure are checked, with further immediate surgical treatment as indicated. With a satisfactory reduction and no evidence of neurovascular compromise, it is expeditious to leave the provisional cast intact. If the reduction is not satisfactory or closed treatment is, for some other reason, less desirable, definitive fixation may be carried out electively after the initial swelling has begun to resolve, but without excessive delay.

An alternative to gravity reduction and cast application is the use of skeletal traction applied by way of either the distal end of the tibia or the calcaneus. A centrally threaded external fixator pin or a smooth Kirschner wire with ample padding between the skin and tractor bow arms may be used. Another alternative is a "pinless" external fixator clamp.[214, 624] The leg is supported on a Böhler-Braun or equivalent frame, and traction is limited to the least force needed to maintain length and stability. The traction can be continued for several weeks until early consolidation makes an initially unstable reduction manageable in a cast. For optimal provisional stabilization that does not require bed-bound skeletal traction, we occasionally apply in the emergency department a minimal external fixator with transfixion pins in the distal end of the femur and calcaneus, radiolucent rods with adjustable articulating connectors, and a supplementary well-padded posterior splint.

### Tibial Cast Application

Advance preparation is a great aid to reduction and cast application. Before beginning, it is necessary to have close at hand ample cast padding, usually as 4-inch rolls, plaster or fiberglass rolls 4 to 6 inches wide, plaster splints or fiberglass cast material if desired, a bucket of cool water, and a cast saw. The patient's radiographs should be visible on a viewbox. A seat is helpful for the person applying the cast. The task requires at least two people: one to hold the leg and another to apply the cast. The patient must be as comfortable as possible, and cooperation and understanding should be encouraged. An intravenous line should be in place. Analgesia is often best provided with intravenous narcotics (e.g., morphine sulfate, 3 to 8 mg, titrated as needed). Naloxone and medications and equipment for resuscitation should be readily available. A hematoma block with 1% lidocaine may be considered, with scrupulous attention to sterile technique and awareness of the risk of systemic effects (myocardial depression, seizures).

The patient is positioned recumbent on an examining or operating table. Both legs are evaluated so that that rotational alignment and contours of the normal limb can guide reduction and cast molding. Such evaluation can be facilitated by hanging both legs over the end of the table. Alternatively, the injured leg can be abducted at the hip and hung over the table's side. Enough room must remain to allow padding and plaster to be rolled around the upper portion of the calf. The cast is applied in two parts. Almost always (except for very proximal fractures), the lower part is applied first. The assistant holds the forefoot to steady the leg and maintain its alignment, especially with regard to rotation and plantigrade foot position. With knee flexion, the tibia can rotate significantly on the femur. It is therefore important to assess rotational alignment by using the relationship of the second toe to the tibial tubercle, as demonstrated by the opposite limb. The assistant's fingers are placed under the plantar surface, with the thumb over the dorsum of the foot. Thus, plantar flexion and inversion (supination) are controlled, both of which tend to occur and subsequently interfere with weight bearing in this cast. Although ankle equinus is occasionally the alternative to apex-posterior angulation of a distal tibial fracture site, it can usually be avoided if as Sarmiento suggests, the initial cast is applied with the foot in neutral.[504]

The assistant maintains foot position as chosen while ample cast padding is rolled onto the foot (including the thumb and fingers of the assistant) and up as high on the leg as the flexed knee will allow (Fig. 57–15). Developing soft tissue edema and the leg's characteristic bony prominences argue for thick padding, as does the likelihood that the cast will need to be cut in the near future while the leg is still swollen. Because the patient will be supine, extra padding is required posterior to the heel, where much of the limb's weight will be borne during recumbency. The malleoli, the fibular head and neck with the surrounding peroneal nerve, and the subcutaneous tibial border also require extra padding. The padding is palpated to ensure its adequacy and supplemented if necessary, and then a thin cast (8 to 10 layers of plaster or 5 to 8 layers of fiberglass) is rolled on from the metatarsophalangeal joints to an inch or two below the top of the padding at the knee. The plantar surface may be extended to support the toes, but the dorsum should be placed or trimmed proximal to all five metatarsophalangeal joints.

Some surgeons believe that plaster is easier to apply and mold than fiberglass. However, it should be left thin to simplify alterations and avoid unnecessary weight. Overlying fiberglass reinforcement can be applied in 1 or 2 days once it is clear that the cast will be left in place. As the plaster sets, molding is carried out to make the shape of the medial border of the cast concave, similar to the patient's opposite leg; a straight cast produces valgus malalignment. The surgeon should ensure that foot position has been maintained. Improved water-activated fiberglass casting tape offers a lighter and more durable alternative to plaster. I believe that it is now quite acceptable as an initial tibial fracture cast, although like plaster, adequate padding and careful application are essential.

Once the lower leg portion of the cast is firm, it can be lifted and held horizontally with the knee flexed 10° to 15° and the thigh sufficiently clear of the table surface to allow padding to be extended proximally an inch beyond the intended top of the cast, approximately two thirds of the way up the thigh (see Fig. 57–15B). Cast material is then rolled on, with the top of the previously applied lower portion overlapped 4 to 6 inches. It is essential that adequate padding be placed at the junction of the two segments, but no padding should lie between the layers of the cast material.

As soon as practical, AP and lateral radiographs of the entire tibia within the cast are obtained and a decision made regarding provisional adequacy of the reduction and

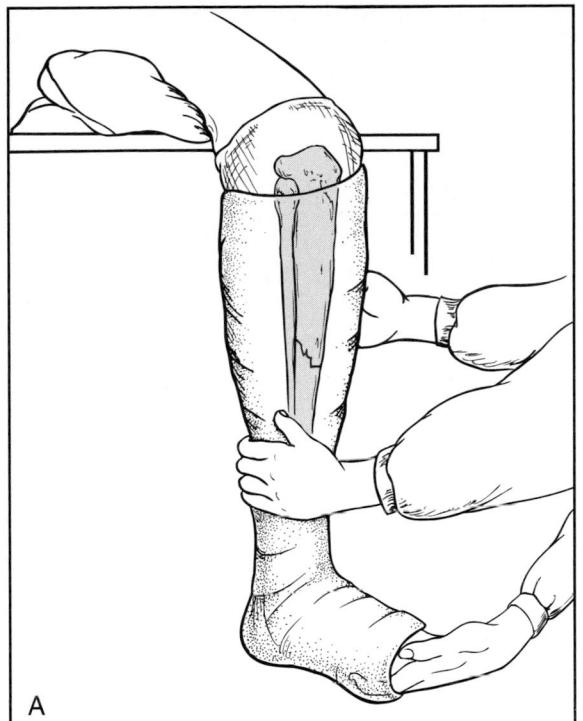
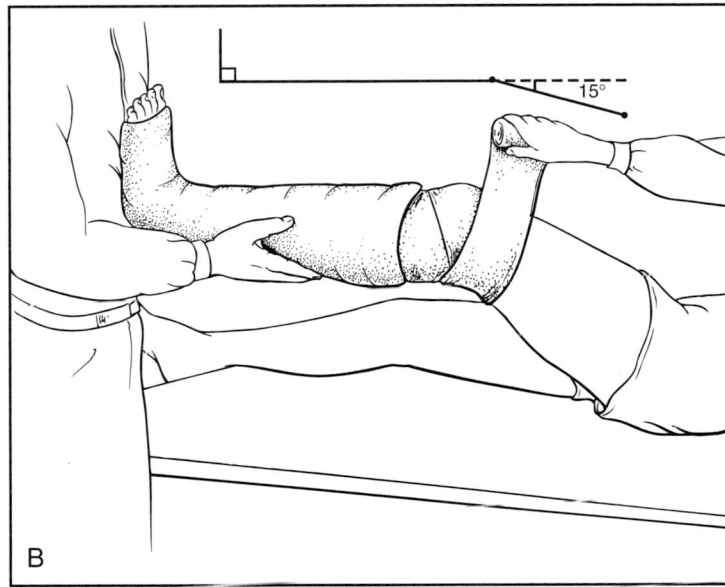

**FIGURE 57–15.** Gravity reduction and cast application. Most acute tibial shaft fractures will reduce fairly satisfactorily when hung over the side of an examining table with the foot correctly rotated and supported in neutral position. *A,* The leg must hang far enough away from the table to allow circumferential access. A pad under the proximal aspect of the thigh helps. An assistant must hold the foot and steady the leg. The surgeon ensures that the alignment is correct and applies ample cast padding, especially over the posterior of the heel, the malleoli, the proximal end of the fibula, the fracture site, and the point where the cast will be cut. Plaster or fiberglass casting tape is rolled over the padding with a segment of padding left exposed just below the knee to be overlapped later by the above-knee part of the cast. Gentle molding by the surgeon often improves alignment, especially by making the medial tibial surface slightly concave to match that of the normal leg. Six to eight layers of plaster, or a bit less fiberglass tape, is usually sufficient, perhaps with extra reinforcement at the knee and ankle. *B,* Once the lower portion of the cast is firm, it is used to hold the limb in correct rotation and with the knee flexed approximately 15°. Cast padding is then rolled over the thigh on top of a proximal segment of stockinette to provide a well-padded top cuff. The patella and hamstring tendons need extra padding. Cast material is then applied approximately two thirds of the way up the thigh, with the cast material overlapping the lower part of the cast by 4 to 6 inches. The stockinette and padding are turned down over the top of the cast and secured with a turn of the casting tape to avoid a sharp edge. The leg must be supported until the cast is hard. Rotational alignment is then checked by comparison with the opposite leg. Anteroposterior and lateral radiographs of the full tibia are obtained and assessed for angulation, displacement, and shortening.

cast application. Only in patients with marked deformity or a risk of skin compromise should the appearance of these radiographs lead to changing the cast. Adjustments such as wedging, applying a new cast, or changing to another mode of treatment are better deferred until the swelling has resolved.

The long leg cast just applied may need to be loosened to accommodate potential or actual swelling of the injured limb. Although it is wise to always anticipate such swelling, many low-energy tibial fractures can remain in an intact, well-padded cast. Routine splitting of all initial tibial casts results in unnecessary manipulation and may compromise the cast's stability.

A cast may be loosened in several ways. If the swelling is severe and likely to progress, the cast should be converted to a posterior trough splint, which is accomplished by removing the *anterior third* of the cast and bending both sides outward, wide enough to permit removal of the leg and avoid any pressure on the sides of the limb. The padding is cut anteriorly and folded outward as well so that the padding is not a source of constriction and to allow examination of the limb. Removal of part of the medial cast wall at the ankle can allow assessment of the posterior tibial pulse, if needed (Fig. 57–16). A

practical concern about removing strips and windows from casts is that the stability of the cast may be compromised. The result can be a plaster cast that fails to immobilize the injured limb and thus does not prevent pain and additional tissue trauma. Fiberglass used as the

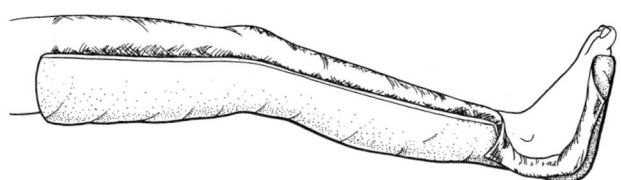

**FIGURE 57–16.** A cast can be loosened somewhat by cutting its anterior surface from top to bottom, using a cast spreader to open the cut, and bending the sides out and stretching the cast padding to loosen it as well. However, this technique may not accommodate significant swelling. If swelling is a concern or if it is necessary that a severely injured limb be observed while maintaining an adequate splint, the long leg cast can be converted into a trough splint, after it has hardened, by removing an anterior strip approximately one third of the cast's circumference. The cast padding is cut and turned back, and the sides of the cast are bent outward to eliminate pressure on the leg. The trim line is placed posteriorly, if needed, in the area of the posterior tibial pulse to permit palpation of it in case of potential vascular injury.

initial cast material or as reinforcement can improve the mechanical properties of the initial cast. Whatever material is used, the adequacy of immobilization must be frequently reassessed.

Removal of an anterior strip of plaster interferes with ongoing use of the cast. An alternative is to split the cast anteriorly after it has hardened, which usually takes 1 or 2 hours for plaster, and then widen this cut sufficiently with cast spreaders so that the padding is stretched and subsequent loosening of the cast will be easy. This "univalved" cast may be salvaged after the swelling recedes by squeezing it together and encircling it with adhesive tape just tightly enough to provide adequate support. Once a final adjustment has been made, fiberglass reinforcement is added to make the cast strong enough to begin ambulation. It is important to realize that this technique of cast spreading does not provide adequate decompression in the presence of serious swelling, nor if the cast material cannot be bent open. Somewhat better decompression may be provided by "bivalving" the cast, with medial and lateral longitudinal cuts placed just a bit anterior to the midlateral lines of the cast to maximize stiffness and durability of the posterior portion, but not so far anterior that the opening is too narrow for removal of the leg. A bivalved cast can be loosened as needed and held securely together with several encircling loops of adhesive tape. In addition to longitudinal cuts in the cast, windows may be removed to check questionable areas of skin, relieve pressure over a bony prominence, or assess pulses. The removed cast window should be retained and taped securely in place when the opening is not in use. Doing so adds to the strength of the cast and maintains enough overlying pressure to avoid "window edema"—swelling of the soft tissues into the window defect.

If a cast is left intact around a fresh tibial fracture, fail-safe arrangements for it to be released must be made if significant pain or neurovascular compromise develops. Although tibial fracture patients typically require hospitalization, a patient may occasionally be sent home with a low-energy injury if able to use crutches and perform transfers and if adequate assistance and prompt transportation back to the hospital are available. Whether as an outpatient or in the hospital, the patient should keep the injured leg slightly elevated and should be observed closely for increasing pain, decreasing sensation, and loss of palpable toe muscle strength. Pain after a tibial fracture is largely relieved by adequate splinting. Narcotic analgesics are usually required, but standard doses of parenteral or oral drugs should be effective and should be needed progressively less frequently. After 1 or 2 days, oral narcotics should be sufficient, perhaps with a timed-release capsule form that may last through the night. Lack of response to analgesia suggests neurovascular problems.

## Definitive Treatment of Tibial Fractures

### NONOPERATIVE (FUNCTIONAL CAST OR BRACE)

Sarmiento, perhaps the most eloquent advocate and teacher of nonoperative functional treatment of tibial fractures, reports impressive results in selected patients with less displaced, usually lower energy tibial shaft fractures. He advises that functional closed treatment be limited to closed injuries that have no more than 15 mm of initial shortening or are axially stable, reduced transverse fractures.[509] Displacement in his series averaged only $28\% \pm 25\%$. He stated that high-energy tibial fractures and fractures in patients with multiple injuries or ipsilateral femoral fractures were usually treated with surgical fixation, which was also indicated for fractures with excessive initial shortening, segmental bone loss, and neurovascular damage and for those whose alignment was not maintained satisfactorily in the initial cast or subsequent brace.

Functional treatment of tibial fractures has proved very satisfactory for properly selected patients and has yielded low rates of nonunion, infection, and significant malunion.[505] However, it is important to recognize that this treatment protocol has been effective only for *selected* low-energy tibial fractures.[26, 441, 509, 575–577] When other alternatives are available, this protocol is inappropriate for tibial fractures with significant associated soft tissue injury. In accordance with the modified Ellis classification system described earlier, functional bracing, as a primary treatment, should be restricted to tibial fractures of minor severity. Rarely, more severe injuries can also be managed in this way, but only if they are axially stable and can be easily controlled during weight bearing in the cast or brace.

Functional bracing begins with closed gravity realignment and application of an initial cast, as described earlier. In addition to injury severity, the adequacy of reduction in this cast and the patient's subsequent clinical course are the most important determinants of whether closed functional treatment is appropriate. The amount of soft tissue damage determines the shortening that may occur. Ultimate shortening is usually predictable from the amount of shortening apparent on the initial radiographs. Brace treatment is rarely appropriate in fractures with more than 15 mm of shortening, as measured by fragment overlap or by a scanogram in the cast. Poor control of angulation in a long leg cast is also a contraindication to functional bracing unless it is corrected by reapplication of a cast or brace. Angulation on either the AP or lateral radiograph should not exceed 5°.

Significant comminution and displacement of more than 30% of the shaft diameter are further contraindications to closed functional treatment because of their association with delayed healing when this treatment is used.[577] Closed functional treatment should be used with caution for distal tibial fractures because maintenance of satisfactory alignment may prove difficult. It is also not optimal for patients with bilateral lower extremity injuries who could walk sooner on a tibial fracture if it were fixed with an IM nail, for patients with high-energy injuries and extensive closed or open soft tissue injuries, and for patients with ipsilateral femoral fractures. Elderly and infirm patients may be better able to care for themselves after fracture fixation if it permits weight bearing sooner with greater comfort and less encumbrance.[218] Unreliable patients who may not return faithfully for follow-up visits during the 4 to 7 months typically required for fracture healing may have a lower risk if internal fixation can be performed in a manner that permits unrestricted weight bearing. If such fixation is not possible, internal fixation may not be as safe as closed treatment.[67, 284, 412]

Fracture braces and functional casts rely on soft tissues, primarily the interosseous membrane, to prevent shortening while the surrounding cast controls angulation and rotation.[507] When the soft tissue disruption is considerable, simple closed reduction cannot stabilize a displaced oblique or spiral fracture or one with significant comminution. Exceptionally, a displaced transverse fracture may have its length and stability restored by closed reduction and cast application under anesthesia if end-on-end apposition can be maintained. This technique has been advocated for such injuries. However, because these injuries are well treated with closed IM nailing (described later), it seems generally inappropriate to subject a patient to anesthesia for closed reduction without offering the benefit of stable fixation as well. Toivanen and co-workers have demonstrated that IM nailing is less costly than closed reduction if an anesthetic is required.[575]

Functional cast or brace treatment is also advisable after removal of an external fixator. Its use for this purpose is discussed in the section on external fixation.

### Fracture-Bracing Technique

The following protocol for closed functional treatment of tibial shaft fractures is similar to that developed by Sarmiento and co-workers.[507, 509] The first stage involves the application of a gravity reduction cast, as previously described. Acceptable reduction must be confirmed. Initially, the patient's leg is resting and slightly elevated above heart level. Ice packs applied to the cast may increase comfort, but narcotic analgesics are usually required. Progressively increasing ambulation is encouraged, with weight bearing as tolerated in a removable cast boot and crutches or a walker as needed. The patient is asked to elevate the limb when not walking and to perform isometric exercises with the immobilized muscles and active and passive exercises with the toes. The patient should be reassured about the inevitable motion of fracture fragments felt inside the cast and the benefits of progressive weight bearing on the fractured limb. In addition to the exercise program, physical therapy may help with gait training on level surfaces, on stairs, and for transfers. Once patients are comfortable and mobile enough to manage at home and after any necessary assistance has been arranged, they are discharged to outpatient follow-up. Patients are instructed to promptly report any cast problems, increasing pain, motor or sensory deficit, or excessive swelling that is not rapidly relieved by rest, elevation, and milder analgesics. An office or clinic visit 1 or 2 weeks after discharge permits reassessment of comfort, gait, swelling, neuromotor function, cast integrity, and clinical and radiographic alignment.

Although some patients may benefit from a PTB walking cast, as originally advocated by Sarmiento, a prefabricated functional PTB brace from knee to foot with a hinged ankle has largely replaced this cast unless a satisfactorily fitting brace is not available or offers inadequate control, as may happen with a very distal fracture (Fig. 57–17). The PTB cast or brace is applied when the patient can comfortably bear partial weight in the long leg cast and early fracture consolidation has begun, usually between 3 and 5 weeks after injury. Proximal tibial fractures may be better controlled in a long leg cast. If knee motion is desired for such patients, hinges and a thigh cuff can be added to the below-knee portion of the cast. An effective method is to use a fiberglass below-knee cast, molded as shown in Figure 57–17A, to which are attached the hinges and adjustable thigh cuff of a commercially available modular fracture brace. A prefabricated fracture brace that follows Sarmiento's principles usually provides excellent fracture control while permitting satisfactory function for most patients with low-energy tibial shaft fractures. Alternatively, a custom-molded, bivalved, total-contact brace can be fabricated by an orthotist. It may have either a fixed or a hinged ankle, depending on the degree of immobilization desired. Such braces can be helpful for patients who are hard to fit with prefabricated ones. For experimental midshaft tibial fractures, Zagorski showed equivalent stabilizing efficiency of plaster casts, custom braces, and prefabricated fracture braces, plus no additional benefit from the classic PTB proximal extensions.[642]

Radiographs through the cast or brace are initially checked every 2 to 3 weeks to ensure maintenance of satisfactory alignment. Minor degrees of angulation can be corrected with cast changes or wedging. However, the latter may render the cast less suitable for weight bearing, so once the fracture is "sticky" enough to permit only bending rather than translation of fragments, it is better to change the cast or proceed to a brace rather than adjust alignment with wedging. Significant difficulty in obtaining or maintaining satisfactory fracture alignment with a cast or brace suggests the advisability of surgical reduction and fixation.

The fracture brace is applied when the patient can walk in a long leg cast and satisfactory fracture alignment has been maintained. The cast is removed, a thick elastic fracture brace sock is applied, and the fracture brace is secured snugly over the sock. Trimming of this brace and occasionally padding or molding with the aid of a heat gun may be needed for comfort and optimal fracture control. The heel cup and ankle hinge must be sized and adjusted correctly. A lace-up athletic shoe helps hold the brace in place. Brace tightness is adjusted as needed by the patient to provide support with comfort. Progressive weight bearing is again encouraged. Crutches and cane can be discarded when comfort and a satisfactory gait permit. Many believe that significant weight bearing within 6 weeks of injury is very beneficial for healing of tibial fractures.[508, 509]

Radiographs are obtained in the brace initially and again in 1 or 2 weeks, at which time it is also essential to confirm that the brace fits well, without skin or nerve irritation, and that the patient is maintaining and adjusting it properly. Thereafter (usually from 6 to 8 or more weeks after a low-energy tibial shaft fracture), it is usually possible to monitor the patient with visits and radiographs every 4 to 6 weeks. Use of the brace is continued until the patient is fully weight bearing without discomfort, tenderness and warmth are absent at the stable fracture site, and radiographs in the AP, lateral, and both oblique projections confirm union with mature bridging callus (see later discussion of assessment of fracture healing).

At this point, some residual muscle weakness and atrophy persist, the patient's endurance is not yet normal, and the skeleton is weaker than normal as a result of disuse atrophy. Therefore, a continuing rehabilitation program with avoidance of risk and contact sports is advised while encouraging repetitive loading increased as rapidly as tolerated. These graded, progressively increasing exercises should continue until the patient's activity level and tolerance reach an appropriate goal, which often requires 6 to 12 months from the time of injury.

Skin problems associated with braces are usually rare but should be watched for. If they develop, padding or other brace adjustments may be required. All patients need at least two socks, one to wash and the other to wear.

### Loss of Reduction in a Cast or Brace

Acceptable alignment may be gained and lost during treatment of a fracture. It occasionally occurs with failure of internal fixation but is more common with a cast or brace. Loss of alignment is a significant risk after removal of an external fixator because stability is hard to assess and less control is provided by a cast.

During nonoperative treatment of a tibial fracture, periodic radiographs are required to identify loss of satisfactory alignment. Reduction goals are usually set more strictly than guidelines for acceptable deformity after healing. Stricter reduction goals are reasonable because osteotomy of a healed fracture usually has a higher risk-benefit ratio than does correction of deformity in an ununited one. Most references give guidelines of 5° to 10° maximal varus-valgus angulation, 10° to 20° sagittal-plane angulation, up to 1.5 or even 2 cm shortening, and up to 15° internal or 20° external rotation.[455, 456, 572, 604] Appearance of the limb and unwillingness to accept any visible deformity have become issues for some patients. It is important to acknowledge that some, usually slight, deformity is an expected outcome of closed treatment of tibial shaft fractures and, if within the parameters just described, seems to be of little consequence to long-term outcome.

Any question about adequacy of alignment should lead to a comprehensive assessment of limb alignment, according to the principles set forth by Paley and others (see Chapter 62). If the leg's mechanical axis is abnormal on a long radiograph with the patellar shadow in the midline or with the knee in a true lateral projection, the angles of the

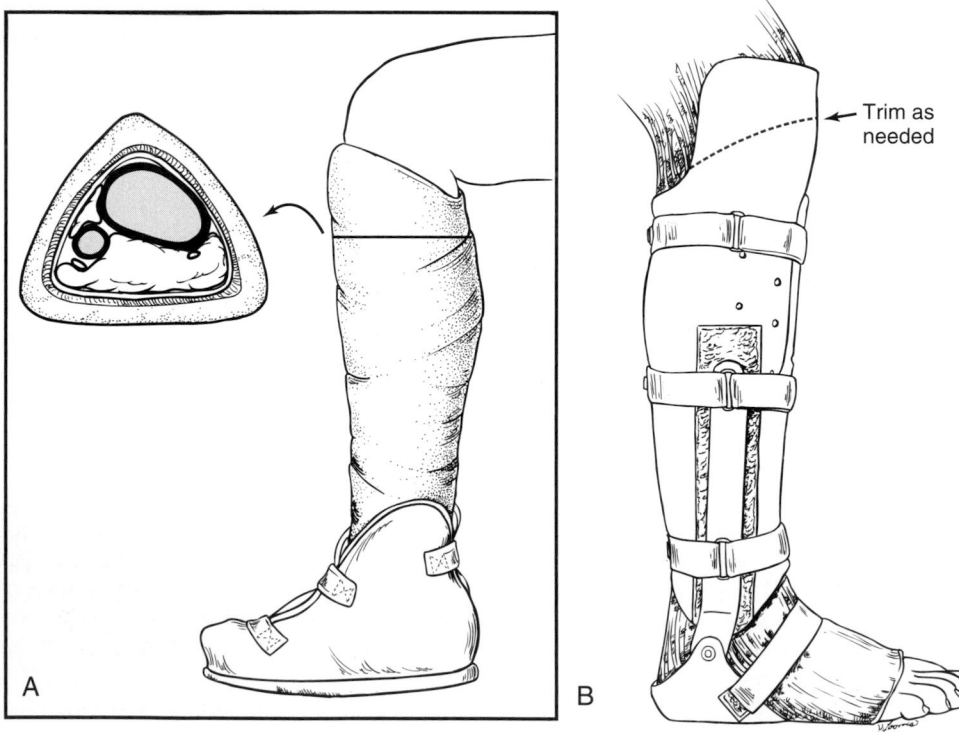

**Figure 57–17.** *A,* A patellar tendon–bearing (PTB) functional cast is applied after the soft tissue swelling has resolved and the fracture has become somewhat "sticky" and less tender. If a neutral ankle position was achieved with the initial cast, it should be easy to maintain in the PTB cast. Such a walking cast is pointless unless the foot is plantigrade, for the patient will not otherwise be able to bear weight. The top of the cast is trimmed anteriorly at the level of the distal portion of the patella, a little lower than originally described by Sarmiento and low enough posteriorly to permit 90° knee flexion. The upper part of the PTB cast is molded into a triangular cross section so that it flares upward and outward over the anterior surfaces of the tibial plateau (*inset*). This alteration produces a bulge over the proximal end of the fibula and peroneal nerve while providing a molded fit for the anterior surfaces of the proximal part of the tibia, thus supporting it and gaining rotational control. The PTB cast is used chiefly for distal fractures in which a brace with ankle motion might not provide adequate control and for patients in whom commercially available prefabricated braces do not fit. *B,* A prefabricated fracture brace is usually applied to tibia fractures instead of a PTB cast. It may not fit well or provide adequate support for a distal fracture, and it typically requires proximal trimming or padding for comfort and fracture support. The brace is applied over a thick Spandex stocking. A sneaker or walking shoe goes on over the heel cup and helps maintain alignment of the brace on the leg.

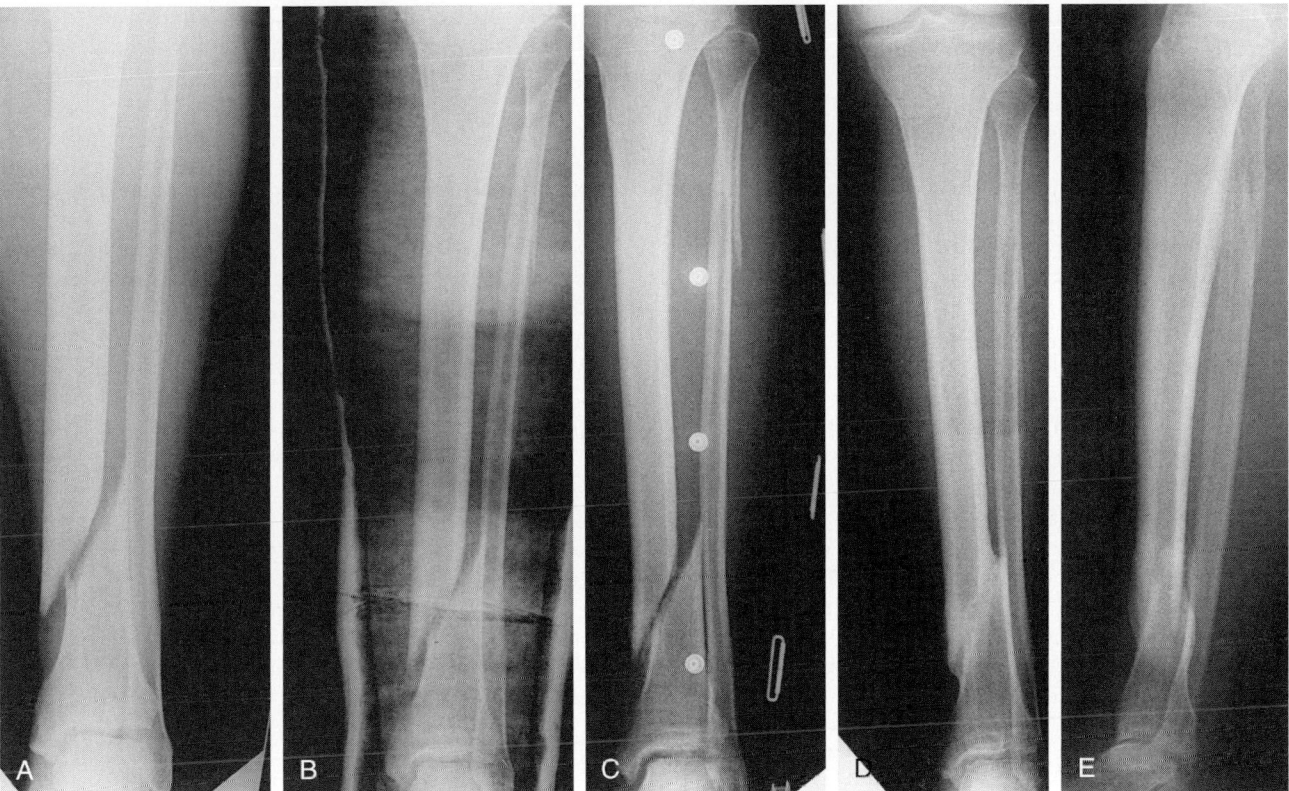

FIGURE 57–18. Successful functional brace treatment of a minor-severity, distal tibiofibular shaft fracture. *A,* Initial injury caused by a slip and fall. *B,* Appearance after gravity reduction and a medially based opening wedge. *C,* Twelve weeks after injury. The patient was fully weight bearing in a fracture brace since its application at 6 weeks. *D, E,* Healed fracture, 1 cm short 9 months after injury. The patient was fully functional and without complaint.

joint surfaces with the femoral and tibial axes must be assessed for deviation from normal. If any such deviation is noted, one must determine the true plane of deformity, as well as the degree of any displacement at the site of deformity, which is not typically in the same plane. Rotation must be separately assessed because it is not well shown by radiographs unless the specific limb position is known. A CT scan or C-arm fluoroscopy with the use of angle readings from the C-arm can be used to document rotational alignment, which can generally be satisfactorily assessed during a careful physical examination.

If alignment of a tibial fracture becomes unacceptable during closed treatment, correction may be possible by manipulation and revision of the cast or brace. Such correction may require return to a long leg cast, perhaps with temporary restriction of weight bearing. If adequate correction cannot be obtained and maintained, an alternative treatment should be selected and carried out before the fracture heals in unsatisfactory alignment. Depending on the deformity, its mobility, and the fracture configuration, a carefully planned open reduction may be required. If so, bone grafting should be considered. Closed reduction plus fixation with an IM nail is a better option, if possible. Rarely, an external fixator may be used to realign a healing fracture.[201, 495]

### Results of Fracture Brace Treatment

The results of functional cast and brace treatment of tibial fractures are generally very good with appropriate patient selection and management. Sarmiento reported a 1.1% incidence of nonunion, shortening under 13 mm in 95% of fractures, essentially unchanged from that present at the beginning of treatment, and angulation of less than 7° in all but 10% of patients. Spiral, oblique, and transverse fractures healed at an average of 17.5 weeks. Comminuted and segmental fractures required 19.4 and 21.4 weeks, respectively. Fractures with minimal initial displacement averaged 17 weeks to heal; those with 100% displacement (28 fractures) required 21 weeks. The conclusions from this study must be regarded with some caution because its actual follow-up rate is just under 40%. Complications are rare. Functional recovery will be adequate, within a year or so, in approximately 80% of patients, although many will have at least some residual symptoms.[26, 136, 253, 422, 441] Pun and associates reported that 2 years after injury, 25% of patients treated in PTB braces still had limited ankle motion and 30% had stiff subtalar joints.[453] Slow improvement in very common ankle and hindfoot stiffness was typical for most patients. Examples of closed functional treatment of tibial fractures are shown in Figures 57–18 and 57–19.

### INTRAMEDULLARY NAILING

IM nailing has become the favored fixation technique for tibial diaphyseal fractures (Fig. 57–20). However, it requires operative fluoroscopy, sophisticated implants and instruments, and an experienced surgeon. A variety of modern tibial IM nails are available. Nails are often categorized as reamed and nonreamed, depending on whether enlargement of the medullary canal with power reamers is an intended part of the nail insertion procedure. The designation reamed or unreamed is, of course, not a property of the nail but of the surgical technique used. Nails for which reaming is generally required have outside diameters of 11 mm or more, whereas those intended for insertion without nailing may be as small as 8 mm in outside diameter. Most are now cannulated, so they can be inserted over a guide wire. Some smaller nails are solid. Current tibial IM nails have holes in various configurations for locking screws at both the proximal and distal ends. Depending on the tibia's intramedullary diameter, reaming may or may not be required for any given nail. Many surgeons, as will be discussed later, prefer nonreamed nails for more severe open fractures. They believe that this nailing technique will reduce the risk of infection and the difficulty of treating it. Surgical judgment, without strong clinical evidence, is the basis for deciding whether to use locking screws at both ends (static locking) or one end (dynamic locking) of IM nails. Fatigue failure of smaller diameter locking screws, as typically used for nonreamed

nails, is common but rarely leads to significant problems unless a fracture is very unstable. Most statically locked tibial fractures heal with the locking screws in place, but when they do not, removal of screws from the more stable end of the nail (longer tibial segment, usually) may promote union. Should the screws be removed too soon in mechanically unstable fractures, loss of alignment is possible.

IM nails control diaphyseal fractures with an interference fit against the internal surface of the medullary canal and with an interference fit and locking bolts in the proximal and distal ends of the tibia. Fracture location and working length and the typically short isthmic portion of the tibial medullary canal limit the tightness of IM nail fit in the tibial diaphysis. A nail is generally effective at controlling bending and lateral displacement; its longitudinal shape and diameter affect stability and fracture alignment. Most of the tibial medullary canal is relatively straight, so a straight IM nail usually restores axis alignment for fractures in the mid and distal diaphysis. Because of variable precision in creation of the entry site and less stable fixation in the larger diameter proximal metadiaphyseal region, IM nails are less successful in

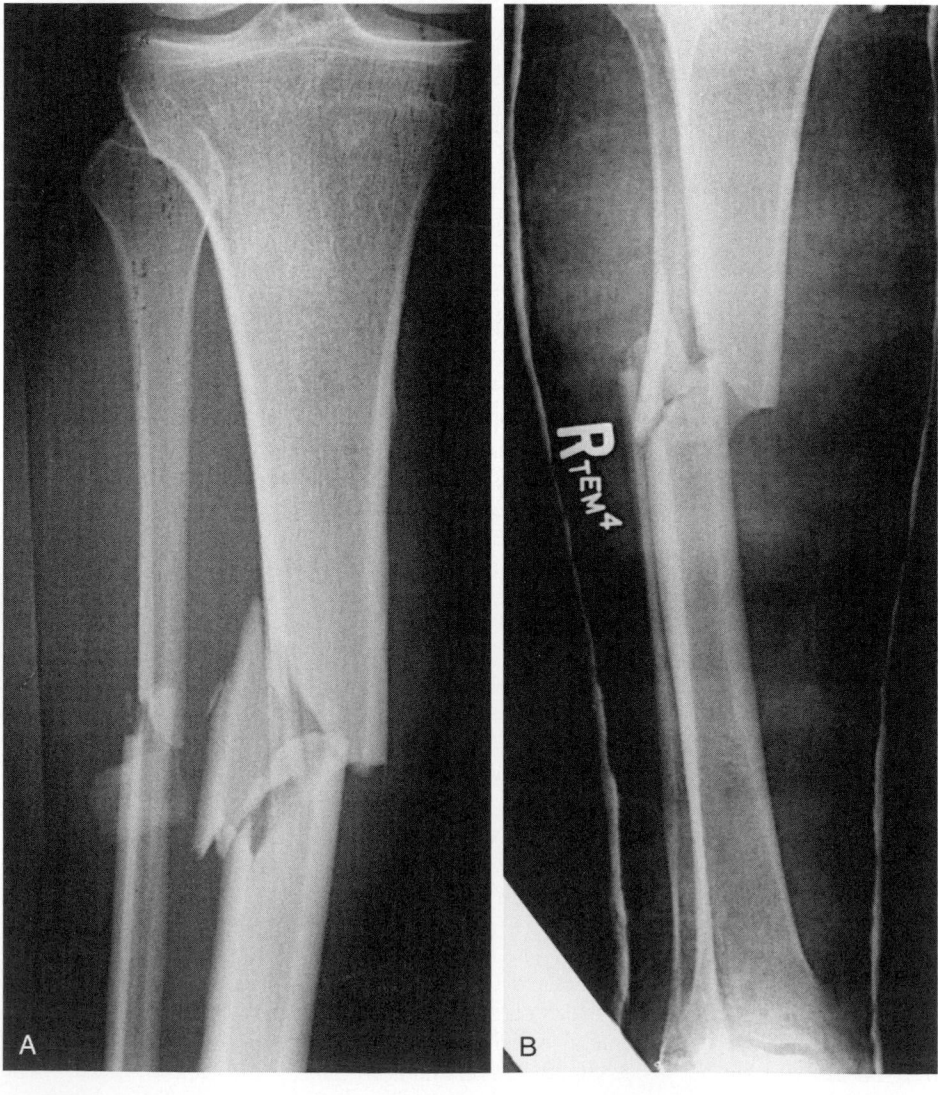

**FIGURE 57–19.** *A, B,* Unsatisfactory reduction 3 weeks after injury in a well-molded, long leg cast. This 79-year-old patient was unable to walk in the cast but readily became ambulatory and healed uneventfully after closed intramedullary nailing.

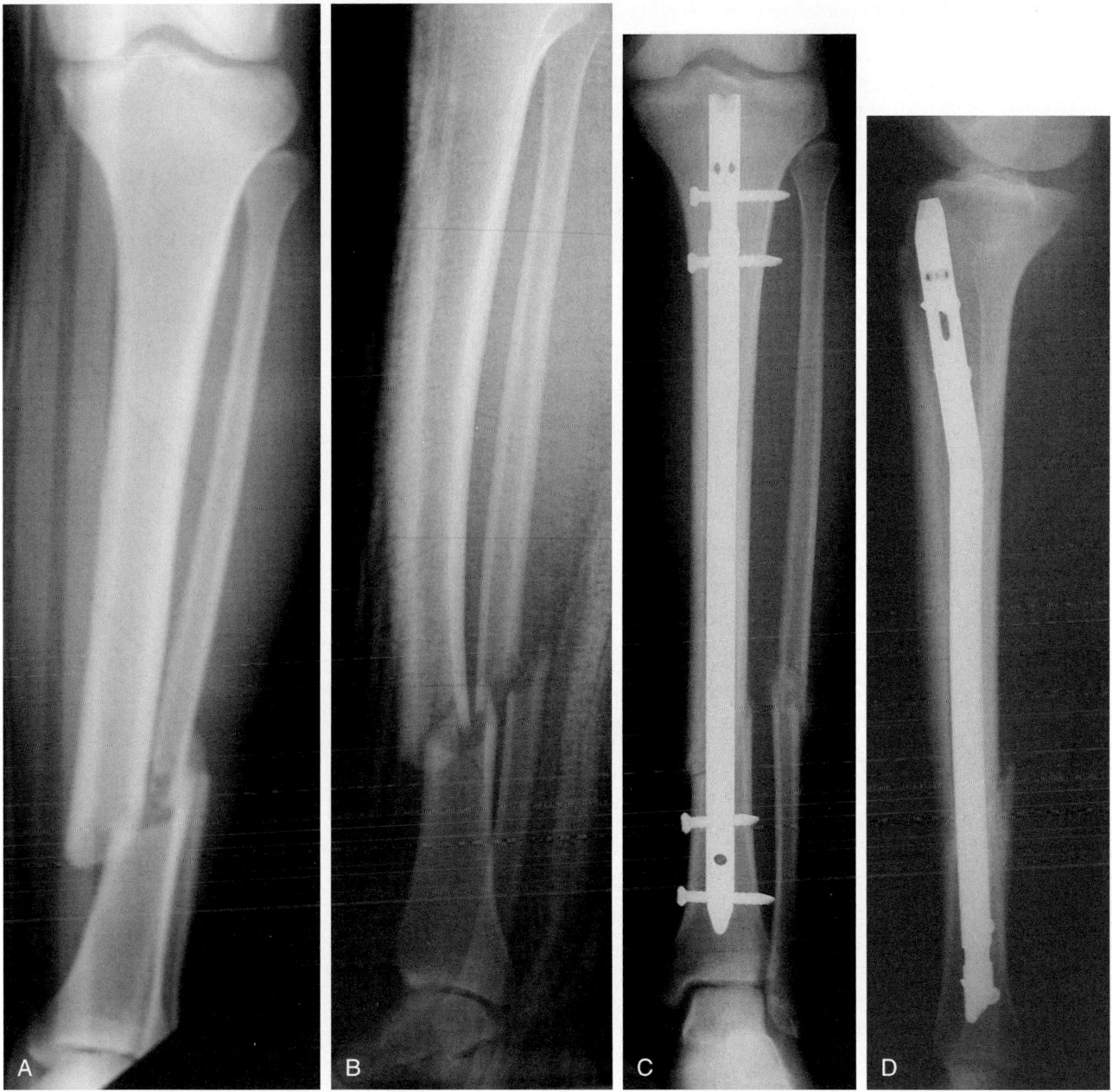

**FIGURE 57–20.** Intramedullary nail treatment of a tibia-fibula shaft fracture of moderate severity. *A, B,* Injury radiographs. *C, D,* After closed reduction and reamed, statically locked intramedullary nailing.

controlling proximal third tibial fractures.[179, 326, 596] More rigid tubular or solid nails, especially if inserted with a tight fit into a reamed canal, allow less motion, but all IM nails act as splints and limit motion rather than provide rigid fixation. Thus, fracture healing occurs mostly through the proliferation of peripheral callus, which may be delayed if the surrounding soft tissues or tibial blood supply is badly injured. With axial loading, the fracture ends telescope together until weight is borne by the bone, unless both the proximal and distal ends of the nail are locked to the tibia. If the tibia has significant comminution or obliquity with a canal diameter greater than the nail's, excessive shortening, bending, or rotation may occur with an unlocked nail. The use of both proximal and distal

locking screws in a statically locked pattern requires that the nail and screws endure whatever forces are not borne by the healing tibia.

The several components of a statically locked nail are thus at risk for fatigue failure, which is most likely at the distal interlocking screw holes or in the screws themselves.[241, 488, 620] Clinically, distal tibial fractures close to the nail's distal locking screws are most at risk of causing nail failure.[219] Implant material and design, especially the outside diameter, determine the strength and endurance of IM nails and locking screws. Tibial nails in general and nonreamed tibial nails in particular have a small margin of safety, which may be improved by limiting the use of nonreamed tibial nails and protecting them from excessive loading and extremes of bending by using crutches and functional braces until fracture consolidation has progressed enough that fracture callus protects the nail.[405] Once fracture healing is sufficiently advanced, removal of the locking screws may avoid screw failure. Leaving screws in the shorter tibial fragment may contribute to fracture stability. Another way to deal with problems of fatigue and weakness of a small tibial nail is to exchange it for one of larger size if the fracture has not healed after several months has elapsed. Exchanging the nail is not usually technically difficult. However, the necessary reaming may risk infection if bacterial contamination remains from the original injury, so it is wise to obtain a routine culture of the reamed material and continue antibiotic coverage until the culture is reported negative. A positive culture is an indication for several weeks of antibiotic treatment.

Optimally, an IM nail is inserted along the anatomic or mechanical axis of a long bone. In the tibia, these axes are identical but run through both the knee and ankle joints. Therefore, it is necessary to insert a slightly bent nail (the so-called Herzog curve) from a compromise site outside the tibial axis. This anterior proximal tibial entry site may vary with differences in proximal tibial anatomy, but it is usually on the anterior edge of the tibial plateau, approximately aligned with the lateral tibial spine (discussed later).

IM nailing, with or without reaming, affects endosteal blood circulation. Immediate loss of medullary arterial flow takes place, along with a variable thickness of bone necrosis around the nail. To compensate, the periosteal blood supply assumes a larger role in perfusing the cortex. If immobilization is sufficient and adequate space is left between the nail and the internal surface of the cortex, the medullary arterial system regenerates within a few weeks.[81, 466] Cortical necrosis is significantly less when a smaller diameter IM nail is inserted without reaming than when a larger diameter nail is inserted after reaming the medullary canal,[466] which is the main reason that nonreamed IM nails have been advocated for open tibial fractures.[18, 151, 213, 318, 347, 381, 499, 511] Clinical experience, however, has not shown any better outcome for nonreamed IM tibial nails.[17, 125, 176, 293, 599]

The systemic effects of IM nailing, perhaps more of a concern regarding femoral fractures, have also been raised as a reason for using nonreamed IM tibial nails. However, although it is clear that medullary fat and debris enter the circulation during IM nailing, there is little evidence that they have any significant consequences. Systemic hemodynamic effects—increased central venous and pulmonary artery pressure and relative hypoxia—are related more to the tibial fracture than to IM nail insertion.[239]

### Indications

IM nailing has increasingly become the usual treatment of displaced tibial shaft fractures in institutions with the necessary equipment and experienced staff. Except for fractures that are too proximal or distal and those in patients with tibial anatomy that precludes IM nailing, it has proved its effectiveness for these injuries, both open and closed. IM nails without locking screws became well recognized in the 1980s as especially suitable for closed, displaced, transverse mid-diaphyseal tibial fractures with

little comminution.[61] When interlocking is used routinely, nailing provides excellent stability for most tibial shaft fractures,[124, 280, 631, 635] with a low risk of infection and other treatment complications. It is necessary that a satisfactory reduction be achieved and that secure fixation be obtained in the proximal and distal fragments because the technique does not automatically provide good results (Fig. 55–21).

Nailing is advantageous for any patient with an anatomically suitable acute tibial shaft fracture that has a significant risk of delayed union or malalignment. It may simplify rehabilitation and is of special benefit to patients with floating knees, contralateral injuries that will delay

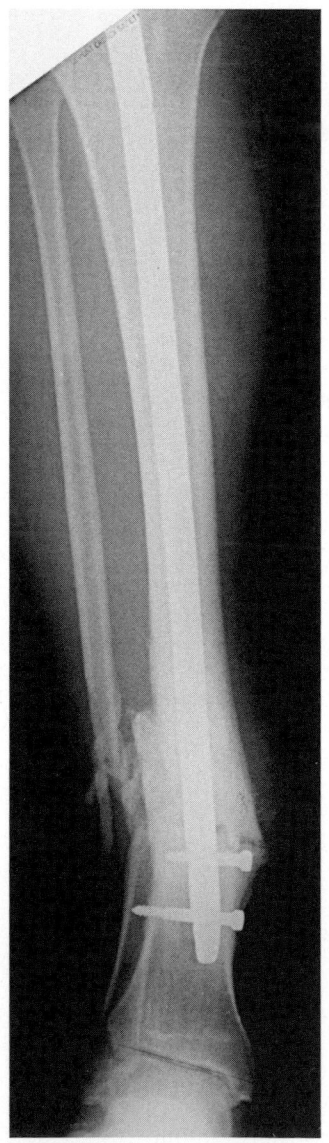

**FIGURE 57–21.** Proper technique is important for intramedullary nailing. The nail must be long enough and adequately fixed at both ends. This 6-ft 6-inch, 270-lb patient was initially treated with a nail too short, even with distal locking screws, to control his comminuted distal fracture. Posterolateral bone grafting during progressive angulation did not help either. Better external support and avoidance of unprotected weight bearing might have maintained his initially satisfactory reduction, but proper initial fixation or early revision as soon as instability is recognized is recommended (see Fig. 57–67 for reconstruction).

weight bearing on the opposite side, or upper extremity injuries that interfere with crutch use. Segmental tibial fractures, which have a very high risk of nonunion, are especially amenable to nailing, but technical details are important.[257, 633, 635] IM nailing can simplify the management of tibial fractures with intact fibulas that angulate in a cast (approximately 25% of such injuries). Because alignment is usually secure after technically satisfactory IM nailing of the tibia and because patients rarely need much supervision during rehabilitation, this technique may be beneficial for less compliant patients who might fail to keep follow-up appointments or to abide by the restricted weight bearing needed after plate fixation. IM nailing is also valuable as a reconstructive technique for appropriately selected patients with nonunion and malunion of the tibia, as discussed later.

### Reamed versus Nonreamed Nails

Tibial IM nails intended for insertion without reaming have smaller diameters and thus require smaller diameter locking screws. Both nail and screws thus have an increased risk of mechanical failure, which might lead to loss of fracture fixation and alignment. Therefore, limited weight bearing is advisable until healing of the fibula or tibia (or both) is advanced enough to protect the IM fixation. In practice, fatigue fracture of nonreamed IM tibial nails rarely occurs, and the much more common occurrence of locking screw failure rarely leads to significant problems.[488] However, the surgeon must include such possibilities when planning treatment. Not to be forgotten are the problems of removal of broken locking screws, particularly retrieval and removal of a broken solid IM nail. More difficult for the surgeon than mechanical failure of nonreamed tibial nails is the challenge of inserting them into a medullary canal that may be a poor fit because of its inner diameter, mismatched curvature, or both. Uhlin and Hammer[599] found that not even 8-mm nails could be inserted without reaming in a significant percentage of their adult Swedish patients and that the smaller diameter nails and locking screws designed for use without reaming demonstrated no benefit, but more frequent mechanical failure. In a randomized, prospective study comparing reamed with nonreamed nailing for fixation of closed Tscherne grade I injuries, Court-Brown and colleagues reported faster healing and fewer reoperations when reaming was used.[125] Court-Brown, Keating and colleagues, and others have also reported no detrimental effects from reamed IM nailing for open fractures.[124, 292, 293] It therefore seems that the potential theoretical benefits of smaller diameter IM nails for fixation of tibial fractures without reaming have not as yet been confirmed by clinical experience, even though such nails have been used successfully by a number of authors.[48] Schmelling and co-workers have shown that IM nail insertion is easier after "minimal" medullary reaming.[513] Although the relative biologic benefits of this practice have not been established, it does help the surgeon avoid jamming a nonreamed nail into a tibia that is too small to accept it.

A major advantage of a reamed nail for a closed tibial fracture is that it permits more secure interlocking than usually obtained with less durable, smaller diameter nails and locking bolts of nonreamed medullary devices.

Reamed IM nails offer comparatively better stability and strength and thus earlier unsupported weight bearing.

Nonreamed IM nails have been advocated for use in selected closed fractures with significant soft tissue injury or compartment syndrome. They are also valuable as an option, usually with at least some reaming, for patients with smaller diameter medullary canals. However, when compared with larger diameter nails designed for insertion with reaming, their smaller diameter shafts, proportionately larger locking screw holes, and smaller locking screw diameters typically result in reduced ultimate strength and shorter fatigue life. They appear to have more problems with fracture healing.[48] It has not yet been established that they offer any benefits beyond those of reamed nails, even for open fractures and closed fractures with severe soft tissue injuries. Nassif and colleagues' prospective randomized study showed no difference in compartment pressure between reamed and nonreamed nailing.[405] Reaming had no effect on soft tissue perfusion either.[340] The possibility that solid IM nails, without internal "dead space," might be beneficial in contaminated or infected tibias has been suggested, but not established. Infection rates after IM nail fixation are typically under 2%.[121] It must be acknowledged that studies comparing IM nailing with external fixation for open tibial fractures were performed with nonreamed nails. Several studies have demonstrated that nonreamed nails have fewer problems than external fixation does for the treatment of open tibial fractures, although the evidence is not quite as strong for the more severe type IIIB injuries.[8, 47, 71, 137, 240, 581]

From the information currently available, it appears that medullary reaming is a beneficial part of IM nailing for most, if not all closed tibial fractures. Furthermore, it is acceptable practice for open tibial fractures, and surgeons who choose to avoid reaming because of concern that it might pose problems with infection must take into account issues of obstruction to nail insertion and fixation failure, which are both more frequent without reaming.

### Intramedullary Nailing after External Fixation

External fixation offers a quick and less invasive means of stabilizing tibial shaft fractures that might benefit a patient with multiple injuries or severe soft tissue wounding or one who will be transferred elsewhere for definitive care. The stability provided by external fixation promotes recovery of significant soft tissue injuries that might be prone to complications when treated with a cast or splint, and external fixation allows easier, safer patient transfers within and between hospitals than might occur with traction or less stable splints and casts. Temporary external fixation has thus been proposed as an initial stage in the care of patients with open or severe closed soft tissue injuries.[51] However, insertion of any IM nail *after an external fixator has been used for more than a few days* appears to increase the risk of infection of the intramedullary canal, although this risk might be moderated by delaying several weeks or more between removal of the external fixator and insertion of the nail, by using a solid nail without the internal dead space found in tubular implants, and possibly when reaming can be avoided.[19, 471, 583] If infection of the fracture wound or at pin sites occurs during external fixation, even if treated successfully, recurrence of the infection after subsequent IM nailing must be a real concern. Therefore, it seems wise to make an early choice between external fixation and IM nailing for stabilization of an open tibial fracture while keeping in mind that current evidence favors IM fixation when an experienced surgeon is available and the configuration of the fractured bone is appropriate. When planning treatment of a tibial fracture, the surgeon should remember the problems that may result from the use of external fixator pins before IM nails and take steps to avoid these problems by choosing alternative initial stabilization options such as a temporary bridging external fixator from the distal end of the femur to the calcaneus or the AO/ASIF pinless fixator, discussed later.

Tornetta and DeMarco have pointed out that nailing after external fixation can be separated into early cases, done by protocol as planned "sequential" treatment, and into later, "reconstructive" cases.[583] Problems with infection are more likely in the reconstructive setting and should be less frequent if IM nailing is avoided when pin wounds have been infected or heavily contaminated, at least until the pin sites have been débrided and have healed.

Although problems with infection are more frequent when IM nailing is used after external fixation, in cautiously selected patients, the ability to gain durable, weight-bearing stability with an IM nail permits functionally successful salvage of an infected nonunion. Thus, it may still be appropriate to treat a previously externally fixed tibial nonunion with an IM nail if it is the most satisfactory alternative and steps are taken to minimize the risk of infection.[274, 383] When such treatment is successful and healing occurs, any recurrent infection typically responds to nail removal and medullary canal débridement with reaming.

**Timing.** Fractures that need immediate surgery for soft tissue considerations (open fractures, compartment syndromes, and perhaps significantly unstable fractures with higher grade soft tissue injury) may be fixed initially with IM nails. It is important to be aware that restoration of length decreases muscular compartment volume, which in theory may precipitate a compartment syndrome, especially if the fascial compartments remain intact (as they may with closed nailing).[361, 389, 521] The actual incidence of this complication is not clear. McQueen and colleagues found only a 1.5% incidence of compartment syndrome with continuous pressure monitoring during and after IM nailing of acute tibial fractures.[375] Tornetta and French found transient elevation of pressure during nail passage, but no compartment syndromes in 58 patients treated by nailing without traction.[584] Moehring and Voigtlander, however, studied 26 fractures in 25 patients and found compartment syndromes requiring fasciotomy in 35%.[394] Clearly, the surgeon must be aware of this risk and monitor neuromuscular function after IM nailing. Whether routine continuous compartmental pressure monitoring is of value has not been firmly established.[376, 587] Closed fractures that would benefit from reamed nailing do not usually need immediate fixation and can be provisionally stabilized with a cast. Therefore, reamed nailing can typically be delayed until the soft tissue swelling is resolving and the patient's neurovascular status is secure. Bhandari and

colleagues' retrospective study of two small groups of selected patients raises the possibility that delaying surgical treatment, even beyond 12 hours, might be associated with a higher frequency of complications, as well as an increased length of hospitalization.[45] However, this observation has not as yet been confirmed by a prospective study, and it may be hard to identify confounding variables. Too long a delay can also be a problem in fractures with significant shortening. Temporary skeletal traction on a Böhler-Braun frame with a calcaneal pin can be used after the acute swelling resolves to maintain or restore length before surgery, but a bridging external fixator provides better mobility. Progressive distraction with such a fixator, followed by nailing after length is restored, may be helpful if the callus is stiffer after a longer delay. Preliminary external fixation and distraction may avoid a difficult intraoperative reduction with the resultant risk of compartment and peripheral nerve problems.

**Preoperative Preparation.** Adequate radiographs of the injured limb are needed to ensure that the injury is suitable for IM nailing and to identify knee or ankle involvement. Occasionally, an undisplaced metaphyseal fracture can be fixed with cancellous lag screws before IM nailing. Measurement of the opposite intact tibia with a measuring tape from the apex of the tibial tubercle to the tip of the medial malleolus is a good guide to nail length, better than the use of radiographic rulers or proprietary overlay templates.[111, 314] Especially when marked comminution of the tibia and fibula has occurred such that radiographic interpretation is difficult, measuring the uninjured limb is essential. Radiographic determination of medullary canal diameter is similarly unreliable. It is better done with an IM reamer or a "sound" of known outside diameter. Acrylic templates can be helpful in assessing configuration and the location of locking screws for proximal and distal fractures.

Because it may be hard to obtain an appropriate IM nail for very short or very tall patients, preoperative measurements are especially important for such individuals to ensure that the proper range of implants is available when needed in the operating room. It is valuable to have a broad selection of IM nails so that intraoperative problems do not preclude some form of satisfactory IM fixation. All instruments required for nail insertion must be on hand and in working order. The surgeon should review and know the technical details of the selected implant system. Image intensification fluoroscopy and an appropriate operating table, as discussed later, are also essential. If an operating room table is used instead of a fracture table, it is helpful to have some form of radiolucent support for the leg so that the knee can be flexed during nail insertion and on which to rest the leg during distal interlocking. Abundant folded sterile linen may suffice.

Careful inspection of the patient's uninjured leg is helpful as a guide to correct alignment, particularly rotation (e.g., foot-thigh angle with the knee at 90°).

**Anesthesia and Positioning.** General or spinal anesthesia is appropriate. Perioperative antibiotics are routinely administered in accordance with the local protocol for either open or closed fractures. A tourniquet may aid in exposure but must never be used during reaming because the absence of blood flow increases the extent of

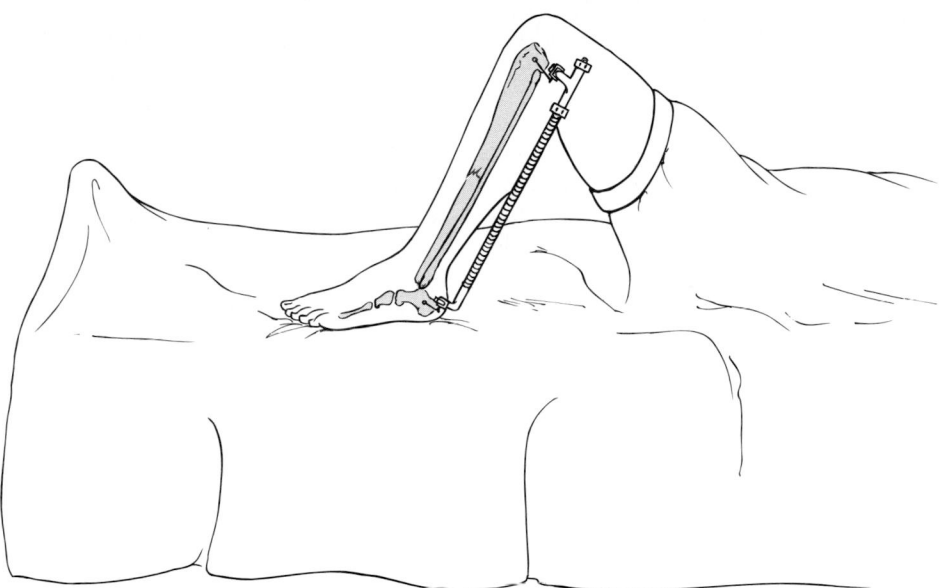

**FIGURE 57–22.** Tibial intramedullary nailing is now usually performed on a radiolucent operating room table with the leg free or supported with a distractor or external fixator. Bridging external fixation helps with provisional reduction of the fracture and permits the knee and hip to be flexed with the foot on the table during reaming and nail insertion. Some manual support of the fracture is usually needed to control angulation. The surgeon stands on the medial side of the injured leg with the C-arm placed on the lateral side. After nailing, the leg is supported on a "bump" of folded sterile linen, or its equivalent, to elevate it above the opposite side for the fluoroscopic lateral view. The distractor can be placed on either the medial or the lateral side of the limb, with care taken to avoid injury to vital structures and to position the distractor so that it does not interfere with nail insertion (including the insertion instruments). Placing the distractor's distal pin in the tibia just above the plafond may give better control of the fracture.

thermal necrosis. The patient is positioned supine on a radiolucent operating table (Fig. 57–22) or on a fracture table set up for IM nailing of the tibia (Fig. 57–23). As experience has accrued with tibial IM nailing, many surgeons have discarded the fracture table in favor of the radiolucent table.[368] On such a table, the leg can be free or supported with an external fixator or large distractor.[151, 356, 390, 391, 486]

If a fracture table is used, the proximal leg support must be well padded. It is positioned posterior to the distal femoral shaft, not in the popliteal fossa, to avoid excessive pressure on neurovascular structures. With a fracture table, rotational alignment must be assessed before draping, as well as intraoperatively. Fluoroscopic visualization and provisional reduction should also be checked before draping. Open fractures cannot be débrided adequately with the leg affixed to a fracture table, so if this option is chosen, débridement must be performed on another surface with the leg free, after which the foot is attached to the fracture table with a calcaneal pin or taped to a footplate allowing access for distal locking screws.

Typically, the knee must be flexed more than 90° to permit free access to the entry site (unless the patella is displaced enough for the nail to lie within its portion of the knee joint, as discussed later). Adequate fluoroscopic visualization in the AP and lateral planes from the tibial plateaus to the ankle must be ensured. Usually, the opposite leg is extended close to and below the injured one when a fracture table is used. If hip motion is adequate, the uninjured leg may be alternately flexed, abducted, and externally rotated to allow bilateral access. The surgeon stands on the medial side of the injured leg with the fluoroscope on the lateral side because such positioning

simplifies medial-to-lateral insertion of locking screws. Although screws inserted in a lateral-to-medial direction may be theoretically less likely to injure the posterior tibial neurovascular bundle and superficial peroneal nerve, they are not as mechanically stable.[474] When a radiolucent operating table or extension is used, the injured leg is draped free, the fluoroscope with sterile cover is on the lateral side, and the surgeon is on the medial side. Typical nail insertion portals require that the knee be flexed 90° or more. However, such flexion may interfere with reduction of proximal fractures. Tornetta and Collins describe the use of a parapatellar incision and only slight flexion to avoid the apex-anterior angulation associated with knee flexion. With the patella dislocated laterally, the nail can pass along its femoral groove.[582]

**Surgical Techniques.** If the fracture is open, irrigation and débridement are performed first, as previously described; the leg is then reprepared and redraped. The surgeon must decide whether to ream the medullary canal, while at the same time recognizing that some authors have reported acceptably low rates of infection in open tibial fractures treated with reamed IM nails.[124, 292, 293] It may be difficult to insert a nonreamed nail into an unprepared tibial medullary canal. Such insertion can require increased force and can generate greater stress in the bone. A single pass of a reamer of the same diameter as the intended nail significantly eases insertion of the nail, but the biologic consequences of this maneuver are not yet known.[513] Even more reaming to a diameter 1 to 1.5 mm greater than that of the intended IM nail may further ease its insertion.

***Entry Site Preparation.*** The incision is centered over the long axis of the tibia, usually just medial, but occasionally lateral to the patellar ligament, and extended proximally from the tibial tubercle to the midportion of the patella. Distally, the incision is carried to bone, but proximally it is taken only to the deep fascia so that skin flaps can be retracted out of the way of reamers and the nail; the knee joint is not entered. The infrapatellar fat pad is pushed proximally and posteriorly into the knee joint with an elevator to expose the anterior surface of the proximal end of the tibia, from which the periosteum is reflected over a 1-cm-diameter area after incising it with an electrocautery unit. With appropriate retraction and protective sleeves, it is possible to limit the entry incision to a 2-cm length, just below the patella. The patellar ligament is retracted laterally as needed to gain access to this site, which must lie over the long axis of the tibia, just lateral to the tibial tubercle, and on the anterior edge of the tibial plateau.[585] The cortical bone is thin here and is easily perforated with an awl. The AO/ASIF cannulated cutter or a cannulated drill can be used advantageously because both allow the entry site location to be confirmed radiographically before being created. It will be necessary to enlarge the entry site either with a short awl or with IM reamers to accommodate the chosen IM nail, some of which have a larger diameter proximally.

It is important to place the entry site correctly in the proximal end of the tibia because this site, where the AP dimension is the greatest, improves reduction of proximal fractures and is least likely to injure the articular structures of the knee (Fig. 57–24). Such injuries may be a cause of persistent knee pain, which is common after IM nailing of the tibia.[244] McConnell and co-workers demonstrated that radiographically, the optimal tibial nail entry site on the AP image is "just medial to the lateral tibial spine" and, on the lateral image, "immediately adjacent and anterior to the articular surface."[367]

After fluoroscopically confirming the correct entry site, a passage for the nail is prepared by advancing the drill or awl toward the center of the diaphyseal medullary canal (posterior to the anterior tibial crest and parallel to the anterior cortex of the proximal end of the tibia).[84] Fluoroscopy in the AP and, especially, the lateral planes confirms the appropriate entry site and safe passage down the tibial shaft.

***Reaming and Nailing.*** Some surgeons use a tourniquet to prepare the tibial entry site, but a tourniquet is rarely needed. If used, it is essential to deflate it before reaming is begun. Osseous blood flow helps dissipate the heat that may be generated during reaming, which has been shown

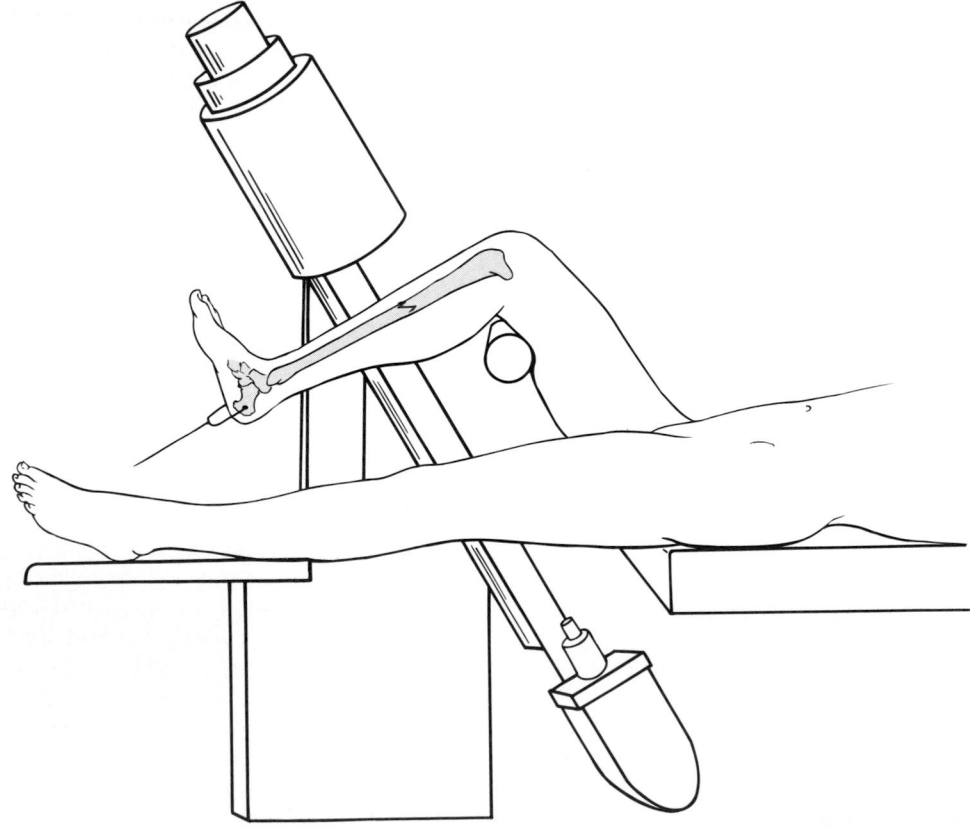

**Figure 57–23.** Position of the patient on a fracture table for closed intramedullary nailing of the tibia. It is important to be familiar with the equipment available to ensure easy, safe positioning and surgery. The patient's knee should be flexed to at least 90°. The thigh rests on a well-padded support proximal to the popliteal fossa. The foot of the injured limb may be secured in a boot, but if distal interlocking is performed, a calcaneal pin is necessary for support, with adequate access to the distal end of the tibia. A good table provides a pin holder with positive control of alignment in all planes. Rotational alignment of the fractured tibia must be assessed and corrected as needed. However, the position of the thigh may affect tibial rotation. The opposite limb must be placed so that it does not interfere with either the surgeon or the fluoroscope. A satisfactory method is to extend the opposite limb beside and below the flexed, injured leg. To place interlocking screws in the medial side of the fractured tibia, the surgeon stands on this side with the C-arm fluoroscope on the same side as the fracture. After positioning the patient and the injured leg, it is important to confirm that fluoroscopic visualization is satisfactory in both the anteroposterior and lateral planes throughout the length of the tibia. Repositioning of the legs and table may be necessary.

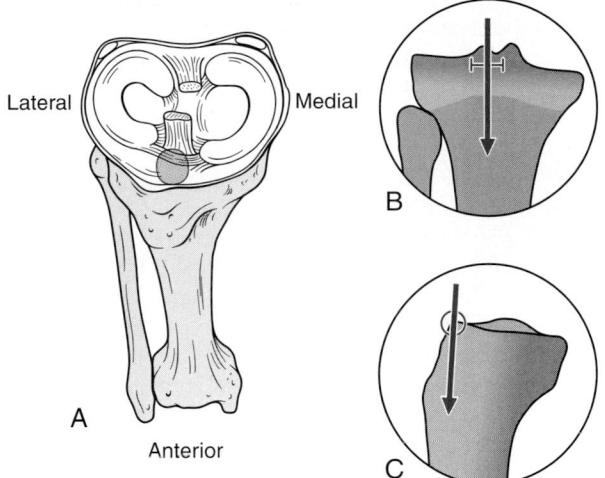

Lateral

Medial

Anterior

A  B  C

**FIGURE 57–24.** *A,* The entry portal for an intramedullary tibial nail is located at the junction of the anterior and proximal (plateau) surfaces of the proximal end of the tibia, posterior to the patellar ligament, and in close proximity to the anterior meniscal horns, which should be avoided. Usually, it can be approached by retracting the patellar ligament laterally, but occasionally, entering lateral to the ligament is easier. The entry site should be confirmed radiographically before it is created. *B,* Anteroposterior fluoroscopic view with the entry marker just medial to the lateral tibial eminence. *C,* Lateral fluoroscopic view with the entry marker at the junction of the proximal and anterior surfaces and directed parallel to the anterior tibial surface.

to cause thermal necrosis, a concern whenever reaming is difficult, particularly in young patients with tight medullary canals and thick cortices.[333, 417] For reaming, an appropriate guide wire with a beaded tip is passed across the fracture site and down into the dense bone of the distal tibial metaphysis. Its location is confirmed on AP and lateral views. Closed manipulation guided by the subcutaneous anterior tibial crest usually makes it an easy procedure in relatively fresh fractures. By subtracting the length of the exposed guide wire from that of another wire of the same length, IM length can be determined, although in comminuted fractures, nail length and ultimate location should be chosen from a radiograph of the intact tibia with an appropriately positioned metal ruler. Reaming is then performed over the guide wire with cannulated power reamers and manual alignment of the fracture as required when the reamers pass through it. Depending on the reamers used and the size and shape of the nail, it is usual to ream 0.5 to 1 mm or even 1.5 mm larger than the nail's nominal diameter. Generally, no more than 2 to 4 mm of reaming is carried out after the first reamer makes contact with the cortex. Nail diameter is thus best chosen during reaming because reaming demonstrates the dimensions of the medullary canal. It is desirable to ream enough to use a nail diameter that provides adequate strength and fit and to enlarge the canal diameter sufficiently to ease insertion of the implant. If the medullary canal has a shape different from that of the nail, additional reaming may be required. It is not necessary to ream all the way into the distal metaphysis, where the nail can usually be embedded into the dense cancellous bone and thus increase distal fixation, though at some risk of fracture distraction.

After reaming, the ball-tipped guide wire may need to

be exchanged for one over which the cannulated IM nail can be inserted. If a noncannulated nail is used, it will be inserted directly after removing the guide wire. The canal is irrigated with antibiotic solution, and the chosen nail, which should be as long as possible without distracting the fracture by impinging on dense distal metaphyseal bone or protruding above the cortex at the insertion site, is inserted with the appropriate instruments. Liberal use of biplanar fluoroscopy helps ensure that reduction is maintained and that the nail is passed across the fracture zone without producing comminution. If the nail does not advance easily with each hammer blow, it should be removed for additional reaming or a smaller diameter nail used. Once the nail has crossed the fracture site, it is advisable to release any traction and provide firm support for the foot to avoid distraction during the last stages of nail insertion. Distraction may occur because of the density of distal tibial metaphyseal bone, which resists penetration by the advancing nail. Because distraction of a tibial shaft fracture interferes with healing, it must be avoided. One way to avoid distraction is to ensure that the nail is not too long, insert it sufficiently distally, and then place the distal interlocking screws. Reversed hammer blows with an insertion-extraction adapter are then used to pull the nail backward until the fracture is impacted, a technique referred to as "back-slapping." At this point, proximal interlocking is carried out after ensuring that the nail is not excessively prominent at the knee.

***Interlocking Screws.*** Although strong clinical data have not indicated which tibial fractures need interlocking, anecdotes abound. For fresh tibial fractures, it is probably best to interlock, proximally and distally, in almost all cases.[562] Such interlocking does not interfere with healing and helps retain alignment. Two distal locking screws are more durable and probably provide better fixation than one does.[305] Two or three locking screws should be chosen for the fixation of a short proximal or distal segment because medullary interference fit is not available as it is for diaphyseal fractures.

Proximal locking screws are easily placed with the insertion guide if the guide is true to the holes in the nail, which should routinely be checked during assembly of the device. Its bolt may loosen during driving and should be tightened again before drilling for locking screws. Proximal locking helps keep the nail from backing out into the knee if it loosens or the fracture telescopes, and it also provides angular and rotational control of a shorter proximal fragment. As discussed earlier, locking first distally and then "back-slapping" the nail can help avoid distraction of the tibial fracture.

Distal locking screws are inserted in a freehand technique with an awl or drill guided by fluoroscopy after careful positioning of the C-arm fluoroscope and the leg to ensure that "perfect circle" images of the distal locking holes can be obtained and maintained during screw insertion (Fig. 57–25). The surgeon should decide preoperatively whether to insert these screws medially or laterally[474] because the direction of insertion determines where to place the C-arm. Screws inserted medially may be slightly more stable, and those inserted laterally are a little further away from neurovascular structures. Whichever direction is selected, use of screws long enough to

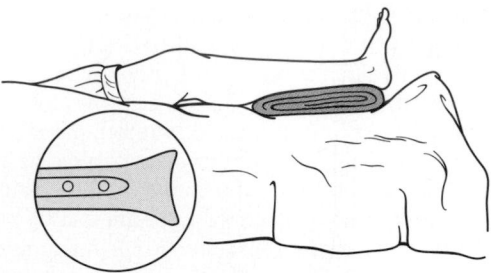

**FIGURE 57–25.** Insertion of distal locking screws is aided by stable positioning of the extended leg on enough padding so that it is above the uninjured limb. (Rotational alignment of the fracture must be maintained.) The essential first step is orienting the C-arm fluoroscope so that its central ray is perpendicular to the nail and centered over the hole for the locking screw. The distal holes must appear to be perfectly round. The skin is marked over the locking hole, and a small incision is made with blunt dissection to bone. An appropriate drill, possibly aided by a radiolucent drive attachment, is placed onto the bone so that the bit is in the center of the hole. The tip is held carefully against the bone while the drill is swung into the position of the central ray, which is confirmed fluoroscopically. It is then advanced through bone and the locking screw hole, with confirmation of the proper site before measuring screw length and inserting the locking screw. Screw position and length (typically with a few threads outside the opposite cortex) are reconfirmed before conclusion of the procedure.

ensure tip protrusion of a few millimeters will facilitate removal of both ends should a screw break.

***Use of the AO Distractor or External Fixator.*** Instead of a fracture table, the longer AO/ASIF distractor or an appropriate external fixator can be used to apply traction and stabilize the fractured tibia during IM nailing, which can then be performed with the leg free on a radiolucent table. The patient may be supine, with the hip and knee flexed during nailing and a bolster or sterile linen "bump"

used to hold the leg in this position. Alternatively, as described by Rubinstein, Duwelius, and co-workers, the patient can be rotated enough toward the injured side so that the flexed leg is supported on the radiolucent table, and distal interlocking is accomplished with the C-arm central ray perpendicular to the table top[151, 486] (Fig. 57–26). The first step after preparation and draping is insertion of the distractor. A proximal Schanz screw is placed horizontally, just below and parallel to the articular surface, parallel with the knee joint axis, and sufficiently posterior to the nail entry site that it will not interfere with reaming and nailing. Fluoroscopy aids in positioning this screw. The distal Schanz screw can be placed at the distal-most point of the tibia for better control of reduction or in the calcaneal tuberosity, where it will not need to be removed during nailing. With the fracture reduced, both screws should be approximately parallel to the coronal plane of the leg. Once the two Schanz screws are in place, the distractor is attached securely, and its length is adjusted to apply traction across the fracture site to stabilize the leg.

After the entry site is prepared, the knee and hip are flexed with the foot or whole leg resting on the table surface, depending on which position was chosen. Typically, mild apex-anterior angulation of the fracture is controlled with manual pressure during reduction, reaming, and nail insertion.

Proximal locking screws are placed through the insertion guide. Distal locking is easier if the foot is positioned neutrally on a stable pile of linen or some form of radiolucent support so that the central ray of the fluoroscope can be easily aligned concentrically with the nail's distal locking holes. The distal screws are then inserted with the surgeon's preferred technique. For example, an incision is made to expose the bone surface,

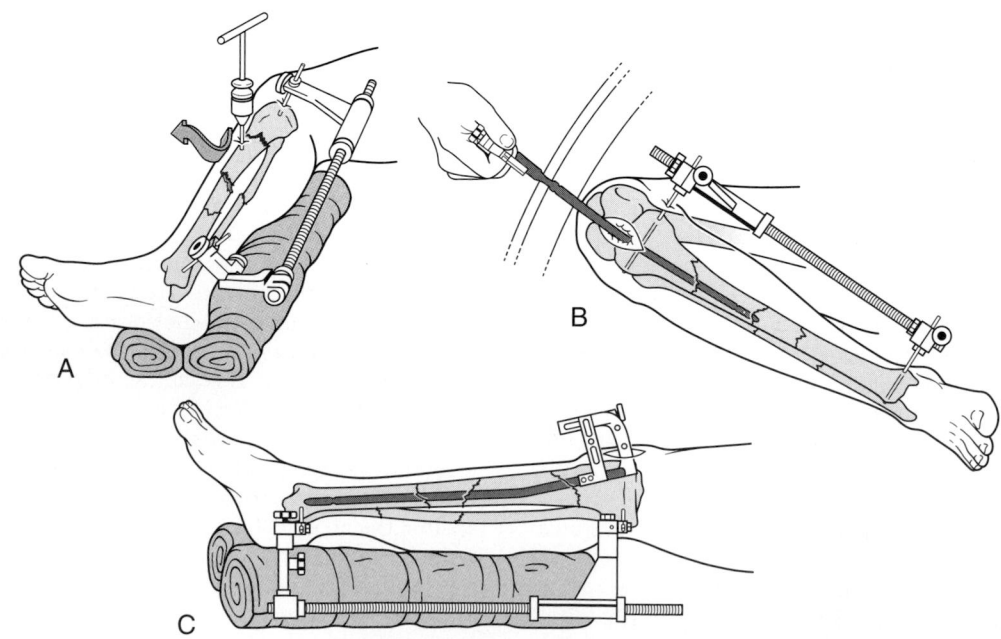

**FIGURE 57–26.** Technique of Duwelius and colleagues for nailing proximal tibial fractures. *A,* The patient is positioned so that the tibia rests on its lateral side on the radiolucent table, with the hip and knee flexed. The distractor is applied posteromedially, and a Schanz screw is used to manipulate the proximal fracture, if necessary. *B,* After the fracture is reduced, an intramedullary nail is introduced while the patient remains in this position, with the C-arm providing a lateral view. *C,* The leg is repositioned in extension to correct the apex-anterior fracture site angulation and to obtain anteroposterior and cross-table lateral fluoroscopic views. (Redrawn from Buehler, K.C., et al.: J Orthop Trauma 22:30, 1997.)

and a sharp awl is then placed with the aid of the fluoroscope in the center of the round image of the locking hole and turned so that it is coaxial with the central x-ray beam. The awl is used to make a pilot hole for drilling the bone, which is easier with a radiolucent drill adapter. The drill bit also follows the central beam. Finally, the length is measured, and the locking screw is inserted and its position confirmed with AP and lateral fluoroscopic views. Particularly with smaller diameter locking screws, which often break, it is wise to choose screws that protrude 5 mm or so beyond the far cortex to facilitate their extraction should it be required.

***Proximal Fracture Reduction and Fixation.*** Proximal tibial shaft fractures are relatively rare, 6% in a recent Edinburgh series of over 500.[596] However, they are challenging because of their severity, with an increased frequency of compartment syndrome, neurovascular injury, damage to the soft tissue envelope, and difficulty related to reduction and fixation.[64] In contrast to the generally reliable results reported with IM nails elsewhere in the diaphyseal tibia, extra-articular proximal tibial fractures are often difficult to reduce and fix with a nail. Thus, proximal tibial fractures should be given special consideration by surgeons who choose IM nail fixation. External fixation may be more appropriate. Plate fixation, perhaps supplemented with a temporary external fixator on the side opposite the plate, is another alternative, but because of the risk associated with plating in patients with severe soft tissue injuries, experience, caution, and delay of definitive fixation are often advisable. Less invasive plate fixation with small incisions and specially designed plates may prove to be an approach that offers the mechanical benefits of plating with less soft tissue and bone healing problems than associated with an open procedure. Successful IM nail fixation of a proximal fracture requires that the fracture be held reduced during nail insertion and that the nail entry site be in line with the diaphyseal medullary canal in its reduced position. Once inserted properly, an IM nail with appropriately placed locking screws and perhaps supplemented with Poller (blocking) screws as described later should stay satisfactorily reduced. Typical errors are an entry site too medial, which results in valgus malalignment, or nail insertion with apex-anterior angulation of the fracture, which occurs when the knee is flexed for easier access to the nail entry portal. Deformity may be avoided by careful entry site selection, which is usually anterior to the lateral intercondylar eminence.[579] Avoidance of deformity may be easier with an incision lateral to or through the patellar tendon rather than medial to it.[84] Nail insertion with the knee in a semiextended (15° flexed) position or the use of an appropriately placed distractor or external fixator with "pinless" clamps or pins outside the nail path (or both) can help prevent deformity.[582] Buehler and colleagues suggest an alternative to nailing in minimal flexion.[84] They use an AO distractor medially, correct any posterior displacement of the diaphyseal fragment with traction and a manipulating Schanz screw or clamp, and make an entry site with the knee in hyperflexion. The entry portal in the proximal segment is anterior to the lateral eminence on the AP view and is confirmed radiographically on the lateral view to start at the anterior edge of the articular surface and progress parallel to the

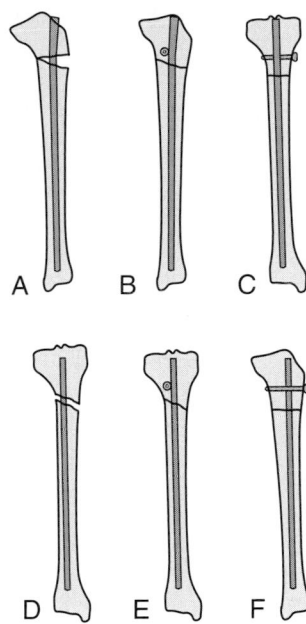

**Figure 57–27.** Poller, or blocking, screws provide improved control of bone alignment by intramedullary (IM) nails by narrowing the medullary canal and preventing displacement of a metaphyseal tibial segment in which the nail does not fit snugly. *A*, Apex-anterior angulation of a proximal tibial fracture after IM nailing. *B, C,* A transverse Poller screw posterior to the desired nail path prevents the nail's passage posteriorly, thus blocking the proximal fragment's relative anterior rotation in the sagittal plane. *D*, Valgus angulation of a proximal tibial fracture after IM nailing. *E and F,* A sagitally directed screw placed lateral to the nail blocks the nail from moving laterally, thus preventing the proximal fragment's relative medial rotation in the frontal plane.

anterior cortex of the proximal fragment. Such a portal helps avoid posterior displacement of the distal piece as a result of impingement of the nail's posteriorly convex curvature on the posterior cortex of the distal segment. This displacement, they suggest, can be avoided by selection of a proper entry path. After nail insertion with the use of proximal locking screw insertion guides, the knee is fully extended and the fracture held reduced while the locking screws are inserted. Open reduction with an anterior unicortical plate can also help in obtaining and maintaining satisfactory alignment of proximal tibial fractures, but it requires an incision through skin that may be compromised.[359]

***Poller (Blocking) Screws.*** Placing positioning screws just outside the desired path of the nail so that the nail is prevented from displacing into an area of comminution or weak metaphyseal bone effectively narrows the metaphyseal tibial medullary canal and can thus help maintain reduction of proximal and distal fractures[317, 319, 469] (Fig. 57–27). Screws provided for interlocking are ideal for use as Poller screws. The value of such screws can often be suspected during preoperative analysis of the fracture pattern, but their need may become evident from difficulty maintaining adequate reduction during nailing. Such screws can be inserted before the nail is passed, or if manipulative over-reduction can be achieved, the screws can be placed so that when the overcorrective forces are discontinued, the blocking screws maintain satisfactory reduction (Fig. 57–28).

***Distal Fracture Reduction and Fixation.*** Careful preoperative planning is required, and the fracture anatomy should be well understood. A CT scan helps identify and define articular involvement. Cross-sectional images facilitate reduction and lag screw insertion, which should be performed before IM nailing. A template or transparent outline drawing of the planned IM nail should be carefully compared with adequate radiographs of both tibias. If the images are digital, appropriate size correction will be needed to ensure that the locking screws and distal nail will provide adequate fixation without encroaching on the preliminary fixation screws or the ankle joint. To restore normal anatomy, it will be necessary to place the IM nail in the center of the distal end of the tibia on both the AP and lateral views. The exact location can be determined with the aid of templates and radiographs of the opposite, intact tibia. Drawing in the fracture lines, which can be done on AP and lateral radiographic tracings of the intact tibia, helps plan secure fixation. Choosing or modifying the nail to obtain proper placement of interlocking screws may be helpful.[146] It is essential to have good mechanical control of the distal tibial segment during nail insertion. A distractor in the talus or calcaneus can help. A pin in the distal end of the tibia provides the best control, but it may be in the way of the advancing nail. Any such pin used for distal control should be positioned perpendicular to the tibial axis, approximately parallel to the ankle joint plafond (mechanical lateral distal tibial angle [mLDTA] = 89°—see Chapter 62). This technique provides an additional check on reduction. When reducing a distal tibial fracture during IM nailing, it is important to remember that the position of the nail is determined by where it emerges from the diaphyseal isthmus proximally. Therefore, it is up to the surgeon to place the distal portion of the tibia so that as the nail is advanced into it, adequate reduction is achieved. Typically, one must adjust this position, including angulation on both the AP and lateral views and rotation as well. Unlike nailing a fracture in the diaphyseal part of the tibia, nail insertion does not reduce a distal fracture. However, with care, good results can be obtained with IM nailing for these fractures, which may be hard to manage without surgical fixation[594] (Fig. 57–29).

***Nailing Proximal and Distal Fractures with Articular Involvement.*** Articular fractures are rarely thought of as

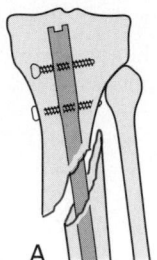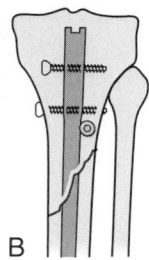

**Figure 57–28.** Use of a Poller screw to correct valgus angulation after intramedullary nailing of a proximal tibial fracture. *A,* The entry site must be properly positioned. The proximal locking screws are removed. *B,* A pointed reduction clamp is applied across the fracture. If satisfactory reduction is achieved, it can usually be maintained by placing a sagittally directed screw just lateral to the nail's desired path. Removal of the nail and reinsertion after placement of a blocking screw may be needed, particularly if over-reduction cannot be achieved with the clamp.

indications for IM nails. Experienced surgeons have learned to look carefully, before IM nailing, for occult articular involvement, which may become displaced during nail insertion.[191] However, particularly in the case of multifocal injuries with one component of a tibia fracture involving either the knee or ankle and in certain comminuted diaphyseal fractures that extend into the knee or ankle, the benefits of IM fixation are worth considering. When articular involvement is relatively limited and the nail entry and locking sites are intact, IM nailing has been shown to be feasible and effective.[307, 398] Preoperative evaluation must identify and characterize the articular fracture. The preplanned fixation is usually best performed before nailing the diaphyseal component. Typically, the fixation involves one or more lag screws and occasionally a plate (Figs. 57–30 and 57–31). Rehabilitation must consider the need for delaying weight bearing while proceeding with joint mobilization, sometimes with a hinged brace.

### Complications Related to Intramedullary Nailing

**Technical Problems.** Technical problems can usually be anticipated and, one hopes, prevented. Such problems include malreduction, fracture comminution, incarceration of a nail, impaired fixation, and neurovascular injury.[215, 309, 322, 502, 621] Familiarity with the technique and attention to detail minimize their occurrence. Deliberate, step-by-step technique ensures that the fracture is satisfactorily aligned while a nail of appropriate size is placed across it. Fluoroscopy in two planes aids in smooth passage of the nail into the medullary canal and across the fracture. Spot images should be checked often. The nail should advance with each hammer blow, but if it fails to advance or if its audible pitch rises, the nail may be about to jam. It should then be withdrawn and exchanged for a smaller one, or the canal should be reamed larger. Proper positioning and padding and avoidance of overly forceful traction with a fracture table will reduce the risk of neurovascular injury.

As mentioned earlier, nailing soon after a tibia fracture, particularly if strong traction must be used to restore length, *may* increase the risk of compartment syndrome.[361, 389, 521] However, reported rates of compartment syndrome after tibial nailing are actually quite low. Because compartment syndrome can occur after any tibial nailing procedure, the patient must be closely monitored during the early postoperative period, with pressure measurement or fasciotomy as indicated. Reduced awareness of pain, as may occur with unconsciousness, peripheral nerve injury, prolonged anesthetic use, or epidural analgesia, may interfere with recognition of a compartment syndrome.[230, 260]

Infection, a worrisome problem if it extends through the medullary canal, is rare if reamed nailing is not used for open fractures and if closed or minimally invasive reductions are used.[61, 121, 288] Some experience and good technique are important to reduce the risk of infection. Alertness should permit early detection of infection by aspiration of the intramedullary canal and culture. Low-virulence intramedullary infections may be managed by administering appropriate antibiotics, retention of a secure nail, or reaming a small amount and inserting a larger

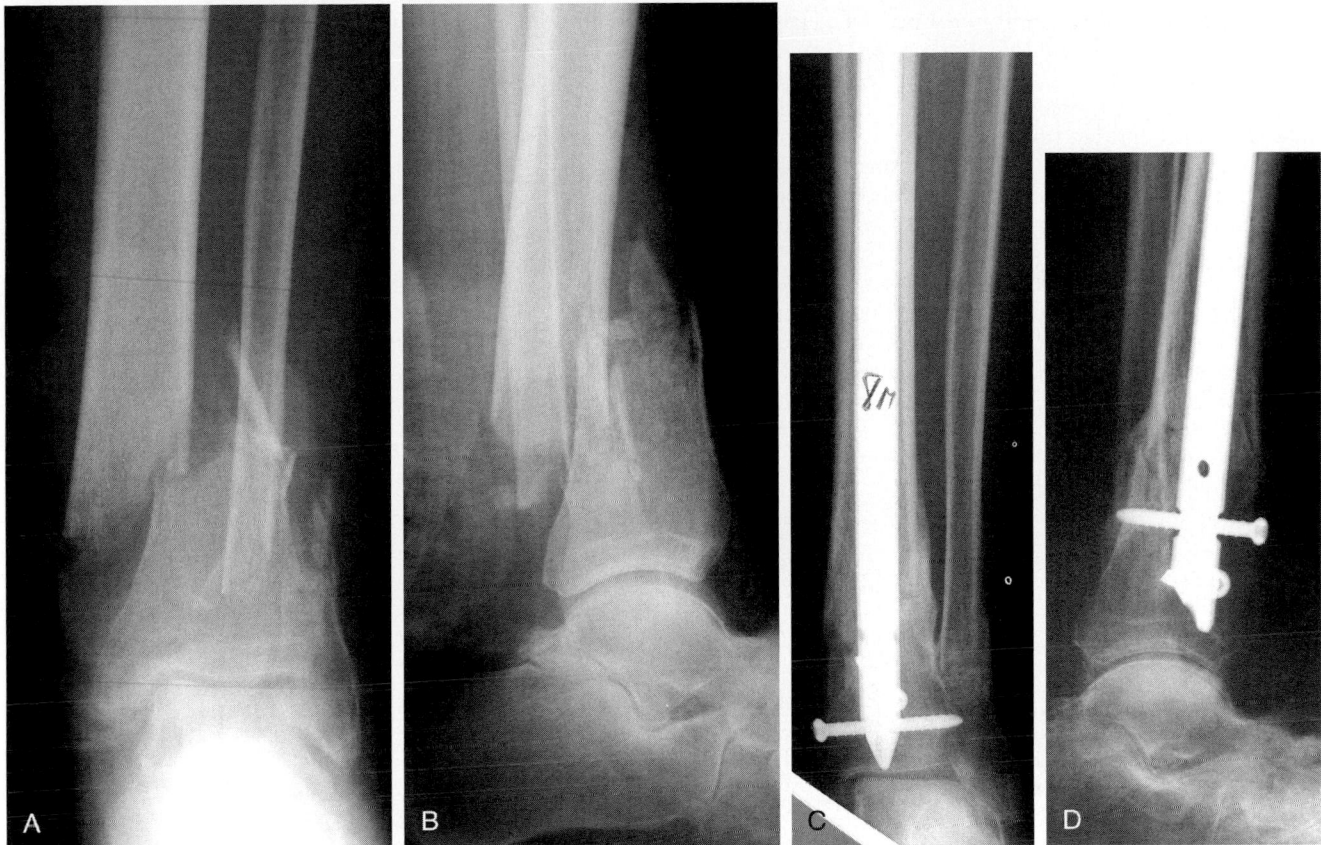

**FIGURE 57–29.** With careful planning and attention to technical details, even very distal tibial fractures can be fixed with intramedullary (IM) nails. *A, B,* Preoperative anteroposterior (AP) and lateral radiographs. *C, D,* Healed fracture after débridement of an open injury, followed by reduction and IM nailing. Sufficient length of the distal segment is required. Reduction must be precise, and the nail must be inserted centrally and as far as possible on both the AP and lateral images. A well-molded cast, fibular fracture fixation, or both may provide helpful additional support.

nail.[121, 645] Rarely, an especially aggressive and unresponsive intramedullary infection occurs and requires nail removal, external fixation, antibiotics, canal irrigation, and often, bone grafting to obtain union (see Infected Nonunion, later).

**Knee Pain.** Pain that persists at the IM nail insertion site after fracture healing is not unusual, especially if any hardware is prominent or the nail was inserted through the patellar ligament.[294] Most surgeons think that such knee pain improves after the nail is extracted. However, Keating and colleagues found that 32 months after nail removal from 49 of 61 patients with anterior knee pain after tibial IM nailing, the pain was completely relieved in 45%, partially relieved in 35%, and unimproved in 20%.[294] In addition to avoiding insertion of the nail through the patellar ligament, effort should be made to minimize the nail's prominence by choosing its length carefully, monitoring insertion with radiographs, and locking it proximally to prevent upward displacement of the nail. Heterotopic bone formation at the insertion site is exceedingly rare.[580]

### Postoperative Care

Nail insertion wounds are closed in layers if an open exposure was used. If a more percutaneous entry was made, only the skin needs closure. Open fracture or fasciotomy wounds are managed as previously described. Splinting is described in the next section. Moderate elevation and observation for neurovascular problems are necessary for the first 1 or 2 days, after which the patient is encouraged to ambulate with crutches or a walker if other problems permit. Weight bearing may be allowed with larger diameter nails and locking screws if the fracture configuration is stable with bone contact that shares axial loading. If stability is uncertain, only limited weight bearing is allowed, typically until about 6 weeks, when the soft tissue and fibula have healed enough to prevent loss of alignment or excessive hardware stress with tibial fracture loading. The role of anticoagulation and venous compression devices for patients with tibia fractures remains unclear. Geerts and co-authors reported evidence of deep venous thrombosis in 66 of 86 (77%) trauma patients with tibia fractures who did not receive prophylaxis.[187] Others have reported deep venous thrombosis rates generally ranging from 20% to 90% in trauma patients, with pulmonary embolism occurring in 2.3% to 22%.[220] Although some form of prophylaxis against thromboembolic disease would seem appropriate, the most effective regimen has not yet been defined. Anticoagulation poses a risk of bleeding with potential local and systemic consequences. Compressive devices are typically hard to use for lower leg injuries.

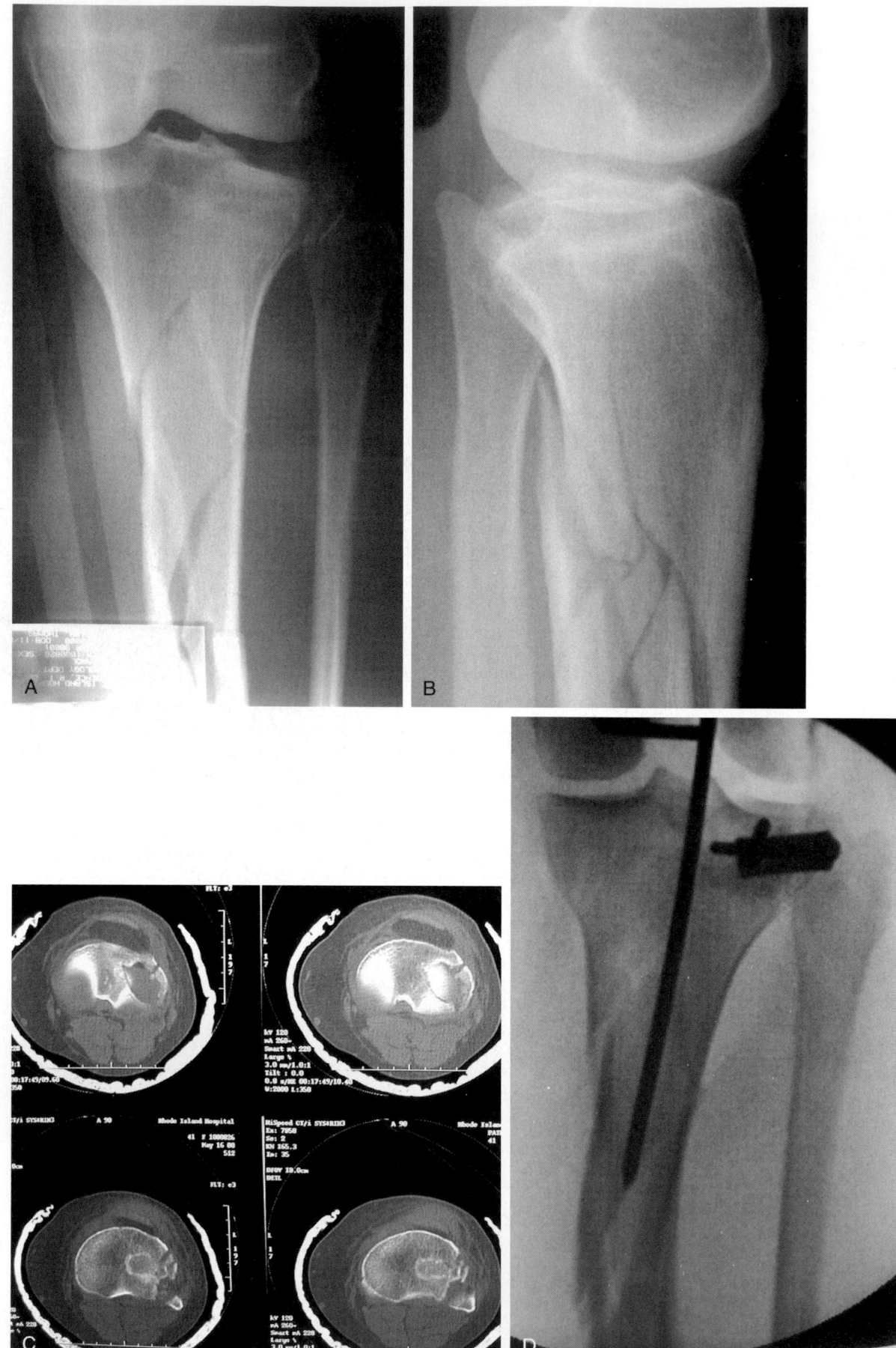

**FIGURE 57–30.** Intramedullary (IM) nail fixation of a complex proximal tibial fracture. *A–C,* Comminuted proximal tibial fracture involving the lateral plateau and shaft. *D, E,* Under distractor and fluoroscopic control, the shallow plateau fracture was elevated and fixed with a plate, "rafter" screws, and coralline hydroxyapatite. Then, as shown, an entry site was prepared for the IM nail. Computed tomography previously showed this region to be intact.

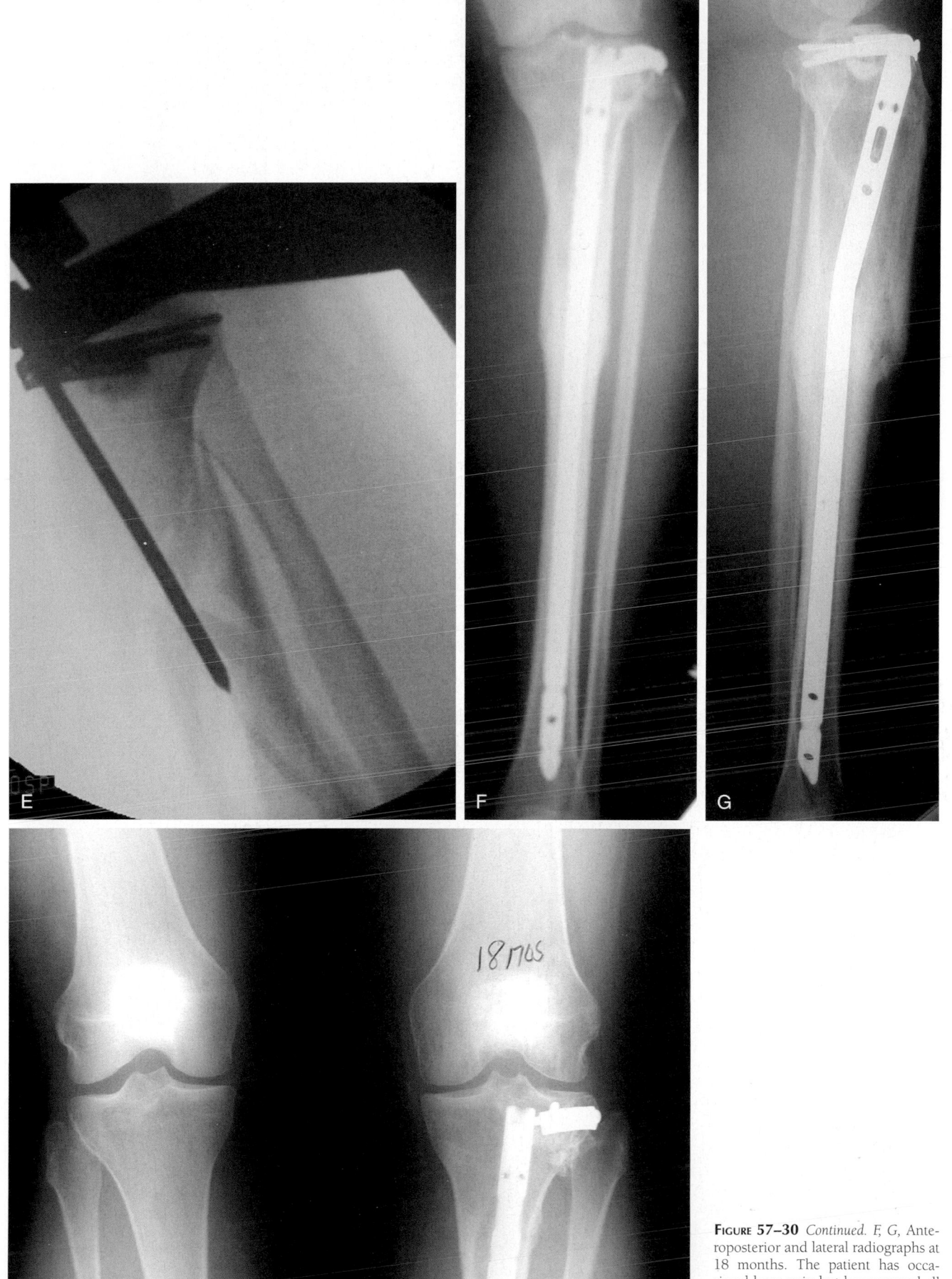

**FIGURE 57–30** *Continued. F, G,* Anteroposterior and lateral radiographs at 18 months. The patient has occasional knee pain but has resumed all activities. *H,* Standing radiograph of both knees, without deformity or arthritis.

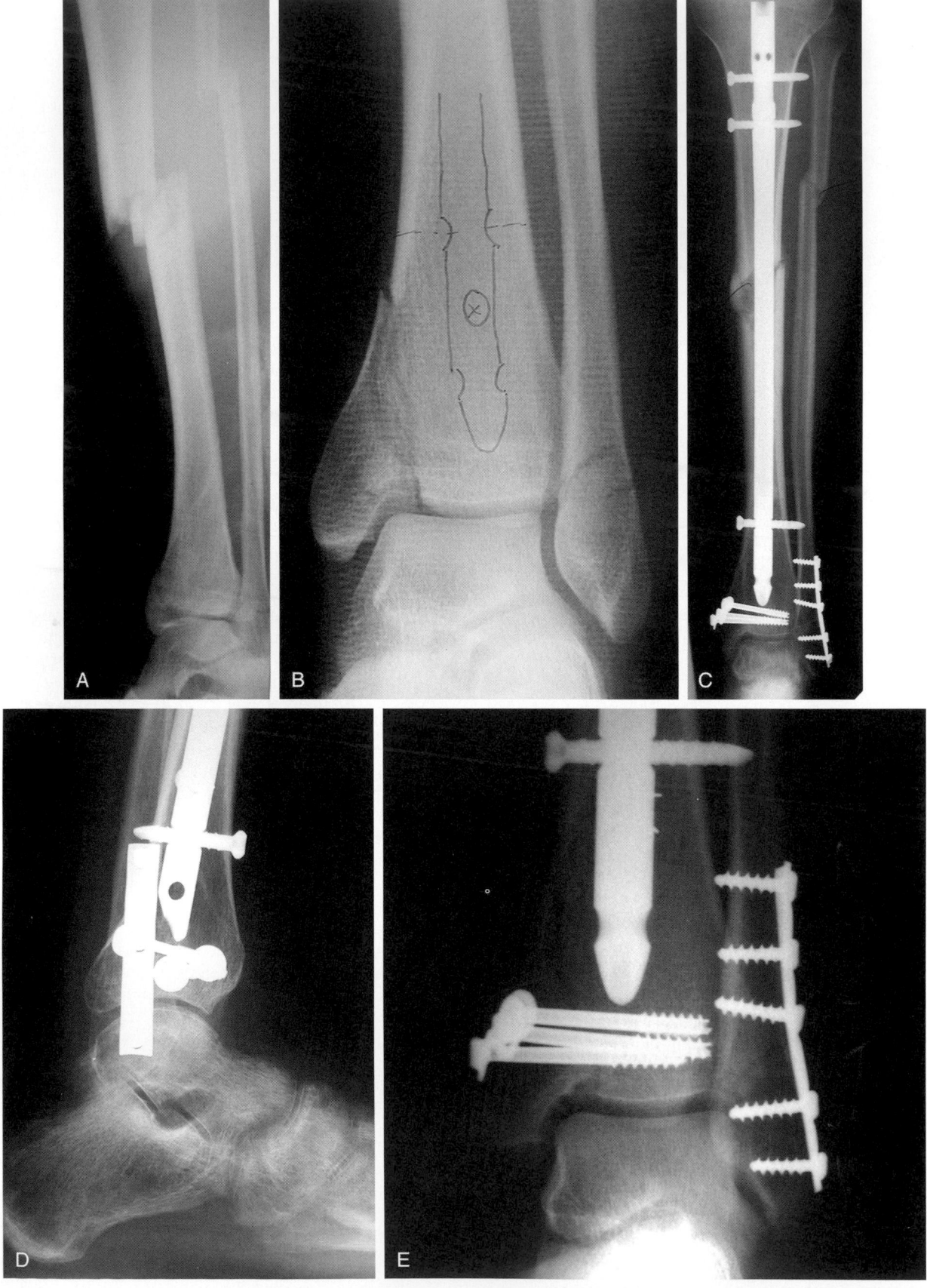

**FIGURE 57–31.** Intramedullary (IM) nail fixation of combined ankle and tibial shaft fractures. *A*, Bimalleolar fracture associated with an open tibial shaft fracture. IM nailing greatly aids in treatment of the combined injury, but preoperative planning (*B*) is essential. *C*, Progressive healing of both fractures. *D*, *E*, Weight-bearing lateral and anteroposterior radiographs a year after injury.

**Splinting.** External support for the injured limb may be advisable. Most patients are more comfortable for the first few days if a posterior splint is used to stabilize the ankle, although such stabilization is not as important with proximal fractures. Continued external support may range from only an elastic stocking, with a strong nail and good bone contact, to a prefabricated fracture brace or even a long leg bent-knee cast if comminution, weaker locking screws and nail, or impaired patient cooperation are issues.

**Weight Bearing.** IM nails vary significantly with regard to strength and stiffness, and their fatigue life is not well known. Tibial anatomy also varies from person to person and from one spot to another in a given tibia. These facts, plus the wide spectrum of tibial fracture configurations, make it essential to individualize postoperative care for patients with nailed tibial fractures.

The surgeon must determine the stability and strength of the fracture montage, which like a chain, is limited by its weakest link. Although more than a PTB fracture brace is rarely necessary, the surgeon must make this decision for each patient and ensure that proper protection is provided. Rarely is it necessary to continue external support for more than 6 weeks, by which time the fibula is usually healed enough to contribute to limb stability. From removal of any initial splint until rehabilitation is advanced, a short leg elastic stocking may be valuable for controlling edema and perhaps reducing the risk of deep vein thrombosis. The amount of weight bearing that can be allowed is similarly an important and individualized decision. When the nail acts primarily as a gliding splint and bone contact allows the tibia to bear compressive loads, full weight bearing can be allowed as soon as the patient can tolerate it. If comminution or poor contact is present, significant weight bearing must be deferred to prevent failure of fixation. With early and progressive healing, as determined by periodic radiographs, weight bearing can be increased progressively, generally after about 6 weeks. At a minimum, all patients should begin isometric and toe mobility exercises as soon as possible in the postoperative period. The patient should not sit with the leg dependent for the first few weeks. Instead, it should be elevated on a couch or footstool when the patient is not walking.

**Outpatient Care.** Once they are comfortable, ambulatory, and without evidence of complications, patients with intramedullary tibial fixation are ready for outpatient management. Instructions are provided for bracing and weight bearing as detailed previously. Follow-up visits are needed at regular intervals until the fracture is healed and the limb rehabilitated. If no problems are apparent, radiographs need not be obtained too soon or too frequently. Robertson and associates found that no radiograph in the first 10 weeks after reamed IM nailing affected patient management.[475] Thereafter, radiographs every 4 to 6 weeks should be monitored for bridging callus, which confirms the appropriateness of continued full weight bearing. Oblique views, as well as AP and lateral views, may be valuable for assessment of fracture healing. When some bridging callus is evident and after the fibula has healed, there is usually little reason to be concerned about persistent, slowly healing fracture lines. If no bridging callus at all is present at 5 or 6 months, it may be wise to change to a larger reamed nail or to add a bone graft. The timing of such a rarely needed procedure is adjusted according to the estimated durability of the patient's nail.

**Hardware Removal.** Removal of locking screws (so-called dynamization) is rarely necessary to gain union, although it may occasionally be helpful if postponed until the nonhealing fracture's stability is ensured. In spite of intraoperative efforts to prevent it, the tibial fracture site may remain distracted after IM nail fixation. If observed during nailing, continued distraction is an indication for the use of a slotted rather than a round proximal locking hole to control rotation while allowing fracture compression from weight bearing. If visible bridging callus does not appear on radiographs by 3 months, removal of the proximal or distal locking screws, generally from the longer segment, may promote fracture impaction and healing. Leaving screws in a shorter metaphyseal segment helps prevent angulation. If alignment is satisfactory but proximal displacement will make the nail prominent, leaving the proximal screws in can prevent protrusion of the nail. If screws are removed before fibular healing, loss of alignment may result. However, once length and rotation are stable, it may be wise to remove at least the distal locking screws from the nonreamed tibial nails to reduce the risk of late failure, which can occur even after fracture healing. The IM nail itself should be left in place until the fracture is well healed, with mature, remodeled callus on four-view radiographs, usually a year or more after injury. Symptoms at the insertion site are common if the nail is prominent, and they occur often enough when it is not. Usually but not always, the symptoms resolve after the nail is removed.[119, 294, 425, 493, 641] Many patients will request nail removal when so informed. At present, removal of asymptomatic nails may be considered optional,[58] but it may be very difficult to remove a slotted nail that has been in place for many years. Therefore, removal at a convenient time after healing might be a reasonable option, at least for symptomatic younger patients and those with prominent hardware. It can be done with an acceptably low rate of complications.[58]

When planning removal of an IM nail, it is important to ensure that healing is complete, which usually requires 12 to 18 months and is signified by obliteration of fracture lines and complete cortical remodeling. The surgeon must correctly identify the type of implant and obtain the necessary instruments for nail extraction. The manufacturer's instructions should be reviewed preoperatively because instrumentation might be used differently during removal than during insertion. Occasionally, IM nail removal may prove so difficult that a longitudinal osteotomy of the entire diaphysis is required to extract the nail without excessive force. The distal segment of a broken nail may pose significant challenges. If it is cannulated, an IM retrieval instrument available from the manufacturer or improvised to fit the broken nail usually succeeds.[178] Solid nail fragments can also be removed with IM techniques, although special equipment provided by the manufacturer is usually required.[195, 238, 295] Most current IM nails are threaded proximally for attaching an insertion/extraction device. If the threads are damaged, another means of grabbing the nail must be devised. Georgiadis and colleagues recommend using a high-speed metal-cutting drill bit to perforate the nail so that a hooked extractor can be used.[192] Bent nails, usually the result of another injury, can generally be removed in the usual manner, often aided by manipulation to straighten the nail.[640]

Broken locking screws are not unusual. They must be removed to extract the nail. Screw fragments can be removed more easily if they protrude enough beyond the cortex to be grabbed with locking pliers, such as those in the AO/ASIF broken screw extraction kit, which also has helpful trephines and screw sleeves. Screw fragments remaining within a nail can be hammered free with a flat-ended Steinmann pin of appropriate diameter.[497] Refracture of the tibia during nail removal is infrequent, but does occur.[276, 557] This complication is probably best treated by inserting a new nail, which typically permits unencumbered return to full weight bearing as soon as comfort permits.

### Results

When patients are appropriately selected and the procedure is technically well executed, satisfactory results are usual for the vast majority of tibial fractures treated by IM nailing.[61, 216, 265, 631] For closed, unstable (i.e., more than 50% displaced) tibial shaft fractures in all but the upper portion of the bone, it is fairly well accepted that closed reamed IM nailing is the best current management. Hooper and associates' randomized prospective study showed significant superiority of the nail over cast treatment.[252] Other comparative reports and case series support this conclusion.[63, 147, 280, 575, 631] However, as Littenberg and colleagues have pointed out, for a variety of reasons, incontrovertible supporting clinical evidence has not been forthcoming.[342] Furthermore, it must be acknowledged that the technique is not without complications.[119, 121, 215, 309, 414, 488, 620, 621] Techniques must be mastered and attention devoted to detail. Infections occur no more frequently than with other treatments.[121, 137, 240, 288] Nonunion, malunion, and fixation failure are exceptional, with an incidence generally well under 5% each. More rapid return to unsupported weight bearing and to work is typical when compared with other methods.[147, 453, 575]

The relative benefits of nonreamed tibial IM nails are not less clear.[17, 217] Bone and colleagues[63] and Singer and Kellam[540] point out that tibial shaft fractures fixed with nonreamed nails heal with the same spectrum of rates seen with other treatments—the use of this type of nail does not change their biologic behavior. The limited durability and risk of fatigue failure of nonreamed nails are well recognized. Improved nails and limited weight bearing have made this problem less of an issue. However, nonreamed nails have not been shown to offer any benefit over reamed nailing for either closed or open acute tibial fractures in several randomized, prospective trials.[52, 125, 176, 292] Mechanical problems during nail insertion occur frequently without reaming.[599] Theoretical benefits from nonreamed nail insertion have not been convincingly demonstrated clinically. The development of smaller diameter nails has, however, made it easier for the surgeon to nail tibia fractures in patients with smaller medullary canals without excessive reaming. With locking screws, these nails offer improved stability, albeit with relatively less durable implants. In a retrospective compar-

ison, Reimer and Butterfield reported that nonreamed, solid nails were associated with a reduced frequency of infection after reconstruction of previously externally fixed tibia fractures.[471] Currently, there does not appear to be any strong indication for avoiding reaming during IM fixation of tibial fractures, closed or open and of any severity. However, little seems to be gained by reaming more than enough to insert a standard-sized (diameter of 10 mm or larger) locked tibial nail. In situations in which infection is present or at risk, the surgeon may reasonably choose a solid nail and insert it with minimal reaming, with the understanding that definitive support for these options is not yet available.

## EXTERNAL FIXATION

External fixation refers to techniques and tools for stabilizing bones and joints in which an external frame is attached to bone with threaded pins or multiple tensioned wires. A variety of external fixators are available for tibial fractures. External fixators and their principles and techniques are discussed in general in Chapter 9, which should be consulted for more basic information.

Treatment of tibial fractures and their complications is greatly aided by the appropriate use of external fixation for the indications listed in Table 57–3. When immediate IM nailing or plate fixation is risky or unfeasible, external fixation is valuable for tibial fractures of moderate and major severity. It is rarely needed for minor-severity tibial fractures. External fixators may be applied rapidly, with little additional soft tissue injury, and can either be replaced by internal fixation or used for definitive management, depending on the situation. A fixator configuration chosen for provisional stabilization, optimal soft tissue access, or both may be less well suited for definitive fixation, particularly if bone transport, tibial lengthening, or other reconstructive applications are planned. Similarly, provisional fixator configurations may be inadequate for weight bearing unless bone healing and the fracture configuration allow the tibia itself to help support the frame. To accommodate these changing roles,

---

**TABLE 57–3**

Indications for Tibial External Fixation

1. Intraoperative reduction aid for fixator-assisted nailing or minimally invasive plating (substitute for bone distractor)
2. Rapid stabilization for associated vascular injury
3. Temporary support of severely injured soft tissue
4. Open fractures with exceptional medullary contamination
5. To permit a second look, through the fracture site, at a posterior soft tissue injury
6. Disaster or battlefield setting
7. Third World, without institutional capabilities for intramedullar nail or plate fixation
8. Definitive fixation for fractures not anatomically suited for intramedullary nailing (e.g., proximal or distal fracture, canal deformity, or previous osteomyelitis)
9. Reconstruction of severe injuries (e.g., compression-distraction or segmental transport)
10. Optionally as definitive fracture fixation
11. Treatment of fracture site infection, typically after previous internal or external fixation

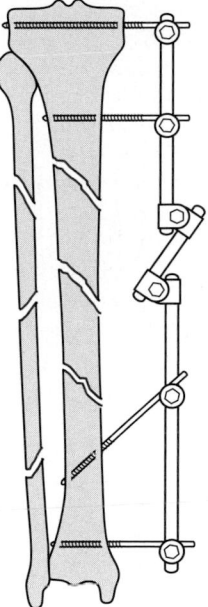

**FIGURE 57–32.** Modular application of a component-style (AO-ASIF) external fixator for emergency stabiliztion of a high-energy, comminuted tibial shaft fracture.

the surgeon may replace the initial fixator with one that is better suited for subsequent therapy.

Early publications about external fixation for tibial fractures strongly suggested that this technique was the answer for open fractures, particularly higher grade ones. Intuitively, one might think that external fixation would reduce the risk of infection in open fractures. It has indeed been shown to do so in comparison to plate fixation.[27] Its superiority to IM nailing has been shown in a short-term goat osteotomy model.[128] However, randomized prospective clinical studies have demonstrated that IM nailing is generally more effective for all grades of open tibial fractures,[240, 581] primarily because external fixation has more problems with maintenance of alignment, slower healing, and pin tract infections, without a lower rate of fracture site infections. Furthermore, soft tissue coverage and bone grafting were easier in nailed fractures. With increasing awareness of its problems, surgeons with access to other options have tended to limit external fixation to temporary support in patients with severe soft tissue or multiple injuries. Early conversion to an IM nail or somewhat later conversion to a plate (once the soft tissues have recovered sufficiently to do so safely) appears to provide the benefits of external fixation while attempting to avoid their longer term problems. Nonetheless, successful definitive treatment of tibial fractures has been demonstrated by several authors, whereas others have been less satisfied with this option.[104, 162, 289, 350, 567]

**Tibial External Fixators.** As discussed in Chapter 9, external fixators may be assembled from sets of components or may be provided as units designed for application to the diaphysis or to the proximal or distal metaphyses. Component fixators can be assembled in a modular fashion, with a pin-frame section for each major tibial segment and a linkage with adjustable connectors

that permits easy multiplane reduction of the fracture (Fig. 57–32). This feature makes them particularly adaptable for joint-spanning applications and unusual fracture configurations. Thus, multicomponent external fixator systems are a good choice for an operating room that will stock only one type of fixator. A great variety of external fixators are available for use on the tibia. Surgeons should be familiar with those available in their operating room and have pre-established plans for how they can be used to accommodate the needs of patients likely to be encountered. Because all fixators cannot be thoroughly described here, this chapter focuses on general principles and illustrates the application of only a typical emergency tibial fixator. Specialized components allow a variety of pin configurations and can include rings for tensioned wires, as well as various pin clamps.[28, 464] As an alternative to a modular configuration, external fixator components can be assembled in a so-called simple configuration, with each pin attached directly to a single frame, thus constructing a more stable, but less adjustable configuration (Fig. 57–33). Monolateral single-unit fixators offer a stable, but adjustable connection between groups of pins placed in the proximal and distal tibial segments (Fig. 57–34). Though not readily adaptable to every fracture situation, these devices can be particularly valuable when the fixator is used for definitive treatment and for stabilization during traction histogenesis, bone transport, and correction of deformity. Many are designed to permit controlled axial loading of the fracture site (EBI, Dynafix, Mefisto, Orthofix DAF, and other models). Some may have problems with axial

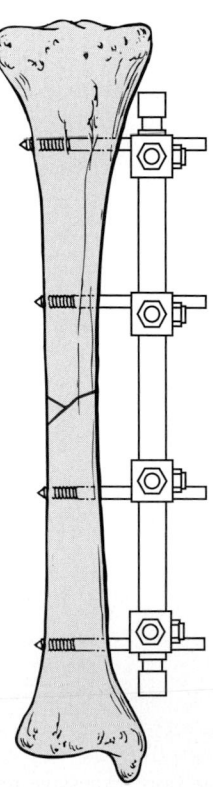

**FIGURE 57–33.** Monolateral, single-bar external fixator assembled from AO-ASIF fixator components, as described by Behrens and colleagues.

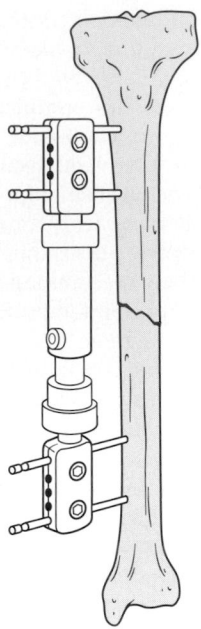

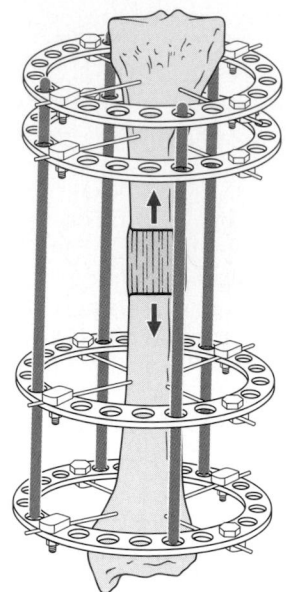

**FIGURE 57–34.** A monolateral, single-unit external fixator (Orthofix DAF) provides good stability, axial fracture loading, and potential for bone transport. However, such single-unit devices may have limited adaptability for complex fractures.

**FIGURE 57–35.** Ilizarov ring fixator with four rings and four connecting rods. A stable, adaptable, component-based fixator used for bone transport is shown. Potentially complex to apply, cumbersome, and ill-suited for soft tissue care, these devices are valuable for reconstructive applications.

sliding[357] or long-term stability, which should be monitored during use.[183]

Ilizarov's circular fixator (see Chapter 21) uses rings with tensioned wires for bone anchorage. Multiple rods link the rings into an often cumbersome, but potentially very stable structure that can be configured at the surgeon's discretion for compression, distraction, bone transport, correction of deformity, or any combination of these purposes (Fig. 57–35). Many surgeons use Ilizarov circular frames with half pins for diaphyseal anchors instead of tensioned wires, although they often prefer the latter for

metaphyseal locations. The term "hybrid fixator" has acquired two different meanings, the first related to the bone fixation technique and the second implying not only that but a simpler frame as well. Thus, "hybrid" can refer to a typical Ilizarov frame with mixed pin and wire anchorage, or it may be referring to an external fixator based on proximal or distal rings attached to a diaphyseal uniplanar simple fixator frame (Fig. 57–36). Though easier to apply than Ilizarov's circular fixator, such frames may be significantly less stable and may thus have correspondingly more frequent problems with loss of

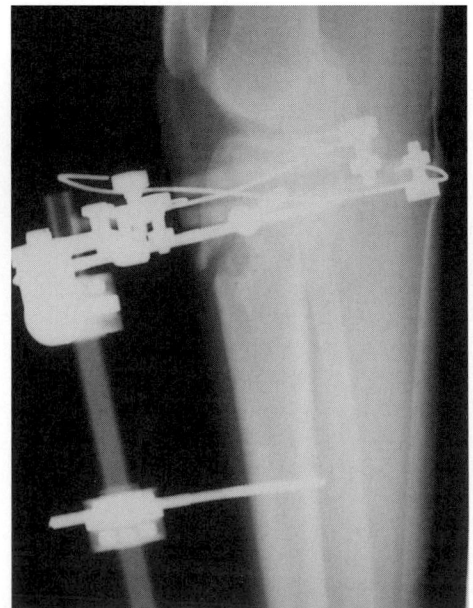

**FIGURE 57–36.** So-called hybrid fixator composed of a single ring attached to a single bar with two diaphyseal pins. Here the fixator is used for a metaphyseal fracture but demonstrates poor control of fracture alignment. Because of their poor stability, such frames are rarely well suited for definitive care.

alignment, pin loosening and infection, and impaired fracture healing.[15, 301]

A special pinless fixator with tong-like clamps instead of pins or wires that penetrate the medullary canal has been developed specifically for temporary use when delayed IM nailing is planned.[516, 555] The pinless fixator's intended use is for provisional fixation before IM nailing. It is not clear whether this device reduces the rate of infection in comparison to traditional pins, nor has it been shown that its potentially greater stability offers any significant benefit over a bridging external fixator that spans the injured tibia with fixation in the distal end of the femur and calcaneus and stabilizes the fracture through fixed traction and usually an adjunctive temporary splint.[16] When compared with the pinless device, both a bridging fixator and a unilateral modular or simple fixator are much more suited for repeated soft tissue débridement.[570] One potential benefit of the pinless fixator is its ability to maintain alignment of a tibial fracture during IM nailing.[624] It may thus be used as an intraoperative reduction aid and then be removed as soon as the IM nail plus locking and perhaps Poller screws can maintain the reduction.

**Optimal Mechanical Behavior of External Fixation.** Fixator stiffness and fracture site load and motion in various planes and at different times in the course of healing are variables under the surgeon's control that are limited by bone quality and fracture morphology. No consensus has been reached, however, on the optimal mechanical environment for fracture healing, nor how to achieve it reliably with external fixation. Kenwright and colleagues suggest the importance of early motion with a subsequently stiffer frame to protect the fracture site during healing. Their studies in humans have shown the efficacy of early controlled motion as a healing stimulus,[297] as have Foxworthy and Pringle.[177] Stiffer fixation tends to suppress callus formation and results in more "direct" bone healing, but no evidence has indicated that direct is better than indirect healing, in which more abundant peripheral callus is formed.[639] The optimal mechanical milieu for healing of an externally fixed fracture remains elusive. Too much axial motion too early in the course of external fixator treatment may impede fracture healing.[409] In addition, stiffer fixators do seem to have fewer problems with pin loosening and pin tract infection.

External fixator stability depends significantly on the type of bone fixation and placement. Periarticular fracture fixation is typically limited by the length of the metaphyseal fragment. To limit the risk of septic arthritis, the surgeon should try to keep pins or wires outside the joint cavity, which proximally, generally requires being at least 1 to 1.5 cm from the joint.[259, 462] Thus, the distance that the fracture is from these levels will determine the segment length. Occasionally, the surgeon must choose between stability and avoiding the joint. The stiffness of tensioned-wire fixation is increased by using thicker wires (1.8 vs. 1.5 mm at higher tension [>100 kilogram-force]) and by using more wires. Using a second level of fixation also adds stiffness.[442] The effect of the angle between wires is different, depending on the force applied. With a single level of fixation, the use of three wires, including more oblique second and third wires, improves sagittal-plane

stability. Calhoun and co-workers state that either one tensioned wire with two or more half pins at least 5 mm in diameter or three or more half pins of similar size in each segment should provide stability similar to that of Ilizarov's fixators.[91, 92] The use of opposed olive-tipped wires improves shear stability.[424] More anterior placement of oblique proximal tibial wires improves sagittal-plane stability.[188] An alternative means of external fixation in the proximal end of the tibia involves the use of a frame with a T configuration, the transverse proximal portion of which holds two half pins placed anteroposteriorly into subchondral bone.[28]

The most effective means of stabilizing the fracture site, however, is by creating interfragmentary compression by loading the fracture site with the fixator. Whether this technique is clinically beneficial remains in question. Such interfragmentary compression can also be provided with a lag screw, but the results of this practice are poorer than when such screws are omitted.[316]

**Uses of Tibial External Fixation.** It is wise to consider external fixation primarily as *part of a treatment plan* for selected tibial fractures rather than as a single "curative" operation. This principle is obvious when the fixator is used for preliminary stabilization before another definitive means of fixation. It is also true when the external fixator is intended as the definitive stabilizer. Series demonstrating successful use of external fixation report a high frequency of early bone grafting to obtain union of severe injuries, as well as a frequent need for procedures to correct problems with pins and alignment.[155, 162, 350] Thus, when considering external fixation for a tibial shaft fracture, the surgeon should also think about early elective bone grafting, conversion to nail or plate fixation, or early weight bearing with frame "dynamization" to permit axial loading. The most common significant complication of external fixation for tibial shaft fractures is late loss of alignment, which typically occurs when the fixator is removed before fracture healing. Because external fixation is generally used for more severe injuries, their risk of delayed or arrested healing must be anticipated in planning and follow-up of treatment.

Although the effectiveness of external fixation is well documented when used for bone transport to deal with large segmental bone loss, it is important to remember that the more frequently encountered smaller defects can usually be managed well with an IM nail and soft tissue flap as needed. It should be expected that patients thus treated may need possible exchange nailing (for incomplete wedge loss of less than 50% in diameter and less than 2.5 cm in length) or open bone grafting at 2 to 3 months for larger defects.[476] An accepted threshold for choosing bone transport instead of IM nailing and grafting has not been convincingly established, but it may be about 5 cm. It is probable that transport does have advantages[107, 351] over external fixation plus a flap with delayed bone grafting,[106] at least if infection has developed. Reconstructive options for dealing with bone defects are discussed in more detail later.

**Planning for Tibial External Fixation.** *Definitive external fixation* may be chosen for metaphyseal fractures, bone transport, and rare diaphyseal fractures not amenable to IM nailing, as well as for unstable severe tibial fractures in skeletally immature patients. For patients who require surgical access and for expediency, application of a definitive fixator may need to be deferred until after the articular fracture components are repaired, soft tissue coverage has been obtained with free or pedicled flaps, or split-thickness skin grafts have been applied. By the time that soft tissue coverage is in place, the definitive fixator should have been adjusted as required to ensure adequate reduction and stability of the fixator-bone composite, with interfragmentary fracture compression if possible. The more stable the fixator-fracture combination, the more likely it is that the device will last long enough to achieve the goal of restoring osseous integrity before it is removed. The recently developed hydroxyapatite-coated pins may be advantageous.[395] Provision for dynamization and early axial loading should be considered when appropriate (adequate bone contact is required).

Selection of a definitive external fixator must be based on the specific problem and proposed solution. Typically, several options exist. For instance, bone transport can be carried out with either a complex circular frame or a stable, specifically designed monolateral half-pin fixator. Access for bone grafting within a few weeks is desirable for many such injuries and is an important consideration when choosing a definitive external fixator and the timing of conversion from the emergency frame to the definitive one.

Occasionally, a fixator is used as temporary additional support for an internally fixed fracture, typically opposite a laterally placed proximal metaphyseal plate to resist a tendency for varus collapse.[59, 193]

**Emergency Tibial External Fixation.** It appears that the benefits of realignment and mechanical stability are advantageous for healing of soft tissue wounds and maximizing viability and infection resistance of threatened, but still viable tissue. Thus, for optimal soft tissue care, stabilization should be considered whenever one is faced with a significant tibial fracture. If IM nailing is not appropriate for the patient, the health care setting, or the injury, the surgeon will want to consider external fixation to help with soft tissue management, not just for open fractures, but for severe closed ones as well, such as those with compartment syndromes, arterial injury, or significant crushing. Such a fixator must provide adequate stability, as well as access for further débridement and wound closure. It must be safe and in particular avoid injury to nerves and blood vessels. Fixators for emergency stabilization can be simply applied, even without radiographs if necessary. In this situation, pins should be placed well proximal and distal to the zone of injury, perhaps in the distal end of the femur and calcaneus to avoid the tibia altogether. They should be placed, as advised by Behrens and Searls, through relatively thin soft tissue and away from nerves and blood vessels[40] (see Fig. 9–11). The frame might be left as an intraoperative reduction aid or removed before definitive fixation. It should allow for soft tissue swelling and care or transfer of the patient. Metallic fixator components should be placed outside the path of necessary x-rays. Equipment needed includes, in addition to sharp drill bits, drill sleeves, and a power drill, except in war or disaster situations, appropriate sterile pins and frame components of sufficient length. Especially for more severe injuries, consideration should be given to extending

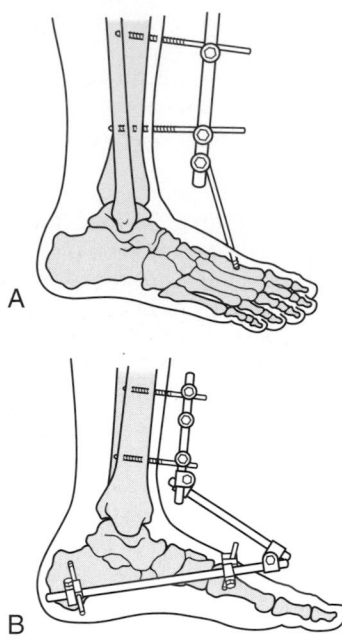

**FIGURE 57–37.** Two ways to stabilize the foot and ankle for control of distal fractures and to provide soft tissue stability for wound care. *A,* Minimal control with a single first metatarsal pin. *B,* More stability is achieved by ligamentotaxis across the ankle, with calcaneal and first metatarsal pins used for distal fixation of the module. The use of pins in both the medial and lateral metatarsals can further improve stability.

the fixator to the foot to stabilize the ankle and distal soft tissues (Fig. 57–37). Emergency frames need not be elaborate. Typically, the surgeon constructs a modular, uniplanar frame with adequate clearance to allow soft tissue care. An anteromedial location usually works well and is compatible with access to most wounds, as well as their closure with local or free flaps as needed. Such fixators should be easily adjustable and removable to accommodate anticipated further care. A suggested technique for temporary emergency external fixation follows.

*Technique for Applying an "Emergency" Tibial External Fixator.* Every surgeon who treats significant tibial fractures must be comfortable with rapid, simple external fixation for such injuries. For severe open and closed soft tissue trauma, including compartment syndromes and crush injuries, the benefits of rapidly applied, minimally invasive external fixation are well recognized. Such fixation, unless IM nailing is applicable, should be routinely considered after débridement of any open tibial fracture. The type of frame selected should be straightforward and easy to apply. It should provide adequate stability, pose minimal risk of additional injury, avoid interference with subsequent wound care, and facilitate conversion to another definitive fixation technique, be it an IM nail, plate, or a more stable external fixator. Particularly for fractures of the proximal or distal tibial metaphysis, a joint-spanning fixator might be needed initially (Fig. 57–38). For diaphyseal fractures, the fixator might be limited to the tibia, although bridging to the foot adds often-beneficial soft tissue stabilization that aids in wound management and simplifies supplementary splinting. A unilateral, modular type of frame is usually recommended (see Fig. 57–32).

PIN INSERTION. Fixation is obtained in each selected segment with a proximal and distal threaded half pin. The pins should be placed near the ends of a bone segment, but at least 1.5 cm away from joints or fractures. More pins might be desirable in the metaphysis, particularly if

osteoporosis is significant. Pins should have relatively similar orientation relative to the limb axis to permit the application of a connecting frame in a reasonable location. Pins designed as self-drilling may be used without predrilling in the metaphysis, but *in the dense bone of the*

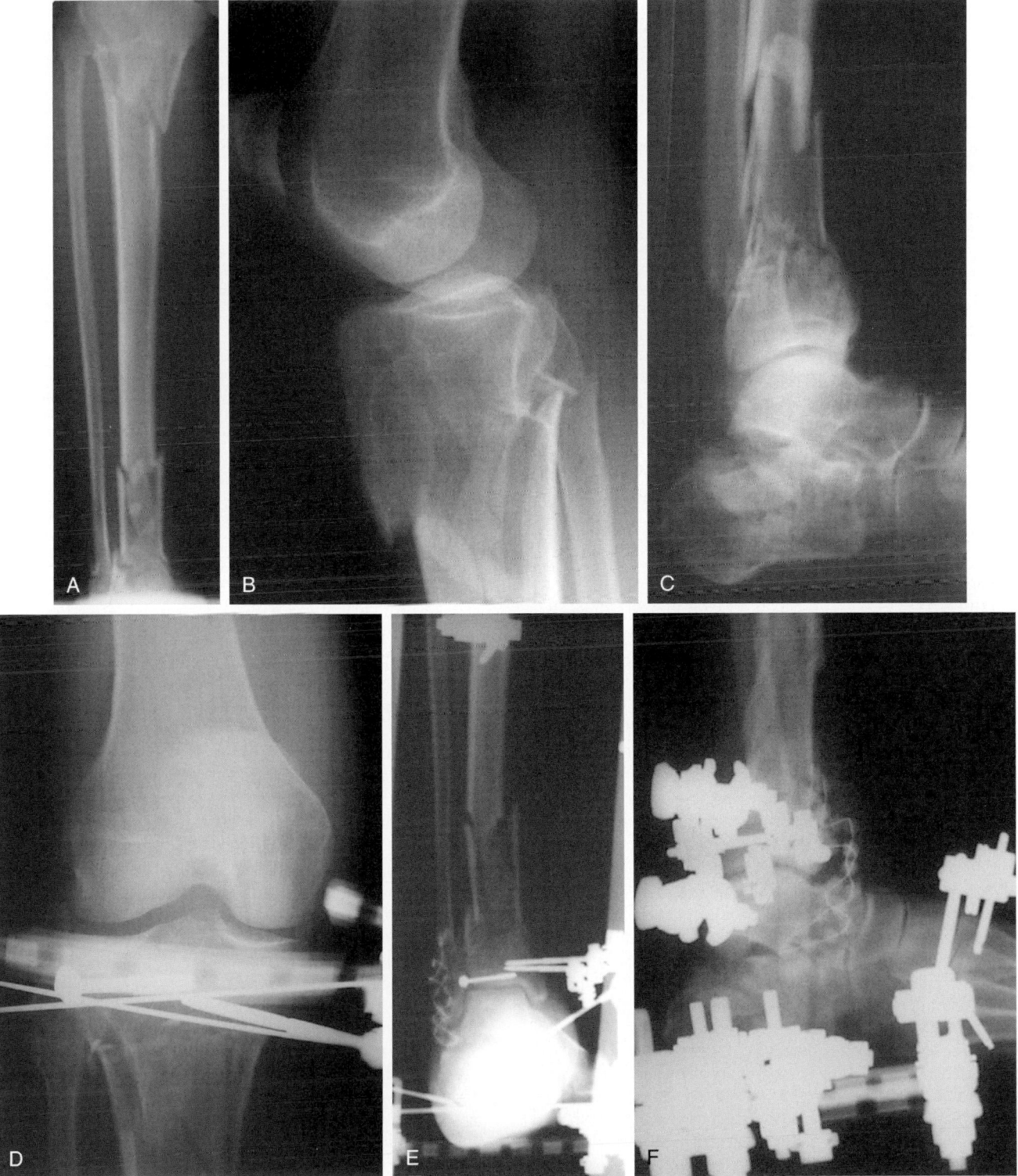

**FIGURE 57–38.** External fixation of a complex multilevel tibial fracture in a middle-aged patient struck by an automobile. *A–C,* Views of the injury showing proximal and distal articular involvement, as well as a calcaneal fracture, which was treated nonoperatively because of the patient's soft tisssue condition. *D–G,* Hybrid external fixator from the tibial plateau through the hindfoot (tensioned wires) and forefoot (metatarsal pins).

*Illustration continued on following page*

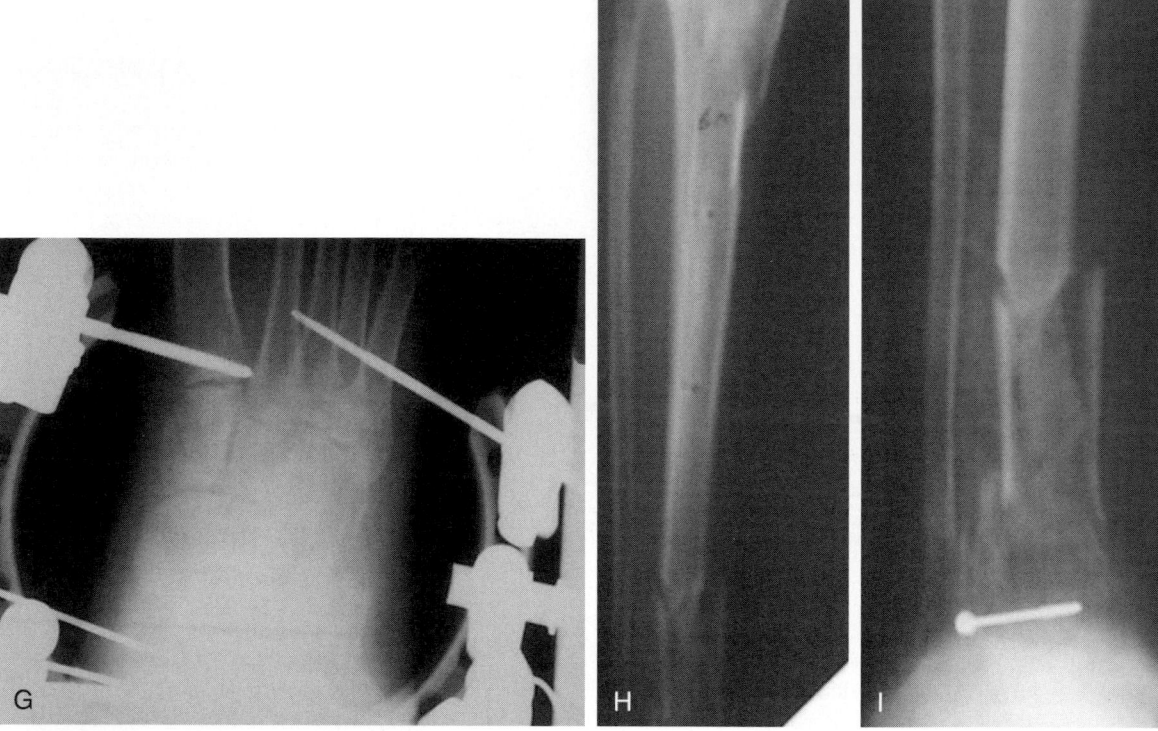

FIGURE 57–38 *Continued. H, I,* The fracture has united and the patient is fully weight bearing 6 months postinjury after a distal posterolateral bone graft at 5 weeks.

*tibial shaft, they too often produce thermal necrosis of skin as well as bone.* In the tibial diaphysis it is therefore essential to predrill for external fixator pins with a sharp drill bit slightly smaller than the chosen pin. A soft tissue sleeve, very limited blunt dissection to bone after incising the skin, irrigation, and a "stop-and-cool" technique all help avoid tibial pin tract complications. If drilling is at all hard, the bit should be removed and cleaned of bone chips. The chips should be white, not brown or black, which signifies burning. If evidence of thermal necrosis is encountered, another pin site should be prepared and used.

FRAME CONSTRUCTION. Each pair of pins is connected with a rod placed close enough to the bone to allow for soft tissue care and dressings. Enough rod should protrude toward the fracture for connection of a third rod that links the two segments by means of rod-rod connecting clamps. This arrangement forms a universal joint that allows fracture reduction and can readily be adjusted or disconnected if required for subsequent débridement. A similarly constructed external fixator can span the knee or the ankle for transarticular fixation. Once the frame has been assembled and the fracture reduced, the pin sites should be checked again and the skin released with a small scalpel if it is tented at all by the pin.

**Pin Care.** Elaborate care of external fixator pin sites is rarely needed for tibial diaphyseal pins. If they penetrate thicker, more mobile soft tissues than the typically thin subcutaneous anteromedial tibial border, a dressing that inhibits motion of the soft tissues around the pin is advisable. Daily pin cleaning rituals are commonly used, but unless significant crusting of exudate has occurred, simple cleaning with perhaps a little antibiotic ointment is all that is usually necessary.[198]

**External Fixator Removal.** By waiting until the tibial fracture is securely healed before removing an external fixator, the surgeon significantly reduces the risk of late loss of alignment and impaired fracture healing. Early bone grafting of externally fixed tibial shaft fractures decreases the time required to heal these usually severe open injuries that often involve loss of bone as well as soft tissue damage. If convincing restoration of cortical bone continuity is not seen on AP, lateral, and oblique radiographs, healing may not be sufficient for stability after fixator removal. Removal of fixator parts that prevent adequate visualization may be needed to evaluate the fracture adequately. The patient's ability to bear significant weight on the fracture site without much local pain (although pin site discomfort may need to be distinguished) provides additional reassurance. Dynamization of the fixator frame, as described earlier, to allow axial weight bearing transfers weight bearing from the frame to the tibia, provides a prolonged provocative loading test, and may promote fracture healing as well. I generally have the patient bear weight for several weeks in such a frame before removing it, usually at least 2 or 3 months after bone grafting or 4 or 5 months after a tibial diaphyseal fracture. Manual assessment of fracture site tenderness and instability may be falsely reassuring immediately after fixator removal because even ununited fractures can feel quite stable for a day or two before "loosening up."

An external fixator can be removed in a doctor's office or clinic with oral narcotic and optional sedative premedication.[20] All necessary tools should be available, including a hand drill or T-handled chuck. Local anesthetic may help a little, but not usually enough to be worth the pain from injecting it. Some patients insist on a general anesthetic, which can make outpatient removal very brief if it is required. After the external fixator pins are removed, the pin site is gently scrubbed with povidone-iodine (Betadine) solution, and a fairly bulky sterile dressing is applied to accommodate the usual limited bleeding. I apply a short leg splint for 2 or 3 days, leave the pin sites covered during that period, and then replace the splint with a weight-bearing brace or cast for the next 4 to 6 weeks and encourage weight bearing to tolerance. Within a few days, most pin sites are nearly healed and need little if any continuing care. Reassessment of fracture stability by the application of manual (bending) stress at this visit a few days after fixator removal is important to confirm healing, but fracture site pain should be regarded as a worrisome sign. Occasionally, a tibial pin site has become infected, with loosening, persistent purulent drainage, radiographic ring sequestrum, or any combination of these signs. Rather than attempting to cleanse the pin tract with a curette, a hand drill with bits large enough to débride the affected bone is a much more efficient and less traumatic instrument. If a need for such débridement is anticipated, an operating room and general anesthetic are advised.

**Results.** The results of external fixation used as temporary stabilization before nail or plate fixation, with or without other procedures, are hard to glean from the literature. These uses have been documented as beneficial.[19, 532] External fixation as the exclusive treatment of tibial shaft fractures is less commonly reported or is limited to fractures that may be difficult to manage with a nail, plate, or cast. Hay has recently reported 50 patients with unstable closed or open tibial fractures treated by protocol with the Orthofix dynamic axial fixator.[232a] All united, but 22% required further surgery; 16% were malaligned, but none desired correction; and in 10%, pin site but no deep infections were encountered. Similar results have been reported by Checketts and colleagues: 4 months' healing time for closed, 5 months for grade II open, and 6 months for grade III open fractures. Pin infections were noted in 34% of this series.[104] De Bastiani and associates and Marsh and co-workers have shown the effectiveness of this device as definitive fixation for severe open fractures.[131, 350] Its cost-effectiveness has been noted by Shaw and Lawton.[526] Other types of fixators have been enthusiastically reported as definitive tibial fracture stabilization techniques.[31, 40, 155, 590] Emami and colleagues offer a more cautionary assessment, with slow healing and frequent need for unplanned secondary operations.[162]

## PLATE FIXATION

Plate fixation, especially for proximal and distal tibial shaft fractures, offers potentially stable fixation in regions difficult to treat with IM nailing, but with a risk of postoperative infection, wound slough, and potential problems with fracture union. Complications were commonly seen after plate fixation of tibial shaft fractures when it first became popular during the 1950s.[90] Their frequency encouraged a strong shift toward nonoperative treatment of closed tibial fractures in the 1960s and 1970s. Plating of tibial shaft fractures was not universally rejected, however. The Swiss AO group developed implants and technical expertise and reported plating results as good as those of any other treatment.[487] However, it soon became apparent that good results were not guaranteed by using the Swiss implants. Considerable experience and expertise are necessary if complications are to be minimized.[541] Proper patient selection is also important. Crushed soft tissues, tenuous skin flaps, severe open wounds, and other signs of high-energy trauma are characteristics of tibial fractures with a high risk of problems after plate fixation. Plating of properly selected tibial fractures can be made considerably safer by delaying plate application until after the soft tissue injury has recovered. Such delay in plate application may involve the use of temporary external fixation placed outside the wound that will be used for plate insertion. Another way to reduce the risk of problems with plate fixation is to use minimally invasive insertion techniques consisting of tunneling the plate under intact skin and placing screws through stab wounds under image intensifier control.[113, 170, 171, 237, 314, 487]

Because less soft tissue stripping is required, the blood supply to the fracture site is better preserved. However, this technique has its own technical challenges. As originally proposed by the AO/ASIF, plate fixation was intended to promote direct bone healing by achieving rigid fixation that prevented interfragmentary motion. Direct healing without callus formation is typically observed when this mechanical objective is achieved. Periosteal callus formation in such situations can be seen as evidence of micromotion at the fracture site. Rigid fixation requires interfragmentary compression, which can be achieved in noncomminuted fractures with the appropriate use of lag screws and preloaded compression plates. It is better to restrict the use of such rigid fixation to minimally comminuted fractures in which the bone fragments can be compressed in a manner that produces absolute stability, the requirement for direct bone healing. More flexible plate fixation without interfragmentary compression tends to not suppress callus formation. If the plate and screws do not fail because of excessive micromotion, this indirect healing with visible peripheral callus may be associated with satisfactory and more rapid fracture healing. A prerequisite is that the surrounding soft tissues be intact and able to provide the necessary blood supply for interfragmentary callus formation.[382] Plates used in this manner are intended to splint the bone, like IM nails. More flexible plates, greater space between screws, leaving some holes empty, and most importantly, great respect for the integrity of all remaining soft tissue attachments to fracture fragments are important aspects of this technique, as described by Mast and co-workers,[356] Bolhofner,[59] and Miclau and Martin,[382] among others. This approach, often called bridge plating or biologic plating to distinguish it from compression plating, has been shown to produce impressive results, but the scientific foundations of its important technical aspects are still being elucidated.[285, 286, 550] The limits of acceptable technique have not yet been defined. Biologic plating remains a surgical art that must be learned and practiced and demands great attention to detail. The reader will note that plating with indirect reduction and preservation of soft tissue integrity is quite similar to closed IM nailing. The hope is that this "extramedullary" approach will be as successful.

In fresh tibial injuries, plates are probably best suited for displaced fractures that involve the articular surface and require more stability than can be provided by lag screws alone. In low-energy injuries and when used with good technique, the results of plates can rival those of IM nails, although patients may have to wait longer before significant weight bearing. The technical aspects of plate fixation are covered in Chapters 56 and 58 on tibial plateau fractures and fractures of the tibial pilon. If significant articular involvement is present, the reader should consult the appropriate section. Treatment and outcome are dictated by articular involvement, with the diaphyseal injury being of secondary importance. Many centers have reported unacceptably high complication rates with plate fixation of severe fractures of the tibial plateaus or pilon. Such complications have been significantly reduced by using ring-type external fixation as either an Ilizarov or hybrid device for control of the metaphyseal segment. The use of such external fixators should be considered whenever one must treat an extensive tibial shaft fracture that involves either the proximal or distal joint. Plates should also be considered when fixation is required for tibial fractures that are not suitable for IM nailing. In these situations as well, one should also consider external fixation as an alternative for acute treatment because of its lower risk of wound problems.

Very rarely, a plate may be the best alternative for an open tibial fracture, but only when its mechanical stability is essential, the overlying soft tissues are adequate, and additional damage will not result from the required exposure. Exceptional surgical experience and skill, as well as careful judgment, help in avoiding complications. Bach and Hansen[27] have shown that the use of a plate rather than external fixation for open fractures carries an increased rate of infection, wound problems, and fixation failure. Bilat and associates agreed, although the effect on ultimate outcome was negligible.[50] Apparently, the additional soft tissue trauma required for plating and the presence of a large foreign body negate any beneficial effect conferred by improved fracture stability. If the mechanical benefits of plating are essential for long-term management of a tibial fracture with a significant soft tissue injury, consideration should be given to provisional external fixation, with plating performed some weeks later when uncomplicated wound healing is more likely.

Plate fixation of closed tibial fractures may be used occasionally after arterial repair, particularly if the needed exposure has been created during the approach to the injured vessels (see Fig. 57–13). Plates should be used with great caution, however, for *open* fractures that require vascular repair because the infection rate is especially high in this setting and external fixation is generally preferred.

Exceptionally, when a long comminuted span of diaphysis is exposed by an open fracture, neither an external fixator nor statically locked IM nailing satisfactorily stabilizes the multiple fragments. If the open fracture wound offers sufficient access for plating without additional soft tissue dissection and if the fracture fragments are viable and not badly contaminated, plate-and-screw fixation may be appropriate. Early plating may be even more appropriate for an occasional highly comminuted *closed* shaft fracture (Fig. 57–39). Such injuries must be treated with great care to avoid additional soft tissue stripping and bone devascularization. If healthy soft tissue flaps do not permit early tension-free wound closure, prompt muscle pedicle or free-flap closure will generally be required. Bone grafting after soft tissue healing may also be advisable for such injuries.

### Surgical Approach

With its triangular external cross section, the tibial shaft offers three potential surfaces for plate application. The medial and lateral surfaces are readily available from an anterior approach. The less accessible posterior surface may also be mechanically less satisfactory for plate fixation (Fig. 57–40).

It is crucial to carefully assess the condition of the skin and soft tissues before choosing plate fixation and

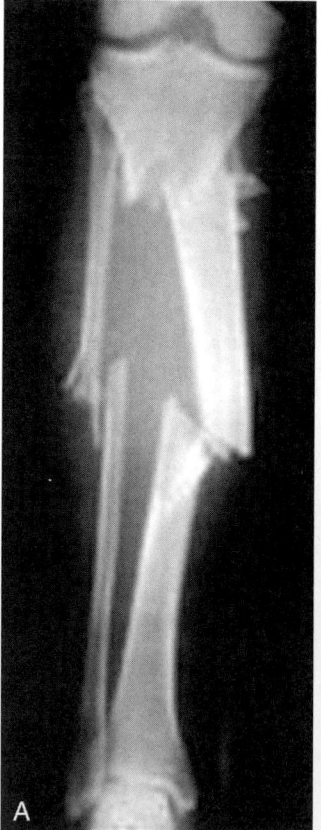
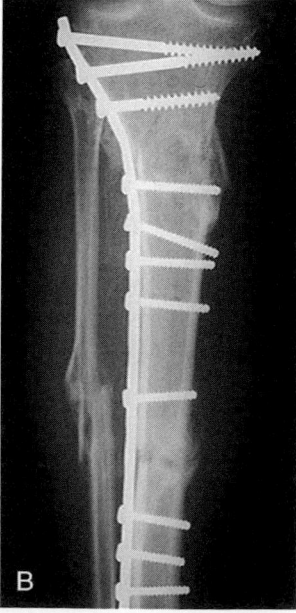

**FIGURE 57–39.** "Biologic" plate fixation. *A,* Segmental comminuted closed tibial shaft fracture. *B,* Fracture alignment was maintained with traction until the soft tissues had recovered. Extraperiosteal plating was performed 8 days after injury, with indirect reduction and minimal soft tissue dissection. Note the callus formation at both fracture sites 8 weeks after injury.

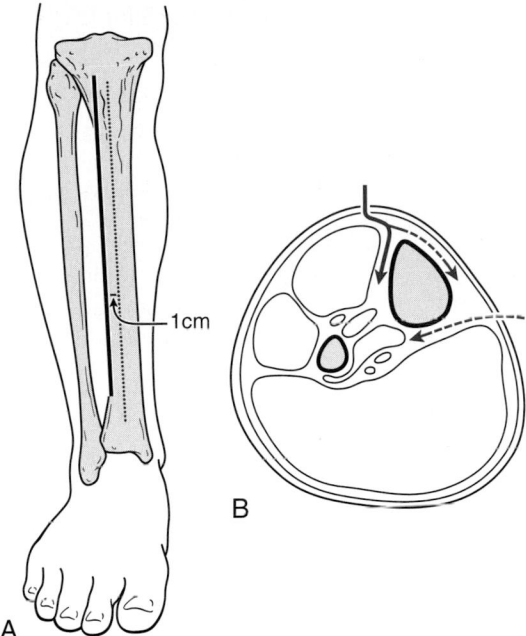

**FIGURE 57–40.** Surgical approaches for plate fixation of tibial shaft fractures. *A,* An anterior skin incision 1 cm lateral to the anterior tibial crest and over the tibialis anterior muscle is used to approach either the anterolateral or the anteromedial surface. Distally, the incision follows the medial border of the tibialis anterior as it crosses the tibia. A posteromedial incision, typically used for a double-incision fasciotomy, should never be combined with an anterior incision because the intervening skin bridge is too narrow and might slough. However, it can be used to plate the tibia on the anteromedial or, rarely, the posterior surface. *B,* The approach to the tibia should be carried directly through and then beneath the fascia. A fasciocutaneous flap is elevated rather than dissecting in the subcutaneous plane. Extraperiosteal plate application is preferred. As much soft tissue as possible should be left attached to the tibia, with only enough of its surface exposed to apply the plate. Although limited fracture exposure may be required to reduce a two-part fracture, comminuted fragments should be left undisturbed and bridged over with a plate that maintains overall alignment and promotes indirect bone healing.

exposing the tibia. The subcutaneous anteromedial surface of the tibia is often injured, and it may not be suitable for plate application, especially after direct local trauma. The risk of wound sloughing is high if an incision is made near or through contusions, lacerations, or abrasions. For this reason, many believe that the anteromedial surface should rarely, if ever be used for acute tibial fractures. A safer alternative may be the anterolateral surface, which is covered by the anterior compartment muscles, although a plate applied here interferes with an important route of blood supply to the healing fracture. Thus, each injured leg should be evaluated on the basis of its own characteristics and those of the injury. The presence of a posteromedial incision for vascular repair or fasciotomy provides easy access to the medial surface of the tibia, which might also be the best site for a plate if extensive soft tissue wounds mandate from the outset the use of a muscle pedicle flap for medial coverage. In such a situation, detachment of any remaining anterior compartment muscles from the bone fragments seems to have little merit. An anterolateral incision risks sloughing of the intervening skin flap if it is combined with one on the posteromedial aspect of the leg.

The tibia is approached with the patient supine and a pneumatic tourniquet in place about the upper part of the thigh. Caution must be exercised regarding use of the tourniquet, however. Salam and associates have shown an increased incidence of wound problems in patients with tibial shaft fractures plated with the use of a tourniquet as compared with those in whom it was not used.[494] We avoid tourniquet use unless absolutely necessary. The leg is prepared sterilely and draped free on a standard or radiolucent operating table. Additional padding under the ipsilateral buttock may aid in access to the lateral part of the calf.

The same skin incision can be used to access both the anteromedial and anterolateral tibial surfaces. This incision should be made over the muscles of the anterior compartment at least 1 cm lateral to the anterior tibial crest (see Fig. 57–40). If significant soft tissue contusion is present, a more lateral incision ensures that bone and hardware will remain covered by soft tissue, even if skin closure is not possible. Similarly, a posteromedial incision can be used to access the tibia's anteromedial surface. The incision is carried down directly through the deep fascia without creating subcutaneous flaps. Preservation of a fasciocutaneous flap composed of skin, subcutaneous tissue, and underlying deep fascia is important because the dermal blood supply depends on vascular connections with the fascia. The resulting anterior flap is elevated from the underlying muscles and reflected only as much as required for exposure. A longer incision is safer than overvigorous retraction. Self-retaining retractors should be used briefly and gently or not at all.

Depending on the surgeon's choice, the tibial shaft is next exposed on *either* its anterolateral or anteromedial aspect. To preserve the blood supply, only minimal soft tissue should be reflected from the other surface. The tibia can be exposed either subperiosteally or extraperiosteally. Fracture healing after plate fixation appears to be equivalent with either exposure, but injured muscles may do better with a subperiosteal dissection.

**Minimally Invasive Approaches.** Interest is growing in the application of plates through very limited incisions to minimize soft tissue injury and preserve the bone's blood supply.[113, 171, 237, 313, 315, 382] Specially designed implants and instruments are being developed for this purpose[315] (Fig. 57–41). The use of periarticular screws threaded into the plate offers the stability of a fixed-angle device (like a blade plate) that controls frontal plane alignment in spite of comminution opposite the plate.

Some evidence has indicated that rigid, precisely anatomic, piece-by-piece reduction devascularizes comminuted bone fragments and delays fracture healing.[34] Whether this problem is clinically relevant for the tibial shaft has not yet been determined. Less invasive plate insertion may, however, offer a lower risk of wound complications for selected patients. The tibia's anteromedial surface is amenable to insertion of a subcutaneous plate. The saphenous vein and nerves, which run from in front of the medial malleolus to just behind the medial tibial plateau, must be remembered and spared. However, the biggest concern regarding this location is the potentially tenuous skin viability. Delayed insertion of anteromedial plates is safer, but some patients have such severely contused anteromedial skin that this location is contraindicated for a plate, even when it is inserted through a small incision and tunneled subcutaneously. Anterolaterally, a plate can be inserted submuscularly under the anterior compartment musculature. Proximally, such plate insertion is relatively safe, including percutaneous screw insertion, but Kregor and colleagues have shown that this approach for a plate inserted from the proximal end of the tibia has an unacceptable risk of injury to the anterior tibial artery and superficial peroneal nerve in the lower half of the tibia, so they recommend the use of an open incision in this area.[312]

### Reduction Techniques

Mast and co-workers led a shift in emphasis from interfragmentary reduction and fixation, which generally require more bone exposure, to "indirect reduction" techniques in which soft tissue attachments are spared and the fracture is reduced by distraction or the application of appropriately precontoured plates.[334, 356] This approach contrasts with the "classic" AO technique for plate fixation, which involves provisional reduction, initial fixation with interfragmentary lag screws, and finally, application of a neutralizing plate contoured to match the reassembled tibia. This technique requires significant exposure to gain reduction and to apply bone-holding clamps. Less invasive approaches offer decreased complications in both wound and fracture healing. Minimally invasive plating preserves the local blood supply.[171, 313, 334]

The AO distractor or an external fixator used in the same way is a very helpful instrument for gaining indirect reduction (Fig. 57–42). Another indirect reduction technique involves the attachment of an appropriately contoured plate to one major fragment, with which it can be manipulated relative to the other, often with the aid of the articulated tension device or a bone spreader and screw (Fig. 57–43).

### Type of Implant

The basic plate for most tibial fractures extending into the diaphysis is the so-called narrow AO/ASIF limited-contact dynamic compression plate (LC-DCP) from the large-fragment set. The plate holes are shaped so that a properly placed screw causes the plate to slide along the bone, thereby increasing compression forces between fracture fragments. Each end hole is slightly larger so that a 6.5-mm-diameter cancellous screw can be directed at a greater angle than it can through the other holes. This feature helps when the plate is used either proximally or distally, but only the end hole is so shaped, and the use of multiple metaphyseal cancellous screws is hindered. It is therefore less suited for buttress applications than the

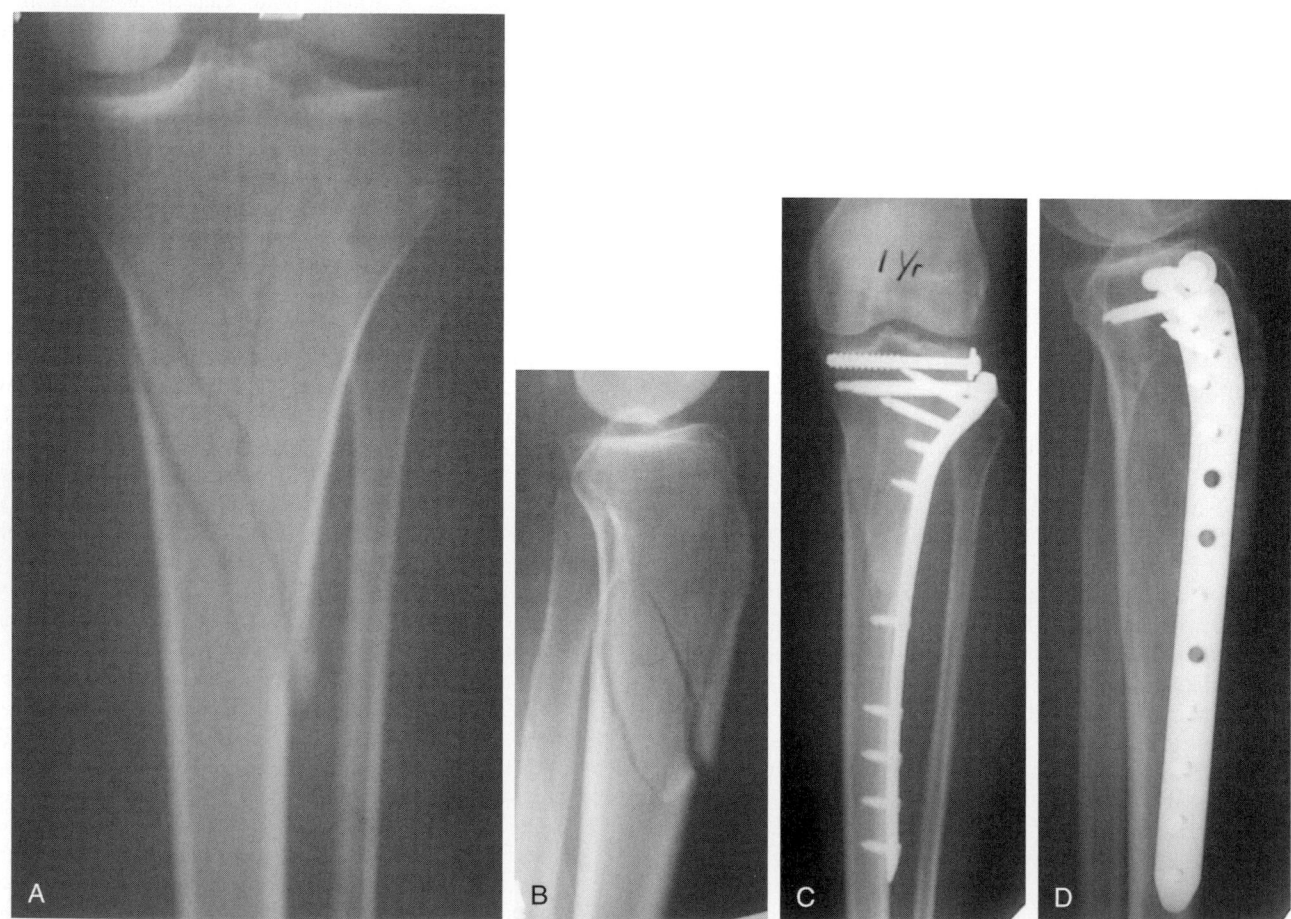

**FIGURE 57–41.** *A, B,* Metadiaphyseal proximal tibial fracture with a slight intra-articular extension. *C, D,* One-year follow-up after intra-articular open reduction–internal fixation and percutaneous, submuscular application of a LISS fixator. (Courtesy of Kenneth Lambert, M.D.)

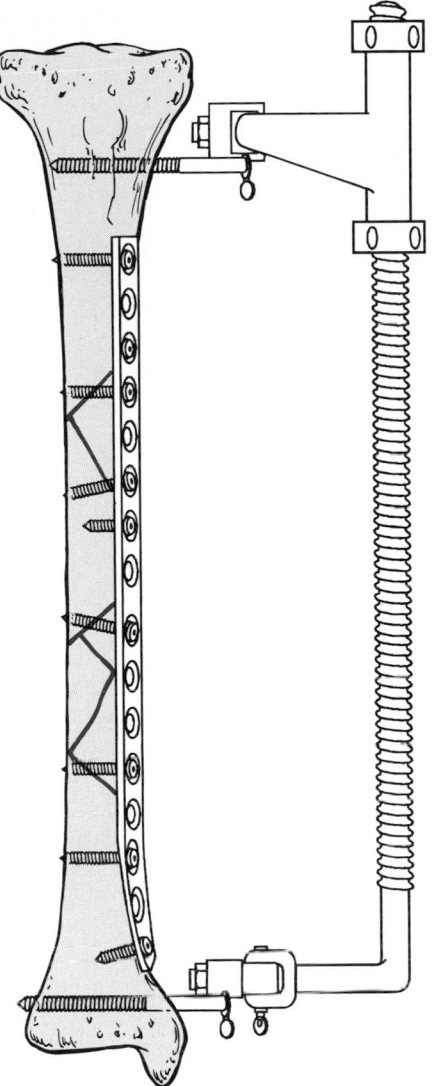

**FIGURE 57–42.** The AO bone distractor permits indirect, less traumatic reduction of a tibial shaft fracture. Traction reduction minimally disturbs the soft tissue attachments of bone fragments and allows less traumatic application of an appropriately contoured plate.

thinner and much more flexible metaphyseal plates are. A plate designed specifically for the proximal tibial condyles combines the features of a narrow dynamic compression plate for the shaft with a thinner, broader proximal segment with multiple holes for cancellous screws to fix and support fractures involving the tibial plateau. Similar plates for the distal end of the tibia are now available; these plates have a diaphyseal portion shaped like an LC-DCP and a distal metaphyseal portion that is thinner and precontoured. Several manufacturers are developing plates designed to fit the periarticular tibia while extending into the diaphysis with an implant suited to the greater forces encountered there. Occasionally, particularly for patients with smaller tibias, the small-fragment (3.5-mm screw series) LC-DCP offers better fit and control for metadiaphyseal tibia fractures, but this plate and its screws are significantly weaker, and although they are less bulky and permit more screws in a short segment of bone, they do require strict protection until fracture healing is quite

advanced. Titanium LC-DCPs have now been available for several years. They have several theoretical advantages, but problems have been reported with fixation failure, particularly through their titanium screws, when these titanium plates are used in the lower extremity.[29] Although experimental evidence suggests that titanium implants may be associated with higher resistance to wound infection, such has not been established by clinical results. Jain has demonstrated the equivalence of titanium and stainless steel plates for fracture healing in a dog spiral tibia fracture model.[263]

The broad, stainless steel dynamic compression plate with staggered holes for 4.5-mm screws is stiffer and more bulky than appropriate for the tibia. However, on occasion it may be chosen to span a significant comminuted zone or an area of segmental bone loss. Rarely, the 95° condylar blade plate is helpful for proximal tibial fractures and nonunion involving the transitional zone between the metaphysis and diaphysis.[95] It provides better control of angulation for comminuted fractures when cortical contact cannot be restored on the side opposite the plate. In a similar fashion, custom-prepared blade plates can be used, with an oblique screw placed from the metaphyseal portion of the plate into the part that is driven into the metaphysis to provide more secure fixation for poorer bone.[432]

A tibial plate should be sufficiently long that at least four secure screws attach each end to the proximal and distal fragments. A longer plate can increase stability. Increasing the span between the most distal and most proximal screw may improve stability more than can be obtained by using more screws in a shorter span. One must be cautious about undisplaced comminution. Poor-quality radiographs and fracture planes visible only on oblique views may significantly compromise a screw's holding power, as may osteopenic bone. In such situations, a longer plate may be safer.[484] When a plate lies over cancellous bone, it is generally preferable to use fully threaded 6.5-mm cancellous screws rather than those with 16- or 32-mm threaded segments. The metaphyseal cortex is usually thin and provides neither additional purchase nor impediment to insertion of a cancellous screw. Purchase in low-density cancellous bone is improved by allowing the screw to cut its own threads. With longer plates, omitting as many as 40% of the screws in an effort to increase surface strain and thereby stimulate indirect bone healing does not appear to compromise fixation. Surgical judgment is required to avoid inadequate fixation in this approach to "biologic" fixation.[174]

**Lag Screws without Plates.** Although plating is the basic extramedullary technique for internal fixation of tibial shaft fractures, in some situations, screws alone may be considered. Long spiral fractures (at least three times the shaft diameter) without comminution are most suited to lag screw fixation. The technique of lag screw insertion is important and has been well defined.[269] In long spiral fractures with good bone quality, three lag screws are inserted perpendicular to the long axis of the tibia and also perpendicular to the fracture line in the transverse plane in which the screw lies. The screws should (1) be spaced evenly, (2) spiral with the fracture, (3) bisect the fracture surface of each fragment, and (4) be well back from the thin, fragile fracture ends. The shorter the obliquity or the greater the presence or likelihood of comminution, the more that lag screw fixation must be protected with a neutralization plate. However, the soft tissue consequences of applying a plate must be balanced against its benefits. External fixation is an alternative means of neutralizing forces applied to such lag screw fixation, but its clinical results in this setting have been disappointing, and it is not recommended.[316] Fixing the tibia with lag screws alone should be done with caution. Limited weight bearing is required until the fracture has healed enough to protect the fixation. Most long spiral fractures have little displacement and can be treated with a weight-bearing cast or brace instead.

### Bone Grafting of Plated Fractures

It is well recognized that a fracture that does not heal soon enough will result in failure of internal fixation. Therefore, bone grafting should be considered for fractures with more than minimal bone loss or with an increased risk for delayed union or nonunion because of a high-energy mechanism of injury. Indirect reduction and atraumatic fixation, which preserve the soft tissue attachments and blood supply needed for healing, obviate the need for bone grafting in most plated fractures. If the injury has caused significant periosteal stripping, bone grafting may be advisable during plate fixation of a closed tibial fracture. To minimize additional soft tissue stripping, surgeons whose preoperative plan includes the use of a bone graft should insert the graft through the mobile fracture site *before the plate is applied.* The optimal location for bone grafting to support the plate is on the opposite cortex, but if the graft must be placed there by stripping soft tissues that bring blood supply to the fracture zone, it may not be as beneficial as desired.

If the fracture is open or significant soft tissue injury has occurred, it is safer to delay grafting (Fig. 57–44). Only in minor wounds should bone grafting be performed through the wound at the time of delayed primary closure. After significant injury, bone grafting should be delayed for several weeks to minimize the risk of wound problems.[38] Occasionally, a young patient will have radiographically evident periosteal callus formation by that time, thus obviating the need for grafting. If not, it is generally best to graft early rather than wait until fixation failure indicates the need.

### Wound Management

After plate fixation of a closed tibial fracture, the wound can usually be closed primarily with suction drains only if the surgeon chooses. The fascia is left open to decrease the risk of compartment syndrome, and sutures are placed as gently as possible in the skin, which should never be grasped directly with forceps. Should one side of the

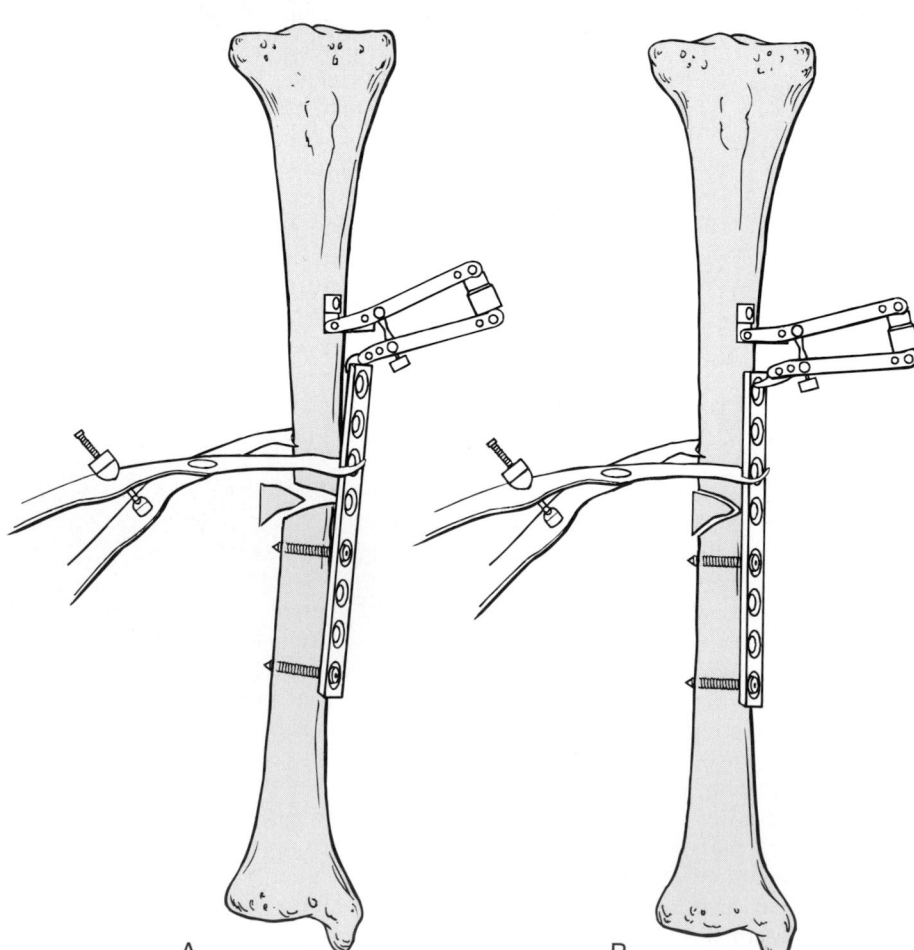

**Figure 57–43.** A plate can be used as a reduction aid. It is first contoured, if necessary, and then attached to one end fragment and used to manipulate it relative to the other, often with the aid of an articulated tension device as shown here. *A,* Tension device used as a distractor. *B,* Tension device used to compress the fracture fragments. It may be possible to tease comminuted fragments into place and gain interfragmentary compression through them for additional stability, but such compression is less important than preserving the soft tissue attachments. (*A, B,* Redrawn from Mast, J.; et al. Planning and Reduction Techniques in Fracture Surgery. New York, Springer-Verlag, 1989.)

A                                        B

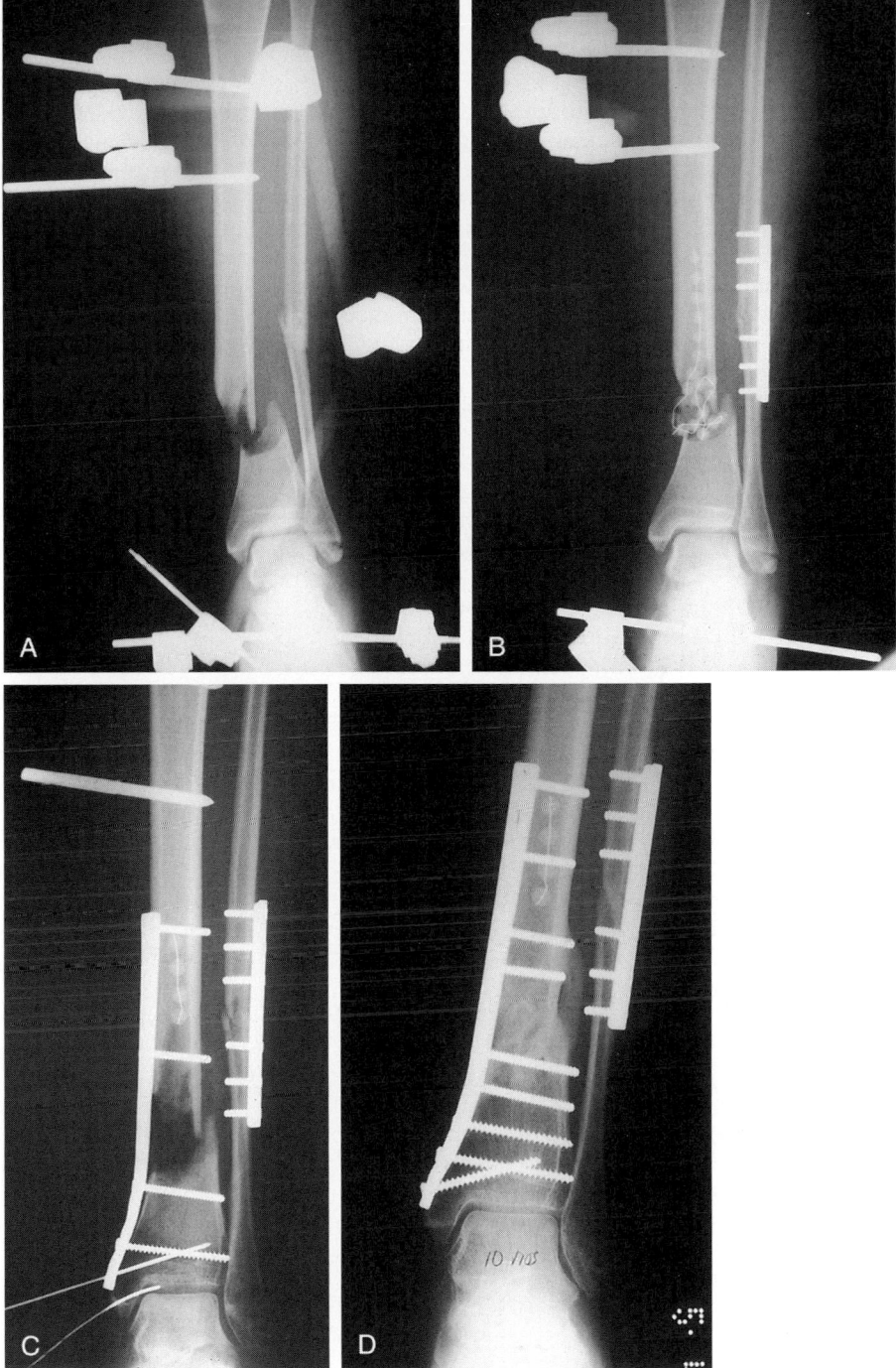

**FIGURE 57–44.** *A,* Open high-energy fracture referred 36 hours after limited initial wound irrigation. The first stage of treatment is thorough débridement and external fixation. *B,* The medial wound is closed over tobramycin-impregnated polymethyl methacrylate beads, external fixation is maintained, and the fibula is fixed with indirect reduction and limited exposure. *C,* Eight weeks later, the benignly healed medial wound is reopened, the beads are replaced with autologous bone graft, and a contoured plate is applied. *D,* Two years later, a standing radiograph shows mature healing and mild arthritic changes in the ankle.

wound be more tenuous, it may be appropriate to use Algöwer's modified Donnati suture technique, in which suture is passed only through subcuticular tissue on the side at greater risk. After application of a sterile dressing and adequate padding, the foot and ankle are splinted in neutral and the leg is moderately elevated during the initial postoperative period. No evidence supports more than brief use of prophylactic antibiotics, although perioperative administration is valuable. Patients are much more comfortable in a splint than with the foot and ankle free after fixation of all but the most proximal tibial fractures. Early motion, if desired, may begin within a few days. A splint may still be helpful between exercise sessions for comfort and to avoid contractures. In some very badly injured limbs in which the knee or ankle requires stabilization, an external fixator might be used provisionally for this purpose after an associated tibial fracture has been plated.

If a plate is used for an open fracture, the wound should not be closed primarily. In some such situations in which the plate is inserted through a completely separate wound, the surgical wound might be closed while the original injury is left open for delayed closure by suture or a skin graft. However, with severe injuries, it is unwise to close any part of the wound until the limb has been reevaluated again in the operating room.

### Rehabilitation after Plating

One of the advantages of plate fixation for tibial fractures is that it should provide sufficient stability for motion of adjacent joints and myotendinous units. Such motion helps prevent stiffness, particularly if it is combined with the use of resting splints until satisfactory dorsiflexion has been achieved. However, it is essential to delay significant weight bearing on the plated tibial fracture until healing is advanced enough to protect the fixation from cyclical loading and resulting failure. Optimally, patients treated in this manner can proceed with limited weight bearing on crutches, with only an elastic stocking used as needed to control edema. However, when patient cooperation is questionable or the fixation is tenuous, additional external support must be used. In the most unreliable patients, such support might be a long leg cast with the knee flexed and the dorsum of the foot portion removed to permit ankle dorsiflexion above neutral. A functional cast or fracture brace could also be used, but no definitive data are available to indicate how much protection braces offer to plated tibial fractures, so crutches and limited weight bearing are the mainstay of mechanical protection.

Periodic outpatient follow-up is required until the fracture is healed and the patient rehabilitated. The patient is instructed to promptly report any pain or wound problems. Unless problems are noted, radiographs are needed only every 4 to 6 weeks until union has occurred. Very limited weight bearing (15 to 20 lb) during the first 6 weeks after internal fixation of a tibial fracture may be gradually increased during the second 6 weeks if radiographs demonstrate maintenance of fixation and progressive obliteration of any fracture lines. Weight bearing should increase more slowly after more severe injuries.

External callus is rarely seen with rigid internal fixation unless bone graft has been used to obtain it or the plate is applied in a (bridging) manner intended to promote indirect bone healing (see Fig. 57–39). When it is observed unexpectedly but does not convincingly support the fracture site, such wispy "irritation callus" may indicate excessive loading and relative instability. This finding is an indication to reduce loading until the callus becomes radiographically mature. If healing of a plated tibial fracture does not progress, serious consideration should be given to *early* revision of fixation rather than delaying the necessary surgery while the tibia becomes more osteoporotic.[182] Ankle and subtalar range-of-motion exercises should begin early after plating of a tibial fracture to minimize late disability resulting from contractures of the ankle joints. Low-resistance strength and endurance exercises are progressively increased as the fracture heals, and functional rehabilitation is completed once bone healing and soft tissues permit. By 4 or 5 months, most plated tibial fractures are healed enough for unsupported weight bearing. Rarely is it wise for a patient to return to contact sports and risk activities in less than 6 to 9 months. Time estimates for tibial fracture healing must be adjusted upward for more severe injuries, with the clinical and radiographic progress of healing critically reassessed to

ensure that union is complete before excessive loading is begun. Local pain, warmth, swelling, and tenderness may indicate mechanical instability or occult infection. Adequate radiographs, wound aspiration, the sedimentation rate, C-reactive protein, and perhaps indium-labeled leukocyte scans may be helpful in questionable cases.

### Plate Removal

Hardware removal should be delayed at least 18 months or more for severe injuries. Dual-energy x-ray absorptiometry (DEXA) studies have not shown any progressive decrease in bone density under the tibial plates in current use, as occurs in stress-protected proximal femurs with some total joint implants.[264] Incomplete healing of severe fractures, continued remodeling of necrotic bone, and the temporary stress riser effect of recently removed screws all predispose to refracture after hardware removal.[89, 298] Delay until completion of both bone union and remodeling, as well as protection from undue stress for 6 to 12 weeks after plate and screw removal, is important to minimize the risk of refracture.

### Results

When plate fixation is performed with great skill in appropriate patients, the results are gratifying, and the relatively few complications are usually manageable. Few series are as impressive as that of Rüedi, Bilat, and associates,[50, 487] who reported good or very good outcomes in 98% of closed and 88% of open fractures. Complications occurred in 6% of closed and 32% of open fractures. However, after successful management, they had little effect on the end result. Nonunion occurred in less than 1% of closed and 7% of open fractures. Infections followed plate fixation after 12% of open fractures. The more recent report by Bilat and associates[50] confirms these findings, with 93% good or excellent ultimate results after plating open fractures versus 94% in closed injuries, as does another report by Rommens and colleagues.[479] Other authors have been enthusiastic about plate fixation, but complication rates have been high (19% to 30%), especially after open fractures.[136, 480] Three randomized trials compared plate fixation with other treatments. Bach and Hansen found external fixation more satisfactory than plating for type II and type III open fractures.[27] Van der Linden and Larsson had better results with plates than with non–weight-bearing cast treatment of closed fractures from predominantly low-energy injuries, but more complications occurred with plates used to treat open injuries.[602]

## CERCLAGE WIRING

Few authors now recommend cerclage wiring for tibial shaft fractures.[216] Injuries for which it may seem most suited (i.e., spiral fractures without comminution) rarely need internal fixation because they are typically low-energy injuries that do well with functional fracture bracing. Unless placed percutaneously with great care to avoid neurovascular injury, cerclage wiring is likely to be more invasive than IM nailing, which is therefore a better choice for unstable, comminuted spiral fractures.[280]

# PRIMARY AMPUTATION

## Indications

Every *appropriate* effort should be made to salvage a severely injured leg and restore its function. Modern fracture care makes such management possible for the vast majority of tibial fractures.[248, 457] However, if limb salvage poses excessive risk to the individual, if the functional end result will be worse than with a prosthesis, or if the duration of treatment will cause intolerable psychosocial problems, amputation may be a better course.[228, 233, 593] The dismal results for salvage of type IIIC open tibial fractures reported by Caudle and Stern raise serious questions about salvage for such injuries.[99] Georgiadis and colleagues found longer and more severe disability, more complications, and poorer outcomes in patients with grade IIIB open tibial fractures treated with limb-sparing salvage procedures, including free-flap coverage, than with amputation.[190] It is especially important to avoid delaying an amputation that is inevitable from the outset of treatment. Mortality, morbidity, extensive treatment, and increased cost are associated with delayed amputation after severe tibial fractures. Early amputation of unsalvageable limbs will reduce futile suffering and expense and expedite rehabilitation. Pozo and associates' 15 patients with infected nonunion and delayed amputation had an average of 12 operations, 8 months' total hospitalization, and more than 50 months before amputation.[448] In contrast, they reported that only 6 months' rehabilitation time was required before employment after a below-knee amputation, although patients could not always return to their previous job. Fairhurst has shown better functional outcomes in patients with severe tibial shaft fractures treated by amputation instead of limb salvage.[168] Hoogendoorn and van der Werken found little difference.[251]

Lange and co-workers proposed two absolute indications for amputation in open tibial fractures associated with arterial injuries: crush injury with a warm ischemia time of 6 hours and anatomic division of the tibial nerve in adults. They also offer the following relative indications: serious associated polytrauma, severe ipsilateral foot injuries, and an anticipated protracted course for salvage.[327, 328] Howe and colleagues proposed a predictive salvage index (PSI) based on the arterial injury level, the severity of bone and muscle injury, and the elapsed time from injury to surgery.[256] Others have also proposed guidelines for which severely injured limbs are best amputated.[206, 207, 267] Tibial nerve disruption as an absolute indication for amputation has been questioned.[249] Limb salvage may occasionally succeed in carefully selected patients with anatomic loss of the tibial nerve, but a plantigrade, supple foot is a crucial requirement. Johansen and colleagues developed the so-called Mangled Extremity Severity Score (MESS),[267] which gives numerical ratings for soft tissue injury, limb ischemia, shock severity, and age. A MESS of 7 or higher predicted 100% of their amputations. A significant amount of subjectivity is involved in assigning the soft tissue severity, which may be one reason why the MESS and similar efforts have not provided a totally successful means of deciding between amputation and limb salvage. McNamara and colleagues attempted to improve the MESS by adding to the score a component that measured nerve injury, thus producing the NISSSA (nerve injury, ischemia, soft tissue injury and contamination, skeletal injury, shock, and age) score.[373] Bonanni and co-workers rigorously reviewed four such scales, including the MESS, and found them all to be without predictive utility.[60] Durham and associates agreed that sensitivity and specificity were low and that no correlation could be found between the severity scores and long-term functional outcome.[150] Bosse and colleagues recently reported their experience with extremity injury severity scores in a prospective multicenter study (part of the Lower Extremity Assessment Project, or "LEAP").[65] The ability to predict amputation was not confirmed for any of the indices studied (MESS, Limb Salvage Index [LSI], PSI, NISSSA, and Hannover Fracture Scale, 1997 version [HFS-97]) for either ischemic or nonischemic limbs.

Without a valid, accepted system for determining the appropriateness of amputation, surgical judgment is required. Therefore, it is wise to seek knowledgeable consultation or to refer such patients to treatment centers with the necessary experience. Although the ideal scoring system eludes us, attention to the factors that their authors have included will help us better evaluate these challenging patients. Injury and patient factors to be considered are age, shock, ischemia time, and damage to bone, muscle, skin, nerves, and deep veins, as well as the severity of contamination. It is important to assess the viability and functionality of all the structures in the calf that contribute to foot and ankle function. Contracted or absent muscles irretrievably damaged by a severe injury may affect function so severely that a prosthesis is a better alternative than a viable, but dysfunctional foot.

## Technique

Amputation for trauma is both a débriding and a function-restoring procedure. After a tibial fracture, modifications of standard amputations can often improve the residual limb. At the outset it is important that all necrotic and contaminated tissue be removed. It is also important to preserve a functional knee, if possible, with sufficient tibial length below it for prosthesis use. See Chapter 64 for a comprehensive discussion. The benefits of a functioning knee are so significant that a stump that includes no more than the tibial tubercle may be worth saving, particularly now that subsequent lengthening procedures are possible. A bony margin 12 to 18 cm below the medial knee joint line is generally adequate. Little benefit is gained by going much below the midportion of the tibia. Healthy, full-thickness skin coverage is desirable, but split-thickness skin over muscle is also satisfactory. It is essential to débride thoroughly and not attempt to preserve unsalvageable tissue. It is also important to not discard valuable tissue below the level of amputation. Uneven skin flaps may take advantage of an asymmetric level of injury. One compartment may contain viable muscle, which can be turned proximally over the end of the bone. A variety of resourceful primary and secondary techniques help provide a longer or more durable stump. Acutely, one should consider fixing rather than amputating through more proximal fracture levels (Fig. 57–45). Soft tissue rather than bony integrity should determine the amputation level. Weight-bearing skin or a composite tissue graft can be transferred from the foot as a neurovascular pedicle flap or, exceptionally, as a free flap.[225, 500] The distal end of the tibia can be turned up into a proximal defect, or a surviving segment of fibula might be used similarly.[232] Delayed options for dealing with a short or poorly covered residual limb after proximal below-knee traumatic amputation include tissue expansion, rotation and free muscle flaps, innervated fasciocutaneous flaps, and traction histo-genesis using limb-lengthening techniques.[363] These techniques require judgment and experience, however.

The amputated part is a valuable tissue bank for reconstructive use. Cancellous bone, tendon, and split-thickness skin can be harvested and used, depending on the patient's injuries; a pure "guillotine" amputation may sacrifice tissue excessively. Primary amputation wounds should not be closed unless performed through more proximal, uninjured tissue. They should instead be

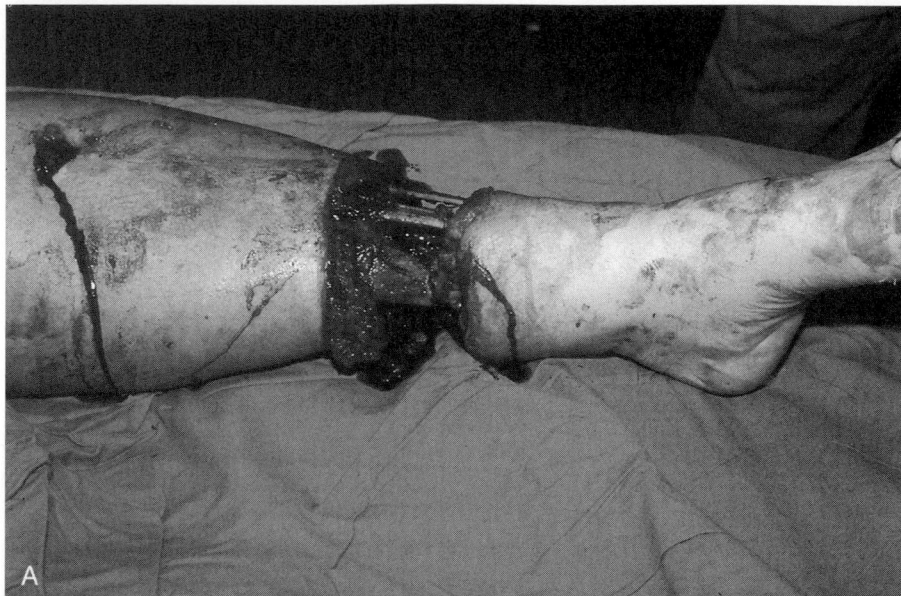

**FIGURE 57–45.** Reconstructive amputation. *A, B,* Leg crushed between a speeding car and a stationary bumper. *C,* Fixation of the proximal fracture provided length for a functional below-knee amputation.

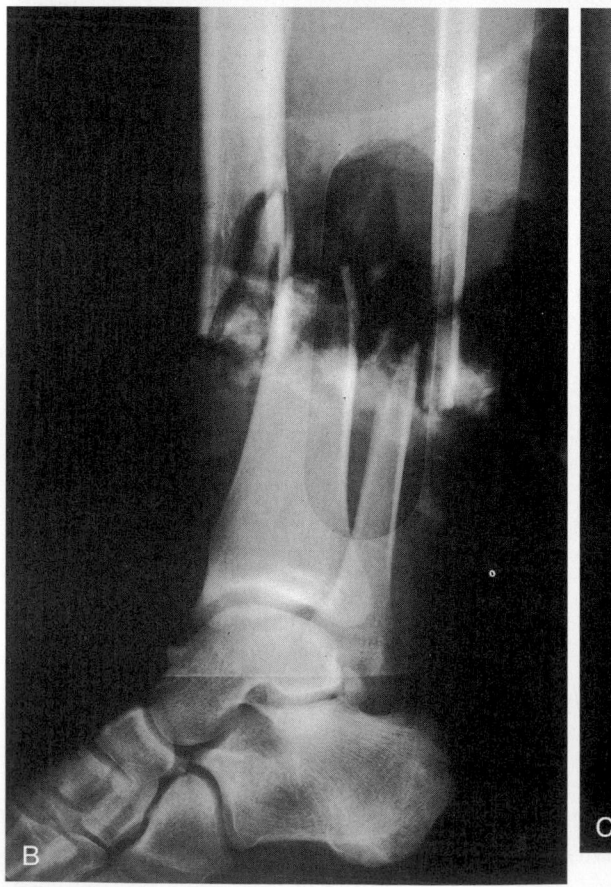

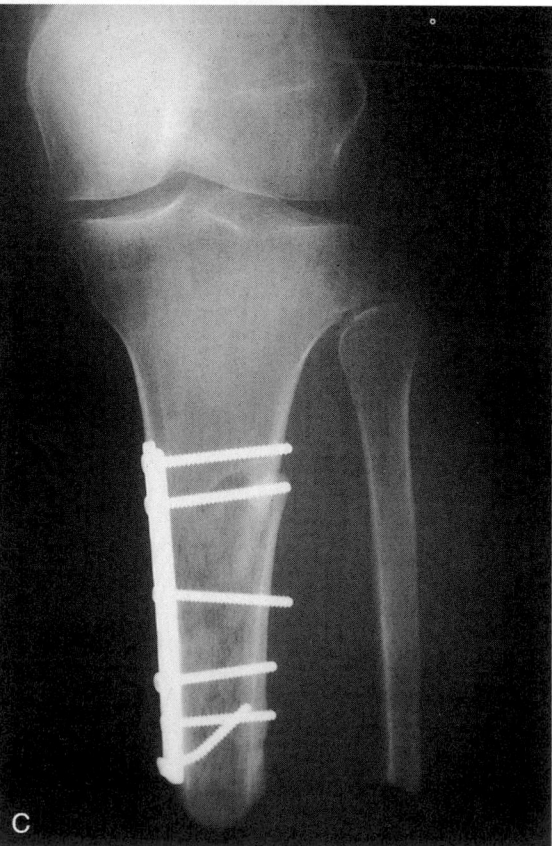

managed like any severe open fracture, with early return to the operating room for repeat débridement as needed and, ultimately, delayed closure. If done within 5 to 7 days, rarely does a problem occur with contraction of the flaps, which could interfere with closure after longer delays. It is usually better to begin with bone and tissue flap lengths that permit delayed closure rather than insist on a transverse amputation that subsequently requires more proximal reamputation. Whenever possible, myofascial flaps anchored to bone under adequate tension and cushioning of the end of the stump will provide an optimal limb. A rigid postoperative dressing protects the residual limb and helps avoid knee flexion contracture during the early stages of recovery.

Heroic attempts to salvage a below-knee level may be rewarded by significantly improved function, but such attempts run the risk of prolonged recovery, skin that may repeatedly break down with weight bearing, and precarious, insensate skin coverage. Heroic attempts should not be considered if they risk the patient's life or threaten salvage of a long above-knee stump.

Function after traumatic lower extremity amputation depends on multiple factors, but with adequate attention to both surgical procedures and rehabilitation, return to more or less normal activities and effective psychosocial and vocational adjustment are usually achieved.[73, 400, 439] In a recent functional outcome assessment, Hoogendoorn and van der Werken demonstrated that severe lower extremity injuries have a tremendous impact on function and quality of life.[251] Although impairment ratings were much more severe for amputees, no significant difference in quality of life between amputees and those who had limb salvage was noted when using the SF-36 and Nottingham Health Profile.

## BONE GRAFTING

Although we are tantalizingly close to clinically useful bone graft alternatives, none of those *currently available* have yet been fully approved by the U.S. Food and Drug Administration (FDA) as equivalent or better than the patient's own cancellous bone in the treatment of diaphyseal fractures.[71, 227, 291] Therefore, autogenous bone graft remains the mainstay for treating tibial shaft fractures that have significant bone loss, predictably impaired healing, or established failure of union. Traditionally, bone grafting was reserved for ununited fractures. Its earlier use to promote union in high-risk fractures has been established as valuable.[38, 54, 85, 94, 548] Complete segmental bone loss is a compelling indication for grafting. The implications of defect size on the need for bone grafting have been evaluated by Robinson and co-workers from Edinburgh. They reviewed 30 tibial fractures with bone loss, all of which were stabilized acutely with IM nails. They proposed a classification of bone loss severity based on length and percentage of circumference lost (Table 57–4). They advocated early (8 to 12 weeks) elective bone grafting for fractures with moderate and severe bone loss (>50% maximal circumference; >2.5-cm maximal defect length). Patients with smaller defects reliably healed with IM nail exchange if they did not after primary IM nail fixation.[476] This study

### TABLE 57–4

Bone Loss Severity

| Bone Loss Grade | Anatomic Loss |
|---|---|
| **Trivial** | Up to 25% wedge fragment |
| **Minor** (nail exchange; 4/9 succeed) | Wedge 25%–50% of circumference Wedge >50% to <100%, under 2.5 cm long |
| **Moderate** (bone graft required in 10/11) | Wedge >50% to <100%, 2.5–10 cm long or circumferential loss <2.5 cm |
| **Severe** (bone graft required in 10/10) | Wedge >50% to <100%, >10 cm long or circumferential loss >2.5 cm |

*Source:* Adapted from Robinson, C.M.; et al. J Bone Joint Surg Br 77:906–913, 1995.

demonstrates the benefits of IM nail fixation for tibial fractures with acute bone loss.

Other authors have encouraged grafting regardless of whether a defect is present after high-energy tibial shaft fractures if external fixation is used. They have shown that such grafting reduces the time to healing, prevents nonunion, and improves the chance of restoring normal strength to the bone.[38, 54, 572] There is probably some point at which repair of a significant bone defect might be done as well or better with bone transport, which has demonstrated effectiveness, but length of time in an external fixator, patient cooperation, and other issues pose potential challenges. Although bone transport is usually performed with either a circular or a specialized monolateral external fixator, it has been shown to work by transport of a segment over an IM nail, with more rapid fixator removal and perhaps improved alignment of regenerate bone.[96, 250, 459] However, inconsistent results make this technique appear to be still experimental.[321]

As alternatives to autogenous bone become available, they may be considered for the treatment of tibial diaphyseal fractures. Osteoconductive materials may help fill partial defects. Coralline hydroxyapatite, for instance, is as effective as cancellous autograft for filling tibial plateau fracture defects. Collagraft, a mixture of calcium phosphate ceramic beads and bovine collagen to which autogenous bone marrow is added, has been claimed to be as effective as iliac crest graft when used for acute fractures at the time of internal or external fixation.[116] However, most commercially available autograft substitutes do not appear to induce healing in ununited fractures, nor do they achieve union across segmental defects. Bone morphogenetic proteins such as BMP-7, also called OP-1, and BMP-2, with appropriate carriers, have shown great promise as osteo-inductive agents and may soon provide valid alternatives.[181] In the meanwhile, the surgeon should recognize the absence of significant supporting evidence for allografts, coralline hydroxyapatite, calcium phosphate ceramic–collagen composites, decalcified bone matrix, or ground-up cortical bone as a stimulus for fracture union in situations in which only cancellous autograft has been shown to work. The same is true for established or inevitable nonunion.

Another potential bone graft substitute that has been

studied is autologous bone marrow aspirated from the iliac crest and injected into the region of either a bone defect or an ununited fracture.[114, 534] Autologous marrow has been claimed to be effective, although an adequate prospective randomized comparative study has not been reported.

### Timing

Recognizing the value of bone grafting, one might advocate the procedure as soon as possible after injury for patients who are likely to need it. Such timing would result in some grafts being applied to tibias that would have healed anyway while at the same time reducing the number of nonunions. However, its major drawback seems to be an increased risk of wound infection, with loss of the grafted bone and development of the very complications that the operation was performed to avoid. The optimal timing remains unclear. Some recommend grafting less severe injuries at the time of delayed wound closure. Behrens and co-workers found a high failure rate, usually because of infection, if such bone grafting was performed during the first week. They pointed out that delayed healing was not unusual for benign-appearing tibial fractures treated with fixators.[38] Blick and colleagues recommend early grafting based on a history of high-energy trauma. They suggest waiting 2 weeks after closure by suture, skin graft, or local muscle flap, but 6 weeks after a free muscle graft.[54] For this reason, Behrens and others have advised delaying bone grafting until the wounds are well healed and sufficient time has elapsed for soft tissue revascularization (e.g., 6 weeks or more). On the other hand, if the soft tissue condition permits, little is to be gained by waiting, except perhaps in very young patients, whose periosteum may produce enough bridging bone to make grafting unnecessary. Unless the area is infected or dysvascular or the patient's nutritional status has not yet been optimized, bone grafting should be considered for most externally fixed severe tibia fractures, except those with evidence of progressive healing on radiographs at 6 to 8 weeks. If an IM nail has been used, bone grafting, also delayed for soft tissue recovery, is reserved for injuries with bone loss, as described earlier, or those that fail to respond to one or more trials of exchange nailing.

### Technique

The optimal graft is autogenous cancellous bone, and it may be obtained in considerable quantity from the iliac crest, especially posteriorly. Alternative sources include the greater trochanter, the femoral condyles, or Gerdy's tubercle of the proximal end of the tibia. Harvesting graft material from the same side as the injury usually promotes more comfortable mobility.

Optimal graft placement spans the fracture zone under a healthy layer of muscle, either preexisting normal tissue or a muscle pedicle flap, if required for coverage. It is unclear whether posterolateral grafting or alternative approaches through native tissue are better than the use of a pocket under a muscle flap. Generally, it is better to avoid injured or healing tissue that is contracted, scarred, and stiff. Christian and associates have shown that space can be reserved for such a bone graft by placing antibiotic-laden PMMA beads under the muscle flap.[105] Once the soft tissues are healed, bone graft is exchanged for the beads.

Collaboration with the surgeon who transferred the flap is essential to avoid damage to its vascular pedicle. It is difficult to place a graft under a muscle flap—either local transposition or a free vascularized flap—unless space is saved for the graft in this manner. The same is true if the patient's local soft tissues have been closed over a bone defect. This difficulty should be considered during wound closure for patients who may need bone grafting.

Preparation of the graft site requires some attention. While protecting the adjacent muscle, the tibial surface is cleared of all soft tissue. Any necrotic cortex is removed, and a sharp osteotome is used to turn up superficial osseous flaps to expose bleeding bone. An alternative is to expose a bleeding bone surface with a well-irrigated power bur. Samples of bone should be sent for culture. The addition of antibiotics to cancellous bone grafts may be of value if the fracture site has become infected or is severely contaminated.[100, 101]

Phemister's technique of raising periosteal flaps from the anterior surfaces of the tibia and placing graft within the pockets thus formed is not well suited to recent injuries. Rarely is the anterior soft tissue stable enough for this procedure until months have elapsed after injury, unless healthier tissue has been provided by free or occasionally muscle transposition flap coverage. However, the posterior soft tissues are often healthy, and early grafting can be accomplished via the posterolateral approach originally described by Harmon[166, 229, 461, 535, 538] (Fig. 57–46). This technique is far easier if the patient is prone because the posteriorly located fibula overhangs the deep posterior compartment when the patient is on his side. An external fixator, if present, is left in place unless its pins are loose. Sterile, folded linen bolsters can be positioned to support an externally fixed tibia. The interval between the lateral and the posterior compartments is identified distally, where the peroneus muscles are tendinous. Dissection is carried medially around the fibula to the interosseous membrane distal and proximal to the zone of injury, which is then exposed by progressing from normal to injured tissue. The large veins of the deep and superficial calf muscle compartments are avoided by retracting rather than entering these spaces. After subperiosteally exposing the posterior tibial surface for 4 to 5 cm proximal and distal to the fracture, the cortex is "petalled" with a sharp osteotome. The fracture site is not taken down or excised, although a small tissue sample is obtained for culture. Previously harvested cancellous graft is then laid against the bleeding tibial cortex, as described previously. Graft should extend along the interosseous membrane to the fibula if fibular reinforcement is desired. Because incorporation of the fibula to form a synostosis may interfere with ankle function, this technique is not chosen unless it is necessary to reinforce a tibial defect. An oblique radiograph is best for assessing placement of the graft and should be obtained intraoperatively. Only the skin is closed over a suction drain, and the ankle is splinted in neutral. Rehabilitation resumes when the wound is healed, with weight bearing as soon as appropriate.

So-called central grafting uses an incision laterally over the fibula that is carried anteriorly around that bone and onto the interosseous membrane, similar to Harmon's

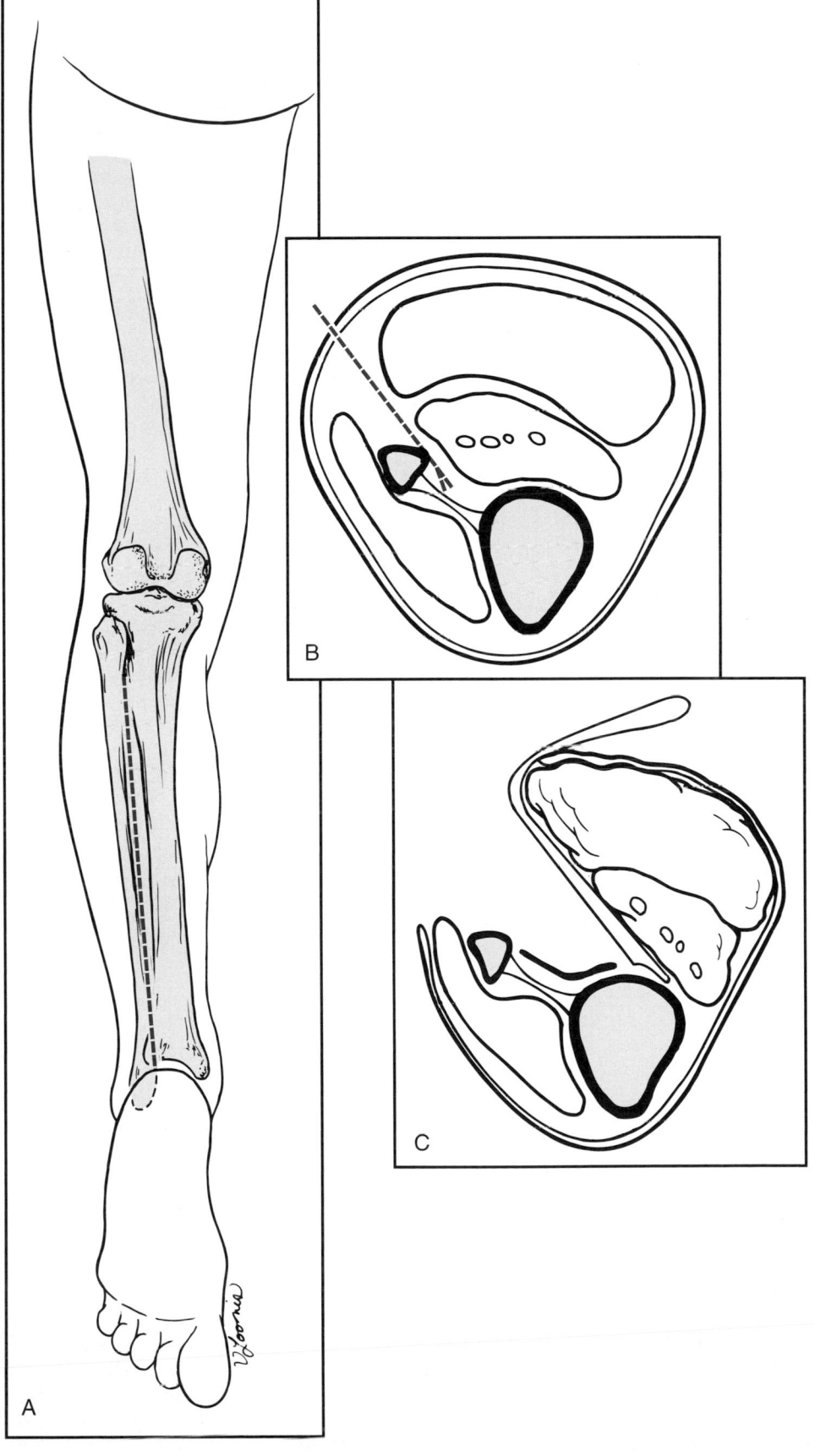

**FIGURE 57–46.** Posterolateral bone grafting is performed through the approach described by Harmon (see text). *A,* The patient is positioned prone, with the posterior of the ilium and entire leg prepared. The leg is exsanguinated by elevation or an Esmarch tourniquet, and the procedure is performed under pneumatic tourniquet control. The skin incision is shown. The peroneal tendons are identified distally and retracted laterally to gain access to the posterior aspect of the fibula. *B,* The deep posterior compartment muscles are elevated from the fibula and retracted medially, with care taken to avoid injuring the large veins of the posterior of the calf, as well as other neurovascular structures. Avoidance of injury is easiest if a long incision is made and the fracture site is approached proximally or distally, through normal tissue. With the intact interosseous membrane identified, it and the posterior surface of the tibia are followed to the fracture site. *C,* After exposing the fracture or nonunion, tissue is routinely taken for culture, and the tibia is bared approximately 5 cm proximally and distally and its surface "feathered" with a sharp osteotome. At this time, the tourniquet is deflated to check for bone perfusion and significant, usually venous bleeding. A separately harvested cancellous or corticocancellous autogenous iliac crest graft is packed in against the tibia and, if synostosis is desired, across the interosseous membrane to the fibula. An oblique radiograph taken perpendicular to the interosseous membrane (internally rotated) is advisable to ensure adequate placement of the graft. A large suction drain is placed under the muscles, and only the skin is closed. Even if the fracture is stable, the foot is initially splinted in neutral position to protect against soft tissue motion.

posterolateral approach. The contents of the anterior compartment are elevated en masse from the interosseous membrane and the lateral surface of the tibia to create a "central compartment" for bone graft material that can be used to gain synostosis or kept more medially along the tibia. The exposed cortices are roughened with an osteotome, and the graft is packed adjacent.[472] After significant anterior soft tissue injury, the anterior compartment may not be as well vascularized or as safe a bed for the graft as the more protected and muscular deep posterior compartment.

## Enhancement of Tibial Fracture Healing

Most patients are frustrated by the prolonged disability associated with tibial shaft fractures, particularly when progress toward healing is retarded or absent. Thus, surgeons continue to seek means that will accelerate or ensure timely fracture union (see Chapter 22). The wide range in healing times and the many factors, some known and some not, that affect the rate of healing make it difficult to demonstrate a clinically relevant effect on recovery time and similarly increase the risk of assuming such an effect when it does not exist. Various means of stimulating fracture union have been reviewed by Bostrom and Camacho and by Hannouche and co-workers.[71, 227] It is well accepted that mechanical stimulation (i.e., production of motion at the fracture site) promotes callus formation. This effect was recognized by Sarmiento and associates, among others, as one of the benefits of early weight bearing.[506, 509] Kenwright and colleagues have confirmed and clarified our understanding of the effects of the mechanical environment on tibial healing. Axial micromotion begun soon after fracture fixation and applied daily for a short period reduced healing time by approximately 6 weeks when compared with externally fixed controls not stimulated in this manner.[297] Although early micromotion seems to stimulate fracture healing, it may have deleterious effects on externally fixed fractures later in their course.[280] Heckman and co-workers showed that low-energy ultrasound treatments applied daily through a cast window for 20 minutes beginning in the first week after injury resulted in faster radiographic and clinical union of minor-severity tibial fractures (average displacement, 33%) treated in casts[234] (Fig. 57–47). Although union occurred 2 to 3 months sooner in the group treated with active ultrasound units, both groups included many patients whose weight bearing was delayed significantly longer than Sarmiento's recommendations. The average time to weight bearing was 45 days in the treated group and 49 days in the control subjects. This study did not report whether the treated patients returned to work and other activities any more rapidly than the control subjects did. Ultrasound treatments seem to counteract the detrimental effects of smoking on healing of tibial fractures.[115] Ultrasound fracture stimulation seems worth pursuing with further clinical investigations. It appears to counteract, at least partially, the detrimental effects of smoking on the healing rate of low-energy fractures. Its effectiveness in comparison to placebo for *ununited* fractures has now been accepted. It may thus be

reasonable to conclude that brief, daily low-energy ultrasound therapy is potentially beneficial for tibial fractures, even if it is started after the first week or if it is selectively applied to fractures that appear to be healing slowly. However, Emami and associates' prospective trial showed no additional benefit from ultrasound treatment of more severe tibia fractures that had been fixed with IM nails.[164] An even more vigorous mechanical stimulus, high-energy extracorporeal shock waves, also appears to stimulate bone union. This effect is more pronounced in nonsmokers and in those with bone scan–positive fracture sites.[482]

Various forms of electrical stimulation have been shown to be more effective than inactive controls as treatment of ununited fractures.[78, 227, 262] However, they are generally less effective than the reported results of surgical treatment. Sharrard studied the effectiveness of pulsating magnetic fields for tibial fractures with delayed union (16 to 32 weeks).[525] Forty-five percent of the stimulated fractures healed versus 12% of the controls. Like mechanical stimuli, electrical energy is more effective if the fracture zone has increased uptake on a Tc 99m MDP bone scan.[212] No studies have shown that electrical stimulation accelerates or ensures the healing of fresh fractures.

Bone graft substitutes currently available in the United States have not been shown to enhance fracture healing. Experimental and clinical evidence indicates that bone morphogenetic proteins promote fracture healing in nonunion models and in patients with ununited fractures.[56, 71, 180, 181, 227] It is not yet clear whether bone morphogenetic protein preparations will accelerate normal fracture healing or will reduce the chance of delayed healing in patients with fractures at risk.

## Assessment of Healing

The decision that a tibial fracture is healed is more a matter of judgment than identifying an obvious end-point. Progressive bone remodeling with eventual obliteration of an apparent fracture zone occurs over a period of many months after union is initially achieved. Functional rehabilitation, as measured by muscle strength and endurance, joint mobility, performance of physical tasks, and patient-perceived outcome measures, also requires an additional 6 to 12 months before reaching a plateau.[186, 542] Therefore, union should be seen as an important threshold rather than termination of the healing and recovery process. Nonetheless, an operational definition is essential, for union implies that external support and restrictions on activity can be progressively discontinued. Conventionally, union is diagnosed when fracture motion is not evident, the patient can walk without pain or support, and radiographs demonstrate bone continuity on multiple views. The presence of stable internal fixation, particularly an IM nail, impairs our ability to determine whether union has occurred. In spite of apparent clinical union, some patients with internally fixed fractures will not have achieved radiographic union. Although radiographic union generally does occur, often over a period of many months, the possibility of delayed fixation failure because of micromotion of an ununited fracture site may raise concern.

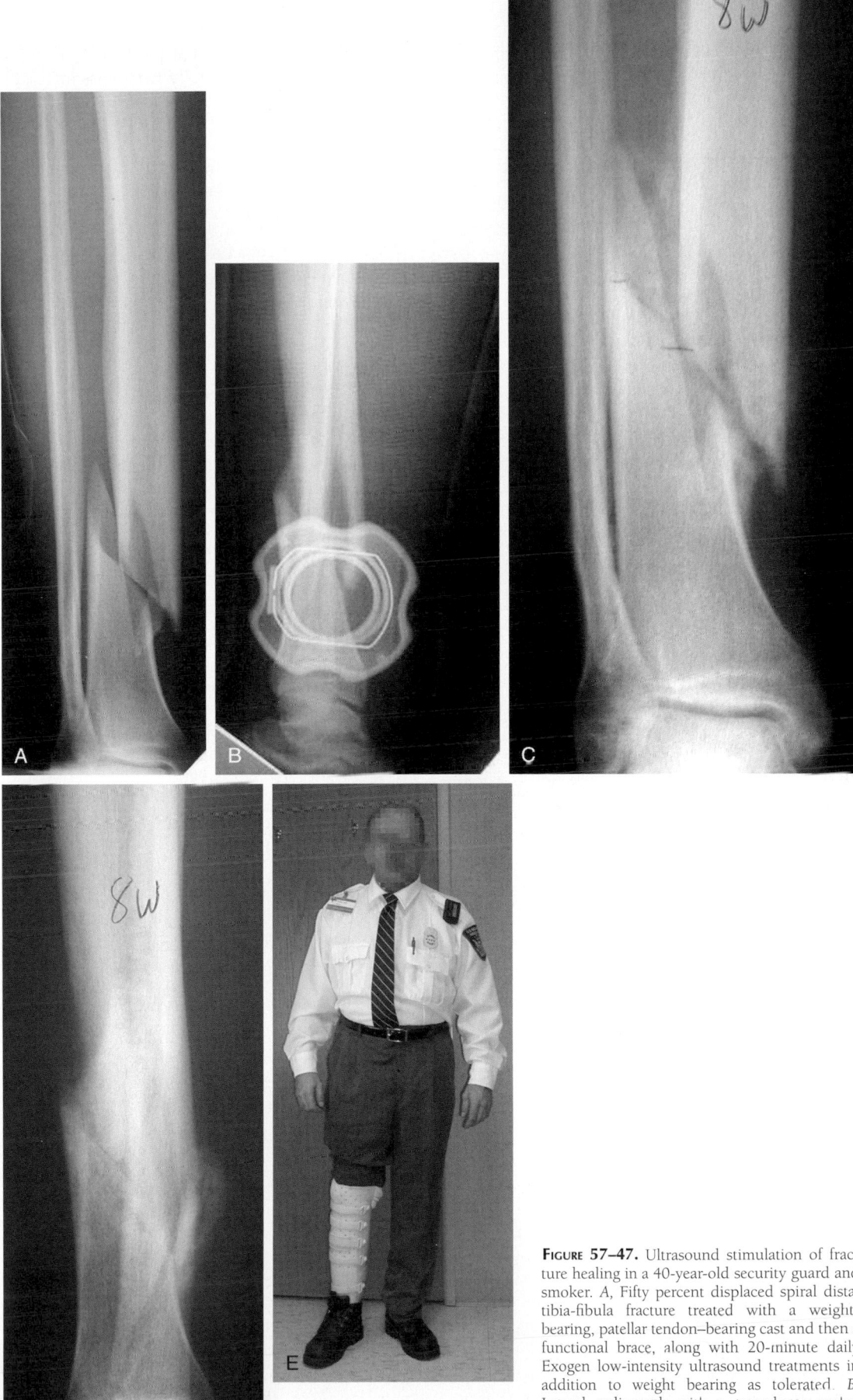

**FIGURE 57–47.** Ultrasound stimulation of fracture healing in a 40-year-old security guard and smoker. *A,* Fifty percent displaced spiral distal tibia-fibula fracture treated with a weight-bearing, patellar tendon–bearing cast and then a functional brace, along with 20-minute daily Exogen low-intensity ultrasound treatments in addition to weight bearing as tolerated. *B,* Lateral radiograph with a transducer socket mounted on the cast. *C, D,* Satisfactory alignment with visible callus at 8 weeks. *E,* Light duty at 4 weeks and full duty 10 weeks after the injury, still in the fracture brace.

The diagnosis of fracture union is based on the history, physical examination, and radiographs. The patient is asked about pain at the fracture site, especially with activities. The pain should have diminished considerably from the first weeks after injury, but it is rarely absent.[130, 253, 541] Patients with united fractures are usually able to bear full weight without the use of crutches or a cane. The elapsed time since injury must be considered, though in reference to the severity of the original injury because more severe injuries typically require more time to heal. In Ellis' series, for example, 80% of minor (undisplaced) tibial fractures had healed by approximately 12 weeks. Eighty percent of moderate (displaced, noncomminuted) fractures healed by 15 weeks, but it took 27 weeks to achieve union in 80% of tibial fractures with major severity (complete displacement with significant comminution or a significant open wound).[161] On physical examination, a healed fracture exhibits no motion or pain with bending stress in any direction. Some local tenderness to direct pressure may be noted. The increased warmth typical of healing fractures is less apparent. Strain gauges attached to external fixator pins can be used to document bending stiffness, the mechanical property assessed manually by the clinician as "fracture site stability." Using such strain gauges, Richardson and co-workers demonstrated that sagittal-plane stiffness of 15 Nm/degree is a threshold that defines tibial fracture union.[470]

AP and lateral radiographs are standard for monitoring alignment of tibial fractures, but the addition of both 45° oblique views aids in the evaluation of healing.[152] New bone formation (radiographic callus) should bridge the fracture defect on each radiograph. Nonunion, if present, will usually be evident on at least one of the four views (see Fig. 57–9). Tomograms and CT may be helpful but are generally no more conclusive than well-exposed standard films. Stress radiographs with manually applied force may be helpful but are rarely convincing unless movement is obvious on physical examination. Panjabi and colleagues demonstrated that physicians are not reliably able to assess bone strength from a single set of radiographs.[433] Hammer and co-workers showed this limitation clearly for tibial fractures.[226] Blokhuis and associates have added further evidence.[56] The patient's *serial* films, taken over a period of 3 or more months, should be reviewed carefully for signs of problems: progressive deformity, hardware failure, lack of maturing callus, and an increasingly evident fracture cleft. Schnarkowski and colleagues demonstrated that change in quantitative fracture callus volume on serial CT scans predicts progress toward union of externally fixed tibial shaft fractures.[515] However, neither the appearance of a tibial fracture on a single CT scan nor its interpretation by a radiologist has proved more helpful in my experience than the history, physical examination, and four-view radiographs, occasionally supplemented by fluoroscopy. It is important to be aware of differences in apparent healing related to different techniques of fracture management. Immediately after removal of a rigid external fixator, a fracture site can feel very stiff, even though minimal radiographic callus is present. When reexamined 1 or 2 days later, obvious motion may be present. As mentioned earlier, fracture mobility and tenderness are abolished by intact internal fixation. Therefore, these important clinical signs of incomplete healing are typically absent after internal fixation, unless it has failed.

Anatomic reduction and interfragmentary compression are hallmarks of rigid internal fixation. If achieved, the fracture line may not be evident on the initial postfixation radiographs. Fractures thus fixed with absolute stability exhibit essentially no external callus formation. In this situation, healing must be diagnosed primarily by the absence of pain and radiographic signs of instability (e.g., external callus, loss of fixation, or bone resorption around implants) as the patient progresses from non–weight bearing to full weight bearing *over an appropriate time period,* according to the surgeon's judgment and experience. Because internal fixation does not accelerate union, 4 or more months must typically elapse before unrestricted activity can be allowed.

## Results of Tibial Fractures

Historically, the results of tibial fractures were reported in relatively simplistic terms: nonunion rate, average healing time, occurrence of infection, and a few radiographic findings such as angulation or shortening. Factors that give a fair picture of the results include final deformity (rotation, length, angulation, location), actual time to both union and completion of rehabilitation, ultimate functional performance, and mobility of the foot and ankle joints. Also important, but rarely included are length of hospitalization, associated cost and complications, number of operations, outpatient rehabilitation, and cost of disability. Clearly, many valid indicators of outcome can be used after a tibia fracture. Efforts to include a number of them have resulted in summary rating scales developed by surgeons, but typically not validated by patients (see Tables 57–6 and 57–7).

Recent progress in outcomes assessment has improved awareness of methodology and interpretation of results. A variety of health status assessment instruments are now available. Their sensitivity and specificity for different outcomes of interest after tibia fractures remain to be defined. For example, a rating system developed to measure lower extremity injury outcome could be expected to provide greater relevant detail for tibial fractures than a general health status instrument would (see Chapter 24). A more detailed assessment instrument might be required to identify relatively small variations in athletic performance that could be very significant for certain patients. However, such outcome measures would not reveal important considerations such as the rate and severity of complications, the cost to the patient and society, the length of time before return to work, or the risk of late complications. Additionally, patients are concerned not only about pain and function but also about the appearance of their leg.

How results are assessed affects the perception of outcome quality, particularly when summary scales such as those discussed later are used. For example, Bridgman and Baird showed that published standards for outcomes of tibial fractures were so variable that they did not permit comparison among different publications. Depending on which criteria were chosen, 4% to 42% of their group of 51 patients could be considered to have suboptimal results.[76] It is clear that nonunion, osteomyelitis, gross deformity, amputation, and severe pain are undesirable outcomes. They are often used as criteria for a poor result. However, after corrective treatment, nonunion or infection may ultimately yield a very satisfactory limb, whereas a united fracture, albeit with deformity, contractures of the foot and ankle, and poor function, might in some series be reported as a satisfactory result. For grade IIIC open fractures, amputation often provides a better result in several ways than limb salvage does. Clearly, which factors are included and which are excluded will have a large bearing on an author's conclusions about treatment efficacy. Similarly, the definitions used for fracture union and for significant deformity affect the interpretation of results. The relative importance of the various factors that affect outcome after tibial fractures is not clear, nor is the way that they are best stratified.[76] For example, how much angulation is acceptable? Merchant and Dietz's and Kristensen and colleagues' long-term follow-up studies failed to show a threshold beyond which angular deformity compromises late results.[320, 379] Others, however, support the well-accepted concept that excessive angulation is a problem.[254, 455, 456, 603] This topic has been reviewed by Tetsworth and Paley.[566] Without confidence in a threshold level of deformity that results in arthritis or interferes with function, any definition of "malunion" must be arbitrary.

The timing of any outcome assessment is important inasmuch as the process of recovery is gradual and lengthy. Evaluation at set intervals after injury offers a truer indication of the time course of recovery than does one based on findings at typical follow-up visits or when a group of patients are recalled for "long-term" assessment. Time needed for healing is an understandable focus of studies on tibial fracture treatment. A figure such as the number of months until union seems concrete and objective, but in reality, judgments are typically made about healing at outpatient visits occurring at intervals of at least several weeks. Furthermore, they are arbitrary and based on symptoms, function, and radiographic appearance. The precision and significance of several-week differences in healing time must therefore be questioned.

The timing of assessment may be particularly important when the parameters studied are slow to recover. An example is mobility of the hindfoot, which may continue to improve for 1 to 2 years after injury.[453] It is unclear how long it takes for various tibial outcome measures to become final. Table 57–5 demonstrates mean times to recovery of various functional abilities in patients treated by the Edinburgh group with reamed IM nails. It should be expected that other treatment protocols and differences among patients might affect a given person's time to achieve one or more of these milestones. DaSilva and colleagues found that time to maximal healing was 10 months for Ellis minor-severity, 12 for moderate-severity, and 17 for major-severity tibial fractures.[130]

Confounding variables—other injuries and other patient-related factors—must be considered before outcome differences are ascribed to differences in injury severity or treatment. It is important to acknowledge that multiple issues affect a given patient's result after a tibial

| TABLE 57–5 | | |

**Ability to Perform Defined Tasks after Tibial Shaft Fractures Treated with Reamed Intramedullary Nailing**

| Task | Mean Number of Weeks* |
|---|---|
| Maintain awkward posture | 7 |
| Prolonged kneeling | 24 |
| Stoop or crawl | 18 |
| Prolonged walking | 6 |
| Climb stairs or slope | 3 |
| Walk over rough ground | 9 |
| Jump | 25 |
| Climb ladder | 18 |
| Run | 27 |
| Restart work | 13 |
| Restart sports training | 25 |
| Restart sports | 41 |

*Mean time to resume listed activity for 93 patients.
*Source:* Data from Gaston, P., et al. J Bone Joint Surg Br 81:71–76, 1999.

shaft fracture in different ways. Gaston and colleagues prospectively investigated the possibility of predicting tibial fracture outcome after reamed IM nailing with several accepted classification systems: AO/OTA, Tscherne closed fracture scale, and the comminution assessment scale of Winquist and Hansen, as well as the amount of displacement, the location of the fracture, and fibular integrity.[185] They considered union rate and time, malunion rate, deep infection rate, and the need for reoperation, as well as the ability to perform a variety of functional tasks (see Table 57–5), and found that the Tscherne scale was somewhat predictive of outcome but that none of the measures had significant predictive value. Although many surgeons, such as Henley and associates and Rommens, support the belief that the severity of the soft tissue injury strongly affects tibial shaft fracture outcome, it may be that our methods of quantitating this injury are too crude to demonstrate the correlation.[240, 481]

Current evidence does, however, suggest some important facts about tibial fracture results: recovery takes many months and is rarely complete, especially in the patient's viewpoint. Complications are common after any form of treatment, and different treatment methods have different types of complications. Thus, it is inherently difficult to establish that one treatment is clearly superior to another for all grades of tibial fracture severity. However, increasing evidence suggests that better results, at least for more severe fractures, are obtained with internal fixation, particularly with reamed IM nailing.[63, 71, 147, 252, 280, 342, 575]

Horne,[253] Skoog,[542] and DaSilva[130] and their colleagues reported residua of tibial shaft fractures and found that restricted ankle motion correlated with symptoms and impaired function. Kyro and co-workers[323] similarly reported a high prevalence of persisting objective and subjective problems after tibial shaft fractures, as did Greenwood and colleagues[203] and Skoog and co-workers.[542]

When assessing a result reported only as a mean time or percentage, one must remember, as pointed out by

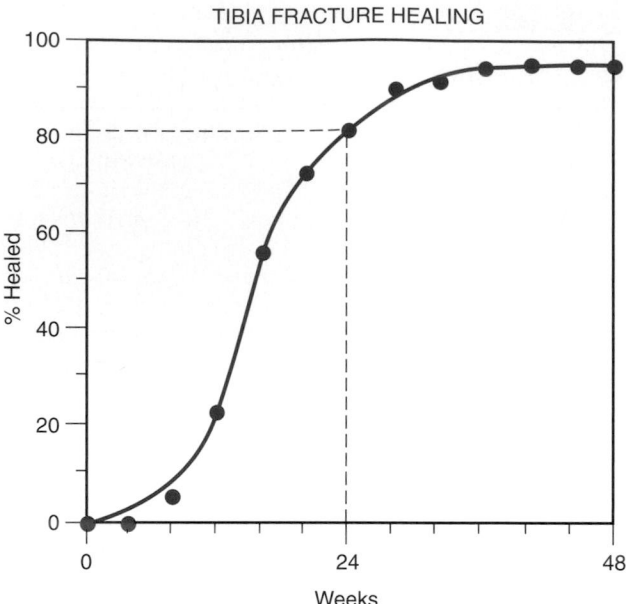

**Figure 57–48.** The time required for union of tibial fractures is best understood when plotted as percent healed against elapsed time. Note that 80% of this pooled series of tibia fractures had healed at 24 weeks. (Redrawn from Austin, R.T. Injury 9:93–101, 1977.)

Austin offers two answers to this problem: stratification of injury severity and the cumulative healing curve, with the percent healed on the ordinate and weeks since injury on the abscissa.[25] Figure 57–48 illustrates this format. Rightward displacement of the healing curve, its more gradual slope, and failure to arrive at 100% healing are typical of patient sets with more severe injuries and less successful treatment. If injury severity is stratified, effects of treatment become clear when groups of patients are presented in this manner. Figure 57–49 demonstrates the importance of both fracture severity and treatment by presenting the nonoperative results of Ellis[161] and Burwell's[90, 161] similarly stratified series of plated tibial fractures. The healing curves graphically display the relatively poorer results of this plated series, especially for more severe injuries. Also apparent is the relatively smaller difference between minor and moderate injuries, as classified by Ellis, in comparison to the difference between his moderate and major injuries. The distinction between minor and moderate, which seems irrelevant with cast treatment, does, however, become apparent in Burwell's plated series.

Another important observation revealed by cumulative healing curves is the often quite substantial overlap in the results of different groups (i.e., some severe injuries do heal within the same length of time as minor ones).

Austin used cumulative healing curves to report his prospective study of Sarmiento's PTB cast for tibial fractures[26] (Fig. 57–50). Of particular note was the marked difference between minor- and moderate-severity groups, although the latter was rather small. Ninety percent of minor fractures had healed by 20 weeks, but it took 47 weeks for 90% of the moderate ones (completely displaced, minor comminution, minor wound) to heal with this treatment. Cumulative percent curves can be

Watson-Jones and Coltart, that "it means nothing to find that 1074 fractures of the tibia had an average time of union of 17 weeks. The figure depends wholly on the proportion of simple uncomplicated fractures uniting in about 10 weeks, difficult fractures uniting in 10 to 20 weeks, infected fractures uniting in 6 to 12 months, and avascular fractures uniting in 1 to 3 years."[614]

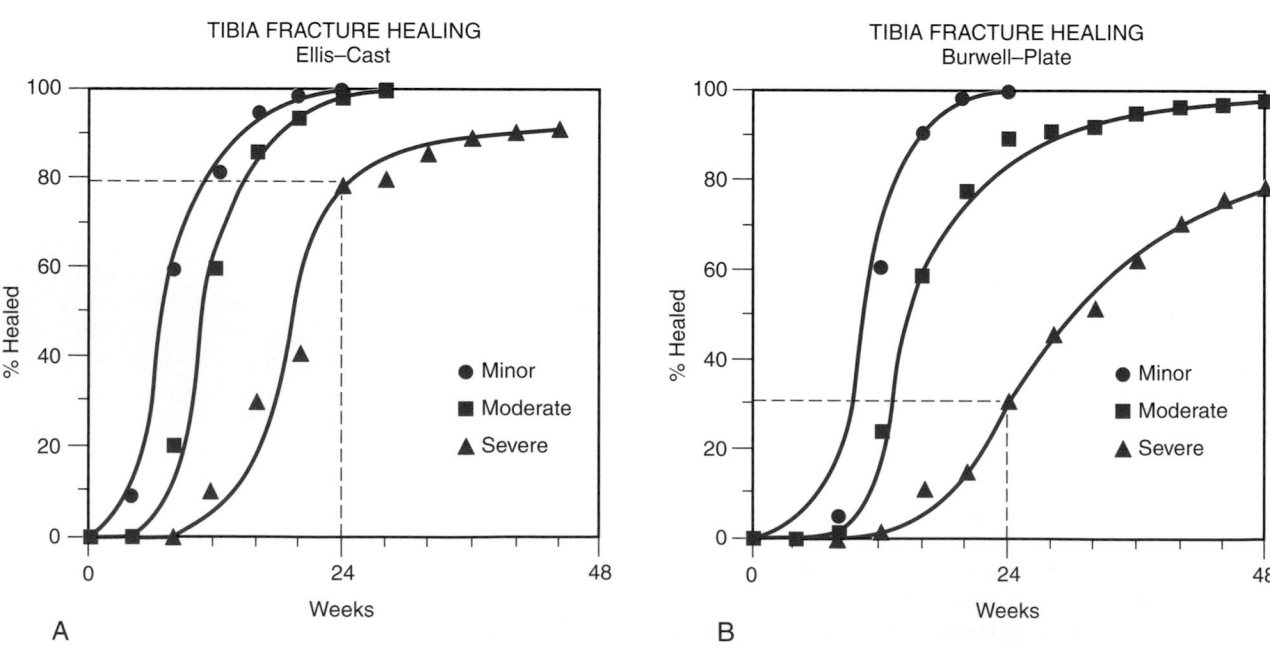

**Figure 57–49.** Austin plotted Ellis' data for cast treatment (A) and Burwell's data for plating (B) of minor-, moderate-, and major-severity tibial shaft fractures, as shown here, with separate curves for cumulative percent healed versus elapsed time for each of the three Ellis severity grades. This chart clarifies differences in outcome and their potential significance for an individual patient's fracture healing. (A, B, Redrawn from Austin, R.T. Injury 9:93–101, 1977.)

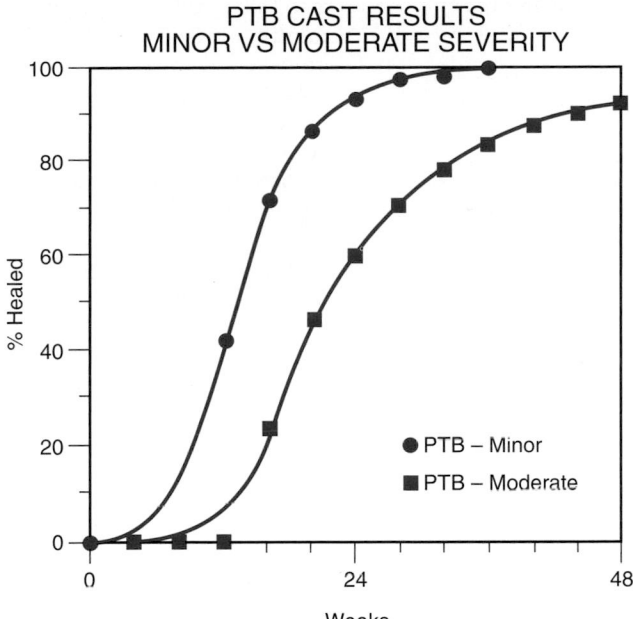

**FIGURE 57–50.** Differences in healing time between minor- and moderate-severity fractures treated by Austin in patellar tendon–bearing casts with early weight bearing. (Data from Austin, R.T. Injury 13:10–22, 1981.)

used to report end-points other than fracture healing, as in Figure 57–51, which shows time until return to work after transverse tibial fracture.[11]

### TIBIAL FRACTURE OUTCOME SCALES

Bauer and colleagues[33] classified the final results of tibial fractures into three grades: good (minimal or no complaints, full or slightly limited function), fair (minor complaints or limitation of function), and poor (major complaints, nonunion, draining wound, amputation, or poor function of the knee or ankle). Edwards expanded on this scheme and used eight different parameters plus nonunion, osteomyelitis, and amputation to classify results.[156] His system, shown in Table 57–6, considers pain; ability to work; gait; sports activity; motion of the knee, ankle, and foot; and leg swelling. Notably absent is any reference to deformity. Edwards reported the following overall results: for 149 spiral fractures: good, 83%; fair, 17%; and poor, 0%; for 149 closed transverse fractures: good, 75%; fair, 20%; and poor, 5%; and for 106 open transverse fractures: good, 59%; fair, 26%; and poor, 14%.

Johner and Wruhs used a four-level scale for classifying the results of tibial fractures[270] (Table 57–7). They included deformity, which has often been omitted, but otherwise assessed factors similar to those of Edwards. Although some overlap exists between categories, their "excellent" and "good" categories correspond fairly well to Edwards' "good." "Poor" has essentially the same criteria in both studies. In this rating system, they reported results at 4 to 8 years for 283 patients with mostly closed injuries (84%) classified by fracture morphology (see Fig. 57–7). All were treated by skeletal fixation with a plate (67%), nail (30%), or external fixator (3%). Eighty-six percent of the

group had good or excellent results, 9% had fair results, and 5% had poor results. When reviewed separately for different categories, however, the proportion with good or excellent results ranged from 50% to 100%. Consistent with other observers, these investigators found that spiral or oblique fractures (A1, A2, B1, C1), caused by typically indirect mechanisms, had the best outcomes (93% to 100% good or excellent results). Transverse fractures resulting from the application of direct force (A3, B2) had slightly poorer outcomes (80% to 92% good or excellent results). Comminuted transverse fractures (B3, C2, C3) caused by the direct application of greater force had the poorest results, ranging from 50% to 75% good or excellent outcomes. It must be emphasized that the cases reported by Johner and Wruhs from the University Orthopaedic Clinic in Bern, Switzerland, were treated by experts in internal fixation and included a higher proportion of closed and low- to moderate-energy injuries than might be seen in a center that deals exclusively with serious polytrauma.

## COMPLICATIONS AND THEIR MANAGEMENT

The essence of treating tibial fractures is the avoidance of complications, most of which have thus already been mentioned. This section reviews the complications of tibial fractures, which are listed comprehensively in Table 57–8.

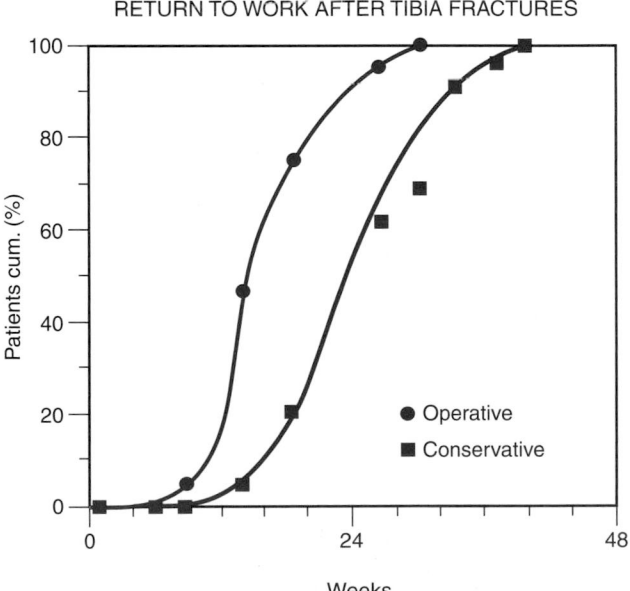

**FIGURE 57–51.** Cumulative percentage of patients returned to work versus time since injury in a retrospectively matched series of transverse tibia fractures from the files of the Swiss National Insurance Company. In this series, 50% of patients treated operatively had returned to work by 14 weeks as compared with 22 weeks for 50% of the nonoperatively managed patients. Note that all patients in both groups did return to work in less than 40 weeks after injury. (Data from Allgöwer, M. AO/ASIF Dialogue 1:1, 1985.)

**Table 57–6** ...............................................................................

Edwards' Classification System for Results after Tibial Fracture Treatment

| | Good | Fair | Poor |
|---|---|---|---|
| 1. Pain | Little or none | Slight | Severe |
| 2. Work capacity | Normal | Difficulty or inability to do heavy work | Markedly decreased, light seated work only |
| 3. Limp | None | Slight with or after severe exercise | Constant |
| 4. Sports activity | Normal | Decreased ability | Short walks only |
| 5. Knee motion | Stable, full extension, loss of flexion less than 20° | Stable, full extension, flexion to at least 90° | Lack of full extension, flexion to less than 90° |
| 6. Ankle motion | Less than 10° loss of dorsiflexion, less than 20° loss of plantar flexion | Dorsiflexion over 90°, less than 30° loss of plantar flexion | Dorsiflexion less than 90°, more than 30° loss of plantar flexion |
| 7. Foot motion | Less than 25% decrease of pronation and supination | Moderately decreased | Severely decreased |
| 8. Swelling of lower part of leg | Slight, only after exercise | Slight | Constant |

Poor results also include
1. Amputation
2. Osteomyelitis with recurrent drainage
3. Pseudarthrosis

................................................................................................

*Source:* Edwards, P. Acta Orthop Scand Suppl 76:33, 1965.

## Fracture Site Problems

### WOUND SLOUGH

Wound-healing difficulties often result from damage sustained at the time of injury, especially if degloving occurs and results in loss of the radially oriented blood supply to the skin. Not unusually, the problem becomes evident after a surgical incision is placed through the injured area. Deep abrasions, crushing, significant swelling, and fracture blisters are some of the indicators of an area at risk. Problems can often be avoided by resisting the temptation to operate through such an area until it has recovered.

The combination of contused and poorly perfused tissue, an open wound, and bacterial contamination predisposes to infection, which may remain superficial or, because of proximity to the fracture site, may involve this site as well. In the absence of significant infection, a superficial wound will heal unless accompanied by an inadequate local blood supply, fracture instability, edema, or external pressure. Early recognition of a skin flap that is in jeopardy is important. Correction of some or all of these factors might salvage it. If full-thickness necrosis does occur and the fracture site is exposed before the formation of well-organized callus, a deep wound infection is likely to develop. Immediate débridement of such a flap and replacement with viable soft tissue coverage may prevent a deep infection and promote fracture healing.

A small wound, especially if it does not communicate with a fresh fracture hematoma, will often heal satisfactorily with minimal treatment. Bone with intact periosteum will rapidly be covered by granulation tissue. If it is bare and necrotic, this process takes much longer, although it may still occur, especially in smaller wounds. Even exposed hardware may be covered by secondary wound

**Table 57–7** ...............................................................................

Johner and Wruhs' Criteria for Evaluation of Final Results after Tibial Shaft Fracture

| | Excellent (Left = Right) | Good | Fair | Poor |
|---|---|---|---|---|
| Nonunion, osteitis, amputation | None | None | None | Yes |
| Neurovascular disturbances | None | Minimal | Moderate | Severe |
| Deformity | | | | |
|   Varus/valgus | None | 2°–5° | 6°–10° | >10° |
|   Anteversion/recurvation | 0°–5° | 6°–10° | 11°–20° | >20° |
|   Rotation | 0°–5° | 6°–10° | 11°–20° | >20° |
|   Shortening | 0–5 mm | 6–10 mm | 11–20 mm | >20 mm |
| Mobility | | | | |
|   Knee | Normal | >80% | >75% | <75% |
|   Ankle | Normal | >75% | >50% | <50% |
|   Subtalar joint | >75% | >50% | <50% | ... |
| Pain | None | Occasional | Moderate | Severe |
| Gait | Normal | Normal | Insignificant limp | Significant limp |
| Strenuous activities | Possible | Limited | Severely limited | Impossible |

................................................................................................

*Source:* Johner, R.; Wruhs, O. Clin Orthop 178:12, 1983.

**TABLE 57–8** ......................................

Complications of Fractures of the Tibia and Fibula

Bone and fracture site
  Deep infection
    Acute
    Chronic osteitis, drainage, or osteomyelitis
  Bone loss
  Delayed union
  Nonunion
  Malunion
  Loss of alignment in cast or brace
  Fixation problems
    Failure of hardware
    Failure of bone
  Refracture
Skin and subcutaneous tissue
  Wound slough
  Wound infection (superficial)
  Pressure sore
Nerve
  Direct injury
  Pressure from cast or brace
  Ischemic damage (compartment syndrome)
  Reflex sympathetic dystrophy
Vascular
  Arterial occlusion
  Venous insufficiency
  Deep venous thrombosis
  Compartment syndrome
Joint motion
  Associated joint surface fracture
  Contracture
    Knee
    Ankle
    Subtalar
    Foot and toe
  Late arthritis (secondary to deformity)
  Fatigue fracture distally
Functional
  Pain
  Disability (temporary vs. permanent)
    Objective
      Muscle strength
      Endurance
    Subjective
    Activities of daily living
    Work
    Sport
  Cosmesis

......................................

healing, but the process is slow and often punctuated by episodes of infection with pain, swelling, erythema, and drainage. Such problems often occur after a draining wound heals completely and may be less frequent if a small opening remains. Although a chronic infection persists around such an exposed plate, bone healing often continues slowly if the fixation is secure. Once the fracture is united, removal of the plate and superficial débridement of its bed are often followed by secondary wound healing and resolution of active or recurrent flares of infection, unless sequestra remain.[88]

It is important to recognize that many fractures with exposed bone or hardware can unite without hardware removal or surgical soft tissue coverage. No well-supported guidelines have been presented for treating established soft tissue sloughing. In many situations, slowly progressive healing may be more acceptable than aggressive débridement and soft tissue coverage. If fixation

is secure, healing is progressing, and infection does not remain active, simple wound care may be all that is required until the fracture is healed, at which point it is often quite simple to proceed with hardware removal, débridement, and delayed coverage. If progress is not satisfactory, especially if the fixation becomes unstable, a change in treatment is required. Such change usually entails hardware removal and radical débridement of necrotic bone and soft tissue. External fixation, muscle flap coverage, and delayed bone grafting offer an effective salvage.[105] Alternatively, the Ilizarov techniques of bone transport and treatment of nonunion may be considered, as discussed earlier in the sections on infection and nonunion.

## ACUTE INFECTION

The presence of a deep infection is usually heralded by increasing pain, drainage from the wound, or the development of a sinus. Wound exploration with deep tissue cultures or, occasionally, aspiration permits early diagnosis. It is important to recognize the significance of these signs of infection because delay in diagnosis or treatment compromises the outcome. Some infections may be chronic and indolent; they interfere little with healing and perhaps respond satisfactorily, after fracture union, to hardware removal, débridement, and a brief course of antibiotics. More often, an acute infection in the first weeks after injury results in progressive tissue necrosis, as well as cessation of fracture healing. Surgical treatment, not just antibiotics, is required to salvage a reasonable result.

Occasionally, an infection is superficial, without deeper extension, but this situation is rare because of the tibia fracture's extensive zone of injury. The surgeon must always suspect the worst. Another potentially confusing issue is soft tissue necrosis resulting from injury or devascularization of wound flaps. Though initially indolent and without obvious signs and symptoms of infection, such problems cannot be ignored because they will typically become infected unless the necrotic tissue is excised and the wound is closed with healthy tissue. Closure often requires a plastic surgical procedure.

Acute deep fracture site infections and chronic osteomyelitis have significant similarities. Both processes involve necrotic, devascularized bone. Effective treatment requires surgical removal of such sequestra. Antibiotics may be helpful, but they are only an adjunct. Stability is crucial and is best provided surgically if the fracture is not united. Usually, external fixation is the best way to stabilize an infected fracture. It avoids an implant that compromises local host resistance and can provide excellent stability. Various host factors, especially local vascularity and systemic nutrition, also play significant roles. The sequence of treatment is usually (1) débridement; (2) stabilization with external fixation; (3) provision of healthy soft tissue coverage, with muscle pedicle or free muscle flap grafts frequently necessary; and (4) repair (with bone graft or traction histogenesis) of any resulting defect.[88, 121, 166, 310, 362, 472, 574, 645] Adequate débridement often produces a defect in the tibia, management of which is discussed later (Fig. 57–52).

**Infection after Intramedullary Nailing.** If an infected tibial fracture remains satisfactorily stabilized by an IM nail and if the infection can be controlled, it may be best to continue with IM stabilization until the fracture is healed.[121, 645] If an abscess is present, it must be drained, and such a finding suggests the need for removal of the nail and reaming of the medullary canal. Radiographic evidence of intramedullary bone erosion is another sign that IM reaming is indicated. If these measures gain control

of infection, one might consider replacement of the nail until the fracture is healed (Fig. 57–53). After control of infection, bone grafting may be advisable to stimulate union, address a defect, or both. Suppressive antibiotics are chosen according to sensitivity studies on cultures from deep tissue specimens. Typically, a medullary infection that is aggressive or has been present a long time results in nail loosening. Removal plus exchange of a loose nail for a

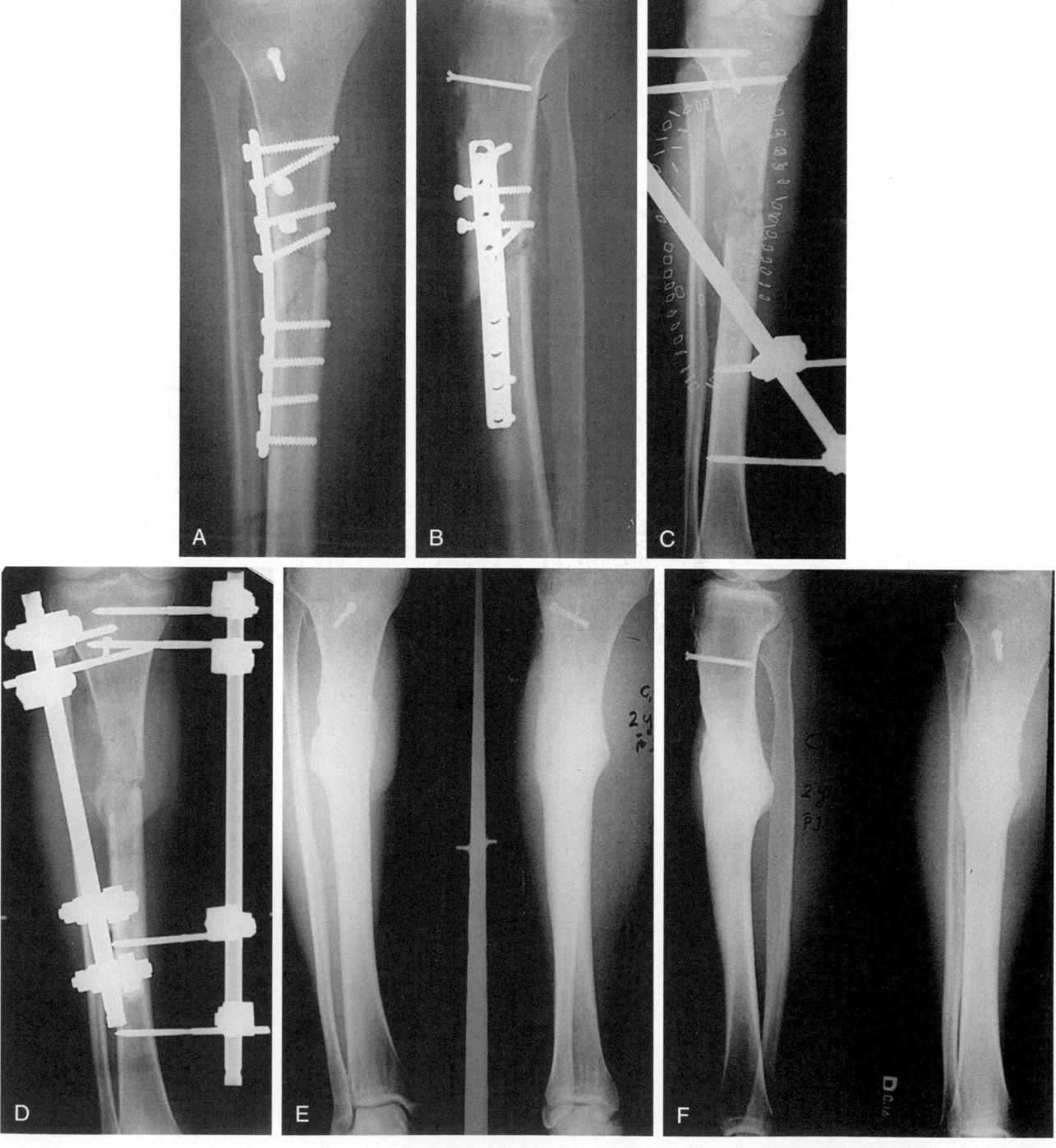

**Figure 57–52.** Infected draining tibial shaft fracture with exposed hardware after plate fixation. *A, B,* The hardware became loose before fracture healing. *C,* The plate and screws were removed, and an external fixator with an oblique frame was applied for stability and easy access for serial wound débridement. This step was followed by development of a medial gastrocnemius muscle pedicle flap and cancellous bone grafting once the wound was clean and the bone entirely covered by healthy granulation tissue. *D,* Once the wounds were healed, the fixator was modified to gain purchase of additional pins in the osteoporotic proximal metaphysis for increased fracture stability. *E, F,* Healed fracture. The wound healed as well, and the patient is minimally symptomatic.

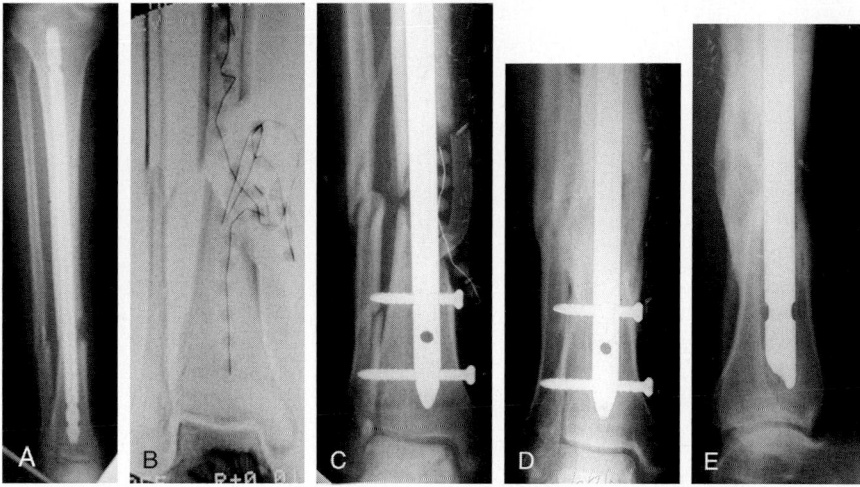

**FIGURE 57–53.** Early infection after intramedullary (IM) nailing. *A,* Purulent drainage from an open fracture wound a month after perfunctory débridement and IM nailing. *B,* Nail removal, débridement to bleeding bone, and temporary external fixation. *C,* Renailing a week later with insertion of tobramycin-loaded polymethyl methacrylate beads and administration of intravenous antibiotics. *D,* Beads replaced with bone graft 6 weeks later. *E,* Two years after injury, the patient has fully recovered without recurrent infection.

larger one provides both increased stability and a measure of débridement by gently reaming the canal to a larger diameter. If used, a tourniquet should be deflated, as always, before reaming. The reamed material is cultured to confirm appropriate antibiotic choices. A flagrant infection after IM nailing may not respond to such treatment. Persisting drainage, aggressive organisms, and recurrent infection all suggest a lack of response. A metaphyseal area of infection that will not be adequately débrided by reaming may predispose to failure. If attempted nail exchange does not succeed, one should proceed with nail removal, more aggressive débridement, and external fixation[121, 645] (Fig. 57–54).

## SUPERFICIAL WOUND INFECTION

Superficial wound infections occasionally develop during open treatment of closed fractures, as well as after open tibial injuries. Definition and diagnosis are important because trivial treatment of a deep infection is usually ineffective. Even worse, failure to identify and treat a deep infection promptly and appropriately may compromise its definitive care. Therefore, pain, tenderness, redness, swelling, and drainage should be seen first as a possible indication of a deep infection if these symptoms persist beyond the normal first few days of wound inflammation.[88] Adequate deep cultures are essential for wounds with any indication of infection extending below the subcutaneous tissue. Tissue samples for culture can usually be obtained by needle aspiration with sterile technique. The fracture hematoma and the area around any hardware should be sampled and studied with Gram stain as well as culture and sensitivity tests. If no fluid can be aspirated, introduction of a small volume of nonbacteriostatic saline may permit culture. A more certain test is operative exploration of the wound, with tissue samples obtained under direct vision for bacteriologic studies. Because it leads to prompt definitive diagnosis and care, formal surgical exploration of a possibly infected wound is safer than merely opening it on the ward and instituting dressing changes. Early aggressive management of a significant infection minimizes recovery time and improves results. However, certain patients with superficial erythema, possibly a bacterial cellulitis, have no signs of

deep infection and respond in a few days to rest, elevation of the extremity, and antibiotic treatment appropriate for gram-positive cocci. Some infections are undoubtedly superficial, although the burden of proof is on the treating surgeon. With time, the presence of a significant deep infection may become evident.

## CHRONIC INFECTION (INCLUDING INFECTED NONUNION)

Chronic osteomyelitis after a tibia fracture exhibits a wide spectrum of severity. A low-grade infection causing little pain and tolerable wound drainage and not associated with significant symptoms from nonunion, malalignment, or dysfunctional contractures may need little, if any treatment. However, any of these potential problems, alone or in combination, is an indication for treatment if they are severe enough. The surgeon and patient together must decide whether the patient's disease is troublesome enough to justify the morbidity associated with a proposed treatment option. The legendary image of chronic post-traumatic tibial osteomyelitis being a lifelong illness unless it is "cured" by amputation has been tempered by remarkable results achieved with expert modern treatment, such as Cierny's recent 99% 2-year success rate for mid-diaphyseal infected nonunion.[106] Although the psychosocial impact of infected tibial nonunion can be profound,[574] significant quality-of-life improvement can be anticipated from successful treatment.[72] One should not delay adequate surgical treatment of an infected tibial fracture in the hope that antibiotics alone will solve the problem. Failure to progress steadily toward union despite adequate débridement and healthy skin coverage should prompt reassessment of the care plans for a patient with an infected tibial fracture (Fig. 57–55).

When planning treatment of established chronic osteomyelitis, with or without fracture union, the surgeon must carefully assess all aspects of the patient's problems. The local and systemic factors of the infection should be classified according to Cierny (see Chapter 19). What, precisely, are the things that bother the patient? How and in what ways is the patient's function impaired? What are the patient's hopes, expectations, and fears? It may be that pain not directly related to the infection, limited function, or appearance is a more significant issue than the infection itself. Successful eradication of osteomyelitis in which a patient is left with a malaligned, dysfunctional limb is not beneficial.

Having defined the patient's disease, the surgeon is in a position to consider the various treatment options. For a relatively benign infection, management might involve only observation, without active treatment unless a "flare-up" of infection occurs. Occasionally, brief courses of oral or parenteral antibiotics can control an episode of acute inflammation. Chronic suppressive oral antibiotics are successful in some patients.

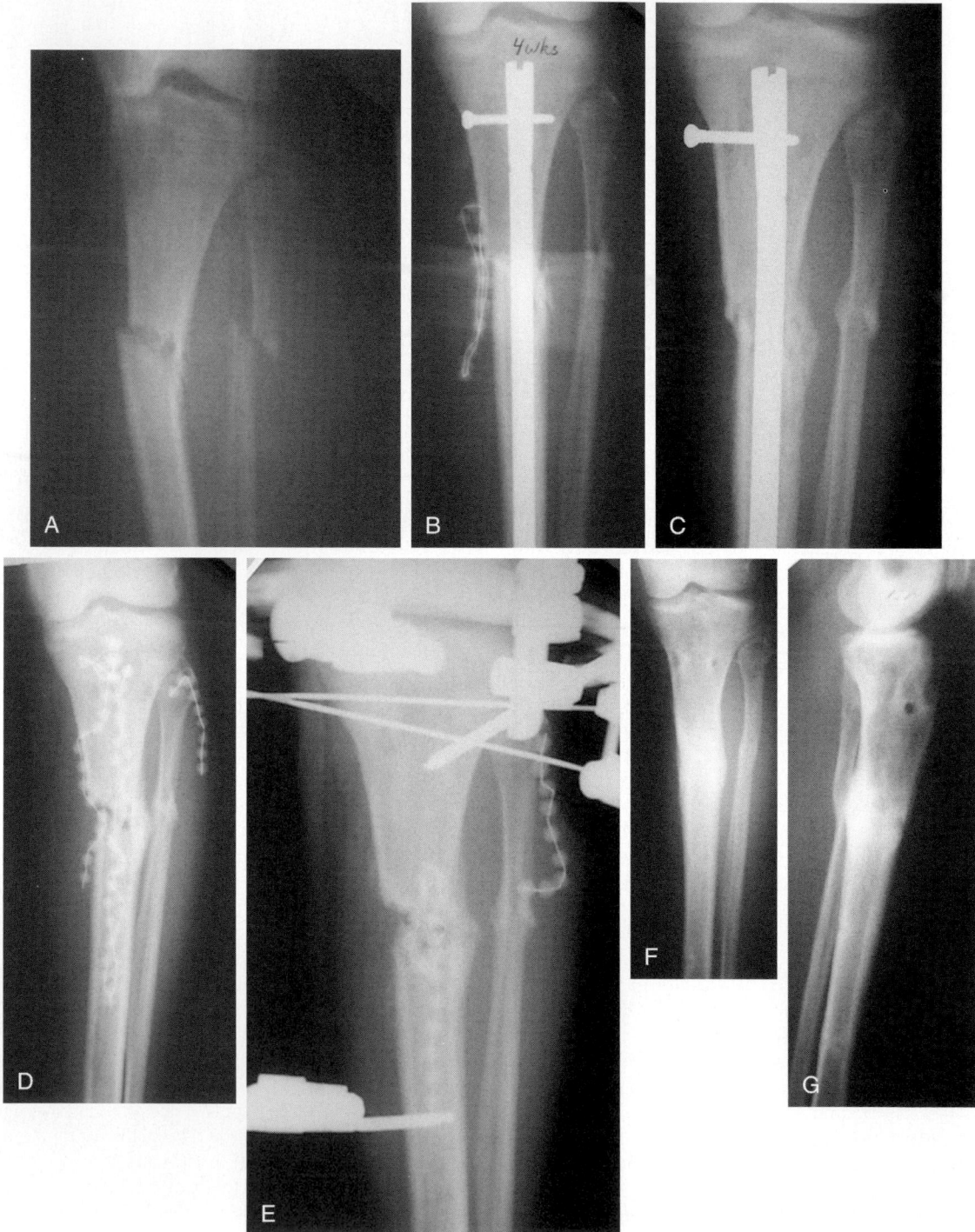

**Figure 57–54.** *A,* Open type IIIA fracture in a pedestrian struck by an automobile and initially treated elsewhere by débridement and intramedullary nailing, with a small wound left open to heal secondarily. *B,* Because of persistent drainage, the wound was débrided, with closure several days later. Cultures were "negative." *C,* Persistent pain with hardware loosening led to aspiration of pus from the closed wound. *D,* The nail was removed and the wounds were extensively débrided and treated initially with beads containing tobramycin. *E,* Hybrid external fixation. *F, G,* Once the wound had healed and become sterile with local and systemic antibiotics, autologous bone grafting was performed. The fixator was left on until union was achieved with full pain-free weight bearing. Anteroposterior and lateral views show mature healing without recurrence of infection at a 2-year follow-up.

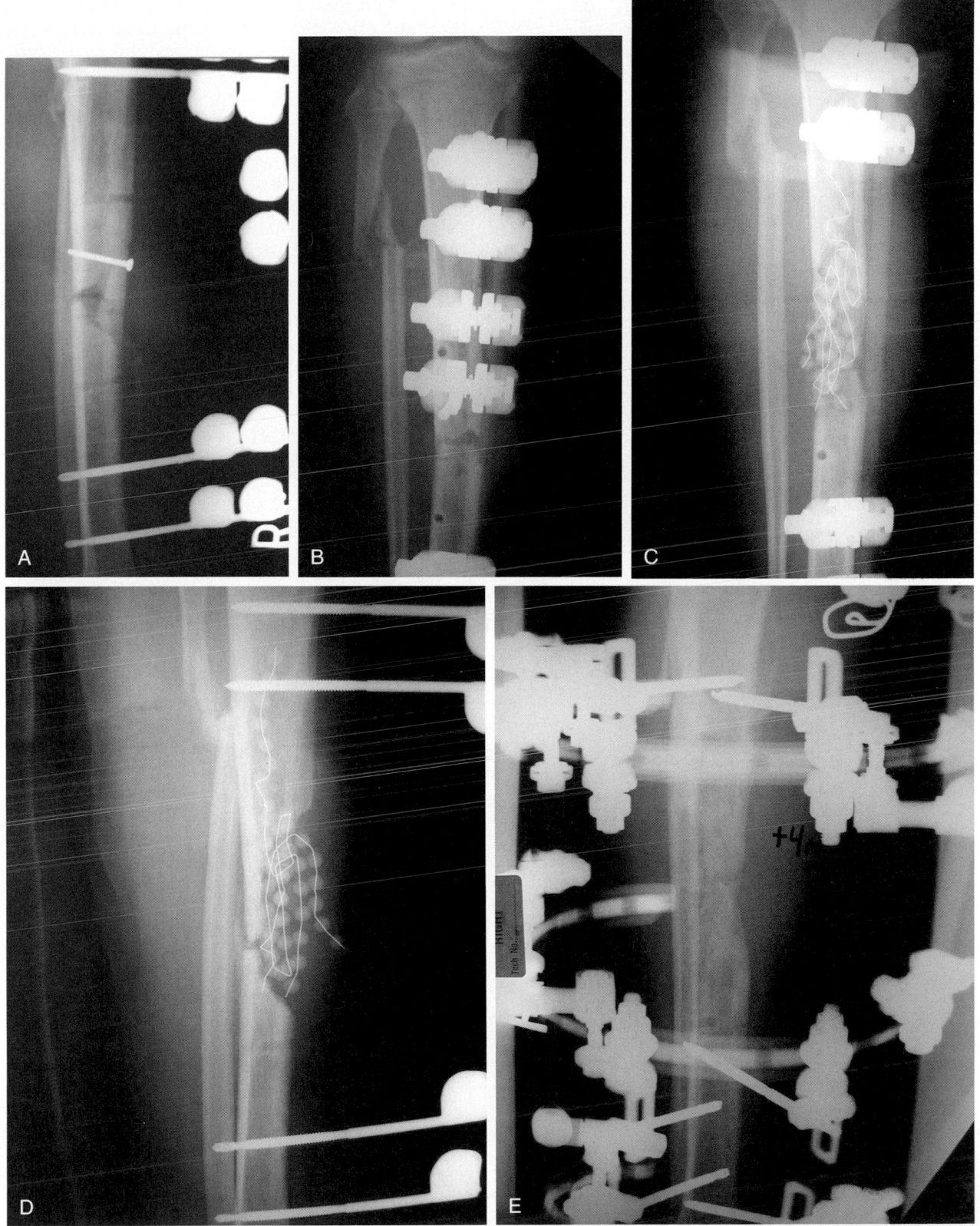

**FIGURE 57–55.** Multiring, multibar external fixator for weight-bearing stability after débridement and grafting. Grade IIIB open tibia fracture treated by débridement, external fixation, and free-flap coverage. *A, B,* Wound drainage began 3.5 months later. *C, D,* After débridement to bleeding bone and tobramycin-containing bead pouch dressing, a more stable external fixator with four rings and three connecting rods was applied. The patient was allowed weight bearing on this side, as the opposite side was incapacitated by femoral shaft fracture and below-knee amputation. *E, F,* Four months after replacement of the beads with autologous bone graft and before fixator removal.

*Illustration continued on following page*

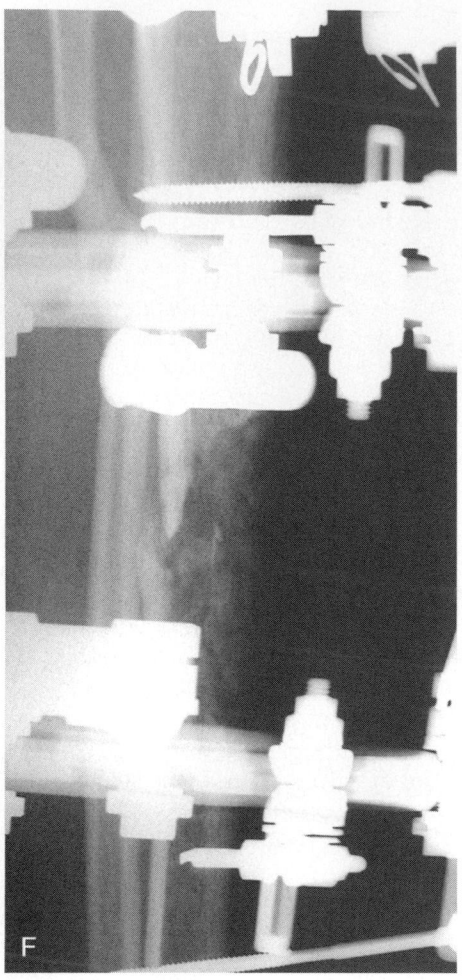

**FIGURE 57–55** *Continued.*

Patients with significantly symptomatic osteomyelitis are candidates for surgery, particularly in the absence of fracture union. Treatment goals may be limited to alleviation of acute symptoms, or they may extend to radical resection of all potentially infected and necrotic or marginally viable tissue and then staged reconstruction in an attempt to gain permanent control of the disease process with normalization of function and anatomy. Surgical treatment is advised if a pointing abscess or necrotic area is present, if pus can be aspirated, or if the patient's local or systemic condition is deteriorating or not improving in spite of optimal antibiotics. The surgeon must choose how extensive a procedure to recommend, with the awareness that intraoperative findings might require modification of the preoperative plan because infected tissue cannot be precisely identified with any imaging study. This need for intraoperative decision making should be discussed beforehand with the patient, who should also participate in the decision about whether the treatment goal should be relief of the acute flare-up or definitive débridement and reconstruction. Sometimes, relatively less aggressive surgery is appropriate. Such surgery may be incision and drainage of a pointing abscess or local débridement of necrotic or poorly perfused soft tissue or bone. A patient with chronic osteomyelitis but good function and infrequent or tolerable recurrences may recover sooner and with less travail from such a limited procedure. However, if significant disability and pain, frequent recurrence, or progressive bone destruction threatening skeletal integrity is found, an attempt at surgical control or "cure" of the infection is warranted. The treatment plan must be individualized for each patient. Chronic post-traumatic tibial osteomyelitis is never limited to bone. The surrounding soft tissues typically hold the key to treatment. Also vitally important are (1) whether the fracture is united, (2) whether the necessary bone débridement will produce a defect that places the bone at risk for pathologic fracture, (3) the functional status of the limb before and after any surgical treatment, (4) the various options for restoration of soft tissue coverage and bone integrity, and (5) the local and systemic status of the patient. These issues are discussed further in Chapter 14.

## SURGICAL TREATMENT OF INFECTED TIBIAL SHAFT FRACTURES

### Preoperative Planning

A careful physical examination is essential. Pulses, the strength and sensation of each local nerve, and the status of the soft tissue envelope must be evaluated and documented because of their influence on outcome and the risk of operative injury. Tissue pliability, vascularity, and scarring must be considered when planning surgical access to the area of infection, as well as when anticipating problems with wound closure that might require tissue transfer to obtain coverage. Appropriate surgical goals should be established. If an infected nonunion is present, control of the infection with adequate débridement and antibiotics must precede bone reconstruction, but both are necessary because in the absence of fracture union, infection usually recurs. If the fracture has healed, surgeons may seek to eradicate infection or merely control a flare-up. The former requires radical excision of all necrotic and contaminated or infected tissue. The latter may be far less aggressive, perhaps only draining a pointing abscess. Relatively limited débridement may be particularly beneficial if a sequestrum of dead bone is identified either on radiographs with multiple views or by CT. These two studies provide the essential images needed to plan débridement. A sinogram, in which radiopaque water-soluble contrast is injected through a small flexible catheter, may help guide débridement. Dilute methylene blue solution similarly injected into a sinus at the beginning of the operation recognizably stains the sinus tissue and thus makes it easier for the surgeon to identify and excise. Neither technetium-labeled phosphonate bone scans nor MRI is very helpful, in my experience, to define the extent of bone infection because they typically show abnormality over a larger area than that of the necrotic infected bone. The gross appearance of the remaining bone and soft tissue during débridement is the most important guide. However, MRI can help in assessing the overlying soft tissue and can exclude intraosseous involvement if no abnormality is seen.

## Incision

Infected tibial fractures usually have scars from traumatic or surgical wounds in the area that needs débridement. Generally, one must select the best of these scars rather than create a new incision to access the area to be débrided. If an adequately mature previous incision must be crossed, it is best to do so at right angles, but using rather than crossing an incision is typically best. Longitudinal incisions are nearly always preferable to transverse ones. As discussed in the helpful article by Tetsworth and Cierny, the surgical approach to débride an osteomyelitic tibia should be extraperiosteal to preserve as much blood supply as possible to the bone that will remain after débridement.[565] Once the area to be débrided is identified, periosteum is reflected only from the area of bone that will be excised. Any avascular or unhealthy soft tissue encountered should be excised, and the tissue that will be retained should be handled gently. The incision should be planned to allow for expansion as necessary to accommodate all needed bone débridement. The goal of creating flaps for a "watertight," tension-free closure, if possible, should be remembered during the approach, but adequate débridement should not be compromised by concern about wound closure. Rather, the surgeon must have other means of wound closure in case of need.

## Débridement

After removal of all detached fragments, necrotic bone should be excised with a well-irrigated power bur back to the level where its surface shows punctate bleeding from canalicular vessels (the "paprika sign"). Reactive, living involucrum should be left unless it prevents débridement. Internal fixation, if present, should usually be removed during débridement and replaced, at least temporarily, with external fixation unless the bone is solidly healed. If infection extends through the diaphyseal medullary canal, IM reaming can usually débride it adequately, although reaming does produce some cortical necrosis. Sharp reamers cleaned frequently and advanced slowly with frequent irrigation may reduce the extent of this necrosis. Reaming should be done with the tourniquet deflated. If the canal is intact, creation of a 4.5-mm drill hole distally to decompress the medullary canal may reduce the extent of debris intravasation. If infection extends from the medullary canal into the metaphyseal bone or if the endosteal surface is significantly "scalloped," reaming will not usually achieve adequate débridement, and an oval cortical window will be required for this task. This window can be extended as a trough 7 to 10 mm wide and as long as needed to remove the necrotic bone. A slightly narrower trough may be preferable if lengths over 10 cm are required. It is unwise to débride both the internal and external tibial surfaces simultaneously because such débridement essentially removes all the local blood supply and thus produces a sequestrum that can neither participate significantly in healing nor resist infection. If required, separating the two procedures by several weeks may be safer.[565] Sometimes, it is impossible to débride an area of tibial osteomyelitis adequately without resecting an entire segment of the bone along with any surrounding dystrophic scar and periosteum. If such extensive resection

is performed, the surgeon must, of course, have a plan for reconstruction of the defect and rehabilitation of the patient within a reasonable period. Reconstruction requires stabilization and bone transport or grafting, as well as possibly microvascular transfer of a soft tissue or composite tissue flap.[107, 407, 431, 492, 546, 598, 613] Smaller defects, 2 cm or less in length, may respond to delayed closure and autologous cancellous bone grafting. Recurrence of infection may be less frequent if appropriate antibiotics are added to the graft.[100, 101]

Staged or serial débridement allows the surgeon to determine viability by observation over time. In years past, such a wound left open, even under a damp dressing, was challenged by bacterial superinfection and desiccation necrosis. Tobramycin-impregnated bead pouch dressings, which retain moisture and deliver locally high antibiotic levels, greatly aid in the care of such wounds.

Once débridement is adequate, the surgeon can choose between early flap coverage and tissue transport. The latter brings healthy bone and soft tissue into the defect but does not provide immediate protection for tissues that cannot withstand exposure in an open wound (vessels, tendons, marginally viable bone, and retained hardware). Rather than a drawn-out process of serial débridement, it is apparent that a well-planned radical débridement, beyond the margins of infected tissue, is more expeditious. Modern reconstructive options make such management a usually reasonable option.[106]

## Cultures

Although microbiologic studies have little to offer in the initial care of an open tibial fracture, once an infection is established, such studies provide essential guidance for appropriate antibiotic therapy. Cultures with Gram stain should always be performed to identify microorganisms. Multiple samples of potentially infected tissue rather than swabs of the wound surface should be sent promptly to the microbiology laboratory. Deep wound cultures are appropriate. Those from a sinus tract or from exudate on the skin are too often contaminated. Excised tissue specimens need be no bigger than 1 cm³. They should be transferred promptly to individual wide-mouthed specimen containers. Aerobic, anaerobic, and fungal cultures should all be obtained—usually all these cultures can be requested for each individual sample. Post-traumatic osteomyelitis may be associated with multiple organisms. The recovery of any bacteria at all may be compromised by preoperative antibiotic treatment, as well as by the nonuniform distribution of viable bacteria in the wound. If possible, antibiotic administration should be stopped 24 to 48 hours before deep cultures are obtained. Likewise, antibiotic-containing irrigation solutions, bacteriostatic injectable solutions, and the like should not be used until specimens have been obtained for all cultures.

## Skeletal Stability

An intraoperative assessment should be made regarding the tibia's stability. When nonunion is present, this decision is easy. One must also remember that the structural integrity of a healed tibia is compromised by aggressive débridement, so a pathologic fracture is a definite risk. Tetsworth and Cierny advise external fixation for prophylactic stabilization if more than 30% of the original cortical volume has been removed.[565] If the need is not certain, a radiolucent external fixator can be applied and the amount of remaining bone assessed by CT after débridement. Internal fixation with a plate or IM nail is another option to consider in the face of significant débridement. The choice will be individualized and based on considerations of infection risk, soft tissue coverage, and plans for reconstruction of the defect.

### Dead Space

Excision of bone leaves a cavity behind that will fill with hematoma. The hematoma is slow to organize and does not resist microbial colonization and recurrent infection. Thus, elimination of dead space has become a key part of surgery for osteomyelitis. Previously, "saucerization" by excision of overlying bone and soft tissue and allowing granulation tissue to form on the wound surface with epithelialization from the periphery was a means of accomplishing this goal. This approach has been supplanted, generally by temporarily filling the dead space with depot antibiotics (e.g., acrylic beads) and subsequently filling the defect with bone graft or graft substitutes (which might be mixed with antibiotics) and muscle flaps, either local or free; for smaller defects, sometimes just leaving the antibiotic carrier in place beyond its expected period of drug elution is effective.[106] It is hard to determine how important a contribution is made to the "sterilization" of dead space with the use of depot antibiotics, but many surgeons believe that this adjunct is a significant one. It should be considered as well for the medullary canal, which is as much a dead space after nail removal and reaming as the extraosseous ones just mentioned. A chain of beads securely anchored to a wire suture can be placed in the canal temporarily, but it may be difficult to remove if left more than a couple weeks.

### Wound Management and Closure

The wound is usually dressed open, at least initially, with Seligson's bead pouch dressing to reduce the risk of contamination and wound surface desiccation. At least one return to the operating room for assessment of the adequacy of débridement is often wise. If possible after adequate débridement and appropriate coverage, the wound should be closed in a watertight tension-free manner with careful use of monofilament mattress sutures to avoid inverting the edges. The skin and subcutaneous tissue may be cautiously mobilized from the underlying fascia while remembering that this fascia may be their major source of blood supply.

Now that usually successful tissue transfer procedures are available, one does not need to leave a wound open for dressing changes and healing by second intention. However, flap closure is not required, and it is possible to manage postdébridement defects as open wounds, which may be closed by Ilizarov traction histogenesis, by open bone grafting, or by healing by secondary intention.

## AMPUTATION

Another option that must be considered in the management of recalcitrant infection of a tibial fracture is amputation. Amputation may be the best possible functional restoration if the injured leg has extensive damage, particularly a dysfunctional foot or neurovascular insufficiency, or if serious systemic consequences are anticipated from aggressive or lengthy treatment of infection. Sometimes, a technically possible limb salvage has significant socioeconomic consequences, as well as the possibility of failure. Some patients in such a situation find that amputation with its more predictable rehabilitation is preferable. Amputation is usually performed as a two-staged procedure in the face of active infection and at the lowest conventional level above the patient's zone of infection (see Chapter 64). Delayed closure after 3 to 5 days of intravenous antibiotics to which the patient's infecting organisms are sensitive and a tobramycin-loaded or alternative bead pouch dressing may reduce the risk of wound infection. Amputation may be more appropriate than an extensive reconstructive protocol for many patients if structure or function of the infected limb is or will be significantly compromised. It is usually the operation of choice for systemically compromised hosts whose infection cannot be controlled with antibiotics and occasional minor surgical procedures. However, the results of salvage are good enough that this option should be seriously considered for most patients with chronic tibial osteomyelitis.[533]

## OCCULT INFECTION

Occasionally, a low-grade infection will be present at the site of a nonunion that appears to be manageable without the problems of a defect. Any nonunion may be found to have positive tissue cultures.[349] One might question whether a positive culture without other signs of infection represents wound contamination or infection, but the frequency of infection in the early postoperative period after fixation of an ununited fracture is high enough that it seems appropriate to address such contamination as a potential infection and treat it with appropriate antibiotics and débridement of obviously necrotic tissue. It is always advisable to at least obtain intraoperative cultures from the nonunion site or from medullary canal reaming if IM nail fixation is chosen. Surgeons who strongly suspect, based on clinical or laboratory evidence, that an ununited fracture is infected may wish to obtain cultures before applying internal fixation or a bone graft or deciding to use external rather than internal fixation. Usually hypertrophic but occasionally atrophic, these ununited tibial fractures with contamination or low-grade or quiescent infection often unite with internal fixation or with internal fixation and bone grafting. If these techniques seem preferable to external fixation, they may be worth considering. Higher rates of infection have been reported with IM nails than with plates in such cases, so more caution and greater perceived benefits might be desired before IM nailing is chosen for a potentially or actually infected nonunion.[563, 627, 629] Nonetheless, for some patients it remains a reasonable consideration.

Experience is very helpful for planning and implementation of treatment for post-traumatic tibial osteomyelitis. However, few fracture surgeons have extensive experience with this disease. It appears to be less frequent in most developed regions of the world, perhaps because of better treatment of initial injuries and acute infections or possibly because of fewer osteomyelitis-prone injuries. As with many unusual and challenging conditions, consultation or referral (or both) of a patient with tibial osteomyelitis should be considered.

Treatment of infected nonunion is discussed further in Chapters 19 through 21.

## Bone Loss

Loss of bone from the tibia is associated with severe open fractures, but it may also result from débridement of infected or necrotic bone. (Management of acute bone loss is discussed earlier.) Most wounds can now be closed with well-perfused local or free microvascular flaps, and bone defects can be filled with cancellous or free vascular bone graft, especially through traction histogenesis (Ilizarov). Therefore, the surgeon need not compromise a totally adequate débridement of either an open fracture or infection for fear that the reconstruction may not succeed.[107, 613] In fact, failure to remove this dead or bacteria-laden bone poses a greater risk of failure than does the occasionally daunting task of reconstructing the defect that remains after débridement. Short defects, particularly if they are partial rather than complete, can usually be managed with internal fixation and bone grafting. If infected, adequate débridement and temporary placement of antibiotic-containing PMMA beads are important first stages in such a reconstruction.

One should consider treating larger combined bone and soft tissue defects with traction histogenesis and transport of both bone and its overlying soft tissue into the defect while leaving the débrided wound open and granulating.[106] Such management does not provide adequate protection when vessels, tendons, hardware, and marginally viable (e.g., reamed) bone are exposed. Thus, these situations call for flap coverage instead of open transport. Some authors believe that transport under coverage of a healthy well-vascularized muscle flap is easier and more successful. It may also provide a better bed for "docking" of the transported segment, which frequently needs a local bone graft to promote union.[446, 463, 546]

It is not necessary, however, to routinely cover defects with free flaps before bone transport, as demonstrated by several series that relied on transport alone to treat defects involving both bone and soft tissue.[22, 402, 431, 446, 546] Several bone transport strategies should be considered as potential treatment of a bone defect. The débrided and viable fracture site can be compressed acutely and then lengthened gradually until leg length is equal.[23] Alternatively, acute compression can be followed by lengthening through a corticotomy outside the zone of injury.[200] The third approach involves transport of a segment into the defect after a distal or proximal corticotomy. A second corticotomy can be used to restore length more rapidly in longer defects.[135, 202, 329, 348, 431, 451, 546]

If no infection is present, transport to fill a defect can be performed over an IM nail to reduce the time spent in an external fixator and to minimize problems with alignment at the docking site.[96, 200, 321, 431, 459] The length of time required for healing a defect by bone transport varies from patient to patient, but reports suggest that it is around 2 months per centimeter. Paley and Maar reported an average of 1.7 months' fixation per centimeter defect, with a range from 0.7 to 4.3.[431] Several problems should be anticipated with bone transport beyond the inevitable ones associated with prolonged use of external fixation. Malalignment or poor healing (or both) at the docking site may require a local bone graft, which many surgeons perform routinely or if union is not evident a month after docking. Slow consolidation of the regenerate bone formed behind the transported segment may be aided by slowing transport, by compressing this tissue through reversal of transport direction, or by both. Foot and ankle contractures, often related to proximal transport from a distal corticotomy, can be prevented by extending the frame distally to hold the foot in neutral. Although patients' ability to tolerate the pain and encumbrance of prolonged external fixation for bone transport is frequently raised as a concern, McKee and colleagues found a marked improvement in health status after this type of treatment.[369] It is important to remember the possibility of late complications such as fractures after traction histogenesis.[537]

Deficient bone can also be replaced with other techniques. Placement of cancellous autograft under a free muscle flap, as described by Christian and coauthors, may require repeat grafting and must be protected by fixation until the graft is maturely healed.[105]

Free fibular microvascular grafts can span a larger defect, but they have problems with durability, later fatigue fractures, and deformity.[287, 339, 346, 589] Interposition of the ipsilateral fibula on its peroneal vascular pedicle is an occasionally good option.[302, 492] The intact ipsilateral fibula is a helpful support for a deficient tibia and can be used, with bone graft under healthy tissue (e.g., posterolaterally), to build a synostosis that bypasses the defect. Such support can also be provided with proximal and distal tibiofibular arthrodeses, the so-called fibula-pro-tibia approach.[134] Adding a synostotic graft hastens the development of a stout bypass around the tibial defect. Fibular hypertrophy progressively increases strength, which might require protection with a brace for 6 to 12 months of progressive weight bearing. Orthotic support may be needed for any patient whose bone strength is significantly compromised.[399]

## Delayed Union

The term *delayed union* describes an ununited fracture that continues to show progress toward healing or has not been present long enough to satisfy an arbitrary time criterion for nonunion. The lack of precision in its definition decreases its value in reports of results. Retarded progress toward union is especially evident after more serious fractures, as in Edwards' series, in which only 23% of grade III open fractures had healed by 6 months.[156] It is essential that the surgeon recognize delayed healing, search for causes, and make appropriate decisions about treatment.

It is usually difficult to identify a definite cause for

retarded healing of a given fracture, but occult infection is a possibility that must always be considered.[349] Poor local blood supply, bone loss, excessive mechanical instability, and for some fractures, insufficient functional use are some of the potential contributors to delayed healing that can be addressed in the treatment of delayed union of the tibia (Fig. 57–56). Fracture malalignment may need correction to prevent potential adverse effects on the mechanical environment, as well as to promote union. The factor most commonly associated with delayed union of tibial fractures is the severity of the original injury. Many other possible local and systemic contributing factors exist,[33, 85, 142, 284, 421, 422, 561] however, and are discussed in Chapters 20 and 22.

Continued weight bearing in an appropriate brace or cast will often lead to union of a fracture that is being treated in closed fashion.[422, 507] The same treatment may be appropriate for fractures that have been fixed with an IM nail, but if union does not occur, the hardware will fail and become more difficult to extract. If the fracture is stable, dynamization (i.e., removal of locking screws from at least one end of the nail) can promote union in 50% or so of cases.

The best treatment of a nailed tibial fracture that is not uniting is usually to insert a reamed nail of larger diameter (Fig. 57–57). Such treatment is advisable if union is not evident by 6 to 9 months. Because the durability of an IM nail depends on several factors, some judgment is necessary, especially for smaller diameter locked nails. The risk of reactivating an infection by substituting a reamed nail for a nonreamed nail originally placed for an open fracture remains uncertain.[120, 563] In a patient at significant risk, an onlay bone graft may be a safer alternative.

If delayed union is noted after plate fixation and no infection is present, IM fixation can be considered.[182] Delayed healing associated with a flagrant infection requires débridement, usually a change of fixation from plate to external fixation, and subsequent bone grafting. Occasionally, with a suppressed or quiescent infection, a secure plate may permit fracture union, especially if a bone graft is added. Control of infection, typically involving débridement, hardware removal, and whatever antibiotic coverage is needed, is accomplished after fracture healing.[88]

Delayed union is especially common after external fixation, perhaps because it is generally used for fractures of greater severity. If the fixator must be removed before a fracture has consolidated, loss of alignment may follow. Therefore, as discussed previously, the physician should routinely consider early bone grafting and progressive weight bearing after appropriate fixator modification. An alternative is conversion from external fixation to a plate as soon as soft tissue healing permits (see Fig 57–44).

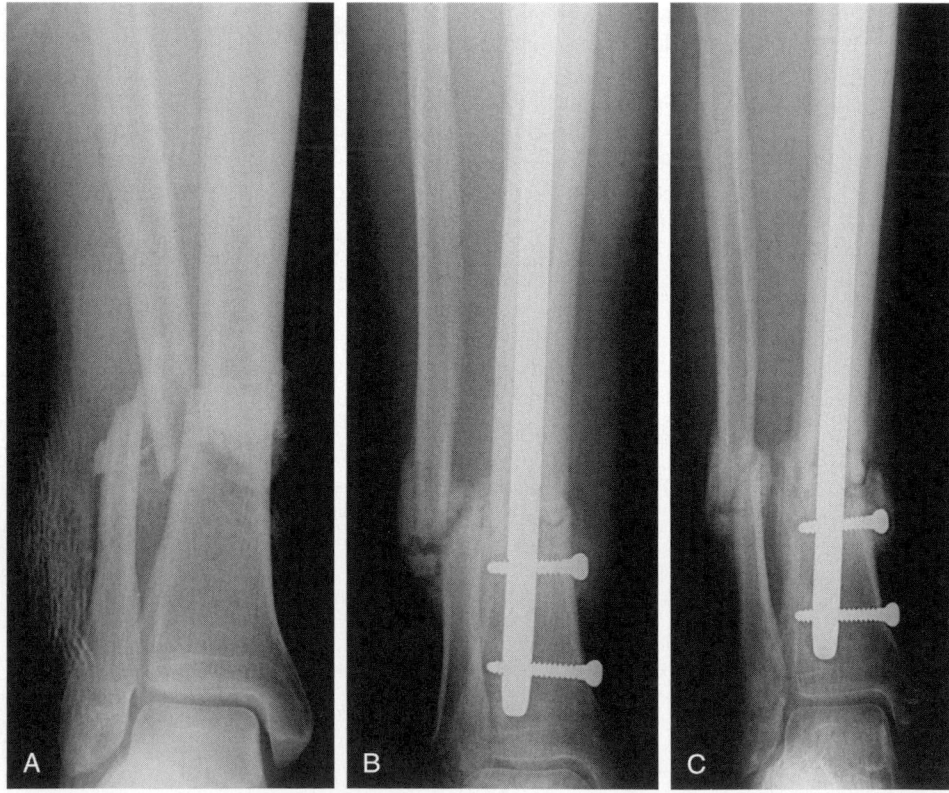

**FIGURE 57–56.** Bracing for delayed union with satisfactory alignment. *A,* An open, moderate-severity distal tibiofibular fracture treated with irrigation and débridement, a distally locked nonreamed intramedullary nail, and delayed split-thickness skin grafting. *B,* Five months after injury, the patient had mild pain on weight bearing, slight tenderness, questionable motion at the fracture site, fluffy callus without union, and some resorption about his hardware distally. Fatigue failure of the 9-mm intramedullary nail was a concern, especially because the fracture site was so close to the upper of the two distal locking screws. An orthosis was prescribed. *C,* Six weeks later, he was bearing full weight in his ankle-foot orthosis without any pain and had a stable, nontender fracture. Sclerosis of the proximal fracture end probably represents avascular necrosis caused by the fracture or by interference with medullary diaphyseal blood flow by the snugly fitting, nonreamed nail. The fracture subsequently healed, after which a fracture of the nail was noted at the upper distal locking hole.

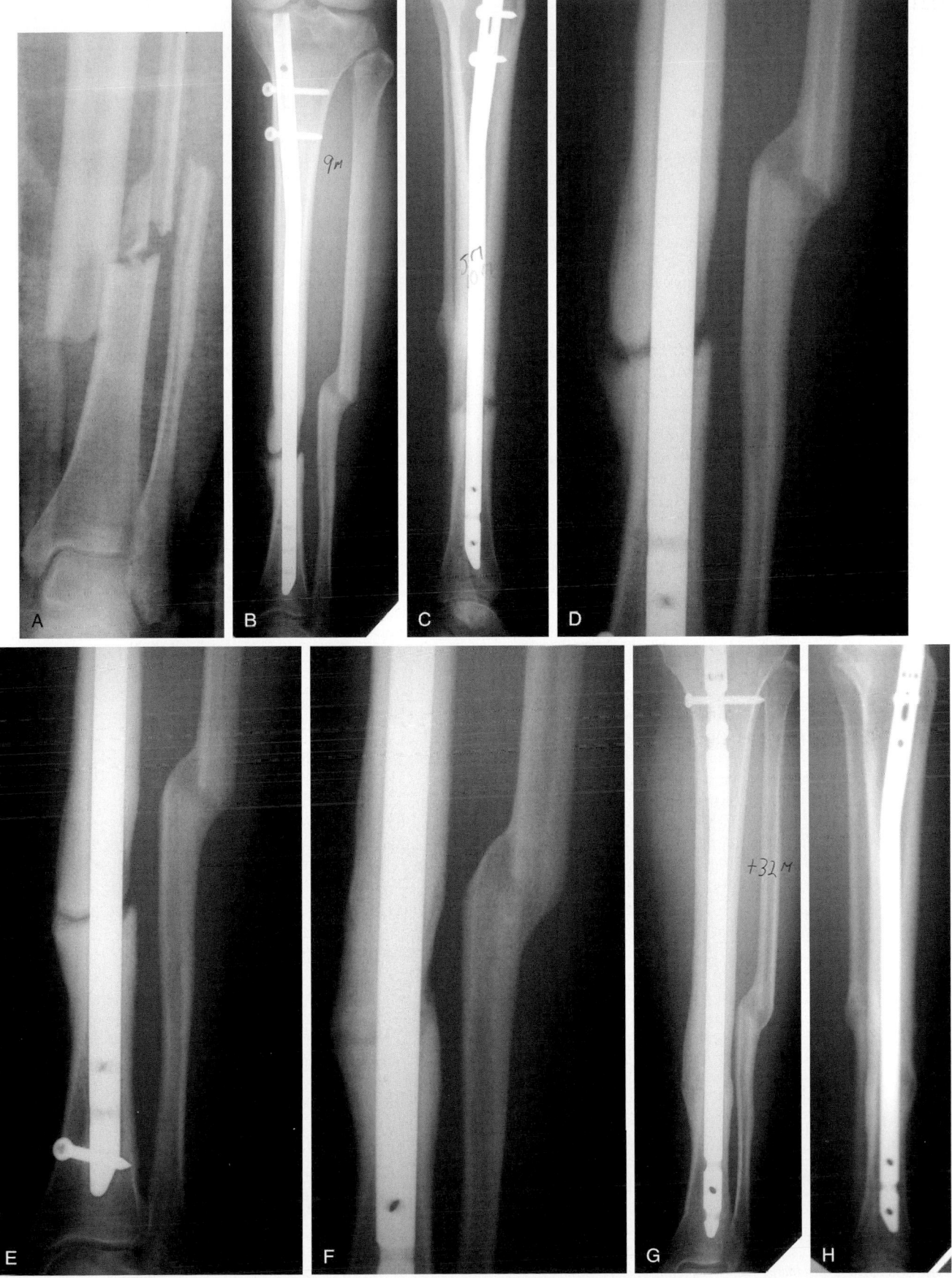

**Figure 57–57.** Nail exchange for nonunion after intramedullary (IM) nail fixation. *A,* Grade IIIA open tibia-fibula fracture in a 55-year-old pedestrian struck by an automobile. She was treated with débridement, including removal of a devascularized butterfly fragment, reamed 9-mm IM nail fixation, and delayed closure. *B, C,* Internal oblique and lateral radiographs 9 months later. She has persisting pain at the fracture site. Nail exchange was performed, with reaming to 11 mm and insertion of a 10-mm nail locked proximally (slotted hole) and distally. *D,* Six weeks later. *E,* Seven months after nail exchange, the fracture is clinically united. *F,* Nineteen months after renailing. *G, H,* Anteroposterior and lateral radiographs 32 months after injury show reconstitution of missing bone and functional recovery.

Fibular osteotomy has been recommended as a stimulus for tibial fracture union. Although it might counteract a tendency to varus deformity produced by an intact fibula and might produce more loading of a tibial fracture, osteotomy of the fibula is not a very successful means of achieving union. It may also increase instability and deformity.

Various types of electrical stimulation have been advocated for problems of fracture healing. Sharrard's study demonstrated that magnetic stimulation was more effective than placebo treatment of delayed union, though markedly less so than in most reports of surgical treatment.[525]

Another, more recently recognized stimulus for fracture healing is low-intensity pulsed ultrasound. Initially approved by the U.S. FDA for stimulating bone healing in acute fractures, this treatment has recently been accepted for delayed union and nonunion.[134, 218, 234, 365, 408, 485] Ultrasound treatments are delivered for 20 minutes daily with a device that includes a transducer readily applied to the fracture site through a cast window or strapped directly on an unencumbered fracture site (Exogen). Though not effective when applied to acute higher energy tibial fractures after IM nailing, the currently available low-energy pulsed ultrasound units do appear to be beneficial for lower energy acute tibial fractures, as well as ununited fractures. They thus seem reasonable to use for satisfactorily aligned delayed union in patients whose function is acceptable and who wish to defer surgical treatment. To date, no studies have compared the effectiveness of magnetic stimulation with that of ultrasound.

As long as a tibial fracture is satisfactorily aligned, progressing toward union, and not causing more pain or disability than the patient can tolerate, the physician should continue the treatment course or increase functional weight bearing with appropriate external support, unless the risk of fixation failure prevents such management. However, if unacceptable deformity, an excessively prolonged course, or a high likelihood of nonunion becomes evident, it is appropriate to reexamine the alternatives and perhaps select another treatment option. The choice must meet the patient's needs, especially correction of any deformity, but it should also have a high likelihood of achieving union within a reasonable period. It should interfere as little as possible with the patient's activities and have a low risk of complications when compared with the other alternatives.

## Fixation Failure

Fracture fixation depends on the mechanical behavior of a composite of bone and hardware. Either or both may fail and result in loss of fixation. Bone may be deficient, most often because of osteoporosis or unrecognized comminution. Internal fixation may prove inadequate as a result of insufficient length, too few screws, too weak an implant, poor technique, or too much cyclical or single-episode loading or because the fracture does not heal within a reasonable time. Clues to failing fixation are provided by increased local inflammation, by the development of

deformity, by loosening or plastic deformation of implants, and by the appearance of peripheral callus in a fracture that was initially thought to be rigidly fixed. The possibility of fixation failure must be anticipated whenever progressive fracture healing is not radiologically evident.

Treatment generally requires at least decreased loading and, if failure has occurred, revision of the fixation. Unless infection is present, failed diaphyseal plate fixation without infection is often best revised with an IM nail.[182] If the problem is metaphyseal, new lag screws and a plate are usually needed. External fixators must often be replaced, perhaps after dealing with pin site infection. Reaming plus insertion of a larger nail is generally the best choice when healing does not progress after IM fixation, but if a larger or longer nail with improved interlocking and perhaps position screws will not control alignment, another form of fixation must be used.[135] Various methods have been devised to help remove retained fragments of a broken IM nail.[149, 178, 195, 238, 295, 354, 497] Most IM nail manufacturers have instrumentation available for removing retained portions of their nails.

Whenever a fracture is not healing as expected, the possibility of a deep infection must be excluded by appropriate tissue culture during operative repair.[349, 645] Cultures should be obtained before revision of fixation if sepsis appears likely.

When fixation is not adequate and mobility of the fracture fragment is noted, some mechanical change is warranted, usually revision of the fixation. If failure has not yet occurred, onlay bone grafting may provide the necessary stimulus for healing. In such cases, ultrasound or electromagnetic stimulation of the healing fracture may also have a role. IM nailing after external fixation is risky because of the likelihood of bacterial contamination from pin sites or the initial injury.[352, 617] Adequate débridement, prolonged delay, and preoperative or intraoperative medullary cultures with appropriate antibiotic coverage are all ways to decrease the risk of intramedullary canal sepsis when an IM nail is chosen for treatment of a nonunion.[274, 304, 382]

## Nonunion

Like the diagnosis of delayed union, labeling a tibial fracture a nonunion is also an arbitrary decision. It is more readily supported once the radiographic evidence is clear, such as sclerotic or atrophic bone ends with obvious separation. However, radiographic confirmation of nonunion often requires many months that should have been devoted to treating the patient's ununited fracture. Time limits that have been used to define nonunion range from 5 months to more than 1 year. A good working definition is a fracture that has shown no radiographic progress toward union during a 3-month period. Requiring longer may unnecessarily delay treatment. However, if a patient is functional, comfortable, and not losing alignment or fixation, nonoperative weight-bearing management may reasonably be continued for prolonged periods. Noninvasive electrical or ultrasound stimulation may also be considered.[218, 227, 365, 408, 485, 491] High-energy extracorporeal shock wave treatment has recently been described as another potentially beneficial adjunct to stimulate healing in ununited tibial fractures.[482]

Although adjunctive treatments, including "watchful waiting," are appropriate for ununited fractures in asymptomatic patients, the presence of disability, pain, malalignment (especially if progressive), and actual or impending hardware failure should lead to a prompt change in treatment. Healing "stimulators" are not an answer for unacceptable deformity, uncontrolled infection, or a mobile pseudarthrosis. Several risk factors make nonunion difficult to treat. In addition to infection, smoking, previous unsuccessful surgery, impaired vascularity, osteopenia that hinders fixation, arterial insufficiency, and obesity are all noteworthy.*

It is important to determine whether an ununited tibial fracture is infected.[347] Low-grade infected nonunion can be managed in much the same way as noninfected nonunion if débridement and antibiotic coverage are adequate. However, if the presence of a dormant infection is missed, the situation can flare out of control, with local abscesses and bone necrosis, as well as a systemic response. In such cases, healing becomes less likely, and further surgical treatment will be required. An ununited tibial fracture with active infection is a major problem that requires a more aggressive approach, including drainage of all abscesses, débridement of all necrotic, infected, and questionably viable tissue, and usually removal of internal fixation. Stability is then provided with external fixation, coverage and débrided bone are restored, and union is gained through grafting, bone compression (after Ilizarov), or both.[98, 202, 276, 351, 437, 574, 613] Treatment of infected nonunion of the tibia is discussed earlier and in Chapter 20.

Noninfected tibial nonunion may be classified as atrophic or hypertrophic, depending on the amount of bone that has formed at the fracture ends. An intermediate category, so-called oligotrophic nonunion, typically behaves more like hypertrophic nonunion. Abundant bone suggests good vascularity, which correlates with healing potential. Minimal bone implies that vascularity is poor or that local osteogenesis is otherwise suppressed, or both. Atrophic nonunion usually requires bone grafts for healing, whereas hypertrophic nonunion has good potential for healing with any of a range of treatments.

A variety of treatments can be used to promote healing in ununited fractures. None are totally successful, and each has its drawbacks and advantages. The surgeon should be familiar with several options because a given patient and fracture might be much more suited to one treatment than another. Ideally, the treatment will have a high success rate and low potential for risk and will permit rapid functional rehabilitation with weight bearing as soon as possible. These goals are readily accepted by the patient and surgeon. However, they may not be coexistent. Options for treating noninfected ununited tibial fractures include onlay bone grafts, perhaps to gain a tibiofibular synostosis,[472, 535, 538] fibula-pro-tibia,[23, 134] free vascularized bone grafts,[261, 524, 559, 597, 598, 638] IM

nailing,† plate fixation,[96, 236, 626] and the use of Ilizarov techniques.[97, 103, 329, 404, 495, 630] Bone grafting, often a valuable adjunct to the repair of nonunion and occasionally used as the only operative procedure, is further discussed in the earlier section Bone Defects and Need for Grafting.

The choice of a surgical protocol for aseptic nonunion is affected by several factors. In particular, one should consider fracture alignment, previous treatment, including whether any fixation devices remain in place, and the status of the overlying soft tissues and how well they might withstand the challenges of surgical exposure, reduction, and fixation. Fractures that are well aligned with an open, "nailable" medullary canal can often be treated optimally with closed reamed IM nailing (Fig. 57–58).

However, if significant periosteal soft tissue stripping is required to correct deformity or to apply a bone graft to an atrophic nonunion, the surgeon should consider plating or possibly external fixation instead. When endosteal callus significantly plugs the medullary canal, both the technical challenges of reestablishing an adequate medullary canal and the possibility of thermal bone necrosis from difficult reaming suggest that another form of fixation might be preferable. In patients with previous infections or significant contamination from open fractures or prolonged use of external fixation, IM nailing should be used cautiously because it is associated with recurrence of infection. However, for some high-risk patients, even those with quiescent infected nonunion, IM nailing may be the best of several problematic alternatives.[274, 383] Long delay between contamination or infection and IM nailing reduces, but does not eliminate the risk of infection.

IM nailing is usually easy if a nail is already in place. Such "exchange nailing" is a very successful technique for promoting union if it is not achieved as expected after primary IM nailing[120, 123, 335, 563, 636] (see Fig. 57–57). Because exchange nailing is so successful in treating tibial nonunion and does not involve bone grafts, exposure of the fracture site, significantly delayed weight bearing, or even fibular osteotomy, IM nailing is very attractive as primary treatment. Nailing may also be an appropriate treatment after failed plate fixation (Fig. 57–59). If still in place, the plate and screws will have to be removed first. Ideally, removal can be accomplished without formally exposing and devascularizing the tibia. Several short incisions along the plate may allow screw removal without significant exposure. A longer distal or proximal incision over the end of the plate will typically permit withdrawal from its soft tissue pocket, perhaps after being loosened with an old osteotome driven between the plate and bone and rotated to loosen the plate. If the plate is broken, both the proximal and distal ends will need to be exposed.

## INTRAMEDULLARY NAILING FOR TIBIAL NONUNION

It is important that the canal accept the planned IM nail to avoid poor fixation, cortical perforation, or both. Suitability for IM nailing can be judged preoperatively by careful

---

*See references 79, 103, 140, 142, 199, 278, 450, 458, 514, 574.

†See references 10, 209, 273, 296, 378, 390, 544, 563, 629, 636.

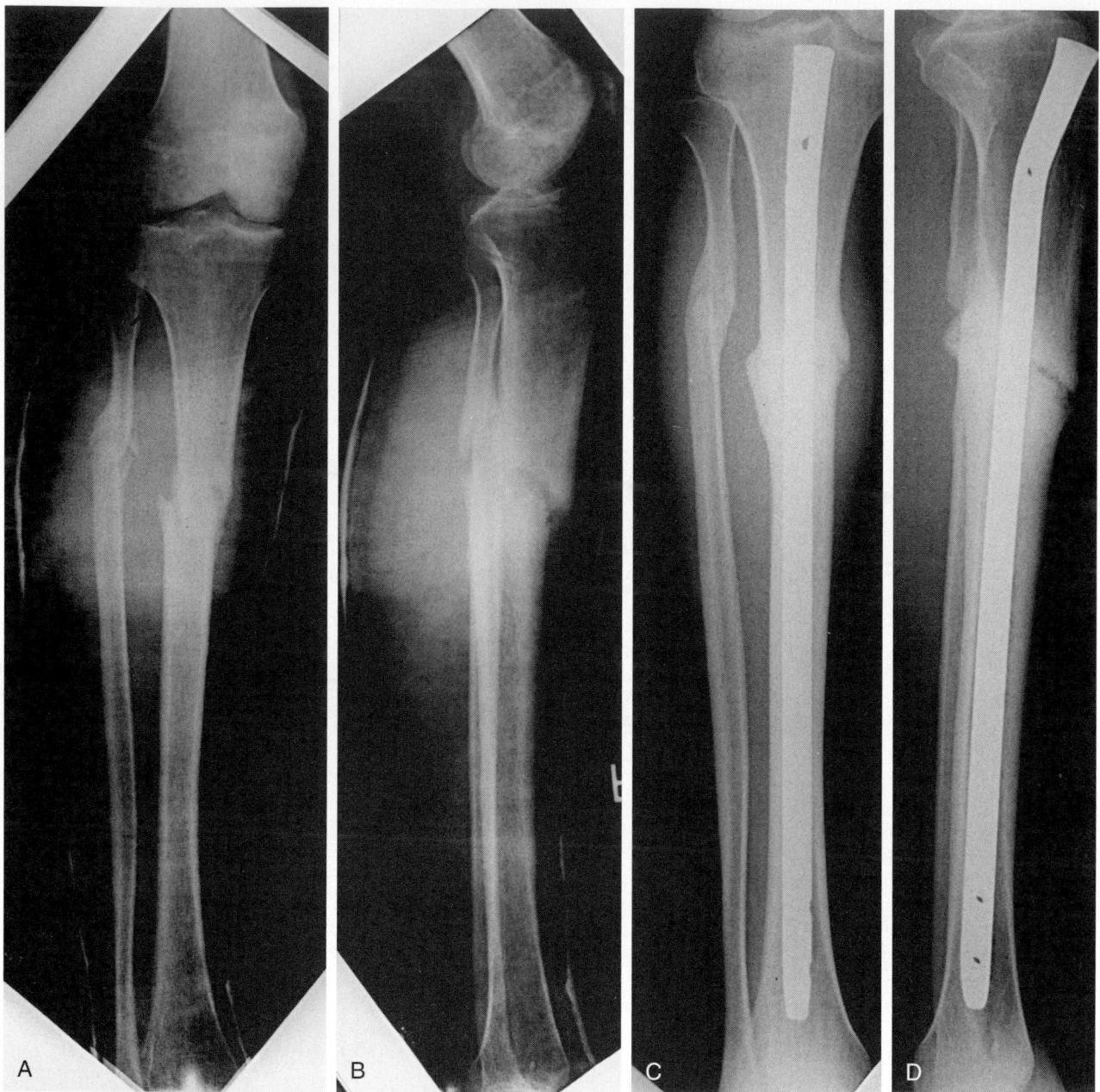

**FIGURE 57–58.** Closed intramedullary nailing for well-aligned nonunion. *A, B,* Six months after closed fracture treatment and weight bearing in a patellar tendon–bearing cast, this patient still had pain at his somewhat mobile fracture site. *C, D,* The fracture was clinically united 3 months after nailing. This radiograph was taken 12 months after injury and 3 months after he returned to work.

review of AP, lateral, and oblique radiographs of the entire tibia, perhaps including stress films to assess reducibility. A zone of totally or partially occlusive callus in the medullary canal is almost always present and must be perforated to allow passage of a guide wire and reamers to prepare for nail insertion. A sharp, stout (approximately ¼ inch in diameter) "wire" with a bent tip, similar to Küntscher's "pseudarthrosis chisel," is good for such perforation. After reaming of the proximal end of the canal to gain room for manipulation of this instrument, it must be advanced carefully with controlled, but persistent hammer blows under biplanar radiographic control to ensure that it stays within the medullary canal. If this sharp-tipped wire perforates the cortex, it is nearly impossible to successfully

prepare the canal for nailing without exposing and "taking apart" the fracture. Once the fracture site's callus has been negotiated successfully, the canal can be enlarged with sharp hand reamers in progressively increasing diameters or with end- and then side-cutting power reamers over a guide wire. If reaming is difficult, cleaning the reamer flutes and allowing the instruments and bone to cool help avoid problems with thermal necrosis. Usually, 1 to 2 mm beyond cortical bone contact is all the reaming required. If a secure fit of the nail is not achieved or if the fracture is proximal or distal, locking screws are not generally needed when nonunion is treated with closed IM nailing. However, if the fracture is rendered unstable by exposure and reduction, locking may be important to gain adequate stability. Although some authors have more or less routinely performed fibular osteotomies with exchange nailing or closed nailing of well-aligned tibial nonunion, no evidence has shown that such management is needed to achieve union. Even if little callus formation is evident (atrophic nonunion), unless bone loss is present, the stimulus of reaming and renailing is often enough to promote healing without adding a bone graft. However, a second nail exchange or the addition of a bone graft may be needed if healing does not occur after the first nail exchange.

IM nail fixation may also be helpful for ununited fractures with moderate deformity (Fig. 57–60). However, such fixation may require significant exposure of the fracture, along with stripping and separation of the bone ends, as well as opening the medullary canal to permit realignment, reaming, and passage of the nail through the medullary canal. If much shortening has occurred at the nonunion, it can be a major challenge to regain the length required to achieve the end-to-end contact needed to pass an IM nail. Some shortening of the bone ends may help, but if a length discrepancy of more than 1 to 2 cm is produced, shortening may detract from the overall outcome. Many surgeons recommend applying autologous bone graft or a substitute around the denuded tibial fracture to compensate for the devascularizing effects of this procedure. Fibular osteotomy is typically needed to achieve reduction. It is better to perform the osteotomy proximal or distal to the tibial nonunion to minimize local soft tissue injury and to preserve an intact segment of fibula at the tibial fracture site so that it can be used for a salvage synostotic bone graft in the future if necessary. An IM nail may be chosen over plate or external fixation in such a situation because it may be a safer form of fixation for patients who are unable to comply with limited weight bearing or because the surgeon believes that the more durable nail will remain intact long enough for the fracture to heal (Fig. 57–61).

## PLATE FIXATION FOR NONUNION

Some ununited fractures are much easier to fix with a plate than with an IM nail, particularly acceptably aligned fractures for which the medullary canal cannot be prepared for IM nailing unless the fracture is completely taken apart, a fibular osteotomy is performed, and the soft tissues are extensively stripped. The typical situation is a patient who has maintained acceptable alignment, with slight shortening, but has not healed during treatment with a functional cast or brace (Fig. 57–62). Another typical scenario is a patient who was initially treated with an external fixator and the fracture has failed to unite, perhaps with some progressive angulation. Such patients might have already had a bone graft that is producing hypertrophic nonunion. A plate is more attractive than an IM nail for many patients with previous external fixation because it is an effective form of fixation and has a lower risk of stirring up infection than IM nailing does, which inevitably passes through previously contaminated and possibly infected pin sites.[627]

Plate fixation of ununited tibial fractures should be considered as an alternative to IM nailing in several clinical situations. In all cases, for plating to be an acceptable alternative, healthy enough soft tissue must remain to cover the plate after insertion. Rarely, this technique may involve replacing poor-quality skin with a pedicle or free flap that provides secure coverage.

**Tension Band Plating.** Plates are particularly useful in patients with an angulated hypertrophic nonunion. A plate applied under sufficient tension on the convex side of such a deformity will not only correct the deformity but will also compress the nonunion tissue and thus stabilize it so that union typically occurs during the next few weeks, and its stability is such that weight bearing can rapidly progress even during this period (Fig. 57–63). If this technique is chosen, the AO external tension device is required, even if a dynamic compression plate with compressing screw holes is used. The plate is undercontoured and securely attached to one end of the ununited fracture so that it crosses the nonunion site parallel to the tibia's anatomic axis. The tension device is then attached to the other end of the plate. When it is tightened maximally ("into the red" indicators), the plate and bone are brought together as the deformity is corrected and the fracture is compressed. The opposite side of the nonunion may open up a bit as the tension band is tightened, but because of the usually broad tibial transverse diameter at this level, the width of the bone is ample to provide cyclical plate loading. For an appropriately shaped nonunion with sufficiently healthy local soft tissues, this technique is reliable. The nonunion site is not "taken down," and bone grafting is not necessary.

**Wave or Bridge Plating.** Plate fixation can be valuable and effective for tibial nonunion even when the preceding tension band model is not applicable. Depending on the nonunion configuration, the plate may be applied to neutralize a lag screw that is compressing an oblique nonunion, to compress a transverse nonunion site, or even as a tension band on the convex side of a not quite corrected deformity, but more typically it bridges across the nonunion, which may have been realigned to correct deformity at the fracture site.[236] Although IM nailing, as discussed earlier, is attractive in many such situations, the challenges of inserting a nail and the fact that exposure for the plate has already been achieved during lysis of the malaligned nonunion make plating an attractive alternative, particularly for cooperative patients. Typically, bone grafts will be used as well in this setting. Graft material can be placed adjacent to a plate that is apposed to the tibial cortex or underneath one that has been contoured to lie, like a wave, away from the nonunion site[53, 285] (Fig. 57–64). Specialized plates, usually standard or customized blade plates, are very helpful for metadiaphyseal nonunion because they usually provide more secure compressive fixation in these sites than can be achieved with standard plates or plates designed for the proximal or distal end of the tibia (Fig. 57–65). Newer plates with screws that thread into and thus lock onto plates may be equivalently valuable and easier to use.

The vast majority of uninfected tibial shaft nonunions that I currently encounter can be managed with nails or plates as described. Such was not always true, however. More serious deformities were frequent in the past when severe tibial fractures were treated with casts or external fixators that were removed before union. Such practice too often resulted in severely malaligned nonunion, often with

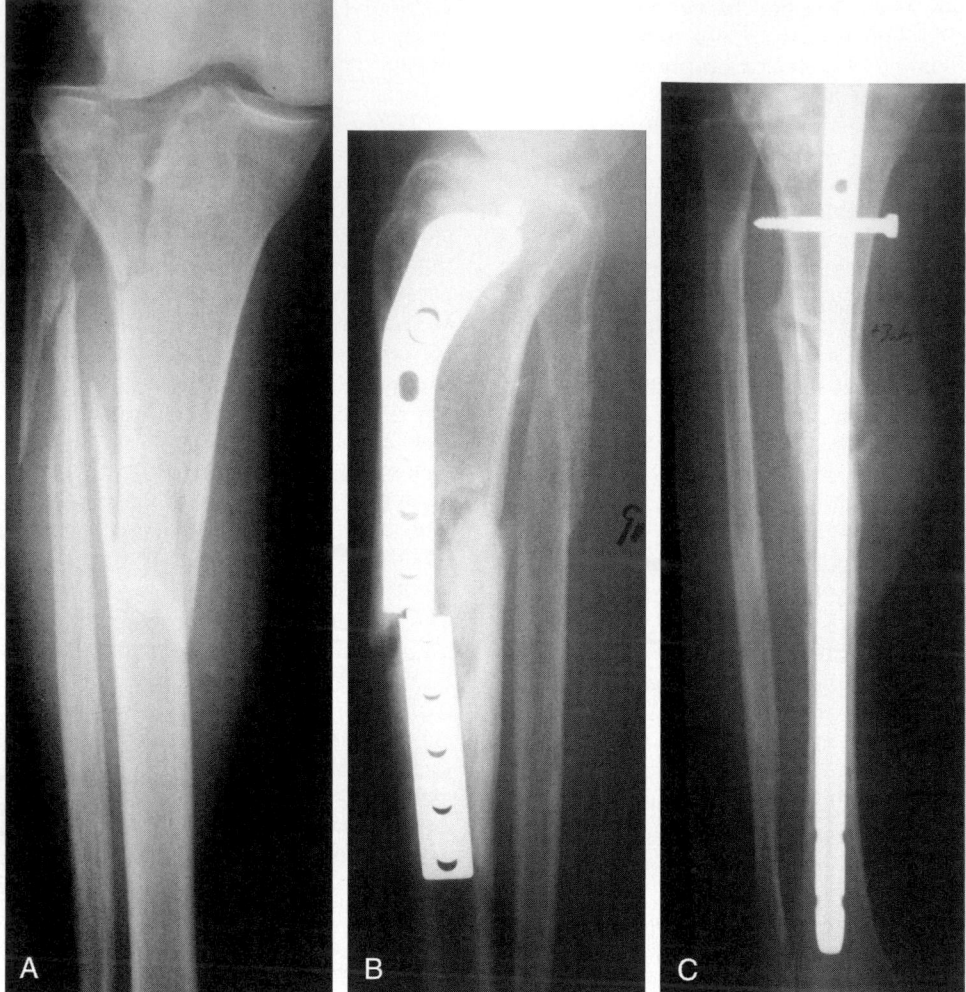

**FIGURE 57–59.** Intramedullary (IM) nailing for diaphyseal nonunion with a failed plate. *A,* Complex proximal tibia-fibula fracture involving the lateral plateau and shaft. *B,* Six months after open reduction and internal fixation with a tibial head plate, which failed at an ununited shaft fracture just before this radiograph. *C,* Healed fracture after hardware removal and IM nail fixation.

a locally compromised skin envelope. When significant deformity is noted, particularly if shortening is more than 1 to 2 cm, the surgeon should consider external fixation with distraction/compression as a means of correcting the deformity. The techniques of Ilizarov and his disciples have inestimable value for infected nonunion and nonunion with bone loss.[103, 329, 348, 404, 430, 495, 496] However, they can be used for almost any nonunion and should thus be considered not only for restoring missing length but also whenever nailing or plating is not safely applicable because of the patient's soft tissues, the surgeon's experience, or institutional capabilities. Ilizarov techniques are further discussed in Chapter 21. Treatment of nonunion is also considered in Chapter 20.

## Malunion

### INDICATIONS

The significance of residual deformity after union of a tibial fracture remains uncertain. It is generally addressed in terms of single parameters: angulation in the coronal or sagittal planes, shortening, or rotational deformity. Little information is available regarding combinations of these elements. Puno and co-workers[455] and others[566, 610] have pointed out that the location of the deformity is important. Angulation is more significant, in terms of its effect on ankle loading, with more distal fracture sites. Kettlekamp and colleagues investigated knee joint arthritis and demonstrated abnormal joint loading as a result of tibial deformity.[299] Such loading seemed more of a problem with varus than with valgus deformities. They pointed out that very long-term studies are needed to demonstrate the relationship between deformity and arthritis because more than 30 years had elapsed between fracture and arthrosis in their small series of patients. Merchant and Dietz were unable to demonstrate a long-term risk of problems from malalignment of healed tibial fractures.[379] Kristensen and colleagues, in a similar long-term follow-up study, concluded that deformity of up to 15° did not produce ankle complications.[320] However, Puno and colleagues, van der Schoot and co-workers, and other evidence reviewed by

Tetsworth and Paley strengthen the case that malalignment of tibial fractures probably increases the long-term risk for arthrosis.[455, 566, 603] Certainly, some patients with deformity after tibial shaft fractures are symptomatic. Perhaps as Olerud has pointed out, the ability to compensate varies and is related to the range of subtalar joint motion, among other factors.[420]

Because it is not possible to predict which patients with deformity will be symptomatic, it remains appropriate to strive for restoration of normal alignment during treatment of tibial fractures. Kyro reported on 64 patients with nailed tibial fractures, 17 of whom healed in malalignment (>5° angulation or rotation, >10-mm shortening).[322] Symptoms were significantly more frequent in those with malalignment. However, the evidence that aggressive treatment of asymptomatic malalignment reduces the risk of late post-traumatic arthrosis is not yet conclusive. Thus, for truly asymptomatic patients, I discuss the techniques, risks, and potential benefits of correction of deformity and the alternatives of activity modification and accommodative shoes. Osteotomy is considered on a case-by-case basis. Occasionally, cosmetic deformity is a significant consideration for the patient.

## EVALUATION AND PLANNING

Assessment and correction of skeletal deformity are reviewed extensively in Chapter 62, to which the reader is referred. Tibial diaphyseal deformity is due to alterations in length, rotation, angulation, and transverse-plane displacement. Usually, more than one of these factors is significantly present. Deformity that is symptomatic or sufficiently severe is an indication for osteotomy. Before undertaking an osteotomy, however, the surgeon must consider multiple issues and make an individualized assessment and treatment plan. The condition of the surrounding soft tissues may significantly affect the healing potential of incisions for osteotomy and fixation. Arteries and nerves may be at risk during surgery or from tension produced by correction of the deformity. Mobility and alignment of the foot and ankle need to be assessed because tibial alignment may affect, for better or worse, their ability to function during gait. When planning an osteotomy for tibial malunion, one should strive to restore the mechanical axis of the lower extremity by placing the foot in a neutral position at the end of a line beginning at the center of the femoral head and passing through the

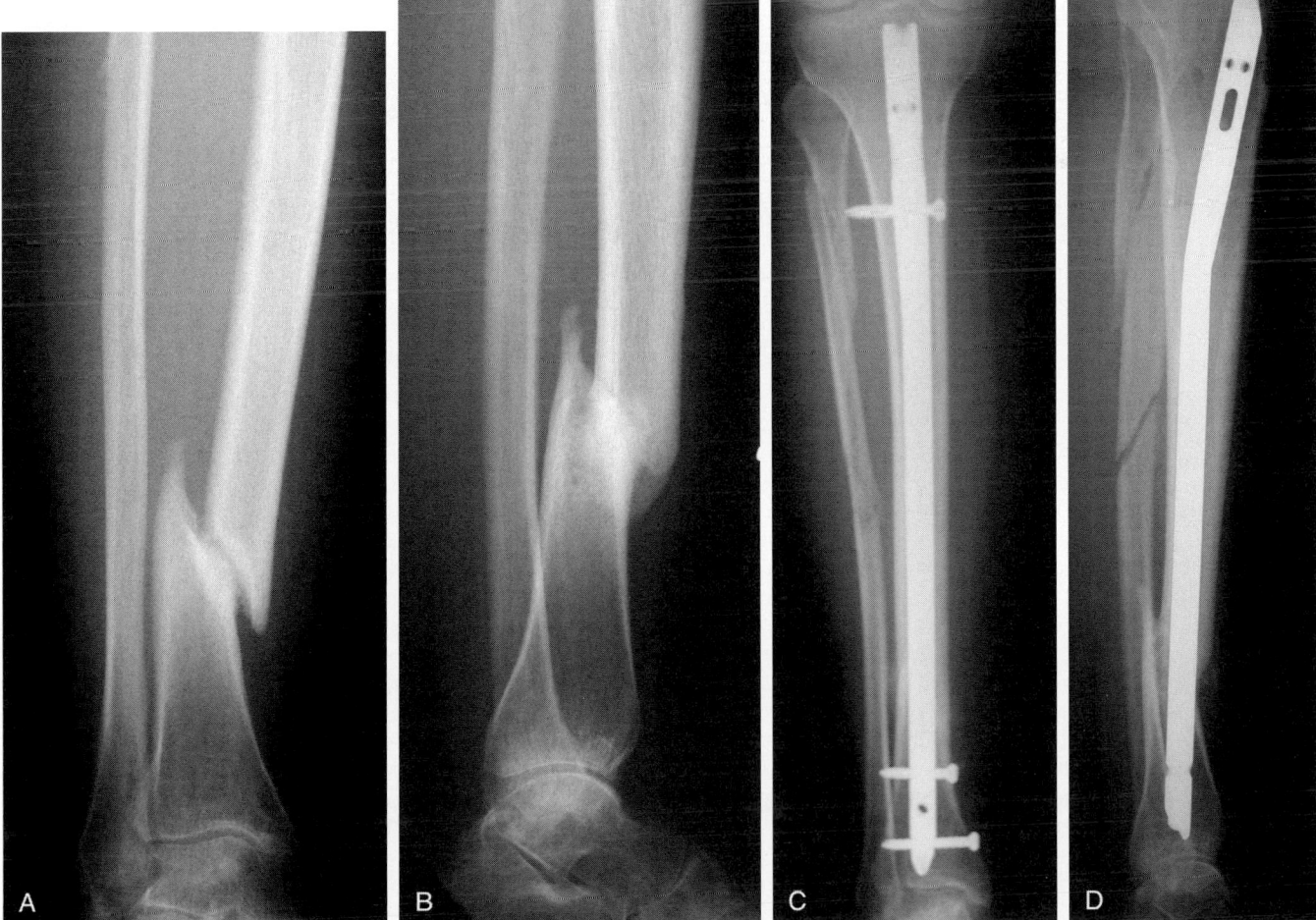

**FIGURE 57–60.** Intramedullary (IM) nailing for nonunion with moderate deformity. *A, B,* Twelve months after a low-energy, moderately displaced distal tibia fracture. The patient is fully weight bearing but experiencing pain after much walking, and a progressive varus deformity is present. *C, D,* After release of the nonunion through a small incision, oblique fibular osteotomy, distraction, and antegrade IM nailing. Stout, sharp guide wires were driven through the endosteal callus under fluoroscopic control before reamed IM nail fixation. Slight recurvatum was accepted in lieu of additional soft tissue release.

center of the knee on the AP view and through a point on the proximal tibial articular surface one fifth the distance posteriorly from its anterior edge (see Fig. 62–2E). The mechanical and anatomic axes of the tibia are parallel, with the anatomic axis a little medial and posterior. The anatomic axis connects the midpoints of the "outside-diameter" lines crossing the diaphysis transversely on AP or lateral radiographs. The mechanical axis connects the midpoints of the knee and ankle joints. The angles that the axes make with the joint surfaces of knee and ankle and the points where they cross these joints can be determined from properly positioned radiographs of both the normal and deformed sides to provide the information necessary for planning. Length and rotational alignment must be separately determined. With this information, the nature of a deformity can be determined and options for its correction assessed. To restore normal alignment, the surgeon should not merely correct angulation but should also realign the axes of the proximal and distal segments, as well as equalize length and correct malrotation. By determining the center of rotation of angulation, the point where the axes of the proximal and distal tibial segments meet, the surgeon can select the location and type of osteotomy for realignment. Limitations of the surrounding soft tissue may dictate the safety of a potential osteotomy site or means of fixation. The surgeon must have a variety of options available. Osteotomies can be performed percutaneously, with comparatively little soft tissue exposure, or with a much more extensile incision. Correction of deformity can be completed at the time of osteotomy, or it can be carried out progressively with an appropriately adjustable hinged external fixator. Acute correction may compromise soft tissues and precipitate a compartment syndrome or nerve traction injury.[358] Bone defects resulting from correction of deformity can be filled with bone graft acutely, which may be of value in promoting osteotomy healing as well, or the defects can be filled with the regenerate bone that forms in response to traction histogenesis with appropriately paced deformity correction in a sufficiently stable external fixator (see Chapter 21). If correction of deformity cannot be accomplished by an osteotomy that has a high probability of uncomplicated healing of both soft tissue and bone, consideration must be given to improving soft tissue coverage simultaneously or before proceeding. Such coverage might be accomplished with either local or free tissue transfer or through traction histogenesis concurrent with correction of the deformity (for example, a shortening osteotomy that might remove marginally viable tissue, followed by lengthening from another focus).

Rarely, if ever, is it possible to correct post-traumatic tibial diaphyseal deformity with a closing wedge metaphyseal osteotomy similar to that used to treat knee arthritis. Failure to address all aspects of a patient's deformity may increase some components of malalignment while correcting the one that the surgeon is focusing on. Adequate analysis and preoperative planning will prevent such surprises.

For symptomatic patients with significant deformity, an osteotomy is the appropriate treatment. A complete preoperative evaluation and careful planning are essential for best results.[39, 254, 272, 355, 356, 358, 498] Details of defor-

mity assessment and planning for osteotomy are reviewed in Chapter 62. When planning an osteotomy, it is important to consider not only the effect that it will have on the deformity, but also how it will be fixed, whether a fibular osteotomy will be required, and especially whether previous bacterial contamination, vascular impairment, or tenuous soft tissue coverage will increase the risk of infection, wound slough, and impaired healing. One might need to avoid an otherwise suitable region of the bone to not create a wound that may heal poorly. Internal fixation, particularly IM nailing, may be less appropriate than external fixation. Slow correction of deformity with Ilizarov techniques to permit soft tissue accommodation may be safer than immediate, complete correction.

A number of authors have described various techniques for tibial osteotomy.* For primarily uniplanar deformities, the oblique osteotomy described by Sangeorzan and colleagues, by Johnson, and by Sanders and co-workers is attractive if the surrounding soft tissue is sufficiently healthy.[272, 498, 501] Oblique osteotomies can be very helpful for properly selected tibial deformities. An appropriately oriented oblique osteotomy allows correction of both angulation and rotation by rotating the distal tibial fragment around an axis perpendicular to the osteotomy plane.[501] A fibular osteotomy is required as well. When carried out before placing a screw in the axis of rotation, distraction can often restore some additional length as well. A long oblique osteotomy surface provides good bone contact and promotes secure fixation, as well as reliability and speed of union. Grafting is not usually required. Surface trimming with a cooled saw blade can adjust the osteotomy if required before final fixation (Fig. 57–66).

Complex deformities can be corrected by osteotomy through the site of the malunion and then fixed, usually with a plate and occasionally with an IM nail (Fig. 57–67).[272] IM nail fixation is durable and generally easier for patients to tolerate because it avoids both the external fixation and prolonged limitation of weight bearing that may be advisable after plating.[364, 370, 634] However, it may be difficult to align and open the medullary canal to permit nail fixation. Extensive soft tissue stripping may be required, but such stripping devascularizes the tibia, delays healing, and makes bone grafting advisable. Length may be difficult to restore, even with the AO distractor, which is a necessary aid. Interlocking nails offer more secure control of alignment than simple nails do and are thus preferable after tibial osteotomy. The surgeon may need to use position screws (see Figs. 57–27 and 57–28).

Deformity and callus in the medullary canal may preclude nail insertion. In such cases, nailing is not a good option, and plating is thus the only reasonable choice for internal fixation. The possibilities of plate fixation might be extended with percutaneous osteotomies and minimal-incision plating.[39] However, soft tissue health and pliability set limits on plated osteotomies. If the skin envelope will not tolerate osteotomy and plating, Ilizarov techniques should be chosen instead.[97, 348, 404]

---

*See references 39, 254, 271, 364, 370, 498, 501, 552, 634, 637, 639.

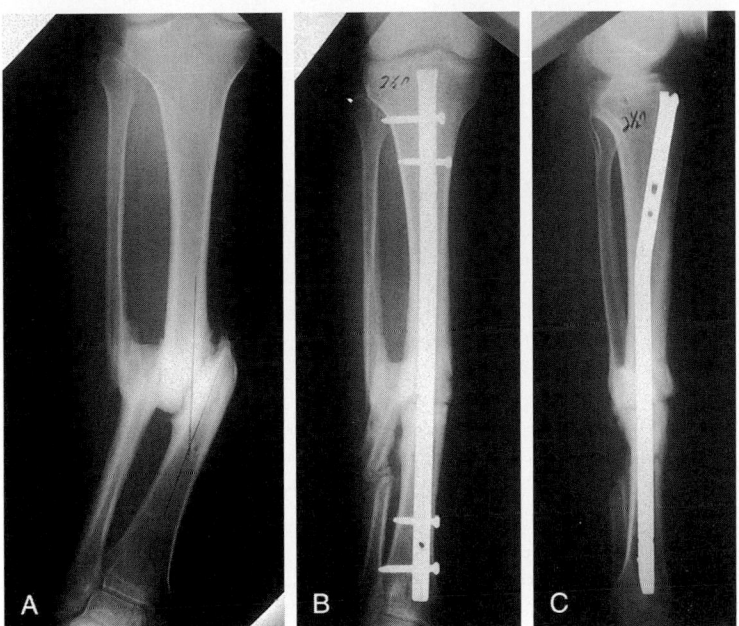

**FIGURE 57–61.** Intramedullary (IM) nailing for nonunion with severe deformity. *A,* Malaligned, ununited tibia-fibula fracture after external fixation of an originally open fracture and premature transition to a cast. *B, C,* Anteroposterior and lateral radiographs after a difficult open reduction involving fibular osteotomy and "take-down" of the nonunion with distraction and nailing after removal of medullary callus. IM nail fixation of fresh fractures and bone grafting with external fixator retention until union are two ways to avoid this degree of deformity.

### Length

Shortening of up to 2 cm can be tolerated by most patients, although a shoe lift or insole may improve comfort and function.[208, 548] Many patients are unhappy about this possibility, however. Correction can be obtained, if appropriate, with traction histogenesis or with osteotomy and acute lengthening in the 1.5- to 3.0-cm range.[271] Patients who undergo osteotomy for angular deformities often regain some length in the process and usually desire length correction if at all possible. Thus, the surgeon should assess leg length and the effect that osteotomy will have on it and consider additional measures to restore length if necessary.

### Rotation

Minor rotational deformities are not a problem, but van der Werken and Marti advise osteotomy if external rotation is greater than 20° or internal rotation is greater than 15°.[604] Rotation is often a component of a deformity that has other important aspects as well. Occasionally, it is the predominant problem, particularly after IM nailing when rotational alignment was not restored or was lost because of the absence of static locking. Purely rotational deformity can usually be corrected by percutaneous osteotomy and fixation with an IM nail appropriately locked with both proximal and distal locking screws. If the nail used has a slotted hole for so-called dynamic locking, it will control rotation while allowing load bearing across the osteotomy site. I have been happy using the Afghan percutaneous Gigli saw osteotomy for this purpose because it maximizes bone contact.[429] A good location, unless the osteotomy must be directed elsewhere to deal with related deformity, is the proximal metadiaphyseal area, sufficiently distal to the proximal locking screws. The osteotomy should be oriented exactly perpendicular to the tibial axis unless some angular correction is desired as well. A fibular osteotomy is almost always required to allow rotational correction (Fig. 57–68).

## Refracture

Excessive loading before fracture healing may result in deformation of an incompletely healed fracture. White and co-workers defined four stages of fracture healing and demonstrated flexible and then more rigid failure, followed by high-energy failure through the fracture site, and finally, failure adjacent to the healed fracture.[618] The clinical relevance of such refracture from torsional loading of healed spiral tibial fractures has been demonstrated by Bostman.[69]

Refracture can also occur when hardware is removed too early, which is more likely with plate fixation, especially if direct bone healing predominates with little visible callus. Although waiting at least 18 months is generally sufficient, higher energy fractures and those with greater devascularization may heal more slowly. Removal of screws and external fixator pins transiently weakens bone, so a cast or brace with progressive weight bearing and avoidance of early torsional loading is recommended to protect against fracture through diaphyseal screw holes.[89] The length of time for the human tibial diaphysis to regain its strength after screw removal is not known for certain, but a waiting period of at least 6 weeks before unsupported weight bearing and a delay of 12 weeks before initiating contact or risk activities are conventional restrictions. It has been asserted that plates cause progressive disuse osteopenia as a result of stress protection.

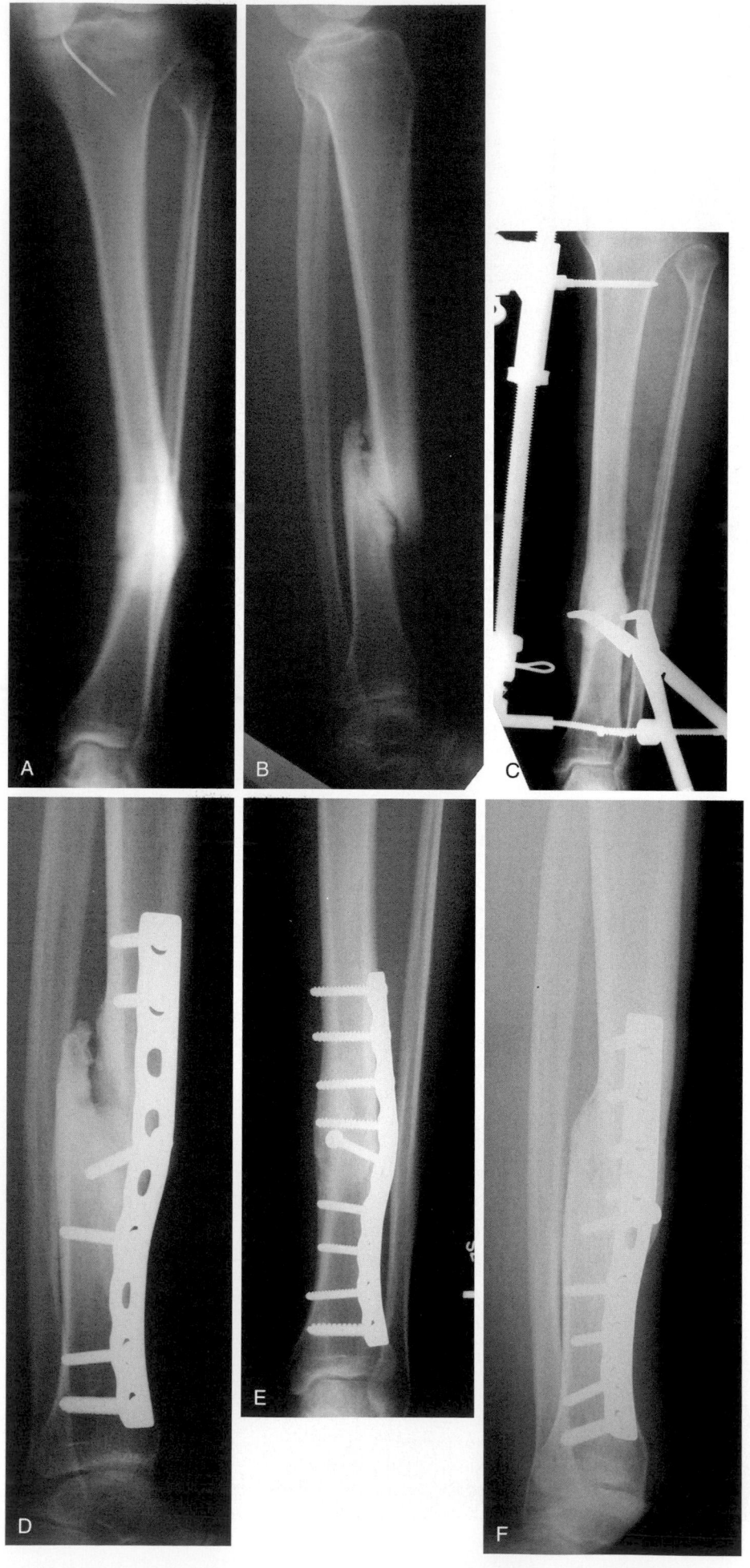

FIGURE 57–62. Plate for repair of nonunion. *A, B,* Anteroposterior and lateral radiographs of a moderately deformed tibial nonunion after unsuccessful fracture brace treatment. The short spiral fracture was initially 60% displaced after closed reduction under anesthesia. The initially satisfactory axial alignment was gradually lost. Although the patient was weight bearing and working, persistent pain and progressive deformity persuaded the patient to undergo operative treatment. *C,* Open reduction with a distractor and just enough exposure to allow release for correction of deformity and application of a reduction clamp. *D,* After replacing the clamp with a lag screw, a neutralization plate was applied. *E* and *F,* Healed nonunion 4 months later.

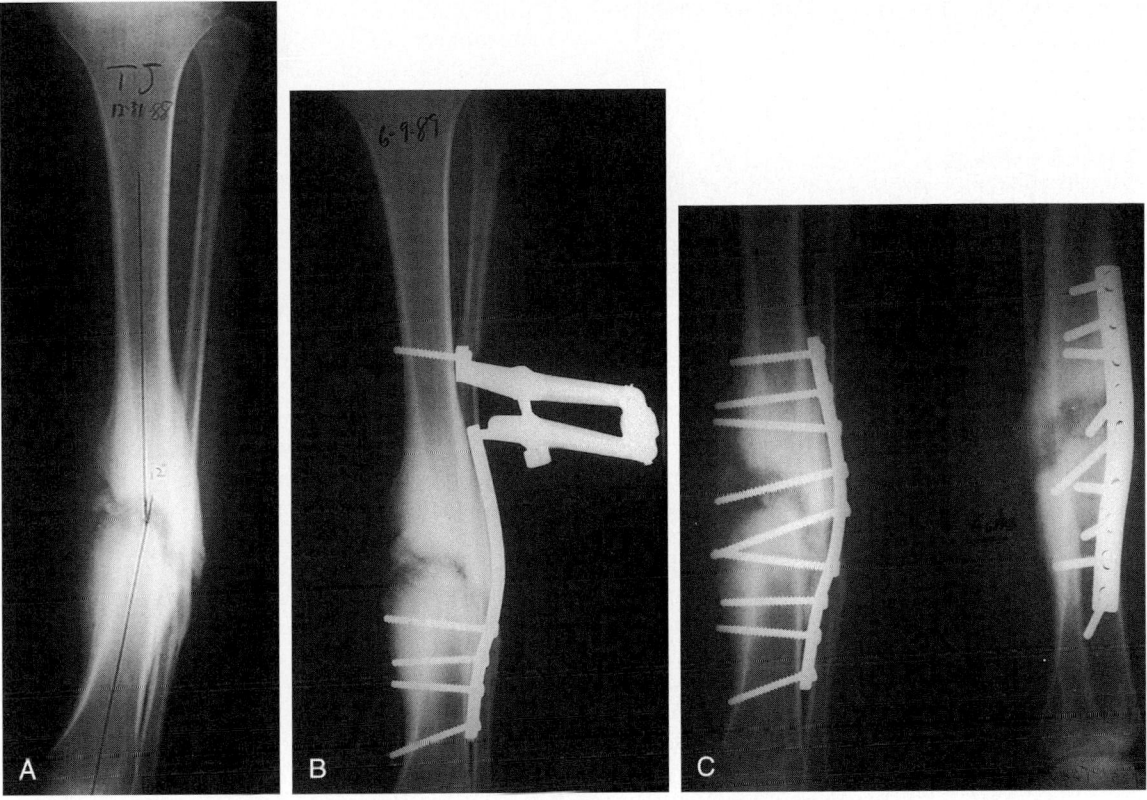

**FIGURE 57–63.** Tension band plate for hypertrophic nonunion. *A,* Angulated, hypertrophic nonunion. *B,* Plate applied to a convex surface, with an external tension device used to correct the deformity. *C,* Healing in satisfactory alignment.

However, studies indicate that the osteopenia, which is well localized under the plate, is probably a result of interference with local vascularity and is not progressive.[264, 298] Therefore, leaving an appropriately chosen plate in place long enough to achieve complete healing should cause no concern because it reduces, rather than increases the risk of refracture. Karlsson and associates have shown a higher long-term incidence of subsequent fractures in patients who initially had a tibial fracture. Because new fractures did not involve the originally injured tibia any more than they did bones in other limbs, they concluded that the cause was the patient being

**FIGURE 57–64.** *A, B,* Nonunion after a midshaft osteotomy with wound slough and infection. The fracture is still ununited, but free of infection 6 months after free-flap coverage. *C, D,* Repair with open reduction and a wave plate. Bone graft was placed between the plate and the lateral tibial cortex.

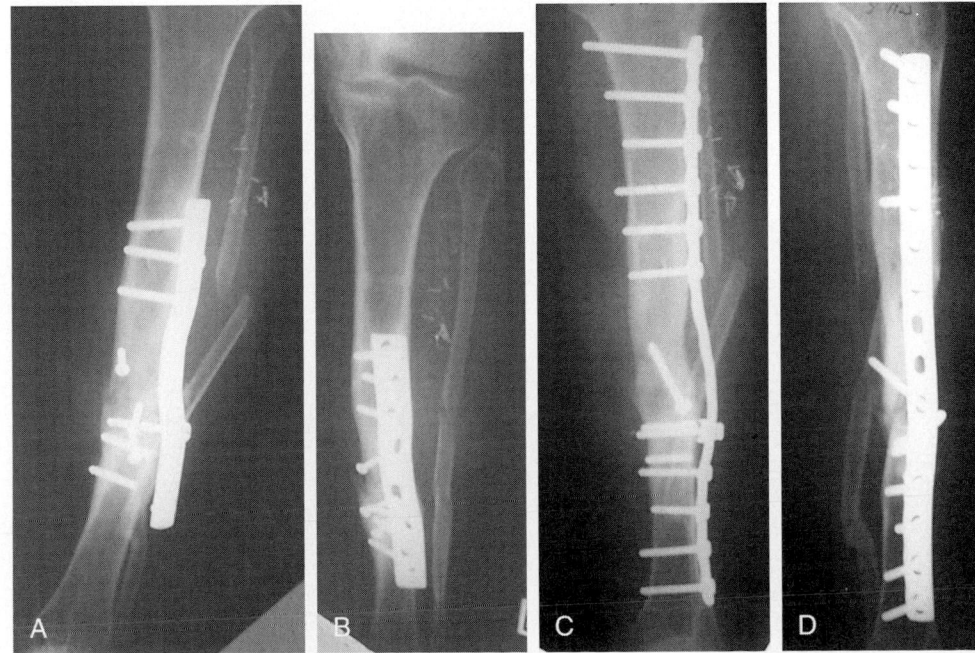

"fracture prone" rather than having structural weakness from residual tibial osteoporosis.[282]

## Pressure Sores

The use of casts and splints always risks development of a pressure sore, which typically occurs over a bony prominence. It is crucial to be aware of this complication, especially if the patient has an impaired level of consciousness or peripheral sensation or has poor nutrition. The risk of pressure sores can be reduced by appropriately padding all areas at risk, including the fibular head and neck, the posterior of the heel and the Achilles tendon, the malleoli, the anterior tibial crest, and the fracture site. Early inspection of such areas by bivalving the cast or looking through a cast window may permit correction of a problem before major tissue loss occurs. It is important to manage such a window with care. It should be well placed and be large enough to see the area in question. After windowing a cast, the piece of plaster removed should be replaced over adequate padding. Adhesive-backed foam padding can be directly applied to the removed piece of plaster. Failure to close a window can lead to localized swelling ("window edema") and more pressure problems around the edge of the window. Replaced or not, a window weakens a cast, usually too much for weight bearing and sometimes so much that the cast is no longer a satisfactory splint. Reinforcement, preferably with fiberglass cast tape, or replacement of the cast may be needed.

Although pressure sores are usually associated with casts and splints, they may also occur during treatment with external fixation. Occasionally, sores are caused by the pressure of a malpositioned frame component, but more often they occur because the entire weight of the leg is borne by the patient's heel on an inadequately padded bed surface. Because of obtundation, pain, or other impediments to moving the leg, a pressure sore develops on the posterior of the heel. Such sores may be prevented by suspending the leg from the fixator frame or by using padding that distributes the weight over the entire posterior surface of the leg. Should a pressure sore develop, immediate relief of pressure and appropriate wound care techniques must be initiated.

## Nerve Injuries

Direct injuries to the peripheral nerves of the leg may result from laceration, contusion, traction, or a combination of these mechanisms at the same time as the tibial fracture. It is thus vital to perform and document a detailed neurologic examination as soon as possible during the patient's care. If a complete examination is impossible, the possibility of an occult nerve injury must be kept in mind and precautions taken, including a complete documented examination as soon as feasible. Nerve injuries can occur during treatment, as well as from the initial trauma.[309, 502, 609, 621] Obviously, care must be taken during surgical approaches and the application of fixation, including percutaneous pins or wires for external fixators. Pressure injury from a cast, particularly over the peroneal nerve as it rounds the proximal end of the fibula, is a well-known complication. The same may occur from pressure of a splint, traction frame, fracture table, and even the hospital bed. If loss of peroneal nerve function occurs, the subcutaneous course of this nerve must be inspected. It is important to never blame a nerve injury, including "tourniquet palsy," for loss of motor or sensory function in a patient in whom a compartment syndrome is developing. Although pain is usually present with compartment syndromes, if a sensory deficit is already present or if the

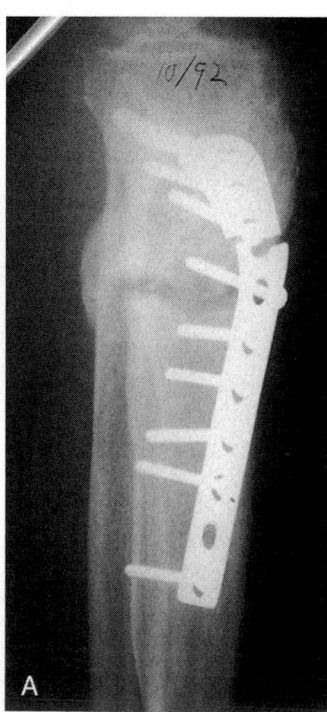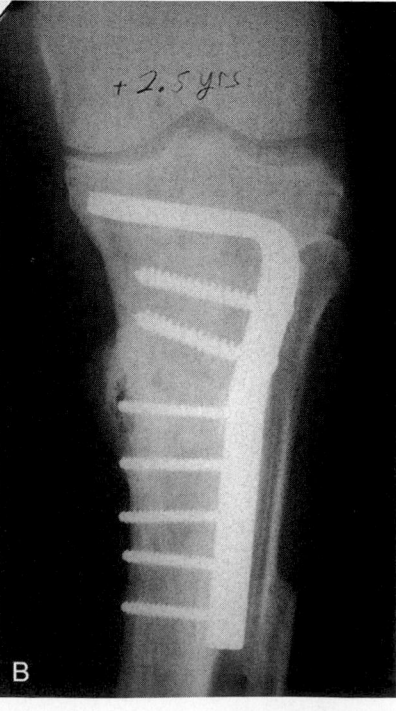

FIGURE 57–65. Blade plate for periarticular nonunion. *A,* Nonunion and a failed tibial head plate. *B,* Repair with a blade plate applied with axial compression.

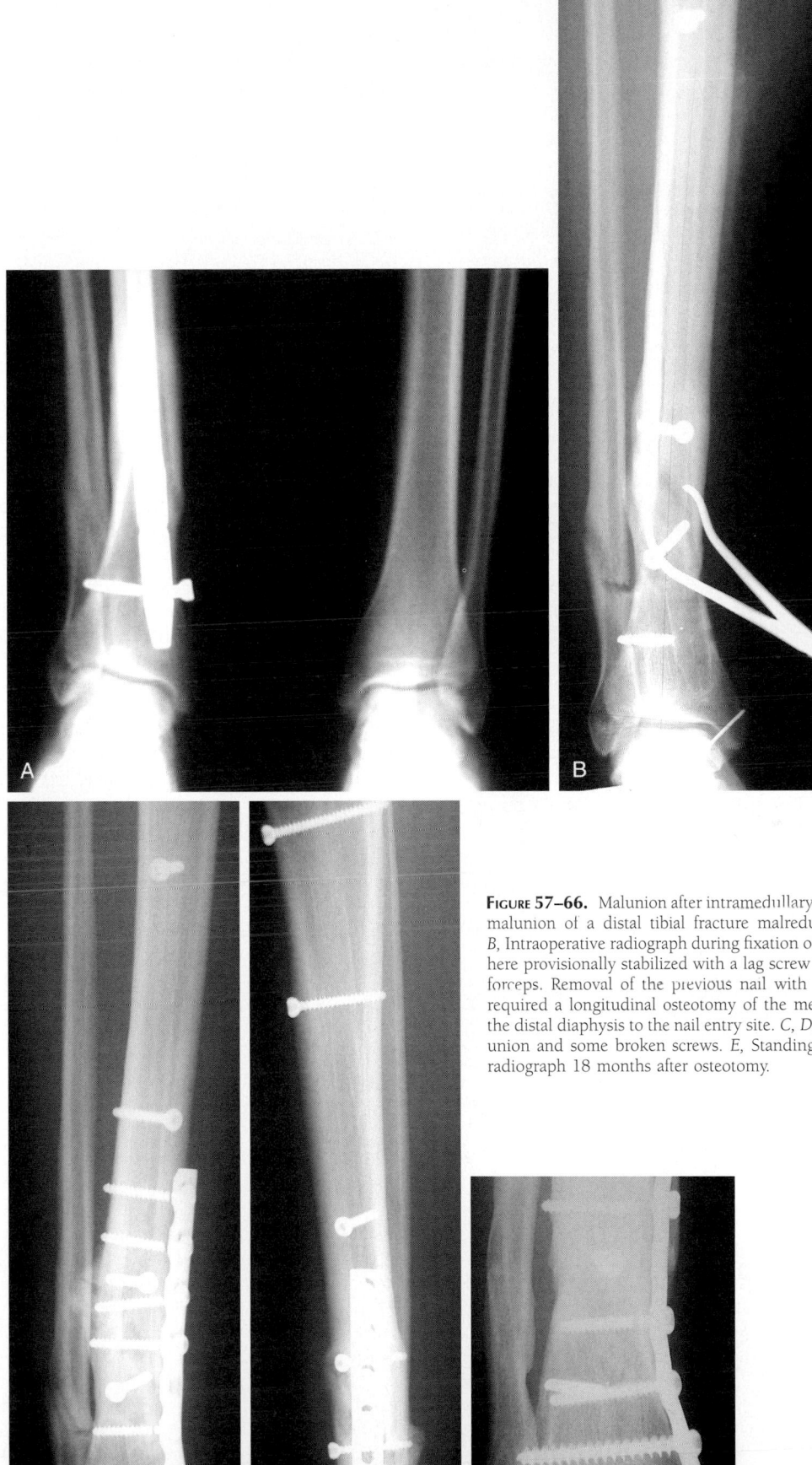

**FIGURE 57–66.** Malunion after intramedullary (IM) nailing. *A,* Valgus malunion of a distal tibial fracture malreduced with an IM nail. *B,* Intraoperative radiograph during fixation of an oblique osteotomy, here provisionally stabilized with a lag screw and pointed reduction forceps. Removal of the previous nail with its bulbous distal end required a longitudinal osteotomy of the medial tibial cortex from the distal diaphysis to the nail entry site. *C, D,* Six-month views with union and some broken screws. *E,* Standing ankle anteroposterior radiograph 18 months after osteotomy.

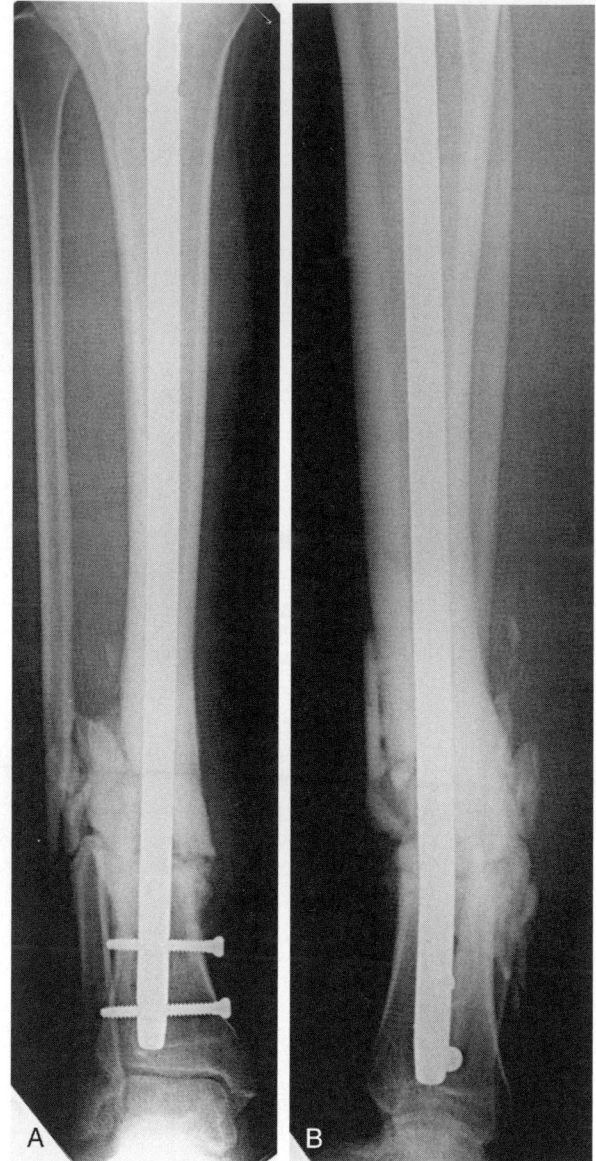

**FIGURE 57–67.** Malunion after intramedullary (IM) nailing. Anteroposterior (*A*) and lateral (*B*) radiographs after osteotomy of the tibia and fibula with IM nail fixation. (The preoperative radiograph is shown in Figure 57–21.) A posterolateral bone graft had been inserted before the fracture healed in a valgus position, which was intolerable to this active man with a previous subtalar arthrodesis.

painful period is missed for some reason, this initially treatable cause of impaired neural function may be ignored.[230, 260] Impaired strength or sensation can also be a sign of arterial injury.

## Vascular Problems

The diagnosis and treatment of arterial injuries associated with tibial fractures have been discussed previously, as well as in Chapter 11. The onset of vascular occlusion can be delayed, so adequate patient monitoring must include continued assessment of vascular status. Invasive fracture treatment can result in arterial injuries.[601, 623] Later, false aneurysms and arteriovenous fistulas may be found.

Venous insufficiency may be the result of an associated acute injury, as well as deep venous thrombosis, which is common and probably occurs in a significant percentage of shaft fractures.[411, 632] Abelseth and associates reported a 22% incidence (95% confidence interval, 12% to 36%) in surgically treated patients without risk factors or preoperative delay.[1] The insufficiency is most often limited to the deep veins of the calf and is not typically recognized. It usually has no evident sequelae, but occasionally, thrombosis may progress proximally or pulmonary embolism may occur. Risk factors for pulmonary embolism should be assessed and anticoagulation considered for high-risk patients after the early stages of injury. To date, there appear to be no accepted guidelines for anticoagulation in patients with isolated tibial shaft fractures, although some have suggested its advisability, even for those who are mobilized immediately in a cast.[1, 306] Certainly, any symptoms or signs that suggest a pulmonary embolism after a tibial fracture must be seriously evaluated with a ventilation-perfusion scan, spiral CT, pulmonary angiogram, or any combination of these techniques if indicated. Patients with more leg swelling than expected should be considered for color duplex Doppler ultrasonography or leg venography. Routine anticoagulation for all patients with tibial fractures is not without risk, as demonstrated by a report of compartment syndrome 12 days after injury in a prophylactically anticoagulated patient.[371]

Chronic venous stasis is a potentially challenging problem after tibia shaft fractures complicated by venous thrombosis.[6, 452] The relative rarity of chronic swelling is fortunate given the prevalence of venous occlusion, but it is usual for a patient to have some degree of foot and calf edema during the months after a tibial fracture. Elastic support stockings are thus frequently beneficial until the tendency for swelling abates.

## Reflex Sympathetic Dystrophy ("Algodystrophy")

omplex regional pain syndrome is a diffuse limb pain response to injury whose character is often described as "burning." It is typically, but variably associated with diffuse trophic changes in skin and bone, as well as autonomic, sensory, and motor neurologic abnormalities. Joint involvement may additionally compromise outcomes.[324] Sarangi reported radiographic evidence of diffuse osteoporosis characteristic of reflex sympathetic dystrophy (RSD) that was unrelated to the type of treatment in 30% of 60 patients with unilateral tibial fractures.[503] Smith and co-workers suggest that external fixation may predispose to RSD.[545] Tandon and colleagues found that earlier functional rehabilitation that included weight bearing reduced its frequency.[559] Patients may have a predisposing personality pattern.[139] If a patient with a tibial fracture seems to be having a particularly difficult time with pain and an inability to use the injured limb and if other causes have been adequately excluded, RSD should be considered. It can usually be addressed effectively with more vigorous supportive rehabilitation, but medications and nerve blocks may need to be considered (see Chapter 7).

## Compartment Syndromes

Compartment syndromes, listed here for completeness, have been discussed previously in this chapter and more thoroughly in Chapter 12. Tibial fracture patients who have had compartment syndromes, even after prompt diagnosis and decompression, often have persisting symptoms, but it is hard to correlate them with the duration of elevated pressure.[402, 587]

## Associated Fatigue Fracture

During rehabilitation and after a period of prolonged non–weight bearing, some patients will have pain and well-localized tenderness in a metatarsal, the calcaneal tuberosity, or the distal end of the fibula. Radiographs are usually normal initially. The results of other studies may become positive and confirm a fatigue fracture. The usual treatment is temporary reduction of weight bearing rather than external immobilization.

## Limited Joint Motion

Injuries to the articular surfaces of the knee, ankle, subtalar joint, or foot are obvious causes of impaired motion, post-traumatic arthritis, and pain. They are discussed in Chapters 55 and 61 and are mentioned here only to remind the reader that early recognition is necessary for effective treatment of these injuries[68, 605] (see Fig. 57–48). Bowing of an intact fibula associated with a shortened tibial fracture may cause ankle symptoms.[279]

*Contractures* also involve these same joints after tibial fractures, even without direct articular injury. Such problems are rare at the knee, but most are probably the result of unrecognized knee injuries.[568] Some loss of knee motion may result from prolonged immobilization. Contractures are more significant problems in the ankle and foot, as demonstrated and discussed by McMaster after closed treatment[372] and Merriam and Porter after open treatment[380] and confirmed by Horne and associates.[253] Most common is subtalar stiffness without bony damage, which was present in 72% of patients in McMaster's series and in 50% of Merriam and Porter's. Motion was better preserved after internal fixation and in both groups was only occasionally severe enough to be a functional problem (12% after closed treatment and 16% after open treatment). Operative fracture fixation followed by early motion does appear to decrease foot and ankle stiffness (Fig. 57–69). Some studies suggest that the severity of a contracture is related to the amount of soft tissue damage, especially in the lower half of the leg. Unrecognized deep posterior compartment syndrome can also cause contrac-

tures, especially of the forefoot and toes.[283] Rupture or loss of the posterior tibial tendon may cause a pes planus deformity.

Failure to immobilize the foot and ankle in a functional position results in far more disability than mere loss of motion does. A fixed equinovarus deformity is to be avoided at all cost, which can usually be accomplished with a cast or splint. More severe open injuries are especially well managed by extending the external fixator out to the foot. In patients with severe open tibial fractures, Edwards and associates reported only a 5% incidence of major problems with foot and ankle contractures.[155] Toe flexion contractures can often be prevented by repeated passive manipulation, but they occasionally persist or recur and, if symptomatic, benefit from surgical correction.

Recovery of ankle and, especially, foot mobility is slow after tibial fractures but often occurs if a patient can initiate weight bearing with the foot in a functional position. If weight bearing must be delayed, maintenance of a neutral position is important, as are early vigorous, active range-of-motion exercises for the toes and ankle.

## Late Arthritis

Direct joint damage is a well-accepted cause of post-traumatic arthritis. Post-traumatic skeletal deformity also contributes to the development of arthritis, although the details of this association and the acceptable limit of malalignment remain uncertain, as discussed earlier. Long-term follow-up studies of tibial fractures are rare. If significant deformity is present with radiologically mild arthritis, an osteotomy, as discussed previously, may relieve the symptoms.

Once severe arthritis develops, correction of deformity may still be advisable, but arthrodesis of the symptomatic distal joints is the best method for managing disabling symptoms that do not respond to conservative therapy consisting of well-cushioned footgear, bracing of the foot and ankle, oral anti-inflammatory agents, and reduced activity.

## Functional Disabilities

Few reports detail the functional results after tibial fractures, and it is not clear how long complete recovery takes. Depending on the severity of injury, the frequency of reported good or excellent results ranges from 50% to 100%, although one must remember Bridgman and Baird's demonstration that the same group of patients could be considered to have a prevalence of suboptimal results ranging from 4% to 42%, depending on which criteria are chosen.[33, 76, 156, 270] At 5 years, Peter and colleagues found minimal problems after low-energy fractures treated with functional braces, but only half had returned to skiing by 1 year after injury.[441] Horne and co-workers reported that after a 68-month follow-up, only 21% of patients were asymptomatic and only 40% could participate in all activities without difficulty. Nineteen percent had severe, constant pain, 60% had visible deformity, 24% had modified their work, and 52% had reduced walking tolerance. Symptoms correlated best with reduced ankle rather than subtalar motion, and disability was more common with more distal fractures.[253] DaSilva and associates provided confirmatory evidence.[130] Further work is necessary to adequately document the relationship between functional results and fracture severity and treatment, including rehabilitation.

## Poor Cosmetic Result

Deformity of bone and soft tissues can produce an unsightly leg that may be more or less objectionable to the patient. Injury severity and problems during treatment are major determinants of the leg's appearance. Some improvement may be achieved with delayed plastic and recon-

structive surgery involving the skin and soft tissues, as well as the bones of the leg.

## Fibular Fractures

The anatomy and function of the fibula have been discussed previously in the section on anatomy. Weight bearing is not a major function of the fibula under normal conditions.[558] It has been claimed to carry approximately 17% of body weight, but the figure may be closer to 6%.[325, 558] Proximally, it anchors the lateral supports of the knee. Distally, it is the crucial lateral buttress for the talus and ankle joint. Although structural continuity of the fibula is not important if the tibia is intact, patients with tibial fractures are often aided by fibular union, and occasionally fixation of the fibula is indicated as a means of

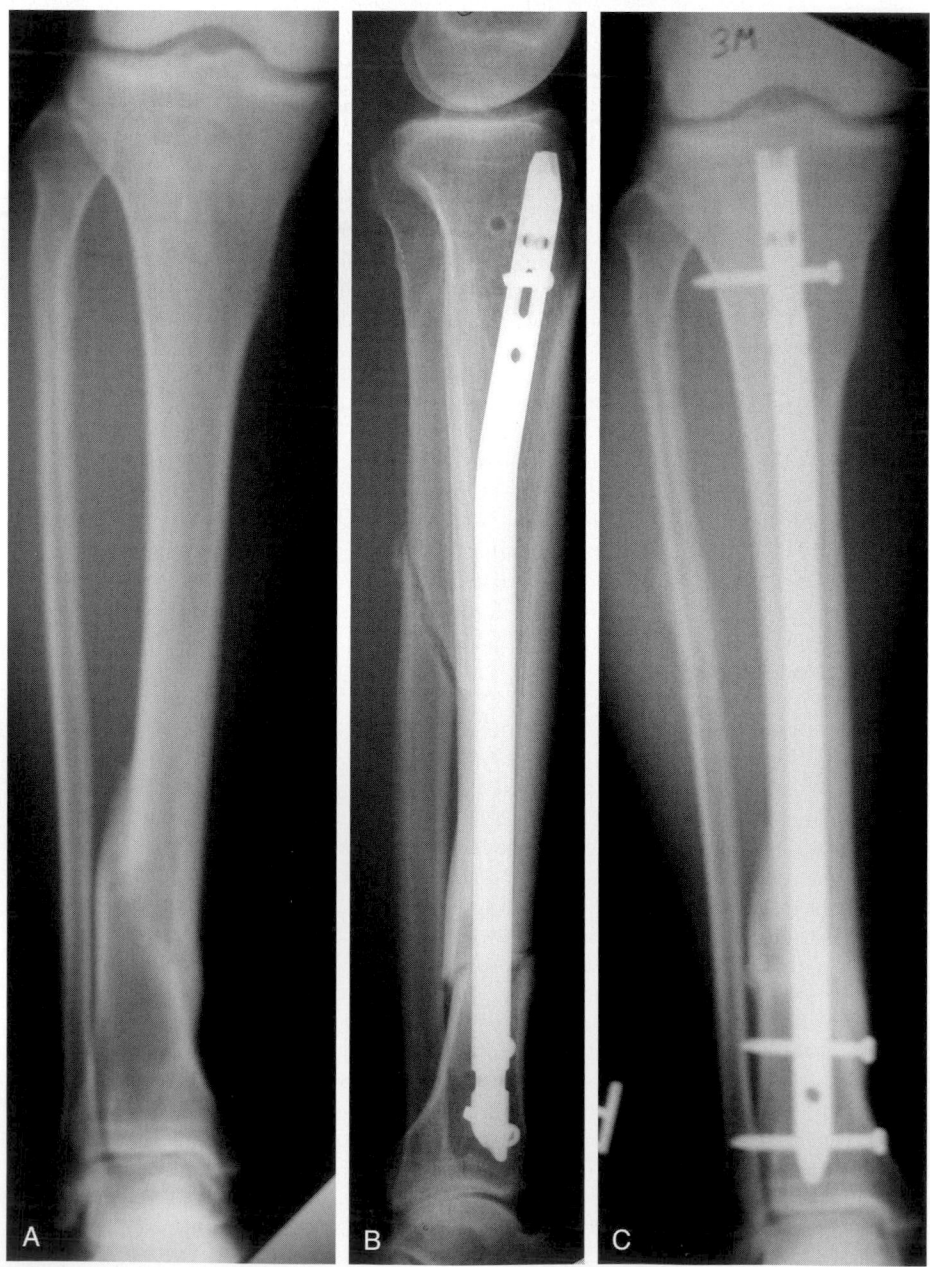

**Figure 57–68.** Rotational malunion. A 30° externally rotated malunion of a tibia-fibula shaft fracture was corrected with a percutaneous "Afghan" osteotomy using a Gigli saw, a long oblique fibular osteotomy, and closed intramedullary nail fixation. *A*, Preoperative anteroposterior view showing slight varus angulation in addition to rotation. *B*, Lateral view 6 weeks after reamed nail fixation. Note the similar lateral views of both the knee and ankle, slight obliquity of the osteotomy to correct the varus deformity, and early callus. *C*, Radiographically and clinically healed at 3 months.

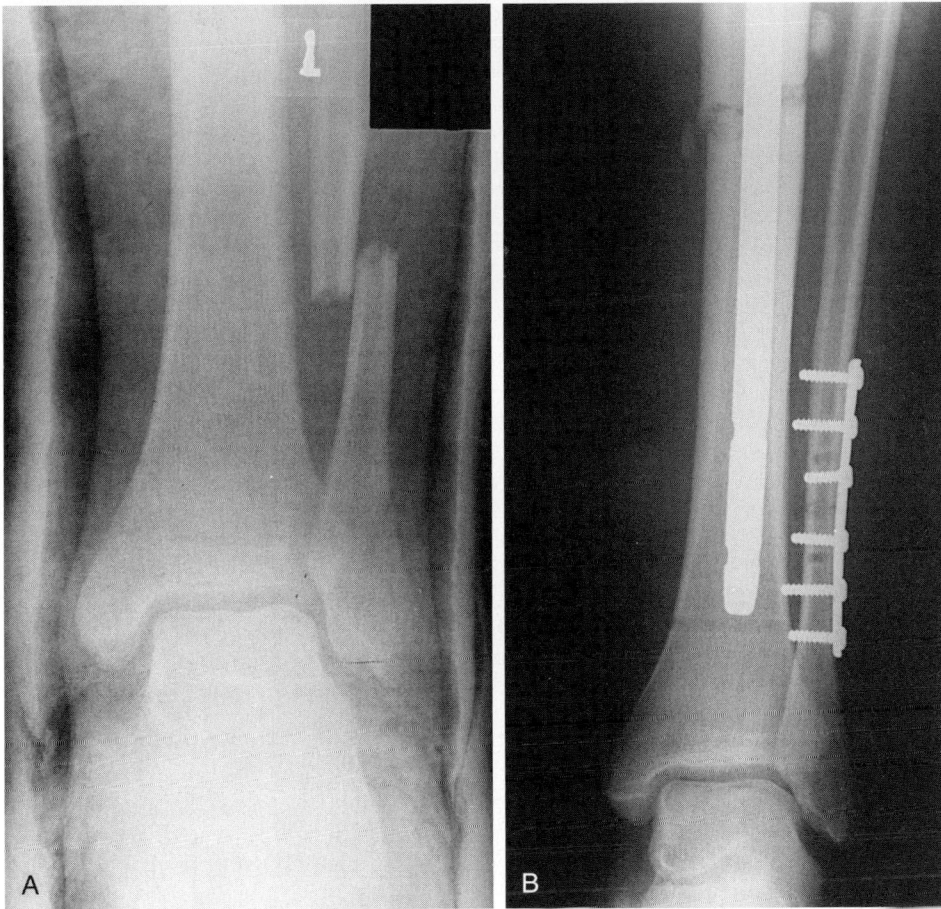

**FIGURE 57–69.** An ankle joint injury is occasionally associated with a tibial shaft fracture. Anatomic reduction and fixation provide the best opportunity for normal function of the ankle and may be required to gain satisfactory reduction of both fractures. *A,* Radiograph obtained when patient was first seen, 3 weeks after injury. *B,* After open reduction and internal fixation of both fractures. The transverse radiolucency distal to the tibial nail is from the bone distractor used to restore length.

restoring stability and alignment.[615] If used to substitute for the tibia in one of the so-called fibula-pro-tibia operations, it can hypertrophy significantly, albeit gradually. As helpful as an intact fibula can be, it will occasionally disturb the healing of a tibia shaft fracture and produce a varus deformity or possibly delayed union.[561] However, the presence of an intact fibula in association with a tibial shaft fracture is actually a marker for a less severe injury and thus an improved prognosis.[415, 416] IM nail fixation of an isolated tibial fracture counteracts the detrimental effects of the intact fibula.

Isolated acute fractures of the fibula should be evaluated carefully to exclude an occasionally associated significant injury. Truly isolated fibular fractures are almost always minor, and only symptomatic treatment is required. However, the situation may not be as it seems. Common associated injuries involve nerves and vessels, ligaments of the knee or ankle, and compartment syndromes, in addition to tibial shaft fractures.[7, 222, 279] Indirectly produced fibular fractures are caused by external rotation of the foot, which often produces a distal fibular fracture at or slightly above the ankle syndesmosis, but occasionally the fracture is much higher. This so-called Maisonneuve fracture is discussed further in Chapter 59. If the medial ankle disruption is purely ligamentous and if the talus is not displaced very far laterally, this injury complex may not be suspected. A spiral fracture pattern, ankle pain, tenderness, and instability are clues to the diagnosis of a

Maisonneuve fracture. Clearly, the ankle must be examined carefully when the fibula is fractured at any level.

Proximal fibular fractures may be caused by avulsion of the attachments of the fibular collateral ligament and biceps femoris tendon.

If the injury involves a blow to the lateral aspect of the calf during weight bearing, the resulting valgus force on the knee may tear the medial collateral ligament. The superficial, deep, or common peroneal nerves may be injured initially or may become involved as a result of progressive elevation of compartmental pressure in the anterior and lateral compartments. Because the fibula is contiguous with all four compartments, the deep and superficial posterior spaces are potentially involved as well. Even if the knee is stable, the possibility of a vascular injury, especially to the anterior tibial artery, must be considered.[7] Therefore, assessment of a patient with a fibular fracture must include a detailed neurovascular examination, repeated if symptoms increase or the patient's consciousness is compromised. Knee and ankle stability must be confirmed as well. Occasionally, especially in the young, the fibula may be bowed rather than fractured, and this bowing may interfere with reduction of an angulated tibial fracture.[196, 279]

Treatment of truly isolated fibular shaft fractures need only be symptomatic. A well-padded splint or cast may be useful briefly for comfort, but is not required. If the patient is comfortable, a lightly wrapped elastic bandage support is applied over adequate padding. Elevation, ice, crutches (with weight bearing as tolerated), and analgesics as needed are all helpful. Once the pain and swelling have largely resolved (usually in 1 to 2 weeks), progressive weight bearing is encouraged, and activities are allowed as the patient's capacity permits. Functional recovery is usually nearly complete by 6 to 8 weeks if the foregoing scheme is followed.

Rare indications do exist for fixation of fractures of the fibular shaft, typically to augment other fixation for a severe tibial fracture.[397] If required, fixation is best performed with a 3.5-mm, small-fragment dynamic compression plate with a minimum of three secure screws on each side of the fracture. If comminution or significant devascularization is present, bone grafting may be valuable as well. One must be careful to not injure the common peroneal nerve with an operation on the proximal end of the fibula. It is worth noting that fibular fixation is not an essential part of the surgical treatment of tibial plafond fractures.[622]

Complications after fibular shaft fracture include the neurovascular problems and associated injuries mentioned previously. Prompt recognition and treatment of arterial injuries and compartment syndrome are essential. Mino and Hughes reported late entrapment and palsy of the superficial peroneal nerve by fracture callus.[384] Nonunion occurs occasionally but is rarely symptomatic.[66, 153, 529] If treatment is indicated, fibular nonunion should respond to compression plate fixation, with or without a bone graft, depending on the pattern and vascularity of the fracture. Closed IM nailing of a fibular nonunion may be considered.[2] Resection of symptomatic hypertrophic nonunion has also been reported as successful.[529] Fibular malunion may affect the ankle mortise, typically because of shortening, which results in widening of the mortise because the lateral malleolus has a larger diameter distally. Malrotation is also possible. A CT scan plus comparison with the opposite ankle helps in planning treatment. Fibular osteotomy with a bone graft if needed to regain length should be performed before irreversible changes occur in the ankle joint.

## Injuries to the Proximal Tibiofibular Joint

The proximal tibiofibular joint is not a frequent site of recognized injuries, but it is at risk from both indirect and direct trauma.[13, 109, 245, 483, 571] Ogden's and Resnick and colleagues' comprehensive reviews have established our understanding of these injuries, which may occur with or be independent of tibial shaft fractures.[419, 465] Awareness is necessary so that early appropriate treatment can be carried out. Recurrent dislocations are rare.[194, 616] Reports and reviews of proximal tibiofibular joint injuries tend to focus on isolated injuries. It is important to look for disruption of this joint whenever a displaced tibial fracture is associated with an intact fibula.

Anatomically, the proximal tibiofibular joint has two major patterns: horizontal and oblique. Ogden used 20° as the dividing point between the two, though acknowledging a continuum from horizontal to 76°.[419] The more vertical joints had a smaller contact area. He believed that

an important role of the proximal tibiofibular joint is to permit slight rotation and relieve rotational stress at the ankle, a function that is lost after tibiofibular synostosis. The more vertical joints, perhaps because of less ability to accommodate rotation, seemed more frequent in those with dislocations. It is not clear how much weight is borne by the proximal joint, but it may be that the variation in joint anatomy signifies a similar variability in its loading.[157]

Four types of proximal tibiofibular joint injury can occur: subluxation, anterolateral dislocation, posteromedial dislocation, and superior (or proximal) dislocation. Their mechanisms, consequences, and treatments are different. Common to all are complaints of local pain, tenderness, and frequent distally radiating paresthesias, with or without objective peroneal nerve involvement. Local deformity may initially be masked by soft tissue swelling, and subtle findings may render early diagnosis difficult (see Fig. 57–49).

Subluxation of the proximal tibiofibular joint is associated with generalized ligamentous laxity. Hypermobility of the joint is associated with local tenderness. If symptoms do not resolve with observation or a brief period of splint or cast immobilization and especially if peroneal nerve palsy does not recover promptly, resection of the fibular head is indicated.

Anterolateral dislocation of the proximal tibiofibular joint is usually caused by an acute indirect injury produced by a relative internal rotation of the proximal aspect of the shank on the inverted talus with the knee flexed and the anterior and lateral compartment muscles contracting.[523] The fibular collateral ligament and biceps tendon are relaxed, and the rotational stress, combined with tension in the anterolateral muscle groups, tends to spring the proximal end of the fibula laterally and forward. Examination reveals prominence of the fibular head and an abnormal, anteriorly curving course of the biceps tendon.[169] Associated injuries may interfere with recognition of the dislocation.

Treatment is by closed reduction unless the diagnosis is excessively delayed.[126, 277, 419, 436] The knee is flexed to at least 70°, and the foot is dorsiflexed, pronated, and externally rotated. Direct pressure on the fibular head (but not over the peroneal nerve) then displaces it abruptly posteriorly over the lateral tibial ridge and back into its sulcus on the proximal end of the tibia. The reduction is usually quite stable. Ogden recommends active rehabilitation after 2 to 3 weeks of immobilization. However, 8 of his 14 patients had recurrent pain and subjective instability, for which he advises fibular head resection, which was successful in the 4 patients thus treated. Proximal arthrodesis is not recommended because it is associated with the development of subsequent ankle joint symptoms, presumably because of loss of rotation of the lateral malleolus. Difficulty obtaining fusion was also noted, along with hardware failure and symptomatic nonunion. Should ankle symptoms occur after proximal tibiofibular synostosis, a segmental fibulectomy distal to the synostosis or resection of the fibular head is Ogden's recommendation.[419] However, if delayed too long, ankle arthrosis may progress to the point that the symptoms are not relieved. Posteromedial proximal tibiofibular joint dislocation is a rare injury that is usually caused by direct, high-energy trauma. It is likely to be associated with damage to the lateral supporting structures of the knee joint. Nonoperative treatment has poor results. Surgical repair of the injured structures, including open reduction and temporary screw fixation of the proximal end of the fibula, is likely to offer the best results. It is essential to identify and protect the peroneal nerve during any such procedure.

Superior proximal tibiofibular joint dislocations are the result of a severe leg injury with a displaced tibial shaft fracture and an intact fibula[74, 86, 245, 483, 528] (Fig. 57–70). Although most isolated tibial shaft fractures are caused by lower energy injuries and thus have an overall improved prognosis, it is important to look for these rare injuries that have failed through the proximal tibiofibular joint rather than the fibular shaft. This dislocation, because of the force required to produce it, is associated with neurovascular injuries and compartment syndromes.[337] Anatomic reduction and secure stabilization of the tibial fracture usually reduce the proximal tibiofibular joint. If unsuccessful, closed or open reduction, perhaps with provisional stabilization, is probably warranted. Occasionally, impaction of the proximal tibiofibular joint blocks reduction of a tibial fracture.[530] Retention of the proximal part of the fibula at this time seems wise because it may be needed to reconstruct the leg. Persistent local symptoms may require later resection of the fibular head. In spite of a generally benign result, late instability can occur.[607]

## Fatigue and Insufficiency Fractures

Fatigue fractures occur when repetitive loading exceeds a bone's capacity to remodel in response to the application of cyclical stress.[87] They are often called "stress fractures," but "fatigue" more correctly emphasizes the role that cyclical loading plays in their etiology. They are most commonly seen in individuals who place significant demands on their lower extremities, such as soldiers, dancers, and runners.* A careful history usually reveals recently increased impact loading, such as an intensified or altered training schedule or a change in footgear or exercise surface. In distance runners, high mileage alone, without an increase, may be sufficient cause.[308] The increase in activity may not be remarkable—perhaps just repetitive twisting loads, as reported by Clayer and coauthors.[108] Occasionally, aggressive resumption of weight bearing after a period of disability provokes a fatigue fracture in a patient recovering from a previous injury.[442, 644] Both disuse osteopenia and increased mechanical stress may be involved in the occasional tibial fatigue fracture seen after ankle arthrodesis.[338, 385] There may be a relationship to decreased bone mass.[447] Another noteworthy pair of risk factors are dietary problems and menstrual abnormalities in female athletes.[43, 578] Fatigue fractures tend to involve the

---

*See references 36, 43, 138, 148, 366, 396, 410, 423, 460, 553.

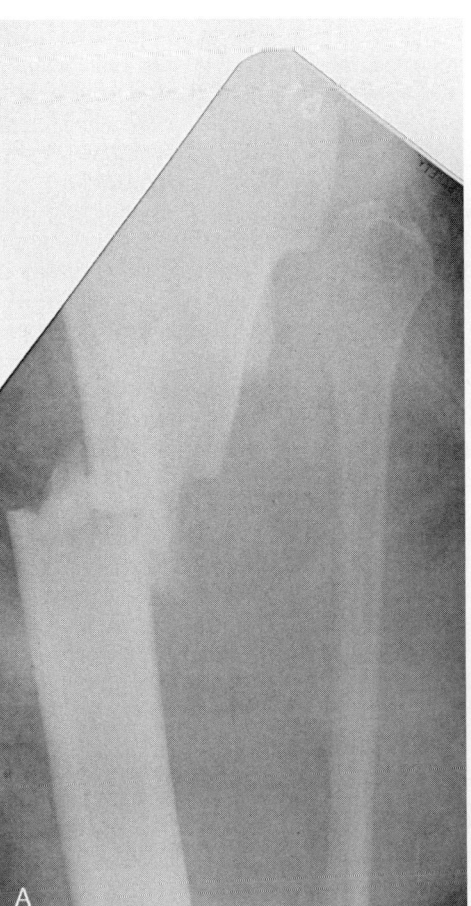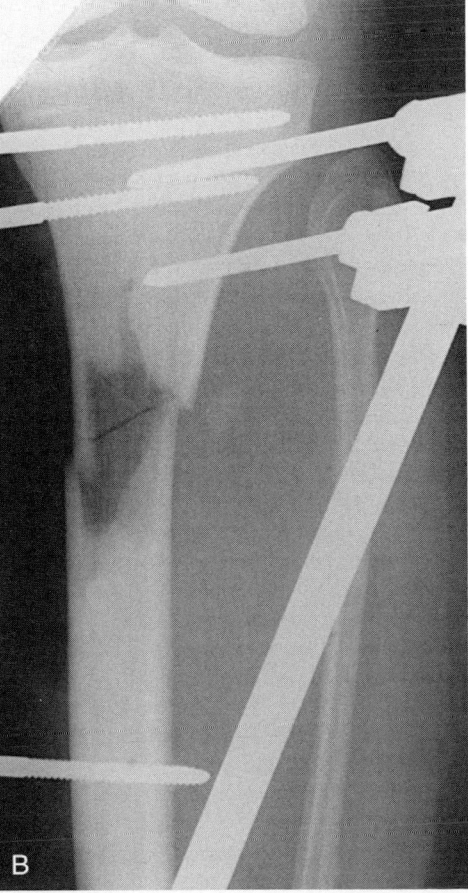

**FIGURE 57–70.** Dislocation of the fibula associated with a severe proximal tibial fracture. *A,* After provisional casting. *B,* After débridement and external fixation.

"push-off" leg.[159] In soldiers, an association was found between tibial fatigue fractures and shorter tibial length, relatively greater valgus knee alignment, right leg dominance, and increased external rotation range of the hip, as well as membership in specific military units.[175] Emery and colleagues reported tibial fatigue fractures occurring after harvest of an ipsilateral segmental fibular bone graft.[165] In patients with reduced bone tolerance for cyclical loading—generally, reduced mineral content or increased brittleness—the term *insufficiency fracture* is often applied.[12, 83, 438] Typically, this variety of fatigue fracture occurs in patients with generalized osteopenia. Patients with rheumatoid arthritis, especially if taking steroids, or with angular deformity of their lower extremities are also at risk.[341] Such fatigue fractures may be confused with a flare-up of the patient's arthritis.[521] Bone scans may be positive before the onset of symptoms.[386]

The location of fatigue fractures is typical and is perhaps related to specific activities.[489] The location of maximal tibia deformation (strain) varies with a person's activity.[158] Thus, a relationship between activity and the typical location of fatigue fractures might be expected. The bones of the foot, particularly the metatarsals, are often reported as the most frequent site of fatigue fractures, but the tibia and fibula are also significantly involved.[553] The posterior surface of the tibial diaphysis from the proximal third to the junction of the middle and distal thirds is the usual location. The anterior tibial cortex can be involved, particularly in "leaping athletes," and typically heals slowly with a risk of the fracture completing unless activities are sharply curtailed.[35, 423, 441] Occasionally, fatigue fractures involve the supramalleolar aspect of the tibia.[386, 401] Although most fatigue fractures are transverse or short oblique defects, they are occasionally oriented longitudinally.[14, 41, 266, 311, 527, 600, 606] The fibula may also be affected by fatigue fractures, particularly its distal third.

The osseous failure of a fatigue fracture may be only microscopic, with pain, swelling, tenderness, and increased warmth as its clinical manifestations. Usually, no radiologic abnormality is noted until periosteal or intraosseous new bone formation is evident. A very fine radiolucent defect may be present. A Tc 99m MDP bone scan generally shows well-localized uptake of radionuclide in the area of a fatigue fracture.[410, 489, 552] Increased temperature by thermography and pain induction by ultrasound are noninvasive, economical tests, one or both of which will have positive results in most patients with fatigue fractures and normal radiographs.[138, 478] This combination can be used instead of the frequently requested bone scan if objective confirmation is desired. MRI shows edema and often fracture lines as well. It is assuming an increasing role in the diagnosis of fatigue fractures and may be most helpful in excluding other potential diagnoses.[14, 353, 595, 600]

Elimination of other conditions in the differential diagnosis of fatigue fractures is important to ensure timely, appropriate treatment. Tumor, infection, exertional compartment syndrome, and so-called medial tibial stress syndrome must be considered. The history, physical examination, and radiographs should allow each of these conditions to be distinguished. Medial tibial stress syndrome is characterized by a more diffuse area of hyperactive bone resorption and remodeling without microfractures. These features are demonstrated by a more diffusely increased uptake of Tc 99m MDP. Chronic recurrent exertional compartment syndromes show typical activity-related changes in physical findings and compartmental pressure measurements. Infections and tumors may have only localized morphologic findings evident on high-quality radiographs or CT scans. A typical clinical and radiologic course is often the best confirmation for a diagnosis of fatigue fracture. Only very exceptionally will a biopsy be necessary for tissue diagnosis.

Because fatigue fractures develop in mechanically weakened bone, catastrophic failure may occur with an obvious displaced fracture and may perhaps be preceded by local pain and be associated with radiolucency or new bone formation, which might generate concern about other types of pathologic fractures. Early recognition and appropriate treatment consisting of reduced activity and external support, if needed, should prevent catastrophic failure of fatigue fractures. Anterior tibial cortical fatigue fractures are "high-risk" fatigue fractures that may readily proceed to catastrophic failure and thus deserve more aggressive treatment.[57]

The best treatment of fatigue fractures of the tibia and fibula is usually conservative. Even if displacement occurs, the fracture is generally a result of low-energy trauma and is typically amenable to nonoperative treatment with a cast or brace and early weight bearing.[143, 553, 619] If failure has not occurred but is thought to be a risk because of an obvious radiolucent defect, external support may be advisable, just as it is if activity restriction does not control the symptoms. In a high-risk anterior tibial fatigue fracture and perhaps in other recalcitrant situations, reamed IM nail fixation might be considered.[32, 102, 443] Otherwise, weight bearing is restricted with crutches, and less demanding activities are gradually resumed while avoiding those that produce pain. It has been suggested that low-intensity ultrasound treatment can accelerate recovery from tibial fatigue fractures.[75] Once the patient's symptoms have resolved and radiographs show progressive healing of any defect, a carefully monitored, gradually increased rehabilitation program will help the patient return to the desired level of performance. Good coaching regarding technique and proper footgear are important aspects of such a rehabilitation program. Two to 3 months may be required for resolution of the symptoms and risk of fracture, but the problem can recur if resumption of activity is too vigorous. Fatigue fractures occasionally develop in patients with arthritis and tibial deformity. Such patients have a significant risk of nonunion and should be considered for appropriate total-knee replacement.[505, 510]

## REFERENCES

1. Abelseth, G.; Buckley, R.E.; Pineo, G.E.; et al. Incidence of deep-vein thrombosis in patients with fractures of the lower extremity distal to the hip. J Orthop Trauma 10:230–235, 1996.
2. Abhaykumar, S.; Elliott, D.S. Closed interlocking nailing for fibular nonunion. Injury 29:793–797, 1998.
3. Adams, C.I.; Keating, J.F.; Court-Brown, C.M. Cigarette smoking and open tibial fractures. Injury 32:61–65, 2001.
4. Adamson, G.J.; Wiss, D.A.; Lowery, G.L.; Peters, C.L. Type II floating knee: Ipsilateral femoral and tibial fractures with intraarticular extension into the knee joint. J Orthop Trauma 6:333–339, 1992.

5. Agarwal, S.; Agarwal, R.; Jain, U.K.; Chandra, R. Management of soft-tissue problems in leg trauma in conjunction with application of the Ilizarov fixator assembly. Plast Reconstr Surg 107:1732–1738, 2001.

6. Aitken, R.J.; Mills, C.; Immelman, E.J. The postphlebitic syndrome following shaft fractures of the leg. A significant late complication. J Bone Joint Surg Br 69:775–778, 1987.

7. al Awami, S.M.; Sadat Ali, M.; ad Sankaran-Kutty, M. Arterial injury complicating fracture of the fibula: A case report. Injury 18:214–215, 1987.

8. Alberts, K.A.; Loohagen, G.; Einarsdottir, H. Open tibial fractures: Faster union after unreamed nailing than external fixation. Injury 30:519–523, 1999.

9. Alho, A.; Benterud, J.G.; Hogevold, H.E.; et al. Comparison of functional bracing and locked intramedullary nailing in the treatment of displaced tibial shaft fractures. Clin Orthop 277:243–250, 1992.

10. Alho, A.; Ekeland, A.; Stromsoe, K.; Benterud, J.G. Nonunion of tibial shaft fractures treated with locked intramedullary nailing without bone grafting. J Trauma 34:62–67, 1993.

11. Allgöwer, M. Modern concepts of fracture treatment. AO/ASIF Dialogue 1:1, 1985.

12. Alonso-Bartolome, P.; Martinez-Taboada, V.M.; Blanco, R.; Rodriguez-Valverde, V. Insufficiency fractures of the tibia and fibula. Semin Arthritis Rheum 28:413–420, 1999.

13. Andersen, K. Dislocation of the superior tibiofibular joint. Injury 16:494–498, 1985.

14. Anderson, M.W.; Ugalde, V.; Batt, M.; et al. Longitudinal stress fracture of the tibia: MR demonstration. J Comput Assist Tomogr 20:836–838, 1996.

15. Anglen, J.O. Early outcome of hybrid external fixation for fracture of the distal tibia. J Orthop Trauma 13:92–97, 1999.

16. Anglen, J.O.; Aleto, T. Temporary transarticular external fixation of the knee and ankle. J Orthop Trauma 12:431–434, 1998.

17. Anglen, J.O.; Blue, J.M. A comparison of reamed and unreamed nailing of the tibia. J Trauma 39:351–355, 1995.

18. Angliss, R.D.; Tran, T.A.; Edwards, E.R.; Doig, S.G. Unreamed nailing of tibial shaft fractures in multiply injured patients. Injury 27:255–260, 1996.

19. Antich-Adrover, P.; Marti-Garin, D.; Murias-Alvarez, J.; Puente-Alonso, C. External fixation and secondary intramedullary nailing of open tibial fractures. A randomised, prospective trial. J Bone Joint Surg Br 79:433–437, 1997.

20. Arangio, G.A.; Lehr, S.; Reed, J.F., 3rd. Reemployment of patients with surgical salvage of open, high-energy tibial fractures: An outcome study. J Trauma 42:942–945, 1997.

21. Ashcroft, G.P.; Evans, N.T.; Roeda, D.; et al. Measurement of blood flow in tibial fracture patients using positron emission tomography. J Bone Joint Surg Br 74:673–677, 1992.

22. Atesalp, A.S.; Basbozkurt, M.; Erler, E.; et al. Treatment of tibial bone defects with the Ilizarov circular external fixator in high-velocity gunshot wounds. Int Orthop 22:343–347, 1998.

23. Atkins, R.M.; Madhavan, P.; Sudhakar, J.; Whitwell, D. Ipsilateral vascularised fibular transport for massive defects of the tibia. J Bone Joint Surg Br 81:1035–1040, 1999.

24. Atkins, R.M.; Sudhakar, J.E.; Porteous, A.J. Distraction osteogenesis through high energy fractures. Injury 29:535–537, 1998.

25. Austin, R.T. Fractures of the tibial shaft: Is medical audit possible? Injury 9:93–101, 1977.

26. Austin, R.T. The Sarmiento tibial plaster: A prospective study of 145 fractures. Injury 13:10–22, 1981.

27. Bach, A.W.; Hansen, S.T., Jr. Plates versus external fixation in severe open tibial shaft fractures. A randomized trial. Clin Orthop 241:89–94, 1898.

28. Bal, G.K.; Kuo, R.S.; Chapman, J.R.; et al. The anterior T-frame external fixator for high-energy proximal tibial fractures. Clin Orthop 375:234–240, 2000.

29. Banovetz, J.M.; Sharp, R.; Probe, R.A.; et al. Titanium plate fixation: A review of implant failures. J Orthop Trauma 10:389–394, 1996.

30. Barquet, A.; Masliah, R. Large segmental necrosis of the tibia with deep infection after open fracture. Acta Orthop Scand 59:443–446, 1988.

31. Barquet, A.; Massaferro, J.; Dubra, A.; et al. The dynamic ASIF-BM tubular external fixator in the treatment of open fractures of the shaft of the tibia. Injury 23:61–66, 1992.

32. Barrick, E.F.; Jackson, C.B. Prophylactic intramedullary fixation of the tibia for stress fracture in a professional athlete. J Orthop Trauma 6:241–244, 1992.

33. Bauer, G.C.H.; Edwards, P.; Widmark, P.H. Shaft fractures of the tibia: Etiology of poor results in a consecutive series of 173 fractures. Acta Chir Scand 124:386–395, 1962.

34. Baumgaertel, F.; Buhl, M.; Rahn, B.A. Fracture healing in biological plate osteosynthesis. Injury 29(Suppl 3):C3–C6, 1998.

35. Beals, R.K.; Cook, R.D. Stress fractures of the anterior tibial diaphysis. Orthopedics 14:869–875, 1991.

36. Beck, T.J.; Ruff, C.B.; Shaffer, R.A.; et al. Stress fracture in military recruits: Gender differences in muscle and bone susceptibility factors. Bone 27:437–444, 2000.

37. Bednar, D.A.; Parikh, J. Effect of time delay from injury to primary management on the incidence of deep infection after open fractures of the lower extremities caused by blunt trauma in adults. J Orthop Trauma 7:32–35, 1993.

38. Behrens, F.; Johnson, J.; Guntzburger, T.; et al. Early bone grafting for tibial fractures. J Orthop Trauma 3:156, 1989.

39. Behrens, F.F.; Sabharwal, S. Deformity correction and reconstructive procedures using percutaneous techniques. Clin Orthop 375:133–139, 2000.

40. Behrens, F.; Searls, K. External fixation of the tibia. Basic concepts and prospective evaluation. J Bone Joint Surg Br 68:246–254, 1986.

41. Belzunegui, J.; Plazaola, I.; Maiz, O.; et al. Longitudinal stress fractures of the tibia: Report of three cases. Br J Rheumatol 36:1130–1131, 1997.

42. Bengner, V.; Ekbom, T.; Johnell, O.; et al. Incidence of femoral and tibial shaft fractures. Acta Orthop Scand 61:251–254, 1990.

43. Bennell, K.L.; Malcolm, S.A.; Thomas, S.A.; et al. Risk factors for stress fractures in female track-and-field athletes: A retrospective analysis. Clin J Sport Med 5:229–235, 1995.

44. Bhandari, M.; Adili, A.; Lachowski, R.J. High pressure pulsatile lavage of contaminated human tibiae: An in vitro study. J Orthop Trauma 12:479–484, 1998.

45. Bhandari, M.; Adili, A.; Leone J.; et al. Early versus delayed management of closed tibial fractures. Clin Orthop 368:230–239, 1999.

46. Bhandari, M.; Guyatt, G.H.; Swiontkowski, M.F.; Schemitsch, E.H. Treatment of open fractures of the shaft of the tibia. J Bone Joint Surg Br 83:62–68, 2001.

47. Bhandari, M.; Guyatt, G.H.; Swiontkowski, M.F.; et al. Surgeons' preferences for the operative treatment of fractures of the tibial shaft. An international survey. J Bone Joint Surg Am 83:1746–1752, 2001.

48. Bhandari, M.; Guyatt, G.H.; Tong, D.; et al. Reamed versus nonreamed intramedullary nailing of lower extremity long bone fractures: A systematic overview and meta-analysis. J Orthop Trauma 14:2–9, 2000.

49. Bhandari, M.; Schemitsch, E.H.; Adili, A.; et al. High and low pressure pulsatile lavage of contaminated tibial fractures: An in vitro study of bacterial adherence and bone damage. J Orthop Trauma 13:526–533, 1999.

50. Bilat, C.; Leutenegger, A.; Rüedi, T. Osteosynthesis of 245 tibial shaft fractures: Early and late complications. Injury 25:349–358, 1994.

51. Blachut, P.A.; Meek, R.N.; O'Brien, P.J. External fixation and delayed intramedullary nailing of open fractures of the tibial shaft. A sequential protocol. J Bone Joint Surg Am 72:729–735, 1990.

52. Blachut, P.A.; O'Brien, P.J.; Meed, R.N.; Broekhuyse, H.M. Interlocking intramedullary nailing with and without reaming for the treatment of closed fractures of the tibial shaft. A prospective, randomized study. J Bone Joint Surg Am 79:640–646, 1997.

53. Blatter, G.; Weber, B.G. Wave plate osteosynthesis as a salvage procedure. Arch Orthop Trauma Surg 109:330–333, 1990.

54. Blick, S.S.; Brumback, R.J.; Lakatos, R.; et al. Early prophylactic bone grafting of high energy tibial fractures. Clin Orthop 240:21–41, 1989.

55. Blick, S.S.; Brumback, R.J.; Poka, A.; et al. Compartment syndrome in open tibial fractures. J Bone Joint Surg Am 68:1348–1353, 1986.

56. Blokhuis, T.J.; de Bruine, J.H.; Bramer, J.A.; et al. The reliability of plain radiography in experimental fracture healing. Skeletal Radiol 30:151–156, 2001.

57. Boden, B.P.; Osbahr, D.C. High-risk stress fractures: Evaluation and treatment. J Am Acad Orthop Surg 8:344–353, 2000.

58. Boerger, T.O.; Patel, G.; Murphy, J.P. Is routine removal of intramedullary nails justified. Injury 30:79–81, 1999.

59. Bolhofner, B.R. Indirect reduction and composite fixation of extraarticular proximal tibial fractures. Clin Orthop 315:75–83, 1995.

60. Bonanni, F.; Rhodes, M.; Lucke, J.F. The futility of predictive scoring of mangled lower extremities. J Trauma 34:99–104, 1993.

61. Bone, L.B.; Johnson, K.D. Treatment of tibial fractures by reaming and intramedullary nailing. J Bone Joint Surg Am 68:877–887, 1986.

62. Bone, L.B.; Kassman, S.; Stegemann, P.; France, J. Prospective study of union rate of open tibial fractures treated with locked, unreamed intramedullary nails. J Orthop Trauma 8:45–49, 1994.

63. Bone, L.B.; Sucato, D.; Stegemann, P.M.; Rohrbacher, B.J. Displaced isolated fractures of the tibial shaft treated with either a cast or intramedullary nailing. An outcome analysis of matched pairs of patients. J Bone Joint Surg Am 79:1336–1341, 1997.

64. Bono, C.M.; Levine, R.G.; Rao, J.P.; Behrens, F.F. Nonarticular proximal tibia fractures: Treatment options and decision making. J Am Acad Orthop Surg 9:176–186, 2001.

65. Bosse, M.J.; MacKenzie, E.J.; Kellam, J.F.; et al. A prospective evaluation of the clinical utility of the lower-extremity injury-severity scores. J Bone Joint Surg Am 83:3–14, 2001.

66. Böstman, O.; Kyro, A. Delayed union of fibular fractures accompanying fractures of the tibial shaft. J Trauma 31:99–102, 1991.

67. Böstman, O.M. Body-weight related to loss of reduction of fractures of the distal tibia and ankle. J Bone Joint Surg Br 77:101–103, 1995.

68. Böstman, O.M. Displaced malleolar fractures associated with spiral fractures of the tibial shaft. Clin Orthop 228:202–207, 1988.

69. Böstman, O.M. Rotational refracture of the shaft of the adult tibia. Injury 15:93–98, 1983.

70. Böstman, O.M. Spiral fractures of the shaft of the tibia. Initial displacement and stability of reduction. J Bone Joint Surg Br 68:462–466, 1986.

71. Bostrom, M.P.; Camacho, N.P. Potential role of bone morphogenetic proteins in fracture healing. Clin Orthop 335:(Suppl):274–282, 1998.

72. Bowen, C.V.; Botsford, D.J.; Hudak, P.L.; Evans, P.J. Microsurgical treatment of septic nonunion of the tibia. Quality of life results. Clin Orthop 332:52–61, 1996.

73. Bowker, J.H. Surgical techniques for conserving tissue and function in lower-limb amputation for trauma, infection, and vascular disease. Instruct Course Lect 39:355–360, 1990.

74. Brana Vigil, A.; Mieres Barredo, P.; Montes Mortera, S. Traumatic luxation of the proximal tibiofibular joint, superior variety. A case report. Acta Orthop Belg 49:479–482, 1983.

75. Brand, J.C. Jr.; Brindle, T.; Nyland, J.; et al. Does pulsed low intensity ultrasound allow early return to normal activities when treating stress fractures? A review of one tarsal navicular and eight tibial stress fractures. Iowa Orthop J 19:26–30, 1999.

76. Bridgman, S.A.; Baird, K. Audit of closed tibial fractures: What is a satisfactory outcome? Injury 24:85–89, 1993.

77. Brien, E.W.; Long, W.T.; Serocki, J.H. Management of gunshot wounds to the tibia. Orthop Clin North Am 26:165–180, 1995.

78. Brighton, C.T.; Shaman, P.; Heppenstall, R.B.; et al. Tibial nonunion treated with direct current, capacitive coupling, or bone graft. Clin Orthop 321:223–234, 1995.

79. Brinker, M.R.; Bailey, D.E., Jr. Fracture healing in tibia fractures with an associated vascular injury. J Trauma 42:11–19, 1997.

80. Brinker, M.R.; Caines, M.A.; Kerstein, M.D.; Elliott, M.N. Tibial shaft fractures with an associated infrapopliteal arterial injury: A survey of vascular surgeons opinions on the need for vascular repair. J Orthop Trauma 14:194–198, 2000.

81. Brinker, M.R.; Cook, S.D.; Dunlap, J.N.; et al. Early changes in nutrient artery blood flow following tibial nailing with and without reaming: A preliminary study. J Orthop Trauma 13:129–133, 1999.

82. Brumback, R.J.; Jones, A.L. Interobserver agreement in the classification of open fractures of the tibia. The results of a survey of two hundred and forty-five orthopaedic surgeons. J Bone Joint Surg Am 76:162–166, 1994.

83. Buckwalter, J.A.; Brandser, E.A. Stress and insufficiency fractures. Am Fam Physician 56:175–182, 1997.

84. Buehler, K.C.; Green, J.; Woll, T.S.; Duwelius, P.J. A technique for intramedullary nailing of proximal third tibia fractures. J Orthop Trauma 11:218–223, 1997.

85. Burgess, A.R.; Poka, A.; Brumback, R.J.; et al. Pedestrian tibial injuries. J Trauma 27:596–601, 1987.

86. Burgos, J.; Alvarez-Montero, R.; Gonzalez-Herranz, P.; Rapariz, J.M. Traumatic proximal tibiofibular dislocation. J Pediatr Orthop B 6:70–72, 1997.

87. Burr, D.B.; Milgram, C.; Boyd, R.D.; et al. Experimental stress fractures of the tibia: Biological and mechanical aetiology in rabbits. J Bone Joint Surg Br 72:370–375, 1990.

88. Burri, C. Posttraumatic Osteomyelitis. Bern, Switzerland, Hans Huber, 1975.

89. Burstein, A.H.; Currey, J.; Frankel, V.H.; et al. Bone strength. The effect of screw holes. J Bone Joint Surg Am 54:1143–1156, 1972.

90. Burwell, H.N. Plate fixation of tibial shaft fractures. J Bone Joint Surg Br 53:258–271, 1971.

91. Calhoun, J.H.; Li, F.; Bauford, W.L.; et al. Rigidity of half-pins for the Ilizarov external fixator. Bull Hosp Jt Dis 52:21–26, 1992.

92. Calhoun, J.H.; Li, F.; Ledbetter, B.R.; Gill, C.A. Biomechanics of the Ilizarov fixator for fracture fixation. Clin Orthop 280:15–22, 1992.

93. Canovas, F.; Bonnel, F.; Faure, P. Extensive bone loss in an open tibial shaft fracture (immediate bone boiling reimplantation). Injury 30:709–710, 1999.

94. Carmack, D.B.; Kaylor, K.L.; Yaszemski, M.J. Structural stiffness and reducibility of external fixators placed in malalignment and malrotation. J Orthop Trauma 15:247–253, 2001.

95. Carpenter, C.A.; Jupiter, J.B. Blade plate reconstruction of metaphyseal nonunion of the tibia. Clin Orthop 332:23–28, 1996.

96. Carrington, N.C.; Smith, R.M.; Knight, S.L.; Matthews, S.J. Ilizarov bone transport over a primary tibial nail and free flap: A new technique for treating Gustilo grade 3b fractures with large segmental defects. Injury 31:112–115, 2000.

97. Catagni, M.A.; Guerreschi, F.; Holman, J.A.; Cattaneo, R. Distraction osteogenesis in the treatment of stiff hypertrophic nonunions using the Ilizarov apparatus. Clin Orthop 301:159–163, 1994.

98. Cattaneo, R.; Catagni, M.; Johnson, E.E. The treatment of infected nonunions and segmental defects of the tibia by the methods of Ilizarov. Clin Orthop 280:43–52, 1992.

99. Caudle, R.J.; Stern, P.J. Severe open fractures of the tibia. J Bone Joint Surg Am 69:801–807, 1987.

100. Chan, Y.S.; Ueng, S.W.; Wang, C.J.; et al. Management of small infected tibial defects with antibiotic-impregnated autogenic cancellous bone grafting. J Trauma 45:758–764, 1998.

101. Chan, Y.S.; Ueng, S.W.; Wang, C.J.; et al. Antibiotic-impregnated autogenic cancellous bone grafting is an effective and safe method for the management of small infected tibial defects: A comparison study. J Trauma 48:246–255, 2000.

102. Chang, P.S.; Harris, R.M. Intramedullary nailing for chronic tibial stress fractures. A review of five cases. Am J Sports Med 24:688–692, 1996.

103. Chatziyiannakis, A.A.; Verettas, D.A.; Raptis, V.K.; Charpantitis, S.T. Nonunion of tibial fractures treated with external fixation. Contributing factors studied in 71 fractures. Acta Orthop Scand Suppl 275:77–79, 1997.

104. Checketts, R.G.; Moran, C.G.; Jennings, A.G. 134 tibial shaft fractures managed with the Dynamic Axial Fixator. Acta Orthop Scand 66:271–274, 1995.

105. Christian, E.P.; Bosse, M.J.; Robb, G. Reconstruction of large diaphyseal defects, without free fibular transfer, in grade-IIIB tibial fractures. J Bone Joint Surg Am 71:994–1004, 1989.

106. Cierny, G., 3rd. Infected tibial nonunions (1981–1995). The evolution of change. Clin Orthop 360:97–105, 1999.

107. Cierny G, Zorn, K.E. Segmental tibial defects: Comparing conventional and Ilizarov methodologies. Clin Orthop 301:118–123, 1994.

108. Clayer, M.; Krishnan, J.; Lee, W.K.; Tamblyn, P. Longitudinal stress fracture of the tibia: Two cases. Clin Radiol 46:401–404, 1992.

109. Clews, A.G. Dislocation of the upper end of the fibula. Can Med Assoc J 98:169–170, 1968.

110. Cole, J.D.; Ansel, L.J.; Schwartzberg, R. A sequential protocol for management of severe open tibial fractures. Clin Orthop 315:84–103, 1995.

111. Colen, R.P.; Prieskorn, D.W. Tibial tubercle–medial malleolar distance in determining tibial nail length. J Orthop Trauma 14:345–348, 2000.

112. Coles, C.P.; Gross, M. Closed tibial shaft fractures: Management and treatment complications. A review of the prospective literature. Can J Surg 43:256–262, 2000.

113. Collinge, C.A.; Sanders, R.W. Percutaneous plating in the lower extremity. J Am Acad Orthop Surg 8:211–216, 2000.

114. Connolly, J.F.; Guse, R.; Tiedeman, J.; Dehne, R. Autologous marrow injection as a substitute for operative grafting of tibial nonunions. Clin Orthop 266:59–70, 1991.

115. Cook, S.D.; Ryaby, J.P.; McCabe, J.; et al. Acceleration of tibia and distal radius fracture healing in patients who smoke. Clin Orthop 337:198–207, 1997.

116. Cornell, C.N.; Lane, J.M.; Chapman, M.W.; et al. Multicenter trial of Collagraft as bone graft substitute. J Orthop Trauma 5:1–8, 1991.

117. Costa-Ferreira, A.; Reis, J.; Pinho, C.; et al. The distally based island superficial sural artery flap: Clinical experience with 36 flaps. Ann Plast Surg 46:308–313, 2001.

118. Court-Brown, C.M. Reamed tibial nailing in Edinburgh (1985–1995). Bull Hosp Jt Dis 58:24–30, 1999.

119. Court-Brown, C.M.; Gustilo, T.; Shaw, A.D. Knee pain after intramedullary tibial nailing: Its incidence, etiology, and outcome. J Orthop Trauma 11:103–105, 1997.

120. Court-Brown, C.M.; Keating, J.F.; Christie, J.; McQueen, M.M. Exchange intramedullary nailing. Its use in aseptic tibial nonunion. J Bone Joint Surg Br 77:407–411, 1995.

121. Court-Brown, C.M.; Keating, J.F.; McQueen, M.M. Infection after intramedullary nailing of the tibia. Incidence and protocol for management. J Bone Joint Surg Br 74:770–774, 1992.

122. Court-Brown, C.M.; McBirnie, J. The epidemiology of tibial fractures. J Bone Joint Surg Br 77:417–421, 1995.

123. Court-Brown, C.M.; McQueen, M.M. High success rate with exchange nailing to treat tibial shaft aseptic nonunion. J Orthop Trauma 13:274, 1999.

124. Court-Brown, C.M.; McQueen, M.M.; Quaba, A.A.; Christie, J. Locked intramedullary nailing of open tibial fractures. J Bone Joint Surg Br 73:959–964, 1991.

125. Court-Brown, C.M.; Will, E.; Christie, J.; McQueen, M.M. Reamed or unreamed nailing for closed tibial fractures. A prospective study in Tscherne C1 fractures. J Bone Joint Surg Br 78:580–583, 1996.

126. Crothers, O.D.; Johnson, J.T.H. Isolated acute dislocation of the proximal tibiofibular joint. J Bone Joint Surg Am 55:181–183, 1973.

127. Cunningham, J.L.; Evans, M.; Kenwright, J. Measurement of fracture movement in patients treated with unilateral external skeletal fixation. J Biomed Eng 11:118–122, 1989.

128. Curtis, M.J.; Brown, P.R.; Dick, J.D.; Jinnah, R.H. Contaminated fractures of the tibia: A comparison of treatment modalities in an animal model. J Orthop Res 13:286–295, 1995.

129. Darouiche, R.O.; Farmer, J.; Chaput, C.; et al. Anti-infective efficacy of antiseptic-coated intramedullary nails. J Bone Joint Surg Am 80:1336–1340, 1998.

130. DaSilva, M.F.; Voss, L.; Khon, R.; et al. Functional outcome after tibial shaft fractures: A 4-year follow-up study. Orthop Trans 22:86, 1999.

131. De Bastiani, G.; Aldegheri, R.; Renzi Brivio, L. Dynamic axial fixation. A rational alternative for the external fixation of fractures. Int Orthop 10:95–99, 1986.

132. DeFranzo, A.J.; Argenta, L.C.; Marks, M.W.; et al. The use of vacuum-assisted closure therapy for the treatment of lower-extremity wounds with exposed bone. Plast Reconstr Surg 108:1184–1191, 2001.

133. DeLong, W.G.; Jr.; Born, C.T.; Wei, S.Y.; et al. Aggressive treatment of 119 open fracture wounds. J Trauma 46:1049–1054, 1999.

134. De Meulemeester, C.; Verdonk, R.; Bongaerts, W. The fibula pro tibia procedure in the treatment of nonunion of the tibia. Acta Orthop Belg 58(Suppl 1):187–189, 1992.

135. Dendrinos, G.K.; Kontos, S.; Lyritsis, E. Use of the Ilizarov technique for treatment of non-union of the tibia associated with infection. J Bone Joint Surg Am 77:835–846, 1995.

136. Den Outer, A.J.; Meeuwis, J.D.; Hermans, J.Z.A. Conservative versus operative treatment of displaced noncomminuted tibial shaft fractures. A retrospective comparative study. Clin Orthop 252:231–237, 1990.

137. Dervin, G.F. Skeletal fixation of grade IIIB tibial fractures. The potential of meta-analysis. Clin Orthop 332:10–15, 1996.

138. Devereaux, M.D.; Parr, G.R.; Lachmann, S.M.; et al. The diagnosis of stress fractures in athletes. JAMA 252:531–533, 1984.

139. De Vilder, J. Personality of patients with Sudeck's atrophy following tibial fracture. Acta Orthop Belg 58(Suppl 1):252–257, 1992.

140. Dickson, K.; Katzman, S.; Delgado, E.; Contreras, D. Delayed unions and nonunions of open tibial fractures. Correlation with arteriography results. Clin Orthop 302:189–193, 1994.

141. Dickson, K.F.; Hoffman, W.Y.; Delgado, E.D.; Contreras, D.M. Unreamed rod with early wound closure for grade IIIA and IIIB open tibial fractures: Analysis of 40 consecutive patients. Orthopedics 21:531–535, 1998.

142. Dickson, K.F.; Katzman, S.; Paiement, G. The importance of the blood supply in the healing of tibial fractures. Contemp Orthop 30:489–493, 1995.

143. Dickson, T.B., Jr.; Kichline, P.D. Functional management of stress fractures in female athletes using a pneumatic leg brace. Am J Sports Med 15:86–89, 1987.

144. DiStasio, A.J., 2nd.; Dugdale, T.W.; Deafenbaugh, M.K. Multiple relaxing skin incisions in orthopaedic lower extremity trauma. J Orthop Trauma 7:270–274, 1993.

145. Dodenhoff, R.M.; Howell, G.E. The shoelace technique for wound closure in open fractures: Report of early experience. Injury 28:593–595, 1997.

146. Dogra, A.S.; Ruiz, A.L.; Thompson, N.S.; Nolan, P.C. Diametaphyseal distal tibial fractures—treatment with a shortened intramedullary nail: A review of 15 cases. Injury 31:799–804, 2000.

147. Downing, N.D.; Griffin, D.R.; Davis, I.R. A comparison of the relative costs of cast treatment and intramedullary nailing for tibial diaphyseal fractures in the UK. Injury 28:373–375, 1997.

148. Dugan, R.C.; D'Ambrosia, R. Fibular stress fractures in runners. J Fam Pract 17:415–418, 1983.

149. Dugdale, T.W.; Degnan, G.G.; Bosse, M.J.; Reinert, C.M. A technique for removing a fractured interlocking tibial nail. J Orthop Trauma 2:39–42, 1988.

150. Durham, R.M.; Mistry, B.M.; Mazuski, J.E.; et al. Outcome and utility of scoring systems in the management of mangled lower extremities. Am J Surg 172:569–574, 1996.

151. Duwelius, P.J.; Schmidt, A.H.; Rubinstein, R.A.; Green, J.M. Nonreamed interlocked intramedullary tibial nailing. One community's experience. Clin Orthop 315:104–113, 1995.

152. Ebraheim, N.A.; Savolaine, F.R.; Patel, A.; et al. Assessment of tibial fracture union by 35–45 degrees internal oblique radiographs. J Orthop Trauma 5:349–350, 1991.

153. Ebraheim, N.A.; Savolaine, E.R.; Skie, M.C.; Jackson, W.T. Fibular nonunion in combination with fractures of the tibia. Orthopedics 16:1229–1232, 1993.

154. Edlich, R.F.; Rogers, W.; Kasper, G.; et al. Studies in the management of the contaminated wound. I. Optimal time for closure of contaminated wounds. II. Comparison of resistance to infection of open and closed wounds during healing. Am J Surg 117:323–329, 1969.

155. Edwards, C.C.; Simmons, S.C.; Browner, B.D.; Weigel, M.C. Severe open tibial fractures. Results treating 202 injuries with external fixation. Clin Orthop 230:98–115, 1988.

156. Edwards, P. Fracture of the shaft of the tibia: 492 consecutive cases in adults: Importance of soft tissue injury. Acta Orthop Scand Suppl 76:1–83, 1965.

157. Eichenblat, M.; Nathan, H. The proximal tibio fibular joint: An anatomical study with clinical and pathological considerations. Int Orthop 7:31–39, 1983.

158. Ekenman, I.; Halvorsen, K.; Westblad, P.; et al. Local bone deformation at two predominant sites for stress fractures of the tibia: An in vivo study. Foot Ankle Int 19:479–484, 1998.

159. Ekenman, I.; Tsai-Fetlander, L.; Westblad, P.; et al. A study of intrinsic factors in patients with stress fractures of the tibia. Foot Ankle Int 17:477–478, 1996.

160. Ellis, H. Disabilities after tibial shaft fractures: With special references to Volkmann's ischaemic contracture. J Bone Joint Surg Br 40:190–197, 1958.

161. Ellis, H. The speed of healing after fracture of the tibial shaft. J Bone Joint Surg Br 40:42–46, 1958.

162. Emami, A.; Mjoberg, B.; Karlstrom, G.; Larsson, S. Treatment of closed tibial shaft fractures with unilateral external fixation. Injury 26:299–303, 1995.

163. Emami, A.; Mjoberg, B.; Ragnarsson, B.; Larsson, S. Changing epidemiology of tibial shaft fractures. 513 cases compared between 1971–1975 and 1986–1990. Acta Orthop Scand 67:557–561, 1996.

164. Emami, A.; Petren-Mallmin, M.; Larsson, S. No effect of low-

intensity ultrasound on healing time of intramedullary fixed tibial fractures. J Orthop Trauma 13:252–257, 1999.

165. Emery, S.E.; Heller, J.G.; Petersilge, C.A.; et al. Tibial stress fracture after a graft has been obtained from the fibula: A report of five cases. J Bone Joint Surg Am 78:1248–1251, 1996.

166. Esterhai, J.L.; Sennett, B.; Gelb, H.; et al: Treatment of chronic osteomyelitis complicating nonunion and segmental defects of the tibia. J Trauma 30:49–54, 1990.

167. Faergemann, C.; Frandsen, P.A.; Rock, N.D. Expected long-term outcome after a tibial shaft fracture. J Trauma 46:683–686, 1999.

168. Fairhurst, M.J. The function of below-knee amputee versus the patient with salvaged grade III tibial fracture. Clin Orthop 301:27–32, 1994.

169. Falkenberg, P.; Nygaard, H. Isolated anterior dislocation of the proximal tibiofibular joint. J Bone Joint Surg Br 65:310–311, 1983.

170. Farouk, O.; Krettek, C.; Miclau, T.; et al. Minimally invasive plate osteosynthesis and vascularity: Preliminary results of a cadaver injection study. Injury 28(Suppl 1):A7–A12, 1997.

171. Farouk, O.; Krettek, C.; Miclau, T.; et al. Minimally invasive plate osteosynthesis: Does percutaneous plating disrupt femoral blood supply less than the traditional technique? J Orthop Trauma 13:401–406, 1999.

172. Feliciano, D.V.; Cruse, P.A.; Spjut-Patrinely, V.; et al. Fasciotomy after trauma to the extremities. Am J Surg 156:533–536, 1988.

173. Ferraro, S.P., Jr.; Zinar, D.M. Management of gunshot fractures of the tibia. Orthop Clin North Am 26:181–189, 1995.

174. Field, J.R.; Tornkvist, H.; Hearn, T.C.; et al. The influence of screw omission on construction stiffness and bone surface strain in the application of bone plates to cadaveric bone. Injury 30:591–598, 1999.

175. Finestone, A.; Shlamkovitch, N.; Eldad, A.; et al. Risk factors for stress fractures among Israeli infantry recruits. Mil Med 156:528–530, 1991.

176. Finkemeier, C.G.; Schmidt, A.H.; Kyle, R.F.; et al. A prospective, randomized study of intramedullary nails inserted with and without reaming for the treatment of open and closed fractures of the tibial shaft. J Orthop Trauma 14:187–193, 2000.

177. Foxworthy, M.; Pringle, R.M. Dynamization timing and its effect on bone healing when using the Orthofix Dynamic Axial Fixator. Injury 26:117–119, 1995.

178. Franklin, J.L.; Winquist, R.A.; Benirschke, S.K.; Hansen, S.T., Jr. Broken intramedullary nails. J Bone Joint Surg Am 70:1463–1471, 1988.

179. Freedman, E.L.; Johnson, E.E. Radiographic analysis of tibial fracture malalignment following intramedullary nailing. Clin Orthop 315:25–33, 1995.

180. Friedlaender, G.E. OP-1 clinical studies. J Bone Joint Surg Am 83(Suppl 1):160–161, 2001.

181. Friedlaender, G.E.; Perry, C.R.; Cole, J.D.; et al. Osteogenic protein-1 (bone morphogenetic protein-7) in the treatment of tibial nonunions. J Bone Joint Surg Am 83(Suppl 1):151–158, 2001.

182. Galpin, R.D.; Veith, R.G.; Hansen, S.T. Treatment of failures after plating of tibial fractures. J Bone Joint Surg Am 68:1231–1236, 1986.

183. Gardner, T.N.; Evans, M.; Kenwright, J. A biomechanical study on five unilateral external fracture fixation devices. Clin Biomech (Bristol, Avon) 12:87–96, 1997.

184. Garland, D.E.; Saucedo, T.; Reiser, T.V. The management of tibial fractures in acute spinal cord injury patients. Clin Orthop 213:237–240, 1986.

185. Gaston, P.; Will, E.; Elton, R.A.; et al. Fractures of the tibia. Can their outcome be predicted? J Bone Joint Surg Br 81:71–76, 1999.

186. Gaston, P.; Will, E.; McQueen, M.M.; et al. Analysis of muscle function in the lower limb after fracture of the diaphysis of the tibia in adults. J Bone Joint Surg Br 82:326–331, 2000.

187. Geerts, W.H.; Code, K.I.; Jay, R.M.; et al. A prospective study of venous thromboembolism after major trauma. N Engl J Med 331:1601–1606, 1994.

188. Geller, J.; Tornetta, P., 3rd.; Tiburzi, D.; et al. Tension wire position for hybrid external fixation of the proximal tibia. J Orthop Trauma 14:502–504, 2000.

189. Georgiadis, G.M. Tibial shaft fractures complicated by compartment syndrome: Treatment with immediate fasciotomy and locked unreamed nailing. J Trauma 38:448–452, 1995.

190. Georgiadis, G.M.; Behrens, F.F.; Joyce, M.J.; et al. Open tibial fractures with severe soft-tissue loss. Limb salvage compared with below-the-knee amputation. J Bone Joint Surg Am 75:1431–1441, 1993.

191. Georgiadis, G.M.; Ebraheim, N.A.; Hoeflinger, M.J. Displacement of the posterior malleolus during intramedullary tibial nailing. J Trauma 41:1056–1058, 1996.

192. Georgiadis, G.M.; Heck, B.E.; Ebraheim, N.A. Technique for removal of intramedullary nails when there is failure of the proximal extraction device: A report of three cases. J Orthop Trauma 11:130–132, 1997.

193. Gerber, A.; Ganz, R. Combined internal and external osteosynthesis: A biological approach to the treatment of complex fractures of the proximal tibia. Injury 29(Suppl 3):C22–C28, 1998.

194. Giachino, A.A. Recurrent dislocations of the proximal tibiofibular joint: Report of two cases. J Bone Joint Surg Am 68:1104–1116, 1986.

195. Giannoudis, P.V.; Matthews, S.J.; Smith, R.M. Removal of the retained fragment of broken solid nails by the intra-medullary route. Injury 32:407–410, 2001.

196. Golimbu, C.; Firooznia, H.; Rafii, M. Acute traumatic fibular bowing associated with tibial fractures. Clin Orthop 182:211–214, 1984.

197. Gopal, S.; Majumder, S.; Batchelor, A.G.; et al. Fix and flap: The radical orthopaedic and plastic treatment of severe open fractures of the tibia. J Bone Joint Surg Br 82:959–966, 2000.

198. Gordon, J.E.; Kelly-Hahn, J.; Carpenter, C.J.; Schoenecker, P.L. Pin site care during external fixation in children: Results of a nihilistic approach. J Pediatr Orthop 20:163–165, 2000.

199. Goulet, J.A.; Templeman, D. Delayed union and nonunion of tibial shaft fractures. Instr Course Lect 46:281–291, 1997.

200. Granhed, H.P.; Karladani, A.H. Bone debridement and limb lengthening in type III open tibial shaft fractures: No infection or nonunion in 9 patients. Acta Orthop Scand 72:46–52, 2001.

201. Green, S.A.; Garland, D.E.; Moore, T.J.; Barad, S.J. External fixation for the uninfected angulated nonunion of the tibia. Clin Orthop 190:204–211, 1984.

202. Green, S.A.; Jackson, J.M.; Wall, D.M.; et al. Management of segmental defects by the Ilizarov intercalary bone transport method. Clin Orthop 280:136–142, 1992.

203. Greenwood, D.C.; Muir, K.R.; Doherty, M.; et al. Conservatively managed tibial shaft fractures in Nottingham, UK: Are pain, osteoarthritis, and disability long-term complications? J Epidemiol Community Health 51:701–704, 1997.

204. Greer, S.; Kasabian, A.; Thorne, C.; et al. The use of a subatmospheric pressure dressing to salvage a Gustilo grade IIIB open tibial fracture with concomitant osteomyelitis to avert a free flap. Ann Plast Surg 41:687, 1998.

205. Gregory, P.; DiCicco, J.; Karpik, K.; et al. Ipsilateral fractures of the femur and tibia: Treatment with retrograde femoral nailing and unreamed tibial nailing. J Orthop Trauma 10:309–316, 1996.

206. Gregory, P.; Sanders, R. The management of severe fractures of the lower extremities. Clin Orthop 318:95–105, 1995.

207. Gregory, R.T.; Gould, R.J.; Peclet, M.; et al. The mangled extremity syndrome (M.E.S.): A severity grading system for multisystem injury of the extremity. J Trauma 25:1147–1150, 1985.

208. Gross, R.H. Leg length discrepancy: How much is too much? Orthopedics 1:307–310, 1978.

209. Gualdrini, G.; Rollo, G.; Montanari, A.; Zinghi, G.F. Aseptic nonunion of the tibia treated by intramedullary osteosynthesis. Chir Organi Mov 81:275–278, 1996.

210. Gualdrini, G.D. Zati, A.; Degli Esposti, S. [The effects of cigarette smoke on the progression of septic pseudarthrosis of the tibia treated by Ilizarov external fixator.] Chir Organi Mov 81:395–400 1996.

211. Guercio, N.; Orsini, G. Fractures of the limbs complicated by ischaemia due to lesions of the major vessels. Ital J Orthop Traumatol 10:163–165, 1984.

212. Gunalp, B.; Ozguven, M.; Ozturk, E.; et al. Role of bone scanning in the management of non-united fractures: A clinical study. Eur J Nucl Med 19:845–847, 1992.

213. Haas, N.; Krettek, C.; Schandelmaier, P.; et al. A new solid unreamed tibial nail for shaft fractures with severe soft tissue injury. Injury 24:49–54, 1993.

214. Haas, N.; Schutz, M.; Wagenitz, A.; et al. Routine application of the pinless external fixator. Injury 25(Suppl 3):C3–C7, 1994.

215. Habernek, H.; Kwasny, O.; Schmid, L.; Ortner, F. Complications of interlocking nailing for lower leg fractures: A 3-year follow up of 102 cases. J Trauma 33:63–69, 1992.

216. Habernek, H.; Walch, G.; Dengg, C. Cerclage for torsional fractures of the tibia. J Bone Joint Surg Br 71:311–313, 1989.

217. Haddad, F.S.; Desai, K.; Sarkar, J.S.; Dorrell, J.H. The AO unreamed nail: Friend or foe. Injury 27:261–263, 1996.

218. Hadjiargyrou, M.; McLeod, K.; Ryaby, J.P.; Rubin, C. Enhancement of fracture healing by low intensity ultrasound. Clin Orthop 355:(Suppl)216–229, 1998.

219. Hahn, D.; Bradbury, N.; Hartley, R.; et al. Intramedullary nail breakage in distal fractures of the tibia. Injury 27:323–327, 1996.

220. Hak, K.J. Prevention of venous thromboembolism in trauma and long bone fractures. Curr Opin Pulm Med 7:338–343, 2001.

221. Hak, D.J.; Johnson, E.E. The use of the unreamed nail in tibial fractures with concomitant preoperative or intraoperative elevated compartment pressure or compartment syndrome. J Orthop Trauma 8:203–211, 1994.

222. Hall, R.F.J.; Gonzales, M. Fracture of the proximal part of the tibia and fibula associated with an entrapped popliteal artery: A case report. J Bone Joint Surg Am 68:941–944, 1986.

223. Hallock, G.G.; Sussman, D., Rhodes, M. Lower limb salvage with autoclaved autogenous tibial diaphysis: Case report. J Trauma 29:528–530, 1989.

224. Hamilton, F.H.: A Practical Treatise on Fractures and Dislocations. Philadelphia, Blanchard & Lea, 1860.

225. Hamm, J.C.; Stevenson, T.R.; Mathes, S.J. Knee joint salvage utilising a plantar musculocutaneous island pedicle flap. Br J Plast Surg 39:249–254, 1986.

226. Hammer, R.R.; Hammerby, S.; Lindholm, B. Accuracy of radiologic assessment of tibial shaft fracture union in humans. Clin Orthop 199:233–238, 1985.

227. Hannouche, D.; Petite, H.; Sedel, L. Current trends in the enhancement of fracture healing. J Bone Joint Surg Br 83:157–164, 2001.

228. Hansen, S.T.J. The type IIIC tibial fracture. Salvage or amputation. Editorial. J Bone Joint Surg Am 69:799–800, 1987.

229. Harmon, P.H. A simplified posterior approach to the tibia for bone grafting and fibular transference. J Bone Joint Surg Am 27:496, 1945.

230. Harrington, P.; Bunola, J.; Jennings, A.J.; et al. Acute compartment syndrome masked by intravenous morphine from a patient-controlled analgesia pump. Injury 31:387–389, 2000.

231. Harris, I. Gradual closure of fasciotomy wounds using a vessel loop shoelace. Injury 24:565–566, 1993.

232. Hartford, J.M.; Abdu, W.A.; Mayor, M.B. Reconstructive amputation after grade IIIC open tibial fracture. One method of preserving residual limb length. J Orthop Trauma 8:354–358, 1994.

232a. Hay, S.; Richman, M.; Saleh, M. Fracture of the tibial diaphysis treated by external fixation and the axial alignment grid: A single surgeon's experience. Injury 28:437–443, 1997.

233. Heatley, F.W. Severe open fractures of the tibia: The courage to amputate. Editorial. BMJ 296:229, 1988.

234. Heckman, J.D.; Ryaby, J.P.; McCabe, J.; et al. Acceleration of tibial fracture-healing by non-invasive, low-intensity pulsed ultrasound. J Bone Joint Surg Am 76:26–34, 1994.

235. Heckman, M.M.; Whitesides, T.E., Jr.; et al. Compartment pressure in association with closed tibial fractures. The relationship between tissue pressure, compartment, and the distance from the site of the fracture. J Bone Joint Surg Am 76:1285–1992, 1994.

236. Helfet, D.L.; Jupiter, J.B.; Gasser, S. Indirect reduction and tension-band plating of tibial non-union with deformity. J Bone Joint Surg Am 74:1286–1297, 1992.

237. Helfet, D.L.; Shonnard, P.Y.; Levine, D.; Borrelli, J., Jr. Minimally invasive plate osteosynthesis of distal fractures of the tibia. Injury 28(Suppl 1):A42–A47, 1997.

238. Hellemondt, F.J.; Haeff, M.J. Removal of a broken solid intramedullary interlocking nail. A technical note. Acta Orthop Scand 67:512, 1996.

239. Helttula, I.; Karanko, M.; Gullichsen, E. Central hemodynamics during reamed intramedullary nailing of unilateral tibial fractures. J Trauma 48:704–710, 2000.

240. Henley, M.B.; Chapman, J.R.; Agel, J.; et al. Treatment of type II, IIIA, and IIIB open fractures of the tibial shaft: A prospective comparison of unreamed interlocking intramedullary nails and half-pin external fixators. J Orthop Trauma 12:1–7, 1998.

241. Henley, M.B.; Meier, M.; Tencer, A.F. Influences of some design parameters on the biomechanics of the unreamed tibial intramedullary nail. J Orthop Trauma 7:11–19, 1993.

242. Henry, S.L.; Osterman, P.; Seligson, D. Prophylactic management of open fractures with the antibiotic bead pouch technique. Orthop Trans 13:748, 1989.

243. Heppenstall, R.B.; Sapega, A.A.; Scott, R.; et al. The compartment syndrome. An experimental and clinical study of muscular energy metabolism using phosphorus nuclear magnetic resonance spectroscopy. Clin Orthop 226:138–155, 1988.

244. Hernigou, P.; Cohen, D. Proximal entry for intramedullary nailing of the tibia. The risk of unrecognised articular damage. J Bone Joint Surg Br 82:33–41, 2000.

245. Herscovici, D. Jr.; Fredrick, R.W.; Behrens, F. Superior dislocation of the fibular head associated with a tibial shaft fracture. J Orthop Trauma 6:116–119, 1992.

246. Heitel, R.; Lambert, S.M.; Muller, S.; et al. On the timing of soft-tissue reconstruction for open fractures of the lower leg. Arch Orthop Trauma Surg 119:7–12, 1999.

247. Hertel, R.; Pisan, M.; Jacob, R.P. Use of the ipsilateral vascularized fibula for tibial reconstruction. J Bone Joint Surg Br 77:914–921, 1995.

248. Hertel, R.; Strebel, N.; Ganz, R. Amputation versus reconstruction in traumatic defects of the leg: Outcome and costs. J Orthop Trauma 10:223–229, 1996.

249. Higgins, T.F.; DeLuca, P.A.; Ariyan, S. Salvage of open tibial fracture with segmental loss of tibial nerve: Case report and review of the literature. J Orthop Trauma 13:380–385, 1999.

250. Hofmann, G.O.; Gonschorek, O.; Buhren, V. Segment transport employing intramedullary devices in tibial bone defects following trauma and infection. J Orthop Trauma 13:170–177, 1999.

251. Hoogendoorn, J.M.; van der Werken, C. Grade III open tibial fractures: Functional outcome and quality of life in amputees versus patients with successful reconstruction. Injury 32:329–334, 2001.

252. Hooper, G.J.; Keddell, R.G.; Penny, I.D. Conservative management or closed nailing for tibial shaft fractures. A randomised prospective trial. J Bone Joint Surg Br 73:83–85, 1991.

253. Horne, G.; Iceton, J.; Twist, J.; Malony, R. Disability following fractures of the tibial shaft. Orthopedics 13:423–426, 1990.

254. Horster, G. Corrective osteotomies of the tibial shaft. In: Hierholzer, G.; Müller, K.H., eds. Corrective Osteotomies of the Lower Extremity after Trauma. Berlin, Springer-Verlag, 1985, pp. 127–139.

255. Howard, P.W., Jr.; Poole, G.V., Jr.; Hansen K.J.; et al. Lower limb fractures with associated vascular injuries. J Bone Joint Surg Br 72:116–120, 1990.

256. Howe, H.R., Jr.; Poole, G.V., Jr.; Hansen, K.J.; et al. Salvage of lower extremities following combined orthopedic and vascular trauma. A predictive salvage index. Am Surg 53:205–208, 1987.

257. Huang, C.K.; Chen, W.M.; Chen, T.H.; Lo, W.H. Segmental tibial fractures treated with interlocking nails. A retrospective study of 33 cases. Acta Orthop Scand 68:563–566, 1997.

258. Hung, S.H.; Chen, T.B.; Cheng, Y.M.; et al. Concomitant fractures of the ipsilateral femur and tibia with intra-articular extension into the knee joint. J Trauma 48:547–551, 2000.

259. Hutson, J.J., Jr.; Zych, G.A. Infections in periarticular fractures of the lower extremity treated with tensioned wire hybrid fixators. J Orthop Trauma 12:214–218, 1998.

260. Hyder, N.; Kessler, S.; Jennings, A.G.; De Boer, P.G. Compartment syndrome in tibial shaft fracture missed because of a local nerve block. J Bone Joint Surg Br 78:499–500, 1996.

261. Ikeda, K.; Tomita, K.; Hashimoto, F.; Morikawa, S. Long-term follow-up of vascularized bone grafts for the reconstruction of tibial nonunion: Evaluation with computed tomographic scanning. J Trauma 32:693–697, 1992.

262. Ito, H.; Shirai, Y. The efficacy of ununited tibial fracture treatment using pulsing electromagnetic fields: Relation to biological activity on nonunion bone ends. J Nippon Med Sch 68:149–153, 2001.

263. Jain, R.; Podworny, N.; Hearn, T.; et al. Effect of stainless steel and titanium low-contact dynamic compression plate application on the

vascularity and mechanical properties of cortical bone after fracture. J Orthop Trauma 11:490–495, 1997.

264. Janes, G.C.; Collopy, D.M.; Price, R.; Sikorski, J.M. Bone density after rigid plate fixation of tibial fractures. A dual-energy x-ray absorptiometry study. J Bone Joint Surg Br 75:914–917, 1993.

265. Jenny, J.Y.; Jenny, G.; Kempf, I. Infection after reamed intramedullary nailing of lower limb fractures. A review of 1,464 cases over 15 years. Acta Orthopa Scand 65:94–96, 1994.

266. Jeske, J.M.; Lomasney, L.M.; Demos, T.C.; et al. Longitudinal tibial stress fracture. Orthopedics 19:263–270, 1996.

267. Johansen, K.; Daines, M.; Howey, T.; et al. Objective criteria accurately predict amputation following lower extremity trauma. J Trauma 30:568–572, 1990.

268. Johansen, K.; Lynch, K.; Paun, M.; et al. Non-invasive vascular tests reliably exclude occult arterial trauma in injured extremities. J Trauma 31:515–519, 1991.

269. Johner, R.; Joerger, K.; Cordey, J.; Perren, S.M. Rigidity of pure lag-screw fixation as a function of screw inclination in an in vitro spiral osteotomy. Clin Orthop 178:74–79, 1983.

270. Johner, R.; Wruhs, O. Classification of tibial shaft fractures and correlation with results after rigid internal fixation. Clin Orthop 178:7–25, 1983.

271. Johnson, E.E. Acute lengthening of shortened lower extremities after malunion or non-union of a fracture. J Bone Joint Surg Am 76:379–389, 1994.

272. Johnson, E.E. Multiplane correctional osteotomy of the tibia for diaphyseal malunion. Clin Orthop 215:223–232, 1987.

273. Johnson, E.E.; Marder, R.A. Open intramedullary nailing and bone-grafting for non-union of tibial diaphyseal fracture. J Bone Joint Surg Am 69:375–380, 1987.

274. Johnson, E.E.; Simpson, L.A.; Helfet, D.L. Delayed intramedullary fixation after external fixation of the tibia. Clin Orthop 253:251–257, 1990.

275. Johnson, E.E.; Urist, M.R.; Finerman, G.A. Resistant nonunions and partial or complete segmental defects of long bones. Treatment with implants of a composite of human bone morphogenetic protein (BMP) and autolyzed, antigen-extracted, allogeneic (AAA) bone. Clin Orthop 279:229–237, 1992.

276. Jones, D.H., 4th.; Schmeling, G. Tibial fracture during removal of a tibial intramedullary nail. J Orthop Trauma 13:271–273, 1999.

277. Joshi, R.P.; Heatley, F.W. Dislocation of superior tibio-fibular joint in association with fracture of the tibia: 'Monteggia' injury of the leg. Injury 28:405–407, 1997.

278. Jupiter, J.B.; Ring, D.; Rosen, H. The complications and difficulties of management of nonunion in the severely obese. J Orthop Trauma 9:363–370, 1995.

279. Karkabi, S.; Reis, N.D. Fibular bowing due to tibial shortening in isolated fracture of the tibia: Failure of late segmental fibulectomy to relieve ankle pain. Arch Orthop Trauma Surg 106:61–63, 1986.

280. Karladani, A.H.; Granhed, H.; Edshage, B.; et al. Displaced tibial shaft fractures: A prospective randomized study of closed intramedullary nailing versus cast treatment in 53 patients. Acta Orthop Scand 71:160–167, 2000.

281. Karladani, A.H.; Granhed, H.; Fogdestam, I.; Styf, J. Salvaged limbs after tibial shaft fractures with extensive soft-tissue injury: A biopsychosocial function analysis. J Trauma 50:60–64, 2001.

282. Karlsson, M.K.; Nilsson, B.E.; Obrant, K.J. Fracture incidence after tibial shaft fractures. A 30-year follow-up study. Clin Orthop 287:87–89, 1993.

283. Karlstrom, G.; Lonnerholdm, T.; Olerud, S. Cavus deformity of the foot after fracture of the tibial shaft. J Bone Joint Surg Am 57:893–900, 1975.

284. Karlstrom, G.; Olerud, S. The management of tibial fractures in alcoholics and mentally disturbed patients. J Bone Joint Surg Br 56:730–734, 1974.

285. Karnezis, I.A. Biomechanical considerations in 'biological' femoral osteosynthesis: An experimental study of the 'bridging' and 'wave' plating techniques. Arch Orthop Trauma Surg 120:272–275, 2000.

286. Karnezis, I.A.; Miles, A.W.; Cunningham, J.L.; Learmonth, I.D. "Biological" internal fixation of long bone fractures: A biomechanical study of a "noncontact" plate system. Injury 29:689–695, 1998.

287. Kasashima, T.; Minami, A.; Kutsumi, K. Late fracture of vascularized fibular grafts. Microsurgery 18:337–343, 1998.

288. Keating, J.F.; Blachut, P.A.; O'Brien, P.J.; et al. Reamed nailing of open tibial fractures: Does the antibiotic bead pouch reduce the deep infection rate? J Orthop Trauma 10:298–303, 1996.

289. Keating, J.F.; Gardner, E.; Leach, W.J.; et al. Management of tibial fractures with the Orthofix dynamic external fixator. J R Coll Surg Edinb 36:272–277, 1991.

290. Keating, J.F.; Kuo, R.S.; Court-Brown, C.M. Bifocal fractures of the tibia and fibula. Incidence, classification and treatment. J Bone Joint Surg Br 76:395–400, 1994.

291. Keating, J.F.; McQueen, M.M. Substitutes for autologous bone graft in orthopaedic trauma. J Bone Joint Surg Br 83:3–8, 2001.

292. Keating, J.F.; O'Brien, P.I.; Blachut, P.A.; et al. Reamed interlocking intramedullary nailing of open fractures of the tibia. Clin Orthop 338:182–191, 1997.

293. Keating, J.F.; O'Brien, P.J.; Blachut, P.A.; et al. Locking intramedullary nailing with and without reaming for open fractures of the tibial shaft. A prospective, randomized study. J Bone Joint Surg Am 79:334–341, 1997.

294. Keating, J.F.; Orfaly, R.; O'Brien, P.J. Knee pain after tibial nailing. J Orthop Trauma 11:10–13, 1997.

295. Kelley, S.S.; Morrison, J.A.; Templeman, D.C. Techniques for the removal of broken small-diameter tibial nails: A report of two cases. J Orthop Trauma 9:523–525, 1995.

296. Kempf, I.; Grosse, A.; Rigaut, P. The treatment of noninfected pseudarthrosis of the femur and tibia with locked intramedullary nailing. Clin Orthop 212:142–154, 1986.

297. Kenwright, J.; Richardson, J.B.; Cunningham, J.L.; et al. Axial movement and tibial fractures. A controlled randomised trial of treatment. J Bone Joint Surg Br 73:654–659, 1991.

298. Kessler, S.B.; Deiler, S.; Schiffl-Deiler, M.; et al. Refractures: A consequence of impaired local bone viability. Arch Orthop Trauma Surg 111:96–101, 1992.

299. Kettelkamp, D.B.; Hillberry, B.M.; Murrish, D.E.; Heck, D.A. Degenerative arthritis of the knee secondary to fracture malunion. Clin Orthop 234:159–169, 1988.

300. Khalily, C.; Behnke, S.; Seligson, D. Treatment of closed tibia shaft fractures: A survey from the 1997 Orthopaedic Trauma Association and Osteosynthesis International—Gerhard Küntscher Kreis meeting. J Orthop Trauma 14:577–581, 2000.

301. Khalily, C.; Voor, M.J.; Seligson, D. Fracture site motion with Ilizarov and "hybrid" external fixation. J Orthop Trauma 12:21–26, 1998.

302. Kim, H.S.; Jahng, J.S.; Han, D.Y.; et al. Immediate ipsilateral fibular transfer in a large tibial defect using a ring fixator. A case report. Int Orthop 22:321–324, 1998.

303. Kindsfater, K.; Jonassen, E.A. Osteomyelitis in grade II and III open tibia fractures with late debridement. J Orthop Trauma 9:121–127, 1995.

304. Klemm, K.; Schnettler, R. The use of gentamicin-PMMA chains in the treatment of infected tibial nonunion. Acta Orthopa Belg 58(Suppl 1):222–226, 1992.

305. Kneifel, T.; Buckley, R. A comparison of one versus two distal locking screws in tibial fractures treated with unreamed tibial nails: A prospective randomized clinical trial. Injury 27:271–273, 1996.

306. Kock, H.J.; Schmit-Neuerburg, K.P.; Hanke, J.; et al. Thromboprophylaxis with low-molecular-weight heparin in outpatients with plaster-cast immobilisation of the leg. Lancet 346:459–461, 1995.

307. Konrath, G.; Moed, B.R.; Watson, J.T.; et al. Intramedullary nailing of unstable diaphyseal fractures of the tibia with distal intraarticular involvement. J Orthop Trauma 11:200–205, 1997.

308. Korpelainen, R.; Orava, S.; Karpakka, J.; et al. Risk factors for recurrent stress fractures in athletes. Am J Sports Med 29:304–310, 2001.

309. Koval, K.J.; Clapper, M.F.; Brumback, R.J.; et al. Complications of reamed intramedullary nailing of the tibia. J Orthop Trauma 5:84–89, 1991.

310. Koval, K.J.; Meadows, S.E.; Rosen, H.; et al. Posttraumatic tibial osteomyelitis: A comparison of three treatment approaches. Orthopedics 15:455–460, 1992.

311. Krauss, M.D.; Van Meter, C.D. Longitudinal tibial stress fracture. Orthop Rev 23:163–166, 1994.

312. Kregor, P.J.; Christensen, R.; Nemecek, D.; et al. Neurovascular risk associated with submuscular fixation of the proximal tibia: A cadaveric study, Paper #2. Paper presented at the 17th Annual

Meeting of the Orthopaedic Trauma Association, San Diego, CA, 2001.

313. Krettek, C. Foreword: Concepts of minimally invasive plate osteosynthesis. Injury 28(Suppl 1):A1–A2, 1997.

314. Krettek, C.; Blauth, M.; Miclau, T.; et al. Accuracy of intramedullary templates in femoral and tibial radiographs. J Bone Joint Surg Br 78:963–964, 1996.

315. Krettek, C.; Gerich, T; Miclau, T. A minimally invasive medial approach for proximal tibial fractures. Injury 32(Suppl 1):A4–A13, 2001.

316. Krettek, C.; Haas, N.; Tscherne, H. The role of supplemental lag-screw fixation for open fractures of the tibial shaft treated with external fixation. J Bone Joint Surg Am 73:893–897, 1991.

317. Krettek, C.; Miclau, T.; Schandelmaier, P.; et al. The mechanical effect of blocking screws ("Poller screws") in stabilizing tibia fractures with short proximal or distal fragments after insertion of small-diameter intramedullary nails. J Orthop Trauma 13:550–553, 1999.

318. Krettek, C.; Schandelmaier, P.; Tscherne, H. Nonreamed interlocking nailing of closed tibial fractures with severe soft tissue injury. Clin Orthop 315:34–47, 1995.

319. Krettek, C.; Stephan, C.; Schandelmaier, P.; et al. The use of Poller screws as blocking screws in stabilising tibial fractures treated with small diameter intramedullary nails. J Bone Joint Surg Br 81:963–968, 1999.

320. Kristensen, K.D.; Kiaer, T.; Blicher, J. No arthrosis of the ankle 20 years after malaligned tibial shaft fracture. Acta Orthop Scand 60:208–209, 1989.

321. Kristiansen, L.P.; Steen, H. Lengthening of the tibia over an intramedullary nail, using the Ilizarov external fixator. Major complications and slow consolidation in 9 lengthenings. Acta Orthop Scand 70:271–274, 1999.

322. Kyro, A. Malunion after intramedullary nailing of tibial shaft fractures. Ann Chir Gynaecol 86:56–64, 1997.

323. Kyro, A.; Tunturi, T.; Soukka, A. Conservative treatment of tibial fractures: Results in a series of 163 patients. Ann Chir Gynaecol 80:294–300, 1991.

324. Lagier, R.; Van Linthoudt, D. Articular changes due to disuse in Sudeck's atrophy. Int Orthop 3:1–8, 1979.

325. Lambert, K.L. Weightbearing function of the fibula. J Bone Joint Surg Am 54:507–513, 1971.

326. Lang, G.J.; Cohen, B.E.; Bosse, M.J.; Kellam, J.F. Proximal third tibial shaft fractures. Should they be nailed? Clin Orthop 315:64–74, 1995.

327. Lange, R.H. Limb reconstruction vs. amputation. Decision making in massive lower extremity trauma. Clin Orthop 243:92–99, 1989.

328. Lange, R.H.; Bach, A.W.; Hansen, S.T., Jr.; Johansen, K.H. Open tibial fractures with associated vascular injuries: Prognosis for limb salvage. J Trauma 25:203–208, 1985.

329. Laursen, M.B.; Lass, P.; Christensen, K.S. Ilizarov treatment of tibial nonunions results in 16 cases. Acta Orthop Belg 66:279–285, 2000.

330. Leach, R.E. Fracture of the tibia. In: Rockwood, C.A., Jr.; Green, D.P., eds. Fractures. Philadelphia, J.B. Lippincott, 1975, pp. 1285–1259.

331. Lee, E.H.; Goh, J.C.H.; Helm, R.; Pho, R.W.H. Donor site morbidity following resection of the fibula. J Bone Joint Surg Br 72:129–131, 1990.

332. Lee, J. Efficacy of cultures in the management of open fractures. Clin Orthop 339:71–75, 1997.

332a. Lehman, W.B.; Paley, D.; Atar, D. Operating Room Guide to Cross-Sectional Anatomy of the Extremities and Pelvis. New York, Raven Press, 1989.

333. Leunig, M.; Hertel, R. Thermal necrosis after tibial reaming for intramedullary nail fixation: A report of three cases. J Bone Joint Surg Br 78:584–587, 1996.

334. Leunig, M.; Hertel, R.; Siebenrock, K.A.; et al. The evolution of indirect reduction techniques for the treatment of fractures. Clin Orthop 375:7–14, 2000.

335. Levin, P.E. Exchange reamed intramedullary nailing for delayed union and nonunion of the tibia. Clin Orthop 332:304–305, 1996.

336. Levy, A.S.; Bromberg, J.; Jasper, D. Tibia fractures produced from the impact of a baseball bat. J Orthop Trauma 8:54–58, 1994.

337. Levy, M. Peroneal nerve palsy due to superior dislocation of the head of the fibula and shortening of the tibia (Monteggia-like fracture dislocation of the calf). Acta Orthop Scand 46:1020–1025, 1975.

338. Lidor, C.; Ferris, L.R.; Hall, R.; et al. Stress fracture of the tibia after arthrodesis of the ankle or the hindfoot. J Bone Joint Surg Am 79:558–564, 1997.

339. Lin, C.H.; Wei, F.C.; Chen, H.C.; Chuang, D.C. Outcome comparison in traumatic lower-extremity reconstruction by using various composite vascularized bone transplantation. Plast Reconstr Surg 104:984–992, 1999.

340. Lindstrom, T.; Gullichsen, E.; Lertola, K.; Niinikoski, J. Leg tissue perfusion in simple tibial shaft fractures treated with unreamed and reamed nailing. J Trauma 43:636–639, 1997.

341. Lingg, G.M.; Soltesz, I.; Kessler, S.; Dreher, R. Insufficiency and stress fractures of the long bones occurring in patients with rheumatoid arthritis and other inflammatory diseases, with a contribution on the possibilities of computed tomography. Eur J Radiol 26:54–63, 1997.

342. Littenberg, B.; Weinstein, L.P.; McCarren, M.; et al. Closed fractures of the tibial shaft. A meta-analysis of three methods of treatment. J Bone Joint Surg Am 80:174–183, 1998.

343. Lonner, J.H.; Jupiter, J.B.; Healy, W.L. Ipsilateral tibia and ankle fractures. J Orthop Trauma 7:30–37, 1993.

344. Lynch, K.; Johansen, K. Can Doppler pressure measurement replace "exclusion" arteriography in the diagnosis of occult extremity arterial trauma? Ann Surg 214:737–741, 1991.

345. MacKenzie, E.J.; Cushing, B.M.; Jurkovich, G.J.; et al. Physical impairment and functional outcome six months after severe lower extremity fractures. J Trauma 34:528–538, 1993.

346. Malizos, K.N.; Nunley, J.A.; Goldner, R.D.; et al. Free vascularized fibula in traumatic long bone defects and in limb salvaging following tumor resection: Comparative study. Microsurgery 14:368–374, 1993.

347. Markmiller, M.; Tjarksen, M.; Mayr, E.; Ruter, A. The unreamed tibia nail. Multicenter study of the AO/ASIF. Osteosynthesefragen/Association for the Study of Internal Fixation. Langenbecks Arch Surg 385:276–283, 2000.

348. Marsh, D.R.; Shah, S.; Elliott, J.; Kurdy, N. The Ilizarov method in nonunion, malunion and infection of fractures. J Bone Joint Surg Br 79:273–279, 1997.

349. Marsh, J.; Nepola, J.; Seabold, J. Subclinical infection in delayed union of fractures. J Orthop Trauma 3:169, 1988.

350. Marsh, J.L.; Nepola, J.V.; Wuest, T.K.; et al. Unilateral external fixation until healing with the dynamic axial fixator for severe open tibial fractures. J Orthop Trauma 5:341–348, 1991.

351. Marsh, J.L.; Prokuski, L.; Biermann, J.S. Chronic infected tibial nonunions with bone loss. Conventional techniques versus bone transport. Clin Orthop 301:139–146, 1994.

352. Marshall, P.D.; Saleh, M.; Douglas, D.L. Risk of deep infection with intramedullary nailing following the use of external fixators. J R Coll Surg Edinb 36:268–271, 1991.

353. Martin, S.D.; Healey, J.H.; Horowitz, S. Stress fracture MRI. Orthopedics 16:75–78, 1993.

354. Marwan, M.; Ibrahim, M. Simple method for retrieval of distal segment of the broken interlocking intramedullary nail. Injury 30:333–335, 1999.

355. Mast, J.W. Preoperative planning in the surgical correction of tibial nonunions and malunions. Clin Orthop 178:26–30, 1987.

356. Mast, J.; Jakob, R.; Ganz, R. Planning and Reduction Technique in Fracture Surgery. New York, Springer-Verlag, 1989.

357. Matsushita, T.; Nakamura, K.; Ohnishi, I.; Kurokawa, T. Sliding performance of unilateral external fixators for tibia. Med Eng Phys 20:66–69, 1998.

358. Matsushita, T.; Nakamura, K.; Okazaki, H.; Kurokawa, T. A simple technique for correction of complicated tibial deformity including rotational deformity. Arch Orthop Trauma Surg 117:259–261, 1998.

359. Matthews, D.E.; McGuire, R.; Freeland, A.E. Anterior unicortical buttress plating in conjunction with an unreamed interlocking intramedullary nail for treatment of very proximal tibial diaphyseal fractures. Orthopedics 20:647–648, 1997.

360. Maurer, D.J.; Merkow, R.L.; Gustilo, R.B. Infections after intramedullary nailing of severe open tibial fractures initially treated with external fixation. J Bone Joint Surg Am 71:835–838, 1989.

361. Mawhinney, I.N.; Maginn, P.; McCoy, G.F. Tibial compartment syndromes after tibial nailing. J Orthop Trauma 8:212–214, 1994.

362. May, J.W., Jr.; Jupiter, J.B.; Weiland, A.J.; Byrd, H.S. Current concepts review. Clinical classification of post-traumatic tibial osteomyelitis. J Bone Joint Surg Am 71:1422–1428, 1989.

363. May, J.W., Jr.; Sheppard, J. Reconstruction of the stump after below-the-knee amputations. Soft tissue expansion and local muscle rotation flaps: A case report. J Bone Joint Surg Am 69:1240–1245, 1987.

364. Mayo, K.A.; Benirschke, S.K. Treatment of tibial malunions and nonunions with reamed intramedullary nails. Orthop Clin North Am 21:715–724, 1990.

365. Mayr, E.; Frankel, V.; Ruter, A. Ultrasound—an alternative healing method for nonunions? Arch Orthop Trauma Surg 120:1–8, 2000.

366. McBride, A.M. Stress fractures in runners. Clin Sports Med 4:737–752, 1985.

367. McConnell, T.; Tornetta, P., 3rd.; Tilzey, J.; Casey, D. Tibial portal placement: The radiographic correlate of the anatomic safe zone. J Orthop Trauma 15:207–209, 2001.

368. McKee, M.D.; Schemitsch, E.H.; Waddell, J.P.; Yoo, D. A prospective, randomized clinical trial comparing tibial nailing using fracture table traction versus manual traction. J Orthop Trauma 13:463–469, 1999.

369. McKee, M.D.; Yoo, D.; Schemitsch, E.H. Health status after Ilizarov reconstruction of post-traumatic lower-limb deformity. J Bone Joint Surg Br 80:360–364, 1998.

370. McLaren, A.C.; Blokker, C.P. Locked intramedullary fixation for metaphyseal malunion and nonunion. Clin Orthop 265:253–260, 1991.

371. McLaughlin, J.A.; Paulson, M.M.; Rosenthal, R.E. Delayed onset of anterior tibial compartment syndrome in a patient receiving low-molecular-weight heparin. A case report. J Bone Joint Surg Am 80:1789–1790, 1998.

372. McMaster, M. Disability of the hindfoot after fracture of the tibial shaft. J Bone Joint Surg Br 58:90–93, 1976.

373. McNamara, M.G.; Heckman, J.D.; Corley, F.G. Severe open fractures of the lower extremity: A retrospective evaluation of the Mangled Extremity Severity Score (MESS). J Orthop Trauma 8:81–87, 1994.

374. McQueen, M.M.; Christie, J.; Court-Brown, C.M. Acute compartment syndrome in tibial diaphyseal fractures. J Bone Joint Surg Br 78:95–98, 1996.

375. McQueen, M.M.; Christie, J.; Court-Brown, C.M. Compartment pressures after intramedullary nailing of the tibia. J Bone Joint Surg Br 72:395–397, 1990.

376. McQueen, M.M.; Court-Brown, C.M. Compartment monitoring in tibial fractures. The pressure threshold for decompression. J Bone Joint Surg Br 78:99–104, 1996.

377. McQueen, M.M.; Gaston, P.; Court-Brown, C.M. Acute compartment syndrome. Who is at risk? J Bone Joint Surg Br 82:200–203, 2000.

378. Megas, P.; Panagiotopoulos, E.; Skriviliotakis, S.; Lambiris, E. Intramedullary nailing in the treatment of aseptic tibial nonunion. Injury 32:233–239, 2001.

379. Merchant, T.C.; Dietz, F.R. Long term follow-up after fractures of the tibial and fibular shafts. J Bone Joint Surg Am 71:599–606, 1989.

380. Merriam, W.F.; Porter, K.M. Hindfoot disability after a tibial shaft fracture treated by internal fixation. J Bone Joint Surg Br 65:326–328, 1983.

381. Mertens, P.; Broos, P.; Reynders, P.; Deswart, R. The unreamed locked intramedullary tibial nail: A follow-up study in 51 patients. Acta Orthop Belg 64:277–283, 1998.

382. Miclau, T.; Martin, R.E. The evolution of modern plate osteosynthesis. Injury 28(Suppl 1):A3–A6, 1997.

383. Miller, M.E.; Ada, J.R.; Webb, L.X. Treatment of infected nonunion and delayed union of tibia fractures with locked intramedullary nails. Clin Orthop 245:233–238, 1989.

384. Mino, D.E.; Hughes, E.C., Jr. Bony entrapment of the superficial peroneal nerve. Clin Orthop 185:203–206, 1984.

385. Mitchell, J.R.; Johnson, J.E.; Collier, B.D.; Gould, J.S. Stress fracture of the tibia following extensive hindfoot and ankle arthrodesis: A report of three cases. Foot Ankle Int 16:445–448, 1995.

386. Miyakoshi, N.; Sato, K.; Murai, H.; Tamura, Y. Insufficiency fractures of the distal tibiae. J Orthop Sci 5:71–74, 2000.

387. Moda, S.K.; Kalra, G.S.; Gupta, R.S.; et al. The role of early flap coverage in the management of open fractures of both bones of the leg. Injury 25:83–85, 1994.

388. Moed, B.R.; Kim, E.C.; van Holsbeeck, M.; et al. Ultrasound for the early diagnosis of tibial fracture healing after static interlocked nailing without reaming: Histologic correlation using a canine model. J Orthop Trauma 12:200–205, 1998.

389. Moed, B.R.; Strom, D.E. Compartment syndrome after closed intramedullary nailing of the tibia: A canine model and report of two cases. J Orthop Trauma 5:1–7, 1991.

390. Moed, B.R.; Watson, J.T. Intramedullary nailing of aseptic tibial nonunions without the use of the fracture table. J Orthop Trauma 9:128–134, 1995.

391. Moed, B.R.; Watson, J.T. Intramedullary nailing of the tibia without a fracture table: The transfixion pin distractor technique. J Orthop Trauma 8:195–202, 1994.

392. Moed, B.R.; Watson, J.T.; Goldschmidt, P.; van Holsbeeck, M. Ultrasound for the early diagnosis of fracture healing after interlocking nailing of the tibia without reaming. Clin Orthop 310:37–44, 1995.

393. Moehring, H.D.; Gravel, C.; Chapman, M.W.; Olson, S.A. Comparison of antibiotic beads and intravenous antibiotics in open fractures. Clin Orthop 372:254–261, 2000.

394. Moehring, H.D.; Voigtlander, J.P. Compartment pressure monitoring during intramedullary fixation of tibial fractures. Orthopedics 18:631–635, 1995.

395. Moroni, A.; Faldini, C.; Marchetti, S.; et al. Improvement of the bone-pin interface strength in osteoporotic bone with use of hydroxyapatite-coated tapered external-fixation pins. A prospective, randomized clinical study of wrist fractures. J Bone Joint Surg Am 83:717–721, 2001.

396. Morris, J.M.; Blickenstaff, L.D. Fatigue Fractures—A Clinical Study. Springfield, IL, Charles C Thomas, 1967.

397. Morrison, K.M.; Ebraheim, N.A.; Southworth, S.R.; et al. Plating of the fibula. Its potential value as an adjunct to external fixation of the tibia. Clin Orthop 266:209–213, 1991.

398. Mosheiff, R.; Safran, O.; Segal, D.; Liebergall, M. The unreamed tibial nail in the treatment of distal metaphyseal fractures. Injury 30:83–90, 1999.

399. Moshirfar, A.; Showers, D.; Logan, P.; Esterhai, J.L., Jr. Orthotic management for posttraumatic nonunion of the tibia complicated by osteomyelitis. Clin Orthop 360:106–109, 1999.

400. Moshirfar, A.; Showers, D.; Logan, P.; Esterhai, J.L., Jr. Prosthetic options for below knee amputations after osteomyelitis and nonunion of the tibia. Clin Orthop 360:110–121, 1999.

401. Müller, M.E.; Nazarian, S.; Koch, P.; et al. The Comprehensive Classification of Fractures of Long Bones. Berlin, Springer-Verlag, 1990.

402. Mullett, H.; Al-Abed, K.; Prasad, C.V.; O'Sullivan, M. Outcome of compartment syndrome following intramedullary nailing of tibial diaphyseal fractures. Injury 32:411–413, 2001.

403. Mulligan, M.E.; Shanley, D.J. Supramalleolar fatigue fractures of the tibia. Skeletal Radiol 25:325–328, 1996.

404. Murray, J.H.; Fitch, R.D. Distraction histiogenesis: Principles and indications. J Am Acad Orthop Surg 4:317–327, 1996.

405. Nassif, J.M.; Gorczyca, J.T.; Cole, J.K.; et al. Effect of acute reamed versus unreamed intramedullary nailing on compartment pressure when treating closed tibial shaft fractures: A randomized prospective study. J Orthop Trauma 14:554–558, 2000.

406. Nicoll, E.A. Fractures of the tibial shaft: A survey of 705 cases. J Bone Joint Surg Br 46:373–387, 1964.

407. Nieminen, H.; Kuokkanen, H.; Tukiainen, E.; Asko-Seljavaara, S. Free flap reconstructions of tibial fractures complicated after internal fixation. J Trauma 38:660–664, 1995.

408. Nolte, P.A.; van der Krans, A.; Patka, P.; et al. Low-intensity pulsed ultrasound in the treatment of nonunions. J Trauma 51:693–702, 2001.

409. Noordeen, M.H.; Lavy, C.B.; Shergill, N.S.; et al. Cyclical micromovement and fracture healing. J Bone Joint Surg Br 77:645–648, 1995.

410. Nussbaum, A.R.; Treves, S.T.; Micheli, L. Bone stress lesions in ballet dancers: Scintigraphic assessment. AJR Am J Roentgenol 150:851–855, 1988.

411. Nylander, G.; Semb, H. Veins of the lower part of the leg after tibial fractures. Surg Gynecol Obstet 134:974–976, 1972.

412. Nyquist, F.; Berglund, M.; Nilsson, B.E.; Obrant, K.J. Nature and healing of tibial shaft fractures in alcohol abusers. Alcohol Alcohol 32:91–95, 1997.

413. O'Brien, E.D.; Denton, J.R. Open tibial fracture infections in asymptomatic HIV antibody–positive patients. Orthop Rev 23:662–664, 1994.

414. O'Dwyer, K.J.; Chakravarty, R.D.; Esler, C.N. Intramedullary nailing technique and its effect on union rates of tibial shaft fractures. Injury 25:461–464, 1994.

415. O'Dwyer, K.J.; DeVriese, L.; Feys, H.; Vercruysse, L. Tibial shaft fractures with an intact fibula. Injury 24:591–594, 1993.

416. O'Dwyer, K.J.; Devriese, L.; Feys, H.; et al. The intact fibula. Injury 23:314–316, 1992.

417. Ochsner, P.E.; Baumgart, F.; Kohler, G. Heat-induced segmental necrosis after reaming of one humeral and two tibial fractures with a narrow medullary canal. Injury 29(Suppl 2):B1–B10, 1998.

418. Oestern, H.J.; Tscherne, H. Pathophysiology and classification of soft tissue injuries associated with fractures. In: Tscherne, H.; Golzen, L. Fractures with Soft Tissue Injuries. Berlin, Springer-Verlag, 1994, pp. 1–9.

419. Ogden, J.A. Subluxation and dislocation of the proximal tibiofibular joint. J Bone Joint Surg Am 56:145–154, 1974.

420. Olerud, C. The pronation capacity of the foot—its consequences for axial deformity after tibial shaft fractures. Arch Orthop Trauma Surg 104:303–306, 1985.

421. Oni, O.A.O.; Fenton, A.; Iqbal, S.J.; Gregg, P.J. Prognostic indicators in tibial shaft fractures: Serum creatinine kinase activity. J Orthop Trauma 3:345–347, 1989.

422. Oni, O.O.; Hui, A.; Gregg, P.J. The healing of closed tibial shaft fractures. The natural history of union with closed treatment. J Bone Joint Surg Br 70:787–790, 1988.

423. Orava, S.; Karpakka, J.; Hulkko, A.; et al. Diagnosis and treatment of stress fractures located at the mid-tibial shaft in athletes. Int J Sports Med 12:419–422, 1991.

424. Orbay, G.L.; Frankel, V.H.; Kummer, F.J. The effect of wire configuration on the stability of the Ilizarov external fixator. Clin Orthop 279:299–302, 1992.

425. Orfaly, R.; Keating, J.E.; O'Brien, P.J. Knee pain after tibial nailing: Does the entry point matter? J Bone Joint Surg Br 77:976–977, 1995.

426. Orthopaedic Trauma Association Committee for Coding and Classification: Fracture and Dislocation Compendium. J Orthop Trauma 10(Suppl 1):1–154, 1996.

427. Ostermann, P.A.; Seligson, D.; Henry, S.L. Local antibiotic therapy for severe open fractures: A review of 1085 consecutive cases. J Bone Joint Surg Br 77:93–97, 1995.

428. Ostrum, R.F. Treatment of floating knee injuries through a single percutaneous approach. Clin Orthop 375:43–50, 2000.

429. Paktiss, A.S.; Gross, R.H. Afghan percutaneous osteotomy. J Pediatr Orthop 13:531–533, 1993.

430. Paley, D. Treatment of tibial nonunion and bone loss with the Ilizarov technique. Instr Course Lect 39:185–197, 1990.

431. Paley, D.; Maar, D.C. Ilizarov bone transport treatment for tibial defects. J Orthop Trauma 14:76–85, 2000.

432. Palmer, S.H.; Handley, R.; Willett, K. The use of interlocked 'customised' blade plates in the treatment of metaphyseal fractures in patients with poor bone stock. Injury 31:187–191, 2000.

433. Panjabi, M.D.; Lindsey, R.W.; Walter, S.D.; White, A.A.I. The clinician's ability to evaluate the strength of healing fractures from plain radiographs. J Orthop Trauma 3:29–32, 1989.

434. Pare, A. The classic: Compound fracture of leg, Pare's personal care. Clin Orthop 178:3–6, 1983.

435. Park, S.; Lee, T.J. Strategic considerations on the configuration of free flaps and their vascular pedicles combined with Ilizarov distraction in the lower extremity. Plast Reconstr Surg 105:1680–1686, 2000.

436. Parkes, J.C.; Zelko, R.R. Isolated acute dislocation of the proximal tibiofibular joint. J Bone Joint Surg Am 55:177–180, 1973.

437. Patzakis, M.J.; Scilaris, T.A.; Chon, J.; et al. Results of bone grafting for infected tibial nonunion. Clin Orthop 315:192–198, 1995.

438. Pease, C.T. Insufficiency fractures of the distal tibia. Br J Rheumatol 33:1056–1059, 1994.

439. Pedersen, P.; Damholt, V. Rehabilitation after amputation following lower limb fracture. J Trauma 36:95–97, 1994.

440. Peltier, L.F. Fractures. A History and Iconography of Their Treatment. San Francisco, Norman Publishing, 1990.

441. Peter, R.E.; Bachelin, P.; Fritschy, D. Skiers' lower leg shaft fracture. Outcome in 91 cases treated conservatively with Sarmiento's brace. Am J Sports Med 16:486–491, 1988.

442. Petje, G.; Landsiedl, F. Stress fracture of the tibia after total knee arthroplasty. Arch Orthop Trauma Surg 116:514–515, 1997.

443. Plasschaert, V.F.; Johansson, C.G.; Micheli, L.J. Anterior tibial stress fracture treated with intramedullary nailing: A case report. Clin J Sport Med 5:58–61, 1995.

444. Podolsky, A.; Chao, E.Y. Mechanical performance of Ilizarov circular external fixators in comparison with other external fixators. Clin Orthop 293:61–70, 1993.

445. Pollak, A.N.; McCarthy, M.L.; Burgess, A.R. Short-term wound complications after application of flaps for coverage of traumatic soft-tissue defects about the tibia. The Lower Extremity Assessment Project (LEAP) Study Group. J Bone Joint Surg Am 82:1681–1691, 2000.

446. Polyzois, D.; Papachristou, G.; Kotsiopoulos, K.; Plessas, S. Treatment of tibial and femoral bone loss by distraction osteogenesis. Experience in 28 infected and 14 clean cases. Acta Orthop Scand Suppl 275:84–88, 1997.

447. Pouilles, J.M.; Bernard, J.; Tremollieres, F.; et al. Femoral bone density in young male adults with stress fractures. Bone 10:105–108, 1989.

448. Pozo, J.L.; Powell, B.; Andrews, B.G.; et al. The timing of amputation for lower limb trauma. J Bone Joint Surg Br 72:288–292, 1990.

449. Praemer, A.; Furner, S.; Rice, D.P. Incidence of Musculoskeletal Disorders in the United States. Rosemont, IL, American Academy of Orthopaedic Surgeons, 1999.

450. Pretre, R.; Peter, R.E.; Kursteiner, K. Limb revascularization to stimulate bone fracture healing. Am Surg 63:836–838, 1997.

451. Prokuski, L.J.; Marsh, J.L. Segmental bone deficiency after acute trauma. The role of bone transport. Orthop Clin North Am 25:753–763, 1994.

452. Pun, W.K.; Chow, S.P.; Fang, D.; et al. Posttraumatic oedema of the foot after tibial fracture. Injury 20:232–235, 1989.

453. Pun, W.K.; Chow, S.P.; Fang, D.; et al. A study of function and residual joint stiffness after functional bracing of tibial shaft fractures. Clin Orthop 267:157–163, 1991.

454. Puno, R.M.; Teynor, J.T.; Nagano, J.; Gustilo, R.B. Critical analysis of results of treatment of 201 tibial shaft fractures. Clin Orthop 212:113–121, 1986.

455. Puno, R.M.; Vaughan, J.J.; Stetten, M.L.; Johnson, J.R. Long-term effects of tibial angular malunion on the knee and ankle joints. J Orthop Trauma 5:247–254, 1991.

456. Puno, R.M.; Vaughan, J.J.; Von Fraunhofer, J.A.; et al. A method of determining the angular malalignments of the knee and ankle joints resulting from a tibial malunion. Clin Orthop 223:213–219, 1987.

457. Quirke, T.E.; Sharma, P.K.; Boss, W.K., Jr.; et al. Are type IIIC lower extremity injuries an indication for primary amputation? J Trauma 40:992–996, 1996.

458. Raikin, S.M.; Landsman, J.C.; Alexander, V.A.; et al. Effect of nicotine on the rate and strength of long bone fracture healing. Clin Orthop 353:231–237, 1998.

459. Raschke, M.; Oedekoven, G.; Ficke, J.; Claudi, B.F. The monorail method for segment bone transport. Injury 24(Suppl 2):54–61, 1993.

460. Read, M.T. Runner's stress fracture produced by an aerobic dance routine. Br J Sports Med 18:40–41, 1984.

461. Reckling, F.W.; Waters, C.H., 3rd. Treatment of non-unions of fractures of the tibial diaphysis by posterolateral cortical cancellous bone-grafting. J Bone Joint Surg Am 62:936–941, 1980.

462. Reid, J.S.; Van Slyke, M.A.; Moulton, M.J.; Mann, T.A. Safe placement of proximal tibial transfixation wires with respect to intracapsular penetration. J Orthop Trauma 15:10–17, 2001.

463. Reigstad, A. Soft tissue defects and bone loss in tibial fractures—treatment with free flaps and bone transport. Acta Orthop Scand 68:615–622, 1997.

464. Remiger, A.R.; Miclau, T.; Neuer, W. A simple technique for creating hybrid fixators using a modified AO single adjustable clamp. J Orthop Trauma 11:54–56, 1997.

465. Resnick, D.; Newell, J.D.; Guerra, J., Jr.; et al. Proximal tibiofibular

joint: Anatomic, pathologic and radiologic correlation. Am J Radiol 131:133, 1978.

466. Rhinelander, F.W. The vascular response of bone to internal fixation. In: Browner, B.D.; Edwards, C.C., eds. The Science and Practice of Intramedullary Nailing. Philadelphia, Lea & Febiger, 1987, pp. 25–29.

467. Rhinelander, F.W. Tibial blood supply in relation to fracture healing. Clin Orthop 105:34–81, 1975.

468. Rhinelander, F.W.; Wilson, J.W. Blood supply to developing, mature and healing bone. In: Sumner-Smith, G., ed. Bone in Clinical Orthopedics. Philadelphia, W.B. Saunders, 1982.

469. Ricci, W.M.; O'Boyle, M.; Borrelli, J.; et al. Fractures of the proximal third of the tibial shaft treated with intramedullary nails and blocking screws. J Orthop Trauma 15:264–270, 2001.

470. Richardson, J.B.; Cunningham, J.L.; Goodship, A.E.; et al. Measuring stiffness can define healing of tibial fractures. J Bone Joint Surg Br 76:389–394, 1994.

471. Riemer, B.L.; Butterfield, S.L. Comparison of reamed and non-reamed solid core nailing of the tibial diaphysis after external fixation: A preliminary report. J Orthop Trauma 7:79–85, 1993.

472. Rijnberg, W.J.; van Linge, B. Central grafting for persistent nonunion of the tibia. A lateral approach to the tibia, creating a central compartment. J Bone Joint Surg Br 75:26–31, 1993.

473. Ring, D.; Jupiter, J.B.; Gan, B.S.; et al. Infected nonunion of the tibia. Clin Orthop 369:302–311, 1999.

474. Roberts, C.S.; King, D.; Wang, M.; et al. Should distal interlocking of tibial nails be performed from a medial or a lateral direction? Anatomical and biomechanical considerations. J Orthop Trauma 13:27–32, 1999.

475. Robertson, A.; Sutherland, M.; Keating, J.F. Intramedullary nailing of tibial fractures: How often are post-operative radiographs needed? J R Coll Surg Edinb 45:220–222, 2000.

476. Robinson, C.M.; McLauchlan, G.; Christie, J.; et al. Tibial fractures with bone loss treated by primary reamed intramedullary nailing. J Bone Joint Surg Br 77:906–913, 1995.

477. Robla, J.; Zych, G.A.; Matos, L.A. Assessment of soft tissue injury in open tibial shaft fractures by transcutaneous oximetry. Clin Orthop 304:222–228, 1994.

478. Romani, W.A.; Perrin, D.H.; Dussault, R.G.; et al. Identification of tibial stress fractures using therapeutic continuous ultrasound. J Orthop Sports Phys Ther 30:444–452, 2000.

479. Rommens, P.; Broos, P.; Gruwez, J.A. [Follow-up results of 102 tibial shaft fractures stabilized by dynamic compression plate osteosynthesis]. Unfallchirurgie 12:320–326, 1986.

480. Rommens, P.; Schmit-Neuerburg, K.P. Ten years of experience with the operative management of tibial shaft fractures. J Trauma 27:917–927, 1978.

481. Rommens, P.M. The significance of soft tissue trauma for fracture healing: A prospective study on 70 tibial shaft fractures. Acta Chira Belg 92:10–18, 1992.

482. Rompe, J.D.; Rosendahl, T.; Schollner, C.; Theis, C. High-energy extracorporeal shock wave treatment of nonunions. Clin Orthop 387:102–111, 2001.

483. Roy, N.; Halliwell, P.; Taylor, L. Superior dislocation of the superior tibiofibular joint associated with fracture of the tibial shaft. Injury 29:486–488, 1998.

484. Rozbruch, S.R.; Muller, U.; Gautier, E.; Ganz, R. The evolution of femoral shaft plating technique. Clin Orthop 354:195–208, 1998.

485. Rubin, C.; Bolander, M.; Ryaby, J.P.; Hadjiargyrou, M. The use of low-intensity ultrasound to accelerate the healing of fractures. J Bone Joint Surg Am 83:259–270, 2001.

486. Rubinstein, R.A., Jr.; Green, J.M.; Duwelius, P.J. Intramedullary interlocked tibia nailing: A new technique (preliminary report). J Orthop Trauma 6:90–95, 1992.

487. Rüedi, T.H.; Webb, J.K.; Allgöwer, M. Experience with a dynamic compression plate (DCP) in 418 recent fractures of the tibial shaft. Injury 7:252–257, 1976.

488. Ruiz, A.L.; Kealey, W.D.; McCoy, G.F. Implant failure in tibial nailing. Injury 31:359–362, 2000.

489. Rupani, H.D.; Holder, L.E.; Espinola, D.A.; et al. Three-phase radionuclide bone imaging in sports medicine. Radiology 156:187–196, 1985.

490. Russell, G.G.; Henderson, R.; Arnett, G. Primary or delayed closure for open tibial fractures. J Bone Joint Surg Br 72:125–131, 1990.

491. Ryaby, J.T. Clinical effects of electromagnetic and electric fields on fracture healing. Clin Orthop 355:(Suppl):205–215, 1998.

492. Safoury, Y. Use of a reversed-flow vascularized pedicle fibular graft for treatment of nonunion of the tibia. J Reconstr Microsurg 15:23–28, 1999.

493. Sala, F.; Binda, M.; Lovisetti, G. Anterior gonalgic syndrome after intramedullary nailing: Ultrasound and radiologic study. Chir Organi Mov 83:271–275, 1998.

494. Salam, A.A.; Eyres, K.S.; Cleary, J.; el-Sayed, H.H. The use of a tourniquet when plating tibial fractures. J Bone Joint Surg Br 73:86–97, 1991.

495. Saleh, M.; Royston, S. Management of nonunion of fractures by distraction with correction of angulation and shortening. J Bone Joint Surg Br 78:105–109, 1996.

496. Saleh, M.; Yang, L.; Sims, M. Limb reconstruction after high energy trauma. Br Med Bull 55:870–884, 1999.

497. Sancineto, C.F.; Rubel, I.F.; Seligson, D.; Ferro, G.V. Technique for removal of broken interlocking screws. J Orthop Trauma 15:132–134, 2001.

498. Sanders, R.; Anglen, J.O.; Mark, J.B. Oblique osteotomy for the correction of tibial malunion. J Bone Joint Surg Am 77:240–246, 1995.

499. Sanders, R.; Jersinovich, I.; Anglen, J.; et al. The treatment of open tibial shaft fractures using an interlocked intramedullary nail without reaming. J Orthop Trauma 8:504–510, 194.

500. Sanders, W.E. Amputation after tibial fracture: Preservation of length by use of a neurovascular island (fillet) flap of the foot. A brief note. J Bone Joint Surg Am 71:435–437, 1989.

501. Sangeorzan, B.J.; Sangeorzan, B.P.; Hansen, S.T., Jr.; Judd, R.P. Mathematically directed single-cut osteotomy for correction of tibial malunion. J Orthop Trauma 3:267–275, 1989.

502. Sarangi, P.P.; Karachalios, T. Posterior tibial nerve palsy after intramedullary nailing. Int Orthop 17:25–26, 1993.

503. Sarangi, P.P.; Ward, A.J.; Smith, E.J.; et al. Algodystrophy and osteoporosis after tibial fractures. J Bone Joint Surg Br 75:450–452, 1993.

504. Sarmiento, A.; Latta, L.L. Closed Functional Treatment of Fractures. Berlin, Springer-Verlag 1981.

505. Sarmiento, A. On the behavior of closed tibial fractures: Clinical/radiological correlations. J Orthop Trauma 14:199–205, 2000.

506. Sarmiento, A., ed. Tibial fractures. Clin Orthop 105:2–282, 1974.

507. Sarmiento, A.; Latta, L.L. Functional fracture bracing. J Am Acad Orthop Surg 7:66–75, 1999.

508. Sarmiento, A.; McKellop, H.A.; Llinas, A.; et al. Effect of loading and fracture motions on diaphyseal tibial fractures. J Orthop Res 14:80–84, 1996.

509. Sarmiento, A.; Sharpe, F.E.; Ebramzadeh, E.; et al. Factors influencing the outcome of closed tibial fractures treated with functional bracing. Clin Orthop 315:8–24, 1995.

510. Sawant, M.R.; Bendall, S.P.; Kavanagh, T.G.; Citron, N.D. Nonunion of tibial stress fractures in patients with deformed arthritic knees. Treatment using modular total knee arthroplasty. J Bone Joint Surg Br 81:663–666, 1999.

511. Schandelmaier, P.; Krettek, C.; Rudolf, J.; et al. Superior results of tibial rodding versus external fixation in grade 3B fractures. Clin Orthop 342:164–172, 1997.

512. Schandelmaier, P.; Krettek, C.; Rudolf, J.; Tscherne, H. Outcome of tibial shaft fractures with severe soft tissue injury treated by unreamed nailing versus external fixation. J Trauma 39:707–711, 1995.

513. Schmeling, G.J.; McCallum, S.; Havey, R. The effect of single-pass reaming on tibial nail insertion load and stress. J Orthop Trauma 10:569–574, 1996.

514. Schmitz, M.A.; Finnegan, M.; Natarajan, R.; Champine, J. Effect of smoking on tibial shaft fracture healing. Clin Orthop 365:184–200, 1999.

515. Schnarkowski, P.; Redei, J.; Peterfy, C.G.; et al. Tibial shaft fractures: Assessment of fracture healing with computed tomography. J Comput Assist Tomogr 19:777–781, 1995.

516. Schutz, M.; Sudkamp, N.; Frigg, R.; et al. Pinless external fixation. Indications and preliminary results in tibial shaft fractures. Clin Orthop 347:35–42, 1998.

517. Seabold, J.E.; Nepola, J.V.; Conrad, G.R.; et al. Detection of osteomyelitis at fracture nonunion sites: Comparison of two scintigraphic methods. AJR Am J Roentgenol 152:1021–1027, 1998.

518. Seale, K.S. Reflex sympathetic dystrophy of the lower extremity. Clin Orthop 243:80–85, 1989.

519. Segal, D.; Brenner, M.; Gorczyca, J. Tibial fractures with infrapopliteal arterial injuries. J Orthop Trauma 1:160–169, 1987.

520. Seligson, D.; Ostermann, P.A.; Henry, S.L.; Wolley, T. The management of open fractures associated with arterial injury requiring vascular repair. J Trauma 37:938–940, 1994.

521. Shakespeare, D.T.; Henderson, N.J. Compartmental pressure changes during calcaneal traction in tibial fractures. J Bone Joint Surg Br 64:498–499, 1982.

522. Shapira, D.; Scharf, Y. Insufficiency fracture of the distal tibia mimicking arthritis in a rheumatoid arthritis patient. The possible role of methotrexate treatment. Clin Exp Rheumatol 13:130–131, 1995.

523. Sharma, P.; Daffner, R.H. Case report 389: Idiopathic, anterolateral dislocation of the fibula at the proximal tibiofibular joint. Skeletal Radiol 15:505–506, 1986.

524. Sharma, S.; Tiwari, P.; Kasabian, A.K.; Longaker, M.T. Reconstruction of a tibial defect with microvascular transfer of a previously fractured fibula. Ann Plast Surg 45:202–206, 2000.

525. Sharrard, W.J.W. A double-blind trial of pulsed electromagnetic fields for delayed union of tibial fractures. J Bone Joint Surg Br 72:347–355, 1990.

526. Shaw, D.L.; Lawton, J.O. External fixation for tibial fractures: Clinical results and cost effectiveness. J R Coll Surg Edinb 40:344–346, 1995.

527. Shearman, C.M.; Brandser, E.A.; Parman, L.M.; et al. Longitudinal tibial stress fractures: A report of eight cases and review of the literature. J Comput Assist Tomogr 22:265–269, 1998.

528. Shelbourne, K.D.; Pierce, R.O.; Ritter, M.A. Superior dislocation of the fibular head associated with a tibia fracture. Clin Orthop 160:172–174, 1981.

529. Shen, W.J.; Shen, Y.S. Fibular nonunion after fixation of the tibia in lower leg fractures. Clin Orthop 287:231–232, 1993.

530. Shenolikar, A.; Hoddinott, C. Tibiofibular impaction: Obstruction to tibial fracture reduction. J Bone Joint Surg Br 77:158–159, 1995.

531. Siebenrock, K.A.; Gerich, T.; Jakob, R.P. Sequential intramedullary nailing of open tibial shaft fractures after external fixation. Arch Orthop Trauma Surg 116:32–36, 1997.

532. Siebert, C.H.; Lehrbass-Sokeland, K.P.; Rinke, F.; Hansis, M. Compression plating of tibial fractures following primary external fixation. Arch Orthop Trauma Surg 116:390–395, 1997.

533. Siegel, H.J.; Patzakis, M.J.; Holtom, P.D.; et al. Limb salvage for chronic tibial osteomyelitis: An outcomes study. J Trauma 48:484–489, 2000.

534. Sim, R.; Liang, T.S.; Tay, B.K. Autologous marrow injection in the treatment of delayed and non-union in long bones. Singapore Med J 34:412–417, 1993.

535. Simon, J.P.; Stuyck, J.; Hoogmartens, M.; Fabry, G. Posterolateral bone grafting for nonunion of the tibia. Acta Orthop Belg 58:308–313, 1992.

536. Simpson, A.H.; Andrews, C.; Giele, H. Skin closure after acute shortening. J Bone Joint Surg Br 83:668–671, 2001.

537. Simpson, A.H.; Kenwright, J. Fracture after distraction osteogenesis. J Bone Joint Surg Br 82:659–665, 2000.

538. Simpson, J.M.; Ebraheim, N.A.; An, H.S.; Jackson, W.T. Posterolateral bone graft of the tibia. Clin Orthop 251:200–206, 1990.

539. Sinclair, J.S.; McNally, M.A.; Small, J.O.; Yeates, H.A. Primary free-flap cover of open tibial fractures. Injury 28:581–587, 1997.

540. Singer, R.W.; Kellam, J.F. Open tibial diaphyseal fractures. Results of unreamed locked intramedullary nailing. Clin Orthop 315:114–118, 1995.

541. Singh, S.; Ng, K.C.; Chia, P. Plating of displaced mid-tibial fractures—a retrospective review of 80 cases. Singapore Med J 38:58–61, 1997.

542. Skoog, A.; Soderqvist, A.; Tornkvist, H.; Ponzer, S. One-year outcome after tibial shaft fractures: Results of a prospective fracture registry. J Orthop Trauma 15:210–215, 2001.

543. Skraba, J.S.; Greenwald, A.S. The role of interosseous membrane on tibiofibular weight bearing. Foot Ankle 4:301–304, 1984.

544. Sledge, S.L.; Johnson, D.D.; Henley, M.B.; Watson, J.T. Intramedullary nailing with reaming to treat non-union of the tibia. J Bone Joint Surg Am 71:1004–1019, 1989.

545. Smith, E.J.; Ward, A.J.; Watt, I. Post-traumatic osteoporosis and algodystrophy after external fixation of tibial fractures. Injury 24:411–415, 1993.

546. Song, H.R.; Cho, S.H.; Koo, K.H.; et al. Tibial bone defects treated by internal bone transport using the Ilizarov method. Int Orthop 22:293–297, 1998.

547. Stanitski, D.F. Limb-length inequality: Assessment and treatment options. J Am Acad Orthop Surg 7:143–153, 1999.

548. Stegemann, P.; Lorio, M.; Soriano, R.; Bone, L. Management protocol for unreamed interlocking tibial nails for open tibial fractures. J Orthop Trauma 9:117–120, 1995.

549. Sterett, W.I.; Ertl, J.P.; Chapman, M.W.; Moehring, H.D. Open tibia fractures in the splenectomized trauma patient: Results of treatment with locking, intramedullary fixation. J Trauma 38:639–641, 1995.

550. Stoffel, K.; Klaue, K.; Perren, S.M. Functional load of plates in fracture fixation in vivo and its correlate in bone healing. Injury 31(Suppl 2):B37–B50, 2000.

551. Strachan, R.K.; McCarthy, I.; Fleming, R.; Hughes, S.P.F. The role of tibial nutrient artery. Microsphere estimation of blood flow in the osteotomized canine tibia. J Bone Joint Surg Br 72:391–397, 1990.

552. Stuyck, J.; Nelen, G.; Feys, H.; Devlies, Y. Corrective osteotomy for mal- and nonunion of the tibia using the posterolateral approach. Acta Orthop Belg 58(Suppl 1):194–196, 1992.

553. Sullivan, D.; Warren, R.F.; Pavlov, H.; Kelman, G. Stress fractures in 51 runners. Clin Orthop 187:188–192, 1984.

554. Swiontkowski, M.F. Criteria for bone debridement in massive lower limb trauma. Clin Orthop 243:41–47, 1989.

555. Swiontkowski, M.F. The pinless fixator—part II. Injury 25(Suppl 3):C1–C2, 1994.

556. Swiontkowski, M.F.; Agel, J.; McAndrew, M.P.; et al. Outcome validation of the AO/OTA fracture classification system. J Orthop Trauma 14:534–541, 2000.

557. Takakuwa, M.; Funakoshi, M.; Ishizaki, K.; et al. Fracture on removal of the ACE tibial nail. J Bone Joint Surg Br 79:444–445, 1997.

558. Takebe, K.; Nakagawa, A.; Minami, H.; et al. Role of the fibula in weight bearing. Clin Orthop 185:289–292, 1984.

559. Tandon, S.C.; Gregson, P.A.; Thomas, P.B.; et al. Reduction of post-traumatic osteoporosis after external fixation of tibial fractures. Injury 26:459–462, 1995.

560. Taylor, G.I.; Gianoutsos, M.P.; Morris, S.F. The neurovascular territories of the skin and muscles. Anatomic study and clinical implications. Plast Reconstr Surg 94:1–36, 1994.

561. Teitz, C.C.; Carter, D.R.; Frankel, V.H. Problems associated with tibial fractures with intact fibulae. J Bone Joint Surg Am 62:770–776, 1980.

562. Templeman, D.; Larson, C.; Varecka, T.; Kyle, R.F. Decision making errors in the use of interlocking tibial nails. Clin Orthop 339:65–70, 1997.

563. Templeman, D.; Thomas, M.; Varecka, T.; Kyle, R. Exchange reamed intramedullary nailing for delayed union and nonunion of the tibia. Clin Orthop 315:169–175, 1995.

564. Templeman, D.C.; Gulli, B.; Tsukayama, D.T.; Gustilo, R.B. Update on the management of open fractures of the tibial shaft. Clin Orthop 350:18–25, 1998.

565. Tetsworth, K.; Cierny, G., 3rd. Osteomyelitis debridement techniques. Clin Orthop 360:87–96, 1999.

566. Tetsworth, K.; Paley, D. Malalignment and degenerative arthropathy. Orthop Clin North Am 25:367–377, 1994.

567. Thakur, A.J.; Patankar, J. Open tibial fractures. Treatment by uniplanar external fixation and early bone grafting. J Bone Joint Surg Br 73:448–451, 1991.

568. Thiagarajan, P.; Ang, K.C.; Das De, S.; Bose, K. Ipsilateral knee ligament injuries and open tibial diaphyseal fractures: Incidence and nature of knee ligament injuries sustained. Injury 28:87–90, 1997.

569. Thomas, K.A.; Harris, M.B.; Willis, M.C.; et al. The effects of the interosseous membrane and partial fibulectomy on loading of the tibia: A biomechanical study. Orthopedics 18:373–383, 1995.

570. Thomas, S.R.; Giele, H.; Simpson, A.H. Advantages and disadvantages of pinless external fixation. Injury 31:805–809, 2000.

571. Thomason, P.A.; Linson, M.A. Isolated dislocation of the proximal tibiofibular joint. J Trauma 26:192–195, 1986.

572. Tile, M. Fractures of the tibia. In: Schatzker, J.; Tile, M., eds. The Rationale of Operative Fracture Care. Berlin, Springer-Verlag, 1987, pp. 297–341.

573. Ting, A.J.; Tarr, R.R.; Sarmiento, A.; et al. The role of subtalar motion and ankle contact pressure changes from angular deformities of the tibia. Foot Ankle 7:290–299, 1987.

574. Toh, C.L.; Jupiter, J.B. The infected nonunion of the tibia. Clin Orthop 315:176–191, 1995.

575. Toivanen, J.A.; Hirvonen, M.; Auvinen, O.; et al. Cast treatment and intramedullary locking nailing for simple and spiral wedge tibial shaft fractures—a cost benefit analysis. Ann Chir Gynaecol 89:138–142, 2000.

576. Toivanen, J.A.; Honkonen, S.E.; Koivisto, A.M.; Jarvinen, M.J. Treatment of low-energy tibial shaft fractures: Plaster cast compared with intramedullary nailing. Int Orthop 25:110–113, 2001.

577. Toivanen, J.A.; Kyro, A.; Heiskanen, T.; et al. Which displaced spiral tibial shaft fractures can be managed conservatively? Int Orthop 24:151–154, 2000.

578. Tomten, S.E.; Falch, J.A.; Birkeland, K.I.; et al. Bone mineral density and menstrual irregularities. A comparative study on cortical and trabecular bone structures in runners with alleged normal eating behavior. Int J Sports Med 19:92–97, 1998.

579. Tornetta, P., 3rd. Technical considerations in the surgical management of tibial fractures. Instr Course Lect 46:271–280, 1997.

580. Tornetta, P., 3rd.; Barbera, C. Severe heterotopic bone formation in the knee after tibial intramedullary nailing. J Orthop Trauma 6:113–115, 1992.

581. Tornetta, P., 3rd.; Bergman, M.; Watnik, N.; et al. Treatment of grade-IIIb open tibial fractures. A prospective randomised comparison of external fixation and non-reamed locked nailing. J Bone Joint Surg Br 76:13–19, 1994.

582. Tornetta, P., 3rd.; Collins, E. Semiextended position of intramedullary nailing of the proximal tibia. Clin Orthop 328:185–189, 1996.

583. Tornetta, P., 3rd.; DeMarco, C. Intramedullary nailing after external fixation of the tibia. Bull Hosp Jt Dis 54:5–13, 1995.

584. Tornetta, P., 3rd.; French, B.G. Compartment pressures during nonreamed tibial nailing without traction. J Orthop Trauma 11:24–27, 1997.

585. Tornetta, P. 3rd.; Riina, J.; Geller, J.; Purban, W. Intraarticular anatomic risks of tibial nailing. J Orthop Trauma 13:247–251, 1999.

586. Trabulsy, P.P.; Kerley, S.M.; Hoffman, W.Y. A prospective study of early soft tissue coverage of grade IIIB tibial fractures. J Trauma 36:661–668, 1994.

587. Triffitt, P.D.; Konig, D.; Harper, W.M.; et al. Compartment pressures after closed tibial shaft fracture. Their relation to functional outcome. J Bone Joint Surg Br 74:195–198, 1992.

588. Tscherne, H.; Gotzen, L. Fractures with Soft Tissue Injuries. Berlin, Springer-Verlag, 1984.

589. Tu, Y.K.; Yen, C.Y.; Yeh, W.L.; et al. Reconstruction of posttraumatic long bone defect with free vascularized bone graft: Good outcome in 48 patients with 6 years' follow-up. Acta Orthop Scand 72:359–364, 2001.

590. Tucker, H.L.; Kendra, J.C.; Kinnebrew, T.E. Management of unstable open and closed tibial fractures using the Ilizarov method. Clin Orthop 280:125–135, 1992.

591. Tukiainen, E.; Asko-Seljavaara, S. Use of the Ilizarov technique after a free microvascular muscle flap transplantation in massive trauma of the lower leg. Clin Orthop 297:129–134, 1993.

592. Turen, C.H.; Burgess, A.R.; Vanco, B. Skeletal stabilization for tibial fractures associated with acute compartment syndrome. Clin Orthop 315:163–168, 1995.

593. Turen, C.H.; DiStasio, A.J. Treatment of grade IIIB and grade IIIC open tibial fractures. Orthop Clin North Am 25:561–571, 1994.

594. Tyllianakis, M.; Megas, P.; Giannikas, D.; Lambiris, E. Interlocking intramedullary nailing in distal tibial fractures. Orthopedics 23:805–808, 2000.

595. Tyrrell, P.N.; Davies, A.M. Magnetic resonance imaging appearances of fatigue fractures of the long bones of the lower limb. Br J Radiol 67:332–338, 1994.

596. Tytherleigh-Strong, G.M.; Keating, J.F.; Court-Brown, C.M. Extra-articular fractures of the proximal tibial diaphysis: Their epidemiology, management and outcome. J R Coll Surg Edinb 42:334–338, 1997.

597. Ueng, S.W.; Chuang, D.C.; Cheng, S.L.; Shih, C.H. Management of large infected tibial defects with radical debridement and staged double-rib composite free transfer. J Trauma 40:345–350, 1996.

598. Ueng, S.W.; Wei, F.C.; Shih, C.H. Management of large infected tibial defects with antibiotic beads local therapy and staged fibular osteoseptocutaneous free transfer. J Trauma 43:268–274, 1997.

599. Uhlin, B.; Hammer, R. Attempted unreamed nailing in tibial fractures: A prospective consecutive series of 55 patients. Acta Orthop Scand 69:301–305, 1998.

600. Umans, H.R.; Kaye, J.J. Longitudinal stress fractures of the tibia: Diagnosis by magnetic resonance imaging. Skeletal Radiol 25:319–324, 1996.

601. Urban, W.P., Jr.; Tornetta, P., 3rd. Vascular compromise after intramedullary nailing of the tibia: A case report. J Trauma 38:804–807, 1995.

602. Van Der Linden, W.; Larsson, K. Plate fixation versus conservative treatment of tibial shaft fractures. A randomized trial. J Bone Joint Surg Am 61:873–878, 1979.

603. van der Schoot, D.K.; Den Outer, A.J.; Bode, P.J.; et al. Degenerative changes at the knee and ankle related to malunion of tibial fractures. 15-year follow-up of 88 patients. J Bone Joint Surg Br 78:722–725, 1996.

604. van der Werken, C.; Marti, R.K. Post-traumatic rotational deformity of the lower leg. Injury 15:38–40, 1983.

605. van der Werken, C.; Zeegers, E.V. Fracture of the lower leg with involvement of the posterior malleolus; a neglected combination? Injury 19:241–243, 1988.

606. Verlhac, B. Longitudinal stress leg fracture in the elderly. Biomed Pharmacother 51:213–216, 1997.

607. Veth, R.P.; Klasen, H.J.; Kingma, L.M. Traumatic instability of the proximal tibiofibular joint. Injury 13:159–164, 1981.

608. Vitkus, K.; Vitkus, M. Reconstruction of large infected tibia defects. Ann Plast Surg 29:97–106, 1992.

609. Vives, M.J.; Abidi, N.A.; Ishikawa, S.N.; et al. Soft tissue injuries with the use of safe corridors for transfixion wire placement during external fixation of distal tibia fractures: An anatomic study. J Orthop Trauma 15:555–559, 2001.

610. Wagner, K.S.; Tarr, R.R.; Resnick, C.; et al. The effect of simulated tibial deformities on the ankle joint during the gait cycle. Foot Ankle 5:131–141, 1984.

611. Waikakul, S.; Sakkarnkosol, S.; Vanadurongwan, V. Vascular injuries in compound fractures of the leg with initially adequate circulation. J Bone Joint Surg Br 80:254–258, 1998.

612. Watson, J.T. Treatment of unstable fractures of the shaft of the tibia. J Bone Joint Surg Am 76:1575–1584, 1994.

613. Watson, J.T.; Anders, M.; Moed, B.R. Management strategies for bone loss in tibial shaft fractures. Clin Orthop 315:138–152, 1995.

614. Watson-Jones, R.; Coltart, W.D. Slow union of fractures, with a study of 804 fractures of the shafts of the tibia and femur. Clin Orthop 168:2–16, 1982.

615. Weber, T.G.; Harrington, R.M.; Henley, M.B.; Tencer, A.F. The role of fibular fixation in combined fractures of the tibia and fibula: A biomechanical investigation. J Orthop Trauma 11:206–211, 1997.

616. Weinert, C.R., Jr.; Raczka, R. Recurrent dislocation of the superior tibiofibular joint: Surgical stabilization by ligament reconstruction. J Bone Joint Surg Am 68:126–128, 1986.

617. Wheelwright, E.F.; Court-Brown, C.M. Primary external fixation and secondary intramedullary nailing in the treatment of tibial fractures. Injury 23:373–376, 1992.

618. White, A.A.I.; Panjabi, M.M.; Southwick, W.O. The four biomechanical stages of fracture repair. J Bone Joint Surg Am 59:188–192, 1977.

619. Whitelaw, G.P.; Wetzler, M.J.; Levy, A.S.; et al. A pneumatic leg brace for the treatment of tibial stress fractures. Clin Orthop 270:301–305, 1991.

620. Whittle, A.P.; Wester, W.; Russell, T.A. Fatigue failure in small diameter tibial nails. Clin Orthop 315:119–128, 1995.

621. Williams, J.; Gibbons, M.; Trundle, H.; et al. Complications of nailing in closed tibial fractures. J Orthop Trauma 9:476–481, 1995.

622. Williams, T.M.; Marsh, J.L.; Nepola, J.V.; et al. External fixation of tibial plafond fractures: Is routine plating of the fibula necessary? J Orthop Trauma 12:16–20, 1998.

623. Williamson, D.M.; Kershaw, C.J. Serious vascular complication of locked tibial nailing. Injury 20:310–312, 1989.

624. Winkler, H.; Hochstein, P.; Wentzensen, A. Experience with the pinless fixator in the treatment of fractures of the lower leg. Injury 25(Suppl 3):C8–C14, 1994.

625. Winquist, R.A.; Hansen, S.T., Jr. Comminuted fractures of the femoral shaft treated by intramedullary nailing. Orthop Clin North Am 11:633–648, 1980.

626. Wiss, D. Symposium: The treatment of tibial fractures. Clin Orthop 315:1–198, 1995.

627. Wiss, D.A.; Johnson, D.L.; Miao, M. Compression plating for non-union after failed external fixation of open tibial fractures. J Bone Joint Surg Am 74:1279–1285, 1992.

628. Wiss, D.A.; Sherman, R.; Oechsel, M. External skeletal fixation and rectus abdominis free-tissue transfer in the management of severe open fractures of the tibia. Orthop Clin North Am 24:549–556, 1993.

629. Wiss, D.A.; Stetson, W.B. Nonunion of the tibia treated with a reamed intramedullary nail. J Orthop Trauma 8:189–194, 1994.

630. Wiss, D.A.; Stetson, W.B. Tibial nonunion: Treatment alternatives. J Am Acad Orthop Surg 4:249–257, 1996.

631. Wiss, D.A.; Stetson, W.B. Unstable fractures of the tibia treated with a reamed intramedullary interlocking nail. Clin Orthop 315:56–63, 1995.

632. Wolfe, J.H. Postphlebitic syndrome after fractures of the leg. BMJ 295:1364–1365, 1987.

633. Woll, T.S.; Duwelius, P.J. The segmental tibial fracture. Clin Orthop 281:204–207, 1992.

634. Wu, W.J.; Chen, W.J.; Shih, C.H. Tibial shaft malunion treated with reamed intramedullary nailing: A revised technique. Arch Orthop Trauma Surg 120:152–156, 2000.

635. Wu, C.C.; Shih, C.H. Segmental tibial shaft fractures treated with interlocking nailing. J Orthop Trauma 7:468–472, 1993.

636. Wu, C.C.; Shih, C.H.; Chen, W.J.; Tai, C.L. High success rate with exchange nailing to treat a tibial shaft aseptic nonunion. J Orthop Trauma 13:33–38, 1999.

637. Yadav, S.S. Double oblique diaphyseal osteotomy. A new technique for lengthening deformed and short lower limbs. J Bone Joint Surg Br 75:962–966, 1993.

638. Yajima, H.; Tamai, S.; Mizumoto, S.; et al. Vascularized fibular grafts in the treatment of osteomyelitis and infected nonunion. Clin Orthop 293:256–264, 1993.

639. Yasui, N.; Nakase, T.; Kawabata, H.; et al. A technique of percutaneous multidrilling osteotomy for limb lengthening and deformity correction. J Orthop Sci 5:104–107, 2000.

640. Yip, K.M.; Leung, K.S. Treatment of deformed tibial intramedullary nail: Report of two cases. J Orthop Trauma 10:580–583, 1996.

641. Yu, S.W.; Tu, Y.K.; Fan, K.F.; Su, J.Y. Anterior knee pain after intramedullary tibial nailing. Chang Keng I Hsueh Tsa Chih 22:604–608, 1999.

642. Zagorski, J.B.; Latta, L.L.; Finnieston, A.R.; Zych, G. Tibial fracture stability. Analysis of external fracture immobilization in anatomic specimens in casts and braces. Clin Orthop 291:196–207, 1993.

643. Ziv, I.; Zeligowski, A.; Mosheiff, R.; et al. Split-thickness skin excision in severe open fractures. J Bone Joint Surg Br 70:23–26, 1988.

644. Zlatkin, M.D.; Bjorkengren, A.; Sartoris, D.J.; Resnick, D. Stress fractures of the distal tibia and calcaneus subsequent to acute fractures of the tibia and fibula. AJR Am J Roentgenol 149:329–332, 1987.

645. Zych, G.A.; Hutson, J.J., Jr. Diagnosis and management of infection after tibial intramedullary nailing. Clin Orthop 315:153–162, 1995.

# CHAPTER 58

# Fractures of the Tibial Pilon

Craig S. Bartlett III, M.D.
Lon S. Weiner, M.D.

Fractures of the distal end of the tibia that involve a significant portion of the weight-bearing articular surface and overlying metaphysis are notoriously difficult to treat.* They occur when the talus is driven up into the tibial articular surface. In 1905, Albin Lambotte[100] was perhaps the first to perform open reduction and internal fixation (ORIF) of this type of fracture. The term *tibial pilon* was later introduced by the French radiologist Destot[45] in 1911 to describe the distal tibial metaphysis, which is shaped like a pharmacist's pestle ("pilon"). Another French term was contributed to the fracture lexicon for this region by Bonin,[18] who used the word *plafond* ("ceiling") to refer to the horizontal distal tibial articular surface. The spelling "pylon" should be avoided because it means "bridge" or "stone archway" and has nothing to do with the distal part of the tibia.[52, 76]

Although the articular component will involve some combination of the medial, lateral, and posterior malleoli, the defining character of a tibial pilon fracture is supra-articular metaphyseal involvement, which typically exhibits varying degrees of impaction. This impaction, combined with comminution, instability, primary articular cartilage damage, and persistent joint surface incongruity, contributes to the uncertain outcome of these injuries.

Pilon fractures are often of a high-energy nature. As a result, one third to one half are associated with concomitant fractures or other organ system injuries. Approximately 10% to 30% (in some series as many as 50%) are open injuries with degloving and crushing of the skin.[†] Treatment is fraught with complications, including infection, necrosis of the soft tissue envelope, nonunion, malunion, and post-traumatic arthrosis.

Fortunately, pilon fractures account for only 3% to 10% of all fractures of the tibia and less than 1% of all fractures of the lower extremity.[‡]

## MECHANISM OF INJURY

The injury is most commonly caused by a fall from a height, a motor vehicle accident with a sudden stop, a skiing injury ("boot-top fracture"), or a fall forward with a trapped foot.[13, 17, 92, 148, 149, 166, 168, 193, 196]

Several authors have emphasized the importance of foot position at the time of injury because it relates to the ensuing fracture pattern[17, 63, 87, 104, 105, 124, 164, 168, 189] (Fig. 58–1). If the foot is plantar flexed, the posteriorly directed compressive forces result in separation of a large posterior tibial fragment (see Fig. 58–1A). With a neutral foot, purely vertical forces lead to involvement of the entire articular surface or the creation of a Y-shaped fracture with large anterior and posterior fragments (see Fig. 58–1B). Should the foot be forced into dorsiflexion, the broader anterior portion of the talus becomes snugly engaged in the ankle mortise. This position may result in compression and fracture of the anterior tibial margin, which often produces a large anterior fragment (see Fig. 58–1C). Abduction injuries tend to cause lateral fractures, and adduction injuries tend to cause medial disruption.

The fracture pattern is also influenced by two main forces acting either separately or together.[§] Axial compression occurs as the talus is driven into the tibial plafond. In addition, a shearing or rotational component produces variable degrees of separation of the fracture fragments. However, clear distinction should be made between these two mechanisms because the extent of their contribution to the injury affects the severity of the fracture, soft tissue damage, and the prognosis for treatment.[12, 92, 112, 119, 164, 166–168] High-energy injuries

---

*See references 4, 6, 9, 24, 28, 31, 39, 44, 45, 63, 92, 112, 148, 152, 191, 200, 214, 217.

†See references 9, 10, 13, 16, 40, 76, 94, 130, 138, 148, 149, 155, 188, 189, 206, 207.

‡See references 6, 17, 23, 24, 112, 124, 133, 164, 166, 168, 189.

§See references 26, 63, 105, 107, 112, 124, 125, 133, 152, 164, 166–170, 189.

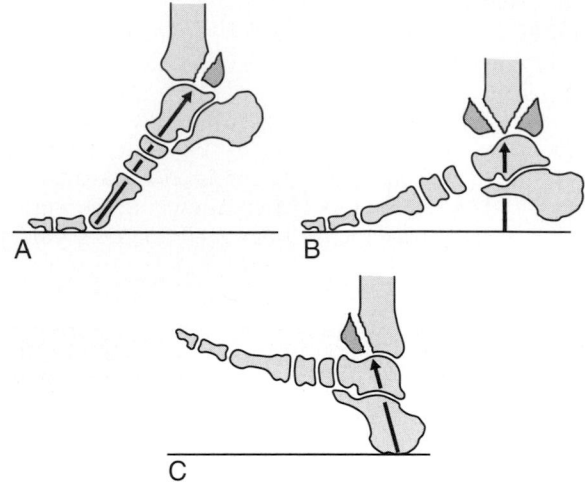

**FIGURE 58–1.** Mechanism of injury. Ankle position as it relates to fracture pattern. *A,* A plantar flexion injury results in a posterior lip fragment. *B,* A neutral ankle injury results in anterior and posterior fragments. *C,* A dorsiflexion injury results in an anterior lip fragment. (Redrawn from Gay, R.; Evrard, J. Rev Chir Orthop 49:397–512, 1963.)

are generally the result of tremendous axial loading forces imparted to the extremity during a motor vehicle accident or fall from a significant height. Accordingly, they tend to be associated with greater degrees of articular and metaphyseal impaction and comminution, along with more severe soft tissue disruption. The more impacted or complex a fracture of the tibial metaphysis, the more likely the presence of axial malalignment.[76] Axial loading has also been shown to cause cartilage necrosis and may be responsible for poor outcomes despite anatomic radiographic joint reconstruction.[22] In contrast, torsional injuries tend to be lower-energy injuries that occur most commonly during sporting activities such as skiing accidents.

An associated fibula fracture is present in approximately 70% to 85% of cases.[9, 13, 115, 125, 149, 166, 191, 195, 217] Its presence implicates valgus shear forces, which usually result in damage to the lateral articular surface, valgus deformity, and a greater likelihood of axial malalignment because of the absence of an intact lateral column.[76, 92, 144, 193] Open injuries are more commonly associated with displacement into valgus (see Fig. 58–33),[76] primarily related to the extremely thin medial soft tissue envelope. In contrast, an intact fibula is more likely to be associated with a varus compression force, crushing of the medial articular surface, and varus angulation[76, 92, 193] (Fig. 58–2; see Figs. 58–23, 58–24, and 58–27).

## CLASSIFICATION

One of the earliest attempts to classify pilon fractures was published in the French literature by Gay and Evard[63] in 1963. Though still used widely in French-speaking countries, this complicated system has for the most part been abandoned.

Lauge-Hansen's classification[104, 105] of ankle fractures aided understanding of the forces involved in producing various injury patterns. One pattern, the pronation dorsiflexion injury, was described by studying radiographs but never duplicated experimentally.[74, 105] It has many of the features of a pilon fracture but without comminution. The pattern evolves in four stages. First, the medial malleolus is split off, which may be a transverse fracture but is more commonly oblique. In stage 2, the anterior lip of the tibial plafond is crushed, and a large fragment is produced. In the third stage, a fibula fracture occurs above the level of the syndesmosis. Finally, the tibia fractures transversely above the anterior lip fracture.

The system proposed by Ruëdi and Allgöwer[166–168] (Fig. 58–3) is descriptive, like Lauge-Hansen's, and makes a distinction between nondisplaced, low-energy injuries and severely comminuted and impacted fractures. A Ruëdi type I fracture (see Fig. 58–3A) is a cleavage fracture of the distal end of the tibia without significant displacement of the articular surface. A type II fracture (see Fig. 58–3B) has significant displacement of the articular surface cleavage lines, but the joint surface is neither crushed nor grossly comminuted. The more severe type III fracture (see Fig. 58–3C) involves both comminution and impaction of the distal tibial articular surface and its overlying metaphysis. Maale and Seligson[112] modified Ruëdi's scheme by identifying a spiral fracture of the distal tibial diaphysis with intra-articular extension as a separate injury (Figs. 58–4 and 58–5). This low-energy tibial plafond variant is a rotational fracture with a relatively good prognosis.

Ovadia and Beals[148] also modified Ruëdi's system. Their type I and type V fractures correspond to Ruëdi types I and III. However, they further subdivided Ruëdi type II injuries into minimally displaced fractures, moderately displaced fractures with several large fragments, and moderately displaced fractures with metaphyseal defects (types II, III, and IV, respectively). Although this system is more descriptive, it does not contribute additional information regarding the treatment of pilon fractures.

Mast and co-workers[124, 125] suggested a composite classification in which the prognosis worsens from type I through type IIIC fractures.[125, 126, 168, 178] A type I fracture has large malleolar and posterior lip fragments similar to a severe trimalleolar fracture. A type II fracture is equivalent to the spiral extension fracture described by Maale and Seligson.[112] A type III fracture is a central compression injury and is classified A, B, and C as in the Ruëdi and Allgöwer system.[124, 125, 168, 178]

The current AO classification[141, 142] (Fig. 58–6), adopted by the Orthopaedic Trauma Association, is the most descriptive system in the literature. Fractures of the distal end of the tibia are divided into extra-articular fractures (type A), partial articular fractures (type B), and complete articular fractures with metaphyseal-diaphyseal dissociation (type C). Although variations occur, most pilon fractures are type C. Fracture types are further subdivided into three groups (1, 2, 3). Simple patterns (no comminution or impaction) in both the articular and metaphyseal areas constitute a C1 fracture. A simple articular pattern with impaction involving only the supra-articular metaphysis represents a C2 injury. In addition to metaphyseal impaction, a type C3 fracture involves comminution and impaction of the articular surface. Type B2 (partial articular fracture with split depression) and B3 (partial articular fracture with multifragmentary depression) patterns should also be included in the spectrum of pilon fractures (Fig. 58–7; see Figs. 58–14 and 58–19).

Unfortunately, recent studies involving plain films have demonstrated poor to moderate interobserver and intraob-

server reliability of both the AO[119, 187] and the Ruëdi-Allgöwer classification systems.[48, 119] The AO system is reliable as well as superior to that of Ruëdi and Allgöwer when classifying by type (A, B, C),[119, 187] but agreement becomes poor when it is used to further subdivide fractures into groups (1, 2, 3).[119] Although experience may improve the ability to more consistently classify pilon fractures, its effect has not been shown to be significant.[48, 119] Even with the addition of computed tomogra-

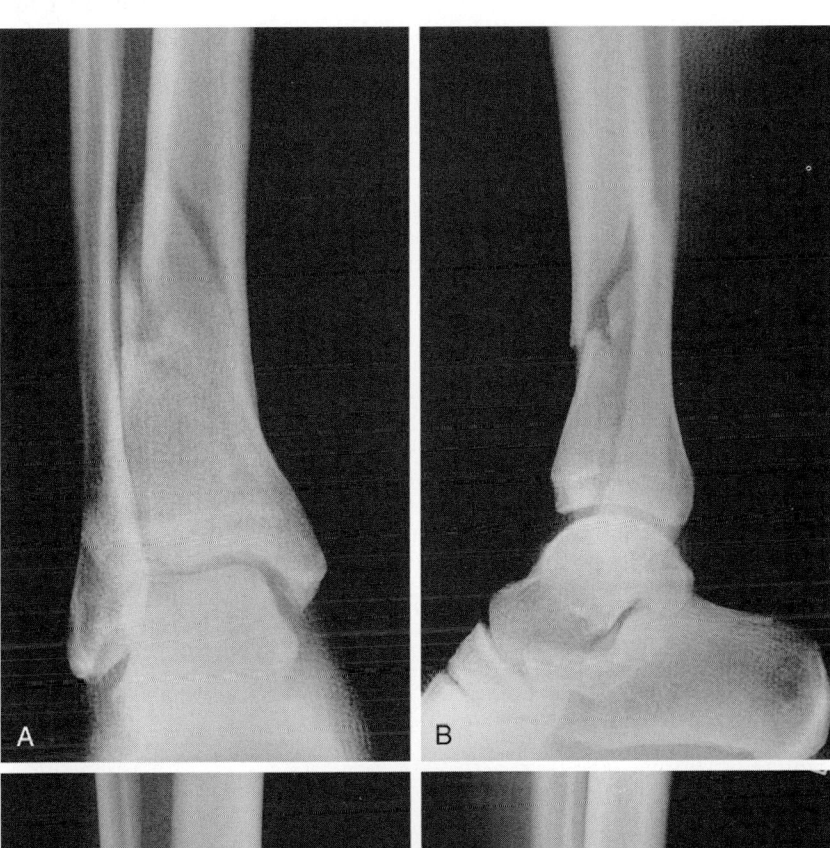

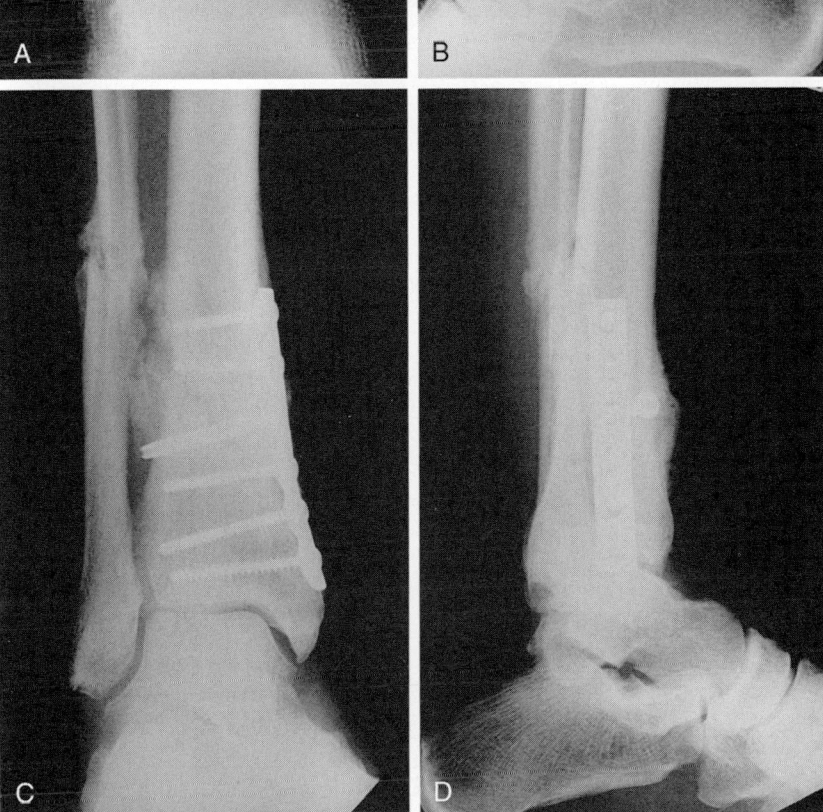

**FIGURE 58–2.** *A, B,* Closed treatment of a C1 pilon fracture with an intact fibula has led to a varus nonunion. *C, D,* A fibular osteotomy was required for proper reduction and correction of the deformity.

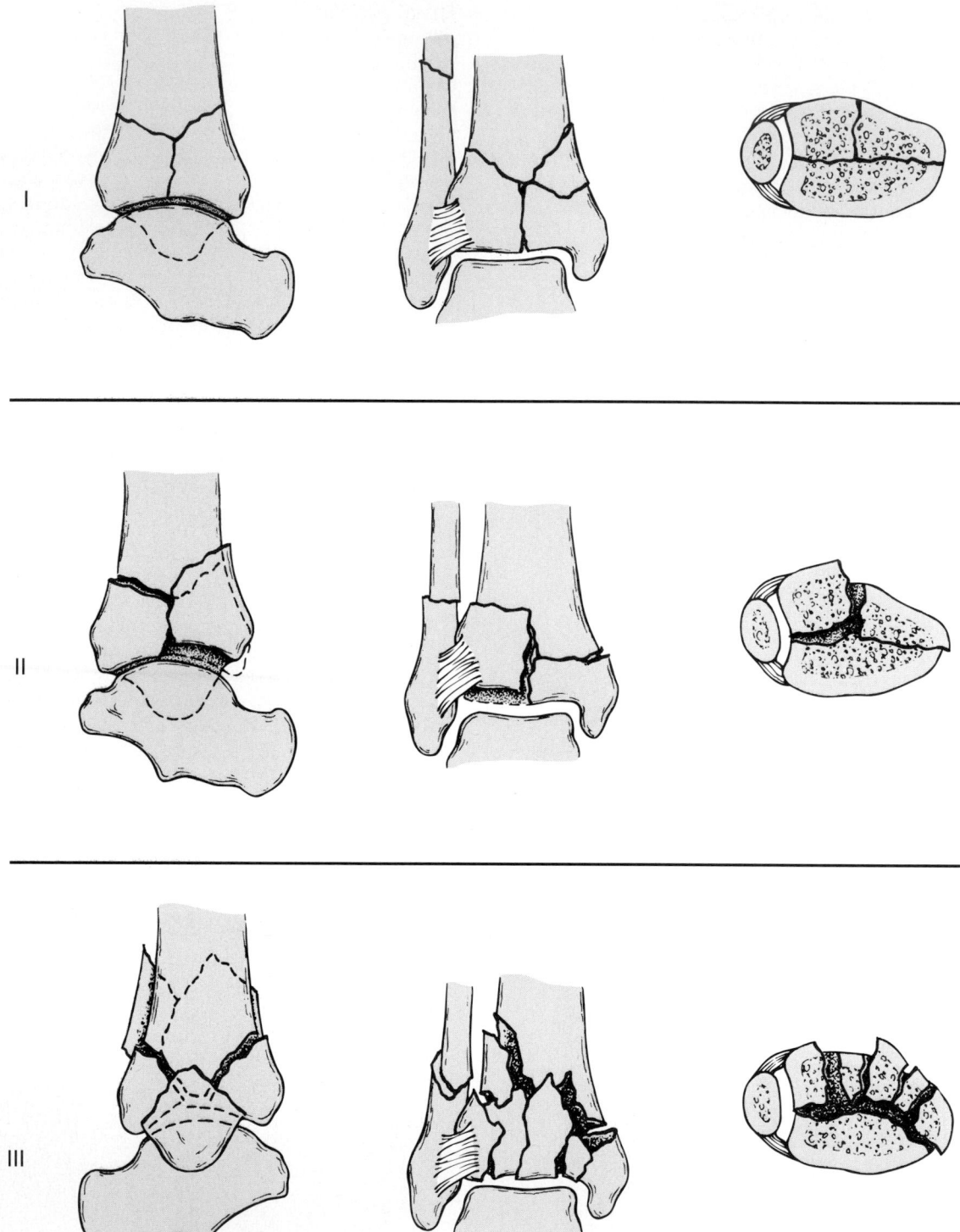

I

II

III

**FIGURE 58–3.** Ruĕdi and Allgöwer's classification of pilon fractures (see text). (Redrawn from Ruĕdi, T.P.; Allgöwer, M. Clin Orthop 138:105–110, 1979.)

phy (CT) to plain films, one study failed to note an improvement in the ability to diagnose displacement, count the number of articular pieces present, or reliably classify the fracture.[119]

These findings should not condemn fracture classification systems, experience of the surgeon, or the use of CT—all of which can still have some utility in the management of individual patients and serve as a framework for decision making.[187, 194] However, it is important for both the clinician and the academic orthopaedic surgeon to understand the limitations of any classification system.

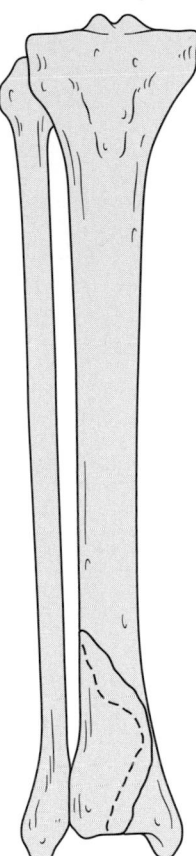

**FIGURE 58–4.** Maale and Seligson–type spiral extension fracture. (Redrawn from Meyer, M.H. The Multiply Injured Patient with Complex Fractures, 1st ed. Philadelphia, Lea & Febiger, 1984, p. 299.)

# DIAGNOSIS AND EVALUATION

Patients with pilon fractures often have associated injuries.[9, 76, 80, 125, 149, 170, 207] Blauth and colleagues[13] noted that one third of their patients had injuries to the contralateral leg and foot, 6% had polytrauma, and 6% suffered peroneal nerve damage. Patterson and Cole[149] reported a 64% incidence of associated injuries in their series of AO type C3 pilon fractures. Although in some reports the most commonly associated fractures have been to the calcaneus (often contralateral) and tibial shaft,[76] transmission of an axial load up the entire extremity can result in virtually any fracture from the foot to the lumbar spine.[13, 17, 21, 76, 80, 92, 130, 149, 188]

Examination of the ankle should include a careful evaluation of the soft tissues, the presence or absence of an open injury, the amount of swelling, the patient's neurologic status, and the status of the peripheral pulses. The amount of soft tissue damage should be graded according to the system of Tscherne and Gotzen[201] and open fractures according to the system of Gustilo and Anderson.[73] The size, location, and extent of contamination of each wound must be documented. Care must be taken to immediately recognize the presence of an impending open fracture, most commonly a concern when the distal fragment is displaced posteriorly and the anterior aspect of the tibial shaft tents the skin anteriorly.[21] This deformity must be reduced as soon as possible to prevent further soft tissue compromise, necrosis, and subsequent fracture contamination. When the deformity involves posterior and medial displacement of the distal fragment, the deep and superficial peroneal nerves are at risk for injury.[21]

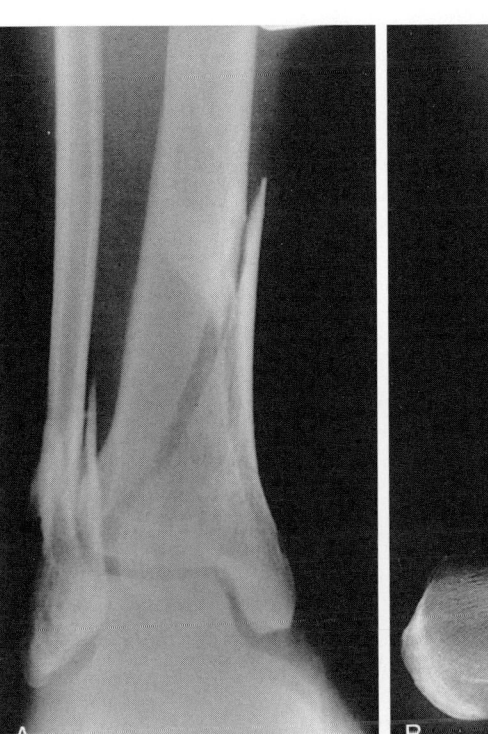
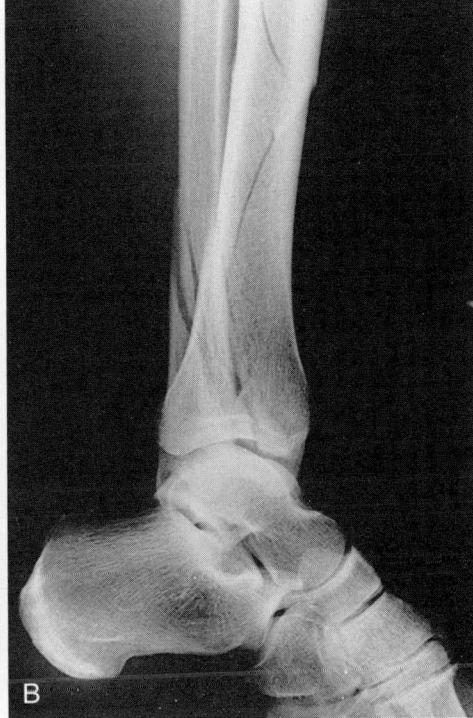

**FIGURE 58–5.** *A, B,* Clinical example of a Maale and Seligson–type spiral extension injury.

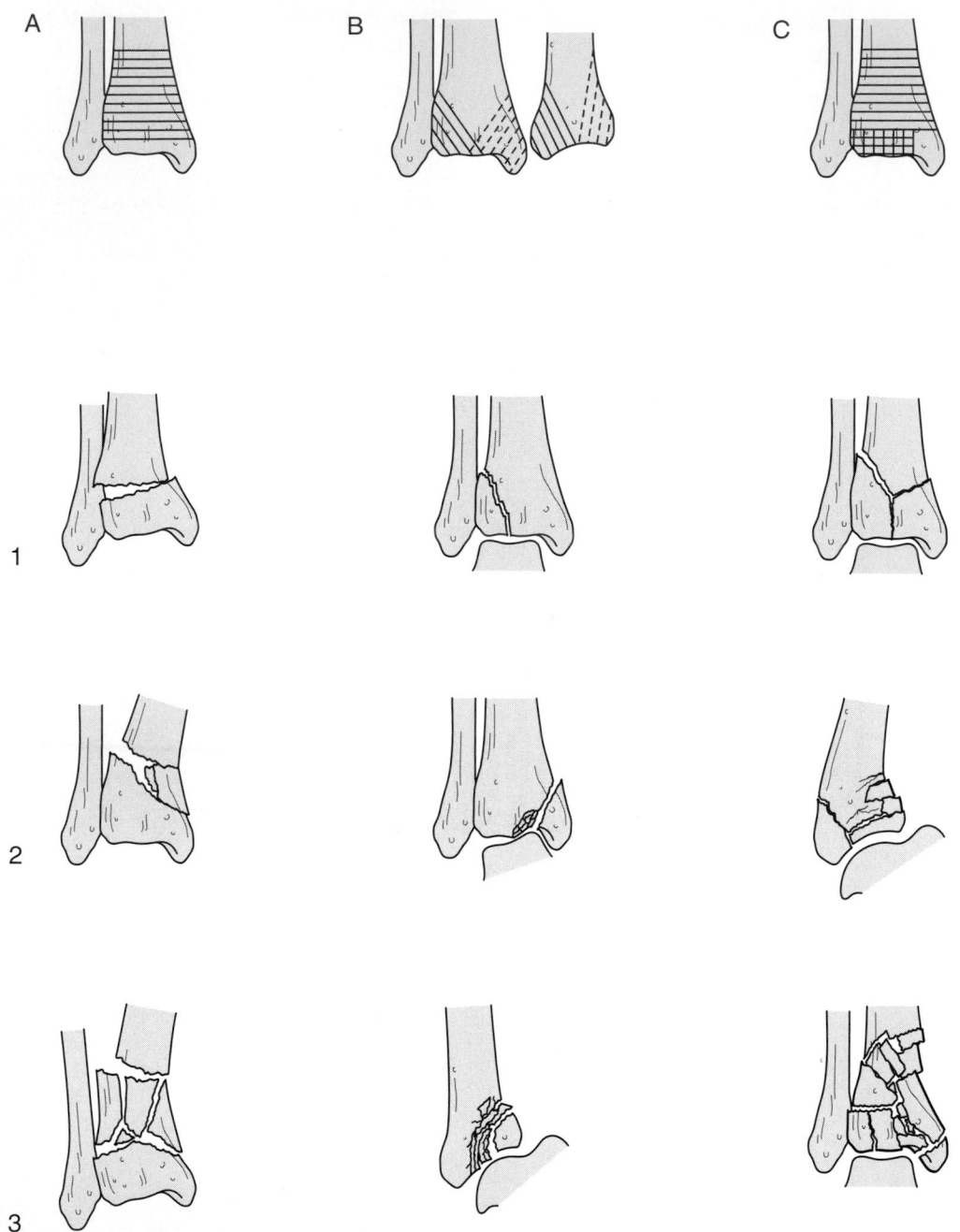

**FIGURE 58–6.** *A–C,* The comprehensive AO classification system for pilon fractures (see text). (Redrawn from Müller, M.E.; et al. Manual of Internal Fixation, 3rd ed. New York, Springer-Verlag, 1991, p. 147.)

Particularly important is observation for any early signs or symptoms of compartment syndrome. Severe pain, first webspace sensory changes, and weakness of toe dorsiflexion suggest a developing anterior compartment syndrome. Subclinical signs are more likely in a slowly progressing deep posterior compartment syndrome, which can be confirmed by pain on passive toe dorsiflexion, weakness of toe flexion, and plantar hypesthesia.[76]

The patient's medical history should be reviewed to identify the presence of any preexisting medical conditions, which are associated with poor healing and might require modification of the treatment plan. These conditions include alcoholism, peripheral vascular disease,

diabetes mellitus, osteoporosis, or other causes of poor bone stock.[148]

An adequate preoperative plan requires a clear understanding of the fracture's geometry. Acquisition of such knowledge begins with the standard three views of the ankle and a 45° external rotation view to delineate the anteromedial and posterolateral surfaces of the tibia.[121, 203] Mortise and lateral radiographs of the contralateral ankle can provide a model for templating and reduction. Traction radiographs often allow better visualization of individual fracture fragments.[50, 59]

Although some have questioned its value,[119] most authors agree that a CT scan provides valuable information with regard to the fracture pattern, especially the location of fracture lines, the location and number of cortical fragments, the extent of articular comminution, and the degree of impaction or displacement[53, 59, 194, 195, 209] (Figs. 58–7C and 58–8). The addition of sagittal and coronal reconstructions completes the three-dimensional representation of the fracture. Such imaging allows the surgeon to make specific preoperative decisions about optimal placement of the incision and the position of screws and other implants. Tornetta and Gorup[194] found that the use of CT provided additional information in 82% of cases and led to a change in the surgical plan in 64% of pilon fractures undergoing operative stabilization. When obtained after placement of traction or a provisional bridging external fixator, a CT scan is easier to read and provides the most useful information because of improvement in fragment alignment through ligamentotaxis.[209]

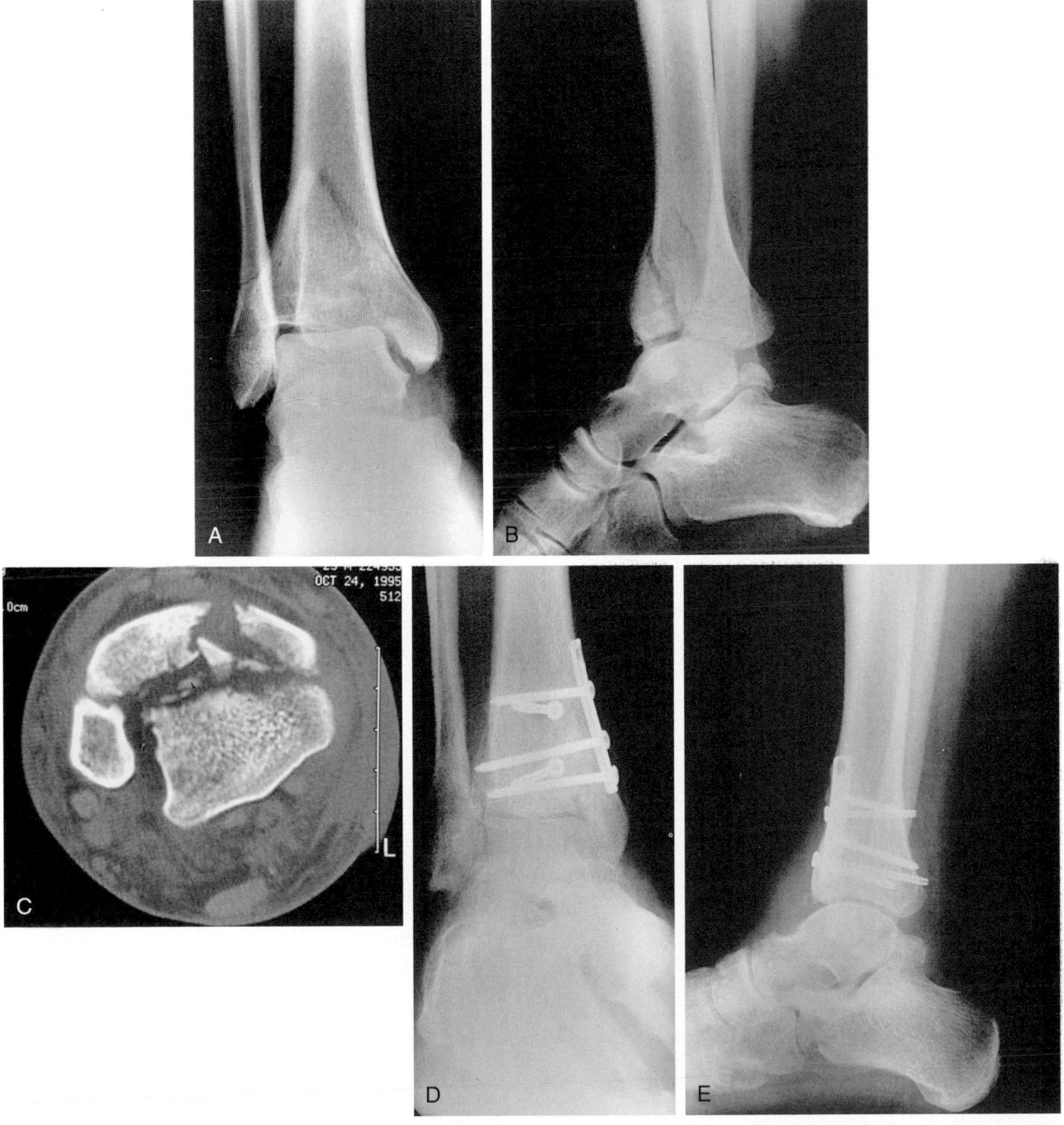

**FIGURE 58–7.** *A, B,* A type B3 pilon fracture with anterior comminution has allowed forward subluxation of the talus. *C,* A computed tomographic scan delineates the extent of the fragmentation and the morphology of the major fragments. *D, E,* Nine-month follow-up after surgical fixation. The talus is well reduced, and the fracture has healed.

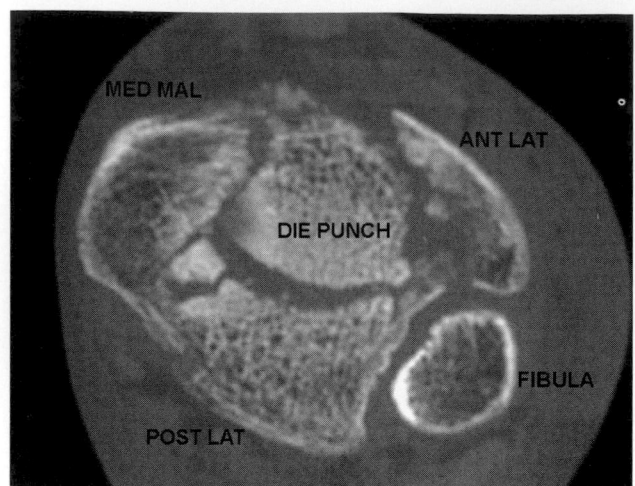

**FIGURE 58–8.** Axial computed tomography. Classically, the major ("key") fragments of the pilon fracture that can be identified are the anterolateral (Tillaux-Chaput) fragment, the posterior (Volkmann's) fragment, the medial malleolus, and a variable degree of comminution and impaction of the articular surface (die punch).

## EVOLUTION OF CARE AND RESULTS OF TREATMENT

Before 1963, reported outcomes of surgical treatment of severely comminuted and impacted fractures of the distal tibial articular surface were dismal (Table 58–1). Good results were achieved in only 43% to 50% of cases.[19, 44, 57, 63] Frustrated with the typical surgical results, Jergesen[88] described these fractures as "not being amenable to internal fixation." Therefore, a preference for nonoperative treatment was established.* Unfortunately, nonoperative treatment also produced generally poor results.[19, 23, 24, 44, 51, 92, 168, 213]

In 1963, the AO/Association for the Study of Internal Fixation (ASIF) group introduced its principles of ORIF.[2, 141] From these initial guidelines for operative fixation have evolved modern "biologic principles" that

---

*See references 19, 36, 38, 41, 44, 57, 63, 87, 88, 105, 168, 169, 213.

---

**TABLE 58–1**

Evolution and Results of Treatment

| Author(s) | Year | Cases | Treatment | Good-Excellent Results (%) |
|---|---|---|---|---|
| Fourquet[57] | 1959 | 20 | Mostly ORIF | 55 |
| Bonier[19] | 1961 | 30 | Mostly closed | 43 |
| Decoulx et al.[44] | 1961 | 49 | Closed or ORIF | 45 |
| Gay and Evrard[63] | 1963 | 142 | Closed or ORIF | 50 |
| Scheck[176] | 1965 | 5 | Ltd ORIF & ExFix | 100 |
| Ruëdi et al.[166] | 1969 | 84 | ORIF | 74 |
| Ruëdi[164] | 1973 | 54 | ORIF | 85 |
| Heim[76, 77] | 1976 | 128 | ORIF | 90 |
| Ruëdi and Allgöwer[168] | 1979 | 75 | ORIF | 69 |
| Kellam and Waddell[92] | 1979 | 26 | Ltd ORIF | 68 |
| Pierce and Heinrich[152] | 1979 | 14 | ORIF | 7 |
| Moller and Krebs[133] | 1982 | 23 | ORIF | 54 |
| Ovadia and Beals[148] | 1986 | 80 | ORIF | 74 |
| Ovadia and Beals[148] | 1986 | 65 | Other methods | 54 |
| Ayeni[6] | 1988 | 11 | ORIF | 81 |
| Bourne[23] | 1989 | 33 | ORIF | 64 |
| Bone et al.[16] | 1993 | 20 | ExFix | 30 |
| Leone et al.[109] | 1993 | 9 | ORIF | 56 |
| Beck[10] | 1993 | 256 | ORIF | 82 |
| Waddell[207] | 1993 | 38 | ORIF | 74 |
| Saleh et al.[171] | 1993 | 9 | Ltd ORIF & ExFix | 67 |
| Teeny and Wiss[191] | 1993 | 60 | ORIF | 25 |
| Tornetta et al.[196] | 1993 | 17 | Ltd ORIF & ExFix | 71 |
| Helfet et al.[80] | 1994 | 34 | ORIF | 62 |
| Rommens et al.[163] | 1994 | 64 | ORIF | 56 |
| Marsh et al.[115] | 1995 | 30 | ExFix | 60 |
| DiChristina et al.[46] | 1996 | 9 | Ltd ORIF & ExFix | 89 |
| Barbieri et al.[9] | 1996 | 37 | Ltd ORIF & ExFix | 62 |
| Wyrsch et al.[217] | 1996 | 19 | ORIF | Clinical score, 61/100 |
| Wyrsch et al.[217] | 1996 | 20 | Ltd ORIF & ExFix | Clinical score, 73/100 |
| Kim et al.[94] | 1997 | 21 | Ltd ORIF/PercFix & ExFix | 71* |
| Patterson and Cole[149] | 1999 | 22 | Staged ORIF | 77 |
| Raikin and Froimson[156] | 1999 | 20 | Ltd ORIF & ExFix | 70 |
| Anglen[3] | 1999 | 29 | Ltd ORIF & ExFix | 52 |
| Anglen[3] | 1999 | 19 | ORIF | 79 |
| Watson et al.[209] | 2000 | 41 | ORIF | 75 |
| Watson et al.[209] | 2000 | 64 | Ltd ORIF & ExFix | 81 |
| Blauth et al.[13] | 2001 | 51 | ORIF/Staged Ltd ORIF/staged PercFix | 80 |

*R-I, 100%; R-II, 71%; R-III, 60%.

*Abbreviations:* ExFix, external fixation; Ltd, limited; ORIF, open reduction and internal fixation; PercFix, percutaneous fixation; Staged, staged protocol with provisional spanning external fixator.

emphasize meticulous soft tissue dissection, limited stripping of fracture fragments, indirect reduction techniques, and stable fixation,[122, 123, 125] followed by early active motion with delayed weight bearing.

In 1969, Ruëdi and Allgöwer[166] reported 74% good to excellent functional results in a series of 84 pilon fractures monitored for 4.2 years. Ninety percent of patients returned to their previous occupation. By 9 years, 85% had a good to excellent outcome. However, in ankles with inadequate reconstruction of the articular surface or unstable internal fixation, progressive arthritic changes and painful limitation of motion almost always developed.[164] Heim and Naser[77] echoed these admirable results and reported good function in 90% and a wound infection rate of only 1.4% for 128 patients. However, 75% and 90% of patients, respectively, in each of these two studies had sustained lower-energy, skiing-type injuries. In addition, only 6% of the fractures in the series of Ruëdi and Allgöwer[166] were open. Nonetheless, both groups concluded that if a pilon fracture could be reconstructed anatomically and stabilized by rigid internal fixation, a predictably good long-term outcome was possible.

Other authors have been less optimistic, with dismal complication rates and frequently suboptimal end results reported when attempting to apply AO techniques to the treatment of high-energy pilon fractures.* Pierce and Heinrich[152] were unable to reproduce the respectable results of Ruëdi and Allgöwer in their small series of 21 pilon fractures, 7 of which were open. They reported seven cases of skin sloughing, three infections, and five cases of metal erosion. Kellam and Waddell[92] obtained only 53% good or excellent results for severe pilon fractures. Moller and Krebs[133] reported unacceptable results of ORIF in all six of their patients with severely comminuted intra-articular pilon fractures and, like Jergesen[88] 23 years before, concluded that primary operative reduction should not be performed.

Ruëdi and Allgöwer[168] themselves obtained only a 69% rate of good to excellent results in a new group of 75 patients (average follow-up of 6 years) operated on primarily by senior orthopaedic residents at a major university trauma center. Dillin and Slabaugh[47] encountered disastrous results, including a 36% rate of skin sloughing and a 55% incidence of osteomyelitis in a series of 11 patients with pilon fractures treated by resident staff. Only one fracture was adequately stabilized with plate fixation of the tibia, whereas eight others underwent ORIF with a combination of Kirschner wires, lag screws, and fibular stabilization (the fibular fracture was plated in only four cases). Two other patients had closed treatment of their tibial fracture. As a result, the authors' postoperative rate of osteomyelitis and chronic wound drainage was actually closer to 89%, with a 56% rate of soft tissue complications. Two nonunions developed, and one patient required amputation for chronic osteomyelitis and septic arthritis. After reviewing their results, these authors concluded that in the presence of severe comminution and open wounds, "the efficacy of rigid internal fixation performed by surgeons without great experience with these types of fracture is dubious [and that] the results of

closed reduction and immobilization are preferable" in such circumstances.

In 1986, Ovadia and Beals[148] reviewed 145 pilon fractures, most of which were caused by high-energy trauma. Good to excellent outcomes were obtained in 74% of the 80 patients treated with ORIF as compared with 54% of those treated with all other methods. However, when only the severe injuries were evaluated, ORIF yielded good or better results in only 38%. Their overall complication rates were significant and included 10 superficial wound infections, 10 cases of osteomyelitis, 5 cases of wound sloughing, 17 cases of delayed arthrodesis or arthroplasty, and 3 amputations. Nine of the 25 open wounds became infected, and type II and III open fractures had significantly higher complication rates, consistent with other reports.[31, 58, 63, 131, 173, 179]

Formal ORIF of Ruëdi type III injuries by Bourne and associates[23, 24] yielded only a 44% rate of satisfactory results, with a high rate of complications consisting of nonunion in 25%, deep infection in 13%, malunion in 25%, and post-traumatic arthrosis in 63%. They therefore expressed little enthusiasm for this form of treatment. Providing some optimism, Helfet and colleagues[80] reported 65% excellent results in 26 Ruëdi type II fractures and 50% excellent outcomes in 8 Ruëdi type III fractures. In addition, Rommens and co-workers[163] evaluated 64 severe pilon fractures treated with ORIF and noted 56% good or better subjective results in the group with severe soft tissue lesions (48% objective results) versus 86% good or better results in those without soft tissue injury (75% objective results). Treatment with plate osteosynthesis was associated with both a greater number of delayed complications and a greater number of secondary procedures. McFerran and colleagues[130] reported a 54% rate of complications in severe pilon fractures treated by surgery at a Level I trauma center, including a 24% rate of wound breakdown and a 17% rate of infection. Most of these complications were major.

Teeny and Wiss[191] noted even more dismal results of ORIF in a series of 60 pilon fractures, with unacceptable clinical outcomes in 75%. Not surprisingly, complication rates increased from 30% in Ruëdi type I and II fractures to 70% in type III fractures—with many patients having more than one complication. These complications included a 37% rate of skin sloughing and dehiscence and a 37% rate of infection in 30 Ruëdi type III fractures as compared with respective rates of 17% and 0% for lower-energy fractures. Ruëdi type III fractures were also four times more likely to result in nonunion (27% versus 7%), seven times more likely to lead to malunion (23% versus 3%), six times more likely to have problems with unstable fixation and hardware failure, and nearly three times more likely to ultimately require arthrodesis (26% versus 10%). Rather than correlating infection with the presence of an open fracture, these authors found that it was the presence of wound problems that increased the incidence of deep infection sixfold to 44% (7 of 16 patients)! Still, only 17% of the open fractures went on to have a good or better outcome as compared with 27% of the closed injuries. The authors recommended that "if anatomic reduction without soft tissue complications cannot be predicted preoperatively, consideration should be given to alternative types of treatment."

---

*See references 17, 23, 24, 47, 92, 130, 133, 148, 152, 188, 191, 217.

Because most poor results after a formal open approach and ORIF appeared to be linked to soft tissue complications, investigators began to compare the outcomes of this technique with those of more limited approaches. Nast-Kolb and associates[145] found that delayed wound healing occurred twice as often with plating of the tibia (27% versus 14%) as with limited ORIF. A greater incidence of severe post-traumatic arthrosis was also associated with the use of tibial plate fixation (43% versus 18%).

In a prospective study of severe pilon fractures (44% Ruĕdi type III, 26% open), Wyrsch and colleagues[217] compared the results of ORIF and bridging external fixation with or without limited internal fixation. Although ankle scores for the two groups were equivalent, complications were more frequent and severe in patients treated with ORIF. Fifteen complications occurred in 7 of 19 patients treated with ORIF and necessitated 28 additional procedures. These complications included wound breakdown requiring a free flap in 33%, deep infection in 33%, and amputation in 16%. In contrast, only four complications occurred in 4 of 20 patients treated with external fixation, including a 5% rate of skin sloughing, a 5% rate of infection, and no amputations. A critical caveat to these findings is that 13 patients undergoing ORIF (68%) had operative stabilization between 3 and 5 days after their injury and 5 (26%) were treated within 24 hours—time periods when soft tissue edema would probably be substantial. Furthermore, primary wound closure was not possible in seven patients, who required additional procedures for débridement and closure or coverage. In the external fixation group, 11 patients were treated during the first 24 hours, only 2 between 3 and 5 days, and 7 (35%) at 1 week or more after injury.

In an effort to improve on the poor results associated with more severe pilon fractures, Tornetta and co-workers[195, 196] proposed an alternative method of treatment. They reported 81% good to excellent results overall for 26 fractures of the distal end of the tibia treated with limited internal fixation and hybrid external fixation, including a rate of 69% for 13 Ruĕdi type III pilon fractures. Complications were fewer and less severe than typical for cases treated with ORIF. They reported one varus malunion (10°), one superficial infection, and three pin tract infections that resolved after the administration of oral antibiotics, pin removal, or both. Only one deep infection occurred, and it was eliminated by débridement and removal of the fixator and lag screws. This method yielded anatomic and early functional results comparable to those of previous studies, but without the related soft tissue complications. Marsh and associates[115] similarly reported satisfactory results in a group of patients with 49 severe pilon fractures treated with an articulated external fixator and limited internal fixation.

Raikin and Froimson[156] applied the concepts of hybrid fixation to a group of 20 patients with mostly high-energy pilon fractures. All but three were Ruĕdi type II or III, eight were type II or III open fractures, and three other closed fractures had significant soft tissue contusion. Twelve patients had additional limited internal fixation of the tibia, fibula, or both bones. Although 18 of 20 fractures healed at an average of 4.8 months, with 70% good or better results, the rate of complications was high; however,

most complications were minor and easily treated. Delayed bone grafting was required in five patients, and varus malunion eventually developed in five (average of 5.2°). The authors observed a 15% rate of superficial infection, which responded to local wound care and short-term antibiotics, and a 10% rate of deep infection, which required removal of the fixator, irrigation and débridement, and 10 weeks of antibiotics. Although radiographic signs of early arthrosis were present in 30% of patients at a follow-up of nearly 1 year, ankle range of motion still averaged from 5° dorsiflexion to 26° plantar flexion.

Combining limited internal fixation with external immobilization is not a new concept. Limited internal fixation of the fibula with Rush rods combined with external immobilization in plaster was proposed by Leach in 1964.[107] However, varus deformity was common because of inadequate medial buttress support for the tibial metaphysis. Limited open reduction plus external fixation was introduced by Scheck in 1965.[176] He used this technique in five patients with comminuted distal tibial fractures (two were open) and reported satisfactory results in all cases. After identification, reduction, and fixation of "key fragments" with minimal soft tissue stripping, he maintained alignment by applying a dual-pin fixator from the calcaneus to the proximal end of the tibia.

Other investigators have endorsed the concept of limited surgery for severe pilon injuries to avoid the poor results associated with formal ORIF, and a variety of techniques were used,[87, 92, 124, 139, 160, 169, 177, 191] including hybrid fixators,[9] Ilizarov-type fixators,[5, 86, 94, 129, 144, 209] bridging external fixation,[15, 115, 116, 171] and percutaneous screw or plate fixation.[13, 81] Kim and colleagues[94] achieved 71% good results (Ruĕdi type I, 100%; Ruĕdi type II, 71%; Ruĕdi type III, 60%) when using Ilizarov techniques with or without limited ORIF or arthroscopy. McDonald and colleagues[129] reviewed 13 pilon fractures (1 type I, 8 type II, 4 type III) treated with the Ilizarov method alone and noted 91% good to excellent results.

However, external fixation is not a panacea. Anatomic and functional results still depend to some degree on the soft tissues and fracture pattern, as shown by Bone and co-workers.[16] Although soft tissue complications were minimal, they noted only 30% good or better results after treatment of severe open pilon fractures with limited internal fixation and a spanning triangular external fixator.

Further dampening enthusiasm for external fixation is Anglen's recent observation[3] that hybrid external fixation with or without limited internal fixation often fails to solve the problems inherent in severe pilon fractures. In his retrospective review, 29 of 63 patients treated by such techniques had lower clinical scores, slower return to function, and a higher rate of complications (nonunion, malunion, infection) than did a group of 19 patients treated with ORIF. Good to excellent results were obtained in only 52% of the hybrid group versus 79% of the ORIF group. Whereas only three patients in the ORIF group had complications, 15 patients in the hybrid group had 16 complications, including 7 wire site infections, 3 half-pin site infections, 3 wound-healing problems, 1 case of septic arthritis, 1 tethered flexor tendon, and 1 patient with numb toes. Seven infections resolved with oral antibiotics and three required long-term intravenous antibiotics.

Three of the patients with pin site infections ultimately required surgical treatment. Although all the patients undergoing ORIF achieved union, 7 of 34 patients (21%) in the hybrid group had a diagnosis of nonunion at 6 months. Unlike other researchers, Anglen found that wound problems after internal fixation were minimal and did not require additional surgery. He attributed this outcome to careful patient selection and a long delay before definitive fixation (11 days for the ORIF group versus 7 days for the hybrid group). However, treatment was biased toward the use of hybrid fixation for patients with more severely damaged soft tissues (eight open fractures versus one in the ORIF group), highly comminuted or longitudinally extensive fracture patterns, and significant systemic injury.

Pugh and co-workers[155] followed with a retrospective review of 60 patients with high-energy pilon fractures treated by one of three methods (21 by ankle-spanning external fixators, 15 by hybrid fixation, 24 by formal ORIF). Twenty-six fractures were open and 41 were AO type C. No significant differences in complication rates were noted between the groups, although two below-knee amputations were required in the ORIF group. A greater number of malunions occurred after external fixation, with fractures showing a significant tendency to lose their initial adequate reduction either while in the fixator or after its removal and conversion to a partial weight-bearing cast. A trend for patients in the hybrid fixation group to require late bone grafting for impending metaphyseal-diaphyseal nonunion was also observed.

Other authors have noted problems with fixators, particularly pin site problems[9, 62, 71, 86, 94, 209, 210] (see Complications). In a recent review of 14 patients treated with hybrid external fixation, Gaudinez and colleagues[62] reported one varus malunion (7°), eight superficial pin tract infections, no deep infections, and one pin placed in the ankle joint. Barbieri and associates[9] noted that 35% of their patients had at least one complication, such as skin sloughing, pin tract infection (15%), osteomyelitis, nonunion, loss of reduction, or the presence of degenerative changes at the tibiotalar joint. Many patients had more than one complication.

Unfortunately, although external fixation and limited surgical approaches have been able to minimize wound necrosis and skin sloughing, they have not eliminated deep infections and are associated with high rates of pin tract infection, malalignment, nonunion, malunion, arthritis, and chronic pain. Furthermore, techniques that rely on ligamentotaxis for fracture reduction do little to reduce depressed articular fragments and routinely provide inadequate visualization to anatomically align the articular surface, particularly in the face of increasing comminution. On the other hand, it has been noted that steps in the articular surface after surgical stabilization are more frequently associated with post-traumatic arthritis than are comparable steps in fractures treated non-operatively, perhaps because of further devascularization of bone fragments.[13, 158] Therefore, the potential trade-off between a formal open approach to achieve a perfect reduction and a more limited approach remains a dilemma.

In an effort to maximize the advantages of both ORIF and percutaneous techniques such as external fixation, Watson and colleagues[209] established a staged prospective treatment protocol based on the severity of soft tissue injury. All fractures were stabilized immediately by the application of calcaneal traction, and a distraction CT scan was obtained. Open fractures and those with associated polytrauma were treated by urgent operative stabilization with a spanning external fixator ("traveling traction"). Patients with open fractures returned to the operating room an average of 2.5 days later for a second irrigation and débridement procedure and definitive stabilization. Those with closed injuries underwent definitive fracture treatment an average of 5 days after the initial injury, when the soft tissues had improved. Forty-one patients with Tscherne and Gotzen[201] grade 0 or I closed injuries underwent ORIF, whereas 64 patients with grade II and III injuries and all those with open fractures underwent definitive stabilization using a small circular wire external fixator with or without a limited open approach. Seven soft tissue coverage procedures (four flaps, three skin grafts) were required in the external fixation group.

At an average follow-up of 4.9 years, 36 patients who had undergone ORIF and 58 treated with external fixation had achieved good to excellent results in 75% and 81% of cases, respectively. When stratified by AO fracture type, good or excellent results were obtained after ORIF in 91% of type A, 68% of type B, and 60% of type C fractures. For the external fixation group, good to excellent results were achieved in 93% of type A, 86% of type B, and 62% of type C fractures. Patients in the open plating group had a significantly higher rate of nonunion, malunion, and severe wound complications than did those who had undergone external fixation for type C fracture patterns. Although patients treated with external fixation tended to have lower radiographic scores and the quality of reduction tended to predict clinical results, clinical outcomes were influenced to a greater degree by the soft tissue damage than the skeletal injuries. Other variables adversely affecting clinical outcome included the presence of articular incongruity, an articular defect greater than 2 mm, and malalignment of the mechanical axis greater than 5°.

Complications after ORIF included wound dehiscence or skin breakdown (14%), deep infection (5%), nonunion (11%), malunion (4%), post-traumatic arthrosis requiring late arthrodesis (8%), and symptomatic hardware requiring removal (27%). In contrast, after external fixation, wound complications were minimal (4%) and resolved with local wound care, no deep infections were noted, and rates of nonunion (3%), malunion (5%), and late arthrodesis (7%) were low. However, 100% of patients in the later group had at least one instance of major pin tract infection that resolved with either a change in pin care, a short course of oral antibiotics, or removal of the pin (10%). The authors suggested that their failure to associate delayed union or nonunion with external fixation, as in other recent studies, was due to their use of a complete circular construct to minimize cantilever-bending forces. Though acknowledging that ORIF was still the treatment of choice for AO type A and B fractures with low-grade soft tissue injury, the authors recommended external fixation for open or closed type C fractures because of their increased incidence of bony and soft tissue complications. This practice has been advocated by other authors.[42, 59, 196]

Because ORIF provides the best chance of obtaining anatomic reduction of the articular surface, a desirable alternative to the protocol of Watson and colleagues[209] would be to convert the condition of severely damaged soft tissues from a Tscherne and Gotzen[201] grade II or III to that of 0 or I. To this end, recent retrospective reviews have promoted staged protocols for the treatment of higher-energy pilon fractures.[3, 13, 149, 180] These protocols combine the advantages of ORIF, limited surgical exposure, external fixation, and delayed treatment. In the initial stage, the fibula is usually stabilized with plate fixation, and an external fixator that spans the ankle joint is used. Once the soft tissues have healed, formal or limited ORIF of the tibia is undertaken.

Sirkin and associates[180] treated 56 patients with such a protocol, and definitive treatment of the tibia was achieved at an average of 13 days after the initial surgery. Thirty-four patients had closed fractures and 22 had open fractures (three type I, six type II, eight type IIIA, five type IIIB). Four fractures were AO type C1, 10 were C2, and 43 were C3 (3 Ruëdi type I, 13 type II, and 40 type III). All the wounds healed with no cases of wound dehiscence or full-thickness necrosis requiring secondary soft tissue coverage (by definition, type IIIB open fractures required secondary soft tissue coverage). Partial-thickness necrosis developed in 17% of patients with closed fractures and in 10.5% with open fractures and healed with local wound care and oral antibiotics. Osteomyelitis developed in one patient with a closed fracture and in two with open fractures, one of these injuries resulting in amputation.

Using a similar protocol, except with a preference for intramedullary fixation of the fibula and definitive stabilization of the tibia with a slightly greater delay (average of 24 days), Patterson and Cole[149] treated 22 consecutive AO type C3 pilon fractures (6 were open). They obtained 77% good, 14% fair, and 9% poor results, with all but one fracture healing at an average of 4.2 months. No infections or soft tissue complications developed. At follow-up, two patients required tibiotalar arthrodesis.

Blauth and colleagues[13] separated 51 patients (4 AO type B, 2 C1, 26 C2, and 19 C3; 19 open fractures) into three different treatment groups: 15 patients underwent formal ORIF, and two other groups of patients were treated with minimally invasive osteosynthesis of the articular surface (short anteromedial approach or stab incisions with placement of screws and Kirschner wires), followed by transarticular external fixation of the ankle. Fibular fractures were routinely stabilized with a plate and screws. Of the later two groups, 28 were kept in their fixator for an average of 43 days before conversion to a cast (average total immobilization time, 60 days; range, 40 to 87 days), and 8 underwent a second-stage procedure consisting of fixator removal and percutaneous plate fixation of the tibia 17 days (average) after their initial surgery. Primary wound closure was not possible in 25 patients (49%). After temporary coverage with artificial skin, 10 patients subsequently underwent split-thickness skin grafting, and

2 received free muscle flaps. Overall, 80% of patients resumed their former employment, 86% resumed their former sporting activities at the same or a reduced level, and 92% were satisfied with their results.

Infection requiring surgical débridement occurred in 13 patients (25%), with a trend toward a greater risk of infection noted in the formal ORIF group (33%) versus the staged treatment group (12.5%). Although this difference was not statistically significant, it is important to consider that all the patients in the formal ORIF group had lower-energy closed injuries. Of the five patients (10%) in whom osteomyelitis developed, all were AO type C and four had sustained a type II open fracture. Although post-traumatic arthrosis did not correlate with the type of procedure, none of the patients requiring arthrodesis (23% of patients) were in the group that had undergone the two-stage procedure. Though not statistically significant, the staged group also had less pain, more frequently returned to their previous occupation, and had fewer limitations of leisure activities. In the group undergoing single-stage minimal osteosynthesis and external fixation, poorer outcomes were attributed to the long period of immobilization needed. Other reports have attributed poor outcomes to the long periods of immobilization required for external fixation and minimal osteosynthesis.[7]

Unfortunately, most of the studies to date have been rather small, retrospective, uncontrolled, and without consistent classification of injuries or outcomes, which makes comparisons very difficult. There is little disagreement that treatment of pilon fractures remains challenging. Nonsurgical methods, ORIF, and various combinations of limited internal and external fixation have all met with varying degrees of success. It is apparent that no specific method is ideal for all pilon fractures, so it is up to the individual surgeon to determine the most appropriate form of treatment for a particular patient.

## INITIAL TREATMENT

Care should begin at the scene of the injury. Some form of immobilization is imperative before the patient is moved to prevent further damage to the tenuous soft tissue sleeve. Once radiographs are obtained and the severity of the fracture is documented, preliminary reduction and more rigid immobilization should be obtained.

While awaiting definitive treatment, three basic principles should be followed: the fracture must be reduced and length restored, the ankle must be stabilized, and the limb must be moderately elevated.[125, 193, 195] Maintenance of neutral alignment is an important detail not to be forgotten because an unsupported ankle typically falls into an equinus position.

A Ruëdi type I fracture may be placed in a well-padded splint. However, with more extensive injuries, reduction and stability are best obtained with some form of external fixation or calcaneal traction.[3, 13, 149, 175, 178, 180, 193, 209] Early motion in traction may help decrease edema and reduce scarring and stiffness around the joint as the soft tissues heal.[195, 196] This immediate ligamentotaxis reduction is also advantageous in reducing the metaphyseal and fibular components of the fracture and may subsequently decrease the necessity to perform gross manipulation of these large fragments, thereby decreasing the amount of stripping required at surgery.[209] It is unclear when the absolute immobilization of a bridging external fixator extended onto the forefoot is of greater benefit for severely injured soft tissues. If the soft tissues never return to an acceptable state, traction or external fixation becomes the definitive treatment.[193]

## OPEN FRACTURES

Open fractures are treated on an emergency basis using accepted principles.[35, 58, 73, 99, 128, 150, 180, 209, 217] These principles emphasize tetanus prophylaxis, initiation of appropriate antibiotics,[73, 150] and early surgical débridement. If surgery will be delayed, some benefit may be derived from irrigating the wound in the emergency room, although the potential for increased contamination is a concern.

Franklin and co-workers[58] recommend a standardized protocol for the treatment of open ankle fractures. Prophylactic antibiotics are started in the emergency room and continued for 48 hours. The patient is brought immediately to the operating room for irrigation and débridement of the wound. Rigid fixation is then achieved with the AO principles and techniques of internal fixation; delayed primary closure follows 5 days later.

Some studies have shown a link between open pilon fractures and infection,[13, 31, 58, 63, 131, 173, 179, 188, 206] whereas others have found comparable rates of infection in both open and closed fractures.[16, 35, 58, 76, 94, 99, 190, 191] Swiontkowski and colleagues[188] noted an 11% overall rate of deep infection after ORIF in 26 open pilon fractures as compared with 4% in 58 closed pilon fractures. However, LaDuca and colleagues[99] reported a 4% rate of infection when staged wound débridement was used to convert an open contaminated wound to a sterile operative field before definitive rigid fixation of ankle fractures. Moreover, Bone and associates[16] saw no infection in their 12 patients, and Tassler[190] had only six infections in 54 patients with type III open pilon fractures. Heim[76] noted that his 21 cases of osteomyelitis (3.4% of 615 cases overall) were evenly distributed between open and closed fractures. Finally, reports of staged ORIF of open pilon fractures have yielded rates of infection between 0% and 9%, which compare favorably with rates after ORIF of closed fractures.[149, 180] Therefore, open wounds of the ankle per se are not necessarily contraindications to ORIF.

More severe open injuries associated with extensive soft tissue compromise are candidates for tibial-calcaneal external fixation with or without extension to the forefoot (see Half-Pin Frames). This construct provides length, alignment, and stability until the soft tissues allow definitive treatment to be performed. In some cases, the combination of severe soft tissue and bony injury may require salvage-type procedures (see Unreconstructible Pilon Fractures).[173]

## TREATMENT OPTIONS

Most surgeons agree that anatomic reduction of the articular surface, proper alignment, and a stable construct to allow early joint motion are desirable goals of treatment for pilon fractures,* the belief being that such treatment results in a more rapid return to premorbid lower extremity function, a lower incidence of post-traumatic arthrosis, and a subsequently better functional outcome. However, the ability to achieve these goals is directly related to the severity of the injury and avoidance of iatrogenic complications. Fundamental factors influencing treatment include the presence or absence of shaft extension, the amount of displacement or comminution, the quality of the bone stock, the condition of the soft tissues, the presence or absence of an open fracture, and patient factors.

Treatment options can be divided into nonoperative and surgical methods. The nonoperative methods include closed reduction with immobilization in plaster[6, 16, 37, 92, 130, 133, 148, 169, 213] or traction with early range of motion,[36, 37, 87, 92, 125] generally by way of calcaneal pin placement. Of historical note, various closed and percutaneous procedures for stabilizing these fractures have been devised and discarded throughout the years. These procedures include pins and plaster,[148, 169] intramedullary fixation of the fibula,[107, 161] and percutaneous transarticular fixation with a vertical calcaneal-talar-tibial pin.[31]

Surgical management options include internal fixation, external fixation, or a combination of the two. Internal fixation can be achieved through a classic formal ORIF carried out with a variety of plates and screws,† on a more limited basis with minimal soft tissue stripping,[6, 13, 37, 81, 92, 112, 130, 152] or as a staged procedure.[3, 13, 149, 180] External fixation may be combined with limited internal fixation of the fibula or tibial articular surface.‡

Arthrodesis§ and amputation‖ are salvage procedures that have limited indications in primary fracture treatment. Amputation, however, should be strongly considered in patients with severe soft tissue and bony injury, particularly if associated with ischemia, hypotension, polytrauma, advanced age, or significant neurologic injury[69, 79, 173, 183] (see Fig. 58–30).

## Closed Treatment

Various forms of skeletal traction and immobilization with plaster have been used to treat pilon fractures.[31, 40, 76, 87, 169, 170] Common to these measures is the

---

*See references 3, 6, 13, 16, 18, 24, 25, 28, 39, 51, 59, 78, 80, 88, 92, 96, 104–106, 113, 122, 123, 125, 133, 144, 149, 151, 152, 159, 164–169, 180, 184, 193, 197, 204, 206, 213.

†See references 2, 23, 26, 28, 80, 92, 109, 123, 130, 141, 152, 155, 164–168, 176, 188, 191, 209, 217.

‡See references 3, 6, 9, 13, 15–17, 46, 59, 85, 87, 94, 108, 109, 115, 116, 130, 144, 155, 160, 171, 176, 193, 195–197, 209, 217.

§See references 30, 41, 69, 72, 88, 117, 134–136, 140, 148, 152, 170, 173, 183, 185.

‖See references 20, 69, 70, 76, 79, 131, 148, 152, 173, 178, 183, 190.

reliance on ligamentotaxis to reduce and maintain alignment of the fracture fragments. The strong medial ligaments, when intact, may transmit enough force to stabilize the medial plafond.

However, the lax anterior and posterior capsules are not generally capable of disengaging and reducing their associated fragments.[125] Even when anatomic reduction is achieved, plaster usually fails to maintain the alignment, and late displacement is common because of associated comminution and metaphyseal bone loss.[24, 59] Furthermore, immobilization prevents joint motion, which is important in promoting cartilage nutrition and healing.[132, 172] The end result is often joint stiffness and trophic impairment (osteodystrophy), which further complicate an already difficult rehabilitative course.[24, 76]

Closed treatment is therefore recommended only for nondisplaced fractures, for fractures in debilitated patients, or as a temporary measure to allow for soft tissue healing before definitive surgical management.[17, 80, 112, 124, 170, 193] Undisplaced fractures of the tibial plafond generally do well with either operative or nonoperative treatment.[6, 42, 141, 148, 159] Although it has not been proved that surgical intervention benefits patients with such injuries, we suspect that if fixation can be achieved without excessive risk, earlier motion may be of value.

## Traction

Skeletal traction remains a viable treatment to assist with reduction, particularly in the presence of severe comminution or significantly compromised soft tissues.[41, 87, 121, 144, 169, 176, 209, 213] It may be used as either a temporary or a definitive method of treatment, is easy to apply, allows access to wounds for inspection and care, and permits ankle motion while preventing further shortening or displacement of the fracture fragments. As length is maintained, vascular inflow and outflow are improved because vessels and lymphatics are unkinked. Such unkinking decreases swelling and may promote more rapid healing of the soft tissues. However, severely comminuted and impacted articular fragments that lack capsular attachments will not be reduced by traction across the ankle. Furthermore, traction may open gaps in the impacted metaphysis that will not heal without bone grafting and may lead to shortening or angulation later.

If severe and inoperable disintegration is present, acceptable long-term results may be achieved by traction, especially if it is combined with external fixation.[87, 108] Fifteen to 20 lb of skeletal traction transmitted through a calcaneal pin has been the recommended technique.[125, 170] In patients with an associated calcaneal fracture, a traction pin may be placed into the neck of the talus.

## Surgical Management

The goals of surgical reconstruction of the pilon are to preserve bone and soft tissue viability, perform an anatomic reduction of the articular surface, and provide fixation that is stable enough to allow early range of motion.* Unfortunately, surgical exposure of this difficult fracture is risky because of the associated soft tissue injury.[24, 47, 148, 152, 191, 195, 209, 217] Generally, operative treatment should be considered for open fractures, compartment syndrome, and any fracture with joint space incongruity greater than 2 mm or malalignment greater than 10° in any plane.[92, 166, 217] However, the authors of a recent study found that clinical outcome was adversely affected when malalignment of greater than 5° was present.[209]

Because of soft tissue involvement and variable fracture patterns, preoperative planning is vital. Important details that affect decision making include joint displacement and comminution, metaphyseal comminution, and diaphyseal extension of the fracture. Surgical options include ORIF—either a formal or limited approach—external fixation with a small-wire frame or bridging external fixator (static or articulated), and a combination of external fixation with limited ORIF.

Although each case must be evaluated and treated separately, the following guidelines, with the AO classification system used to define fracture types, are helpful in providing a focused approach to treatment of pilon injuries. However, the surgeon needs to appreciate that the severity of the soft tissue injury cannot be separated from the degree of skeletal involvement but, instead, should be combined to create an overall injury pattern.[209]

*Type B* pilon fractures are partial articular fractures without metaphyseal-diaphyseal dissociation and are usually best treated with low-profile plates and screws (see Figs. 58–7 and 58–19).

*Type C1 and C2* pilon fractures *without* diaphyseal extension can be approached with the use of indirect reduction techniques and low-profile implants (Fig. 58–9; see Figs. 58–22 and 58–23). The use of very thin implants, such as a one-third tubular plate, should be contemplated only in type B fractures or those with good cortical apposition in the area of the metaphysis.

*Type C1 and C2* pilon fractures *with* diaphyseal extension (Fig. 58–10) are essentially pilon fractures with concomitant shaft fractures and may be more suited for hybrid external fixation (see Fig. 58–10C). Fixation of the joint can be performed with standard or cannulated screws through a small arthrotomy (see Fig. 58–10C). An alternative to the external fixator is a precontoured, percutaneously placed plate, which can provide many of the advantages of classic plate fixation while avoiding extensive soft tissue dissection.[13, 81]

*Type C3* pilon fractures are treated according to fragmentation and diaphyseal extension of the fracture and require careful preoperative planning. Optimal operative visualization of anatomic restoration of the joint must be weighed against the risk of further insult to the soft tissues. Type C3 fractures *without* diaphyseal extension can be approached with the use of indirect reduction techniques and low-profile implants (see Fig. 58–24).

*Type C3* fractures *with* diaphyseal extension (Fig. 58–11)

---

*See references 23, 24, 28, 35, 51, 108, 133, 148, 164, 166, 191.

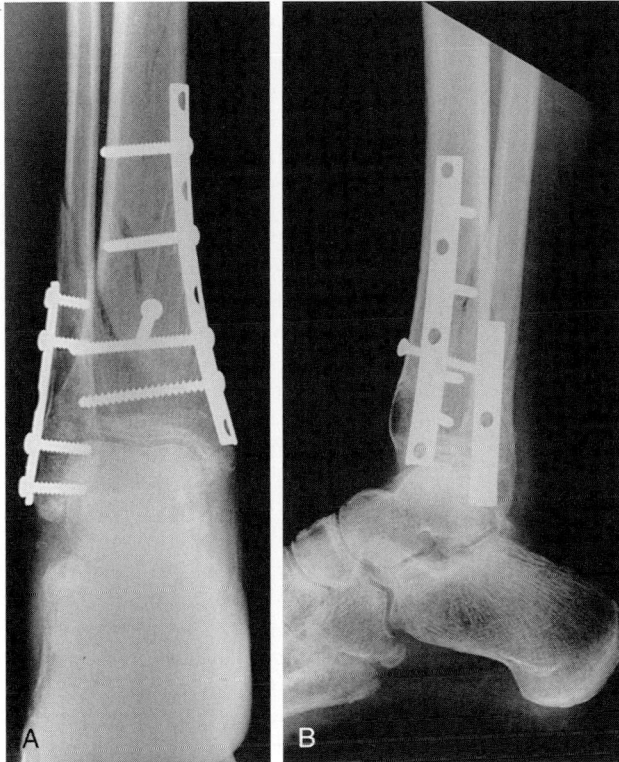

**FIGURE 58–9.** *A, B,* A type C2 pilon fracture was stabilized with a one-third tubular plate and indirect reduction techniques. In this case, plating of the fibula helped reduce the lateral column of the tibia.

fixation (see Fig. 58–11C to E) or percutaneous plate fixation.[13, 81]

*Type C3* fractures with severe comminution (Fig. 58–12; see Fig. 58–32) require a joint-spanning external fixator with or without augmented fixation.

As advocated by Watson and colleagues[209] and others,[13, 42, 50, 59, 149, 180, 196] the soft tissues also play a critical role, and severe soft tissue disruption or contusion may mitigate more for percutaneous techniques such as external fixation, regardless of the fracture pattern. The alternative is a staged treatment protocol to allow time for healing of the soft tissues[13, 50, 149, 180] (see Timing of Surgery and Staged Treatment). French and Tornetta[59] noted that a relative contraindication to hybrid fixation is the presence of a type IIIB open fracture because soft tissue reconstructive efforts are made more difficult by the presence of metaphyseal wires.

An important consideration is whether the fracture is amenable to percutaneous treatment. Ideal fractures for percutaneous treatment include pilon fractures with simple joint patterns (AO type C1 or perhaps C2; see Fig. 58–22) or with minimally displaced articular fragments and diaphyseal extension. Preoperative traction imaging studies or intraoperative fluoroscopic evaluation must demonstrate restoration of the ankle mortise by ligamentotaxis or demonstrate fracture fragments that are amenable to reduction by percutaneously placed clamps or other instruments (see Fig. 58–22D). It is important to realize that fracture fragments may herniate through fascial layers and that soft tissues may be interposed and preclude the use of "ligamentotaxis" to achieve reduction. If ORIF of the joint is not required and metaphyseal bone loss is not significant, percutaneous fixation of the metaphysis with screws can be performed, followed by either a small-wire fixator, bridging external fixator, or percutaneous plate to

are transitional injuries and require anatomic restoration of the joint and neutralization of the tibial shaft fracture. This goal can often best be achieved with combined limited ORIF of the joint and hybrid external

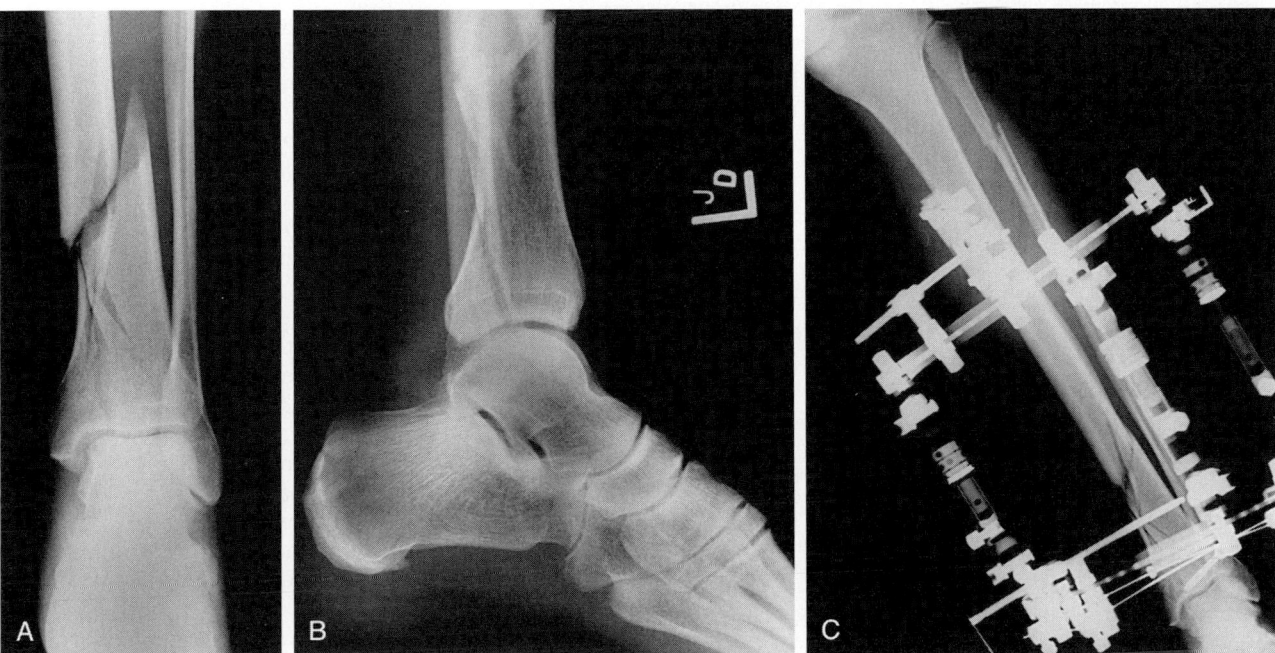

**FIGURE 58–10.** *A, B,* A type C2 pilon fracture with diaphyseal extension. *C,* The articular surface was reduced with a miniarthrotomy ("mini-open" approach) and internal fixation with cannulated screws, followed by neutralization of the shaft to the metaphysis with a hybrid external fixator.

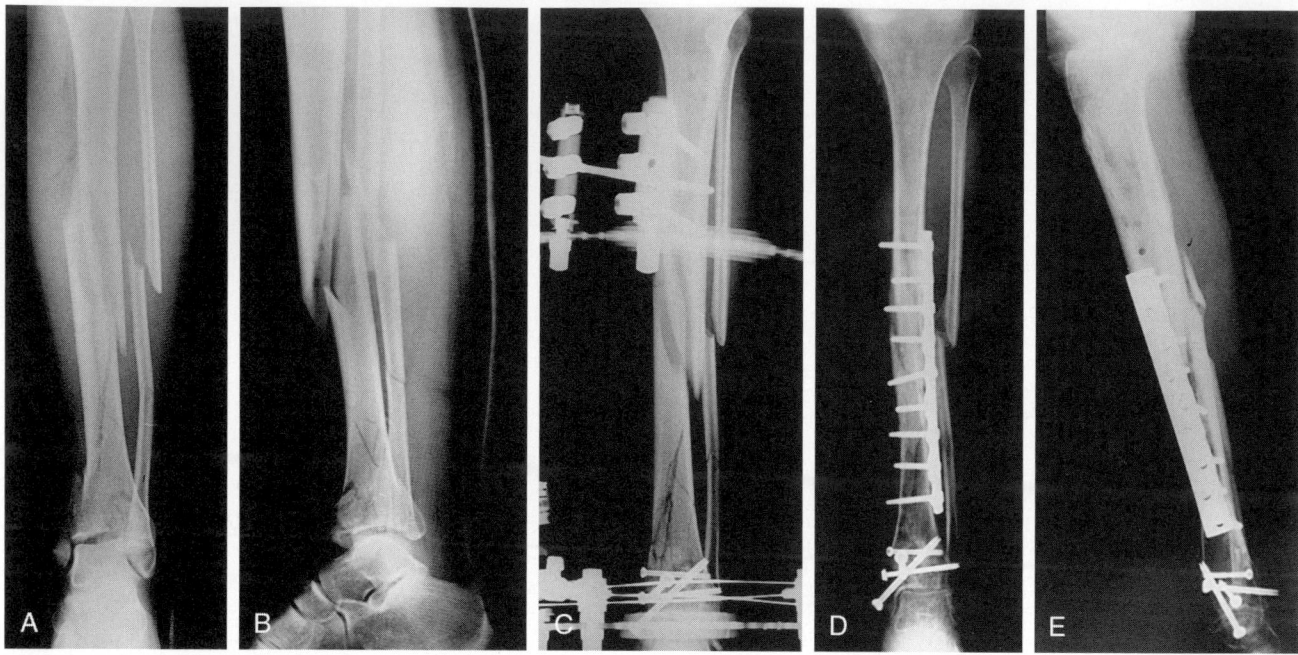

**FIGURE 58–11.** *A, B,* Type C3 fracture with diaphyseal extension. *C,* Limited open reduction and internal fixation restored the joint surface and metaphysis. Next, the shaft was neutralized to the metaphysis with a hybrid external fixator. *D, E,* At 4 months, minimal diaphyseal callus was present. However, the periarticular area had healed, thereby allowing removal of the fixator and rigid fixation of the delayed union of the shaft.

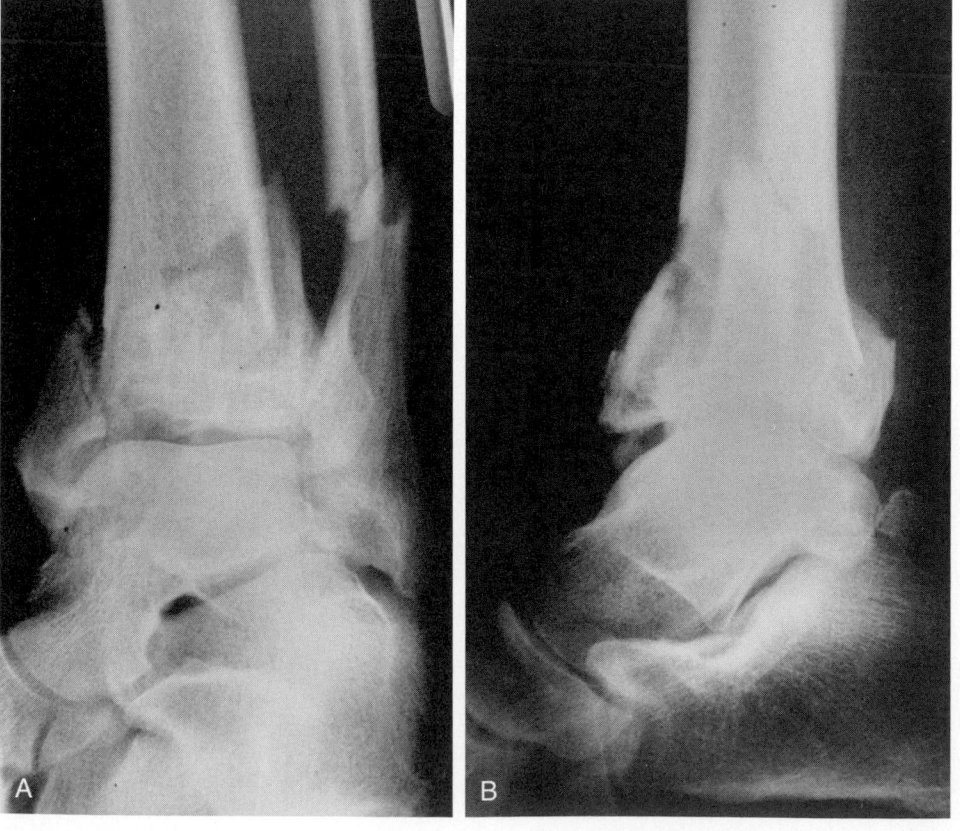

**FIGURE 58–12.** *A, B,* Type C3 pilon fracture with extreme comminution. The fracture is limited to the metaphysis. Stable fixation is difficult to achieve and should be augmented with a joint-spanning external fixator.

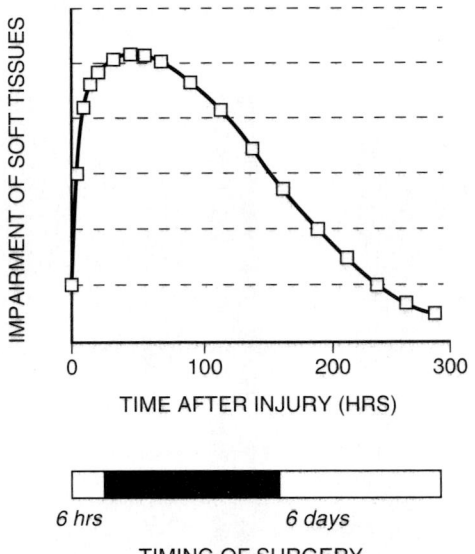

**FIGURE 58–13.** Timing of surgery. Soft tissue conditions as a function of time after injury. Two surgical "windows" may be used—the early period, within 6 hours after injury, and the late period, between 6 and 12 days after the injury. (Redrawn from Trentz, O.; Friedl, H.P. In: Tscherne, H.; Schatzker, J., eds. Major Fractures of the Pilon, the Talus, and the Calcaneus. Heidelberg, Germany, Springer-Verlag, 1993, pp. 59–64.)

stabilize the metaphyseal-diaphyseal junction. Though not universally accepted, arthroscopy may serve as an adjunct in these circumstances.[82, 94]

## Timing of Surgery and Staged Treatment

Because it has a significant effect on the incidence of wound-healing problems, the timing of surgical intervention is critical (Fig. 58–13). It is important to operate when the risk of additional soft tissue compromise is as small as possible. After the injury, the initial swelling is due to the fracture hematoma and the effect of shortening on the extremity.[125] After 8 to 12 hours, swelling is primarily due to interstitial edema, which increases the likelihood of postoperative wound problems.[80, 121, 125, 170] This edema is perhaps the single most important factor to control for successful wound healing.[13, 109, 149, 180]

Fracture blisters are common and can occur as early as 6 to 8 hours after injury[17] (Fig. 58–14). Varela and associates[204] reported an incidence of 29.4% with pilon fractures, which was higher than at any other area that they studied. Two types of fracture blisters may develop: those filled with clear fluid and those with bloody fluid. The former represents a partial and the later a complete separation of the epidermis from the dermis. Giordano and Koval[65] noted that all seven complications in a series of 53 cases involved only blood-filled blisters and concluded that incisions should not be placed through this type of blister until it has reepithelialized. Once the blister has ruptured, reepithelialization may take from 4 to 21 days (average of 16 days).[65, 204]

Marked edema, skin blistering, deep abrasions, and contusions of skin, subcutaneous fat, and muscle are significant indicators of soft tissue compromise. In addi-

tion, a broad transitional zone may exist in patients with severe fractures, so the soft tissue injury can extend far from the fracture site.[109] Evidence of soft tissue swelling or injury suggests the need to delay an open approach for a pilon fracture (open fractures and those with a developing compartment syndrome require urgent surgery to deal with these emergency conditions). It is important to remember that even when the leg is appropriately elevated and immobilized, a degree of progressive soft tissue ischemia usually develops after severe distal lower extremity injuries. Although maximal ischemia can exist as early as the initial 24 hours, it may progress over the first 3 to 6 days[76, 126, 198, 199] (see Fig. 58–13). If a surgical approach through the compromised soft tissue envelope is initiated during this high-risk period, a disastrous outcome is all too common.[112, 121, 126, 130, 170, 191, 217] Responding to such concerns, Kim and associates[94] used primarily percutaneous fixation and arthroscopy when operating on closed pilon fractures at an average of 5.3 days after injury; they did not encounter any soft tissue complications. Therefore, if percutaneous techniques are applicable, the timing of surgery is less critical.

In general, however, operative intervention should be deferred until the soft tissues have healed and the swelling has started to subside, usually a period of 7 to 14 days, but ranging from 5 days to 7 weeks.* This improved status is generally heralded by the reappearance of normal skin creases and the absence of a shiny appearance of the skin. With delay beyond 3 weeks, the onset of granulation tissue, organization of the hematoma, and development of disuse osteoporosis and bone resorption at the fracture site make the operation more technically difficult, jeopardize the vitality of articular cartilage, and reduce the probability of achieving an anatomic reduction.[56, 76, 126]

Because of the considerable risk of soft tissue complications when performing formal surgical approaches in the acute period, we and other authors[13, 50, 149, 180] prefer a staged protocol (see Fig. 58–14). The initial procedure is typically performed within 24 hours of injury. If the lateral soft tissues permit, routine fibular stabilization is carried out, followed by placement of a bridging fixator (see Joint-Spanning Frames). Although many configurations are possible, the simplest is easily achieved with two pins in the tibia and a transfixion pin through the tuberosity of the calcaneus. The bridging external fixator maintains proper length and axial alignment while immobilizing the limb and protecting the soft tissues from further injury. After the initial procedure, the patient is discharged if applicable and returns to the office at weekly intervals. Once the edema has resolved, the patient returns to the operating room for the second stage of the procedure, typically a formal ORIF. Additional theoretical advantages of such a protocol include reducing the length of hospitalization and decreasing cost. A caveat to the use of a staged protocol is that pilon fractures are an incredibly diverse group of injuries that require individualized treatment. Strict adherence to a single methodology will not routinely accomplish the same desired outcome in all cases.

*See references 3, 9, 13, 17, 21, 27, 28, 35, 46, 50, 80, 83, 85, 88, 112, 144, 149, 165, 166, 170, 175, 180, 193, 195, 200.

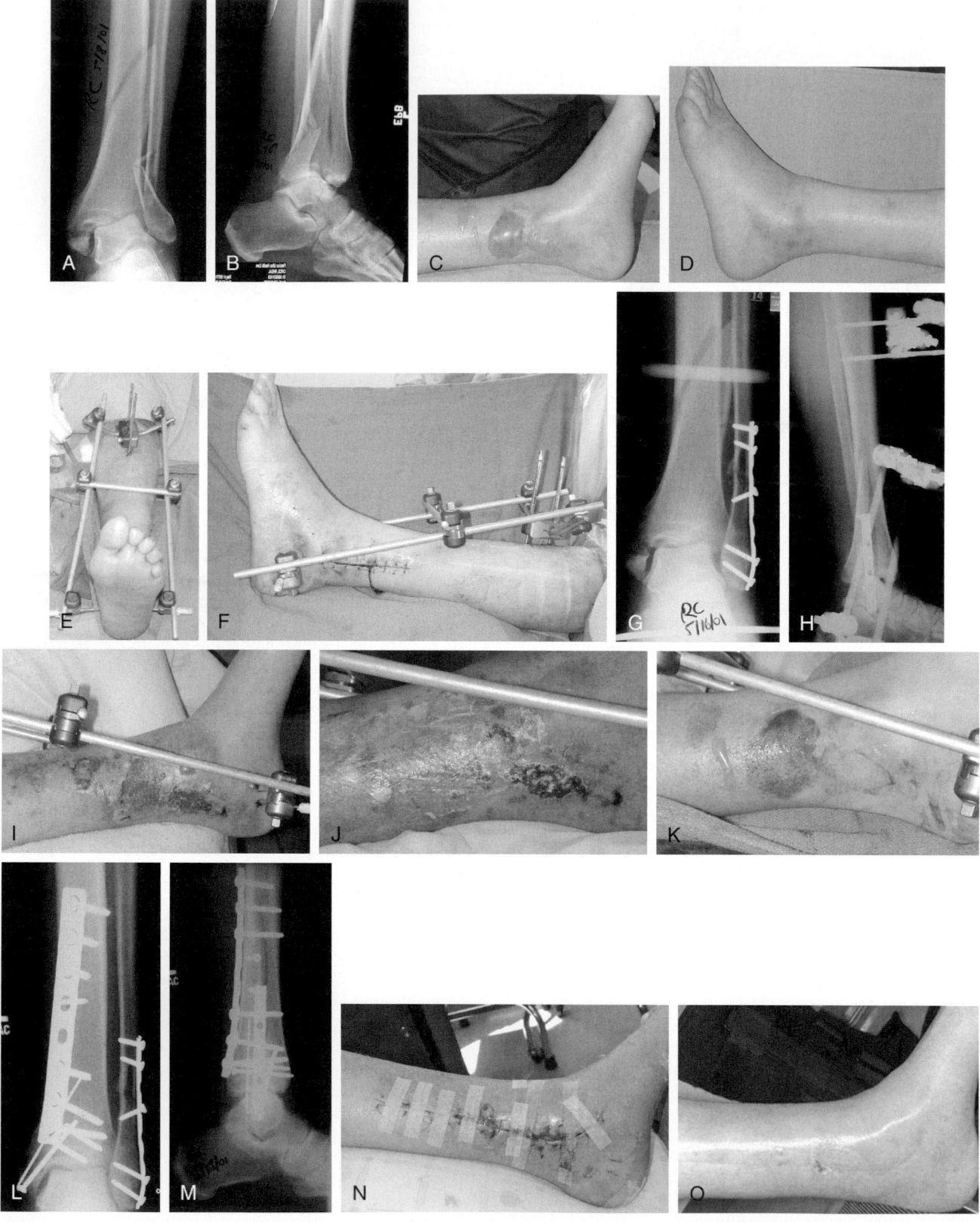

**FIGURE 58–14.** Staged protocol for reconstruction. A healthy active 69-year-old man sustained this type B3 fracture with significant diaphyseal extension and displacement when falling 8 ft off a ladder. *A, B,* Anteroposterior and lateral radiographs. *C,* Medial clinical view within 8 hours of injury demonstrating rapid formation of a fracture blister with edema. *D,* Lateral clinical view. *E–H,* Placement of a spanning external fixator has partially reduced the fracture by ligamentotaxis. *I,* Medial view at 1 week demonstrating soft tissue compromise/edema. *J,* Medial view at 2 weeks demonstrating resolving edema. *K,* Medial view at 3 weeks demonstrating healing soft tissues and reduction of the edema. *L, M,* Reconstruction of the fracture at 3 weeks. Although a 4.5-mm low-contact dynamic compression plate (DCP) was used, a 3.5-mm DCP or lower-profile implant could have been considered. *N,* Postoperative · marginal necrosis still developed within 1 week of open reduction and internal fixation, thus highlighting both the importance of a delay before operative fixation and the difficulty in dealing with the tenuous soft tissues in this area. *O,* The marginal necrosis resolved with simple local wound care.

Another potential concern of the staged protocol is inclusion of the fixator and pins in the operative field. However, at the time of the secondary procedure, several authors[46, 180] have removed the fixator, cleansed the pins in the operative field, and replaced the resterilized fixator without encountering an increased rate of infection. Although this method is probably optimal, in some cases it may be desirable to retain the entire fixator apparatus. Watson and associates[210] evaluated a standardized surgical cleansing protocol for in situ fixators in 96 patients (55% initially had an open fracture) undergoing 108 secondary procedures (ORIF, bone grafting, wound coverage). At the time of the secondary procedure, 21% had some evidence of mild pin tract infection, but none had purulent drainage. Their protocol consisted of initially cleansing the entire limb and fixator pins with 95% isopropyl alcohol. The external fixator was then cleansed with a routine aqueous povidone-iodine (Betadine) scrub solution for 6 minutes, followed by similar preparation for the limb. Both the fixator and the extremity were then coated with spray Betadine paint solution and draped into the operative field. A deep postoperative infection developed in only two patients (2.1%), and both initially had type IIIB open fractures. The duration of application of the frame before surgery, the presence of mild pin tract infection (serous drainage, erythematous skin around the pin, or frank loosening), and preoperative cultures were not predictive of postoperative infection.

## Surgical Approach

The standard surgical approach to the tibial pilon region is through a two-incision technique: a posterolateral incision for the fibula and an anteromedial incision for the tibia.[141, 166] A pneumatic tourniquet is used but inflated only if bleeding interferes with visualization during reduction of the articular surface. Ischemia time should be kept to less than 1 hour whenever possible.[109, 191, 195]

Fractures of the fibula are best approached through a straight posterolateral skin incision. By placing the incision anterior to the peroneal tendons but near the posterior border of the fibula, delayed wound closure may be performed without risking exposure of either the implants or the tendons.[193, 199] Proximally, one must be wary of the superficial peroneal nerve because it pierces the lateral intermuscular septum and crosses the incision in an anterior direction. The posterolateral incision should also provide an adequate anterior soft tissue bridge for the anteromedial incision to approach the tibia (Fig. 58–15). Although some investigators have accepted a bridge as small as 5 cm[109, 180] and others have required one as large as 12 cm, a minimum of 7 to 8 cm has generally been advised to prevent skin sloughing.[17, 21, 50, 80, 109, 125, 141, 193, 198]

The classic AO anteromedial incision begins proximally, 5 to 10 mm lateral to the anterior tibial crest, crosses over the tibialis anterior muscle belly, and curves medially distal to the medial malleolus[17, 80, 125, 141] (see Fig. 58–15). Increasingly popular is a straighter and more extensile modified medial incision that follows the medial border of the tibialis anterior tendon distally toward the talona-

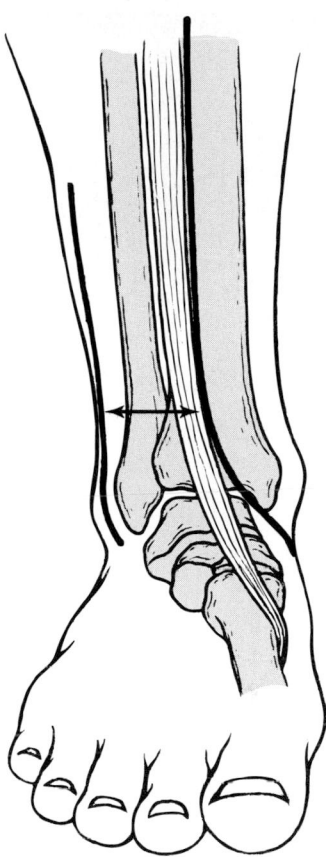

**FIGURE 58–15.** Placement of skin incisions. A minimum of a 7-cm skin bridge must be maintained between the medial and the lateral skin incisions to avoid flap devascularization and necrosis. (Redrawn from Müller, M.E.; et al. Manual of Internal Fixation, 2nd ed. New York, Springer-Verlag, 1979.)

vicular joint.[21, 121, 149, 180] Full-thickness flaps must be created and retracted with minimal trauma to the skin edges. The paratenon of the tibialis anterior tendon should not be violated because it, unlike the tendon itself, will accept a skin graft should soft tissue problems arise.[67, 121, 125, 170, 180] The deep portion of the dissection is made in a transretinacular fashion distally and is extended at the level of the joint capsule as far laterally as necessary up to the tubercle of Chaput.[121, 149]

A limited open approach is most appropriate for nondisplaced fractures and for a joint surface with major fragments that become reduced after the application of distraction (see Fig. 58–10; see also Figs. 58–22 and 58–27). Also advantageous with the limited approach is that the incision can be tailored to the fracture by positioning it anteromedially or anterolaterally over the major fracture line as seen on a CT scan.[9, 46, 59, 155, 194, 195] In this way, optimal exposure can be achieved while reducing the risk of soft tissue complications and thereby improving the likelihood of good results. The anterolateral incision (interval between the extensor digitorum communis and peroneus tertius) has been recommended by Tornetta and Gorup[194] when considering a limited open approach to fractures with more laterally based primary fracture lines ("fracture angle" <90°). On CT, the "fracture angle" is defined as the angle between a line drawn across the tibiofibular axis and a line oriented from the center of the joint to the anterior cortical exit of the primary fracture line (angles >90° indicate a medial exit). The main limitation of the anterolateral incision is that it precludes making an additional incision over the fibula.

Other approaches are also at the disposal of the surgeon. The classic posterolateral approach to the ankle has been reported to have some utility for select pilon fractures.[97] A posteromedial-anterior approach, in which a posteromedial incision is carried under the medial malleolus and anteriorly, has been reported to provide excellent exposure of the anterior, medial, and posterior aspects of the ankle joint with a clear view of the articular surface and minimal soft tissue complications[91] (see Fig. 58–14; see also Fig. 58–18).

## TECHNIQUE OF ORIF

It was Ruëdi and Allgöwer[166] who first proposed four sequential principles as a guide for successful surgical reconstruction of a pilon fracture (Fig. 58–16). With some modification in terminology, these principles can be referred to as follows: (1) restoration of length of the extremity, (2) reconstruction of the metaphyseal shell, (3) bone grafting, and (4) reattachment of the metaphysis to the diaphysis. A fifth principal, achieved by strict adherence to the previous four steps, is early postoperative range of motion while maintaining alignment.

Waddell[207] described these steps in greater detail: (1) restoration of fibular length, (2) anterior ankle

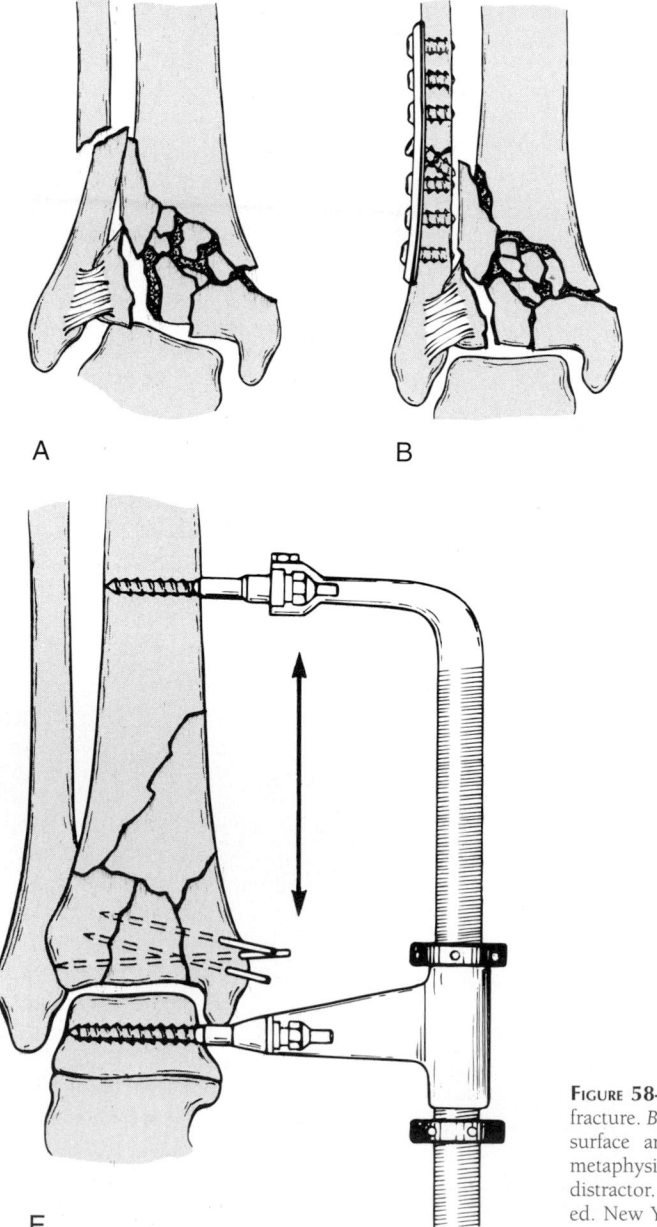
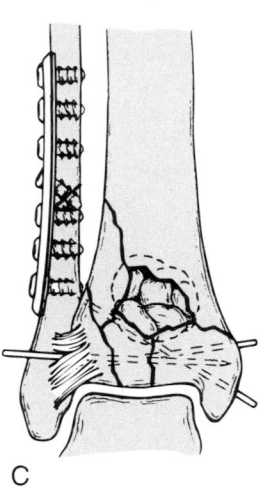
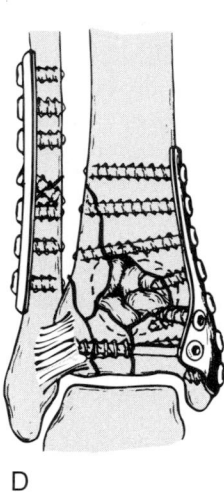

**A**    **B**    **C**    **D**

**E**

**Figure 58–16.** Surgical technique. Principles of fracture management. *A,* The initial fracture. *B,* Restoration of length and fibular fixation. *C,* Reconstruction of the articular surface and bone grafting of the metaphyseal defect. *D,* Reattachment of the metaphysis to the diaphysis. *E,* Alternative means of restoring length with the AO distractor. (*A–D,* Redrawn from Müller, M.E.; et al. Manual of Internal Fixation, 2nd ed. New York, Springer-Verlag, 1979. *E,* Redrawn from Mast, J.; et al. Planning and Reduction Technique in Fracture Surgery. New York, Springer-Verlag, 1989.)

arthrotomy, (3) external fixation for ankle joint distraction, (4) restoration of the lateral articular and metaphyseal fragments, (5) restoration of the central fragment, (6) supporting bone graft, (7) restoration of the medial pillar (column), (8) anterior or medial buttress plating, (9) early motion, and (10) delayed weight bearing.

From radiographs, anteroposterior and lateral tracings of the fracture fragments are prepared and then reassembled to fit the outline of the normal ankle, as advocated by Müller and co-workers[141] and illustrated by Mast and colleagues.[122, 123] After the fracture fragments are sketched in a reduced position, the selected implants are drawn in their expected locations. The sequence of steps to obtain reduction and fixation are also documented to allow the procedure to be broken down into a series of tasks. Each of these steps must then be evaluated and questioned as necessary. Alternatives must be considered for each portion of the procedure.

## Restoration of Length (Step 1)

### FIBULAR FIXATION

In 1956, Rieunau and Gay[161] were the first to recognize that alignment and, potentially, reduction of the tibial articular surface could be achieved by stabilization of the fibula alone. Since then, reduction plus fixation of the fibula has become the classic first step in the treatment of a pilon fracture.* Ruëdi and Allgöwer[168] acknowledged that such was the case in 60% of their fractures; in the other 40%, the tibia was reconstructed first. Yablon and associates[218] demonstrated the fibula's importance in clinical and cadaver studies of bimalleolar ankle fractures. They found that anatomic reduction of the fibula fracture restored stability to the ankle joint by eliminating talar tilt and indirectly reducing the talus and medial malleolar fragment. Tile[193] noted that "failure to reconstruct the fibula at all is a major error in judgment and may jeopardize the tibial reconstruction, as the tendency of the ankle to drift into valgus will be difficult to overcome."

In general, a well-buttressed fibular fracture functioning as a lateral column helps prevent secondary valgus deformity. The distal end of the fibula is usually attached to some of the lateral tibial metaphyseal-articular fragments and talus.[76, 104, 161] Therefore, anatomic reduction plus rigid fixation of the fibula restores the lateral column and often reduces the anterolateral and posterior fragments. Such treatment improves overall limb length, alignment, and stability. In patients with soft tissue compromise, early fixation of the fibula preserves length and allows definitive ORIF of the pilon to be delayed until the soft tissue status has improved.[13, 149, 170, 180, 193]

More recently, the decision to reduce and fix associated fibular fractures has become more controversial.[6, 115, 170, 195, 196, 208, 215] Although reestablishing the relationship of the distal end of the fibula to the ankle mortise is a priority, an inability to anatomically reduce a comminuted fibula fracture interferes with each subsequent stage of reconstruction of the pilon.[21, 121, 141, 166, 215] Failure to restore fibular length will result in valgus alignment of the distal part of the tibia and excessive loading of the lateral articular surface, thereby potentially increasing the risk of degenerative arthritis.[21] Furthermore, rigid stabilization of the fibula with external fixation in the presence of tibial comminution may distract the metaphyseal portion of the tibial fracture and lead to varus collapse, which can result in malunion, delayed union, or nonunion[59, 208, 215] (Fig. 58–17). Late collapse is of particular concern with early removal of an external fixator. A final consideration before proceeding with stabilization of the fibula is that a second incision increases the risk of wound complications and potentially delays healing.[59, 115, 196, 215]

The implant of choice is usually a one-third tubular plate (see Fig. 58–16B) with two or three screws on each side of the fracture.[21, 141] In higher diaphyseal fractures, a 3.5-mm dynamic compression plate can be considered in anticipation of slower fracture healing. Antiglide plate techniques are also an option if applicable. Should the fibula fracture be transverse, a Steinmann pin, Rush rod, or other intramedullary device may be used[9, 149, 193] (see Fig. 58–23). These devices have the added advantage of producing a smaller incision and less soft tissue dissection. Tile[193] has noted that less than perfect rotational stability is acceptable when treating pilon fractures, in contrast to bimalleolar and trimalleolar ankle fractures, in which rotational stability is vital.

### USE OF THE AO DISTRACTOR

In patients with severe tibial shortening, an intact fibula allowing the fracture to tilt into varus, metaphyseal comminution, a segmental fibular fracture, or a comminuted fibular fracture, the application of tibiocalcaneal or tibiotalar distraction may be particularly helpful.† It may be performed with either the AO distractor (see Fig. 58–16E) or a spanning external fixator (see Fig. 58–14; see also Figs. 58–24, 58–26, and 58–28). These devices restore extremity length and alignment by increasing tension on the soft tissue sleeve. If enough soft tissue remains attached to comminuted fragments, ligamentotaxis has the potential to restore joint anatomy. Distraction can also be used to open up the joint space and allow direct inspection of the quality of the reduction.

After a 3.5-mm hole is drilled, a 5.0-mm Schanz pin is placed proximally, perpendicular to the anatomic axis and therefore almost parallel with the distal tibial joint surface. A second pin is placed through the talus or calcaneus.[17, 123, 170] The ideal location for talar pin placement is in the neck, just behind the rim of cartilage that extends medially, just anterior to the medial malleolus, and just proximal to the neurovascular bundle. The hole should be drilled up to but not through the far cortex.[123] Valgus of the foot must be avoided because it may lead to malreduction of the lateral aspect of the plafond.[59]

---

*See references 2, 9, 17, 23, 92, 121–125, 141, 164, 166–168, 193, 217.

†See references 13, 21, 81, 83, 92, 94, 122, 123, 125, 149, 180, 209, 217.

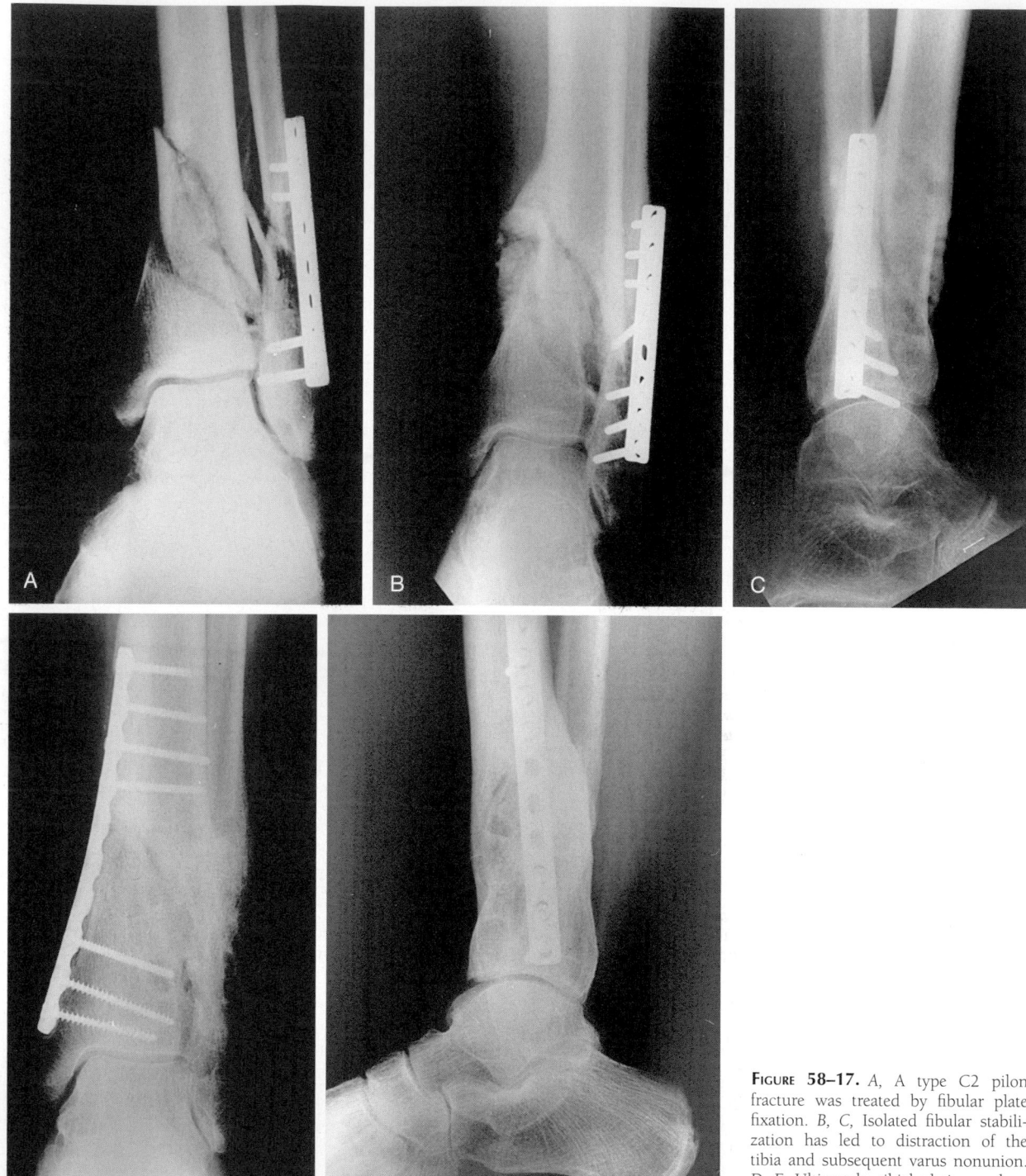

**FIGURE 58–17.** *A,* A type C2 pilon fracture was treated by fibular plate fixation. *B, C,* Isolated fibular stabilization has led to distraction of the tibia and subsequent varus nonunion. *D, E,* Ultimately, tibial plating and an iliac crest bone graft were required to achieve union.

## Reconstruction of the Metaphyseal Shell (Step 2)

After addressing the fibula, contemplating use of the distractor, and exposing the tibia, the surgeon now reconstructs the major fragments of the metaphysis and distal tibial articular surface (see Fig. 58–16C). Despite the wide variety of possible fracture patterns, three major fragments can generally be identified for fixation: the medial malleolus, the anterolateral (Tillaux-Chaput, tubercle of Chaput) fragment, and the posterior lip (Volkmann's triangle) fragment (see Figs. 58–7, 58–8, and 58–16; see also Fig. 58–23). These fragments will vary in size and position, thus necessitating a careful surgical plan, including CT. The anterolateral corner fragment attaches to the fibula by means of the anterior tibiofibular ligament and, if intact, can provide a reference point to the anatomic level of the joint surface. The posterolateral fragment is attached to the lateral malleolus by the posteroinferior tibiofibular and deep transverse ligaments and is generally preferred as the initial template for reconstruction.[125, 141, 149, 175] The fibula and these lateral fragments are used to restore the lateral column of the distal end of the tibia, whereas the large medial malleolar fragment facilitates reduction of the medial column.[175]

In addition to an arthrotomy extended across the front of the tibia with distraction of the joint, the metaphyseal fracture fragments can be opened like a book to expose the impacted articular fragments, which are then reduced to the reconstituted lateral column fragments. Reduction of the anterolateral portion of the plafond can be difficult, particularly if the fracture is being treated on a delayed basis and a medial incision has been used.[59] In these cases, limited exposure over the anteromedial border of the fibula may be necessary. Because a significant amount of soft tissue dissection is required to fit a plate on the lateral surface of the tibia, lag screw fixation of large anterolateral fragments has been recommended.[149]

The articular surface of the talus can serve as a template for reduction of the tibial articular surface, particularly if comminuted.[59, 76, 141, 149, 166, 175, 193] Major fragments are reduced and can usually be held in place with a large bone tenaculum or pelvic reduction forceps. If a small-wire external fixator is planned, the articular reduction can be facilitated by the use of counter-opposed olive-tipped wires as long as the primary fracture line is not in the coronal plane (placement of transfixion wires in an anterior-to-posterior direction is limited by anatomic constraints).[209]

Provisional fixation of the metaphyseal shell and articular surface is of great value. We usually attain such fixation with 1.6-mm Kirschner wires (see Fig. 58–16C). Articular fragments that are too small for Kirschner wire fixation and too large to be discarded may be held in place between cancellous bone graft and the dome of the talus.[193] At this point, both visual inspection and radiographic confirmation of joint reduction are necessary to determine that length and articular congruity have been restored.

It is critical to have a firm understanding of the fracture pattern and optimal visualization of the joint because anteroposterior radiographs tend to primarily characterize the anterior portion of the joint and even substantial posterior defects may not be readily apparent.[49] Therefore, if the articular damage or displacement is primarily posterior, close attention to this area is required during reconstruction, including consideration of additional oblique views.

Precise and adequate screw fixation of the major periarticular fragments is critical. Once adequate reduction has been confirmed, the Kirschner wires are replaced with small-fragment screws (4.0-mm partially threaded cancellous or 3.5-mm cortical lag screws). Whenever possible, interfragmentary compression should be obtained for stability. Figure 58–18 demonstrates a case in which the posterior fragment was not captured by the screws. This shortcoming led to late displacement, which required revision surgery with a plate and screws.

## Bone Grafting of Metaphyseal Defects (Step 3)

Because joint surface fragments have typically been driven up into the softer metaphyseal bone, reconstruction of the articular surface often produces defects in this transitional area between the joint and the shaft. Autologous cancellous bone grafting of these metaphyseal defects is critical and must be done meticulously. Because cancellous bone grafting of metaphyseal defects contributes to the stability of the construct, it is generally recommended at the time of the original procedure—especially when an open reduction is performed.[121, 208, 209] Open fractures with contaminated wounds are contraindications to early grafting. Because of the wide range of soft tissue injuries, variable fracture patterns, and the use of more limited or percutaneous techniques, recent reports have noted the need for primary bone grafting in 12% to 73% of cases when performing ORIF[3, 13, 149, 155, 209, 217] and in 0% to 48% when using external fixation.[3, 9, 94, 155, 209, 217]

Although the iliac crest is considered the gold standard for autologous graft, the proximal tibial metaphysis[46, 76] and distal femoral metaphysis[3] have also served as suitable sources. Other alternatives include cancellous allograft chips[13, 180] or bone substitutes[149] (e.g., coralline hydroxyapatite). Delayed primary grafting may be needed to prevent late angulation of the fracture if delayed union of the metaphyseal-diaphyseal junction is present (see Late Complications).

## Reattachment of the Metaphysis to the Diaphysis (Step 4)

The final step in reconstruction is to reconnect (neutralize) the metaphysis to the diaphysis, usually with a plate applied medially. Medial metaphyseal cortical comminution requires a supportive buttress to prevent varus deformity. Plating techniques, external fixation, or a combination of internal and external fixation can produce such support. Because of the wide spectrum of severity of soft tissue and osseous disruption, no single treatment modality is applicable to all pilon fractures. Therefore, a variety of factors should be considered when selecting the method of metaphyseal-diaphyseal fixation, which must be stable regardless of the technique.

### PLATE FIXATION

Formal open reduction plus plate fixation has been shown to provide good clinical results for properly selected pilon fractures* (see Figs. 58–7 and 58–9; Fig. 58–19; see also Fig. 58–23). Plate fixation is ideal for fractures confined to the metaphysis and fractures in which neutralization of key fragments stabilizes the medial column, provided that the required incision is through tissues healthy enough to heal. Some have recommended that metaphyseal-diaphyseal

---

*See references 6, 17, 23, 24, 28, 92, 120, 124, 125, 148, 149, 164, 166–168, 180, 189, 193.

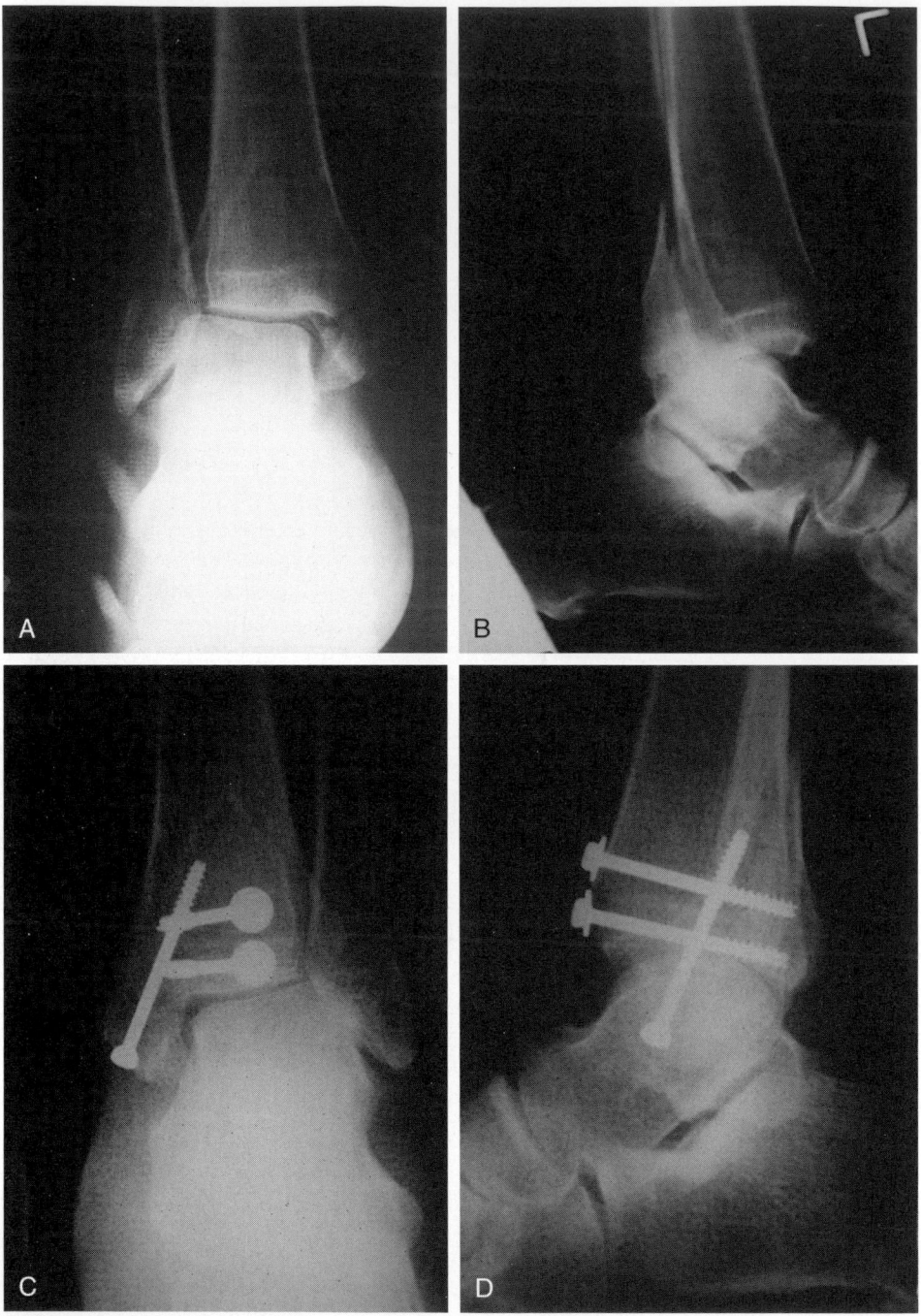

**FIGURE 58–18.** A 50-year-old man sustained a pilon fracture in a motor vehicle accident. *A, B,* Anteroposterior and lateral radiographs of a pilon fracture with posterior fracture dislocation. *C, D,* The patient underwent a miniarthrotomy ("mini-open" approach), reduction, and internal fixation. Loss of fixation became apparent 4 weeks after the initial procedure.

junction fractures be stabilized initially by lag screws before placement of the plate.[149]

The type of plate selected depends on the fracture configuration. A cloverleaf small-fragment plate (Fig. 58–20) or T plate has classically provided excellent fixation, especially for fractures with a short distal main fragment.* If the fracture is in the sagittal plane, these plates may be used as a medial buttress to prevent varus deformity and allow lag screws to be placed in a medial-to-lateral direction across the fracture.[17, 50] Failure to properly contour this plate to the medial cortex typically leads to undesirable valgus angulation.[76] When placed medially, the posterior projection of the cloverleaf plate can easily be removed with a wire cutter to provide a better fit. To facilitate anterior positioning of this plate, the central projection can be removed (Fig. 58–21).

A long fracture zone in a larger patient may be fixed with a 3.5-mm dynamic compression plate contoured to fit the medial aspect of the distal end of the tibia. Because of their extreme bulk, the older spoon plates have no current role in internal fixation of a pilon fracture. In contrast, advanced plating concepts include smaller implants such as one-third or semitubular plates, newer anatomic-specific precontoured plates designed for the distal end of

*See references 3, 17, 21, 50, 76, 109, 123, 141, 180, 193, 217.

the tibia (see Figs. 58–18, 58–22, 58–23, and 58–28), "spring plating" with less soft tissue dissection, and indirect reduction techniques.[3, 21, 122, 123, 125, 149, 180, 209] Especially promising is the use of indirect reduction and application of a percutaneous anatomic-specific, semitubular, or dynamic compression plate contoured to the medial border of the tibia[13, 81] (Fig. 58–22). In this later technique, the plate essentially functions as an "internal external fixator" by achieving metaphyseal-diaphyseal fixation with less soft tissue stripping than required during formal open reduction and plate fixation.

However, these newer implants should in no way give the surgeon carte blanche when it comes to soft tissue considerations. More than ever it has become apparent that the status of the soft tissue, the timing of surgery, and the amount of fracture stripping dictate much of the treatment.[209] Once the soft tissue swelling has resolved enough to contemplate surgery, the fracture pattern should be used to determine the best location for dissection and the length of incision. The surgeon must balance the desire to restore anatomy with the least amount of soft tissue

stripping. Figures 58–23 and 58–24 illustrate the concept of a minimally invasive approach to pilon fractures. The former required an anteromedial approach with anterior and medial plates. The later demonstrates a posteriorly displaced pilon fracture that required a spanning external fixator to reduce the ankle joint. A posteromedial approach was used to apply a small one-third tubular plate and percutaneous anterior-to-posterior lag screws.

For patients with severe medial soft tissue damage, some authors have recommended an anterolateral approach with laterally applied internal fixation.[61, 205] One technique, called *en peigne* ("like a comb"), involves screws placed in a lateral-to-medial direction through a plate applied to the fibula[76, 89, 198] (Fig. 58–25).

## METAPHYSEAL-DIAPHYSEAL EXTERNAL FIXATION

If soft tissue injury or severe comminution precludes ORIF, less invasive techniques such as external fixation should be considered. External fixation of a severe pilon fracture with

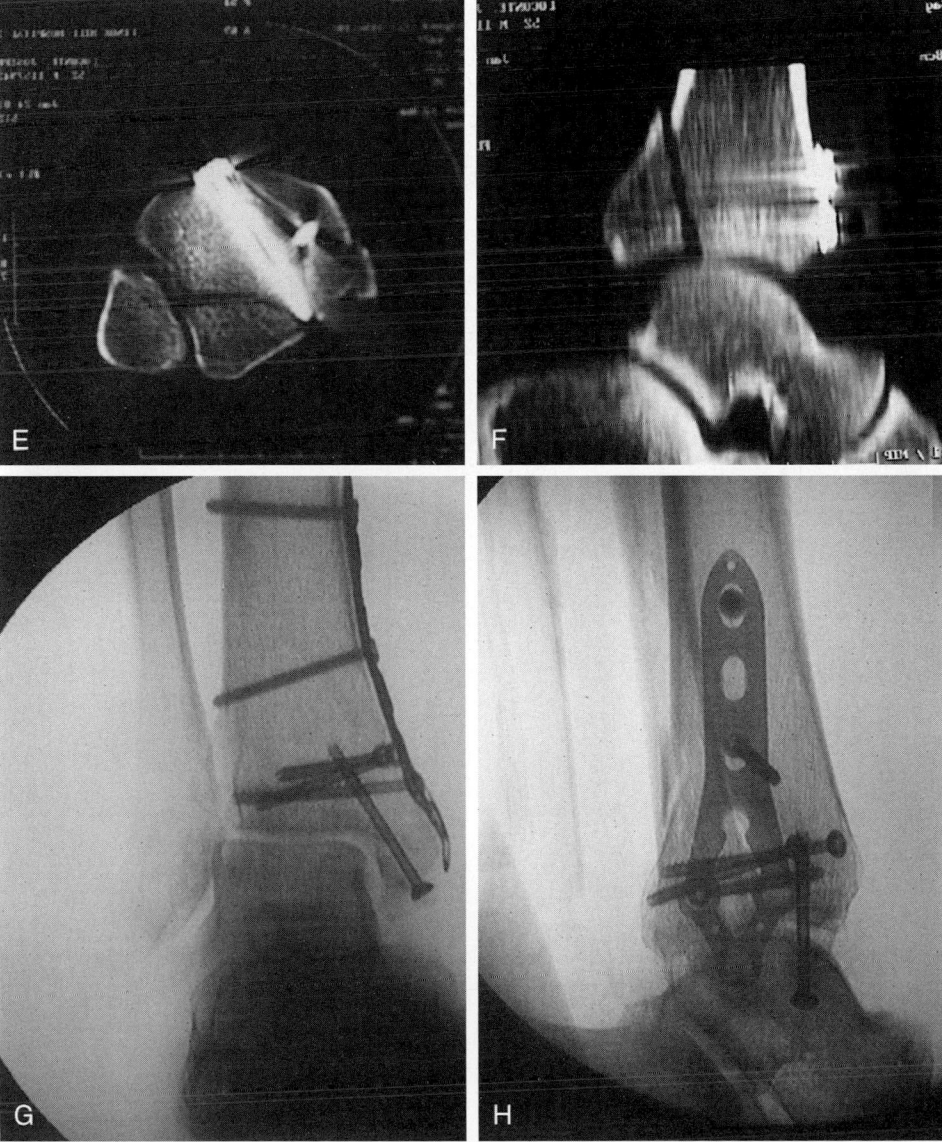

FIGURE 58–18 *Continued. E, F,* Computed tomography reveals that the posterior fragment was not secured by the fixation and redisplacement resulted. *G, H,* Revision open reduction plus internal fixation through a posteromedial approach allowed for stable anatomic fixation with incorporation of the "key" posterior fragment. Note the use of an anatomic-specific (precontoured low-profile) plate. Proper use of percutaneous or "mini-open" techniques necessitates that adequate fixation be obtained and the major fracture fragments of the articular surface be captured. Augmentation with a spanning external fixator may be useful in certain cases.

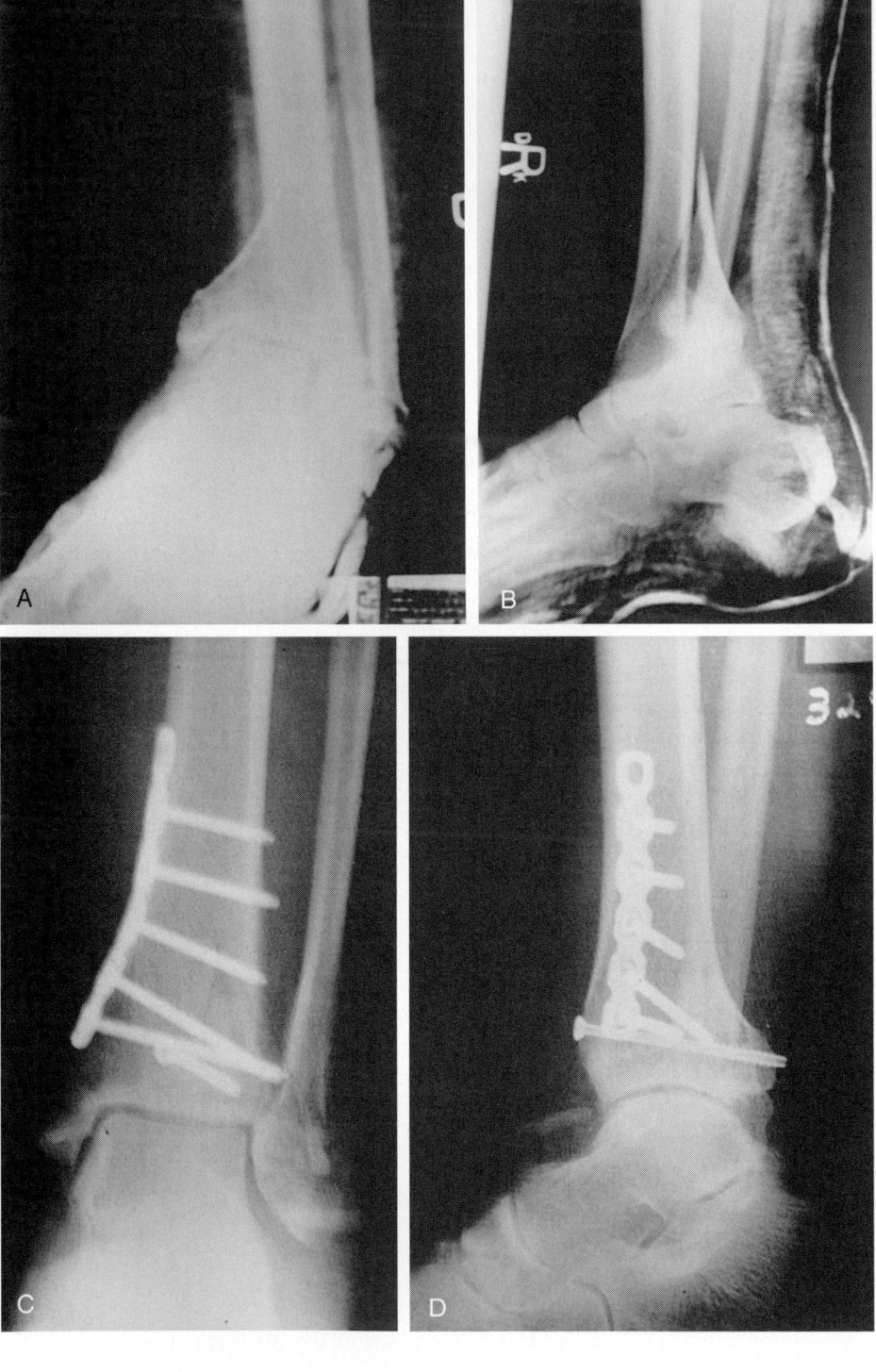

**Figure 58–19.** *A, B,* Type B2 pilon fracture (displaced) with shortening and dislocation of the talus from the anterior portion of the articular surface. The lateral radiograph reveals shortening of the tibia. The talus is displaced with the posterior fragment. *C, D,* Reduction was performed through an anteromedial exposure. Note the use of a reconstruction plate. Proper positioning of the plate allows for a lag effect between the two main fragments, thereby increasing stability.

soft tissue compromise has the capability of producing excellent outcomes.* External fixators are easy to apply, provide excellent stability, and have the ability to achieve indirect reduction of the fracture to restore limb length and proper alignment without soft tissue stripping. Such versatility makes external fixators useful for preoperative maintenance of limb length, intraoperative traction, or part of definitive treatment. They also allow immediate uninhibited access to wounds for inspection, wound care, and soft tissue coverage procedures.

Three basic categories of fixator design are available (Fig. 58–26; also see Figs. 58–10, 58–11, 58–14, and 58–23; Figs. 58–27 and 58–28): the joint-spanning static fixator,† the joint-spanning articulated fixa-

---

*See references 16, 83, 86, 101, 108, 114, 121, 123, 125, 138, 147, 160, 165, 209, 217.

†See references 3, 13, 16, 17, 35, 83, 108, 149, 155, 157, 160, 176, 180, 217.

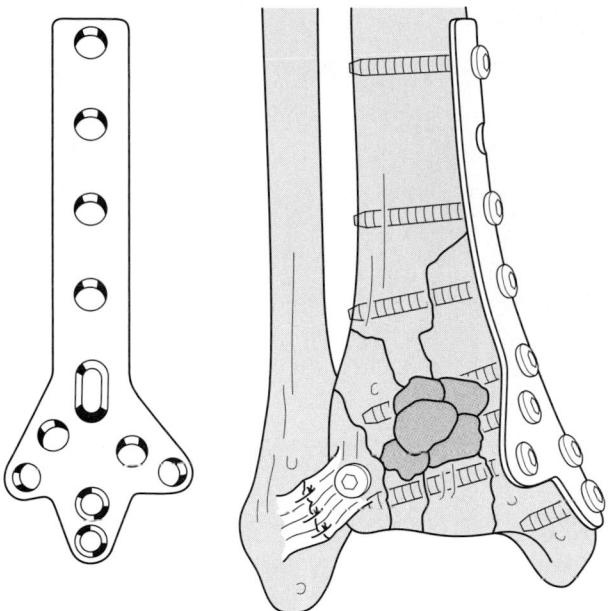

**FIGURE 58–20.** Surgical technique. The cloverleaf plate. (Redrawn from Müller, M.E.; et al. Manual of Internal Fixation, 3rd ed. New York, Springer-Verlag, 1991.)

tor,[15, 46, 55, 115, 116, 171, 197] and the non–joint-spanning (hybrid or Ilizarov type) fixator.* The unique merit of the later is its ability to use acute shortening and bone transport to achieve union and normal length.[86]

The biomechanical profile for the ideal external fixator has not been defined. However, too rigid a system may produce nonunion, delayed union, or disuse porosis by stress shielding, and too flexible a system can result in malunion, nonunion, and problems with the device–bone interface.[29] In general, greater stability is desirable. External fixators are best supplemented with some form of limited internal fixation of the distal end of the tibia.† The fixator, when combined with interfragmentary lag screws, can eliminate the need for a large buttress plate, which lessens the likelihood of skin sloughing, infection, and the necessity for delayed closure. In general, supplementary screws are not recommended for metaphyseal-diaphyseal fixation in combination with an external fixator.[59]

Solitary plate fixation of the fibula,[27, 107, 148, 169] though no longer acceptable, can be a viable form of limited internal fixation when combined with a bridging external fixator.[176, 200]

### Joint-Spanning Frames

Application of a joint-spanning rigid external fixator in the acute setting reduces and stabilizes the metaphyseal and fibular fracture fragments by ligamentotaxis. The immediate benefits are substantial: the fixator increases patient comfort, helps prevent further soft tissue injury, encourages more rapid healing of soft tissues, helps avoid dysfunctional equinus contracture, and permits mobilization of the patient. Furthermore, its presence facilitates radiographic evaluation of the fracture, reconstruction of

---

*See references 3, 9, 60, 86, 94, 121, 144, 155, 156, 195, 196.
†See references 3, 9, 13, 15–17, 46, 59, 87, 109, 115, 116, 130, 144, 155, 156, 160, 171, 176, 195–197, 209, 217.

the articular surface, and incorporation of bone graft. In general, the spanning construct can be maintained for 6 to 10 weeks to allow consolidation of the fracture and then be replaced with plate fixation of the tibia or immobilization in a cast or brace.[13, 17, 165, 217]

Spanning constructs vary and may be tibial-talar,[16, 17, 89] tibial-calcaneal,[3, 8, 13, 16, 89, 121, 149, 209, 217] or a combination of both.‡ Based on the surgeon's preference and the fracture pattern, the fixator configuration can be unilateral, triangular (see Figs. 58–14 and 58–26A; see also Fig. 58–33), circular, or semicircular[114] (see Figs. 58–24 and 58–28) with half pins, transfixion pins, or wires. Certain pitfalls must be avoided.[85] The leg should be brought out to length but not distracted because distraction can create multiple problems, including deformity, neurovascular compromise, and even compartment syndrome. An attractive technique is the use of a posterior semicircular frame, which allows for balanced traction, correction of deformity, and easy access for wound treatment and surgical exposure.

A more simple configuration consists of a triangular frame with 5.0-mm half pins placed in the tibia and a 5.0-mm centrally threaded transfixion pin in the calcaneal tuberosity. This later pin must be carefully inserted well posterior and inferior to avoid injury to the neurovascular bundle. The talar neck will also accept a pin if required. To prevent equinus and provide additional stability, smaller pins may be placed in the first and fifth metatarsals (see Fig. 58–33G to J). Increased frame stiffness is achieved by adding extra sidebars, decreasing the distance of the sidebar or sidebars to the center of the bone, moving half pins out of plane with one another, increasing the separation of pins across fracture fragments, and increasing the number or diameter of the pins.[11, 192] Although

---

‡See references 15, 46, 55, 83, 89, 108, 115, 116, 180, 217.

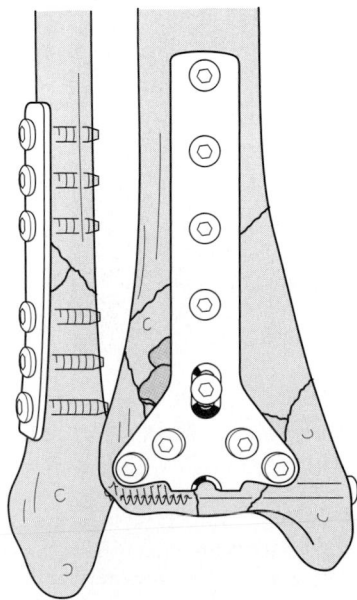

**FIGURE 58–21.** Surgical technique. The modified cloverleaf plate. The distal central flange has been removed to facilitate anterior placement. (Redrawn from Müller, M.E.; et al. Manual of Internal Fixation, 3rd ed. New York, Springer-Verlag, 1991.)

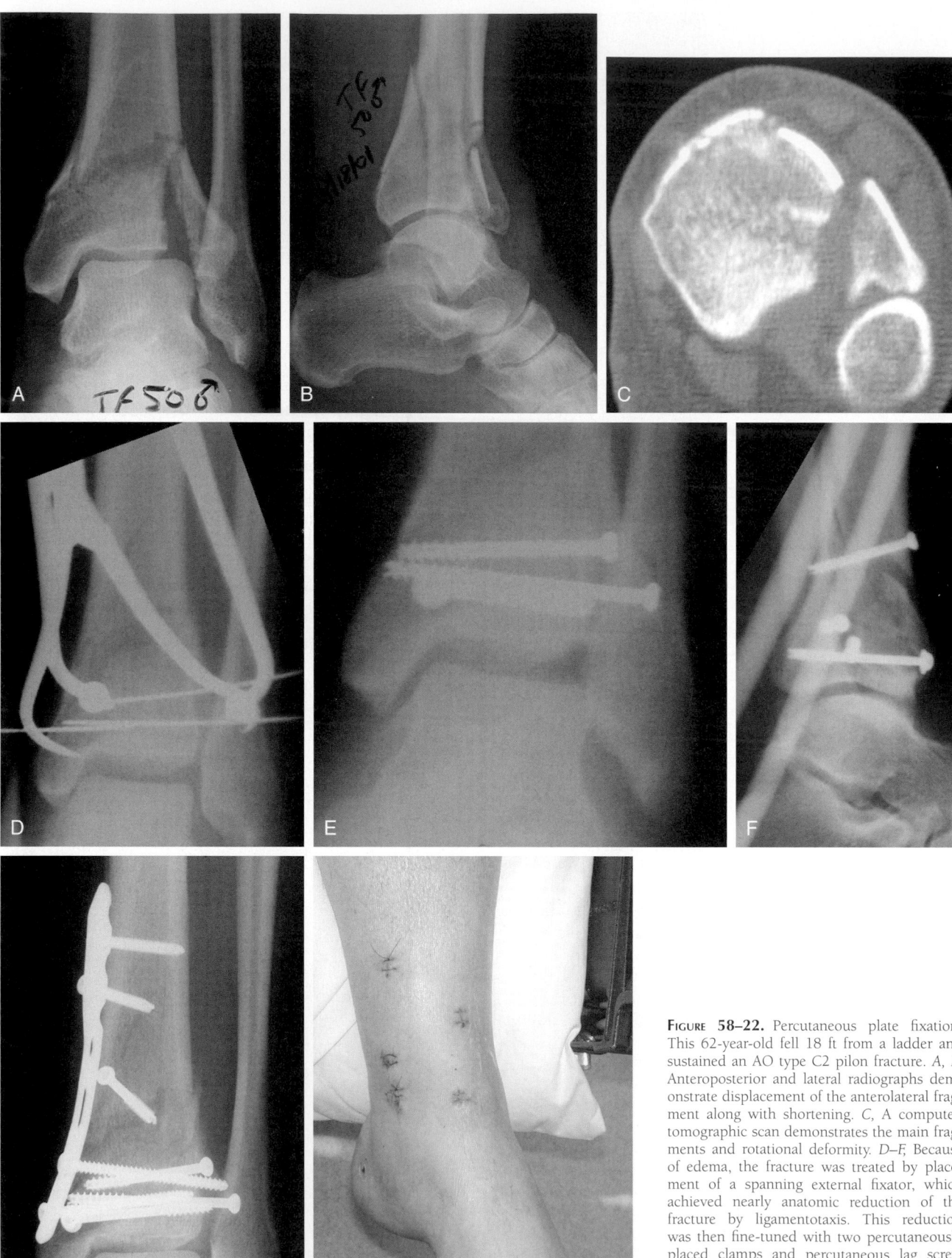

**FIGURE 58–22.** Percutaneous plate fixation. This 62-year-old fell 18 ft from a ladder and sustained an AO type C2 pilon fracture. *A, B,* Anteroposterior and lateral radiographs demonstrate displacement of the anterolateral fragment along with shortening. *C,* A computed tomographic scan demonstrates the main fragments and rotational deformity. *D–F,* Because of edema, the fracture was treated by placement of a spanning external fixator, which achieved nearly anatomic reduction of the fracture by ligamentotaxis. This reduction was then fine-tuned with two percutaneously placed clamps and percutaneous lag screw fixation of the metaphyseal shell. *G,* Two weeks later, the patient returned to the operating room for percutaneous plate fixation of the metaphysis to the diaphysis with an anatomic-specific (precontoured low-profile) plate. *H,* Wounds 1 week after plate fixation.

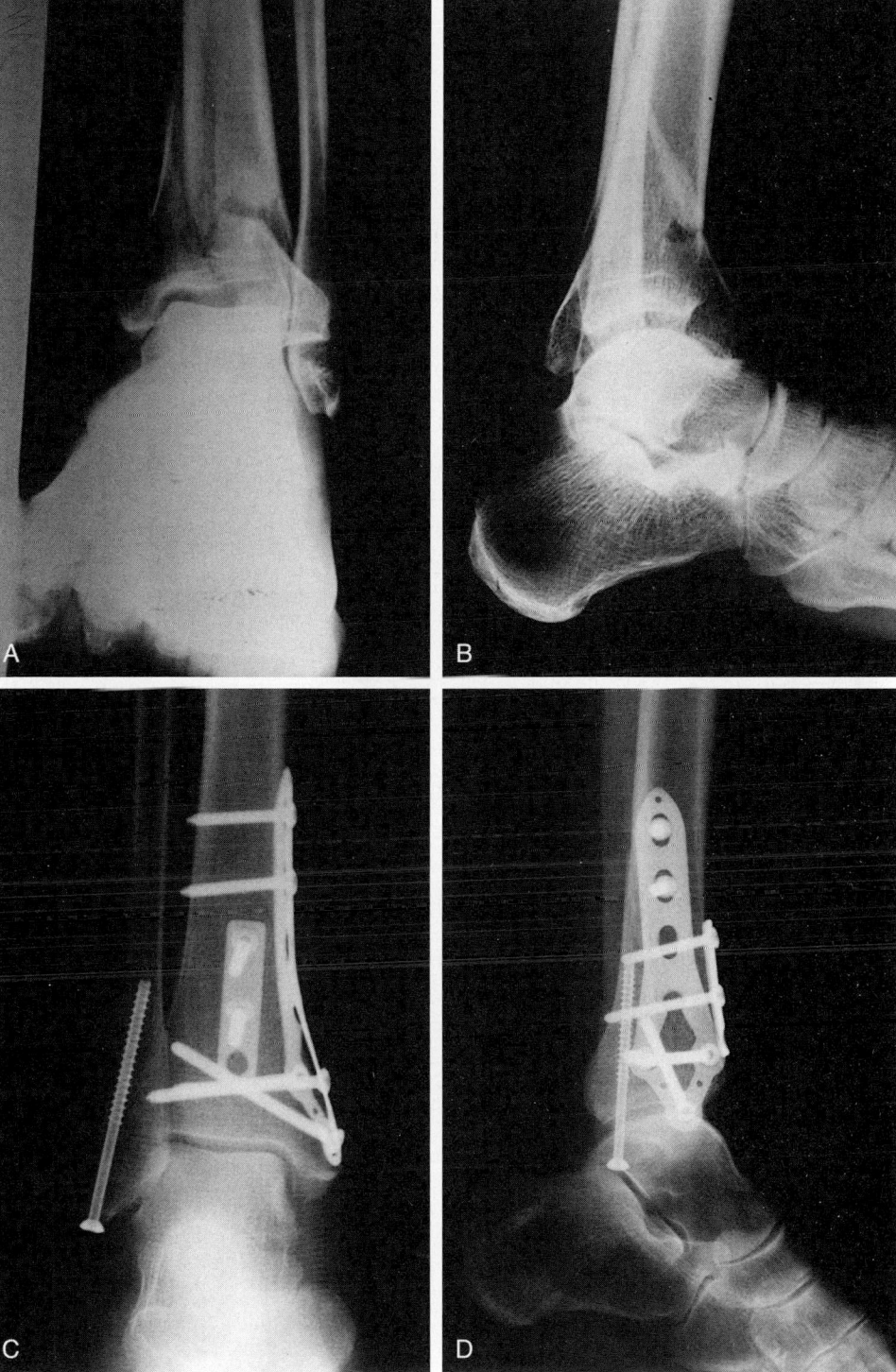

**FIGURE 58–23.** A 62-year-old fell from a height and sustained this AO type C2 pilon fracture, which was splinted for 8 days to allow for resolution of soft tissue edema. *A, B,* Anteroposterior and lateral radiographs show a C2 type pilon fracture with displacement and shortening. *C, D,* Open reduction plus internal fixation (ORIF) was performed through an anteromedial exposure. Note the specialized low-profile medial implant designed specifically for this indication. This case is an ideal indication for ORIF because the major fragments of the epiphysis could be keyed into the metaphysis and comminution did not extend into the diaphysis.

6.0-mm pins can be used, they create a larger stress riser. For example, placement of a 6.0-mm pin in the calcaneus has been shown to create a 22% reduction in compressive load to failure when compared with the intact bone.[90] Therefore, a period of protected weight bearing is recommended after removal of a spanning fixator to allow for healing of the pin defect or defects.

The obvious drawback of spanning the ankle joint is an inability to initiate the early tibiotalar mobilization needed to encourage healing of the articular surface.[172, 202]

Subtalar joint stiffness can also result from prolonged immobilization in a tibial-calcaneal construct. Such concerns were highlighted by Blauth and colleagues,[13] who attributed poor outcomes to immobilization in a spanning external fixator and cast for an average of 60 days. However, at a follow-up of 18 months, Bone and colleagues[16] reported good or better range of motion in 15 of 20 ankles that had been immobilized in a spanning fixator for 10 weeks (range, 6 to 12). They attributed this improvement to their slight distraction of the joint, which

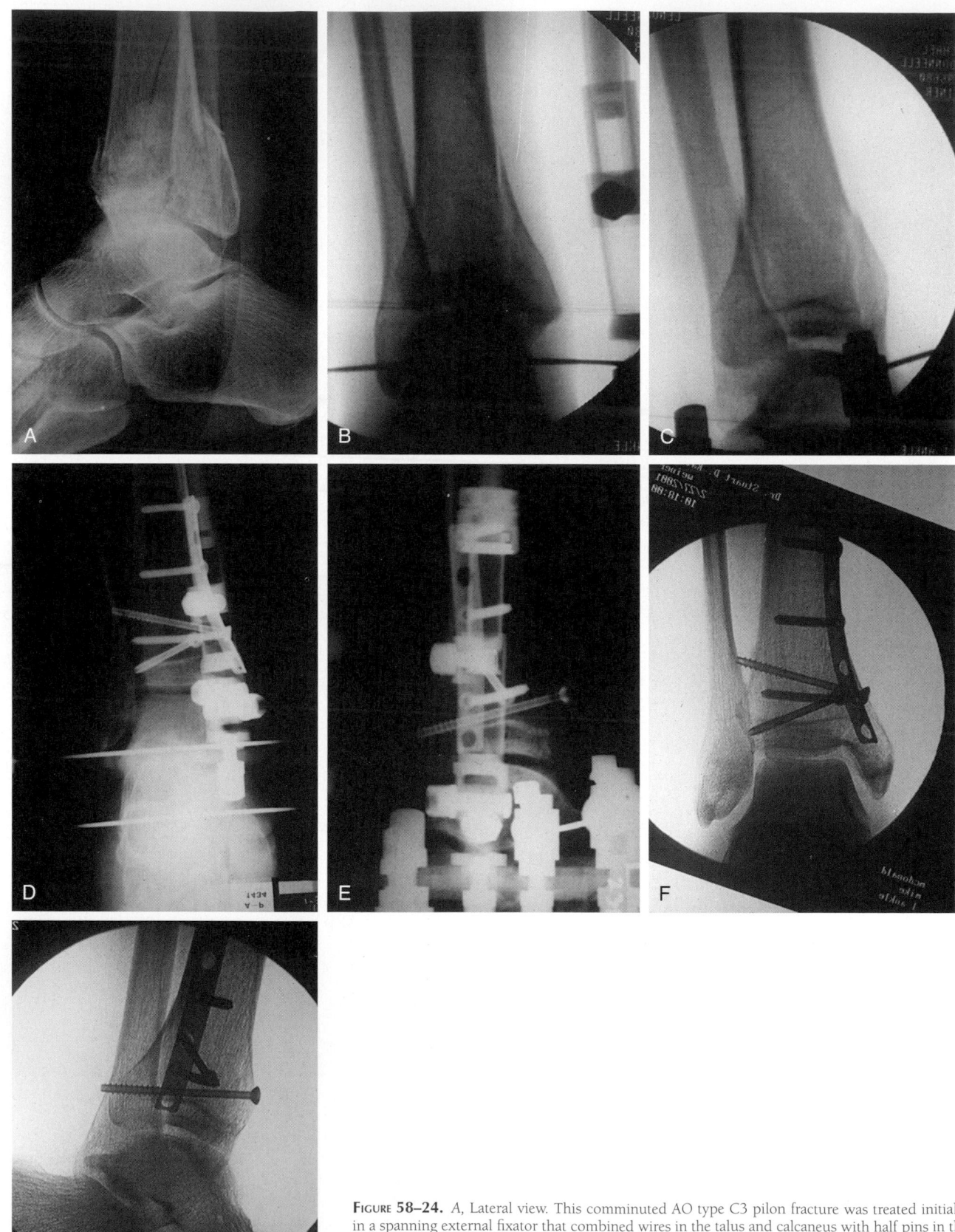

**FIGURE 58–24.** *A,* Lateral view. This comminuted AO type C3 pilon fracture was treated initially in a spanning external fixator that combined wires in the talus and calcaneus with half pins in the tibia. Rings were used on the posterior aspect of the leg. *B, C,* Distraction allows for provisional reduction and healing of the soft tissues. The definitive procedure was performed 11 days later. *D, E,* Postoperative radiographs after open reduction and internal fixation. The fixator was maintained to augment the fixation because it allows for easy wound access and increased stability. *F, G,* After fixator removal, anatomic reduction was maintained.

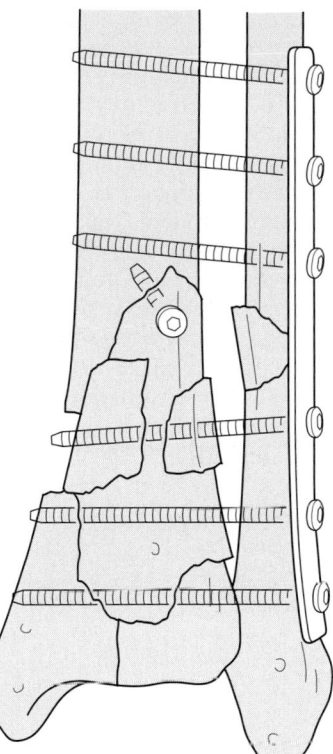

FIGURE 58–25. Surgical technique. The technique known as *en peigne* ("like a comb") is useful in fractures with soft tissue compromise. Tibial fixation is achieved through the fibular plate with screws directed in a lateral-to-medial direction. (Redrawn from Heim, U. The Pilon Tibial Fracture: Classification, Surgical Techniques, Results. Philadelphia, W.B. Saunders, 1995.)

kept the soft tissues stretched. Similarly, Wyrsch and co-workers[217] maintained their spanning construct for an average of 10 weeks (range, 6 to 14) until radiographic evidence of callus was apparent. Although some stiffness was present in all ankles, patients immobilized in the spanning fixator still had better ankle scores than did those treated by ORIF. Other authors have noted an acceptable range of motion after spanning the ankle joint for 6 to 10 weeks.[86, 94, 160, 217] DiChristina and co-workers[46] found that immobilization of the ankle (spanning fixator and cast) for even longer periods of 13 to 22 weeks resulted in an average range of motion of 3.7° dorsiflexion, 24° plantar flexion, 12° inversion, and 7° eversion. Although the issue is unresolved, prolonged immobilization should be avoided if possible.

While providing all the benefits of a bridging external fixator, a hinged (articulated) fixator offers the additional theoretical advantage of early ankle motion. As described by Marsh and colleagues,[115] application of this device begins with placement of distal half pins into the hindfoot. The pins are inserted from the medial side of the ankle into the neck of the talus and tuberosity of the calcaneus under fluoroscopic guidance. These pins determine the alignment of the fixator hinge, so care is taken to ensure that they are placed parallel to the dome of the talus. A template is used to insert the proximal half pins into the medial border of the tibial diaphysis. The fixator is then connected to the pins, the talus is reduced, and the

proximal ball joint is locked. Distraction is applied across the ankle joint with the fixator to facilitate fracture reduction, which is then checked with fluoroscopy.

Any further reduction maneuvers can be performed through open or closed means with the fixator in place. Supplemental internal fixation, fibular fixation, and bone grafting of metaphyseal defects can also be accomplished at this time. Finally, distraction across the ankle is slowly released until a normal joint space is achieved. The articulated hinge is then locked in neutral alignment for the first 1 to 2 weeks to allow soft tissue healing.[55, 115] Once the hinge is opened, the patient can begin passive and active-assisted range-of-motion exercises. In one report, the fixator was usually dynamized between 4 and 12 weeks and removed at an average of 15 weeks (range, 8 to 25)[15]; however, the authors reported removal at approximately 10 to 12 weeks in a more recent study.[115]

At present, although small changes in their design have allowed orientation of the hinge closer to the true ankle joint axis,[55] articulated external fixators do not completely reconstitute normal ankle joint kinematics. Even though the clinical significance of such alterations is unknown, with less than perfect alignment of the fixator, motion through the fracture site rather than the ankle joint can occur and lead to a high rate of pin tract infection and loosening. Even when the articulated hinge was not used, DiChristina and associates[46] reported that articulated external fixators in all seven of their AO type C fractures had to be removed at an average of 8 weeks because of calcaneal pin loosening or infection; draining ceased after pin removal in each case. These authors also noted that the articulated fixator failed to resist persistent anterior subluxation of the ankle joint in two AO type B3 fractures and thus necessitated placement of a vertical calcaneal-talar-tibial pin to maintain reduction of the joint.[31, 46] Nevertheless, the early range of motion allowed with this device may be of some value. Marsh and associates[115] found that at a 30-week follow-up, 30 patients thus treated had achieved on average 8° of dorsiflexion and 28° of plantar flexion as compared with 18° and 36° for the contralateral ankle.

As an alternative to spanning the joint, some authors[17, 121] have used a nonbridging external fixator with 4.0-mm Schanz pins proximally in the diaphysis and distally in the reconstructed articular block. This supplementary buttressing external fixator may be removed at 6 to 8 weeks.

### Small-Wire Frames

Circular frames with skinny wires (Ilizarov) and hybrid fixators have the advantage of not crossing the ankle joint and therefore allowing early motion. They are useful for AO type C1 and C2 fractures with minimally displaced joint surfaces that can be treated percutaneously. In addition, this construct becomes an attractive alternative if diaphyseal extension or significant comminution requires an excessively long plate (see Figs. 58–5, 58–10, 58–11, and 58–24).

Frame stiffness can be maximized by using stainless steel or aluminum rings, using stainless steel wires and pins, increasing the wire diameter and their angle of convergence, using olive-tipped wires, increasing the number of pins and wires at each level of fixation, placing wires above and below the ring, creating a construct with two levels of fixation at the periarticular segment (usually impractical because of the segment's small size), obtaining appropriate tension, decreasing the working length of the wires with smaller-diameter rings or by moving the ring-wire clamps to the inner portion of the ring (if room permits), and adding connecting bars in different planes.*

More important than the material properties of the fixator are host factors. Calhoun and associates[29] have shown that stiffness is more dependent on bone preload (compression at the fracture site, which depends on both the fracture pattern and the reduction) than wire number, wire type, or frame design.[29] Furthermore, the metaphyseal segment must have solid enough bone stock (minimal comminution and bone loss) to provide adequate fixation. If fixation in this region is tenuous or articular damage is severe, an ankle-bridging fixator might be the preferred alternative.[59] Another option is to use hybrid fixation but

*See references 3, 9, 29, 59, 98, 110, 146, 154, 196, 208.

temporarily unload the tenuous periarticular areas by extending the construct across the ankle joint (see Joint Spanning Frames) for approximately 6 to 8 weeks.[86, 94, 144] Kim and colleagues[94] added a hinge to their foot mounting to allow range of motion as early as the third postoperative day. Although this construct ultimately yielded good to excellent ankle range of motion in 74% of their patients and fair to poor motion in only 26%, the former group did not outnumber the later until approximately 9 months.

The small-wire frame is not usually removed until the fracture has healed, somewhere between 8 and 28 weeks (approximately 16 weeks on average).[59, 94, 144, 156, 196, 209] Patients are generally dynamized for 1 to 2 weeks before removal and then wear a walking boot brace for an additional 4 weeks after removal of the fixator.

**Skinny-Wire Technique.** The specifics will differ depending on the system used, but adherence to certain principles is important.[59, 154, 195, 196] Generally, wound closure is performed first to avoid interference by the frame and minimize soft tissue tension around the wires. Application of the metaphyseal ring of the fixator usually

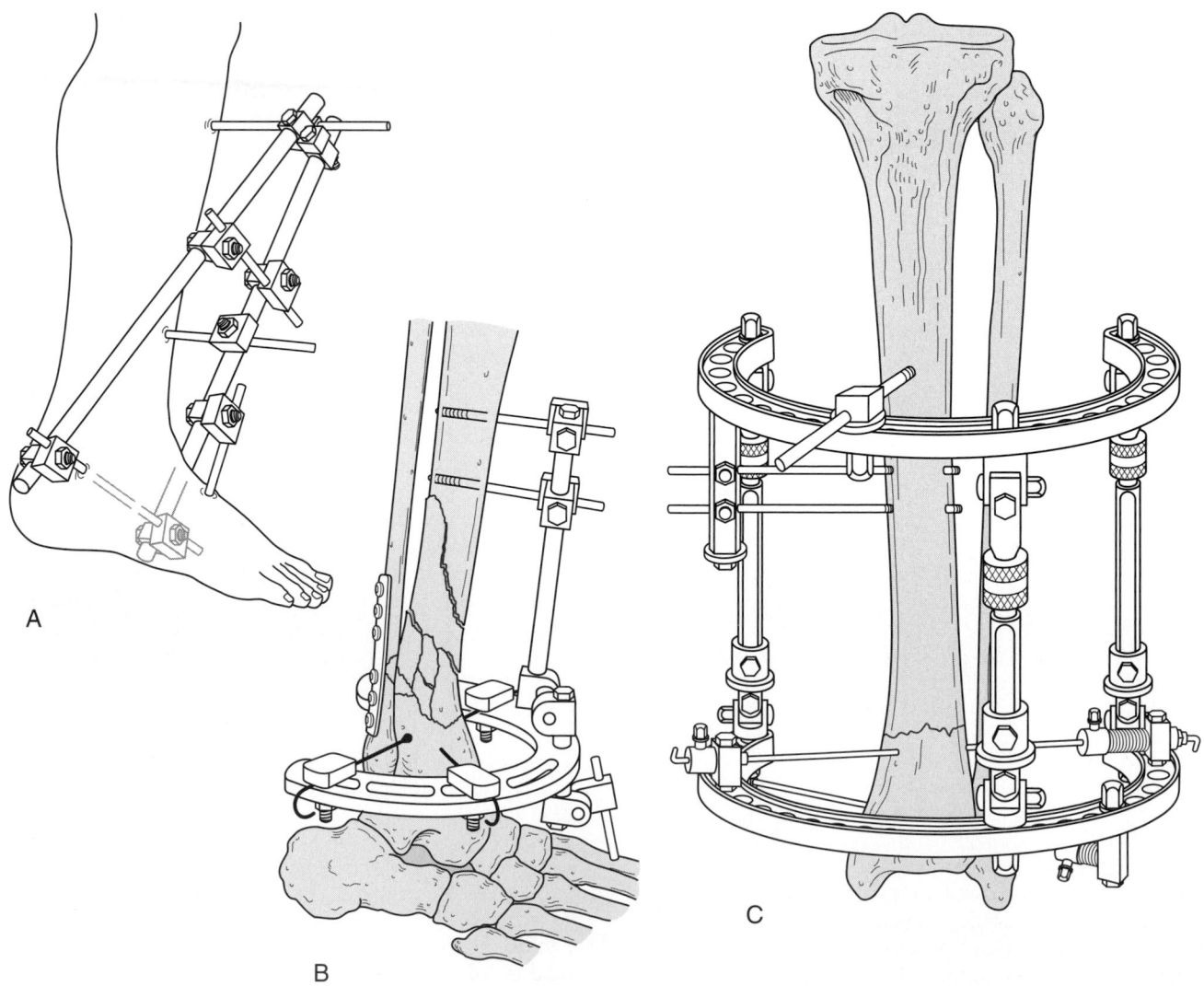

A

B

C

**FIGURE 58–26.**  Surgical technique. *A–C,* Various external fixators. (*A,* Redrawn from Ries, M.D.; Meinhard, B.P. Clin Orthop 256:215–224, 1990. *B, C,* Redrawn from Heim, U. The Pilon Tibial Fracture: Classification, Surgical Techniques, Results. Philadelphia, W.B. Saunders, 1995.)

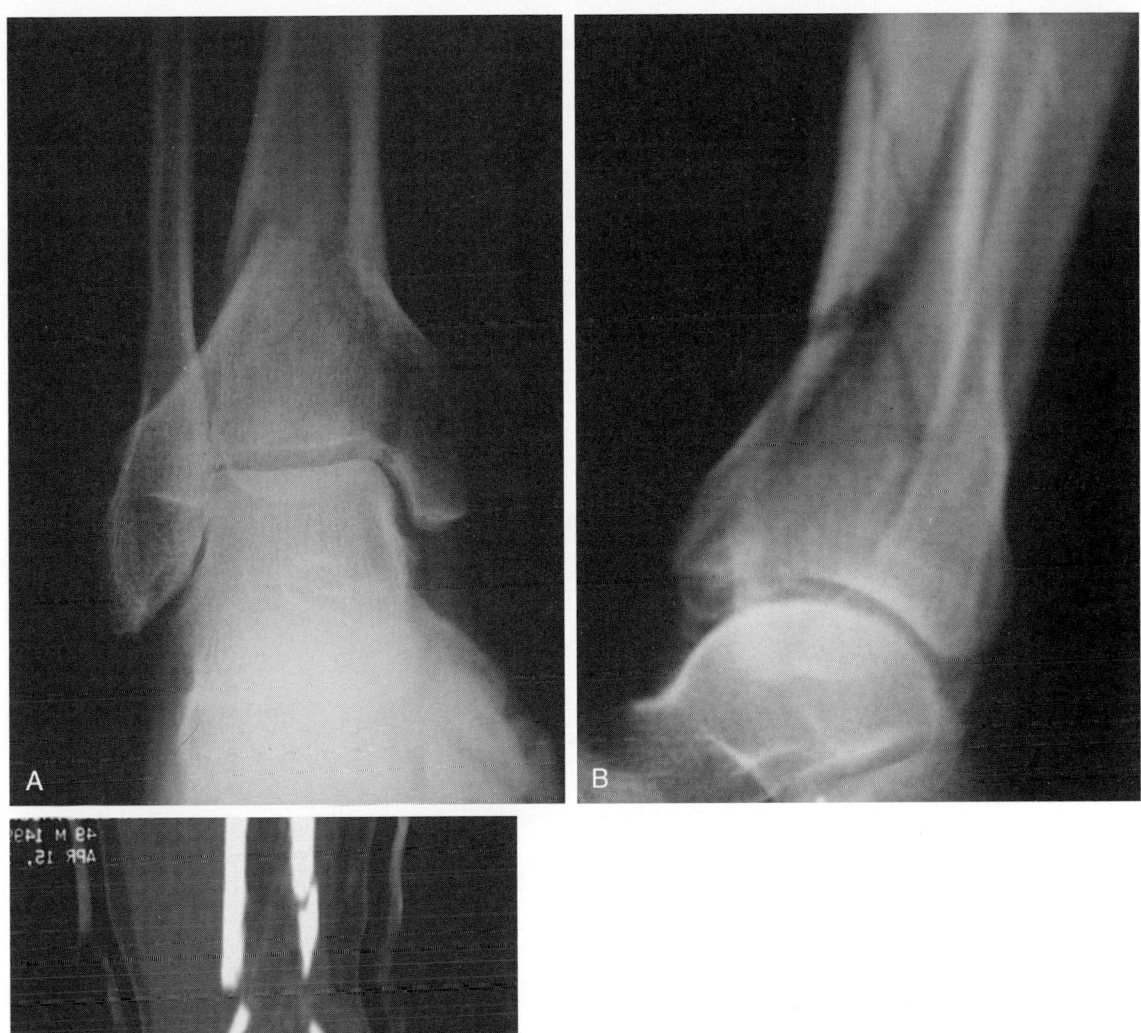

**FIGURE 58–27.** This type C3 pilon fracture was sustained by a 40-year-old man who fell off his bicycle at high speed. *A, B,* Anteroposterior and lateral radiographs reveal a displaced pilon fracture with comminution extending well into the diaphysis. *C,* A computed tomographic scan (coronal reconstruction) shows articular comminution, displacement, and impaction.

*Illustration continued on following page*

begins by inserting a 1.8- or 2.0-mm wire (olive-tipped wires may enhance fixation)[29, 59, 85, 98, 146, 183, 209] in a posterolateral-to-anteromedial direction and exiting medial to the anterior tibial tendon (Fig. 58–29). This wire can be inserted through the fibula and should travel parallel to the plafond and pass either above or below the screws in the reconstructed metaphyseal shell. It should also lie at a distance of at least 5 to 10 mm from the articular surface to minimize the possibility of communicating with the ankle joint. However, although this limit tends to define the fairly regular proximal extent of the

joint capsule, proximal extension of an isolated synovial pocket in the tibiofibular recess varies from 9 to 15 mm (up to 20 mm in the sagittal plane).[143] Therefore, intra-articular placement of wires may be more frequent than thought. After exiting the bone, each wire is tapped through the soft tissues with a mallet to minimize damage to neurovascular structures and limit cortical thermal necrosis. Care must also be taken to avoid skewering the tendons of the tibialis anterior or toe extensors, which can be checked by flexing the toes and ankle.

A semicircular ring is connected to the first wire, which

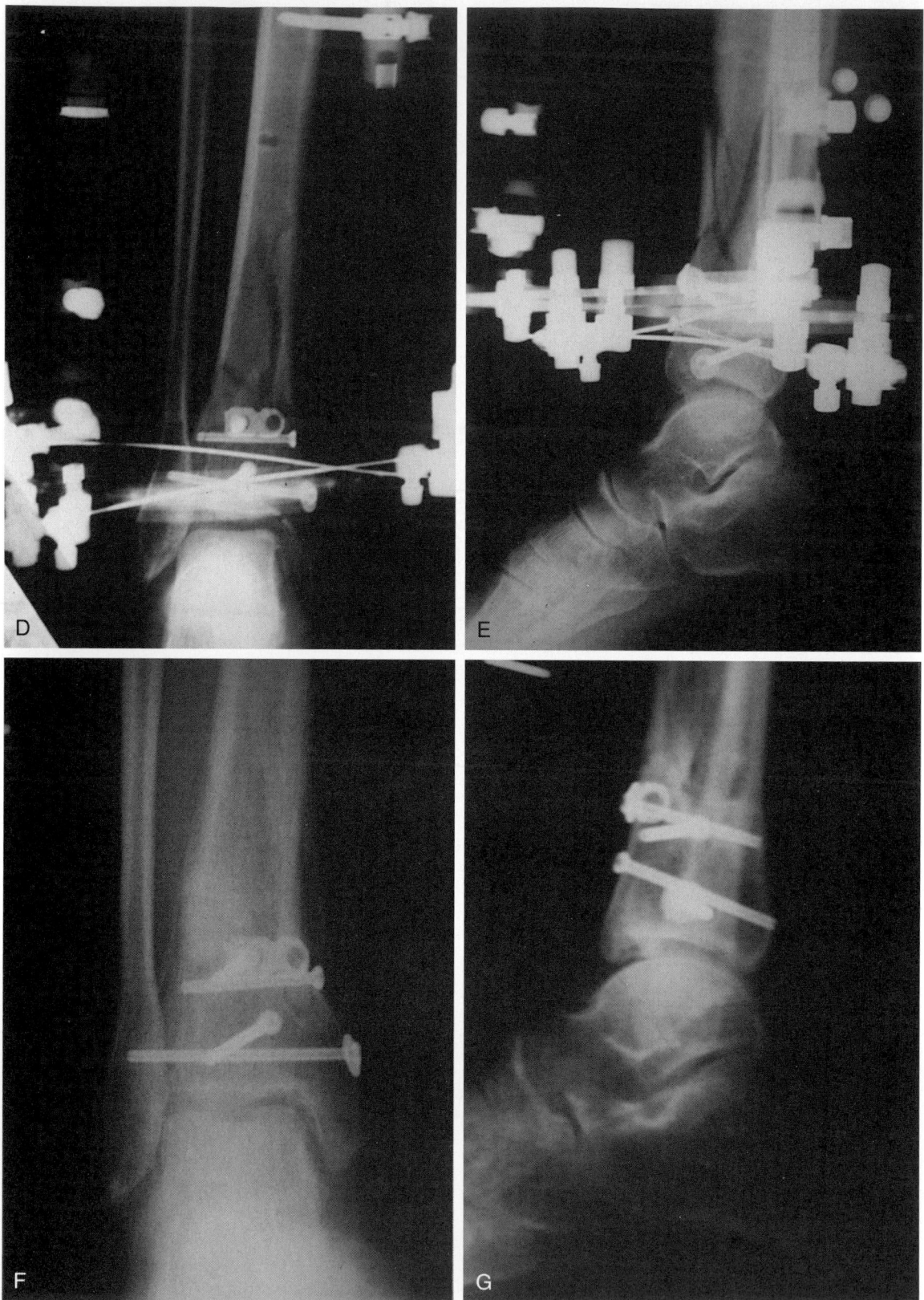

**FIGURE 58–27** *Continued. D, E,* The patient underwent open reduction and internal fixation (ORIF) plus hybrid external fixation. Because formal ORIF was performed, nearly anatomic reduction of the metaphysis and articular surface was achieved. The hybrid external fixator was used to reduce and stabilize the reconstructed metaphysis to the diaphysis. The comminution in the transitional area was reduced indirectly with the fixator. *F, G,* Nine months after injury, the fracture is well healed with maintenance of the reduction.

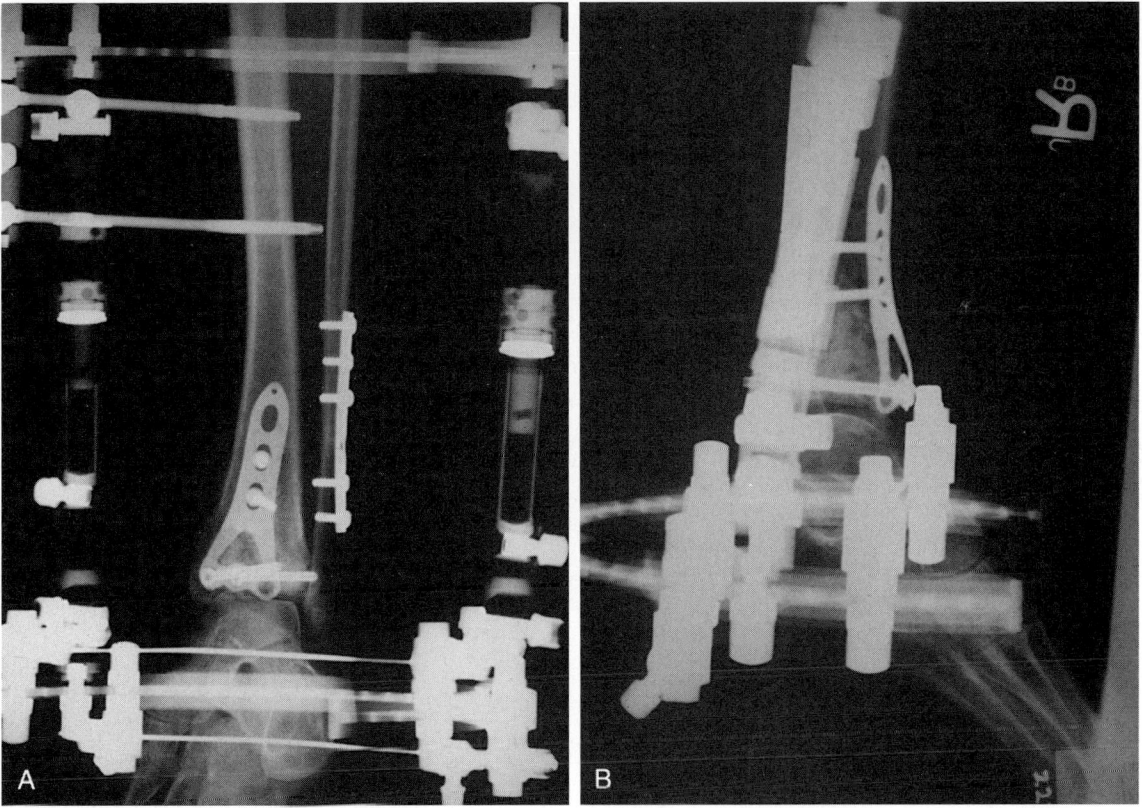

**FIGURE 58–28.** Posterior spanning external fixator that can be used preoperatively for traction, intraoperatively for distraction, and postoperatively as augmented fixation. For this particular construct, parallel wires are used in the talar neck and calcaneus. A beaded wire can be used to prevent translation. A two-thirds ring is placed on the posterior aspect of the foot and ankle. The wires are tensioned to 100 kg and locked. Half pins are placed in the medial aspect of the tibia, and a posterior ring is attached behind the calf. Connecting rods are used to connect the rings. The advantage of this technique is balanced distraction with the ability to correct multiplanar deformities. The posterior placement of the rings provides easy access to the anterior, medial, and lateral aspects of the ankle.

is tensioned according to the particular system (usually 100 to 130 kg).[98] The ring should be placed so that it does not block radiographic evaluation of the mortise. With the ring used as a template or drill guide, a second wire is inserted posteromedially, just anterior to the tibialis posterior tendon, and it exits anterolaterally. Convergence of the two wires should be at least 60° for optimal

strength.[146] The second wire is then tensioned in a similar fashion as the first. Wires placed above and below the ring segment achieve the best stability. If the fracture pattern requires wire placement on the same side of the ring, they must be placed at different heights to avoid impinging on each other. Some devices have the ability to separately adjust the starting heights for the wires, whereas others

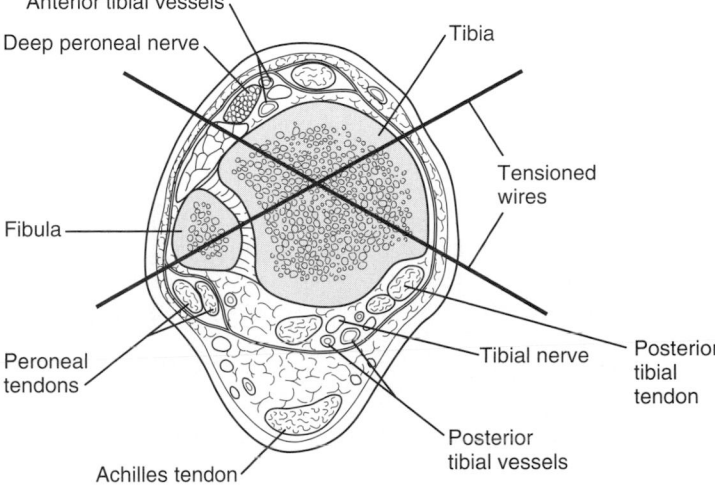

**FIGURE 58–29.** Surgical technique. An axial cross section displays the critical anatomy related to the placement of skinny wires and pins. (Redrawn from Tornetta, P.; et al. J Orthop Trauma 7:489–496, 1993.)

use small washers. In most situations, a half pin or third wire (bisecting the first two) should be added for greater stability of fixation of the epiphyseal segment.[3, 9, 59, 85, 110, 196, 208] Once the distal construct has been assembled, it should be tested with varus and valgus stress under fluoroscopy to evaluate the stability of fixation. Motion of a wire within the bone indicates inadequate fixation and necessitates exchange of the wire.[59]

Proximally in the diaphyseal area, hybrid frame devices commonly use three biplanar 5.0-mm half pins, placement of which typically starts 2 to 3 cm proximal to the fracture site (in very low fractures, pin placement will probably be much higher to allow attachment of the connecting rods). A common configuration includes two pins placed in the standard anterior position and a third "off plane" to the others at 60° to 90°.[59] These pins are attached to a frame construct (unilateral or triangular) or second ring. More complex, the Ilizarov fixator can use any number of combinations of wires and pins connected to circular rings proximally.

Once proximal and distal fixation has been achieved, the reconstructed metaphyseal shell is realigned to the diaphysis by manipulating the proximal fixation and distal ring. After this indirect reduction has been performed, the fixator is locked into place and any incremental adjustments are made in accordance with the capabilities of the particular device.

## Closure and Coverage

Meticulous soft tissue handling helps reduce the incidence of complications. Dead space and fluid collections are avoided by atraumatic closure over small suction drains. After repair of the capsule, the anterior tibial wound is closed meticulously in layers, with absorbable sutures used for the deep tissues (2–0 polyglactin 910 [Vicryl]) and 3–0 or 4–0 nylon Allgöwer-Donati sutures used for the skin wounds.[21, 121, 125, 141] Skin staples should be avoided because the inability to adjust tension at the wound edge leads to an increased incidence of necrosis.[199] The absence of skin wrinkles, the presence of fracture blisters, and the loss of palpable bony landmarks are considered relative contraindications to primary closure.[109, 193] Open wounds, poor capillary refill, and blanching of skin flaps on attempted approximation are absolute contraindications.[109, 199]

If the anterior wound permits closure without undue tension, the same technique is used for the posterolateral wound. Should primary closure of the posterolateral wound be unobtainable, the epimysium and paratenon of the peroneal musculature are sutured to the deep fascia and deep subcutaneous layers of the anterior and posterior flaps.[109, 121] This technique provides coverage of both bone and implant while reducing the risk of medial flap necrosis. Primary skin grafting or delayed primary closure can then be performed, often as early as 3 to 5 days after surgery[17, 58, 109, 121] but, in some cases, as long as 10 days later.[193]

After closure, a large, bulky soft dressing is applied. For patients treated by ORIF, a U splint or brace is applied to maintain the ankle at 90° and avoid equinus deformity. If the patient has undergone external fixation and the construct has not been extended to the metatarsals, such support can be provided by an external footplate attached to the frame. Full-length anteroposterior and lateral films must be obtained before leaving the operating room.

Any significant skin sloughing should prompt consideration of a soft tissue transfer procedure such as a free muscle flap, which is required in as many as 35% of cases.[128] If a flap procedure becomes necessary, which is more likely with an open fracture, it should be performed within 5 to 10 days after injury, but only in patients with no evidence of infection.[35] Rotation flaps in this area are ineffective because of their low perfusion.[199] Although free flaps have a tendency to be bulky and therefore impair the ability to comfortably fit and wear shoes, they typically provide the best coverage. A radial forearm flap with a pedicle of up to 12 cm has been suggested as a good choice.[199] Other useful flaps for the ankle region have included tensor fasciae latae, scapular, latissimus dorsi, internal oblique, rectus, sural island, and various fasciocutaneous flaps.[61, 67, 179, 199]

## POSTOPERATIVE CARE

Postoperative care varies to some extent, depending on the type of treatment. Strict elevation of the extremity for at least 2 to 3 days is crucial, and its importance cannot be overemphasized. In fact, Ruëdi and Allgöwer[166] recommended an initial 5 days of bedrest with elevation.

Antibiotic coverage should continue for 24 to 72 hours postoperatively, depending on the condition of the wounds. In addition, prophylaxis against thromboembolism should be considered. If an external fixator has been used, we advise pin cleaning at least two to three times daily with a half-strength hydrogen peroxide solution, followed by a bulky dry dressing at the pin–skin interface. The use of hydrogen peroxide is controversial, with some surgeons advocating cleansing with only a simple saline solution.[85] Once the wound and pin sites have matured, the patient is encouraged to shower daily with soap.

Early, active range of motion of the ankle joint is considered vital for improved healing and a good functional result.[132, 172] This recommendation is somewhat controversial in that several series have failed to note an advantage of early postoperative ankle motion after ORIF of ankle fractures.[54, 75, 181] However, most patients in these studies had low-energy injuries—many with only an isolated fibular fracture. If early ankle motion is to be instituted, it is important that it not begin until the soft tissues appear healthier and the surgical wounds have sealed, usually a minimum of 48 hours but often 5 to 7 days or more. The patient is then encouraged to begin active dorsiflexion in a splint. After ORIF of a pilon fracture, some authors have even recommended that the patient be discharged in a short leg, non–weight-bearing cast for 3[180] or 6[209] weeks before beginning range-of-motion activities.

After the soft tissues have healed and postoperative swelling is diminished, the patient is allowed non–weight-bearing ambulation with crutches. Elastic stockings are helpful to minimize edema if an external fixator is not in place.[76, 125] Once good ankle control has been obtained, cooperative patients may discard their splint and begin more aggressive active range of motion, usually at about 10 days to 2 weeks.[17, 125] Although exceptionally compliant patients may be allowed minimal (20-lb) foot-flat weight bearing in a brace as early as 2 weeks,[125, 170, 196] most authors have recommended that a non–weight-bearing (or "toe-touch") status be maintained for 6 to 8 weeks.[21, 59, 209]

Fracture consolidation is monitored with monthly radiographs. Union of a tibial pilon fracture usually requires 10 to 16 weeks.[9, 21, 149, 180, 193, 217] Therefore, by 3 months and guided by radiographic evidence of union, the patient can usually be advanced to full weight bearing. For severely comminuted fractures and those with significant chondral damage, a longer period of protected weight bearing (up to 14 to 26 weeks) has been suggested.[76, 92, 156, 166, 168, 193, 196] This longer period may allow time for defects to fill in with repair tissue, mostly fibrocartilage.[166]

## UNRECONSTRUCTABLE PILON FRACTURES

With the use of modern biologic techniques, the orthopaedic surgeon and microsurgeon have dramatically increased the capabilities of limb reconstruction.[33-35, 66, 69, 173, 183, 211] Most pilon fractures are now recognized as salvageable. However, in certain injuries with a severe degree of trauma, reconstruction is still considered impossible. In these cases, alternative methods such as arthrodesis and amputation must be entertained.

When the injury involves severe comminution and articular damage or results in the loss of a sufficiently large degree of bone stock that satisfactory reduction cannot be obtained by closed or open means, arthrodesis has been suggested by numerous authors.*

Indications for primary arthrodesis remain controversial. To achieve arthrodesis in a badly comminuted injury with significant bone loss is often a difficult task.[76, 173, 185] Complications can affect as many as half of the cases, with the incidence of both infection and failure of primary fusion ranging from 0% to 23% (see Complications).† It is often better to obtain alignment, provide length, preserve bone stock, and defer fusion until after bony consolidation and soft tissue recovery. In addition, some patients regain a considerable degree of painless motion or adapt well with a stiff ankle despite marked residual deformity and subsequent arthrosis.‡ Therefore, primary arthrodesis should be performed rarely, if ever, in these injuries.[10, 51, 124, 141, 193, 217]

If early arthrodesis is deemed necessary, various limb salvage procedures are applicable (see the sections Post-

traumatic Arthrosis and Chronic Osteomyelitis under Late Complications). Sanders and colleagues[173] salvaged six type IIIB open pilon fractures by using a staged protocol of wound débridement, temporary placement of antibiotic-impregnated beads, temporary coverage with a synthetic biologic dressing, intravenous antibiotics (initially cephalothin, tobramycin, and penicillin) for up to 6 weeks depending on final bone cultures, soft tissue coverage (three free muscle flaps and one osseocutaneous flap), and tibiotalar arthrodesis. Iliac crest bone grafting plus stabilization with a contoured anterior 4.5-mm dynamic compression plate was performed at the time of delayed primary wound closure or skin grafting or at 4 to 6 weeks after free tissue transfer to allow incorporation and healing of the flap. When distal fixation in the talus was tenuous, it was first extended to the calcaneus and then, if needed, also to the navicular. Although eradication of infection and fusion were achieved in all cases, a minimum of five procedures were needed for each patient (average of nine), costs were high, and major impairments in physical and psychosocial function persisted. The authors advocated consideration of delayed primary amputation as the "conservative" treatment of choice, although all their patients continued to refuse this option.

Despite the best possible care, a few patients ultimately require amputation[76, 79, 131, 173, 183, 190] (Fig. 58–30). Arterial reconstruction is rarely accomplished at this site.[76, 102, 162] Even when successful, the functional results after salvage of the more severe pilon fractures are often poor.[69, 117, 173, 183, 188] In contrast, the use of modern lower extremity prostheses allows for early and nearly normal return to function after below-knee amputations. Therefore, consideration of primary amputation must be entertained in the most severe of injuries. As Hansen has noted, salvage of a useless limb is "the triumph of technique over reason."

## COMPLICATIONS

Complications after operative treatment of pilon fractures, especially those caused by high-energy injuries, are frequent and often severe.§ In the operating room, it is important to avoid malalignment and malreduction and minimize the soft tissue injury that inevitably accompanies surgical treatment. Failure to obtain stable internal fixation because of bone loss or comminution can be prevented by augmentation with an external fixator and bone grafting. Postoperatively, complications can be grouped as either early or late.

Although deep venous thrombosis is not usually thought of in association with a fracture of the tibial pilon, it has been reported to occur in 12.5% of such cases, with rates reportedly as high as 77% for all fractures of the tibia.[1, 64] Associated risk factors include advanced age, longer operating times, and a prolonged interval before fracture fixation. Prophylaxis or adequate screening has been advocated for such high-risk

---

*See references 30, 41, 72, 88, 134, 136, 140, 148, 170, 173, 185.
†See references 34, 51, 69, 76, 111, 135, 137, 153, 186, 189.
‡See references 13, 36, 37, 43, 51, 92, 103, 118, 149, 153, 168, 177, 216.

§See references 9, 14, 23, 24, 26, 47, 76, 92, 130, 133, 138, 148, 152, 155, 164, 177, 188, 191, 195, 199.

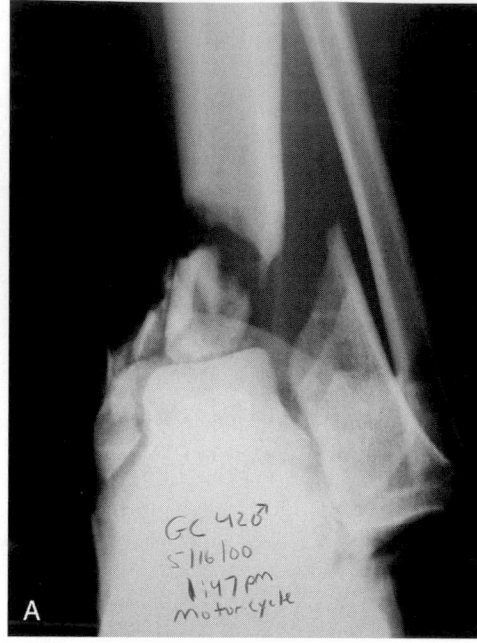

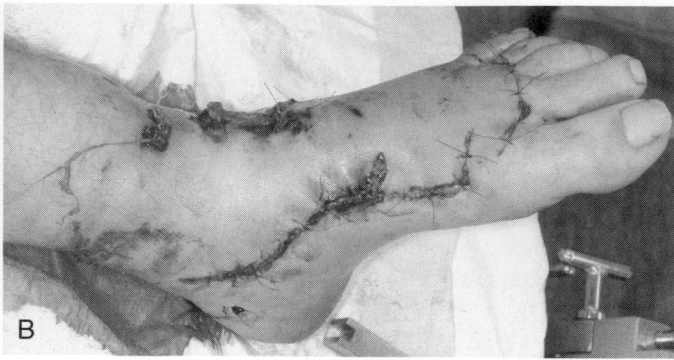

**FIGURE 58–30.** *A, B,* Anteroposterior radiograph of an AO type C3, type IIC open pilon fracture in a polytrauma patient who also sustained a forearm fracture and complex open pelvic fracture. On admission, only a posterior tibial pulse could be obtained by ultrasound (Mangled Extremity Severity Score of 6). Initial treatment included irrigation, débridement, loose approximation of the wounds, and a spanning external fixator. Pulses were completely absent the following day. Because of the patient's critical condition, the severity of the pilon injury, and the question of a warm ischemic time of approximately 7 hours, a below-knee amputation was performed.

patients to avoid the devastating sequelae of pulmonary embolism.

## Early Complications

Soft tissue problems are common, range in incidence from 0% to 37%,* and correlate closely with the severity of injury. The occurrence of soft tissue injury may be attributed to the poor vascularity (watershed effect) of the skin over the anteromedial surface of the tibia, which has no underlying muscle to provide perforating arteries.[199] The classic anteromedial and posterolateral incisions isolate the perforating arteries that contribute to skin vascularity from the peroneal and posterior tibial arteries. Unfortunately, although the cutaneous branches from the anterior artery are preserved during these approaches, these fragile vessels are often damaged at the time of the initial injury.[199] When combined with the additional soft tissue dissection and periosteal stripping of surgery, this tenuous condition increases the risk of hematoma formation, wound dehiscence, skin sloughing, chronic edema, stasis ulceration, and infection.[24, 76, 77, 126, 130, 153, 193, 198, 199]

The incidence of skin sloughing and dehiscence generally varies from 5% to 14%[20, 76, 148, 205, 209, 212, 217] but has distressingly affected over one third of patients in several studies in which surgical approaches were probably performed through compromised tissues.[47, 152, 191, 217] Even when the condition of the soft tissues is optimal, marginal necrosis of the medial wound edge is not uncommon.[121, 180] Fortunately, such marginal necrosis generally heals with local wound care.

Postoperative infections tend to originate in the soft tissues and spread down to bone later.[76] Superficial infection rates range from 8% to 20%.[24, 34, 109, 130, 133, 138, 156]

Deep infection rates have been reported to be 0% to 55%.† The presence of contamination and an increased severity of injury are the crucial factors that prejudice the use and timing of internal fixation. Teeny and Wiss[191] noted that infection was characteristic of comminuted fractures (rising from 0% to 37% in Ruëdi type III fractures) and those with soft tissue problems (rising sixfold to 43%). Higher rates of infection also appear to be related to ORIF during the acute period.[20, 76, 77, 217] Another critical factor is the level of skill of the operating team, where inexperience has often led to disastrous results.[47, 168, 191]

Wound complications can be minimized by the judicial use of staged protocols,[3, 13, 50, 149, 180] which generally involve early ORIF of the fibula and spanning external fixation until the soft tissues subside, followed by delayed ORIF. These biologic approaches have resulted in infection rates of 0% to 3% in closed injuries and up to 10.5% in open fractures, which compares favorably with historical rates for pilon fractures.[13, 149, 180]

Although external fixation has helped minimize some of the problems associated with ORIF, it has also added a new category of complications. Placement of external fixation wires or pins through tendons, vessels, and nerves damages these structures and increases the risk of infection. Pin tract infections in particular are among the most common complications after external fixation, with rates generally ranging from 5% to 20%.[3, 46, 59, 62, 71, 85, 195, 196, 212] Inconsistent with these figures are other studies that have reported much higher frequencies of up to 100%.[46, 85, 209] Part of the problem lies in the definition of what constitutes a pin site infection. Fortunately, most of these "infections" tend to respond well to local wound care and the administration of oral antibiotics, usually a first-generation cephalosporin such as cephalexin.[85] Despite such treatment, some have encountered high rates of pin drainage and

---

*See references 24, 33, 40, 47, 60, 76, 109, 130, 133, 138, 139, 148, 151, 152, 155, 209, 217.

†See references 23, 33, 47, 130, 138, 145, 148, 156, 188, 191, 209, 217.

loosening requiring removal of the offending hardware,[46, 94] and one recent study reported poor outcomes after hybrid external fixation, with 15 complications being noted, including wound problems and infections in 34 patients.[3] Of particular concern is the juxta-articular nature of hybrid or Ilizarov fixator wires, where a pin tract infection can extend into and through the fracture site and involve the metaphyseal screws or the joint.[9, 62, 85, 129, 196, 212]

In a prospective cohort study of 145 fractures (56 pilon fractures) treated with tensioned hybrid fixator wires, Hutson and Zych[85] observed an overall pin site infection rate of 13% (defined as an infectious complication that failed to respond to local wound care and antibiotics). However, all their patients required oral antibiotics at some point during treatment. The average time for occurrence of pin tract inflammation requiring intravenous antibiotics was 14 weeks (range, 6 to 32). In the pilon fracture group, eight of nine pin tract infections improved with intravenous antibiotics (two cases), irrigation and débridement of the pin site (five cases), or débridement of a deep infection (one case at 23 weeks). One case of septic arthritis (at 24 weeks) required irrigation and débridement of the joint and late arthrodesis. The authors recommended early antibiotic treatment of superficial erythema surrounding the pins, aggressive irrigation and débridement with intravenous antibiotics for deep infections, and arthrotomy and intravenous antibiotics for septic arthritis.

## Late Complications

Late complications are usually osteoarticular in nature and related to a combination of the severity of the injury itself and the degree of soft tissue disruption by both the initial trauma and the surgeon. These complications include nonunion, malunion, traumatic arthrosis, and chronic osteomyelitis. A rare complication after the use of a tensioned fixator is vasculitis and lipodermatosclerosis, which was observed by Hutson and Zych in three patients.[85] Findings associated with this process included chronic edema and extremity pain persisting for many months after frame removal, a normal white blood cell count, a mildly elevated sedimentation rate, ineffective oral antibiotics, and a good patient response to corticosteroid therapy.

### NONUNION AND MALUNION

Rates of delayed union and nonunion have ranged from 4% to 36%.* Teeny and Wiss[191] found the highest rates in Ruëdi type III fractures (27% as compared with 7% in Ruëdi type I and II fractures), with 55% requiring bone grafting. Salvage of a pilon nonunion is challenging because it often requires multiple techniques, including correction of deformity, bone grafting, and stabilization.

An increasingly recognized problem associated with

the use of external fixation is the occurrence of malunion, delayed union, or nonunion at the metaphyseal-diaphyseal junction[3, 9, 155, 156, 208, 212, 217] (see Fig. 58–32). Anglen observed that nonunion developed in 7 of 34 patients treated by hybrid external fixation as compared with none of 25 patients treated by ORIF.[3] Five of these nonunions occurred at the metaphyseal-diaphyseal junction and two occurred in the metaphysis. Although it is unclear to what extent this phenomenon is related to the diaphyseal extension itself, failure to bone graft, or the method of fixation,[3] it appears to result from overdistraction or failure to properly dynamize a markedly comminuted fracture[16, 76, 83, 138, 206, 208] (see Figs. 58–2, 58–17, and 58–32).

In an analysis of 39 cases of failed fixation after external fixation of pilon fractures, Watson and co-authors[208] noted that 64% (25 patients) were related to malunion or nonunion of the tibial-metadiaphyseal junction. They attributed this problem to the presence of unrecognized comminution or bone loss in this area, failure to bone graft, and an intact or plated fibula that prevented compression of the fracture site after frame dynamization, with subsequent varus collapse of the fracture. Additional sources of fixation failure included failure to bone graft, inadequate stabilization of the metaphyseal region with only two wires (15%) or the diaphyseal region with only two Schanz pins (7%), and malreduction of either the metaphysis or the articular surface (12% of cases). Although no inherent mechanical failure could be attributed to monolateral ankle-bridging frames, 55% of the circular fixators had frame instability as a direct cause of their complications. Other authors have noted that early removal of a hybrid frame can lead to late varus collapse of the fracture, particularly if the fibula has been plated.[59]

To improve the chance for union and decrease the likelihood of malunion, delayed primary bone grafting should be performed in patients with significant metaphyseal-diaphyseal comminution or bone loss. Grafting is usually best performed between 4 and 8 weeks,[9, 155, 212, 217] although some authors have waited up to 10 to 16 weeks.[59, 155, 217] Recalcitrant nonunion associated with severe comminution, necrotic bone, or post-traumatic arthritis will require consideration of limb salvage procedures (see the sections Post-traumatic Arthrosis and Chronic Osteomyelitis).

Depending on the form of treatment, malunion rates range from 2% to 58%.[23, 24, 130, 133, 148, 155, 164, 191, 209] Metaphyseal malunion can lead to chronic pain and may require a realignment procedure.[68] Articular malunions are often recognized too late to avoid post-traumatic arthrosis,[7, 21] and even if surgical treatment is considered, intra-articular osteotomies for reconstitution of the articular surface after malreduction are very challenging. Babis and colleagues[7] reviewed 67 pilon fractures treated by operative fixation and found that outcomes were affected by the personality of the fracture, the quality of reduction, and the form of surgical management. Because good long-term results were obtained in only one third of patients with a moderate to poor reduction, they concluded that it is important to achieve as near an anatomic reduction as possible at the time of the initial surgery.

---

*See references 3, 9, 20, 23, 24, 60, 76, 92, 130, 133, 148, 149, 156, 191, 205, 209.

## POST-TRAUMATIC ARTHROSIS

Because of a combination of articular damage, immobilization, and soft tissue scarring, some degree of joint stiffness is unavoidable. However, fracture fixation that permits early motion may minimize this problem and improve function.[6, 55, 115, 125, 217] Post-traumatic arthrosis, probably related to a combination of trauma, mechanical wear, and avascular necrosis of subchondral bone, is reported to range from 13% to 54%.[23, 24, 76, 92, 130, 133, 148, 164] Bourne and colleagues[24] recognized this complication in 100% of patients with poor reductions. Comminution can be so severe that small avascular pieces of articular cartilage and subchon-

dral bone must be discarded, with gaps left in the articular surface.[193] Evidence of avascular necrosis is difficult to identify but easy to suspect in the face of early signs of arthrosis after anatomic reduction of a complex fracture.[10, 76, 92, 101, 139, 148, 159]

Treatment of ankle arthritis begins with nonoperative measures, including modification of activity, nonsteroidal anti-inflammatory medications, and bracing. The later usually involves either a laced-up ankle brace, an orthotic, or (in more severe situations) a solid ankle-foot orthosis with a rocker-bottom sole.[21] Once these options have failed, tibiotalar arthrodesis should be considered for pain relief (Fig. 58–31). Many patients with post-traumatic

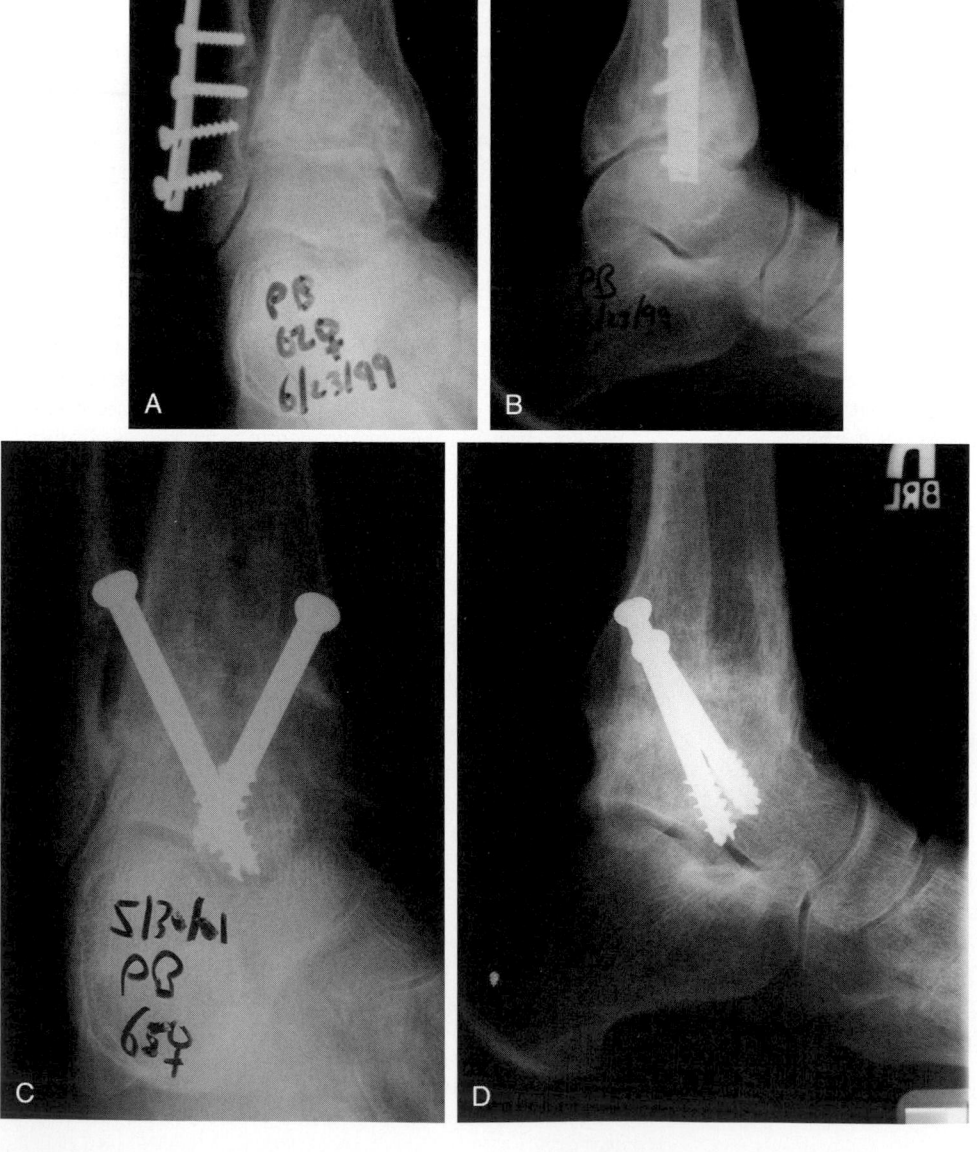

**FIGURE 58–31.** A 64-year-old woman presented with ankle pain 8 years after sustaining this pilon fracture. The fracture was originally treated by open reduction plus internal fixation and grafting with a bone substitute, followed by later removal of the tibial implants. *A, B,* Anteroposterior (AP) and lateral radiographs reveal severe tibiotalar arthrosis, but normal alignment and no bony defects. *C, D,* AP and lateral radiographs demonstrate a successful tibiotalar fusion 2 years later. However, the patient returned because of increasing anterolateral pain related to the distal tibiofibular joint, which was effectively treated by simple resection of the distal end of the fibula.

ankle arthropathy wait at least 1 year before fusion is considered.*

In patients with severe post-traumatic arthritis, tibiotalar arthrodesis is the treatment of choice. When successful, long-term follow-up after this procedure has usually revealed good function in activities of daily living, with the most common restriction being difficulty in running.[111, 127, 135, 137, 186] Morrey and Wiedeman[137] found that more than half (58%) of their post-traumatic ankle arthrodesis procedures were required within the first 12 months. Although satisfactory results were achieved in 83% of cases, complications still occurred frequently, including infection (23%), nonunion (23%), delayed union (7%), inadequate alignment or loss of position (15%), and malunion (12%). Arthrodesis rates after pilon fractures range from 6% to 26% for the more severe injuries.[13, 23, 24, 92, 138, 149, 164, 191] When considering only Ruëdi type III fractures, Bourne and colleagues[23, 24] and Teeny and Wiss[191] reported respective arthrodesis rates of 32% and 26%. All five of the type III open pilon fractures treated by Sanders and associates[173] required arthrodesis.

Although various methods have been described† (see Figs. 58–31 to 58–33), no single procedure is applicable to all patients because of the heterogeneity of pilon fractures and their associated soft tissue injuries, including the possibility of persistent metaphyseal-diaphyseal nonunion (Fig. 58–32). (See also Chapter 61.)

The use of blade-plate fixation for arthrodesis of the ankle joint has been described by several authors[30, 72, 136, 182] (see Fig. 58–32). However, prominence of the hardware, infection, and fracture of the talus have complicated its use. To minimize such problems Gruen and Mears[72] advocated a posterior approach, which avoids compromised tissue from previous incisions and allows for significant soft tissue coverage of the hardware. Morgan and colleagues[136] used a modified posterior approach with a 90° cannulated blade plate and autogenous bone grafting to obtain arthrodesis in five patients after a pilon fracture (a lateral approach was performed in one case). In their preliminary report, all six patients eventually achieved uncomplicated bony union within 26 weeks. Another option for arthrodesis is a retrograde intramedullary nail.[134] However, this procedure is limited by the need to additionally fuse the subtalar joint and presents concerns regarding infection, particularly when an external fixator has been present.

For post-traumatic arthrosis complicated by an associated supramalleolar nonunion, Marsh and co-workers[117] have advocated one of two treatment protocols. In a group of seven patients, they performed either ORIF and fusion with medial and lateral plates or a combination of internal and external fixation. Selection of the surgical procedure was based on the radiographic appearance of the area of injury and the presence or absence of infection. Two patients with a hypertrophic nonunion underwent fixation with medial and lateral one-third tubular plates. Three patients with an atrophic nonunion and an associated

history of infection were treated with external fixation and bone grafting. Two patients with active draining wounds required resection of the distal end of the tibia below the nonunion, removal of cartilage from the talar dome, and compression of the talus into the distal end of the tibia with a monolateral external fixator. Later, distraction osteogenesis was used to regain length. Although bony union was obtained in six of seven patients, the authors noted a prolonged treatment time (7.5 months to achieve union, fixator removal at 6 months, and bracing until 11 months), frequent complications (two patients required additional débridement for recurrent infection and two needed a second arthrodesis for recurrent nonunion), a high cost of care, and functional outcome measurements (SF-36) that were strikingly inferior to those of age-matched controls. Even though their techniques were an effective alternative to amputation, the authors recommended careful patient selection as well as consideration of amputation (particularly in the presence of infection) before undertaking surgery for this demanding treatment problem.

## CHRONIC OSTEOMYELITIS

The development of chronic osteomyelitis is among the most devastating of complications associated with a pilon fracture (Fig. 58–33), with rates as high as one third to one half of cases when a formal surgical approach has been performed through compromised soft tissue.[47, 130, 145, 148, 191, 217] The outcome of treatment can be unpredictable, and a functional ankle is often difficult to achieve, with arthrodesis or even amputation being the end result. Prevention, through sound judgment and the use of established surgical principles and techniques, is the best method of handling chronic osteomyelitis.

The basic principles of management of chronic osteomyelitis include aggressive radical débridement of all infected and necrotic bone and surrounding soft tissues, removal of any remaining hardware, immobilization, appropriate antibiotic therapy (including the use of antibiotic-impregnated polymethyl methacrylate beads), and filling of the resulting dead space.[33, 34, 66, 69, 84, 95, 183, 211] For small defects, local autologous bone grafting can be used to fill the bony gaps and promote healing. To address large defects, treatment options include massive bone grafting, tricortical bone blocks, vascularized bone grafts, bone transport techniques, local flaps, and a variety of free tissue transfers.[32–34, 69, 173, 174, 183, 211] Treatment with massive autologous bone grafting is lengthy and requires multiple procedures and the sacrifice of both iliac crests; failure of such treatment usually results in amputation.[32, 173, 183] Treatment with free vascularized bone grafts has been reported to yield successful results in 60% to 83% of cases, with failures usually resulting in amputation.[66, 93, 211] Preservation of the contralateral fibula is desirable because the patient is left with one normal lower extremity—an important consideration should ipsilateral amputation ultimately be required. Therefore, other surgical options should be ruled out before proceeding with this technique.

Green and Roesler[69] approached the problem of

---

*See references 16, 23, 26, 27, 34, 36, 67, 101, 137, 148, 166, 173, 185.

†See references 30, 41, 69, 72, 84, 88, 117, 134, 136, 140, 148, 170, 173, 182, 183, 185.

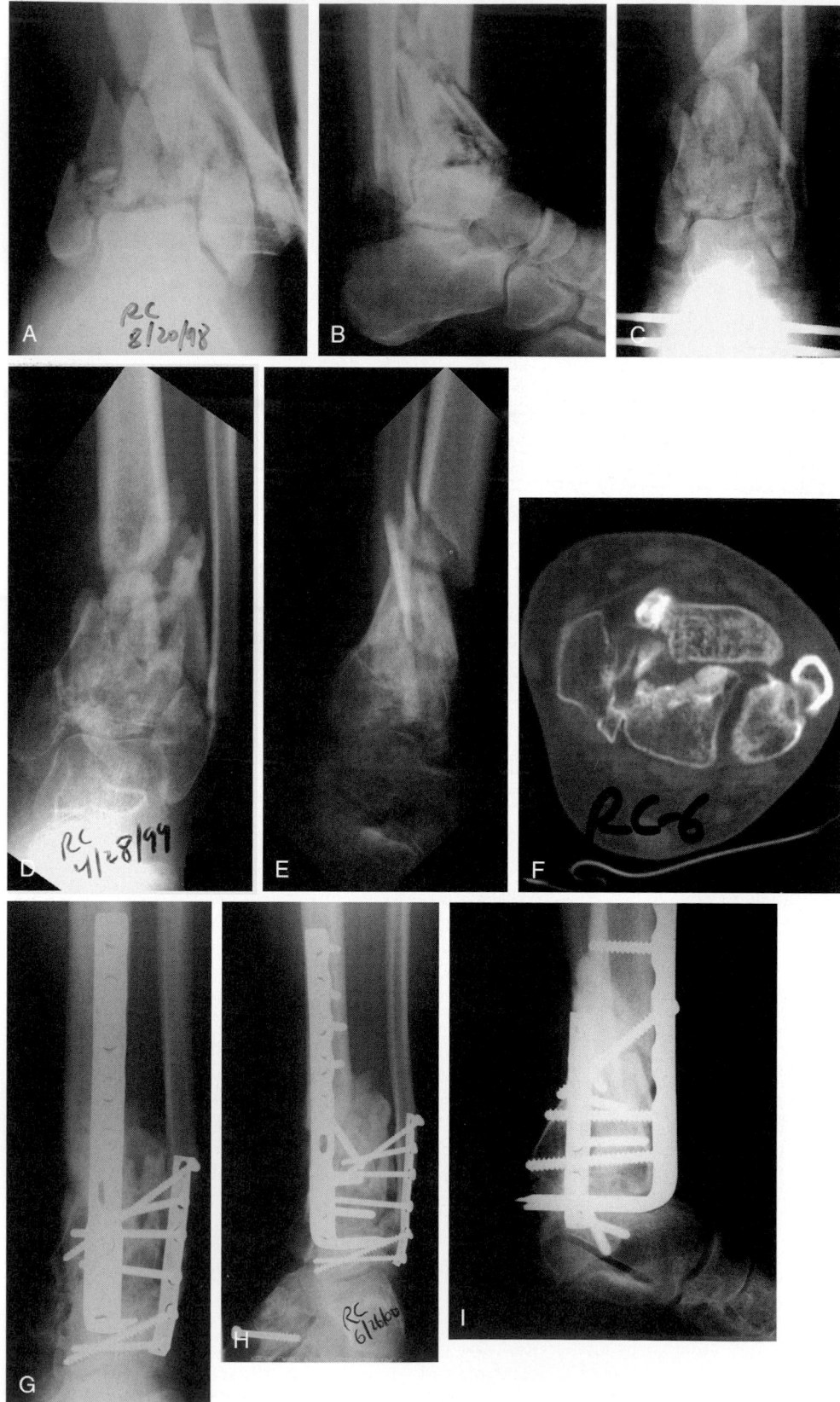

FIGURE 58–32. A 42-year-old woman had pain and instability 9 months after sustaining this AO type C3, type IIIA open pilon fracture. *A, B,* Anteroposterior (AP) and lateral views reveal severe comminution and impaction. *C,* AP view demonstrating improved alignment by ligamentotaxis with a spanning external fixator. Because of multiple other fractures, severe comminution, and poor soft tissue status, the treating physician elected to definitively manage the fracture with the fixator. *D, E,* AP and lateral radiographs show nonunion and severe post-traumatic arthrosis at 9 months. *F,* A computed tomographic scan confirms the articular destruction and incongruity. Open reduction plus internal fixation (ORIF) was performed from an anteromedial approach with a cannulated blade plate and autologous bone graft. For additional stability, supplementary ORIF of the fibula and tibiofibular and talofibular joints was obtained through a lateral approach. *G,* Postoperative follow-up at 13 months. *H, I,* AP mortise and lateral views reveal successful tibiotalar fusion and progressive consolidation of the metaphyseal shell. Alignment was anatomic.

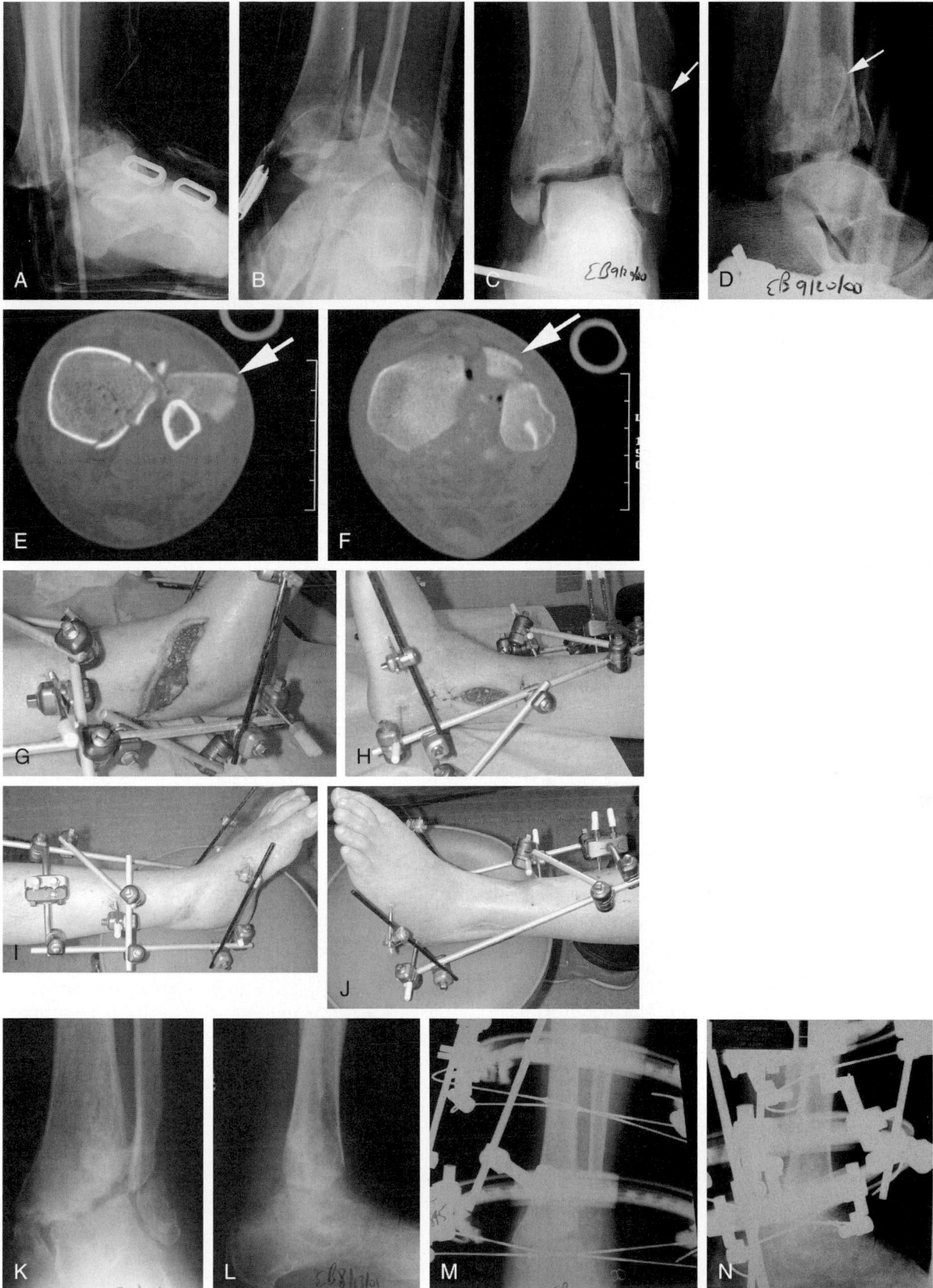

**Figure 58–33.** A 45-year-old man fell from a height and sustained an AO type C3, type IIIA open pilon fracture. *A, B,* Anteroposterior (AP) and lateral views after injury show the fracture dislocation and severe comminution. *C, D,* AP and lateral views after irrigation and débridement along with placement of a spanning external fixator at the time of patient referral. The initial displacement and disruption were so severe that the posterior malleolus actually lies anterior to the fibula (*arrows*). *E, F,* A computed tomographic scan confirms the size and position of the fragments, including the posterior malleolus (*arrows*). *G, H,* Even with repeated débridement and placement of an antibiotic bead pouch, a mixed microbial infection rapidly developed and necessitated aggressive débridement of bone and plastic surgery consultation. *I, J,* The wounds were allowed to granulate and healed with local wound care and 6 weeks of intravenous antibiotics. The spanning fixator was maintained to facilitate healing and wound care. *K, L,* Because of prolonged edema, fragile soft tissues, and pin loosening, the fixator was removed, and a trial of bracing with an ankle-foot orthosis and an anterior clamshell was attempted. The ankle quickly drifted into valgus. *M, N,* Postoperative AP and lateral views after tibiotalar fusion through a lateral approach. A small-wire fixator was used to improve alignment and obtain compression across the tibiotalar joint.

infection in a stepwise fashion in the recognition that all patients are not managed similarly. In some cases, infection can be manifested as localized skin sloughing over a screw head or other prominent piece of hardware several weeks or months after the original surgery. If the fixation is stable, exposure of the hardware is minimal, the inflammatory changes are limited to the skin immediately surrounding the sloughing, the bone is viable, and evidence of progressive healing is apparent, these exposed implants can occasionally be retained until bony union has occurred. Serial radiographs are important and should reveal evidence of disuse osteopenia of all bone fragments. Nonviable bone will remain radiodense. Most patients, however, will require hardware removal to ensure eradication of infection because of deep tissue involvement. When early removal of the implants is necessary for persistent infection and lack of progressive healing, a bridging external fixator or non–weight-bearing cast is needed to resist the propensity of the fracture to collapse into varus or apex posterior angulation. The patient should be told that the external fixator might have to remain in place for 8 to 12 months.

When infection persists despite thorough débridement and removal of hardware, the possibility of joint infection must be entertained. A septic ankle joint draining to the surface might not demonstrate the usual clinical signs of joint infection (swelling, fever, intense pain) and instead suffer from slow, progressive bacterial degradation of articular cartilage manifested as joint space narrowing and, possibly, juxta-articular bone erosion.[69] In these cases, tibiotalar arthrodesis may be the only option for salvage of the limb.[69, 84, 138, 173, 183] However, the surgeon needs to appreciate that these are not typical ankle fusion procedures.

Osteomyelitis will probably have created large cavitary defects that must be filled with bone graft and free or composite tissue transfer. Unfortunately, full incorporation and corticalization of a cancellous bone graft takes 2 to 5 years, and bracing must ultimately be instituted after removal of external fixation.[69] To prevent undue motion that may lead to nonunion, Green and Roesler[69] advocated incorporation of the distal end of the fibula into the site to "corticalize" the graft. To preserve this option, they recommend against excision of the fibula when undertaking ankle arthrodesis for an infected pilon fracture. In some cases, although extensive anterior cortical débridement is required, the infection has spared the posterior and posterolateral aspects of the distal end of the tibia, which allows abutment against the posterior edge of the remaining upper part of the talus and thereby enhances the stability of the construct.

In spite of their best efforts to salvage infected pilon fractures, Green and Roesler[69] noted that a substantial number of patients had unfavorable outcomes.[69] Although 8 of 13 fractures went on to union, 2 demonstrated persistent sepsis that could not be eradicated. Two nonunions occurred, one patient needed a below-knee amputation, and four patients required ankle fusion to control chronic pyarthrosis. All six patients whose fractures united with eradication of infection had stiff ankles with scarred, dystrophic skin around the distal end of the tibia. For this reason, the authors recommended that each

patient with a dystrophic leg be offered the option of below-knee amputation and that the patient be made to understand that reconstruction of the leg might require 1 or more years in an external fixator—with an uncertain outcome at best.

Stasikelis and coauthors[183] treated six infected pilon nonunions with an Ilizarov fixator and bone transport techniques to eradicate infection and obtain a tibiotalar arthrodesis. Necrotic and infected bone was resected adequately enough to reveal viable bleeding bone at both the tibial and talar surfaces. Dead space management consisted of either filling the resultant defect with antibiotic-impregnated beads, performing an immediate shortening of the extremity, or shortening the extremity over a period of several weeks (the advantages of acute shortening include closure of associated soft tissue defects and earlier docking between the intercalary segment and talus, which decreases the time required to achieve arthrodesis). Distraction osteogenesis was then used to correct any significant limb length inequality. All patients received initial doses of intravenous tobramycin and clindamycin. Intravenous antibiotics were terminated after 5 days in patients with implanted antibiotic beads, but most patients continued with some form of intravenous antibiotics for 4 weeks. In all cases, the infections were eradicated and solid arthrodesis attained. Patients required an average of 1.3 additional procedures, and their time in a fixator averaged 8 months (range, 3 to 13 months). Every patient experienced at least a minor complication during treatment (e.g., superficial pin tract infections), two patients healed with residual deformities, and one patient required occasional analgesics for pain control. These authors recommended consideration of amputation as an alternative reconstructive procedure before undertaking limb salvage.

Hulscher[84] advocated a step-by-step approach to both eradicate the infection and obtain arthrodesis of the ankle joint. Treatment begins with implant removal, synovectomy, and thorough débridement of nonvital and poorly vascularized soft tissue and bone. Antibiotic beads are added to increase the local concentration of antibiotics. Next, a local or free muscle transfer is performed when indicated. Finally, arthrodesis is achieved with internal fixation, external fixation, or a combination of the two techniques. In his small series, successful fusion was achieved in all 10 patients (8 had either a type II or type III open fracture) with septic arthritis after a pilon fracture. Consolidation occurred at an average of 11.7 weeks, with half the patients noting a satisfactory functional outcome (two of the five with less than satisfactory results had other sequelae of polytrauma). Unfortunately, the author provided no specifics with respect to timing or technique.

## CLINICAL EVALUATION

Marked variation in the severity and classification of pilon fractures makes evaluation and comparison of the different treatment methods difficult. Ovadia and Beals[148] considered an excellent result to be pain-free movement and the ability to return to all activities without a limp. A good result involved mild pain after vigorous activity, slightly modified recreational activities, and return to other preinjury activities without a limp or medication.

Many systems have been devised for evaluating both the radiographic and the clinical results of treatment of pilon fractures.* Among the first was that of Burwell and Charnley,[28] who defined radiographic criteria for reduction (Table 58–2). Tornetta and co-workers[196] suggested criteria for clinical results (Table 58–3).

Teeny and Wiss[191] fashioned a more complicated system similar to the Harris hip score and modified the system of Mazur and colleagues[127] to create a functional ankle scoring system. In addition, they modified an objective scoring system proposed by Ovadia and Beals[148] to measure the quality of reduction.

# PROGNOSIS

Ruëdi and Allgöwer[164, 166] and others[23, 24, 28, 51, 76, 133, 159, 191, 207] have directly correlated the adequacy of reduction with functional and radiographic results at long-term follow-up. Similarly, Teeny and Wiss[191] noted that outcomes in patients with anatomic reductions were good to excellent in 41%, fair in 31%, and poor in 27%. In contrast, for those with nonanatomic reductions, outcomes were good to excellent in 16%, fair in 21%, and poor in 63%. When reductions were rated good or better, 10% required arthrodesis as compared with 32% of those whose reductions were graded inadequate.

However, regardless of the reduction, the presence of

---

*See references 6, 28, 43, 96, 118, 152, 156, 191, 196, 205, 216.

---

**TABLE 58–2** ...................................

Radiographic Criteria of Reduction

**ANATOMIC**

No medial or lateral displacement of the medial and lateral malleoli
No angulation
Not more than 1-mm longitudinal displacement of the medial and lateral malleoli
Not more than 2-mm proximal displacement of a large posterior fragment
No displacement of the talus

**FAIR**

No medial or lateral displacement of the medial and lateral malleoli
No angulation
2- to 5-mm posterior displacement of the lateral malleolus
2- to 5-mm proximal displacement of a large posterior fragment
No displacement of the talus

**POOR**

Any medial or lateral displacement of the medial and lateral malleoli
More than 5-mm posterior displacement of the lateral malleolus or more than 5-mm displacement of the posterior malleolus
Any residual displacement of the talus

..............................................

*Source:* Burwell, H.N., Charnley, A.D. J Bone Joint Surg Br 47:634–660, 1965.

---

**TABLE 58–3** ...................................

Criteria for Clinical Results

| Grade | Pain | Range of Motion | Angulation (°) |
|---|---|---|---|
| Excellent | None | D > 5 P > 40 | <3 |
| Good | Intermittent, relieved by NSAID | D = 0–5 P = 30–40 | 3–5 valgus <3 varus |
| Fair | Pain during activities of daily living relieved by narcotics | D = –5–0 P = 25–30 | 5–8 varus 3–5 varus |
| Poor | Intractable | D < –5 P < 25 | >8 valgus >5 varus |

.................................................

*Abbreviations:* D, dorsiflexion; NSAID, nonsteroidal anti-inflammatory drug; P, plantar flexion.
*Source:* Tornetta, P.; et al. J Orthop Trauma 7:489–496, 1993.

---

avascular necrosis,[10, 22, 76, 92, 148, 159] plafond chondral damage,[22, 36, 42, 101, 106, 148, 209] or associated talar chondral damage[22, 51, 103, 133, 164, 196] increases the likelihood of post-traumatic arthritis. Furthermore, when cartilage is traumatized, it is much more susceptible to the effects of malalignment,[76] which explains why AO type C1 and C2 fractures have much better outcomes than do type C3 (Ruëdi type III) fractures regardless of treatment. Wyrsch and colleagues[217] observed that no matter what type of fixation is used, all patients who had a Ruëdi type II or III fracture had some degree of osteoarthrosis at an average follow-up of 39 months.[217] In addition, although clinical scores did not correspond with the fracture type, a general trend was noted for lower scores in patients with Ruëdi type II and III fractures. When retrospectively reviewing three different treatment options in 38 patients with pilon fractures, Crutchfield and colleagues[42] found that in general, simple fractures had good outcomes whereas complex patterns did not and that the fracture severity appeared to be the key variable affecting outcome, regardless of the means of stabilization. Barbieri and associates[9] reported that six AO type C1 fractures had 100% good to excellent results as compared with 18 C2 and C3 fractures, which had 45% good to excellent results, 22% fair results, and 33% poor results. Watson and colleagues[209] noted that their patients with severe pilon fractures (AO type C) had poor outcomes irrespective of the means of stabilization (60% good to excellent results for ORIF vs. 62% for external fixation); the poor outcomes were thus more indicative of the nature of the injury than the treatment methodologies.

Other prognostic factors adversely affecting treatment and outcome include the presence of an open injury, soft tissue damage, loss of bone stock, preexisting medical problems, inexperience of the surgeon,[47, 168, 191] and associated injuries to other physiologic systems. Of final interest is the observation that steps in the articular surface after operative treatment are more frequently associated with post-traumatic arthritis than are comparable steps in fractures treated nonoperatively, perhaps because of devascularization of bone fragments at the time of surgery.[13, 158]

In contrast to the aforementioned reports are studies

that highlight the difficulties in predicting medium- and long-term outcomes after fractures of the tibial pilon. Williams and colleagues[216] used a clinical ankle score, a radiographic arthrosis score, the SF-36, and the patient's ability to return to work to evaluate 32 pilon fractures treated by limited ORIF and a cross–ankle-bridging external fixator. Although the severity of the injury as measured on preoperative radiographs and the accuracy of reduction strongly correlated with the development of arthrosis, neither demonstrated any significant relationship with the three outcome measurements. A statistically significant relationship was, however, noted between the patient's level of education and the ability to return to work. Decoster and associates[43] further investigated the effects of the severity of the initial fracture pattern and the quality of the articular reduction by using the rank-order method for 25 patients with pilon fractures. Although this method reliably stratified the severity of injury and the quality of the reduction, with the later predicting the development of radiographic arthrosis, neither the injury nor the accuracy of reduction correlated with the clinical ankle score. The authors concluded that other factors such as soft tissue injury (not evaluated in their study) are important in determining outcome.

Blauth and associates[13] noted that although 84% of patients had radiographic signs of arthritis at a follow-up of 84 months, more than half still had greater than 75% of their normal range of motion and 92% were satisfied with their results. No significant relationship could be found between the soft tissue damage and the degree of arthritis or between the type of surgical treatment and the extent of post-traumatic arthritis. Other authors have failed to correlate the development of radiographic arthrosis with clinical function.[118, 156, 209] In a long-term follow-up study (average, 79 months; range, 60 to 169 months) of 52 patients managed by external fixation with limited ORIF, Marsh and colleagues[118] found that the injury severity and the quality of reduction predicted the development of radiographic osteoarthritis. However, no correlation was found between radiographic osteoarthritis and clinical measures of function and health-related quality of life. In fact, although the patients had poorer scores than did age-matched controls and most ankles demonstrated radiographic arthrosis, a reasonable amount of motion remained (average of 10° dorsiflexion, 29° plantar flexion, 10° inversion, and 9° eversion), and patients reported continued improvement for an average of 2.4 years.

From the studies just presented, it can be concluded that fractures of the tibial pilon have a detrimental long-term effect on ankle function, pain, and health-related quality of life. However, subjective results do not always deteriorate and actually tend to improve in some patients over time, despite persistent restriction of motion.[118, 168] Although arthrosis develops in most patients, it does not routinely correlate with clinical outcome. Still, the presence of minimal articular damage, anatomic reduction with early range of motion, and a lack of complications generally foretells satisfactory results.[92, 148, 164, 168] Ruëdi[164] noted that a lack of joint arthrosis 1 to 2 years after injury forecasts further absence for another 5 to 10 years. Jahna and co-workers[87] and

others[76, 207] concurred and have documented that the degree of severity of the injury can be reliably assessed at 4 to 5 years, with late changes being minor.

## SUMMARY

As techniques of biologic fixation and external fixation are refined, they are playing an increasingly important role in the management of severe fractures. Adherence to these principles has been shown to increase healing rates and decrease infection while providing stable fixation. Excellent functional long-term results are often obtained with minimal soft tissue and bony complications. The goals of ORIF and external fixation with limited internal fixation are identical: anatomic reduction and rigid stabilization to achieve early motion. In general, their results are comparable. Expert ORIF of tibial pilon fractures as developed by Ruëdi and Allgöwer[164, 166–168] has been accepted as a means to obtain superior results for most pilon fractures. However, in a patient whose fracture is marked by significant displacement, severe articular comminution, metaphyseal or diaphyseal comminution (or comminution of both regions), a long fracture type, compromised soft tissues, or an open wound, alternative treatment strategies must be considered. In these cases, staged reconstruction or a combination of internal fixation and percutaneous techniques (external fixation or percutaneous plating) provides the best chance of a good clinical result without any undue risk of disaster.

### REFERENCES

1. Abelseth, G.; Buckley, R.E.; Pineo, G.E.; et al. Incidence of deep-vein thrombosis in patients with fractures of the lower extremity distal to the hip. J Orthop Trauma 10:230–235, 1996.
2. Allgöwer, M.; Müller, M.E.; Willenegger, H. Technik der Operativen Frakturbehandlung. New York, Springer-Verlag, 1963.
3. Anglen, J.O. Early outcome of hybrid external fixation for fracture of the distal tibia. J Orthop Trauma 13:92–97, 1999.
4. Ashhurst, A.P.C.; Bromer, R.S. Classification and mechanism of fractures of the leg bones involving the ankle. Arch Surg 4:51, 1922.
5. Atkins, R.M.; Sudhakar, J.E.; Porteous, A.J. Use of modified Ilizarov olive wires as pushing wires. J Orthop Trauma 12:436–438, 1998.
6. Ayeni, J.P. Pilon fractures of the tibia: A study based on 19 cases. Injury 19:109–114, 1988.
7. Babis, G.C.; Vayanos, E.D.; Papaioannou, N.; Pantazopoulos, T. Results of surgical treatment of tibial plafond fractures. Clin Orthop 341:99–105, 1997.
8. Babst, R.; Renner, N.; Rosso, R.; et al. [Stable joint-bridging extension of malleolar dislocations and pilon fractures with the AO pinless external fixator] [German]. Helv Chir Acta 60:833–838, 1994.
9. Barbieri, R.; Schenk, R.S.; Koval, K.; et al. Hybrid external fixation in the treatment of tibial plafond fractures. Clin Orthop 332:16–22, 1996.
10. Beck, E. Results of operative treatment of pilon fractures. In: Tscherne, H.; Schatzker, J., eds. Major Fractures of the Pilon, the Talus, and the Calcaneus. Heidelberg, Springer-Verlag, 1993, pp. 49–51.
11. Behrens, F.; Johnson, W.D. Unilateral external fixation. Methods to increase and reduce frame stiffness. Clin Orthop 241:48–56, 1989.
12. Bistrom, O. Conservative treatment of severe ankle fractures. Acta Chir Scand Suppl 168:1–57, 1952.
13. Blauth, M.; Bastian, L.; Krettek, C.; et al. Surgical options for the treatment of severe tibial pilon fractures: A study of three techniques. J Orthop Trauma 15:153–160, 2001.

14. Bohler, L. Die Technik der knochenbruch Behandlung. Vienna, Mudrich, 1951.

15. Bonar, S.K.; Marsh, J.L. Unilateral external fixation for severe pilon fractures. Foot Ankle 14:57–64, 1993.

16. Bone, L.; Stegeman, P.; McNamara, K.; Seibel, R. External fixation of severely comminuted and open tibial pilon fractures. Clin Orthop 292:101–107, 1993.

17. Bone, L.B. Fractures of the tibial plafond: The pilon fracture. Orthop Clin North Am 18:95–104, 1987.

18. Bonin, J.G. Injuries to the Ankle. London, William Heinemann, 1950, pp. 248–260.

19. Bonnier, P. Les Fractures du Pilon Tibial [thesis]. University of Lyon. Lyon, France, 1961.

20. Borner, M. Einteilung, Behandlung und Ergennisse der Frakturen des Pilon tibial. Unfallchirurgie 8:230–235, 1982.

21. Borrelli, J., Jr.; Catalano, L. Open reduction and internal fixation of pilon fractures: Current controversies in orthopaedic trauma. J Orthop Trauma 13:573–582, 1999.

22. Borrelli, J.; Torzilli, S. Effect of impact load on articular cartilage. J Orthop Trauma 11:319–326, 1997.

23. Bourne, R.B. Pylon fractures of the distal tibia. Clin Orthop 240:42–46, 1989.

24. Bourne, R.B.; Rorabec, C.H.; McNab, J. Intra-articular fractures of the distal tibia: The pilon fracture. J Trauma 23:591–596, 1983.

25. Braustein, P.W.; Wade, P.A. Treatment of unstable fractures of the ankle. Ann Surg 149:217–226, 1959.

26. Brennan, M.J. Tibial pilon fractures. Instr Course Lect 39:167–170, 1990.

27. Brumback, R.J.; McGarvey, W.C. Fractures of the tibial pilon: Evolving treatment concepts for the pilon fracture. Orthop Clin North Am 26:273–285, 1995.

28. Burwell, H.N.; Charnley, A.D. The treatment of displaced fractures of the ankle by rigid internal fixation and early joint movement. J Bone Joint Surg Br 47:634–660, 1965.

29. Calhoun, J.H.; Ledbetter, B.R.; Gill, C.A. Biomechanics of the Ilizarov fixator for fracture fixation. Clin Orthop 280:15–22, 1992.

30. Carpenter, C.A.; Jupiter, J.B. Blade plate reconstruction of meta-physeal nonunion of the tibia. Clin Orthop 332:23–28, 1996.

31. Childress, H.M. Vertical transarticular-pin fixation for unstable ankle fractures. J Bone Joint Surg Am 47:1323–1334, 1965.

32. Christian, E.P.; Bosse, M.J.; Robb, G. Reconstruction of large diaphyseal defects, without free fibular transfer, in grade IIIB tibial fractures. J Bone Joint Surg Am 71:994–1004, 1989.

33. Cierny, G.; Byrd, H.S.; Jones, R.E. Primary versus delayed soft tissue coverage for severe open tibial fractures. Clin Orthop 178:54–63, 1983.

34. Cierny, G.; Cook, W.G.; Mader, J.T. Ankle arthrodesis in the presence of ongoing sepsis. Orthop Clin North Am 20:709–721, 1989.

35. Collins, D.N.; Temple, S.D. Open joint injuries. Clin Orthop 243:48–56, 1989.

36. Colton, C.L. Injuries of the ankle. In: Watson-Jones, R., ed. Fractures and Joint Injuries. London, E.S. Livingstone, 1982, pp. 1130–1133.

37. Connolly, J.F. Pronation-dorsiflexion injuries. In: Connolly, J.F., ed. The Management of Fractures and Dislocations. Philadelphia, W.B. Saunders, 1981, pp. 1898–1914.

38. Conwell, H.E.; Reynolds, F.C. Key and Conwell's Management of Fractures, Dislocations, and Sprains, 7th ed. St. Louis, C.V. Mosby, 1961.

39. Coonrad, R.W. Fracture-dislocations of the ankle joint with impaction injury to the lateral weight bearing surface of the tibia. J Bone Joint Surg Am 52:1337–1343, 1970.

40. Copin, G.; Nerot, G. Les fractures recentes du pilon tibial de l'adulte. Rev Chir Orthop 78(Suppl 1):34–83, 1992.

41. Cox, F.J. Fractures of the ankle involving the lower articular surface of the tibia. Clin Orthop 42:51–55, 1965.

42. Crutchfield, E.H.; Seligson, D.; Henry, S.L.; Warnholtz, A. Tibial pilon fractures: A comparative clinical study of management techniques and results. Orthopaedics 18:613–617, 1995.

43. Decoster, T.A.; Willis, M.C.; Marsh, J.L.; et al. Rank order analysis of tibial plafond fractures: Does injury or reduction predict outcome? Foot Ankle Int 20:44–49, 1999.

44. Decoulx, P.; Razemon, J.P.; Rousselle, Y. Fractures du pilon tibiale. Rev Chir Orthop 47:563, 1961.

45. Destot, E. Traumatismes du pied et rayons x malleoles. In: Astragale, Calcaneum, Avant-pied. Paris, Mason, 1911.

46. DiChristina, D.; Riemer, B.L.; Butterfield, S.L.; Burke, C.J. Pilon fractures treated with an articulated external fixator: A preliminary report. Orthopedics 19:1019–1024, 1996.

47. Dillin, L.; Slabaugh, P. Delayed wound healing, infection, and nonunion following open reduction and internal fixation of tibial plafond fractures. J Trauma 26:1116–1119, 1986.

48. Dirschl, D.R.; Adams, G.L. A critical assessment of factors influencing reliability in the classification of fractures, using fractures of the tibial plafond as a model. J Orthop Trauma 11:471–476, 1997.

49. Ebraheim, N.; Sabry, F.F.; Mehalik, J.N.: Intraoperative imaging of the tibial plafond fracture: A potential pitfall. Foot Ankle Int 21:67–72, 2000.

50. Egol, K.A.; Wolinsky, P.; Koval, K.J. Open reduction and internal fixation of tibial pilon fractures. Foot Ankle Clin 5:873–885, 2000.

51. Ettei, C.; Ganz, R. Long-term results of tibial plafond fractures treated with open reduction and internal fixation. Arch Orthop Trauma Surg 110:277–283, 1991.

52. Fekete, G. [Pilon or Pylon? (letter)] [Hungarian]. Magy Traumatol Ortop Helyreallito Seb 34:236, 1991.

53. Feldman, F.; Singson, R.D.; Rosenberg, Z.S.; et al. Distal tibial fractures: Diagnosis with CT. Radiology 164:429–435, 1988.

54. Finsen, V.; Saetermo, R.; Kibsgaard, L.; et al. Early weight-bearing and muscle activity in patients who have a fracture of the ankle. J Bone Joint Surg Am 71:23–27, 1989.

55. Fitzpatrick, D.C.; Marsh, J.L.; Brown, T.D. Articulated external fixation of pilon fractures: The effects on ankle joint kinematics. J Orthop Trauma 9:76–82, 1995.

56. Fogel, G.R.; Morrey, B.F. Delayed open reduction and fixation of ankle fractures. Clin Orthop 215:187–195, 1987.

57. Fourquet, D. Contribution a l'Etude des Fractures Recentes du Pilon Tibial [thesis]. University of Paris. Paris, 1959.

58. Franklin, J.L.; Johnson, K.D.; Hansen, S.T. Immediate internal fixation of open ankle fractures. Report of thirty-eight cases treated with a standard protocol. J Bone Joint Surg Am 66:1349–1356, 1984.

59. French, B.; Tornetta, P., 3rd. Hybrid external fixation of tibial pilon fractures. Foot Ankle Clin 5:853–871, 2000.

60. Froimson, M.I.; Raikin, S. Combined internal and circular frame external fixation for intra-articular tibial fractures. Paper presented at the 63rd Annual Meeting of the American Academy of Orthopaedic Surgeons, Atlanta, Georgia, 1996.

61. Ganzoni, N.; Jirecek, V. Muscle-flap plasty in fractures of the tibial pilon. Helv Chir Acta 56:255–258, 1989.

62. Gaudinez, R.F.; Mallik, A.R.; Szporn, M. Hybrid external fixation in tibial plafond fractures. Clin Orthop 329:223–232, 1996.

63. Gay, R.; Evrard, J. Les fractures recentes du pilon tibial chez l'adulte. Rev Chir Orthop 49:397–512, 1963.

64. Geerts, W.H.; Code, K.I.; Jay, R.M.; et al. A prospective study of venous thromboembolism after major trauma. N Engl J Med 331:1601–1606, 1994.

65. Giordano, C.P.; Koval, K.J. Treatment of fracture blisters: A prospective study of 53 cases. J Orthop Trauma 9:171–176, 1995.

66. Gordon, L.; Chiu, E.J. Treatment of infected nonunions and segmental defects of the tibia with staged microvascular muscle transplantation and bone grafting. J Bone Joint Surg Am 66:181–193, 1984.

67. Gould, J.S. Reconstruction of soft tissue injuries of the foot and ankle with microsurgical techniques. Orthopedics 10:151–157, 1987.

68. Graehl, P.M.; Hersh, M.R.; Heckman, J.D. Supramalleolar osteotomy for the treatment of symptomatic tibial malunion. J Orthop Trauma 1:281–292, 1988.

69. Green, S.A.; Roesler, S. Salvage of the infected pilon fracture. Techn Orthop 2:37–41, 1987.

70. Gregory, R.T.; Gould, R.J.; Peclet, M.; et al. The mangled extremity syndrome (M.E.S.): A severity grading system for multisystem injury of the extremity. J Trauma 25:1147–1150, 1985.

71. Griffiths, G.P.; Thordarson, D.B. Tibial plafond fracture: Limited internal fixation and hybrid external fixation. Foot Ankle Int 17:444–448, 1996.

72. Gruen, G.S.; Mears, D.C. Arthrodesis of the ankle and subtalar joints. Clin Orthop 268:15–20, 1991.

73. Gustilo, R.B.; Anderson, J.T. Prevention of infection in the treatment of one thousand and twenty-five open fractures of the long bones. Retrospective and prospective analysis. J Bone Joint Surg Am 58:453–458, 1976.

74. Hamilton, W.C. Comminuted fractures of the tibial plafond. In: Traumatic Disorders of the Ankle. New York, Springer-Verlag, 1984.

75. Hedstrom, M.; Torbjorn, A.; Dalen, N. Early postoperative ankle exercise. Clin Orthop 300:193–196, 1994.

76. Heim, U. The Pilon Tibial Fracture: Classification, Surgical Techniques, Results. Philadelphia, W.B. Saunders, 1995.

77. Heim, U.; Naser, M. Die operative Behandlung der Pilon tibial-Fractures. Technik der Osteosynthesis und der Resultate bei 128 Patienten. Arch Orthop Unfallchir 86:341, 1976.

78. Heim, U.; Naser, M. Fractures du pilon tibial. Rev Chir Orthop 63:5, 1977.

79. Helfet, D.L.; Howey, T.; Sanders, R.; Johansen, K. Limb salvage versus amputation: Preliminary results of the mangled extremity severity score. Clin Orthop 256:80–86, 1990.

80. Helfet, D.L.; Koval, K.; Pappas, J.; et al. Intra-articular "pilon" fractures of the tibia. Clin Orthop 298:221–228, 1994.

81. Helfet, D.L.; Shonnard, P.; Levine, D.; Borrelli, J. Minimally invasive plate osteosynthesis of distal fractures of the tibia. Injury 28 (Suppl 1):SA42–SA48, 1997.

82. Holt, E.S. Arthroscopic visualization of the tibial plafond during posterior malleolar fracture fixation. Foot Ankle Int 15:206–208, 1994.

83. Hontzsch, D.; Karnatz, N.; Jansen, T. One- or two-step management (with external fixator) of severe pilon-tibial fractures. Aktuel Traumatol 20:199–204, 1990.

84. Hulscher, J.B.; te Velde, E.A.; Schuurman, A.H.; et al. Arthrodesis after osteosynthesis and infection of the ankle joint. Injury 32:145–152, 2001.

85. Hutson, J.J., Jr.; Zych, G.A. Infections in periarticular fractures of the lower extremity treated with tensioned wire hybrid fixators. J Orthop Trauma 12:214–218, 1998.

86. Hutson, J.J.; Zych, G.A. The treatment of 100 tibia/fibula, distal segment fractures with circular tensioned wire fixators. Paper presented at the 16th Annual Meeting of the Orthopaedic Trauma Association, San Antonio, Texas, 2000.

87. Jahna, H.; Wittich, H.; Hartenstein, H.: Der distale Stauchungs-bruch der Tibia. Unfallheilkunde 137(Suppl):1, 1980.

88. Jergesen, F. Open reduction of fractures and dislocations of the ankle. Am J Surg 98:136, 1959.

89. Judet, J.; Judet, R.; Letournel, E. Un procede d'osteosynthesis pour fracture multifragmentaire du pilon tibial. Mem Acad Chir 17–18:547–549, 1967.

90. Juliano, P.J.; Yu, J.R.; Schneider, D.J.; Jacobs, C.R. Evaluation of fracture predilection in the calcaneus after external fixator pin removal. J Orthop Trauma 11:430–434, 1997.

91. Kao, K.F.; Huang, P.J.; Chen, Y.C.; et al. Postero-medial-anterior approach of the ankle for the pilon fracture. Injury 31:71–74, 2000.

92. Kellam, J.F.; Waddell, J.P. Fractures of the distal tibial metaphysis with intra-articular extension: The distal tibial explosion fracture. J Trauma 19:593–601, 1979.

93. Kelly, P.J.; Fitzgerald, R.H.; Cabenella, M.E.; et al. Results of treatment of tibial and femoral osteomyelitis in adults. Clin Orthop 259:295–303, 1990.

94. Kim, H.S.; Jahn, J.S.; Kim, S.S.; et al. Treatment of tibial pilon fractures using ring fixators and arthroscopy. Clin Orthop 334:244–250, 1997.

95. Klemm, K.; Seligson, D. Treatment of chronic osteomyelitis of the foot and ankle with gentamicin-PMMA beads and mini-beads. Techn Orthop 2:89–95, 1987.

96. Klossner, O. Late results of operative and nonoperative treatment of severe ankle fractures. Acta Chir Scand 293(Suppl):1–93, 1962.

97. Konrath, G.A.; Hopkins, G. Posterolateral approach for tibial pilon fractures: A report of two cases. J Orthop Trauma 13:586–592, 1999.

98. Kummer, F.J. Biomechanics of the Ilizarov external fixator. Clin Orthop 280:11–14, 1992.

99. LaDuca, J.; Bone, L.; Seibel, R.; et al. Primary open reduction and internal fixation of open fractures. J Trauma 20:580–589, 1980.

100. Lambotte, A. Chirurgie Operatioire des Fractures. Paris, Masson, 1913.

101. Lamprecht, E.; Ochsner, P.E. Spatprobleme nach konservativ und operativ Behandelten, "pilon tibial" Frakturen. Helv Chir Acta 51:629–631, 1984.

102. Lange, R.H.; Bach, A.W.; Hansen, S.T.; Johansen, K.H. Open tibial fractures with associated vascular injuries: Prognosis for limb salvage. J Trauma 25:203–208, 1985.

103. Lanz, B.A.; McAndrew, M.; Scioli, M.; et al. The effect of concomitant chondral injuries accompanying operatively reduced malleolar fractures. J Orthop Trauma 5:125–128, 1991.

104. Lauge-Hansen, N. Fractures of the ankle III: Genetic roentgenologic diagnosis of fractures of the ankle. AJR Am J Roentgenol 71:456, 1954.

105. Lauge-Hansen, N. Fractures of the ankle V: Pronation-dorsiflexion fractures. Arch Surg 67:813–820, 1953.

106. Leach, R.E. Fractures of the tibial plafond. In: Yablon, I.G.; Segal, D.; Leach, R., eds. Ankle Injuries. New York, Churchill Livingstone, 1983.

107. Leach, R.E. A means of stabilizing comminuted distal tibial fractures. J Trauma 4:722–725, 1964.

108. Lechevallier, J.; Thomine, J.M.; Biga, N. Le fixator externe tibio-calcareen dans le traitement des fracture du pilon tibial. Rev Chir Orthop 74:52–60, 1989.

109. Leone, V.J.; Ruland, R.; Meinhard, B. The management of soft tissue in pilon fractures. Clin Orthop 292:315–320, 1993.

110. Lundy, D.W.; Albert, M.J.; Hutton, W.C. Biomechanical comparison of hybrid external fixators. J Orthop Trauma 12:496–503, 1998.

111. Lynch, A.F.; Bourne, R.B.; Rorabeck, C.H. The long-term results of ankle arthrodesis. J Bone Joint Surg Br 70:113–116, 1988.

112. Maale, G.; Seligson, D. Fractures through the distal weight-bearing surface of the tibia. Orthopedics 3:517–521, 1980.

113. MacKinnon, A.P. Fracture of the lower articular surface of the tibia in fracture dislocation of the ankle. J Bone Joint Surg 10:352, 1928.

114. Marsh, J.L. External fixation is the treatment of choice for fractures of the tibial plafond. J Orthop Trauma 13:583–585, 1999.

115. Marsh, J.L.; Bonar, S.; Nepola, J.V.; et al. Use of an articulated external fixator for fractures of the tibial plafond. J Bone Joint Surg Am 77:1498–1509, 1995.

116. Marsh, J.L.; Nepola, J.V.; Wuest, T.K.; et al. Unilateral external fixation until healing with dynamic axial fixator for severe open tibia fractures. J Orthop Trauma 5:341–348, 1991.

117. Marsh, J.L.; Rattay, R.E.; Dulaney, T. Results of ankle arthrodesis for treatment of supramalleolar nonunion and ankle arthrosis. Foot Ankle Int 18:138–143, 1997.

118. Marsh, J.L.; Weigel, D.; Dirschl, D. Tibial plafond fractures—do these ankles function over time? Paper presented at the 16th Annual Meeting of the Orthopaedic Trauma Association, San Antonio, Texas, 2000.

119. Martin, J.S.; Marsh, J.L.; Bonar, S.K.; et al. Assessment of AO/ASIF fracture classification for the tibial plafond. J Orthop Trauma 11:477–483, 1997.

120. Martsa, B.; Fekete, G.; Renner, A. [Experience with management of fractures of the distal tibial end penetrating the joint] [Hungarian]. Magyar Traumatologia Ortopedia Kezsebeszet Plaztikai Sebeszet 36:269–276, 1993.

121. Mast, J. Pilon fractures of the distal tibia: A test of surgical judgement. In: Tscherne, H.; Schatzker, J., eds. Major Fractures of the Pilon, the Talus, and the Calcaneus. Heidelberg, Springer-Verlag, 1993, pp. 7–27.

122. Mast, J.W. Reduction techniques in fractures of the distal tibial articular surface. Techn Orthop 2:29–36, 1987.

123. Mast, J.W.; Jacobs, R.; Ganz, R. Planning and Reduction Techniques in Fracture Surgery. Berlin, Springer-Verlag, 1989, pp. 139, 182–184.

124. Mast, J.W.; Spiegal, P.G. Complex ankle fractures. In: Meyers, M.H., ed. The Multiply Injured Patient with Complex Fractures. Philadelphia, Lea & Febiger, 1984, pp. 291–312.

125. Mast, J.W.; Spiegal, P.G.; Pappas, J.N. Fractures of the tibial pilon. Clin Orthop 230:68–82, 1988.

126. Mast, J.W.; Teipner, W.A. A reproducible approach to the internal fixation of adult ankle fractures: Rationale, technique, and early results. Orthop Clin North Am 11:661–679, 1980.

127. Mazur, J.M.; Schwartz, E.; Simon, S.R. Ankle arthrodesis: Long-term follow-up with gait analysis. J Bone Joint Surg Am 61:964–975, 1979.

128. McAndrew, M.P.; Lantz, B.A. Initial care of massively traumatized lower extremities. Clin Orthop 243:20–29, 1989.

129. McDonald, M.G.; Burgess, R.C.; Bolano, L.E.; Nicholls, P.J. Ilizarov treatment of pilon fractures. Clin Orthop 325:232–238, 1996.

130. McFerran, M.A.; Smith, S.W.; Boulas, H.J.; Schwartz, H.S. Complications encountered in the treatment of pilon fractures. J Orthop Trauma 6:195–200, 1992.

131. McNamara, M.G.; Heckman, J.D.; Corley, F.G. Severe open fractures of the lower extremity: A retrospective evaluation of the mangled extremity severity score (MESS). J Orthop Trauma 8:81–87, 1994.

132. Mitchell, N.; Shepard, N. Healing of articular cartilage in intra-articular fractures in rabbits. J Bone Joint Surg Am 62:628–635, 1980.

133. Moller, B.N.; Krebs, B. Intra-articular fractures of the distal tibia. Acta Orthop Scand 53:991–996, 1982.

134. Moore, T.; Prince, R.; Pochatko, D.; et al. Retrograde intramedullary nailing for ankle arthrodesis. Foot Ankle Int 16:433–436, 1995.

135. Morgan, C.D.; Henke, J.A.; Bailey, R.W.; Kaufer, H. Long-term results of tibiotalar arthrodesis. J Bone Joint Surg Am 67:546–555, 1985.

136. Morgan, S.J.; Thordarson, D.B.; Shepherd, L.E. Salvage of tibial pilon fractures using fusion of the ankle with a 90 degrees cannulated blade-plate: A preliminary report. Foot Ankle Int 20:375–378, 1999.

137. Morrey, B.F.; Weideman, G.P. Complications and long term results of ankle arthrodesis following trauma. J Bone Joint Surg Am 62:777–784, 1980.

138. Muhr, G.; Breitfuss, H. Complications after pilon fractures. In: Tscherne, H.; Schatzker, J., eds. Major Fractures of the Pilon, the Talus, and the Calcaneus. Heidelberg, Springer-Verlag, 1993, pp. 65–67.

139. Muller, K.H.; Presscher, W. Posttraumatische Osteomyelitis nach distalen intraarticularen Unterschenkelfrakturen. Hefte Unfall-heilkd 131:163–183, 1978.

140. Müller, M.E.: Les fractures du pilon tibial. Rev Chir Orthop 50:557, 1964.

141. Müller, M.E.; Allgöwer, M.; Schneider, R.; Willenegger, H. In: Tscherne, H.; Schatzker, J., eds. Manual of Internal Fixation Techniques Recommended by the AO Group. New York, Springer-Verlag, 1979, pp. 146, 147, 208–210, 214–215, 586–612.

142. Müller, M.E.N.; Nazarian, S.; Koch, P.; Schatzker, J. The Comprehensive Classification of Fractures of Long Bones. New York, Springer-Verlag, 1987, pp. 170–179.

143. Muller-Gerble, M.; Putz, R. The lower segment of the tibia. Functional anatomy of the ankle joint. In: Heim, U., ed. The Pilon Tibial Fracture: Classification, Surgical Techniques, Results. Philadelphia, W.B. Saunders, 1995, pp. 2–25.

144. Murphy, C.P.; D'Ambrosia, R.; Dabezies, E.J. The small pin circular fixator for distal tibial pilon fractures with soft tissue compromise. Orthopedics 14:283–290, 1991.

145. Nast-Kolb, D.; Betz, A.; Rodel, C.; Schweiberer, L. [Minimal osteosynthesis of the tibial pilon fracture] [German]. Unfallchirurg 96:517–523, 1993.

146. Orbay, G.L.; Frankel, V.H.; Kummer, F.J. The effect of wire configuration on the stability of the Ilizarov external fixator. Clin Orthop 279:299–302, 1992.

147. Ordway, C.B.; Weiner, L.; Bergman, M.; et al. Wire tension techniques combined with minimal internal fixation for treatment of juxta-articular fractures. Exhibit 3608. Presented at the 58th Annual Meeting of the American Academy of Orthopaedic Surgeons, Anaheim, California, 1991.

148. Ovadia, D.N.; Beals, R.K. Fractures of the tibial plafond. J Bone Joint Surg Am 68:543–551, 1986.

149. Patterson, M.J.; Cole, J.D. Two-staged delayed open reduction and internal fixation of severe pilon fractures. J Orthop Trauma 13:85–91, 1999.

150. Patzakis, M.J.; Wilkins, J. Factors influencing infection rate in open fracture wounds. Clin Orthop 243:36–40, 1989.

151. Picanza, J. Poor results mark ORIF of tibia plafond fractures. Orthop Today 10:1, 1990.

152. Pierce, F.O.; Heinrich, J.H. Comminuted intra-articular fractures of the distal tibia. J Trauma 19:828–832, 1979.

153. Pillsbury, S.L. Complications of foot and ankle fractures. In: Gossling, H.R.; Pillsbury, S.L., eds. Complications of Fracture Management. Philadelphia, J.B. Lippincott, 1984, pp. 531–534.

154. Pugh, K.J.; Wolinsky, P.; Pienkowski, D.; et al. Comparative biomechanics of hybrid external fixation. J Orthop Trauma 13:418–425, 1999.

155. Pugh, K.J.; Wolinsky, P.R.; McAndrew, M.P.; Johnson, K.D. Tibial pilon fractures: A comparison of treatment methods. J Trauma 47:937–941, 1999.

156. Raikin, S.; Froimson, M.I. Combined limited internal fixation with circular frame external fixation of intra-articular tibial fractures. Orthopedics 22:1019–1025, 1999.

157. Ralston, J.L.; Brown, T.D.; Nepola, J.V.; et al. Mechanical analysis of the factors affecting dynamization of the Orthofix dynamic axial fixator. J Trauma 4:449–457, 1990.

158. Resch, H. Die Entwicklung der posttraumatischen Arthrose nach Pilon-Tibialfrakturen. Unfallchirurg 89:8–15, 1986.

159. Resch, H.; Pechlaner, S.; Benedetto, K.P.: Long-term results after conservative and surgical treatment of fractures of the distal end of the tibia [German abstract]. Aktuel Traumatol 16:117–123, 1986.

160. Ries, M.D.; Meinhard, B.P. Medial external fixation with lateral plate internal fixation in metaphyseal tibia fractures: A report of eight cases associated with severe soft-tissue injury. Clin Orthop 256:215–224, 1990.

161. Rieunau, G.; Gay, R. Enclouge du perone dans les fractures supra-malleolaires. Lyon Chir 51:594–600, 1956.

162. Rogge, D. Gelenktransfixation bei Gelenkuerletzungen mit schwerem Weichteilschaden. Hefte Unfallheilkd 162:97–110, 1983.

163. Rommens, P.M.; Claes, P.; De Boodt, P.; et al. [Therapeutic procedure and long-term results in tibial pilon fracture in relation to primary soft tissue damage] [German]. Unfallchirurg 97:39–46, 1994.

164. Ruëdi, T. Fractures of the lower end of the tibia into the ankle joint: Results nine years after open reduction and internal fixation. Injury 5:130–134, 1973.

165. Ruëdi, T. Treatment of pilon tibial fractures: State of the art. In: Tscherne, H.; Schatzker, J., eds. Major Fractures of the Pilon, the Talus, and the Calcaneus. Heidelberg, Springer-Verlag, 1993, pp. 3–5.

166. Ruëdi, T.; Allgöwer, M. Fractures of the lower end of the tibia into the ankle joint. Injury 1:92–99, 1969.

167. Ruëdi, T.; Matter, P.; Allgöwer, M. Die intra-artikularen Frakturen des distalen Unterschenkelendes. Helv Chir Acta 35:556, 1968.

168. Ruëdi, T.P.; Allgöwer, M. The operative treatment of intra-articular fractures of the lower end of the tibia. Clin Orthop 138:105–110, 1979.

169. Ruoff, A.C.; Snider, R.K. Explosion fractures of the distal tibia with major articular involvement. J Trauma 11:866–873, 1971.

170. Ruwe, P.A.; Randall, R.L.; Baumgaertner, M.R. Pilon fractures of the distal tibia. Orthop Rev 22:987–996, 1993.

171. Saleh, M.; Shanahan, M.D.; Fern, E.D.: Intra-articular fractures of the distal tibia: Surgical management by limited internal fixation and articulated distraction. Injury 24:37–40, 1993.

172. Salter, R.; Simmonds, D.F.; Malcolm, B.W.; et al. The biologic effect of continuous passive motion on the healing of full-thickness defects in articular cartilage. An experimental investigation in the rabbit. J Bone Joint Surg Am 62:1232–1251, 1980.

173. Sanders, R.; Pappas, J.; Mast, J.; Helfet, D. The salvage of open grade IIIB ankle and talus fractures. J Orthop Trauma 6:201–208, 1992.

174. Sangeorzan, B.J.; Hansen, S.T. Early and late posttraumatic foot reconstruction. Clin Orthop 243:86–91, 1989.

175. Schatzker, J. Compression in surgical treatment of fractures of the tibia. Clin Orthop 105:220–239, 1974.

176. Scheck, M. Treatment of comminuted distal tibial fractures by combined dual-pin fixation and limited open reduction. J Bone Joint Surg Am 47:1537–1553, 1965.

177. Shelton, M.; Anderson, R.L. Complications of fractures and dislocations of the ankle. In: Epps, C.H., ed. Complications in Orthopaedic Surgery. Philadelphia, J.B. Lippincott, 1986, pp. 599–648.

178. Shelton, M.; James, R.; Shelton, Y. Pilon fractures—a new classification and treatment. Orthop Trans 13:762, 1959.

179. Sherman, R.; Wellisz, T.; Wiss, D.; et al. Coverage of type III open ankle and foot fractures with temporoparietal fascial free flap. Orthop Trans 14:265, 1990.

180. Sirkin, M.; Sanders, R.; DiPasquale, T.; Herscovici, D. A staged protocol for soft tissue management in the treatment of complex pilon fractures. J Orthop Trauma 13:77–84, 1999.

181. Sondenaa, K.; Hoigaard, U.; Smith, D.; Alho, A. Immobilization of operated ankle fractures. Acta Orthop Scand 57:59–61, 1986.

182. Sowa, D.T.; Krackow, K.A. Ankle fusion: A new technique of internal fixation using a compression blade plate. Foot Ankle 9:232–240, 1989.

183. Stasikelis, P.J.; Calhoun, J.H.; Ledbetter, B.R.; et al. Treatment of infected pilon nonunions with small pin fixators. Foot Ankle 14:373–379, 1993.

184. Steadman, J.R. Rehabilitation of tibial plafond fractures after stable internal fixation. Am J Sports Med 9:71–72, 1981.

185. Stiehl, J.B.; Dollinger, B. Primary ankle arthrodesis in trauma: Report of three cases. J Orthop Trauma 2:277–283, 1988.

186. Sward, L.; Hughs, J.S.; Howell, C.J.; et al. Posterior internal compression arthrodesis of the ankle. J Bone Joint Surg Br 74:752–756, 1992.

187. Swiontkowski, M.F. Interobserver variation in the AO/OTA fracture classification system for pilon fractures: Is there a problem? J Orthop Trauma 11:467–470, 1997.

188. Swiontkowski, M.F.; Sands, A.; Grujic, L.; et al. Open reduction with screw/plate fixation for pilon fractures: Complications and functional outcome. Paper presented at the 11th Annual Meeting of the Orthopaedic Trauma Association, Tampa, Florida, 1995.

189. Szyszkowitz, R.; Reschauer, R.; Seggl, W. Pilon fractures of the tibia. In: Chapman, M.W., ed. Operative Orthopaedics. Philadelphia, J.B. Lippincott, 1988, pp. 461–470.

190. Tassler, H. Behandlungsprinzipien bei drittgradig offenen Frakturen des distalen Unterschenkels. Unfallheilkunde 84:509–513, 1981.

191. Teeny, S.M.; Wiss, D.A. Open reduction and internal fixation of tibial plafond fractures. Variables contributing to poor results and complications. Clin Orthop 292:108–117, 1993.

192. Tencer, A.F.; Johnson, K.D. Biomechanics in Orthopaedic Trauma. Philadelphia, J.B. Lippincott, 1994.

193. Tile, M. Fractures of the distal tibial metaphysis involving the ankle joint: The pilon fracture. In: Schatzker, J.; Tile, M., eds. The Rationale of Operative Fracture Care. Berlin, Springer-Verlag, 1987, pp. 343–369.

194. Tornetta, P., 3rd; Gorup, J. Axial computed tomography of pilon fractures. Clin Orthop 323:273–276, 1996.

195. Tornetta, P.; Weiner, L. Severe fractures of the distal tibia. Complications Orthop Nov/Dec:75–78, 1993.

196. Tornetta, P.; Weiner, L.; Bergman, M.; et al. Pilon fractures: Treatment with combined internal and external fixation. J Orthop Trauma 7:489–496, 1993.

197. Treadwell, J.R.; Fallat, L.M. Dynamic unilateral distraction fixation: Surgical management of tibial pilon fractures. J Foot Ankle Surg 33:438–442, 1994.

198. Trentz, O.; Friedl, H.P. Critical soft tissue conditions and pilon fractures. In: Tscherne, H.; Schatzker, J., eds. Major Fractures of the Pilon, the Talus, and the Calcaneus. Heidelberg, Springer-Verlag, 1993, pp. 59–64.

199. Trumble, T.E.; Benirschke, S.K.; Vedder, N.B. Use of radial forearm flaps to treat complications of closed pilon fractures. J Trauma 6:358–365, 1992.

200. Tschere, H.; Gotzen, L. External articular transfixation of joint injuries with severe soft tissue damage. In: Tscherne, H.; Gotzen, L., eds. Fractures with Soft Tissue Injuries. Berlin, Springer-Verlag, 1984, pp. 103–117.

201. Tscherne, H.; Gotzen, L. Fractures with Soft-Tissue Injuries. Berlin, Springer-Verlag, 1984, pp. 1–58.

202. Vander Griend, R.A.; Michelson, J.D.; Bone, L.B. Fractures of the ankle and distal part of the tibia. J Bone Joint Surg Am 78:1772–1783, 1996.

203. Vander Griend, R.A.; Savoie, F.H.; Hughs, J.L. Fractures of the ankle. In: Rockwood, C.A.; Green, D.P.; Bucholz, R.W., eds. Fractures in Adults. Philadelphia, J.B. Lippincott, 1991, pp. 2030–2033.

204. Varela, C.D.; Vaughan, T.K.; Carr, J.B.; Slemmons, B.K. Fracture blisters: Clinical and pathological aspects. J Orthop Trauma 7:417–427, 1993.

205. Vasli, S. Operative treatment of ankle fractures. Acta Chir Scand 226(Suppl):1–74, 1957.

206. Vives, P.; Hourlier, H.; De Lestang, M.; et al. Etude de 84 fractures du pilon tibial de l'adulte. Rev Chir Orthop 70:129–139, 1984.

207. Waddell, J.P. Tibial plafond fractures. In: Tscherne, H.; Schatzker, J., eds. Major Fractures of the Pilon, the Talus, and the Calcaneus. Heidelberg, Springer-Verlag, 1993, pp. 43–48.

208. Watson, J.T.; Karges, D.E.; Cramer, K.E.; Moed, B.R. Analysis of failure of hybrid external fixation techniques for the treatment of distal tibial pilon fractures. Presented at the 16th Annual Meeting of the Orthopaedic Trauma Association, San Antonio, Texas, 2000.

209. Watson, J.T.; Moed, B.R.; Karges, D.E.; Cramer, K.E. Pilon fractures. Treatment protocol based on severity of soft tissue injury. Clin Orthop 375:78–90, 2000.

210. Watson, J.T.; Occhietti, M.J.; Moed, B.R.; et al. Perioperative external fixator management during secondary surgical procedures. Paper presented at the 15th Annual Meeting of the Orthopaedic Trauma Association, Charlotte, North Carolina, 1999.

211. Weiland, A.J.; Moore, J.R.; Daniel, R.K. The efficacy of free tissue transfer in the treatment of osteomyelitis. J Bone Joint Surg Am 66:181–193, 1984.

212. Weiner, L.S.; Mirsky, E.; Karas, E. Complications of composite fixation in juxtaarticular tibial fractures. Paper presented at the 11th Annual Meeting of the Orthopaedic Trauma Association, Tampa, Florida, 1995.

213. Welz, K. Besondere Aspekte und Ergebnisse der Behandlung von Pilon-tibial-frakturen. Orthop Traumatol 29:632–643, 1982.

214. Williams, C.W.; Langston, J.; Sanders, A. Comminuted fractures of the distal tibia into the ankle joint. J Bone Joint Surg Am 49:192, 1967.

215. Williams, T.M.; Marsh, J.L.; Nepola, J.V.; et al. External fixation of tibial plafond fractures—is routine plating of the fibula necessary? J Orthop Trauma 12:16–20, 1998.

216. Williams, T.M.; Marsh, J.L.; Nepola, J.V.; et al. Factors affecting outcome in tibial plafond fractures. Paper presented at the 14th Annual Meeting of the Orthopaedic Trauma Association, Vancouver, British Columbia, 1998.

217. Wyrsch, B.; McFerran, M.A.; McAndrew, M.; et al. Operative treatment of fractures of the tibial plafond: A randomized prospective study. J Bone Joint Surg Am 78:1646–1657, 1996.

218. Yablon, I.G.; Heller, F.G.; Shouse, L. The key role of the lateral malleolus in displaced fractures of the ankle. J Bone Joint Surg Am 59:169–173, 1977.

# CHAPTER 59

# Malleolar Fractures and Soft Tissue Injuries of the Ankle

James B. Carr, M.D.

No unequivocal boundary marks the proximal or distal limits of the ankle region. Structure, function, and injuries have no borders here and often require that the leg and foot be included in any regional assessment or treatment. This chapter considers malleolar fractures, related ligament injuries, and other soft tissue injuries of the ankle region. Pilon fractures are discussed in Chapter 58. Talar injuries are reviewed in Chapter 60.

The ankle is a complex hinge in which both bones and ligaments play important and inseparable parts.[127] Satisfactory function depends significantly on its precise structural integrity. As a weight-bearing joint, the ankle is exposed to forces that transiently exceed 1.25 times body weight with normal gait and that may exceed 5.5 times body weight with vigorous activities. Normal gait requires adequate dorsiflexion and plantar flexion. Inversion and eversion, as well as accommodation to rotational stresses, are provided by the subtalar joint, whose function is linked closely with that of the ankle.[112, 159] The ankle is not intrinsically stable in any position and requires support from the muscles that cross it.

The overlying skin is thin, with a tenuous blood supply.[251] Tendons rather than muscle bellies cross the joint and provide no coverage for it. After severe injuries, ankle wounds, both traumatic and surgical, may have problems healing. An injury of the ankle region can affect—in addition to bone, articular surface, and ligament—any of the tendons, nerves, or blood vessels that cross it.

Management of ankle injuries requires a thorough evaluation identifying both the anatomic structures involved and the severity of the damage.[96, 248] Once the injuries have been defined, optimal treatment generally entails as anatomic a repair as possible while avoiding any additional compromise to the region.

## ANATOMY AND BIOMECHANICS

### Anatomy

Ankle anatomy has been thoroughly reviewed by several investigators.[96, 238] Distally, the tibial shaft flares

and the bone changes from tubular cortical to metaphyseal and cancellous (Fig. 59–1). In the young, active adult, the distal tibia may be exceptionally dense. The AO/Association for the Study of Internal Fixation (AO/ASIF) has contributed to our awareness of the distinction between *malleolar fractures*, which may have associated involvement of the plafond, and *pilon fractures*, in which the focus of the injury is primarily supramalleolar.[235] The latter are discussed in the previous chapter.

The anteromedial aspect of the distal tibia is notable for the prominent medial malleolus, which carries the medial articular surface of the ankle mortise. It is smaller than the lateral malleolus and can be divided into an anterior colliculus, covered laterally with articular cartilage, and a posterior colliculus. The superficial deltoid (medial collateral) ligament is attached at the anterior colliculus and distally goes to the talus, calcaneus, and navicular, but it provides little stability to the ankle joint itself. The primary medial stabilizer is the deep portion of the deltoid ligament, which is attached to the posterior colliculus, the somewhat shorter posterior part of the malleolus. This nearly transverse, synovium-covered, essentially intra-articular ligament is not accessible from outside the joint unless the talus is displaced laterally or the medial malleolus can be turned distally through a fracture or osteotomy (Fig. 59–2). Any repair of the deltoid ligament that does not include this structure does not restore ligamentous stability.

The articular surface of the distal tibia is concave, with the anterior and, especially, posterior lips projecting more distally. The posterior lip of the plafond is the anchorage for the posterior part of the inferior tibiofibular syndesmotic ligaments. It does not limit movement of the talus as the medial and lateral malleoli do. However, it is not uncommonly injured along with the lateral and medial malleoli, becoming the "third malleolus." This injury is the basis for the term *trimalleolar fracture* to describe injuries involving both the medial and the lateral malleoli along with the posterior lip.[96]

Because of the clinical observation that trimalleolar fractures with a large postmalleolar component tend to heal with posterolateral talar subluxation, it has been assumed that the posterior malleolus is a restraint to

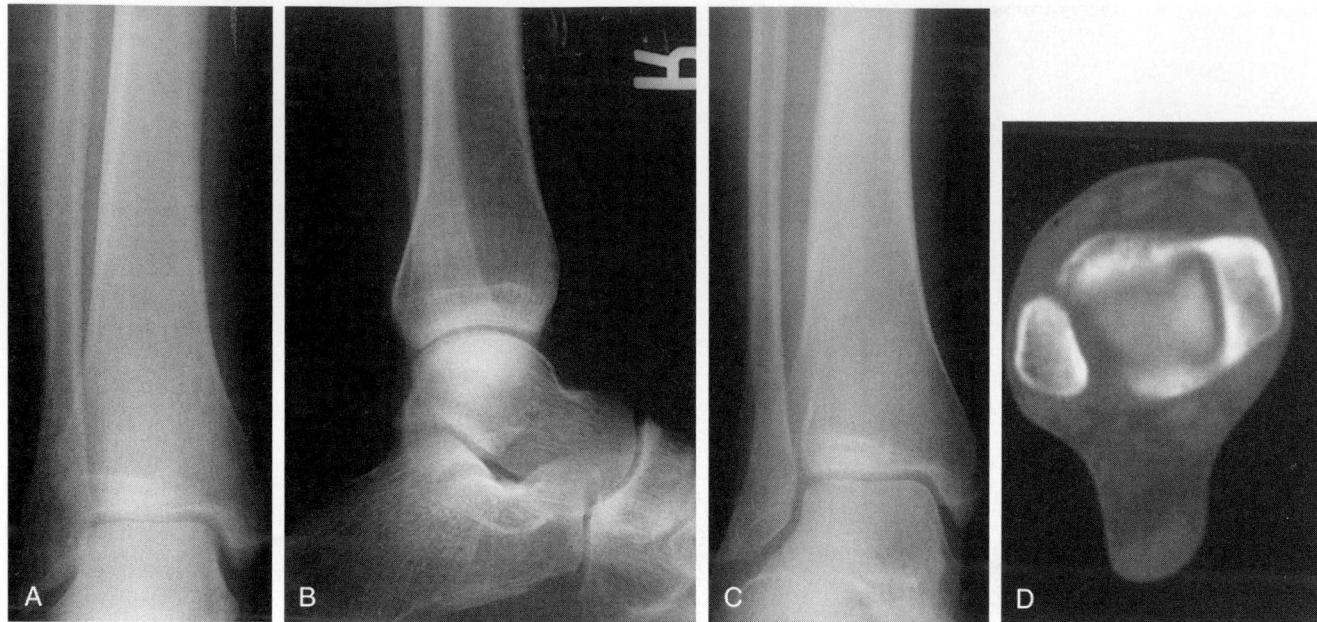

**FIGURE 59–1.** Normal anteroposterior (A), lateral (B), and mortise (C) views of the ankle. The tibiotalar joint demonstrates congruent articular surfaces, normal subchondral bone outline, and uniform width of cartilage space. The overlap of the tibia and the fibula at the incisural notch is evident. D, Computed tomographic scan through another patient's ankle shows that the medial and lateral joint spaces are not necessarily parallel. Note again the congruent fit of the talus in mortise.

posterior translation of the talus.[292] It is unclear to what extent fibular malunion contributed to this finding. Using cadaver specimens, Harper[99] and Raasch and colleagues[216] noted no posterior talar instability with fractures involving up to 40% of the tibial surface. Somewhat contradictory findings were noted by Scheidt and co-workers.[244] Using an axially loaded experimental model, they noted increased posterior drawer and internal rotation with posterior malleolar fractures involving 25% of the distal tibial articular surface. The posterior malleolus also contributes to the weight-bearing surface, with a loss of 35% of contact pressure seen with a fracture involving half of the joint surface.[216] Thus, the posterior malleolus fracture must be evaluated regarding its effect on articular congruity. Although the posterior tibia's contribution to

posterior talar stability is less clear, a sizable (>25%) posterior malleolar fracture demands careful assessment regarding whether it should be repaired.

The tibial joint surface has a central prominence oriented in the sagittal plane. The size of this ridge is variable. The articular surface contour of the talar dome very closely matches the curved plafond and sagittal ridge. Slight lateral displacement of the talus results in a considerable reduction of the contact area between the two bones. According to Ramsey and Hamilton,[218] a 1-mm lateral shift produces a 42% decrease in joint contact area. It is presumed that increased joint pressure, caused by the same amount of force being borne by a smaller area, results in degenerative changes of the articular cartilage, a common problem after severe injuries in which loss of the

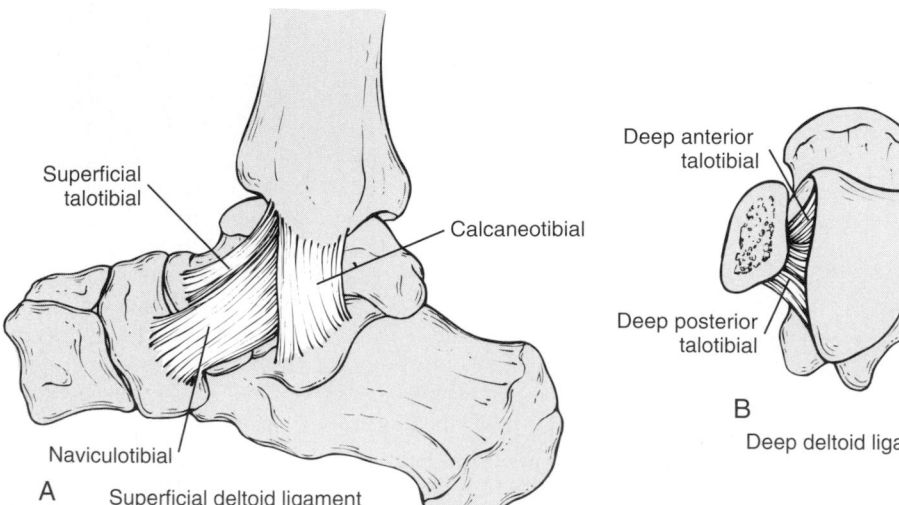

**FIGURE 59–2.** The medial collateral ligament of the ankle. A, The superficial fibers connecting the medial malleolus to the talus, calcaneus, and navicular have a roughly triangular appearance and suggest the name *deltoid*. B, The much more important deep fibers run nearly transversely from the posterior colliculus to the talus posterior to its medial articular facet.

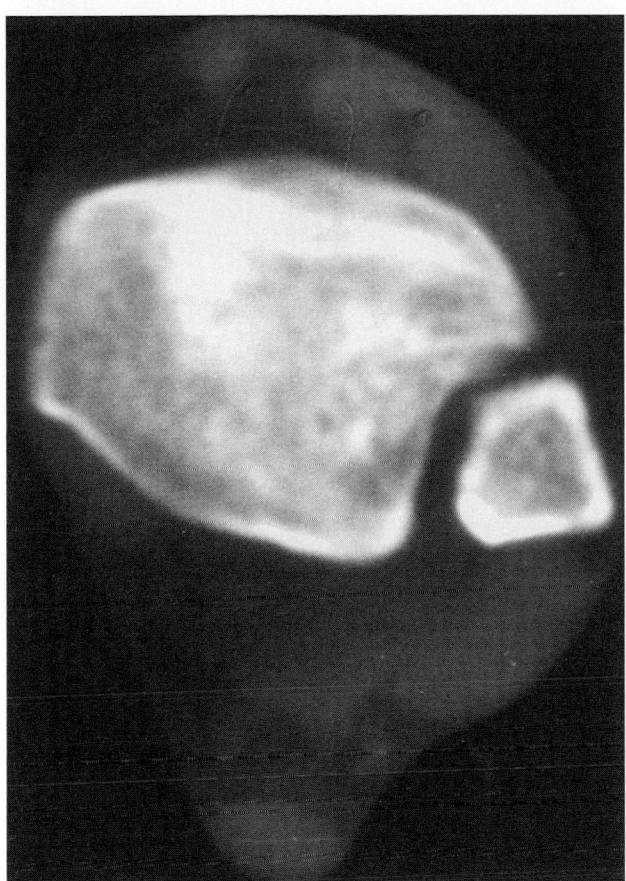

**FIGURE 59–3.** Computed tomographic scan just above the ankle shows the prominent anterior tubercle, which overlaps the more posterior fibula and helps form the incisural notch.

congruent relationship between talus and tibia occurs. Other studies have utilized contact pressure film technology to investigate alterations in joint contact pressures.[41, 155, 285] Although they failed to replicate the dramatic results of Ramsey and Hamilton, these studies demonstrated increased stresses with lateral talar shift and large posterior malleolar fragments. Despite these findings, the primary cause of post-traumatic arthrosis remains unknown.

Laterally, the distal tibia is indented by a shallow groove or incisura for the fibula (Fig. 59–3). This groove is formed by a larger anterior tubercle (Chaput or Tillaux-Chaput) and a significantly smaller posterior tubercle.

The most significant ligamentous complex of the ankle is that which unites the distal tibia and fibula. This so-called syndesmosis comprises four distinct portions (Fig. 59–4). Anteriorly, the *anterior inferior tibiofibular ligament* (AITFL) runs obliquely slightly distally from the anterolateral tubercle of the tibia (Chaput's) to the anterior portion of the lateral malleolus, where its attachment is occasionally referred to as Wagstaffe's tubercle. The *posterior inferior tibiofibular ligament* (PITFL) runs obliquely distally from the posterior tubercle (Volkmann's or third or posterior malleolus). It is distinguished from a fibrocartilaginous but otherwise similar connection between the tibia and the fibula that lies just distally and is called the *inferior transverse tibiofibular ligament*. A short and variable distance above the ankle, the *tibiofibular interosseous membrane* thickens and becomes the *interosseous ligament*. These four structures collectively make up the *syndesmosis* and are largely responsible for the structural integrity of the ankle mortise. If they fail and the fibular malleolus displaces laterally, the talus follows it and loses its normal

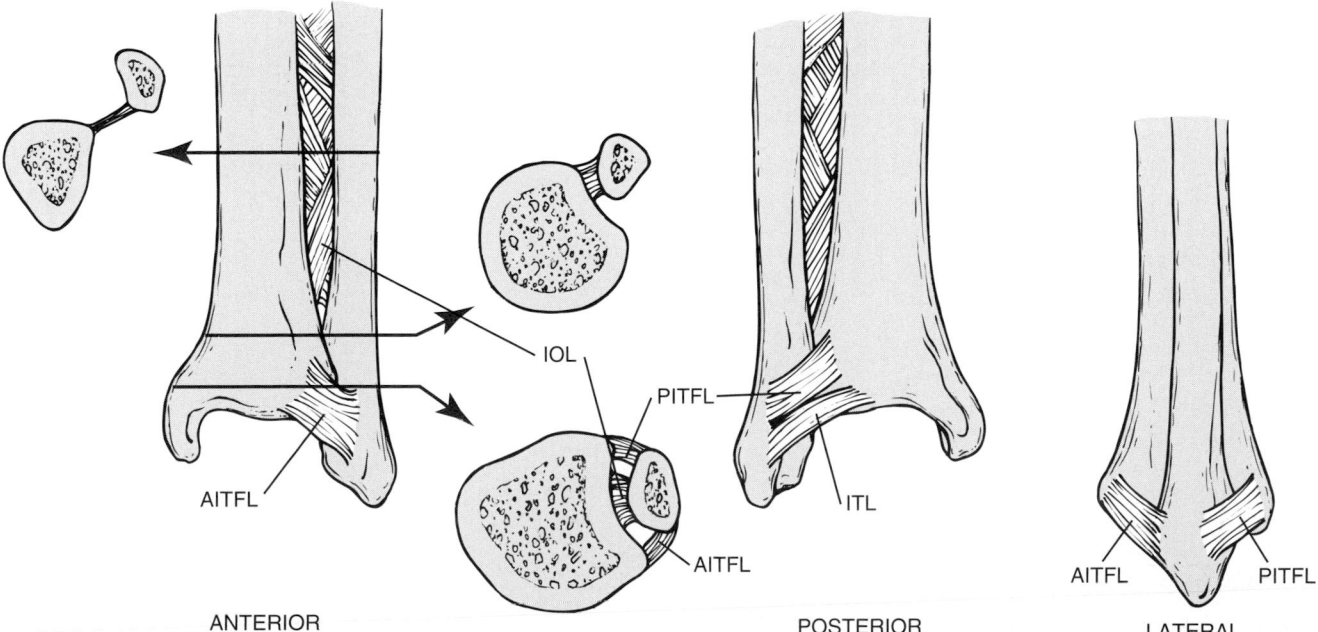

ANTERIOR                    POSTERIOR                    LATERAL

**FIGURE 59–4.** The ligaments of the distal tibiofibular syndesmosis. The lower part of the interosseous membrane thickens to form the interosseous ligament (IOL). Just above the plafond lie the anterior inferior tibiofibular ligament (AITFL) and the posterior inferior tibiofibular ligament (PITFL), with more distal fibers called the *inferior transverse ligament* (ITL). (Redrawn from Hamilton, C.C. Traumatic Disorders of the Ankle. New York, Springer-Verlag, 1984, Fig. 1–7.)

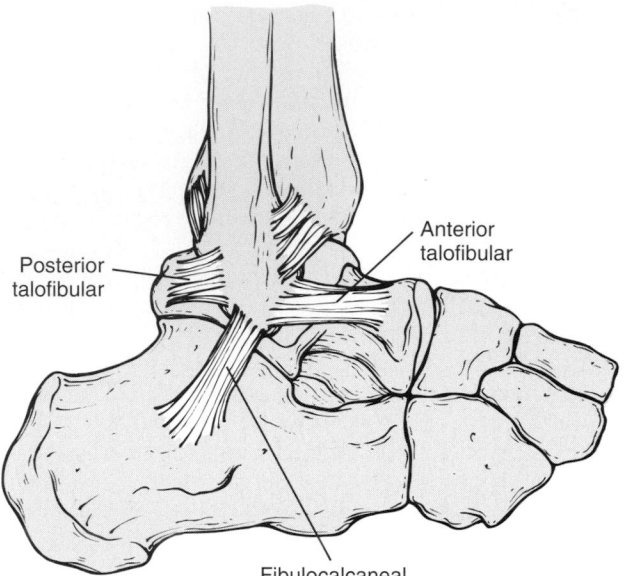

**FIGURE 59–5.** The three components of the lateral collateral ligament are the anterior and posterior talofibular ligaments and, between them, the fibulocalcaneal ligament, which crosses the talus. The orientation of anterior talofibular and fibulocalcaneal ligaments is demonstrated in Figure 54–14.

relationship with the weight-bearing surface of the tibial plafond.[140, 211, 292] This lateral talar shift is not reliably prevented by an apparently intact deltoid ligament and forms the basis for the now well-appreciated need to reestablish the anatomic relationship of the lateral malleolus to the distal tibia when it has been disrupted in a malleolar injury.

The lateral collateral ligament (LCL) complex is made up of three portions (Fig. 59–5). The *anterior talofibular ligament* is directed anteromedially to the lateral neck of the talus. The bulky and stout *posterior talofibular ligament* is posteromedially attached to the posterior process of the talus. Both of these are essentially thickenings, along with

the superficial deltoid ligament medially, in an otherwise structurally unimpressive and redundant ankle joint capsule. The middle part of the ankle's LCL complex is the *fibulocalcaneal ligament.* It runs obliquely posteriorly and distally deep to the peroneal tendons, more or less perpendicularly across the posterior facet of the subtalar joint, and attaches to the calcaneus just posterior to the proximal extent of its peroneal tubercle. An additional, inconstant, posterolateral extracapsular ligamentous structure is the so-called fibulotalocalcaneal ligament, a local thickening of the deep aponeurosis of the leg that resists extreme foot dorsiflexion.[238]

A number of important structures cross the ankle joint and must be considered with any approach to diagnosis and treatment of ankle injuries.

Superficially and posteriorly, the powerful plantar flexor of the ankle, the tendo calcaneus or Achilles tendon, is prominent, with a thin tendon sheath and little subcutaneous tissue between it and the overlying skin. Just lateral to the Achilles tendon lies the sural nerve, which supplies the skin of the lateral heel and midfoot and is at risk of painful entrapment in a surgical scar. The plantaris tendon runs along the medial border of the Achilles tendon and attaches to the calcaneus just medial to it. This slender tendon may be used for tendon or ligament repairs in the ankle region and elsewhere.

On the lateral side of the ankle, the peroneus brevis and peroneus longus tendons, the latter more posteriorly, course around the posterior surface of the lateral malleolus (Fig. 59–6). They are tethered there by the superior peroneal retinaculum, which, with its fibrocartilaginous attachment, may be avulsed from the fibula, permitting anterior dislocation of the tendons. Such a dislocation is not prevented by the more anteriorly located inferior peroneal retinaculum, a prolongation of the inferior extensor retinaculum. The peroneal tendons are superficial to the fibulocalcaneal ligament. As they reach the lateral border of the foot, the peroneus longus crosses plantarward under the peroneus brevis and traverses the foot under the long plantar ligament to insert on the proximal

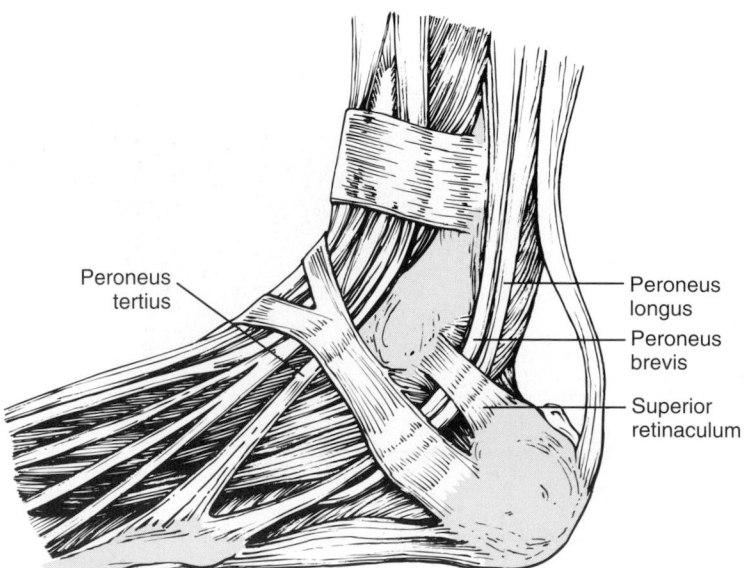

**FIGURE 59–6.** The lateral ankle is crossed posteriorly by the peroneus brevis and peroneus longus tendons, restrained primarily by the superior retinaculum posterior to the distal part of the lateral malleolus. The Achilles tendon is most posterior. The peroneus tertius and toe extensors are anterior.

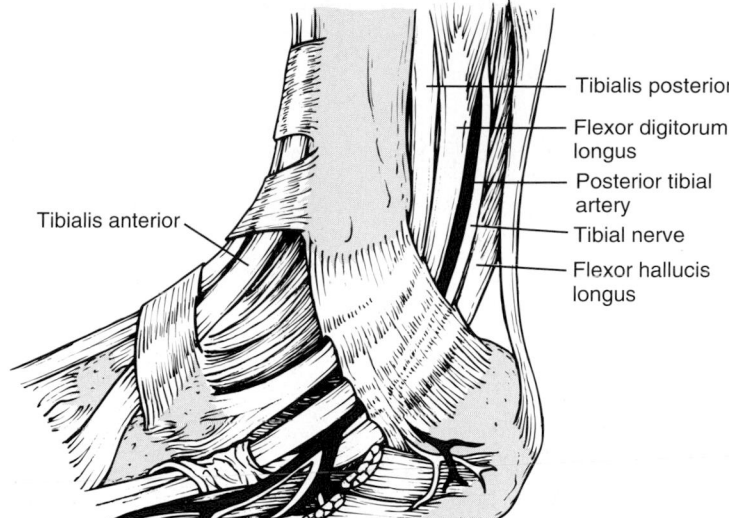

**FIGURE 59–7.** The structures crossing the medial ankle anteriorly include the tibialis anterior tendon, saphenous vein, and saphenous nerve. Behind the medial malleolus lie the important tibialis posterior, the flexor digitorum longus, the posterior tibial artery and veins, the tibial nerve, and the posteriorly located flexor hallucis longus.

first metatarsal and first cuneiform. The peroneus brevis inserts on the base of the fifth metatarsal, from which, with an inversion injury, it may be avulsed with a small bone fragment.

On the medial side of the ankle, several important structures lie posterior to the medial malleolus, anchored there by the flexor retinaculum, which runs from the posteroinferior surface of the malleolus to the medial surface of the tuberosity of the calcaneus. Its malleolar attachment is a fibrocartilaginous pulley for the most anterior of the flexor tendons, the tibialis posterior, behind which lie, in order, the flexor digitorum longus; the posterior tibial artery and associated veins with the tibial nerve; and most posteriorly, crossing the posterior surface of the ankle joint, the flexor hallucis longus (Fig. 59–7). Each tendon lies in a well-developed tunnel. Should a flexor tendon rupture or be lacerated, it may retract beyond the surgeon's view, with the result that the injury is not recognized. Posterior tibial tendon laceration occurs frequently enough with medial malleolus fractures that the surgeon should identify this tendon when the fracture exposes its tunnel.

A centimeter or two anterior to the medial malleolus lies the saphenous vein with its accompanying saphenous nerve (usually two or more small branches). The vein is valuable for fluid administration, as it is rapidly available by cutdown regardless of whether a patient is in shock. It is also important for venous drainage of an injured foot and should be spared in such situations whenever possible. The saphenous nerves are at risk of entrapment in a local surgical or traumatic scar, with resultant formation of painful neuromas. They should be identified and preserved or resected in a manner that allows the proximal end to retract well away from any wound.

On the anterior aspect of the ankle, the extensor retinacula restrain the extensor tendons, anterior tibial vessels, and deep peroneal nerve as they leave the anterior compartment of the leg and cross onto the dorsum of the foot (Fig. 59–8). Proximal to the ankle, the transverse fibers of the superior extensor retinaculum run from the anteromedial subcutaneous surface of the tibia to the

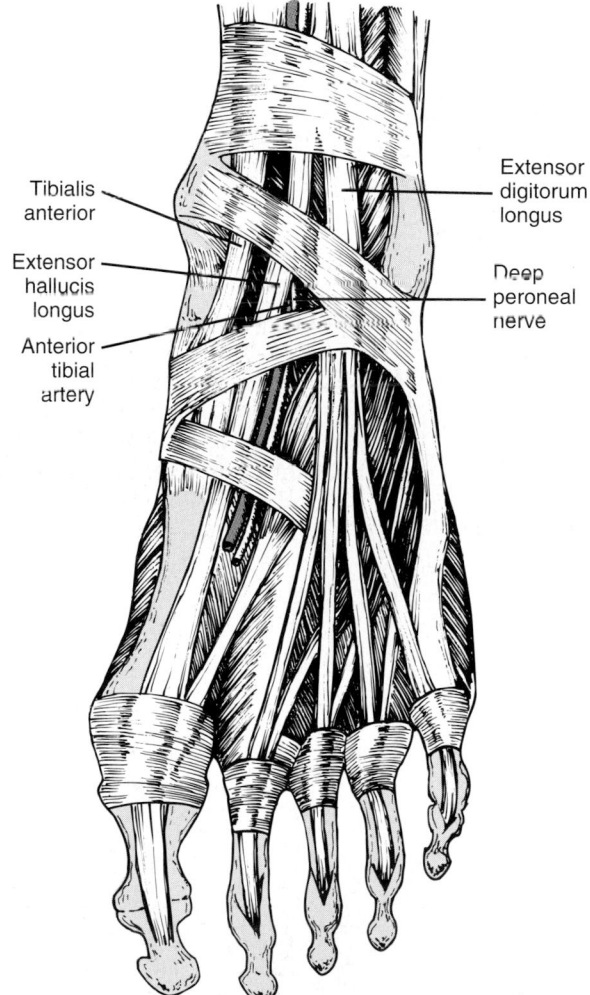

**FIGURE 59–8.** The anterior ankle is crossed by the dorsiflexors: tibialis anterior, extensor hallucis longus, extensor digitorum longus, and the occasionally absent peroneus tertius tendons. The anterior tibial vessels and deep peroneal nerve are just lateral to the extensor hallucis longus. The superior (transverse) and inferior (cruciate) retinacula provide pulleys for the dorsiflexors. The origin of the short extensors is from the anterolateral calcaneus beneath the long toe extensor tendons.

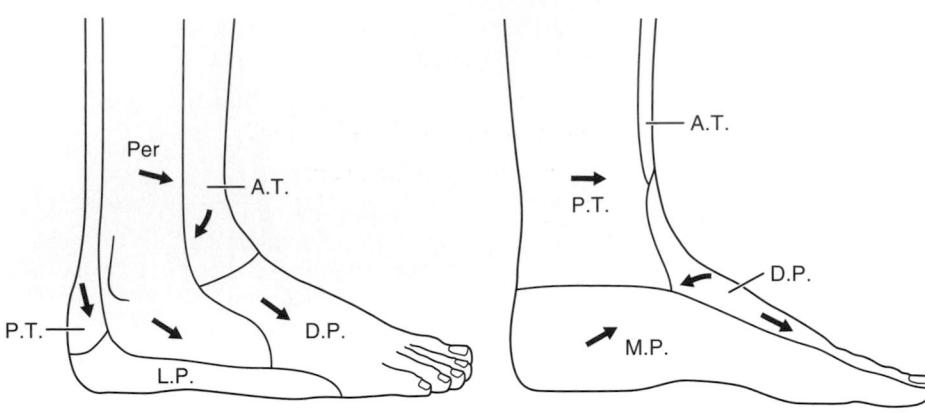

FIGURE 59–9. The angiosomes of the foot and ankle. Cutaneous blood flow is in the direction indicated by the *arrows*. Surgical incisions should not interrupt cutaneous blood flow to the distal portion of an angiosome. The cutaneous arterial territories are supplied by the following arteries: A.T., anterior tibial; D.P., dorsalis pedis; P.T., posterior tibial; Per, peroneal; M.P., medial plantar; and L.P., lateral plantar. (Redrawn from Salmon, N. Arteries of the Skin. New York, Churchill Livingstone, 1988.)

anterolateral surface of the distal fibula. The inferior extensor retinaculum is Y shaped. Its base attaches to the calcaneus laterally. The proximal medial limb attaches to the medial malleolus and the distal limb to the deep fascia medial to the navicular. The inferior extensor retinaculum thus lies over the anterior ankle joint capsule. Under it, from lateral to medial, are the peroneus tertius, the extensor digitorum longus tendon, the deep peroneal nerve, the anterior tibial artery (becoming the dorsalis pedis), the extensor hallucis longus tendon, and the tibialis anterior tendon. The last runs somewhat obliquely to insert on the medial surface of the first cuneiform and the base of the first metatarsal.

The cutaneous blood supply of the ankle comes from the three major lower extremity arteries.[236] Each delivers segmental branches that perforate the overlying fascia, branch superficial to it, and supply the skin[95] (Fig. 59–9). Anastomotic vessels link the segmental perforators. Each of these three arteries has a "zone of distribution" termed an *angiosome*. Ideally, incisions should follow the approximate borders of these angiosomes. In addition, dissection should be done below the enveloping deep fascia to avoid

damage to the cutaneous vessels, which inevitably occurs when subcutaneous flaps are created. These two principles are most important when treating high-energy fractures with damaged soft tissues. Finally, if wound breakdown occurs, fasciocutaneous flaps based on these angiosomes may offer a solution.[95]

Significant individual variation in ankle joint anatomy and mechanics should be recognized and considered in attempts to define normality and to treat injuries. The use of the opposite ankle as a control is helpful, but it is important to recognize the normal range of asymmetry that may account for some differences. For example, 3% of normal individuals have a 10° difference between ankles in talar tilt measured on inversion stress radiographs.[96]

## Biomechanics

### ANKLE JOINT MECHANICS

The "empirical" ankle axis can be estimated by palpating the tips of the medial and lateral malleoli.[112, 159] It passes just below these, directed both posteriorly and inferiorly from the medial side (Fig. 59–10). In 80% of ankles, normal motion is simple rotation around this axis.

The obliquity of the empirical ankle joint axis varies from person to person. Its angle with the midline of the tibia in the coronal plane averages 82° (i.e., 8° varus angulation). This angle varies from 74° to 94°, with a standard deviation of 3.6°. External tibial torsion in the transverse plane increases during childhood. In the adult, it measures approximately 22° relative to the midpoints of the proximal tibial condyles, ranging from 4° to 56°, with a standard deviation of 10°.[112]

The "actual" axis of the ankle joint is more oblique than the joint surface. The joint surface of the tibial plafond is also angled in the coronal plane relative to the midline of the tibia but in the *opposite* direction to the ankle joint axis. Its average is 3° of valgus angulation, ranging from 2° to 10°. The angle between the two, the talocrural angle, is an indicator of normal lateral malleolar alignment. It measures 83° ± 4° and is normally within 2° of the angle in the opposite ankle (Fig. 59–11).[111, 209]

The fit of talus in mortise is precise, making it the most congruent of the weight-bearing joints.[112] Both mortise and talar trochlea are narrower posteriorly. Both this

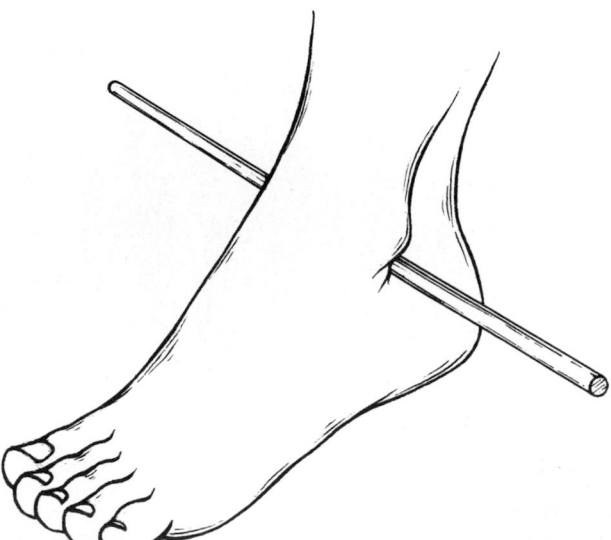

FIGURE 59–10. A line joining the tips of the medial and lateral malleoli is a close approximation of the axis of the ankle joint. Inman (1976) called this the *empirical axis of the ankle*.

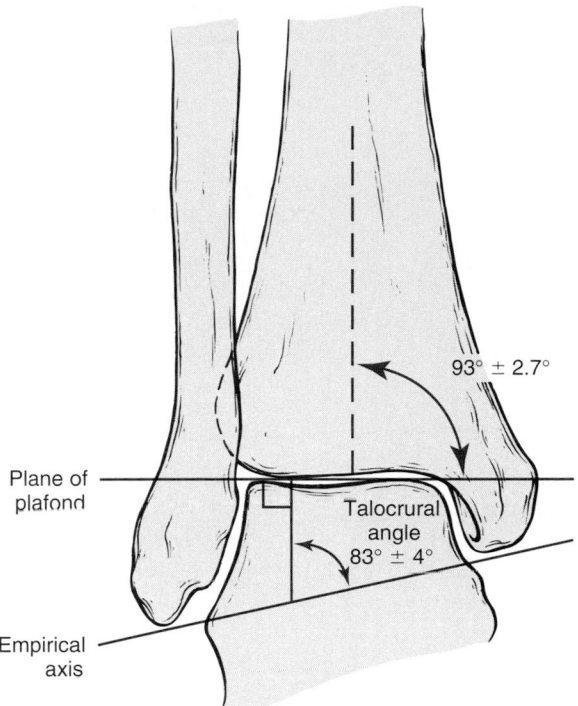

**FIGURE 59–11.** The tibiotalar articular surface (plafond) usually has a slight lateral tilt, averaging 3 degrees. The empirical axis is in a relatively varus position, as indicated by the talocrural angle, formed by the intersection of a line perpendicular to the plafond with the empirical axis. This averages 83 ± 4 degrees and is a reliable radiographic indicator of the relationship among malleoli and plafond. It should be similar to that of the opposite ankle.

diminution of width and the degree of parallelism of the malleolar articular surfaces vary among individuals. The fit of talus in mortise remains congruent throughout the ankle's range of motion, as Inman[112] demonstrated, because the joint surface is a portion of a frustum of a cone, the axis of which is the ankle's axis of rotation (Fig. 59–12). Therefore, there is little if any change in mortise width during ankle motion (0 to 2 mm, according to Inman).[112] The effect of the ankle's oblique axis is an obligatory internal and external rotation of the foot with plantar flexion and dorsiflexion, respectively (Fig. 59–13).

Lindsjö and associates[151] measured motion of the loaded ankle, noting, with hip and knee flexed and the foot on a 30-cm-high stool, a mean of 32° dorsiflexion and 45° plantar flexion. They stated that, although normal gait required at least 10° dorsiflexion, athletic activities were limited if loaded dorsiflexion was less than 20° to 30°.

Because the medial and lateral facets of the ankle mortise vary in their relationship to each other and to the ankle joint axis, a mortise view radiograph does not necessarily show symmetric width of the ankle joint's "cartilage space."

Average in vivo subtalar motion is approximately 40°, ranging from 20° to 62°.[111] The orientation of the subtalar joint is 23° ± 11° (range 4° to 47°), internally rotated relative to the long axis of the foot in the transverse plane and elevated anteriorly from the horizontal by 42° ± 9° (range 20.5° to 68.5°) relative to the horizontal in the

sagittal plane.[112] During walking on level ground, average subtalar motion for a normal foot is 6°.[159]

## ANKLE LIGAMENT MECHANICS

### Medial Collateral Ligament

The deltoid ligament lies near the apex of the cone on which the surface of the ankle joint lies. It is thus able to accommodate to the relatively smaller distance the talus travels on this side of the joint.[112, 159, 222]

The deltoid ligament functions to restrain external rotation of the talus in the mortise. On the basis of biomechanical studies, it may provide up to 57% of this function.[259] As discussed later in this chapter, the presence of a deltoid ligament tear in the setting of other

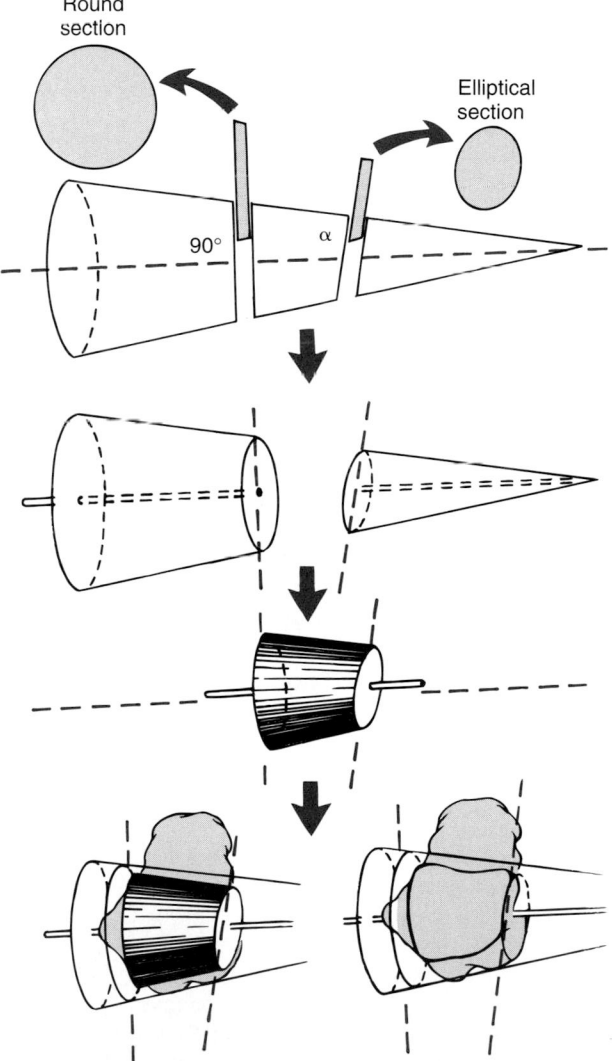

**FIGURE 59–12.** The puzzling shape of the talus and mortise, which maintain a congruent fit throughout the range of ankle motion, is explained by Inman's demonstration that the joint surface is a segment (frustum) of a cone, the axis of which lies on the ankle's empirical axis. The smaller fibular facet is elliptical because of its obliquity. The larger medial articular facet is round because it is perpendicular to the axis of the cone. (Redrawn from Inman, V.T. The Joints of the Ankle. Baltimore, Williams & Wilkins, 1976.)

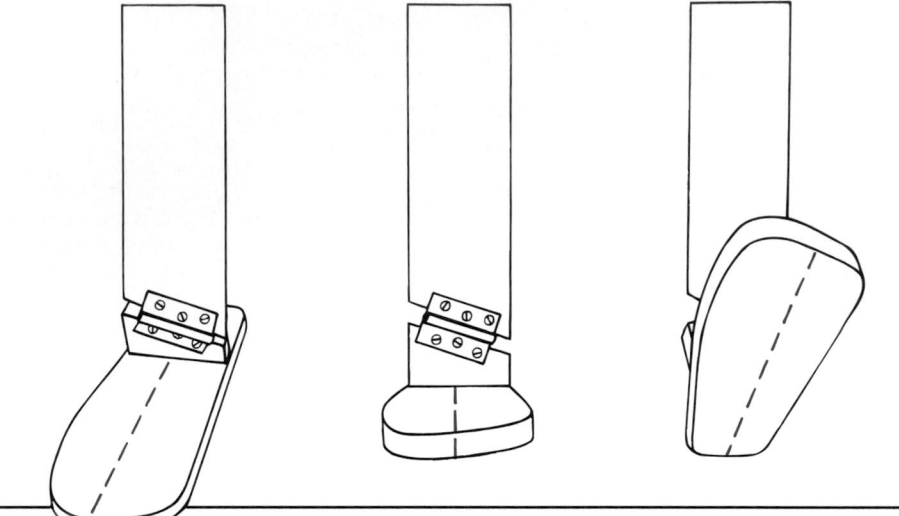

**Figure 59–13.** The obliquity of the ankle axis produces relative medial deviation of the foot (internal rotation) with plantar flexion and relative lateral deviation of the foot (external rotation) with dorsiflexion. (Redrawn from Mann, R., ed. Surgery of the Foot, 5th ed. St. Louis, C.V. Mosby, 1986, Fig. 1–12.)

malleolar lesions demands particular care in assessing talar stability.

### Lateral Collateral Ligament

Because the lateral side of the joint has a greater radius of curvature, a larger distance is traveled on this side during the same arc of rotation. The LCL is thus more complex, comprising three portions.[220] The anterior part, the anterior talofibular ligament, lines up with the fibula during plantar flexion and, in this position, functions as a true collateral ligament, resisting inversion of the talus in the mortise. With dorsiflexion, the fibulocalcaneal ligament is brought into alignment with the fibula and becomes the functional collateral ligament. Inman[112] demonstrated considerable variation (70° to 140°) in the relationship between these two portions of the LCL complex (see Fig. 54–14). He hypothesized that ankle inversion laxity may be present in individuals with a relatively greater arc between the anterior talofibular and the anterior fibulocalcaneal ligaments, as a significant part of their ankle range of motion would be without an appropriately positioned LCL.

An important corollary of the relative positions of the components of the ankle's LCL complex is that assessment of stability must be done with regard to the position of the ankle joint. The anterior talofibular ligament resists inversion in plantar flexion. It also resists anterior subluxation of the talus when the ankle is in neutral, as demonstrated by the so-called anterior drawer test. The fibulocalcaneal ligament resists inversion when the ankle is dorsiflexed. Because either or both components may be incompetent, an adequate examination requires testing inversion instability in both dorsiflexion and plantar flexion.

The relationship of the fibulocalcaneal ligament to the subtalar joint is important. Normally, it lies on the conical plane of motion of this joint and thus does not interfere with it.[112] If it is to be reconstructed surgically, deviation from its normal location may compromise subtalar joint movement.

### Syndesmosis

The syndesmosis firmly binds the fibula to the tibia and along with the deltoid ligament guides talar motion within the mortise. The syndesmosis allows minor lateral motion and rotation of the fibula during normal gait. Anatomic fibular length and rotation are a prerequisite to normal

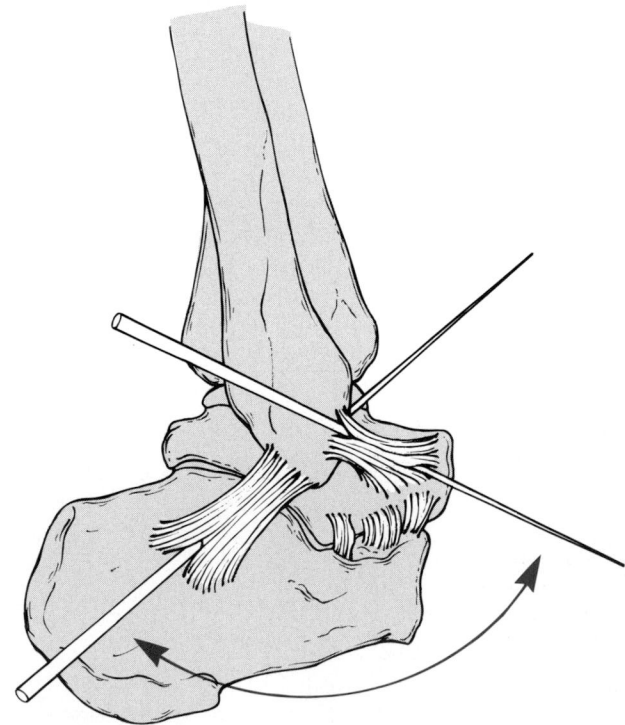

**Figure 59–14.** The angle between the fibulocalcaneal and the anterior talofibular components of the lateral collateral ligament varies in normal individuals from less than 80 degrees to more than 130 degrees. In ankles with a wide spread between the two, there may be a less effective check to inversion of the ankle joint. Note that dorsiflexion brings the fibulocalcaneal ligament into position to resist inversion and that plantar flexion does the same for the anterior talofibular ligament. (Redrawn from Inman, V.T. The Joints of the Ankle. Baltimore, Williams & Wilkins, 1976.)

**TABLE 59–1**

Progressive Increase in External Rotation Instability in Stages of Simulated Weber C Malleolar Injury

| Ankle Injury | Mean External Rotation (deg) | Total Instability (%) |
|---|---|---|
| Intact ankle | 8 | 0 |
| Medial malleolus fracture | 14 | 25 |
| Medial malleolus + AITFL | 19 | 46 |
| Medial malleolus + AITFL + interosseous membrane + PITFL | 24 | 67 |
| Medial malleolus + AITFL + interosseous membrane + PITFL + lateral malleolus fracture | 32 | 100 |

*Abbreviations:* AITFL, anterior inferior tibiofibular ligament; PITFL, posterior inferior tibiofibular ligament.
*Source:* Data from Solari, J.; et al. J Orthop Trauma 5:1990, 1991.

syndesmotic function. Thus, "syndesmotic stability" is a term that requires evaluation of both osseous and ligamentous structures. In particular, fibular length and rotation must be anatomic to ensure proper position of the talus (Fig. 59–11).

Syndesmotic instability is recognized by movement of the talus in the mortise—most commonly demonstrated by medial clear space widening. Although it appears as a lateral movement of the talus, external rotation and varying degrees of posterior translation are also present.

Using a model of a Weber C fibula fracture with a disrupted deltoid ligament, the relative contribution of each syndesmotic structure to talar stability has been studied by Solari and colleagues[259] (Tables 59–1 and 59–2). With a similar model, Boden and co-workers[28] concluded that in the presence of a deltoid ligament tear, the critical zone of syndesmotic disruption leading to talar instability is 3 to 4.5 cm above the mortise. In each study, the presence of an intact deltoid ligament contributed significantly to talus stability and, in many instances, obviated the need for syndesmotic fixation. I believe these guidelines cannot be strictly applied to the clinical situation.[204] In the final analysis, syndesmotic stability, which comes into question primarily during treatment of lateral malleolar fractures, must be assessed on an individual case-by-case basis.

## BIOMECHANICS OF GAIT

The ankle helps to smooth the vertical movement of the body's center of gravity and to decrease the transient ground reaction force during forward progression.[159] This function minimizes the energy cost of walking and moderates the impact on the lower extremity. At heel strike, the ankle begins to plantar flex against the force of the anterior compartment muscles contracting eccentrically. As the leg accepts weight, foot pronation and knee flexion decelerate the body's fall. The plantar flexed ankle begins to dorsiflex. With further plantar flexion, the heel elevates and the foot supinates, thus becoming rigid and propelling the body upward and forward (Fig. 59–15). During this process the tibia rotates—internally during swing and externally during stance—about its long axis. Inman pointed out that because of the obliquity of the subtalar joint axis, internal and external rotations of the tibia are linked, respectively, to pronation and supination of the foot.[112] It is important to remember that during the stance phase, the foot is fixed on the ground and becomes the fixed point of reference for movements of the leg and body.

Mann[159] described three intervals of the stance phase. In the first portion, from heel strike to foot flat, the initially slightly dorsiflexed ankle plantar flexes to approximately 18° and then begins to dorsiflex, reaching neutral by the end of this phase. The anterior tibial muscles contract throughout this phase, the foot progressively pronates through the subtalar joint, and internal rotation of the tibia continues.

In the second part, or foot flat period of stance, the ankle moves from neutral to approximately 18° of dorsiflexion, with heel rise beginning just before plantar flexion starts to end this phase. During the second phase, the plantar flexors of the superficial and deep posterior calf

**TABLE 59–2**

External Rotation Instability after Repair of Various Structures in Simulated Weber C Malleolar Fracture Model

| Repair | Mean External Rotation (deg) | Increase in Stability (%) |
|---|---|---|
| None | 32 | — |
| Lateral malleolus plate | 24 | 32 |
| Lateral malleolus plate + syndesmosis screw | 22 | 51 |
| Lateral malleolus plate + medial malleolus screw | 14 | 73 |
| Lateral malleolus plate + syndesmosis screw + medial malleolus screw | 8 | 100 |
| Medial malleolus screw | 18 | 56 |

*Source:* Data from Solari, J.; et al. J Orthop Trauma 5:1990, 1991.

compartments are active, controlling the forward motion of the tibia on the talus (i.e., contracting eccentrically while the ankle dorsiflexes). Early in this phase, the internally rotated tibia begins to rotate externally, and the foot supinates, becoming more rigid, supported also by the intrinsic muscles of the foot.

In the third and final portion of the stance phase, the ankle plantar flexes from its extreme of dorsiflexion to a little more than 10° plantar flexion, with continuing contraction of the posterior calf muscles. The tibia remains externally rotated and the foot supinated; the latter is made even more rigid by the windlass action of the dorsiflexed toes, tightening the plantar fascia and elevating the longitudinal arch of the foot.

Mann[159] emphasized that the ankle joint's oblique axis determines relative motion of the leg. Heel strike and plantar flexion produce apparent in-toeing. In midstance, the ankle dorsiflexes as the tibia moves forward, resulting in internal rotation of the leg. When the heel begins to rise and plantar flexion occurs, the tibia externally rotates. The amount of observed rotation of the leg is greater than that accounted for by ankle joint obliquity and is in fact accomplished through motion of the subtalar joint, which is also oblique.

# EVALUATION OF THE INJURED ANKLE

## History

The major points to be gained from the history of a patient with an injured ankle are (1) how, when, and where the injury happened; (2) the preexisting status of the injured part; and (3) the overall medical condition of the individual.

The mechanism of injury is only occasionally presented in a way that provides definitive understanding of the direction and magnitude of applied force and a good clue to the diagnosis ("I stepped on a pebble and my foot turned inward until I felt a pop on the outside of my ankle"). More often, the actual details are more vague but still helpful ("motorcycle crash"; "tripped and fell down the stairs"; "jumped off a deck and landed flatfooted"). The location is important in assessing the likely extent of contamination of an open wound. Elapsed time, correlated with the extent of swelling, helps in assessing the patient's suitability for certain types of surgery.

The status of the leg before the present injury is also important. It includes, for example, whether the part was

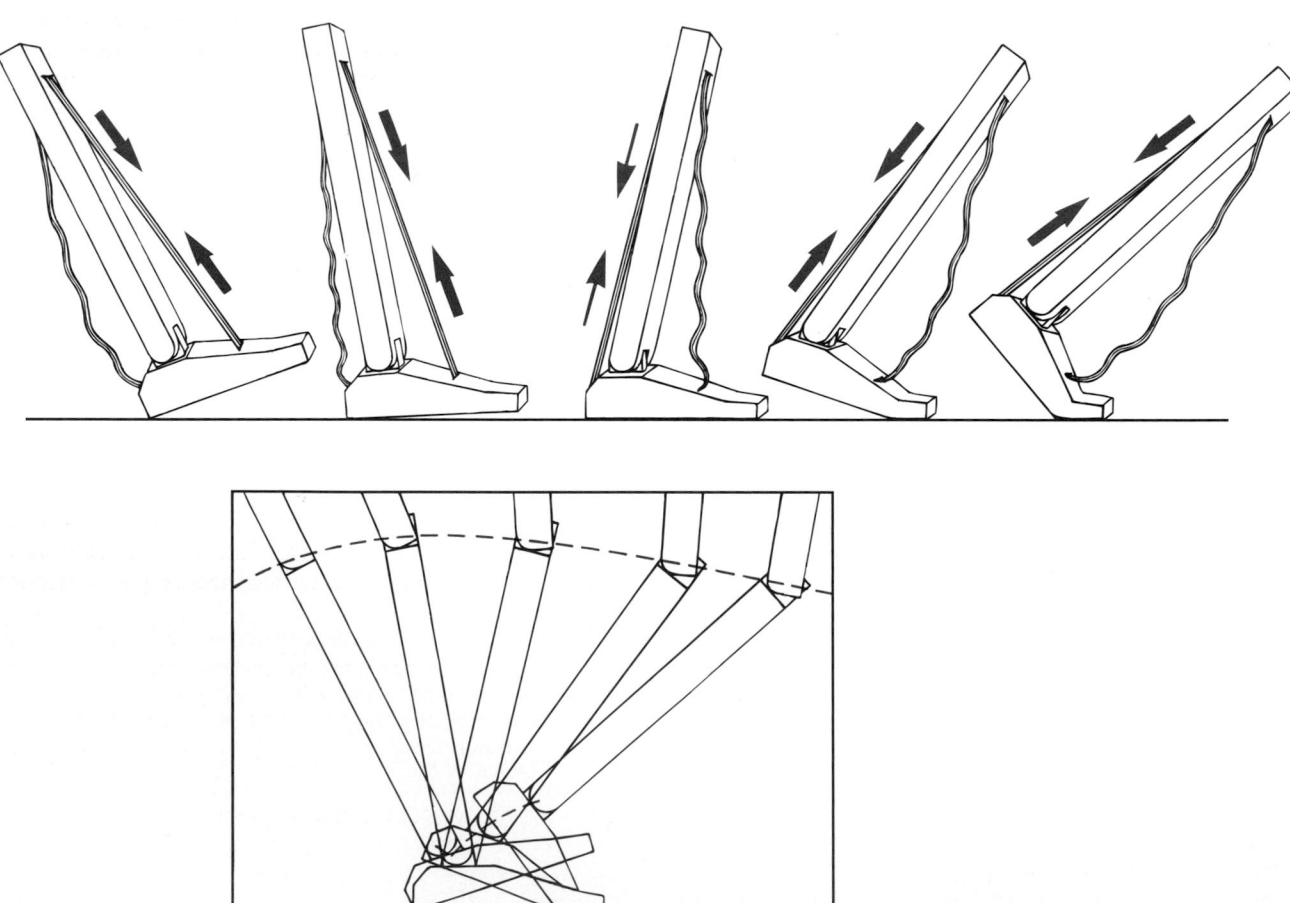

**FIGURE 59–15.** Ankle mechanics during gait. At heel strike, the dorsiflexors slow plantar flexion produced by the moment arm of the heel. Forward momentum of the body next produces ankle dorsiflexion. This is restrained by the plantar flexors, which stabilize the foot during terminal stance. (Redrawn from Inman, V.T.; Ralston, H.J.; Todd, F. Human Walking, Vol. 1. Baltimore, Williams & Wilkins, 1981, Fig. 1–9.)

normal, incompletely recovered from a prior injury, subject to recurrent instability or pain, or untrustworthy since a stroke. Symptoms to be sought are those suggestive of neurologic difficulty, especially peripheral neuropathy, most often caused by diabetes mellitus. Similarly critical is evidence of vascular disease, venous stasis ulcers, claudication, or chronic infection. Other factors include pain, deformity, or altered function affecting the ankle or any other part of the leg. Choice of treatment may be profoundly altered by these factors.

Systemic illness clearly has an impact on overall management and often on local treatment choice as well.[49] Smokers have a higher risk of problems with wound and fracture healing. An alcoholic person may not be able to cooperate with limited weight bearing. A patient with cardiorespiratory disease may not be able to handle the energy cost of walking with crutches or a cast. A patient with injuries of the opposite leg that prevent weight bearing requires rehabilitation plans different from those of a patient with an isolated unstable fracture. Information on medications, drug allergies, and familial problems must be obtained from the patient or from family members or friends.

## Physical Examination

Physical examination of the injured ankle is conducted differently depending on the injury. A brief inspection may reveal severe deformity or an open wound. The challenge then is to identify all elements of the injury and to proceed rapidly with the treatment required to reduce a dislocation, relieve tension on overlying soft tissues, or decontaminate and appropriately treat an open wound. Some parts of the examination may not be possible to perform or may even be inappropriate until later in the patient's course. (For instance, an adequate distal motor examination may be unobtainable while a fracture dislocation is markedly displaced. Exploration of any significant wound should be deferred until the patient is in the operating room.)

Conversely, if the patient complains of an ankle injury but the problem is not obvious, it is necessary to carry out a systematic assessment of each structure in the region before an injury can be excluded or identified. Because injuries often occur in constellations but may coexist seemingly at random, it is especially important not to terminate the evaluation after the first positive finding on either physical examination or radiography.

The ankle should be inspected circumferentially for open or impending wounds; crushed, abraded, or swollen areas; and bone deformity. Pallor may suggest ischemia. Any open wound, even a small one, may communicate with underlying crushed tissues, a fracture, or a joint, or a combination of these. It is vital to correlate the appearance of the wound with the patient's history. For example, a small opening in the skin of a patient whose ankle was run over by a car is *not* a grade I open fracture. A transverse, seemingly shallow laceration along the lateral surface of the ankle, just distal to the lateral malleolus, may be the result of rupture of the overlying

skin with a severe inversion injury and complete failure of the LCLs. Such a laceration extends into the ankle joint.

The vascular examination must include palpation of the posterior tibial and dorsalis pedis pulses. Swelling or deformity may interfere with this. A Doppler device can help identify the pulses, but it reliably assesses flow only if local arterial pressure is measured with a pneumatic cuff on the calf. Skin temperature, capillary filling after blanching pressure, venous engorgement, and edema should each be noted. A decision must be made about the adequacy of perfusion, both before and after any treatment, with measures taken to identify and correct the cause of ischemia rapidly.

The nerves that cross the ankle are assessed by testing light touch and pain sensation in each of their sensory areas. The sural nerve supplies the lateral heel and lateral border of the foot. The sole of the foot is innervated by the medial and lateral plantar nerves, branches of the tibial nerve, which also gives medial calcaneal branches. The plantar intrinsic muscles of the foot are supplied by this system but are hard to test because of the long motors of the toes. Pain produced in the sole of the foot by forced passive dorsiflexion of the toes may indicate ischemia of the intrinsic muscles.

The medial border of the foot is innervated by the saphenous nerve. The dorsal webspace between the great and second toes is the territory of the deep peroneal nerve. This nerve gives motor branches to the short extensors on the dorsum of the foot. Their contraction can be palpated locally if swelling is not excessive. The superficial peroneal nerve provides sensation for the majority of the dorsum of the foot.

Function of the tendons crossing the ankle may be difficult to assess but must be checked initially and then reviewed as a more thorough examination becomes possible. It is necessary to assess the strength generated, not just the apparent motion of the part.

The Achilles tendon is checked by palpation for tenderness or a defect and by means of Thompson's test. In Thompson's test, plantar flexion is produced in response to the examiner's squeezing the calf of a relaxed (usually kneeling) individual (Fig. 59–16). Definitive assessment of integrity and muscle strength of the gastrocsoleus muscle-tendon unit requires checking the patient's ability to rise repeatedly on tiptoe, as this powerful muscle group normally must exert forces far in excess of what is required to move the examiner's hand.

The peroneus longus and peroneus brevis lie behind the lateral malleolus and may be locally tender or palpably displaced if they have been dislocated from their superior retinaculum. The peroneals evert the foot and should be checked, if possible, before a cast is applied that prevents this maneuver.

The anterior compartment muscles dorsiflex the ankle and toes. Extension of both the hallux and the lesser toes should be confirmed. A palpable contraction of the tibialis anterior is often present. This tendon rarely ruptures because of attrition, but it may be tender and nonpalpable if this has occurred.

The deep posterior compartment muscles are the long

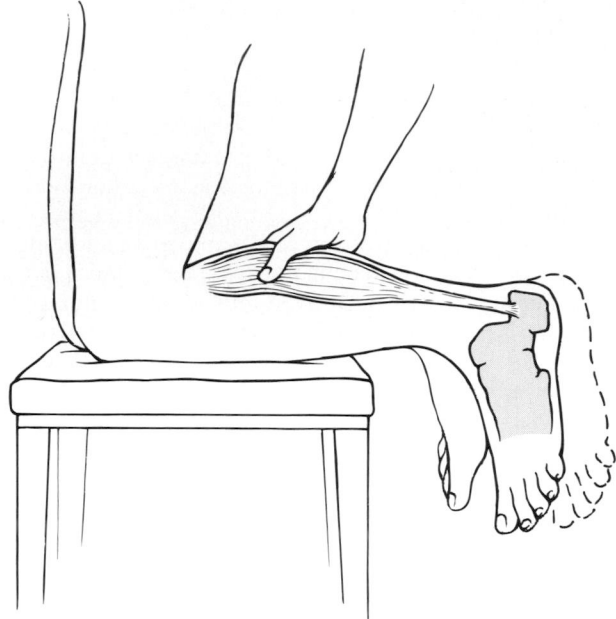

**FIGURE 59–16.** Thompson's test. Compression of the calf muscles normally produces plantar flexion of the ankle. If the Achilles tendon is ruptured, this response is greatly diminished or absent.

flexors of the hallux and lesser digits as well as the tibialis posterior. This important support for the longitudinal arch of the foot may be injured along with other ankle structures and may also rupture on an attritional basis or in association with inflammatory arthritis. It inverts and plantar flexes the foot and should be palpable during performance of these tasks. The toe flexors are tested by checking the strength of that activity. These tendons should be palpated for tenderness behind the medial malleolus, where dislocation from beneath the flexor retinaculum occurs occasionally.

It is essential to realize that ankle pain may be the complaint of a patient with a developing calf compartment syndrome.[11] The pain of compartment syndrome is very severe and poorly responsive to immobilization. Impaired distal motor and sensory function may be the early manifestation of such a problem, which should suggest a careful search for calf tenderness, induration, and stretch-induced pain within involved muscle groups. When doubt exists, measurement of calf compartment pressures may be diagnostic.

When assessing an ankle with less severe injuries, systematic palpation to localize tenderness is especially important. The cooperative patient with normal sensation and no overbearing pain can often define the injured area quite precisely because of the superficial location of most of the ankle's structures.

Each of the traversing structures reviewed previously must be checked for tenderness. Each bony prominence should be assessed as well. Is a malleolus diffusely tender or tender only where a ligament attaches to it? Is tenderness localized over one or more parts of the LCL, the nearby anterior syndesmosis, or the superficial deltoid ligament? The deep deltoid ligament is intra-articular and nonpalpable, and may be ruptured without much medial

tenderness—a vital point to remember in assessing its integrity. The posterior syndesmotic ligaments are also buried more deeply and may be ruptured without well-localized tenderness. The entire fibula must be palpated because standard ankle radiographs do not demonstrate the occasional fracture of the upper fibula associated with disruption of the ankle joint (Maisonneuve's fracture).

Examinations for range of motion and stability should be deferred if an obvious injury is present on the basis of either physical examination or radiographs, which are often obtained before the orthopaedist is asked to see a patient with an ankle injury. Otherwise, joint motion should be checked. Active and passive dorsiflexion and plantar flexion must be compared with those of the contralateral side because of the wide range of normal values. The average is about 30° dorsiflexion and about 30° to 45° plantar flexion.[146, 248] In assessing the ankle's range of motion, it is important to recognize that a surprising amount of dorsiflexion and plantar flexion occurs in the tarsal and tarsometatarsal joints. A better estimate of true ankle motion is obtained, as Segal suggested, by measuring the angle between the tibia and the weight-bearing surface of the foot while the patient dorsiflexes maximally. The angle between the plantar surface of the heel (only) and the tibia is the measure of plantar flexion.[248] By measuring the angle between the leg and the surface on which the foot rests, tibiotalar motion can be better distinguished from that of more distal joints.

Inversion and eversion are intimately associated with ankle motion and should be assessed as well. They normally occur at the subtalar joint, although an ankle with LCL insufficiency may invert at the tibiotalar joint as well. Inversion stress radiographs are necessary to make this distinction and are thus required if excessive inversion is noted on examination or a history of recurrent inversion injuries is obtained. Anterior displacement of the foot relative to the tibia can be produced by performing an anterior drawer test (Fig. 59–17). This finding implies laxity of the anterior fibulotalar component of the LCL complex. The test may be easier to perform with the patient prone.[94]

Instability of the mortise, with laxity or rupture of the syndesmotic ligaments, is suggested by sideways movement of the talus within the mortise. This movement may produce pain and may also be associated with a sensation of the talus' moving laterally or clicking back against the medial malleolus after having been subtly displaced away from it. A stress view mortise radiograph may be helpful in confirming such talar instability. The tibia is rotated internally to bring the malleoli into a plane parallel with the film. The talus is then pulled laterally or externally rotated and is held in this position while the radiograph is exposed. A control view of the other side may be helpful. Remember that even a 1-mm lateral shift of the talus significantly decreases ankle joint contact area.[218]

It is important to check other regional structures that might be injured in association with the ankle or that might lead the patient to complain of ankle symptoms in spite of the tibiotalar joint's not being directly involved. In particular, fractures of the anterior process of the calcaneus, the lateral process of the talus, or the base of the fifth

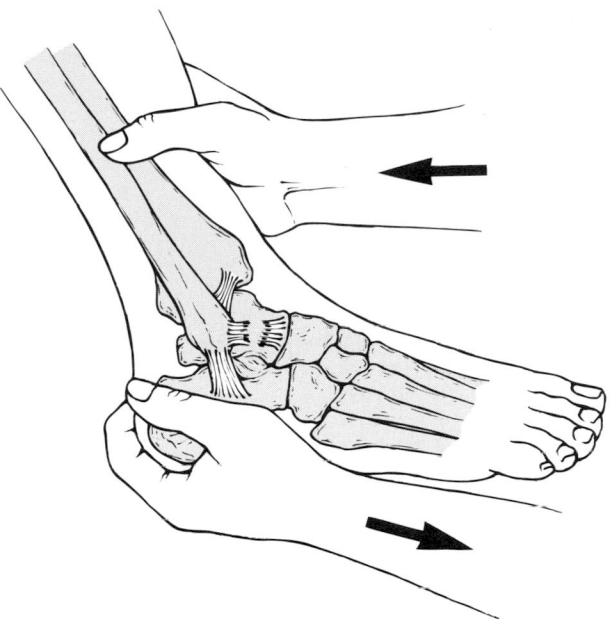

**FIGURE 59–17.** Anterior displacement of the foot relative to the tibia by the so-called anterior drawer test indicates insufficiency of the anterior talofibular ligament. This finding should be compared with that on the opposite side and may be quantified radiographically.

metatarsal may be missed, as might a fracture elsewhere in the calcaneus or talus, a fracture of the navicular, or osteoligamentous injuries of the midfoot (e.g., a tarsometatarsal dislocation) (see Chapter 60).[125] Any findings suggesting foot abnormalities should lead to a request for additional radiographic projections of the foot,

as routine ankle radiographs poorly demonstrate foot abnormalities.

## Radiographic Imaging

Localized malleolar tenderness or inability to bear weight is the best indication to obtain ankle radiographs.[210, 271] Protocols exist to guide decision making on whether to obtain a radiograph in the first place.[184] Routine studies for the ankle typically include anteroposterior (AP), lateral, and internally rotated mortise views.[54, 83, 180, 181] Evidence suggests that a mortise and a lateral view are sufficient for intraoperative use.[189] The mortise view is a true AP radiograph of the ankle joint in a plane parallel to its intermalleolar empirical axis. The traditional AP view, in the anatomic coronal plane, may provide additional evaluation of medial malleolar screws.[89] If proximal tenderness has been noted, full-length views of the fibula are essential, as are all other radiographs necessary to evaluate symptoms and signs of other potential injuries proximal to the ankle. The same holds true, as just noted, for radiographs of the foot.

Additional radiographic studies of the ankle may include one or more of several views. Forty-five degree oblique radiographs can help identify and assess articular involvement and anatomic details of fractures affecting the distal tibial metaphysis. Weight-bearing views of the ankle demonstrate the thickness of articular cartilage as well as joint congruity during loading. They are a valuable part of follow-up evaluations after ankle fractures (Fig. 59-18). Stress views are the basis for confirming ligamentous instability. Comparison with the opposite ankle is helpful, but symmetric laxity is not reliably present in normal

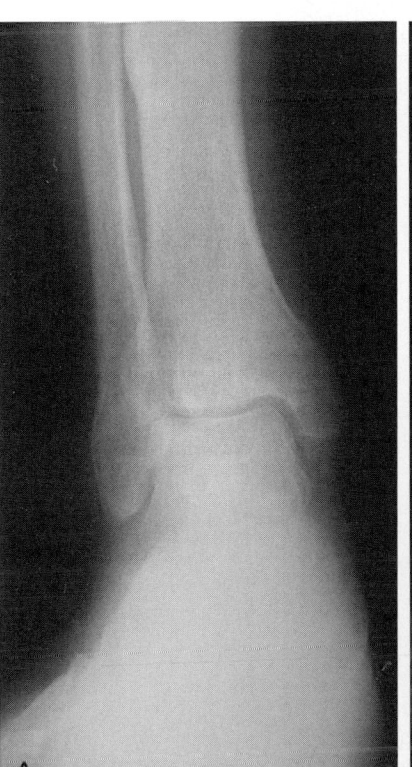
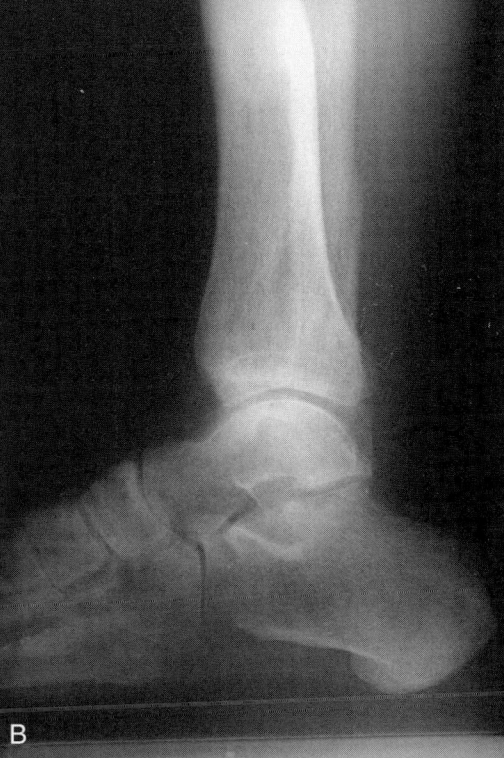

**FIGURE 59–18.** Weight-bearing radiographs demonstrate the true thickness of the articular cartilage and the congruence of the loaded ankle joint. Anteroposterior (A) and lateral (B) views.

individuals. Furthermore, in normal ankles, the range of inversion laxity varies considerably.[225, 233] Therefore, judgment must be used in interpreting stress radiographs. In general, they are not indicated for assessment of an acute ligamentous injury but can be helpful in planning the appropriate management of a chronically unstable ankle.

For assessment of the LCL complex, an anterior drawer lateral view is obtained with the foot supported by a pad under the heel and a posteriorly directed force applied to the distal tibia. Broström[36] claimed that as little as 3 mm anterior talar displacement indicates rupture of the anterior talofibular ligament.

Inversion instability of the tibiotalar joint is demonstrated by inversion stress radiographs.[54, 107, 225, 282] These are perhaps most consistently obtained with specific positioning and loading jigs, but the clinical value of such devices has not been established. As noted in the section on biomechanics, an inversion stress radiograph in plantar flexion demonstrates the competence of the anterior talofibular ligament, and one in dorsiflexion demonstrates the fibulocalcaneal ligament. Gross instability (more than 25° talar inversion) in neutral strongly suggests incompetence of both the anterior and the middle portions of the LCL complex. Inversion instability may also be caused by excessive laxity of the subtalar joint. This may be demonstrated with appropriate stress radiographs.[33, 302]

Ankle arthrograms and peroneal tenograms have been advocated for assessment of collateral ligament integrity.[282] Leakage of dye occurs when there is a complete tear of the joint capsule, such as that produced by an LCL rupture.[26] This rupture can also produce an abnormal communication between the ankle joint and the peroneal tendon sheath, which lies immediately superficial to the fibulocalcaneal ligament. With the present trend toward functional management of LCL injuries, clinical justification for confirming a complete LCL rupture is lacking, and these studies are rarely indicated unless some special indication exists for surgical repair.[62]

Standard tomography (laminagrams) in AP and lateral projections may be helpful in documenting articular surface deformity, fracture comminution, and osteochondral lesions of the talus (Fig. 59–19).[40]

Computed tomography (CT), especially if carefully done with thin sections and maintenance of the patient's positioning, can be even more informative, as it provides a cross section of the joint that clarifies the relationship of the fibula to the tibia as well as the fit of the talus within the mortise and the status of soft tissue structures.[229–231, 272] Precise measurements are readily obtainable. The extent and location of articular surface involvement are obvious, and planning of surgical approaches is facilitated. Computer reconstructions in sagittal and coronal planes currently provide essentially as much information as standard tomography, which does not offer the cross-sectional view (Fig. 59–20). Although CT scans are rarely needed for evaluation and treatment of routine malleolar injuries, they are very helpful for assessing plafond involvement.[156, 180, 181] CT scans can accurately determine the size and location of posterior malleolar fractures. Regular radiographs underestimate the size of the latter lesion.[71] If a CT scan is desired after an ankle has been externally fixed, replacement of the metal connecting rods with radiolucent carbon fiber composite rods makes it possible to obtain high-quality CT studies. CT cuts through the ankle region can be made transversely, parallel to the tibiotalar articular surface, or coronally, nearly perpendicular to the injury, by flexing the knee and tilting the CT gantry. The first are best for assessment of the mortise and pilon region. The last are now standard for calcaneal fractures and subtalar joint visualization. CT studies may also aid the evaluation of patients with chronic pain after inversion injuries.[177]

Magnetic resonance imaging can be valuable for assessing some ankle region injuries, especially occult tendon ruptures and articular surface disruptions (see Fig. 59–19).[55, 228, 237, 239, 301]

Bone scanning with Tc 99m diphosphonate or an equivalent agent can be helpful in localizing stress or other occult fractures, infections, and neoplastic lesions.[40, 166, 170, 207]

## Other Studies

Ankle arthroscopy through anteromedial, anterolateral, or posterolateral portals may be helpful for diagnosing and treating osteophytes, loose bodies, osteochondral fractures, ligamentous laxity, and synovitis.[15, 153, 154, 205, 215] Smaller arthroscopes are helpful; the technology continues to develop. Some means of ankle distraction aids entry and visualization.[279] Arthroscopy is at present of greatest value for assessing ankles that remain painful after injury, often because of anterolateral soft tissue impingement or osteochondritis dissecans.[69, 101, 164, 206]

Arteriography, noninvasive vascular studies, and pulse oximetry can be helpful for assessing and monitoring perfusion distal to an injured ankle. Compartment pressures may need to be measured in the leg or foot. Nerve conduction velocities and electromyography may be helpful for assessing lesions of the tibial nerve, such as tarsal tunnel syndrome.

## Essential Studies to Exclude Other Injuries

A careful history and physical examination are the basis for identifying all of a trauma patient's injuries. Assessment (and documentation) of peripheral pulses is essential to avoid missing limb-threatening ischemia. If the patient is not conscious or is not able to cooperate, routine radiographs of the pelvis and spine are essential. An ankle fracture may be the only outward sign of a fall from a height or a high-velocity motor vehicle crash. Inspection, palpation, and assessment of range of motion and stability of the lower extremity proximal to the ankle are fundamental. Radiographs up to and including the pelvis should be obtained unless the physical examination is completely normal.

## Differential Diagnosis

It is wise to modify the traditional concept of differential diagnosis when dealing with trauma, especially in the

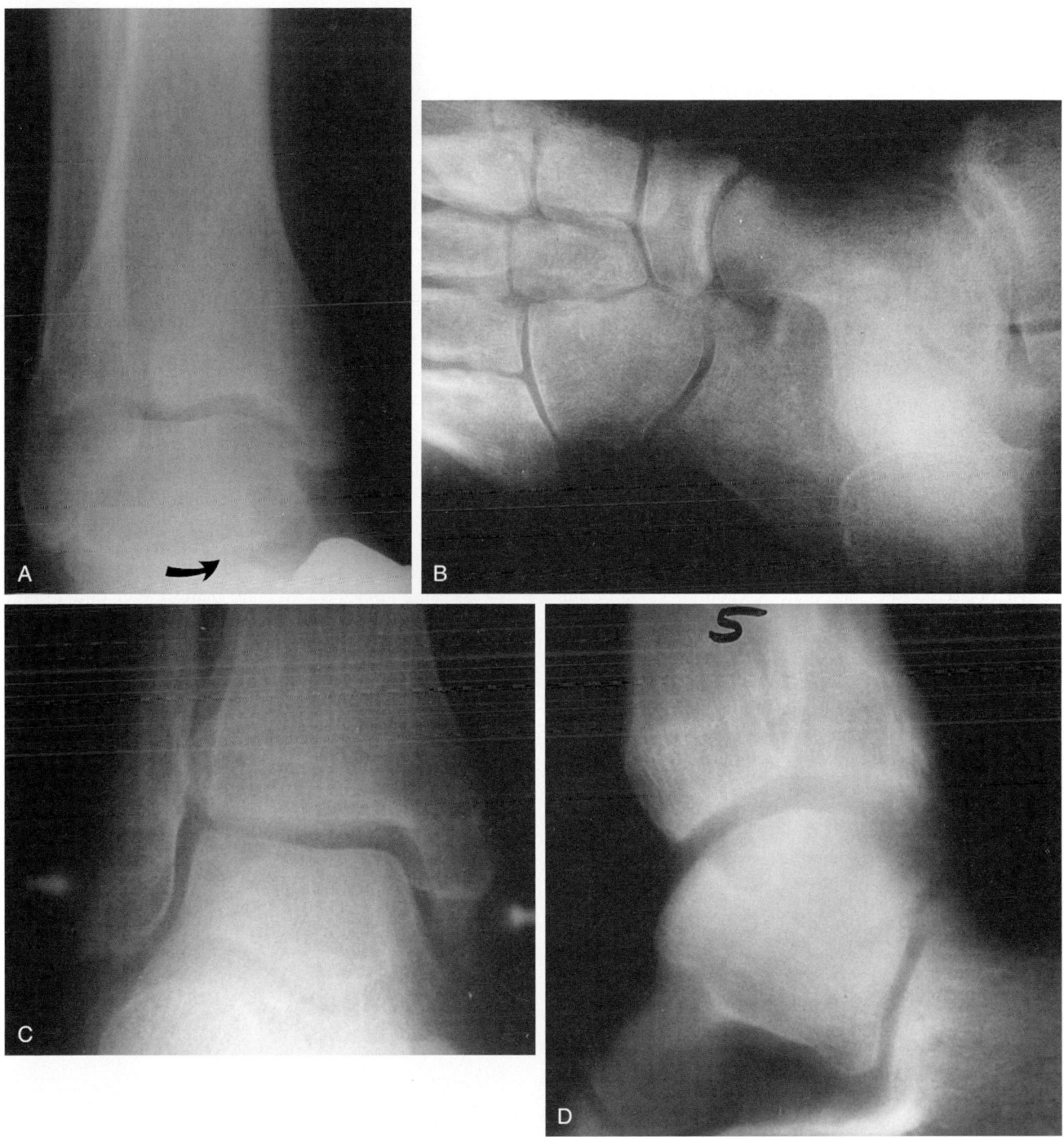

**FIGURE 59–19.** Painful episodes of giving way developed 9 months after ankle and tibia fractures sustained in a fall from a scaffold. Weight-bearing radiographs are shown in Figure 59–18. *A,* No instability is evident on an inversion stress *(arrow)* radiograph. *B,* An oblique radiograph of the foot shows no abnormality of the anterior process of the calcaneus. *C,* A repeated plain film taken 2½ months later suggests a defect in the lateral talar dome. *D,* Lateral tomogram reveals a cystic lesion of the talar dome.

*Illustration continued on following page*

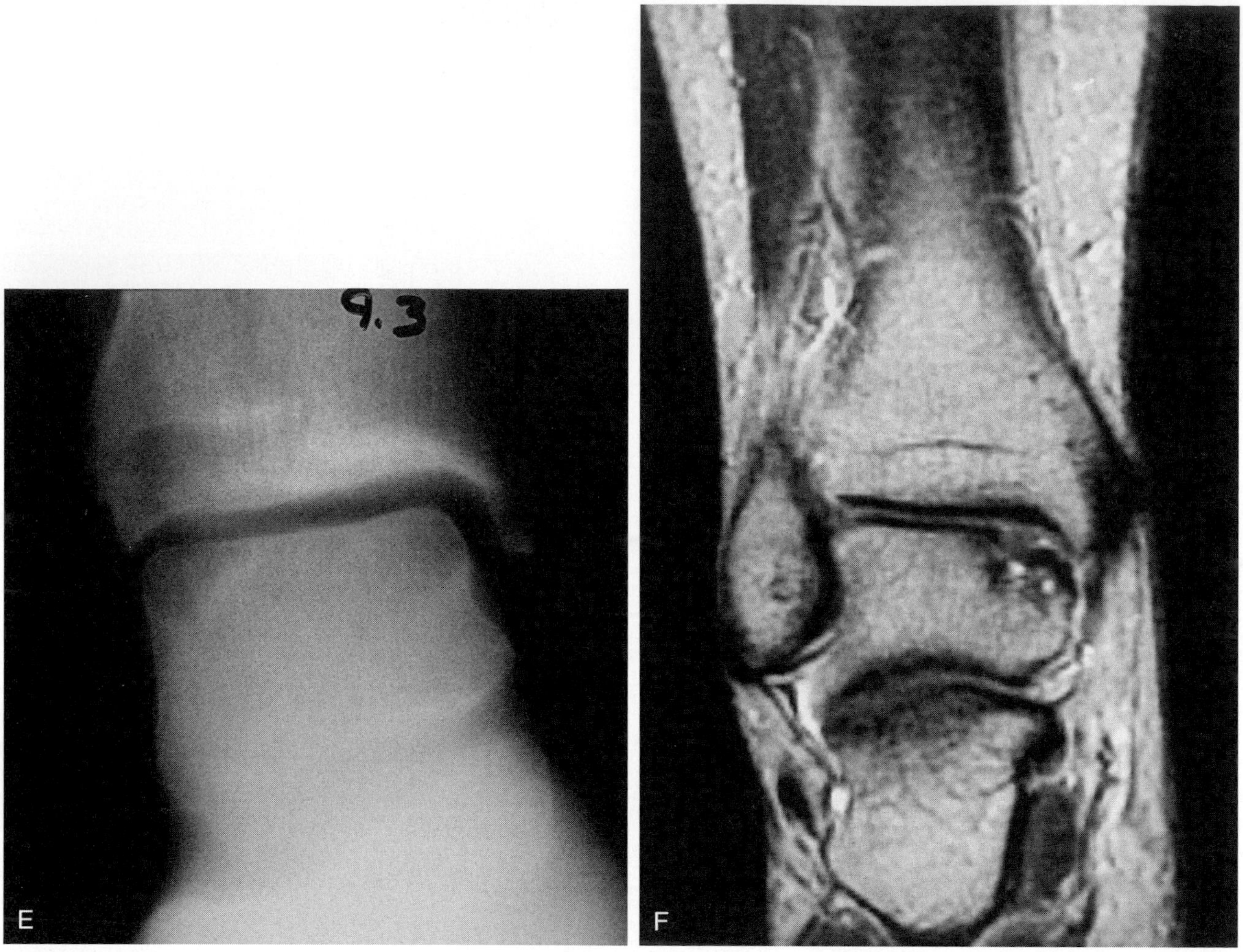

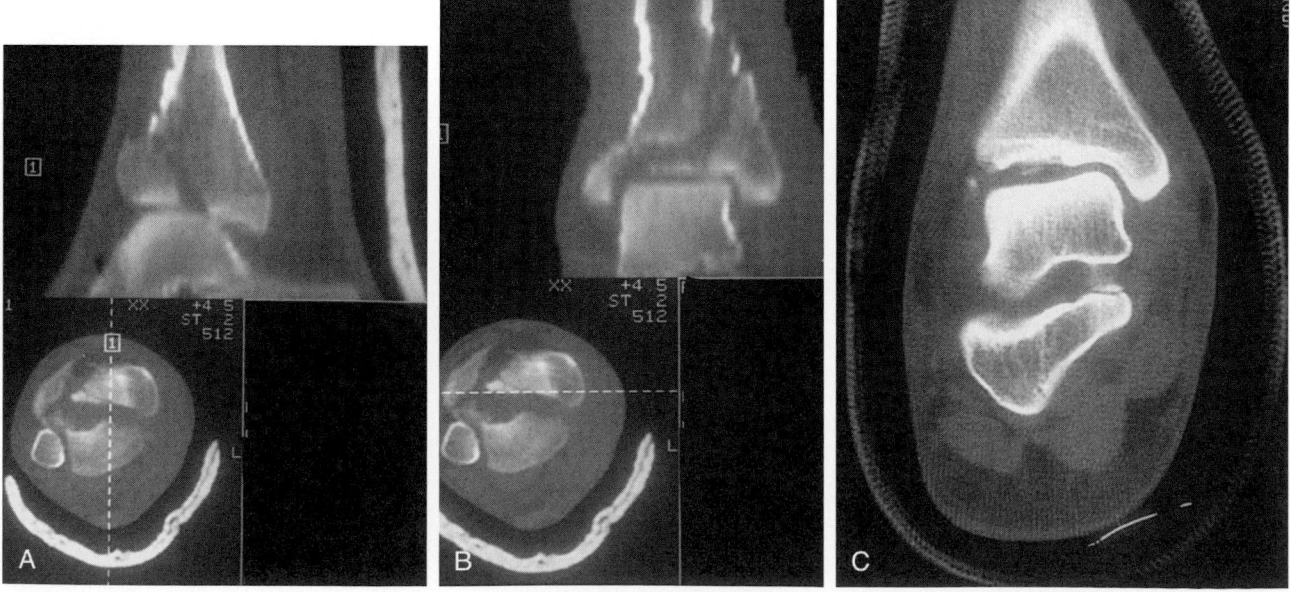

**FIGURE 59–19** *Continued. E,* Anteroposterior tomogram further localizes the lesion. This underlay a typical small osteochondral fracture, which responded to excision and drilling of the defect. *F,* Magnetic resonance imaging coronal view of *another patient* clearly shows an osteochondral lesion of the talar dome.

**FIGURE 59–20.** Computed tomographic (CT) scan of the ankle provides helpful detailed views of the pathologic anatomy of ankle injuries. *A, B,* A transverse CT scan with sagittal and coronal plane reconstructions. *C,* Coronal plane CT scan of *another patient* shows impaction of the anterior lateral margin of the distal tibia.

ankle region. Rather than thinking in terms of a list of potential diagnoses to be excluded one by one, the surgeon must remain constantly aware of the likelihood of more than one lesion.[85, 136, 185, 193, 289] In addition to indicating local structural damage, ankle pain may be the complaint of a patient with a leg compartment syndrome, proximal neurovascular compromise, or a foot injury. Table 59–3 is a list of various injuries that can affect the structures of the ankle.

## MANAGEMENT OF ANKLE FRACTURES

### General Principles

Adequate assessment and treatment of the entire patient and the entire injured limb generally have a higher priority than assessment and treatment of the ankle (see Chapter 5). However, significant permanent disability, including that from amputation, can be prevented by adequate care of an ankle injury. After lifesaving and limb-saving measures are under way, the ankle injury must not be neglected. Priorities for the ankle itself include both diagnosis and treatment, in the following order: (1) assurance of adequate blood flow; (2) provisional reduction of marked deformity or dislocation; (3) care of any open wound or other injury to the skin and soft tissue envelope; (4) precise reduction of skeletal deformity, which must be maintained throughout healing; (5) repair of tendons and nerves; (6) rehabilitation; and (7) identification and treatment of any complications that develop.

Without adequate perfusion, the foot cannot survive. Therefore, it is crucial to recognize ischemia. Except in the case of a mangled foot and ankle, it is unusual for an ankle level arterial injury to be limb threatening, probably because three arteries cross the region. Thus, if the foot is ischemic, one must look for a more proximal arterial lesion. Some injuries are unsalvageable, or an attempt at salvage may pose too much of a threat to the patient. For such patients, an early amputation is the best treatment. This topic is discussed in further detail in Chapter 57. An exceptional patient with an injury that is more of a laceration than a crush may be a candidate for local microvascular reconstruction or even replantation of a traumatic incomplete or complete amputation.

Marked deformity, usually resulting from a dislocation, fracture-dislocation, or severely displaced fracture, poses a threat to the local perfusion of skin stretched over bony prominences. It promotes local swelling and may also interfere with distal blood circulation. In addition, it is often quite painful and may injure articular cartilage impinged on by a sharp bony edge. Therefore, provisional reduction to improve local perfusion and prevent further injury is urgent. Application of a very well padded splint should follow. Although not always successful, an attempted manipulation in the emergency department often yields at least some improvement and is an appropriate part of applying a splint. It is better to return exposed and contaminated bone to the wound than to splint it in a position of excessive deformity. Because urgent operative wound care must soon follow, the benefits of correcting

| TABLE 59–3 |
| --- |
| **Injuries of the Ankle Region** |

**BONE INJURIES (FRACTURES)**

Malleolar
Metaphyseal—split
Metaphyseal—impacted
Ligamentous avulsion
Joint capsule avulsion
Other nearby fractures
   Base of fifth metatarsal
   Lateral process of talus
   Anterior process of calcaneus
   Tarsometatarsal complex
   Many other possibilities

**ARTICULAR SURFACE INJURIES**

Fractures, as above, with articular involvement
Osteochondral fractures (predominantly talus)

**LIGAMENT INJURIES**

Lateral collateral complex injuries
Syndesmosis injuries
Medial collateral injuries
Injuries to other nearby ligaments
   Subtalar
   Tarsometatarsal
   Midtarsal

**SOFT TISSUE ENVELOPE INJURIES**

Laceration
Contusion extending to crush injury
Avulsion or degloving
Foreign body retention
Edema
Preexisting compromise

**TENDON INJURIES**

Intrinsic injury
   Rupture
   Laceration
Retinacular injury
Rupture; tendon dislocation

**NERVE INJURIES**

Laceration
Contusion
Entrapment

**VASCULAR INJURIES**

Arterial
Venous

deformity outweigh the theoretical risks of introducing additional contamination into an already dirty wound.

Care of the soft tissues, including any open wound, is a vital element in the management of an injured ankle. There is a surprising spectrum of both open and closed soft tissue injuries.[281] Some low-energy ankle injuries have so little soft tissue damage that it may be ignored. There is little swelling, and surgery, if indicated, can be carried out safely any time after the injury. These injuries may lull the surgeon into thinking that all ankle injuries can be similarly treated. A high-energy injury with extensive displacement of comminuted, impacted, and transverse fractures may not exhibit much swelling during the first few hours, especially if the patient is in shock. However, such fractures are accompanied by a high degree of soft tissue trauma, even if there is no open wound, and have very low tolerance for extensive surgical approaches. Although all operations on ankle fractures must be done as atraumatically as possible, such severe crushing injuries should be approached with trepidation, if at all.[32, 61, 273, 275] Certainly, if there is evidence of soft tissue compromise—marked swelling, blistering, abrasions, or early eschar formation—whatever the fracture pattern, the surgeon must consider external fixation and should be willing to delay open reduction for several weeks if necessary until the soft tissues recover.

Open wounds involving fractures and dislocations of the ankle represent only a part of the soft tissue damage. The zone of injury extends beyond the open wound.[51, 281] Each such open wound should be treated as any open fracture, with sterile dressing, splint, tetanus prophylaxis, and urgent intravenous antibiotics (generally a first-generation cephalosporin for less severe wounds, with an aminoglycoside or substitution of a third-generation cephalosporin for those that are more severe). In addition to these adjuncts, prompt surgical débridement and irrigation in an operating room are crucial to minimizing the risk of serious infection. If a fracture is present, immediate fixation with appropriate techniques offers better results.[23, 35, 77, 89, 269, 294] With less severe injuries, fixation techniques are essentially the same as for closed injuries. For more severe injuries, it may be appropriate to minimize the extent of surgical exposure and to employ external fixation, at least provisionally, to immobilize both the foot and the ankle. In either case, the original open wound is left open for delayed closure.

Articular fractures of the ankle have the best prognosis when they heal in an alignment as close as possible to their original anatomy. It is generally accepted that the quality of the reduction is more important than whether it was achieved with an open or a closed technique. With this recognition and with the development of internal fixation methods that reliably maintain the tibiotalar relationship, open treatment of malleolar fractures has become more popular. When AO principles and techniques are properly applied to malleolar fractures, good results can be obtained in up to 90% of supination–external rotation malleolar fractures.[59, 110, 150] Other fixation techniques have their proponents, but they are now less widely favored, at least in North America.[1, 2, 30, 44, 104, 172, 200] As Olerud and Molander[200] have shown, less rigid fixation with wires, pins, or staples works well for more stable unilateral injuries, but when there is involvement of both sides of the ankle, reduction is more likely to be lost.

Fractures of the ankle vary widely in severity. Their effect on ankle stability and on the articular surface may range from minimal to profound. Treatment of the fracture itself depends on its location, size, displacement, and effects on joint stability. Opinions and recommendations for management of ankle fractures range equally widely, from nonoperative management to anatomic repair of every fragment. Clearly, the treating surgeon must make a decision on the basis of the reported results of injuries and treatment, the patient's injury and other characteristics, and his or her own personal experience and expertise. Stable restoration of normal anatomy in the safest and most reliable way ought to be the basic guideline for treatment of articular fractures about the ankle.[44, 45, 96, 275]

If any tendon injury accompanies or is the major component of ankle trauma, its surgical repair must be considered.[73, 268] In some patients, closed nonoperative treatment of a ruptured Achilles tendon may be appropriate.[10, 143] Unless repaired early, failure of the posterior tibial tendon usually results in a symptomatic flatfoot deformity.[159, 160] Lacerations or ruptures of other tendons may also prove less disabling if they are repaired. Therefore, such tendon injuries often require surgical treatment, but only if there is an open wound is such treatment urgent.

The most disabling nerve injury of the ankle region is loss of the tibial nerve, which provides sensation for the sole of the foot. Some have advocated amputation when adults sustain this injury along with an otherwise treatable arterial injury because of the high risk of neurotrophic ulcers and their complications.[137] Such problems are more common when the foot and ankle are stiff and deformed and do not necessarily accompany absence of plantar sensation. If nerve continuity is present, functional recovery may occur, even after many months. A temporary but prolonged period of dysesthesia may accompany recovery of tibial nerve function, either spontaneously or after repair. It may also persist after an injury to the nerve and may respond to nerve repair. Experience with treatment of lower extremity nerve injuries is rare. Sedel[247] recommended that microsurgical repair be considered for complete lesions of the major lower extremity nerves. Seddon,[246] reviewing a large number of patients, few of whom were treated surgically, recommended against nerve repair but emphasized the good functional result that can be obtained, even with a complete tibial nerve palsy.[48]

Injuries of the other nerves crossing the ankle can become painful because of neuromas that are caught in the scar. This problem may be prevented by transecting the injured nerve and burying it deeply in soft tissue, away from scar and moving structures.

The ankle's ligaments are frequently damaged. The syndesmosis (distal tibiofibular ligaments) may be disrupted in association with a fibular fracture. If it is unstable after the associated fracture has been repaired, surgical fixation of the syndesmosis is the safest way of ensuring healing with stability in the correct configuration. Syndesmosis fixation may not be required, especially if the AITFL or PITFL has caused an avulsion fracture that permits stable repair of the ligament's attachment. Assessment of the stability of the tibiofibular relationship (as discussed later) is an essential part of the operative treatment of any malleolar injury with a fibular fracture above the level of the plafond.

Acute surgical repair of the completely ruptured LCL complex has been advocated by a number of authors.[3, 36, 67, 116] Although this repair may improve apparent stability, it does not seem to provide a better result than functional treatment, which has now become the more favored approach, even for vigorous athletes.[66, 262] Should late instability occur, delayed repair is as successful as primary suture, but it is not frequently required after adequate functional management and rehabilitation.[42, 140]

The medial collateral ligament (MCL) is rarely injured

without a malleolar fracture.[113] When it occurs, deltoid ligament failure is often the equivalent of a medial malleolar fracture, and unless the talus is visibly displaced when radiographs are taken, the injury may be missed. Its repair has been advocated for unstable malleolar injuries, but this does not effectively stabilize the talus. Moreover, it is unnecessary if the lateral malleolus has been restored securely to its anatomic location.[2, 13, 59, 98, 297] Isolated late insufficiency of the deltoid ligament is practically unheard of in spite of nonoperative treatment, so skepticism about the need for primary repair of ruptured deltoid ligaments seems warranted.

Rehabilitation of ankle injuries emphasizes maintenance of a neutral functional position, protection of the injured area from excessive forces, restoration of motion, and progressive resumption of weight bearing as soon as safe. Many different approaches and recommendations exist. Whether one is better than another remains questionable.[1, 249] The surgeon who has managed the entire treatment of a patient with an ankle fracture and knows the quality of bone and fixation is best equipped to manage the rehabilitation phase, as this information is not as readily conveyed to therapists and other personnel. Finally, restoration of strength, endurance, and agility is necessary before a patient completes her or his recovery.

Complications that may develop during care of ankle injuries are discussed later. Especially important to avoid, and to recognize if they occur, are infection, skin slough, malalignment, loss of fixation, nonunion, and reflex sympathetic dystrophy with its variants.[45, 251, 276, 295] Infection after open injury or surgical treatment may be occult and may involve the ankle joint itself. Diagnosis requires a high index of suspicion and aspiration of the joint for Gram stain, cell count, and culture and sensitivity testing. Wound exploration in the operating room may also be required. Skin sloughs, unless very small, usually require plastic surgical repair, typically with a free flap in this region, which has limited local soft tissue. Malalignment can be identified with adequate intraoperative radiographs. Patients being treated with cast immobilization require regular follow-up radiographs with strict assessment according to standard criteria for reduction. Fixation loss can be prevented by good technique and appropriate postoperative management. If it should occur, reoperation is usually indicated. Nonunions, if symptomatic, need open reduction and often bone grafting. Reflex sympathetic dystrophy should be considered as a potential cause of pain. Even after apparently satisfactory fracture healing with an anatomic reduction, minor degrees of arthrosis are common, and 25% to 30% of patients have at least some degree of subjective complaints.[20]

## Special Considerations for Polytrauma Patients

As noted previously, most other injuries take precedence over definitive treatment of the ankle. Evaluation with as much history as possible, a brief physical examination, and application of a well-padded splint with provisional reduction of dislocation or gross deformity may be all that can be done for some time. Adequate radiographs are necessary for definitive diagnosis and treatment. If life- or limb-threatening injuries require urgent attention, radiographs of the ankle should be deferred until the earliest appropriate time and can certainly be obtained in the operating room. Although operative treatment of an open wound should be accomplished as soon as possible, fracture fixation may need to be deferred for some time.

If soft tissue injury is severe or if a distraction force is needed to maintain reduction, an external fixator including the tibia, calcaneus, and metatarsals is advisable and can be applied rapidly. This fixator maintains a neutral foot position, provides access to soft tissue wounds, and permits suspension and continuous elevation of the injured limb. For less severe injuries, a plaster cast or splint maintains a provisional reduction and allows the patient to be mobilized in bed and chair while maintaining as much elevation as possible of the injured leg. It is important to use a great deal of padding, especially posterior to the heel. If the injury is rotationally unstable, a short extension onto the thigh with the knee moderately flexed improves the effectiveness of such a cast or splint. It is important to gain the best possible provisional reduction and immobilization, for the multiply-injured patient may not be able to return to the operating room as soon as initially planned for definitive care of the ankle. Marked displacement or instability may cause further damage to the soft tissues. Ankle injuries for which operative treatment is optimal can often have this deferred for up to a week or two without significantly compromising the ultimate result, if the patient's overall condition makes this advisable and if adequate interim management is provided for the ankle.[132]

## CLASSIFICATION

Hamilton thoroughly and lucidly discussed malleolar fractures in his text *Traumatic Disorders of the Ankle*.[96] A number of other helpful summaries are also available.[56, 275, 287, 291–294] This section reviews the pathophysiologic findings of Lauge-Hansen and others to provide an understanding of injury patterns as related to mechanism. It then offers the Danis-Weber (AO) classification as a practical clinical scheme and uses it as the basis for discussing treatment of malleolar fractures.[149] As will become evident, the details of treatment depend more on the actual anatomy of a bone and ligament injury than on its classification according to any system. However, the more thoroughly the surgeon understands the fracture anatomy, the better he or she can plan and carry out effective treatment.

### Lauge-Hansen

It is important to clarify Lauge-Hansen's terminology before considering his experiments and classification. His names for fracture types refer to how he caused them in experiments with cadaver legs that were secured proximally while he manipulated the foot. The first part of the name is the position of the foot—either supination or pronation. The second part of the name indicates the force that was applied to cause the observed injury—external rotation, abduction, or adduction. Unfortunately, Lauge-Hansen used the word *eversion* to mean external rotation and thus magnified the complexity of his terminology.[141, 142] Figure 59–21 illustrates the Lauge-Hansen malleolar fracture classification and the corresponding Danis-Weber categories.

## SUPINATION-ADDUCTION

Adducting the supinated (inverted) foot, usually from unanticipated weight bearing on the lateral border, is the most common mechanism of injury to the ankle. Failure occurs first on the lateral side, which is under tension, and is usually limited to the LCL, which may be avulsed with a portion of the distal fibula. This mechanism thus produces the typical inversion sprain. Avulsion fractures are recognizable as characteristically transverse, perpen-

dicular to the applied force. The second stage of this injury, produced by continued adduction of the supinated foot, is a shearing, medially displaced fracture of the medial malleolus, which is pushed medially by the talus. This mechanism causes a vertical fracture line that is distinct from the horizontal failure produced by tensile loading. It accounts for 10% to 20% of malleolar fractures (Fig. 59–22).[96]

The characteristic vertical appearance of the medial malleolar fracture reveals the injury mechanism, even if the lateral failure is purely ligamentous. It is important to note that an undisplaced or minimally displaced medial malleolus fracture may be produced by this mechanism without lateral failure if sufficient preexisting lateral laxity is present. Because of the compressive forces applied medially, supination-adduction may produce impaction of the medial plafond in addition to the medial malleolus fracture (Fig. 59–23).

*Oblique* fractures of the medial malleolus are not often differentiated from vertical ones. Giachino and Ham-

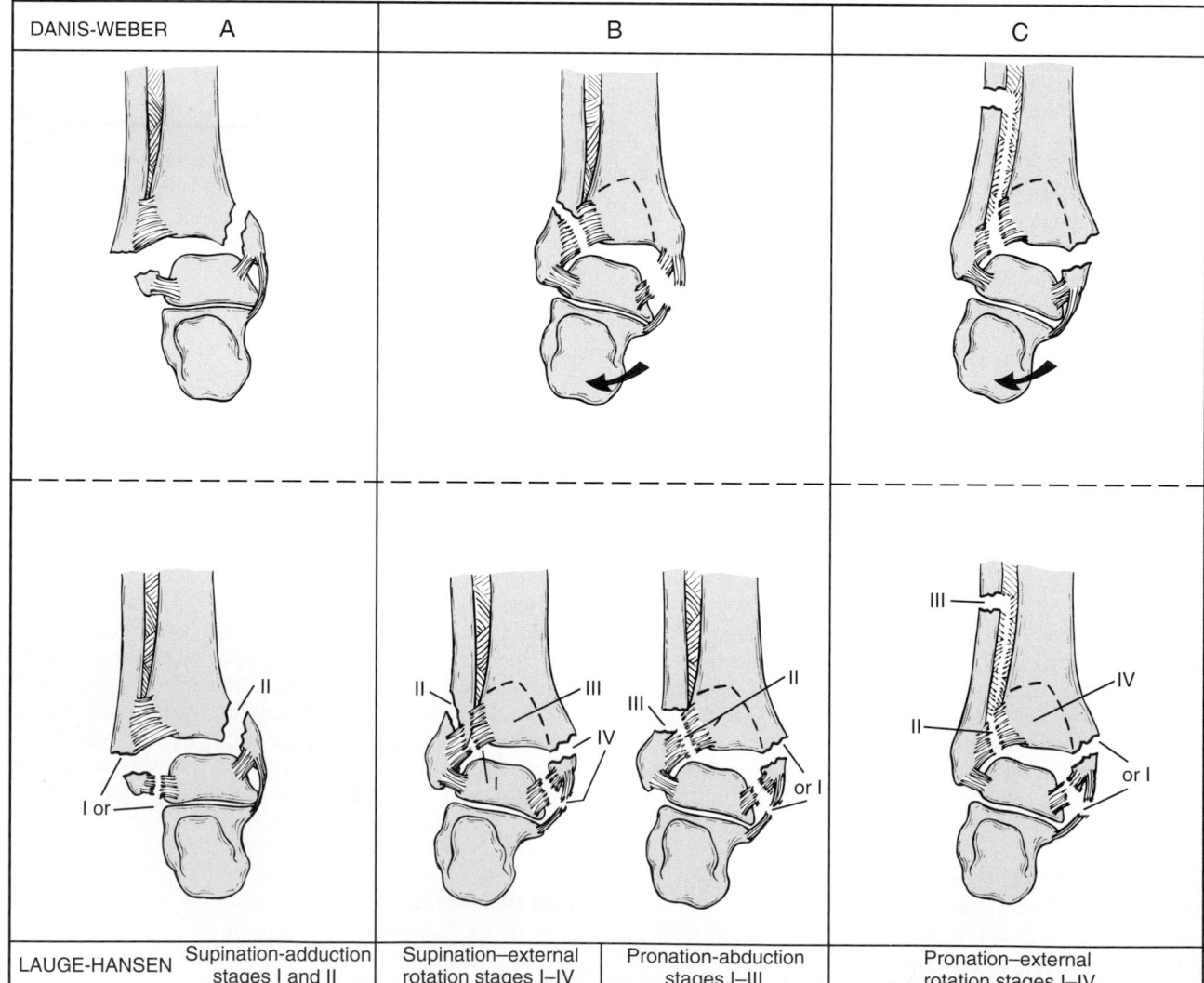

**FIGURE 59–21.** Correlation of the Danis-Weber (AO/ASIF [Association for the Study of Internal Fixation]) and the Lauge-Hansen classification systems for malleolar fractures. The Danis-Weber system is based on the level of the fibular fracture, and the Lauge-Hansen system is based on experimentally verified injury mechanisms. Type B injuries can be produced by two mechanisms: supination–external rotation and pronation-abduction. See text.

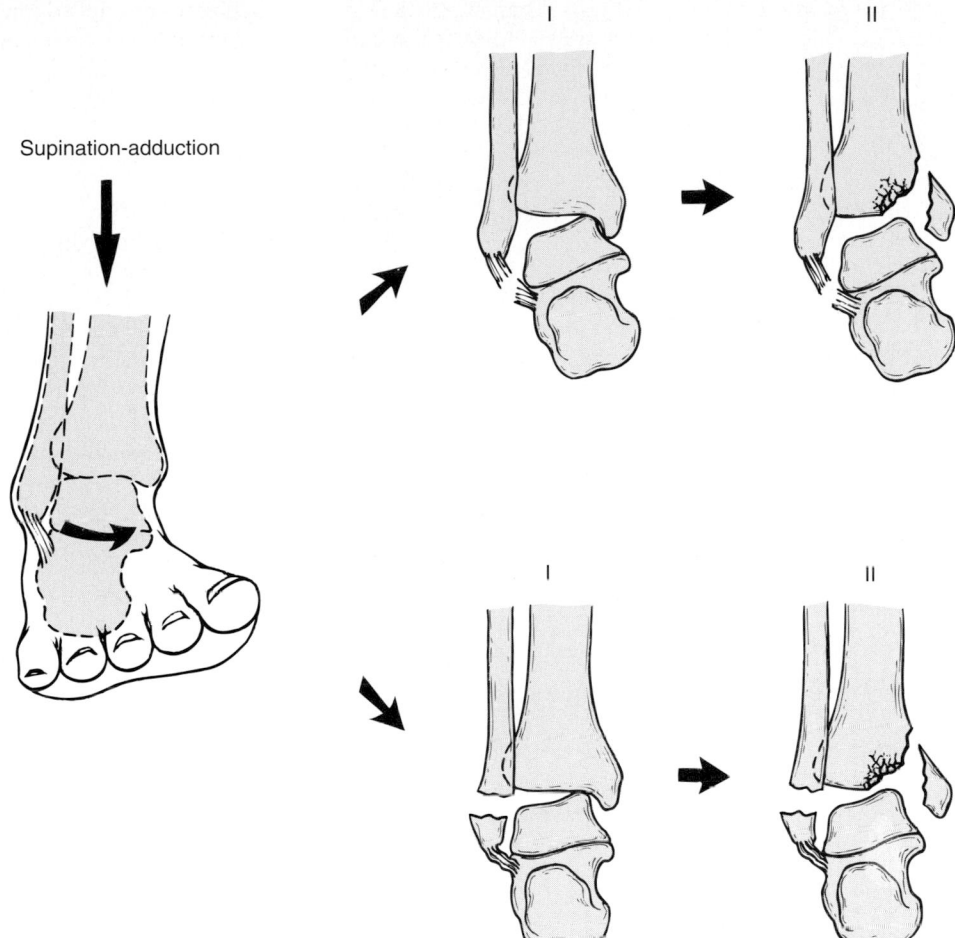

**FIGURE 59–22.** Supination-adduction injury pathology. The first stage is lateral failure of either the malleolus or the collateral ligament. The second stage is a vertical fracture of the medial malleolus, which may be associated with medial plafond impaction, as shown here.

mond[82] pointed out that they should be, because of their mechanism involving dorsiflexion as well as abduction and external rotation, which also produces a frequently occult, impacted anterolateral tibial plafond fracture. These oblique medial malleolus fractures are avulsion injuries rather than impacted ones and therefore are unstable in tension and better treated with internal fixation.

## SUPINATION–EXTERNAL ROTATION

External rotation of the supinated foot produces a common fracture pattern and is the cause of 40% to 75% of malleolar fractures.[96] The pattern is a spiral oblique fracture of the lateral malleolus, beginning at the level of the tibial plafond and extending a variable distance proximally (Fig. 59–24). The plane of this injury is predominantly frontal, so it is typically more evident on the lateral than on the AP or mortise radiograph, unless there is significant displacement. The mechanism of the fibular fracture is a rotational shearing force produced by pressure on the fibula by the talus while the tibia internally rotates, usually because of the body's falling to the opposite side.[161]

Lauge-Hansen demonstrated that during external rotation injuries, failure of structures around the ankle occurs sequentially in a characteristic order. In supination–external rotation injuries, the first to fail is the AITFL,

followed by the fibula, then the PITFL, and then the medial side of the ankle mortise, where tensile failure may produce either a rupture of the deltoid ligament or a generally transverse avulsion fracture of the medial malleolus (Fig. 59–25). Knowledge of the several components and sequence of injury brings some order to an otherwise chaotic collection of bone and ligament injuries. This can help the surgeon identify an occult ligamentous injury or guide treatment.

Note that in supination–external rotation injuries, the fibular fracture is at or just above the level of the plafond, so that even with failure of the AITFL and the PITFL, the more proximal syndesmotic components stabilize the fibular shaft. Thus, open reduction and internal fixation (ORIF) of the fibular fracture should restore the proper relationship of the lateral malleolus to the distal tibia. Stability is not guaranteed, however, because it depends on integrity of the interosseous tibiofibular membrane above the fracture. Occasionally, this structure is disrupted, explaining why mortise-syndesmotic stability needs a case-by-case analysis.

Although the general pattern of each type of malleolar fracture is usually consistent, a moderate amount of variation is seen.[199] Thus, the supination–external rotation injury can be identified by its typical fibular fracture pattern. If it is explored surgically, the AITFL disruption is obvious. The disruption may be through the substance of

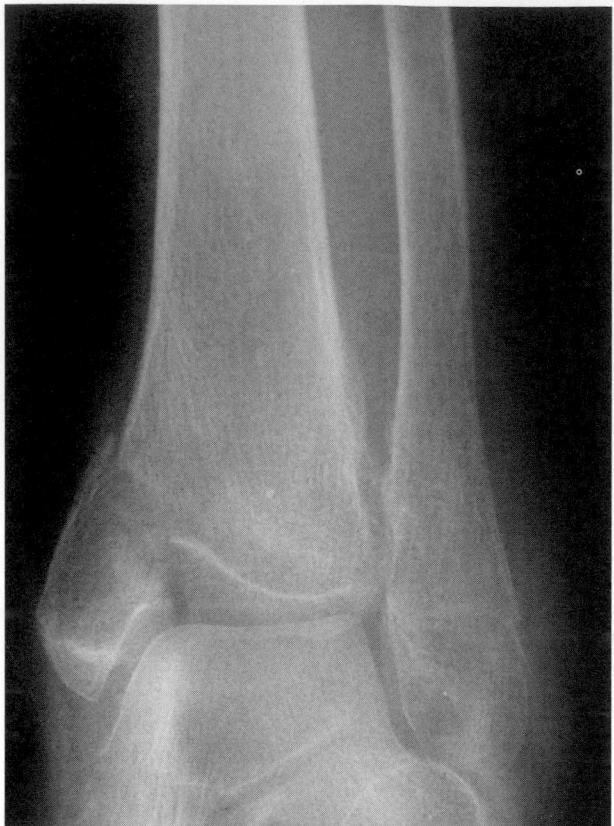

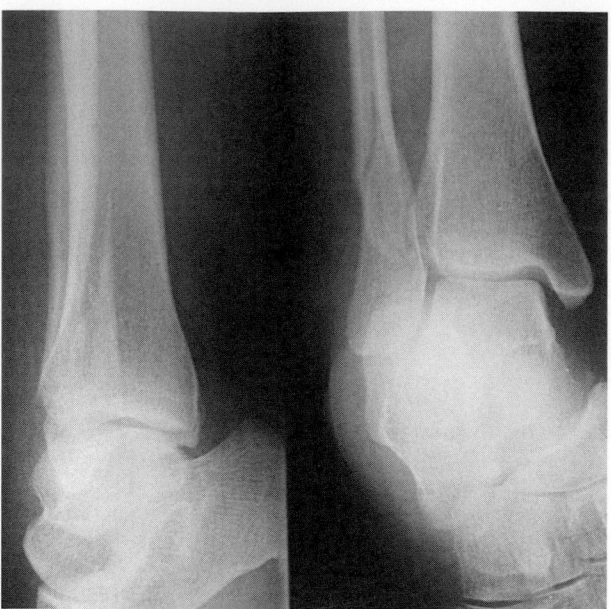

**FIGURE 59–24.** A slightly displaced supination–external rotation fracture of the lateral malleolus shows the typical pattern of fibular fractures caused by this mechanism. The overall plane of the fracture is oblique, from low anteriorly to high posteriorly, so that displacement is more evident on the lateral than on the anteroposterior view.

**FIGURE 59–23.** A supination-adduction stage II fracture with significant impaction of the medial tibial plafond. The type A lateral malleolus fracture is undisplaced on this radiograph but was unstable to examination during surgery.

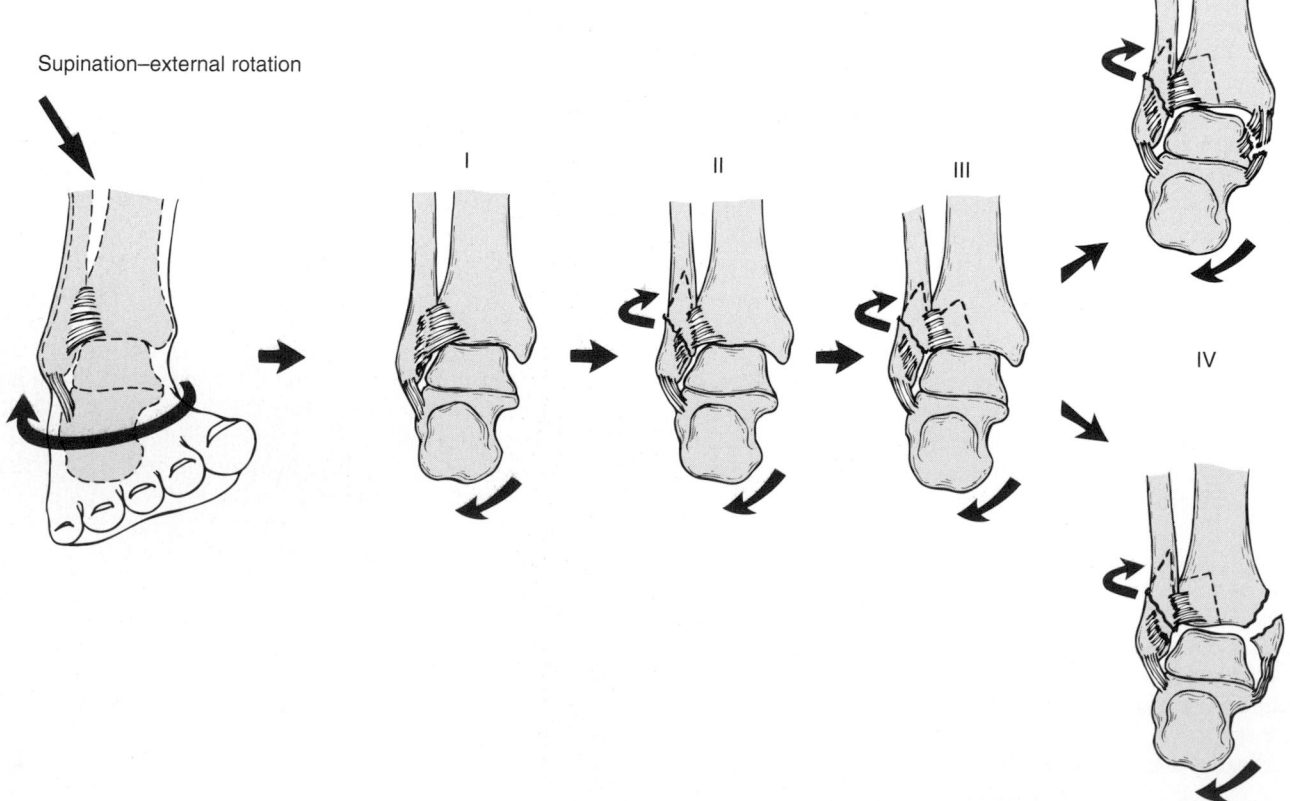

**FIGURE 59–25.** Supination–external rotation injury pathology. The first stage is failure of the anterior inferior tibiofibular ligament (AITFL). The second stage is a spiral lateral malleolar fracture at the level of the plafond. The third stage is posterior inferior tibiofibular ligament (PITFL) failure. The fourth stage is medial failure of either malleolus or the deltoid ligament.

the ligament, by avulsion of a bone fragment from Chaput's tubercle on the tibia, or by avulsion of its fibular attachment, called the *Wagstaffe (Le Fort) tubercle*. This ligament can guide reduction of the normal tibiofibular relationship, and its repair may aid in the secure healing of the syndesmosis. Although most supination–external rotation fibular fractures are at the level of the ankle joint, the same pattern, resulting from the same mechanism, is occasionally seen at a higher level.[202]

After the fibula, the PITFL is next in order of failure. Because of its posterior location, it is not exposed as often during surgical treatment of malleolar fractures. It may fail in substance or by avulsion of its tibial attachment, often as a small, extra-articular "posterior malleolar" fragment but occasionally as a large, intra-articular one. These postero-lateral tibial tubercle avulsion fractures are sometimes referred to as *Volkmann's fragments*.

The medial and final component of the supination–external rotation injury may be either a fracture of the medial malleolus or a rupture of the deltoid ligament.[119] Rarely, a hybrid lesion is seen, with fracture of the anterior colliculus representing superficial deltoid ligament failure and rupture of the fibers of the deep deltoid ligament while the posterior colliculus remains intact[253] (see Fig. 59–32).

The surgeon must remember that an ankle with a radiologically apparent supination–external rotation fracture of the lateral malleolus may have a completely unstable stage IV injury, with the deltoid ligament ruptured medially, or a stable stage II injury, with an intact posterior syndesmosis and medial complex. Lateral talar shift, a posterior lip fragment, and significant displacement of the fibular fracture are all evidence for more than a stage II injury. Differential diagnosis is important because true stage II injuries do well with nonoperative weight-bearing treatment, even though the potential for some lateral mobility of the talus is present.[19, 44, 107, 134] However, if the injury is an unrecognized stage IV, then talar subluxation, malunion, and arthrosis are potential sequelae that are preventable with surgery. If doubt exists, follow-up radiographs should help identify an initially unrecognized deltoid ligament disruption.

## PRONATION-ABDUCTION

Forced abduction of the pronated foot is responsible for this category of ankle injuries and typically fractures the fibula at the level of the plafond. This pattern accounts for 5% to 21% of malleolar fractures.[96] Pronation-abduction fibular fractures are distinguished from supination–external rotation injuries by their different pattern, which is transverse and often laterally comminuted, as bending forces applied to the fibula result in medial tension and lateral compression (Fig. 59–26). Some such injuries may be hybrids, with initiation by abduction followed by rotation externally about the axis of the PITFL.[84] The transverse orientation and lateral comminution, which may be extensive, make ORIF of pronation-abduction injuries more difficult than it usually is for supination–external rotation injuries.

Lauge-Hansen demonstrated that the initial stage of failure (essentially a mirror image of the supination-adduction pattern) is medial tensile failure, either through

the deltoid ligament or with a transverse avulsion fracture of the medial malleolus. The second stage is rupture or avulsion of the AITFL and PITFL of the syndesmosis. The third stage is the fibular fracture (Fig. 59–27). Limbird and Aaron[148] emphasized that these injuries may have an associated impaction fracture of the lateral plafond, also analogous to the supination-adduction pattern. Although the syndesmotic fibers proximal to the level of a pronation-abduction fracture are usually intact, the fracture itself may be proximal enough that these fibers offer little stability to the tibiofibular relationship. Therefore, after repair of a pronation-abduction fibular fracture, as with a supination–external rotation fracture, it is important to assess the stability of the syndesmosis.

## PRONATION–EXTERNAL ROTATION

With external rotation of the pronated foot, Lauge-Hansen produced another pattern of malleolar injury (Fig. 59–28). In this case, because the medial structures are placed under tension by pronation, the initial failure occurs on the medial side with either deltoid ligament rupture or avulsion of the medial malleolus. In the second stage, the AITFL fails. The pathognomonic third stage is a spiral or oblique fracture, which typically runs from anterior proximally to posterior distally, rather than the reverse pattern seen in supination–external rotation fractures.[202] The location of the pronation–external rotation fibular fracture is its most important characteristic, for it is above the level of the ankle joint plafond. This level of fibular fracture is the hallmark of the Danis-Weber type C malleolar injury (Fig. 59–29). A pronation–external rotation mechanism can produce a fibular fracture in the proximal leg in conjunction with other malleolar lesions—the Maisonneuve fracture. Thus, an apparently isolated

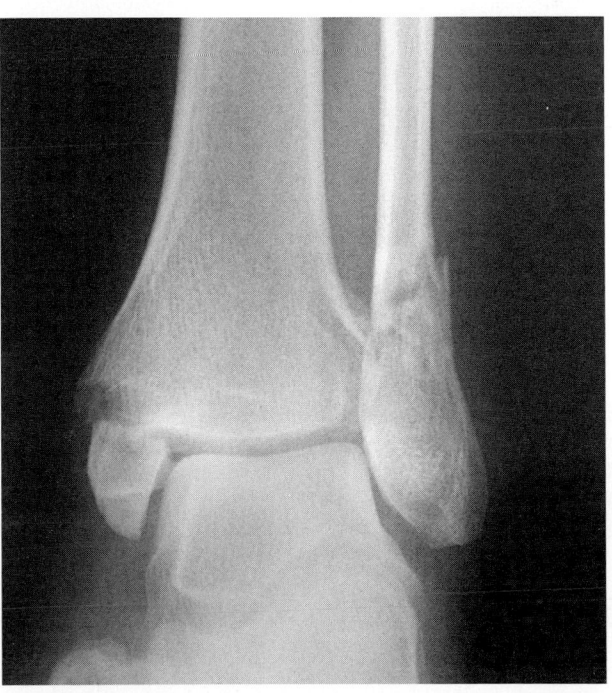

**FIGURE 59–26.** Pronation-abduction fracture demonstrating a laterally comminuted, fairly transverse fibular fracture just above the plafond.

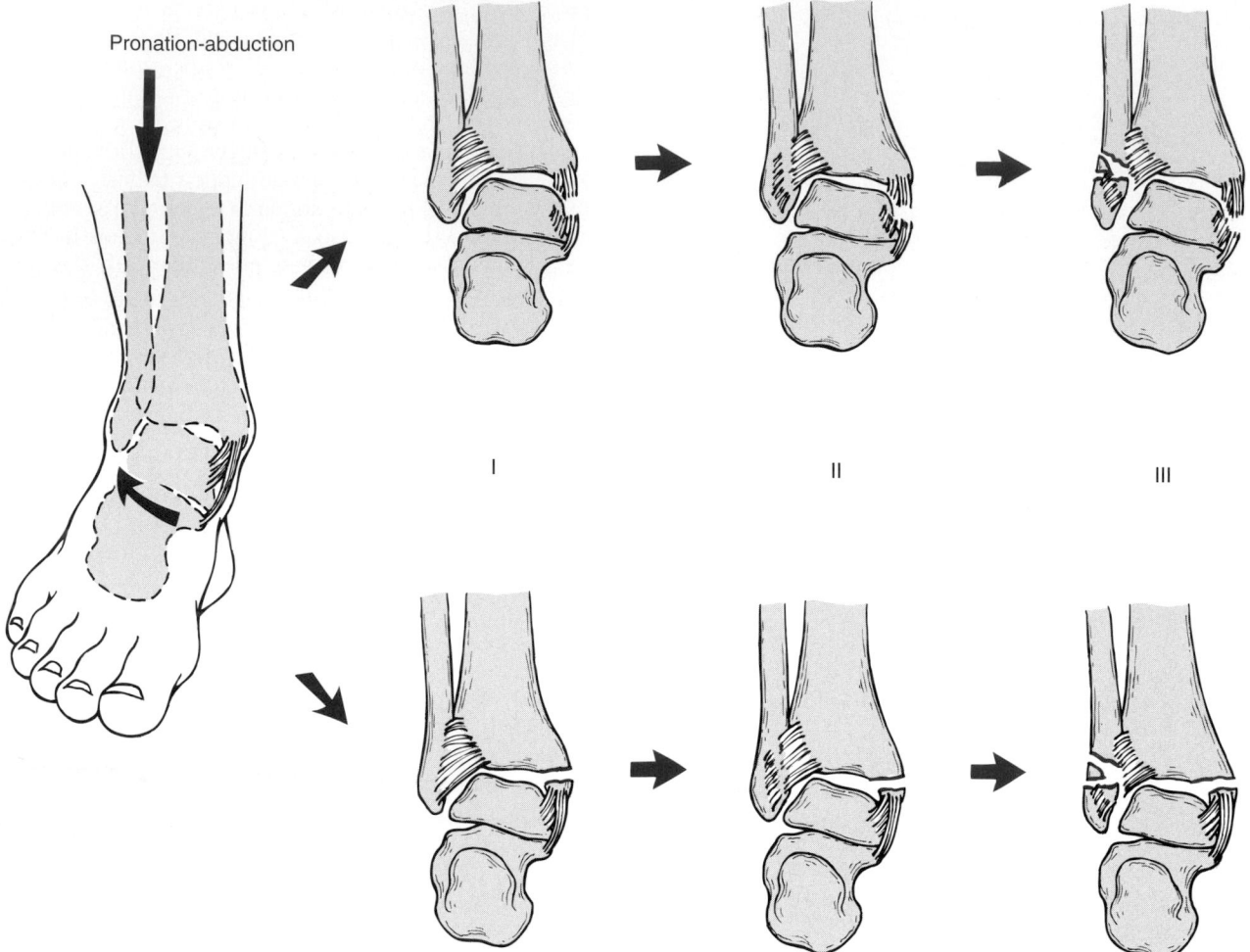

**Figure 59–27.** Pronation-abduction injury pathology. The first stage is medial failure of either malleolus or the deltoid ligament. The second stage is syndesmosis (anterior inferior tibiofibular ligament and posterior inferior tibiofibular ligament) disruption. The third stage is a bending fracture of the lateral malleolus with a transverse, laterally comminuted pattern.

medial or posterior malleolar fracture should lead to a search for a proximal fibular fracture. The fourth stage is disruption of the PITFL osteoligamentous complex. Pronation–external rotation injuries account for 7% to 19% of malleolar fractures.[96]

Thus, disruption occurs in the same direction around the ankle as it does with supination–external rotation injuries, but the starting point is medial instead of anterolateral. Because supra-articular fibular fractures can also be produced by supination–external rotation, a stage IV injury may be assigned to one category or the other on the basis of the appearance of the fibular fracture.[202, 203] Furthermore, a type C fibular fracture with little displacement may be a stable stage II supination–external rotation fracture.

## Danis-Weber

This system classifies ankle fractures into three groups, A, B, and C, on the basis of the level of the fibula fracture in relation to the tibial plafond.[188]

Type A fractures involve the fibula distal to the level of the tibial plafond. Supination-adduction would be a typical mechanism. Therefore, the syndesmosis is rarely damaged. The fibula fracture pattern tends to be transverse, with medial pathology that is seen with supination-adduction forces.

Type B fractures involve the fibula at the level of the plafond. Supination–external rotation and pronation-abduction both cause fractures at this level. Although components of the syndesmosis are routinely injured, functional instability is unusual. This stability is due to sparing of the tibiofibular interosseous membrane proximal to the fibula fracture. Medial pathology is that seen with either of these two mechanisms.

Type C fractures involve the fibula above the level of the plafond. Pronation–external rotation is the typical force involved. Thus, all syndesmotic ligaments at the plafond are torn. Tearing of the tibiofibular interosseous membrane extends at least to the level of the fibula fracture. Syndesmotic stability of the ankle once again is related to the level of the tearing of the tibiofibular interosseous membrane as previously discussed.

## AO–Orthopaedic Trauma Association

This classification is essentially a detailed, numerically based expansion of the Danis-Weber classification. However, as with other detailed classifications, it probably suffers from interobserver and intraobserver variability. It is cumbersome for day-to-day usage. It is an important research and publication tool. The reader is encouraged to use it for such purposes. It can be found as Supplement I, Volume 10, 1996 in the *Journal of Orthopaedic Trauma.*

## Significance of Classification

An important point about the supra-articular type C fibular fracture is that the entire ligamentous connection between the distal tibia and the distal fibula may have failed, whether through the radiolucent ligaments or by avulsion of a bone fragment. The need for operative stabilization of the syndesmosis is more likely with type C injuries and may be confirmed by a stress test after fixation of the malleolar fracture.

Occasionally, with type C fibula fractures, remaining ligamentous connections are sufficient and additional syndesmosis fixation is not necessary. If the supra-articular fibular fracture is caused by a stage II supination–external rotation mechanism, as demonstrated by Pankovich,[202] displacement is less and the ankle may be quite stable.[276] The *potential* for instability of the syndesmosis is the

rationale for the separate category of type C injuries in the Danis-Weber classification system.[223]

Neither the Lauge-Hansen nor the Danis-Weber classification provides with the categories a complete indication of the pathology present and the treatment required.[149] A Lauge-Hansen grade IV supination–external rotation injury may or may not have an unstable syndesmosis, a posterior articular lip fracture, an unstable fracture-dislocation, or a medial malleolus fracture. It may even have a high fibular fracture. A Danis-Weber type A injury may or may not have a lateral malleolus fracture, a medial malleolus fracture, or a medial articular plafond impaction. However, with a little more anatomic detail, such classification systems provide an efficient means of categorizing and describing malleolar injuries and developing a treatment plan.

## Atypical Malleolar Fractures

A certain number of malleolar fractures are not classifiable according to the schemes presented. Those caused by direct crushing or angulating forces, as seen often in open injuries, frequently fall into this category.[77, 195] The so-called Bosworth fracture-dislocation has a fracture just above the plafond with marked external rotation of the foot. The end of the proximal fibular segment is incarcerated behind the tibia and usually requires open reduction.[105] Rarely, the fibula may be dislocated anteriorly.[243]

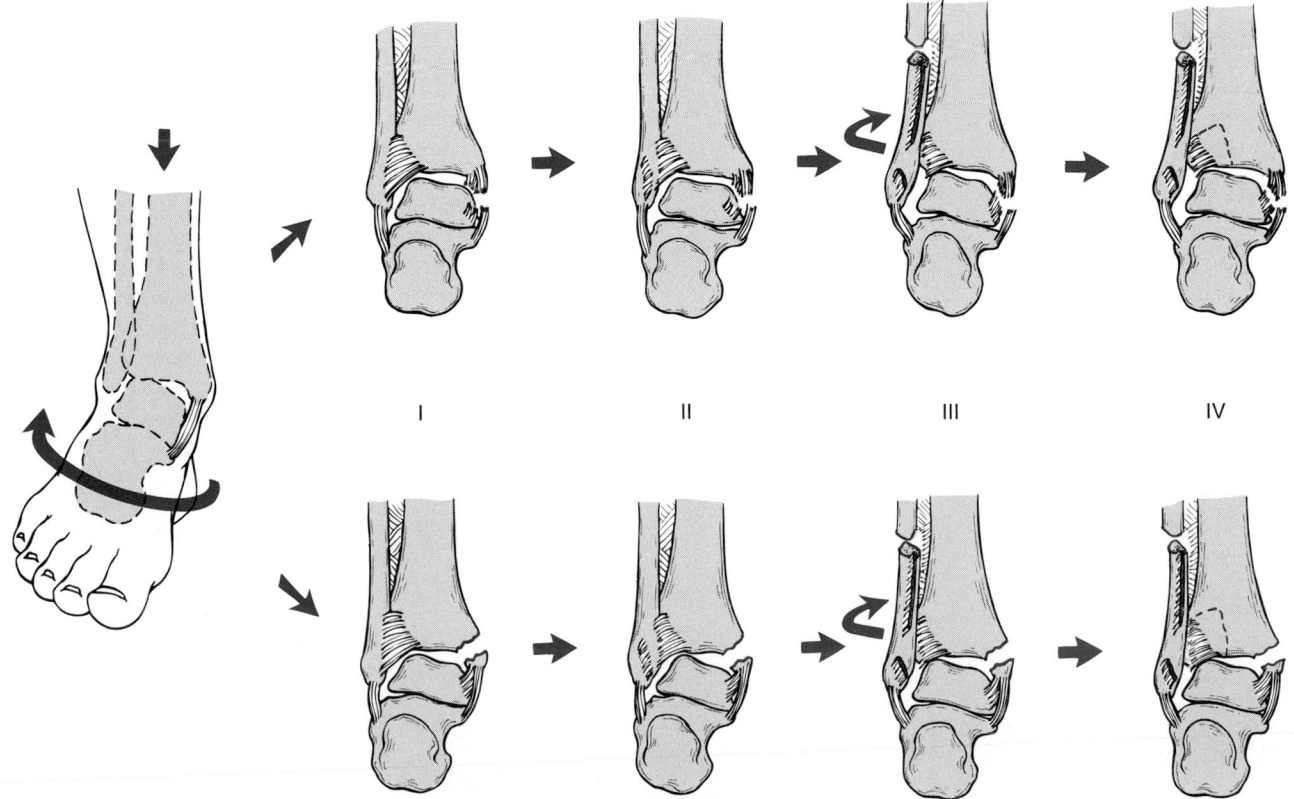

**FIGURE 59–28.** Pronation–external rotation injury pathology. The first stage is medial failure of either malleolus or the deltoid ligament. The second stage is anterior inferior tibiofibular ligament disruption. The third stage is a spiral fracture of the fibula above the level of the plafond. The fourth stage is posterior inferior tibiofibular ligament failure, demonstrated as a posterior malleolar failure.

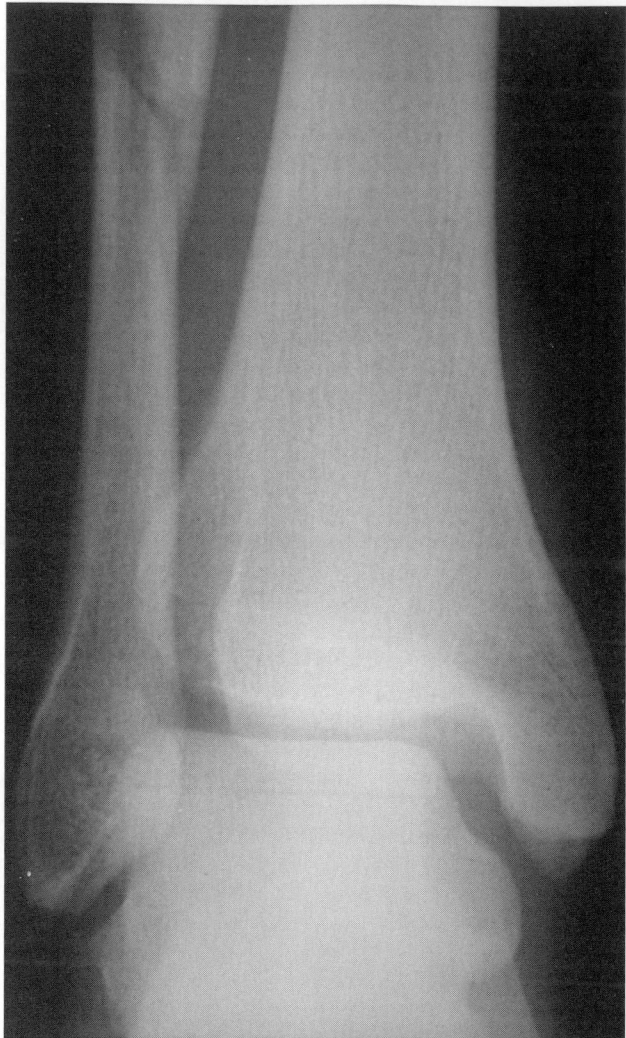

**FIGURE 59–29.** Radiograph of pronation–external rotation ankle fracture. This stage IV injury has a ruptured deltoid ligament; a laterally displaced fibula, indicating complete syndesmosis disruption; and a supra-articular short spiral fracture of the fibula, with orientation from low medial to high lateral.

In cases of atypical malleolar fractures, careful analysis of the pathoanatomy should lead to appropriate anatomic reduction.[197]

## DEFINITIVE TREATMENT

### Malleolar Fractures

Malleolar injuries are the most common significant lower extremity fracture.[57] Thus, most orthopaedic surgeons are frequently called on to treat them. The understanding and philosophy of management of these injuries have changed significantly since the 1970s. Current approaches appear to produce better results with fewer problems and more rapid rehabilitation. However, some controversies remain, and complications still occur.

Using the Danis-Weber classification, this section reviews the general principles of treatment for each injury pattern. Thereafter, details of operative management are provided. The basis of treatment for malleolar fractures is the secure restoration of a normal tibiotalar relationship. This means anatomic repositioning of the talus under the plafond, with anatomic realignment of the articular surface of the lateral malleolus to the plafond as well. In a displaced malleolar fracture, the lateral malleolus follows the talus. If it is reduced and heals in its anatomic relationship with the ankle plafond, it restores and maintains the proper tibiotalar relationship.

Assessing the reduction of the talus requires adequate radiographs and careful scrutiny of the relationships between the plafond and the talar dome, between the lateral articular surface of the talus and the lateral malleolus, and between the lateral malleolus and the distal tibial articular surface.[208, 267] Reduction of the fibular fracture site is, of course, helpful. However, the lateral malleolar fracture is extra-articular, and it is the restoration of *articular* congruence that is our primary goal. Length, rotation, and obliquity of the distal fibula are all-important aspects of a successful reduction. The fibula must be appropriately seated in its incisural notch. Because of its greater distal diameter, proximal displacement of the lateral malleolus interferes with the fit of the malleolus in this notch, displacing the fibula laterally and thus widening the mortise. A comparison radiograph of the opposite ankle and, occasionally, a CT scan are helpful tools for assessing the adequacy of lateral malleolus reduction.

Figure 59–30 demonstrates the radiologic landmarks for assessing the relationship of the lateral malleolus to both the talus and the distal tibia. It is important to remember that a good closed reduction and a well-molded cast often align the talus satisfactorily. However, unless the lateral malleolus heals anatomically, it cannot maintain talar position after the cast is removed. Therefore, the surgeon must assess the position not only of the talus but also of the lateral malleolus. Failure to reduce the fibula anatomically with a closed reduction is a prime justification for opening an unstable malleolar fracture in an effort to minimize the risk of post-traumatic arthrosis. This goal is more relevant in the young, active, healthy individual, for slight deviations from an anatomic alignment are often well tolerated by an older, more sedentary patient. There are as yet no conclusive and well-accepted criteria, based on long-term clinical outcome studies, for the limits of a satisfactory reduction. Other factors also affect the results.[20] The importance of an accurate reduction has been convincingly demonstrated for more severe injuries,[149] but minor degrees of displacement in relatively stable injuries do not have dire consequences, as shown by two long-term follow-up studies.[19, 44, 134] Rarely, if ever, is primary ankle arthrodesis recommended for malleolar fractures.[270]

### Treatment Principles

#### TYPE A INJURIES

Type A injuries, caused by supination-adduction mechanisms, produce a tensile failure on the lateral side with either LCL disruption or a transverse distal fracture of the lateral malleolus. On the medial side, an oblique medial malleolus fracture may be present, rarely in isolation. The medial malleolar fracture may be more or less displaced, may extend into the posterior articular surface, and may be associated with an impacted fracture of the medial plafond beginning just lateral to the malleolar fracture line. The syndesmosis is rarely affected.

Truly undisplaced fractures of either malleolus do not require surgical treatment and can be managed well with a short leg cast. Some displaced supination-adduction fractures of the medial malleolus with either a fracture or a ligament rupture laterally can be reduced with a maneuver that reverses the mechanism of injury and corrects both angulation and displacement by abducting the hindfoot. Overreduction is not likely, so a significant

force can be applied and the position maintained with a well-padded short leg cast molded medially over the talus and calcaneus to maintain a valgus alignment of the hindfoot. Radiographic monitoring of the reduction is necessary.

If there is significant articular surface impaction, plafond incongruity resulting from a posteromedial fracture line, or an inadequate closed reduction, ORIF is indicated. Isolated, purely ligamentous lateral injuries can be managed satisfactorily nonoperatively (see "Lateral Collateral Ligament Injuries"). However, repair of the LCL is a relatively minor procedure that may protect an unstable medial reconstruction. A type A lateral malleolus fracture should generally be fixed for similar reasons unless the medial side is very secure and the lateral

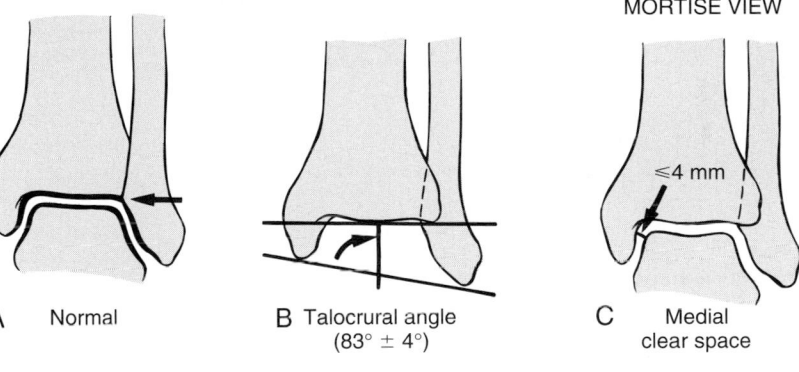

**FIGURE 59-30.** Restoration of the ankle mortise requires anatomic reduction of the lateral malleolus so that its articular surface is congruous with the reduced talus. *A,* On a mortise view radiograph, the condensed subchondral bone should form a continuous line around the talus, and there should be no proximal displacement, malrotation, or angulation of the lateral malleolus. *B, C,* A proper talocrural angle and normal joint space width also indicate normality. The medial joint space should be less than 4 mm and the superior joint space within 2 mm medially of its width laterally. *D,* Adequate tibiofibular overlap on the anteroposterior view indicates a proper syndesmotic relationship. The space between the medial wall of the fibula and the incisural surface of the tibia should be less than 5 mm. The anterior tubercle of the tibia should overlap the fibula by at least 10 mm. *E, F,* Talar malalignment is indicated by its lateral displacement or tilt into valgus. *G,* Although the talus may be reduced by external pressure, its alignment is not maintained by a shortened, malrotated lateral malleolus, as shown.

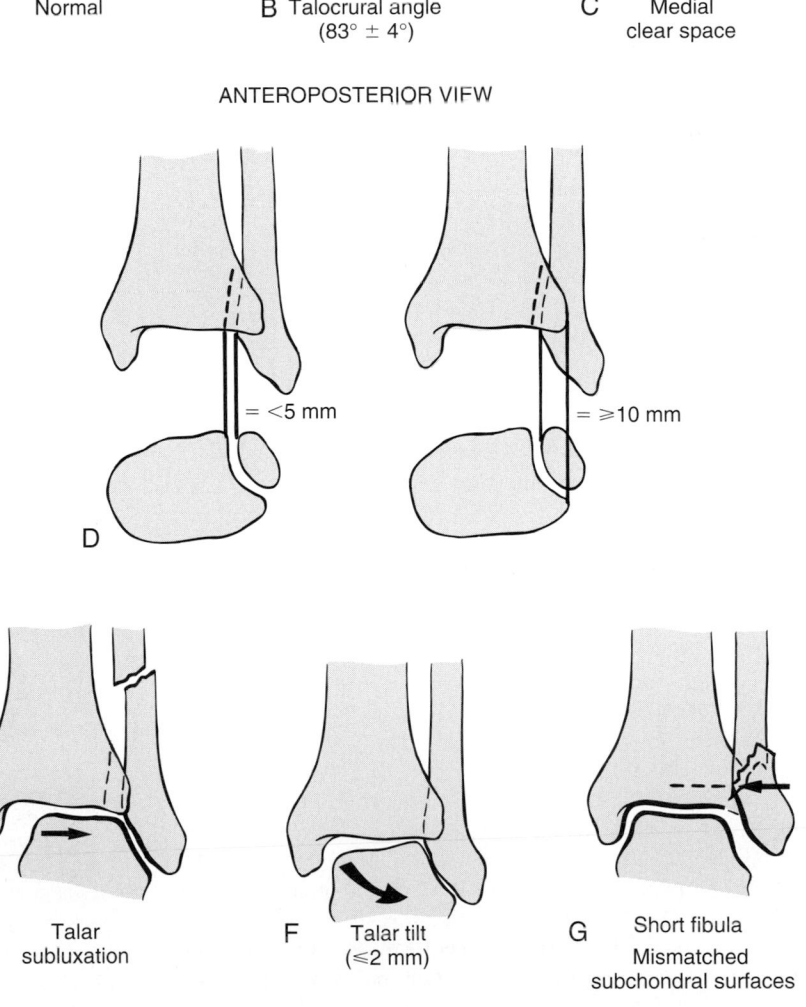

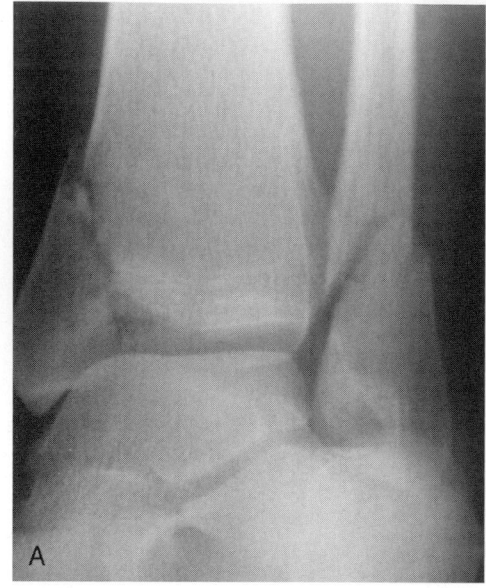
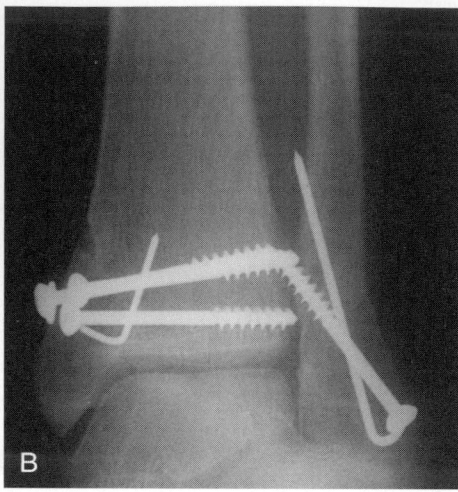

**FIGURE 59–31.** *A,* This stage II supination-adduction fracture has significant plafond impaction medially. *B,* The impacted fragment was reduced through the medial malleolar fracture plane. The defect was filled with local cancellous graft, and the fracture was stabilized with cancellous screws and a K-wire.

malleolus is completely undisplaced. Displaced medial malleolar fractures should be fixed unless an anatomic closed reduction is obtained and preserved. The same is true if there is plafond distortion by either a posteromedial fragment or an impacted area that requires elevation, usually with bone grafting of the resulting defect (Fig. 59–31). Depending on bone quality, security of fixation, and extent of plafond involvement, postoperative weight bearing may need to be restricted.

## TYPE B INJURIES

Type B injuries may be caused by either a supination–external rotation or a pronation-abduction mechanism. The syndesmosis is occasionally disrupted. The medial injury may be an avulsion fracture of the medial malleolus, an MCL rupture, or occasionally a combined lesion. Anatomic reduction and fixation of the medial malleolus cannot be counted on to reduce and maintain talar alignment (Fig. 59–32).[13, 76, 98, 145, 297] Depending on the mechanism and stage, either or both of the inferior tibiofibular ligaments may be ruptured, but above the level of injury, the ligamentous connections between the tibia and the fibula are usually maintained. Often, but not always, they adequately stabilize the syndesmosis after the distal fibular fragment is securely and anatomically reattached to the proximal one.

As discussed previously, the fibular fracture configuration depends significantly on the mechanism of injury. In supination–external rotation fractures, the characteristic spiral oblique fracture usually begins in an almost transverse plane distally on the anterior surface of the fibula. It then spirals lazily externally, extending a variable length up the fibula to exit proximally on its posterior surface. Occasionally, the long posterior spike of the distal fragment may be comminuted. The more transverse, often laterally comminuted, pronation–external rotation fibular fracture is usually recognizable as different, even though its primary location is the same. Transitional forms incorporating some external rotation about the intact PITFL are

typically spiral but are oriented differently, from low medial to high lateral, and begin above the plafond level.

In addition to the constant pathognomonic fibular fracture and the possibility of some form of medial side disruption, type B injuries may have associated posterior lip fractures of larger or smaller size, with or without articular surface involvement. Also, with pronation-abduction injuries, there may occasionally be impaction of the lateral tibial plafond. Elevation and bone grafting may be required if a significant portion of the plafond is involved. Fragments and deformation of the tibia may prevent satisfactory reduction of the fibula unless they are corrected. Anteriorly, the AITFL may be avulsed with a bone fragment of the anterior tibia or fibula or may be a pure soft tissue injury.

Treatment of type B malleolar fractures is determined by the severity and anatomy of the injury. Undisplaced injuries usually represent lesser degrees of severity and are well suited to nonoperative management.[284] Grade I supination–external rotation injuries, with damage limited to the AITFL, are hard to confirm but are recognized injuries. Such anterior syndesmosis sprains are slow to

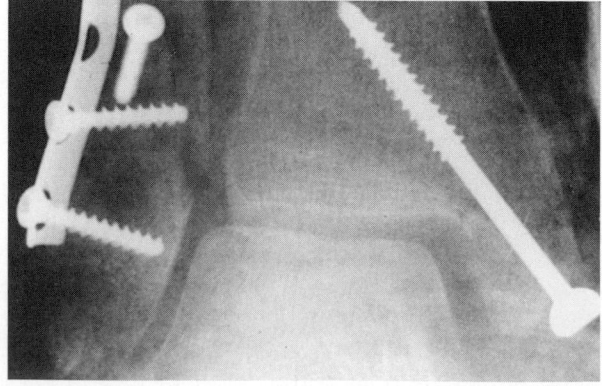

**FIGURE 59–32.** In spite of anatomic reduction of the medial malleolus, the talus is laterally subluxated, as it is not stabilized by the malreduced lateral malleolus. The deep deltoid ligament is disrupted.

heal. A more common example is the undisplaced or minimally displaced (up to 2 or 3 mm) spiral fracture of the lateral malleolus exhibiting the pattern described previously but unassociated with lateral displacement or tilt of the talus or evidence of medial side injury. Because the radiographic appearances are similar, it is essential to differentiate this injury from unstable stage IV injuries with MCL disruption. A short leg walking cast or brace for 6 weeks permits functional treatment of stable type B supination–external rotation fractures of the lateral malleolus. Radiographs taken in the cast about 10 to 14 days after injury can be checked for talar shift to aid in identifying a missed supination–external rotation stage IV deltoid ligament injury.

Closed reduction may succeed for management of displaced supination–external rotation injuries. The knee is flexed, and the foot is distracted, pulled anteriorly, and *internally rotated*. Assessment of reduction should ensure not only reposition of the talus relative to the plafond but also anatomic reduction of the lateral and (if present) medial malleolar fracture. More than 2 to 3 mm of displacement of a malleolus or of a plafond fragment is a reason to consider ORIF.

When local and systemic conditions permit, ORIF of displaced external rotation fibular fractures usually provides the best results and the quickest restoration of function. In general, the most secure fixation is with an interfragmentary lag screw and a small plate for added strength. The plate may be applied posterolaterally, as advocated by Brunner and Weber,[38, 242] or directly laterally. Syndesmosis stability must be confirmed, for occasionally such marked tibiofibular instability is present that it is necessary to employ syndesmosis transfixation or repair the inferior tibiofibular ligaments, if this is possible with security. Syndesmosis instability is more likely to occur with malleolar fractures that involve a ruptured deltoid ligament than in those with medial malleolar fractures that are amenable to stable fixation.

With anatomic reduction of the lateral malleolus and a stable syndesmosis, talar position is maintained; there is no benefit from repair of a torn deltoid ligament.[13, 59, 98, 297, 300] To avoid the occasional symptomatic medial malleolus nonunion and improve stability, most surgeons prefer to fix all but the smallest medial malleolar fractures associated with displaced ankle injuries.

It is helpful to recognize the mechanism of type B injuries, for pronation-abduction fractures require a different technique of closed reduction and may pose different surgical challenges from those with fractures associated with supination–external rotation. Stage I pronation-abduction injuries have only isolated medial side lesions. If the injury is ligamentous, repair is not required, and functional treatment is appropriate. The same is true for undisplaced medial malleolar fractures, which may deserve fixation if there is more than 2 to 3 mm of displacement. Stage II injuries add complete distal syndesmosis disruption, but unless a large avulsed fragment results in plafond or syndesmosis incongruity, treatment is the same. Stage III injuries may be markedly displaced and usually require fixation of the fibular fracture, although closed reduction by supination and adduction may be successful. In pronation-abduction fractures, lateral comminution

of the fibular fracture is frequently seen. It may be so severe as to defy anatomic reduction by reassembly of the fragments. In such a situation, it is best to realign the talus and reduce the lateral malleolus to it with provisional Kirschner wire (K-wire) fixation to the tibia or talus. The reduction is confirmed with a mortise view radiograph checked against a control view of the other side. Then one can proceed with buttress plate fixation and possibly bone grafting of a very comminuted fibular fracture. If possible, these comminuted lateral malleolar fractures should be reduced indirectly, without exposing the fracture fragments. The intact soft tissue sleeve aids reduction and promotes fracture healing (see Fig. 59–46). Often, initial reduction and fixation of the much less complex medial malleolus fracture can aid repair of the comminuted lateral side of the ankle. In true pronation-abduction lateral malleolus fractures, it is rarely possible to use a lag screw between the proximal and the distal fragments, and as a result, lateral fixation may be less secure.

## TYPE C INJURIES

The mechanism of type C malleolar injuries is classically pronation–external rotation. Stage I involves bone or ligamentous failure medially. In stage II, the AITFL fails, along with the interosseous ligament and some of the interosseous membrane. Stage III is the supra-articular fibular fracture at a variable height above the plafond. In significantly higher fractures, such as the Maisonneuve, it is probably unlikely that the interosseous membrane tear ascends as high as the fibular fracture. Rather, the intact proximal interosseous membrane does not interfere with torsional failure of the proximal fibula after the more distal soft tissues rupture. Finally, stage IV involves PITFL rupture. Anterior and especially posterior tubercular fractures may be a part of inferior syndesmotic ligament failure. Such posterior malleolus fractures may involve the articular plafond.

Rarely, a type C malleolar fracture is stable, undisplaced, and amenable to nonoperative management. Much more frequently, there are displacement and syndesmosis instability. Restoration of stability requires anatomic ORIF of the fibular fracture. Next, the syndesmosis is assessed and, if it is unstable or remains displaced, fixed in a position of anatomic alignment. Reduction and fixation of a large or destabilizing plafond fragment and of a medial malleolar fracture complete the reconstruction of displaced type C injuries. When the fibular fracture is very proximal, it is sufficient to regain length and rotation with only a distal exposure. After anatomic reduction of the lateral malleolar articular surface, confirmed by a comparison radiograph, one or two transfixion screws are placed to maintain this position during ligamentous healing of the syndesmosis. Type C malleolar injuries have a greater risk of syndesmosis disruption and instability, even after fixation of the fibular fracture. This category therefore serves to warn the surgeon of the need to assess syndesmosis stability. Particularly deceiving is the high Maisonneuve fracture with only a deltoid ligament tear medially.[203] On a routine ankle radiograph, only subtle malalignment of the fibular malleolus indicates the existence and nature of the injury.

## NONOPERATIVE TREATMENT OF MALLEOLAR FRACTURES

Undisplaced malleolar fractures can usually be satisfactorily treated with the ankle in neutral in a short leg walking cast, which should extend nearly to the knee. Rotational control is improved with triangular proximal molding of the cast to fit the proximal tibia without pressure on the peroneal nerve. Medial or lateral distal molding of the cast can resist varus or valgus angulation. It is important to distribute the contact area widely over the hindfoot rather than just around the malleoli and to avoid focal pressure on bony prominences with thin overlying soft tissues.

For fractures seen acutely, 10 ml of local anesthetic injected into the joint can provide excellent pain relief and allow a satisfactory closed reduction.[5] Alternatively, a general or regional anesthetic provides total relaxation and relief of pain.

A satisfactory closed reduction becomes harder to achieve if more than a day or so has elapsed since injury. Closed reduction is usually best achieved by reversing the mechanism of injury that produced the displacement and fracture pattern evident on initial radiographs. Some distraction as well helps to disengage fragments and eases the realignment of the talus with the mortise. Reduction of the talus, rather than direct pressure on the malleoli, brings the malleoli back into position and maintains alignment.

Thus, a type A *supination-adduction* fracture is reduced by abducting (everting) the hindfoot and molding the medial side of the distalmost part of the cast to retain this position. Three-point fixation is provided by a lateral mold proximal to the ankle and another molded area extending medially along the proximal medial tibial shaft.

Type B *supination–external rotation* fractures are reduced with (1) distraction, (2) anterior traction, (3) internal rotation, and (4) medial displacement of the talus. A long leg cast with the knee flexed is necessary to maintain the foot's internally rotated position that resists redisplacement. Upward traction on the big toe with posterior pressure on the distal medial tibia helps maintain the reduction while the cast is applied. Pronation is not necessary, and the foot should be in a relatively neutral position. Although it may be tempting to supinate the hindfoot in an effort to restore fibular length, this rarely works and may result in difficulties regaining a plantigrade foot. The long leg cast for a supination–external rotation ankle fracture is best applied with the patient supine, the hip and knee flexed, the hip abducted, and the foot held in internal rotation as shown in Figure 59–33. The entire cast from toes to midthigh can be applied at one time, after the reduction maneuver, if the foot and leg are held in the proper position by an assistant. The weight of the externally rotated leg counteracts the internal rotation moment applied to the foot and stabilizes the reduction. With adequate padding, molding of the cast is primarily over the lateral foot, around but not directly on top of the lateral malleolus (Fig. 59–34).

Type B *pronation-abduction* fractures are reduced by distraction and adduction. The presence of an intact medial malleolus or at least an overhanging remnant thereof often prevents overcorrection and provides a template for anatomic reduction. If there is no medial buttress (i.e., the medial malleolar fracture is at or above

the plafond), the ankle may be so unstable that a satisfactory closed reduction is not possible. Although rotation does not usually need to be corrected, its control may enhance stability; thus, a long leg, bent-knee cast is better if the reduction is unstable. The weight of the leg can be positioned to maintain a varus force on the ankle during reduction and cast application.

Type C *pronation–external rotation* fractures are best reduced with (1) distraction, (2) anterior displacement, (3) internal rotation, and (4) medial displacement, similarly to supination–external rotation injuries. A long leg cast with the knee bent and the foot in internal rotation is applied, as shown in Figure 59–33, with the foot held gently internally rotated but otherwise as neutral as possible.

Although a closed manipulation usually restores the talotibial relationship, for type C fractures, it rarely reduces the lateral malleolus anatomically. Because some shortening or malrotation is likely to remain, the lateral malleolus is not able to maintain the precise alignment of the talus after a cast is removed and normal weight bearing is resumed. Thus, ORIF is generally preferred.

If closed reduction is chosen for treatment of a displaced malleolar fracture, it is important to monitor the reduction until healing is secure, for if it is lost, prompt rereduction or ORIF may still provide a satisfactory result. In general, adequate monitoring of an unstable malleolar fracture requires radiographs in the cast at 7 to 10 days and again at 3 weeks. If reduction is maintained at 3 weeks, it is unlikely to be displaced during the next 3 weeks in a non–weight-bearing cast. Many regimens have been proposed for immobilization after closed reduction of a displaced malleolar fracture. We generally

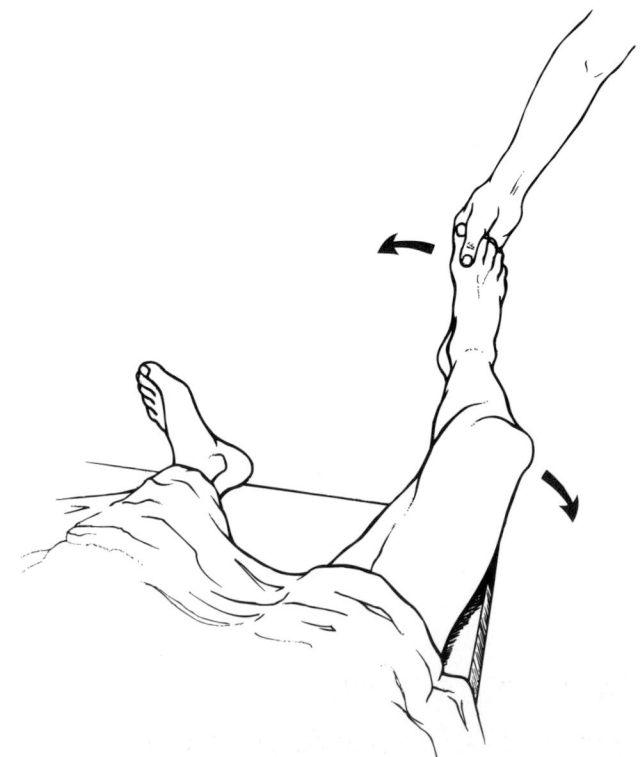

**Figure 59–33.** External rotation deformity can be reduced by internally rotating the foot relative to the abducted and flexed proximal leg. A well-padded long leg cast is applied while the leg is held in this position.

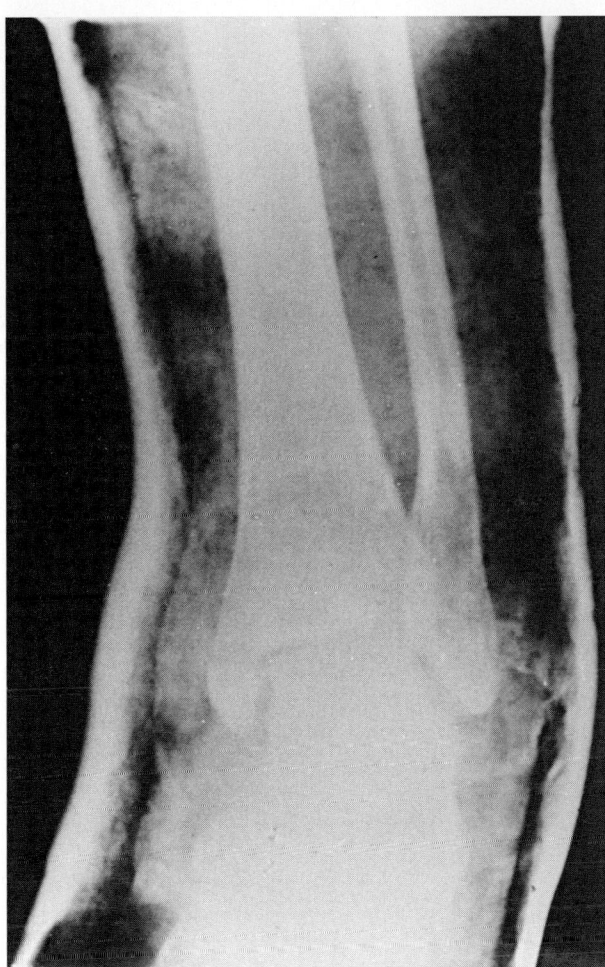

**FIGURE 59–34.** Molding of this cast over the lateral hindfoot, combined with moderate internal rotation, holds the talus anatomically reduced. The malleoli reduce with it, as they are attached by the collateral ligaments.

advocate 6 weeks in a non–weight-bearing cast molded primarily to preserve the reduction. Following this, another 2 to 3 weeks in a plantigrade short leg walking cast or brace provides additional protection and helps with rehabilitation. Variations from this protocol may be advisable on the basis of bone quality, fracture stability, and the patient's characteristics.

When the cast is removed, the patient may need to resume crutch use for a while, even if he or she was able to manage without them while in the cast. Stretching, progressive strengthening, endurance, and agility exercises are required for several months if optimal results are to be achieved as rapidly as possible. After cast removal, an elastic stocking may be needed for a month or two to control edema. Elevation of the leg when the patient is not actually walking also helps.

## Operative Treatment

### INITIAL CARE AND TIMING OF SURGERY

Displaced malleolar fractures often involve significant subluxation or dislocation of the tibiotalar joint. To minimize pain, swelling, and additional local trauma, such injuries should be treated with a prompt provisional reduction and immobilization in a safe, effective splint. Evaluation of skin and neurovascular status precedes this, with follow-up reassessment periodically thereafter.

If possible, a formal closed reduction maneuver is carried out in the emergency department with appropriate analgesia. Then a very well padded cast is applied. This cast provides the best possible splint. Extra padding is necessary to accommodate swelling and protect the skin from the cast saw blade. Once hard, the cast can be split and spread or bivalved, if necessary, to accommodate swelling and facilitate removal in the operating room. Radiographs are obtained in the cast to assess reduction, which should be repeated immediately only if there is gross deformity with skin or neurovascular compromise. An *anatomic* reduction obtained without the foot's being placed in an extreme position suggests consideration of nonoperative management unless the fracture is very unstable. Unsuccessful closed reduction in this setting may still be improved with a manipulation under anesthesia, but if an anesthetic is required, we feel that only strong local contraindications would dissuade us from ORIF of an unstable malleolar fracture.

If an abrasion of any significance is present about an injured ankle, ORIF can be done urgently, as with open fractures, or delayed until the skin has healed.[132] A povidone-iodine dressing over such a superficial skin wound may reduce the rate of bacterial colonization. If there is only slight soft tissue injury, indicated by mild initial displacement and little swelling, ORIF can be done essentially electively during the early postinjury period, although it becomes progressively less easy after about 10 days and is often quite difficult after 3 weeks because of early fracture healing and disuse osteoporosis, which is a potentially severe problem in older women.[22, 43]

Because it is associated with a reduced likelihood of anatomic reduction, delay in ORIF of malleolar fractures beyond 2 weeks is associated with poorer results. If an anatomic reduction is achieved, however, the outcome may closely approach that obtainable by early surgery.[75] It is wise to remember that unappreciated swelling may increase the risk of such procedures during the first several days after injury. Therefore, during the early postinjury period, the skin should be reassessed just prior to inducing anesthesia for ORIF of an ankle fracture. If significant soft tissue injury with marked swelling and blisters is evident, ORIF should be delayed until the local tissues have recovered, which may take 7 to 10 days or more of strict elevation. The return of cutaneous wrinkles indicates the resolution of edema. If soft tissue trauma is exceptionally severe, it is often best to treat the ankle with closed reduction and external fixation, deferring open reduction, if it is required, until the risk of wound slough has diminished.

It is important not to accept poor ankle alignment and an inadequate splint because early surgery is planned. The opportunity to operate may be lost for a variety of reasons, and the ankle may suffer additional insult without proper early care.

Konrath and colleagues[132] compared early versus delayed (mean of 14 days) fixation of severe ankle fractures and found that a shorter postoperative hospital stay in the delayed fixation group was the only significant difference.

## CHOICE AND PLANNING OF FIXATION

A satisfactory fixation technique must have a low risk of failure, must resist the forces that are likely to cause redisplacement of the fracture, and must not be likely to increase comminution or cause displacement during its application. Many techniques of malleolar fracture fixation have been advocated.[18] The ones described here are essentially those advocated by AO/ASIF.[103, 187, 234, 287] They have been generally accepted and work well for us.[186] Less rigid techniques have also been advocated, and although they are often successful, especially in more stable injuries, they are not as reliable as those of the AO in maintaining reduction of bimalleolar or trimalleolar and equivalent fractures.[200] Absorbable implants have also been used, but they have not yet won a place in our armamentarium.[30, 31, 39, 78]

Adequate preoperative radiographs are required for planning fixation. Comparison views of the uninjured ankle can be very helpful. An explicit preoperative plan guides positioning and choice of incision and also provides a shared operative strategy that increases the efficiency of the entire surgical team.[169]

## OPERATIVE ADJUNCTS

A plan for intraoperative radiographic control should be made—either fluoroscopic or plain films. The patient is typically positioned on a radiolucent table. A roll is placed under the ipsilateral pelvic area (proximal to the sciatic nerve) to rotate the leg medially and facilitate exposure of the fibula. If fixation of a posterior malleolus is anticipated, this position can be exaggerated even more to allow posterolateral access. Tourniquet use is optional. There is some evidence that its use can increase postoperative pain and swelling and lead to wound complications. Long-acting local anesthetic with epinephrine is a good alternative and assists with postoperative pain control.

## LATERAL MALLEOLUS FRACTURES

A secure anatomic repair of a displaced lateral malleolus fracture is one of the most important steps in operative management of a malleolar fracture because of the role this structure plays in maintaining tibiotalar alignment.

Because of its posterior location, the fibula is easier to approach if a cushion is placed under the supine patient's ipsilateral buttock to rotate the trunk and leg internally. A safety strap about the pelvis allows the table to be tilted further if needed. A pneumatic tourniquet is a conventional adjunct but may wisely be omitted in patients with impaired perfusion or vascular disease.

A longitudinal lateral incision provides adequate access to the distal fibula. Because the primary purpose of the procedure is to reconstruct the alignment and integrity of the ankle joint, not to improve the appearance of the fibular fracture, it is important that the lateral incision also permit exposure of the anterior syndesmosis, in particular the AITFL and the superolateral corner of the anterior ankle joint (Fig. 59–35). Exposure of the AITFL requires incision of the extensor retinaculum—a structure potentially confused with the AITFL. Inspection of the relation-

ship of the talus, tibial plafond, and lateral malleolus reveals the congruity or lack thereof of the articular surfaces. This area is better seen if the distal end of the incision is angled slightly anteriorly and carried sufficiently distally. The distal end of the incision permits an arthrotomy for irrigation and inspection of the ankle joint to identify and remove loose osteochondral fragments and intra-articular clot. The proximal extent of the incision is determined by the requirements for fixation of the fibular fracture.

Flaps should be kept as thick as possible and handled gently. A more extensive fasciotomy may be wise in patients with more soft tissue swelling. If an anteromedial incision is also used, the lateral incision must be more posterior, as it also should for access to the posterolateral tibia through the interval between the peronei and the Achilles tendon or for posterior plate fixation of a supination–external rotation fibular fracture. The sural and superficial peroneal nerves have branches in the region of this lateral incision and should be protected or resected and buried away from the scar to avoid a painful neuroma.

Through this lateral incision, it is possible to repair the lateral ligaments as well as to fix fractures of the lateral malleolus. The torn LCL complex is reapproximated with interrupted, medium-weight sutures. A small, very distal fibular avulsion fracture can be reattached with sutures to bone or soft tissue or with a small fragment or minifrag-

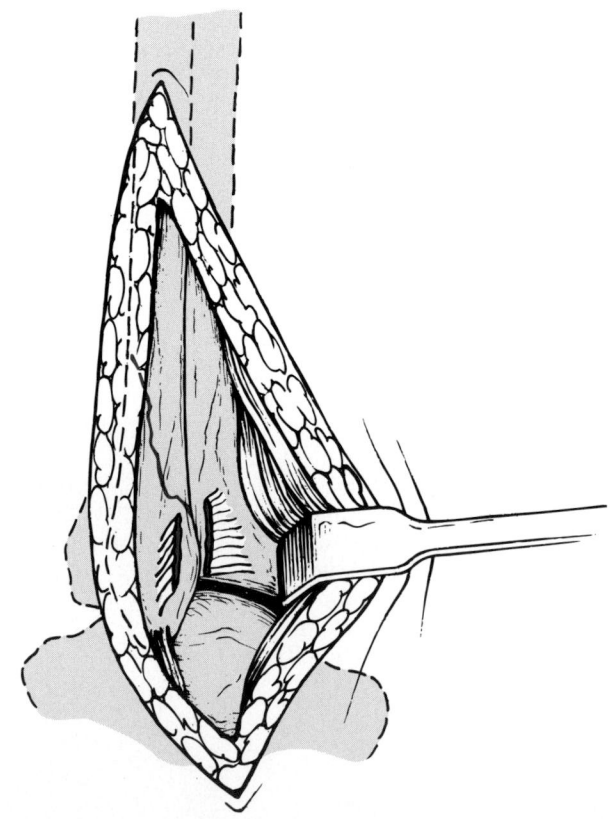

**FIGURE 59–35.** The incision to repair a lateral malleolar fracture should provide access to the anterolateral ankle joint, as well as the anterior inferior tibiofibular ligament. This access is necessary to search for osteochondral injuries and especially to ensure anatomic repair of the mortise.

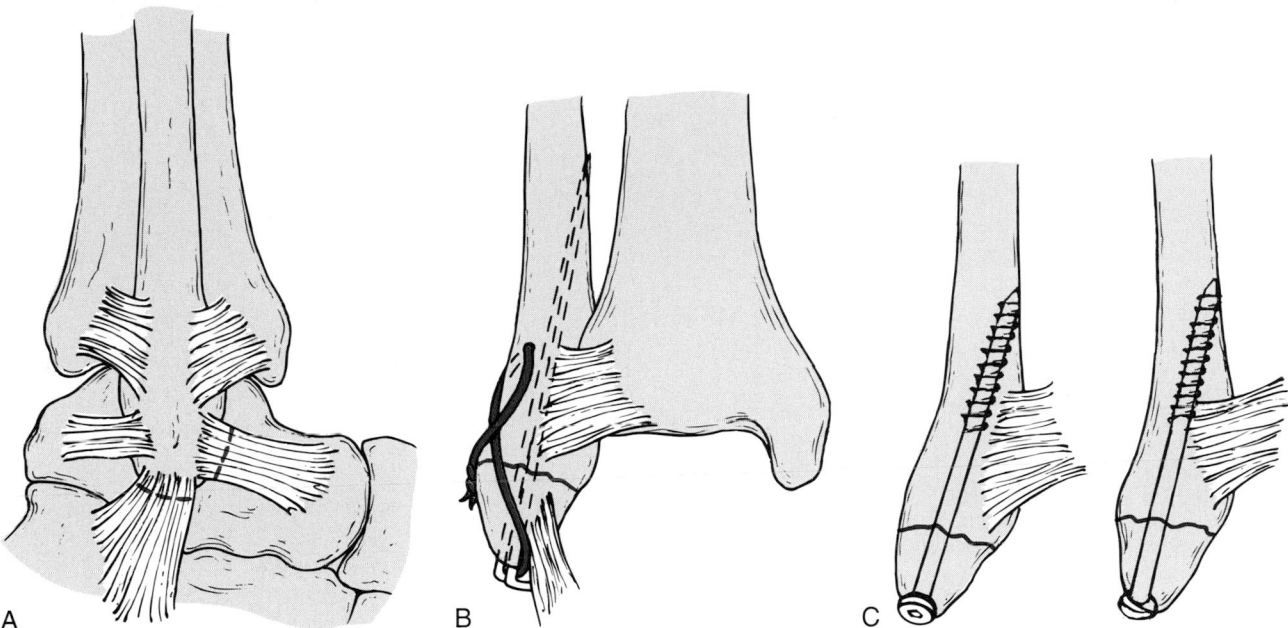

**FIGURE 59–36.** Repair of type A lateral ankle injuries. *A,* Ligament tears are sutured. Low transverse fibular fractures are reduced anatomically and fixed with K-wires and a tension band *(B)* or a small oblique lag screw *(C)* that penetrates and anchors in the medial cortex proximally. *(A,* Redrawn from Müller, M.E.; et al. Manual of Internal Fixation. 2nd ed. New York, Springer-Verlag, 1979. *B,* Redrawn from Heim, U.; Pfeiffer, K.M. Small Fragment Set Manual: Technique Recommended by the ASIF Group, 2nd ed. New York, Springer-Verlag, 1982.)

ment screw and plastic ligament washer, whose small spikes prevent pressure necrosis of the soft tissue it secures to bone.[111, 227] A larger avulsed fragment of the distal lateral malleolus, typical of type A injuries, is best fixed with either a tension band wire or a small oblique screw. Fixation must resist distraction forces produced by inversion of the hindfoot (Fig. 59–36).

Reduction is begun by clearing clot and minimally reflecting the periosteum to see the bone apposition. The distal fragment is grasped with a small forceps, guided into place, and held with a sharp dental probe. For tension band wiring, it is fixed with two 1.25- or 1.6-mm K-wires, which may be oblique or intramedullary. Advancing and then withdrawing them permits their impaction

into the bone after the exposed ends are cut and bent into a **J** shape (Fig. 59–37). The figure-of-eight 1.25-mm tension band wire can be anchored proximally by passage through a transverse drill hole in the fibula or, more easily, around a small cortical screw. If an oblique lag screw is chosen instead, provisional fixation of the fragment with a small K-wire aids in holding position during screw insertion.

Supination–external rotation type B injuries, as discussed previously, generally cause a spiral fracture that exits the anterior surface of the fibula distally at or just above the level of the plafond. The malleolar fragment carries the lateral attachment of the AITFL. This structure can often be a guide to reduction. Comminution produced

**FIGURE 59–37.** *A,* Type A bimalleolar fracture with significant comminution of a small medial malleolar fragment. *B,* K-wires with tension bands provide fixation.

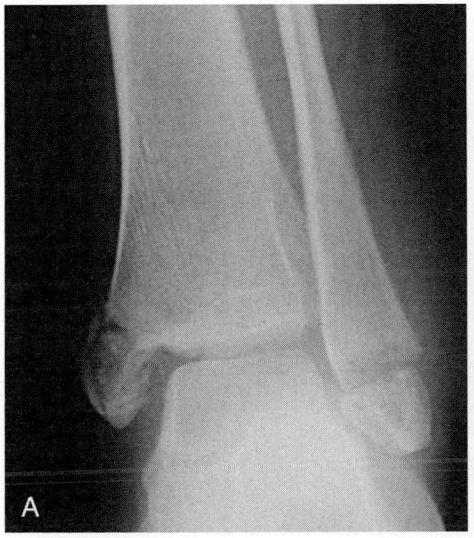
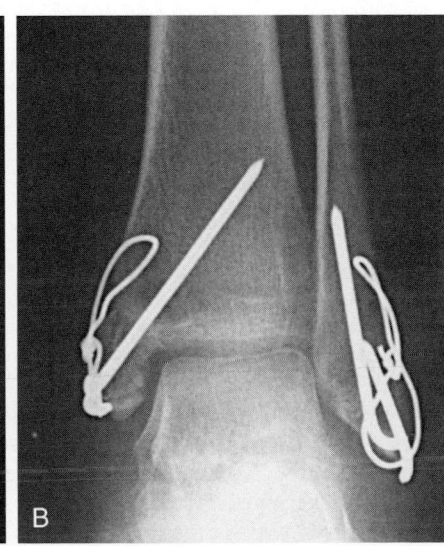

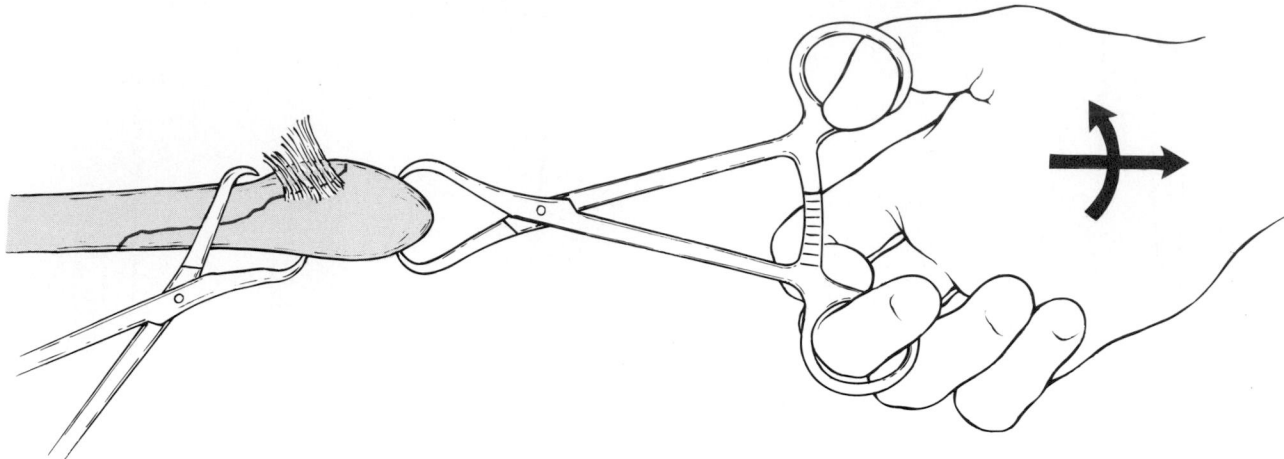

**Figure 59–38.** Reduction of the common supination–external rotation lateral malleolar fracture requires grasping the distal fragment (cautiously if the patient is osteopenic) and bringing it into precise alignment with the proximal fragment, after which a reduction forceps is tightened, perpendicular to the fracture plane.

by its avulsion from either the tibia or the fibula may add another element of complexity.

The incision previously described is used for lateral malleolus ORIF. It should extend sufficiently proximal to provide easy access to the posterior proximal end of the distal fragment. Unless excessively comminuted, this posterior spike can guide restoration of length and rotational alignment. It can often be repositioned first and held in place while the reduction is completed. After exposure of the fracture and the anterior surface of the fibula proximal to it, the joint is explored, aided by an intra-articular angled retractor anteriorly. Then the distal fibula is grasped with a pointed forceps, such as a towel clip, and teased into place with traction and repositioning of both foot and fracture fragment as needed (Fig. 59–38). Be cautious with strong forces if the bone is osteopenic. Simultaneous control of the proximal fibular fragment with a bone clamp may aid reduction.

A small, pointed, or lobster-claw reduction forceps is used to appose the bone edges as proximal and distal pieces are realigned. The reduction forceps should be applied perpendicular to the fracture plane or it may cause redisplacement. It should not interfere with placing an AP lag screw perpendicular to the fracture, and it should not be so close to the end of the proximal piece that it produces comminution. A satisfactory reduction results in good apposition at the fracture line on the anterior and lateral surfaces of the fibula, restores the position of the proximal spike, places the AITFL so that its ends lie anatomically, and restores the relationship of the lateral malleolus, lateral plafond, and lateral edge of the talar dome, as seen in the anterolateral corner of the mortise. If reduction is not readily achieved, the possibility of a medial obstruction—fracture fragments or an intra-articular flexor tendon—must be excluded by exploration of the medial side of the joint.

If a truly anatomic reduction has been achieved, a lag screw is applied perpendicular to the fracture using a 3.5-mm cortical screw with the anterior cortex overdrilled. Two or more such lag screws can be used as the entire fixation if the bone is of excellent quality and a cast will be used for protection. More secure fixation is achieved with a one-third tubular plate contoured to fit the concave, slightly spiral, lateral surface of the fibula. This plate is usually applied with three or four screws proximal to the fracture's distal obliquity and at least two in the distal fragment, placed carefully and checked with radiographs to ensure that they do not enter the joint space (Figs. 59–39 and 59–40).

Alternatively, as proposed by Brunner and Weber,[38] a similar plate can be applied on the posterolateral surface of the fibula, where it overlies the posterior fracture spike of the distal fragment and prevents its gliding proximally.[242] This plate is less prominent laterally and may be better tolerated, although it requires more posterior exposure (Fig. 59–41). Any technique that is used for fixation of the lateral malleolus must resist proximal migration or rotation of the distal fragment. Therefore, most intramedullary techniques are risky, although special devices such as the Inyo nail may be successful.[173, 174]

Pronation-abduction type B injuries cause a transverse and often comminuted fracture at or just above the level of the plafond. Depending on the extent of comminution, reduction of the lateral malleolus may be quite difficult. Preoperative radiographs usually define the pathology and allow a modified operative plan.[148] Lateral plafond impaction may need to be elevated through or around the fibular fracture; a CT scan may be a considerable aid to planning. The medial side of the ankle is a helpful guide to reduction. If its malleolus is intact, the talus can be pushed back medially against it. If there is a transverse fracture that can readily be fixed, it, too, can provide support. With the talus reduced against the medial side of the mortise, the lateral shoulder of the talus provides a template for reduction of the lateral malleolus. Provisional fixation with K-wires to the talus or tibia, or both, permits radiographic confirmation of reduction (Fig. 59–42). This view is compared with a mortise view of the opposite ankle, and if reduction is satisfactory, a plate (either a one-third tubular or, if the fracture is very comminuted and the patient is large, a stouter 3.5-mm dynamic compression

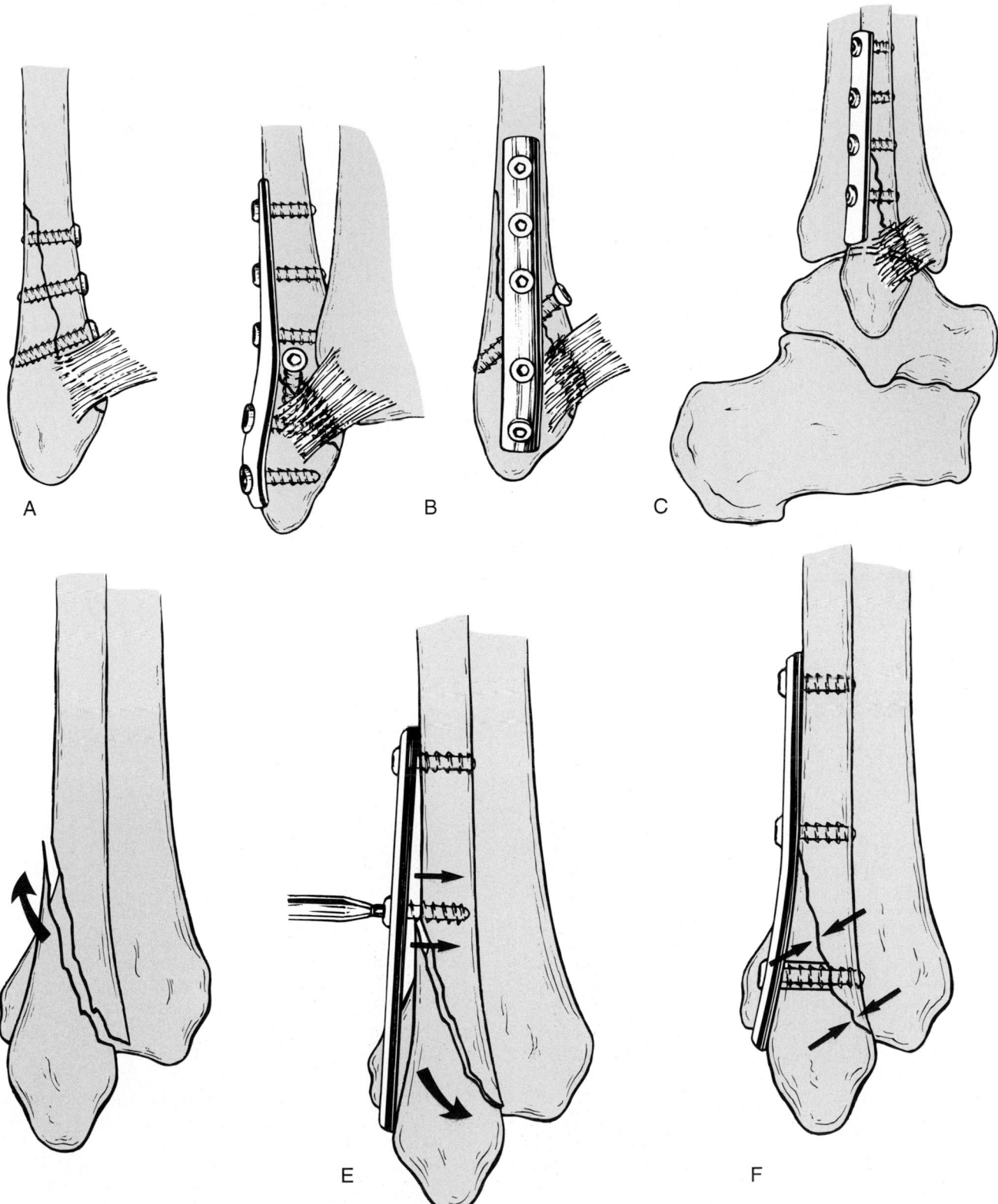

**FIGURE 59–39.** Repair of type B lateral malleolar injuries. *A*, A long spiral fracture can be repaired with two or more lag screws. External protection is required. *B, C,* A single lag screw and a one-third tubular neutralization plate are more secure. *D, E,* An antiglide plate (one-third tubular) can be applied posteriorly, where it resists proximal displacement of the distal fragment. *F,* A lag screw can be used with a posterior plate, either through the plate, as illustrated, or previously placed from anterior to posterior (see Fig. 59–41). The principle of the posterior antiglide plate is illustrated. (*A*, Redrawn from Müller, M.E.; et al. Manual of Internal Fixation, 2nd ed. New York, Springer-Verlag, 1979. *B*, Redrawn from Heim, U.; Pfeiffer, K.M. Small Fragment Set Manual: Technique Recommended by the ASIF Group, 2nd ed. New York, Springer-Verlag, 1982. *D–F*, Modified from Brunner, C.F.; Weber, B.G. Special Techniques in Internal Fixation. New York, Springer-Verlag, 1982.)

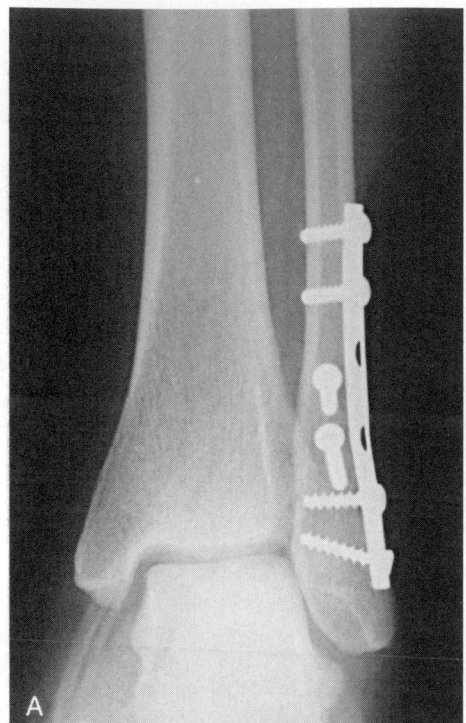
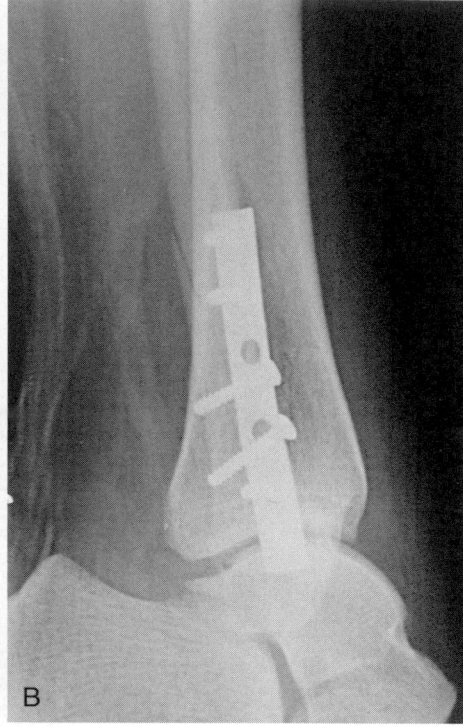

FIGURE 59–40. *A, B,* This type B lateral malleolar fracture was fixed anatomically with two lag screws across the fracture line, barely visible at its most proximal extent on the lateral view. A one-third tubular plate adds support to the fracture, with cortical screws proximally and cancellous fully threaded screws distally. Screws could probably have been placed through the empty holes and into the anterior portion of the proximal fibular fragment.

FIGURE 59–41. This type B fracture was reduced anatomically and fixed with a single anteroposterior (AP) lag screw perpendicular to the fracture plane. An antiglide plate was applied to the posterolateral surface of the malleolus, avoiding prominent lateral hardware. With an undisplaced medial malleolus fracture, the patient is fully weight bearing in a patellar tendon–bearing cast. *A,* AP radiograph. *B,* Lateral radiograph.

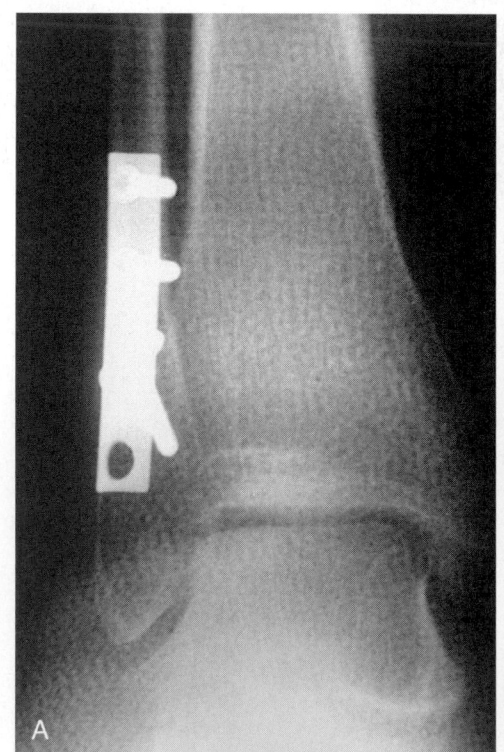
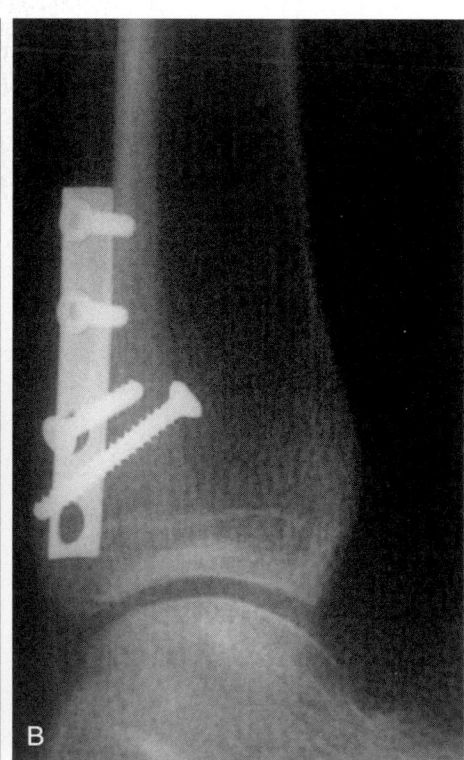

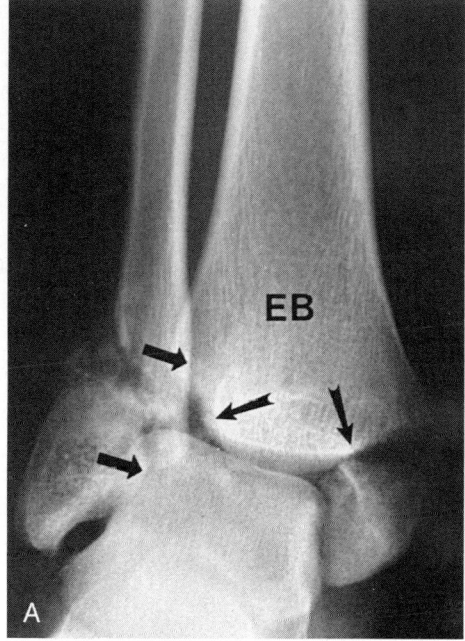

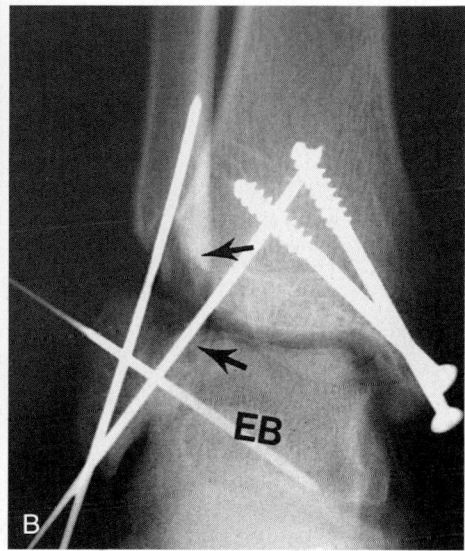

**FIGURE 59–42.** *A,* A pronation-abduction type B fracture with lateral plafond impaction. *Arrows* show marginal lateral impaction and medial malleolar fracture. *B,* The fracture has been realigned by reduction and fixation of the medial malleolus, followed by provisional K-wire fixation of the lateral malleolus. Radiographic confirmation of this reduction precedes definitive internal fixation and bone grafting of the fibula. *Arrows* show marginal lateral impaction. (*A,* From Limbird, R.S.: Aaron, R.K. J Bone Joint Surg Am 69:881, 1987.)

plate) is applied as a buttress. Bone graft may aid healing of a comminuted fibular fracture. Indirect reduction techniques can help with these challenging fracture reductions (see Fig. 59–46).[167, 168]

The AITFL disruption should be repaired, at least to confirm appropriate reduction of the syndesmosis. Avulsion of the ligament with or without a fragment of bone from the Wagstaffe (Le Fort) or the Chaput tubercles can often be repaired with a small screw or ligament washer. A mechanically insecure horizontal mattress suture apposes the ends of a rupture in substance and may improve the ultimate quality of the healed ligament (Fig. 59–43).

Repair of the PITFL is not as easy but has been recommended as justification for reduction and fixation of

all posterolateral tibial lip (Volkmann's) fragments, even those that are extra-articular, because of the presumed benefit of immediate syndesmosis stabilization (Fig. 59–44).[102] Possibly this may eliminate the need for syndesmosis transfixation. Strong evidence that refixation of the PITFL to the distal tibia makes a difference in outcome has not yet been provided.[100] The value of fixation of a small Volkmann fragment thus remains controversial.

After fixation of the lateral malleolus, it is important to assess stability of the syndesmosis by externally rotating the foot and pulling the repaired fibula laterally with an encircling clamp. The anterolateral corner of the malleolus is observed, and demonstrable laxity of more than 3 or 4 mm with such maneuvers should be

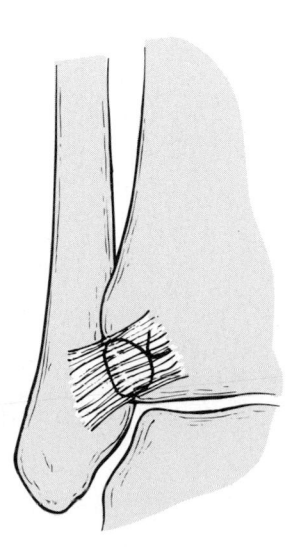

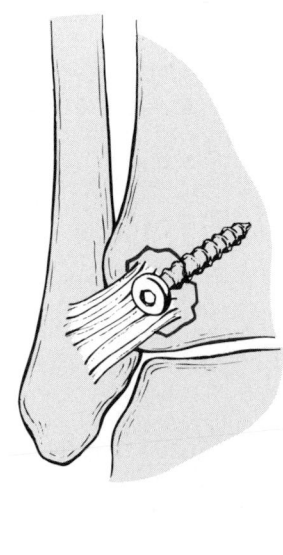

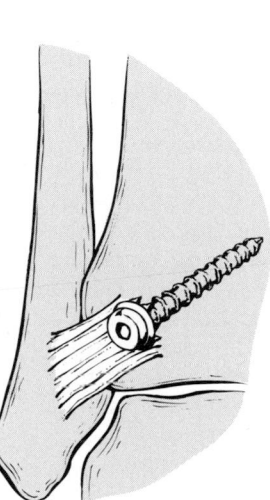

**FIGURE 59–43.** The anterior inferior tibiofibular ligament ends should appose perfectly if reduction is precise. The ligament can be repaired with a horizontal mattress suture, with a screw through an avulsed bone fragment, or with a small, spiked, plastic ligament washer.

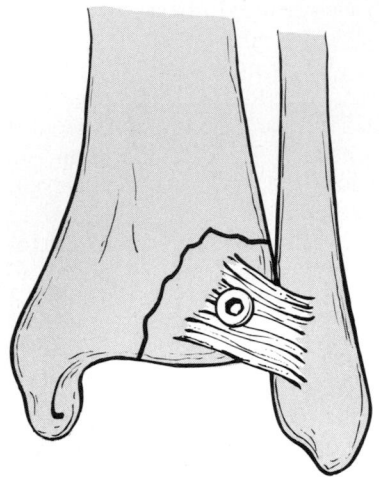

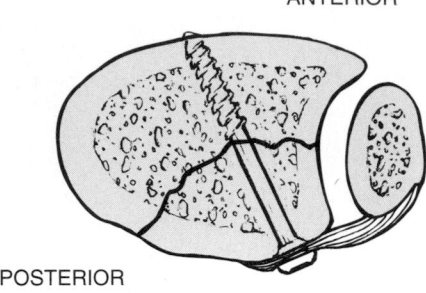

ANTERIOR

POSTERIOR

**FIGURE 59–44.** The posterior inferior tibiofibular ligament can be repaired by reduction and fixation of a posterolateral avulsion fracture (Volkmann's fragment) of the distal tibia.

considered an indication for use of a syndesmosis transfixation screw.[84, 96, 122, 124, 191, 267]

In higher lateral malleolus fractures (those classified as type C injuries), the fracture is often relatively transverse. Fixation with an interfragmentary lag screw may be impossible, but comminution is not as frequent a problem as it is in typical pronation-abduction injuries (Fig. 59–45). If comminution and shortening of the fibula are significant, indirect reduction using a small distractor or a plate with a tension device or bone spreader to regain length may be very helpful (Fig. 59–46).[168] Provisional fixation and confirmation of reduction by radiographs and direct visualization of the ankle joint are essential. The surgeon should resist the temptation to reduce the high lateral malleolus fracture without exposing the joint and should not be misled by an apparent reduction of a comminuted fracture site. Ankle joint restoration, not fibular fracture reduction, is the goal (Figs. 59–47 and 59–48). Use of a syndesmosis transfixation screw without precise fibular fracture reduction is unlikely to provide an anatomic reduction because of difficulty in assessing and obtaining length and rotational alignment. Therefore, this approach should also be avoided.

Only very proximal fibular fractures (upper third) with mortise disruption are reasonably treated without direct reduction and fixation, but mortise reconstruction and transfixation must still be done with great care.

## SYNDESMOSIS TRANSFIXATION

Syndesmosis stability is checked by laterally displacing the distal fibula from the tibia while observing the relationship of the two bones. If more than 3 to 4 mm of lateral shift of the talus occurs, instability is present. This check has been called the *Cotton test* (Fig. 59–49).[267] Gross displacement indicates the need for surgical stabilization of the syndesmosis. As previously discussed, laboratory studies point to a disruption of the interosseous membrane 3.5 to 4.0 cm above the mortise as leading to syndesmotic instability if the MCL is disrupted.[28, 41, 259]

Various beliefs exist regarding indications and technique for stabilizing a disrupted syndesmosis. Few hard data support them, so skepticism is warranted. As with

other controversial topics, it may be that controversy flourishes because there is little difference in outcome. The problem is that sometimes, after seemingly satisfactory reduction of the medial and lateral malleoli, the space between the tibia and the fibula widens and the talus fits

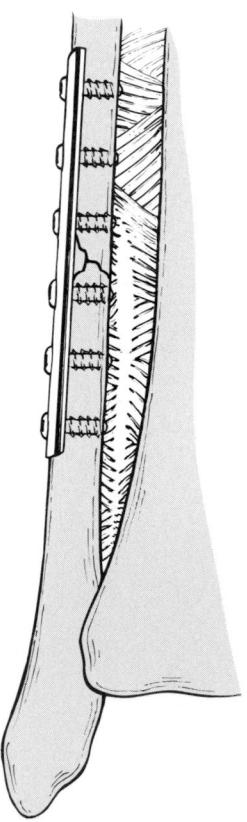

**FIGURE 59–45.** Repair of type C lateral malleolar fractures requires precise anatomic reduction of the articular fragment and usually plate-and-screw fixation of the fracture. Occasionally, the fracture permits use of a lag screw as well, but more often it is transverse or comminuted. A one-third tubular, small fragment plate or a 3.5-mm dynamic compression plate may be used, with three or four screws above and below the fracture. (Redrawn from Heim, U.; Pfeiffer, K.M. Small Fragment Set Manual: Technique Recommended by the ASIF Group, 2nd ed. New York, Springer-Verlag, 1982.)

loosely in the mortise. Pain, instability, and post-traumatic arthrosis may follow. It is clear that the fibula bears some weight and that in some individuals, at least, it moves slightly relative to the tibia with normal gait.[112, 191, 267] The strength of the forces that displace the fibula laterally is not known. Significantly controversial issues include (1) when syndesmosis fixation is necessary (e.g., internal fixation between the tibia and the fibula that prevents diastasis), (2) how such fixation should be carried out, (3) what activities should be permitted when the distal tibia and fibula are fixed together, and (4) how long such fixation should be retained.

Obvious distal tibiofibular diastasis on initial or subsequent radiographs or gross mechanical instability of the syndesmosis signals the possible need for syndesmosis transfixation. The amount of fibular motion that indicates critical instability is not certain.[111, 122, 124, 191] Slight laxity

(up to 2 to 3 mm) of a well-reduced fibula, especially if there is a good end-point, rarely indicates a significant risk of late diastasis. Adjunctive syndesmosis stabilization through repair of avulsed inferior tibiofibular ligaments may improve such a situation. There is some evidence that stability increases over time.[200] The use of a long leg, non–weight-bearing cast for a few weeks may also prevent loss of alignment in questionable cases. It is vital to remember that if the fibula is not first reduced satisfactorily, transfixation of the syndesmosis is unlikely to yield an acceptable result.

## TECHNIQUES

Inman,[112] who agreed with Grath,[91] cited Grath's study as evidence that only slight lateral motion (0 to 2 mm) of the lateral malleolus occurred with full ankle dorsiflex-

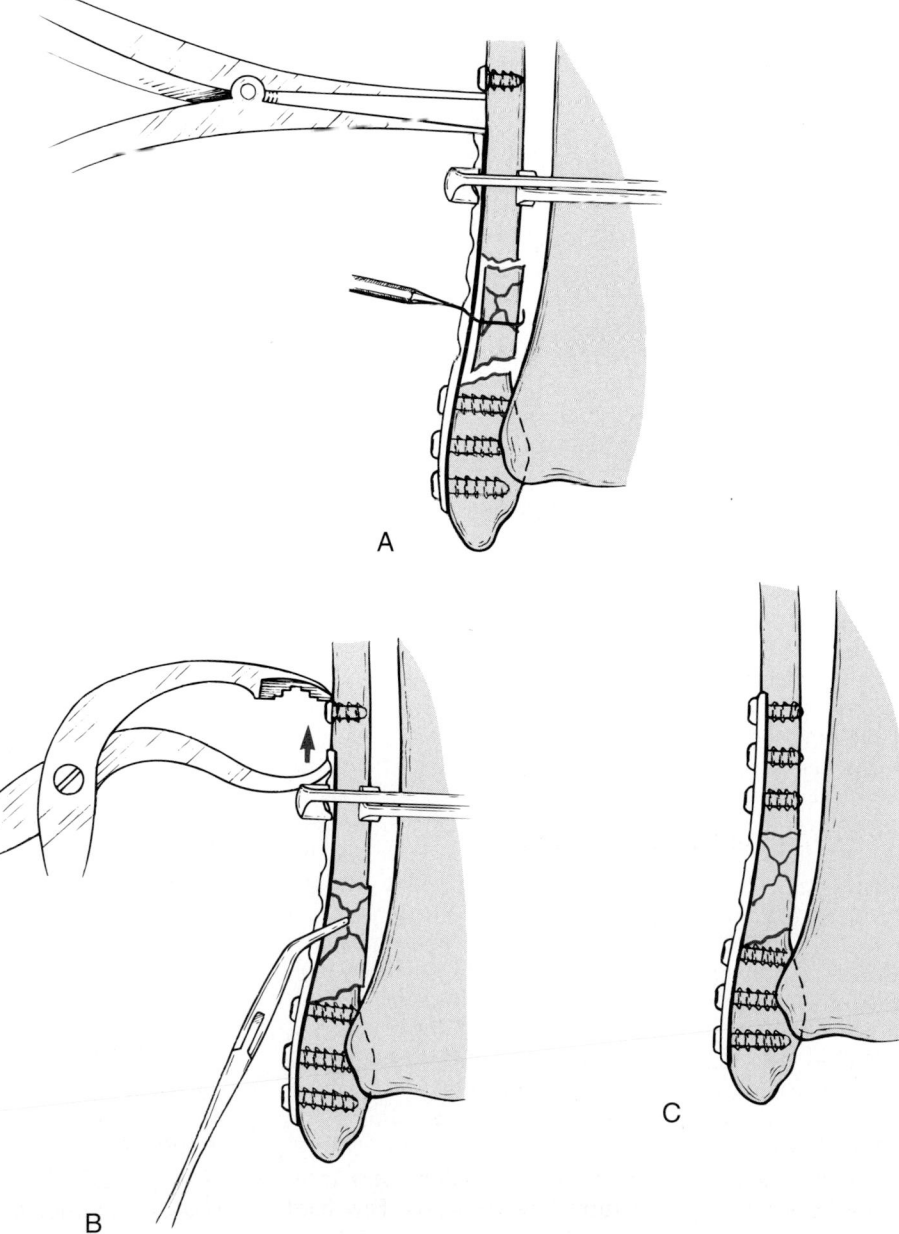

**FIGURE 59–46.** When a type C fibular fracture is comminuted, a plate can be used for indirect reduction while leaving soft tissue attachments on comminuted fragments. A, The plate is contoured and attached distally and controlled proximally with a clamp, and a bone spreader is used against a more proximal, temporary screw to push the distal fragment into a reduced position. Comminuted fragments may be teased gently into place. B, If fracture configuration permits, compression across it may be obtained with a small Verbrugge clamp hooked over the proximal screw. Lateral malleolar length *must* be maintained. C, The plate is then attached proximally. It is not necessary to place screws into small comminuted fragments. (A–C, Redrawn from Mast, J.; et al. Planning and Reduction Techniques in Fracture Surgery. New York, Springer-Verlag, 1989, Fig. 3–18.)

A

B

C

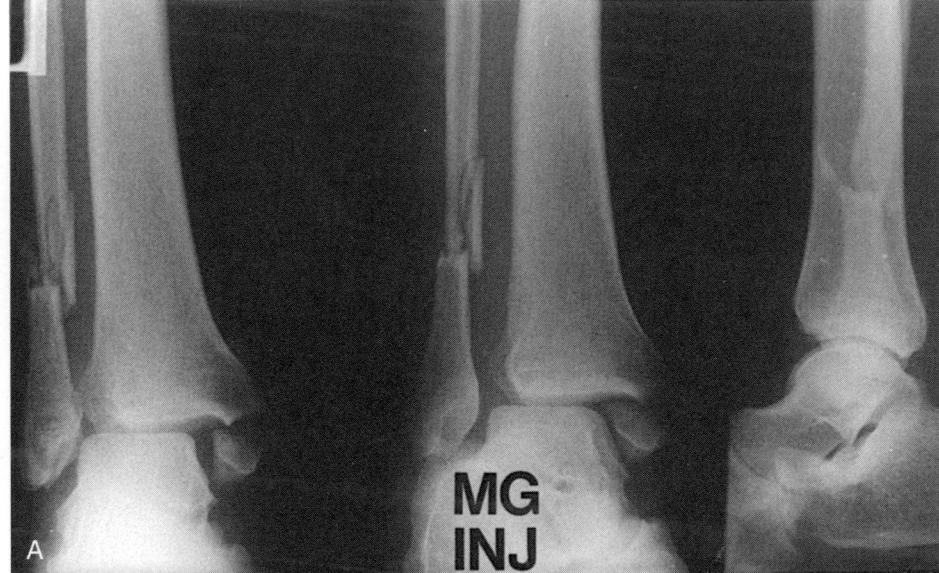

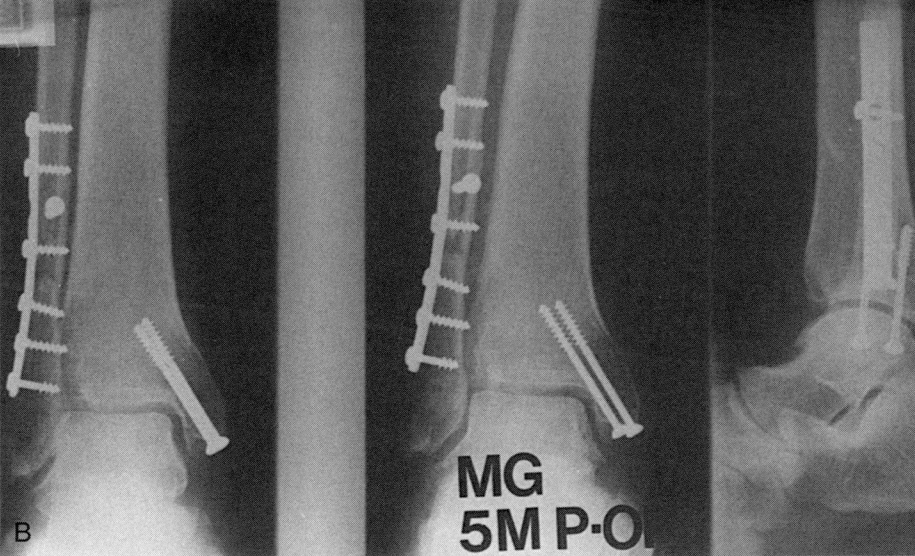

**FIGURE 59–47.** *A,* Type C bimalleolar fracture. *B,* Typical fixation with a one-third tubular plate and lag screw for a comminuted fragment and two 4.0-mm cancellous lag screws for the medial malleolus.

ion.[91, 112] Olerud[198] demonstrated loss of 0.1° of dorsiflexion for every degree of plantar flexion the ankle was in at the time the syndesmosis was fixed. For this reason, it seems wise to fix the syndesmosis with the talus held fully dorsiflexed. Fixation is usually obtained by placing one or two screws from posterolaterally in the fibula to anteromedially in the tibia about 1.5 to 3.0 cm above the plafond (Fig. 59–50). Direct observation of the ankle joint provides assurance that the screw is at the desired distance from it. It is essential that the tibiofibular relationship be anatomic when such screws are inserted. Provisional K-wire fixation or an appropriate clamp may help with this (Fig. 59–51).

The AO group advocated use of a fully threaded screw, a "position screw," with threads tapped in a pilot hole in both the fibula and the tibia. This procedure allows essentially no motion between the two bones unless the screw loosens, as it often does. It avoids the risk of overtightening inherent with a lag screw but permits no adjustment of the relationship between the fibula and the

tibia from that existing when the screw is placed between the bones. The optimal type of screw is also debated and is as yet unproved. Generally, a 4.5- or 3.5-mm cortical screw is chosen. Some advocate its insertion only part way through the tibia, so that the screw soon loosens. There is a small incidence of screw fracture, and removal of a retained fragment in the tibia is traumatic. Use of a stronger screw, limited weight bearing, early screw removal, provision for some motion around the screw, and use of other devices are various ways to avoid screw failure.[68, 108, 112, 122, 124, 191]

Aware of the risks of overtightening a lag screw, one might use the original AO 4.5-mm malleolar screw for syndesmosis fixation (Fig. 59–52). With the fibula reduced, a 3.2-mm drill is used to prepare a hole through the fibula and tibia. The screw length is chosen to penetrate deeply into the tibial metaphysis, approximately 3 cm above the plafond. The fibula and tibia are held reduced with the ankle fully dorsiflexed. Reduction is ascertained

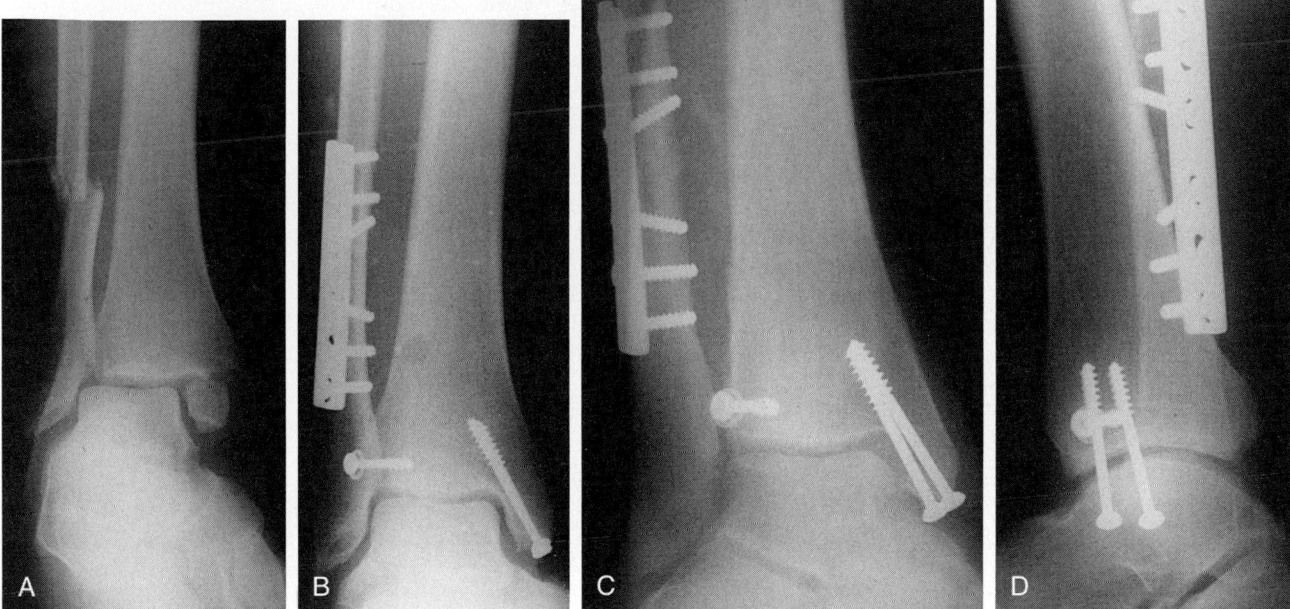

**FIGURE 59–48.** *A,* Type C, atypically high pronation-abduction fracture, indicated by a transverse, laterally comminuted fracture. Injury was caused by a heavy blow to the lateral leg, just above the ankle. *B,* Intraoperative mortise radiograph shows 3.5-mm dynamic compression plate fixation, additional repair of the syndesmosis with a screw and ligament washer to reattach the anterior inferior tibiofibular ligament to the tubercle of Chaput, and two 4.0-mm cancellous lag screws for the medial malleolus. *C, D,* Ten weeks later, both fractures had healed. Note heterotopic ossification of the torn lower interosseous membrane.

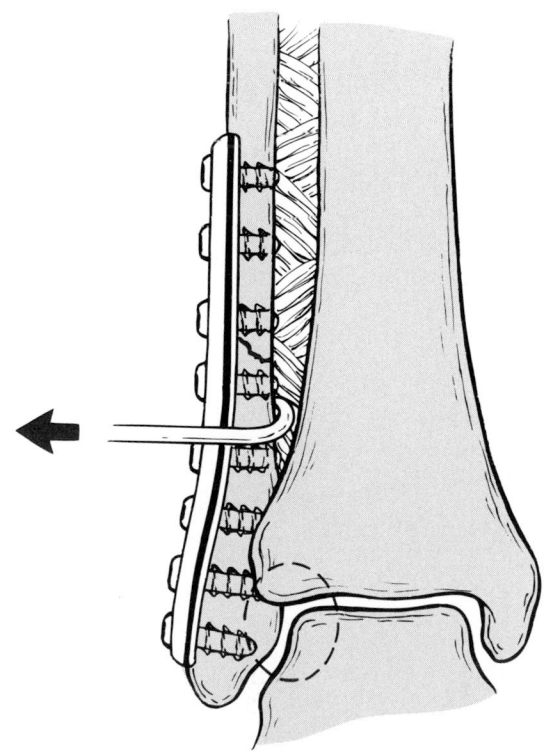

**FIGURE 59–49.** After repair of the fibula fracture, syndesmosis stability is confirmed by attempting to displace the malleolus laterally while observing the anterolateral corner of the joint for excessive movement of the fibula and talus. (Redrawn from Müller, M.E.; et al. Manual of Internal Fixation, 2nd ed. New York, Springer-Verlag, 1979.)

by inspection of the superolateral corner of the mortise, which is observed as the screw is inserted. The screw is tightened only enough to prevent lateral displacement of the fibula without compression of the mortise, which can be observed through the arthrotomy. The screw head stabilizes the fibula, preventing lateral displacement. Its nonthreaded shaft is slightly loose within the fibula, permitting a small amount of fibular motion around the screw, which is anchored securely in the tibia.

The purpose of transfixing the syndesmosis with a screw is to maintain the distal tibiofibular relationship until the syndesmotic ligaments have healed enough to do so on their own. How long it takes for sufficient ligament healing is not certain, but inference from clinical and experimental studies of the healing of other ligaments suggests that at 6 weeks little strength has returned. Therefore, the frequent recommendation of only 6 weeks of transfixation seems risky (Fig. 59–53). A related issue is the weight-bearing regimen prescribed during and after syndesmosis screw fixation, ranging from no weight bearing to full weight bearing.

In attempting to choose the best approach, the surgeon finds an opinionated literature with few supporting data. One author used 4.5- or 3.5-mm cortical position screws and delayed weight bearing for the first 6 weeks, without routinely removing the screws. This approach has an approximately 10% incidence of screw breakage. Leaving a few screw threads through the medial cortex can assist later retrieval if breakage occurs. Another author generally used a 4.5-mm malleolar screw, encouraged full weight bearing in a short leg cast if the fibula was fixed securely, and left the screw in place for a minimum of 3 months.

## POSTERIOR TIBIAL LIP FRACTURE REDUCTION AND FIXATION

A posterior lip fracture may be associated with essentially any mechanism of malleolar fracture and may be caused by the interplay between tensile forces applied through the PITFL and compressive weight-bearing forces applied by the talar dome (Fig. 59–54). The posteromedial lip of the mortise may also be fractured by the supination-adduction mechanism.[96] Posterior lip fragments are often difficult to assess in fracture dislocations until a provisional reduction has been achieved. They are best demonstrated by a transverse CT scan (Fig. 59–55). On the AP or mortise radiograph, the posterior lip fragment can often be observed as a double density superimposed on the tibial metaphysis. These views help in assessing the proximal extent and width of the fragment and in determining whether it is posteromedial or posterolateral. Comminution and obliquity of the posterior lip fragment may not be easily appreciated on the lateral ankle radiograph. Because of obliquity, the apparent size of the fragment may differ from reality. A transverse CT scan provides an explicit

image of the size, location, comminution, and displacement of posterior lip fractures. The ankle should be inspected carefully for posterior subluxation of the talus relative to the tibia; this subluxation is more common with larger posterior lip fragments.

Occasionally, loss of the posterior lip in combination with fibula fracture produces such instability that the talus redislocates posteriorly and cannot be held reduced in a cast (Fig. 59–56). Dorsiflexion tends to worsen this situation by increasing the tension on posterior myotendinous units. Small posterior lip fragments may be extra-articular avulsions. Larger ones, however, involve the joint. Most authors agree that if more than 25% to 35% of the joint surface is involved, the fragment should be reduced and fixed to stabilize the ankle and decrease the risk of post-traumatic arthrosis caused by irregularity of the joint surface.[96, 155, 172, 292, 293] Although closed reduction of a displaced posterior lip fragment is rarely successful, such fragments are usually connected to the distal fibular fragment by the PITFL. Therefore, precise open reduction of the lateral malleolus often results in a close, if not anatomic, realignment of the posterior tibial

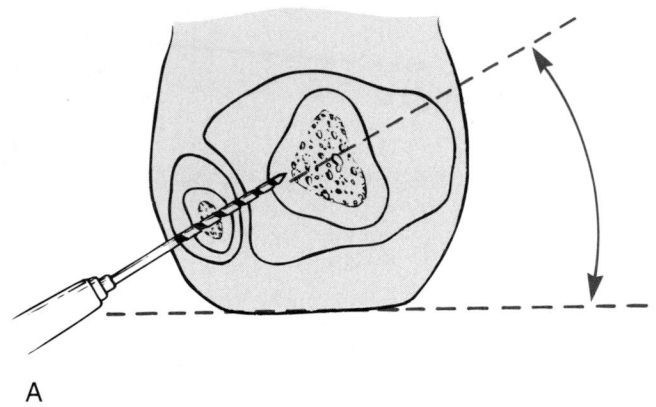

A

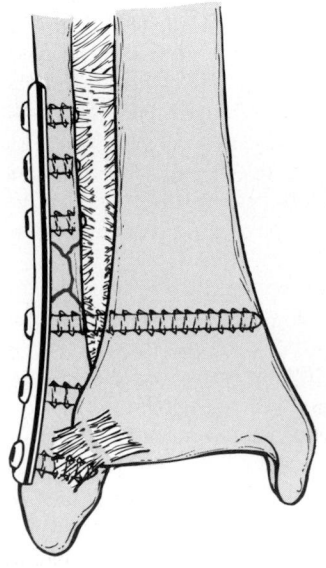

B

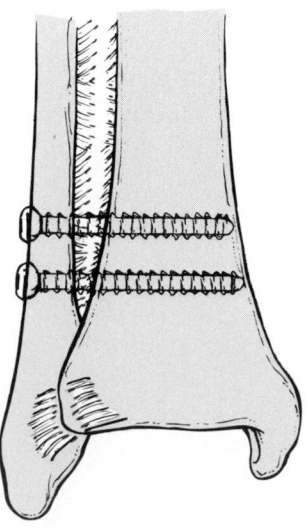

C

**FIGURE 59–50.** *A,* A syndesmosis transfixation screw must be inserted with care from posterolaterally in the fibula to anteromedially in the tibia. The appropriate angle is approximately 30 degrees from the coronal plane. *B,* The fibula must be held reduced during screw placement, and the ankle should be fully dorsiflexed. In this example, the screw is inserted through the fibular plate. *C,* Two screws are used for improved control when a proximal fibular fracture is not internally fixed. (*A–C,* Redrawn from Heim, U.; Pfeiffer, K.M. Small Fragment Set Manual: Technique Recommended by the ASIF Group, 2nd ed. New York, Springer-Verlag, 1982.)

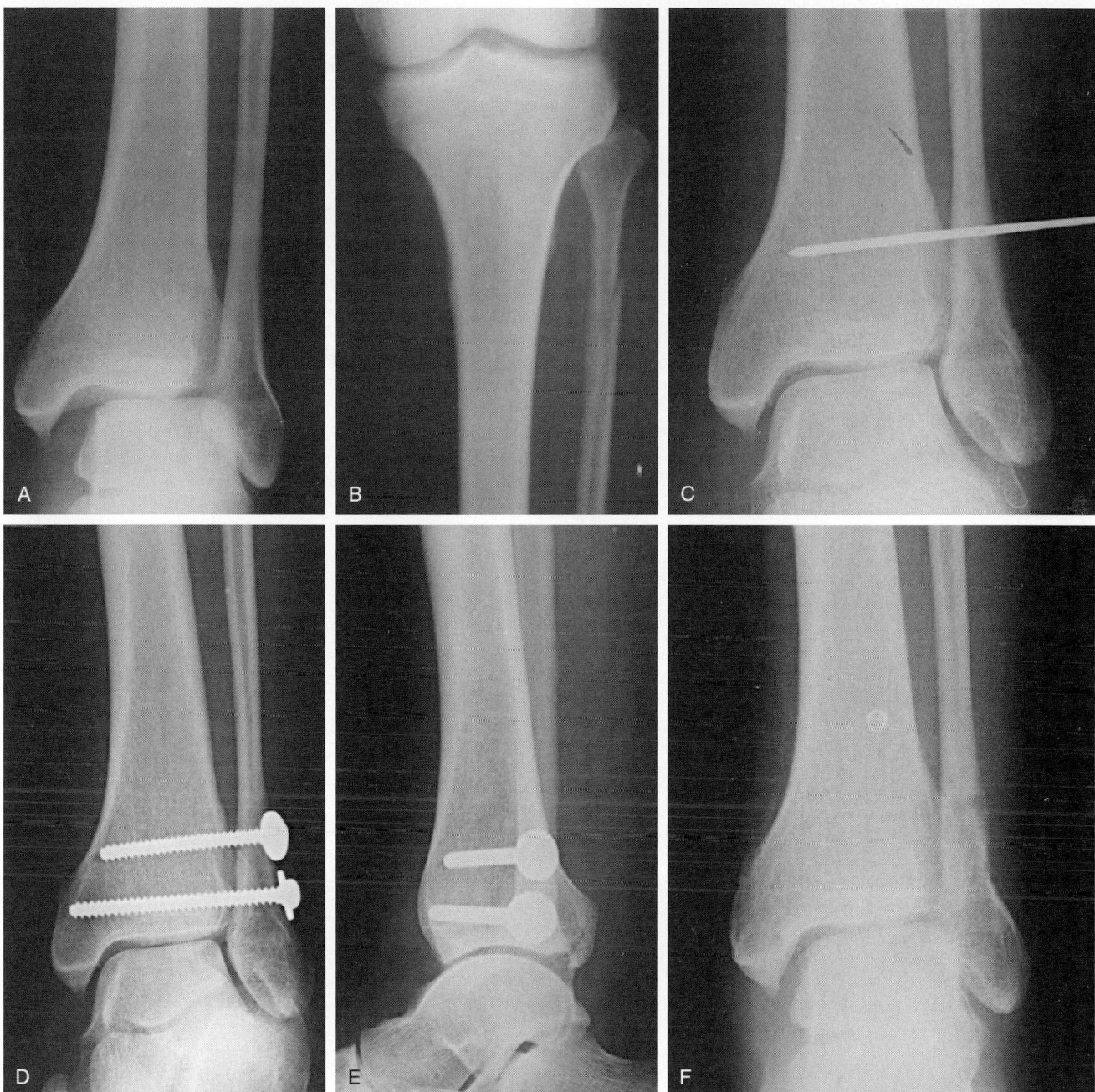

**Figure 59–51.** Maisonneuve fracture. *A,* Ankle radiograph shows mortise widening and lateral displacement of the talus. *B,* A spiral fracture of the proximal fibula is present. *C,* Intraoperative radiograph confirms satisfactory reduction of a provisionally fixed syndesmosis. *D, E,* Definitive fixation with two 4.5-mm cortical position screws threaded into both the fibula and the tibia. *F,* One year after injury, fixation has been removed and the ankle mortise remains congruent.

lip fragment. Some suggest that this is all that is necessary unless the weight-bearing surface of the plafond is distorted or posterior subluxation of the talus persists.[101] Others advise routine fixation of all posterior lip fragments.[102] The optimal approach remains controversial.

Indications and techniques for reduction and fixation of posterior lip fragments thus depend significantly on the judgment of the surgeon. Posterior talar subluxation or dislocation, plafond articular incongruity, and possibly stabilization of the syndesmosis are the usual reasons for ORIF of a posterior lip fragment.

The surgical approach should be guided by the location of the fragment, by the incisions required for treatment of associated components of the ankle injury, and by the preoperative plan for fixation.[103] Generally, some direct access to the posterior fragment is necessary, although often the articular surface reduction is not fully visualized. When the joint surface is not seen and its reduction is judged by the extra-articular portion of the fracture line, it is wise to obtain an intraoperative lateral radiograph after provisional K-wire or clamp fixation of the fragment before definitive screws are inserted.

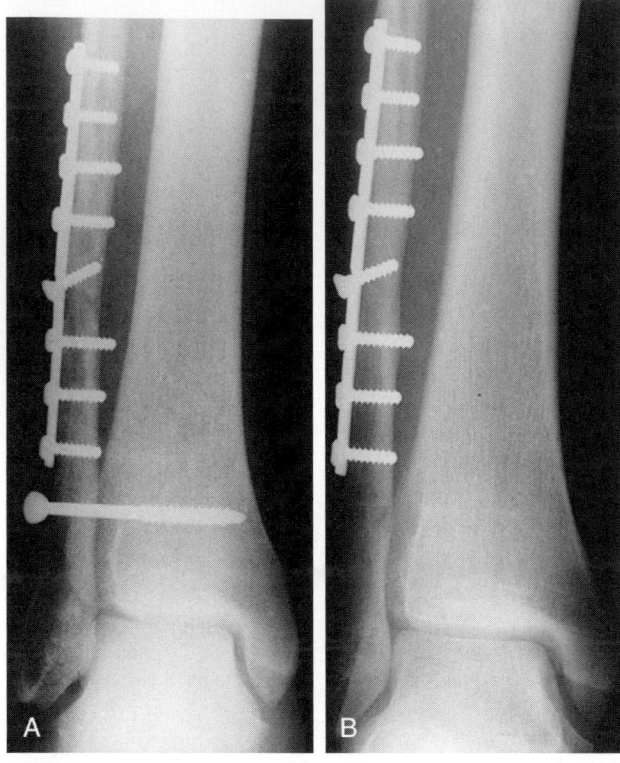

**Figure 59–52.** The syndesmosis was unstable after reduction and fixation of this type C supra-articular lateral malleolus fracture. *A,* The syndesmosis was stabilized with a 4.5-mm malleolar screw inserted with the syndesmosis held reduced and the ankle fully dorsiflexed. The screw was tightened just enough to retain the position of the fibula in the incisural notch, with direct inspection of the ankle to ensure that it was not compressed. *B,* The patient was allowed to bear weight with the screw in place; it was removed at 3 months. A year after injury, the patient had a stable syndesmosis and normal, pain-free ankle function.

Revision of fixation may not be possible after lag screws have been placed.

Posterior lip fragments can best be reattached with one or two lag screws, occasionally supplemented with K-wires, washers, or, rarely, a small buttress plate. It is important to avoid penetrating the ankle joint with such implants, but they must be close to it to obtain good fixation, as the distal base of the wedge-shaped fragment is thickest. The most secure fixation is provided by interfragmentary fixation with lag screws, which must glide through the fragment adjacent to their head and be threaded only into the opposite fragment. Such screws can be placed from posterior to anterior if the fragment is exposed using a posterolateral incision. Otherwise, they must be inserted from anterior to posterior using the anteromedial incision or a small anterolateral stab incision. Screws placed from posteriorly can be either 4.0- or, rarely, 6.5-mm cancellous lag screws or fully threaded screws inserted through a predrilled sliding hole in the posterior fragment. Lag screws inserted from anteriorly pose the problem of gaining maximal purchase in the posterior fragment without having threads on both sides of the fracture line. It is rare, and difficult to ensure, that a partially threaded lag screw is appropriate for this. Sometimes cutting off a portion of the screw's tip permits these screws to be used this way.

A better technique is to overdrill a gliding hole and place the appropriate insert drill sleeve in the anterior metaphyseal fragment before reduction. Then the posterior lip fragment is reduced and provisionally fixed, its alignment is confirmed by a lateral radiograph, and the threaded hole is drilled through the sleeve and tapped if necessary. Finally, the fragments are lagged together with a fully threaded 3.5- or 4.5-mm cortical screw of appropriate

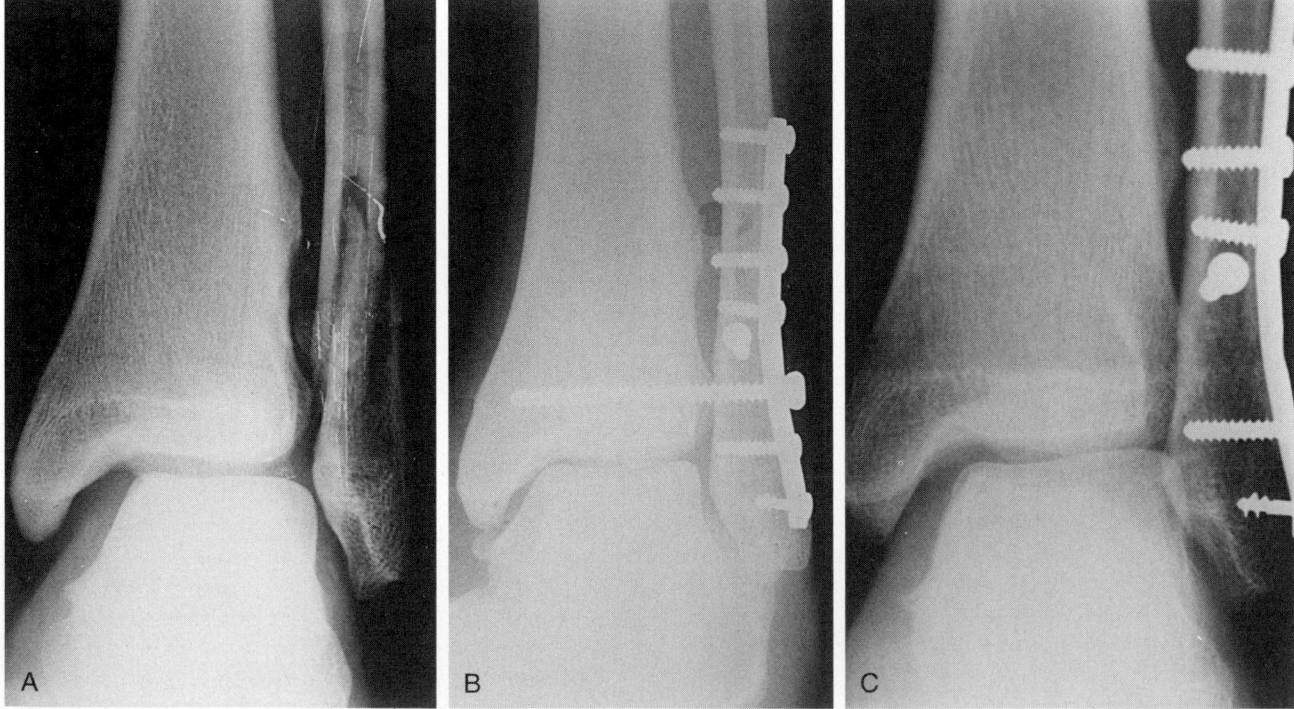

**Figure 59–53.** *A,* The danger of too early removal (at 6 weeks) of a syndesmosis screw is demonstrated by this type B malleolar fracture with a deltoid ligament rupture. *B,* Postoperative view demonstrates excellent reduction. *C,* Eight weeks after screw removal, medial joint space widening was noted, and a syndesmotic reconstruction was required.

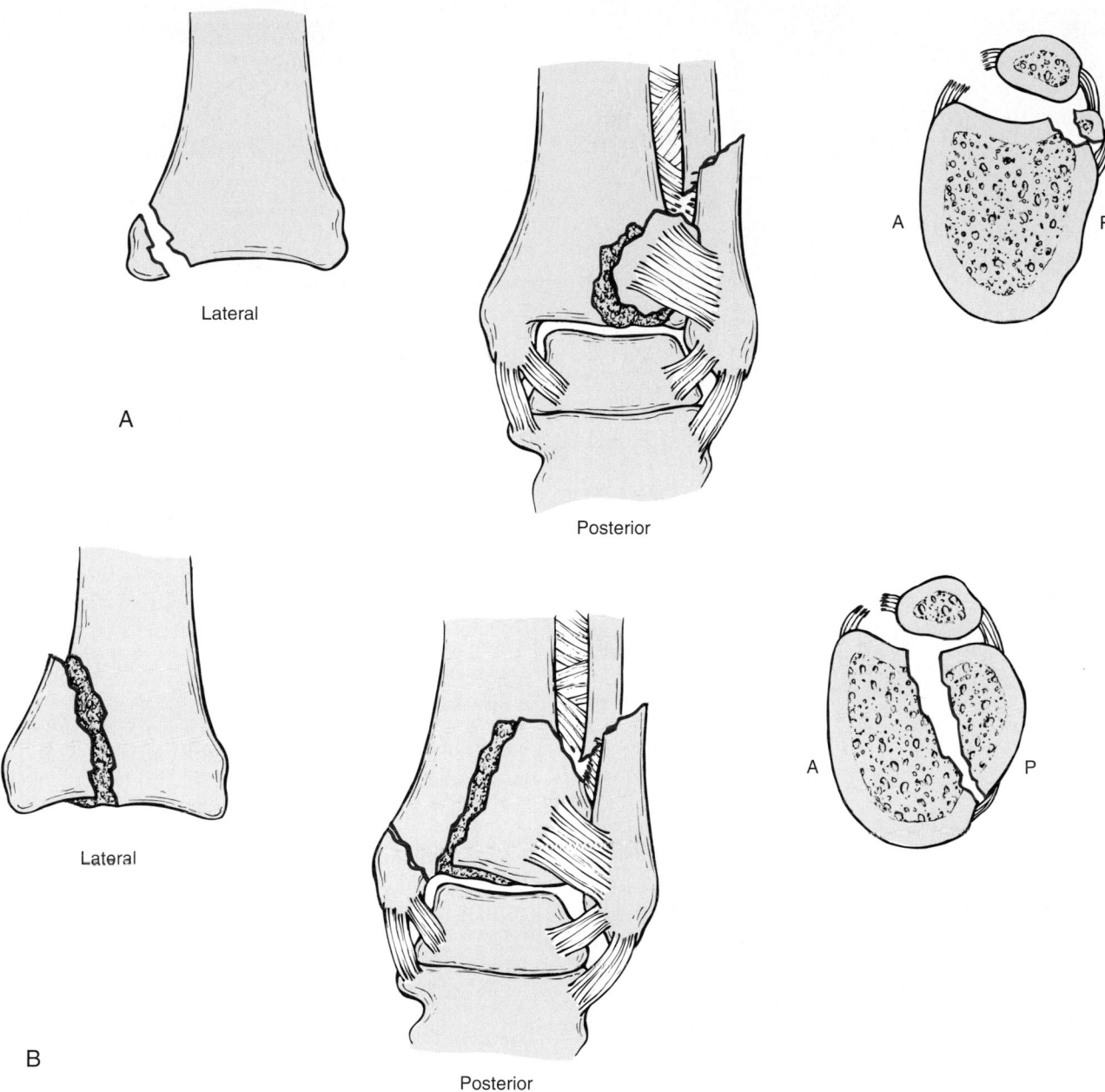

**FIGURE 59–54.** Posterior malleolar fractures may be small (*A*), often extra-articular, or there may be large articular fragments that require reduction to prevent posterior dislocation of the talus (*B*). Careful inspection of anteroposterior and mortise radiographs often reveals whether the fragment is more medial or lateral in location. (*A, B,* Redrawn from Heim, U.; Pfeiffer, K.M. Small Fragment Set Manual: Technique Recommended by the ASIF Group, 2nd ed. New York, Springer-Verlag, 1982.)

length. In general, AP screws are better suited for larger posterior fragments. The choice of whether to use a medial or a lateral insertion site can be made according to the obliquity of the fragment and the need for other incisions. Unless the piece is small, a second screw or at least a heavy K-wire may be advisable to prevent rotation around a single implant. Small posterior fragments are best fixed with screws inserted from posterior to anterior, with care taken to avoid the joint surface, which is convex proximally.

Reduction of posterior lip fragments can be done indirectly through either posteromedial or posterolateral incisions. The choice is often best made by the location of the fragment on the AP radiograph. Posteromedial exposure is by retraction of the flexor tendons and neurovascular bundle from the posteromedial tibial cortex (Fig. 59–57). As illustrated in Figure 59–57, it may be possible to insert a posteroanterior screw in such a fragment through a plane between the deep flexors and the Achilles tendon.

Posterolateral exposure of a posterior lip fragment is through the interval between the peroneal tendons and the Achilles tendon (Fig. 59–58). Attention must be paid to protect the sural nerve. This approach is greatly facilitated by having the patient lie prone or on the unaffected side. Unfortunately, both these positions hamper medial exposure and interfere with reduction and fixation of the medial malleolus. With the prone patient, internal rotation of the leg, aided by a cushion anterior to the opposite

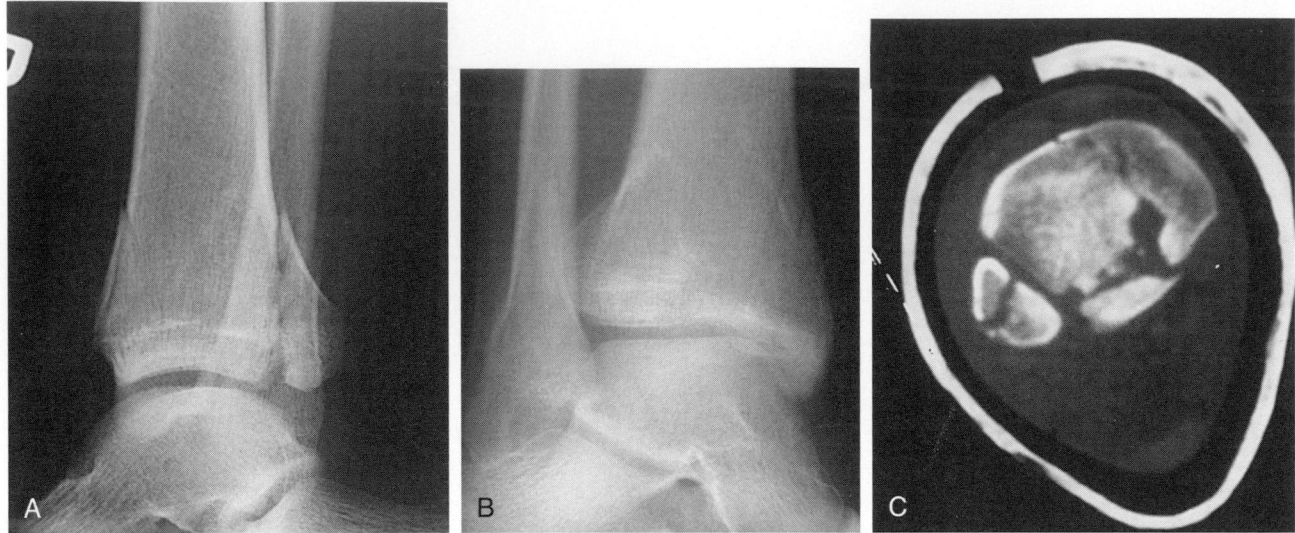

**FIGURE 59–55.** Lateral (*A*) and oblique (*B*) radiographs demonstrate a small, displaced posterior lip fracture. *C*, The computed tomographic scan shows impaction, interposed fragments, and significant displacement just above the articular surface.

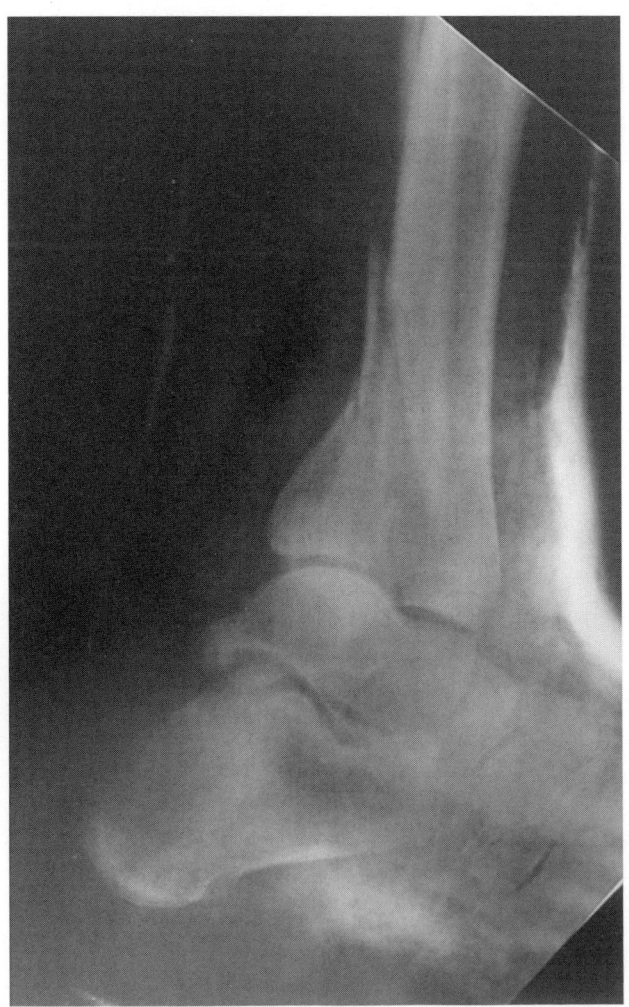

**FIGURE 59–56.** After an attempted closed reduction, posterior dislocation persists. Note that the ankle has been dorsiflexed to neutral, probably increasing the tension in posterior soft tissues and adding to the difficulty of regaining tibiotalar alignment.

hip, eases access to the medial malleolus if it must also be fixed.

Through either a posterolateral or a posteromedial approach, the fragment is retracted and hematoma removed from the fracture cleft with irrigation and suction. The peripheral margin of the fracture is used as a guide to fragment reduction, perhaps aided by a small arthrotomy or occasionally by visualization of the plafond through the bed of an as yet unreduced medial or lateral malleolar fracture. A sharp dental pick, K-wires, and the three-hole pointed drill guide aid reduction. Provisional fixation from the anterior tibia to the posterior lip fragment is achieved with K-wires or, occasionally, large, pointed reduction forceps. Unless the articular surface is well seen, a lateral radiograph of the provisional reduction should be obtained before definitive fixation. Final intraoperative radiographs are routinely obtained after all fixation is in place but before the sterile field is broken in case changes are required (Figs. 59–59 through 59–61).

Clearly, in view of the many options and multiple steps involved in fixing a trimalleolar fracture, the surgical team is aided and the result often improved by careful preoperative assessment and a detailed, explicit preoperative plan for positioning, exposure, reduction, fixation, and radiographic documentation. If many radiographs are needed or if parts of the reduction and fixation are to be done without direct visualization, the use of image intensification fluoroscopy is helpful, and appropriate positioning and use of the table should be planned. Image quality, however, may lack the detail obtained with standard radiographs, which are the best confirmation of final reduction and fixation.

When there is a large posterior lip fracture, extensive visualization of the plafond is possible by delivering the distal tibia through a medial incision, as advocated by Shelton and described by Grantham.[90] Both advised release of the posterior lip fragment from its attached PITFL and a careful search for any comminuted fragments of articular surface in the joint. The entire distal tibial

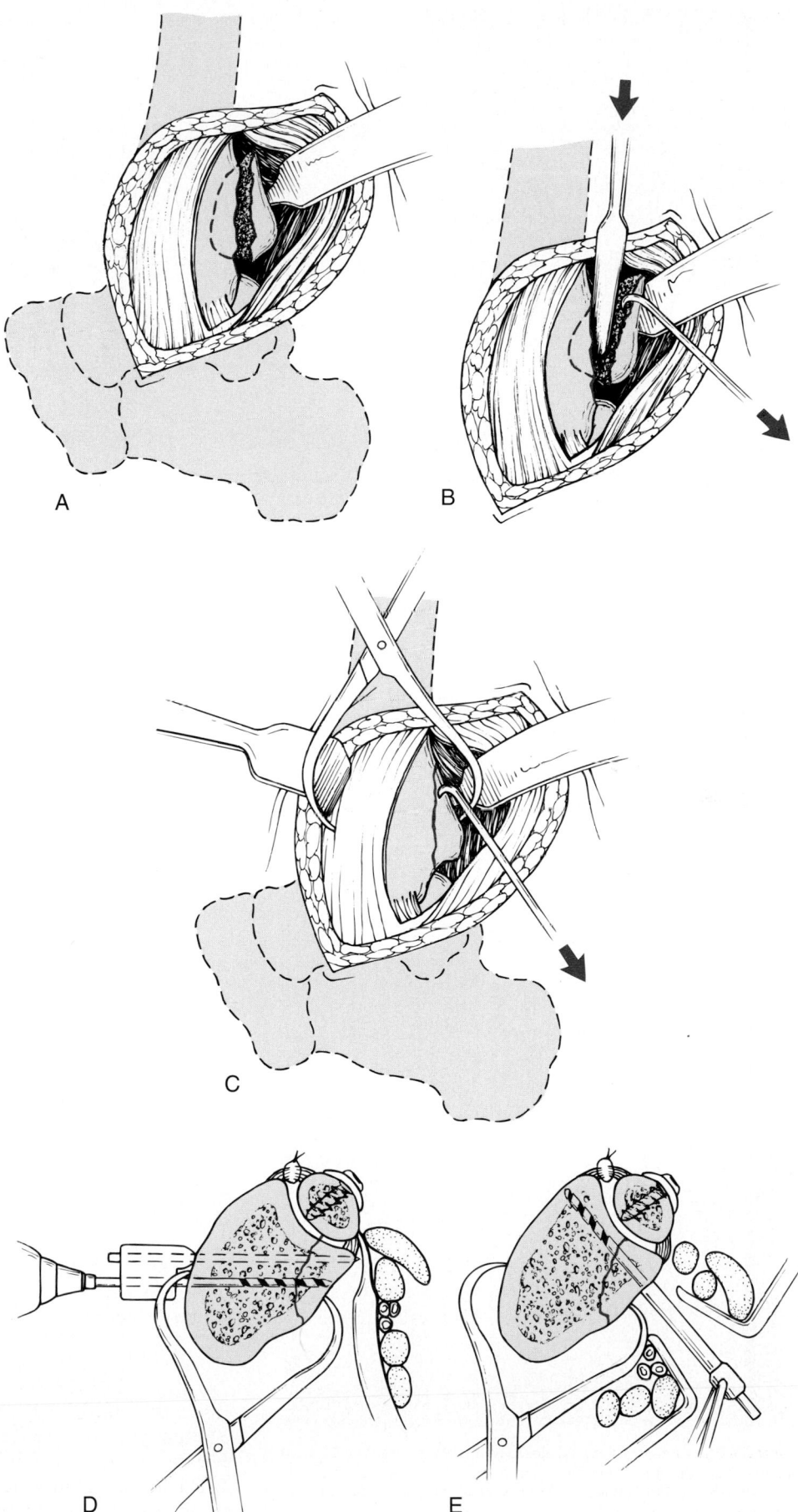

**FIGURE 59–57.** Reduction and fixation of a posterior malleolar fragment through a posteromedial approach. The flexor tendons and neurovascular bundle are retracted posteriorly with a Hohmann retractor (A), the fragment is manipulated into place (B), and provisional fixation is made, often with a pointed reduction clamp (C). Occasionally, the articular surface reduction can be seen directly through an unreduced medial malleolar fracture. A confirmatory radiograph should be taken. Definitive fixation is obtained with anteroposterior lag screws (D) or occasionally, as also shown, with a screw inserted through the interval between the Achilles tendon and the structures behind the medial malleolus (E). (A–E, Redrawn from Heim, U.; Pfeiffer, K.M. Small Fragment Set Manual: Technique Recommended by the ASIF Group, 2nd ed. New York, Springer-Verlag, 1982.)

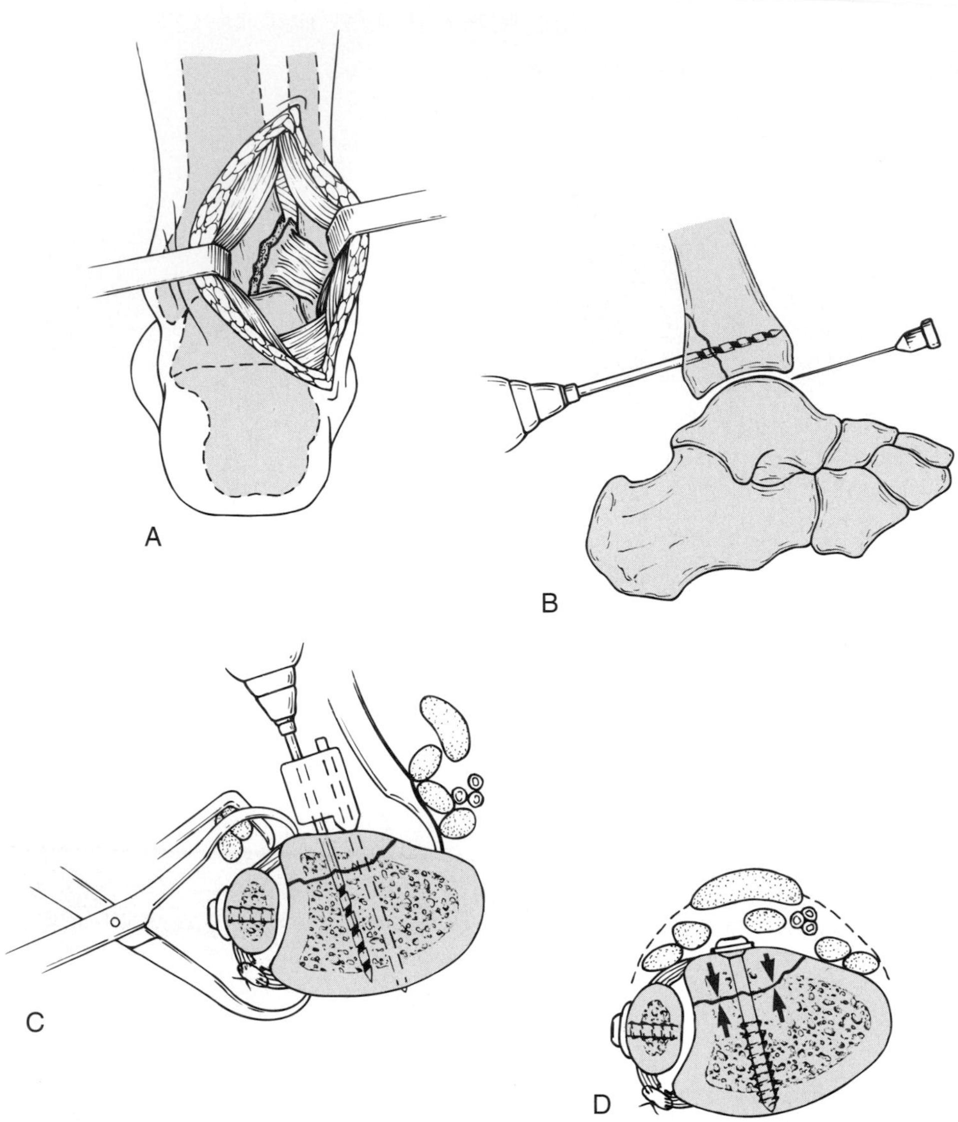

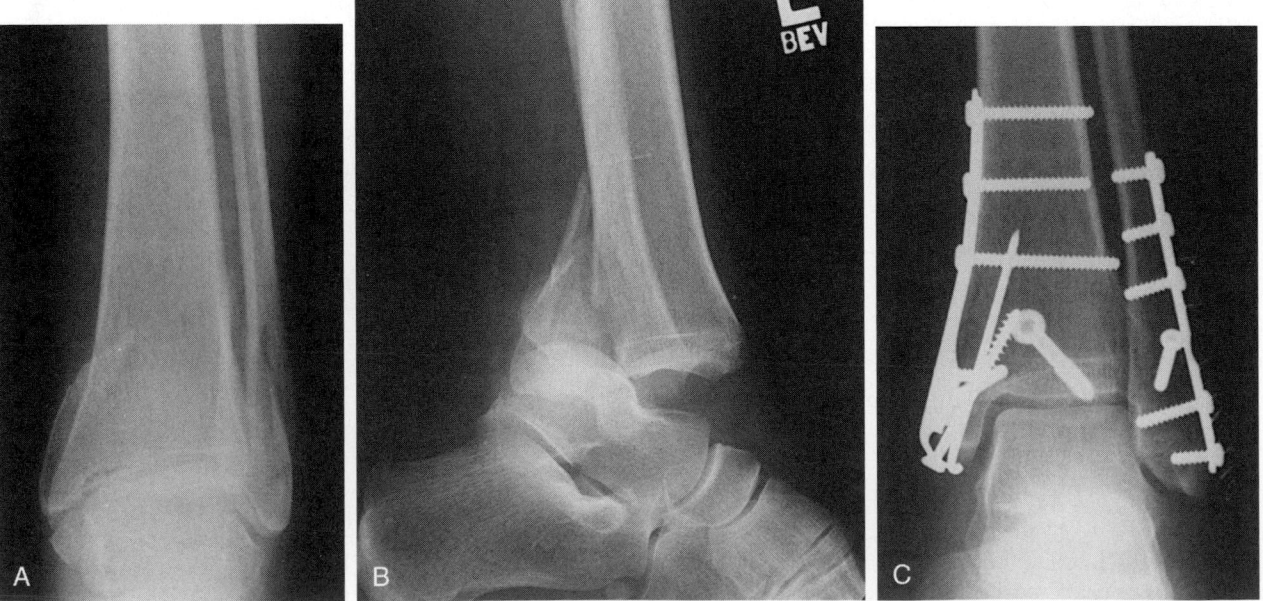

**FIGURE 59–58.** Reduction and fixation of a posterior tibial fragment through a posterolateral approach. *A,* The extra-articular fracture line is used for reduction because the joint cannot usually be directly visualized. *B,* Fixation is with a lag screw inserted posteriorly, with attention to aiming proximally enough to avoid the convex joint surface. *C,* The approach is between the peroneal tendons and the flexor hallucis longus. *D,* A partially threaded 4.0-mm cancellous lag screw provides interfragmentary compression. (*A–D,* Redrawn from Heim, U.; Pfeiffer, K.M. Small Fragment Set Manual: Technique Recommended by the ASIF Group, 2nd ed. New York, Springer-Verlag, 1982.)

**FIGURE 59–59.** *A, B,* Fracture-dislocation of the ankle with a large posterior lip fragment and extensive medial malleolar comminution. *C,* A cannulated screw inserted over a provisional K-wire fixes the posterior lip fragment. A medial cloverleaf plate and standard lateral malleolar construct complete the fixation.

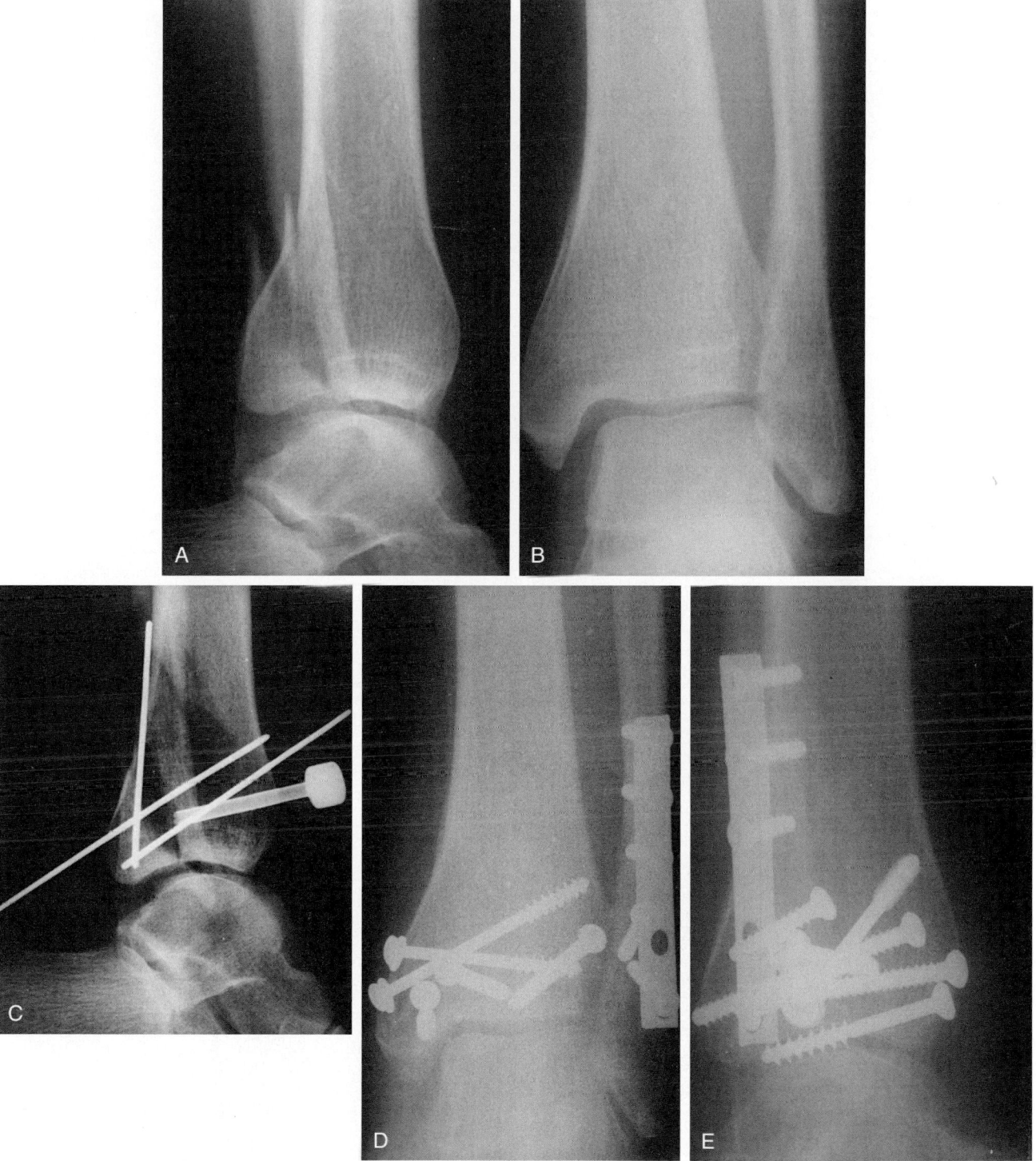

**FIGURE 59–60.** *A,* Articular incongruence is primarily caused by a large, displaced, posterior malleolar fragment. *B,* A comminuted medial malleolar fracture is also present. *C,* After predrilling the anterior distal tibia for a 3.5-mm sliding hole, the insert drill sleeve is placed, and a provisional reduction is accomplished with K-wire fixation. This radiograph confirms anatomic realignment of the joint surface. *D, E,* Fixation is completed with multiple lag screws and a fibular plate. The fracture healed uneventfully.

plafond is delivered through an approximately 7-inch medial incision while the talus, lateral and medial malleolar fragments, and foot are dislocated laterally. This delivery requires release and posterior retraction of the posterior tibial tendon sheath. According to the technique's proponents, comminution and bone grafting, if needed, can readily be dealt with through this approach. After reconstruction of the plafond, the talus is relocated, and the lateral and medial malleoli are fixed in the usual fashion.

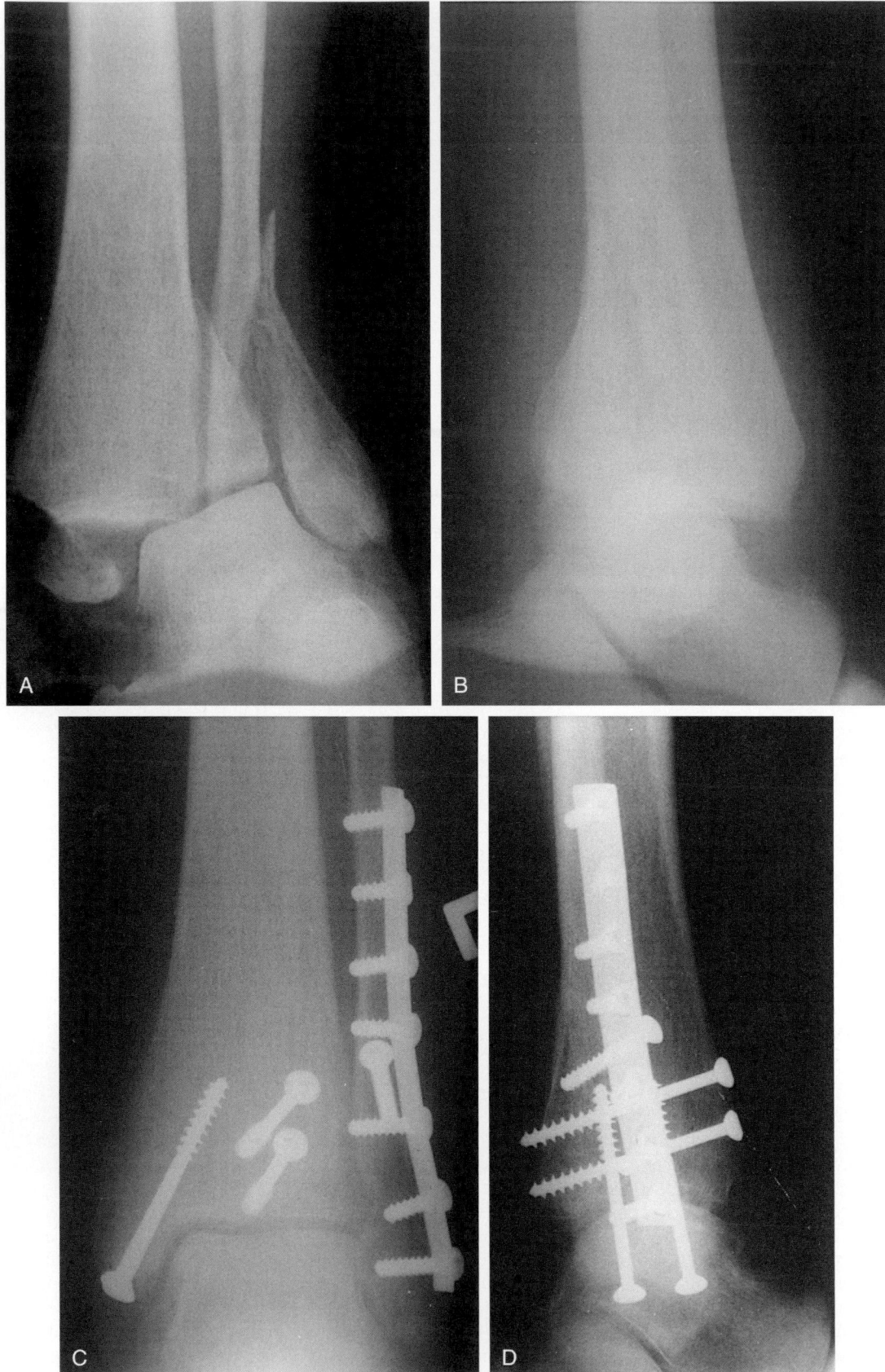

**Figure 59–61.** *A, B,* Trimalleolar fracture-dislocation with a significant posterior lip fragment. *C, D,* Fixation with two 4.0-mm cancellous lag screws inserted from front to back. It was fortunate that the threads were the right length for this fixation, which would have been impaired had they crossed the fracture plane.

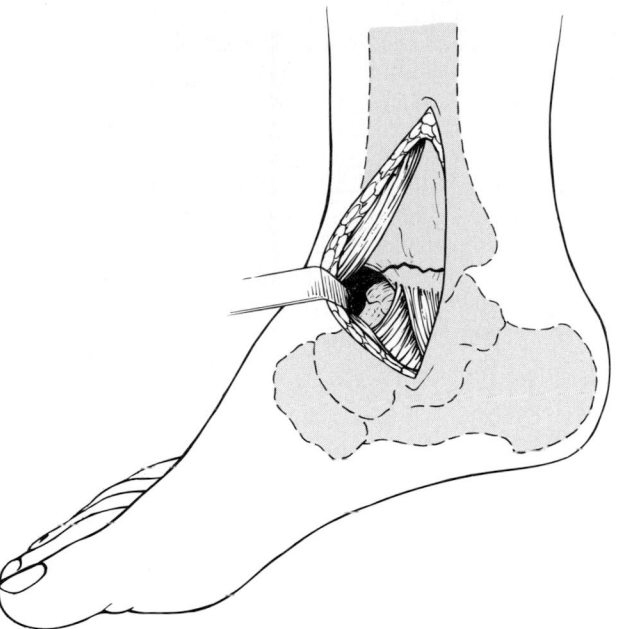

**FIGURE 59–62.** The medial malleolus is approached through a longitudinal incision that allows access to the anteromedial corner of the ankle joint and as much of the distal tibia as required. A longer incision is better than too vigorous retraction. Attention is paid to the saphenous nerve branches; a painful neuroma may result if they are caught in the scar.

## ANTERIOR LIP FRACTURES

The location and character of anterior lip injuries determine the approach and fixation. A CT scan may be helpful for preoperative planning. If extensive comminution of the anterior lip is a relatively isolated injury, an anterolateral arthrotomy lateral to the extensor tendons may provide the best access. Extensive comminution may require buttress fixation with a small plate. An avulsed Tillaux fragment (anterolateral articular surface) should be reduced and fixed with a lag screw. An impacted anterolateral fragment may be excised, if small, or elevated with bone grafting if it involves a significant part of the articular surface.

## MEDIAL MALLEOLAR AND LIGAMENTOUS INJURIES

Operative treatment of medial ligamentous disruptions in malleolar injuries may not always be necessary. Since recognition of the vital role of the lateral malleolus, many authors have reported satisfactory results with anatomic repair of the lateral malleolus and nonoperative management of complete deltoid ligament disruptions. In general, fractures of the medial malleolus should be reduced and fixed to add stability, maintain joint congruity, and decrease the rather low risk of a symptomatic medial malleolar nonunion.

A straight, slightly oblique, or curving incision is made according to the surgeon's preference and the planned fixation (Fig. 59–62). Anteriorly, the saphenous vein and its accompanying cutaneous nerve branches should be protected. The incision should permit an anteromedial ankle arthrotomy as well as visualization of both the

anterior and the medial aspects of any malleolar fracture. The joint is inspected, and any loose osteochondral shards are removed. Retraction of the malleolar fragment demonstrates the flexor tendons, which are occasionally injured. The tibialis posterior is most commonly involved, and it should be checked to exclude injury.[60, 241, 257] Local comminution may be associated with posterior tibial tendon involvement.[266]

The medial surface of the plafond should be assessed through the fracture site, especially in supination-adduction injuries, to search for an impacted area that may need elevation and bone grafting of any resulting defect. Usually, only a small amount of graft is required, and this can be obtained from the more proximal part of the tibial pilon or, through a separate incision, from Gerdy's tubercle (Figs. 59–63 and 59–64).

If repair of the deltoid ligament is desired, its deep portion must be visualized, usually posteriorly after retraction of the tendons, and sutures placed before the lateral side has been fixed. The talus must be displaced laterally to permit this. Depending on the location of the tear, sutures may be placed through drill holes in the malleolus or talus to provide secure reattachment. A few sutures in the superficial deltoid ligament may improve the appearance of the repair but probably add little to stability of the ankle.

Avulsion fractures of the medial malleolus are best reduced after exposing both the anterior and the medial aspects of the fracture by sharply turning back the periosteum and attached fascia. The fragment is grasped with a small towel clip or pointed reduction forceps and maneuvered into place with this and a sharp dental pick. It can be held in place with this or with a bone hook while two fixation points are achieved. For smaller fragments, especially if comminuted, two small K-wires (1.2 or 1.6 mm) may be chosen. For intermediate-sized fragments, one wire and a 2.0- or 2.5-mm drill bit are used to prepare a hole for a 4.0-mm partially threaded cancellous screw. For larger fragments, two such drills are used for provisional fixation and replaced one at a time with the 4.0-mm partially threaded screws.

Cancellous screws for fixation of medial malleolar fractures should be inserted to avoid comminution of the fragment (i.e., not too close to its edge and not overtightened). They should be oriented perpendicular to the plane of the fracture. To obtain a lag effect, their threads must not cross the fracture. They should be seated in the dense bone of the central distal tibial metaphysis and thus should be approximately 40 mm long. The surgeon must not attempt to anchor them in the far cortex, which is too thin to provide much purchase. Doing so can cause either the drill or the screw to deviate during the insertion process and thus lead to malreduction or comminution of the malleolar fragment. Although tapping of cancellous bone is not needed and may reduce the pull-out strength of screws, the use of an appropriate tap through the malleolus and just across the fracture may ease screw insertion and reduce risk of comminution. A preliminary small incision of the superficial deltoid ligament fibers before drilling the pilot hole is helpful.

When the medial malleolar fragment is too small for screws or if comminution develops, the use of K-wires with a figure-of-eight tension band can provide satisfactory fixation. The ends of the K-wires are bent over and gently impacted over the tension band.[81] Proximal anchorage for the wire can be over a screw head rather than through a transverse drill hole (Figs. 59–65 and 59–66). Tension banding is also useful in osteopenic bone.

If the medial malleolar fracture is vertical or oblique, as in supination-adduction type A injuries, the orientation of lag screws to fix the fracture must be different from that used for horizontal plane avulsion fractures. They must be inserted perpendicular to the fracture and thus are fairly transverse. Washers are more likely to be needed because of the thinner medial cortex, and occasionally even a small medial buttress plate is advisable if the bone is osteopenic or excessively comminuted. Three or more screws may be needed for vertical fractures with large medial fragments.

## INTRAOPERATIVE RADIOGRAPHS

Adequate intraoperative radiographs must be obtained to confirm the reduction and fixation of any periarticular fracture, and this holds true for malleolar injuries. In general, AP, lateral, and mortise exposures are made during or just prior to wound closure, although the need for an AP view as well as a mortise view has not been proved. The ankle should be in neutral during these radiographs, which should be carefully checked for adequate positioning and exposure, malleolar fracture reduction (especially the talotibial relationship), the tibiofibular relationship (syndesmosis), the articular surfaces, the length and rotation of the lateral malleolus, and the location of any inserted hardware.

## WOUND CLOSURE AND POSTOPERATIVE CARE

After fixation has been confirmed, the wounds are irrigated and closed atraumatically, usually with interrupted nonabsorbable skin sutures, although some advise that deeper tissues be approximated as well. Small suction drains may decrease problems from hematomas. Generally, a very well padded, loosely wrapped short leg splint is applied to hold

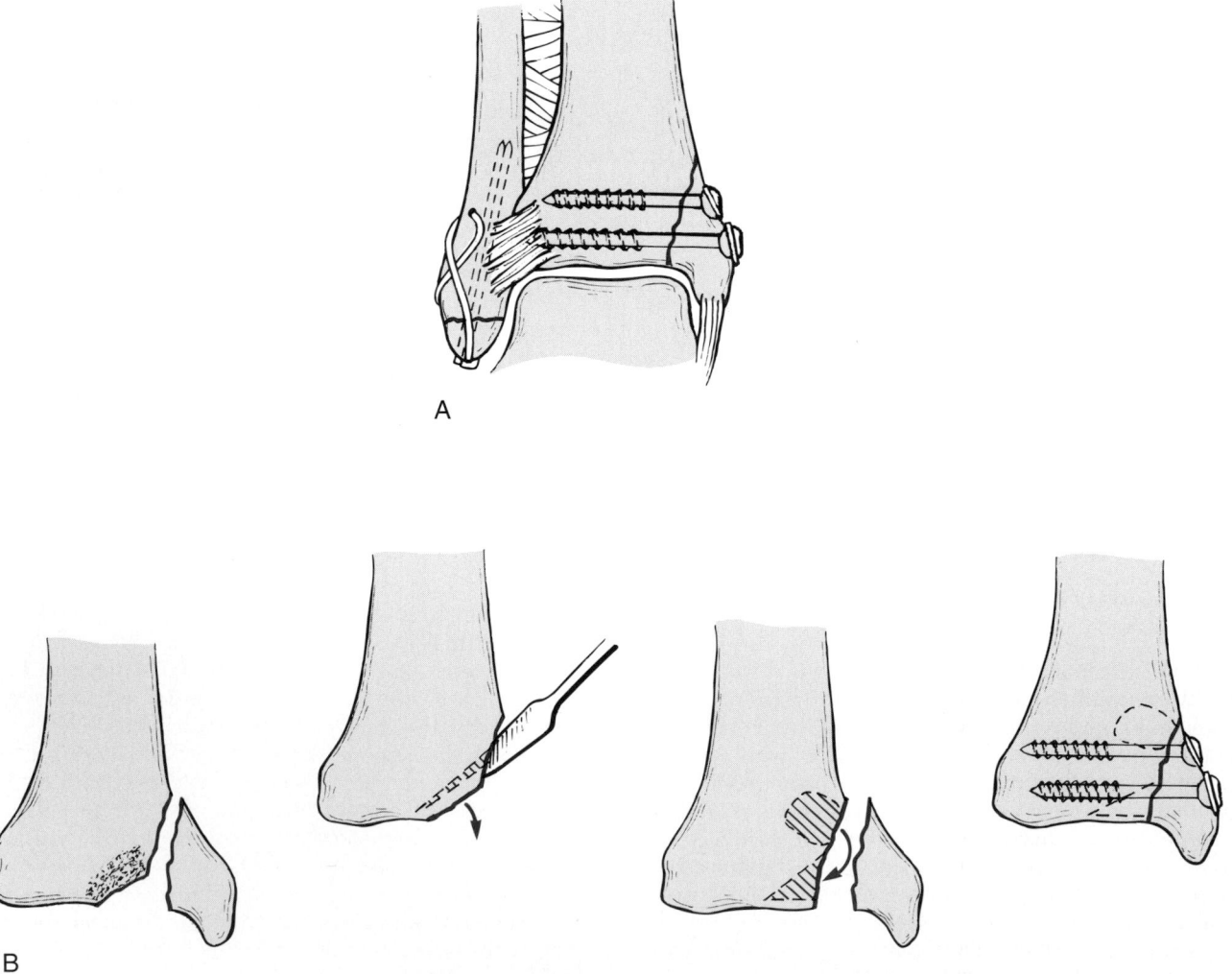

**FIGURE 59–63.** *A,* The vertical type A medial malleolar fracture is fixed with two or more lag screws inserted perpendicular to the fracture. The use of washers or, rarely, a buttress plate is wise. *B,* If there is impaction of the medial plafond, the articular cartilage and subchondral bone are carefully pried en masse back into place against the reduced talus, and bone graft is inserted into the defect before the medial malleolus is repaired. (*A,* Redrawn from Heim, U.; Pfeiffer, K.M. Small Fragment Set Manual: Technique Recommended by the ASIF Group, 2nd ed. New York, Springer-Verlag, 1982. *B,* Redrawn from Müller, M.E.; et al. Manual of Internal Fixation, 2nd ed. New York, Springer-Verlag, 1979.)

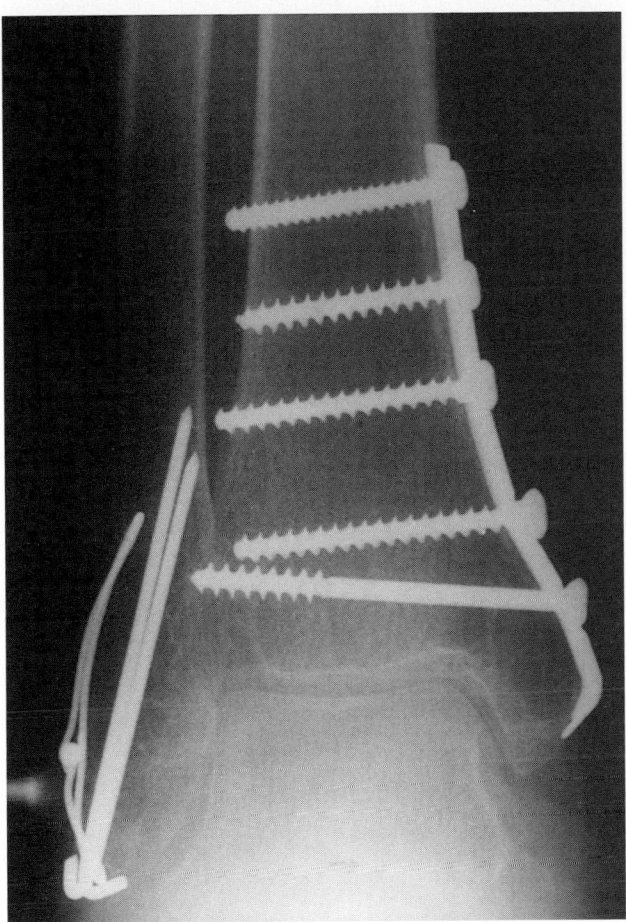

**FIGURE 59–64.** Occasionally, the supination-adduction medial malleolus fracture requires buttress support, analogous to an impacted tibial plateau fracture. A one-third tubular plate has been flattened, cut through the distal hole to provide prongs for additional fixation, and secured with multiple screws. This weight-bearing radiograph was taken 9 months after fixation of the fracture seen in Figure 59–23.

appropriate until the patient is walking well without a limp and radiographic healing is advanced. Range-of-motion, strengthening, endurance, and agility exercises are also necessary elements of the rehabilitation program, which usually lasts several months before the patient can successfully return to vigorous work and athletics. Some swelling of the soft tissues frequently persists for months.[63]

## Special Treatment Groups

### OSTEOPENIA

As the population ages, the incidence of fractures with osteopenia will rise. One needs to weigh carefully the risks and benefits of operative fixation in light of the chances of securing stability. If ORIF is chosen, standard techniques can be used. Alternative methods such as tension band wiring or intramedullary fibula fixation and cerclage can be used. Placing the fibular plate posteriorly is one method to obtain longer and typically stronger screw purchase.

the ankle fully dorsiflexed. Such a splint can be used until the sutures are removed and the surgeon's choice of subsequent immobilization is applied. It seems wise to splint the ankle in as much dorsiflexion as possible, for this is hard to regain if an equinus contracture is allowed to develop.

According to Ahl and co-workers,[1] it makes little difference to most patients what postoperative immobilization regimen is followed, although with tenuous fixation, osteopenic bone, or an uncooperative or neuropathic patient, more rather than less protection may be advisable. Accordingly, the ankle may be placed in a long or short leg non–weight-bearing cast, a short leg walking cast, a hinged brace, a removable bivalved cast, or an elastic support with crutches to limit weight bearing.* One study has documented improved early outcomes with early range of motion versus casting.[65] In the neuropathic patient, most commonly with diabetes, a bent-knee long leg cast may be required to prevent weight bearing for as long as 8 weeks.[49] After the first 6 weeks (if the fracture is only malleolar) or longer (if there is plafond involvement), progressive unrestricted weight bearing can usually be allowed with safety. Crutches are

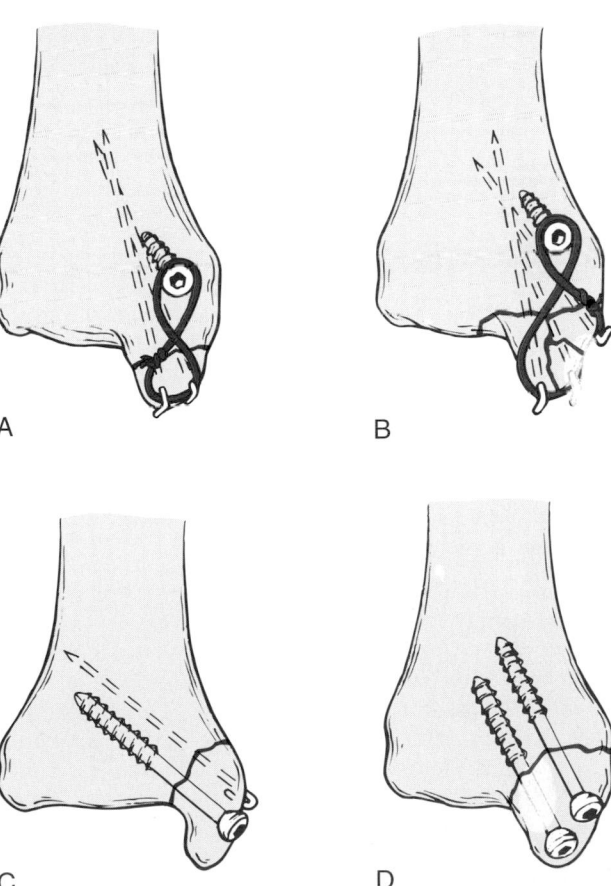

**FIGURE 59–65.** Fixation of avulsion fractures of the medial malleolus depends on their size and comminution. *A, B,* Small or comminuted fragments are best repaired with K-wires and a tension band wire. *C,* A larger piece can be fixed with a single K-wire and a lag screw or two lag screws. *D,* Usually, 4.0-mm partially threaded lag screws are used. They are inserted perpendicular to the fracture line. Provisional fixation of a medial malleolar fragment is often better done with K-wires or 2.5-mm drill bits rather than clamps, which might comminute or displace it.

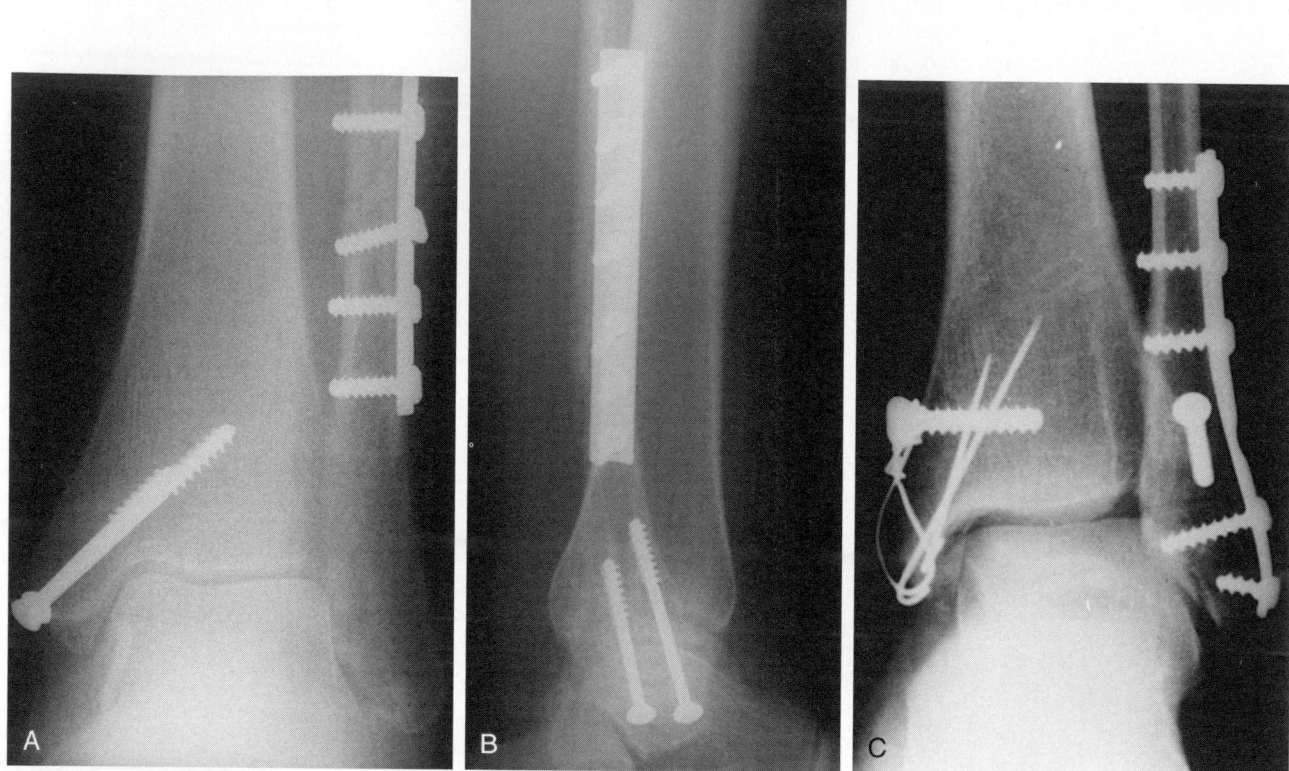

**FIGURE 59–66.** Medial malleolus fixation with two 4.0-mm cancellous lag screws. On mortise (*A*) and lateral (*B*) radiographs, note insertion of the threads into only the densest bone of the central metaphysis and their posterior orientation to accommodate the anteriorly situated medial malleolus. *C*, K-wires and a tension band loop are more appropriate for a small or comminuted medial malleolar avulsion. Note the use of a screw for proximal anchorage of the wire.

## DIABETIC PATIENTS

A severe ankle fracture in the diabetic patient places the treating surgeon directly on the uncomfortable horns of a dilemma. The literature documents a significant increase in complications with either operative or nonoperative treatment.[27, 74] In particular, skin ulceration, infection, and malunion occur much more frequently than in the general population.[27, 74] The literature fails to provide a guiding consensus. We approach these injuries with the following guidelines:

1. One needs to ensure that the fracture represents an acute injury and not part of an ongoing Charcot process. With a Charcot process there is typically a history of weeks of swelling and pain in the ankle. A misdiagnosis of cellulitis or deep vein thrombosis may have been made. A Charcot ankle generally requires casting, elevation, and non–weight bearing to reduce the hyperemic process. Once this process "quiets down," surgical treatment, if needed, can be considered.
2. Fixation must be rigid. We tend to overuse syndesmotic fixation simply as a means to stabilize the mortise.
3. Postinjury immobilization is typically a bent-knee long leg cast for 6 weeks, followed by a short leg walking cast for 1 month. The patient is kept in bed to chair with short-distance ambulation only. A wheelchair is provided. In our experience, neuropathy with loss of protective proprioception is the major factor that leads

to early weight bearing despite strict instructions otherwise. This early weight bearing results in a reddened, hyperemic wound accompanied by early fixation failure. Although this regimen places a hardship on the patient in the short run, it can help to minimize long-term complications.

4. Despite the surgeon's best efforts, problems do occur. Early intervention for developing complications is warranted.

## Results of Treatment

The outcome of an injury is best judged by how much it affects the patient.[190] Pain, impaired function, deformity, and loss of motion are all-important factors. A variety of rating systems have been proposed for the subjective and objective components of clinical results of ankle injuries. Results are usually stratified into groups for analysis. Outcome criteria are not uniform, so it is unwise to compare published series directly. Rating and scoring systems often give different levels of importance to different variables, and most include several interrelated aspects of ankle function or anatomy. Some systems consider only functional outcome; others include clinical examinations and radiographic findings. Some rely heavily on the ability to work or participate in sports, criteria that are irrelevant to certain categories of patients. The American Orthopaedic Foot and Ankle Society has devised a rating scale based largely on function (Table 59–4). Its use is recommended.

Radiographic results may be assessed separately or combined with subjective and objective clinical data.[13, 120, 208] Both the quality of reduction after healing and the presence of degenerative changes are pertinent. Joy and co-workers[120] presented objective techniques for

---

**TABLE 59–4** ..................................................

American Orthopaedic Foot and Ankle Society Rating Scale for Ankle Injury

| Feature | Hindfoot Scale (100 Points Total) |
|---|---|
| **PAIN (40 POINTS)** | |
| None | 40 |
| Mild, occasional | 30 |
| Moderate, daily | 20 |
| Severe, almost always present | 0 |
| **FUNCTION (50 POINTS)** | |
| Activity limitations, support requirement | |
| No limitations, no support | 10 |
| No limitation of daily activities, limitation of recreational activities, no support | 7 |
| Limited daily and recreational activities, cane | 4 |
| Severe limitation of daily and recreational activities, walker, crutches, wheelchair, brace | 0 |
| Maximal walking distance, blocks | |
| Greater than 6 | 5 |
| 4–6 | 4 |
| 1–3 | 2 |
| Less than 1 | 0 |
| Walking surfaces | |
| No difficulty on any surface | 5 |
| Some difficulty on uneven terrain, stairs, inclines, ladders | 3 |
| Severe difficulty on uneven terrain, stairs, inclines, ladders | 0 |
| Gait abnormality | |
| None, slight | 8 |
| Obvious | 4 |
| Marked | 0 |
| Sagittal motion (flexion plus extension) | |
| Normal or mild restriction (30 degrees or more) | 8 |
| Moderate restriction (15–29 degrees) | 4 |
| Severe restriction (less than 15 degrees) | 0 |
| Hindfoot motion (inversion plus eversion) | |
| Normal or mild restriction (75%–100% normal) | 6 |
| Moderate restriction (25%–74% normal) | 3 |
| Marked restriction (less than 25% normal) | 0 |
| Ankle-hindfoot stability (anteroposterior, varus valgus) | |
| Stable | 8 |
| Definitely unstable | 0 |
| **ALIGNMENT (10 POINTS)** | |
| Good, plantigrade foot, ankle-hindfoot well aligned | 10 |
| Fair, plantigrade foot, some degree of ankle-hindfoot malalignment observed, no symptoms | 5 |
| Poor, nonplantigrade foot, severe malalignment, symptoms | 0 |

..................................................

*Source:* Kitaoka, H.B.; et al. Foot Ankle Int 15:349, 1994.

---

measurement of malleolar and talar displacement. Goergen and associates[83] emphasized the value of adequately positioned radiographs for such assessments. Pettrone and colleagues[208] demonstrated the predictive validity of radiographic criteria—particularly displacement of either malleolus, syndesmosis widening, and increased clear space between the medial malleolus and the medial surface of the talus. In a prospective study, Phillips and co-workers[209] noted that the significant indicators of a poor result after severe external rotation ankle fractures were talar subluxation on the lateral radiograph and lateral malleolar shortening, as measured directly or by a talocrural angle different from that on the normal side (see Fig. 59–11).

Osteoarthritis of the ankle joint, rare except after injury, is manifested by osteophyte formation, narrowing of the radiolucent cartilage space, and subchondral sclerosis and cyst formation. Radiographs taken during weight bearing have not always been used to diagnose joint narrowing. The changes of osteoarthritis tend to develop early (within 2 to 3 years) after injury and may not progress.[150] Although the significance of slight joint narrowing is not clear, poor clinical results are associated with more advanced osteoarthritis.

A number of factors affect the outcome of ankle fractures.[303] An important one is the severity of the original injury. The severity is indicated primarily by the amount of damage to the plafond and by the amount of impaction, comminution, or displacement of the posterior lip fracture. Involvement of multiple structures is also pertinent, as higher grade injuries, in the Lauge-Hansen system, have a poorer prognosis, as do trimalleolar fractures when compared with those involving a single malleolus. Some, but not all, reports suggest that women and older patients experience poorer results. The fracture type (Lauge-Hansen or AO/ASIF) carries variable prognostic weight, depending on the study.[96, 150] The presence of a posterior lip fracture, even when small, adversely affects the prognosis of malleolar fractures.[103, 117]

A well-established finding is the benign nature and good outcome of supination–external rotation grade II lateral malleolar fractures.[19, 43, 134, 284] Prolonged follow-up after nonoperative treatment in a short leg weight-bearing cast reveals an extremely low incidence of arthrosis and symptoms in spite of an initial 2- to 3-mm displacement of many of these isolated injuries. It is important to distinguish these from the similar supination–external rotation type IV injuries with deltoid ligament ruptures medially, as the latter have a much worse prognosis.

The adequacy of reduction after fracture healing is a significant determinant of outcome. Lindsjö[150] reported 87% good to excellent results in 217 patients with well-reduced, originally displaced malleolar fractures, compared with 68% good to excellent results in 89 patients with inadequate reductions. These patients were treated with AO fixation techniques and had a higher incidence of maintained reduction and of good outcomes than those in a series reported by Cedell[43] with less rigid fixation. Similar good results after anatomic reduction and rigid fixation were reported by others, including Hughes and associates, from several Swiss centers.[59, 110, 157] Satisfactory outcomes were achieved in 78% to 83% of type A,

76% to 83% of type B, and 62% to 85% of type C malleolar injuries. A comparable group of patients with similar injuries treated nonoperatively had satisfactory results in 71% to 75% of type A, 35% to 43% of type B, and 23% to 37% of type C fractures.

Results with less satisfactory approaches to reduction and internal fixation (i.e., medial fixation alone, approximate reduction, or avoidance of lateral plates) are generally poorer as well, although they are not strictly compared in the literature.[120, 172, 201, 208, 209] Subjective complaints are common after malleolar fractures, even after several years. Many authors reported an approximately 30% incidence of such symptoms, although there is evidence that the symptoms gradually resolve.[19, 20, 146] Removal of prominent implants can relieve symptoms from this source.[114, 226] The reported incidence of significant post-traumatic osteoarthritis after malleolar fractures ranges from negligible in supination–external rotation type II injuries to 37% or more in more severely displaced patterns, especially if posterior malleolar involvement is present.[19] It is also clear that the incidence of arthritis is much greater if a malleolar fracture heals with significant displacement.[105, 201, 296]

# SOFT TISSUE INJURIES OF THE ANKLE

## Lateral Collateral Ligament Injuries

Ankle "sprains" are frequent injuries and are thus familiar to both patients and physicians.[219, 240] They are the most common injury resulting from recreational sports, have a considerable socioeconomic impact, and have generated an abundant literature that has been extensively reviewed.[123, 140, 235, 258] According to Bröstrom,[36] common ankle sprains have complete ligament ruptures in 75% of cases. Two thirds of these are isolated injuries of the anterior talofibular ligament.[36, 221]

This section emphasizes (1) the need for appropriate diagnosis, (2) the currently favored nonoperative management of essentially all closed LCL ruptures, and (3) late instability resulting from functional or mechanical causes and its management.

### DIAGNOSIS

The complaint of a sprain by a patient with a swollen, tender ankle is so common in the urgent care setting that it is often disregarded if ankle radiographs fail to reveal a fracture. Systematic evaluation is necessary to avoid missing a less obvious injury.[184] The patient's description of the injury is important, and it should be determined whether the onset was sudden, with an injury episode, or gradual.

An inversion mechanism, with the foot forcibly supinated, as has been previously discussed, produces failure of the LCL complex. The anterior talofibular ligament is the structure most likely to be partially or completely torn. If the foot was dorsiflexed, the fibulocalcaneal ligament may also be involved. If it was plantar flexed, the anterior capsule is often torn as well. If the applied force *externally* rotated the foot (often in a pronated position), the injury is

likely to involve the tibiofibular syndesmosis and possibly the deltoid ligament (see the discussion of pronation–external rotation in the previous section "Malleolar Fractures"). If no fracture is present on the ankle radiographs, this injury may be mistaken for an LCL sprain in spite of syndesmotic involvement and the risk of a higher fibular fracture or talar instability in the mortise. Tendon ruptures or dislocations have a characteristic history of failure under load, without extreme twisting of the ankle. It is important to ask about prior difficulties with the ankle to identify tendon degeneration and other chronic conditions.

Physical examination is often difficult because of tenderness.[179] Status of the skin and neurovascular function is important. Very forceful inversion injuries may rupture the lateral ankle skin, producing a characteristic transverse wound that looks almost as though it were made with a scalpel. Peroneal nerve palsies and occasionally delayed compartment syndromes accompany inversion sprains.[11, 136, 193] Localization of tenderness is essential to identify the injured structures. If the LCL complex is involved, there is tenderness over the anterior talofibular ligament and possibly over the fibulocalcaneal ligament, the anterior capsule, and the MCL. LCL injuries should not produce tenderness over the syndesmosis, the malleoli themselves, the proximal fibula, or the Achilles or other tendons, although the nearby peroneal tendons may be rather sensitive. Rarely, an LCL disruption occurs in company with a lateral malleolar fracture.[289]

Assessment of stability is the basis for confirming and grading a ligament injury. The assessment is often difficult in the case of an acute ankle injury and is even harder after a day or two have elapsed. Anterior drawer motion of the plantigrade foot is a sign of anterior fibulotalar laxity, which can be confirmed and quantitated by stress radiography. Inversion laxity may be caused by deficiencies of the fibulocalcaneal ligament (in dorsiflexion) or the anterior talofibular ligament (in plantar flexion). It is hard to judge because of the patient's discomfort and the normal motion of the subtalar joint, which itself may be unstable in as many as 10% of patients with inversion laxity.

Confirmation of ligament rupture is possible with peroneal tenography or ankle arthrography, but neither defines the degree of instability. This definition can be made with stress films, with or without special apparatus or anesthesia.[4, 138] With general anesthesia, stress radiographs are quite accurate (92%), but accuracy with local anesthesia falls to 68% (Fig. 59–67).[107] Although academically interesting, such studies do not convincingly improve the patient's outcome after acute ankle sprains, so they are rarely indicated.

It is vital to inspect carefully the standard radiographs of a patient with a presumed ankle sprain. Osteochondral fractures of the talus may be present on either the lateral or the medial dome; their identification is necessary for proper management (see Chapter 60).[96, 299] A fracture of the lateral process of the talus may simulate an LCL sprain, as may a fracture of the anterior process of the calcaneus. The latter is hard to see without oblique radiographs of the foot, although its characteristic tenderness is more anterior. Avulsion of the base of the fifth metatarsal may occur with an inversion injury with or without associated ankle LCL rupture.

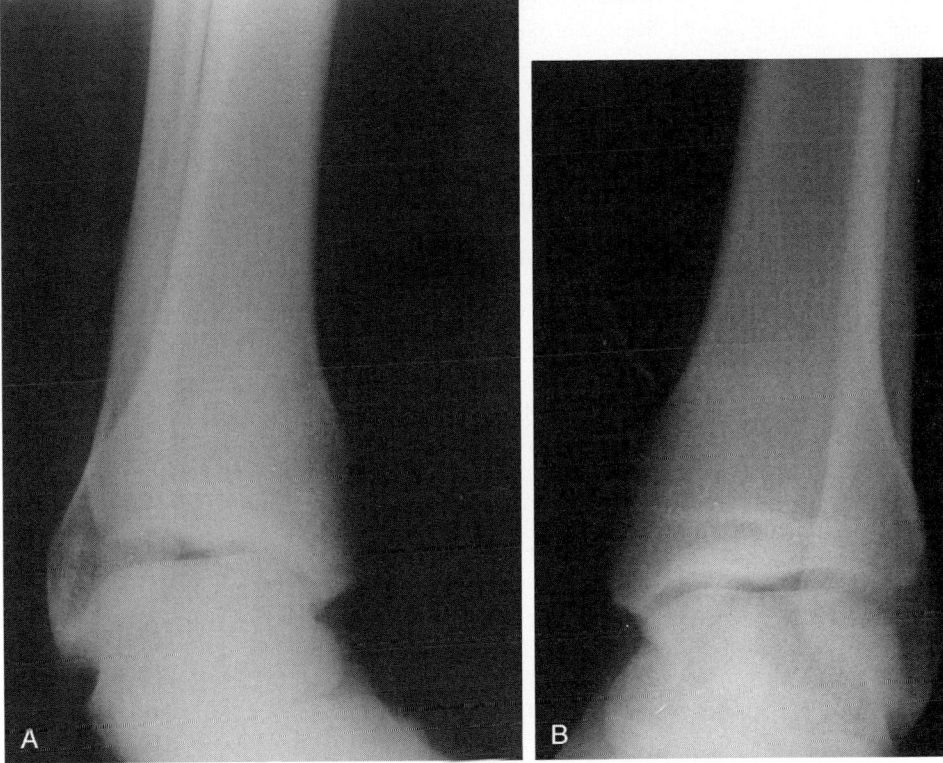

**FIGURE 59–67.** Inversion stress radiographs demonstrate 14 degrees of varus tilt of the right talus (*A*) versus 2 degrees of varus on the left (*B*).

Small ligamentous avulsion fractures from the lateral malleolus or ankle capsular attachments are occasionally seen with sprains and should not affect treatment or outcome. Bröstrom[36] found these in 14% of patients using standard radiographs. Meyer and colleagues,[177] using high-resolution CT, reported them in 42% of patients.

## TREATMENT

The goals of treatment for LCL injuries are to achieve rapid and complete rehabilitation with minimal morbidity and cost and the lowest possible risk of late instability. Many approaches, with a great number of variations, have been reported.[97] At present, there appears to be little justification for primary surgical repair, which has been shown by several randomized prospective studies not to improve the outcome of either isolated ruptures of the anterior talofibular ligament or those with concomitant fibulocalcaneal rupture.[66, 132, 262] Furthermore, late reconstructions for those who need them are no less successful than early repair.[42]

Optimal nonoperative management of ankle LCL sprains should involve functional aftercare.[23, 212, 255, 258, 262] Because late instability may be caused by functional or anatomic factors[9, 140, 237] and may respond to appropriate rehabilitation measures, including exercises for muscle strength and agility, such measures may have a role in the management of acute injuries, as may various physical modalities that increase comfort and provide support for the ankle. On the other hand, many patients with these common injuries do so well with independent rehabilitation programs that routine prescription of phys-

ical therapy and long-term bracing carries a significant unnecessary economic burden.

The patient with an acute ankle LCL sprain may have a *minor injury* with tenderness, slight swelling, and little difficulty walking. More demanding activities may be symptomatic, and the risk of reinjury is probably significant if she or he returns immediately and without protection to challenging activities. The patient with a *moderate injury* has significant swelling and tenderness, walks with difficulty on the ankle, and is unable to participate in vigorous work or sports. The patient with a *severe LCL injury* has such significant pain and tenderness that he or she is unable to bear weight without rigid immobilization or crutches and usually has documentable evidence of a complete disruption of both the anterior talofibular ligament and the fibulocalcaneal ligament.

Treatment of minor ankle sprains is directed at relief of symptoms and prevention of further injury. It consists of reduced activity, stretching and strengthening exercises, and the use of a training-type brace that provides proprioceptive input. Moderate and severe ankle sprains are difficult to differentiate precisely without anesthesia. Therefore, similar treatment regimens are advised. Although a more precise diagnosis might expedite rehabilitation for athletes under pressure to return to competition earlier, it is unnecessary and not cost effective in the majority of cases. Progressive return to normal activity can be determined by the patient's clinical course.

The acutely injured ankle with a moderate or severe sprain is best immobilized in a well-padded plaster splint. Ice, elevation, and crutch walking are advised. Within 2 or 3 days, as the acute swelling diminishes, the patient is reassessed. Generally, a stirrup splint with pneumatic or other cushions (e.g., Aircast or equivalent) is applied over a sock or a light, loose elastic wrap, and the patient is encouraged to bear weight progressively as tolerated and to discard the crutches as soon as comfort and security permit (Fig. 59–68).[23, 217] For a noncompliant patient with a severe injury, a cast may be considered. Generally, however, it is withheld unless the patient is so disabled that rigid external support is necessary for comfort. In such a case, a short leg walking cast can be applied as soon as swelling permits and used for 1 to 3 weeks until full weight bearing is possible in the cast. At this point, the functional brace is substituted.

An important part of the aftercare of an acute LCL ankle sprain is a functional rehabilitation program. This program usually consists of progressive resumption of activity, stretching and strengthening exercises, functional bracing or taping, and proprioceptive drills. Many such regimens have been described and are reported in the literature.[6, 14, 21, 47, 53, 80, 140, 183]

## Late Inversion Instability

Chronic instability has been reported to follow 20% to 40% of acute inversion ankle sprains.[106] The patient reports recurring inversion sprains or the feeling that the ankle will "give way" in this manner. Prospective randomized studies provide little support for the belief that acute surgical treatment reduces this risk.[66, 133, 140, 262] More effective early nonoperative management may be beneficial, however.

Instability may be mechanical with documentable inversion laxity of the ankle or subtalar joint.[9, 33, 140, 176, 302] It may also have functional causes, such as impaired proprioception and balance or, rarely, peroneal rupture or palsy.[80, 93, 131, 280] History, examination, and stress radiographs usually permit diagnosis of the cause of ankle instability. If a trial of intensive rehabilitation is unsuccess-

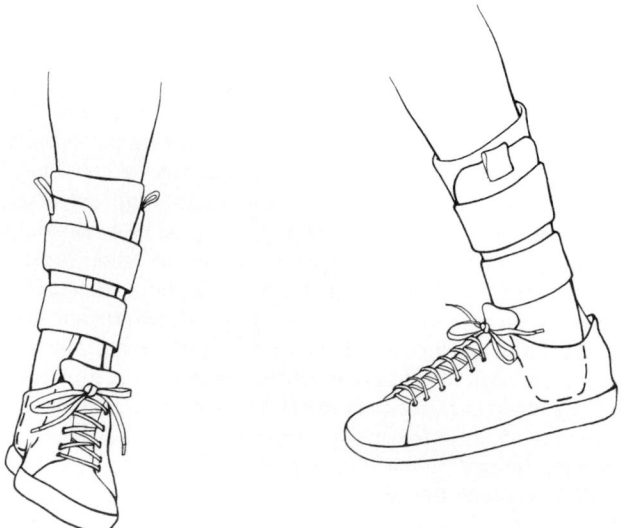

**Figure 59–68.** A stirrup splint with air-filled cushions and Velcro fasteners provides secure, functional support for a lateral collateral ligament injury after the acute pain and swelling have resolved.

ful and mechanical instability is present, some form of lateral ligamentous reconstruction is appropriate. High success rates have been reported for treatment of recalcitrant mechanical instability by most of these various procedures, which range from repair of the residual ligament to its advancement or to its augmentation with local or more distant tendon grafts. If subtalar instability is present, the ligament reconstruction must address it. Anatomic repairs (e.g., Bröstrom) are currently in favor, but acceptable results can be obtained with a number of operations.*

## Persistent Pain

Occasionally, ankle pain, rather than a sensation of instability per se, is a residual problem after an ankle inversion injury. It may be the result of one or more of several factors. An osteochondral fracture of the talus should be considered.[96, 297] There may be impingement on the talus by a synovial thickening or hypertrophic AITFL.[17] Another possibility is a post-traumatic sinus tarsi syndrome with damage to the restraining ligaments of the subtalar joint, which can be demonstrated by posterior subtalar arthrography.[178] CT or magnetic resonance imaging evaluation, bone scan, or ankle arthroscopy may help with the evaluation and management of these often puzzling injuries.

## Ankle Dislocations

### ANKLE DISLOCATIONS WITHOUT FRACTURE

Although most ankle dislocations are part of a complex malleolar injury, the tibiotalar joint rarely dislocates without a fracture.[52, 278] Approximately one third are open, with an associated risk of infection that can be diminished with appropriate wound care and delayed closure.[129] Neurovascular injuries are frequently associated with these dislocations. Closed reduction is usually successful, with a generally satisfactory result and little risk of long-term functional instability or arthritis. The results of open dislocations are poorer.

Occasionally, there is a complete dislocation of the talus with dislocation from the subtalar and talonavicular joints as well. These *extruded talus* lesions are usually open and have a high risk of sepsis, avascular necrosis, and ultimate amputation. Despite these problems, an attempt at salvage of the talus is warranted. If complications ensue, talectomy and early tibiotalar arthrodesis may be the best means of salvaging a functional foot.[129]

### SPRAINS OF THE SYNDESMOSIS—THE "HIGH ANKLE SPRAIN"

Sprains of the syndesmotic ligaments are reported in 1% to 11% of all ankle sprains. They are identified by a history of external rotation with tenderness over the AITFL. In the absence of concomitant fibular fracture, compression of

---

*See references 7, 8, 25, 37, 118, 121, 194, 224, 237, 256, 283, 290.

the fibula to the tibia in the proximal half of the leg produces pain in the syndesmotic area (squeeze test).[109] These less frequent ligamentous injuries of the ankle are slower to recover and may benefit from a somewhat more restrictive approach to management, including a period of a few weeks in a non–weight-bearing cast.[23, 236] Disability for sports participation can extend to 3 to 4 months.

It is important to exclude the diagnosis of complete ligamentous disruption with displacement of the fibula from the incisural notch. This diagnosis is suggested by mortise widening or by a separation of 5 mm or more between the fibula and the lateral border of the notch on mortise radiographs. Remember that a high fibula fracture or plastic deformation of the fibula may accompany these injuries. Precise documentation of the distal tibiofibular anatomy is readily obtained with a CT scan. If displacement is present, closed management is not likely to replace the fibula, and ORIF is indicated. In the absence of displacement of the fibula, protection and progressive rehabilitation are advised.

## TIBIOFIBULAR DIASTASIS

Widening of the ankle mortise occurs occasionally without obvious fracture.[158, 166] It may be occult, with a syndesmosis disruption that requires stress radiographs for confirmation. It may also be frank and visible on routine radiographs (Fig. 59–69). Edwards and DeLee[64] described four types of this rare injury. In type I, there is a direct lateral displacement of the otherwise normal fibula. This type is best treated with open reduction and syndesmosis transfixation. Type II injuries are similar but have plastic deformation of the fibula and may need an osteotomy as well as open reduction of the distal fibula. Type III injuries have posterolateral rotatory subluxation. Type IV have interposition of the superiorly dislocated talus. Types III and IV are usually managed well with closed reduction and cast immobilization, according to Edwards and DeLee.[64]

## Medial Collateral (Deltoid) Ligament Ruptures

The deltoid ligament is usually injured as a component of a malleolar fracture, and this has been discussed previously. Rarely, it appears as an isolated injury.[99] Nonoperative management should provide satisfactory stability unless unrecognized syndesmosis disruption is present.

## Achilles Tendon Ruptures

A myriad of pathologic conditions may affect the Achilles tendon, including Achilles tendinitis, partial or incomplete ruptures of the tendon, bursitis, and tenosynovitis. Because of the large mass of the triceps surae and its importance in control of the tibiotalar relationship during walking, running, and jumping, the Achilles tendon is subjected to large loads on a regular, recurrent basis. Achilles tendinitis is an overuse syndrome and must be differentiated from more acute problems such as tears, partial tears, muscle strains, and thrombophlebitis. Radio-

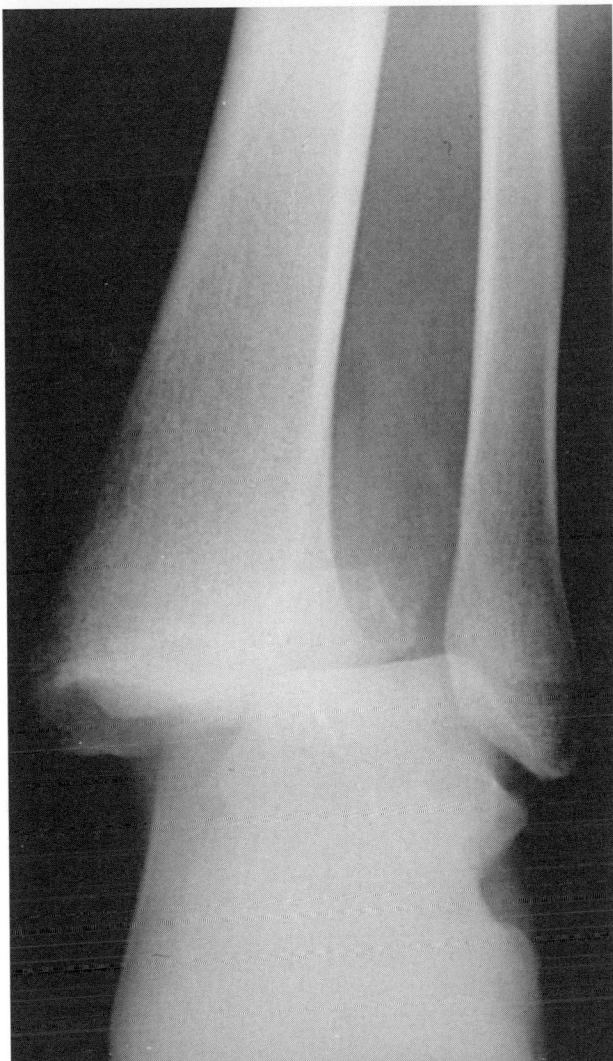

**FIGURE 59–69.** Tibiofibular diastasis with a small posterior avulsion fracture of the tibia in a teenaged patient. Plastic deformation of the fibula required osteotomy and fibular fixation.

graphic examinations are usually noncontributory except in the case of a large posterosuperior calcaneal spur. Most of the overuse syndromes respond to activity modification, a heel lift, stretching exercises, night splints, and oral anti-inflammatory agents. Injections with steroid preparations should be discouraged as they damage the collagen matrix and may result in iatrogenic tendon ruptures.

Ruptures of the Achilles tendon are usually secondary to forced dorsiflexion of the plantar flexed foot. Typical patients are middle-aged "weekend athletes." Not uncommonly, rupture occurs in high-demand sports such as basketball, football, or tennis. A possible contributory factor may be failure to stretch and warm up appropriately for the sporting event. Rarely, these ruptures accompany fractures of the ankle.[165]

Examination of the patient with an acute Achilles tendon rupture usually demonstrates a defect in the heel cord with exquisite pain and inability to plantar flex the ankle completely. Swelling may obscure the tendon defect. The Thompson test is performed by manually squeezing the calf while the patient is kneeling. This action normally produces passive plantar flexion of the ankle. The injured Achilles tendon demonstrates less plantar flexion than the normal calf when the test is performed (see Fig. 59–16).

The treatment for Achilles tendon rupture includes conservative management with the foot held in the plantar flexed position for at least 8 to 12 weeks, open management with primary repair and preservation of the tenosynovium, percutaneous repair through small stab incisions, and open repair with or without augmentation. The literature offers various opinions about the results of treatment.[92, 143] A large, randomized study demonstrated little difference in outcome, and similar complication rates, between nonoperative and operative treatments.[192] However, it is usually suggested that "serious athletes" should be treated with operative repair, which may offer a more functional result than conservative management. The reported risk of rerupture is lower after surgical treatment unless care is taken with nonoperative treatment.[22, 29, 128]

Surgical technique should include a posteromedial skin incision rather than one in the midline, which could be associated with shoe wear problems as well as skin sloughs. The paratenon should be preserved and repaired, if possible, to prevent adhesions between the skin and the tendon repair. The tendon ends are reapproximated with appropriate suture techniques in the manner of Bunnell or Kessler.[277] Loose ends of the tendon can be sutured into bundles before being reconnected.[24] The plantaris tendon can be used to augment the primary repair if it does not appear strong enough. Dacron mesh or other fabric can also be used to reinforce an Achilles tendon repair. An alternative technique relies on a suture placed percutaneously through the tendon ends, which are not exposed in an effort to avoid skin complications, which may be a problem with open repairs. After primary repair or augmentation, short leg immobilization for 6 to 8 weeks is usually adequate, followed by use of a heel lift to protect the repair for an additional 6 weeks.

Late repairs of neglected Achilles tendon ruptures can be augmented with a turndown of the gastrocsoleus fascia, a strip of fascia lata, plantaris tendon, or flexor hallucis longus.[16]

## Less Common Tendon Injuries

Other less common tendon injuries around the ankle include ruptures and dislocations of the peroneal or posterior tibial tendons.[147, 211, 245, 269] Posterior tibial tendon rupture or dysfunction is usually due to attritional failure. It typically results in a painful flatfoot deformity of fairly sudden onset in middle-aged or elderly individuals. Any ankle tendon is at risk of laceration in an open wound. Loss of peroneal tendon function may be manifested as inversion instability.[131, 274]

### PERONEAL TENDON DISLOCATIONS

Dislocations of the peroneal tendon are fairly rare and usually result from forced dorsiflexion or forced inversion.[12, 50, 196] The injury is easily misdiagnosed as an ankle sprain and treated with early mobilization, with attendant risk of redislocation or chronic dislocation. Radiographic

evaluation of a patient with a peroneal tendon dislocation reveals a small fleck of bone off the posterior aspect of the lateral malleolus. This is well seen by CT.[229, 230, 261, 272] Such an avulsion fragment, in association with the classic physical findings of pain *behind* the lateral malleolus and localized swelling, is the hallmark of the diagnosis.

If reduction of the dislocated tendons is stable, these injuries can be treated with closed reduction of the tendons and a below-knee walking cast for 6 to 8 weeks. In some cases, little intrinsic stability exists after retinacular rupture, and open reduction with retinacular repair or reconstruction is advisable.

Recurrent dislocation (or subluxation), however, poses a more difficult reconstructive problem. Surgical alternatives include transfer of the lateral Achilles tendon sheath, fibular osteotomy to create a deeper pulley for the tendons, and rerouting peroneal tendons under the fibulocalcaneal ligament.*

### POSTERIOR TIBIAL TENDON RUPTURES

Acute posterior tibial tendon ruptures are difficult to diagnose and are frequently unrecognized for long periods of time.[2, 37, 79, 130, 133, 247] Occasionally, they accompany malleolar fractures.[126, 241, 266] They are usually found in patients in the fourth to sixth decades of life who present with a recently developed, painful flatfoot deformity. Standing radiographic evaluations classically show a flatfoot deformity with asymmetry of the talonaviculocuneiform arch. The tendon can be visualized by CT and especially well by magnetic resonance imaging, which greatly aid diagnosis.[115, 228, 231] Complete ruptures that have been diagnosed early can be treated with repair, usually with augmentation from the adjacent toe flexors.[160] However, chronic posterior tendon ruptures may require a subtalar or triple arthrodesis, depending on the severity of symptoms. Rarely, dislocations of the posterior tibial tendon may occur.[182, 260, 264]

## COMPLICATIONS

Shelton and Anderson[251] provided a thorough and exceptionally detailed analysis of the complications of ankle injuries and their treatment. On the basis of our review of the literature and extensive personal experience, this definitive work is strongly recommended.[251, 275, 276, 291, 296, 303]

Most complications of ankle injuries are related to one of three basic areas: infection, soft tissue problems, or malunion and arthrosis (osteoarthritis).

### Wound Sloughs

Soft tissue wounds around the ankle usually result from high-energy trauma. Open ankle fractures should be treated as mentioned previously with aggressive surgical débridement, immediate internal fixation, and delayed wound closure. In the event of a superficial skin loss, the

---

*See references 47, 58, 87, 139, 162, 179, 213, 214, 254, 265.

wound can be treated with wet to dry dressing changes for a 5- to 7-day period, followed by split-thickness skin grafting with a 1:1.5 mesh. Alternatively, skin substitutes (e.g., Epigard) or Seligson's bead pouch technique can be used, especially if there is exposed bone and tendon, to prevent desiccation and infection. Local fasciocutaneous flaps are useful in selected cases.[95]

With the sophistication of microvascular transfer techniques, consultation with a microvascular surgeon well versed in orthopaedic injuries can provide reconstructive options not previously available.[86, 252] Small, well-perfused free tissue transfers may be more cosmetic and more functional than the split-thickness skin graft that was previously placed on granulating periosteum. Such free tissue transfer can salvage the ankle after a potentially catastrophic injury, especially in the event of an open joint. If severe cartilage injury has occurred to either the tibial or the talar articular surface, ankle arthrodesis may be required.[46] Such free tissue transfers provide a much more appropriate surgical soft tissue environment for arthrodesis.

# Infection

The open ankle fracture is at highest risk for developing an infection after internal fixation. However, in several large series of open ankle fractures treated with immediate internal fixation, rates of infection were acceptable. The main reason for this success is a combination of compulsive surgical technique, open-wound management, and perioperative antibiotics. The improved outcome of open ankle fractures treated with appropriate wound care and immediate internal fixation justifies this change from traditional orthopaedic teaching.[34, 35, 51, 77, 89, 294]

Infection may be difficult to identify after surgical treatment of an ankle fracture. It may be limited to a surgical wound but often involves the ankle joint. Aspiration of the joint and proper evaluation of its fluid are thus mandatory whenever an infection is possible. Studies should include Gram stain, cell count, and culture and sensitivity.

If an infection ensues after ORIF of the ankle, an aggressive approach must be undertaken with immediate surgical débridement, multiple deep wound cultures, initially open-wound management, and appropriate antibiotics. The ankle joint should not be left open but should be closed over a suction tube to prevent any accumulation of pus under pressure. If the ankle joint cannot be closed, serious consideration must be given to early local soft tissue transfers or free microvascular tissue transfer.

There may be disagreement between infectious disease consultants and orthopaedic surgeons concerning the necessity of hardware removal in the event of an infection. If the hardware is providing stability, even in the presence of gross infection, it should generally not be removed until the fracture has united. Instability of the infected fracture fragments provides a less desirable biologic environment in which to fight infection. Obtaining a durably functional ankle without chronic infection requires a combination of adequate débridement of necrotic and infected bone and soft tissue, anatomic reduction, rigid stability, appropriate antibiotics, occasional soft tissue coverage (which might entail a free muscle flap), and ultimately an aggressive postoperative ankle rehabilitation program.[92] If internal fixation does not provide adequate stability, external fixation should be used instead, generally with distal purchase in both calcaneus and forefoot.

# Malunion

Malunion of an ankle fracture may be caused by an inadequate closed reduction or by loss of such a reduction. If it is caused by one of these, early recognition and correction, usually with ORIF, may resolve the problem, although the difficulties of a late operation must be remembered. Malalignment may follow ORIF if reduction is inadequate and not recognized or if it is lost because of failure of fixation. It may result from an uncooperative or neuropathic patient or from mechanical problems of fixation or bone quality. The risk of inadequate reduction of an ankle fracture is significantly increased in severe injuries with comminution, impaction, bone loss, and obscured landmarks for reduction.

The operating surgeon must compulsively examine the intraoperative radiographs to be absolutely certain that an anatomic reduction has been achieved. Failure to do so is a not infrequent source of error. Well-positioned and satisfactorily exposed AP, lateral, and mortise views must be obtained intraoperatively and carefully reviewed, perhaps by comparison with the opposite side, to be sure that the bone relationships are appropriate.

The most common malunion of the ankle has been reported to be shortening and malrotation of the fibula. Weber and Simpson[288] described a corrective osteotomy to bring the fibula back to length and restore appropriate rotation. This procedure requires preoperative planning, the use of intraoperative distraction, bone grafting, and rigid fixation.[296] If the fibula has been brought to appropriate length and reduced, aggressive physical therapy should follow. This osteotomy may have limited application, as many malunions of the ankle are associated with pain and severe degenerative changes. If loss of motion, pain, and severe degenerative changes are present, the lengthening distraction osteotomy may not be enough to provide the patient with a functional ankle. However, such a procedure, along with correction of all other deformities affecting the ankle, should be seriously considered unless end-stage functional impairment is present, as nearly three fourths of such patients can have significant, long-lasting improvement.[163, 286, 288, 298]

# Post-traumatic Arthrosis

Post-traumatic arthrosis may be manageable with reduced activity, nonsteroidal anti-inflammatory medication, a well-cushioned shoe with a heel lift, or a fixed-ankle short leg brace with a cushioned rocker heel. If these measures are inadequate, arthrodesis is a reasonable consideration (Fig. 59–70).[171, 232] Ankle replacement arthroplasties have

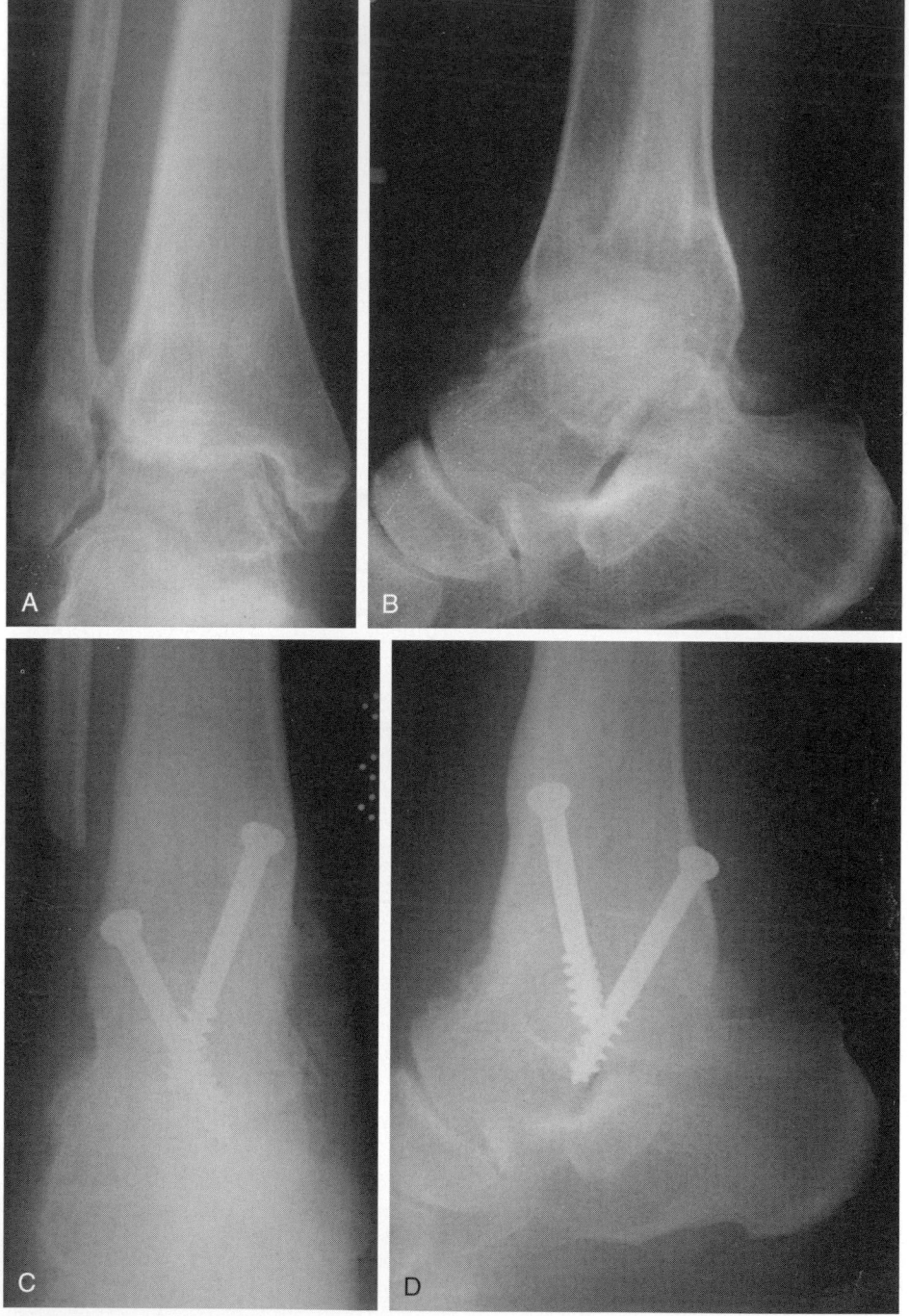

**FIGURE 59–70.** *A, B,* Post-traumatic arthrosis several years after a malleolar ankle fracture. *C, D,* Because of progressive severe symptoms, unresponsive to conservative treatment, an arthrodesis was performed with good result.

not proved as successful as arthrodesis for most patients with post-traumatic arthrosis. Occasionally, however, removal of osteophytes, especially from the anterior ankle, with open or arthroscopic techniques can significantly relieve symptoms.

Total ankle replacement is receiving renewed attention. It offers the promise of preserved motion with pain relief. Initial reports are encouraging for this technically demanding procedure. Caution is warranted given the previous history of ankle replacement. This topic is discussed further in Chapter 61.

## Late Syndesmotic Instability

Occasionally, following an ankle fracture and despite normal bone anatomy, medial clear space widening with concomitant pain and swelling develops. In most cases, the deltoid ligament is insufficient, along with the lateral syndesmotic complex. A method of surgical reconstruction was detailed by Kelikian and Kelikian.[127] In this procedure, both the medial and the lateral ankle are exposed. Debris must be cleared from the tibial incisura and the medial joint space. The syndesmosis is reduced and clamped, and stability confirmed visually and radiographically. The anterior tibiofibular ligament is reconstructed with the extensor tendon to the fifth toe. Two staples are used for fixation of the tibiofibular joint. Alternatively, screws can be used. The patient is kept non–weight bearing for 6 weeks.

## Tibiofibular Synostosis

After disruption of the tibiofibular syndesmosis, heterotopic bone occasionally forms in the soft tissues between the tibia and the fibula and may unite with both to produce a synostosis. It occurs with and without syndesmosis transfixation screws and is probably dependent primarily on the severity of the original injury. It may be completely asymptomatic or may be associated with pain during push-off.[175] If so, its excision may help relieve symptoms.[88, 102, 154]

## Nonunion

Nonunions of the ankle, albeit rare, are usually treated with small autogenous cancellous bone grafts and stable internal fixation. Medial malleolar nonunions with interposed periosteum have been successfully treated with curettage of the fibrous interface, packing of cancellous bone grafting, and rigid screw fixation. Fibular nonunions result from unreduced significant displacement, comminution, or bone loss. In the case of bone loss or comminution, bone grafting should be considered. When grafting is anticipated, the iliac crest should be prepared. An alternative is Gerdy's tubercle in the proximal tibia, where a small to moderate amount of cancellous graft is readily available.

*Acknowledgments*

   The author acknowledges the contributions, insights, and expertise of Timothy J. Bray, M.D., Lex A. Simpson, M.D., and Peter G. Trafton, M.D., who were coauthors of this chapter in the previous editions of this book. Some of their cases are illustrated herein.

## REFERENCES

1. Ahl, T.; Dalen, N.; Holmberg, S.; Selvik, G. Early weight bearing of displaced ankle fractures. Acta Orthop Scand 58:535, 1987.
2. Ahl, T.; Dalen, N.; Selvik, G. Ankle fractures. A clinical and roentgenographic stereophotogrammetric study. Clin Orthop 245:246, 1989.
3. Ahlgren, O.; Larsson, S. Reconstruction for lateral ligament injuries of the ankle. J Bone Joint Surg Br 71:300, 1989.
4. Ahovuo, J.; Kaartinen, E.; Slatis, P. Diagnostic value of stress radiography in lesions of the lateral ligaments of the ankle. Acta Radiol 29:711, 1988.
5. Alioto, R.J.; Furia, J.P.; Marquardt, J.D. Hematoma block for ankle fractures: A safe and efficacious technique for manipulations. J Trauma 9:113, 1995.
6. Allen, M.J.; McShane, M. Inversion injuries to the lateral ligament of the ankle joint. A pilot study of treatment. Br J Clin Pract 39:282, 1985.
7. Andersen, E.; Hvass, I. Treatment of lateral instability of the ankle—A new modification of the Evans repair. Arch Orthop Trauma Surg 106:15, 1986.
8. Anderson, M.E. Reconstruction of the lateral ligaments of the ankle using the plantaris tendon. J Bone Joint Surg Am 67:930, 1985.
9. Anonymous. Residual disability after ankle joint injury. Editorial. Lancet 1:1056, 1989.
10. Anonymous. Achilles tendon rupture. Editorial. Lancet 1:1427, 1989.
11. Arciero, R.A.; Shishido, N.S.; Parr, T.J. Acute anterolateral compartment syndrome secondary to rupture of the peroneus longus muscle. Am J Sports Med 12:366, 1984.
12. Arrowsmith, S.R.; Fleming, L.L.; Allman, F.L. Traumatic dislocations of the peroneal tendons. Am J Sports Med 11:142, 1983.
13. Baird, R.A.; Jackson, S.T. Fractures of the distal part of the fibula with associated disruption of the deltoid ligament. Treatment without repair of the deltoid ligament. J Bone Joint Surg Am 69:1346, 1987.
14. Balduini, F.C.; Vegso, J.J.; Torg, J.S.; Torg, E. Management and rehabilitation of ligamentous injuries to the ankle. Sports Med 4:364, 1987.
15. Barber, F.A.; Britt, B.T.; Ratliff, H.W.; Sutker, A.N. Arthroscopic surgery of the ankle. Orthop Rev 17:446, 1988.
16. Barnes, M.J.; Hardy, A.E. Delayed reconstruction of the calcaneal tendon. J Bone Joint Surg Br 68:121, 1986.
17. Bassett, F.H., III; Gates, H.S., III; Billys, J.B.; et al. Talar impingement by the anteroinferior tibiofibular ligament. A cause of chronic pain in the ankle after inversion sprain. J Bone Joint Surg Am 2:55, 1990.
18. Bauer, M.; Johnell, O.; Redlund-Johnell, I.; Johnsson, K. Ankle fractures. Foot Ankle 8:23, 1987.
19. Bauer, M.; Jonsson, K.; Nilsson, B. Thirty-year followup of ankle fractures. Acta Orthop Scand 56:103, 1985.
20. Bauer, M.; Bergstrom, B.; Hemborg, A.; Sandegard, J. Malleolar fractures: Nonoperative versus operative treatment: A controlled study. Clin Orthop 199:17, 1985.
21. Baxter, D.E. Ligamentous injuries. In: Mann, R.A., ed. Surgery of the Foot, 5th ed. St. Louis, C.V. Mosby, 1986, p. 456.
22. Beauchamp, C.G.; Clay, N.R.; Thexton, P.W. Displaced ankle fractures in patients over 50 years of age. J Bone Joint Surg Br 65:329, 1983.
23. Bergfeld, J.A.; Cox, J.S.; Drez, D.; et al. Symposium: Management of acute ankle sprains. Contemp Orthop 13:83, 1986.
24. Beskin, J.L.; Sanders, R.A.; Hunter, S.C.; et al. Surgical repair of Achilles tendon ruptures. Am J Sports Med 15:1, 1987.
25. Bjorkenhelm, J.M.; Sandelin, J.; Santavirta, S. Evans' procedure in the treatment of chronic instability of the ankle. Injury 19:70, 1988.
26. Bleichrodt, R.P.; Kingma, L.M.; Binnendijk, B.; Klein, J.P. Injuries of the lateral ankle ligaments: Classification with tenography and arthrography. Radiology 173:347, 1989.
27. Blotter, R.H.; Connolly, E.; Wasan, A.; Chapman, M.W. Acute complications in the operative treatment of isolated ankle fractures with diabetes mellitus. Foot Ankle Int 20:687, 1999.
28. Boden, S.D.; Labropaulos, P.A.; McCowin, P.; et al. Mechanical considerations for the syndesmotic screw. A cadaver study. J Bone Joint Surg Am 71:1548, 1989.
29. Bomler, J.; Sturup, J. Achilles tendon rupture. An 8-year followup. Acta Orthop Belg 55:307, 1989.
30. Böstman, O.; Hirvensalo, E.; Vainionpaa, S.; et al. Ankle fractures treated using biodegradable internal fixation. Clin Orthop 238:195, 1989.
31. Böstman, O.; Partio, E.; Hirvensalo, E.; Rokkanen, P. Foreign-body reactions to polyglycolide screws. Observations in 24/216 malleolar fracture cases. Acta Orthop Scand 74:1021, 1992.
32. Bourne, R.B. Pylon fractures of the distal tibia. Clin Orthop 240:42, 1989.
33. Brantigan, J.W.; Pedegana, L.R.; Lippert, F.G. Instability of the subtalar joint. J Bone Joint Surg Am 59:321, 1977.
34. Bray, T.J. Soft-tissue techniques in the management of open ankle fractures. Tech Orthop 2:20, 1987.
35. Bray, T.J.; Endicott, M.; Capra, S.E. Treatment of open ankle fractures. Immediate internal fixation vs closed immobilization and delayed fixation. Clin Orthop 240:47, 1989.
36. Broström, L. Sprained ankles. Anatomic lesions in recent sprains. Acta Chir Scand 128:483, 1964.
37. Broström, L. Sprained ankles. VI. Surgical treatment of chronic ligament ruptures. Acta Chir Scand 132:551, 1966.
38. Brunner, C.F.; Weber, B.G. Special Techniques in Internal Fixation. Berlin, Springer-Verlag, 1982.

39. Bucholz, R.W.; Henry, S.; Henley, M.B. Fixation with bioabsorbable screws for the treatment of fractures of the ankle. J Bone Joint Surg Am 76:319, 1994.

40. Burkus, J.K.; Sella, E.J.; Southwick, W.O. Occult injuries of the talus diagnosed by bone scan and tomography. Foot Ankle 4:316, 1984.

41. Burns, W.C.; Prakash, K.; Adelaar, R.S.; et al. Tibiotalar joint dynamics: Indications for the syndesmotic screw. A cadaver study. Foot Ankle 14:153, 1993.

42. Cass, J.R.; Morrey, B.F.; Katoh, Y.; Chao, E.Y. Ankle instability: Comparison of primary repair and delayed reconstruction after long-term follow-up study. Clin Orthop 198:110, 1985.

43. Cedell, C.A. Supination–outward rotation injuries of the ankle. Acta Orthop Scand Suppl 110:1, 1967.

44. Cedell, C.A. Is closed treatment of ankle fractures advisable? Editorial. Acta Orthop Scand 56:101, 1985.

45. Chapman, M.W. Fractures and fracture-dislocations of the ankle. In: Mann, R.A., ed. Surgery of the Foot, 5th ed. St. Louis, C.V. Mosby, 1986, pp. 568–591.

46. Cierny, G., III; Cook, W.G.; Mader, J.T. Ankle arthrodesis in the presence of ongoing sepsis. Indications, methods, and results. Orthop Clin North Am 20:709, 1989.

47. Clancy, W.G., Jr. Specific rehabilitation for the injured recreational runner. Instr Course Lect 38:483, 1989.

48. Clawson, D.K.; Seddon, H.J. The late consequences of sciatic nerve injury. J Bone Joint Surg Br 42:213, 1960.

49. Clohisy, D.R.; Thompson, R.C., Jr. Fractures associated with neuropathic arthropathy in adults who have juvenile-onset diabetes. J Bone Joint Surg Am 70:1192, 1988.

50. Cohen, I.; Lane, S.; Koning, W. Peroneal tendon dislocations: A review of the literature. J Foot Surg 22:15, 1983.

51. Collins, D.N.; Temple, S.D. Open joint injuries: Classification and treatment. Clin Orthop 243:48, 1989.

52. Colville, M.R.; Colville, J.M.; Manoli, A., II. Posteromedial dislocation of the ankle without fracture. J Bone Joint Surg Am 69:706, 1987.

53. Cox, J.S. Surgical and nonsurgical treatment of acute ankle sprains. Clin Orthop 198:118, 1985.

54. Daffner, R.H. Ankle trauma. Radiol Clin North Am 28:395, 1990.

55. Daffner, R.H.; Riemer, B.L.; Lupetin, A.R.; Dash, N. Magnetic resonance imaging in acute tendon ruptures. Skeletal Radiol 15:619, 1986.

56. Dahners, L.E. The pathogenesis and treatment of bimalleolar ankle fractures. Instr Course Lect 39:85, 1990.

57. Daly, P.J.; Fitzgerald, R.H., Jr.; Melton, L.J.; Ilstrup, D.M. Epidemiology of ankle fractures in Rochester, Minnesota. Acta Orthop Scand 58:539, 1987.

58. Das, De S.; Balasubramaniam, P. A repair operation for recurrent dislocation of peroneal tendons. J Bone Joint Surg Br 67:585, 1985.

59. DeSouza, L.J.; Gustillo, R.B.; Meyer, T.J. Results of operative treatment of displaced external rotation-abduction fractures of the ankle. J Bone Joint Surg Am 67:1066, 1985.

60. DeZwart, D.E.; Davidson, J.S.A. Rupture of the posterior tibial tendon associated with fracture of the ankle. J Bone Joint Surg Am 65:260, 1983.

61. Dillin, L.; Slabaugh, P. Delayed wound healing, infection, and nonunion following open reduction and internal fixation of tibial plafond fractures. J Trauma 26:1116, 1986.

62. Dory, M.A. Arthrography of the ankle joint in chronic instability. Skeletal Radiol 15:291, 1986.

63. Drabu, K.J. Soft-tissue swelling following fractures of the ankle. Injury 18:401, 1987.

64. Edwards, G.S.; DeLee, J.C. Ankle diastasis without fracture. Foot Ankle 4:305, 1984.

65. Egol, K.A.; Dolan, R.; Koval, K.J. Functional outcome of surgery for fractures of the ankle: A prospective, randomized comparison of management in a cast or a functional brace. J Bone Joint Surg Br 82:246, 2000.

66. Evans, G.A.; Hardcastle, P.; Frenyo, A.D. Acute rupture of the lateral ligament of the ankle. To suture or not to suture? J Bone Joint Surg Br 66:209, 1984.

67. Eyring, E.J.; Guthrie, W.D. A surgical approach to the problem of severe lateral instability at the ankle. Clin Orthop 206:185, 1986.

68. Farhan, M.J.; Smith, T.W. Fixation of diastasis of the inferior tibiofibular joint using the syndesmosis hook. Injury 16:309, 1985.

69. Ferkel, R.D.; Fischer, S.P. Progress in ankle arthroscopy. Clin Orthop 240:210, 1989.

70. Fernandez, G.N. Internal fixation of the oblique, osteoporotic fracture of the lateral malleolus. Injury 19:257, 1988.

71. Ferries, J.S.; DeCoster, T.A.; Firoozbakhsh, K.K.; et al. Plain radiographic interpretation in trimalleolar ankle fractures poorly assesses posterior fragment size. J Orthop Trauma 8:328, 1994.

72. Finsen, V.; Saetermo, R.; Kibsgaard, L.; et al. Early postoperative weight-bearing and muscle activity in patients who have a fracture of the ankle. J Bone Joint Surg Am 71:23, 1989.

73. Floyd, D.W.; Heckman, J.D.; Rockwood, C.A., Jr. Tendon lacerations in the foot. Foot Ankle 4:8, 1983.

74. Flynn, J.M.; Rodriguez-del Rio, F.; Piza, P.A. Closed ankle fractures in the diabetic patient. Foot Ankle Int 21:311, 2000.

75. Fogel, G.R.; Morrey, B.F. Delayed open reduction and fixation of ankle fractures. Clin Orthop 215:187, 1987.

76. Fowler, P.J.; Regan, W.D. Management of the deltoid ligament disruption in fracture-dislocation of the ankle. J Bone Joint Surg Br 69:504, 1987.

77. Franklin, J.L.; Johnson, K.D.; Hansen, S.T. Immediate internal fixation of open ankle fractures. J Bone Joint Surg Am 66:1349, 1984.

78. Frokjaer, J.; Moller, B.N. Biodegradable fixation of ankle fractures. Complications in a prospective study of 25 cases. Acta Orthop Scand 63:434, 1992.

79. Funk, D.A.; Cass, J.R.; Johnson, K.A. Acquired adult flat foot secondary to posterior tibial-tendon pathology. J Bone Joint Surg Am 68:95, 1986.

80. Gauffin, H.; Tropp, H.; Odenrick, P. Effect of ankle disk training on postural control in patients with functional instability of the ankle joint. Int J Sports Med 9:141, 1988.

81. Georgiadis, G.M.; White, D.B. Modified tension band wiring of medial malleolar ankle fractures. Foot Ankle Int 16:64, 1995.

82. Giachino, A.A.; Hammond, D.I. The relationship between oblique fractures of the medial malleolus and concomitant fractures of the anterolateral aspect of the tibial plafond. J Bone Joint Surg Am 69:381, 1987.

83. Goergen, T.G.; Danzig, L.A.; Resnick, D.; Owen, C.A. Roentgenographic evaluation of the tibiotalar joint. J Bone Joint Surg Am 59:874, 1977.

84. Golterman, A.F.L. Diagnosis and treatment of tibiofibular diastasis. Arch Chir Neerl 16:185, 1964.

85. Goris, R.J. Irreducible subluxation of the tibiotalar joint due to a fracture of the calcaneus. Injury 18:358, 1987.

86. Gould, J.S. Reconstruction of soft tissue injuries of the foot and ankle with microsurgical techniques. Orthopedics 10:151, 1987.

87. Gould, N. Technique tips: Footings. Repair of dislocating peroneal tendons. Foot Ankle 6:208, 1986.

88. Gould, N.; Flick, A.B. Postfracture, late débridement resection arthroplasty of the ankle. Foot Ankle 6:70, 1985.

89. Gourinemi, P.V.; Knuth, A.E.; Nuber, G.F. Radiographic evaluation of the position of the implantation in the medial malleolus in relation to the ankle joint: Anteroposterior compared with mortise radiographs. J Bone Joint Surg Am 81:364, 1999.

90. Grantham, S.A. Trimalleolar ankle fractures and open ankle fractures. Instr Course Lect 39:105, 1990.

91. Grath, G.B. Widening of the ankle mortise: A clinical and experimental study. Acta Chir Scand Suppl 263:1, 1960.

92. Green, S.A.; Roesler, S. Salvage of the infected pilon fracture. Tech Orthop 2:37, 1987.

93. Gross, M.T. Effects of recurrent lateral ankle sprains on active and passive judgments of joint position. Phys Ther 67:1505, 1987.

94. Gungor, T. A test for ankle instability: Brief report. J Bone Joint Surg Br 70:487, 1988.

95. Hallock, G.G. Local fasciocutaneous flap skin coverage for the dorsal foot and ankle. Foot Ankle 11:274, 1991.

96. Hamilton, W.C. Traumatic Disorders of the Ankle. New York, Springer-Verlag, 1984.

97. Harper, M.C. An anatomic study of the short oblique fracture of the distal fibula and ankle stability. Foot Ankle 4:23, 1983.

98. Harper, M.C. The deltoid ligament: An evaluation of need for surgical repair. Clin Orthop 226:156, 1988.

99. Harper, M.C. Posterior instability of the talus: An anatomic evaluation. Foot Ankle 10:36, 1989.

100. Harper, M.C.; Hardin, G. Posterior malleolar fractures of the ankle associated with external rotation-abduction injuries: Results with and without internal fixation. J Bone Joint Surg Am 70:1348, 1988.

101. Hawkins, R.B. Arthroscopic treatment of sports-related anterior osteophytes in the ankle. Foot Ankle 9:87, 1988.

102. Heim, U.F. Trimalleolar fractures: Late results after fixation of the posterior fragment. Orthopedics 12:1053, 1989.

103. Heim, U.; Pfeiffer, K.M. Small Fragment Set Manual: Technique Recommended by the ASIF Group, 2nd ed. New York, Springer-Verlag, 1981.

104. Hirvensalo, E. Fracture fixation with biodegradable rods. Forty-one cases of severe ankle fractures. Acta Orthop Scand 60:601, 1989.

105. Hoblitzell, R.M.; Ebraheim, N.A.; Merrit, T.; Jackson, W.T. Bosworth fracture-dislocation of the ankle. A case report and review of the literature. Clin Orthop 255:257, 1990.

106. Homminga, G.N.; Kluft, O. Long-term inversion stability of the ankle after rupture of the lateral ligaments. Neth J Surg 38:103, 1986.

107. Hoogenband, C.R.; Moppes, F.I.; Stapert, J.W. Clinical diagnosis, arthrography, stress examination and surgical girding after inversion trauma of the ankle. Arch Orthop Trauma Surg 103:115, 1984.

108. Hooper, J. Movement of the ankle joint after driving a screw across the inferior tibiofibular joint. Injury 14:493, 1983.

109. Hopkinson, W.J.; St. Pierre, P.; Ryan, J.B.; et al. Syndesmosis sprains of the ankle. Foot Ankle 10:325, 1990.

110. Hughes, J.L.; Weber, H.; Willenegger, H.; Kuner, E.H. Evaluation of ankle fractures: Nonoperative and operative treatment. Clin Orthop 138:111, 1979.

111. Hurson, B.J.; Sheehan, J.M. Use of spiked washers in the repair of avulsed ligaments. Acta Orthop Scand 52:23, 1981.

112. Inman, V.T. The Joints of the Ankle. Baltimore, Williams & Wilkins, 1976.

113. Jackson, R.; Wills, R.E.; Jackson, R. Rupture of deltoid ligament without involvement of the lateral ligament. Am J Sports Med 16:541, 1988.

114. Jacobsen, S.; Honnens de Lichtenberg, M.; Jensen, C.M.; Torholm, C. Removal of internal fixation—The effect on patients' complaints: A study of 66 cases of removal of internal fixation after malleolar fractures. Foot Ankle Int 15:170, 1994.

115. Jahss, M.H. Spontaneous rupture of the tibialis posterior tendon: Clinical findings, tenographic studies, and a new technique of repair. Foot Ankle 3:158, 1982.

116. Jaskulka, R.; Fischer, G.; Schedl, R. Injuries of the lateral ligaments of the ankle joint. Operative treatment and long-term results. Arch Orthop Trauma Surg 107:217, 1988.

117. Jaskulka, R.A.; Ittner, G.; Schedl, R. Fractures of the posterior tibial margin: Their role in the prognosis of malleolar fractures. J Trauma 29:1565, 1989.

118. Javors, J.R.; Violet, J.T. Correction of chronic lateral ligament instability of the ankle by use of the Brostrom procedure. A report of 15 cases. Clin Orthop 198:201, 1985.

119. Johnson, D.P.; Hill, J. Fracture-dislocation of the ankle with rupture of the deltoid ligament. Injury 19:59, 1988.

120. Joy, G.; Patzakis, M.J.; Harvey, J.P. Precise evaluation of the reduction of severe ankle fractures. J Bone Joint Surg Am 56:979, 1974.

121. Karlson, J.; Bergsten, T.; Lansinger, O.; Peterson, L. Reconstruction of the lateral ligaments of the ankle for chronic lateral instability. J Bone Joint Surg Am 70:581, 1988.

122. Katznelson, A.; Lin, E.; Militiano, J. Ruptures of the ligaments about the tibiofibular syndesmosis. Injury 15:170, 1983.

123. Kay, D.B. The sprained ankle: Current therapy. Foot Ankle 6:22, 1985.

124. Kaye, R.A. Stabilization of ankle syndesmosis injuries with a syndesmosis screw. Foot Ankle 9:290, 1989.

125. Keene, J.S.; Lange, R.H. Diagnostic dilemmas in foot and ankle injuries. JAMA 256:247, 1986.

126. Kelbel, M.; Jardon, O.M. Rupture of tibialis posterior tendon in a closed ankle fracture. J Trauma 22:1026, 1982.

127. Kelikian, H.; Kelikian, A.S. Disorders of the Ankle. Philadelphia, W.B. Saunders, 1985.

128. Kellam, J.F.; Hunter, G.A.; McElwain, J.P. Review of the operative treatment of Achilles tendon rupture. Clin Orthop 201:80, 1985.

129. Kelly, P.J.; Peterson, F.P. Compound dislocations of the ankle without fractures. Am J Surg 103:170, 1986.

130. Kerr, H.D. Posterior tibial tendon rupture. Ann Emerg Med 17:649, 1988.

131. Konradsen, L.; Sommer, H. Ankle instability caused by peroneal tendon rupture. A case report. Acta Orthop Scand 60:723, 1989.

132. Konrath, G.; Karges, D.; Watson, J.T.; et al. Early versus delayed treatment of severe ankle fractures: A comparison of results. J Orthop Trauma 9:377, 1995.

133. Korkala, O.; Rusanen, M.; Jokipii, P.; et al. A prospective study of the treatment of severe tears of the lateral ligament of the ankle. Int Orthop 11:13, 1987.

134. Kristensen, K.D.; Hansen, T. Closed treatment of ankle fractures. Stage II supination-eversion fractures followed for 20 years. Acta Orthop Scand 56:107, 1985.

135. Kristiansen, B. Results of surgical treatment of malleolar fractures in patients with diabetes mellitus. Dan Med Bull 30:272, 1983.

136. Kym, M.R.; Worsing, R.A., Jr. Compartment syndrome in the foot after an inversion injury to the ankle. A case report. J Bone Joint Surg Am 72:138, 1990.

137. Lange, R.H.; Back, A.W.; Hansen, S.T., Jr.; Johansen, K.H. Open tibial fracture with associated vascular injuries. Prognosis for limb salvage. J Trauma 25:203, 1985.

138. Larsen, E. Experimental instability of the ankle. A radiographic investigation. Clin Orthop 204:193, 1986.

139. Larsen, E.; Flink-Olsen, M.; Seerup, K. Surgery for recurrent dislocation of the peroneal tendons. Acta Orthop Scand 55:554, 1984.

140. Lassiter, T.E., Jr.; Malone, T.R.; Garrett, W.E., Jr. Injury to the lateral ligaments of the ankle. Orthop Clin North Am 20:629, 1989.

141. Lauge-Hansen, N. Fractures of the ankle. Analytic historic survey as basis of new experimental roentgenologic and clinical investigations. Arch Surg 56:259, 1948.

142. Lauge-Hansen, N. Fractures of the ankle. II. Combined experimental-surgical and experimental-roentgenologic investigation. Arch Surg 60:957, 1950.

143. Lea, R.B.; Smith, L. Non-surgical treatment of tendo Achilles rupture. J Bone Joint Surg Am 54:1398, 1972.

144. Leddy, J.J.; Smolinski, R.J.; Lawrence, J.; et al. Prospective evaluation of the Ottawa Ankle Rules in a university sports medicine center: With a modification to increase specificity for identifying malleolar fracture. Am J Sports Med 26:158, 1998.

145. Leeds, H.C.; Ehrlich, M.G. Instability of the distal tibiofibular syndesmosis after bimalleolar and trimalleolar ankle fractures. J Bone Joint Surg Am 66:490, 1984.

146. Lehto, M.; Tunturi, T. Improvement 2–9 years after ankle fracture. Acta Orthop Scand 61:80, 1990.

147. LeMelle, D.P.; Janis, L.R. Longitudinal rupture of the peroneus brevis tendon: A study of eight cases. J Foot Surg 28:132, 1989.

148. Limbird, R.S.; Aaron, R.K. Laterally comminuted fracture dislocation of the ankle. J Bone Joint Surg Am 69:881, 1987.

149. Lindsjö, U. Classification of ankle fractures: The Lauge-Hansen or AO system? Clin Orthop 199:12, 1985.

150. Lindsjö, U. Operative treatment of ankle fracture-dislocations: A follow-up study of 306/321 consecutive cases. Clin Orthop 199:28, 1985.

151. Lindsjö, U.; Danckwardt-Lillieström, G.; Sahlstedt, B. Measurement of the motion range in the loaded ankle. Clin Orthop 199:68, 1985.

152. Litchfield, J.C. The treatment of unstable fractures of the ankle in the elderly. Injury 18:128, 1987.

153. Lundeen, R.O. Arthroscopic evaluation of traumatic injuries to the ankle and foot. Part II: Chronic posttraumatic pain. J Foot Surg 29:59, 1990.

154. Lundeen, R.O. Medial impingement lesions of the tibial plafond. J Foot Surg 26:37, 1987.

155. Macko, V.M.; Matthews, L.S.; Zwerkoski, P.; Goldstein, S.A. The joint contact area of the ankle. The contribution of the posterior malleolus. J Bone Joint Surg Am 73:347, 1991.

156. Magid, D.; Michelson, J.D.; Ney, D.R.; Fishman, E.K. Adult ankle fractures: Comparison of plain films and interactive two- and three-dimensional CT scans. AJR 154:1017, 1990.

157. Mak, K.H.; Chan, K.M.; Leung, P.C. Ankle fracture treated with the AO principle—An experience with 116 cases. Injury 16:265, 1985.

158. Manderson, E.L. The uncommon sprain. Ligamentous diastasis of the ankle without fracture or bony deformity. Orthop Rev 15:664, 1986.

159. Mann, R.A. Biomechanics of the foot and ankle. In: Mann, R.A. Surgery of the Foot and Ankle, 5th ed. St. Louis, C.V. Mosby, 1986, p. 3.

160. Mann, R.A.; Thompson, F.M. Rupture of the posterior tibial tendon causing flat foot. Surgical treatment. J Bone Joint Surg Am 67:556, 1985.

161. Markolf, K.L.; Schmalzried, T.P.; Ferkel, R.D. Torsional strength of the ankle in vitro. The supination-external-rotation injury. Clin Orthop 246:266, 1989.

162. Martens, M.A.; Noyez, J.F.; Mulier, J.C. Recurrent dislocation of the peroneal tendons. Results of rerouting the tendons under the calcaneofibular ligament. Am J Sports Med 14:148, 1986.

163. Marti, R.K.; Raaymakers, E.L.F.B.; Nolte, P.A. Malunited ankle fractures. The late results of reconstruction. J Bone Joint Surg Br 72:709, 1990.

164. Martin, D.F.; Curl, W.W.; Baker, C.L. Arthroscopic treatment of chronic synovitis of the ankle. Arthroscopy 5:110, 1989.

165. Martin, J.W.; Thompson, G.H. Achilles tendon rupture. Occurrence with a closed ankle fracture. Clin Orthop 210:216, 1986.

166. Marymont, J.V.; Lynch, M.A.; Henning, C.E. Acute ligamentous diastasis of the ankle without fracture. Evaluation by radionuclide imaging. Am J Sports Med 14:407, 1986.

167. Mast, J.W. Reduction techniques in fractures of the distal tibial articular surface. Tech Orthop 2:29, 1987.

168. Mast, J.W.; Jakob, R.; Ganz, R. Planning and Reduction Technique in Fracture Surgery. New York, Springer-Verlag, 1989.

169. Mast, J.W.; Spiege, P.G.; Pappas, J.N. Fractures of the tibial pilon. Clin Orthop 230:68, 1988.

170. Maurice, H.; Watt, I. Technetium-99m hydroxymethylene diphosphonate scanning of acute injuries to the lateral ligaments of the ankle. Br J Radiol 62:31, 1989.

171. Mazur, J.M.; Schwartz, E.; Simon, S.R. Ankle arthrodesis: Long-term follow-up with gait analysis. J Bone Joint Surg Am 61:964, 1979.

172. McDaniel, W.J.; Wilson, F.C. Trimalleolar fractures of the ankle. Clin Orthop 122:37, 1977.

173. McLennan, J.G.; Ungersma, J. Evaluation of the treatment of ankle fractures with the Inyo nail. J Orthop Trauma 2:272, 1988.

174. McLennan, J.G.; Ungersma, J.A. A new approach to the treatment of ankle fractures. The Inyo nail. Clin Orthop 213:125, 1986.

175. McMaster, J.H.; Scranton, P.E. Tibiofibular synostosis. A cause of ankle disability. Clin Orthop 111:172, 1975.

176. Meyer, J.M.; Garcia, J.; Hoffmeyer, P.; Fritschy, D. The subtalar sprain. A roentgenographic study. Clin Orthop 226:169, 1988.

177. Meyer, J.M.; Hoffmeyer, P.; Savoy, X. High resolution computed tomography in the chronically painful ankle sprain. Foot Ankle 8:291, 1988.

178. Meyer, J.M.; Lagier, R. Posttraumatic sinus tarsi syndrome. Acta Orthop Scand 48:121, 1977.

179. Micheli, L.J.; Waters, P.M.; Sanders, D.P. Sliding fibular graft repair for chronic dislocation of the peroneal tendons. Am J Sports Med 17:68, 1989.

180. Mitchell, M.J.; Ho, C.; Howard, B.A.; et al. Diagnostic imaging of trauma to the ankle and foot: I. Fractures about the ankle. J Foot Surg 28:174, 1989.

181. Mitchell, M.J.; Ho, C.; Howard, B.A.; et al. Diagnostic imaging of trauma to the ankle and foot: Part II. J Foot Surg 28:266, 1989.

182. Mittal, R.L.; Jain, N.C. Traumatic dislocation of the tibialis posterior tendon. Int Orthop 12:259, 1988.

183. Molnar, M.E. Rehabilitation of the injured ankle. Clin Sports Med 7:193, 1988.

184. Montague, A.P.; McQuillan, R.F. Clinical assessment of apparently sprained ankle and detection of fracture. Injury 16:545, 1985.

185. Montane, I.; Zych, G.A. An unusual fracture of the talus associated with a bimalleolar ankle fracture. A case report and review of the literature. Clin Orthop 208:278, 1986.

186. Morris, M.; Chandler, R.W. Fractures of the ankle. Tech Orthop 2:10, 1987.

187. Müller, M.E.; Allgöwer, M.; Schneider, R.; Willenegger, H. Manual of Internal Fixation. New York, Springer-Verlag, 1979.

188. Müller, M.E.; Nazarian, S.; Koch, P. Classification AO des Fractures. New York, Springer-Verlag, 1987.

189. Musgrove, D.J.; Frankhauser, R.A. Intraoperative radiographic assessment of ankle fractures. Clin Orthop 351:186, 1998.

190. Nasell, H.; Bergman, B.; Tomkvist, H. Functional outcome and quality of life in patients with type B ankle fractures: A two year follow-up study. J Orthop Trauma 13:363, 1999.

191. Needleman, R.L.; Skrade, D.A.; Stiehl, J.B. Effect of the syndesmotic screw on ankle motion. Foot Ankle 10:17, 1989.

192. Nistor, L. Surgical and nonsurgical treatment of Achilles tendon rupture. J Bone Joint Surg Am 63:394, 1981.

193. Nitz, A.J.; Dobner, J.J.; Kersey, D. Nerve injury and grades II and III ankle sprains. Am J Sports Med 13:177, 1985.

194. Noyez, J.F.; Martens, M.A. Secondary reconstruction of the lateral ligaments of the ankle by the Chrisman-Snook technique. Arch Orthop Trauma Surg 106:52, 1986.

195. Nugent, J.F.; Gale, B.D. Isolated posterior malleolar ankle fractures. J Foot Surg 29:80, 1990.

196. Oden, R.R. Tendon injuries about the ankle resulting from skiing. Clin Orthop 216:63, 1987.

197. O'Leary, C.; Ward, F.J. A unique closed abduction–external rotation ankle fracture. J Trauma 29:119, 1989.

198. Olerud, C. The effect of the syndesmotic screw on the extension capacity of the ankle joint. Arch Orthop Trauma Surg 104:299, 1985.

199. Olerud, C.; Molander, H. Atypical pronation-eversion ankle joint fractures. Arch Orthop Trauma Surg 102:201, 1984.

200. Olerud, C.; Molander, H. Bi- and trimalleolar ankle fractures operated with nonrigid internal fixation. Clin Orthop 206:253, 1986.

201. Ovadia, D.N.; Beals, R.K. Fractures of the tibial plafond. J Bone Joint Surg Am 68:543, 1986.

202. Pankovich, A.M. Fractures of the fibula proximal to the distal tibiofibular syndesmosis. J Bone Joint Surg Am 60:221, 1978.

203. Pankovich, A.M. Maisonneuve fracture of the fibula. J Bone Joint Surg Am 58A:337, 1976.

204. Parfenchuck, T.A.; Frix, J.M.; Bertrand, S.L.; Corpe, R.S. Clinical use of a syndesmosis screw in stage IV pronation–external rotation ankle fractures. Orthop Rev Suppl August:23, 1994.

205. Parisien, J.S. Ankle and subtalar joint arthroscopy. An update. Bull Hosp Jt Dis Orthop Inst 47:262, 1987.

206. Parisien, J.S.; Vangsness, T. Operative arthroscopy of the ankle. Three years' experience. Clin Orthop 199:46, 1985.

207. Paulos, L.E.; Johnson, C.L.; Noyes, F.R. Posterior compartment fractures of the ankle. A commonly missed athletic injury. Am J Sports Med 11:439, 1983.

208. Pettrone, F.A.; Gail, M.; Pee, D.; et al. Quantitative criteria for prediction of results after displaced fracture of the ankle. J Bone Joint Surg Am 65:667, 1983.

209. Phillips, W.A.; Schwartz, H.S.; Keller, C.S.; et al. A prospective, randomized study of the management of severe ankle fractures. J Bone Joint Surg Am 67:67, 1985.

210. Pigman, E.C.; Klug, R.K.; Sanford, S.; Joly, B.T. Evaluation of the Ottawa clinical decision rules for the use of radiography in acute ankle and midfoot injuries in the emergency department: An independent site assessment. Ann Emerg Med 24:41, 1994.

211. Plattner, P.F. Tendon problems of the foot and ankle. The spectrum from peritendinitis to rupture. Postgrad Med 86:155, 167, 1989.

212. Pointer, J. Using an Unna's boot in treating ligamentous ankle injuries. West J Med 139:257, 1983.

213. Poll, R.G.; Duijfjes, F. The treatment of recurrent dislocation of the peroneal tendons. J Bone Joint Surg Br 66:98, 1984.

214. Pozo, J.L.; Jackson, A.M. A rerouting operation for dislocation of peroneal tendons: Operative technique and case report. Foot Ankle 5:42, 1984.

215. Pritsch, M.; Horoshovski, H.; Farine, I. Ankle arthroscopy. Clin Orthop 184:137, 1984.

216. Raasch, W.G.; Larkin, J.J.; Draganich, L.F. Assessment of the posterior malleolus as a restraint to posterior subluxation of the ankle. J Bone Joint Surg Am 74:1201, 1992.

217. Raemy, H.; Jakob, R.P. Functional treatment of fresh fibular ligament injuries using the Aircast ankle brace. Swiss J Sports Med 31:53, 1983.

218. Ramsey, P.; Hamilton, W. Changes in tibiotalar area of contact caused by lateral talar shift. J Bone Joint Surg Am 58:356, 1976.

219. Rasmussen, O. Stability of the ankle joint. Analysis of the function and traumatology of the ankle ligaments. Acta Orthop Scand Suppl 211:1, 1985.

220. Rasmussen, O.; Jensen, I.T.; Hedeboe, J. An analysis of the function of the posterior talofibular ligament. Int Orthop 7:41, 1983.

221. Rasmussen, O.; Kromann-Andersen, C. Experimental ankle injuries. Analysis of the traumatology of the ankle ligaments. Acta Orthop Scand 54:356, 1983.

222. Rasmussen, O.; Kromann-Andersen, C.; Boe, S. Deltoid ligament. Functional analysis of the medial collateral ligamentous apparatus of the ankle joint. Acta Orthop Scand 54:36, 1983.

223. Riegels-Nielsen, P.; Christensen, J.; Greiff, J. The stability of the tibiofibular syndesmosis following rigid internal fixation for type C malleolar fractures: An experimental and clinical study. Injury 14:357, 1983.

224. Riegler, H.F. Reconstruction for lateral instability of the ankle. J Bone Joint Surg Am 66:336, 1984.

225. Rijke, A.M.; Jones, B.; Vierhout, P.A. Stress examination of traumatized lateral ligaments of the ankle. Clin Orthop 210:143, 1986.

226. Roberts, R.S. Surgical treatment of displaced ankle fractures. Clin Orthop 172:164, 1983.

227. Robertson, D.B., Daniel, D.M.; Biden, E. Soft tissue fixation to bone. Am J Sports Med 14:398, 1986.

228. Rosenberg, Z.S.; Cheung, Y.; Jahss, M.H.; et al. Rupture of posterior tibial tendon: CT and MR imaging with surgical correlation. Radiology 169:229, 1988.

229. Rosenberg, Z.S.; Feldman, F.; Singson, R.D. Peroneal tendon injuries: CT analysis. Radiology 161:743, 1986.

230. Rosenberg, Z.S.; Feldman, F.; Singson, R.D.; Kane, R. Ankle tendons: Evaluation with CT. Radiology 166:221, 1988.

231. Rosenberg, Z.S.; Jahss, M.H.; Noto, A.M.; et al. Rupture of the posterior tibial tendon: CT and surgical findings. Radiology 167:489, 1988.

232. Ross, S.D.; Matta, J. Internal compression arthrodesis of the ankle. Clin Orthop 199:54, 1985.

233. Rubin, G.; Witten, M. The talar tilt angle and fibular collateral ligaments. J Bone Joint Surg Am 42:311, 1960.

234. Rüedi, T.P.; Allgöwer, M. The operative treatment of intra-articular fractures of the lower end of the tibia. Clin Orthop 138:105, 1979.

235. Ryan, J.B.; Hopkinson, W.J.; Wheeler, J.H.; et al. Office management of the acute ankle sprain. Clin Sports Med 8:477, 1989.

236. Salmon, N. Arteries of the Skin. New York, Churchill Livingstone, 1988, pp. 62, 151.

237. Sammarco, G.J.; DiRaimondo, C.V. Surgical treatment of lateral ankle instability syndrome. Am J Sports Med 16:501, 1988.

238. Sarrafian, S.K. Anatomy of the Foot and Ankle. Philadelphia, J.B. Lippincott, 1983.

239. Sartoris, D.J.; Resnick, D. Magnetic resonance imaging of tendons in the foot and ankle. J Foot Surg 28:370, 1989.

240. Schaap, G.R.; de Keizer, G.; Marti, K. Inversion trauma of the ankle. Arch Orthop Trauma Surg 108:273, 1989.

241. Schaffer, J.J.; Lock, T.R.; Salciccioli, G.G. Posterior tibial tendon rupture in pronation–external rotation ankle fractures. J Trauma 27:795, 1987.

242. Schaffer, J.J.; Manoli, A., II. The antiglide plate for distal fibular fixation. A biomechanical comparison with a lateral plate. J Bone Joint Surg Am 69:596, 1987.

243. Schatzker, J.; Johnson, R.G. Fracture-dislocation of the ankle with anterior dislocation of the fibula. J Trauma 23:420, 1983.

244. Scheidt, K.B.; Stiehl, J.B.; Skrade, D.A.; Barnhardt, T. Posterior malleolar ankle fractures: An in vitro biomechanical analysis of stability in the loaded and unloaded states. J Orthop Trauma 6:96, 1992.

245. Scheller, A.D.; Kasser, J.R.; Quigley, T.B. Tendon injuries about the ankle. Clin Sports Med 2:631, 1983.

246. Seddon, H.J. Surgical Disorders of Peripheral Nerves, 2nd ed. London, Churchill Livingstone, 1975.

247. Sedel, L. The surgical management of nerve lesions in the lower limbs. Clinical evaluation, surgical technique and results. Int Orthop 9:159, 1985.

248. Segal, D. Introduction. In: Yablon, I.G.; Segal, D.; Leach, R.E., eds. Ankle Injuries. New York, Churchill Livingstone, 1983, p. 21.

249. Segal, D.; Wiss, D.A.; Whitelaw, G.P. Functional bracing and rehabilitation of ankle fractures. Clin Orthop 199:39, 1985.

250. Segal, D.; Yablon, I.G. Bimalleolar fractures. In: Yablon, I.G.; Segal, D.; Leach, R.E., eds. Ankle Injuries. New York, Churchill Livingstone, 1983, p. 31.

251. Shelton, M.L.; Anderson, R.L., Jr. Complications of fractures and dislocations of the ankle. In: Epps, C.H., Jr., ed. Complications in Orthopaedic Surgery, 2nd ed., Vol. 1. Philadelphia, J.B. Lippincott, 1986, p. 599.

252. Sherman, R.; Wellisz, T.; Wiss, D.; et al. Coverage of type III open ankle and foot fractures with the temporoparietal fascial free flap. Orthop Trans 14:265, 1990.

253. Skie, M.; Woldenberg, L.; Ebraheim, N.; Jackson, W.T. Assessment of collicular fractures of the medial malleolus. Foot Ankle 10:118, 1989.

254. Slatis, P.; Santavirta, S.; Sandelin, J. Surgical treatment of chronic dislocation of the peroneal tendons. Br J Sports Med 22:16, 1988.

255. Smith, R.W.; Reischl, S. The influence of dorsiflexion in the treatment of severe ankle sprains: An anatomical study. Foot Ankle 9:28, 1988.

256. Snook, G.A.; Chrisman, O.D.; Wilson, T.C. Long-term results of the Chrisman-Snook operation for reconstruction of the lateral ligaments of the ankle. J Bone Joint Surg Am 67:1, 1985.

257. Soballe, K.; Kjaersgaard-Anderson, P. Ruptured tibialis posterior tendon in a closed ankle fracture. Clin Orthop 231:140, 1988.

258. Soboroff, S.H.; Pappius, E.M.; Komaroff, A.L. Benefits, risks, and costs of alternative approaches to the evaluation and treatment of severe ankle sprain. Clin Orthop 183:160, 1984.

259. Solari, J.; Benjamin, J.; Wilson, J.; et al. Ankle mortise stability in Weber C fractures: Indications for syndesmotic fixation. J Orthop Trauma 5:1990, 1991.

260. Soler, R.R.; Gallart Castany, F.J.; Riba Ferret, J.; et al. Traumatic dislocation of the tibialis posterior tendon at the ankle level. J Trauma 26:1049, 1986.

261. Solomon, M.A.; Gilula, L.A.; Oloff, L.M.; Oloff, J. CT scanning of the foot and ankle: 2. Clinical applications and review of the literature. AJR 146:1204, 1986.

262. Sommer, H.M.; Arza, D. Functional treatment of recent ruptures of the fibular ligament of the ankle. Int Orthop 13:157, 1989.

263. Sondenaa, K.; Hoogaard, U.; Smith, D.; et al. Immobilization of operated ankle fractures. Acta Orthop Scand 57:59, 1986.

264. Stanish, W.D.; Vincent, N. Recurrent dislocation of the tibialis posterior tendon—A case report with a new surgical approach. Can J Appl Sport Sci 9:220, 1984.

265. Stein, R.E. Reconstruction of the superior peroneal retinaculum using a portion of the peroneus brevis tendon. A case report. J Bone Joint Surg Am 69:298, 1987.

266. Stein, R.E. Rupture of the posterior tibial tendon in closed ankle fractures. Possible prognostic value of a medial bone flake: Report of two cases. J Bone Joint Surg Am 67:493, 1985.

267. Stiehl, J.B. Ankle fractures with diastasis. Instr Course Lect 39:95, 1990.

268. Stiehl, J.B. Concomitant rupture of the peroneus brevis tendon and bimalleolar fracture. A case report. J Bone Joint Surg Am 70:936, 1988.

269. Stiehl, J.B. Open fractures of the ankle joint. Instr Course Lect 39:113, 1990.

270. Stiehl, J.B.; Dollinger, B. Primary ankle arthrodesis in trauma: Report of three cases. J Orthop Trauma 2:277, 1988.

271. Stiell, I.G.; Greenberg, G.H.; McKnight, R.D.; et al. Decision rules for the use of radiography in acute ankle injuries. Refinement and prospective validation. JAMA 269:1127, 1993.

272. Szczukowski, M., Jr.; St. Pierre, R.K.; Fleming, L.L.; Somogyi, J. Computerized tomography in the evaluation of peroneal tendon dislocation. A report of two cases. Am J Sports Med 11:444, 1983.

273. Teeny, S.; Wiss, D.A.; Hathaway, R.; Sarmiento, A. Tibial plafond fractures: Errors, complications, and pitfalls in operative treatment. Orthop Trans 14:265, 1990.

274. Thompson, F.M.; Patterson, A.H. Rupture of the peroneus longus tendon. Report of three cases. J Bone Joint Surg Am 71:293, 1989.

275. Tile, M. Fractures of the distal tibial metaphysis involving the ankle joint: The pilon fracture. In: Schatzker, J.; Tile, M., eds. The Rationale of Operative Fracture Care. New York, Springer-Verlag, 1987, p. 343.

276. Tile, M. Fractures of the ankle. In: Schatzker, J.; Tile, M., eds. The Rationale of Operative Fracture Care. New York, Springer-Verlag, 1987, p. 371.

277. Tonino, P.; Shields, C.L.; Chandler, R.W. Rupture of the Achilles tendon. Tech Orthop 2:6, 1987.

278. Toohey, J.S.; Worsing, R.A., Jr. A long-term follow-up study of tibiotalar dislocations without associated fractures. Clin Orthop 239:207, 1989.

279. Trager, S.; Frederick, L.D.; Seligson, D. Ankle arthroscopy: A method of distraction. Orthopedics 12:1317, 1989.

280. Tropp, H.; Odenrick, P.; Gillquist, J. Stabilometry recordings in functional and mechanical instability of the ankle joint. Int J Sports Med 6:180, 1985.

281. Tscherne, H.; Gotzen, L. Fractures with Soft Tissue Injuries. Berlin, Springer-Verlag, 1984.

282. Van den Hoogenband, C.R.; van Moppes, F.I.; Stapert, J.W.; Greep, J.M. Clinical diagnosis, arthrography, stress examination and surgical findings after inversion trauma of the ankle. Arch Orthop Trauma Surg 103:115, 1984.

283. Van der Rijt, A.J.; Evans, G.A. The long-term results of Watson-Jones tenodesis. J Bone Joint Surg Br 66:371, 1984.

284. Veldhuizen, J.W.; van Thiel, T.P.; Oostvogel, H.J.; Stapert, J.W. Early functional treatment of supination-eversion stage-II ankle fractures: Preliminary results. Neth J Surg 40:155, 1988.

285. Vrahas, M.; Veenis, B.; Nudert, S.; et al. Intra-articular contact stress with simulated ankle malunions. Orthop Trans 14:265, 1990.

286. Ward, A.J.; Ackroyd, C.E.; Baker, A.S. Late lengthening of the fibula for malaligned ankle fractures. J Bone Joint Surg Br 72:714, 1990.

287. Weber, B.G. Die Verletzungen des Oberen Sprunggelenkes. Bern, Hans Huber, 1966.

288. Weber, B.G.; Simpson, L.A. Corrective lengthening osteotomy of the fibula. Clin Orthop 199:61, 1985.

289. Whitelaw, G.P.; Sawka, M.W.; Wetzler, M.; et al. Unrecognized injuries of the lateral ligaments associated with lateral malleolar fractures of the ankle. J Bone Joint Surg Am 71:1396, 1989.

290. Williams, J.G. Plication of the anterolateral capsule of the ankle with extensor digitorum brevis transfer for chronic lateral ligament instability. Injury 19:65, 1988.

291. Wilson, F.C. The pathogenesis and treatment of ankle fractures: Classification. Instr Course Lect 39:79, 1990.

292. Wilson, F.C. The pathogenesis and treatment of ankle fractures, historical studies. Instr Course Lect 39:73, 1990.

293. Wilson, F.C. Fractures and dislocations of the ankle. In: Rockwood, C.A., Jr.; Green, D.P., eds. Fractures in Adults, 2nd ed. Philadelphia, J.B. Lippincott, 1984.

294. Wiss, D.A.; Gilbert, P.; Merritt, P.O.; Sarmiento, A. Immediate internal fixation of open ankle fractures. J Orthop Trauma 2:265, 1988.

295. Yablon, I.G. Complications and their management. In: Yablon, G.; Segal, D.; Leach, R.E., eds. Ankle Injuries. New York, Churchill Livingstone, 1983, p. 103.

296. Yablon, I.G. Treatment of ankle malunion. Instr Course Lect 33:118, 1984.

297. Yablon, I.G.; Keller, F.G.; Shouse, L. The key role of the lateral malleolus in displaced fractures of the ankle. J Bone Joint Surg Am 59:169, 1977.

298. Yablon, I.G.; Leach, R.E. Reconstruction of malunited fractures of the lateral malleolus. J Bone Joint Surg Am 71:521, 1989.

299. Yablon, I.G.; Segal, D.; Leach, R.E. Ankle Injuries. New York, Churchill Livingstone, 1983.

300. Zeegers, A.V.; van der Werken, C. Rupture of the deltoid ligament in ankle fractures: Should it be repaired? Injury 20:39, 1989.

301. Zeiss, J.; Saddemi, S.R.; Ebraheim, N.A. MR imaging of the peroneal tunnel. J Comput Assist Tomogr 13:840, 1989.

302. Zell, B.K.; Shereff, M.J.; Greenspan, A.; Liebowitz, S. Combined ankle and subtalar instability. Bull Hosp Jt Dis Orthop Inst 46:37, 1986.

303. Zenker, H.; Nerlich, M. Prognostic aspects in operated ankle fractures. Arch Orthop Trauma Surg 100:237, 1982.

# CHAPTER 60

## Foot Injuries

Christopher W. DiGiovanni, M.D.
Stephen K. Benirschke, M.D.
Sigvard T. Hansen, Jr., M.D.

*Man's foot is all his own. It is unlike any other foot. It is the most distinctly human part of his whole anatomical makeup. It is a human specialization and, whether he be proud of it or not, it is his hallmark and so long as Man has been Man and so long as he remains Man, it is by his feet that he will be known from all other members of the animal kingdom.*
—*Frederick Wood Jones, 18th century British anatomist*

The foot, an amazingly complicated adaptation that has taken 30 million years to produce in humans, demands maintenance of its evolved anatomic relationships for normal gait and function. It remains incredibly underappreciated by both the medical and the nonmedical communities. No other structure in our body relies on the interdependence of 28 bones and 31 articulations to support daily biomechanical loads of up to three to seven times body weight. Any injury to the foot that alters these bones, joints, soft tissues, or their relationships to one another can have a devastating impact on the ability to use the entire lower extremity, regardless of the status of the ipsilateral hip, knee, or surrounding structures.

Foot injuries requiring orthopaedic attention have been rising almost exponentially in recent years according to recent U.S. crash statistics.[35] This increase is partly due to our improved ability to protect vital structures and improve survival through better restraints and the advent of airbag support, which saves lives during motor vehicle crashes. These data suggest, however, that we are still not effectively protecting the lower extremity in such collisions, especially the foot and ankle. Therefore, the distal end of the tibia and the foot absorb the brunt of the impact. In a recent retrospective study of 1107 consecutive trauma center admissions with motor vehicle accident–related orthopaedic injuries, 164 patients (15%) had 253 foot and ankle injuries. The report identified that when these patients sustained a foot and ankle injury, they were often more severely injured than those without trauma to this region (Injury Severity Score of 17.9 versus 11.6, $P < .001$).[355] Furthermore, recent statistics highlight the fact that the foot is more vulnerable than any other part of the body in an industrial injury.[109] It remains widely recognized that most long-term post-traumatic disabilities in the lower extremity result from fractures in the foot and ankle, and because most of these blunt trauma victims are also quite young, research and training in care of the injured foot have become paramount. Forefoot injuries frequently account for the long-term disability and pain suffered by multitrauma patients.[342] In fact, foot and ankle trauma seems to result in a higher functional loss and a greater negative psychosocioeconomic impact on quality of life than any other orthopaedic injury does, including injury to all four extremities and the pelvis. Some evidence suggests that multiply injured patients with foot involvement have lower physical, emotional, and social scores and higher body pain scores than do similar patients devoid of traumatic foot problems.[337, 342]

Advances in fracture treatment related to open reduction and internal fixation (ORIF) have demonstrated that function in the lower extremities can be markedly improved when normal anatomy is restored and prolonged casting is avoided.[283] These principles also apply to the foot, where excellent functional results have been realized with ORIF. Because it is impossible for the lower extremity to function normally without a sound foot, the increased interest in optimal stabilization and rapid mobilization of foot injuries is most welcome. This chapter provides an update on the operative and nonoperative management of the injured foot. Emphasis is placed on internal fixation techniques, instrumentation, avoidance of pitfalls during surgery, and overall perioperative care of a traumatized foot. The importance of effective management after foot trauma on restoration of function and prevention of fracture disease cannot be overemphasized. The fact remains that foot complaints, many of which are post-traumatic in nature, are a leading cause of patient visits to an orthopaedic surgeon's office today.

Readers seeking information about relevant anatomy, biomechanics, or history or a review of treatment of foot fractures are referred to excellent overviews by authors such as Heckman,[128] Sangeorzan,[285] and Myerson.[225] Inman and colleagues,[145] Mann and Coughlin,[194] and others have outlined the complex biomechanics of the foot, which relies on normal motion, alignment, and stability. DeLee[64] has contributed a monumental historical work on the treatment of fractures, dislocations, and other foot injuries in Mann and Coughlin's text.[194] From a historical standpoint, one of the most pertinent studies of foot function was published by the anatomist Dudley Morton in 1935.[218] Although much of his work has been neglected or falsely discredited, his studies on the anthropology of the most advanced human musculoskeletal structure, the foot, provide a comprehensive overview of the specifics of foot structure and function that are important to consider when planning a reconstruction or ORIF. The anatomy of the foot is actually complex and often understudied by orthopaedic residents during training. It is advisable to have a skeletal foot model available for evaluation both before and during surgery to aid in understanding the proximity and three-dimensional relationships of these many structures when considering internal fixation or surgical exposure. We encourage our residents to use these simple models because they seem to cut down on the operative time required for safe exposure, proper hardware placement, and efficient C-arm use.

Adaptation of internal fixation techniques to fractures in the foot is consistent with the fundamental principles of fracture treatment described by the AO/ASIF in the *Manual of Internal Fixation*.[219] Four goals of internal fixation are identified by the AO group: (1) anatomic reduction of the fracture, (2) preservation of the blood supply during surgery, (3) application of stable internal fixation that addresses the biomechanical demands of the affected region, and (4) mobilization of the injured limb as soon after injury as possible. The last point is particularly salient to the foot because it spends its entire "life" supporting a tremendous amount of weight in comparison to its size and thus seems to function even more poorly than other parts of the musculoskeletal system if this environment is altered for prolonged periods. By virtue of its location, function, distribution of stress per unit area, and articular interdependence, the foot cannot tolerate some of the smaller discrepancies in alignment or instability that can easily be withstood in many of the more proximal lower or upper extremity regions. Consider the fact that, for example, the metatarsal heads are normally in contact with the ground up to 80% of the time during the stance phase of normal gait. Thus, although 5° of extra-articular malalignment might be well tolerated in many other parts of the body, this same amount of sagittal or even coronal incongruity in the metatarsal heads, calcaneus, or talus after foot injury can translate to significant disability in active individuals on their feet much of the day.[43, 115]

Not all fractures require internal fixation to heal with satisfactory functional results. For example, treatment of diaphyseal tibia and humerus fractures by cast immobilization frequently results in satisfactory healing. Intra-articular fractures, on the other hand, require anatomic reduction of the joint surfaces and repair of surrounding torn ligaments, tendons, and joint capsules if full functional recovery is to be expected. Precise anatomic restoration to maintain the postural axis described by Morton and repair of surrounding tissues cannot be achieved without ORIF. The trend in fracture care of an injured foot has recently evolved toward use of smaller and more low-profile devices; they not only have been found to provide adequate fixation but have also been less symptomatic than their larger predecessors. Their support of periarticular surfaces has been acceptable and has resulted in negligible subsidence over time.

Full range of motion is required for normal function in some joints in the foot, but no correlation between movement and normal function has been found in others. In general, joint motion may be sacrificed in the flat joints of the midfoot without risk of functional impairment. Loss of motion in the intertarsal and tarsometatarsal (TMT) joints, which are predominantly flat joints, has little effect on the overall function of the foot. In marked contrast to the fingers, loss of motion in the interphalangeal (IP) joint of the great toe and the proximal and distal IP joints of the lesser toes has very few consequences unless the toes are significantly deformed or cannot contact the ground. Injuries to these joints do not require precise open reduction.

Two fundamental considerations should be kept in mind when choosing the appropriate treatment of a foot fracture: motion is essential in some joints but not in others, and early motion with at least some weight bearing is necessary for return of normal motion. These principles are particularly important in navicular fractures and TMT and subtalar fracture-dislocations. Many of the bones and joints in the foot are closely interrelated, and some joints must have nearly full range of motion for the rest to function normally. ORIF is indicated in articular injuries and in areas that indirectly affect articular congruity. The hindfoot joints, for example, must retain normal motion to evert and unlock and thereby provide a cushioned heel-strike, but they must later be able to act as a rigid platform during inversion to shift weight smoothly to the forefoot during the late stance phase and push-off. The midfoot, on the other hand, is required to remain stiff at all times to provide a fairly rigid and immobile arch through which weight can be effectively transferred from posterior to anterior and under which the neurovascular bundle can be protected from impact during stance. The forefoot acts as the platform on which we generate formal locomotion, and it must contact the ground evenly to allow a normal distribution of weight. During normal barefoot gait, the forefoot actually encounters three times as much load distribution as the hindfoot.[115] This load increases further in the event of a gastrocnemius contracture, which can occur as a purely atavistic trait and not necessarily as a result of any traumatic event or pathologic process in the lower extremity[71, 218] (Fig. 60–1).

The "essential" joints in the foot that require normal or near-normal motion for proper foot function because their motion is obligatorily coupled to that of the other surrounding joints are the ankle (fibulotalar and tibiotalar), subtalar, talonavicular, and lesser metatarsophalangeal

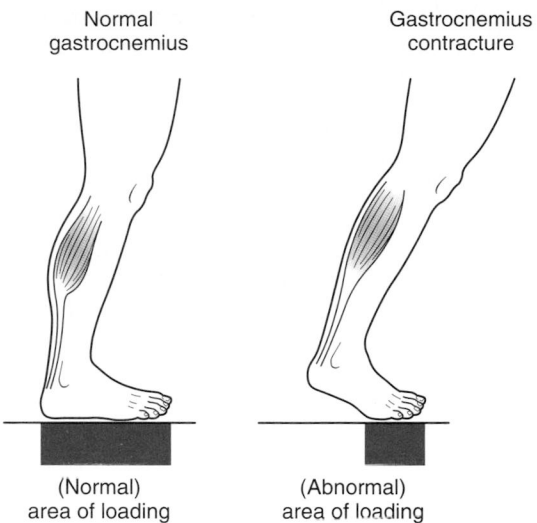

Normal
gastrocnemius

Gastrocnemius
contracture

(Normal)
area of loading

(Abnormal)
area of loading

**FIGURE 60–1.** Patients who exhibit evidence of gastrocnemius contracture on initial evaluation may have an increased risk for failure of fixation or nonunion in reconstructed midfoot and forefoot fractures or for instability patterns because of undue stress on the foot during gait in their recovery period. A tight gastrocnemius muscle transfers greater stress to the midfoot and forefoot during the stance phase of ambulation, as depicted here in the normal versus abnormal (i.e., tight gastrocnemius) situation. Such tightness may have an impact on the outcome of injury fixation in this region, and affected patients should be considered for concomitant gastrocnemius release.

(MTP) joints. The small translational ability of the flat calcaneocuboid and the cuboid–fourth/fifth metatarsal articulations is also important for optimal foot function.[242] However, uninhibited motion of the calcaneocuboid joint is not needed for significant inversion and eversion of the hindfoot through the talocalcaneal and talonavicular joints. In fact, incongruity or post-traumatic arthritis of the calcaneocuboid joint is relatively well tolerated in most individuals, as opposed to other joints in the foot. Astion and associates[10] found by cadaveric study that simulated fusion of the talonavicular joint eliminated all but 2% of motion in the hindfoot joint complex whereas subtalar fusion resulted in a 74% decrease in talonavicular and a 44% decrease in calcaneocuboid motion. Fusion of the calcaneocuboid joint, on the other hand, resulted in only minor impairment of motion (33%) in the talonavicular joint and almost no change in subtalar joint motion.[10] The remainder of the joints in the foot can be sacrificed or fused with little effect on overall function. For example, fusion of the first MTP joint in an optimal position is compatible with near-normal function of the forefoot.

When fixing fractures or joint incongruity of the midfoot or forefoot in particular, attention should also be directed toward identification of concomitant gastrocnemius contracture. Gastrocnemius equinus is actually common in non-neurologically impaired adults and, if left untreated in a trauma patient, might lead to a compromised long-term outcome by virtue of its potentially detrimental effect on midfoot and forefoot function, as suggested in a recent study by DiGiovanni and colleagues.[71] When identified in a trauma patient who is considered at risk because of a midfoot or forefoot injury that is either potentially unstable or anticipated to require

a prolonged period of healing, gastrocnemius contracture should be released concomitantly during treatment of the foot injuries. This procedure, called a gastrocnemius slide, is fast, safe, simple, and very effective in decreasing load across the front of the foot during gait (Fig. 60–2), and it is especially important in trauma patients who have been bedridden or off their feet (in or out of the hospital) for a prolonged period before discovery of a significant foot injury. Because foot injuries often initially take a back seat to more severe life-threatening injuries or are subtle in nature and not noticed on admission of a multiply injured patient, this scenario is not uncommon. Such a period of time in an unsplinted state predisposes patients to the development of gastrocnemius or Achilles contracture if they did not have preexistent gastrocnemius tightness, and it can be devastating for normal gait or foot recovery if not promptly addressed.

Because the foot is in a dependent position, it is prone to impaired circulation with inadequate venous and lymphatic return and, consequently, fracture disease. These conditions may lead to the gradual development of secondary complications such as joint stiffness, disuse osteoporosis, and muscle atrophy. Early motion and protected weight bearing, even if allowed in only just a portion of the foot during the healing phase, may mitigate these conditions. The foot is also prone to significant swelling immediately after a major operation and must be elevated slightly for 36 to 72 hours after surgery. This

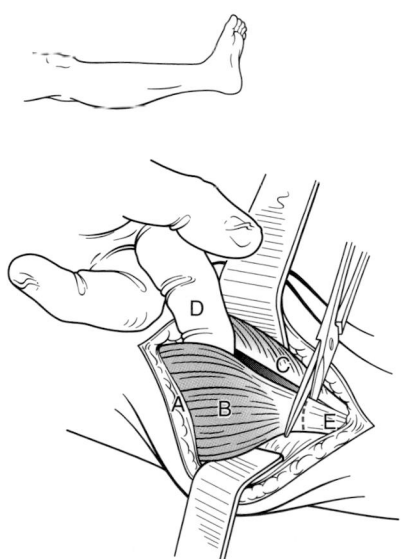

**FIGURE 60–2.** Gastrocnemius release (the "gastrocnemius slide" procedure) can be quickly and easily performed during the course of any foot procedure with the patient either supine or prone. This figure depicts the standard location of the 1- to 2-inch posteromedial incision located at the gastrocnemius-soleus musculotendinous interval. This incision placement minimizes postoperative scarring around the sural nerve. It is deepened through the superficial posterior compartment musculature, and the interval between the gastrocnemius (B) and soleus (C) is identified anteriorly, along with the interval between the gastrocnemius muscle (B) and its tendinous attachment (E) distally. This interval is most easily identified with the surgeon's finger in a sweeping motion from proximal to distal (D). The sural nerve (A) is protected posteriorly while the release is made.

phase of recovery is called *bed exercise* rather than bedrest because patients are encouraged to perform gentle isometric foot exercises of the plantar intrinsic musculature as soon as tolerable to prevent the development of edema. These muscles surround the large venous plexus located in the plantar compartments of the foot, and their activity can effectively improve venous outflow and decrease swelling. The amount of elevation must be monitored carefully; slight elevation is beneficial, but more is not better. Ideally, the foot is elevated 6 to 12 inches above the bed or just above the level of the patient's heart when lying in bed. Greater elevation does not further decrease venous pressure but instead decreases arterial pressure. The cause of a compartment syndrome is commonly believed to be high intracompartmental pressure; however, it is in fact caused by a decreased differential between arterial and tissue pressure. Lack of arterial circulation in tissues is the pathogenic factor in necrosis. Elevation of the leg does not affect tissue pressure, but it decreases arterial pressure and may severely decrease arterial flow to the foot. This condition is called *elevation ischemia,* and it frequently occurs in patients who are in shock and in those with normally low blood pressure.[353] Excessive elevation of the foot, possibly combined with extrinsic pressure, can cause ischemia. An early sign that this process has begun is the onset of discomfort when the leg is elevated and relief of the discomfort when it is lowered, the same as for a typical compartment syndrome.

We do not generally use ice as a mainstay of therapy for patients with foot injuries. Although ice is certainly a common adjunct to decrease swelling in a traumatized patient, it is doubtful that it has much of an effect through any padded splint or cast. Furthermore, ice bags can often be heavy and uncomfortable for the patient and are frequently not changed often enough to be of value. Ice is probably much more useful in the absence of the dense external splinting or padding required for soft tissue immobilization in most trauma cases. The point here is that there is no better substitute for settling the soft tissue envelope after foot injury than adequate external immobilization, elevation, pain control, and an appropriate observation period. The presence of skin wrinkles is often the best way to determine that a soft tissue envelope is amenable to surgical intervention. Early experience with foot pumps that can be placed directly around the foot or even within a posterior splint to decrease edema has also been encouraging.[327] Patients seem to tolerate these devices fairly well, and they have been particularly effective in alleviating the swelling associated with hindfoot and midfoot injuries to permit earlier surgical intervention.

Some general radiographic principles in treating foot fractures should be mentioned. For any fracture of the midfoot or hindfoot, a set of three standard plain radiographs should always be obtained: an anteroposterior (AP) view, a lateral view, and a medial oblique view of the entire foot. Calcaneal fractures should also always have an axial heel view (Harris) and a cone-down lateral view of the heel, and fractures or dislocations involving the talus or subtalar joint should always include specialized oblique projections of the foot as described in their respective sections of this chapter, as well as AP and mortise views of the ankle. Any suspected Lisfranc injury should have stress views obtained in both the sagittal and transverse planes. The standard set of three "trauma views" as just described is usually adequate for all forefoot injuries unless the injury is clearly limited to a single toe, in which case a toe series is acceptable. When dealing with pathology of the first MTP joint, consideration should be given to both an internal and an external oblique view, as well as an axial sesamoid view. The last-named is also useful in determining displacement in a multiply injured forefoot. Computed tomography (CT) scans should be obtained for all calcaneus, talus, and midfoot fractures or fracture-dislocations and for any complicated foot trauma that is poorly understood on the radiographs available. Sections 1 to 3 mm in thickness can be taken, depending on what the surgeon is looking for. Axial views are the basic "workhorse" plane for reconstruction and are most indicated for Lisfranc's joints, the calcaneocuboid joint, and the talonavicular axis. Coronal cuts are most useful for imaging the dome of the talus, the ankle mortise, tibiotalar joint loose bodies, and the subtalar joint. Sagittal reconstruction views are best for visualizing talar neck fractures.

The following sections outline the causes of injury, commonly seen complications, and the recommended treatment of various foot fractures, dislocations, or soft tissue injuries. The sections on rehabilitation emphasize the importance of early motion and partial weight bearing throughout the healing phase in joints in which normal motion is essential for foot function.

## INITIAL EVALUATION OF A PATIENT WITH A FOOT INJURY

The foot is probably the most frequently overlooked aspect of a patient's musculoskeletal system on arrival at the emergency department. One of the keys to identification of subtle foot injuries is understanding the mechanism of injury and taking a good history from the patient, if possible, or those responsible for transport. This information serves to elevate the caregiver's index of suspicion, when appropriate, regarding the likelihood and pathogenesis of foot injury. Knowledge of the magnitude, duration, mechanism, and location of trauma is imperative to permit efficient and accurate assessment of foot and ankle injury, as well as, of course, other associated injuries. A thorough history of any previous injury or disease that could or has already affected the feet is also helpful, including querying about previous trauma, diabetes, venous stasis disease, deformity, use of assistive devices, and other conditions. If possible, a patient's ability to localize the pain with a single finger is extremely helpful in establishing a correct diagnosis because patients will often be vague in their descriptions if allowed to be and many injuries are frequently misdiagnosed as another, possibly more common pathology in an adjacent area (some less common injuries often diagnosed late include lateral process talus fractures, anterior process calcaneal fractures, subtalar instability, Lisfranc injury, navicular fracture, and compartment syndrome). Both feet and ankles should always be

**FIGURE 60–3.** Fracture blisters around the foot as shown here are a hallmark of severe injury to the soft tissue envelope. They should be considered a major risk factor for infection or wound complications if surgery is performed too quickly in their vicinity before they have had a chance to develop completely in terms of size and severity, as well as to epithelialize. This process can often take up to 7 to 10 days. Note the clear versus the red blistering in this patient. Clear blistering represents more superficial separation of the epidermal layers from the underlying skin with resultant serous fluid formation within. Hemorrhagic blisters, however, are an indication of more severe injury because they occur when the entire epidermal layer has separated from the dermis beneath. Thus, these latter blisters take a longer period to epithelialize. The best way to manage them is still controversial; some surgeons prefer to leave these blisters intact, whereas others prefer unroofing them and coating the underlying layer with silver sulfadiazine (Silvadene), xeroform, or other coating agents.

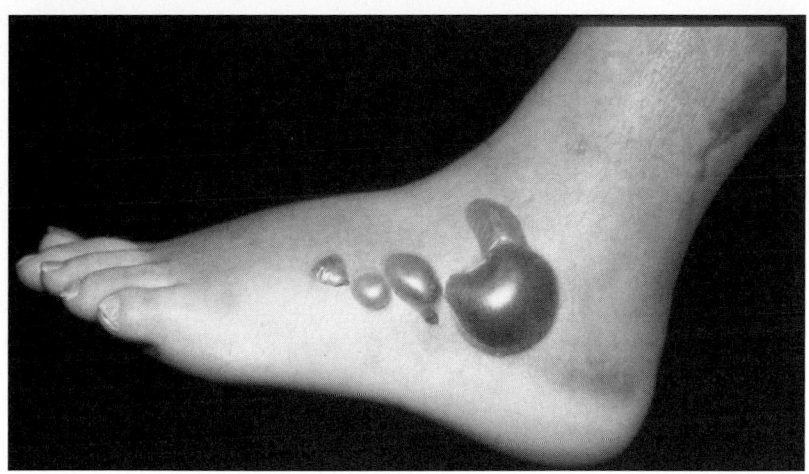

completely exposed and evaluated in the course of examination.

Physical examination of the foot must be meticulous and well documented in the chart. Pain control is important to allow the patient to assist the physician and cooperate with the clinical assessment. The skin is checked for puncture wounds, abrasions, blisters, skin tenting, lacerations, erythema, and swelling (Fig. 60–3). The examination includes checking less obvious places such as the plantar aspect of the feet, the back of the heels, and between the toes. Open wounds should generate a reflexive response to administer first-generation cephalosporins (grade 1 and 2 injury) with the addition of an aminoglycoside (grade 3 injury) or clindamycin (barnyard injury, severe contamination) as wound severity increases, after first verifying any drug allergies. Probing of wounds is not necessary and is best done in a sterile operative environment, except when determining the depth of a plantar puncture wound or deciding whether a wound violates a nearby joint space (in which case, saline should be sterilely instilled into the joint and observed for extravasation). Tetanus prophylaxis should also be administered when necessary. Any open areas should be covered with a sterile povidone-iodine (Betadine)-soaked dressing and wrapped to minimize further contamination. Foot wound cultures in an emergency department setting are unreliable and amount to a useless, unnecessary expense. Any deformity of the foot in comparison to the opposite side should be noted. The neurovascular status of the limb should be documented, including assessment of (1) the integrity and amplitude of the dorsalis pedis and posterior tibialis pulses with performance of an ankle-brachial index and comparison to the opposite side if necessary, (2) capillary refill of the toes, (3) proprioceptive status, (4) sensation of all five nerves with a light touch examination using a paperclip or alternative instrument (and sometimes two-point discrimination if indicated), and (5) motor function of all muscle groups in both the foot and leg. Any irregularity in this portion of the examination should be followed by an immediate similar examination of the more proximal portion of the limb to determine causality and the severity of involvement. Compartments should be

carefully examined and compared with those on the other side. Pain on passive extension (and flexion) of the toes should be checked. *Any* suggestion of pathologic or worsening pain, swelling, numbness and tingling, or coolness in the foot should be followed by prompt reassessment of its neurovascular status and, if suspected, measurement of compartment pressure and comparison with the patient's current pressure. Stability and alignment of the foot and ankle should be checked, after which an appropriate routine radiographic trauma series (three views) of the foot or ankle (or both) should be obtained. This examination should not be impeded by dressings, pants, casting material, or other objects, if possible, if high-quality films can be obtained. Poor films should be immediately discarded and followed by a request for repeat radiographic examination. In busy emergency departments, if one gets in the habit of accepting only quality radiographic views, they will eventually become routine (and vice versa).

Once this evaluation has been completed, the injured extremity is splinted, braced, placed in a cast, or left alone as the injury dictates, and the patient and family are counseled about the severity of the problem, its prognosis, and the various treatment options available. Multiply injured patients and their families should also be told that roughly 10% of occult traumatic injuries can go undetected on initial evaluation (primary survey) and that in the course of hospitalization and recovery (with secondary and tertiary surveys), other injuries may be identified. Interestingly, studies have documented as high as a 30% incidence of delayed identification of foot and ankle injuries in polytrauma patients.

## FRACTURES OF THE TALUS

Of all the bones in the foot, the most important one to stabilize anatomically with internal fixation and to mobilize soon after injury is the talus.[134, 250] It alone provides the link between the foot and the leg and is responsible for transferring all weight from the body to the foot and coupling much of the motion and function from the foot to the body. The surgical approach to a talar fracture, if indicated, is determined by the fracture pattern and the status of the soft tissue envelope. In general, four working approaches to the talus are used: the medial utility approach with or without medial malleolar osteotomy, the anterolateral approach, the posterior approach, and a combined approach. Rarely, a fibular osteotomy or window, as described by Hansen,[120] can be used to access the posterolateral body of the talus. When faced with decisions regarding treatment of a talus fracture, one must always consider the fracture pattern, the soft tissues, the tibiotalar joint, and the talocalcaneal joint. For displaced talar fractures, a strong case can be made in favor of ORIF. When compared with closed treatment, this method results in a lower rate of nonunion, shorter time to union, earlier return to motion, earlier return to weight bearing, precise reduction of articular anatomy, enhanced revascularization, lower rate of detectable avascular necrosis, and lower rate of infection in the presence of open wounds. Talar fractures are open 15% to 20% of the time. Bone grafting of major injuries is frequently required, about 65% of the time in our experience. The goals of operative management of these fractures are to restore joint congruity, prevent deformity, and avoid infection.

## ANATOMY

The articular surfaces of the head, the superior body, and the inferior body of the talus make flexion and extension of the ankle, inversion and eversion of the hindfoot, pronation during early stance, supination during late stance, and normal push-off possible. Most hindfoot motion is dependent on the integrity of the acetabulum pedis, a confluence of the talonavicular joint and anterior facet of the subtalar joint. More than 60% of the surface of the talus is covered by cartilage and articulates in at least seven different places with other bones; thus, normal gait mechanics may be seriously disrupted by loss of motion in these joints.[163] The unique structure, weight-bearing function, and articular anatomy of the talus demand individualized treatment for the multiple potential fracture locations and patterns that can occur in this single bone.[93, 317] It is wider anteriorly than posteriorly and broader inferiorly than superiorly as it fits within the ankle mortise. The bone is extremely dense; accordingly, any injury to its neck or body should immediately suggest a high-energy mechanism. The neck is angled 15° to 20° medially in a proximal-to-distal direction and is one of the few areas of the talus without cartilage; this area is also distinguished as being the major source of vascular inflow to the talus and, in addition, its most vulnerable site of injury. Because most of the bone must articulate with the surrounding facets of the ankle, talonavicular, and subtalar joints, it has no muscular or tendinous attachments.[200, 321] Moreover, the relatively small perfusion zones of the talus render it susceptible to disturbances in perfusion with many injuries, especially dislocations (see Table 60–1). Its two processes, posterior and lateral, help provide articular and ligamentous support to the surrounding structures and will be discussed further in their fracture sections.

## BLOOD SUPPLY

Talar blood supply is limited and easily compromised by trauma. Thus, the talus is prone to vascular insufficiency

---

**TABLE 60–1**

### Susceptibility to Avascular Necrosis*

| | | |
|---|---|---|
| **Type I** | | |
| *Peripheral fractures* | Circulation intact | No necrosis |
|     Processus fibularis | | |
|     Processus posterior | | |
|     Distal neck | | |
|     Head | | |
| **Type II** | | |
| *Central fractures without displacement* | Circulation mainly intact | Seldom necrosis |
|     Proximal neck | | |
|     Body | | |
| **Type III** | | |
| *Central fractures with displacement* | Intraosseous circulation interrupted, auxiliary circulation intact | Often necrosis |
|     Proximal neck | | |
|     Body | | |
| **Type IV** | | |
| *Dislocation fractures* | Interosseous and auxiliary circulation interrupted | Nearly always necrosis |
|     Proximal neck | | |
|     Body dislocated in the ankle and/or subtalar joint | | |

*As noted by Szyszkowitz and colleagues, the degree of avascular necrosis in the talus really depends on the "personality" of the fracture; thus when trying to predict the eventuality of osteonecrosis, one must consider not only the energy that went into the fracture but also its location.
Source: Szyszkowitz, R.; et al: Clin Orthop 197:97–107, 1985.

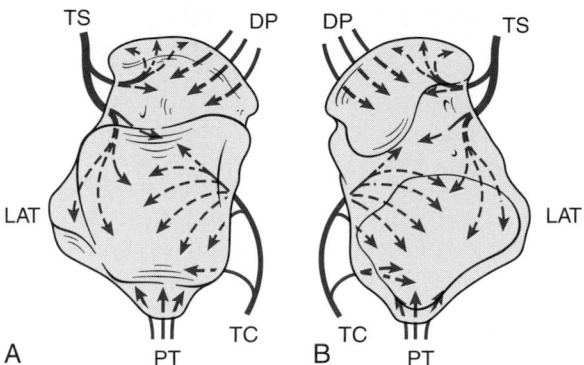

FIGURE 60–4. Knowledge of arterial perfusion to the injured talus is imperative when considering exposure for open reduction and internal fixation. These illustrations show the five major arterial supplies (variably from each of the three major leg vessels) from dorsal (A) and plantar (B) views: the artery of the tarsal sinus (TS) from the dorsalis pedis or peroneal artery; the artery of the tarsal canal, usually from the posterior tibial artery; the deltoid artery from the artery of the tarsal canal (TC) or the posterior tibial artery; the posterior direct branches (PT), usually from the peroneal artery; and the superomedial direct branches of the dorsalis pedis (DP). Note that the talus is a largely cartilage-covered articular surface and that important blood supply enters it wherever soft tissues are attached to the bone.

## IMAGING

Talar injuries can usually be identified on a routine set of ankle plain films. Care should be taken to obtain a true lateral of the talus so that a nondisplaced talar neck fracture is not missed because of radiographic obliquity. With this latter view, the fracture line can often be seen at the point where it exits the talus superiorly along the neck or inferiorly into the talocalcaneal joint. Foot views, however, should also be obtained because the talus articulates with both the ankle and the foot and injury can disrupt the anatomic relationships of both. Canale and Kelly have also described an additional view to visualize the entire talar neck and shoulder as a true AP projection[37] (Fig. 60–5). The foot is maximally plantar flexed and everted (pronated 15°) to swing the calcaneus under and away from the overlying talus, thereby allowing an unimpeded radiographic view of the talus in the AP plane.

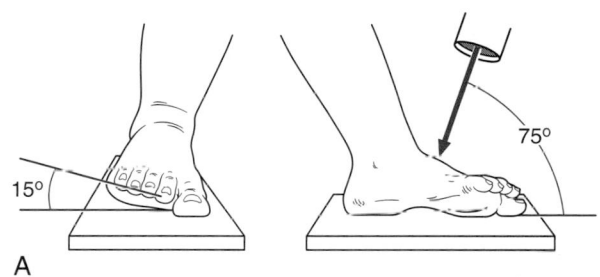

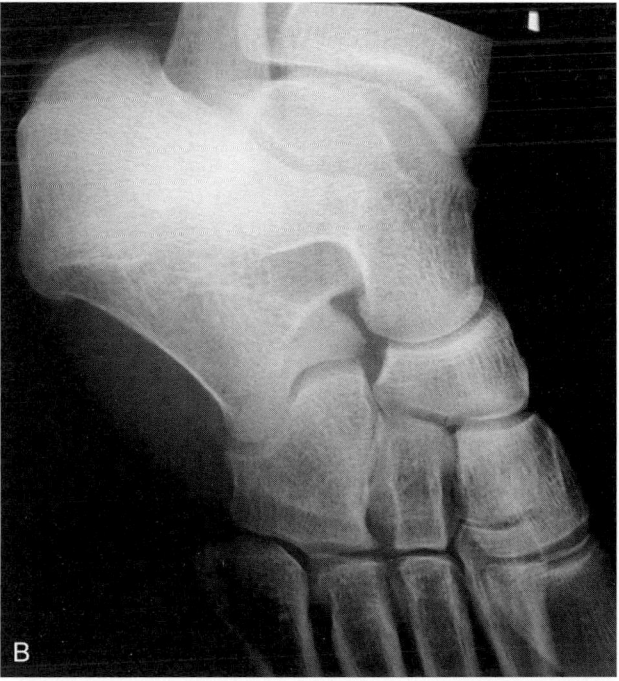

FIGURE 60–5. The Canale view, as described by Canale and Kelly, is a useful en face image of the talus used to most accurately identify step-off or malalignment in talar neck fractures. When obtained correctly, it should correct for the 15° declination of the talus and its overlap of the calcaneus by everting and plantar flexing the foot in relation to the image machine as shown (A). This view brings the talus into a more orthogonal position to the image plane and swings the calcaneus out from underneath to get an unimpeded view of the medial cortex and lateral aspect of the shoulder of the talar neck (B).

and avascular necrosis, especially after subluxation or dislocation of the body.[255] Evidence suggests that immediate compression fixation may reduce the ultimate extent of avascular necrosis, and ORIF should be considered for treatment of all talar fractures. Blood flow to the talus is supported to some extent by all three major vessels that course through the leg en route to the ankle. Because branches of these vessels traverse the talus to form an anastomotic sling around its neck in the region of the sinus tarsi and tarsal canal, most blood flow must travel in a distal-to-proximal direction in the bone, and hence talar neck injuries result in a high level of avascular necrosis within the talar body. Although inflow support is variable and the talus enjoys only limited entry regions (neck and body), multiple extraosseous sources are available, and intraosseous and extraosseous anastomoses are rich. In order of importance, the talus relies on the artery of the tarsal canal and deltoid branches (off the posterior tibial artery) to supply the body and on the dorsalis pedis artery (off the anterior tibial artery) and the artery of the tarsal sinus (off the perforating peroneal artery) to supply the head, neck, and posterior process, respectively (Fig. 60–4). Preservation of even one of these three major arteries can at times provide enough collateral flow to sustain healing and viability of the talus, depending on patient and injury factors, although in general, viability of the talar body requires integrity of the posterior tibial artery.[102, 163, 220, 221, 295] The capsular and ligamentous supports also contribute a rich vascular plexus of vessels supplying collateral flow through the periarticular attachments, and tributaries between the three major arteries provide an intraosseous network. Medial malleolar osteotomy or fracture manipulation for fixation of talus fractures must be done with care to avoid injury to the deltoid artery.

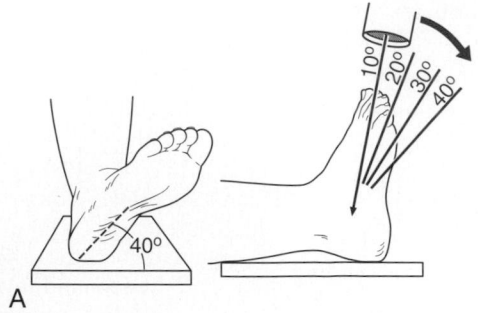

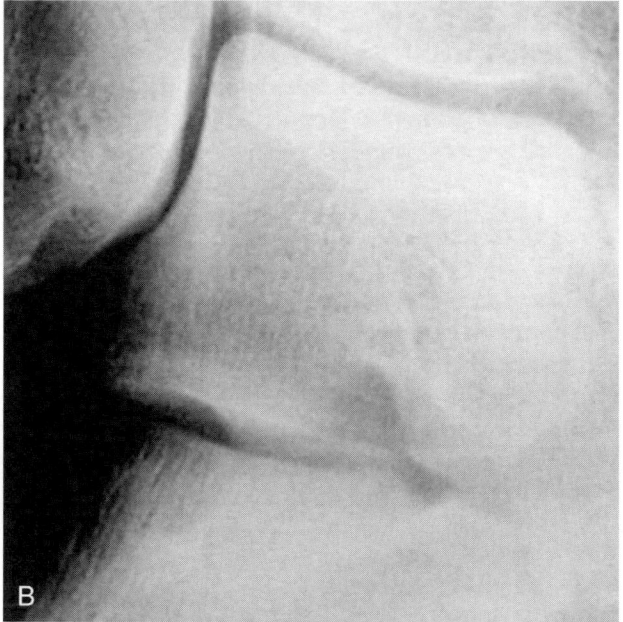

**FIGURE 60–6.** The Broden view is taken best fluoroscopically because it often requires multiple reposition attempts to get a "perfect view" of the subtalar joint—varying both angulation with the C-arm from a vertical position and rotation of the foot by the surgeon (A). This radiograph is most useful to identify congruity of the posterior facet of the subtalar joint, but with experience, it can also be used to evaluate the anterior and middle facets as well (B). Although the view provided shows a normal posterior facet, irregularity at the subchondral margin of the subtalar joint can also easily be identified in this view, such as occurs after intra-articular displacement from a calcaneal fracture.

The x-ray tube is angled at 75° up from the horizontal toward the center of the ankle joint (talus). Another view that can be used to examine articular congruity of the posterior facet is a Broden view (Fig. 60–6). The foot is internally or externally rotated 45° and the beam angled sequentially between 10° and 40° cephalad until an accurate image of the posterior or middle facet (or both) is obtained.[28] Because of the need to vary beam position and rotation, these views are most easily obtained intra-operatively with a C-arm to minimize the need for repetitive positioning and plain radiographs until an optimal view is obtained. Despite the utility and reliability of routine plain films in the identification of talar injuries, more precise definition of talar injuries has been greatly facilitated by the use of CT scans. CT is particularly helpful for preoperative assessment of complex fractures, when it can supplement the findings seen on plain radiographs, including oblique views of the ankle and foot. Magnetic

resonance imaging (MRI) and bone scans are not of particular value in most acute foot injuries but become more useful in the chronic setting (6 weeks or more) when patients have unremitting ankle or hindfoot pain despite negative studies. Often, these patients can have a previously difficult-to-recognize osteochondral talar injury, peroneal tear, or anterior process calcaneal fracture, all of which can be manifested as swelling or discomfort around the talus. Subtalar or ankle instability can also result from the same injury that affected the talus, although stiffness is frequently a more common scenario in the subacute or chronic setting. AP and lateral stress views with comparison with the opposite foot are ideal in this situation (Fig. 60–7).

When evaluating fractures of the talar neck or body, it is important to remember that plain radiographs can be deceptive. As a general rule of thumb, if one "sees" a fracture line, it is generally "displaced." Because closed treatment of these injuries is reserved for truly nondisplaced variants, this caveat plays a role in the workup of any "borderline" fracture in this region.

## Fractures of the Neck of the Talus

Fractures in the body and neck of the talus usually result from high-energy injuries. Fractures involving the head, midbody, and posterior body are less common but may occur after certain types of axial loading or high-energy injuries. Osteochondral fractures are frequently associated with ankle sprains, subtalar sprains, and fracture-dislocations. The type of talar fracture that is most commonly seen in trauma centers, however, is a fracture of the neck and the anterior body,[52, 321] which occurs in over 50% of talar injuries.[165] Injury is usually caused by dorsiflexion impaction of the foot during a high-energy collision (the so-called aviator's astragalus as described by Coltart in 1952 after evaluation of over 200 talar injuries of the Royal Air Force during World War II).[51] Excessive dorsiflexion and axial loading are also applied to the foot when it rests on the pedal of an automobile at the moment of a head-on collision or when it strikes the ground after a fall from a height. These mechanisms lead to medial malleolar fracture 20% to 25% of the time.[126] Talar fractures in this region can also occur as a result of forced inversion, eversion, or rotation. Inokuchi and associates defined a talar neck fracture as one whose fracture line exits laterally on the interior surface of the talus in front of the lateral process, regardless of its course anteromedially.[148] Although the evidence suggesting that these injuries should be considered surgical emergencies when displaced is indeterminate, it is recommended that salvageable displaced talar neck fractures be treated within 4 to 6 hours of identification to minimize complications.[281]

### CLASSIFICATION

Many authors such as Coltart (1952), Mindell (1963), and Marti-Weber (1978) have provided classifications of talar fractures, but the Hawkins classification (1970) has withstood the test of time as being the most useful to grade the severity of injury and determine the best type of treatment of talar neck fractures.[126] This classification is traditionally used to grade talar neck fractures by the amount of dislocation that has occurred between the body fragments and the neck, the ankle, or the subtalar joint. It is also used to predict the amount of avascular necrosis that may be expected.[126] Depending on the severity of the injury, the risk of avascular necrosis in the talar body runs from less than 5% to 90% or more. Although roughly 20% of talar injuries can be open with an anterolateral ankle wound, almost 50% of Hawkins type III injuries occur as open wounds, and infection rates have been as high as 40%.[52, 198] The force necessary to create a talar neck fracture experimentally is extremely high, so any fracture of this remarkably hard bone needs to be recognized and aggressively treated. The extreme foot position and energy

dissipation resulting in Hawkins type IV injuries cause extrusion of the talar body fragment posteromedial to the medial malleolus. In these circumstances, the skin is often tented or open with concomitant impingement of the neurovascular bundle, thus making this injury a true orthopaedic emergency. Extreme care should be taken to avoid injury to the deltoid ligament in these situations because it is usually both the only remaining soft tissue attachment to this fragment and the most important prognostically regarding viability of the talar body.[251] The Hawkins classification is as follows:

*Type I:* The talar neck fracture is undisplaced; the risk of avascular necrosis in the body is less than 10% (0% to 13%).

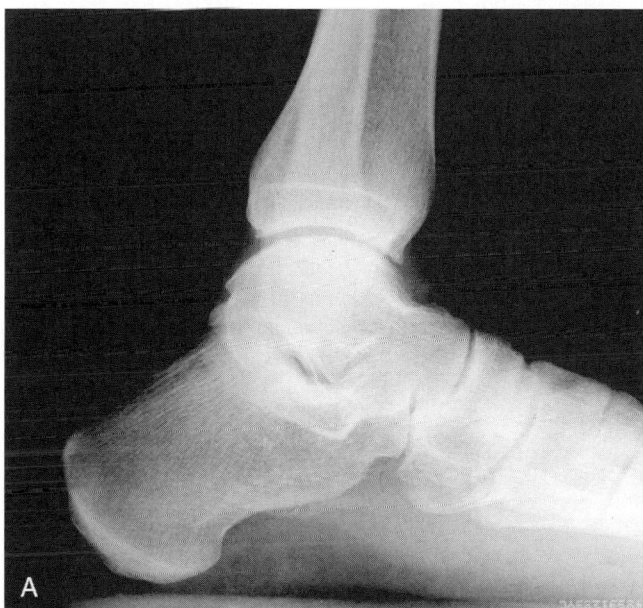

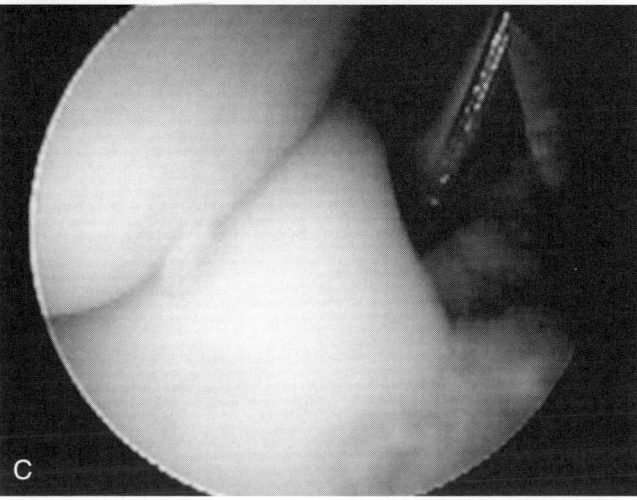

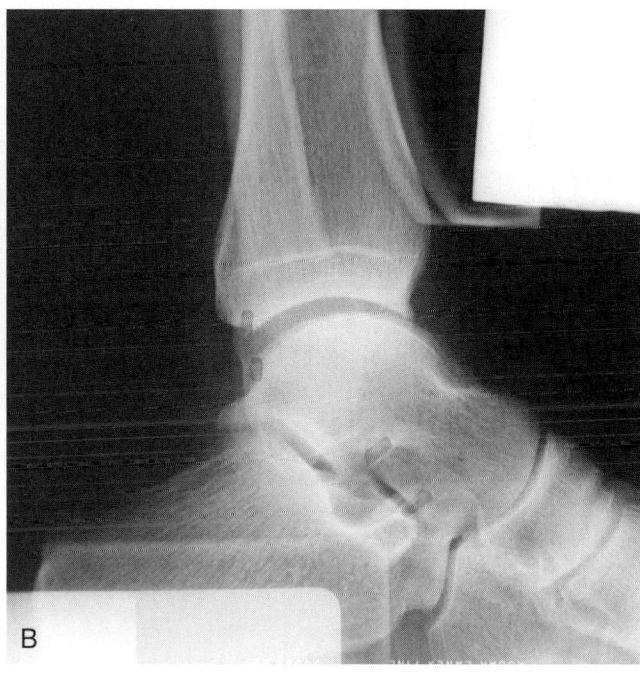

**FIGURE 60–7.** Subtalar instability is often subtle and can accompany hindfoot injury or fracture. Although no absolute criteria can be used to reliably confirm its existence when not overt (i.e., dislocation), it is best identified by taking stress films when radiographs are otherwise normal and the clinical examination is equivocal. These views are similar to the anterior drawer and varus stress views of the ankle, although in this case, different parameters are being evaluated. Lateral gapping of the posterior facet of over 1 cm, or greater than 5 mm when compared with the opposite side, and 1 cm of anterior (forward) translation of the anterior process of the calcaneus away from the lateral process of the talus suggest instability of the subtalar joint. Such findings may require reconstruction of the interosseous ligament or subtalar fusion if symptoms warrant. The images are from a 20-year-old college student with a vague history of low-energy trauma (sprains) to the foot but persistent complaints of unsteadiness on uneven ground. He had no complaints about the ankle—only the sinus tarsi. His unstressed (*A*) and anterior drawer (*B*) stress films suggest a stable ankle but excessive subtalar laxity, as indicated by lower markers. He eventually underwent subtalar arthroscopy to determine the nature of his problem and was found to have abundant synovitis along the posterior facet with a small tear in the interosseous ligament. Intraoperative arthroscopic images of the lateral aspect of the posterior facet during translational and varus stress showed abnormal motion when compared with the unstressed view shown here (*C*), where the edges of the talar (above) and calcaneal (below) facets line up normally. The probe lies in the lateral gutter adjacent to the reflection of the lateral talocalcaneal and calcaneofibular ligaments.

*Type II:* The body is slightly displaced or dislocated from the subtalar joint; the risk of avascular necrosis in the body is less than 40% (20% to 50%).

*Type III:* The body is displaced from both the ankle and the subtalar joints; the risk of avascular necrosis in the body is greater than 90% (75% to 100%).

*Type IV:* This category, added by Canale and Kelly[37] and not part of Hawkins' original classification, includes subluxation of the head at the talonavicular joint, dislocation of the body from the ankle and subtalar joints, and extrusion of the body; the risk of avascular necrosis in the body approaches 100%.

It is important to note that many talar injuries are unclassifiable, even with this scheme; therefore, results are difficult to compare when looking at published series' rates of avascular necrosis (multiple authors' ranges are in parentheses).

## CLOSED REDUCTION

Closed treatment is rarely advisable, even though it has been recommended for undisplaced fractures.[250, 254] A nondisplaced Hawkins type I fracture, confirmed by tomography or CT, may be managed through a posterior approach with lag screw fixation. This fracture is the one instance when the posterior approach is ideal (described in more detail in the section on percutaneous fixation).[200] Rarely, nondisplaced fractures can be treated by closed manipulation: the foot is distracted, plantar flexed, inverted or everted to reduce the varus or valgus malposition, and subsequently compressed as it is returned to a neutral position. If maintenance of reduction requires a plantar flexed position, application of a non–weight-bearing below-knee cast should be maintained for 3 weeks, after which it can usually be safely changed to a neutral position. Even when this reduction is perfect, prolonged positioning in a plantar flexed posture is not optimal, and surgical intervention is usually warranted. Any residual skin tenting, at-risk soft tissue, or malreduction demands rapid operative intervention. In any case of closed management, non–weight-bearing cast immobilization should be pursued for at least 4 to 6 weeks and followed by 4 to 6 weeks of protected weight bearing until both radiographic and clinical evidence of bony union. Usually, casting of nondisplaced or minimally displaced (less than 1 mm) talar neck fractures should be used only as a temporary measure to immobilize the foot until internal fixation can be carried out or in cases in which surgery is contraindicated, such as in very elderly or nonambulatory patients. Regardless of the chosen form of treatment, the vast majority of nondisplaced or minimally displaced fractures enjoy a favorable long-term outcome. Although some authors suggest that up to 5° of malposition or 5 mm of displacement is an acceptable parameter for closed reduction, we advocate consideration of closed reduction only when it can be anatomic (<1 mm).[59] In fact, one laboratory group created a 2-mm displacement in simulated talar neck fractures with a saw and found that they could not identify the fracture on plain radiographs.[294]

## PERCUTANEOUS FIXATION (HAWKINS TYPE I)

Percutaneous fixation should be considered only if the fracture is nondisplaced or the resultant reduction is anatomic, and the use of a Canale view or CT should accompany routine foot and ankle views to accurately determine displacement and reduction because the accuracy of closed reduction is quite hard to verify. This plain film view permits assessment of angulation and shortening not noticeable on the other films, and it is also important to know how to obtain this view intraoperatively to assess reduction, which often requires a team effort with the imaging technician (see Fig. 60–5). With evidence of even 1 mm of step-off or rotation in a talar neck fracture, it is recommended that it be openly reduced and fixed for best results. It can be argued that even nondisplaced talar neck fractures should be stabilized with screws to allow earlier mobilization and range-of-motion exercises. Displacement of as little as 2 mm can significantly alter contact loads within the subtalar joint and affect motion of the hindfoot. A recent cadaveric biomechanical study by Sangeorzan and colleagues found that displacement of 2 mm resulted in significant weight-bearing shifts of the talus on the calcaneal facets and subsequent changes in contact pressure that thereafter overloaded the posterior facet.[294] Malalignment in the dorsomedial or varus position resulted in the greatest displacement, the combination of which happens to be the most common malposition after union. Another recent anatomic study also supports altered foot mechanics with varus hindfoot positioning, forefoot adduction, or both after talar neck malunion.[59]

If the talar neck fracture is truly nondisplaced either before or after reduction and surgery is anticipated, it can be performed percutaneously either from an anterior approach with the patient supine on an image table or from a posterior approach with the patient prone. Some biomechanical evidence suggests that fixation is improved with posteriorly directed screws, and this method of insertion avoids potential disruption of the major blood supply to the talar neck. Its disadvantages include limited inspection of the fracture site and limited (no) access to the subtalar joint. Anterior-to-posterior insertion allows visualization of the fracture edges (open anatomic reduction) and subtalar débridement and is less prone to penetration of the subtalar joint, plantar flexion impingement, or flexor hallucis longus injury.[320] However, it does require dissection in the area of the blood supply, requires transchondral screw placement, and by laboratory standards, provides weaker fixation in comparison. Posterior fixation can be performed through a vertical posterolateral or posteromedial approach. In either case, an incision is made just to one side of the Achilles tendon to avoid the adjacent lateral sural nerve or medial posterior bundle, and regardless of the choice of approach, during deeper dissection the flexor hallucis longus is swept to the medial side once the deep posterior compartment is located. Although these screws can be introduced through stab incisions, it is desirable to make the incisions slightly larger for visualization and more accurate placement. The posterior approach does not allow direct visualization of the fracture, but it does provide an avenue for relatively "percutaneous" screw application if indicated. Because the talus is aligned in a posterosuperolateral-to-anteroinferomedial direction about 25° (10° to 40°) in the transverse plane and about 15° (5° to 50°) in the sagittal plane, the posterolateral approach is preferred.

A countersunk, subchondral screw is introduced from either side of the posterior process of the talus so that it misses the flexor hallucis longus. The tendency in recent years has been toward smaller, lower profile fixation in the foot to minimize the incidence of hardware irritation, and 2.7- or 3.5-mm screws are thus ideal for this purpose. Despite their seemingly shallow thread configuration, these small screws have strong shanks and a tremendous number of threads, which results in a high surface area and allows excellent compressive strength in the typically dense bone of the talus. Newer 2.4- and 4.0-mm screw designs may also be amenable to this application. Alternatively, the smaller 3.5- or 4.0-mm cannulated screws can be ideal for this purpose if limited exposure is required. Moreover, the head profile does not interfere with the ankle or subtalar joints, and in the case of cannulated screws, definitive fixation can be placed directly over the K-wires if the reduction is anatomic. Although cannulated screws in this size range can make the insertion process quicker, greater strength can be obtained with solid-core screws inserted after preliminary reduction with two parallel K-wires, the holes of which can often be used for sequential screw insertion when wires averaging 0.062 to 0.125 inch in diameter are used. They must be preliminarily drilled with a gliding hole and an appropriately sized bit, however, for compressive lag fixation. These newer solid screws are available as self-tapping screws, which can save operative time. One wire should be left in place during insertion of the initial screw to prevent rotation at the fracture site, not uncommon with the amount of torque generated during screw placement in this good bone stock. Placement of only one screw is not recommended because little time is required for a second one and the extra compression and resistance to rotation are certainly worthwhile. If an anterior approach is preferred, a screw can reliably be placed percutaneously through stab incisions on both the medial and lateral aspects unless some displacement warrants larger incisions. A small longitudinal medial utility incision between the posterior and anterior tibial tendons and a oblique one laterally in Langer's lines (Ollier incision) can be used. A longitudinal lateral incision can similarly be used if extension is considered likely. Anteriorly placed hardware is less dangerous and more accurate than posteriorly placed hardware with proper percutaneous insertion, although care must be taken during insertion to avoid interference with talonavicular function. If anterior, the screw heads must be recessed within the head of the talus or at the junction of the head and neck. One screw from each side is probably more ideal fixation, although parallel screws from only one side can be considered (Fig. 60–8). Regardless of the direction of screw placement, the point of screw insertion is paramount in enabling anatomic and concentric compression. Eccentrically inserted screws from either direction, when tightened for compression, will allow

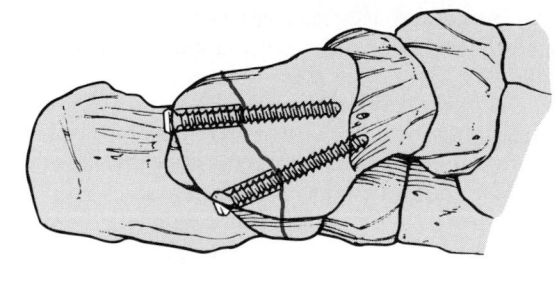

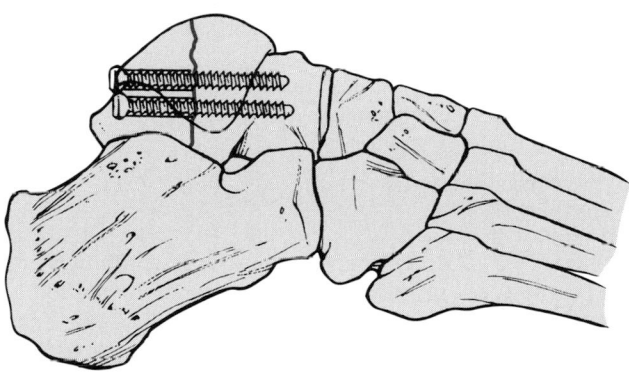

**FIGURE 60–8.** The ideal fixation of a talar neck fracture without significant comminution that has been reduced consists of one 3.5-mm lag screw for compression and another placed nearly parallel to it for rotatory control. Although K wires can be used as alternative fixation, they do not provide acceptable enough compression to permit early range of motion and limited weight bearing. Standard AO technique is used during drilling to lag these cortical screws. They provide the best means of fixation in this dense bone and, because of their thinner outer diameter, produce less torque across the fracture site during introduction than noted with other screws. A vertical posteromedial or preferably a posterolateral incision (because of talar angulation) provides the best access. One or both screws can be placed through these incisions; occasionally, the second screw must be introduced through a nearby stab incision on the other side of the Achilles tendon.

gapping of the fracture edges on the side opposite their location if they are not placed in the midaxial plane of the talus.

If comminution is noted intraoperatively despite minimal displacement, use of a 2.0-mm blade plate as a fixed-angle device should be considered to maintain length and rotation, which cannot be accomplished by screws under these circumstances. It is easily placed from the lateral side along the shoulder of the talus, and the entrance of the blade can be predrilled with a 1.5-mm drill bit or similar-diameter K-wire. Plate holders can position the device along the long axis of the talus, and a small bone tamp can be used to gently impact the fixed-angle blade into the predrilled hole. This hole should be made about 1 cm proximal to the talonavicular joint, centered in the AP plane. Imaging can be used to facilitate proper placement through the center of the anatomic neck of the talus. A fracture fixed firmly by this approach can adjust to stresses caused by early motion and rarely becomes displaced. Although stainless steel hardware is the strongest and easiest to remove, one can consider titanium implants if avascular necrosis is a substantial risk. The latter will allow subsequent unimpeded MRI evaluation. This situation is probably the only time that titanium is advantageous during fracture fixation in the foot. Titanium's high biocompatibility with bone and its tendency to strip at the head during removal can add unnecessary time and worry to otherwise routine hardware removal.

## OPEN REDUCTION (HAWKINS TYPES II TO IV)

In the absence of skin at risk, displaced talar neck fractures are considered injuries of orthopaedic urgency and should ideally be reduced and stabilized within approximately 6 hours of injury to minimize further vascular insult to the talus or surrounding soft tissue. Skin tension, impending necrosis, or open wounds should be considered an orthopaedic emergency, and the patient should be taken to the operating room as soon as possible. Closed anatomic reduction is not usually feasible in a displaced or comminuted talar fracture (Hawkins types II through IV), and these types of fractures must be exposed through at least two incisions. When the talar body has not been extruded, a standard medial utility incision should be combined with a lateral Ollier oblique-type or anterolateral longitudinal incision. The patient is probably best managed in a supine position on an image table for this procedure, with a bump placed under the buttock to keep the patella pointing straight up and therefore providing equal access to both sides of the foot. The medial approach allows good access to the medial tibiotalar joint, the middle facet of the subtalar joint, and the talonavicular joint. This incision begins just distal to the tip of the medial malleolus and extends along the medial border of the foot to approximately the naviculocuneiform joint. It is deepened through the retinaculum, and the posterior tibial tendon is brought inferiorly and the saphenous vein and anterior tibial tendon dorsally. Direct access to the medial talar neck can then be obtained by sharp dissection, but care must be taken to retain all dorsal and plantar capsular attachments to the talar neck because they provide much of its remaining blood flow if the deltoid or tarsal canal has been disrupted. If intact, the deltoid should be carefully protected from iatrogenic injury. This exposure is extensile to the medial malleolus and more proximally if it needs to be combined with medial malleolar osteotomy in unusual circumstances (unexpected extension proximal to the lateral process and into the body). If an osteotomy is required, the incision is extended proximoposteromedially and the medial malleolus is initially predrilled with a 2.0-mm drill bit, tapped, and then "fixed" with two 4.0-mm cancellous screws, which are thereafter removed. It is then cut but not completed with a thin microsagittal saw at a 45° obliquity just infratectal to the shoulder of the plafond. This osteotomy is then completed with an osteotome to leave an "irregular" margin at the chondral level to improve a "keyed-in" fit on fixation after the talus is accessed and treated. A common error is to rely only on the medial approach to treat such injuries. Doing so leaves lateral debris in the sinus tarsi and subtalar joint and increases the risk of malreduction of the neck secondary to incomplete assessment of rotation and alignment. The lateral incision begins just distal to the ankle joint along the course of the peroneus tertius and just above the sinus tarsi. It extends distally to the level of the midfoot and exposes the anterolateral articular surface of the body and the posterior facet of the subtalar joint and lateral talonavicular joint. The lateral tibiotalar joint can also be accessed with a proximal extension. The subtalar joint can be débrided of small osteocartilaginous fragments through this approach, which stays anterosuperior to the sinus tarsi canal to avoid vascular compromise and brings the peroneus tertius dorsal to expose the capsule of the talar neck. Sometimes, the tertius can be released for the purpose of exposure of the lateral talar shoulder and then repaired during closure. Similar care should be taken on this side with regard to the dorsal and plantar blood supply, and manipulation of fragments should be gentle (Fig. 60–9).

By using this recommended combination of incisions, a surgeon may open the fracture and observe it directly without disrupting the blood supply in the dorsal part of the talar neck. The deltoid ligament, which is attached to the medial body and may be observed through the medial incision, is a very important source of blood to the talus and must be left intact. More accurate reduction is possible through the combined incisions, and consequently, fractures heal with fewer rotatory and angular deformities, particularly comminuted fractures, which frequently heal with a varus and dorsiflexion deformity if they are reduced through a medial incision alone. Such deformity is caused by the talar settling within the dorsomedial comminution as a result of the typical dorsiflexion moments that produce these injuries. Fracture comminution can cause gaps in cortical bone that may allow the head to drift into varus, and these gaps should be filled with cancellous bone graft at the time of fixation.

Similar lag screws and hardware are used as described for fixation of minimally displaced fractures if significant comminution is not preventing compression and a good read can be obtained for accurate reduction. Otherwise, a neutralization plate can be applied either medially, laterally, or both to maintain proper length, angulation, and rotation. Under these circumstances, a 2.0-mm blade, straight, or T plate or even the stouter new 2.4-mm plates are ideal for this purpose (Fig. 60–10). They are low profile, fairly rigid, and easily contoured to apply along the walls of the talus. On the lateral side, they can be positioned just proximal to the cartilage of the head (extra-articular) and contoured along the shoulder up to the edge of the lateral process to provide spanning fixation extending from the posterior body all the way to the anterior neck and head of the talus. On the medial side where the neck is relatively straight, they can be positioned similarly adjacent to the head and extend proximally to the edge of the medial malleolus (Fig. 60–11). The ankle should be dorsiflexed and plantar flexed in the course of applying the medial plate to ensure that abutment does not occur in the medial gutter as a result of the hardware. One can typically get much further posteriorly than initially anticipated with these fractures and thus achieve far better purchase and balanced fixation. If an accurate reduction can be made on one side despite comminution on the other, screws would be acceptable fixation on that side. The requisite buttress plate fixation on the opposite side

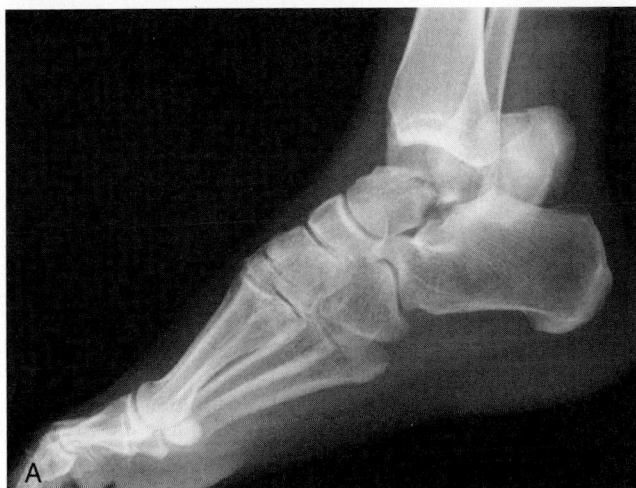

**FIGURE 60–9.** The medial and lateral approaches to the talar neck should be used in all displaced talar neck fractures. The lateral exposure allows evaluation of the subtalar joint for reduction of the inferior talar facets and débridement; the medial approach allows excellent visualization of the ankle and talonavicular joints and can also be extended across the medial malleolus by osteotomy if necessary. Reduction of the talar fracture often requires looking through both incisions to identify where the best "read" is for assessing anatomic alignment and preventing malreduction. This Hawkins type III talar neck posteromedial fracture-dislocation in a young woman required posteromedial exposure in addition to standard medial and lateral exposure to gain reduction. The almost extruded talus was causing an unusual neurovascular compromise. In this instance, good fixation was obtained with a screw placed through two of the three required incisions.

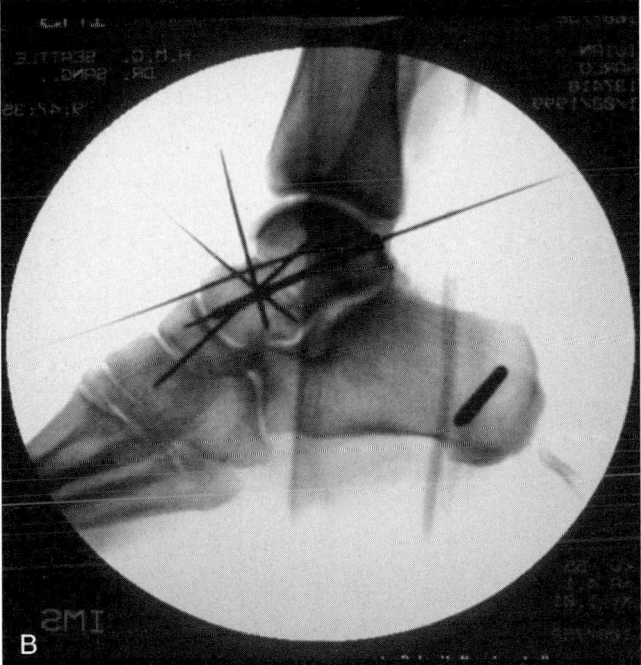

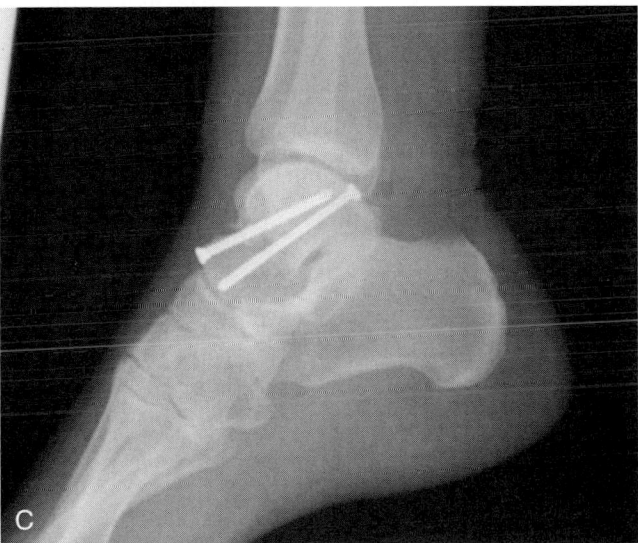

under these circumstances helps maintain stable alignment. It should be kept in mind that these fractures often fail (malunite) in varus, thereby leading to a supination deformity, so the positioning of both bone graft and plates should confer rigid structural integrity to support early motion. Often, a shoulder hook, much like the awls used in shoulder surgery, and a headlight can facilitate reduction; the former has less of a tendency to break than the less stout dental picks traditionally used. Any screws used outside of a plate must be placed as perpendicular as possible to the fracture line to provide firm anatomic compression (Fig. 60–12). A lateral screw can be inserted extra-articularly if the lateral flare of the neck is attached to the distal fragment. This usually dense cortical bone provides good fracture definition and accurate reduction. A medial screw obtains good purchase when it is placed through the tubercle in the neck or countersunk into the medial edge of the articular surface of the talonavicular

joint. These two incisions allow wide separation of the fixation and no intervening disruption in blood supply, as well as optimal immobilization. It is ideal to maintain K-wire fixation of the fracture until the lag screws are well across the fracture site and compression is noted.

Reduction of the body of the talus may be very difficult in displaced Hawkins type III or type IV (Canale and Kelly) fractures because visualization of the partially extruded body is obstructed by the flexor digitorum, the flexor hallucis, or the posterior tibial tendon. Nevertheless, an attempt should be made to replace the talus and to apply compression fixation. It is possible that the body may still be attached to the deltoid ligament even if it is completely extruded and no soft tissue attachments are evident. In this situation, the patient can be positioned prone if it also facilitates treatment of concomitant injuries and subsequently turned over after the talar body is repositioned, or a bump can be placed under the contralateral greater trochanter to permit easy exposure posteromedially to reduce the body fragment, followed by removal and replacement of the bump under the ipsilateral buttock to allow equal anterior medial and lateral exposure for later fixation. Such reduction should be performed on an image table with use of the C-arm. After positioning, the displaced body is directly exposed through a vertical posteromedial incision as previously described, with care taken to avoid the neurovascular bundle, which is often tented toward the incision from pressure of the fragment. The posterior tibial artery is a major source of blood to the body of the talus, and it must not be disrupted after dislocation of the talar body at the subtalar joint. The risk of avascular necrosis increases if this artery is severed. Vascularization of the body by vessels in the deltoid ligament may eliminate the need for major arthrodesis in the future. A temporary large K-wire or Schanz pin may be used as a joystick to manipulate the fracture fragments back into anatomic position. Often, a femoral distractor or external fixator frame can be a useful adjunct; if applied, these devices can be attached to pins in the tibial crest and calcaneus from the medial side and subsequently used to widen the volume of the ankle joint for ease of talar relocation.

Instability in the ankle or subtalar joint that persists after screw fixation can be corrected by placement of a ⅛-inch Steinmann pin buried under the skin, through the calcaneus, across the subtalar and tibiotalar joints, and into the distal end of the tibia from below. The pin should be left in place for approximately 4 weeks to provide supplementary fixation; it may be removed when motion is initiated. However, if direct observation reveals severe damage to the articular surface of the subtalar joint, primary arthrodesis can be carried out with screw fixation.[112] When these fragments are reconstructible, however, as in the case of a large lateral process fracture, this fixation can often prevent further dislocation and impart stability (Fig. 60–13).

## POSTOPERATIVE CARE

Postoperative wound closure can be performed in layered fashion if soft tissue swelling permits. As is typical for high-energy injuries involving the talus, calcaneus, and ankle (pilon fractures), once the tourniquet is deflated, approximately one-half hour is available for closure before reperfusion edema prevents safe reapproximation of skin edges. In any of these cases, skin should not be handled with forceps and, after closure, should be protected with individually laid, uncut (full length) Steri-Strips without application agents such as benzoin. It makes no sense to use Steri-Strips for an expanded distribution of pressure across the skin and wound and concomitantly cut them in half, which decreases their effectiveness in half. Similarly, using substances such as benzoin across the skin before Steri-Strip application prevents their ability to allow skin movement underneath them should the swelling become too great. The worse alternative (in this case) instead forces

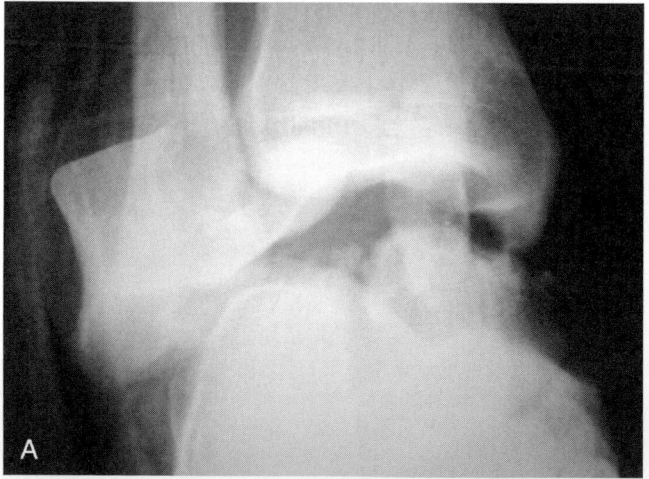

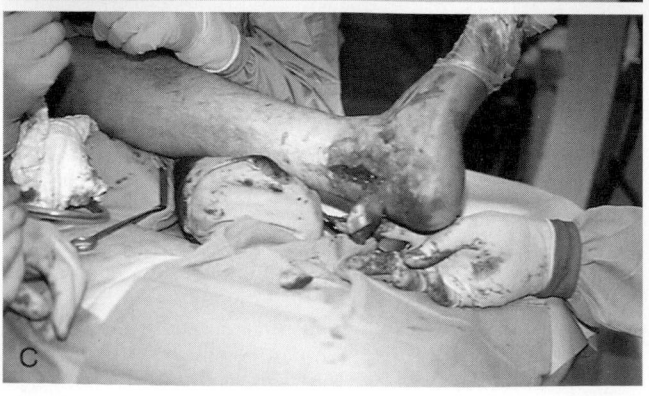

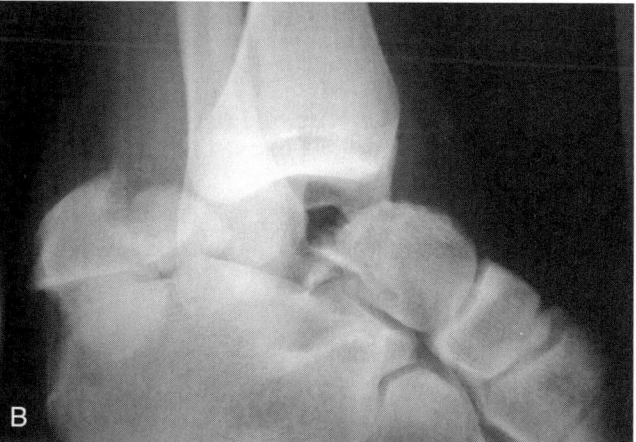

**FIGURE 60–10.** Comminuted or severely displaced talar neck fractures require formal open reduction and internal fixation through a two-incision technique for best visualization and reduction. Often, a combination of plate-and-screw fixation provides rigid fixation to allow safe early range of motion and maximize the chance for revascularization, which is probably best with early, anatomic, rigid internal fixation. A 2.0-mm blade plate, as used in this case, can be nicely contoured along the lateral aspect of the shoulder or medial part of the neck of the talus as a strong construct, and 2.0-mm screws can be fanned out along the talar neck and body for maximal, balanced fixation. Small 1.5- or, preferably, 2.0-mm minifragment plates can alternatively be used if the fracture anatomy is not amenable to simple screw placement. These plates allow maintenance of length, rotation, and alignment that is frequently not possible with screw fixation alone. This case involved an open talar neck fracture-dislocation, as well as a small body fragment (*A, B*), and the open wound was extended intraoperatively to both débride and facilitate reduction of the fragments (*C*).

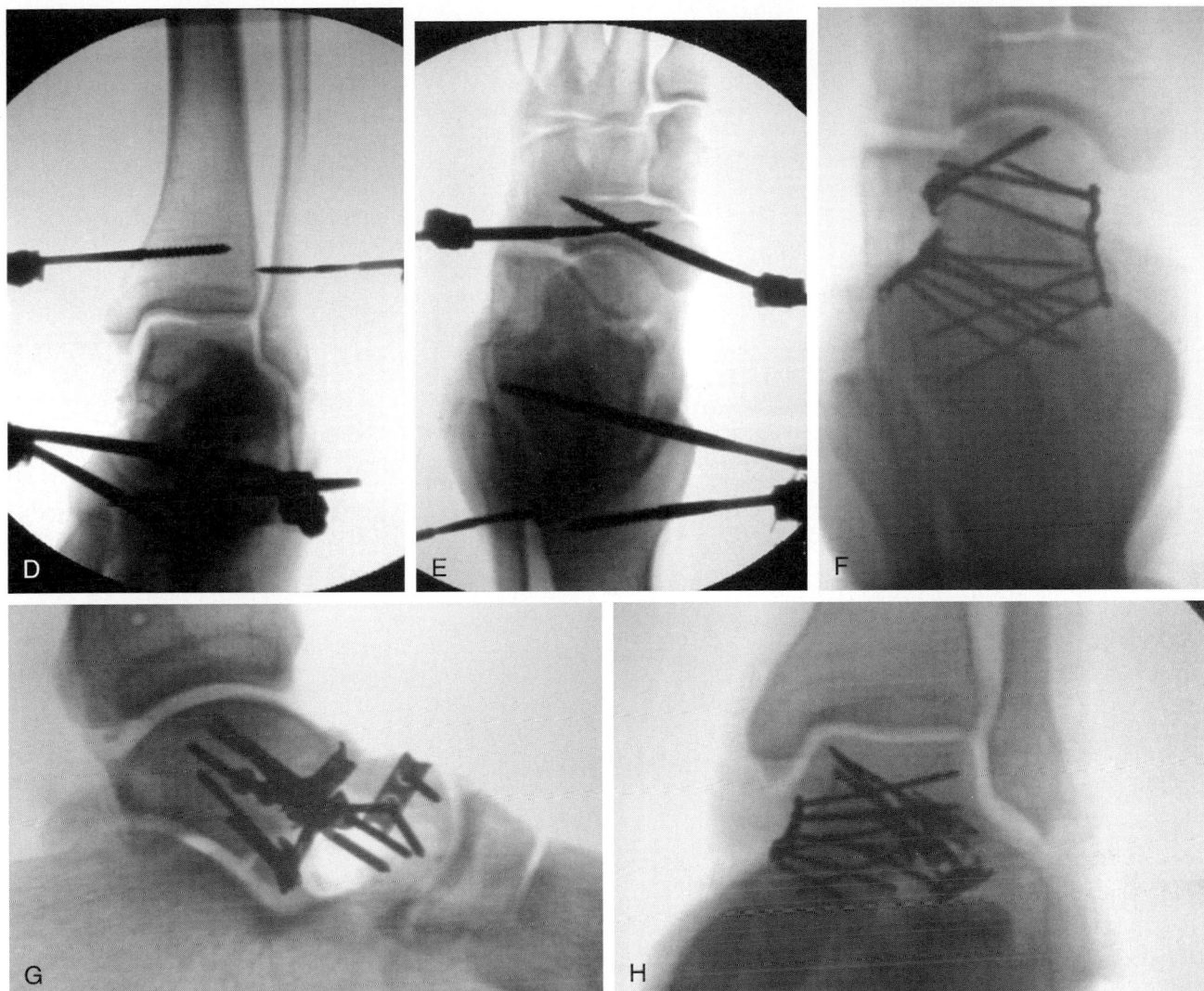

**FIGURE 60–10** *Continued.* External fixation across the ankle to the midfoot also facilitated reduction of the dislocated fragments (*D, E*) and can be an important adjunct in these cases to avoid the temptation of larger incisions and more devascularization (dissection) to alternatively obtain reduction. Postfixation images in the operating room should include an anteroposterior and lateral views of the foot, a Canale view, and a mortise view of the ankle to verify appropriate position of the implants (*F–H*).

motion between the dermal and epidermal layers of the skin, which frequently results in massive blisters that can compromise the integrity of the skin envelope and increase the likelihood of infection. The patient should eventually be placed in a bulky Jones-type dressing and a well-padded posterior splint in neutral position. Sutures should be removed 2 to 3 weeks after surgery and non–weight bearing maintained until evidence of early healing is identified both radiographically and clinically at around 8 to 10 weeks. This period is within the time frame at which the first sign of revascularization in subchondral bone is seen, approximately 6 weeks after surgery. At this time, a mortise view of the talus should be examined for the Hawkins sign—evidence of disuse osteoporosis of the subchondral bone of the superior talar dome. This osteolysis is an excellent indication of revascularization, and weight bearing may be increased after it occurs. Sometimes, osteolysis appears only in the medial half of the talar body, but even this finding is an optimistic sign.

As noted by Canale and Kelly in follow-up of over 70 talar neck fractures, avascular necrosis developed in only 1 of 23 with a Hawkins sign versus 20 of 26 without a Hawkins sign.[37] Once union of a talar fracture is demonstrated radiographically at between 8 and 12 weeks after surgery, the patient is allowed to proceed gradually to full weight bearing. If weight bearing is increased in the absence of a Hawkins sign, partial collapse of the talus may result. However, usually no amount of discouragement keeps patients from gradually increasing weight bearing after 8 weeks if the foot is not symptomatic, and data correlating early weight bearing with the risk of avascular bone collapse are lacking for the talus, hip, or knee. Fortunately, good function is usually regained despite partial collapse and minor arthrosis if it occurs.[52]

Like all injuries involving periarticular structures, the importance of early range of motion should be considered when deciding on how to fix a talus. Early motion is especially important for this bone because every part of the foot rotates around it and motion of the ankle, subtalar, and transverse tarsal joints is coupled to its function. Outcome can be significantly affected by improper alignment, stiffness, or residual pain. Thus, as soon as the soft tissues permit, fixation should allow active range-of-motion exercises, edema control, and physiotherapy. This program can usually be started between 2 and 4 weeks after surgery, and to facilitate mobilization, the patient can be placed in a short leg bivalved removable cast. If avascular necrosis is suspected, as heralded by the absence

of a Hawkins sign or the presence of subchondral collapse, the patient can alternatively be fitted with a patellar tendon–bearing (PTB) cast or double-upright ankle-foot orthosis (AFO) to provide, at least in theory, some added protection against premature weight bearing until revascularization is complete. A limited amount of avascular necrosis is expected in all severely displaced talar neck fractures. If part of the deltoid ligament and its branch of the posterior tibial artery remain attached to the medial body and the blood supply has not been disrupted, medial

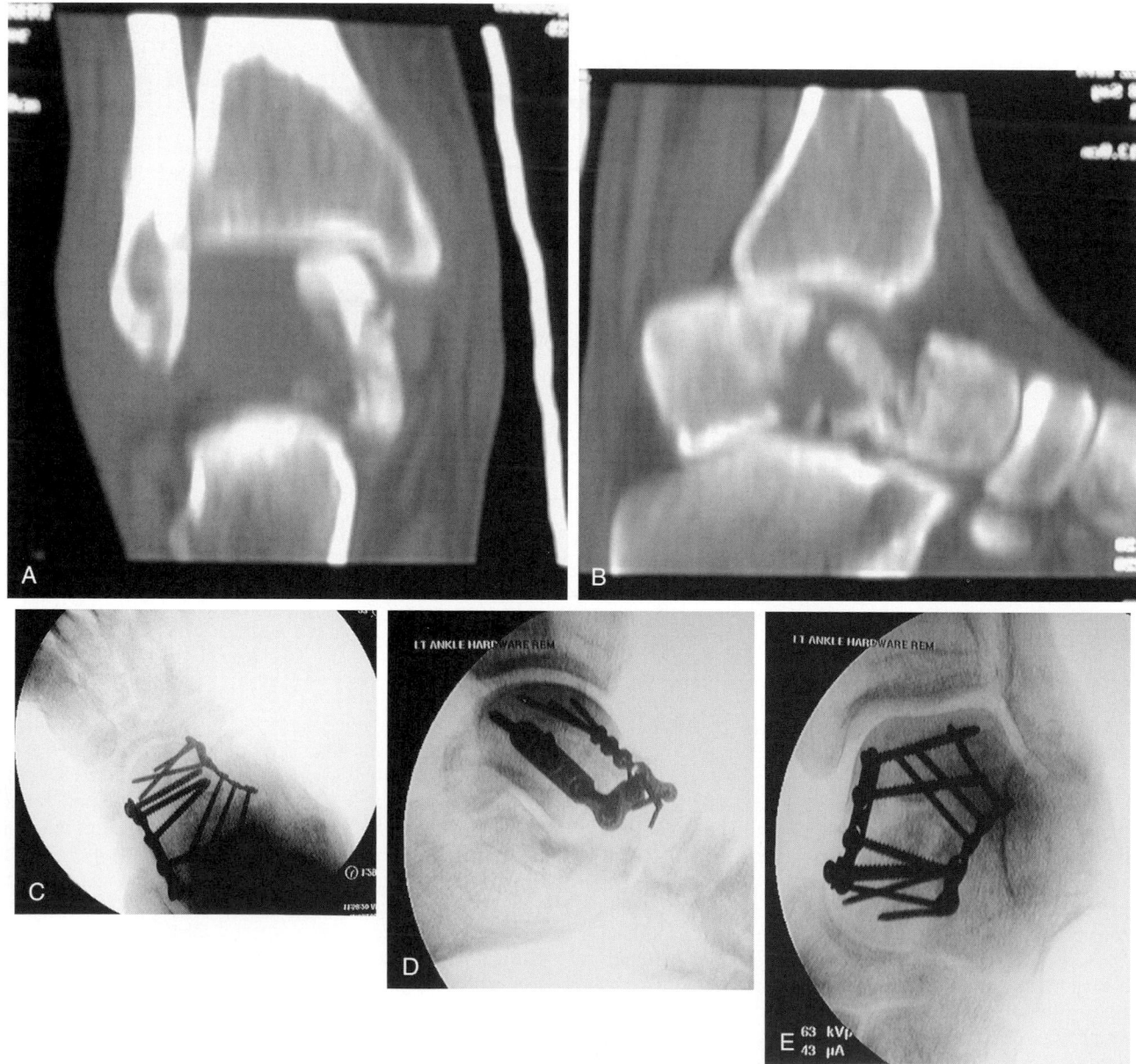

**Figure 60–11.** Typical stable fixation that can be obtained during plate fixation of comminuted talar neck or body fractures (*A, B*). Note the proximal extension of the hardware along both the medial portion of the neck and the lateral aspect of the shoulder of the talus, without ankle impingement (*C–E*). This patient fell 25 ft because of a drug addiction and came in with a moderately comminuted Hawkins type III talar neck fracture that required a minifragment 2.0-mm blade plate and 2.7-mm L plate along the neck of the talus for rigid fixation. Motion was begun within a week of surgery because of the stability of the construct.

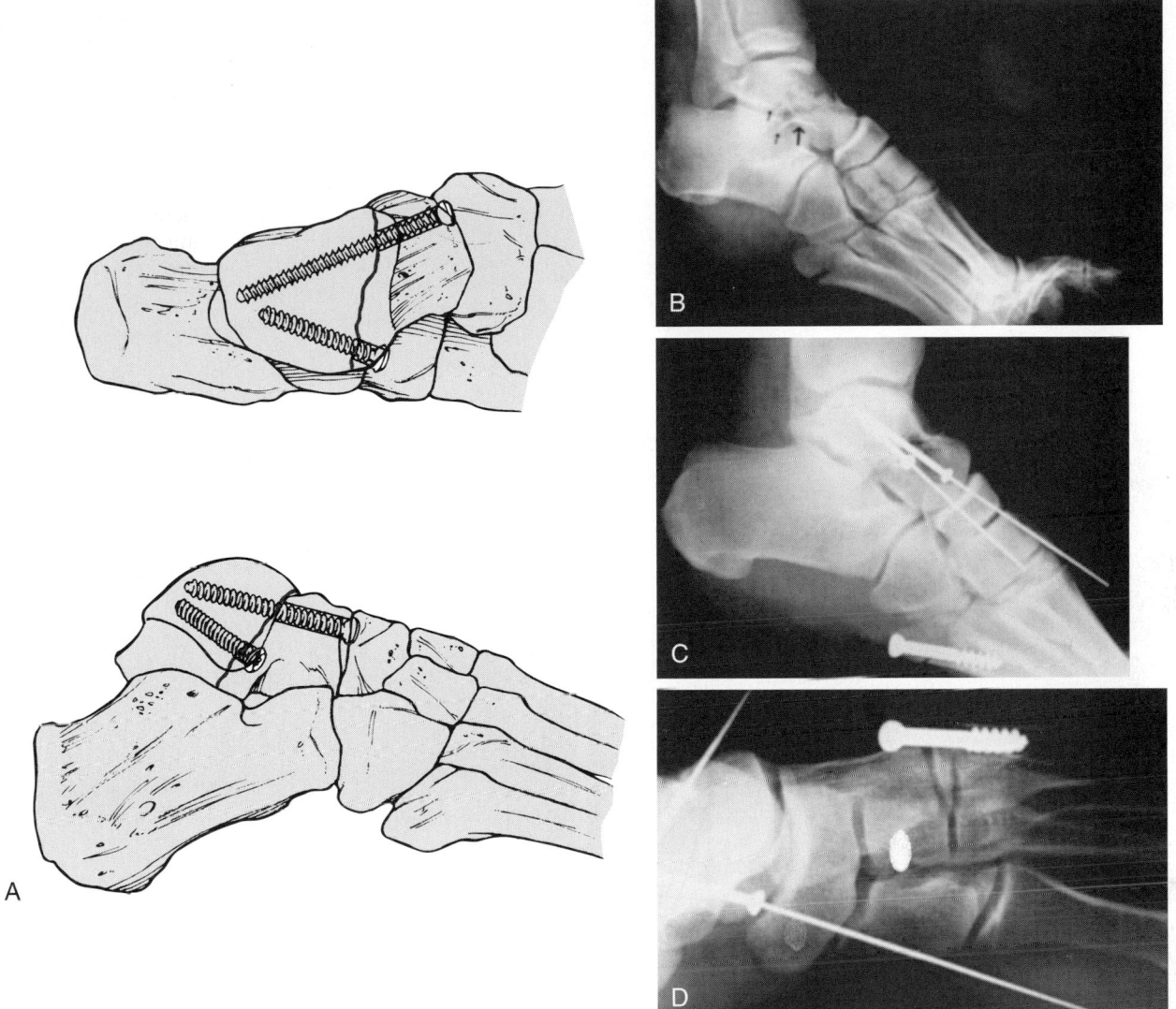

**FIGURE 60–12.** Two 3.5-mm cortical screws are placed across a fracture located at the base of the neck of the talus. The first screw, which is placed medially, is countersunk into the articular surface. The second screw is placed through a 3.5-mm gliding hole in the sinus tarsi and a 2.5-mm thread hole in the body. *A,* In this case, both screws are inserted approximately perpendicular to the fracture line and along the midaxial line of the talar neck to avoid creating dorsal or plantar gapping along the fracture line during compression. *B,* Lateral radiograph showing the talar neck fracture. *C, D,* Intraoperative lateral and dorsoplantar anteroposterior views showing screw location.

vascularity may gradually spread and maintain the normal anatomy of the talus (i.e., prevent collapse) even after partial weight bearing has been started.

## COMPLICATIONS

Complications are common after talar neck fractures, even when reduction and fixation are performed in a timely and stable anatomic fashion. Their frequency is related to the initial severity of the soft tissue injury, fracture and articular displacement, vascular embarrassment, and time elapsed before treatment.[58] Most patients with these injuries, however, enjoy an acceptable outcome with appropriate treatment. No prospective studies have investigated outcome after ORIF of talar neck injuries, nor has

any compared open and closed treatment.[15, 95] The literature is replete with studies basing conclusions on small numbers, short follow-up, and comparisons of apples and oranges. Data do suggest, however, that the Hawkin's classification is prognostic with regard to overall outcome.

**Avascular Necrosis.** Too much emphasis is placed on osteonecrosis of the talus after fracture fixation. Fortunately, avascular necrosis is usually an incomplete phenomenon, and the presence of partial necrosis guarantees neither collapse nor a poor result. In fact, rigid lag screw fixation of the talar fragments may permit early revascularization of the fracture site and limit the ultimate amount of avascular necrosis that occurs in the body. Traditionally, K-wires were used to immobilize talar neck fractures, but they are no longer recommended because they do not provide sufficiently stable fixation for revascularization to occur. In addition, the fixation accomplished by K-wires alone is not sufficient to preclude cast immobilization.[320] Optimal conditions for revascularization are obtained when the fracture interfaces are completely immobilized

by compression screws or by plate fixation with a fixed-angle device through two approaches to the talus as soon as possible after injury. Fixation with this combination of hardware is significantly stronger than fixation with K-wires alone. Moreover, screw fixation is more beneficial to ultimate joint function because it allows early motion in

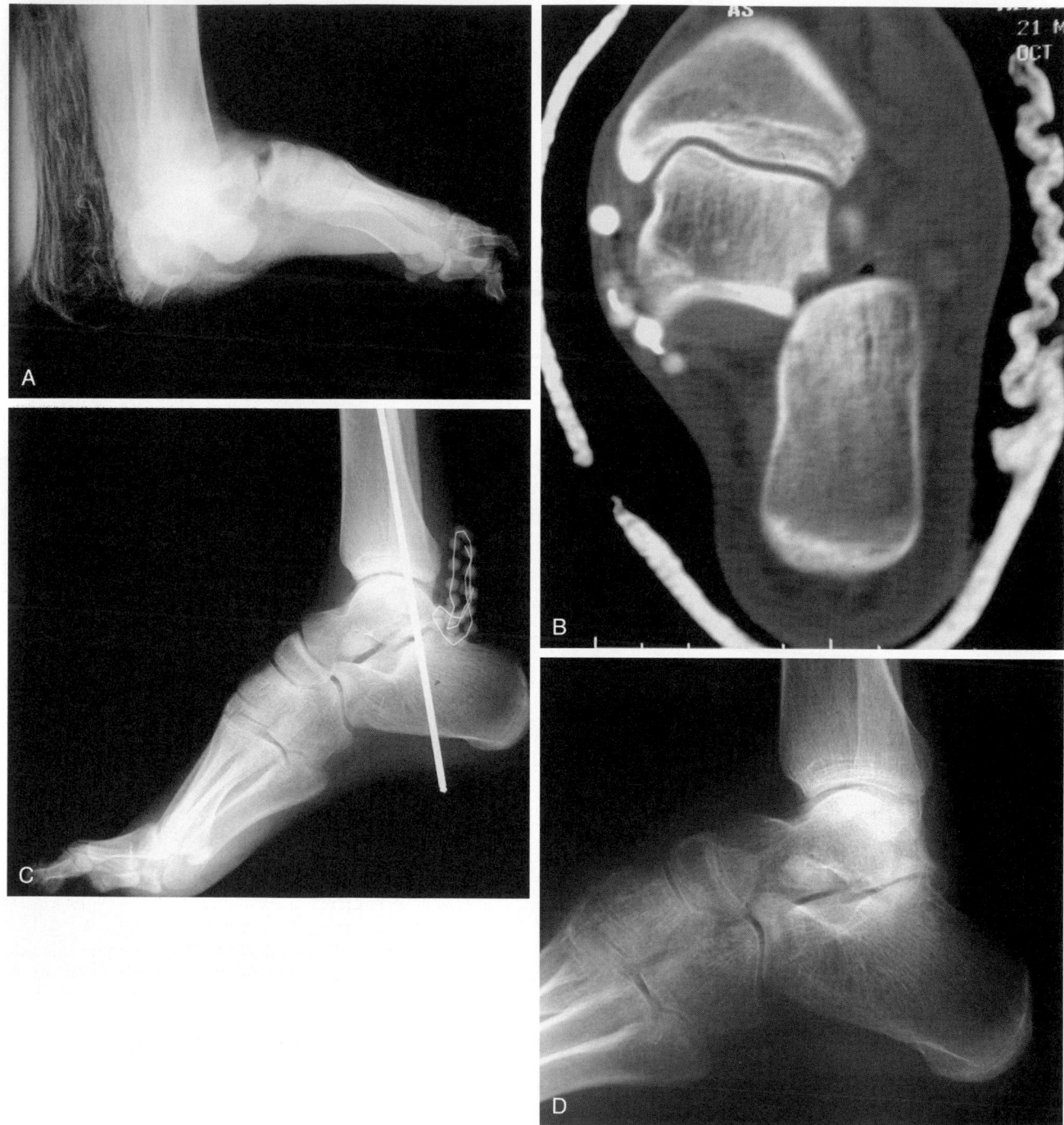

**FIGURE 60–13.** This patient sustained an open lateral subtalar fracture-dislocation with a medial wound and a large lateral process fracture after a high-energy motorcycle crash; closed reduction in the emergency department was unsuccessful (A). Initial operative open reduction was accompanied by plaster immobilization, but neither fixation of the lateral process nor pin stabilization. Within a few days of surgery, the joint was found to have redislocated laterally directly into the defect made by the persistently displaced lateral process because of incompetent medial soft tissue restraints (B). This case is an example of the degree to which fixation of body fragments of the talus such as the lateral process can impart stability to a peritalar injury and prevent recurrent instability. Stabilized large lateral process fractures can effectively functionalize their many lateral ligamentous attachments and intrinsic bony restraint in lieu of alternative Steinmann pin fixation across the subtalar joint from the heel, as was eventually used here on return to the operating room (C). It should be noted that the lateral process can still be seen to be malunited, along with some subtalar joint space narrowing, on the latest follow-up film only 6 months after injury (D).

the peritalar joints. It is not uncommon for a healed but avascular talus to remain asymptomatic for years and require no bracing or other interventional treatment, probably because the avascular process in the post-traumatic as opposed to the systemic (for example, steroid induced) setting is spotty and leaves enough healthy bone behind to support the structure and function of the talus. MRI is probably the most accurate means of assessing the presence and severity of avascular necrosis in a talus after fracture. Its usefulness is facilitated by using titanium hardware at the time of initial treatment.[329]

If symptomatic avascular necrosis develops, the avascular portion of the talus can be replaced with a large tricortical block of bone from the posterior iliac crest or other cancellous bone. Either limited arthrodesis or pan-arthrodesis can then be performed with screw fixation. An anterior Blair fusion or in situ arthrodesis with the remaining vascularized portion of talus can also be considered, depending on how much viable bone remains. Recent encouraging results suggest that total-ankle arthroplasty may be beneficial when the volume of necrosis is small and significant ankle arthrosis and pain exist. These devices are still undergoing a process of design evolution, even for patients without a dysvascular talus, and should therefore be considered experimental under these particular circumstances. Tibiotalocalcaneal fusion results in a fairly rigid hindfoot and produces disability in heavy patients and in those in whom accurate alignment was not originally achieved; a pan-talar arthrodesis maintains the normal size and shape of the hindfoot and preserves the midtarsal joints. Much of the symptomatic discomfort that remains may be alleviated by a well-cushioned rocker-bottom shoe or a solid-ankle, cushioned-heel (SACH) appliance. However, significant arthrosis will occur in adjacent joints over the long run.

**Infection.** The risk of infection increases with increased fracture displacement, open wounds, and attempts to close swollen tissues too early. Prompt reduction and treatment can minimize many of these factors, and aggressive débridement of all open wounds should always be performed. Any open wound or questionable wound flaps after ORIF of an initially closed injury are better left open with antibiotic bead pouches and splinting, elevation, and return to the operating room in 3 to 5 days for repeat débridement and delayed closure. Infection of a talar fracture almost always results in a poor outcome and salvage surgery in the form of partial or total talectomy combined with fusion.[37]

**Nonunion and Malunion.** Although talar neck fractures can often take 3 to 6 months or even longer to heal, the incidence of actual nonunion is quite low, between 0% and 4%, and delayed union occurs in under 10%.[126, 186] Protected weight bearing in this situation is advised and should be followed by clinical examination and eventually evaluated by CT scanning if no progress is identified on plain films within 6 months. In our experience, it typically takes on average about 11 weeks for these injuries to heal. Symptomatic nonunion or nonunion persisting for over 12 to 18 months can be effectively treated with either local cancellous bone grafting or the use of a corticocancellous dowel graft obtained from the iliac crest and inserted across the nonunion site by transtalar drilling above the sinus tarsi. This grafting can be accompanied by appropriate hardware for stability of the construct to allow early range of motion.

Malunion is usually avoidable with stable and anatomic fixation through direct open medial and lateral approaches for any displaced talus fracture. Typically, malunion results from impaction and shortening in a dorsal (especially) and medial direction, with subsequent varus deformity, dorsiflexion impingement at the ankle, shortening of the medial column (adduction of the foot), and impaired peritalar motion (Fig. 60–14). Malunion can occur from settling after fixation of a comminuted fracture, inadequate initial fixation, malreduction as a result of incomplete visualization of the fracture (for example, from only one side), or placement of fixation on only one side of the talus, which can cause compression and shortening through the fracture on that side. The resultant foot deformity usually creates an abnormal lateral weight-bearing pattern and a painful gait. If the initial anatomic reduction is lost on serial films, early intervention with revision reduction and fixation can circumvent these problems before requiring a relatively higher risk osteotomy of the talus or a limited fusion procedure.[59] Sometimes, simple exostectomy can eliminate the symptoms if they are localized.[37]

**Arthrofibrosis.** Stiffness after talar neck injury is also common, particularly with higher energy injuries or those that required prolonged periods of immobilization. Early range-of-motion exercises should begin as soon as possible, with a goal of maintaining at least 50% of preinjury peritalar motion. Some degree of stiffness is inevitable with any displaced talar fracture requiring ORIF. Most patients should be able to obtain at least 50% of subtalar and 75% to 100% of ankle motion after injury. Post-traumatic arthritis is also common in this setting, although it is more likely to be the result of initial osteoarticular damage at the subtalar, ankle, and talonavicular joints. Adjacent joint stiffness can make the other, less affected joints around the talus more subject to wear and accelerated degeneration. Hindfoot fusion is thus not an uncommon salvage procedure after talar injury.

## SALVAGE

Talar neck injuries with poor results can be salvaged with a number of treatment options, depending on the reason for failure and the joints involved. Options include subtalar arthrodesis, tibiotalar arthrodesis, pan-talar arthrodesis, and in rare cases, talectomy.

## Fractures of the Body of the Talus

Fractures of the talar body come in many shapes and sizes and are usually the result of axial compression. They account for over 25% of talar injuries and are probably best described as being located within or behind the lateral process of the talus, which distinguishes them from neck fractures, where the inferior fracture line runs anterior to this anatomic landmark.[1, 126] Fractures extending behind the lateral talar process obligatorily involve the posterior facet of the subtalar joint and are hence most aptly considered body fractures. Although these injuries have

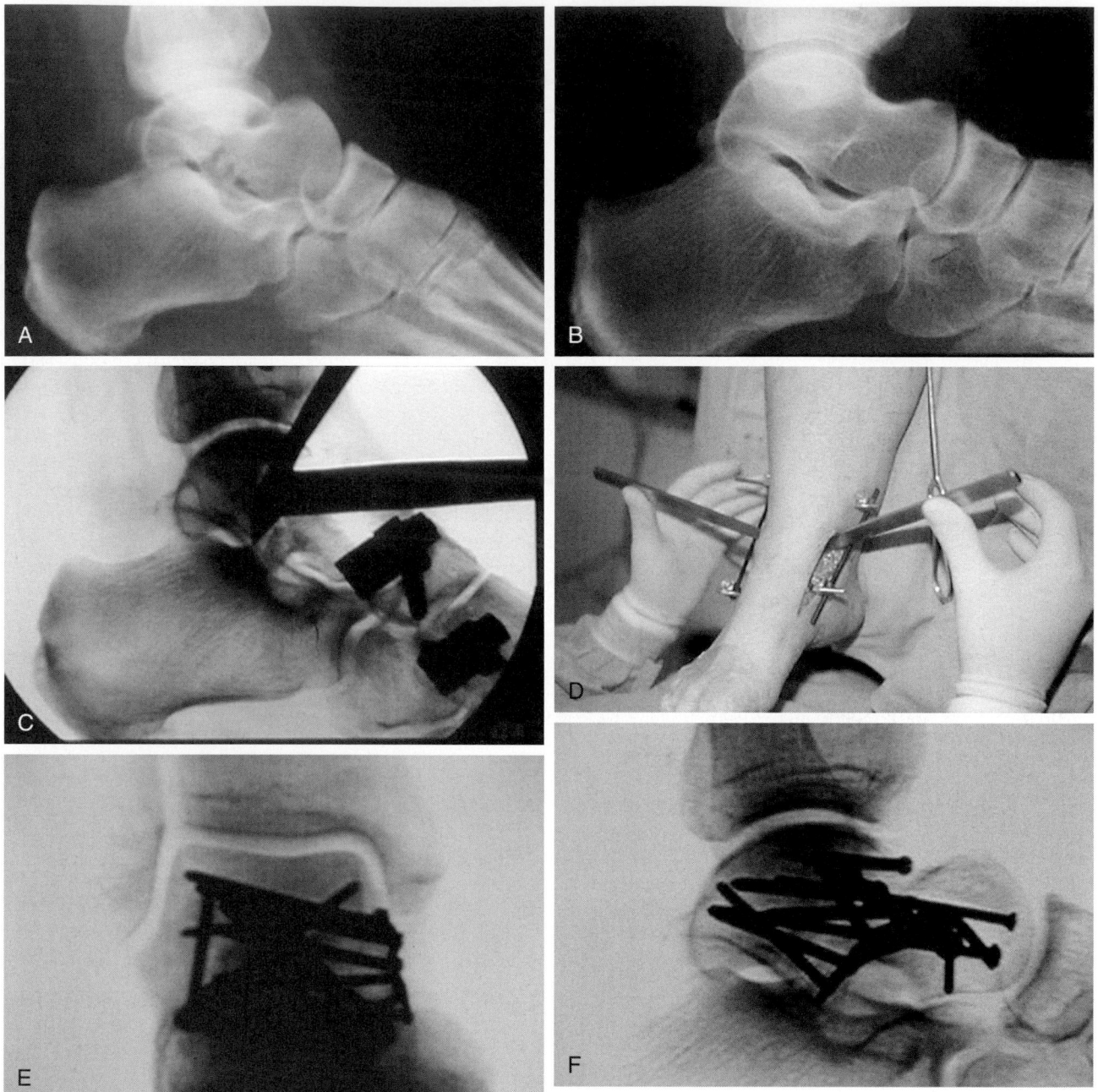

**FIGURE 60–14.** Malunion of a talar neck fracture usually results in medial column shortening, varus malposition of the foot, and abnormal joint mechanics (*A, B*). Because a reduced talonavicular joint defines a "neutral foot," it seems obvious that attention needs to be paid to reduction of talar injuries and the surrounding articulations. This case is an example of such a problem. It required a high-risk takedown osteotomy of the talar neck with bone grafting of the defect to restore proper length and alignment (*C, D*). Follow-up on this patient is short, however, and her ultimate response to this surgery remains unknown (*E, F*). This case is a good example of how an ounce of prevention is worth a pound of cure.

been classified in the past, it seems most utilitarian to just perform a CT scan on them and base treatment on their location and the extent of comminution instead of describing the fracture configuration. They can occur in a coronal, sagittal, transverse, or comminuted (crushed) pattern. As with all talar injuries, prolonged casting is counterproductive to outcome, and thus the vast majority of these body fractures require ORIF through a standard set of exposures and instrumentation. Occasionally, a talar body fracture is rendered non-reconstructible by virtue of comminution, in which case it is best left closed to allow

consolidation with the understanding that future reconstruction in the form of hindfoot or ankle fusion (or fusion of both) may be necessary.[331]

## TREATMENT

The lateral and medial approaches described previously may not provide sufficient exposure of fractures in the midbody or posterior body of the talus. In this event, other approaches should be used to avoid excessive dissection and keep the blood supply safe from injury. A fracture in the midbody can be adequately visualized through a medial transmalleolar approach (Fig. 60–15). The surgical approach is made through a posterior extension of the medial utility incision that curves proximal and cephalad over the malleolus itself, followed by an osteotomy into the axilla of the medial malleolus. The malleolus should be predrilled and fixed with two 4.0-mm cancellous screws before performing the osteotomy to facilitate later reduction. Once these screws are removed, the cut can be made with a small microsagittal saw and completed with an osteotome so that the intra-articular area is protected and the mobile segments key in well during fixation. Obviously, if the malleolus is concomitantly fractured, this plane can be alternatively extrapolated for exposure of the talus.

A fracture of the posterior body may be visualized through a vertical posterolateral or posteromedial approach as described earlier. The lateral body is approached through a vertical incision just lateral to the heel cord and continued behind the sural nerve. Screws inserted from this posterolateral location are directed anteriorly and slightly medially and follow the normal anatomy of the head and neck of the talus. A posteromedial talar body fracture is visualized through a posteromedial approach, with the neurovascular bundle and flexor hallucis longus lifted to access the subtalar joint. Small screws (2.0 and 2.4 mm) are necessary to avoid the ankle and subtalar articulations. Care must be taken to protect the calcaneal branch of the tibial nerve during this procedure. A 4-mm half pin can be placed in the talar head from a medial approach to assist in maintaining both length and alignment.

A high-energy Hawkins type III or IV fracture can result in posteromedial or posterolateral extrusion of the body and is frequently associated with an open injury (40% to 50%) necessitating aggressive irrigation, débridement, and antibiotic bead pouch placement. A long, vertical posteromedial incision provides the best approach for reduction of these injuries. As mentioned previously, the deltoid ligament's attachment to the medial body must not be damaged because it carries the blood supply to this portion of the talus. Often, calcaneal pin traction on a femoral distractor can facilitate reduction of the extruded fragment. The surgeon should also ensure that the patient is paralyzed during surgery, if possible, to help relieve any tension in the surrounding soft tissue.

The size of the fracture fragments and the density of the bone determine the diameter of the screws to be inserted

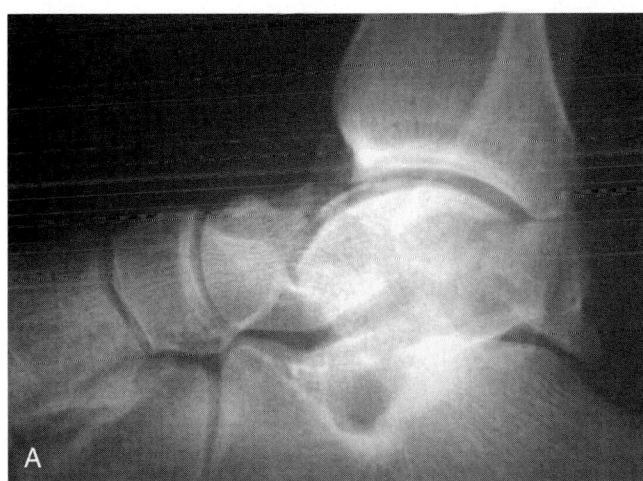

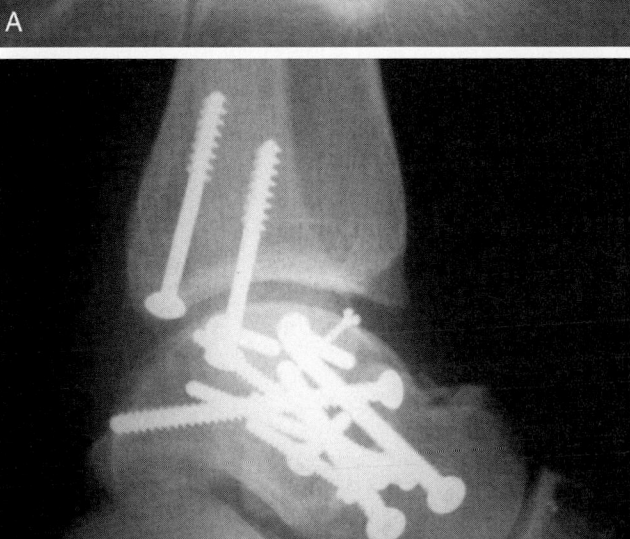

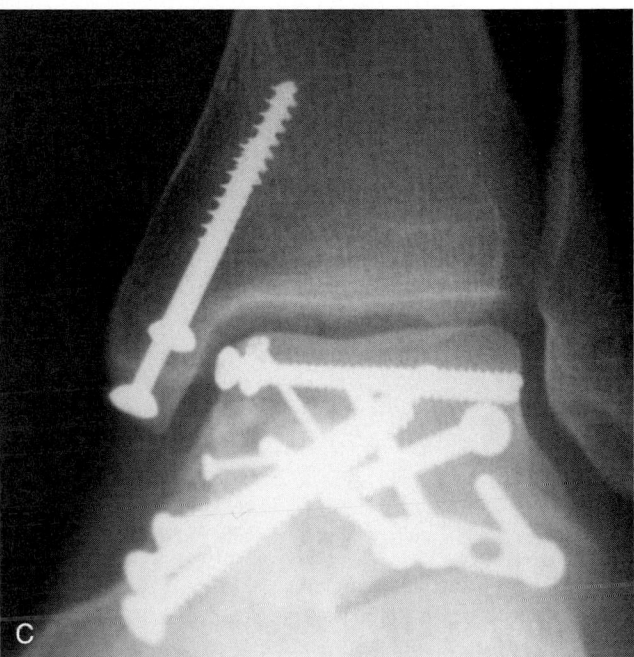

**FIGURE 60–15.** Talar body fractures often require a medial malleolar osteotomy to adequately visualize the area of injury and reduce and stabilize it, often with countersunk subchondral screws. As opposed to when the medial malleolar osteotomy is performed at or above the level of the malleolar shoulder for vertical access and transplantation of the autogenous osteoarticular graft harvest during mosaicplasty for talar dome osteochondritis dissecans, in this case the osteotomy should be performed just below the level of the shoulder because it not only allows sufficient access for open reduction and internal fixation but also becomes a more stable construct after fixation. There remains a small intact shoulder against which the talus can safely sit without stress to the repair, and weight bearing is thus also away from the area of osteotomy, theoretically decreasing the risk of symptomatic osteoarthritis. This case of a talar body fracture (A) required medial malleolar osteotomy and osteoarticular screw fixation for adequate reduction (B, C). The typical location of the osteotomy is well visualized.

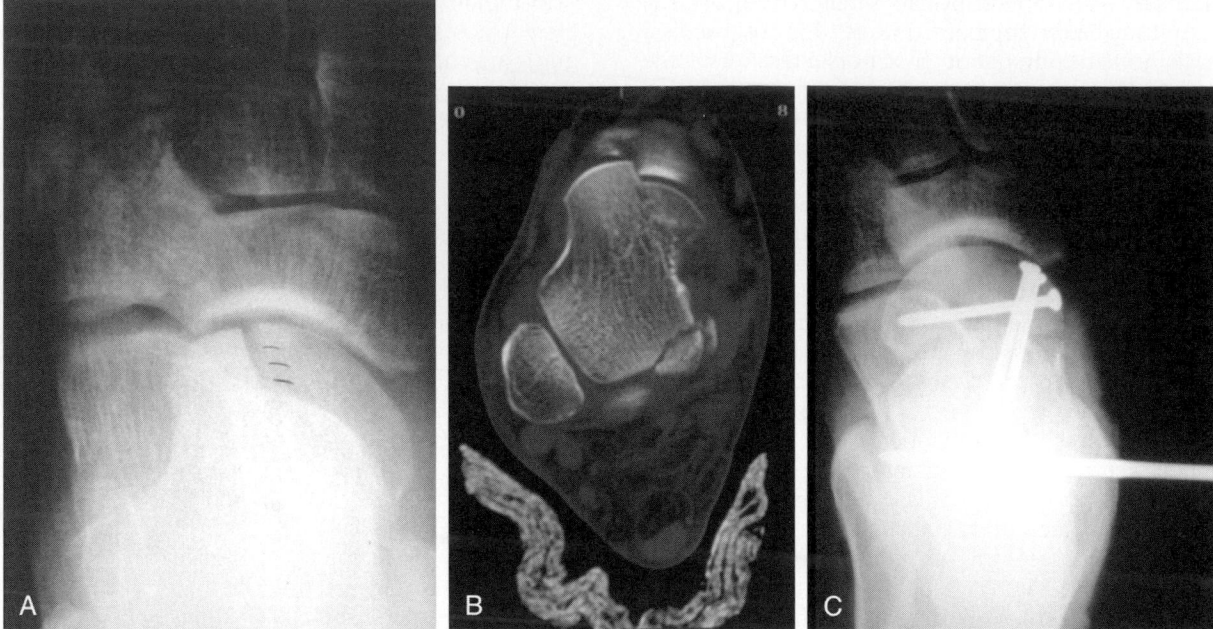

**Figure 60–16.** Talar head fractures are uncommon and easily missed. In this case, the patient sustained a significant abduction and impaction loading injury to the foot that caused a shear fracture through the talar head and an associated impaction fracture of the cuboid with loss of length of the lateral column and abduction and peritalar subluxation through the medial column (*A*). An axial computed tomographic cut shows this shear injury well (*B*). The fracture of the talar head was disimpacted, reduced, and fixed, and the cuboid fracture was disimpacted, bone grafted, and plated (*C*).

and the size of the holes to be drilled. A large fragment may accept 2.7- or 3.5-mm screws for compression and immobilization of the fracture, as well as rotatory control. A small fragment may be adequately secured with a 2.4- or 2.0-mm screw inserted through a gliding hole in the proximal fragment. All the screws are allowed to self-tap into the cancellous bone. Any large defects should be concomitantly filled with bone graft harvested from the iliac crest or Gerdy's tubercle, depending on size requirements. This procedure should be done primarily only when the soft tissue bed is considered healthy.

## OUTCOME

The high incidence of complications with major talar body fractures has been well documented.[51, 315] These complications are similar to those listed for talar neck fractures and follow the same treatment guidelines.[149] Open fractures are associated with a markedly inferior overall prognosis. Avascular necrosis can be anticipated in at least 50% of patients, and in many, post-traumatic arthrosis will develop in the ankle, subtalar, or both joints and lead to chronic pain of varying severity.

## Fractures of the Head of the Talus

Fractures of the head of the talus are uncommon but may occur from compressive axial loads, extreme dorsiflexion moments, or high-energy injuries such as motor vehicle accidents.[51] These fractures typically occur in conjunction with more complex injuries, and partial dislocation or subluxation of the talus is common. Capsular and ligamentous injuries may occur with subluxation or

dislocation and are frequently associated with fractures of the talar head. The talonavicular joint is often damaged and can be rendered unstable if this fracture involves half of the talar head.[332] A Chopart joint injury can also extend into the lateral column and involve the calcaneocuboid articulation, thus suggesting an even more severe injury. These injuries are frequently missed on routine radiographs.

## TREATMENT

Small, impacted articular fragments or nondisplaced fractures are best treated conservatively with a short period of casting for 4 to 6 weeks, followed by early mobilization and progressive weight bearing. Consideration can be given to orthotic arch support after full weight-bearing status and cast removal to decompress stress across the talonavicular joint until the patient is asymptomatic.

Surgery is indicated when fragments are displaced, in association with talonavicular incongruity, or are large in size. The surgical approach for the treatment of fractures and dislocations of the head of the talus is similar to that used for other talar fractures and is typically anteromedial. Depending on size, fracture fragments are secured to the head with 1.5-, 2.0-, 2.4-, or 2.7-mm cortical screws or even headless (Herbert or Accutrax) or bioresorbable screws inserted perpendicular to the fracture line and countersunk into the cartilage (Fig. 60–16). Bone grafting may be necessary for severely impacted fragments to prevent settling and articular incongruity after fixation. Fragments that are too small to be replaced or held securely by fixation because of comminution should be excised. Impacted articular fragments, usually caused by navicular impression, may be buttressed by miniplates

(2.0, 1.5 mm) after support by cancellous bone grafts. By itself, a fracture in the head of the talus does not threaten vascularity in the body, although a dislocation associated with a fracture may present this risk. Occasionally after reconstruction of the talar head, the talonavicular joint may still be unstable and can be secured in anatomic position with a large axial K-wire at least 0.062 inch in diameter, and the capsule is sutured in place for additional stability. As a last resort, talonavicular fusion may be required in the event of persistent instability, nonunion, or post-traumatic arthrosis.

A fracture or dislocation of the talar head requiring operative intervention usually heals after 6 to 8 weeks of immobilization in a partial weight-bearing cast. If mobilization can be permitted with this or other talar injuries after fixation, a dorsiflexion night splint or similar device that is easily removable can help prevent a resting equinus contracture, protect the limb during healing, and provide free access during therapy.

## Chip and Avulsion Fractures

These small fractures involve various segments of the talus and are usually the result of a twisting-type sprain of the foot or ankle. They are typically low energy and account for 25% of talar fractures. Usually, these fractures are clinically insignificant in size and result from the pull of a ligamentous attachment. They are more important to identify as a radiographic sign of a potentially significant soft tissue or ligamentous injury that might require further evaluation, as opposed to worrying about a bony abnormality that might require ORIF.

## Osteochondral Fractures of the Talus

Small osteochondral fractures of the talus are not always visible on standard radiographs. They may also be missed on physical examination because their symptoms sometimes mimic those of a sprain syndrome. However, the presence of osteochondral fracture fragments should be suspected in all type III ankle sprains or syndesmotic injuries and all partial or complete subtalar fracture-dislocations.[5] Furthermore, a recent retrospective study of 50 supination–external rotation type IV ankle fractures identified osteochondral fractures in 38% of cases.[317] No difference was noted between bony and ligamentous injury patterns, and inspection of the talar dome was recommended in all ankle fractures. The presence of osteochondral fragments may be confirmed by Broden's radiographic views and by careful palpation of the ankle[28] (see Fig. 60–6). Additionally, mortise views of the ankle in maximal dorsiflexion and plantar flexion should also be obtained because of their increased sensitivity and because these injuries are often posterolateral or anteromedial on the talar dome. If left untreated, even small, undisplaced fragments may precipitate symptoms of internal derangement of the ankle or secondary subtalar arthritis that can eventually necessitate subtalar fusion. CT, scintigraphy, and MRI are helpful in making a difficult diagnosis.

## TREATMENT

Small osteochondral fractures 5 mm or smaller in diameter may occur along the margins of the talar dome or around the head. These fragments are composed primarily of cartilage and should be removed by open surgery or arthroscopy. If they are anterior enough, they can easily be removed by a medial or lateral arthrotomy. Most of them, however, are best managed by arthroscopic intervention through standard anterior, lateral, and sometimes posterolateral ankle portals with a 30°, 2.7-mm scope camera[12, 87] (Fig. 60–17). Occasionally, a 1.9-mm, 30° or a 2.7-mm, 70° angled camera is required for osteochondral fragments in difficult positions. Once the area is débrided, its base should be either curetted or drilled transmalleorally with 0.054- or 0.062 inch K-wires because smaller wires run the risk of intra-articular breakage. Various vector guides are available to facilitate this technique through a single portal that violates the cartilage only once. Larger fragments may be anatomically repositioned and secured with 2.0-, 2.4-, or 2.7-mm cortical screws or Herbert screws as soon as possible after injury. The screws are countersunk under the articular surface. Every effort should be made to débride free non-reconstructible osteochondral or chondral fragments if surgically accessible.

Postoperatively, patients are kept in a removable controlled ankle motion (CAM) walker and kept non–weight bearing for 4 to 6 weeks, during which time they undergo aggressive mobilization and therapy. Such management allows sufficient time for a fibrocartilage healing response, after which patients can begin weight-of-leg weight bearing, which can rapidly progress to unrestricted ambulation guided by patient comfort. Mosaicplasty, a recently described technique to replace injured or displaced hyaline cartilage in a defined anatomic region with similar cartilage from the knee, remains experimental but promising. It requires a fair amount of surgery, usually through a windowing osteotomy of either the medial malleolus or distal end of the fibula, and should probably be reserved as salvage if the arthroscopic intervention as outlined earlier fails. Thus, it is best considered in the more chronic situation.[119] Newer techniques relying on cartilage restoration by osteoarticular allograft transplantation[113] or cartilage regeneration through host chondroblast injection beneath periosteal flaps sewn over the articular surface defects[45, 213] are promising but as of yet unproven methods of managing this difficult problem around the talus (Fig. 60–18). Patients frequently remain symptomatic, not so much because of the size of these defects (most of them are actually quite small and are surrounded by otherwise normal hyaline tissue), but rather because of the location of these defects in a major weight-bearing area.

## Fractures of the Posterior Process of the Talus

Acute osteochondral fractures involving the subtalar joint are usually more difficult to diagnose and treat, partly because of the confusing anatomy and more limited imaging. CT scanning and a high index of clinical suspicion are most helpful in this regard. The presence of fragments here, if left untreated, usually leads to late arthrosis in the subtalar joint and eventually necessitates subtalar arthrodesis. A fracture in this location is generally caused by a direct plantar flexion compressive injury resulting in impaction or by an indirect tension injury (sprain) resulting in avulsion by pull of the posterior talofibular ligament.[249] They are frequently missed on initial examination.

## ANATOMY

The posterior process is probably the most commonly injured region of the talus, although it is rare for it to be fractured in its entirety and injury almost always involves one of its adjacent tubercles, primarily the lateral one.[44, 234] This prominence is composed of a larger, lateral tubercle (so-called Shepherd's fracture) and a smaller medial one; the sulcus between these tubercles provides

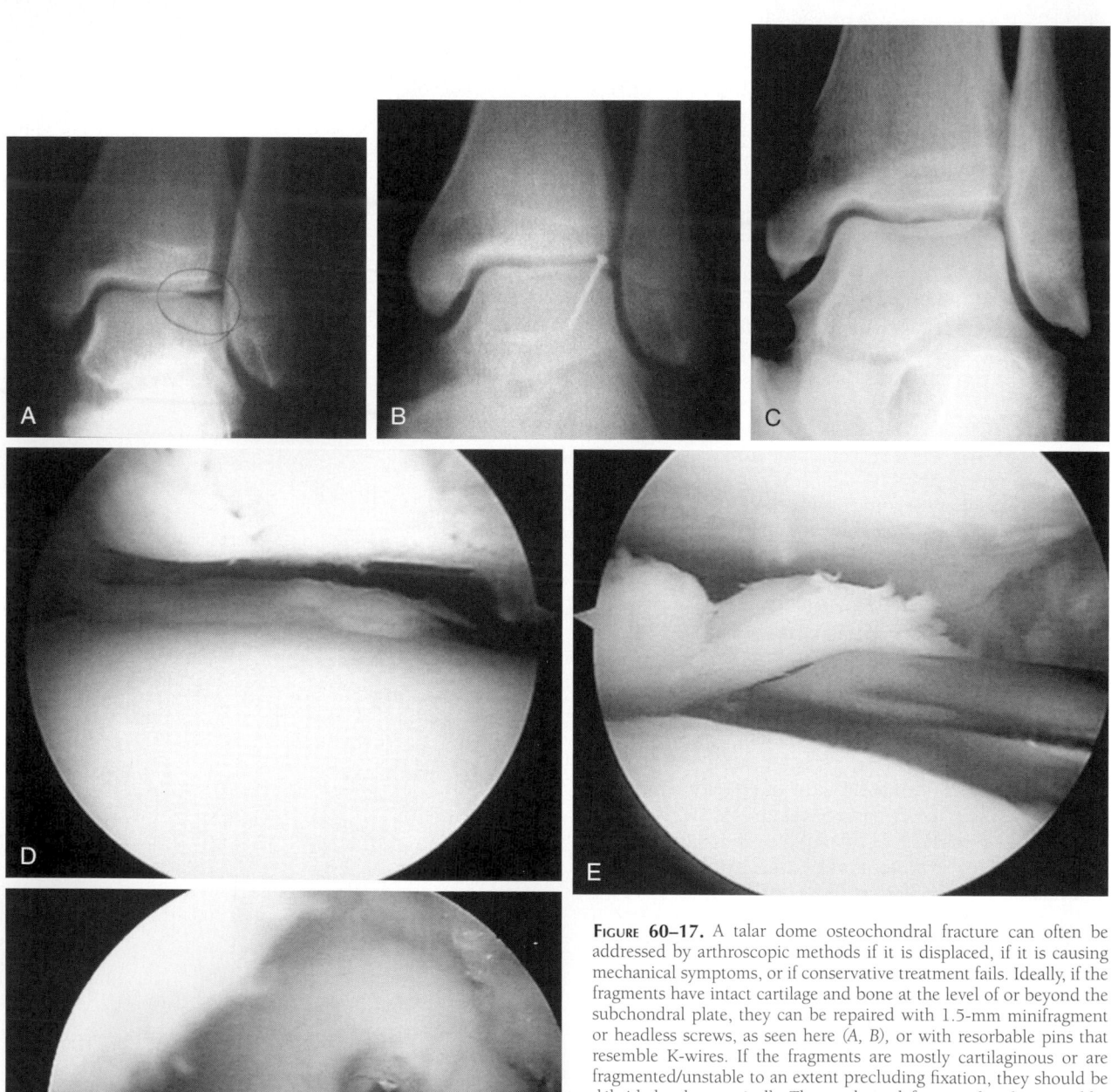

**Figure 60–17.** A talar dome osteochondral fracture can often be addressed by arthroscopic methods if it is displaced, if it is causing mechanical symptoms, or if conservative treatment fails. Ideally, if the fragments have intact cartilage and bone at the level of or beyond the subchondral plate, they can be repaired with 1.5-mm minifragment or headless screws, as seen here (A, B), or with resorbable pins that resemble K-wires. If the fragments are mostly cartilaginous or are fragmented/unstable to an extent precluding fixation, they should be débrided arthroscopically. The resultant defect can then be treated by either drilling, curettage, or a microfracture technique. The latter situation was found in this semiprofessional football player who had chronic locking and pain in his ankle after a bad ankle sprain a few months before the initial evaluation. His displaced osteochondral fracture can be identified on the initial plain radiograph at the lateral aspect of the shoulder of the talus (C) and is better seen as a step-off on the initial arthroscopic evaluation (D). After excision of a large, unstable lateral defect (E), this patient was treated by drilling (F). To date, he still has some intermittent pain and swelling in his ankle, but the procedure has relieved 80% of his pain and all of his mechanical symptoms, and he is back playing football.

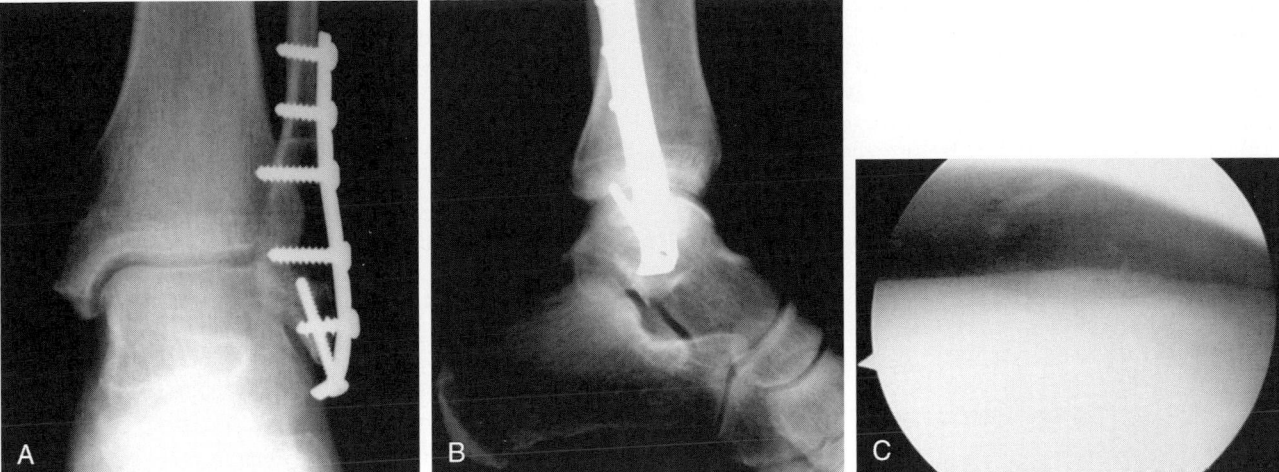

**FIGURE 60–18.** Osteochondral transplantation is a relatively new and promising technique for treating chronic and possibly acute full-thickness cartilage defects or osteochondral fractures. In the foot, it has been most widely used for contained talar dome injuries. Experiments are being performed with osteocartilaginous allograft transplantation, chondral regeneration, and most commonly, autograft mosaicplasty as seen here. With the last-named technique, dowel-type autogenous donor grafts composed of cartilage, subchondral plate, and cancellous bone approximately 1 mm longer and thicker than the cored-out receiver site defects are harvested from the ipsilateral knee and inserted into the talar dome recipient sites. Malleolar osteotomies are usually necessary to provide access during these procedures. The grafts are left proud approximately 1 mm, and non–weight-bearing, early range-of-motion exercises are begun to nourish the cartilage and avoid stiffness. Although computed tomography best identifies the exact anatomy of the defect, it is less sensitive than magnetic resonance imaging in predicting an intact cartilaginous surface preoperatively or identifying the edematous changes that correlate with subclinical impaction injuries not seen on plain films. The case provided shows the typical lateral fibular window and postoperative fixation used to treat a posterolateral osteochondral defect in the talus (*A, B*). The arthroscopic picture (*C*) was taken 6 months after transplantation during hardware removal and demonstrates a nicely filled-in defect at the talar level.

passage for the flexor hallucis longus before it traverses underneath the sustentaculum. The process can be described by various terms, depending on its appearance. Acute fracture must be distinguished from a congenital os trigonum, essentially a well-rounded synchondrosis of this process to the posterior talar body that is found just behind the lateral tubercle.[99, 235, 296] An os trigonum is present bilaterally in 50% to 60% of patients, and comparison views are therefore often helpful. Both can be symptomatic after an extreme plantar flexion moment on the foot that drives the posterior process into the inferior tibial plafond (posterior malleolus), an injury best described as "posterior impingement syndrome of the ankle." Pain in this case results from a combination of soft tissue impingement and inflammation, as well as from bone bruises or fracture as a consequence of the impaction. The patient can have a fracture, symptomatic os trigonum, or simply soft tissue swelling and tenderness to palpation located posterolaterally or posteromedially in the soft spot behind the ankle. It may be more common with two alternative variations of this anatomy, for example, when the posterior process is large, the so-called Stieda process or, if the os trigonum is fused, the so-called trigonal process. Both these processes are joined to the posterior talar body by synostosis. The best test is probably a positive provocative plantar flexion maneuver of the foot in the face of a negative dorsiflexion maneuver. Patients are often locally tender to palpation in either the medial or lateral posterior fossa of the ankle joint. Acute fractures can be differentiated from these other congenital abnormalities by an irregular contour on radiographs or by use of a bone scan, CT, or MRI.

## TREATMENT

All causes of posterior impingement syndrome except displaced, large articular fragments are best treated acutely with a RICE (rest, ice, compression, elevation) protocol for 2 to 3 weeks with immobilization, followed by rapid progression of weight bearing and range-of-motion exercises over the ensuing few weeks. Full recovery is usually the rule, but sometimes a diagnostic (and occasionally therapeutic) injection, as advocated by Hamilton,[118] or even open or arthroscopic excision of a symptomatic os trigonum or ununited tubercle fracture is necessary for maximal relief.[10, 346] Arthroscopically, either tubercle can be accessed through a two-portal posterior approach (trans-Achilles and posterolateral or superoposterolateral and inferoposterolateral), although if a limited open approach is preferred, direct exposure on the side of the injury through either a small posterolateral or posteromedial exposure is recommended. Excision is typically very successful in relieving pain and restoring motion and a more normal gait pattern.[201, 346]

Large displaced fragments have strong ligamentous attachments superolaterally with the posterior talofibular ligament and the fibuloastragalocalcaneal ligament of Rouvière and Canela Lazaro (on the lateral tubercle) and inferomedially with the flexor retinaculum, posterior talocalcaneal ligament, and deltoid ligament (on the medial tubercle). Thus, fractures of the posterior process not only represent significant intra-articular involvement of the ankle and subtalar joints (25% of the facet) but may affect joint stability as well. These fractures are therefore probably best fixed openly through a posteromedial or, preferably, a posterolateral vertical incision. Small 1.5- or 2.0-mm screws are best, and occasionally a minifragment T plate is required.[234]

The posteromedial talar body is often involved in a subtalar dislocation or high-energy axial load on a varus-positioned foot. The medial subtalar dislocation that results is often open anterolaterally because the skin is literally torn by the force of the dislocation. Access to the posteromedial body is difficult and requires elevation of the neurovascular bundle and flexor hallucis longus, with limited visualization of the subtalar joint. Large fragments should be repaired to facilitate subtalar stability and potentially limit the often rapid onset of subtalar arthritis. Fixation is usually with small screws (2.0 or 2.4 mm) to avoid transgressing the ankle and subtalar joints because of the limited room for implants in this area (Fig. 60–19).

## Fractures of the Lateral Process of the Talus

Lateral process fractures (the so-called snowboarder's fracture) are frequently mistaken for sprains and diagnosed late in the course of treatment.[129, 238] They are missed about 33% of the time at initial examination. The tip-off to these injuries is often a history of an inversion sprain that never seems to become pain free. Late symptoms are common after these injuries, regardless of the initial method of treatment. The ability to successfully treat these fractures with ORIF, if necessary, to maximize the outcome

decreases after approximately 4 weeks from injury. After this period, excision becomes the only feasible treatment alternative in symptomatic patients and is usually successful in alleviating some, but not all symptoms of pain and stiffness in the hindfoot. Symptomatic nonunion is unfortunately common and usually requires operative intervention.

The lateral process or "shoulder" of the talus forms the posterior wall of the sinus tarsi and the anterolateral corner of the posterior facet of the talus. This structure is underappreciated functionally, but it incorporates some major ligamentous attachments of the lateral talocalcaneal ligament, the anterior talofibular ligament, and the posterior talofibular ligament.[296] It also provides some bony structural support and resistance to valgus stress through its superior articulation with the lateral malleolus and inferior articulation with the posterior facet of the calcaneus. It is frequently larger than appreciated on plain films and represents some of the biggest osteochondral fractures surrounding the talus. These fractures are typically caused by axial loading with elements of dorsiflexion and eversion and have been identified to have a high prevalence in snowboarders as a result of the particular stresses put on the foot and ankle in the boot-binding complex.[170] Physical examination usually reveals point tenderness over the anteroinferior aspect of the distal end of the fibula, in the immediate vicinity of the lateral ligament complex of the ankle. Although these fractures can usually be seen on plain films of the ankle,

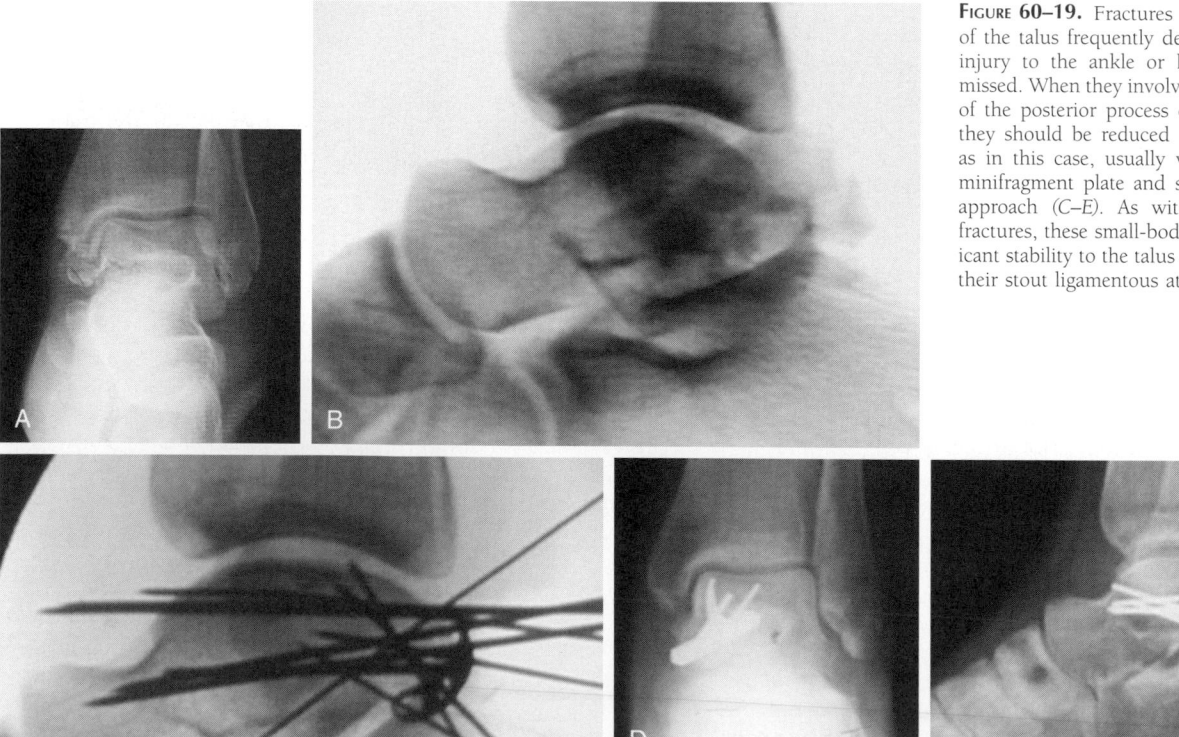

**FIGURE 60–19.** Fractures of the posterior process of the talus frequently denote a more significant injury to the ankle or hindfoot and are often missed. When they involve a considerable portion of the posterior process or are displaced (*A, B*), they should be reduced anatomically and fixed, as in this case, usually with a 1.5- or 2.0-mm minifragment plate and screws from a posterior approach (*C–E*). As with lateral process talus fractures, these small-body fragments lend significant stability to the talus after fixation because of their stout ligamentous attachments.

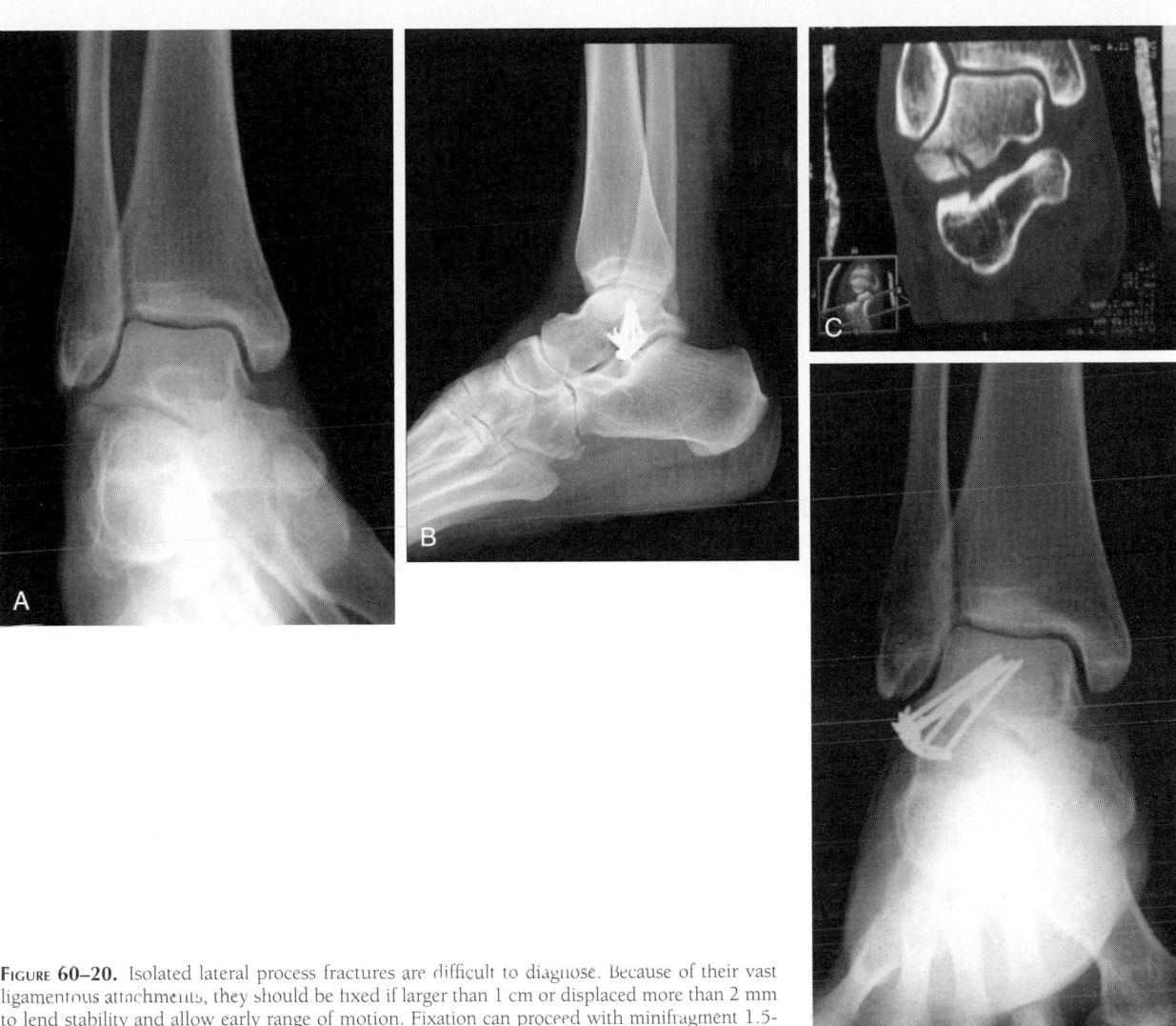

**FIGURE 60–20.** Isolated lateral process fractures are difficult to diagnose. Because of their vast ligamentous attachments, they should be fixed if larger than 1 cm or displaced more than 2 mm to lend stability and allow early range of motion. Fixation can proceed with minifragment 1.5- or 2.0-mm lag screws or, as in this case, with a small, straight minifragment 2.0-mm plate through an Ollier approach and early motion.

especially on a mortise view with a plantar flexed foot, a CT scan may be warranted in those with a high index of clinical suspicion or to detect the presence of an undisplaced body fracture. Hawkins has classified these injuries into three groups: (1) an extra-articular avulsion fracture, (2) a large fragment with a single fracture line traversing both the superior and inferior articular surfaces, and (3) a large fragment that is comminuted.[125]

## TREATMENT

Small or minimally displaced (less than 2 mm) fractures of the lateral process can be treated with short leg cast immobilization and non–weight bearing for 4 to 6 weeks.[129] Because this fracture fragment transfers much of the 16% to 17% of weight borne in the leg through the fibula, early weight bearing risks further displacement. Generally good results can be expected with nondisplaced fragments treated according to this regimen. Closed reduction is usually difficult when displacement is present.

A large osteochondral fracture that is not comminuted or one that may be smaller but significantly displaced

(greater than 2 mm) requires anatomic open reduction and compression with one or two 1.5-, 2.0-, or 2.4-mm screws or a small miniplate (Fig. 60–20). Consideration should be given to primary excision of comminuted fracture fragments, especially those associated with an undisplaced body fracture, because of the ill effects that closed treatment of such injuries can have on subtalar motion.[217] Excision should also be considered in the event of a delay in diagnosis (chronic). If a body fracture is present, it should be repaired at the same operation. Frequently, patients are seen with chronic ankle or sinus tarsi pain after a previous sprain, with unremarkable plain films, but in actual fact these patients have ununited, often undisplaced lateral process fractures. Unless the fragments are very large and the joint space is in good shape, they should probably be excised for symptomatic relief.[340] Instability is not usually a problem at this juncture (although it certainly can be in the acute setting) because most of these patients have some degree of stiffness that overrides the instability. As with all talar fractures, any gap after fixation should be treated by autogenous bone grafting.

Despite appropriate management in many of these cases, a large number of patients treated by both closed and open means remain persistently painful and stiff through their subtalar joint and require either subtalar arthroscopy or even subtalar fusion for minimization of their symptoms. Subtalar arthrosis is a common eventuality in this scenario.

## Postoperative Care and Rehabilitation

In general, the postoperative regimen for talar fractures is the same as for other major injuries in the foot. The foot is either wrapped in a bulky compression splint or immobilized in a cast. The patient is restricted to bed exercise with the leg slightly elevated for 2 to 3 days.

Patients should actively wiggle their toes (intrinsic muscle exercises) and perform isometric exercises of the ankle and other parts of the foot to stimulate circulation and control swelling. On the third postoperative day, a removable splint may be applied and patients may begin active range-of-motion exercises of the ankle and subtalar joints, provided that these joints are stable. Weight-of-leg weight bearing is also begun if the fixation is strong enough to tolerate the weight. The foot must be elevated frequently during the next 2.5 to 3 weeks. The original cast and sutures are removed at the scheduled time, and a well-molded short leg bivalved cast or a commercially made removable splint is applied. A bivalved cast or removable splint should be used only on a reliable patient who is expected to follow the exercise regimen and replace it afterward. The splint or cast must be applied firmly in a neutral position at night to prevent the foot from dropping into an equinus posture during sleep. Weight-of-leg weight bearing and active motion of the toes, ankle, and subtalar joint should be continued, if fixation and bone stock are reliable, until healing is complete, usually at about 10 to 12 weeks after surgery. Passive range of motion of the MTP joints, especially in extension, can help prevent long toe flexor clawing. Early motion is extremely important for a satisfactory result. Active, but nonresistive inversion-eversion exercises are performed at first, followed by inversion-eversion exercises with the use of rubber tubing for resistance. If a length of rubber tubing is looped over the toes of both feet, one foot can work against the other in eversion. If the loop of tubing is wrapped around a solid object such as a table leg, the foot may be inverted against resistance. Return of normal motion in the foot is very gradual and may take up to a year.

Fractures that are susceptible to avascular necrosis should be evaluated by radiograph at 6 weeks to look for Hawkins' sign.[126] If disuse osteoporosis, which is associated with intact vascularity, occurs only in the medial part of the talar body, the patient should continue partial weight bearing until evidence is seen of either healing and increased vascularity progressing laterally or slight collapse. Some surgeons rely on a PTB brace to prevent excessive weight bearing. A brace does not guarantee prevention of excessive weight bearing because patient compliance is difficult to ensure and these orthoses are not easy to fit. The brace creates an obligatory leg length discrepancy that makes normal gait essentially impossible.

It is hard to keep a patient on crutch-protected weight bearing for longer than a few months anyway, although enough vascularity usually remains in the body fragments to heal the fracture even when weight-bearing restrictions are disregarded. In fact, Szyszkowitz and associates[321] and others have demonstrated that complete avascular necrosis is rare when immediate reduction and compression fixation are followed by an active, but low-impact postoperative regimen. A removable bivalved cast or splint should be used at night for at least 3 months to prevent the development of an equinus contracture under these circumstances. Thereafter, the act of weight bearing passively continues to stretch the gastrocnemius-soleus complex, and splinting can be more safely terminated. Anatomic reduction, stable fixation, and early motion can achieve near-normal function in many cases.

## TARSAL DISLOCATIONS

### Subtalar Dislocation

#### ANATOMY AND DIAGNOSIS

About 1% to 2% of all dislocations involve the subtalar joint.[176] Isolated subtalar dislocations classically involve incongruity of the talocalcaneal and talonavicular joints, whereas the calcaneocuboid and ankle joints remain unaffected.[47, 66] Occasionally, surrounding hindfoot injuries such as a talar neck fracture can accompany the dislocation and should be carefully looked for on plain films, although more commonly, simple avulsion or impaction fractures of the talar processes or head, hindfoot tarsals, fifth metatarsal base, or malleoli are identified in at least half of cases.[66] Osteochondral fractures can be found in most of these injuries, particularly lateral dislocations, thus making a "pure" dislocation fairly unusual.

Subtalar dislocations are the result of a high-energy mechanism 75% of the time, and their description is based on the relationship of the resultant foot to the remaining leg and ankle. When compared with low-energy mechanisms, the high-energy variant is associated with a poorer prognosis and a higher incidence of lateral dislocation, intra-articular fracture, and open injury.[142] The subtalar joint can dislocate in any direction, most commonly in a medial (80%) and, to a lesser extent, a lateral (15%) direction. These injuries can also have posterior or anterior components to them, although pure sagittal plane dislocations are rare. The main ligamentous support involves the interosseous, superficial deltoid, and fibulocalcaneal ligaments, all of which need to tear for a typical coronal plane dislocation. The calcaneonavicular ligament is often spared during this injury because of its increased tensile strength and thus may also indirectly contribute to the reason why the talocalcaneal and not other surrounding tarsal joints dislocate with such frequency in the hindfoot/midfoot.

Typically, these injuries cause marked deformity of the foot, regardless of the direction of dislocation; the appearance can mimic an ankle dislocation at initial evaluation, especially when the injury is accompanied by significant soft tissue swelling (see Fig. 60–13). In fact, with injuries due to extreme force, ankle dislocation can represent a continuation of a subtalar dislocation and be a precursor to total talar dislocation (extrusion). Medial dislocations result from a plantar flexion inversion moment around the sustentaculum that initially disrupts the talonavicular before the talocalcaneal joint; these injuries can even result from such injuries as a sprain because of the fewer anatomic constraints against this direction. In this case, the injured foot looks like a clubfoot on initial examination. The foot is inverted, adducted, and plantar flexed, usually with tented skin or an open wound laterally. Lateral dislocations, on the other hand, have the opposite deformity, and more than half are associated with open wounds. In general, this dislocation pattern can be expected to carry a worse prognosis.[339] The foot is abducted and pronated and, in contradistinction to medial dislocations, looks much like a flatfoot. The injury in this circumstance usually rotates around the anterior process of the calcaneus. Although neurovascular injury is rare except in open injuries, the tented skin in closed injuries remains at high risk and therefore represents a surgical urgency. Avascular necrosis is unusual, and infection can occur in up to one third of open cases.[132]

Standard foot radiographs should be obtained before attempts at reduction to assess for any associated fracture and thus aid in diagnosis and reduction, although the diagnosis is usually obvious. These films should ideally include an ankle series as well if injury at that level is also suspected. Remember that it is impossible to "sprain" the ankle without using the foot as a lever arm, and it is equally difficult to twist the foot without some degree of torque on the ankle. Concomitant injuries are not uncommon and should be expected and evaluated.

## CLOSED REDUCTION

The important point in understanding the nature of a subtalar dislocation and thus how best to treat it is the talonavicular relationship and the direction of its displacement because it guides reduction. The reduction maneuver depends on the direction of displacement. In any case, the following initial sequence helps facilitate this process: (1) adequate anesthesia is induced, (2) the hip and knee are flexed to relax the pull of the gastrocnemius muscle and held for countertraction, (3) the heel is manually distracted longitudinally, and (4) the deformity is initially exaggerated to "unlock" the foot.[319] Thereafter, if the dislocation is medial, the now inverted and plantar-flexed foot (in line with the deformity) is subsequently everted and dorsiflexed to achieve relocation. As with any subtalar dislocation, the talonavicular joint is key to this reduction because it guides the talar head distally and brings the foot from a plantar-medial to a dorsolateral position. In the case of lateral dislocations, after similarly exaggerating the position of the initial deformity, plantar-medial pressure is placed on the foot from a dorsolateral direction while stabilizing the talar head distally, until relocation occurs.

Any component of posterior translation is concomitantly corrected by first disimpacting the plantarly displaced navicular from the talar neck with forefoot plantar flexion and then distracting the foot and applying anterior longitudinal and dorsal pressure on the foot. Again, the talus must be stabilized through manual positioning of its prominent head to facilitate this technique.[147] Remember, everything in the foot always moves around the talus, not vice versa. Any component of anterior translation is oppositely reduced with plantar flexion and anterior longitudinal translation to disengage the posterior calcaneal facet from being perched underneath the lateral talar process, much like a jumped facet in the cervical spine.[146] The foot is then allowed to translate posteriorly in a reduced fashion. Conscious sedation is often all that is required for reduction of these injuries if caught early, although 10% to 15% of dislocations remain irreducible without surgery. As the time between injury and treatment increases, the inevitable peritalar swelling makes closed reduction increasingly more difficult. If reduction can be successfully achieved, it is recommended that immediate postreduction radiographs of the ankle and foot be obtained to verify the reduction before splinting. Occasionally, CT scanning is warranted to assess for intra-articular osteochondral injury.

## OPEN REDUCTION

Approximately 10% of medial and 20% of lateral dislocations cannot be reduced by closed means.[132] When surgery is required for medial dislocations, the cause may be anatomic constraints such as an interposed deep peroneal neurovascular bundle; talar head buttonholing through its surrounding retinaculum (the extensor retinaculum being the most common offender), the calcaneonavicular ligament (medial portion of the bifurcate ligament), the capsule, or the extensor brevis musculature; peroneal interposition; or a talonavicular impaction fracture (or any combination of these mechanisms).[127] The latter occurs particularly with prolonged dislocation times, when the navicular cannot be disimpacted from the talar head, and it forms a kind of Hill-Sachs lesion here as in the shoulder. Reduction of lateral dislocations is often impeded by a mirror image impaction injury of the talonavicular region or by interposition of the flexor digitorum longus or, most commonly, the posterior tibial tendon around the talar neck. For medial dislocations, an anteromedial incision should be made starting just distal to the talar head and extending proximally. Such an incision allows access to all potential obstructions, including any locked impression fractures. Care should be taken to avoid the talocalcaneal joint, unless imaging suggests incarceration of fragments at that site, because it is not usually impeding reduction and contains a significant vascular contribution to the talus. For irreducible lateral dislocations, a medial utility incision or, less preferably, a longitudinal approach to the sinus tarsi and tip of the fibula is made. The former approach is useful for access to the incarcerated posterior tibial or flexor tendons, whereas the latter approach can be used for any irreducible anterior or posterior subluxation. Any non-reconstructible bony or cartilaginous fragments should be concomitantly excised before reduction while visualization is best, and any large periarticular fractures should be anatomically reduced and fixed.

## REHABILITATIVE PROTOCOL

Reduction is usually stable after closed or open treatment and does not require internal fixation because of the innately stable nature of the hindfoot complex; it should, however, be verified by passive pronation and supination before placement in a short leg cast in neutral position. For an easily reduced, closed injury without fracture, weight-of-leg weight bearing can be progressed slowly for 4 to 6 weeks until full weight bearing, followed by cast removal and aggressive physical therapy for range of motion of the ankle, subtalar, and transverse tarsal joints. Good results can typically be expected. For more severe injuries requiring open reduction or those accompanied by significant fractures, casted weight-of-leg weight bearing for the first 4 to 6 weeks followed by progressive weight bearing in a cast for another 2 to 4 weeks is usually an appropriate postreduction regimen. Cast removal is followed by early mobilization exercises if the foot is stable. Sooner mobilization can result in recurrent dislocation (particularly in the presence of ligamentous laxity), although more prolonged immobilization has been reported to result in increased stiffness.[47] The optimal duration of immobilization has yet to be determined. If the joint is found to be unstable after reduction, CT scanning should be considered if no bony reason for the instability can be identified on plain radiographs. If a large osteochondral fracture is identified or if persistent instability or incongruity of the joints is noted after closed reduction, open treatment with appropriate ORIF is the preferred method of treatment. Surgical excision of smaller fragments should be considered if they are found to be intra-articular or interposed, regardless of stability. Open injuries are best treated as surgical urgencies with standard irrigation and débridement, appropriate treatment of any associated fracture fragments, and bead pouch placement with delayed primary closure if possible. Delay in arrival at the operating room should not preclude attempts at closed reduction in the emergency department to protect the surrounding soft tissues. Intraoperative instability despite ORIF and repair of the ligamentous and capsular anatomy is common and should be treated by external fixation or 1/8-inch smooth Steinmann pin fixation from the heel up through the talus and into the ankle to ensure maintenance of reduction. An additional stout K-wire across the talonavicular joint is also sometimes necessary. These pins should be kept in place for about 6 weeks, and they also render the patient non–weight bearing during that time. If closure does not seem feasible or if skin on initial inspection is clearly nonviable, early involvement of a plastic surgeon is advisable, and it is frequently helpful to have one see the wound at the time of initial débridement if possible.

## PROGNOSIS AND COMPLICATIONS

The prognosis is worse with infection or wound slough, high-energy injury, delayed reduction, open wounds, lateral dislocation, or intra-articular fracture.[105] In addition, patients with ligamentous laxity should probably be immobilized for an additional 2 to 3 weeks to minimize the risk of recurrent instability. Most patients will have some degree of subtalar stiffness, and some arthritis of the subtalar joint often develops long-term with this injury, regardless of its mechanism or direction, although medial dislocation tends to fare far better than lateral dislocation, probably because of the injury mechanism. The need for immediate initial subtalar or talonavicular fusion is rare, but if subtalar dislocation is diagnosed later than 1 month after injury, the likelihood of requiring triple arthrodesis to obtain a stable, reduced hindfoot is high. Avascular necrosis of the talus is rare because it is not dissociated from its position in the mortise and thus maintains some of its major blood supply through at least the deltoid ligament. Recurrent subluxation is also relatively uncommon, except as noted earlier.

## Total Talar Dislocation

Total talar dislocation or "in vivo extrusion" without fracture is rare, but has been reported[69] (Fig. 60–21). Here

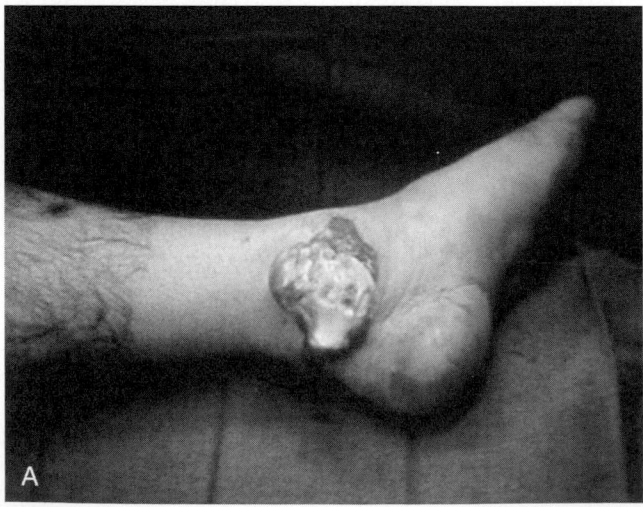
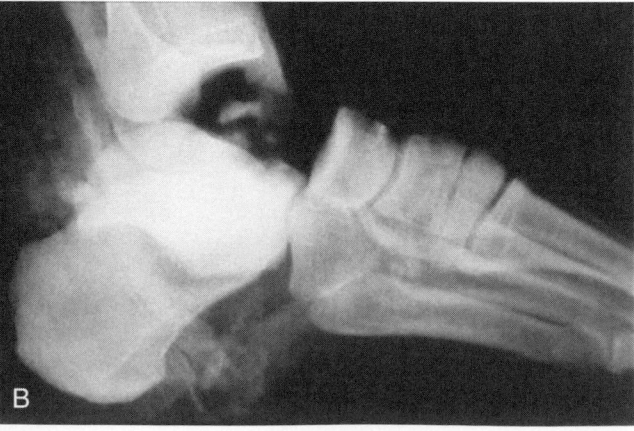

**FIGURE 60–21.** Rare example of total talar dislocation. No significant fracture was present in this case (*A*), and the talus was almost completely extruded in its entirety (*B*). The outcome of these injuries can be expected to be poor regardless of treatment. They are usually associated with open wounds, as can be seen here.

too, the talus can dislocate in virtually any direction as a result of continuation of the aforementioned forces to the limits of the soft tissues. Thus, most are open injuries and have poor outcomes. Rates of avascular necrosis, infection, and post-traumatic arthrosis are extremely high, with talectomy and tibiocalcaneal fusion often being necessary.

Although closed reduction can be attempted with manual traction and manipulation, it is highly likely that open reduction through either an anteromedial or antero-lateral approach will be required. The surrounding anterior or posterior compartment tendons must often be exposed and disentangled to facilitate reduction, depending on the direction of dislocation.[205]

Although some authors advocate early removal of the talus, if the bone and soft tissue bed can be effectively débrided, it seems most prudent to maintain the talus in a reduced position and allow healing of the peritalar tissues. If unstable after reduction, an ⅛-inch Steinmann pin inserted through the heel, a 0.062-inch K-wire through the talonavicular joint, or both can be effective in holding the reduction for 6 weeks and then safely removed. Replacement of the talus in its bed preserves length, restores anatomic relationships, and if healing occurs without a major soft tissue complication or infection, allows for easier and more functional salvage should any peritalar fusions be necessary at a later date because of collapse, avascular necrosis, or pain. These patients can be protected in a PTB AFO for upward of 1 to 2 years to minimize the chances of collapse during revascularization, although it remains controversial whether such bracing or protected weight bearing has any effect on the natural history of avascular necrosis.

## Isolated Tarsal Dislocations

Isolated tarsal dislocations are rare, and the literature consists mostly of isolated case reports.[212, 356] In each case, care should be taken to evaluate for other fractures or tarsal instability patterns that might require ORIF. Careful physical examination and CT scanning are strongly recommended, in addition to routine radiographic views of the foot.

### CALCANEUS

Fewer than 10 cases of isolated calcaneal dislocation, defined as subtalar and calcaneocuboid dissociation in the face of an intact talonavicular joint and no major fracture, have been reported.[348] Dislocation is predominantly lateral. Closed reduction in usually possible, followed by 6 to 8 weeks of immobilization in a short leg weight-bearing cast. Open reduction is performed through a lateral approach if required.

### TALONAVICULAR

Isolated talonavicular dislocation is also rare. It occurs through rotation of the calcaneocuboid joint when the forefoot is used as a fulcrum in the coronal plane. The interosseous talocalcaneal ligament remains intact. Closed reduction is typically followed by 6 to 8 weeks of progressive weight bearing in a short leg cast. When required, open reduction is performed through the medial utility approach. The navicular can be extruded with high-energy plantar flexion forces on the forefoot.[70] This mechanism typically results in a dorsal dislocation, probably related to lack of substantial dorsal ligamentous support and the overall trapezoidal, curvilinear morphology of the navicular, with the wider portion based dorsally (Fig. 60–22). Such injuries should be treated by ORIF to minimize the risk of skin or neurovascular compromise, avascular necrosis, or post-traumatic midfoot collapse.

### CALCANEOCUBOID

Pure calcaneocuboid dislocation is also rare and can occur only plantarly because of the structural anatomy of the cuboid, which has a hook-shaped plantar prominence and strong ligamentous attachments. It requires a high-energy mechanism.[172] Total dislocation of the cuboid has been reported but is also rare.[73, 85] It prevents dorsal excursion of the cuboid across the joint. Treatment is similar to that for the other dorsal dislocations, with a dorsolateral approach advocated in the event that closed reduction plus short leg casting is not possible. If the joint remains unstable after anatomic reduction, it should be fixed with a spanning minifragment plate or crossing K-wires, either of which should be removed after sufficient time (8 to 12 weeks) has passed to heal the ligamentous complex.

### CUNEIFORM

Cuneiform dislocations are similarly rare and also tend to occur dorsally, probably secondary to the stronger plantar ligamentous and tendinous attachments and the bony structural anatomy of the midfoot. Specifically, the Roman arch design of the midfoot results in stability in dorsal compression (from cephalad to caudad, as in normal weight bearing), but much lower resistance to disturbances that result in load transmission from a caudocranial direction. These dislocations are nonfracture variants of Lisfranc (who originally described amputations through this joint level) injuries and can coexist with them.[29] The diagnosis can be difficult to make in the event of subtle subluxation or instability and thus requires a high index of suspicion. It should be accompanied by stress views or a CT scan as in Lisfranc disruptions. Treatment is similar and requires ORIF.

## HINDFOOT SPRAIN

Many severe sprains of the hindfoot complex do not result in dislocation or subluxation, but they can cause significant ligamentous disruption. In the past, pain typically located in the sinus tarsi was called a "sinus tarsi syndrome." This phrase has been a wastebasket term for over a decade and should be used with less frequency in lieu of a more accurate alternative diagnosis. By definition, sinus tarsi syndrome is focal pain, as described earlier, with a repetitive clinical response to sinus tarsi injection. Frey and co-workers[99] and others have demonstrated that any number of clinical entities can be responsible for these symptoms and should be evaluated for interosseous

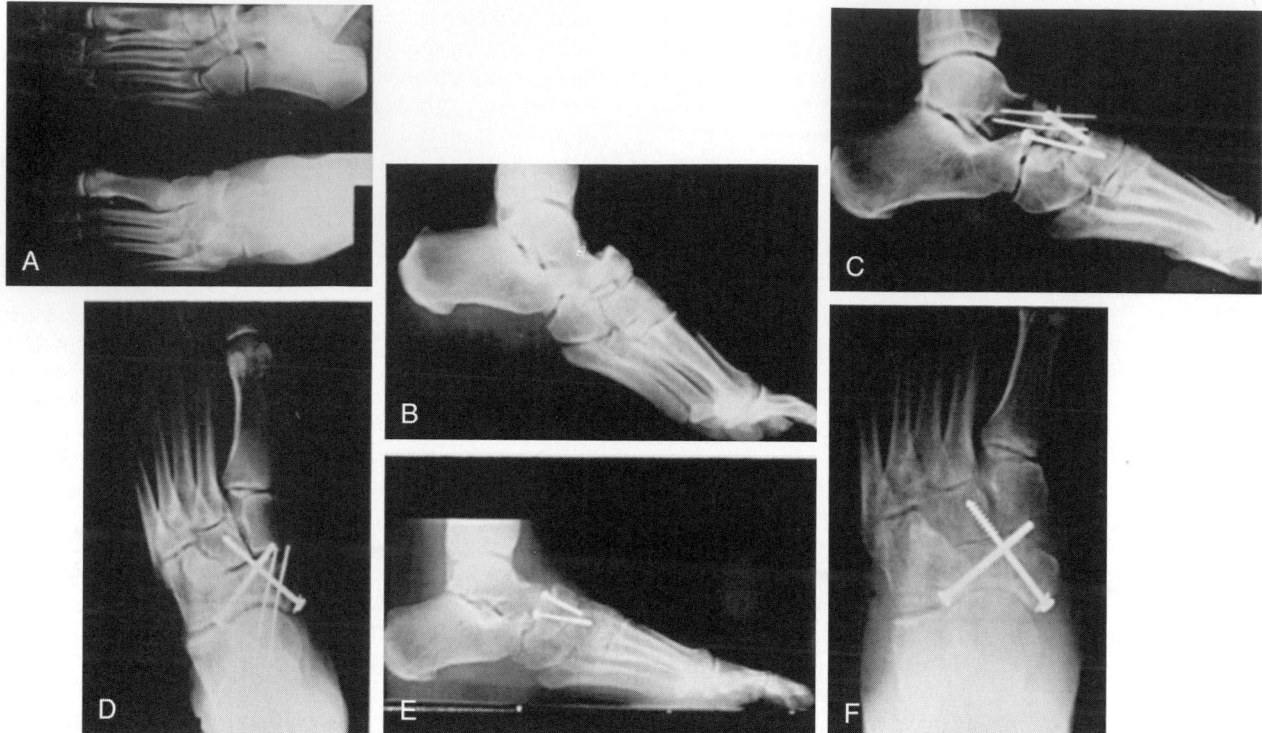

**FIGURE 60–22.** Anteroposterior (AP) and oblique (A) and lateral (B) radiographs show a talonavicular joint fracture-dislocation in a 24-year-old man who was injured when he fell off a roof. The patient experienced immediate pain, dorsomedial swelling, and deformity in his left foot. The dislocated talonavicular joint had a large intact dorsomedial fragment riding over the head of the talus and a comminuted inferolateral fragment from a type II crushing injury. On postoperative lateral (C) and AP (D) views of the fracture after open reduction, the large dorsomedial fragment is held in position by screws attached to the distal tarsal row. Note that the large medial tubercle fragment is fixed with a screw that extends into the second cuneiform. The second screw, placed from a lateral stab incision, crosses the comminuted lateral fragment and enters the intact medial fragment after it crosses the first naviculocuneiform joint. Two K-wires placed across the talonavicular joint hold the reduction intact while the capsular attachments heal. A congruent joint seen on the AP view at the end of the procedure indicates that the talonavicular joint was successfully restored. Lateral (E) and AP (F) radiographs taken approximately 10 weeks after surgery show a well-healed fracture. The K-wires were removed 6 weeks after surgery.

ligament tears (subtalar impingement or "STIL" lesions), hindfoot fracture such as the lateral talar process or anterior process of the calcaneus, osteochondral injuries, arthrofibrosis, hindfoot arthrosis, tarsal coalition, loose bodies, subtalar joint synovitis, or even ankle pathology such as anterolateral impingement syndrome. It should be remembered that people who twist their ankle must also twist their foot and vice versa. Thus, because the anterolateral gutter and sinus tarsi are separated by only 1 cm, on physical examination it is not only difficult to distinguish between them but also not uncommon to have symptoms emanating from both regions after a traumatic sprain. Treatment of both these problems is conservative and includes a RICE protocol, nonsteroidal anti-inflammatory drugs (NSAIDs), activity modification, gradual progressive weight bearing, and in patients with severe discomfort, a short period (2 to 3 weeks) of cast or walking boot immobilization. Symptoms usually resolve within weeks to 1 to 3 months, and if they do not, arthroscopic evaluation of either the subtalar, ankle, or both joints is indicated and frequently fruitful. Often, a ligamentous tear in the subtalar or anterolateral ankle joint that has been ignored or incompletely rested results in recalcitrant synovitis or scarring that is symptomatic (Fig. 60–23) and responds well to injection or arthroscopic decompression. It is also not unusual to find an osteochondral injury that prevents complete resolution of symptoms in these patients. Such

an injury can be seen in the form of a bone marrow edema pattern on MRI (typically in the talus or midfoot) or as an osteochondral fracture on arthroscopic evaluation.

Although most foot sprains occur on the lateral side of the ankle and hindfoot because of the tendency to roll the foot inward, an eversion stress to the foot occasionally occurs and results in a partial tear or strain of the deep deltoid ligament. This injury can also be managed successfully with conservative care, but 4 to 8 weeks may be required for resolution of symptoms. In any of these cases and particularly in someone with a history of recurrence, a predisposing hindfoot or forefoot malalignment should be carefully considered.

## CALCANEAL FRACTURES

Calcaneal fractures can result in severe functional disability if they disrupt the subtalar joint, and many patients who sustain subtalar injuries are unable to return to work. Undeniably, a high-energy calcaneal fracture is a life- and potentially career-changing injury for the vast majority of people who sustain them. The high incidence of these injuries and the serious nature of the disabilities that they produce constitute a serious socioeconomic problem. Calcaneal fractures account for 60% of all tarsal fractures and involve working individuals in their peak earning years (20 to 40) up to 90% of the time.[239, 323] Cotton and Henderson summed up their difficult experience with conservative calcaneal fracture management in 1916: "The man who breaks his heel bone is done." This view has been substantiated by a number of subsequent authors, including Conn in 1926: "Calcaneus fractures are serious and disabling injuries in which the end results continue to be incredibly bad," and Bankart in 1942: "The results of crush fractures of the os calcis are rotten."[84] In fact, on average only about 15% of patients in available studies were pain free at follow-up. Despite our best efforts and advances in fracture care of the calcaneus over the past 100 years, we still have room for improvement based on these realities, and thus to date the calcaneus still remains an "unsolved fracture" to some extent. One famous calcaneal fracture surgeon is quoted as saying: "It would seem that the best results that can be expected from the fracture of the os calcis involving the sub-astragaloid joint is a completely stiff but painless foot of a good shape, and the free movement of the ankle joint."

Fracture of the calcaneus is usually caused by a sudden, high-velocity impact on the heel.[164] The most common mechanisms of injury are motor vehicle accidents and industrial injuries involving falls of 6 ft or more.[298] Rarely, they are caused by explosions that come through a floor from below. A variety of injuries can result. Fractures may be extra-articular or intra-articular, and the articular surface of the subtalar joint is involved approximately 75% of the time. Most intra-articular injuries result from a direct axial load, whereas those that are extra-articular often result from more of a twisting or avulsive force. Bilateral fractures or spine injuries can occur in 10% to 15% of patients in reported series, and associated injuries may include axial compression fractures in other areas of the musculoskeletal system, such as the proximal end of the femur. Damage to the subtalar joint frequently eliminates

motion in this joint; consequently, the foot's ability to conform to uneven surfaces is impaired, and cushioning during gait is reduced. As a result, greater impact is transferred to all the other weight-bearing joints. Interestingly, however, although normal subtalar motion is rare, loss of subtalar motion does not equate with the overall functional result. Function is most dependent on normal architecture and anatomic structure above and beyond simply restoration of the subtalar articular surface. A vast majority of the time, deformation of the calcaneus (either untreated or late collapse of the talus into the calcaneus) results in a change in ankle joint mechanics as well that predisposes this joint to abnormal stress if the os calcis injury is left untreated. Of course, the subtalar joint and its motion must not be ignored because preservation of this function is responsible for the cushioning of heel-strike (particularly for accommodating on uneven ground) and stabilization of the midfoot during toe-off. It is vitally important for protecting the proximal and distal joints from impact overload and long-term secondary arthrosis.

Although most descriptions and much of the discussion surrounding the treatment of calcaneal fractures emphasize the posterior facet of the subtalar joint complex,[76, 330] the outcome of calcaneal fracture treatment probably depends just as much if not more on other aspects of disrupted hindfoot anatomy. Without a doubt, reduction of the posterior facet is important; however, restoration of calcaneal length, height, and width is equally necessary to minimize functional impairment. This relationship is emphasized by Infante and colleagues in their evaluation of 635 displaced intra-articular calcaneal fractures treated by formal ORIF through a lateral approach.[90] The stiffness that accompanies calcaneal fractures and their treatment may undermine any advantage of anatomic reduction of the posterior facet. Thus, although we strongly advocate rigid anatomic fixation of both the calcaneus and its posterior facet, it is probably much easier to salvage the

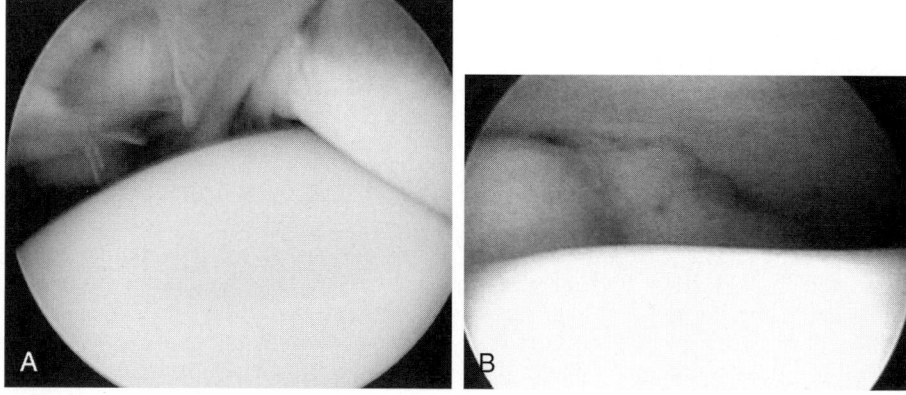

**FIGURE 60–23.** Anterolateral impingement syndrome of the ankle is a common cause of persistent post-traumatic "hindfoot" pain and is frequently seen as a late sequela of a significant antecedent hindfoot or ankle fracture or ligamentous injury. Because any sprain of the ankle requires a concomitant sprain of the foot, symptoms in these regions often coexist. Thus, although patients may have a history of only "foot" trauma or complain of pain along the sinus tarsi region with dorsiflexion or weight bearing, this entity should be considered. Symptoms emanate from a synovitis and scar build-up in the anterolateral gutter of the ankle, much like the "cyclops" lesion in the knee after an anterior cruciate ligament injury. Injection or, if necessary, arthroscopic débridement is frequently successful in rapidly restoring function. This tissue build-up is easily seen along the inferior border of the anterior inferior tibiofibular ligament and often obscures visualization of the lateral malleolus on arthroscopic inspection (*A*). It is occasionally associated with a similar build-up of tissue more posterior at the syndesmotic origin in the region of the trifurcation (*B*), which is treated in similar fashion. These patients should probably undergo concomitant arthroscopic evaluation of the subtalar joint during surgery, which takes only an additional 20 minutes in experienced hands and can help rule out concomitant hindfoot pathology.

subtalar arthrosis and hindfoot pain associated with a well-aligned calcaneus in which it was impossible to obtain an exact reduction of the articular surface as opposed to trying to salvage one with an anatomic posterior facet but malaligned heel—in which case the weight-bearing pattern of the entire foot and the status of many of the surrounding joints and their interrelationships can also be affected. In fact, Infante and colleagues also reiterated the prudence of primary subtalar fusion in the setting of severe articular disruption. Hansen has previously outlined the main functions of the calcaneus, all of which can be severely impaired by this injury: maintenance and support of the lateral column of the foot, a dynamically stable but accommodative foundation for body weight, and the lever arm for propulsive gait through the gastrocnemius-soleus complex.[120] The point here is that equal effort needs to be directed toward both overall skeletal alignment and anatomic relationships in the heel and toward what the posterior facet looks like. For example, the anterior process, middle facet, calcaneocuboid joint, and weight-bearing segment and alignment of the calcaneal tuber must not be ignored in the course of treatment. Laboratory data do suggest, however, that intra-articular displacement greater than 2 mm results in a significant decrease in the joint area available for function in the subtalar joint, with a concomitant increase in pathologic load concentration across any remaining facet articulations.[286] Restoration of heel height improves tibiotalar position, restores the interrelationships between the facets, and may decrease long-term degeneration of the ankle. Restoration of heel length may improve the ability to wear a shoe and the lever arm of the gastrocnemius-soleus complex. Maintenance of horizontal length helps support the lateral column to control any abnormal abduction or adduction of the forefoot. With pathologic forefoot rotation (usually abduction), dorsolateral peritalar subluxation results in a reduction in push-off efficiency and overloads the posterior tibial tendon. Narrowing of the heel relieves subfibular impingement, and restoration of valgus inclination permits unlocking of the subtalar complex to cushion gait and also stabilize the foot and ankle during weight bearing. Such anatomic realignment should effectively decrease the pain and stiffness commonly associated with treatment of calcaneal fractures and often related to incomplete success in achieving these goals. The basic goals of treatment thus remain restoration of function (subtalar motion, ankle motion, painless heel-to-toe gait), avoidance of deformity, and normal shoe wear, as stated by Böhler in 1935: "Fractures of the calcaneus should be treated like all other fractures, i.e., exact reduction must be made and the reduced fragments must be fixed in position until bony union has occurred, and during this period of fixation as many joints as possible should be exercised." In untreated calcaneal fractures, one can expect some degree of decreased function in the ankle and subtalar joint, a shorter heel with a decreased lever arm, varus inclination, a widened position, and a requirement for a wider shoe.

Displacement associated with a calcaneal fracture is not always limited to the subtalar joint. For example, fractures in the sagittal plane may originate in the subtalar joint and continue forward into the calcaneocuboid joint. If this type

of fracture is not reduced, it may heal in a very incongruous manner and create major deformities in the subtalar joint, as well as the foot in general. Related deformities may include flattening of the heel and the arch, dorsiflexion of the talus in the ankle mortise, and lateral displacement of the calcaneal tuberosity, which can be tilted into either varus or valgus.[41] Although we believe that accurate ORIF of displaced, intra-articular calcaneal fractures is paramount for an optimal result, the literature remains confusing on this issue, mostly because of the limited scope of previous randomized trials comparing operative and nonoperative management.[179] For example, a multicenter Canadian study prospectively compared the two treatments and ultimately favored nonoperative management of these injuries; however, many of the surgeons experienced in operative management of calcaneal fractures opted out of the study before its completion, which may have skewed the results, and a greater proportion of the nonoperated group required late fusion.[33] Fractures with higher levels of comminution or smaller Böhler angles had poorer outcomes regardless of the treatment method. Buckley and Meek encouraged nonoperative management in patients older than 40 years, smokers, noncompliant or sedentary individuals, and worker's compensation recipients.[33] Sanders recently reviewed all previous randomized trials on treatment of calcaneal fractures.[280] Although pooling such results can introduce error in data interpretation, there appeared to be no difference in residual pain between operatively and nonoperatively treated groups (odds ratio, 0.90; 95% confidence interval [CI], 0.34 to 2.36). Greater numbers of operated patients than nonoperated patients were able to return to their same work (odds ratio, 0.30; 95% CI, 0.13 to 0.71) and were able to wear the same shoes as in their preinjury status (odds ratio, 0.37; 95% CI, 0.17 to 0.84). Pain on a visual analog scale in one study did appear to favor the operated group at 1 year (mean difference, 1.40; 95% CI, 0.02 to 2.82), with greater subtalar motion and earlier return to work at 3 months in the impulse compression group (mean difference, 14°; 95% CI, 3.2 to 24.6). Sanders concluded that operative treatment seems to have a slight benefit over nonoperative treatment of calcaneal fractures but that these benefits remain small statistically and might be outweighed by the risks involved in surgical intervention. These conclusions are also supported by another recent meta-analysis in the literature.[264] The conflicting literature on the superiority of open versus closed treatment of intra-articular calcaneal fractures is based on antiquated techniques. Newer methods of management, treatment algorithms, fracture classifications, instrumentation, imaging procedures, and education on handling of the surrounding soft tissues have resulted in surgical outcomes that compare favorably with nonoperative management of intra-articular injuries.[239, 277, 323] Although open treatment is considered the standard of care for many other intra-articular fractures of the lower extremity, this matter can be answered definitively only with a larger scale, randomized, multicenter, controlled study involving surgeons well versed in both operative and nonoperative fracture care of the calcaneus. It is reasonable to expect, however, that patients in whom infection or severe wound complications develop after

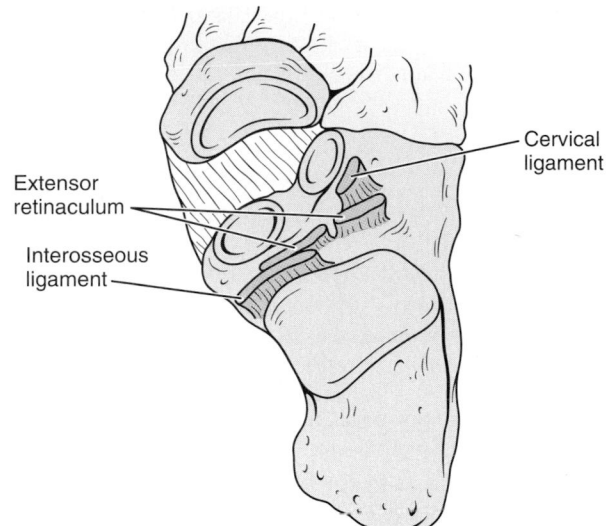

**FIGURE 60–24.** When looking from the lateral side within the sinus tarsi through either a subtalar arthroscope or a lateral exposure during fixation of a calcaneal fracture, it is impossible to visualize the anterior and middle facets of the subtalar joint if the interosseous ligament complex is intact. This structure normally separates the subtalar joint into two separate compartments—anterior and posterior—and must be either torn or removed to visualize the anatomy of both compartments at the same time. Thus, during fixation of a calcaneal fracture, one can see only the posterior facet, unless it is taken down, which can and should be done to permit more accurate fracture reduction because postoperative subtalar instability is rarely an issue after calcaneal injury. In contradistinction, it is recommended that the ligament be left intact for stability during routine subtalar arthroscopy unless partial débridement or repair is required after identification of a tear.

open treatment are usually worse off than if they had been treated in closed fashion, and thus this decision must be seriously weighed on a case-by-case basis. Similar controversy exists in the treatment of calcaneal fractures in children and teenagers, although the consensus is that the indications for open intervention are similar to those for older adults and should be based on fracture displacement, malalignment, degree of intra-articular involvement, status of the soft tissue envelope, and confounding host factors.[30, 326]

## ANATOMY

The anatomy of the calcaneus has been well described.[17, 188] The subtalar joint has two compartments that are separated by the interosseus ligamentous complex in the sinus tarsi and tarsal canal. As described by Frey and DiGiovanni, the posterior compartment contains the posterior facet of the calcaneus, and the anterior compartment contains the anterior and middle facets, which are often confluent.[98] These latter two facets bear more weight per unit area than the larger posterior one.[294] During exposure of the calcaneus from a traditional lateral approach, if this ligamentocapsular structure remains intact, one will not be able to visualize the anterior and middle facets or the anterior process unless it is at least partially taken down[77] (Fig. 60–24). We believe that nonvisualization of these structures is a common cause of malreduction in calcaneal fracture treatment, and the

surgeon must be alert to this pitfall and diligent in the course of this exposure, which can often take the largest portion of time during surgery. Whereas the posterior facet is convex and somewhat saddle shaped in its support of the talar body, the anterior and middle facets are flatter and support the talar neck and head. Medially, the sustentaculum supports the middle facet and acts as a fulcrum for travel of the flexor hallucis longus. Immediately dorsal to this structure lie the neurovascular bundle and other deep posterior compartment tendons, all of which are vulnerable to injury or incarceration with the typically used lateral-to-medial drilling or screw placement in this area. Laterally and inferiorly along the lateral wall of the calcaneus, the peroneal tubercle acts as a fulcrum or groove for the peroneal tendons as they traverse across the hindfoot. It separates the two, the peroneus brevis lying superiorly and the longus lying inferiorly. The tubercle can come in many shapes and sizes, and if congenitally large or allowed to remain significantly displaced (malunited), it can become a cause of stenosing tenosynovitis of the peroneal tendons. This condition is mistaken for or contributes to the painful os peroneum syndrome or "cuboid syndrome" recently popularized in the literature.[253, 316] As a whole, the calcaneus serves as an important lever arm and vertical support during gait, as well an important horizontal support of the lateral column during stance phase. It must maintain its normal height to preserve leg length and alignment directly under the tibia to avoid tilt stress in the ankle.

Five major areas in the calcaneus provide structural rigidity to the bone and are therefore amenable to screw fixation (Fig. 60–25). The most important is the area

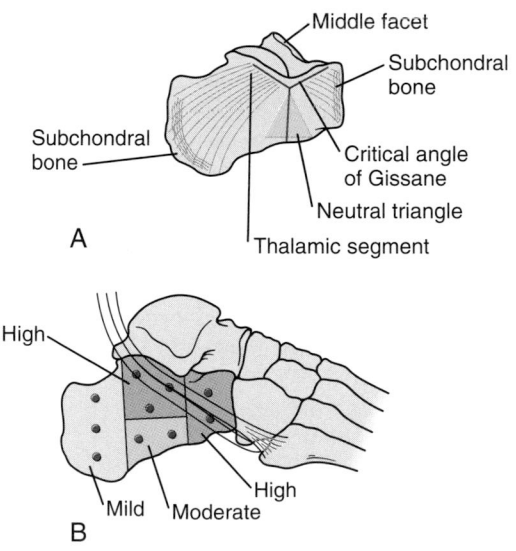

**FIGURE 60–25.** The calcaneus has five major areas of dense bone that are amenable to hardware placement during fracture fixation (*A*). Being familiar with these areas assists in guiding appropriate screw placement and cuts down on operative time and fixation failure if early motion is encouraged. These areas include the posterior tuber, the thalamic region beneath the critical angle, the subchondral bone of the posterior facet, the anteromedial-most aspect of the anterior process, and the sustentaculum. In addition, familiarity with Albert and colleagues' cadaveric study of danger zones during screw placement in a lateral-to-medial direction helps avoid inadvertent injury to the neurovascular bundle and adjacent tendons (*B*).

known as the thalamic region, which exists beneath the calcaneal facets as a confluence of compression trabeculae in support of the weight and structure of the talus. In addition, the critical angle (of Gissane) beneath the lateral process of the talus, the plantar posterior tubercle of the calcaneus, the anterior-most aspect of the anterior process along the calcaneocuboid and calcaneonavicular articulations, and the medial sustentaculum are the areas of increased bone density that should be considered during screw placement or plate application. Centrally, the neutral triangle is typically devoid of any significant bone and should be avoided. This triangle is often the area in which the posterior facet is rotated and compressed by the weight of the body and, after appropriate reduction, becomes a potential space because of the surrounding bony impaction. Böhler's angle, as seen on a lateral radiograph of the calcaneus, represents the angle formed by the intersection of a line joining the tip of the posterior tuber with the posterior facet and one joining the tip of the posterior facet to the tip of the anterior process. Typically, it measures 25° to 40° with little variation between sides and is a good indication of loss of calcaneal inclination and joint depression.[22] Changes such as these, including fractures that are purely extra-articular, can functionally alter the relationships between the facets of the subtalar joint analogous to an intra-articular fracture and should thus be treated as such.

## FRACTURE PATTERNS

All suspected calcaneal injuries should be initially evaluated with non–weight-bearing plain radiographs of the foot in standard AP, lateral, and oblique projections. The AP view is helpful in evaluating calcaneocuboid joint involvement or subluxation, talonavicular joint subluxation, and lateral wall "blowout." The lateral view is useful for measuring Böhler's angle, assessing loss of calcaneal inclination (or ankle dorsiflexion impingement), and evaluating involvement of the subtalar joint. The oblique view can provide some assistance in visualizing the degree of displacement of the primary fracture line and the lesser facets. An axial view should also accompany these views to assess the primary fracture line, any varus malposition, step-off of the posterior facet, the relationship between the posterior facet and the sustentacular fragment, or significant lateral wall displacement and fibular abutment. Comparison lateral and axial views of the uninjured heel are also helpful in assessing the degree of displacement and quality of reduction. This set of films is useful because it can provide a rapid determination of the severity of the injury and is an excellent screening tool for concomitant assessment of foot injury, which is often masked on the initial examination by diffuse swelling and pain. Sometimes, an AP view of the ankle is helpful in assessing subfibular impingement as a result of lateral displacement of the lateral wall of the calcaneus, but because any significantly displaced calcaneal fracture under consideration for operative intervention should undergo CT scanning, this last radiograph is often redundant. In addition, oblique views of the ankle and foot, known as Broden's views, are helpful in assessing congruity of the subtalar joint (see Fig. 60–6). These views have been well

described and are not really indicated as part of the initial workup for a calcaneal injury.[28] Their use lies in the intraoperative evaluation of articular reduction of the posterior facet, and they can easily be obtained by using the C-arm with 45° of both internal and external rotation of the foot and a cephalad projection of the beam between 10° and 40° centered over the sinus tarsi.[28]

Most fracture pattern classifications for the calcaneus have focused on being of assistance in describing and managing intra-articular calcaneal fractures, which represent not only 75% of the fractures seen in the calcaneus but also the vast majority that will require operative intervention. Palmer[245] and, later, McReynolds[203] and Burdeaux[34] described common fracture patterns in the calcaneus before modern imaging techniques were available. Letournel (Judet) and Rowe have also described classification systems in the past. Today's CT scans clearly define fracture patterns and have verified the analyses of earlier authors. Carr[39] has previously summarized the principal fracture patterns of the calcaneus, although some more recent classifications may prove useful in determining which fracture patterns should be operated on (Sanders) and the method of operative treatment (Tornetta).[280, 335] None are reliably prognostic, and none consider displacement that disturbs the relationship between the three facets of the subtalar joint complex despite their interdependency.

The Essex-Lopresti classification, though best determined by CT scan, can be fairly easily identified on plain films alone and seems to be the most universally used[83, 84] (Fig. 60–26). It is easily understood and helps guide treatment decisions, but it does not correlate well with prognosis. Fracture patterns are divided into a "joint depression" type of injury, in which the posterior facet has disassociated from the remaining posterior tuber by a secondary fracture line, and a "tongue-type" injury, in which some continuity of the posterior facet with the tuber remains. This difference aids the surgeon in determining the most appropriate method of fracture reduction when indicated; many of the tongue-type injuries can be percutaneously reduced with a joystick through the intact tuber/facet fragment, but the discontinuous joint depression injuries always require formal ORIF to disengage and reduce the impacted posterior facet. When this method is used, approximately 50% of calcaneal fractures are considered joint depressive, 35% are tongue type, and 10% to 15% are unclassified.

The Sanders classification uses CT evaluation of the posterior facet and may correlate better with prognosis. The coronal sections on CT reconstruction are used for assessment because they are most useful in evaluating step-off of the posterior facet (Fig. 60–27). The other cuts routinely obtained in CT assessment of calcaneal fractures are also useful. Sagittal reconstruction views provide important information about the status of anterior and middle facet involvement, loss of calcaneal inclination, and whether the injury is a joint-depressive or tongue-type injury. Transverse cuts are useful in evaluating the primary and secondary fracture patterns within the calcaneus, as well as calcaneocuboid joint involvement. All CT cuts should be approximately 3-mm sections to provide an adequate description of changing fracture anatomy. It is

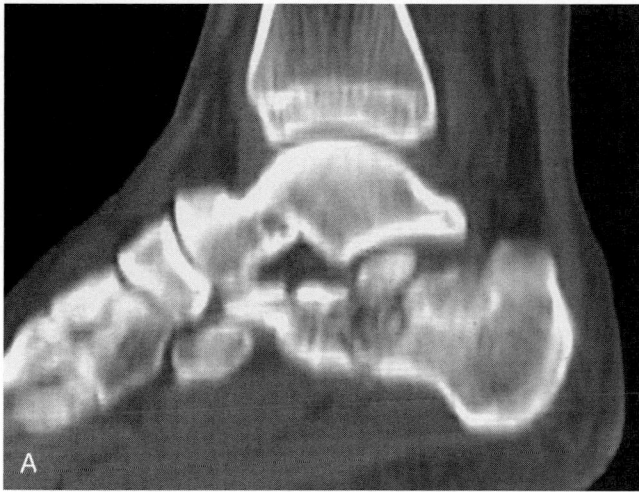
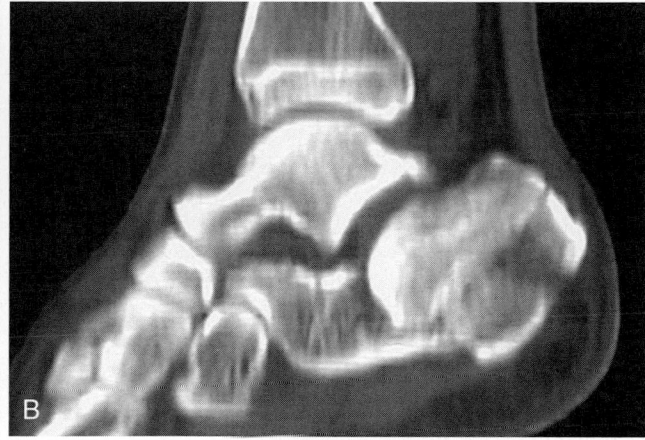

**FIGURE 60–26.** The Essex-Lopresti classification remains the most widely used, easiest, and helpful classification of calcaneal fractures to assist in guiding treatment approaches, and it may have some prognostic significance. Although not all calcaneal fracture patterns fit this description, it divides them into the two most common types: joint-depressive (*A*) and tongue (*B*) types. These types can usually be distinguished on plain films alone, although sagittal computed tomographic (CT) cuts, as shown here, are often very helpful in carefully distinguishing which pattern is present and thus how best to proceed with reduction and fixation. The basic difference is where the secondary fracture line exits the tuber posteriorly: the former exits superiorly, with no connection left between the posterior tuber and the facet fragment; the latter extends and exits posteriorly, with a large manipulable fragment left connected to the major fragment of the posterior facet. Interestingly, the sagittal CT cuts in this case came from the same patient, a laborer who sustained a tongue-type fracture on one side and a joint-depressive fracture on the other after a 30-ft fall.

also a useful study to evaluate peroneal subluxation or dislocation, seen best in the soft tissue windows. In general, less posterior facet remaining attached to the middle facet correlates with a higher degree of comminution and hence a poorer prognosis.[243]

Several injuries have been identified as typical components of a calcaneal fracture. As described by Letournel, the primary fracture line begins in the sinus tarsi at the crucial angle (of Gissane) and lateral wall, beneath the lateral process of the talus.[177] The lateral process creates this separation fracture on impact with a wedge-like action, and the fracture line always lies behind the interosseous liga-

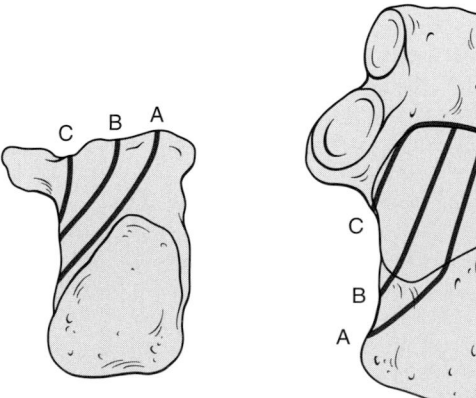

**FIGURE 60–27.** The Sanders classification is a more recent calcaneal fracture classification based on the fracture pattern through the posterior subtalar facet as identified on coronal computed tomographic cuts. It is being used with increasing frequency and is helpful in preoperatively detecting patterns that are going to require substantially more effort to reduce the posterior facet, as determined by the location of the fracture fragments in relation to an observer accessing them from an extended lateral approach to reduce them.

ment. This force propagates the fracture line posteromedially across the posterior facet at varying angles until it reaches the medial wall. Thus, two major fracture fragments remain, a posterolateral tuber with the posterior facet and an anteromedial remnant of the posterior facet with the anterior process and anterior and middle facets. In reality, the fracture often emanates in multiple directions from the crucial angle, usually leading to multiple "secondary" fracture patterns extending in a radial direction from this site. Typically, these fractures can extend anteriorly to divide the anterior process or medially to divide the middle from the posterior facet. Secondary fracture lines can also result in either the so-called tongue-type injury or the joint depression–type injury based on their exit behind and beneath the posterior facet. Typically, these patterns result in additional fracture fragments such as an anterolaterally displaced tuber fragment and a downwardly rotated and impacted sustentacular fragment in relation to the posterior facet. Usually, a triangular sustentacular fragment of variable size and comminution is located on the medial side of the calcaneus. Over half of intra-articular calcaneal fractures involve the calcaneocuboid joint, about one third involve the anterior facet, and about 9% involve the middle facet.[214] Over 90% of the time, a primary fracture line extends anterior to the angle of Gissane and results in an anterolateral and a posteromedial fragment seen best by CT. The anterior portion of the posterior facet may be impacted farther into the body than the posterior portion is. As a result, the posterior facet may seem to be rotated 30° to 90° in a plantar direction, and the posterior end may appear to be hinged on the intact calcaneal tuber. A long posterior extension of the posterior body may be fractured and rotated upward and produce the so-called tongue fracture. The lateral wall of the calcaneal body may burst and be displaced laterally under the fibula and the peroneal tendons, thereby significantly widening the heel and impinging on tendons and the lateral malleolus. The vertical force produces a fracture lateral to the sustentaculum, and further collapse forces the body of the calcaneus into varus and displaces it in a lateral direction. On clinical examination, the laterally displaced calcaneus may appear to be in valgus.

## INITIAL ASSESSMENT

Initial evaluation of patients with calcaneal fractures should include a careful assessment of neurovascular status, any open wounds or skin at risk, and the status of the soft tissue compartments. Other injuries should also be suspected and searched for, particularly in the spine, foot, and ankle—on both sides. In the absence of findings promulgating emergency operative intervention, these injuries should be supported with a Jones-type dressing and splinted in either a plaster splint, sponge Buck's boot, or preferably, a prefabricated dorsiflexion splint that permits maintenance of a neutral position to prevent Achilles contracture during the period of soft tissue observation. Although this initial positioning will help in eventual restoration of calcaneal height and length, it should not be excessive or performed at the risk of challenging the thin posterior soft tissue envelope—if too much pressure is placed here with dorsiflexion, it is better to leave the foot in a plantar-flexed position and avoid skin necrosis. The patient should have three standard radiographic views of the foot, including an axial calcaneal (Harris) view of the heel and an opposite axial and lateral view for comparison. The lateral view must be a true lateral, defined as one with no superimposition of the talus on itself; thus, because everything revolves around the talus in the foot, a true lateral of the talus gives a true representation of current foot alignment and interrelationships. This view is the only way that an accurate assessment of calcaneal alignment relative to itself and to surrounding structures can be made. A CT scan with reconstructive views should always be obtained for all intra-articular calcaneal fractures, including sagittal, axial, and coronal sections 2 to 3 mm in thickness. Views of the ankle should be obtained to assess for any associated ankle or talar injury. These patients should be admitted to the hospital at least overnight for observation of soft tissue status, compliance with instructions, pain control, and elevation. Patients should be taught how to perform intrinsic flexion exercises to decrease edema and be given temporary deep venous thrombosis (DVT) prophylaxis (many options exist), and depending on the patient's overall injury status, consideration of treatment options and timing can then be discussed once it is thought that the tissues have stabilized and begun to improve. The four major determinants used for deciding whether to operate on a closed calcaneal fracture include (1) the degree of distortion in the relationship between the posterior facet and the middle and anterior facets, which may contribute to the development of restricted subtalar motion; (2) the amount of displacement of the posterior facet; (3) the amount of lateralization of the tuberosity; and (4) the degree of widening of the foot and other factors such as displacement of the tuberosity, the calcaneocuboid joints, or both.[189]

## Nonoperative Treatment of Intra-articular Calcaneal Body Fractures

Closed reduction rarely restores normal anatomy and does not usually prevent the onset of severe functional disability. It can be considered for patients with calcaneal body fractures that do not change the weight-bearing surface of the foot or alter normal hindfoot biomechanics or for those with a simple fracture pattern (two fragments) and 2 mm or less of intra-articular displacement at the level of the posterior facet.[192] In unusual cases, closed reduction may be the best choice for treatment of fractures with severe comminution when adequate reconstruction is deemed impossible or in patients in whom operative reduction is contraindicated for other reasons.[244] When indicated, closed reduction can be attempted by plantarly displacing both the forefoot and hindfoot at the same time to induce a reversal of the injury mechanism and elevation of the posterior facet. Transverse compression can be added to narrow the heel. The knee should be flexed during these maneuvers to relax the pull of the gastrocnemius-soleus complex.[184] These patients are most commonly elderly or low-demand patients, but consideration should even be given to younger patients who have either minimal deformity or any of the following premorbid risk factors: diabetes, intravenous drug use, peripheral vascular disease, neuropathy, sedentary lifestyle, a poor soft tissue envelope, a significant smoking history, or noncompliance. Patients who are also considered to be at risk for a suboptimal outcome after open treatment of a calcaneal fracture include those with open fractures, blisters, compartment syndrome, worker's compensation claims, or bilateral injuries. Flap necrosis and an infected calcaneus are far graver problems to handle than a suboptimally healed calcaneal fracture, especially in light of the fact that the ideal treatment of these injuries is still being debated. Furthermore, these calcaneal fractures, regardless of treatment, should not be immobilized in a cast.[83, 184] These injuries become comfortable within a week or two with a simple posterior, removable, well-padded splint that prevents equinus, and most patients tolerate early motion at this time quite nicely. Obviously, non–weight-bearing status must still be maintained until evidence of healing, unless the fracture does not involve the body and is, for example, a simpler anterior process fracture. Such injuries should be treated with CAM walker immobilization and early weight bearing. Early mobilization allows maximal preservation of subtalar, ankle, and Chopart motion. Some stiffness is inevitable, but any preserved motion (preferably 50% or greater than normal) should help protect the other joints and allow some accommodative motion on uneven ground over the long term. Most calcaneal fractures that are treated nonoperatively heal in 8 to 12 weeks, and pain resolves to a tolerable level after 12 to 18 months. Subtalar motion can be decreased or absent after closed reduction, and patients treated in this manner frequently have a permanent limp, are often unable to perform certain activities (e.g., running), and rarely return to a normal level of activity. Pain-free joint motion in the hindfoot can be maximized only by anatomic reduction of the subtalar and calcaneocuboid joints. Some severe associated injuries, such as soft tissue damage to the heel pad, are impossible to correct and may produce disability that is unrelated to restoration of subtalar joint motion. It should also be mentioned that nonoperative management of calcaneal fractures should be seriously considered in anyone older than 50 years, as affirmed by numerous authors.[244]

Although it is still emphasized in some current literature that "conservative" (nonoperative) management of calcaneal fractures and operative management are equally successful, caution must be exercised in interpreting these statements because such comparisons truly depend on how we *define* success. In terms of major potential complications (an infected calcaneus or flap sloughing is certainly worse than a nonoperated and malaligned calcaneus after fracture), this statement is probably true, but in the hands of an experienced calcaneal fracture surgeon and a patient without significant risk factors and a displaced intra-articular calcaneal fracture, it can be reasonably argued that restoration of anatomic relationships with ORIF will always fare better than not doing so in the absence of major complications.

## Open Treatment of Intra-articular Calcaneal Body Fractures

Until recently, treatment of calcaneal fractures by ORIF was not routinely successful. The technique was associated with a high incidence of infection and wound breakdown and was thought by some surgeons to be dangerous. Exposure and visualization are difficult, the bone has a complex shape and anatomy, fixation devices have not been optimal, the surgical technique is complex, and much of the bone is soft cancellous bone that is not amenable to fixation. However, surgical protocols for the treatment of calcaneal fractures by ORIF have been established in several trauma centers, and these centers have reported better results with this technique than with nonoperative treatment.[17, 18, 123, 178, 179, 270, 282, 305, 318, 363] Most studies suggest that functional outcome is directly related to several factors: the accuracy of reduction of the talocalcaneal joint with early subtalar motion exercises, restoration of normal morphology in the heel (height, width, and alignment), accurate repositioning of the midfoot in relation to the forefoot, subfibular decompression, and implementation of measures to minimize swelling.[143, 156] A recent randomized, prospective evaluation also found the preoperative Böhler angle to be highly prognostic of outcome: those with significantly depressed angles had much poorer results at 2 years, regardless of the treatment method.[187] This finding probably reflects the fact that higher energy injuries have a worse prognosis because of fracture and soft tissue disruption. The level of ankle function after open treatment of displaced calcaneal fractures supports the thesis that restoration of calcaneal shape does make a difference.

The advent of several technologic advances explains why ORIF is more successful now than it was in the past. Better operative equipment and imaging techniques, particularly CT, are available to help define fracture patterns more accurately and to plan anatomic reduction more efficiently.[187] New techniques have been developed to handle damaged soft tissue without inflicting more harm.[42] Equally important is the learning curve for fixing calcaneal fractures: experienced surgeons performing 30 or more a year should be the ones responsible for caring for these injuries, a qualification that is increasingly being recognized. Successful results with ORIF have led musculoskeletal traumatologists to believe that previous failures and the high rate of infection associated with open reduction were not directly related to the technique itself but rather to lack of skill on the part of surgeons handling the injured tissues. Historically and even today, it is probable that we often accept less than we can actually obtain intraoperatively with these injuries. Recent data also suggest that host factors may play an important role in overall risk and outcome. A retrospective review of almost 200 operatively treated calcaneal fractures identified smoking, diabetes, and open fractures to be the greatest predictors of postoperative wound complications.[92] Impairment in wound healing was thought to be additive to these factors, and their presence suggested that conservative measures be strongly considered in such patients in lieu of surgical management. Recently in Switzerland, subtalar arthroscopy has been combined with more limited calcaneal fracture treatment as a less invasive reduction technique, but these results are as yet unpublished; because subtalar arthroscopy introduces a relatively novel and demanding technique to an already complicated management problem, it is not advised until further data document its safety and efficacy[263] (Fig. 60–28).

### TIMING

The amount of function that may be expected after open reduction is directly related to the accuracy of reduction, and the accuracy of reduction is related to the timing of the operation. Surgery is not usually feasible immediately after injury because all the information necessary (radiographs, CT scan) and appropriate counseling of the patient are difficult to complete within a 4- to 6-hour time frame. It should be understood that surgery, much as in a pilon fracture, is an additional soft tissue injury. Until swelling is finished, it is hard to tell how severe the injury is and whether the patient can withstand additional surgical trauma. A mistake in judgment with premature surgery can result in disastrous soft tissue problems, such as necrosis or infection (or both), that may be salvaged only with free soft tissue transfer or amputation. While awaiting surgery, the patient is splinted with the ankle in neutral position and elevated to the level of the heart for as much of the time as possible. Icing and, in particular, intrinsic exercises of the deep plantar flexors in the foot are also useful in controlling edema. An intermittent pneumatic pedal compression device (foot pump) has also been shown to be effective in accelerating resolution of edema before surgery.[327] It is surprisingly well tolerated by patients. If fracture blisters develop, which usually occurs medially, they should be treated until completely reepithelialized. If they are present on the lateral side of the foot, surgery should be postponed as well. In many instances, these blisters herald a much more serious soft tissue injury, and perhaps only a late reconstructive procedure is appropriate.

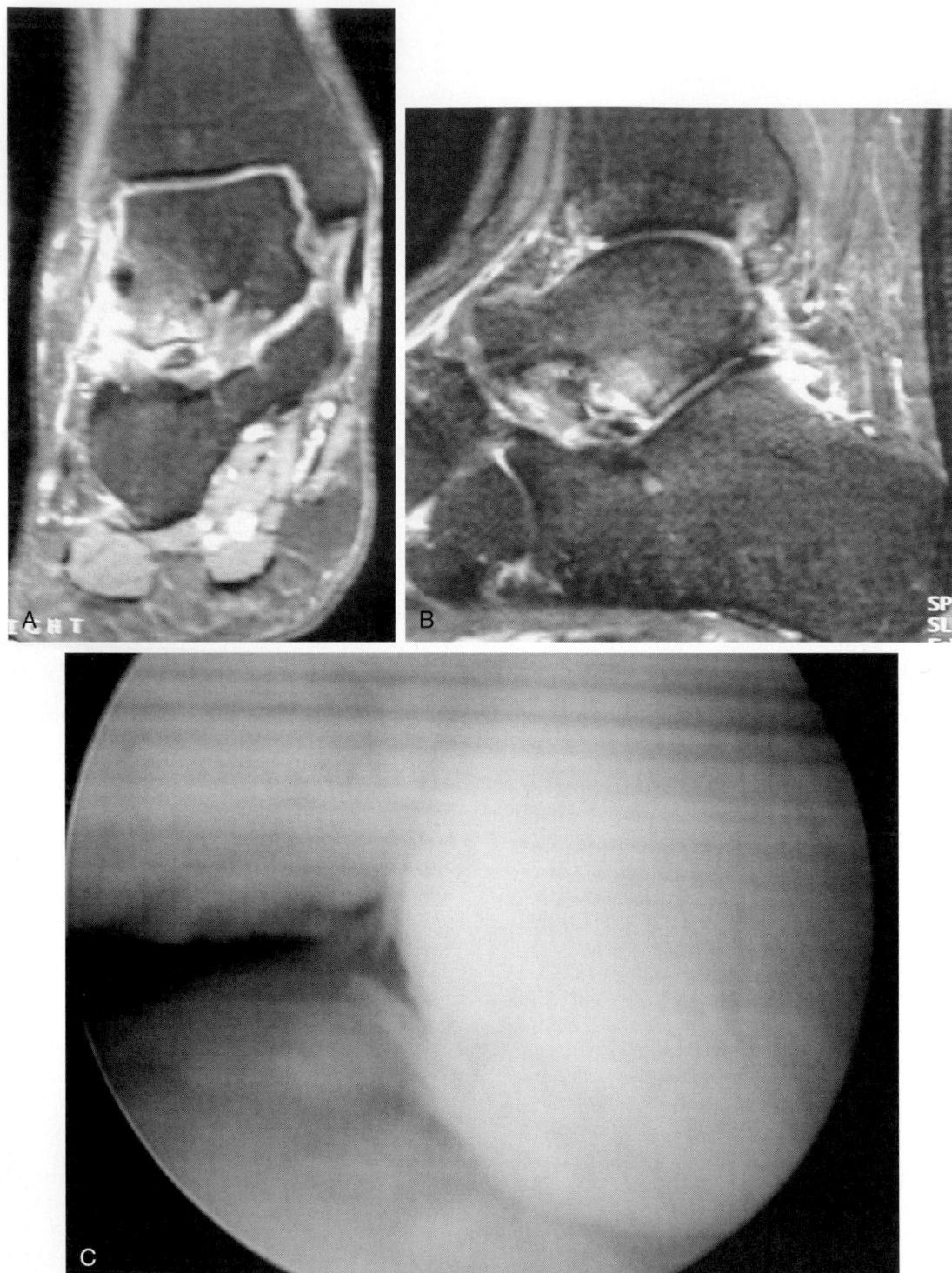

**FIGURE 60–28.** Subtalar arthroscopy is a relatively novel way of evaluating the subtalar joint for loose bodies, interosseous ligament tears, arthrofibrosis, synovectomy, tarsal coalition, and degenerative disease and, most recently, for assisting with fracture reduction or fixation. In the past, most of these findings were simply lumped together as "sinus tarsi syndrome." In this case, a patient was evaluated for a missed lateral process fracture 2 years after a fall; symptomatic nonunion had developed along with mechanical symptoms in his subtalar joint and sinus tarsi pain. These T2-weighted magnetic resonance image findings (*A, B*) are typical of "sinus tarsi syndrome": edema in the sinus tarsi and signal change within the ligamentous complex of the subtalar joint. One can easily see the loose body at the anterior-most aspect of the posterior subtalar compartment, as well as where it came from on the lateral talar process in both cuts. During arthroscopic examination, the patient was confirmed to have two large loose bodies and a matching defect in the lateral process, abundant synovitis, and a subtalar impingement lesion ("STIL") along the posterior facet—probably the result of scar build-up from an interosseous ligament tear. The arthroscopic picture (*C*) identifies one joint mouse anteromedially and some early degenerative changes in the posterior facet posteriorly during visualization from the anterior (and lateral) portal.

Primary reduction is possible for only 3 (or in unusual circumstances, 4) weeks after injury; it then becomes progressively more difficult. The optimal time for surgery is when consistent and persistent skin wrinkling occurs around the entire foot, a finding indicating that venous and lymphatic drainage is returning, usually between 10 and 21 (average of 14) days after injury if appropriate splinting and elevation have been carried out. After a delay of 4 weeks, it is probably best to allow the heel to consolidate and to plan late reconstruction by osteotomy or subtalar joint fusion, or both.[41] If open reduction is contemplated after 4 weeks, the dissection must be more aggressive because early callus healing will have begun and reduction will necessitate taking this consolidation down to manipulate the fracture fragments.

## SURGICAL APPROACH

Open reduction is commonly becoming accepted as the best treatment of intra-articular calcaneal fractures, but general agreement is not as forthcoming regarding the ideal surgical approach to use. Whereas some surgeons still use the medial approach popularized by McReynolds[203] and Burdeaux,[34] most prefer to use one of the many lateral approaches that have been devised, and some occasionally use both. The medial approach is advantageous in facilitating reduction of the tuber and narrowing of the heel; however, one cannot reduce the facets directly, assess the rest of the subtalar joint, address any lateral pathology, or apply appropriate fixation, and the neurovascular bundle remains a significant risk. Thus, we espouse the extensile lateral approach popularized by Palmer-Letournel,[177, 245] Regazzoni,[266] and Benirschke and Sangeorzan.[17, 287] It consists of an L-shaped (right heel) or J-shaped (left heel) lateral incision through which the entire fracture may be visualized and anatomic reduction may be performed (Fig. 60–29). This incision provides excellent visualization and eliminates the need for a medial incision in most cases. After gaining extensive experience with this approach, most authors have reported a very low incidence of complications.[108] The lateral approach allows direct treatment of the entire calcaneal morphology, including lateral wall blowout, reduction of the tuberosity to the anterior process and the calcaneocuboid joint, visualization and reduction of the entire subtalar joint, and finally, indirect reduction of the tuberosity to the sustentacular fragment at the medial wall.

Good arguments may be presented for stabilization of the calcaneus from the medial aspect, where the weight-bearing medial wall is located and where fracture patterns are usually simple. However, the soft tissue approach from this side is more complex and may threaten the medial neurovascular structures, especially the calcaneal branch of the tibial nerve. It is, however, very difficult to reduce the burst component of this fracture on the lateral side through this approach, and therefore it is considered to rarely be indicated. Thus, indirect reduction of the medial wall through the lateral approach is recommended. The lateral incision may also be extended in an anterior direction to visualize and reduce fractures extending into the calcaneocuboid joint.

## HARDWARE

Various devices are used for internal fixation of calcaneal fractures, and each has its own advocates. Theoretically, ideal fixation of calcaneal fractures uses compression screws alone. However, most surgeons prefer to use some sort of plate construct that facilitates compression of the lateral wall to the medial wall and more effectively maintains length and alignment in the presence of comminution. A plate construct thereby increases stability and maintenance of the reduction until healing. Initially, the use of 3.5-mm reconstruction plates was popular, but the thickness of this implant necessitated removal nearly 75% of the time because of hardware prominence. Thinner plates have evolved, including 2.7-mm reconstruction plates, long H plates, C plates, and plates shaped to the peripheral contour of the calcaneus. The intent of the implant should be to maximize the stability possible, yet

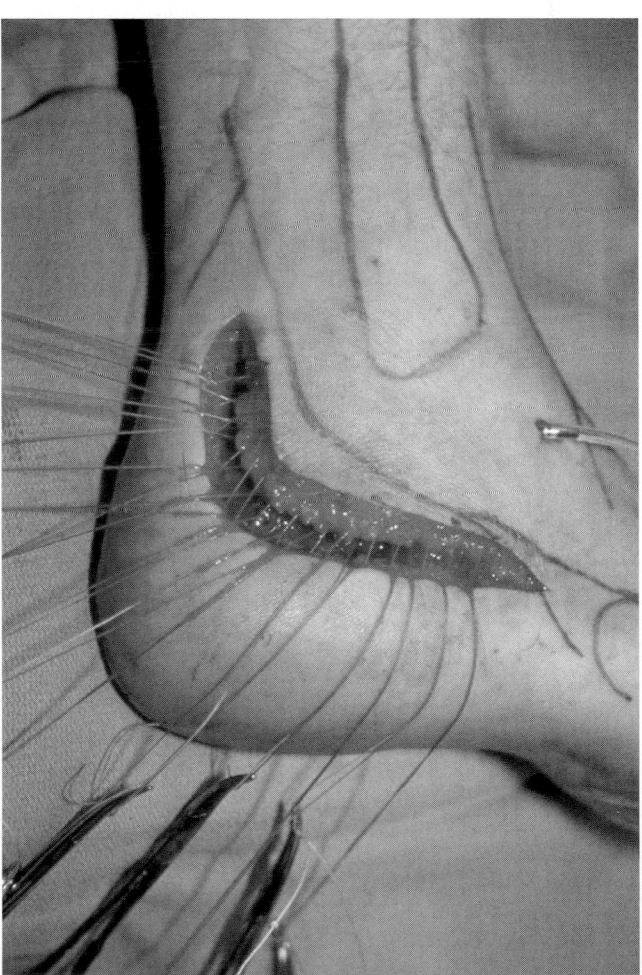

**FIGURE 60–29.** The extensile lateral incision advocated by both Regazzoni and Benirschke is carried straight through the soft tissues, deep into the subperiosteal layer. The incision may be extended in an anterior direction to the calcaneocuboid joint and then in a posterosuperior direction to the top of the calcaneus. The anterior flap containing the sural nerve and the peroneal tendons is lifted up intact. When performed correctly, this incision is safe and allows complete reconstruction under direct observation. The flap is closed in layered fashion over a drain after all deep sutures are inserted and then tied sequentially.

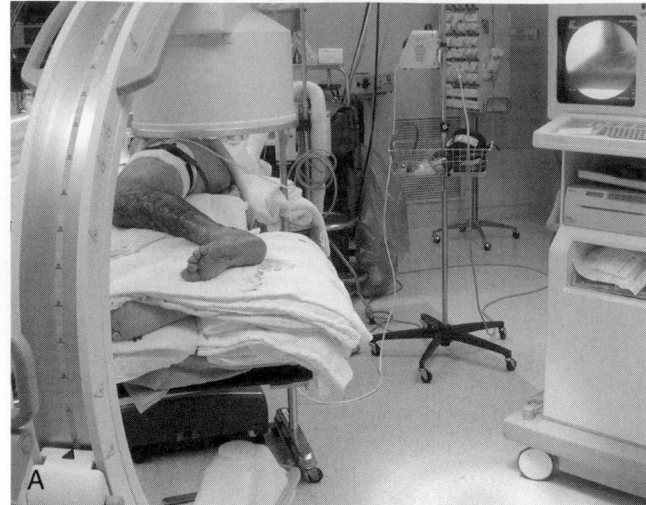
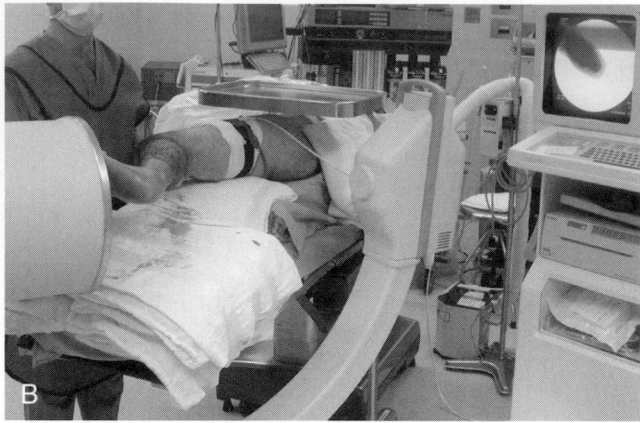

FIGURE 60–30. In preparation for fixing a calcaneal fracture, the patient should be positioned carefully in a lateral decubitus position on an image table with multiple folded blankets or a prefabricated foam sandwich. The goals of this setup are to (1) protect superficial areas at risk during a prolonged procedure, (2) have a durable "workbench" on which one can facilitate reduction and fixation, and (3) obtain easily reproducible intraoperative images of the heel in lateral (*A*) and axial (*B*) projections without having to move anything or anyone except a simple rotation of the C-arm on its axis, as shown here. Note that the operated leg is both superior and posterior on the image bed for both unimpeded imaging of the heel and proximity of the heel to the operating surgeon on that side. The respective images can easily be seen in the background on the image screen.

be as low profile as possible to avoid hardware prominence. Although hardware removal is a relatively safe procedure in comparison with its insertion, it is nevertheless another operative procedure and has the inherent risks of flap compromise, iatrogenic sural nerve injury, and peroneal irritation. Current designs of plates are thinner and stronger, with smaller screws and lower profile heads to reduce the need for removal, yet strong enough to maintain the reduction achieved until healing of the bone is complete.

## PREFERRED OPERATIVE MANAGEMENT

The primary goals (steps) of operative management are (1) open reduction and anatomic reconstruction of all articular surfaces under direct visualization, (2) rigid internal fixation, (3) bone grafting of defects, and (4) early functional treatment. The posterior, middle, and anterior facets should be realigned and oriented appropriate to one another so that the subtalar joint complex can function.[286] The calcaneal portion of the calcaneocuboid joint should be reconstructed to restore length of the lateral column. Finally, tuberosity alignment is critical to position the foot for normal gait. Even with open treatment, these objectives are difficult to achieve.

**Positioning.** Because optimal visualization and fixation can be achieved through the lateral approach, the patient is ideally placed in the lateral decubitus position on a radiolucent table. Great care should be taken to pad the dependent flank and lower extremity, with additional padding at the greater trochanter, thigh, and 1 handbreadth beneath the downside leg to protect the peroneal nerve at its vulnerable position 2 fingerbreadths below the fibular head. An axillary roll should also be used to decompress the brachial plexus. The upper part of the arm is placed on an arm holder to support but not stretch the shoulder. A combination of blankets or custom precut

foam padding is placed around the dependent extremity, as well as additional blankets or foam to provide a flat surface on which to place the operated extremity (Fig. 60–30). This surface is used to position the limb to optimize the headlight-facilitated view in the sinus tarsi after the initial surgical incision. A thigh-high tourniquet is applied and the pressure selected (usually 200 to 250 mm Hg).

**Exposure.** The optimal method for exposure and fixation of the vast majority of calcaneal fractures is through the lateral extensile approach. Unlike other approaches, this method can address the entire calcaneal morphology, including that in lateral wall blowout, malalignment from the tuberosity to the anterior process, the calcaneocuboid joint, and the entire subtalar joint, and it can facilitate indirect reduction of the tuberosity fragment to the sustentacular fragment at the medial wall. After making the skin incision, the dissection is carried down to the lateral wall at the apex of the J or L incision to expose the lateral wall, and a periosteal-cutaneous flap is elevated. Care must be taken to not disturb the interval between the skin and periosteum, but to maintain it as an undisturbed flap. As the flap is lifted, the fibulocalcaneal ligament is brought up with the subperiosteal dissection. Care must be taken to avoid injury to the abductor digiti quinti when developing the plantar limb of the incision. Additional elevation of the flap exposes the long peroneal at the level of the crucial angle of Gissane, and just beneath the peroneal is the osseous reflection of the peroneal sheath. This sheath is elevated sharply off the lateral wall to expose the sinus tarsi and protect the peroneus brevis beneath it. The sural nerve is in direct proximity to these tendons and must also be protected. The flap may be retracted with skin hooks or Senn retractors by grasping the periosteum, and the flap may be held open with deeper oral surgery Langenbeck retractors or K-wires into the fibula and lateral talar neck, as popularized by Sangeorzan.[284] Understanding the vascularity of the lateral flap is critical for proper soft tissue dissection and minimizing postoperative wound complications. The blood supply of the flap is predicated on the peroneal artery and is well described in a recent cadaveric injection study.[23] Three major arterial sources provide flap viability: the lateral calcaneal artery, the lateral malleolar artery, and the lateral tarsal artery. The first of these provides the greatest flow to the tip of the flap and is also most at risk for injury from the apex of the vertical limb of the incision.

As the exposure continues, additional visualization of the posterior facet can be achieved superolateral to the joint, which is an aid to later posterior facet articular reduction. The dissection then involves lifting the origin of the extensor digitorum brevis and Sharpey's fibers off the anterior process superiorly to the most medially displaced fracture line (seen on the AP cuts of the CT scan). Distal exposure out to the level of the calcaneocuboid joint is achieved by elevation of the long and short peroneals in the flap. Once the fracture has been visualized in this way, the reduction can ensue. From this point forward, it is extremely helpful to have a bright headlight to illuminate the recesses of the joints and sinus tarsi region. A bump placed beneath the foot medially and just proximal to the sustentaculum allows varus tilting of the exposed subtalar joints to increase visualization of the more medial structures, such as the middle facet and interosseous ligament. To assist in reduction and visualization, a 4.0/5.0 mm Schanz screw is inserted in the posterior body (tuberosity) in a lateral-to-medial direction to facilitate distraction and manipulation of the tuberosity fragment. This manipulative Schanz screw is placed for joint depression–type injuries. The tuberosity can be pulled distally and posteriorly to restore height and length. Varus/valgus control and medial translation of the tuberosity are also possible with this manipulative pin, and the position of the tuberosity is held with axially placed 0.062-inch or 2.0-mm K-wires, with the wires anchored into the cancellous bone of the medial sustentacular fragment. This manipulation provides space for the reduction to proceed, especially when the posterior facet is reconstructed. The reduction begins with reconstruction of the anterior process, and characteristically the process proceeds medially to laterally and anteriorly to posteriorly. Because the medial sustentacular fragment is often still intact, with dense ligamentous attachments from the medial side, the lateral fragment or fragments of the anterior process are sequentially reduced by using the superior cortex as a guide to reduction. If the morphology of the superior surface is accurately reduced, most of the fracture lines extending into the calcaneocuboid joint are thereby indirectly reduced. Most calcaneocuboid joint displacement is secondary to rotation of the anterior process fragments. Very rarely is there direct impaction of the anterior os calcis by the cuboid, which would necessitate direct visualization and reduction. The reduction of the anterior process fragments is held with a combination of K-wires, some placed percutaneously through the sinus tarsi, and the summation K-wires are directed in a lateral-to-medial direction as close as possible to the superior edge of the lateral cortical reconstruction. This technique leaves space available for

the buttress plate to be inserted later without necessitating that the K-wire "jail" be removed during plate application.

Once the anterior process is anatomically reduced (which can be the most time-consuming part of the procedure), reduction of the posterior facet can proceed. Because the anterior process has now been reconstructed, better assessment of the posterior facet's position and fixation can be ascertained; the anterior orientation of the joint can now be linked to the restored anterior process. Visualization of the posterior facet can be achieved through the sinus tarsi, and the posterolateral view, above the tuberosity, can permit direct visualization of the posteromedial part of the posterior facet. Because the joint is saddle shaped and curves in multiple planes, multiple views are necessary to effect an anatomic reduction. Distraction with a Schanz screw in the tuberosity facilitates viewing the posterior facet. Once again, K-wires are placed at the subchondral level to hold the articular reduction but still allow unencumbered lateral buttress plate placement. Reduction of the posterior facet oftentimes includes reduction of the middle facet because displacement of the posterior facet will also depress a posterior segment of the middle facet. The view for this reduction is through the sinus tarsi, and the portion of the posterior-middle facet complex at the level of the critical angle of Gissane often needs *elevation* from below to reconstruct it to the anterior process, which had to be *depressed* to reduce its morphology because it was driven up into the sinus tarsi (lateral to the talar head). After the posterior facet is reduced, the proper position of the tuberosity can finally be determined and achieved by manipulation (usually small amounts of height, length, and varus/valgus correction) with the Shanz pin and then anchored to the reconstructed posterior facet with axially placed wires (Fig. 60–31). Plain lateral and Harris axial radiographic views are taken to corroborate the direct reduction achieved and monitor the indirect reduction of the tuberosity to the medial wall reduction on the axial projection. Once the surgeon is satisfied with the reduction, fixation can then ensue. The lateral wall, repositioned and wired in place, gives another assessment of the reconstructed height and length. A modification of the Shanz pin placement in the tuberosity is needed in the case of a tongue-type fracture. Because the gastrocnemius-soleus complex is responsible for rotation of the posterior

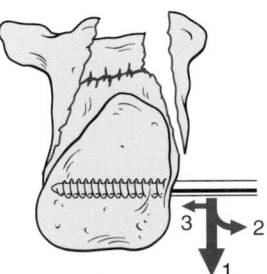

**FIGURE 60–31.** It is imperative that the maneuver selected for reducing depressed calcaneal fractures restore length, decrease width, and eliminate varus of the heel during restoration of the articular surface of the subtalar joint. Often, an osteotome can be used as a lever within the primary fracture line to help facilitate this process. Alternatively, a traction bow can be placed in the posteroinferior tuber to provide traction and disimpaction during reduction.

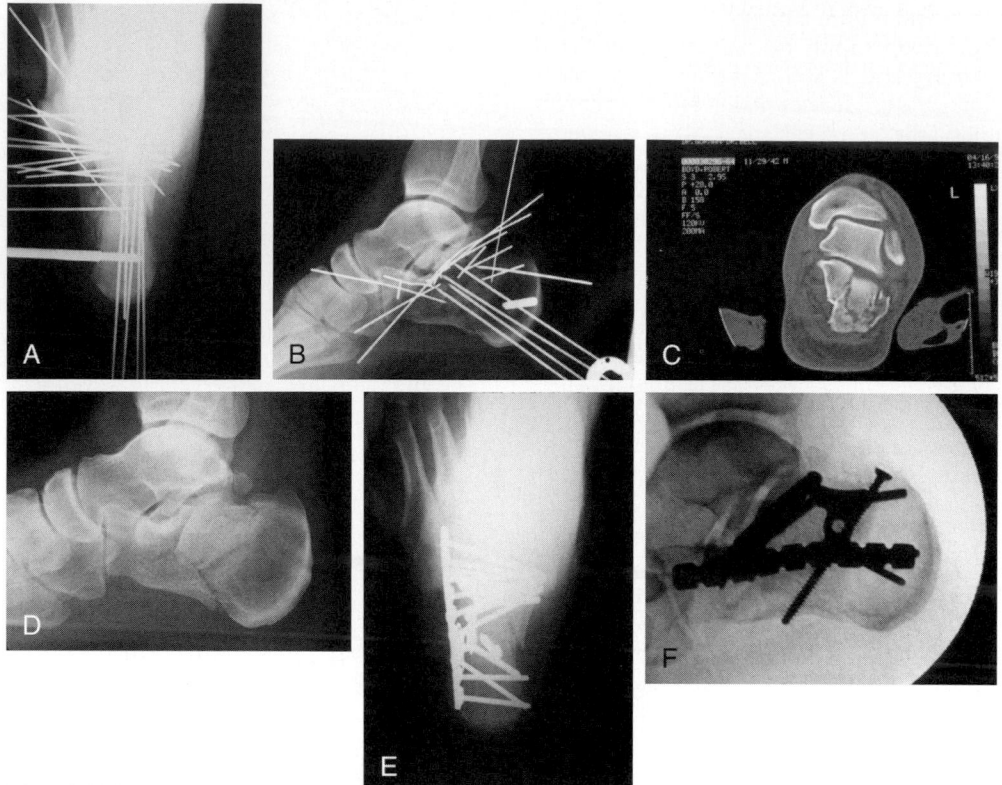

**FIGURE 60–32.** Example of a joint depression–type fracture with typical open reduction and internal fixation with a plate. *A, B,* The initial fracture pattern visualized on a lateral radiograph and coronal computed tomographic scan, respectively. *C, D,* Reduction should be preliminarily carried out with provisional K-wire fixation and verified on both axial and lateral images intraoperatively. *E, F,* Once reduction is acceptable, a Y-shaped Letournel, 3.5-mm reconstruction, or other appropriate plate is applied to the lateral wall and contoured. In this case, subthalamic and posterior tuber interlocking plates are used to take advantage of the better bone in these regions to improve the strength and rigidity of the construct so that early motion is possible. Through 3.5-mm gliding holes in the near fragment and 2.5-mm threaded holes in the sustentacular (medial triangular) fragment, 3.5-mm cortical screws can be inserted parallel and rather close to the articular surface of the subtalar joint posterior facet. These screws can be placed either through or above the plate. The smaller minifragment plates are used to aid maintenance of calcaneal length or alignment, as a buttress to the posterior facet, or as neutralization to the pull of the Achilles on any tuber fragments. The lateral plate bridges the transverse fracture lines, thereby separating the anterior calcaneus from the tuberosity, and buttresses the lateral wall comminution to correct pathologic widening and lateral impingement. Screws through the plate lag the sustentacular fragment to increase stability of the longitudinal fracture line.

facet fragment (it is attached to a superior fragment of the posterior tuberosity), a percutaneous posterior Schanz pin is placed through the heel cord attachments and into this fragment. The pin is inserted directly beneath the posterior facet so that manipulation of this fragment can safely progress. The remaining plantar tuberosity fragment often requires secondary manipulation with the standard lateral-to-medial Schanz screw because it will migrate superiorly and follow the rotation of the superior posterior tongue fragment.

If the reconstruction of the calcaneus is satisfactory after placement of the K-wire "jail," the surgeon may proceed with definitive fixation (Fig. 60–32). The implant chosen should be as low profile as possible, and choices include the Letournel Y plate, the 2.7-mm custom reconstruction plate, the cervical H plate, minifragment plates, the AO calcaneal locking plate, and small or minifragment screws. Often, use of a combination of these plates, such as interlocking them over the posterosuperior tuber fragment or beneath the posterior facet, is helpful to form a rigid construct that can endure early range of motion and possibly weight bearing. Bone grafting, if necessary, should be performed and the lateral wall replaced and held with K-wires.

A lateral 2.7/3.5-mm reconstruction plate is then contoured to fit the lateral wall, with an approximately 5° supination twist being made on the very anterior portion of the plate (at the calcaneocuboid joint level) to correspond to the shape of the anterior process where the long peroneal wraps around and under the foot. The plate should be placed as close as possible to the superior portion of the lateral cortex, just beneath the reduction K-wires, to produce direct lateral-to-medial compression (without shear). The screws in the plate are placed in an anterior-to-posterior direction, with each subsequent implant helping compress the lateral wall to the medial sustentacular cortex. Great care must be taken when drilling through the medial cortex because the medial neurovascular bundle and flexor hallucis longus tendon are in close proximity to the medial cortex.[3] To provide additional stabilization in a joint depression injury, a cervical H plate can be placed beneath the reconstruction plate to facilitate locking the interval between the posterior facet and the tuberosity. This additional plate provides extra stability to the tuberosity fragment, which will migrate superiorly, and the posterior facet, which will migrate plantarly, if healing is not rapid enough. Custom calcaneal plate constructs have provided this additional fixation so that composite plate constructs can be avoided.[167] The last screws to be placed are the posterior facet lag screws because they are the easiest to get good purchase with and the more difficult screws in the remainder of the fixation will have been completed. The lateral posterior facet fragment or fragments are drilled with a 3.5-, 2.7-, or 2.4-mm bit, the medial sustentacular segment is drilled with its corresponding 2.5-, 2.0-, or 1.8-mm bit, and screws of the appropriate length and size are inserted. Good compression is possible, often facilitated by lateral washers or the washer effect of the buttress plates now commercially available. After insertion of the hardware is completed, all K-wires no longer necessary to hold fracture fragments are removed. The goal of the provisional K-wires and Schanz screw placement is to correct the morphologic displacement. If the hardware is placed correctly and effectively, it compresses the reduced articular surfaces, maintains axial alignment of the tuberosity, and narrows the heel to its premorbid position in the process.

Positioning and exposure for ORIF of tongue-type fractures, if this method of treatment is chosen by the surgeon, are as described earlier for joint depression injury. After reduction, a tongue-type fracture can be stabilized with a Y plate as popularized by Letournel, with additional neutralization of the superior tuberosity fragment to the plantar cortex of the anterior process with an axially placed lag screw, usually 50 to 60 mm in length.[178] With either plate construct, final lateral and axial radiographs should be taken to monitor screw length and alignment because many screws will have become in effect too long by virtue of the compression achieved by the washer compression effect of the plate. Additionally, an AP view of the foot should also be taken to monitor the calcaneocuboid joint reduction and the length of the anterior process screws anterior to the sustentaculum, which is not visible on the axial view. Also, the travel of the flexor hallucis longus should be checked to make sure that its mobility has not been encumbered by a screw piercing it through the medial wall.

## BONE GRAFTING

Most surgeons believe that bone grafting is not necessary in every case, particularly because after reduction of a fracture, the defect that remains is similar in location to the neutral triangle of the calcaneus, where little structural bone integrity is normally found (Fig. 60–33). However, if the stability of the reconstruction is jeopardized by the lack of support provided by a bone graft, some thought should be entertained regarding its use. Large osseous defects do invite the possibility of late collapse. Occasionally, posterior facet reductions sag after weight bearing is started, and improved fixation can be obtained with some form of compressible filler. To prevent this eventuality, a cancellous bone graft or morselized allograft can be added whenever a large gap occurs under the posterior facet after reduction. Because it may take many months for consolidation, sagging of the reduction may take place if adequate healing has not occurred by the time that weight bearing has begun. To help prevent this complication, we bone graft 80% to 90% of fractures, especially the high-energy joint depression and tongue types. Autogenous bone graft may be harvested from Gerdy's tubercle or the anterior or posterior iliac crest, all accessible with the patient in the lateral position. More recently, the use of allograft cancellous chips (nonirradiated), bone substitutes (Pro-Osteon, DBX bone matrix, Norian SRS), and other bone graft substitutes has been popularized to avoid autogenous bone harvest and its attendant complications.[358] Morselized cancellous allograft is a relatively inexpensive, readily available, easily handled, compressible substance that is excellent for these purposes and causes no donor site morbidity. It is an excellent mechanical filler that demonstrates good incorporation, promotes scaffolding, and has an infection risk less than 1 in 1 million. No negative impact on infection rates or nonunion has been documented with this approach. Recent cadaveric and prospective clinical studies suggest using Norian because of improved loading characteristics and a much earlier postoperative return to weight-bearing status, as early as 3

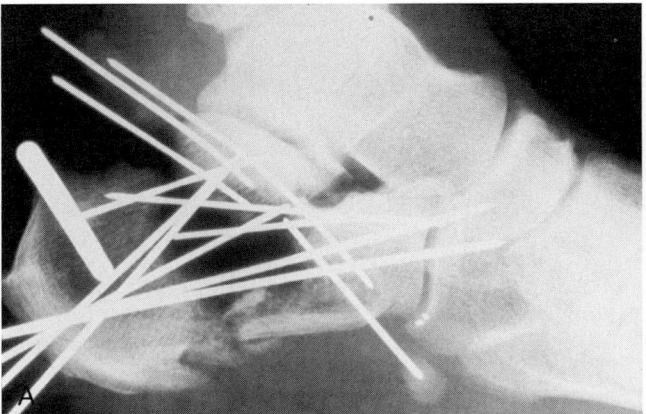
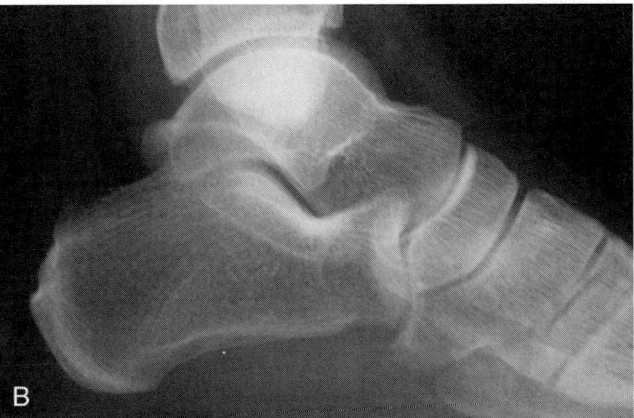

**FIGURE 60–33.** After calcaneal fracture reduction, a large void is usually left beneath the posterior facet as a result of its disimpaction from the crushed underlying cancellous bone during impact (*A*). Normally, the neutral triangle slightly posteroinferior to this region has a similar "hole" appearance on plain lateral radiographs (*B*). Thus, it is still controversial whether these postreduction voids should be filled during surgery; although it has not been verified to make a difference, optimal compressive fixation is probably best obtained when the voids in these constructs are filled with bone graft or a compressible bone graft substitute.

weeks after surgery without loss of reduction.[300, 328] Their infection rate of 11% is in pace with that of other studies of calcaneal fixation without such substances. Although no difference in clinical outcome was noted between those bearing full weight before and those bearing full weight after 6 weeks postoperatively, we believe that earlier weight bearing probably has many advantages not necessarily measurable, such as joint nutrition, limb conditioning, and prevention of fracture disease. The rationale for bone grafting or other substrates is to provide support for the elevated posterior facet–anterior process interval and provide volumetric filling so that the lateral plate has something tangible to compress against. The volume of bone usually necessary is approximately 10 to 15 cc, but it can range up to 60 cc!

## WOUND CLOSURE

Closure of the wound is as important and often as demanding as the surgical procedure itself. A small suction drain (⅛ inch) is placed and exits in a safe internervous zone in the sinus tarsi (between the sural and superficial peroneal nerves). Once the flap has been closed, an additional light compression dressing and splint will facilitate the drain's efforts to decompress the flap and prevent a significant hematoma from developing between the lateral wall and the periosteum of the periosteal cutaneous flap. It can be removed when less than 10 mL drains over an 8-hour shift or if it clots. These drainage measures helps prevent the postoperative complication of hematoma, a risk exacerbated by the concomitant use of DVT prophylaxis. A 2–0 absorbable suture is placed at the apex of the flap (at the corner), through the periosteum and then the subcutaneous layer of the flap, and next through the subcutaneous layer and then the periosteum of the matching location of the unelevated lateral skin. This suture positions the location of the flap so that subsequent sutures can help match the skin edges up. All the sutures are placed, each held with a provisional snap and designed to sequentially advance the flap to minimize tension at its vulnerable apex. Once these deep sutures have been placed, the flap is digitally reduced to its origin and the sutures are tied. The knots of the sutures are effectively under the periosteum to minimize subsequent suture abscess formation. Horizontal Allgöwer (Donati) skin 4–0 Dermalon sutures can then be placed with minimal tension because effective tension of the flap reduction has been already achieved by the deep sutures. Avoiding excessive tension on the cutaneous closure is critical to avoid skin necrosis, which can lead to wound contamination and infection. Elastic Steri-Strips can be placed between the skin sutures to further aid in closure of the skin and facilitate more rapid wound sealing. At the conclusion of the skin closure, both sides of the incision edges should be perfused to avoid blister formation or frank skin necrosis. Oxygen is given by nasal cannula starting in the recovery room to reinforce the principle of wound healing over nicotine drive.

## DRESSING

After wound closure, a light absorptive dressing is placed (Adaptic, fluffs), followed by Webril dressings applied with the foot and ankle in the neutral position. A well-padded plaster splint in the neutral position is then placed, with care taken to have no anterior compression. Alternatively, a compressive Jones-type dressing and elastic wrap are applied postoperatively, with careful padding along the fibular prominence to avoid skin ulceration. The patient can then be put in a removable 90° well-padded splint or prefabricated orthosis, with ankle range of motion allowed in 24 to 48 hours and subtalar range of motion within 3 to 5 days or as soon as wound healing permits. Under ideal situations, percutaneous sciatic blockade with a long-lasting anesthetic (0.5% bupivacaine [Marcaine] with epinephrine) is then induced to provide immediate pain relief, which may last 12 to 18 hours, and additionally induce a sympathetic blockade, ideal for perfusion of the flap.[272] Alternatively, an epidural provides bilateral pain relief for a similar period. Once the block has resolved, patient-controlled analgesia or other form of pain relief can be chosen, with the avoidance of NSAIDs, which have contributed to wound- and bone-healing problems.[103, 130]

## PRIMARY SUBTALAR FUSION

Primary fusion of the subtalar joint during operative treatment of an acute calcaneal fracture is difficult and should be reserved for severely comminuted fractures whose joint surfaces are not amenable to operative reconstruction. The appropriate indications for this decision are poorly defined, and some surgeons would argue that such patients should be treated nonoperatively from the outset with plans to perform subtalar fusion later if necessary.[90, 284] If primary reconstruction is chosen, the goal is to not only commit the posterior facet to subtalar fusion but also correct malalignment of the hindfoot complex, which affects other structures such as the talus and peroneals. Anterior ankle impingement from a horizontal talus and peroneal impingement from subluxation or dislocation remain two of the most common complaints when a calcaneus is left malpositioned. Because of its rare and ill-defined indications, the technique is best described as late salvage of post-traumatic subtalar arthrosis after calcaneal fracture.[328]

## Closed Reduction and Percutaneous Treatment of Intra-articular Calcaneal Body Fractures

### INDICATIONS

The technique of limited open or closed manipulation of the calcaneus with percutaneous fixation has recently been popularized by Sangeorzan and Tornetta.[335, 336] This method, however, lacks long-term follow-up. Although formal ORIF remains the best way to reduce and fix most displaced calcaneal fractures, this revisited technique initially described by Essex-Lopresti does have a role in certain cases and carries with it a lower risk of wound complications, a shorter operative time, and a faster healing phase by virtue of less soft tissue stripping. Hardware removal is less often necessary in such patients as well because of the lack of plate fixation. With these advantages, however, come inherent risks. Incomplete exposure can result in incomplete reduction and fixation. Thus, this technique is indicated for patients in whom ORIF would be a significant risk because of soft tissue compromise or impaired healing as a result of heavy smoking, diabetes, or soft tissue or adjacent bony trauma. Most important, it should be considered only for fracture patterns amenable to the technique, specifically, true tongue-type fracture patterns with a tuber attachment to the posterior facet that can be used as a reduction tool. A patient should therefore be considered a candidate for percutaneous fixation as determined by both the fracture pattern (tongue type or Sanders type 2C) and host factors.

It is not always possible to achieve absolutely anatomic reduction of the calcaneus with the percutaneous technique because of its limited exposure, but one can often get surprisingly close. Though a distinct disadvantage of this approach, it needs to be anticipated by the surgeon. The goals of this operation are improvement in alignment of the heel and reduction of the posterior calcaneal facet to the limits of both anatomy and exposure. If a perfect reduction is desired or expected, inordinate time should not be spent in attempting to do so, and a formal open approach needs to be performed.

## POSITIONING

Standard positioning of the patient in the lateral decubitus position on an image table should be done as described for the open technique. Care should be taken to use an axillary roll and pad all pressure points carefully. Gel pads can be used but should not be in the image field because they will disrupt radiographic visualization of the fracture. A "workbench" should be created with the operated leg posterior to the nonoperated downside one and both knees flexed on the image table. The peroneal nerve in the nonoperated extremity should be protected with folded blankets at least 2 inches distal to and underneath the fibular neck (see Fig. 60–30). The operated limb should be bumped higher (closer to the surgeon) than its counterpart so that its position allows for easy C-arm access to obtain true unimpeded lateral, AP, and axial views of the foot without having to move the foot at all. It cannot be accomplished with the limb either in front of or below the dependent side. With proper positioning, the image technician does not need to resort to any complicated maneuvering with the machine other than sagittal rotation. Because the adequacy of any percutaneous technique is dependent on good images, positioning should be carefully verified before proceeding further with preparation and draping of the leg.

## SURGICAL TECHNIQUE

Once the setup is complete, an attempt at closed reduction should be made. A bump can be placed (usually three folded sterile towels) beneath the heel for improved access and manipulation of the fracture. Images can be used to locate the proper insertion site for placement of a 4-mm Schanz pin into the tuber fragment attached to the posterior facet and avoid errant and unnecessary incisions. A vertical or horizontal stab incision can then be made directly posterior and over the portion of tuber that remains continuous with the displaced posterior facet, as determined by the preoperative sagittal CT images. Thus, this position may be central, medial, or lateral to the midline. Care should also be taken to place this incision such that it can also eventually be used for lag screw insertion to hold the tuber fragment reduced to the remaining body. This joystick should ideally be introduced approximately 5 mm beneath the superior rim of the tuber fragment and advanced to the subchondral bone of the posterior facet for best purchase during manipulation. Once it has been placed, the surgeon can then perform a reduction as described by Essex-Lopresti and Tornetta[83, 335] (Fig. 60–34). Gentle longitudinal distraction (with countertraction by an assistant) and disimpaction of the fragment are required, followed by a valgus moment on the heel and subsequent reimpaction medially to the sustentacular fragment to aid in reduction of the primary fracture line. Concomitantly, the surgeon can plantar flex the pin with a T-handled chuck, and the assistant can plantar flex the midfoot-forefoot to facilitate reduction of the secondary fracture line through the tuber fragment. Entertain caution in performing this maneuver, as well as during screw placement, so that the flexor hallucis longus or medial neurovascular bundle is not caught between the fracture fragments. If a lateral image verifies anatomic reduction of the posterior facet, a smooth 0.054- or 0.062-inch K-wire should be inserted axially and longitudinally to hold the fragment reduced while an axial view can be taken to verify the reduction in two planes. If the reduction remains unsatisfactory but still seems possible, a 1-cm Ollier incision should be made just proximal to the critical angle of Gissane for introduction of a dull, rounded elevator to aid in disimpaction and reduction of the facet. If the fracture is a joint depression injury, the proximolaterally displaced outer wall often prevents percutaneous elevation of the posterior facet, which is hidden far beneath this fragment. Caution should be exercised when making subsequent stab incisions during this limited approach because their location and direction can impair the surgeon's ability to make a formal lateral exposure if ultimately deemed necessary. Care should also be taken to avoid the sural nerve and peroneal tendons in this approach; the incision can alternatively be made parallel to these structures if necessary. The reduction tool will usually easily find its way just underneath the facet with fluoroscopic guidance, will often provide some decompression of hematoma, and can then be used in conjunction with the previous maneuvers to achieve calcaneal alignment.

When percutaneous reduction can be acceptably obtained, fixation is usually performed with 2.7- or 3.5-mm cortical screws through selected stab incisions (see Fig. 60–34). The sequence of insertion is determined by the fracture anatomy. The first screws are typically placed obliquely axially to neutralize the primary fracture line. They can be inserted from the heel all the way to the anterior process, just underneath the critical angle and posterior facet. These screws concomitantly serve as a buttress underneath the reduced, elevated facet. Often, two screws are then also placed, in lag fashion, across the posterosuperior lip of the tuber into the inferior body to counteract the pull of the Achilles postoperatively on the

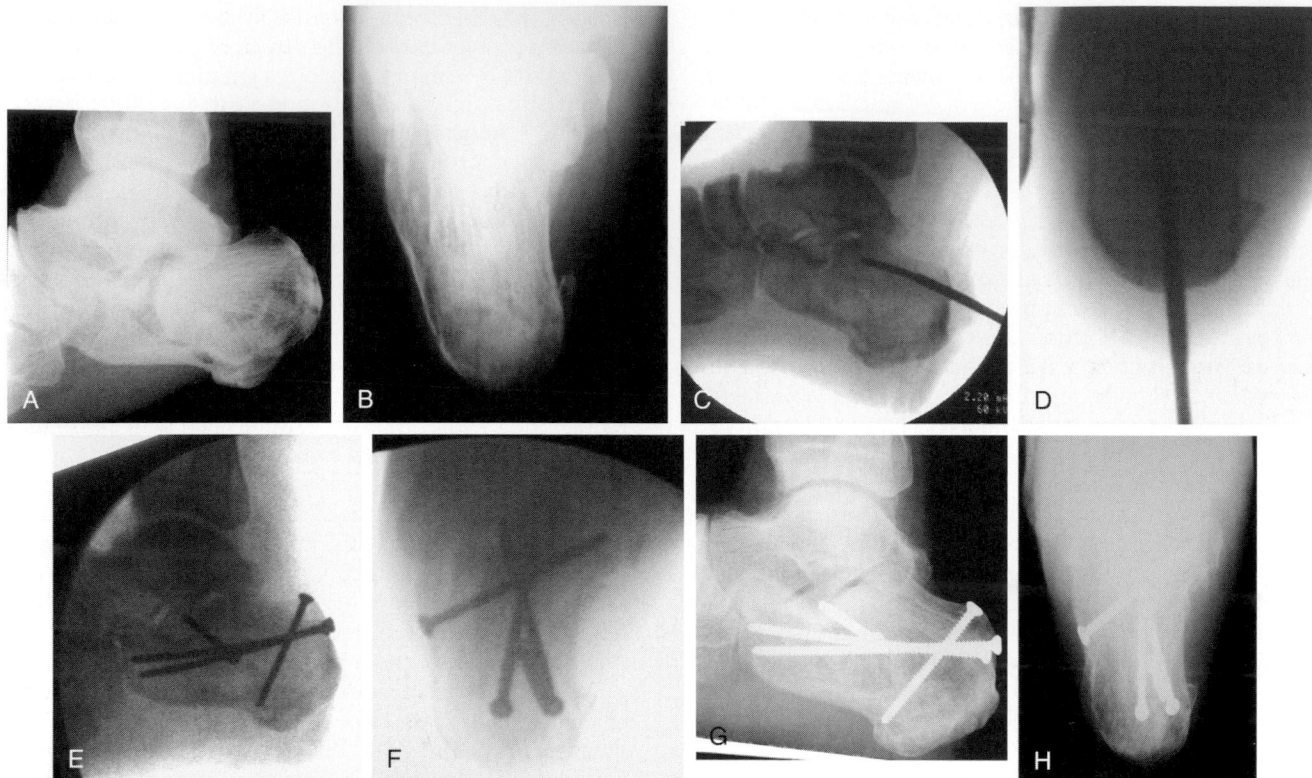

**FIGURE 60–34.** The Essex-Lopresti maneuver is useful for percutaneous reduction and fixation of tongue-type calcaneal fractures (*A, B*). As shown here, the combination of a curved AO elevator to pry beneath the primary fracture line and a 4.5-mm Schanz pin within the posterior tuber as a joystick is very helpful in facilitating this reduction (*C, D*). Imaging should be used to assist in this procedure and to then verify acceptable reduction, which can subsequently be held with K-wire fixation. Thereafter, percutaneous fixation of the tongue-type fracture with 3.5-mm cortical screws can provide a very successful and minimally invasive means of restoring length, height, and width of the calcaneus and also to satisfactorily restore the anatomy of the posterior facet of the subtalar joint (*E, F*). Two screws are usually inserted longitudinally into the subthalamic region without compression to maintain length and alignment, as well as to buttress the reduced posterior facet. One is inserted lateromedially to maintain compression of the primary fracture line and restore width, and the other is inserted in a posterosuperior-to-inferior direction to reduce the tongue fragment attached to the Achilles and counteract its tendency to redisplace this fragment. These patients can often be moved within 1 to 2 weeks for active and passive range-of-motion exercises and can enjoy near-normal return of hindfoot motion and alignment without the major risks of formal open reduction and internal fixation. This patient was doing nicely at 6 months after injury, with approximately 75% of his subtalar motion, no pain, and part-time return to heavy construction work (*G, H*).

previously displaced tongue fragment. These fragments can sometimes become redisplaced within a few weeks after surgery from pull or tightness of the gastrocnemius-soleus complex if care is not taken to get good bicortical fixation. Consideration should also be given to intraoperative gastrocnemius recession if it is determined preoperatively or intraoperatively that the gastrocnemius is a potential confounder to reduction or its maintenance. Finally, one or two screws can be placed in lag fashion through the lateral sinus tarsi exposure to maintain reduction and compression of the posterior facet to the intact medial sustentacular fragment. As in open fixation, care must be taken to not overdrill or insert screws that are too long. The medial wall of the calcaneus is concave, and transcalcaneal drilling or fixation can exit earlier than anticipated into the surrounding soft tissue without caution. Once these final screws are placed, the Schanz pin and K-wires can be removed to allow optimal imaging in all three projections, as well as good manipulation under image control to assess the quality of reduction and fixation. It is important to obtain a true lateral view of the talus, best determined by having no superimposition of the talar neck or dome, before assessing anything on images.

Remember that everything rotates around the talus. When a true lateral projection of this bone is visualized, one then has the best view of how well reduced the calcaneus will be in the standing, anatomic position. Such visualization is particularly relevant when using imaging, which is notorious for underdepicting the true anatomy.

## WOUND CLOSURE AND POSTOPERATIVE PROTOCOL

On completion, the skin incisions are simply closed with nylon and a soft compressive Jones-type dressing applied under a posterior, removable splint to hold the foot in neutral. Early range of motion is begun within a few days, as soon as comfort permits, and weight bearing is prohibited until signs of early healing are seen, usually in 6 to 10 weeks (Fig. 60–35). The functional results of percutaneous treatment of tongue-type calcaneal fractures have been better than those of the more traditional open technique for joint depression injuries. Complications such as infection, wound-healing problems, and postoperative stiffness are also significantly less frequent. This reduction in complication rate is probably multifactorial and related most to the nature of the articular, bony, and soft tissue injury (its "personality") as opposed to merely surgical technique, although the latter no doubt plays some role.

## Postoperative Care and Rehabilitation of Intra-articular Calcaneal Fractures

Postoperatively, the neutral or 90° splint that is applied at the time of wound closure is maintained for approximately 3 days. The drain is removed when less than 10 mL is evacuated in an 8-hour shift. The patient is confined to a bed exercise regimen for 2 to 3 postoperative days, with the foot at or slightly above cardiac level. Active isometric exercise of the toes is encouraged. Passive flexion and especially hyperextension of the toes are begun once the sciatic block has resolved and the patient can tolerate such movement, to help prevent the development of long toe flexor contracture.

Between 3 days and 2 weeks after surgery (depending on soft tissue status), the splint is changed for a removable, commercial, well-padded lightweight one and the incision covered with a dry sterile dressing until the sutures are removed. Alternatively, a short leg bivalved fiberglass cast can be fabricated if the patient's anatomy prohibits commercial splint application. Once the incision has sealed (often within 48 hours), active range-of-motion exercises are begun, with flexion-extension of the ankle and inversion-eversion or circumduction exercises of the subtalar complex. A below-knee compressive (thromboembolic disease [TED]) stocking is useful and important in relieving dependent edema in the extremity. The goal of the rehabilitative program is to mimic the range of motion of the opposite foot and be able to obtain this motion before weight bearing. This goal requires a reliable patient who is willing to perform these exercises on a consistent basis a specified number of times a day and then to place the foot back in the splint at night to avoid equinus contracture. Active range-of-motion exercises should not disrupt the fracture fixation, so the internal fixation used should be solid enough to withstand the rehabilitation program.

Adequate healing of incisions to permit suture removal is usually noted between 2 and 3 weeks after surgery. Persistent hematoma drainage is managed by frequent dressing changes and additional Steri-Strips on the incision when necessary. Oral antibiotics (trimethoprim-sulfamethoxazole [Bactrim DS], ciprofloxacin) should be used prophylactically in this circumstance. Aggressive range-of-motion exercises are not started until the incision has completely sealed to avoid sinus formation at the apex of the flap, where most persistent hematoma drainage occurs. Six weeks after surgery, an elastic stocking is applied, and the first postoperative lateral and axial radiographs are taken. Progressive healing with consolidation of the medial wall is seen on the axial view. On the lateral view, revascularization of the posterior facet can be monitored, which can also be seen on Broden's views. Critical radiographic assessment of fracture healing is necessary because callus healing is characteristically not seen, but the fracture lines gradually soften and the homogeneous ground-glass appearance returns to the cancellous architecture of the calcaneus.

Full weight bearing is delayed for at least 3 months, and when weight bearing is begun, it is done in 10- to 20-lb increments. If the patient does not experience pain with the level of weight bearing used, it is increased at regular intervals. Progression to full weight bearing is followed by removal of the crutches, first on the uninvolved side and then the involved side, with advance to a cane. At each stage of weight bearing, encouragement of a normal foot progression angle and gait cycle is stressed so that a permanent limp does not develop, which in many instances is not secondary to analgesia but more a habit. Adherence to the postoperative regimen is very important for restoration of motion in the subtalar joint. When the patient is compliant and actively participates in the rehabilitation, restoration of full ankle motion is expected, and 50% to 75% of subtalar joint motion is possible.

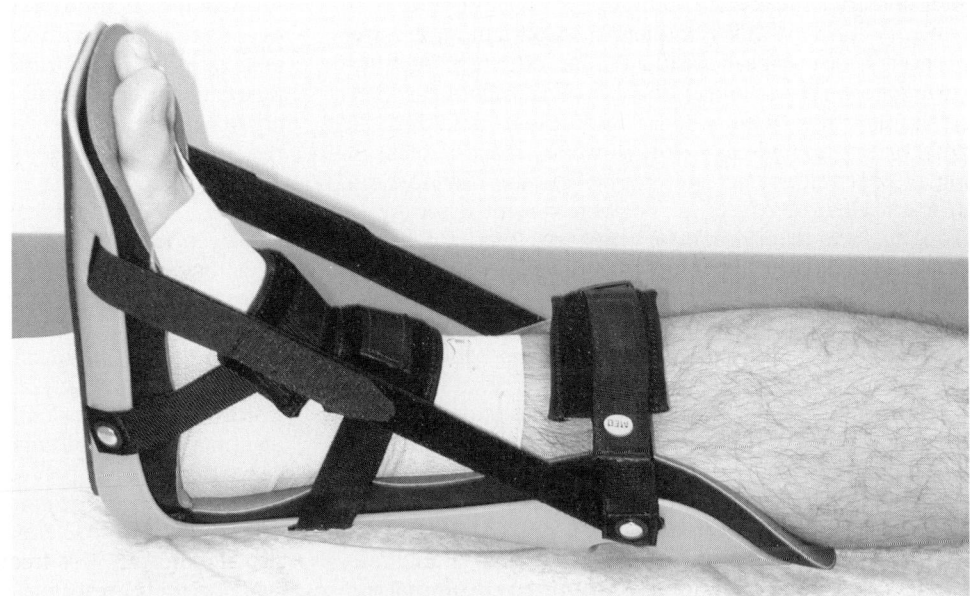

**FIGURE 60–35.** A well-padded dorsiflexion night splint is an excellent way of managing an acute calcaneal fracture. It is lightweight, maintains a neutral ankle position, allows for observation of fracture blisters and swelling, and can also be used in the postoperative setting to permit early non–weight-bearing range-of-motion exercises of the ankle and subtalar joint.

Greater subtalar range of motion occurs in the most motivated patients and less in more passive individuals. Physical therapy intervention is often helpful in the latter group, with more advanced balance and proprioceptive exercises begun in the motivated group. At 6 months postoperatively, once solid healing and revascularization have occurred, joint mobilization exercises can be initiated to achieve the extremes of subtalar and ankle motion.[345]

These patients will never have a "normal" heel again and therefore should be educated early about this fact (preferably before surgery), as well as about the possible long-term necessity of alternative shoe wear and modifications, including shock-absorbing (e.g., Vibram) soles, arch supports with heel cups to "bunch up" the fat pad beneath the injured heel, and cushioned heel supports.

## Outcome

Deriving a reliable conclusion regarding the outcome of calcaneal fracture treatment is impossible because of the difficulty in gleaning meaningful information from so many studies with different patient populations, fracture classifications, surgical approaches, and inadequate follow-up or small numbers. No definitive, unbiased prospective studies on calcaneal fracture management and outcome have yet been performed. Letournel found that 47% of his 99 operatively treated intra-articular calcaneal fracture patients at a 2-year follow-up had useful subtalar motion, with only 56% having good or very good results.[177] Sanders and colleagues reviewed 120 patients treated by a combination of the lateral and modified lateral approach and, according to the Sanders CT classification system of the posterior facet, found that 73% of those with mild to moderate comminution had good or excellent results but only 9% with severe comminution had such results.[282] Tscherne and Zwipp used a combined medial, lateral, and bilateral approach during their treatment of 157 displaced fractures; with the use of their scoring and fracture classification systems, they identified an inverse relationship between fracture severity and clinical outcome.[338] A review at Harborview Medical Center in Seattle of over 100 displaced intra-articular calcaneal fractures with follow-up for longer than 2 years suggests a 70% satisfaction rate with surgery and shows that 65% of patients are limited only in their ability to participate in vigorous activities and sports and 50% are able to walk comfortably on any surface.[192] Sixty percent reported no pain medication requirement, but 40% were unable to return to their previous employment because of functional limitations. The very steep learning curve involved in the preoperative decision-making process and the intraoperative management of calcaneal fractures probably has an effect on outcome in these injuries more than any other factor except the "personality" (bony and soft tissue damage) of the fracture itself. It does appear that although most patients can expect some degree of functional limitation, reconstruction of normal calcaneal anatomy and restoration of hindfoot biomechanics should be the surgeon's goal to achieve an optimal outcome of these potentially devastating injuries. Final determination of the most appropriate treatment algorithm will be decided by the results of a well-controlled, multicenter, prospective randomized clinical trial.

## Complications of Intra-articular Calcaneal Fractures

### PREOPERATIVE COMPLICATIONS

One must be vigilant about preventing and screening for a number of preoperative complications, depending on host and injury factors. Such complications include (1) fracture blisters or eschars (particularly occurring laterally), which should be observed as they develop, be débrided early, and be allowed to epithelialize before surgery; (2) swelling, which should be carefully evaluated for compartment syndrome and, in most cases, simply observed with elevation until wrinkling occurs; (3) "cellulitis," which can be either chemically induced or secondary to a skin lesion; (4) DVT, which although rare in this situation, should be screened for with duplex ultrasound by an experienced ultrasonographer if symptoms are suggestive or if the patient is multiply injured and has been at bedrest without prophylaxis for a short time, or has been transferred from elsewhere, immobilized for a prolonged period, and is considered an "at risk" patient; (5) occult open fractures— look medially for even punctate holes; and (6) occult nerve injury, particularly the posterior tibial nerve branches, which should be evaluated for cause and documented in the record before undertaking ORIF.

### PERIOPERATIVE COMPLICATIONS

The complication rate after ORIF of a calcaneal fracture through a lateral approach ranges from 10% to 20%. Compartment syndrome occurs in approximately 10% of all calcaneal fractures[230] and can lead to clawtoe deformity or neurologic sequelae and pain in about half of affected patients. Vigilance is imperative for early diagnosis and rapid decompression when indicated. Many other soft tissue injuries need to be carefully considered when formulating an appropriate treatment plan, most of which occur before surgery and can be increasingly problematic after surgery if not initially addressed, such as peroneal dislocation, skin blistering (often medial), open wounds, and tendon entrapment.[180] Iatrogenic intraoperative injuries to the sural nerve or medial neurovascular bundle injury can be minimized by careful dissection, ORIF, and closure.[3] By far the most feared complications related to any open treatment of a calcaneal fracture remain tissue infection or sloughing.[180] Infection occurs 2% to 3% of the time but usually resolves after healing and hardware removal.[114] Wound necrosis has been found to be the most common complication after fixation of a calcaneal fracture. It occurs in 8% to 9% of patients, typically a wound edge necrosis that resolves with local expectant wound care and dressing changes. Necrosis has decreased with the advent of a sharper L-shaped incisional modification to Palmer and Letournel's more gradually curved lateral approach, as described by Benirschke and Sangeorzan.[17] Once identification is made, operative débridement must be early and aggressive, and potential plastic surgery involvement must be rapid for successful salvage because the consequences can otherwise be disastrous. Even an initially benign-appearing hematoma beneath the flap should be rapidly decompressed if flap viability is at all in question, or it could become a nidus for infection. These problems represent the few complications that can be extremely difficult and sometimes impossible to salvage with a good result.[18] The best treatment for this problem is prevention, facilitated by proper patient selection, consideration of nonoperative or percutaneous techniques, and if formal ORIF is required, the use of meticulous surgical technique and soft tissue handling with minimization of tourniquet time and adequate postoperative soft tissue relaxation before mobilization.

## POSTOPERATIVE COMPLICATIONS

A number of problems, if they occur after open treatment of a fairly well-aligned calcaneus, can be fairly easily treated, including delayed union or nonunion, reorientation of the tuberosity, subtalar fusion, and loss of calcaneal inclination with dorsiflexion ankle impingement. Reconstructive procedures for these problems have been described by Hansen.[120] In-house review of 36 cases of calcaneal ORIF at Harborview Medical Center in Seattle suggested a 3% to 4% incidence of infection, 8% to 9% incidence of wound problems (excluding infection), 3% incidence of nerve complications, and a requirement for secondary procedures (excluding implant removal) in 7% to 8%. One case of heterotopic ossification and one case of DVT occurred. Overall, the postoperative complication rate was 16.5%. Only 2% of the patients in this evaluation required subtalar fusion, which results in predictable pain relief but probable ankle arthrosis 5 to 10 years after fusion.

## HARDWARE REMOVAL

At 12 to 18 months postoperatively, the patient is counseled regarding hardware removal. If prominence is noted, the implants can be removed on an outpatient basis, with 3 days of splint immobilization and progression to full weight bearing if healing has been complete. Thinner hardware constructs have decreased the need for removal, and many patients truly do not have hardware symptoms, although the spectrum ranges from exquisite symptoms, to mechanical irritation, to barometric changes alone. Hardware removal can cause injury to the sural nerve or peroneal artery if enveloped in scar during exposure, and caution must be exercised.[279]

## STIFFNESS

Most patients maintain excellent functional range of motion of the ankle if early exercises are begun pending soft tissue stability. Two thirds of patients maintain approximately 50% of their preinjury subtalar motion, whereas the other third is split between having almost complete recovery (>75%) or loss (<25%) of their subtalar motion postoperatively. In the experience of Sangeorzan and Benirschke with these aforementioned protocols, more than 85% of injured workers were able to return to work within 9 months of injury, and 30% had significant activity

modification. Shoe wear does not usually require an alteration in size, but it does require an adjustment in cushioning.

## PAIN

Patients with intra-articular calcaneal fractures can expect some degree of long-term swelling, stiffness, intermittent and sometimes constant heel pain, and functional deficit. Multiple authors have documented a prolonged recovery for this injury, as long as 10 years after surgery.[208, 258] Typically, however, 1 year is a good rule of thumb to observe patients until they can be presumed to have reached maximal medial improvement. Any further intervention based purely on symptoms should therefore at least be reserved for after this time frame. Frequently, patients can be helped and may be better off with conservative measures such as oral and topical anti-inflammatory medications, UCBL heel orthotics, or a double-upright PTB offloading brace. Pain is frequently multifactorial in cause, and surgery for these patients is not always the answer. If its suspected cause is presumed to be intra-articular, a simple subtalar injection with a 1- to 2-mL mixture of 0.5% bupivacaine or lidocaine can be diagnostic. Imaging may be required to ensure cannulation of the joint. A short course of immobilization can also be helpful in deciding whether further intervention such as subtalar fusion is warranted. Great care must be taken in determining the exact cause of the pain because in many instances, it is unlikely to be alleviated regardless of an orthopaedist's management.

## AVASCULAR NECROSIS

Rarely, necrosis of the avascular posterior facet fragments may occur, but if enough time is allowed for revascularization, collapse is rare. The joint may sag from bearing weight too early, which is usually heralded by pain. These complications develop in a small number of patients despite appropriate care, and specific factors can usually be attributed to the failures, including displacement of the original fracture, dislocation, open fracture, infection, or premorbid factors such as systemic health problems (diabetes, peripheral vascular disease, or immunocompromised status) and smoking. Successful salvage, when indicated by symptoms, usually requires excision of necrotic bone, restoration of calcaneal alignment, and limited hindfoot fusion.[231, 279] Bone grafting may be necessary.

## NONUNION

Nonunion is extremely rare, which is why we call it the "heel" bone. When nonunion does occur, it is challenging to treat and requires aggressive débridement of dead, fibrous, or infected bone. Staged revision fixation with bone grafting is recommended.

## FAILURE OF FIXATION OR POST-TRAUMATIC ARTHROSIS

Patients with failure of fixation or post-traumatic arthrosis can be treated by subtalar fusion. Late arthrodesis is

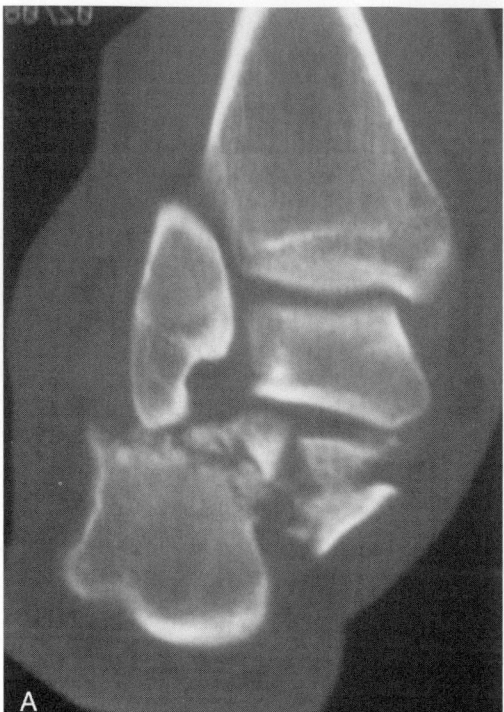

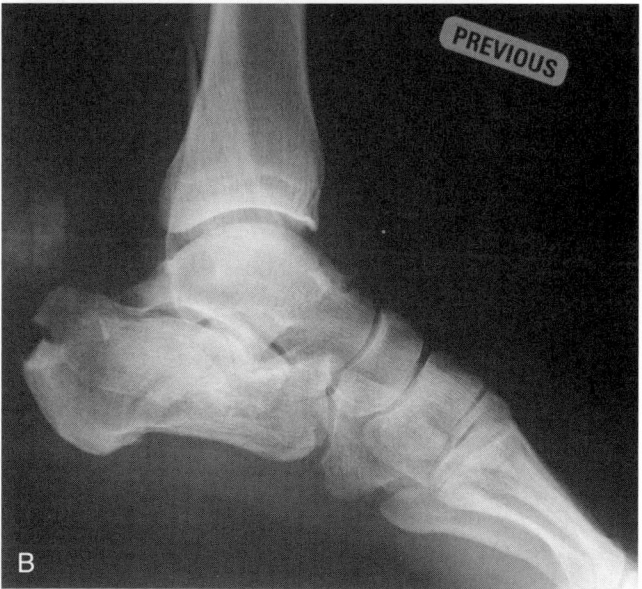

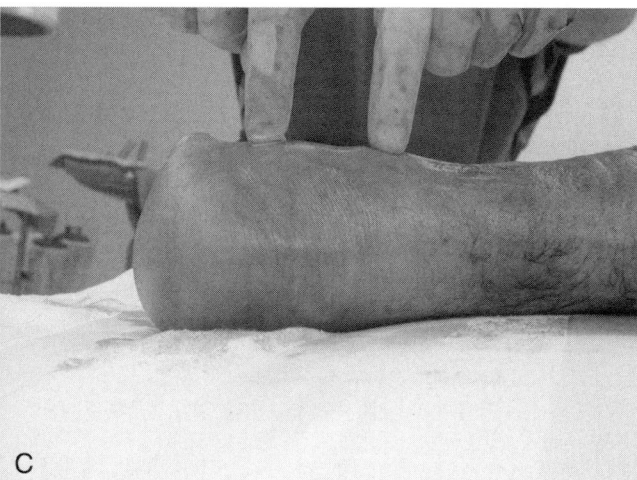

**FIGURE 60–36.** Subfibular impingement after a calcaneal fracture results from a lateral "blowout" of the lateral wall of the calcaneus (A). The impingement usually occurs because of the compressive, wedgelike forces of the lateral process and body of the talus on the critical angle and posterior facet of the calcaneus (B). It is often accompanied by shortening of the calcaneus, loss of height, and lateral subluxation of the posterior facet fragments and lateral wall, all of which contribute to peroneal impingement or subluxation and subfibular pain. These findings are usually an indication for surgery and can be seen nicely in this patient before operative reduction, fixation, and decompression (C).

relatively simple in the presence of arthrosis alone if the overall morphology has been restored in the index procedure. Avascular segments should be replaced with corticocancellous blocks to maintain height and length of the heel and preserve normal ankle mechanics and function. Reconstructive effort must be tailored so that every attempt is made to keep the ankle and Chopart joints functional because they will bear the brunt of the stress once arthrodesis has been performed on the talocalcaneal joints.[40, 271] Incongruity or arthrosis of the calcaneocuboid joint is actually fairly well tolerated, and isolated fusion of this joint is rarely indicated. Occasionally, double or triple hindfoot fusions can be performed if indicated.

## PERONEAL OR ANKLE IMPINGEMENT

Impingement of the peroneal tendons can be caused by residual lateral wall displacement or calcaneal malunion that constricts the peroneal tunnel and results in symptomatic tendonitis or restricted and painful inversion/eversion[275] (Fig. 60–36). The tendons are effectively subluxated in this instance, but they can also be frankly dislocated. If selective injection, casting, and shoe wear modification are not helpful, a decompressive lateral wall exostectomy is often successful in relieving symptoms.[27] Anterior ankle pain with dorsiflexion impingement can also occur with settling of the calcaneus or incomplete restoration of height through Böhler's angle. Carr and associates have described a technique of subtalar arthrodesis through a posterior approach in which a large piece of tricortical iliac crest graft is used to distract the joint and restore calcaneal inclination.[41] An alternative technique involves calcaneal osteotomy with plantar displacement before fixation.[271] Both methods are capable of addressing subtalar arthrosis through fusion and decompression of the anterior ankle joint, and both run the risk of soft tissue complications from skin stretching; the latter, however, has the added advantage of being able to correct malalignment in the sagittal plane by virtue of mediolateral heel shift as well.

## MALUNION

Various reconstructive techniques are available for correction of hindfoot malalignment or impingement as a result of calcaneal malunion.[279] These techniques are described in depth in the subsequent chapter on post-traumatic reconstruction. Surgery is rarely helpful for plantar exostosis or malunion along the weight-bearing portion of the posterior tuber and is not advised except in situations of extreme prominence or displacement.

## Extra-articular Calcaneus Fractures

About one third of calcaneal fractures are extra-articular. They can involve the anterior process ("beak"), tuber, body, or sustentaculum. Most of them result from a twist or direct impact (not necessarily compressive) on the foot, although avulsion injuries of the posterior tuber are occasionally seen, particularly in diabetics.[20] The avulsion is probably due to a combination of abnormalities in collagen crosslinking in these patients that results in extremely tight Achilles tendons, as well as the often weaker bone that such patients have. We suspect that gastrocnemius tightness is the most important determinant of this injury in diabetics and believe that it is rare to find a diabetic patient without a tight superficial posterior compartment.

Minimally displaced nonarticular calcaneal fractures of any size may be treated nonoperatively. As with other foot fractures, large displaced fragments in the calcaneus should be repaired and small fragments excised. Small nonarticular fractures may occur as posterosuperior beak fractures; they do not involve the Achilles tendon and may be excised. Operative reduction may be indicated for large nonarticular fractures that involve the Achilles tendon, particularly when they are displaced or are tenting the thin posterior soft tissue envelope. They are best managed with screw or wire fixation and careful attention to soft tissue handling because of the tenuous posterior soft tissue envelope.

## Anterior Process Calcaneal Fractures

All but the smallest anterior process or "beak" fractures of the calcaneus involve the calcaneocuboid joint. Symptoms of this injury may be identical to those of a chronic ankle sprain, and the mechanism of injury can be identical.[224] Typically, the bifurcate ligament or, on occasion, the extensor digitorum brevis pulls off a fragment of bone during a plantar flexion inversion moment. Remember that one cannot sprain the ankle without twisting the (hind) foot. The presence of an anterior beak fracture must always be suspected if after an injury a patient complains of persisting pain or swelling in the region of the calcaneocuboid joint or the sinus tarsi. This diagnosis is commonly missed because the fracture fragments can be quite small and identification can be hindered by talocalcaneal overlap on routine plain films. Their small size and location also usually result in little functional disability aside from chronic pain, although the pain itself can be quite limiting. It is usually located in the sinus tarsi or directly over the anterior process, a superficial and usually easily identifiable anatomic structure. Often, this pain is very reproducible on repetitive examination, and careful attention during palpation with the foot inverted and plantar flexed can aid in transposing the area of interest away from the lateral ankle ligament complex to facilitate the differential diagnosis. Thus, any patient with persistent pain in this region attributed to an "ankle sprain" or otherwise should have a set of standard foot films taken in addition to typical ankle films. If the diagnosis remains difficult but a high index of suspicion remains, bone scan and CT evaluation are both fairly sensitive and specific tests that may demonstrate the fracture (Fig. 60–37).

Anterior beak fractures are best visualized on a lateral or oblique view of the foot as a small avulsion off the anterior process of the calcaneus, often with an adjacent radiolucency suggestive of nonunion. They are usually minimally displaced. These fractures should be distinguished from the os calcaneum secondarium, a small accessory bone that can be seen in this proximity and has all the hallmarks of a secondary ossification center as opposed to a fracture. When these fractures are detected early, treatment should be supportive for all but those with unusually large fragments, which can involve a considerable portion of the calcaneocuboid joint and should be fixed. Depending on symptoms and swelling, either a supportive postoperative shoe or a short leg cast is applied with instructions for progressive weight bearing as tolerated. Most importantly, however, one must explain to the patient that although these fractures are not generally considered operative or severe injuries by virtue of their location and size, they occasionally remain symptomatic despite any conservative measures and may require excision later, which usually results in a very acceptable functional outcome and good pain relief.[63]

If the anterior process fracture is identified in the chronic setting, the aforementioned procedures are usually unsuccessful, and instead, sinus tarsi injection can be attempted with a 1- to 2-mL mixture of 0.5% bupivacaine and a steroid derivative such as betamethasone (Celestone) or triamcinolone (Kenalog). If symptoms persist, resulting in a situation often mimicking the findings in "sinus tarsi syndrome," as described by Frey and DiGiovanni, excision is also recommended.[98] Open or arthroscopic excision can be performed, depending on the experience and preference of the surgeon. The open approach is best performed through an oblique Ollier incision, with care taken to avoid the superficial peroneal nerve, the extensor tendons, and the peroneus tertius superiorly, as well as the sural nerve and peroneal tendons inferiorly. The arthroscopic approach is performed through anterior, middle, and posterior portals as previously described for subtalar arthroscopy. The two anterior-most portals in this instance are the most utilitarian for visualization and removal (see Fig. 60–28). Even in the chronic situation, excision usually results in significant improvement in comfort and function for the patient.

## Medial Sustentacular Fractures of the Calcaneus

Sustentacular fractures are uncommon and occur from a direct impact on an inverted foot. Patients have an antalgic gait and medial swelling plus pain that, in the absence of ecchymosis, often resembles the fullness and pain identified in a patient with a tarsal coalition of the subtalar joint. Pain can be exacerbated by a resistive maneuver of the flexor hallucis longus, which stresses the fracture site as it courses beneath the sustentaculum. Care must be taken to not misdiagnose an ankle fracture or sprain because the

pain is in direct proximity to the deltoid ligament, which partially envelopes the medial sustentaculum. Routine plain films of the foot are indicated, including an axial calcaneal view, which is most reliable in detecting this fracture. Ankle films, CT scanning, or both should also be considered to rule out other injuries or for further evaluation. The ankle should be carefully inspected to ensure that the neurovascular bundle, which courses directly medial and just superior to this structure, is functional.

Because this fracture is by definition an intra-articular injury and involves a portion of bone responsible for significant support of the talus above, serious consideration should be given to anatomic ORIF of larger fragments displaced more than 2 mm (Fig. 60–38). We have also seen stenosing tenosynovitis of the flexor hallucis longus tendon, as well as a symptomatic compressive irritation of the neurovascular bundle with untreated displaced fractures in this region. ORIF should be performed through a horizontal medial utility approach. After incising the flexor retinaculum, the posterior tibial tendon and flexor digitorum longus (which is often directly medial to this structure) should be raised superiorly and the neurovascular bundle and flexor hallucis

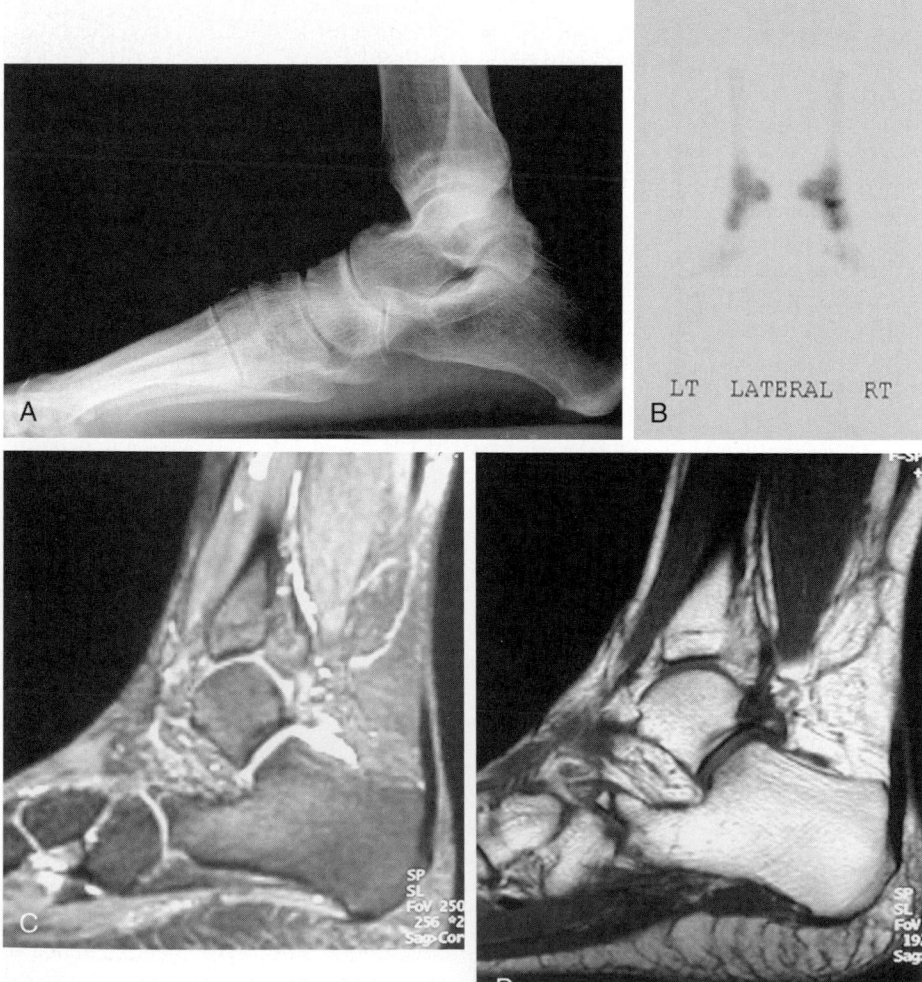

**Figure 60–37.** Although isolated anterior process calcaneal avulsion fractures are rarely of sufficient functional significance to warrant primary surgical treatment, they are frequently identified after the fact as a result of persistent sinus tarsi pain, which can be debilitating. As seen in this case, these fractures are often subtle on initial radiographs, any displacement being the result of pull by the bifurcate ligament or the extensor digitorum brevis (A). Despite a lack of findings on plain films, however, persistent pain and reproducible tenderness to palpation along the anterior process of the calcaneus should prompt further testing. This patient had an abnormality in this region detected on a bone scan (B), followed by clear identification of the problematic nonunion on both T2-weighted (C) and T1-weighted (D) magnetic resonance imaging sequences. Such abnormalities require excision when persistently symptomatic, and the result is usually excellent. This patient's injury occurred as a result of a twisting basketball injury, and it was not diagnosed until over a year after injury. Excision resulted in complete resolution of symptoms.

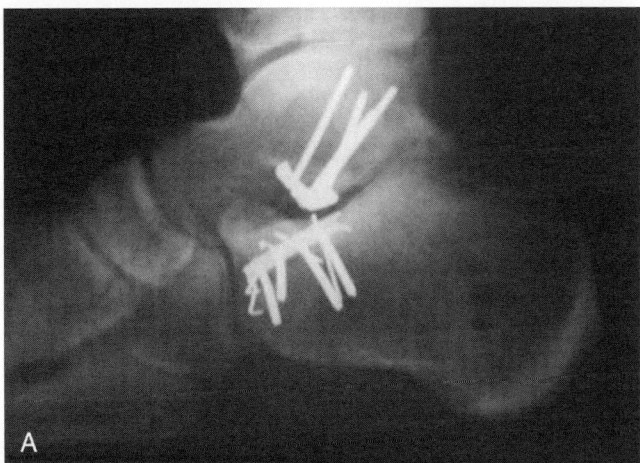

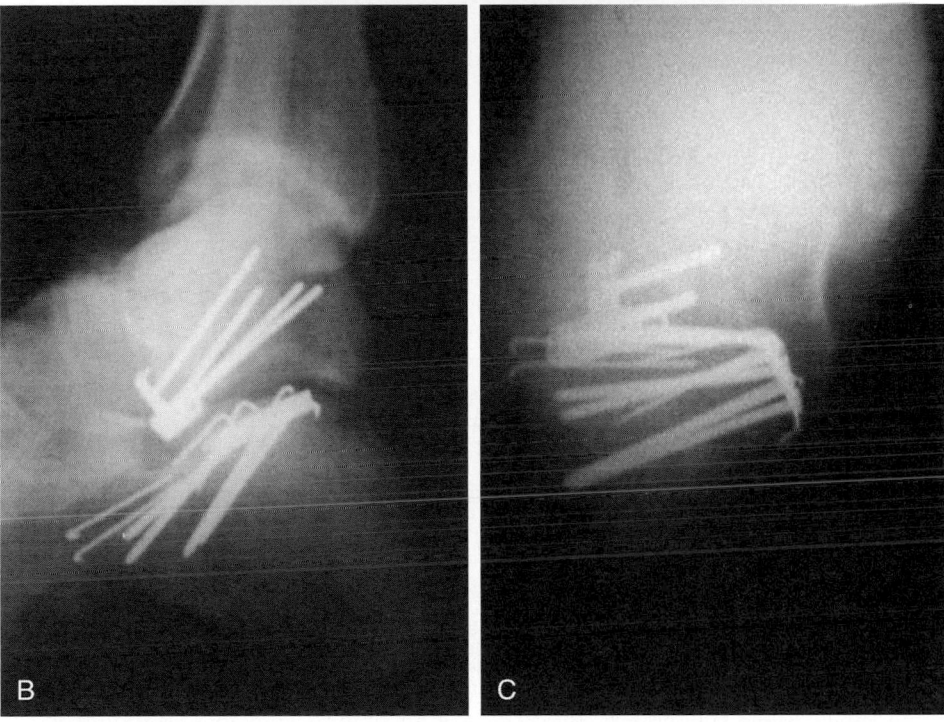

FIGURE 60–38. Medial sustentacular fractures of the calcaneus are unusual injuries to sustain alone. A search for other nearby bony or ligamentous injuries is imperative. This case is such an example; this patient also sustained a lateral process talar fracture, and an acute abduction moment to the foot probably caused this injury pattern. Open reduction plus internal fixation was carried out through an incision medially and laterally. Note the reduction and fixation of the sustentaculum with a minifragment plate on the lateral (*A*), Broden (*B*), and axial (*C*) views. These injuries by definition involve the medial/anterior facets of the subtalar joint and also have major ligamentous attachments (deltoid) and should thus be fixed in most circumstances.

longus tendon raised inferiorly. The deltoid insertion and capsule can then be split at the level of the subtalar joint and middle facet for ease of visualization and to minimize injury and dissection of the ligamentous complex. This complex can initially be localized with a needle or image intensification if soft tissue disruption has not already allowed direct access by virtue of the injury. The best indication for fixation is often visualization of the inferior edge of the fracture fragment against the medial wall of the calcaneus, best seen with placement of a Hohmann retractor gently against the bundle and flexor. Once keyed in, the middle facet is usually reduced anatomically in the absence of comminution or a rotatory component. Fixation can proceed with small 1.5-, 2.0-, or 2.4-mm screws and sometimes with a washer. The latter is not typically needed in this very dense bone. All non-reconstructible intra-articular fragments should be removed before closure. Postoperatively, these patients can be splinted for 2 weeks in neutral dorsiflexion to relax the soft tissues,

followed by immobilization in a removable splint or bivalved cast to allow aggressive range-of-motion exercises of the ankle, the toes, and especially the subtalar joint to minimize stiffness. This plan of course assumes rigid intraoperative fixation, which should be the goal in addition to anatomic reduction for this reason. Progressive weight bearing should begin approximately 4 to 6 weeks after surgery if clinical and radiographic parameters permit. These fractures are usually healed within 8 to 10 weeks after surgery, and patients typically do quite well.

Nondisplaced or minimally displaced fractures can be immobilized in a short leg cast for 6 weeks, followed by early mobilization and progressive weight bearing and physical therapy.[38] Closed reduction in the case of displaced fractures can be attempted with plantar flexion and inversion of the foot to impact the sustentacular fragment, but this technique is not recommended in lieu of operative fixation because of the required prolonged dysfunctional position of the foot in a cast for healing.

Nonunion is unusual and can be treated by excision in much the same way that an incomplete tarsal coalition of the middle facet is treated when the remaining articulation is well preserved.

## Extra-articular Body Fractures of the Calcaneus

Most extra-articular fractures involving the calcaneus occur in its body.[277] Because the mechanism of injury is similar to that for intra-articular fractures, these injuries seem to represent a lower energy variant with a better prognosis. The primary fracture line in this circumstance can travel in any of several planes, although it typically courses through the body and exits behind the posterior facet while avoiding the subtalar joint. Deformity is often minimal and usually less severe than in typical intra-articular fractures, although it can be quite significant and have many of the components of its relative with regard to malalignment. The features, evaluation, and workup of these particular injuries are identical to those for intra-articular calcaneal body injuries, although in this case, if subtalar joint involvement can be reliably excluded on the basis of plain films and surgery is not contemplated, CT evaluation is not needed. Not uncommonly, however, subtalar joint involvement cannot be appreciated on the initial plain films, and its presence may change the course of treatment. When any question arises in this circumstance, formal CT scanning should be performed.

As might be suspected from the fact that it remains controversial whether operative or nonoperative treatment of intra-articular calcaneal fractures has a better impact on functional outcome, the outcome of extra-articular injuries is usually quite good and improved in comparison to the former. Casting is contraindicated in these patients, and they should be protected from any weight bearing and initially splinted for soft tissue swelling and pain in the acute setting. Within a few weeks, however, these patients are frequently quite comfortable and capable of tolerating an early regimen of physical therapy for range of motion, edema control, and eventually weight-bearing mobilization as soon as early healing occurs at around 4 to 6 weeks after injury. If significant widening of the heel or loss of calcaneal inclination has occurred, strong consideration should be given to a closed reduction maneuver accompanied by casting or even percutaneous pinning. Heckman has advocated closed reduction when Böhler's angle is decreased by 10° or more.[128] Closed reduction can avoid the potential complications of peroneal impingement, heel counterirritation, and anterior ankle impingement. In this case, the postoperative protocol is similar and is guided by patient comfort and signs of early healing. In either case, the vast majority of these patients can expect a good long-term functional result, although their heel may never be exactly the same and they should not expect such. Intermittent soreness, some stiffness, and occasional activity-dependent swelling can occur, but they are not nearly as troublesome as with intra-articular fractures. Again, nonunion is rare,[247] which is why it is called the "heel" bone.

## Posterior Tuberosity Fractures of the Calcaneus

The posterior tuber of the calcaneus can be injured superiorly or inferiorly, although the former is more common. In either case, patients have pain, difficulty walking, and weakness in heel-rise, or they avoid heel contact with the ground. Swelling is usually present posteriorly, and care must be taken to inspect the thin soft tissue envelope because any skin tenting, breach, or necrosis necessitates rapid operative decompression and débridement. The only other time that these fractures require operative intervention is when the fracture fragment is large and significantly displaced.

Fracture of the tuber superiorly most often results from an avulsion-type injury in response to a sudden contractile force of the gastrocnemius-soleus complex, although we believe that chronic tightness of the gastrocnemius in particular can also play a role in predisposing to this injury.[83, 190] In addition, bone weakness probably plays a role in this injury because it is more common in the older and, in particular, diabetic population.[20] Nondisplaced or small fragments associated with little weakness and no threatened skin can be treated by progressive weight bearing in a neutral or slightly plantar-flexed short leg cast for 6 to 8 weeks. Patients should be serially observed for fracture displacement. Consideration should also be given to prophylactic gastrocnemius recession if this muscle is considered to be of pathologic significance in the etiology of the injury. The Silfverskiöld maneuver is the best physical examination determinant for establishing this component. Large, displaced fragments or those threatening skin viability should be openly reduced (the latter urgently) through either a small vertical posterolateral or posteromedial approach. A direct posterior approach can also be used, depending on the location of this fracture fragment or the area of skin at risk (or both). Fixation can be achieved with 2.7- or 3.5-mm screws placed in lag fashion across the fracture (Fig. 60–39). Typically, one or two of these screws are placed orthogonal to the line of Achilles insertion to offset its pull, and the other one or two are inserted vertical to the fracture for optimal compression. In our experience, the screw heads are small and rarely become sufficiently symptomatic to require removal if recessed slightly into the tuber. Alternatively, a cerclage method can be used, although more soft tissue dissection may be required, placing the skin at greater risk of wound complications. Any difficulty in mobilizing the fragment plantarly for anatomic reduction should alert the surgeon to the possibility of a predisposing gastrocnemius contracture and be accompanied by gastrocnemius recession. The recession is easily performed well proximal to the potentially at-risk skin or incision, in the region of the gastrocnemius musculotendinous interval with the Achilles. Typically, a 1- to 2-inch posteromedial incision is made in the calf at the junction of the distal and middle third of the leg to identify the sural nerve and gastrocnemius-soleus muscular interval. The gastrocnemius can then be effectively isolated above its insertion and released under direct visualization. It is sometimes amazing how much this step improves mobility of the distal fracture fragment and places less tension on the

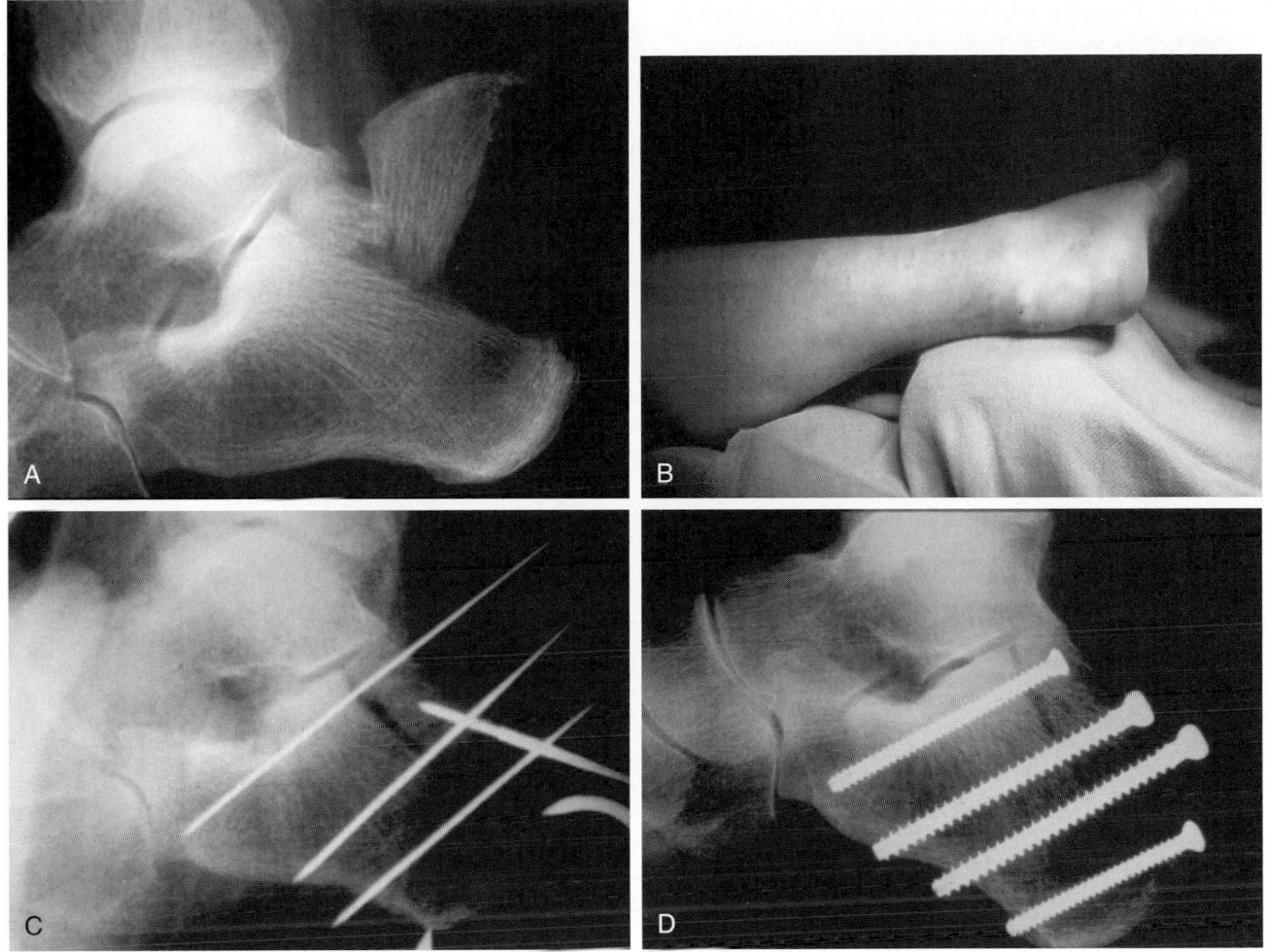

**FIGURE 60–39.** Isolated fractures of the posterior tuber of the calcaneus are unusual and frequently occur in the diabetic population, as with this patient (A). When displaced, they often tent the posterior skin as seen here (B) and should thus be considered an injury of a surgical urgency and fixed with either lag screws (C, D), a compression plate, or cerclage wire. Such fixation restores the integrity of the Achilles tendon and decompresses the skin against pressure necrosis, which can be a catastrophe in the diabetic population. Such patients should also be inspected for gastrocnemius tightness at the time of surgery because it is often the reason for their avulsion, is common in diabetics, and can be easily treated with a proximal release that would concomitantly provide stress relief on the repair—particularly valuable for someone with poor bone stock.

repair through a full range of knee and ankle motion. The postoperative protocol is similar to that for nonoperative treatment of this fracture type, although progression of weight bearing should be slower. In both cases, the decision to place patients in either a plantar flexion or neutral cast is governed in part by tightness of the gastrocnemius (as a potential factor in future displacement) and can be influenced by recession.

Rarely, the inferior-most aspect of the calcaneus is fractured. It typically involves the proximal medial weight-bearing portion of the calcaneus where the abductor hallucis, plantar fascia, and flexor digitorum brevis originate.[22, 296] The area of involvement has also been called the posteromedial tubercle (process) of the calcaneus and corresponds to the site where the fracture line can be seen to exit on an axial or lateral radiograph. It is rarely significantly displaced, and the vast majority of these injuries can be treated symptomatically with good result. Immobilization is not required, although it may be preferred by some patients for comfort. The mainstay of treatment is a 2- to 3-week course of non–weight bearing,

followed by gradually progressive weight bearing in a cast or well-cushioned sneaker or shoe over a period of 2 to 4 weeks. Operative intervention is rare, and patients should again be warned that although the functional results are generally very good after treatment of this injury, it does involve the major weight-bearing portion of a bone that must support full body weight. Thus, some discomfort or the sensation of an "irregularity" or tightness in the base of the heel occasionally persists.

## COMPARTMENT SYNDROME

Compartment syndrome of the foot should be suspected in any foot injury associated with soft tissue swelling.

### ANATOMY AND DIAGNOSIS

The foot has nine anatomic compartments (Fig. 60–40) surrounded by thick fascial confines that are resistant to volume expansion by the hemorrhage or interstitial edema created through trauma. Though often the result of fracture, dislocation, or crushing during high-energy injury mechanisms, compartment syndrome can occur after even minor bony or soft tissue trauma in the foot. It can also develop in isolated or multiple compartments at one time. Compartment syndrome can be exacerbated iatrogenically by untreated hypotension or, more commonly, by elevation ischemia, when the foot is elevated too high.[353] Use of a Gatch bed, ice, and too many pillows under the foot can further impair arterial inflow in the face of injury. Ideally, 12 to 18 inches of elevation above the heart is adequate. Thus, compartment syndrome does not result from reaching some absolute amount of pressure in the foot. Rather, it occurs when the pressure within the tissue of this confined system (compartments) for any reason approaches or exceeds arterial inflow pressure to an extent that oxygen demand exceeds supply.

The diagnosis of foot compartment syndrome requires a high index of suspicion; the foot has the notorious distinction of being a most difficult site in which to identify this problem because symptoms can often be silent. As such, the diagnosis can be missed more often than in other parts of the body and can occur, for example, in 10% of calcaneal fractures.[230] Any severe injury, tense swelling, exaggerated pain in the foot, or loss of two-point discrimination (diagnostically superior to diminished light touch sensation) should alert the orthopaedist to the possibility of impending vascular compromise and myoneural necrosis in the foot. Particular attention should be paid to pain out of proportion during passive extension stretch of the intrinsic musculature of the toes. Open wounds in foot injuries by no means guarantee adequate decompression of elevated tissue fluid pressure. Loss of pedal pulses, poor capillary refill, or the onset of identifiable paralysis or paresthesia frequently occurs late in this phenomenon and beyond the time when decompression is most effective.[19] This condition remains one of the true orthopaedic emergencies and requires direct measurement of compartment pressure and, if necessary, rapid operative decompression. Irreversible damage is usually present beyond 12 hours.[227] Failure of timely treatment can have catastrophic consequences on subsequent foot function, most notably the commonly involved

calcaneal compartment, and can result in contracture, pain, scarring, and nerve dysfunction.

The confluence of the plantar compartment with the deep posterior compartment along the long flexor tendons going to the toes can give rise to concomitant deep posterior compartment syndrome of the leg. This relationship is important to remember when evaluating any injury seemingly isolated to the leg or foot.

## PRESSURE MEASUREMENT

Four plantar compartments run the length of the foot: the medial, lateral, superficial, and calcaneal compartments (see Fig. 60–40). Dorsally, four interosseous compartments and the deeper adductor compartment make up the remaining groups of confined muscles, for a total of nine separate compartments. Measurement, description, and release of these compartments have been well described by Manoli,[195, 196] although the presence of a clinically significant calcaneal compartment at risk for a compartment syndrome remains controversial.[116] Many pressure-monitoring systems are now commercially available. They are portable and simple to operate and have disposable needles, but require accurate knowledge of foot anatomy to use reliably. Local skin infiltration with an anesthetic is recommended, although care should be taken to not infiltrate the subdermal tissues for fear of a falsely elevated pressure measurement. One or two of the dorsal compartments can be measured between the metatarsals, and if one of these measurements is taken in the second webspace, the needle can be subsequently advanced through the interosseous fascia to also access the adductor compartment. This technique also avoids a risk of injury to the dorsal neurovascular bundle. Pressure in the abductor hallucis can then be measured in the medial hindfoot compartment by introducing the needle 4 cm inferior to the medial malleolus and 6 cm anterior to the back of the heel. Here too, the needle can be advanced through the intermuscular septum to measure another compartment through the same needle stick, the calcaneal compartment, in which the quadratus and intrinsic toe flexors are located. Thereafter, the superficial plantar compartment with the flexor digitorum brevis can be checked by introducing the needle into the midplantar aspect of the

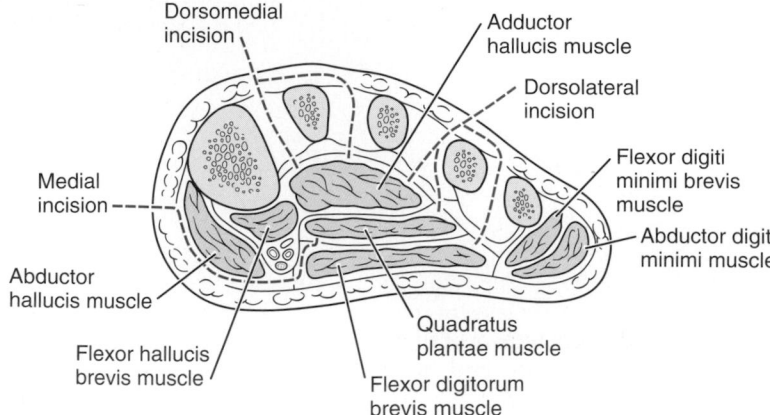

**Figure 60–40.** The foot has nine individual muscle compartments, as described by Manoli. Medially, they can communicate with the deep posterior compartment of the leg, and thus swelling in one area can affect the other. Any surgeon treating traumatic foot injuries should be familiar with the deep compartmental anatomy of the foot in the event that a compartment syndrome requires release.

**FIGURE 60–41.** A compartment syndrome of the foot is frequently caused by hemorrhage into the muscles in the sole of the foot. The nine compartments of the foot can be checked with four different needle sticks and an appropriate pressure measurement instrument such as a Stryker, and if pathologically elevated pressure (ΔP) is identified, all nine compartments can be adequately and safely released through three separate incisions (A). The two dorsal ones, similar to those for Lisfranc fracture fixation in the second and fourth webspaces, are responsible for releasing the four interosseous and the one adductor compartments. The medial one (B) is responsible for decompressing the remaining four deep longitudinal compartments (the medial, lateral, calcaneal, and plantar superficial compartments). These incisions relieve pressure and pain by evacuating hemorrhage. Delayed primary closure may be performed after 3 to 5 days, and a dynamic toe extension brace can be worn if contracture is a concern.

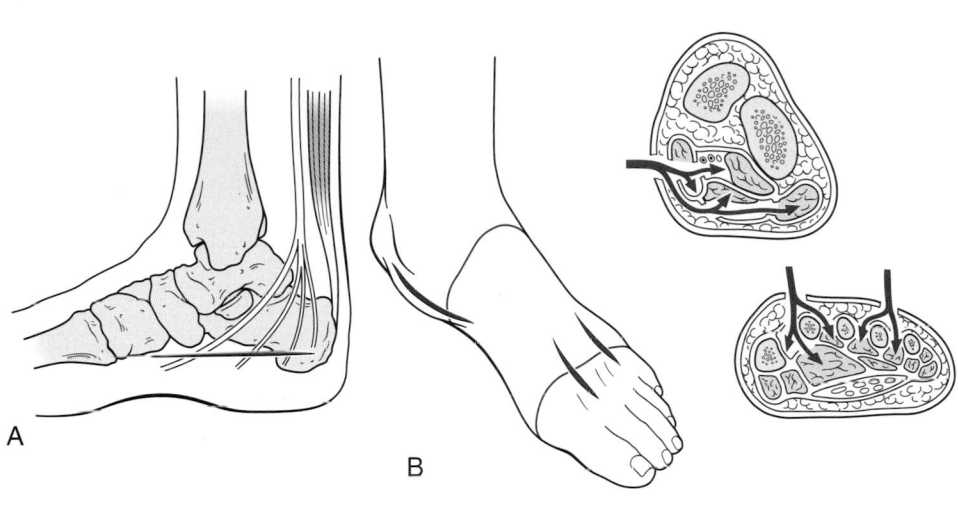

arch of the foot. A last needle stick just below the fifth metatarsal will check pressure in the lateral compartment, which contains the abductor digiti minimi.

## OPERATIVE DECOMPRESSION

Indications for compartment release are varied, and no absolute consensus on a single critical threshold has been reached. We suggest operative decompression when the pressure exceeds mean arterial pressure by 30 mm (i.e., ΔP, which is the most reliable indicator available), reaches an absolute of 40 mm or greater, or is borderline but trending upward on repeated examination. Manoli has nicely described a three-incision technique for operative decompression of these compartments[195] (Fig. 60–41). Although some surgeons advocate no tourniquet for this procedure, it is recommended as a helpful adjunct for safely identifying the posterior tibial neurovascular bundle. The first incision is located in the medial portion of the hindfoot and is used to release the medial, lateral, superficial, and calcaneal compartments. It begins 4 cm from the back of the heel and 3 cm from the plantar surface, and although it is described as extending 6 cm, for ease of visualization it is recommended that the incision be carried an additional 2 to 4 cm, depending on patient size and swelling. The abductor hallucis fascia is released and the muscle is then elevated dorsally to open the medial intermuscular septum and decompress the calcaneal compartment. Decompression should be done bluntly with an elevator or digit when possible once a nick in the fascia is made. Care needs to be taken because the lateral plantar neurovascular bundle is directly subfascial or intrafascial here as it traverses the foot. The medial plantar bundle has variable anatomy and can be found in the calcaneal or superficial compartment or within their fascial separation because it too courses across the plantar aspect

of the foot and can be found at various locations, depending on the exact placement of one's incisions and the patient's particular anatomy. After release of the calcaneal compartment, the initial skin incision is then elevated plantarly and the abductor with its fascia is elevated superiorly to reveal the plantarly and medially based superficial compartment for fascial release. Once this release is performed, the flexor digitorum brevis can be retracted plantar-ward away from the dorsal transverse septum to release the laterally based abductor and flexor digiti minimi through the lateral intermuscular septum. A headlight is useful for this exposure.

Attention is then turned dorsally to make two longitudinal interosseous incisions located between the first and second metatarsals and the fourth and fifth metatarsals. These incisions can be altered, depending on the exposure anticipated for any fracture fixation, but an adequate skin bridge of at least 7 cm should be maintained. The incisions need not be longer than 2 to 4 cm and can even be staggered such that they overlap less and therefore have less of a tendency to compromise vascularity to the flap. Flap necrosis is rare as long as the bridge has not been significantly traumatized before surgery or undermined at the time of surgery. If this complication is a concern, an alternative pie-crusting technique as advocated by Benirschke and described in the next paragraph can be used. Through any of these dorsal incisions, first the fascia is released, followed by release of the interosseous musculature on the flanking metatarsals. In the medial incision, the adductor muscle is exposed and released by elevating a portion of the interosseous from the medial aspect of the second metatarsal and then identifying and opening the deeper fascia over this compartment. Wounds are left open after release, and either a bead pouch or vacuum-assisted closure device can be applied with a posterior splint or fixator to stabilize the soft tissue, and the swelling is allowed to subside before return to the operating room for later closure in 3 to 5 days.[7, 62] Skin grafting is occasionally needed, particularly for one or both of the dorsal incisions. Any fracture fixation, especially in the metatarsals or midfoot, can be performed at the time of decompression if needed; wounds located over hardware should also be primarily closed in preference to others if it is anticipated that skin grafting will be required at one of these sites. ORIF of calcaneal, navicular, or cuboid fractures can be performed at a later date when the soft tissue are more amenable, but talar fractures should be stabilized at the time of decompression to limit their vascular embarrassment. Ziv and colleagues have described one-stage management of crush injuries of the foot with compartment syndrome using split-thickness skin excision to confirm dermal viability, fasciotomies, fracture reduction and fixation, and closure with muscle transposition and the excised split-thickness skin.[360]

The dorsal "pie-crusting" technique espoused by Benirschke may also be used to decompress the skin when swelling and pain extend into the forefoot (Fig. 60–42). It is ideal in dorsally traumatized tissues or a foot that seems to be amenable to dorsal release alone based on compartment pressure measurements and clinical examination.

Occasionally, release through this technique can decompress a hematoma successfully and thereby relax all the surrounding tissues of the foot. Remember, however, that the calcaneal compartment is most commonly involved and most difficult to see, so measurement of pressure in this compartment is recommended after this technique is completed. These skin incisions are 5 to 10 mm long and situated about the dorsal surface of the forefoot and midfoot with well-separated skin bridges. Blunt dissection is then carried out in each with the use of a small hemostat through the superficial fascia and deepened to the intermetatarsal area to relieve any accumulated pressure or hematoma. Here too, consideration should be given perioperatively to skeletal stabilization with either internal or, preferably, external fixation to further rest the soft tissue envelope and prevent progressive soft tissue swelling or damage. Confirmatory pressure readings should be rechecked after decompression if the adequacy of compartmental release is at all uncertain.

If the late development of toe contracture is a concern, a nighttime dynamic splint fashioned to the dorsum of the foot can be used to minimize this risk. It has slings that individually hold each toe in extension, much like a radial nerve splint for the hand, and active or contractural flexion

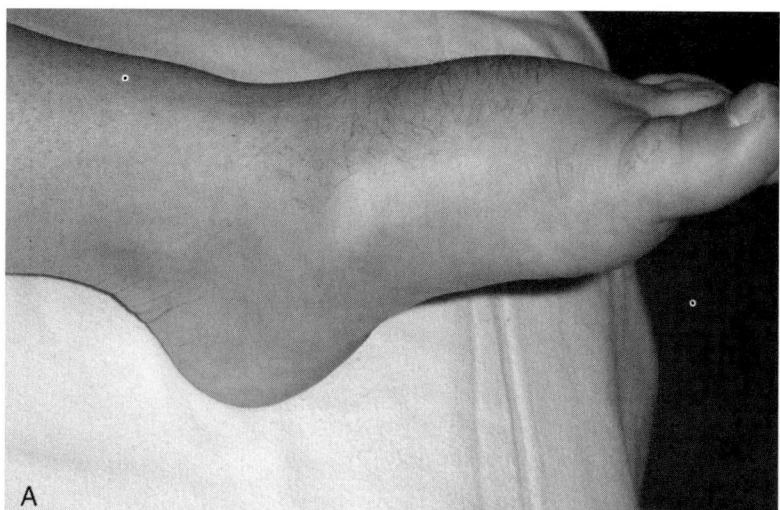
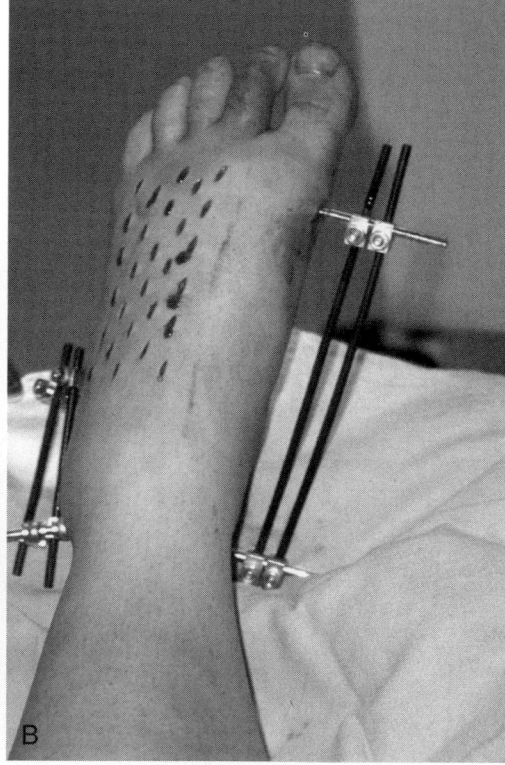

**FIGURE 60–42.** Benirschke has recently popularized a dorsal pie-crusting technique for release of foot compartmental pressure that is indicated when (1) a subacute hematoma is suspected and can be released through multiple stab wounds on the dorsum of the skin, (2) the soft tissue envelope is not amenable to the larger standard incisions described for compartmental release, or (3) prophylactic release is performed "percutaneously" because compartment syndrome is considered imminent. This technique should be used cautiously; it has the advantage of limited soft tissue violation/flaps, as well as ease of subsequent treatment because it does not require formal closure (granulation tissue forms between the swollen edges of skin), but it also has the disadvantage of unreliable release of the four longitudinal deeper compartments of the foot, which are most commonly responsible for foot compartment syndrome. If these areas are a major concern, formal open exposure and release should be preferentially performed. This patient (A) had severe soft tissue swelling, discomfort, and midfoot instability after a Lisfranc injury from a motorcycle accident. Although he did not have an overt compartment syndrome, his impending one was headed off by initial soft tissue stabilization and realignment with external fixation, as well as by hematoma decompression with the pie-crusting technique (B), which worked nicely to avert progressive fascial compartment compromise and minimize hematoma beneath an already compromised soft tissue envelope. Note that the pie crust incisions have been placed in a vertical manner such that they could later easily be extended into formal exposure for open reduction and internal fixation if necessary. They can be situated across the entire dorsum of the foot if needed.

can be counteracted by both active and passive extension exercises.

## NAVICULAR FRACTURES

### ANATOMY

The navicular bone, or scaphoid, is the keystone of the medial arch of the foot. It is a dense, ovoid, saucer-shaped bone that makes up half of the very important talonavicular joint on its concave posterior or proximal surface. On the distal end, it articulates with the first, second, and third cuneiforms on three distinct facets. In some instances, a small lateral facet may articulate with the cuboid. All these articulations are relatively immobile and nonessential. The blood supply is a radial one, which makes the bone prone to vascular disturbances with injury, especially at the center, where most stress fractures occur. The only muscular attachment to the navicular is through a variable portion of the posterior tibial tendon called the anterior component by Sarrafian[296]; this component inserts into the inferomedial tuberosity. The strong inferior calcaneonavicular or bifurcate ligament originates on the calcaneus and attaches to the inferior surface of the navicular. Just medial to this attachment is the superomedial calcaneonavicular ligament, which also connects the calcaneus and the navicular. These ligaments, together with the posterior surface of the navicular and the anterior facet of the calcaneus, form the acetabulum pedis around the head of the talus.

To maintain normal gait mechanics after injury, it is essential to restore anatomic integrity to this complex joint. The talonavicular articulation is the key joint that allows pronation (which cushions heel-strike) and supination (which strengthens push-off). It works in concert with the subtalar (talocalcaneal) joint and is essential for inversion and eversion of the hindfoot as the foot adapts to sloped surfaces. Alignment of the navicular is thus crucial in maintaining length of the medial column to ensure that these interrelationships are not disturbed.

### ETIOLOGY

The navicular is susceptible to two major types of fracture: acute and stress fractures. Acute fractures result primarily from high-energy axial loading injuries such as a motor vehicle crash or, less commonly, from forced eversion causing tension failure transmitted through either the posterior tibial tendon or the capsuloligamentous support of the talonavicular joint. Stress fractures are commonly seen in running or jumping athletes. By virtue of the morphology of the bone, the vast majority of navicular fractures are intra-articular. They are often missed on the initial evaluation without careful physical examination and radiographic inspection.[79, 191]

The standard series of foot films is sufficient for diagnosing most of these injuries, although CT is indicated for better fracture delineation in the more displaced or high-energy body fractures requiring operative repair. Just as with cuboid injuries, one must look to the opposite column (laterally, in this case) for failure in tension or compression along the hindfoot. The failure mode depends on the mechanism of injury.

## Acute Fractures

Little has been published about the treatment of traumatic navicular fractures because isolated fractures are relatively rare. Most reports include very few cases or just a single case.[79] They have been described as two main types, avulsion and body fractures, the incidence rates of which are fairly equal. Half of body fractures occur vertically in the midportion of the bone and roughly the other half occur through the navicular tuberosity.

### AVULSION FRACTURES

These fracture are typically quite small and, despite being articular, rarely require operative intervention. They account for almost 50% of navicular fractures.[79] Usually dorsal in nature as a result of pull of the stout superficial deltoid ligament insertion here, these fractures can be confused with accessory bones such as the os supranaviculare. They can also occur plantarly or medially, the latter of which results from pull of the posterior tibial tendon or spring ligament. A history of recent twisting-type trauma and identification of sharp margins on radiographs permit easy distinction between the two. Avulsion fractures of the navicular are caused by excessive plantar flexion or eversion forces applied to the midfoot. A flake of bone from the dorsal side may be avulsed by the capsule with excessive plantar flexion, and the interomedial tuberosity may be avulsed by the posterior tibial tendon with excessive eversion. In all but the rare case of a large, intra-articularly displaced fragment (which really ends up falling into the subsequent classification of navicular fractures), these injuries are treated symptomatically. Depending on swelling, chronicity of the injury, and patient comfort, both postoperative wooden shoe wear and short leg casting for 3 to 6 weeks are acceptable. Results are often excellent, although residual displacement or abundant callus can occasionally cause dorsal impingement similar to a tarsal boss and require excision of the small nonarticular dorsal lip or medial tubercle fragments. An anterior tarsal tunnel syndrome can also result, and if injection, modification of shoe wear (dorsal lacing change, soft leather upper), or both are unsuccessful, treatment by excision is also indicated and usually successful. If the fragment is large, the capsule or the posterior tibial tendon should be reattached with a compression screw and a soft tissue washer or by means of drill holes through bone with nonabsorbable suture similar to fixation of greater tuberosity fractures of the humerus[297] (Fig. 60–43). Severe associated midfoot sprain or injury often requires longer periods of immobilization and recovery, upward of 3 to 4 months.

### BODY FRACTURES AND BLOOD SUPPLY

Navicular body fractures are by far the most complicated and challenging variety to treat. They can occur in multiple sites and directions along the arc of the navicular and usually result from higher energy axial loading mechanisms than seen with avulsion fractures.[79] Typically, the

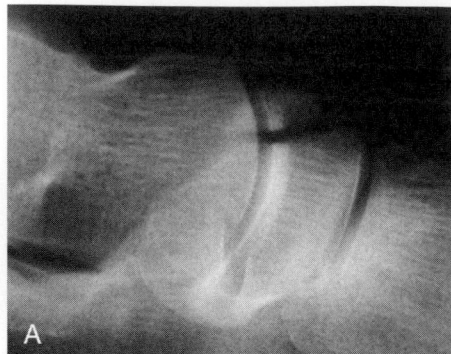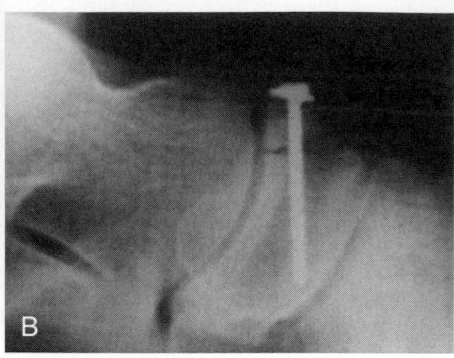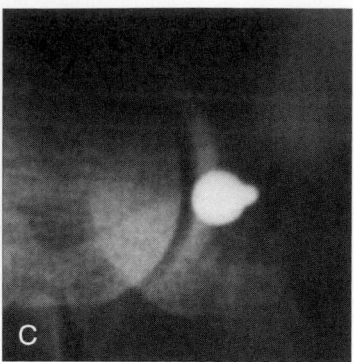

**Figure 60–43.** Trauma to the accessory navicular or posterior tibial insertion can result in navicular avulsion and proximal migration necessitating treatment. Although smaller fragments are readily excised and the posterior tibial tendon advanced as in the Kidner procedure, Sangeorzan has recently described a way of fixing the larger fragments with screws if they are amenable, as in this case (*A–C*). Fractures can be lagged back with a 2.7- or 3.5-mm cortical screw, often with a ligament or metal washer.

axial loading is delivered with a component of abduction and flexion. Here too, confusion with accessory bones such as the common os tibiale externum is possible, particularly with regard to isolated tuberosity injury. A good history and set of plain films can easily make this distinction. Injury involving the accessory navicular can also occur, however, and must be carefully evaluated on physical examination, as discussed in more detail later. Most simple, nondisplaced tuberosity or body fractures can be managed nonoperatively for 6 weeks in a weight-of-leg weight-bearing short leg cast molded beneath the longitudinal arch for extra support. Any significant displacement of a primarily extra-articular tuberosity fragment should be reduced with minifragment or small-fragment lag screw fixation because of its attachment to the posterior tibial tendon.[60] Residual displacement can have a major impact on the integrity of the longitudinal arch, as well as overall gait function, as seen with long-standing posterior tibial tendon insufficiency. Midbody fractures are entirely articular and involve a significant portion of the important talonavicular joint. Thus, any displacement greater than 1 to 2 mm should be openly reduced and fixed. They are often associated with other fractures or joint injuries in the foot.[191] The trick with fixing these injuries is avoiding devascularization during exposure and reduction. The blood supply is radial in nature and nonarticular. The navicular relies primarily on the dorsalis pedis and medial plantar arteries for inflow, which decreases with age. Because of the intrinsically poor blood supply and central watershed area that this bone has, the central segment of the navicular can be considered increasingly avascular and at risk of not healing after fracture. Interestingly, it is not unusual to also see evidence of navicular collapse or avascularity in older patients without a history of acute trauma, probably for similar reasons. Thus, navicular body fractures are often deceivingly difficult to anatomically reduce and fix through the limited exposure necessary to avoid avascular necrosis or nonunion, and they are therefore discussed in detail later. Because of these facts, some authors have advocated primary fusion of such injuries, whereas others consider ORIF the initial treatment of choice.

**Classification of Body Fractures.** Sangeorzan and colleagues[288] reported on the operative results of 21 displaced intra-articular navicular fractures. They reviewed the existing literature and devised a classification system based on the type and direction of displacement, which they then related to treatment. They divided displaced navicular fractures into three types of injuries and described them as follows:

*Type 1 navicular fractures* are caused by a force running along the central axis of the foot. The fracture line is usually located in the transverse (coronal) plane and separates the dorsal and plantar sections of the navicular, but comminution is minimal. No forefoot malalignment is present, and a lateral view often shows a dorsally displaced fragment of the navicular.

*Type 2 navicular fractures* are the most common. They are caused by axial compression and dorsomedial forces exerted on the forefoot and result in a fracture line running in a dorsolateral–to–plantar-medial direction. The talonavicular joint is frequently subluxated or dislocated by this injury, and the larger, relatively intact dorsomedial navicular fragment is displaced dorsomedially. As a result, the forefoot appears adducted or medially translated, and an AP view often shows a large navicular fragment displaced medially.

*Type 3 navicular fractures* are caused by axial and laterally directed forces. The naviculocuneiform joint is disrupted, and the middle or lateral portion of the navicular is impacted. Comminuted and displaced fracture patterns are common, and associated fractures may occur in the cuboid, the anterior of the calcaneus, and the calcaneocuboid joint. Here, the forefoot assumes a more lateral malposition, and on all views significant comminution is evident in the central body of the navicular, often with loss of height of the medial longitudinal arch or shortening of the medial column as a result of the impaction and joint incongruity.

Displaced intra-articular navicular fractures are treated by stable anatomic internal fixation. Open reduction of displaced fractures allows anatomic reduction of the joint surface, but every attempt must be made to not further disrupt its tenuous blood supply. The navicular is unique among bones in having a large articular surface in its proximal or posterior articular surface, which is the only essential joint. The distal or anterior facets against the medial, middle, and lateral cuneiforms are nonessential joints. They are much less critical to restore because they are relatively immobile and can eventually be fused with minimal residual disability.

**Surgical Technique.** Type I fractures heal with the best prognosis. The surgical approach to expose the talonavicular joint is made through an anteromedial incision between the anterior and the posterior tibial tendons. A small capsulotomy is performed in the talonavicular joint to visualize the fracture and the talonavicular articular surfaces. Large, sharp-pointed forceps may be inserted through stab incisions to grip the major fracture fragments perpendicular to the fracture line, and the fracture is reduced by longitudinal traction. Alternatively, indirect reduction may be carried out by means of a distractor or a small external fixation device that spans the area between the talus or the medial malleolus and the base of the proximal first metatarsal or cuneiforms. Distraction provides the capability of visualizing the articular reduction of the navicular surface of the talonavicular joint before, during, and after reduction and facilitating more precise reduction of impacted articular fragments. Fixation is provided by two compression screws inserted through dorsal stab incisions. If the fragments are large, the ideal fixation uses two 3.5-mm cortical screws placed in a dorsal-to-plantar direction. The larger core diameter of the 3.5-mm screws is stronger than that of the older 4.0-mm cancellous design and minimizes the chance of screw breakage, especially in recalcitrant nonunion or screw removal (rarely indicated). The dorsal and plantar fragments of displaced intra-articular navicular fractures are rarely severely comminuted and can be stabilized with screws. It is not usually necessary to extend the fixation into the distal cuneiforms (Fig. 60-44). Do not forget the integral use of washers as effective, compressive, "one-hole plates" for these constructs.

Type II fractures are more difficult to reduce because the lateral plantar fragment may be comminuted and the dorsomedial fragment may be dislocated at the talonavicular joint. A similar dorsomedial approach can be used. Indirect reduction maneuvers are ideal in these circumstances, if possible. The dorsomedial fragment may be reduced with screws aimed obliquely into the second or third cuneiform (Fig. 60-45). This procedure provides satisfactory fixation of the dorsomedial fragment, but the talonavicular joint requires separate fixation with smooth K-wires. In many instances, comminution of the lateral and plantar fragments precludes the use of lag screws alone. Because the capsular attachments to the peripheral navicular fragments are still often attached, it is ideal to work through the fracture surfaces to obtain reduction and use K-wires just tangential to the articular surface to provisionally maintain the articular reduction. Small washer plates, a one-quarter tubular plate with 2.7-mm screws, 2.4-mm miniplates with 2.4-mm screws, and 2.0-mm miniplates and T plates with 2.0-mm screws are ideal for navicular fixation, especially the 2.0-mm plates, because they are low profile and can be oriented to provide good compression without iatrogenic fragmentation. Self-tapping screws are ideal and can be placed with the K-wires still orienting the articular reduction. Once sufficient stability is achieved, the superfluous wires are removed. In the face of severe comminution, fixation of the lateral, plantar, and medial fragments can be secured into the cuneiforms or cuboid in a medial-to-lateral direction with the intent of restoring talonavicular morphology. It is critical that complete congruity of the talonavicular joint be obtained to facilitate restoration of pronation and supination without shortening the medial column. Complete congruity involves reduction of not only the articular surface but also the overall morphology so that Chopart's joint will function as well. If the medial column is not reduced to anatomic length, abnormal midfoot and hindfoot mechanics will result. Often, placement of an exterior small fixator or minifixator spanning the medial column (base of the first metatarsal to the talar neck) can facilitate reduction and visualization of these difficult injuries. Bone grafting should be readily performed if the articular surface requires buttressing to maintain stable anatomic reduction. Because of the relative avascularity of the navicular, this bone should be autogenous.

Like type II navicular fractures, type III fractures also have comminution of the plantar lateral fragment and cannot be securely reduced by screw fixation. Once again, the large medial or dorsomedial fragment must be fixed in anatomic position by anchoring the screw into the cuneiforms. Fixation by this method reduces both the navicular fracture and the naviculocuneiform joint disrup-

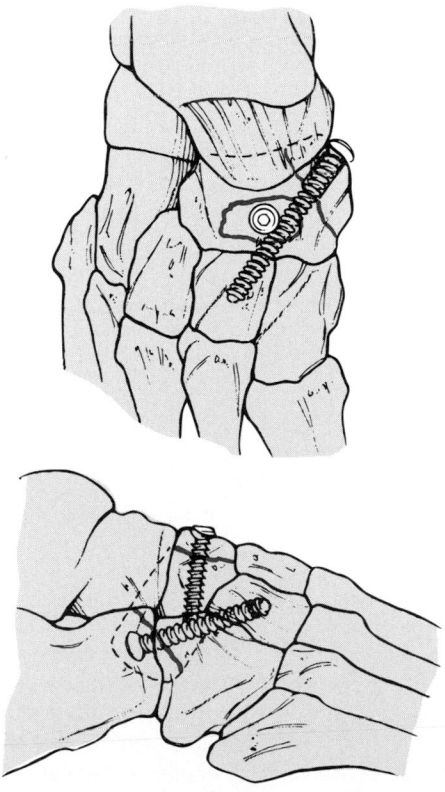

**FIGURE 60-44.** Methods of placing screws in a dorsal avulsion fracture and a tuberosity avulsion fracture. In the latter example, the screw is placed across the navicular and into a cuneiform bone for resistance. A small plastic washer can be used to secure the posterior tibial tendon.

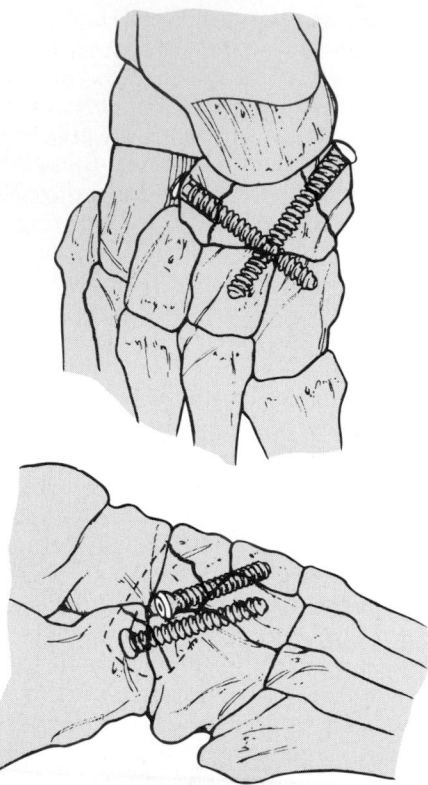

**Figure 60–45.** Screws placed across a comminuted navicular fracture are usually insufficient by themselves to adequately stabilize the navicular despite its dense subchondral bone. Serious consideration should therefore be given to using the adjacent cuneiforms for supplemental fixation. The naviculocuneiform (NC) joint should be concomitantly taken down and fused with bridging screws, if possible, to help hold the navicular fragments in place, improve stability and maintain length of the medial column repair, and improve vascular inflow to an already compromised vascular bed encompassing the navicular. Reduction efforts are always concentrated along the talonavicular joint to maintain anatomic integrity and maximize the longevity of this important articulation. The NC joint can be sacrificed with little, if any compromise in foot motion or function. Typical fixation is usually more elaborate than that shown here. Generally, three 2.7- or 3.5-mm cortical screws are used to cross the NC joint to capture the navicular fragments proximomedially and are lagged across the NC joint distally, with extension to the distal subchondral region of the first and third cuneiforms for maximal fixation. The more dorsal of these screws should be aimed at the lateral cuneiform because the medial malleolus will prevent the drill from allowing entrance into the first cuneiform. The more plantarly inserted screw can easily be placed here because more adduction is possible for drilling along the medial column. A third screw can then extend from the distal medial aspect of the medial cuneiform and lagged across the NC joint into the most lateral aspect of the navicular. Additional fixation, as necessary, can be added from the medial utility incision or a separate lateral one to lag the remaining navicular fragments together.

tion. In this instance, the use of miniplates is ideal because they can maintain the naviculocuneiform reduction, buttress the talonavicular articular surface, and provide stable fixation in the face of severe comminution. Injury extending into the calcaneocuboid joint should be fixed separately with small screws. A cuboid "nutcracker" fracture may be reduced by distraction and stabilized with an H plate or mini T plate (Fig. 60–46). According to Pinney and Sangeorzan, preservation or restoration of at least 60% of the articular surface of the navicular is

required to prevent subluxation of the talonavicular joint after healing.[256]

**Postoperative Care and Rehabilitation.** Postoperatively, the patient is confined to bed exercise with the foot elevated for 2 days. The foot is immobilized in a short leg cast for up to 6 weeks. If stable fixation is achieved, early active range-of-motion and pronation and supination exercises can help restore motion without the axial loading brought on by weight bearing. At approximately 10 to 12 weeks, if radiographic evidence of consolidation is seen, progressively increased weight bearing may begin. The amount of weight bearing that may be allowed depends on the strength of fixation. Patients who sustained type I fractures may tolerate limited weight bearing from the start and gradually progress to full weight bearing by week 8 to 10 postoperatively. Type II and type III fractures are characterized by joint disruption and comminution; weight bearing after these injuries is limited to the weight of the leg because the fixation cannot support full weight bearing. Any K-wires placed across a persistently unstable talonavicular joint to maintain congruous reduction after fixation may be removed after 7 to 8 weeks. Range-of-motion exercises may be initiated at this time, and only partial weight bearing is allowed until 10 to 12 weeks after surgery. Weight bearing is gradually increased after radiographs show evidence of union.

**Complications.** Partial avascular necrosis, late partial collapse of the bone, and narrowing of the joint cartilage are common in type II and III navicular fractures even after optimal treatment (see Fig. 60–22). Symptomatic arthrosis and even collapse can occur in displaced fractures, and late bone block fusion or a triple arthrodesis may be indicated.

A late progressive hindfoot varus deformity may develop after collapse of the lateral side of the navicular. This syndrome is managed by talonavicular fusion or triple arthrodesis. Varus deformity in the hindfoot and subsequent problems with shoe breakdown frequently cause more incapacity than the post-traumatic arthritis that precedes it. The goal of talonavicular fusion or triple arthrodesis is not simply to fuse the involved joints but to also correct the varus deformity by restoring the normal talocalcaneal angle and the length of the medial column before fusion.

## ACCESSORY NAVICULAR INJURY

The accessory navicular is a nonunited ossification in the plantar medial tuberosity that is the attachment site of the anterior component of the posterior tibial tendon. It may be partially or wholly avulsed from its navicular attachments by a sudden pronation stress. Kidner[169] suggested that injury to the accessory navicular may be associated with a weak arch or flatfoot deformity. In some cases, almost the entire posterior tibial tendon is attached to this tubercle, and if it is excised, the foot collapses, much as it does from posterior tibial tendon rupture syndrome.

An augmented Kidner procedure may be carried out to treat the accessory navicular if it is symptomatic after injury. The accessory bone and any other large plantar medial tuberosities may be excised and the posterior tibial tendon reattached to the navicular. The flexor digitorum communis is transected at the master knot of Henry and reinserted through a drill hole in the plantar surface of the first cuneiform. This procedure restores normal posterior tibial tendon dynamics in the arch without significantly weakening plantar flexion in the toes. If the accessory navicular is large enough, Malicky and colleagues have described an alternative procedure to excision whereby the opposing edges of the os and navicular are débrided back to bone and then fixed with one or two 2.7- or 3.5-mm screws[193] (see Fig. 60–43). Ligament washers can be helpful as well in maintaining compression during fixation. A weakened posterior tibial tendon can also be augmented with the nearby flexor tendon.[121] Postoperatively, patients are protected by means similar to those used after formal ORIF. The presence of gastrocnemius tightness must be ruled out during the examination. If tightness is present, a gastrocnemius recession may improve the long-term result (see p. 2377). This very important procedure should be considered for any traumatic injury that might predispose the foot to eventual midfoot breakdown. Because a tight gastrocnemius over-loads the forefoot and the midfoot in particular, any fracture or disruption of the navicular or Lisfranc articulations, for example, may be susceptible to chronic stress and accelerated breakdown or arthrosis. Gastrocnemius contracture is best tested by using the Silfverskiöld maneuver.[312]

**Postoperative Care and Rehabilitation.** Postoperative rehabilitation of accessory navicular injuries is similar to that for acute fractures.

## Stress Fractures

Stress fractures of the navicular frequently occur in running or jumping athletes who increase the intensity of their training too rapidly. The cause of stress fractures in the navicular is unclear, although several theories have been proposed to explain how they develop. Stress fractures may occur with more frequency in persons with a cavus foot deformity and in those with conditions that restrict normal motion of the navicular, such as a fibrous or

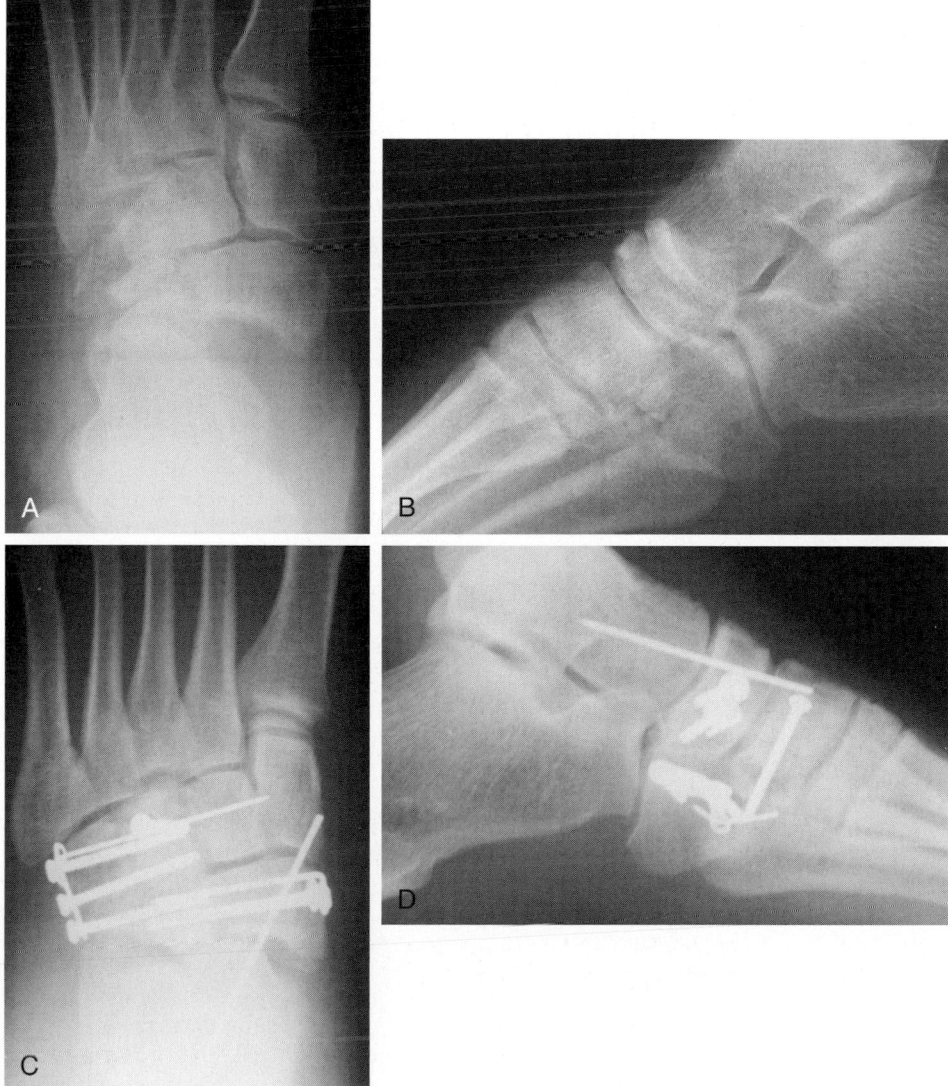

**FIGURE 60–46.** Navicular body fractures are difficult fractures to treat if they are significantly displaced or comminuted, especially when accompanied by shortening or peritalar subluxation of the medial column. This case represented a relatively easy navicular body fracture to fix, although the energy required to create this midfoot instability pattern is evident from the pattern of global disruption of the midtarsal and tarsometatarsal joints (A, B). The lateral column compression injury is probably the result of an abduction impaction injury to the foot, as evidenced by overlap of the cuboid and fourth and fifth articulations before fixation. It is important to note that *both* columns of the foot must be restored to proper length with open reduction and internal fixation. Usually, compression plus fixation of the navicular is adequate for the medial side, as in this case, because of its dense bone stock, but the cuboid is markedly cancellous and frequently requires disimpaction and bone grafting before plate fixation to restore normal integrity of the column (C, D).

osseous calcaneonavicular coalition. Several factors seem to aggravate stress fractures, but how these conditions relate to actual causes is uncertain.[59, 141] It is apparent that a long second ray or a functionally short first ray leads to overload of the lateral third of the navicular by transmission of force through the second metatarsal, and this overload is associated with an increased risk of navicular stress fracture.[88, 334]

## DIAGNOSIS

Stress fractures almost always occur in the sagittal plane in the middle third of the bone and usually start on the dorsal surface. Stress fractures are frequently misdiagnosed as anterior tibial tendinitis because such patients have similar symptoms (e.g., pain in the dorsomedial and medial aspect of the midarch). In addition, these usually vertical fractures are frequently undisplaced or only partial fractures, thus making radiographic diagnosis even more difficult unless the beam is directed perfectly co-linearly with the fracture line on the AP view. To make an accurate early diagnosis, the origin of the pain must be determined clinically, by scintigraphy, by MRI, or by a combination of these methods. Plain radiographs may not reveal a fracture in the early stages; if scintigraphy or MRI and clinical examination suggest the presence of a stress fracture, a CT scan may be indicated to aid in management decisions. CT can ascertain whether the fracture is partial or complete and can assess adjacent sclerosis, joint degeneration, or cyst formation not appreciated as well on plain films.[171]

Secondary changes such as cystic degeneration, partial avascular necrosis (especially in the lateral fragment), sclerosis at the edges of the fracture, and secondary arthritis in the talonavicular joint commonly occur in chronic, complete, or separated fractures. Clearly, a stress fracture of the navicular can end an athlete's career if it is not diagnosed and treated early.

## NONOPERATIVE MANAGEMENT

Torg and co-workers[334] studied these injuries and noted that in the very early stages, when a fracture is imminent but still incomplete, it may be treated successfully by immobilization of the foot in a short leg, non–weight-bearing cast for 4 to 6 weeks, followed by gradual resumption of activity. This regimen differs from the traditional treatment of incomplete stress fractures in the lower extremity, which simply calls for discontinuation of training for a time and then a gradual return to the previous level of activity. Surgical treatment is advisable when an incomplete stress fracture is not diagnosed early and goes on to become a complete or displaced fracture. Delay in diagnosis has been associated with refracture or nonunion.[334] Time to return to sports for an athlete can be prolonged, between 3 months to upward of 3 years (average of 10 months).[334]

## OPERATIVE MANAGEMENT

Meticulous surgical technique is required to reduce a navicular stress fracture absolutely anatomically and to restore motion in the talonavicular joint. Dissection of soft tissues must be kept to a minimum to preserve the blood

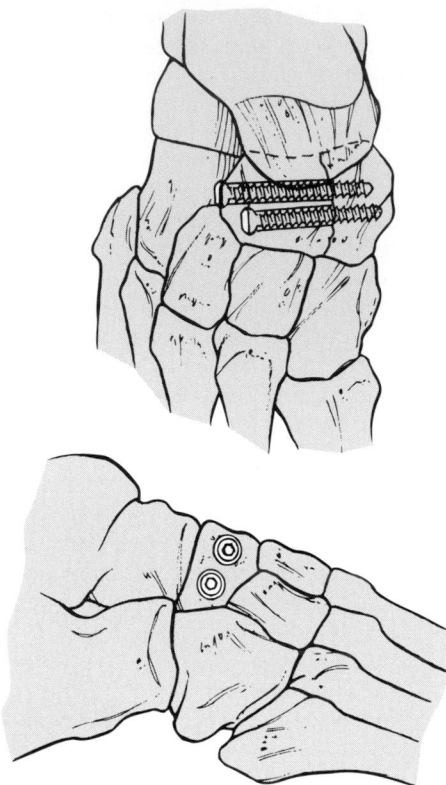

**FIGURE 60–47.** A fracture line is seen in the sagittal plane in the middle of the navicular bone in this navicular stress fracture. The screws should be placed in a lateral-to-medial direction for this type of fracture. A 3.5-mm gliding hole is drilled into the lateral fragment, and a 2.5-mm thread hole is drilled into the medial fragment.

supply going to the navicular and to prevent avascular necrosis. Indications for ORIF include fractures that are complete, comminuted, persistently ununited, or associated with marginal sclerosis or cyst formation.

A dorsomedial incision is made to expose the superior end of the fracture, and a short talonavicular capsulotomy is performed to visualize the joint surface. A stab incision is made over the upper tuberosity and a small linear incision just over the lateral aspect of the navicular. After the fracture site has been débrided with a small curette or bur to remove all marginal sclerosis or intramedullary cysts, the area is bone grafted with autogenous cancellous graft. A large, pointed (Weber) forceps is then inserted through the small incisions to grip the medial and lateral sides of the bone. The fracture is compressed with force applied perpendicular to the fracture line, and the joint is anatomically realigned. Ideally, the reduction at the talonavicular articulation should be visualized and provisionally held with one or two K-wires just distal and tangential to the articular surface. Next, the fracture site is perforated with small holes drilled in a lateral-to-medial direction. It is particularly important to drill the fracture edges if they are sclerotic. After this step, two 3.5-mm cortical compression screws are placed perpendicular to the fracture with image intensifier guidance (Fig. 60–47). Gliding holes for the screws are drilled through the lateral fragment (usually the smaller of the two fragments) with a 3.5-mm drill bit and through the medial fragment with a

2.5-mm drill bit. The screws are inserted from the small lateral incision and guided through these holes. They self-tap in the dense, cancellous bone and obtain purchase in the larger medial fragment (Fig. 60–47). If the lateral fragment's cortex is soft, a small three-hole one-quarter or two-hole one-third tubular plate may alternatively be used as a "washer" to effect greater compression without comminuting the smaller fragment. A 4.5-mm screw may be used as one of the fixation screws in a large bone. If a larger screw is used, the gliding hole in the near fragment is drilled with a 4.5-mm bit and the far fragment with a 3.2-mm bit. A shear strain–relieved cancellous bone graft may be inset into the dorsal part of the fracture after fixation to further bridge the fracture edges.

## SEVERE COMMINUTION

Fusion of the navicular to the first and second cuneiforms may be required for unstable or chronic conditions such as flatfoot. It is also an excellent procedure for comminution at the naviculocuneiform joint or tarsal navicular in the acute setting to salvage maintenance of length of the medial column. Navicular fusion is a very good way to improve vascular inflow to a non-reconstructible or severely devascularized navicular, and it stabilizes the midfoot and results in little loss of foot function. It can be performed with a small-fragment plate placed along a medial utility incision, ideally a 2.7-mm dynamic compression or reconstruction plate. These plates allow a greater number of screws per unit area to achieve better mediolateral purchase in the small-dimension bones of the midfoot. They are stout and provide rigid fixation of the medial column, as well as transnavicular bridging of a comminuted navicular, the center of which can later be filled with bone graft through a separate dorsal incision (see Fig. 60–45). Accurate anatomic alignment and restoration of the talonavicular joint are essential during this process, regardless of the alignment of the naviculocuneiform joint, and are vital for successful fusion.[120]

## BONE GRAFTING

In the acute setting, autogenous bone grafting is indicated for any complete or comminuted fracture. It is also advisable in the chronic setting of nonunion regardless of etiology.[88]

## POSTOPERATIVE CARE AND REHABILITATION

A short leg cast is applied postoperatively, and the patient is confined to bed exercise with the foot elevated for 2 days. Weight bearing is limited to the weight of the leg for approximately 6 weeks. The cast is then removed, but protected weight bearing is continued for 4 more weeks. Vigorous range-of-motion exercises are started at that time to strengthen the muscles responsible for supination and pronation. After bony union has been confirmed by radiographs, a more strenuous training program that includes walking may be initiated, and the patient may gradually progress to a running training program, not to begin before at least 3 to 4 months postoperatively. If the stress fracture was precipitated or

exacerbated by a preexisting condition such as a fibrous coalition, that abnormality should be addressed at the same operation.

Fusion may be indicated if significant post-traumatic arthritis develops after a tarsonavicular stress fracture is overlooked. A tricortical bone block graft harvested from the iliac crest may be inserted into the injured joint to appropriately align and lengthen the medial column. Permanent stiffness in the hindfoot and lack of normal pronation-supination and eversion-inversion are inevitable results of fusion, which may still be beneficial for relief of pain.

## TARSOMETATARSAL INJURIES (LISFRANC JOINTS)

The incidence of Lisfranc injuries is reported as being only 1 in 55,000 per year. Although with that figure these injuries can be considered uncommon, the true incidence is probably higher and increasing in frequency because of motor vehicle crashes and the overall increase in athletic activity in our society across all ages.[2] The five TMT joints of the foot are very stable and immobile structures that usually sustain acute injuries from high-energy forces or crush injuries. Lisfranc injury can be caused by direct or indirect mechanisms. Isolated lesions are more common in sports injuries and occur as a result of a sudden torque on the foot when a portion of it is fixed or by axially loading the foot in a vertical position.[197] For example, a runner may sustain an isolated TMT joint fracture by stumbling into a hole, a football player may be injured if another player falls on the heel of his dorsiflexed foot, or a motorcyclist or horseback rider can wrench the foot through its midtarsal region when it is only partially restrained in a stirrup or pedal. Traumatic TMT injuries are usually a component of multiple injuries and may be caused by high-energy motor vehicle or industrial accidents. Such injuries are frequently open fractures that have associated soft tissue injuries, such as degloving or bone and cartilage loss.[228] They can vary from being pure fractures or fracture-dislocations to pure ligamentous disruptions and correspondingly seem to have a progressively worsening prognosis.[86] Regardless of the nature of this injury or its treatment, kinesiologic studies of patients with displaced Lisfranc fractures suggest that no patient will ever enjoy a normal gait after injury.[357] This "limp" usually results from a shortened stance phase and period of weight transfer through the midfoot. These injuries should also always be suspected in a multiply injured patient because of their frequency.[106]

### ANATOMY

The TMT articulations have very little intrinsic mobility by design.[243] Midfoot motion has probably lessened over the course of ages because of the fact that the foot has evolved from a mobile "extra hand" in quadrupeds into a present-day stable platform for bipeds. Thus, the midfoot supports a rigid arch to allow safe passage of the neurovascular structures and tendons into the foot without being crushed by the weight of stance. Such injuries threaten the integrity of this structure and therefore its function. Whereas the more lateral articulations are most mobile (the lateral column) and need to be for accommodative gait, the first TMT joint remains atavistically predisposed to instability because of its lateral migration away from being a "thumb." This change has resulted in no intrinsic proximal intermetatarsal ligamentous support along the first ray akin to that found between the other four bones, and in fact the Lisfranc ligament runs from the base of the medial cuneiform to the base of the second metatarsal without a counterpart across the first ray, which helps explain the frequency of bunions and hypermobility along the first ray that we treat so commonly in uninjured patients.

It is the plantar ligaments, much more so than those dorsally, that account for most of the soft tissue restraint in the midfoot.[8] Their job is supplemented by insertions of the peroneus longus at the base of the first ray and the plantar fascia. All five bones have stout intermetatarsal ligaments between their distal necks, but these supporting structures lend more stability and resistance to displacement of distal metatarsal fractures than they do for proximally based injuries. When viewed in cross section, the bony architecture of the midfoot also lends great rigidity and strength to this area (Fig. 60–48) in the form of the so-called Roman arch; the trapezoidal shape of both the bases of the metatarsals and their respective cuneiforms is ideal for supporting weight from above. Additionally, the second metatarsal base, or "keystone," is recessed between the first and third cuneiforms, so that pure shear across the midfoot cannot merely stress the capsuloligamentous support for failure but must also fracture the second metatarsal as a bony restraint.

The dorsalis pedis artery crosses the midfoot just above the second TMT articulation, after which it sends the first intermetatarsal branch between the first interspace as part of the plantar arterial arcade. This branch, in particular, is therefore prone to damage during Lisfranc injuries and has been associated with the onset of compartment syndrome.

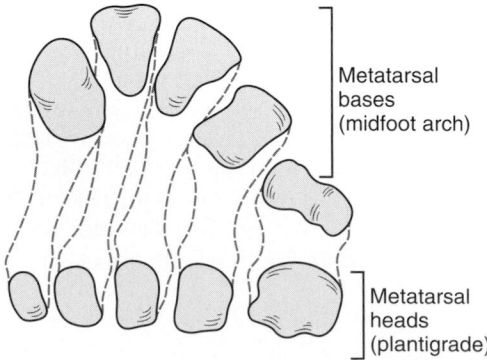

**Figure 60–48.** In cross section, the midfoot mimics the rigid, self-supporting architectural design of the Roman arch. It is stable by virtue of both its ligamentous and, most important, its bony anatomy. The recessed nature and trapezoidal configuration of the metatarsal bases lend bony support to compressive loads in both the coronal and transverse planes, and its configuration also prevents us from walking on our neurovascular bundle during weight bearing—a situation that can change with, for example, an untreated Lisfranc injury that heals in dorsiflexion and abduction.

Care must also be taken to avoid injury to the deep peroneal nerve, which travels just lateral to this artery to supply sensation to the first webspace.

## DIAGNOSIS

Lisfranc injuries can be quite subtle, but they are typically easily identified with a history of an appropriate mechanism and a good physical examination. These individuals generally have dorsal swelling or ecchymosis about the midfoot and significant tenderness to palpation through the TMT articulations. Each of these symptoms can be separately isolated and tested for accurate interpretation, and clinical stress can be gently applied in dorsiflexion and abduction to elicit a "chandelier" or "apprehension" sign. Some authors suggest passive pronation and supination of the foot as being very specific for TMT injury if pain is elicited.[210] Ecchymosis identified on the plantar aspect of the midfoot is also suggestive.[86, 276] In extreme cases, the foot can be grossly malaligned in a shortened, widened, and abducted position, often unstable with any attempt at midfoot palpation. A careful neurovascular examination as well as examination of the opposite foot, which can be similarly injured, should be performed, with a very high index of clinical suspicion maintained for compartment syndrome.

Most TMT fractures are clearly seen on standard AP, lateral, and oblique radiographs. The AP radiographic view should be taken tangential to the TMT joints so that even a subtle dislocation can be seen. Even if no fracture line is visible, the presence of a TMT fracture should be suspected if a small fracture is seen at the base of the second metatarsal on the AP view (the "fleck" sign) or if the second or third metatarsal is displaced dorsally on the lateral view (Fig. 60–49). Generally, a line drawn on the AP view joining the medial border of the first cuneiform and the navicular should bisect the base of the first metatarsal, as described by Coss and associates.[53] Although radiographic obliquity can alter the accuracy of this measurement, any medial or lateral translation can be identified. Any widening larger than 2 mm between the metatarsal bases should be viewed with suspicion.[228] The best way to identify subtle Lisfranc disruptions is to remember that on the AP view, the medial base of the first and second metatarsals should line up with the medial bases of their respective cuneiforms and the lateral base of the third metatarsal should line up with the lateral aspect of the lateral cuneiform.[94] Thus, an extension of the medial border of the second metatarsal, for example, should line up with the medial border of the middle cuneiform. On the oblique view, the medial base of the fourth metatarsal should be continuous with the medial edge of the cuboid, and the lateral flare of the fifth metatarsal base should gradually slope to the point of articulation with the cuboid, with the base straightening out in line with the cuboid facet. Additionally, the medial border of the third metatarsal should line up with the medial border of the lateral cuneiform. Finally, on a lateral view, no dorsal step-off in TMT alignment should be seen, and Meary's line should be straight.[291] Here, the first and second metatarsal cortices should be in continuity with the medial and middle cuneiforms, respectively. It is important to beware

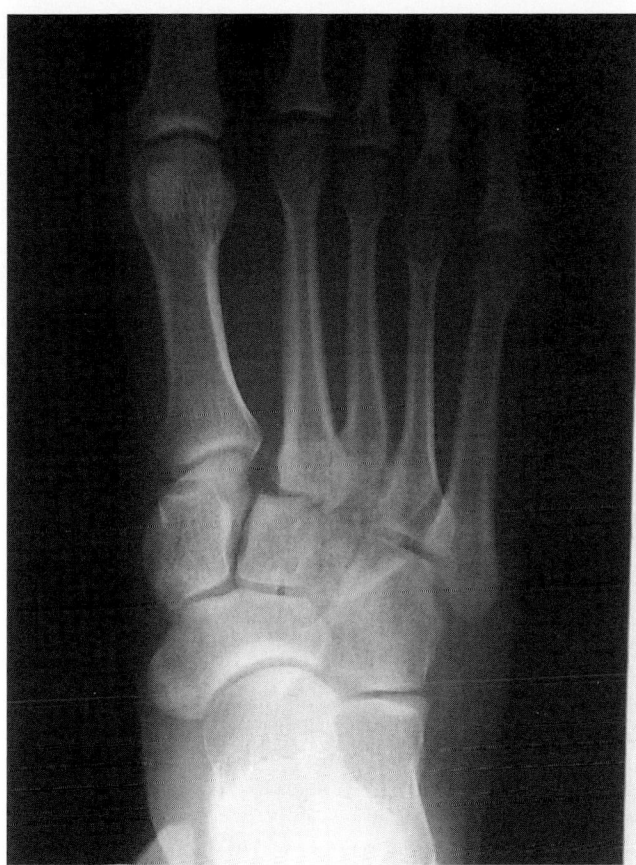

**FIGURE 60–49.** The fleck sign is an often subtle indication of underlying midfoot instability through the Lisfranc articulations. It is located between the first and second metatarsal bases on an anteroposterior view of the foot and represents a bony avulsion off the base of the second metatarsal base from pull of the plantar Lisfranc ligament originating from the medial cuneiform. Even if the radiographs look otherwise normal, these patients should undergo stress examination of the midfoot to rule out occult midfoot instability.

that multiple fractures at the bases of the metatarsals can also mimic a Lisfranc injury clinically, either by themselves or in conjunction with articular subluxation or dislocation, and they should be considered of similar severity and be treated accordingly.

Adjunctive imaging techniques are not typically required for either diagnosis or treatment of these injuries. CT scanning with three-dimensional reconstructive sections can be considered for subtle or complicated injuries when better definition is required to aid in diagnostic or operative intervention, and a bone scan can also be helpful in identifying more occult Lisfranc injuries or simply severe midfoot sprains that may not require surgery but frequently result in prolonged disability.[259] Although it is likely that midfoot (Lisfranc) sprains are an early continuum of frank Lisfranc disruption and do not require surgery because of a lack of demonstrable instability, Meyer and colleagues and others have suggested that they can still result in prolonged disability in athletes, especially when the medial column is involved (as compared with the lateral column).[209, 308] It is doubtful that current MRI techniques are useful for aiding in diagnosis or guiding treatment beyond established methods, although its use is being researched and has been described.[257]

**Stress Views.** When displacement is minimal but tenderness or swelling is noted during the clinical examination, further investigation with a stress radiograph is warranted, and consideration should be given to comparison views of the normal foot. Although some midfoot sprains are intrinsically stable and safe for early weight bearing, they are along a continuum of injury through the midfoot that can result in occult instability requiring operative intervention. This injury must be diagnosed early for optimal outcome and warrants stress view examination if it is clinically suspected because of the mechanisms of injury, appearance of the foot, or degree of discomfort exhibited by the patient, regardless of what the initial standard radiographs demonstrate.

The manipulation required for performing a stress radiograph may be painful, but the presence of pain is indicative of a fracture or sprain. This type of manipulation may be done under a regional (ankle block) or general anesthetic, the same as for an ankle sprain. The AP view is taken with the forefoot held in abduction under pressure and the fulcrum based laterally at the anterior process of the calcaneus at the level of the calcaneocuboid joint. The lateral view is taken with the forefoot in plantar flexion, whereas the midfoot and hindfoot are held in neutral position. In the case of subtle or unclear injuries, comparative views of the opposite foot are helpful. Radiographic continuity is seen on the various views. Any significant abduction of the first metatarsal, along with subluxation of the metatarsal cuneiform joint, is a pathognomonic finding (Fig. 60–50). Operative intervention is indicated if displacement of the TMT joints is greater than 2 mm.

## CLASSIFICATION

A number of classification systems have been proposed to rate the severity of TMT fractures, but none is helpful in choosing treatment. For example, the classic Quenu and Kuss system[261] describes several combinations of injuries that commonly occur together, but it neither rates the injuries by severity nor indicates optimal treatment or prognosis. Quenu and Kuss outline three major patterns of disruption as defined by metatarsal subluxation or dislocation in varying number and direction: isolated (unidirectional displacement of at least one but not all the metatarsals, typically the first or second rays), homolateral (uniform medial or, more typically, lateral subluxation or dislocation of all the metatarsals), and divergent (separation of any combination of metatarsals in different directions or in more than one plane). A more useful classification of TMT injuries, however, is difficult to devise because so many fracture combinations are possible. The amount of displacement in a TMT disruption can vary from a subtle pure dislocation, which can be difficult to diagnose, to severe displacement with associated fractures in the metatarsal bases, the cuneiforms, or the distal metatarsals. Other associated injuries may involve fracture or dislocation of the cuneiforms and the cuboid. Although many other classification systems have been reported, they are predominantly descriptive and do not permit prognostic assessment or direct treatment decisions.[122, 229] For example, Hardcastle and co-workers divided the types of injury into partially incongruent, totally incongruent, and divergent patterns.[122] None of the classifications discuss the other fractures that commonly occur with these injuries and often require recognition and treatment for optimal outcome. Most commonly and in decreasing order of frequency, these fractures include the metatarsals, cuneiforms, and the cuboid.

Kuo and colleagues have recently performed a long-term follow-up of outcome after ORIF of Lisfranc injuries and suggest that the pattern of disruption may have prognostic significance.[174] We used an anatomic description that based operative intervention on fracture displacement, ligamentous involvement, or demonstrable instability. Lisfranc injuries that are purely ligamentous may indeed be more prone to failure of fixation or loss of alignment than ones with identifiable fractures that can be fixed. These latter injuries seem to have a more predictable healing potential. What is most important about trying to classify a Lisfranc injury is deciding whether the medial column (first, second, and third metatarsals and TMT joints), the lateral column (fourth and fifth metatarsals and corresponding joints), the intertarsal joints (the intercuneiform and naviculocuneiform joints), or any combination of these structures is involved because the pattern of involvement affects treatment. It is also more important to focus on how many of the TMT joints are disrupted rather than trying to distinguish exactly which direction each may have been displaced.

## MIDFOOT SPRAIN

Midfoot sprains do occur, although not all acknowledge the existence of such sprains. These injuries are along a continuum of midfoot ligamentous damage and result from enough force to stretch or partially tear the plantar restraints of the midfoot but not enough so that instability results. Thus, patients initially have a great deal of swelling, ecchymosis, and pain, but no instability can be demonstrated on physical examination or documented on

radiographs. Like the variations that can be seen for ankle sprains, these injuries can recover in a matter of weeks or months and do not require surgical intervention. After appropriate observation to rule out an impending compartment syndrome and stress views to rule out occult instability, these injuries can be managed by a RICE protocol, protected crutch walking with weight-bearing advancement guided by comfort, and possibly physical therapy. Full recovery is the rule, but patients should be warned that symptoms can linger, often for 2 to 4 months. Care should also be taken to evaluate for concomitant foot injury as well if symptoms do not abate in a time frame that coincides with the injury mechanism. Such injuries include talar neck fractures, midtarsal fractures, or subtalar interosseous ligamentous tears.

## TREATMENT

Closed reduction plus casting of unstable Lisfranc fractures or fracture-dislocations remains unrewarding. Historically, treatment of TMT fractures has progressed from closed reduction and percutaneous K-wire fixation or casting to open reduction with screw fixation and either smooth or threaded K-wires. Although K-wire fixation has its proponents,[122, 322] it has been associated with a high failure rate in some series.[293] No general consensus exists about the optimal treatment of these injuries, but evidence is clear that a satisfactory final result is directly related to the accuracy of the reduction and its successful maintenance through healing.[9, 229, 245] For this reason, most authors, including us, recommend open reduction and screw fixation for treatment of all TMT fractures and dislocations.[8, 36, 273] It is much more difficult to salvage a collapsed foot with disrupted midfoot alignment and post-traumatic Lisfranc arthrosis than one with normal anatomic relationships. Furthermore, the anatomic alignment of the metatarsal heads (on which the body's weight is borne) is equally, if not more important than alignment of the TMT articulations. Obviously, metatarsal head position

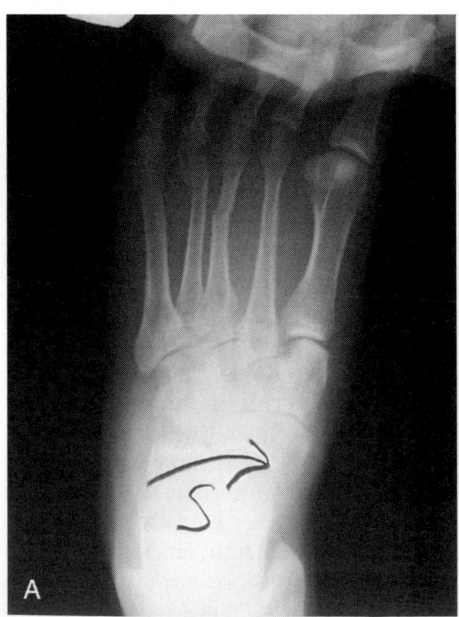 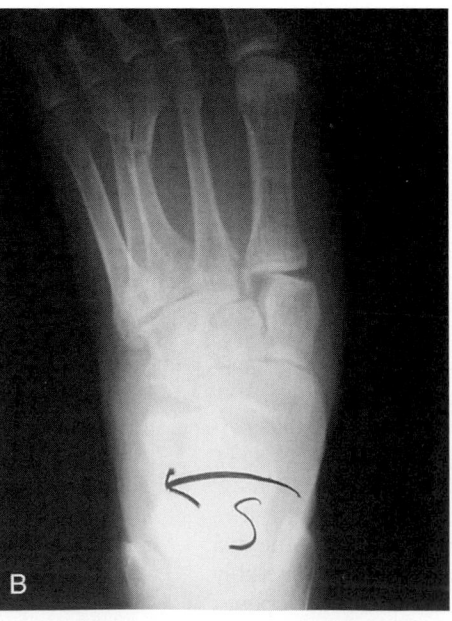

**Figure 60–50.** Stress examination of the midfoot is performed in the two planes most likely to demonstrate instability (subluxation). The examiner first stresses the forefoot on an anteroposterior projection with lateral stress to the second through fifth metatarsals and medial stress to the first ray. The second stress view is obtained with dorsiflexion stress on the forefoot in a lateral projection. Comparison views of the opposite foot can be obtained to clarify any ambiguity regarding the diagnosis. The plantar ligamentous support of the foot is powerful and must be disrupted for this instability to occur, in contradistinction to the weak dorsal ligamentous complex. A break in Meary's line whereby the talus and first ray are no longer in co-linear apposition can also be visualized on positive stress examinations.

in space is directly related to proper proximal alignment, and even small differences proximally can be magnified distally by the length of the metatarsal itself. Isolated disruption of the Lisfranc ligament identified by fracture or MRI, if not associated with overt or radiographic instability, has reportedly been successfully treated with 6 weeks of casting and nonoperative management.

Some surgeons have expressed concern about the possibility of complications arising from the use of ORIF in closed TMT fractures and dislocations. They argue that screw fixation may stiffen the joints and that the risks of additional surgery to remove the fixation screws far outweigh any advantages that ORIF may offer. The disadvantages of closed reduction, however, occur far more commonly than any theoretical complications that may result from ORIF. Many patients treated by closed reduction have sustained malalignment deformities, disability from secondary arthritis, and shoe-fitting problems if the original reduction was not accurate or the reduction was lost during rehabilitation. Conversely, after normal anatomy has been restored, patients regain normal function for routine activities and, in some cases, even for demanding sports activities. In one of the largest series of Lisfranc injury fixation and outcome, Kuo and associates suggested that anatomic reduction was associated with a significantly lower rate of post-traumatic arthritis ($P$ = .004) and a significantly better average American Orthopaedic Foot and Ankle Society (AOFAS) outcome score ($P$ = .05). Patients with pure ligamentous injury had a trend toward a higher prevalence of post-traumatic arthritis, roughly 40% at an average 52 months of follow-up ($P$ = .11).[174]

Stiffness after screw fixation is a minor concern in the medial three TMT joints because the three medial joints normally have very little motion; arthrosis seen on radiographs does not correlate with functional disability or discomfort in the TMT joints. We recommend screw fixation in two or three medial joints for all TMT (Lisfranc) joint dislocations or fracture-dislocations. The fourth and, most commonly, the fifth metatarsal may be fixed with K-wires. Sometimes, after stabilization of the medial column, the lateral column falls into place nicely and remains stable during examination and fluoroscopy. In these cases, fixation may not be required in the fourth or fifth ray, and thus some stiffness can be avoided here because these joints typically require some motion for proper function, in contrast to the medial column. Surgery for hardware removal 3 months after the initial operation constitutes an expense, but the risks related to this procedure are minor and disability time is short. It is possible to leave the hardware in place, however, particularly in older or more sedentary individuals. Such patients should be warned of the possibility of hardware breakage, which can often be asymptomatic.

General agreement does exist about the need for stable anatomic fixation in open or markedly displaced fractures.[229] The advantages of ORIF in these fractures are clear: ORIF protects soft tissues, facilitates general healing, alleviates pain, and minimizes the chance of late deformity. In acute injuries, ORIF also decompresses potential compartment syndromes in the forefoot. It is incredibly easier to anatomically fix these injuries initially as opposed to trying to realign them after incorrect healing has already taken place and resulted in symptoms that necessitate operative intervention.

**Timing.** The timing of an operation on the TMT joints is of major importance in open injuries and those with severely damaged soft tissues. Reduction is easiest to accomplish within 4 to 6 hours after injury. Moreover, a dislocation in the foot may damage the arterial and venous circulation, so early restoration of circulation in this dependent limb is critical to promote healing in soft tissue and bone. The dorsalis pedis is frequently disrupted in TMT injuries, but disruption of this single artery is not a major problem because it is only one of many branches of the anterior and posterior tibial arterial system. However, disruption of the first intermetatarsal branch off the dorsalis pedis located in the first intermetatarsal space is common in these injuries and can be the cause of a foot compartment syndrome. One needs to be alert to this potential problem when faced with any variation of this injury. More extensive vascular disruption can occur when the distal bony and soft tissue structures are crushed. A significant injury here could destroy all sources of blood to the TMT region, and unless blood flow is restored, a midfoot-level amputation may be unavoidable. Actual vascular disruption is less common than elevated tissue pressure. Tissue pressure can be reduced and circulation restored by open reduction. All dislocations should be considered an indication for emergency reduction by either direct open reduction or, in patients with severe soft tissue damage or swelling, indirect reduction techniques with external fixation along the medial and lateral columns. Compartment syndrome should be carefully watched for and, if identified, is also an indication for emergency treatment.

**Operative Management.** The surgical approach to correct an isolated TMT fracture-dislocation is made through two longitudinal incisions, one in the interspace between the first and second metatarsals and the other in the interspace between the third and fourth metatarsals or over the fourth metatarsal. These incisions are approximately 4 to 6 cm long and should go straight down to the bone; they should undermine the tendons and neurovascular structures as little as possible (Fig. 60–51). The intervening soft tissue flap should be meticulously preserved to avoid wound slough or necrosis. Care should be taken to avoid the cutaneous nerves during dissection, as well as the deep peroneal nerve in the medial incision.

All the TMT joints should be inspected for injury before any fixation devices are applied. The first and second TMT joints are inspected first, through the first incision. Direct investigation may reveal greater damage to the capsules of these joints than had been anticipated; for example, an oblique fracture may be found around the ligamentous attachments at the base of the second TMT joint. The first and second joints are replaced in their anatomic positions at this time with the use of pointed reduction forceps and K-wire stabilization, but definitive fixation is delayed until the third and fourth TMT joints have been examined and relocated through the second incision. To facilitate complete reduction of the first metatarsal, inspection of not only the dorsal articulation but also the medial articulation with the medial cuneiform can ensure that the best

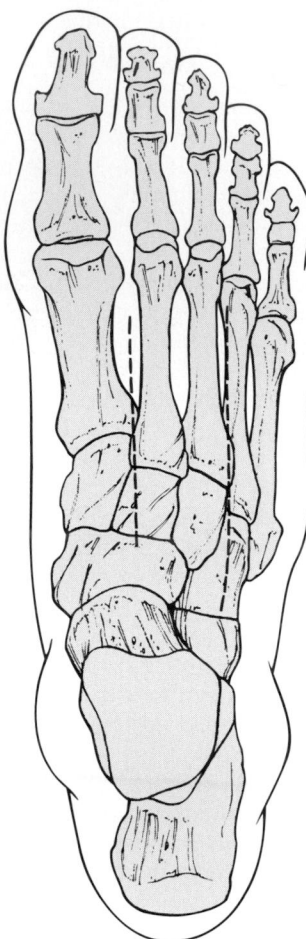

**FIGURE 60–51.** Two parallel dorsal incisions are usually needed to completely stabilize a tarsometatarsal fracture-dislocation. The incisions are carried straight down to bone, with a flap at least 7 to 9 cm wide kept between them, and do not undermine or separate the skin or the subcutaneous tissue from the fascia, particularly between the flap. Usually, these incisions can be closed primarily, although a skin graft is occasionally required for the lateral side (also the side with typically less hardware to cover).

reduction possible is obtained. Fragments of bone or cartilage too small to be repaired may be removed. After the third and fourth TMT joints have been explored and realigned, attention is turned to formal fixation of the first and second. The screws used in reduction of these injuries are not lag (compression) screws; they are "set" screws.

***Medial Column.*** The key to successful internal fixation of a TMT joint is correct placement of the screws. Small holes are drilled or burred into the metatarsal bases and the cuneiforms, and a sharp-pointed forceps is inserted through them to grip the joints tightly and reduce them accurately. The base of the second metatarsal is reduced first, if it is intact. It is pulled securely into anatomic position against the lateral first cuneiform and the distal second cuneiform and pinned with a K-wire. It is then stabilized with a 2.7- or 3.5-mm lag screw inserted percutaneously from the medial side of the first cuneiform and directed obliquely through a gliding hole drilled toward the base of the second metatarsal; the second metatarsal must be predrilled to create an appropriately

sized distally threaded hole (Fig. 60–52). This screw enters the base of the second metatarsal at the proximal medial corner and penetrates the lateral cortex at an angle of approximately 45°. A longer screw may be extended

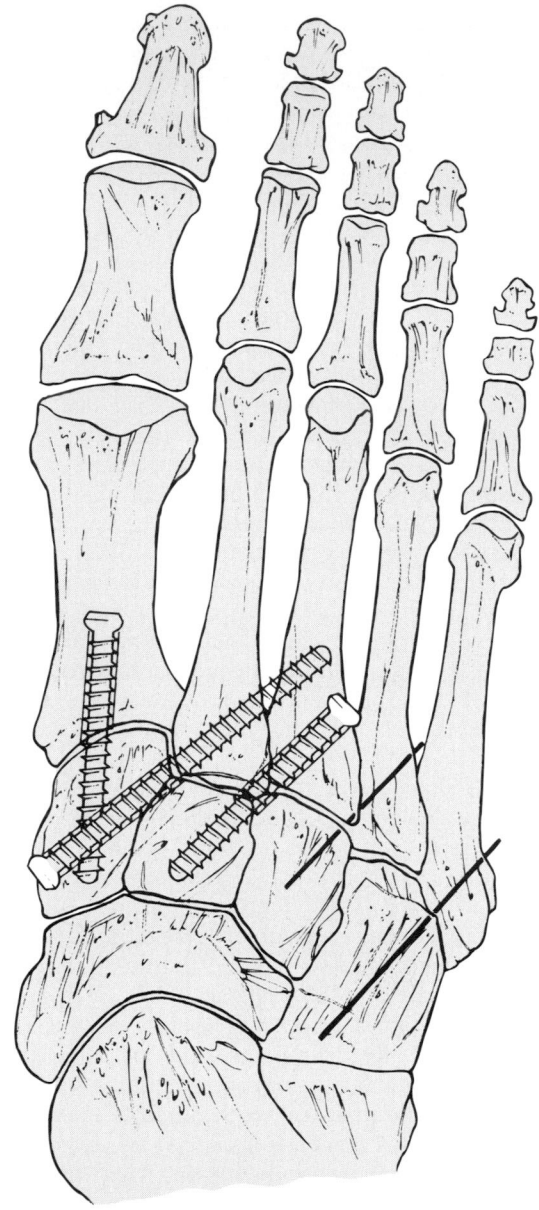

**FIGURE 60–52.** Screw placement for fixation of acute tarsometatarsal fracture-dislocations, delayed treatment of acute fractures, and realignment and fusion of old tarsometatarsal fracture-dislocations. One screw is placed from the base of the first metatarsal into the first cuneiform through a notch in the dorsum of the metatarsal. The principal screw is placed from the proximal medial first cuneiform into the base of the second and sometimes also the third metatarsal. It is angled from a gliding hole in the cuneiform directly into the proximal medial corner of the base of the second metatarsal, which has been predrilled with a 2.5-mm bit. This screw provides very stable fixation by compressing the base of the second metatarsal into the notch between the first and the second cuneiforms as it is tightened. Another screw can be placed at the same angle from the dorsolateral surface of the third metatarsal into the second cuneiform through the more lateral dorsal incision. It also pushes the bases of the second and third metatarsals snugly into their corrected positions. K-wires may be used in the fourth and fifth metatarsals, but they must be angled in a lateral-to-medial direction and slightly dorsally to ensure proximal fixation.

through the base of the third metatarsal for greater stability. This technique is used in late reconstructions and in Charcot (neuropathic) TMT joint dislocations, which are always fused.

After the second TMT joint has been reduced, the first may be fixed. The size of the screw to be used for the first TMT joint is determined by the diameter of the bone; a 3.5-mm cortical screw is used in large bone, whereas a 2.7-mm cortical screw is used in smaller bone. A small notch or trough is made in the dorsal cortex of the first metatarsal at least 2 cm distal to the joint (Fig. 60–53) with a 3-mm bur. This notch serves two purposes. It prevents the screw head from striking the inclined surface of the metatarsal and splitting the proximal side of the dorsal cortex, and it provides an indentation into which the head of the screw can be countersunk. A gliding hole is aimed into the middle of the joint and drilled through the upper half of the notch (not through the base of the notch). The threaded hole is continued into the first cuneiform with a smaller appropriate drill bit. After the holes have been drilled, a screw is inserted and allowed to self-tap in the dense cancellous bone. Because the screws are meant to be positional, precise reduction of the articular surfaces against each other is necessary before tapping or placing a self-tapping screw across them. We have found, however, that preparing them in lag fashion during drilling allows for gentle coaptation of the joints during insertion that sometimes cannot be as effectively maintained with the occasionally awkward grip of reduction forceps in the midfoot. Screws inserted in this manner should therefore be finger tightened so that the joint is not overcompressed and the cartilage crushed. The threads in each bone grip and maintain the reduction without shifting. It is ideal in the first metatarsal–cuneiform joint to use two screws in a crisscross fashion to neutralize the dorsal and plantar aspects of this large joint. Single-screw fixation, especially in purely ligamentous injuries, has resulted in medial column failure.[174] In large or very active patients or those with a purely ligamentous injury, serious consideration should be given to placing a second screw across each TMT joint to improve the rigidity of the construct, especially the first ray, which bears a third of body weight all by itself. This second screw can be placed in a proximal-to-distal direction, does not have to be lagged, and does not require a preburred entry site because the bone of the medial cuneiform is softer and more accommodative than the metatarsal base. As for the second metatarsal, a similar second point of fixation can be established if desired with a longitudinal, distal-to-proximal screw. The third metatarsal often requires only one screw when the remainder of the medial column is rigidly fixed because of the intrinsic stability conferred by the distal intermetatarsal ligaments and proximal bony alignment flanking both its sides.

*Intertarsal Instability.* Intertarsal instability should always be assessed intraoperatively during treatment of these injuries, and it is not uncommon. If instability is identified at the level of the intercuneiform or naviculocuneiform articulations, it is probably easiest to stabilize these joints before addressing the TMT region so that a stable proximal segment can act as a building block for more distal fixation. K-wires can hold these joints aligned

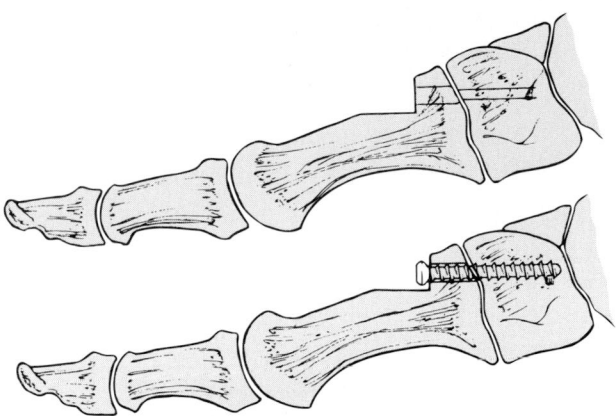

**FIGURE 60–53.** A special technique is required for notching and drilling the proximal metatarsal bones. This technique is not usually required elsewhere in the midfoot (in the cuneiforms, for example) because the bone is softer and more amenable to drill and screw placement. A notch is first made in the base of a metatarsal with a 3-mm bur just through the superficial dorsal cortex. It should begin as a small circle at least 1 cm away from the joint and tail off distally for about 5 mm so that it has the appearance of a comet. A hole is then made with a 3.5-mm drill bit stabilized in the proximal indentation and drilled across the base of the metatarsal to the joint; it is continued into the cuneiform with a 2.5-mm bit. The hole is drilled above the base of the notch, not at the bottom of the notch. The screw may then be inserted without a risk of splitting the dorsum of the base of the metatarsal by striking the head on the metatarsal shaft and angulating it. The screw head is countersunk so that it will not protrude from underneath the skin.

initially, after which either 2.7- or 3.5-mm screws can be inserted transtarsally from the medial side, or a longer screw can be placed longitudinally starting from the aligned metatarsals and crossing both the TMT and naviculocuneiform joint (Fig. 60–54). If this technique is used, it is important to ensure initial anatomic reduction because the interdependent anatomy of these tightly packed joints can otherwise lead to sequential malreduction. Longer screws used for this purpose require a good understanding of the architecture of the midfoot arch because one needs to aim dorsally from any medial or distal starting point to not exit plantarly from the bone. Like the TMT joint, the naviculocuneiform and intercuneiform joints normally have little mobility, and screw fixation across them does not compromise function.

Fixation of the third TMT joint is a bit trickier than the other medial two by virtue of its anatomy. The angle of entry is different from that used in the first and second TMT joints because the transverse arch in the third and fourth TMT joints slopes downward and laterally. The base of the metatarsal is also significantly shallower than that of the adjacent first or second metatarsal bases. The screw is inserted from the lateral side in a slightly dorsal direction and angled medially through the base of the metatarsal and into the tarsus. This approach ensures placement of the screw into the cuneiform instead of underneath it because the second and third cuneiforms are less deep than the first cuneiform on the plantar side.

*Lateral Column.* Once anatomic alignment of the medial column is ensured by C-arm imaging, fixation then proceeds with placement of smooth 0.054-inch or, preferably, 0.062-inch K-wires, if necessary, across the fourth and fifth TMT joints under direct vision (see Fig. 60–52). Unless the injury requires open reduction, the fourth and fifth TMT joints are usually fixed with a percutaneous K-wire because they generally subluxate dorsally. A K-wire placed through an open approach enters the joint from the lateral side and angles slightly upward into the medial cuboid and the tarsus. These wires can be left out of the skin or buried, depending on surgeon preference. They should be removed at about 6 weeks, which can be done in an office or operatory setting. Any significant swelling

after surgery should be appropriately addressed with compartment decompression, bead pouch placement with delayed primary closure, or vacuum-assisted closure. This latter technique has been popularized by plastic surgeons and has proved very effective in closing dead space and filling soft tissue defects with abundant granulation tissue[7, 62] (Fig. 60–55). Amazingly, this effect can occur even in the presence of exposed hardware or bone, and large or severe defects can be effectively closed with split-thickness skin grafts. If permissible, the incisions

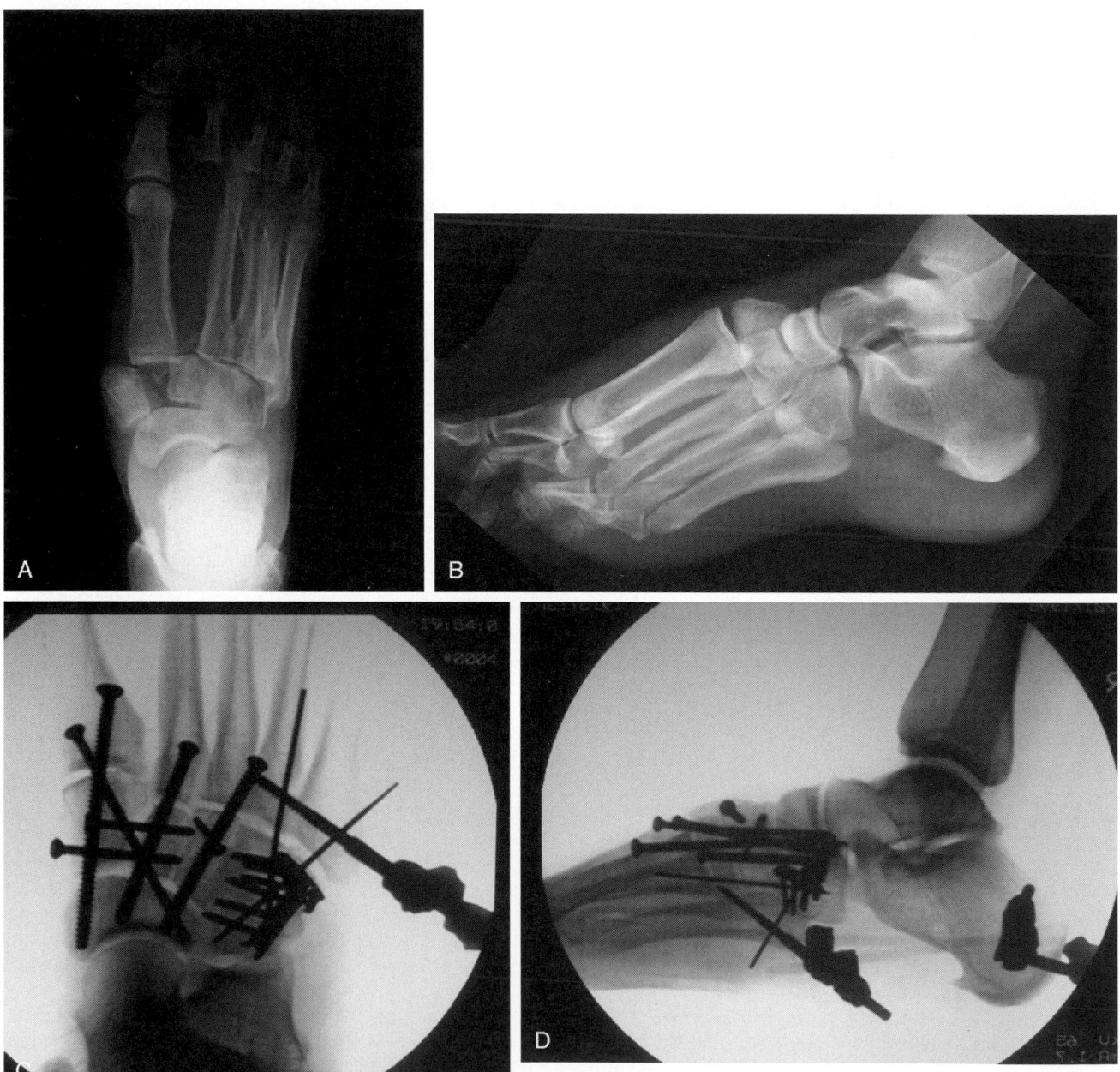

**FIGURE 60–54.** Commonly, intertarsal instability accompanies a Lisfranc (tarsometatarsal) injury. Sometimes it is occult, so a high index of suspicion should always be maintained intraoperatively and both clinical and radiographic stress examinations performed. Usually, however, it is overt (as in this case—*A, B*), and treatment is the same and demands rigid anatomic open reduction and internal fixation (ORIF) (*C, D*). The intertarsal instability can often be initially aligned with a medial or lateral column external fixator, as was used for this patient, after which fixation is made easier for the surgeon and should begin proximally and proceed distally so that abnormal anatomy can be realigned to normal anatomy in a sequential manner. Note that this technique also helped with disimpaction of the lateral cuboid nutcracker injury in this patient, which also required ORIF with bone grafting to restore integrity to the lateral column.

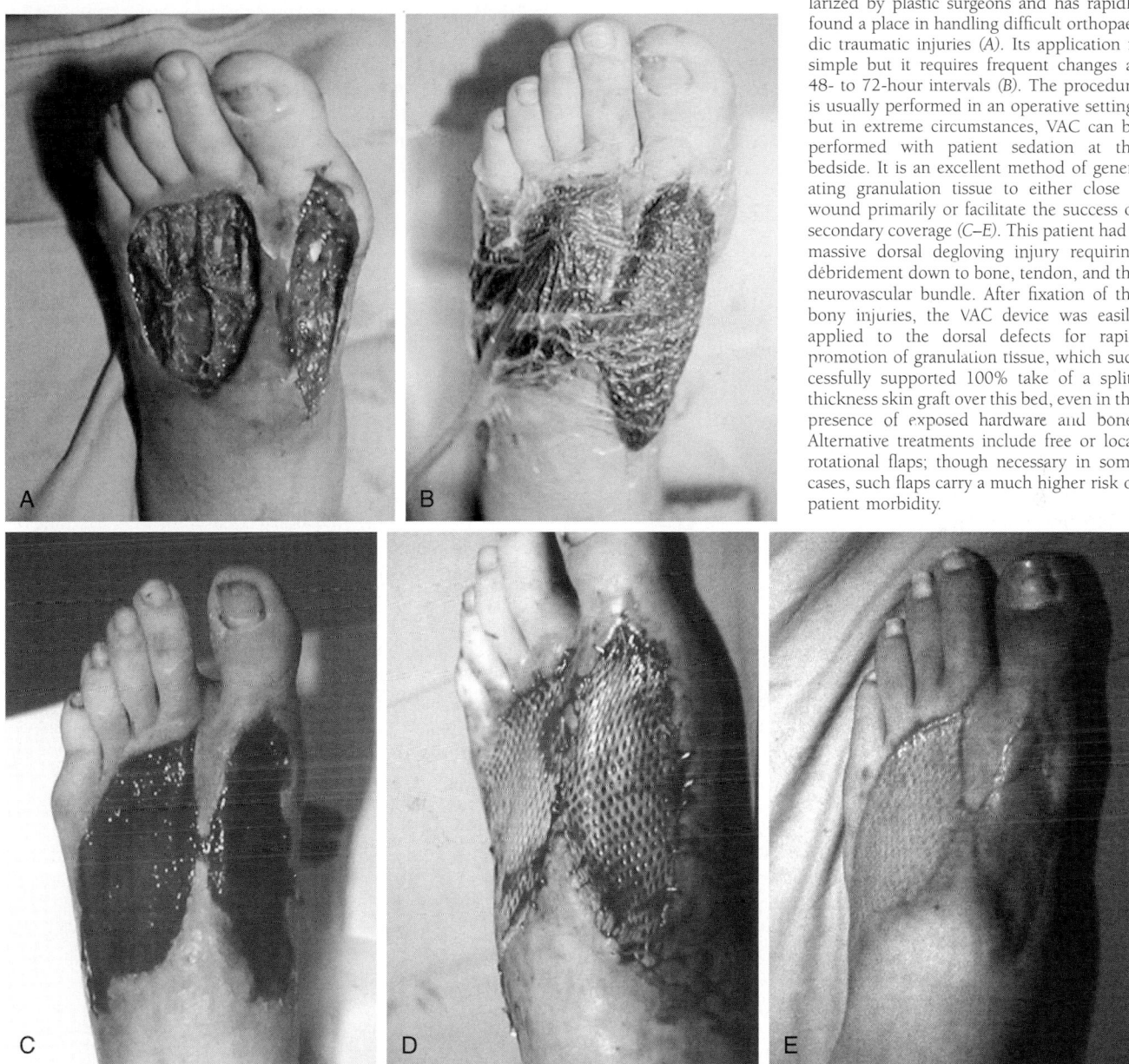

**FIGURE 60–55.** The "vacuum-assisted closure" device (VAC) has recently been popularized by plastic surgeons and has rapidly found a place in handling difficult orthopaedic traumatic injuries (*A*). Its application is simple but it requires frequent changes at 48- to 72-hour intervals (*B*). The procedure is usually performed in an operative setting, but in extreme circumstances, VAC can be performed with patient sedation at the bedside. It is an excellent method of generating granulation tissue to either close a wound primarily or facilitate the success of secondary coverage (*C–E*). This patient had a massive dorsal degloving injury requiring débridement down to bone, tendon, and the neurovascular bundle. After fixation of the bony injuries, the VAC device was easily applied to the dorsal defects for rapid promotion of granulation tissue, which successfully supported 100% take of a split-thickness skin graft over this bed, even in the presence of exposed hardware and bone. Alternative treatments include free or local rotational flaps; though necessary in some cases, such flaps carry a much higher risk of patient morbidity.

should alternatively be primarily closed and a posterior splint applied to rest the soft tissues. Compartment syndrome can commonly occur after this injury, but it is unusual after operative fixation because of the decompression and hematoma evacuation obtained during surgery.

Beware of a cuboid impaction fracture with these injuries. This fracture is often subtle and, if left untreated, can result in residual subluxation or instability of the cuboid–metatarsal base articulations regardless of K-wire reduction attempts. More importantly, it can exacerbate the lateral column shortening that frequently occurs with the dorsiflexion/abduction forces that cause a Lisfranc injury. Progressive weight borne on such a deformity can lead to progressive peritalar subluxation, posterior tibial tendon insufficiency, talonavicular collapse, and sinus tarsi

impingement. Thus, when identified, significant impaction or nutcracker injuries of the cuboid should be fixed, with restoration of articular congruity by using the metatarsal bases as a template, restoration of lateral column length, bone grafting of the residual defect, and dorsal plating with usually a 2.0-mm T plate, an external minifixator, or both.

***Associated Metatarsal Fracture.*** Associated metatarsal fractures conferring segmental instability are also common with these injuries. They can involve the metatarsal shaft, neck, or head. If the shafts are fractured, maintenance of anatomic length and rotation of the metatarsal with concomitant alignment of the TMT joints may be impossible with screw fixation, and plates may be required. In larger bones, 2.4-, 2.7-, or even 3.5-mm plates are ideal for this purpose. The smaller implants are low profile, can be very stout as dynamic compression or reconstruction plates if need be, and have multiple holes per size that allow many points of fixation to neutralize these fractures. They can be placed along the length of the metatarsal or used to bridge the TMT joint, depending on need. Distal metatarsal neck or head fractures can usually be treated separately from the proximal screw fixation just described for the TMT region. In this case, standard reduction and fixation are facilitated with the use of K-wires or small minifragment plates.

***Gastrocnemius Recession.*** One should not forget to examine for superficial posterior compartment tightness of the leg when treating these injuries. Such examination is especially important for identifying gastrocnemius contracture, which can commonly exist in isolation without Achilles equinus; it is a much more subtle finding and can predispose to midfoot and forefoot overload that tensions the reconstruction and causes potential loss of reduction or late deformity if not initially identified and treated. Gastrocnemius recession can easily be identified by the Silfverskiöld maneuver and treated intraoperatively by posteromedial exposure at the level of the gastrocnemius-soleus musculotendinous interval. Release is performed through a small 1- to 2-inch incision that enters the superficial posterior compartment fascia and allows separation of the gastrocnemius from the soleus and release of the gastrocnemius at the musculotendinous junction. Such release results in significant relaxation of forefoot and midfoot pressure during knee extension in the stance phase of gait and is thought to be vital to protecting this repair if the gastrocnemius is thought to be pathologically tight.

**External Fixation.** External fixation can have a useful role in the preliminary management of midfoot fractures or dislocations. Any small-bone external fixator system, similar to that used in the radius, for example, can be spanned along either the medial or the lateral column of the foot for realignment and stability. For severely unstable injuries, it can be placed on both sides of the foot (Fig. 60–56). The side of application depends on the mechanism of injury and the direction of displacement. Thus, homolateral Lisfranc dislocations require a lateral application for optimal reduction, and divergent injuries often require application on both sides. Four-millimeter Schanz pins can be placed in the calcaneus, talus, or navicular proximally (as determined by the injury location) and in the base of the first metatarsal or fourth and fifth metatarsals distally. These devices have a tremendous ability to realign a deformed foot and stabilize traumatized soft tissues. Reestablishment of anatomy can also alleviate an impending compartment syndrome. External fixation is most indicated in the face of severe soft tissue injury precluding operative fixation, as preliminary alignment of a grossly unstable midfoot injury until more definitive management can be rendered, or as an adjunct to internal fixation when, for example, the bone is comminuted or of poor quality.

**Primary Fusion.** Primary fusion of the Lisfranc or intertarsal joints is occasionally indicated in the acute trauma setting, and the technique has recently been well described.[289] When the joints are found to be severely comminuted or the patient is elderly, consideration should be given to anatomic realignment, primary fusion, and bone grafting to prevent an early return to the operating room for pain secondary to post-traumatic arthrosis. Hansen has also recently espoused consideration of primary fusion for grossly unstable, purely ligamentous injuries because of their presumed poorer outcome with

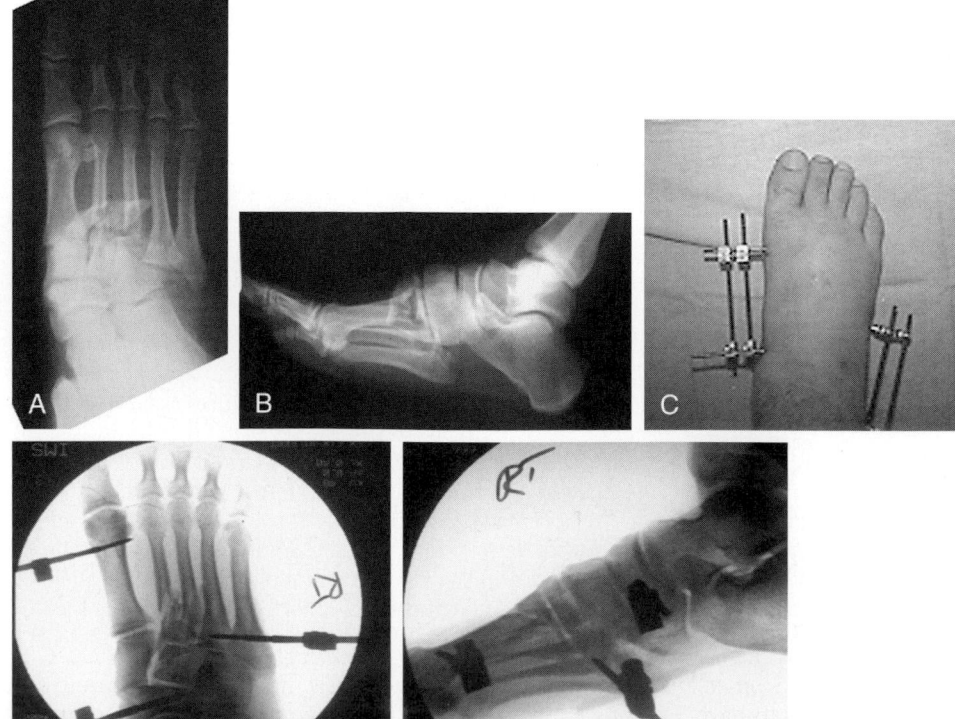

**Figure 60–56.** External fixation for foot injuries is underused. A small fixator is an excellent means of obtaining and maintaining alignment in the foot. It can be used for reduction or distraction of either the medial or lateral column, or both. This case demonstrates the value of this technique. A motorcyclist got his foot caught in the pedal during a head-on collision, flipped over the handlebars, and sustained a gross deformity of foot, a severe Lisfranc disruption (*A*, *B*), and impending compartment syndrome (*C*). Rapid realignment in a bicolumn external fixator (*D*, *E*) easily stabilized his injuries and averted the need for compartmental release. Once the soft tissues had settled down, the patient was returned to the operating room for definitive fixation.

standard ORIF.[120] This treatment is technically more complicated than traditional fixation, although the technique and means of fixation are similar. It is ideally performed with a 2.7-mm dynamic compression plate placed medially along the length of the medial column, and the plate can be advanced as far proximally as the talar neck to provide adequate compression between the first TMT, naviculocuneiform, and talonavicular joints, if necessary.

## POSTOPERATIVE CARE AND REHABILITATION

Postoperative care and rehabilitation are similar to that for other midfoot injuries. If the injury is to be treated conservatively (a midfoot sprain or stable injury), a short leg cast with a well-molded longitudinal and transverse arch support and weight-of-leg weight bearing are recommended in the initial 3 to 4 weeks for swelling and comfort measures. The cast can be followed by transition to a well-molded supportive shoe or wooden postoperative shoe for an additional 3 to 5 weeks with progressive weight bearing until full activity is tolerated. During this time, the patient should be seen at regular intervals and undergo radiographic examination to ensure that progressive displacement has not occurred, which might warrant surgical intervention. Additionally, consideration should be given to an accommodative orthotic to support the arch and midfoot during healing, a process that can take upward of 3 to 6 months to become asymptomatic.

If surgery is required, the initial emphasis should be on soft tissue preservation and minimization of swelling, which typically requires 1 to 3 days of bed exercises and elevation, followed by gradual mobilization in a short leg reinforced splint or cast. Individuals should be observed for evidence of late compartment syndrome. All sutures are left in place for 2 to 3 weeks postoperatively, after which patients are permitted weight-of-leg weight bearing until 6 weeks postoperatively, at which time radiographs are taken. If the clinical and radiographic findings suggest maintained alignment and early signs of healing, the patient can be weaned into a rigidly soled, rocker-bottom shoe for another 6 weeks, during which time aggressive physical therapy is begun. At this time, any indwelling K-wires meant to initially stabilize the lateral column can be removed. Removal is imperative to minimize toe stiffness at the IP and MTP joints, as well as prohibit extrinsic extensor contracture. At this point, the patient should be fully weight bearing and placed in a well-cushioned shoe or sneaker if a repeat set of films suggests complete healing and the arch remains well aligned. Hardware can be removed anytime between 3 and 18 months after injury—on the earlier side for the lateral column to allow preservation of motion and on the later side for the medial column to allow maturity of healing, which can take up to 1 year. Any stiffness associated with this period does not tend to cause any functional impairment. Patients can certainly retain their medial column hardware, but they should be warned about the frequency of breakage. Breakage is often asymptomatic, however, and rarely of clinical significance if it occurs. Recent data by Kuo and others suggest that these patients will take up to 2 years to have full functional recovery.[174, 343, 344]

## OUTCOME

In the most recent study of outcome after Lisfranc injury with approximately 50 patients and over 4 years' mean follow-up, the mean AOFAS score was 77 (range, 40 to 100), and points were lost for mild pain, decreased recreational function, and shoe wear modification.[174] With the Multifunctional Assessment Examination (MFA) scoring system, the mean was 19 (range, 0 to 55). Most higher (worse) scores resulted from osteoarthritis, rheumatoid arthritis, or other associated lower extremity trauma. Patients who had primary ORIF fared better in scoring than did those with primary fusions (80 versus 58, 18 versus 26). Although the data supported the well-documented and clinically significant experience that anatomic reduction results in the best outcomes, a trend toward worse results was noted in purely ligamentous injury, open injury, involvement of all five TMT joints, associated midfoot fracture, and delayed diagnosis (longer than 4 weeks). Interestingly, no difference was found in multiply injured patients, those with ipsilateral lower extremity trauma, or patients with work-related injuries. The mean time from primary ORIF to secondary fusion was approximately 1 year for 6 patients, although 12 (25%) had post-traumatic arthrosis. The incidence of post-traumatic arthrosis was higher in patients with nonanatomic reduction ($P = .004$), purely ligamentous injury ($P = .11$), open injuries, involvement of all five TMT joints, and isolated or work-related injuries. Thus, the best outcomes were found in patients with closed, anatomically reduced bony injuries.

**Short-Term Complications.** Associated midfoot injuries, including cuboid impaction fractures and intertarsal instability, are common with these injuries and should be concomitantly treated when identified. Soft tissue complications such as severe swelling or blistering can lead to compartment syndrome or skin slough, respectively. Vascular insult can also occur, but it typically does not threaten the viability of the foot; it can, however, evolve into a compartment syndrome.

**Long-Term Complications.** Often, some residual swelling, stiffness, and pain are present long-term, and patients need to be made aware of this possibility on initial evaluation.[354] Overall, however, function seems to be optimal with early anatomic realignment and stabilization of these difficult injury patterns. Primary or delayed fusion of the TMT joints also does not always result in an excellent outcome. Komenda and colleagues identified an average AOFAS score of 78 (out of 100) after monitoring Lisfranc arthrodesis for post-traumatic arthritis over a period of 4 years.[173] In general, however, selective TMT fusion for post-traumatic arthrosis in these patients provides a good clinical outcome over time with significant relief of pain and no change in overall stiffness appreciated through the foot. Regarding the more commonly involved medial column, it is relatively easy to fuse one involved joint, but if at least two must be fused, it is recommended that the third be included for ease of reduction during fusion (and little advantage is gained by not including it). Care must be taken to align the metatarsal heads distally during this procedure, which can be deceivingly difficult; concomitant autogenous bone grafting is always recommended. Accurate restoration of Meary's line should also be verified before acceptance of reduction or insertion of any fixation. The incisions and hardware used for fusion of these joints are similar to those used for ORIF in the acute setting. The lateral column joints do not respond well to fusion or rigidity and, when arthritic, should be treated conservatively with bracing and activity modification; in rare instances, however, one can perform an interpositional arthroplasty at the metatarsocuboid articulations.

## CUBOID AND CUNEIFORM FRACTURES

Tarsal injuries may occur in conjunction with hindfoot or metatarsal fractures. For example, a TMT joint fracture may occur when the first cuneiform is separated from the second. A compression fracture of the cuboid may result from lateral displacement of a TMT fracture, a subtalar fracture-dislocation, a type III navicular fracture, or a Chopart dislocation.[292] Radiographs of major injuries in the midfoot should always be closely inspected for these injuries. Some occult or complex tarsal fractures may be apparent only on CT scans.

Although major cuboid injuries are unusual, the cuboid frequently sustains some degree of axial impaction by these injury mechanisms that is often missed on initial radiographs. The impaction can be as subtle as a small increase in density or irregularity along the cuboid–fourth or cuboid–fifth metatarsal articulations, or it can be as obvious as a true "nutcracker" injury when the cuboid buckles in fracture along its midaxis because of lateral compression.[133] The impaction can be intra- or extra-articular and can be associated with lateral subluxation or even dislocation of the midtarsal joint. Remember that the lateral and medial columns of the foot work in concert, much like the anatomy of the pelvis. It is difficult, if not impossible to have severe compression on the lateral side (as in this case) without similar disruption (through the caspuloligamentous structures, joints, or fractures) along the medial side. For example, Hunter and Sangeorzan have described an associated navicular avulsion fracture or posterior tibial tendon tear in conjunction with this injury.[140] This situation is also true in reverse, and as such, any injury to the normally quite rigid and resistant midfoot should alert the physician to look on all sides of the foot for concomitant damage. Midfoot fractures have been reported to result from forced eversion, inversion, plantar flexion or dorsiflexion, or crushing of the foot. Such injury patterns typically require a fair amount of force to disrupt the extremely stable midfoot complex.

Cuneiform fractures are unusual, especially in isolation.[248] When they do occur, they generally involve the medial cuneiform, but most commonly a more global midfoot injury complex is present as part of a Lisfranc disruption.[137] As such, the presence of a cuneiform fracture should spawn efforts to carefully evaluate and identify concomitant fractures or instability patterns. When they do occur in isolation, they often result from a crush injury or direct impact, as opposed to the high-energy mechanisms responsible for the more diffuse injury patterns.

## TREATMENT

Lateral column sprains without evidence of articular incongruity or instability and small impaction fractures either within the substance of the cuboid or along its fourth and fifth metatarsal articulations should be treated conservatively. Short leg casting, removable CAM walker immobilization, or even postoperative wooden shoe wear is appropriate under these circumstances; both the choice and duration of treatment are dependent on patient symptoms, which can last from weeks to months.

Surgical intervention is indicated for severely displaced or impacted cuboid fractures and for those with significant intra-articular involvement or one in which any of these injuries is associated with articular incongruity along the medial column because of relative shortening or displacement laterally. If residual shortening or instability of the lateral column is left unaddressed, significant long-term disability can result.[191] The best outcomes in these circumstances are probably obtained with reestablishment of articular congruity and length, bone grafting, and stable ORIF.[292] Lateral dislocations in the forefoot may be reduced by placement of a small distractor that reaches from the calcaneus to the base of the fifth metatarsal on the lateral side of the foot. Distraction not only reduces the fracture but also dislodges impacted fracture fragments in the cuboid region and helps restore length and normal alignment of the lateral column.[42] Restoration of length in the cuboid after a compression injury is essential to reestablish normal alignment of the foot and preserve the arch (Fig. 60–57). Autogenous bone grafting or use of a similar bone substitute such as morselized allograft is usually required to fill the gaps created in the tarsal bone after distraction and disimpaction along the articular surface. Grafting is performed after articular reduction with K-wire fixation and verification of anatomic alignment by C-arm visualization. Either an oblique Ollier approach or, preferably, a longitudinal lateral approach can be used in the midfoot to access both the cuboid and the bases of the fourth and fifth metatarsals for evaluation. Care must be taken to avoid the sural nerve and peroneal tendons in the course of this approach, which are typically brought plantar-ward during the course of exposure as the extensor digitorum brevis is brought dorsally. Sural nerve injury is a common complication of this surgery and should be avoided. After reduction of significantly impacted or displaced cuboid fractures, *grafting* (as though one were treating a pilon fracture of the ankle) *is imperative* to provide articular buttressing and help maintain length. Fixation can then be achieved with small 2.0-mm minifragment T plates faced juxta-articularly along the site of injury and extending proximally along the cuboid beyond the graft site to maintain length of the lateral column as a bridging plate (Fig. 60–58). These plates are also low profile and infrequently require removal as a result of peroneal or sural irritation if exposure was meticulous. In rare cases of severe comminution or post-traumatic arthrosis of the calcaneocuboid joint, it can be fused with reasonable results and some loss of hindfoot motion.[10, 291] Fusion of the articulation of the cuboid and fourth and fifth metatarsals is poorly tolerated and should be avoided. In the event that these joints become progressively symptom-

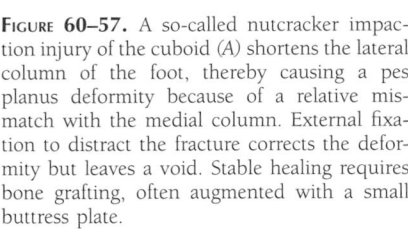

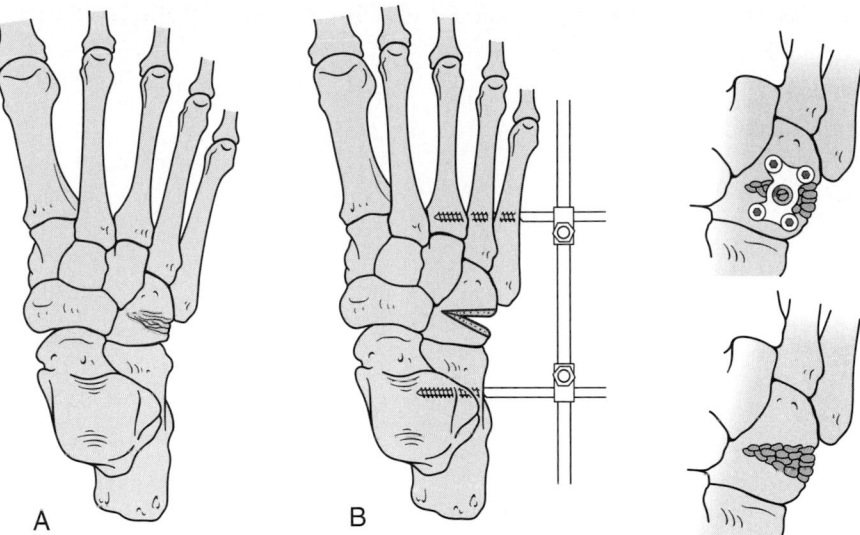

**FIGURE 60–57.** A so-called nutcracker impaction injury of the cuboid (*A*) shortens the lateral column of the foot, thereby causing a pes planus deformity because of a relative mismatch with the medial column. External fixation to distract the fracture corrects the deformity but leaves a void. Stable healing requires bone grafting, often augmented with a small buttress plate.

atic, they can be salvaged with resectional arthroplasty and interposition of fat, muscle, or tendon. In general, however, arthrosis along the lateral column articulations is better tolerated than along their medial equivalents.

Irregularity beneath the cuboid along the cuboid tunnel should also be evaluated at the time of surgery or corrected operatively if identified by preoperative assessment or CT scan. This irregularity can be the result of fracture displacement or joint subluxation and can give rise to peroneal (longus) tenosynovitis, scarring, tearing, or symptomatic pain at the accessory bone or its articulation beneath the cuboid (Fig. 60–59). Such a syndrome is better known as painful os peroneum syndrome or cuboid syndrome and can be more debilitating than any intra-articular pathology over the long term.[316] In fact, in our experience, post-traumatic arthrosis of the calcaneocuboid or cuboid-metatarsal articulations is frequently well tolerated by patients. These joints seem to be very forgiving. Any significant displacement or subluxation of the cuboid

at this level warrants open reduction of the articular surface and joint, as well as appropriate débridement of the cuboid canal plantarly. At the same time, the peroneus longus should be inspected, and in the 10% of individuals with an os peroneum, normal tracking and continuity of this surface should be ensured. Minimal or asymptomatic amounts of displacement or subluxation should be treated conservatively with a short course of below-knee casting. Excursion of the peroneus longus is best tested through recruitment of the peroneal by asking the patient to actively plantar flex the big toe against resistance. The examiner's thumbs can be placed beneath the first and fifth metatarsal heads to accurately determine whether excursion is present; thereafter, palpation along the peroneal groove and cuboid tunnel during this maneuver can provide an indirect indication of tracking through the tunnel. Any significant pain, locking, or clicking during this examination is suggestive of pathology along the canal and may warrant further evaluation with a CT scan.

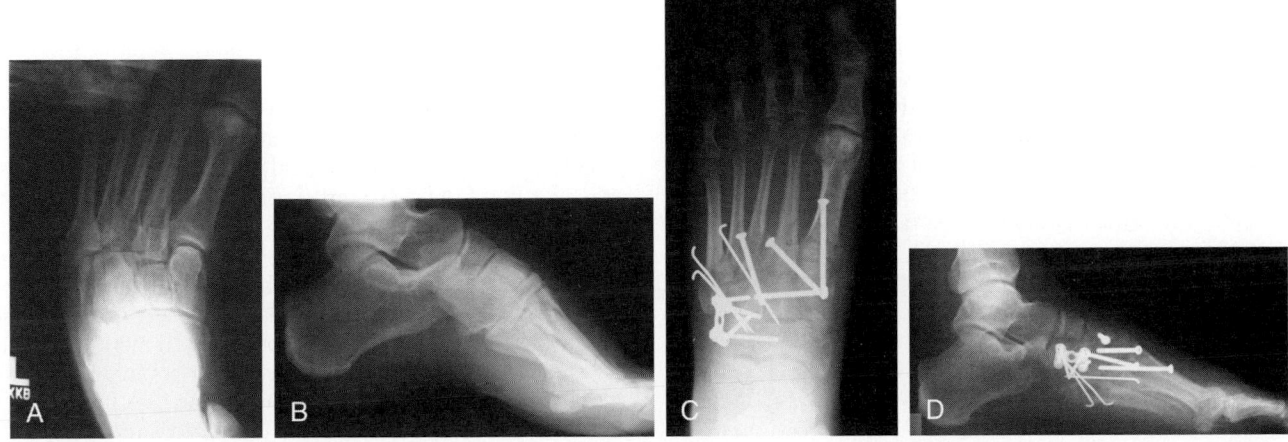

**FIGURE 60–58.** Cuboid fractures can occur alone or in combination with other midfoot or forefoot injury. This patient sustained a Lisfranc injury that included direct crushing of the cuboid; open reduction plus internal fixation, bone graft, and a lateral plate were required to reduce the "blowout" component of this fracture. Generally, all components of these combined injuries should receive stable fixation.

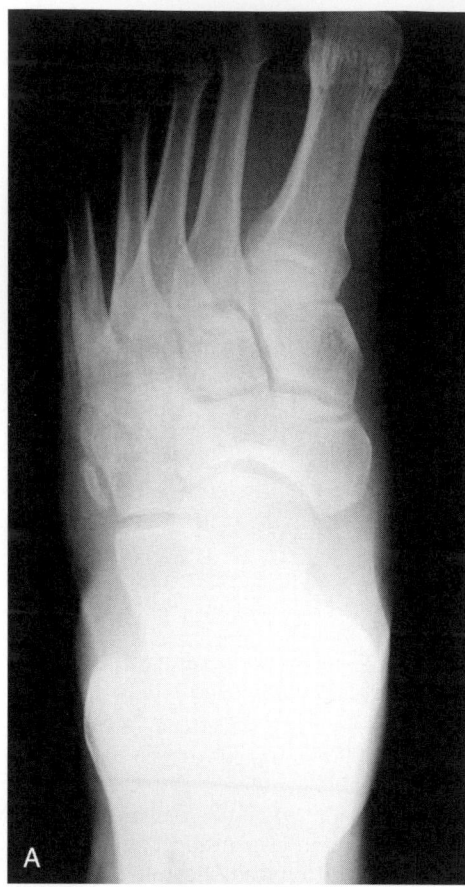 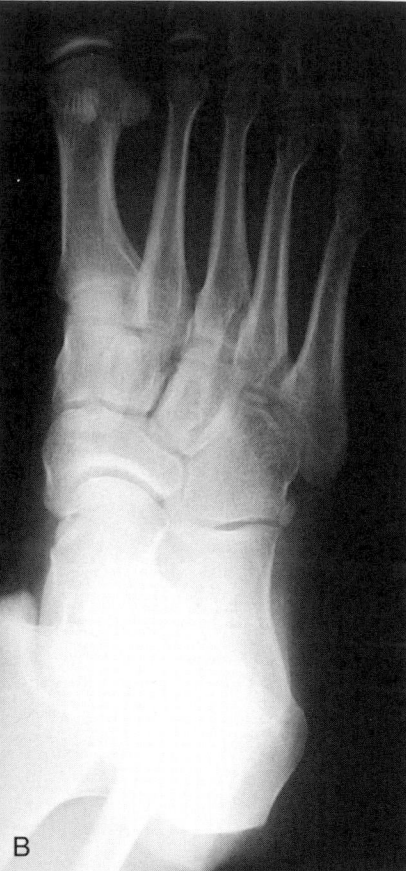

**FIGURE 60–59.** Painful os peroneum syndrome is a recently recognized post-traumatic entity that results in pain along the cuboid tunnel and peroneus longus tendon. It often responds to a RICE (rest, ice, compression, elevation) protocol along with a nonsteroidal anti-inflammatory drug or an injection, but in some cases, excision of the painful accessory bone is necessary for symptomatic relief. This patient was involved in a high-speed motor vehicle crash and sustained a tension injury to the lateral column of the foot that resulted in fracture of the fifth metatarsal and probably a traction injury of the os peroneum. The metatarsal healed uneventfully and became asymptomatic at examination; however, pain persisted proximally in the region of the cuboid tunnel with weight bearing, and the patient had a positive provocative maneuver to peroneus longus stress. His follow-up radiographs suggested abnormal morphology of the os peroneum (*A*) not appreciated on the initial films or on the normal, contralateral side (*B*).

Excision can be performed at a later date when the condition is chronic, symptoms persist, or fibrous union of an os peroneum fracture has occurred.[253]

Treatment of high-energy instability patterns or fractures involving the cuneiforms is usually operative and has already been discussed in the section on TMT injury because these injuries are most typically identified in this scenario. Treatment of isolated closed fractures is usually casting unless the skin is at risk or the displacement is significant.[248] When surgical exposure is required, it can be performed through a medial utility incision between the anterior tibialis and the posterior tibialis or through a dorsal incision centered over the medial and middle cuneiforms. The latter approach should be exposed cautiously to avoid damage to the nearby neurovascular bundle of the deep peroneal nerve and dorsalis pedis artery. The anterior tibialis can be incarcerated in the naviculocuneiform joint when the disruption is significant, but it will require relocation before joint reduction. As with Lisfranc variants, fixation should be rigid with screws and kept in for at least 3 to 4 months to allow stable ligamentous healing.

## POSTOPERATIVE CARE AND REHABILITATION

Postoperatively, a right-angle splint or a padded cast is applied to the foot if significant swelling is anticipated. A soft compression dressing under a posterior plaster slab provides adequate immobilization, but we prefer to apply a standard padded short leg cast and use a minimal amount of plaster. After the cast is dry, a 1.0-cm strip is removed from the anterior section over the dorsum of the foot and anterior of the leg and expanded slightly over the instep. This gap allows the cast to accommodate edema and provides access to the underlying soft dressing if it also needs to be split because of swelling.

The patient is confined to bed exercise with the leg slightly elevated for 2 full days. The cast is then overwrapped lightly, and the patient is instructed in limited weight bearing (15 or 20 lb or the weight of the leg) on crutches, with most of the weight rested on the hindfoot. The cast and sutures are removed at the scheduled time, and a well-molded short leg walking cast is applied. Weight bearing is gradually increased, and more weight may be transferred to the anterior part of the foot over the next 8 to 10 weeks. After appropriate reduction and pinning, a pure tarsal dislocation is treated by casting for approximately 10 to 12 weeks. Fractures of the bases of the cuneiforms and midbody of the cuboid unite quickly, and the cast may be removed after 8 weeks in most cases. Primary fusion may be an alternative treatment of isolated dislocations in elderly patients, particularly on the medial side. The decision is more difficult laterally because some motion is required for proper gait.

After the second cast 6 to 8 weeks postsurgery, any K-wires placed across the fourth, fifth metatarsal–cuboid or any of the cuneiform articulations are removed, and the patient is allowed to bear partial weight on crutches while wearing elastic hose. Nonresistive range-of-motion exercises in the ankle and the foot are begun at this time. Full weight bearing may be started 2 weeks after the final cast has been removed. A custom semirigid insert is fabricated for the shoe, which is worn for at least a year or until full lower extremity strength has returned while maintaining the reduction achieved. Exercises against resistance are started to strengthen the ankle and subtalar joint, and the patient gradually returns to normal activities. Implant removal is delayed for at least 6 to 9 months because in many instances, ligamentous disruption will take at least this long to consolidate. Screw removal is usually performed on an outpatient basis for prominence of the screw head, if entertained at all. In many instances, the screws are left in permanently if asymptomatic.

# STRESS FRACTURES

Although stress fractures are by definition not truly the result of an acute traumatic episode, they are included in this chapter because of the frequency of their occurrence. They do in fact result from trauma, but it is typically repetitive microtrauma, that if singular in occurrence, would not be of sufficient force to generate an acute fracture. Over time, however, this persistent force leads to cumulative stress injury in bone whose resorptive and repair response (which can often take 2 to 4 weeks) cannot keep pace. Stress patterns in bone have increased in recent years as a result of not only the increased interest in personal fitness but also its popularity in older age groups whose bone stock is less capable of adapting to such stress.[80, 210] Stress fractures have been described in every bone of the lower extremity, including the pelvis, but they occur most commonly in the tibia, fibula, metatarsals, and navicular and less so in the hindfoot and sesamoids.[252] The second metatarsal remains the most common site, probably related to medial column shortening or instability of the first ray with transfer of stress to the therefore relatively or functionally longer second ray, a typical pattern in the so-called Morton foot.[218]

The differential diagnosis must include acute fracture, osseous tumor, infection, Paget's disease, rheumatoid arthritis or other metabolic bone disorders, crystalline disease, and shin splints. The vast majority of stress fractures in the lower extremity are the result of running. Stress fractures are given a very appropriate name, and the most important consideration in choosing a treatment regimen is determining the actual reason for why a sudden change in stress occurred. Although traumatic overuse is almost inevitably the cause, other predisposing factors must not be overlooked, including metabolic abnormalities,[124] calcium deficiency,[223] and amenorrhea in athletic females.[350] If these other factors are not corrected, the stress fracture may successfully heal over time, but the likelihood of its recurrence is still high. At best, such a complication can be very frustrating and time consuming for a patient; at worst, however, incomplete treatment or misdiagnosis can lead to completion or displacement of a fracture, which in some cases can have a devastating effect on the prognosis. Often, an underlying condition can be identified that over time contributed to the gradual overload, fatigue, and eventual "fracture" of the bone.

One of the nice things about the foot, compared with other parts of the body, is that even subtle pathologic changes are often magnified on clinical or radiographic examination because the foot is constantly subjected to high loads and must concomitantly obey the laws of physics. Thus, foot radiographs can demonstrate abnormal biomechanics by virtue of their ability to show what is being stressed and what is not. As a structure submitted to essentially constant weight bearing, the foot reacts very differently to even small degrees of malalignment that are easily tolerated, for example, in the hand or other non–weight-bearing or low-stress joints. Although plain radiographs can frequently be negative on gross inspection, subtle reactive changes such as sclerosis, linear cortical resorption or trabecular condensation, which can be transverse or oblique across the bone, and periostitis can often be found to identify the problem. Comparison views of the other foot under these circumstances are also very helpful. The diagnosis can also be made by repeating plain films 2 to 4 weeks after the initial evaluation, when they can be positive for a fracture or healing response. Occasionally, bone scan, CT, or MRI is required for definitive diagnosis. MRI is quite sensitive in identifying marrow edema on T2-weighted images or a linear area of low signal intensity on all images. One must be cautious to differentiate other causes of marrow edema, however, which can occur under myriad circumstances.

By history, the patient will typically be able to indicate a relatively focal area of pain in the foot that is associated with localized swelling; this area should correlate with a similar region of point tenderness on clinical examination. Frequently, patients have a prolonged prodrome of symptoms consisting of a dull ache in the area of the stress reaction that lasts weeks to months before an actual stress fracture of the bone occurs, at which point symptoms escalate and cause the patient to seek medical attention. On physical examination, areas of diffuse tenderness or pain in the foot are usually soft tissue mediated, such as in periostitis or tendonitis, and not the result of stress fracture. Alterations in the weight-bearing pattern of the foot can lead to stress fractures by inducing multiple biomechanical imbalances (picked up by the history or on physical examination), such as varus or valgus hindfoot malalignment, hyperpronation, peroneus longus overdrive or brevis weakness, or clawtoe and other deformities that keep the toes from contacting the ground to unload the metatarsal heads; alterations can also be induced by hormonal imbalances or by acute changes in training conditions (such as surfaces or regimen) or activity common in athletes (deconditioning injury). An individual description of these factors, however, is beyond the scope of this chapter. A good clinical examination and routine weight-bearing foot films or an axial sesamoid view (or both) can often identify most of these problems. The important point to remember is that these underlying conditions should be corrected at the same time that the fracture is repaired. Plain films are frequently negative in the early stage of this process (before 2 to 3 weeks), but repeat films taken shortly thereafter or those taken beyond the 2- to 3-week bone-remodeling process during a stress reaction or after a stress fracture can easily show diagnostic areas of callus. A bone scan or MRI is most helpful in diagnosis when repeated radiographs remain negative but suspicion of stress injury remains high.[295]

## Treatment

A symptomatic stress injury without fracture that is identified early can usually be successfully treated with a few weeks of protected weight-bearing ambulation, reduction in activity, and the RICE protocol. Either short leg casting or postoperative wooden shoe wear is an appropriate but less important adjunct in this recovery process. Gradual resumption of activity is allowed after symptoms resolve. Most foot stress fractures remain nondisplaced or minimally displaced and can be treated with activity restriction in a molded cast or orthosis, although pneumatic (CAM) walkers allow physical therapy mobilization and prevent atrophy and deconditioning. The vast majority of these injuries heal well but can require prolonged periods of rest and activity restriction. Occasionally, electrical stimulation can be useful for recalcitrant cases, but its value remains questionable in more difficult cases such as stress fractures of the sesamoid, navicular, or fifth metatarsal.[344] Anatomic reduction plus internal fixation is recommended in patients with a complete break or when the fracture is displaced. Intramedullary callus should be removed and a bone graft applied to encourage early union. A stress fracture may require a longer time to heal than an acute fracture, but normal distribution of weight in the forefoot can be ensured only after anatomic reconstruction has been performed and appropriate bony and soft tissue balance in the foot (including the hindfoot, midfoot, and forefoot) has been restored.

Treatment of high-risk foot stress fractures is dictated by their specific location, although the mainstay of treatment is always rest and elimination of the incipient cause (stress), immobilization, institution of dietary modification or metabolic treatment when necessary, and occasionally, surgery.[21] Some surgeons prefer the addition of electrical stimulation or electromagnetic field treatment as an adjunct to these methods for improving healing rates. Calcium or estrogen deficiency as a result of dietary or menstrual irregularities also needs to be identified. These deficiencies are often easily treated by supplementation with 1200 mg/day of calcium and 400 mg/day of vitamin D, a contraceptive regimen, or alendronate sodium.

Calcaneal stress fractures can be caused by many of the typical biomechanical abnormalities leading to stress injury, including trauma and mechanical overload (Fig. 60–60). They are best diagnosed by cupping the heel with one hand on each side and performing a manual compression test. Plain radiographs often denote a linear density perpendicular to the trabecular pattern of the tuber in adults or sclerotic abnormalities of the apophysis in adolescents (Sever's disease). Confirmation can be obtained by bone scan, CT, or in some cases, MRI. These problems can be chronic and debilitating and are best treated by rapid short leg cast immobilization in neutral for adults but with 5° of equinus for adolescents to relax the pull of the Achilles on the apophysis. Non–weight bearing

for 6 to 8 weeks is enforced, followed by a progressive return to activity/weight bearing with the use of cross-training and heel pads. Any contributory biomechanical factor must also be eliminated to prevent recurrence.

Talar stress fractures most commonly occur at the lateral process, but they can develop in the neck or body as well. They are very unusual, probably because of the density and strength of the bone found in the talus. Talar stress fractures typically cause sinus tarsi pain and result from abnormal stress induced by a pronatory or supinatory deformity or from a tarsal coalition that transfers undue stress to the talus,[26] most commonly hyperpronation, as found with lateral process impingement. Plain films are usually unremarkable, and CT or MRI is required for accurate diagnosis. Treatment is with 6 to 8 weeks of non–weight bearing in a short leg cast, followed by appropriate orthotic management. Navicular stress fractures are common, but often difficult to diagnose because of a very nondescript constellation of prodromal symptoms. These fractures are often related to overuse phenomena in athletes, but they can also be seen in diabetics or adolescents (Köhler's disease). Patients often have vague tenderness in the medial arch or anterior of the ankle, and they are frequently unable to identify a specific focal site. Point tenderness over the midnavicular region, known as the "N" sign, is a very helpful clinical indicator but must be specifically considered and evaluated for successful identification. The fractures can be identified on plain films as linear sagittal splits in the midbody of the navicular.[168] One must be careful to also look for calcaneonavicular coalition because it is sometimes a cause of navicular stress

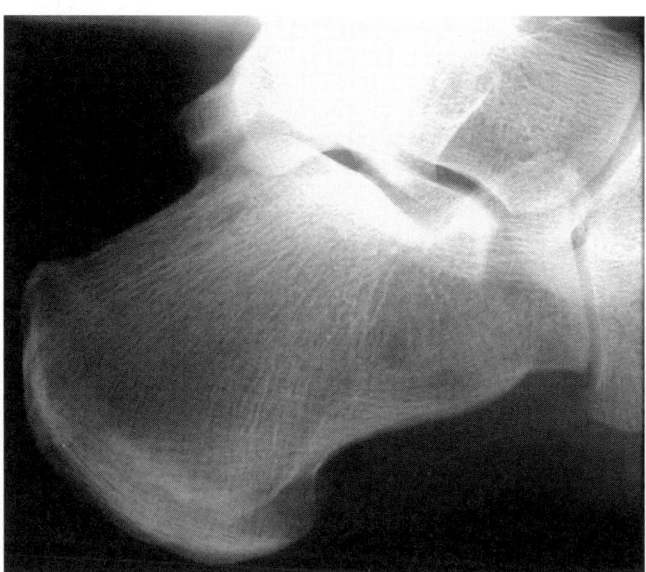

**Figure 60–60.** Calcaneal stress fractures are not common and are probably overdiagnosed in patients with recalcitrant "heel pain" after a positive bone scan, which is often simply abnormal as a result of plantar fasciitis or heel pad atrophy and edema. The most reliable way to diagnose a calcaneal stress fracture is (1) an appropriate history of repetitive overload on the heel or osteoporosis of the heel, (2) a positive compression test of the heel consisting of simply cupping it on each side with both hands and gently squeezing (this maneuver does not hurt a patient with other forms of heel pain at all), and (3) a lateral radiograph of the calcaneus with a linear density traversing the tuber consistent with compression (stress) fracture.

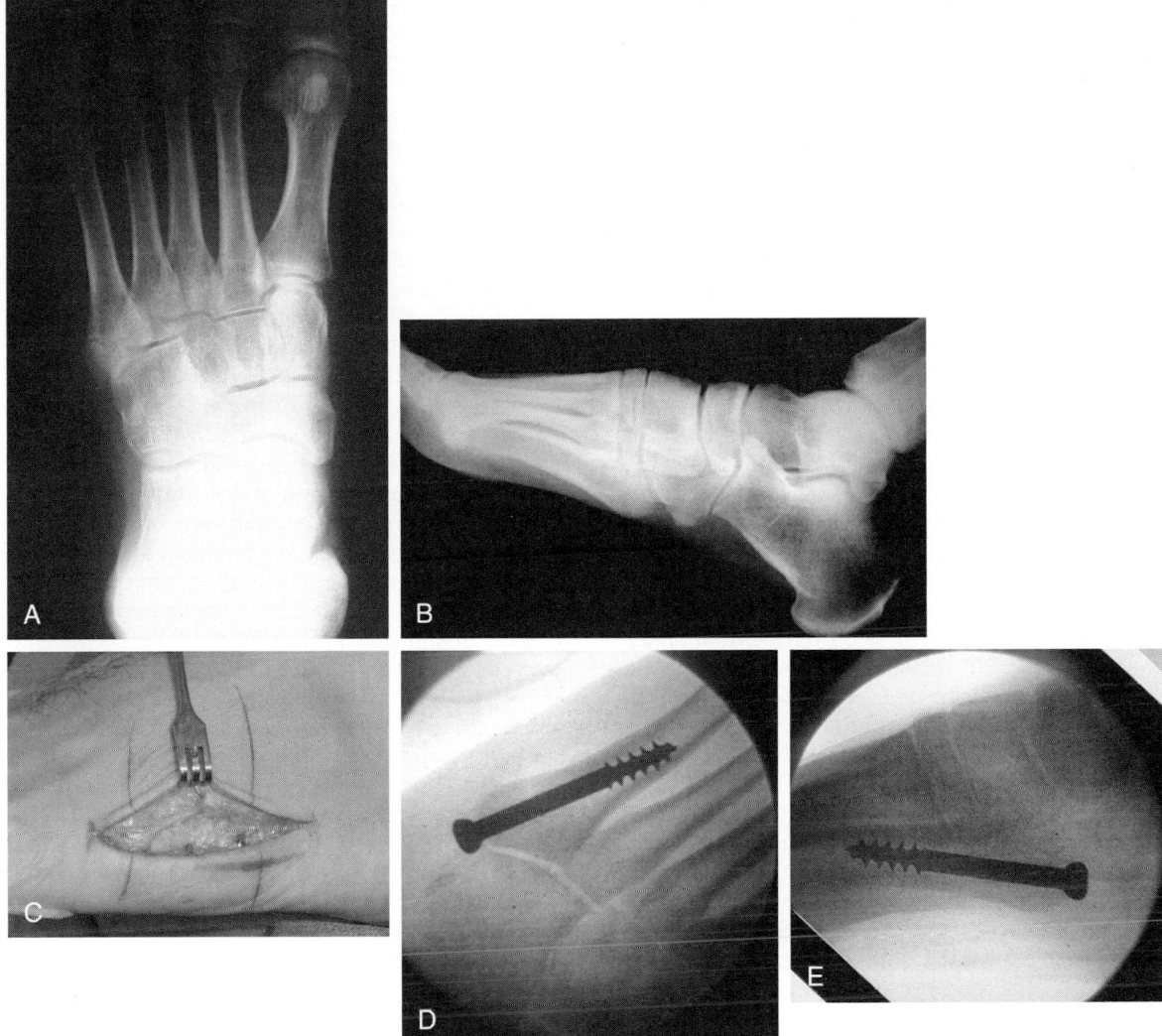

**FIGURE 60–61.** Metatarsal stress fractures are quite common, especially in runners or "weekend" athletes after a sudden change or burst in activity. They are easy to identify because of their localized swelling and point tenderness. Although initial radiographs can be negative, a high index of suspicion should prompt the clinician to have the patient protect the foot and return in 2 to 3 weeks, when repeat radiographs often show signs of early healing. This runner with a fifth metatarsal stress fracture (*A, B*) had symptoms for 2 years and treated himself with activity modification until he could no longer tolerate the pain. His nonunion was exposed laterally, fixed with a 6.5-mm lag screw inserted through a small split in the peroneus brevis tendon insertion, and augmented with a shear strain–relieved bone graft at the nonunion site (*C*). A bur was used to create this recipient site, with care taken to avoid injury to the dorsally located sural nerve, as seen here. Bone graft was taken from the calcaneus and inserted into the donor area, after which intraoperative films were obtained (*D, E*) to confirm appropriate screw placement.

fracture. The navicular midbody also corresponds to the area where force concentration is greatest and vascular inflow lowest. Frequently, similar adjunct radiologic studies are required if plain films are negative but clinical suspicion remains high. Non–weight bearing for 6 to 8 weeks in a short leg cast is usually all that is required if the diagnosis is made quickly, followed by orthotic management and progressive weight-bearing activity.[334] These fractures, if not detected initially, can proceed to rapid displacement, sclerosis, and midfoot collapse because of the forces across them, particularly in diabetics. ORIF with bone grafting should be considered in high-level athletes, patients with late progressive collapse, patients with displaced fractures, or those with chronic changes. Interestingly, stress injury very rarely develops in the other midfoot tarsal bones such as the cuboid or cuneiforms.

Cuboid stress fractures are rare.[16, 237] They probably occur from repetitive compression between the bases of the lateral metatarsals and the calcaneus as a result of forefoot abduction. They can also result from foot malalignment, such as hindfoot varus when persistent undue stress is borne by the lateral column during gait. This condition can be misdiagnosed as peroneal tendonitis.[16] Treatment is similar to that for all stress-related injuries to the foot: rest, activity modification, short-term immobilization, and gradual reintegration into weight-bearing activity as symptoms permit. If an anatomic abnormality is considered causative in this regard, it too should be addressed.

The metatarsals remain the most common site for stress injury in the foot (Fig. 60–61). Metatarsal stress fractures, particularly fractures of the fifth, are also common overuse injuries in athletes.[57] A prodrome of symptoms lasting weeks to months and accompanied by nonfocal forefoot swelling and pain often help differentiate these injuries from acute fractures. Because of the superficial nature of these bones, however, point tenderness can usually be elicited on clinical examination to identify the site of injury. The chance of successful union lessens with increased intramedullary sclerosis. Treatment varies from conservative cast immobilization, to functional bracing, to ORIF with intramedullary screws, depending on the chronicity of the fracture, radiographic changes, and predisposing host factors.

Sesamoid stress fractures have a greater preponderance in the medial sesamoid by virtue of the extra weight that it supports by being centered under the first metatarsal head.[344] These fractures most commonly result from repetitive dorsiflexion moments on the MTP joint. They must be distinguished from a bipartite sesamoid (which is also more common medially), chronic sesamoiditis, or osteochondritis. Comparison views of the opposite foot and bone scans are most valuable in making these determinations. Conservative treatment should be attempted initially. Non–weight-bearing immobilization for 6 to 8 weeks in 5° to 10° of foot dorsiflexion along with restricted dorsiflexion (neutral) of the great toe to relax the sesamoidal complex is necessary. Similar to the metatarsals, treatment of the fracture itself must be accompanied by elimination of any poorly supportive shoe wear, hard surfaces during training, predisposing changes in work- or home-related activity, or malalignment of the foot.[139]

Any patient with a stress fracture of the foot that is accompanied by osteopenia on radiographs and no other identifiable risk factor should be considered a candidate for bone density and metabolic profiles. Activity restriction is also a necessary adjunct for successful management. Surgery for unsuccessful, persistently symptomatic cases consists of either bone grafting or, preferably, complete sesamoid excision.

## METATARSAL FRACTURES

Metatarsal fractures are common injuries, but the amount of disability that they can produce is often underestimated. In high-performance athletes, a fifth metatarsal stress fracture can ruin performance or end a career. The five metatarsals all function differently from one another and require different types of treatment to heal with a satisfactory result. Fractures of the first metatarsal, the middle three metatarsals, and the fifth metatarsal are presented in separate sections to provide an adequate discussion of the various treatments. Displacement of metatarsal shaft fractures is unusual because of the tremendous muscle and ligamentous attachments surrounding them. On the other hand, fractures at the metatarsal neck separate the ligamentous attachments to the head from the muscular attachments of the shaft and thereby result in apex-dorsal angulation at the fracture site. Any metatarsal base fracture should be viewed with suspicion for Lisfranc disruption because of its proximity and inherent stability.[307] The metatarsals can be fractured

through many different mechanisms, although direct impact and twisting-type injuries are considered most frequent. Certain fracture patterns are common to different metatarsals by virtue of their location and surrounding soft tissue constraints, and they will be discussed in more detail later.

Soft tissue injuries, such as crushing or degloving injuries over the metatarsals, are not unusual because of the thin soft tissue envelope surrounding the dorsum of the foot. These injuries can require special skin coverage techniques. The procedure originally described by Ziv and associates[361] as split-thickness skin excision is helpful for degloving injuries. In this technique, avulsed skin is tacked loosely into position and thin split-thickness grafts are removed from areas of questionable viability. Viability of avulsed skin is demonstrated by dermal bleeding. If the skin in the injured area bleeds, it may be left in place, and the split-thickness graft is replaced on its bed. If bleeding does not occur, the dermal layer is excised and the split-thickness skin placed onto the underlying tissue. The temporoparietal fascial free-flap technique described by Sherman and co-workers[311] is recommended when a free graft is required. This type of tissue transfer is well vascularized and may be covered with a split-thickness skin graft. The chief advantage of this type of graft is that the foot heals with a normal contour and fits into normal shoes. Newer fascial grafts taken from more acceptable donor sites may be preferable.

Patients sustaining a metatarsal fracture usually complain of pain that they can isolate to a focal site in the forefoot. They typically have dorsal swelling because the thick fibrous septa distributed within the plantar skin pad are specialized tissue that permits little swelling regardless of the location of injury, except in the case of significant bony or soft tissue trauma. A careful and sequential assessment of each individual metatarsal and TMT joint is very reliable for identifying the site of injury. This evaluation can be performed both by longitudinal palpation along each shaft, or sagittal-plane "shuck" of each metatarsal with palpation of each TMT joint, and by axial loading of each toe. Particularly in the acute setting, this examination has been an accurate way of locating the site of injury along the metatarsal—its TMT joint, shaft, neck, head, or MTP joint. Careful and serial assessment of neurovascular status should be performed in such patients because of the vulnerability of these structures across the superficial arch and between the adjacent metatarsals as they course through the foot.[309] The standard set of non–weight-bearing foot radiographs in the AP, lateral, and oblique projections is sufficient for diagnosing metatarsal fractures. Radiographs of the forefoot or a single toe are inadequate because they often miss the entire zone of injury and do not allow the physician to assess for concomitant fractures or malalignment of adjacent joints.

Fractures through the shafts are frequently minimally displaced because of the abundance of balanced soft tissue constraints (intrinsic interosseous muscles and ligaments) around the bones, particularly when these fractures occur within the central rays of the foot. Fractures of the metatarsal necks can result in proximal and plantar displacement requiring operative intervention as a result of pull of the extrinsic tendons, although mediolateral displacement is unusual because of the strong intermetatarsal ligaments.[310] Metatarsal head fractures can also occasionally require operative intervention because the fracture line separates the head from any bony, muscular, or capsuloligamentous support, thus relying only on the intrinsic stability of the fracture and adjacent toes to prevent displacement. These latter fractures are often the result of a direct impact or transverse force across the foot that causes either an abduction or adduction force through this region. Multiple fractures in this case are not unusual and generally heal with minimal difficulty in 6 to 8 weeks if alignment can be maintained by either operative or nonoperative means.

The literature discussing indications for the treatment of metatarsal fractures or their long-term outcome is limited, and much of our decision-making processes have been based on anecdotal experience. Although most metatarsal fractures are effectively treated conservatively, surgery is typically considered in the face of severe displacement, multiple fractures, intra-articular injury, open wounds, compartment syndrome, skin at risk, significant sagittal displacement in any ray, or significant transverse displacement in the border rays. Ideal fixation is usually with axial intramedullary K-wires, if possible, because of their ease of use and limited exposure/soft tissue disruption. In general, plate fixation is required when length or rotation is unstable. Occasionally, an intramedullary screw can be used for fixation, particularly for the fifth ray. The biggest pitfall in treating metatarsal fractures by open or closed means remains sagittal plane angulation (either dorsal or plantar) because it is least tolerated and most likely to result in intolerable symptoms in the weight-bearing foot. When in doubt, do not forget that open reduction plus rigid internal fixation is the most precise and most reliable in the long term. It is much easier to accomplish such treatment initially than have to correct it after the fact, when suboptimal healing has already taken place.

# First Metatarsal

## ANATOMY

The first metatarsal is unique in several ways. It is considerably wider, shorter, and stronger than the lesser metatarsals. It is also slightly more mobile because the ligaments that attach to its base are less extensive and it has had to evolve from the mobility of a thumb into the stability of a great toe. This process remains in a state of continued transformation in humans, and although the medial metatarsal heads normally bear more weight than the lateral ones do, such is frequently found to not be the case in the pathologic situation of medial column hypermobility. It also does not have the same stout transverse intermetatarsal ligament at the webspace between adjacent metatarsal necks that the other lesser metatarsals do. Two powerful extrinsic muscles that attach into the first metatarsal influence its position and that of the entire forefoot. The first is the anterior tibial tendon, which attaches to a tubercle on the inferomedial base of the first metatarsal. Its function is to elevate the first metatarsal and

supinate the forefoot. The second is the peroneus longus, which attaches to a tubercle on the proximal lateral base of the first metatarsal. The peroneus longus plantar flexes the first metatarsal and pronates the forefoot. Both these muscles help stabilize the longitudinal arch.

The first metatarsal bears approximately one third of the body's weight through the forefoot on two subjacent sesamoid bones, a distinctly disproportionate amount for its size. The sesamoids are held in position under the head of the first metatarsal by the medial and lateral flexor brevis muscles, which originate in the ligaments and tendon sheaths underneath the cuneiforms. Two heads of the adductor hallucis muscle attach into the lateral side of the fibular sesamoid, and a section of the abductor hallucis inserts into the medial side of the tibial sesamoid. The sesamoids are also tethered to the deep transverse intermetatarsal ligament, and their relation to the lesser metatarsals is fixed. Thus, a small malalignment can have potentially huge effects on weight-bearing distribution and ambulation. Very little displacement should be tolerated in either the coronal or, in particular, the sagittal plane.

Injuries to the first metatarsal are frequently caused by directly applied force, and open or comminuted fracture patterns are common. Displacement of the first metatarsal head in any direction disturbs the major weight-bearing complex of the anterior portion of the foot and impairs forefoot function. Musculoskeletal trauma protocols call for anatomic fixation of all open fractures and all fractures that threaten joint function directly or indirectly. Displaced fractures of the first metatarsal are included in this category.

The goal of ORIF in a first metatarsal fracture is to maintain normal distribution of weight under all the metatarsal heads. In normal feet, the body's total weight is distributed over six contact points: the two sesamoids under the first metatarsal head and the four lesser metatarsal heads. Weight bearing is not strictly divided among the six contact points, and the actual distribution may vary slightly among individuals. The second and third metatarsals frequently bear more weight than the fourth and fifth. Morton's concept that the postural and anatomic axes of the forefoot are in balance when half the weight goes to the first and second metatarsal heads (three points) and half goes to the third, fourth, and fifth metatarsal heads (three points) is probably quite accurate.[218]

## NONOPERATIVE MANAGEMENT

Nondisplaced or minimally displaced first metatarsal fractures can be successfully treated in a short leg cast with gradually progressive weight bearing for 4 weeks. If they are considered very stable injuries at the time of initial evaluation, consideration can be given to either a CAM walker boot or even a wooden rocker shoe initially. In the latter case, follow-up should perhaps be more regimented to identify the possibility of significant displacement early, although some authors have suggested that a more aggressive mobilization protocol actually enhances healing and recovery and that we are often overtreating these injuries based on the rarity of adverse sequelae with such fracture patterns.[158] Regardless of which method of treatment is chosen by the physician and the patient, weaning into a regular well-cushioned shoe should take place as soon as symptoms permit. These injuries usually do quite well with little functional deficit, and the patient should be encouraged to engage in active and passive motion exercises of the toes during this recovery process.

## OPERATIVE MANAGEMENT

Metatarsal fracture displacement should be least tolerated in the first ray. Although attention need not be paid to moderate transverse plane displacement of the second, third, or fourth rays (except in the case of multiple ray involvement), the fifth and, in particular, the first ray must be carefully evaluated for displacement in either the transverse or the sagittal plane because of their location and the well-documented ill effects of malunion on shoe fitting and weight bearing long-term.[150] The anatomy of the first metatarsal limits the types of fixation that are suitable for a fracture in this area. The diaphysis of the first metatarsal is small in relation to those in the long bones, and the thin layer of soft tissue surrounding it necessitates the use of a low-profile device. A one-third tubular plate with 3.5-mm cortical screws or a 2.7-mm dynamic compression or reconstruction plate with 2.7-mm screws is ideally suited for fixation of fractures in this area (Fig. 60–62). A low-profile one-quarter tubular plate held by 2.7-mm screws is appropriate for smaller bones. The position of the plate on the metatarsal is determined by the kind of injury that has been sustained and by placement of the incision. In general, placement of a plate on the tension side of a metatarsal bone is unfortunately not possible. K-wire fixation can also be used in adolescents with open growth plates, and occasionally just lag screw fixation with 2.4-, 2.7-, or 3.5-mm cortical screws is indicated for long spiral fractures. These screws are superior to cancellous or partially threaded screws for two reasons: first, the bone is primarily cortical in nature with little metaphyseal bone, and second, it is typically hard to judge the thickness of the bone on either side of the fracture to ensure that the full length of the threaded screw is across the fracture site for optimal lag fixation and compression. Thus, it is more prudent to use a cortical screw drilled in lag fashion, and the number of threads on these screws can generate impressive compression and rigid fixation when placed in this manner.

Finally, bridged fixation across the TMT joint or external fixation is occasionally needed. In the former case, the principle in treatment remains maintenance of both length and plantar presence of the first metatarsal, which are extremely important for proper stress distribution during ambulation. Sometimes with a very comminuted shaft fracture or one that involves the TMT joint to an extent that it cannot be salvaged, it is best to simply bridge this area in proper alignment to allow healing. This situation is not uncommon in severe trauma or Lisfranc injury variants. These patients may eventually require TMT fusion, and although it can be done at the time of initial surgery if the periarticular comminution is manageable, it can also be easily performed at a later date after consolidation has occurred and the soft tissues are more amenable to a more involved procedure. Sacrificing this joint has little if any effect on foot function, and in fact it

can be argued that the instability of this ray, as opposed to stiffness, accounts for much of the pathology that we see in some common foot deformities such as hallux valgus and transfer metatarsalgia. When the proximal joint requires bridging but the joint is in good condition, the hardware can either be removed at a later date or simply be left in, although the former is preferable. In this case, screw fixation occurs in a dorsal-to-plantar direction both above

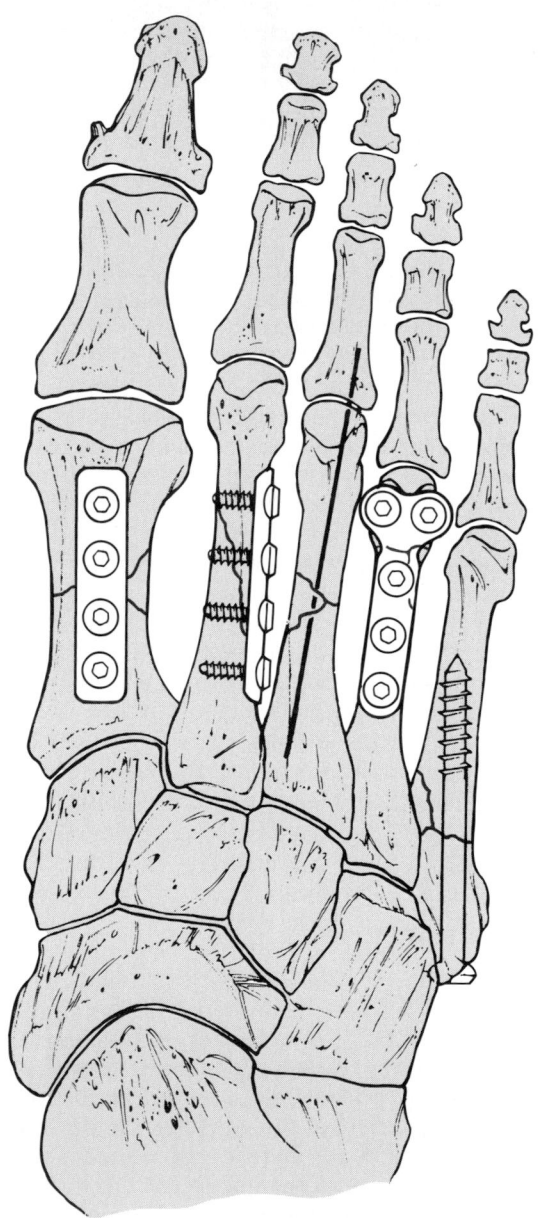

**Figure 60–62.** Various fixation devices for metatarsal fractures. A one-third tubular plate placed either straight dorsally or slightly dorsomedially is suitable for fixation of a displaced fracture of the first metatarsal. A quarter-tubular plate may be used for fixation of a fracture or an osteotomy in a second metatarsal fracture with significant displacement. It may be placed either straight dorsally or dorsolaterally, as depicted here. K-wires are ideal for fixation of midshaft fractures in the lesser metatarsals. A quarter-tubular T plate and 2.7-mm screws may be used to stabilize an extremely distal neck fracture in a lesser metatarsal. A straight quarter-tubular plate with four holes may be used for fixation of an osteotomy. A malleolar screw, seen here in the fifth metatarsal, may be used for fixation in a typical Jones fracture, to treat delayed union, or for acute fixation in a high-performance athlete.

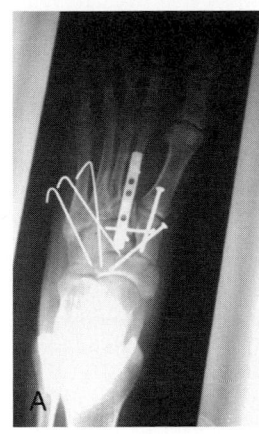
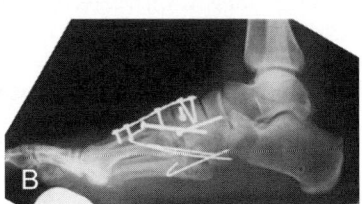

**FIGURE 60–63.** When instability of the tarsometatarsal (TMT) joint or proximal comminution accompanies a metatarsal fracture, it is often prudent to bridge fixation across the TMT joint, particularly for the first ray. It can be done with a one-third or one-quarter tubular, 2.7-mm reconstruction, or 3.5-mm dynamic compression plate The postoperative radiographs here represent the fixation required for the patient seen in Figure 60–70, where the second metatarsal basilar comminution precluded maintenance of length, rotation, and alignment with screws alone. Thus, a bridging plate was used and the screws kept above and below the TMT joint to avoid further injury to the joint. The plate is not applied in compression (even if a dynamic compression plate is used) unless primary fusion of the TMT joint is desired because of the severity of the injury. Postoperative stiffness in either case is not an issue in these joints because they require some degree of stiffness to impart midfoot stability during gait.

and below the joint, but not across it. Proper rotation of the metatarsal, established by using the great toe and imaging as a guide, is also important in these circumstances to allow congruent motion of the sesamoidal apparatus with the metatarsal head during gait (Fig. 60–63). Fixation of the first ray is typically performed through a longitudinal approach between the first and second rays, with care taken to not injure the superficial peroneal nerve in the subcutaneous tissue or the deep peroneal nerve and dorsalis pedis artery with its first intermetatarsal branch in the deeper planes. This approach is very versatile and can concomitantly be used for decompression of a compartment syndrome, cuneiform injury, TMT instability, or second metatarsal fracture. It can be combined with or supplanted by a medial utility approach along the midaxial aspect of the medial column as well, another very safe and even more extensile approach that can access the entire medial aspect of the foot and ankle. In this case, care must be taken to avoid injury to the saphenous vein and nerve, which should be brought dorsal in the dissection, because all tributaries travel in a dorsal-to-plantar direction. These venous branches, particularly the deeper ones forming part of the deep venous plexus, can bleed significantly and retract into the depths of the foot if care is not taken to expose and cauterize them as they are identified. Though rarely a problem, they can be difficult to access after inadvertent laceration if they retract, and hematoma can develop if these vessels are not identified.

Any dorsal foot incisions such as these in the setting of traumatic injury should be carefully closed in layered fashion with a no-touch technique on the skin. Skin

retraction during the procedure should also be minimized, and the paratenon of the extensors should not be opened to minimize contracture and scarring. Dissection should always be directed beneath the fascial layer above the extensor tendons to protect skin perfusion above, and after any periarticular capsular closure with a 4–0 monofilament absorbable suture, the facial layer can be reapproximated with similar 3–0 suture to relieve tension. Thereafter, the skin can be closed with a running 3–0 monofilament nylon or with interrupted vertical mattress sutures. If a flap has questionable viability, Donati sutures should be used.

## POSTOPERATIVE MANAGEMENT

Postoperatively, patients should be placed in a short leg splint, well padded, to permit some swelling. Intrinsic muscle exercises incorporating early active and passive motion of the first MTP joint are performed in the postoperative splint, which holds the ankle in correct position during healing and helps control dependent edema. The dorsal trim line of the splint must not interfere with dorsiflexion of the MTP joint on the distal side. Sutures can be removed 2 to 3 weeks postoperatively, during which time weight-of-leg weight bearing can be permitted through the heel only. A lightweight short leg cast can then be applied for an additional 4 weeks to allow gradual and progressive weight bearing with range of motion of the great toe, after which the patient can be placed in a postoperative hard-soled rocker shoe if clinical and radiographic parameters suggest early healing. Physical therapy at this time can be rapidly advanced. Most of these injuries will heal in 8 to 12 weeks and usually have a good functional outcome.

## Second, Third, and Fourth Metatarsals

A traumatic fracture in the second, third, or fourth metatarsal is usually caused by direct application of force. The resulting fracture is frequently open with a comminuted or transverse fracture pattern. Indirect force such as twisting is also a common mechanism of fracture in the middle metatarsals and usually results in a spiral fracture pattern. In most cases, fracture displacement in a middle metatarsal is minimal and the injury heals quickly, so the likelihood of a serious complication is frequently overestimated. However, complications such as shortening may occur, although problems may not be evident until many months after the original injury. As little as 2 to 4 mm of elevation or shortening in a metatarsal can exacerbate metatarsalgia or produce intractable plantar keratoses in the metatarsal heads that still bear weight.[299] Lesser metatarsal neck fractures should be openly pinned if plantar angulation develops to prevent weight-bearing callosities or transfer lesions. Plantar and proximal migration is not unusual in these injuries because of the strong pull of the flexors, their proximity to the fracture site, and the thin cross-sectional area of the metatarsal necks predisposing to instability.[183] When not significantly displaced, they can be similarly treated with use of a wooden-soled or semirigid rocker-bottom shoe or sneaker and early weight bearing. Lesser metatarsal head fractures are usually minimally displaced and not amenable to significant improvement with operative intervention. Closed treatment and reduction with finger traps can be valuable in the presence of significant displacement. K-wire fixation is usually necessary under these circumstances. Although some authors accept closed management for metatarsal shaft fractures with up to 4 mm of displacement and 10° of angulation, such treatment can lead to significant long-term disability in the form of metatarsalgia or intractable plantar keratoses.[309] Thus, these parameters are probably more appropriately accepted in the coronal as opposed to the sagittal plane. Even transverse plane motion can lead to pain as a result of interdigital nerve impingement.[309] Gross displacement of all the metatarsal heads through, for example, unilateral metatarsal neck fractures can be successfully treated with nonoperative management if all the metatarsal heads move in the same direction and their relationship to the weight-bearing surface and to each other remains unchanged.

## NONOPERATIVE MANAGEMENT

To ensure a good prognosis, a metatarsal fracture must be reduced anatomically, and the length, rotation, and declination of the metatarsal must be maintained throughout healing. As mentioned earlier, hanging of the toes in finger traps with gravity reduction from the weight of the leg is often helpful in facilitating reduction of initially displaced fractures and avoiding surgery. Cast immobilization is appropriate for all closed, undisplaced, or minimally displaced lesser metatarsal fractures. Healing is typically evident 4 to 6 weeks after injury, at which point the patient can be placed in a wooden-soled postoperative or rigid-soled well-cushioned shoe. Such management can also be considered as an initial form of treatment if the fracture pattern is deemed stable and not associated with multiple forefoot fractures that might increase the instability of reduction.[217]

## OPERATIVE MANAGEMENT

Intramedullary K-wire fixation is frequently used in open fractures and produces satisfactory results if the wire is placed correctly. For fixation of an open or displaced fracture in a single middle metatarsal, a K-wire is run into the medullary canal of the distal segment, through the metatarsal head and the base of the phalanx, and out through the plantar skin at the base of the toe. It is driven back into the proximal fragment when the fracture is reduced (Fig. 60–64). This technique has some inherent problems. Plantar angulation of the K-wire in the distal fragment may over-reduce or elevate the head of the metatarsal when the wire is drilled retrograde into the proximal fragment. To avoid excessive angulation and over-reduction, the K-wire is routed distally just within and parallel to the dorsal cortex, through the MTP joint, and out the plantar surface of the proximal phalanx. The forefoot must be palpated carefully at the end of the operation to verify that the metatarsal head is not elevated or depressed in relation to the other metatarsal heads. Alternatively, DeLee has described a means of closed

manipulation and transverse K-wire fixation of the distal fracture fragment to its adjacent metatarsal, particularly for the fifth ray.[65]

Closed reduction and K-wire fixation of closed, displaced lesser metatarsal shaft fractures can be more difficult than is usually anticipated. An alternative technique engages fixation from a distal-to-proximal direction, ideally with a starting point through one of the webspaces along the flare of the condyle beyond the metatarsal neck. C-arm imaging is frequently required to facilitate this process to prevent multiple passes and avoid injury to the neurovascular bundle. Because of this risk, it is not recommended that this technique be tried on both sides of a given metatarsal. Vascular embarrassment is unusual, but possible. Regardless of the closed method, fixation wires should be at least 0.062 inch in size to minimize the chance of breakage, although in smaller bones, 0.045- or 0.054-inch wires are needed. With either

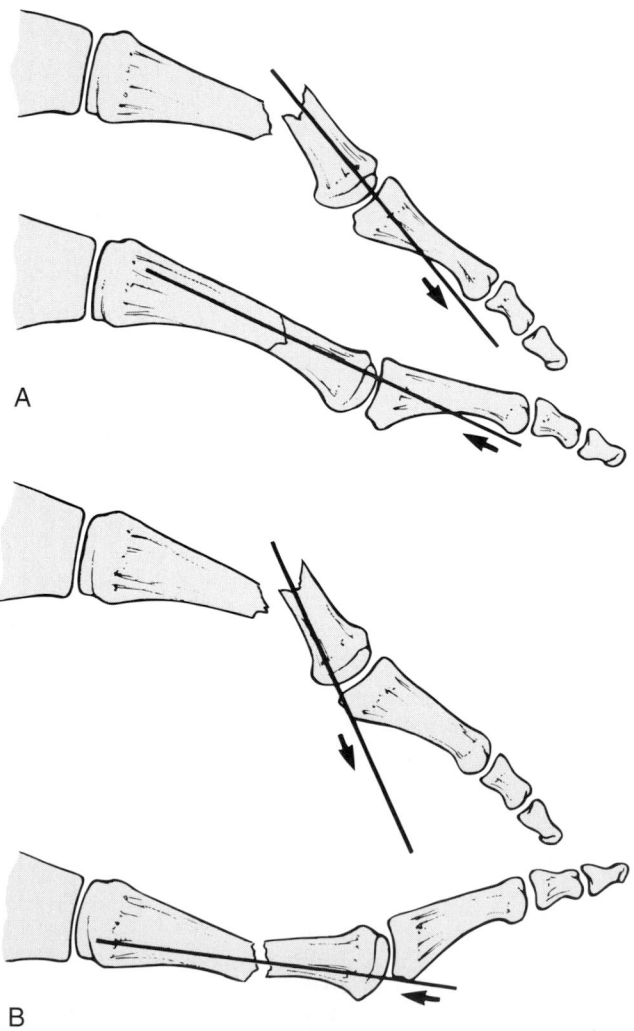

**FIGURE 60–64.** *A,* A K-wire is used to reduce and fix a metatarsal fracture. Note that the metatarsal head is not elevated. *B,* The K-wire elevates the distal metatarsal head when it is drilled back into the proximal fragment. This error commonly occurs when a surgeon tries to miss the phalanx in the metatarsophalangeal joint and inadvertently angles out too far plantar in the distal fragment. Fixation in this position produces malunion and, subsequently, metatarsalgia and a transfer lesion under the adjacent metatarsals.

the antegrade or retrograde approach, the wire must be aimed proximal and dorsal to match the normal declination of the metatarsal and not exit plantarly or dorsally. Usually, one K-wire provides adequate fixation, and it can be removed 4 to 6 weeks after injury, when early healing is evident. Another technique if these methods are not successful or cannot be performed because of the distal nature of some fractures (head, neck) is to start in the plantar aspect of the base of the proximal phalanx and pass the K-wire retrogradely across the MTP joint and into the metatarsal shaft. This technique is frequently facilitated by a stab incision dorsal to the metatarsal neck and the use of a freer elevator with C-arm guidance to manipulate these fragments into appropriate position. Longitudinal traction on the toe can help as well. The wire can also be inserted from the tip of the toe, which is much easier to do but also obviates early motion of the IP and MTP joints and can lead to some postoperative stiffness. Such stiffness is not a major problem if the toe is pinned in a slightly plantar position (maximally 10°) because the function of toes over evolution has become one of simple contact through the MTP joint to help unload the metatarsal heads and not so much one of grasp through the IP joints. However, some motion at these distal articulations to enhance traction and offload stress is, of course, always better than none. If the wire driver is placed on oscillate during introduction of the wire, the wire will have less tendency to exit the cortex while traversing the intramedullary canal of each bone. When these methods are insufficient to produce an anatomic result, consideration should be given to formal open plate fixation with minifragment 1.5- or 2.0-mm T, C, or straight-configured plate fixation. Alternatively, open reduction and K-wire fixation can also be considered, but if the joint needs to be formally opened for fixation, it may be more advantageous to plate it rigidly so that no joints are immobilized and early motion at all sites can begin as soon as possible. This scenario is typical for most metatarsal neck and head fractures if significantly displaced, shortened, or rotated.

If more than one middle metatarsal is broken, anatomic plate-and-screw fixation with or without a primary cancellous bone graft to equalize weight bearing under the metatarsal heads is recommended with any displacement greater that 1 to 2 mm, rotational abnormality of the toes, or gross shortening that is asymmetric and therefore changes the distal "parabolic" relationships of the metatarsal heads on an AP radiograph. A view of the opposite foot is frequently helpful in making this decision. Because of the intermetatarsal ligaments, however, shortening often cannot occur significantly in one metatarsal in comparison to the others. Thus, in the case of multiple metatarsal fractures, uniform shortening may be noted, but normal distal anatomic relationships are maintained. Because weight is borne in this area and most attention should therefore be directed here, such a case does not require any operative intervention. In addition to using the AP view, the best way to assess metatarsal positioning in or out of the operating room is to use an axial sesamoid view, which identifies any abnormal plantar displacement of one metatarsal with respect to another (Fig. 60–65). Both views are easy to obtain in an emergency department or operative setting. The decision for fixation should really

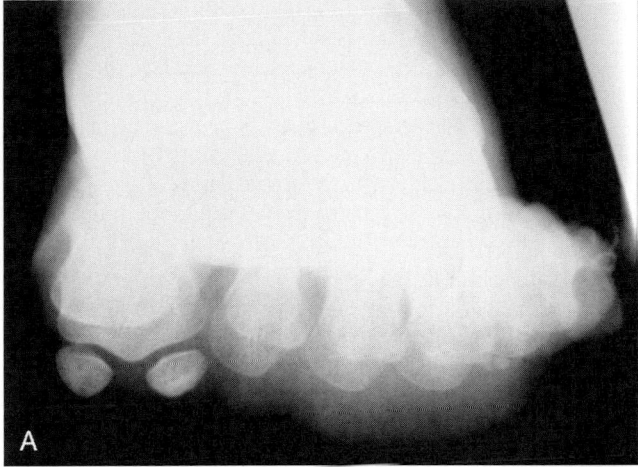

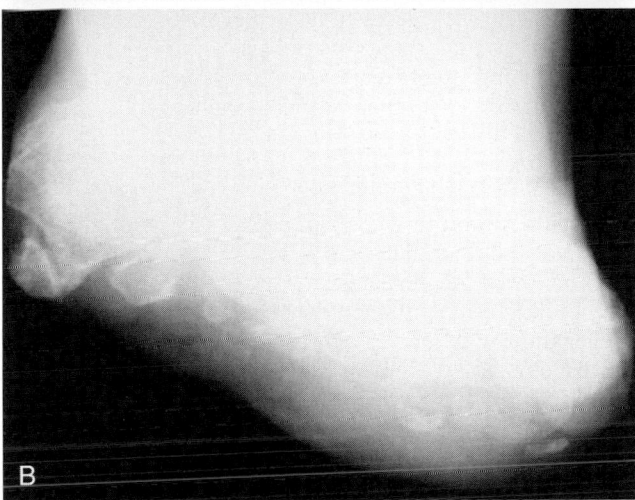

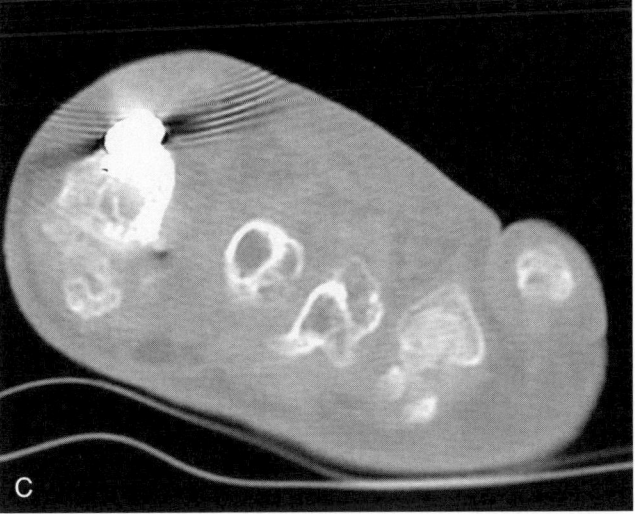

**FIGURE 60–65.** The axial sesamoid view (*A, normal*) is an underused and excellent way of evaluating the sesamoidal articulation beneath the first metatarsal, the plantar (ground) contact relationships between each of the metatarsal heads, or any pathology that exists at this level. It significantly improves the surgeon's ability to assess proper position of the metatarsals during fracture or joint reconstruction in the forefoot and can be taken either preoperatively or intraoperatively. The abnormal axial sesamoid radiograph (*B*) and respective computed tomographic cut (*C*) shown here demonstrate the pathologic relationship between the metatarsal heads in a patient who sustained a crush injury to the forefoot that resulted in multiple metatarsal shaft, neck, and head fractures; these injuries eventually led to deformity in the sagittal plane and transfer metatarsalgia. He required operative realignment to resolve his plantar discomfort.

depend more on the interrelationship and anatomic alignment of the metatarsal heads in the sagittal, transverse, and longitudinal planes rather than alignment more proximally in the forefoot.

Intra-articular metatarsal head fractures can usually be treated conservatively by closed reduction and application of a short leg cast for 3 to 4 weeks unless significant instability of the fracture or articular incongruity is present. In this circumstance, ORIF with K-wire fixation plus attention to the periarticular soft tissues to avoid avascular necrosis of the metatarsal head is indicated.[74] Bone grafting may be needed once the articular congruity is restored. K-wires can be removed in 4 weeks with early range of motion and mobilization.

## Stress Fractures of the Medial Four Metatarsals

Stress fractures of the metatarsals rarely occur as a result of the same acute trauma that causes most metatarsal injuries. A prodrome of symptoms is often accompanied by a preexistent deformity in the foot or extremity or an acute change in a patient's activity that alone would not normally be identified as causing a foot fracture. Thus, stress fractures of the metatarsals can result from various bony or soft tissue abnormalities that have been at work over a prolonged period before culminating in bony fracture. Some abnormalities can be identified on clinical examination, for example, lack of callus under the first metatarsal head (which should be bearing about one third of body weight) or abnormally large callus under the second head. Radiographically, one can also often depict incompetence of the first ray by significant shortening on the AP view or dorsiflexion through either a previous malunion or TMT sag on the lateral view. Meary's talus–first metatarsal line will be disrupted in this instance. Alternatively, the patient can have a Morton foot with an abnormally long second ray in relation to the first. Patients can be putting too much stress over a certain part of the foot (instead of equally distributing it) as a result of obesity, foot or leg malalignment, or a sudden change in activity level, shoe wear, or walking surface. Another common cause of stress fracture is a tight gastrocnemius, which forces too much weight onto the forefoot. This phenomenon is grossly underrecognized and can easily be identified by the Silfverskiöld test, which compares relative ankle dorsiflexion obtained when the foot is held neutrally reduced through the talonavicular joint and the knee is first straight and then brought to 90°. This muscle requires a gastrocnemius slide if it is found to be pathologically tight in patients with symptoms of chronic forefoot overload. Any overly long, dorsiflexed, plantar flexed, or otherwise translated metatarsal may bear too much weight or cause adjacent ones to do so if it becomes incompetent and may thus predispose to stress fracture. The pathoanatomy as well as the biology behind the causation of stress fractures is very different from that of a normal metatarsal fracture, and therefore treatment and recovery are also quite different. These concepts are discussed in more detail in the section on stress fractures.

## Fifth Metatarsal Fractures

The fifth metatarsal is unique in comparison to the other lesser metatarsals for a number of reasons: it is the only one with extrinsic tendinous attachments (namely, the peroneus brevis and tertius at its base), it has a strong ligamentous attachment of the plantar aponeurosis, and it enjoys little soft tissue coverage plantar-laterally. These differences have an impact on the mechanisms causing fracture, their location, their healing potential, and their duration of symptoms. Fifth metatarsal fractures account for almost one quarter of all metatarsal injuries.[128]

Four major groups of fractures involve the fifth metatarsal bone: basilar or avulsion fractures, metadiaphyseal (Jones) fractures, metadiaphyseal stress fractures, and diaphyseal fractures.[222, 262, 274] Each implies a separate causality, location, treatment, and prognosis[57] (Fig. 60–66). The former three represent the vast majority of fifth metatarsal fractures, which primarily occur in the proximal half of the ray. Dameron,[56] Kavanaugh and colleagues,[161] and Torg and associates[334] separately pointed out the many different types of injuries that can occur in the proximal end of the fifth metatarsal. Dameron, for example, divided the proximal half of the fifth ray into three distinct fracture zones: zone I comprised the styloid process (avulsion fracture), zone II comprised the metadiaphyseal region (Jones fracture), and zone III comprised the proximal diaphyseal region (stress fracture). Over 90% of the injuries in his study occurred in zone I. DeLee and co-workers have also classified these fractures[67]: type IA consists of acute, nondisplaced, metadiaphyseal fractures; type IB includes acute, comminuted metadiaphyseal fractures; type II consists of chronic metadiaphyseal fractures with either a clinical prodrome of symptoms or

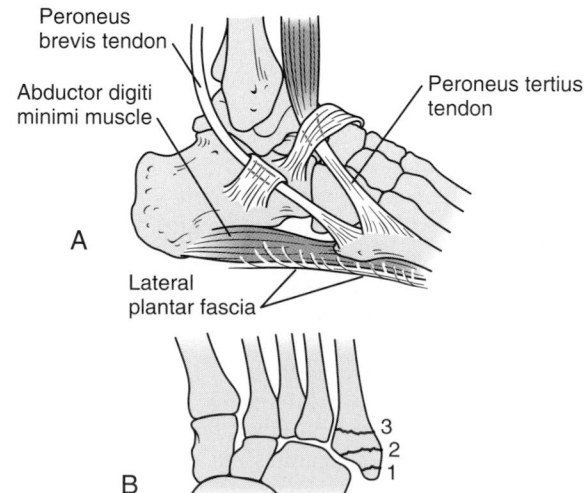

**FIGURE 60–66.** The base of the fifth metatarsal has a complex anatomy that probably accounts for the many variations in fracture location and outcome that we now appreciate. As shown in *A*, multiple forces are at work across a relatively short segment of bone by virtue of the several tendinous and fascial insertions. The watershed vascularity to the fifth metatarsal base and its propensity for load bearing also play a role. Note the three different fracture patterns in *B* and their respective involvement of either the fifth metatarsal styloid, the cuboid articulation, or the fourth metatarsal articulation.

radiologic evidence of stress reaction; type IIIA includes extra-articular avulsion fractures of the styloid process; and type IIIB consists of intra-articular avulsion fractures of the styloid process. Torg and colleagues' classification is discussed in the section on stress fractures. Although these classifications are helpful in diagnosing and understanding such injuries, opinions vary in the literature regarding how to best manage them, and historically, treatment decisions seem to really depend most on surgeon experience and host factors or expectations. These injuries must not be confused with accessory bones, which occur commonly in this region, such as the os peroneum located within the substance of the peroneus longus at the level of the cuboid tunnel or the os vesalianum located within the substance of the peroneus brevis as it courses lateral and superior to the peroneal tubercle of the calcaneus just proximal to the styloid of the fifth metatarsal base. Assessment of comparison views and radiographic margins of the bone in question can be helpful in this regard.

## AVULSION FRACTURES

The most common fracture that occurs in the fifth metatarsal is an avulsion of the proximal apophysis. This type of injury was once thought to be caused by avulsion of the fifth metatarsal by the peroneus brevis. Richli and Rosenthal[268] examined the mechanism of this injury and suggested that the avulsion is probably caused by the lateral plantar aponeurosis, which inserts proximal to the insertion of the peroneus brevis. Implication of the lateral plantar aponeurosis explains why fifth metatarsal fractures are seldom displaced. A number of authors, however, consider the peroneus brevis to be the major deforming force in this injury.[182] The mechanism of injury is usually acute inversion, possibly with an element of plantar flexion, the same mechanism that produces an anterior talofibular ligament injury or a sprain or avulsion fracture of the anterior tubercle in the calcaneus. The presence of an inversion injury is first suggested by palpation of the lateral aspect of the foot and ankle during the physical examination. The location of tenderness or pain indicates whether a radiograph of the foot or ankle should be obtained to look for an avulsion fracture or, for example, an occult fracture on the anterior beak of the calcaneus.

**Treatment.** Avulsion fractures of the fifth metatarsal tuber are typically treated nonoperatively in a walking cast, walking boot, or even a stiff-soled but well-cushioned shoe, depending on patient preference and comfort. In fact, treatment should be based on clinical rather than radiographic union because the latter correlates less reliably with outcome and can frequently be prolonged (up to 4 to 9 months) or absent. Uneventful healing within 6 to 8 weeks is the rule regardless of the initial degree of displacement or intra-articular involvement. Symptoms may linger for months after injury but usually abate with symptomatic care, and even in the unusual event of nonunion, painful nonunion is actually rare. If it occurs, it is best treated by excision of the fragment and repair of the peroneus brevis or by fixation and grafting with an intramedullary screw if the fragment is large enough.[175, 267] Rarely, the nonunion can remain uncorrected because of sural nerve entrapment.[110]

Primary internal fixation that consists of a narrow tension band wire or a lag screw should be used only in significantly displaced, large fractures. Indications for such treatment are rare. For example, a transverse fracture at the proximal end of the fifth metatarsal resulting in a large fragment may involve the cuboid–fifth metatarsal joint and thus be intra-articular. Internal fixation of this type of injury is indicated if the fifth metatarsal is displaced more than 2 mm.

## JONES FRACTURE

An acute traumatic injury to the proximal metaphysis is caused by a different type of inversion force than that causing an avulsion at the base of the fifth metatarsal. The mechanism is an upwardly directed force or a direct blow to the planted fifth metatarsal. This injury, known as a "Jones fracture," is an acute fracture of the proximal end of the shaft near the metadiaphyseal junction of the fifth metatarsal and was originally described by Jones for basal fractures of the fifth metatarsal resulting from an adduction moment and an element of axial loading on a plantar flexed foot.[159] He noted that the intrinsic ligamentous support surrounding the base of the fifth metatarsal makes it more amenable to fracture than dislocation. Anatomically, however, it can be distinguished from a simple avulsion fracture because a true Jones fracture exits the intermetatarsal facet rather than the cuboid–fifth metatarsal articulation. There is great confusion in the literature regarding what a true Jones fracture is, and thus much of the notoriety received by this injury for its propensity for nonunion is undeserved because many previous papers had inadequate selection criteria to distinguish between stress and Jones fractures in the fifth ray. Thus, much of the data that we have used to determine the treatment and prognosis of Jones fractures was probably based on pooled data that included many fractures that were actually stress injuries and not acute metadiaphyseal fractures. Some data suggest, however, that the intraosseous vascularity in the metadiaphyseal area is fairly poor and may contribute to a delayed healing response.[314, 333]

The Jones fracture in general actually has a 72% to 93% chance of healing and very few complications after closed management if not significantly displaced. Whether we even need to protect these injuries differently from an avulsion fracture of the base of the fifth ray remains a matter of debate. Treatment should be guided by whether the fracture is an acute injury or a stress fracture. In most cases, this distinction can be accurately determined by the chronicity of symptoms, elapsed time since injury and its mechanism (if any), location of pain, radiographic evaluation, including an assessment of sclerosis or nonunion at the fracture margins, and the presence or absence of any predisposing factors that can result in a stress fracture. With so many variables, to call all these fractures by one name can be confusing. The term "Jones fracture" will probably persist, but a detailed description of the injury should be included whenever an individual case is discussed.

**Nonoperative Management.** Nondisplaced or minimally displaced fractures can be treated for 6 weeks in a non–weight-bearing short leg cast, after which weight bearing is gradually increased over the next 2 weeks. Most fractures treated with this regimen go on to successful union. It is suspected that these injuries would heal equally well with no change in outcome even if treated with the protocol used for avulsion injuries, but until a large, prospective, randomized controlled study using rigid descriptive parameters to properly classify these injuries for comparison is performed, the time-honored protocol of both prolonged casting and non–weight bearing stands.[57, 175] Depending on signs of healing, patients can have their weight bearing advanced and eventually progressed to wearing a hard-soled shoe, fracture brace, or orthosis for another 4 weeks. If no sign of healing is noted, consideration should be given to ORIF.

**Operative Management.** For acute, displaced fractures or those in high-performance athletes, intramedullary screw fixation plus supplementation with a strain-relieved bone graft on the dorsomedial surface of the fracture is recommended.[131] The procedure is described later and is identical to management of chronic nonunion. The risks associated with this intervention, however, in the setting of a relatively nondisplaced or minimally displaced fracture in an elite athlete who demands the most rapid return to training must be weighed against the fact that most such injuries do heal well with excellent functional outcomes, albeit more slowly than zone I injuries do. Alternatively, a tension band construct with screws or a hook plate construct can be used to reduce the fracture and neutralize the forces around the metatarsal to promote a rapid healing response (Fig. 60–67).

## PROXIMAL DIAPHYSEAL STRESS FRACTURES

Stress fractures of the proximal fifth metatarsal can be troublesome. Unlike other fractures involving the fifth ray, this injury has a high propensity for painful nonunion. The key to treating these injuries is to always ask *"why?"* Such proximal diaphyseal fractures are not usually acute or the result of an acute traumatic injury (although the patient may finally seek medical care as the result of one), and premorbid factors are frequently associated with their occurrence. These same factors can be detrimental to healing or result in recurrence if not addressed at the time of initial evaluation. A stress fracture is most typical in a young male athlete[19] and may result from a mild biomechanical abnormality such as genu varum or a varus deformity in the heel or from a sudden increase in training intervals or demand on the foot. If such is the case, the abnormality should be corrected when the fracture is treated. Sometimes, it is simply a matter of education regarding the importance of conditioning and varying training patterns to avoid the excessive overload of one area so common in repetitive use–type injury.

DeLee and colleagues defined a stress fracture of the fifth metatarsal by three criteria: (1) a *prodrome* of symptoms over the lateral aspect of the foot, (2) radiographic evidence of a proximal fifth metatarsal *stress reaction,* and (3) *no* previous treatment of a fifth metatarsal fracture.[67] The fracture probably occurs in the metadiaphyseal region because it is the transition zone between a change in both vascularity and tendon forces. The bone here remains relatively avascular in comparison to its proximal and distal ends (a watershed area), and its area is an interface between the proximal attachment and pull of the peroneus brevis and the distal influence of the adductors.

**Nonoperative Management.** Treatment of an "acute," nondisplaced stress fracture without evidence of sclerosis is similar to that for a Jones fracture, but a long period of inactivity and rehabilitation is also required. It can be unattractive to patients who must remain active, especially high-performance athletes. As mentioned earlier, treatment in this case must be extended to any risk factors to avoid persistent nonunion or recurrence after the bone is successfully healed and activity is resumed.

**Operative Management.** For chronic nonunion or the more unusual displaced or "acute" stress fracture with sclerosis, intramedullary screw fixation plus supplementation with a strain-relieved tricortical inlay bone graft on the dorsomedial surface of the fracture is performed. The size of the screw used for fixation is determined by the size of the bone. Precise surgical technique and image intensifier guidance are required to ascertain whether the screw is of the proper size and whether it has been placed directly through the canal from the tip of the fifth metatarsal base (see Fig. 60–62). This procedure has been well-described by Glasgow[104] and Torg[334] and their colleagues and can be complicated by fifth metatarsal or screw fracture after fixation.

To help guide treatment, Torg and co-workers[334] have classified these injuries as (1) acute (thin fracture line visible), (2) delayed union (marginal sclerosis at the fracture edges), and (3) nonunion (sclerosis of the entire medullary canal). They pointed out that after sclerosis or intramedullary callus has developed in a stress fracture (i.e., types 2 and 3), the likelihood of healing without surgery is greatly reduced. The surgical procedure they recommend is designed to reestablish the medullary canal in a delayed union or nonunion. The bone is drilled or scraped with a bur, and an onlay bone graft is inserted without hardware. Hansen advocates a stress-relieving, inlayed cancellous bone graft in addition to intramedullary screw fixation with a 4.5-mm malleolar screw.[120] The bone is harvested from the calcaneus or from the base of the fifth metatarsal or the proximal lateral tibial head. A short segment of hard cortical bone on the dorsomedial side of the fracture is drilled with a small (5 to 8 mm) burr, and the gap is filled with a bone graft.

Kavanaugh and colleagues[161] and DeLee and associates[67] recommend intramedullary screw fixation for fractures with sclerosis, for patients with a history of stress fracture, and for patients with a poor prognosis related to delayed union or nonunion (see Fig. 60–62). It is important to understand the serpiginous anatomy of the fifth metatarsal and base selection of the intramedullary screw accordingly. Factors affecting selection include the site of fracture (length), the size of the entry area (size), and the curvature of the metatarsal (width).[78] Smaller, shorter metatarsals and very serpiginous ones require smaller screws such as a 4.0-mm cancellous or, preferably, a 4.5-mm malleolar screw if possible, which is typically ideal in the average-sized patient.[162] For larger bones,

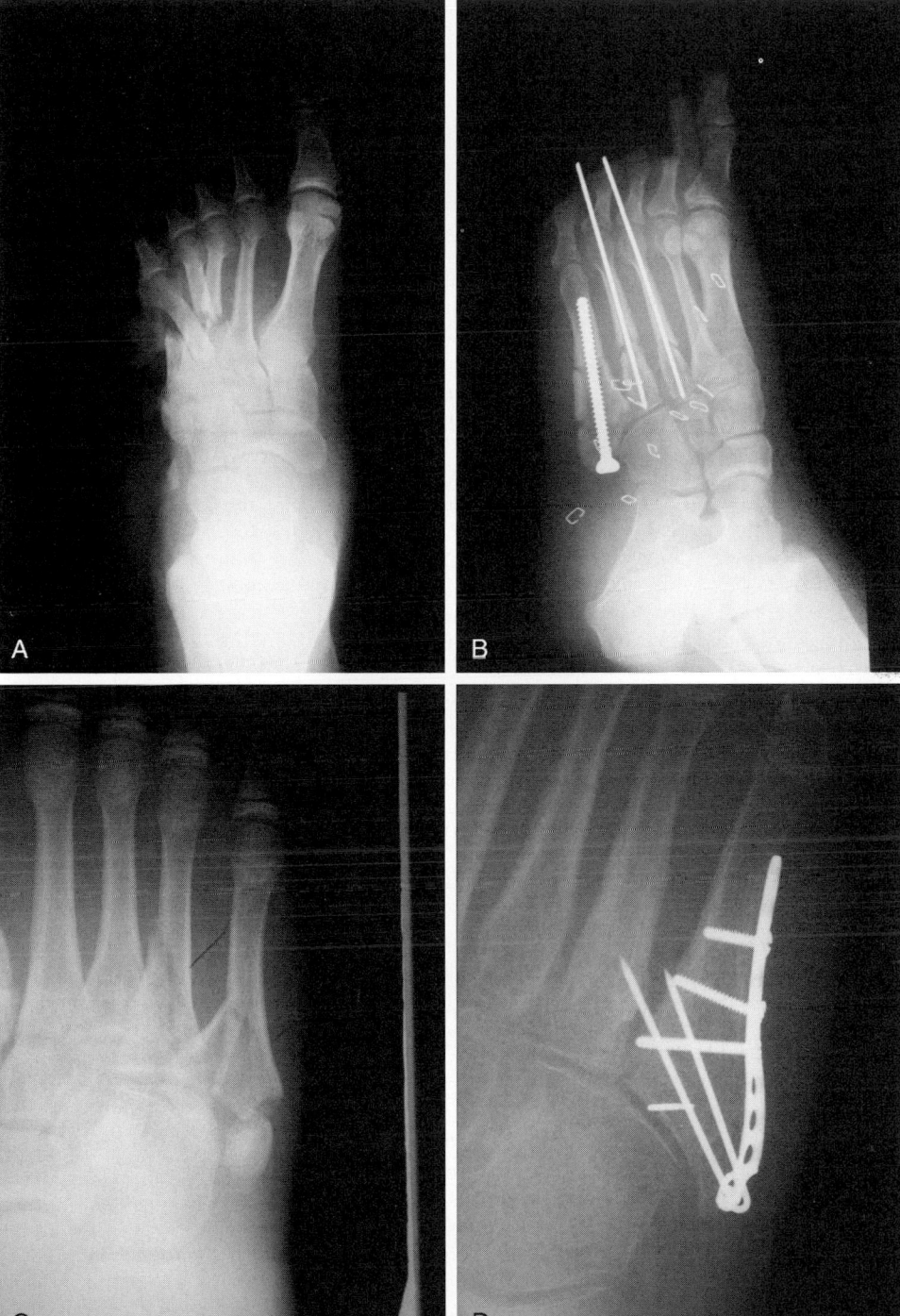

**FIGURE 60–67.** Fractures of the fifth metatarsal vary in location, healing potential, and fracture pattern. Those that require operative intervention are best treated with either intramedullary fixation for compressible basilar or comminuted diaphyseal fractures (*A, B*), tension band constructs for comminuted, noncompressible metadiaphyseal fractures, or open plating for midshaft fractures that are comminuted or unstable (*C, D*). Because of the tenuous blood supply to portions of the fifth metatarsal, fixation should be chosen that devitalizes as little tissue as possible while imparting stability.

6.5-mm screws can be used, but care must be taken to look at the limitations of sagittal width on the lateral radiograph, which often limits screw diameter more than the width identified on the AP view.[307] Care must be taken to not exit the cortex, which is quite easy to do. In all cases, the entry site must be immediately adjacent to the cuboid articulation and should be verified on AP and lateral projections before insertion.

Hens and Martens[131] and Dameron[57] have also described modifications to grafting: a reversed trapezoidal and a sliding bone graft, respectively. Recently, electrical stimulation (pulsed electromagnetic field radiation) has been alternatively advocated in chronically symptomatic nonunion with encouraging early healing at 4 months.[135]

Postoperatively, the foot is immobilized in a short leg cast with protected weight-bearing restrictions for 6 weeks. After this period, a walking cast is used for 2 to 4 more weeks before the patient gradually returns to normal activity. Emphasis is placed on serial clinical and radiographic examination to demonstrate union before permitting return to unrestricted sports or any predisposing activities. Gradual reconditioning in athletes is important to prevent recurrence.

## ACUTE DIAPHYSEAL (SHAFT) FRACTURE

Traumatic fractures are common in the diaphysis ("dancer's fracture") and the distal end of the fifth metatarsal, and they are managed in the same manner as for acute fractures in the other lesser metatarsals.[240] The fifth metatarsal is more flexible and less crucial to weight bearing than the first and medial metatarsals are and warrants internal fixation only if the fracture is significantly displaced. Moderate displacement in the transverse and oblique planes is common and, as a rule, well tolerated because it is usually associated with satisfactory alignment and length in the sagittal plane. Most distal fifth metatarsal fractures with little or no displacement heal successfully in a walking cast. A stiff-soled boot such as a hiking boot provides adequate protection if this type of shoe wear is acceptable to the patient.

# INJURY TO THE METATARSOPHALANGEAL JOINTS

Normal gait and lack of pain in the forefoot are dependent on mobility in the MTP joints. Mobility in the TMT or IP joints may be sacrificed without incurring significant functional losses, but every effort should be made to maintain motion in the MTP joints. Fusion of the first MTP joint should be undertaken only as a salvage procedure under extraordinary circumstances, and the lesser MTP joints should never be fused. Though unusual, persistent pain as a result of injury to one of these joints, especially the first ray, can be quite problematic. Hughes and co-workers identified the importance of minimizing stiffness in the toes to enable ground contact during gait. They noted that the toes contact the ground for 75% of the stance phase of gait and generate pressure approaching that underneath the metatarsal heads.[138]

## First Metatarsophalangeal Joint

### ANATOMY

The first MTP joint is larger than the lesser MTP joints, and several strong muscles (the abductor hallucis, the extensor brevis, the adductor hallucis, and the two flexor brevis tendons) attach into the base of the first proximal phalanx with the strong plantar plate. The plantar plate has a much stronger attachment to the base of the proximal phalanx than it does to the metatarsal neck.[81] In addition to musculotendinous attachments, it is also reinforced by the lateral transverse metatarsal ligament. The abductor and medial short flexor attach medially into the MTP joint, and the adductor and lateral short flexor attach laterally, frequently as conjoined tendons. These tendons contain the sesamoidal apparatus, the bones of which help support weight beneath the first metatarsal head. Dorsally, the

extensor hallucis longus converges with the extensor hallucis brevis to expand over the base of the proximal phalanx and lend additional stability. Injury to the first MTP joint is usually the result of severe dorsiflexion with an axial loading component and can range from a mild sprain to turf toe (severe sprain) to overt dislocation.[269] Normal motion in this joint ranges from as high as 90° of dorsiflexion to 45° of plantar flexion.

## INJURY CLASSIFICATION

The first MTP joint is subject to compression injuries, sprains, and hyperextension injuries (turf toe)[25]; these injuries can result in various combinations of fracture, subluxation, or dislocation. Cartilage damage is common in this area and may lead to hallux valgus or hallux limitus and, if progressive, eventually to hallux rigidus or the development of a dorsal bunion. Significant disability can result from these "minor-appearing" sprains.[25, 48] Routine foot views are preferred over selected toe radiographs in evaluating these patients. Patients typically have exquisite pain, swelling, and stiffness, sometimes in conjunction with an open wound or gross deformity of the toe.

## TURF TOE

Field athletes such as football or soccer players frequently sustain turf toe, which can be debilitating enough to keep the athlete out of play for a season.[50] In general, however, most of these inferior and medial capsular tears and joint injuries are successfully treated nonoperatively. It has not been proved whether more aggressive open repair is superior. In addition to hyperdorsiflexion (really a subluxation) of the first MTP joint, turf toe has a varus or valgus impaction component on the joint as well. Disruption of the sesamoid complex may also accompany this injury. To help guide treatment, Clanton and co-workers have classified these injuries as grade I (stretch of the capsulo-ligamentous complex with minimal swelling and perhaps plantar-medial tenderness), grade II (soft tissue disruption of the complex with moderate swelling and diffuse tenderness), and grade III (including dorsal impaction of the first MTP articular surface with severe swelling, tenderness to palpation, and stiffness about the first MTP joint).[48] The cartilaginous and bony impaction resulting from the latter stages of this injury tend to have a worse prognosis. Although most injuries remain stable, stress dorsiflexion and mediolateral radiographs are also helpful in classifying this injury and detecting any sesamoid component to assist in management decisions.

**Treatment.** Sprain or a small capsular avulsion (turf toe equivalent) can be treated by wearing hard-soled shoes or custom graphite orthoses to limit dorsiflexion for 2 to 4 weeks. With a grade I or II injury, a CAM walker or postoperative shoe plus physical therapy is preferable for 3 to 4 weeks, followed by return to sports with protective steel shank shoes or graphite insoles. Strapping of the hallux in plantar flexion is also useful. Further treatment can include a total-contact insole or Morton's extension to prevent further injury. Grade III injury can take two to three times as long for recovery. Surgery is indicated in the event of large or incarcerated intra-articular fragments or joint incongruity. With most injuries of this nature, the patient is comfortable enough to permit early range-of-motion exercises and progressive weight-bearing activity within 2 to 3 weeks to minimize stiffness. These injuries have been associated with late arthrosis and stiffness.[269]

## METATARSOPHALANGEAL DISLOCATION

First MTP dislocations are rare, and most occur in a dorsal direction and as a result of a high-energy hyperextension mechanism; rarely, the phalanx can be plantar or lateral in location[31, 155] (Fig. 60–68). Usually, plain films in two views are adequate to make this diagnosis, although three views are recommended. Jahss classified dorsal dislocation according to involvement of the plantar plate sesamoidal complex.[155] The plantar plate is disrupted at its proximal attachment beneath the metatarsal and, together with the phalanx and sesamoids, becomes situated above the metatarsal head. Relocation is prevented by the intact collateral ligaments and mediolateral conjoint tendons, which incarcerate the metatarsal head plantarly and prevent reduction. In a type I dislocation, the intersesamoidal ligamentous complex remains intact dorsally and fixed and is avulsed from its weaker origin at the metatarsal neck; through this linear defect and thus beneath the plantar plate, the metatarsal head is sandwiched between the transverse intermetatarsal ligament, conjoint tendon, flexor hallucis brevis, and adductor hallucis. These injuries usually require open reduction and can be diagnosed by the presence of an intact (unseparated and unfractured) sesamoidal apparatus interposed between the two articular surfaces instead of beneath them.[202] This type of dislocation is considered a "complex" one. Higher energy type II dislocations disrupt the intersesamoidal ligament, which allows either divergence of the sesamoids medially or laterally (type IIA) or a transverse fracture and distal displacement of one or both sesamoids,

which is typically the medial one (type IIB). In type II injuries, a lack of dorsal restraint usually permits closed reduction. Some authors have noted other unusual injury combinations, such as distal disruption of the sesamoidophalangeal ligaments during dislocation, with the sesamoids left plantarly and proximally retracted.[233]

**Treatment.** Skin is often compromised in many of these dislocations, although few are open, and thus prompt reduction should be performed. Postreduction films and a range-of-motion examination should also be done to confirm stability, congruency, and lack of soft tissue or bony interposition.

If closed reduction is attempted, adequate anesthesia is required, usually in the form of a toe block. The IP joint is extended, longitudinal traction is applied, and finally, plantar translation is accomplished. Impedance to reduction is typically caused by hinging of the plantar aspect of the proximal phalangeal base above the dorsal lip of the metatarsal head (where the cartilage ends and the neck begins). An exaggeration of this deformity to unlock this impaction, followed by gentle distraction, is usually successful for relocation. In most cases, the reduction is generally successful and stable and can be followed by restricted dorsiflexion in wooden-soled shoe wear or short leg casting for 3 to 4 weeks. The prognosis is good. If, however, the joint is unstable or incongruent as a result of bony or soft tissue interposition after attempted reduction, open reduction with 1.6-mm K-wire fixation is required. The wire can be removed at 3 to 4 weeks.

Sometimes, closed reduction of dorsal dislocations is impossible because the head of the first metatarsal "buttonholes" through the sesamoid–short flexor mechanism.[31] Thus, the metatarsal head is incarcerated dorsally by the base of the proximal phalanx, transverse metatarsal ligament, and plantar plate; medially by the medial collateral ligament, medial flexor hallucis brevis tendon, and abductor tendon; plantarly by the plantar aponeurosis; and laterally by the lateral collateral ligament, lateral flexor hallucis brevis tendon, adductor tendon, and usually the flexor hallucis longus. When incarceration or postreduction incongruity, crepitance, or instability is encountered, open reduction of the first MTP joint is indicated. It is carried out through either a transverse plantar or, preferably, a safer dorsal first webspace approach to extricate the interposed plantar plate. The intermetatarsal (deep transverse metatarsal) ligament and both heads of the adductor should be released from the lateral side to facilitate this process, both of which must be repaired after reduction. K-wire immobilization of the joint can be used in the presence of any residual instability. After open reduction, the foot and the great toe are immobilized with a cast in neutral position for 2 to 3 weeks, and the joint is thereafter gradually rehabilitated with range-of-motion exercises, strengthening, and edema control. For plantar dislocation, a medial approach is preferable to a plantar or lateral one.

Postoperative radiographs should always be taken to ensure acceptable joint alignment and removal of any incarcerated fragments. First MTP arthroscopy with a 1.9-mm small-joint arthroscope has also recently been described for pathology of this joint, although the only indication in this setting would be a residual loose body or

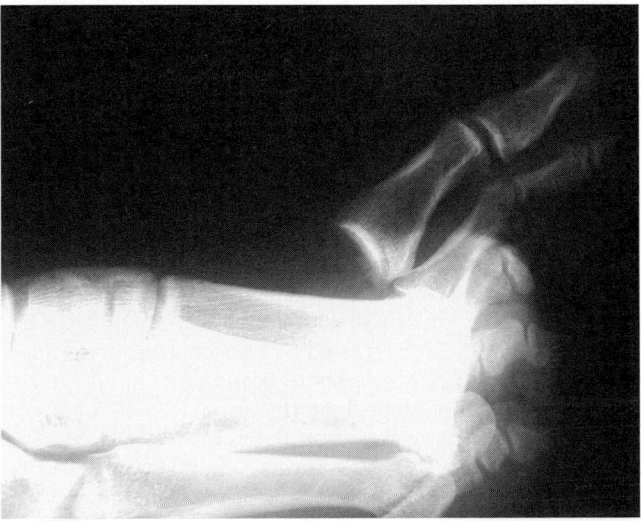

**FIGURE 60–68.** First metatarsophalangeal dislocations are easily recognizable injuries that should always be reduced anatomically to minimize postinjury debility. Reduction may require operative intervention with inspection and repair of periarticular tissues if it cannot be achieved in closed fashion.

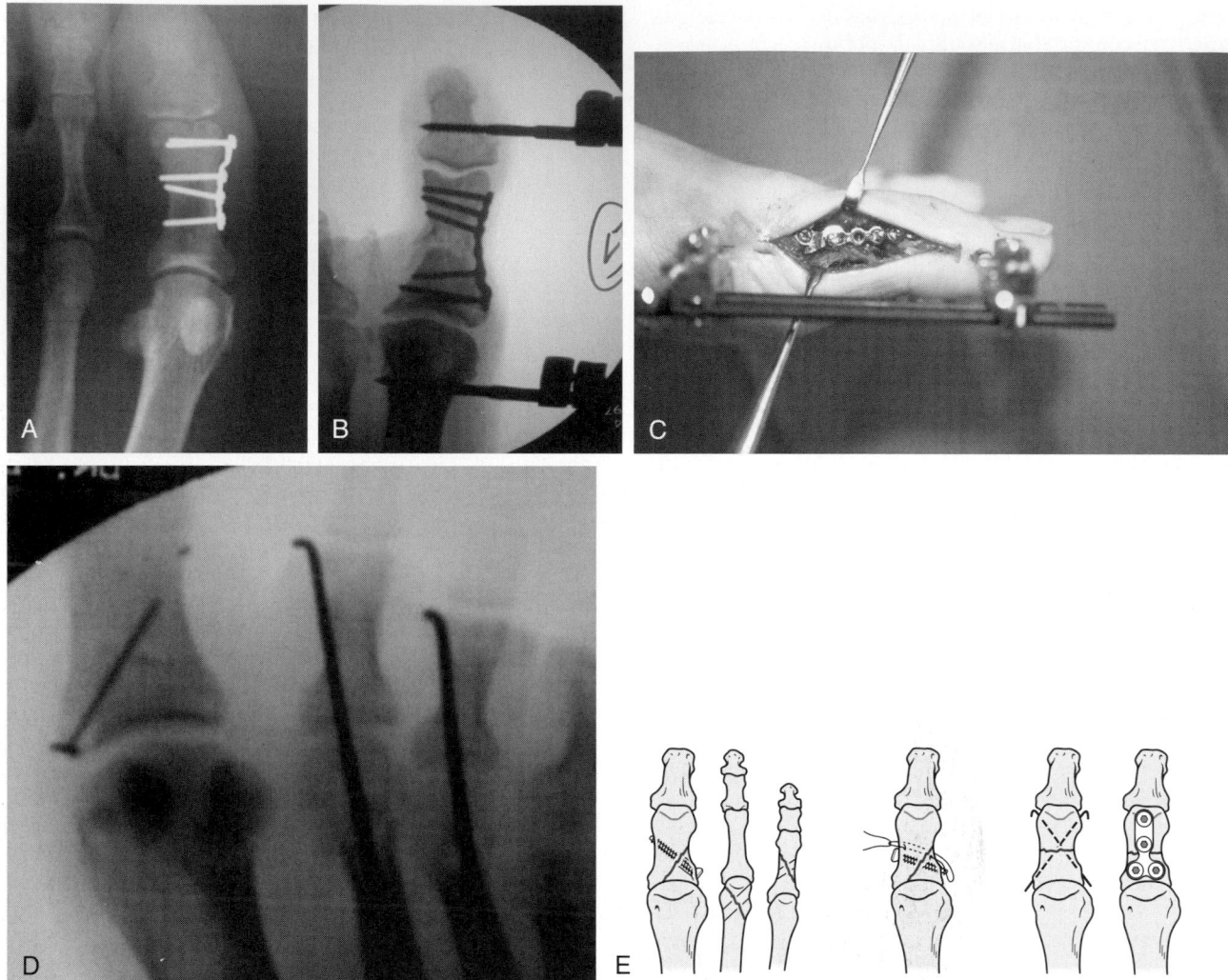

**FIGURE 60–69.** Fixation techniques for metatarsophalangeal and proximal phalangeal fractures are shown. Fractures in the proximal phalanx of the great toe and the first metatarsal head are typically stabilized with 2.0-, 2.4-, or 2.7-mm screws, tension band wiring, or both, depending on size, but K-wires may be used in the smaller heads of the lesser metatarsals. At the level of the hallux, bony avulsion is often accompanied by the deforming force of the conjoined tendon of the lateral short flexor and abductor. The dorsal view shows the two surgical incisions through which the fracture is reduced and stabilized—a lateral webspace incision and a medial midline incision over the intact medial proximal phalangeal cortex. The screw protrudes 2.0 to 3.0 mm through the lateral fragment so that a tension band wire can be passed through a midaxial drill hole in a medial-to-lateral direction and then passed underneath the phalanx and around the tip of the screw before tensioning on itself. Alternatively, two small lag screws (2.7 and 2.0 mm) can be used in opposite directions to compress this fracture fragment. In the case provided, the patient sustained an unstable, shortened, displaced intra-articular transcondylar fracture of the proximal phalanx of the hallux that required fixation with a 2.0-mm minifragment plate-and-screw construct to maintain length and alignment (A). Note the medial utility incision and external fixator placement, which together allowed easy reduction and fixation with minimal devascularization of the comminuted diaphyseal region before plate application (B, C). The fixator was removed after completion of the internal fixation, and the construct allowed early range of motion.

Phalangeal fractures of the lesser toes do not require fixation unless the fracture is open or tends to angulate. In that case, K-wires or, preferably, minifragment 1.5- or 2.0-mm cortical lag screws are used, much like in the case shown here of a basilar hallux phalangeal fracture with metatarsophalangeal joint subluxation that was stabilized by lag fixation of the fragment (D). A lateral basilar fracture of the hallux's proximal phalanx is more plantar and easier to fix with a screw inserted superomedially, perhaps supplemented with a tension band wire as shown (E).

Note that in E this screw is placed from the lateral side but that the lateral base of the first proximal phalanx is frequently located in a more plantar lateral position than depicted here. In that case, the screw should be placed through a gliding hole in the dorsomedial surface of the proximal phalanx and angled perpendicular to the fracture line to compress the plantar lateral fragment in its anatomic position.

an incarcerated fragment preventing congruent reduction. Familiarity with this technique is recommended before use, and caution should be exercised in arthroscopy of any acutely injured joint because extravasation of fluid and compartment syndrome have been documented.

## OSTEOCHONDRAL FRACTURE

Osteochondral fractures may also occur as a result of traumatic injuries. A traumatic injury can avulse the lateral

conjoined tendon together with a large section of the lateral base of the proximal phalanx. If the resultant fracture is displaced by several millimeters, ORIF is required with a lag screw or a tension band device (Fig. 60–69). Some metatarsal head fractures are best left alone—particularly comminuted ones. If the fracture is allowed to remain displaced, however, muscle imbalance may force the great toe into varus.

**Treatment.** Small osteochondral fragments of the first MTP joint may be excised, but large fragments should be replaced by ORIF. K-wires are sometimes used to stabilize large osteochondral fractures, but better results are achieved by fixation of the joint surface with small compression screws or double-threaded headless Herbert or Accufex screws. Fractures at the base of the proximal phalanx, those in the first metatarsal head, and all acutely displaced fractures and dislocations should be reduced as soon after injury as possible.

## HALLUX RIGIDUS TREATMENT

Hallux rigidus is a common sequela of first MTP injury, but is usually seen in the chronic setting. Operative treatment of isolated hallux rigidus consists of cheilectomy and careful remobilization of the sesamoidal joint complex. Nonoperative treatment by immobilization of the foot in a stiff, rocker-soled shoe or through use of a rigid, graphite shoe insert is satisfactory in some cases.

## Lesser Metatarsophalangeal Joints

### ANATOMY

From an anatomic standpoint, the lesser MTP joints are all very similar. Each MTP joint has simple collateral ligaments, a volar plate mechanism, and intrinsic tendons that attach to the dorsal hood. The long flexors attach to the bases of the distal phalanges, the short flexors attach to the middle phalanges, and the long extensors run along the dorsal hoods and attach to the dorsal aspects of the distal phalanges. The plantar fat pads of the MTP joints are properly positioned under the metatarsal heads when the proximal phalanges are in a neutral position or in slight flexion relative to the metatarsal heads.

The actions of the intrinsic and extrinsic flexor tendons are complementary during normal gait. Gait mechanics requires 30° to 40° of passive dorsiflexion in the toes as the foot rolls forward past heel-off. The toes require between 60° and 90° of passive dorsiflexion for kneeling or squatting. When they function properly, the intrinsic and extrinsic flexor tendons flex the toes, elevate the metatarsal heads slightly, and assume weight from the MTP joints during stance and early push-off.

Sprain of the lesser MTP joints is essentially unbroached in the orthopaedic literature. Though possibly the result of under-recognition, it is suspected that the injury is unusual because most axial stubbing injuries causing MTP sprains affect the longer medial rays (first and second) and probably never reach the smaller lateral ones. By virtue of the difference in anatomy between the first and second rays, the same mechanism resulting in a "turf toe" of the first ray may cause fracture or extreme IP joint flexion in the second.

Dislocation of the lesser MTP joints is also rare and usually occurs dorsolaterally as a result of a sudden lateral force on the forefoot, as in stubbing or jamming the toe.

### MANAGEMENT

Treatment of dislocations, sprains, and fractures in the lesser MTP joints is intended to restore maximal motion in the joint. Two thirds of lesser MTP dislocations are easily reducible with longitudinal traction or hanging finger traps. They are also typically stable after reduction. Occasionally, the metatarsal head can also buttonhole through the plantar plate and become trapped between the lumbrical medially and the flexor laterally.[32, 265]

Treatment and indications for open reduction of such irreducible dislocations are similar to those for hallux MTP dislocation, with a straight dorsal approach over the base of the proximal phalanx and metatarsal head recommended when needed.[55] The plantar plate and deep transverse metatarsal ligament are thus divided in line with the metatarsal before it is relocated under the metatarsal head. Small K-wires and screws are used in metatarsal head fractures for anatomic reduction (see Fig. 60–69). When no fracture is present, K-wire fixation is rarely necessary after reduction. This incision is preferred regardless of the direction of dislocation because of the absence of a sesamoidal complex to contend with in the lesser joints. In the unusual case of multiple distal metatarsal fractures or MTP dislocations, closed reduction can be prevented by any number of interposed intrinsic or extrinsic tendons as a result of the deformity, and formal open reduction will be required. Open reduction or, in the case of extreme chronic deformity, metatarsal head excision may also be indicated for lesser MTP dislocations initially seen late after injury, depending on the clinical setting (beyond 3 weeks).

The articular surface of the MTP joint bears no weight, and sufficient motion for most activities may be restored by anatomic reduction and early mobilization. Gentle passive dorsiflexion is applied to the foot 2 to 3 days postoperatively, while it is still protected in a neutral splint. Active motion and more vigorous passive motion are started 3 to 4 weeks later, after evidence of bony healing has been demonstrated on radiographs.

## INJURY TO THE PROXIMAL PHALANX AND INTERPHALANGEAL JOINT OF THE HALLUX

The first proximal phalanx and the first IP joint are discussed separately because these structures are anatomically different from the lesser phalanges. Most of these injuries are caused by direct impact on an unprotected foot, either by falling objects or stubbing the toe. Fractures can easily be identified on routine plain films of the foot, and most are nondisplaced or minimally displaced. A concomitant crush component involving the surrounding soft tissue and nail bed is not uncommon and should always be checked for. A higher frequency of malunion is noted with these transverse proximal phalanx fractures because of the strong intrinsic and extrinsic musculature imbalance created after injury.

## First Proximal Phalanx

Diaphyseal fractures in the first proximal phalanx may be treated more aggressively than fractures in the lesser toes. The short flexor complex is stronger than the short extensor complex, and instability in a proximal phalangeal fracture may produce plantar angulation, subsequent late keratosis formation, and shoe-fitting problems. For these reasons, unstable or significantly displaced fractures in the first proximal phalanx should be treated by anatomic reduction and fixation with 0.045- or 0.054-inch crossed K-wires or 1.5- or 2.0-mm minifragment lag screws rather than by simple splinting. Finger traps are often helpful in maintaining reduction of displaced fracture ends during this process. Nondisplaced or minimally displaced fractures typically do very well with 2 to 3 weeks of buddy-taping and wooden-soled shoe wear until comfort levels permit transition to a well-cushioned flexible shoe.

## First Interphalangeal Joint

Although IP joint dislocation is very rare, when it occurs it usually involves the first ray. The mechanism is similar to that of other forefoot toe injuries (jamming). These dislocations can be reduced easily and are usually stable thereafter, with only a few weeks of buddy-taping immobilization required before rapid resumption of function and motion exercises. Cases of flexor hallucis longus, plantar plate, and IP sesamoidal interposition requiring open reduction for this injury have been reported.[211, 351] In such cases, a dorsal approach is preferred and usually results in stable reduction, followed by 4 weeks of weight-bearing cast immobilization. K-wire fixation is indicated if the reduction is unstable after an open approach.

Near-normal anatomic open reduction is not required in a fracture of the first IP joint. Normal range of motion in this joint varies from 20° to 60°, and stiffness is the most common complication of intra-articular involvement. Disability resulting from ankylosis of the first IP joint, however, is minimal in most cases. Restoration of motion in the IP joint is important only if the MTP joint is ankylosed and will require late fusion. In this event, mobility in the IP joint can compensate somewhat for stiffness in the MTP joint. Any large or displaced intra-articular fracture involving the first IP joint should be anatomically reduced, which can often be performed in closed fashion with gentle traction and casting, but if not, ORIF with a longitudinal incision based over the fracture site (medial or lateral), minifragment screw or K-wire fixation, and early motion are required. In either case, protected weight bearing can be performed in a postoperative short leg cast or wooden shoe.[100]

## INJURY TO THE LESSER PHALANGES AND INTERPHALANGEAL JOINTS

### Dislocation

Dislocation of the lesser IP joints is even more unusual than in the great toe. Most are easily reducible with longitudinal traction and manipulation plus a few weeks of buddy-taping in a wooden-soled shoe before return to activity, including active and passive motion or flexible

shoe wear. Interposition of the long toe flexor or plantar plate requiring open reduction has been described.[100, 160] As with most toe dislocations, a dorsal longitudinal approach is most appropriate for achieving reduction.

Motion in the proximal and distal IP joints is not essential for normal toe function, although a dislocation left unreduced can lead to chronic deformity, pain, and shoe-fitting problems, as evidenced by the widespread use of IP joint fusions for treatment of clawtoes. It is unusual to have sequelae after fractures in these sites unless the displacement is significant, and surgery for these injuries is rarely required.

## Fracture

The most common fracture in the forefoot involves the toe.[64] Diaphyseal fractures in the proximal and middle phalanges ("night walker's fracture") commonly occur as closed injuries from a direct impact and may be treated nonoperatively by splinting or buddy-taping (Fig. 60–70). These injuries are typically the result of stubbing and occur most commonly at the proximal phalanx of the fifth toe.[153] The injured toe is taped lightly to an adjacent toe with a piece of gauze or lamb's wool inserted between them. The tape should be applied without excessive pressure for the first 2 or 3 days after injury, when significant swelling is expected. Sometimes, a metatarsal bar or stiff-soled shoe is preferred.[49] A fracture that extends into the IP joint is splinted with the shaft straight. These injuries require no surgical intervention unless the fracture is markedly displaced or open. Displaced fractures can often be reduced manually or with the use of finger traps. Muscle forces across the proximal phalanx can predispose this injury to plantar angulation. Deformity in the middle and

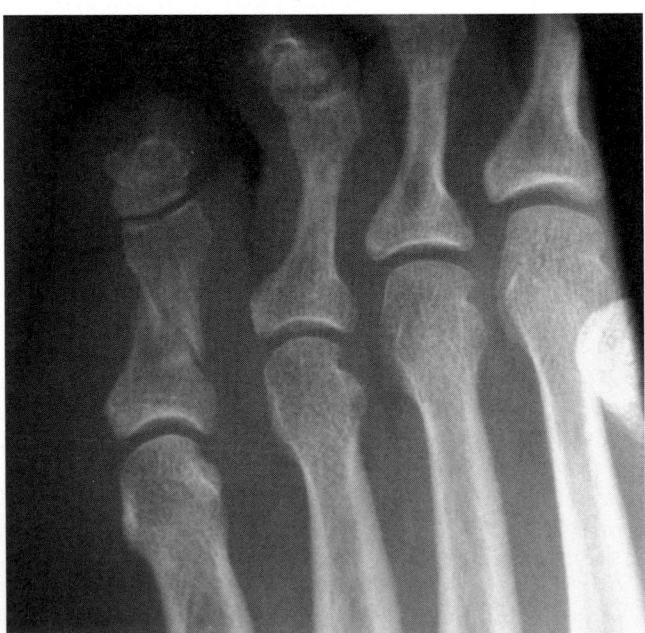

**FIGURE 60–70.** Phalangeal fractures of the toes frequently result from a direct impact or stubbing. Often appropriately dubbed "night walker's fracture," they are usually easily treated conservatively with a splint or buddy-taping, heal with few sequelae, and rarely require reduction.

distal phalanges is more dependent on the mechanism of injury. Regardless of what the radiograph looks like, treatment should be based on what the toe looks like clinically in comparison to the surrounding toes. Often, significant deformity on a radiograph is accompanied by a benign-appearing forefoot and is best treated with a few weeks of rest, buddy-taping, and wooden-soled shoe wear for a good functional result. Residual instability of the fifth ray can be troublesome because it catches on socks, shoes, or the ground during daily use.[152] This problem can be corrected by exostectomy, syndactylization, or even amputation, depending on the patient's medical status and functional demands.

Failure to anatomically realign a lesser toe by closed means may warrant open reduction with K-wire fixation. Much of the stiffness that results after fusion of an IP joint can be prevented by early fixation of the large fracture fragments with K-wires. A serious complication that may occur in a toe that heals in an angulated position is the development of a lateral prominence. This prominence may rub against an adjacent toe and produce an interdigital corn that can eventually become macerated. A macerated corn not only is painful but may become infected and require later surgery to eradicate the infection and eliminate any deformity. Surgery in such cases is rarely indicated and can often be controlled with appropriate shoe wear and padded inserts. When necessary, management usually requires only exostectomy, osteotomy, or resectional arthroplasty and pinning.

## DISTAL PHALANX AND NAIL BED INJURIES

Injuries to the distal tuft and the nail bed are extremely common. In the fingers, such injuries are caused by a blow (e.g., from a hammer) or by trapping of the fingers in a door. In the toes, they are typically caused by a heavy object falling on the foot.[341] Nail bed problems are common in long-distance runners, whose toenails may be completely disrupted when they are subjected to repeated trauma from running downhill in loose shoes.

## Nail Bed Injuries

One of the simplest nail bed injuries is a subungual hematoma. The hematoma may be very painful and tender at first and result in loss of a section of the nail bed, but complete healing can usually be expected. As in the fingernails, a hematoma in a toenail may be drained after the area has been prepared. The blood should be evacuated if greater than 25% of the nail bed is involved. A hole is bored through the nail into the middle of the hematoma with a heated paper clip, small bur, or electrocautery device. The area should be kept clean and sterile to prevent infection in the nail bed and distal tuft. With hematoma involving 50% or more of the nail bed area, some authors suggest that treatment may be required for laceration of the nail bed (present two thirds of the time) or a phalangeal fracture.[313] A prospective study with almost 1 year of follow-up in 48 patients who underwent simple hematoma evacuation regardless of its size, however, resulted in no cases of osteomyelitis, other infection, or nail plate deformity.[306] Open injuries should be treated by nail plate removal, irrigation and débridement, nail bed repair, and standard open fracture management of any tuft fracture. If the injury is not open, however, the nail should be maintained as a concomitant splint for the tuft fracture and a biologic protectant for the nail bed injury.[324]

## Crushing Injuries

Crushing injuries resulting from high-energy trauma can cause severe damage to the nail bed, and the matrix and bed must be treated with meticulous care. A disrupted nail bed or nail matrix must be carefully cleaned and débrided, even if the injury appears to be merely a laceration, and if desired, the nail bed must be carefully reapproximated with absorbable 5–0 or 6–0 catgut suture.[362] The foot is wrapped in a bulky, soft compression dressing to protect the area around the nail tuft from hematoma and is kept elevated for 2 or 3 days. Continuing protection is provided by a bunion shoe with an extension that reaches past the toes or by a cast with an extended toeplate. Injury to the nail bed or underlying phalanx can result in mild deformities such as ridging, pitting, incurvation, discoloration, or thickening, but such deformities are unusual. Unlike the situation in the hand, however, in which scarring and erratic nail growth are possible if the eponychium and nail bed are not separated by something in the absence of the removed nail plate until partial nail regrowth, normal nail growth in the feet does not require any such special precautions. In fact, hand surgeons frequently advocate coverage of any repair with the residual nail plate to protect the repair, guide new nail growth, and prevent scar formation, although scarring rarely seems to be an issue in the lower extremity regardless of how these injuries are protected. Obviously, the quality of future nail growth will be influenced by the severity of the original injury to the germinal matrix and nail bed, and thus in some cases, complete surgical ablation (matricectomy) of the nail or a distal Syme amputation may be indicated.

## SESAMOID INJURIES

### ANATOMY

The sesamoids are an integral component of the two-headed short flexor mechanism in the great toe, and their function is similar to that of the patella in the quadriceps mechanism of the knee. They cushion the first metatarsal head and the MTP joint from the pressure of weight bearing and provide leverage to the short flexors to pull the proximal phalanx.

Each sesamoid is approximately 7 to 10 mm long and slightly oblong. Their dorsal surfaces articulate with the plantar aspect of the first metatarsal head. A midline crista that runs beneath the metatarsal head divides the medial and lateral articular surfaces and holds the sesamoids in correct position under the head. A strong intersesamoid ligament connects the two sesamoids and extends to the deep transverse intermetatarsal ligament. The extensions of the medial and lateral short flexors combine with the abductor and adductor muscles to become conjoined tendons and attach into the inferior medial and lateral bases of the first proximal phalanx. Typically, the medial sesamoid is more centrally located beneath the first metatarsal head and as a result probable bears more weight and is more prone to injury such as sesamoiditis or fracture.[54, 154]

## ETIOLOGY AND EVALUATION

Injury to a first MTP sesamoid, though rare, can cause tremendous pain and disability. Dancers and runners are susceptible to traumatic stress fractures in the sesamoids from repeated impact and tension. Dancers who train and perform in thin-soled shoes are most vulnerable to this injury because they land on a hard surface with the toes dorsiflexed. Sesamoidal injuries can be properly evaluated with a routine set of three views of the foot, including an axial sesamoidal view. The latter radiograph enables the physician to independently assess the congruity of each metatarsosesamoid articulation, the status of the cartilage surfaces, and any fracture displacement. Patients typically have mild swelling, stiffness of the MTP joint, and point tenderness over the specifically involved sesamoid, which can usually be accurately determined by a careful, deliberate examination. Active or passive hyperextension exacerbates their pain by putting the entire sesamoidal apparatus on stretch. An acute fracture needs to be differentiated from a symptomatic partite sesamoid, which can be partitioned into two, three, or even multiple ossification centers. Many features of partitioned sesamoids can be distinguished on plane films with comparison views: bilaterality (85%), medial location (10×), smooth edges, large size, obliquity of the radiolucency (rather than transverse), and lack of callus.[154]

## SESAMOIDITIS

Sesamoiditis is a syndrome characterized by pain, tenderness, inflammation, and possible cartilage injury in the metatarsal head–sesamoid articulation. It is similar to chondromalacia in the patellofemoral joint in the knee, which in turn is very similar to traumatic chondritis or chondrosis and arthrosis. Sesamoiditis is typically caused by some form of repetitive stress on the MTP apparatus, such as with dancers or runners. It is aggravated by improper tracking of the sesamoids under the metatarsal head and by progressive metatarsus varus, which may arise from an atavistic condition in the TMT joint. Plantar flexion of the first metatarsal and overactivity in the long peroneal tendon (peroneal overdrive) can overload the sesamoids and produce pain similar to that associated with sesamoiditis. These underlying problems must be identified and treated.

## SESAMOID FRACTURES

Potential problems from a sesamoid fracture may be graver than simple discomfort. Half of the flexor mechanism and conjoined tendon may be disrupted when the great toe drifts to the opposite side. For example, if the medial sesamoid–short flexor complex is disrupted, lateral drift of the great toe produces a hallux valgus deformity.[359] The crista that normally separates the medial and lateral articular surfaces on the anterior metatarsal head is worn away as the medial sesamoid moves underneath it, and as a result the head shifts medially. Sesamoiditis commonly progresses to complete dislocation of the fibular sesamoid and to a painful condition in which only the tibial sesamoid remains centered under the metatarsal head. Fracture of a sesamoid can result from either tension force on the sesamoidal apparatus or a direct impact force on the sesamoid itself. Most sesamoidal fractures have simple transverse patterns with minimal displacement and sharp fracture edges.

## MANAGEMENT

Acute fractures and suspected stress fractures of the sesamoids are commonly treated by placing soft padding underneath the arch and the first metatarsal head and strapping the MTP joint in a neutral position or in slight flexion. The foot is then immobilized in a cast or a bunion shoe for 4 to 8 weeks. This course of treatment should be the first step in management of acute sesamoid fractures. If a sesamoid does not heal with casting (and it frequently does not) or if pain persists (which may take 4 to 6 months to resolve), sesamoidectomy or bone grafting is indicated. Sesamoiditis can be treated in a similar fashion and followed by orthotic decompression of the first MTP joint with load transfer to the lesser MTP joints and medial longitudinal arch.

**Sesamoidectomy.** Sesamoidectomy requires extremely precise surgical technique. In this procedure, the broken sesamoid is removed from its capsule without disturbing the tendon. If the fracture is not through the midbody of the sesamoid and a much smaller pole exists, only partial excision of the lesser sesamoid fragment can be performed. For lateral (fibular) sesamoid excision, a plantar approach is recommended between the first and second metatarsal heads to minimize the painful scar formation that can occur in about 10% of cases (Fig. 60–71). Care must be taken to avoid the digital nerve, which traverses the MTP joint immediately adjacent to the sesamoid, because injury to this nerve can be quite debilitating by virtue of the location of the neuroma. This approach seems to be significantly easier than a dorsal exposure. For medial (tibial) sesamoid excision, a direct medial approach is performed, again avoiding the dorsal and plantar digital sensory nerve branches. After the bone has been enucleated, the tendon is repaired or imbricated, and the wound is closed. The toe is splinted in a protected position for 4 to 6 weeks before rehabilitation with dorsiflexion exercises and full weight bearing is begun. The foot may be splinted at night for several more months to ensure that the great toe does not drift out of position. It may be impossible to perform this operation on some patients because of differences in individual anatomy.

Serious disability is occasionally associated with sesamoidectomy, and every attempt should be made to salvage the sesamoids. Pain-free normal function is not always

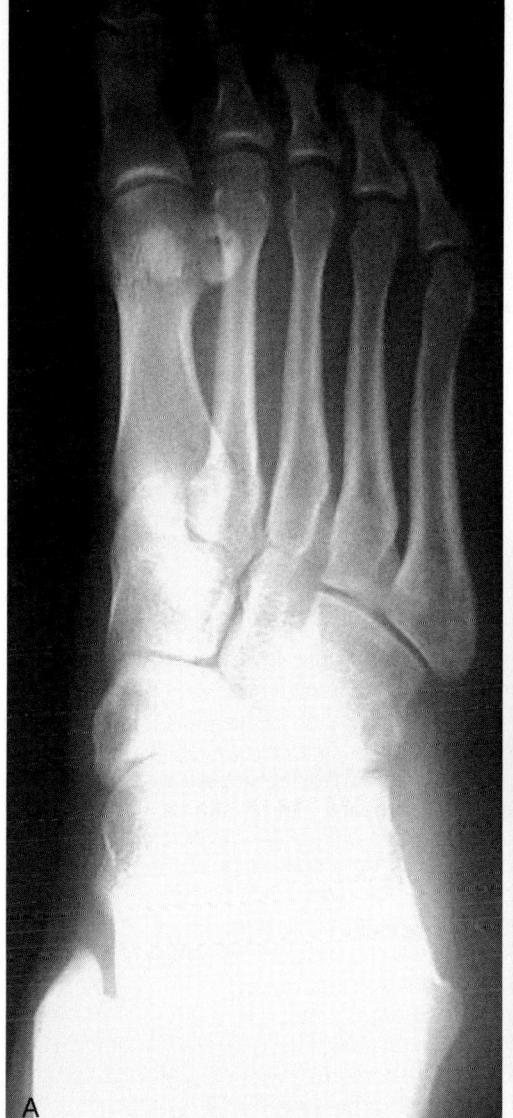

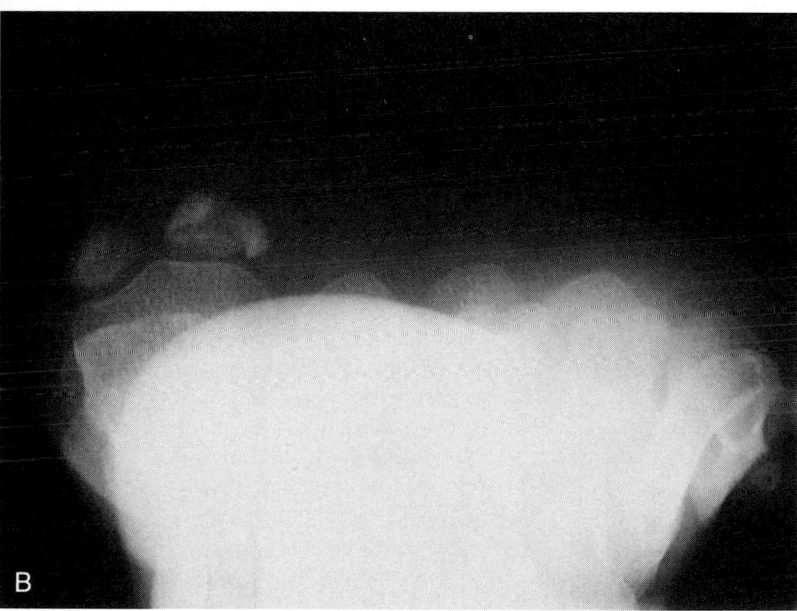

**FIGURE 60–71.** Sesamoid fractures frequently do not heal despite appropriate care and can remain persistently symptomatic. Exhaustive attempts should be made to avoid operative intervention. When necessary, excision is probably the most reliable treatment choice and consists of carefully shelling out the involved sesamoid, followed by meticulous restoration of the flexor and adductor/abductor mechanism. This young patient was a catcher for a division 1 softball team and sustained a fracture of her sesamoid because of her chronically crouched position (*A, B*). Her symptoms were not alleviated with prolonged conservative treatment, and she eventually required excision to relieve her symptoms and resume playing softball.

restored by sesamoidectomy. Excision of the lateral sesamoid causes medial drift and a cock-up deformity called hallux varus, a complication associated with the McBride bunionectomy, in which the lateral sesamoid is excised. Another possible complication is the development of a transfer lesion on the rest of the metatarsals. A transfer lesion may form when the remaining sesamoid becomes painful from the extra weight that it must support despite an intact flexor mechanism. Removal of the remaining sesamoid may be necessary, but before removal, the surgeon must rule out the possibility that the excessive loading on the sesamoids and the first metatarsal head is being caused by a plantar flexion deformity in the first metatarsal or by hyperactivity or recruitment of the long peroneal tendon as a result of triceps surae weakness.

**Bone Grafting.** Experience and published results after ORIF and bone grafting of a sesamoid nonunion are scant. If a decision is made to graft and fix a sesamoid fracture that resists healing, the rate of union is higher than it is with splinting alone. A small hole is drilled into the center of the fracture site with a bur and filled with cancellous bone graft. If the fracture fragments are large enough, compression could be obtained with a 1.5-mm screw, but experience with this technique is limited. Alternatively, if the articular surface is not disrupted on inspection (i.e., incomplete union), the plantar nonunion site can be treated by curettage or drilled and subsequently filled with bone graft. This situation is seemingly the best indication for this technique in lieu of complete excision. Postoperatively, the great toe and the short flexor mechanism are splinted in neutral position, as in routine nonoperative treatment. This type of bone graft is a variation of a strain-relieved graft and can be successful.

## DEEP VENOUS THROMBOSIS AND PROPHYLAXIS

DVT in the perioperative setting after foot trauma is fairly unusual, but not nonexistent and should therefore be considered in all patients with predisposing risk factors. The topic is poorly documented in the literature and does not seem to have been formally studied in foot and ankle trauma patients.[216] Only a couple of papers in the literature have discussed this topic, and prophylaxis for DVT in foot and ankle patients in general has essentially been ignored by most because of the low incidence of symptomatic DVT and pulmonary embolism (PE). The one large, prospective multicenter study that evaluated DVT in general foot and ankle patients after surgery identified a 0.22% incidence of DVT and a 0.15% incidence of nonfatal symptomatic PE in 2733 patients, thus suggesting that routine prophylaxis in this setting was not warranted.[213] Meissner and colleagues[207] have also studied the incidence of venous thromboembolism in trauma patients. They monitored multitrauma patients with varying levels of extremity, axial, and head injury admitted to a major academic trauma center and used lower extremity duplex ultrasound in addition to levels of prothrombin fragments F1 and F2 and quantitative D dimer for measurement of thrombin and fibrin levels to assess the overall risk of venous thromboembolism. They noted that 63% of thrombi occurred within the first 7 days of injury in these patients and over 90% occurred in individuals immobilized for longer than 3 days. Most importantly, they found that neither the specific regional injury pattern (location) nor its severity (Abbreviated Injury Score) served as a good predictor of venous thromboembolism. The duration of immobilization (>3 days) and obesity were determined to be the only significant predictors of thromboembolism in injured patients.[206, 207]

Because tremendous outside forces over the past 10 to 15 years have increasingly resulted in a switch to early postoperative discharge and outpatient elective surgery in most cases of foot and ankle trauma, many of these patients are thrust into an unsupervised, somewhat immobile position and are thus at increased risk for DVT or PE. At Brown University School of Medicine, we are currently completing a survey of members of the AOFAS and the Orthopaedic Trauma Association regarding their DVT prophylaxis regimens for such patients. No consistent pattern of practice exists, and often no anticoagulation is given. Although the incidence of DVT and PE in this population is unknown, we suspect that the risk is significant for patients with acute foot and ankle injuries by virtue of their increased immobilization, decreased activity, and injured tissues. We therefore currently recommend some form of prophylaxis for any foot and ankle trauma patient whose injury requires some form of immobilization that exceeds their ability to be active, as well as those with risk factors such as multiple trauma, head or spinal cord injury, obesity, previous DVT or PE, oral contraceptive use, active malignancy, and other factors. Our current practice usually involves the use of 5000 U of subcutaneous heparin twice a day in the hospital setting, combined with intrinsic muscle exercises, early mobilization, and either foot pumps or a TED/sequential compression device if possible. Alternative outpatient measures to consider in addition to the preceding are low-molecular-weight heparin, low-dose aspirin (80 mg/day), and warfarin (Coumadin). The choice should depend on host risk factors and the duration of immobilization. Management of this unusual but potentially fatal calamity in foot and ankle trauma patients continues to be researched and discussed because the data are inconclusive. The fact remains that to date, most surgeons decide to treat or not to treat based on purely anecdotal evidence.

## MUTILATING INJURIES AND AMPUTATIONS

High-energy mechanisms cause various degrees of damage to skeletal and soft tissue, depending on the degree of compressive, shear, or degloving component incurred and for how long.

Lawn mower injuries, typically from sit-down mowers that have tipped over, and road burns on the foot as a result of a spinning tire can be devastating injuries. Since 1993, the AOFAS has developed a position statement on this topic because of its public health risk. According to some recent data and the U.S. Consumer Product Safety Commission, between 50,000 and 160,000 lawn mower injuries occur and result in 75 deaths every year and a devastating number of toe or partial foot amputations. Sixty percent of these fatalities occur in children younger than 5 years and adults older than 67.[136] Fifteen percent of these injuries occur in preadolescent bystanders, and 80% occur as a result of private, weekend use. Almost 75% of childhood injuries occur in bystanders, with amputation eventually being necessary in 16% to 78% of them.[72] The worst combination seems to be a riding mower with more than one person aboard on a sloped or wet piece of property. Lack of shoe wear and insufficient soles have also been implicated.[260] Lawn mower injuries cost the health care industry $475 million annually. Such high-energy injuries are contaminated wounds caused by a 2100-ft-lb rotary force[246] (Fig. 60–72). Patients often have severe dorsal soft tissue loss, exposed bone, instability, mangled tissues, and sometimes partial loss of a limb.[246] At least 50% of these injuries require flap coverage or skin grafting. Although each injury is obviously very different, depending on the mechanism of injury, shoe wear, and host factors, certain important steps should be taken in each case to optimize care.[82, 349] Plantar or posterior wounds have the worst prognosis.[14, 349] Trauma protocols should be followed, although salvage is typically more difficult in this situation than in open injuries elsewhere in the extremities because of the degree of damage and intrinsic lack of soft tissue coverage and vascular flow in the region.

Any decision regarding ultimate treatment should not be made until adequate débridement and inspection are performed in an operating room. Heckman has recently nicely outlined prioritization in managing a multiply injured foot: preserve the circulation, preserve sensation (especially plantar), maintain a plantigrade foot position, control infection, preserve the plantar skin and fat pads, preserve gross motion in all planes (both active and passive), achieve bony union, and preserve fine motion.[128] He points out that as espoused by Jacobs,[151] achievement of bony union is of relatively less import in management of a mangled foot.

Because these injuries are usually isolated and open, appropriate films should be obtained, antibiotic coverage administered for at least 3 days for gram-positive (grade I), gram-negative (grade II and III), or anaerobic (barnyard, severe contamination) organisms, and tetanus status verified and updated if necessary. Tissue culture has no role in the emergency department because of the degree of contamination and sampling error. Instead, wounds should be covered with a povidone-iodine (Betadine) dressing, compartment pressures should be checked if necessary, appropriate and adequate films unimpeded by splints should be taken in the emergency department to document the extent of bony injury, and the patient should then be splinted and urgently transported to the operating room for definitive irrigation, débridement, fasciotomy, and antibiotic bead pouch placement, if necessary. In wounds grossly contaminated with dirt, grass, pavement, or other debris, continuous irrigation is probably better than a pulsatile method because the latter can drive particulate matter further into the surrounding soft tissue bed and has not been shown to have increased efficacy. Jet lavage is clearly better than bulb syringe irrigation for removing necrotic material and bacteria, as long is it remains at a low to moderate setting. Anglen's review of animal data on wound irrigation during musculoskeletal injury suggests that volume is an important factor in decreasing the overall bacterial load in tissues, although the ideal volume to infuse remains unknown.[6] At least 3 L of fluid should be used for each Gustilo grade in an open fracture. High-pressure irrigation has been shown to improve removal of debris and lessen the incidence of infection, although it may also damage both surrounding osseous and soft tissues and delay fracture healing. Thus, it is best when wounds are heavily contaminated or treatment has been delayed. Repetitive trips to the operating room or healthy wounds at initial evaluation are probably better managed with bulb syringe irrigation because the mechanical effects of higher pressure are not required in this situation and the gentle effect of the lower pressure on surrounding tissue is amenable to wound healing. The usefulness of antibiotic solutions such as bacitracin, polymyxin, or neomycin during this process remains unproved in the clinical setting; in view of their cost and the possibility of allergic reaction or bacterial resistance, they are also not recommended for routine use. Antiseptic additives such as alcohol, povidone-iodine, chlorhexidine gluconate, hexachlorophene, or sodium hypochlorite, though broadly toxic to bacteria, viruses, and fungi, can be equally toxic to host tissue. They should probably not be used because their toxicity has been documented more extensively than their benefit. More research is required to establish the clinical efficacy of detergent agents, such as soaps (surfactants) or benzalkonium chloride, that physically remove bacteria and debris

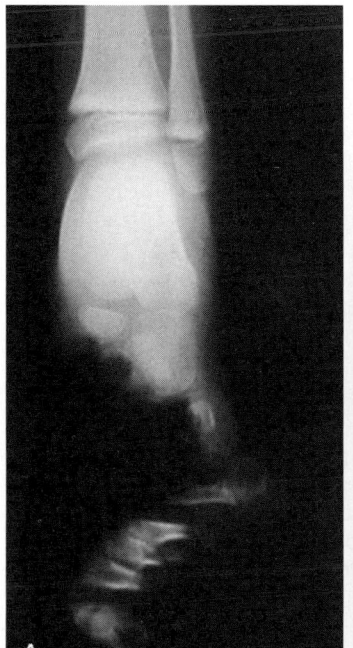
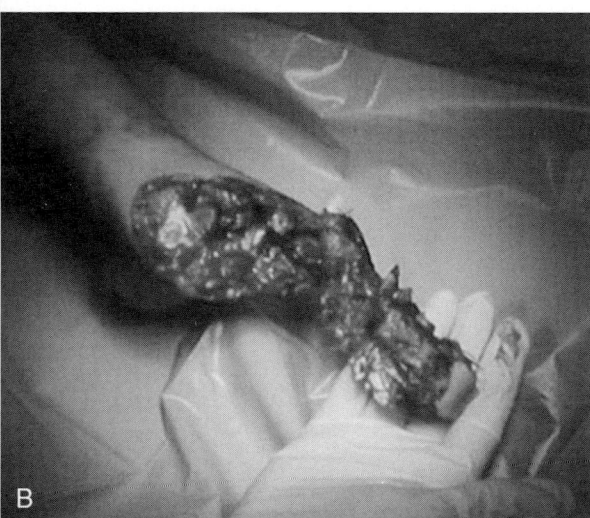
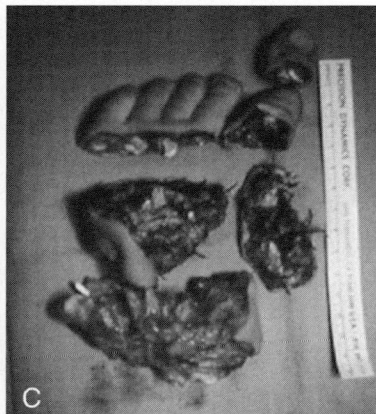

**FIGURE 60–72.** Management of a mutilated foot requires incorporation of all aspects of musculoskeletal trauma care and taxes the ability of even the most experienced trauma surgeons. Unfortunately, many of these injuries, particularly those involving lawn mower accidents such as the one seen here (*A–C*), go beyond the limits of our reconstructive technology and are best served by completion amputation. Thus, good foot and ankle care also necessitates a thorough knowledge of how and when to perform amputation surgery.

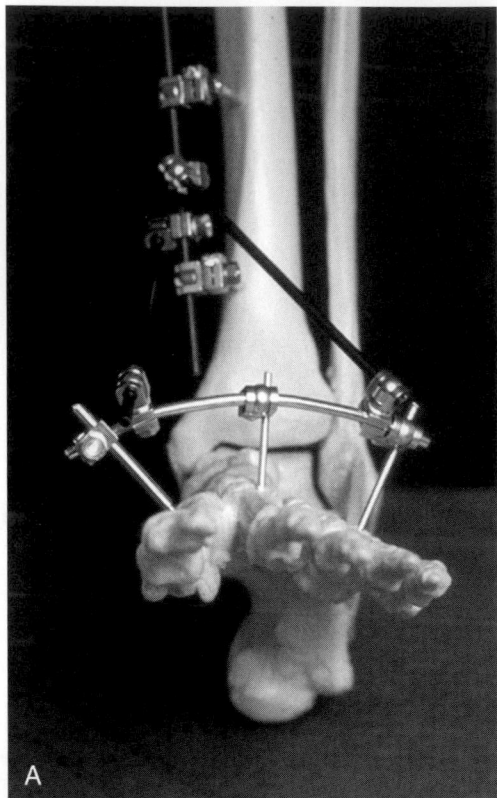
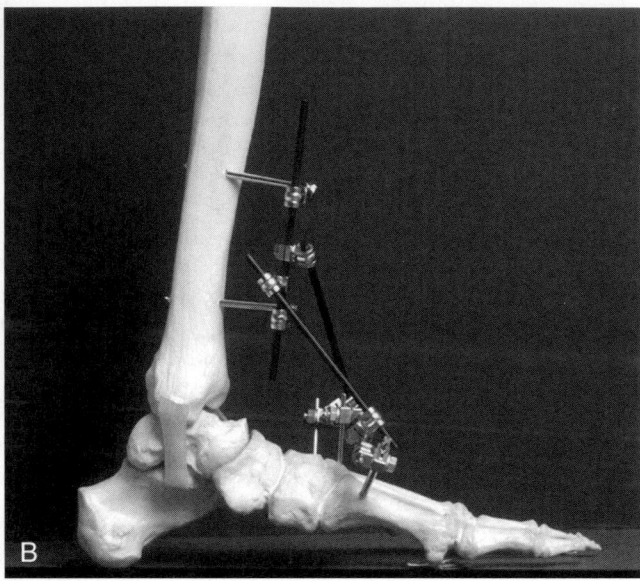

**FIGURE 60–73.** Use of an external fixator frame across the foot is an excellent way of stabilizing bony and soft tissue disruption in the acute setting. Although many constructs are possible, either a small or a large fixator set can be used to bridge the medial distal aspect of the tibia to the hindfoot, midfoot, or forefoot. The front (*A*) and side (*B*) views of a frame are presented that can effectively reduce and stabilize injuries to the ankle and foot even when present at multiple levels. Isolated forefoot injuries rarely require external fixation, although more simple constructs along the lateral or medial column can be used to maintain length in patients with areas of extensive bone loss.

or prevent adhesion because current animal models have supported their usefulness in highly contaminated wounds.

Skeletal stabilization at the initial surgery should usually be temporizing and consist of K-wires, Schanz pins, or external fixators from the leg to the foot or the hindfoot to the forefoot because the degree of tissue damage ("zone of injury") is often greater than initially recognized and generally requires repeated débridement before an accurate assessment of viable bone and soft tissue can be made[150] (Fig. 60–73). In fact, the rate of subsequent infection is very high if wounds are closed primarily. Many recently described techniques such as fluorescein labeling, Doppler flowmetry, and split-thickness skin excision can aid the surgeon in assessing tissue viability if necessary.[226, 357] More complicated soft tissue procedures have also been used with limited success.[107, 199] Decisions regarding the placement of incisions in these compromised soft tissue envelopes should follow the known angiosomal patterns in the foot.[11, 325] These five areas represent the supply network of their respective arterial source: the calcaneal branch of the posterior tibial artery, the dorsalis pedis, the calcaneal branch of the peroneal artery, and the medial and lateral plantar arterial branches. Although these vascular channels are connected by a rich anastomotic framework, even with disruption at some level, placement of an incision is safest

when it respects the interface between angiosomes. Thus, healing is most reliable when incisions or extensions of open wounds are directed longitudinally along these border regions: at the glabrous junctions along the medial and lateral sides of the foot, at the midline of the heel and Achilles tendon, and along the center of the plantar foot.

Kenzora and associates described the usefulness of external fixation of severe lower extremity trauma injuries to stabilize fractures and dislocations, maintain length in the presence of bony loss, prevent contracture, perform ligamentotaxis in periarticular injuries, and allow soft tissue stability and unimpeded access in the event that serial soft tissue observation or further fixation is necessary.[166] If the soft tissues permit, Sangeorzan and Hansen advocate early internal fixation in the management of such injuries.[290] When possible, such treatment may allow more rapid definitive wound closure and postoperative mobilization of the injured extremity and joints. Once internal fixation can be established, preferably within 3 to 5 days to minimize the chance of bacterial colonization and eventual treatment failure, the surgeon is able to make better decisions about appropriate definitive hardware for stabilization and should also have already introduced this patient and the wounds to a plastic surgeon or other qualified personnel and can then schedule management of the soft tissue injury around care of the fracture. Ideally, this process is completed as rapidly as débridement permits. It is advantageous to use either serial bead pouches or, preferably, serial vacuum-assisted closure devices to maximize the débridement effort and viable soft tissue bed for future closure or coverage as necessary (see Fig. 60–55). These techniques are usually required at 48- to 72-hour intervals but can be performed daily if the wounds mandate such treatment. This system, popularized by plastic surgeons, has proved incredibly effective in filling large soft tissue defects or degloving injuries with exuberant granulation tissue.[7, 204] DeFranzo and colleagues recently demonstrated successful wound closure in 71 of 75 major orthopaedic trauma injuries, including those with exposed bone or hardware, with use of the vacuum-assisted closure device with a 6-month to 6-year follow-up.[62] Most of these wounds either closed primarily or required split-thickness skin grafting or local rotational flaps for closure over the granulated bed. Its success is supported by numerous other authors over the last several years, and it has rapidly become a valuable adjunctive tool in handling difficult traumatic lower extremity wounds or degloving injuries. Vacuum-assisted closure can even be done under intravenous sedation at the bedside if absolutely necessary or mandated by the patient's clinical status. Daily physical therapy should be performed at the bedside both actively and passively to minimize postinjury stiffness or contracture in the toes and adjacent joints as soon as the soft tissues and patient can tolerate such therapy. Early mobilization and protected weight bearing with graduated progression should begin as soon as possible after definitive fixation and wound closure. At the earliest, such rehabilitation is safe within 2 to 4 weeks after closure when the soft tissues appear amenable. Not uncommonly, patients require future reconstructive surgery in the form of ligament repair, fusion, or soft tissue tendon balancing once the initial foot injury has healed and rehabilitated to its fullest potential—which can take 1 to 2 years.

Occasionally, amputation is required for an optimal result, but in general, if salvage of an aligned, sensate, mobile plantigrade foot can reasonably be accomplished, the result is probably better than after formal amputation. The choice for primary amputation is a difficult one, and no ideal criteria or algorithms are available to make this decision because although many have attempted to identify such predictive factors, they are usually based on open tibia fractures and not on foot and ankle injuries.[111] One of the most commonly used scores is the Mangled Extremity Severity Score (MESS). Assessment includes evaluation of skeletal and soft tissue injury, limb ischemia, shock, and age. A score of 7 or greater is a positive predictor of amputation (100% in this study), although the presence of ischemic time longer than 6 hours doubles its point value and also suggests an increased likelihood of amputation.[157] It should be based on neurovascular status, degree of soft tissue and bony injury, the presence of concomitant injuries, ischemia time, and host factors. Deciding on the level of amputation in the foot is also a difficult issue that is based on many factors. Although such discussion is beyond the scope of this text, some excellent references on the subject outline both technique and decision making.[46] In general, as much of the foot should be salvaged as possible, provided that it

has adequate soft tissue coverage, at least protective sensation, sufficient vascularity, and a reasonable chance of any necessary bony fixation healing without major complications. One should ensure that what remains can effectively serve as a durable, stable, long-term platform capable of assisting with weight support, balance, and propulsive gait, ideally with little or no pain.[157] Replantation efforts are anecdotal in the foot and ankle, and the benefits of these heroic efforts remain poorly understood. Prosthetic management in the lower extremity is quite good and may be part of the reason for the low frequency of replantation. An extensive evaluation of over 300 replantations involving the lower extremity and toes has been conducted in Japan.[101] The most difficult salvage remains feet that are insensate, poorly vascularized, or severely degloved on the plantar surface. A patient's health status, expectations, and age at injury must also be taken into account before making this decision. Medical costs are 50% less with primary versus delayed amputation.

## CRUSH INJURIES

A crush injury in the foot, such as an industrial injury from a forklift or power machine, is another severe injury that is unfortunately fairly common and mostly due to gravity. These injuries are usually closed, but they can also have a great deal of underlying bone and soft tissue damage, the results of which some liken to a "closed degloving."[89] Compartment syndrome should be carefully monitored in such patients, and it is wise to admit these individuals and elevate and splint the foot with daily neurovascular examination, as well as evaluation of pain control. Treatment of fractures and dislocations follows similar protocols as outlined in this chapter, but one must keep in mind that these patients have a significantly poorer prognosis beyond what can be attributed to the pure bone or articular damage. This poor prognosis is due to their underlying mechanism, which causes a tremendous amount of ill-identified damage to all the soft tissues in the zone of injury, including nerves and vessels. Thus, it is not uncommon for such individuals to have signs and symptoms consistent with causalgia or complex regional pain syndrome. In these instances, prompt recognition and referral to a pain specialist and physical therapist tend to produce better long-term outcomes. Such injuries frequently result in some degree of long-term stiffness, pain, and disability that is hard to initially predict.[225] Evolution of these sequelae can also take 1 to 2 years. In most cases, early mobilization and soft tissue coverage, rigid skeletal stabilization, avoidance and treatment of compartment syndrome or reflex sympathetic dystrophy, avoidance of prolonged non–weight-bearing status, minimization of soft tissue edema, and encouragement of rapid return to use of the limb and previous lifestyle, if possible, seem to significantly improve the outcome.[231] It is clear that preservation of a stable, plantigrade, sensate foot after severe injury still provides better long-term function than does even the most well-performed amputation and state-of-the-art prosthetic design.

# CHEMICAL AND THERMAL BURNS

Because of the small surface area represented by the foot (3.5% each), the potentially devastating functional impairment created by burns in this region is often underestimated. The American Burn Association actually classifies burns of the foot as "major" despite their overall size, probably because the area of contracture and skin breakdown is subject to weight bearing and high shear stress.[301] These sequelae obviously eliminate any hope of a painless gait. The resultant scarring often leads to arthrofibrosis and tendon impairment, which significantly alter the biomechanics of coupled foot and ankle motion. The severity of the injury is mostly related to the fact that the foot has very little soft tissue depth, and thus burns are quick to involve the nearby underlying neurovascular and tendinous structures either directly or through subsequent scarring as part of the healing process. Treatment of burns in the foot is similar to that in other parts of the body, although when isolated, they are not subject to the same massive fluid shifts that sometimes need to be addressed. The damage to skin, subcutaneous tissues, and vital structures, however, often requires the combined efforts of both the orthopaedic and general surgical services. In the absence of ongoing injury, the soft tissues should be assessed for the degree or level of tissue involvement and compartment syndrome. Appropriate treatment includes judicious operative débridement and removal or reversal of the causative agent when necessary. Further reconstructive procedures after initial healing are common.

# GUNSHOT WOUNDS

Gunshot wounds of the foot are treated similar to those in other parts of the body. Whereas handgun injuries are usually of low velocity (less than 2000 ft/sec), rifles tend to cause higher energy injuries (>2000 ft/sec). Shotguns typically create low-velocity wounds that should be considered high-energy injuries by virtue of diffuse projectile damage.[24] With low-velocity missile damage, wounds are best managed by local wound care and débridement in the emergency department, assessment of neurovascular status, and appropriate treatment of any associated fractures. Unlike traditional open injuries, fractures that are the result of low-energy or small-caliber guns require surgery only if the fracture pattern or articular disruption indicates such management.[13] Otherwise, these fractures can be treated in closed fashion with immobilization in an appropriate postoperative shoe, splint, or cast, a short course (3 to 7 days) of antibiotic coverage with a first-generation cephalosporin, and early follow-up for examination of the wound. Some controversy remains regarding the advantage of administering intravenous versus oral antibiotics over this period. Lead toxicity or synovitis is not a concern when these injuries are nonarticular, but if a significant amount of debris is found within a joint, consideration should be given to formal operative débridement to minimize the chance of post-traumatic synovitis and arthritis. Recovery from these

injuries is often complete. High-velocity gunshot wounds (Fig. 60–74), on the other hand, need to be treated aggressively with standard open wound management, fracture care, and broad-spectrum intravenous antibiotics.[24] As expected, the degree of soft tissue and bone damage is usually much greater than can be appreciated on radiographs or by examination of the entrance or exit wounds. This greater damage is due to the missile's own cavitation effect on the surrounding soft tissue in its path, as well as concomitant destruction by adjacent structures, which can be broadly dispersed depending on the missile's kinetic energy.[68] Compartment syndrome is also a significant risk with these injuries and needs to be carefully ruled out by measurement of compartment pressure if necessary. Any soft tissue coverage or bony stabilization required should be performed as soon as, but not before the soft tissues permit because of the time-dependent increase in bacterial contamination and infection, preferably within the first 5 to 7 days.

# PUNCTURE, ANIMAL, AND MARINE WOUNDS

Very little science governs how best to manage puncture wounds of the foot. The foot frequently sustains puncture wounds that usually look innocuous initially (Fig. 60–75). Despite the fact that these wounds often result in bone (1%), soft tissue (10%), or joint infection (1%), punctures of the foot are still commonly undertreated. Such wounds run the spectrum of developing into major deep space abscesses or simply inciting a minor foreign body reaction from dermal penetration by wood, glass, or other debris.[347] Over 90% of these injuries occur as a result of a nail, and the vast majority that result in osteomyelitis or pyarthrosis are pseudomonal in origin, probably because of the affinity of *Pseudomonas* for synthetic shoe wear and its predilection for cartilaginous tissue. *Staphylococcus* and *Streptococcus,* common pathogens in many soft tissue infections, account for most of the more superficial tissue infections, although these infections can frequently be polymicrobial.

Factors associated with an increased likelihood of infection are a retained foreign body, deep penetration (below the plantar fascia), immunosuppression, absence of tetanus immunization, and probably delay in time to treatment. One should also take into consideration the type or absence of shoe wear, the site of the puncture (near a joint or deep compartment not easily examined), the mechanism or object of injury, and the overall medical condition of the patient. Plain radiographs should always be taken, regardless of injury description or time after injury, because they provide a rapid, inexpensive, and valuable tool to help identify a retained foreign body or deep space infection (gas), which would favor surgical exploration. Simple puncture wounds of the foot seen within the first 24 hours should be managed with appropriate antibiotic and tetanus coverage and radiographs to examine for any residual foreign bodies in the soft tissues.[304] Probing of wounds in the emergency department runs the risk of advancing foreign bodies more

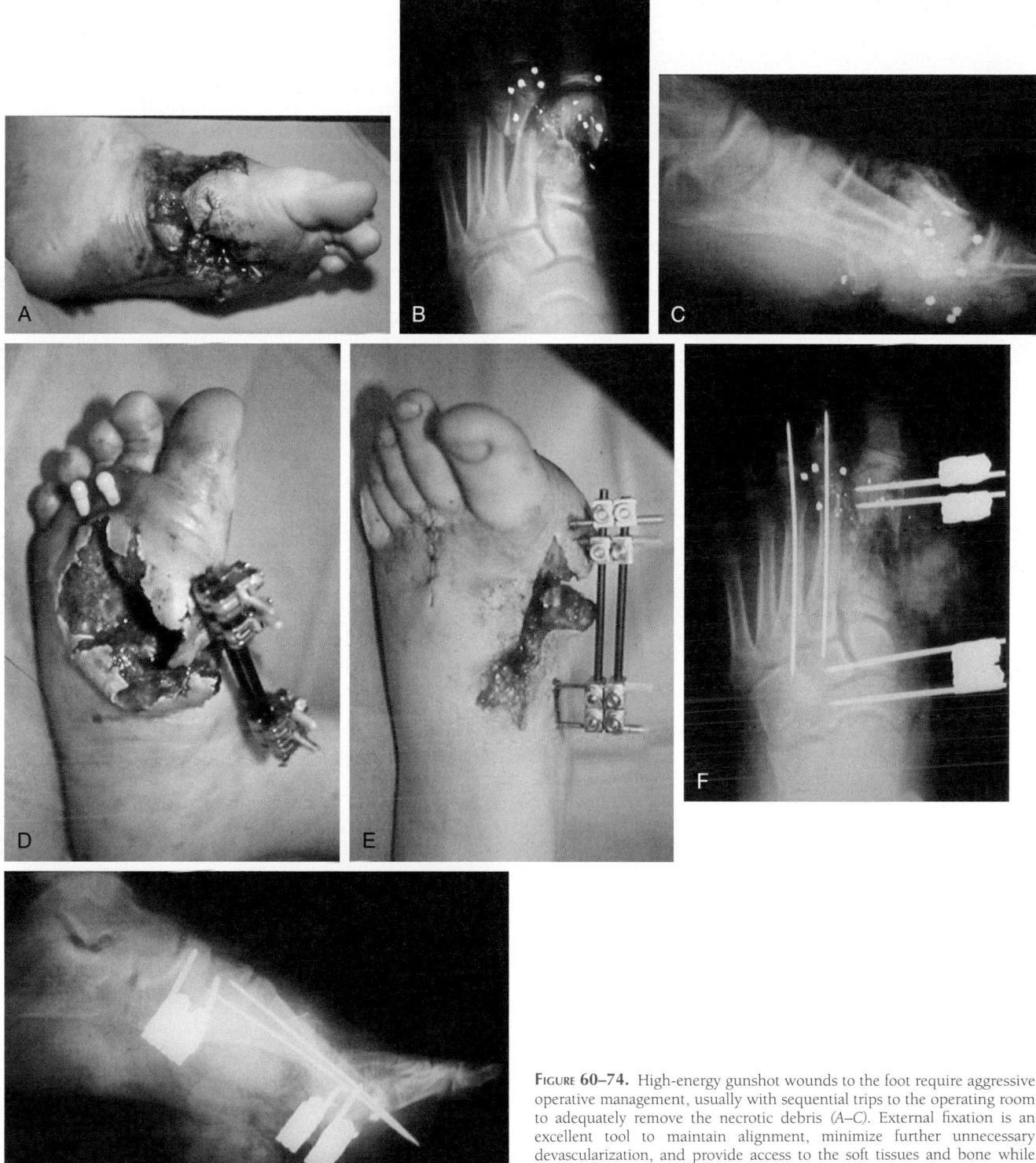

**FIGURE 60–74.** High-energy gunshot wounds to the foot require aggressive operative management, usually with sequential trips to the operating room to adequately remove the necrotic debris (*A–C*). External fixation is an excellent tool to maintain alignment, minimize further unnecessary devascularization, and provide access to the soft tissues and bone while débridement is carried out (*D–G*). The status of the remaining tissues is then assessed to determine the requirements for safe, definitive bony stabilization and soft tissue coverage.

deeply into the soft tissues and should probably be reserved for the operating room.

If the injury is caught acutely, initial treatment should consist of local cleansing, wound débridement, and a course of non–weight-bearing immobilization in a splint or Jones dressing. A follow-up visit should be scheduled within 48 to 72 hours. The presence of symptoms at this latter time is associated with a high rate of complications. Foreign body reactions, on the other hand, are typically manifested long after inoculation, even months to years later, as a granulomatous reaction. Polymicrobial infection should be suspected in all diabetics, and pseudomonal infection and osteomyelitis should be ruled out in any patient with persistent symptoms after plantar penetration through a sneaker because the organism has been found in the glue used to sole this type of shoe wear. This injury is best managed by operative irrigation, débridement, and broad-spectrum antibiotics that include pseudomonal coverage, followed by a 4- to 6-week course of bacteria-specific intravenous antibiotics as determined by culture.[144] If a patient is initially examined late after injury (beyond 24 to 48 hours) and has erythema, swelling, or pain in the foot, serious consideration should be given to operative exploration, culture, and débridement of any abscess, foreign body, granulomatous reactive tissue, or pyarthrosis. It is often difficult at this point to radiographically or visually establish the presence of osteomyelitis, but any confirmation of bony infection (including the use of adjunctive nuclear medicine or magnetic resonance studies) requires aggressive surgical débridement of involved bone and consideration of a staged procedure and placement of a antibiotic bead pouch.

A good history is imperative to establish any environmental risk at the time of puncture or after it if the patient is not seen early after injury. Environmental risk can affect the choice of antibiotic and, in the case of severe contamination, a decision for surgery. Signs of cellulitis, lymphadenopathy, and, most important, fluctuance or Kanavel's sign, all suggestive of deep space or tendon sheath infection (abscess), should be ruled out by physical examination and either ultrasound or MRI if necessary.[215] The presence of a deep space infection or soft tissue gas seen on radiographs (suggestive of clostridial necrotizing fasciitis) in any of the plantar compartments of the foot requires rapid decompression, débridement, and good cultures for subsequent antibiotic coverage. Most puncture

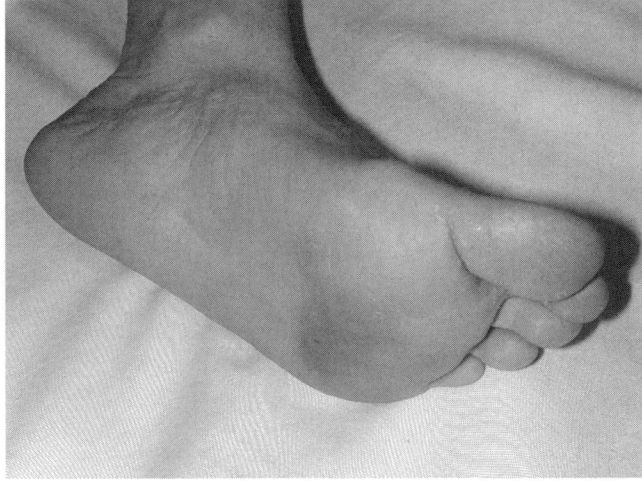

**Figure 60–75.** Puncture wounds in the foot usually look very innocuous at initial examination. They are, however, notorious for causing persistent symptoms resulting from deep space or bony infection if not initially treated aggressively, particularly when they are evaluated late after injury, as in this case. Despite their appearance, the physician should be alert to the possible need for operative débridement, removal of any foreign body identified by imaging studies, and long-term intravenous antibiotic coverage. This patient required eventual metatarsal head excision because the puncture wound entered the lesser metatarsophalangeal joint and resulted in septic arthritis and osteomyelitis.

wounds initially seem fairly innocuous, and in the absence of significant signs or symptoms, a worrisome history or radiograph, or penetration beneath the plantar fascia, they can be treated with local wound care and a 10- to 14-day course of antibiotics with one of the newer broad-spectrum drugs effective against gram-positive and, if suspected, gram-negative, anaerobic, or marine organisms. The administration of antibiotics is controversial, however; some literature suggests that antibiotic prophylaxis in the absence of documented infection may actually be a risk factor for infection, possibly by selecting out certain flora. It remains controversial whether antipseudomonal agents should be used with deeper puncture wounds. Special attention to these benign-looking wounds should be afforded to at-risk or immunologically compromised hosts such as persons with diabetes, human immunodeficiency virus infection, alcohol abuse, or chronic immunosuppressive therapy. They have an increased risk of necrotizing fasciitis. Such cases rarely respond to antibiotics alone, and patients often appear to be in a toxic state. An underlying abscess or deep space infection can frequently be masked in these individuals, and the diagnosis can be aided by adjunctive laboratory tests such as a complete blood count, erythrocyte sedimentation rate, and C-reactive protein, as well as with some of the noninvasive measures previously mentioned. Culture of the entrance wound, unless frank pus can be expressed after topical cleansing, is usually of little to no value initially, but if symptoms persist after 10 days, it is strongly recommended. Avoidance of weight bearing on the affected area should be maintained for a few weeks after treatment to allow healing.

Cat and dog bites often introduce *Pasteurella multocida* and are best treated with a first-generation cephalosporin, amoxicillin-clavulanate (Augmentin), or tetracycline-clindamycin if the patient is penicillin allergic. As with any other bite or puncture wound, these injuries should be reevaluated within a few days after initial treatment.

Marine bites, coral-induced injuries, or open wounds from any source in a similar environment are common along coastal areas and introduce an entirely different set of organisms that may require treatment.[97]

## HEEL PAD INJURY

Heel pad avulsion is usually the result of high-energy injury and can have severe consequences regardless of the status of the neurovascular bundle or skeletal integrity. The dense fibrous septa that normally hold the fat pad to the undersurface of the calcaneus and resist migration, as well as the specialized epidermal and dermal tissue exteriorly, render this part of the foot anatomy somewhat irreplaceable in the event of injury. When heel pad viability is evident, sensation is present, and detachment is incomplete, it is reasonable to consider débridement and reattachment[181] (Fig. 60–76). Such salvage does not tend to work well in the event of a more global avulsion, however, and in such cases, the possibility of either Syme or below-knee amputation needs to be discussed with the patient.[61] The application of free flaps to this area has been

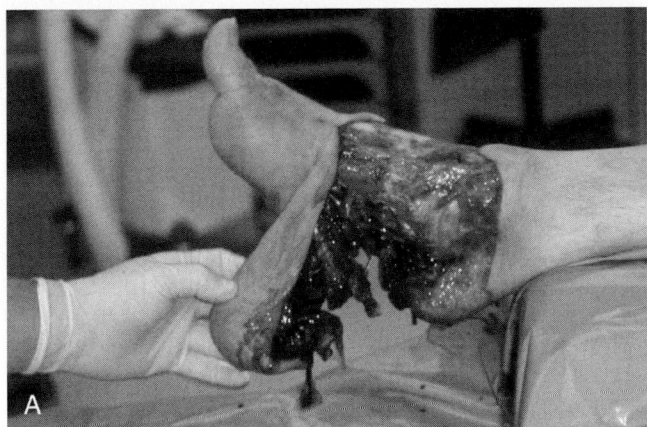
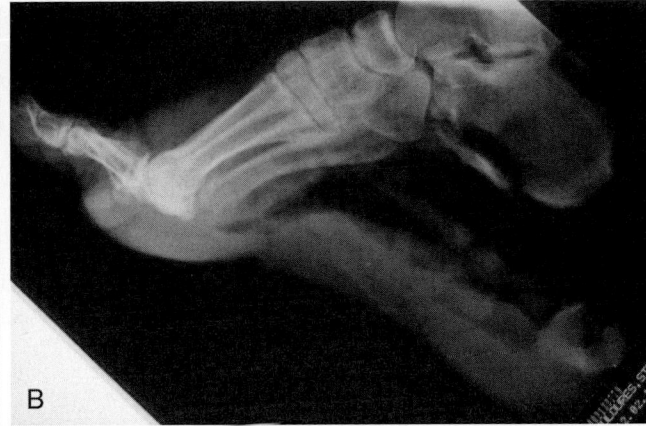

FIGURE 60–76. Heel pad avulsions tend to have a poor prognosis regardless of the bony or neurovascular status of the limb because it is impossible to restore the specialized fibrous septa at the plantar aspect of the heel that are designed to withstand the shear stress of daily standing and walking. This patient caught his foot in an industrial machine, and his entire heel pad was avulsed in a proximal-to-distal direction (A). Interestingly, it was well perfused, and although he was warned that a Syme or below-knee amputation was possible, an attempt was made to salvage this avulsion given its minimal bony injury and no significant neurologic deficit (B). By the 1-month follow-up, this flap appeared viable, but the functional outcome of this repair remains questionable and will be determined only after progressive weight bearing has begun.

reported, but the amount of pressure and shear that this transferred and insensate (or avulsed and repaired but traumatized) tissue must endure during stance or ambulation is often too overwhelming to allow a good functional result. If a free flap is undertaken, a stress-relieving insert is imperative to decrease the almost certain pressure sore at the most plantar aspect of the tuberosity. To date, no good salvage procedure is available for this difficult problem.

## NEUROPATHIC FOOT FRACTURE

Recovery from neuropathic fracture of the foot is plagued by difficulty in diagnosis and treatment, primarily because of impaired pain sensation, which often results in both delayed diagnosis and counterproductive overuse of an injured extremity.[4] In today's society, diabetes is by far the most common condition responsible for this scenario. Diabetes itself should not be considered a contraindication to surgical treatment of a foot fracture or dislocation that would otherwise warrant operative intervention. Special precautions after treatment, however, should be enacted to prevent the onset of neuroarthropathy.[303] The rate of Charcot neuropathy after foot fracture in the diabetic population is actually fairly low (0% to 1%). It occurs most commonly after a delay in treatment or diagnosis, especially in the presence of premature weight bearing or lack of the extended immobilization usually necessary regardless of operative or nonoperative management. As a general rule, Schon and Marlen recommend doubling the length of cast time normally required for the management of any diabetic patient with a fracture.[185, 303] The midtarsal and TMT region are by far the most frequently affected by this process. Interestingly, calcaneal tuberosity avulsion fractures are also rare in patients without peripheral neuropathy.[20]

On initial evaluation, diabetic patients with Charcot joints or acute fractures often have signs and symptoms that mirror an infectious process. With a careful history and physical examination and in the absence of a skin breach, however, osteomyelitis or soft tissue infection is not only quite unusual but also fairly easily ruled out. A brief period of immobilization and rest can also quickly differentiate between these diagnoses because infection will show little sign of improvement. A good clinical indication of being safely in the post-healing phase is resolution of all warmth and swelling in the affected foot or ankle. Moreover, foot trauma in diabetics poses a more challenging set of problems beyond the concerns of fracture and traumatized soft tissue management. Although these injuries are often low energy, they are to be treated with the same respect as their high-energy counterparts. Occasionally, diabetic patients can have spontaneous subluxation or dislocation of the pedal joints without a documented traumatic event.[236] Bone in diabetics is often more osteopenic and prone to subtle comminution not appreciated on initial radiographs, which can become an issue when considering operative management of these injuries. As a result of impaired perception of pain, the often periarticular and initially trivial injuries (fractures) in diabetic patients are underappreciated by them, stressed by weight bearing, and unable to form a successful reparative healing response with bridging callus.

If the fracture is caught early, cast immobilization and non–weight-bearing rest are usually conducive to healing, but if the process is allowed to continue, it results in haphazard and fruitless deposition of callus, swelling, and eventually progressive instability and collapse of the midfoot. Fixation often requires either a more stable construct than traditionally used or, more commonly, a longer period of protected mobilization. These patients frequently have longer healing times (up to 1.5 to 2 times normal) and higher rates of infection, nonunion, and amputation, so increased diligence is required during soft tissue handling and progression of postoperative weight bearing.[302] Traumatic episodes can also incite a Charcot arthropathy in diabetic patients that can be very difficult to manage. This complication can be heralded by the onset or persistence of excessive swelling, warmth, or rubor in the extremity, often with an exuberant but erratic bony healing response on radiographs. The mainstay of treatment in these circumstances is prolonged, protected immobilization, control of edema, gradual progression of weight bearing, modification of activity, and serial evaluation. Bedrest is contraindicated. Any type of splint, cast, or orthotic applied to these patients should be placed with neuropathic risks in mind. Removable devices such as bivalved total-contact casts are advised to allow both the patient and the physician visual access to the injured site. If non-removable casting is required, it should be placed so that pressure is equally distributed along the affected limb and then checked and changed at weekly intervals to keep up with the fluctuations in leg edema and avoid ulceration.

In general, conservative management of hindfoot injuries requires 2 months of restricted/non–weight-bearing activity, followed by 6 to 12 months in a cast and then use of a custom UCBL or AFO brace; the midfoot requires 6 weeks of restricted/non–weight-bearing activity, followed by cast or boot immobilization with increased weight bearing for an additional 4 to 6 months and, finally, a custom orthosis with an extra-deep shoe; the ankle, in comparison, may require up to 2 years of immobilization and eventually an AFO to reach a stable state. The decision for surgery in these patients can be a difficult one, and the poor bone quality can result in suboptimal fixation.[278] Most patients do not require a formal vascular workup before surgery unless there is a specific reason to do so. The vast majority of diabetics have sufficient blood flow to heal any standard foot or ankle incision in the absence of severe soft tissue trauma. In most cases, unless the patient has a medical contraindication to surgery, the same criteria for surgical intervention in nondiabetic foot trauma should be followed. However, in patients with borderline criteria, serious consideration should be given to nonoperative management, particularly in the absence of any instability or soft tissue injuries. High-risk incisions and fracture care such as for calcaneal fractures should also be given a second thought before ORIF, especially in the presence of other risk factors such as smoking or noncompliance.

Indications for acute operative intervention in diabetics with foot injuries are similar to those in the nondiabetic population,[4] but potential skin breakdown, if deemed probable, needs to be avoided by the use of casting or other immobilization. Surgery should be avoided if patients are in florid diabetic ketoacidosis or are otherwise seriously ill, unless the foot is deemed to be the source of this problem, or if they are initially seen more than 6 to 8 weeks after injury and a neuropathic process is suspected. Avoidance of surgery is necessary because of the horrific decrease in bone quality that rapidly accompanies this process. Often, ORIF alone is not sufficient stabilization, and primary fusion should be considered as the best definitive long-term management (Fig. 60–77). External fixation can also be used as an adjunctive stabilizer to ORIF or in patients with a concomitant ulcer or infection. Incision and exposure should be rapid, directly to bone, and entail minimal soft tissue dissection. The length of surgery should be kept as short as possible, preferably below 2 hours and without the use of a tourniquet to minimize further soft tissue trauma and handling of an already compromised soft tissue bed; such management also cuts down on postoperative edema. The skin should never be handled with forceps, and similarly, self-retainers should be used sparingly. Closure should be performed in layered fashion with monofilament, and vertical mattress 3–0 or 4–0 nylon suture should be used for the skin. Uncut elastic Steri-Strips can be placed over the incisions to distribute any tension on the skin from edema as widely as possible. No diabetic incision should ever be closed in tension or without the wound edges everted, both of which can almost guarantee a poor result. Benzoin should not be used because it decreases the ability of the skin to slide beneath the Steri-Strips in response to swelling and thus causes dermal-epidermal separation and severe blistering, which will significantly increase the risk of contamination and infection after surgery. A total-contact splint should be applied after closure with a Hemovac drain if necessary, and all patients should be kept in the hospital with at least 2 to 3 days of strict bed exercises and elevation before mobilized non–weight bearing with physical therapy. Antibiotic coverage during this period is preferred. These concepts are important to keep in mind when treating such patients because the available salvage procedures for alternative management of potential midfoot collapse are difficult and fraught with complications, particularly in inexperienced hands.[75]

Most important, one must recognize the need for a comprehensive educational and management program for diabetics, even long after their injury. Although their fractures will usually heal, their feet will remain at risk from diabetic neuropathy for the rest of their lives, and some of these injuries may predispose them to future problems such as midfoot breakdown after a Lisfranc disruption. Chronic foot care issues need to be discussed with these patients long after recovery, and consideration should be given to diabetic, extra depth, accommodative

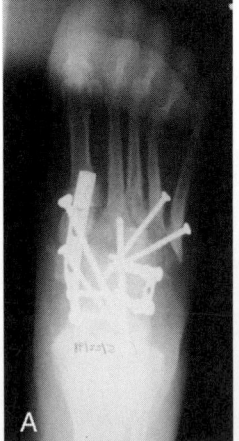
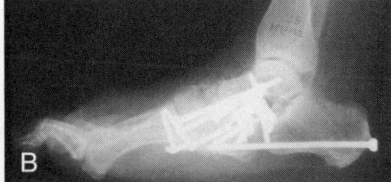

**Figure 60–77.** Charcot fractures or dislocations of the foot are difficult problems to stabilize and are fraught with complications (A, B). Patients often require more than one procedure for bony consolidation, including bone grafting, revision fixation, or antibiotic–polymethyl methacrylate augmentation. Amputations are possible in the face of severe concomitant soft tissue or bony injuries.

shoe wear or orthotic inserts, or even bracing, for long-term protection.

## TRAUMATIC TENDON RUPTURE OR DISLOCATION

Traumatic rupture or dislocation of tendons coursing the foot and studies discussing the indications for treatment are both rare in comparison to such injuries and studies in the hand. Though more frequent at the ankle level, it remains unusual there as well. The most common reason to treat discontinuity of a foot tendon is a laceration, which often occurs from a direct blow or sharp object. Rupture occurs rarely, and systemic causes leading to persistent weakening of the tendon or mechanical imbalance, such as gastrocnemius equinus causing prolonged wear and tear, should be sought. Under these circumstances, treatment should be directed not only at the rupture but also at its cause. The diagnosis is usually straightforward with a good history and examination.

The extensor tendons support much lower loading and enjoy a more robust blood supply than the flexors do, and they thus have a lower incidence of injury. Treatment depends on the functional expectations and health status of the patient. Laceration of the anterior tibialis or extensor hallucis longus should probably be repaired after appropriate irrigation and débridement to avoid stubbing or difficulty donning shoe wear.[91, 241] In the setting of chronic rupture, treatment consisting of primary operative repair, tendon transfer with alternative extensors, or bracing must be based on individual patient demands and depends on how separated the ends are. Both can lead to acceptable functional results, depending on the clinical setting. Injury to an isolated common extensor tendon can usually be treated conservatively in the absence of clinical deformity, and some authors also support conservative management of extensor hallucis longus tears with 4 weeks of splinting and limitation of MTP plantar flexion to neutral.[352]

Most disruptions of the foot flexors are also caused by laceration. Although these injuries have historically been treated conservatively with little functional deficit, new attention has been given to their management because of concern regarding long-term function of the windlass mechanism and hyperextension deformity of the toe.[91, 352] Operative repair of a lacerated flexor hallucis longus has been advocated because of the high incidence of concomitant injury (50%). Good results with operative repair have been reported. As with the extensors, laceration of an individual lesser toe flexor can be effectively treated conservatively in most cases with reasonable results, unless the associated wound demands operative intervention. Rupture of the foot flexors is quite rare.[96]

Acute laceration or dislocation of the posterior tibial or peroneal tendons is usually associated with ankle and not foot injuries. Dislocation is seen far more commonly than tear or rupture in the acute traumatic setting. Because the degree of functional deficit can be considerable over the long term in these injuries as a result of the demands placed on these tendons as they course into the foot, early operative repair, retinacular reconstruction, or both are recommended under most circumstances. A good result can usually be expected with early diagnosis and treatment.[91, 253]

Painful os peroneum syndrome is a recently recognized and poorly understood phenomenon that is manifested as either acute or insidious laterally based foot pain[253, 316] (see Fig. 60–59). Although multiple causes exist, in the acute setting this entity can be associated with traumatic rupture (type IV) of the peroneus longus or fracture/diastasis of the os peroneum (type I). Even though some believe that this bone exists in some form (bony, cartilaginous, or fibrous) within the substance of the peroneus longus, a bony and radiographically identifiable os peroneum occurs in only approximately 10% of the population. It can be bipartite or multipartite and is designed to enhance excursion of the peroneal as it courses through the cuboid tunnel at an acute angle. Anterior process fractures of the calcaneus, lateral process fracture of the talus, and fracture or impingement within the peroneal tubercle of the calcaneus are all notoriously difficult to diagnose but must be ruled out in the setting of acute lateral foot pain and swelling, particularly before the diagnosis of painful os peroneum syndrome is entertained. The strength of the peroneus longus in all but an acute complete rupture or laceration is usually good and can be verified by a provocative maneuver consisting of resisted plantar flexion of the first ray. This syndrome has also been identified in association with a fifth metatarsal fracture, presumably as a result of a concomitant injury to the peroneal or accessory itself along the lateral column (see Fig. 60–59). Oblique plain radiographs of the foot with comparison views should be obtained to aid in diagnosis. MRI is occasionally helpful for better soft tissue or tendon evaluation. If patients have had less than 1 month of symptoms, nonoperative management with 4 weeks of short leg casting is recommended. Good outcomes with this technique have been reported, although the data are scant. With more chronic symptoms, operative exploration of the cuboid tunnel with either repair, débridement, or excision of the os peroneum and peroneus longus is usually indicated. In some cases, consideration should be given to peroneus brevis transfer or peroneus longus tenodesis.

## REFERENCES

1. Adelaar, R.S. Fractures of the talus. In: Gould, J.S.; Thompson, F.M.; Cracchiolo, A.; et al. Operative Foot Surgery. Philadelphia, W.B. Saunders, 1990, pp. 147–156.
2. Aitken, A.P.; Poulson, D. Dislocations of the tarsometatarsal joint. J Bone Joint Surg Am 45:246–260, 1963.
3. Albert, M.J.; Waggoner, S.M.; Smith, J.W. Internal fixation of calcaneal fractures: An anatomical study of structures at risk. J Orthop Trauma 9:107–112, 1995.
4. Alpert, S.W.; Koval, K.J.; Zuckerman, J.D. Neuropathic arthropathy: Review of current knowledge. J Am Acad Orthop Surg 4:100–108, 1996.
5. Anderson, I.F.; Crichton, K.J.; Grattan-Smith, T.; et al. Osteochondral fractures of the dome of the talus. J Bone Joint Surg Am 71:1143–1152, 1989.
6. Anglen, J.O. Wound irrigation in musculoskeletal injury. J Am Acad Orthop Surg 9:219–226, 2001.
7. Argenta, L.C.; Morykwa, M.J. Vacuum assisted closure: A new method for wound closure and treatment: Clinical experience. Ann Plastic Surg 38:563–576, 1997.

8. Arntz, C.; Hansen, S.T. Dislocations and fracture dislocations of the tarsometatarsal joints. Orthop Clin North Am 18:105–114, 1987.

9. Arntz, C.T.; Veith, R.G.; Hansen, S.T. Fractures and fracture-dislocations of the tarsometatarsal joint. J Bone Joint Surg Am 70:173–181, 1988.

10. Astion, D.J.; Deland, J.T.; Otis, J.C.; Kenneally, S. Motion of the hindfoot after simulated arthrodesis. J Bone Joint Surg Am 79:241–246, 1997.

11. Attinger, C.T. How to avoid skin problems with incisions around the foot/ankle. Paper presented at the 32nd Annual Meeting of the American Orthopaedic Foot and Ankle Society, Dallas, Texas, February 16, 2002.

12. Baker, C.L., Jr.; Morales, R.W. Arthroscopic treatment of transchondral talar dome fractures: Long term follow up study. Arthroscopy 15:197–202, 1999.

13. Bartlett, C.S.; Helfet, D.L.; Hausman, M.R.; Strauss, E. Ballistics and gunshot wounds: Effect on musculoskeletal tissues. J Am Acad Orthop Surg 8:21–36, 2000.

14. Baumhauer, J.E. Mutilating injuries. In: Myerson, M., ed. Foot and Ankle Disorders, Vol. 2. Philadelphia, W.B. Saunders, 2000, pp. 1245–1264.

15. Baumhauer, J.F.; Alvarez, R.G. Controversies in treating talus fractures. Orthop Clin North Am 26:335–351, 1995.

16. Beaman, D.N.; Roeser, W.M.; Holmes, J.R.; Saltzman, C.L. Cuboid stress fractures. A report of 2 cases. Foot Ankle Int 14:525–528, 1993.

17. Benirschke, S.K.; Sangeorzan, B.J. Extensive intraarticular fractures of the foot: Surgical management of calcaneal fractures. Clin Orthop 292:128–134, 1993.

18. Bezes, H.; Massart, P.; Delveaux, D.; et al. The operative treatment of intraarticular calcaneal fractures: Indications, technique, and results in 257 cases. Clin Orthop 292:55–59, 1993.

19. Bibbo, C.; Lin, S.S.; Cunningham, F.J. Acute traumatic compartment syndrome in the foot in children. Pediatr Emerg Care 16:244–248, 2000.

20. Biehl, W.C., III; Morgan, J.M.; Wagner, F.W., Jr.; Gabriel, R. Neuropathic calcaneal tuberosity avulsion fractures. Clin Orthop 296:8–13, 1993.

21. Boden, B.P.; Osbahr, D.C. High risk stress fractures: Evaluation and treatment. J Am Acad Orthop Surg 8:344–353, 2000.

22. Böhler, L. Diagnosis, pathology, and treatment of factures of the os calcis. J Bone Joint Surg 13:75–89, 1931.

23. Borrelli, J., Jr.; Lashgari, C. Vascularity of the lateral calcaneal flap: A cadaveric injection study. J Orthop Trauma 13:73–77, 1999.

24. Boucree, J.B., Jr.; Gabriel, R.A.; Lezine-Hanna, J.T. Gunshot wounds to the foot. Orthop Clin North Am 26:191–197, 1995.

25. Bowers, K.D., Jr.; Martin, R.B. Turf toe: A shoe-surface related football injury. Med Sci Sports 8:81–83, 1976.

26. Bradshaw, C.; Khan, K.; Bruckner, P. Stress fractures of the body of the talus in athletes demonstrated with CT. Clin J Sports Med 6:48–51, 1996.

27. Braly, W.G.; Bishop, J.O.; Tullos, H.S. Lateral wall decompression for malunited os calcis fractures. Foot Ankle 6:90–96, 1987.

28. Broden, B. Roentgen examination of the subtaloid joint in fractures of the calcaneus. Acta Radiol 3:85–91, 1949.

29. Brown, D.C.; McFarland, G.B., Jr. Dislocation of the medial cuneiform bone in tarsometatarsal fracture-dislocation: A case report. J Bone Joint Surg Am 57:858–859, 1975.

30. Brunet, J.A. Calcaneal fractures in children: Long term results of treatment. J Bone Joint Surg Br 82:211–216, 2000.

31. Brunet, J.A. Pathomechanics of complex dislocation of the first metatarsophalangeal joint. Clin Orthop 332:126–131, 1996.

32. Brunet, J.A.; Tubin, S. Traumatic dislocation of the lesser toes. Foot Ankle Int 18:406–411, 1997.

33. Buckley, R.E.; Meek, R.N. Comparison of open versus closed reduction of intraarticular calcaneal fractures: A matched cohort in workmen. J Orthop Trauma 6:216–222, 1992.

34. Burdeaux, B.D. The medial approach for calcaneal fractures. Clin Orthop 292:96–107, 1993.

35. Burgess, A. Personal communication, July 1999.

36. Buzzard, B.M.; Briggs, P.J. Surgical management of acute tarsometatarsal fracture-dislocation in the adult. Clin Orthop 353:125–133, 1998.

37. Canale, S.T.; Kelly, F.B. Fractures of the neck of the talus: Long term evaluation of seventy one cases. J Bone Joint Surg Am 60:143–156, 1978.

38. Carey, E.J.; Lance, E.M.; Wade, P.A. Extra-articular fractures of the os calcis. J Trauma 5:362–372, 1965.

39. Carr, J.B. Mechanism and pathoanatomy of the intraarticular calcaneus fracture. Clin Orthop 290:36–40, 1993.

40. Carr, J.B.; Hamilton, J.J.; Bear, L.S. Experimental intraarticular calcaneal fractures: Anatomic basis for a new classification. Foot Ankle 10:81–87, 1989.

41. Carr, J.B.; Hansen, S.T.; Benirschke, S.K. Subtalar distraction bone block fusion for late complications of os calcis fractures. Foot Ankle 9:81–86, 1988.

42. Carr, J.B.; Hansen, S.T.; Benirschke, S.K. Surgical treatment of foot and ankle trauma: Use of indirect reduction techniques. Foot Ankle 9:176–178, 1989.

43. Cavanaugh, P.R.; Rogers, M.M.; Iboshi, A. Pressure distribution under symptomatic free feet during barefoot standing. Foot Ankle 7:262–276, 1987.

44. Cedell, C.A. Rupture of the posterior talotibial ligament with the avulsion of a bone fragment from the talus. Acta Orthop Scand 45:454–461, 1974.

45. Chen, F.S.; Frenkel, S.R.; DiCesare, P.E. Chondrocyte transplantation and experimental treatment options for articular cartilage defects. Am J Orthop 26:396–406, 1997.

46. Chordhury, S.N.; Kitaoka, H.B. Amputations of the foot and ankle: Review of techniques and results. Orthopedics 20:446–457, 1997.

47. Christensen, S.B; Lorentzen, J.E.; Krogsoe, O.; Sneppen, O. Subtalar dislocation. Acta Orthop Scand 48:707–711, 1977.

48. Clanton, T.O.; Butler, J.E.; Eggert, A. Injury to the first metatarsophalangeal joint in athletes. Foot Ankle 14:435–442, 1993.

49. Cobey, J.C. Treatment of undisplaced toe fractures with a metatarsal bar made from tongue blades. Clin Orthop 103:56, 1974.

50. Coker, T.P., Jr.; Arnold, J.A.; Weber, D.L. Traumatic lesions of the metatarsophalangeal joint of the great toe in athletes. J Ark Med Soc 74:309–317, 1978.

51. Coltart, W.D. Aviator's astragalus. J Bone Joint Surg Br 34:545–566, 1952.

52. Comfort, T.H.; Behrens, F.; Garthe, D.W.; et al. Long term results of displaced talar neck fractures. Clin Orthop 199:81–87, 1985.

53. Coss, H.S.; Manos, R.E.; Buoncristiani, A.; Mills, W.J. Abduction stress and AP weightbearing radiographs of purely ligamentous injury to the tarsometatarsal joint. Foot Ankle Int 19:537–541, 1998.

54. Coughlin, M.J. Sesamoid pain: Cases and surgical treatment. Inst Course Lect 39:23–35, 1990.

55. Coughlin, M.J. Subluxation and dislocation of the second metatarsophalangeal joint. Orthop Clin North Am 20:535–551, 1989.

56. Dameron, T.B. Fractures and anatomical variations of the proximal portion of the fifth metatarsal. J Bone Joint Surg Am 57:788–792, 1975.

57. Dameron, T.B., Jr. Fractures of the proximal fifth metatarsal: Selecting the best treatment option. J Am Acad Orthop Surg 3:110–114, 1995.

58. Daniels, T.R.; Smith, J.W. Talar neck fractures. Foot Ankle 14:225–234, 1993.

59. Daniels, T.R.; Smith, J.W.; Ross, T.I. Varus malalignment of the talar neck: Its effect on the position of the foot and on subtalar motion. J Bone Jont Surg Am 78:1559–1567, 1996.

60. Davis, C.A.; Lubowitz, J.; Thordarson, D.B. Midtarsal fracture-subluxation: Case report and review of the literature. Clin Orthop 292:264–268, 1993.

61. DeCoster, T.A.; Miller, R.A. Management of traumatic foot wounds. J Am Acad Orthop Surg 2:226–230, 1994.

62. DeFranzo, A.J.; Argenta, L.C.; Marks, M.W.; et al. The use of vacuum assisted closure therapy for the treatment of lower extremity wounds with exposed bone. Plast Reconst Surg 108:1184–1191, 2001.

63. Degan, T.J.; Morrey, B.F.; Braun, D.P. Surgical excision for anterior process fractures of the calcaneus. J Bone Joint Surg Am 64:519–524, 1982.

64. DeLee, J. Fractures of the calcaneus. In: Mann, R.A.; Coughlin, M.J., eds. Surgery of the Foot, 6th ed. St. Louis, C.V. Mosby, 1993, p. 592.

65. DeLee, J. Surgery of the foot. In: Mann, R., ed. Fractures and Dislocations of the Foot. St. Louis, C.V. Mosby, 1980, pp. 729–749.

66. DeLee, J.; Curtis, R. Subtalar dislocation of the foot. J Bone Joint Surg Am 64:433–437, 1982.

67. DeLee, J.C.; Evans, J.P.; Julian, J. Stress fractures of the fifth metatarsal. Am J Sports Med 5:349–353, 1983.

68. Demuth, N.E., Jr. Bullet velocity and design as determinants of wounding capacity: An experimental study. J Trauma 8:744–754, 1966.

69. Detenbeck, L.C.; Kelly, P.J. Total dislocation of the talus. J Bone Joint Surg Am 51:283–288, 1969.

70. Dhillon, M.S.; Nagi, O.N. Total dislocations of the navicular: Are they ever isolated injuries? J Bone Joint Surg Br 81:81–85, 1999.

71. DiGiovanni, C.W.; Kuo, R.; Tejwani, N.; et al. Isolated gastrocnemius tightness. J Bone Joint Surg Am 84:962–970, 2002.

72. Dormans, J.P.; Azzoni, M.; Davidson, R.S.; Drummond, D.S. Major lower extremity lawnmower injuries in children. J Pediatr Orthop 15:78–82, 1995.

73. Drummond, D.S.; Hastings, D.E. Total dislocation of the cuboid bone. J Bone Joint Surg Br 51:716–718, 1969.

74. Dutowsky, J.; Freeman, B.L., III. Fracture dislocation of the articular surface of the metatarsal head. Foot Ankle 10:43–44, 1989.

75. Early, J.S.; Hansen, S.T. Surgical reconstruction of the diabetic foot: A salvage approach for midfoot collapse. Foot Ankle Int 17:325–330, 1996.

76. Eastwood, D.M.; Gregg, P.J.; Atkins, R.M. Intraarticular fractures of the calcaneum: Part I. Pathological anatomy and classification. J Bone Joint Surg Br 75:183–188, 1993.

77. Eastwood, D.M.; Langkamer, V.G.; Atkins, R.M. Intraarticular fractures of the calcaneum: Part II. Open reduction and internal fixation by the extended lateral approach. J Bone Joint Surg Br 75:189–195, 1993.

78. Ebraheim, N.A.; Haman, S.P.; Lu, J.; et al. Anatomical and radiological considerations of the fifth metatarsal bone. Foot Ankle Int 21:212–215, 2000.

79. Eichenholtz, S.N.; Levine, D.B. Fractures of the tarsal navicular bone. Clin Orthop 34:142–157, 1964.

80. Eisele, S.A.; Sammarco, G.J. Fatigue fractures of the foot and ankle in the athlete. J Bone Joint Surg Am 75:290–298, 1993.

81. Enna, C.D. The denervated great toe: A review of anatomy and functions as they relate to the deformity. Orthop Rev 6:29, 1977.

82. Erdmann, D.; Lee, B.; Roberts, C.D.; Levin, S. Management of lawnmower injuries to the lower extremity in children and adolescents. Ann Plastic Surg 45:595–600, 2000.

83. Essex-Lopresti, P. The mechanism, reduction technique, and results of fractures of the os calcis. Br J Surg 39:395–419, 1952.

84. Essex-Lopresti, P. The mechanism, reduction technique, and results of fractures of the os calcis. Clin Orthop 290:3–16, 1993.

85. Everson, L.I.; Galloway, H.R.; Suh, J.S.; et al. Cuboid subluxation. Orthopedics 14:1044–1048, 1991.

86. Faciszewski, T.; Burks, R.T.; Manaster, B.J. Subtle injuries of the Lisfranc joint. J Bone Joint Surg Am 72:1519–1522, 1990.

87. Ferkel, R.D. Arthroscopic Surgery: The Foot and Ankle. Philadelphia, Lippincott-Raven, 1996, pp. 145–184.

88. Fitch, K.D.; Blackwell, J.B.; Gilmour, W.N. Operation for nonunion of stress fracture of the tarsal navicular. J Bone Joint Surg Br 71:105–110, 1989.

89. Flaherty, J.D.; Evans, D.A.; Danahy, P.R. The empty toe phenomenon: A type of closed degloving injury. Am J Orthop 27:524–525, 1998.

90. Flemister, A.S., Jr.; Infante, A.F.; Sanders, R.W.; Walling, A.K. Subtalar arthrodesis for complications of intraarticular calcaneal fractures. Foot Ankle Int 21:392–399, 2000.

91. Floyd, D.W.; Heckman, J.D.; Rockwood, C.A., Jr. Tendon lacerations of the foot. Foot Ankle 4:8–14, 1983.

92. Folk, J.W.; Starr, A.J.; Early, J.S. Early wound complications of operative treatment of calcaneal fractures: Analysis of 190 fractures. J Orthop Trauma 13:369–372, 1999.

93. Fortin, P.T.; Balazsy, J.E. Talus fractures: Evaluation and treatment. J Am Acad Orthop Surg 9:114–127, 2001.

94. Foster, S.C.; Foster, R.R. Lisfranc's tarsometatarsal fracture dislocation. Radiology 120:79–83, 1976.

95. Frawley, P.A.; Hart, J.A.; Young, D.A. Treatment outcome of major fractures of the talus. Foot Ankle Int 16:339–345, 1995.

96. Frenette, J.P.; Jackson, D.W. Laceration of the FHL in the young athlete. J Bone Joint Surg Am 59:673–676, 1977.

97. Frey, C. Marine injuries: Prevention and treatment. Orthop Rev Aug:645–649, 1994.

98. Frey, C.; DiGiovanni, C.W. Gross and arthroscopic anatomy of the foot. In: Guhl, J.F.; Parisien, J.S.; Boynton, M.D., eds. Foot and Ankle Arthroscopy, 3rd ed. New York, Springer-Verlag, 2003.

99. Frey, C.; Feder, K.S.; DiGiovanni, C.W. Arthroscopic evaluation of the subtalar joint: Does sinus tarsi syndrome exist? Foot Ankle Int 20:185–191, 1999.

100. Fugate, D.S.; Thompson, J.D.; Christensen, K.P. An irreducible fracture dislocation of a lesser toe: A case report. Foot Ankle 11:317–318, 1991.

101. Fukui, A.; Tamai, S. Present status of replantation in Japan. Microsurgery 15:842–847, 1994.

102. Gelberman, R.H.; Mortensen, W.W. The arterial anatomy of the talus. Foot Ankle 4:64–72, 1983.

103. Giannardis, P.V.; MacDonald, D.P.J.; Matthews, S.J.; et al. Nonunion of the femoral diaphysis. The influence of reaming and nonsteroidal anti-inflammatory agents. J Bone Joint Surg Br 82:655–658, 2000.

104. Glasgow, M.T.; Naranja, R.J., Jr.; Glasgow, S.G.; Torg, J.S. Analysis of failed surgical management of fractures of the base of the fifth metatarsal distal to the tuberosity: The Jones fracture. Foot Ankle Int 17:449–457, 1996.

105. Goldner, J.L.; Poletti, S.C.; Gates, H.S., 3rd.; Richardson, W.J. Severe open subtalar dislocations: Long term results. J Bone Joint Surg Am 77:1075–1079, 1995.

106. Goosens, M.; DeStoop, N. Lisfranc fracture dislocation: Etiology, radiology, and results of treatment. A review of 25 cases. Clin Orthop 176:154–162, 1983.

107. Gould, J.S. Reconstruction of soft tissue injury of the foot and ankle with microsurgical techniques. Orthopedics 10:151–157, 1987.

108. Gould, N. Lateral approach to the os calcis. Foot Ankle 4:218–220, 1984.

109. Gould, N. Safety shoes for industry. In: Bateman, J., ed. Foot Science. Philadelphia, W.B. Saunders, 1976.

110. Gould, N.; Trevino, S. Sural nerve entrapment by avulsion of the base of the fifth metatarsal bone. Foot Ankle 32:153–155, 1981.

111. Gregory, R.T.; Gould, R.J.; Peclet, M.; et al. The mangled extremity syndrome (M.E.S.): A severity rating system for multisystem injury of the extremity. J Trauma 25:1147–2250, 1985.

112. Grob, D.; Simpson, L.A.; Weber, B.G.; et al. Operative treatment of displaced talus fractures. Clin Orthop 199:88–96, 1985.

113. Gross, A.E.; Agnidis, Z.; Hutchinson, C.R. Osteochondral defects of the talus treated with fresh osteochondral allograft transplantation. Foot Ankle Int 22:385–391, 2001.

114. Grujic, L.; Macey, L.R.; Early, J.S.; et al. Incidence of morbidity associated with open reduction internal fixation of displaced intraarticular calcaneal fractures using a lateral approach. Abstract. Paper presented at the 61st Annual Meeting of the American Academy of Orthopaedic Surgeons, Rosemont, Illinois, 1994, p. 259.

115. Grundy, M.; Tosh, P.A.; McLeish, R.D.; Smidt, L. An investigation of the centers of pressures under the foot while walking. J Bone Joint Surg Br 57:98–103, 1975.

116. Guyton, G.P.; Sheerman, C.M.; Saltzman, C.L. The compartments of the foot revisited. Rethinking the validity of cadaver infusion experiments. J Bone Joint Surg Br 83:245–249, 2001.

117. Hall, R.L.; Shereff, M.J. Anatomy of the calcaneus. Clin Orthop 290:27–35, 1993.

118. Hamilton, W.G. Stenosing tenosynovitis of the flexor hallucis longus tendon and posterior impingement upon the os trigonum in ballet dancers. Foot Ankle 3:74–80, 1982.

119. Hangody, L.; Kish, G.; Modis, L.; et al. Mosaicplasty for the treatment of osteochondritis dissecans of the talus: 2–7 year results in thirty six patients. Foot Ankle Int 22:552–558, 2001.

120. Hansen, S.T. Functional Reconstruction of the Foot and Ankle. Philadelphia, Lippincott Williams & Wilkins, 2000, pp. 1–512.

121. Hansen, S.T., Jr.; Clark, W. Tendon transfer to augment the weakened tibialis posterior mechanism. J Am Podiatr Med Assoc 78:399–402, 1988.

122. Hardcastle, P.H.; Reschauer, R.; Kutscha-Lissberg, E.; Schoffmann, W. Injuries to the tarsometatarsal joint. Incidence, classification, and treatment. J Bone Joint Surg Br 64:349–356, 1982.

123. Harding, D.; Waddell, J.P. Open reduction in depressed fractures of the os calcis. Clin Orthop 199:124–131, 1985.

124. Harper, M.C. Metabolic bone disease presenting as multiple recurrent metatarsal fractures. A case report. Foot Ankle 9:207–209, 1989.

125. Hawkins, L.G. Fracture of the lateral process of the talus. J Bone Joint Surg Am 47:1170–1175, 1965.

126. Hawkins, L.G. Fractures of the neck of the talus. J Bone Joint Surg Am 52:991–1002, 1970.

127. Heck, B.E.; Ebraheim, N.A.; Jackson, W.T. Anatomic considerations of irreducible medial subtalar dislocation. Foot Ankle Int 17:103–106, 1996.

128. Heckman, J.D. Fractures and dislocations of the foot. In: Rockwood, C.A.; Green, D.P.; Bucholtz, R.W.; Heckman, J.D., eds. Rockwood and Green's Fractures in Adults, 4th ed. Lippincott-Raven, Philadelphia, 1996, pp. 2267–2405.

129. Heckman, J.D.; McLean, M.R. Fractures of the lateral process of the talus. Clin Orthop 199:108–113, 1985.

130. Henley, M.B.; Chapman, J.R.; Agel, J.; et al. Treatment of type II, IIIa, IIIb open fractures of the tibial shaft: Prospective comparison of undreamed interlocking intramedullary nails and half pin external fixators. J Orthop Trauma 12:1–7, 1998.

131. Hens, J.; Martens, M. Surgical treatment of Jones fractures. Arch Orthop Trauma Surg 109:277–279, 1990.

132. Heppenstall, R.B.; Farahvar, H.; Balderston, R.; Lotke, P. Evaluation and management of subtalar dislocations. J Trauma 20:494–497, 1980.

133. Hermel, M.B.; Gershon-Cohen, J. The nutcracker fracture of the cuboid by indirect violence. Radiology 60:850–854, 1953.

134. Higgins, T.F.; Baumgaertner, M.R. Diagnosis and treatment of fractures of the talus: A comprehensive review of the literature. Foot Ankle Int 20:595–605, 1999.

135. Holmes, G.B., Jr. Treatment of delayed unions and nonunions of the proximal fifth metatarsal with pulsed electromagnetic fields. Foot Ankle 15:552–556, 1994.

136. Horowitz, J.H.; Nichter, L.S.; Kenney, J.G.; Morgan, R.F. Lawn-mower injuries in children: Lower extremity reconstruction. J Trauma 25:1138–1146, 1985.

137. Hubbell, J.D.; Goldhagen, P.; O'Connor, D.; Denton, J. Isolated plantar fracture dislocation of the middle cuneiform. Am J Orthop 27:1234–1236, 1998.

138. Hughes, J.; Clarke, P.; Kleneman, L. The importance of the toes in walking. J Bone Joint Surg Br 72:245–251, 1990.

139. Hulkko, A.; Orava, S.; Pellinen, P.; Puranen, J. Stress fractures of the sesamoid bones of the first metatarsophalangeal joint in athletes. Arch Orthop Trauma Surg 104:113–117, 1985.

140. Hunter, J.C.; Sangeorzan, B.J. A nutcracker fracture: Cuboid fracture with an associated avulsion fracture of the tarsal navicular. AJR Am J Roentgenol 166:888, 1996.

141. Hunter, L.Y. Stress fracture of the navicular: More frequent than we realize? Am J Sports Med 9:217–219, 1981.

142. Hurwitz, S. Severe open subtalar dislocation: Long term results. J Bone Joint Surg Am 78:313–314, 1996.

143. Ibister, J.F. Calcaneofibular abutment following crush fracture of the calcaneus. J Bone Joint Surg Br 56:274–278, 1974.

144. Inaba, A.S.; Zukin, D.D.; Perro, M. An update on the evaluation and management of plantar puncture wounds and pseudomonal osteomyelitis. Pediatr Emerg Care 8:38–44, 1992.

145. Inman, V.T.; Ralston, H.J.; Todd, F. Human Walking. Baltimore, Williams & Wilkins, 1981.

146. Inokuchi, S.; Hashimoto, T.; Usami, N. Anterior subtalar dislocation. J Orthop Trauma 11:235–237, 1997.

147. Inokuchi, S.; Hashimoto, T.; Usami, N. Posterior subtalar dislocation. J Trauma 212:310–313, 1997.

148. Inokuchi, S.; Ogawa, K.; Usami, N. Classification of fractures of the talus: Clear differentiation between neck and body fractures. Foot Ankle Int 17:748–750, 1996.

149. Inokuchi, S.; Ogawa, K; Usami, N. Long-term follow up of talus fractures. Orthopedics 19:477–481, 1966.

150. Irwin, C.G. Fractures of the metatarsals. Proc R Soc Med 31:789–793, 1938.

151. Jacobs, L.G. The land mine foot: Its description and management. Injury 22:463–466, 1991.

152. Jahss, M.H. Chronic and recurrent dislocation of the fifth toe. Foot Ankle 1:275–278, 1981.

153. Jahss, M.H. Stubbing injuries to the hallux. Foot Ankle 1:327–332, 1981.

154. Jahss, M.H. The sesamoids of the hallux. Clin Orthop 157:88–97, 1981.

155. Jahss, M.H. Traumatic dislocation of the first metatarsophalangeal joint. Foot Ankle 1:15–21, 1980.

156. Janzan, D.L.; Connell, D.G.; Munk, P.L.; et al. Intraarticular fractures of the calcaneus: Value of CT findings in determining prognosis. AJR Am J Roentgenol 158:1271–1274, 1992.

157. Johansen, K.; Daines, M.; Havey, T.; et al. Objective criteria accurately predict amputation following lower extremity trauma. J Trauma 30:568–572, 1990.

158. Johnson, V.S. Treatment of fractures of the forefoot in industry. In: Bateman, J.E., ed. Foot Science. Philadelphia, W.B. Saunders, 1976, pp. 257–265.

159. Jones, R. Fracture of the base of the fifth metatarsal bone by indirect violence. Ann Surg 35:697–700, 1902.

160. Katayama, M.; Murakami, Y.; Takahashi, H. Irreducible dorsal dislocation of the toe: Report of three cases. J Bone Joint Surg Am 70:769–770, 1988.

161. Kavanaugh, J.H.; Brower, T.D.; Mann, R.V. The Jones fracture revisited. J Bone Joint Surg Am 60:776–782, 1978.

162. Kelly, I.P.; Glisson, R.R.; Fink, C.; et al. Intramedullary screw fixation of Jones fractures. Foot Ankle Int 22:585–589, 2001.

163. Kelly, P.J.; Sullivan, C.R. Blood supply of the talus. Clin Orthop 30:37–44, 1963.

164. Kenwright, J. Fractures of the calcaneum. J Bone Joint Surg Br 75:176–177, 1993.

165. Kenwright, J.; Taylor, R.G. Major injuries of the talus. J Bone Joint Surg Br 52:36–48, 1970.

166. Kenzora, J.E.; Edwards, C.C.; Browner, B.D.; et al. Acute management of major trauma involving the foot and ankle with Hoffman external fixation. Foot Ankle 1:348–361, 1981.

167. Kerr, P.S.; Pape, M.; Jackson, M.; et al. Early experiences with the AO calcaneal fracture plate. Injury 27:39–41, 1996.

168. Khan, K.M.; Fuller, P.J.; Bruckner P.D.; et al. Outcome of conservative and surgical management of navicular stress fractures in athletes; 86 cases proven with CT. Am J Sports Med 20:657–666, 1992.

169. Kidner, F.C. The prehallux (accessory scaphoid) in its relation to flatfoot. J Bone Joint Surg 11:831, 1929.

170. Kirkpatrick, D.P.; Hunter, R.E.; Janes, P.C.; et al. The snowboarder's foot and ankle. Am J Sports Med 26:271–277, 1998.

171. Kiss, Z.S.; Khan, K.M.; Fuller, P.J. Stress fractures of the tarsal navicular bone: CT findings in 55 cases. AJR Am J Roentgenol 160:111–115, 1993.

172. Kollmannsberger, A.; DeBoer, P. Isolated calcaneocuboid dislocation. Brief report. J Bone Joint Surg Br 71:323, 1989.

173. Komenda, G.A.; Myerson, M.S.; Biddinger, K.R. Results of arthrodesis of the tarsometatarsal joints after traumatic injury. J Bone Joint Surg Am 78:1665–1676, 1996.

174. Kuo, R.S.; Tejwani, N.C.; DiGiovanni, C.W.; et al. Outcome after ORIF of Lisfranc joint injuries. J Bone Joint Surg Am 82:1609–1618, 2000.

175. Lawrence, S.J.; Botte, M.J. Jones fractures and related fractures of the proximal fifth metatarsal. Foot Ankle 14:358–365, 1993.

176. Leitner, B. Obstacles to reduction in subtalar dislocation. J Bone Joint Surg Am 36:299–306, 1954.

177. Letournel E. Open reduction and internal fixation of calcaneal fractures. In: Spiegel, P., ed. Topics in Orthopaedic Trauma. Baltimore, University Park Press, 1984, pp. 173–192.

178. Letournel E. Open treatment of acute calcaneal fractures. Clin Orthop 290:60–67, 1993.

179. Leung, K.S.; Yuen, K.M.; Chan, W.S. Operative treatment of displaced intraarticular fractures of the calcaneum: Medium-term results. J Bone Joint Surg Br 75:196–201, 1993.

180. Levin, L.S.; Nunley, J.A. The management of soft-tissue problems associated with calcaneal fractures. Clin Orthop 290:151–156, 1993.

181. Libermanis, O. Replantation of the heel pad. Plast Reconstr Surg 92:537–539, 1993.

182. Lichtblau, S. Painful nonunion of a fracture of the fifth metatarsal. Clin Orthop 59:171–175, 1968.

183. Lindholm, R. Operative treatment of dislocated simple fractures of the neck of the metatarsal bone. Ann Chir Gynaecol 50:328–331, 1961.

184. Lindsay, W.R.N.; Dewar, F.P. Fractures of the calcaneus. Am J Surg 95:555–576, 1958.

185. Loder, R.T. The influence of diabetes mellitus on the healing of closed fractures. Clin Orthop 232:210–216, 1988.

186. Lorentzen, J.E.; Christensen, S.B.; Krogsoe, O.; Sneppen, O. Fractures of the neck of the talus. Acta Orthop Scand 48:115–120, 1977.

187. Loucks, C.; Buckley, R. Böhler's angle: Correlation with outcome in displaced, intraarticular calcaneal fractures. J Orthop Trauma 13:554–558, 1999.

188. Lowery, R.B.W.; Calhoun, J.H. Fractures of the calcaneus: Part I. Anatomy, injury mechanism, and classification. Foot Ankle Int 17:230–235, 1996.

189. Lowery, R.B.W.; Calhoun, J.H. Fractures of the calcaneus: Part II. Treatment. Foot Ankle Int 17:360–366, 1996.

190. Lowy, M. Avulsion fractures of the calcaneus. J Bone Joint Surg Br 51:494–497, 1969.

191. Main, B.J.; Jowett, R.L. Injuries to the midtarsal joint. J Bone Joint Surg Br 57:89–97, 1975.

192. Macey, L.R.; Benirschke, S.K.; Sangeorzan, B.J.; Hansen, S.T., Jr. Acute calcaneal fractures: Treatment options and results. J Am Acad Orthop Surg 2:36–43, 1994.

193. Malicky, E.S.; Levine, D.S.; Sangeorzan, B.J. Modification of the Kidner procedure with fusion of the primary and accessory navicular bone. Foot Ankle Int 20:53–54, 1999.

194. Mann, R.A.; Coughlin, M.J., eds. Surgery of the Foot, 6th ed. St. Louis, C.V. Mosby, 1993, pp. 1–30.

195. Manoli, A. Compartment releases of the foot. In: Johnson, K.A., ed. Master Techniques in Orthopaedic Surgery, The Foot and Ankle. New York, Raven, 1994, pp. 257–270.

196. Manoli, A. Compartment syndromes of the foot: Current concepts. Foot Ankle Int 10:340–344, 1990.

197. Markowitz, H.D.; Chase, M.; Whitelaw, G.P. Isolated injury of the second tarsometatarsal joint. A case report. Clin Orthop 248:210–212, 1988.

198. Marsh, J.L.; Saltzman, C.L.; Iverson, M.; Shapiro, D.S. Major open injuries of the talus. J Orthop Trauma 9:371–376, 1995.

199. Maxwell, G.P.; Hoopoes, J.E. Compound injuries of the lower extremity. Plast Reconstr Surg 63:176–185, 1979.

200. Mayo, K.A. Fractures of the talus: Principles of management and techniques of treatment. Tech Orthop 2:42, 1987.

201. McDougall, A. The os trigonum. J Bone Joint Surg Br 37:257–265, 1955.

202. McKinley, L.M.; Davis, G.L. Locked dislocation of the great toe. J La State Med Soc 127:389–390, 1975.

203. McReynolds, I.S. Fractures of the os calcis involving the subastragalar joint: Treatment by open reduction and internal fixation with staples using a medial approach. J Bone Joint Surg Am 58:733, 1976.

204. Meara, J.G.; Guo, L.; Smith, J.D.; et al. Vacuum assisted closure in the treatment of degloving injuries. Ann Plast Surg 42:589–594, 1999.

205. Meinhard, B.P.; Girgis, I.; Moriarty, R.V. Irreducible talar dislocation with entrapment by the posterior tibial and flexor digitorum longus tendon: A case report. Clin Orthop 286:222–224, 1993.

206. Meissner, M.H. Deep venous thrombosis in the trauma patient. Semin Vasc Surg 11:274–282, 1998.

207. Meissner, M.H.; Chandler, W.C.; Elliot, J. The pathophysiology of venous thromboembolism after injury. Submitted for publication.

208. Melcher, G.; Degonda, F.; Leutenegger A.; Reudi, T. Ten year follow-up after operative treatment for intra-articular fractures of the calcaneus. J Trauma 38:713–716, 1995.

209. Meyer, S.A.; Callaghan, J.J.; Albright, J.P.; et al. Midfoot sprains in collegiate football players. Am J Sports Med 22:392–401, 1994.

210. Meyer, S.A.; Saltzman, C.L.; Albright, J.P. Stress fractures of the foot and leg. Clin Sports Med 12:395–413, 1993.

211. Miki, T.; Tamamuro, T.; Kitai, T. An irreducible dislocation of the great toe: Report of two cases and review of the literature. Clin Orthop 230:200–206, 1988.

212. Miller, C.M.; Winter, W.G.; Bucknell, A L.; Johanssen, E.A. Injuries to the midtarsal joint and lesser tarsal bones. J Am Acad Orthop Surg 6:249–258, 1998.

213. Minas, T.; Nehrer, S. Current concepts in treatment of articular cartilage defects. Orthopedics 20:525–538, 1997.

214. Miric, A.; Patterson, B.M. Pathoanatomy of intraarticular fractures of the calcaneus. J Bone Joint Surg Am 80:207–212, 1998.

215. Mizel, M.S.; Steinmetz, N.D.; Trepman, E. Detection of wooden foreign bodies in muscle tissue: Experimental comparison of CT, MRI, and ultrasound. Foot Ankle Int 15:437–443, 1994.

216. Mizel, M.S.; Temple, H.T.; Michelson, J.D.; et al. Thromboembolism after foot and ankle surgery. A multicenter study. Clin Orthop 348:180–185, 1998.

217. Morrissey, E. Metatarsal fractures. J Bone Joint Surg Am 28:594–602, 1946.

218. Morton, D.J. The Human Foot: Its Evolution, Physiology and Functional Disorders. Morningside Heights, NY, Columbia University Press, 1935.

219. Mueller, M.E.; Allgöwer, M.; Schneider, R.; et al. Manual of Internal Fixation, 3rd ed. Berlin, Springer-Verlag, 1991.

220. Mukherjee, S.K.; Pringle, R.M.; Baxter, A.D. Fractures of the lateral process of the talus. A report of 13 cases. J Bone Joint Surg Br 56:263–273, 1974.

221. Mulfinger, G.L.; Trueta, J. The blood supply of the talus. J Bone Joint Surg Br 52:160–167, 1970.

222. Munro, T.G. Fractures of the base of the fifth metatarsal. J Can Assoc Radiol 40:260–261, 1989.

223. Myburgh, K.H.; Hutchin, J.; Fataar, A.B.; et al. Low bone density as an etiologic factor for stress fractures in athletes. Ann Intern Med 113:754–759, 1990.

224. Myers, S.R.; Fadale, P.D.; Trafton, P.G. Fracture of the anterior process of the calcaneus as a cause of lateral foot pain. Contemp Orthop 18:445–449, 1989.

225. Myerson, M. Management of crush injuries and compartment syndromes of the foot. In: Meyerson, M., ed. Foot and Ankle Disorders, Vol. 2. Philadelphia, W.B. Saunders, 2000, pp. 1223–1244.

226. Myerson, M. Split-thickness skin excision: Its uses for immediate wound care in crush injuries of the foot. Foot Ankle 10:54–60, 1989.

227. Myerson, M.S. The diagnosis and treatment of compartment syndrome of the foot. Orthopaedics 13:711–717, 1990.

228. Myerson, M.S. The diagnosis and treatment of injuries to the Lisfranc joint complex. Orthop Clin North Am 20:655–664, 1989.

229. Myerson, M.S.; Fisher, R.T.; Burgess, A.R.; Kenzora, J.E. Fracture-dislocations of the tarsometatarsal joints: End results correlated with pathology and treatment. Foot Ankle 6:225–242, 1986.

230. Myerson, M.; Manoli, A. Compartment syndromes of the foot after calcaneal fractures. Clin Orthop 290:142–151, 1993.

231. Myerson, M.S.; McGarvey, W.C.; Henderson, M.R.; Hakim, J. Morbidity after crush injuries to the foot. J Orthop Trauma 8:343–349, 1994.

232. Myerson M.; Quill, G.E., Jr. Late complications of fractures of the calcaneus. J Bone Joint Surg Am 75:331–341, 1993.

233. Nabarro, M.N.; Powell, J. Dorsal dislocation of the metatarsophalangeal joint of the great toe: A case report. Foot Ankle 16:75–78, 1995.

234. Nadim, Y.; Tosic, A.; Ebraheim, N. Open reduction internal fixation of the posterior process of the talus: Case report and review of the literature. Foot Ankle Int 20:250–252, 1999.

235. Nasser, S.; Manoli, A., III. Fracture of the entire posterior process of the talus. A case report. Foot Ankle 10:235–238, 1990.

236. Newman, J.H. Spontaneous dislocation in diabetic neuropathy: A report of 6 cases. J Bone Joint Surg Br 61:484–488, 1979.

237. Nicastro, J.F.; Haupt, H.A. Probable stress fracture of the cuboid in an infant. J Bone Joint Surg Am 66:1106–1108, 1984.

238. Nicholas, R.; Hadley, J.; Paul, C.; James, P. Snowboarder's fracture: Fracture of the lateral process of the talus. J Am Board Fam Pract 7:130–133, 1994.

239. O'Connell, F.; Mital, M.A.; Rowe, C.R. Evaluation of modern management of fractures of the os calcis. Clin Orthop 83:214–223, 1972.

240. O'Malley, M.J.; Hamilton, W.G.; Munyak, J. Fracture of the distal shaft of the fifth metatarsal dancer's fracture. Am J Sports Med 24:240–243, 1996.

241. Ouzounian, T.J.; Anderson, R. Anterior tibial tendon rupture. Foot Ankle Int 16:406–410, 1995.

242. Ouzounian, T.J.; Shereff, M.J. In vitro determination of midfoot motion. Foot Ankle 10:140–146, 1989.

243. Paley, D.; Hall, H. Calcaneal fracture controversies: Can we put Humpty Dumpty back together again? Orthop Clin North Am 20:665–677, 1989.

244. Paley, D.; Hall, H. Intraarticular fractures of the calcaneus: A critical analysis of results and prognostic factors. J Bone Joint Surg Am 75:342–354, 1993.

245. Palmer, I. The mechanism and treatment of fractures of the calcaneus. J Bone Joint Surg Am 30:2, 1948.

246. Park, W.H.; DeMuth, W.E., Jr. Wounding capacity of rotary lawn mowers. J Trauma 15:36–38, 1975.

247. Parkes, J.C., II. The conservative management of fractures of the os calcis. In: Leach, R.E.; Hoaglund, F.T.; Riseborough, E.J., eds. Controversies in Orthopaedic Surgery. Philadelphia, W.B. Saunders, 1982, pp. 229–231.

248. Patterson, R.H.; Petersen, D.; Cunningham, R. Isolated fracture of the medial cuneiform. J Orthop Trauma 7:94–95, 1993.

249. Paulos, L.E.; Johnson, C.L.; Noyes, F.R. Posterior compartment fractures of the ankle. A commonly missed athletic injury. Am J Sports Med 11:439–443, 1983.

250. Pennal, G.F. Fractures of the talus. Clin Orthop 30:53, 1963.

251. Penny, J.N.; Danis, L.A. Fractures and fracture-dislocations of the neck of the talus. J Trauma 20:1029–1037, 1980.

252. Penstrom, P.A.F.H. Mechanisms, diagnosis, and treatment of running injuries. Instr Course Lect 42, 1993.

253. Peterson, D.A.; Stinson, W. Excision of the fractured os peroneum: A report on five patients and review of the literature. Foot Ankle 13:277–281, 1992.

254. Peterson, L.; Goldie, I.F.; Irstam, L. Fracture of the neck of the talus. A clinical study. Acta Orthop Scand 48:696–706, 1977.

255. Peterson, L.; Goldie, I.F.; Lindell, D. The arterial supply of the talus. A study on the relationship to experimental talar fractures. Acta Orthop Scand 46:1026–1034, 1975.

256. Pinney, S.J.; Sangeorzan, B.J. Fractures of the tarsal bones. In: Sangeorzan, B.J., ed. The Traumatic Foot. Rosemont, IL, American Academy of Orthopaedic Surgeons, 2001, pp. 41–53.

257. Potter, H.G.; Deland, J.T.; Gusmer, P.B.; et al. Magnetic resonance imaging of the Lisfranc ligament of the foot. Foot Ankle Int 19:438–446, 1998.

258. Pozo, J.L., Kirwan, E.O.; Jackson, A.M. The long term results of conservative management of severely displaced fractures of the calcaneus. J Bone Joint Surg Br 66:386–390, 1984.

259. Preidler, K.W.; Peicha, G.; Lajtai, G.; et al. Conventional radiography, CT, and MRI imaging in patients with hyperflexion injuries of the foot: Diagnostic accuracy in the detection of bony and ligamentous changes. AJR Am J Roentgenol 173:1673–1677, 1999.

260. Preventing Lawnmower Injuries. American Orthopaedic Foot and Ankle Society Position Statement, Rosemont, IL, 2001.

261. Quenu, E.; Kuss, G. Etude sur les luxations du metatarse. Rev Chir 39:1, 1909.

262. Quill, G.E., Jr. Fractures of the proximal fifth metatarsal. Orthop Clin North Am 26:353–361, 1995.

263. Rammelt, S.; Gavlik, J.M.; Zwipp, H. Value of subtalar arthroscopy in the management of intraarticular calcaneus fractures. Paper presented at the American Orthopaedic Foot and Ankle Society 17th Summer Meeting, San Diego, California, July 2001.

264. Randle, J.A.; Kreeder, H.J.; Stephen, D.; et al. Should calcaneal fractures be treated surgically: A metaanalysis. Clin Orthop 377:217–227, 2000.

265. Rao, J.P.; Banzon, M.T. Irreducible dislocation of the metatarsophalangeal joints of the foot. Clin Orthop 145:224–226, 1979.

266. Regazzoni, P. Technik der stabilen Osteosynthese bei Calcaneusfrakturen. Hefte Unfallheilkd 200:432, 1988.

267. Rettig, A.C.; Shelbourne, K.D.; Wilckens, J. The surgical treatment of symptomatic nonunions of the proximal (metaphyseal) fifth metatarsal in athletes. Am J Sports Med 210:50–54, 1992.

268. Richli, W.R.; Rosenthal, D.I. Avulsion fracture of the fifth metatarsal: Experimental study of pathomechanics. Am J Radiol 143:889–891, 1984.

269. Rodeo, S.A.; O'Brien, S.; Warren R.F.; et al. Turf toe: An analysis of metatarsophalangeal joint sprains in pro football players. Am J Sports Med 8:280–285, 1990.

270. Romash, M.M. Calcaneal fractures: Three-dimensional treatment. Foot Ankle 8:180–197, 1988.

271. Romash, M.M. Reconstructive osteotomy of the calcaneus with subtalar fusion for malunited calcaneal fractures. Clin Orthop 290:157–167, 1993.

272. Rongstad, K.; Mann, R.A.; Prieskorn, D.; et al. Popliteal sciatic nerve block for postoperative analgesia. Foot Ankle Int 17:378–382, 1996.

273. Rosenberg, G.A.; Patterson, B.M. Tarsometatarsal (Lisfranc's) fracture-dislocation. Am J Orthop Suppl, pp. 7–16, 1995.

274. Rosenberg, G.A.; Sferra, J.J. Treatment strategies for acute fractures and nonunions of the proximal fifth metatarsal. J Am Acad Orthop Surg 8:332–338, 2000.

275. Rosenberg, Z.S.; Feldman, F.; Singson, R.D.; Price, G.J. Peroneal tendon injury associated with calcaneal fractures: CT findings. AJR Am J Roentgenol 149:125–129, 1987.

276. Ross, G.; Cronin, R.; Howzenblas, J.; Juliano, P. Plantar ecchymosis sign: A clinical aid to diagnosis of occult Lisfranc tarsometatarsal injuries. J Orthop Trauma 10:119–122, 1996.

277. Rowe, C.R.; Sakellarides, H.T.; Freeman, P.A.; Sorbie, C. Fractures of the os calcis: A long term follow up study of 146 patients. JAMA 184:920–923, 1963.

278. Sammarco, G.J.; Conti, S.F. Surgical treatment of neuroarthropathic foot deformity. Foot Ankle Int 19:102–109, 1998.

279. Sanders, R., guest ed. Calcaneal fractures (multiauthor symposium). Clin Orthop 290:2–167, 1993.

280. Sanders, R. Displaced intraarticular fractures of the calcaneus. J Bone Joint Surg Am 82:225–250, 2000.

281. Sanders, R. Fractures and fracture-dislocations of the talus. In: Coughlin, M.J.; Mann, R.A., eds. Surgery of the Foot and Ankle, 7th ed, Vol 2. St Louis, Mosby–Year Book, 1999, pp. 1465–1518.

282. Sanders, R.; Fortin, P.; DiPasquale, T.; et al. Operative treatment in 120 displaced intraarticular calcaneal fractures: Results using a prognostic computed tomography scan classification. Clin Orthop 290:87–95, 1993.

283. Sangeorzan, B.J. Foot and ankle joint. In: Hansen, S.T., Jr.; Swiontowski, M.F., eds. Othopaedic Trauma Protocols. New York, Raven, 1993.

284. Sangeorzan, B.J. Salvage procedures for calcaneal fractures. Instr Course Lect 46:339–346, 1997.

285. Sangeorzan, B.J., ed. The Traumatized Foot. Rosemont, IL, American Academy of Orthopaedic Surgeons, 2001.

286. Sangeorzan, B.J.; Ananthakrishnan, D.; Tencer, A.F. Contact characteristics of the subtalar joint after a simulated calcaneus fracture. J Orthop Trauma 9:251–258, 1995.

287. Sangeorzan, B.J.; Benirschke, S.K.; Carr, J.B. Surgical management of fractures of the os calcis. Instr Course Lect 44:359–370, 1995.

288. Sangeorzan, B.J.; Benirschke, S.K.; Mosca, V.; et al. Displaced intraarticular fractures of the tarsal navicular. J Bone Joint Surg Am 71:1504–1510, 1989.

289. Sangeorzan, B.J.; Hansen, S.T., Jr. Cuneiform-metatarsal arthrodesis (Lisfranc). In: Johnson, K.A., ed. Master Techniques in Orthopaedic Surgery, The Foot and Ankle. New York, Lippincott-Raven, 1994, pp. 231–246.

290. Sangeorzan, B.J.; Hansen, S.T. Early and late posttraumatic foot reconstruction. Clin Orthop 243:86–91, 1989.

291. Sangeorzan, B.J.; Mosca, V.; Hansen, S.T., Jr. Effect of calcaneal lengthening on relationships among the hindfoot, midfoot, and forefoot. Foot Ankle Int 14:136–141, 1993.

292. Sangeorzan, B.J.; Swiontkowski, M.F. Displaced fractures of the cuboid. J Bone Joint Surg Br 72:376–378, 1990.

293. Sangeorzan, B.J.; Veith, R.G.; Hansen, S.T., Jr. Salvage of Lisfranc tarsometatarsal joints by arthrodesis. Foot Ankle Int 10:193–200, 1990.

294. Sangeorzan, B.J.; Wagner, U.A.; Harrington, R.M.; Tencer, A.F. Contact characteristics of the subtalar joint: The effect of talar neck misalignment. J Orthop Res 10:544–551, 1992.

295. Santi, M.; Sartoris, D.J.; Resnick, D. Diagnostic imaging of tarsal and metatarsal stress fractures. Orthop Rev 18:178–185, 1989.

296. Sarrafian, S.K. Anatomy of the Foot and Ankle. Philadelphia, J.B. Lippincott, 1983.

297. Schaffer, J.J.; Lock, T.R.; Salciccioli, G.G. Posterior tibial tendon rupture in pronation external rotation ankle fractures. J Trauma 27:795–796, 1987.

298. Schatzker, J.; Tscherne, H. Major Fractures of the Pilon, Talus, and Calcaneus. New York, Springer-Verlag, 1992.

299. Schenck, R.C., Jr.; Heckman, J.D. Fractures and dislocations of the forefoot: Operative and nonoperative management. J Am Acad Orthop Surg 3:70–78, 1995.

300. Schildhauer, T.A.; Bauer, T.W.; Josten, C.; Muhr, G. Operative reduction and augmentation of internal fixation with an injectable skeletal cement for treatment of complex calcaneal fractures. J Orthop Trauma 14:309–317, 2000.

301. Schoen, N.S.; Gottlieb, L.J.; Zachary, L.S. Distribution of pedal burns by source and depth. J Foot Ankle Surg 35:194–198, 1996.

302. Schon, L.C.; Easley, M.E.; Weinfeld, S.B. Charcot neuroarthropathy of the foot and ankle. Clin Orthop 349:116–131, 1998.

303. Schon, L.C.; Marlen, R.M. The management of neuropathic fracture dislocation in the diabetic patient. Orthop Clin North Am 26:375, 1995.

304. Schwab, R.A.; Powers, R.D. Conservative therapy of plantar puncture wounds. J Emerg Med 13:291–295, 1995.

305. Sclamberg, E.L.; Davenport, K. Operative treatment of displaced intraarticular fracture of the calcaneus. J Trauma 28:510–516, 1988.

306. Seaberg, D.C.; Angelos, W.J.; Paris, P.M. Treatment of subungual hematoma with nail trephination: A prospective study. Am J Emerg Med 9:209–210, 1991.

307. Shah, S.N.; Knoblich, G.O.; Lindsey, D.P.; et al. Intramedullary screw fixation of proximal fifth metatarsal fractures: A biomechanical study. Foot Ankle Int 22:581–584, 2001.

308. Shapiro, M.S.; Wascher, D.C.; Finerman, G.A. Rupture of Lisfranc ligament in athletes. Am J Sports Med 22:687–691, 1994.

309. Shereff, M.J. Complex fractures of the metatarsals. Orthopedics 13:875–882, 1990.

310. Shereff, M.J. Fractures of the forefoot. Instr Course Lect 39:133–140, 1990.

311. Sherman, R.; Wellisz, T.; Wiss, D.; et al. Coverage of type III open ankle and foot fractures with the temporoparietal fascial free flap. Paper presented at the 4th Annual Meeting of the Orthopaedic Trauma Association Meeting, Philadelphia, Pennsylvania, October 18–21, 1989.

312. Silfverskiöld, N. Reduction of the uncrossed two joint muscles of the leg to one joint muscles in the spastic condition. Acta Chir Scand 56:315–330, 1923.

313. Simon, R.R.; Wolgin, M. Subungual hematoma: Association with occult laceration requiring repair. Am J Emerg Med 5:302–304, 1987.

314. Smith, J.W.; Arnoczky, S.P.; Hersh, A. The intraosseous blood supply of the fifth metatarsal: Implications for proximal fracture healing. Foot Ankle 13:143–152, 1992.

315. Sneppen, O.; Christensen, S.B.; Krogsoe, O.; Lorentzen, J. Fractures of the body of the talus. Acta Orthop Scand 48:317–324, 1977.

316. Sobel, M.; Pavlov, H.; Thompson, F.M.; et al. Painful os peroneus syndrome: A spectrum of conditions responsible for plantar lateral foot pain. Foot Ankle Int 15:112–124, 1994.

317. Sorrento, D.L.; Mlodzienski, A. Incidence of lateral talar dome lesions in SER IV ankle fractures. J Foot Ankle Surg 39:354–358, 2000.

318. Stephenson, J.R. Surgical treatment of displaced intraarticular fractures of the calcaneus: A combined lateral and medial approach. Clin Orthop 290:68–75, 1993.

319. Straus, D.C. Subtalar dislocation of the foot. Am J Surg 30:427–434, 1935.

320. Swanson, T.V.; Bray, T.J.; Holmes, G.B., Jr. Fractures of the talar neck: A mechanical study of fixation. J Bone Joint Surg Am 74:544–551, 1992.

321. Szyszkowitz, R.; Reschauer, R.; Seggl, W. Eighty-five talus fractures treated by open reduction internal fixation with five to eight year follow-up of sixty nine patients. Clin Orthop 199:97–107, 1985.

322. Tan, Y.H.; Chin, T.W.; Mitra, A.K.; Tan, S.K. Tarsometatarsal (Lisfranc) injuries—results of open reduction and internal fixation. Ann Acad Med Singapore 24:816–819, 1995.

323. Tanke, G.M. Fractures of the calcaneus. A review of the literature together with some observations on methods of treatment. Acta Chir Scand Suppl 505:1–103, 1982.

324. Taylor, G. Treatment of fracture at the great toe. BMJ 1:724–725, 1943.

325. Taylor, G.I.; Pan, W.R. Angiosomes of the leg: Anatomic study and clinical implications. Plast Reconstr Surg 102:599–618, 1998.

326. Tejwani, N.; DiGiovanni, C.W.; Kuo, R.; et al. Fractures of the os calcis in children: A study of 43 fractures. Presented, 67th AAOS Meeting, Orlando, FL, 3/00. Submitted for publication.

327. Thordarson, D.B.; Greene, N.; Shepherd, L.; Perlman, M. Facilitated edema resolution with a foot pump after calcaneus fracture. J Orthop Trauma 13:43–46, 1999.

328. Thordarson, D.B.; Hedman, T.P.; Yetkinlen, D.N.; et al. Superior compressive strength of calcaneal fracture construct segments with remodellable cancellous bone cement. J Bone Joint Surg Am 81:239–246, 1999.

329. Thordarson, D.B.; Triffon, M.J.; Terk, M.R. Magnetic resonance imaging to detect avascular necrosis after open reduction internal fixation of talar neck fractures. Foot Ankle Int 17:742–747, 1996.

330. Thoren, O. Os calcis fractures. Acta Orthop Scand Suppl 70:1–116, 1964.

331. Tile, M. Fractures of the talus. In: Schatzker, J.; Tile, M, eds. The Rationale of Operative Fracture Care. Berlin, Springer-Verlag, 1987, p. 407.

332. Toolan, B.C.; Sangeorzan, B.J. Fractures of the talus. In: Sangeorzan, B.J., ed. The Traumatic Foot. Rosemont, IL, American Academy of Orthopaedic Surgeons, 2001, pp. 1–14.

333. Torg, J.S. Fractures of the base of the fifth metatarsal distal to the tuberosity: A review. Contemp Orthop 19:497, 1988.

334. Torg, J.S.; Pavlov, H.; Cooley, L.H., et al. Stress fractures of the tarsal navicular. A retrospective review of 21 cases. J Bone Joint Surg Br 64:700–712, 1982.

335. Tornetta, P., III. Percutaneous treatment of calcaneal fractures. Clin Orthop 375:91–96, 2000.

336. Tornetta, P., III. The Essex-Lopresti reduction for calcaneal fractures revisited. J Orthop Trauma 12:469–473, 1998.

337. Tran, T.; Thordarson, D.B. Functional outcome of multiply injured patients with associated foot injury. Paper presented at the 32nd Annual Meeting of the American Orthopaedic Foot and Ankle Society, Dallas, Texas, February 16, 2002.

338. Tscherne, H.; Zwipp, H. Calcaneal fracture. In: Tscherne, H.; Schatzker, J., eds. Major Fractures of the Pilon, the Talus, and the Calcaneus: Current Concepts of Treatment. Berlin, Springer-Verlag, 1993, pp. 153–174.

339. Tucker, D.J.; Burian, G.; Boylan, J.P. Lateral subtalar dislocation: Review of the literature and case presentation. J Foot Ankle Surg 37:239–247, 1998.

340. Tucker, D.J.; Feder, J.M.; Boylan, J.P. Fractures of the lateral process of the talus: 2 case reports and a comprehensive review of the literature. Foot Ankle Int 19:641–646, 1998.

341. Tucker, D., Jules, K.; Raymond, F. Nailbed injuries with hallucal phalangeal fractures. J Am Podiatr Med Assoc 86:170–173, 1996.

342. Turchin, D.C.; Schemitsch, E.H.; McKee, M.E.; Waddell, J.P. Do foot injuries significantly affect the functional outcome of multiply injured patients? J Orthop Trauma 13:1–4, 1999.

343. Twerino, S.G.; Kodros, S. Controversies in tarsometatarsal injuries. Orthop Clin North Am 26:229–238, 1995.

344. Van Hal, M.E.; Keene, J.S.; Lange, T.A.; Clancy, W.G., Jr. Stress fractures of the great toe sesamoids. Am J Sports Med 10:122–128, 1982.

345. Varga, T. In: Department of Orthopaedics, Harborview Medical Center Trauma Protocols, Seattle.

346. Veazy, B.L.; Heckman, J.D.; Galindo, M.J.; McGanity, P.L. Excision of ununited fractures of the posterior process of the talus: A treatment for chronic posterior ankle pain. Foot Ankle 12:453–457, 1991.

347. Verdile, V.P.; Freed, H.A.; Gerard, J. Puncture wounds to the foot. J Emerg Med 7:193–199, 1989.

348. Viswanath, S.S.; Shephard, E. Dislocation of the calcaneum. Injury 9:50–52, 1977.

349. Vosburgh, C.; Gruel, C.P.; Herndon, W.A.; Sullivan, J.A. Lawnmower injuries of the pediatric foot and ankle: Observations on prevention and management. J Pediatr Orthop 15:504–509, 1995.

350. Warren, M.P.; Brooks-Gunn, J.; Fox, R.P.; et al. Lack of bone accretion and amenorrhea: Evidence for relative osteopenia in weightbearing bones. J Clin Endocrinol Metab 72:847–853, 1991.

351. Weiss, A.P.; Yates, A.J. Irreducible dorsal dislocation of the IP joint of the great toe. Orthopedics 15:480–482, 1992.

352. Wicks, M.H.; Harbison, J.S.; Paterson, D.C. Tendon injury about the foot and ankle in children. Aust N Z J Surg 50:158–161, 1980.

353. Wiger, P.; Styf, J.R. Effects of limb elevation on abnormal increased intramuscular pressure, blood perfusion pressure, and foot sensation: An experimental study in humans. J Orthop Trauma 12:343–347, 1998.

354. Wilppula, E. Tarsometatarsal fracture-dislocation: Late results in 26 patients. Acta Orthop Scand 44:335–345, 1973.

355. Wilson, L.S., Jr.; Mizel, M.S.; Michelson, M.D. Foot and ankle injuries in motor vehicle accidents. Foot Ankle Int 22:649–652, 2001.

356. Wilson, P.D. Fractures and dislocations of the tarsal bones. South Med J 26:833, 1933.

357. Wiss, D.A.; Kull, D.M.; Perry, J. Lisfranc fracture-dislocations of the foot: A clinical-kinesiological study. J Orthop Trauma 1:267–274, 1988.

358. Younger, E.M.; Chapman, M.W. Morbidity at bone graft donor sites. J Orthop Trauma 3:192–195, 1989.

359. Zinman, H.; Keret, T.; Reis, N.D. Fractures of the medial sesamoid bone of the hallux. J Trauma 21:581–582, 1981.

360. Ziv, I.; Mosheiff, R.; Zeligowski, A.; et al. Crush injuries of the foot with compartment syndrome: Immediate one stage management. Foot Ankle 9:185–189, 1989.

361. Ziv, I.; Zeligowski, A.; Mosheiff, R.; et al. Split-thickness skin excision in severe open fractures. J Bone Joint Surg Br 70:23–26, 1988.

362. Zook, E.G. Treatment of nail bed injuries. Surg Rounds Orthop 3:20, 1989.

363. Zwipp, H.; Tscherne, H.; Thermann, H.; et al. Osteosynthesis of displaced intraarticular fractures of the calcaneus: Results in 123 cases. Clin Orthop 290:76–86, 1993.

# CHAPTER 61

## Post-traumatic Reconstruction of the Foot and Ankle

Sigvard T. Hansen, Jr., M.D.

Residuals of trauma are a major cause of symptoms in the foot and ankle. The reason for this is that, until recently, foot injuries were not treated as aggressively and expertly at the time of initial trauma as were the long bone and other joint injuries. Moreover, the foot and the ankle are less prone to pure degenerative arthritis or osteoarthritis than are the knee, the hip, the spine, or even the hands.

It is widely recognized that injuries to soft tissues, including the ligaments and tendons, can lead to significant arthrosis in the ankle and in the foot itself. Many case reports of ankle fusion or arthroplasty list osteoarthritis as the primary diagnosis. However, upon careful evaluation of their histories and physical examinations, it is clear that ankle arthrosis was caused by old lateral ligament injuries. In the same way, posterior tibial tendon trauma or degeneration leads to valgus malalignment and secondary arthrosis in the foot and, eventually, the ankle. Even peroneus brevis or brevis and longus tears or ruptures lead to increased varus and eventual arthrosis. Trauma involving the joints of the ankle and foot is the most common cause of symptoms leading to the need for ankle and foot reconstruction.

Pilon fractures in the ankle, in which the weight-bearing articular surfaces have been damaged, are the most susceptible to arthrosis either with or without good initial treatment. In most other ankle fractures (except chondral injuries), deformity and late complications can be significantly reduced by good initial treatment. Severe intra-articular calcaneal fractures can lead to arthrosis in the subtalar joint with or without good initial treatment. Naturally, treatment is simplified when the body of the calcaneus has been anatomically reconstructed and maintained. Trauma to the talus resulting in a type III or IV fracture may lead to avascular necrosis (AVN) in spite of good initial treatment and present a reconstructive challenge. In types I and II talar fractures, as well as in many body and peripheral fractures, optimal initial treatment minimizes complications and the need for reconstruction.

Intra-articular fractures in non-essential joints, for example, the naviculocuneiform, the intercuneiform, and the 1-2-3 tarsometatarsal joints, are easier to treat or reconstruct because, by definition, stability is important in these joints but motion is not. Fusions can provide very adequate treatment here if anatomy has been restored.

## PRINCIPLES

An important principle in reconstructive foot surgery is to identify the cause of a problem. It might seem obvious that, if a patient develops midfoot arthrosis following a Lisfranc injury, arthrosis and collapse are caused by inadequate fixation of the Lisfranc injury. However, it is less commonly recognized that a tight gastrocnemius might be a contributing factor by applying a strong plantar flexion force to the hindfoot and stressing the healing midfoot and its supportive plantar ligaments. Prior to a Lisfranc injury, the plantar fascia, the long plantar ligament, and the plantar articular ligaments can resist this force but once damaged, they no longer can. Treatment by realignment and fusion of the affected Lisfranc joints might be inadequate, and gastrocnemius lengthening should be included in the treatment.

## PHYSICAL EXAMINATION

The purpose of the initial physical examination of a symptomatic foot is to ascertain the underlying condition causing the problem. Evaluation begins with a careful examination of the noninjured or asymptomatic foot, assuming that the other side was spared injury. With this information, the surgeon can make theoretical assumptions about the condition of the foot before it was injured and answer some basic questions, such as, did the patient have a tight gastrocnemius or heel cord (Fig. 61–1), varus or valgus heel alignment, a low or high arch, was muscle balance in the long toe flexors and extensors good or was it disordered (Fig. 61–2), does the long peroneal show

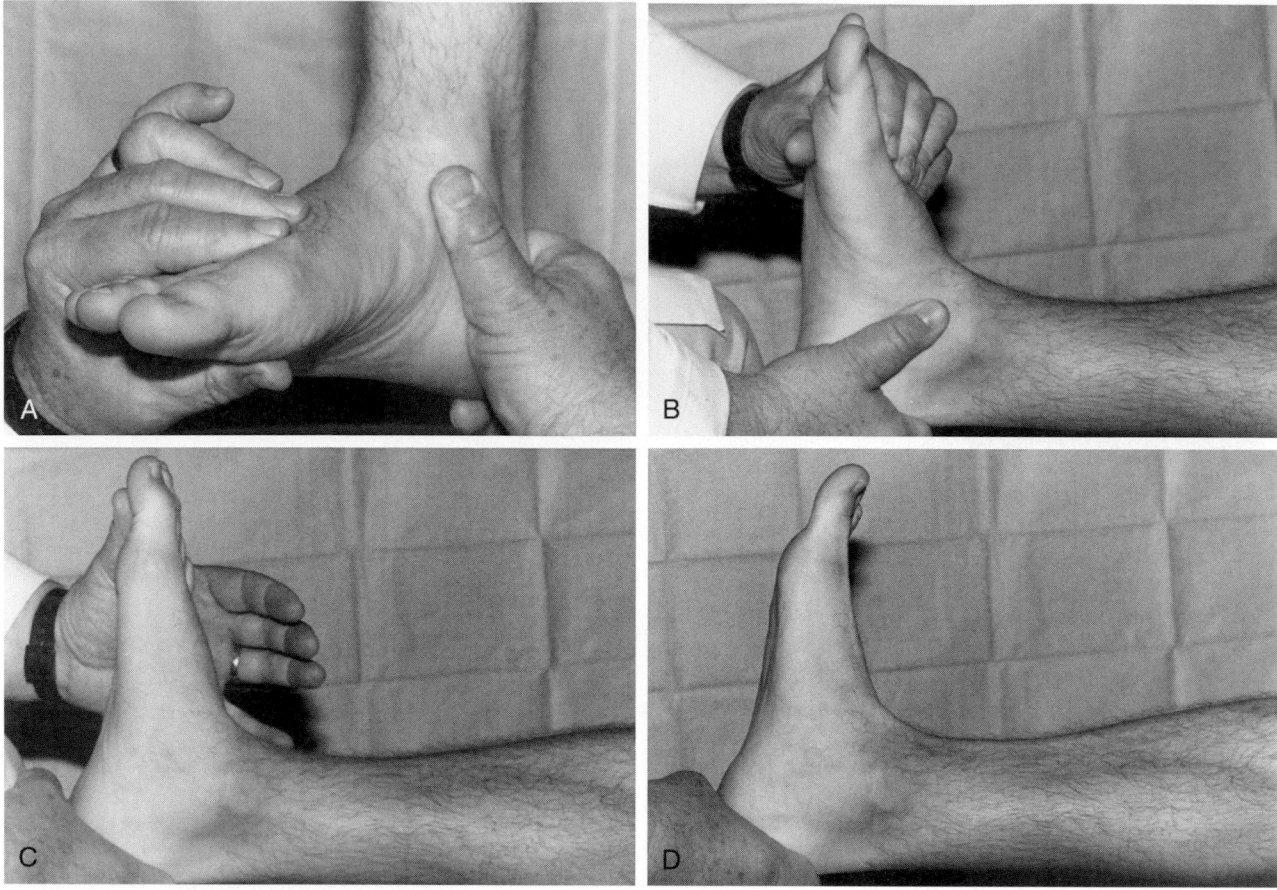

FIGURE 61–1. *A,* To inspect for gastrocnemius equinus, the examiner sits in front of the patient on the examining table and stabilizes the hindfoot and medial column in a neutral anatomic position. Using the right hand for the right foot, the examiner places the thumb on the head of the talus just proximal to the navicular tubercle while the fingers grasp the heel to keep the hindfoot out of valgus. The examiner's opposite hand holds the forefoot in adduction and the lateral metatarsals plantar flexed in line with the hindfoot. *B,* The patient is asked to relax, neither assisting nor resisting the examiner, and passive range of dorsiflexion is tested with the knee straight (gastrocnemius on stretch proximally) and with the knee bent (proximal end of gastrocnemius relaxed). If dorsiflexion from neutral is essentially absent with the knee straight or, in fixed equinus, if dorsiflexion with the knee bent is greater than 20 ± 5°, the gastrocnemius is probably pathologically short or tight and adds functional stress to the heel cord, plantar fascia, plantar ligaments, and the posterior tibial muscle and tendon. *C,* Confusion can arise if the examination is done inconsistently or incorrectly. Unless the foot is stabilized with the medial column locked, the ankle may appear to be in approximately 10° of dorsiflexion. *D,* When a patient actively dorsiflexes the foot while it is not stabilized, it may dorsiflex 10° or more. The test must be done with the muscles relaxed and the foot stabilized in exactly the same way each time. Each examiner develops a feel for the range between normal and abnormal in this examination. I think gastrocnemius lengthening is warranted when there is essentially no dorsiflexion with the knee straight and the foot stabilized and (with the foot held in exactly the same way) when dorsiflexion reaches or exceeds 15° with the knee bent.

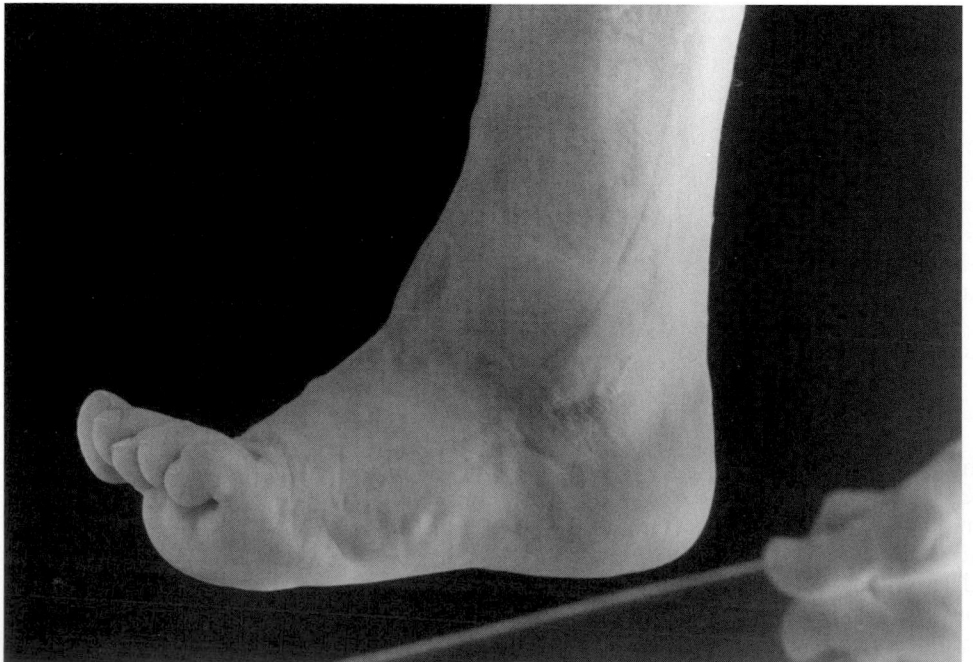

FIGURE 61–2. The patient is attempting to dorsiflex the ankle with the knee straight. Notice that the toes are all maximally extended. Such recruited activity indicates a very tight gastrocnemius. In this situation, it is common for "extensor recruitment" to occur—the toe extensors help the tibialis anterior and the peroneus tertius (the primary dorsiflexors) to dorsiflex the ankle. When the intrinsics are weak, denervated (e.g., diabetic neuropathy), or destroyed by inflammation (e.g., rheumatoid arthritis), subluxation and eventual dislocation of the toes will occur. Treatment consists of lengthening the gastrocnemius and transferring the long toe extensors into the midfoot or the peroneus tertius.

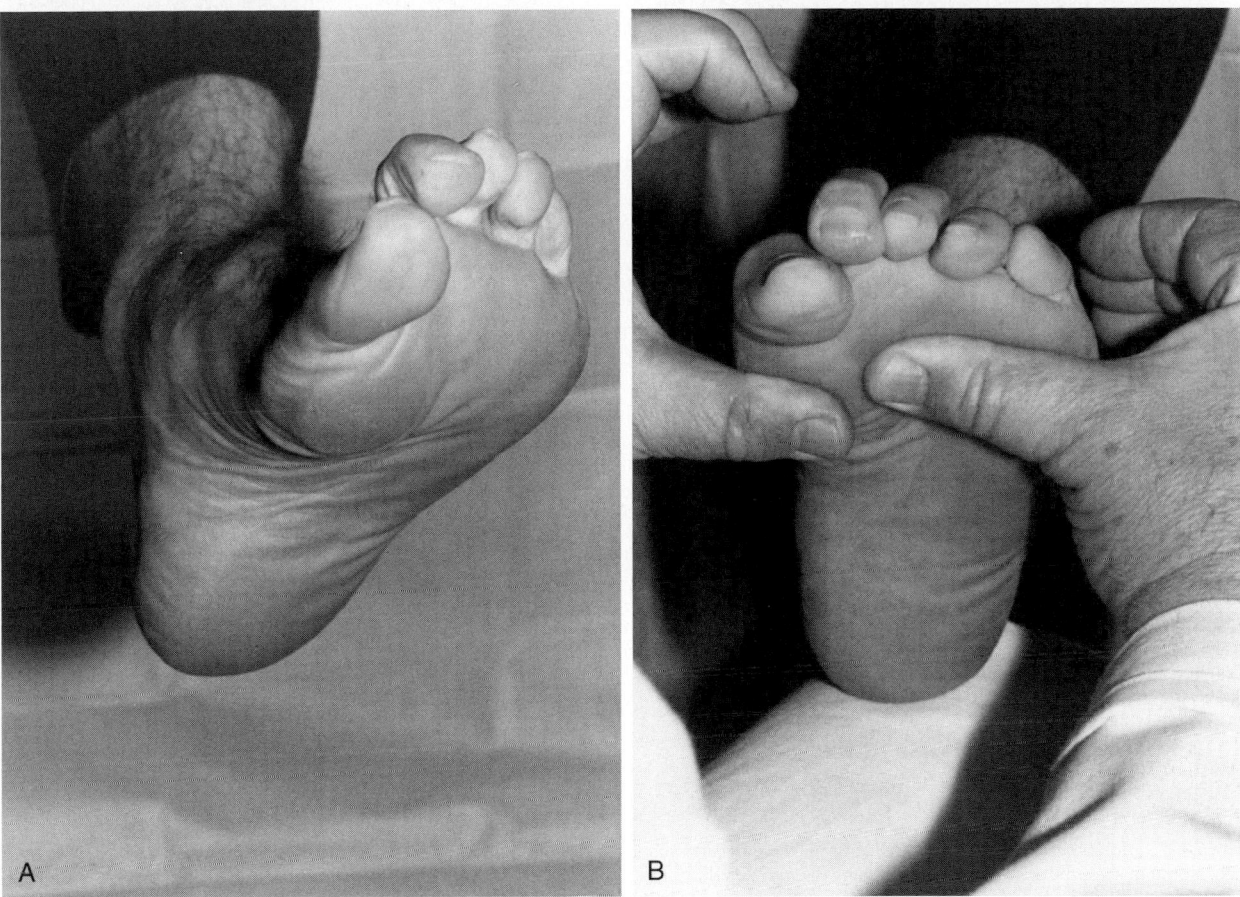

**FIGURE 61–3.** *A,* This patient has a plantar-flexed first metatarsal. Notice the dorsiflexed lesser toes and the presence of heavy callus primarily under the first metatarsal head. A dynamic deformity exists when the apparent medial cavus can be reduced by passively pushing the first metatarsal up to the level of the lesser metatarsals. If this maneuver does not correct the deformity, it is determined to be static or bony. *B,* To ascertain whether first metatarsal plantar flexion deformity is static or dynamic, the examiner places one thumb under the lesser metatarsal heads and the other thumb under the first. If the first metatarsal head plantar flexes below the lesser heads only when the patient plantar flexes the ankle and foot, the cause is dynamic overactivity of the peroneus longus.

signs of overuse or overdrive, is plantar flexion in the first metatarsal dynamic or static (Fig. 61–3), is there evidence of forefoot-driven hindfoot varus or valgus (Figs. 61–4 and 61–5).

With knowledge of the probable preinjury status in mind, the examiner turns next to the affected foot. Other injuries in the same extremity, such as post-traumatic tibial varus or valgus, extension or malrotation, a shortened leg, a longer leg, must be noted. The injured foot must be evaluated for adequate circulation and sensation as well as muscle power and balance. Circulation can be evaluated by noting the quality of the skin and soft tissues and capillary refill. Pulses are palpated and lower extremity pressures are compared with those in the upper extremity. If circulatory capacity appears to be inadequate, Doppler studies or angiography might be needed before major reconstruction is planned.

Neuropathy caused by nerve injury, diabetes, excessive height in older patients, or other diseases or idiopathic causes can greatly affect the type of treatment that should be prescribed. For example, ankle joint replacement is contraindicated in a neuropathic foot, but gastrocnemius lengthening is more strongly indicated here than in a foot without neuropathy. Motor power in all intrinsic and extrinsic muscles should be evaluated, as well as any limitation in range of motion that might be related to tethering or chronic compartment syndromes. Intrinsic flexor deformity and fixed claw toes are commonly seen in patients with calcaneal fractures.

Muscle imbalance between the plantar flexors and dorsiflexors of the ankle, the plantar flexors and dorsiflexors of the first metatarsal, and the inverters and evertors must be noted and corrected. Peroneus brevis or combined peroneus brevis and peroneus longus ruptures, for example, frequently go undiagnosed and lead to a progressive cavovarus deformity in the foot and instability in the ankle (Fig. 61–6). More commonly, deficits in the posterior tibial tendon lead to progressive valgus deformity in the foot and, eventually, to lateral erosion in the ankle.

Whether the heel is in neutral, varus, or excessive valgus, weight-bearing alignment in the hindfoot must be evaluated, in addition to the relative position of the midfoot and forefoot to the hindfoot. The relative length of the medial and lateral columns controls the position of the forefoot relative to the hindfoot. Rigid plantar flexion in the first metatarsal can cause forefoot-driven hindfoot varus, whereas a hypermobile first metatarsal or medial column allows the arch to sink and the hindfoot to go into secondary valgus. This condition is frequently called excessive pronation.

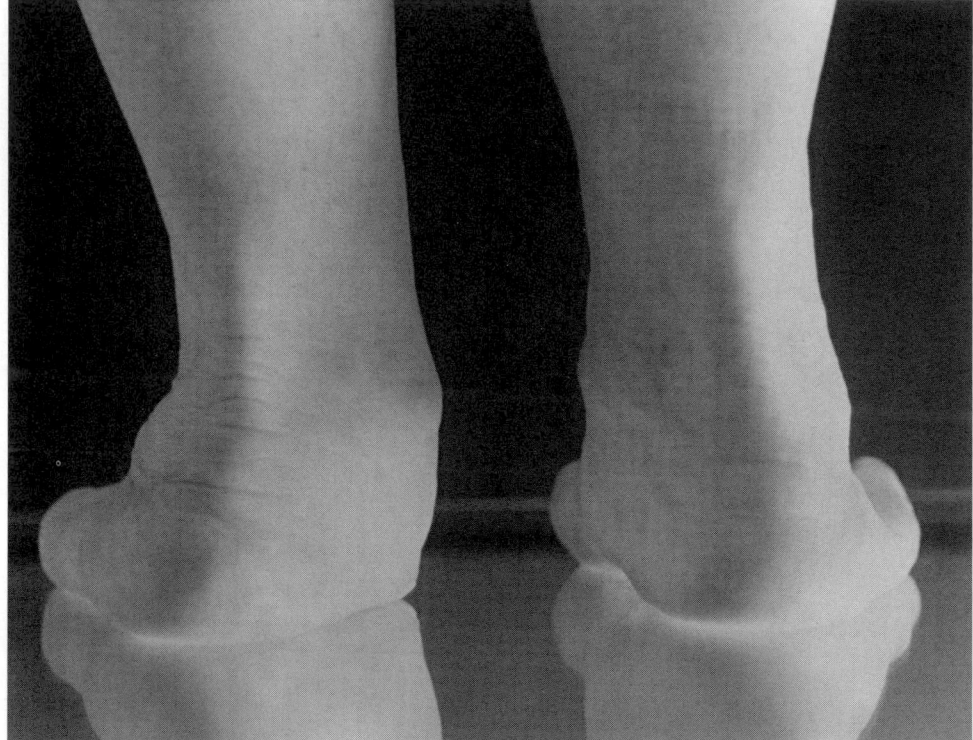

**FIGURE 61–4.** A standing view from behind shows a patient with long-standing flatfeet and mild heel valgus. A couple of years earlier, he experienced proximal medial arch pain on the left side and progressive flattening of the arch with severe heel valgus. Examination of that side revealed a very tight gastrocnemius, inability to do a single-leg heel rise, and inability to plantar flex and invert the foot. The first metatarsal is hypermobile and elevated. These symptoms are classic indications of rupture of the posterior tibial tendon.

**FIGURE 61–5.** Both heels of this young woman are in varus, more pronounced on the right than on the left. She was more symptomatic on the right and experienced pain and swelling behind the lateral malleolus. On a Coleman block test, the hindfoot straightened out to near normal but did not go into valgus. The peroneus brevis was very tender. These findings are all consistent with a combined forefoot-driven and fixed hindfoot varus deformity, commonly seen with a longitudinal tear of the peroneus brevis. Treatment involves moving the peroneus longus into the distal brevis on the lateral side of the foot, carrying out a lateralizing calcaneal osteotomy, and repairing the peroneus brevis.

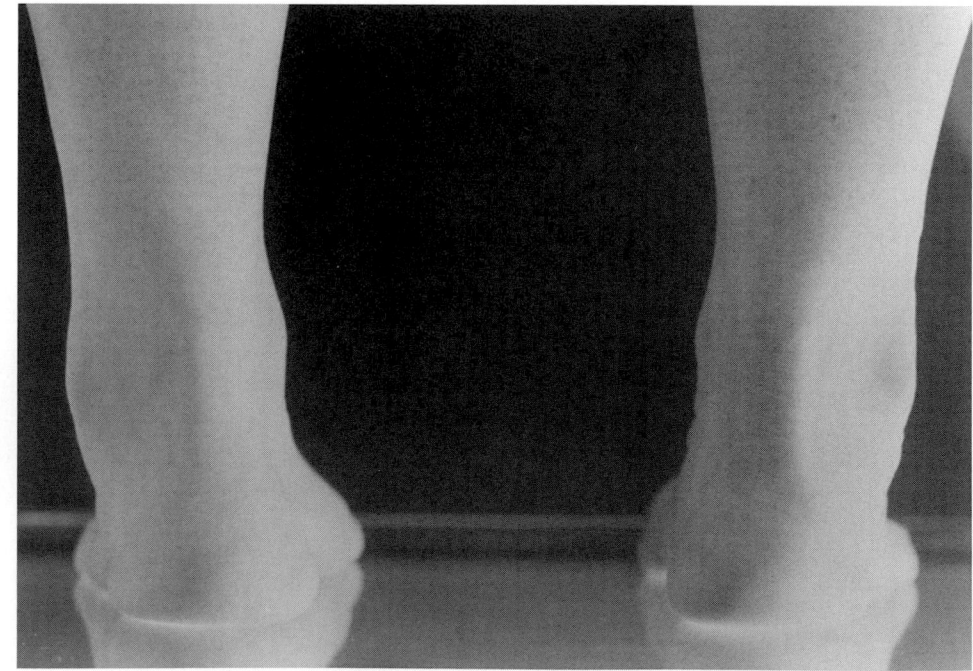

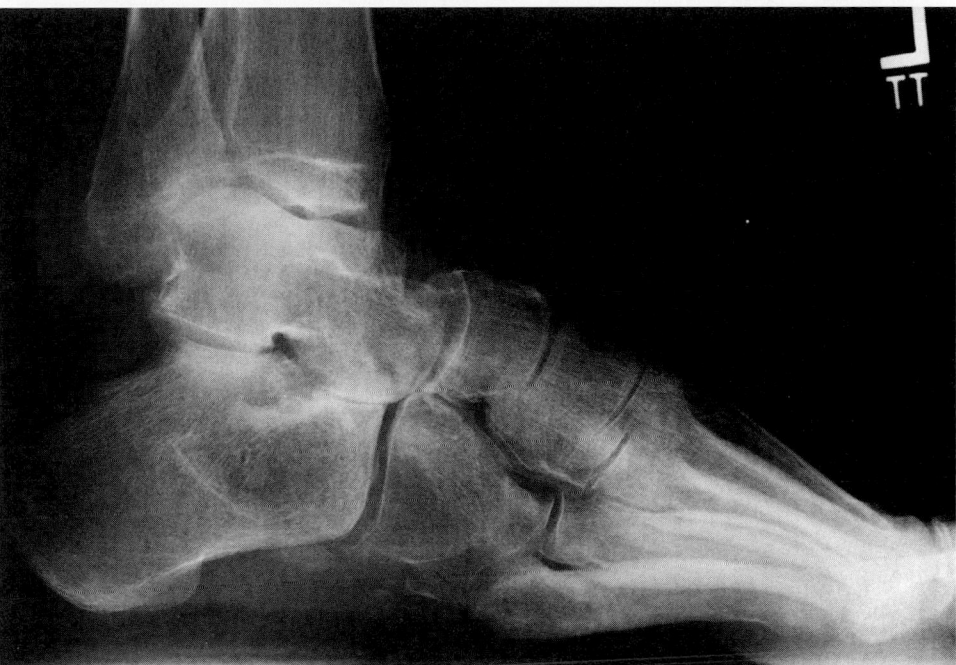

**FIGURE 61–6.** The left foot of a 50-year-old man with a long history of moderately severe cavovarus feet abruptly became more symptomatic and the ankle unstable after rupture of the long and short peroneal tendons. Notice the proximal displacement of the os peroneum. Muscle balancing plus calcaneal and first metatarsal osteotomies resulted in a satisfactory outcome.

After all information is gathered from the physical examination, appropriate radiographs should be taken and a treatment plan formulated.

## RADIOLOGY

Radiographs of the foot are taken with the patient standing with full weight bearing and the knee extended to reveal if the gastrocnemius is a contributing factor to the abnormality. Voluntary attempts by the patient or the radiographer to correct the position of the foot should not be allowed. The goal is to show the deformity or functional problem, including sag or subluxation at the normally stable midfoot joints, on the radiographs. The radiography series should include at least weight-bearing anteroposterior (AP) and lateral projections of the foot, and oblique views are needed if abnormalities are suspected in the more lateral cuneiform or cuneiform-metatarsal joints. In the ankle, weight-bearing lateral, AP, and mortise views are obtained. A computerized axial tomography (CAT) scan may be helpful before reconstruction of complex malunions in the talus or the calcaneus and, rarely, of pilon fractures.

Magnetic resonance imaging (MRI) is sometimes used for evaluation of soft tissue injuries, but they usually can be diagnosed perfectly well by physical examination alone. In my experience, MRIs produce many false-positive pathologic diagnoses in the foot and ankle. Malunions frequently require complex osteotomies, particularly in the talus and calcaneus, and CAT scans can be very useful there. They are less necessary for diagnosing ankle or pilon fractures but can be helpful for planning reconstruction.

Nonunions are easier to treat if they are not malpositioned. Avascular necrosis takes time to stabilize and may take as long as 18 to 36 months. MRI tends to overread AVN, and usually indicates a larger area of necrosis than actually exists. I base my diagnosis on evaluation of the initial injuries and watch what happens over time, especially with weight bearing. Good plain films and, to some extent, CAT scans provide an idea of how much bone is necrotic and interferes with function, requiring removal. Post-traumatic AVN tends to be irregular and incomplete when compared with AVN caused by use of steroids or other drugs, and it is compatible with fusion, arthroplasty procedures, or both.

## MALUNION, NONUNION, AND DEGENERATIVE SPUR FORMATION ON THE TALUS, INCLUDING OS TRIGONUM AND OSTEOCHONDROSIS

The key to correction of many problems in the talus is an adequate surgical exposure. Surgery in this area requires visualization of the affected part of the talus with enough room to manipulate a fragment. It is important not to disturb the blood supply, the local nerves, or the ligamentous structures in the course of making the incision. These are general requirements of all surgical exposures, but access to the talus is more demanding because it is hidden under the malleoli medially and laterally, is covered by deep soft tissues over its posterior aspect, and the major neurovascular structures and tendon groups to the foot are located at its posteromedial corner.

I recommend anteromedial and anterolateral surgical incisions for access to the talar neck and virtually always use a combination of these approaches. For the posterior body, I prefer a transmalleolar (medial) approach through an extended medial utility incision. For an approach to the lateral body that entails a double osteotomy of the fibula, I use a fibular "window" approach made through a vertical-lateral skin incision. For the posteromedial corner fragments, I make an inferomedial approach, which, in fact, is the upper end of a medial utility incision and allows access to the talus between the posterior tibial and flexor digitorum longus tendons and neurovascular structures. To approach the os trigonum and the posterior aspect of the talus and posterior degenerative spurs, I make a vertical posteromedial incision well in front of the heel cord. I go in laterally through the deep posterior compartment fascia and lateral to the neurovascular structures and the flexor hallucis longus. The sheath of the flexor hallucis longus can be loosened and the tendon pulled medially along with the neurovascular structures to provide excellent exposure of the posterior subtalar joint and the posterior talus.

A screw is inserted through the posterior talus, down through the neck, and into the head through a posterolateral approach, because the alignment of these structures is posterolateral to anteromedial. The screw can be placed through a posterolateral stab wound made with image intensifier guidance or by direct vision through the wide open posteromedial approach. Débridement of the anterior aspect of the ankle, including spurs or bossing on the neck of the talus, is carried out through slightly more proximal anteromedial and anterolateral surgical approaches in order to visualize the ankle joint from both sides. Care must be taken on the lateral side to avoid coming in too low and inadvertently dividing the anterior talofibular ligament in the sinus tarsi. Either or both of these incisions may be used, depending on whether the abnormalities are located more medially or more laterally. For extensive reconstruction, I frequently make both exposures and use a 5/8- or 3/4-inch gouge to completely redevelop the neck of the talus and provide adequate clearance at the ankle joint. Bone wax is placed on raw bone in this area.

Débridement of the sinus tarsi is done through a short section of the Ollier approach. This oblique surgical approach is made along the skin line and can be placed directly over the sinus tarsi. The approach is made after lifting the proximal end of the extensor digitorum brevis off the anterior calcaneus and removing some fat and possibly part of the cervical ligament from the sinus tarsi. Débridement of any prominence or excrescence and fracture stabilization of the anterolateral shoulder of the talus can be done then as needed. Again, care is taken to avoid going in too high in this approach and risking division of the anterior talofibular ligament.

## OSTEOCHONDRITIC LESIONS ON THE DOME OF THE TALUS

We have begun to use osteochondral plugs to repair osteochondritic defects in the talus that are up to 1.5 centimeters in diameter. The ipsilateral knee is used as the donor site and the talus is visualized through an arthroscope both to determine an indication for the procedure and to assess the size of the plug that will be needed.[1] The operation is carried out through an open surgical approach. On the medial side, a medial malleolar osteotomy is carried out and the talar dome is tilted out. This is followed by the standard approach and placement of an osteochondral plug taken from the lateral condyle of the ipsilateral knee. This approach is less common on the lateral side for getting a vertical look at a lesion on the lateral dome of the talus. However, it can easily be done through the fibular window approach.[2] A straight vertical and lateral incision is made over the fibula to expose it, and the fibula is transected just below and approximately 6 to 8 centimeters proximal to the dome of the talus. The fibula is rotated posteriorly on its peroneal tendon and sheath attachments. A Schanz pin is placed into the anterior body of the talus, and the talus is pulled slightly to the lateral side and tilted, then flexed or extended until the lesion presents in the fibular notch of the tibia. This approach allows direct vertical visualization of the lesion as well as simple removal of the defect and implantation of the osteochondral plug in the standard manner.

## CALCANEAL MALUNION AND NONUNION

Good visualization of the calcaneus is much easier to achieve than visualization of the talus. The lateral extensile incision commonly used for open reduction and internal fixation (ORIF) of the calcaneus also works very well for reconstruction. However, for other procedures, such as medializing or lateralizing osteotomies perpendicular to the tuber, other incisions are smaller and safer. I use extensile lateral L- or J-incisions for triplane osteotomies and to correct intra-articular malunions without subtalar fusion. A small lateral oblique incision over the tuber is satisfactory for simple medial, lateral, or plantar displacement osteotomies of the tuber. For subtalar fusion with bone block distraction, I frequently make a long vertical posterolateral incision and occasionally sacrifice the sural nerve. A femoral distractor is used on the medial side to be sure that the distracted joint is not pushed into varus, a common event with distraction from the lateral side.

Every malunion is unique and only general principles can be described in a discussion of nonspecific conditions. However, some guidelines apply to all calcaneal malunions. The original fracture line or a composite of the original fracture lines must be recreated by an osteotomy and the original anatomy of the calcaneus restored as best possible. Common findings in many os calcis fractures that were not restored by immediate ORIF include a tuber that is tilted into varus but displaced laterally and a heel that is shortened in terms of lateral column length and vertical height. All these abnormalities can be corrected by an oblique osteotomy started more anteriorly on the lateral side of the heel and angled posteriorly and medially (Fig. 61–7). Usually, the obliquity is located closer to the frontal plane than to the sagittal plane and, in this case, the amount of valgus that is corrected is greater than the amount of lateral column lengthening that occurs. This is usually desirable.

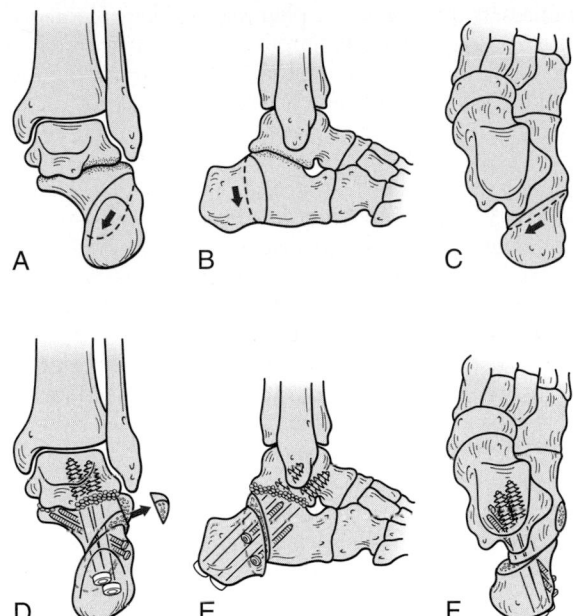

**FIGURE 61–7.** Osteotomy for triplane correction. *A,* A posterior illustration depicts residuals of a calcaneal fracture displaced in valgus. Notice the impingement under the tip of the fibula and lateral displacement in relation to the weight-bearing line of the tibia. *Solid and dotted lines* outline the osteotomy for correction. Displacement of the tuber medially will correct the valgus. *B,* Seen from the lateral side, the hindfoot demonstrates loss of height and calcaneal pitch as a result of a crushing fracture through the subtalar joint. *Solid and dotted lines* indicate the plane of the potential corrective osteotomy. The osteotomy line helps the surgeon to visualize how plantar translation of the tuber can correct height and calcaneal pitch. *C,* Seen from above, it is clear how medial translation of the heel, the third (transverse) plane of correction, will add overall length to the heel. *D,* After osteotomy and fixation, the posterior tuber is displaced medially, inferiorly, and posteriorly. Two 3.5-mm or, preferably, 4.0-mm cortical screws are placed in lag fashion perpendicular to the osteotomy. Two 6.5-mm cancellous screws are placed from the tuber across the osteotomy and nearly perpendicular to the posterior facet, where the joint has been curetted and packed with cancellous bone chips removed from the expanded lateral wall. *E,* The position of the tuber has been corrected in three planes and stabilized with screw fixation. Plantar displacement and increased height and pitch angle of the heel are obvious. *F,* Medial and posterior translation of the heel and the angles of the fixation screws are seen from above.

In addition to the osteotomy, the local soft tissues should be carefully stretched without inflicting damage to the nerves or blood supply going to the bony fragments. Sometimes the tendo Achilles should be lengthened; in other cases, just the scarred sheath and periosteal tissues should be stretched. This allows the surgeon to slide the posterior or tuber fragment in three directions along a single plane. The tuber can be moved medially and posteriorly and/or it can be displaced inferiorly. After the heel cord is lengthened, the fragment can be rotated slightly out of varus tilt. Rotation is simple when the osteotomy is transverse but becomes quite complex when the osteotomy is made oblique to the frontal plane to obtain lateral calcaneal length. The osteotomy is then stabilized with at least two screws placed into the os calcis perpendicular to the osteotomy plane. When the subtalar joint is severely arthritic, a small amount of cartilage may

be curetted from the subtalar joint or a divot or bur hole made in the joint and filled with cancellous bone. Bone can be taken from the Gerdes tubercle area or the expanded lateral wall that was excised at the beginning of the procedure. Two additional screws may be placed from the tuber and angled across the osteotomy and up through the subtalar joint.

Intra-articular malunions that can be reconstructed require a surgical approach similar to that used for an os calcis fracture. The joint is visualized and appropriate osteotomies are made to simulate the initial fracture and realign the articular surface in its original anatomic position. This is not always possible, and this procedure is difficult at best. The same precautions that are observed during a lateralizing calcaneal osteotomy apply: the surgeon must be very careful to avoid the neurovascular structures, particularly the lateral plantar nerve when it is entrapped in scar. This nerve runs close to the medial calcaneus in the area of the usual osteotomy and is sandwiched between the quadratus plantae and the flexor digitorum brevis, which may be damaged by fracture and scar down the nerve. The nerve can be damaged easily by pinching or stretching, and it can be inadvertently cut by an osteotome. When possible nerve damage is anticipated, it may be prudent to add a medial approach, similar to that used for a tarsal tunnel release, to protect the neurovascular structures by direct observation and mobilization.

## NAVICULAR NONUNION AND MALUNION AND TALONAVICULAR ARTHROSIS

As in the talus, the blood supply of the navicular must be protected during a surgical approach to the navicular. The navicular is vascularized through peripheral soft tissue attachments and periosteum, so stripping of these structures must be minimized. The approach should be made directly over the fracture or nonunion site, usually on the dorsal or dorsolateral side. An incision in this area should be longitudinal and in line with the neurovascular structures, which must be identified and moved aside. The fracture or nonunion site can be entered directly, and any hematoma or fibrous tissue can be removed with little or no stripping of soft tissue attachments.

When a nonunion is to be taken down, a slightly longer incision is made to open the talonavicular joint (and possibly the naviculocuneiform joint) wider to determine where to make the osteotomy cuts. The objective here is to reconstruct the talonavicular joint as anatomically as possible without much concern for the naviculocuneiform joint, which moves very little and can be fused without loss of function. The fracture can be reduced by direct visualization and compressed with a Weber or other sharp-tipped (towel clip-like) forceps. Appropriate drill holes are made and lag screws are inserted through stab wounds, usually from the lateral side and with the help of image intensifier guidance, if desired. The peripheral tissues on the lateral side should not be stripped more to make room for placing the screws under direct vision.

This technique works particularly well for treatment of displaced or nonunited stress fractures, which generally are more or less vertical fracture lines lying slightly lateral to the midline. In recurrent or persistent navicular stress fractures, the presence of a calcaneonavicular coalition should be ruled out by careful inspection of an oblique radiographic view and possibly a CAT scan. In my experience, other types of nonunions are rare, but the same principles would apply to their correction. The site at which the surgical approach is made varies with the site of the nonunion, as does the direction from which the screw is inserted. Unfortunately, the lateral portion of the navicular is extremely comminuted in some nonunions and cannot be reduced as a block to the medial column. In such cases, it is important to position the medial (usually larger) block in precise relationship to the first and possibly the second cuneiform. These bones (the navicular and the 1–2 cuneiforms) are fused without shortening but rather by inserting a bone block graft or chips of cancellous bone into a shear strain–relieved site. Alternatively, a block or cylinder rotated at 90° may be used. This technique can be used in acute situations to keep the usually intact larger medial fragment correctly positioned and to allow the comminuted lateral segments to be trapped in place and to regenerate. The articular surface fragments may be pushed up against the head of the talus, and the talonavicular joint may be stabilized temporarily with large K-wire fixation for 2 to 6 weeks. Fusion of the navicular and the 1 and 2 cuneiforms is particularly advantageous in the treatment of nonunion because it provides stability and possibly enhances blood flow to the healing site (Fig. 61–8).

After temporary fixation and placement of the bone grafts, at least three (and possibly four) screws should be placed. I generally use 2.7- or 3.5-mm screws, depending on the size of the patient, running one screw from the tubercle of the navicular across to each of the first and second cuneiforms. The third, and possibly the fourth, screw is placed retrograde from the distal medial first cuneiform into the lateral navicular. Newly available 4.0-mm Lisfranc screws are ideal for use in larger patients.

## Talonavicular Fusion for Arthrosis

The major difficulty in the treatment of talonavicular arthrosis is attaining the correct alignment. Basically, the talus, the navicular, and the first cuneiform-first metatarsal should be aligned almost exactly straight in both AP and lateral radiographic projections. The next consideration is not to shorten the medial column, which would be similar to over-reducing the navicular medially on the head of the talus and placing the foot into supination. Subchondral bone is preserved on the joint to avoid shortening. At least two shear strain–relieved bone graft sites are made by burring evenly spaced divots into the joint surfaces on each side and packing them with cancellous bone. As a result, the screws transfixing the joint need not be

compressed, and function as position screws that maintain the foot in exact position.

A supinated foot is rigid and can produce significant disability. Patients frequently walk on the base of the fifth metatarsal, often with the heel in varus and with a stiff, uncushioned gait. A small amount of pronation is preferable, but excessive pronation stresses the deltoid ligament and the posterior tibial tendon and eventually causes failure in the lateral portion of the ankle, just as excessive varus or valgus does in the knee.

Talonavicular fusion without repair of a navicular fracture, nonunion, or malunion is done through a medial utility incision. It is carried along the medial side of the joint between the anterior and posterior tendons, far from

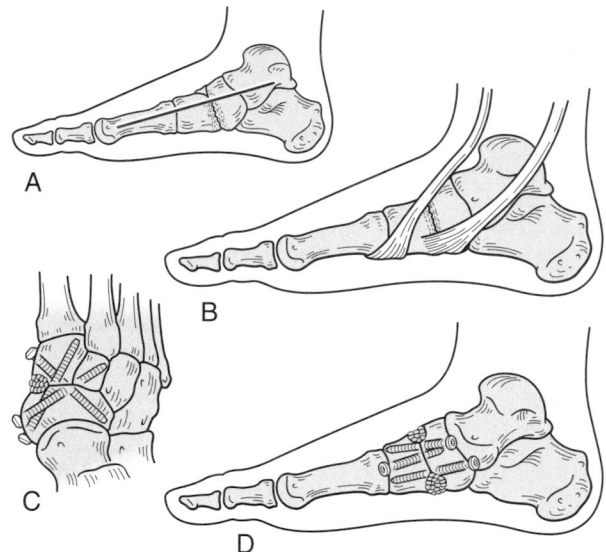

**FIGURE 61–8.** Naviculocuneiform joint fusion. *A,* The *solid line* shows the location of the medial utility incision, which is used to expose the naviculocuneiform joints for arthrodesis. *B,* Arthrosis (with sag) is seen in the naviculocuneiform joint. Notice the anterior tibial tendon, which is used as a guide to the joint and which must be protected during exposure of the medial cuneiform while placing screws. The anterior tibial tendon attaches on the medial plantar surface of the base of the first metatarsal and can be moved distally or proximally on the medial cuneiform. Cartilage at the first and second naviculocuneiform joints is débrided with small osteotomes and curettes, and the subchondral bone is perforated at multiple sites with a 2.0-mm drill. The bones are then aligned and stabilized. *C,* A dorsal-plantar view of the area depicts the screw configuration we have found to be most successful. Because these joints are hard to fuse, they must be rigidly stabilized. Shear strain–relieved bone grafts are placed at least in dorsomedial and plantar medial sites (not shown). The more plantar screw (3.5- or 4.0-mm cortical) runs from the tubercle of the navicular nearly parallel to the medial border of the foot and into the lower half of the first cuneiform. The second screw runs from a site more dorsal on the tubercle across and into the shallower second cuneiform. The third screw is started distal to the crossed anterior tibial tendon and angled across and into the lateral navicular. In some cases, a fourth screw is angled from the medial border of the cuneiform back across and into the navicular. *D,* The screw configuration across the reduced naviculocuneiform joints is depicted on a medial view. The same principles apply when this fusion is done in conjunction with nonunion at the mid to lateral third of a navicular fracture with comminution of the lateral navicular body. (Adapted from Hansen, S.T. Functional Reconstruction of the Foot and Ankle. Philadelphia, Lippincott Williams & Wilkins, 2000.)

any significant neurovascular structures other than veins with multiple branches (see Fig. 61–19).

## CUBOID MALUNIONS AND NONUNIONS WITH AND WITHOUT LATERAL COLUMN SHORTENING

Problems with the surgical approach and the blood supply are not as significant in the cuboid because the proportion of soft tissue attachment to articular surface is greater there than in the talus and the navicular. The major problem with cuboid fractures is to regain the length of the lateral column, since lateral column shortening causes forefoot abduction and progressive disruption of normal function. The amount of abduction, and possibly pain from arthrosis, in the calcaneocuboid and/or cuboid 4–5 metatarsal joints is directly related to the amount of shortening.

A dorsolateral linear incision is used to approach the cuboid, taking care to protect the sural nerve, and a lateral external fixation device or a distractor is attached from the lateral os calcis to the base of the fifth metatarsal. If the fracture has united short, the distractor can be lengthened gradually as the osteotomized fracture is manipulated to length. The incision must be low enough along the border to enable the surgeon to reach underneath to reapproximate the joint surfaces. Sometimes the calcaneocuboid joint requires bone block fusion to restore adequate or anatomic lateral column length. The surgeon must decide whether to lengthen the lateral column through the cuboid or the calcaneonavicular joint by evaluating the radiograph to determine where the shortening exists. It is usually better to lengthen the cuboid and preserve the calcaneo-cuboid joint if lateral column shortening is caused by a compression fracture.

### Cuboid-Metatarsal 4–5 Arthrosis

Treatment of arthrosis in the cuboid-fourth and -fifth metatarsal joints is an enigma. These joints do not fuse readily and, when they do, they frequently remain symptomatic because the small amount of motion they normally have is needed to provide cushioning along the lateral border. Normally there is no lateral arch, and the only soft tissue structure to enter the foot from the lateral side is the long peroneal coming through a groove in the cuboid.

It seems that the lateral side of the foot requires a certain amount of cushioning or expansion joint function and, when the calcaneocuboid joint is fused, the cuboid 4–5 metatarsal joints are pressed into service. These joints can be symptomatic when they are overstressed, and discomfort can be alleviated by use of orthotics or a thick, soft-soled shoe. Fusion here is unreliable and probably unwise. In rare cases, arthroplasty by a type of "anchovy" procedure is helpful, but there is no definitive solution to cuboid 4–5 metatarsal joint arthrosis.

## METATARSAL NONUNIONS AND MALUNIONS

Significant malunion in major metatarsal fractures, particularly multiple fractures, can disrupt forefoot alignment significantly and disturb normal forefoot weight bearing. Disabling symptoms can develop whenever weight bearing is concentrated under one or two metatarsals or any number fewer than the normal six contact points. These contact points are the tibial and fibular sesamoids under the first metatarsal head and the four lesser metatarsal heads. Contrary to what was taught about anatomy a couple of decades ago, there is no such thing as a transverse metatarsal arch at the metatarsal head level and, ideally, all the metatarsal heads should make contact with the ground upon forefoot weight bearing, distributing the weight equally among the six contact surfaces. In fact, however, the second, third, and possibly fourth metatarsals commonly bear slightly more weight than the others do. More concentrated weight bearing on fewer contact surfaces results in earlier and more severe symptoms.

A metatarsal head takes its proper share of weight when its length and inclination are appropriate to the adjacent metatarsals. Fractured metatarsals may heal in an elevated position, less frequently in a depressed position, and commonly with dysfunctional shortening. Metatarsal heads that bear an increased share of weight gradually can develop a number of abnormalities, including painful plantar keratosis, metatarsophalangeal synovitis with swelling, metatarsal stress fracture, or synotivis and eventual arthrosis at the tarsometatarsal joint. These various manifestations can occur independently or in any combination in a given patient. Long-term metatarsophalangeal synovitis in a foot with a congenitally long and stable second metatarsal and a hypermobile first metatarsal can cause synovitic damage in the capsule and the intrinsic muscles, an extensor (intrinsic minus) clawing deformity and, eventually, dislocation of the metatarsophalangeal joint with severe dorsal clawing. Rarely, the exuberant synovitis presents as a "tumor" between the metatarsal heads.

Each abnormality calls for specific treatment. Correction is most important in the first metatarsal, which is prone to excessive motion and tends to transfer weight to the second metatarsal. Fusion of the first tarsometatarsal joint and appropriate osteotomies may be needed to reconstruct anatomic length, inclination, and rotation before normal weight bearing can be restored to the six weight-bearing points in the forefoot (Fig. 61–9).

Osteotomy in the lesser metatarsals generally is done at the site of malunion or nonunion and then plated and grafted. Intramedullary K-wire fixation does not provide precise enough positioning or stability for healing, and intrafragmental screws alone may not be strong enough to maintain position, although they can be used together with a neutralization plate (Fig. 61–10). I generally use a bur to remove dorsal callus and reestablish the normal cortex across the osteotomy site. Next, I place cancellous autograft bone taken from the proximal tibia into the fusion site, particularly when an opening wedge is done. A ¼-tubular four- to six-hole plate on the dorsal side of the

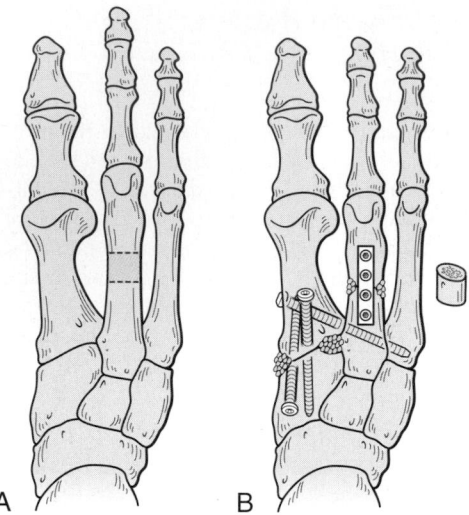

**FIGURE 61–9.** Stabilization of the first metatarsal and shortening osteotomy of the second metatarsal. *A,* The forefoot has a short first metatarsal and a long, obviously hypertrophied, and overloaded second metatarsal. In general foot reconstruction, this is called a Morton foot, and it is usually associated with gastrocnemius equinus. Symptoms usually include pain around the second metatarsal head, with heavy callus formation or a painful plantar keratosis under the head. In later stages, symptomatic synovitis, eventual dislocation of the second metatarsophalangeal joint, and arthrosis can mimic a missed Lisfranc injury at the second tarsometatarsal joint. *B,* The problem is treated by removing the cartilage from the first tarsometatarsal joint and stabilizing the first metatarsal in appropriate inclination with three 4.0-mm cortical screws. Cancellous grafting is usually necessary at two sites on the dorsal side of the joint. The overly long second metatarsal is managed by a diaphyseal shortening osteotomy with plating and grafting. Weight bearing should become equalized across the metatarsal heads at the six weight-bearing points: the medial and lateral sesamoids and four lesser metatarsal heads. (Adapted from Hansen, S.T. Functional Reconstruction of the Foot and Ankle. Philadelphia, Lippincott Williams & Wilkins, 2000.)

metatarsal provides fixation. In large patients with good soft tissue coverage, a stronger plate (such as a 2.7-mm DCP plate) may be preferable. For osteotomies located near the metatarsal neck or head, small T-plates or L-plates may be needed to get at least two screws into the distal fragment. Grafting and protected weight bearing are required for up to 8 weeks.

Finally, patients requiring forefoot or midfoot reconstruction must be evaluated for gastrocnemius equinus, which may have been asymptomatic in the foot before injury. However, once a foot has sustained an injury, gastrocnemius tightness may compromise treatment. A simple Strayer-type gastroc slide can be carried out to relieve forces on the anterior side of the foot and the midfoot (Fig. 61–11). After healing and rehabilitation, patients inevitably regain adequate strength for virtually any activity short of competitive sprinting.

## PHALANGEAL MALUNIONS AND NONUNIONS

Symptomatic malunions are uncommon in the lesser phalanges unless they press against the adjacent bones

and cause intradigital corns. These must be straightened out or shaved. Malunions are more serious in the first proximal phalanx. In contrast to the other phalanges, the first proximal phalanx is vulnerable to deformation from significant dynamic forces. The two heads of the flexor brevis attach to its proximal plantar base, and the extensor brevis attaches more diffusely and weakly to its dorsal aspect. The strong pull of the flexor brevis can cause plantar angulation of a phalangeal shaft fracture or osteotomy and result in plantar prominence and keratosis that is frequently very symptomatic. Occasionally, poor execution or inadequate stabilization of an Akin osteotomy has the same result. Symptomatic malunions can be straightened by osteotomy and plating, usually through a medial incision and dorsal flap elevation. Plates from the hand set can be bent to fit the bone, and fixation with at least two, ideally three, screws, provides adequate stabilization on either side of the osteotomy. The addition of cancellous autograft is important to ensure union.

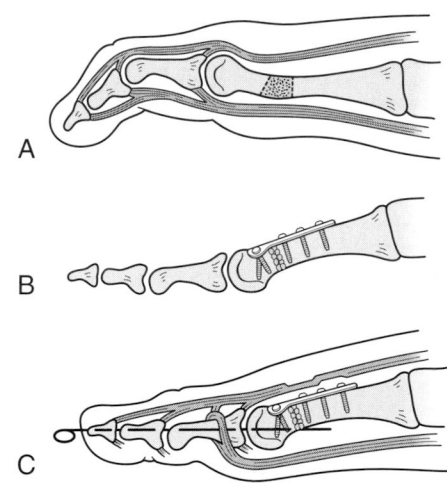

**FIGURE 61–10.** Lesser metatarsal osteotomy for distal metatarsal malunion in extension. *A,* A lateral view of a lesser metatarsal and toe depicts a malunion in extension. This can occur in any metatarsal after an acute metatarsal neck fracture, but it occurs commonly in the second metatarsal after a stress fracture. When the metatarsal head heals in an elevated position, it no longer takes its share of weight. The adjacent metatarsal heads become overloaded and develop symptoms of metatarsalgia, with or without intractable keratosis or metatarsophalangeal joint synovitis. On physical examination, an empty space can be felt on the plantar surface when all the toes are flexed at the metatarsophalangeal joints. A "bump" is seen on the dorsum of the foot over the affected head. *B,* The dorsal callus is burred away to the original dorsal cortex, and the osteotomy is carried out. Depending on what length the metatarsal should be in relation to the neighboring metatarsals, an opening or closing wedge can be done. A T plate and 2.7-mm screws are applied after alignment, length, and shared weight bearing are restored on the plantar surface. Cancellous bone grafting is necessary for timely healing. *C,* Adjunctive procedures may be needed to straighten a clawed toe. Z lengthening of the extensor tendons and a Girdlestone flexor-to-extensor transfer or intrinsicplasty may be done to straighten the toe. A K-wire holds the toe straight and crosses the metatarsophalangeal joint to stabilize the joint in appropriate position. The K-wire is removed after 4 or 5 weeks. (Adapted from Hansen, S.T. Functional Reconstruction of the Foot and Ankle. Philadelphia, Lippincott Williams & Wilkins, 2000.)

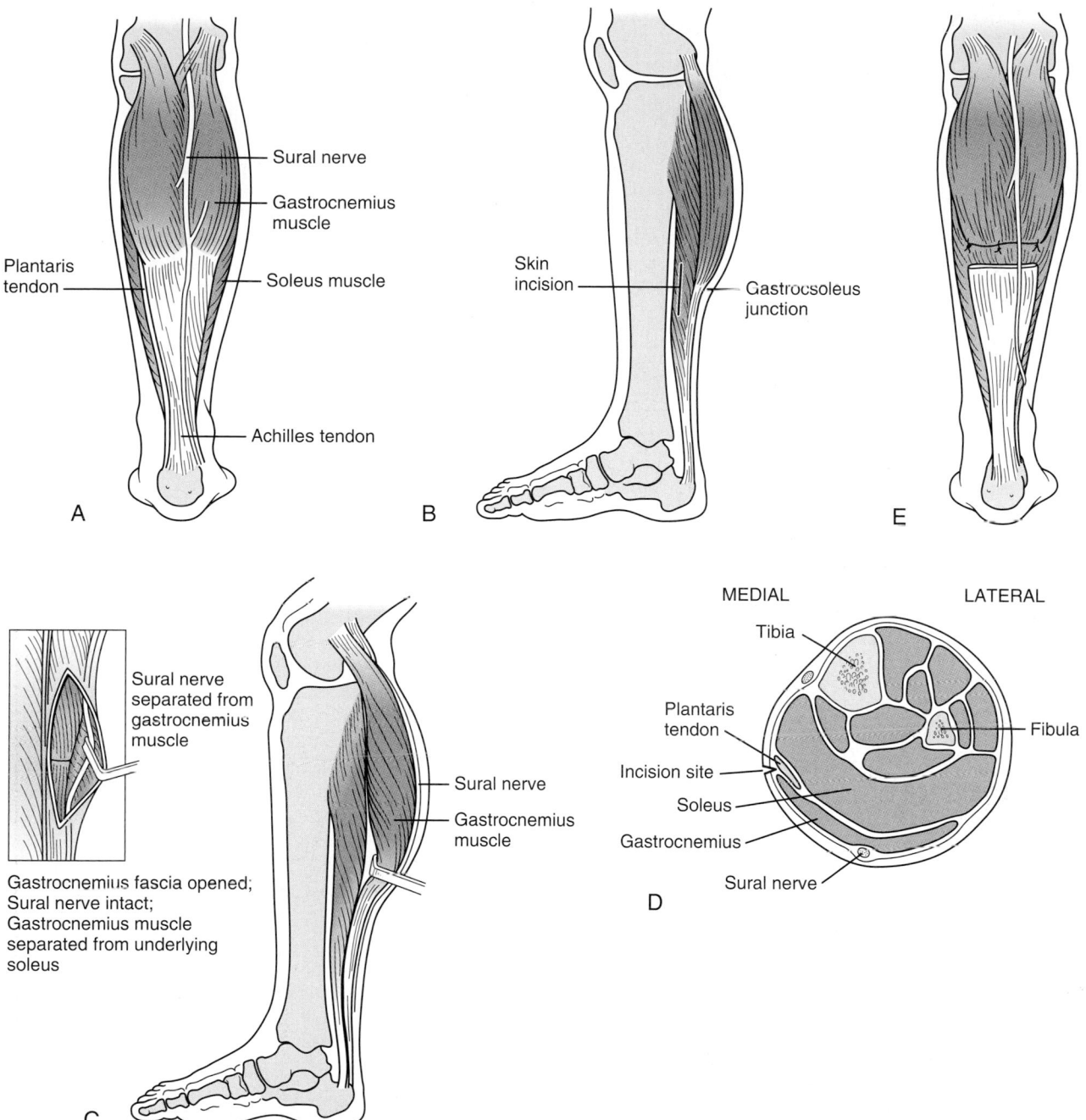

**FIGURE 61–11.** Gastrocnemius slide. *A,* In the posterior view of the calf musculature and sural nerve in the superficial posterior compartment, notice the medial and lateral heads of the gastrocnemius arising from the back of the femur above the knee and tapering to flat fascia beyond the middle leg. It joins here together with the posterior fascia of the soleus. The sural nerve lies in delicate fascia just on the surface of the muscle. *B,* The dark line indicates the recommended site for the posteromedial incision for separating the gastrocnemius fascia from the posterior soleus muscle. *C,* The gastrocnemius muscle is separated from the underlying soleus with a retractor. Separation is easiest when it is done approximately 1 to 3 cm above the gastrocnemius musculotendinous junction and the coalescence of the gastrocnemius and soleus fascias. Separation becomes progressively more difficult when it is attempted at or beyond the musculotendinous junction. The *inset* shows a transverse incision made in the deep, filmy, investing fascia of the musculature with the enclosed sural nerve pulled back from the incision in the gastrocnemius fascia. The fascia is closed separately at the end of the procedure to prevent the cut muscle-tendon from dimpling the skin. *D,* A cross section of the leg is depicted at the level of or just proximal to the level of gastrocnemius transection. The incision is made medially, slightly posterior to the midline, and over the plantaris tendon that lies at the interval between the gastrocnemius and soleus. *E,* The gastrocnemius muscle is released, retracted proximally for 2 to 3 cm, and may be reattached to the posterior soleus fascia. Substantive suturing is seldom necessary here, and frequently, just the medial corner is tacked down. (Adapted from Hansen, S.T. Functional Reconstruction of the Foot and Ankle. Philadelphia, Lippincott Williams & Wilkins, 2000.)

# POST-TRAUMATIC ARTHROSIS

## Ankle Arthrosis

In my experience, most cases of ankle arthrosis are attributable to residuals of trauma. Certainly, this is true when arthrosis develops after a history of multiple and/or severe ankle sprains and when there is a finding of lateral instability. This is post-traumatic arthrosis, not primary degenerative joint disease. Intra-articular fractures, especially pylon fractures, commonly result in post-traumatic arthrosis. A small number of malleolar fractures also go on to arthrosis, and those that deteriorate after apparently anatomic ORIF probably had sustained undiagnosed osteochondral injuries. This is true of some trimalleolar fractures with relatively large or unreduced posterior malleolar fragments. If the original injury were associated with axial loading, they should have been more accurately diagnosed as pilon fractures. Another type of malleolar fracture with a consistently poor outcome is one with lateral displacement and an associated but unrecognized tubercle of Chaput fracture or lateral plafond impaction. Such injuries can develop significant arthrosis when they are not accurately reduced. Apparently, relatively simple malleolar fractures, particularly those with displacement of the medial malleolus, a shortened fibula, a widened mortise, or some combination of these deformities, can go on to arthrosis if they are not accurately reduced. Treating physicians tend to be complacent in the treatment of ankle sprains and malleolar fractures because they are common injuries and many heal well with simple routine treatment. However, even though the percentage of patients who go on to post-traumatic arthrosis is small, the number they comprise is large.

Osteochondral fractures are frequently classified as osteochondrosis or osteochondritis dissicans and treated with observation or benign neglect. These fractures, many of which occur in young patients, can go on to early and serious arthrosis and cause lifelong ankle disability. Acute osteochondral injuries resulting from major trauma should be cause for immediate, complete, and aggressive diagnosis and treatment.

## Evaluation and Nonoperative Management

The symptoms of early ankle arthrosis can be treated nonoperatively in many cases. However, by applying the first principle of accurate diagnosis and finding the cause of the problem, the surgeon might determine that nonoperative treatment is contraindicated because arthrosis would only continue to worsen, since the underlying cause would not be corrected. For example, arthrosis can be caused by instability and lead to anterior extrusion or jamming, which is then further aggravated (if not primarily caused) by gastrocnemius equinus. In these circumstances, an early gastroc slide with anterior débridement and stabilization by the Brostrum procedure or anatomic ligament reconstruction is indicated (see Fig. 61–11). A history of recurrent ankle sprains, anterior displacement of the talus on radiograph, and clinical signs of gastrocnemius equinus or anterior drawer instability, or both, will confirm this diagnosis.

Ankle arthrosis may be caused by long-term varus or valgus and subsequent eccentric loading in the ankle, similar to a long-term varus or valgus deformity in the knee. Ankle arthrosis caused by traumatic posterior tibial tendon rupture occurring with medial column collapse, valgus heel, and tendo-Achilles tendon or gastrocnemius contracture may require early midfoot reconstruction. Reconstruction should include heel cord lengthening, posterior tibial augmentation, and possibly a medializing calcaneal osteotomy to realign and preserve the ankle. Medial column stabilization also may be needed to control the valgus attitude of the hindfoot (Fig. 61–12).

Varus and subsequent varus talar tilt is evident in patients with Charcot-Marie-Tooth disease who have a muscle imbalance, such as an overpowering posterior tibial or long peroneal tendon, or an old deep posterior compartment syndrome. Early foot reconstruction that includes realignment of the foot, muscle balancing, and ligament stabilization is required to prevent further deterioration of the ankle. Even when these measures fail to preserve the ankle, they are essential for successful ankle fusion or arthroplasty.

In the absence of aggravating problems, when the ankle is painful secondary to loss of cartilage and range of motion, nonoperative treatment can be helpful. The least onerous recommendation is to wear clogs or another type of rocker-bottom shoe with a stiff sole and a wide base that will allow relatively normal gait requiring minimal ankle function (particularly dorsiflexion). When pain is caused primarily by anterior impingement, but the patient is relatively comfortable between 5° and 10° to 30° of plantar flexion, temporary relief can be attained by elevating the heel in a rocker-bottom shoe and positioning the ankle in its mid-range (approximately 20° of flexion) while standing.

If these measures fail to alleviate pain, the next nonoperative step is to use an ankle-foot orthosis (AFO) molded into neutral or, if necessary, into plantar flexion near the patient's midrange. Here, the goal is to nearly immobilize the ankle and to protect it from varus or valgus tilt stresses. In severe cases, use of an AFO may replace or postpone a surgical solution.

## Surgical Treatment of Ankle Arthrosis

When surgical treatment becomes necessary, the choice of procedures is not limited to arthroplasty or arthrodesis. As noted earlier, conditions apart from the ankle itself can be improved to reduce stresses in the ankle. Pain in ankles with eccentric erosion, such as those in valgus or varus, may be temporized by an osteotomy in the supramalleolar area. Supramalleolar osteotomies are done when varus or valgus is seen in the plafond. The principle applied in this operation is the same as that in a high tibial osteotomy, that is, to transfer force away from the eroded cartilage and toward the more normal side of the joint. If there is excessive heel valgus but the plane of the plafond is correct, a medializing calcaneal osteotomy may be carried

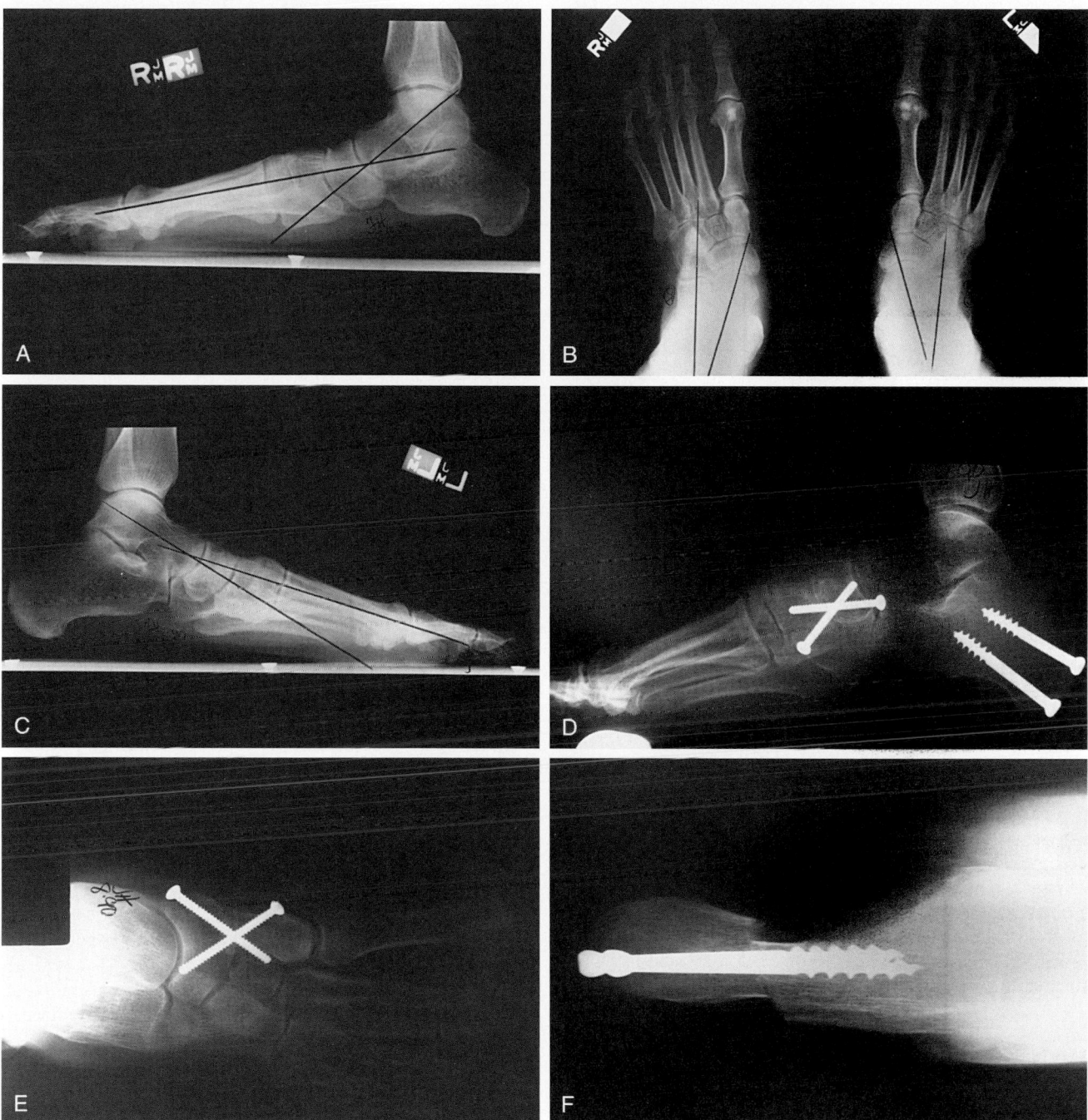

**FIGURE 61–12.** Valgus hindfoot. *A,* A weight-bearing medial radiograph shows the right foot of a 35-year-old woman with long-term "achy" feet. Her heel is in valgus, and she experienced a sudden increase in medial arch pain and pronation. Clinical findings revealed a rupture of the posterior tibial tendon. The radiograph shows a marked sag in the medial column at the naviculocuneiform joint, a decreased calcaneal pitch angle, a closed-up sinus tarsi, and a plantar-flexed talus. *B,* Weight-bearing anteroposterior (AP) views of both feet show an increased talocalcaneal angle and a break in the talar–first metatarsal alignment. The less symptomatic (right) foot had the same predispositions, but hindfoot valgus was less severe, and the arch was better maintained there. The posterior tibial tendon was intact on the left, but both gastrocnemii were very tight. *C,* A weight-bearing medial view of the left foot shows a slight sag at the naviculocuneiform joint, but the calcaneal pitch and talocalcaneal angle are better than on the right side, and the sinus tarsi is open. *D,* Surgery on the right foot included fusion of the naviculocuneiform joint in corrected alignment, a medializing osteotomy of the heel, lengthening of the gastrocnemius, and augmentation of the posterior tibial tendon by the flexor digitorum longus. Compared with *A,* the calcaneal pitch is improved, talar–first metatarsal alignment has been corrected, and the sinus tarsi is open. *E,* A weight-bearing AP view taken several weeks postoperatively shows the fixation at the naviculocuneiform joint, corrected talar–first metatarsal alignment, and more normal coverage of the talar head by the navicular. *F,* An axial calcaneal view shows the medializing calcaneal osteotomy fixed with two 6.5-mm cancellous screws.

*Illustration continued on following page*

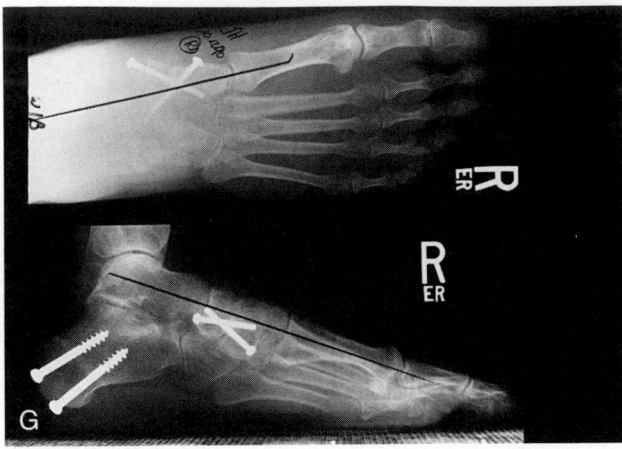

FIGURE **61–12** *Continued. G,* Composite weight-bearing AP and lateral views taken 3 months postoperatively show a normally aligned foot. By this time, the foot was nearly asymptomatic. Similar procedures were carried out prophylactically on the moderately symptomatic left foot, eliminating all symptoms on that side. (Adapted from Hansen, S.T. Functional Reconstruction of the Foot and Ankle. Philadelphia, Lippincott Williams & Wilkins, 2000.)

out. Both procedures may be done for arthrosis with lateral erosion and valgus talar tilt and can delay the need for arthrodesis or arthroplasty for several years. For varus talar tilt and medial ankle plafond erosion, a lateral closing wedge supramalleolar osteotomy or a lateral translational calcaneal osteotomy in conjunction with realignment of the foot by muscle balancing may preserve ankle function for several years (Fig. 61–13).

## ARTHRODESIS VERSUS ANKLE ARTHROPLASTY

### Problems with Ankle Fusion

Ankle arthrodesis has long been the gold standard for ankle salvage. During my training, I was led to believe that it was a permanent solution and that patients continued to function well indefinitely. Needless to say, we saw bad results in the form of nonunions and malpositioned and painful ankles as well as a significant incidence of infection. Because early attempts at ankle arthroplasty in the 1970s were unsuccessful, confidence in the effectiveness of ankle fusion continues today. I was a strong advocate of that belief for the first 15 or 20 years of my practice and worked diligently to perfect a reliable arthrodesis operation. My goals were to attain early union in order to mobilize the subtalar joint, to get it into ideal position (which I believed was between 0° and 5° of plantar flexion and approximately 5° to 7° of valgus) and, of course, to avoid infection. In spite of attaining all these goals, (and I still believe they are optimal) I was disappointed to find that patients with excellent early results developed first, subtalar and later, midtarsal arthrosis approximately 10 years postoperatively. The time it took for arthrosis to develop was unpredictable, but

ranged between one to 20 years with an average of 10. I usually describe the time as 10 ± 9 years. It became clear that ankle motion is essential to long-term preservation of other joints in the midfoot and hindfoot.

For this reason, I became interested in the newer generation of ankle prostheses and found them to be significantly better in terms of implant design. In the meantime, we have also learned much more about the importance of anatomic alignment of the ankle and foot to enhance the function and longevity of any arthroplasty. Another important factor affecting foot function is muscle balancing, primarily gastrocnemius or heel cord lengthening with or without posterior medial and lateral ligament release and long and short peroneal adjustment. However, we still may not have an ankle prosthesis that is closely comparable in function to a normal ankle or one that will last with confidence for 10 years or longer in a wide range of cases.

Many excellent and long-lasting results have been reported with ankle arthroplasty, but most of these take place in ideal cases. An ideal patient is one with good bone stock, good alignment and muscle balance, strong medial and (hopefully) lateral ankle ligaments, and an adequate bone size to body weight ratio. The last criterion generally describes a patient who is not significantly overweight. Finally, a good result also requires a compliant patient who

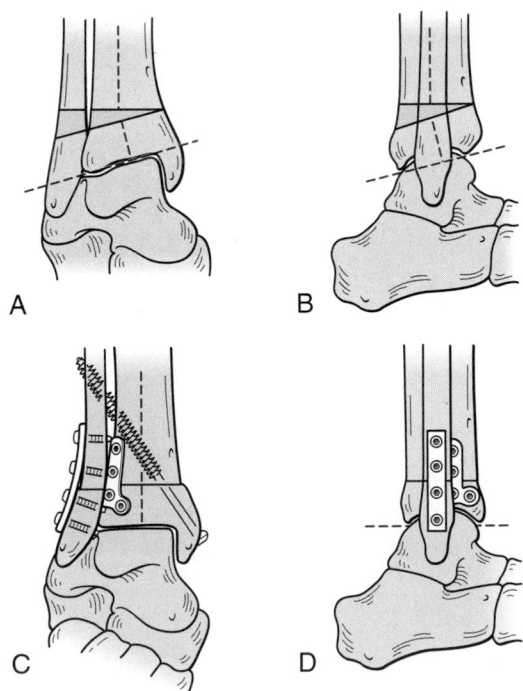

FIGURE **61–13.** Distal tibial and fibular osteotomy for varus. *A,* An anteroposterior view depicts varus and extension malunion resulting from an old pilon fracture in an ankle with reasonably normal joint congruency. *B,* Joint extension is depicted on a lateral view. The *shaded wedges* in the supramalleolar area represent the closing wedge osteotomy needed to correct the plane of the ankle joint and decrease eccentric or shear loading of the cartilage. *C* and *D,* The osteotomy is closed and fixed in the plane of the ankle, assumedly correcting the alignment of the hindfoot with the leg. Correction of alignment delays progressive ankle arthrosis. (Adapted from Hansen, S.T. Functional Reconstruction of the Foot and Ankle. Philadelphia, Lippincott Williams & Wilkins, 2000.)

does not smoke and will not bear weight prematurely or with excessive impact or shear force in the 6 or 8 weeks needed for implant bonding. The bottom line is that we still do not have a permanent or even a long-term answer to severe ankle arthrosis in young patients.

However, much progress has been made, and some older ideas have been proved untrue. First of these is that a failed ankle fusion cannot be salvaged. This problem can be treated and the ankle can be salvaged in a number of ways. When fusion fails from poor alignment in equinus, anterior extrusion, or varus, it can be revised by repositioning. More surprising to many, an ankle fusion can be taken down and changed to an arthroplasty if adequate anatomy, including both malleoli and the deltoid ligament, have been left intact during the original fusion. Many fusions do so, including one we have recommended for many years.[3] A large number of ankle fusions fail from secondary subtalar arthrosis. Here, treatment is a choice between a pantalar arthrodesis and takedown of the ankle fusion in conjunction with ankle arthroplasty and subtalar fusion. We have had significantly good results with these procedures, although there are two down sides to a pantalar fusion. The first is that the resulting hindfoot is very stiff, a condition that many patients find so unsatisfactory they request an amputation. The second is that complete hindfoot fusion can be difficult to attain, especially in heavy patients, because motion tends to break down the fusion hardware and/or the fusion site itself. This is more likely to occur when the second fusion is in the ankle. Even primary ankle fusion can be difficult to obtain in patients over 6 feet tall and those weighing more than 250 pounds, because high stresses frequently cause persistent or recurrent nonunions, or both.

Another myth surrounding total ankle arthroplasty is that, if the prosthesis is painful or loose, it must be removed and a complex ankle fusion must be carried out. This clearly has been proved to be incorrect, at least with the Agility Ankle. In general, the most common cause of pain and failure of an ankle prosthesis is bony overgrowth around the talar component as a result of incomplete or lack of talar bonding. Generally, the arthroplasty can be revised by extensive débridement of the ankle and replacement of the talar component with a larger implant or one with an expanded base, this time with a contrite patient who neither smokes nor bears weight too early. The resulting arthroplasty can be excellent. Exchanging a worn or loose prosthesis is also surprisingly easy with available revision components or using the next larger size prosthesis.

## Arthrodesis Techniques

In view of the previous discussion, several basic principles should be applied when choosing a surgical approach and fixation technique for ankle fusion. Ideally, fusion generates early union with minimal damage to the bone stock. Subchondral bone and full bony contours are to be preserved along with the malleoli and the deltoid ligament whenever possible. The malleoli may be narrowed slightly, but there is no reason to remove them. They will not impinge on shoe counters if the hindfoot is shortened only

slightly by minimal bone removal. When the malleoli are left intact, the normal anatomy is preserved and the sheaths through which the posterior tibial tendon and the peroneal tendons pass are retained. It is particularly important to keep the width of the lateral malleolus nearly normal to make sure that a prosthesis of adequate size can be placed during later revision. Application of these principles results not only in a normal looking and functional hindfoot following ankle fusion, but also ensures easier conversion to ankle arthroplasty at a later time.

The arthrodesis technique I use when the ankle is in a nonanatomic position, particularly anterior subluxation, involves making an incision over the fibula to free up the fibula laterally and anteriorly, then transecting the anterior syndesmosis and the anterior talofibular ligament (Fig. 61–14). An osteotomy is carried out approximately 3 inches above the tip of the fibula in an oblique plane going from proximal lateral to distal medial. Unless the fibula has already been shortened, it is slightly shortened by making a second cut and removing 5 to 10 mm of bone. The fibula is rotated posteriorly on this peroneal sheath hinge to expose the ankle and subtalar joints laterally. This approach is particularly useful when the ankle is to be repositioned by posterior translation, since the posterior malleolus can be easily thinned or resected under direct vision. All the ankle cartilage is removed and multiple holes are drilled in the subchondral bone with a 2.0-mm drill. A small anteromedial vertical incision is made just in front of the medial gutter to clear cartilage from the medial talus and the medial malleolus and to push the talus against the medial malleolus.

After the joint has been denuded, shaped, and drilled, it is placed into ideal position (in 5° to 7° of valgus and 0° to 5° of equinus) and temporary fixation is applied. This consists of an anterolateral 3.5- or 4.0-mm cortical screw directed downward vertically from the tubercle of Chaput into the lateral talar body. A lateral radiographic view is taken of the entire foot under simulated load to confirm the exact position of the ankle. If the alignment is satisfactory, permanent fixation can be applied. The first fixation screw is placed by direct vision through a stab wound just lateral to the heel cord, well proximal to the ankle. A 4.5-mm drill is inserted into the posterolateral tibia high on the posterior malleolus approximately three centimeters above the ankle. It is directed downward and slightly medially and aimed to cross the anterior half of the ankle joint first, then to enter the neck, and continue into the lower head of the talus. A 4.5-mm drill is used in the tibia and a long 3.5-mm drill is used into the talus. A 6.5-mm screw that is approximately 75 mm long with 16 mm of thread is appropriate in most patients. Alternatively, a cannulated screw of similar size may be used.

Next, a 6.5-mm screw of appropriate length is placed from the upper medial malleolus and aimed at a 45° angle into the midbody of the talus. Another screw is placed from the anterior tibia down into the posterior talus, taking care not to penetrate the subtalar joint. After the medial cortex of the osteotomized fibula has been denuded, it is placed back against the lateral talus and the distal tibia at appropriate length and position and fixed there with 3.5- or 4.0-mm cortical screws. The angled proximal end of the distal fibular fragment traps the fibula

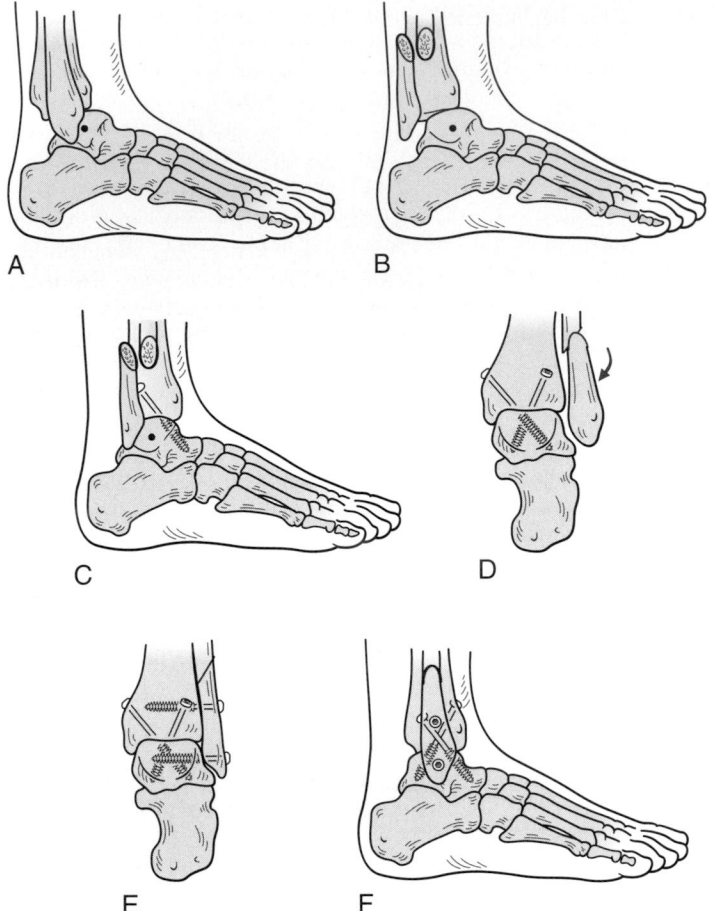

A    B

C    D

E    F

FIGURE 61–14. First ankle fusion technique. *A,* An arthritic ankle rsulting from chronic anterior talofibular ligament sprain or anterior pilon fracture with anterior extrusion of the foot relative to the weight-bearing line of the tibia is depicted on a lateral illustration. *B,* The fibula is transected approximately 3 cm above the joint through a lateral, vertical transfibular approach. Anterior, medial, and lateral soft tissues are removed, leaving the fibula hinged posteriorly on the peroneal tendon sheath. This approach maintains blood supply and provides adequate visibility to prepare and reduce the ankle. The medial malleolar gutter may be cleaned through a small, vertical, anteromedial incision. *C,* The posterior malleolus may be exposed through the lateral incision to provide an entry point for the first fixation screw. A positioning screw (usually a 3.5- or 4.0-mm cortical screw) may be placed directly down into the lateral talus from above the tubercle of Chaput to help maintain position during the check radiograph and placement of the fixation screw. The entry point for the screw running from posterior superior to the joint (home run screw) is a stab wound made higher on the leg just lateral to the heel cord. The screw enters the posterior tibia approximately 1 cm medial to the lateral border and angles slightly medially and downward in the direction of the talar neck and lower head. A 4.5-mm gliding hole in the tibia and 3.5-mm tap hole in the talus prepare the track for the screw. Image intensifier guidance may be used for accuracy. *D,* After the first screw is in place, another screw is placed percutaneously from the medial malleolus across the midbody. *E,* The partially detached fibula is replaced and held in place with 3.5- or 4.0-mm cortical screws. *F,* The final screw is placed from the anterior tibia and crosses back to the posterior talar body to complete the very stable fixation. Patients with good bone stock may have the cast replaced with a CAM walker at 2.5 postoperative weeks to allow bathing, mobilization of the subtalar joint, and sleeping out of a cast. Walking is not permitted until radiographs show evidence of healing, usually at about 8 weeks postoperatively. (Adapted from Hansen, S.T. Functional Reconstruction of the Foot and Ankle. Philadelphia, Lippincott Williams & Wilkins, 2000.)

from above and will not protrude under the skin because that area has been beveled.

Any bone that has been removed can be used as graft between the anterior fibula and the tibia. Approximately two shear strain relieved graft sites, each approximately one centimeter in diameter, are burred into the anterior joint and filled with cancellous autograft from the proximal anterior tibia (Gerdy's tubercle) site. Radiographs are taken prior to closure to check ankle position and screw length.

Postoperatively, the foot is casted for 2 to 3 weeks and, at that time, the cast is exchanged for a commercial walking boot with a rocker sole. The patient is limited to weight-of-leg or slightly more weight bearing and may remove the boot for bathing, sleeping, and mobilizing the subtalar joint. Healing usually takes place in 8 to 12 weeks, and the patient continues to wear a shoe with mild rocker modification in the sole indefinitely.

Another technique, described by Zwipp, may be preferable when conversion to arthroplasty is planned at a later date[4] (Fig. 61–15). An anterior surgical approach is made with this technique. Preparation and positioning are similar to the first technique described, that is, the foot is brought into neutral flexion-extension and slight valgus with the dome of the talus at or slightly posterior to the mid-axial line of the tibia. Two 6.5-mm lag screws are placed side by side from the well-exposed distal anterior tibia, starting at least three centimeters proximal to the joint and going into the midbody of the talus. The

all-important third screw is inserted through a stab wound made over the posteromedial crest of the tibia above the medial malleolus and drilled anterolaterally into the neck and inferior head of the talus. The tibial-fibular syndesmosis is also denuded and grafted, then stabilized with

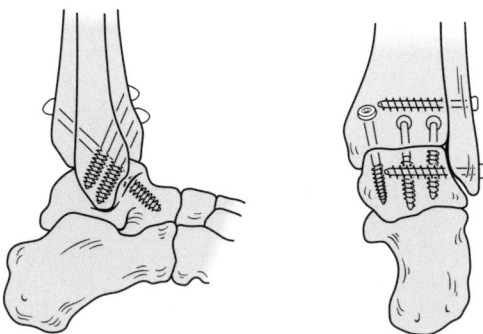

FIGURE 61–15. Second ankle fusion technique. This alternative ankle fusion may be done when future takedown for arthroplasty is anticipated. It is done through an anterior incision, which may be used again to accomplish takedown and arthroplasty. Two 6.5-mm lag screws are placed through an anterior incision from the anterior distal tibia into the midbody of the talus. One screw is placed through a stab wound at the posteromedial tibia above the medial malleolus and angled forward into the neck and head of the talus. This screw configuration provides excellent stability for early ankle fusion and is easy to remove for subsequent takedown of the fusion and ankle arthroplasty. (Adapted from Hansen, S.T. Functional Reconstruction of the Foot and Ankle. Philadelphia, Lippincott Williams & Wilkins, 2000.)

3.5- or 4.0-mm screws placed from the fibula to the tibia and from the fibula to the talus. Syndesmotic fusion facilitates the future arthroplasty procedure.

Postoperative management is identical to the previous technique. The advantages of this technique are that later arthroplasty can be done through the same incision and that the screws that will have to be removed are easily accessible through the standard anterior approach used to perform the arthroplasty.

Ankle fusion is only a temporary solution that demonstrates a typical mode of failure. Fusion of the ankle forces the subtalar joint to accommodate flexion and extension forces and, in some cases, the amount of motion it assumes may nearly mimic normal ankle motion. However, such a demand on the subtalar joint is abnormal and eventually it deteriorates and becomes severely symptomatic.

## Total Ankle Arthroplasty Technique

The ideal patient for ankle arthroplasty of any type would be one who is older than 55 years. The primary damage sustained would be to the articular surfaces of the ankle, but muscle and ligament balance would be good, and foot alignment would be normal. These conditions are rarely met. Unfortunately, many cases of post-traumatic arthrosis occur in young people, some under the age of 20, and are associated with scarring in the soft tissues, malalignment of the distal tibia, varus or valgus hindfoot, and retained intact or broken hardware. The lateral ligaments frequently are incompetent and/or the deltoid and posterior musculature is contracted. Ankle fusion is not a good solution in these less than optimal cases, because malalignment and young age both are contraindications to this procedure. A more realistic solution seems to be either fusion with planned later arthroplasty or arthroplasty with the understanding that a revision or revisions will be needed.

The various types of ankle arthroplasties currently used in North America include the Beuchel-Pappas, the S.T.A.R. (Link), and the Agility Ankle (DePuy Orthopaedics, Warsaw, IN), all of which have been used widely for the past three or four years. A close likeness of the current Agility device was first introduced in about 1984. It was approved by the FDA and released to a small number of surgeons for further evaluation in 1995. I was one of those who were taught the technique at that time by Dr. Frank Alvine, the developer of the prosthesis. My experience of approximately 400 cases is limited to the Agility prosthesis.

The S.T.A.R. and Agility prostheses are similar in that they require removal of just one centimeter or so of the distal tibia. Both devices consist of three parts and neither has a medullary extension. The Agility Ankle is a partially constrained device with a polyethylene component fixed within the metallic tibial component that conforms to the smaller talar component. The S.T.A.R. is mobile bearing and slightly less constrained, and both the S.T.A.R. and the Agility are press fit bone-to-metal bonding types that do not need methylmethacrylate. The Agility technique requires removal of 6 to 10 mm of the upper talus, whereas the S.T.A.R. prosthesis covers the talus after the joint surface has been removed and uses the anatomic malleoli for medial-lateral stabilization. The Agility tibial component has attached simulated ears or malleoli that provide partial medial and lateral constraint of the talar component. The tibial-fibular syndesmosis is fused in anatomic position to securely support the Porecoat (titanium bead) covered tibial component. Because the design of the tibial component does not rely on the presence of a patient's normal malleoli, this arthroplasty is amenable to a wide range of indications. In fact, this half of the prosthesis has virtually never failed in my experience. The talar component, which has occasionally failed due to talar subsidence or loosening, has recently been redesigned with a wider base or a larger overall size to offset some of these problems.

The technique used for arthroplasty is quite demanding and it really is not an operation for the occasional operator. In my opinion, a surgeon who does fewer than 15 ankle arthroplasties per year should probably not do any but the most straightforward cases, which, as I noted above, are rare. Learning the technique is best done at a hands-on course and/or by doing a visiting preceptorship with an experienced operator. Agility learning courses are put on at the Orthopaedic Learning Center several times a year.

By far the most difficult ankles to treat by arthroplasty are those with residual varus problems. These require a number of specialized muscle and ligament balancing procedures in addition to bony realignment. Experience with numerous cases is essential, because almost every case has unique features that must be recognized and definitively treated.

## SUBTALAR ARTHROSIS

The majority of patients with symptomatic subtalar arthrosis have sustained intra-articular calcaneal fractures and may have associated malalignment. Other post-traumatic causes include talar fractures or subtalar fracture-dislocations. Rarely, an untreated post-traumatic deep posterior compartment syndrome can cause the subtalar joint to go into varus and subsequently develop arthrosis over time. Post-traumatic malalignment from tibial fractures left in varus or valgus can go on to ankle and subtalar arthrosis as well, but it may take many years, up to 40 or more, before treatment may be required. Subtalar arthrosis can also occur from neuromuscular conditions in long-term varus and from untreated posterior tibial tendon rupture with severe valgus, but these problems are degenerative, not post-traumatic.

## Nonoperative Treatment

Nonoperative or temporizing care may consist of nonsteroidal anti-inflammatory drugs and immobilization. Devices to mobilize the subtalar joint may include a rigid posterior plastic AFO or a double-upright brace with a flexion-extension hinge attached to a supportive shoe. The latter device allows ankle motion while blocking inversion and eversion. Orthotics are not very effective in my experience. Injection with local anesthetic and steroids is a diagnostic measure and may provide short-term relief from symptoms.

## Surgical Treatment

Currently, a subtalar joint prosthesis is unavailable, and arthrodesis of the joint is the primary treatment when the foot is symptomatic and nonoperative care is ineffective or unacceptable to a patient. There are some concerns associated with arthrodesis of the subtalar joint. Because it is an essential joint, loss of motion here changes gait mechanics and stresses nearby joints. Together with the tibiotalar or ankle joint, the subtalar joint comprises one-half of a "universal" joint, and its absence means that the ankle will be overworked and subjected to tilt forces.

As with any arthrodesis, the subtalar joint must be fused in optimal position, that is, in exact neutral or in physiologic alignment. In fact, this position is in 5° to 7° of valgus and not in the midrange of the joint. A valgus position is physiologically appropriate here because the deltoid ligament on the medial side provides much stronger support and resistance to tilt of the ankle than the lateral ligaments do. The subtalar joint must not be fused in supination, which limits compensatory motion at Chopart's joints and makes the patient walk on the lateral border of the foot. This would increase impact loading in general and eventually cause pain at the base of the fifth metatarsal.

A common misconception by surgeons is that correct alignment can be attained by adding or removing wedges of bone from the subtalar joint. In fact, it is much simpler to attain correct alignment by manipulating the foot in the same rotatory motion it normally undergoes with pronation and supination. In other words, to position the foot in valgus or pronation, the surgeon externally rotates it through the subtalar-talonavicular complex to close up the space in the sinus tarsi. Greater varus can be obtained by internally rotating the foot or placing it into supination, thereby opening up the space in the sinus tarsi. The sinus tarsi space is a very important feature to note and measure on weight-bearing films.

Once appropriate alignment has been attained, it must be held in place rigidly with at least two screws. In a common technique, a screw is placed across the joint near the normal axis of rotation of the subtalar joint either from the talar neck downward or from the tip of the heel upward and forward. This single screw can lose position by allowing a small amount of rotation or micromotion to take place and produce shear strain, resulting in a fibrous union. The problem with a single screw is that it is very near the axis of rotation of the subtalar joint, and we see nonunions after single screw fixation on a regular basis.

Subtalar arthrosis is a common sequela of calcaneal fractures. Another problem is distortion of overall hindfoot anatomy resulting from an unreduced calcaneal fracture. In some cases, the calcaneus is compressed, resulting in subsequent shortening of the leg, loss of inclination of the talus, and a reduced range of dorsiflexion in the ankle with anterior ankle joint impingement. More typically, the posterior tuber is tilted into varus and laterally displaced with functional valgus and impingement of the exploded lateral wall under the fibula. The calcaneus may have been shortened as a result of lateral column shortening. Rarely, the joint is minimally displaced with a small ridge of impinging bone. Sometimes most of the symptoms a

patient experiences may be due to simple impingement on the fibula from the lateral blowout of the lateral wall of the calcaneus.

## Surgical Techniques

Because of the problems associated with subtalar fusion, less final or detrimental procedures should be considered. For example, if a CAT scan indicates that the joint surface is largely intact except for a ridge of bone laterally, open débridement and arthrolysis may be attempted, possibly by arthroscopy. A tuber that is elevated or malaligned in varus or valgus can be repositioned by osteotomy at the same time.

A special problem exists when subtalar arthrosis occurs in young patients. Because serious problems are associated with having the subtalar joint fused for many years, an intraarticular calcaneal osteotomy may be warranted. When subtalar joint fusion is done in ideal alignment, secondary ankle arthrosis may not appear for many years, particularly if patients are of light weight, spend most of their time on level surfaces, and have no genetic predisposition to arthrosis. However, when patients are overweight, work on uneven surfaces, or have a predisposition to arthrosis or when there was injury to the ankle, secondary ankle arthrosis frequently occurs within 2 to 5 years. Arthrosis develops more rapidly in the absence of a normal subtalar joint motion, which provides cushioning and protection from tilt stresses.

The greatest potential problem associated with calcaneal osteotomies is the potential for posterior tibial nerve damage, particularly to the lateral plantar division. The nerve can be trapped in scar tissue or constricted by an old plantar compartment syndrome. Even when the nerve is not injured directly by an osteotome, moving part of the heel can result in traction or a compression injury, which is usually transient but can be persistent. Opening the medial side, as is done in a tarsal tunnel release, may be a consideration at the time of the osteotomy or, at least, the patient should be prepared for the need to do this preoperatively.

Arthrosis can develop in the subtalar joint without gross structural malalignment and in spite of stabilization by ORIF. If hardware removal and arthrolysis had been already attempted without success or if it seems that these procedures might fail, arthrodesis *in situ,* the simplest of the various arthrodesis techniques, is the treatment of choice (Fig. 61–16).

All remaining cartilage is removed with a curette either through the original extensile lateral surgical approach or through a limited sinus tarsi approach. A bur is used to create a divot 10- to 12-mm wide across the joint surface of the mid-posterior facet and this cavity, along with any other crevices or gaps in the joint, is filled with cancellous autograft bone. Cancellous autograft may be taken from Gerdy's tubercle, the proximal tibial graft site, or another preferred site. Two 6.5-mm screws with 16 mm of thread are placed from the posterior inferior heel into the midbody and anterior neck of the talus, respectively. The screws are started well lateral in the heel when aiming for the body, but must be angled toward the midline from the

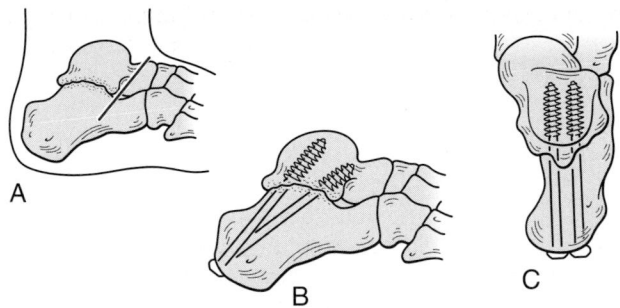

**FIGURE 61–16.** Subtalar arthrodesis in situ. *A,* A hindfoot with subtalar arthrosis but no significant distortion of overall anatomy is depicted on a lateral illustration. The *solid black line* indicates the Ollier incision used to approach the subtalar joint through the sinus tarsi. After the origin of the extensor brevis is lifted out and fat is removed, the synovium, cervical ligament, and posterior facet can be seen and easily accessed using straight and curved curettes and a bur. *B,* Two large lag screws (usually 6.5-mm screws that are 85 ± 5 mm long with 16 mm of thread) are placed. We prefer to use noncannulated screws. The first screw is inserted through a stab wound over the point of the heel and aimed into the posterior body, nearly perpendicular to the posterior facet. The screw can be aimed accurately using a triangulation technique with the help of an assistant surgeon or an image intensifier for sighting the second plane to position the 4.5- and 3.5-mm drills. Alternatively, cannulated screws may be used. The entry point for the second screw is near the midline of the heel. This screw is aimed slightly medially and more anteriorly so that it is well separated from the first screw to prevent rotation. It should enter the talus in the region of the anterior neck or head. Intraoperative radiographs, including anteroposterior views of the foot and the ankle, a lateral view of the foot and ankle, and an axial view of the heel, are taken before wounds are closed. *C,* Ideal placement of the screws and positioning of the talocalcaneal angle results in a foot that is neither supinated (narrow talocalcaneal angle) nor pronated (increased talocalcaneal angle). (Adapted from Hansen, S.T. Functional Reconstruction of the Foot and Ankle. Philadelphia, Lippincott Williams & Wilkins, 2000.)

lateral position to avoid the lateral gutter. The screw to be placed into the anterior talus is started in the midline and then angled medially to avoid insertion lateral to the neck in the sinus tarsi. The screw going into the body is usually about 80 mm long and the more anterior screw is 85 to 90 mm long. The shank-thread junction will be too close to the fusion line and subject to breakage if the compression screw has more than 16 mm of thread. Screws are not started medial to the midline of the heel to avoid penetration of the neurovascular indent in the medial tuber.

With this type of very stable fixation in place, the foot is casted and the patient is allowed touchdown weight bearing for 2-½ weeks until the sutures are removed. After the cast has been removed, a CAM walker is used to provide protection during continued weight-of-leg ambulation, but it may be removed for bathing and sleeping and to mobilize the ankle. Weight-of-leg weight-bearing restrictions continue with use of crutches until there is evidence of solid union, usually in 8 to 12 weeks.

Treatment is more difficult when the heel is deformed and/or was not stabilized earlier by ORIF. Here, the surgeon must carry out the arthrodesis while also restoring the normal anatomic shape of the calcaneus. Subtalar fusion with bone block distraction is also recommended for impaction fractures caused by forces that have gone

straight up into the body of the calcaneus and exploded the lateral wall, especially in patients with inadequate bone stock. The goal here is to restore height or leg length and the inclination of the talus, which means restoration of the radiological (and anatomic) talar–first metatarsal alignment. One can assume that normal structural anatomy has been restored when a straight line can be drawn through the axis of the talus, the navicular, the cuneiform, and the first metatarsal in both AP and lateral weight-bearing radiographs of the foot.

The technical requirements to attain proper alignment and solid fusion are somewhat demanding. The patient is placed in a lateral position on the operating table to allow posterolateral access to the subtalar joint and the posterior pelvic graft donor site. It is helpful, albeit awkward in this position, to attach a femoral distractor from the tibia to the posterior tuber on the medial side. The distractor helps ensure that the joint is not wedged open more laterally than medially, a development that would rotate the calcaneal tuber into varus and subsequently produce an unsatisfactory result (Fig. 61–17).

After preparation and positioning, a long vertical posterolateral surgical approach is made. It must be noted that this approach can damage the sural nerve. I sometimes tell patients that I might transect the nerve and bury the proximal end in muscle. This works well, but some surgeons find it unacceptable and prefer to make attempts to protect it. The joint is located, cleaned, and wedged open with osteotomes and curettes. Neurovascular and tendinous structures from the deep posterior compartment must be protected on the medial side. The compartment may be released slightly on the distal side to allow greater flexibility. A medial distractor is attached and serially tightened to keep the heel from distracting into neutral or varus malalignment due to the scarred tissues on the medial side of the joint. These must be excised and removed carefully because of their proximity to the neurovascular structures.

Joint preparation is limited to the posterior facet, and anterior dissection is avoided to prevent damage to the blood supply going to the talus. The expanded lateral wall of the calcaneus is excised, and this bone is set aside to be used as additional bone graft. A normal talocalcaneal angle usually can be restored by making a gap 1.0 to 1.5 cm in height. The size of the actual gap is measured, and attention is turned to the posterior iliac crest, where one or two wedges of tricortical bone are harvested to fit into the gap. Additional cancellous bone can be taken to pack around the blocks.

The graft is packed into place, and two position screws (not lag screws) are placed across the distracted joint. The best fixation hardware for this purpose is a fully-threaded 6.5-mm cancellous screw or, better yet, a 6.5-mm bolt with a large core diameter. Those who prefer them may use cannulated screws of appropriate size. However, a fully-threaded screw that will not impact the talus to the calcaneus is needed to act as a position screw and maintain distraction.

One screw is placed from the lateral tuber into the midbody and another through the midline of the tuber into the neck. Good angular separation provides ideal fixation. The screws are placed through a single diameter

3.5-mm drill hole in the calcaneus and the talus to preclude a lag effect from taking place and to ensure that they function as position screws. Intraoperative radiographs include an AP projection of the foot to check the talocalcaneal and talar–first metatarsal joint alignments in that plane and to verify accurate positioning of the foot. A narrow talocalcaneal angle would indicate that the foot has been placed into supination. Lateral and axial views of the heel are taken to inspect reduction, alignment, and the lengths of the screws. A mortise ankle view must be obtained to be sure that no screw has wandered into a gutter. This usually occurs when the body screw angles over laterally into the talofibular joint space.

Postoperative management consists of casting and minimal weight bearing for 8 to 10 weeks.

## Combination Fusion and Osteotomy

In recent years, I have done fewer fusions by bone block distraction and more by combinations of fusion and calcaneal osteotomy (Fig. 61–18). This operation avoids morbidity associated with block bone grafts, awkward placement of the medial distractor, and poses less risk to the sural nerve. The operation corrects calcaneal malalignment, but it does require that the remaining bone in the calcaneus be of good quality. It is slightly less reliable for restoring talar inclination and alignment.

Fusion with concomitant transverse osteotomy is effective in patients with calcaneal varus or lateral displacement and/or dorsal compression of the heel. When rotation is not a problem but more length is desired in the sagittal plane, a more oblique osteotomy can be carried

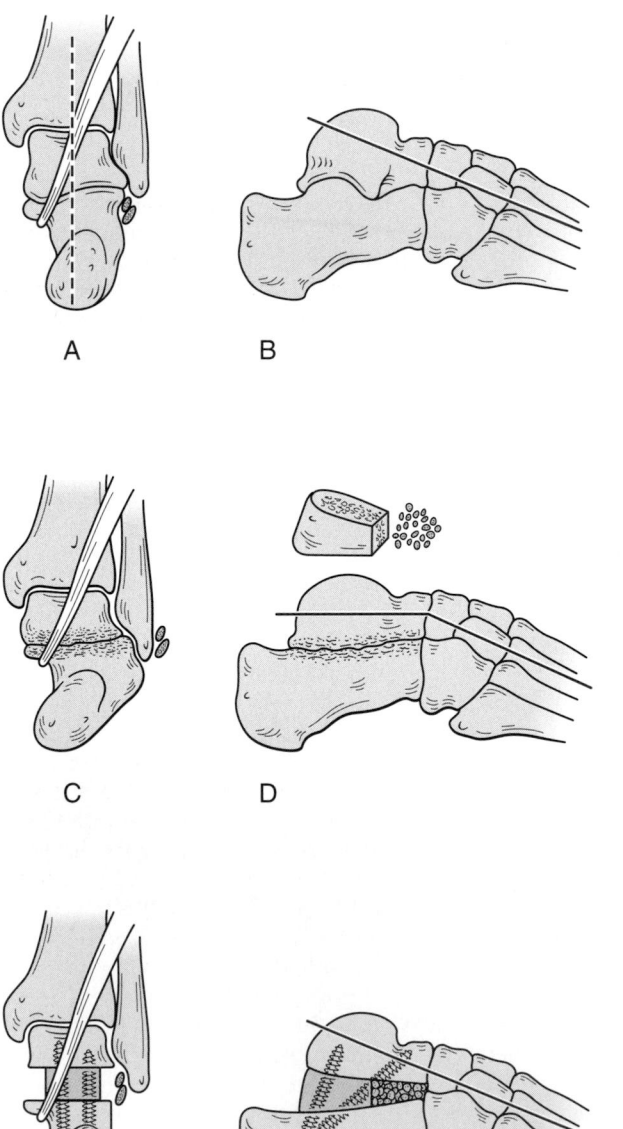

A  B

C  D

E  F

**Figure 61–17.** Subtalar fusion with distraction. *A,* The *dotted line* shows the alignment of the tibia through the tuber, the area where the flexor hallucis longus crosses at the back of the joint, and the location of the peroneal tendons under the fibular tip. *B,* Normal alignment of the subtalar joint and inclination of the talus are depicted. Notice that the all-important midaxial line of the talus continues directly through the midfoot and the apex of the first metatarsal in the medial column. *C,* After a typical high-energy calcaneal crush injury, the tuber is angled into varus while the lateral wall is angled and has exploded laterally toward valgus and impinges on the distal fibula, pushing the peroneal tendons out of their normal position. The subtalar joint is crushed, and the hindfoot has lost height. *D,* The inclination of the talus is out of line with the medial column and markedly limits the range of dorsiflexion in the anterior dome of the talus. A wedge of posterior iliac crest tricortical bone will be used to open the talocalcaneal joint and restore height. *E,* Two large, 6.5-mm bolts or fully threaded screws are positioned much as they would be for subtalar arthrodesis in situ. In this case, however, they serve as positioning screws rather than lag screws and maintain distraction of the talus from the calcaneus instead of compressing the graft. The exploded lateral wall is excised, and the tuber repositioned with less varus tilt and in slight valgus alignment to the weight-bearing line of the tibia. *F,* Reconstruction restores ideal talar inclination and talar–naviculocuneiform–first metatarsal axial alignment. An anteroposterior radiographic view of the foot should be taken intraoperatively to be sure that the talocalcaneal alignment is correct in the transverse plane and that the foot is not significantly pronated or supinated. (Adapted from Hansen, S.T. Functional Reconstruction of the Foot and Ankle. Philadelphia, Lippincott Williams & Wilkins, 2000.)

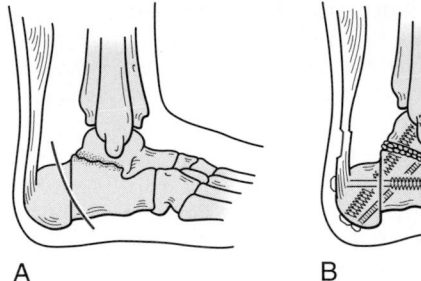

**FIGURE 61–18.** Calcaneal osteotomy. *A,* Some loss of height and talar inclination with decreased calcaneal pitch and arthrosis in the subtalar joint is seen in the right ankle and hindfoot. The *dotted line* indicates placement of the skin incision at the lateral border of the heel behind the peroneal tendons and the main branch of the sural nerve. The incision usually crosses a small posterior branch of the sural nerve. The *dark line* marks the osteotomy site. On the dorsal side, it starts just at the back of the subtalar joint, and on the plantar aspect, it is in front of the weight-bearing portion of the tuber. The incision must not overly penetrate the medial side of the foot. *B,* The osteotomy is completed and plantarly displaced, the subtalar joint is cleared of cartilage and grafted, and both areas are stabilized with large, 6.5-mm screws. Z lengthening of the Achilles tendon has been carried out as well. Notice the increased talar inclination and calcaneal pitch angles. These are easier to see than the talocalcaneal angle in the transverse plane that controls supination and pronation and which also must be corrected before inserting screws across the joint. (Adapted from Hansen, S.T. Functional Reconstruction of the Foot and Ankle. Philadelphia, Lippincott Williams & Wilkins, 2000.)

out. In a valgus heel, the obliquity usually runs from lateral anterior to medial posterior and, along with lateral translation of the tuber, the heel lengthens slightly.

An extended lateral surgical incision is made to expose the lateral wall and tuber. The posterior extent of the subtalar joint is located and the joint is cleared of residual cartilage. The expanded or blown out lateral wall is excised, and the bone is set aside to pack into the subtalar joint later.

Unless the heel is to be lengthened along the lateral column, a straight vertical cut is marked out from the posterior border of the posterior facet to the plantar surface of the calcaneus just in front of the weight-bearing tuber. These two criteria usually can be met by making a straight vertical cut. If they are not, the cut is moved forward slightly into the subtalar joint, because the subtalar joint is to be fused in any case and the weight-bearing area of the heel should not be violated. A Tuke or another type of oscillating saw is used to make the osteotomy up to and just penetrating the medial cortical bone. Overpenetration and damage to the medial neurovascular structures must be avoided.

The osteotomy is then carefully stretched open using broad osteotomes or broad-bladed lamina spreaders. The periosteal tissues and scar dorsally and medially are divided sharply when they can be visualized or they can be stripped with a large blunt curved AO elevator. The heel cord may require Z-lengthening. The posterior tuber is repositioned as required to restore original anatomy. It may be rotated out of varus, then translated medially out of valgus and plantarly to restore leg length and talar inclination. The tuber is then stabilized temporarily with a large K-wire and its position is verified by x-ray to confirm that the position attained is the one desired.

Fixation is achieved with one large 6.5-mm lag screw placed perpendicular to the osteotomy from the posterior to the anterior calcaneus. Next, two fully threaded 4.0-mm cortical or 6.5-mm cancellous position screws are placed perpendicular to the subtalar joint. The screws are started at the posteroinferior tuber and cross the osteotomy and the joint into the talar body and neck. Additional cancellous bone can be harvested from the proximal tibia to pack into the subtalar joint.

Like all subtalar fusions, this operation has two major objectives. They are to obtain reliable solid fusion and to restore normal shape and alignment to the hindfoot. Loss of motion in the critical subtalar joint and, consequently, the foot's ability to adapt to uneven surfaces, cushion gait, and protect the ankle from additional stress can be ameliorated only by fusing it in its optimal neutral position.

## TALONAVICULAR AND CALCANEOCUBOID (CHOPART'S) JOINT ARTHROSIS

Injuries to Chopart's joints are frequently missed, treated nonoperatively, or treated inadequately, resulting in a high rate of post-traumatic arthrosis in this area after injury. One reason for this is that a Chopart's injury may be occult initially if it occurs in association with a more obvious injury. Another is that operative treatment might seem unfeasible in some common types of injury, namely those in which the lateral third of the navicular is very comminuted or almost pulverized and those with partial dislocation of the medial tuber and subtle impaction of the cuboid. Whatever the reason for inadequate operative treatment, the result is often a very compromised foot. Arthrosis in the talonavicular joint affects the all-important subtalar motion, and impaction through the cuboid-lateral column causes lateral column shortening. These conditions place the forefoot in abduction and prevent normal supination necessary for pushoff, making the patient walk with a significant limp. Discomfort and swelling cause problems with shoe fitting.

Joint reconstruction possibilities for this area are as yet unavailable, and the recommended treatment is arthrodesis. A major disadvantage of arthrodesis of Chopart's joints is loss of nearly 90% of essential subtalar joint motion. This results in limited supination and pronation during normal gait and decreased cushioning and pushoff strength. It also eliminates inversion and eversion or adaptation of the foot to tilted surfaces, deflecting this motion to the ankle. Since the ankle tolerates these stresses poorly over the long term, arthrosis frequently develops here. To minimize these negative effects, fusion of these joints must be precise, and any existing muscle imbalance, for example, gastrocnemius equinus, must be corrected.

The same criteria described for subtalar fusion apply to fusion of Chopart's joints: to restore the talar–first metatarsal line in both weight-bearing AP and lateral radiographic projections and to balance medial and lateral column length by restoring the normal talocalcaneal angle in both planes. In a way, having two criteria is redundant, because they are mutually inclusive. When the foot is perfectly aligned and balanced, it looks and feels quite normal when the patient is standing. That is, the heel will be in 5° to 10° of valgus, the arch will be normal, and the alignment of the forefoot with the hindfoot and the midfoot will be straight. Weight should be evenly distributed from the heel to the metatarsals and between the medial and lateral columns. The negative effects of fusion at least can be minimized with perfect alignment.

## Surgical Technique

To fuse the talonavicular joint, the patient is placed supine on the operating table with a roll under the ipsilateral hip so that the affected foot rests straight up in a relaxed position. After appropriate preparation and draping, a tourniquet is applied and a medial utility incision is made to approach the talonavicular joint medially just above the posterior tibial tendon. The medial capsule is removed and, if better joint exposure is needed, the posterior tibial tendon attachments may be sharply dissected just from the medial side of the cuneiforms. The medial capsule is sharply dissected so it can be lifted dorsally, but excessive stripping must be avoided to protect blood supply going to the navicular, which enters radially from the capsule. Like the talus, the navicular surface is largely articular and entry for blood supply is therefore limited (Fig. 61–19).

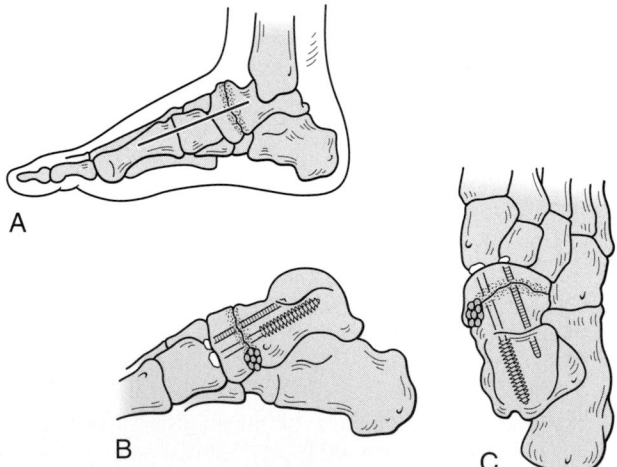

**Figure 61–19.** Talonavicular fusion. *A,* Hypertrophic arthrosis is seen at the talonavicular joint, but the basic alignment in this plane is acceptable. In a normal medial column, the talus, navicular, first cuneiform, and first metatarsal fall in nearly a straight line through the axis of the bones during full weight bearing on anteroposterior and lateral x-ray projections. *B,* Spurs are removed from the edges of the joint, and a shear strain–relieved bone graft is inserted in the plantar-medial joint line. Fixation is applied as depicted. Notice that the talar–first metatarsal alignment is straight. *C,* A 6.5-mm cancellous screw typically is used for compression. The second screw, which may be smaller, is applied to prevent rotational shear strain. It is placed in lag mode through a 4.0-mm gliding hole in the navicular and 2.5-mm tap hole in the talus. Occasionally, a third screw is placed from the proximal side of the talar head across to the lateral navicular. This is done when bone quality is questionable. (Adapted from Hansen, S.T. Functional Reconstruction of the Foot and Ankle. Philadelphia, Lippincott Williams & Wilkins, 2000.)

The articular cartilage is removed sharply using a curved osteotome and curettes, and any large spurs or bony excrescencies resulting from trauma are removed. In some cases, the medial navicular extrudes medially and curves around the medial head of the talus. It may be necessary to remove a portion of the medial navicular in order to pull the head of the talus medially, position the navicular more laterally, and restore talar-navicular-cuneiform–first metatarsal alignment and a neutral foot position.

After removing the cartilage, the surgeon perforates the subchondral bone at multiple sites with a 2.0-mm drill tip. The talonavicular joint is then aligned as ideally as possible by judging the clinical appearance of the foot. A large K-wire is inserted into the mid-distal navicular tubercle adjacent to the first cuneiform or even into a small notch drilled into it. To drill through this notch, the drill bit is directed parallel to the first metatarsal and up into the talar head and neck. A radiograph may be taken or an image intensifier may be used to confirm alignment. A final set of intraoperative radiographs are taken with the foot held under a simulated load, that is, with the head of a mallet held under the metatarsal heads, to ensure that the foot is in a neutral position at the ankle. AP and lateral views are taken to verify correct alignment. When the alignment is correct, two screws (6.5-mm cancellous or 4.0-mm cortical screws or one of each) are placed across the joint. A bur is used to make two divots in the joint line dorsomedial and plantar medial for a shear strain–relieved bone graft site. The bone graft is usually taken from the proximal tibia.

Fusion of the calcaneocuboid joint can be carried out with or without fusion of the navicular through a longitudinal lateral foot incision just dorsal to the peroneus brevis and the sural nerve (Fig. 61–20). The extensor brevis is lifted out of the sinus tarsi and off the top of the joint, and spurs and bony fragments are removed. The medial side of the extensor brevis must be protected to preserve the nerves and its blood supply. The joint is cleared of cartilage and perforated as described for the talonavicular joint. A critical decision at this point is whether to distract the joint to equalize the medial and lateral columns, keeping in mind that overdistraction produces supination and results in serious functional disability. When both joints require fusion, neither is fixed until both have been prepared. Distraction balancing, an essential part of realigning the talonavicular joint, is carried out before the screws are placed across the talonavicular joint.

If distraction is needed, it is done with a small external fixation device with the pins placed into the calcaneus and proximal fifth metatarsal. A block bone graft can be taken from the lateral calcaneus or the anterior iliac crest. When the surgeon knows in advance that a large block graft will be needed, it may be taken from the posterior iliac crest at the start of the operation with the patient in a lateral position.

The joint can be stabilized in one of several ways. A medium-sized cervical plate can be applied laterally to bridge the calcaneus and the cuboid. One or two screws can be inserted from the sinus tarsi to the cuboid, or a long (approximately 100 mm) 6.5-mm screw may be inserted

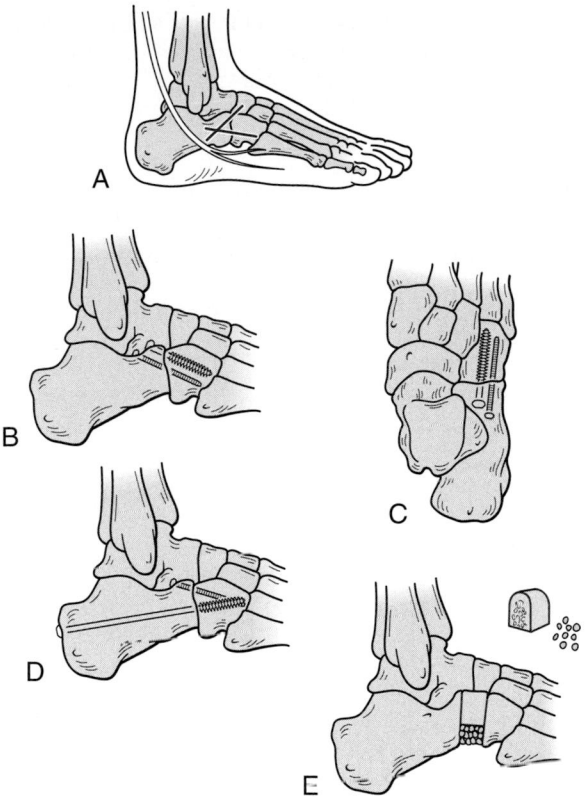

**FIGURE 61–20.** Calcaneocuboid joint fusion. *A,* Arthrosis is seen at the calcaneocuboid joint. The *dark lines* depict longitudinal and Ollier-type incisions. A longitudinal incision is generally used if arthrodesis distraction is planned. *B,* This method of fixation is carried out when there is no need to lengthen the lateral column. Cartilage is removed, and the subchondral bone is perforated. Although not shown here, a shear strain–relieved bone graft is always necessary. *C,* A dorsoplantar view confirms appropriate alignment with equal medial and lateral column lengths. *D,* This alternative form of fixation is stronger and is appropriate in the absence of a strong anterior process of the calcaneus. *E,* Forefoot abduction or a short lateral column caused by compression and shortening through the cuboid or calcaneocuboid joint may be found in old Chopart injuries. The technique commonly used to correct these abnormalities includes a block graft taken from the posterior iliac crest of the calcaneus. Extra cancellous chips are placed medially and inferiorly, and at least two screws are used for fixation. The screws should be as long as possible to provide good leverage. Screws placed from distal to proximal may provide even better fixation by virtue of the length they extend into the calcaneus. Placement in this manner requires careful exposure over the distal cuboid to avoid the sural nerve and the peroneus tertius. (Adapted from Hansen, S.T. Functional Reconstruction of the Foot and Ankle. Philadelphia, Lippincott Williams & Wilkins, 2000.)

from the posterior lateral calcaneus into the cuboid. A lag screw with 16 mm of thread may be placed in primary bone-to-bone fusion, but a fully threaded 6.5-mm screw or a bolt is preferable when the position screw must hold the distraction. I generally use a plate and at least one screw from either the sinus tarsi or the heel.

Notice that the dorsal-plantar position of the cuboid on the anterior calcaneus must be carefully controlled prior to fixation. Distraction may make this difficult, as it can displace the cuboid dorsally. The surgeon can control distraction by twisting the external fixation device into correct alignment during screw insertion. In primary fusions, shear strain–relieved grafts are made, the same as in talonavicular fusions. Fusions with bone block distrac-

tion have extra cancellous bone packed around the bone block.

## LISFRANC JOINT ARTHROSIS

The incidence of post-traumatic arthrosis and deformity in the midfoot seems to be increasing. This might be due to an increase in the number of foot injuries caused by motor vehicle accidents, where the rest of the body is protected by complex belts or air bags, or it may be that treating physicians are more aware of foot problems and are better able to diagnose them.

Increased awareness has resulted in diagnosis that is more accurate. It is clearly evident that Lisfranc joint arthrosis does not always result from traumatic injuries, such as a Lisfranc sprain or fracture-dislocation, but can be a late-stage manifestation of "Morton's foot" with associated gastrocnemius equinus. Briefly, this condition is caused by chronic overload of the second metatarsal by a functionally short or hypermobile first metatarsal. As a result, the second metatarsal becomes very thickened, hyperostotic, or both. Arthrosis and instability gradually develop at the cuneiform–second metatarsal joint and overload the third tarsometatarsal (or cuneiform–third metatarsal) joint. As this process repeats itself, the forefoot eventually angulates into dorsiflexion and abduction relative to the midfoot. The clinical appearance of this deformity is nearly identical to a foot with post-traumatic Lisfranc joint arthrosis.

Differentiation between the two problems can become a medical-legal problem, and a physician may be accused of missing or inadequately treating a Lisfranc joint sprain, thereby causing the subsequent arthrosis. Evidence that the etiology of Lisfranc joint arthrosis is chronic degeneration and not a post-traumatic condition is clear when the patient has a very thickened, dense, second metatarsal. It is even more convincing when the patient demonstrates a Morton's foot with a tight gastrocnemius on the contralateral side. Post-traumatic arthrosis is associated with a clear history of diagnosis and treatment of a Lisfranc joint injury. Radiographs taken long after the injury occurred demonstrate a variable pattern of arthrosis that may include injury into the cuneiform level or an old metatarsal fracture with or without malunion.

Treatment of individual cases varies, but the goal always remains the same, that is, to restore normal anatomy and alignment and fuse the arthritic or painful joints. Only the first, second, and third tarsometatarsal joints are fused in most cases. These three joints normally have only minimal, if any, motion, and patients experience virtually no functional loss after their fusion. The 4–5 metatarsal-cuboid joints, which have a small amount of motion essential for normal gait, usually are not as susceptible to arthritis.

## Surgical Technique

The patient is positioned supine on the operating table with a roll under the ipsilateral hip so that the affected foot rests with the toes pointing nearly straight up. After appropriate preparation and draping, a tourniquet is applied, and two incisions are drawn on the midfoot and forefoot (Fig. 61–21). The medial incision goes in a longitudinal direction in the interval between the first and second metatarsals, that is, on the lateral dorsum of the first metatarsal extending proximally over the first and second cuneiforms. The second incision is made essentially in line with the fourth metatarsal and extends up and over the third cuneiform. The first cuneiform–metatarsal joint, the 1–2 intercuneiform joint, and the medial side of the second cuneiform can be visualized through the medial incision. I routinely excise the residual cartilage with a narrow oscillating saw and take out wedges of bone so that the joint surfaces are in good apposition with the realigned joints. Alignment cannot be corrected until all the joints have been exposed and freed up through both incisions. Dissection is deepened to the joint level through the second incision by going through an interval between the muscle bellies of the extensor hallucis brevis and the extensor digitorum brevis to the lesser toes. The lateral second cuneiform-metatarsal joint, the third cuneiform–metatarsal joint, and the medial side of the fourth cuboid–metatarsal joint can be visualized through this

interval. In cases of long-standing arthrosis, spurs or hypertrophic bone frequently obscure the joints. These excrescencies can be excised with an osteotome to get a clear view of the remaining joint.

Alignment and apposition are achieved after cartilage and subchondral bone have been removed and all adhesions have been loosened around the joints. The relative length of the metatarsals also must be corrected, usually by shortening the second and possibly third metatarsal bases. (This is more common in degenerative arthrosis, where the second and third metatarsals are frequently longer than the first.)

The joints frequently cannot be completely closed or placed in apposition at the first attempt for several possible reasons. Some interposed bone may remain deep in the joint. The intermetatarsal ligaments between the lesser metatarsals may require division, especially those between the third and fourth metatarsals. Occasionally, the joints cannot be realigned until the ligaments between the second and third or the first and second metatarsals also have been divided, because they might have adapted to an angulated position. Division of the intermetatarsal ligaments is carried out with a ½-inch or 1.0-cm osteotome. The osteotome is inserted deeply between the proximal ends of the metatarsals, aligned parallel to the metatarsals, and advanced distally. This motion divides the tethers between the metatarsals, usually with the sound of cutting celery, and the metatarsals can be shortened to appose the surfaces to be fused.

Now comes the most technically difficult part of the operation. The surgeon must hold the metatarsals in correct alignment in both transverse (abduction/adduction) and sagittal (plantar flexion-dorsiflexion) planes while an assistant places screws across the joints. The first screw (a 3.5- or 4.0-mm cortical screw) is routinely placed through a stab wound at an angle of approximately 45° from the medial side of the first cuneiform and across the axilla between the first and second cuneiforms. It is continued into the base of the second metatarsal, lagging the base of the second metatarsal compactly into this notch. Normally, the strength and stability of the Lisfranc joints can be attributed to the secure position of the second metatarsal base against the face of the second cuneiform and the lateral side of the first cuneiform.

The second screw is inserted through a countersunk hole or trough made 2 cm distal to the joint on the cortical dorsum of the first metatarsal. The screw used here is always a 4.0-mm cortical screw that is approximately 45 mm long (the Lisfranc screw, Synthes USA). During placement of both screws, the surgeon must hold the alignment securely while keeping the metatarsal heads level.

The third screw is usually started from the dorsolateral third metatarsal. It is aimed proximally and medially and inserted into the third or second cuneiform. After each metatarsal-cuneiform joint is stabilized, the accuracy of its position and alignment are verified clinically and, if desired, by radiographs. If the position is correct, a 2.7-mm screw is added across each joint, usually going from proximal to distal. The second screw may be smaller

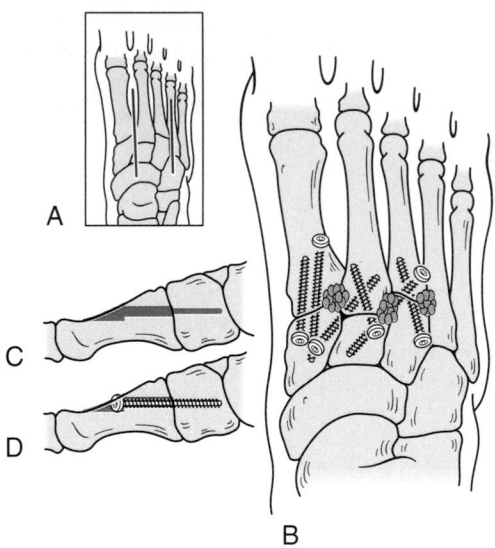

**FIGURE 61–21.** Lisfranc's arthrodesis (forefoot triple arthrodesis). *A,* The *dark lines* depict the placement of the two incisions recommended for reduction and fusion of a Lisfranc or 1-2-3 tarsometatarsal arthrodesis. Dorsal neurovascular structures lie in the bridge of soft tissue between the incisions. The more lateral incision exposes the interval between the extensor brevis going to the great toe medially and extensor brevis going to the lesser toes laterally as well as the third tarsometatarsal joint. *B,* The tarsometatarsal joints are reduced and two screws are placed across each joint to be fused. The screws should be as long as possible to attain sufficient leverage to stabilize these joints. *C,* A trough for the screw head is burred into the dorsal cortex of the first metatarsal, ideally about 2.0 cm distal to the joint. Next, a 3.5-mm or 4.0-mm gliding hole is drilled into the base of the metatarsal, and a 2.5-mm tap hole is drilled into the first cuneiform. *D,* This allows a 3.5-mm or, preferably, a 4.0-mm cortical screw to be lagged, compressing the surface to be fused. A screw that is 45 ± 5 mm long generally provides adequate leverage. At least one shear strain–relieved bone graft site is made at the junction of the first and second metatarsal bases and their respective cuneiforms. (Adpted from Hansen, S.T. Functional Reconstruction of the Foot and Ankle. Philadelphia, Lippincott Williams & Wilkins, 2000.)

because its purpose is to control rotation, not provide leverage for holding power.

At the end of this procedure, a neutralization screw may be placed upward and laterally from the plantar metaphysis of the first metatarsal into the second cuneiform. A neutralization screw is particularly useful when the naviculocuneiform joint also has been fused. This is done because of traumatic arthrosis there or for correction of sag or a break in the talar–first metatarsal alignment at the naviculocuneiform level. In this case, the screw is advanced into the lateral navicular. Although plates are not routinely used as fixation in this area, they are fine if they are needed to provide adequate fixation.

After fixation, I always add cancellous autograft at each joint using the shear strain–relief technique. To do this, divots between 6 and 8 mm in diameter are burred across the dorsal aspect of each joint, with two divots in the first tarsometatarsal joint, and are filled with cancellous bone chips. The cancellous bone used for grafting usually is bone that was removed in the course of shaping the joints. If this amount of bone is inadequate, more cancellous bone may be removed from the proximal tibial metaphysis.

The tourniquet is removed and AP and lateral radiographs are taken with simulated loading and the foot in a neutral position. The purpose of these radiographs is to verify the position of the screws and the alignment of the metatarsals. The actual level of the metatarsals cannot be established on a radiographic view and must be determined by clinical examination. Skin closure may be started while awaiting the results of the radiographs and after the hyperemic effect has resolved and/or bleeding arteries have been controlled. A light plaster cast is applied with the foot in a neutral position and, an hour or two later, a strip 1 cm wide is removed from the anterior aspect of the cast to accommodate any swelling that may develop. Surgery in this area is usually associated with significant swelling and pain, and I keep the patient in the hospital with the foot elevated for 2 or 3 days.

At 2½ to 3 postoperative weeks, the cast is changed, the sutures are removed, and the wound is checked. The patient is allowed to ambulate on crutches with weight-of-leg weight bearing but must avoid any forefoot pushoff for 8 to 10 weeks. It may take as long as 3 to 6 months before swelling and discomfort completely resolve. If a patient is still uncomfortable after 6 months and no other problem, such as a nonunion or malunion, is evident, the hardware may be removed. Should one of the metatarsals heal in greater plantar flexion than the others, a shoe with a thick, cushioning fixed sole and soft accommodative orthoses may alleviate discomfort. The metatarsal may be surgically repaired by a proximal metaphyseal dorsal closing wedge osteotomy.

It is important to note that a tight gastrocnemius aggravates stress across the midfoot. The surgeon decides whether to carry out a gastroc slide by examining the patient's contralateral foot. If a gastroc slide is planned, it is done after fusing the Lisfranc joint. A gastrocnemius release should be considered whenever a patient cannot move the foot easily to 10° or 15° of dorsiflexion with the knee straight during the postoperative phase.

# RESIDUALS OF COMPARTMENT SYNDROMES

Post-traumatic compartment syndromes in the leg or the foot can affect the foot and ankle significantly. Most commonly, they occur in the anterior, deep posterior, and mid-plantar compartments of the leg. An anterior compartment syndrome can develop after a tibial fracture, from reperfusion syndrome following injury to a more proximal artery, or any other injury that interrupts the flow of blood for several hours. Reperfusion syndrome occurs when circulation is restored after a delayed repair.

A deep posterior compartment syndrome may develop following a tibial fracture, a talar fracture, a calcaneal fracture, or upon reperfusion. Typically, only very high-energy foot and ankle fractures cause deep posterior compartment syndromes. Plantar medial compartment syndromes generally are associated with calcaneal fractures and, in advanced cases, they are difficult to differentiate from direct muscle injuries. It is very easy to miss a deep posterior or plantar compartment syndrome in the leg in the acute stage. In general, an anterior compartment syndrome is easier to diagnose immediately following trauma, because its symptoms are easier to elicit. Treatment is fairly simple and effective when it is carried out early. Surprisingly, an anterior compartment syndrome can be the least devastating of the three if the necrotic tissue does not become infected.

Scarring and contracture are sequelae of intercompartment necrosis. Marked dropfoot or severe equinus deformity that is aggravated by sleeping posture might be expected with simple paralysis of the anterior compartment muscles (the anterior tibial, the extensor hallucis longus, the extensor digitorum longus, and the peroneus tertius). However, scar contracture here tends to dorsiflex the foot, and the foot and ankle often are raised to a few degrees short of neutral. A calcaneal deformity could result, but gravity and sleeping posture prevent continued dorsiflexion. Because the inverter and evertor muscles continue to stabilize the foot and the plantar flexors still provide pushoff, the amount of disability may be slight, especially in women who wear high-heeled shoes. A slight limp is usually unavoidable, as the patient has to "hip hike" to clear the toe and avoid tripping, especially when walking barefoot or in low-heeled shoes.

Treatment, if needed, consists of transferring the posterior tibial muscle and tendon to the dorsum of the foot to replace the anterior tibialis and the peroneus tertius. The flexor digitorum longus is transferred to the navicular or to the stump of the posterior tibialis to prevent collapse of the medial arch.

Various techniques have been described for transfer of the posterior tibialis to the dorsum. After trying several over many years, I prefer to splice a section of the posterior tibial tendon into the anterior tibialis tendon and the extensor digitorum longus tendon above the ankle after it has been routed anterior through the interosseous membrane. This technique is contraindicated when the peroneal nerve is injured or in the presence of neuromuscular disease, when the peroneals are paralyzed. Under these circumstances, posterior tibial tendon contraction would dorsiflex and invert the foot through the anterior tibial action, which is unopposed by the peroneals. For example, patients with Charcot-Marie-Tooth disease tend toward varus, and the posterior tibial tendon should be transferred only to the lateral side of the foot through the extensor digitorum longus and the peroneus tertius to avoid aggravating this condition.

## Old, Deep Posterior Compartment Syndrome

In contrast, a deep posterior compartment syndrome can cause marked deformity and disability in the foot. Here, some combination of the posterior tibial, flexor hallucis longus, and flexor digitorum longus muscle functions will be affected. All the muscle bellies of all three muscles may be involved, all of one or two muscles, or only part of one or two. In this case, gravity and sleeping posture in equinovarus aggravate the contractures rather than minimize them. The posterior tibial muscle inverts and internally rotates the foot and may cause equinus at the ankles as well. Occurring in association with a tibial fracture, it may be mistaken for a malunion in internal rotation when actually it is just the foot internally rotated on the leg by the posterior tibial muscle.

Contractures in the long toe flexors cause flexor contracture at the interphalangeal and the metatarsophalangeal joints and may contribute to equinocavovarus posturing of the foot and ankle. Sleeping posture in a supine or prone position may make the foot go into internal rotation and equinocavovarus, and this position can gradually become fixed as the muscles scar and contract during the night. Clearly, this posture is not well adapted for ambulation, and numerous remedies from tenotomies to dorsiflexion eversion osteotomies of the distal tibia have been suggested for treatment.

For obvious reasons, I prefer to completely excise the heavily scarred muscles and the adhered tendons so that they cannot rejoin and deformity cannot recur. This procedure is similar to the treatment described by Volkmann for volar compartment syndromes in the forearm. Removal of the contracted muscles allows dorsiflexion, eversion, and external rotation out of the deformity, and enables the foot to assume a plantar grade position. Residually scarred plantar medial capsules may be divided carefully to attain complete correction, but overly aggressive division can lead to overcorrection and pronation due to absence of the posterior tibial tendon.

Since any individual muscle or parts of a muscle may have been spared necrosis and scar contracture, the remaining healthy muscle and tendon is placed into the stump of the posterior tibial tendon to restore some inversion or at least to protect it against excessive pronation. In other words, this is done in an attempt to retain arch support. The presence of even slight gastrocnemius contracture is an indication for lengthening to prevent aggravating pronation. It is possible that the plantar and forefoot intrinsics have been spared and can supply normal toe flexion, but frequently they are damaged as well. In any case, some fixed toe flexion contracture usually has developed by the time the syndrome has been diagnosed and treatment carried out. Simple Girdlestone flexor extensor transfers and plantar capsulotomies can straighten the toes. If the toes are pulled into extension at the metatarsophalangeal joints over time, they can be straightened by transfer of the extensor digitorum longus to the peroneus tertius and possibly extensor substitution (transfer of the extensor digitorum brevis to the distal extensor digitorum longus).

A central plantar compartment syndrome results in toe flexion contracture that is very similar to that produced by a deep posterior compartment syndrome in the leg. This is not surprising, as the affected flexor accessorius or quadratus plantar muscle inserts into the long extrinsic flexors in the forefoot and exerts flexion through its distal tendon. The result is a fixed flexion deformity in the interphalangeal and metatarsophalangeal joints. Claw toes caused by intrinsic minus deformity or extensor recruitment are very different in that here, the metatarsophalangeal joint is extended while the interphalangeal joints are flexed.

I have no experience with deep débridement of necrotic scarred muscle in the plantar compartments, and treat this problem simply by removing the distal contracted flexor tendons from the toes through a medial surgical approach, the same as the Girdlestone flexor-extensor approach. The distal tendon cannot flex or extend, and this section of tendon should be removed to prevent reattachment and repeat contracture. The forefoot intrinsics (lumbricals and interossei) may be unaffected and remain supple enough to provide some metatarsophalangeal joint flexion.

## REFERENCES

1. Hansen, S.T. The Fibular Window. In: Functional Reconstruction of the Foot and Ankle. Philadelphia, Lippincott Williams & Wilkins, 2000, pp. 496–497.
2. Holt, E.S.; Hansen, S.T.; Mayo, K.A.; et al. Ankle arthrodesis using internal screw fixation. Clin Orthop 268:21–28, 1991.
3. Scranton, P.E.; McDermott, J.E. Treatment of type V osteochondral lesions of the talus with ipsilateral knee osteochondral autografts. Foot Ankle Int 22:380–384, 2001.
4. Zwipp, H. Arthodese OSG. In: Chirurgie des Fusses. Wien, Springer-Verlag, 1994, pp. 188–191.

# Principles of Deformity Correction

Dror Paley, M.D.

## LOWER LIMB ALIGNMENT AND JOINT ORIENTATION

Bones, joints, and bone and joint segments can be two-dimensionally characterized using axis lines. A *mechanical axis line* connects the center of a proximal joint to the center of a distal joint (Fig. 62–1). An *anatomic axis line* is the mid-diaphyseal line (see Fig. 62–1). The anatomic axis is used in the frontal and sagittal planes, whereas the mechanical axis is used only in the frontal plane. The orientation of each joint can be measured between frontal and sagittal-plane *joint orientation lines* and the mechanical and anatomic axes (Fig. 62–2). The mechanical and anatomic axes of the tibia are parallel to each other (see Fig. 62–1A). The tibial anatomic axis is normally a few millimeters medial to the tibial mechanical axis. In the femur, the mechanical and anatomic axes are convergent with each other (see Fig. 62–1B).

The *mechanical axis of the lower limb* extends from the center of the hip to the center of the ankle (Fig. 62–3A). In the normally aligned limb, the mechanical axis of the lower limb passes through or slightly medial to the center of the knee joint line. The distance between the mechanical axis of the lower limb and the center of the knee joint is called the *mechanical axis deviation* (MAD) (see Fig. 62–3A). Deformities of the femur and tibia in the frontal plane lead to a MAD outside this normal range. Medial and lateral MADs can lead to arthrosis of the knee joint. To determine objectively whether the MAD results from femoral or tibial deformity, the mechanical joint orientation angles (i.e., lateral distal femoral angle and medial proximal tibial angle) are measured and compared with the normal range (85° to 90°) (see Fig. 62–3B and C). This assessment is called the *malalignment test*. Values outside the normal range indicate the source of MAD to be femoral, tibial, or both. When the femoral and tibial joint orientation lines in the frontal plane are not parallel to each other, this *joint line convergence angle* is another source of MAD (see Fig. 62–3D). Angular deformities near the hip and ankle have little effect on MAD (Figs. 62–4 and 62–5).

It is therefore important to check the orientation of the ankle and hip to the individual bone mechanical or anatomic axis in the frontal plane. The orientation of the ankle and hip can be checked relative to the mechanical axis line in the frontal plane and the *overall anatomic axis line,* a line between the normal intersection points of the anatomic axis with the proximal and distal joints, in the sagittal plane. Alternatively, it can be checked relative to a segmental anatomic or mechanical axis line. Both are called *malorientation tests.*

## CHARACTERISTICS OF DEFORMITY

### Level of Angulation

Angular deformity leads to a bend or break in the anatomic and mechanical axis lines (Fig. 62–6). The intersection point of the proximal and distal axis lines is the *center of rotation of angulation* (CORA) (Fig. 62–7). Multiple levels of angulation have one CORA for each apex. The CORA can be found by drawing proximal and distal mechanical or anatomic axis lines. The anatomic axis line method of planning is illustrated in Figures 62–8 to 62–11. The mechanical axis method of planning can also be used and is explained in other publications.[3, 5] Anatomic axis planning can be used in the frontal and sagittal planes and easily identifies single-level or multilevel angular deformities (see Figs. 62–8 to 62–11).

### OSTEOTOMY RULES

The relationship of an osteotomy to the CORA determines the effect of an osteotomy on limb alignment. A line passing through the CORA dividing the transverse angle into two equal parts is called the *transverse bisector line* (Fig. 62–12A). Each point on this line can be considered a CORA (see Fig. 62–12B). When the osteotomy line passes through the convex cortex CORA and an opening wedge angular correction of the magnitude of deformity is performed, the proximal and distal anatomic and mechanical

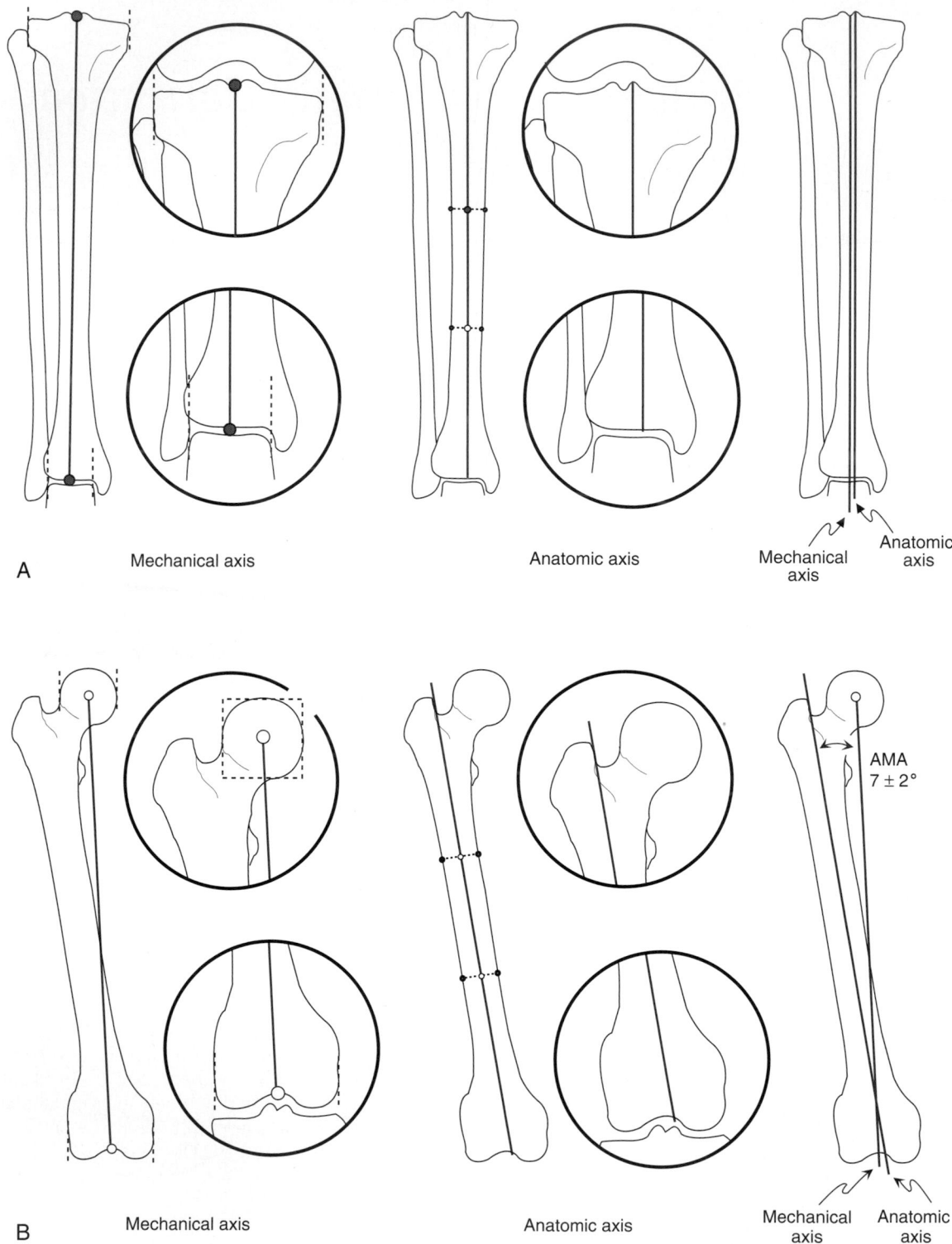

**FIGURE 62–1.** *A,* The tibial mechanical and anatomic axes are parallel but not the same. The anatomic axis is slightly medial to the mechanical axis. The mechanical axis of the tibia is actually slightly lateral to the midline of the tibial shaft. Conversely, the anatomic axis does not pass through the center of the knee joint. It intersects the knee joint line at the medial tibial spine. *B,* The femoral mechanical and anatomic axes are not parallel. The femoral anatomic axis intersects the knee joint line generally 1 cm medial to the knee joint center, in the vicinity of the medial tibial spine. When extended proximally, it usually passes through the piriformis fossa, just medial to the greater trochanter medial cortex. The angle between the femoral mechanical and anatomic axes is 7±2°. (Redrawn from Paley, D. Principles of Deformity Correction. Heidelberg, Germany, Springer-Verlag, 2002.)

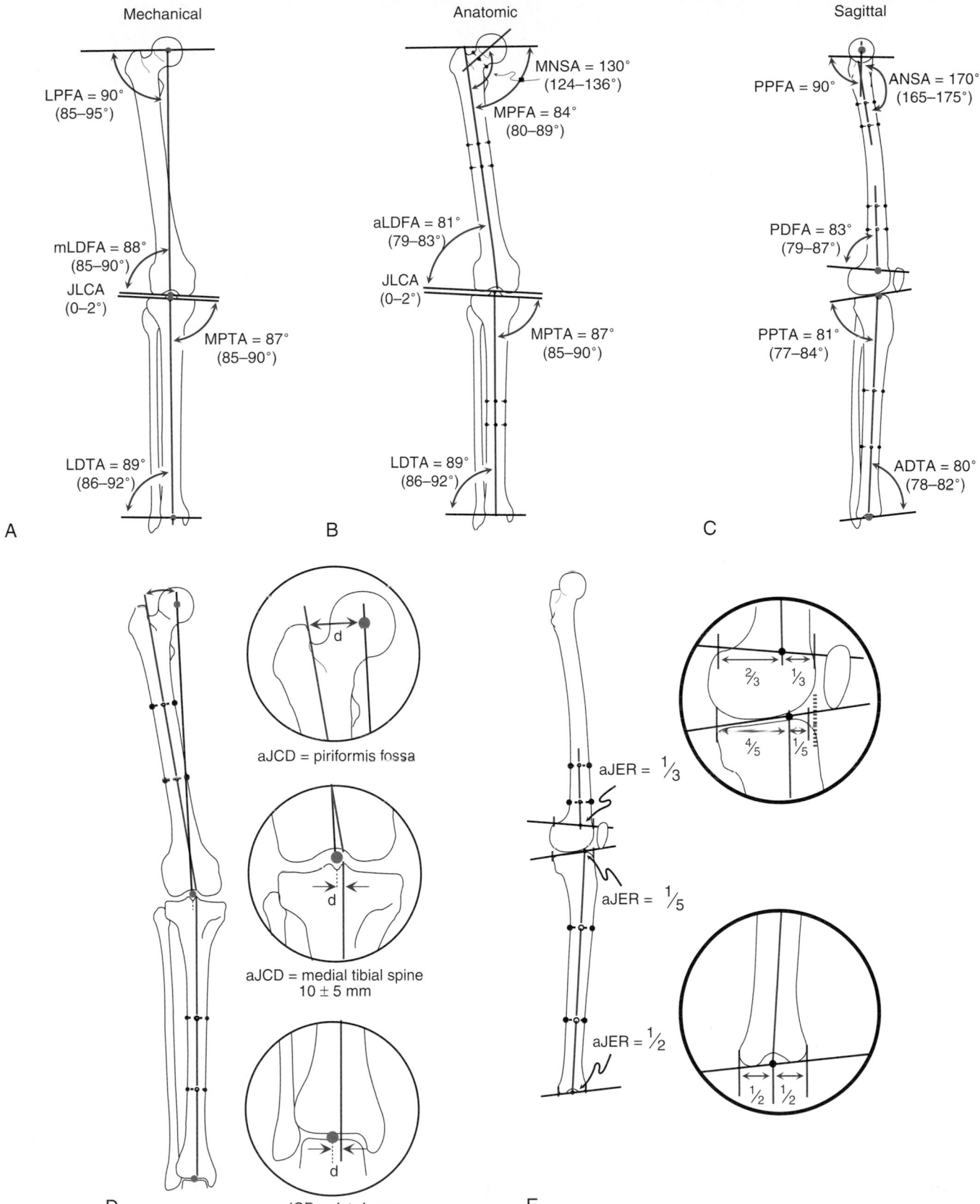

**FIGURE 62–2.** Lower extremity axes. *A*, Frontal-plane joint orientation angle nomenclature and normal values are given relative to the mechanical axis. *B*, Frontal-plane joint orientation angle nomenclature and normal values are given relative to the anatomic axis. *C*, Sagittal-plane joint orientation angle nomenclature and normal values relative to the anatomic axis. *D*, Anatomic axis–joint line intersection points. Anatomic joint center distances (aJCD) for the frontal plane are shown. *E*, Anatomic axis–joint line intersection points. The anatomic joint edge ratio (a-JER) for the sagittal plane is shown. ADTA, anterior distal tibial angle; aLDFA, anatomic lateral distal femoral angle; ANSA, anterior neck shaft angle; d, distance; JLCA, joint line convergence angle; LDTA, lateral distal tibial angle; LPFA, lateral proximal femoral angle; mLDFA, mechanical lateral distal femoral angle; MNSA, medial neck shaft angle; MPFA, medial proximal femoral angle; MPTA, medial proximal tibial angle; PDFA, posterior distal femoral angle; PPFA, posterior proximal femoral angle; PPTA, posterior proximal tibial angle. (Redrawn from Paley, D. Principles of Deformity Correction. Heidelberg, Germany, Springer-Verlag, 2002.)

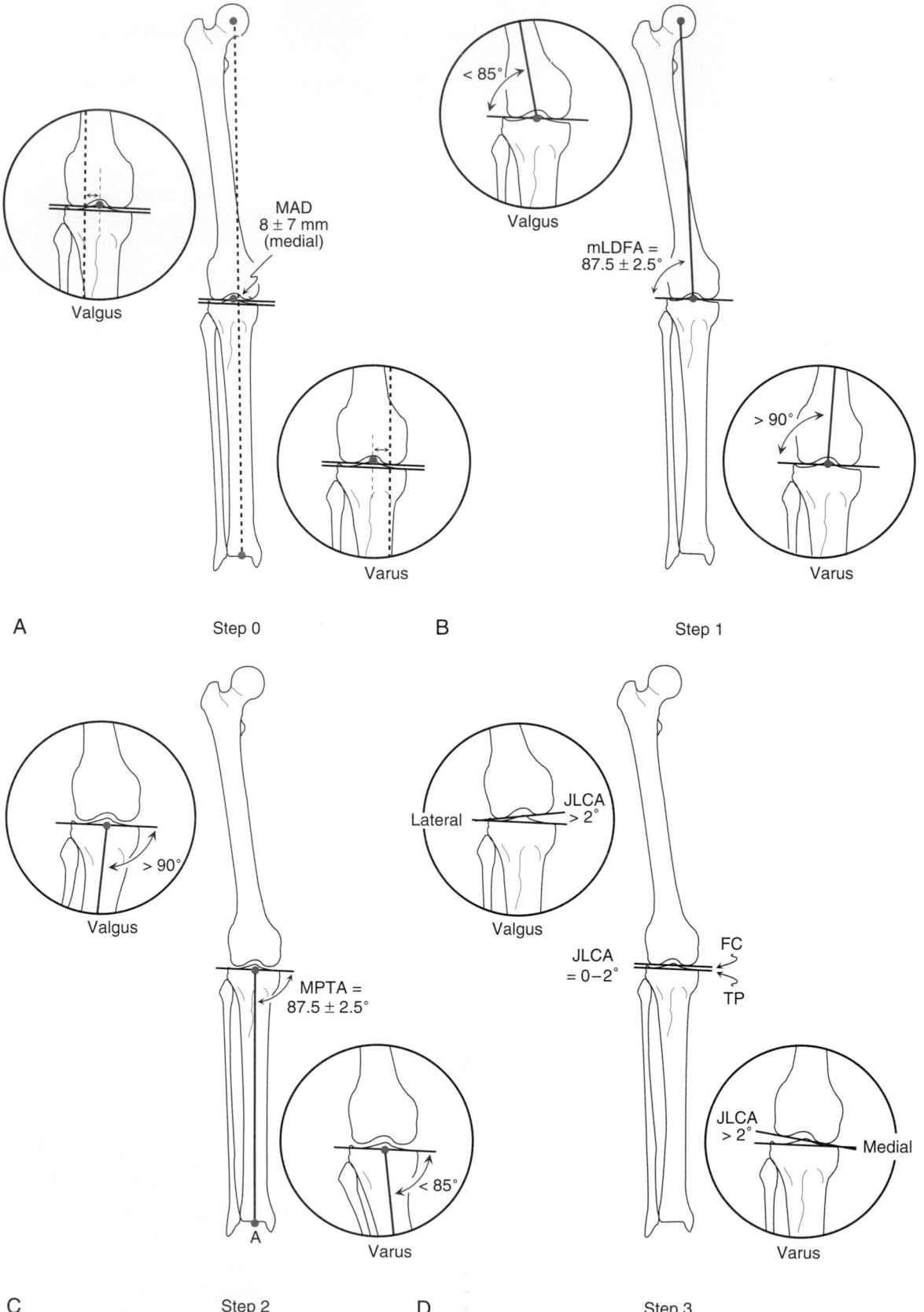

**Figure 62–3.** Malalignment test to identify and locate a deformity. *A,* Step 0: Measure the mechanical axis deviation (MAD). The normal range is 1 to 15 mm medial relative to the center of the joint. A medial MAD greater than 15 mm is considered varus, and a lateral MAD is considered valgus *(insets)*. *B,* Step 1: Measure the lateral distal femoral angle. The normal range is 85° to 90°. A lateral distal femoral angle less than 85° means that femoral bone deformity is a source of lateral MAD (i.e., valgus), and a lateral distal femoral angle greater than 90° means that femoral bone deformity is a source of medial MAD (i.e., varus). *C,* Step 2: Measure the medial proximal tibial angle. The normal range is 85° to 90°. A medial proximal tibial angle greater than 90° means that tibial deformity is a source of lateral MAD (i.e., valgus), and a medial proximal tibial angle less than 85° means that tibial deformity is a source of medial MAD (i.e., varus). *D,* Step 3: Measure the joint line convergence angle. The normal range is 0° to 2° of medial convergence of the joint lines. A medial joint line convergence angle greater than 2° means that lateral ligamentocapsular laxity or medial cartilage loss is a source of medial MAD (i.e., varus), and a lateral joint line convergence angle means that medial ligamentocapsular laxity or lateral cartilage loss is a source of lateral MAD (i.e., valgus). JLCA, joint line convergence angle; FC, femoral condyle; mLDFA, mechanical lateral distal femoral angle; MPTA, medial proximal tibial angle; TP, tibial plateau. (Redrawn from Paley, D. Principles of Deformity Correction. Heidelberg, Germany, Springer-Verlag, 2002.)

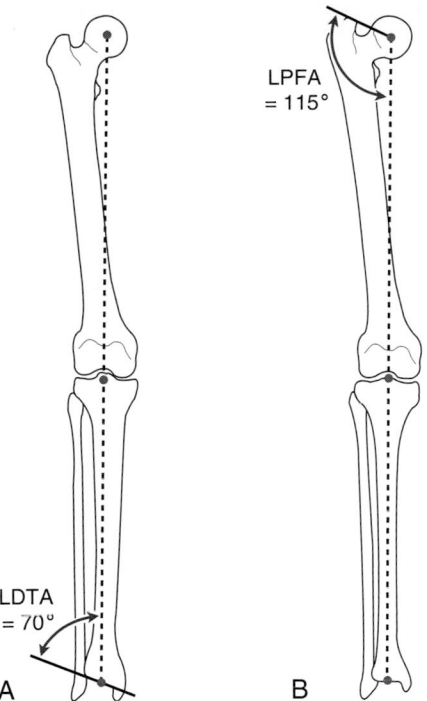

**FIGURE 62–4.** A deformity near the ankle or hip may not affect the mechanical axis. *A,* Malorientation of the ankle joint at or near the level of the plafond produces no mechanical axis deviation (MAD). *B,* Malorientation of the hip joint at or near the level of the femoral head produces no MAD. LDTA, lateral distal tibial angle; LPFA, lateral proximal femoral angle. (Redrawn from Paley, D. Principles of Deformity Correction. Heidelberg, Germany, Springer-Verlag, 2002.)

converges on the concave cortex CORA. Both are examples of osteotomy rule 1 (Fig. 62–13).

If the opening and closing wedge osteotomies are made at a level different from that of the CORA, the proximal and distal axis lines are realigned in angulation but become translated to each other (osteotomy rule 3) (Fig. 62–14). Osteotomy rule 3 demonstrates that angulation through the osteotomy with an ACA *different from* the CORA will angulate the osteotomy but leave the bone segment anatomic axes translated instead of aligned. This condition is called a *secondary translation deformity.* To avoid secondary translation deformity when the osteotomy is performed at a level different from that of the CORA, the osteotomy line can be angulated by the magnitude of angulation and translated by the amount of secondary translation expected (i.e., osteotomy rule 2) (see Fig. 62–14). The bone axes are realigned in a co-linear fashion, and the joint orientation of the distal to the proximal joint is normal.

## FOCAL DOME OSTEOTOMY

Circular (cylindrical) bone cuts are called dome osteotomies. The dome osteotomy has its axis of correction of angulation at the center of the circular cut. Because the osteotomy is at a distance (radius) from the center of the circle, the osteotomy line angulates and translates. If the center of the circular cut is matched to a CORA of an angular deformity, complete realignment of the bone ends will result according to osteotomy rule 2. This approach is called a *focal dome osteotomy.*[5]

If the center of the circular cut is at a level different from that of the CORA, the proximal and distal axis lines will translate to each other according to osteotomy rule 3. The Maquet osteotomy[2] of the proximal tibia (Fig. 62–15) is an example of mismatching the center of the circular cut and the CORA. If the circular cut is made concave proximal instead of distal, the axis of correction of

axes of the bone become co-linear, and normal joint orientation is restored between the distal and proximal joints of that bone. The same correction is achieved when a closing wedge osteotomy of the magnitude of angulation

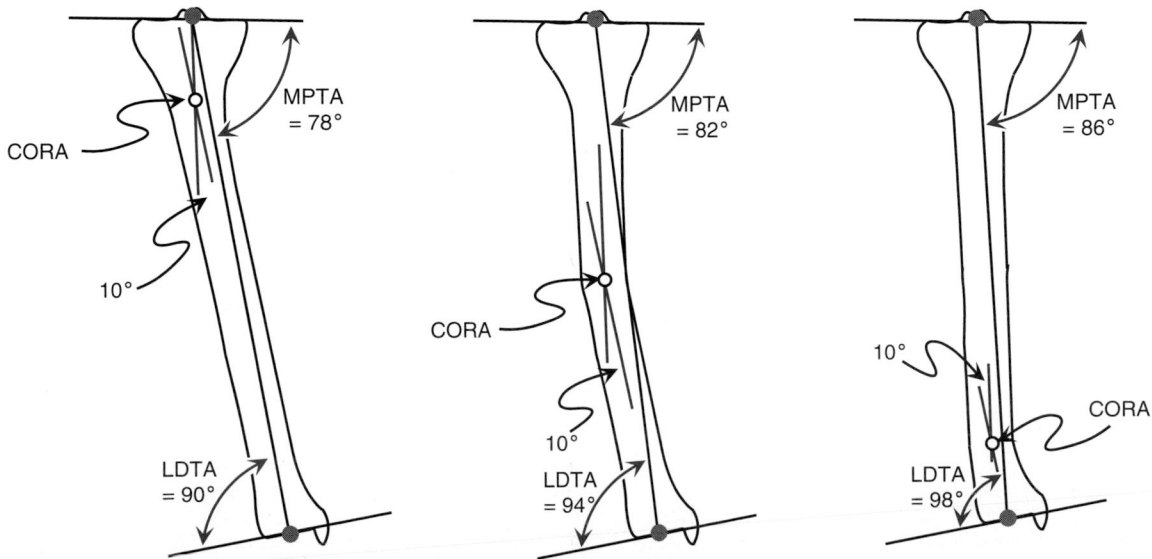

**FIGURE 62–5.** The location of deformities affects the joints. Three tibial 10° angular deformities. When the center of rotation of angulation (CORA) is near the ankle, the ankle joint orientation relative to the mechanical axis is affected (lateral distal tibial angle [LDTA]), but the knee joint orientation is unaltered (medial proximal tibial angle [MPTA]). The converse is true when the CORA is near the knee. Mid-diaphyseal deformities alter the joint orientation of the proximal and distal joints. (Redrawn from Paley, D. Principles of Deformity Correction. Heidelberg, Germany, Springer-Verlag, 2002.)

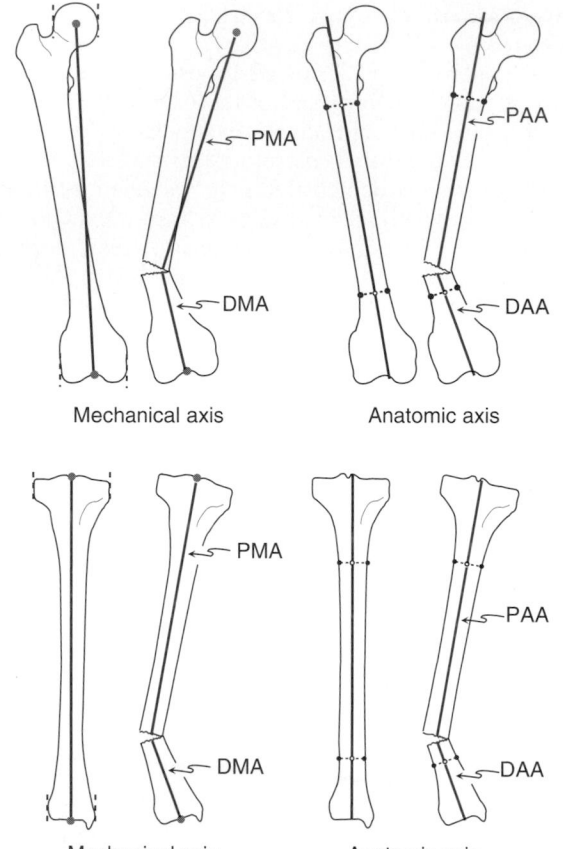

Mechanical axis          Anatomic axis

Mechanical axis          Anatomic axis

**Figure 62–6.** A deformity may be expressed as mechanical or anatomic axis angulation. When the femur or tibia is angulated, the axis line is also angulated. Where there was one axis line to represent the bone, there are now two axis lines: proximal and distal. In the tibia, because mechanical and anatomic axes are almost the same, the proximal mechanical axis (PMA) and proximal anatomic axis (PAA) lines are almost the same, as are the distal mechanical axis (DMA) and distal anatomic axis (DAA) lines. In the frontal-plane femur, because the mechanical and anatomic axis lines are not the same, the proximal mechanical axis and proximal anatomic axis lines and the distal mechanical axis and distal anatomic axis lines, respectively, are not the same. (Redrawn from Paley, D. Principles of Deformity Correction. Heidelberg, Germany, Springer-Verlag, 2002.)

the dome osteotomy and the CORA are matched (see Fig. 62–15).

The dome osteotomy is very useful for correction of deformities with intramedullary nailing because it is adjustable and has a large surface area of bone contact, allowing load sharing with the nail. The technique with intramedullary nailing is called fixator-assisted nailing[4] (Figs. 62–16 to 62–19).

## Plane of Angulation

A single-level angular deformity when reduced to two dimensions exists in only one plane. I have so far considered angulation only in the two anatomic reference planes: frontal and sagittal. Between the frontal and sagittal planes exist oblique planes. Clinical and radiographic assessments of deformity are conducted in two anatomic reference planes. Angulation seen on the anteroposterior (AP) and lateral views (i.e., biplanar) is evidence of an oblique-plane angulation (Fig. 62–20). The plane of

angulation can be calculated trigonometrically (Fig. 62–21) or determined graphically (Fig. 62–22). The graphic analysis is an approximation and is accurate within 2° to 4° when both angles are less than 45°.[3] For larger angles, the trigonometric formulas should be used. The orientation of the plane of angulation is expressed relative to the frontal or sagittal plane. Each plane of angulation contains two possible apical directions. For example, in the frontal plane, varus and valgus can exist, correlating with lateral and medial apical directions, respectively. The apical direction must be stated in addition to the orientation of the plane of angulation. The magnitude of angulation in the oblique plane of deformity is always greater than the magnitude of its frontal- and sagittal-plane projections.

In summary, there are four parameters that characterize an angular deformity: the level of the CORA, the orientation of the plane, the direction of the apex, and the magnitude of angulation. The graphic method of planning provides three of these parameters. The CORA method of anatomic or mechanical axis planning yields the remaining parameter.

## Multiapical Angulation

When more than one CORA is identified, the deformity is considered multiapical. The osteotomy solution for multiapical angular deformities can be resolved into a single-level solution or a multilevel solution. The single-level solution is obtained by extending the mechanical or anatomic axis lines of the proximal and distal joints toward each other. The intersection of the two axis lines is the resolution-point CORA. This point can be used to resolve the multiple CORA levels into one level to achieve a single-level osteotomy solution (Figs. 62–23 and 62–24). Alternatively, a separate osteotomy can be performed for each CORA. This is the multilevel osteotomy solution (Figs. 62–23 to 62–25). If the proximal and distal axis lines intersect between the proximal and distal ends of the

*Text continued on page 2536*

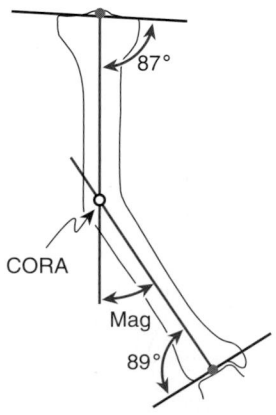

**Figure 62–7.** Center of rotation of angulation. The intersection point of the proximal and distal mechanical axis lines is the center of rotation of angulation (CORA). The magnitude of angulation (Mag) is measured between the proximal and distal axis lines. The CORA corresponds to the obvious apex of angulation. The knee and ankle are normally orientated to the proximal and distal axis lines, respectively. This is a uniapical angular deformity (i.e., single site of deformity). (Redrawn from Paley, D. Principles of Deformity Correction. Heidelberg, Germany, Springer-Verlag, 2002.)

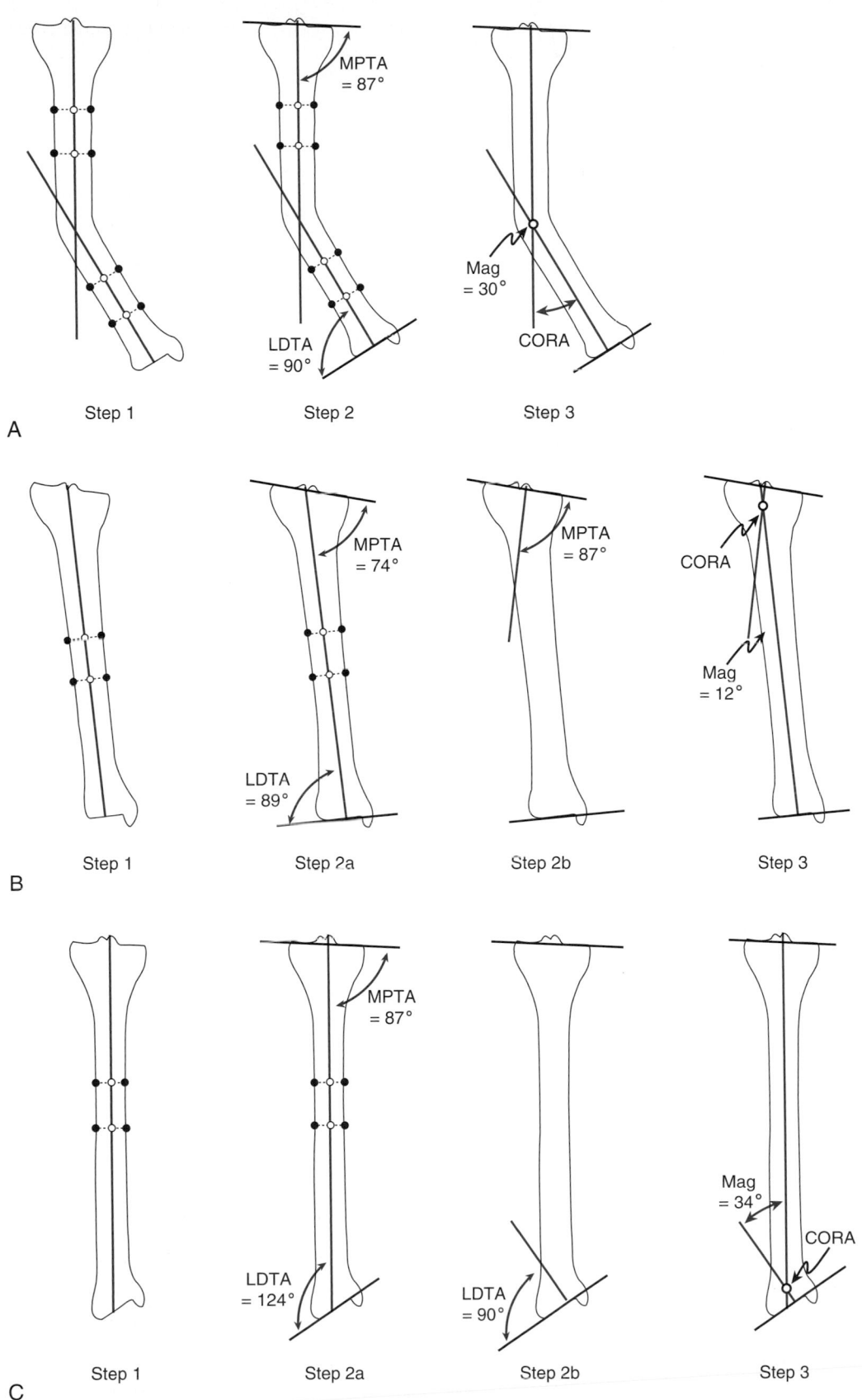

**FIGURE 62–8.** Tibial anatomic axis planning. *Step 1,* Draw the mid-diaphyseal lines to represent the diaphysis of the tibia. In examples *A* through *E,* each mid-diaphyseal line segment is the anatomic axis line for that segment of bone. *Step 2,* Perform the malorientation test between the proximal and distal-most mid-diaphyseal lines and the knee and ankle joint lines, respectively. Measure the medial proximal tibial angle (MPTA) to the proximal-most tibial mid-diaphyseal line.

*Illustration continued on following page*

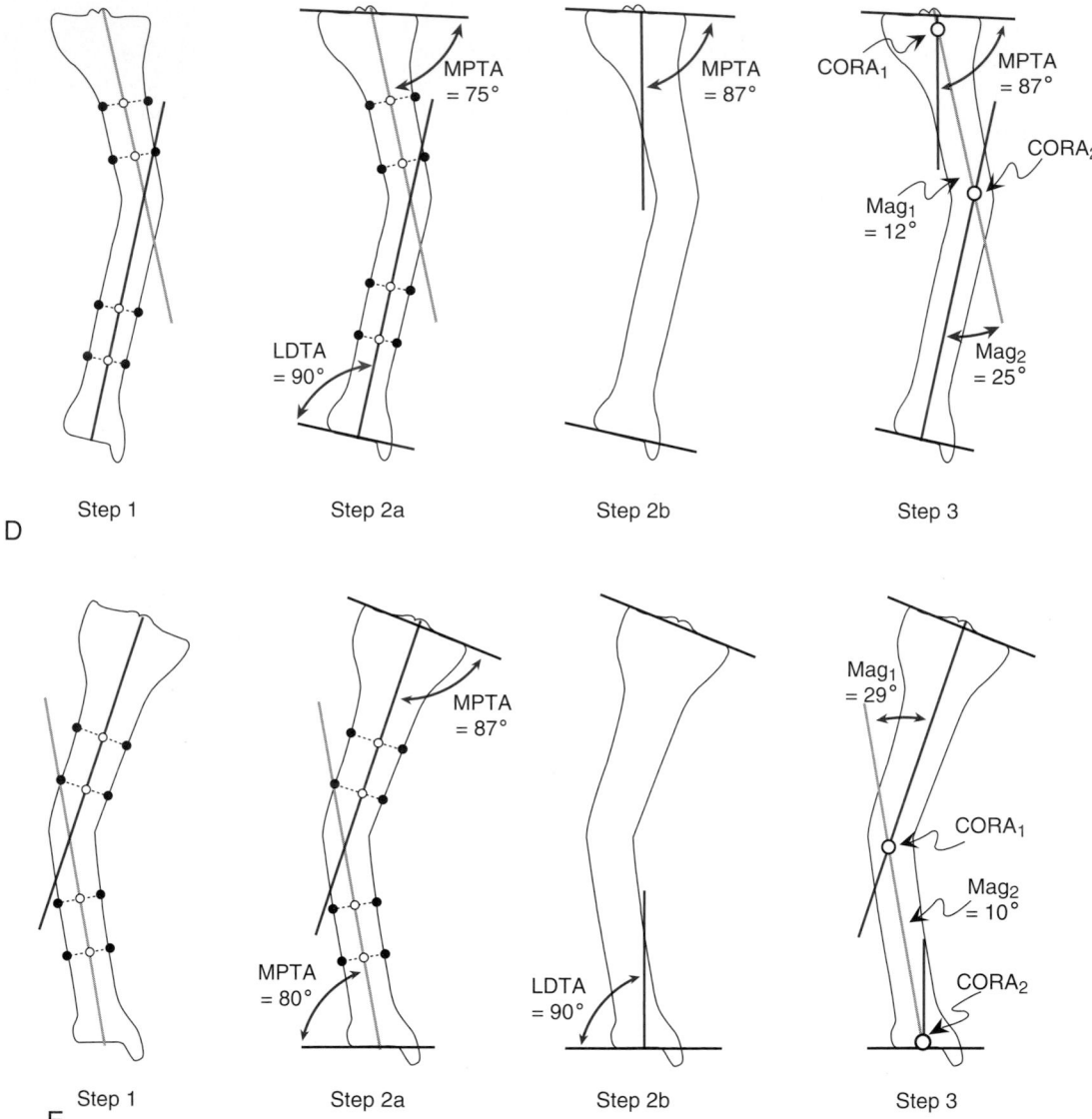

**FIGURE 62–8** *Continued.* In *A, C,* and *E,* if the MPTA is normal, there is no more proximal center of rotation of angulation (CORA)or anatomic axis line. In *B* and *D,* if the MPTA is abnormal, draw an anatomic axis line referenced to the knee joint orientation line. The starting point can be obtained from the opposite, normal side, if available, or in an adult, this line can be drawn from the apex of the medial tibial spine. Use the MPTA of the contralateral normal side, if available, as a template angle. If the opposite MPTA is unavailable or abnormal, the average normal MPTA of 87° is used instead. Measure the lateral distal tibial angle (LDTA) to the distal-most tibial mid-diaphyseal line. In *A, B,* and *D,* if the LDTA is normal, there is no distal CORA. In *C* and *E,* if the LDTA is abnormal, draw an anatomic axis line referenced to the ankle joint orientation line. The starting point can be obtained from the opposite, normal side, if available, or in an adult, this line can be drawn from a point 4 mm medial to the ankle joint's center point. Use the LDTA of the contralateral normal side, if available, as a template angle. If the opposite LDTA is unavailable or abnormal, the average normal LDTA of 90° is used instead. *Step 3,* Decide whether the case is uniapical (*A, B, C*) or multiapical (*D, E*) angulation. Mark the CORAs, and measure the magnitudes of angulation (Mag). (Redrawn from Paley, D. Principles of Deformity Correction. Heidelberg, Germany, Springer-Verlag, 2002.)

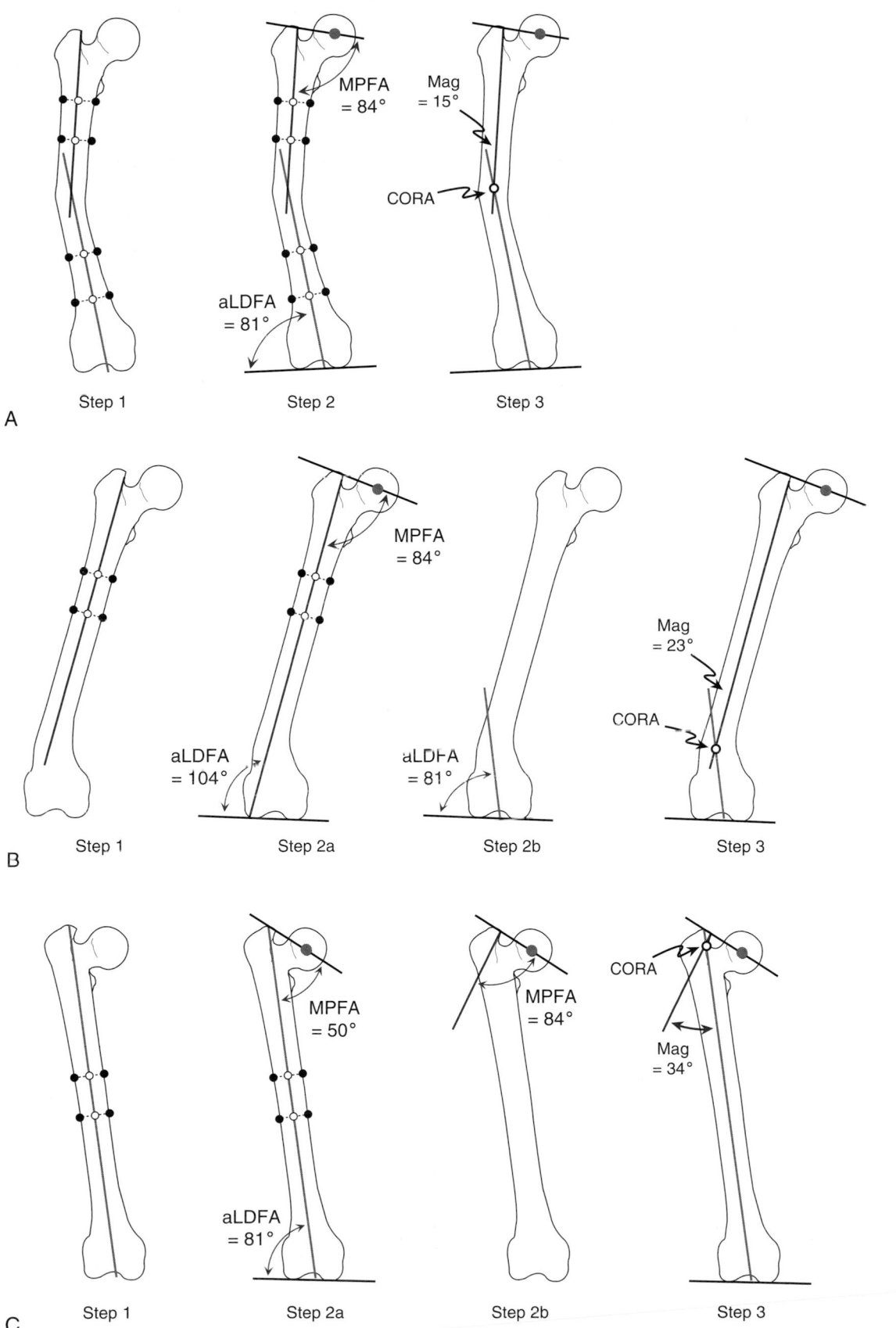

**FIGURE 62–9.** Femoral anatomic axis planning. *Step 1,* Draw the mid-diaphyseal line to represent the diaphysis of the femur. In examples *A* through *E,* each mid-diaphyseal line segment is the anatomic axis line for that segment of bone. *Step 2,* Perform the malorientation test between the distal-most and proximal-most mid-diaphyseal lines and the knee and hip joint lines, respectively. Measure the anatomic lateral distal femoral angle (aLDFA) to the distal-most femoral mid-diaphyseal line.

*Illustration continued on following page*

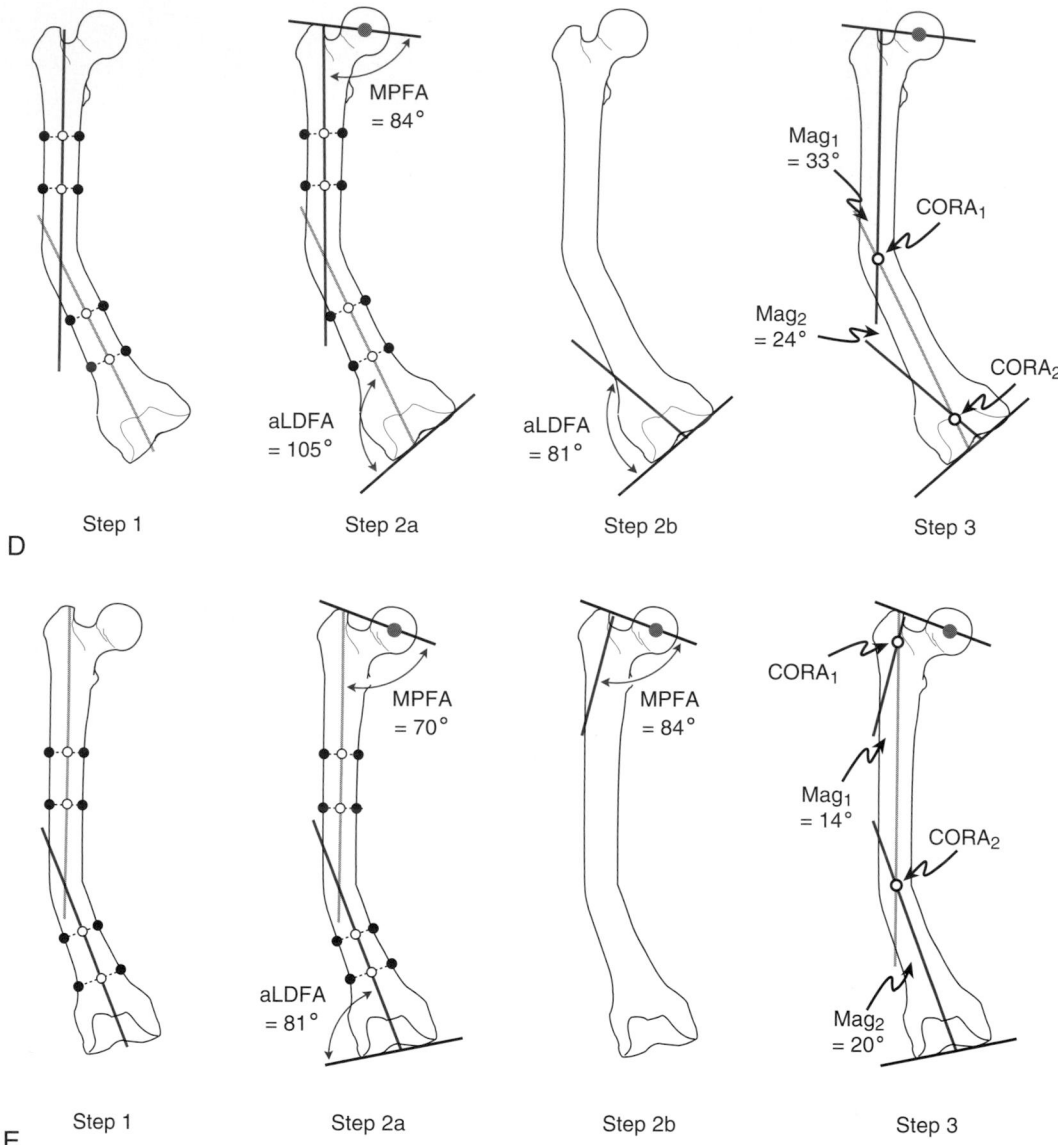

**Figure 62–9** *Continued.* In *A, C,* and *E,* if the aLDFA is normal, there is no more distal center of rotation of angulation (CORA) or anatomic axis line. In *B* and *D,* if the aLDFA is abnormal, draw an anatomic axis line referenced to the knee joint orientation line. The starting point can be obtained from the opposite, normal side, if available, or in an adult, this line can be drawn starting 1 cm medial to the center point of the knee joint. Use the aLDFA of the contralateral normal side, if available, as a template angle. If the opposite aLDFA is unavailable or abnormal, the average normal aLDFA of 81° is used instead. Measure the medial proximal femoral angle (MPFA) to the proximal-most femoral mid-diaphyseal line. In *A, B,* and *D,* if the MPFA is normal, there is no more proximal CORA. In *C* and *E,* if the MPFA is abnormal, draw an anatomic axis line referenced to the hip joint orientation line. The starting point can be obtained from the opposite, normal side, if available, or in an adult, this line can be drawn passing through the piriformis fossa. Use the MPFA of the contralateral normal side, if available, as a template angle. If the opposite MPFA is unavailable or abnormal, the average normal MPFA of 84° is used instead. *Step 3,* Decide whether this is uniapical (*A, B, C*) or multiapical (*D, E*) angulation. Mark the CORAs, and measure the magnitudes of angulation (Mag). (Redrawn from Paley, D. *Principles of Deformity Correction.* Heidelberg, Germany, Springer-Verlag, 2002.)

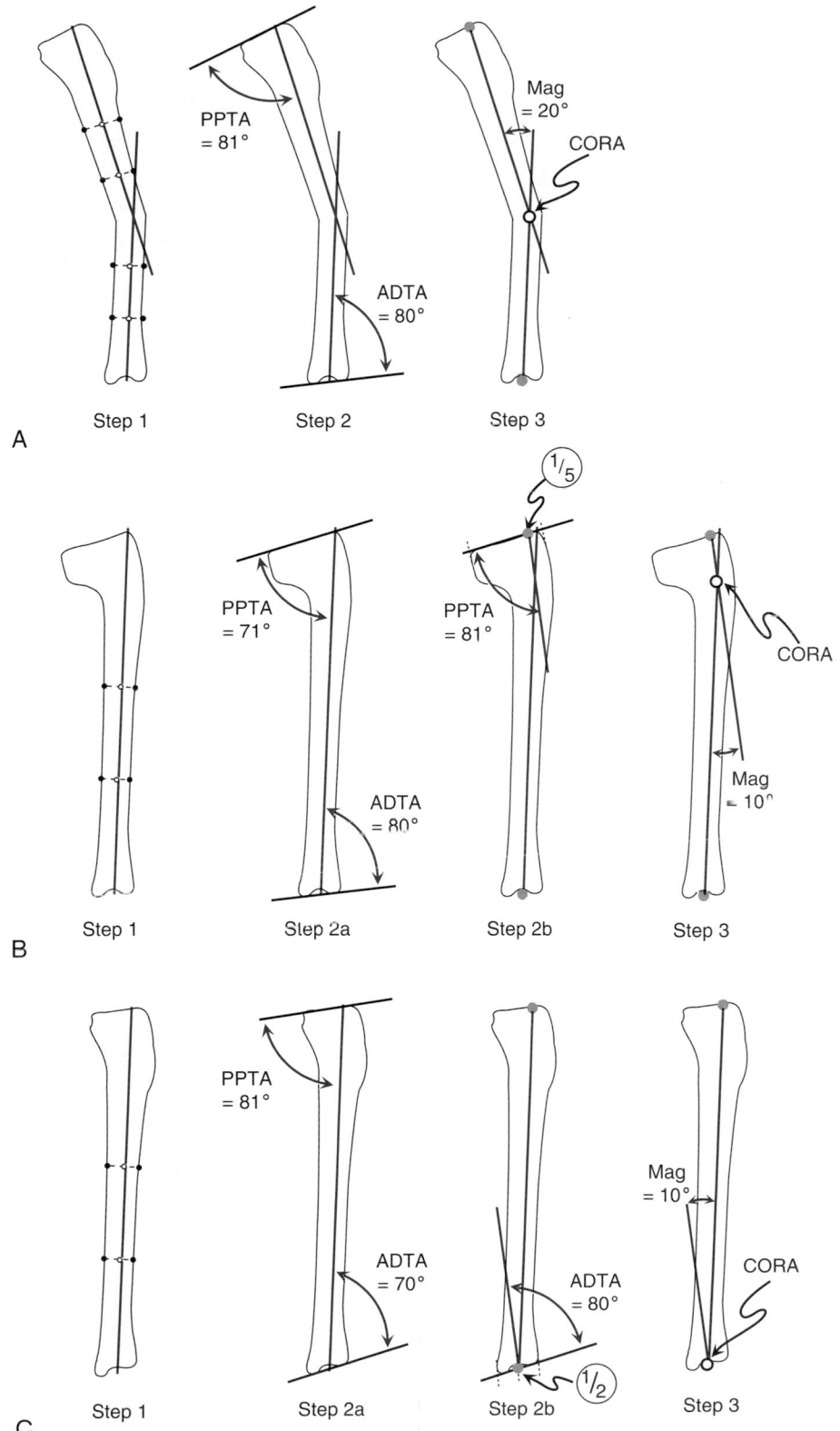

**FIGURE 62–10.** Sagittal-plane anatomic axis planning of tibial deformity correction. *Step 1,* Draw the mid-diaphyseal line to represent the diaphysis of the tibia. In examples *A* through *F,* each mid-diaphyseal line segment is the anatomic axis line for that segment of bone. *Step 2,* Perform the malorientation test between the proximal and distal-most mid-diaphyseal lines and the knee and ankle joint lines, respectively. Measure the posterior proximal tibial angle (PPTA) to the proximal-most tibial mid-diaphyseal line.

*Illustration continued on following page*

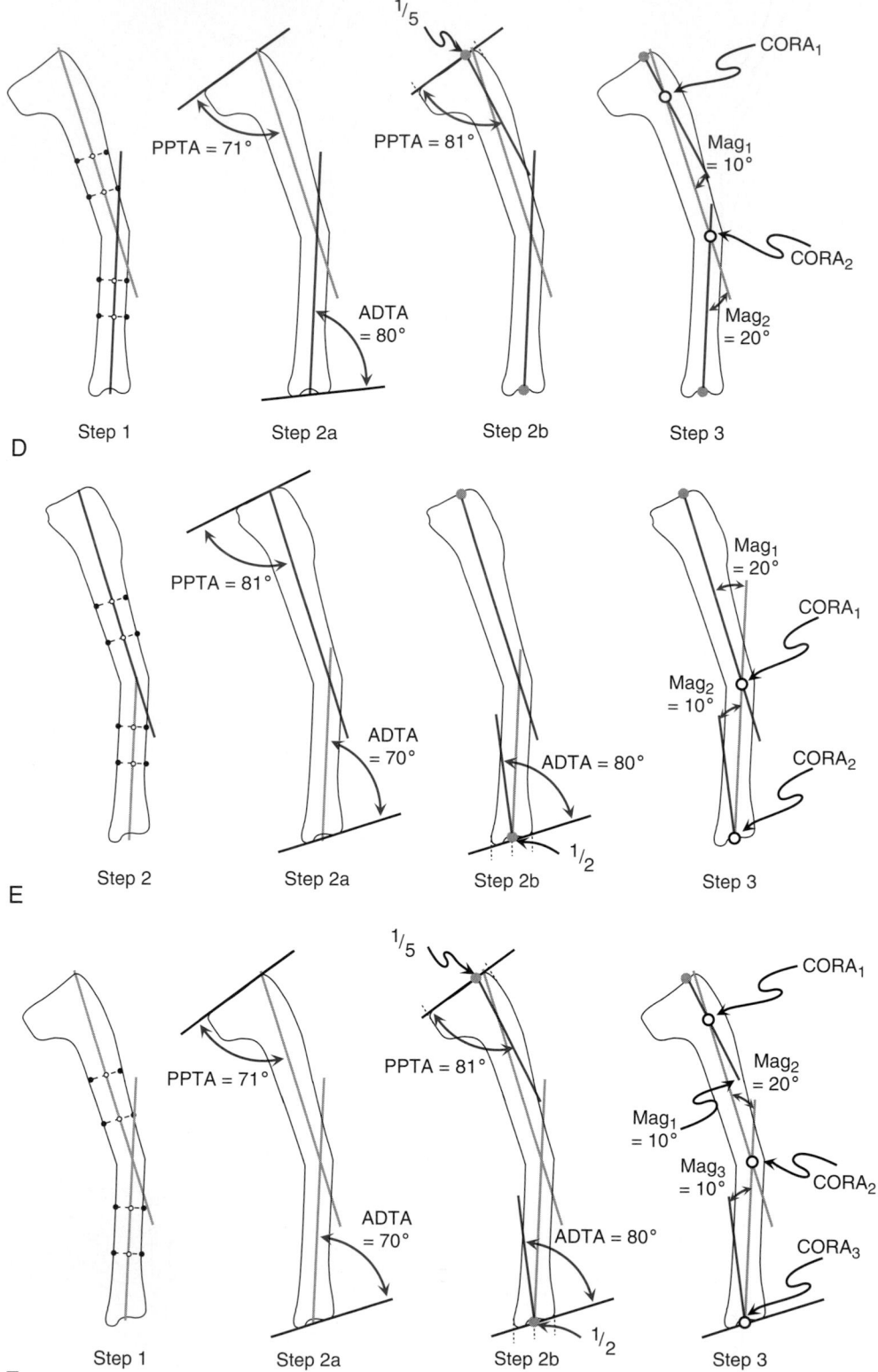

**Figure 62–10** *Continued.* In *A, C,* and *E,* if the PPTA is normal, there is no more proximal center of rotation of angulation (CORA) or anatomic axis line. In *B, D,* and *F,* if the PPTA is abnormal, draw an anatomic axis line referenced to the knee joint orientation line. The starting point can be obtained from the opposite, normal side, if available, or in an adult, this line can be drawn from the point that is one fifth of the way back from the anterior edge of the joint. Use the PPTA of the contralateral normal side, if available, as a template angle. If the opposite PPTA is unavailable or abnormal, the average normal PPTA of 80° is used instead. Measure the anterior distal tibial angle (ADTA) to the distal-most tibial mid-diaphyseal line. In *A, B,* and *D,* if the ADTA is normal, there is no more distal CORA. In *C, E,* and *F,* if the ADTA is abnormal, draw an anatomic axis line referenced to the ankle joint orientation line. The starting point can be obtained from the opposite, normal side, if available, or in an adult, this line can be drawn from the mid point of the ankle joint line on the lateral view. Use the ADTA of the contralateral normal side, if available, as a template angle. If the opposite ADTA is unavailable or abnormal, the average normal ADTA of 90° is used instead. *Step 3,* Decide whether this is uniapical (*A, B, C*) or multiapical (*D, E, F*) angulation. Mark the CORAs, and measure the magnitudes of angulation (Mag). (Redrawn from Paley, D. Principles of Deformity Correction. Heidelberg, Germany, Springer-Verlag, 2002.)

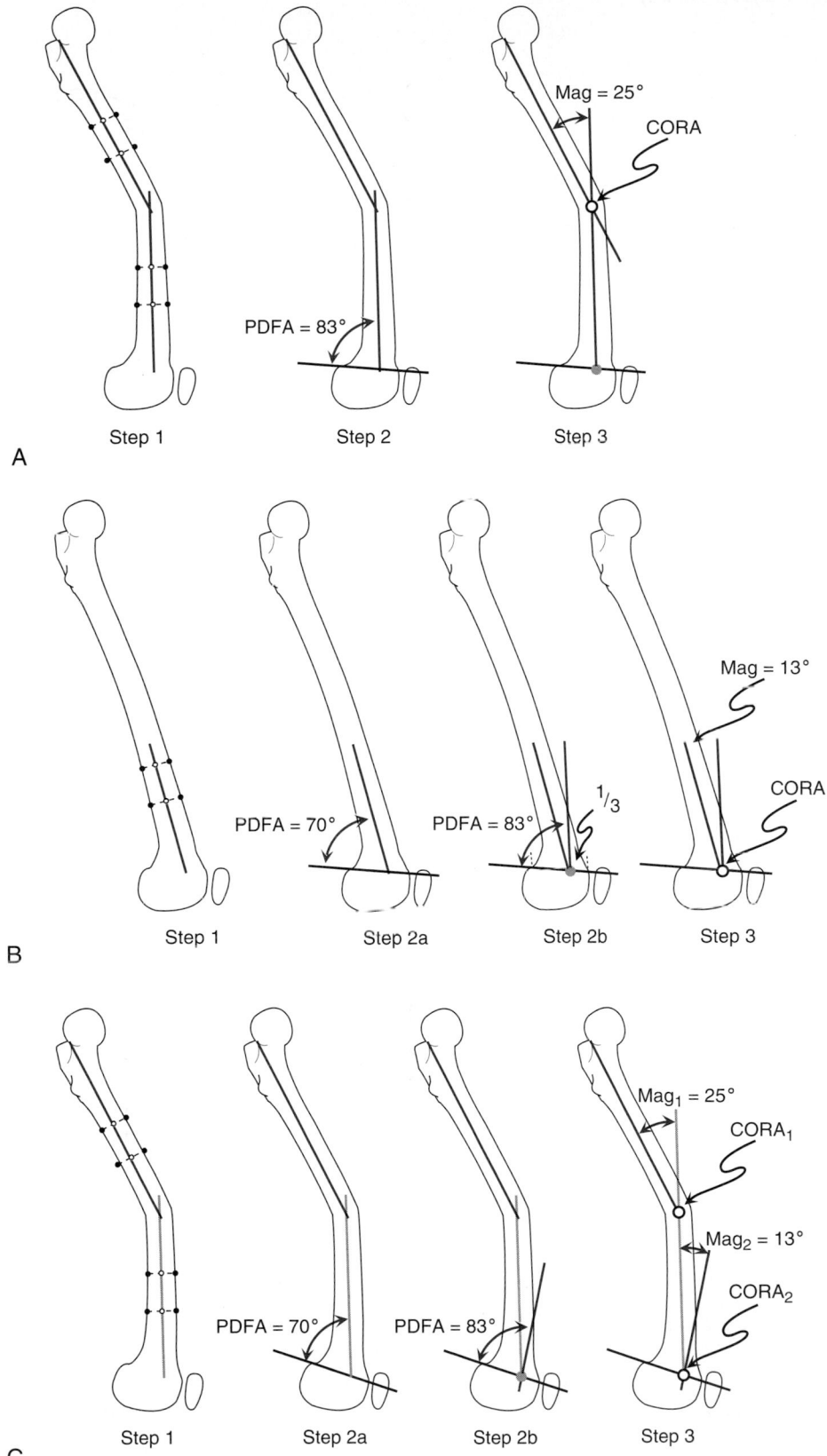

**Figure 62–11.** Sagittal-plane anatomic axis planning for femoral deformity correction. *Step 1,* Draw the mid-diaphyseal line to represent the diaphysis of the femur. In examples *A–C,* each mid-diaphyseal line segment is the anatomic axis line for that segment of bone. *Step 2,* Perform the malorientation test between the distal mid-diaphyseal line and the knee joint line. Measure the posterior distal femoral angle (PDFA) to the distal-most femoral mid-diaphyseal line. In *A,* if the PDFA is normal, there is no more distal center of rotation of angulation (CORA) or anatomic axis line. In *B* and *C,* if the PDFA is abnormal, draw an anatomic axis line referenced to the knee joint orientation line. The starting point can be obtained from the opposite, normal side, if available, or in an adult, this line can be drawn starting one third of the way back from the anterior edge of the joint line. Use the PDFA of the contralateral normal side, if available, as a template angle. If the opposite PDFA is unavailable or abnormal, the average normal PDFA of 83° is used instead. *Step 3,* Decide whether this is uniapical (*A, B*) or multiapical (*C*) angulation. Mark the CORAs, and measure the magnitudes of angulation (Mag). (Redrawn from Paley, D. Principles of Deformity Correction. Heidelberg, Germany, Springer-Verlag, 2002.)

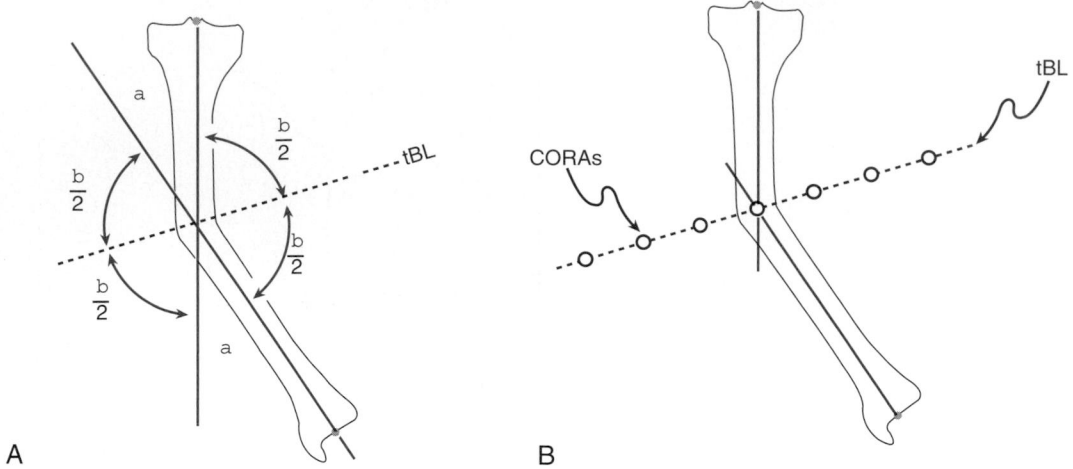

**FIGURE 62–12.** Transverse bisector line. *A,* The axis lines create two transverse angles (β) and two longitudinal angles (α). A bisector line divides an angle into two equal halves. The transverse bisector line (tBL) divides the transverse angle into two equal halves. *B,* All the points on the transverse bisector line are centers of rotation of angulation (CORAs). (Redrawn from Paley, D. Principles of Deformity Correction. Heidelberg, Germany, Springer-Verlag, 2002.)

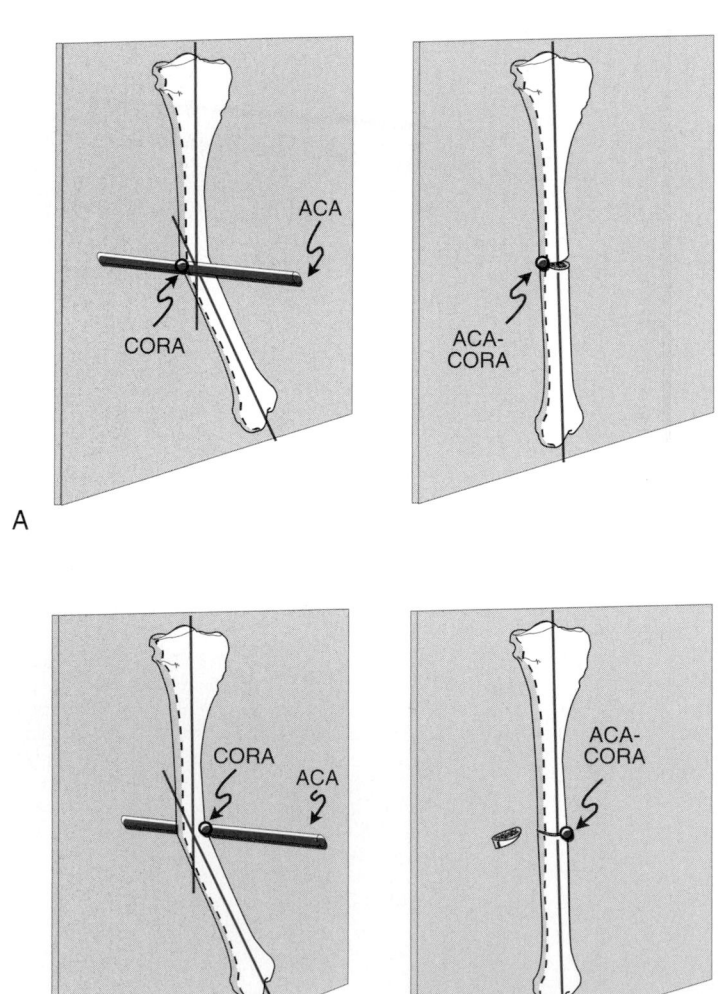

**FIGURE 62–13.** Osteotomy rule 1. Angulation is changed by rotation of a bone segment around an axis, the axis of correction of angulation (ACA). The ACA *(rod)* can pass through the opening wedge center of rotation of angulation (CORA) *(circle),* a point is referred to as an ACA-CORA. If an osteotomy passes through the ACA-CORA, correction produces pure angulation at the osteotomy site, and the proximal and distal axis lines of the bone become co-linear. *A,* Opening wedge axis of angulation. If the ACA-CORA is on the convex cortex, an opening wedge angulation results. *B,* Closing wedge axis of angulation. If the ACA-CORA is on the concave cortex, a closing wedge angulation occurs. (Redrawn from Paley, D. Principles of Deformity Correction. Heidelberg, Germany, Springer-Verlag, 2002.)

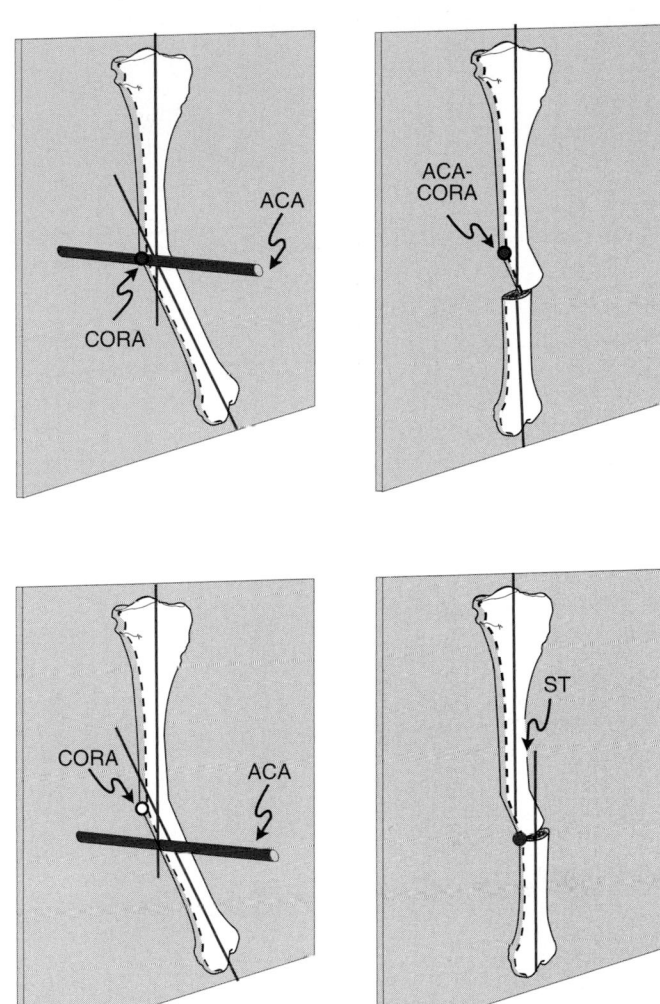

**FIGURE 62–14.** Osteotomy rules 2 and 3. *A,* Osteotomy rule 2. When the osteotomy is at a level different from that of the center of rotation of angulation (CORA) but the axis of correction of angulation (ACA) passes through the CORA (ACA-CORA), the correction produces angulation and translation at the level of the osteotomy site. *B,* Osteotomy rule 3. When the osteotomy and the ACA are at the same level but are at a level different from that of the CORA, the axis lines become parallel but translated to each other (i.e., secondary translation [ST]) after angular correction, even though the bone ends at the osteotomy site angulate without translation. The translation is a secondary deformity produced by angular correction at a level different from that of the CORA. (Redrawn from Paley, D. Principles of Deformity Correction. Heidelberg, Germany, Springer-Verlag, 2002.)

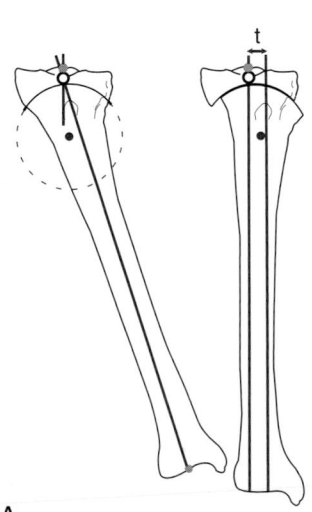
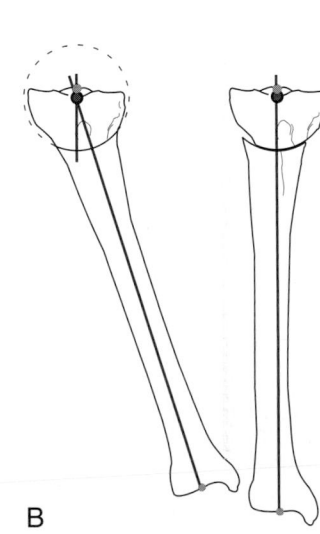

**FIGURE 62–15.** Dome osteotomy. *A,* The Maquet dome osteotomy (concave distal) is used for a varus tibia with the apex of the dome osteotomy passing through the center of rotation of angulation (CORA), even though the osteotomy passes through the CORA. The bone ends translate medially at the osteotomy line, producing a secondary medial translation deformity and incomplete correction of the varus due to the translational deformity (i.e., osteotomy rule 3). *B,* Focal dome osteotomy for this CORA should be done with the concavity proximal. Realignment of the axis lines with angulation and lateral translation of the osteotomy line is shown (i.e., osteotomy rule 2). (Redrawn from Paley, D. Principles of Deformity Correction. Heidelberg, Germany, Springer-Verlag, 2002.)

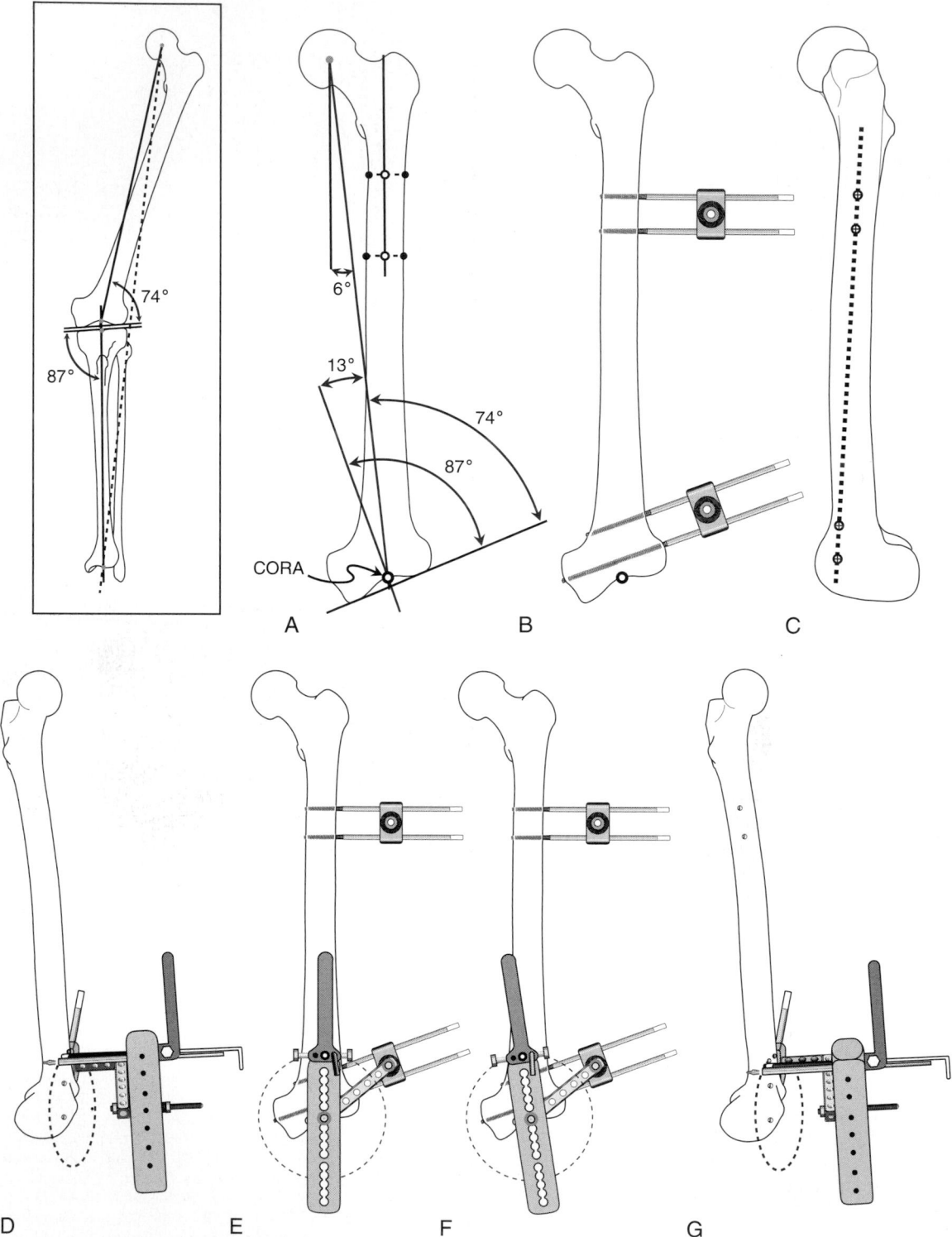

**Figure 62–16.** Fixator-assisted nailing of a distal femoral valgus deformity: retrograde technique. *A,* Valgus deformity of the distal femur (13°), with the center of rotation of angulation (CORA) at the joint line level. *B,* Two pairs of external fixation pins are inserted from the lateral side. *C,* Distally, the pins are anterior in the femur to keep them out of the planned nail path. Proximally, the pins are mid-diaphyseal because the retrograde nail will stop short of the pins. *D,* The focal dome drill guide is attached to the distal pair of pins. The drill guide is suspended above the soft tissues of the thigh. *E,* Frontal view of the focal dome drill guide assembly. The pivot point of the guide is over the CORA. The outrigger shown here creates this pivot point in space. The outrigger is adjusted, using the image intensifier, until the pivot point on the outrigger matches the CORA. The focal dome drill guide can rotate side to side on the CORA. The hole chosen for the osteotomy must leave a sufficiently large segment distally to allow locking screw fixation. A transverse incision is made in the skin, and a longitudinal split is made in the quadriceps muscle. Using a drill guide for protection, multiple drill holes are drilled into the femur with a 4.8- or 3.8-mm drill bit. The holes follow a circular pattern of a set radius determined by the focal dome drill guide. *F, G,* It is difficult to drill the edge holes. The drill bit tends to walk on the sloping surface of the bone. By using the constrained guide probe, it is easier to drill the edge holes.

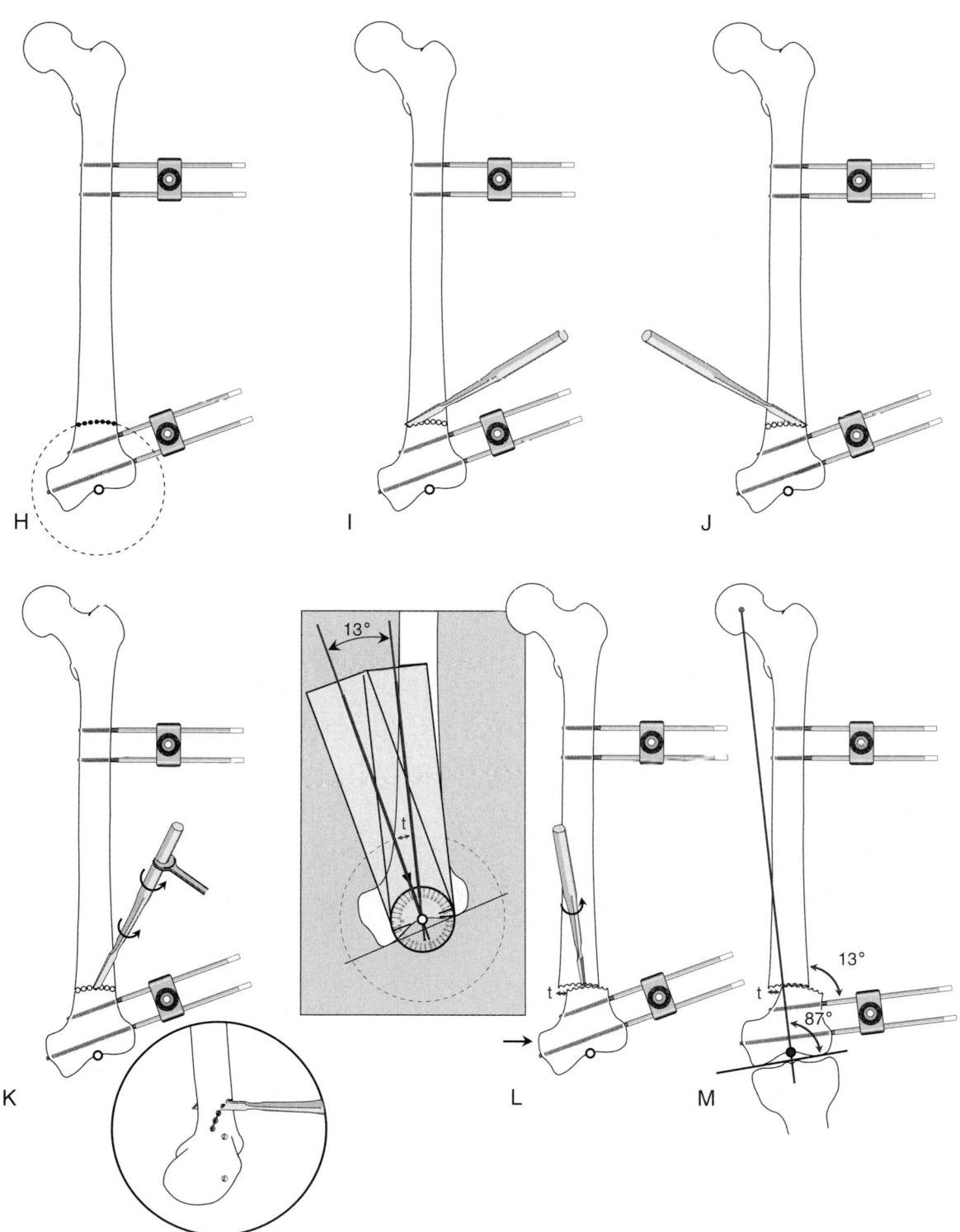

**FIGURE 62–16** *Continued. H,* Circular pattern of holes after completion of drilling. *I, J,* An osteotome is used to cut the medial and lateral edges of the bone. *K,* The osteotome is then inserted into the center of the bone, going through both cortices. The osteotome is twisted to spread and crack the bone, and the direction of twisting is based on the direction of displacement desired. For medial translation, the osteotome is twisted clockwise; for lateral translation, it is twisted counterclockwise. *L,* The osteotomy is displaced laterally before any angulation is performed. The amount of translation is determined preoperatively using a goniometer. The surgeon centers the goniometer over the CORA, and it is opened to the desired degrees of correction. The necessary translation at the level of the osteotomy is the distance between the two arms of the goniometer at that level. *M,* The osteotomy is then angulated.

*Illustration continued on following page*

bone, a single-level angulation osteotomy solution may be practical, although a multilevel osteotomy solution may be preferable (see Fig. 62–23). If the proximal and distal axis lines intersect proximal or distal to the proximal or distal joints of the deformed bone, the osteotomy solution can be resolved into a combination of angulation and translation at one level or into multiple levels of angular correction (see Fig. 62–24). If the proximal and distal axis lines are parallel (i.e., do not intersect), the deformity can be considered a translation and be treated by translation osteotomy at a single level, if possible. This single-level solution may not be practical when the distance between the proximal and distal axis lines is large, because bone contact across the osteotomy would be too little or lost (see Fig. 62–25). The preferable solution is equal and opposite angulation at two levels (see Fig. 62–25).

The proximal and distal axis lines of a bone are linked to the proximal and distal joints. To maintain normal joint orientation, the proximal and distal axis lines cannot be altered. The middle axis line represents the orientation of the diaphyseal segments of the bone. Middle lines can be redrawn, altering the levels of the CORAs and therefore the osteotomy levels. This property of multiapical deformity planning can be used to change the levels of osteotomies without producing a secondary translation deformity and can be useful when the CORAs are at undesirable levels. By altering the middle lines, the levels of the CORAs can be moved to the levels chosen (e.g., from diaphyseal to metaphyseal levels) (Fig. 62–26).

## Translation Deformity

Translation deformity most commonly results from displacement after a fracture or osteotomy. The proximal and distal bone axes are parallel but displaced to each other, with isolated translation deformity (Fig. 62–27). The direction of displacement is described as the distal segment relative to the proximal segment. The magnitude of translation is measured as the distance between the proximal and distal axis lines. The level of translation depends on the level of discontinuity of the bone. Two equal but opposite levels of angulation are equivalent to a translation deformity (Fig. 62–28). Conversely, a translation deformity from a fracture can be resolved into two opposite and equal angular deformities (see Fig. 62–28). The levels of these deformities are adjustable (e.g., adjusting the middle axis line). The osteotomy solutions for translation deformity are a single-level translation or two levels of angulation (see Fig. 62–28).

The plane of translation deformity can be determined

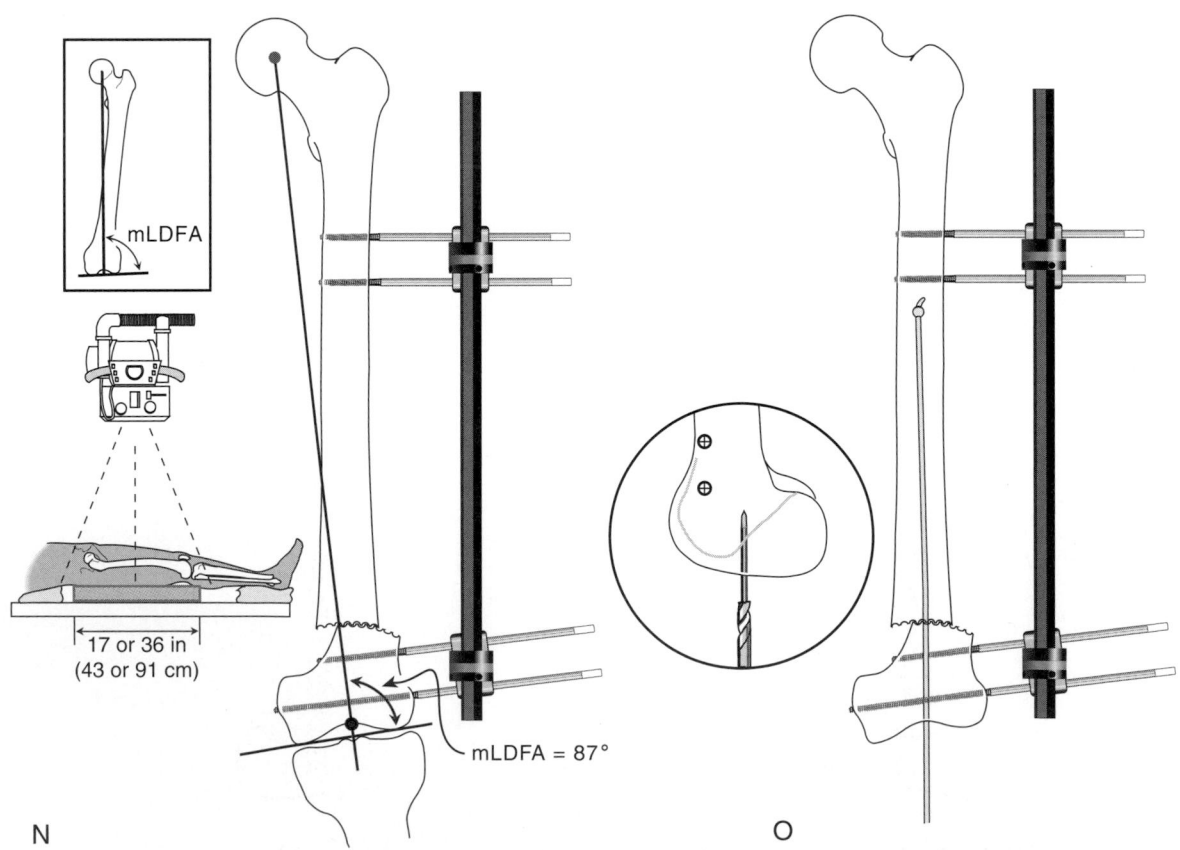

**N**    **O**

**FIGURE 62–16** *Continued. N,* To confirm that the desired correction has been achieved, an intraoperative radiograph is obtained and the LDFA measured. If the desired correction has been achieved, nailing can begin. If the correction obtained provides an LDFA of more than 1° from the goal, the fixator needs to be readjusted and the radiography repeated. *O,* A supracondylar nail is then inserted. The starting point is at the edge of Blumensaat's line, which is in the intercondylar notch region. A wire is inserted percutaneously into the correct starting site and checked on the anteroposterior and lateral radiographic images. The wire is over-reamed with a 4.8-mm cannulated drill bit. The reamer ball-tipped guide wire is then inserted through the hole.

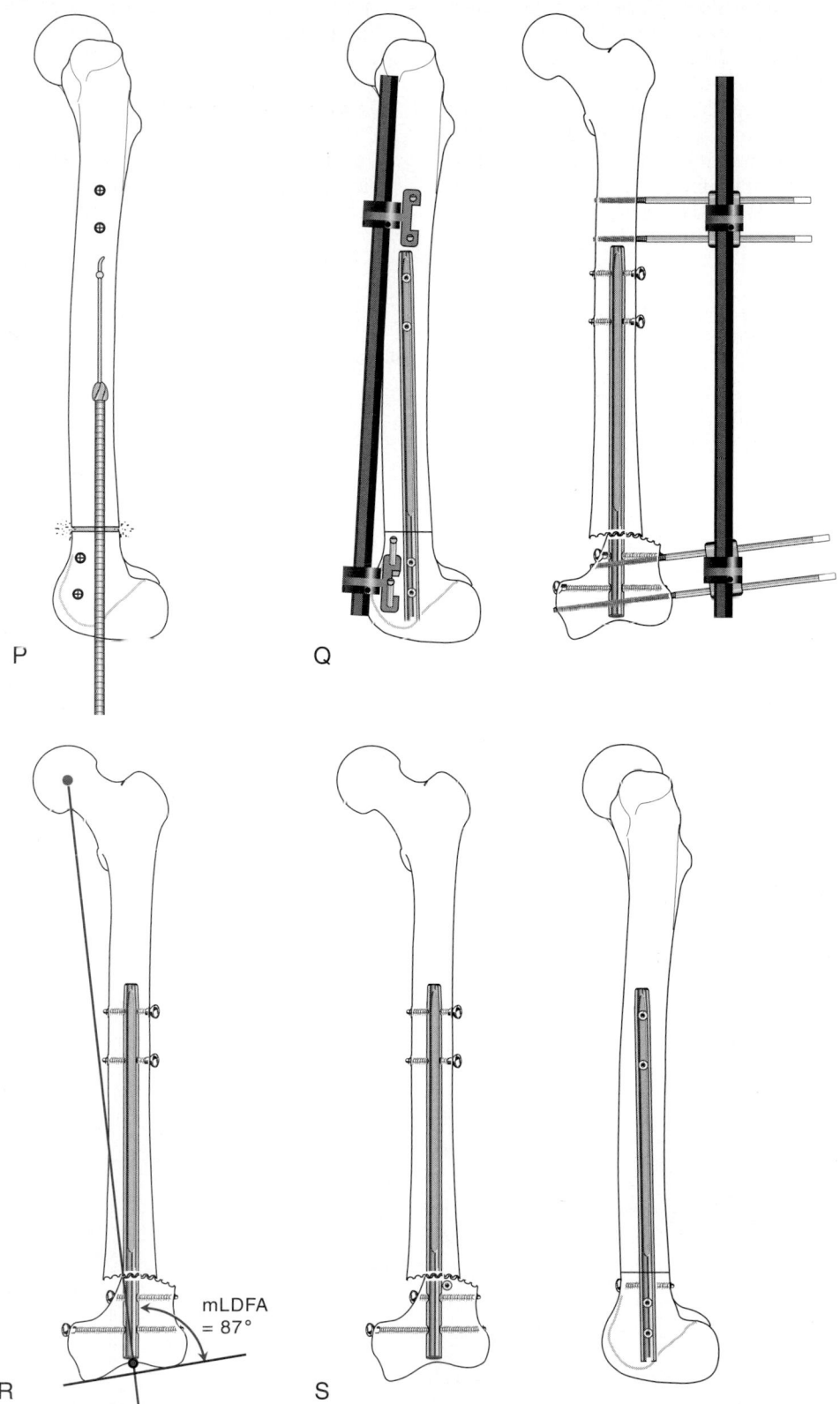

**FIGURE 62–16** *Continued.* *P,* The femur is reamed in a retrograde direction. The reamings exit the osteotomy site and serve as an auto bone graft. *Q,* A nail is inserted and locked proximally and distally. The distal screws are easier to insert from the medial side to avoid collision between the locking guide and the fixator. The fixator body is anterior to the femur so that it does not obstruct visualization of the femur by the image intensifier. *R,* The fixator is then removed, and the nail maintains the correction. *S,* For additional stability, interference screws can be inserted to narrow the medullary canal. Ideally, this should be done before removing the external fixator. (Redrawn from Paley, D. Principles of Deformity Correction. Heidelberg, Germany, Springer-Verlag, 2002.)

graphically or trigonometrically (Fig. 62–29). The magnitude of translation in the oblique plane can be measured from the graph. As with oblique-plane angulation, the magnitude of oblique-plane translation is greater than the translation measured on the AP and lateral views. Unlike angulation assessment, graphic analysis of oblique-plane translation is accurate rather than approximate. The translation graph determines the orientation of the plane and the direction and magnitude of translation.

## Angulation and Translation

When angulation and translation deformities occur together, the CORA of the angulation is moved proximal or distal to the level of the original fracture. The closer the CORA is moved toward the knee, the greater is the effect of angulation on knee joint orientation. Conversely, the farther the CORA is moved away from the knee, the greater is the effect of angulation on the hip or ankle. The effect of

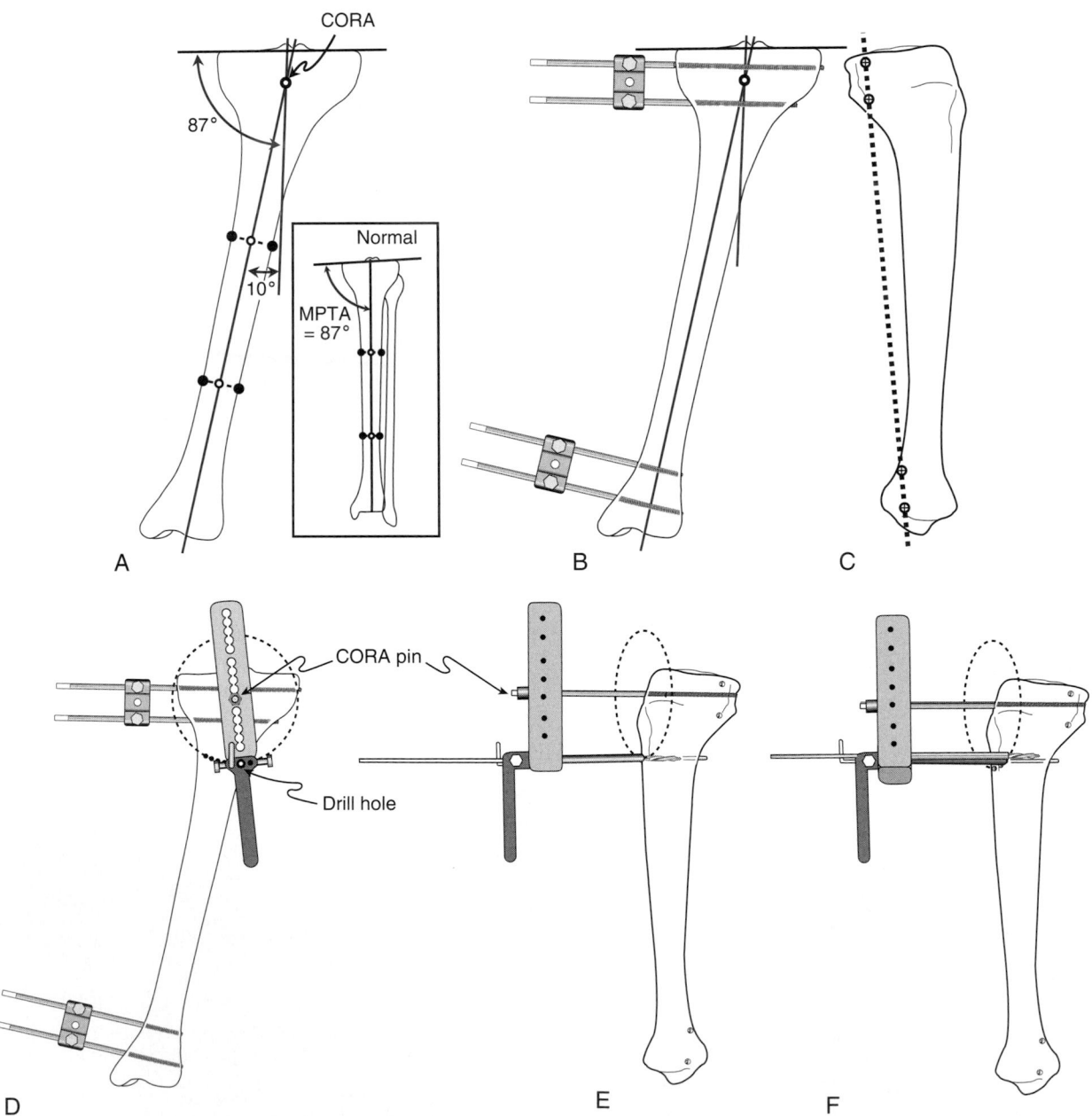

**FIGURE 62–17.** Fixator-assisted nailing of a tibial varus deformity. *A,* Tibial varus deformity correction is planned by using the anatomic axis method. The center of rotation of angulation (CORA) is in the proximal metaphysis. The magnitude of angulation is 10°. The normal, opposite tibia shows the anatomic axis (i.e., mid-diaphyseal line). Because the nail must follow the mid-diaphyseal line, the point at which this line intersects the knee joint is the optimal starting point (in this case, the medial tibial spine). *B,* Two pairs of fixator pins are inserted very proximally and very distally in the tibia. *C,* The pins are located posteriorly in the tibia, outside the path of the intramedullary nail. *D,* A half pin is inserted into the CORA, perpendicular to the frontal plane. The focal dome drill hole guide pivots around the pin. Multiple drill holes are made in a circular pattern. *E,* Lateral view of focal dome construct. *F,* With the constrained guide, the edge holes are easier to drill.

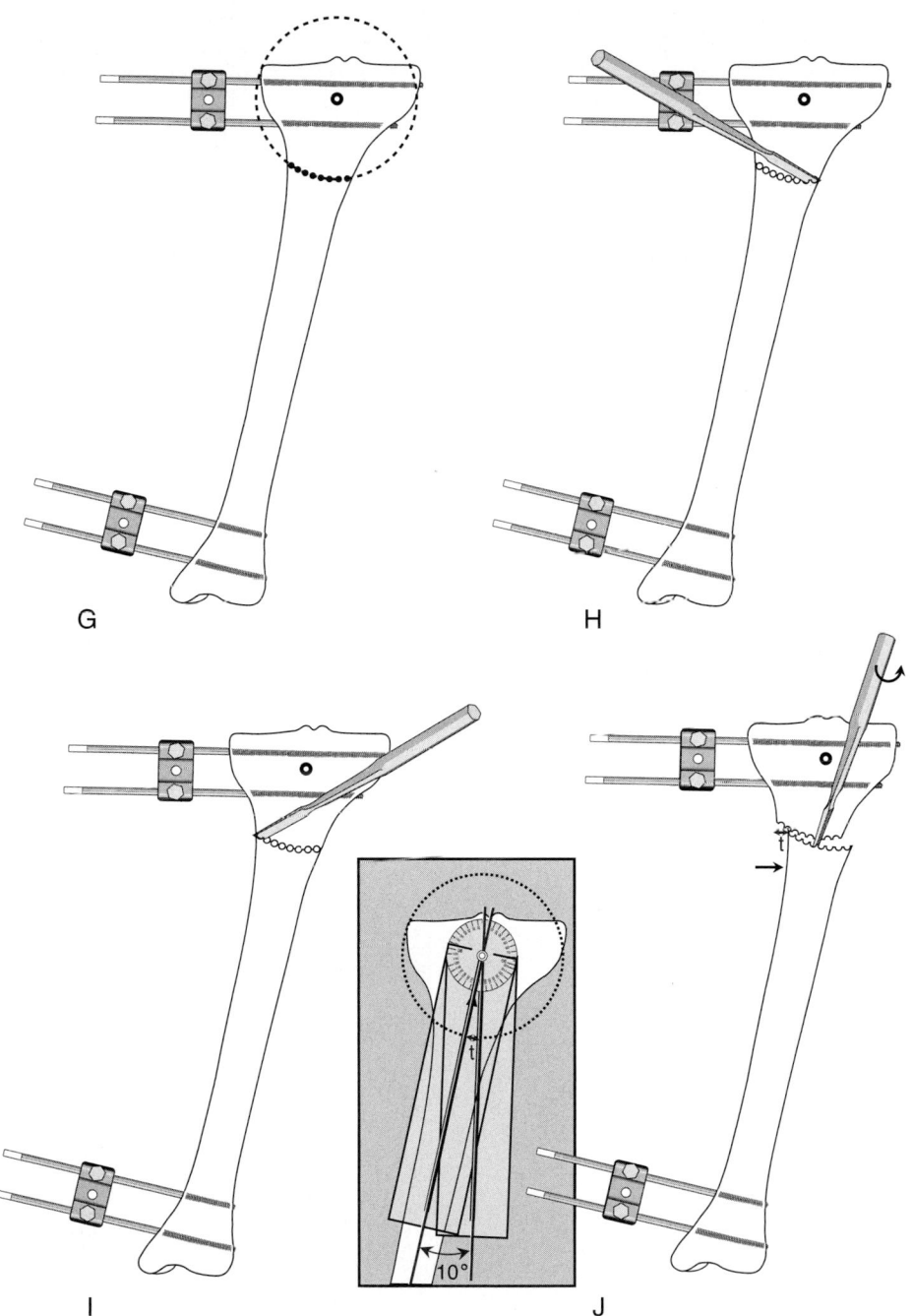

**FIGURE 62–17** *Continued. G,* The circular pattern of the drill holes after completion. *H, I,* The edge holes are cut first with the osteotome. *J,* The osteotome is inserted into the center and then twisted to complete the osteotomy. The osteotome is twisted counterclockwise to translate the bone laterally. The amount of initial translation (T) required can be estimated by using the goniometer method preoperatively.

*Illustration continued on following page*

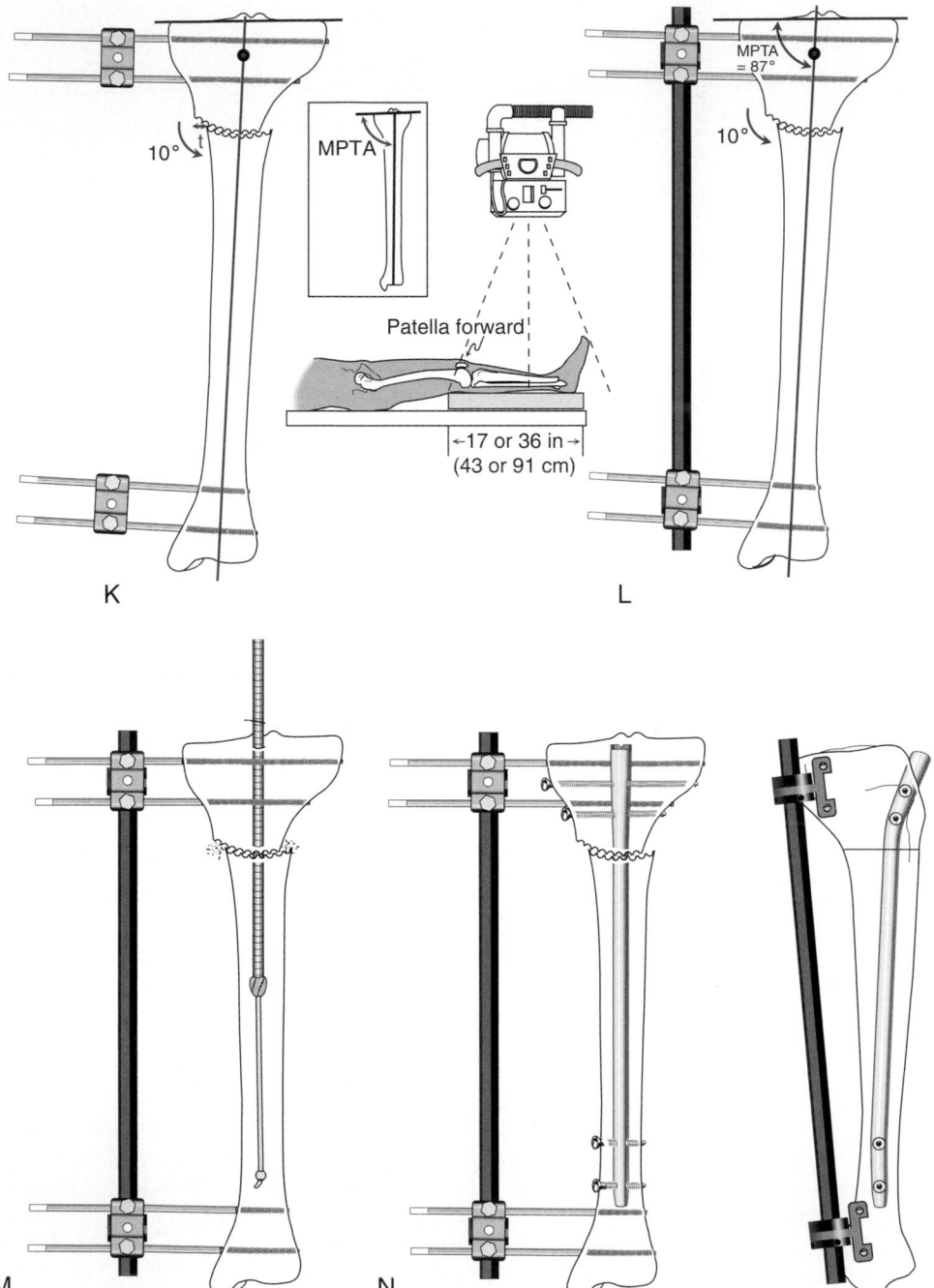

**FIGURE 62–17** *Continued. K,* The osteotomy is then angulated. *L,* The fixator is applied to the pins to hold the correction. An anteroposterior radiograph of the tibia is obtained and the medial proximal tibial angle (MPTA) measured. If the desired correction has been achieved, the nail is inserted. If the desired correction has not been achieved, the fixator is adjusted and the radiography repeated. *M,* The tibia is then reamed. *N,* The nail is inserted and locked proximally and distally. The fixator body is posterior to the pins to avoid interfering with the locking screws and the image intensifier view.

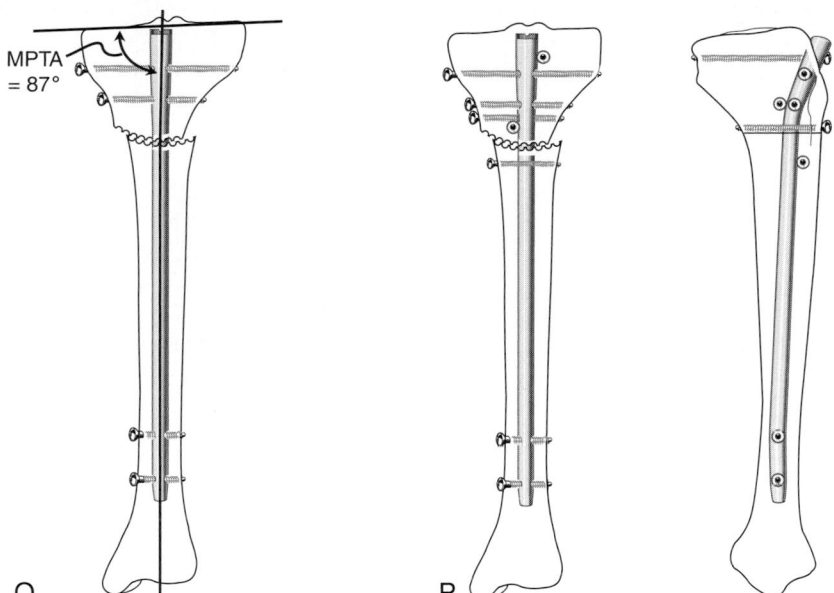

**Figure 62–17** *Continued. O,* The fixator is removed, and the nail maintains the correction. *P,* For added stability, interference screws may be inserted to narrow the medullary canal. This is more important for proximal tibial fixator-assisted nailing than for distal femoral fixator-assisted nailing. These interference screws may be inserted before removing the fixator. (Redrawn from Paley, D. Principles of Deformity Correction. Heidelberg, Germany, Springer-Verlag, 2002.)

translation can be additive or compensatory to the MAD (Fig. 62–30).

The magnitude of translation in the face of angulation is measured at the proximal end of the distal fragment (Fig. 62–31). For an oblique-plane deformity, the translation should be measured at the same level in the bone on the AP and lateral views. Angulation and translation can be plotted on the same graph. Graphic representation of the plane of orientation of angulation and translation permits comparison of the two planes. The plane of angulation may be the same as that of translation (Figs. 62–32 and 62–33), or it may be different (Figs. 62–34 and 62–35). When angulation and translation are in the same plane, the CORAs on the AP and lateral views are at the same levels (see Figs. 62–32 and 62–33). When angulation and translation are in different planes, the AP and lateral view CORAs are at different levels (see Figs. 62–34 and 62–35).

When angulation and translation are in the same plane, there are two osteotomy solutions. First, the two can be treated as a single-level deformity at the level of the CORAs using a single-level opening or closing wedge osteotomy (i.e., osteotomy rule 1) (see Fig. 62–32). Alternatively, the osteotomy can be performed at the original fracture level with angulation and translation (i.e., osteotomy rule 2) (see Fig. 62–33). In the former scenario, the original fracture level is avoided. This may be advantageous when the original level is at risk for poor bone healing and infection. The disadvantage is that an intramedullary nail cannot be used because of the translation at the original fracture level. In the second scenario, the osteotomy is at the level of the original fracture and therefore needs angulation and translation.

When angulation and translation are in different planes, the AP and lateral CORAs are at different levels. If the osteotomy is made at the level of the AP or lateral CORA and all the angulation is corrected at that level, secondary translation will occur in the other plane (see Fig. 62–34). Alternatively, the fracture, malunion, or nonunion can be reduced through the original fracture site (with osteotomy if the site is united). If the CORAs are widely separated, the deformity can be considered biplanar, with angulation at one level in the frontal plane and at another level in the sagittal plane (see Fig. 62–35H). Understanding the relationship between angulation and translation can also be useful for fracture reduction (see Fig. 62–35C).

## Rotational Deformity

Rotational deformity is defined as angulation around the long axis of the bone. The axis of correction of a rotational deformity is perpendicular to the axis of correction of an angulation deformity. The axis of correction of angulation deformity is in the transverse plane. To determine the axis of correction of a combined angulation and rotational deformity, the orthopaedist can use graphic analysis (Fig. 62–36). This yields an inclined axis of correction, which can be used to correct angulation with rotation together with an inclined osteotomy.[1, 6–8] Resolving angulation and rotation into a single axis in space is also the basis of correction with the Taylor Spatial Frame external fixator (Smith & Nephew, Inc., Memphis, TN). A simpler strategy to correct rotational deformity is to realign angulation and translation first and then rotate the bone around its long axis.

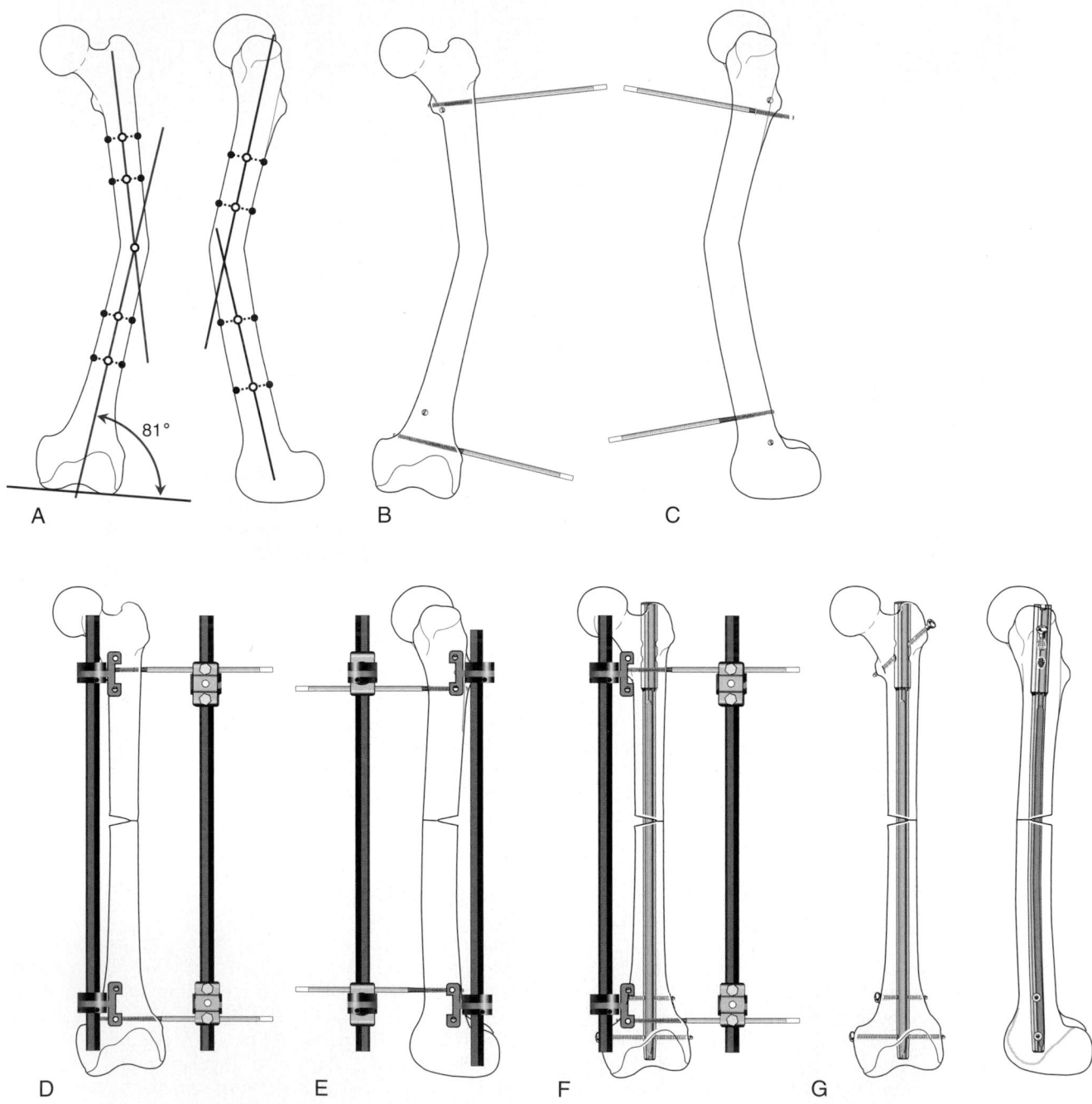

**Figure 62–18.** Fixator-assisted nailing. *A–G,* The biplanar fixator method of fixator-assisted nailing can be used to correct angular deformities that have elements in two planes (i.e., oblique-plane deformities). (Redrawn from Paley, D. Principles of Deformity Correction. Heidelberg, Germany, Springer-Verlag, 2002.)

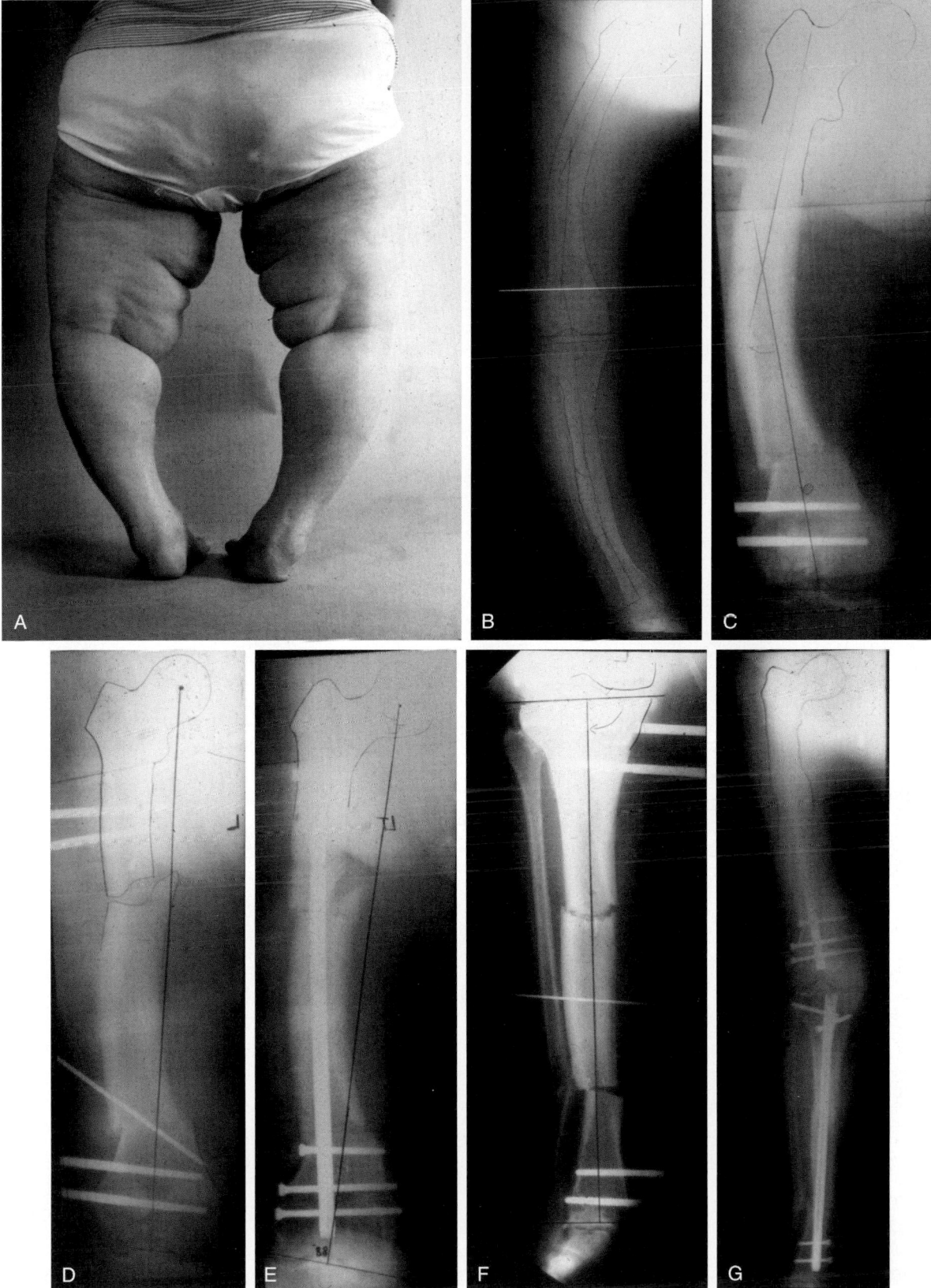

**FIGURE 62–19.** *A,* The clinical photograph shows a bowleg deformity in a 40-year-old, obese woman with chondrometaphyseal dysplasia. *B,* The long, standing radiograph of the right side of the same woman shows planning of the multiapical deformity correction. *C,* The intraoperative anteroposterior radiograph of the femur was obtained after application of a monolateral external fixator and distal focal dome correction. The level of the second center of rotation of angulation (CORA) is confirmed, with repeat planning conducted in the operating room directly on the radiograph. *D,* After the first osteotomy was stabilized with a temporary Steinmann pin, the second osteotomy was made and immediately corrected. The bone was valgusized and derotated at the second osteotomy level. For this reason, the second osteotomy is a straight cut, not a dome cut. After complete correction of the deformities was achieved and maintained with the external fixator, this intraoperative radiograph was obtained and the lateral distal femoral angle (LDFA) measured. The LDFA is 88°. *E,* Because the LDFA goal was achieved, the bone was nailed through a retrograde approach. The final LDFA is 88°. *F,* Six weeks after femoral fixator-assisted nailing, a similar procedure was performed on the tibia with a proximal diaphyseal focal dome and distal diaphyseal Gigli saw cut. The distal osteotomy was made transversely for the purpose of acute external rotation correction. The intraoperative radiograph confirmed a 90° medial proximal tibial angle (MPTA). *G,* The radiograph was obtained after nailing and healing of the femoral and tibial osteotomies. (From Paley, D. Principles of Deformity Correction. Heidelberg, Germany, Springer-Verlag, 2002.)

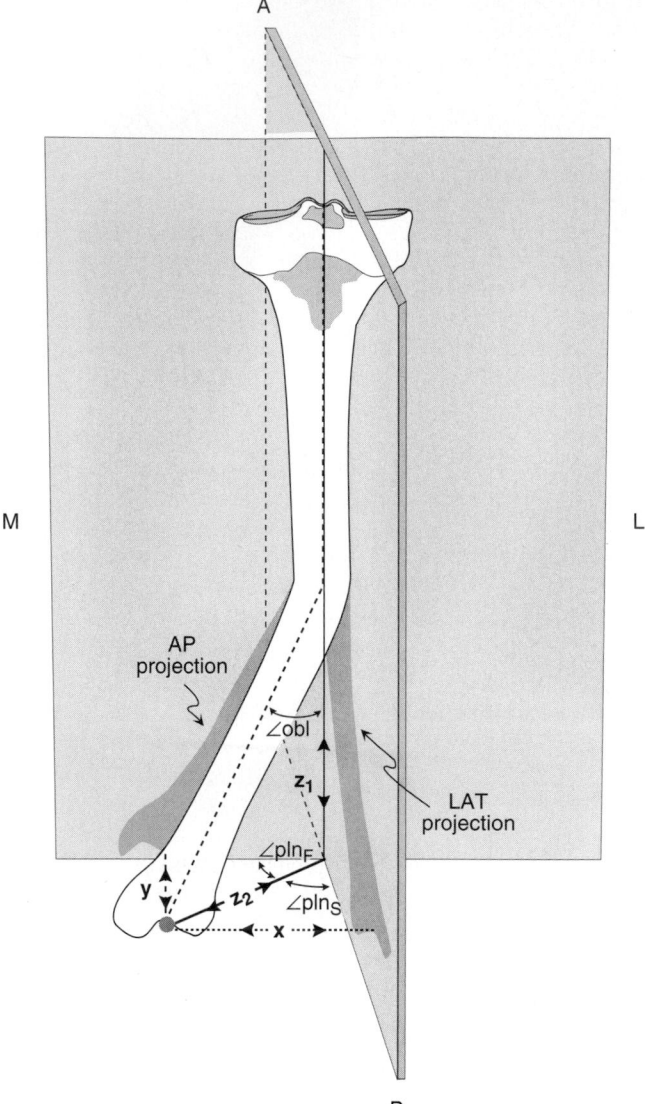

**FIGURE 62–20.** Oblique-plane angulation. Angulation is seen on the anteroposterior and lateral projections. The true plane of angulation is oriented in an oblique plane between the frontal and sagittal planes ($\angle pln_F$ to the frontal plane and $\angle pln_S$ to the sagittal plane). The magnitude of angulation in the oblique plane ($\angle obl$) is greater than that measured from the frontal- or sagittal-plane projections. A, anterior; P, posterior; L, lateral; M, medial. (Redrawn from Paley, D. Principles of Deformity Correction. Heidelberg, Germany, Springer-Verlag, 2002.)

## Length Deformity

Limb-length discrepancy is caused by a deformity of the length of the bone. Because it is a length measurement, it is similar to translation deformity. Translation deformity can be resolved graphically with length deformity, as was done for rotation with angulation. This is the basis of correction with the Taylor Spatial Frame external fixator. Rather than resolve these together, it is often easier to correct length separately from the correction of angulation and translation.

## JOINT CONSIDERATIONS FOR CORRECTION OF DEFORMITY

When the adjacent joint has motion in the plane and direction of angulation, the joint motion can be used to compensate for the angular deformity (Fig. 62–37). For example, recurvatum deformity of the tibia is compensated by flexion of the knee joint. Procurvatum deformity of the knee can be compensated by hyperextension of the knee joint. Because hyperextension is limited, fixed flexion deformity arises from even small amounts of procurvatum bone deformity. This is why recurvatum deformity of the femur and tibia is better tolerated than procurvatum deformity. Before correction of bone deformity in the plane of motion of a joint, the surgeon should ensure that no contracture has developed in association with the compensatory motion. For example, with recurvatum of the knee, if the passive hyperextension of the knee joint is less than the amount of angular deformity, a secondary fixed flexion contracture of the knee occurs. If the bone recurvatum were fully corrected, the flexion contracture would be uncovered. Measuring the joint orientation of the proximal tibia and distal femur (posterior proximal tibial angle and posterior distal femoral angle, respectively) and comparing it with the maximal extension position of the knee allows the orthopaedist to separate bone deformity from joint contracture and to identify the presence of fixed contracture or joint hyperlaxity that has developed to compensate for bone deformity (Figs. 62–38 and 62–39).

The ankle and subtalar joints compensate for tibial deformities near the ankle. Dorsiflexion of the ankle compensates for procurvatum, and plantar flexion compensates for recurvatum (Figs. 62–40 and 62–41). Because the range of plantar flexion is so much greater, recurvatum deformity of the distal tibia is more easily compensated for than procurvatum deformity. Paradoxically, recurvatum is more likely to lead to degenerative changes around the ankle because the dome of the talus becomes uncovered. Procurvatum is often more symptomatic because of anterior tibiotalar impingement. Similarly, valgus is more easily compensated for than varus because of the normally greater range of inversion than eversion of the subtalar joint. Hindfoot valgus is better tolerated than hindfoot varus. However, valgus increases the contact forces on the ankle, whereas varus decreases them. Valgus is more likely to lead to late degeneration of the ankle than varus. Well-compensated recurvatum deformity is often associated with secondary ankle equinus contracture, whereas procurvatum deformity may develop a dorsiflexion contracture. Varus deformity may develop an eversion contracture, whereas valgus deformity develops an inversion contracture of the subtalar joint. These contractures are occult, and to identify them, the foot should be placed into the deformed position of the tibia. For example, for a valgus distal tibial deformity, the heel should be placed in maximal eversion (Fig. 62–42). If the heel cannot be placed in valgus to the extent of the angular deformity, there is a fixed inversion contracture. To fully correct the tibial bone deformity, the subtalar joint must also be corrected out of varus.

# IMPROVEMENTS IN DEFORMITY CORRECTION: DEVELOPMENT AND APPLICATION

During the 20th century, limb deformity correction was performed using the "eyeball" technique. Such ballpark estimates are no longer acceptable in the 21st century. Limb deformities can be classified according to cause (e.g., congenital, developmental, post-traumatic), location (e.g., bone or joint contracture, extra-articular or intra-articular), geometry (e.g., angulation, translation, rotation, length discrepancy), severity (i.e., magnitude), and progression (i.e., static or progressive). Orthopaedic surgical correction must consider all of these factors.

Limb deformities may lead to dysfunction, pain, and joint degeneration. To patients, appearance may be a primary concern. For bone deformities, the mainstay of treatment has been osteotomy, whereas for joint contracture deformities, extra-articular and intra-articular soft tissue releases have been the standard treatment. Many innovative osteotomies have been developed to treat limb deformities. The results are frequently subjectively acceptable but objectively inaccurate. Secondary deformities often result from primary correction. The significance of this has only recently been recognized.[5] Inaccuracy of correction has often been excused by the time-honored orthopaedic mottos of "it will remodel with time" (in children) and "it's not bad" (in adults). In some cases, this advice has been true, but in many cases, residual and secondary translation and angulation deformities have gone untreated, suggesting the corollary of the last statement: "it's not good either."

Although most residual and secondary deformities are asymptomatic initially, many lead to degenerative changes and disability with time. During the 20th century, high postoperative complication rates were often reported, such as for neurovascular complications due to acute correction with stretch injury and compartment syndromes and bone complications due to extensive exposure and methods of fixation.

During the last decade of the 20th century, a revolution occurred in the management of deformities because of improved biologic and mechanical techniques. Thanks to

*Text continued on page 2552*

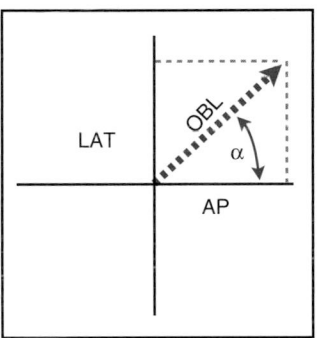

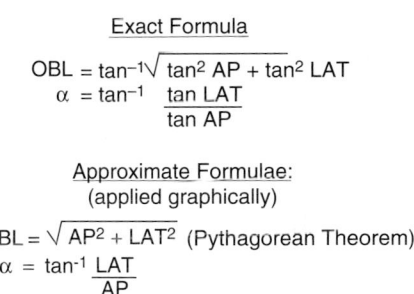

Exact Formula

$$OBL = \tan^{-1}\sqrt{\tan^2 AP + \tan^2 LAT}$$
$$\alpha = \tan^{-1}\frac{\tan LAT}{\tan AP}$$

Approximate Formulae:
(applied graphically)

$$OBL = \sqrt{AP^2 + LAT^2} \text{ (Pythagorean Theorem)}$$
$$\alpha = \tan^{-1}\frac{LAT}{AP}$$

**FIGURE 62–21.** Determining the plane and magnitude of deformity from anteroposterior (AP) and lateral (LAT) radiographs. The trigonometric formula for the magnitude of the oblique-plane correction (OBL) can be approximated using the graphic method. The graphic method calculation of the oblique-plane correction is equivalent to using the Pythagorean theorem with the magnitude of AP and LAT angulation. Similarly, the trigonometric formula for the orientation of the oblique plane to the frontal plane ($\alpha$) can be approximated as $\tan^{-1}$ LAT/AP based on the graphic method. The trigonometric formulas provide the exact values, whereas the graphic method provides the approximate values. The errors of the oblique plane of correction and $\alpha$ using the graphic method are plotted. For the orientation of the oblique plane of angulation, there is less than 2° of error until both angles are greater than 30°. The largest error of $\alpha$ is 4° when AP = 20° and LAT = 45°. The error of the magnitude of angulation in the oblique plane exceeds 5° only when both AP and LAT angles are greater than 30°. The oblique-plane formulas are based on the tangent function. The tangent is approximately linear from 0° to 45°. For this reason, the graphic approximation can be used with little error from 0° to 45°. (Redrawn from Paley, D. Principles of Deformity Correction. Heidelberg, Germany, Springer-Verlag, 2002.)

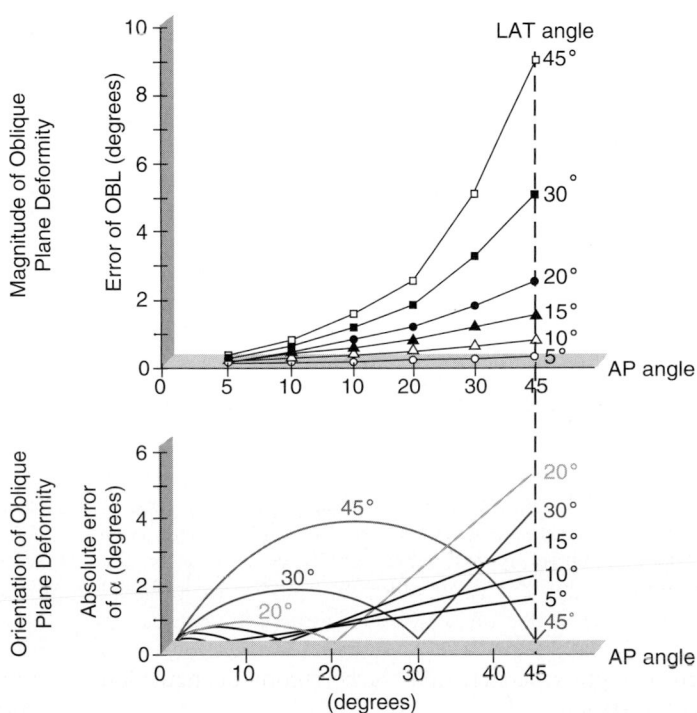

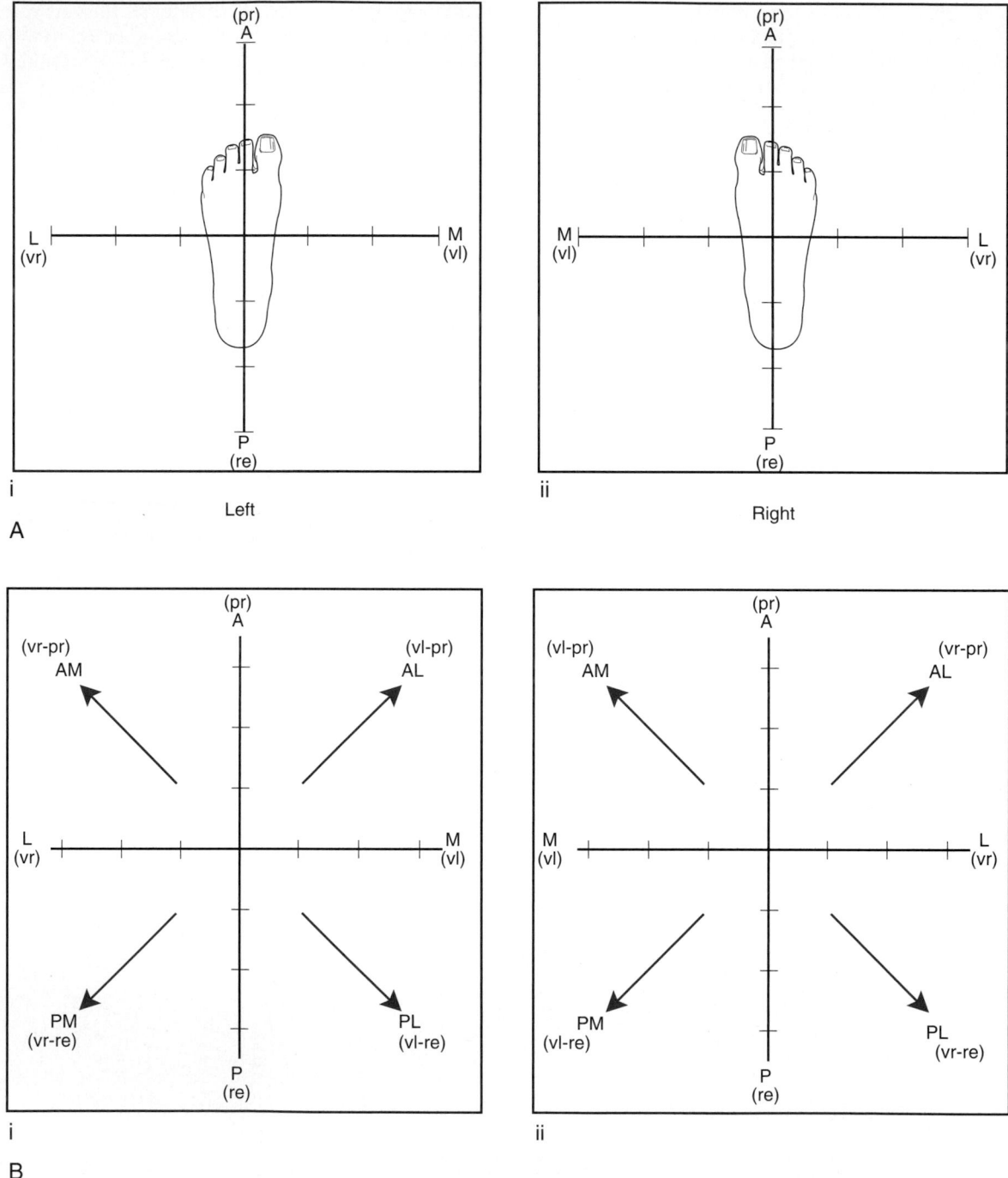

**FIGURE 62–22.** Graphic method of oblique-plane analysis. *A,* Apical direction graphs are drawn for the right and left legs. The graphs are drawn and labeled as if looking down at one's feet. Anterior is drawn at the top of the graph and posterior at the bottom. Medial and lateral are labeled as mirror images to each other for right and left legs. *B,* Each quadrant of the graph defines a different oblique-plane apex of angulation: anteromedial (AM), anterolateral (AL), posteromedial (PM), and posterolateral (PL); pr, procurvatum; re, recurvatum; vl, valgus; vr, varus.

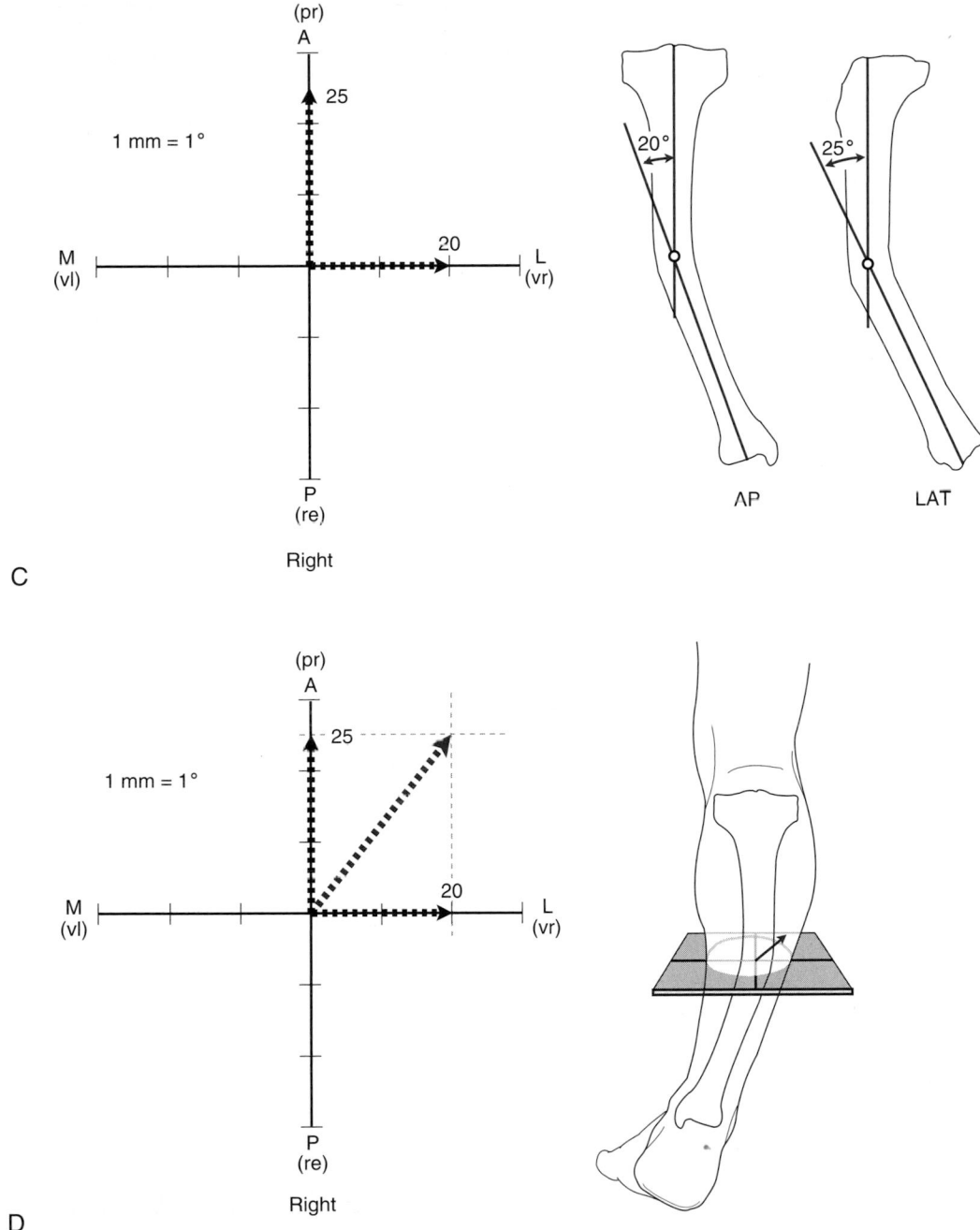

C

D

**Figure 62–22** *Continued. C,* The magnitude of the frontal-plane deformity is marked on the x-axis, and the magnitude of the sagittal-plane angulation is marked on the y-axis (scale of 1 mm = 1°). In the example shown, the angulation on the AP radiograph is 20° apex lateral (i.e., varus), and on the LAT radiograph, it is 25° apex anterior (i.e., procurvatum). *D,* The oblique plane of angulation is the line connecting the origin of the graph (0,0) to the point (AP,LAT) = (20°,25°). This graph represents a transverse cross section of the leg at the level of the axis of angulation.

*Illustration continued on following page*

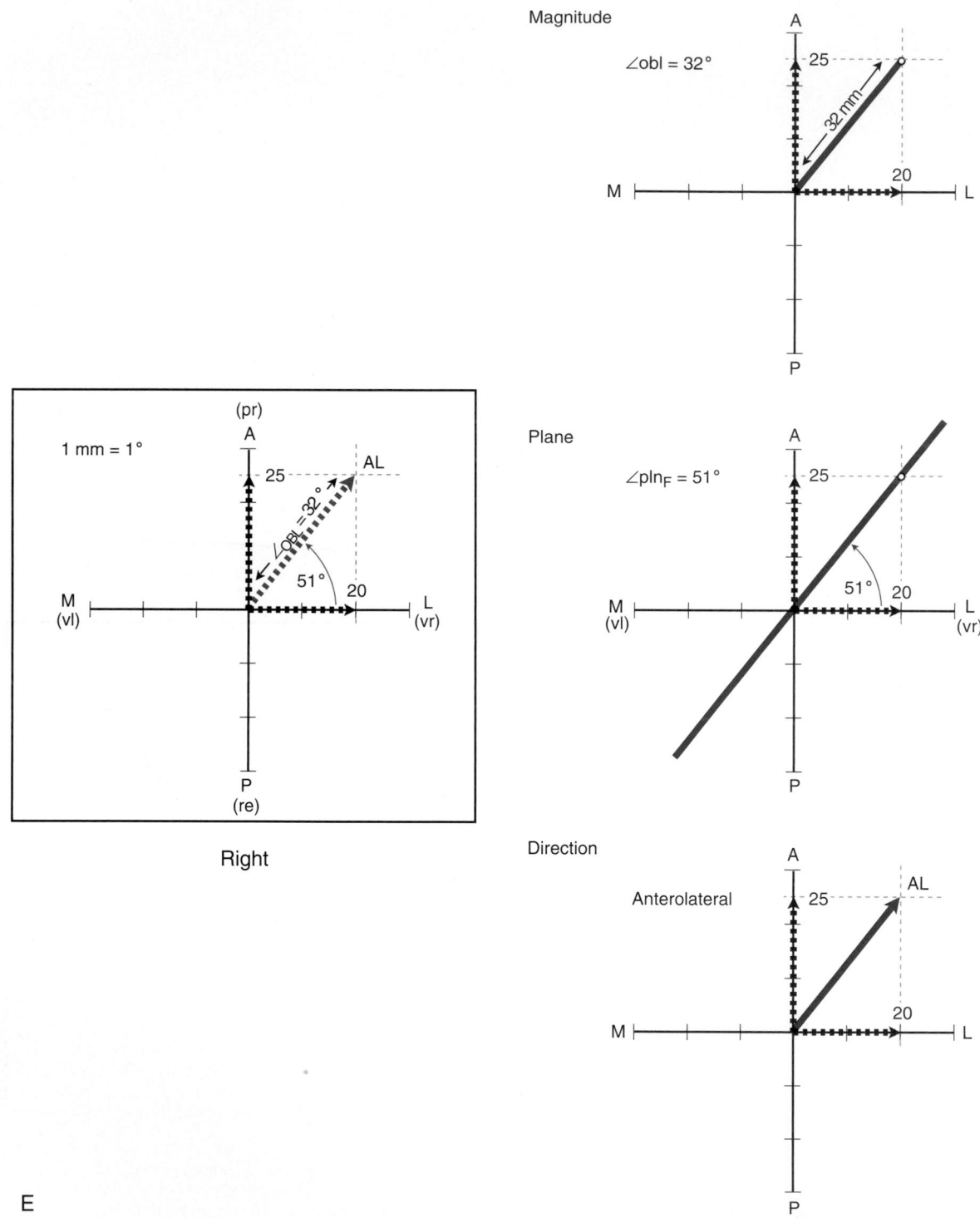

**E**

FIGURE 62–22 *Continued. E,* The final graph presents the magnitude, plane orientation, and apical direction of the oblique-plane deformity (*left box*). The magnitude of the oblique-plane angulation (∠obl) in degrees is the length of the third line in millimeters (32 mm = 32°) (*top*). The orientation of the oblique plane of angulation relative to the frontal plane (∠pln$_F$) can be measured off the graph (51°) (*middle*). The direction of the apex of angulation is marked with an *arrow* (*bottom*).

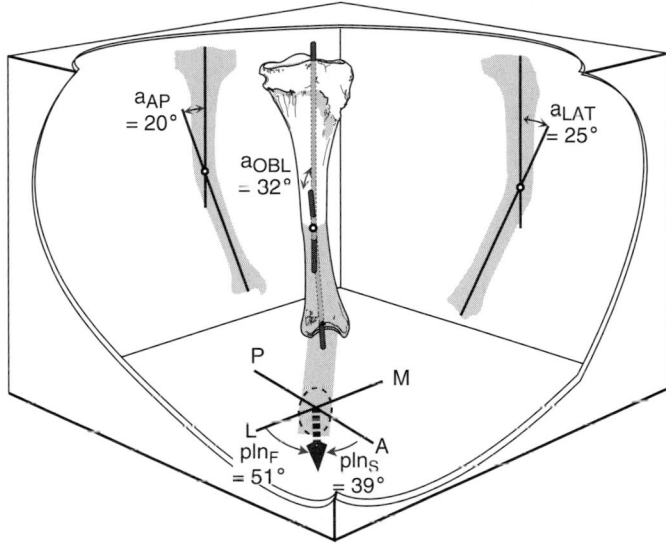

**Figure 62–22** *Continued. F,* The box diagram *(above)* can be compared with the final graphic method result *(below).* A, anterior; $a_{AP}$, anteroposterior angulation; AL, anterolateral; $a_{LAT}$, lateral angulation; $a_{OBL}$, oblique angulation; L, lateral; M, medial; P, posterior; $pln_F$, plane of angulation oriented to the frontal plane; $pln_S$, plane of angulation oriented to the sagittal plane. (Redrawn from Paley, D. *Principles of Deformity Correction.* Heidelberg, Germany, Springer-Verlag, 2002.)

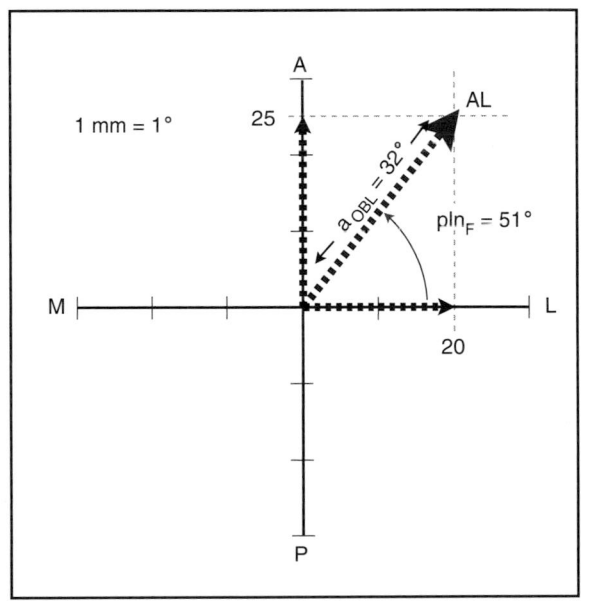

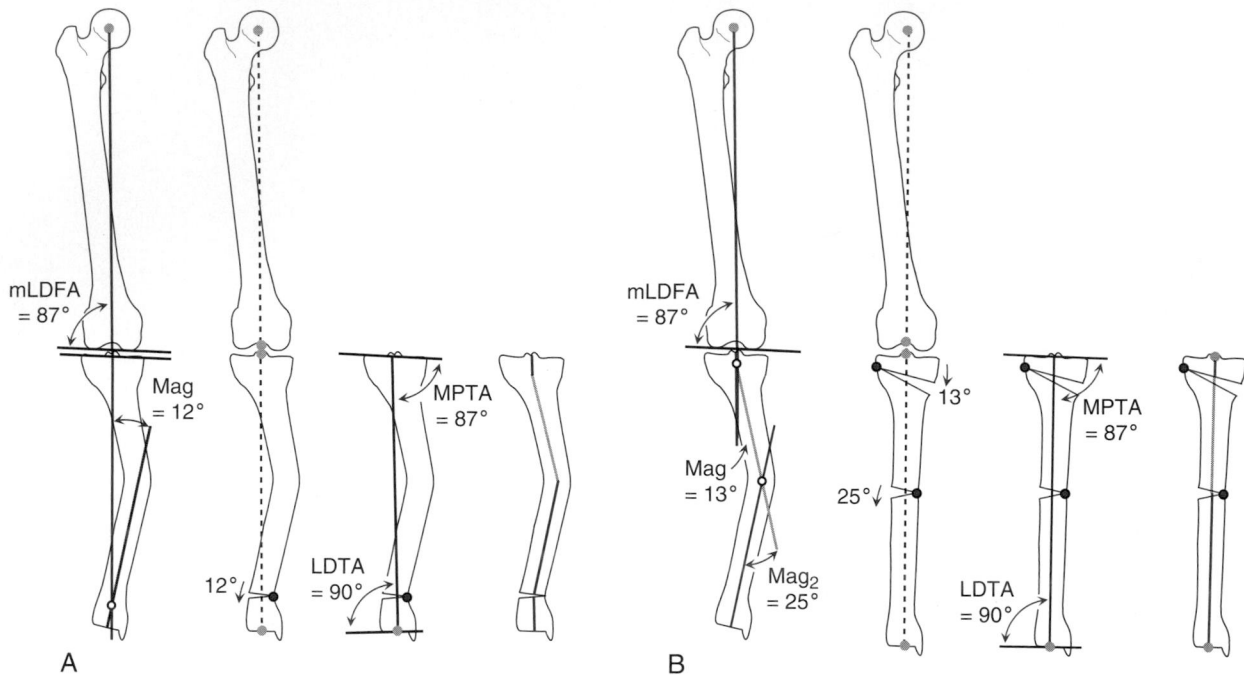

**FIGURE 62–23.** Tibial multiapical deformity. Single-level and multilevel osteotomy solutions use opening wedge-type osteotomies. Closing wedge and dome osteotomy solutions are not shown but are equally applicable and yield the same mechanical and anatomic axis and joint orientation results. *A,* In the single-level osteotomy solution, the proximal and distal mechanical axis lines intersect in the distal tibia at a level of no obvious angular deformity (resolved-apex center of rotation of angulation [CORA]). The magnitude at the resolved CORA is 12°. An osteotomy performed at this level with 12° angulation realigns the mechanical axis (i.e., osteotomy rule 1). The knee and ankle joint orientations are returned to normal. The anatomic axis is zigzagged. *B,* In the multilevel osteotomy solution, a third middle axis line is drawn, identifying the two true CORAs. The magnitude at the proximal CORA is 13° and at the distal CORA is 25°. The mechanical axis is realigned by angular correction of 13° valgus and 25° varus around the proximal and distal CORAs, respectively. The knee and ankle joint orientations are returned to normal, and the anatomic axis is completely realigned. LDFA, lateral distal femoral angle; Mag, magnitude of angulation; MPTA, medial proximal tibial angle. (Redrawn from Paley, D. Principles of Deformity Correction. Heidelberg, Germany, Springer-Verlag, 2002.)

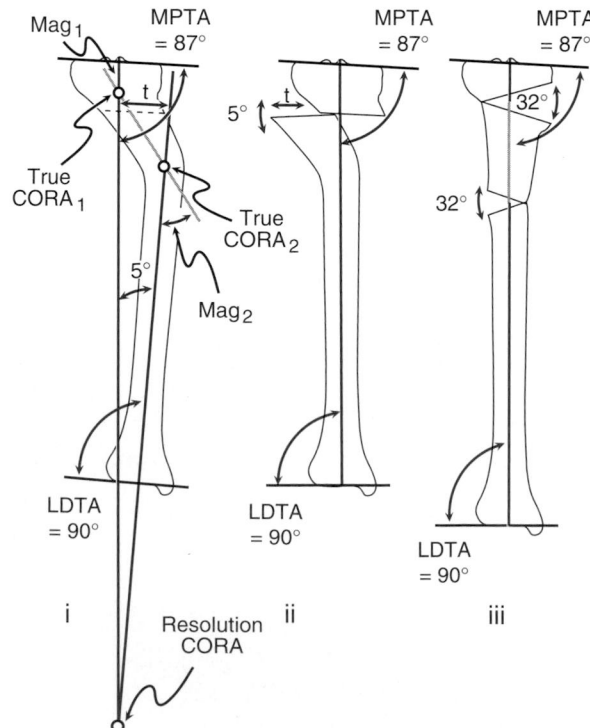

**FIGURE 62–24.** Translation versus angulation. The proximal and distal axis lines intersect distal to the ankle joint (i). The deformity can be considered as translation (t) with mild angulation or as double-level angulation in opposite directions. The single-level osteotomy solution achieves predominantly translation with slight angulation (ii). The multilevel osteotomy solution achieves opposite-direction angulation at two levels (iii). Mag, magnitude of angulation. (Redrawn from Paley, D. Principles of Deformity Correction. Heidelberg, Germany, Springer-Verlag, 2002.)

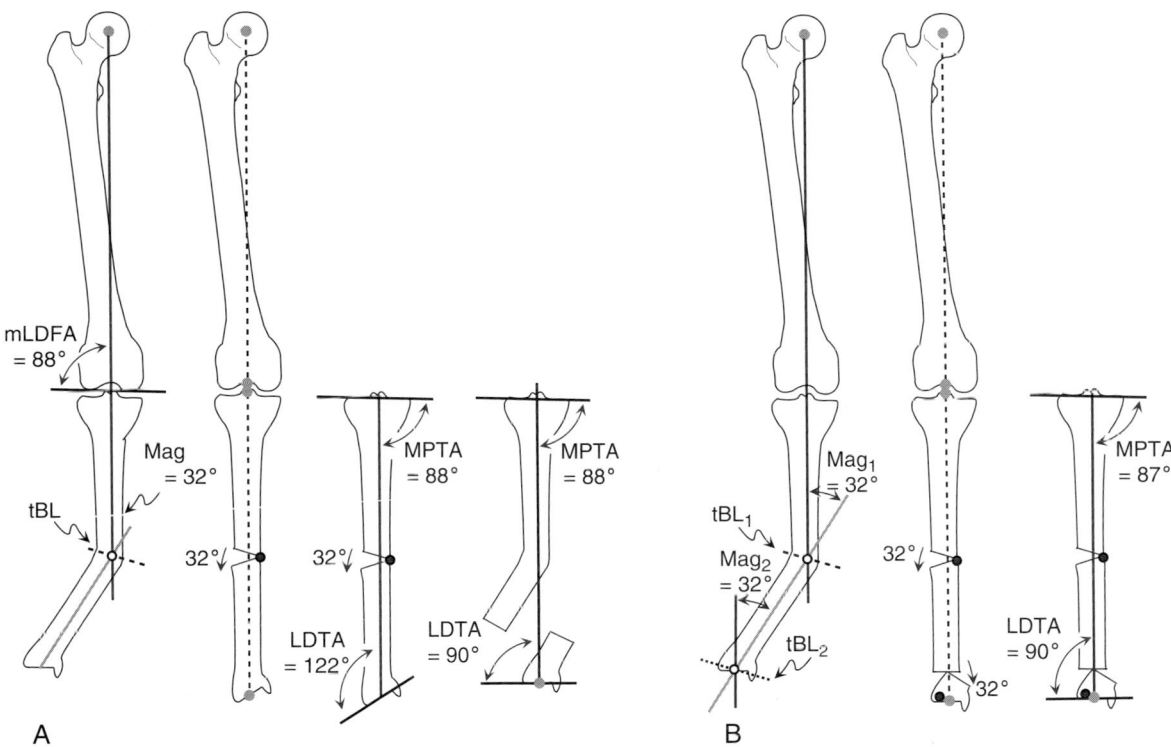

**FIGURE 62–25.** Tibial multiapical deformity. Opening wedge-type single-level and multilevel osteotomy solutions are shown. Closing wedge and dome solutions are not shown but are equally applicable and yield the same mechanical axis, anatomic axis, and joint orientation results. *A*, In the single-level osteotomy solution. the proximal and distal mechanical axis lines intersect at the level of the obvious diaphyseal valgus deformity. The magnitude of this deformity is 32°. The osteotomy and 32° angular correction of the obvious angular deformity realign the mechanical axis. The knee joint orientation is normal, but the ankle joint orientation is abnormal (lateral distal tibial angle = 122°). The ankle is in varus. This single-level osteotomy solution uncovers the ankle varus and should be avoided. *B*, In the multilevel osteotomy solution, the proximal and distal mechanical axis lines intersect at the level of the obvious diaphyseal valgus deformity. The magnitude of this deformity is 32°. The ankle is maloriented to the distal axis line. There is a second center of rotation of angulation (CORA) at the level of the ankle joint. The magnitude of the ankle deformity is 32°. The proximal and distal axis lines are parallel. This could be considered a translation deformity. A single-level translation osteotomy solution is not practical because the amount of translation required to fully correct the alignment cannot be physically achieved and would result in no bone-to-bone contact at the osteotomy site (*A*). The preferred option is to realign the mechanical axis using two equal and opposite 32° angular correction osteotomies around the proximal and distal CORAs, respectively. The knee and ankle joint orientation is returned to normal (lateral distal tibial angle = 90°). There is no malorientation of the ankle to the anatomic axis. LDFA, lateral distal femoral angle; tBL, transverse bisector line; Mag, magnitude; LDTA, lateral distal tibial angle; MPTA, medial proximal tibial angle. (Redrawn from Paley, D. Principles of Deformity Correction. Heidelberg, Germany, Springer-Verlag, 2002.)

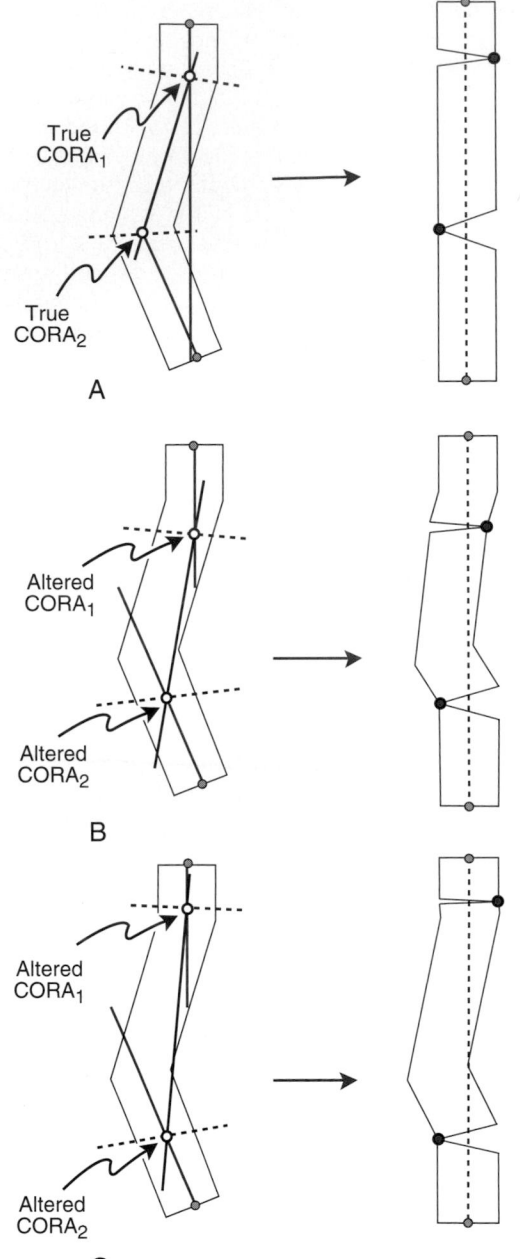

**FIGURE 62–26.** Corrective osteotomies need not be a the mid-diaphyseal apex for multiapical deformity. *A,* Original middle line. Multilevel osteotomy leads to realignment of the mechanical and anatomic axes. *B* and *C,* The middle line orientation can be altered. Multilevel osteotomy leads to mechanical axis and joint line realignment but residual anatomic axis malalignment. Altering the location of the third line moves the center of rotation of angulation (CORA) levels. (Redrawn from Paley, D. Principles of Deformity Correction. Heidelberg, Germany, Springer-Verlag, 2002.)

Gavril Abramovich Ilizarov, a Soviet orthopaedic surgeon, our understanding of bone and soft tissue regeneration has led to a plethora of devices and techniques that use gradual correction methods to correct simple or complex deformities. Gradual correction reduces the operative exposure

once needed to cut the bone to a percutaneous procedure. Acute surgical morbidity is greatly reduced by these techniques. Progressive correction avoids stretch damage to the neurovascular structures that are at risk. The magnitude of correction, which was previously the limiting factor in how much deformity correction could be achieved, is no longer an obstacle with gradual correction of bone or joint deformities. The accuracy of correction, which was usually only ±5°, improved greatly with gradual correction because of postoperative adjustability of external fixation. Although Ilizarov recommended circular external fixation, others attempted to achieve gradual correction of deformities with monolateral external fixation. The monolateral external fixators had more limited adjustability. Later designs became more modular and adjustable, and they can even incorporate rings. The circular fixator, previously perceived as bulky and difficult to apply, has become a more user-friendly device, hybridized with half pins and monolateral components.

The direction in this new century is toward minimally invasive surgery. Newer designs of plates and nails and their instrumentation are extending the application of such techniques to deformity correction in adults.[4] Modular and expandable rods and subcutaneous plates will allow orthopaedists to use stable, minimally invasive internal fixation techniques to achieve results similar to those achieved with external fixation. For example, the accuracy of fixator-assisted nailing for correction of deformities can offer the accuracy of external fixation while using internal fixation.

With the advent of radiography more than 100 years ago, our understanding of the geometry of deformities increased greatly. A wide variety of configurations of osteotomy were developed to correct these deformities. The opening and closing wedge osteotomy and the dome osteotomy have been the most commonly used techniques. Computed tomography can obtain more accurate images of rotational and intra-articular deformities than previously available.

Despite improvements in imaging techniques and methods of internal and external fixation, the study of the geometry of deformities remained greatly unexplored until the past 10 years. The level of the apex of deformity was always considered intuitive, and the level of osteotomy relative to the apex depended mostly on the space needed for the hardware. This approach more often than not created secondary translation deformities. Paley and co-workers[5] described the concept of the CORA. They demonstrated that secondary translation deformities occur when the axis of correction and the osteotomy are at a level different from that of the CORA. They developed a simple method to rapidly and accurately identify the level of the CORA. Because the concepts of the CORA and the axis of correction are basic principles of deformity correction, they are independent of the method of fixation used. Although the tendency in the past was to make the osteotomy accommodate the fixation, the current concept is to consider the principles of deformity correction as preeminent and to make the fixation and osteotomy adhere to the principles. Instead of osteotomy being slave to fixation, fixation becomes a slave to osteotomy. With this approach, surgeons can eliminate secondary deformities after osteotomy.

This chapter provides a set of techniques for defining and analyzing lower extremity deformity in terms of angulation, translation, and rotation. To correct a deformity, it is important to fully understand its details. Post-traumatic deformities typically involve more than one of these parameters. They rarely lie in the usual anatomic and radiographic planes and are typically in an oblique plane and therefore seen on AP and lateral radiographs. Another frequently confusing factor is that angulation and translation are in different planes, indicated by different CORA levels on AP and lateral radiographs. Shortening is also typically present.

The tools presented in this chapter can help in planning for correction of deformity, which can be done in several ways. Limb-length equalization (not reviewed here) must be considered and addressed. Before making a recommendation for a given patient, the surgeon should consider other factors: tissue viability relative to wound and bone healing, the type of fixation to be employed, whether to correct the deformity totally in one procedure or progressively with an adjustable device, status of blood vessels and nerves and whether prophylactic release is indicated, associated and compensatory contractures, and cosmesis. Compromises may be advisable, especially if chosen after a complete analysis, understanding, and consideration of all of the deformities and correction strategies for each case. This chapter serves as an introduction the field of deformity correction and its principles, and more detailed material is available elsewhere.[3]

*Text continued on page 2576*

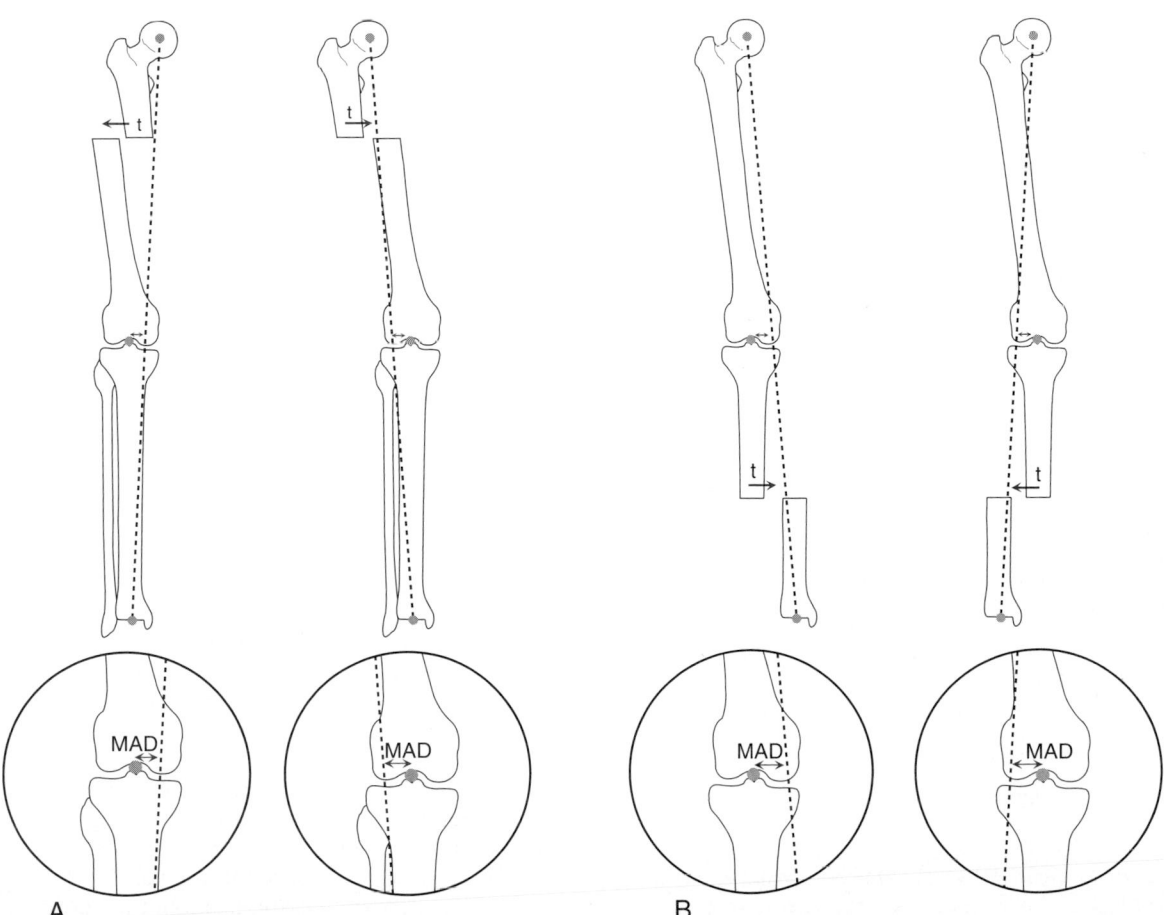

**FIGURE 62–27.** Effects of translation of the frontal plane. *A,* Lateral and medial translation (t) of the femur leads to medial and lateral mechanical axis deviation (MAD), respectively. *B,* Medial and lateral translation of the tibia leads to medial and lateral MAD, respectively. (Redrawn from Paley, D. Principles of Deformity Correction. Heidelberg, Germany, Springer-Verlag, 2002.)

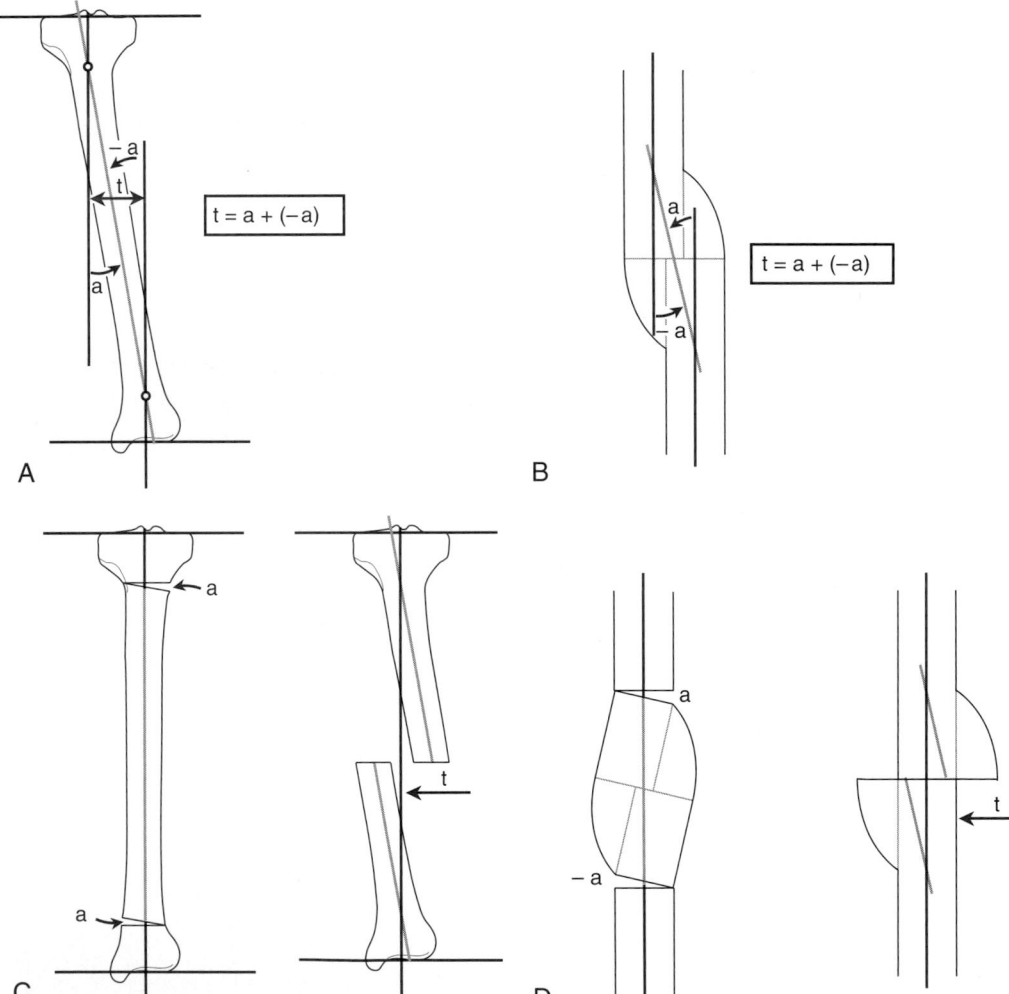

**FIGURE 62–28.** Osteotomies for translation deformity. *A,* Two angular (a) deformities in the same plane, of equal magnitudes and in opposite directions, have the net effect of a single translation (t) deformity. *B,* Translation deformity at a single level can be resolved into two equal-magnitude and opposite-direction angular deformities in the same plane. *C, D,* Correction of these deformities can be achieved by performing a single-level osteotomy with translation of the bone ends or by performing two levels of osteotomy with angulation at each level. (Redrawn from Paley, D. Principles of Deformity Correction. Heidelberg, Germany, Springer-Verlag, 2002.)

Translation graphs

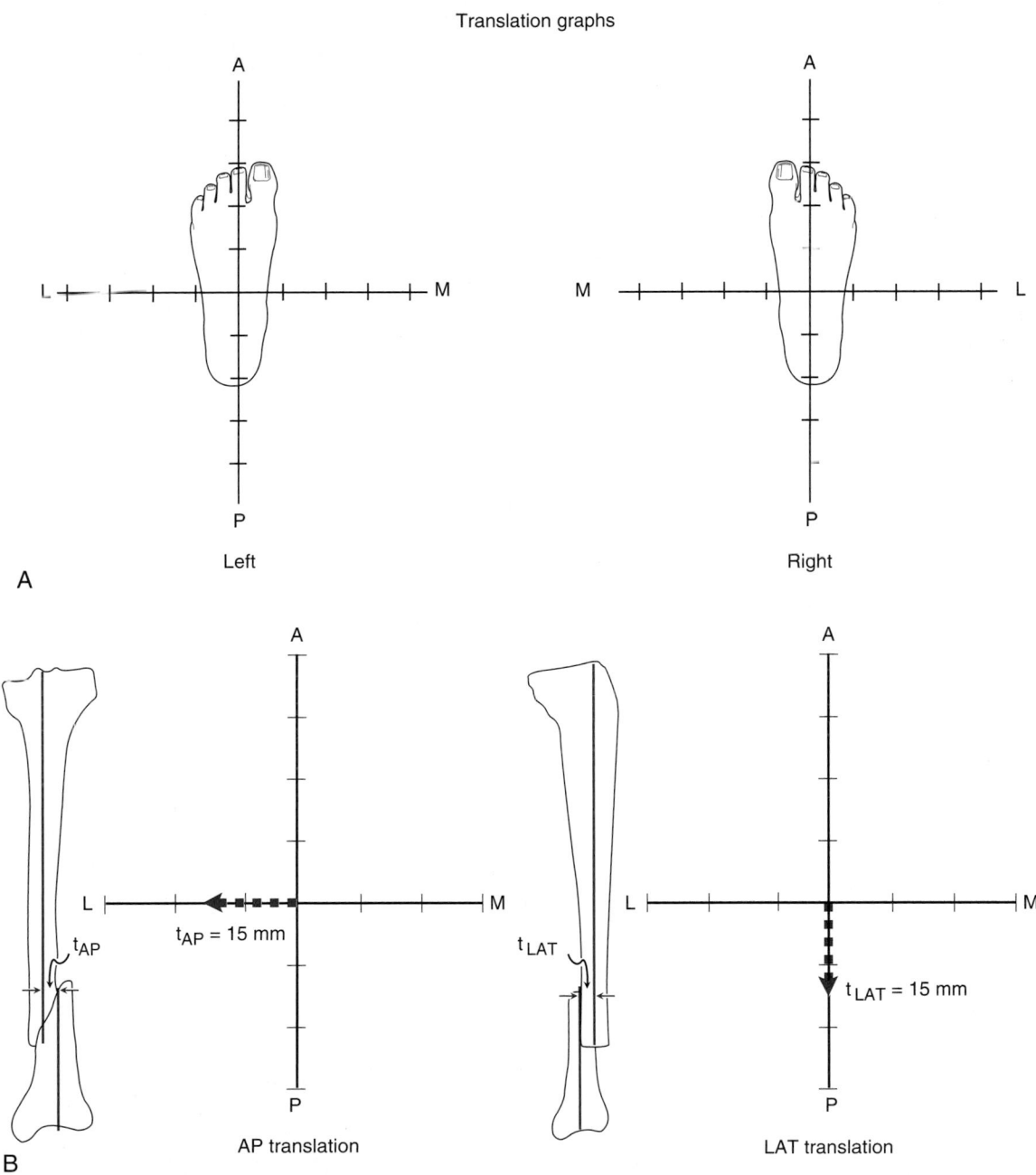

**FIGURE 62–29.** Translation graphs. *A*, The graphs for translation are labeled the same as for angulation. The directions of anterior (A), posterior (P), lateral (L), and medial (M) refer to directions of translation of the distal segment relative to the proximal segment. The graphs are mirror images for right and left legs. *B*, Left tibia. Lateral frontal-plane translation (15 mm) is shown graphically (*left*). Posterior sagittal-plane translation (15 mm) is shown graphically (*right*).

*Illustration continued on following page*

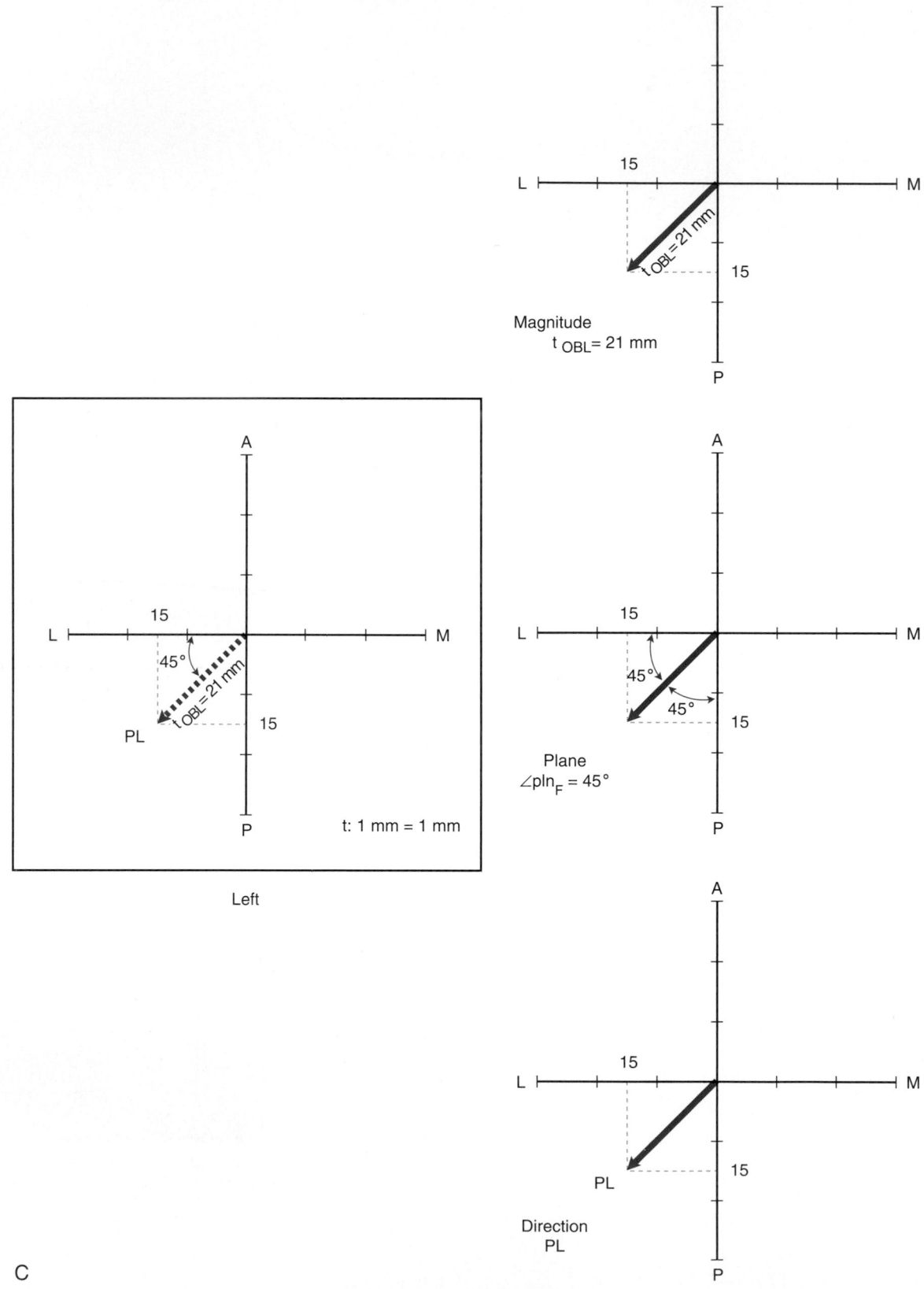

**C**

**Figure 62–29** *Continued. C,* The oblique-plane graph shows the magnitude, orientation of plane, and direction of translation deformity (*left box*). The magnitude of oblique-plane translation ($t_{OBL}$ = 21 mm) is the length of the line measured from the origin of the graph to the point (–15, –15). The magnitude can be measured directly in millimeters if the graph is labeled so that 1 mm on the graph equals 1 mm of translation ($t_{OBL}$ = 21 mm). This corresponds to the distance between the midaxial lines on the axial projection of the box diagram (*see D*). The plane of translation relative to the frontal or sagittal plane is the angle between the vector above and the x-axis or y-axis, respectively (45°) (*middle*). The direction of translation is indicated by an *arrow* on the end of the line. In this case, the direction is posterolateral (*bottom*).

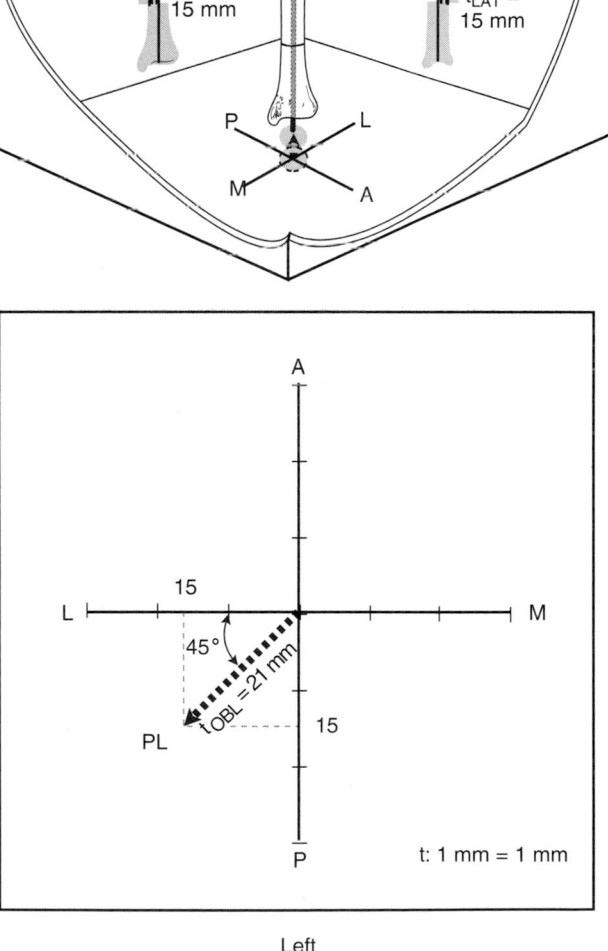

**FIGURE 62–29** *Continued. D,* Oblique-plane translation is shown in a three-dimensional box diagram. In the center is the true deformity. Because the direction of translation is posterolateral and because the view into the box is from the anteromedial side, the bone segments appear to be overlapped and aligned in the same oblique plane. On the left wall is the anteroposterior (AP) projection; on the right wall is the lateral (LAT) projection; and on the floor is the axial projection. The axial projection shows the graph, which is labeled according to the perspective of the box diagram. The plane of angulation is measured relative to the frontal or sagittal plane.

*Illustration continued on following page*

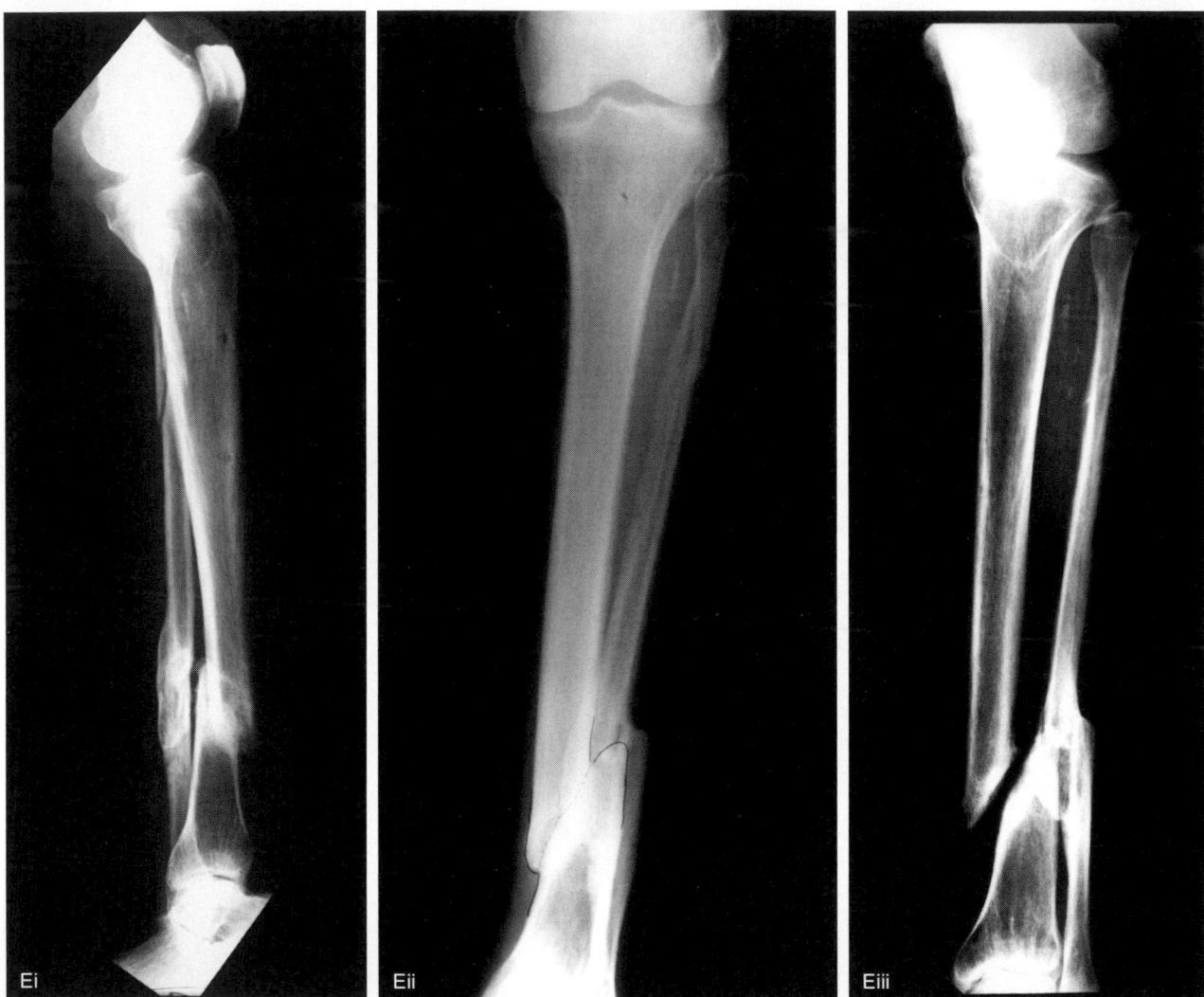

**Figure 62–29** *Continued. E,* The radiographs show examples of translation. The AP radiograph (*i*) shows lateral translation with approximately 50% overlap, which appears to be a malunion. The LAT radiograph (*ii*) shows posterior translation with approximately 50% overlap, which appears to be a malunion. The oblique radiograph (*iii*) shows maximal translation and reveals this to be a nonunion. PL, posterolateral; pln$_F$, plane of angulation in the frontal plane; t, translation; t$_{AP}$, anteroposterior translation; t$_{LAT}$, lateral translation. (Redrawn from Paley, D. Principles of Deformity Correction. Heidelberg, Germany, Springer-Verlag, 2002.)

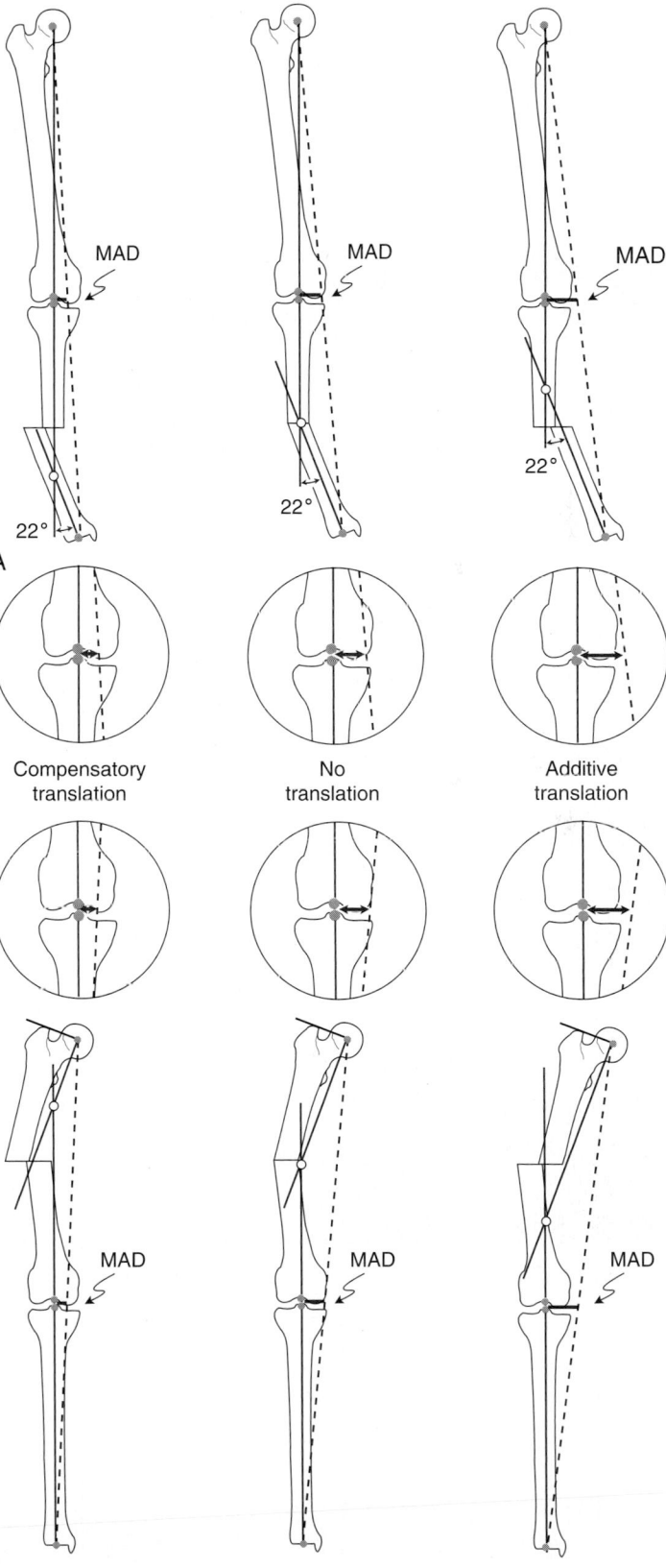

**FIGURE 62–30.** The mechanical axis deviation (MAD) is affected by angulation and translation. Some combinations are compensatory and reduce the MAD, whereas others are additive and increase the MAD. *A,* In the tibia, translation in the apical direction is compensatory, and translation away from the apex of angulation is additive. *B,* In the femur, translation in the apical direction is additive, and translation away from the apex of angulation is compensatory. (Redrawn from Paley, D. Principles of Deformity Correction. Heidelberg, Germany, Springer-Verlag, 2002.)

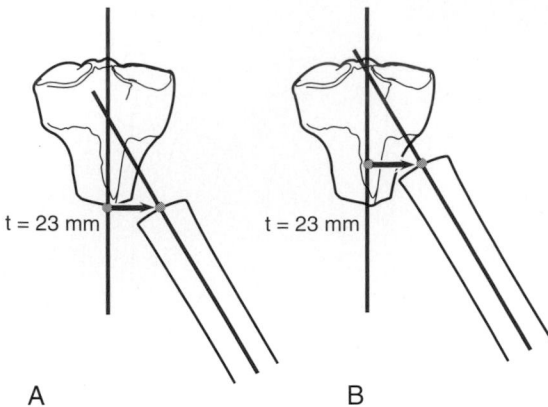

A                B

**FIGURE 62–31.** Measurement of translation (t) magnitude in the presence of angular deformity. *A,* The translation can be measured as the perpendicular distance from the proximal axis line to the distal axis line at the level of the proximal end of the distal segment. *B,* If there is shortening and the shortening is referred to the proximal axis line, the amount of shortening relative to the proximal axis line does not change with changes in length. (Redrawn from Paley, D. Principles of Deformity Correction. Heidelberg, Germany, Springer-Verlag, 2002.)

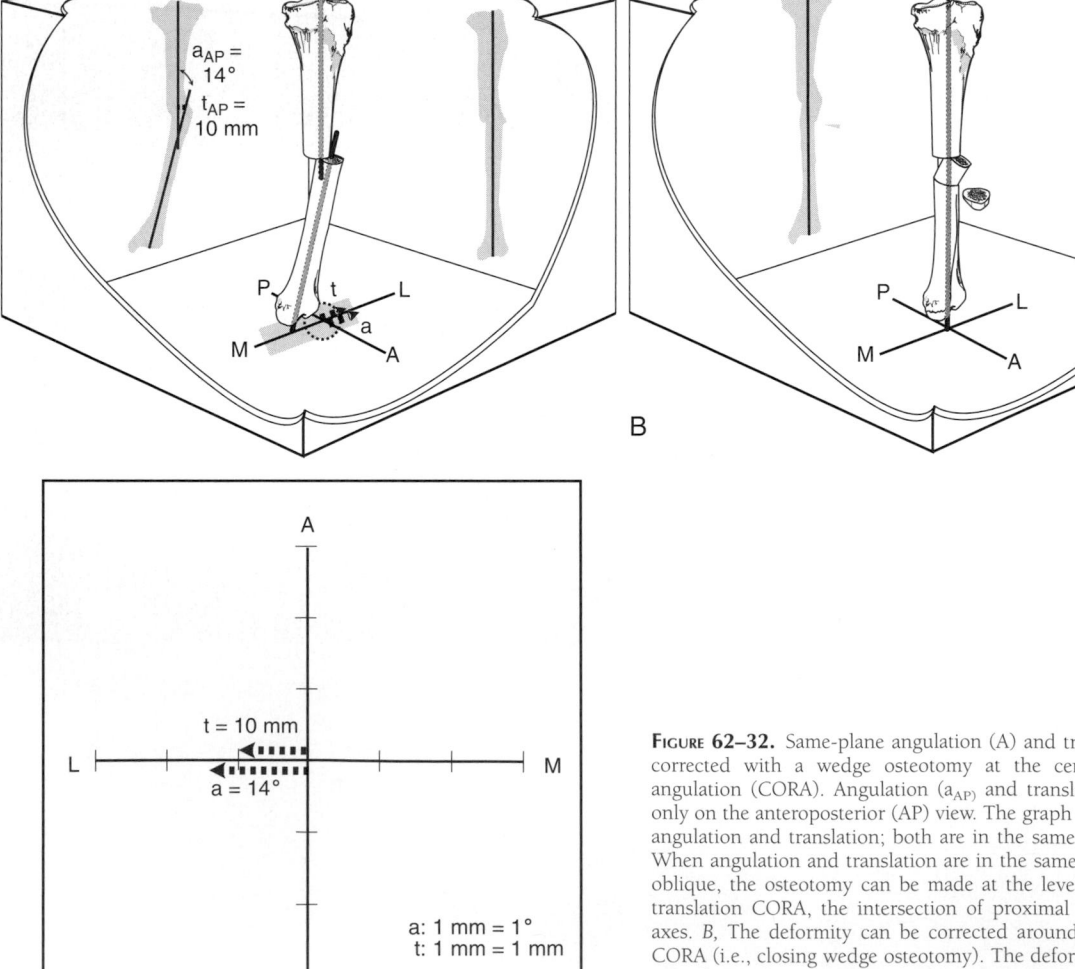

**FIGURE 62–32.** Same-plane angulation (A) and translation (t) can be corrected with a wedge osteotomy at the center of rotation of angulation (CORA). Angulation ($a_{AP}$) and translation ($t_{AP}$) are seen only on the anteroposterior (AP) view. The graph depicts the plane of angulation and translation; both are in the same anatomic plane. *A,* When angulation and translation are in the same plane, anatomic or oblique, the osteotomy can be made at the level of the angulation-translation CORA, the intersection of proximal and distal segment axes. *B,* The deformity can be corrected around the closing wedge CORA (i.e., closing wedge osteotomy). The deformity is corrected by a single angular maneuver. The fracture site is not disturbed, and the bump from the translation is therefore left on the bone. Because the bump is on the lateral side of the tibia in this case, it is covered by the anterior compartment muscles and is not visible.

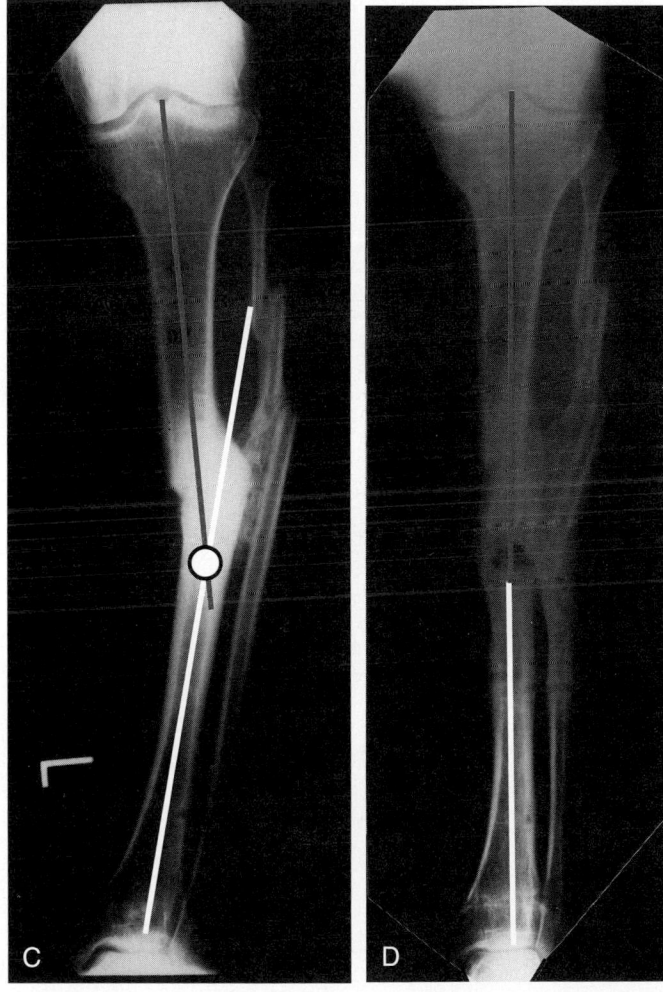

**FIGURE 62–32** *Continued. C,* The preoperative radiograph shows a similar deformity. *D,* The radiograph was obtained after osteotomy correction at the angulation-translation point with the opening wedge method; this case was treated with the Ilizarov apparatus. A, anterior; L, lateral; M, medial; P, posterior. (Redrawn from Paley, D. Principles of Deformity Correction. Heidelberg, Germany, Springer-Verlag, 2002.)

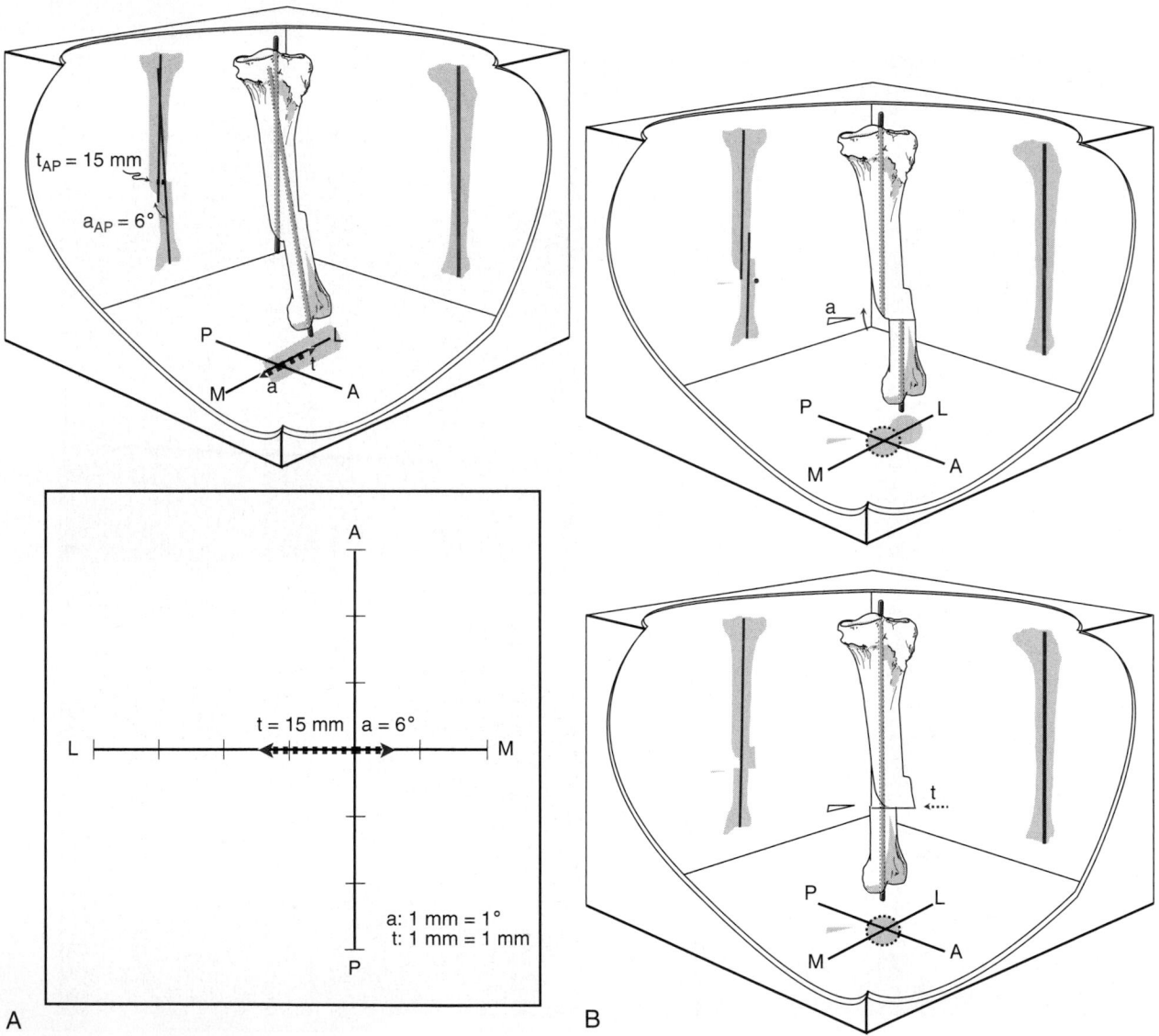

**FIGURE 62–33.** Same-plane angulation (a) and translation (t) can be corrected with angulation and translation. *A*, When the bump is on the medial subcutaneous border of the tibia, it is obvious. To avoid leaving a bump, it is necessary to perform the osteotomy at the original fracture site. The correction involves angulation and translation, in either order. There is no residual bump with this treatment strategy. In acute corrections, it is preferable to perform translation first and then angulation. With gradual correction, the reverse order is preferred. *B*, For the closing wedge osteotomy, angulation occurs first and then translation.

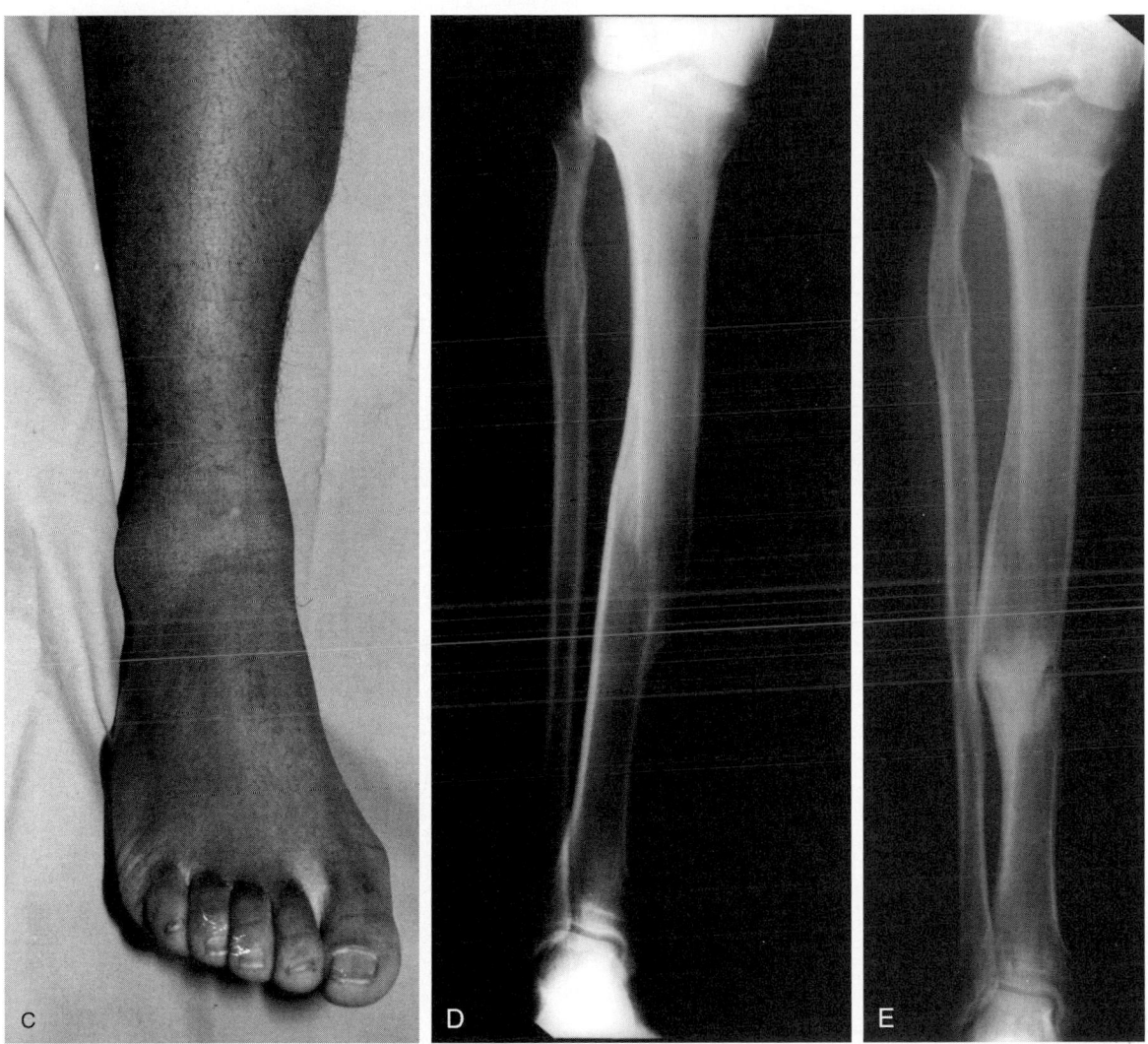

**FIGURE 62–33** *Continued. C,* The clinical photograph shows a bump on the medial border of the tibia from malunion. *D,* Anteroposterior radiographs show the deformity. *E,* The radiograph was obtained after correction was performed, eliminating the medial bump. This case was treated using the Ilizarov apparatus. A, anterior; $a_{AP}$, anteroposterior angulation; L, lateral; M, medial; P, posterior; $t_{AP}$, anteroposterior translation. (Redrawn from Paley, D. Principles of Deformity Correction. Heidelberg, Germany, Springer-Verlag, 2002.)

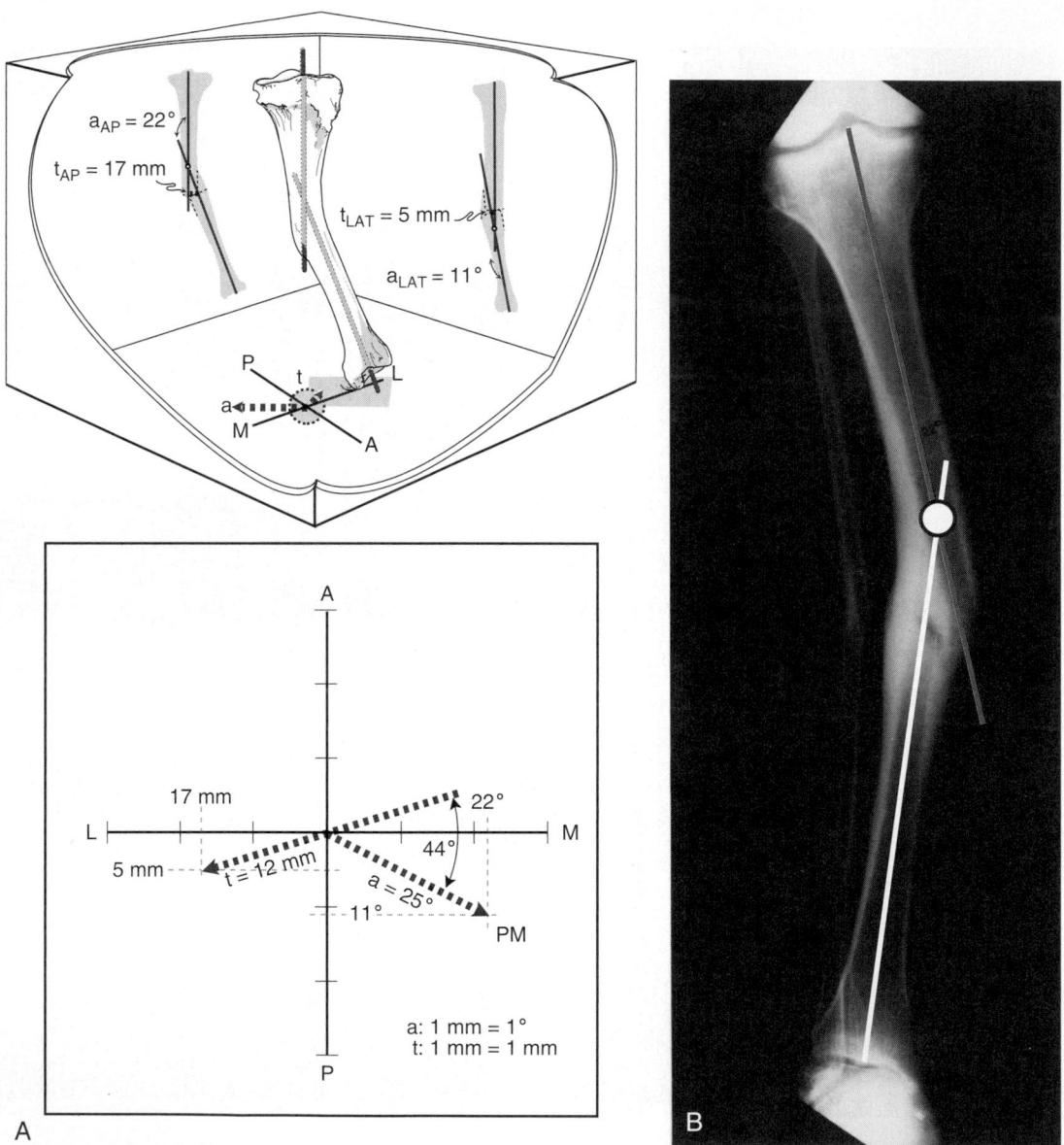

**FIGURE 62–34.** Angulation (a) and translation (t) are in different planes that are less than 90° apart. *A,* Angulation and translation are seen on the anteroposterior (AP) and lateral (LAT) radiographic views. The center of rotation of angulation (CORA) of each view is at a different level, indicating that angulation and translation are in different planes. The graph depicts the plane of angulation and translation. Both plane lines are in oblique planes, and the angle between the two plane lines is less than 90°. *B,* Angulation and translation are in different oblique planes less than 90° apart. On the AP radiograph, there is valgus angulation and lateral translation, with the CORA proximal to the fracture site.

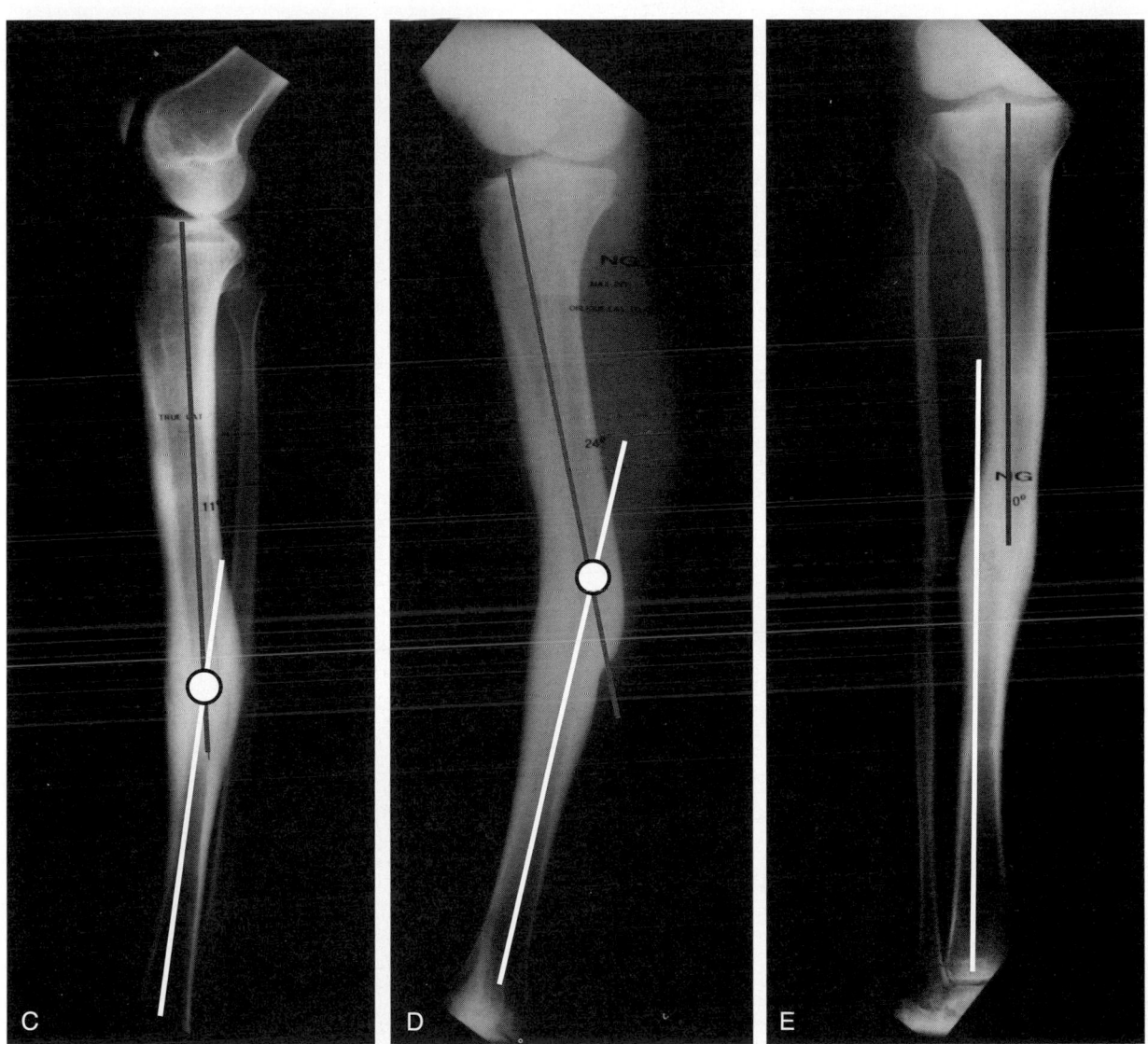

**FIGURE 62–34** *Continued. C,* On the LAT radiograph, there is recurvatum angulation and posterior translation, with the CORA distal to the fracture site. *D,* The oblique radiograph shows the maximal angulation and some remaining translation. *E,* The oblique radiograph obtained at 90° to that shown in *D* shows no angulation but some translation. Because some translation is seen on both oblique radiographs, the plane of translation cannot be 90° to the plane of angulation. If angulation and translation were 90° apart, there would be no translation seen in the plane of maximal angulation.

*Illustration continued on following page*

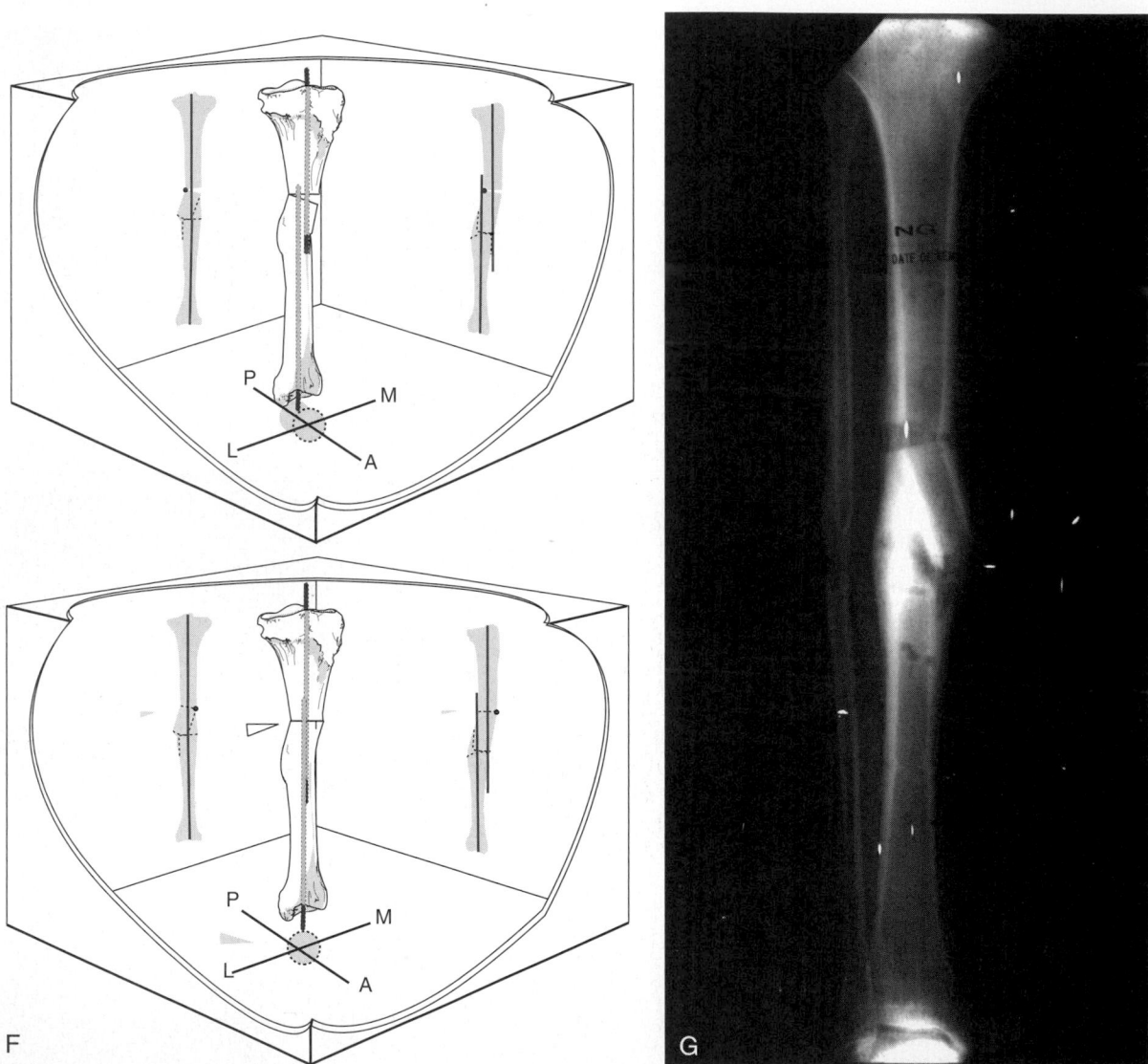

**FIGURE 62–34** *Continued. F,* In the first example, angulation and translation are in different planes, and the translation deformity on the LAT view is considered clinically insignificant. The oblique-plane angular correction opening wedge is performed at the AP angulation-translation CORA. The translation on the AP view is automatically corrected. This leaves some residual translation deformity on the LAT view, which is considered insignificant and is therefore not corrected. In the second example, a similar correction can be achieved with a closing wedge osteotomy. *G, H,* AP and LAT radiographs of the tibia were obtained after gradual opening wedge correction using an Ilizarov device. The opening wedge osteotomies are filled with maturing regenerate bone.

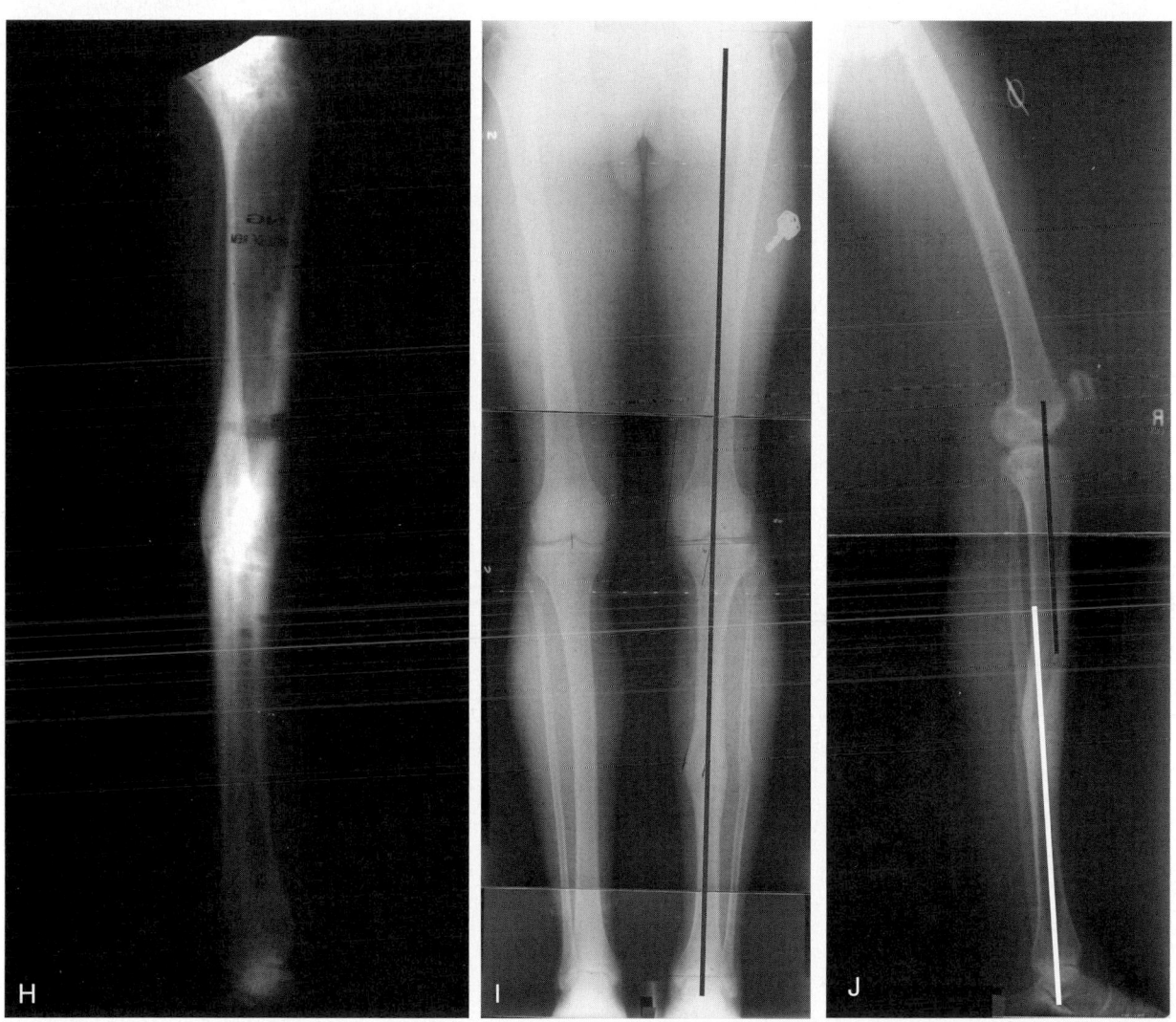

**FIGURE 62–34** *Continued. I,* Complete realignment of the mechanical axis is seen on the long, standing AP radiograph. *J,* On the long LAT radiograph, the clinical insignificance of the residual translation can be appreciated. A, anterior; $a_{AP}$, anteroposterior angulation; $a_{LAT}$, lateral angulation; L, lateral; M, medial; P, posterior; PM, posteromedial; $t_{AP}$, anteroposterior translation; $t_{LAT}$, lateral translation. (Redrawn from Paley, D. Principles of Deformity Correction. Heidelberg, Germany, Springer-Verlag, 2002.)

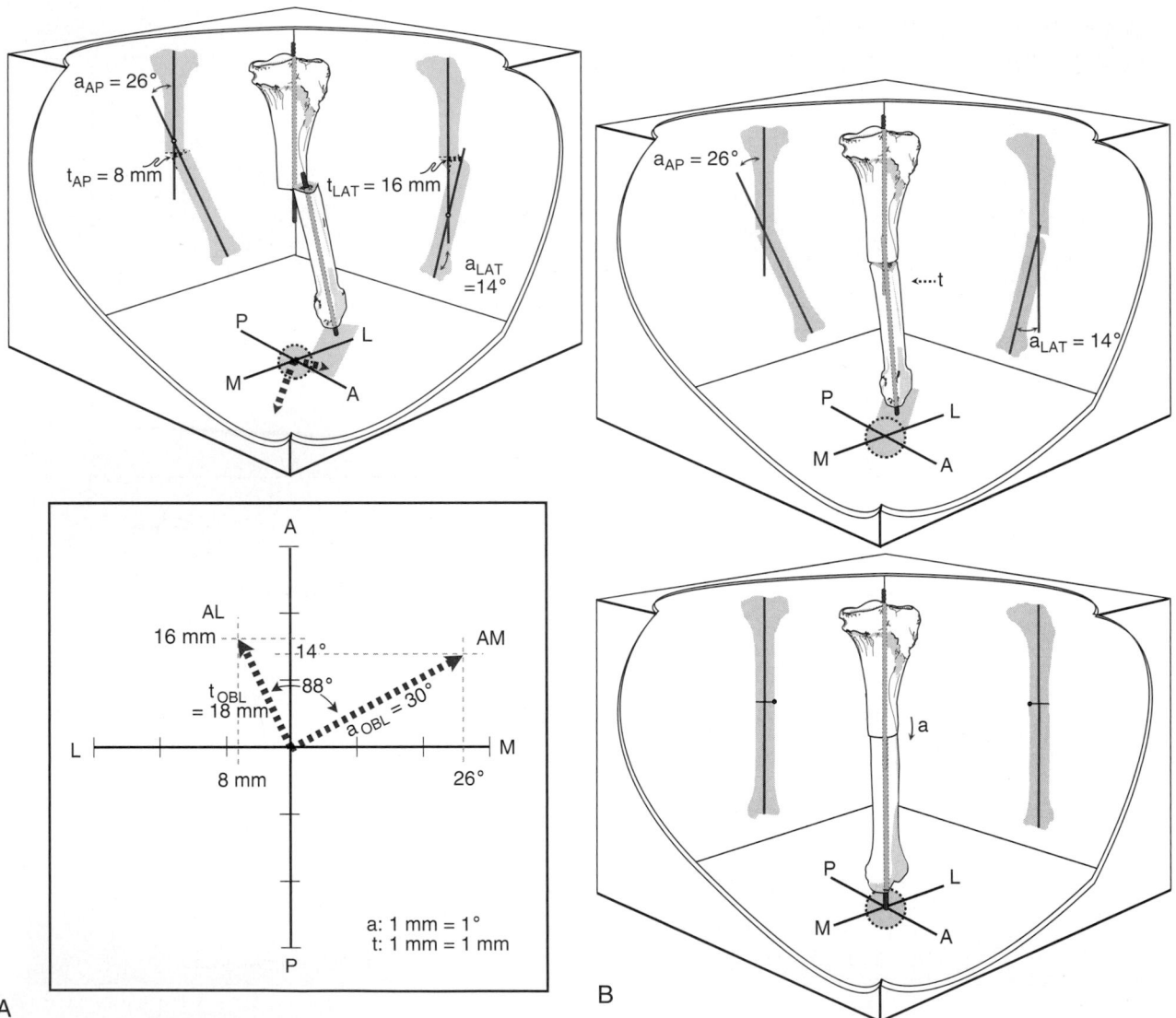

**Figure 62–35.** Angulation (a) and translation (t) are both in oblique planes that are approximately 90° apart. *A*, In this series, correction is performed through the original fracture site. *B*, The angulation is corrected in its oblique plane, and the translation is corrected in its oblique plane. This eliminates the bump. Translation is corrected first and then angulation; this is the most practical solution.

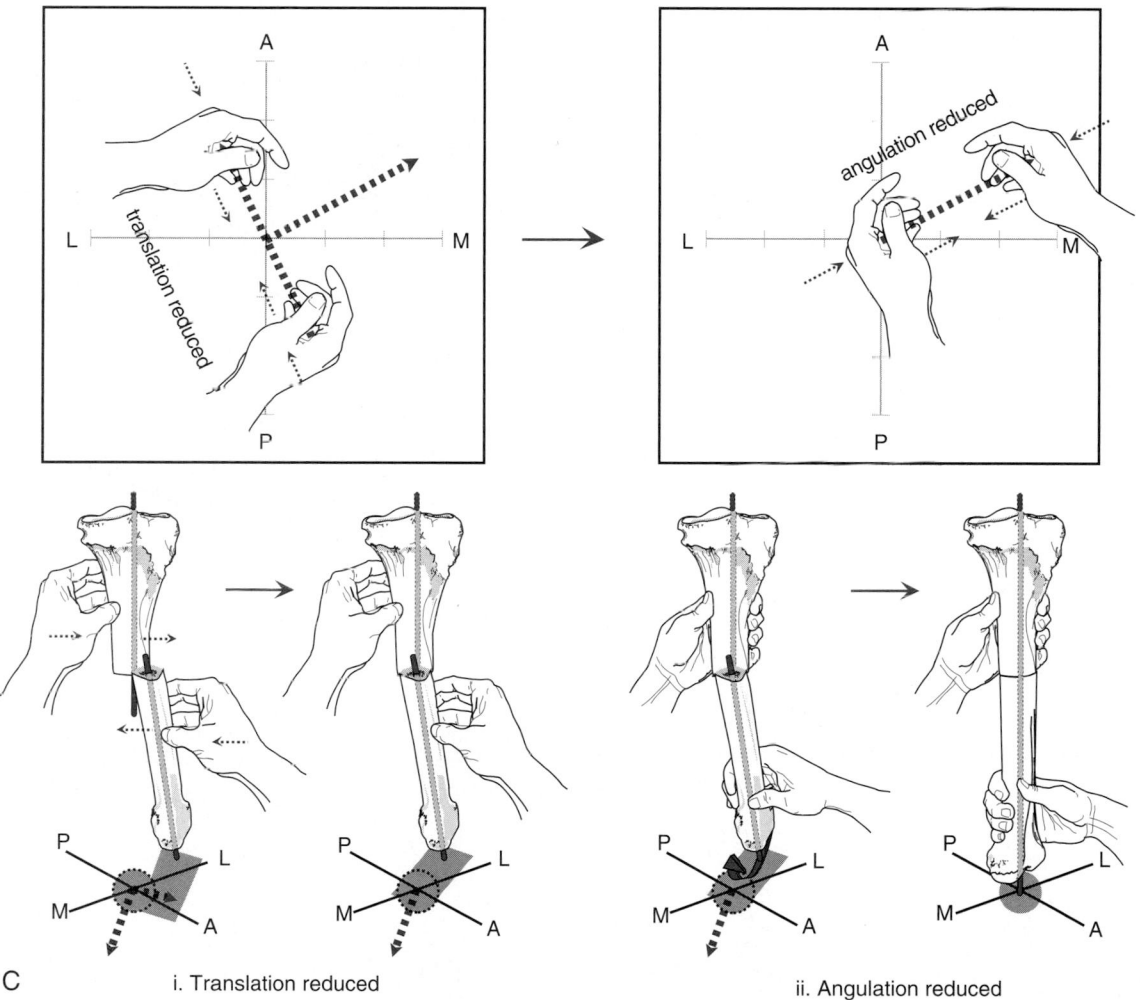

C      i. Translation reduced              ii. Angulation reduced

**Figure 62–35** *Continued. C,* Fracture reduction follows the same strategy as that presented previously: translation first and then angulation. Hands are placed along the plane of translation to reduce translation (*i*). Hands are manipulated in the plane of angulation to correct the angular deformity (*ii*).
*Illustration continued on following page*

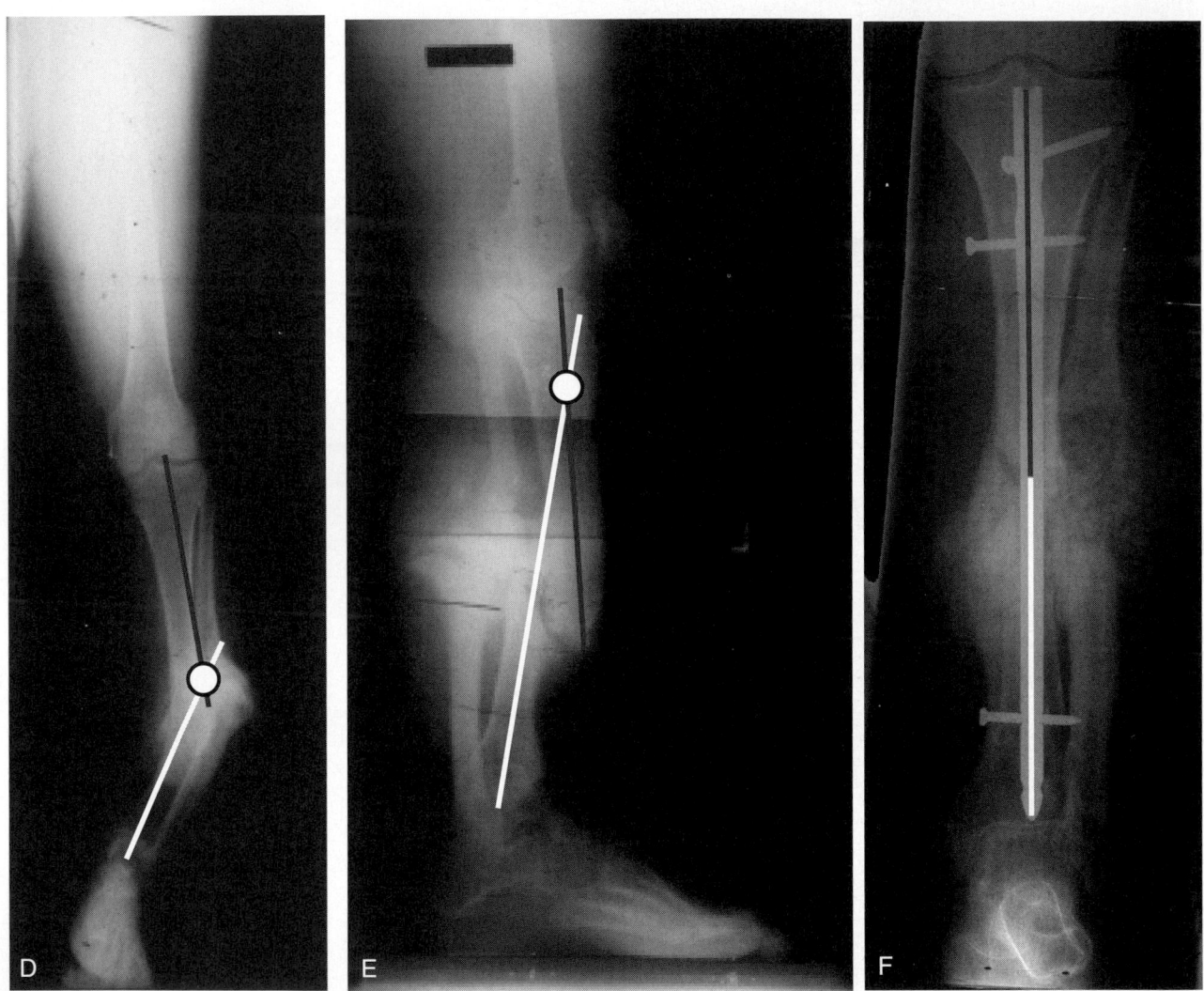

**FIGURE 62–35** *Continued. D, E,* Nonunion with angulation and translation in two different oblique planes. The anteroposterior (AP) radiograph shows varus angulation with lateral translation. The lateral (LAT) view shows procurvatum angulation with posterior translation. The centers of rotation of angulation (CORAs) are at different levels. *F, G,* AP and LAT radiographs show complete realignment through the original fracture site, which was achieved by angulation and translation of the bone ends in different planes. Reduction is facilitated by an understanding of the plane of the two components of deformity; the nonunion site could not have been reduced.

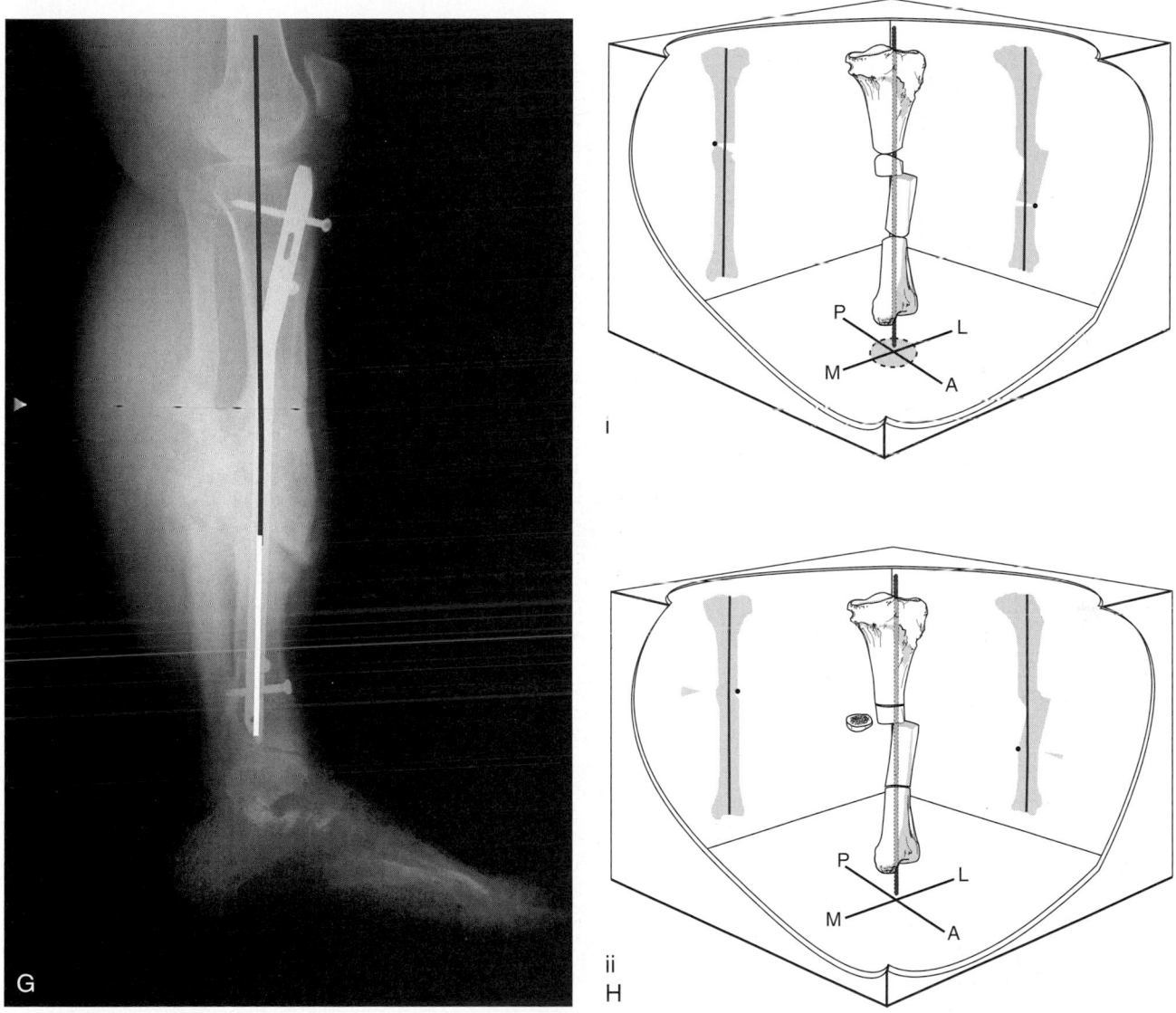

**FIGURE 62–35** *Continued. H,* An alternative solution is possible for the deformity shown in *A.* Because the two CORAs are far apart from each other, the correction can be performed using two osteotomies. One osteotomy is made at the AP CORA, and the other is made at the LAT CORA. Angulation at the AP CORA is performed for frontal-plane correction only and at the LAT CORA for sagittal-plane correction only. The deformity is treated as a double-level, biplanar angular deformity (i.e., two single-level, uniplanar angular deformities) with an opening wedge solution (*i*) or closing wedge solution (*ii*). A, anterior; AL, anterolateral; $a_{LAT}$, lateral angulation; AM, anteromedial; $a_{AP}$, anteroposterior angulation; L, lateral; M, medial; P, posterior; $t_{AP}$, anteroposterior translation; $t_{LAT}$, lateral translation. (Redrawn from Paley, D. Principles of Deformity Correction. Heidelberg, Germany, Springer-Verlag, 2002.)

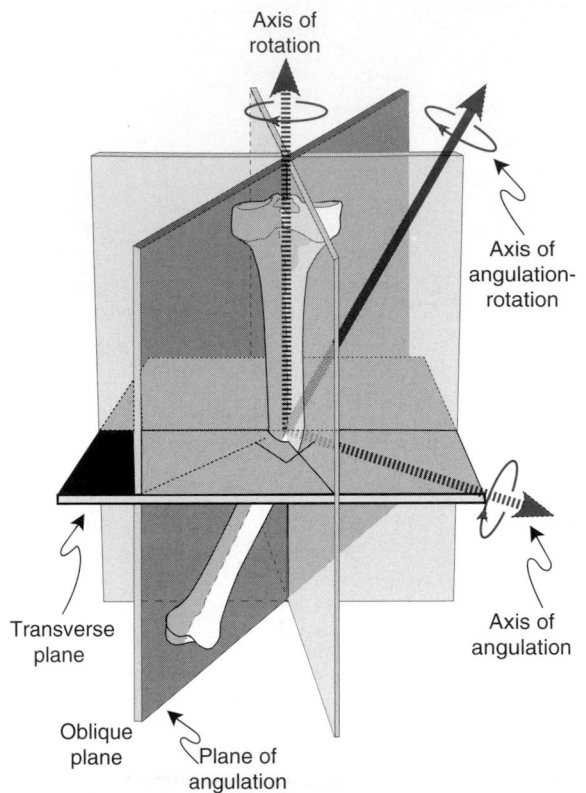

**FIGURE 62–36.** Rotational deformity. The axis of deformation for angulation is in the transverse plane. The axis of deformation for rotation is longitudinal (axial) and perpendicular to the transverse plane. The axes of angulation and rotation can be resolved into a single axis in a longitudinally inclined orientation. (Redrawn from Paley, D. Principles of Deformity Correction. Heidelberg, Germany, Springer-Verlag, 2002.)

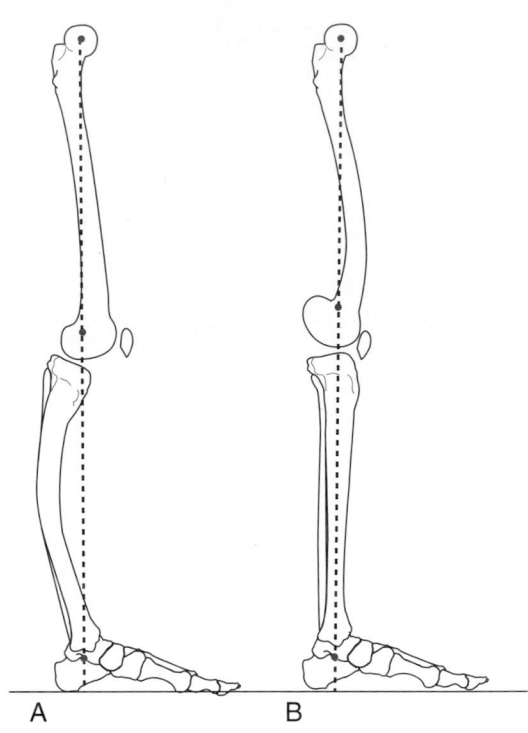

**FIGURE 62–37.** A joint can compensate for deformity in its plane of motion. *A,* Recurvatum deformity of the tibia is easily compensated by flexion of the knee joint. *B,* Flexion deformity of the femur can be compensated, to a limited extent, by hyperextension of the knee joint. (Redrawn from Paley, D. Principles of Deformity Correction. Heidelberg, Germany, Springer-Verlag, 2002.)

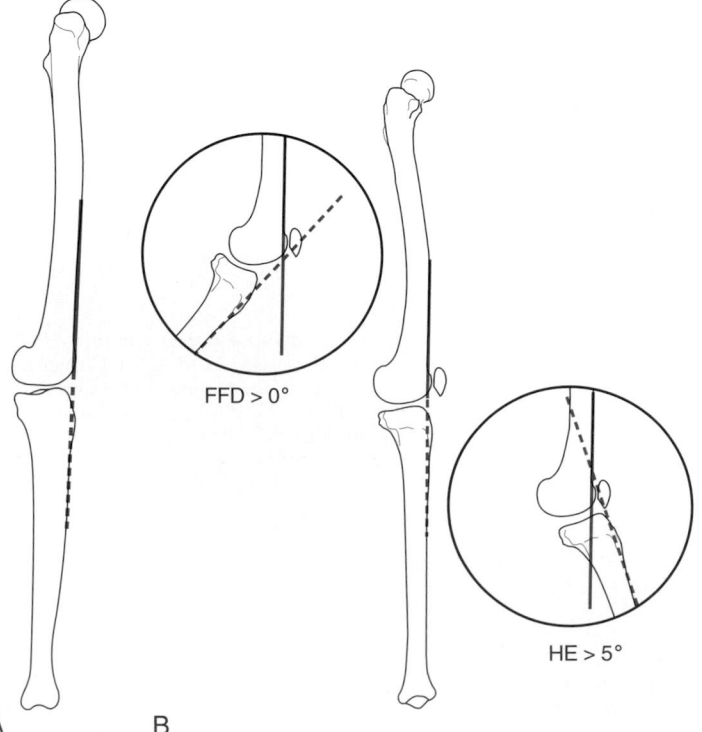

**FIGURE 62–38.** Check for contractures before correcting a deformity. *A,* The anterior cortical line of the proximal tibia and the anterior cortical line of the distal femur are co-linear when the knee is in 0° flexion. *B,* The knee is radiographed in maximal extension. If the anterior cortical lines cross in flexion when the knee is in maximal extension, there is a fixed flexion deformity (FFD). If they cross in extension, there is knee hyperextension (HE). More than 5° of hyperextension represents a hyperextension deformity.

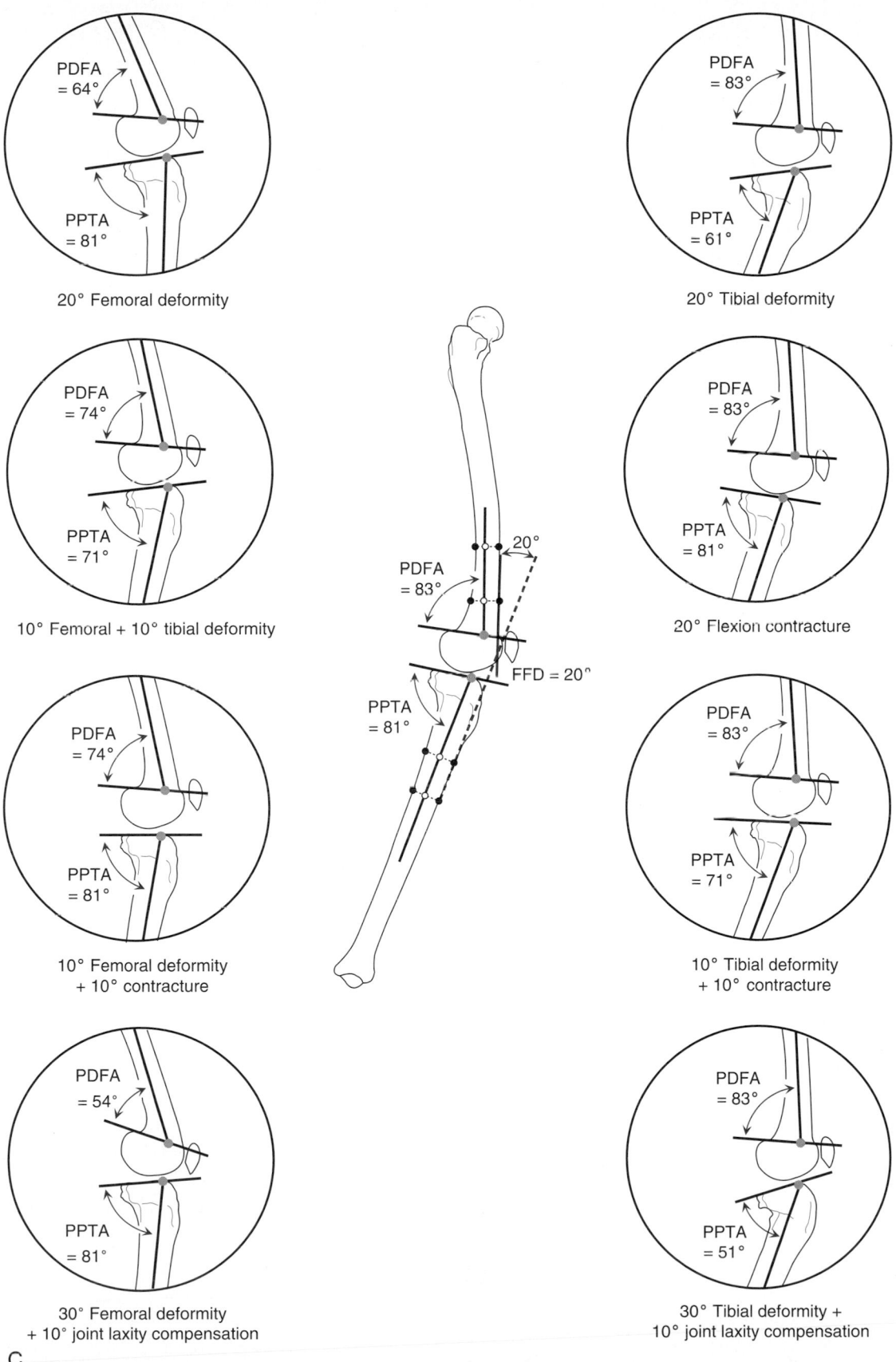

**FIGURE 62–38** *Continued. C,* Knee-level sagittal-plane malorientation test. Compare the amount of fixed flexion deformity or hyperextension with the amount of bone deformity identified. If they correspond, the bone deformity is the sole cause of the fixed flexion deformity or hyperextension. If femoral or tibial deformity is present, but there is a discrepancy between the fixed flexion deformity or hyperextension and the bone recurvatum or procurvatum, respectively, knee joint laxity or contracture is compensating or adding to the fixed flexion deformity or hyperextension. Multiple examples of combinations of problems are shown, and all result in a FFD of 20°. PDFA, posterior distal femoral angle; PPTA, posterior proximal tibial angle. (Redrawn from Paley, D. Principles of Deformity Correction. Heidelberg, Germany, Springer-Verlag, 2002.)

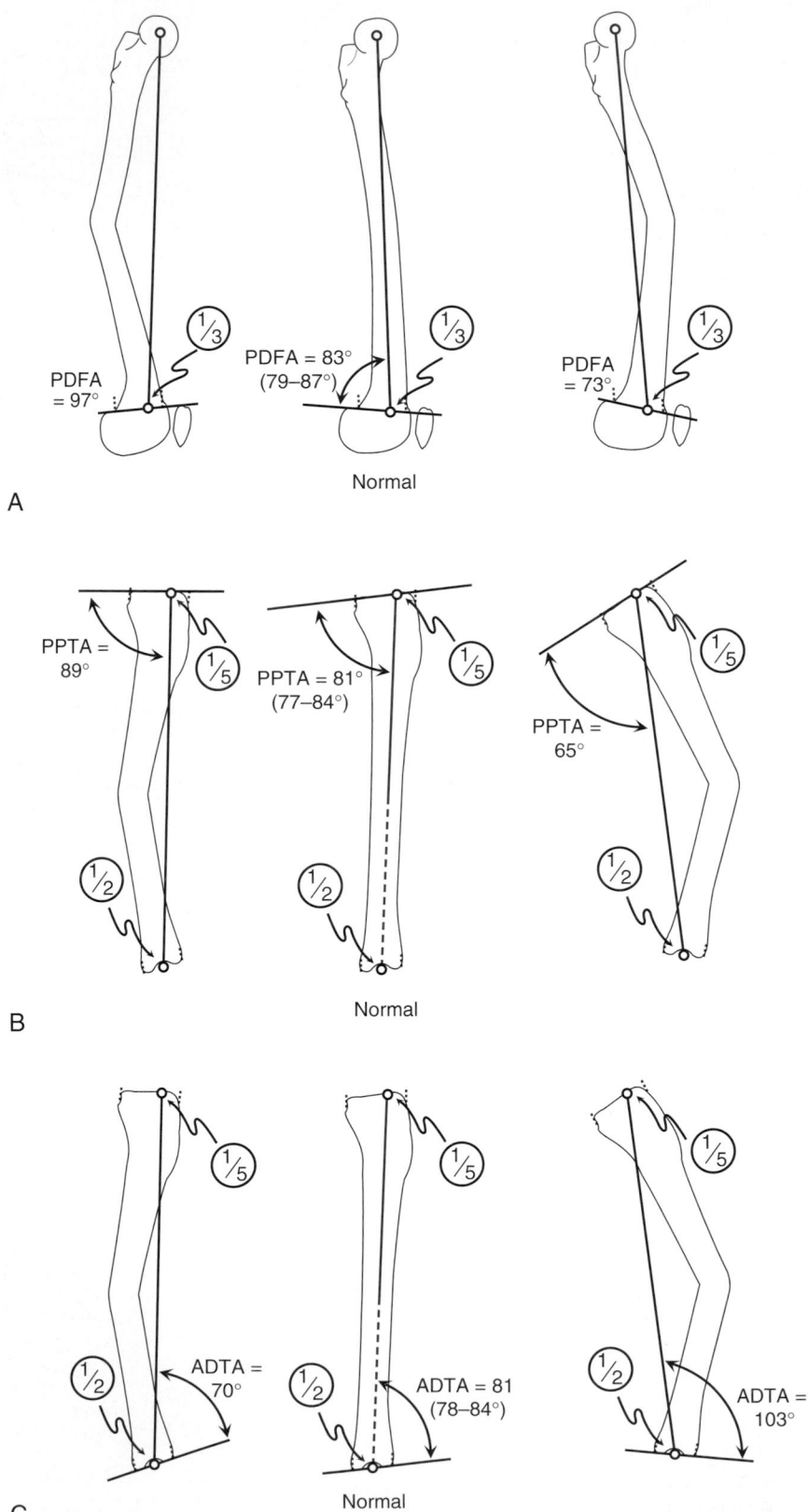

**FIGURE 62–39.** The effect on joint orientation of deformity at any level in the bone is assessed with the "overall" saggital plane malorientation test. *A,* Distal femur. *B,* Proximal tibia. *C,* Distal tibia. The anterior distal tibial angle is measured relative to the modified tibial anatomic axis line, which is determined from normal joint-intersection points. This represents the effect of an angular deformity on the orientation of the proximal or distal joint. ADTA, anterior distal tibial angle; PDFA, posterior distal femoral angle; PPTA, posterior proximal tibial angle. (Redrawn from Paley, D. Principles of Deformity Correction. Heidelberg, Germany, Springer-Verlag, 2002.)

**FIGURE 62–40.** Sagittal-plane deformity of a distal tibia. *A,* The normal anatomic anterior distal tibial angle (aADTA) is 80°. *B,* The 20° recurvatum deformity of the distal tibia is compensated by 20° of plantar flexion of the ankle joint. This uncovers the talus and produces a net anterior displacement shear force on the ankle. The center of rotation of the ankle is displaced anteriorly, elongating the length of foot to be stepped over. *C,* The 20° procurvatum deformity of the distal tibia is compensated by 20° of dorsiflexion of the ankle joint. This covers the talus to the point that there is impingement with the neck of the talus in maximal dorsiflexion. The center of rotation of the ankle is displaced posteriorly, shortening the length of foot to be stepped over. (Redrawn from Paley, D. Principles of Deformity Correction. Heidelberg, Germany, Springer-Verlag, 2002.)

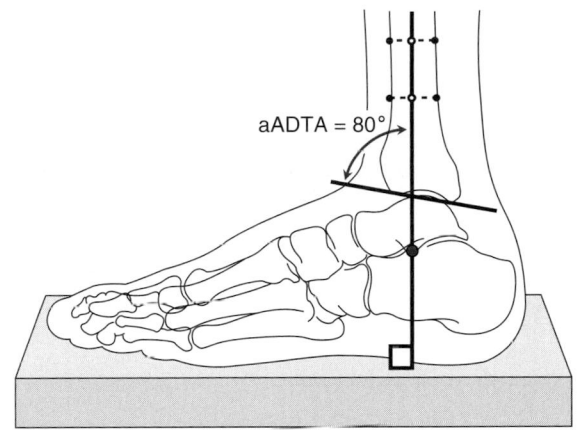

A      Normal

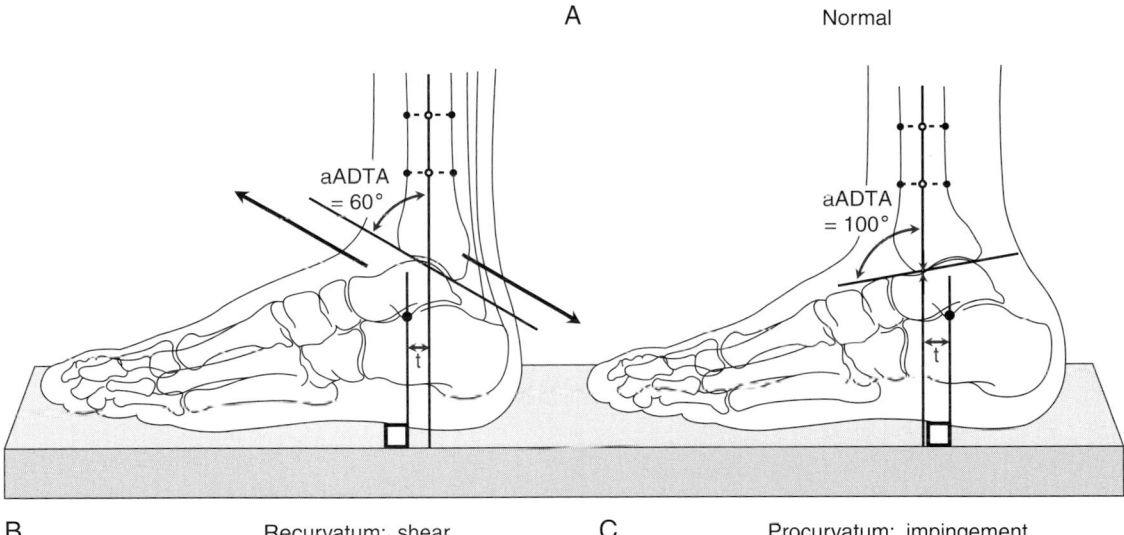

B      Recurvatum: shear      C      Procurvatum: impingement

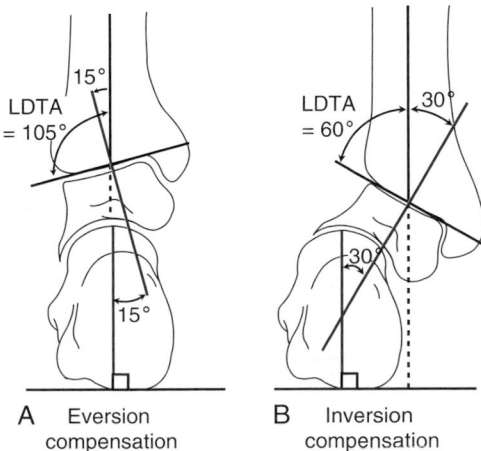

A   Eversion compensation      B   Inversion compensation

**FIGURE 62–41.** Frontal-plane deformity of the distal tibia. *A,* Varus deformity of the distal tibia is 15°, and the subtalar joint is in 15° of eversion to compensate for the varus angulation. This moves the midline of the calcaneus medially, more in line with the mid-diaphyseal line of the tibia, and decreases the loading moment arm on the ankle joint. *B,* Valgus deformity of the distal tibia is 30°, and the subtalar joint is in 30° of inversion to compensate for the valgus angulation. Despite the compensation, the midline of the calcaneus is laterally displaced farther away from the mid-diaphyseal line of the tibia. This condition increases the loading moment arm on the ankle joint. *LDTA,* lateral distal tibial angle. (Redrawn from Paley, D. Principles of Deformity Correction. Heidelberg, Germany, Springer-Verlag, 2002.)

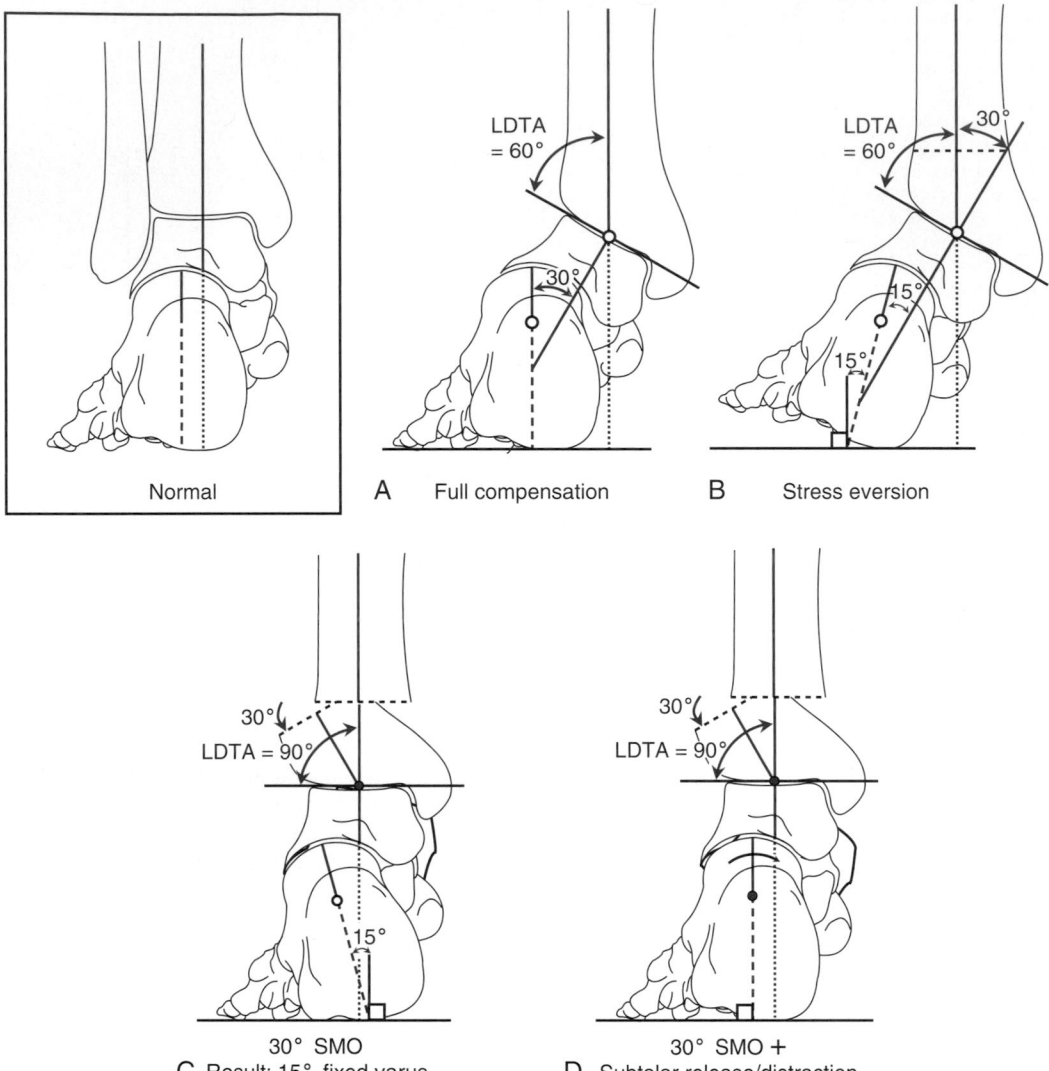

**FIGURE 62–42.** Hindfoot varus contracture resulting from a distal tibial valgus deformity. *A,* The 30° valgus deformity of the distal tibial is well-compensated with 30° compensatory subtalar varus. The foot is plantigrade. The compensated angular deformity results in a net lateral translation deformity of the heel. *B,* Maximal stressed eversion reveals a fixed, 15° compensatory subtalar varus contracture. The position of the heel is in 15° valgus relative to the tibia. It would be 30° valgus if there were no contracture. *C,* Full correction of the 30° distal tibial deformity with a supramalleolar osteotomy (SMO) in the presence of 15° of fixed subtalar varus puts the foot into 15° of hindfoot varus. *D,* To realign the heel, the subtalar joint is released or distracted. *LDTA,* lateral distal tibial angle. (Redrawn from Paley, D. Principles of Deformity Correction. Heidelberg, Germany, Springer-Verlag, 2002.)

## REFERENCES

1. Johnson, E.E. Multiplane correctional osteotomy of the tibia for diaphyseal malunion. Clin Orthop 215:223–232, 1987.
2. Maquet, P. Valgus osteotomy for osteoarthritis of the knee. Clin Orthop 120:143–148, 1976.
3. Paley, D. Principles of Deformity Correction. Berlin, Springer-Verlag, 2002.
4. Paley, D; Herzenberg, J.E.; Bor, N. Fixator-assisted nailing of femoral and tibial deformities. Tech Orthop 12:260–275, 1997.
5. Paley, D.; Herzenberg, J.E.; Tetsworth, K.; et al. Deformity planning for frontal- and sagittal-plane corrective osteotomies. Orthop Clin North Am 25:425–465, 1994.
6. Sanders, R.; Anglen, J.O.; Mark, J.B. Oblique osteotomy for the correction of tibial malunion. J Bone Joint Surg Am 77:240–246, 1995.
7. Sangeorzan, B.P.; Judd, R.P.; Sangeorzan, B.J. Mathematical analysis of single-cut osteotomy for complex long bone deformity. J Biomech 22:1271–1278, 1989.
8. Sangeorzan, B.J.; Sangeorzan, B.P.; Hansen, S.T.; Judd, R.P. Mathematically directed single-cut osteotomy for correction of tibial malunion. Orthop Trauma 3:267–275, 1989.

# Periprosthetic Fractures of the Lower Extremities

Jay D. Mabrey, M.D.

## ASSESSING PATIENTS AT RISK

The largest population at risk for perioperative fractures about a total-joint replacement is the millions of patients already walking around with one or two implanted. Although it is impossible to predict whether an individual patient will sustain any given fracture, it is possible to identify patients who have one or more risk factors for periprosthetic fracture and attempt to ameliorate that risk. Osteoporotic patients with total-joint replacements should undergo at least a basic metabolic bone disease workup. Routine radiographic surveys of each total-joint prosthesis will alert the surgeon to potential problems with loosening and osteolysis. Clinical trials are now under way to treat osteolytic lesions with alendronate after animal models have demonstrated the efficacy of oral bisphosphonate therapy in inhibiting bone resorption mediated by wear debris.[7, 242]

## PREOPERATIVE PLANNING

Preoperative planning is a critical element in the prevention of periprosthetic fractures and, along with meticulous intraoperative technique, the one over which the surgeon has the most control. Identification of potential pitfalls ahead of time, on all sides of the joint, allows the surgeon to develop solutions to these problems in addition to backup plans should the original approach fail. A careful medical history and full assessment of the available bone stock should be carried out before each procedure. A younger patient with severe osteoporosis may fare better with a cemented femoral stem than one that is porous coated. If the physical examination reveals severe scarring and stiffness about the hip or arthrofibrosis about the knee, soft tissue releases may be called for to ease dislocation of the hip or exposure of the knee. Full-length anteroposterior and lateral radiographs of the lower extremities may reveal unexpected bony deformities that can lead to breaching of the cortex, especially in canal-filling, uncemented implants. The surgeon should plan to bypass obvious cortical defects by at least two cortical diameters,[140] although such technique has been shown to prevent fractures only with cemented stems, not uncemented stems.[154] Retained hardware about the femur may need to be removed before performing a total-hip replacement, especially if it will leave a stress concentrating screw hole[33] near the tip of a prosthesis.

Most importantly, the surgeon should assess the following four main areas when addressing a periprosthetic fracture: patient function, component function, patient history, and tools.

**Patient Function.** How well was the patient functioning before the fracture? Was the patient a community ambulator, house confined, or bedridden? Heroic measures directed at making the radiograph look good will not benefit a patient who cannot appreciate the effort. Medically unstable patients or those with severe chronic health problems that may significantly increase their perioperative mortality may benefit from a functional brace to facilitate bed-to-chair transfers.

**Component Function.** How well are *all* the involved components functioning, and are they all stable? Patients with periprosthetic fractures of the femur associated with osteolysis may also have osteolysis of the pelvis around a worn acetabular component. The surgeon should be ready to revise both components if necessary.

**Patient History.** A careful history may elicit prefracture complaints of pain about the prosthesis suggesting that one or more components were loose before fracture. Bethea and colleagues[20] reported that up to 75% of the periprosthetic fractures in their series had evidence of loosening before fracture. In many cases, especially at a referral center such as ours, these patients are unknown to us before their admission for fractures. Contacting the original surgeon who was monitoring the patient may provide important information with respect to the need for revision of what appear to be otherwise stable components. If revision has been considered in the past, the surgeon should address this issue during fixation of the fracture.

**Tools.** What techniques for fixation and revision are available to the surgeon? It is not advisable to tackle any revision of a periprosthetic fracture without the appropriate instruments and personnel. I always have at least one or two backup plans available should the fracture turn out to be more complex at surgery than was anticipated by the preoperative radiographs. It is imperative that the surgeon address these fractures with the most experienced team that can be assembled. Revision total-hip procedures typically take longer,[11] reportedly 77% longer on average than primary hip replacement,[219] and a periprosthetic fracture often adds to that time. Waiting for appropriate equipment or graft material only prolongs the time that the incision is open and may increase the risk of infection and blood loss.[12]

## METICULOUS TECHNIQUE

Anticipation of problems before reaching the operating room ensures that the surgeon will have the appropriate equipment and personnel available. Intraoperative fluoroscopy or radiographs are especially important in avoiding problems during revision procedures. Any hardware remaining about the hip should be left in place until the hip is dislocated so that the femur is not weakened before manipulation.[104]

Revision arthroplasty has become increasingly complex, so it is extremely important to approach the joint in a safe and rational manner. New extensile approaches about the hip have significantly simplified the removal of solidly fixed components without compromising bone stock.[162]

Any intraoperative cracks in the cortex should be protected with cerclage wires or cables.[50, 84, 90, 174, 261] Protective cerclage cables or wires are also useful during the insertion of extensively porous-coated implants into a femoral shaft after an extended osteotomy. The cable is placed 2 cm distal to the distal portion of the extended osteotomy before the insertion of any broaches or reamers.[287]

Proper templating ensures that the appropriate broaches are used during preparation of the femoral canal. Oversized broaches can breach the cortex or weaken it distally by over-reaming. Under-reaming distally may create a wedging effect and split the femur during insertion of the final prosthesis. Any doubts about the position of the broaches or trial implants should be addressed with intraoperative radiographs or fluoroscopy.[104]

## POSTOPERATIVE PROTOCOLS

Postoperative radiographs should be carefully examined by the surgeon to assess any potential complications. Significant defects should be addressed sooner rather than later.

Patients and their families need to be carefully instructed on all precautions with respect to appropriate weight bearing, ambulatory aids, rehabilitation, and the extent of exercises. Home nursing services may also be helpful in analyzing the patient's postoperative home environment and eliminating various hazards, as well as improving safe access.

## FRACTURES ABOUT TOTAL-HIP ARTHROPLASTIES

## Incidence and Etiology

### FEMUR

Intraoperative fractures associated with cemented femoral stems occur in an average of 1% of patients overall, with a range of 0.3% to 6.9%.* Berry, referring to the Mayo Clinic Joint Registry, reported a total of 1249 intraoperative and postoperative femoral fractures occurring during or after 30,329 primary and revision arthroplasties, cemented and uncemented, in the past 30 years for an overall incidence of 4%.[17]

Modifications in the design of total-hip prostheses over the years have changed the nature of periprosthetic fractures. Cortical penetration by sharp broaches during cemented total-hip implantation procedures has resulted in stress risers that subsequently lead to fracture through the defect.[259] Later, revision of loose cemented components required the creation of cortical windows, which led to intraoperative[125] and postoperative[125, 127] fractures. Implantation of porous ingrowth and press-fit femoral components creates hoop stresses within the proximal end of the femur that can easily fracture the cortex during surgery.[90, 94, 122, 174, 204] Table 63–1 summarizes the risk factors for intraoperative and postoperative periprosthetic fractures about total-hip prostheses.

Intraoperative femoral fractures are more likely to occur with uncemented, press-fit components.[94] The prevalence in these cases ranges from 2.6% to 4% for primary hip replacements[39, 98, 174, 235] to as high as 17.6% for uncemented revisions.[30, 50, 77, 90, 177] Only 0.3% of the 20,859 cemented primary total-hip arthroplasties in the Mayo Clinic Joint Registry sustained an intraoperative fracture, as opposed to 5.4% of the 3121 uncemented primary total-hip replacements.[17]

The true incidence of postoperative fractures is reflected best in studies that report on fractures around both cemented and uncemented stems, and it ranges from 0.8% to 2.3%.[3, 20, 22, 84, 150, 261, 292]

The number of postoperative periprosthetic femoral fractures is expected to continue to increase as the population of patients with total-hip revisions continues to grow, current patients are living longer, and younger patients are being offered implants.[17] Recent technologic advances in total-hip arthroplasty still fall short of providing the "lifetime hip,"[26] thus ensuring a steady supply of periprosthetic fractures.

---

*See references 16, 28, 47, 73, 75, 76, 81, 82, 109, 138, 145, 165, 172, 181, 193, 265, 278.

**TABLE 63–1** ...............................................

## Risk Factors for Fractures about Total-Hip Replacements

**MECHANICAL**

| | |
|---|---|
| Previous hip surgery | Stress risers within cortex |
| | Screw holes |
| | Plates |
| Associated hip surgery | Subtrochanteric osteotomy |
| | Proximal femoral focal deficiency |
| Previous arthroplasty | Revision arthroplasty |
| | Loose prosthesis |
| | Localized osteolysis |
| | Femoral bone loss |
| Cortical perforation | Narrow femoral canal |
| | Developmental dysplasia of the hip |
| | Over-reaming distally |
| Uncemented prosthesis | Large-diameter implants |
| | Long, straight stems |

**MEDICAL**

| | |
|---|---|
| Osteoporosis | Primary |
| | Secondary to steroids or other medications |
| | Female gender |
| Osteopenia | Rheumatoid arthritis |
| | Osteomalacia |
| | Paget's disease |
| | Osteopetrosis |
| | Osteogenesis imperfecta |
| | Thalassemia |
| Neuromuscular disorders | Parkinsonism |
| | Neuropathic arthropathy |
| | Poliomyelitis |
| | Cerebral palsy |
| | Myasthenia gravis |
| | Seizures |
| | Ataxia |
| Juvenile rheumatoid arthritis | Osteoporosis |
| | Narrow femoral canal |
| | Periacetabular adhesions |

*Source:* Haddad, F.; et al. In: Duncan, C.; Callaghan, J., eds. Periprosthetic Fractures after Major Joint Replacement. Philadelphia, W.B. Saunders, 1999, pp. 191–208.

### Etiology of Femoral Fractures

**Cortical Defects.** Bony abnormalities of the femur are a major cause of intraoperative and postoperative periprosthetic fractures.* These defects can occur as a result of removal of previous fixation devices or cement, or they can result directly from the motion of a loose implant or improper broaching and reaming techniques.

Surgically generated cortical defects have a high association with periprosthetic fractures occurring less than a year after arthroplasty.[56, 236] Figure 63–1A and B is an example of eccentric reaming of the femoral shaft that subsequently led to fracture. Primary cemented hips have a reported intraoperative femoral perforation rate of up to 2.8% with simple broaching.[196, 259] Screws removed from the femur generate stress risers that weaken the bone for at least 4 weeks.[33] Larger defects involving 50% of the cortical width can reduce torsional strength to 44% of the original value,[140] but bypassing such a defect with a cemented stem doubles the bone's strength.[140] Data from our laboratory

---

*See references 14, 55, 56, 70, 90, 94, 104, 125, 147, 202, 230, 236, 241.

suggest that smooth, uncemented stems do not, however, provide torsional stability.[154] Table 63–2 lists some of the precautionary measures that can be taken against mechanical risk factors associated with periprosthetic fractures of the femur.[153]

**Revision Arthroplasty.** Femoral fractures induced by revision arthroplasty were first reported by Charnley[48] and are associated with high morbidity and prolonged convalescence.[50] Some authors have reported either no fractures in their series of revisions[78] or no difference in fracture rates between revision and primary surgery.[235] However, many authors note that a large percentage of their periprosthetic fractures are associated with revision.[30, 66, 77, 257] One study reported a fivefold increase in fractures during revision as compared with primary arthroplasty,[90] and other studies have reported a nearly sixfold increase in fractures during uncemented revisions as compared with cemented revisions.[177, 178] Risk factors specific to revision arthroplasty include penetration of the cortex during cement removal,[127, 241] creation of cortical windows for cement removal,[125, 258] attempts to dislocate the femur in the face of a scarred joint capsule,[4, 125] and sepsis.[157] It is likewise possible that the trauma of previous surgery on the proximal part of the femur weakens it by disrupting its blood supply or inducing osteoporosis.[3] Previous arthroplasties, osteotomy, and fractures can also alter the geometry of the proximal end of the femur and increase the risk of fracture.[90]

**Mismatched Components.** Oversized femoral broaches or prostheses may cause fractures secondary to increased hoop stress within the femur. These fractures are necessarily intraoperative in nature but may be detected postoperatively only on careful review of radiographs. Such fractures have been associated with cemented arthroplasty during the initial reaming for or seating of the component[4, 125, 236, 261] and with malalignment of the broaches.[151] Unusual anatomy can be a significant factor, with Dunn and Hess[71] reporting a 27% intraoperative fracture rate while seating a curved Charnley prosthesis into the relatively narrow, straight femoral shafts of patients with chronically dislocated hips. Charnley[48] has indicated that intraoperative fractures heal in the presence of fresh cement, provided that it does not become interposed between the fracture surfaces.

Uncemented femoral stems require initial stability to promote proper osseous integration or bony ingrowth,[37, 70, 92, 94, 104, 105] and any micromotion between the implant and bone can lead to the formation of fibrous tissue at the interface.[204] Thus, these implants and their broaches and reamers come into intimate contact with cortical bone and may result in increased assembly stress during insertion that can approach the yield stress of cortical bone.[122] Components that are oversized with respect to the femur create significant assembly strain, or hoop stress, whereas same-sized components produce only moderate strain.[122] Intraoperative fracture rates for uncemented components vary from 4.2% to 15.2%, depending on the type of prosthesis[90]; according to one report,[174] three fourths of these fractures occur during preparation of the femoral canal and the remainder are noted during insertion of the component.

In their analysis of 93 periprosthetic fractures, Beals and

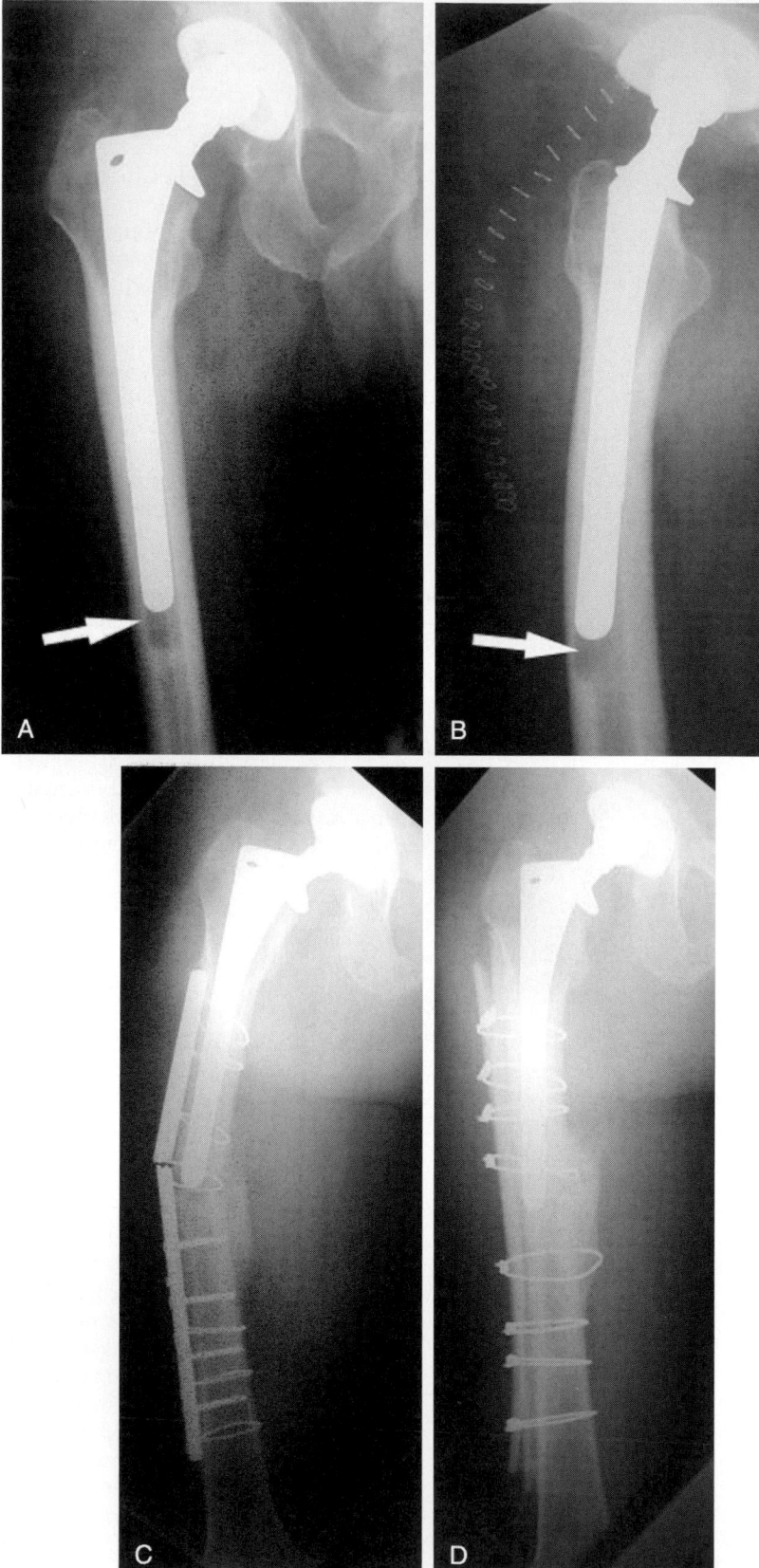

**FIGURE 63–1.** Immediate postoperative radiographs, anteroposterior (*A*) and lateral (*B*), demonstrating eccentric reaming of a straight-stemmed femoral component, with generation of a stress riser at the tip of the component (*white arrows*). Within a year after the hip replacement, the patient sustained a Vancouver B1 fracture of the femur at the stress riser that was repaired by implanting a 4.5-mm side plate with screws and cables. This repair subsequently failed at the level of the original fracture (*C*). Final treatment consisted of an osteotomy through the abundant callus and placement of a femoral allograft strut along the length of the patient's femur (*D*).

## TABLE 63–2

Mechanical Risk Factors and Precautionary Measures

| Factor | Precautionary Measures |
|---|---|
| **Cortical defect** | |
| Screw hole | Bypass by 2 cortical diameters; allow to remodel |
| Instrument penetration | Careful orientation of device; adequate operative exposure |
| Cortical window | Use other removal techniques*; bypass by 2 cortical diameters; cortical strut graft |
| Osteolysis | Bypass and bone graft |
| **Oversized broach/ prosthesis** | Accurate preoperative template silhouetting |
| | Intraoperative radiographs |
| | Familiarity with technique; cerclage cable or wire |
| **Nonanatomic femur** | |
| Developmental | Custom broach/prosthesis |
| | Extra small broach/prosthesis; osteotomy/shortening |
| | 3-D model reconstruction |
| Osteotomy or fracture | Custom broach/prosthesis |
| | 3-D CT reconstruction |
| **Pericapsular pathology** | |
| Periarticular scarring | Careful capsulectomy |
| Heterotopic ossification | Careful resection of heterotopic ossification |

*Ultrasonic cement removal, direct visualization from above with high-speed bur, Segles cement removal system (Zimmer, Warsaw, In.).

*Abbreviations:* CT, Computed tomography; 3-D, three-dimensional.

*Source:* Mabrey, J.D. In: Heckman, J.D.; Bucholz, R.D., eds. Rockwood and Green's Fractures in Adults. Philadelphia, Lippincott Williams & Wilkins, 2001.

Tower[14, 266] observed that femurs with ingrowth prostheses tended to fracture within the first 6 months after implantation because of cortical stress risers created by reaming and broaching. They also noted no late fractures associated with ingrowth prostheses, except in association with violent trauma.[14, 266]

Experience plays a significant role in the successful implantation of these devices. Separate authors report markedly different fracture rates for the same prosthesis,[6, 160] whereas others note marked reductions in fracture rates after several hundred procedures or several months of training.[235, 243]

Among the latest generation of uncemented femoral components are those that use a milling or tapered reaming technique to prevent hoop stress in the proximal part of the femur.[41, 61, 280]

**Pericapsular Pathology.** Fractures of the femoral neck or shaft that occur while attempting to dislocate the femoral head may be due to failure to adequately release a tight or scarred hip capsule. This situation can be encountered in cases of primary total-hip replacement involving acetabular protrusion, ankylosing spondylitis, previous osteotomy[48] or proximal femoral fracture, or previous fracture of the acetabulum. Fracture caused by manipulation of the femur during revision arthroplasty has been reported in several series,[50, 125, 235, 236] with the riskiest maneuver being initial dislocation of the femoral

component from the acetabulum. Heterotopic ossification, which usually arises from previous trauma, can also make dislocation hazardous.

**Loose Components.** One third to three fourths of periprosthetic fractures are associated with loose femoral components.[14, 20, 22, 66, 94, 96, 104, 123, 266] In a general population of patients with total-hip replacements, only 0.2% of cemented femoral components were loose at over 11 years of follow-up,[63] and only 2% had been revised for loosening at 20 years of follow-up,[234] which suggests that mechanical failure plays a significant role in these fractures. In one series,[123] loose, cemented prostheses were more likely to fracture around the proximal part of the femur, whereas well-fixed cemented components fractured around the tip. A loose component is more likely to transmit stress at relatively few contact points, thus overloading the femur, than to distribute the force over the wide contact area afforded a well-fixed component. Figure 63–2 highlights the benign appearance of a loose, long-stem uncemented femoral component that eventually led to a periprosthetic fracture.

**Osteoporosis.** Osteoporosis is the one constitutional risk factor that is mentioned frequently in association with periprosthetic fracture of the hip and over which the orthopaedist has little control.* More than half of all periprosthetic fractures in one Swedish study occurred in patients who had undergone arthroplasty for hip fracture, but only 1 in 10 primary total-hip arthroplasties were performed for hip fracture.[3] This finding is not surprising inasmuch as more patients with femoral neck fractures have osteoporosis than do age-matched control subjects.[233]

**Osteolysis.** Osteolysis is rarely cited as a primary cause of periprosthetic fracture of the hip,[56, 112, 194, 283] but an increasing number of clinical reviews of periprosthetic fractures have begun to mention it as a risk factor.[70, 94, 104, 130] Figure 63–3 illustrates such a fracture through an osteolytic lesion of the greater trochanter, and Figure 63–4 presents an osteolytic fracture through the femoral shaft. As Pazzaglia and Byers[194] have noted, osteolytic lesions can leave the cortex dangerously weak and susceptible to intraoperative fracture during manipulation or instrumentation.

## ACETABULUM

Intraoperative acetabular fractures are primarily due to insertion of an uncemented, metal-backed component with so-called press-fit techniques to achieve initial stability.[36, 38] Sharkey and coauthors[244] reported on 13 intraoperative acetabular fractures collected from three separate institutions and noted that 11 of the 13 occurred in women. When all cups were cemented, intraoperative fractures of the acetabulum were almost nonexistent. McElfresh and Coventry[164] reported only one periprosthetic fracture of the acetabulum in 5400 total-hip replacements performed at their institution with cement.

Postoperative fracture of the acetabulum after total-hip arthroplasty is also relatively rare.[17, 36, 38] In a recent study, Peterson and Lewallen[201] reported on 11 patients who

---

*See references 5, 14, 48, 50, 94, 104, 143, 156, 261, 291, 292.

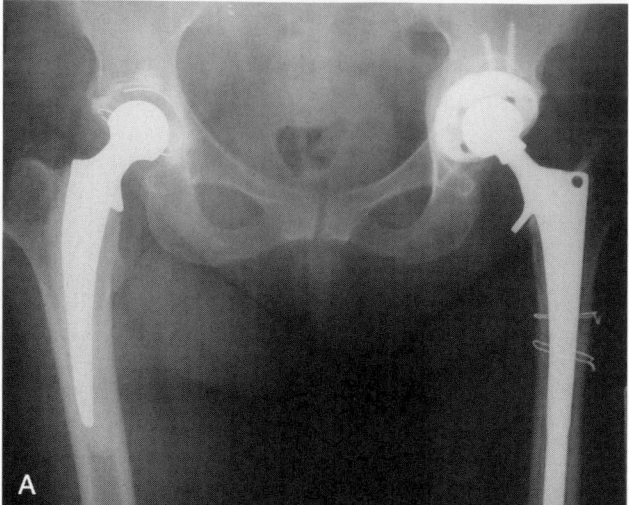

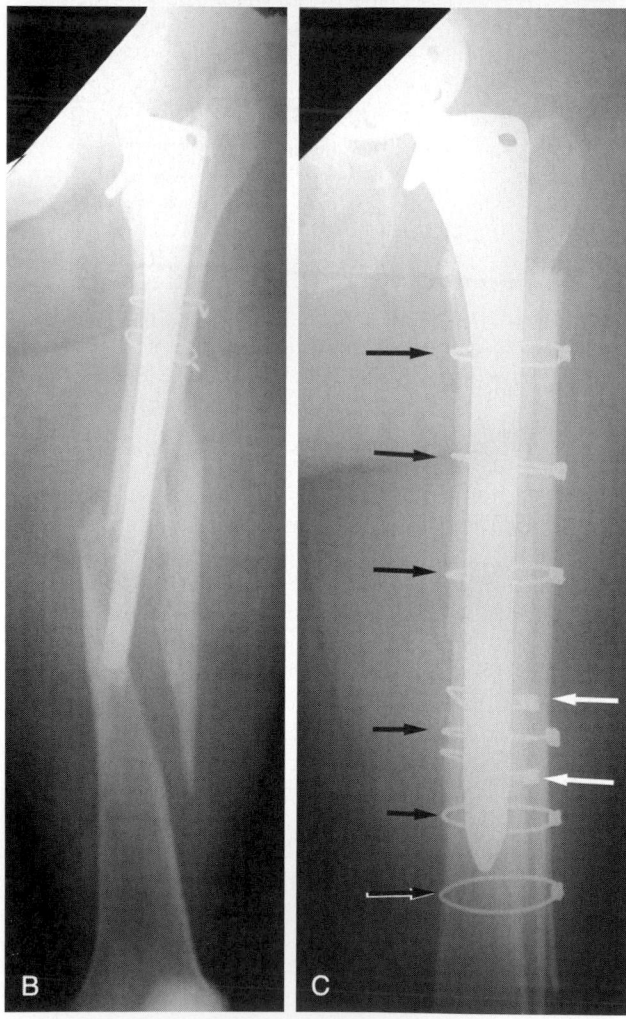

sustained a periprosthetic fracture of the acetabulum an average of 6 years after total-hip arthroplasty. Eight fractures were caused by blunt trauma or a fall, and three occurred spontaneously. Eight of the 10 surviving patients underwent revision of the components because of pain or loosening. Sanchez-Sotelo and colleagues[227] reported three cases of periprosthetic acetabular fracture associated with severe pelvic osteolysis and stated that the fractures occurred with little or no trauma. Berry notes an additional category of postoperative acetabular fracture, pelvic discontinuity, which was identified in 29 of 3505 acetabular revisions at the Mayo Clinic. These fractures were characterized by a transverse acetabular fracture nonunion that the authors suggested began as a stress fracture.[17]

### Etiology of Acetabular Fractures

Whereas early clinical studies of press-fit acetabular components reported no fractures associated with their use,[179, 231, 232] periprosthetic fractures of the acetabulum have increased in primary total-hip replacements over the last several years because of the increased popularity of uncemented, press-fit components.[104] In revision arthroplasties, pelvic osteolysis, stress shielding, and severe bony defects all contribute to the risk of periacetabular fracture.[9, 38, 158, 201] In one multicenter study of intraoperative

**FIGURE 63–2.** Anteroposterior radiograph of the pelvis demonstrating a well-fixed, cemented right hip and a loose, uncemented left hip (A). While being evaluated for possible revision of her painful, loose hip, the patient sustained a Vancouver B2 fracture about the long-stem component (B). The fracture was reduced about a fully porous-coated revision stem with cerclage cables (white arrows) and then supplemented with femoral allograft stabilized with additional cables (black arrows) (C).

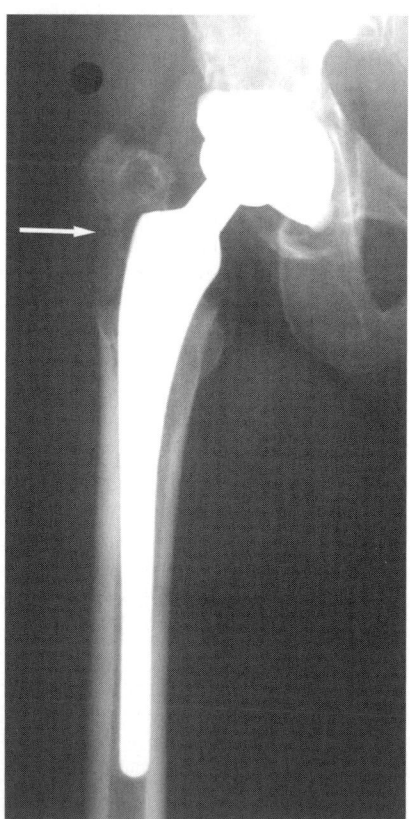

**FIGURE 63–3.** Fracture of the greater trochanter (white arrow) through an osteolytic cyst in an otherwise well-fixed uncemented total-hip replacement. Note the eccentric alignment of the femoral head within the anteroposterior aspect of the acetabulum, indicative of significant polyethylene wear.

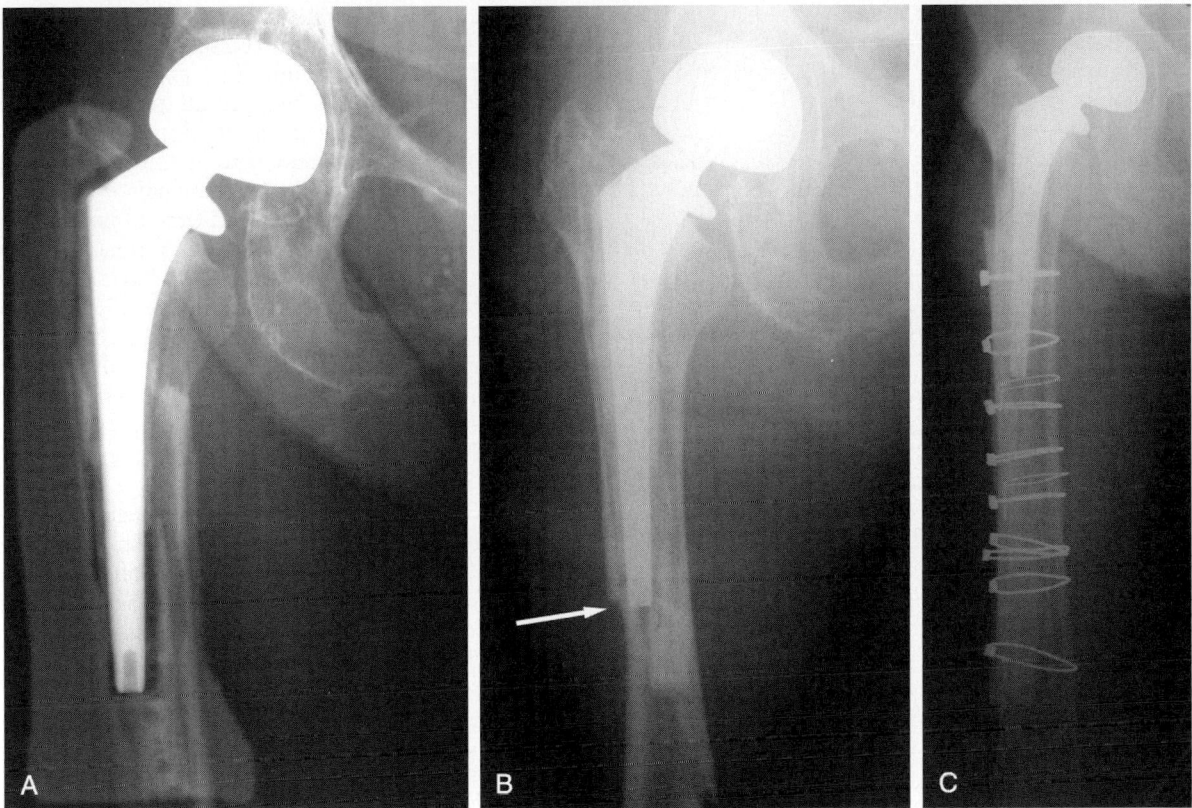

**FIGURE 63–4.** Prefracture radiograph of a loose hemiarthroplasty in a patient being assessed for possible revision, although she had minimal symptoms at the time of evaluation (*A*). The patient's health deteriorated and her revision was delayed. She subsequently fell and sustained a Vancouver B2 fracture about the loose stem (*B*). Rather than attempt an involved revision of the prosthesis, the minimally displaced fracture was reduced and stabilized with a contoured femoral allograft and cables (*C*).

acetabular fractures occurring after the insertion of components in under-reamed acetabula, 11 of 13 fractures occurred in women with osteopenic bone.[244]

**Over-reaming of the Acetabulum.** Excessive reaming of the acetabulum may weaken the supporting bone to such an extent that the increased hoop stress seen with impaction of the cup may cause the pelvis to dissociate.[104] This etiology is predominantly seen in primary cases involving osteoporosis and in revisions associated with extensive pelvic osteolysis.

**Under-reaming of the Acetabulum.** Oversized press-fit acetabular components have been favored in the past to avoid screw fixation and its associated risk of vessel perforation[129, 133, 274] and fretting.[116, 129, 133, 274] No screws also means no screw holes to channel polyethylene wear debris into the pelvis.[200] In an in vitro study of acetabular components inserted into human cadaveric specimens, Callaghan reported fractures in 4 of 15 acetabula that had been under-reamed by 2 mm and in 4 of 15 that had been under-reamed by 4 mm.[36, 38, 131, 132, 244] Other investigations suggest that inadequately reaming the acetabulum by as much as 3 mm less than the component is safe, but that inadequately reaming it by 4 mm leads to some fractures of the pelvis.[64, 137] Although these fractures typically occur during impaction of the prosthesis, they may not be noted until much later. Simple rim fractures should not affect the overall stability of the cup, but an oversized component that splits and distracts the acetabulum can lead to a painful fibrous union.

Callaghan's work suggests that the most common fracture pattern involves the peripheral rim of the acetabulum and that these rim fractures occur only in larger specimens in the range of 56 to 58 mm.[36, 38, 132] Displaced split fractures running from the anterior to the posterior wall were seen exclusively in smaller-sized specimens in the range of 50 to 54 mm. The authors also noted that one third of the fractures were visible only on special cup oblique views.[36, 38, 132] Callaghan currently discourages excessive under-reaming, defined as greater than 1 mm, especially in patients with osteopenic bone,[38] and instead prefers to manage these patients with line-to-line reaming and augmentation of fixation with screws through the dome of the component.

**Trauma to the Pelvis.** Unlike periprosthetic femoral fractures, periprosthetic fractures of the acetabulum after total-hip arthroplasty have been the subject of relatively few reports.[164, 201, 236, 246] This paucity of reports may in part be due to the fact that the forces across the acetabulum are primarily compressive, in contrast to the torsional and bending moments applied to the femur during the activities of daily living.

Peterson and Lewallen[201] studied 11 patients who sustained a periprosthetic fracture of the acetabulum 1 month to 13 years after total-hip arthroplasty. Four fractures were caused by blunt trauma, four patients had simply fallen, and the etiology was unknown in the remaining three. Nine of the 11 had fractures about a cemented component. Five patients had fractures of the medial wall, three fractures involved the posterior column, two were transverse fractures, and one involved the anterior column. Eight of the 10 surviving patients underwent revision of the acetabular component because of pain, loosening, or nonunion.[201]

**Fractures of the Pubic Ramus.** Fracture of the pubic ramus in association with arthroplasty of the hip is rare (0.06%)[164] when compared with rates for femoral fractures. A review of the available case reports[60, 142, 161, 164, 187, 202] reveals several common factors: (1) just as in the first reports of pubic ramus fractures in military recruits,[240] these patients experienced an unusual increase in activity; (2) the fractures often appeared within the first year or so of the arthroplasty; (3) many of the patients had osteoporosis; (4) persistent groin pain was a typical symptom; (5) symptoms in all cases resolved after 4 to 6 weeks of protected weight bearing; and (6) fracture healing was often documented on follow-up radiographs of the pelvis. A bone scan of the pelvis greatly assists in establishing the diagnosis and ruling out infection of the joint.[60]

# Classification

## FEMORAL FRACTURES

Whittaker and colleagues[281] proposed one of the earliest classification schemes, based primarily on their experience with hemiarthroplasties. Johansson and associates[125] presented their more familiar classification in 1981, one based on both intraoperative and postoperative fractures associated with cemented total-hip arthroplasties. Type I fractures were proximal to the tip of the prosthesis, with the stem remaining in the medullary canal. In type II fractures, the fracture line extended from the proximal portion of the femoral shaft to beyond the distal portion of the prosthesis, with the prosthetic stem dislodged from the medullary canal of the distal fragment, and in type III fractures, the fracture line was entirely distal to the tip of the prosthesis.[125] Later, Bethea and colleagues[20] proposed a system that excluded all fractures distal to the tip of the prosthesis. In their scheme, type A was a fracture at the tip of the component, type B was a spiral fracture around the component, and type C was a comminuted fracture around the stem. More recently, Mont and Maar[173] proposed a six-part classification based on a review of almost 500 cases reported in the literature.

The American Academy of Orthopaedic Surgeons (AAOS) Committee on the Hip[1] proposed a six-part classification in 1990 that divided the femur into three separate regions, with level I defined by the proximal end of the femur distally to the lower extent of the lesser trochanter. Level II included the 10 cm of the femur distal to level I, and level III covered the remainder of the femur distal to level II.

AAOS type I is a fracture proximal to the intertrochan-

teric line that usually occurs during dislocation of the hip. It can also result from a partial saw cut that is completed with an osteotome. Often, this fracture requires only revision of the neck cut, but it could become a problem for a prosthesis that relies on the femoral neck for fixation. Type II is a vertical or spiral split that does not extend past the lower extent of the lesser trochanter, whereas type III does extend past the lesser trochanter but not beyond level II, usually the junction of the middle and distal thirds of the femoral stem. Type IV fractures traverse or lie within the area of the femoral stem tip in level III, with type IVA being a spiral fracture around the tip and type IVB being a simple transverse or short oblique fracture, similar to a Bethea[20] type A or a Johansson[125] type II fracture. Type V fractures are severely comminuted fractures around the stem in level III, and type VI fractures are fractures distal to the stem tip, also in level III.

Beals and Tower[14, 266] proposed a similar five-stage classification scheme in 1996. After analyzing the outcomes of 93 periprosthetic fractures classified with their system, Beals and Tower[14, 266] suggested that treatment of these fractures be selected with knowledge of the prefracture interface status, site of the fracture, and the patient's general medical condition.

### Vancouver Classification

One of the most recent and, in the author's opinion, one of the most comprehensive instruments for evaluation of periprosthetic hip fractures is the Vancouver classification.[26, 70, 286] It is notable for the manner in which it directs the surgeon toward the most appropriate reconstructive procedure for a variety of fracture scenarios. Recent investigations by Dunwoody and co-workers[26, 72] have shown the classification to be both a reliable and valid construct (Fig. 63–5).

The Vancouver classification incorporates three important factors that must be considered in the management of periprosthetic femoral fractures: the site of the fracture, stability of the implant, and assessment of surrounding bone stock.

**Fracture Site.** The fractures are divided into A, B, or C, depending on their location. Type A fractures are proximal to the prosthesis and occur in either the greater ($A_G$) (see Fig. 63–3) or lesser ($A_L$) trochanter. Type B fractures occur around or just below the stem, whereas type C fractures are found well below the distal tip of the prosthesis.

**Implant Stability.** Type A fractures are further subdivided into stable and unstable fractures, depending on the need for surgical stabilization. In type B1 fractures, the femoral component is well fixed, as opposed to type B2 fractures (see Fig. 63–2B), in which the component is loose.[26] The stability of the implant in type C fractures is usually considered independently of management of the fracture itself.

**Bone Stock Assessment.** The quality of the surrounding bone stock further subdivides the type B group. Type B1 and type B2 fracture classifications assume that the surrounding bone stock is adequate. Type B3 assumes a loose component with severe bone stock loss, either from osteopenia, osteolysis, or comminution.

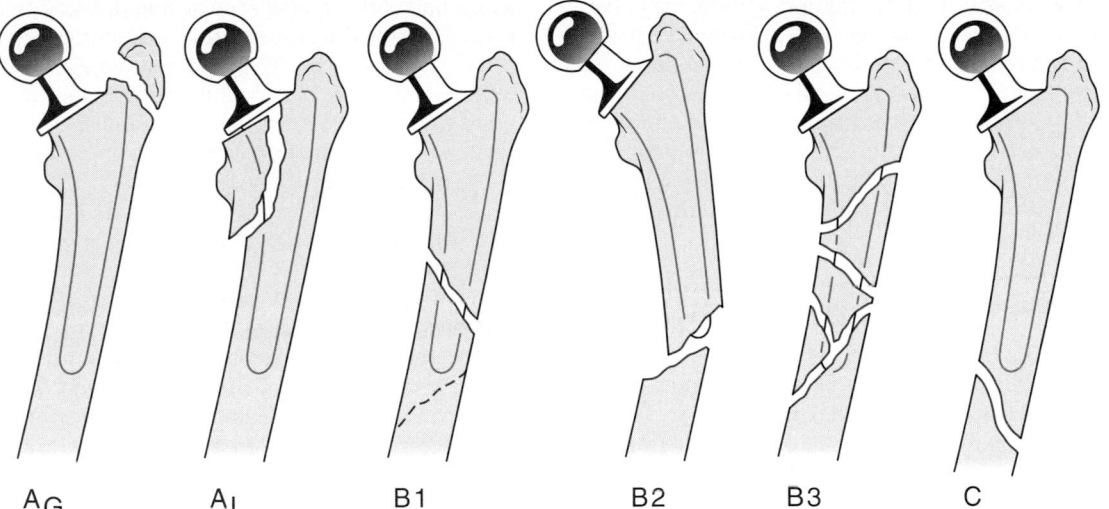

**FIGURE 63–5.** Vancouver classification scheme for periprosthetic femoral fractures. (After Duncan, C.; Masri, B. Instr Course Lect 44:293–304, 1995.)

## ACETABULAR FRACTURES

Fractures of the acetabulum, though rare, can occur both intraoperatively and postoperatively and give rise to differing clinical findings. Callaghan and associates noted that most of the fractures in their in vitro study were peripheral, although column and transverse fractures also occurred.[36, 38, 131]

Peterson and Lewallen[201] developed a simple classification scheme based on their observations of 11 postoperative periprosthetic fractures of the acetabulum after total-hip arthroplasty: type 1 fractures had a clinically and radiographically stable acetabular component, and type 2 fractures had an unstable component. Although the authors treated all type 1 fractures nonsurgically at their initial evaluation, half were associated with eventual loosening of the component and required revision.

## Special Considerations

### INFECTED FRACTURES

The differential diagnosis in cases of sudden onset of pain about a total-hip replacement should always include infection. The erythrocyte sedimentation rate, white blood cell count, and C-reactive protein level can assist the surgeon in making the distinction between fracture and infection. However, when a patient experiences acute pain in the groin after total-hip arthroplasty, one should also consider periprosthetic fracture of the acetabulum or insufficiency fracture of the pubic ramus.[38]

Infection has been implicated as a contributory factor in postoperative periprosthetic fractures,[56, 171] in addition to being associated with intraoperative fractures occurring during revision for sepsis.[50, 157] With an infected revision, the hip should be débrided of all old cement and reactive tissue, but the prosthesis should not be replaced, although it may be necessary to stabilize the fracture with internal fixation.[50] The patient is then treated in traction and with antibiotics, depending on culture results. Delayed reimplantation is performed at a time determined by the individual surgeon's protocol. Removal of a well-fixed implant as the initial step of a two-stage revision may be complicated by fracture of the femoral shaft during extraction. It is important to stabilize the fracture and allow it to heal while at the same time treat the initial infection.

## FRACTURES ABOUT TOTAL-HIP/TOTAL-KNEE REPLACEMENT COMBINATIONS

Patients with multiple joint involvement, such as those with rheumatoid arthritis, often have ipsilateral total-hip and total-knee replacements. If the femoral component of the knee replacement has an intramedullary stem (e.g., Guepar, rotating hinge, or a modular revision stem), a greater concentration of stress occurs between the tips of the hip and knee components.[59] Urch and Moskal[269] reported on their treatment of an elderly woman with severe rheumatoid arthritis and distal femoral nonunion; management involved placement of an entire femoral allograft and simultaneous ipsilateral revision total-hip and total-knee arthroplasty. The woman's fracture subsequently healed, and she returned to her prefracture level of ambulation. Dave and colleagues[65] reported on another case of an elderly woman with rheumatoid arthritis who sustained a spiral fracture of the femur between her cemented hip and her cemented, stemmed, constrained total-knee prosthesis. They used a Mennen plate[168] and interfragmentary screws to stabilize the fracture.

Walker and co-workers[273] described a reconstruction involving a combined hip and stemmed knee that was designed to be rigidly connected during the surgical procedure, thus preserving the entire femur with its muscle attachments. Their three examples of the technique proved that this technique could be successful in this difficult situation.

Total-femur replacement is another option in these rare,

but troublesome cases. Porsch and colleagues[203] reported on two cases of total femoral replacement, both in male patients with rheumatoid arthritis who had sustained a femoral fracture after ipsilateral total-hip and total-knee replacements. Both men suffered from severe osteoporosis caused by long-term steroid therapy, and their radiographs demonstrated refracture of the femur with loosening. After replacement with total femoral prostheses, both patients were able to walk.

## BILATERAL PERIPROSTHETIC FRACTURES

Simultaneous fracture of both femurs places great stress on patients in terms of blood loss, pain, and mobilization. Zuber and associates[291] reported one case of bilateral periprosthetic femoral fracture treated by bilateral cementless revision stems staged 4 days apart. This procedure was followed by 8 weeks in a rehabilitation hospital. Systemic disease, whether neurologic or hematologic, can place a patient at even greater risk for bilateral periprosthetic fracture. Van Heest and colleagues[270] reported on a patient with bilateral central acetabular fracture-dislocations secondary to sustained myoclonus. Because of ongoing myoclonus, the patient was initially treated nonoperatively but eventually underwent successful staged bilateral total-hip arthroplasty 15 months after injury. Timon and coauthors[262] reported bilateral femoral shaft fractures in a 49-year-old woman with β-thalassemia minor who had undergone bilateral hybrid total-hip arthroplasty in a single sitting. The fractures were discovered immediately postoperatively on routine radiographs and were found to be minimally displaced longitudinal fractures extending below the level of the cement plugs. Treatment entailed restricted weight bearing for 6 weeks, with subsequent healing.

## POST-TRAUMATIC TOTAL-HIP ARTHROPLASTY

The flip side of treating fractures about total-hip replacements is performing total-hip arthroplasty about a previously fractured joint. Scarring from a previous procedure, retained hardware, heterotopic bone, and residual osseous deformity and deficiency may make the procedure more complex than routine total-hip arthroplasty.[275]

On the femoral side, deformities may occur about the greater trochanter, femoral neck, metaphysis, diaphysis, or any combination thereof.[19] Not only do these cases require removal of the previous fixation, but rotational or angular osteotomies may also be necessary.

Skeide and colleagues[249] reported on nearly 4000 total-hip arthroplasties performed for previous hip fracture and compared them with a cohort of nearly 20,000 patients who received total-hip arthroplasties because of osteoarthrosis. Five years after the index replacement, the fracture patients were shown to have a 1.35 times higher risk of revision than the osteoarthrosis patients did ($P = .008$). More of the fracture patients than the osteoarthrosis patients had to undergo additional operations because of dislocation or femoral shaft fracture, whereas fewer needed reoperations because the acetabular component had loosened.

Because the acetabulum may be surrounded by fixation plates and riddled with screws, a more extensive exposure is often needed just to remove penetrating hardware (Fig. 63–6). Fortunately, Weber and colleagues[275] reported that none of the 22 acetabular components they inserted without cement in previously fractured acetabula had to be revised or demonstrated radiographic loosening at a 10-year follow-up.

## Diagnosis

The diagnosis of intraoperative fracture of the femur may not be apparent if the prosthesis remains stable within the shaft; however, most of these fractures are readily picked up either by a sudden change in stability of the shaft or by a change in the sound of impact of the prosthesis. Any suspicions on the part of the surgeon warrant an immediate intraoperative radiograph. In cases in which a shaft fracture is obvious, I begin my extended exposure while the radiology technician is being summoned to the operating room. Intraoperative fractures of the acetabulum may be detected by the lowered pitch and hollowness of the sound of impact of the cup into the pelvis. Judet views are indicated if the fracture line is not apparent. Intraoperative fluoroscopy may also be helpful as one pans around the cup in search of fracture lines.[38]

The diagnosis of postoperative periprosthetic fracture about total-hip arthroplasties may be obscured if the fracture occurs within the scenario of an already loosened prosthesis or in a mentally compromised patient. Postoperative fracture of the acetabulum may be suspected in cases of violent trauma or a sudden onset of pain after a fall. Judet views offer a first look, but it may be necessary to conduct a detailed examination with spot fluoroscopy films.[38] Computed tomography[93] or magnetic resonance imaging (MRI)[83] of total-joint prostheses has been reported for other reasons and provides reasonable resolution, especially if the implants are made of titanium. Recent work with MRI venography about total-hip arthroplasties[139, 205] suggests that signal voids about the prosthesis may not obscure the essential details of periprosthetic tissue.

As always, the most helpful radiographic view may be the one obtained before the patient's current symptoms began. Comparison of prefracture with postfracture radiographs may reveal subtle changes in alignment or subsidence suggestive of an occult fracture. Full-length images of the femur are essential in ruling out a Vancouver type C fracture distal to the tip of the prosthesis.

## Treatment Options

Up to three quarters of periprosthetic fractures have evidence of femoral loosening on prefracture radiographs.[20] It is also possible for the prosthesis to become loose at a later time even if the femoral component is stable at the time of fracture fixation. Such loosening can be associated with both intraoperative fractures[125, 236] and those that occur after primary arthroplasty.[3, 20, 56]

Fracture healing is paramount to success in these types of injuries. Nonunion of a periprosthetic fracture, regard-

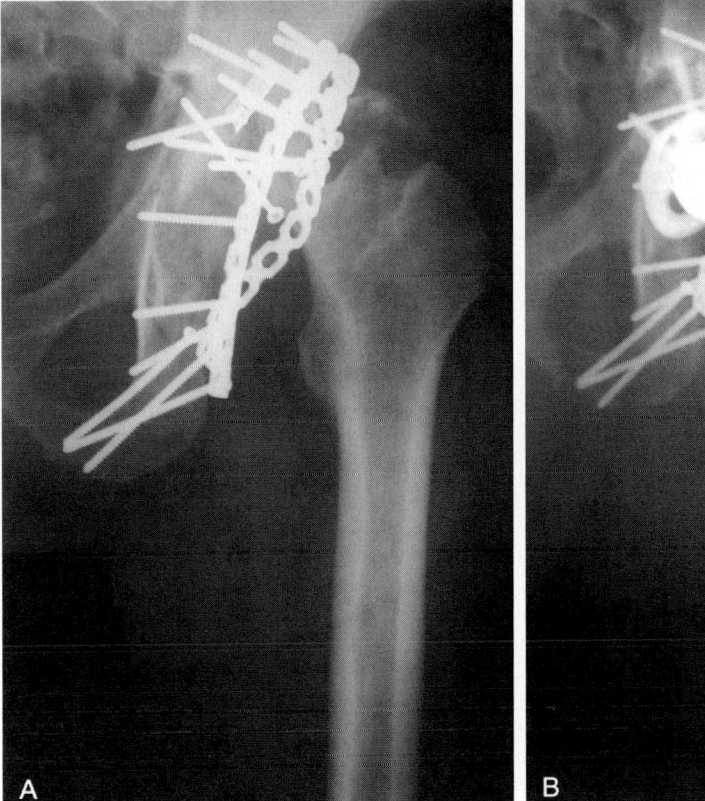

**FIGURE 63–6.** *A,* Severe traumatic arthritis of the left acetabulum and subsequent osteonecrosis of the femoral head. *B,* Insertion of a total-hip replacement required extended trochanteric osteotomy for exposure of acetabulum. Note that the proximal aspect of the posterior plate was cut (*white arrow*) to allow placement of an uncemented cup, thus avoiding unnecessary exposure.

less of treatment, places an added burden on an already compromised patient, and reoperation is frequently necessary in these cases.[20, 45, 247, 250] Allowing a patient to ambulate with a pseudarthrosis, even if it is not painful, places constant stress on the remaining components and can result in fracture of the stem.[241] Delayed union not only prolongs the patient's convalescence[56, 281] but can also result in fatigue failure of the component.[20]

Proximal fractures that are stable and incomplete are almost certain to heal,[235] and fractures that are stabilized by a well-fixed prosthesis also have a high union rate.[20, 56, 125] Fractures distal to the tip of the prosthesis, however, are inherently unstable and have a high nonunion rate when treated without surgery.[20] Duncan and Masri[70] have outlined a comprehensive treatment algorithm, as shown in Figure 63–7.

## NONOPERATIVE TECHNIQUES

Only a few absolute indications exist for nonoperative management of periprosthetic fractures of the hip. Stress fractures of the pubic ramus after total-hip arthroplasty, as noted earlier, invariably heal without complication.[60, 142, 161, 187] Incomplete, proximal, longitudinal split fractures that occur early after surgery or that were missed during surgery do not require operative fixation[235] but should be observed carefully. Relative indications include patients who are at high risk for surgical procedures and fractures that can be maintained readily with either casting or traction[56, 125, 202] or those in which the prosthesis provides significant stability.[125]

### Observation or Protected Weight Bearing

Observation or protected weight bearing should be reserved for stable, incomplete, proximal split fractures that are identified either during surgery or soon thereafter.[3, 160, 235, 236, 266, 281] A prosthesis that relies on distal fixation for stability is less likely to require intraoperative stabilization of a proximal split than one that relies on proximal fit and fill.[235]

### Traction

Traction management of periprosthetic fractures of the hip is considered here more for its historical perspective than overall utility. Treatment in traction can last from 9 weeks to 4 months,[3, 91, 261] with the added risk that prolonged bedrest can result in increased mortality and still not prevent surgery.[96] In one series, nearly one third of the patients treated with traction required subsequent operative correction for malalignment of the fracture.[3] In other series, patients treated with traction have had to undergo revision to long-stem femoral components.[185, 197] Complications associated with traction therapy include refracture,[91] decubitus ulcers,[108] gangrene,[3] and death.[3, 108, 281] Conversely, traction may be the only option in medically unstable patients.

Certain fracture patterns around prostheses have slightly better results. Long oblique fractures[4] and fractures associated with well-fixed stems[124] fare better than do those around loose stems[124] or those located at or distal to the tip of the prosthesis.[108]

Skin traction can be used as temporary stabilization while awaiting surgery or casting, but pin traction should

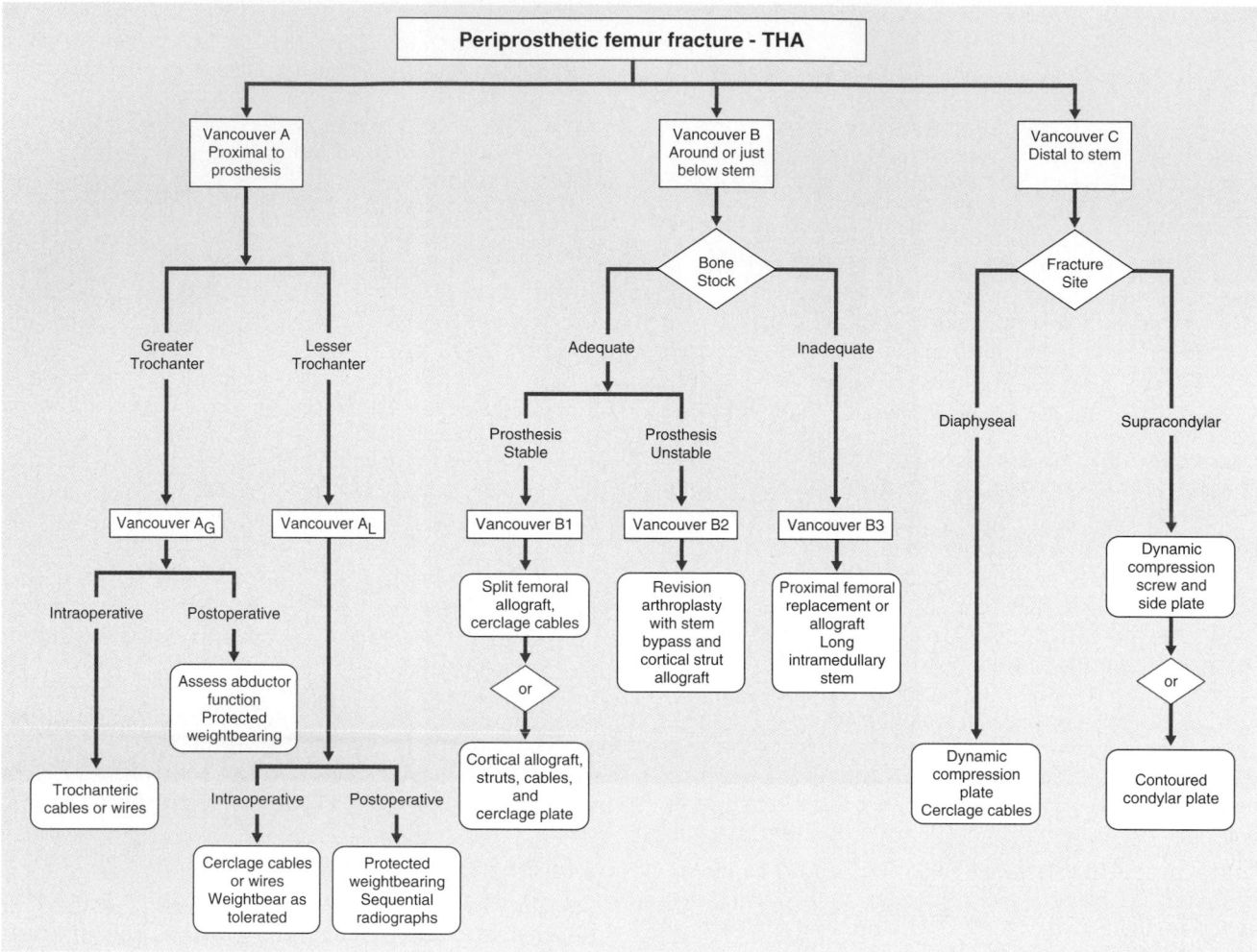

**FIGURE 63–7.** Hip fracture algorithm. (After Duncan, C.; Masri, B. Instr Course Lect 44:293–304, 1995.)

be considered for the long-term management of unstable fractures. Careful consideration should be given to pin placement around the knee because a knee arthroplasty may be present as well and placement of a femoral pin may contaminate the femur for future procedures. The orthopaedist should consider the use of an air-supported mattress as an essential component of this technique for the prevention of decubitus ulcers.

### Casting or Bracing

Casting and bracing of periprosthetic femoral fractures have been used both as adjuncts to traction and as primary modes of treatment. Preliminary traction for 4 to 7 weeks can be followed by the application of either a long leg cast[3] or a hip spica cast.[281] Primary spica cast treatment works better with fractures that are minimally displaced and easily controlled.[74, 235]

## OPERATIVE TECHNIQUES

### Indications

Intraoperative fractures are an absolute indication for operative management of periprosthetic fractures around the femur and may call for nothing more than a simple cerclage wire or cable about the femur[70, 94] or a short

pelvic reconstruction plate behind the cup.[38] Unless other, more pressing circumstances intervene, there is no better time to stabilize the femur or acetabulum than during the initial exposure. Strong relative indications for operative management of postoperative fractures include loose or fractured prostheses,[20, 56, 69, 70, 94, 95, 123, 266] malalignment of the fracture,[3] and fractures distal to the femoral stem tip.[20, 125, 266, 290] Much like the complications associated with routine revision surgery, reported complications associated with operative treatment of fractures about total-hip replacements include infection,[45, 59, 125] malunion,[125, 271] nonunion,[45, 125, 250] and subsequent loosening of the prosthesis.[52, 55, 125]

Although the femur is most frequently involved in periprosthetic fractures, the surgeon should address the acetabulum as well and determine whether it should also be revised for loosening, malposition, or wear. Dislocation is common after revision arthroplasty, and a poorly positioned cup should be revised. The modularity of current acetabular components allows the liner to be replaced without removing the metal shell. If the acetabulum is to be spared but the femoral component revised, it is important to have the proper size of femoral head available to fit the cup. Postoperative fractures about the acetabulum can be difficult to assess, and even if most do heal uneventfully without surgical intervention, the majority still end up as revisions for pain and loosening.[201]

### Acetabular Fractures

Thirteen cases of acetabular fracture associated with the insertion of cementless acetabular components were reported by Sharkey and colleagues.[244] Nine of these fractures were identified intraoperatively, and six were treated with both additional screws for stability and autograft from the femoral head. Two patients were treated with non–weight bearing for 6 to 8 weeks. Of the four cases not identified until after surgery, two failed and required revision and a third demonstrated migration of the cup. The fourth was treated with non–weight bearing for 6 weeks. Two of the nine patients with fractures identified intraoperatively complained of significant groin pain at follow-up, as did two of the four patients with fractures identified postoperatively. Ideally, one should attempt to stabilize the cup within the acetabulum and place a bone graft at the same time. Autografting is also strongly suggested to speed the healing process, as is a period of delayed weight bearing.[244]

The surgeon is more likely to encounter postoperative acetabular fractures, and they have a more varied fracture pattern. In their review of 11 such fractures, Peterson and Lewallen[201] noted five medial wall fractures, three involving the posterior column, two transverse fractures, and one of the anterior column. One should not attempt to revise these fractures by using the uncemented cup and its screws as an internal fixation plate.[201] It is better to stabilize the pelvis through traditional plating techniques and then revise the acetabulum. If bone loss is severe, bone graft and an antiprotrusio cage may be necessary. In some cases, it may be necessary to stabilize the fracture within the dome of the acetabulum with pelvic fixation plates and then rebuild a new acetabulum over the fracture, again using allograft and a protrusio cage.

### Femoral Fractures

**Surgical Exposure.** An extended trochanteric osteotomy enables controlled access to the femoral component and is a useful technique for revision of solidly fixed femoral components.[8, 162, 288] The trochanteric slide allows comprehensive exposure of the acetabulum and femur comparable to trochanteric osteotomy, but with a diminished risk of trochanteric escape. The vastus slide allows wide exposure of the femoral shaft when using an anterolateral approach.[162] An extended femoral osteotomy is very useful in the revision of long-stemmed, cemented components.[287, 288] The anterolateral aspect of the proximal end of the femur is cut for one third of its circumference, extended distally, and levered open on an anterolateral hinge of periosteum and muscle. This technique creates an intact muscle-osseous sleeve composed of the gluteus medius, greater trochanter, anterolateral femoral diaphysis, and vastus lateralis and exposes the fixation surface, as well as distal cement.[287] This technique is also useful in exposing and removing the femoral and acetabular components after severe intrapelvic protrusion.[89]

It is important to protect the femur adjacent to these osteotomies with cerclage cables or wires to avoid potential hoop stress fractures.[174] Any intraoperative cracks in the cortex should also be protected with cerclage wires or cables.[50, 84, 90, 174, 261] Protective cerclage cables or wires are likewise useful during the insertion of extensively porous-coated implants into a femoral shaft after an extended osteotomy. The cable is placed 2 cm distal to the distal portion of the extended osteotomy before insertion of any broaches or reamers.[287]

**Intramedullary Techniques.** Long-stem femoral revisions accounted for a significant percentage of the operative treatment in several studies.[66, 91, 96, 124, 185, 197, 261, 264, 281] In most cases, long-stem revision is used as a primary mode of treatment, but in some cases, it is used after more conservative measures have failed.[185, 197] Some authors consider revision arthroplasty to be the treatment of choice for periprosthetic fractures if the femoral component is loose,[123] and the length of hospitalization is considerably shorter than with traction management[91]; however, problems with healing may require reoperation with bone grafting.[3] When these longer stems are inserted, it is important to bypass any cortical defects by at least two cortical widths to decrease stress concentrations[170] (see Fig. 63–2C).

Fluted or "ribbed" stems add significant rotational control to the distal fragment, and their success has been well documented in the European literature.[229, 272, 277, 291, 292] These devices eliminate the need for extramedullary stabilization in many cases. Modular, ribbed-stem designs allow the insertion of a longer stem to bypass fracture sites while maintaining the integrity of a proximal fixation collar.[51]

Flexible intramedullary devices have been used successfully to treat fractures primarily around uncemented hemiarthroplasties,[52, 134, 192] but they have also been used in more distal fractures around cemented total-hip prostheses.[134, 135] Küntscher nails have been inserted in antegrade fashion around both cemented hips[4] and uncemented hemiarthroplasties.[31] In addition, rigid nails have been used as extensions of standard total-hip prostheses when longer revision components were not immediately available.[155, 188, 189, 285] This experience led Luck and colleagues[151] to suggest the development of modular stems for hip prostheses as early as 1972.

Proximal femoral replacement has been used in cases in which simple revision arthroplasty was not stable enough, either for acute fractures[215, 247, 264] or for cases of chronic nonunion around prostheses.[247] Although the Harris Hip Scores for one series of patients undergoing proximal femoral replacement averaged 91 after surgery,[247] leg length discrepancies ranged from 1.5 cm long to 2.5 cm short on the affected side, and half the patients had moderate to marked abductor weakness.[247]

**Extramedullary Techniques.** Stabilization of periprosthetic fractures with metal plates allows accurate reduction and early mobilization.[241] Plate fixation around hip arthroplasty owes its popularity to the ready availability of the materials and the nearly universal familiarity of orthopaedic surgeons with the technique. Success with this procedure has been reported in several series,[241, 250, 281, 290] with union rates as high as 100%.[241] Loss of cortical bone beneath broad cerclage bands has interfered with bridging callus and led to refracture in one series.[126] Narrow cerclage cables do not appear to have this problem and are widely available.

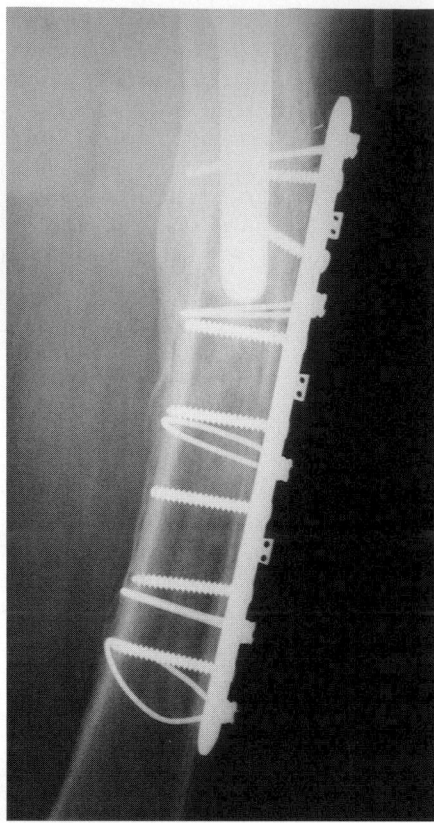

**FIGURE 63–8.** Varus angulation of a Vancouver B1 fracture fixed with a 4.5-mm side plate with special crimps incorporated for the cables.

Plate fixation is particularly useful in fractures distal to the tip of the prosthesis.[22, 50] An excellent review of the subject by Serocki and colleagues[241] recommends using a broad AO dynamic compression plate with at least eight cortices of fixation on each side of the fracture. Screws occasionally need to be angled more than the 7° to 25° allowed by the AO plates to avoid the stem, which leaves the screw heads incompletely seated.[241] After surgery, some authors recommend 3 months of no weight bearing followed by another 6 months of progressive weight bearing.

Complications associated with this technique include fracture of the plate (see Fig. 63–1C) or failure of fixation with subsequent varus angulation at the fracture site (Fig. 63–8). These failures are more likely to occur when an insufficient length of plate is used proximal to the fracture site.

Cortical allograft struts have also proved successful in periprosthetic fractures[27, 44–46, 198, 284] (see Fig. 63–4C). Chandler and colleagues[45] reported on a series of fractures around or below well-fixed femoral components. Nearly 90% of the fractures united, and the patients returned to their preinjury status within less than 5 months. The fractures are first reduced and temporarily stabilized with cerclage wires (see Fig. 63–2C). Two equal struts of fresh frozen femoral shaft allograft from an ipsilateral femur are then contoured to fit with a high-speed bur and are held to the host bone with 2-mm cerclage cables at 4-cm intervals. Autograft from the pelvis is always added to the fracture site.[45] The average hospital stay is only 12 days.

Advantages of this technique include the ability to customize the graft to any femur and the low modulus of elasticity of the graft.[32, 159, 195, 254] Experimental studies have shown that stiffer plates lead to a significant reduction in bone mass under the plate; such is not the case with flexible plates.[180] In addition, the cortical plate may even stimulate healing of the periprosthetic fracture.[159] Disadvantages include the cost of the allograft, as well as the possibility of disease transmission.[263] Finally, with any delay in healing, the struts can fail because they become weaker by 4 to 6 months as they are incorporated into the fracture site.[254]

**Combined Techniques.** Several authors report success with a combination of techniques, usually a long-stem prosthesis in conjunction with cerclage fixation alone or with plates.[4, 20, 66, 91, 123, 125, 189, 236, 281]

In Johansson and colleagues' series,[125] the six fractures treated with long-stem revision and either cerclage fixation or dynamic compression plating all did well, whereas only one of five periprosthetic fractures treated with a long-stem revision alone had a satisfactory result. Long oblique fractures treated with long-stem revision are more readily stabilized with cerclage fixation than are transverse fractures, which offer little purchase. In this situation, the addition of an extramedullary cortical strut provides additional rotational stability (see Fig. 63–2C).

## Preferred Management

### FEMUR

Intraoperative proximal femoral fractures are readily identified during the procedure and should be dealt with at that time (Table 63–3). They are generally a result of using press-fit or porous ingrowth components with tight tolerances. Components that rely on an extensive porous coating and distal incorporation are reported to be stable in this situation,[235] especially with a simple vertical split, but all other noncemented components can be expected to increase the hoop stress around the proximal part of the femur under load and should be stabilized with a cerclage wire or cable. Cemented cases should be stabilized with wire or cable before cement injection, primarily to prevent extravasation of cement into the fracture. For stable patterns, the postoperative regimen consists of protected weight bearing while monitoring the position of the prosthesis on radiographs.

Fractures can occur at the tip of an extensively coated prosthesis if the femoral canal was reamed eccentrically. If a longer, bowed stem cannot be used to replace the original implant because it is well fixed, these fractures can be reduced anatomically in the operating room and stabilized with cables and a cerclage plate. Based on more recent experience, however, I would suggest supplementing this fixation with femoral allograft struts if the material is available.

Immediate postoperative fractures in this region are usually intraoperative fractures that were missed. Treatment of stable patterns involves protected weight bearing and careful observation. If the prosthesis remains loose and symptomatic, it can be revised once the fracture has healed.

**TABLE 63–3**

Treatment Regimen for Intraoperative Periprosthetic Fractures about Total-Hip Replacements

| Fracture Site | Bone Quality | Implant Stability | Treatment |
|---|---|---|---|
| Proximal end of femur | Good | Stable | Cerclage |
| | Good | Unstable | Bypass fx with longer component; cerclage |
| | Poor | Stable/unstable | Proximal femoral allograft; bypass fx with longer component; cerclage |
| Periprosthetic, femoral shaft | Good | Stable | Dall-Miles plate[70] or bicortical onlay femoral shaft allograft; cerclage |
| | Good | Unstable | Bypass fx with longer component; bicortical onlay femoral shaft allograft; cerclage |
| | Poor | Unstable | Proximal femoral allograft; bypass fx with longer component; cerclage |

*Abbreviation:* fx, fracture.

Fractures about the stem are often associated with either a previous stress riser or a loose prosthesis. Intraoperative fractures in this region typically occur during revision surgery and are treated with a long-stem prosthesis that bypasses the cortical defect by two cortical diameters. Note that existing data support such treatment only for cemented stems[140] and that smooth, uncemented stems provide no protection against torsional fractures.[134] Fluted and extensively porous-coated stems that provide an interference fit distally should provide some protection.

Postoperative fractures can be associated with either a loose stem or a well-fixed component (Table 63–4). The femoral component is revised to a long stem if it is loose, and supplemental extramedullary fixation may be required. Well-fixed stems can be retained, especially if they provide some stability, and extramedullary stabilization is achieved with cortical allograft (see Fig. 63–2C).

Fractures involving the proximal and middle regions offer little support to the new component and warrant consideration of either a proximal femoral replacement or a long-stem component in a proximal femoral allograft.[70, 94] An alternative is to stabilize the femur with a contoured, split, ipsilateral femoral allograft.[27, 42, 43, 46, 70, 147, 266]

## ACETABULAR FRACTURES

As with intraoperative femoral fractures, intraoperative acetabular fractures should be addressed at the time of surgery. Occasionally, one encounters a crack in an osteophyte about the rim of the acetabulum, but such cracks are usually of no consequence. Small defects in the medial wall should be addressed with bone graft and stabilization of the cup with screws. Cracks about the anterior or posterior columns should be repaired with pelvic reconstruction plates. Major defects should be protected with an antiprotrusio cage[18, 99] and bone graft. Intraoperative fluoroscopy is helpful in assessing the integrity of the acetabulum by panning through an arc around the cup and providing multiple views of the pelvis.

## FRACTURES ABOUT TOTAL-KNEE ARTHROPLASTIES

### Incidence and Etiology

The overall prevalence of periprosthetic knee fractures is 1.2% in the combined results of five series[10, 42, 58, 141, 183]

**TABLE 63–4**

Treatment Regimen for Postoperative Periprosthetic Fractures about Total-Hip Prostheses

| Fracture Site | Bone Quality | Implant Stability | Treatment |
|---|---|---|---|
| Proximal end of femur | Good | Stable | Observe[235] |
| | Good | Unstable | Bypass fx with longer component; cerclage |
| Periprosthetic femoral shaft | Good | Stable | Bicortical onlay femoral shaft allograft; cerclage |
| | Good | Unstable | Bypass fx with longer component; bicortical onlay femoral shaft allograft; cerclage |
| | Poor | Unstable | Proximal femoral allograft; bypass fx with longer component; cerclage |
| Tip of component | Good | Stable/unstable | Bypass fx with longer component; bicortical onlay femoral shaft allograft; cerclage |
| | Poor | Stable/unstable | Consider proximal femoral allograft; bypass fx with longer component; cerclage |
| Distal to tip of femoral component | Good/poor | Stable | Treat fx with standard fixation techniques; cerclage if necessary; bone graft |
| | Good/poor | Loose | Bypass fx with longer component if fx in diaphysis; bicortical onlay femoral shaft allograft; cerclage |

*Abbreviation:* fx, fracture.

with a total of 2178 patients, although some series report rates as high as 5.6% associated with revision cases.[54] Periprosthetic knee fractures have been reported to occur at any time from during surgery to up to 10 years afterward,[35, 169] and most result from minimal trauma.[62, 67, 113, 221, 245, 248] Manipulation of total-knee prostheses under anesthesia to improve range of motion has also led to periprosthetic fractures.[62, 248] Cases resulting from motor vehicle accidents or other violent force are more difficult to treat, especially when they are bilateral.[106]

Most recently, Berry[17] reported a 2.8% overall incidence (573 cases) of periprosthetic fractures in the entire 19,810 primary and revision total-knee prostheses in the Mayo Clinic Joint Registry. Of these 573 cases, 256 (45%) occurred in the femur, 139 (24%) occurred in the tibia, and 178 (31%) involved the patella.[17]

## FEMUR

The Mayo Clinic Joint Registry lists a postoperative femoral fracture rate of 0.9% after primary knee arthroplasty and a much higher rate of 1.6% after revision knee arthroplasty.[17]

Intraoperative femoral fractures in total-knee arthroplasty may occur in association with posterior cruciate–substituting implants that require a notch to be cut for the femoral "box" that receives the tibial post.[17] Fractures may result if the slot is not cut wide enough for the box or if the femoral condyle is extremely narrow and the notch cut comes dangerously close to the medial or lateral cortex.

Initial exposure of the joint during revision arthroplasty is responsible for some intraoperative fractures, but they are more likely to occur during implant removal, especially if the femoral component is well fixed. Fracture may also occur during the insertion of a stemmed component[79] or even during some reduction maneuvers if the flexion and extension gaps are not well balanced. In many cases, the bone around these revisions is compromised by osteoporosis or osteolysis.[79] Berry[17] reported 23 intraoperative femoral fractures in 16,906 primary cases (0.1%) as compared with 24 such fractures in only 2904 revision arthroplasties (0.8%).

Postoperative femoral fractures, however, tend to occur in the supracondylar region.[17] Most of them are sustained after relatively minor trauma, usually because the patient has one or more of the risk factors listed in Table 63–5.

## TIBIA

The Mayo Clinic Joint Registry reports an incidence of 0.4% for postoperative primary fractures of the tibia versus 0.9% for postoperative revision fractures of the tibia.[17]

The incidence of periprosthetic tibial fractures is approximately half that of periprosthetic femoral fractures.[17] Felix and colleagues[85] reported on a series of 102 tibial fractures around total-knee arthroplasties and noted that 19 of them occurred intraoperatively. Intraoperative tibial fractures occurred during tibial preparation, during trial reductions, and at the time of cement removal during revisions. In contrast to the increased incidence of

| TABLE 63–5 |
| :--- |
| Risk Factors for Periprosthetic Fractures about Total-Knee Arthroplasties |

| | |
| :--- | :--- |
| Systemic | Osteoporosis |
| | Rheumatoid arthritis |
| | Neurologic disorders |
| Local | Cortical defect |
| | Adjacent total-hip stem |
| | Osteolysis |

intraoperative periprosthetic femoral fractures during revision, the Mayo Clinic Joint Registry reports similar incidences for primary and revision arthroplasty at 0.8% and 0.9%, respectively.[17]

In one recent study,[85] periprosthetic tibial fractures were identified in 83 postoperative cases and 19 intraoperative cases involving 73 women and 29 men. Fifty of them involved the tibial plateau, mostly around a loose implant. An additional 15 fractures involved the metaphysis or the proximal diaphysis and were also associated with a loose implant. A few developed after a major traumatic event, but most were associated with only minor trauma.

## PATELLA

In the Mayo Clinic Joint Registry, intraoperative fractures accounted for only 4.5% of all patellar fractures.[17] No intraoperative fractures were noted in the primary total-knee replacements, and only 8 of the 2904 total-knee revisions (0.2%) sustained an intraoperative patellar fracture.[17]

Resurfaced patellas are more likely to fracture than unresurfaced patellas.[101] The prevalence of these fractures ranges from 0.1% to 8.5%.* The Mayo Clinic Joint Registry reports a postoperative incidence of 0.7% for primary total-knee prostheses and a significantly greater value of 1.8% for revision arthroplasties.[17]

## Etiology

### BONY DEFECTS

#### Osteotomies

Osteotomy of the tibial tubercle can provide excellent exposure for a very stiff primary or revision knee, although the technique lowers the structural integrity of the proximal end of the tibia. Ritter and coauthors[218] reported two cases of proximal tibial fracture out of a total of nine tibial tubercle osteotomies. In both cases, the fractures occurred 1 to 2 months after surgery, and both healed without further operative intervention.[218]

Conversion of a proximal tibial osteotomy to a total-knee replacement also carries a certain degree of risk. Wedge osteotomies tend to make exposure of the knee more difficult than for a standard primary knee replace-

---

*See references 29, 53, 101, 111, 118, 152, 207, 217, 237, 267.

ment. Not only can they be associated with cortical defects from hardware removal, but the osteotomy site can also create an internal plane of denser trabecular bone. This layer of denser bone, when unexpected, may interfere with broaching of the proximal end of the tibia and create new cortical cracks or deflect the stem tip of the trial implant.

### Preexisting Deformities

Merkel and Johnson[169] found that two of the three men in their series of periprosthetic fractures had no other risk factors for fracture except for having had a healed supracondylar fracture before their initial total-knee arthroplasty.[169] They also reported a nearly threefold increase (0.6% versus 1.6%) in the incidence of periprosthetic supracondylar fractures in patients with previous total-knee arthroplasty.[169] Twenty-five percent of the patients in another series of fractures had undergone a revision arthroplasty before their periprosthetic femoral fracture.[35] This fracture may have been caused in part by residual cortical defects from earlier procedures, as well as by disruption of the epiphyseal and intramedullary blood supply to the distal end of the femur.[211] Retained hardware from earlier open reduction and internal fixation of a tibial plateau fracture can leave stress risers when removed. Iatrogenic defects, such as drill holes from tibial cutting jigs, can also lead to fractures about the plateau.

Revision of a previously inserted prosthesis may lead to an intraoperative fracture, especially if the surrounding bone has been damaged by osteolysis or loosening of the implant.[79] Fractures may also occur in cases in which the implant remains well fixed, as in the first stage of revision of an infected arthroplasty. Anticipation of these problems through extensive preoperative planning is essential for avoiding these problems.

Bony defects about the tibia can appear in several forms. Obvious developmental deformities such as the severe genu varum seen with Blount's disease can alter the proximal tibial geometry such that the implant may impinge on the cortex and create a defect.

### Anterior Cortical Notching

Surgical infringement on the anterior aspect of the distal femoral cortex,[2] or notching, has been implicated as a major cause of supracondylar fracture of the femur after total-knee arthroplasty.[2, 35, 62, 87, 169, 176, 184] The incidence of fractures associated with notching is around 40% in some series[2, 87] and less than 1% in others.[216]

Resection of this bone to accommodate the patellar flange of the femoral component poses the risk of cutting too deeply and interrupting the transfer of stress from the metaphysis to the diaphysis.[2] Anterior referencing guides will prevent this problem from occurring unless the intramedullary guide rod is angled too far posteriorly. Fracture of the anterior femoral cortex at this transition zone may also occur as a result of accidental perforation of the cortex during instrumentation with an intramedullary alignment rod.[79]

Culp and colleagues[62] calculated the effect of the thickness of anterior cortex removed on torsional strength of the distal end of the femur. Reductions in the polar moment of inertia for this region were 23.8% for a 1.5-mm loss of cortex and 29.2% for a 3-mm loss.[62]

## OSTEOLYSIS

"Osteolysis . . . is an important and common cause of bone loss after TKA [total-knee arthroplasty]."[148] Osteolysis of the femur or tibia after total-knee arthroplasty may run as high as 11% to 16% in some series, depending on the type of implant and fixation.[34, 200] Peters and co-workers[199] reported on a series of 57 revision knee arthroplasties and listed osteolysis as the reason for revision in 7% of their cases and supracondylar femoral fracture in 4%. Case reports of fracture through aggressive pseudotumors secondary to wear debris[15] and even fracture through femoral components secondary to osteolysis[115] underscore the significance of the problem.

## OSTEOPOROSIS

Osteopenia is a major contributing factor to periprosthetic fractures in total-knee arthroplasty.[2, 35, 62, 110, 169] Women are at much greater risk for osteoporosis than men,[13] so it is not surprising that between 75% and 100% of the patients in these series are female.[62, 102, 110, 113, 206] Patients with rheumatoid arthritis,[2, 23, 35, 113, 190] especially those taking corticosteroids,[35, 169, 184] have an increased risk of fracture. Women dominate these groups as well because they are two and a half times more likely to have rheumatoid arthritis than men are.[282]

## DESIGN FACTORS

Resurfacing the distal end of the femur with a cobalt-chromium shell renders the composite structure stiffer and concentrates stress at the junction of the metaphysis and the femoral component.[23] This area is the same one where notching is most likely to occur, as well as the site of origin of the major metaphyseal trabeculae.

Constrained or semiconstrained components are more likely to transmit rotational forces directly to the femur.[62, 184, 253] Hinged devices, which make up 10% to 25% of the components in some series,[62, 184] are extremely rigid and transmit high loads to the implant–cement–bone junction instead of relying on the patient's ligaments to absorb some of the energy.[253]

Total-knee arthroplasties that incorporate intramedullary stems, especially those that are cemented along their length, concentrate torsional and bending forces at the tip of that stem. Several stemmed total-knee implants, such as the Waldius,[176] Guepar,[35, 67, 121, 226] variable axis,[245, 276] Gschwend-Scheier-Bähler,[103] and spherocentric,[54, 253] have been associated with fractures at the tip of the femoral stem. Although most of these prostheses are no longer in use, current modular designs allow the addition of a variety of stem lengths and diameters to both the tibial and femoral components.

Posteriorly stabilized devices have their own unique risks. Fracture of a femoral condyle can occur with inadvertent medialization or lateralization of the femoral box cut for housing of the stabilization peg.[223, 225] Vigorous impaction of trial or final components can also lead to fracture of the condyle, especially if the bone cuts are off or if the implant is malaligned.[225]

Intraoperative fractures of the tibia, though rare, are often the result of design-related factors, either in the instrumentation or in the final implant configuration. Inadequate preparation of the seating holes for the fins or pegs of the tibial tray may create a split on impaction of the prosthesis.[79, 85, 223]

Long, modular stems added to tibial components, especially during revision arthroplasty, may lead to fracture of the tibial shaft as the stem impinges on the diaphysis.[223] Cementing these longer modular stems in revision situations will inject cement into the fracture site if the diaphysis breaks.

Of 102 periprosthetic tibial fractures in a report from the Mayo Clinic,[85] 83 were postoperative, with 15 of them being associated with a loose-stemmed implant. These fractures typically involved the metaphysis or proximal diaphysis.

## NEUROLOGIC DISORDERS

More than one third of the patients reported by Culp and colleagues[62] had a preexisting neurologic disorder such as seizure, cerebral ataxia, or Parkinson's disease. These patients may have been predisposed to fracture secondary to disuse osteoporosis,[62] an ataxic gait,[62, 106] or osteoporosis resulting from prolonged phenytoin (Dilantin) use. Gait abnormalities could subject the bone–implant interface to higher stress or lead to an increased incidence of falls.

## IPSILATERAL HIP ARTHROPLASTY

The presence of a total-hip arthroplasty on the same side as a total-knee prosthesis increases the torsional rigidity of the femur and reduces the mean energy absorption of the femur in torsion[67]; this situation could result in a fracture between the two components. The few cases reported in the literature list additional risk factors, including rheumatoid arthritis,[203, 221] femoral total-knee components with intramedullary stems,[59] and osteoporosis.[67]

## STRESS FRACTURE

Because they are so rare, stress fractures about the proximal end of the femur after total-knee arthroplasty are difficult to readily diagnose.[40, 60, 88, 107, 136, 146, 191, 210] With no other history of trauma, these patients often complain of tenderness about the groin within weeks of resuming full weight bearing after their total-knee arthroplasty.[107, 136] Bone scintigrams and radiographs often demonstrate a stress fracture of the femoral neck[107] or, in rarer instances, the subtrochanteric region of the hip.[136] Conservative management is usually successful, although some of these cases have progressed to complete fracture.[136] The increase in activity after total-knee arthroplasty may be a factor in the incidence of these stress fractures of the hip. Another contributing factor may be a

decrease in the tension band effect of the iliotibial tract in combination with coxa vara and changes in static and dynamic forces of the femur.[136]

Patients who have been immobilized for an extended period may sustain stress fractures about the femur or tibia when they are suddenly mobilized after total-knee arthroplasty.[79] These patients may complain of a sudden onset of pain about the knee during rehabilitation; appropriate radiographs and additional studies are required to rule out a stress fracture.

Rand and Coventry[209] reported 15 patients who sustained stress fractures of the tibia after geometric and polycentric total-knee arthroplasty. The chief causes of the stress fractures were axial malalignment and improper orientation of the component. All 15 patients experienced loosening of the prosthesis and required revision arthroplasty for a satisfactory result. Revision at the time of diagnosis of the fracture did not adversely affect fracture healing.

## ARTHROFIBROSIS

Limited preoperative range of motion, whether in a primary or revision situation, renders the tibial tubercle vulnerable to avulsion during exposure,[223] especially in cases involving osteoporotic bone. Several surgical approaches are available to improve access to the knee and limit intraoperative complications and fractures. In addition to a formal tibial tubercle osteotomy,[25, 162] which is useful in the appropriate situation, available procedures include the rectus snip,[117] V-Y–plasty,[268] and quadriceps turndown.[57, 141]

## PATELLA

Although some periprosthetic patellar fractures may be due to direct trauma,[24] they are most commonly a result of fatigue,[207] which can be related to excessive resection of bone,[101] malalignment,[86] or avascularity of the patella.[128, 167, 237, 238, 279] Le and colleagues[144] recently reviewed 22 patellar fractures about total-knee arthroplasties and suggested that lateral release, fat pad excision, quadriceps tendon release, and previous surgery were also implicated. Scuderi and co-workers[238] performed postoperative bone scans and demonstrated cold scans in over half of all patellas that had undergone lateral retinacular release, although Ritter and Campbell[217] were unable to replicate these findings. Patient-related factors such as osteoporosis and rheumatoid arthritis are similar to those for supracondylar femoral fractures,[223] whereas other factors such as male gender and increased activity level are unique (Table 63–6).

# Classification

## FEMUR

In 1985, Sisto and colleagues[248] published the first formal grouping of periprosthetic knee fractures and classified their cases as nondisplaced, displaced, and displaced-

**TABLE 63–6**

Factors Predisposing to Patellar Fracture after Total-Knee Arthroplasty

**PATIENT FACTORS**

Osteoporosis
Rheumatoid arthritis (related to osteoporosis)
Male gender (increased stress related to increased activities)
Increased activities
Increased range of motion (increased stress on patella)

**IMPLANT FACTORS**

Central peg
Metal-backed cementless
PCL-substituting design
Countersunk design (excessive bony resection)
Osteolysis (related to titanium backing)

**TECHNICAL FACTORS**

Excessive resection
Inadequate resection (overstuffed patellofemoral compartment)
Revision arthroplasty
Perforation of patella anteriorly
Malalignment
Patellar subluxation
Devascularization (extensive lateral release, quadriceps turndown)

*Abbreviation:* PCL, posterior cruciate ligament.
*Source:* Data from Rorabeck, C.H.; et al. Instr Course Lect 47:449–458, 1998; Bourne, R.B. Orthop Clin North Am 30:287–291, 1999.

comminuted. The following year, Merkel and Johnson[169] proposed classifying their series of fractures according to the system described by Neer and colleagues[183] for supracondylar fractures of the femur. The Neer system, which is based on fracture displacement and the degree of comminution, was later modified by DiGioia and Rubash[68] to apply to supracondylar fractures about total-knee prostheses.

This chapter will refer to a classification scheme recently proposed by Lewis and Rorabeck[119, 224] that takes into account both fracture displacement and prosthesis stability. As with the Vancouver classification for fractures about total-hip prostheses,[26, 70, 286] the principal factor that makes this classification so useful is its assessment of the stability of the implant. Type I femoral fractures are essentially nondisplaced, and the bone–prosthesis interface remains intact. In type II fractures, the interface remains intact, but the fracture is displaced. Finally, type III fractures all have a loose or failing prosthesis in the face of either a displaced or nondisplaced fracture (Table 63–7).

## TIBIA

After studying 102 tibial fractures associated with total-knee arthroplasties, Felix and colleagues[85, 256] proposed a classification scheme based on three factors: location of the fracture, stability of the implant, and whether the fracture occurred intraoperatively or postoperatively. Type I fractures occur in the tibial plateau, type II fractures are adjacent to the stem, type III fractures are distal to the prosthesis, and type IV fractures involve the tubercle. The stability of the implant is then used to further classify the fractures: subtype A is a well-fixed implant, subtype B

**TABLE 63–7**

Lewis and Rorabeck Classification of Supracondylar Periprosthetic Fractures Proximal to Knee Arthroplasty

| Fracture Type | Fracture Quality | Prosthesis |
|---|---|---|
| Type I | Undisplaced | Intact |
| Type II | Displaced | Intact |
| Type III | Displaced or undisplaced | Loose<br>Failing (significant polyethylene or metal wear) |

*Source:* Rorabeck, C.H.; Taylor, J.W. Orthop Clin North Am 30:209–214, 1999.

is loose, and subtype C is an intraoperative fracture (Table 63–8).

## PATELLA

Hozack and co-workers[114] reviewed 21 periprosthetic patellar fractures and proposed a classification scheme based on fracture location, displacement, and the presence of extensor lag. That same year, Goldberg and colleagues[100] proposed a five-part classification system for patellar fractures based on 36 fractures in 35 patients. They also included the location of the fracture, disruption of implant fixation, dislocation of the patella, and the status of the extensor mechanism (Table 63–9).

## Diagnosis

The femoral component may obscure intraoperative fractures of the distal end of the femur if the fracture occurs during impaction. Fractures of the tibial plateau may also be masked by the platform of the prosthesis, as well as by surrounding soft tissue. Intramedullary stems used during revision arthroplasty may impinge on and fracture the diaphysis, with a subsequent sudden change in stability. As with periprosthetic fractures about the hip, any suspicions warrant an immediate intraoperative radiograph, fluoroscopy, or both.

**TABLE 63–8**

Felix, Stuart, and Hanssen Classification of Periprosthetic Tibia Fractures

| | Location | Component Fixation |
|---|---|---|
| Type I | Tibial plateau | A—well fixed<br>B—loose<br>C—intraoperative fx |
| Type II | Adjacent to stem | A—well fixed<br>B—loose<br>C—intraoperative fx |
| Type III | Distal to prosthesis | A—well fixed<br>B—loose<br>C—intraoperative fx |
| Type IV | Tibial tubercle | |

*Abbreviation:* fx, fracture.
*Source:* Felix, N.A.; et al. Clin Orthop 345:113–124, 1997.

**TABLE 63–9**

Goldberg Classification of Periprosthetic Patellar Fractures

| | |
|---|---|
| Type I | Marginal fracture |
| | Extensor mechanism intact |
| | Implant–bone interface intact |
| Type II | Disruption of extensor mechanism or implant–bone interface |
| Type III | Fracture of inferior pole of patella |
| | With patellar ligament rupture |
| | Without patellar ligament rupture |
| Type IV | Fracture associated with patellar dislocation |

*Source:* Goldberg, V.M.; et al. Clin Orthop 236:115–122, 1988.

A loosened prosthesis or a mentally compromised patient may obscure the diagnosis of postoperative fracture of a total-knee arthroplasty. Computed tomography may prove useful in delineating the complexity of the fracture site, but the cheapest and most useful films are prefracture radiographs, which allow the surgeon to make comparisons with current radiographs for changes in alignment or subsidence. Full-length femur and tibia films are essential for ruling out diaphyseal fractures. Bone scans may be helpful in delineating stress fractures of the proximal end of the femur and hip.

## Treatment Options

### FEMORAL FRACTURES

#### Intraoperative

**Condylar Fractures.** Intraoperative fracture of a femoral condyle is one of the more common intraoperative fractures associated with primary total-knee arthroplasty.[225] Typically, it occurs when the surgeon inadvertently medializes or lateralizes the box cut for the housing of the stabilization peg, with the medial condyle most frequently being involved.[223, 225] Rorabeck and Taylor[225] recommend immediate and extensive exposure of the fracture to determine its extent and direction. Condylar fractures can usually be treated with a simple lag screw, with care taken to avoid contact with the implant. Soft metaphyseal bone may require the addition of a washer to improve fixation.[79] The addition of a stem to the implant will help decrease stress on the fracture site.[79]

**Femoral Shaft Fractures.** Severely osteoporotic bone may lead to perforation of the anterior femoral cortex with the intramedullary alignment rod.[79, 223] Bypassing the defect with a long-stemmed fluted implant is advisable if the prosthesis is available; otherwise, Engh and Ammeen recommend protected weight bearing for a minimum of 6 to 8 weeks.[79]

However, the surgeon should take into account that a long femoral stem may impinge on the anterior bow of the femur and initiate a crack. In such cases, it is difficult to bypass the fracture unless a curved stem is available, but a split femoral allograft stabilized with cerclage fixation will provide adequate fixation. Newer stem designs also incorporate a transverse cut in the end of the stem, the "clothespin" configuration, which allows for some deformation of the device during impaction.

#### Postoperative

**Type I: Undisplaced Fracture, Stable Prosthesis.** The Lewis and Rorabeck[149] classification provides an excellent foundation on which to build a treatment plan. This approach assumes that the surgeon has taken great care to assess the stability of the implant and the quality of the bone around the prosthesis before embarking on a course of therapy.

*Nonoperative Management.* If one plans to use nonoperative management, it is most successful in type I fractures. Chen and associates[49] reviewed 195 fractures in 12 studies of ipsilateral supracondylar femoral fractures occurring about a total-knee arthroplasty and divided the fractures into nonoperative and operative treatment groups. The fracture types were also subclassified into nondisplaced and displaced. Satisfactory results were noted in 83% of the patients with nondisplaced fractures that were treated without surgery,[49] in contrast to only a 64% satisfactory outcome rate in all patients with displaced fractures that were treated with or without surgery. Chen and colleagues[49] estimated a 5% incidence of life- and limb-threatening complications from open treatment, as opposed to only 1% for closed techniques. McLaren and co-workers[166] noted that satisfactory results were achieved in 57% of all cases treated in closed fashion. Moran and associates[175] treated five nondisplaced fractures nonoperatively in their series of 29 supracondylar fractures and reported satisfactory results in all five. In a case report of one type I fracture treated successfully with nonoperative management, Sochart and Harding[252] argued vigorously against surgery for these types of fractures; they cited the absence of potential operative risks while still maintaining the option of later surgical intervention if necessary. It should be noted that in this case, no evidence of coexisting loosening, osteolysis, or significant wear could be found, and satisfactory bony reduction was achieved, with correct alignment of the prosthetic components being maintained.[252]

*Operative Management.* Open reduction plus internal fixation of periprosthetic knee fractures is particularly challenging because of the proximity of the prosthesis to the cement mantle, as well as the lack of intramedullary support. Fixation is further compromised by the fact that many of these patients have osteoporosis and some also have rheumatoid arthritis being treated with corticosteroids. Reduction is best maintained by some type of rigid internal fixation.

The surgeon should never hesitate to fix intraoperative, nondisplaced fractures about the femur. Even a simple nondisplaced split just above the femoral component should be stabilized with one or two lag screws. The exposure will never be as good as it is at the primary procedure, and it is always possible that this nondisplaced fracture will become displaced during a minor fall.

PLATES AND SCREWS. Healy and colleagues[110] reported a series of 20 cases treated successfully with open reduction and internal fixation through a lateral approach and noted that bone grafting of the fracture site was a key factor in their success. On average, the patients maintained their prefracture knee scores. The authors preferred using the blade plate over the condylar screw plate because it removed less bone and provided better rotational control of the distal fragment.[110] However, they noted that placement of the blade between the anterior femoral flange and the condylar lugs could be a tight fit. Blade plates have also been used in several other series,[87, 113, 248] with generally good results. Another reported option is fixation with buttress plates or dynamic compression plates.*

Ochsner and Pfister[186] recently reported on six cases of periprosthetic fracture of the distal end of the femur treated with a newly developed fork plate. Instead of the blade of the condylar plate, this implant features two prongs that are adaptable in length and space between the prongs, and the implant can surround the anchorage pegs of the prosthesis and grip the distal fragment near the joint line.[186]

Other reports of fixation of supracondylar fractures with plates and screws have not had as great a success as that of Healy and colleagues.[110] Figgie and associates[87] reported 5 nonunions in 10 supracondylar fractures treated with plates and screws, with failure occurring at the bone–plate junction. Varus angulation complicated the three patients whom Cordeiro and co-workers[58] managed with plate and screw fixation, and similar treatment by Nielsen and associates[184] failed in three of three patients because of infection, fistula formation, and a loose plate.

INTRAMEDULLARY DEVICES. Several types of intramedullary devices have been proposed for stabilization of supracondylar femoral fractures, including standard intramedullary nails, supracondylar nails, Rush pins, and Zickel devices.† The advantage of this technique lies in the minimal soft tissue dissection necessary for reduction and insertion of the devices. Rorabeck and Taylor[225] caution that these devices are simply not reliable enough to provide adequate fixation for early weight bearing.

Experience with intramedullary fixation of these fractures has expanded tremendously over the last 5 years (see Fig. 10–55). One series reported good results in three patients treated with an antegrade interlocking nail in which the fracture was at least 8 cm from the joint line.[106] Another group used a Huckstep intramedullary nail to engage the tip of a stemmed femoral component.[239] Retrograde nailing of certain fractures is also effective,[119, 166, 251] but the surgeon must check to ensure clearance of the device with the femoral component. The intercondylar distance of commonly used knee arthroplasties ranges from 12 to 20 mm,[119] whereas supracondylar nails are available in diameters of 11 and 12 mm. Table 63–10 lists the intercondylar distances of commonly used knee implants. Posteriorly stabilized devices may not allow passage of the nail because the containment box is completely enclosed. When faced with this situation, I have had no problem in creating a passage with a carbide-tipped bur. More importantly, adequate bone must remain distally for fixation with screws to stabilize the rod.

McLaren and co-workers[166] leave the distal end of the nail exposed by a centimeter to permit optimal screw

position and use a carbide-tipped bur to remove the prominent nail. I have had one case of collapse of a fracture into a stable position several weeks postoperatively; the nail was left protruding only a few millimeters into the patellofemoral joint, and resection of the prominent nail with the carbide-tipped bur solved the problem.

Ries[212] notes that removal of a plate from the distal end of the femur creates a risk of fracture through the screw holes during total-knee arthroplasty and suggests prophylactic intramedullary rodding at the time of total-knee arthroplasty. This method permits simultaneous plate removal and total-knee arthroplasty while protecting the femur from postoperative fracture.

Combining intramedullary fixation with autogenous grafting, Tani and colleagues[260] described a case of intramedullary fibular grafting in a patient with a comminuted supracondylar fracture of the femur after total-knee arthroplasty. A free autogenous fibular graft was inserted into the medullary cavity from the intercondylar region and fixed to the proximal fragment of the femur with augmented fixation consisting of a small plate and screws.

### Type II: Displaced Fracture, Stable Prosthesis

*Nonoperative Management.* Nonoperative management can be recommended for type II fractures of the femur only in patients with an overriding medical reason to avoid surgery. It is simply not possible in today's health care environment to maintain a patient in traction for several weeks. It also places the patient at risk for all the complications associated with prolonged bedrest. Even attempting to place the knee in an immobilizer for any length of time ensures that many of these elderly patients will essentially be confined to bed for the duration of treatment.[225]

Closed treatment of displaced fractures with nonoperative methods yields notoriously poor results. Neer and colleagues,[183] after treating most of their nonprosthetic supracondylar femoral fractures with traction, reported that the most common deformities were varus and internal rotation. Malunion in varus or valgus orientation is common with this technique.[23, 58, 87, 248]

Seven of 10 fractures treated with traction followed by casting in Figgie and colleagues' series[87] healed with the femoral component in an average of 7° of varus orientation relative to the long axis of the femur. Of particular note is

**TABLE 63–10** ...........................................

Intercondylar Distances of Condylar Knee Implants

| Component | Intercondylar Distance (mm) |
| --- | --- |
| Miller-Galante (Zimmer) | 12 |
| Insall-Burstein II (Zimmer) | 14–19 |
| Biomet | 22 |
| Intermedics | 18 |
| AMK (DePuy) | 14–17 |
| Osteonics | 19 |
| PFC (Johnson & Johnson) | 20 |
| Genesis (Smith & Nephew) | 20 |
| Duracon (Howmedica) | 12–16 |

••••••••••••••••••••••••••••••••••••••••••••

*Source:* Data from Jabczenski, F.F.; Crawford, M. J. Arthroplasty 10:95–101, 1995; Engh, G.A.; et al. J Bone Joint Surg Am 79:1030–1039, 1997.

---

*See references 23, 35, 58, 62, 87, 169, 184, 214, 245, 276, 289.
†See references 10, 106, 119, 166, 182, 216, 220, 222, 228, 251.

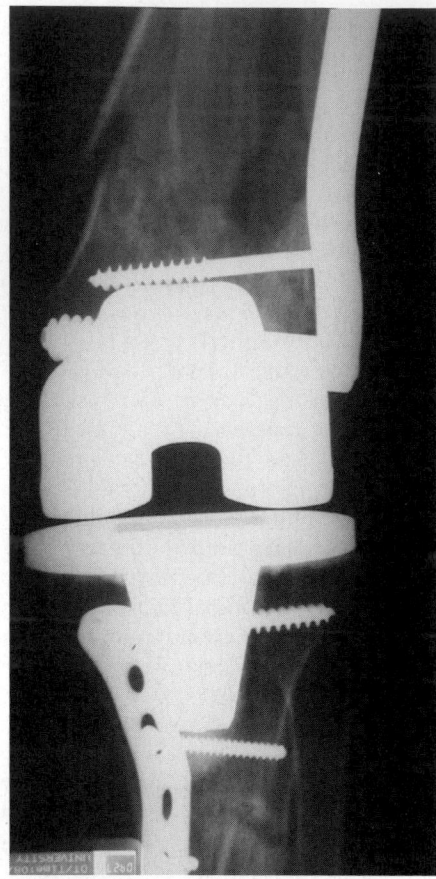

FIGURE 63–9. A high-speed motor vehicle accident resulted in comminuted fractures about the metaphysis of the femur (type II) and the metaphyseal-diaphyseal junction of the tibia (type III); both components were well fixed. The femur was repaired with a long dynamic compression screw and side plate and the tibia with a condylar molded plate.

that new and progressive lucent lines around the tibial components had developed in four of those seven knees on follow-up radiographs.[87] Overall, these patients lost 19° of motion and 13 points on their knee scores.[87] In the same series, the operative patients lost 15° of motion and 22 points on their knee scores.

### Operative Management

PLATES AND SCREWS. The approach is the same as for type I fractures, although one is more likely to encounter a larger hematoma with type II fractures. In addition, displacement of the fracture often occurs as a result of the increased energy applied to the femur, so one should expect more comminution and therefore be prepared to use provisional fixation to maintain alignment while the final construct is being applied. Displaced fractures may also have more than one fracture component. Because the femoral component can act as an internal splint, it is not uncommon to see a vertical split or other fracture pattern within the distal end of the femur once the fracture site is exposed (Fig. 63–9).

ALLOGRAFT. Bone graft is the key to success as Healy and colleagues[110] noted in their series. Allograft bone is used as an adjunct to other forms of fixation in most type II

fractures. Supplementation with cancellous chips at the fracture site, especially if augmented with autogenous bone, will improve the chance of bony union.

Just as they are used about hip stem, split femoral allograft struts may serve as the primary form of fixation about stemmed knee implants. The inner surface of the graft should be flared out with a bur to improve contact with the host bone. I find such flaring harder to achieve about the distal metaphysis of the femur than the proximal diaphysis because of the variable geometry in the metaphyseal region. Cerclage cables or wires provide stable fixation of the graft.

INTRAMEDULLARY DEVICES. It is imperative that the fracture be reduced in both planes before passage of the nail if an intramedullary device is planned for use in a type II fracture. Because of the distal nature of supracondylar fractures and the wide flare of the metaphysis, it is relatively easy to pass the intramedullary guide wire and reamers without achieving an accurate reduction. Proper reduction, if possible, before passage of the guide wire ensures that the dense cancellous bone about the metaphysis will be reamed appropriately (Figs. 63–10 and 63–11).

The femoral component can also mask the true nature of the fracture and give the surgeon a false sense of security when attempting simple intramedullary nailing. The surgeon should be prepared to stabilize such splits with interfragmentary cannulated screws.

EXTERNAL FIXATION. Only a few cases of external fixation of periprosthetic fractures of the knee have been reported, usually with mixed results.[21, 62, 87, 169] One fixation became infected and was converted to fusion,[87] and the others were reported to have either good or excellent results.[169] Thin-wire fixators hybridized with half-pin devices may prove useful in specific cases. Sepsis from the pin site, however, may affect not only the fracture but also the implant, thus posing a continued risk for this type of treatment.[225]

**Type III: Displaced or Undisplaced Fracture, Loose or Failing Prosthesis.** The combination of a loose prosthesis with a fracture is the most challenging, and all such cases should be treated operatively unless prohibited by the patient's medical condition. Good bone stock will allow for revision of the fracture with a stemmed implant, whereas poor bone stock may require an allograft composite or a segmental femoral replacement prosthesis such as those used in musculoskeletal tumor reconstruction.

*Primary Revision Arthroplasty.* Immediate revision arthroplasty of the knee preserves alignment of the extremity and allows early weight bearing.[58] In many cases, defects can be accommodated with segmental metal blocks that screw into or are cemented to the revision implant. In all such cases, it is important to stabilize the implant with a longer intramedullary stem.[54, 58, 253] McLaren and associates[166] reported that 24 of 25 periprosthetic fractures treated with standard long-stemmed revision components had a satisfactory outcome.

Replacement of the distal end of the femur with structural allograft and a long-stem prosthesis may be the only option in cases of periprosthetic distal femoral fracture and significant loss of bone stock.[42, 79, 80, 87, 97, 135, 208, 284]

Treatment with a distal femoral allograft is associated with instability of the knee in some cases.[135] Wong and Gross[284] emphasize the importance of retaining the origins of the collateral ligaments of the host bone and suggest longitudinally splitting the femur distal to the fracture in an anteroposterior direction. The new stemmed implant is cemented into the distal allograft, but no cement is inserted into the host femur.[163, 284] A step cut between the allograft and the host femur, as well as onlay grafts of the split distal host femur, enhance the union.[97, 163]

***Staged Revision Arthroplasty.*** Some femoral fractures about loose or failing total-knee components, especially those of the diaphysis, may lend themselves to fixation and union of the fracture first, followed by definitive revision after union.[223] Such staged treatment reduces the extent of the overall surgical exposure and operative time while getting patients back on their feet faster. These cases often involve multiple trauma in which several fractures have to be addressed at once during off hours, when the full total-joint team and equipment are not immediately available.

***Distal Femoral Replacement.*** Distal femoral replacement is an option in isolated cases.[120, 214, 255] Instability is not usually a problem with these implants because the distal prosthetic replacements rely entirely on mechanical linkage for stability. In some cases, because of multiple previous revision arthroplasties, distal femoral replacement may be the only alternative to amputation.[255]

## TIBIAL FRACTURES

### *Intraoperative Fractures*

**Type IC—Tibial Plateau Fractures.** These fractures are most likely to be encountered during removal of cement in a revision or during trial reduction of a primary component. Often minimally displaced, these fractures may not be noticed by the surgeon until review of the postoperative radiographs.[256] Fixation with a cancellous screw before insertion of the final component will stabilize the fracture. Stuart and Hanssen[256] suggest that a longer stem may also be used to bypass the fracture site. Stabilization of a displaced fracture noted after insertion of the final component may require plate fixation (Fig. 63–12).

**Type IIC—Fracture Adjacent to the Stem.** Though just as likely to occur during primary as revision procedures, these fractures are most likely to occur if a long tibial stem is used.[223, 256] Bypassing the fracture site with a longer stem and bone grafting are recommended if the fracture is discovered intraoperatively; bracing accompanied by limited weight bearing for 6 weeks is advised if the fracture is discovered in the recovery room.[256]

**Type IIIC—Fracture Distal to the Prosthesis.** Stuart and Hanssen[256] reported only 2 such cases in their review of 102 tibial fractures associated with total-knee arthroplasty. One fracture in a patient with rheumatoid arthritis and severe osteopenia was treated with casting

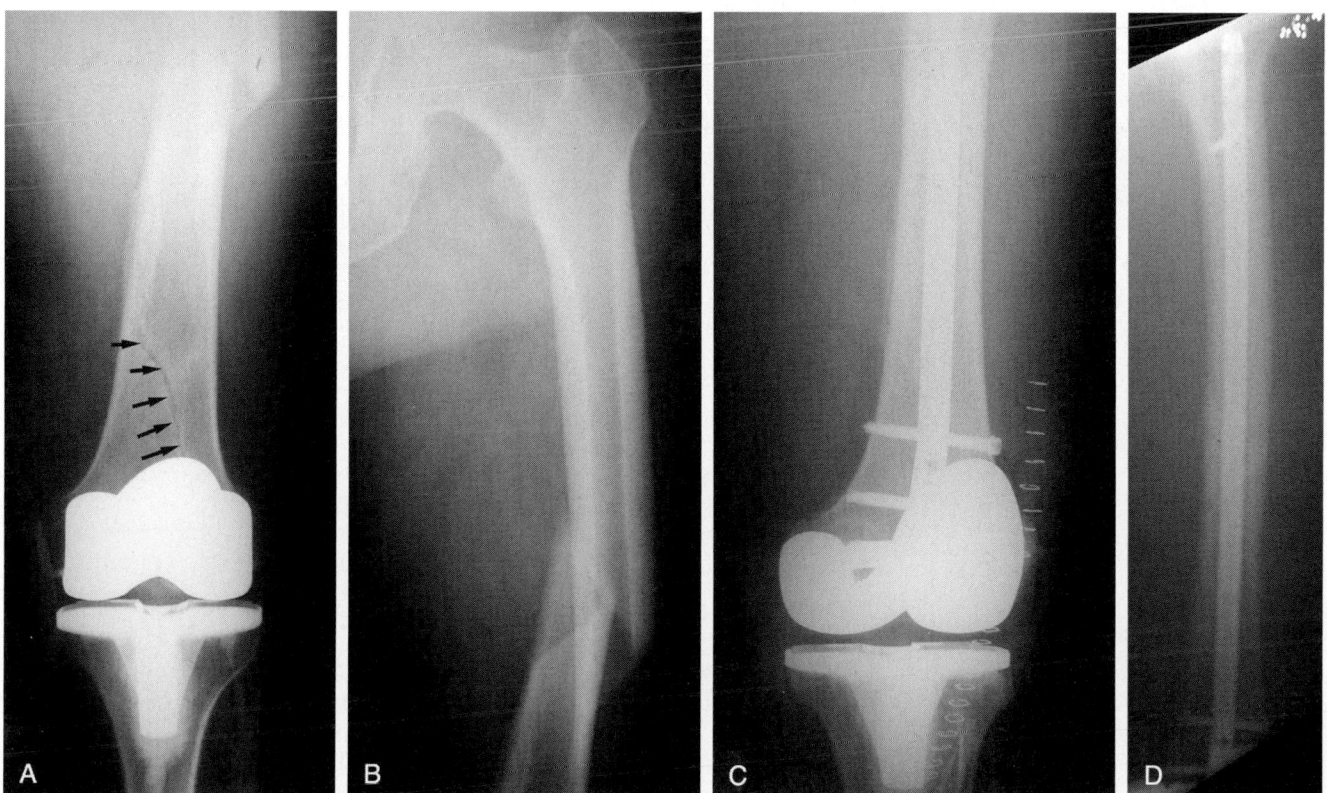

**FIGURE 63–10.** Spiral diaphyseal femoral fracture (type II) with well-fixed components (*A* and *B*). Note the secondary crack extending past the metaphysis toward the intercondylar notch (*black arrows*). The fracture was stabilized with a retrograde nail and distal (*C*) and proximal (*D*) interlocking screws.

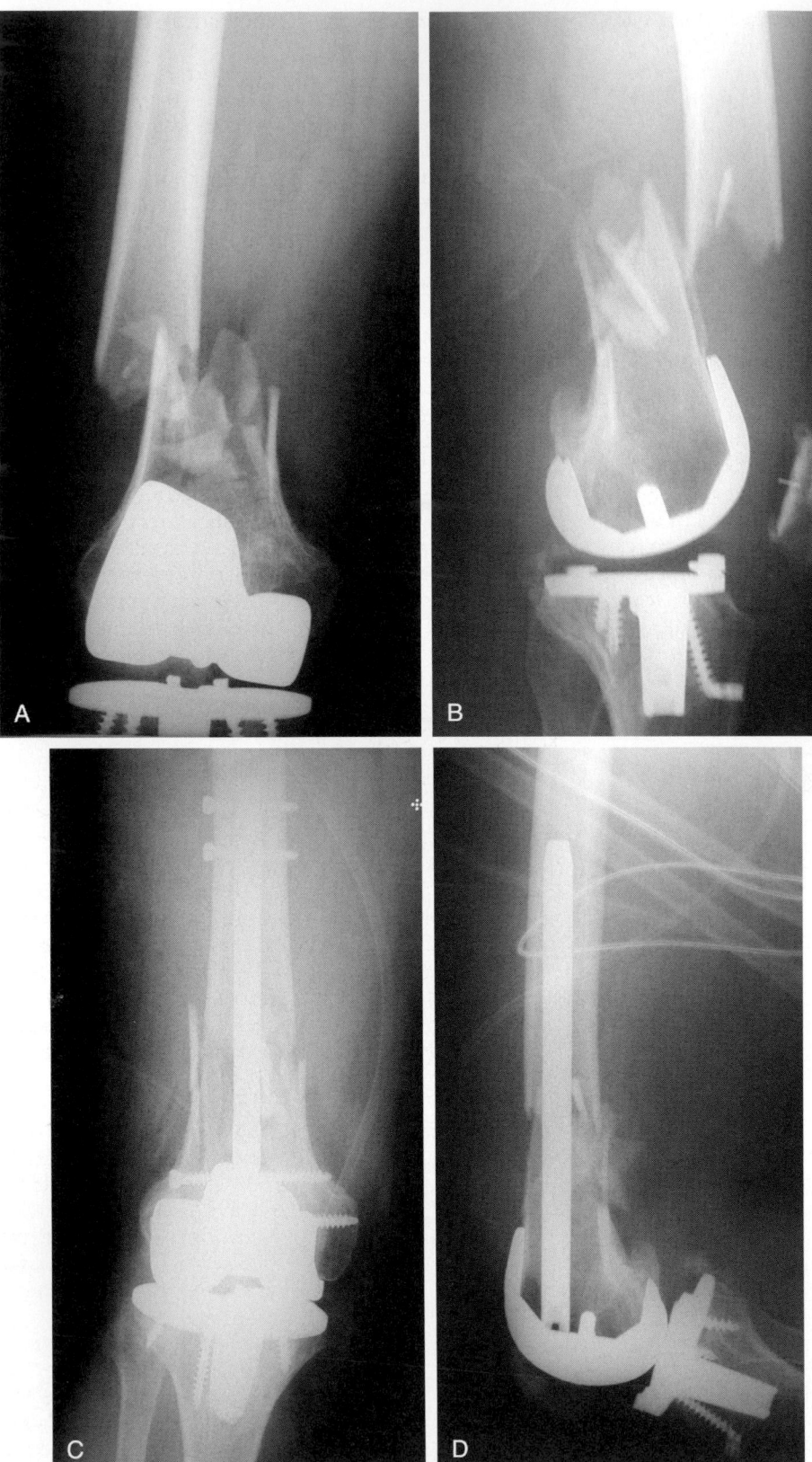

**Figure 63–11.** Anteroposterior (AP) (*A*) and lateral (*B*) radiographs of a comminuted type II supracondylar femur fracture involving a well-fixed uncemented femoral component. A key to successful treatment in this case is establishing that enough distal femoral length remains to support the distal screws of the nail. Postoperative AP (*C*) and lateral (*D*) views demonstrate appropriate fixation of the proximal and distal screws in this supracondylar nail.

and non–weight bearing for 7 weeks.[256] The other required excision of extruded cement and stabilization with a plate and screws.[256] Such fractures are a challenge to deal with because they are more likely to occur after insertion of the final component, thus making revision to a longer component much more difficult. The tibial baseplate also restricts positioning of a longer stem within the shaft, unlike total-hip prostheses, in which some flexibility is created through an extended trochanteric osteotomy.

**Type IVC—Tibial Tubercle Fracture.** Only one intraoperative fracture of the tubercle was noted in Stuart and Hanssen's series,[256] and it occurred during extraction of an infected prosthesis. They repaired the fracture with suture and placed the patient in a cast until the fracture healed.[256] Ironically, this complication may best be avoided by performing a tibial tubercle osteotomy,[162, 213] while keeping in mind the risks that it poses to later fracture of the tibia.[218]

*Postoperative Fractures*

**Type I—Tibial Plateau Fracture.** These fractures should be treated with revision of the loose prosthesis and stabilization of the fracture; nonoperative treatment is not an attractive option in this type of fracture. Stuart and Hanssen treated 21 of 53 type IB tibia fractures without surgery to allow consolidation of the fracture fragments, but 83% of these patients eventually required revision arthroplasty.[256]

**Type II—Fracture Adjacent to the Stem.** Fractures adjacent to the stem of a well-fixed prosthesis postoperatively heal with rigid immobilization with no untoward effect on knee function.[256] In contrast, fractures adjacent to a loose stem often involve large cavitary and segmental defects of the proximal end of the tibia and may require

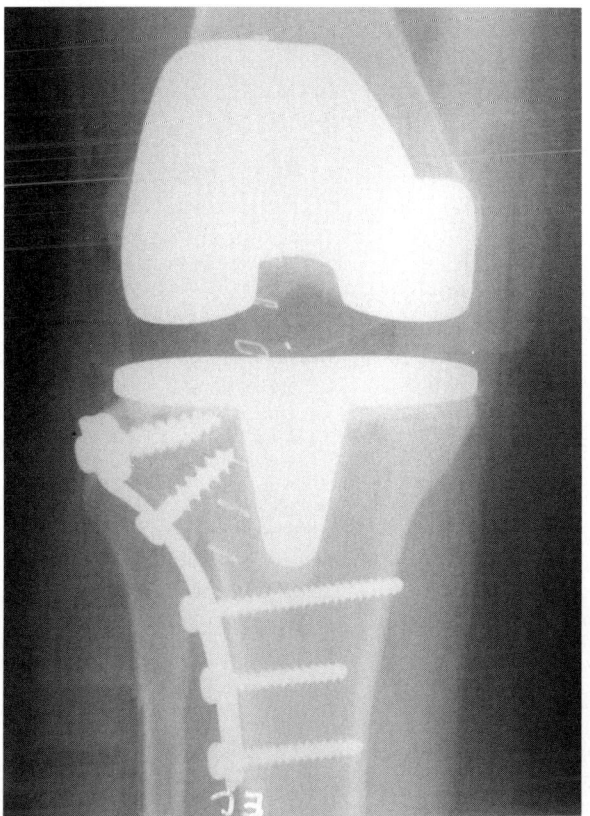

**FIGURE 63–12.** Postoperative anteroposterior view of a type I fracture of the tibial plateau. The fracture was noted and repaired intraoperatively with an L plate. The postoperative regimen consisted of touch-down weight-bearing for 6 weeks while continuing active and passive range-of-motion exercises. The final result was a full range of pain-free motion.

structural bone grafting in addition to revision with a long-stemmed component.[256]

**Type III—Fracture Distal to the Prosthesis.** These fractures tend to occur adjacent to a well-fixed prosthesis.[85, 256] Type IIIA fractures can be treated as isolated tibial fractures while ensuring that proper limb alignment is maintained. In the largest series reported to date, 14 type IIIA fractures were all treated with casting and limited weight bearing, and most healed without revision.

If the component is loose (type IIIB), the surgeon has several choices. If possible, diaphyseal fractures may be treated with immobilization first, followed by delayed revision after the fracture has healed. Type IIIB fractures about the metaphysis may benefit from a combined approach consisting of revision of the total-knee prosthesis and bypassing the fracture with a long, modular stem.[256] In severe cases, proximal tibial replacement may be necessary.

**Type IV—Tibial Tubercle Fracture.** The two type IVA fractures reported by Felix and colleagues[85] occurred after minor falls. One was minimally displaced and was treated by immobilization in extension, whereas the other, a displaced fracture, healed with internal fixation with a tension band wire.[85] Stuart and Hanssen reported an additional type IVB fracture that was treated by revision and internal fixation.[256]

## PATELLAR FRACTURES

### Intraoperative Fractures of the Patella

Overzealous resection of the patella to less than 10 mm in thickness or over-reaming of an inset patella may precipitate an intraoperative fracture.[24] Revision surgery also places the patella at risk for fracture if it is already thinned from the previous procedure. These fractures are best repaired with tension band wire without resurfacing the patella itself and then allowing the fracture to heal. Later, if the patient is symptomatic and the fracture healed, one may consider resurfacing with a biconvex patella to minimize further patellar resection and restore patellar height.[24]

### Postoperative Fractures of the Patella

Most postoperative patellar fractures associated with total-knee arthroplasty are vertical and occur laterally without disrupting the extensor mechanism.[24] Rand[207] suggests that patellar fractures that are not associated with loosening and have an intact quadriceps mechanism are best treated without surgery. Dislocation, loosening, and disruption of the extensor mechanism are all indications for open treatment.[207]

Fractures not associated with extensor disruption or loosening of the patellar implant are candidates for nonoperative treatment. All 15 such fractures (13 type I and 2 type IIIB) in Goldberg and colleagues' report[100] were treated successfully with immobilization, partial weight bearing, and rehabilitation.

If the patellar component is loose, it is advisable to remove or revise this component, with additional repair to the extensor mechanism as necessary.[24] Overall, only one third of patients with disruption of the extensor mechanism in Goldberg and associates' series[100] had a satisfactory result.

## POST-TRAUMATIC TOTAL-KNEE ARTHROPLASTY

Treatment of post-traumatic arthritis of the knee with total-knee arthroplasty presents a special set of problems that include intraoperative planar and rotational alignment of the prosthesis, accommodation of bony defects, stress risers resulting from previous fixation devices, and the possibility of infection arising from previous episodes associated with an open injury. Deformities within the plane of the knee joint, such as the one illustrated in Figure 63–13, are readily dealt with by using intraoperative fluoroscopy to place a standard, posteriorly stabilized prosthesis. Angular fractures are best assessed on long cassettes preoperatively and on a full radiolucent table intraoperatively, as was done for the case in Figure 63–14.

## Preferred Management

### FEMUR

Nondisplaced periprosthetic fractures (type I) can be managed safely with casting or bracing, provided that they are observed closely for displacement. Patients who cannot follow instructions and those who have difficulty using crutches or a walker should not be considered for this modality. I prefer to manage subsequent displacement with internal fixation rather than traction to avoid the problems of prolonged bedrest.

Displaced (type II) fractures are almost always managed with internal fixation because of the difficulty in obtaining and maintaining acceptable alignment after displacement. For fractures close to the joint line, blade plate fixation is an excellent choice because it does not remove much metaphyseal bone and provides some rotational control in the sagittal plane.[110] Bone grafting is an essential component of the procedure, preferably with autologous bone. My personal preference is retrograde nailing through the notch[251] and avoidance of extensive exposure of the distal end of the femur, which can destroy an already tenuous blood supply. It is important to check for proper clearance of the intramedullary device through the notch of a trial implant before proceeding.[166, 251] Type II fractures at the tip of the intramedullary stem of a well-fixed femoral component are treated with a split femoral shaft allograft and cerclage fixation, just as one would for a Vancouver B2 fractures about a hip stem. Fractures of the femoral diaphysis not involving any aspect of the prosthesis may be treated according to the surgeon's preference. I have found that the retrograde approach is much quicker than antegrade nailing, blood loss is minimal, and I have better control of fixation distally about the femoral component (see Fig. 63–10).

Special consideration is reserved for type II fractures through an area of distal osteolysis. With no metaphyseal bone available for fixation, it is possible to replace the entire distal part of the femur with an oncology management prosthesis.[120] This option tends to work best with severely debilitated patients who might otherwise not tolerate a prolonged period of rehabilitation. If at all possible, however, I would attempt to reconstruct the distal end of the femur with allograft and a long-stemmed

component, followed by early range-of-motion exercises and protected weight bearing.[163, 284]

I always schedule type III fracture cases as elective but urgent surgery so that I have full access to the necessary bone graft and revision implants. Care is taken to preserve as much bone stock as possible and then bypass the fracture site with a modular stem. I do not cement the stem in this situation because the cement could extrude through the fracture site and interfere with healing. Extensive comminution of the fracture site requires structural bone graft,[135, 284] in addition to a well-fitting intramedullary stem. Figure 63–15 presents an algorithm for the treatment of periprosthetic femoral fractures about total-knee arthroplasties.

### TIBIA

Intraoperative type I fractures of the plateau about a well-fixed prosthesis are stabilized with interfragmentary cancellous screws with or without supplemental plate fixation (see Fig. 63–12). Percutaneous screw fixation has the advantage of minimizing soft tissue dissection, especially during primary or revision arthroplasty.

Type I fractures about a loose prosthesis are prime candidates for revision arthroplasty with an extended intramedullary stem. Fixation of the fracture may require additional structural bone graft. Care must be exercised during insertion of the revision stem to avoid creating a type II fracture of the diaphysis. Type IA fractures are more likely to be encountered as intraoperative fractures picked up on routine postoperative radiographs. I would treat these fractures with limited weight bearing but carefully maintain range of motion.

Type II fractures about a loose prosthesis with otherwise good bone stock are best treated with revision arthroplasty. The challenge here is to remove the loose prosthesis without extending or further comminuting the fracture. I avoid cement in the diaphysis to prevent extrusion of cement into the fracture site.

Type III fractures tend to be minimally displaced and occur about well-fixed prostheses, conditions that make nonoperative management the treatment of choice. Younger patients may tolerate simple cast immobilization, but I prefer a cast brace in patients with fragile skin that has a tendency to break down.

Fortunately, type IV fractures of the tibial tubercle are rare. Intraoperatively, I prefer wire fixation through drill holes and avoid a prominent screw head near the tubercle. Postoperatively, if the fracture is minimally displaced and the extensor mechanism intact, I will treat these patients with immobilization in extension. Displaced fractures require reduction and internal fixation. Figure 63–16 presents an algorithm for the treatment of periprosthetic fractures of the tibia.

### PATELLA

I treat type I patellar fractures with immobilization and limited weight bearing for 6 weeks. Such management can pose its own risks in already debilitated patients, who may require home health care or transfer to a rehabilitation center until they can ambulate independently. Type II

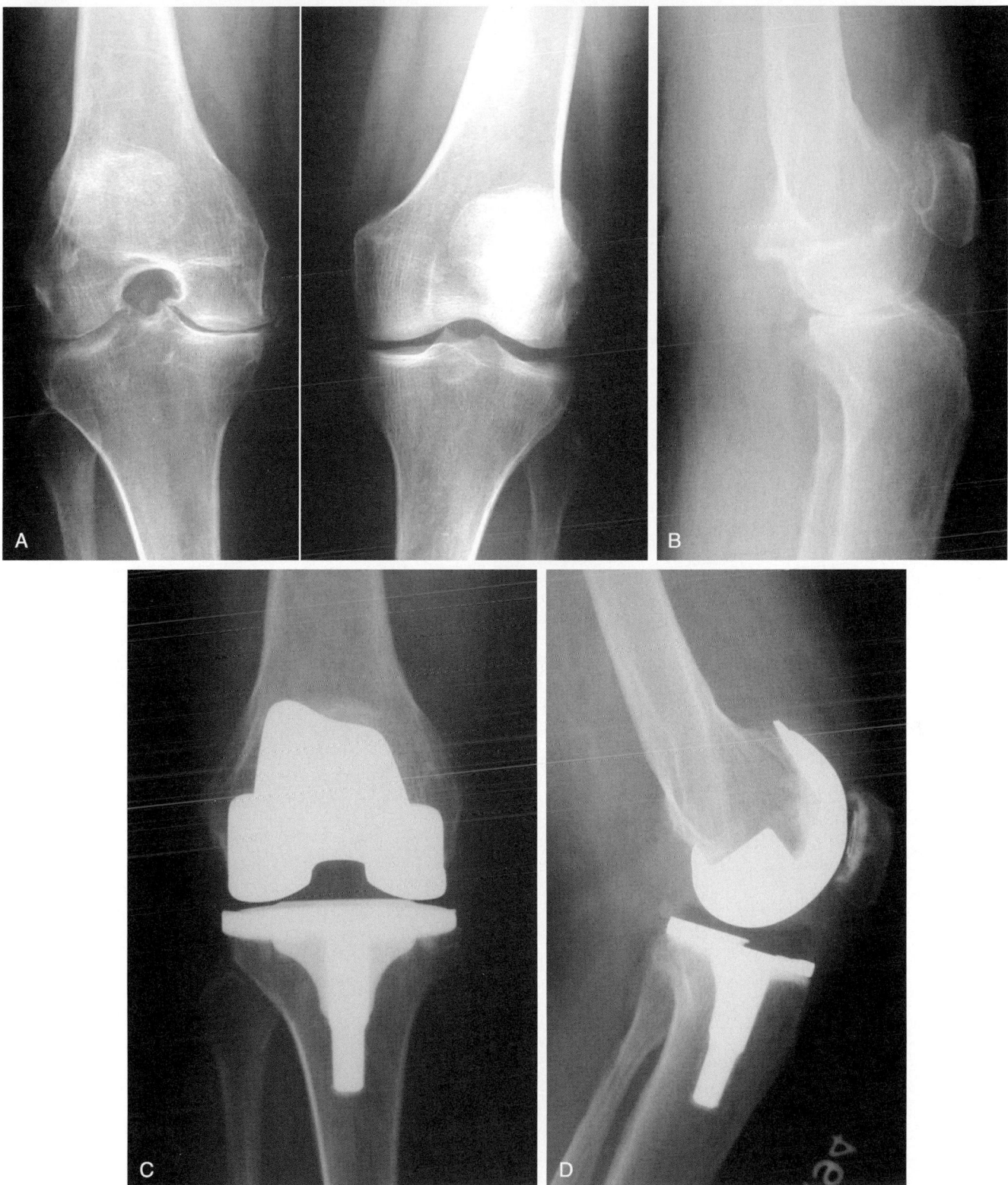

**FIGURE 63–13.** Traumatic arthritis of the knee after an epiphyseal fracture as a teen. *A,* A standing anteroposterior radiograph of both knees reveals a notch view of the affected right knee in comparison to the normal left knee. *B,* Lateral radiograph demonstrating the hyperextended position of the distal end of the femur. *C, D,* Posterior stabilization of the total-knee prosthesis was performed by splitting the difference between the anatomic position and the hyperextended position.

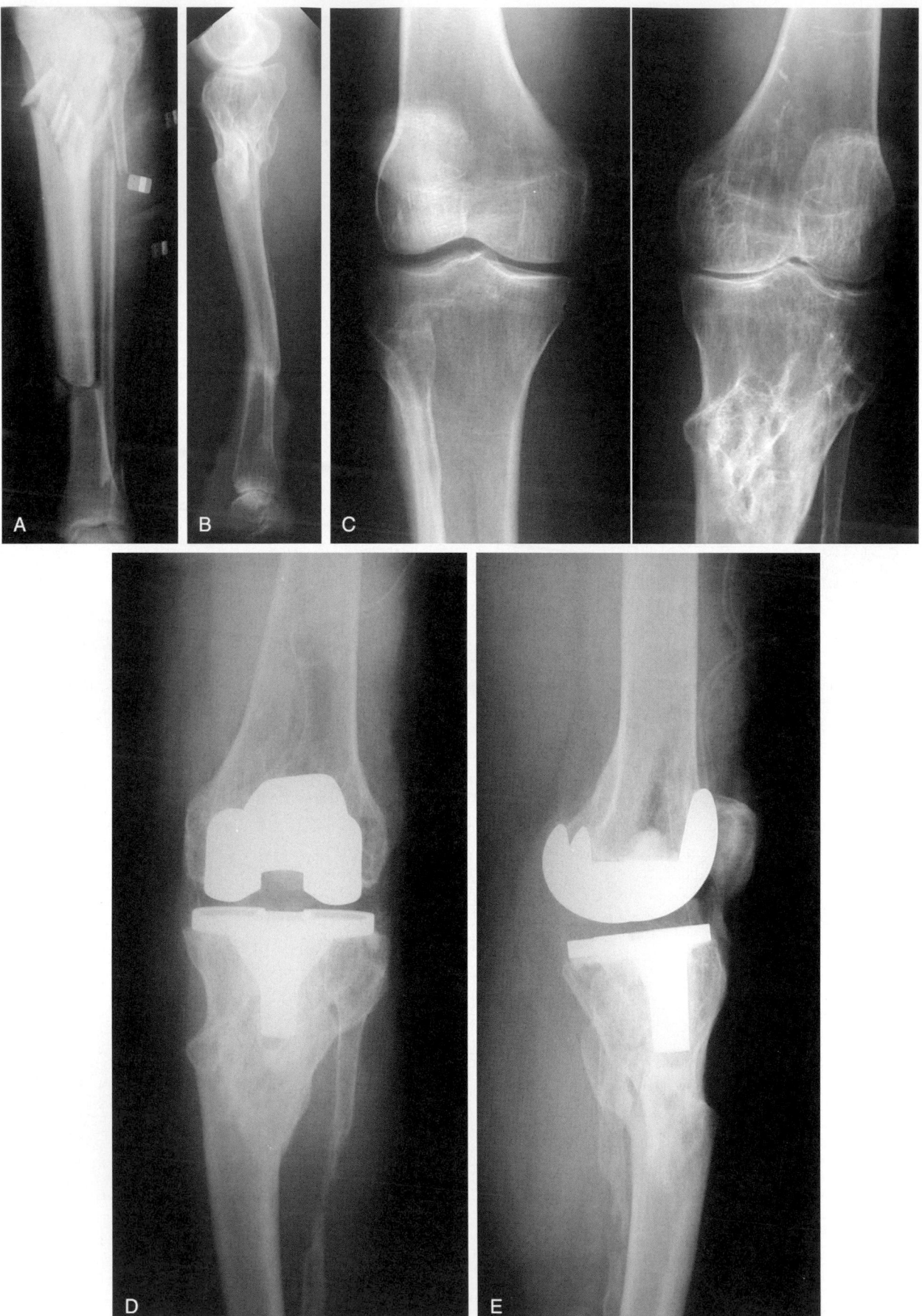

**FIGURE 63–14.** *A,* Initial injury film of a comminuted proximal tibial fracture and distal diaphyseal fracture. *B,* Immediate preoperative lateral view of the tibia 10 years after the initial injury. The recurvatum is within the plane of the knee joint. *C,* Anteroposterior view of the affected left knee in comparison to the uninvolved right knee. The mechanical axis passes through the center of the joint. *D,* Postoperative anteroposterior radiograph demonstrating alignment of the components. *E,* Lateral postoperative radiograph of the posteriorly stabilized component. Intraoperative alignment was checked by fluoroscopy before making the final cuts.

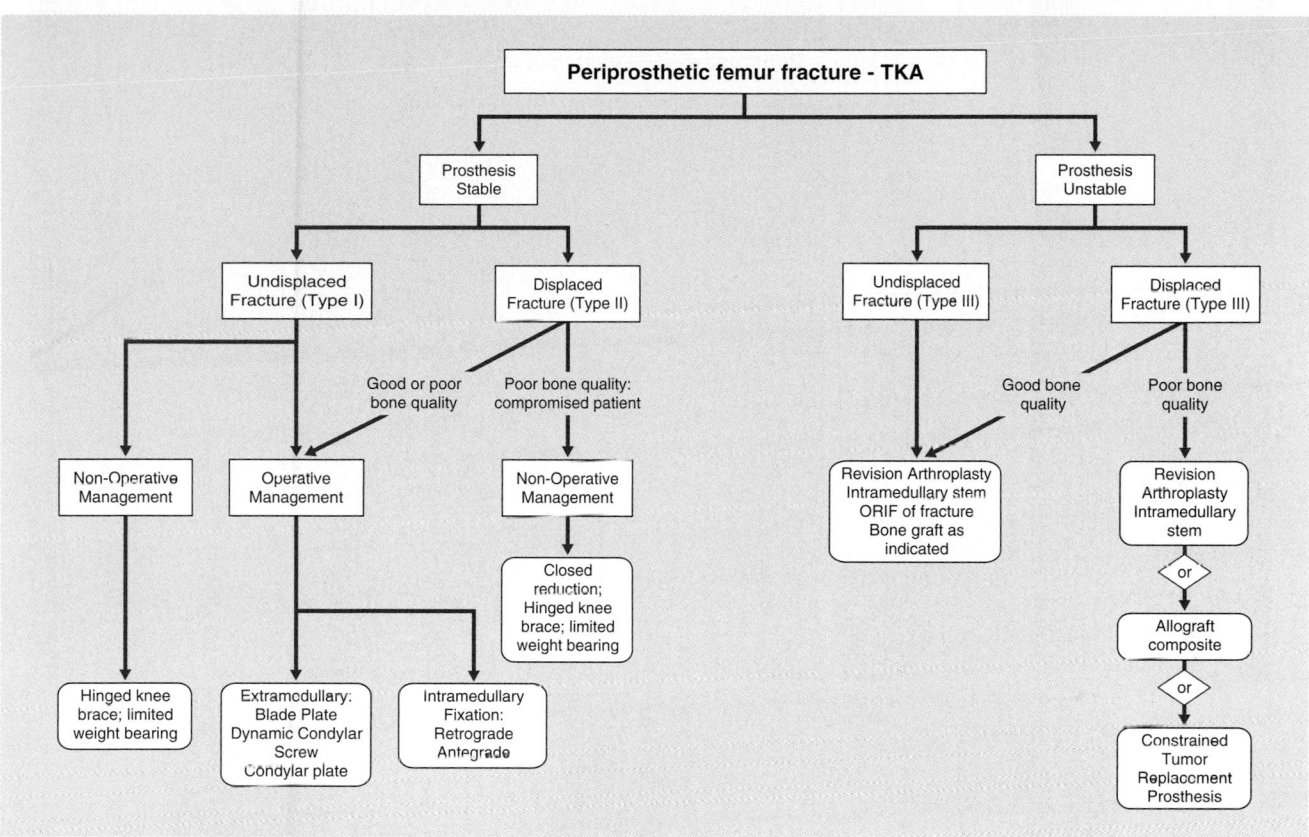

**FIGURE 63–15.** Algorithm for the treatment of periprosthetic femoral fractures about total-knee arthroplasties. (After Rorabeck, C.H.; Taylor, J.W. Orthop Clin North Am 30:265–277, 1999.)

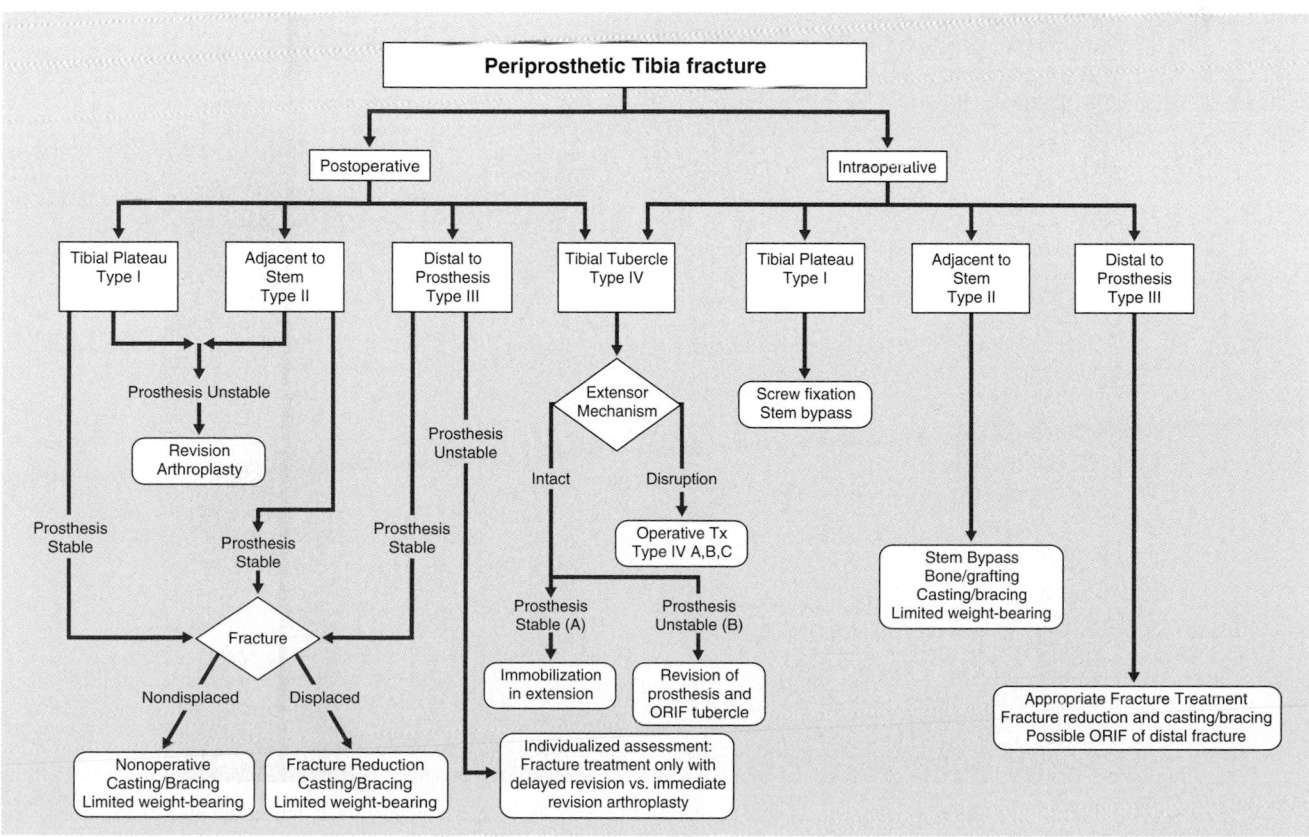

**FIGURE 63–16.** Algorithm for the treatment of periprosthetic tibial fractures about total-knee arthroplasties. (After Stuart, M.J.; Hanssen, A.D. Orthop Clin North Am 30:279–286, 1999.)

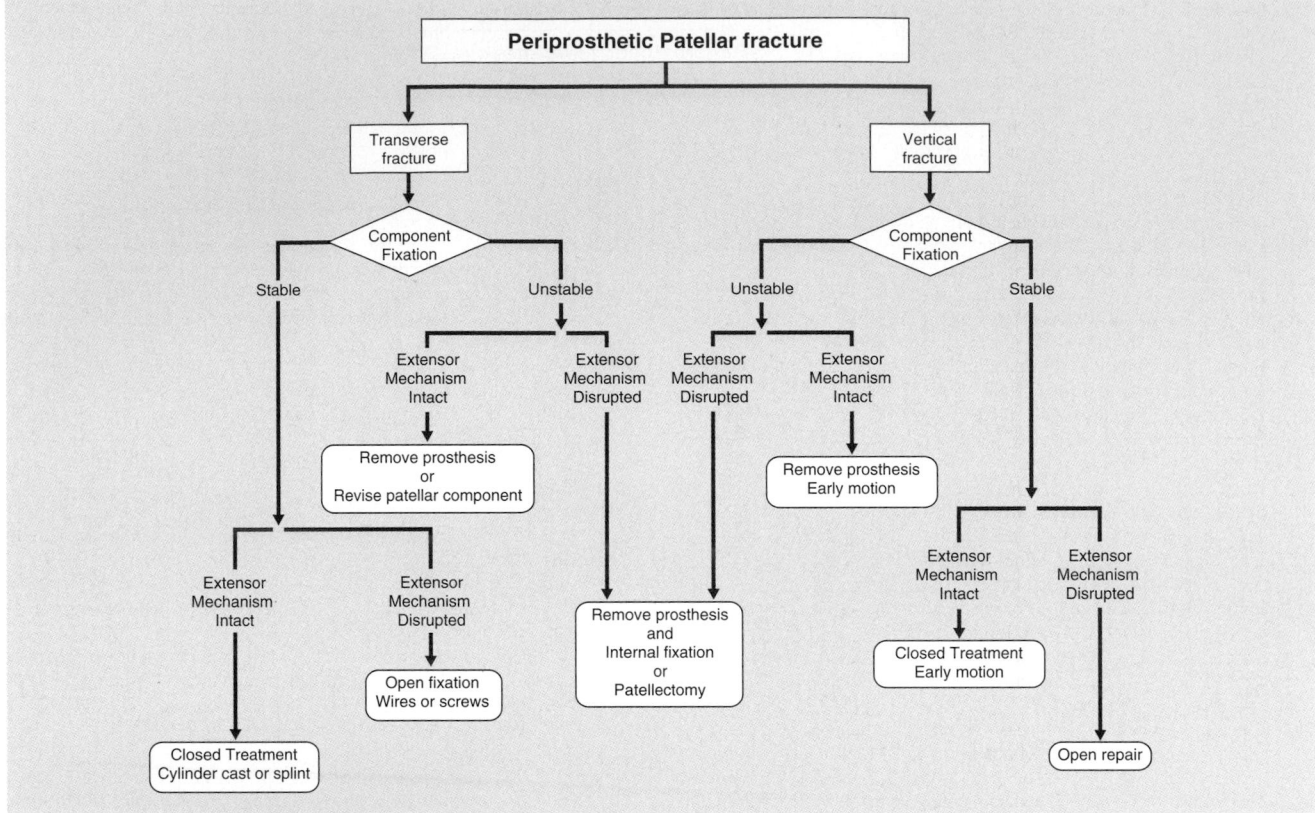

**Figure 63–17.** Algorithm for the treatment of periprosthetic patellar fractures about total-knee arthroplasties. (After Bourne, R.B. Orthop Clin North Am 30:287–291, 1999.)

fractures can be managed with a standard tension band wire technique. Type III fractures with disruption of the extensor mechanism require additional protection with a cerclage wire around the superior pole of the patella, but secured to a transtibial screw distal to the tubercle (Fig. 63–17).

## REFERENCES

1. AAOS, Committee on the Hip. Classification and management of femoral defects in total hip replacement. Paper presented at the 57th Annual Meeting of the American Academy of Orthopaedic Surgeons, New Orleans, 1990.
2. Aaron, R.K.; Scott, R.S. Supracondylar fracture of the femur after total knee arthroplasty. Clin Orthop 219:136–139, 1987.
3. Adolphson, P.; Jonsson, U.; Kalen, R. Fractures of the ipsilateral femur after total hip arthroplasty. Arch Orthop Trauma Surg 106:353–357, 1987.
4. Ali Khan, M.A.; O'Driscoll, M. Fractures of the femur during total hip replacement and their management. J Bone Joint Surg Br 59:36–41, 1977.
5. Anderson, L.D.; Hamsa, W.R.J.; Waring, T.L. Femoral-head prostheses. A review of three hundred and fifty-six operations and their results. J Bone Joint Surg Am 46:1049–1065, 1964.
6. Andrew, T.A.; Flanagan, J.P.; Gerundini, M.; Bombelli, R. The isoelastic, noncemented total hip arthroplasty. Preliminary experience with 400 cases. Clin Orthop 206:127–138, 1986.
7. Antoniou, J.; Huk, O.; Zukor, D.; et al. Collagen crosslinked N-telopeptides as markers for evaluating particulate osteolysis: A preliminary study. J Orthop Res 18:64–67, 2000.
8. Aribindi, R.; Paprosky, W.; Nourbash, P.; et al. Extended proximal femoral osteotomy. Instr Course Lect 48:19–26, 1999.
9. Astion, D.J.; Saluan, P.; Stulberg, B.N.; et al. The porous-coated anatomic total hip prosthesis: Failure of the metal-backed acetabular component. J Bone Joint Surg Am 78:755–766, 1996.
10. Ayers, D.C. Supracondylar fracture of the distal femur proximal to a total knee replacement. Instr Course Lect 46:197–203, 1997.
11. Barrack, R.L. Economics of revision total hip arthroplasty. Clin Orthop 319:209–214, 1995.
12. Barrack, R.L.; Hoffman, G.J.; Tejeiro, W.V.; Carpenter, L.J., Jr. Surgeon work input and risk in primary versus revision total joint arthroplasty. J Arthroplasty 10:281–286, 1995.
13. Barth, R.W.; Lane, J.M. Osteoporosis. Orthop Clin North Am 19:845–858, 1988.
14. Beals, R.K.; Tower, S.S. Periprosthetic fractures of the femur. An analysis of 93 fractures. Clin Orthop 327:238–246, 1996.
15. Benevenia, J.; Lee, F.Y.; Buechel, F.; Parsons, J.R. Pathologic supracondylar fracture due to osteolytic pseudotumor of knee following cementless total knee replacement. J Biomed Mater Res 43:473–477, 1998.
16. Bergstrom, B.; Lindberg, L.; Persson, B.M.; Onnerfalt, R. Complications after total hip arthroplasty according to Charnley in a Swedish series of cases. Clin Orthop 95(Sep):91–95, 1973.
17. Berry, D. Epidemiology: Hip and knee. In: Duncan, C.; Callaghan, J., eds. Periprosthetic Fractures after Major Joint Replacement. Philadelphia, W.B. Saunders, 1999, pp. 183–190.
18. Berry, D.J. Acetabular anti-protrusio rings and cages in revision total hip arthroplasty. Semin Arthroplasty 6(2):68–75, 1995.
19. Berry, D.J. Total hip arthroplasty in patients with proximal femoral deformity. Clin Orthop 369:262–272, 1999.
20. Bethea, J.S., III; DeAndrade, J.R.; Fleming, L.L.; et al. Proximal femoral fractures following total hip arthroplasty. Clin Orthop 170:95–106, 1982.
21. Biswas, S.P.; Kurer, M.H.; Mackenney, R.P. External fixation for femoral shaft fracture after Stanmore total knee replacement. J Bone Joint Surg Br 74:313–314, 1992.
22. Blatter, G.; Fiechter, T.; Magerl, F. Peri-prosthesis fractures in total hip endoprostheses. Orthopade 18:545–551, 1989.
23. Bogoch, E.; Hastings, D.; Gross, A.; Gschwend, N. Supracondylar fractures of the femur adjacent to resurfacing and MacIntosh arthroplasties of the knee in patients with rheumatoid arthritis. Clin Orthop 229:213–220, 1988.

24. Bourne, R.B. Fractures of the patella after total knee replacement. Orthop Clin North Am 30:287–291, 1999.

25. Bourne, R.B.; Crawford, H.A. Principles of revision total knee arthroplasty. Orthop Clin North Am 29:331–337, 1998.

26. Brady, O.; Garbuz, D.; Masri, B.; Duncan, C. Classification of the hip. In: Duncan, C.; Callaghan, J., eds. Periprosthetic Fractures after Major Joint Replacement. Philadelphia, W.B. Saunders, 1999, pp. 215–220.

27. Brady, O.; Garbuz, D.; Masri, B.; Duncan, C. The treatment of periprosthetic fractures of the femur using cortical onlay allograft struts. In: Duncan, C.; Callaghan, J., eds. Periprosthetic Fractures after Major Joint Replacement. Philadelphia, W.B. Saunders, 1999, pp. 249–258.

28. Breck, L.W. Metal to metal total hip joint replacement using the wrist socket: An end result. Clin Orthop 95(Sep):38–42, 1973.

29. Brick, G.W.; Scott, R.D. The patellofemoral component of total knee arthroplasty. Clin Orthop 231:163–178, 1988.

30. Brindley, G.W.; Kavanagh, B.F.; Fitzgerald, R.H. Intraoperative fractures during uncemented total hip arthroplasty. Orthop Trans 11:463, 1987.

31. Broad, C.P.; Hamami, M.N. Küntscher nailing of femoral fractures associated with Austin Moore's prosthesis. Injury 12:252–255, 1980.

32. Burchardt, H. Biology of bone transplantation. Orthop Clin North Am 18:187–196, 1987.

33. Burstein, A.H.; Currey, J.; Frankel, V.H.; et al. Bone strength: The effect of screw holes. J Bone Joint Surg Am 54:1143–1156, 1972.

34. Cadambi, A.; Engh, G.A.; Dwyer, K.A.; Vinh, T.N. Osteolysis of the distal femur after total knee arthroplasty. J Arthroplasty 9:579–594, 1994.

35. Cain, P.R.; Rubash, H.E.; Wissinger, H.A.; McClain, E.J. Periprosthetic femoral fractures following total knee arthroplasty. Clin Orthop 208:205–214, 1986.

36. Callaghan, J.; Kim, Y.; Pederson, D.; Brown, T. Periprosthetic fractures of the acetabulum. In: Duncan, C.; Callaghan, J., eds. Periprosthetic Fractures after Major Joint Replacement. Philadelphia, W.B. Saunders, 1999, pp. 221–234.

37. Callaghan, J.J. The clinical results and basic science of total hip arthroplasty with porous-coated prostheses. J Bone Joint Surg Am 75:299–310, 1993.

38. Callaghan, J.J. Periprosthetic fractures of the acetabulum during and following total hip arthroplasty. Instr Course Lect 47:231–235, 1998.

39. Callaghan, J.J.; Heekin, R.D.; Savory, C.G.; et al. Evaluation of the learning curve associated with uncemented primary porous-coated anatomic total hip arthroplasty. Clin Orthop 282:132–144, 1992.

40. Cameron, H. Femoral neck stress fracture after total knee replacement: A case report. Am J Knee Surg 5:41–43, 1992.

41. Cameron, H.U.; Jung, Y.K.; Noiles, D.G.; McTighe, T. Design features and early clinical results with a modular proximally fixed low bending stiffness uncemented total hip replacement. Paper presented at the 55th Annual Meeting of the American Academy of Orthopaedic Surgeons, Atlanta, 1988.

42. Chandler, H.; Tigges, R. The role of allografts in the treatment of periprosthetic femoral fractures. J Bone Joint Surg Am 79:1422–1432, 1997.

43. Chandler, H.; Tigges, R. The role of allografts in the treatment of periprosthetic femoral fractures. Instr Course Lect 47:257–264, 1998.

44. Chandler, H.P. Use of allografts and prostheses in the reconstruction of failed total hip replacements. Orthopedics 15:1207–1218, 1992.

45. Chandler, H.P.; King, D.; Limbird, R.; et al. The use of cortical allograft struts for fixation of fractures associated with well-fixed total joint prostheses. Semin Arthroplasty 4:99–107, 1993.

46. Chandler, H.P.; Penenberg, B.L., eds. Bone Stock Deficiency in Total Hip Replacement. Thorofare, N.J., Slack, 1989.

47. Chapchal, G.J.; Sloof, J.J.; Nollen, A.D. Results of total hip replacement: A critical follow-up study. Clin Orthop 95(Sep):111–117, 1973.

48. Charnley, J. The healing of human fractures in contact with self-curing acrylic cement. Clin Orthop 47(Jul–Aug):157–163, 1966.

49. Chen, F.; Mont, M.A.; Bachner, R.S. Management of ipsilateral supracondylar femur fractures following total knee arthroplasty. J Arthroplasty 9:521–526, 1994.

50. Christensen, C.M.; Seger, B.M.; Schultz, R.B. Management of intraoperative femur fractures associated with revision hip arthroplasty. Clin Orthop 248:177–180, 1989.

51. Christie, M.J.; DeBoer, D.K.; Tingstad, E.M.; et al. Clinical experience with a modular noncemented femoral component in revision total hip arthroplasty: 4- to 7-year results. J Arthroplasty 15:840–848, 2000.

52. Clancey, G.J.; Smith, R.F.; Madenwald, M.B. Fracture of the distal end of the femur below hip implants in elderly patients. J Bone Joint Surg Am 65:491–494, 1983.

53. Clayton, M.L.; Thirupathi, R. Patellar complications after total condylar arthroplasty. Clin Orthop 170:152–155, 1982.

54. Convery, F.R.; Minteer-Convery, M.; Malcom, L.L. The spherocentric knee: A re-evaluation and modification. J Bone Joint Surg Am 62:320–327, 1980.

55. Cooke, P.H.; Newman, J.H. Femoral fractures in relation to cemented hip prostheses. J Bone Joint Surg Br 66:278, 1984.

56. Cooke, P.H.; Newman, J.H. Fractures of the femur in relation to cemented hip prostheses. J Bone Joint Surg Br 70:386–389, 1988.

57. Coonse, J.; Adams, J. A new operative approach to the knee joint. Surg Gynecol Obstet 77:334, 1943.

58. Cordeiro, E.N.; Costa, R.C.; Carazzato, J.G.; Silva, J. dos S. Periprosthetic fractures in patients with total knee arthroplasties. Clin Orthop 252:182–189, 1990.

59. Courpied, J.P.; Watin-Augouard, L.; Postel, M. Fractures du femur chez les sujets porteurs de prostheses totales de hanche ou de genou. Int Orthop 11:109–115, 1987.

60. Cracchiolo, A. Stress fractures of the pelvis as a cause of hip pain following total hip and knee arthroplasty. Arthritis Rheum 24:740–742, 1981.

61. Cuckler, J. Richards Modular Hip System. Memphis, TN, Smith & Nephew Richards, 1994.

62. Culp, R.W.; Schmidt, R.G.; Hanks, G.; et al. Supracondylar fracture of the femur following prosthetic knee arthroplasty. Clin Orthop 222:212–222, 1987.

63. Cupic, Z. Long term follow-up of Charnley arthroplasty of the hip. Clin Orthop 141:28–43, 1979.

64. Curtis, M.J.; Jinnah, R.H.; Wilson, V.D.; Hungerford, D.S. The initial stability of uncemented acetabular components. J Bone Joint Surg Br 74:372–376, 1992.

65. Dave, D.J.; Koka, S.R.; James, S.E. Mennen plate fixation for fracture of the femoral shaft with ipsilateral total hip and knee arthroplasties. J Arthroplasty 10:113–115, 1995.

66. De Beer, J.D.V.; Learmonth, I.D. "Pathological" fracture of the femur—a complication of failed total hip arthroplasty. S Afr Med J 79(16):202–205, 1991.

67. Delport, P.H.; Van Audekercke, R.; Martens, M. Conservative treatment of ipsilateral supracondylar femoral fracture after total knee arthroplasty. J Trauma 24:846–849, 1984.

68. DiGioia, A.M.; Rubash, H.E. Periprosthetic fractures of the femur after total knee arthroplasty: A literature review and treatment algorithm. Clin Orthop 271:135–142, 1991.

69. Duncan, C.; Callaghan, J., eds. Periprosthetic Fractures after Major Joint Replacement. Philadelphia, W.B. Saunders, 1999.

70. Duncan, C.; Masri, B. Fractures of the femur after hip replacement. Instr Course Lect 44:293–304, 1995.

71. Dunn, H.K.; Hess, W.E. Total hip reconstruction in chronically dislocated hips. J Bone Joint Surg Am 58:838–845, 1976.

72. Dunwoody, J.; Duncan, C.P.; Younger, A.; et al. A review of the reliability and validity of a new classification system for periprosthetic fractures of femur in hip arthroplasty. J Bone Joint Surg Br 80(Suppl):17, 1998.

73. Dupont, J.A.; Charnley, J. Low friction arthroplasty of the hip for the failures of previous operations. J Bone Joint Surg Br 54:77–87, 1972.

74. Dysart, S.H.; Savory, C.G.; Callaghan, J.J. Nonoperative treatment of a postoperative fracture around an uncemented porous-coated femoral component. J Arthroplasty 4:187–190, 1989.

75. Eftekhar, N.S.; Smith, D.M.; Henry, J.H.; Stinchfield, F.E. Revision arthroplasty using Charnley low friction arthroplasty technique. Clin Orthop 95(Sep):48–59, 1973.

76. Eftekhar, N.S.; Stinchfield, F.E. Experience with low friction arthroplasty. Clin Orthop 95(Sep):60–68, 1973.

77. Ejested, R.; Olsen, N.J. Revision of failed total hip arthroplasty. J Bone Joint Surg Br 69:57–60, 1987.

78. Engh, C.A.; Glassman, A.H.; Griffin, W.L.; Mayer, J.G. Results of cementless revision for failed cemented total hip arthroplasty. Clin Orthop 235:91–110, 1988.

79. Engh, G.A.; Ammeen, D.J. Periprosthetic fractures adjacent to total knee implants: Treatment and clinical results. Instr Course Lect 47:437–448, 1998.

80. Engh, G.A.; Herzwurm, P.J.; Parks, N.L. Treatment of major defects of bone with bulk allografts and stemmed components during total knee arthroplasty. J Bone Joint Surg Am 79:1030–1039, 1997.

81. Evanski, P.M.; Waugh, T.R.; Orofino, C.F. Total hip replacement with the Charnley prosthesis. Clin Orthop 95(Sep):69–72, 1973.

82. Evarts, C.M.; DeHaven, K.E.; Nelson, C.L.; et al. Interim results of Charnley-Muller total hip arthroplasty. Clin Orthop 95(Sep):193–200, 1973.

83. Exner, G.U.; Malinin, T.I.; Weber, D.; Hodler, J. Titanium implant for the osteosynthesis of massive allograft reconstruction to improve follow-up by magnetic resonance imaging. Bull Hosp Jt Dis 54:140–145, 1996.

84. Federici, A.; Carbone, M.; Sanguineti, F. Intraoperative fractures of the femoral diaphysis in hip arthroprosthesis surgery. Ital J Orthop Traumatol 14:311–321, 1988.

85. Felix, N.A.; Stuart, M.J.; Hanssen, A.D. Periprosthetic fractures of the tibia associated with total knee arthroplasty. Clin Orthop 345:113–124, 1997.

86. Figgie, H.E., 3rd.; Goldberg, V.M.; Figgie, M.P.; et al. The effect of alignment of the implant on fractures of the patella after condylar total knee arthroplasty. J Bone Joint Surg Am 71:1031–1039, 1989.

87. Figgie, M.P.; Goldberg, V.M.; Figgie, H.E., 3rd. The results of treatment of supracondylar fracture above total knee arthroplasty. J Arthroplasty 5:267–276, 1990.

88. Fipp, G. Stress fractures of the femoral neck following total knee arthroplasty. J Arthroplasty 3:347–350, 1988.

89. Firestone, T.P.; Hedley, A.K. Extended proximal femoral osteotomy for severe acetabular protrusion following total hip arthroplasty. A technical note. J Arthroplasty 12:344–345, 1997.

90. Fitzgerald, R.H., Jr.; Brindley, G.W.; Kavanagh, B.F. The uncemented total hip arthroplasty. Intraoperative femoral fractures. Clin Orthop 235:61–66, 1988.

91. Fredin, H.O.; Lindberg, H.; Carlsson, A.S. Femoral fracture following hip arthroplasty. Acta Orthop Scand 58:20–22, 1987.

92. Friedman, R.J.; Black, J.; Galante, J.O.; et al. Current concepts in orthopaedic biomaterials and implant fixation. J Bone Joint Surg Am 75:1086–1109, 1993.

93. Fruhwald, F.; Fellinger, E.; Hubsch, P.; et al. Computerized tomography analysis of cement-free total hip endoprostheses. Rontgenblatter 41:313–319, 1988.

94. Garbuz, D.S.; Masri, B.A.; Duncan, C.P. Periprosthetic fractures of the femur: Principles of prevention and management. Instr Course Lect 47:237–242, 1998.

95. Garbuz, D.S.; Penner, M.J. Role and results of segmental allografts for acetabular segmental bone deficiency. Orthop Clin North Am 29:263–275, 1998.

96. Garcia-Cimbrelo, E.; Munuera, L.; Gil-Garay, E. Femoral shaft fractures after cemented total hip arthroplasty. Int Orthop 16:97–100, 1992.

97. Ghazavi, M.T.; Stockley, I.; Yee, G.; et al. Reconstruction of massive bone defects with allograft in revision total knee arthroplasty. J Bone Joint Surg Am 79:17–25, 1997.

98. Giacometti, R.C.; Pace, A. CLS femoral component. Orthopedics 12:1195–1200, 1989.

99. Gill, T.J.; Sledge, J.B.; Muller, M.E. The Burch-Schneider anti-protrusio cage in revision total hip arthroplasty: Indications, principles and long-term results. J Bone Joint Surg Br 80:946–953, 1998.

100. Goldberg, V.M.; Figgie, H.E.; Inglis, A.E.; et al. Patellar fracture type and prognosis in condylar total knee arthroplasty. Clin Orthop 236:115–122, 1988.

101. Grace, J.N.; Sim, F.H. Fracture of the patella after total knee arthroplasty. Clin Orthop 230:168–175, 1988.

102. Graves, E.J.; Owings, M.F. 1996 Summary: National Hospital Discharge Survey. Advance data from Vital and Health Statistics 11, Vol. 301, 1998.

103. Grob, D.; Gschwend, N. Periprothetische Frakturen nach Totalersatz des Kniegelenkes. Orthopade 11:109, 1982.

104. Haddad, F.; Masri, B.; Garbuz, D.; Duncan, C. The prevention of periprosthetic fractures in total hip and knee arthroplasty. In: Duncan, C.; Callaghan, J., eds. Periprosthetic Fractures after Major Joint Replacement. Philadelphia, W.B. Saunders, 1999, pp. 191–208.

105. Haddad, R.J., Jr.; Cook, S.D.; Thomas, K.A. Biological fixation of porous-coated implants. J Bone Joint Surg Am 69:1459–1466, 1987.

106. Hanks, G.A.; Mathews, H.H.; Routson, G.W.; Loughran, T.P. Supracondylar fracture of the femur following total knee arthroplasty. J Arthroplasty 4:289–292, 1989.

107. Hardy, D.C.; Delince, P.E.; Yasik, E.; Lafontaine, M.A. Stress fracture of the hip. An unusual complication of total knee arthroplasty. Clin Orthop 281:140–144, 1992.

108. Harrington, I.J.; Tountas, A.A.; Cameron, H.U. Femoral fractures associated with Moore's prosthesis. Injury 11:23–32, 1979.

109. Harris, W.H. Preliminary report of results of Harris total hip replacement. Clin Orthop 95(Sep):168–173, 1973.

110. Healy, W.L.; Siliski, J.M.; Incavo, S.J. Operative treatment of distal femoral fractures proximal to total knee replacements. J Bone Joint Surg Am 75:27–34, 1993.

111. Healy, W.L.; Wasilewski, S.A.; Takei, R.; Oberlander, M. Patellofemoral complications following total knee arthroplasty. Correlation with implant design and patient risk factors. J Arthroplasty 10:197–201, 1995.

112. Heekin, R.D.; Engh, C.A.; Herzwurm, P.J. Fractures through cystic lesions of the greater trochanter. A cause of late pain after cementless total hip arthroplasty. J Arthroplasty 11:757–760, 1996.

113. Hirsh, D.M.; Bhalla, S.; Roffman, M. Supracondylar fracture of the femur following total knee replacement. Report of four cases. J Bone Joint Surg Am 63:162–163, 1981.

114. Hozack, W.J.; Goll, S.R.; Lotke, P.A.; et al. The treatment of patellar fractures after total knee arthroplasty. Clin Orthop 236:123–127, 1988.

115. Huang, C.H.; Yang, C.Y.; Cheng, C.K. Fracture of the femoral component associated with polyethylene wear and osteolysis after total knee arthroplasty. J Arthroplasty 14:375–379, 1999.

116. Huk, O.L.; Bansal, M.; Betts, F.; et al. Polyethylene and metal debris generated by non-articulating surfaces of modular acetabular components. J Bone Joint Surg Br 76:568–574, 1994.

117. Insall, J.N.; Haas, S.B. Complications of total knee arthroplasty. In: Insall, J., ed. Surgery of the Knee. New York, Churchill Livingstone, 1993, pp. 891–934.

118. Insall, J.N.; Lachiewicz, P.F.; Burstein, A.H. The posterior stabilized condylar prosthesis: A modification of the total condylar design. Two to four-year clinical experience. J Bone Joint Surg Am 64:1317–1323, 1982.

119. Jabczenski, F.F.; Crawford, M. Retrograde intramedullary nailing of supracondylar femur fractures above total knee arthroplasty. A preliminary report of four cases. J Arthroplasty 10:95–101, 1995.

120. Jacobs, P.; Williams, R.; Mabrey, J.D. Segmental skeletal replacement for periprosthetic fractures about the knee in debilitated patients. Orthop Trans 19:812, 1995.

121. Jahn, K.; Siegling, C.W. Femurfrakturen bei Totalondoprothesen-plastiken. Zentralbl Chir 106:463–468, 1981.

122. Jasty, M.; Henshaw, R.M.; O'Connor, D.O.; Harris, W.H. High assembly strains and femoral fractures produced during insertion of uncemented femoral components. J Arthroplasty 8:479–487, 1993.

123. Jensen, J.S.; Barfod, G.; Hansen, D.; et al. Femoral shaft fracture after hip arthroplasty. Acta Orthop Scand 59:9–13, 1988.

124. Jensen, T.T.; Overgaard, S.; Mossing, N.B. Partridge Cerclene system for femoral fractures in osteoporotic bones with ipsilateral hemi/total arthroplasty. J Arthroplasty 5:123–126, 1990.

125. Johansson, J.E.; McBroom, R.; Barrington, T.W.; Hunter, G.A. Fracture of the ipsilateral femur in patients with total hip replacement. J Bone Joint Surg Am 63:1435–1442, 1981.

126. Jones, D.G. Bone erosion beneath Partidge bands. J Bone Joint Surg Br 68:476, 1986.

127. Kavanagh, B.F.; Ilstrup, D.M.; Fitzgerald, R.H. Revision total hip arthroplasty. J Bone Joint Surg Am 67:517–526, 1985.

128. Kayler, D.E.; Lyttle, D. Surgical interruption of patellar blood supply by total knee arthroplasty. Clin Orthop 229:221–227, 1988.

129. Keating, E.M.; Ritter, M.A.; Faris, P.M. Structures at risk from medially placed acetabular screws. J Bone Joint Surg Am 72:509–511, 1990.

130. Kelley, S.S. Periprosthetic femoral fractures. J Am Acad Orthop Surg 2:164–172, 1994.

131. Kim, Y.S.; Callaghan, J.J.; Ahn, P.B.; Brown, T.D. Acetabular fracture during oversized component insertion. Paper presented at the 41st Annual Meeting of the Orthopaedic Research Society, Orlando, Florida, 1995.

132. Kim, Y.S.; Callaghan, J.J.; Ahn, P.B.; Brown, T.D. Fracture of the acetabulum during insertion of an oversized hemispherical component. J Bone Joint Surg Am 77:111–117, 1995.

133. Kirkpatrick, J.S.; Callaghan, J.J.; Vandemark, R.M.; Goldner, R.D. The relationship of the intrapelvic vasculature to the acetabulum. Implications in screw-fixation acetabular components. Clin Orthop 258:183–190, 1990.

134. Kolmert, L. A method for fixation of femoral fractures below previous hip implants. J Trauma 27:407–410, 1987.

135. Kraay, M.J.; Goldberg, V.M.; Figgie, M.P.; Figgie H.E., III. Distal femoral replacement with allograft/prosthetic reconstruction for treatment of supracondylar fractures in patients with total knee arthroplasty. J Arthroplasty 7:7–16, 1992.

136. Kumm, D.A.; Rack, C.; Rutt, J. Subtrochanteric stress fracture of the femur following total knee arthroplasty. J Arthroplasty 12:580–583, 1997.

137. Kwong, L.M.; O'Connor, D.O.; Sedlacek, R.C.; et al. A quantitative in vitro assessment of fit and screw fixation on the stability of a cementless hemispherical acetabular component. J Arthroplasty 9:163–170, 1994.

138. Langenskiold, A.; Paavilainen, T. Total replacement of 116 hips by the McKee-Farrar prosthesis: A preliminary report. Clin Orthop 95(Sep):143–150, 1973.

139. Larcom, P.G.; Lotke, P.A.; Steinberg, M.E.; et al. Magnetic resonance venography versus contrast venography to diagnose thrombosis after joint surgery. Clin Orthop 331:209–215, 1996.

140. Larson, J.E.; Chao, E.Y.S.; Fitzgerald, R.H.J.; et al. Bypassing femoral cortical defects with cemented intramedullary stems. J Orthop Res 9:414–421, 1991.

141. Laskin, R.S. Management of the patella during revision total knee replacement arthroplasty. Orthop Clin North Am 29:355–360, 1998.

142. Launder, W.J.; Hungerford, D.S. Stress fracture of the pubis after total hip arthroplasty. Clin Orthop 159:183–185, 1981.

143. Lazansky, M.G. Complications in total hip replacement with the Charnley technic. Clin Orthop 72:40–45, 1970.

144. Le, A.X.; Cameron, H.U.; Otsuka, N.Y.; et al. Fracture of the patella following total knee arthroplasty. Orthopedics 22:395–398, discussion 398–399, 1999.

145. Leinbach, I.S.; Barlow, F.A. 700 total hip replacements. Clin Orthop 95(Sep):174–192, 1973.

146. Lesniewski, P.J.; Testa, N.N. Stress fracture of the hip as a complication of total knee replacement. Case report. J Bone Joint Surg Am 64:304–306, 1982.

147. Lewallen, D.G.; Berry, D.J. Periprosthetic fracture of the femur after total hip arthroplasty: Treatment and results to date. Instr Course Lect 47:243–249, 1998.

148. Lewis, P.L.; Brewster, N.T.; Graves, S.E. The pathogenesis of bone loss following total knee arthroplasty. Orthop Clin North Am 29:187–197, 1998.

149. Lewis, P.L.; Rorabeck, C.H. Periprosthetic fractures. In: Engh, G.A.; Rorabeck, C.H., eds. Revision Total Knee Arthroplasty. Baltimore, Williams & Wilkins, 1997, pp. 275–295.

150. Lowenhielm, G.; Hansson, L.I.; Karrholm, J. Fracture of the lower extremity after total hip replacement. Arch Orthop Trauma Surg 108:141–143, 1989.

151. Luck, J.V.; Brannon, E.W.; Luck, J.V.J. Total hip replacement arthroplasties: Causes, orthopaedic management, and prevention of selected problems. J Bone Joint Surg Am 54:1569–1571, 1972.

152. Lynch, A.F.; Rorabeck, C.H.; Bourne, R.B. Extensor mechanism complications following total knee arthroplasty. J Arthroplasty 2:135–140, 1987.

153. Mabrey, J.D. Periprosthetic fractures about total hips, and fractures about total knees and total ankles. In: Heckman, J.D.; Bucholz, R.D., eds. Rockwood and Green's Fractures in Adults. Philadelphia, Lippincott Williams & Wilkins, 2001.

154. Mabrey, J.D.; Foote, J.; Kose, N.; et al. Smooth uncemented femoral stems do not provide torsional stability of femurs with cortical defects. Orthop Trans 22:236–237, 1998.

155. Mackechnie-Jarvis, A.C. Fractures below a femoral prosthesis—a report on two cases treated by conservative surgery. Injury 17:271–273, 1986.

156. Malchau, H.; Herberts, P.; Wang, Y.X.; et al. Long-term clinical and radiological results of the Lord total hip prosthesis. A prospective study. J Bone Joint Surg Br 78:884–891, 1996.

157. Mallory, T.H.; Kraus, T.J.; Vaughn, B.K. Intraoperative femoral fractures associated with cementless total hip arthroplasty. Orthopaedics 12:231–239, 1989.

158. Maloney, W.J.; Peters, P.; Engh, C.A.; Chandler, H. Severe osteolysis of the pelvis in association with acetabular replacement without cement. J Bone Joint Surg Am 75:1627–1635, 1993.

159. Mankin, H.J.; Friedlander, G.E. Biology of bone grafts: In: Chandler, H.P.; Penenberg, B.L., eds. Bone Stock Deficiency in Total Hip Replacement. Thorofare, N.J., Slack, 1989.

160. Marega, T.; Feroldi, G.; Marega, L. Our experience with the uncemented isoelastic total hip prosthesis. Arch Putti Chir Organi Mov 37:65–75, 1989.

161. Marmor, L. Stress fracture of the pubic ramus simulating a loose total hip replacement. Clin Orthop 121:103–104, 1976.

162. Masri, B.A.; Campbell, D.G.; Garbuz, D.S.; Duncan, C.P. Seven specialized exposures for revision hip and knee replacement. Orthop Clin North Am 29:229–240, 1998.

163. McAuley, J.; Sanchez, F. Knee: Role and results of allografts. In: Duncan, C.; Callaghan, J., eds. Periprosthetic Fractures after Major Joint Replacement. Philadelphia, W.B. Saunders, 1999, pp. 293–304.

164. McElfresh, E.C.; Coventry, M.B. Femoral and pelvic fractures after total hip arthroplasty. J Bone Joint Surg Am 56:483–492, 1974

165. McKe, G.K.; Chen, S.C. The statistics of the McKee-Farrar method of total hip replacement. Clin Orthop 95(Sep):26–33, 1973.

166. McLaren, A.C.; Dupont, J.A.; Schroeber, D.C. Open reduction internal fixation of supracondylar fractures above total knee arthroplasties using the intramedullary supracondylar rod. Clin Orthop 302:194–198, 1994.

167. McMahon, M.S.; Scuderi, G.R.; Glashow, J.L.; et al. Scintigraphic determination of patellar viability after excision of infrapatellar fat pad and/or lateral retinacular release in total knee arthroplasty. Clin Orthop 260:10–16, 1990.

168. Mennen, U. The paraskeletal clamp-on plate. Part I. A new alternative for retaining the surgically reduced position of bone fractures. S Afr Med J 66(5):167–170, 1984.

169. Merkel, K.D.; Johnson, E.W. Supracondylar fracture of the femur after total knee arthroplasty. J Bone Joint Surg Am 68:29–43, 1986.

170. Mihalko, W.M.; Beaudoin, A.J.; Cardea, J.A.; Krause, W.R. Finite-element modelling of femoral shaft fracture fixation techniques post total hip arthroplasty. J Biomech 25:469–476, 1992.

171. Miller, A.J. Late fracture of the acetabulum after total hip replacement. J Bone Joint Surg Br 54:600–606, 1972.

172. Moczynski, G.; Abraham, E.; Barmada, R.; Ray, R.D. Evaluation of total hip replacement arthroplasties. Clin Orthop 95(Sep):213–216, 1973.

173. Mont, M.A.; Maar, D.C. Fractures of the ipsilateral femur after hip arthroplasty: A statistical analysis of outcome based on 487 patients. J Arthroplasty 9:511–519, 1994.

174. Mont, M.A.; Maar, D.C.; Krackow, K.A.; Hungerford, D.S. Hoop-stress fractures of the proximal femur during hip arthroplasty: Management and results in 19 cases. J Bone Joint Surg Br 74:257–260, 1992.

175. Moran, M.C.; Brick, G.W.; Sledge, C.B.; et al. Supracondylar femoral fracture following total knee arthroplasty. Clin Orthop 324:196–209, 1996.

176. Moreland, J.R. Mechanisms of failure in total knee arthroplasty. Clin Orthop 226:49–77, 1988.

177. Morrey, B.F.; Kavanagh, B.F. Comparison of cemented and uncemented femoral revision total arthroplasty: Analysis of complications and reoperations. Orthop Trans 13:496, 1989.

178. Morrey, B.F.; Kavanagh, B.F. Complications with revision of the femoral component of total hip arthroplasty. Comparison between cemented and uncemented techniques. J Arthroplasty 7:71–79, 1992.

179. Morscher, E.; Masar, Z. Development and first experience with an uncemented press-fit cup. Clin Orthop 232:96–103, 1988.

180. Moyen, B.J.-L.; Lahey, P.J.; Weinberg, E.H.; Harris, W.H. Effects on intact femora of dogs of the application and removal of metal plates. A metabolic and structural study comparing stiffer and more flexible plates. J Bone Joint Surg Am 60:940–947, 1978.

181. Murray, W.R. Results in patients with total hip replacement arthroplasty. Clin Orthop 95(Sep):80–90, 1973.

182. Murrell, G.A.; Nunley, J.A. Interlocked supracondylar intramedullary nails for supracondylar fractures after total knee arthroplasty. A new treatment method. J Arthroplasty 10:37–42, 1995.

183. Neer, C.S., 2nd.; Grantham, S.A.; Shelton, M.L. Supracondylar fracture of the adult femur. A study of one hundred and ten cases. J Bone Joint Surg Am 49:591–613, 1967.

184. Nielsen, B.F.; Petersen, V.S.; Varmarken, J.E. Fracture of the femur after knee arthroplasty. Acta Orthop Scand 59:155–157, 1988.

185. Nolan, D.R.; Fitzgerald, R.H., Jr.; Beckenbaugh, R.D.; Coventry, M.B. Complications of total hip arthroplasty treated by reoperation. J Bone Joint Surg Am 57:977–981, 1975.

186. Ochsner, P.E.; Pfister, A. Use of the fork plate for internal fixation of periprosthetic fractures and osteotomies in connection with total knee replacement. Orthopedics 22:517–521, 1999.

187. Oh, I.; Hardacre, J.A. Fatigue fracture of the inferior pubic ramus following total hip replacement for congenital hip dislocation. Clin Orthop 147:154–156, 1980.

188. Olerud, S. Reconstruction of a fractured femur following total hip replacement. Report of a case. J Bone Joint Surg Am 61:937–938, 1979.

189. Olerud, S. Hip arthroplasty with extended femoral stem for salvage procedures. Clin Orthop 191:64–81, 1984.

190. Oni, O.O. Supracondylar fracture of the femur following Attenborough stabilized gliding knee arthroplasty. Injury 14:250–251, 1982.

191. Palance-Martin, D.; Albareda, J.; Seral, F. Subcapital stress fracture of the femoral neck after total knee arthroplasty. Int Orthop 18:308–309, 1994.

192. Pankovich, A.M.; Thrabishy, I.; Barmada, R. Fractures below non-cemented femoral implants. Treatment with Ender nailing J Bone Joint Surg Am 63:1024–1025, 1981.

193. Patterson, F.P.; Brown, C.S. The McKee-Farrar total hip replacement: Preliminary results and complications of 368 operations performed in five general hospitals. J Bone Joint Surg Am 54:257–275, 1972.

194. Pazzaglia, U.; Byers, P.D. Fractured femoral shaft through an osteolytic lesion resulting from the reaction to a prosthesis: A case report. J Bone Joint Surg Br 66:337–339, 1984.

195. Pelker, R.R.; Friedlaender, G.E. Biomechanical aspects of bone autografts and allografts. Orthop Clin North Am 18:235–239, 1987.

196. Pellicci, P.M.; Inglis, A.E.; Salvati, E.A. Perforation of the femoral shaft during total hip replacement: Report of 12 cases. J Bone Joint Surg 62:234–240, 1980.

197. Pellicci, P.M.; Wilson, P.D., Jr.; Sledge, C.B.; et al. Revision total hip arthroplasty. Clin Orthop 170:34–41, 1982.

198. Penenberg, B.L. Femoral fractures below hip implants. A new and safe technique of fixation. Orthop Trans 13:496, 1989.

199. Peters, C.L.; Hennessey, R.; Barden, R.M.; et al. Revision total knee arthroplasty with a cemented posterior-stabilized or constrained condylar prosthesis: A minimum 3-year and average 5-year follow-up study. J Arthroplasty 12:896–903, 1997.

200. Peters, P.C., Jr.; Engh, G.A.; Dwyer, K.A.; Vinh, T.N. Osteolysis after total knee arthroplasty without cement. J Bone Joint Surg Am 74:864–876, 1992.

201. Peterson, C.A.; Lewallen, D.G. Periprosthetic fracture of the acetabulum after total hip arthroplasty. J Bone Joint Surg Am 78:1206–1213, 1996.

202. Petty, W., ed. Total Joint Replacement. Philadelphia, W.B. Saunders, 1991, pp. 291–314.

203. Porsch, M.; Galm, R.; Hovy, L.; et al. Total femur replacement following multiple periprosthetic fractures between ipsilateral hip and knee replacement in chronic rheumatoid arthritis. Case report of 2 patients. Z Orthop Ihre Grenzgeb 134:16–20, 1996.

204. Poss, R.; Walker, P.; Spector, M.; et al. Strategies for improving fixation of femoral components in total hip arthroplasty. Clin Orthop 235:181–194, 1988.

205. Potter, H.G.; Montgomery, K.D.; Padgett, D.E.; et al. Magnetic resonance imaging of the pelvis. New orthopaedic applications. Clin Orthop 319:223–231, 1995.

206. Praemer, A.; Furner, S.; Rice, D.P. Musculoskeletal Conditions in the United States, 1st ed. Park Ridge, IL, American Academy of Orthopaedic Surgeons, 1992.

207. Rand, J.A. The patellofemoral joint in total knee arthroplasty. J Bone Joint Surg Am 76:612–620, 1994.

208. Rand, J.A. Supracondylar fracture of the femur associated with polyethylene wear after total knee arthroplasty. J Bone Joint Surg Am 76:1389–1393, 1994.

209. Rand, J.A.; Coventry, M.B. Stress fractures after total knee arthroplasty. J Bone Joint Surg Am 62:226–233, 1980.

210. Rawes, M.L.; Patsalis, T.; Gregg, P.J. Subcapital stress fractures of the hip complicating total knee replacement. Injury 26:421–423, 1995.

211. Rhinelander, F.W. Circulation in bone. In: Bourne, G.H., ed. The Biochemistry and Physiology of Bone, ed. 2 Vol. 2. New York, Academic, 1972, pp. 1–77.

212. Ries, M.D. Prophylactic intramedullary femoral rodding during total knee arthroplasty with simultaneous femoral plate removal. J Arthroplasty 13:718–721, 1998.

213. Ries, M.D.; Richman, J.A. Extended tibial tubercle osteotomy in total knee arthroplasty. J Arthroplasty 11:964–967, 1996.

214. Rinecker, H.; Hailbock, H. Surgical treatment of peri-prosthetic fractures after total knee replacement. Arch Orthop Unfallchir 87:23, 1977.

215. Ritschl, P.; Kotz, R. Fractures of the proximal femur in patients with total hip endoprostheses. Arch Orthop Trauma Surg 104:392–397, 1986.

216. Ritter, M.; Faris, P.; Keating, E. Anterior femoral notching and ipsilateral supracondylar femur fracture in total knee arthroplasty. J Arthroplasty 3:185–187, 1988.

217. Ritter, M.A.; Campbell, E.D. Postoperative patellar complications with or without lateral release during total knee arthroplasty. Clin Orthop 219:163–168, 1987.

218. Ritter, M.A.; Carr, K.; Keating, E.M.; et al. Tibial shaft fracture following tibial tubercle osteotomy. J Arthroplasty 11:117–119, 1996.

219. Ritter, M.A.; Carr, K.D.; Keating, E.M.; et al. Revision total joint arthroplasty: Does Medicare reimbursement justify time spent? Orthopedics 19:137–139, 1996.

220. Ritter, M.A.; Keating, E.M.; Faris, P.M.; Meding, J.B. Rush rod fixation of supracondylar fractures above total knee arthroplasties. J Arthroplasty 10:213–216, 1995.

221. Ritter, M.A.; Stiver, P. Supracondylar fracture in a patient with total knee arthroplasty. A case report. Clin Orthop 193:168–170, 1985.

222. Rolston, L.R.; Christ, D.J.; Halpern, A.; et al. Treatment of supracondylar fractures of the femur proximal to a total knee arthroplasty. A report of four cases. J Bone Joint Surg Am 77:924–931, 1995.

223. Rorabeck, C.H.; Angliss, R.D.; Lewis, P.L. Fractures of the femur, tibia, and patella after total knee arthroplasty: Decision making and principles of management. Instr Course Lect 47:449–458, 1998.

224. Rorabeck, C.H.; Taylor, J.W. Classification of periprosthetic fractures complicating total knee arthroplasty. Orthop Clin North Am 30:209–214, 1999.

225. Rorabeck, C.H.; Taylor, J.W. Periprosthetic fractures of the femur complicating total knee arthroplasty. Orthop Clin North Am 30:265–277, 1999.

226. Roscoe, M.W.; Goodman, S.B.; Schatzker, J. Supracondylar fracture of the femur after Guepar total knee arthroplasty: A new treatment method. Clin Orthop 222:221–223, 1989.

227. Sanchez-Sotelo, J.; McGrory, B.J.; Berry, D.J. Acute periprosthetic fracture of the acetabulum associated with osteolytic pelvic lesions: A report of 3 cases. J Arthroplasty 15:126–130, 2000.

228. Schatzker, J. Fractures of the distal femur revisited. Clin Orthop 347:43–56, 1998.

229. Schenk, R.K.; Wehril, U. Reaction of bone to a cement-free SL femoral stem used in revision arthroplasty. Orthopade 18:454–462, 1989.

230. Scher, M.A. Fractures of the femoral shaft following total hip replacement. J Bone Joint Surg Br 63:472, 1981.

231. Schmalzried, T.P.; Harris, W.H. The Harris-Galante porous-coated acetabular component with screw fixation. Radiographic analysis of

eighty-three primary hip replacements at a minimum of five years. J Bone Joint Surg Am 74:1130–1139, 1992.

232. Schmalzried, T.P.; Wessinger, S.J.; Hill, G.E.; Harris, W.H. The Harris-Galante porous acetabular component press-fit without screw fixation. Five-year radiographic analysis of primary cases. J Arthroplasty 9:235–242, 1994.

233. Schnitzler, C.M. Bone formation, bone resorption and bone mineralisation in osteoarthritis and osteoporosis. J Bone Joint Surg Br 61:257, 1979.

234. Schulte, K.R.; Callaghan, J.J.; Kelley, S.S. The outcome of Charnley total hip arthroplasty with cement after a minimum twenty year follow-up. The results of one surgeon. J Bone Joint Surg Am 75:961–975, 1993.

235. Schwartz, J.J.; Mayer, J.G.; Engh, C.A. Femoral fracture during non-cemented total hip arthroplasty. J Bone Joint Surg Am 71:1135–1142, 1989.

236. Scott, R.D.; Turner, R.H.; Leitzes, S.M.; Aufranc, O.E. Femoral fractures in conjunction with total hip replacement. J Bone Joint Surg Am 57:494–501, 1975.

237. Scott, R.D.; Turoff, N.; Ewald, F.C. Stress fracture of the patella following duopatellar total knee arthroplasty with patellar resurfacing. Clin Orthop 170:147–151, 1982.

238. Scuderi, G.; Scharf, S.C.; Meltzer, L.P.; Scott, W.N. The relationship of lateral releases to patella viability in total knee arthroplasty. J Arthroplasty 2:209–214, 1987.

239. Sekel, R.; Newman, A.S. Supracondylar fractures above a total knee arthroplasty. A novel use of the Huckstepp nail. J Arthroplasty 9:445–447, 1994.

240. Selakovich, W.; Love, L. Stress fractures of the pubic ramus. J Bone Joint Surg Am 36:573–576, 1954.

241. Serocki, J.H.; Chandler, R.W.; Dorr, L.D. Treatment of fractures about hip prostheses with compression plating. J Arthroplasty 7:129–135, 1992.

242. Shanbhag, A.S.; Hasselman, C.T.; Rubash, H.E. The John Charnley Award. Inhibition of wear debris mediated osteolysis in a canine total hip arthroplasty model. Clin Orthop 344:33–43, 1997.

243. Sharkey, P.F.; Hozack, W.J.; Booth, R.E.; Rothman, R.H. Intraoperative femoral fractures in cementless total hip arthroplasty. Orthop Rev 21:337–342, 1992.

244. Sharkey, P.F.; Hozack, W.J.; Callaghan, J.J.; et al. Acetabular fracture associated with cementless acetabular component insertion: A report of 13 cases. J Arthroplasty 14:426–431, 1999.

245. Short, W.H.; Hootnick, D.R.; Murray, D.G. Ipsilateral supracondylar femur fractures following knee arthroplasty. Clin Orthop 158:111–116, 1981.

246. Silvello, L.; Scarponi, R.; Lucia, G.; Guazzetti, R. Traumatic loosening of a prosthetic acetabular cup in a young patient. Ital J Orthop Traumatol 11:237–239, 1985.

247. Sim, F.H.; Chao, E.Y.S. Hip salvage by proximal femoral replacement. J Bone Joint Surg Am 63:1228–1239, 1981.

248. Sisto, D.J.; Lachiewicz, P.F.; Insall, J.N. Treatment of supracondylar fractures following prosthetic arthroplasty of the knee. Clin Orthop 196:265–272, 1985.

249. Skeide, B.I.; Lie, S.A.; Havelin, L.I.; Engesaeter, L.B. Total hip arthroplasty after femoral neck fractures. Results from the national registry on joint prostheses. Tidsskr Nor Laegeforen 116:1449–1451, 1996.

250. Sleeswijk Visser, S.V. Accidental femoral shaft fractures following hip arthroplasty of the same leg. Ned Tijdschr Geneeskd 124:962–964, 1980.

251. Smith, W.J.; Martin, S.L.; Mabrey, J.D. Use of a supracondylar nail for treatment of a supracondylar fracture of the femur following total knee arthroplasty. J Arthroplasty 11:210–213, 1996.

252. Sochart, D.H.; Hardinge, K. Nonsurgical management of supracondylar fracture above total knee arthroplasty. Still the nineties option. J Arthroplasty 12:830–834, 1997.

253. Sonstegard, D.A.; Kaufer, H.; Matthews, L.S. The spherocentric knee: Biomechanical testing and clinical trial. J Bone Joint Surg Am 59:602–616, 1977.

254. Springfield, D.S. Massive autogenous bone grafts. Orthop Clin North Am 18:249–256, 1987.

255. Steinbrink, K.; Engelbrecht, E.; Fenelon, G.C.C. The total femoral prosthesis. A preliminary report. J Bone Joint Surg Br 64:305–312, 1982.

256. Stuart, M.J.; Hanssen, A.D. Total knee arthroplasty: Periprosthetic tibial fractures. Orthop Clin North Am 30:279–286, 1999.

257. Stuchin, S.A. Femoral shaft fracture in porous and press-fit total hip arthroplasty. Orthop Rev 19:153–159, 1990.

258. Sydney, S.V.; Mallory, T.H. Controlled perforation. A safe method of cement removal from the femoral canal. Clin Orthop 253:168–172, 1990.

259. Talab, Y.A.; States, J.D.; Evarts, C.M. Femoral shaft perforation. A complication of total hip reconstruction. Clin Orthop 141:158–165, 1979.

260. Tani, Y.; Inoue, K.; Kaneko, H.; et al. Intramedullary fibular graft for supracondylar fracture of the femur following total knee arthroplasty. Arch Orthop Trauma Surg 117:103–104, 1998.

261. Taylor, M.M.; Meyers, M.H.; Harvey, J.P. Intraoperative femur fractures during total hip replacement. Clin Orthop 137(Nov–Dec):96–103, 1978.

262. Timon, S.; O'Flynn, H.M.; Tate, D.E.; Sculco, T.P. Bilateral pathologic fractures in a patient with beta-thalassemia undergoing total hip arthroplasty. J Arthroplasty 13:217–220, 1998.

263. Tomford, W.W.; Thongphasuk, J.; Mankin, H.J.; Ferraro, M.J. Frozen musculoskeletal allografts. A study of the clinical incidence and causes of infection associated with their use. J Bone Joint Surg Am 72:1137–1143, 1990.

264. Toni, A.; Giunti, A.; Graci, A.; et al. Fratture post-operatorie del femore prossimale con protesi d'anca. Chir Organi Mov 70:53–65, 1985.

265. Torgerson, W.R. Three years experience with total hip replacement. Clin Orthop 95:151–157, 1973.

266. Tower, S.; Beals, R. Fractures of the femur after hip replacement: The Oregon experience. In: Duncan, C.; Callaghan, J., eds. Periprosthetic Fractures after Major Joint Replacement. Philadelphia, W.B. Saunders, 1999, pp. 235–248.

267. Tria, A.J., Jr.; Harwood, D.A.; Alicea, J.A.; Cody, R.P. Patellar fractures in posterior stabilized knee arthroplasties. Clin Orthop 299:131–138, 1994.

268. Trousdale, R.T.; Hanssen, A.D.; Rand, J.A.; Cahalan, T.D. V-Y quadricepsplasty in total knee arthroplasty. Clin Orthop 286:48–55, 1993.

269. Urch, S.E.; Moskal, J.T. Simultaneous ipsilateral revision total hip arthroplasty and revision total knee arthroplasty with entire femoral allograft. J Arthroplasty 13:833–836, 1998.

270. Van Heest, A.; Vorlicky, L.; Thompson, R.C., Jr. Bilateral central acetabular fracture dislocations secondary to sustained myoclonus. Clin Orthop 324:210–213, 1996.

271. Vicenzi, G.; Moroni, A.; Ponziani, L. An unusual case of proximal femoral fracture in a patient with a total hip prosthesis. Chir Organi Mov 73:161–163, 1988.

272. Wagner, H. Revisionsprothese fur das Huftgelenk. Orthopade 18:438–453, 1989.

273. Walker, P.S.; Yoon, W.W.; Cannon, S.R.; et al. Design and application of combined hip-knee intramedullary joint replacements. J Arthroplasty 14:945–951, 1999.

274. Wasielewski, R.C.; Cooperstein, L.A.; Kruger, M.P.; Rubash, H.E. Acetabular anatomy and the transacetabular fixation of screws in total hip arthroplasty. J Bone Joint Surg Am 72:501–508, 1990.

275. Weber, M.; Berry, D.J.; Harmsen, W.S. Total hip arthroplasty after operative treatment of an acetabular fracture. J Bone Joint Surg Am 80:1295–1305, 1998.

276. Webster, D.A.; Murray, D.G. Complications of variable axis total knee arthroplasty. Clin Orthop 193:160–167, 1985.

277. Wehrli, U. Wagner cement-free revision stem. Z Unfallchir Versicherungsmed 84:216–224, 1991.

278. Welch, R.B.; Charnley, J. Low-friction arthroplasty of the hip in rheumatoid arthritis patients and ankylosing spondylitis. Clin Orthop 72:22–32, 1972.

279. Wetzner, S.M.; Bezreh, J.S.; Scott, R.D.; et al. Bone scanning in the assessment of patellar viability following knee replacement. Clin Orthop 199:215–219, 1985.

280. Whitesides, L.A. Impact Modular Total Hip System. Warsaw, IN, Biomet, 1994.

281. Whittaker, R.P.; Sotos, L.N.; Ralston, E.L. Fractures of the femur about femoral endoprostheses. J Trauma 14:675–694, 1974.

282. Wilder, R.L. Rheumatoid arthritis: Epidemiology, pathology, and pathogenesis. In: Schumacher, H.R., ed. Primer on Rheumatic Disease. Arthritis Foundation. Atlanta, 1993, pp. 86–89.

283. Wirganowicz, P.Z.; Thomas, B.J. Massive osteolysis after ceramic on ceramic total hip arthroplasty. A case report. Clin Orthop 338:100–104, 1997.

284. Wong, P.; Gross, A.E. The use of structural allografts for treating periprosthetic fractures about the hip and knee. Orthop Clin North Am 30:259–264, 1999.

285. Wroblewski, B.M.; Browne, A.O.; Hodgkinson, J.P. Treatment of fracture of the shaft of the femur in total hip arthroplasty by a combination of a Küntscher nail and a modified cemented Charnley stem. Injury 23:225–227, 1992.

286. Younger, A.S.; Dunwoody, I.; Duncan, C.P. Periprosthetic hip and knee fractures: The scope of the problem. Instr Course Lect 47:251–256, 1998.

287. Younger, T.I.; Bradford, M.S.; Magnus, R.E.; Paprosky, W.G. Extended proximal femoral osteotomy. A new technique for femoral revision arthroplasty. J Arthroplasty 10:329–338, 1995.

288. Younger, T.I.; Bradford, M.S.; Paprosky, W.G. Removal of a well-fixed cementless femoral component with an extended proximal femoral osteotomy. Contemp Orthop 30: 375–380, 1995.

289. Zehntner, M.K.; Ganz, R. Internal fixation of supracondylar fractures after condylar total knee arthroplasty. Clin Orthop 293:219–224, 1993.

290. Zenni, E.J.; Pomeroy, D.L.; Caudle, R.J. Ogden plate and other fixations for fractures complicating femoral endoprostheses. Clin Orthop 231:83–90, 1988.

291. Zuber, K.; Jutzi, J.; Ganz, R. Bilateral femoral fracture at the site of bilateral hip prostheses. A case report. Unfallchirurg 95:240–242, 1992.

292. Zuber, K.; Koch, P.; Lustenberger, A.; Ganz, R. Femoral fractures following total hip prosthesis. Unfallchirurg 93:467–472, 1990.

# CHAPTER 64

## Amputations in Trauma

Michael S. Pinzur, M.D.

One of the most important changes today in the practice of orthopaedic surgery is the change in focus from results to outcomes. Whether performing surgical arthroscopy, open reduction of an acetabular fracture, or amputation of a nonsalvageable limb, the astute surgeon understands that the surgery is only the first step of the treatment. The process of managing illness entails making a reasonable estimation of outcome expectation at the initiation of treatment.

What is a good result? The vascular surgeon measures "outcomes" on the basis of graft patency and limb salvage. The man in Figure 64–1 returned to his cherished avocation shortly after transtibial amputation. He is considered a "bad" result. If he underwent vascular surgery, had a patent bypass graft, but was functionally limited to walking across the room because of claudication, he would be considered a "good" result. The orthopaedic surgeon measures outcomes in amputation surgery on the basis of wound failure rates and ambulatory capacity. The physiatrist measures outcomes on the basis of a measure of functional independence, the so-called Functional Independence Measure or FIM score. When we determine outcomes, we need to measure meaningful indicators. We need to have a reasonable estimation at the initiation of treatment of what we are going to get at the completion of treatment. What are our goals? Is the goal limb salvage, or is the goal the resumption of the lifestyle of the individual before injury or disease? (See Fig. 64–1.)

Following World War II, Ernest Burgess applied Polish physician Marion Weiss' concepts of immediate postoperative prosthetic limb fitting to the great number of traumatic amputees returning from battle. The introduction of an aggressive rehabilitation approach was the first step in changing the principles of amputation surgery from destructive to constructive surgery. He taught us that the surgical amputation should be the first step in treatment, forcing us to focus on surgical decision making and techniques that would optimize functional outcomes as opposed to simply obtaining surgical wound healing. As surgical and rehabilitation techniques improved, he stimulated engineers to use modern technology to develop lightweight, dynamic, and comfortable prosthetic limbs. The focus became assisting the reentry of the amputee into normal functional activities, setting achievable goals. Rather than accept the concept of disability, his programs focused on adapting to functional limitations and allowing the amputee to reenter mainstream society. This chapter is dedicated to his efforts and attempts to provide an outcomes method of approaching amputation surgery in the arena of traumatic injury.[1, 2, 22]

## LIMB SALVAGE VERSUS AMPUTATION

Amputation of an extremity can be performed for gangrene, trauma, infection, neoplastic disease, or congenital deformity. Irrespective of the disease process or etiology, the following issues should be addressed before undertaking an attempt at limb salvage or performing an amputation:

1. Will the salvaged limb outperform a prosthesis? If all transpires as one could *reasonably* predict, will the functional independence of the patient following limb salvage and reconstruction be greater or less than that after amputation and prosthetic limb fitting? The answer varies greatly with age, vocation, medical health, lifestyle, education, and social status. Impairment and disability are dependent on both patients' abilities and the demands of their workplace. An attorney or accountant might well return to full work capacity in a wheelchair, whereas a laborer might become fully disabled and not capable of returning to work with even a small functional impairment. For the laborer, amputation surgery might be the more "conservative" alternative, allowing him or her to perform at a significantly higher work level. The same question may need to be addressed quite differently in upper extremity trauma, in which a sensate hand with minimal prehensile ability may be more capable of performing the individual's necessary tasks than an

**Figure 64–1.** Is this patient a good result or a bad result? See text. He returned to the golf course 17 days following his second transtibial amputation for peripheral vascular disease.

insensate prosthesis. Functional expectations need to be tailored to the specific needs and capabilities of the individual patient.

2. What is a realistic functional outcome expectation? Not every patient is going to achieve the best result ever achieved by that surgeon. Most patients achieve an average, middle of the bell-shaped curve, result, mostly dependent on the injury but certainly influenced by the experience of the treating surgeon. At the outset of treatment, a realistic long-term appreciation of expected functional capacity following both limb salvage and amputation makes decision making objective as opposed to emotional. If the decision is not clear on the day of injury, the final decision may be deferred by combining débridement with provisional bone stabilization so that an informed decision can be made when the "smoke has cleared."

3. What is the time and effort commitment required from both the patient and the treatment team? Initially, patients for whom limb salvage is considered have greatly increased potential morbidity because of the risk of infection and the potential retention of nonviable tissue. Retained dead tissue can lead to sepsis, rhabdomyolysis with renal failure, or simple wound failure. These patients often require multiple surgical procedures over a prolonged period of months, often including the harvest of free tissue to effect wound closure. Both the patient and the physician need to be cognizant of the process, the duration, and the end results. This awareness may tip the scales in a borderline situation.

4. What are the relative costs of limb salvage to both the patient and the health care system? The most obvious costs are the financial cost to the patient and resource consumption of the health care system. What about the medical cost to the patient? Seriously injured patients with multiple organ system involvement can be placed at appreciable risk of mortality and morbidity during prolonged surgical procedures to achieve bone stability and soft tissue reconstruction. Limb salvage may exact too great a physiologic cost in these critically ill

patients. One must remember that open tibia fractures frequently occur in young men who work at the heavy end of the workforce. Experienced trauma surgeons have often witnessed trauma patients exhaust their medical benefits, bankrupting the family and producing psychologic stress leading to divorce.[3, 4] In the current medical-economic climate, one must address these issues realistically from both the patient's and the health care system's perspectives.

Once everyone involved has reconciled each of these issues, a logical individualized treatment algorithm can be initiated.[3, 4, 10]

## FUNCTIONAL INDEPENDENCE MEASURE

Whether we embark on a course of limb salvage or amputation following trauma, our major focus is the resumption of a lifestyle approaching the patient's capacity before the injury. To appreciate the magnitude of injury and recovery, we must have an objective measuring tool. The "industry standard" in the domain of physical medicine and rehabilitation is the FIM score. Health care professionals, that is, nurses, physical therapists, and social workers, can be quickly trained to provide an objective measure of severity of disease. Its inherent value lies in its ease of training and implementation, which can be applied to large populations of patients.

The FIM instrument includes a seven-level scale that designates major gradations in behavior from dependence to independence. It is a measure of disability, not impairment, measuring what the person with disability actually does, not what the person is capable of doing. Table 64–1 outlines the domains measured as well as the scoring system.[5]

## METABOLIC COST OF WALKING WITH AN AMPUTATION

We each walk at an energy-efficient individualized self-selected walking speed. With injury, arthritis, motor, or joint abnormality, our walking becomes less efficient. We compensate by walking slower to consume less energy. Anatomic joints of the lower limb act as energy couples. Prosthetic joints (neither endoprosthetic nor extraskeletal limb replacement) are never as efficient as the original equipment. The amount of energy consumed, that is, the metabolic cost of walking, is increased proportionally with proximal level amputations, being inversely proportional to the length of the residual limb and the number of joints preserved (Fig. 64–2).[11, 20, 21] With more proximal level amputation, amputees have a decreased self-selected, and maximal, walking speed and consume relatively more oxygen per meter walked. This demand exacts such a toll on proximal level amputees that dysvascular transfemoral amputees often utilize their maximal energy expenditure in walking on level ground. This limits them to a single

TABLE 64–1 ...................................................................................................

Functional Independence Measurement (FIM)

| Score (1–7) | | Score (1–7) | |
|---|---|---|---|
| **SELF-CARE** | | **TRANSFERS** | |
| | Eating | | Bed, Chair, Wheelchair |
| | Bathing | | Toilet |
| | Dressing Upper Body | | Tub, Shower |
| | Dressing Lower Body | **COMMUNICATION** | |
| | Toileting | | |
| | Bladder Management | | Comprehension |
| | Bowel Management | | Expression |
| **LOCOMOTION** | | | Social Interaction |
| | | | Problem Solving |
| | Walking, Wheelchair | | Memory |
| | Stairs | | |

| Scoring Guidelines | | |
|---|---|---|
| **COMPLETE DEPENDENCE** | | |
| 1 | Total Assist (Subject = 0%+) | |
| 2 | Maximal Assist (Subject = 25%+) | |
| **MODIFIED DEPENDENCE** | | HELPER |
| 3 | Moderate Assist (Subject = 50%+) | |
| 4 | Minimal Assist (Subject = 75%+) | |
| 5 | Supervision | |
| 6 | Modified Independence (Device) | NO HELPER |
| 7 | Complete Independence (Timely, Safety) | |

Patient Name: ___ _____
Rater: _____     Date: ___ / ___ / ___     ___ : ___
.........................................................................................................

References: *Guide for the Uniform Data Set for Medical Rehabilitation (including the FIM™ instrument), Version 5.1.* Buffalo, NY 14214: State University at Buffalo; 1997; *Getting Started with the Uniform Data System for Medical Rehabilitation, Version 5.0.* Buffalo, NY 14214: State University of New York at Buffalo; 1996.

slow walking speed and a distance restriction depending on their limited energy reserve.

From an outcomes perspective, their ultimate independence (FIM score) is closely associated with amputation level, with distal level amputees achieving proportionally higher FIM scores. With patients who are likely to be able to walk with a prosthesis, every effort should be made to perform lower extremity amputation surgery at the most distal amputation level commensurate with the creation of a reasonable terminal weight-bearing end-organ.

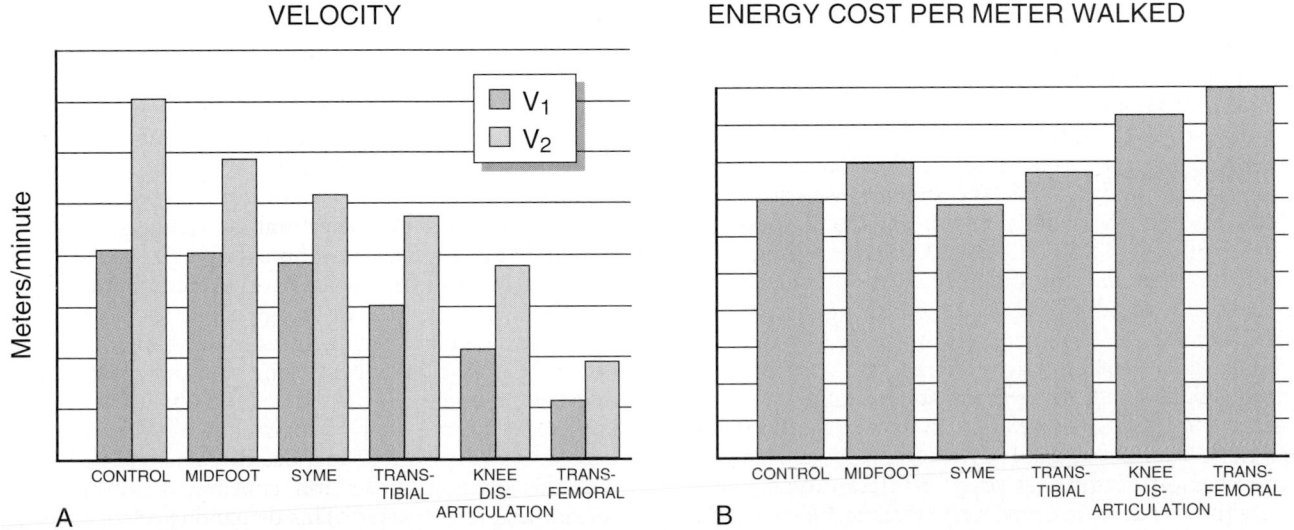

FIGURE 64–2. Metabolic cost of walking with an amputation. *A,* Walking speed compared with surgical amputation level. V1 is the subject's self-selected walking speed. V2 is the subject's maximal walking speed. *B,* Oxygen consumption per meter walked compared with resting oxygen consumption. (Adapted from Pinzur, M.S.; Gold, J.; Schwartz, D.; Gross, N. Orthopedics 15:1033–1037, 1992.)

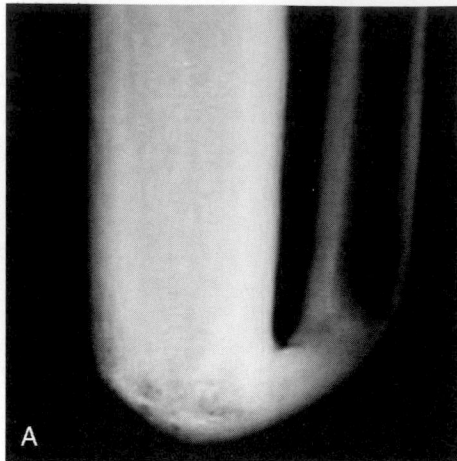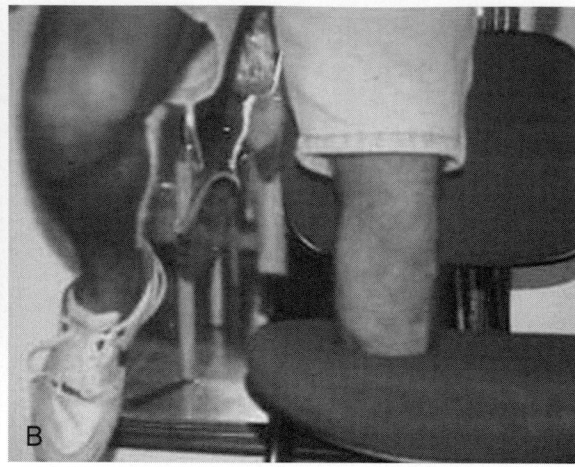

**FIGURE 64–3.** *A,* Bone bridge between tibia and fibula in transtibial amputation, the Ertl procedure. The goal of this surgical modification is to create a larger, more stable platform for weight bearing in transtibial amputation (*B*). (Courtesy of Dr. Marco Guedes.)

## LOAD TRANSFER AND WEIGHT BEARING

Our feet act as uniquely adapted end-organs of weight bearing, cushioning impact and adapting to uneven surfaces. Following amputation, the residual limb must assume the tasks of load transfer, adapting to uneven terrain, and providing a stable platform for propulsion, utilizing tissues that are not biologically engineered for those purposes. In an effort to create an optimal end-organ for weight bearing, the surgeon should have an appreciation of the load transfer requirements as well as the compensatory methods that the prosthetist can utilize when the prosthetic limb is prescribed and fabricated.

The weight-bearing surfaces of long bones are substantially wider than the corresponding diaphysis. This increased surface area dissipates the forces applied during weight bearing over a larger surface area. Those forces are further dissipated by the biomechanical characteristics of articular cartilage and metaphyseal bone, these tissues being substantially less stiff than diaphyseal bone and utilizing a more "shock-absorbing" elastic modulus during the loading periods of walking and running. The final ultimate stress dissipater is the foot, whose multibone linked weight-bearing mechanism and unique plantar soft tissues absorb and dissipate the forces of weight bearing while providing a stable platform to affect propulsion. Following lower extremity amputation, the residual limb has to compensate for these tasks using one of two methods of load transfer: direct (end bearing) and indirect (total contact).

The fibula appears to be far more important than previously assumed. Its presence appears to be critical in creating a sufficient surface area for transferring the load of weight bearing. Proximal tibiofibular instability occurring with the initial trauma should be addressed by stabilization with a syndesmosis-type screw that can be removed at a later date if prominent. Late instability can be treated with proximal tibiofibular fusion with a similar stabilization technique. Classical teaching advises cutting the fibula

at a level 1 cm proximal to the tibial level. Experience has shown that optimal load transfer is achieved by transecting the fibula at a level just proximal to the tibia. This approach achieves an optimal surface area while avoiding the bony prominence of an overly long fibula.

As we understand more about creating a sufficient surface area for load transfer, a controversial procedure from the past, the Ertl procedure, has resurfaced. This procedure attempts to create a stable "platform" for transferring the weight-bearing load by fusing the distal residual tibia and fibula. Preliminary results are very encouraging, warranting further study (Fig. 64–3).[8, 9, 12] When the fibula is lost, creative load transfer solutions are difficult to achieve.

Direct load transfer, that is, end bearing, is achieved in disarticulation amputations at the knee and ankle joint levels (Fig. 64–4). This method takes advantage of the normal weight-bearing characteristics of joints, as discussed before. At these amputation levels, the mechanical load of weight bearing is directly applied to the end of the bone. The overlying soft tissue envelope then simply acts to cushion the impact of loading, much as the heel pad and plantar tissues function in the foot. Walking on level surfaces is well compensated with disarticulation amputations. The demands on the prosthetic socket are minimal, primarily confined to aligning the loading forces and maintaining suspension, that is, keeping the prosthesis from falling off. Intimate socket fit is not essential. As patients gain or lose weight, the volume within the socket can be adjusted with liners or additional prosthetic socks.

Indirect load transfer, or total contact weight bearing, is necessary at the diaphyseal transtibial and transfemoral amputation levels. At these through-bone amputation levels, the surface area of the terminal residual limb is small and the elastic modulus of the bone is much stiffer than that of the metaphyseal region. End bearing would concentrate forces to a small surface area of dynamically rigid bone, leading to soft tissue breakdown and ulceration. The terminal residual limb is unloaded by applying the forces of weight bearing over the entire surface of the

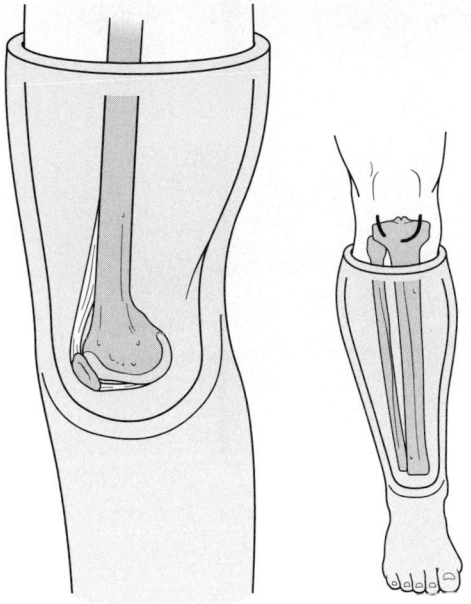

**FIGURE 64–4.** Load transfer and weight bearing in knee or ankle disarticulation amputation. This bone is adapted for weight bearing, so individuals can bear weight by direct load transfer or end bearing. (Adapted from Pinzer, M.S. New concepts in lower-limb amputation and prosthetic management. Instr Course Lect 39:361–366, 1990.)

residual limb (Fig. 64–5). The prosthetist attempts to position the residual tibia at 7 to 10 degrees of knee flexion in transtibial amputations and place the femur in the normally occurring adducted weight-bearing position at transfemoral amputation levels. Surgically created hip or knee flexion contractures or deformities allowed to occur during the rehabilitation period limit the ability of the prosthetist to optimize the mechanical transfer of weight bearing. Appropriate splinting and mobilization during rehabilitation are essential. The prosthetic socket fit must now be intimate. If patients gain more than a few pounds, they are not able to get "in," and if they lose a corresponding amount of weight or volume, they "bottom out" and break down because of direct pressure applied to the residual diaphyseal bony end.

## SOFT TISSUE ENVELOPE

The soft tissue envelope acts as the interface, or cushion, between the bone of the residual limb and the prosthetic socket. It functions both to cushion the underlying bone and to dissipate the pressures and forces applied during weight bearing. Iatrogenic joint contractures should be avoided by performing muscle repair with the residual limb in a neutral position. Placing a bolster under the buttock, rather than under the residual limb, and achieving muscle repair with the affected joint neutrally positioned lessen the potential for repairing the antagonist muscle groups at different tensions and creating an iatrogenic joint contracture. Avoiding joint contracture allows the prosthetist to position the residual limb ideally within the prosthetic socket.

Ideally, the soft tissue envelope should be composed of a mobile, nonadherent muscle mass and full-thickness skin. It should be durable enough to tolerate the direct pressures of weight bearing and the shearing forces that occur with moving ("pistoning") within the prosthetic socket (Fig. 64–6). This objective is accomplished by creating a myofasciocutaneous flap, being careful not to dissect the tissue plane between the gastrocnemius muscle and the subcutaneous tissue. The muscle is cut with a sharp amputation knife and is beveled only if retention would create a too bulky residual limb.

When the soft tissue envelope has adequate muscle mass between the skin and bone, the bone moves within the soft tissue envelope. In total-contact prosthetic limb fittings, the intimacy of the prosthetic socket is never absolutely perfect. Because of this lack of perfect intimate fit, there is always some degree of pistoning of the residual limb within the prosthetic socket. When the skin is adherent to the residual bone, the pistoning occurs between the skin and the prosthetic socket, leading to blister formation, ulceration, and tissue breakdown.

Split-thickness skin grafts should be avoided in areas overlying the anterior leg and the distal tip of residual tibia because of the significant shear forces applied in these regions during load transfer. When transtibial amputees develop late blistering or shearing tissue breakdown of the residual limb because of an inadequate adherent soft tissue envelope, the surgeon must go back to basic principles necessary to create a better terminal end weight-bearing organ. With adequate residual limb length, the bone can be shortened and a local soft tissue envelope can create a more functional residual limb. Free tissue transfer and the

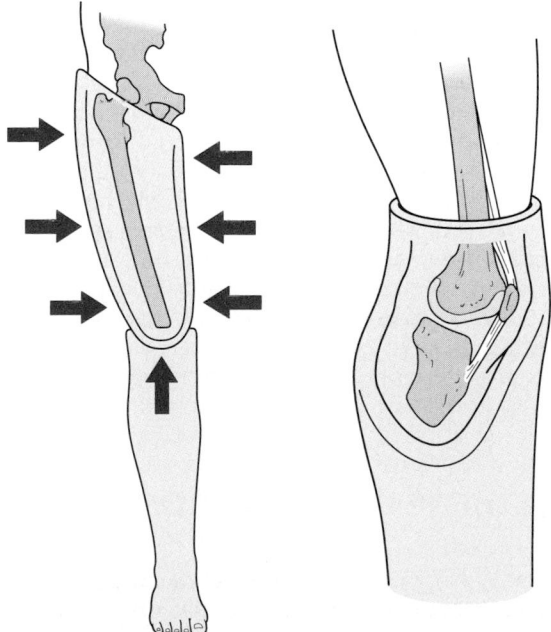

**FIGURE 64–5.** Load transfer in transfemoral or transtibial amputation. The ends of the cortical diaphyseal bone must be unloaded. The weight bearing is accomplished by total residual limb contact or indirect load transfer. (Adapted from Pinzer, M.S. New concepts in lower-limb amputation and prosthetic management. Instr Course Lect 39:361–366, 1990.)

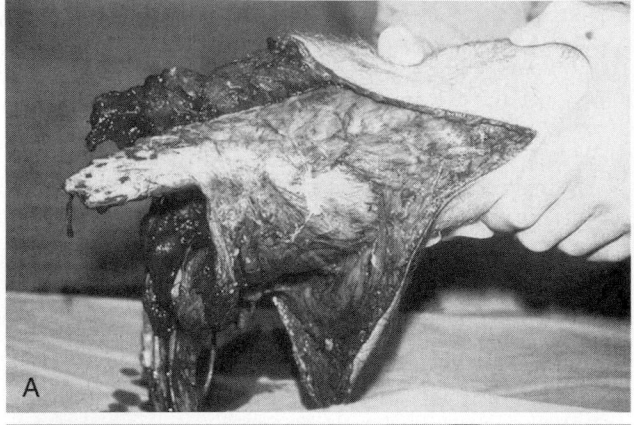

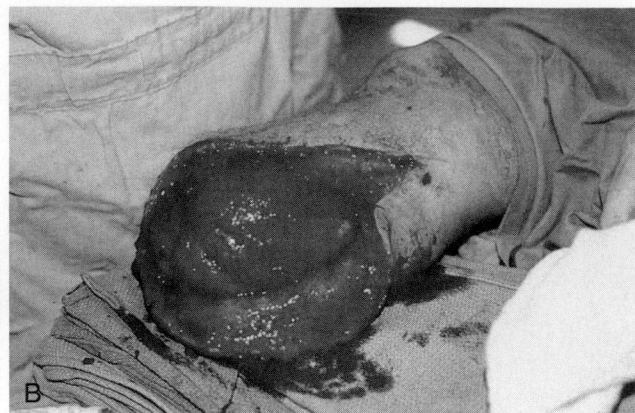

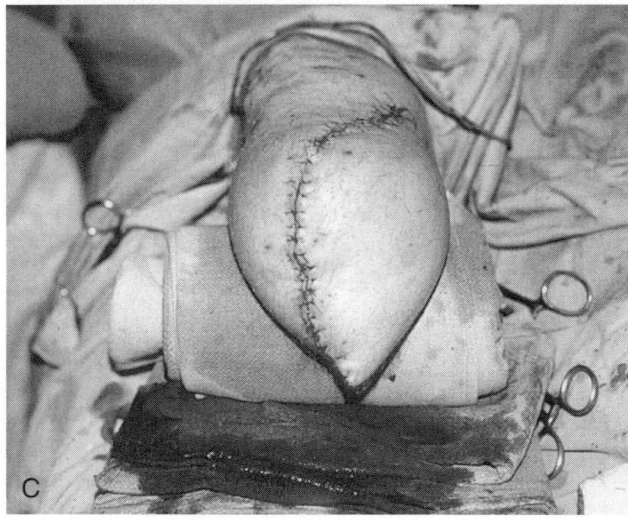

**FIGURE 64–6.** *A,* This grade IIIC open tibia fracture was not a candidate for limb salvage. The patient underwent débridement of all infected and nonviable tissue. *B,* He returned to surgery for serial débridements prior to wound closure. *C,* Wound closure. The patient was able to return to construction labor. In spite of the wound being anterior, the patient has not had any episodes of residual limb ulceration in more than 15 years following amputation and prosthetic limb fitting.

use of tissue expanders have limited roles and should be employed only by those experienced in their application.

Disarticulation at the knee and ankle levels allows end bearing or direct load transfer. At these amputation levels, the muscle mass simply acts to provide a cushion interface between the residual limb bone and the prosthetic socket. Pistoning and shearing forces do not affect these amputation levels. End-bearing residual limbs with less than optimal cushioning can occasionally be accommodated with silicone gel end pads within the prosthetic socket. Split-thickness skin grafting is better tolerated. Because of the mechanism of loading, these patients sustain less soft tissue envelope morbidity.

## PROSTHETIC CONSIDERATIONS

If we accept the premise that amputation surgery is the first step in the rehabilitation process, the surgeon must understand the interaction between the residual limb and the prosthesis. Lower extremity prosthetic limbs have three components: (1) prosthetic socket, (2) shank, and (3) foot. A knee hinge is necessary in knee disarticulation and transfemoral prostheses. The prosthetic socket accepts the load transfer and suspends the limb. The shank makes up

for the loss in limb length, and the foot interfaces with the floor.

The prosthetic socket accepts the load of weight bearing. With an appropriate soft tissue envelope, cushioning requirements are minimal. Adequate residual limb length is essential for both suspension and providing an adequate surface area for weight bearing. A good rule of thumb is the 5-inch rule. The optimal transtibial residual limb has 5 inches (10 to 12 cm) of retained tibia. The optimal transfemoral residual limb is a similar distance above the knee joint in order to provide adequate space for a prosthetic knee joint. In this way, the knee centers of the amputated and remaining limb are maintained at similar levels, which limits limping and inefficient walking patterns. A shortened residual limb requires augmentative suspension. A less than optimal soft tissue envelope requires augmentative cushioning. Both adaptations lessen the ultimate performance of the prosthetic limb, add weight, and require more complex modification.

The shank simply makes up for loss of limb length. The prosthetic limb is fabricated ¼ to ½ inch shorter than the contralateral limb to centralize the body mass over the prosthesis during the stance phase of gait.

Early prosthetic feet were "dead," simply absorbing the load of weight bearing. Current dynamic elastic response, "energy-storing" prosthetic feet deform with the load of weight bearing and recoil during push-off to simulate normal walking propulsion. On the basis of the individual activities and requirements of the amputee, the unique characteristics of the prosthetic foot are prescribed. These can combine variable amounts of dynamic elastic response, shock absorption, stability, and adaptability to uneven surfaces (Fig. 64–7).

## SURGICAL CONSIDERATIONS

Following injury, amputation can be performed initially, early in treatment when it is determined that amputation is preferable to limb salvage, or late with a goal of functional reconstruction.[19] Traumatic amputation can be considered as a Gustillo-Anderson grade IIIC open fracture. Therefore, the initial treatment is débridement combined with open-wound management (see Fig. 64–6). Any clearly nonviable tissue and devascularized bone should be removed. It is unlikely that one can "resurrect" dead tissue.

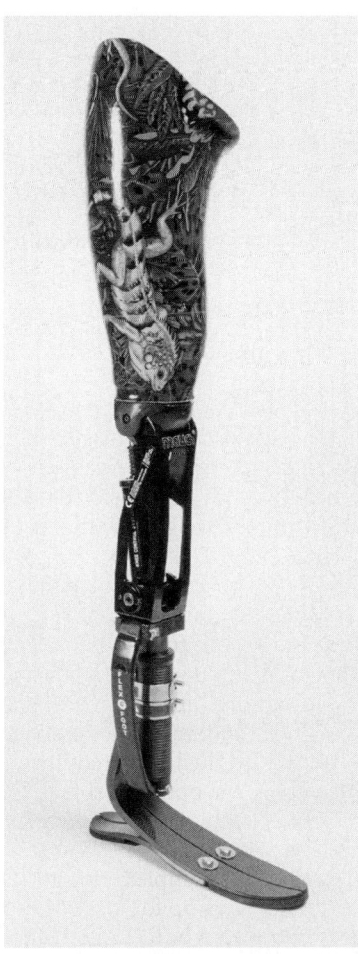

**FIGURE 64–7.** "High-technology" transfemoral prosthesis. This lightweight prosthesis has a flexible ischial containment socket, high-performance hydraulic knee, and dynamic elastic response prosthetic foot with a shock absorber to dissipate the stresses of weight bearing. (Flex-Foot Re-Flex VSP foot on a Mauch Gaitmaster Low Profile Prosthetic Knee, Flex-Foot, Inc. and Mauch, Inc., a subsidiary of Flex-Foot, Aliso, CA.)

There is always an element of crush in these injuries, so the zone of injury may not be clearly delineated at the initial surgery. Bone stabilization can be accomplished to save limb length if there appears to be adequate soft tissues for the creation of a functional soft tissue envelope (Fig. 64–8). Wounds should be managed with open care, returning the patient to the operating room every 2 to 3 days for repeated débridement, until a healthy wound is secured. Skin traction should be avoided, as this treatment method applies tension within the zone of injury. Contrary to previous beliefs, muscle length can easily be reestablished.

Most investigators advocate early wound closure. Because of the unacceptable infection rate associated with early wound closure within the theoretical zone of injury, I advise delayed wound closure when the tissues appear secure, usually by 5 to 7 days after injury. Soft tissue envelope principles should be applied. Bone should be covered with healthy muscle to provide a good cushion and full-thickness skin in areas that will need to tolerate weight-bearing pressure and shearing forces. Use of plastic surgery reconstruction and limb lengthening can be considered as a method of later reconstruction.

Arteries should be double ligated with a suture ligature. The use of surgical clips and electrocautery for venous bleeding is efficient. Nerves should never be clamped, as this crush injury often leads to late neurogenic pain even if the crushed nerve is removed. Once identified, the nerve can be gently grasped with a surgical sponge, retracted distally, and transected proximally with a fresh surgical scalpel. All transected nerves develop a neuroma. If cut with a fresh scalpel and with retraction within the muscle mass, they rarely lead to late neuroma pain.

Muscles should be secured to bone by means of drill holes or suture to periosteum at their normal functional length. Muscle retraction or redundancy makes prosthetic control of the residual limb difficult, lessening the efficiency and comfort of the prosthetic limb. Wounds should not be repaired under tension, as this leads to wound failure, wound infection, or a nonresilient residual limb.

Intermediate amputation is performed in the early postinjury period when it is determined, on the basis of the principles discussed earlier, that amputation is appropriate. Optimal limb length and soft tissue coverage can be planned in these situations. Remember that the optimal residual limb has adequate bone length and stability combined with a mobile, padded soft tissue envelope. Occasionally, methods of internal or external fixation allow preservation of residual limb length (see Fig. 64–8). This treatment is advised only when adequate soft tissues are available for creating a functional residual limb. In healthy patients, free tissue transfer or tissue expanders can be used to utilize retained bone that has an inadequate soft tissue envelope. When trauma patients have multiple organ system involvement, planned staged treatment can be considered. In this situation, the initial treatment is early soft tissue coverage. When the patient has less medical and anesthetic risk, a planned revision of the soft tissue envelope with local or distant tissue can be accomplished with far less morbidity.

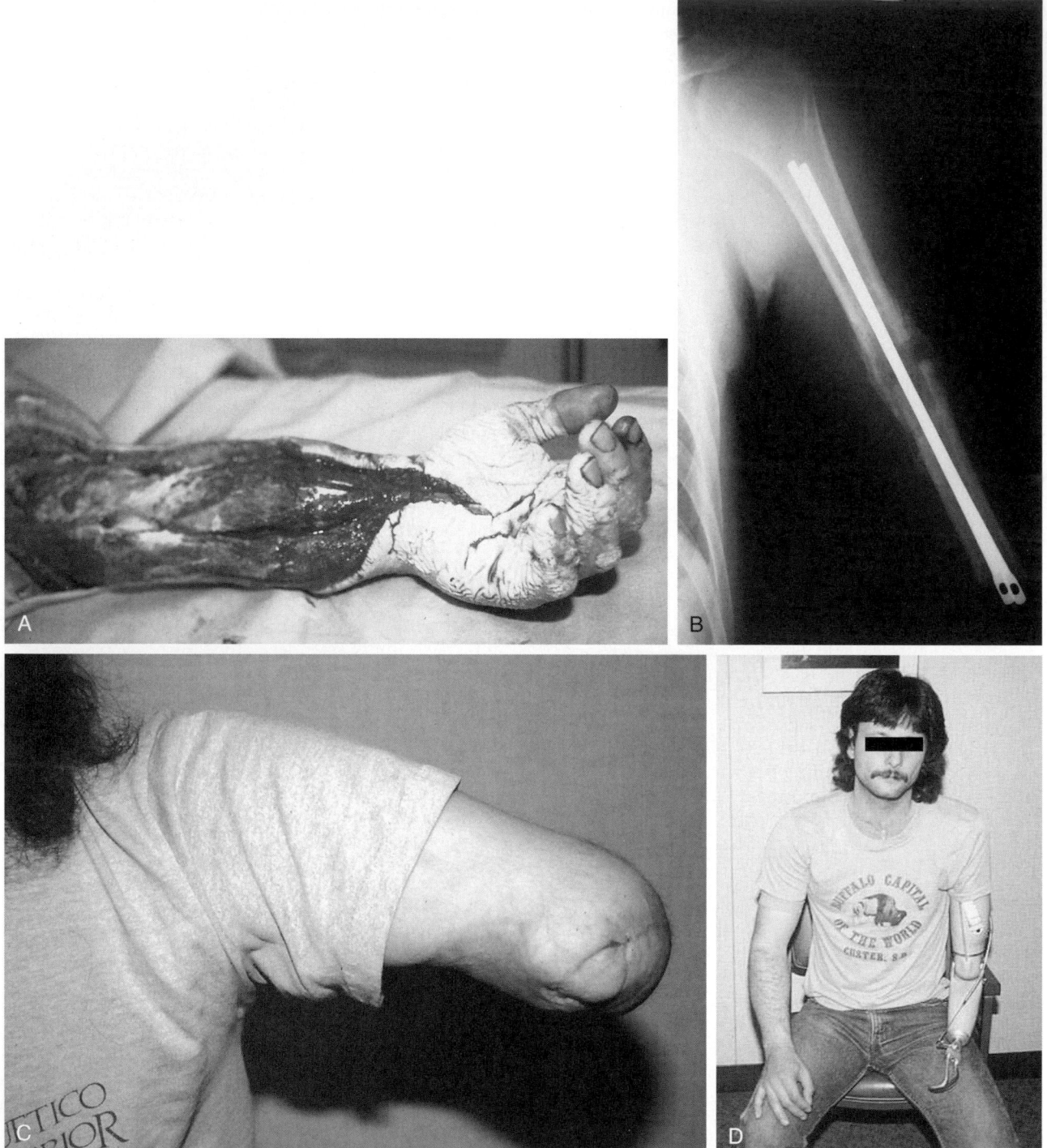

**FIGURE 64–8.** *A,* This patient sustained a burn and crushing injury of his forearm combined with a closed humerus fracture. Limb salvage was not feasible. *B,* Distal transhumeral amputation was combined with intramedullary nailing of the humerus to save residual limb length. *C,* Eventual range of motion. *D,* Prosthetic fitting with myoelectric prosthesis.

Late amputation is performed for infection, deformity, or inadequate function. The surgery can be performed in a single stage if it can be done above the level of infection. If it is performed through the zone of infection, the wound closure should be staged and combined with parenteral antibiotic therapy.

## POSTOPERATIVE MANAGEMENT

If amputation surgery is the first step in the rehabilitation process, postoperative management becomes essential. The steps should include pain control, early ambulation, and early weight bearing. Preemptive pain control is important in trauma patients, as there is almost always a crush component of their injury. Crushing injury is one of the hallmarks of causalgia and neurogenic pain, for which preemptive pain management is essential. The most productive method of preemptive pain control is postoperative pain management with continuous epidural or continuous regional anesthesia[13] (Fig. 64–9). Augmentative epidural, lumbar sympathetic, or regional nerve blocks may be necessary in the early postoperative period. Although successful in the early postoperative period, these methods do not decrease the risk of late pain, which appears to be more dependent on the injury and the technical surgery.[13] Adults who undergo amputation all experience phantom limb sensation, but few (with good technical surgery) experience late phantom limb pain.

Early ambulation is valuable in the trauma population for both systemic and local reasons. When patients lie or sit, they aerobically decompensate and are susceptible to joint contractures and pressure ulcers. Contrary to long-held beliefs, weight bearing in transtibial and transfemoral amputations, not stump wrapping, shrinks residual limbs. Immediate postoperative prosthetic limb fitting (IPOP, or immediate postsurgical limb fitting) has not gained wide acceptance because of unacceptable rates of wound complications. The explanation is related to the IPOP prosthesis, which was fabricated from plaster. During the early postoperative period, the residual limb swelling or volume decreased and the plaster IPOP lost intimate fit. Pistoning led to wound breakdown. It became too labor intensive to change IPOP sockets constantly, so weight bearing has generally been delayed until the wound is more secure and the volume of the residual limb more stable (early postoperative prosthetic limb fitting or early postsurgical limb fitting). Technology advances with silicone-lined or volume-adaptable sockets may allow IPOP (Fig. 64–10).

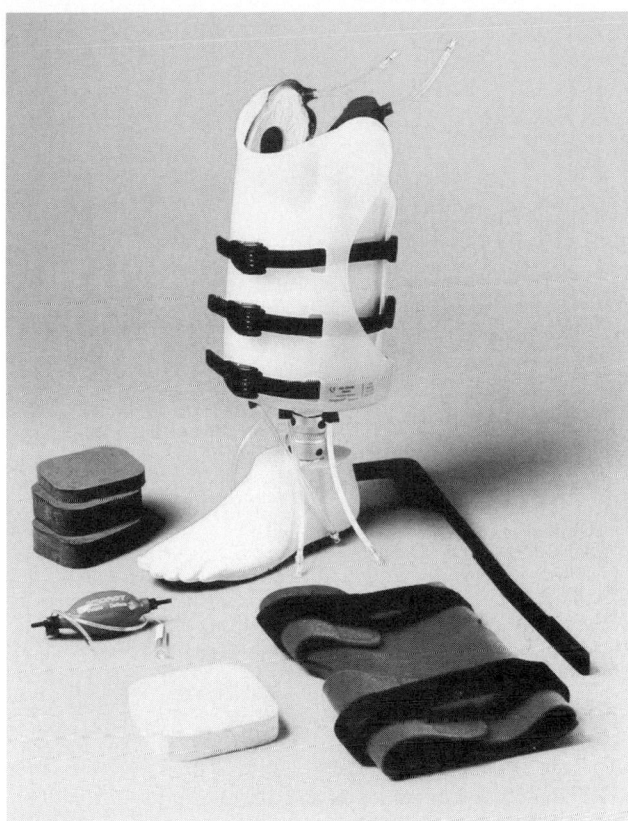

**FIGURE 64–10.** Volume-adaptable pneumatic preparatory transtibial prosthetic limb. This commercial device is applied in the operating room. Weight bearing is initiated in the early postoperative period. (Aircast Air-Limb, Aircast Inc., Summit, NJ.)

## COMMON SURGICAL TECHNIQUES

When performing an amputation for trauma, one needs to work with the available tissues and skin flaps dictated by the zone of injury and any surgical attempts at limb salvage. Creativity and application of plastic surgery tissue transfer principles enhance the quality of the eventual residual limb. Distal lower extremity amputations allow retention of some normal weight-bearing tissue. The functional loss is often directly correlated with the amount of the foot removed.

**Toe Amputation.** Hallux (great toe) amputation does not appear to impair walking greatly, as evidenced by the relatively normal functioning of patients after toe-to-hand transfer. The functional deficit seen with hallux amputation is a mild decrease in walking stability during the terminal stance phase of gait. Optimally, one prefers to perform the amputation distal to the insertion of the flexor hallucis brevis (Fig. 64–11). This level both retains the stability of the medial column of the foot during the stance phase of gait and centralizes the sesamoids, decreasing the risk of late sesamoid pain. The long plantar flap is preferred but not essential. When second toe amputation is necessary, one should strive to retain the base of the proximal phalanx. This "space occupier" prevents the drift of the hallux to a severe hallux valgus position, which

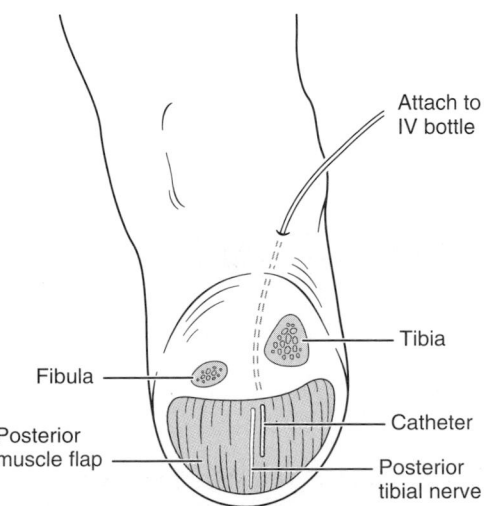

**FIGURE 64–9.** A 19-gauge epidural catheter is placed next to the transected posterior tibial nerve in transtibial amputation. The catheter is brought through the skin, where it is attached to a medication pump. Bupivacaine 0.5% is injected through the catheter through a drug pump at 1 ml/hr for 48 hours following surgery.

Attach to IV bottle

Tibia

Fibula

Catheter

Posterior muscle flap

Posterior tibial nerve

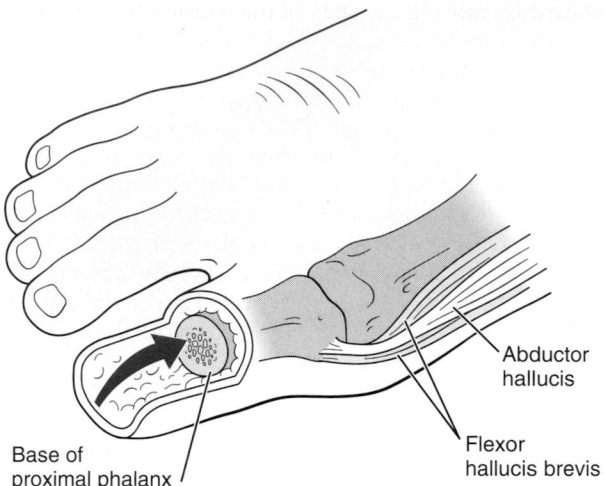

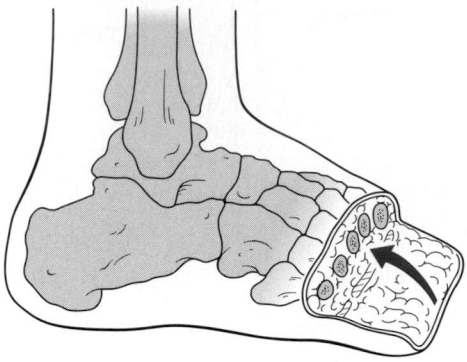

FIGURE 64–13. Midfoot amputation. Functionally, midfoot amputations at the transmetatarsal level (as depicted) and the tarsal-metatarsal level function equally well. (Redrawn from Kelikian, A.S., ed. Operative Treatment of the Foot and Ankle. Stamford, CT, Appleton & Lange, 1999, p. 616.)

FIGURE 64–11. Hallux amputation. An attempt is made to preserve the proximal aspect of the proximal phalanx in order to preserve the insertion of the flexor hallucis longus. Doing so improves walking stability during the terminal stance phase of gait and centralizes the sesamoids, decreasing the potential for late pain. (Redrawn from Kelikian, A.S., ed. Operative Treatment of the Foot and Ankle. Stamford, CT, Appleton & Lange, 1999, p. 613.)

increases pressure on the medial aspect of the first metatarsal. The goal of lesser toe amputation is to maintain a reasonable contour within the shoe, as there is essentially no functional loss with lesser toe amputation.

**Ray Resection.** Ray resection involves the removal of the metatarsal and corresponding toe. A single, outer ray is preferred. Lateral (fifth) ray resection produces virtually no disability, but medial (first) ray resection decreases the stability of the medial column of the foot during the terminal stance phase of gait. With central ray resection it is difficult to achieve wound healing; hence, it is rarely applicable to the trauma patient. When more than one ray is resected, the residual forefoot is so narrow and susceptible to the development of equinus that midfoot level amputation is preferred. The incision is longitudi-

nal, with a "tennis racket" incision around the base of the corresponding toe. A postoperative healing shoe can be used until standard footwear can be attempted (Fig. 64–12).

**Midfoot Amputation.** Midfoot amputation can be performed at either the transmetatarsal or tarsal-metatarsal (Lisfranc) level depending on the available tissue. Although the long plantar flap is preferred, other variants can easily be accommodated in protective footwear. Tarsal-metatarsal amputation should include percutaneous tendon Achilles lengthening to prevent late ankle equinus (Figs. 64–13 and 64–14). If a late varus deformity develops, the tibialis anterior muscle can be transferred to a neutral dorsiflexion point in the residual midfoot. Postoperatively, a below-knee walking cast should be used

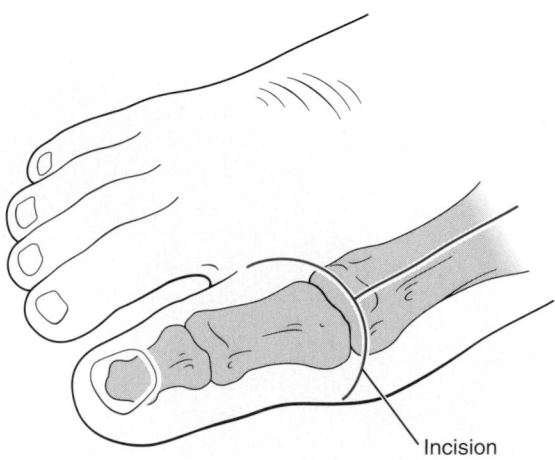

FIGURE 64–12. Resection of a single outer ray (metatarsal and corresponding toe) leaves the individual with minimal disability. The incision is carried to the toe, where a tennis racquet modification is used to remove the toe.

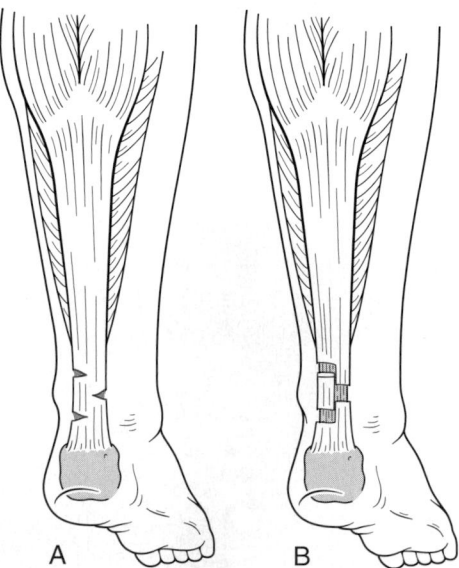

FIGURE 64–14. When amputation is performed at the tarsal-metatarsal (Lisfranc) level, there is a significant risk of the late development of ankle equinus. This development can be avoided with percutaneous tendon Achilles lengthening combined with a short leg walking cast for 4 weeks. (Redrawn from Kelikian, A.S., ed. Operative Treatment of the Foot and Ankle. Stamford, CT, Appleton & Lange, 1999, p. 615.)

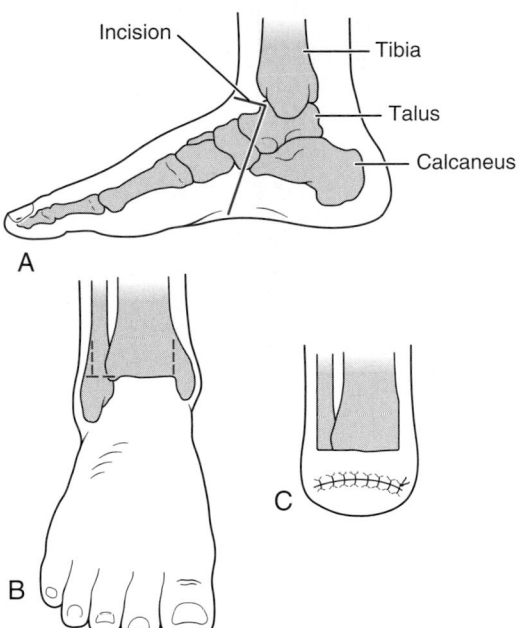

**FIGURE 64–15.** *A,* Incision. *B,* Bone cuts for one-stage ankle disarticulation (Syme's) amputation. (Redrawn from Kelikian, A.S., ed. Operative Treatment of the Foot and Ankle. Stamford, CT, Appleton & Lange, 1999, p. 617.)

for 4 weeks. A neoprene toe filler retains the contour of the shoe.

**Hindfoot Amputation.** Hindfoot amputation (Boyd, Chopart) should be avoided, as late equinus is inevitable. Even if late equinus could be avoided, the lever arm available for walking is short and leads to an apropulsive gait.

**Ankle Disarticulation (Syme's).** Ankle disarticulation provides an excellent end-bearing residual limb that rarely has late complications. The surgery combines ankle disarticulation with removal of the malleoli at the joint line. Although Wagner originally advocated malleolar removal at a second surgery, the amputation is now performed in a single surgery. The "dog ears" that were removed with the malleoli at the second surgery are now

avoided by moving the apex of the incision to a point just anterior to the midanterior border of both the medial and lateral malleoli (Fig. 64–15). The talus and calcaneus are removed by sharp dissection. The posterior tibial artery must be carefully protected, as this artery provides the blood supply necessary to keep the skin flaps viable. Traction is applied to the talus with a bone hook or bone-holding clamp to facilitate exposure. The malleoli are removed at the joint level, and the flares of the distal tibia and fibula are narrowed to facilitate prosthetic fitting. The heel pad is secured to the tibia by suturing the anterior edge fascial to the anterior rim of the tibia through drill holes.[14, 15] A below-knee walking cast with rubber walking heel can be applied at 10 to 14 days. Prosthetic fitting with a dynamic response foot is accomplished when the residual limb volume has stabilized and the wound has become secure.

**Transtibial Amputation.** Use of the posterior myofasciociocutaneous flap has long been the standard technique in the United States.[16] The optimal length of the residual tibia should be 5 inches (10 to 12 cm), although functional transtibial prosthetic limb fitting can be accomplished if the residual tibia retains the tibial tubercle and patellar tendon attachment. The length of the posterior flap is equal to a diameter at the level of bone transection plus 1 cm. The posterior part of the retained gastrocnemius fascia should be secured to the beveled distal tibia through drill holes or directly to the periosteum of the distal tibia and the retained anterior compartment fascia (Fig. 64–16). Many Europeans favor the so-called skew flap in dysvascular amputations, as it appears to be based on anatomic defined vascular regions[18] (Fig. 64–17). Both techniques allow production of a cushioned soft tissue interface to alleviate the shear forces of weight bearing and control the residual tibial position for prosthetic function. Americans who favor the standard posterior flap as popularized by Burgess argue that the avoidance of dissecting the layer between skin and muscle lessens the risk of tissue breakdown. In traumatic amputation, the blood supply of the flap should be well established at the time of definitive amputation surgery. A rigid plaster dressing is applied in the operating room. The cast is changed at 5 to 7 days and weekly until prosthetic fitting.[1] Typically, weight bearing

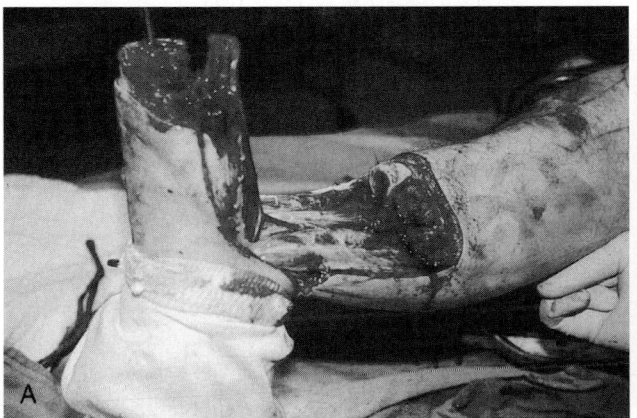

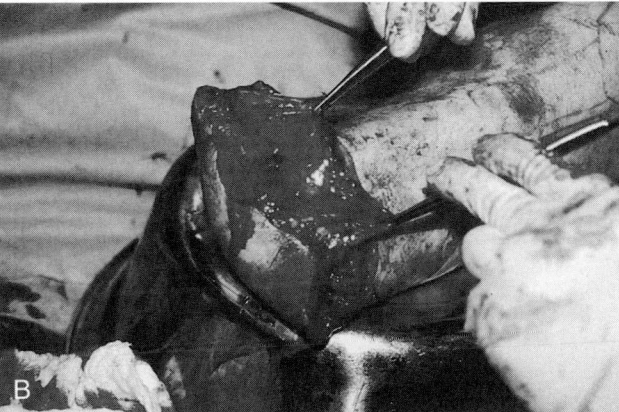

**FIGURE 64–16.** *A,* Soft tissue flap. *B,* Closure of transtibial amputation performed with a long posterior myocutaneous flap. The posterior fascia of the gastrocnemius should be secured to the tibia through drill holes or sutured to the periosteum of the tibia and retained anterior compartment fascia.

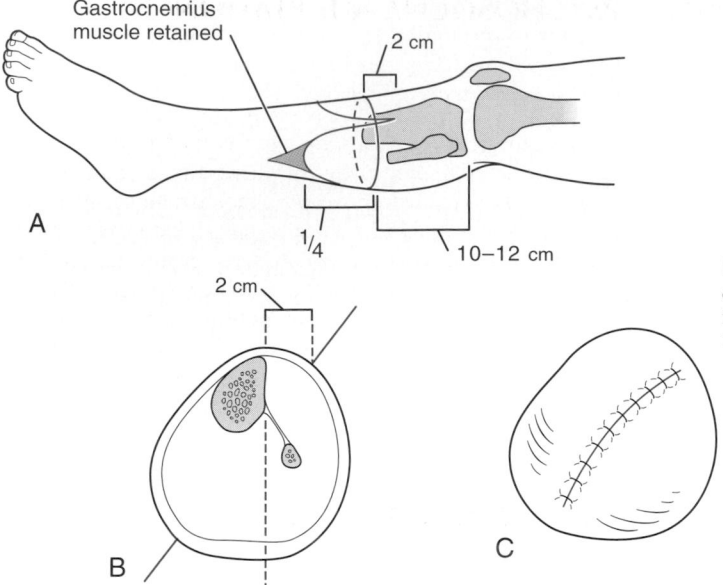

A

Gastrocnemius
muscle retained

2 cm

1/4    10–12 cm

2 cm

B

C

Figure 64–17. The skew flap method of transtibial amputation based on the vascular supply of the leg compartments and skin. (Modified from Robinson, K.P.; Hoile, R.; Coddington, T. Br J Surg 69:554–557, 1982.)

with a preparatory prosthesis is initiated at 5 to 21 days after surgery, depending on the experience of the local rehabilitation team. As discussed earlier, newer technology may allow safe immediate prosthetic limb fitting and weight bearing[19] (see Fig. 64–10).

**Knee Disarticulation.** This level has a limited application in trauma, as the length of the soft tissue myocutaneous flap is similar to that in transtibial amputation and a patient can be fit functionally by a transtibial amputation with a residual tibial length just distal to the tibial tubercle attachment of the quadriceps tendon.[1]

**Transfemoral Amputation.** Unlike the dysvascular population, post-traumatic transfemoral amputees are likely to walk with a prosthesis. Gottschalk and colleagues[6,7] have clearly shown that the method of surgical construction of the transfemoral residual limb is the determining factor in positioning the femur for optimal load transfer. Standard transfemoral amputation with a fish-mouth incision disengages the action of the adductor musculature, leading to abduction of the residual femur. This dynamic motor imbalance produces apparently weak abductors and an "adductor lurch" gait pattern. By using a medial, adductor-based myocutaneous flap, the adductor muscles can be secured to the residual femur, allowing the femur to be appropriately prepositioned within the prosthetic socket[6,7] (Fig. 64–18). Elastic compression dressings are used until the residual limb appears secure. Prefabricated volume-adjustable preparatory or custom-fabricated prosthetic sockets can be fit at 5 to 21 days, depending on the experience and expertise of the local rehabilitation team.

**Hip Disarticulation.** Few hip disarticulation amputees become functional prosthetic users. Extracapsular amputation at the lesser trochanter level provides the optimal weight-bearing platform for sitting in a chair or prosthetic socket. The platform needs to be cushioned by whichever muscle group is available for coverage. Full-thickness skin is preferred.

# UPPER EXTREMITY AMPUTATION

The lower extremity is an organ of locomotion, with lower extremity prostheses functioning reasonably well in substituting for the amputated body part. The upper extremity in humans is an organ of prehension and sensory interaction with the individual's world. After amputation, the prosthesis encases the sensate residual limb, eliminating much sensory feedback. It must be operated by coordinating motor control with visual guidance. If the

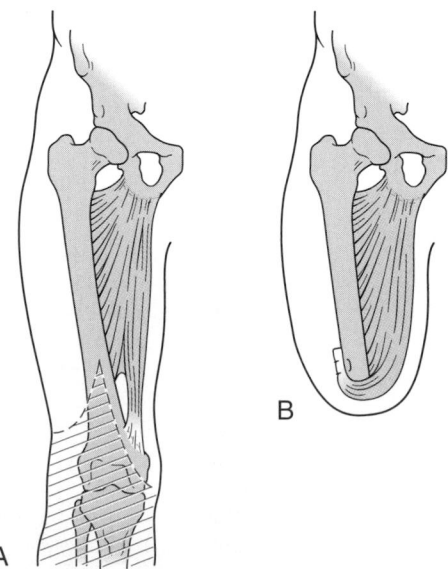

A

B

Figure 64–18. *A*, Surgical incision for medial-based flap technique of transfemoral amputation. *B*, Adductor myodesis is accomplished to control the position of the residual femur in order to optimize weight bearing. (Modified from Gottschalk, F. In: Bowker, J.H.; Michael, J.W., eds. Atlas of Limb Prosthetics. St. Louis, Mosby–Year Book, 1992, pp. 501–507.)

prosthesis is positioned in full pronation, visual cues may be blocked, limiting the function of the prosthesis. A sensate hand with even minimal prehensile function is likely to outperform a prosthesis. Functionally, one can think of the shoulder as the center of a functional sphere. The hand accomplishes its prehension functions at the extremes of the sphere. The elbow acts as a caliper to position the hand within the functional sphere.

Retention of limb length is even more crucial in the upper extremity but for different reasons. We normally operate multiple joints in the same limb simultaneously, whereas the upper extremity amputee must operate joints sequentially. We normally preposition our hand while simultaneously opening or closing it to prepare for performing a task. The amputee must perform these tasks sequentially, making timely prosthetic response less efficient as more tasks are required. The weight and cumbersomeness of the prosthesis also increase as more joint functions need to be accomplished.

Suspension, as in the lower extremity, is enhanced with a longer residual limb. Increased surface area for load distribution (weight bearing in the lower extremity) is now useful to drive the prosthesis in space and to provide resistance to pressures applied to the prosthesis during the performance of tasks.[17]

Optimal transradial function occurs when the residual forearm bones retain one half to two thirds of their normal length. Soft tissue management is similar to that in the lower extremity except that areas of split-thickness skin graft are better tolerated. Preparatory prosthetic fitting should be initiated at 5 to 7 days following surgery. Early myoelectric fittings are advised. Unilateral upper limb amputees are unlikely to use a prosthesis if their preparatory fitting is delayed beyond 30 days.

Transhumeral amputees are less likely to obtain a high level of prosthetic competence. The limb is heavy and cumbersome. Because the amputee now must operate two visually cued joints, the prosthesis is slow to respond. Retaining length and providing a good soft tissue envelope are essential if there is a realistic goal of functional prosthetic limb fitting.[17]

Late wound complications are unusual, as the applied loads are far less than in lower extremity amputation. Although neuromas are somewhat more likely to occur in the upper limb, they can generally be avoided by careful attention at the initial surgery. When painful point-tender, palpable neuromas do not respond to trigger point and steroid injections, sharp proximal resection can often achieve resolution of symptoms.

Brachial plexus and severe shoulder injuries are closely related. Remember that the upper limb, especially if replaced with a prosthesis, functions within the functional sphere. Upper brachial plexus injury may make a functional hand useless because of inability to preposition. Body-powered prostheses that are controlled with shoulder harnesses do not allow overhead activity. A novel approach can be taken to the severe, nonreconstructable lower brachial plexus injury; where shoulder function is lost, scapulothoracic motor control is maintained. In this situation, shoulder fusion combined with transhumeral amputation at a sensate level can allow limited prosthetic function.

## PSYCHOSOCIAL ADAPTATION

Patients need to mourn the loss of a limb. Some accomplish their mourning during the acute hospitalization. Many go through a mourning period several months later. As with treating patients with other medical conditions, those with better support mechanisms fare better. Local support groups act both to provide psychologic support and as a local consumers' group to facilitate interaction with the prosthetists. The Amputee Coalition of America is the only truly national group that can provide these services to patients. It has a great many local chapters. It can be reached at 1-888-AMP-KNOW (267-5669) and at www.amputee-coalition.org.[10]

## LATE COMPLICATIONS

Amputees return to the physician for infection, ulceration, pain, or functional impairment. Most of these problems can be resolved with the help of a knowledgeable prosthetist. Prosthetic technology is rapidly advancing, providing lighter weight prosthetic limbs that are more able to cushion the residual limb and absorb the shock of weight-bearing loading as well as being more adaptable to uneven walking, running, and climbing surfaces. Many ulcers occur because of a change in the residual limb volume or shape. These issues can be resolved with prosthetic socket modification. The first step in the evaluation of most late problems in amputees is a careful evaluation by the prosthetist.

Residual limb pain can be caused by poor socket fit over a bony prominence or growth of heterotopic bone. Both issues can usually be resolved by modification of the prosthetic socket, limb alignment, or the addition of a shock-absorbing dynamic elastic response prosthetic foot. When these modifications do not control the symptoms or when patients develop phantom limb pain (pain in the amputated body part), pain clinic modalities are in order. Every adult who undergoes amputation has a phantom limb sensation. This sensation might be an awareness of the amputated limb in space or the presence of paresthesias. True phantom limb pain is unusual but is characterized by burning, searing, or throbbing pain in the amputated part. Pain clinic modalities or nerve blocks generally control these symptoms.

Indications for revision amputation surgery are based on an extension of the principles of initial amputation surgery. Deep infection is managed with standard surgical techniques. When a bony prominence cannot be accommodated, bony remodeling combined with plastic surgery techniques can be applied.

Dermatologic rashes are usually the result of less than optimal hygiene or allergy. Keeping the residual limb clean and dry, changing soaps, and using lanolin skin cream generally resolve these issues. Hydrocortisone ointment or cream can be used locally to resolve rashes. Acneform lesions and deep carbuncles are managed with oral tetracycline therapy and occasional surgical drainage. Verrucous hyperplasia is a condition that is due to venous congestion, swelling, and loss of total-contact prosthetic socket fit. The terminal tissue of the residual limb is bulbous and swollen. It has villous projections with serous weeping. The tissue develops a "brawny" edema, much like that in the leg of a patient with severe venous insufficiency leg ulcers. The treatment is improved socket fit, often requiring repeated socket modifications by the prosthetist.

## SUMMARY

Burgess taught us that amputation is constructive surgery. It should be performed as the first step in the rehabilitation process when it has been determined that amputation offers a more functional outcome than an attempt at limb salvage and reconstruction. If one views construction of the residual limb with the same reverence as the preparation and placement of a total joint component (which is being used after amputating a joint that cannot be adequately reconstructed), many patients are able to perform tasks similar to those that they could achieve before their injury.

**REFERENCES**

1. Bowker, J.H.; San Giovanni, T.P.; Pinzur, M.S. North American experience with knee disarticulation with use of a posterior myofasciocutaneous flap. Healing rate and functional results in seventy-seven patients. J Bone Joint Surg Am 82:1571–1574, 2000.
2. Burgess, E.M.; Romano, R.L.; Zettl, J.H. The Management of Lower Extremity Amputations. Washington, DC, Government Printing Office, 1969.
3. Dirschl, D.R.; Dahners, L.E. The mangled extremity: When should it be amputated? J Am Acad Orthop Surg 4:182–190, 1996.
4. Fairhurst, M.J. The function of below-knee amputee versus the patient with salvaged grade III tibial fracture. Clin Orthop 301:227–232, 1994.
5. Functional Independence Measure. Buffalo, NY, Center for Functional Assessment Research, School of Medicine and Biomedical Sciences, State University of New York at Buffalo, 1996.
6. Gottschalk, F.; Kourosh, S.; Stills, M. Does socket configuration influence the position of the femur in above-knee amputation? J Prosthet Orthot 2:94–102, 1989.
7. Gottschalk, F. Transfemoral amputation. In: Bowker, J.H.; Michael, J.W., eds. Atlas of Limb Prosthetics. St. Louis, Mosby–Year Book, 1992, pp. 501–507.
8. Guedes, M.A.; Filho, N.A.; Guedes, J.P.B.; Yamahoka, M.S.O. Free paper 68: Bone bridge in transtibial amputation. Paper presented at the Seventh World Congress of the International Society for Prosthetics and Orthotics, Amsterdam, June 28–July 3, 1998.
9. Guedes S. Pinto, M.A.; De Luccia, N.; Filho, N.A.; Yamahoka, M.S. Osteoperiosteal bone bridge in transtibial amputation. Video presentation at the Fifth World Congress of the International Society for Prosthetics and Orthotics, Chicago, July 1992.
10. Lerner, R.K.; Esterhai, J.L.; Polomano, R.C.; et al. Quality of life assessment of patients with posttraumatic fracture nonunion, chronic refractory osteomyelitis, and lower extremity amputation. Clin Orthop 295:28–36, 1993.
11. Pinzur, M.S.; Gold, J.; Schwartz, D.; Gross, N. Energy demands for walking in dysvascular amputees as related to the level of amputation. Orthopedics 15:1033–1037, 1992.
12. Pinzur, M.S. New concepts in lower-limb amputation and prosthetic management. Instr Course Lect 39:361–366, 1990.
13. Pinzur, M.S.; Garla, P.G.; Pluth, T.; Vrbos, L. Continuous postoperative infusion of a regional anesthetic after an amputation of the lower extremity. J Bone Joint Surg Am 78:1501–1505, 1996.
14. Pinzur, M.; Morrison, C.; Sage, R.; et al. Syme's two-stage amputation in insulin-requiring diabetics with gangrene of the forefoot. Foot Ankle 11:394–396, 1991.
15. Pinzur, M.S.; Smith, D.; Osterman, H. Syme ankle disarticulation in peripheral vascular disease and diabetic foot infection: The one-stage versus two-stage procedure. Foot Ankle Int 16:124–127, 1995.
16. Pinzur, M.S.; Gottschalk, F.; Smith, D.; et al. Functional outcome of below-knee amputation in peripheral vascular insufficiency. Clin Orthop 286:247–249, 1993.
17. Pinzur, M.S.; Angelats, J.; Light, T.R.; et al. Functional outcome following traumatic upper limb amputation and prosthetic limb fitting. J Hand Surg Am 19:836–839, 1994.
18. Robinson, K.P.; Hoile, R.; Coddington, T. Skew flap myoplastic below-knee amputation. A preliminary report. Br J Surg 69:554–557, 1982.
19. Schon, L.; Short, K.W.; Rheinstein, J.; et al. Benefits of early prosthetic management of transtibial amputees: A prospective clinical study of a prefabricated prosthesis. In press.
20. Waters, R.L. The energy expenditure of amputee gait. In: Bowker, J.H.; Michael, J.W., eds. Atlas of Limb Prosthetics, 2nd ed. St. Louis, Mosby–Year Book, 1992, pp. 381–388.
21. Waters, R.L.; Perry, J.; Antonelli, D.; et al. Energy cost of walking of amputees: The influence of level of amputation. J Bone Joint Surg Am 58:42–46, 1976.
22. Wilson, A.B., Jr. History of amputation surgery and prosthetics. In: Bowker, J.H.; Michael, J.W., eds. Atlas of Limb Prosthetics, 2nd ed. St. Louis, Mosby–Year Book, 1992, pp. 3–16.

# INDEX

Note: Page numbers followed by f indicate figures; page numbers followed by t indicate tables.